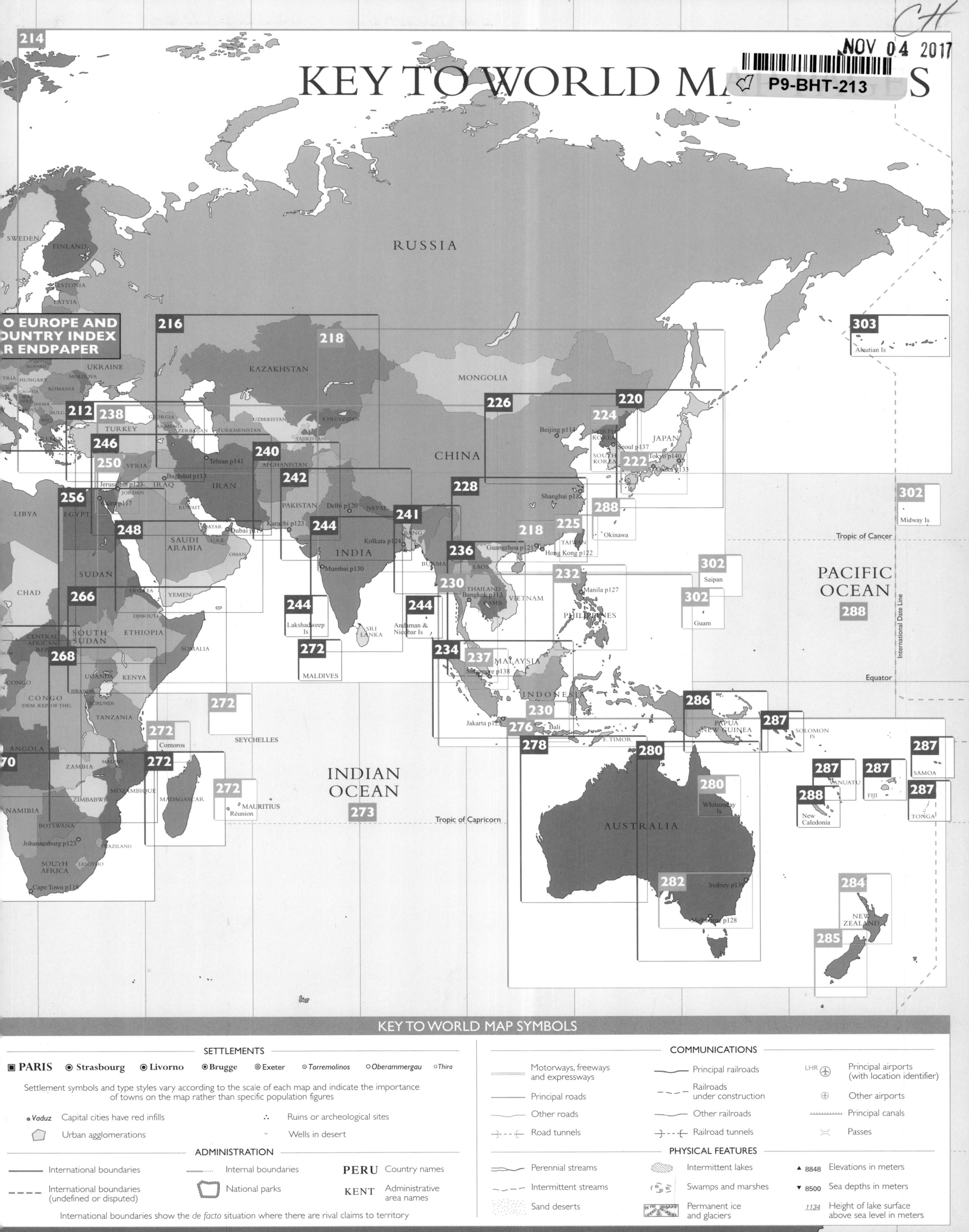

KEY TO WORLD MAPS

KEY TO WORLD MAP SYMBOLS

SETTLEMENTS

■ **PARIS** ◉ **Strasbourg** ◎ **Livorno** ◉ **Brugge** ⊚ **Exeter** ∘ *Torremolinos* ∘ *Oberammergau* ∘ Thira

Settlement symbols and type styles vary according to the scale of each map and indicate the importance
of towns on the map rather than specific population figures

• *Vaduz* Capital cities have red infills

▭ Urban agglomerations

∴ Ruins or archeological sites

˅ Wells in desert

ADMINISTRATION

―――― International boundaries

- - - - International boundaries
(undefined or disputed)

⋯⋯⋯ Internal boundaries

⬠ National parks

PERU Country names

KENT Administrative
area names

International boundaries show the *de facto* situation where there are rival claims to territory

COMMUNICATIONS

―――― Motorways, freeways
and expressways

―――― Principal roads

―――― Other roads

+⋅−⋅+ Road tunnels

―――― Principal railroads

- - - - Railroads
under construction

+―+ Other railroads

+―+ Railroad tunnels

LHR ⊕ Principal airports
(with location identifier)

⊕ Other airports

⋯⋯⋯ Principal canals

⋈ Passes

PHYSICAL FEATURES

―――― Perennial streams

- - - - Intermittent streams

⋰⋱ Sand deserts

▨ Intermittent lakes

⬚ Swamps and marshes

▨ Permanent ice
and glaciers

▲ 8848 Elevations in meters

▼ 8500 Sea depths in meters

1134 Height of lake surface
above sea level in meters

OXFORD
ATLAS
OF THE
WORLD

3 1336 10298 0860

TWENTY-FOURTH EDITION

GAZETTEER OF NATIONS
TEXT Keith Lye/Philip's

PHOTOGRAPHIC ACKNOWLEDGEMENTS
Alamy /*AlamyCelebrity* 82, /*Jon Arnold Images Ltd* 91,
/*B.A.E. Inc.* 79, /*Jens Benninghofen* 11 (center),
/*Chessocampo* 8, 9, /*Mark Conlin* 85 (bottom), /*David R.
Frazier Photolibrary, Inc.* 98, /*Søren Lund Hviid* 103,
/*Images and Stories* 94, /*Galen Rowell/Mountain Light*
11 (bottom), /*Kevin Schafer* 85 (top), /*Travel Pix* 13 (top),
/*Xinhua* 107;
Copernicus Sentinel data 2017/NPA Satellite Mapping,
  CGG Services (UK) Ltd 11 (top);
Corbis /*Jay Dickman* 109 (top), /*Gideon Mendel* 89 (top),
  /*Liba Taylor* 104, /*David Turnley* 109 (bottom);
© Crown copyright 2007. Published by the Met Office,
  UK 80;
Galaxy Picture Library/*Robin Scagell* 73;
Getty Images /*Hannele Lahti* 85 (center);
Garrett Nagle 87;
NASA 13 (bottom), /*GSFC* 81 (bottom), /*Jacques Descloitres*,
  /*ESA, S. Beckwith (STScI), and The Hubble Heritage Team
  (STScI/AURA)* 68;
NSIDC courtesy J. Maslanik and M. Tschudi, University
  of Colorado 81 (top);
NPA Satellite Mapping, CGG Services (UK) Ltd 14–33,
  66–67, 110–111, 144–145, 156–157, 208–209, 252–253,
  274–275, 290–291, 324–325;
Science Photo Library /*Sputnik* 97.

STAR CHARTS (PAGE 69)
Wil Tirion

CARTOGRAPHY BY PHILIP'S

WORLD CITIES

PAGE 121, EDINBURGH,
AND PAGE 125, LONDON:
This product includes mapping data licensed from
Ordnance Survey® with the permission of the Controller
of Her Majesty's Stationery Office. © Crown copyright
2017. All rights reserved. Licence number 100011710.

Copyright © 2017 Philip's
www.philips-maps.co.uk

Philip's, a division of Octopus Publishing Group Limited
(www.octopusbooks.co.uk)
Carmelite House, 50 Victoria Embankment, London EC4Y 0DZ
An Hachette UK Company (www.hachette.co.uk)

Published in North America by
Oxford University Press USA
198 Madison Avenue
New York, NY 10016

www.oup.com/us

OXFORD Oxford is a registered trademark
UNIVERSITY PRESS of Oxford University Press

Library of Congress Cataloging-in-Publication Data available

ISBN 978–0–19–084362–5

Printing (last digit): 9 8 7 6 5 4 3 2 1

Printed in Hong Kong

FOREWORD

AN AUTHORITATIVE AND SERIOUS REFERENCE WORK, the Oxford *Atlas of the World* is one of the finest atlases available anywhere in the world. The atlas incorporates computer-derived maps that have been produced using the very latest in digital cartographic techniques. Country names are shown in conventional English form and are those that are in common usage. They are the forms used by publications such as *Newsweek* and *The Washington Post*, and by the BBC and the British Foreign Office. Alternative country names appear in parentheses on the maps where space permits – for example, Burma (Myanmar) – and are cross-referenced in the index, for example, Côte d'Ivoire = Ivory Coast.

HOW TO USE THE ATLAS
The atlas is divided into a number of sections which are explained below.

WORLD STATISTICS AND "A DIVIDED WORLD: LAND AND MARITIME BOUNDARIES"
World statistics on topics such as area and population for every country in the world. Also included in this section is a listing of the world's largest cities by population, arranged in country alphabetical order. This section is followed by the highly topical "*A Divided World*" feature, which examines some of the major issues concerning land and maritime boundaries.

IMAGES OF EARTH
A beautifully illustrated satellite imagery section showing 17 of the world's major cities and regions in the Americas, Europe, Africa, Asia, and Australasia.

GAZETTEER OF NATIONS
A comprehensive A–Z reference providing concise profiles of every country's geography, climate, history, politics, and economy, together with ready-reference tables, and illustrated with flags and locator maps.

WORLD GEOGRAPHY
A richly informative section comprising 42 pages of maps, charts, graphs, and diagrams that explain key themes about the world in which we live. The topics covered include the Solar System, climate, the natural world, population, energy, and trade. Explanatory text on each spread describes the patterns shown by the data.

WORLD CITIES
A detailed selection of maps for 70 urban areas around the world. These are useful for planning trips abroad as well as for comparative studies of cities worldwide.

WORLD MAPS
An outstanding collection of 179 pages of distinctive Philip's cartography. The highly acclaimed physical world maps combine relief shading with layer-colored contours to give a striking visual picture of the Earth's surface. Roads, railroads, canals, and airports are accurately depicted on the maps, and towns and cities are clearly marked. More information on the key features employed in the construction and presentation of the maps is given on the facing page.

GEOGRAPHICAL GLOSSARY AND INDEX
The 86,000-name index to the world maps includes geographical features as well as towns and cities, with both latitude/longitude and letter/figure grid references. Preceding the index is a list of geographical terms from various foreign languages that may be found in the place names on the maps and also in the index, together with their meanings.

SPECIALIST GEOGRAPHY CONSULTANTS

THE EDITORS are grateful to the following for their contributions to the '*World Geography*' section in this atlas:

Dr Dibyesh Anand	Keith Lye	Robin Scagell
John Burden	Garrett Nagle	John Woodruff
Peter Grego	Ross Reynolds	

THE EDITORS would also like to thank **Richard Chiles** and the staff at NPA Satellite Mapping, **CGG Services (UK) Ltd**, Edenbridge, Kent, UK (www.npa.cgg.com) for sourcing and processing the satellite imagery that appears in the atlas.

USER GUIDE

The reference maps which form the main body of this atlas have been prepared in accordance with the highest standards of international cartography to provide an accurate and detailed representation of the Earth. The scales and projections used have been carefully chosen to give balanced coverage of the world, while emphasizing the most densely populated and economically significant regions. A hallmark of Philip's mapping is the use of hill shading and relief coloring to create a graphic impression of landforms: this makes the maps exceptionally easy to read. However, knowledge of the key features employed in the construction and presentation of the maps will enable the reader to derive the fullest benefit from the atlas..

MAP SEQUENCE

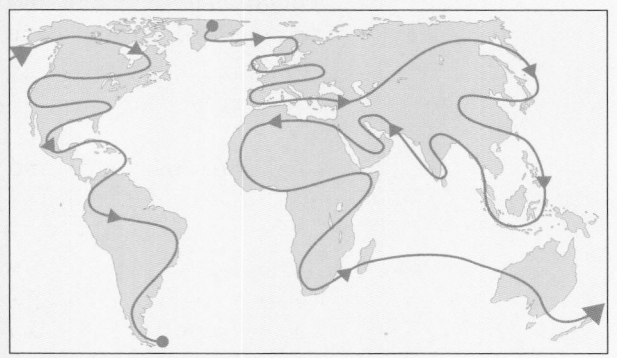

The atlas covers the Earth continent by continent: first Europe; then its land neighbor Asia (mapped north before south, in a clockwise sequence), then Africa, Australia and Oceania, North America, and South America. This is the classic arrangement adopted by most cartographers since the 16th century. For each continent, there are maps at a variety of scales. First, physical relief and political maps of the whole continent; then a series of larger-scale maps of the regions within the continent, each followed, where required, by still larger-scale maps of the most important or densely populated areas. The governing principle is that by turning the pages of the atlas, the reader moves steadily from north to south through each continent, with each map overlapping its neighbors.

MAP PRESENTATION

With very few exceptions (for example, for the Arctic and Antarctica), the maps are drawn with north at the top, regardless of whether they are presented upright or sideways on the page. In the borders will be found the map title; a locator diagram showing the area covered; continuation arrows showing the page numbers for maps of adjacent areas; the scale; the projection used; the degrees of latitude and longitude; and the letters and figures used in the index for locating place names and geographical features. Physical relief maps also have a height reference panel identifying the colors used for each layer of contouring.

MAP SYMBOLS

Each map contains a vast amount of detail which can only be conveyed clearly and accurately by the use of symbols. Points and circles of varying sizes locate and identify the relative importance of towns and cities; different styles of type are employed for administrative, geographical, and regional place names to aid identification. A variety of pictorial symbols denote landforms such as glaciers, marshes, and coral reefs, and man-made structures including roads, railroads, airports, and canals. Where neighboring borders are shown by red lines. Where neighboring countries are in dispute, for example in parts of the Middle East, the maps show the *de facto* boundary between nations, regardless of the legal or historical situation.

The symbols are explained on the front endpapers of the atlas.

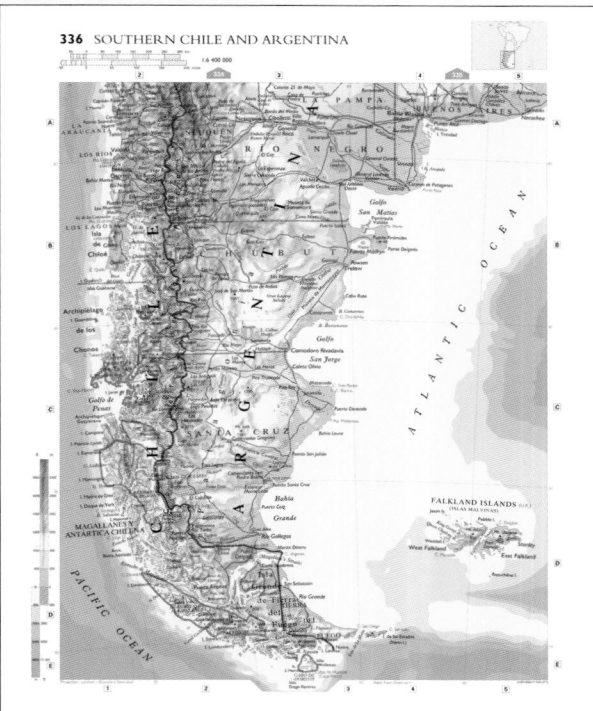

MAP SCALES

1:16 000 000
1 inch = 252 statute miles

The scale of each map is given in the numerical form known as the "representative fraction." The first figure is always one, signifying one unit of distance on the map; the second figure, usually in millions, is the number by which the map unit must be multiplied to give the equivalent distance on the Earth's surface. Calculations can easily be made in centimeters and kilometers, by dividing the Earth units figure by 100 000 (i.e. deleting the last five 0s). Thus 1:1 000 000 means 1 cm = 10 km. The calculation for inches and miles is more laborious, but 1 000 000 divided by 63 360 (the number of inches in a mile) shows that 1:1 000 000 means approximately 1 inch = 16 miles. The table below provides distance equivalents for scales down to 1:50 000 000.

LARGE SCALE		
1:1 000 000	1 cm = 10 km	1 inch = 16 miles
1:2 500 000	1 cm = 25 km	1 inch = 39.5 miles
1:5 000 000	1 cm = 50 km	1 inch = 79 miles
1:6 000 000	1 cm = 60 km	1 inch = 95 miles
1:8 000 000	1 cm = 80 km	1 inch = 126 miles
1:10 000 000	1 cm = 100 km	1 inch = 158 miles
1:15 000 000	1 cm = 150 km	1 inch = 237 miles
1:20 000 000	1 cm = 200 km	1 inch = 316 miles
1:50 000 000	1 cm = 500 km	1 inch = 790 miles
SMALL SCALE		

MEASURING DISTANCES

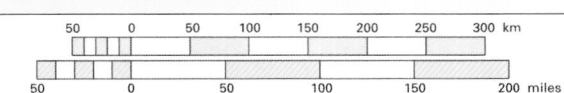

Although each map is accompanied by a scale bar, distances cannot always be measured with confidence because of the distortions involved in portraying the curved surface of the Earth on a flat page. As a general rule, the larger the map scale, the more accurate and reliable will be the distance measured. On small-scale maps such as those of the world and of entire continents, measurement may only be accurate along the "standard parallels," or central axes, and should not be attempted without considering the map projection.

MAP PROJECTIONS

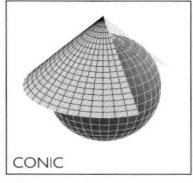 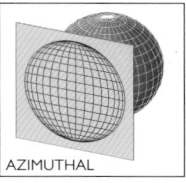 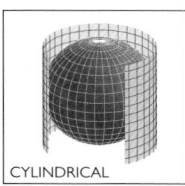

CONIC   AZIMUTHAL   CYLINDRICAL

Unlike a globe, no flat map can give a true scale representation of the world in terms of area, shape, and position of every region. Each of the numerous systems that have been devised for projecting the curved surface of the Earth on to a flat page involves the sacrifice of accuracy in one or more of these elements. The variations in shape and position of land masses such as Alaska, Greenland, and Australia, for example, can be quite dramatic when different projections are compared.

For this atlas, the guiding principle has been to select projections that involve the least distortion of size and distance. The projection used for each map is noted in the border. Most fall into one of three categories – conic, azimuthal, or cylindrical – whose basic concepts are shown above. Each involves plotting the forms of the Earth's surface on a grid of latitude and longitude lines, which may be shown as parallels, curves, or radiating spokes.

LATITUDE AND LONGITUDE

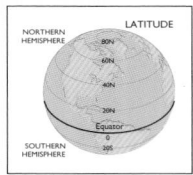 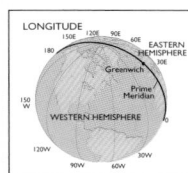 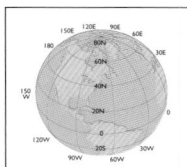

Accurate positioning of individual points on the Earth's surface is made possible by reference to the geometrical system of latitude and longitude. Latitude *parallels* are drawn west–east around the Earth and numbered by degrees north and south of the Equator, which is designated 0° of latitude. Longitude *meridians* are drawn north–south and numbered by degrees east and west of the *prime meridian*, 0° of longitude, which passes through Greenwich in England. By referring to these coordinates and their subdivisions of minutes (1/60th of a degree) and seconds (1/60th of a minute), any place on Earth can be located to within a few hundred meters. Latitude and longitude are indicated by blue lines on the maps; they are straight or curved according to the projection employed. Reference to these lines is the easiest way of determining the relative positions of places on different maps, and for plotting compass directions.

NAME FORMS

For ease of reference, both English and local name forms appear in the atlas. Oceans, seas, and countries are shown in English throughout the atlas; country names may be abbreviated to their commonly accepted form (for example, Germany, not The Federal Republic of Germany). Conventional English forms are also used for place names on the smaller-scale maps of the continents. However, local name forms are used on all large-scale and regional maps, with the English form given in brackets only for important cities – the large-scale map of Russia and Northern Asia thus shows Moskva (Moscow). For countries which do not use a Roman script, place names have been transcribed according to the systems adopted by the British and US Geographic Names Authorities. For China, the Pin Yin system has been used, with some more widely known forms appearing in brackets, as with Beijing (Peking). Both English and local names appear in the index, the English form being cross-referenced to the local form.

CONTENTS

WORLD STATISTICS

COUNTRIES 6
CITIES 7

A DIVIDED WORLD

LAND BOUNDARIES 10–11
MARITIME BOUNDARIES 12–13

IMAGES OF EARTH

PARIS, FRANCE 16
BARCELONA, SPAIN 17
ATHENS, GREECE 18
JERUSALEM, ISRAEL 19
DUBAI, UAE 20
KOCHI, INDIA 21
BANGKOK, THAILAND 22
BRAZZAVILLE, CONGO/
    KINSHASA, DEM. REP. CONGO 23
DAR ES SALAAM, TANZANIA 24
CHRISTCHURCH, NEW ZEALAND 25
ANCHORAGE, USA 26
OTTAWA, CANADA 27
BOSTON, USA 28
MEMPHIS, USA 29
MEXICO CITY, MEXICO 30
SÃO PAULO, BRAZIL 31

GAZETTEER OF NATIONS

AN A–Z GAZETTEER OF
    COUNTRIES 34–65

WORLD GEOGRAPHY

THE UNIVERSE 68–69
THE SOLAR SYSTEM 70–71
SEASONS, TIME AND
    MOTION 72–73
GEOLOGY OF THE EARTH 74–75
THE ATMOSPHERE 76–77
CLIMATE 78–79
CLIMATE CHANGE AND
    GLOBAL WARMING 80–81
WATER AND VEGETATION 82–83
OCEANS AND SEAS 84–85
BIODIVERSITY AND THE
    NATURAL WORLD 86–87
POPULATION 88–89
CITIES 90–91
THE HUMAN FAMILY 92–93
CONFLICT AND
    CO-OPERATION 94–95
ENERGY 96–97
MINERALS 98–99
EMPLOYMENT AND
    INDUSTRY 100–101
TRADE 102–103
HEALTH 104–105
WEALTH 106–107
STANDARDS OF LIVING 108–109

WORLD CITIES

AMSTERDAM 112
ATHENS 112
ATLANTA 113
BAGHDAD 113
BANGKOK 113
BARCELONA 114
BEIJING 114
BERLIN 115
BOSTON 116
BRUSSELS 116
BUDAPEST 117
BUENOS AIRES 117
CAIRO 117
CAPE TOWN 118
COPENHAGEN 118
CHICAGO 119
DUBAI 119
DALLAS-FORT WORTH 120
DELHI 120
EDINBURGH 121
GUANGZHOU 121
HELSINKI 121
HONG KONG 122
ISTANBUL 122
JAKARTA 122
JERUSALEM 123
JOHANNESBURG 123
KARACHI 123
KOLKATA 124
LAGOS 124
LAS VEGAS 124
LIMA 124
LONDON 125
LISBON 126
LOS ANGELES 126
MADRID 127
MANILA 127
MELBOURNE 128
MEXICO CITY 128
MILAN 128
MIAMI 129
MOSCOW 129
MONTRÉAL 130
MUMBAI 130
MUNICH 131
NEW ORLEANS 131
NEW YORK 132
ORLANDO 133
OSAKA 133
OSLO 133
PARIS 134
PRAGUE 135
RIO DE JANEIRO 135
ROME 136
SAN FRANCISCO 136
ST PETERSBURG 137
SANTIAGO 137
SÃO PAULO 137
SEOUL 137
SHANGHAI 138
SINGAPORE 138
STOCKHOLM 139
SYDNEY 139
TOKYO 140
TEHRAN 141
TORONTO 141
VENICE 142
VIENNA 142
WARSAW 143
WASHINGTON 143

WORLD MAPS

THE WORLD

MAP SYMBOLS FRONT ENDPAPER
THE WORLD: PHYSICAL 146–147
1:76 000 000
THE WORLD: POLITICAL 148–149
1:76 000 000
ARCTIC OCEAN 150
1:28 000 000
ANTARCTICA 151
1:28 000 000
ATLANTIC OCEAN 152
1:41 000 000
ISLANDS OF THE
    ATLANTIC 153
BERMUDA 1:400 000
NEW PROVIDENCE ISLAND 1:400 000
MADEIRA 1:800 000
AZORES 1:1 600 000
CANARY ISLANDS 1:1 600 000
FALKLAND ISLANDS 1:6 400 000
ASCENSION ISLAND 1:400 000
ST HELENA 1:400 000
CAPE VERDE ISLANDS 1:8 000 000
GREENLAND 154
1:10 000 000
ICELAND 155
1:2 000 000

EUROPE

EUROPE: PHYSICAL 158
1:16 000 000
EUROPE: POLITICAL 159
1:16 000 000
SCANDINAVIA 160–161
1:4 800 000
ICELAND 1:4 800 000
FÆROE ISLANDS 1:4 800 000
DENMARK AND
    SOUTHERN SWEDEN 162–163
1:2 000 000
SOUTHERN NORWAY 164
1:2 000 000
BRITISH ISLES 165
1:4 000 000
IRELAND 166
1:1 600 000
SCOTLAND 167
1:1 600 000
ENGLAND AND WALES 168–169
1:1 600 000
NETHERLANDS, BELGIUM
    AND LUXEMBOURG 170
1:2 000 000
FRANCE 171
1:4 000 000
NORTHERN FRANCE 172–173
1:2 000 000
SOUTHERN FRANCE 174–175
1:2 000 000
CENTRAL EUROPE 176–177
1:4 000 000
GERMANY AND
    SWITZERLAND 178–179
1:2 000 000
AUSTRIA, CZECHIA
    AND SLOVAKIA 180–181
1:2 000 000
HUNGARY, ROMANIA
    AND THE LOWER
    DANUBE 182–183
1:2 000 000
POLAND AND THE
    SOUTHERN BALTIC 184–185
1:2 000 000
EASTERN EUROPE 186–187
1:8 000 000
BALTIC STATES,
    BELARUS AND
    UKRAINE 188–189
1:4 000 000
THE VOLGA BASIN
    AND THE CAUCASUS 190–191
1:4 000 000
SOUTHERN EUROPE 192–193
1:8 000 000
WESTERN SPAIN AND
    PORTUGAL 194–195
1:2 000 000
EASTERN SPAIN 196–197
1:2 000 000
NORTHERN ITALY,
    SLOVENIA AND
    CROATIA 198–199
1:2 000 000
SOUTHERN ITALY 200–201
1:2 000 000
THE BALKANS 202–203
1:2 000 000
SOUTHERN GREECE AND
    WESTERN TURKEY 204–205
1:2 000 000
MEDITERRANEAN
    ISLANDS 206–207
IBIZA, MAJORCA,
    MINORCA 1:800 000
MALTA 1:400 000
CORFU 1:800 000
RHODES 1:800 000
LEVKAS, ZANTE,
    CEPHALONIA 1:800 000
CRETE 1:1 000 000
CYPRUS 1:1 000 000

ASIA

ASIA: PHYSICAL 210
1:40 000 000
ASIA: POLITICAL 211
1:40 000 000
TURKEY AND
    TRANSCAUCASIA 212–213
1:4 000 000
RUSSIA AND
    NORTHERN ASIA 214–215
1:16 000 000

CONTENTS

KAZAKHSTAN
AND CENTRAL ASIA 216–127
1:8 000 000

CHINA AND
THE FAR EAST 218–219
1:12 000 000
HONG KONG, MACAU
AND SHENZHEN 1:800 000

JAPAN 220–221
1:4 000 000
RYUKYU ISLANDS 1:4 000 000

SOUTHERN JAPAN 222–223
1:2 000 000

KOREA 224
1:3 100 000
JEJU-DO 1:3 100 000

TAIWAN 225
1:1 400 000
CHINMEN 1:1 400 000
MATSU 1:1 400 000

NORTHERN CHINA
AND KOREA 226–227
1:4 800 000

SOUTHERN CHINA
AND TAIWAN 228–229
1:4 800 000
HAINAN 1:4 800 000

SOUTH-EAST ASIA 230–231
1:10 000 000
JAVA AND MADURA 1:6 000 000
BALI 1:1 600 000

PHILIPPINES 232–233
1:3 200 000

WESTERN INDONESIA
AND MALAYSIA 234–235
1:5 600 000

MAINLAND
SOUTH-EAST ASIA 236–237
1:4 800 000
KO PHUKET 1:800 000
KO SAMUI 1:800 000
PINANG 1:800 000
SINGAPORE 1:800 000

SOUTHERN ASIA AND
THE MIDDLE EAST 238–239
1:14 000 000

AFGHANISTAN
AND PAKISTAN 240
1:5 600 000

BANGLADESH, NORTH-EASTERN
INDIA AND BURMA 241
1:4 800 000

NORTHERN INDIA,
PAKISTAN AND NEPAL 242–243
1:4 800 000
JAMMU AND KASHMIR 1:4 800 000

SOUTHERN INDIA
AND SRI LANKA 244–245
1:4 800 000
LAKSHADWEEP ISLANDS 1:4 800 000
ANDAMAN AND
NICOBAR ISLANDS 1:4 800 000

THE MIDDLE EAST 246–247
1:5 600 000

SOUTHERN ARABIAN
PENINSULA 248–249
1:5 600 000
EMIRATES OF THE
U.A.E. 1:5 600 000

EASTERN
MEDITERRANEAN 250–251
1:2 000 000

AFRICA

AFRICA: PHYSICAL 254
1:33 600 000

AFRICA: POLITICAL 255
1:33 600 000

THE NILE VALLEY 256–257
1:6 400 000
THE NILE DELTA 1:3 200 000

CENTRAL NORTH
AFRICA 258–259
1:6 400 000

NORTH-WEST AFRICA 260–261
1:6 400 000

WEST AFRICA 262–263
1:6 400 000

CENTRAL AFRICA 264–265
1:6 400 000
SÃO TOMÉ AND
PRÍNCIPE 1:6 400 000

ETHIOPIA AND THE
HORN OF AFRICA 266–267
1:6 400 000

EAST AFRICA 268–269
1:6 400 000

SOUTHERN AFRICA 270–271
1:6 400 000

MADAGASCAR 272
1:6 400 000
COMOROS 1:2 000 000
MAYOTTE 1:800 000
SEYCHELLES 1:2 000 000
RÉUNION 1:800 000
MAURITIUS 1:800 000
MALDIVES 1:6 400 000

INDIAN OCEAN 273
1:40 000 000

AUSTRALIA
AND OCEANIA

AUSTRALIA AND OCEANIA:
PHYSICAL
AND POLITICAL 276–277
1:16 000 000

WESTERN AUSTRALIA 278–279
1:6 400 000

EASTERN AUSTRALIA 280–281
1:6 400 000
WHITSUNDAY GROUP 1:2 000 000
TASMANIA 1:6 400 000
TORRES STRAIT 1:6 400 000

SOUTH-EASTERN
AUSTRALIA 282–283
1:3 200 000

NEW ZEALAND –
NORTH ISLAND 284
1:2 800 000

NEW ZEALAND –
SOUTH ISLAND 285
1:2 800 000
CHATHAM ISLANDS 1:2 800 000

PAPUA NEW GUINEA 286
1:5 200 000

ISLANDS OF THE
SOUTH-WEST PACIFIC 287
FIJI 1:4 000 000
VANUATU 1:4 000 000
SOLOMON ISLANDS 1:4 000 000
TONGA 1:4 000 000
YAP 1:830 000
CHUUK 1:830 000
SAMOAN ISLANDS 1:4 000 000

PACIFIC OCEAN 288–289
1:43 200 000
OKINAWA 1:1 550 000
IWO-JIMA 1:200 000
PALAU 1:1 550 000
NEW CALEDONIA 1:5 750 000
TAHITI 1:1 150 000
FRENCH POLYNESIA 1:26 000 000
NIUE 1:830 000
RAROTONGA 1:415 000

NORTH
AMERICA

NORTH AMERICA:
PHYSICAL 292
1:28 000 000

NORTH AMERICA:
POLITICAL 293
1:28 000 000

CANADA 294–295
1:12 000 000
NORTHERN CANADA 1:12 000 000

WESTERN CANADA 296–297
1:5 600 000

EASTERN CANADA 298–299
1:5 600 000

UNITED STATES 300–301
1:12 000 000
ALASKA 1:12 000 000
HAWAI'I 1:12 000 000

HAWAI'I AND THE
U.S. PACIFIC ISLANDS 302
1:2 500 000
HAWAIIAN ISLANDS 1:21 000 000
O'AHU 1:500 000
NORTHERN MARIANAS 1:17 500 000
WAKE ISLAND 1:200 000
MIDWAY ISLANDS 1:200 000
GUAM 1:800 000
SAIPAN AND TINIAN 1:800 000
TUTUILA 1:640 000
MANU'A ISLANDS 1:640 000

ALASKA 303
1:8 000 000

UNITED STATES – WEST 304–305
1:5 360 000

CENTRAL AND
SOUTHERN CALIFORNIA
AND WESTERN
WASHINGTON 306–307
1:2 000 000

UNITED STATES –
MIDWEST AND
NORTH-EAST 308–309
1:5 360 000

CHICAGO AND
THE MIDWEST 310–311
1:2 000 000

NORTH-EASTERN
UNITED STATES 312–313
1:2 000 000

UNITED STATES –
SOUTH 314–315
1:5 360 000

SOUTH-EASTERN
UNITED STATES 316–317
1:2 000 000

MEXICO 318–319
1:6 400 000

CENTRAL AMERICA AND
THE WEST INDIES 320–321
1:6 400 000
PUERTO RICO AND THE
VIRGIN ISLANDS 1:1 600 000
JAMAICA 1:1 600 000
PANAMA CANAL 1:800 000

LESSER ANTILLES 322–323
NORTHERN LEEWARDS 1:600 000
ANTIGUA AND BARBUDA 1:600 000
ST KITTS AND NEVIS 1:600 000
GUADELOUPE 1:600 000
ABC ISLANDS 1:600 000
MARTINIQUE 1:600 000
DOMINICA 1:600 000
ST LUCIA 1:600 000
ST VINCENT AND
THE GRENADINES 1:600 000
MONTSERRAT 1:600 000
GRENADA 1:600 000
BARBADOS 1:600 000
TRINIDAD AND TOBAGO 1:600 000

SOUTH
AMERICA

SOUTH AMERICA:
PHYSICAL 326
1:28 000 000

SOUTH AMERICA:
POLITICAL 327
1:28 000 000

SOUTH AMERICA –
NORTH-WEST 328–329
1:6 400 000
MARGARITA 1:600 000

SOUTH AMERICA –
WEST 330–331
1:6 400 000
GALAPAGOS ISLANDS 1:3 200 000
EASTER ISLAND 1:400 000
ROBINSON CRUSOE
ISLAND 1:400 000

EASTERN BRAZIL 332–333
1:6 400 000

CENTRAL
SOUTH AMERICA 334–335
1:6 400 000

SOUTHERN CHILE AND
ARGENTINA 336
1:6 400 000

GEOGRAPHICAL
GLOSSARY 337–338

INDEX TO
WORLD MAPS 339–448

WORLD STATISTICS: COUNTRIES

This alphabetical list includes the principal countries and territories of the world. If a territory is not completely independent, the country it is associated with is named. The area figures give the total area of land, inland water, and ice. The population figures are 2016 estimates where available. The annual income is the Gross Domestic Product per capita (PPP) in US dollars; the figures are the latest available, usually 2016 estimates.

Country/Territory	Area km² Thousands	Area miles² Thousands	Population Thousands	Capital	Annual Income US $
Afghanistan	652	252	33,332	Kabul	2,000
Albania	28.7	11.1	3,039	Tirana	11,900
Algeria	2,382	920	40,264	Algiers	15,000
American Samoa (US)	0.20	0.08	54	Pago Pago	13,000
Andorra	0.47	0.18	86	Andorra La Vella	37,200
Angola	1,247	481	20,172	Luanda	6,800
Anguilla (UK)	0.10	0.04	16	The Valley	12,200
Antigua & Barbuda	0.44	0.17	94	St John's	24,100
Argentina	2,780	1,074	43,887	Buenos Aires	20,200
Armenia	29.8	11.5	3,051	Yerevan	8,900
Aruba (Netherlands)	0.19	0.07	114	Oranjestad	25,300
Australia	7,741	2,989	22,993	Canberra	48,000
Austria	83.9	32.4	8,712	Vienna	47,900
Azerbaijan	86.6	33.4	9,873	Baku	17,700
Azores (Portugal)	2.2	0.86	246	Ponta Delgada	15,197
Bahamas	13.9	5.4	327	Nassau	24,600
Bahrain	0.69	0.27	1,379	Manama	50,300
Bangladesh	144	55.6	156,187	Dhaka	3,900
Barbados	0.43	0.17	291	Bridgetown	17,200
Belarus	208	80.2	9,570	Minsk	17,500
Belgium	30.5	11.8	11,409	Brussels	44,900
Belize	23.0	8.9	354	Belmopan	8,200
Benin	113	43.5	10,741	Porto-Novo	2,200
Bermuda (UK)	0.05	0.02	71	Hamilton	85,700
Bhutan	47.0	18.1	750	Thimphu	8,100
Bolivia	1,099	424	10,970	La Paz/Sucre	7,200
Bosnia-Herzegovina	51.2	19.8	3,862	Sarajevo	11,000
Botswana	582	225	2,209	Gaborone	16,900
Brazil	8,514	3,287	205,824	Brasília	15,200
Brunei	5.8	2.2	437	Bandar Seri Begawan	79,700
Bulgaria	111	42.8	7,145	Sofia	20,100
Burkina Faso	274	106	19,513	Ouagadougou	1,800
Burma (Myanmar)	677	261	56,890	Yangon/Naypyidaw	6,000
Burundi	27.8	10.7	11,099	Bujumbura	800
Cabo Verde	4.0	1.6	553	Praia	6,700
Cambodia	181	69.9	15,957	Phnom Penh	3,700
Cameroon	475	184	24,361	Yaoundé	3,300
Canada	9,971	3,850	35,363	Ottawa	46,200
Canary Is. (Spain)	7.2	2.8	2,105	Las Palmas/Santa Cruz	19,900
Cayman Is. (UK)	0.26	0.10	57	George Town	43,800
Central African Republic	623	241	5,507	Bangui	700
Chad	1,284	496	11,852	Ndjaména	2,600
Chile	757	292	17,650	Santiago	24,000
China	9,597	3,705	1,373,541	Beijing	15,400
Colombia	1,139	440	47,221	Bogotá	14,200
Comoros	2.2	0.86	795	Moroni	1,500
Congo	342	132	4,852	Brazzaville	6,800
Congo (Dem. Rep. of the)	2,345	905	81,331	Kinshasa	800
Cook Is. (NZ)	0.24	0.09	10	Avarua	12,300
Costa Rica	51.1	19.7	4,873	San José	16,100
Croatia	56.5	21.8	4,314	Zagreb	22,400
Cuba	111	42.8	11,180	Havana	11,600
Curaçao (Netherlands)	0.44	0.17	149	Willemstad	15,000
Cyprus	9.3	3.6	1,206	Nicosia	34,400
Czechia	78.9	30.5	10,645	Prague	33,200
Denmark	43.1	16.6	5,594	Copenhagen	46,600
Djibouti	23.2	9.0	847	Djibouti	3,400
Dominica	0.75	0.29	74	Roseau	11,400
Dominican Republic	48.5	18.7	10,607	Santo Domingo	15,900
East Timor	14.9	5.7	1,261	Dili	4,200
Ecuador	284	109	16,081	Quito	11,000
Egypt	1,001	387	94,667	Cairo	12,100
El Salvador	21.0	8.1	6,157	San Salvador	8,900
Equatorial Guinea	28.1	10.8	749	Malabo	38,700
Eritrea	118	45.4	5,870	Asmara	1,300
Estonia	45.1	17.4	1,259	Tallinn	29,500
Ethiopia	1,104	426	102,374	Addis Ababa	1,900
Falkland Is. (UK)	12.2	4.7	3	Stanley	55,400
Faroe Is. (Denmark)	1.4	0.54	50	Tórshavn	36,600
Fiji	18.3	7.1	915	Suva	9,400
Finland	338	131	5,498	Helsinki	41,800
France	552	213	66,836	Paris	42,400
French Guiana (France)	90.0	34.7	250	Cayenne	8,300
French Polynesia (France)	4.0	1.5	285	Papeete	26,100
Gabon	268	103	1,739	Libreville	19,300
Gambia, The	11.3	4.4	2,010	Banjul	1,700
Georgia	69.7	26.9	4,928	Tbilisi	10,100
Germany	357	138	80,723	Berlin	48,200
Ghana	239	92.1	26,908	Accra	4,400
Gibraltar (UK)	0.006	0.002	29	Gibraltar Town	43,000
Greece	132	50.9	10,773	Athens	26,800
Greenland (Denmark)	2,176	840	58	Nuuk	37,900
Grenada	0.34	0.13	111	St George's	14,100
Guadeloupe (France)	1.7	0.66	402	Basse-Terre	7,900
Guam (US)	0.55	0.21	163	Agana	30,500
Guatemala	109	42.0	15,190	Guatemala City	7,900
Guinea	246	94.9	12,093	Conakry	1,300
Guinea-Bissau	36.1	13.9	1,759	Bissau	1,600
Guyana	215	83.0	736	Georgetown	7,900
Haiti	27.8	10.7	10,486	Port-au-Prince	1,800
Honduras	112	43.3	8,893	Tegucigalpa	5,300
Hungary	93.0	35.9	9,875	Budapest	27,200
Iceland	103	39.8	336	Reykjavik	48,100
India	3,287	1,269	1,266,884	New Delhi	6,700
Indonesia	1,905	735	258,316	Jakarta	11,700
Iran	1,648	636	82,802	Tehran	18,100
Iraq	438	169	38,146	Baghdad	16,500
Ireland	70.3	27.1	4,952	Dublin	69,400
Israel	20.6	8.0	8,175	Jerusalem	34,800
Italy	301	116	62,008	Rome	36,300
Ivory Coast (Côte d'Ivoire)	322	125	23,740	Yamoussoukro	3,600
Jamaica	11.0	4.2	2,970	Kingston	9,000
Japan	378	146	126,702	Tokyo	38,900
Jordan	89.3	34.5	8,185	Amman	11,100
Kazakhstan	2,725	1,052	18,360	Astana	25,700
Kenya	580	224	46,791	Nairobi	3,400
Kiribati	0.73	0.28	107	Tarawa	1,800
Korea, North	121	46.5	25,115	Pyo'ngyang	1,800
Korea, South	99.3	38.3	50,924	Seoul	37,900
Kosovo	10.9	4.2	1,883	Pristina	10,000
Kuwait	17.8	6.9	2,833	Kuwait City	71,300
Kyrgyzstan	200	77.2	5,728	Bishkek	3,500
Laos	237	91.4	7,019	Vientiane	5,700
Latvia	64.6	24.9	1,966	Riga	25,700
Lebanon	10.4	4.0	6,238	Beirut	18,500
Lesotho	30.4	11.7	1,953	Maseru	3,100
Liberia	111	43.0	4,300	Monrovia	900
Libya	1,760	679	6,542	Tripoli	14,200
Liechtenstein	0.16	0.06	38	Vaduz	89,400
Lithuania	65.2	25.2	2,854	Vilnius	29,900
Luxembourg	2.6	1.0	582	Luxembourg	102,000
Macedonia (FYROM)	25.7	9.9	2,100	Skopje	14,500
Madagascar	587	227	24,430	Antananarivo	1,500
Madeira (Portugal)	0.78	0.30	289	Funchal	25,800
Malawi	118	45.7	18,570	Lilongwe	1,100
Malaysia	330	127	30,950	Kuala Lumpur/Putrajaya	27,200
Maldives	0.30	0.12	393	Malé	15,300
Mali	1,240	479	17,467	Bamako	2,300
Malta	0.32	0.12	415	Valletta	37,900
Marshall Is.	0.18	0.07	73	Majuro	3,300
Martinique (France)	1.1	0.43	386	Fort-de-France	14,400
Mauritania	1,026	396	3,677	Nouakchott	4,400
Mauritius	2.0	0.79	1,348	Port Louis	20,500
Mayotte (France)	0.37	0.14	213	Mamoudzou	4,900
Mexico	1,958	756	123,167	Mexico City	18,900
Micronesia, Fed. States of	0.70	0.27	105	Palikir	3,000
Moldova	33.9	13.1	3,510	Kishinev	5,200
Monaco	0.002	0.0008	31	Monaco	78,700
Mongolia	1,567	605	3,031	Ulan Bator	12,200
Montenegro	14.0	5.4	645	Podgorica	17,000
Montserrat (UK)	0.10	0.39	5	Brades	8,500
Morocco	447	172	33,656	Rabat	8,400
Mozambique	802	309	25,930	Maputo	1,200
Namibia	824	318	2,436	Windhoek	11,800
Nauru	0.02	0.008	10	Yaren	14,800
Nepal	147	56.8	29,034	Katmandu	2,500
Netherlands	41.5	16.0	17,017	Amsterdam/The Hague	50,800
New Caledonia (France)	18.6	7.2	275	Nouméa	38,800
New Zealand	271	104	4,475	Wellington	37,100
Nicaragua	130	50.2	5,967	Managua	5,300
Niger	1,267	489	18,639	Niamey	1,100
Nigeria	924	357	186,053	Abuja	5,900
Northern Mariana Is. (US)	0.46	0.18	53	Saipan	13,300
Norway	324	125	5,265	Oslo	69,300
Oman	310	119	3,355	Muscat	43,700
Pakistan	796	307	201,996	Islamabad	5,100
Palau	0.46	0.18	21	Melekeok	15,300
Panama	75.5	29.2	3,705	Panamá	22,800
Papua New Guinea	463	179	6,791	Port Moresby	3,500
Paraguay	407	157	6,863	Asunción	9,400
Peru	1,285	496	30,741	Lima	13,000
Philippines	300	116	102,624	Manila	7,700
Poland	323	125	38,523	Warsaw	27,700
Portugal	88.8	34.3	10,834	Lisbon	28,500
Puerto Rico (US)	8.9	3.4	3,578	San Juan	37,700
Qatar	11.0	4.2	2,258	Doha	129,700
Réunion (France)	2.5	0.97	845	St-Denis	6,200
Romania	238	92.0	21,600	Bucharest	22,300
Russia	17,075	6,593	142,355	Moscow	26,100
Rwanda	26.3	10.2	12,988	Kigali	1,900
St Kitts & Nevis	0.26	0.10	52	Basseterre	25,500
St Lucia	0.54	0.21	164	Castries	12,000
St Vincent & Grenadines	0.39	0.15	102	Kingstown	11,300
Samoa	2.8	1.1	199	Apia	5,400
San Marino	0.06	0.02	33	San Marino	65,300
São Tomé & Príncipe	0.96	0.37	198	São Tomé	3,300
Saudi Arabia	2,150	830	28,160	Riyadh	54,100
Senegal	197	76.0	14,320	Dakar	2,600
Serbia	77.5	29.9	7,144	Belgrade	14,200
Seychelles	0.46	0.18	93	Victoria	28,000
Sierra Leone	71.7	27.7	6,019	Freetown	1,700
Singapore	0.68	0.26	5,782	Singapore City	87,100
Slovakia	49.0	18.9	5,446	Bratislava	31,200
Slovenia	20.3	7.8	1,978	Ljubljana	32,000
Solomon Is.	28.9	11.2	635	Honiara	2,000
Somalia	638	246	10,817	Mogadishu	400
South Africa	1,221	471	54,301	Cape Town/Pretoria	13,200
Spain	498	192	48,563	Madrid	36,500
Sri Lanka	65.6	25.3	22,235	Colombo	11,200
Sudan	1,886	728	36,730	Khartoum	4,500
Sudan, South	620	239	12,531	Juba	1,700
Suriname	163	63.0	586	Paramaribo	15,200
Swaziland	17.4	6.7	1,451	Mbabane	9,800
Sweden	450	174	9,881	Stockholm	49,700
Switzerland	41.3	15.9	8,179	Bern	59,400
Syria	185	71.5	17,185	Damascus	2,900
Taiwan	36.0	13.9	23,465	Taipei	47,800
Tajikistan	143	55.3	8,331	Dushanbe	3,000
Tanzania	945	365	52,483	Dodoma	3,100
Thailand	513	198	68,201	Bangkok	16,800
Togo	56.8	21.9	7,757	Lomé	1,500
Tonga	0.65	0.25	107	Nuku'alofa	5,300
Trinidad & Tobago	5.1	2.0	1,220	Port of Spain	31,900
Tunisia	164	63.2	11,135	Tunis	11,700
Turkey	775	299	80,275	Ankara	21,100
Turkmenistan	488	188	5,291	Ashkhabad	17,300
Turks & Caicos Is. (UK)	0.43	0.17	51	Cockburn Town	29,100
Tuvalu	0.03	0.01	11	Fongafale	3,500
Uganda	241	93.1	38,319	Kampala	2,100
Ukraine	604	233	44,210	Kiev	8,200
United Arab Emirates	83.6	32.3	5,927	Abu Dhabi	67,700
United Kingdom	242	93.4	64,430	London	42,500
United States of America	9,629	3,718	323,996	Washington, DC	57,300
Uruguay	175	67.6	3,351	Montevideo	21,600
Uzbekistan	447	173	29,474	Tashkent	6,500
Vanuatu	12.2	4.7	278	Port-Vila	2,600
Vatican City	0.0004	0.0002	1	Vatican City	
Venezuela	912	352	30,912	Caracas	15,100
Vietnam	332	128	95,261	Hanoi	6,400
Virgin Is. (UK)	0.15	0.06	28	Road Town	42,300
Virgin Is. (US)	0.35	0.13	103	Charlotte Amalie	36,100
Yemen	528	204	27,393	Sana'	2,500
Zambia	753	291	15,511	Lusaka	3,900
Zimbabwe	391	151	14,547	Harare	2,000

This list shows the principal cities with more than 900,000 inhabitants. The figures are taken from the most recent census or estimate available and as far as possible are the population of the metropolitan area or urban agglomeration. The list includes Metropolitan Statistical Areas from the United States Census Bureau. All the figures are in thousands. Local name forms have been used for the smaller cities (for example, Antwerpen).

AFGHANISTAN
Kabul 4,842
ALGERIA
Algiers 2,632
ANGOLA
Luanda 5,737
Huambo 1,337
ARGENTINA
Buenos Aires 16,000
Córdoba 1,519
Rosario 1,395
Mendoza 1,020
San Miguel de Tucumán 922
ARMENIA
Yerevan 1,040
AUSTRALIA
Sydney 4,540
Melbourne 4,258
Brisbane 2,238
Perth 1,896
Adelaide 1,265
AUSTRIA
Vienna 1,763
AZERBAIJAN
Baku 2,429
BANGLADESH
Dhaka 17,900
Chittagong 4,640
Khulna 1,013
BELARUS
Minsk 1,925
BELGIUM
Brussels 2,061
Antwerpen 998
BOLIVIA
Santa Cruz 2,181
La Paz 1,834
Cochabamba 1,273
BRAZIL
São Paulo 21,900
Rio de Janeiro 12,700
Belo Horizonte 5,766
Brasília 4,235
Fortaleza 3,944
Recife 3,767
Salvador 3,623
Pôrto Alegre 3,621
Curitiba 3,537
Campinas 3,091
Goiânia 2,327
Belém 2,209
Manaus 2,069
Vitória 1,655
São Luís 1,460
Maceió 1,286
Joinville 1,237
Florianópolis 1,212
Natal 1,186
Santos 1,151
João Pessoa 1,109
Teresina 969
BULGARIA
Sofia 1,230
BURKINA FASO
Ouagadougou 2,923
BURMA (MYANMAR)
Rangoon 4,904
Mandalay 1,196
Naypyidaw 1,045
CAMBODIA
Phnom Penh 1,779
CAMEROON
Yaoundé 3,204
Douala 3,051
CANADA
Toronto 6,083
Montréal 4,014
Vancouver 2,523
Calgary 1,365
Ottawa 1,346
Edmonton 1,298
CHAD
Ndjamena 1,310
CHILE
Santiago 6,544
Valparaiso 913
CHINA
Shanghai 24,484
Beijing 21,240
Chongqing 13,744
Guangzhou, Guangdong 13,070
Tianjin 11,558
Shenzhen 10,828
Wuhan 7,979
Chengdu 7,820
Nanjing, Jiangsu 7,609
Dongguan, Guangdong 7,469
Hong Kong 7,365
Foshan 7,089
Hangzhou 6,658
Shenyang 6,438
Xi'an, Shaanxi 6,220
Suzhou, Jiangsu 5,788
Harbin 5,565
Xiamen 4,738
Qingdao 4,686
Dalian 4,612
Zhengzhou 4,539
Jinan, Shandong 4,138
Shantou 4,011
Zhongshan 3,908
Changsha 3,882
Kunming 3,860
Changchun 3,835
Ürümqi 3,639
Taiyuan, Shanxi 3,549
Hefei 3,398
Fuzhou, Fujian 3,380
Shijiazhuang 3,370
Nanning 3,358
Wenzhou 3,319
Ningbo 3,250
Wuxi, Jiangsu 3,109
Guiyang 2,944
Tangshan 2,853
Lanzhou 2,782
Changzhou, Jiangsu 2,653
Nanchang 2,590
Zibo 2,465
Huizhou 2,425
Weifang 2,269
Yantai 2,182
Shaoxing 2,151
Huai'an 2,108
Luoyang 2,076
Nantong 2,058
Baotou 1,996
Haikou 1,988
Xuzhou 1,956
Hohhot 1,846
Yangzhou 1,803
Linyi 1,744
Handan 1,703
Yinchuan 1,698
Taizhou, Zhejiang 1,695
Liuzhou 1,663
Daqing 1,661
Jiangmen 1,591
Zhuhai 1,578
Anshan 1,570
Datong 1,567
Xiangyang 1,554
Jilin 1,534
Putian 1,512
Yancheng 1,502
Qiqihar 1,469
Quanzhou 1,447
Jining, Shandong 1,403
Xining 1,359
Cixi 1,356
Chaozhou 1,349
Huainan 1,346
Hengyang 1,341
Fushun 1,295
Tai'an 1,239
Taizhou, Jiangsu 1,211
Anyang 1,191
Zhanjiang 1,172
Lianyungang 1,143
Qinhuangdao 1,139
Yiwu 1,124
Baoding 1,120
Suqian 1,111
Zhuzhou 1,100
Rizhao 1,096
Benxi 1,085
Mianyang 1,085
Nanchong 1,084
Zhenjiang 1,070
Yingkou 1,057
Guilin 1,056
Jinzhou 1,053
Chifeng 1,043
Zaozhuang 1,038
Nanyang 1,035
Xiangtan 1,032
Puning 1,032
Jinhua 1,030
Baoji 1,028
Pingdingshan 1,022
Jiaxing 1,016
Huaibei 1,007
Xinxiang 1,006
Ruian 1,005
Zhangjiakou 996
Tengzhou 995
Dongying 992
Jingzhou 976
Yueyang 969
Suzhou 968
Jieyang 947
Liuan 929
Fuyang 916
Wenling 901
Yueqing 901
Jixi 900
COLOMBIA
Bogotá 9,968
Medellín 3,972
Cali 2,682
Barranquilla 2,009
Bucaramanga 1,235
Cartagena 1,113
CONGO
Brazzaville 1,949
Pointe-Noire 999
CONGO (DEM. REP. OF THE)
Kinshasa 12,071
Lubumbashi 2,097
Mbuji-Mayi 2,097
Kananga 1,219
Kisangani 1,079
COSTA RICA
San José 1,183
CUBA
Havana 2,129
CZECHIA
Prague 1,324
DENMARK
Copenhagen 1,281
DOMINICAN REPUBLIC
Santo Domingo 3,020
ECUADOR
Guayaquil 2,756
Quito 1,754
EGYPT
Cairo 17,100
Alexandria 4,863
EL SALVADOR
San Salvador 1,102
ETHIOPIA
Addis Ababa 3,316
FINLAND
Helsinki 1,190
FRANCE
Paris 11,300
Lyon 1,622
Marseilles 1,616
Lille 1,030
Nice 973
Toulouse 950
Bordeaux 901
GEORGIA
Tbilisi 1,145
GERMANY
Berlin 3,578
Hamburg 1,839
Munich 1,454
Cologne 1,042
GHANA
Kumasi 2,718
Accra 2,316
GREECE
Athens 3,046
GUATEMALA
Guatemala City 2,994
GUINEA
Conakry 1,989
HAITI
Port-au-Prince 2,507
HONDURAS
Tegucigalpa 1,146
HUNGARY
Budapest 1,712
INDIA
Delhi 27,200
Mumbai 23,600
Kolkata 16,200
Bengaluru 10,800
Chennai 10,300
Hyderabad 9,218
Ahmedabad 7,571
Surat 5,902
Pune 5,882
Jaipur 3,549
Lucknow 3,295
Kanpur 3,044
Nagpur 2,715
Coimbatore 2,641
Calicut 2,582
Indore 2,503
Kochi 2,484
Thrissur 2,443
Malappuram 2,342
Kannur 2,278
Patna 2,247
Bhopal 2,151
Thiruvananthapuram 2,029
Agra 2,017
Vadodara 2,011
Vishakhapatnam 1,982
Nashik 1,829
Vijayawada 1,822
Ludhiana 1,739
Rajkot 1,647
Madurai 1,623
Meerut 1,579
Varanasi 1,566
Kollam 1,482
Jamshedpur 1,477
Srinagar 1,464
Raipur 1,433
Aurangabad 1,380
Jabalpur 1,352
Asansol 1,330
Jodhpur 1,318
Allahabad 1,313
Tiruppur 1,295
Ranchi 1,293
Amritsar 1,283
Dhanbad 1,269
Gwalior 1,248
Kota 1,200
Chandigarh 1,159
Bhilainagar-Durg 1,144
Bareilly 1,141
Tiruchchirapalli 1,125
Mysore 1,105
Aligarh 1,067
Guwahati 1,059
Moradabad 1,054
Hubli-Dharwad 1,037
Bhubaneswar 1,026
Salem 1,022
Solapur 994
Jalandhar 973
INDONESIA
Jakarta 10,483
Surabaya 2,878
Bandung 2,578
Medan 2,230
Semarang 1,648
Makassar 1,522
Batam 1,498
Palembang 1,460
Denpasar 1,177
Pekanbaru 1,168
Bogor 1,102
Bandar Lampung 984
Padang 919
IRAN
Tehran 8,516
Mashhad 3,088
Esfahan 1,915
Karaj 1,861
Shiraz 1,716
Tabriz 1,594
Ahvaz 1,245
Qom 1,234
Kermanshah 909
IRAQ
Baghdad 6,811
Mosul 1,749
Arbil 1,200
Basra 1,041
As Sulaymaniyah 1,041
Najaf 919
IRELAND
Dublin 1,185
ISRAEL
Tel Aviv-Yafo 3,661
Haifa 1,105
ITALY
Rome 3,738
Milan 3,104
Naples 2,198
Turin 1,769
IVORY COAST (CÔTE D'IVOIRE)
Abidjan 5,020
JAPAN
Tokyo–Yokohama 39,800
Osaka–Kobe 17,800
Nagoya 10,500
Fukuoka–Kitakyushu 5,494
Shizuoka–Hamamatsu 3,493
Sapporo 2,564
Hiroshima 2,180
Sendai 2,071
Kyoto 1,474
JORDAN
Amman 1,159
KAZAKHSTAN
Almaty 1,535
KENYA
Nairobi 4,070
Mombasa 1,141
KOREA, NORTH
Pyongyang 2,872
KOREA, SOUTH
Seoul 9,779
Busan 3,200
Incheon 2,711
Daegu 2,241
Daejeon 1,578
Gwangju 1,550
Suwon 1,106
Yongin 1,090
Changwon 1,036
Seognam 973
Goyang 951
Ulsan 907
KUWAIT
Kuwait City 2,874
LAOS
Vientiane 1,050
LEBANON
Beirut 2,263
LIBERIA
Monrovia 1,305
LIBYA
Tripoli 1,128
MADAGASCAR
Antananarivo 2,739
MALAWI
Lilongwe 945
MALAYSIA
Kuala Lumpur 7,047
Johor Bahru 933
MALI
Bamako 2,651
MAURITANIA
Nouakchott 990
MEXICO
Mexico City 22,300
Guadalajara 4,920
Monterrey 4,589
Puebla 3,032
Toluca 2,207
Tijuana 2,032
León 1,845
Ciudad Juárez 1,401
Torreón 1,354
Querétaro 1,300
San Luis Potosí 1,168
Mérida 1,086
Mexicali 1,053
Aguascalientes 1,050
Cuernavaca 1,006
Chihuahua 957
Saltillo 953
Tampico 932
Morelia 931
Acapulco 907
MONGOLIA
Ulan Bator 1,421
MOROCCO
Casablanca 3,544
Rabat 2,004
Fès 1,197
Marrakesh 1,168
Tangier 1,016
MOZAMBIQUE
Maputo 1,203
Matolo 977
NEPAL
Katmandu 1,224
NETHERLANDS
Amsterdam 1,099
Rotterdam 994
NEW ZEALAND
Auckland 1,360
NICARAGUA
Managua 963
NIGER
Niamey 1,125
NIGERIA
Lagos 13,661
Kano 3,676
Ibadan 3,243
Abuja 2,586
Port Harcourt 2,465
Benin City 1,543
Onitsha 1,165
Kaduna 1,064
Aba 972
NORWAY
Oslo 1,002
PAKISTAN
Karachi 17,121
Lahore 8,990
Faisalabad 3,677
Rawalpindi 2,582
Gujranwala 2,193
Multan 1,969
Hyderabad 1,812
Peshawar 1,787
Islamabad 1,433
Quetta 1,148
Bahawalpur 952
PANAMA
Panamá 1,708
PARAGUAY
Asunción 2,406
PERU
Lima 10,072
PHILIPPINES
Manila 24,100
Davao 1,662
Cebu 965
Zamboanga 959
POLAND
Warsaw 1,727
PORTUGAL
Lisbon 2,902
Porto 1,304
PUERTO RICO
San Juan 2,158
ROMANIA
Bucharest 1,865
RUSSIA
Moscow 12,260
St Petersburg 5,001
Novosibirsk 1,498
Yekaterinburg 1,381
Nizhniy Novgorod 1,200
Samara 1,162
Kazan 1,163
Omsk 1,161
Chelyabinsk 1,160
Rostov 1,095
Ufa 1,069
Volgograd 1,020
Krasnoyarsk 1,013
Perm 978
Voronezh 913
RWANDA
Kigali 1,293
SAUDI ARABIA
Riyadh 6,540
Jedda 4,161
Mecca 1,799
Medina 1,303
Dammam 1,085
SENEGAL
Dakar 3,653
SERBIA
Belgrade 1,183
SIERRA LEONE
Freetown 1,029
SINGAPORE
Singapore City 5,717
SOMALIA
Mogadishu 2,265
SOUTH AFRICA
Johannesburg 9,616
Cape Town 3,698
Durban 2,914
Pretoria 2,125
Port Elizabeth 1,186
Vereeniging 1,164
SPAIN
Madrid 6,264
Barcelona 5,309
SUDAN
Khartoum 5,265
SWEDEN
Stockholm 1,507
SWITZERLAND
Zürich 1,259
SYRIA
Aleppo 3,641
Damascus 2,586
Homs 1,695
Hamah 1,297
TAIWAN
Taipei 2,669
Kaohsiung 1,525
T'aichung 1,241
TANZANIA
Dar es Salaam 5,409
THAILAND
Bangkok 9,444
Samut Prakan 1,980
TOGO
Lomé 985
TUNISIA
Tunis 2,010
TURKEY
Istanbul 14,600
Ankara 4,852
Izmir 3,090
Bursa 1,974
Adana 1,879
Gaziantep 1,528
Konya 1,226
Antalya 1,100
Diyarbakir 938
Kayseri 919
UGANDA
Kampala 2,012
UKRAINE
Kiev 2,966
Kharkov 1,438
Odessa 1,011
Dnepropetrovsk 947
Donetsk 928
UNITED ARAB EMIRATES
Dubai 2,504
Sharjah 1,332
Abu Dhabi 1,179
UNITED KINGDOM
London 10,434
Manchester 2,668
Birmingham 2,533
Glasgow 1,227
UNITED STATES OF AMERICA
New York 22,200
Los Angeles 13,262
Chicago 9,800
Dallas–Fort Worth 6,954
Houston 6,490
Philadelphia 6,051
Washington, DC 6,034
Miami 5,930
Atlanta 5,614
Boston 4,732
San Francisco 4,594
Phoenix–Mesa 4,489
Riverside–San Bernardino 4,442
Detroit 4,297
Seattle 3,671
Minneapolis–St Paul 3,495
San Diego 3,263
Tampa–St Petersburg 2,916
St Louis 2,806
Baltimore 2,786
Denver 2,754
Charlotte 2,380
Pittsburgh 2,356
Portland 2,348
San Antonio 2,329
Orlando 2,321
Sacramento 2,244
Cincinnati 2,149
Kansas City 2,071
Las Vegas 2,070
Cleveland 2,064
Columbus 1,995
Indianapolis 1,971
San Jose 1,953
Austin 1,943
Nashville 1,793
Virginia Beach–Norfolk 1,717
Providence 1,609
Milwaukee 1,572
Jacksonville 1,419
Memphis 1,343
Oklahoma 1,337
Louisville 1,270
Richmond 1,260
New Orleans 1,252
Raleigh 1,243
Hartford 1,214
Salt Lake City 1,153
Birmingham 1,144
Buffalo 1,136
Rochester 1,083
Grand Rapids 1,028
Tucson 1,005
Honolulu 992
Tulsa 969
Fresno 966
Worcester 930
Albuquerque 905
Omaha 904
URUGUAY
Montevideo 1,716
UZBEKISTAN
Tashkent 2,264
VENEZUELA
Caracas 2,923
Maracaibo 2,229
Valencia 1,757
Maracay 1,186
Barquisimeto 1,044
VIETNAM
Ho Chi Minh City 7,498
Hanoi 3,790
Can Tho 1,242
Haiphong 1,110
Da Nang 979
YEMEN
Sana' 3,094
Aden 910
ZAMBIA
Lusaka 2,285
ZIMBABWE
Harare 1,511

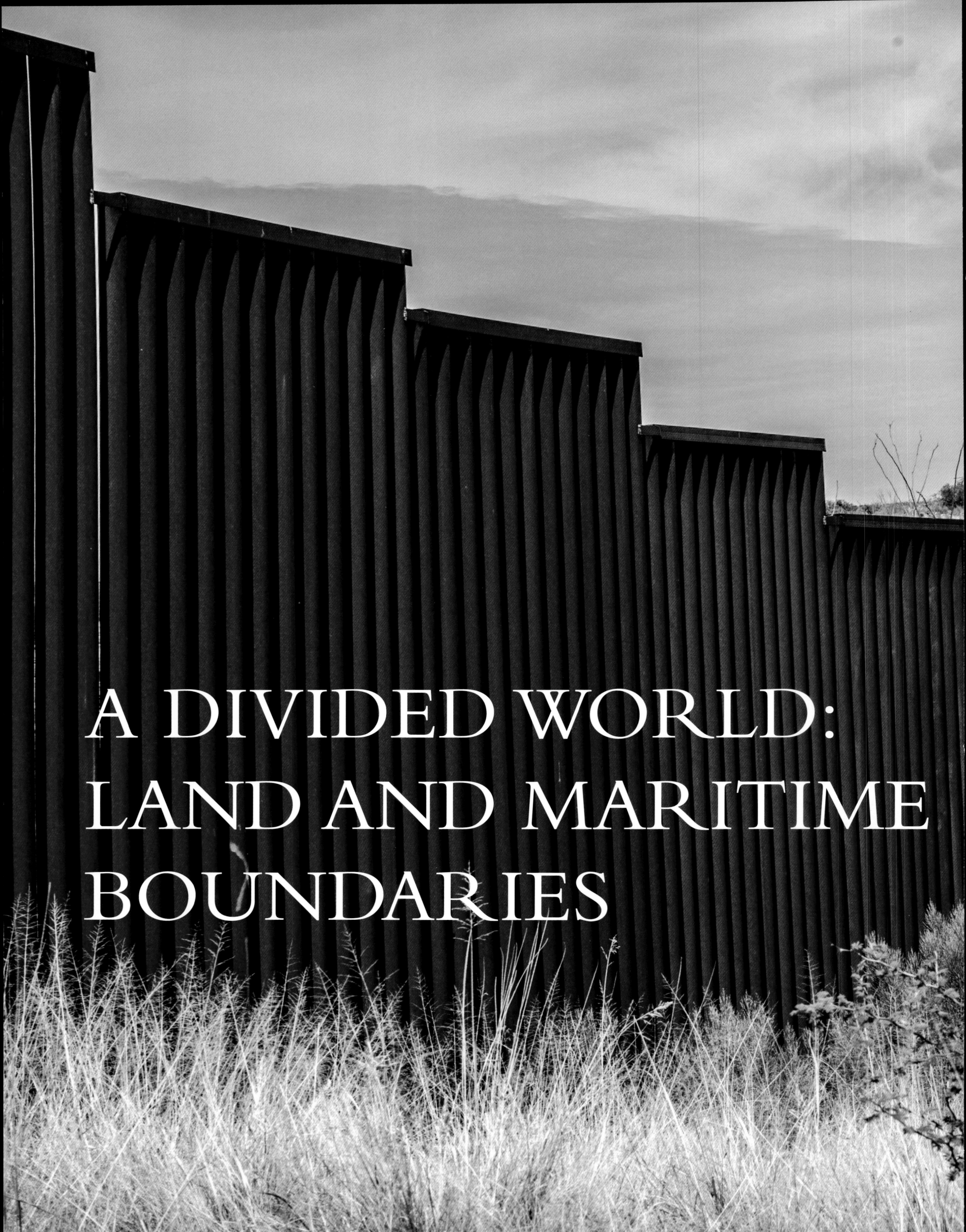

A DIVIDED WORLD: LAND AND MARITIME BOUNDARIES

"Good fences make good neighbors." Many people, in many languages, have expressed this sentiment as they contemplate their neighbors across a boundary line. The established political map of the world in the 21st century shows a mosaic of political units that fit together with no space unoccupied. The defined areas of nation states create boundaries that can be a focus for either cooperation or conflict. In areas where conflict is in the past and people on both sides of the fence can benefit from the free flow of goods and people, a boundary marker may be no more than a ceremonial sign. In more contentious areas, where it is seen necessary to control movement, formidable and physical barriers may be erected. The fence shown in this image marks the division between the United States and Mexico.

For more information:

148 World Political Map

151 Antarctica

In order to establish order, and impose control over territory, humans have long wanted to divide land and sea into areas that are exclusively owned and ruled – that are "sovereign." The great, early empires exerted their control through conquest, and later by imposing their form of civilization over a territory. In the era of European exploration, colonies were established on the coasts of the southern continents and, from these trading posts, influence was extended inland. Boundaries were often ill-defined and large areas of land were beyond the effective control of colonial outposts.

It was from the 17th century that the concept of sovereignty and territory became linked. From this concept evolved the notion of nation-states being the

building blocks of the world political map as we now see it. However, even in the 21st century, we know not to look at a map of the world with political boundaries and think that it is static and unchanging.

The majority of boundaries in Africa were imposed by European powers (see feature below). Boundaries were often drawn with scant regard for the needs of the indigenous population. The 20th century saw many new states emerging after World War I with the breakup of the Ottoman and Austro-Hungarian empires. This creation of new, and smaller, states continued into the 1980s and 1990s with the fragmentation of Yugoslavia, followed by the breakup of the USSR. Since the year 2000, five new countries have gained independence (East Timor, Montenegro,

Serbia, Kosovo, and South Sudan).

Boundaries can change, sometimes gradually, and peacefully, by agreement; sometimes cataclysmically through war or invasion. The purpose and function of boundaries also varies. Boundaries can be used to control immigration, and to mark divisions between religions, language, and culture. Very "closed" boundaries, such as that between North Korea and its neighbors, severely restrict the movement of people and goods. The more open boundaries between many countries in the European Union promote freer movement. Looking beyond the confines of single nation-states, some countries are willing to surrender a degree of individual sovereignty in exchange for greater collective economic or military power.

BREAKDOWN OF EMPIRES SINCE 1945

In 1939, large areas of the world were still under colonial rule, although in India and Africa especially, the colonial powers depended on indigenous political rulers to administer at the local level. Immediately after the end of World War I, the League of Nations had established mandates. Countries that were victorious in the war, such as Great Britain and France, undertook to administer regions that had previously been colonies of Germany or of the Ottoman Empire. Eventual independence was the goal. Japan was the only country to expand its empire during the inter-war period.

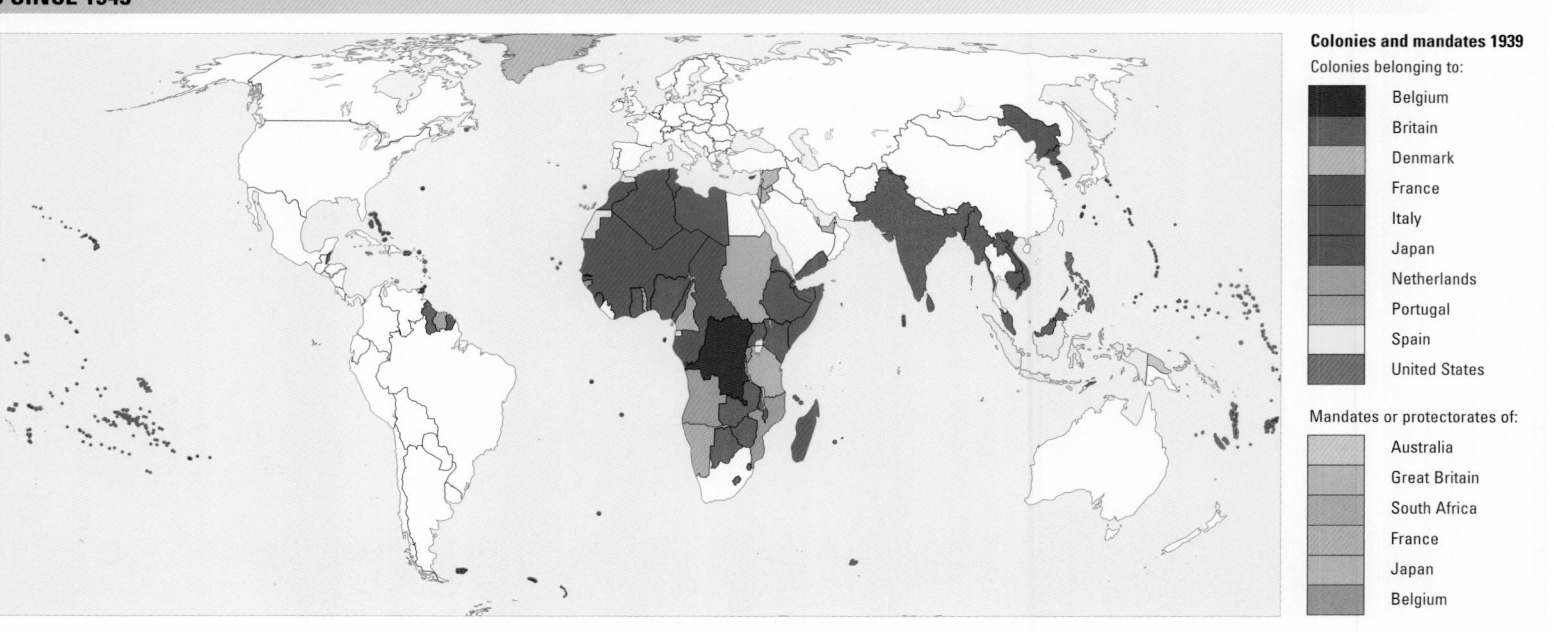

Colonies and mandates 1939

Colonies belonging to:
- Belgium
- Britain
- Denmark
- France
- Italy
- Japan
- Netherlands
- Portugal
- Spain
- United States

Mandates or protectorates of:
- Australia
- Great Britain
- South Africa
- France
- Japan
- Belgium

INDEPENDENT AFRICA

Africa is where the profound effects that boundaries can have on people, society, and economic development are most evident. It retains the legacy of its colonial past: over 80% of its boundaries were created by European powers. First came contact through trade along the coasts followed, in the mid-19th century, by exploration of the interior. The often-forceful acquisition of territory by European colonizers was based

on establishing trade links to exploit natural resources. From the early coastal settlements, spheres of influence were established. The independence granted to India, and other countries in Asia, in the 1940s, encouraged African nationalists to press for similar political freedoms in their own continent. Gradually, throughout the 20th century, states gained independence from their former colonial powers.

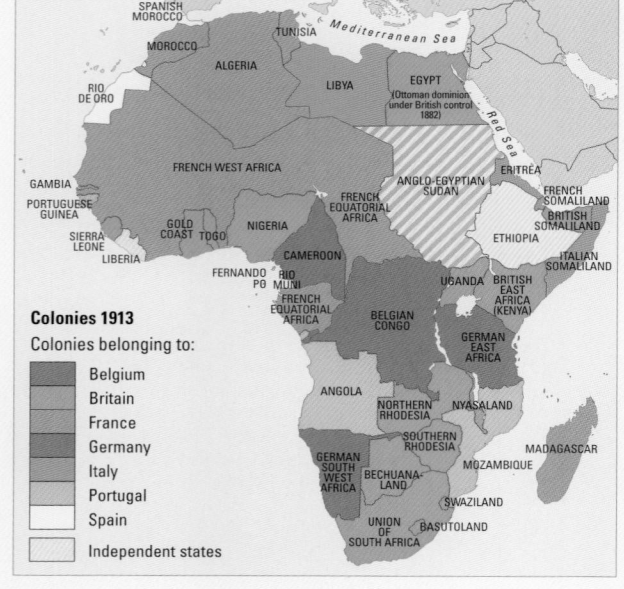

Colonies 1913

Colonies belonging to:
- Belgium
- Britain
- France
- Germany
- Italy
- Portugal
- Spain
- Independent states

◄ The boundaries of the African continent were mainly of European construction. France and Great Britain were the dominant colonial powers, and their influence lingers in their former territories with the use of French and English as official languages.

► In the main, the boundaries of colonial Africa, quickly drawn during the "scramble for Africa" between 1881 and 1914, survived into modern times as the boundaries of the new independent countries. In more recent times, Eritrea and South Sudan have broken away as separate states. The final status of Western Sahara is yet to be resolved.

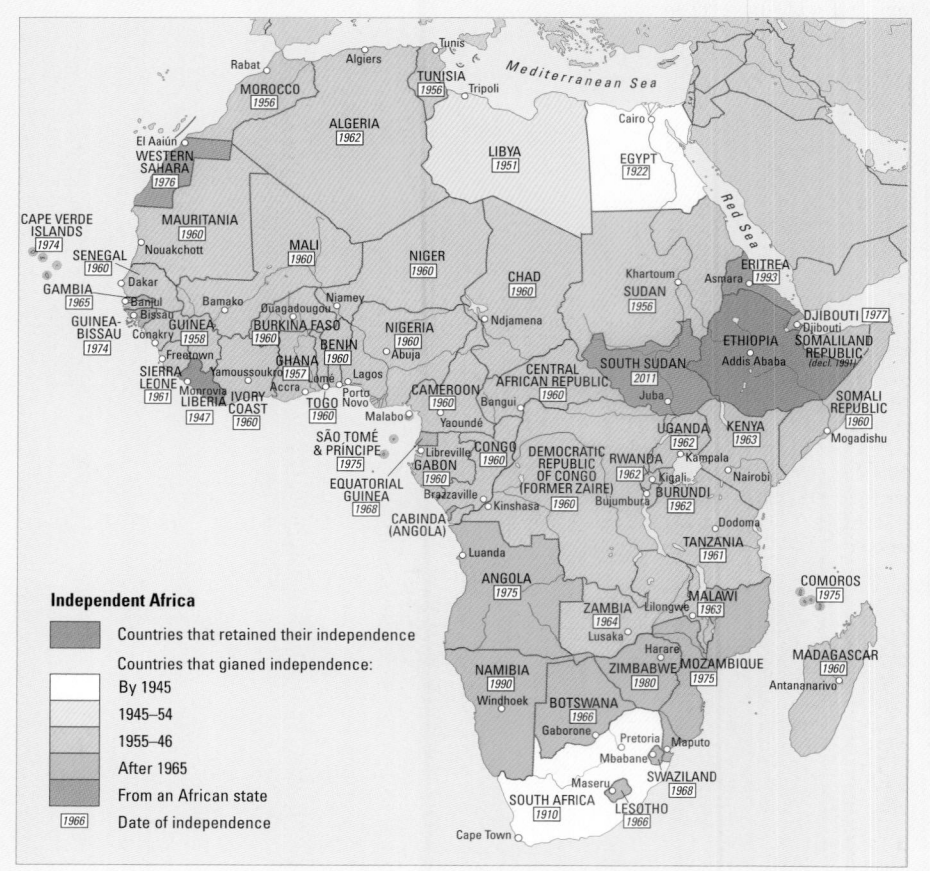

Independent Africa
- Countries that retained their independence
- Countries that gianed independence:
  - By 1945
  - 1945–54
  - 1955–46
  - After 1965
  - From an African state
- *1966* Date of independence

HARD AND SOFT BOUNDARIES

The conventional way of showing an international boundary on an atlas map is to draw a solid line. However, this symbol can conceal myriad differences in the strength and function of a boundary. A "hard" boundary may physically prevent the free movement of people with solid barriers and armed guards. A "soft" boundary may have little effect on people and vehicles as they cross from one country to another. An example of where international boundaries can be considered soft, are those between the European countries that have joined the Schengen Area. The Schengen Agreement aims to reduce border checks, and to ease the movement of goods, and people, between the participating nations. In many places, the only indication that you have crossed a boundary will be a small sign by the side of a road. However, restrictions can be reintroduced, as was the case in 2016, when seven countries put in place border controls in response to the flood of migrants entering southern Europe. In contrast, where a nation wants to control movement, a boundary may be formed of a physically impermeable barrier. The Berlin Wall (1961-89) that divided the city is an example of a hard border. Many people risked their lives to cross this boundary. In the 21st century, some countries, such as Israel and the United States, are extending existing barriers in response to perceived threats from other nations.

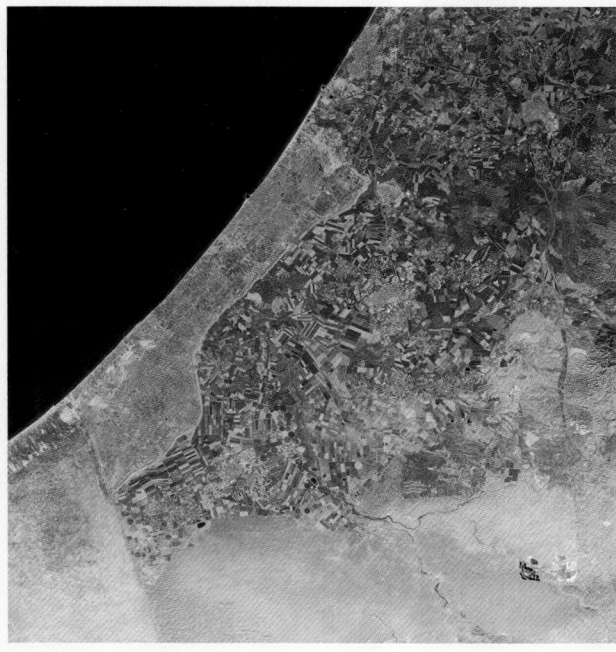

▲ On this satellite image of the Mediterranean coast of Israel, the shape of the Gaza Strip is clearly visible. A security barrier stretches along the entire boundary and all cross-border movements are strictly controlled. The barrier is reinforced by a buffer zone.

▶ Boundary crossing points can provide an opportunity for elaborate ceremonies. Every evening at sunset since 1959, the gates at the crossing point at Wagah, between India and Pakistan, are closed with a colorful military display.

◀ There are 26 countries in Europe are party to the Schengen agreement. This means that, in most cases, border controls have been removed and no checks are made on passengers traveling by road, rail, and air once they are within the Schengen area.

Schengen states

Existing Schengen states

Existing Schengen states not part of the EU

Non-Schengen EU states

DRAWING THE LINE

Where to draw the line? Historically, physical features presented themselves as an obvious place to establish a boundary. They were seen as self-evident and natural. Boundaries could follow rivers and mountain ranges. France can be seen as a good example of this – it is bounded by coasts, the Pyrenees, the river Rhine, and the Alps. Physical features can also act as a line of defense and, theoretically, can be easily described in treaties. However, they can have drawbacks. Where does the boundary lie in a river – in the middle, or following just one bank? River courses are not static and will migrate across the landscape. So it has to be decided if the boundary will remain with the original line of the river, or follow any new course. Around one-quarter of all boundaries follow mountain ranges. Conflict can arise from imprecise definitions in treaties over whether the border is to follow the line of the highest peaks, or the watershed. Allied to this are difficulties of surveying in mountainous terrain.

The world political map also displays boundaries that appear to have been drawn with a ruler, as indeed they were. Straight-line boundaries were often hastily drawn and imposed in Africa and the Middle East without much concern over cutting across existing tribal and linguistic barriers.

All political boundaries are artifical constructions in some way. Divisions following language and ethnic divides were attempted in eastern Europe in the postwar era in the 20th century, but this still led to conflict. There is no perfect solution.

ANTARCTIC TREATY

Most maps of Antarctica in atlases will omit the boundary lines shown on the map to the right. However, these claims to the continent are still valid—although now "frozen." Antarctica has been protected for 50 years by a unique international agreement: the Antarctic Treaty. In 1959, 12 nations signed the original treaty, and this number has now risen to 52 signatories. Prior to the Treaty, disputes over sovereignty were escalating. The seven nations shown here have formal claims to the territory. The United States and Russian Federation have reserved their rights to submit similar claims. The basis of the claims is discovery, geographical proximity, and occupation. The Treaty effectively puts all territorial claims on hold and no new claims can be made. The main purpose of the Treaty is to ensure that the continent is used for peaceful purposes with freedom for scientific investigation and cooperation. There are also agreements on environmental safeguards, management of fishing, and conservation of wildlife. Commercial exploitation of minerals is not allowed. More than 40 permanent, year-round scientific research stations are maintained by 28 of the Treaty nations, with more operating in the Antarctic summer. The Treaty is considered to be one of the most successful international agreements.

▲ The flags of the Antarctic Treaty nations around the ceremonial South Pole.

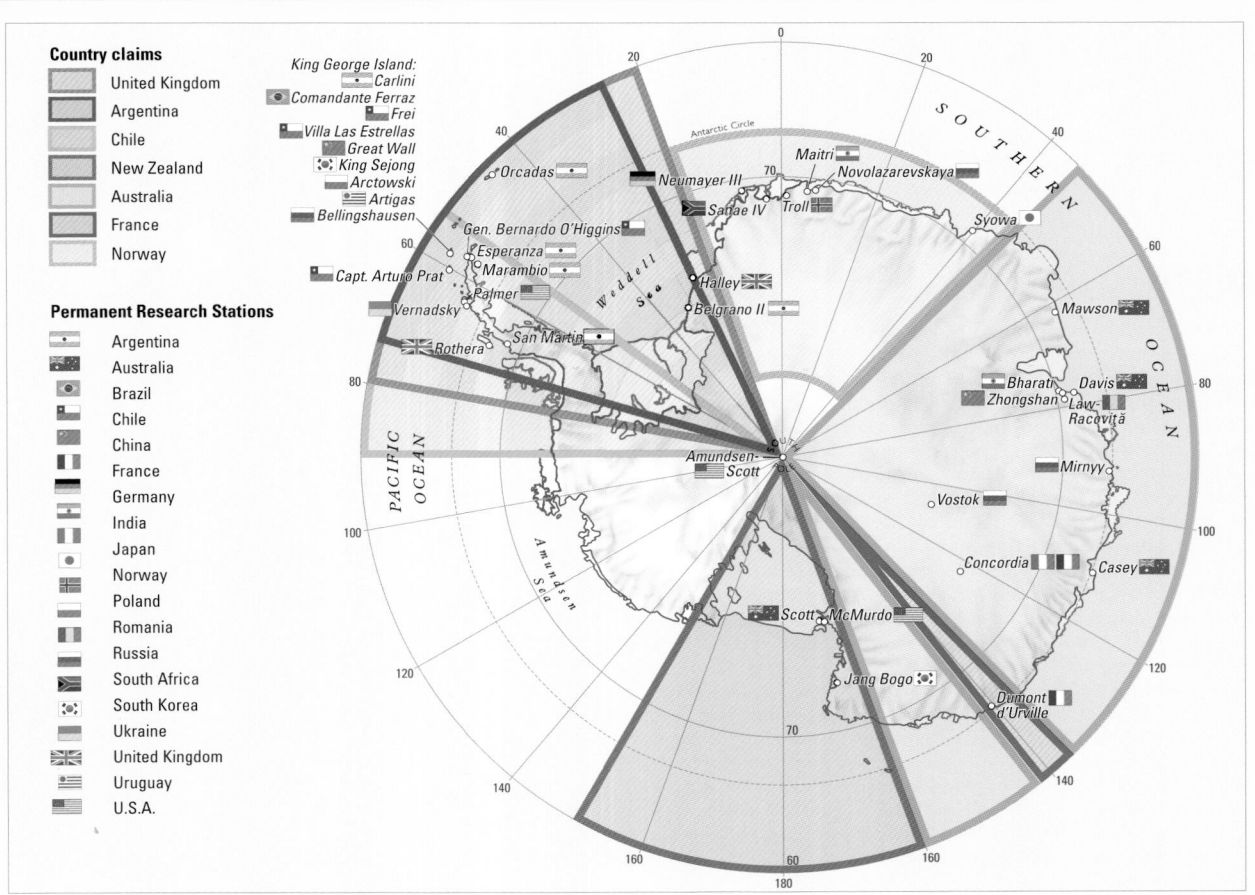

Country claims

United Kingdom
Argentina
Chile
New Zealand
Australia
France
Norway

Permanent Research Stations

Argentina
Australia
Brazil
Chile
China
France
Germany
India
Japan
Norway
Poland
Romania
Russia
South Africa
South Korea
Ukraine
United Kingdom
Uruguay
U.S.A.

King George Island:
Carlini
Comandante Ferraz
Villa Las Estrellas
Great Wall
King Sejong
Arctowski
Artigas
Bellingshausen

For more information:
84 Oceans and Seas
150 Arctic Ocean

As on land, the seas and oceans can be subject to territorial claims. On most atlas maps, maritime boundaries are rarely shown in anything other than a simplified form. Any boundary lines on the maps may just be indicating which offshore islands belong to a particular state. However, because nations want to be able to harvest and exploit the valuable natural resources of the seas and ocean beds, there needs to be a plan to establish sovereignty.

For coastal states, sovereignty does not end at the coastline, but it graduates and changes, moving through a series of zones outward to the high seas. From early times, control of waters close to the coast, or access through narrow straits, was largely dependent on having a strong naval power. Over time, the acceptance of international customary law codified acceptable limits to maritime sovereignty, especially in regard to territorial seas. However, it was the coming into force, in 1994, of the United Nations Convention on the Law of the Sea (UNCLOS) that has provided an internationally accepted program for making and approving national claims to maritime territory. In addition to providing a framework for defining maritime boundaries, UNCLOS has established obligations for protecting the marine environment and controlling the exploitation of mineral resources in the deep seabed, and ocean floor, lying beyond national jurisdiction. This relies on the principle of international law of the "common heritage of mankind" that holds that certain defined territorial areas should be held in trust for future generations.

COASTAL STATE WATERS

Coastal states can claim jurisdiction over a series of maritime zones. Internal waters lie landward of the territorial sea baseline (an officially agreed low-water line). The width of the territorial sea has been set by UNCLOS at 12 nautical miles (nm) from the baseline. The contiguous zone acts as a buffer to the territorial sea and stretches out to 24 nm from the coast. Beyond that, states can claim up to 200 nm as an exclusive economic zone (EEZ). This allows states sovereign rights for exploring, exploiting, conserving, and managing natural resources. The high seas are open to all states, both coastal and landlocked.

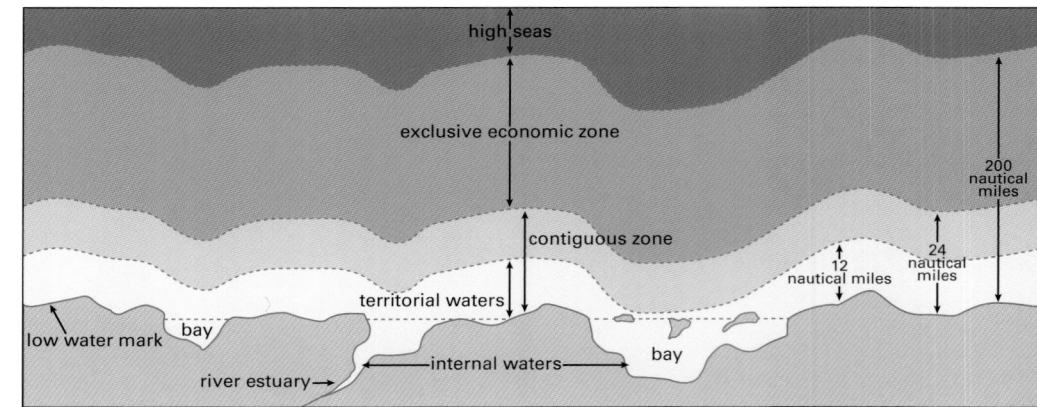

TERRITORIAL SEA

UNCLOS states that "every state has the right to establish the breadth of its territorial sea up to a limit not exceeding 12 nautical miles (nm)." Traditionally, most states had claimed a territorial sea of 3 nm. This program was known as "the canon shot" rule, because it was about the limit of the area that could be controlled from the shore by firepower. However, because UNCLOS allows claims of up to 12 nm, many states now claim this—or more. To help mitigate the need for excessive claims for territorial seas, other zones, such as the exclusive economic zone (EEZ), have been developed within UNCLOS to provide some protection for national economic interests farther out from the coast.

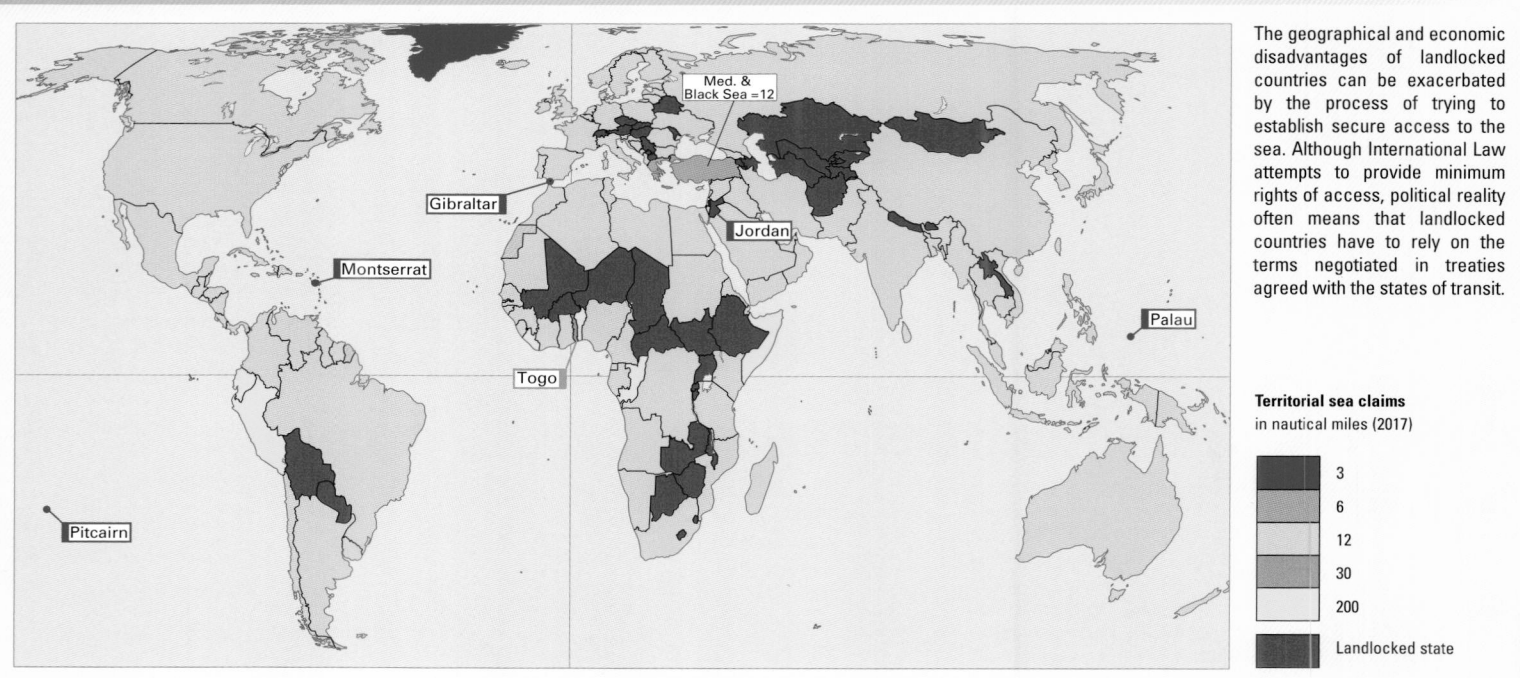

The geographical and economic disadvantages of landlocked countries can be exacerbated by the process of trying to establish secure access to the sea. Although International Law attempts to provide minimum rights of access, political reality often means that landlocked countries have to rely on the terms negotiated in treaties agreed with the states of transit.

Territorial sea claims
in nautical miles (2017)

- 3
- 6
- 12
- 30
- 200

- Landlocked state

SOUTH CHINA SEA

UNCLOS establishes clear guidelines on the limits of the maritime boundaries that states may claim. Complications arise when applying the theory in the real world. The twists and turns of coastlines, the relative importance of offshore islands, and the distance between opposite states all need to be taken into account. Boundaries need to be agreed between adjacent, and neighboring, states. Because having the rights to exploit natural resources in zones controlled by a state are so economically important, nations are willing to go to great lengths to press their claims to maritime territory. One highly contested area lies in the South China Sea around the Spratly Islands. This territorial dispute involves Brunei, China, Malaysia, the Philippines, Taiwan, and Vietnam. At stake are potentially significant oil and gas reserves, rich fishing grounds, and strategic control of shipping lanes. China's ambitious, but ill-defined, claims in the South China Sea are depicted on the map by what China calls the "Nine-dash line." This assertion of sovereignty clashes with the claims for EEZs by the neighboring states. Although the Spratly Islands are far from China's coast, China claims them on the basis of historic occupation. In recent years, China has been artificially strengthening and extending more than half a dozen reefs, including building an airfield on Fiery Cross Reef. The other parties in this dispute have also undertaken reclamation work, but it is the scale of China's efforts that is causing concern. The United States wants to preserve the right of free passage through the South China Sea and deploys aircraft and ships in this area despite objections from China.

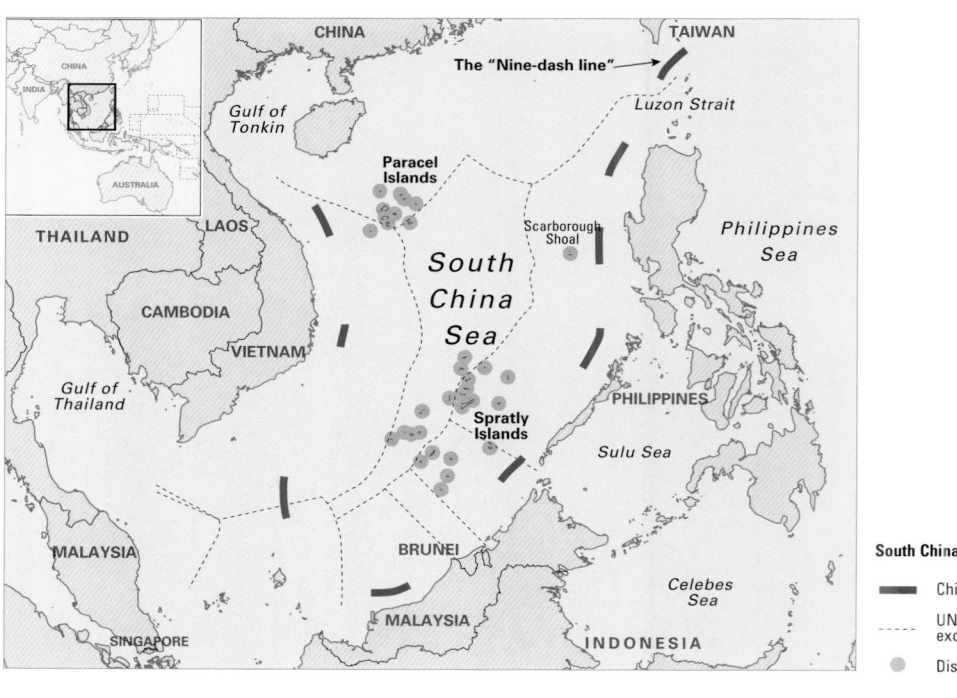

South China Sea

- China's claim line
- --- UNCLOS 200 nautical mile exclusive economic zone
- Disputed islands

CONTINENTAL MARGIN

In addition to the zones that can be claimed up to 200 nautical miles from a state's coastline (see page 12), nations can claim certain rights over their continental shelf. The continental shelf is defined as the natural prolongation of a state's land territory into, and under, the sea. Establishing the legally acceptable outer edge of this geographical feature is technically complex and expensive to research. However, it can be worth the investment, because it allows a state to exploit minerals and nonliving material in the subsoil of the seabed. It does not, however, confer exclusive fishing rights.

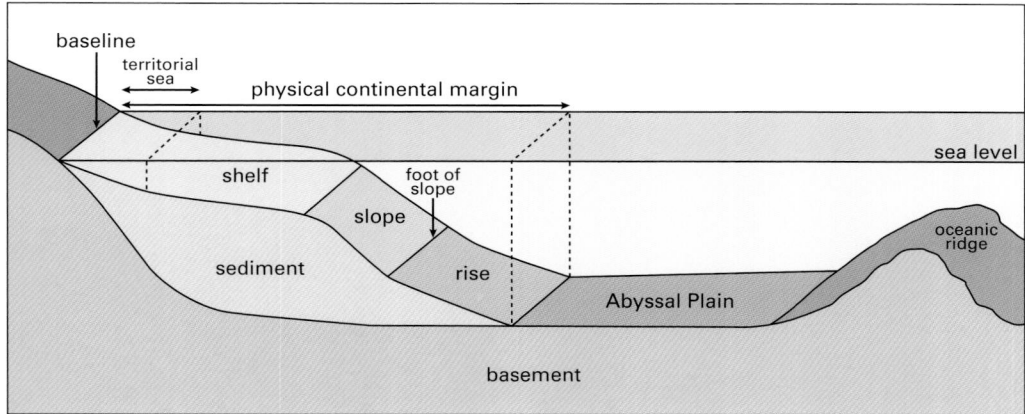

ARCTIC REGION

The map, below, produced by IBRU, the Centre for Borders Research at Durham University in the UK, shows some of the complexity involved in establishing areas of maritime jurisdiction in the Arctic region. Although there are a number of disagreements, all of the Arctic states have followed the rules and procedures for defining their areas of the seabed as set out in UNCLOS. The states involved are Russia, Norway, and Denmark (who have formally submitted their claims), plus Canada and the United States who are continuing to gather data in preparation to submit their claims.

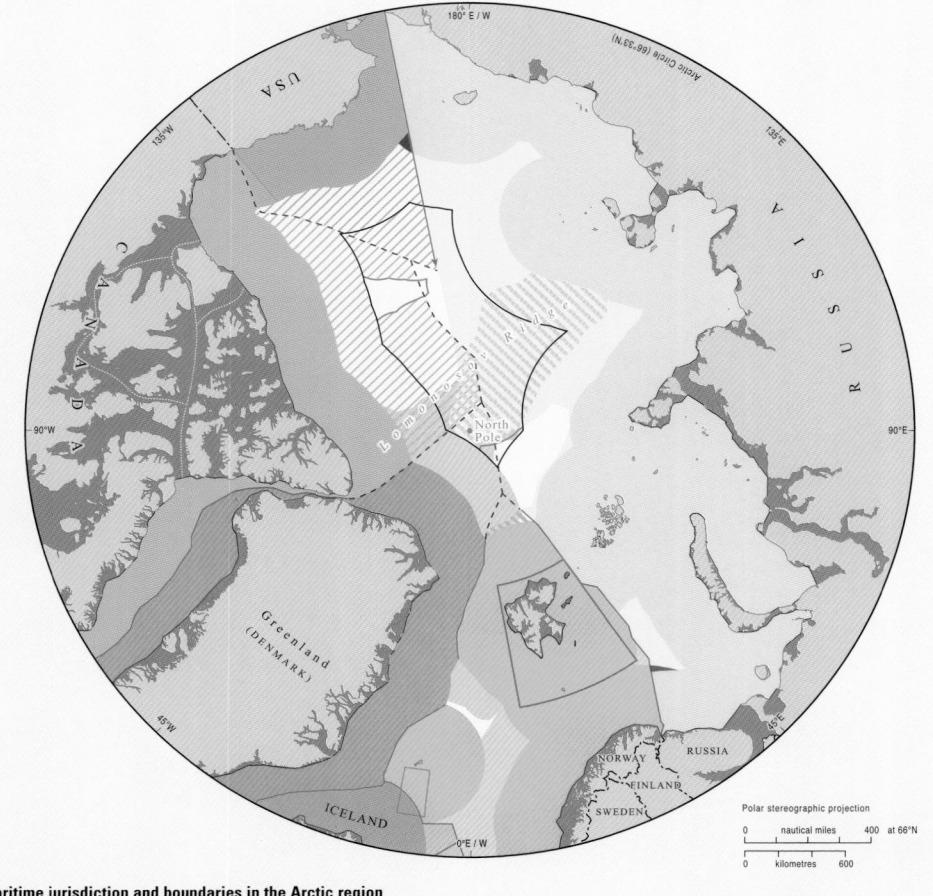

Maritime jurisdiction and boundaries in the Arctic region

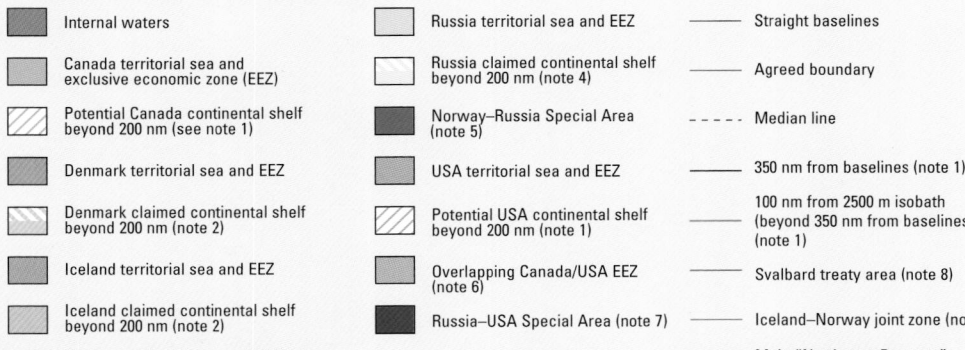

Internal waters

Canada territorial sea and exclusive economic zone (EEZ)

Potential Canada continental shelf beyond 200 nm (see note 1)

Denmark territorial sea and EEZ

Denmark claimed continental shelf beyond 200 nm (note 2)

Iceland territorial sea and EEZ

Iceland claimed continental shelf beyond 200 nm (note 2)

Norway territorial sea and EEZ/Fishery zone (Jan Mayen)/ Fishery protection zone (Svalbard)

Norway claimed continental shelf beyond 200 nm (note 3)

Russia territorial sea and EEZ

Russia claimed continental shelf beyond 200 nm (note 4)

Norway–Russia Special Area (note 5)

USA territorial sea and EEZ

Potential USA continental shelf beyond 200 nm (note 1)

Overlapping Canada/USA EEZ (note 6)

Russia–USA Special Area (note 7)

Unclaimed or unclaimable continental shelf (note 1)

——— Straight baselines

——— Agreed boundary

- - - - - Median line

——— 350 nm from baselines (note 1)

——— 100 nm from 2500 m isobath (beyond 350 nm from baselines) (note 1)

——— Svalbard treaty area (note 8)

——— Iceland–Norway joint zone (note 9)

Main "Northwest Passage" shipping routes through Canada claimed internal waters

Source: IBRU, Durham University, UK
For explanation of notes: www.durham.ac.uk/ibru/resources/arctic

DISPUTED ISLANDS

Islands, large or small, can allow a state to claim significant areas of ocean and the seabed. Islands, as defined by UNCLOS, must be clearly capable of inhabitation and of economic life. If it can be established that an island satisfies this criteria, and is part of the territory of a state, the state may claim all the maritime zones, as outlined on page 12, radiating out from the island's coastline. There are approximately half a million pieces of land that might be considered islands, and 27 states that are entirely insular in nature. If states satisfy farther criteria, they can be considered an "archipelagic sovereign state" under the terms of UNCLOS. This confers the right to construct the baselines that are the starting point for their maritime zones, as joining the outermost points of their outermost islands.

In the quest to establish maritime territory, conflict can arise out of the disputed sovereignty of islands, and over the definition of what legally constitutes an island. Some of the geographic criteria to be evaluated are that islands should be permanent features, above water at high tide, and not reliant on ice cover to be above water. In order to try to strengthen the case of a geographical feature that might not satisfy the conditions to be a legitimate island under the regime of UNCLOS, countries may artificially augment what land is available. This has happened in the Spratly Islands in the South China Sea (see page 20). If an "island" fails to satisfy the criteria, it might be categorized as a rock. One case is Rockall, lying 290 miles (460 km) west of Great Britain in the Atlantic Ocean. It lies within the UK's EEZ, but does not generate its own EEZ or continental shelf claim.

▲ Rock or island? Known as Tok-do to South Korea, and Takeshima to Japan (and internationally as the Liancourt Rocks), these sharp rocks lying in the Sea of Japan are at the root of a long-running dispute between the two countries.

OUTER SPACE

Who owns the Moon? By being the first to step on the Moon's surface in the 1960s does this confer any rights? Where does the boundary lie between air space and outer space—and does it matter? International law recognizes the rights of states to control their own air space and to exclude, or even attack, unauthorized aircraft. The Outer Space Treaty of 1967, and the 1979 Moon Treaty, tried to address some of these issues by recognizing the freedom of using outer space for peaceful purposes. The development of the law in this context owes much to the doctrine of the common heritage of mankind, as embodied in the concept of the "high seas" in UNCLOS, and in the Antarctic Treaty. The Outer Space Treaty states that "Outer space, including the Moon and other celestial bodies, is not subject to national appropriation by claim of sovereignty, by means of use or occupation, or by any other means."

▲ Commander Eugene Cernan from the Apollo 17 mission stands by the U.S. flag on the surface of the Moon in 1972. Commander Cernann said that the astronauts were leaving as they came, "with peace and hope for all mankind."

IMAGES
OF
EARTH

Capital city and teeming metropolis, Seoul lies on the Han river 37 miles (60 km) upstream from the Yellow Sea and can be right of center in this image. In a scenic setting at the foot of Mt Pukhan, the ancient city was formerly enclosed by a high wall of which some remnants remain. After the end of Japanese colonial rule, it became the capital of the Republic of Korea. During the Korean War (1950–53) the city was occupied by invading Communist armies from the north, and severely bombed. The population shrank to 50,000. Following post-war reconstruction the city's expansion has been dynamic, fueled by migration from the countryside. Seoul has embraced all that modern technology has to offer and this modern, vibrant city now houses up to half the country's population.

[Map page 137] *Copernicus Sentinel data 2016 / NPA Satellite Mapping, CGG Services (UK) Ltd*

The capital and largest city in France, Paris is considered one of the world's most elegant cities. Spanning both banks of the river Seine as it flows northwest toward the English Channel, the pattern of wide 19th century boulevards is easily visible. Railroads, built in the same century, radiate from the city, further strengthening its position as the hub of France. By the end of the 20th century, the metropolitan area had spread across much of the land within a 20 mile (30 km) radius of the Île de la Cité. However, many old neighborhoods remain and Parisians say their city is really a collection of 100 villages. The alleyways of the Latin Quarter, on the left (or south) bank, with their many bookshops and cafés comprise a district with a typically Bohemian air.

[Map page 134] *Copernicus Sentinel data 2016 / NPA Satellite Mapping, CGG Services (UK) Ltd*

Barcelona is the chief city of Catalonia and lies on the northeast coast of Spain facing the Mediterranean Sea. As well as being the second largest city in Spain, it is also the country's largest seaport and main industrial and commercial center. The large harbor is clearly visible in this image, as is the airport, close to the coast, in the south. Inland from the northern dock area lies the heart of the old city – the Barri Gòtic. Bounding the western edge of the old town is the wide tree-lined boulevard of La Rambla. This was once a riverbed, but is now a river of perambulating local residents and tourists. The old dock area at the seaward end of La Rambla, and the nearby hill of Montjuïc, were transformed when Barcelona hosted the 1992 Summer Olympics. Modern architects, such as Antonio Gaudi, have also left their mark on the city.

[Map page 114] *Copernicus Sentinel data 2016 / NPA Satellite Mapping, CGG Services (UK) Ltd*

Studded with reminders of the many
civilizations which have left their mark on
the city, Athens remains an important and
powerful focus in southeast Europe.
Despite recent financial difficulties in
Greece, Athens remains a center for
commerce, culture, tourism, and
international trade. It is its location in the
far south of Europe, and the eastern
Mediterranean, that has led to its port at
Piraeus (seen in the far left of the image)
to be one of the largest passenger ports
in the world. One legacy of hosting the
Olympic Games in 2004, was a vast
improvement in transport infrastructure
including expansion of the metro system
and the Eleftherios Venizelos International
Airport which can be seen in the far
right of the image.
[Map page 112] *Planet Labs,
distributed by NPA Satellite Mapping,
CGG Services (UK) Ltd*

Jerusalem lies about 20 miles (30 km) west of the northern end of the Dead Sea on a rocky ridge in the Judean Hills. Both Israelis and Palestinians proclaim the city to be their capital, though neither claim has wide international recognition. One of the world's oldest cities, it is considered to be the holy city of the three major Abrahamic religions of Christianity, Islam, and Judaism. Jerusalem has a typical hot-summer, Mediterranean climate with hot, dry summers and mild, wet winters. Light snow showers can be experienced in most winters and the occasional heavy fall of snow adds much to the Christmas image of the Holy Land. Bethlehem, reputed to be the birthplace of Christ, lies about 6 miles (10 km) south of Jerusalem.

[Map page 123] ©KARI 2017, Distribution (SI Imaging Services, Republic of Korea), all rights reserved / NPA Satellite Mapping, CGG Services (UK) Ltd

Dubai is the capital city of the second
largest of the seven states that make up
the United Arab Emirates. Although the
state does have some oil reserves, Dubai's
current wealth has grown out of trade and
financial services. In the 1960s the town
consisted of low houses of only one or two
storeys. In contrast, the city is now known
for its iconic high-rise towers including the
Burj Khalifa, currently the world's tallest
building soaring to 2,722 ft (828.8 m).
The most striking features seen along the
coast in this image are the artificial islands
in the shape of palm trees (Palm Jumeirah
and Palm Jebel Ali) and a world map.
The aim behind these massive construction
projects is to make Dubai a major
tourist destination.
[Map page 119]   *Planet Labs,
distributed by NPA Satellite Mapping,
CGG Services (UK) Ltd*

The city has had many forms of its name over the years, with Cochin prevailing from the arrival of the Portuguese in the early 16th century until 1996 when Kochi became the official name form. A more romantic description has been attached to this city on the Malabar Coast of the Indian sub-continent: the Queen of the Arabian Sea. This name alludes to its importance as a trading post with merchants from Arabia. An extensive development scheme allowed the natural harbor to be made accessible to seagoing vessels from the 1930s. This was followed by land reclamation schemes and the building of modern harbor facilities. Now a fast growing industrial city and financial center, Kochi is also an important tourist destination.

[Map page 245] *Copernicus Sentinel data 2017 / NPA Satellite Mapping, CGG Services (UK) Ltd*

The old city of Bangkok at the head of the Gulf of Thailand, once known as the "Venice of the East", is a place of "klongs" (canals) and "wats" (temples or monasteries). This core has now been overwhelmed by an ever-expanding and chaotic megalopolis of over nine million people. Until recently, transport infrastructure has failed to keep pace with the needs of the population, but there has been a major investment in public transport and four rapid transit lines are now in operation. The loops of the Chao Phraya river can be seen meandering through the centre of the image. Much of the land surrounding the city was once swamp, but has now been drained for agriculture.
[Map page 113]   *USGS / NPA Satellite Mapping, CGG Services (UK) Ltd*

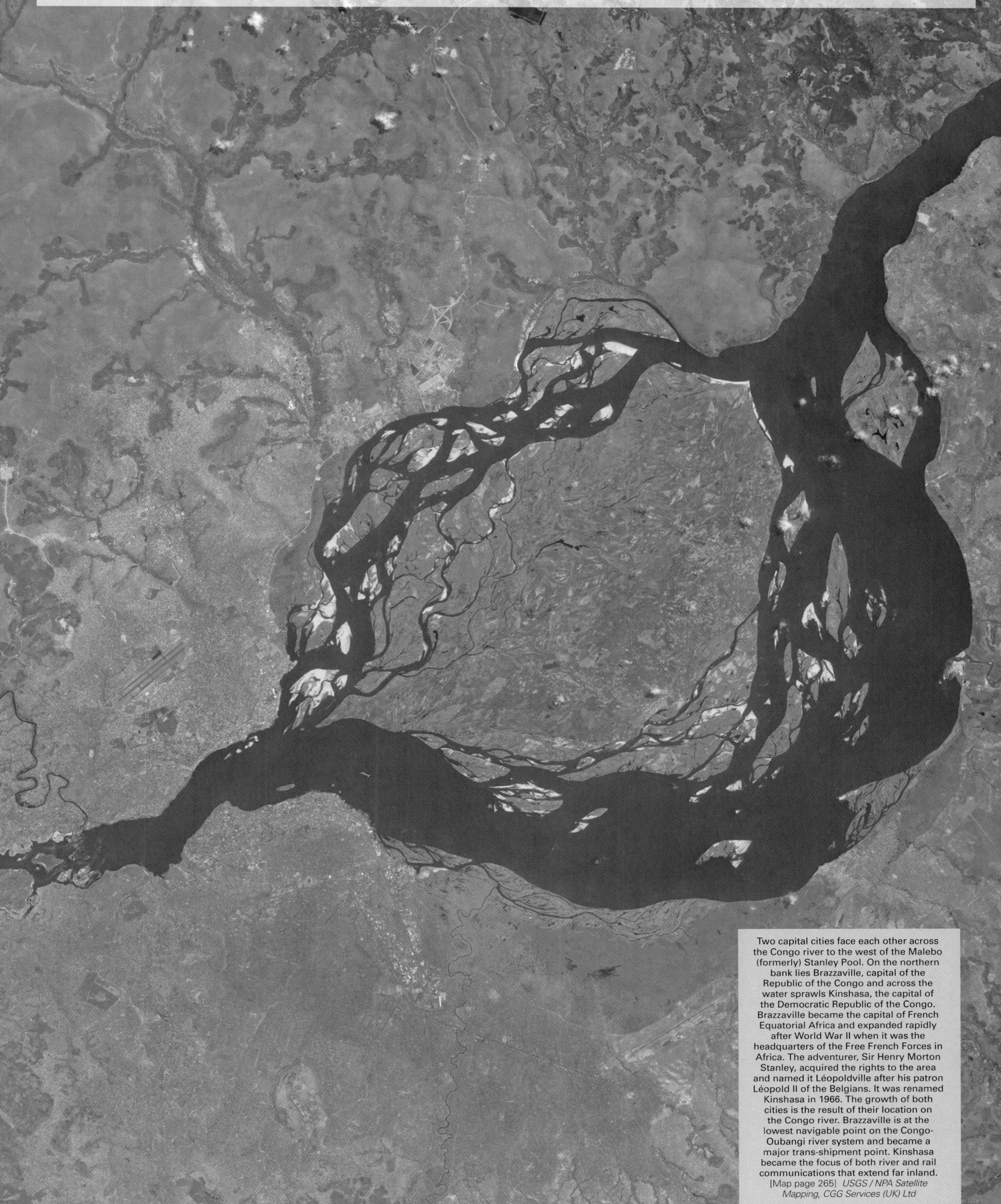

Two capital cities face each other across the Congo river to the west of the Malebo (formerly) Stanley Pool. On the northern bank lies Brazzaville, capital of the Republic of the Congo and across the water sprawls Kinshasa, the capital of the Democratic Republic of the Congo. Brazzaville became the capital of French Equatorial Africa and expanded rapidly after World War II when it was the headquarters of the Free French Forces in Africa. The adventurer, Sir Henry Morton Stanley, acquired the rights to the area and named it Léopoldville after his patron Léopold II of the Belgians. It was renamed Kinshasa in 1966. The growth of both cities is the result of their location on the Congo river. Brazzaville is at the lowest navigable point on the Congo-Oubangi river system and became a major trans-shipment point. Kinshasa became the focus of both river and rail communications that extend far inland.

[Map page 265] *USGS / NPA Satellite Mapping, CGG Services (UK) Ltd*

Dar es Salaam, no longer the capital of
Tanzania, is the largest town and main
seaport in the country. It handles most
of Tanzania's exports and also those of
neighboring, landlocked, Zambia. Founded
in 1862 by the Sultan of Zanzibar its name,
which is of Arabic-Swahili origin, means
"haven of peace". Maybe not so peaceful
in 1916 when it was captured
from Germany by the British during World
War I and, as Tanganyika, remained a
British territory until independence in 1961.
In 1964, Tanganyika and Zanzibar united to
establish the United Republic of Tanzania.
Although the city lost its place as the
capital city to Dodoma in 1974, it has
remained the focus of government and
trade in the country.
[Map page 268] *Planet Labs,
distributed by NPA Satellite Mapping,
CGG Services (UK) Ltd*

Christchurch nestles at the base of Banks Peninsula on South Island, New Zealand. It is the largest city on South Island and is the center of one of the country's most productive wheat, grain, and sheep-rearing areas. It was founded in 1851 as a Church of England settlement and until recently some fine buildings from that era could still be seen. However, one building that has not survived intact is the Gothic-style cathedral that was severely damaged in the earthquake of 2011. New Zealand's location on the Pacific rim means that it is vulnerable to earthquakes. This earthquake, which followed one in September of the previous year, resulted in 185 deaths. Following these earthquakes, a program of wholesale demolition and reconstruction has begun with plans for extensive expansion of residential areas. Christchurch remains as a tourist hub acting as a stopover point for trips to the Southern Alps.

[Map page 285]   *Copernicus Sentinel data 2016 / NPA Satellite Mapping, CGG Services (UK) Ltd*

Anchorage is the largest city in Alaska, but is not the state capital. (Juneau is the capital). It lies some 290 miles (465 km) from the Canadian border at the head of Cook Inlet. The city can be seen at the end of the peninsula in the center of the image with the Knik Arm of the inlet to the north and the Turnagain Arm to the south. It is an important defense center, and communications, commercial, and distribution center for a wide area of the state. Also visible are the extensive mud-flats which, coupled with a high tidal range, can prove deadly for the unwary. Although Anchorage has a subarctic climate, extremes of temperature are moderated by maritime influences.

Due to its location on the "Great Circle" route between Asia and the USA, the international airport (on the tip of the peninsula) is the third busiest in the world for cargo traffic.

[Map page 303] *Copernicus Sentinel data 2016 / NPA Satellite Mapping, CGG Services (UK) Ltd*

Ottawa was founded in 1826 by Colonel By and was subsequently named Bytown. Its name was changed to Ottawa in 1854, a few years before the British queen, Victoria, chose it as the capital of Canada. The city stands on the south bank of the Ottawa river that can be seen flowing across the middle of this image. Most of the major public buildings, including the inspiring gothic-style Parliament complex, cluster round the Rideau Canal. This historic canal was declared to be an UNESCO World Heritage Site in 2007. The city has a wealth of world-class museums, as well as attractive parks and gardens, all of which contribute to Ottawa offering a high quality of living for its residents and visitors.

[Map page 313] *Copernicus Sentinel data 2016 / NPA Satellite Mapping, CGG Services (UK) Ltd*

The largest city of New England, Boston is the focus of a metropolitan region containing around half of the population of Massachusetts. One of the oldest cities in the USA, founded by settlers from England, it played a pivotal role in the American Revolution in the 18th century. Originally occupying the Shawmut Peninsula, the city is sheltered by Boston Harbor, part of the larger Massachusetts Bay. The shoreline of the harbor stretches for 180 miles (290 km) and contains over 30 islands. Boston Logan International airport can be seen occupying one of the peninsulas jutting into the northern part of the bay. The area available for constructing the airport was augmented by land reclamation schemes.

[Map page 116] *Copernicus Sentinel data 2016 / NPA Satellite Mapping, CGG Services (UK) Ltd*

Memphis, on the mighty Mississippi river, conjures up images from the past of steamboats from the plantation era. Also evoked are sounds of blues and rock'n'roll from its musical past. Graceland, the former mansion home of Elvis Presley, to the south of the city center, is still a major tourist attraction. It is the second most visited house in the US – the White House in Washington being the first. The Mississippi, running down the image, separates the main part of the city in the extreme southwest corner of Tennessee from Arkansas on the western bank. Its geographic location has been central to the city's growth: firstly using the river for transport then becoming an intersection point for five major railroads.
In more recent times the airport, lying southeast of the city center, became the world's second busiest cargo airport.

[Map page 315] *Copernicus Sentinel data 2017 / NPA Satellite Mapping, CGG Services (UK) Ltd*

30 MEXICO CITY, MEXICO

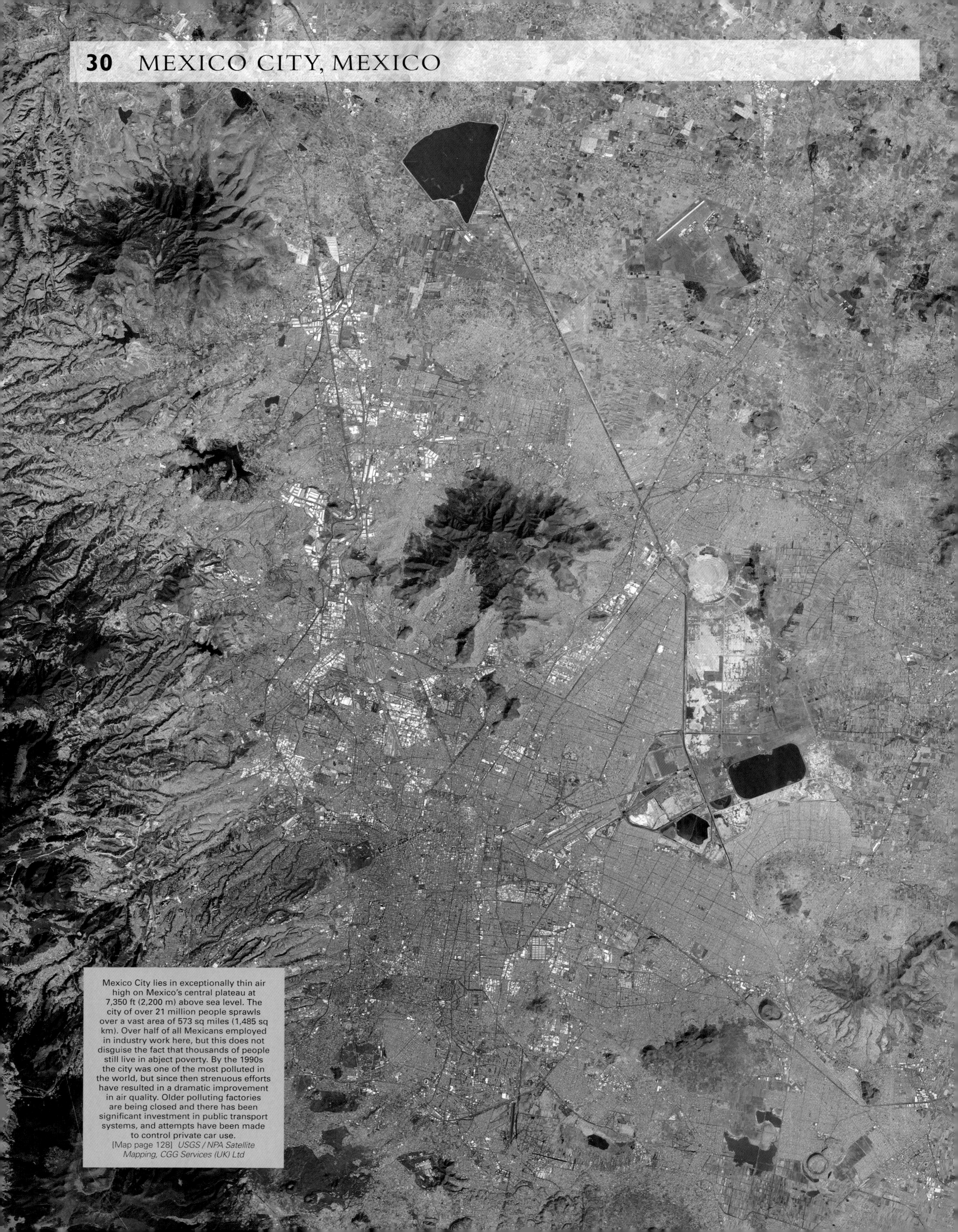

Mexico City lies in exceptionally thin air high on Mexico's central plateau at 7,350 ft (2,200 m) above sea level. The city of over 21 million people sprawls over a vast area of 573 sq miles (1,485 sq km). Over half of all Mexicans employed in industry work here, but this does not disguise the fact that thousands of people still live in abject poverty. By the 1990s the city was one of the most polluted in the world, but since then strenuous efforts have resulted in a dramatic improvement in air quality. Older polluting factories are being closed and there has been significant investment in public transport systems, and attempts have been made to control private car use.

[Map page 128] *USGS / NPA Satellite Mapping, CGG Services (UK) Ltd*

Lying almost exactly on the Tropic of Capricorn, and about 220 miles (350 km) southwest of Rio de Janeiro, is the industrial city of São Paulo. It also acts as Brazil's main financial center. It does not, however, neglect the arts, and it is home to many great museums and hosts the renowned São Paulo Art Biennial. The city is separated from the coast by the escarpment of Serra de Mar which can be seen at the bottom of this image. It rivals Mexico City as one of the fastest growing cities in the world.

[Map page 137] *USGS / NPA Satellite Mapping, CGG Services (UK) Ltd*

GAZETTEER
OF
NATIONS

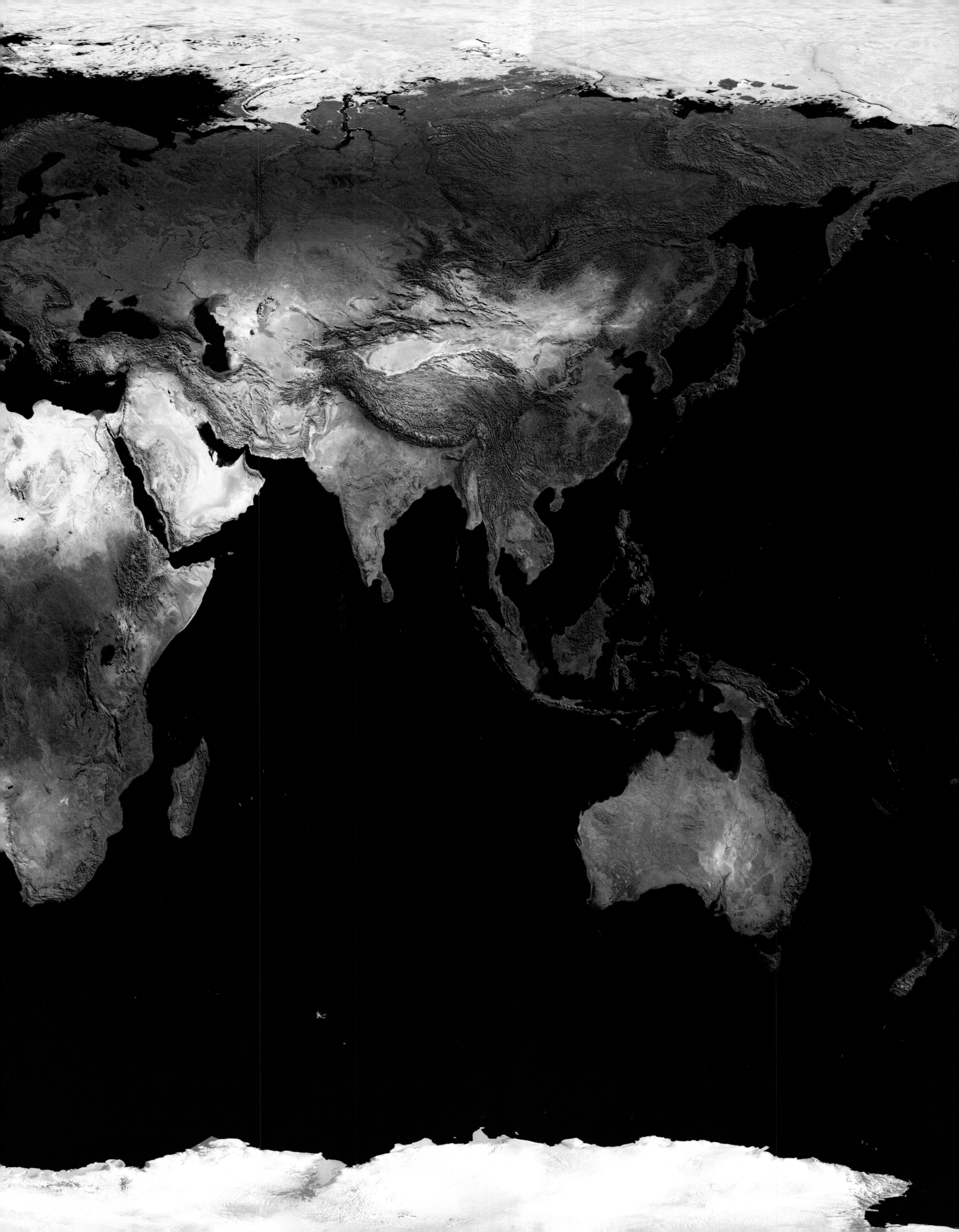

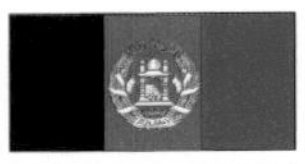
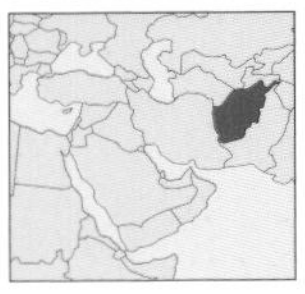

AFGHANISTAN

GEOGRAPHY The Republic of Afghanistan is a landlocked, mountainous country in southern Asia. The central highlands reach a height of more than 22,966 ft [7,000 m] in the east and make up nearly three-quarters of Afghanistan. The main range is the Hindu Kush. In winter, northerly winds bring cold, snowy weather to the mountains, but summers are hot and dry.

POLITICS & ECONOMY The modern history of Afghanistan began in 1747, with the unification of local tribes. In the 19th century, Russia and Britain struggled for control of the country. Following Britain's withdrawal in 1919, Afghanistan became fully independent. Soviet troops invaded in 1979 to support a socialist regime in Kabul, but they withdrew in 1989. By 2001, a group called the Taliban ("Islamic students") controlled 90% of the country. In 2001 an international force invaded Afghanistan. This NATO-led military force ultimately failed to quell the extremist Taliban and the rising toll of deaths of occupying forces led to the withdrawal of all combat troops in 2014. Presidential elections held in the same year resulted in Ashraf Ghani being sworn in as president, leading a unity government. Since then, Afghan forces have been facing a Taliban insurgency.

Decades of conflict have left Afghanistan as one of the world's poorest countries. Until the economy can be rebuilt, the country will continue to be heavily reliant on foreign aid.

AREA 251,772 sq mi [652,090 sq km]
POPULATION 32,332,000 **CAPITAL** Kabul
GOVERNMENT Islamic Republic **ETHNIC GROUPS** Pashtun (Pathan) 42%, Tajik 27%, Hazara 9%, Uzbek 9%, others 13%
LANGUAGES Pashtu, Dari/Persian (both official), Uzbek
RELIGIONS Islam (Sunni Muslim 80%, Shi'ite Muslim 19%), others 1%
CURRENCY Afghani = 100 puls

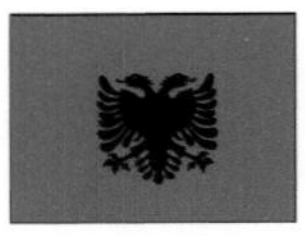
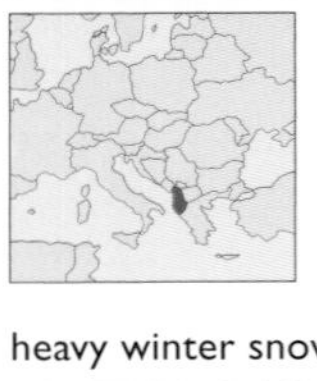

ALBANIA

GEOGRAPHY The Republic of Albania lies in the Balkan peninsula, facing the Adriatic Sea. About 70% of the land is mountainous, with most Albanians living on the western coastal lowlands.

The coastal areas of Albania experience a typical Mediterranean climate, with fairly dry, sunny summers and cool, moist winters. The mountains have a severe climate, with heavy winter snowfalls.

POLITICS & ECONOMY Albania is one of Europe's poorest nations. A former Communist country, Albania adopted a multi-party system in the early 1990s. Although the transition to democracy has been challenging, a socialist government committed to a market system took office in 1997. In 2013 elections, a Socialist-led coalition regained control from the center-right one in place since 2005. A member of NATO since 2009, Albania was granted EU candidate status in 2014.

In 2014, agriculture employed about 42% of the people. Since 1991, private ownership of land has been encouraged, replacing the former state farm and collective system. Albania has some oil, gas, and minerals: chromite, copper, and nickel are exported.

AREA 11,100 sq mi [28,748 sq km]
POPULATION 3,038,000 **CAPITAL** Tirana
GOVERNMENT Multiparty republic **ETHNIC GROUPS** Albanian 95%, Greek 3%, Macedonian, Vlach, Roma **LANGUAGES** Albanian (official)
RELIGIONS Islam 70%, Christianity 30% (Orthodox 20%, Roman Catholic 10%)
CURRENCY Lek = 100 qindars

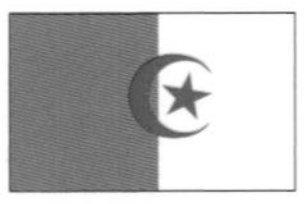
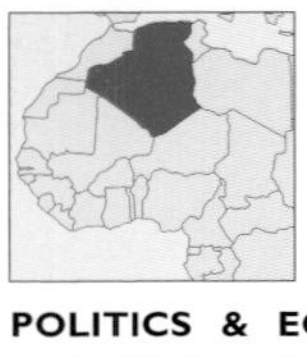

ALGERIA

GEOGRAPHY The People's Democratic Republic of Algeria is Africa's largest country. Most Algerians live in the north, on the fertile coastal plains and hill country bordering the Mediterranean Sea. Four-fifths of Algeria is in the Sahara, the world's largest desert. The coast has a Mediterranean climate but the arid Sahara is hot by day and cold at night.

POLITICS & ECONOMY France ruled Algeria from 1830 until 1962, when the socialist FLN (National Liberation Front) formed a one-party government. Following the recognition of opposition parties in 1989, a Muslim group, the FIS (Islamic Salvation Front), won an election in 1991. The FLN canceled the elections and civil conflict broke out. About 100,000 people were killed in the 1990s. Abdelaziz Bouteflika has been elected president four times: the last being in 2014. In 2011, protests broke out over food prices and unemployment, but the protests did not lead to the overthrow of the government, as elsewhere in North Africa.

Algeria is a developing country, whose chief resources are oil and natural gas, which account for more than 95% of export revenue. Its gas reserves are the largest in Africa. The challenge for the future is to diversify the economy. Cement, iron and steel, textiles, and vehicles are manufactured with barley, citrus fruits, dates, potatoes, and wheat being the major crops.

AREA 919,590 sq mi [2,381,741 sq km]
POPULATION 40,264,000 **CAPITAL** Algiers
GOVERNMENT Socialist republic **ETHNIC GROUPS** Arab-Berber 99%
LANGUAGES Arabic and Berber (official), French **RELIGIONS** Sunni Muslim 99% **CURRENCY** Algerian dinar = 100 centimes

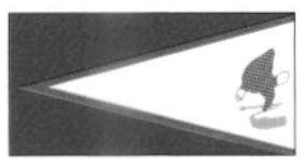
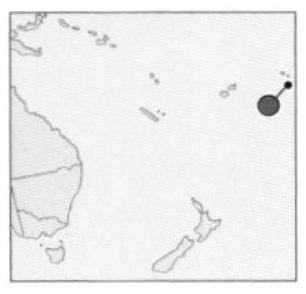

AMERICAN SAMOA

An "unincorporated territory" of the United States, American Samoa lies in the south-central Pacific Ocean.

AREA 77 sq mi [199 sq km]
POPULATION 54,000 **CAPITAL** Pago Pago

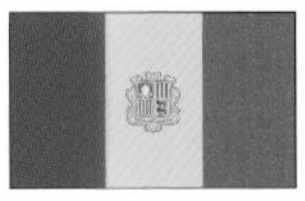
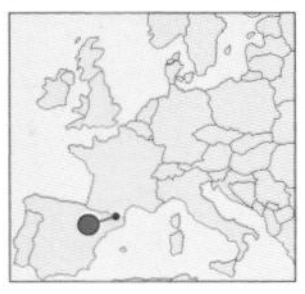

ANDORRA

In this prosperous mini-state, situated in the Pyrenees Mountains, tourism (especially winter sports) accounts for almost 80% of GDP. Most Andorrans live in the six valleys (the Valls) that drain into the River Valira.

AREA 181 sq mi [468 sq km]
POPULATION 86,000 **CAPITAL** Andorra La Vella

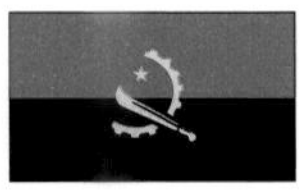
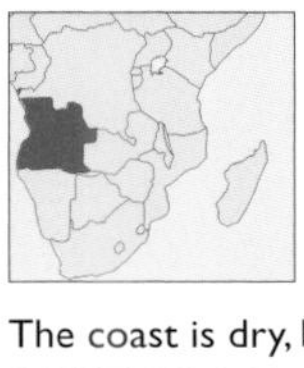

ANGOLA

GEOGRAPHY Situated in southwestern Africa, the Republic of Angola is the seventh largest country on the continent. Much of Angola lies on the South African plateau, with only a narrow coastal plain in the west.

Angola has a tropical climate, with temperatures of over 68°F [20°C] throughout the year, though the highest areas are cooler. The coast is dry, but the rainfall increases to the north and east.

POLITICS & ECONOMY Portugal controlled the coastal slave trade from the 17th century and extended its control inland in the 19th century. Independence, gained from Portugal in 1975, was followed by 27 years of civil war which only finally ended when the rebel leader, Jonas Savimbi, was killed in 2002. Elections in 2008 began a transition toward a more democratic system. After 38 years in power, Jose Eduardo dos Santos announced that he would be standing down ahead of elections in August 2017.

Angola is a developing country, where 85% of the people are poor farmers. The main food crops are cassava and maize with coffee being exported. Angola has important oil reserves, mainly located in the northern exclave of Cabinda. Angola also mines diamonds and has reserves of copper, manganese, and phosphates. Foreign loans and oil revenue have fueled a building boom.

AREA 481,351 sq mi [1,246,700 sq km]
POPULATION 20,172,000 **CAPITAL** Luanda
GOVERNMENT Multiparty republic
ETHNIC GROUPS Ovimbundu 37%, Kimbundu 25%, Bakongo 13%, others 25% **LANGUAGES** Portuguese (official), many others
RELIGIONS Traditional beliefs 47%, Roman Catholic 38%, Protestant 15%
CURRENCY Kwanza = 100 cêntimos

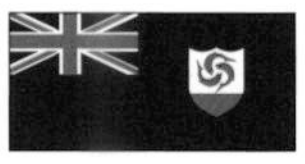
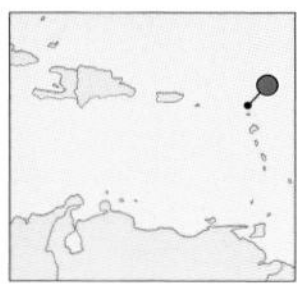

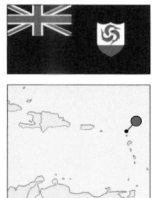

ANGUILLA

Formerly part of St Kitts and Nevis, Anguilla, the most northerly of the Leeward Islands, became a British dependency (now a British overseas territory) in 1980. The main source of revenue is now tourism, though lobster still accounts for half the island's exports.

AREA 37 sq mi [96 sq km]
POPULATION 16,000 **CAPITAL** The Valley

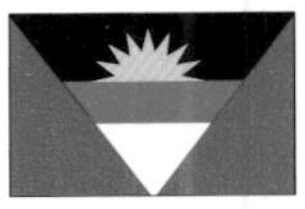
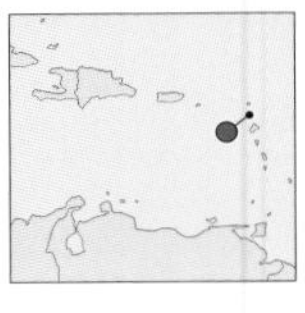

ANTIGUA & BARBUDA

A former British dependency in the Caribbean, Antigua and Barbuda became independent in 1981. Tourism and offshore banking are vital to its service-based economy.

AREA 171 sq mi [442 sq km]
POPULATION 94,000 **CAPITAL** St John's

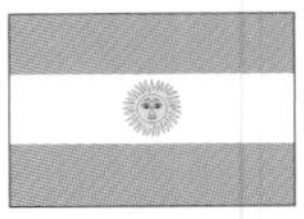
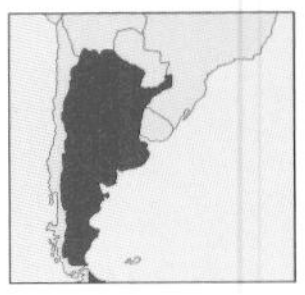

ARGENTINA

GEOGRAPHY The Argentine Republic is South America's second largest and the world's eighth largest country. In the west, the high Andes range contains Mount Aconcagua, the highest peak in the Americas. In southern Argentina, the Andes Mountains overlook Patagonia, a plateau region. The fertile plain of the Pampas occupies the east-central area.

The climate varies from subtropical in the north to temperate in the south. Rainfall is abundant in the north-east but lower to the west and south. Patagonia is largely desert.

POLITICS & ECONOMY The earliest people were American Indians, but 86% of the people are now of European ancestry. After Spanish rule ended in 1816, Argentina experienced periods of regional instability and spells of military rule. In 1982, Argentina's military regime invaded the Falkland (Malvinas) Islands, but Britain regained the islands later that year. In 1983 Argentina restored civilian rule. Since 2015, Mauricio Macri has been both president and the head of government. The ongoing dispute with Britain over the sovereignty of the Falkland Islands continues to cloud diplomatic relations.

The World Bank classifies Argentina as a "high-income" economy. Manufactures include food products, cars, electrical equipment, and textiles. Oil is the main resource and the chief farm products are beef, maize, and wheat. Exports include oil, meat, wheat, maize, vegetable oils, hides and skins, and wool. In 1991, Argentina was a founding member of Mercosur, an alliance of South American countries aimed at creating a common market. Following the economic, social, and political crisis of 2001, government policies have barely allowed fitful recovery, and the country defaulted on repayment of its international debt again in 2014.

AREA 1,073,512 sq mi [2,780,400 sq km]
POPULATION 43,887,000 **CAPITAL** Buenos Aires
GOVERNMENT Federal republic **ETHNIC GROUPS** European 97%, Mestizo, Amerindian **LANGUAGES** Spanish (official)
RELIGIONS Roman Catholic 92%, Protestant 2%, Jewish 2%, others **CURRENCY** Argentine peso = 100 centavos

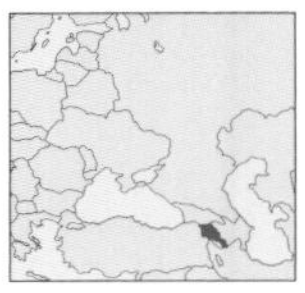

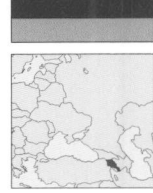

ARMENIA

GEOGRAPHY The Republic of Armenia is a landlocked country in southwestern Asia. Most of Armenia consists of a rugged plateau, crisscrossed by long faultlines which make the area prone to earthquakes. The highest point, just northwest of Yerevan, is Mount Aragats, at 13,419 ft [4,090 m] above sea level.

The height of the land gives rise to severe winters and cool summers. The highest peaks are snow-capped, but the total yearly rainfall is generally low.

POLITICS & ECONOMY In 1920, Armenia became a Communist republic and, in 1922, it became, with Azerbaijan and Georgia, part of the Transcaucasian Republic within the Soviet Union. But the three territories became separate Soviet Socialist Republics in 1936. After the breakup of the Soviet Union in 1991, Armenia became an independent republic. The ongoing dispute over Nagorno-Karabakh, an area enclosed by Azerbaijan where most people are Armenians, has been a major cause of conflict and instability which has hampered the economic development of both countries. The issue also sours relations with Turkey and this needs to be resolved to end Armenia's economic isolation.

Armenia's economy has suffered because of its former dependency on a centrally planned Soviet system. In 2015, the country joined the Russian-led Eurasian Customs Union in order to boost trade.

AREA 11,506 sq mi [29,800 sq km]
POPULATION 3,051,000 **CAPITAL** Yerevan
GOVERNMENT Multiparty republic
ETHNIC GROUPS Armenian 98%, Yezidi 1%
LANGUAGES Armenian (official) **RELIGIONS** Armenian Apostolic 95%
CURRENCY Dram = 100 luma

NOTE: This alphabetical list includes the principal countries and territories of the world. The area figures give the total area of land, inland water, and ice. The population figures are 2016 estimates where available.

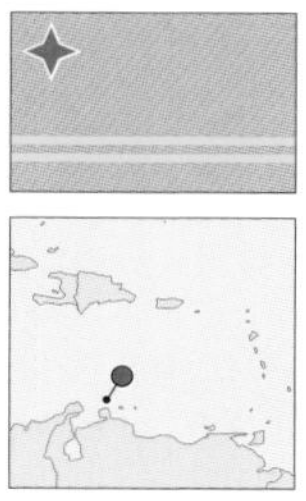

ARUBA

Formerly part of the Netherlands Antilles, Aruba (the most westerly of the Lesser Antilles) became a separate self-governing Dutch territory in 1986.

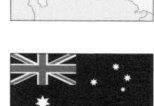

AREA 75 sq mi [193 sq km]
POPULATION 114,000 **CAPITAL** Oranjestad

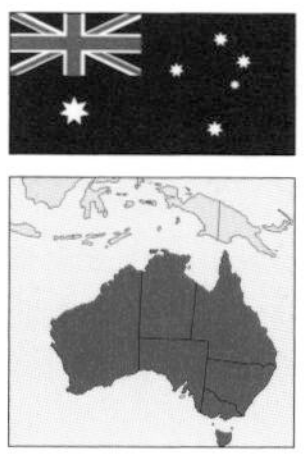

AUSTRALIA

GEOGRAPHY The Commonwealth of Australia, the world's sixth largest country, is also a continent. Australia is the flattest of the continents with its main highlands lying in the east. Here the Great Dividing Range separates the eastern coastal plains from the Central Plains. This range extends from Cape York Peninsula to Victoria in the far south. The longest rivers, the Murray and Darling, drain the southeastern part of the Central Plains. The Western Plateau makes up two-thirds of Australia. A few mountain ranges break the monotony of the generally flat landscape. Only 10% of Australia, notably the tropical north, the northeast coast and the southeast, has an average annual rainfall of more than 39 inches [1,000 mm]. But extreme weather events, including a prolonged drought in the Murray–Darling basin in the early 21st century and severe flooding in Queensland in 2010–12, cause periodic problems.

POLITICS & ECONOMY The Aboriginal people of Australia entered the continent from Southeast Asia more than 50,000 years ago. The first European explorers were Dutch in the 17th century, but they did not settle. In 1770, the British Captain Cook explored the east coast and, in 1788, the first British settlement was established for convicts on the site of what is now Sydney. Whilst maintaining links with the British Isles, the last 50 years, has seen people from other parts of Europe and, most recently, from Asia settling in the country. Ties with Britain were also weakened by Britain's membership of the European Union and Australia has now forged stronger links with the nations of eastern Asia, especially China, Indonesia, and Japan. The issue of retaining the monarch of the UK as the head of state is a recurring theme but, in a referendum in 1999, the majority of Australians voted to remain a constitutional monarchy. The conservative Liberal-National coalition swept into power in 2013, ending six years of Labor Party rule. They won again in 2016, by a very narrow margin.

Australia is a prosperous country. Crops can be grown on only 6% of the land, with dry pasture covering another 58%. Yet the country remains a major producer and exporter of farm products, particularly cattle, wheat, and wool. Grapes grown for wine-making are also important. The country is rich in a wide range of minerals, and Australia also produces oil and natural gas. Metals, minerals and farm products account for the bulk of exports. Australia's imports are mostly manufactured goods, though its own manufacturing industry is growing. The service sector contributes over 70% of total GDP.

AREA 2,988,885 sq mi [7,741,220 sq km] **POPULATION** 22,993,000
CAPITAL Canberra **GOVERNMENT** Federal constitutional monarchy
ETHNIC GROUPS Caucasian 92%, Asian 7%, Aboriginal 1%
LANGUAGES English (official) **RELIGIONS** Non-Christian 36%, Roman Catholic 26%, Anglican 19%, other Christian 19%
CURRENCY Australian dollar = 100 cents

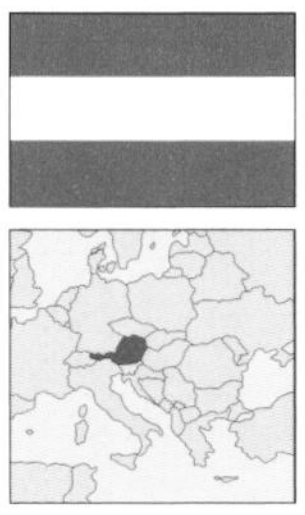

AUSTRIA

GEOGRAPHY Austria is a landlocked country at the heart of Europe. The River Danube flows across northern Austria on its way from Germany to the Black Sea. Southern Austria contains ranges of the Alps, reaching their highest point at Grossglockner, 12,457 ft [3,797 m] above sea level.

The climate is temperate in the west and more continental in the east. Winters are cold and snowy. Summers are warm and dry in the east.

POLITICS & ECONOMY Formerly part of the Austro-Hungarian Empire, Austria was annexed by Germany in 1938. After World War II, the Allies partitioned and occupied the country. In 1955, Austria became a neutral federal republic later joining the European Union in 1995. In recent years, Austria has been governed by coalitions. Since 2013 the government has been formed of an alliance of the left-wing Social Democratic Party and the right-wing Austrian People's Party. Presidential elections in 2016 resulted in victory for Alexander Van der Bellen of the Austrian Greens.

Austria has a highly developed economy, with plenty of hydroelectric power and some oil, gas, and coal reserves. Although manufacturing, metals and metal products are important to the economy, banking and insurance services predominate. Dairy and livestock farming are the leading agricultural activities. Major crops include barley, potatoes, rye, sugar beet, and wheat. Tourism is an important activity in this scenic country.

AREA 32,378 sq mi [83,859 sq km] **POPULATION** 8,712,000
CAPITAL Vienna **GOVERNMENT** Federal republic
ETHNIC GROUPS Austrian 91%, Croatian, Slovene, others
LANGUAGES German (official) **RELIGIONS** Roman Catholic 74%, Protestant 5%, Islam and others 21% **CURRENCY** Euro = 100 cents

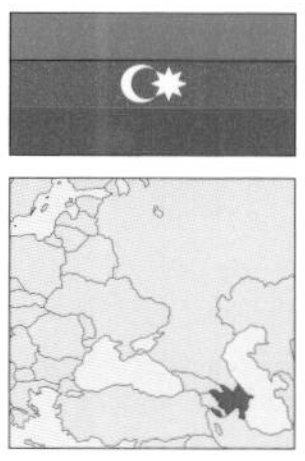

AZERBAIJAN

GEOGRAPHY The Azerbaijani Republic is a country in the southwest of Asia, facing the Caspian Sea to the east. It includes the area of the Naxçivan Autonomous Republic, which is completely cut off from the rest of Azerbaijan by Armenian territory. The Caucasus Mountains border Russia in the north.

Azerbaijan has hot summers and cool winters. The plains are fairly dry, but the mountains are rainy.

POLITICS & ECONOMY For a short period after the Russian Revolution of 1917, Azerbaijanis set up an independent state before the area was occupied by Russian forces in 1920. In 1922, the Communists set up a Transcaucasian Republic consisting of Armenia, Azerbaijan, and Georgia under Russian control. In 1936, the three areas became separate Soviet Socialist Republics within the Soviet Union. In 1991, following the breakup of the Soviet Union, Azerbaijan became an independent nation again. After independence, Azerbaijan clashed with Armenia over the enclave of Nagorno-Karabakh, a region in Azerbaijan where the majority of the people are Armenian. A ceasefire in 1994 left Armenia in control of 20% of Azerbaijan's area, including Nagorno-Karabakh.

Azerbaijan has huge oil reserves. Oil extraction and manufacturing, including oil refining, and the production of chemicals, are vital for the export earnings which are funding investment in the country's infrastructure. Problems remain with corruption and the government has been accused of authoritarianism.

AREA 33,436 sq mi [86,600 sq km] **POPULATION** 9,873,000
CAPITAL Baku **GOVERNMENT** Federal multiparty republic
ETHNIC GROUPS Azeri 91%, Dagestani 2%, Russian 2%, Armenian, others **LANGUAGES** Azerbaijani (official), Lezgi, Russian, Armenian
RELIGIONS Islam 93%, Russian Orthodox 2%, Armenian Orthodox 2%
CURRENCY Azerbaijani manat = 100 qapik

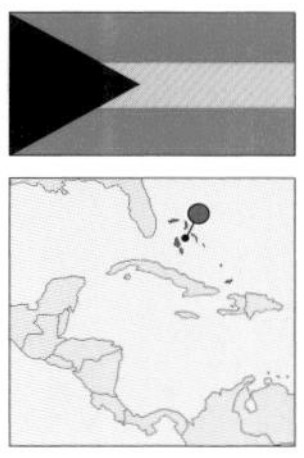

BAHAMAS

A coral-limestone archipelago off the coast of Florida, the Bahamas became independent from Britain in 1973, and has since developed strong ties with the United States. Tourism and banking are major activities.

AREA 5,358 sq mi [13,878 sq km]
POPULATION 327,000 **CAPITAL** Nassau

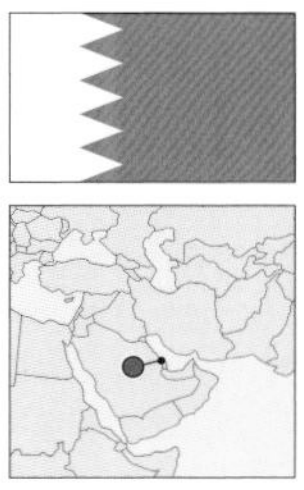

BAHRAIN

The Kingdom of Bahrain, an island nation in the Persian Gulf, became independent from the UK in 1971. An important financial services center, it is less dependent on oil than other Gulf states. Oil accounts for 60% of its exports.

There has been agitation for political reform and the tensions between pro-democracy campaigners and the authorities continue.

AREA 268 sq mi [694 sq km]
POPULATION 1,379,000 **CAPITAL** Manama

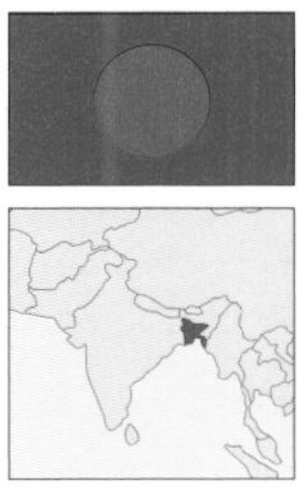

BANGLADESH

GEOGRAPHY The People's Republic of Bangladesh is one of the world's most densely populated countries. Apart from hilly regions in the far northeast and southeast, most of the land is flat and covered by fertile alluvium spread over the land by the Ganges, Brahmaputra, and Meghna rivers. These rivers overflow when they are swollen by the annual monsoon rains. Floods also occur along the coast, 357 mi [575 km] long, when cyclones (hurricanes) drive seawater inland. Bangladesh has a tropical monsoon climate. Dry northerly winds blow in winter, but moist southerly winds bring heavy rain in summer.

POLITICS & ECONOMY In 1947, British India was partitioned between the mainly Hindu India and the Muslim Pakistan. Pakistan consisted of two parts, West and East Pakistan, which were separated by about 1,000 mi [1,600 km] of Indian territory. Differences developed between West and East Pakistan and after a nine-month civil war, East Pakistan declared itself to be the new nation of Bangladesh in 1971. A famine in 1974 and a coup in 1975 were followed by political upheavals. The army took control in 2007, but elections in 2008 returned Sheikh Hasina's Awami League to power. Hasina was re-elected for a third term in 2014.

Bangladesh is one of the world's poorest countries. Its economy depends mainly on agriculture, which employs about 47% of the population. Bangladesh is the world's fourth largest producer of rice.

AREA 55,598 sq mi [143,998 sq km]
POPULATION 156,187,000 **CAPITAL** Dhaka
GOVERNMENT Multiparty republic **ETHNIC GROUPS** Bengali 98%, tribal groups **LANGUAGES** Bengali (official), English
RELIGIONS Islam 89%, Hinduism 10% **CURRENCY** Taka = 100 paisas

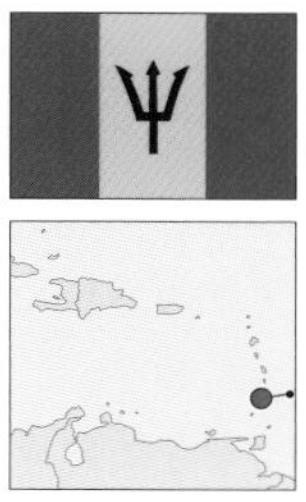

BARBADOS

The most easterly Caribbean country, Barbados became independent from the UK in 1960. A densely populated island, Barbados is prosperous by comparison with most Caribbean countries.

AREA 166 sq mi [430 sq km]
POPULATION 291,000 **CAPITAL** Bridgetown

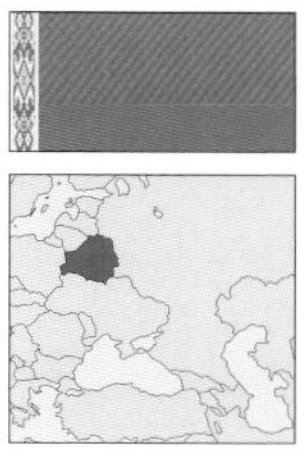

BELARUS

GEOGRAPHY The Republic of Belarus is a landlocked country in Eastern Europe. The land is low-lying and mostly flat. In the south, much of it is marshy and this area contains Europe's largest marsh and peat bog, the Pripet Marshes. The climate is affected by both the moderating influence of the Baltic Sea and continental conditions to the east. The winters are cold and the summers warm.

POLITICS & ECONOMY In 1918, Belarus (White Russia) became an independent republic, but Russia invaded the country and, in 1919, a Communist state was set up. In 1922, Belarus became a founder republic of the Soviet Union. In 1991, Belarus again became an independent republic, and though Belarus continued to support reunification with Russia, any surrender of sovereignty was not expected. President Alexander Lukashenko, who has been re-elected five times between 1994 and 2015 has been criticized for his autocratic rule, his poor record on human rights, and his disregard for freedom of speech. Despite protests, no credible opposition candidates have been allowed to stand.

According to the World Bank, Belarus has an "upper-middle-income" economy. Most economic activities remain under government control and, from the 1990s, the economy has stagnated. Mining and manufacturing are the most valuable activities.

AREA 80,154 sq mi [207,600 sq km]
POPULATION 9,570,000 **CAPITAL** Minsk
GOVERNMENT Multiparty republic **ETHNIC GROUPS** Belarusian 84%, Russian 8%, Polish, Ukrainian, others **LANGUAGES** Belarusian, Russian (both official) **RELIGIONS** Eastern Orthodox 80%, others 20% **CURRENCY** Belarusian ruble = 100 kapyeyka

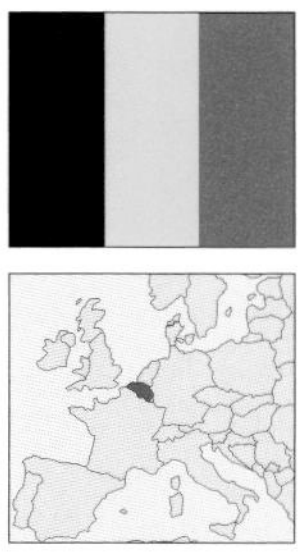

BELGIUM

GEOGRAPHY The Kingdom of Belgium is a densely populated country in western Europe. Behind the coastline on the North Sea, which is 39 mi [63 km] long, lie its coastal plains. Central Belgium consists of low plateaux and the only highland region is the Ardennes in the southeast.

Belgium has a cool, temperate climate. Moist winds from the Atlantic Ocean bring fairly heavy rain, especially in the Ardennes. In January and February much snow falls on the Ardennes.

POLITICS & ECONOMY In 1815, Belgium and the Netherlands united as the "low countries," but Belgium became independent in 1830. Belgium's economy was weakened by the two World

Wars, but, from 1945, the country recovered quickly, first through collaboration with the Netherlands and Luxembourg, which formed a customs union called Benelux, and later through its membership of the European Union.

Tension between the Dutch-speaking Flemings in the north and the French-speaking Walloons in the south is an ongoing political problem. In the 1970s, the government divided the country into three economic regions: Flanders, Wallonia, and bilingual Brussels. In 1993, Belgium adopted a federal constitution, giving each region its own parliament. However, in 2010, differences between the parties led to the collapse of the coalition government. Since 2014, Charles Michel has led a four-party coalition. King Philippe succeeded to the throne in 2013. In March 2016, Islamic State terrorists targeted Brussels' Zaventem Airport and Maalbeek station.

Belgium is a major trading nation, though, with few natural resources, most materials used in manufacturing are imported. Major products include chemicals, processed food, and steel. Flanders has a long history of textile production. Agriculture employs less than 2% of the people, but farmers produce most of the country's food. Barley and wheat are major crops, followed by flax, hops, potatoes, and sugar beet. But the most valuable agricultural activities are dairy farming and livestock rearing.

AREA 11,787 sq mi [30,528 sq km]
POPULATION 11,409,000 **CAPITAL** Brussels
GOVERNMENT Federal constitutional monarchy
ETHNIC GROUPS Belgian 89% (Fleming 58%, Walloon 31%), others 11% **LANGUAGES** Dutch, French, German (all official)
RELIGIONS Roman Catholic 75%, others 25%
CURRENCY Euro = 100 cents

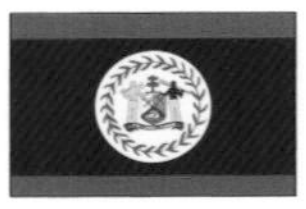
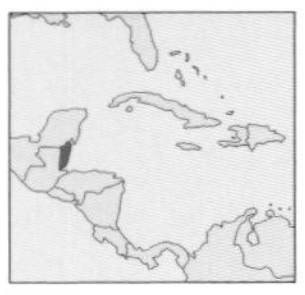

BELIZE

GEOGRAPHY Behind the southern coastal plain, the land rises to the Maya Mountains, which reach 3,674 ft [1,120 m] at Victoria Peak. The north is mostly low-lying and swampy. Temperatures are high all year round, while the average annual rainfall ranges from 51 inches [1,300 mm] in the north to over 150 inches [3,800 mm] in the south. Hurricanes caused much damage in the 1990s and 2000s, but tourist numbers have continued to increase.

POLITICS & ECONOMY From 1862, Belize (then called British Honduras) was a British colony. Full independence was achieved in 1981, but Guatemala, which had claimed the area since the early 19th century, opposed this. Relations improved in the 1990s, when Guatemala recognized Belize's independence although there are still tensions over a boundary dispute. In 2011, the United States added Belize and El Salvador to its list of illegal drug producers.

The World Bank classifies Belize as an "upper-middle-income" developing country. Its economy is based on agriculture, and sugarcane is the chief commercial crop. Other crops include bananas, citrus fruits, maize, and rice. Forestry, fishing, and tourism are other important economic activities, with the last being Belize's chief foreign earner.

AREA 8,867 sq mi [22,966 sq km] **POPULATION** 354,000
CAPITAL Belmopan **GOVERNMENT** Constitutional monarchy
ETHNIC GROUPS Mestizo 49%, Creole 25%, Mayan Indian 11%, Garifuna 6%, others 9%
LANGUAGES English (official), Spanish, Creole, Maya
RELIGIONS Roman Catholic 39%, Protestant 27%, others
CURRENCY Belizean dollar = 100 cents

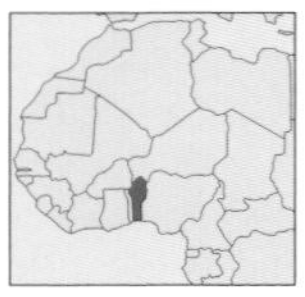

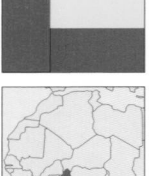

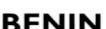

BENIN

GEOGRAPHY The Republic of Benin is one of Africa's smallest countries. It extends north–south for about 390 mi [620 km]. Lagoons line the short coastline, and the country has no natural harbors.

Benin has a hot, wet climate. The average annual temperature on the coast is about 77°F [25°C], and the average rainfall is around 52 inches [1,330 mm]. The inland plains are wetter than the coast.

POLITICS & ECONOMY After slavery was ended in the 19th century, the French gained influence in the area. Benin became self-governing in 1958 and fully independent as Dahomey in 1960. After much instability and many changes of government, a military group took over in 1972. The country, renamed Benin in 1975, became a one-party socialist state. Socialism was abandoned in 1989 and former coup leader Mathieu Kérékou served as president until 2006, when a former banker, Thomas Yayi Boni, was elected president. In 2016 elections, businessman Patrice Talon defeated the ruling party candidate.

Benin is a poor developing country. About half of the people live by subsistence farming. Exports include cotton, petroleum, and palm products. Cocoa, coffee, groundnuts (peanuts), tobacco, and shea nuts are also grown for export.

AREA 43,483 sq mi [112,622 sq km]
POPULATION 10,741,000 **CAPITAL** Porto-Novo
GOVERNMENT Multiparty republic **ETHNIC GROUPS** Fon, Adja, Bariba, Yoruba, Fulani **LANGUAGES** French (official), Fon, Adja, Yoruba
RELIGIONS Christianity 43%, traditional beliefs 30%, Islam 27%
CURRENCY CFA franc = 100 centimes

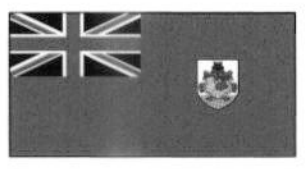
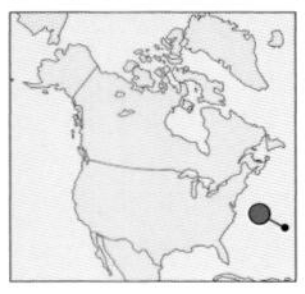

BERMUDA

A group of about 150 small islands situated 570 mi [920 km] east of the USA. Bermuda remains Britain's oldest overseas territory, but it has a long tradition of self-government.

AREA 21 sq mi [53 sq km]
POPULATION 71,000 **CAPITAL** Hamilton

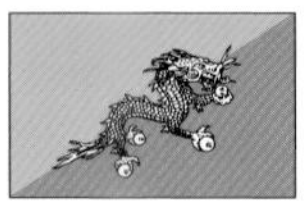
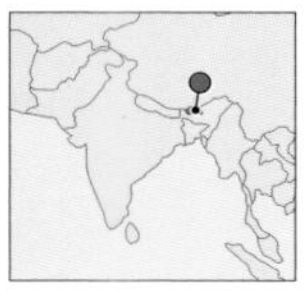

BHUTAN

GEOGRAPHY A mountainous, isolated Himalayan country located between India and Tibet. The climate is similar to that of Nepal, being dependent on altitude and affected by monsoonal winds.

POLITICS & ECONOMY The monarch of Bhutan is head of both state and government, and this predominantly Buddhist country remains, even in the Asian context, both conservative and poor. In 2008, Bhutan held its first ever democratic elections, ending over a century of absolute royal rule and turning Bhutan into a constitutional monarchy.

AREA 18,147 sq mi [47,000 sq km] **POPULATION** 750,000
CAPITAL Thimphu **GOVERNMENT** Constitutional monarchy
ETHNIC GROUPS Bhutanese 50%, Nepalese 35%
LANGUAGES Dzongkha (official) **RELIGIONS** Buddhism 75%, Hinduism 25% **CURRENCY** Ngultrum = 100 chhertum

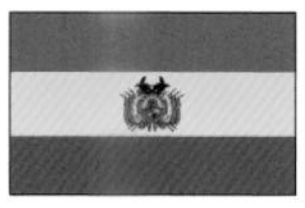
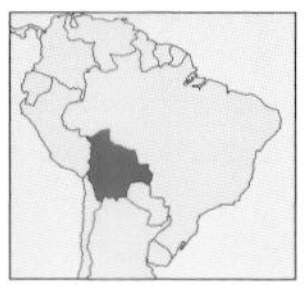

BOLIVIA

GEOGRAPHY The Plurinational State of Bolivia, as the country is officially called, is an isolated and landlocked South American country which straddles the Andes Mountains. The highest point is 21,391 ft [6,520 m] at Nevado Sajama in the west. About 40% of Bolivians live on the Altiplano, a high plateau in the Andes. The sparsely populated east consists of a vast lowland plain.

The Bolivian climate is greatly affected by altitude, with the Andean peaks permanently snow-covered and the eastern plains remaining hot and humid.

POLITICS & ECONOMY American Indians have lived in Bolivia for at least 10,000 years. The main groups today are the Aymara and Quechua people.

In the last 50 years, Bolivia has been ruled by a succession of civilian and military governments. Democracy was restored in 1982. Economic problems have led to a widening of the gap between rich and poor and, in 2005, Evo Morales, an Aymara farmer, was elected president. His policies of nationalization and redistributing wealth to peasants aroused opposition. Re-elected in 2009 and 2014, Morales was a keen advocate of state control and nationalized energy production. In 2016, he failed to win a referendum that would have allowed him to stand again.

Although one of South America's poorest countries, it has its second largest reserves of natural gas. Other resources include silver, tin, zinc, and lithium, but the main activity is agriculture.

AREA 424,162 sq mi [1,098,581 sq km]
POPULATION 10,970,000 **CAPITAL** La Paz (seat of government); Sucre (legal capital/seat of judiciary)
GOVERNMENT Multiparty republic **ETHNIC GROUPS** Mestizo 30%, Quechua 30%, Aymara 25%, White 15% **LANGUAGES** Spanish, Aymara, Quechua (all official) **RELIGIONS** Roman Catholic 95%
CURRENCY Boliviano = 100 centavos

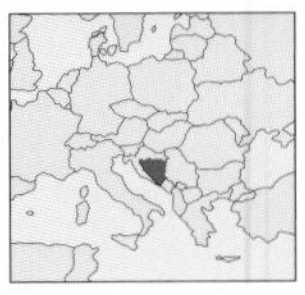

BOSNIA-HERZEGOVINA

GEOGRAPHY The Republic of Bosnia-Herzegovina is one of the seven republics to emerge from the former Federal People's Republic of Yugoslavia. Much of the country is mountainous or hilly, with an arid limestone plateau in the southwest. The River Sava, which forms most of the northern border with Croatia, is a tributary of the River Danube. Because of the country's odd shape, the coastline is limited to a short stretch of 13 mi [20 km] on the Adriatic coast.

A Mediterranean climate, with dry, sunny summers and moist, mild winters, prevails only near the coast. Inland, the weather is more severe, with hot, dry summers and bitterly cold, snowy winters.

POLITICS & ECONOMY In 1918, Bosnia-Herzegovina became part of the Kingdom of the Serbs, Croats, and Slovenes, which was renamed Yugoslavia in 1929. Germany occupied the area during World War II (1939–45). From 1945, Communist governments ruled Yugoslavia as a federation containing six republics, one of which was Bosnia-Herzegovina. In the 1980s, the country faced problems as Communist policies proved unsuccessful.

In 1990, free elections were held in Bosnia-Herzegovina and the non-Communists won a majority. A Muslim, Alija Izetbegovic, was elected president. In 1991, Croatia and Slovenia, other parts of the former Yugoslavia, declared themselves independent. In 1992, Bosnia-Herzegovina held a vote on independence. Most Bosnian Serbs boycotted the vote, while the Muslims and Bosnian Croats voted in favor. Many Bosnian Serbs, opposed to independence, started a war against the non-Serbs. They soon occupied more than two-thirds of the land. The Bosnian Serbs were accused of "ethnic cleansing" – that is, the killing or expulsion of other ethnic groups from Serb-occupied areas. The war spread when Croat forces seized other parts of the country.

In 1995, the country retained its external boundaries, but it was divided into two self-governing provinces – one Bosnian Serb and the other Muslim Croat. Stability was restored with the help of NATO, but the country remained divided. In December 2011, Muslim Croat and Serb leaders agreed on the formation of a central government after 14 months of political crisis. In 2016, the country formally requested membership of the European Union.

The infrastructure and economy of the country were shattered by the war in the early 1990s. Although some stability has been regained it is still considered one of the most corrupt European states. The economy relies on exporting metals and receiving foreign aid. Farm products include fruits, maize, tobacco, vegetables, and wheat, but food has to be imported.

AREA 19,767 sq mi [51,197 sq km]
POPULATION 3,862,000 **CAPITAL** Sarajevo
GOVERNMENT Federal republic **ETHNIC GROUPS** Bosnian 48%, Serb 37%, Croat 14% **LANGUAGES** Bosnian, Serbian, Croatian
RELIGIONS Islam 40%, Serbian Orthodox 31%, Roman Catholic 15%, others 14% **CURRENCY** Convertible marka = 100 convertible pfenniga

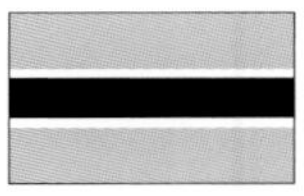
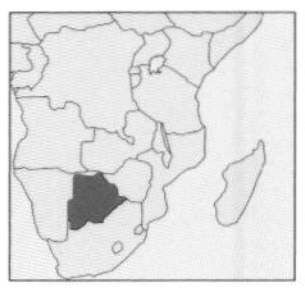

BOTSWANA

GEOGRAPHY The Republic of Botswana is a landlocked country in southern Africa. The Kalahari, a semidesert area covered mostly by grasses and thorn scrub, covers much of the country. Most of the south has no permanent streams but large depressions in the north form inland drainage basins. In one of them, the Okavango River, which rises in Angola, forms a large, swampy delta.

Temperatures are high in the summer months (October to April), but the winter months are much cooler. In winter, nighttime temperatures sometimes drop below freezing point. The average annual rainfall ranges from over 16 inches [400 mm] in the east to less than 8 inches [200 mm] in the southwest.

POLITICS & ECONOMY The earliest inhabitants of the region were the San, sometimes known as Bushmen. They had a nomadic way of life, hunting wild animals and collecting wild plant foods.

Britain ruled the area as the Bechuanaland Protectorate between 1885 and 1966. When the country became independent, it was renamed Botswana. Since then, the country has been a stable, multiparty democracy. However, in a setback to development, the UN has said that around 25% of the adult population are infected with HIV/AIDS, although this is improving.

In 1966, Botswana was extremely poor, but since then per capita income has grown quickly. The discovery of minerals, including coal, cobalt, copper, diamonds, and nickel, has boosted the economy. About 25% of the people depend on agriculture, raising cattle, and growing crops. Industries include the processing of farm products. Safari-based tourism, often upmarket, is important.

AREA 224,606 sq mi [581,730 sq km] **POPULATION** 2,209,000
CAPITAL Gaborone **GOVERNMENT** Multiparty republic
ETHNIC GROUPS Tswana (or Setswana) 79%, Kalanga 11%, Basarwa 3%, others **LANGUAGES** English (official), Setswana
RELIGIONS Christianity 72%, Badimo 6%, others 2%
CURRENCY Pula = 100 thebe

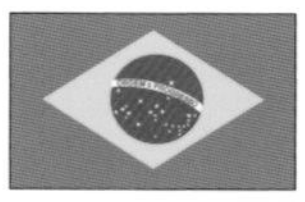
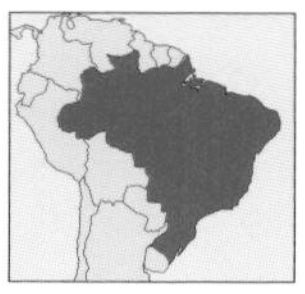

BRAZIL

GEOGRAPHY The Federative Republic of Brazil is the world's fifth largest country. It contains three main regions. The Amazon basin in the north covers more than half of Brazil. The Amazon, the world's second longest river, has a far greater volume than any other river. The second region, the northeast, consists of a coastal plain and the sertão, which is the name for the inland plateaux and hill country. The main river in this region is the São Francisco.

The third region is made up of the plateaux in the southeast. This area, which covers about a quarter of the country, is the most developed and densely populated part of Brazil. Its main river is the Paraná, which flows south through Argentina.

Manaus, on the Amazon, has high temperatures all through the year. Rainfall is heavy, though the period from June to September is drier than the rest of the year. The capital, Brasília, and the city Rio de Janeiro in the south also have tropical climates, with much more marked dry seasons than Manaus. The far south has a temperate climate. The northeastern interior is the driest region, with an average annual rainfall of only 10 inches [250 mm] in places. Rainfall is also unreliable and severe droughts are common in this region.

POLITICS & ECONOMY The Portuguese explorer Pedro Alvarez Cabral claimed Brazil for Portugal in 1500. The Portuguese developed their colony by enslaving many local Amerindian people and introducing about 4 million African slaves. Brazil declared itself an independent empire in 1822 and a republic in 1889. From the 1930s, Brazil faced periods of military rule and widespread corruption. However, civilian rule was restored in 1985.

After two unpopular presidencies, financial stability was established under President Itamar Franco. One of the "BRICS" nations (Brazil, Russia, India, China, and South Africa), Brazil has a rapidly industrializing economy. But many people, including poor farmers and residents of the favelas (city slums), do not share in the country's economic boom. Poverty led to the election of President Luíz Inácio Lula da Silva (generally called "Lula") in 2002. In 2010, he was succeeded by Dilma Roussef, who became Brazil's first female president. She was re-elected for a second term in 2014, but was impeached in 2016 over financial irregularities and replaced by Michel Temer.

Brazil is Latin America's leading economy, with industry as the most important economic sector. It is among the world's top producers of bauxite, chrome, diamonds, gold, iron ore, manganese, and tin. It is also a major manufacturing country, with products including aircraft, cars, chemicals, processed food, iron and steel, paper, and textiles. It is self-sufficient in oil.

Brazil is a major farming nation and agriculture employs 16% of the work force. Coffee is a leading export. Other products include bananas, citrus fruits, cocoa, maize, rice, soybeans, and sugarcane. Brazil is also South America's top producer of eggs, meat, and milk. The rate of deforestation, whilst remaining a global concern as it may accelerate global warming, has been reduced in recent years.

AREA 3,287,338 sq mi [8,514,215 sq km]
POPULATION 205,824,000 **CAPITAL** Brasília
GOVERNMENT Federal republic **ETHNIC GROUPS** White 54%, Mixed 38%, Black 6%, others 2% **LANGUAGES** Portuguese (official)
RELIGIONS Roman Catholic 80%
CURRENCY Real = 100 centavos

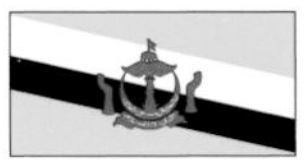
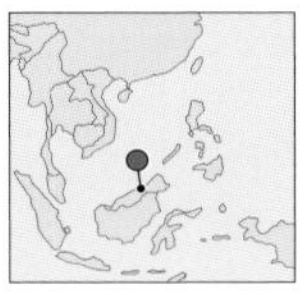

BRUNEI

The Islamic Sultanate of Brunei, a British protectorate until 1984, lies on the north coast of Borneo. The climate is tropical and rain forests cover large areas. Brunei is a prosperous country because of its oil and natural gas production, and the Sultan is said to be among the world's richest men.

AREA 2,226 sq mi [5,765 sq km]
POPULATION 437,000 **CAPITAL** Bandar Seri Begawan

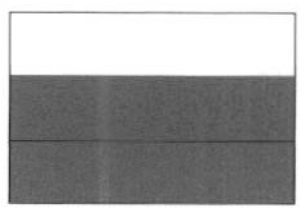
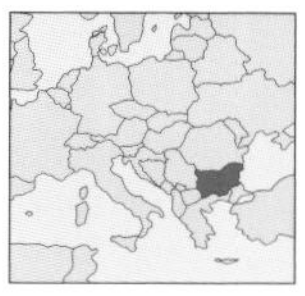

BULGARIA

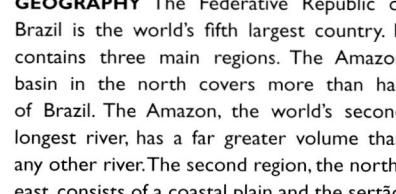

GEOGRAPHY The Republic of Bulgaria is a country in the Balkan peninsula, facing the Black Sea in the east. The heart of Bulgaria is mountainous. The main ranges are the Balkan Mountains in the center and the Rhodope (or Rhodopi) Mountains in the south.

Summers are hot and winters are cold, though seldom severe. The rainfall is moderate.

POLITICS & ECONOMY Ottoman Turks ruled Bulgaria from 1396 and ethnic Turks still form a sizable minority in the country. In 1879, Bulgaria became a monarchy, and in 1908 it became fully independent. Bulgaria was an ally of Germany in World War I (1914–18) and again in World War II (1939–45). In 1944, Soviet troops invaded Bulgaria and, after the war, the monarchy was abolished and the country became a Communist ally of the Soviet Union. Reforms in the Soviet Union in the late 1980s led Bulgaria's government to introduce a multi-party system in 1990. A non-Communist government was elected in 1991, in the first free elections in 44 years. Throughout the 1990s, Bulgaria faced many problems and it sought to become aligned to the West. Bulgaria became a member of NATO in 2004 and a member of the European Union in 2007. Presidential elections in 2016 were won by Socialist-backed independent Ruman Radev, prompting the PM's resignation and early elections.

Bulgaria has an "upper-middle economy." It has some mineral deposits, including brown coal, manganese, gold, and iron ore. Manufacturing is the leading activity, with principal products including chemicals, processed foods, metal products, machinery, and textiles. Corruption and the prevalence of organized crime still hinders economic growth.

AREA 42,823 sq mi [110,912 sq km] **POPULATION** 7,145,000
CAPITAL Sofia **GOVERNMENT** Multiparty republic
ETHNIC GROUPS Bulgarian 77%, Turkish 8%, Roma 4%, Macedonian, Armenian, others **LANGUAGES** Bulgarian (official), Turkish
RELIGIONS Eastern Orthodox 59%, Islam 8%, others
CURRENCY Lev = 100 stotinki

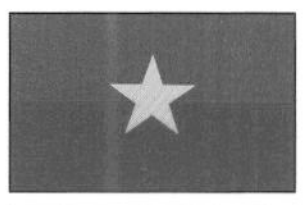
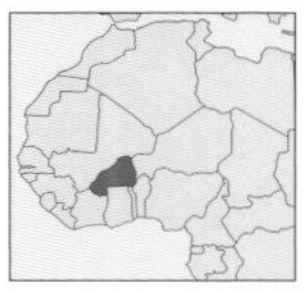

BURKINA FASO

GEOGRAPHY The Democratic People's Republic of Burkina Faso is a landlocked country, a little larger than the United Kingdom, in West Africa. However, Burkina Faso has only a quarter of the population of the UK. The country consists of a plateau, between about 650 ft and 2,300 ft [300 m to 700 m] above sea level. The plateau is cut by several, mainly seasonal, rivers.

The capital city, Ouagadougou, in central Burkina Faso, has high temperatures throughout the year. Most of the rain falls between May and September, but the rainfall is erratic and droughts are common.

POLITICS & ECONOMY The people of Burkina Faso are divided into two main groups: the Voltaic group which includes the Mossi, who form the largest single group, and the Bobo. The French conquered the Mossi capital of Ouagadougou in 1897 and they made the area a protectorate. In 1919, the area became a French colony called Upper Volta. After independence in 1960, Upper Volta became a, sometimes violent and unstable, one-party state. Following a coup in 1983, Thomas Sankara took power and, in 1984, renamed the country Burkina Faso. Four times elected president, Blaise Compaoré was ousted in 2014 and replaced by Marc Kabore, a former prime minister.

Burkina Faso is one of the world's poorest countries and has become very dependent on foreign aid. Most of the land is dry with thin soils. The country's main food crops are beans, maize, millet, rice, and sorghum. Cotton, groundnuts (peanuts), and shea nuts, whose seeds produce a fat used to make cooking oil and soap, are grown for sale abroad. Livestock are also an important export.

The country has few resources and manufacturing is on a small scale. There are some deposits of manganese, zinc, lead, and nickel in the north of the country, but lack of infrastructure hinders development. Many young men seek jobs abroad in Ghana and Ivory Coast and the money they send home to their families is important to the country's economy.

AREA 105,791 sq mi [274,000 sq km]
POPULATION 189,513,000 **CAPITAL** Ouagadougou
GOVERNMENT Multiparty republic **ETHNIC GROUPS** Mossi 40%, Gurunsi, Senufo, Lobi, Bobo, Mande, Fulani **LANGUAGES** French (official), Mossi, Fulani **RELIGIONS** Islam 61%, Christianity 23%, traditional beliefs 16% **CURRENCY** CFA franc = 100 centimes

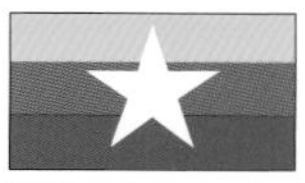
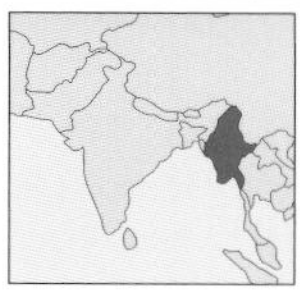

BURMA (MYANMAR)

GEOGRAPHY The Union of Burma has been officially known as the Union of Myanmar since 1989. However, it is more usually referred to as Burma. Mountains border the country in the east and west, with the highest mountains in the north. Burma's highest mountain is Hkakabo Razi, which is 19,294 ft [5,881 m] high. Between these ranges is central Burma, which contains the fertile valleys of the Irrawaddy and Sittang rivers. The Irrawaddy delta is a leading rice-growing area.

Burma has a tropical monsoon climate with three seasons. The rainy season runs from late May to mid-October. A cool, dry season follows, between late October and the middle part of February. The hot season lasts from late February to mid-May. In May 2008, cyclone Nargis devastated the south, including the Irrawaddy delta, killing more than 80,000 people.

POLITICS & ECONOMY The ancestors of the country's main ethnic group today, the Burmese, arrived in the 9th century AD. They encroached on areas occupied since ancient times by a variety of indigenous tribes. Britain conquered Burma in the 19th century making it a province of British India until, in 1937, they granted Burma limited self-government. Japan then invaded and occupied Burma from 1942 until the end of World War II in 1945. Burma became a fully independent country in 1948.

Revolts by Communists and various hill people led to instability in the 1950s. In 1962, Burma became a military dictatorship and, in 1974, a one-party state. The National League for Democracy led by Aung San Suu Kyi won the elections in 1990, but the military continued their repressive rule by ignoring the results.

In 2010, the military released Aung San Suu Kyi from house arrest. A military-backed party was victorious in elections in 2010, and in 2011 a civilian government, backed by the military, took power. In 2012, Aung San Suu Kyi won a parliamentary seat, while her party, the National League for Democracy (NLD), won 43 of the 44 contested seats. The general elections held in 2015 were a victory for the NLD, although constitutional rules have barred Aung San Suu Kyi from becoming president. Violent confrontations continue to erupt between the Buddhist majority and minority groups, notably the Muslim Rohingya, leading to international accusations of ethnic cleansing.

Agriculture is the main activity, employing 70% of the people. The chief crop is rice with maize, pulses, oilseeds, and sugarcane also important. Burma is the world's largest exporter of teak and, together with rice, this makes up about two-thirds of the total value of exports. Burma has many mineral resources including offshore oil and gas deposits. Manufacturing is mostly on a small scale. Tourism is set to become increasingly important.

AREA 261,227 sq mi [676,578 sq km] **POPULATION** 56,890,000
CAPITAL Rangoon (Yangon); Naypyidaw (administrative capital)
GOVERNMENT Military regime **ETHNIC GROUPS** Burman 68%, Shan 9%, Karen 7%, Rakhine 4%, Chinese, Indian, Mon
LANGUAGES Burmese (official); minority ethnic groups have their own languages **RELIGIONS** Buddhism 89%, Christianity, Islam
CURRENCY Kyat = 100 pyas

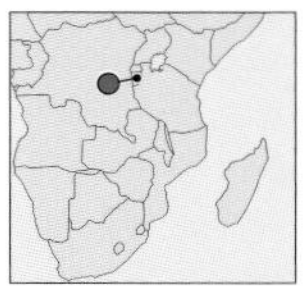

BURUNDI

GEOGRAPHY The Republic of Burundi is the fifth smallest country in mainland Africa. It is also the second most densely populated after its northern neighbor, Rwanda. Part of the Great African Rift Valley, which runs throughout eastern Africa into southwestern Asia, lies in western Burundi. It includes part of Lake Tanganyika. Bujumbura, the capital city, lies on the shore of Lake Tanganyika and has a warm climate. A dry season occurs from June to September, but the other months are fairly rainy. The mountains and plateaux to the east are cooler and wetter, but the rainfall generally decreases to the east.

POLITICS & ECONOMY The Twa, a pygmy people, were the first known inhabitants of Burundi. About 1,000 years ago, the Hutu, a people who speak a Bantu language, gradually began to settle the area, pushing the Twa into remote areas.

From the 15th century, the Tutsi, a cattle-owning people from the northeast, gradually took over the country. The Hutu, though greatly outnumbering the Tutsi, were forced to serve the Tutsi overlords.

Germany conquered the area that is now Burundi and Rwanda in the late 1890s. This was followed by Belgian control during World War I (1914–18). Full independence was achieved in 1962. Since this time rivalry between the Hutu and Tutsi has led to periodic outbreaks of appalling violence, most notably in 1972 and 1993. Many thousands of civilians have been massacred. A cease-fire and power-sharing agreement was reached in 2001. This was

followed, in 2005, by the first parliamentary elections since the beginning of the civil war. The government of President Pierre Nkurunziza, a Hutu, who was first elected in 2005 faces many political and economic challenges. Protests broke out when he sought a third term as president.

Burundi is one of the world's poorest countries. About 94% of the people live by farming, mostly at subsistence level. Food crops include beans, cassava, maize, and sweet potatoes. Livestock are raised and fishing is important. A lack of basic infrastructure and a poorly educated population are hindering development.

AREA 10,747 sq mi [27,834 sq km] **POPULATION** 11,099,000
CAPITAL Bujumbura **GOVERNMENT** Republic **ETHNIC GROUPS** Hutu 85%, Tutsi 14%, Twa (Pygmy) 1% **LANGUAGES** French and Kirundi (both official) **RELIGIONS** Roman Catholic 62%, traditional beliefs 23%, Islam 10%, Protestant 5% **CURRENCY** Burundi franc = 100 centimes

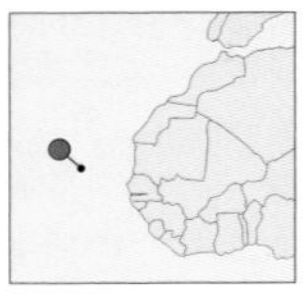

CABO VERDE

Cabo Verde consists of ten large and five small islands, and is situated 350 mi [560 km] west of Dakar in Senegal. The islands have a tropical climate, with high temperatures all year round. Cabo Verde became independent from Portugal in 1975 and is rated as a "low-income" country by the World Bank.

AREA 1,557 sq mi [4,033 sq km]
POPULATION 553,000 **CAPITAL** Praia

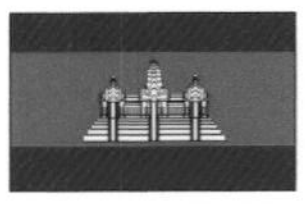
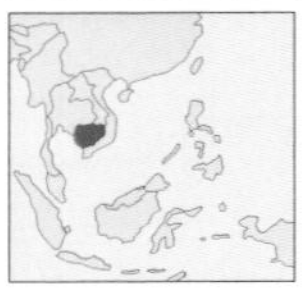

CAMBODIA

GEOGRAPHY The Kingdom of Cambodia is a country in Southeast Asia. Low mountains border the country except in the southeast. Most of Cambodia consists of plains drained by the River Mekong, which enters Cambodia from Laos in the north and exits through Vietnam in the southeast. The northwest contains Tonlé Sap (or Great Lake). In the dry season, this lake drains into the River Mekong. But in the wet season, the level of the Mekong rises and water flows in the opposite direction from the river into Tonlé Sap – the lake then becomes the largest freshwater lake in Asia.

Cambodia has a tropical monsoon climate, with high temperatures throughout the year. The dry season, when winds blow from the north or northeast, runs from November to April. During the rainy season (May to October), moist winds blow from the south or southeast. The high humidity and heat often make conditions unpleasant. Rainfall is heaviest near the coast, and rather lower inland.

POLITICS & ECONOMY From 802 to 1432, the Khmer people ruled a great empire, which reached its peak in the 12th century. The Khmer capital was at Angkor. The Hindu stone temples built there and at nearby Angkor Wat form the world's largest group of religious buildings. France ruled the country between 1863 and 1954, when the country became an independent monarchy. The monarchy was abolished in 1970 and Cambodia became a republic.

In 1970, the Communists under Prime Minister Lon Nol staged a military coup and proclaimed the Khmer Republic, which plunged the country into a civil war. The Khmer Rouge took control in 1975, renaming the country Kampuchea, and launched a reign of terror in which between 1 million and 2.5 million people were killed. In 1979, Vietnamese and Cambodian troops overthrew the Khmer Rouge government. Vietnam withdrew in 1989, and in 1991 Prince Sihanouk was recognized as head of state. Elections were held in May 1993, and in September 1993 the monarchy was restored. In 2004, King Sihanouk abdicated because of ill health and his son, Prince Norodom Sihamoni, became king. Between 2008 and December 2011, Cambodian and Thai troops clashed periodically over a border dispute involving an area near the ancient Preah Vihear temple, a World Heritage Site.

Cambodia is a poor country whose economy, although devastated by war, has now had over 20 years of relative stability. Garment manufacture is the main activity, accounting for 70% of total exports, and rice, rubber, and maize are leading agricultural products. In 2005 offshore oil reserves were discovered and there is potential to mine bauxite, iron, and gold. Tourism is growing rapidly. However, there are still many obstacles to development.

AREA 69,898 sq mi [181,035 sq km] **POPULATION** 15,957,000
CAPITAL Phnom Penh **GOVERNMENT** Constitutional monarchy
ETHNIC GROUPS Khmer 90%, Vietnamese 5%, Chinese 1%, others
LANGUAGES Khmer (official), French, English
RELIGIONS Buddhism 96%, others 4% **CURRENCY** Riel = 100 sen

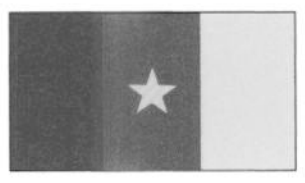
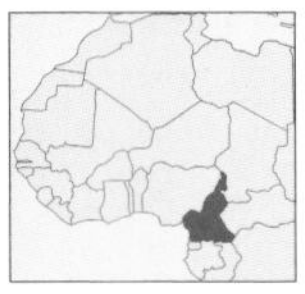

CAMEROON

GEOGRAPHY The Republic of Cameroon in West Africa derived its name from the Portuguese word camarões, or prawns. This name was used by Portuguese explorers who fished for prawns along the coast.

Behind the narrow coastal plains on the Gulf of Guinea, the land rises to a series of plateaux, with a mountainous region in the southwest where the volcano Mount Cameroun is situated. In the north, the land slopes down toward the Lake Chad basin.

The rainfall is heavy, especially in the highlands, but it becomes drier to the north. Temperatures are high on the coast, while the inland plateaux are cooler.

POLITICS & ECONOMY Germany lost Cameroon after World War I (1914–18). The country was then divided into two parts, one ruled by Britain and the other by France. In 1960, French Cameroon became the independent Cameroon Republic. In 1961, after a vote in British Cameroon, part of the territory joined the Cameroon Republic to become the Federal Republic of Cameroon – the other part joined Nigeria. It adopted the name Republic of Cameroon in 1984, but the country had two official languages. In 1995, partly to placate the English-speaking people, Cameroon became the 52nd member of the Commonwealth. In 2008, parliament passed a controversial amendment enabling President Paul Biya, to run successfully for election for a third term in 2011. The country has faced insurgency from Boko Haram since 2014.

Like most countries in tropical Africa, Cameroon's economy is based on agriculture, which employs 70% of the work force. The chief food crops include cassava, maize, millet, sweet potatoes, and yams. Cocoa and coffee are exported, along with oil and bauxite. In 2002, Cameroon's claim over the disputed oil-rich Bakassi peninsula was upheld and the handover by Nigeria was finally completed in 2008. Cameroon has few manufacturing industries, but it is self-sufficient in food. Despite a high literacy rate, economic development is marred by endemic corruption.

AREA 183,568 sq mi [475,442 sq km] **POPULATION** 24,361,000
CAPITAL Yaoundé **GOVERNMENT** Multiparty republic
ETHNIC GROUPS Cameroon Highlanders 31%, Bantu 27%, Kirdi 11%, Fulani 10%, others **LANGUAGES** French and English (both official)
RELIGIONS Christianity 40%, traditional beliefs 40%, Islam 20%
CURRENCY CFA franc = 100 centimes

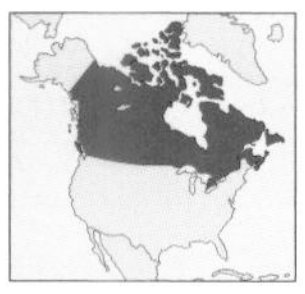

CANADA

GEOGRAPHY Canada is the world's second largest country after Russia but with only 15% of its population. Much of the land is too cold or too mountainous for human settlement. Around 90% of Canadians live within 124 mi [200 km] of the southern border.

Western Canada is rugged: it includes the Pacific ranges and the mighty Rocky Mountains. East of the Rockies are the interior plains. In the north lie the bleak Arctic islands, while to the south lie the densely populated lowlands around lakes Erie and Ontario and in the St Lawrence River valley. The melting of Arctic ice, attributed to global warming, has led to concern about international rights over the Arctic waters off northern Canada.

Canada has a cold climate. In winter, temperatures fall below freezing point throughout most of Canada. But the southwestern coast has a relatively mild climate. Along the Arctic Circle, mean temperatures are below freezing for seven months a year. The west and southeast have high rainfall, but the prairies are dry with 10 inches to 20 inches [250 mm to 500 mm] of rain every year.

POLITICS & ECONOMY Canada's first people, the ancestors of the Native Americans, or Indians, arrived in North America from Asia around 40,000 years ago. The Inuit (Eskimos) were later arrivals from Asia. Europeans first reached Canada in 1497 and soon Britain and France began to compete for control.

France gained an initial advantage, and the French founded Québec in 1608. The British later occupied eastern Canada and, in 1867, they passed the British North America Act, which set up the Dominion of Canada, which was made up of Québec, Ontario, Nova Scotia, and New Brunswick. Other areas were added, the last being Newfoundland in 1949. Canada is a constitutional monarchy, and the British monarch is Canada's head of state. The provinces have a high level of autonomy.

In 1995, the people of Québec voted narrowly against a move to make Québec a sovereign state. In 2006, the national parliament voted to recognize Québec as a nation within a united Canada – a symbolic act of reconciliation. Another major issue concerns the rights of Aboriginal minorities. In 1999, Canada created the territory of Nunavut for the Inuit population. Nunavut covers 64% of what was formerly the eastern part of the Northwest Territories. Nine years of Conservative party rule was ended in late 2015 with an emphatic election victory by the Liberal Party under Justin Trudeau.

Canada is a highly developed and prosperous country. Although farmland covers only 8% of the country, high levels of productivity means that Canada is one of the world's leading producers of barley, wheat, meat, and milk. Forestry and fishing are also important. Canada is rich in natural resources, especially oil and natural gas, and is a major exporter of minerals. The country also produces copper, gold, iron ore, uranium, and zinc. Manufacturing is important in the urban areas, where over 80% of the people live. Manufactures include processed mineral and farm products, cars, chemicals, electronic goods, paper, and timber products. Although the USA is Canada's largest trading partner, increased levels of business involve Asian countries.

AREA 3,849,653 sq mi [9,970,610 sq km]
POPULATION 35,363,000 **CAPITAL** Ottawa
GOVERNMENT Federal multiparty constitutional monarchy
ETHNIC GROUPS British origin 28%, French origin 23%, other European 15%, Amerindian/Inuit 2%, others
LANGUAGES English and French (both official)
RELIGIONS Roman Catholic 43%, Protestant 23%, Judaism, Islam, Hinduism **CURRENCY** Canadian dollar = 100 cents

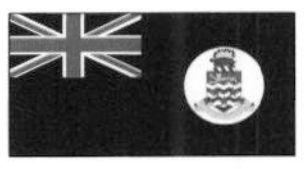
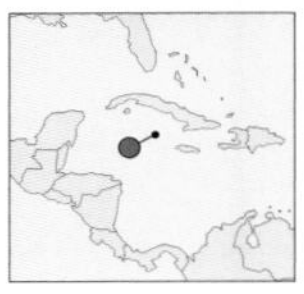

CAYMAN ISLANDS

The Cayman Islands are an overseas territory of the UK, consisting of three low-lying islands. Financial services are the main economic activity and the islands offer a secret tax haven to many companies and banks.

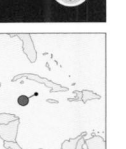

AREA 102 sq mi [264 sq km]
POPULATION 57,000 **CAPITAL** George Town

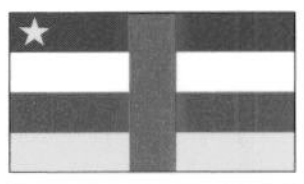
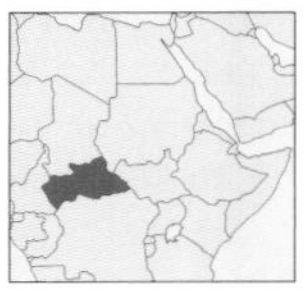

CENTRAL AFRICAN REPUBLIC

GEOGRAPHY The Central African Republic is a remote, landlocked country in the heart of Africa. It consists mostly of a plateau lying between 1,970 ft and 2,620 ft [600 m to 800 m] above sea level. The Oubangi drains the south, while the Chari (or Shari) River flows from the north to the Lake Chad basin. The climate is warm throughout the year, while the annual average rainfall in the capital Bangui totals 62 inches [1,574 mm]. The north is drier, with an average annual rainfall of about 31 inches [800 mm].

POLITICS & ECONOMY France set up an outpost at Bangui in 1889 and ruled the country as a colony from 1894. Known as Ubangi-Shari, the country was ruled by France as part of French Equatorial Africa until it gained independence in 1960.

Central African Republic became a one-party state in 1962, but army officers seized power in 1966. The head of the army, Jean-Bedel Bokassa, made himself emperor in 1976. The country was renamed the Central African Empire, but Bokassa was removed by a military coup in 1979. The country again became a republic.

The election in 1993 ended 12 years of military rule. In 2003 General François Bozizé seized power and served as president from 2005 until he was deposed in 2013 by rebel leader Michel Djotodia. Djotodia resigned in 2014 following international pressure. After an interim period, Faustin-Archange Touadera, a former prime minister, was elected president in February 2016 in largely peaceful eletions. This country has been classified by the UN-based Fund for Peace as a "failed state."

The World Bank classifies Central African Republic as a "low-income" developing country. Over 80% of the people are farmers. The main crops are bananas, maize, manioc, millet, and yams. Coffee, cotton, timber, and tobacco are produced for export. The country has significant natural resources including uranium and diamonds. Development has been impeded by the country's remote position, its poor transport system, and its untrained work force. The country depends heavily on aid.

AREA 240,534 sq mi [622,984 sq km] **POPULATION** 5,507,000
CAPITAL Bangui **GOVERNMENT** Multiparty republic
ETHNIC GROUPS Baya 33%, Banda 27%, Mandjia 13%, Sara 10%, Mboum 7%, Mbaka 4%, others **LANGUAGES** French (official), Sangho
RELIGIONS Traditional beliefs 35%, Protestant 25%, Roman Catholic 25%, Islam 15% **CURRENCY** CFA franc = 100 centimes

CHAD

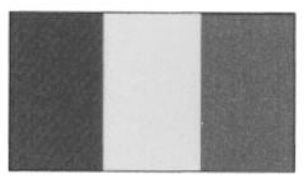
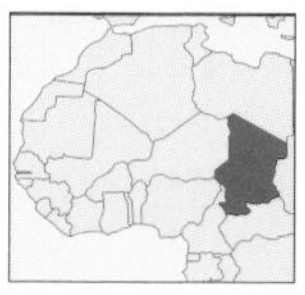

GEOGRAPHY The Republic of Chad is a landlocked country in north-central Africa. It is Africa's fifth largest country and is over twice the size of France, the country which once ruled it as a colony.

Ndjamena in central Chad has a hot, tropical climate, with a marked dry season from November to April. The south of the country is wetter, with an average yearly rainfall of around 39 inches [1,000 mm]. The burning-hot desert in the north has an average yearly rainfall of less than 5 inches [130 mm].

POLITICS & ECONOMY Chad straddles two worlds. The north is populated by Muslim Arab and Berber peoples, while black Africans live in the south. France made Chad a colony in 1902. Chad became independent in 1960, but the 1970s were marked by ethnic conflict that led to civil wars, coups, and conflict with Libya. Chad and Libya agreed a truce in 1987, and in 1994 the International Court of Justice ruled against Libya's claim to the Aozou Strip. From 2004, Chad forces clashed with pro-Sudanese militias as the conflict in Sudan's Darfur province spilled over the border. In 2010 a settlement was agreed with Sudan, and Chad held elections in 2011 when Idriss Deby retained the presidency. He won a fifth term in 2016.

One of the world's poorest countries, Chad has a large refugee population. Farming and fishing employ 83% of the people. Food crops include groundnuts, millet, rice, and sorghum, but cotton is the chief export crop. Chad has few manufacturing industries, but it has had a recent economic boost from oil exports via a pipeline connecting its oilfields to the coast in Cameroon.

AREA 495,752 sq mi [1,284,000 sq km]
POPULATION 11,852,000 **CAPITAL** Ndjamena
GOVERNMENT Multiparty republic **ETHNIC GROUPS** 200 distinct groups: mostly Muslim in the north and center; mostly Christian or animist in the south **LANGUAGES** French and Arabic (both official), many others **RELIGIONS** Islam 53%, Christianity 34%, animist 7%
CURRENCY CFA franc = 100 centimes

CHILE

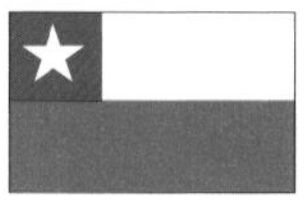
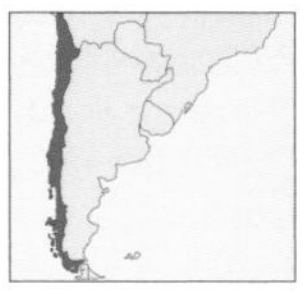

GEOGRAPHY The Republic of Chile stretches about 2,650 mi [4,260 km] from north to south, although the maximum east–west distance is only about 267 mi [430 km]. The high Andes Mountains form Chile's eastern borders with Argentina and Bolivia. To the west are basins and valleys, with coastal uplands overlooking the shore. Most people live in the central valley, where the capital, Santiago, is situated. Earthquakes are common. In February 2010, an earthquake with a magnitude of 8.8 (the biggest in 50 years) struck central Chile, killing more than 400 people.

Santiago has a Mediterranean climate with hot, dry summers and mild, moist winters. The Atacama Desert in the north is extremely arid, while the south is cold and stormy.

POLITICS & ECONOMY Amerindian people reached the southern tip of South America 8,000 years ago. In 1520, Portuguese navigator Ferdinand Magellan was the first European to sight Chile and the country became a Spanish colony in the 1540s. Independent from 1818, Chile won mineral-rich areas from Peru and Bolivia during the War of the Pacific (1879–83).

In 1970, Salvador Allende became the first Communist leader to be elected democratically. He was overthrown in 1973 by army officers, who were supported by the CIA. General Augusto Pinochet then ruled as a dictator until 1989. Since then, government leaders have been democratically elected which has contributed to the country's prosperity and stability. Presidential elections are due in November 2017.

According to the World Bank classifications, Chile has a "high-income" economy, one of the strongest in Latin America. Mining, especially copper, is important and minerals dominate exports. But manufacturing is the most valuable activity. Products include processed foods, metals, iron and steel, transport equipment, and textiles. The chief crop is wheat, while beans, fruits, maize, and livestock products are also important. Chile's fishing industry is one of the world's largest.

AREA 292,133 sq mi [756,626 sq km]
POPULATION 17,650,000 **CAPITAL** Santiago
GOVERNMENT Multiparty republic **ETHNIC GROUPS** Mestizo 95%, Amerindian 4% **LANGUAGES** Spanish (official), English, others
RELIGIONS Roman Catholic 70%, Protestant 17%
CURRENCY Chilean peso = 100 centavos

CHINA

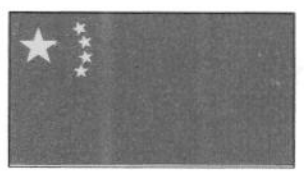
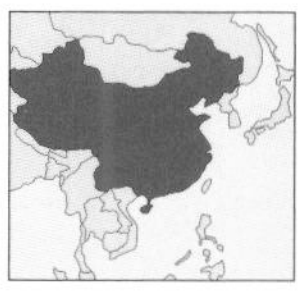

GEOGRAPHY The People's Republic of China is the world's third largest country. Most people live in the east – on the coastal plains or in the fertile valleys of the Huang He (Hwang Ho or Yellow River), the Chang Jiang (Yangtse Kiang), which is Asia's longest river at 3,960 mi [6,380 km], and the Xi Jiang (Si Kiang). Western China is thinly populated. It includes the bleak Tibetan plateau, which is bounded by the Himalaya, the world's highest mountain range. Deserts include the Gobi along the Mongolian border and the Takla Makan in the far west. Earthquakes are common. In May 2008, a major earthquake in the southwest killed more than 69,000 people.

Beijing has cold winters and warm summers with moderate rainfall. To the south, Shanghai has milder winters and more rain. The southeast has a wet, subtropical climate, but the west has a severe climate. Lhasa has very cold winters and a low rainfall.

POLITICS & ECONOMY China is one of the world's oldest civilizations, going back 3,500 years. Mongols conquered China in the 13th century, but Chinese rule was restored in 1368. The Manchu people of Mongolia ruled the country from 1644 to 1912, when the country became a republic.

War with Japan (1937–45) was followed by civil war between the nationalists and the Communists. The Communists triumphed in 1949, setting up the People's Republic of China. In the 1980s, following the death of the revolutionary leader Mao Zedong (Mao Tse-tung) in 1976, China encouraged formerly forbidden policies, namely private enterprise and foreign investment. But the Communist leaders have not permitted political freedom. Opponents are still harshly treated, while attempts to negotiate some degree of autonomy for Tibet have been rejected and central control over Hong Kong has been increased. There remain tensions between China and its neighbours over territorial disputes in the East and South China seas.

China's economy has expanded greatly since the 1970s and many new industries have been set up in the east. Between 1989 and 2011, the economy grew by over 9% per year. China has benefited from its admission to the World Trade Organization. The global financial crisis in 2008 slowed the economic growth rate, though China's grew faster than any other major economy. In 2014 it became the world's largest economy. Since then, however, the economic growth rate has fallen to its lowest level since the 1990s with little prospect of a quick turn around.

China remains a poor country. Agriculture employs around 35% of the work force, although only 10% of the land is farmed. Around 50% of the population lives in urban areas.

Farm products include rice, sweet potatoes, tea, and wheat, and many fruits and vegetables. Livestock farming is important, and China has more than a third of the world's pigs. Resources include coal, iron ore, and other metals. Manufactures include cement, chemicals, fertilizers, machinery, telecommunications equipment, ships, and textiles. China is now a major producer of consumer goods, including cameras, computer products, refrigerators, and television sets, but problems remain such as pollution, inequality, and an inefficient state sector.

AREA 3,705,387 sq mi [9,596,961 sq km]
POPULATION 1,373,541,000 **CAPITAL** Beijing
GOVERNMENT Single-party Communist republic
ETHNIC GROUPS Han Chinese 92%, many others
LANGUAGES Mandarin Chinese (official) **RELIGIONS** Atheist (official)
CURRENCY Renminbi yuan = 10 jiao = 100 fen

COLOMBIA

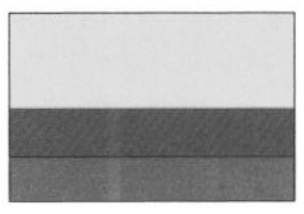
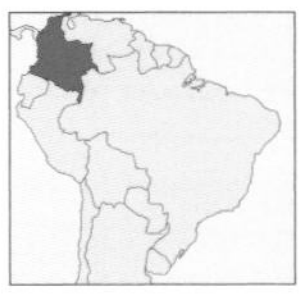

GEOGRAPHY The Republic of Colombia, in northeastern South America, is the only country in the continent to have coastlines on both the Pacific Ocean and the Caribbean Sea. Colombia also contains the northernmost ranges of the Andes Mountains.

There is a tropical climate in the lowlands, but the altitude greatly affects the climate in the Andes. The capital, Bogotá, which stands on a plateau in the eastern Andes at about 9,200 ft [2,800 m] above sea level, has mild temperatures throughout the year. Rainfall is heavy, especially on the Pacific coast.

POLITICS & ECONOMY Amerindian people have lived in Colombia for thousands of years. But today, only a small proportion of the people are of unmixed Amerindian ancestry. Mestizos (people of mixed white and Amerindian ancestry) form the largest group, followed by whites and those of mixed European and African ancestry. Colombia emerged as a republic in 1886.

Although there have been some attempts to quell the violent conflict involving drug cartels, Colombia still faces economic and security problems. Andrés Pastrana, president in 1998–2002, tried to end the guerrilla war, but peace talks collapsed and conflict resumed. His successors, Alvaro Uribe and Juan Manuel Santos, pursued tough policies against the rebels. In 2016, the government and FARC signed a peace agreement, weeks after a previous attempt had been rejected in a public referendum.

Steps have been taken to develop the country's infrastructure to boost employment and the economy was improving strongly until 2015 when the growth of GDP fell back to 2.5% from a high of nearly 5%. Petroleum, coffee, coal, gold, emeralds, cut flowers, and chemicals are exported.

AREA 439,735 sq mi [1,138,914 sq km] **POPULATION** 47,221,000
CAPITAL Bogotá **GOVERNMENT** Multiparty republic
ETHNIC GROUPS Mestizo 58%, White 20%, Mixed 14%, Black 4%
LANGUAGES Spanish (official) **RELIGIONS** Roman Catholic 90%
CURRENCY Colombian peso = 100 centavos

COMOROS

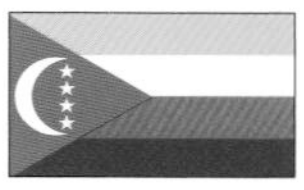
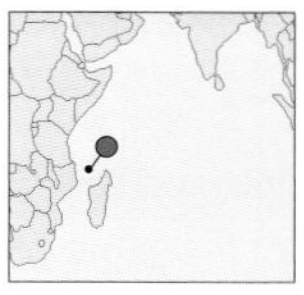

The Union of the Comoros, consists of three large volcanic islands and some smaller ones lying at the north end of the Mozambique Channel in the Indian Ocean. France took over one of the islands, Mayotte, in 1843, and in 1886 the other islands came under French protection. They became independent in 1974, but Mayotte has remained French. Relations between the three remaining islands have been rocky at times and, in the 1990s, the islands of Anjouan and Mohéli tried to secede. The constitution of 2001 granted greater autonomy each island. Very dependent on foreign aid, Comoros is one of Africa's poorest nations. Exports include cloves, perfume oil, copra, and vanilla.

AREA 863 sq mi [2,235 sq km]
POPULATION 795,000 **CAPITAL** Moroni

CONGO

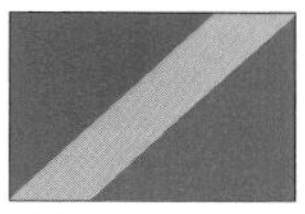
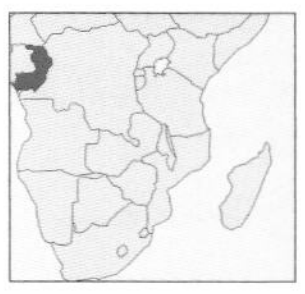

GEOGRAPHY The Republic of the Congo is a country on the River Congo in west-central Africa. The equator runs through the center of the country. Congo has a narrow coastal plain on which its main port, Pointe Noire, stands. Behind the plain are uplands through which the River Kouilou-Niari has carved a fertile valley. Central Congo consists of high plains with the north comprising large swampy areas in the valleys of the tributaries of the River Congo.

Congo has a hot, wet equatorial climate. Brazzaville has a dry season between June and September. The coast is drier and cooler than the rest of the Congo, because of the cold offshore Benguela ocean current.

POLITICS & ECONOMY Part of the huge Kongo kingdom between the 15th and 18th centuries, the coast of the Congo later became a center of the European slave trade. The area came under French protection in 1880 and it was later governed as part of the larger region of French Equatorial Africa. The country remained under French control until 1960.

Congo became a one-party state in 1964 and a military group took over the government in 1968. In 1970, Congo declared itself a Communist country, though it continued to seek aid from Western countries. Multiparty elections were held in 1992, but the elected president, Pascal Lissouba, was overthrown in 1997 by former president Denis Sassou-Nguesso. Civil war broke out with a fragile peace being restored in 2002. Sassou-Nguesso, president for 30 years, is one of Africa's longest serving leaders.

Despite being one of Africa's largest petroleum producers, around 70% of the population live in poverty. Agriculture is the most important activity, employing about 32% of the people, but many farmers produce little more than they need to feed their families. Major food crops include bananas, cassava, maize, and rice, while the leading cash crops are coffee and cocoa. Congo's main exports are oil (which makes up more than 90% of the total), timber, sugar, and diamonds. Manufacturing is still relatively unimportant, hampered by poor transport links, but it is gradually being developed.

AREA 132,046 sq mi [342,000 sq km] **POPULATION** 4,852,000
CAPITAL Brazzaville **GOVERNMENT** Republic
ETHNIC GROUPS Kongo 48%, Sangha 20%, Teke 17%, M'bochi 12%
LANGUAGES French (official), many others **RELIGIONS** Christianity 50%, animist 48%, Islam 2% **CURRENCY** CFA franc = 100 centimes

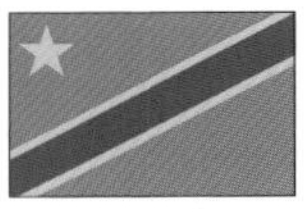

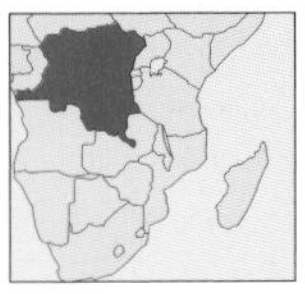

CONGO (DEMOCRATIC REPUBLIC OF THE)

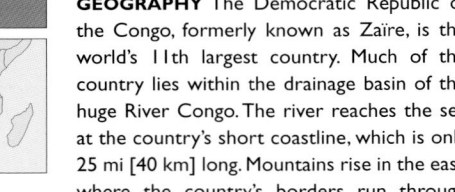

GEOGRAPHY The Democratic Republic of the Congo, formerly known as Zaïre, is the world's 11th largest country. Much of the country lies within the drainage basin of the huge River Congo. The river reaches the sea at the country's short coastline, which is only 25 mi [40 km] long. Mountains rise in the east, where the country's borders run through lakes Tanganyika, Kivu, Edward, and Albert. The equatorial region has high temperatures and heavy rainfall all year.

POLITICS & ECONOMY Portuguese navigators reached the coast in 1482, but the interior was not explored until the late 19th century. In 1885, the country, known as the Congo Free State, became the personal property of King Léopold II of Belgium and was then administered as a Belgian colony from 1908 until 1960.

The country, riven by ethnic rivalries, became a one-party state after a coup by President Mobutu in 1965. Then known as Zaïre, Mobutu held on to power for over 30 years. He was ousted in 1997 by Laurent Kabila, a rebel leader backed by Rwanda and Uganda, who gave the country its present name. Further rifts and violence continued until Kabila was assassinated in 2001. The presidency was taken over by his son, who negotiated the Pretoria Accord with Rwanda which called for an end to fighting and the establishment of a unity government. Presidential elections due at the end of 2016 were deferred after an agreement that gave the opposition cabinets seats.

The Democratic Republic of the Congo is one of the poorest countries in the world. Decades of insurrection and instability since independence have devastated what was once a relatively industrialized economy. It has a vast wealth of natural resources, much of it still to be exploited and, with foreign help, some reform is under way. The economy relies heavily on mining: the country is the world's largest producer of cobalt and a major producer of copper and diamonds. However, the industry is plagued by financial irregularities. Agriculture, mainly at subsistence level, employs 60% of the work force.

AREA 905,350 sq mi [2,344,858 sq km]
POPULATION 81,331,000 **CAPITAL** Kinshasa
GOVERNMENT Single-party republic
ETHNIC GROUPS Over 200; the largest are Mongo, Luba, Kongo, Mangbetu-Azande
LANGUAGES French (official), tribal languages
RELIGIONS Roman Catholic 50%, Protestant 20%, Islam 10%, others
CURRENCY Congolese franc = 100 centimes

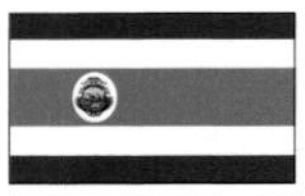

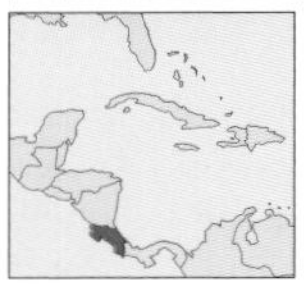

COSTA RICA

GEOGRAPHY The Republic of Costa Rica in Central America has coastlines on both the Pacific Ocean and the Caribbean Sea. Central Costa Rica consists of mountain ranges and plateaux with many volcanoes.

The coolest months of the year are December and January. The northeast trade winds bring heavy rain to the Caribbean coast, while there are lower amounts of rainfall in the highlands and on the Pacific coastlands.

POLITICS & ECONOMY Christopher Columbus reached the Caribbean coast in 1502 and was followed by Spanish settlers. Spain ruled the country until 1821, when the Central American colonies broke away to join Mexico. In 1823, these states then split from Mexico and set up the Central American Federation. Later, this union broke up and Costa Rica became independent in 1838.

From the late 19th century onward, Costa Rica experienced a number of revolutions, with periods of dictatorship alternating with spells of democracy. In 1948, following a revolt, the armed forces were completely abolished and it remains without a standing army today. Since that year, Costa Rica has enjoyed a long period of consistent stable democracy. Luis Guillermo Solis was elected president in April 2014, gaining 78% of votes cast.

Costa Rica is classified by the World Bank as an "upper-middle-income" developing country and one of the most prosperous countries in Central America. There are high educational standards, a high average life expectancy (about 76 years for men and 81 years for women), and the most developed welfare system in Central America. Agriculture employs 14% of the people. Costa Rica's natural resources include its forests, but it lacks minerals apart from some bauxite and manganese. Manufacturing is increasing, with the USA being Costa Rica's main trading partner. Tourism is a fast-growing industry. There are concerns, however, that it is acting as a conduit for drugs and associated corruption.

AREA 19,730 sq mi [51,100 sq km] **POPULATION** 4,873,000
CAPITAL San José **GOVERNMENT** Multiparty republic
ETHNIC GROUPS White (including Mestizo) 94%, Black 3%, Amerindian 1%, Chinese 1%, others **LANGUAGES** Spanish (official), English **RELIGIONS** Roman Catholic 76%, Evangelical 14%
CURRENCY Costa Rican colón = 100 céntimos

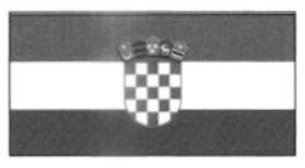

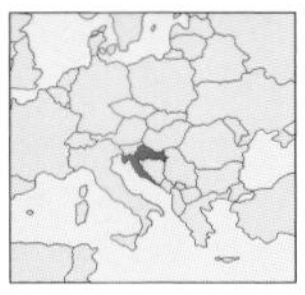

CROATIA

GEOGRAPHY The Republic of Croatia was one of the six republics that made up the former Communist country of Yugoslavia until it became independent in 1991. The region of Dalmatia borders the Adriatic Sea and here are found the coastal ranges of mountains, comprising large tracts of bare limestone. Most of the rest of the country consists of the fertile Pannonian plains.

The coastal area has a typical Mediterranean climate, with hot, dry summers and mild, moist winters. Inland, the climate becomes more continental. Winters are cold, while temperatures often soar to 100°F [38°C] in the summer months.

POLITICS & ECONOMY Once part of the Holy Roman empire, Croatia was an independent kingdom in the 10th and 11th centuries. In 1102, the crowns of Hungary and Croatia were joined, creating a union that lasted 800 years. In 1526, part of Croatia came under the Turkish Ottoman empire, while the rest fell under the control of the Austrian Habsburgs.

After Austria–Hungary was defeated in World War I (1914–18), Croatia became part of the new Kingdom of the Serbs, Croats, and Slovenes. This kingdom was renamed Yugoslavia in 1929. Germany occupied Yugoslavia during World War II (1939–45).

After the war, Communists took power with Josip Broz Tito as the country's leader. Despite ethnic differences between the people, Tito held Yugoslavia together until his death in 1980. In the 1980s, economic and ethnic problems, including a deterioration in relations with Serbia, threatened stability. In the 1990s, Yugoslavia split into five nations, one of which was Croatia, which declared itself independent in 1991.

After Serbia supplied arms to Serbs living in Croatia, war broke out between the two republics, causing great damage. Croatia lost more than 30% of its territory. But in 1992, the United Nations sent a peacekeeping force to Croatia, which effectively ended the war with Serbia. In the same year, when war broke out in Bosnia-Herzegovina, Bosnian Croats occupied parts of the country. But in 1994, Croatia helped to end Croat–Muslim conflict in Bosnia-Herzegovina and, in 1995, after retaking some areas occupied by Serbs, it helped to draw up the Dayton Peace Accord, ending the civil war.

The conflict in the early 1990s badly disrupted the economy. Slow but steady economic growth in the early 2000s was thwarted by the recession of 2008. Various obstacles were overcome and Croatia acceded to membership of the EU in 2013. Problems remain with high unemployment and uneven regional development. Its intricate coastline and islands on the Adriatic Sea are a gift to the tourist industry. Croatia's main exports are manufactures, especially shipbuilding.

AREA 21,829 sq mi [56,538 sq km] **POPULATION** 4,314,000
CAPITAL Zagreb **GOVERNMENT** Multiparty republic
ETHNIC GROUPS Croat 90%, Serb 5%, others
LANGUAGES Croatian 96% **RELIGIONS** Roman Catholic 88%, Orthodox 4%, Islam 1%, others **CURRENCY** Kuna = 100 lipas

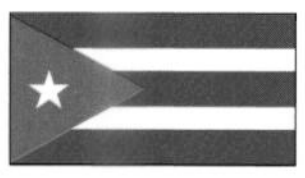

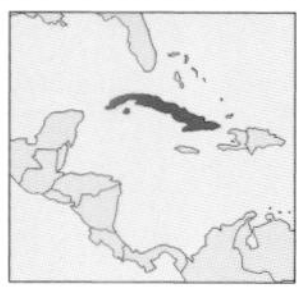

CUBA

GEOGRAPHY The Republic of Cuba is the largest island country in the Caribbean Sea. It consists of one large island, Cuba, the Isle of Youth (Isla de la Juventud), and about 1,600 small islets. Mountains and hills cover about a quarter of Cuba. The highest mountain range, the Sierra Maestra in the southeast, reaches 6,562 ft [2,000 m] above sea level. The rest of the land consists of gently rolling country or coastal plains, crossed by fertile valleys carved by the short, mostly shallow and narrow rivers.

POLITICS & ECONOMY Christopher Columbus discovered the island in 1492 and Spaniards began to settle there from 1511. Spanish rule ended in 1898, when the United States defeated Spain in the Spanish–American War. American influence in Cuba remained strong until 1959, when revolutionary forces under the leadership of Fidel Castro overthrew the dictatorship of Fulgencio Batista.

The United States opposed Castro's policies, when he turned to the Soviet Union for assistance. In 1962, a world crisis occurred when, under intense US pressure, the Soviet Union withdrew missile sites that could have been used to launch nuclear strikes against the United States. The break-up of the Soviet Union in 1991 damaged Cuba's economy and it worked to increase its trade with Latin America and China. Fidel Castro's brother, Raul, took over the leadership in 2008. He introduced reforms in 2009–12. The government still runs the Cuban economy, though, in 2011, a new law allowed people to buy and sell private property. December 2014 saw the start of moves to normalize relations between Cuba and the US. During 2015, banking and diplomatic ties were re-established. The following year, some trade ties with the US were opened, as were diplomatic links with the EU. Fidel Castro died in April 2016.

Sugar cane accounts for more than 60% of the country's exports. The other main crop is tobacco, and citrus fruits, rice, cattle, and milk production all make a contribution to the economy. Nickel oxide is exported and tourism is also important. Cuba has signed an agreement with Russia to exploit off-shore oil deposits.

AREA 42,803 sq mi [110,861 sq km]
POPULATION 11,180,000 **CAPITAL** Havana
GOVERNMENT Socialist republic
ETHNIC GROUPS White 65%, Mestizo 25%, Black 10%
LANGUAGES Spanish (official) **RELIGIONS** Christianity
CURRENCY Cuban peso = 100 centavos

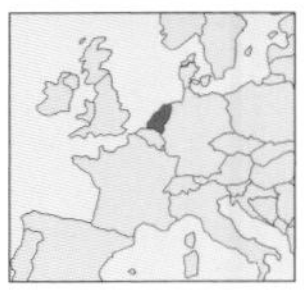

CURAÇAO

Part of the Netherlands Antilles until 2010, Curaçao is a self-governing territory within the Kingdom of the Netherlands. Oil refining, tourism and trade are important.

AREA 171 sq mi [444 sq km]
POPULATION 149,000 **CAPITAL** Willemstad

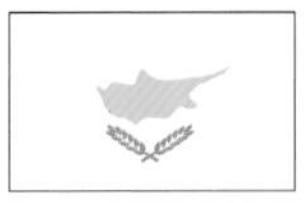

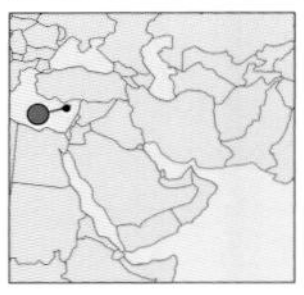

CYPRUS

GEOGRAPHY The Republic of Cyprus is an island nation in the northeastern Mediterranean Sea. Geographers regard it as part of Asia, but it resembles southern Europe in many ways. Its scenic mountain ranges include the southern Troodos Mountains, which reach 6,401 ft [1,951 m] at Mount Olympus, and the Kyrenia range in the north. Between them lies the Mesaoria plain. The climate is Mediterranean, with hot, dry summers and mild, moist winters.

POLITICS & ECONOMY Greeks settled on Cyprus around 3,200 years ago. From AD 330, the island was part of the Byzantine empire until, in the 1570s, Cyprus became part of the Turkish Ottoman empire. Turkish rule continued until 1878 when Cyprus was leased to Britain then went on to be proclaimed a colony in 1925. In the 1950s, Greek Cypriots, who made up four-fifths of the population, began a campaign for enosis (union) with Greece. Their leader was the Greek Orthodox Archbishop Makarios. A secret guerrilla force called EOKA attacked the British, who exiled Makarios in 1956; he returned to Cyprus in 1959.

Cyprus became an independent country in 1960, although Britain retained two military bases. Independent Cyprus had a constitution which provided for power-sharing between the Greek and Turkish Cypriots. But the constitution proved unworkable and fighting broke out between the two communities.

In 1974, Makarios was overthrown by Greek officers and Turkey invaded northern Cyprus. In 1979, the north was proclaimed the Turkish Republic of Northern Cyprus. The only country to recognize this state remains Turkey. In 2002, the European Union invited Cyprus to become a member in 2004. In 2004, the people voted on a UN plan to reunify Cyprus. The Turkish-Cypriots voted in favor, but the Greek-Cypriots voted against, unhappy at limits on their right to return to property located in the north. As a result, only the south was admitted to EU membership on May 1, 2004. Talks on reunification began in 2008, but progress is slow.

Cyprus got its name from the Greek word kypros, meaning copper. But little copper remains and the chief minerals today are asbestos and chromium. However, the most valuable activity in Cyprus is tourism. Manufactures include cement, clothes, footwear, tiles, and wine. Only around 8% of the population are involved in agriculture but 70% are involved in the service industry.

Problems due to the global financial crisis, and the south joining the euro in 2008, resulted in a contraction of the economy and a bailout from the EU at the beginning of 2013. Cypriot banks' substantial exposure to Greek debt is a cause for concern.

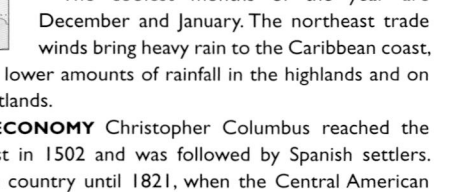

AREA 3,572 SQ MI [9,251 SQ KM]
POPULATION 1,206,000 **CAPITAL** NICOSIA
GOVERNMENT MULTIPARTY REPUBLIC **ETHNIC GROUPS** GREEK CYPRIOT 77%, TURKISH CYPRIOT 18%, OTHERS **LANGUAGES** GREEK AND TURKISH (BOTH OFFICIAL), ENGLISH **RELIGIONS** GREEK ORTHODOX 78%, ISLAM 18%
CURRENCY EURO = 100 CENTS

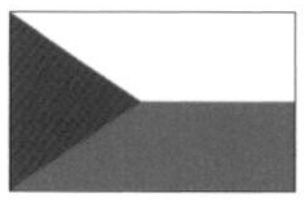
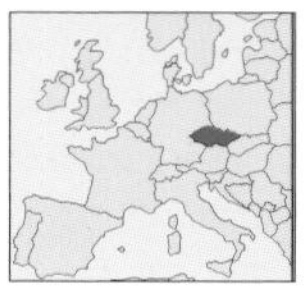

CZECHIA

GEOGRAPHY Until recently known as the Czech Republic, Czechia is the western three-fifths of the former country of Czechoslovakia. It contains two regions: Bohemia in the west and Moravia in the east. Mountains border much of the country in the west. The Bohemian basin in the north-center is a fertile lowland region, with Prague, the capital city, at its heart. Highlands cover much of the center of the country, with lowlands in the southeast.

The climate is influenced by the country's landlocked position in east-central Europe. Summers are warm and winters cold. Rainfall is moderate.

POLITICS & ECONOMY Czechoslovakia was born out of World War I (1914–18) and then occupied by Germany during World War II (1939–45). In 1948, Communist leaders took power and Czechoslovakia was allied to the Soviet Union. In the late 1980s, when democratic reforms were introduced in the Soviet Union, the Czechs also demanded change. Free elections were held in 1990, but differences between the Czechs and Slovaks led to the partitioning of the country (the "velvet divorce") on January 1, 1993. A former dissident, Vaclav Havel, became the first president of the new republic. Czechia became a member of NATO in 1999 and a member of the European Union in 2004. In 2016, Parliament approved a new short form for the country's name, and the Czech Republic became Czechia.

Under Communist rule, Czechia became one of the most industrialized parts of Eastern Europe. Today, it is relatively prosperous although it is still emerging from the recession of 2011-2013. The country has deposits of coal, uranium, iron ore, magnesite, tin, and zinc. Manufacturing employs about 27% of Czechia'a work force.

AREA 30,450 SQ MI [78,866 SQ KM]
POPULATION 10,645,000 **CAPITAL** PRAGUE
GOVERNMENT MULTIPARTY REPUBLIC **ETHNIC GROUPS** CZECH 64%, MORAVIAN 5%, SLOVAK 1%, POLISH, GERMAN, SILESIAN, GYPSY, HUNGARIAN, UKRAINIAN **LANGUAGES** CZECH (OFFICIAL) **RELIGIONS** ATHEIST 40%, ROMAN CATHOLIC 39%, PROTESTANT 4%, ORTHODOX 3%, OTHERS
CURRENCY CZECH KORUNA = 100 HALER

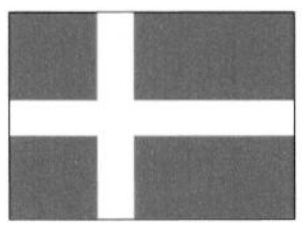
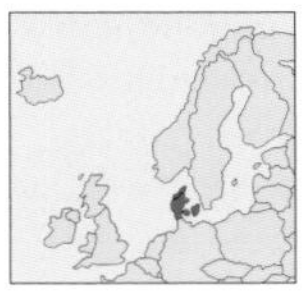

DENMARK

GEOGRAPHY The Kingdom of Denmark is the smallest country in Scandinavia. It consists of a peninsula, called Jutland (or Jylland), which is joined to Germany, and more than 400 islands, 89 of which are inhabited. The land is flat and mostly covered by rocks deposited by huge ice sheets during the last Ice Age. The highest point in Denmark is on Jutland. It is only 561 ft [171 m] above sea level. Denmark has a mild, moist climate, except during cold spells in winter when the Sound (Øresund) between Sjælland and Sweden may freeze over.

POLITICS & ECONOMY Once a Viking stronghold, Denmark formed a union with Norway and Sweden (which included Finland) in the 14th century. Sweden broke away in 1523, while Denmark lost Norway to Sweden in 1814. After 1945, Denmark joined NATO and became a member of the European Economic Community (now the European Union) in 1973. However, the country decided not to join the eurozone in a referendum in 2000. In 2009, Greenland joined the Færoe Islands in becoming a self-governing territory within the Danish realm.

Despite being affected by the global recession of the late 2000s, Denmark is a prosperous country with a generous welfare system. Resources include oil and gas. Manufacturing employs around 12% of the work force. Products include furniture, processed food, machinery, television sets, and textiles. Meat and dairy farming, using intensively scientific methods, employs 3% of the people.

AREA 16,639 SQ MI [43,094 SQ KM] **POPULATION** 5,594,000
CAPITAL COPENHAGEN **GOVERNMENT** PARLIAMENTARY MONARCHY
ETHNIC GROUPS SCANDINAVIAN, INUIT, FÆROESE **LANGUAGES** DANISH (OFFICIAL), GREENLANDIC, ENGLISH, FÆROESE **RELIGIONS** EVANGELICAL LUTHERAN 95% **CURRENCY** DANISH KRONE = 100 ØRE

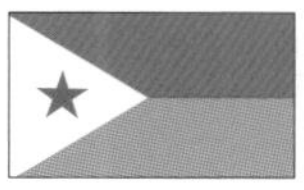
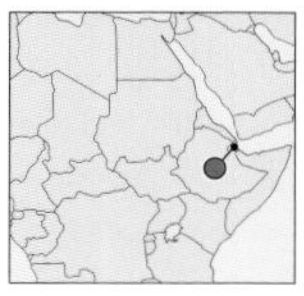

DJIBOUTI

GEOGRAPHY The Republic of Djibouti in eastern Africa occupies a strategic position where the Red Sea meets the Gulf of Aden. Djibouti has one of the world's hottest and driest climates.

POLITICS & ECONOMY Known as the French Territory of the Afars and Issas until 1977, Djibouti owes much of its importance to its rail link to Addis Ababa which allows it to function as a port for Ethiopia and other landlocked African states. It also acts as a regional military base for both France and the USA. The current president, Ismail Omar Guelleh, has been in office since 1999. Djibouti is dominated by one political party, the People's Rally for Progress, with opposition parties having only limited freedom.

Djibouti is a poor country with few natural resources and the climate is unable to support much agriculture. Its economy is based largely on the revenue it gets from its port facilities and it relies heavily on foreign assistance. Unemployment is high at 60%.

AREA 8,958 SQ MI [23,200 SQ KM] **POPULATION** 847,000
CAPITAL DJIBOUTI **GOVERNMENT** MULTIPARTY REPUBLIC
ETHNIC GROUPS SOMALI 60%, AFAR 35% **LANGUAGES** ARABIC AND FRENCH (BOTH OFFICIAL) **RELIGIONS** ISLAM 94%, CHRISTIANITY 6%
CURRENCY DJIBOUTIAN FRANC = 100 CENTIMES

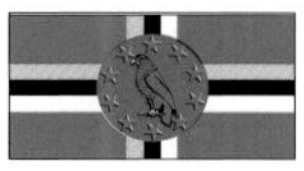
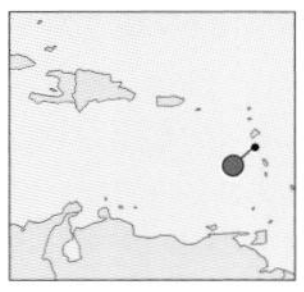

DOMINICA

The Commonwealth of Dominica, a former British colony, became independent in 1978. The island has a mountainous spine and, although less than 10% of the land is cultivated, agriculture employs 40% of the population. The economy has been over-reliant on growing bananas and Dominica is trying to develop its ecotourism business.

AREA 290 SQ MI [751 SQ KM] **POPULATION** 74,000 **CAPITAL** ROSEAU

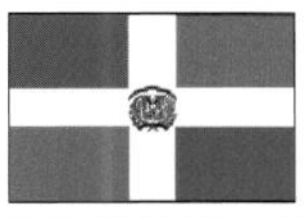
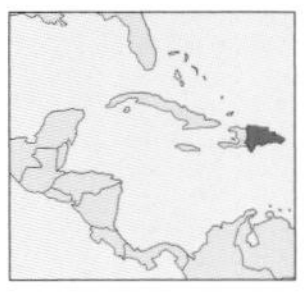

DOMINICAN REPUBLIC

GEOGRAPHY Second largest of the Caribbean nations in both area and population, the Dominican Republic shares the island of Hispaniola with Haiti, with the Dominican Republic occupying the eastern two-thirds. The country is mountainous, and the hot and humid climate eases with altitude.

POLITICS & ECONOMY In 1492, Christopher Columbus landed on Hispaniola and Spaniards soon settled the island, followed by the French, who occupied the western third of the island (which is now Haiti). Civil war broke out in 1966 but US intervention ended the conflict. Since 1966, the young democracy has survived violent elections under the continued watchful eye of the United States.

The Dominican Republic is a developing country and recently tourism and the service industry has overtaken agriculture as the mainstays of the economy. Sugarcane, coffee, rice, bananas, and cocoa are leading crops. Food processing is also important and some ferronickel is produced.

AREA 18,730 SQ MI [48,511 SQ KM] **POPULATION** 10,607,000
CAPITAL SANTO DOMINGO **GOVERNMENT** MULTIPARTY REPUBLIC
ETHNIC GROUPS MULATTO 73%, WHITE 16%, BLACK 11%
LANGUAGES SPANISH (OFFICIAL) **RELIGIONS** ROMAN CATHOLIC 95%
CURRENCY DOMINICAN PESO = 100 CENTAVOS

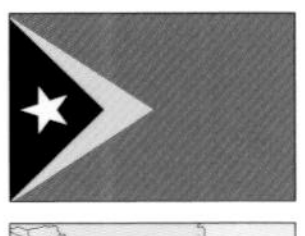
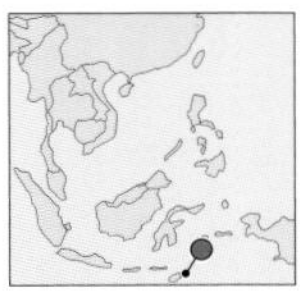

EAST TIMOR

The Republic of East Timor, also known as Timor-Leste, is mainly rugged. Temperatures are generally high and the rainfall is moderate. Portugal, the ruling colonial power, withdrew in 1975 and Indonesia seized control. Brutal suppression by Indonesia led to a vote for independence in 1999 which came into force in 2002. Support from the UN and Australia was crucial in bringing stability and allowing reconstruction. Agriculture is the main activity employing 64% of the work force. In 2006, East Timor and Australia signed a deal to share the revenue from the oil and natural gas deposits under the Timor Sea. The economy is now growing steadily at around 5% per annum.

AREA 5,743 SQ MI [14,874 SQ KM] **POPULATION** 1,261,000 **CAPITAL** DILI

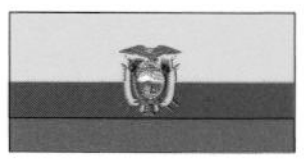
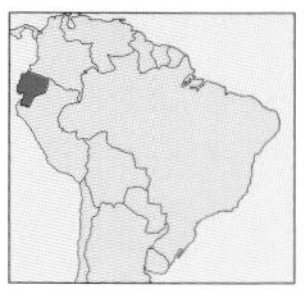

ECUADOR

GEOGRAPHY The Republic of Ecuador straddles the equator on the west coast of South America. Three ranges of the high Andes Mountains form the backbone of the country. Between the towering, snow-capped peaks of the mountains, some of which are volcanoes, lie a series of high plateaux, or basins. Nearly half of Ecuador's population live on these plateaux. The coast has a warm tropical climate, despite the cold offshore Peruvian Current. Inland, the altitude gives the plateaux spring-like weather throughout the year.

POLITICS & ECONOMY The Inca people of Peru conquered much of what is now Ecuador in the late 15th century and their language, Quechua, is still widely spoken today. Spanish forces defeated the Incas in 1533 and took control of Ecuador until 1822.

In the 19th and 20th centuries, Ecuador suffered from political instability, while successive governments failed to tackle the country's social and economic problems. A war with Peru in 1941 led to a loss of territory. Economic crises in the early 21st century led to the adoption of the US dollar as the official currency. Political instability hindered progress and in 2010, a state of emergency was declared following a coup attempt. In 2011, voters approved sweeping reforms and Rafael Correa won a third term in 2013. In 2017, Socialist Lenin Morena became President.

The World Bank classifies Ecuador as an "upper-middle-income" developing country. Much dependent on its oil resources and the fluctuating world price of petrol, Ecuador has tried to diversify its economy. There is a wide disparity in the degree to which some stratas of society benefit from oil revenue: many live in poverty. Agriculture employs 28% of the people and bananas, cocoa, and coffee are all important crops. Fishing, forestry, mining, and manufacturing play a significant part in the economy.

AREA 109,483 SQ MI [283,561 SQ KM]
POPULATION 16,081,000 **CAPITAL** QUITO
GOVERNMENT MULTIPARTY REPUBLIC
ETHNIC GROUPS MESTIZO (MIXED WHITE/AMERINDIAN) 72%, MONTUBIO 7%, AFROECUADORIAN 7%, AMERINDIAN 7%, WHITE 6%
LANGUAGES SPANISH (OFFICIAL), QUECHUA, SHUAR
RELIGIONS ROMAN CATHOLIC 95%
CURRENCY US DOLLAR = 100 CENTS

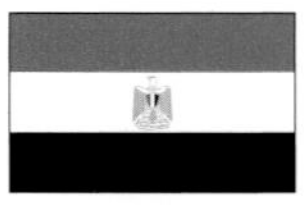
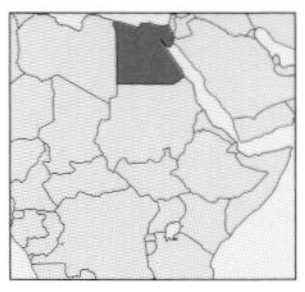

EGYPT

GEOGRAPHY The Arab Republic of Egypt is Africa's third largest country by population after Nigeria and Ethiopia, though it ranks 12th in area. Most of Egypt is desert. Almost all the people live either in the Nile Valley and its fertile delta or along the Suez Canal. This waterway, between the Mediterranean and Red seas, shortens the sea journey between the United Kingdom and India by 6,027 mi [9,700 km]. Recent attempts have been made to irrigate parts of the western desert and thus redistribute the rapidly growing Egyptian population into previously uninhabited regions.

Apart from the Nile Valley, Egypt can be divided into three other main regions. The Western and Eastern deserts are parts of the Sahara. The Sinai peninsula (Es Sina), to the east of the Suez Canal, is a mountainous desert region, falling geographically within Asia. It contains Egypt's highest peak, Gebel Katherîna (8,650 ft [2,637 m]); few people live in this area.

Egypt is a dry country. The low rainfall occurs, if at all, in winter and the country is one of the sunniest places on Earth.

POLITICS & ECONOMY Ancient Egypt, dating from around 5,000 years ago, was one of the great early civilizations. Throughout the country, pyramids, temples, and richly decorated tombs are memorials to its great achievements.

After Ancient Egypt declined, the country came under successive foreign rulers. The Arabs, who first occupied Egypt in the 7th century introducing their language and Islam, had a profound and lasting effect. Their influence was so great that most Egyptians now regard themselves as Arabs.

Egypt came under British rule in 1882, but it gained partial independence in 1922, becoming a monarchy. The monarchy was abolished in 1952, when Egypt became a republic. The creation of Israel in 1948 led Egypt into a series of wars in 1948–9, 1956, 1967, and 1973. In 1979, Egypt signed a peace treaty with Israel and regained the Sinai region, which it had lost in a war in 1967. Extremists opposed contacts with Israel and, in 1981, President Sadat, who had signed the treaty, was assassinated.

While Egypt plays a major part in Arab affairs, most of its people are poor. In February 2011, Hosni Mubarak, Egypt's president since 1981, was forced out of office following huge popular

demonstrations. A Supreme Military Council took power and organized elections in 2011–12. President Muhammed Mursi from the formerly banned Muslim Brotherhood was elected in June 2012. Mursi was removed from power by the military in July 2013 and Abdel Fattah al-Sisi was elected in 2014. Terrorist attacks appear to be primarily aimed at tourist destinations and the Coptic Christian minority.

Egypt is Africa's second most industrialized country after South Africa, but most people are poor. Oil and textiles are the country's main exports with tourism vitally important to the economy. The country is struggling to support its rapidly growing population.

AREA 386,659 SQ MI [1,001,449 SQ KM] **POPULATION** 94,667,000
CAPITAL CAIRO **GOVERNMENT** REPUBLIC
ETHNIC GROUPS EGYPTIANS/BEDOUINS/BERBERS 99%
LANGUAGES ARABIC (OFFICIAL), FRENCH, ENGLISH **RELIGIONS** ISLAM (MAINLY SUNNI MUSLIM) 90%, CHRISTIANITY (MAINLY COPTIC CHRISTIAN) AND OTHERS 10% **CURRENCY** EGYPTIAN POUND = 100 PIASTRES

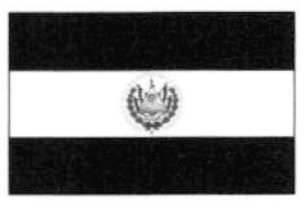
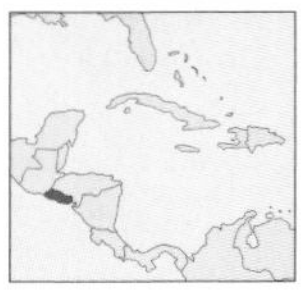

EL SALVADOR

GEOGRAPHY The Republic of El Salvador is the only country in Central America not to have a coast on the Caribbean Sea. El Salvador has a narrow coastal plain along the Pacific Ocean. Behind the coastal plain, the coastal range is a zone of rugged mountains, including volcanoes, which overlooks a densely populated inland plateau. Beyond the plateau, the land rises to the sparsely populated interior highlands. The coast has a hot tropical climate, but inland this is moderated by the altitude. Rain is heavy between May and October.

POLITICS & ECONOMY Amerindians have lived in El Salvador for thousands of years. The ruins of Mayan pyramids, built between AD 100 and 1000, are still found in the western part of the country. Spain first conquered the area in 1524, and ruled until 1821. In 1823, all the Central American countries, except for Panama, set up the Central American Federation, with El Salvador withdrawing in 1840 and declaring its independence in 1841. Suffering from instability throughout the 19th century, the 20th century saw more stable government, although from 1931 military dictatorships alternated with elected governments.

The country remained poor and in the 1970s protesters demanded that the government introduce reforms. Kidnappings and murders committed by left- and right-wing groups were common. A civil war broke out in 1979 between the US-backed government forces and left-wing guerrillas. A ceasefire was agreed in 1992. In 2011, the United States added El Salvador and Belize to its list of countries considered to be major producers or transit routes of illegal drugs. Its murder rate is one of the world's highest.

The World Bank classifies El Salvador as a "lower-middle-income" economy. Often hit by natural disasters, the country relies heavily on remittances from abroad, especially the USA. About three-quarters of the country is farmed. Coffee, grown in the highlands, is the main export, followed by sugar and cotton, which grow on the coastal lowlands. Fishing for lobsters and shrimps is important, but manufacturing is on a small scale.

AREA 8,124 SQ MI [21,041 SQ KM]
POPULATION 6,157,000 **CAPITAL** SAN SALVADOR
GOVERNMENT REPUBLIC **ETHNIC GROUPS** MESTIZO (MIXED WHITE AND AMERINDIAN) 86%, WHITE 13%, AMERINDIAN 1%
LANGUAGES SPANISH (OFFICIAL) **RELIGIONS** ROMAN CATHOLIC 57%, PROTESTANT 21% **CURRENCY** US DOLLAR = 100 CENTS

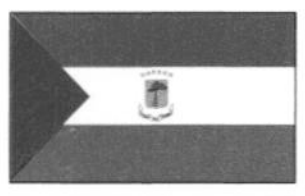
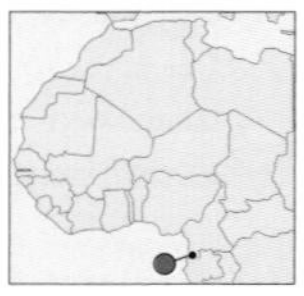

EQUATORIAL GUINEA

GEOGRAPHY The Republic of Equatorial Guinea is a small republic in west-central Africa. It consists of a mainland territory which makes up 90% of the land area, called Rio Muni, between Cameroon and Gabon, and five offshore islands in the Bight of Bonny, the largest of which is Bioko. The island of Annobon lies 350 mi [560 km] southwest of Rio Muni. Rio Muni consists mainly of hills and plateaux behind the coastal plains.

The climate is hot and humid. Bioko is mountainous, with the land rising to 9,869 ft [3,008 m], and hence it is particularly rainy. However, there is a marked dry season between the months of December and February. Mainland Rio Muni has a similar climate, though the rainfall diminishes inland.

POLITICS & ECONOMY Portuguese navigators reached the area in 1471. In 1778, Portugal granted Bioko, together with rights over Rio Muni, to Spain.

In 1959, Spain made Bioko and Rio Muni provinces of overseas Spain and, in 1963, it gave the provinces a degree of self-government. Equatorial Guinea became independent in 1968.

The first president of Equatorial Guinea, Francisco Macias Nguema, proved to be a tyrant. Overthrown in 1979, a Supreme Military Council then took control. In 1991, a democratic system was restored, but alleged human rights abuses continued. A number of organizations categorize Equatorial Guinea as one of worst abusers of human rights.

Agriculture employs two-thirds of the people. The most valuable crop is coffee. Oil, which has been produced since 1966, accounts for most of the export revenue and has fueled recent rapid economic growth. The country is now the third largest oil producer in sub-Saharan Africa.

AREA 10,830 SQ MI [28,051 SQ KM] **POPULATION** 759,000
CAPITAL MALABO **GOVERNMENT** REPUBLIC
ETHNIC GROUPS BUBI (ON BIOKO), FANG (IN RIO MUNI)
LANGUAGES SPANISH AND FRENCH (BOTH OFFICIAL)
RELIGIONS CHRISTIANITY **CURRENCY** CFA FRANC = 100 CENTIMES

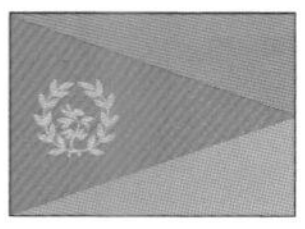
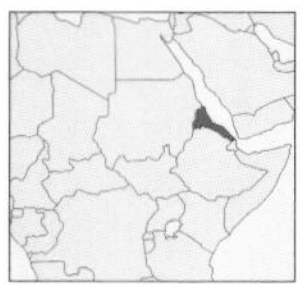

ERITREA

GEOGRAPHY The State of Eritrea consists of a hot, dry coastal plain facing the Red Sea, with a fairly mountainous area in the center. Most people live in the cooler highland area.

POLITICS & ECONOMY From the 1st century AD, Eritrea was part of the ancient Kingdom of Axum, which adopted Christianity in the 4th century AD. The Ottoman Turks took over the area in the 16th century and it became an Italian colony in the 1880s. The Italians were driven out in 1941 and, in 1952, it became part of Ethiopia. A guerrilla struggle launched in 1961 ended in 1993, when Eritrea became independent. Economic recovery was hampered by conflict first with Yemen, over three islands in the Red Sea, and then with Ethiopia. A fragile peace has been negotiated and the country faces the huge task of reconstruction. Unresolved border issues are diverting resources away from development and into the military.

The main economic activities are farming and livestock rearing with some manufacturing based around Asmara. Exploitation of the country's copper and gold resources may drive future economic growth, if very real social problems can be overcome.

AREA 45,405 SQ MI [117,600 SQ KM] **POPULATION** 5,870,000
CAPITAL ASMARA **GOVERNMENT** TRANSITIONAL GOVERNMENT
ETHNIC GROUPS TIGRINYA 55%, TIGRE 30%, SAHO 4%, KUNAMA 2%, OTHERS 16% **LANGUAGES** TIGRINYA, ARABIC, ENGLISH (ALL OFFICIAL), OTHERS **RELIGIONS** ISLAM, COPTIC CHRISTIAN, ROMAN CATHOLIC
CURRENCY NAKFA = 100 CENTS

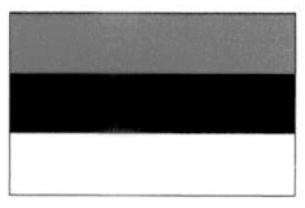
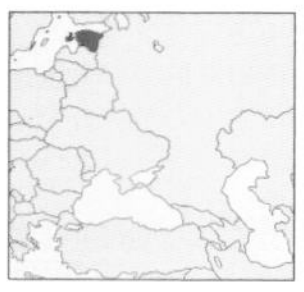

ESTONIA

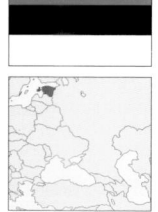

GEOGRAPHY The Republic of Estonia is the smallest of the three states on the Baltic Sea, which were formerly part of the Soviet Union, but became independent in the early 1990s. Estonia consists of a generally flat plain which was covered by ice sheets during the Ice Age. The land is strewn with moraine (rocks deposited by the ice).

The country is dotted with more than 1,500 small lakes. The large Lake Peipus (Ozero Chudskoye) and the River Narva together make up much of Estonia's eastern border with Russia. The largest of the islands is Saaremaa (Ösel). The climate is fairly mild because of the moderating effects of the sea.

POLITICS & ECONOMY The ancestors of the Estonians, who are related to the Finns, settled in the area several thousand years ago. German crusaders, known as the Teutonic Knights, introduced Christianity in the early 13th century. By the 16th century, German noblemen owned much of the land in Estonia. In 1561, Sweden took the northern part of the country and Poland the south. From 1625, Sweden controlled the entire country until Sweden handed it over to Russia in 1721.

Estonian nationalists campaigned for their independence from around the mid-19th century. Finally, Estonia was proclaimed independent in 1918.

In 1939, Germany and the Soviet Union agreed to take over parts of Eastern Europe. In 1940, Soviet forces occupied Estonia, but they were driven out by the Germans in 1941. Soviet troops returned in 1944 and Estonia became one of the 15 Soviet Socialist Republics of the Soviet Union. The Estonians strongly opposed Soviet rule and many of them were deported to Siberia.

Political changes in the Soviet Union in the late 1980s led to renewed demands for freedom. In 1990, the Estonian government declared the country independent and, finally, the Soviet Union recognized this act in September 1991. In January 2011, Estonia became the 17th member of the eurozone.

Under Soviet rule, Estonia was the most prosperous of the three Baltic states. Turning increasingly to the West, it became a member of both the North Atlantic Treaty Organization and the European Union in 2004. From March 2017 NATO made a major deployment of armed forces to Estonia amid reports of a Russian troop build-up across the border.

Estonia's resources include oil shale and its forests. Industries produce fertilizers, processed food, machinery, petrochemical products, wood products, and textiles. Agriculture and fishing are also important activities. Around a quarter of the population are of Russian origin and, due to official language requirements, they can be subject to discrimination.

AREA 17,413 SQ MI [45,100 SQ KM] **POPULATION** 1,259,000
CAPITAL TALLINN **GOVERNMENT** MULTIPARTY REPUBLIC
ETHNIC GROUPS ESTONIAN 69%, RUSSIAN 26%, UKRAINIAN 2%, BELARUSIAN 1%, FINNISH 1% **LANGUAGES** ESTONIAN (OFFICIAL), RUSSIAN
RELIGIONS LUTHERAN, RUSSIAN AND ESTONIAN ORTHODOX, METHODIST, BAPTIST, ROMAN CATHOLIC **CURRENCY** EURO = 100 CENTS

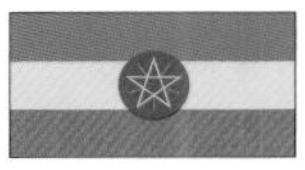
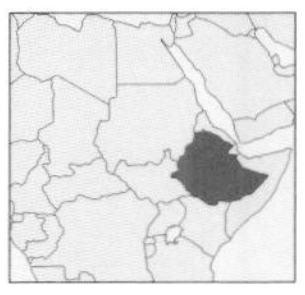

ETHIOPIA

GEOGRAPHY Ethiopia is a landlocked country in northeastern Africa. The land is mainly mountainous, though there are extensive plains in the east, bordering southern Eritrea, and in the south, bordering Somalia. The highlands are divided into two blocks by an arm of the Great Rift Valley which runs throughout eastern Africa. North of the Rift Valley, the land is especially rugged, rising to 14,872 ft [4,533 m] at Ras Dashen. Southeast of Ras Dashen is Lake Tana, source of the River Abay (Blue Nile). The climate is affected by the altitude. The rainfall in the highlands is generally more than 39 inches [1,000 mm]. The lowlands are hot and arid.

POLITICS & ECONOMY Ethiopia was the home of an ancient monarchy, which became Christian in the 4th century. In the 7th century, Muslims gained control of the lowlands, but Christianity survived in the highlands. Ethiopia resisted attempts to colonize it, until Italy invaded the country in 1935. With help from the UK, the Italians were driven out in 1941 and the Emperor Haile Selassie was put back on the throne.

In 1952, Eritrea, on the Red Sea coast, was federated with Ethiopia. But in 1961, Eritrean nationalists demanded their freedom and began a struggle that ended in their independence in 1993. Devastation caused by drought, famine, and war in the 1970s and 1980s led to the overthrow of Haile Selassie in 1974. In 1995, because of Ethiopia's great ethnic diversity, the country was divided into nine provinces. In 1998, boundary disputes with Eritrea led to conflict. A peace agreement was reached in 2001, but tensions mounted in 2005–6 when Ethiopia failed to accept an international ruling over Badme, a border settlement. In 2016, human rights protests broke out across the country.

Ethiopia is one of the world's poorest countries with its economy based on agriculture and at the mercy of a fickle climate. Coffee and the drug "khat" are leading exports. Although still heavily dependent on foreign aid, Ethiopia has one of the fastest growing non-oil economies in Africa.

AREA 426,370 SQ MI [1,104,300 SQ KM] **POPULATION** 102,374,000
CAPITAL ADDIS ABABA **GOVERNMENT** FEDERATION OF NINE PROVINCES
ETHNIC GROUPS OROMO 34%, AMHARA 27%, SOMALI 6%, TIGRAWAY 6%, SIDAMA 4% **LANGUAGES** AMHARIC (OFFICIAL), MANY OTHERS **RELIGIONS** ETHIOPIAN ORTHODOX 43%, ISLAM 34%, PROTESTANT 19% **CURRENCY** BIRR = 100 CENTS

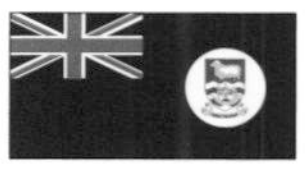
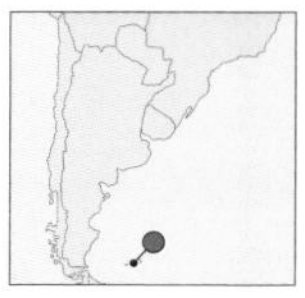

FALKLAND ISLANDS

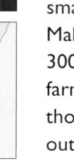

Comprising two main islands and over 200 small ones, the Falkland Islands (or the Islas Malvinas, as they are called in Argentina) lie 300 mi [480 km] from South America. Sheep farming and fishing are the main activities, though the search for oil and diamonds holds out hope for the future. A referendum held in 2013 voted overwhelmingly to stay British.

AREA 4,700 SQ MI [12,173 SQ KM]
POPULATION 3,000 **CAPITAL** STANLEY

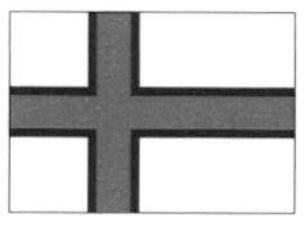

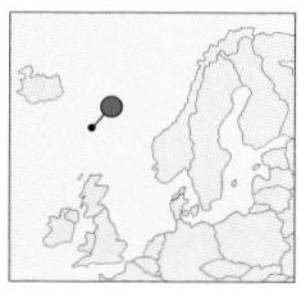

FÆROE ISLANDS

The Færoe Islands are a group of 18 volcanic islands and some reefs in the North Atlantic Ocean. The islands have been Danish since the 1380s, but they became largely self-governing in 1948. The islands are heavily reliant on fishing although the discovery of some oil may allow diversification in the future. Denmark still provides a subsidy.

AREA 540 sq mi [1,399 sq km]
POPULATION 50,000 **CAPITAL** Tórshavn

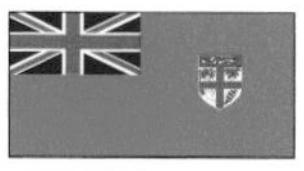

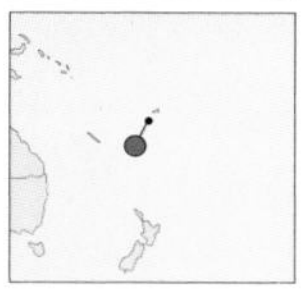

FIJI

The Republic of Fiji (the official name of Fiji since February 2011) consists of more than 800 Melanesian islands, the biggest being Viti Levu and Vanua Levu. The climate is tropical. A former British colony, Fiji became independent in 1970. Its recent history has been marred by efforts of indigenous Fijians to impose their rule, stopping members of the ethnic Indian community from holding senior cabinet posts. Such political instability has harmed the economy.

AREA 7,056 sq mi [18,274 sq km] **POPULATION** 915,000 **CAPITAL** Suva

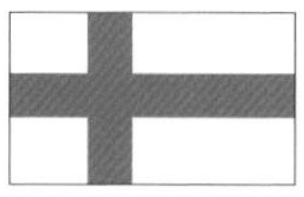

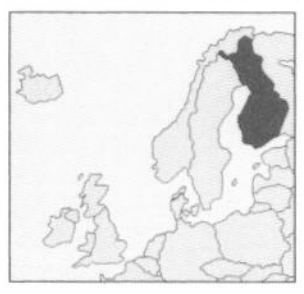

FINLAND

GEOGRAPHY The Republic of Finland is a beautiful country in northern Europe. In the south, behind the coastal lowlands where most Finns live, lies a region of sparkling lakes carved out by ice sheets in the Ice Age. The thinly populated northern uplands cover about two-fifths of the country.

Helsinki, the capital city, has warm summers, but the average temperatures between the months of December and March are below freezing. Snow covers the land in winter. The north has less precipitation than the south, but it is much colder.

POLITICS & ECONOMY Between 1150 and 1809, Finland was under Swedish rule and close links between the countries continue today. Swedish remains an official language in Finland and many towns have Swedish as well as Finnish names.

In 1809, Finland became a grand duchy of the Russian empire. It finally declared itself independent in 1917, following the Russian Revolution. But during World War II (1939–45), the Soviet Union declared war on Finland and took part of Finland's territory. Finland allied itself with Germany, but it lost more land to the Soviet Union at the end of the war.

After World War II, Finland became a neutral country and negotiated peace treaties with the Soviet Union. Finland also strengthened its relations with other northern European countries and became an associate member of the European Free Trade Association (EFTA) in 1961 and a full member in 1986. It then joined the European Union on January 1, 1995, adopting the euro as its currency in 2002.

Forests are the chief resource and wood, wood products, and paper once dominated the economy. They still make up about a quarter of exports, but, since World War II, Finland has set up many new industries, which employ around a quarter of the people. One of Finland's main advantages is a well-qualified work force who enjoy one of the highest rates of per capita income in Western Europe. Major exports include telecommunications equipment, paper products, and iron and steel. However, dealing with a growing aging population is a challenge to be met.

AREA 130,558 sq mi [338,145 sq km] **POPULATION** 5,498,000
CAPITAL Helsinki **GOVERNMENT** Multiparty republic
ETHNIC GROUPS Finnish 93%, Swedish 6%
LANGUAGES Finnish and Swedish (both official)
RELIGIONS Evangelical Lutheran 83% **CURRENCY** Euro = 100 cents

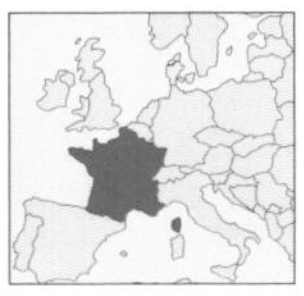

FRANCE

GEOGRAPHY The Republic of France is the largest country in Western Europe. The scenery is extremely varied. The Vosges Mountains overlook the Rhine valley in the northeast, the Jura Mountains and the Alps form the borders with Switzerland and Italy in the southeast, while the Pyrenees straddle France's border with Spain. The only large highland area entirely within France is the Massif Central between the Rhône–Saône valley and the basin of Aquitaine in southern France.

Brittany (Bretagne) and Normandy (Normande) form a scenic region. Fertile lowlands cover most of northern France, including the densely populated Paris basin. Another major lowland area, the Aquitanian basin, is in the southwest, while the Rhône–Saône valley and the Mediterranean lowlands are in the southeast.

The climate of France varies from west to east and from north to south. The west comes under the moderating influence of the Atlantic Ocean, giving generally mild weather. To the east, summers are warmer and winters colder. The climate also becomes warmer as one travels from north to south. The Mediterranean Sea coast has hot, dry summers and mild, moist winters. The Alps, Jura, and Pyrenees mountains have snowy winters. Winter sports centers are found in all three areas. Large glaciers occupy high valleys in the Alps.

POLITICS & ECONOMY The Romans conquered France (then called Gaul) in the 50s BC. Roman rule began to decline in the 5th century AD and, in 486, the Frankish realm (as France was known) became independent under a Christian king, Clovis. In 800, Charlemagne, who had been king since 768, became emperor of the Romans. He extended France's boundaries, but in 843 his empire was divided into three parts and the area of France contracted. After the Norman invasion of England in 1066, large areas of France came under English rule, but this was all but ended in 1453.

France later became a powerful monarchy. But the French Revolution (1789–99) ended absolute rule by French kings. In 1799, Napoleon Bonaparte took power and fought a series of brilliant military campaigns before his final defeat in 1815. The monarchy was restored until 1848, when the Second Republic was founded. In 1852, Napoleon's nephew became Napoleon III, but the Third Republic was established in 1875. France was the scene of much fighting during World War I (1914–18) and World War II (1939–45), causing great loss of life and much damage to the economy.

In 1946, France adopted a new constitution, establishing the Fourth Republic. But political instability and costly colonial wars slowed France's post-war recovery. In 1958, Charles de Gaulle was elected president and he introduced a new constitution, giving the president extra powers and inaugurating the Fifth Republic.

Since the 1960s, France has made rapid economic progress, becoming one of the most prosperous nations in the European Union. But France's government faced a number of problems, including unemployment, pollution, and the growing number of elderly people. France is still facing economic challenges due to lower than expected economic growth and high public spending. A social issue concerns the large numbers of immigrants, including Muslims from North Africa. Since 2015, there have been several terrorist attacks.

In 2002, the euro became France's sole unit of currency, replacing the franc. In 2005, France was rocked by inter-ethnic violence. In 2007, the right-wing Nicolas Sarkozy was elected president and in 2009, he announced that France would rejoin NATO. François Hollande, a socialist, was elected president in 2012. Presidential elections in April-May 2017 were closely fought.

France is one of the world's most developed countries. Its natural resources include its fertile soil, together with deposits of bauxite, coal, iron ore, oil and natural gas, and potash. France is also one of the world's top manufacturing nations, and it has often innovated in bold and imaginative ways. The TGV and hypermarkets are typical examples. Paris is a world center of fashion industries. Manufactures include aircraft, cars, chemicals, electronic and metal products, machinery, processed food, steel, and textiles.

Agriculture employs about 4% of the people, but France is the largest producer of farm products in Western Europe, producing most of the food it needs. Wheat is the leading crop and livestock farming is of major importance. Fishing and forestry are leading industries, while tourism is a major activity.

AREA 212,934 sq mi [551,500 sq km] **POPULATION** 66,836,000
CAPITAL Paris **GOVERNMENT** Multiparty republic
ETHNIC GROUPS Celtic, Latin, Arab, Teutonic, Slavic
LANGUAGES French (official) **RELIGIONS** Roman Catholic 85%, Islam 8%, others **CURRENCY** Euro = 100 cents

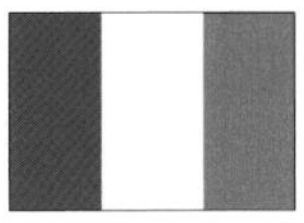

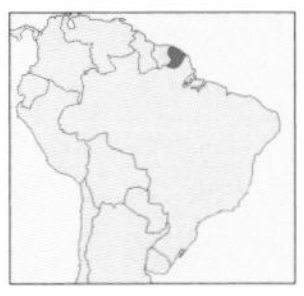

FRENCH GUIANA

GEOGRAPHY French Guiana is the smallest country in mainland South America. The coastal plain is swampy in places, but some dry areas are cultivated. Inland lies a plateau, with the low Serra Tumucumaque in the south. Most of the rivers run north toward the Atlantic Ocean.

French Guiana has a hot, equatorial climate, with high temperatures throughout the year. The rainfall is heavy, especially between December and June, but the climate is dry between August and October. The northeast trade winds blow constantly across the country.

POLITICS & ECONOMY The first people to live in what is now French Guiana were Amerindians. Today, only a few of them survive in the interior. The first Europeans to explore the coast arrived in 1500, and they were followed by adventurers seeking El Dorado, the mythical city of gold. Cayenne was founded in 1637 by a group of French merchants and the area became a French colony in the late 17th century.

France used the colony as a penal settlement for political prisoners from the times of the French Revolution in the 1790s. From the 1850s to 1945, the country became notorious as a place where prisoners were harshly treated. Many of them died, unable to survive in the tropical conditions.

In 1946, French Guiana became an overseas department of France, and in 1974 it also became an administrative region. An independence movement developed in the 1980s, but most people want to retain their links with France. In 2010, the people voted in a referendum to reject plans for increased autonomy.

Although it has rich forest and mineral resources, such as bauxite (aluminum ore), French Guiana is a developing country. It depends greatly on France for money to run its services and the government is the country's biggest employer. Since 1968, Kourou in French Guiana, the European Space Agency's rocket-launching site, has earned money for France by sending communications satellites into space.

AREA 34,749 sq mi [90,000 sq km] **POPULATION** 250,000
CAPITAL Cayenne **GOVERNMENT** Overseas department of France
ETHNIC GROUPS Black or mixed 66%, East Indian/Chinese and Amerindian 12%, White 12%, others 10% **LANGUAGES** French (official)
RELIGIONS Roman Catholic **CURRENCY** Euro = 100 cents

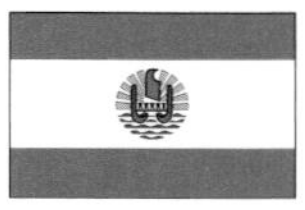

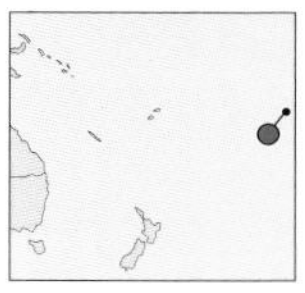

FRENCH POLYNESIA

French Polynesia consists of 130 islands, scattered over 1.5 million sq mi [4 million sq km] of the Pacific Ocean. Tribal chiefs in the area agreed to a French protectorate in 1843. They gained increased autonomy in 1984, but the links with France ensure a high standard of living.

AREA 1,544 sq mi [4,000 sq km]
POPULATION 285,000 **CAPITAL** Papeete

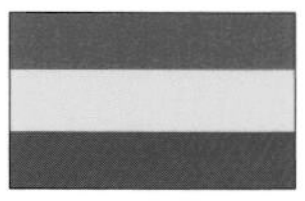

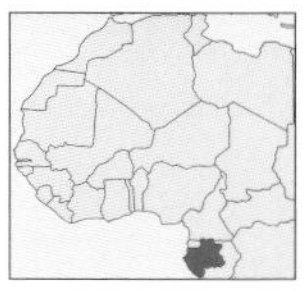

GABON

GEOGRAPHY The Gabonese Republic lies on the equator in west-central Africa. In area, it is a little larger than the United Kingdom, with a coastline 500 mi [800 km] long. Behind the narrow, partly lagoon-lined coastal plain, the land rises to hills, plateaux, and mountains divided by deep valleys carved by the River Ogooué and its tributaries.

Most of Gabon has an equatorial climate, with high temperatures and humidity throughout the year. Rainfall is heavy and the skies are often cloudy.

POLITICS & ECONOMY Gabon became a French colony in the 1880s, but it achieved full independence in 1960. In 1964, an attempted coup was put down when French troops intervened and crushed the revolt. In 1967, Bernard-Albert Bongo, who later renamed himself El Hadj Omar Bongo, became president and remained in power for over 40 years until his death in 2008. He was succeeded by his son, Ali Ben Bongo Ondimba, who was elected in 2009. In 2016, he won a second term.

Gabon's natural resources include its forests, oil and gas deposits, manganese, and uranium. Its mineral deposits make it one of Africa's better-off countries. But agriculture still employs about 30% of the people and many farmers produce little more than they need to support their families. Falling oil revenue means that the economy has to diversify and one growth sector is eco-tourism based round the wildlife in the rain forests.

AREA 103,347 sq mi [267,668 sq km]
POPULATION 1,739,000 **CAPITAL** Libreville
GOVERNMENT Multiparty republic
ETHNIC GROUPS Four major Bantu tribes: Fang, Bapounou, Nzebi and Obamba **LANGUAGES** French (official), Fang, Myene, Nzebi, Bapounou/Eschira, Bandjabi
RELIGIONS Christianity 65%, animist, Islam
CURRENCY CFA franc = 100 centimes

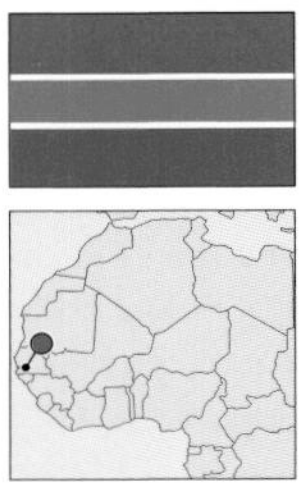

GAMBIA, THE

GEOGRAPHY The Republic of The Gambia is the smallest country in mainland Africa. It consists of a narrow strip of land bordering the River Gambia. The Gambia is almost entirely enclosed by Senegal, except along the short Atlantic coastline.

The Gambia has hot and humid summers, but winter temperatures (November to May) drop to around 61°F [16°C]. In the summer, moist southwesterlies bring rain, which is heaviest on the coast.

POLITICS & ECONOMY English traders established themselves on the River Gambia in the late 16th century and the country was a British colony from 1888 until independence in 1965.

In 1981, an attempted coup in The Gambia was put down with the help of Senegalese troops. Following this in 1982, The Gambia and Senegal set up a defense alliance, called the Confederation of Senegambia. But this alliance was dissolved in 1989. In 1994, a military group led by Captain Yahya Jammeh overthrew the government of Sir Dawda Jawara. Jammeh remained in power until 2016, when he was defeated by Adama Barrow. He refused to accept the result and left only after neighboring countries undertook mediation and threatened armed intervention.

Agriculture is the chief activity employing three-quarters of the population and accounting for around 30% of GDP. Food crops include cassava, millet, and sorghum, but groundnuts (peanuts) and groundnut products are the main exports and the economy is vulnerable to fluctuating world prices for this crop. About one-third of the population live below the poverty line. Tourism is important to the economy, as are remittances sent back from overseas workers. Offshore oilfields were discovered in 2004 but this resource has yet to be developed.

AREA 4,361 sq mi [11,295 sq km] **POPULATION** 2,010,000
CAPITAL Banjul **GOVERNMENT** Republic
ETHNIC GROUPS Mandinka 42%, Fula 18%, Wolof 16%, Jola 10%, Serahuli 9%, others
LANGUAGES English (official), Mandinka, Wolof, Fula
RELIGIONS Islam 90%, Christianity 8%, traditional beliefs 2%
CURRENCY Dalasi = 100 bututs

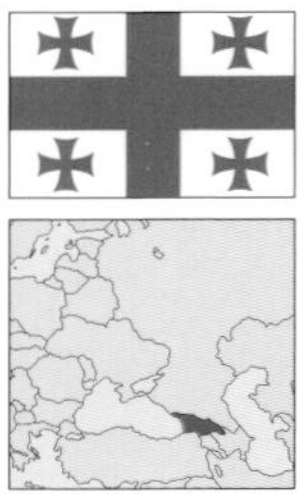

GEORGIA

GEOGRAPHY Georgia is a country on the borders of Europe and Asia, facing the Black Sea. The land is rugged with the Caucasus Mountains forming its northern border.

The highest mountain in this range, Mount Elbrus (18,510 ft [5,642 m]), lies over the border in Russia. The Black Sea plains have hot summers and mild winters. The rainfall is heavy, though inland areas are drier.

POLITICS & ECONOMY The first Georgian state was set up nearly 2,500 years ago but since then has had a chequered history of being overrun by a variety of conquering armies. From the 16th to the 18th centuries, Persia and the Turkish Ottoman empire struggled for control of the area, and in the late 18th century Georgia sought the protection of Russia. By the early 19th century, it was part of the Russian empire. After the Russian Revolution of 1917, Georgia declared its independence, but Russia invaded, making the country part of the Soviet regime. Georgia declared itself independent in 1991 and it became a separate country when the Soviet Union was dissolved in December 1991.

Georgia contains three regions populated by minority peoples: Abkhazia in the northwest, South Ossetia in north-central Georgia, and Ajaria in the southwest. Civil war broke out in South Ossetia in the early 1990s, while fierce fighting continued in Abkhazia until the late 1990s. In 2000, Georgia agreed to recognize Ajaria's autonomy in the country's constitution. In 2003, the pro-Western Mikhail Saakashvili was elected president following the "Rose Revolution." Following Saakashvili's re-election in 2008, relations with Russia deteriorated. In August 2008, Georgia tried to retake South Ossetia by force. Russian troops counterattacked and drove Georgian troops out of South Ossetia and Abkhazia. After parliamentary elections in 2012 were won by the opposition Georgian Dream coalition, Saakashvili resigned and was replaced by Giorgi Margvelashvili. Georgian Dream increased its majority in 2016 elections.

Georgia is a developing country. Agriculture, food processing, and perfume-making are important activities. Products include barley, citrus fruits, grapes for wine-making, maize, tea, tobacco, and vegetables. Sheep and cattle are reared. Hydroelectricity provides most of Georgia's power needs but gas and oil have to be imported. Unemployment remains high.

AREA 26,911 sq mi [69,700 sq km]
POPULATION 4,928,000 **CAPITAL** Tbilisi
GOVERNMENT Multiparty republic
ETHNIC GROUPS Georgian 84%, Azeri 7%, Armenian 6%, Russian 1%, others 2%
LANGUAGES Georgian (official), Russian, Armenian, Azeri; Abkhaz (official in Abkhazia) **RELIGIONS** Georgian Orthodox 84%, Islam 10%, Armenian Gregorian 4% **CURRENCY** Lari = 100 tetri

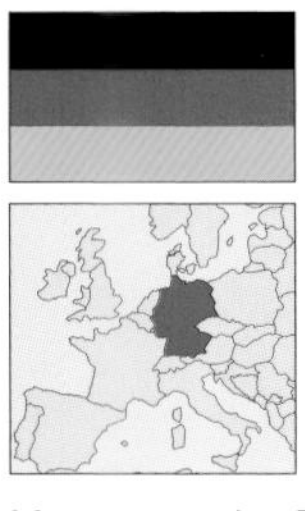

GERMANY

GEOGRAPHY The Federal Republic of Germany is the fourth largest country in Western Europe, after France, Spain, and Sweden. The North German Plain borders the North Sea in the northwest and the Baltic Sea in the northeast. Major rivers draining the plain include the Weser, Elbe, and Oder.

The central highlands include the Harz Mountains, the Thuringian Forest (Thüringer Wald), the Ore Mountains (Erzgebirge), and the Bohemian Forest (Böhmerwald) on the Czech border. The Bavarian Alps in the south contain Germany's highest peak, Zugspitze, at 9,718 ft [2,962 m] above sea level. The Black Forest (Schwarzwald) in the southwest overlooks the River Rhine. Northwestern Germany has a mild climate, but the Baltic coasts are cooler. To the south, the climate becomes more continental, especially in the highlands.

POLITICS & ECONOMY Germany and its allies were defeated in World War I (1914–18) and the country became a republic. Adolf Hitler came to power in 1933 and ruled as a dictator. His order to invade Poland led to the start of World War II (1939–45), which ended with Germany in ruins.

In 1945, Germany was divided into four military zones. In 1949, the American, British, and French zones were amalgamated to form the Federal Republic of Germany (West Germany), while the Soviet zone became the German Democratic Republic (East Germany), a Communist state. Berlin, which had also been partitioned, became a divided city. West Berlin was part of West Germany, while East Berlin became the capital of East Germany. Bonn was the capital of West Germany.

Tension between East and West mounted during the Cold War, but West Germany rebuilt its economy quickly. In East Germany, the recovery was less rapid. In the late 1980s, reforms in the Soviet Union led to unrest in East Germany. Free elections were held in East Germany in 1990 and, on October 3, 1990, Germany was reunited.

In the 1990s, the government faced many problems, especially those arising from reunification. In 1999, the parliament moved from Bonn to the reconstructed Reichstag building in Berlin. In 2005, Angela Merkel became Germany's first female Chancellor. Despite the unpopularity of her policy on welcoming asylum seekers and a series of poor results in regional elections, she announced in 2016 her intention to stand for re-election in 2017.

West Germany's "economic miracle" after World War II was greatly helped by foreign aid. Today, Germany is one of the world's major economic powers. It is a leading member of the European Union and the 19-member eurozone. Since 2011, it has helped to maintain the eurozone by supporting debt-ridden countries, such as Greece. The mainstay of its export-led economy is manufacturing. Exports include machinery, metals, chemicals, and vehicles. Germany has some coal, potash, and rock salt deposits, but it imports many industrial raw materials. Germany also imports food. Leading agricultural products include fruits, grapes for wine-making, potatoes, sugar beet, and vegetables. Livestock include beef cattle and pigs.

AREA 137,846 sq mi [357,022 sq km]
POPULATION 80,723,000 **CAPITAL** Berlin
GOVERNMENT Federal multiparty republic
ETHNIC GROUPS German 92%, Turkish 2%, Serbo-Croatian, Italian, Greek, Polish, Spanish **LANGUAGES** German (official)
RELIGIONS Protestant (mainly Lutheran) 34%, Roman Catholic 34%, Islam 4%, others **CURRENCY** Euro = 100 cents

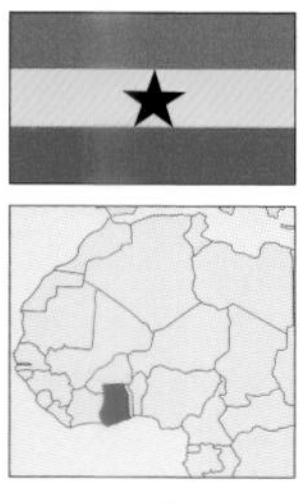

GHANA

GEOGRAPHY The Republic of Ghana faces the Gulf of Guinea in West Africa. This hot country, just north of the equator, was formerly known as the Gold Coast. In the southwest, behind the thickly populated southern coastal plains, which are lined with lagoons, lies a plateau region.

Accra has a hot, tropical climate. Rain occurs all through the year, though Accra is drier than areas inland.

POLITICS & ECONOMY Portuguese explorers reached the area in 1471 and named it the Gold Coast. The area became a center of the slave trade in the 17th century until it was ended in the 1860s and, gradually, the British took control of the area. After independence in 1957, attempts were made to develop the economy by creating large state-owned manufacturing industries. But debt and corruption, together with falls in the price of cocoa, the chief export, caused economic problems. This led to instability and frequent coups. In 1981, power was invested in a Provisional National Defense Council, led by Flight-Lieutenant Jerry Rawlings. The government steadied the economy and introduced reforms. Incumbent John Dramani Mahama lost to human rights lawyer Nana Akufo-Abu in the 2016 presidential elections.

The World Bank classifies Ghana as a "lower-middle-income" developing country. Although the majority of the people are poor and farming employs 56% of the population, Ghana has one of Africa's fastest growing economies. Now exploiting recently discovered offshore oil reserves, the country is benefiting from years of stable government and efficient administration.

AREA 92,098 sq mi [238,533 sq km] **POPULATION** 26,908,000
CAPITAL Accra **GOVERNMENT** Republic
ETHNIC GROUPS Akan 47%, Mole-Dagbon 17%, Ewe 14%, Ga-Dangme 7%, Gurma 6% **LANGUAGES** English (official), Asante, Ewe, Fante, Boron, Dagomba **RELIGIONS** Christianity 71%, Islam 18%, traditional beliefs 5% **CURRENCY** Cedi = 100 pesewas

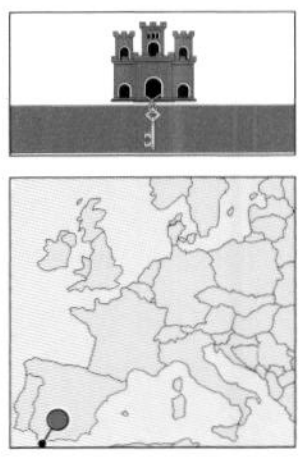

GIBRALTAR

Gibraltar occupies a strategic position on the south coast of Spain where the Mediterranean meets the Atlantic. It was recognized as a British possession in 1713 and, despite Spanish claims, its population has consistently voted to retain its contacts with Britain.

AREA 2.3 sq mi [6 sq km]
POPULATION 29,000 **CAPITAL** Gibraltar Town

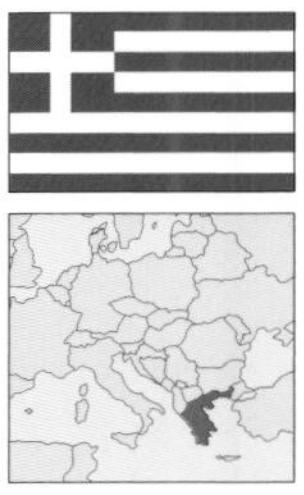

GREECE

GEOGRAPHY The Hellenic Republic, as Greece is officially called, is a rugged country situated at the southern end of the Balkan peninsula. Olympus, at 9,570 ft [2,917 m], is the highest peak. Islands make up about a fifth of the land area.

Low-lying areas in Greece have mild, moist winters and hot, dry summers. The east coast has more than 2,700 hours of sunshine a year and only about half of the rainfall of the west. The mountains have a much more severe climate, with snow on the higher slopes in winter.

POLITICS & ECONOMY Around 2,500 years ago, Greece became the birthplace of Western civilization, and Ancient Greek ruins and art still attract millions of tourists to the country. The first civilization, the Minoan, was centered on Crete. It flourished between about 3000 and 1400 BC. Following the end of the related Mycaenean period on the mainland (1580–1100 BC), a "dark age" lasted until about 800 BC. But from 750 BC, Greeks became rich traders and the city-state of Athens reached its peak in 461–431 BC. Greece became a Roman province in 146 BC and, in 365, it became part of the Byzantine empire.

The Byzantine empire fell to the Turks in 1453. But Greece became an independent monarchy in 1830. After World War II (1939–45), when Germany ruled Greece, a civil war broke out between Greek Communists and nationalists. It ended in 1949 and a military dictatorship seized power in 1967. The monarchy was abolished in 1973 and democracy was restored in 1974. Greece joined the European Community (now the European Union) in 1981 and, on January 1, 2002, the euro became the sole unit of currency. In 2010–13, its government faced a debt crisis and was forced to take drastic emergency economic cuts, amidst growing public unrest.

Greece is one of the EU's less economically developed members. Manufactured products include processed food, cement, chemicals, metal products, textiles, and tobacco. Greece also mines lignite (brown coal), bauxite, and chromite. Crops include barley, grapes, dried fruits, olives, potatoes, sugar beet, and wheat. Livestock farming is important and tourism is a major industry.

AREA 50,949 sq mi [131,957 sq km]
POPULATION 10,773,000 **CAPITAL** Athens
GOVERNMENT Multiparty republic **ETHNIC GROUPS** Greek 93%
LANGUAGES Greek (official) **RELIGIONS** Greek Orthodox 98%
CURRENCY Euro = 100 cents

GREENLAND

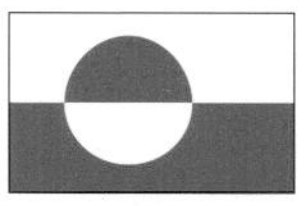
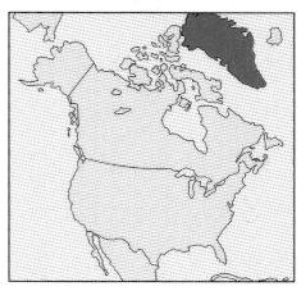

Greenland is the world's largest island. With an ice sheet covering four-fifths of the land, settlements are confined to the coast. Greenland became a Danish possession in 1380. Full internal self-government was granted in 1981 and, in 2009, Greenland became a self-governing territory, though it remains dependent on Danish subsidies.

AREA 838,999 SQ MI [2,175,600 SQ KM]
POPULATION 58,000 **CAPITAL** NUUK

GRENADA

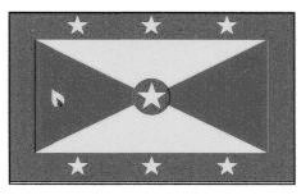
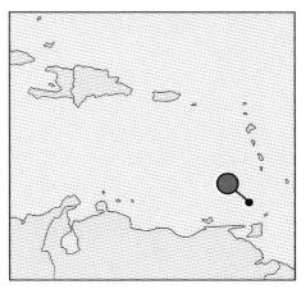

The most southerly of the Windward Islands in the Caribbean Sea, Grenada became independent from the UK in 1974. A military group seized power in 1983, when the prime minister was killed. US troops intervened and restored order and constitutional government.

AREA 133 SQ MI [344 SQ KM]
POPULATION 111,000 **CAPITAL** ST GEORGE'S

GUADELOUPE

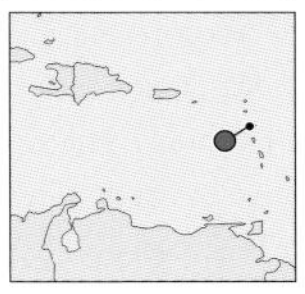

Guadeloupe is a French overseas department which includes seven Caribbean islands, the largest of which is Basse-Terre. French aid has helped to maintain a reasonable standard of living for the people.

AREA 658 SQ MI [1,705 SQ KM]
POPULATION 402,000 **CAPITAL** BASSE-TERRE

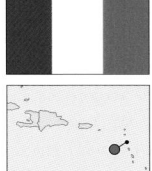

GUAM

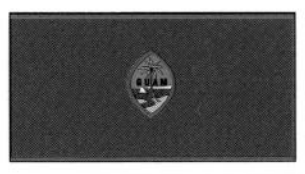
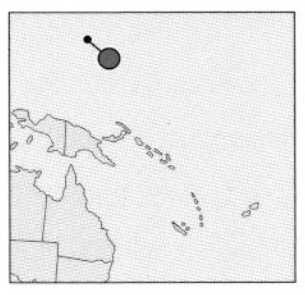

Guam, a strategically important "unincorporated territory" of the USA, is the largest of the Mariana Islands in the Pacific Ocean. Its economy depends on US military spending.

AREA 212 SQ MI [549 SQ KM]
POPULATION 163,000 **CAPITAL** AGANA

GUATEMALA

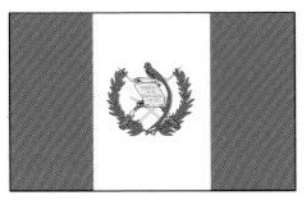
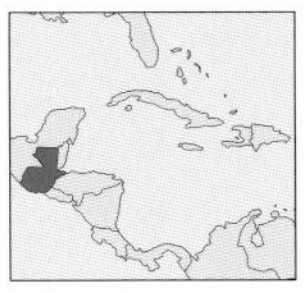

GEOGRAPHY The Republic of Guatemala in Central America contains a densely populated mountain region, with fertile soils. The mountains, which run in an east–west direction, contain many volcanoes, some of which are active. Volcanic eruptions and earthquakes are common in the highlands. South of the mountains lie the thinly populated Pacific coastlands, while a large inland plain occupies the north.

The lowlands of Guatemala are hot and rainy, but the central highlands are cooler and drier. Guatemala City has a pleasant, warm climate with a dry season between November and April.

POLITICS & ECONOMY Much of what is now Guatemala was part of the Maya empire which thrived between AD 300 and 900. Spain ruled the area from the 1520s until 1821, with Guatemala achieving full independence in 1839. Instability and periodic violence have marred its progress. Guatemala has a long-standing claim over Belize, but this was reduced in 1983 to the southern fifth of the country. Between 1960 and 1996, civil war occurred between left-wing groups, including many Amerindians, and government forces. In 2015, Jimmy Morales was elected president following the arrest of the previous incumbent for corruption.

Guatemala is ranked as a "lower-middle-income" economy with agriculture employing 38% of the population. Coffee, sugar, bananas, and beef are exported, and the spice cardamom and cotton are also important. Maize is the main food crop. Poverty is endemic in the countryside and problems of malnutrition, infant mortality, and illiteracy are yet to be overcome.

AREA 42,042 SQ MI [108,889 SQ KM]
POPULATION 15,190,000 **CAPITAL** GUATEMALA CITY
GOVERNMENT REPUBLIC **ETHNIC GROUPS** LADINO (MIXED HISPANIC AND AMERINDIAN) 55%, AMERINDIAN 43%, OTHERS 2%
LANGUAGES SPANISH (OFFICIAL), AMERINDIAN LANGUAGES
RELIGIONS ROMAN CATHOLIC, INDIGENOUS MAYAN BELIEFS
CURRENCY US DOLLAR; QUETZAL = 100 CENTAVOS

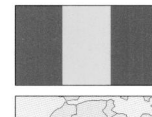

GUINEA

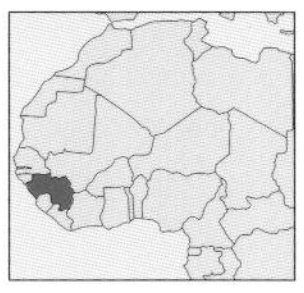

GEOGRAPHY The Republic of Guinea faces the Atlantic Ocean in West Africa. A flat, swampy plain borders the coast. Behind this plain, the land rises to a plateau region called Fouta Djallon. The Upper Niger Plains in the northeast are where the Niger, one of Africa's longest rivers, rises.

Guinea has a tropical climate and Conakry has its rainy period between May and November, the coolest season. In the dry season, hot harmattan winds blow from the Sahara.

POLITICS & ECONOMY Guinea came under the influence of several medieval African states, including Ancient Ghana and Ancient Mali. France began to control the area in the late 19th century with Guinea becoming independent in 1958. Its leaders pursued socialist policies but resorted to repressive measures to hold on to power. A military regime under Lansana Conté took over in 1984, but a multiparty system was restored in 1992. Following Conté's death in 2008, an army group led by Captain Mousa Dadis Camara seized power. But in 2010, Alpha Condé was elected president in Guinea's first democratic election since independence. He was re-elected in 2015.

Guinea is a "low-income" developing country. Its resources include bauxite (aluminum ore), diamonds, gold, iron ore, and uranium. Bauxite and alumina (processed bauxite) account for more than half of the country's exports. Agriculture employs more than 75% of the people, but most farmers are poor. Manufactures include alumina, processed food, and textiles.

AREA 94,925 SQ MI [245,857 SQ KM]
POPULATION 12,093,000 **CAPITAL** CONAKRY
GOVERNMENT MULTIPARTY REPUBLIC
ETHNIC GROUPS PEUHL 40%, MALINKE 30%, SOUSSOU 20%, OTHERS 10% **LANGUAGES** FRENCH (OFFICIAL)
RELIGIONS ISLAM 85%, CHRISTIANITY 8%, TRADITIONAL BELIEFS 7%
CURRENCY GUINEAN FRANC = 100 CAURIS

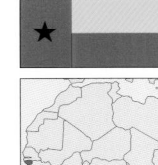

GUINEA-BISSAU

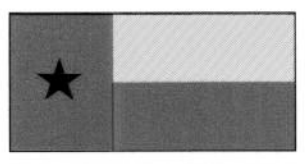
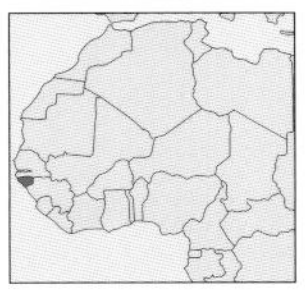

GEOGRAPHY The Republic of Guinea-Bissau, formerly known as Portuguese Guinea, is a small country in West Africa. The land is mostly low-lying, with a broad, swampy coastal plain and many flat offshore islands. The country has a tropical climate, with a dry season (December to May) and a wet season (June to November).

POLITICS & ECONOMY Portuguese explorers reached Guinea-Bissau in 1446 and the area became a center of the slave trade. From 1836, Portugal administered Guinea-Bissau with the Cape Verde Islands, but in 1879 the territories were separated.

In 1956, African nationalists in Portuguese Guinea (as Guinea-Bissau was then known) and Cape Verde founded the African Party for the Independence of Guinea and Cape Verde (PAIGC). The PAIGC began a guerrilla war in 1963 and, by 1968, it held two-thirds of the country. In 1972, a rebel National Assembly, elected by the people in the PAIGC-controlled area, voted to make the country independent as Guinea-Bissau.

The newly independent Guinea-Bissau faced many problems arising from its underdeveloped economy and its lack of trained people to work in the administration. One objective of the leaders of Guinea-Bissau was to unite their country with Cape Verde. But, in 1980, army leaders overthrew Guinea-Bissau's government. The Revolutionary Council, which took over, opposed unification with Cape Verde. Guinea-Bissau ceased to be a one-party state in 1991 and multiparty elections were held in 1994. Civil war and military coups followed until a civilian government was restored in 2004. Following another military coup in 2012, after the death of president Bacai Sanha, a government by Transitional National Council was established. Jose Mario Vaz was elected president in May 2014, vowing to fight the country's endemic poverty.

The economy is massively in debt and relies on foreign aid: Guinea-Bissau is one of the world's poorest countries. Agriculture employs 82% of the people. Crops include coconuts, groundnuts (peanuts), maize, and rice, with cashews becoming more important recently. The country is a major hub for drug trafficking between Latin America and Europe.

AREA 13,948 SQ MI [36,125 SQ KM] **POPULATION** 1,759,000
CAPITAL BISSAU **GOVERNMENT** "INTERIM" GOVERNMENT
ETHNIC GROUPS BALANTA 30%, FULA 20%, MANJACA 14%, MANDINGA 13%, PAPEL 7% **LANGUAGES** PORTUGUESE (OFFICIAL), CRIOULO
RELIGIONS ISLAM 50%, TRADITIONAL BELIEFS 40%, CHRISTIANITY 10%
CURRENCY CFA FRANC = 100 CENTIMES

GUYANA

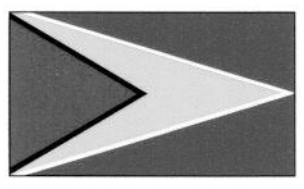
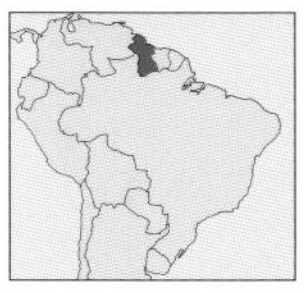

GEOGRAPHY The Cooperative Republic of Guyana is a country facing the Atlantic Ocean in northeastern South America. The coastal plain is flat and much of it is below sea level.

The climate is hot and humid, though the interior highlands are cooler than the coast. Rainfall is heavy, occurring on more than 200 days a year.

POLITICS & ECONOMY Britain gained control of the area in 1814 and ruled British Guiana until it became independent as Guyana in 1966. A black lawyer, Forbes Burnham, was the first prime minister. Under a new constitution adopted in 1980, the president's powers were increased. Burnham became president and served in this post until he died in 1985. The current president is David Granger, who was elected in 2015.

Ethnic tensions persist between the descendants of African slaves and those descended from Indians brought in by the British, spilling over into political rivalries.

Guyana is a poor country. Its resources include gold, bauxite (aluminum ore) and other minerals, forests, and fertile soils. Sugarcane and rice are leading crops. Guyana has potential for producing hydroelectricity from its many rivers.

AREA 83,000 SQ MI [214,969 SQ KM]
POPULATION 736,000 **CAPITAL** GEORGETOWN
GOVERNMENT MULTIPARTY REPUBLIC
ETHNIC GROUPS EAST INDIAN 43%, BLACK 30%, AMERINDIAN 9%, OTHERS 18% **LANGUAGES** ENGLISH (OFFICIAL), CREOLE, HINDI, URDU
RELIGIONS CHRISTIANITY 57%, HINDUISM 28%, ISLAM 7%, OTHERS 8%
CURRENCY GUYANESE DOLLAR = 100 CENTS

HAITI

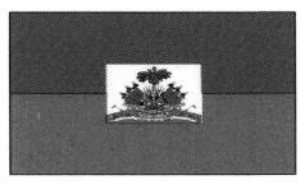
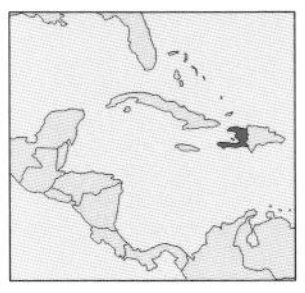

GEOGRAPHY The Republic of Haiti occupies the western third of Hispaniola in the Caribbean. The land is mainly mountainous. The climate is hot and humid, though the northern highlands, with about 79 inches [200 mm], have more than twice as much rainfall as the southern coast.

POLITICS & ECONOMY Visited by Christopher Columbus in 1492, Haiti was later developed by the French. The country became independent in 1804 Haiti subsequently suffered from instability, violence, and dictatorial rule. Elections in 1990 returned Jean-Bertrand Aristide as president, but he was overthrown in 1991. In 1995, René Préval was elected president, but Aristide was again elected in 2000. In 2004, rebel activity forced Aristide to flee the country. Presidential elections in 2016 were won by businessman Jovenal Moise.

In January 2010, an earthquake hit Port-au-Prince, killing up to 230,000 people and devastating the economy. As many as 80% of the people live below the poverty line.

AREA 10,714 SQ MI [27,750 SQ KM]
POPULATION 10,486,000 **CAPITAL** PORT-AU-PRINCE
GOVERNMENT MULTIPARTY REPUBLIC **ETHNIC GROUPS** BLACK 95%, MIXED/WHITE 5% **LANGUAGES** FRENCH AND CREOLE (BOTH OFFICIAL)
RELIGIONS ROMAN CATHOLIC 80%, PROTESTANT 16%, VOODOO
CURRENCY GOURDE = 100 CENTIMES

HONDURAS

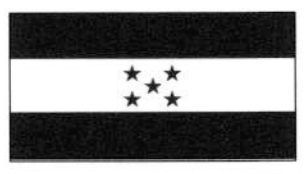
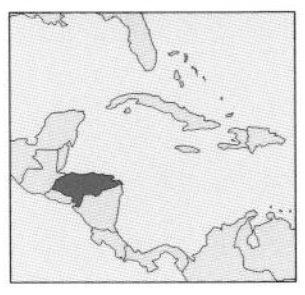

GEOGRAPHY The Republic of Honduras is the second largest country in Central America. The northern coast, on the Caribbean Sea, extends for more than 373 mi [600 km], but the Pacific coast in the southeast is only about 50 mi [80 km] long. Honduras has a tropical climate, but the highlands are cooler. The rainiest months are between May and November. Hurricanes often hit the north coast. Hurricane Mitch in 1998 caused the worst destruction in modern times.

POLITICS & ECONOMY Once part of the Maya empire, Christopher Columbus claimed the area for Spain in 1502 and Spain ruled from 1625 until 1821. Honduras became part of the Central American Federation but withdrew in 1838.

In the 1890s, American companies developed plantations to grow bananas. But instability slowed economic progress. Since 1980, civilian governments friendly toward the United States have ruled Honduras, but in 2008 it joined the "Bolivarian Alternative to the Americas," a left-wing alliance headed by Venezuelan President Hugo Chavez. A military coup in 2009 removed President Manuel Zelaya from office. In elections in January 2014, Juan Orlando Hernández was elected president.

Honduras is one of Central America's least industrialized countries with around 50% of its economy linked to the USA. Its few resources include silver, lead, and zinc. Agriculture is the main activity. Bananas and coffee are exported and maize is the chief food crop. Products include processed food and textiles.

Violent crime (Honduras has the world's highest murder rate) makes the country one of the least secure in Central America.

AREA 43,277 SQ MI [112,088 SQ KM] **POPULATION** 8,893,000
CAPITAL TEGUCIGALPA **GOVERNMENT** REPUBLIC
ETHNIC GROUPS MESTIZO 90%, AMERINDIAN 7%, BLACK (INCLUDING BLACK CARIB) 2%, WHITE 1% **LANGUAGES** SPANISH (OFFICIAL), AMERINDIAN DIALECTS **RELIGIONS** ROMAN CATHOLIC 97%
CURRENCY HONDURAN LEMPIRA = 100 CENTAVOS

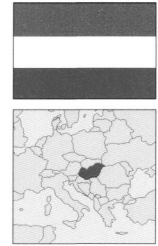

HUNGARY

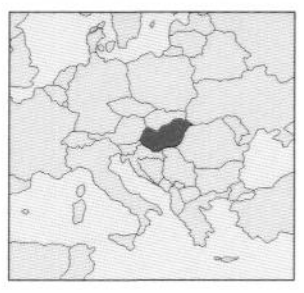

GEOGRAPHY Hungary is a landlocked country in central Europe. The land is mostly low-lying and drained by the Danube (Duna) and its tributary, the Tisza. Most of the land east of the Danube belongs to the region of the Great Plain (Nagy Alföld), which covers about half of Hungary.

Hungary lies far from the moderating influence of the sea, but it does contain Lake Balaton, the largest lake in central Europe. As a result of its position in the European landmass, summers are warmer and sunnier, and the winters colder than in Western Europe.

POLITICS & ECONOMY Following first an alliance, then occupation by Germany during World War II, Hungary was gradually taken over by a Communist government. From 1949, Hungary was an ally of the Soviet Union with Soviet troops crushing an anti-Communist revolt in 1956. But in the 1980s, reforms in the Soviet Union led to the growth of anti-Communist groups and, in 1989, Hungary adopted a new constitution making it a multiparty state and made moves toward a more free market economy. In 2004, Hungary became a member of both the North Atlantic Treaty Organization and the European Union. In recent years there has been a swing toward the right-wing parties with the conservative Fidesz Party of Prime Minister Viktor Orban being re-elected in April 2014 with 44% of the vote.

Before World War II, Hungary's economy was based mainly on agriculture but the Communist era saw the introduction of many manufacturing industries. From the late 1980s, the increase in private ownership of businesses caused problems, including high rates of unemployment and inflation. High levels of government borrowing left the country vulnerable to the recession of 2008 when the country had to ask for outside financial help. Leading manufactures include aluminum, chemicals, electrical and electronic goods, and telecommunications equipment.

AREA 35,920 SQ MI [93,032 SQ KM] **POPULATION** 9,875,000
CAPITAL BUDAPEST **GOVERNMENT** MULTIPARTY REPUBLIC
ETHNIC GROUPS MAGYAR 92%, ROMA, GERMAN, SERB, ROMANIAN, SLOVAK
LANGUAGES HUNGARIAN (OFFICIAL)
RELIGIONS ROMAN CATHOLIC 52%, CALVINIST 16%, LUTHERAN 3%, OTHERS
CURRENCY FORINT = 100 FILLÉR

ICELAND

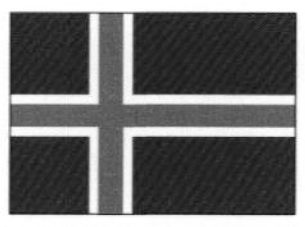

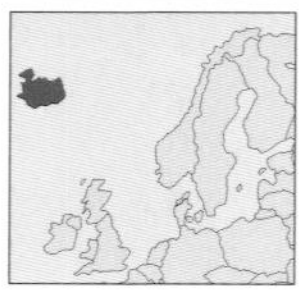

GEOGRAPHY The Republic of Iceland, in the North Atlantic Ocean, is closer to Greenland than Scotland. Iceland sits astride the Mid-Atlantic Ridge and it is slowly getting wider as the ocean is being stretched apart by continental drift.

Iceland has around 200 volcanoes, and eruptions are frequent. An eruption under the Vatnajökull ice cap in 1996 created a subglacial lake which subsequently burst, causing severe flooding. Geysers and hot springs are common, and in 2010 a volcanic eruption and its resulting ash cloud disrupted international air services. Ice caps and glaciers cover about an eighth of the land. The only habitable regions are the coastal lowlands. Despite its northerly position, Iceland's climate is moderated by the warm waters of the North Atlantic Drift. The port of Reykjavik is ice-free all year round.

POLITICS & ECONOMY Norwegian Vikings colonized Iceland in AD 874, and in 930 the settlers founded the world's oldest parliament, the Althing.

Iceland joined forces with Norway in 1262. But when Norway united with Denmark in 1380, Iceland came under Danish rule. Iceland became a self-governing kingdom, still with links to Denmark, in 1918, and a fully independent republic in 1944. Iceland has played a leading part in European affairs. Iceland has few resources besides its fishing grounds, and fishing and fish processing dominate overseas trade. To protect this vital part of its economy, it has been involved in several fishing and whaling disputes. Iceland applied to join the EU in 2009 but in 2013 suspended its application citing potential difficulties over fishing agreements as one reason. Elections in the fall of 2016 resulted in a win for the conservative Bjorni Benediktsson leading a coalition with centrist and center-right parties.

Barely 1% of the land is used to grow crops, but 23% of the country can be used for grazing sheep and cattle. Vegetables and fruit are grown in greenhouses, heated by water from the hot springs. Iceland's economy was badly hit by the global financial crisis of 2008–9, but it is steadily recovering.

AREA 39,768 SQ MI [103,000 SQ KM]
POPULATION 336,000 **CAPITAL** REYKJAVIK
GOVERNMENT MULTIPARTY REPUBLIC
ETHNIC GROUPS ICELANDIC 97%, DANISH 1%
LANGUAGES ICELANDIC (OFFICIAL) **RELIGIONS** EVANGELICAL LUTHERAN 87%, OTHER PROTESTANT 4%, ROMAN CATHOLIC 2%, OTHERS
CURRENCY ICELANDIC KRÓNA = 100 AURAR

INDIA

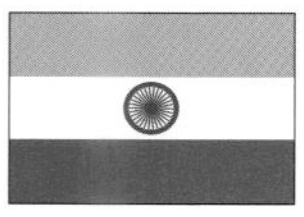

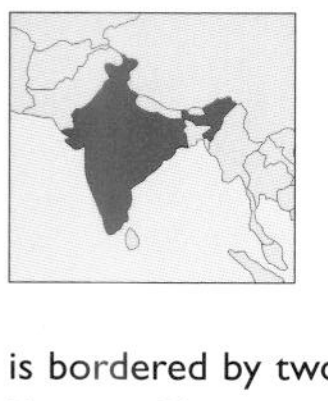

GEOGRAPHY The Republic of India is the world's seventh largest country. In population, it ranks second only to China. The north is mountainous, with mountains and foothills of the Himalayan range. Rivers, such as the Brahmaputra and Ganges (Ganga), rise in the Himalaya and flow across the fertile northern plains. Southern India consists of the Deccan, an extensive plateau. The Deccan is bordered by two mountain ranges, the Western Ghats and the Eastern Ghats.

India has three main seasons. The cool season runs from October to February. The hot season runs from March to June. The rainy monsoon season starts in the middle of June and continues into September. Delhi has moderate rainfall, with about 25 inches [640 mm] a year. The southwestern coast and the north-east have far more rain. Darjeeling in the northeast has an average annual rainfall of 120 inches [3,040 mm]. But parts of the Thar Desert in the northwest have only 2 inches [50 mm] of rain.

POLITICS & ECONOMY In southern India, most of the people are descendants of the dark-skinned Dravidians, who were among India's earliest people. Most northerners are descendants of lighter-skinned Aryans who arrived around 3,500 years ago.

India was the birthplace of several major religions, including Hinduism, Buddhism, and Sikhism. Islam was introduced from about AD 1000. The Muslim Mughal empire was founded in 1526. From the 17th century, Britain began to gain influence and, from 1858 to 1947, India was ruled as part of the British empire. An independence movement began after the Sepoy Rebellion (1857–9), and in 1885 the Indian National Congress was formed. In 1920, Mohandas K. Gandhi became its leader and it soon became a mass movement. When independence was finally achieved in 1947, British India was divided into modern India and Muslim Pakistan. Partition was marred by mass slaughter as Hindus and Sikhs fled from Pakistan, and Indian Muslims poured into Pakistan. In the ensuing disputes, some 1 million people were killed.

India has 15 major languages and hundreds of minor ones, together with many religions. The country remains the world's largest democracy. It has faced many problems, especially with Pakistan, over the disputed territory of Jammu and Kashmir. Two wars in 1965 and 1972 failed to alter greatly the 1948 cease-fire lines. In the late 1980s, Kashmiri nationalists in the Indian-controlled area waged a campaign, demanding either integration into Pakistan or independence. India sent in troops and accused Pakistan of intervention. In the 1990s, Pakistani-backed guerrillas fought to break India's hold on the Srinagar valley, Kashmir's most populous region. Tension mounted following the testing of nuclear devices by both countries in 1998. Relations improved, but an attack on buildings in Mumbai in 2008, allegedly by Pakistanis, caused further tension. In 2009–11, the dispute with Maoists in central and eastern India flared up again.

Classified by the World Bank as a "lower-middle-income" economy, India's economy grew rapidly after 2004 under a government led by the United Progressive Alliance. By 2010–11, India's economy was the world's second fastest growing after China, but growth then slowed. In May 2014, a landslide election was won by the Hindu nationalist Bharatiya Janata Party. The new prime minister, Narendra Modi, has promised to revitalize the economy.

Agriculture employs 53% of the people. Crops include rice, wheat, millet, sorghum, peas, and beans. India has more cattle than any other country. Milk is produced, but Hindus do not eat beef. Resources include coal, iron ore, and oil. Manufacturing has expanded greatly since 1947. Iron and steel, machinery, refined petroleum, textiles, and transport equipment are major products.

AREA 1,269,212 SQ MI [3,287,263 SQ KM]
POPULATION 1,266,884,000 **CAPITAL** NEW DELHI
GOVERNMENT MULTIPARTY FEDERAL REPUBLIC
ETHNIC GROUPS INDO-ARYAN (CAUCASOID) 72%, DRAVIDIAN 25%, OTHERS (MAINLY MONGOLOID) 3%
LANGUAGES HINDI, ENGLISH, TELUGU, BENGALI, MARATHI, TAMIL, URDU, GUJARATI, MALAYALAM, KANNADA, ORIYA, PUNJABI, ASSAMESE, KASHMIRI, SINDHI, AND SANSKRIT ARE ALL OFFICIAL LANGUAGES
RELIGIONS HINDUISM 80%, ISLAM 13%, CHRISTIANITY 2%, SIKHISM 2%, BUDDHISM, AND OTHERS **CURRENCY** INDIAN RUPEE = 100 PAISE

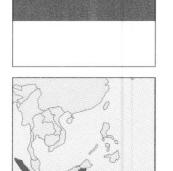

INDONESIA

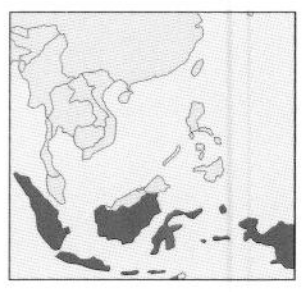

GEOGRAPHY The Republic of Indonesia is an island nation in Southeast Asia. In all, Indonesia contains about 13,600 islands, fewer than 6,000 of which are inhabited. Three-quarters of the country is made up of five main areas: the islands of Sumatra, Java and Sulawesi (Celebes), together with Kalimantan (southern Borneo), and Irian Jaya (western New Guinea). The islands are generally mountainous and volcanic. The larger islands have extensive coastal lowlands. The climate is hot and humid, with a high rainfall. Only Java and the Sunda Islands have relatively dry seasons.

POLITICS & ECONOMY Indonesia is the world's most populous Muslim nation, though Islam was introduced as recently as the 15th century. The Dutch became active in the area in the early 17th century and Indonesia became a Dutch colony in 1799. After a long struggle, the Netherlands recognized Indonesia's independence in 1949. The economy has expanded, but ethnic and religious conflict have slowed down economic progress.

In the early 21st century, Indonesia was facing many problems, arising from widespread corruption in the government and the army. Separatists were operating in Aceh province in northern Sumatra and in West Papua (formerly Irian Jaya), Christian-Muslim clashes led to loss of life in the Moluccas, and East (formerly Portuguese) Timor became an independent country. In December 2004, a tsunami killed more than 100,000 people. Aceh province was granted autonomy in 2006 and separatists in the Papua region continue to agitate for independence.

Indonesia, a developing country, has a growing industrial sector hampered by inadequate infrastructure. It exports oil and natural gas, and mines tin and other minerals. Timber, textiles, rubber, coffee, and tea are also exported. Rice is the main food crop.

AREA 735,354 SQ MI [1,904,569 SQ KM]
POPULATION 258,316,000 **CAPITAL** JAKARTA
GOVERNMENT MULTIPARTY REPUBLIC
ETHNIC GROUPS JAVANESE 41%, SUNDANESE 15%, MADURESE 3%, MINANGKABAU 3%, BETAWI 2%, BUGIS 2%, BANTEN 2%, OTHERS 32%
LANGUAGES BAHASA INDONESIAN (OFFICIAL), MANY OTHERS
RELIGIONS ISLAM 86%, PROTESTANT 6%, ROMAN CATHOLIC 3%, HINDUISM 2%, BUDDHISM 1%
CURRENCY INDONESIAN RUPIAH = 100 SEN

IRAN

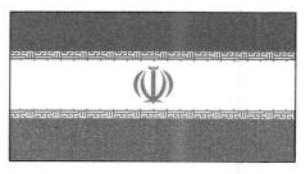

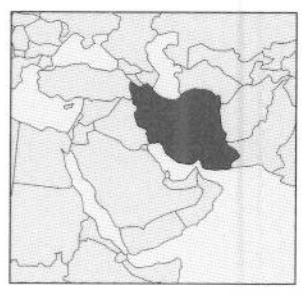

GEOGRAPHY The Republic of Iran contains a barren central plateau which covers about half of the country. It includes the Dasht-e Kavir (Great Salt Desert) and the Dasht-e Lut (Great Sand Desert). The Elburz Mountains north of the plateau contain Iran's highest peak, Damavand, while narrow lowlands lie between the mountains and the Caspian Sea. West of the plateau are the Zagros Mountains, beyond which the land descends to the plains bordering the Persian Gulf.

Much of Iran has a severe, dry climate, with hot summers and cold winters. In Tehran, rain falls on only about 30 days in the year and the annual temperature range is more than 45°F [25°C]. The climate in the lowlands, however, is generally milder.

POLITICS & ECONOMY Iran was called Persia until 1935. The empire of Ancient Persia flourished between 550 and 350 BC. Islam was introduced in AD 641.

Britain and Russia competed for influence in the area in the 19th century, and in the early 20th century the British began to develop the country's oil resources. In 1925, the Pahlavi family took power. Reza Khan became shah (king) and worked to

modernize the country. The Pahlavi dynasty ended in 1979 when a religious leader, Ayatollah Ruhollah Khomeini, made Iran an Islamic republic. In 1980–8, Iran and Iraq fought a war over disputed borders. Khomeini died in 1989. In 2005, a hardliner, Mahmoud Ahmadinejad, was elected president. Iran's nuclear policies led to the application of international sanctions against Iran in 2009–12. The more moderate Hassan Rouhani was elected president in June 2013. Some international economic sanctions were lifted in 2016 after UN inspectors reported satisfactory progress on the nuclear deal. Reformists gained seats in elections to Parliament and the Assembly of Experts.

Iran's prosperity is based on its oil production and oil accounts for more than 80% of the country's exports. However, the economy was severely damaged by the Iran–Iraq war in the 1980s. Oil revenues have been used to develop a growing manufacturing sector. Agriculture is important and the main crops are wheat and barley. Livestock farming and fishing are other important activities, although Iran has to import much of the food it needs.

AREA 636,368 SQ MI [1,648,195 SQ KM]
POPULATION 82,802,000 **CAPITAL** TEHRAN
GOVERNMENT ISLAMIC REPUBLIC **ETHNIC GROUPS** PERSIAN 53%, AZERI 16%, KURD 10%, LUR 6%, ARAB 2%, BALOCH 2%, TURKMEN 2%
LANGUAGES PERSIAN, TURKIC, KURDISH
RELIGIONS ISLAM 98% (SHI'ITE MUSLIM 89%)
CURRENCY IRANIAN RIAL = 100 DINARS

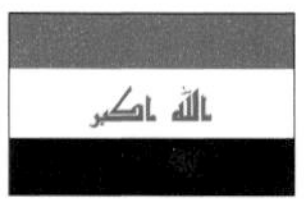

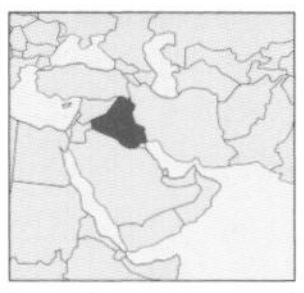

IRAQ

GEOGRAPHY The Republic of Iraq is a southwest Asian country at the head of the Persian Gulf. Rolling deserts cover western and southwestern Iraq, with part of the Zagros Mountains in the northeast, where farming can be practiced without irrigation. The northern plains, across which flow the rivers Euphrates (Nahr al Furat) and Tigris (Nahr Dijlah), are dry. But the southern plains, including Mesopotamia and the delta of the Shatt al Arab, contain irrigated farmland, together with marshland.

The climate of Iraq ranges from temperate in the north to subtropical in the south. Baghdad, in central Iraq, has cool winters, with occasional frosts, and hot summers. The rainfall is generally low.

POLITICS & ECONOMY Mesopotamia was the home of several great civilizations, including Sumer, Babylon, and Assyria. It later became part of the Persian empire. Islam was introduced in AD 637 and Baghdad became the brilliant capital of the powerful Arab empire. But Mesopotamia declined after the Mongols invaded it in 1258. From 1534, Mesopotamia became part of the Turkish Ottoman empire. Britain invaded the area in 1916 and, in 1921, renamed the country Iraq and set up an Arab monarchy. Iraq finally became independent in 1932.

By the 1950s, oil dominated Iraq's economy. In 1952, Iraq agreed to take 50% of the profits of the foreign oil companies. This revenue enabled the government to pay for welfare services and development projects. Since 1958, when army officers killed the king and made Iraq a republic, Iraq has undergone turbulent times. In the 1960s, the Kurds, who live in northern Iraq and also in Iran, Turkey, Syria, and Armenia, pressed for self-rule. The government rejected their demands and war broke out. A peace treaty was signed in 1975, but conflict has continued.

In 1979, Saddam Hussein became Iraq's president. Under his leadership, Iraq invaded Iran in 1980, starting an eight-year war. Iraqi Kurds supported Iran and the Iraqi government attacked Kurdish villages with poison gas. In 1990, Iraqi troops occupied Kuwait, but an international force drove them out in 1991. From 1991, Iraqi troops attacked Shi'ite Marsh Arabs and Kurds. In 1998, Iraq's failure to permit UN inspectors, charged with disposing of Iraq's deadliest weapons, access to suspect sites led to the Western bombardment of Iraqi military sites. Another major offensive occurred in 2001. In 2002–3, pressure mounted on Iraq to dispose of its alleged weapons of mass destruction. In March–April 2003, a coalition force headed by the United States invaded Iraq, overthrowing Saddam Hussein's regime. Despite ongoing violence, elections were held in 2005, and again in 2010. Following a period of deadlock, Nouri al-Maliki continued as prime minister. He was replaced in 2014 by Haider al-Abadi who is trying to improve relations between Iraqi and Kurdish factions.

Civil war, war damage, mismanagement, UN sanctions, and the takeover of large parts of the country by Islamic State militants, have damaged the economy. Oil remains the main resource. Farmland covers about a fifth of the land. Products include barley, cotton, dates, fruit, livestock, wheat, and wool. But Iraq still has to import food. Manufactures include refined oil, petrochemicals, and consumer goods.

AREA 169,235 SQ MI [438,317 SQ KM] **POPULATION** 38,146,000
CAPITAL BAGHDAD **GOVERNMENT** PARLIAMENTARY DEMOCRACY
ETHNIC GROUPS ARAB 77%, KURDISH 19%, ASSYRIAN AND OTHERS
LANGUAGES ARABIC (OFFICIAL), KURDISH (OFFICIAL IN KURDISH AREAS), ASSYRIAN, ARMENIAN **RELIGIONS** ISLAM 97% (SHI'ITE MUSLIM 63%)
CURRENCY IRAQI DINAR = 100 FILS

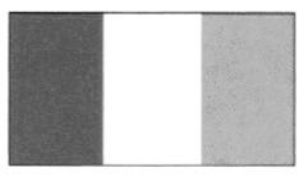

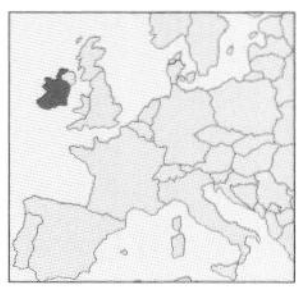

IRELAND

GEOGRAPHY Ireland occupies five-sixths of the island which is also called Ireland. The country consists of a large lowland region surrounded by a broken rim of low mountains. The uplands include the Mountains of Kerry where Carrauntoohill, Ireland's highest peak at 3,415 ft [1,041 m], is situated. The River Shannon is the longest in Ireland, flowing through three large lakes, loughs Allen, Ree, and Derg.

Ireland has a mild, rainy climate influenced by the warm North Atlantic Drift, whose effects are greatest in the west. However, Dublin in the east is cooler than places on the west coast.

POLITICS & ECONOMY In 1801, the Act of Union created the United Kingdom of Great Britain and Ireland. But Irish discontent intensified in the 1840s when a potato blight caused a famine in which a million people died and nearly a million emigrated. Britain was blamed for not having done enough to help. In 1916, an uprising in Dublin was crushed, but between 1919 and 1922 civil war broke out. In 1922, the Irish Free State was created as a Dominion in the British Commonwealth, but Northern Ireland remained part of the UK.

Ireland became a republic in 1949. In 1973, it became a member of the European Community (now the European Union) and, until the global financial crisis of 2008–9, it prospered. In 1998, Ireland took part in the negotiations to produce a constitutional settlement in Northern Ireland. Ireland agreed to give up its claim on Northern Ireland and, in 2007, a power-sharing government was set up in the north. Following elections in 2016, Enda Kenny's Fine Gael formed a minority government.

Major farm products include barley, cattle and dairy products, pigs, potatoes, poultry, sheep, sugar beet, and wheat, while fishing is also important. Manufacturing is the main activity. In 2010, the economy worsened and Ireland sought assistance from the EU and the IMF. But by 2013 austerity measures had borne fruit.

AREA 27,132 SQ MI [70,273 SQ KM]
POPULATION 4,952,000 **CAPITAL** DUBLIN
GOVERNMENT MULTIPARTY REPUBLIC **ETHNIC GROUPS** IRISH 94%
LANGUAGES IRISH (GAELIC) AND ENGLISH (BOTH OFFICIAL)
RELIGIONS ROMAN CATHOLIC 92%, PROTESTANT 3%
CURRENCY EURO = 100 CENTS

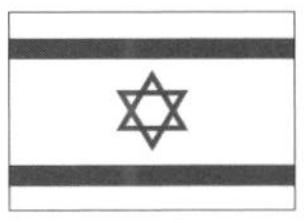

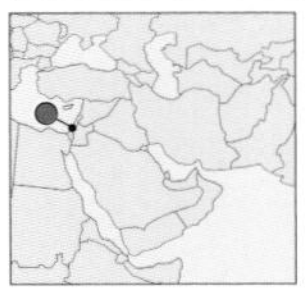

ISRAEL

GEOGRAPHY The State of Israel is a small country in the eastern Mediterranean. It includes a fertile coastal plain, where Israel's main industrial cities, Haifa (Hefa) and Tel Aviv-Jaffa, are situated. Inland lie the Judaeo-Galilean highlands, which run from northern Israel to the northern tip of the Negev Desert. To the east lies part of the Great Rift Valley, which contains the River Jordan, the Sea of Galilee, and the Dead Sea. Summers are hot and dry. Winters on the coast are mild and moist, but rainfall decreases from west to east and from north to south.

POLITICS & ECONOMY Israel is part of a region called Palestine. Some Jews have always lived in the area, though most modern Israelis are descendants of immigrants who began to settle there from the 1880s. Britain ruled Palestine from 1917. Large numbers of Jews escaping Nazi persecution arrived in the 1930s, provoking an Arab uprising against British rule. In 1947, the UN agreed to partition Palestine into an Arab and a Jewish state with the State of Israel coming into being in May 1948. Other Arab–Israeli wars in 1956, 1967, and 1973 led to land gains for Israel.

In 1978, Israel signed a treaty with Egypt which led to the return of the occupied Sinai peninsula to Egypt in 1979. But conflict continued between Israel and the PLO (Palestine Liberation Organization). In 1993, the PLO and Israel agreed to establish Palestinian self-rule in two areas: the occupied Gaza Strip, and in the town of Jericho in the occupied West Bank. The agreement was extended in 1995 to include more than 30% of the West Bank. Israel's prime minister, Yitzhak Rabin, was assassinated in 1995. In 1996, Benjamin Netanyahu was elected prime minister. The peace process stalled until Ehud Barak defeated Netanyahu in 1999. In 2001, Ariel Sharon became prime minister and, in 2005, he handed over the Gaza Strip to the Palestinian Authority. Israeli forces clashed with Palestinians in Gaza and southern Lebanon in 2005–9. In 2010, talks between Israel and the Palestinian Authority collapsed and clashes between Israel and Gaza continued into 2014. Benjamin Netanyahu was re-elected prime minister in 2015.

Israel has developed a very diverse economy. Manufacturing is the most valuable activity with products including chemicals, electronic equipment, plastics, processed food, scientific instruments, and textiles. Fruit and vegetables are major exports. Lacking natural resources, Israel has to import raw materials, crude oil, and grain. Offshore gas fields are now being exploited.

AREA 7,954 SQ MI [20,600 SQ KM] **POPULATION** 8,175,000
CAPITAL JERUSALEM **GOVERNMENT** MULTIPARTY REPUBLIC
ETHNIC GROUPS JEWISH 76%, ARAB AND OTHERS 24%
LANGUAGES HEBREW AND ARABIC (BOTH OFFICIAL)
RELIGIONS JUDAISM 76%, ISLAM (MOSTLY SUNNI) 17%, CHRISTIANITY 2%, DRUZE AND OTHERS 5% **CURRENCY** NEW ISRAELI SHEKEL = 100 AGOROT

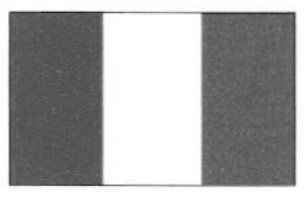

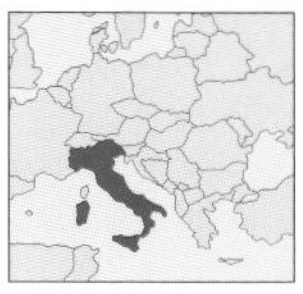

ITALY

GEOGRAPHY The Republic of Italy is famous for its history and traditions, its art and culture, and its beautiful scenery. Northern Italy is bordered in the north by the high Alps, with their many climbing and skiing resorts. The Alps overlook the northern plains – Italy's most fertile and densely populated region – drained by the River Po. The rugged Apennines form the backbone of southern Italy. Bordering the range are scenic hilly areas and coastal plains. Southern Italy contains a string of volcanoes, stretching from Vesuvius, through the Lipari Islands, to Etna on Sicily, the largest Mediterranean island. Northern Italy has cold, often snowy, winters, but the summer months are warm and sunny, with brief summer thunderstorms. Rainfall is abundant. The south has mild, moist winters and warm, dry summers.

POLITICS & ECONOMY Magnificent ruins throughout Italy testify to the glories of the ancient Roman empire, which was founded, according to legend, in 753 BC. Reaching its peak in the AD 100s, it finally collapsed in the 400s, although the Eastern Roman empire, also called the Byzantine empire, survived for another 1,000 years.

In the Middle Ages, Italy was split into many tiny states. These states made a great contribution to Renaissance, the revival of art and learning, in the 14th to 16th centuries. Beautiful cities, such as Florence (Firenze) and Venice (Venézia), testify to the artistic achievements of this period.

Italy finally became a united kingdom in 1861, although the Papal Territories (a large area ruled by the Roman Catholic Church) was not added until 1870. The Pope and his successors disputed this takeover and it was not finally resolved until 1929, when the Vatican City was set up in Rome as a fully independent state.

Italy fought in World War I (1914–18) alongside the Allies – Britain, France, and Russia. In 1922, the dictator Benito Mussolini, leader of the Fascist Party, took power. Under Mussolini, Italy conquered Ethiopia. During World War II (1939–45), Italy at first fought on Germany's side against the Allies until late in 1943 it declared war on Germany. Italy became a republic in 1946. Playing an important part in European affairs, it was a founder member of the North Atlantic Treaty Organization (NATO) in 1949 and also, in 1958, of what has since become the European Union.

After the setting up of the European Union, Italy's economy developed quickly, despite problems such as greater prosperity in the north compared to the south. The greater economic development in the north forced many people to leave the poor south to find jobs in the north or abroad. Social problems, corruption at high levels of society, and a succession of weak coalition governments all contributed to instability. Between 1998 and 2011, power shifted between center left-coalitions led by Romano Prodi and center-right ones under Silvio Berlusconi. In 2016, constitutional changes aimed at creating more stable governments were rejected in a referendum.

Only 50 years ago, Italy was a mainly agricultural society. But today it is a leading industrial power. It lacks mineral resources, and imports most of the raw materials used in industry. Manufactures include textiles and clothing, processed food, machinery, cars, and chemicals. The chief industrial region is in the northwest.

Farmland covers around 42% of the land, pasture 17%, and forest and woodland 22%. Major crops include citrus fruits, grapes which are used to make wine, olive oil, sugar beet, and vegetables. Livestock farming is important, though meat is imported.

AREA 116,339 sq mi [301,318 sq km]
POPULATION 62,008,000 **CAPITAL** Rome
GOVERNMENT Multiparty republic **ETHNIC GROUPS** Italian 94%, German, French, Albanian, Slovene, Greek **LANGUAGES** Italian (official), German, French, Slovene **RELIGIONS** Predominantly Roman Catholic **CURRENCY** Euro = 100 cents

IVORY COAST

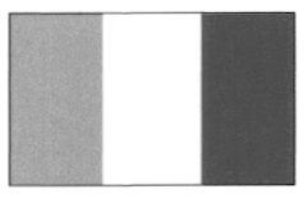
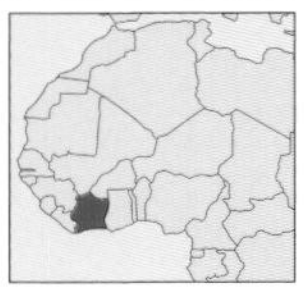

GEOGRAPHY The Republic of the Ivory Coast, in West Africa, is officially known as Côte d'Ivoire. The southeast coast is bordered by sand bars that enclose lagoons. The southwest coast is lined by rocky cliffs.

Ivory Coast has a hot and humid tropical climate, with high temperatures all year. The south has two rainy seasons: between May and July, and from October to November. Inland, the rainfall decreases and the north has one dry and one rainy season.

POLITICS & ECONOMY From 1895, Ivory Coast was governed as part of French West Africa,.

Ivory Coast became fully independent in 1960. Its first president, Félix Houphouët-Boigny, became the longest serving head of state in Africa with an uninterrupted period in office which ended with his death in 1993. Houphouët-Boigny, a pro-Western leader, made Ivory Coast a one-party state. In 1983, the National Assembly voted to make Yamoussoukro, the president's birthplace, the new capital. In 1999, a military coup occurred, but civilian rule was restored in 2000, when Laurent Gbagbo was elected president. By 2004, after an army rebellion, the government held the south, while mainly Muslim rebels held the north. Elections in 2010 were won by Alassane Outtara, but Gbagbo refused to stand down and was finally deposed in 2011. Outtara won an overwhelming 84% of the vote in 2015's elections.

Agriculture employs 68% of the population and the country is the world's largest producer of cocoa beans. Coffee and palm oil are also important exports. Political instability and the lack of modern infrastructure are impeding economic growth.

AREA 124,503 sq mi [322,463 sq km]
POPULATION 23,740,000 **CAPITAL** Yamoussoukro
GOVERNMENT Multiparty republic **ETHNIC GROUPS** Akan 42%, Voltaiques 18%, Northern Mandes 16%, Krous 11%, Southern Mandes 10% **LANGUAGES** French (official), many native dialects
RELIGIONS Islam 39%, Christianity 33%, traditional beliefs 12%
CURRENCY CFA franc = 100 centimes

JAMAICA

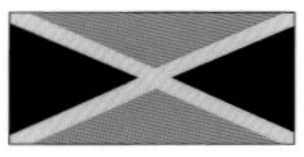
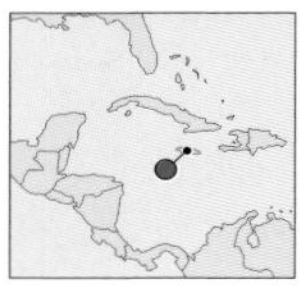

GEOGRAPHY The third largest of the Caribbean islands, half of Jamaica lies above 1,000 ft [300 m] and moist southeast trade winds bring rain to the central mountain range.

The "cockpit country" in the northwest of the island is an inaccessible limestone area of steep broken ridges and isolated basins.

POLITICS & ECONOMY Jamaica gained independence from Britain in 1962. Since then, power has alternated between the People's National Party and the Jamaica Labor Party and, despite some violence, there has been relative political stability. There is some support for becoming a republic. Problems arise from the marked polarization of society between rich and poor, and the murder rate is high. Tourism and sugarcane farming are important, with alumina and bauxite being exported.

AREA 4,244 sq mi [10,991 sq km]
POPULATION 2,970,000 **CAPITAL** Kingston
GOVERNMENT Constitutional monarchy
ETHNIC GROUPS Black 91%, Mixed 7%, East Indian 1%
LANGUAGES English (official), patois English
RELIGIONS Protestant 65%, Roman Catholic 3%
CURRENCY Jamaican dollar = 100 cents

JAPAN

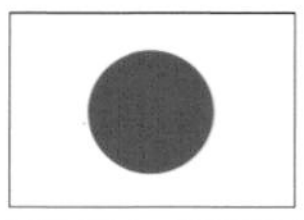
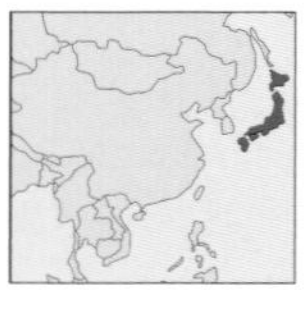

GEOGRAPHY Japan's four largest islands – Honshu, Hokkaido, Kyushu, and Shikoku – make up 98% of the country. But Japan contains thousands of small islands. The four largest islands are mainly mountainous, while many of the small islands are the tips of volcanoes. Japan has more than 150 volcanoes, about 60 of which are active. Volcanic eruptions, earthquakes and tsunamis (powerful sea waves) are common. In March 2011, a massive earthquake, the most powerful recorded in Japan (magnitude 9.0), struck Honshu in the northeast. The tremors and a tsunami caused great loss of life and severe damage to nuclear reactors at Fukushima, shutting down all nuclear power generation at that time.

The climate of Japan varies greatly from north to south. Hokkaido in the north has cold, snowy winters. At Sapporo, temperatures below 4°F [–20°C] have been recorded between December and March. But summers are warm, with temperatures sometimes exceeding 86°F [30°C]. Rain falls throughout the year, though Hokkaido is one of the driest parts of Japan. Tokyo has higher rainfall and temperatures, while the southern islands of Shikoku and Kyushu have warm temperate climates. Summers are long and hot; winters are cold.

POLITICS & ECONOMY In the late 19th century, Japan began a program of modernization. Under its new imperial leaders, it began to look for lands to conquer. In 1894–5, it fought a war with China and, in 1904–5, it defeated Russia. Soon its overseas empire included Korea and Taiwan. In 1930, Japan invaded Manchuria (northeast China), and in 1937 it began a war against China. In 1941, Japan launched an attack on the US base at Pearl Harbor in Hawai'i. This drew both Japan and the United States into World War II.

Japan surrendered in 1945 when the Americans dropped atomic bombs on two cities, Hiroshima and Nagasaki. The United States occupied Japan until 1952, during which time Japan adopted a democratic constitution. The emperor, who had previously been regarded as a god, became a constitutional monarch.

From the 1960s, Japan experienced many changes as the country rapidly built up new industries, becoming the world's second richest economic power after the United States. But economic success has brought problems. For example, the rapid growth of cities has led to housing shortages and pollution. Another problem is that the proportion of people over 65 years of age is steadily increasing. In 2011, China overtook Japan as the world's second largest economy after the US, a position Japan had held since 1968. Japan has managed to retain third place.

The leading activity is manufacturing. Lacking natural resources, Japan imports most of the materials and fuels it needs, and its success has been based on its use of the latest technology, its skilled work force, its vigorous export policies, and the relatively low expenditure on defense. Exports include machinery, electrical and electronic equipment, iron and steel, chemicals, textiles, and ships. Japan's economy suffered a stagnation in the 1990s. Signs of recovery from 2005 were shattered by the global financial crisis in 2008–9, when exports greatly declined. The economy went back into recession following the 2011 earthquake and tsunami, and the consequent extensive reconstruction work that was required. However, since then the economy has largely recovered with Prime Minister Shinzo Abe pursuing proactive policies to stimulate the economy.

Japan is one of the world's top fishing nations and fish is an important source of protein for the Japanese. Because the land is so rugged, only 15% of the country can be farmed. Yet Japan produces about 70% of the food it needs. Rice is the chief crop, taking up about half of the total farmland.

AREA 145,880 sq mi [377,829 sq km] **POPULATION** 126,702,000
CAPITAL Tokyo **GOVERNMENT** Constitutional monarchy
ETHNIC GROUPS Japanese 99%, Chinese, Korean, Brazilian, and others
LANGUAGES Japanese (official) **RELIGIONS** Shintoism and Buddhism 84% (most Japanese consider themselves to be both Shinto and Buddhist), others **CURRENCY** Yen = 100 sen

JORDAN

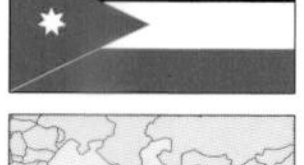
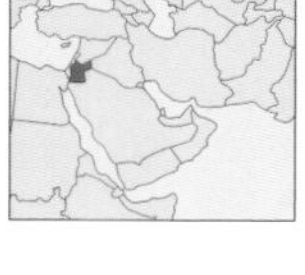

GEOGRAPHY The Hashemite Kingdom of Jordan is an Arab country in southwestern Asia. The Great Rift Valley in the west contains the River Jordan and the Dead Sea, which Jordan shares with Israel. East of the Rift Valley is the Transjordan plateau, where most Jordanians live. To the east and south lie vast areas of desert.

Amman has a much lower rainfall and longer dry season than the Mediterranean lands to the west. The Transjordan plateau, on which Amman stands, is a transition zone between the Mediterranean climate zone and the desert climate to the east.

POLITICS & ECONOMY In 1921, Britain created the territory of Transjordan east of the River Jordan. In 1923, Transjordan became self-governing, but Britain retained control of its defenses, finances, and foreign affairs. This territory became fully independent as Jordan in 1946. Jordan has suffered from instability arising from the Arab–Israeli conflict since the creation of the State of Israel in 1948. After the first Arab–Israeli War in 1948–9, Jordan acquired East Jerusalem and the fertile area of the West Bank. In 1967, Israel occupied this area. In Jordan, the presence of Palestinian refugees led to civil war in 1970–1.

In 1974, Arab leaders declared that the PLO (Palestine Liberation Organization) was the sole representative of the Palestinian people. In 1988, King Hussein of Jordan renounced Jordan's claims to the West Bank and passed responsibility for it to the PLO. Opposition parties were legalized in 1991 and elections were held in 1993. In October 1994, Jordan and Israel signed a peace treaty, ending a state of war that had lasted more than 40 years. Jordan's King Hussein commanded respect for his role in Middle Eastern affairs until his death in 1999. He was succeeded by his eldest son, who became Abdullah II. In 2005, suicide bombings on hotels in Amman damaged Jordan's reputation as a stable country. The king has the power to dissolve parliament and appoint governments. Hani Al-Mulki was appointed Prime Minister in 2016 and won the subsequent elections.

Jordan has an "upper-middle-income" economy. It lacks natural resources, apart from phosphates and potash, and depends on substantial aid. Less than 6% of the land is farmed or used as pasture. The country is currently having to absorb high numbers of refugees from neighboring Syria.

AREA 34,495 sq mi [89,342 sq km]
POPULATION 8,185,000 **CAPITAL** Amman
GOVERNMENT Constitutional monarchy **ETHNIC GROUPS** Arab 98%, of which Palestinians make up roughly half **LANGUAGES** Arabic (official) **RELIGIONS** Islam (mostly Sunni) 92%, Christianity (mostly Greek Orthodox) 6% **CURRENCY** Jordanian dinar = 100 piastre

KAZAKHSTAN

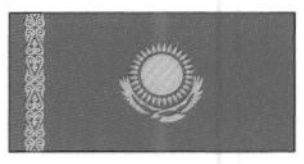
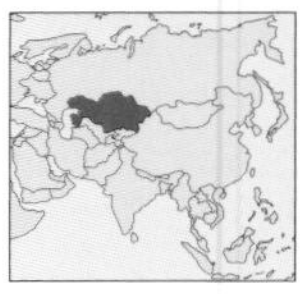

GEOGRAPHY Kazakhstan is a large country in west-central Asia. In the west, the Caspian Sea lowlands include the Karagiye depression, which reaches 433 ft [132 m] below sea level. The lowlands extend eastward through the Aral Sea area. The north contains high plains, but the highest land is along the eastern and southern borders. These areas include parts of the Altai and Tian Shan mountain ranges. Eastern Kazakhstan contains several freshwater lakes, the largest of which is Lake Balkhash. The water in the rivers has been used for irrigation, causing ecological problems. For example, the Aral Sea, deprived of water, shrank from 25,830 sq mi [66,900 sq km] in 1960 to 6,630 sq mi [17,160 sq km] in 2004. Large areas are now barren desert.

Kazakhstan has an extreme climate. Winters are cold and snowy. The rainfall is generally low.

POLITICS & ECONOMY After the Russian Revolution of 1917, many Kazakhs wanted to make their country independent. But the Communists prevailed and in 1936 Kazakhstan became a republic of the Soviet Union, called the Kazakh Soviet Socialist Republic. During World War II and also after the war, the Soviet government moved many people from the west into Kazakhstan. From the 1950s, people were encouraged to work on a "Virgin Lands" project, which involved bringing large areas of grassland under cultivation.

Reforms in the Soviet Union in the 1980s led to its breakup in December 1991. Kazakhstan maintained contacts with Russia through the Commonwealth of Independent States (CIS). In 1997, the government moved its capital from Almaty to Aqmola (later renamed Astana), a town in the north. By the mid-2000s, the economy was in better shape than the other ex-Soviet republics in Central Asia although President Nursultan Nazarbayev was criticized for his authoritarian rule. In 2007, constitutional changes enabled Nazarbaev to stand for the presidency as many times as he wished. He was re-elected in 2011 and 2015 despite allegations of unfair procedures.

The World Bank classifies Kazakhstan as an "upper-middle-income" developing country. Livestock farming, especially sheep and cattle, is an important activity, and major crops include barley, cotton, rice, and wheat. The country is rich in mineral resources, including coal and oil reserves, together with uranium, bauxite, copper, lead, tungsten, and zinc. Manufactures include chemicals, food products, machinery, and textiles. Oil is exported via a pipeline through Russia. However, to reduce the country's dependence on Russia, another pipeline to China was inaugurated in 2009. Other exports include metals, chemicals, grain, wool, and meat.

AREA 1,052,084 sq mi [2,724,900 sq km] **POPULATION** 18,360,000
CAPITAL Astana **GOVERNMENT** Multiparty republic
ETHNIC GROUPS Kazakh 63%, Russian 24%, Uzbek 3%, Ukrainian 2%, others 8% **LANGUAGES** Kazakh (official); Russian, the former official language, is widely spoken **RELIGIONS** Islam 70%, Russian Orthodox 24% **CURRENCY** Tenge = 100 tiyn

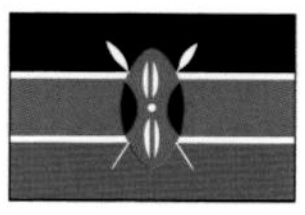

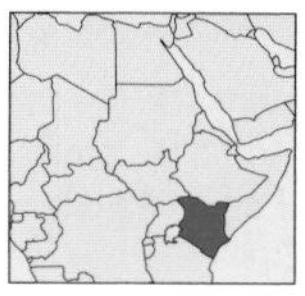

KENYA

GEOGRAPHY The Republic of Kenya is a country in East Africa which straddles the equator. Behind the narrow coastal plain on the Indian Ocean, the land rises to high plains and highlands, broken by volcanic mountains, including Mount Kenya, the country's highest peak at 17,057 ft [5,199 m]. Crossing the country is an arm of the Great Rift Valley, on the floor of which are several lakes, including Baringo, Magadi, Naivasha, Nakuru, and, on the northern frontier, Lake Turkana (formerly Lake Rudolf). Nairobi, in the southwestern highlands, has summer temperatures which are about 10°F [18°C] lower than humid Mombasa. Only about 15% of Kenya has a reliable annual rainfall of 31 inches [800 mm].

POLITICS & ECONOMY The Kenyan coast has been a trading center for more than 2,000 years. Britain took over the coast in 1895 and soon extended its influence inland. In the 1950s, a secret movement, called Mau Mau, launched an armed struggle against British rule. Although Mau Mau was eventually defeated, Kenya became independent in 1963.

Kenya was a one-party state for much of the time after 1963, with democracy restored in 1992. Elections in 2007 led to inter-ethnic violence when the opposition refused to accept the declared results. A deal was agreed by President Mwai Kibaki and Raila Odinga, who became prime minister. In 2011, Somali attacks and kidnappings in northern Kenya provoked Kenya to send forces into Somalia to combat the Islamist al-Shabab group. In March 2013, Uhuru Kenyatta was elected president. Presidential elections are due in August 2017.

Many Kenyans are subsistence farmers. The chief food crop is maize. The main cash crops and the leading exports are coffee and tea. Manufactures include chemicals, leather and footwear, petroleum products, and textiles. Oil was discovered in 2012.

AREA 224,080 sq mi [580,367 sq km]
POPULATION 46,791,000 **CAPITAL** Nairobi
GOVERNMENT Multiparty republic **ETHNIC GROUPS** Kikuyu 22%, Luhya 14%, Luo 13%, Kalenjin 12%, Kamba 11%, others
LANGUAGES Kiswahili and English (both official)
RELIGIONS Protestant 47%, Roman Catholic 23%, Islam 11%, others 19% **CURRENCY** Kenyan shilling = 100 cents

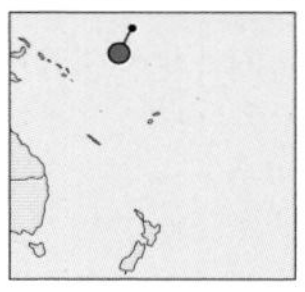

KIRIBATI

The Republic of Kiribati comprises three groups of coral atolls scattered over about 2 million sq mi [5 million sq km]. Kiribati straddles the equator and temperatures are high and the rainfall is abundant.

Formerly part of the British Gilbert and Ellice Islands, Kiribati became independent in 1979. The main export is copra and the country depends heavily on foreign aid.

AREA 280 sq mi [726 sq km] **POPULATION** 107,000 **CAPITAL** Tarawa

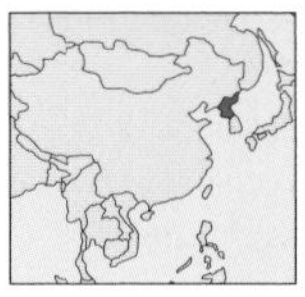

KOREA, NORTH

GEOGRAPHY The Democratic People's Republic of Korea occupies the northern part of the Korean peninsula, which extends south from northeastern China. Mountains form the heart of the country, with the highest peak, Paektu-san, reaching 9,003 ft [2,744 m] on the northern border. North Korea has a fairly severe climate, with cold, snowy winters. In summer, moist winds from the oceans bring rain.

POLITICS & ECONOMY North Korea was created in 1945, when the peninsula, which had been a Japanese colony since 1910, was divided into two parts. Soviet forces occupied the north, with US forces in the south. Soviet occupation led to a Communist government being established in 1948 under the leadership of Kim Il Sung, who effectively became a dictator.

The Korean War began in June 1950 when North Korean troops invaded the south. North Korea, aided by China and the Soviet Union, fought with South Korea, which was supported by troops from the United States and other UN members. The war ended in July 1953. An armistice was signed but no permanent peace treaty was agreed. The end of the Cold War in the late 1990s eased the situation. North and South Korea joined the United Nations in 1991, though North Korea remained isolated from most other countries. In 1993, North Korea withdrew from the Nuclear Non-Proliferation Treaty, arousing suspicions that it was developing nuclear weapons. Kim Il Sung died in 1994 and was succeeded by his son, Kim Jong Il. From 2003, the United States accused North Korea of developing nuclear weapons, and it has since then carried out several tests, resulting in increased international isolation and tension. Kim Jong Il died in 2011, and his son, Kim Jong-Un, succeeded him. He has continued the nuclear program and aggressive stance of his father.

North Korea's resources include coal, copper, iron ore, lead, tin, tungsten, and zinc. Manufactures include chemicals, iron and steel, machinery, processed food, and textiles. Agriculture employs 35% of the people. Rice is the chief food crop, but food shortages have occurred in recent years.

AREA 46,540 sq mi [120,538 sq km]
POPULATION 25,115,000 **CAPITAL** Pyŏngyang
GOVERNMENT Single-party people's republic
ETHNIC GROUPS Korean 99%
LANGUAGES Korean (official)
RELIGIONS Buddhism and Confucianism
CURRENCY North Korean won = 100 chon

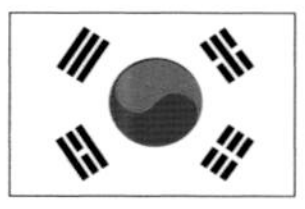

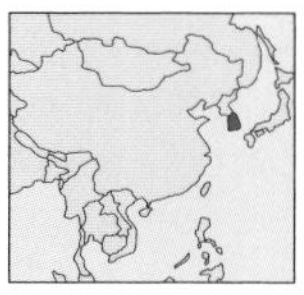

KOREA, SOUTH

GEOGRAPHY The Republic of Korea, as South Korea is officially known, occupies the southern part of the Korean peninsula. Mountains cover much of the country.

The southern and western coasts are major farming regions. Many islands are found along the west and south coasts. The largest of these is Jeju-do, which contains South Korea's highest peak, Hallasan, which rises to 6,398 ft [1,950 m].

Like North Korea, South Korea is chilled in winter by cold, dry winds from central Asia. Summers are hot and wet, especially in July and August.

POLITICS & ECONOMY After Japan's defeat in World War II (1939–45), North Korea was occupied by troops from the Soviet Union, while South Korea was occupied by United States forces. A National Assembly elected in 1948 in South Korea created the Republic of Korea, while North Korea became a Communist state. North Korea invaded the South in June 1950, sparking off the Korean War (1950–3). Despite the destruction caused by the war, South Korea under a series of rather authoritarian governments began to industrialize the economy between the 1960s and 1980s. In 1987, a new constitution permitted the election of presidents every five years. In the 2000s, South Korea worked for closer contacts with the North, but tensions continue.

Until the onset of the global financial crisis in 2008, South Korea had one of the world's fastest growing economies. Its main manufactures are processed food and textiles. Heavy industries produce chemicals, fertilizers, iron and steel, and ships, together with a wide range of consumer products, such as computers, cars, and television sets. The economy relies heavily on exports.

Farming remains important in South Korea. Rice is the chief crop, together with fruits, grains, and vegetables, while fishing provides a major source of protein for Koreans.

AREA 38,327 sq mi [99,268 sq km]
POPULATION 50,924,000 **CAPITAL** Seoul
GOVERNMENT Multiparty republic **ETHNIC GROUPS** Korean 99%
LANGUAGES Korean (official) **RELIGIONS** No affiliation 43%, Christianity 32%, Buddhism 24%, others 1%
CURRENCY South Korean won = 100 jeon

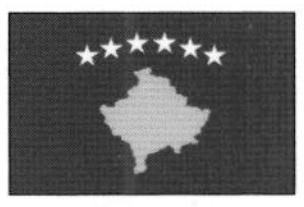

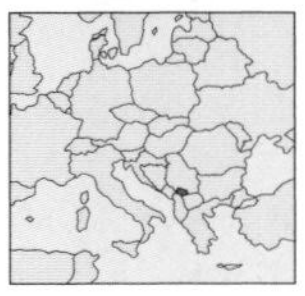

KOSOVO

GEOGRAPHY The Republic of Kosovo in the central Balkans, formerly part of Serbia, declared its independence in February 2008. Its independence was recognized by the United States and major EU countries, but Serbia, and its ally Russia, refused recognition. It is a landlocked country, consisting of a river basin bounded by uplands in the north and southwest. It has cold, snowy winters and hot, dry summers.

POLITICS & ECONOMY Most people are Albanian-speakers who are Muslims, but there is an important Christian Serb minority. In the early 13th century, Kosovo was part of the Serbian empire but, after 1389, it came under Muslim Turkish Ottoman rule.

Serbia regained control of Kosovo in 1912 and, in 1918, it became part of the Kingdom of Serbia. In 1946, it became part of the Socialist Federal Republic of Yugoslavia, becoming an autonomous province within the Republic of Serbia. In 1989, Serbia curtailed Kosovo's autonomy, while Albanian speakers declared their province independent. In 1995, the Albanian speakers set up the Kosovo Liberation Army, which launched an uprising against Serbia. In 1998, Serbia began repressive measures against Kosovo, resulting in massacres and ethnic cleansing of Albanian-speaking Kosovars. In 1999, NATO forces bombed Serbia and placed Kosovo under a temporary administration. Finally, the Kosovo Assembly declared its independence on February 17, 2008. Whilst Serbia still does not recognize Kosovo as an independent state, the two countries are engaged in diplomatic talks.

Kosovo is a poor country, with one of the lowest per capita incomes in Europe. Many people are subsistence farmers and its industries have declined because of lack of investment. The economy is highly dependent on international aid.

AREA 4,203 sq mi [10,887 sq km]
POPULATION 1,883,000 **CAPITAL** Pristina
GOVERNMENT Republic **ETHNIC GROUPS** Albanian 92%, others 8%
LANGUAGES Albanian and Serbian (both official), Turkish
RELIGIONS Islam, Serbian Orthodox, Roman Catholic
CURRENCY Euro = 100 cents

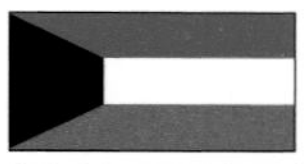

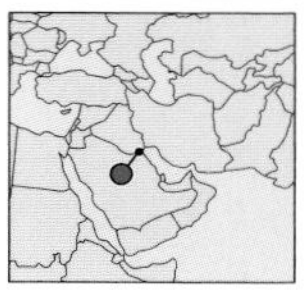

KUWAIT

GEOGRAPHY The State of Kuwait, at the northern end of the Persian Gulf, is an emirate (ruled by an emir, or amir). The land is low-lying and largely desert in nature. Summer temperatures are high but winters are cooler. Rainfall is low.

POLITICS & ECONOMY British influence began in 1775 and, in 1899, the local ruler concluded a treaty with Britain, agreeing to support British interests in return for British protection. Kuwait became independent in 1961. Its revenue from its oil exports made it highly prosperous. Iraq invaded Kuwait in 1990, but it was liberated in 1991 by a coalition force. In 2004, the government announced legislation for women to vote and stand for parliament. In recent years there has been increasing unrest caused by militant Islamists.

AREA 6,880 sq mi [17,818 sq km]
POPULATION 2,833,000 **CAPITAL** Kuwait City

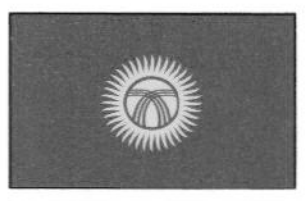

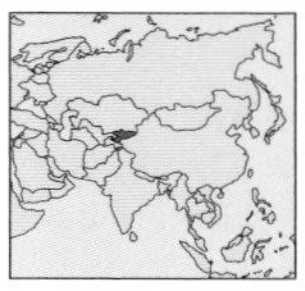

KYRGYZSTAN

GEOGRAPHY The Republic of Kyrgyzstan is a landlocked country between China, Tajikistan, Uzbekistan, and Kazakhstan. The country is mountainous, with spectacular scenery. The highest mountain, Pik Pobedy in the Tian Shan range, reaches 24,406 ft [7,439 m] in the east. The lowlands have warm summers and cold winters. But January temperatures in the mountains plummet to –18°F [–28°C]. Kyrgyzstan has a low annual rainfall.

POLITICS & ECONOMY In 1876, Kyrgyzstan became a province of Russia. In 1916, Russia crushed a rebellion among the Kyrgyz, and many subsequently fled to China. In 1922, the area became an autonomous oblast (self-governing region) of the newly formed Soviet Union, but in 1936 it became one of the Soviet Socialist Republics. Under Communist rule, local customs and religious worship were suppressed, but education and health services were greatly improved.

In 1991, Kyrgyzstan became an independent country following the breakup of the Soviet Union. The Communist Party was dissolved, but the country maintained links with Russia. The first two elections as an independent state produced unpopular presidents who were swept from power and had to flee the country. In 2011, Almazbek Atambayev was elected president in the first peaceful transfer of power since the Soviet era.

As one of the poorest countries of the former Soviet Union, Kyrgyzstan sought to reform its Soviet-style economy in the 1990s. Classified as a "lower-middle income" economy by the World Bank, agriculture is the main activity. Major products include cotton, eggs, fruits, grain, tobacco, vegetables, and wool, but food is imported. Attracting foreign investment and legitimizing business practices will be vital to economic growth.

AREA 77,181 sq mi [199,900 sq km]
POPULATION 5,728,000 **CAPITAL** Bishkek
GOVERNMENT Multiparty republic
ETHNIC GROUPS Kyrgyz 65%, Uzbek 14%, Russian 13%
LANGUAGES Kyrgyz and Russian (both official)
RELIGIONS Islam 75%, Russian Orthodox 20%
CURRENCY Kyrgyzstani som = 100 tyiyn

LAOS

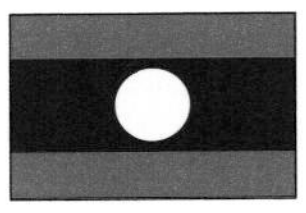
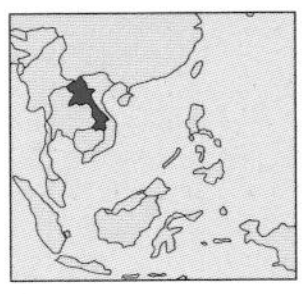

GEOGRAPHY The Lao People's Democratic Republic is a landlocked country in Southeast Asia. Mountains and plateaux cover much of the country. Most people live on the plains bordering the River Mekong and its tributaries. This river, one of Asia's longest, forms much of the country's northwestern and southwestern borders.

Laos has a tropical monsoon climate. Winters are dry and sunny with winds blowing from the northeast. From April, the monsoon season starts with the arrival of moist southwesterly winds.

POLITICS & ECONOMY France made Laos a protectorate in the late 19th century and ruled it, with Cambodia and Vietnam, as part of French Indochina. Laos became an independent kingdom in 1954. After independence, a power struggle between royalist government forces and a pro-Communist group called Pathet Lao caused instability. A civil war broke out and continued into the 1970s. The Pathet Lao took control in 1975 and the king abdicated. In the 1990s, Laos started to open to the world and began tentative reforms. In 2011, a stock exchange was opened in Vientiane, as part of a gradual move toward capitalism.

Laos relies heavily on foreign aid. Agriculture employs nearly 73% of the population and accounts for 26% of the gross domestic product. Rice is the main crop. Timber and coffee are exported. But the most valuable export is electricity, which is produced at hydroelectric power stations on the River Mekong and is exported to Thailand. Laos also produces opium.

AREA 91,428 sq mi [236,800 sq km]
POPULATION 7,019,000 **CAPITAL** Vientiane
GOVERNMENT Single-party republic
ETHNIC GROUPS Lao 55%, Khmou 11%, Hmong 8%, others 26%
LANGUAGES Lao (official), French, English **RELIGIONS** Buddhism 67%, traditional beliefs and others 33% **CURRENCY** Kip = 100 att

LATVIA

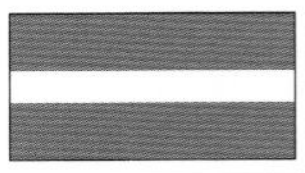
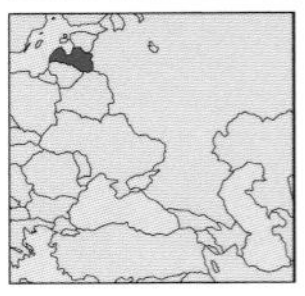

GEOGRAPHY The Republic of Latvia is one of three states on the southeastern corner of the Baltic Sea which were ruled as parts of the Soviet Union between 1940 and 1991. Latvia consists mainly of flat plains separated by low hills, composed of glacial moraine.

Riga has warm summers, but the winter months are sub-zero. The rainfall is moderate.

POLITICS & ECONOMY In 1800, Russia was in control of Latvia, but Latvians declared their independence after World War I. In 1940, under a German-Soviet pact, Soviet troops occupied Latvia, but they were driven out by the Germans in 1941. Soviet troops returned in 1944 and Latvia became part of the Soviet Union. Under Soviet rule, many Russian immigrants settled in Latvia and many Latvians feared that the Russians would become the dominant ethnic group.

In the late 1980s, when reforms were being introduced in the Soviet Union, Latvia's government ended absolute Communist rule and made Latvian the official language. In 1990, it declared the country to be independent, an act which was finally recognized by the Soviet Union in September 1991.

Latvia held the first free elections to its parliament (the Saeima) in 1993. Voting was limited only to citizens of Latvia on June 17, 1940, and their descendants. This meant that about 34% of Latvian residents were unable to vote. In 1994, Latvia restricted the naturalization of non-Latvians, including many Russian settlers, who were not allowed to vote or own land. However, in 1998, the government agreed that all children born since independence should have automatic citizenship. In 2004, Latvia became a member of the North Atlantic Treaty Organization and the European Union. Latvia was hit hard by the global financial crisis in 2009. Maris Kucinskis took over as prime minister in February 2016 as leader of the center-right coalition.

The World Bank classifies Latvia as a "high-income" country. Manufactures include electronic goods, farm machinery, fertilizers, processed food, plastics, radios, and vehicles. Latvia produces only about a tenth of the electricity it needs; it imports the rest from Belarus, Russia, and Ukraine. It adopted the euro in January 2014.

AREA 24,942 sq mi [64,600 sq km] **POPULATION** 1,966,000
CAPITAL Riga **GOVERNMENT** Multiparty republic
ETHNIC GROUPS Latvian 59%, Russian 28%, Belarusian, Ukrainian, Polish, Lithuanian
LANGUAGES Latvian (official), Russian, Lithuanian
RELIGIONS Lutheran, Russian Orthodox, Roman Catholic
CURRENCY Euro = 100 cents

LEBANON

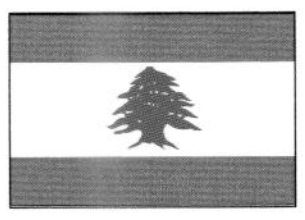
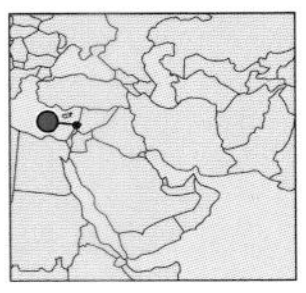

GEOGRAPHY The Republic of Lebanon is a country on the eastern shores of the Mediterranean Sea. Behind the coastal plain are the rugged Lebanon Mountains (Jabal Lubnan), which rise to 10,131 ft [3,088 m]. Another range, the Anti-Lebanon Mountains (Al Jabal Ash Sharqi), forms the eastern border with Syria. Between the two ranges is the Bekaa (Biqa) Valley, a fertile farming region. The coast has hot, dry summers and mild, wet winters. Heavy rain falls on the mountains, with snow at high altitudes.

POLITICS & ECONOMY Lebanon was ruled by Turkey from 1516 until World War I. France then took control from 1923 until independence in 1946. After this date, with the Muslims and Christians agreeing to share power, Lebanon made rapid economic progress. But from the late 1950s, development was slowed by periodic conflict between Sunni and Shia Muslims, Druze, and Christians. The situation was further complicated by the presence of Palestinian refugees, who used bases in Lebanon to attack Israel.

In 1975, civil war broke out as private armies representing the many factions struggled for power. This led to intervention by Israel in the south and Syria in the north. UN peacekeeping forces arrived in 1978, but violence continued in the 1980s. Peace was restored in the 1990s, but, in 2005, the assassination of Rafik Hariri, former prime minister, was blamed on Syria. Under pressure, Syria withdrew its forces from Lebanon. In 2006, a 34-day conflict between Israeli troops and Hezbollah guerrillas caused devastation in southern Lebanon. The civil war in neighboring Syria has had a major destabilizing effect on Lebanese politics. Refugees from Syria now make up one-third of the population.

Lebanon's civil war almost destroyed valuable trade and financial services that had been Lebanon's chief source of income, together with tourism. Manufacturing, formerly a major activity, was badly hit.

AREA 4,015 sq mi [10,400 sq km]
POPULATION 6,237,000 **CAPITAL** Beirut
GOVERNMENT Multiparty republic **ETHNIC GROUPS** Arab 95%, Armenian 4%, others **LANGUAGES** Arabic (official), French, English, Armenian **RELIGIONS** Islam 60%, Christianity 39%
CURRENCY Lebanese pound = 100 piastres

LESOTHO

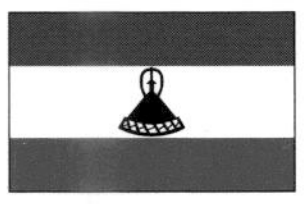
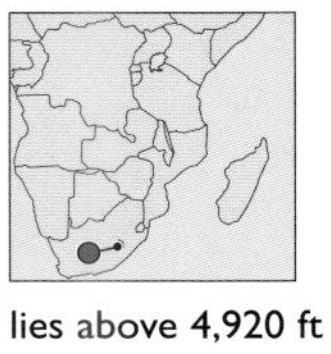

GEOGRAPHY The Kingdom of Lesotho is a landlocked country, completely enclosed by South Africa. The land is mountainous, rising to 11,424 ft [3,482 m] on the northeastern border. The Drakensberg range covers most of the country.

The climate of Lesotho is greatly affected by the altitude, because most of the country lies above 4,920 ft [1,500 m]. Summers are warm but winters are cold. The rainfall averages about 28 inches [700 mm].

POLITICS & ECONOMY The political entity that eventually became Lesotho coalesced under King Moshoeshoe I in the 1820s who united various groups fleeing from tribal wars in southern Africa. Britain made the area a protectorate in 1868 and, in 1871, placed it under the British Cape Colony in South Africa. In 1884, Basutoland, as the area was called, was reconstituted as a British protectorate, where whites were not allowed to own land.

The country finally became independent in 1966 as the Kingdom of Lesotho, with Moshoeshoe II, great-grandson of Moshoeshoe I, as its king. Since independence, times have been turbulent with various factions, including the military, vying for power. Since 2012, a coalition government has been in place. Pakalitha Mosisili became prime minister in 2015, but lost a vote of no confidence in March 2017, leading to early elections

Lesotho faces many problems: agriculture is vulnerable to vagaries of the weather and the population has one of the highest rates of HIV-Aids infection in the world. The UN has classified 40% of the people as "ultra-poor."

Lesotho lacks natural resources with agriculture employing 86% of the people, mostly at subsistence level. Remittances sent home by Basotho working abroad are important to the economy. The textile industry has been a significant employer of women but this has suffered due to competition from Asia.

AREA 11,720 sq mi [30,355 sq km] **POPULATION** 1,953,000
CAPITAL Maseru **GOVERNMENT** Constitutional monarchy
ETHNIC GROUPS Sotho 99% **LANGUAGES** Sesotho and English (both official) **RELIGIONS** Christianity 80%, traditional beliefs 20%
CURRENCY Loti = 100 lisente

LIBERIA

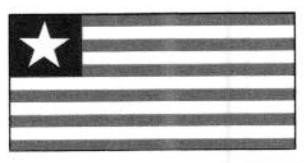
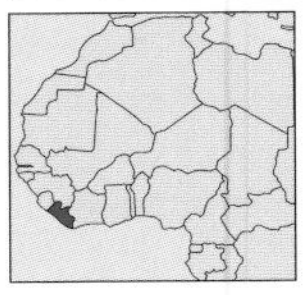

GEOGRAPHY The Republic of Liberia is a country in West Africa. Behind the coastline, 311 mi [500 km] long, lies a narrow coastal plain. Beyond, the land rises to a plateau region, with the highest land along the border with Guinea. Liberia has a tropical climate with high temperatures and high humidity all through the year. Rainfall is abundant all year round, but there is a particularly wet period from June to November. Rainfall generally increases from east to west.

POLITICS & ECONOMY In the late 18th century, some white Americans in the United States wanted to help freed black slaves return to Africa. In 1816, they set up the American Colonization Society, which bought land in what is now Liberia.

In 1822, the Society landed former slaves at a settlement which they named Monrovia after US president Monroe. In 1847, Liberia became a fully independent republic with a constitution much like that of the United States. For many years, Americo-Liberians controlled the country's government with the American Firestone Company, which ran the rubber plantations, being especially influential. Other foreign companies readily exploited Liberia's mineral resources, including its huge iron-ore deposits.

In 1980, a military group composed of people from the local population killed the Americo-Liberian president, William R. Tolbert. An army sergeant, Samuel K. Doe, was made president. Elections held in 1985 resulted in victory for Doe. From 1989, the country was plunged into civil war between various ethnic groups. Doe was assassinated in 1990 and the struggle with rebel groups continued. West African peacekeeping forces arrived in Liberia and, in 1995, a ceasefire was agreed. A council of state, composed of former warlords, was set up in 1997 and Charles Taylor became president. Taylor fled the country in 2003, and in 2006 he was extradited and faced war crimes charges, on several of which he was convicted in 2012. Following elections in 2005, Ellen Johnson-Sirleaf became Africa's first woman president. She and was subsequently re-elected in 2011. Elections are due in October 2017.

Liberia's economy was devastated by the civil war and, more recently, by the outbreak of Ebola in the region. Agriculture is important, but most farmers live at subsistence level. Food crops include cassava, rice, and sugarcane, while rubber, cocoa, and coffee are exported. The most valuable export is rubber.

Liberia also obtains revenue from its "flag of convenience" which is used by about one-sixth of the world's commercial shipping.

AREA 43,000 sq mi [111,369 sq km]
POPULATION 4,300,000 **CAPITAL** Monrovia
GOVERNMENT Multiparty republic **ETHNIC GROUPS** Indigenous African tribes 95% (including Kpelle, Bassa, Grebo, Gio, Kru, Mano)
LANGUAGES English (official), ethnic languages
RELIGIONS Christianity 86%, Islam 12%, traditional beliefs and others 2% **CURRENCY** Liberian dollar = 100 cents

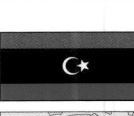

LIBYA

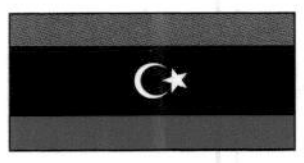
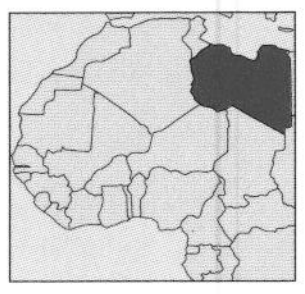

GEOGRAPHY Bordering the Mediterranean Sea, the State of Libya is the fourth largest country in Africa. Most people live on the coastal plains in the northeast and northwest. The Sahara, the world's largest desert, which occupies 95% of Libya, reaches the Mediterranean coast along the Gulf of Sidra (Khalij Surt).

The coastal plains in the northeast and northwest have Mediterranean climates, with hot, dry summers and mild, sometimes wet winters. Hot desert conditions prevail inland.

POLITICS & ECONOMY Italy took possession of Libya in 1911, but lost it during World War II. Britain and France jointly ruled Libya until 1951, when the country became independent.

In 1969, a military group headed by Colonel Muammar Gaddafi deposed the king and set up a military government. Under Gaddafi, the government took control of the economy and used money from oil exports to finance welfare services and development projects. Gaddafi was criticized for supporting terrorist groups around the world, and Libya became isolated from the mid-1980s.

From 2004, relations with the West improved and diplomatic links were restored with many nations, including the United States. However, in February 2011, the arrest of a human rights campaigner sparked off protests in Benghazi which rapidly spread. In October of that year, Gaddafi was killed and a National Transition Council was set up as the de facto government. Libya has struggled to find political stability and the elections held in 2014 produced rival governments, backed by secular and Islamist militias, which are fighting for control of the country.

The discovery of oil and natural gas in 1959 led to a transformation of Libya's economy. This formerly poor country soon became Africa's richest in terms of its per capita income. But it remains a developing country, because oil accounts for nearly all of its export revenues. Agriculture is important, although Libya imports about 80% of its food. Crops include barley, citrus fruits, dates, olives, potatoes, and wheat, while cattle, sheep, and poultry are raised. Libya has oil refineries and petrochemical plants. Development and foreign investment await political stability.

AREA 679,358 SQ MI [1,759,540 SQ KM] **POPULATION** 6,542,000
CAPITAL TRIPOLI **GOVERNMENT** TRANSITIONAL
ETHNIC GROUPS LIBYAN ARAB AND BERBER 97% **LANGUAGES** ARABIC (OFFICIAL), BERBER **RELIGIONS** ISLAM (SUNNI MUSLIM) 97%
CURRENCY LIBYAN DINAR = 1,000 DIRHAMS

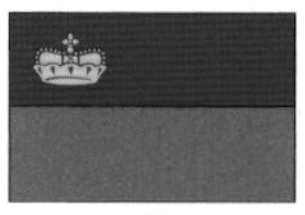
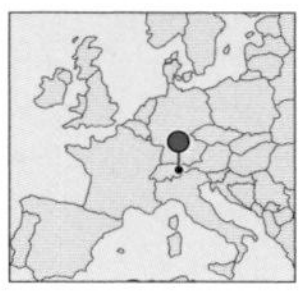

LIECHTENSTEIN

The tiny Principality of Liechtenstein is sandwiched between Switzerland and Austria. The River Rhine flows along its western border, while Alpine peaks rise in the east and south. The climate is relatively mild. Since 1924, Liechtenstein has been in a customs union with Switzerland. Taxation is low and the country is a haven for foreign companies. In 2004, the head of state Prince Hans-Adam II handed over the running of the country to his son, Prince Alois, though he remains titular head of state. In 2009, Liechtenstein agreed to share tax information with a number of countries in order to improve its reputation as a legitimate financial center.

AREA 62 SQ MI [160 SQ KM] **POPULATION** 38,000 **CAPITAL** VADUZ

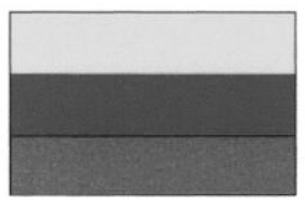
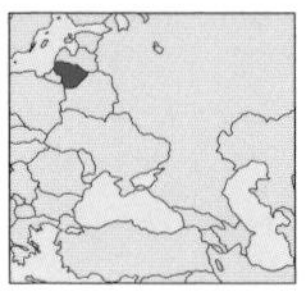

LITHUANIA

GEOGRAPHY The Republic of Lithuania is the southernmost of the three Baltic states which were ruled as part of the Soviet Union between 1940 and 1991. Much of the land is flat or gently rolling, with the highest land in the southeast.

Winters are cold and summers warm. The annual rainfall in the west is about 25 in [630 mm]. Eastern areas are drier.

POLITICS & ECONOMY The Lithuanian people were united into a single nation in the 12th century, and later joined a union with Poland. In 1795, Lithuania came under Russian rule. After World War I (1914–18), Lithuania declared itself independent, and in 1920 it signed a peace treaty with the Russians. In 1940, the Soviet Union occupied Lithuania, but was ousted by Germany a year later. After Soviet forces returned in 1944, Lithuania was integrated into the Soviet Union. However, Lithuanians resisted attempts to suppress their culture and steadfastly clung on to their language and staunch Catholic faith. In 1988, when the Soviet Union was introducing reforms, the Lithuanians demanded independence which was recognized by the Soviet Union in 1991.

Since 1991, Lithuania has sought to reform its economy and introduce a private enterprise system. Lithuania has also drawn closer to the West and, in 2004, it became a member of both the North Atlantic Treaty Organization and the European Union. Its first attempt to join the eurozone in 2007 was rejected due to high inflation but it adopted the euro in 2015.

The World Bank now classifies Lithuania as a "high-income" economy and it is growing faster than most other EU economies. Lithuania lacks natural resources, but manufacturing, based on imported materials, is the most valuable activity.

AREA 25,174 SQ MI [65,200 SQ KM]
POPULATION 2,854,000 **CAPITAL** VILNIUS
GOVERNMENT MULTIPARTY REPUBLIC
ETHNIC GROUPS LITHUANIAN 84%, POLISH 6%, RUSSIAN 5%, BELARUSIAN 1% **LANGUAGES** LITHUANIAN (OFFICIAL), RUSSIAN, POLISH
RELIGIONS MAINLY ROMAN CATHOLIC **CURRENCY** EURO = 100 CENTS

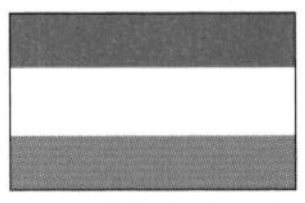
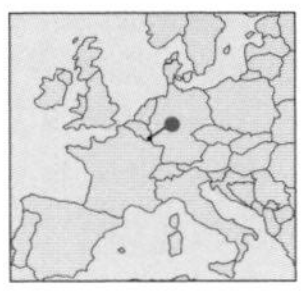

LUXEMBOURG

GEOGRAPHY The Grand Duchy of Luxembourg is one of the smallest and oldest countries in Europe. The north belongs to an upland region which includes the Ardennes in Belgium and Luxembourg, and the Eifel highlands in Germany.

Luxembourg has a temperate climate. The south has warm summers and falls, when grapes ripen in sheltered southeastern valleys. Winters are sometimes severe, especially in upland areas.

POLITICS & ECONOMY Germany occupied Luxembourg in World Wars I and II. In 1944–5; northern Luxembourg was the scene of the Battle of the Bulge. In 1948, Luxembourg joined Belgium and the Netherlands in "Benelux," a customs union, and in the 1950s, it was one of the six founders of what is now the European Union. Its capital is a major financial center and contains several international agencies. In 2008, parliament restricted the monarch to a ceremonial role following the grand duke's refusal to sign a law allowing euthanasia.

Luxembourg has iron-ore reserves and is a major steel producer. It also has many high-technology industries, producing electronic goods and computers. Steel and other manufactures, including chemicals, rubber products, glass, and aluminum, dominate the country's exports. Other major activities include tourism and financial services.

AREA 998 SQ MI [2,586 SQ KM] **POPULATION** 582,000
CAPITAL LUXEMBOURG **GOVERNMENT** CONSTITUTIONAL MONARCHY (GRAND DUCHY) **ETHNIC GROUPS** LUXEMBOURGER 63%, PORTUGUESE 13%, ITALIAN, FRENCH, BELGIAN, SLAVS **LANGUAGES** LUXEMBOURGISH (OFFICIAL), FRENCH, GERMAN **RELIGIONS** ROMAN CATHOLIC 87%, OTHERS 13%
CURRENCY EURO = 100 CENTS

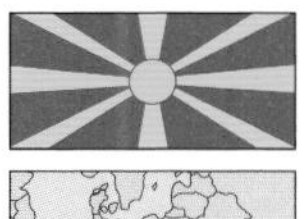
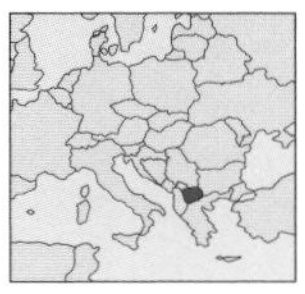

MACEDONIA (FYROM)

GEOGRAPHY The Republic of Macedonia is a country in southeastern Europe, which was once one of the six republics that made up the former Federal People's Republic of Yugoslavia. This landlocked country is largely mountainous or hilly. Macedonia has hot summers, though highland areas are cooler. Winters are cold and snowfalls are often heavy. The climate is fairly continental in character and rain occurs throughout the year.

POLITICS & ECONOMY Until the 20th century, Macedonia's history was closely tied to a larger area, also called Macedonia, which included parts of northern Greece and southwestern Bulgaria. This region reached its peak in power at the time of Philip II (382–336 BC) and his son Alexander the Great (336–323 BC). After Alexander's death, his empire was split up and it gradually declined. The area became a Roman province in the 140s BC and part of the Byzantine empire from AD 395. In the 6th century, Slavs from eastern Europe settled in the area, followed by Bulgars from central Asia in the 9th century. The Byzantine empire regained control in 1018, but Serbia took Macedonia in the early 14th century. In 1371, the Ottoman Turks conquered the area and ruled it for more than 500 years.

In 1913, at the end of the Balkan Wars, the area was divided between Serbia, Bulgaria, and Greece. At the end of World War I, Serbian Macedonia became part of the Kingdom of the Serbs, Croats, and Slovenes, which was renamed Yugoslavia in 1929. After World War II, Yugoslavia became a Communist country under ex-partisan leader Josip Broz Tito.

Tito died in 1980 and, in the early 1990s, the country broke up into five separate republics with Macedonia declaring its independence in 1991. Greece objected to the use of the name Macedonia, which it considered to be a Greek name. It also objected to a symbol on Macedonia's flag and a reference in the constitution to the desire to reunite the three parts of the old Macedonia.

Macedonia adopted a new clause in its constitution rejecting any Macedonian claims on Greek territory and, in 1993, the United Nations accepted the new republic as a member under the name of the Former Yugoslav Republic of Macedonia (FYROM). By the end of 1993, all the countries of the EU, except Greece, were establishing diplomatic relations with the FYROM. In 1995, Greece lifted its trade ban when Macedonia agreed to redesign its flag, though the issue over its name remains unresolved and hinders moves toward EU membership.

The World Bank describes Macedonia as an "upper-middle-income" economy showing steady growth since independence due to conservative government financial policies working toward a more open economy. Manufactures dominate the country's exports. Coal is mined, but oil and natural gas are imported. The country is self-sufficient in its basic food needs and has a low rate of inflation, although it remains one of Europe's poorest economies and unemployment is high.

AREA 9,928 SQ MI [25,713 SQ KM] **POPULATION** 2,100,000
CAPITAL SKOPJE **GOVERNMENT** MULTIPARTY REPUBLIC
ETHNIC GROUPS MACEDONIAN 64%, ALBANIAN 25%, TURKISH 4%, ROMANIAN 3%, SERB 2% **LANGUAGES** MACEDONIAN AND ALBANIAN (OFFICIAL) **RELIGIONS** MACEDONIAN ORTHODOX 65%, ISLAM 33%
CURRENCY MACEDONIAN DENAR = 100 DENI

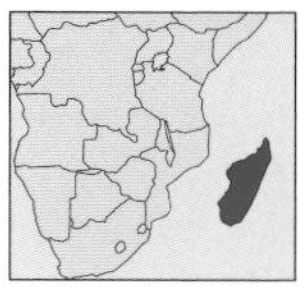

MADAGASCAR

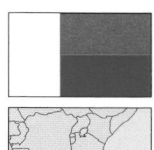

GEOGRAPHY The Democratic Republic of Madagascar, in southeastern Africa, is an island nation, which has an area larger than France. Behind the narrow coastal plains in the east lies a highland zone, mostly between 2,000 ft and 4,000 ft [610 m to 1,220 m] above sea level. Broad plains border the Mozambique Channel in the west.

Temperatures in the highlands are moderated by the altitude. The winters (from April to September) are dry, but heavy rains occur in summer. The eastern coastlands are warm and humid. The west is drier, and the south and southwest are hot and dry. It has a unique fauna and flora.

POLITICS & ECONOMY People from Southeast Asia began to settle on Madagascar around 2,000 years ago. Subsequent influxes from Africa and Arabia added to the island's diverse heritage, culture, and language.

The island was a French colony from 1895 until it achieved independence as the Malagasy Republic in 1960. In 1972, army officers seized control and, in 1975, under the leadership of Lieutenant-Commander Didier Ratsiraka, the country was renamed Madagascar. In 2002, the country came close to civil war when Ratsiraka and his opponent, Marc Ravalomanana, both claimed victory in presidential elections. Ravalomanana became president, but he was deposed in 2009 by Andry Rajoelina. Elections in late 2013 returned Hery Rajaonarimampianina as the new president in the hope that this will resolve the political gridlock which has caused the suspension of foreign aid.

Madagascar is a poor country. Poverty and population growth impose pressure on the dwindling forests and the unique wildlife, as well as causing severe soil erosion. Farming, fishing, and forestry employ about 80% of the people. Food crops include bananas, cassava, rice, and sweet potatoes. Coffee and vanilla are exported.

AREA 226,657 SQ MI [587,041 SQ KM]
POPULATION 24,430,000 **CAPITAL** ANTANANARIVO
GOVERNMENT REPUBLIC **ETHNIC GROUPS** MERINA, BETSIMISARAKA, BETSILEO, TSIMIHETY, SAKALAVA AND OTHERS
LANGUAGES MALAGASY AND FRENCH (BOTH OFFICIAL)
RELIGIONS TRADITIONAL BELIEFS 52%, CHRISTIANITY 41%, ISLAM 7%
CURRENCY MALAGASY ARIARY = 5 IRAIMBILANJA

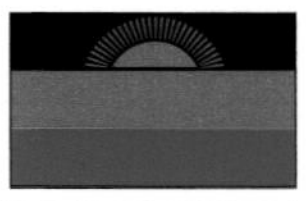
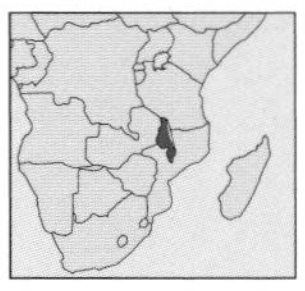

MALAWI

GEOGRAPHY The Republic of Malawi includes part of Lake Malawi, which is drained by the River Shire, a tributary of the River Zambezi. The land is mostly mountainous. The highest peak, Mulanje, reaches 9,849 ft [3,002 m] in the southeast.

While the low-lying areas of Malawi are hot and humid all year round, the uplands have more pleasant weather. Lilongwe has a warm and sunny climate. Frosts sometimes occur in July and August, in the middle of the long dry season.

POLITICS & ECONOMY Malawi, then called Nyasaland, became a British protectorate in 1891. In 1953, Britain established the Federation of Rhodesia and Nyasaland, which also included what are now Zambia and Zimbabwe. Black African opposition, led in Nyasaland by Dr Hastings Kamuzu Banda, led to the dissolution of the federation in 1963. In 1964, Nyasaland became independent as Malawi, with Banda as prime minister. Banda was an autocrat who maintained his control of the country by operating a one-party system and being made "president for life" in 1971 until he retired after elections in 1994. Bakili Muluzi became the first president after Banda and, despite Malawi aspiring toward more open government, subsequent administrations have been mired in accusations of corruption and treason.

Malawi is one of the world's poorest countries with more than half the population living below the poverty line. More than 90% of the people are farmers, but many grow little more than they need to feed their families. Some progress has been made in recent years to grow the economy and Malawi is starting to exploit its uranium deposits, but development is hampered by lack of infrastructure.

AREA 45,747 SQ MI [118,484 SQ KM]
POPULATION 18,570,000 **CAPITAL** LILONGWE
GOVERNMENT MULTIPARTY REPUBLIC
ETHNIC GROUPS CHEWA, LOMWE, YAO, NGONI, TUMBUKA, NYANJA, SENA, TONGA, NGONDE AND OTHERS
LANGUAGES CHICHEWA AND ENGLISH (BOTH OFFICIAL)
RELIGIONS CHRISTIANITY 68%, ISLAM 25%
CURRENCY MALAWIAN KWACHA = 100 TAMBALA

MALAYSIA

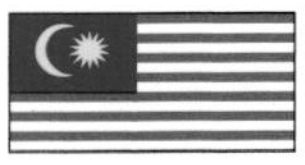

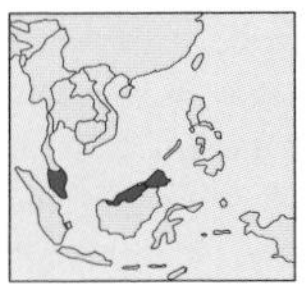

GEOGRAPHY The Federation of Malaysia consists of two main parts. Peninsular Malaysia, which is joined to mainland Asia, contains about 80% of the population. The other main regions, Sabah, and Sarawak, are in northern Borneo, an island which Malaysia shares with Indonesia. Behind the coastal lowlands, the interior is mountainous.

Malaysia has a hot equatorial climate. The temperatures are high all through the year, though the mountains are much cooler than the lowland areas. Rainfall is heavy throughout the year.

POLITICS & ECONOMY Around 1,200 years ago, Indian traders introduced Hinduism and Buddhism into the Malay peninsula, while Arabs introduced Islam in the 15th century. Portuguese traders reached Melaka in 1509, but the Dutch took over in 1641. Britain became established in this region in 1786.

Japan occupied the area during World War II (1939–45), but it reverted to British rule in 1945. In the 1940s and 1950s, Communist guerrillas battled unsuccessfully for power. Malaya (Peninsular Malaysia) became independent in 1957. Malaysia was created in 1963, when Malaya, Singapore, Sabah, and Sarawak agreed to unite, but Singapore withdrew in 1965.

From 1981, Malaysia experienced rapid economic progress under the 22-year term of Prime Minister Mahathir bin Mohamad. Although not unaffected by global financial crises, the government has continued to develop a broad-based economy with an emphasis on manufacturing, tourism, and the service industry.

The World Bank classifies Malaysia as an "upper-middle-income" developing country. Palm oil, rubber, and tin are major products. Manufactures include cars, chemicals, a wide range of electronic goods, plastics, textiles, rubber, and wood products.

AREA 127,320 sq mi [329,758 sq km] **POPULATION** 30,950,000
CAPITAL Kuala Lumpur; Putrajaya (administrative capital)
GOVERNMENT Federal constitutional monarchy
ETHNIC GROUPS Malay and other indigenous groups 61%, Chinese 24%, Indian 7%, others
LANGUAGES Malay (official), Chinese, English
RELIGIONS Islam, Buddhism, Daoism, Hinduism, Christianity, Sikhism
CURRENCY Ringgit = 100 sen

MALDIVES

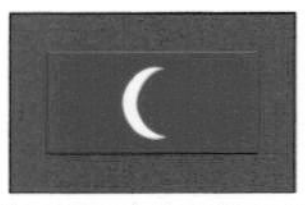

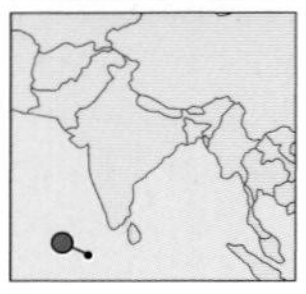

The Republic of the Maldives consists of about 1,200 low-lying coral islands, south of India. The highest point is 79 ft [24 m], but most of the land is only 6 ft [1.8 m] above sea level. It became a British territory in 1887 and independent in 1965. It left the Commonwealth of Nations in 2016. Tourism and fishing are the main industries.

AREA 115 sq mi [298 sq km] **POPULATION** 393,000 **CAPITAL** Malé

MALI

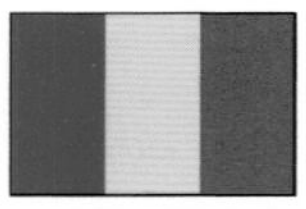

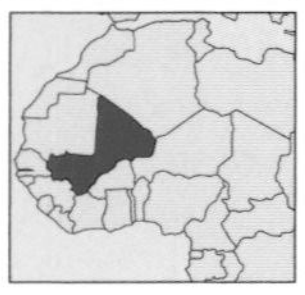

GEOGRAPHY The Republic of Mali is a landlocked country in northwestern Africa. The land is generally flat, with the highest land in the north. Northern Mali is hot and practically rainless. The south has enough rain for farming.

POLITICS & ECONOMY Between the 4th and 16th centuries, Mali was part of three African empires – Ancient Ghana, Ancient Mali and Songhay. However, after 1591, when Songhay was defeated by Morocco, the area was divided into small kingdoms. France ruled the area, then known as French Sudan, from 1893 until the country became independent as Mali in 1960.

The first socialist government was overthrown in 1968 by an army group led by Moussa Traoré, but he was ousted in 1991. Multiparty democracy was restored in 1992 and Alpha Oumar Konaré was elected president. Konaré stood down in 2002 and Ahmadou Touré, who had restored democracy in 1992, was elected president. In 2012, an army coup overthrew Touré, followed by three successive "unity cabinets." The coup leaders said that the government was failing to give them enough arms to tackle a rebellion by ethnic Tuaregs in northern Mali, many of whom had returned from Libya. A fragile peace prevails.

Mali is one of the world's poorest countries and 70% of the land is desert or semi-desert. Only about 2% of the land is used for growing crops, while 25% is used for grazing animals. Agriculture employs more than one-third of the people, many of whom subsist by nomadic livestock rearing.

AREA 478,838 sq mi [1,240,192 sq km] **POPULATION** 17,467,000
CAPITAL Bamako **GOVERNMENT** Multiparty republic **ETHNIC GROUPS** Mande 50% (Bambara, Malinke, Soninke), Peul 17%, Voltaic 12%, Songhai 6%, Tuareg and Moor 10%, others **LANGUAGES** French (official), many African languages **RELIGIONS** Islam 95%, traditional beliefs 3%, Christianity 2% **CURRENCY** CFA franc = 100 centimes

MALTA

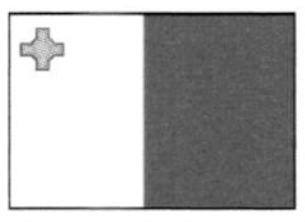

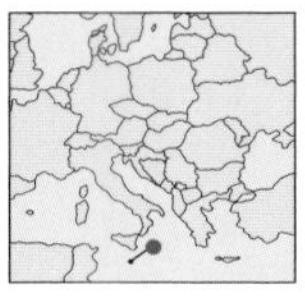

GEOGRAPHY The Republic of Malta consists of two main islands, Malta and Gozo, with a third, much smaller island called Comino lying between the two large islands and two islets. The climate is typically Mediterranean, with hot, dry summers and mild, moist winters.

POLITICS & ECONOMY Malta has fascinating Stone Age and Bronze Age remains. The islands later came under Phoenician, Greek, Carthaginian, Roman, and Arab rule. In about 1090, Malta fell under the Norman kings of Sicily and, from 1530, the Knights Hospitallers (also called the Knights of St John of Jerusalem). France took the islands in 1798, but the British drove them out in 1800. British rule was officially recognized in 1815.

During World War I (1914–18), Malta was an important naval base. In World War II (1939–45), Italian and German aircraft bombed the islands. In recognition of the islanders' bravery, the British King George VI awarded the George Cross to Malta in 1942: the emblem is incorporated into its flag. Malta became independent in 1964 and a republic in 1974. Since the 1980s Malta has pursued a policy of neutrality whilst maintaining links with Europe and the United States. It became a member of the European Union in 2004, and adopted the euro as its official currency in 2008.

The World Bank classifies Malta as a "high-income" developing country. It lacks natural resources, and most people work in the former naval dockyards, which are now used for commercial shipbuilding and repair, in manufacturing industries, and in the tourist industry.

Manufactures include processed food and chemicals. Farming is difficult, because of the rocky soils. Crops include barley, fruits, potatoes, and wheat. Malta also has a small fishing industry.

AREA 122 sq mi [316 sq km] **POPULATION** 415,000
CAPITAL Valletta **GOVERNMENT** Multiparty republic
ETHNIC GROUPS Maltese 96%, British 2% **LANGUAGES** Maltese and English (both official) **RELIGIONS** Roman Catholic 98%
CURRENCY Euro = 100 cents

MARSHALL ISLANDS

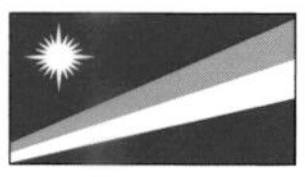

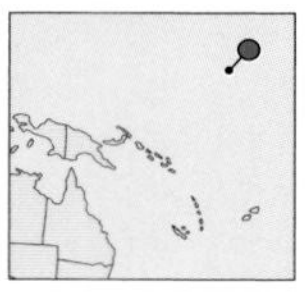

The Republic of the Marshall Islands, a former US territory, became fully independent in 1991. This island nation, lying north of Kiribati in a region known as Micronesia, is heavily dependent on US aid. The main activities are agriculture and tourism.

AREA 70 sq mi [181 sq km]
POPULATION 73,000 **CAPITAL** Majuro

MARTINIQUE

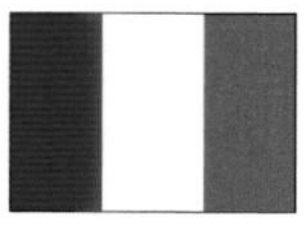

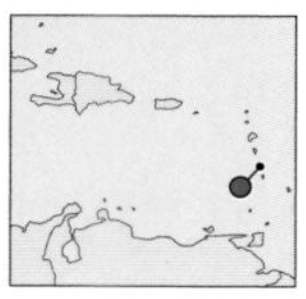

Martinique, a volcanic island nation in the Caribbean, was colonized by France in 1635. It became a French overseas department in 1946. Tourism and agriculture are major activities. About 70% of Martinique's gross domestic product is provided by the French government, allowing for a good standard of living.

AREA 425 sq mi [1,102 sq km]
POPULATION 386,000 **CAPITAL** Fort-de-France

MAURITANIA

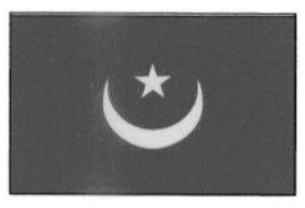

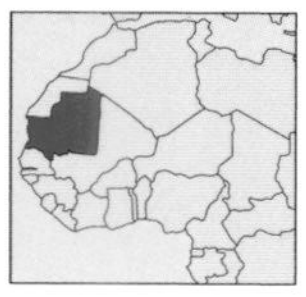

GEOGRAPHY The Islamic Republic of Mauritania in northwestern Africa is nearly twice the size of France. But France has almost 20 times as many people. Part of the world's largest desert, the Sahara, covers northern Mauritania and most Mauritanians live in the southwest. The amount of rainfall and the length of the rainy season increase from north to south. Much of the land is desert, but southwesterly winds bring summer rain to the south.

POLITICS & ECONOMY Originally part of the great African empires of Ghana and Mali, Mauritania became a French protectorate in 1903. In 1920, the country became a territory of French West Africa and a French colony. Mauritania finally became independent in 1960.

In 1976, Spain withdrew from Spanish (now Western) Sahara, a territory bordering Mauritania to the north. Morocco occupied the northern two-thirds of this territory, while Mauritania took the rest. Following this, Saharan guerrillas belonging to POLISARIO (the Popular Front for the Liberation of Saharan Territories) began an armed struggle for independence. In 1979, Mauritania withdrew from the southern part of Western Sahara, which was then occupied by Morocco. Democracy was restored after a new constitution was adopted in 1991. A military group seized power in 2005, but democratic elections were held in 2007. The military again seized control in 2008, and in 2009 its leader, Mohamad Ould Abdel Aziz, was elected president. In 2010–11, al Qaeda militants committed terrorist acts in Mauritania and their presence in the country is having a serious destabilizing effect.

Mauritania is a "lower-middle-income" developing country. Nearly half of the population are engaged in agriculture and at the mercy of frequent droughts. The coastal waters provide good fishing grounds. In 2006, Mauritania became Africa's newest oil producer, when an offshore platform came online for the first time.

AREA 395,953 sq mi [1,025,520 sq km]
POPULATION 3,677,000 **CAPITAL** Nouakchott
GOVERNMENT Multiparty Islamic republic
ETHNIC GROUPS Mixed Moor/Black 40%, Moor 30%, Black 30%
LANGUAGES Arabic (official), Pulaar, Soninke, Wolof, French
RELIGIONS Islam
CURRENCY Ouguiya = 5 khoums

MAURITIUS

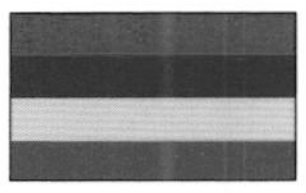

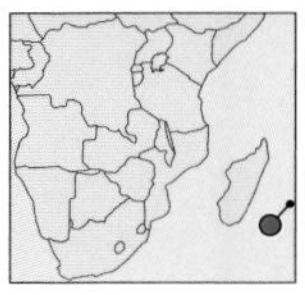

The Republic of Mauritius lies in the Indian Ocean east of Madagascar. It was previously ruled by France and Britain until it achieved independence in 1968. It became a republic in 1992. Sugar production is in decline with tourism and textiles vital to the economy.

AREA 788 sq mi [2,040 sq km]
POPULATION 1,348,000 **CAPITAL** Port Louis

MEXICO

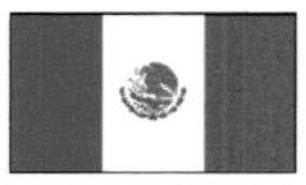

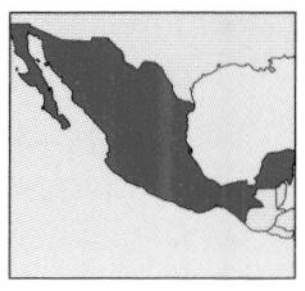

GEOGRAPHY The United Mexican States, as Mexico is officially named, is the world's most populous Spanish-speaking country. Much of the land is mountainous, although most people live on the central plateau. Mexico contains two large peninsulas: Lower (or Baja) California in the northwest, and the flat Yucatán peninsula in the southeast.

The climate varies according to the altitude. The resort of Acapulco on the southwest coast has a dry and sunny climate. Mexico City, at about 7,546 ft [2,300 m] above sea level, is much cooler. Most rain occurs between June and September. Rainfall decreases north of Mexico City and northern Mexico is mainly arid.

POLITICS & ECONOMY In the mid-19th century, Mexico lost land to the United States, and between 1910 and 1921 violent revolutions created chaos. Reforms were introduced in the 1920s and, in 1929, the Institutional Revolutionary Party (PRI) was formed. The PRI ruled Mexico effectively as a one-party state until it was finally defeated in 2001. The new president, Vicente Fox, faced many problems. He was succeeded by Felipe Calderón in 2006, and at the end of 2012 Enrique Peña Nieto was elected president. Since 2008 killings associated with the illegal drug traffic have increased dramatically.

The World Bank classifies Mexico as an "upper-middle-income" developing country. Agriculture is important. Food crops include beans, maize, rice, and wheat, while cash crops include coffee, cotton, fruits, and vegetables.

However, oil and oil products are the chief exports, while manufacturing is the most valuable activity. Mexico is the world's leading silver producer, and it also mines copper, gold, lead, zinc, and other minerals. Many factories near the northern border assemble goods, such as car parts and electrical products, for US companies.

Hopes for the future have lain in increasing cooperation with the US and Canada, possibly through a revitalized North American Free-Trade Agreement (NAFTA). The election of Donald Trump

as US President in 2016 leaves the status of NAFTA and Mexican hopes for more balanced trade uncertain.

AREA 756,061 sq mi [1,958,201 sq km]
POPULATION 123,167,000 **CAPITAL** Mexico City
GOVERNMENT Federal republic
ETHNIC GROUPS Mestizo 60%, Amerindian 30%, White 9%
LANGUAGES Spanish (official)
RELIGIONS Roman Catholic 83%, Protestant 2%, others 15%
CURRENCY Mexican peso = 100 centavos

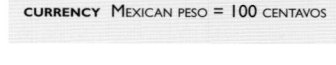

MICRONESIA

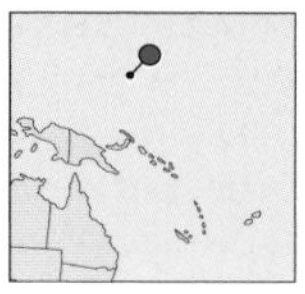

The Federated States of Micronesia, a former US territory covering a vast area in the western Pacific Ocean, became fully independent in 1991. The main export is copra. Fishing and tourism are also important.

AREA 271 sq mi [702 sq km]
POPULATION 105,000 **CAPITAL** Palikir

MOLDOVA

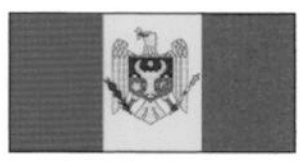
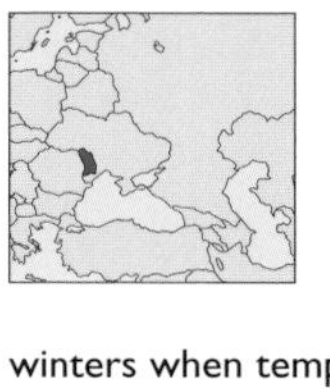

GEOGRAPHY The Republic of Moldova is a small country sandwiched between Ukraine and Romania. It was formerly one of the 15 republics that made up the Soviet Union. Much of the land is hilly and the highest areas are near the center of the country.

Moldova has a moderately continental climate, with warm summers and fairly cold winters when temperatures dip below freezing point. Most of the rain comes in the warmer months.

POLITICS & ECONOMY In the 14th century, the Moldavian people formed a state that comprised part of Romania and the historic region of Bessarabia. Following rule by the Ottoman Turks, Russia took control of Bessarabia in 1812. After World War I (1914–18), Bessarabia declared independence and voted to unite with Romania. This move was not recognized by Russia and in 1940 the area was annexed by the USSR. From 1944, the Moldovan Soviet Socialist Republic became part of the Soviet Union.

In 1989, the Moldovans asserted their independence and ethnicity by making Romanian the official language and, at the end of 1991, Moldova became an independent nation. But Trans-Dniester, an area east of the River Dniester inhabited by mainly Russian and Ukrainian speakers, has sought autonomy. In 2006, its people voted for independence and union with Russia, but this vote was not recognized internationally.

In 2001, Moldovans returned the Communist Party to power. Under President Vladimir Voronin, Moldova enjoyed a period of economic growth. The Communist Party was re-elected in 2005 and 2009. Following allegations of fraud, further elections were held in 2010. In 2014, Moldova signed its Association Agreement with the EU. Russia restricted some agricultural imports in response. In 2016, in the first direct presidential elections in some years, pro-Russian Igor Dodon was elected with 55% of the vote. .

In terms of its GNP per capita, Moldova is one of Europe's poorest countries. Agriculture is the leading activity and products include fruits, maize, tobacco, and wine. Moldova has few natural resources and it imports materials and fuels for its industries.

AREA 13,070 sq mi [33,851 sq km]
POPULATION 3,510,000 **CAPITAL** Kishinev
GOVERNMENT Multiparty republic
ETHNIC GROUPS Moldovan/Romanian 78%, Ukrainian 8%, Russian 6%, Gagauz 4%, others
LANGUAGES Moldovan/Romanian (official), Gagauz, Russian
RELIGIONS Eastern Orthodox 98%
CURRENCY Moldovan leu = 100 bani

MONACO

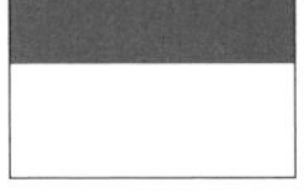
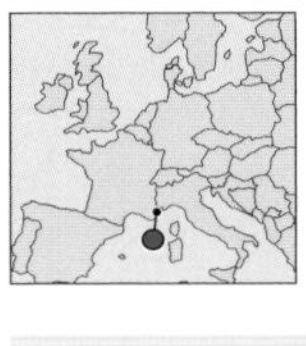

The tiny Principality of Monaco consists of a narrow strip of coastline and a rocky peninsula on the French Riviera. Its considerable wealth is derived largely from banking, finance, gambling, recreation, and tourism. Monaco's citizens do not pay any income tax. The Grimaldi family have ruled the country for over 720 years with Prince Albert II as the current reigning monarch.

AREA 0.4 sq mi [1 sq km] **POPULATION** 31,000 **CAPITAL** Monaco

MONGOLIA

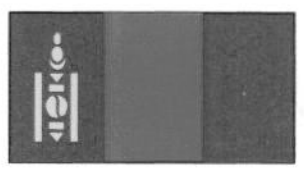
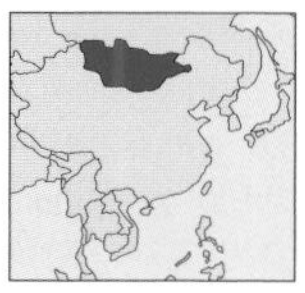

GEOGRAPHY The State of Mongolia is the world's largest landlocked country. It consists mainly of high plateaux, with a cold desert, the Gobi, in the southeast.

Ulan Bator lies on the northern edge of the desert plateau. It has bitterly cold winters. Summer temperatures are moderated by the altitude.

POLITICS & ECONOMY In the 13th century, Genghis Khan united the Mongolian peoples and built up a great empire. Under his grandson, Kublai Khan, the Mongol empire extended from Korea and China to eastern Europe and present-day Iraq.

The Mongol empire broke up in the late 14th century. In the early 17th century, Inner Mongolia came under Chinese control, and by the late 17th century Outer Mongolia had become a Chinese province. In 1911, the Mongolians drove the Chinese out of Outer Mongolia and made the area a Buddhist kingdom. But in 1924, under Russian influence, the Communist Mongolian People's Republic was set up. In 1990, the people demonstrated for more freedom, and free elections in June 1990 were won by the Communist Mongolian People's Revolutionary Party (MPRP). The Democratic Union coalition won in 1996, but the MPRP regained control in 2000. In 2009, the Democratic Union candidate, Tsakhiagiin Elbegdorj, was elected president. He was re-elected in 2013. In 2016 Parliamentary elections, the Mongolian People's Party won a landslide. Presidential elections are due in summer 2017.

The World Bank classifies Mongolia as a "upper-middle-income" developing country. The majority of the population were once nomads but, under Communist rule, most people were moved into permanent homes on government-owned farms. Livestock and animal products remain important, but minerals and fuels now account for more than three-fifths of Mongolia's exports. There is much mineral wealth yet to be exploited.

AREA 604,826 sq mi [1,566,500 sq km]
POPULATION 3,031,000 **CAPITAL** Ulan Bator
GOVERNMENT Multiparty republic **ETHNIC GROUPS** Khalkha Mongol 95%, Kazakh 5% **LANGUAGES** Khalkha Mongolian (official), Turkic, Russian **RELIGIONS** Tibetan Buddhist Lamaism 53%
CURRENCY Mongolian tögrög = 100 möngös

MONTENEGRO

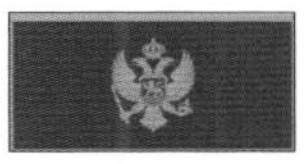
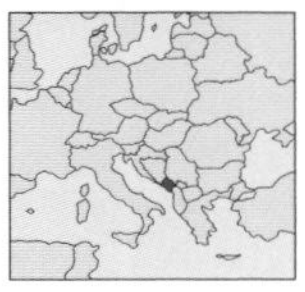

The Republic of Montenegro, on the shores of the Adriatic Sea, became independent in 2006.

The coastal region has a Mediterranean climate. However, inland, the Dinaric Alps, which reach a height of 8,274 ft [2,522 m], have a more severe climate.

Serbia fell under Turkish rule in the 14th century, but Montenegro remained Christian. Montenegro was absorbed into Serbia in 1918 and it later became part of the Kingdom of the Serbs, Croats, and Slovenes, renamed as Yugoslavia in 1929. After World War II, Montenegro was recognized as one of the six republics of Yugoslavia.

Elections were held in 2009 and 2012. In 2016, long-term prime minister Milo Djukanovich was replaced by Dusko Markovic. The presidential election held in April 2013 was won by the incumbent Filip Vujanovic. Montenegro is a candidate for EU membership and in 2015 was invited to join NATO.

Manufacturing is the main activity, and steel and aluminum are major products. Farming also remains important. Montenegro became a member of the World Trade Organization in 2012.

AREA 5,415 sq mi [14,026 sq km] **POPULATION** 645,000
CAPITAL Podgorica **GOVERNMENT** Republic
ETHNIC GROUPS Montenegrin 43%, Serb 32%, Bosnian 8%, Albanian 5%, others **LANGUAGES** Serbian and Montenegrin (both official), Bosnian, Albanian **RELIGIONS** Orthodox, Islam, Roman Catholic **CURRENCY** Euro = 100 cents

MONTSERRAT

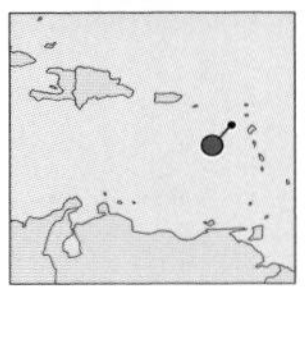

Montserrat is a British overseas territory in the Caribbean Sea. The climate is tropical and hurricanes often cause much damage. Intermittent eruptions of the Soufrière Hills volcano between 1995 and 1998, and again in 2003, led to the emigration of many people and the virtual destruction of Plymouth, the then capital. A new airport was opened in 2005.

AREA 39 sq mi [102 sq km] **POPULATION** 5,000 **CAPITAL** Brades

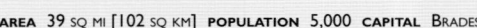

MOROCCO

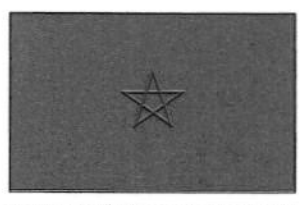
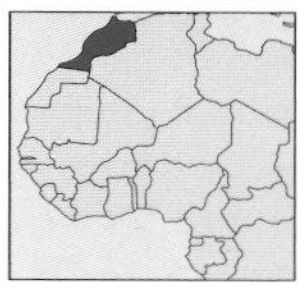

GEOGRAPHY The Kingdom of Morocco lies in northwestern Africa. Its name comes from the Arabic Maghreb-el-Aksa, meaning "the farthest west." Behind the western coastal plain the land rises to a broad plateau and ranges of the Atlas Mountains. The High (Haut) Atlas contains the highest peak, Djebel Toubkal, at 13,665 ft [4,165 m]. East of the mountains, the land descends to the Sahara. The Canaries Current cools the Atlantic coast. Inland, summers are hot and dry. Winters are mild, with moderate rainfall. Snow often falls on the High Atlas Mountains.

POLITICS & ECONOMY The original people of Morocco were the Berbers, but, in the 680s, Arab invaders introduced Islam and the Arabic language. By the early 20th century, France and Spain controlled Morocco, which became an independent kingdom in 1956. Although Morocco is a constitutional monarchy, King Hassan II ruled the country in a generally authoritarian way, from the time of his accession to the throne in 1961 to his death in 1999. His successor, Mohamed VI, faced several problems, including that of Western Sahara, which he claimed for Morocco, and the activities of Islamist extremists. In 2011, the people approved a new constitution, granting the prime minister more power.

Morocco is classified as a "lower-middle-income" developing country. It is the world's third largest producer of phosphate rock, which is used to make fertilizer. One of the reasons why Morocco wants to keep Western Sahara is that it, too, has large phosphate reserves. Farming employs about 45% of Moroccans. Chief crops include barley, beans, citrus fruits, maize, olives, sugar beet, and wheat. Processed phosphates are exported, but most of Morocco's manufactures are for home consumption. Fishing and tourism are also important.

AREA 172,413 sq mi [446,550 sq km]
POPULATION 33,656,000 **CAPITAL** Rabat
GOVERNMENT Constitutional monarchy
ETHNIC GROUPS Arab-Berber 99%
LANGUAGES Arabic (official), Berber dialects, French
RELIGIONS Islam 99% **CURRENCY** Moroccan dirham = 100 centimes

MOZAMBIQUE

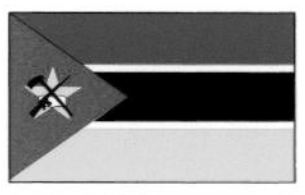
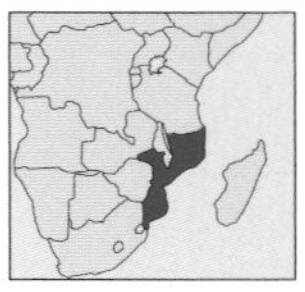

GEOGRAPHY The Republic of Mozambique borders the Indian Ocean in southeastern Africa. The coastal plains are narrow in the north but broaden in the south. Inland lie plateaux and hills, which make up another two-fifths of the country. Mozambique has a mostly tropical climate. The capital Maputo, which lies outside the tropics, has hot and humid summers, though the winters are mild and fairly dry.

POLITICS & ECONOMY In 1885, when the European powers divided Africa, Mozambique was recognized as a Portuguese colony. But black African opposition to European rule gradually increased. In 1961, the Front for the Liberation of Mozambique (FRELIMO) was founded to oppose Portuguese rule. In 1964, FRELIMO launched a guerrilla war, which continued for ten years, until Mozambique became independent in 1975.

After independence, Mozambique became a one-party state. Its government aided African nationalists in Rhodesia (now Zimbabwe) and South Africa. But the white governments of these countries helped an opposition group, the Mozambique National Resistance Movement (RENAMO) to lead an armed struggle against Mozambique's government. Civil war, combined with droughts, caused much suffering in the 1980s. In 1989, FRELIMO ended one-party rule and multiparty elections were held in 1994. In 1995 Mozambique became the 53rd member of the Commonwealth. In January 2015, Filipe Nyusi became the country's 4th president.

In the early 1990s, the UN rated Mozambique as one of the world's poorest countries but the second half of the 1990s saw the start of economic growth. Although hampered by cycles of drought and flood, and the fact that about 80% of the people are poor farmers, the country has one of Africa's strongest growing economies. It will become a major exporter of coal and gas.

AREA 309,494 sq mi [801,590 sq km]
POPULATION 25,930,000 **CAPITAL** Maputo
GOVERNMENT Multiparty republic **ETHNIC GROUPS** Indigenous tribal groups (Shangaan, Chokwe, Manyika, Sena, Makua, others) 99%
LANGUAGES Portuguese (official), many others
RELIGIONS Roman Catholic 28%, Protestant 28%, Islam 18%
CURRENCY Metical = 100 centavos

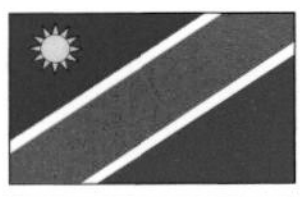
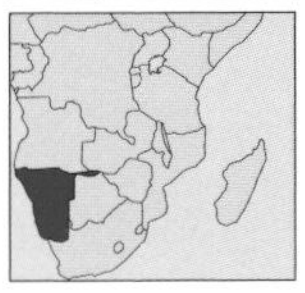

NAMIBIA

GEOGRAPHY When it was ruled by South Africa, the Republic of Namibia was known as South West Africa. The coastal region contains the arid Namib Desert, which is virtually uninhabited. Inland is a central plateau, bordered by a rugged spine of mountains stretching north–south. Eastern Namibia contains part of the Kalahari, a semi-desert area extending into Botswana. Namibia has a warm and arid climate. Windhoek has an average annual rainfall of 15 inches [370 mm], which often occurs in thunderstorms during the hot summer.

POLITICS & ECONOMY During World War I, South African troops defeated the Germans who ruled what is now Namibia. After World War II, many people challenged South Africa's right to govern the territory, and a civil war began in the 1960s between African guerrillas and South African troops. A ceasefire was agreed in 1989 and Namibia became independent in 1990. In the 1990s, the government pursued a policy of "national reconciliation." An enclave on the coast, Walvis Bay (Walvisbaai), remained part of South Africa until 1994, when it was transferred to Namibia. In 2004, the nationalist leader, Sam Nujoma, president since 1990, retired. He was succeeded by Hifikepunye Pohamba, who in turn was followed by Hage Geingob after elections in 2014.

Namibia has reserves of diamonds, uranium, zinc, and copper: minerals make up the bulk of its exports. Agriculture employs 16% of the people and much is at subsistence level. Fishing is important. Namibia has few industries and unemployment is high at around 50%. Oil has been discovered and tourism is expanding.

AREA 318,259 sq mi [824,292 sq km]
POPULATION 2,436,000 **CAPITAL** Windhoek
GOVERNMENT Multiparty republic **ETHNIC GROUPS** Ovambo 50%, Kavango 9%, Herero 7%, Damara 7%, White 6%, Nama 5%
LANGUAGES English (official), Afrikaans, German, indigenous dialects **RELIGIONS** Christianity 90% (Lutheran 51%)
CURRENCY Namibian dollar = 100 cents

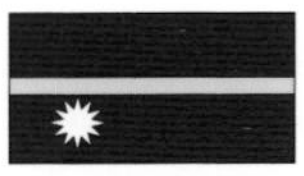
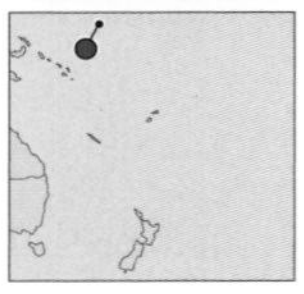

NAURU

Nauru is the world's smallest republic, located in the western Pacific Ocean. Independent since 1968, Nauru's prosperity is based on phosphate mining. Since 2013, Australia has detained asylum-seekers on the island.

AREA 8 sq mi [21 sq km]
POPULATION 10,000 **CAPITAL** Yaren

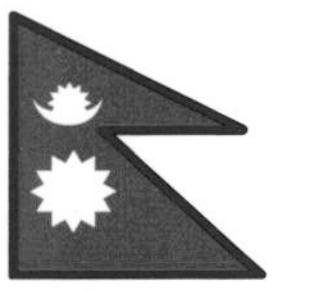
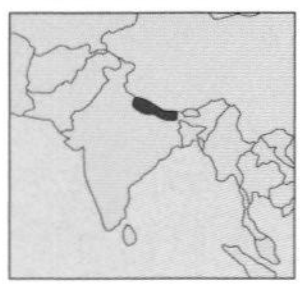

NEPAL

GEOGRAPHY Over three-quarters of Nepal lies in the Himalayan region, culminating in the world's highest peak (Mount Everest, or Chomolongma in Nepali) at 29,035 ft [8,850 m]. As a result, climatic conditions vary widely according to the altitude.

POLITICS & ECONOMY Nepal was united in the late 18th century, although its complex topography has ensured that it remains a diverse patchwork of peoples. From the mid-19th century to 1951, power was held by the royal Rana family. The first democratic elections in 32 years were held in 1991, but, by the early 21st century, Nepal faced many problems, including an uprising of Maoist guerrillas. In 2005, King Gyanendra seized power but failed to stop the conflict. In 2006, the Maoists joined a provisional coalition government. In elections in April 2008, the Maoists became the largest single party. In May, Nepal became a republic after the abolition of the monarchy. A new constitution was adopted in 2015, and Bidhya Devi Bhandari was elected as Nepal's first female president.

Agriculture is the main activity and poverty is rife in this overwhelmingly rural country. Nepal is heavily dependent on aid. Tourism, based on the attractions of the high Himalaya, is growing in importance. There are also ambitious plans to exploit the hydroelectric potential offered by the ferocious Himalayan rivers.

AREA 56,827 sq mi [147,181 sq km] **POPULATION** 29,034,000
CAPITAL Katmandu **GOVERNMENT** Multiparty republic
ETHNIC GROUPS Brahman, Chhetri, Newar, Gurung, Magar, Tamang, Sherpa, and others
LANGUAGES Nepali (official), local languages
RELIGIONS Hinduism 81%, Buddhism 11%, Islam 4%
CURRENCY Nepalese rupee = 100 paisa

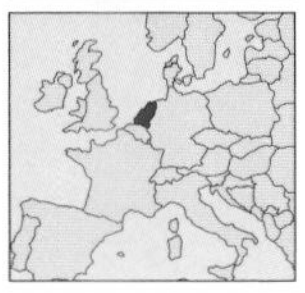

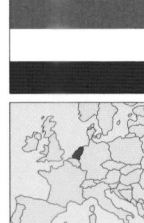

NETHERLANDS

GEOGRAPHY The Netherlands lies at the western end of the North European Plain, which extends to the Ural Mountains in Russia. Except for the far southeastern corner, the Netherlands is flat and about 40% lies below sea level at high tide. To prevent flooding, the Dutch have built dykes (sea walls) to hold back the waves. Large areas which were once under the sea, but which have been reclaimed, are known as polders. Because of its position on the North Sea, the Netherlands has a temperate climate, with mild, rainy winters.

POLITICS & ECONOMY Before the 16th century, the area that is now the Netherlands was under a succession of foreign rulers; including the Romans, the Germanic Franks, the French, and the Spanish. The Dutch declared their independence from Spain in 1581 and their status was finally recognized by Spain in 1648. In the 17th century, the Dutch built up a great overseas empire, especially in Southeast Asia. But in the early 18th century, the Dutch lost control of the seas to England.

France controlled the Netherlands from 1795 to 1813. In 1815, the Netherlands, then containing Belgium and Luxembourg, became an independent kingdom. Belgium broke away in 1830 and Luxembourg followed in 1890.

The Netherlands was neutral in World War I (1914–18), but was occupied by Germany in World War II (1939–45). After the war, the Netherlands Indies became independent as Indonesia. The Netherlands became active in West European affairs and, with Belgium and Luxembourg, it formed the customs union of Benelux in 1948. In 1949, it joined NATO (the North Atlantic Treaty Organization), and the European Coal and Steel Community (ECSC) in 1953. In 1957, it became a founder member of the European Economic Community (now the European Union), and, in 2002, it adopted the euro as its sole unit of currency. After a series of short-lived governments, Mark Rutte's VVD led a stable coalition from 2012–17 and in the latter year's elections remained the largest party. The right-wing Freedom Party did not make the expected gains. In 2013, after a 33-year reign, Queen Beatrix abdicated in favor of her son, Prince Willem Alexander.

2010 saw the dissolution of the Netherlands Antilles, an island territory in the Caribbean. Curaçao and St Maarten became nations in the Kingdom of the Netherlands. The small islands of Bonaire, St Eustatius, and Saba became special municipalities.

The Netherlands is a highly industrialized country, and industry and commerce are the most valuable activities. Its resources include natural gas, some oil, salt, and china clay. But the Netherlands imports many of the materials needed by its industries and it is, therefore, a major trading country. Industrial products are wide-ranging, including aircraft, chemicals, electronic equipment, machinery, textiles, and vehicles. Farming is scientific and yields are high. Dairy farming is the leading farming activity. Major products include barley, flowers and bulbs, potatoes, sugar beet, and wheat.

AREA 16,033 sq mi [41,526 sq km] **POPULATION** 17,017,000
CAPITAL Amsterdam; The Hague (seat of government)
GOVERNMENT Constitutional monarchy
ETHNIC GROUPS Dutch 81%, Indonesian, Turkish, Moroccan, and others **LANGUAGES** Dutch and Frisian (both official)
RELIGIONS Roman Catholic 30%, Protestant 20%, Islam 6%, others
CURRENCY Euro = 100 cents

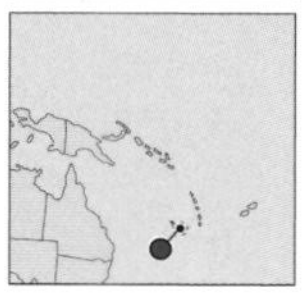

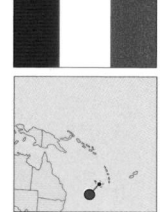

NEW CALEDONIA

New Caledonia is the most southerly of the Melanesian countries in the Pacific. It has been a French possession since 1853 and an Overseas Territory since 1958. In 1998, France announced that a vote on independence would be held before 2018. The country is rich in mineral resources, especially nickel.

AREA 7,172 sq mi [18,575 sq km] **POPULATION** 275,000 **CAPITAL** Nouméa

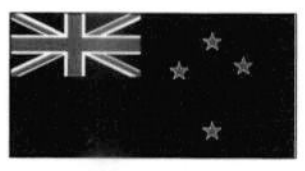
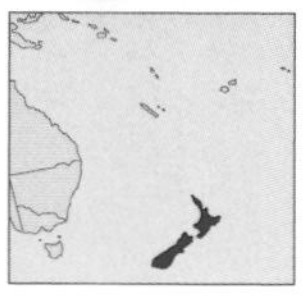

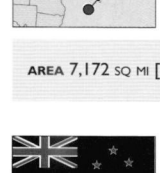

NEW ZEALAND

GEOGRAPHY New Zealand lies about 994 mi [1,600 km] southeast of Australia. It consists of two main islands and several other small ones. Much of North Island is volcanic. Active volcanoes include Ngauruhoe and Ruapehu. Hot springs and geysers are common, and steam from the ground is used to produce electricity. The Southern Alps, which contain the country's highest peak, Aoraki Mount Cook, at 12,217 ft [3,724 m], form the backbone of South Island. This island also has some large, fertile plains.

New Zealand lies on the geologically active "Pacific ring of fire." Most of the 14,000 earthquakes that occur every year have a magnitude of less than 5.0. But, in 2010 and 2011, two earthquakes, with magnitudes of 7.0 and 6.3 respectively, struck Christchurch on South Island, causing great damage. The 2011 earthquake resulted in a death toll of more than 180.

Auckland in the north has a warm, humid climate throughout the year. Wellington has cooler summers, while in Dunedin, in the southeast, temperatures sometimes dip below freezing in winter. The rainfall is heaviest on the western highlands.

POLITICS & ECONOMY Evidence suggests that early Maori settlers arrived in New Zealand more than 1,000 years ago. The Dutch navigator Abel Tasman reached New Zealand in 1642, but his discovery was not followed up. In 1769, the British Captain James Cook rediscovered the islands. During the early 19th century, British settlers arrived and, in 1840, under the Treaty of Waitangi, Britain took possession of the islands. From the 1870s, the Maoris were gradually integrated into colonial society.

In 1907, New Zealand became a self-governing dominion in the British Commonwealth. The country's economy developed quickly and the people became increasingly prosperous. However, after Britain joined the European Economic Community in 1973, New Zealand's exports to Britain shrank and the country had to reassess its economic and defense strategies and seek new markets. The world recession led the government to cut back on welfare spending in the 1990s. The preservation of Maori culture and rights are major issues as the Maoris, a Polynesian people, make up about 15% of the population. Other mainly Polynesian Pacific people make up another 7%. Ties with Britain have been reduced and Helen Clark, leader of the Labor Party and prime minister from 1999–2008, has expressed the view that New Zealand will eventually abolish the monarchy and become a republic. In November 2008, the center-right National Party defeated the Labor Party in elections. John Key was Prime Minister from 2008–16, when he resigned and was replaced by the socially conservative Bill English.

The economy once depended on agriculture, but manufacturing now employs twice as many people as farming. Meat and dairy products are leading commodities. Sheep rearing has declined as the area under cattle, deer, and vines has expanded. In 2008–9, New Zealand's economy entered a period of recession. The economy is now growing but is still fragile.

AREA 104,453 sq mi [270,534 sq km]
POPULATION 4,475,000 **CAPITAL** Wellington
GOVERNMENT Constitutional monarchy
ETHNIC GROUPS European 68%, Maori 15%, Asian 9%, Polynesian 7%
LANGUAGES English and Maori (both official)
RELIGIONS Anglican 24%, Presbyterian 18%, Roman Catholic 15%, others **CURRENCY** New Zealand dollar = 100 cents

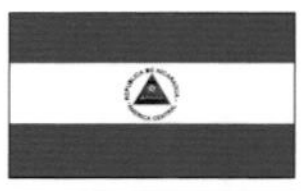
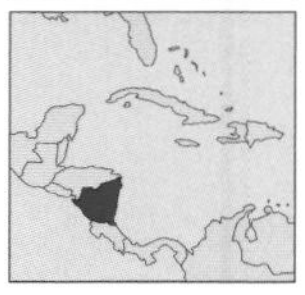

NICARAGUA

GEOGRAPHY The Republic of Nicaragua is a large country in Central America. In the east is a broad plain bordering the Caribbean Sea. The plain is drained by rivers that flow from the Central Highlands. The fertile western Pacific region contains about 40 volcanoes, many of which are active, and earthquakes are common.

Nicaragua has a tropical climate. Managua is hot throughout the year and there is a marked rainy season from May to October. In October 1998, Hurricane Mitch caused great devastation in Nicaragua. The Central Highlands and Caribbean region are cooler and wetter. The wettest region is the humid Caribbean plain.

POLITICS & ECONOMY In 1502, Christopher Columbus claimed the area for Spain, which ruled Nicaragua until 1821. By the early 20th century, the United States had considerable influence in the country and, in 1912, US forces entered Nicaragua. From 1927 to 1933, rebels under General Augusto César Sandino tried to drive US forces out of the country. In 1933, US marines set up a Nicaraguan army, the National Guard, to help to defeat the rebels. Its leader, Anastasio Somoza Garcia, had Sandino murdered in 1934, and from 1937 Somoza ruled as a dictator.

In the mid-1970s, many people began to protest against Somoza's rule and joined a guerrilla force, called the Sandinista National Liberation Front, named after General Sandino. The rebels defeated the Somoza regime in 1979. In the 1980s, US-supported forces, called the "Contras," launched a campaign against the Sandinista government. The US government opposed

the Sandinista regime, under Daniel José Ortega Saavedra, claiming that it was a Communist dictatorship. A coalition, the National Opposition Union, defeated the Sandinistas in 1990. In 2001, the Sandinista candidate, Ortega, was defeated in presidential elections, but he was re-elected in 2006, 2011, and 2016. Ortega's administration has a bias toward Russia and anti-US countries in Latin America.

In the early 1990s, Nicaragua faced many problems in rebuilding its shattered economy. Agriculture employs about 28% of the people with coffee, cotton, sugar and bananas being grown for export, while rice is the main food crop. Attempts are being made to develop the tourist industry.

AREA 50,193 SQ MI [130,000 SQ KM]
POPULATION 5,967,000 **CAPITAL** MANAGUA
GOVERNMENT MULTIPARTY REPUBLIC
ETHNIC GROUPS MESTIZO 69%, WHITE 17%, BLACK 9%, AMERINDIAN 5%
LANGUAGES SPANISH (OFFICIAL)
RELIGIONS ROMAN CATHOLIC 59%, PROTESTANT 23%, OTHERS
CURRENCY NICARAGUAN CÓRDOBA = 100 CENTAVOS

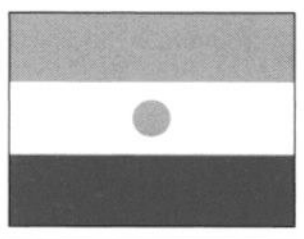
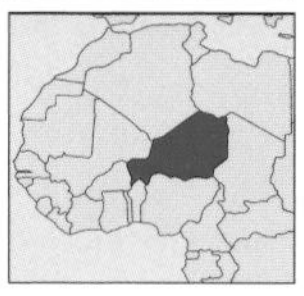

NIGER

GEOGRAPHY The Republic of Niger is a landlocked nation in north-central Africa. The northern plateaux lie in the desert area of the Sahara, while central Niger contains the rugged Aïr Mountains. The most fertile, densely populated region is the Niger valley in the southwest.

Niger has a tropical climate and the south has a rainy season between June and September. The north is practically rainless.

POLITICS & ECONOMY Since independence in 1960, Niger, a French territory from 1900, has suffered severe droughts. Food shortages and the collapse of the traditional nomadic way of life of some of Niger's people have caused political instability. After a period of military rule, a multiparty constitution was adopted in 1992, but the military again seized power in 1996. Later that year, the coup leader, Colonel Ibrahim Barre Mainassara, was elected president. He was assassinated in 1999, but parliamentary rule was restored. After a coup in 2010, Mahamadou Issoufou was elected president in 2011. He gained a second term in a largely uncontested election in 2016.

Niger's chief resource is uranium and the country is the world's fifth largest producer. The export of minerals accounts for 40% of total exports although there is much more to be exploited. Despite its considerable resources, Niger remains one of the world's poorest countries. Only 3% of the land can be used for growing crops but agriculture supports around 90% of the people.

AREA 489,189 SQ MI [1,267,000 SQ KM] **POPULATION** 18,639,000
CAPITAL NIAMEY **GOVERNMENT** MULTIPARTY REPUBLIC
ETHNIC GROUPS HAUSA 55%, DJERMA 21%, TUAREG 9%, FULA 8%, OTHERS **LANGUAGES** FRENCH (OFFICIAL), HAUSA, DJERMA
RELIGIONS ISLAM 80%, INDIGENOUS BELIEFS, CHRISTIANITY
CURRENCY CFA FRANC = 100 CENTIMES

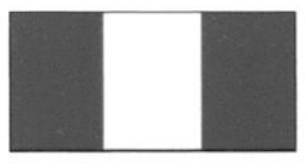
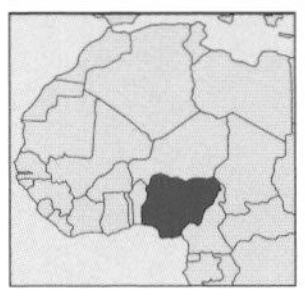

NIGERIA

GEOGRAPHY The Federal Republic of Nigeria is the most populous nation in Africa. The country's main rivers are the Niger and Benue, which meet in central Nigeria. North of the two river valleys are high plains and plateaux. The Lake Chad basin is in the northeast, with the Sokoto plains in the northwest. The south contains hilly uplands and plains. The south has a hot, rainy climate. The north is drier and often hotter than the south.

POLITICS & ECONOMY Nigeria has a long artistic tradition. Major cultures include the Nok (500 BC to AD 200), the Ife, a major Yoruba culture which developed about 1,000 years ago, and the Benin (15th to 17th centuries). Britain gradually extended its influence over the area in the second half of the 19th century.

Nigeria became an independent nation in 1960 and a federal republic in 1963. A federal constitution dividing the country into regions was necessary because Nigeria contains more than 250 ethnic and linguistic groups, as well as several religious ones. Local rivalries have long been a threat to national unity, and six new states were created in 1996 in an attempt to overcome this. Civil war occurred between 1967 and 1970, when the people of the southeast attempted unsuccessfully to secede during the Biafran War. Between 1960 and 1998, Nigeria had only nine years of civilian government.

In 1998–9, civilian rule was restored but Nigeria faced many problems, including violence in the Niger delta region and religious conflict. In 2011–12, northern Nigeria was hit by a series of violent attacks from the Islamist organization, Boko Haram. 2015 saw the first ever democratic change of power in Nigeria when Muhammadu Buhari was elected president.

Nigeria is a developing country with great potential although most of the population currently live in poverty. Its chief natural resource is oil, which accounts for most of its exports. Agriculture employs 70% of the people and the country is a major producer of cocoa, palm oil and palm kernels, groundnuts (peanuts), and rubber. Industry is increasing and manufactures include cement, chemicals, fertilizers, textiles, and timber.

AREA 356,667 SQ MI [923,768 SQ KM] **POPULATION** 186,053,000
CAPITAL ABUJA **GOVERNMENT** FEDERAL MULTIPARTY REPUBLIC
ETHNIC GROUPS HAUSA AND FULANI 29%, YORUBA 21%, IBO (OR IGBO) 18%, IJAW 10%, KANURI 4%, MANY OTHERS
LANGUAGES ENGLISH (OFFICIAL), HAUSA, YORUBA, IBO
RELIGIONS ISLAM 50%, CHRISTIANITY 40%, TRADITIONAL BELIEFS 10%
CURRENCY NAIRA = 100 KOBO

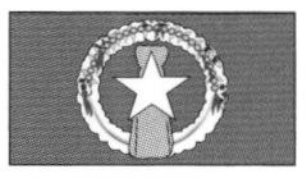
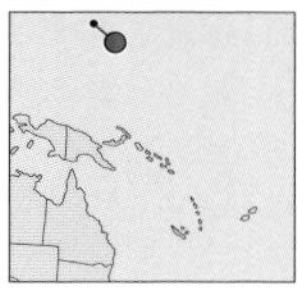

NORTHERN MARIANA ISLANDS

The Commonwealth of the Northern Mariana Islands contains 16 mountainous islands north of Guam in the western Pacific Ocean. In a 1975 plebiscite, the islanders voted for Commonwealth status in union with the United States, and in 1986 they were granted US citizenship.

AREA 179 SQ MI [464 SQ KM] **POPULATION** 53,000 **CAPITAL** SAIPAN

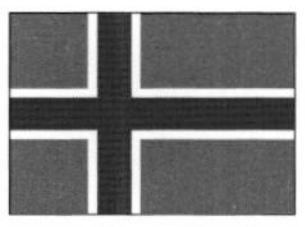
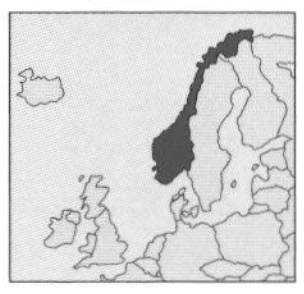

NORWAY

GEOGRAPHY The Kingdom of Norway forms the western part of the rugged Scandinavian peninsula. The deep inlets along the highly indented coastline were gouged out by glaciers during the Ice Age. The warm North Atlantic Drift off the coast of Norway moderates the climate, with mild winters and cool summers. Nearly all the ports are ice-free throughout the year. Inland, winters are colder and snow cover lasts for at least three months a year.

POLITICS & ECONOMY Norway was united with Denmark for over 400 years from the 14th century until 1814 when Denmark handed Norway over to Sweden. Denmark retained control of Norway's colonies – Greenland, Iceland and the Færoe Islands. The union with Sweden ended in 1903 and Norway became independent. Although Germany occupied Norway during World War II (1939–45), the country recovered quickly afterward and it now has one of the world's highest standards of living. In 1960, Norway and six other countries formed the European Free Trade Association (EFTA). However, in 1994, Norway voted against joining the European Union. In 2013, a center-right coalition government was elected with Ema Solberg as prime minister.

Norway's chief resources and exports are offshore oil and natural gas, which are exploited via tightly regulated companies that are largely state owned. To guard against the future decline of oil and gas production, a large sovereign wealth fund has been built up. Farmland covers only 3% of the land. Dairy farming and meat production are important, but Norway has to import food. Norway has many industries powered by cheap hydroelectricity.

AREA 125,049 SQ MI [323,877 SQ KM]
POPULATION 5,265,000 **CAPITAL** OSLO **GOVERNMENT** CONSTITUTIONAL MONARCHY **ETHNIC GROUPS** NORWEGIAN 94%
LANGUAGES NORWEGIAN (OFFICIAL)
RELIGIONS EVANGELICAL LUTHERAN 86%
CURRENCY NORWEGIAN KRONE = 100 ØRE

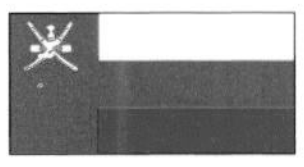
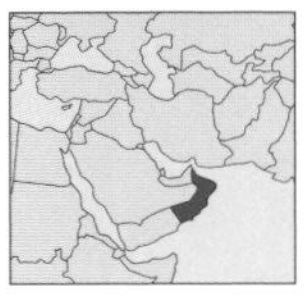

OMAN

GEOGRAPHY The Sultanate of Oman occupies the southeastern corner of the Arabian peninsula. It also includes the tip of the Musandam peninsula, overlooking the strategic Strait of Hormuz.

Oman has a hot tropical climate. In Muscat, temperatures may reach 117°F [47°C] in the summer months.

POLITICS & ECONOMY Although strongly influenced by Britain since the end of the 18th century, Oman never became a colony. Since 1970 when Qaboos ibn Said, the absolute ruler, overthrew his father in a bloodless coup, Oman has followed a path of modernization. In 2000, Oman held elections to its consultative parliament and, in 2004, the Sultan appointed Oman's first woman minister. In 2011, following anti-government demonstrations, Sultan Qaboos promised more reforms linked to jobs and benefits.

Oil and natural gas make up about 80% of Oman's exports although reserves are declining. Agriculture and fishing remain important. Crops include alfalfa, bananas, coconuts, dates, limes, tobacco, vegetables, and wheat, but Oman still has to import food. The tourist industry has grown rapidly in recent years.

AREA 119,498 SQ MI [309,500 SQ KM]
POPULATION 3,355,000 **CAPITAL** MUSCAT
GOVERNMENT MONARCHY WITH CONSULTATIVE COUNCIL
ETHNIC GROUPS ARAB, BALUCHI, INDIAN, PAKISTANI
LANGUAGES ARABIC (OFFICIAL), BALUCHI, ENGLISH
RELIGIONS ISLAM (MAINLY IBADHI), HINDUISM
CURRENCY OMANI RIAL = 1,000 BAISA

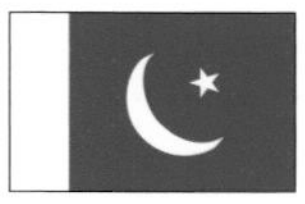
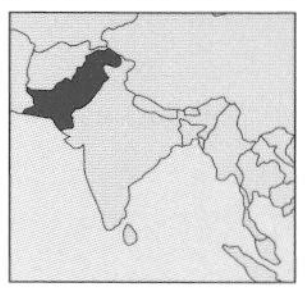

PAKISTAN

GEOGRAPHY The Islamic Republic of Pakistan contains high mountains, fertile plains, and rocky deserts. The Karakoram range, which contains K2, the world's second highest peak, lies in the northern part of Jammu and Kashmir, which is occupied by Pakistan but claimed by India. Other mountains rise in the west. Plains, drained by the River Indus and its tributaries, occupy much of eastern Pakistan. Arid areas include the Thar Desert and the Baluchistan plateau. Most of Pakistan has hot summers and mild winters, though the mountains are cold in winter. The rainfall is generally sparse.

POLITICS & ECONOMY Pakistan was the site of the Indus Valley civilization which developed about 4,500 years ago. However, Pakistan's modern history dates from 1947, when British India was divided into India and Pakistan. Muslim Pakistan was divided into two parts: East and West Pakistan, but East Pakistan broke away in 1971 to become Bangladesh. In 1948–9, 1965, and 1971, Pakistan and India clashed over Kashmir. In 1998, Pakistan responded in kind to India's nuclear weapons tests, but, in 2003–7, Pakistan and India launched a series of initiatives aimed at achieving peace.

Pakistan has been subject to alternating periods of military and civilian rule: the latter often characterized by inefficiency and corruption. The country's leaders have experienced turbulent times: Benazir Bhutto (daughter of the hanged prime minister, Zulfiqar Ali Bhutto) was twice dismissed as prime minister on charges of corruption in 1990 and 1996, and subsequently assassinated during an election campaign in 2007. Narwaz Sharif is serving his third non-consecutive term as prime minister.

Both government and military struggle to control the Afghan border region where Taliban-linked extremists are active. Terrorist activity emanating from this region has hit targets elsewhere in the country. The Christian minority has also been targeted. Talks have resumed to improve relations with India.

Lack of political stability has hindered economic development and discouraged foreign investment. The economy is agrarian, employing nearly half the population. Textiles are the main export and remittances from overseas workers are crucial. Bold moves are needed to overcome economic and social problems.

AREA 307,372 SQ MI [796,095 SQ KM]
POPULATION 201,996,000 **CAPITAL** ISLAMABAD
GOVERNMENT MILITARY REGIME **ETHNIC GROUPS** PUNJABI, SINDHI, PASHTUN (PATHAN), BALUCHI, MUHAJIR
LANGUAGES ENGLISH AND URDU (BOTH OFFICIAL), MANY OTHERS
RELIGIONS ISLAM 97%, CHRISTIANITY, HINDUISM
CURRENCY PAKISTANI RUPEE = 100 PAISA

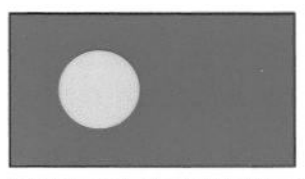
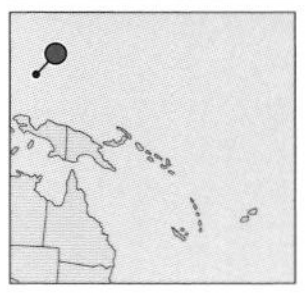

PALAU

The Republic of Palau became fully independent in 1994, after 47 years as a US administered UN Trust Territory. The economy relies heavily on aid from the USA and Taiwan, tourism, fishing, and subsistence agriculture. The main crops include cassava, coconuts, and copra. Palau's low-lying islands are vulnerable to rising sea levels.

AREA 177 SQ MI [459 SQ KM] **POPULATION** 21,000 **CAPITAL** MELEKEOK

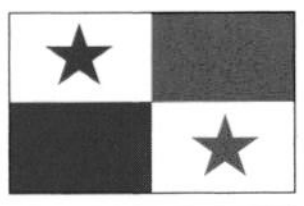
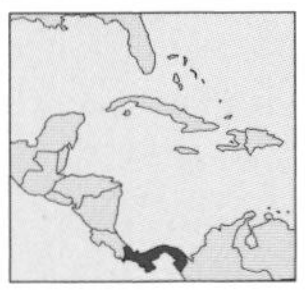

PANAMA

GEOGRAPHY The Republic of Panama forms an isthmus linking Central America to South America. The Panama Canal, which is 50.7 mi [81.6 km] long, cuts across the isthmus. It has made the country a major transport hub.

Panama has a tropical climate. Temperatures are high, though the mountains are much cooler than the coastal plains. The main rainy season is between May and December.

POLITICS & ECONOMY Christopher Columbus landed in Panama in 1502 and Spain soon took the area. In 1821, Panama became independent from Spain and a province of Colombia.

In 1903, Colombia refused a request by the United States to build a canal. Panama revolted against Colombian rule, and became an independent state. The United States then began to build the canal, which was opened in 1914. The United States administered the Panama Canal Zone, a strip of land along the canal. But many Panamanians resented US influence and, in 1979, the Canal Zone was returned to Panama. Control of the canal itself was handed over by the USA to Panama on December 31, 1999.

Panama's government has changed many times since independence, and there have been periods of military dictatorships, including that of General Manuel Antonio Noriega in the 1980s. He was finally convicted of drug offences in the United States in 1992. In May 2014, Juan Carlos Varela of the Panameñista party was elected president. In 2011, the US Congress approved a long-stalled free-trade agreement with Panama.

The Panama Canal is an important source of revenue and, since 2016, new locks and channels have increased capacity and the size of ships that can be accommodated. Away from the canal, the main activity is agriculture, which employs 17% of the work force. The service industry accounts for nearly 80% of GDP.

AREA 29,157 sq mi [75,517 sq km] **POPULATION** 3,705,000
CAPITAL Panamá **GOVERNMENT** Multiparty republic
ETHNIC GROUPS Mestizo 70%, Black and Mixed 14%, White 10%, Amerindian 6% **LANGUAGES** Spanish (official), English
RELIGIONS Roman Catholic 85%, Protestant 15%
CURRENCY US dollar; Balboa = 100 centésimos

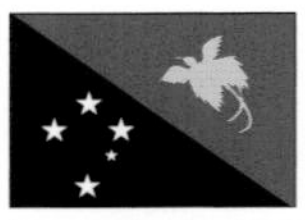
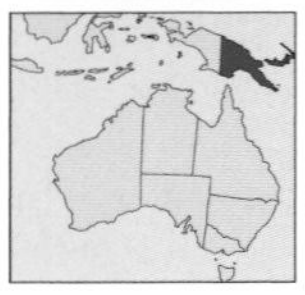

PAPUA NEW GUINEA

GEOGRAPHY Papua New Guinea is an independent country in the Pacific Ocean, north of Australia. Papua New Guinea includes the eastern part of New Guinea, the Bismarck Archipelago, the northern Solomon Islands, the D'Entrecasteaux Islands, and the Louisiade Archipelago. The land is largely mountainous.

Papua New Guinea has a tropical climate, with high temperatures. Most of the rain occurs during the monsoon season (December–April), when northwesterly winds blow. In the dry season, winds blow from the southeast.

POLITICS & ECONOMY The Dutch colonized western New Guinea (now part of Indonesia) in 1828, but it was not until 1884 that Germany appropriated northeastern New Guinea and Britain took the southeast. In 1906, Britain handed the southeast over to Australia when it became known as the Territory of Papua. When World War I broke out in 1914, Australia took German New Guinea, and in 1921 the League of Nations gave Australia a mandate to rule the area, which was named the Territory of New Guinea. In 1949, Papua and New Guinea were combined as one entity, becoming fully independent in 1975.

A secessionist group on the island of Bougainville, lying at the eastern end of the territory, has agitated for independence and has been granted a degree of autonomy, holding elections in 2005.

There was political turmoil in 2011–12, when Prime Minister Michael Somare was replaced by Peter O'Neill, following Somare's absence abroad for medical treatment. O'Neill was finally elected prime minister in August 2012 after a standoff with Somare.

Agriculture employs 85% of the people, mostly at subsistence level. Mining is important with copper a major export. There are large reserves of natural gas and the development of production facilities to convert this to liquidified form for export could have a profound effect on the economy.

AREA 178,703 sq mi [462,840 sq km] **POPULATION** 6,791,000
CAPITAL Port Moresby **GOVERNMENT** Constitutional monarchy
ETHNIC GROUPS Papuan, Melanesian, Micronesian
LANGUAGES English, Tok Pisin, Hiri Motu (all official); more than 800 indigenous languages **RELIGIONS** Traditional beliefs 34%, Roman Catholic 22%, Lutheran 16% **CURRENCY** Kina = 100 toea

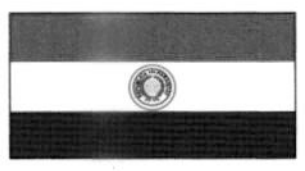
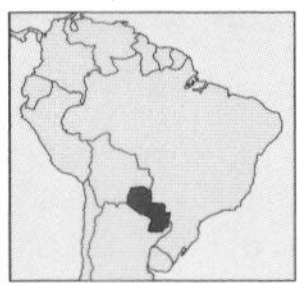

PARAGUAY

GEOGRAPHY The Republic of Paraguay is a landlocked country and rivers, notably the Paraná, Pilcomayo (Brazo Sur), and Paraguay, form most of its borders. The flat region of the Gran Chaco lies in the northwest, while the southeast contains plains, hills and plateaux. Northern Paraguay lies in the tropics, while the south is subtropical. Most of the country has a warm, humid climate.

POLITICS & ECONOMY Paraguayans achieved independence in 1811 after being part of a wider Spanish colonial possession since 1776. For many years, Paraguay was torn by internal strife and conflict with its neighbors. A war against Brazil, Argentina, and Uruguay (1865–70) led to the deaths of more than half of Paraguay's population, and a great loss of territory.

General Alfredo Stroessner took power in 1954 and ruled as a dictator until he was overthrown in 1989 (he died in exile in Brazil in 2006). However, the return of democracy in the years that followed often seemed precarious, because of rivalries between politicians and army leaders, together with economic problems arising partly from the financial crises experienced in neighboring Argentina and Brazil in 1999. In 2008, a former Roman Catholic bishop, Fernando Lugo, who was regarded as a champion of the poor, was elected president. His victory ended more than six decades of rule by the Colorado Party. However, the 2013 presidential election was won by the Colorado Party's representative, Horacio Cartes. In 2017, attempts to change the law to allow Cortes to run again in 2018 led to protests and he backed down.

Agriculture and forestry, employing about a third of the population, are important. Paraguay produces hydroelectricity and exports power to its neighbors although it has few other natural resources. Paraguay is a conduit for smuggling drugs.

AREA 157,047 sq mi [406,752 sq km] **POPULATION** 6,863,000
CAPITAL Asunción **GOVERNMENT** Multiparty republic
ETHNIC GROUPS Mestizo 95% **LANGUAGES** Spanish and Guaraní (both official) **RELIGIONS** Roman Catholic 90%, Protestant 6%
CURRENCY Guaraní = 100 céntimos

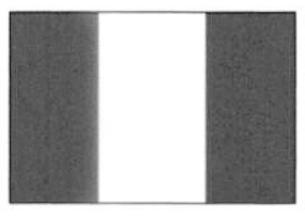
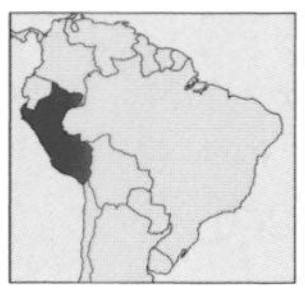

PERU

GEOGRAPHY The Republic of Peru lies in the tropics in western South America. A narrow coastal plain borders the Pacific Ocean in the west. Inland are ranges of the Andes Mountains, which rise to 22,205 ft [6,768 m] at Nevado Huascarán, an extinct volcano. East of the Andes lies the Amazon basin.

Lima, on the coastal plain, has an arid climate. The coastal region is chilled by the cold, offshore Humboldt Current. Rainfall increases inland and many mountains in the high Andes are snow-capped.

POLITICS & ECONOMY Spanish conquistadores conquered Peru in the 1530s. In 1820, an Argentinian, José de San Martín, led an army into Peru and declared it independent although Spain still held large areas. In 1823, the Venezuelan Simon Bolívar led another army into Peru which resulted in surrender by the Spanish in 1826. Peru suffered much instability throughout the 19th century.

Political turmoil continued in the 20th century. In 1980, when civilian rule was restored, a left-wing group called the Sendero Luminoso, or the "Shining Path," instigated guerrilla warfare against the government. In 1990, Alberto Fujimori, son of Japanese immigrants, became president. In 1992, he suspended the constitution and dismissed the legislature. The guerrilla leader, Abimael Guzmán, was arrested in 1992 and, in 2006, he was sentenced to life imprisonment. Fujimori left Peru but was later extradited, and in 2009 he was found guilty of ordering killings and kidnappings and was sentenced to 25 years in jail. Former prime minister Padro Pablo Kuczynski beat Fujimori's daughter, Keiko, in the presidential election of 2016.

Peru's economy benefits from a wide range of mineral resources: lead, silver, zinc, and iron ore, with copper being the most valuable export. Fish products are exported. Although recent economic growth has been strong, lack of basic infrastructure prevents the spread of prosperity away from the coastal areas.

AREA 496,222 sq mi [1,285,216 sq km] **POPULATION** 30,741,000
CAPITAL Lima **GOVERNMENT** Constitutional republic
ETHNIC GROUPS Amerindian 45%, Mestizo 37%, White 15%
LANGUAGES Spanish and Quechua (both official), Aymara, other Amazonian languages **RELIGIONS** Roman Catholic 81%
CURRENCY Nuevo sol = 100 centimos

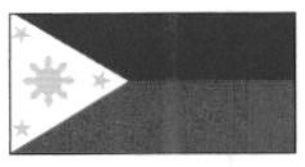
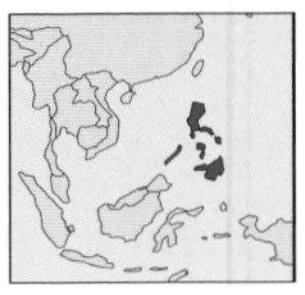

PHILIPPINES

GEOGRAPHY The Republic of the Philippines is an island nation in southeastern Asia. It includes about 7,100 islands, of which 2,770 are named and about 1,000 are inhabited. Luzon and Mindanao, the two largest islands, make up more than two-thirds of the country. The land is mainly mountainous.

The country has a hot tropical climate. The dry season runs from December to April. The rest of the year is wet. Much of the rainfall comes from the typhoons which periodically strike the east coast with devastating effect. In November 2013, Typhoon Haiyan, one of the strongest typhoons ever recorded, resulted in the deaths of over 6,000 people.

POLITICS & ECONOMY The first European to reach the Philippines was the Portuguese navigator Ferdinand Magellan in 1521. Spanish explorers claimed the region in 1565 when they established a settlement on Cebu. The Spaniards ruled the country until 1898, when the United States took over at the end of the Spanish–American War. Japan invaded the Philippines in 1941, but US forces returned in 1944. The country became fully independent as the Republic of the Philippines in 1946.

Since independence, the country's problems have included armed uprisings by left-wing guerrillas demanding land reform, Muslim separatist groups, crime, corruption, and unemployment. The dominant figure in recent times was Ferdinand Marcos, who ruled in a dictatorial manner from 1965 to 1986. His most recent successor, elected in 2016, is the populist Rodrigo Duterte, whose harsh crackdown on drug dealers and users is popular domestically but has led internationally to accusations of human rights abuses. Fighting, killings and kidnappings continued throughout the 2000s, but an outline peace plan was signed in 2012 although not all rebel groups have committed to it.

The Philippines is a developing country and is recovering steadily from the 2008 global financial crisis. Agriculture employs around one-third of the population. The main foods are rice and maize, while bananas, cocoa, coffee, sugarcane, and tobacco are grown commercially. Shellfish and sea fishing are also important, while manufacturing plays an increasingly significant part in the economy. Remittances from overseas workers make a large contribution and attempts are being made to encourage foreign investment.

AREA 115,830 sq mi [300,000 sq km]
POPULATION 102,624,000 **CAPITAL** Manila
GOVERNMENT Multiparty republic
ETHNIC GROUPS Tagalog 28%, Cebuano 13%, Ilocano 9%, Bisaya 8%, and others **LANGUAGES** Filipino (Tagalog) and English (both official), and eight major dialects
RELIGIONS Roman Catholic 83%, Protestant 9%, Islam 5%
CURRENCY Philippine peso = 100 centavos

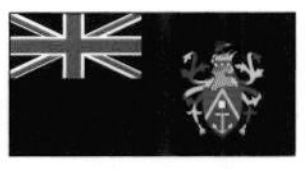
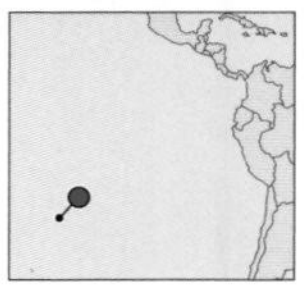

PITCAIRN

Pitcairn Island is a British overseas territory in the Pacific Ocean. Its inhabitants are descendants of the original settlers – nine mutineers from HMS Bounty and 18 Tahitians who arrived in 1790.

AREA 21 sq mi [55 sq km]
POPULATION 54 **CAPITAL** Adamstown

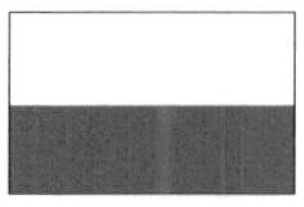
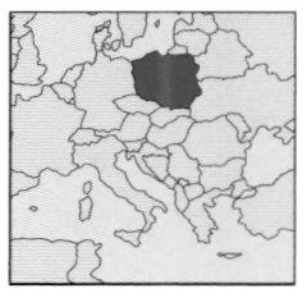

POLAND

GEOGRAPHY The Republic of Poland faces the Baltic Sea and behind its lagoon-fringed coast lies a broad plain. A plateau lies in the southeast, while the Sudeten Highlands straddle part of the border with the Czechia. Part of the Carpathian Range (the Tatra) lies in the southeast.

Poland's climate is influenced by its position in Europe. Warm, moist air masses come from the west, while cold air masses come from the north and east. Summers are warm, but winters are cold and snowy.

POLITICS & ECONOMY Poland's boundaries have changed several times in the last 200 years, partly as a result of its geographical location between the powers of Germany and Russia. It disappeared from the map in the late 18th century, when the Polish state of the Grand Duchy of Warsaw was established. But in 1815, the country was partitioned between Austria, Prussia, and Russia. Poland became independent in 1918, but in 1939 it was divided between Germany and the Soviet Union. The country again became independent in 1945, when it lost land to Russia but

gained some from Germany. Communists took power in 1948, but opposition mounted and eventually became focused through an organization called Solidarity.

A coalition government was formed between Solidarity and the Communists in 1989. In 1990, the Communist Party was dissolved and Lech Walesa, a trade unionist, became president. Facing many problems in developing a market economy, he was defeated in presidential elections in 1995. Poland joined NATO in 1999 and the European Union in 2004. In 2005, a nationalist, Lech Kaczynski, was elected president. But, along with other prominent Poles, he was killed in a plane crash in Russia in 2010. Beata Maria Szydlo was elected prime minister in November 2015.

Poland's economy has grown strongly since the fall of Communism and especially since accession to the EU. It has large reserves of coal, and some oil and gas. Manufactures include chemicals, food, machinery, ships, steel, and textiles. Farming, although important, lacks investment and needs modernization.

AREA 124,807 SQ MI [323,250 SQ KM]
POPULATION 38,523,000 **CAPITAL** WARSAW
GOVERNMENT MULTIPARTY REPUBLIC
ETHNIC GROUPS POLISH 97%, GERMAN, BELARUSIAN, UKRAINIAN.
LANGUAGES POLISH (OFFICIAL) **RELIGIONS** ROMAN CATHOLIC 90%, EASTERN ORTHODOX **CURRENCY** ZLOTY = 100 GROSZY

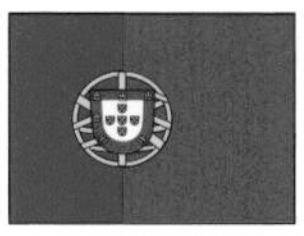
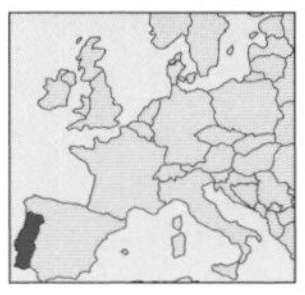

PORTUGAL

GEOGRAPHY The Republic of Portugal is the most westerly of Europe's mainland countries. The land rises from the coastal plains on the Atlantic Ocean to the western edge of the huge plateau, or Meseta, which occupies most of the Iberian peninsula. The climate is moderated by winds blowing from the Atlantic Ocean. Summers are cooler and winters are milder than in other Mediterranean lands. Portugal also contains two autonomous regions: the Azores and Madeira island groups.

POLITICS & ECONOMY Portugal became a separate country, independent of Spain, in 1143. In the 15th century, Portugal led the "Age of European Exploration" resulting in the growth of a large Portuguese empire, with colonies in Africa, Asia, and, most valuable of all, Brazil in South America. Portuguese power began to decline in the 16th century and, between 1580 and 1640, Portugal was ruled by Spain. Portugal lost Brazil in 1822, and in 1910 Portugal became a republic. Instability hampered progress and army officers seized power in 1926. In 1928, they chose Antonio de Salazar to be minister of finance.

Salazar became prime minister in 1932 and ruled as a dictator from 1933 until 1968. In 1974, army officers mounted a coup which led to free elections in 1978. Portugal joined the European Community (now the European Union) in 1986, and in 2002 joined the eurozone. In 2011–12, Portugal experienced many problems and public unrest when it introduced austerity measures in order to obtain an international financial bailout to help its weak economy.

Agriculture and fishing were the economic mainstays until the mid-20th century, when the economy started to diversify and manufacturing became the most valuable activity. Lagging behind the economies of other Western European countries, Portugal faces increasing competition from central Europe and Asia.

AREA 34,285 SQ MI [88,797 SQ KM]
POPULATION 10,834,000 **CAPITAL** LISBON
GOVERNMENT MULTIPARTY REPUBLIC **ETHNIC GROUPS** PORTUGUESE 99%
LANGUAGES PORTUGUESE (OFFICIAL) **RELIGIONS** ROMAN CATHOLIC 85%, PROTESTANT **CURRENCY** EURO = 100 CENTS

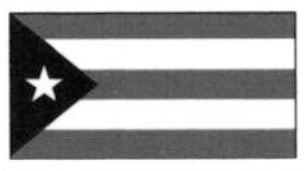
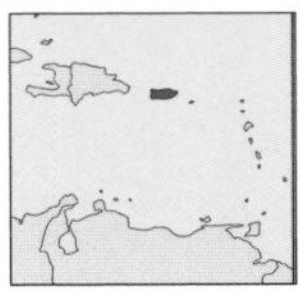

PUERTO RICO

The Commonwealth of Puerto Rico, a mainly mountainous island, is the easternmost of the Greater Antilles chain. The climate is hot and wet. Puerto Rico is a dependent territory of the United States and the people are US citizens. In June 2017, another referendum will be held on changing the island's political status.

Puerto Rico is the most industrialized country in the Caribbean. Tax exemptions attract US companies to the island and manufacturing is expanding. The chief exports are chemicals and chemical products, machinery, and food.

AREA 3,427 SQ MI [8,875 SQ KM]
POPULATION 3,578,000 **CAPITAL** SAN JUAN

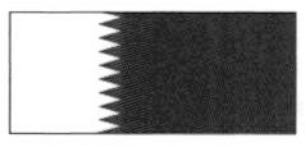
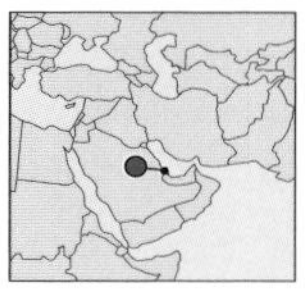

QATAR

The prosperous State of Qatar occupies a low, barren peninsula that extends northward from the Arabian peninsula into the Persian Gulf. The climate is hot and dry. A British protectorate from 1916, Qatar became fully independent in 1971. Oil, first discovered in 1939, is the mainstay of the economy and the country has 13% of the world's known gas reserves.

AREA 4,247 SQ MI [11,000 SQ KM] **POPULATION** 2,258,000 **CAPITAL** DOHA

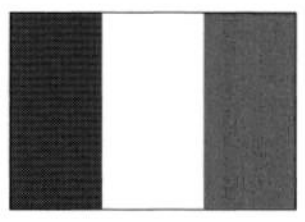
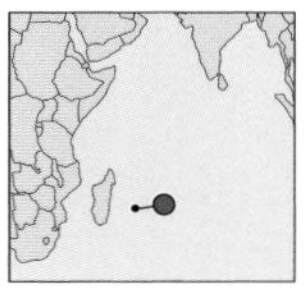

RÉUNION

Réunion is a French overseas department in the Indian Ocean. The land is mainly mountainous, though the lowlands are intensely cultivated. Sugar and sugar products are the main exports, but French aid, given to the island in return for its use as a military base, is important to the economy.

AREA 969 SQ MI [2,510 SQ KM]
POPULATION 845,000 **CAPITAL** ST-DENIS

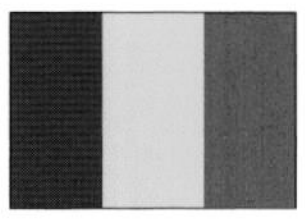
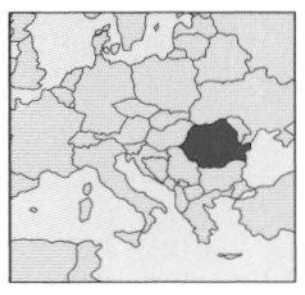

ROMANIA

GEOGRAPHY Romania is a country on the Black Sea in eastern Europe. Eastern and southern Romania form part of the Danube river basin. The delta region, near the mouths of the Danube, where the river flows into the Black Sea, is one of Europe's finest wetlands. The southern part of the coast contains several resorts. At the heart of the country is the region of Transylvania, ringed in the east, south, and west by scenic mountains which are part of the Carpathian mountain system. Romania has hot summers and cold winters. Rainfall is heaviest in spring and early summer.

POLITICS & ECONOMY The entity that has eventually coalesced into modern Romania was born out of the breakup of the Turkish empire in the late 18th century. In 1862 the regions of Wallachia and Moldavia were united under the new heading of Romania. After World War I (1914–18), Romania, which had fought on the side of the Allies, gained territory, including Transylvania, where most people were Romanians. This almost doubled the country's size and population. In 1939, Romania lost territory to Hungary, Bulgaria, and the Soviet Union. Occupied by Soviet troops in 1944, Romania regained northern Transylvania from Hungary in 1945. In 1947, Romania officially became a Communist country.

In 1990, following an uprising which saw the execution of the head of state, Nicolae Ceausescu, Romania held its first free elections since the end of World War II. Initially the government was dominated by former Communists led by Ion Iliescu, but there was a move toward the center-right at the elections in 1996. However, Iliescu again served as president from 2000 until 2004 when the centrist Traian Basescu took office. Romania joined NATO in 2004 and the European Union in 2007. Klaus Iohannis became president in December 2014.

Romania has an "upper-middle-income" economy but growth has been hindered by political instability, lack of reform, corruption, and the international financial crisis of 2008. Following the global downturn, the government was forced to implement austerity measures which led to civil unrest. Exports are increasing and include cars, industrial machinery, metals, textiles, and chemicals. Trade is mainly with other EU states especially Germany and Italy.

AREA 92,043 SQ MI [238,391 SQ KM]
POPULATION 21,600,000 **CAPITAL** BUCHAREST
GOVERNMENT MULTIPARTY REPUBLIC
ETHNIC GROUPS ROMANIAN 89%, HUNGARIAN 7%, ROMA 2%, UKRAINIAN **LANGUAGES** ROMANIAN (OFFICIAL), HUNGARIAN, ROMANY **RELIGIONS** EASTERN ORTHODOX 87%, PROTESTANT 7%, ROMAN CATHOLIC 5% **CURRENCY** LEU = 100 BANI

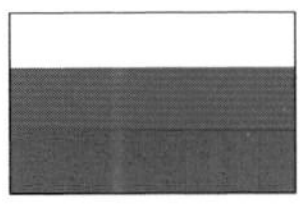
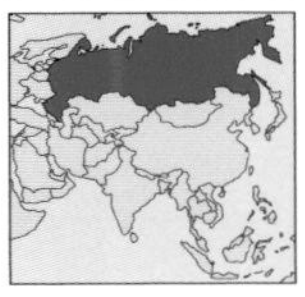

RUSSIA

GEOGRAPHY Russia is the world's largest country. About 25% lies west of the Ural Mountains in European Russia, where 80% of the population lives. It is mostly flat or undulating, but the land rises to the Caucasus Mountains in the south, where Russia's highest peak, Elbrus, at 18,510 ft [5,642 m], is found. Asian Russia, or Siberia, contains vast plains and plateaux, with mountains in the east and south. The Kamchatka peninsula in the far east has many active volcanoes. Russia contains several of the world's longest rivers. It also includes part of the world's largest inland body of water, the Caspian Sea, and Lake Baikal, the world's deepest lake.

Moscow has a continental climate, with cold, snowy winters and hot summers. Siberia has a harsher, drier climate.

POLITICS & ECONOMY In the 9th century AD, a state called Kievan Rus was founded by people known as the East Slavs. Kiev, now capital of Ukraine, became a major trading center, but, in 1237, Mongol armies conquered Russia and destroyed Kiev. Russia was part of the Mongol empire until the late 15th century with Moscow becoming the most important Russian city.

In the 16th century, Moscow's grand prince was retitled "tsar," and the first one, Ivan the Terrible, expanded the Russian territory. In 1613, Michael Romanov became tsar, founding a dynasty which ruled until 1917. In the 18th century, Tsar Peter the Great began to westernize Russia and, by 1812, when Napoleon failed to conquer the country, Russia was a major European power. However, in the 19th century demands for reform were growing.

In World War I (1914–18), the Russian people suffered great hardships and, in 1917, Tsar Nicholas II was forced to abdicate. In November 1917, the Bolsheviks seized power under Vladimir Lenin and set up the Union of Soviet Socialist Republics (also called the USSR or the Soviet Union).

From 1924, Joseph Stalin introduced a socialist economic program, suppressing all opposition. In 1939, the Soviet Union and Germany signed a non-aggression pact, but Germany invaded the Soviet Union in 1941. Soviet forces pushed the Germans back, occupying eastern Europe. They reached Berlin in May 1945. From the late 1940s, tension between the Soviet Union and its allies and Western nations developed into a "Cold War." This continued until 1991, when the Soviet Union was dissolved.

The Soviet Union collapsed due to the failure of its economic policies. From 1991, Boris Yeltsin, as president of the newly independent Russia, introduced democratic and economic reforms. Yeltsin retired in 1999 and, in 2000, was succeeded by Vladimir Putin. Putin, who was re-elected in 2004, sought to develop contacts with the West. Russia's size and diversity make national unity hard to achieve with secessionist movements instigating violent, sometimes fatal, incidents in Chechenia, Dagestan, Ingushetia, and Kabardino-Balkaria. From 2006, relations with the West appeared to deteriorate, with Russia criticizing the expansion of NATO in Eastern Europe.

In 2008, Putin, having served two terms as president, was replaced by Dmitry Medvedev, but Putin was again re-elected in 2012. In August 2008, Russia fought a short war against Georgia, which had attacked the secessionist region of South Ossetia. In early 2014, political unrest in Ukraine allowed pro-Russian forces to bring Crimea under Russian control. Further tensions with the West have arisen over Russia's support for the regime of Syria's President Assad.

Russia's economy was thrown into disarray after the collapse of the Soviet Union. It has now recovered enough to be classified as a "high-income" economy. Russia was admitted to the Council of Europe in 1997 and was also invited to join the G7 group of industrialized countries in 1997.

The Russian economy is underpinned by a wealth of natural resources; in particular, natural gas and coal. Gazprom, the state-run gas corporation, is a major supplier to Europe. Reliance on exporting such commodities makes the economy vulnerable to fluctuations in global prices. Future prosperity needs economic reform and investment in infrastructure.

Russia is a major producer of farm products, though it imports grains. Major crops include barley, flax, fruits, oats, rye, potatoes, sugar beet, sunflower seeds, vegetables, and wheat.

AREA 6,592,812 SQ MI [17,075,400 SQ KM]
POPULATION 142,355000 **CAPITAL** MOSCOW
GOVERNMENT FEDERAL MULTIPARTY REPUBLIC
ETHNIC GROUPS RUSSIAN 80%, TATAR 4%, UKRAINIAN 2%, CHUVASH 1%, MORE THAN 100 OTHERS **LANGUAGES** RUSSIAN (OFFICIAL), MANY OTHERS
RELIGIONS MAINLY RUSSIAN ORTHODOX, ISLAM, JUDAISM
CURRENCY RUSSIAN RUBLE = 100 KOPEKS

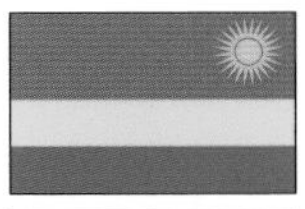
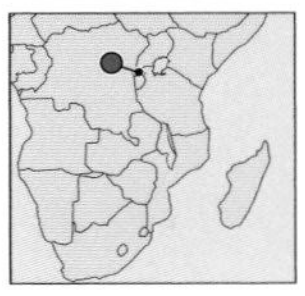

RWANDA

GEOGRAPHY The Republic of Rwanda is a small, landlocked country in east-central Africa. Lake Kivu and the River Ruzizi in the Great African Rift Valley form the country's western border.

Kigali stands on the central plateau of Rwanda. Here, temperatures are moderated by the altitude. Rainfall is abundant, but much

heavier rain falls on the western uplands, while the Rift Valley floor is drier and warmer than the rest of Rwanda.

POLITICS & ECONOMY Germany conquered the area, called Ruanda-Urundi, in the 1890s. However, Belgium occupied the region during World War I (1914–18) and ruled it until 1961 when, after a referendum, it became independent as a republic. This decision followed a rebellion by the majority Hutu people against the Tutsi monarchy which resulted in about 150,000 deaths. Many Tutsis fled to Uganda, where they formed a rebel army. Relations between Hutus and Tutsis deteriorated and, in 1994, between 500,000 and 800,000 people were massacred in Rwanda. After the Tutsis had restored order, Hutu rebels fled into the Democratic Republic of the Congo. In 2009, Rwanda became the 54th member of the Commonwealth.

According to the World Bank, Rwanda is a "low-income" developing country with economic growth driven by exporting tea and coffee. Most people are poor farmers. Food crops include bananas, beans, cassava, and sorghum. Some cattle are raised.

AREA 10,169 SQ MI [26,338 SQ KM]
POPULATION 12,988,000 **CAPITAL** KIGALI
GOVERNMENT REPUBLIC **ETHNIC GROUPS** HUTU 84%, TUTSI 15%, TWA 1% **LANGUAGES** FRENCH, ENGLISH AND KINYARWANDA (ALL OFFICIAL)
RELIGIONS ROMAN CATHOLIC 57%, PROTESTANT 26%, ADVENTIST 11%, ISLAM 5% **CURRENCY** RWANDAN FRANC = 100 CENTIMES

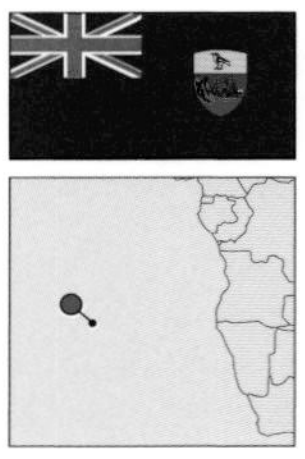

ST HELENA

St Helena, which became a British colony in 1834, is an isolated volcanic island in the South Atlantic Ocean. Now a British overseas territory, it is also the administrative center of Ascension and Tristan da Cunha.

AREA 47 SQ MI [122 SQ KM]
POPULATION 4,000 **CAPITAL** JAMESTOWN

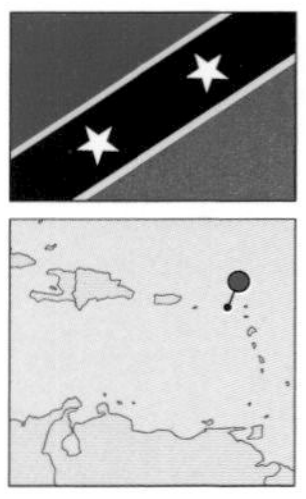

ST KITTS AND NEVIS

The Federation of St Kitts and Nevis comprises two well-watered volcanic islands, whose highest mountain rises to 3,793 ft [1,156 m]. The islands were the first in the Caribbean to be colonized by Britain (in 1623 and 1628), and they became an independent country in 1983. In 1998, a vote for the secession of Nevis fell short of the two-thirds majority required. Tourism, offshore finance, and service industries have replaced sugar as the principal earner.

AREA 101 SQ MI [261 SQ KM]
POPULATION 52,000 **CAPITAL** BASSETERRE

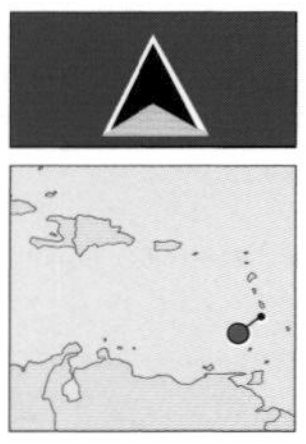

ST LUCIA

St Lucia, which became independent from Britain in 1979, is a mountainous, forested island of extinct volcanoes. It exports bananas and coconuts, and now attracts many tourists.

AREA 208 SQ MI [539 SQ KM]
POPULATION 164,000 **CAPITAL** CASTRIES

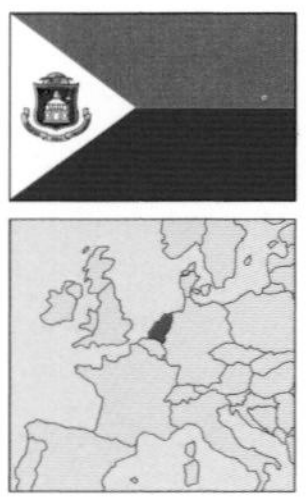

ST MAARTEN

Part of the Netherlands Antilles until 2010, the southern part of the island of St Maarten (called Sint Maarten in Dutch) is a self-governing territory within the Kingdom of the Netherlands.

AREA 13 SQ MI [34 SQ KM]
POPULATION 37,000 **CAPITAL** PHILIPSBURG

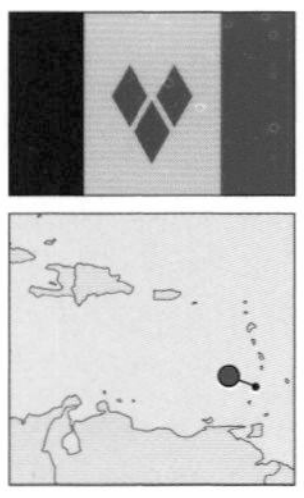

ST VINCENT AND THE GRENADINES

St Vincent and the Grenadines achieved its independence from Britain in 1979. Tourism is growing, but the territory is less prosperous than its neighbors.

AREA 150 SQ MI [388 SQ KM]
POPULATION 102,000 **CAPITAL** KINGSTOWN

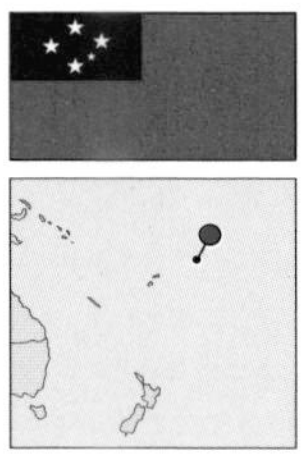

SAMOA

The Independent State of Samoa (formerly Western Samoa) comprises two islands in the south Pacific Ocean. Governed by New Zealand from 1920, the territory became independent in 1962. Exports include coconut cream and beer.

AREA 1,093 SQ MI [2,831 SQ KM]
POPULATION 199,000 **CAPITAL** APIA

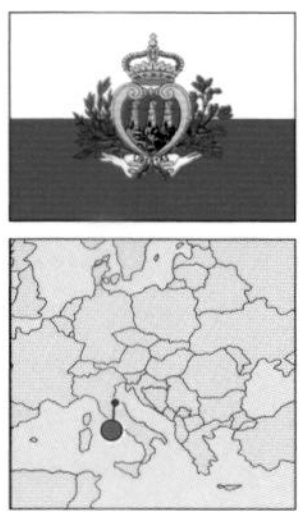

SAN MARINO

San Marino in northern Italy has been independent since 885 and a republic since the 14th century. It is the world's oldest republic. It has a friendship and cooperation treaty with Italy dating back to 1862. The state is governed by an elected council and has its own legal system. It has no armed forces and the police are "hired" from the Italian constabulary. The chief occupations are tourism, limestone quarrying, textiles, and wine-making.

AREA 24 SQ MI [61 SQ KM] **POPULATION** 33,000 **CAPITAL** SAN MARINO

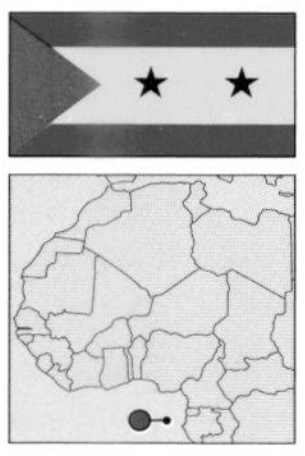

SÃO TOMÉ AND PRÍNCIPE

The Democratic Republic of São Tomé and Príncipe, a mountainous island territory west of Gabon, became a colony of Portugal in 1522. Independent since 1975, the economy has relied heavily on cocoa and foreign aid. Future growth depends on offshore oil.

AREA 372 SQ MI [964 SQ KM] **POPULATION** 198,000 **CAPITAL** SÃO TOMÉ

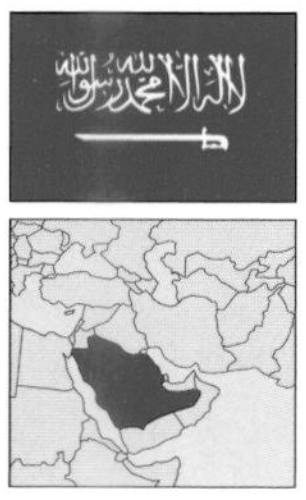

SAUDI ARABIA

GEOGRAPHY The Kingdom of Saudi Arabia occupies about three-quarters of the Arabian peninsula in southwest Asia. Deserts cover most of the land with mountains bordering the Red Sea plains in the west. In the north is the sandy Nafud Desert (An Nafud). In the south is the Rub' al Khali (the 'Empty Quarter'), one of the world's bleakest deserts. Saudi Arabia has a hot dry climate. Summer temperatures in Riyadh often exceed 104°F [40°C]. The nights are cool.

POLITICS & ECONOMY Saudi Arabia contains the two holiest places in Islam – Mecca (or Makka), the birthplace of the Prophet Muhammad in AD 570, and Medina (Al Madinah) where he died in 632. These places are visited by huge numbers of pilgrims.

The monarch has supreme authority and has sought to maintain stability. However, lacking a legitimate outlet, dissident groups have established links with Islamic militants outside the country. In January 2015, Salman bin Abdulaziz Al Saud became king.

Since 1933, oil has been the mainstay of the economy with country having more than 25% of the world's known reserves. Oil products make up about 90% of the exports. Irrigation and desalination projects have increased crop production. Problems have arisen from increasing unemployment, especially among the young, and moves are being made to diversify the economy.

AREA 829,995 SQ MI [2,149,690 SQ KM]
POPULATION 28,160,000 **CAPITAL** RIYADH
GOVERNMENT ABSOLUTE MONARCHY WITH CONSULTATIVE ASSEMBLY
ETHNIC GROUPS ARAB 90%, AFRO-ASIAN 10%
LANGUAGES ARABIC (OFFICIAL)
RELIGIONS ISLAM 100%
CURRENCY SAUDI RIYAL = 100 HALALAS

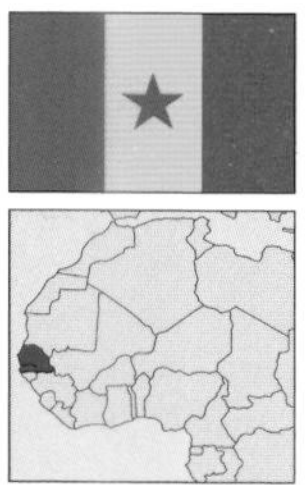

SENEGAL

GEOGRAPHY The Republic of Senegal is on the west coast of Africa. The volcanic Cape Verde (Cap Vert), on which Dakar stands, is the most westerly point in Africa. Plains cover most of Senegal, though the land rises gently in the southeast.

Dakar has a tropical climate, with a short rainy season between July and October.

POLITICS & ECONOMY In 1882, Senegal became a French colony, and from 1895 it was ruled as part of French West Africa, the capital of which, Dakar, developed as a major port and city.

In 1959, Senegal joined French Sudan (now Mali) to form the Federation of Mali. But Senegal withdrew in 1960 and became the separate Republic of Senegal. Its first president, Léopold Sédar Senghor, served until 1981, when he was succeeded by Abdou Diouf. However, in 2000, Diouf was defeated in elections by Abdoulaye Wade which peacefully ended the 40-year rule of the Socialist Party. The current president is Macky Sall.

According to the World Bank, Senegal is a "lower-middle-income" developing country much dependent on foreign aid. It was badly hit in the 1960s and 1970s by droughts. Agriculture still employs 77% of the population, though many farmers produce little more than they need to feed their families. Food crops include groundnuts (peanuts), millet, and rice. Phosphates are the country's chief resource, but Senegal also refines oil, which it imports from Gabon and Nigeria. Dakar is a busy port. Tourism is growing. Economic growth will depend on modernizing infrastructure and guaranteeing reliable power supplies.

AREA 75,954 SQ MI [196,722 SQ KM]
POPULATION 14,320,000 **CAPITAL** DAKAR
GOVERNMENT MULTIPARTY REPUBLIC
ETHNIC GROUPS WOLOF 43%, PULAR 24%, SERER 15%
LANGUAGES FRENCH (OFFICIAL), TRIBAL LANGUAGES
RELIGIONS ISLAM 94%, CHRISTIANITY (MAINLY ROMAN CATHOLIC) 5%, TRADITIONAL BELIEFS 1%
CURRENCY CFA FRANC = 100 CENTIMES

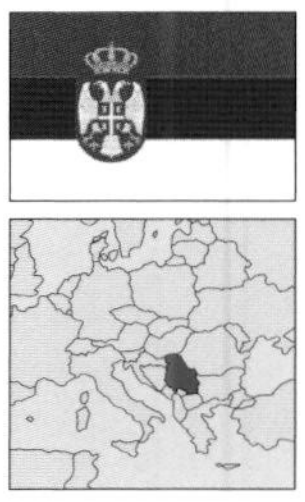

SERBIA

GEOGRAPHY The Republic of Serbia lies in the central Balkan peninsula. A landlocked country, it contains large, fertile lowlands drained by the River Danube and its tributaries, with uplands in the south. Most of Serbia has a continental climate, with cold, snowy winters and hot, dry summers. Heavy rains occur in the spring and the autumn.

POLITICS & ECONOMY Around 1,500 years ago, South Slavs moved into the Balkan peninsula, and each group founded its own state. Serbia came under the Turkish Ottoman empire in the 15th century. In 1918, the South Slavs united as the Kingdom of the Serbs, Croats, and Slovenes, which was renamed Yugoslavia in 1929. Germany invaded in 1941, but Communist partisans, led by Josip Broz Tito, took power in 1945.

From 1945, the country became the Federal People's Republic of Yugoslavia. In 1991–2, the country split apart, with Bosnia-Herzegovina, Croatia, Macedonia and Slovenia proclaiming their independence. The remaining republics, Serbia and Montenegro, retained the name Yugoslavia. In 2003, these two republics agreed to form the loose Union of Serbia and Montenegro. In 2006, the Montenegrins voted for full independence, and Serbia and Montenegro became separate republics. In 2008, the province of Kosovo declared itself independent, an act which Serbia refused to recognize. In 2011, the European Commission recommended Serbia for European Union candidate status, but said talks could start only after it normalized ties with Kosovo. Accession talks started in January 2014 although Serbia still falls short of acknowledging Kosovo as fully independent.

Serbia's resources include bauxite, coal, copper, and other metals, together with oil and natural gas. The country relies on exports and manufacturing, with aluminum, machinery, plastics, steel, textiles, and vehicles being important. Agriculture employs around one-fifth of the work force with crops including fruits, maize, potatoes, tobacco, and wheat. There are serious challenges to development including unemployment and an aging population.

AREA 29,913 SQ MI [77,474 SQ KM]
POPULATION 7,144,000 **CAPITAL** BELGRADE
GOVERNMENT REPUBLIC
ETHNIC GROUPS SERB 83%, HUNGARIAN 4%, OTHERS
LANGUAGES SERBIAN (OFFICIAL), HUNGARIAN
RELIGIONS SERBIAN ORTHODOX, ROMAN CATHOLIC, ISLAM, PROTESTANT
CURRENCY NEW DINAR = 100 PARAS

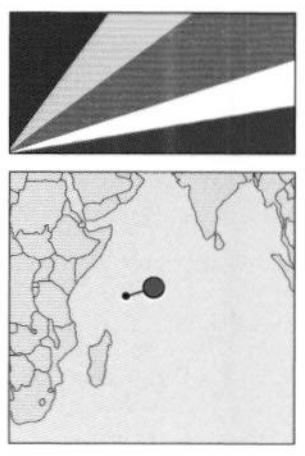

SEYCHELLES

The Republic of Seychelles in the western Indian Ocean achieved independence from Britain in 1976. Coconuts are the main cash crop, and fishing and tourism are important to the country's economy.

AREA 176 SQ MI [455 SQ KM]
POPULATION 93,000 **CAPITAL** VICTORIA

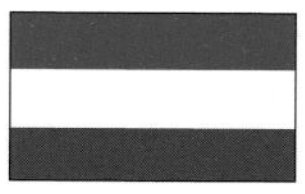

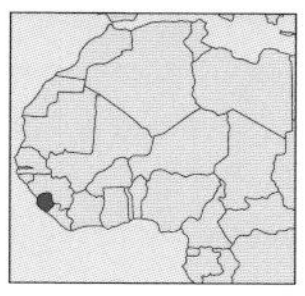

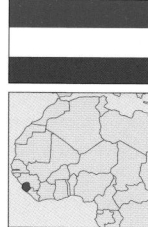

SIERRA LEONE

GEOGRAPHY The Republic of Sierra Leone in West Africa is about the same size as the country of Ireland. The coast contains several estuaries in the north, and extensive mangrove swamps. The most prominent feature is the mountainous Freetown (or Sierra Leone) peninsula.

Sierra Leone has a tropical climate, with heavy rainfall between April and November.

POLITICS & ECONOMY A former British territory, Sierra Leone became independent in 1961 and a republic in 1971. The military seized power in 1992 and the following 11 years of civil war resulted in tens of thousands of deaths and mutilations. The war was only brought to an end in 2002 with the intervention of the UK and a UN peacekeeping force. The last of the UN troops left the country in 2005, and national elections were held in 2007. In 2010, the UN Security Council lifted the last remaining sanctions against Sierra Leone. Ernest Bai Koroma, who was elected president in 2012 for a second term, has pursued free-market policies and encouraged foreign investment.

Sierra Leone has a "low-income" economy and, although it is showing signs of reasonable growth, the legacy of destruction left by the war has still to be overcome. About 59% of the people live by farming, mainly at subsistence level. The leading exports are minerals, including bauxite and rutile (titanium ore), and diamonds. The trade in the latter as "blood diamonds" helped perpetuate the civil war and much diamond mining is still unlicensed.

AREA 27,699 sq mi [71,740 sq km]
POPULATION 6,019,000 **CAPITAL** Freetown
GOVERNMENT Single-party republic **ETHNIC GROUPS** Native African tribes 90% **LANGUAGES** English (official), Mende, Temne, Limba
RELIGIONS Islam 60%, traditional beliefs 30%, Christianity 10%
CURRENCY Leone = 100 cents

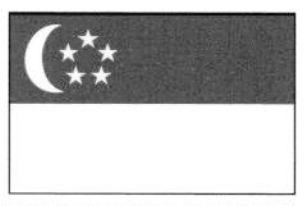

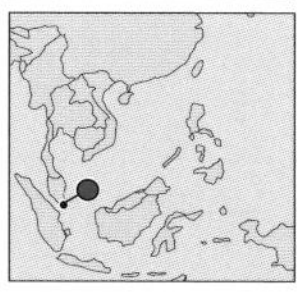

SINGAPORE

GEOGRAPHY The Republic of Singapore is an island country at the southern tip of the Malay peninsula. It consists of the large Singapore Island and 58 small islands, 20 of which are inhabited. The climate is hot and humid. Temperatures are high and rainfall is heavy throughout the year.

POLITICS & ECONOMY In 1819, Sir Thomas Stamford Raffles (1781–1826), agent of the British East India Company, made a treaty with the Sultan of Johor allowing the British to build a settlement on Singapore Island. Singapore soon became the leading British trading center in Southeast Asia and it later became a naval base. Japanese forces seized the island in 1942, but British rule was restored in 1945.

In 1963, Singapore became part of the Federation of Malaysia, which also included Malaya and the territories of Sabah and Sarawak on Borneo. In 1965, Singapore broke away and became independent.

The People's Action Party (PAP) has ruled Singapore since 1959. Its leader, Lee Kuan Yew, served as prime minister from 1959 until 1990, when he was succeeded by Goh Chok Tong. In 2004, Lee Hsien Loong, son of Lee Kuan Yew, became prime minister and has since been re-elected three times, in 2006, 2011, and 2015.

The World Bank classifies Singapore as a "high-income" economy, where a skilled work force has created a fast-growing economy. Trade and finance are major activities. The global financial crisis in 2008–9 caused great concern, but recovery was rapid. Manufactures include electronic products, machinery, scientific instruments, textiles, and ships. Petroleum products and manufactures are the main exports.

AREA 264 sq mi [683 sq km] **POPULATION** 5,782,000
CAPITAL Singapore City **GOVERNMENT** Multiparty republic
ETHNIC GROUPS Chinese 77%, Malay 14%, Indian 8%
LANGUAGES Chinese, Malay, Tamil and English (all official)
RELIGIONS Buddhism, Islam, Christianity, Hinduism
CURRENCY Singapore dollar = 100 cents

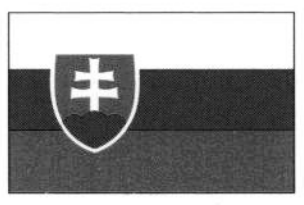

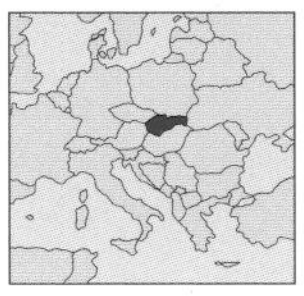

SLOVAKIA

GEOGRAPHY Slovakia is a predominantly mountainous country, consisting of part of the Carpathian range. The highest peak is Gerlachovsky in the Tatra Mountains, which reaches 8,711 ft [2,655 m]. The south is comprised of a fertile lowland. Slovakia has cold winters and warm summers. Kosice, in the east, has average temperatures ranging from 27°F [–3°C] in January to 68°F [20°C] in July. The highland areas are much colder. Snow or rain falls throughout the year. Kosice has an average annual rainfall of 24 inches [600 mm], the wettest months being July and August.

POLITICS & ECONOMY Slavic peoples settled here in the 5th century AD. They were subsequently conquered by Hungary, beginning a millennium of Hungarian rule and suppression of Slovak culture.

In 1867, Hungary and Austria united to form Austria–Hungary, of which the present-day Slovakia was a part. Austria–Hungary collapsed at the end of World War I (1914–18) and the Czech and Slovak people then united to form a new nation, Czechoslovakia. But Czech domination led to resentment by many Slovaks. In 1939, Slovakia declared itself independent, before Germany occupied the country. At the end of World War II, Slovakia again became part of Czechoslovakia.

The Communist Party took control in 1948 and although many people sought reform in the 1960s, they were crushed by the Russians. In the late 1980s, demands for democracy mounted and a non-Communist government took office in 1990. Elections in 1992 led to victory for the Movement for a Democratic Slovakia headed by a former Communist and nationalist, Vladimir Meciar, and Slovakia became independent in 1993.

Independence raised national aspirations among Slovakia's Magyar-speaking community which make up about 10% of the population. Issues about the status of this minority group have soured relations with Hungary, and were not helped by the government making Slovak the only official language. Slovakia became a member of NATO and the European Union in 2004. On January 1, 2009, it became the 16th country to adopt the euro as its official currency. In 2012, the opposition party Smer, led by former Prime Minister Robert Fico, won a landslide election. Since 2016 elections, Smer has been the main party in a four-party coalition.

Before 1948, Slovakia's economy was based on farming, but Communist governments developed manufacturing industries. Economic and social reform, following membership of the eurozone, has resulted in strong economic growth, driven by the export of cars and electronic goods. Since the late 1980s, many state-run businesses have been handed over to private owners.

AREA 18,924 sq mi [49,012 sq km]
POPULATION 5,446,000 **CAPITAL** Bratislava
GOVERNMENT Multiparty republic
ETHNIC GROUPS Slovak 86%, Hungarian 10%
LANGUAGES Slovak (official), Hungarian
RELIGIONS Roman Catholic 69%, Protestant 11%, others
CURRENCY euro = 100 cents

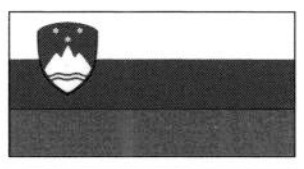

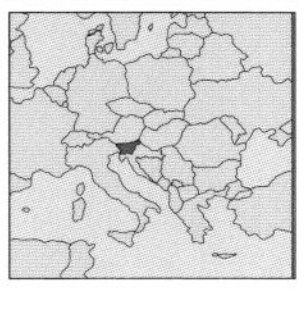

SLOVENIA

GEOGRAPHY The Republic of Slovenia was one of the six republics which made up the former Yugoslavia. Much of the land is mountainous, rising to 9,396 ft [2,864 m] at Mount Triglav in the Julian Alps (Julijske Alpe) in the northwest. Central Slovenia contains the limestone Karst region. The Postojna caves near Ljubljana are among the largest in Europe.

The coast has a mild Mediterranean climate, but inland the climate is more continental.

POLITICS & ECONOMY In the last 2,000 years, the Slovene people have been independent as a nation for less than 50 years. The Austrian Habsburgs ruled over the region from the 13th century until World War I when, in 1918, Slovenia became part of the Kingdom of the Serbs, Croats, and Slovenes (later called Yugoslavia). During World War II, Slovenia was invaded and partitioned between Italy, Germany, and Hungary, but, after the war, Slovenia again became part of Yugoslavia.

From the late 1960s, some Slovenes demanded independence, but the central government opposed the breakup of the country. In 1990, when Communist governments had collapsed throughout Eastern Europe, elections were held and a non-Communist coalition government was set up. Slovenia then declared itself independent. This led to fighting between Slovenes and the federal army, but Slovenia did not become a battlefield. Slovenia's independence was recognized in 1992 and a coalition led by the Liberal Democrats was elected. In 2004, Slovenia became a member of the North Atlantic Treaty Organization and the European Union. In 2013, the coalition government of Janez Jansa collapsed amidst criticisms over its austerity measures and allegations of corruption. Liberal leader Alenka Bratusek took office as prime minister but was replaced in July 2014 by Miro Cerar of the center-left SMC party.

The reform of the formerly state-run economy caused problems for Slovenia. However, since 1993, the country has made considerable economic progress although this stumbled in the European financial crisis of 2012 when tough austerity measures, designed to stave off an international bailout, were unpopular.

Manufacturing is the strongest part of the economy and exports include chemicals, machinery and transport equipment, metal goods, and textiles. Slovenia mines some iron ore, lead, lignite, and mercury. Fruits, maize, potatoes, and wheat are major crops, and livestock are also raised.

AREA 7,821 sq mi [20,256 sq km] **POPULATION** 1,978,000
CAPITAL Ljubljana **GOVERNMENT** Multiparty republic
ETHNIC GROUPS Slovene 83%, Croat 2%, Serb 2%, Hungarian, Bosniak **LANGUAGES** Slovenian (official), Serbo-Croatian
RELIGIONS Roman Catholic 58%
CURRENCY Euro = 100 cents

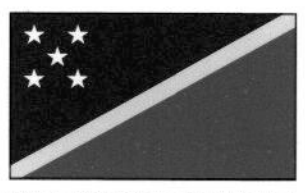

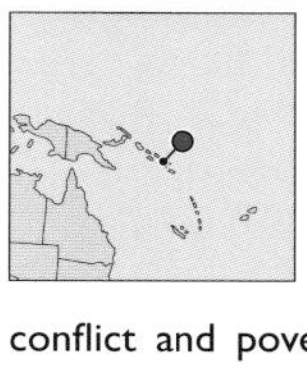

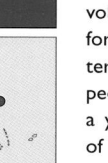

SOLOMON ISLANDS

The Solomon Islands, a chain of mainly volcanic islands in the Pacific Ocean extending for some 1,400 mi [2,250 km], were a British territory between 1893 and 1978. Most people are Melanesians, and the islands have a young population profile, with about 35% of the people aged under 15. The country is struggling to recover from five years of civil conflict and poverty is rife. Fish, coconuts, cocoa, and forestry products underpin the economy.

AREA 11,157 sq mi [28,896 sq km]
POPULATION 635,000 **CAPITAL** Honiara

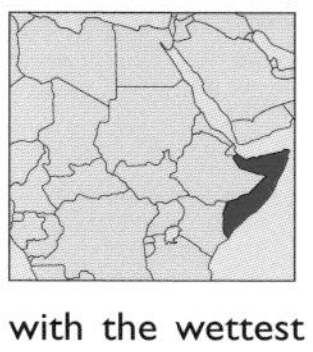

SOMALIA

GEOGRAPHY The Federal Republic of Somalia is in a region known as the "Horn of Africa." It is more than twice the size of Italy, the country which once ruled the southern part of Somalia. The most mountainous part of the country is in the north, behind the narrow coastal plains that border the Gulf of Aden. Rainfall is sparse, with the wettest regions in the south and northern mountains. Droughts are common and temperatures are generally high.

POLITICS & ECONOMY European powers became interested in the Horn of Africa in the 19th century. In 1884, Britain made the northern part of what is now Somalia a protectorate, while Italy took the south in 1905. The new boundaries divided the Somalis into five areas: the two Somalilands, Djibouti (which was taken by France in the 1880s), Ethiopia, and Kenya. Since then, many Somalis have wanted to create a Greater Somalia. Italy invaded British Somaliland in 1940, but was defeated in 1941. Britain ruled both Somalilands until 1950, when the United Nations asked Italy to take over the former Italian Somaliland for ten years. In 1960, the two Somalilands united to become Somalia.

Somalia has faced many problems. Economic difficulties led a military group to seize power in 1969. In the 1970s, Somalia supported an uprising of Somali-speaking people in the Ogaden region of Ethiopia. But, in 1988, Somalia and Ethiopia signed a peace treaty. In the 1990s, Somalia gradually broke apart. In 1991, the people in what was once British Somaliland set up the "Somaliland Republic," but it failed to get international recognition. The northeast, called Puntland, also seceded, while the south was riven by clan warfare. In 2004–5, a Somali parliament was set up in Kenya, moving to Baidoa, in Somalia, in 2006 (Mogadishu was regarded as unsafe). In 2006, Mogadishu was taken over by the Islamist Union of Islamic Courts, but government forces backed by Ethiopian troops defeated the Islamists. Ethiopia finally withdrew all its troops in January 2009. In 2012, the militant group al-Shabab was driven out of central Somalia, but continues to carry out attacks in this country and Kenya.

Somalia's economy has been shattered by war, droughts, and periodic floods. Many Somalis are nomads, who raise livestock. Live animals, meat, and hides and skins are exported. Crops include bananas, citrus fruits, cotton, maize, and sugarcane. Mining and manufacturing are relatively unimportant.

AREA 246,199 sq mi [637,657 sq km] **POPULATION** 10,817,000
CAPITAL Mogadishu **GOVERNMENT** Single-party republic, military dominated **ETHNIC GROUPS** Somali 85%, Bantu, Arab
LANGUAGES Somali (official), Arabic **RELIGIONS** Islam (Sunni Muslim)
CURRENCY Somali shilling = 100 cents

SOUTH AFRICA

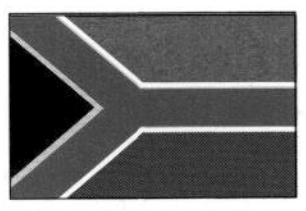

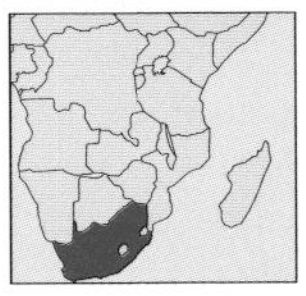

GEOGRAPHY The Republic of South Africa comprises mainly of the southern part of the huge plateau which makes up most of southern Africa. The highest peaks are in the Drakensberg range. Part of the Namib Desert lies in the northwest. The area around Cape Town has a sunny climate with mild, rainy winters. Inland, large areas of the plateau are arid.

POLITICS & ECONOMY Early inhabitants in South Africa were the Khoisa, followed in the last 2,000 years by Bantu-speaking people. Their descendants include the Zulu, Xhosa, Sotho, and Tswana. The Dutch founded a settlement at the Cape in 1652, but Britain colonized the area in the early 19th century. The Dutch, called Boers or Afrikaners, resented British rule and moved inland. Rivalry between the groups led to Anglo–Boer Wars in 1880–1 and 1899–1902.

In 1910, the country was united as the Union of South Africa. In 1948, the National Party won power and introduced the policy of apartheid, under which non-whites could not vote and their human rights were strictly limited. Multiracial elections were held in 1994 and Nelson Mandela, leader of the African National Congress (ANC), became president following 27 years in prison. After Mandela retired, the ANC won elections in 1999 and 2004, led by Thabo Mbeki, and in 2009 when Jacob Zuma became president. The government faces many problems, not least being the fact that one in eight of the population is infected with HIV.

South Africa is Africa's most developed country and is one of the "BRICS" group of emerging global economic powers. However, most of the black people are poor, with farms still white-owned. Unemployment is high at 26% and it has nurtured an associated high crime rate. Natural resources include diamonds and gold; mining and manufacturing are the most valuable activities.

AREA 471,442 sq mi [1,221,037 sq km] **POPULATION** 54,301,000
CAPITAL Cape Town (legislative); Pretoria/Tshwane (administrative); Bloemfontein (judiciary) **GOVERNMENT** Multiparty republic
ETHNIC GROUPS Black 79%, White 10%, Colored 9%, Asian 2%
LANGUAGES Afrikaans, English, Ndebele, Pedi, Sotho, Swazi, Tsonga, Tswana, Venda, Xhosa and Zulu (all official)
RELIGIONS Christianity 68%, Islam 2%, Hinduism 1%
CURRENCY Rand = 100 cents

SPAIN

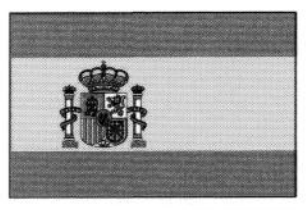

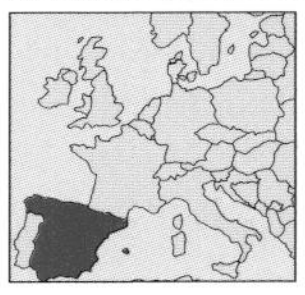

GEOGRAPHY The Kingdom of Spain is the second largest country in Western Europe after France. It shares the Iberian peninsula with the much smaller Portugal. The Meseta, an extensive plateau, covers most of Spain. It is mainly flat, but is crossed by the sierras, a series of mountain ranges.

The northern highlands include the Cantabrian Mountains (Cordillera Cantabrica) and the high Pyrenees, which form Spain's border with France. But Mulhacén, the highest peak on the Spanish mainland, is in the Sierra Nevada in the southeast. Spain also has fertile coastal plains. Other major lowlands include the Ebro river basin in the northeast and the Guadalquivir river basin in the southwest. Spain also encompasses the Balearic Islands in the Mediterranean Sea and the Canary Islands off the northwest coast of Africa.

The Meseta has a continental climate, with hot summers and cold winters, when temperatures often fall below freezing point. Snow frequently covers the mountain ranges on the Meseta. The Mediterranean coasts have hot, dry summers and mild winters.

POLITICS & ECONOMY In the early 16th century, Spain rose to be a world power. At its peak, it controlled much of Central and South America, parts of Africa, and the Philippines in Asia. Spain's influence began to decline in the late 16th century. Its sea power was destroyed by a British fleet in the Battle of Trafalgar (1805), and by the 20th century it was a poor country.

Spain became a republic in 1931, but the republicans were defeated in the Spanish Civil War (1936–9). General Francisco Franco became the country's dictator, though technically Spain remained a monarchy. Juan Carlos was king from Franco's death in 1975 until his abdication in 2014 in favor of his son Felipe.

Within Spain there are several groups, with their own languages and cultures, who have been vocal in their aim to run their own affairs. In the northern Basque region, the separatist group, ETA, has waged a terrorist campaign. In 2012, ETA said it was willing to disarm and enter negotiations. In 2017, it announced its complete disarmament and handed over its weapons.

Spain's regional makeup is complicated and the powers devolved to the regional parliaments since the 1970s are unevenly distributed. There are 17 regions with Catalonia, the Basque Country, and Galicia having gained special status. A non-binding vote held in Catalonia, in late 2014, showed the majority of the region's population were in favor of independence, a move being firmly resisted by central government.

Spain has been badly affected by the global recession of 2008. An unemployment rate of 23% and sluggish economic growth has forced the country to undertake drastic austerity measures. Agriculture employs only 3% of the population, as compared with 15% in industry and 58% in the service sector. Farmland occupies two-thirds of the land area. Manufactures include cars, chemicals, electronic goods, food, metal goods, and textiles. Spain lacks natural resources apart from some iron ore.

AREA 192,103 sq mi [497,548 sq km] **POPULATION** 48,563,000
CAPITAL Madrid **GOVERNMENT** Constitutional monarchy
ETHNIC GROUPS Composite of Mediterranean and Nordic types
LANGUAGES Castilian Spanish (official) 74%, Catalan 17%, Galician 7%, Basque 2% **RELIGIONS** Roman Catholic 94%, others 6% **CURRENCY** Euro = 100 cents

SRI LANKA

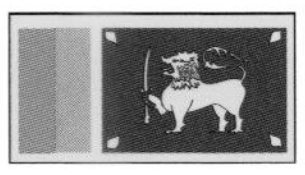

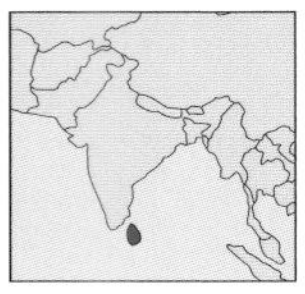

GEOGRAPHY The Democratic Socialist Republic of Sri Lanka is an island nation, separated from the southeast coast of India by the Palk Strait. The land is mostly low-lying, but a mountain region dominates the south-central part of the country.

The western part of Sri Lanka has a wet equatorial climate. Temperatures are high and the rainfall is heavy.

POLITICS & ECONOMY From the early 16th century, Ceylon (as Sri Lanka was then known) was ruled successively by the Portuguese, Dutch, and British. Independence was achieved in 1948 and the country was renamed Sri Lanka in 1972.

After independence, rivalries between the two main ethnic groups, the Buddhist Sinhalese and the minority Hindu Tamils, marred progress. In 1956 Solomon Bandaranaike was elected prime minister on a wave of Sinhalese nationalism, but he was assassinated in 1959 by an extremist Buddhist monk. He was succeeded by his wife. Sirimavo Bandaranaike, the world's first woman prime minister.

Conflict between Tamils and Sinhalese continued in the 1970s and 1980s. In 1987, India helped to engineer a ceasefire but withdrew their troops in 1990 after failing to subdue the main guerrilla group, the Tamil Tigers, who wanted to set up an independent Tamil homeland in the northeast. The Tamil Tigers were finally defeated in May 2009. Promising to fight corruption, Maithripala Sirisena was elected President in January 2015.

In late 2004, a tsunami, caused by a sudden movement of the plates underlying the eastern Indian Ocean, struck parts of the coast of Sri Lanka, killing more than 30,000 people.

Sri Lanka is classed as a "lower-middle-income" economy and growth has been strong since the end of the civil conflict. Agriculture employs about 30% of the people. Coconuts, rubber, and tea are exported, but rice is the main food crop. Factories process farm products and manufacture textiles.

AREA 25,332 sq mi [65,610 sq km]
POPULATION 22,235,000 **CAPITAL** Colombo
GOVERNMENT Multiparty republic
ETHNIC GROUPS Sinhalese 74%, Tamil 9%, Moor 7%
LANGUAGES Sinhala and Tamil (both official)
RELIGIONS Buddhism 69%, Islam 8%, Hinduism 7%, Christianity 6%
CURRENCY Sri Lankan rupee = 100 cents

SUDAN

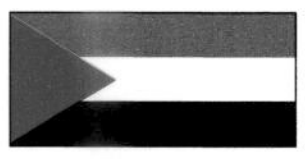

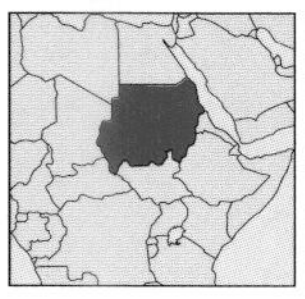

GEOGRAPHY The Republic of Sudan was Africa's largest country until 2011, when the people in the south voted to secede and form the new nation of South Sudan. Sudan is mainly arid, with part of the vast Sahara in the north. The main feature is the fertile River Nile valley, where most people live.

POLITICS & ECONOMY In the 19th century, Egypt gradually took control of Sudan. In 1881, a Muslim religious teacher, the Mahdi ("divinely appointed guide"), led a rebellion which was quashed, in 1898, by Britain and Egypt. In 1899, these two countries agreed to rule Sudan jointly as a condominium. After independence in 1952, the black Africans in the south feared domination by the Muslim north. They objected to Arabic becoming the sole official language and, in 1964, civil war broke out. The war ended in 1972, when the south was granted regional self-government.

In 1983, the announcement that Islamic law would apply throughout Sudan sparked off further resistance from the rebel Sudan People's Liberation Army (SPLA) in the south. In 1998, Sudan's government announced that it accepted the idea of a referendum. In 2005, a peace agreement was signed, and the referendum took place in 2011, when around 99% of the people in the south voted to set up their own country, South Sudan.

Since 2003, another conflict has raged in the western province of Darfur, where government-backed militias battled with local rebel forces. In 2008, the International Criminal Court charged President al-Bashir with war crimes, but he was re-elected president in national elections in 2010 and 2015.

The majority of the population are poor and live by subsistence agriculture. Cotton (the main crop), gum arabic, and sesame seeds are exported, but the most valuable exports are oil and oil products. More than 80% of the oil is produced in South Sudan, but Sudan has the infrastructure to exploit and export it.

AREA 728,222 sq mi [1,886,086 sq km] **POPULATION** 36,730,000
CAPITAL Khartoum **GOVERNMENT** Federal presidential democratic republic **ETHNIC GROUPS** Arab, Black, Beja, others
LANGUAGES Arabic and English (both official), Nubian, Beja
RELIGIONS Islam, traditional beliefs
CURRENCY Sudanese pound = 100 piastres

SUDAN, SOUTH

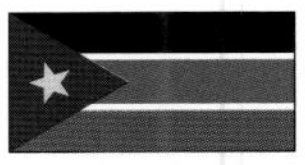

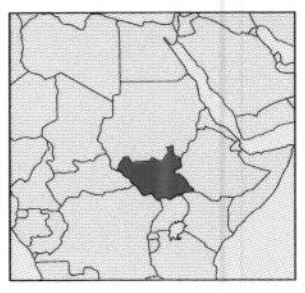

GEOGRAPHY The Republic of South Sudan is a landlocked country in east-central Africa. Much of the land is low-lying and drained by the White Nile and its tributaries. Mountains lie in the far south. The country has a wet tropical climate. Forests, swamps, and grasslands cover large areas.

POLITICS & ECONOMY South Sudan has about 200 ethnic groups. Each group has its own traditional beliefs and languages. The South's deep cultural differences with the mainly Arab-Muslim north led to civil war (1964–1972 and 1983–2005). In January 2011, as part of the peace agreement, a referendum was held in which the vast majority of the people in the south voted to become independent on July 9. Civil war broke out in 2013, displacing millions. In early 2017, famine was declared in parts of the country.

Most people depend on agriculture and forestry, but South Sudan has many mineral resources, including oil.

AREA 239,285 sq mi [619,745 sq km] **POPULATION** 12,531,000
CAPITAL Juba **GOVERNMENT** Republic
ETHNIC GROUPS Dinka, Kakwa, Bari, Azande, Shilluk, others
LANGUAGES English and Arabic (both official), local languages
RELIGIONS Traditional beliefs, Christianity
CURRENCY South Sudanese pound = 100 piastres

SURINAME

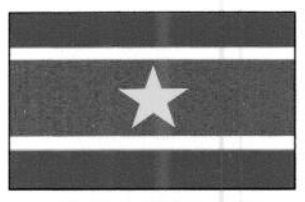

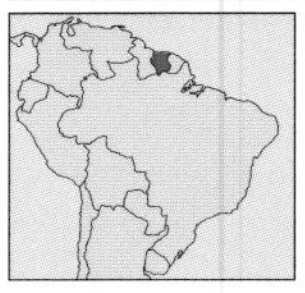

GEOGRAPHY The Republic of Suriname is sandwiched between French Guiana and Guyana in northeastern South America. The narrow coastal plain was once swampy, but it has been drained and now consists mainly of farmland. Inland lie hills and low mountains, which rise to 4,035 ft [1,230 m].

Suriname has a hot, wet and humid climate. Temperatures are high throughout the year.

POLITICS & ECONOMY In 1667, the British handed Suriname to the Dutch in return for New Amsterdam, an area that is now the state of New York. Slave revolts and Dutch neglect hampered development. In the early 19th century, Britain and the Netherlands disputed the ownership of the area with Britain relinquishing its claim in 1813. Slavery was abolished in 1863 and Indian and Indonesian laborers were introduced to work on the plantations.

Suriname became fully independent in 1975, but the economy was weakened when thousands of skilled people emigrated from Suriname to the Netherlands. Following a coup in 1980, Suriname was ruled by a military dictator, Desiré ("Dési") Bouterse. The adoption of a new constitution led to the restoration of democracy in 1988. Ronald Venetiaan was elected president in 2000. The guilder was replaced by the Surinamese dollar in 2004. In 2010, the Mega Combination coalition, led by Bouterse, won parliamentary elections and Bouterse became president. His party won a slim majority in 2015.

Suriname's economy is based on mining and metal processing. It is a leading producer of bauxite, the main ore of aluminum. Offshore oil reserves are ripe for exploitation and gold reserves are attracting foreign investment. Tourism also has potential.

AREA 63,037 sq mi [163,265 sq km]
POPULATION 586,000 **CAPITAL** Paramaribo
GOVERNMENT Multiparty republic
ETHNIC GROUPS Hindustani/East Indian 37%, Creole (mixed White and Black) 31%, Javanese 15%, Black 10%, Amerindian 2%, Chinese 2%, others **LANGUAGES** Dutch (official), Sranang Tongo
RELIGIONS Hinduism 27%, Protestant 25%, Roman Catholic 23%, Islam 20% **CURRENCY** Surinamese dollar= 100 cents

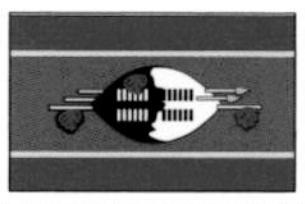
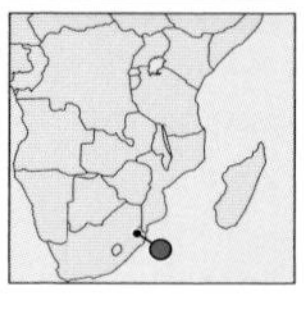

SWAZILAND

GEOGRAPHY The Kingdom of Swaziland is a small, landlocked country in southern Africa. The country has four regions which run north–south. In the west, the Highveld, with an average height of 3,950 ft [1,200 m], makes up 30% of Swaziland. The Middleveld, between 1,150 ft and 3,280 ft [350 m to 1,000 m], covers 28% of the country. The Lowveld, with an average height of 886 ft [270 m], covers another 33%. Finally, the Lebombo Mountains reach 2,600 ft [800 m] along the eastern border. The Lowveld is almost tropical, with average temperatures of 72°F [22°C] and low rainfall.

POLITICS & ECONOMY In 1894, Britain and the Boers of South Africa agreed to put Swaziland under the control of the South African Republic (the Transvaal). But at the end of the Anglo–Boer War (1899–1902), Britain took control of the country. In 1968, when Swaziland became fully independent as a constitutional monarchy, the head of state was King Sobhuza II. Sobhuza died in 1982 and was succeeded by his son, who, in 1986, became King Mswati III. Political parties were banned in elections in 1993 and 1998 and Mswati ruled by decree. In 2005, Mswati signed a new constitution, but Swaziland remains an absolute monarchy.

Swaziland is a developing country. Farm products and processed food and drink, sugar, wood pulp, citrus fruits, and canned fruit are the leading exports. Many farmers live at subsistence level. Swaziland is heavily dependent on South Africa and it shares two problems with its large neighbor – widespread poverty and the world's highest incidence of HIV/AIDS.

AREA 6,704 sq mi [17,364 sq km]
POPULATION 1,451,000 **CAPITAL** Mbabane
GOVERNMENT Monarchy **ETHNIC GROUPS** African 97%, European 3% **LANGUAGES** Siswati and English (both official)
RELIGIONS Zionist (a mix of Christianity and traditional beliefs) 40%, Roman Catholic 20%, Islam 10% **CURRENCY** Lilangeni = 100 cents

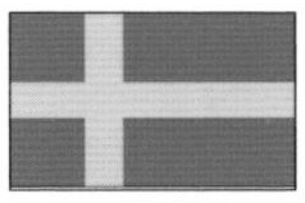
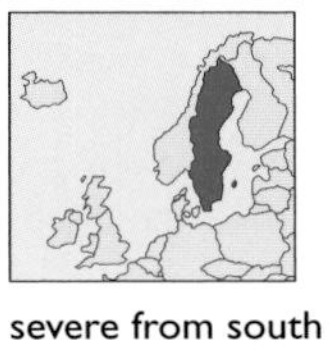

SWEDEN

GEOGRAPHY The Kingdom of Sweden is the largest of the countries of Scandinavia in both area and population. It shares the Scandinavian peninsula with Norway. The western part of the country, along the border with Norway, is mountainous. The highest point is Kebnekaise, which reaches 6,936 ft [2,114 m] in the northwest. The climate becomes increasingly severe from south to north.

POLITICS & ECONOMY Swedish Vikings plundered areas to the south and east between the 9th and 11th centuries. Sweden, Denmark, and Norway were united in 1397, but Sweden regained its independence in 1523. In 1809, Sweden lost Finland to Russia, but, in 1814, it gained Norway from Denmark. The union between Sweden and Norway was dissolved in 1905. Sweden remained neutral in World Wars I and II. Since 1945, Sweden has become a prosperous country and, in 1995, it joined the European Union. However, it did not adopt the euro, nor has it joined NATO.

Sweden has wide-ranging welfare provision but it comes at a high cost to the taxpayer. In 2006, a center-right alliance defeated the Social Democrats, who had governed for 65 of the previous 74 years. The current prime minister, elected in 2014, is Stefan Löfven.

Sweden is a highly developed industrial country: the economy is strong and unemployment low. Major products include steel and steel goods. Steel is used in the country's engineering industry to manufacture aircraft, cars, machinery, and ships. Sweden has some of the world's richest iron ore deposits which are found near Kiruna in the far north. Most of this ore is exported, and Sweden has to import most of the materials needed by its own industries. Forestry is also important and hydroelectricity is a major source of energy. In 1996, Sweden announced the decommissioning of its nuclear power stations with the first reactor closing in 1999, followed by a second in 2005. But in 2009, the government, under pressure to diversify from fossil fuels, reversed this policy and plans to replace the ten remaining reactors.

AREA 173,731 sq mi [449,964 sq km]
POPULATION 9,881,000 **CAPITAL** Stockholm
GOVERNMENT Constitutional monarchy **ETHNIC GROUPS** Swedish 91%, Finnish, Sami **LANGUAGES** Swedish (official), Finnish, Sami
RELIGIONS Lutheran 87%, Roman Catholic, Orthodox
CURRENCY Swedish krona = 100 öre

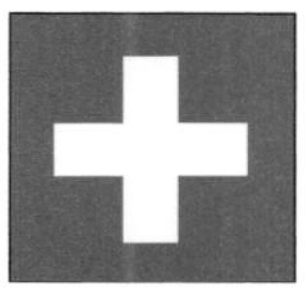
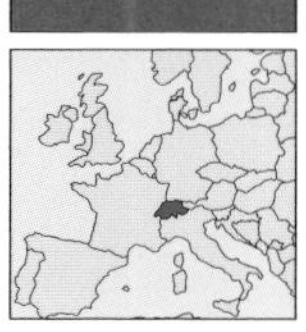

SWITZERLAND

GEOGRAPHY The Swiss Confederation is a landlocked country in Western Europe. Much of the land is mountainous. The Jura Mountains lie along Switzerland's western border with France, while the Swiss Alps make up about 60% of the country in the south and east. Four-fifths of the population live on the fertile Swiss plateau, which contains most of Switzerland's large cities.

The climate of Switzerland varies greatly according to the altitude. The plateau has warm summers and cold, snowy winters. Rain occurs throughout the year.

POLITICS & ECONOMY In 1291, three small cantons (states) united to defend their freedom against the Habsburg rulers of the Holy Roman empire. They were Schwyz, Uri, and Unterwalden, and they called the confederation they formed "Switzerland." Switzerland expanded and, in the 14th century, defeated Austria in three wars of independence. After a defeat by the French in 1515, the Swiss adopted a policy of neutrality, which they still follow. In 1815, the Congress of Vienna expanded Switzerland to 22 cantons and guaranteed its neutrality. Switzerland's 23rd canton, Jura, was created in 1979 from part of Bern.

Neutrality combined with the vigour and independence of its people have made Switzerland prosperous. In 2002, Switzerland became a member of the United Nations, although it has remained outside the EU. In 2010, a fourth female minister was elected by the Federal Assembly to the seven-member Federal Council which acts as the collective head of state. For the first time, women were in the majority in the country's cabinet.

Although lacking in natural resources, Switzerland is a wealthy, industrialized country. Products include chemicals, electrical equipment, machinery and machine tools, precision instruments, processed food, watches, and textiles. Farmers produce about three-fifths of the country's food – the rest is imported. Crops include fruits, potatoes, and wheat. Tourism and banking are also important. Swiss banks attract investors from all over the world.

AREA 15,940 sq mi [41,284 sq km] **POPULATION** 8,179,000
CAPITAL Berne **GOVERNMENT** Federal republic
ETHNIC GROUPS German 65%, French 18%, Italian 10%, Romansch 1%, others **LANGUAGES** German, French, Italian and Romansch (all official) **RELIGIONS** Roman Catholic 42%, Protestant 35% **CURRENCY** Swiss franc = 100 centimes

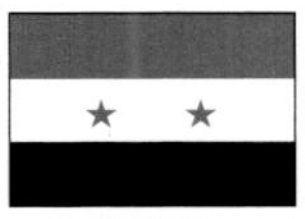
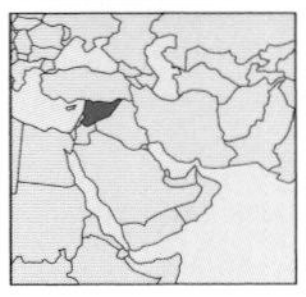

SYRIA

GEOGRAPHY The Syrian Arab Republic is a country in southwestern Asia. The narrow coastal plain is overlooked by a low mountain range which runs north–south. Another range, the Jabal ash Sharqi, runs along the border with Lebanon. To the south are the Golan Heights, which Israel has occupied since 1967.

The coast has a Mediterranean climate, with dry, warm summers and wet, mild winters. The low mountains cut off Damascus from the sea. It has less rainfall than the coastal areas. To the east, the land becomes drier.

POLITICS & ECONOMY After the collapse of the Turkish Ottoman empire in World War I, Syria was governed by France. Since independence in 1946, Syria has been involved in the Arab–Israeli wars, and in 1967 it lost a strategic border area, the Golan Heights, to Israel. In 1970, Lieutenant-General Hafez al-Assad took power, establishing a stable but repressive regime. Syria sent troops into Lebanon in 1976 in an effort to halt the civil war there, but, in 2005, following demonstrations, Syria withdrew. Hafez al-Assad died in 2000 and was succeeded by his son, Bashar al-Assad. Since 2011, civil war, and the occupation of Syrian territory by jihadist militants, has devastated the country with the number of deaths of civilians, rebels and government forces estimated at between 320,000 and 470,000. Millions of people have been internally displaced or sought refuge elsewhere.

Its main resources are oil, hydroelectricity, and fertile land. However, the economy has been crippled by the civil war and the consequent effects of mass emigration into neighboring states.

AREA 71,498 sq mi [185,180 sq km]
POPULATION 17,185,000 **CAPITAL** Damascus
GOVERNMENT Multiparty republic **ETHNIC GROUPS** Arab 90%, Kurdish, Armenian, others **LANGUAGES** Arabic (official), Kurdish, Armenian
RELIGIONS Sunni Muslim 74%, other Islam 16%
CURRENCY Syrian pound = 100 piastres

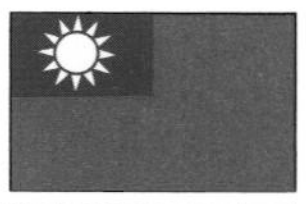
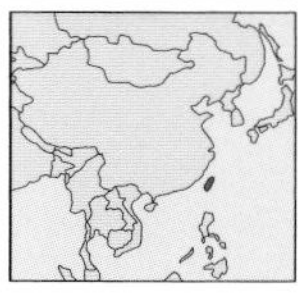

TAIWAN

GEOGRAPHY High mountain ranges run down the length of the island, with dense forest in many areas. The climate is warm, moist, and suitable for agriculture.

POLITICS & ECONOMY Chinese settlers occupied Taiwan from the 7th century. In 1895, Japan seized the territory from the Portuguese, who had named it Isla Formosa, or "beautiful island." China regained the island after World War II and, in 1949, it became the refuge of the Nationalists who had been driven out of China by the Communists. They set up the Republic of China, which, with US help, began to widen its economic base and develop manufacturing industries.

In the early 21st century, the Taiwanese declared full nationhood; however, China has never relinquished its claim of sovereignty over the island. Relations have improved somewhat since Taiwan and China signed a free-trade pact in 2010 although tensions still surface periodically. China is now Taiwan's main export market.

AREA 13,900 sq mi [36,000 sq km]
POPULATION 23,465,000 **CAPITAL** Taipei
GOVERNMENT Unitary multiparty republic
ETHNIC GROUPS Taiwanese 84%, mainland Chinese 14%
LANGUAGES Mandarin Chinese (official), Min, Hakka
RELIGIONS Buddhism, Taoism, Christianity
CURRENCY New Taiwan dollar = 100 cents

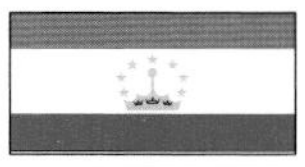
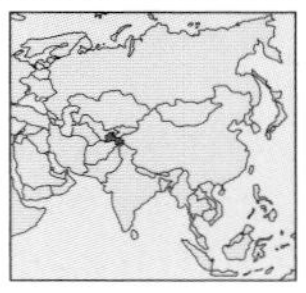

TAJIKISTAN

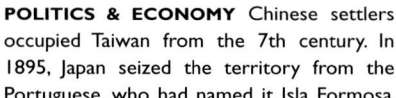

GEOGRAPHY The Republic of Tajikistan is one of the five central Asian republics that formed part of the former Soviet Union. Only 7% of the land is below 3,280 ft [1,000 m], while almost all of eastern Tajikistan is above 9,840 ft [3,000 m]. The highest point is Pik Imeni Ismail Samani (formerly known as Communism Peak or Pik Kommunizma), which reaches 24,590 ft [7,495 m]. The main ranges are the westward extension of the Tian Shan Range in the north and the snow-capped Pamirs in the southeast. Earthquakes are common throughout the country. The climate is continental, with hot, dry summers in the lower valleys and bitterly cold winters, especially in the mountains.

POLITICS & ECONOMY Russia conquered parts of Tajikistan in the late 19th century, and by 1920 Russia took complete control. In 1924, Tajikistan became part of the Uzbek Soviet Socialist Republic, but, in 1929, it was expanded, taking in some areas populated by Uzbeks, becoming the Tajik Soviet Socialist Republic.

While the Soviet Union began to introduce reforms during the 1980s, many Tajiks demanded freedom. In 1989, the Tajik government made Tajik the official language instead of Russian and, in 1990, it stated that its local laws overruled Soviet ones. Tajikistan became fully independent in 1991, following the breakup of the Soviet Union. In 1992, civil war broke out between the government, which was run by former Communists, and an alliance of democrats and Islamic forces. A ceasefire was agreed in 1996. In 2013, Emomali Rahmon, president since 1994, was re-elected for a 4th term. However, his parliamentary elections have been tainted by accusations of fraud.

Tajikistan is the poorest country in Central Asia and many people have left to find work in Russia. Economic hardship is fueling interest in radical Islam, especially amongst the young. Agriculture, mainly on irrigated land, is the main activity and cotton is the chief product. Other crops include fruits, grains, and vegetables. The country has large hydroelectric resources and it produces aluminum. Economic ties are being fostered with China.

AREA 55,521 sq mi [143,100 sq km]
POPULATION 8,331,000 **CAPITAL** Dushanbe
GOVERNMENT Republic
ETHNIC GROUPS Tajik 80%, Uzbek 15%, Russian 1%, Kyrgyz 1%
LANGUAGES Tajik (official), Russian
RELIGIONS Islam (Sunni Muslim 95%, Shia Muslim 3%)
CURRENCY Somoni = 100 dirams

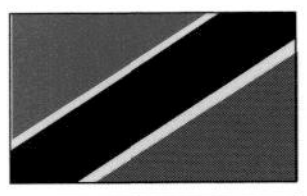
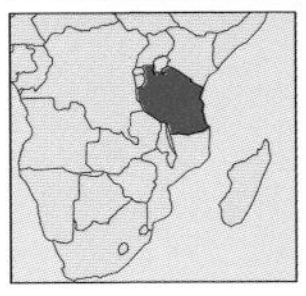

TANZANIA

GEOGRAPHY The United Republic of Tanzania consists of the former mainland country of Tanganyika and the island nation of Zanzibar, which also includes the island of Pemba. Behind a narrow coastal plain, most of Tanzania is a plateau, which is broken by arms of the Great African Rift Valley. In the west, this valley contains lakes Nyasa and Tanganyika. The highest peak is Kilimanjaro, Africa's highest mountain at 19,340 ft [5,895 m].

The coast has a hot and humid climate, with the greatest rainfall in April and May. The inland plateaux and mountains are cooler and less humid.

POLITICS & ECONOMY Mainland Tanganyika became a German territory in the 1880s, while Zanzibar and Pemba became a British protectorate in 1890. Following Germany's defeat in World War I, Britain took over Tanganyika, which remained a British territory until its independence in 1961. In 1964, Tanganyika and Zanzibar united to form the United Republic of Tanzania. The country's president, Julius Nyerere, pursued socialist policies of self-help (ujamaa) and egalitarianism. Many of its social reforms were successful, though the country failed to make economic progress. Nyerere resigned as president in 1985. His successors followed more liberal economic policies.

Tanzania is a poor country in terms of per capita income, but the overall economic growth rate is high, at around 7%, due to gold mining and tourism. Crops are grown on only 4% of the land, yet agriculture employs about 80% of the people and provides 85% of exports. Food crops include bananas, cassava, maize, millet, and rice. Minerals, including gold, as well as cashews, tobacco, coffee, and tea are exported. Offshore gas fields have been discovered.

AREA 364,899 sq mi [945,090 sq km]
POPULATION 52,483,000 **CAPITAL** Dodoma
GOVERNMENT Multiparty republic
ETHNIC GROUPS Native African 99% (of which 95% are Bantu consisting of more than 130 tribes)
LANGUAGES Swahili (Kiswahili) and English (both official)
RELIGIONS Islam 35% (99% in Zanzibar), traditional beliefs 35%, Christianity 30% **CURRENCY** Tanzanian shilling = 100 cents

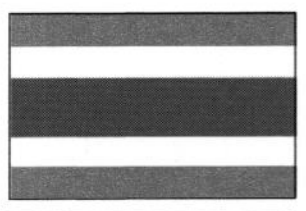
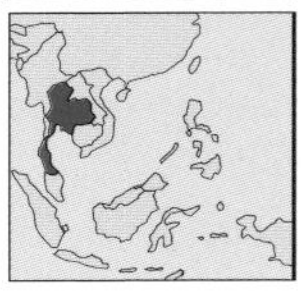

THAILAND

GEOGRAPHY The Kingdom of Thailand, is one of the ten countries in Southeast Asia. The highest land is in the north, where Doi Inthanon, the highest peak, reaches 8,415 ft [2,565 m]. The Khorat plateau, in the north-east, makes up about 30% of the country and is the most heavily populated part of Thailand. In the south, Thailand shares the finger-like Malay peninsula with Burma and Malaysia.

Thailand has a tropical climate. Monsoon winds from the south-west bring heavy rains in May to October. Mountains shelter the central plains from the rain-bearing winds.

POLITICS & ECONOMY The first Thai state was set up in the 13th century and, by 1350, it included most of what is now Thailand. European contact began in the early 16th century, but their interference was unwelcome and, by the late 17th century, all Europeans were forced to leave. In 1782, a Thai General, Chao Phraya Chakkri, became king, founding a dynasty which continues today. The country became known as Siam. From the mid-19th century, contacts with the West were restored. In World War I, Siam supported the Allies against Germany and Austria–Hungary although in 1941 it was aligned with Japan against the UK and US.

After 1967, when Thailand became a member of ASEAN (Association of Southeast Asian Nations), its economy expanded rapidly. In 1997, with other eastern Asian economies, it suffered an economic recession. Thailand has also faced conflict in the south of the country, where the government has clashed with minority Muslim groups. In 2001, Thaksin Shinawatra, a businessman, became prime minister. In 2006, his party won a majority, the result of a boycott of opposition parties. Following mass protests, a military junta took power until civilian rule was restored in 2007. In 2011, Thaksin's sister, Yingluck Shinawatra, was elected prime minister. Elections held in early 2014 were later declared invalid and, in May, the military took control. General Prayath Chan-ocha was appointed prime minister.

Classified as an "upper-middle income country", Thailand has a well-developed infrastructure and an export-led economy. Agriculture employs 32% of the people and rice is the chief crop. Cassava, cotton, maize, rubber, sugarcane, and tobacco are also grown. Tin is mined, but the chief exports are manufactures and food products. Tourism plays a significant part in the economy.

AREA 198,114 sq mi [513,115 sq km]
POPULATION 68,201,000 **CAPITAL** Bangkok
GOVERNMENT Constitutional monarchy
ETHNIC GROUPS Thai 75%, Chinese 14%, others 11%
LANGUAGES Thai (official), English, ethnic and regional dialects
RELIGIONS Buddhism 95%, Islam, Christianity
CURRENCY Thai baht = 100 satang

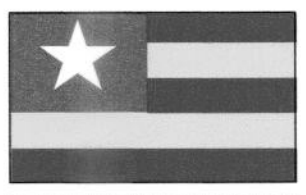
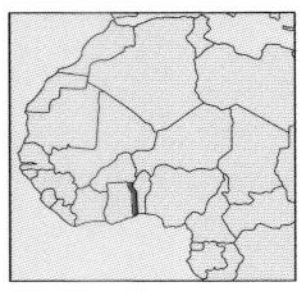

TOGO

GEOGRAPHY The Republic of Togo is a long, narrow country in West Africa. From north to south, it extends about 311 mi [500 km]. Its coastline on the Gulf of Guinea is only 40 mi [64 km] long and it is only 90 mi [145 km] at its widest point.

Togo's climate is generally tropical, and has high temperatures all through the year. The main wet season is from March to July, with a minor wet season in October and November.

POLITICS & ECONOMY Togo became a German protectorate in 1884, but, in 1919, Britain took over the western third of the territory, while France took over the eastern two-thirds. In 1956, the people of British Togoland voted to join Ghana, while French Togoland became an independent republic in 1960.

A military regime took power in 1963. In 1967, General Gnassingbé Eyadéma became head of state, a position he maintained until his death in 2005. Elections held during this period were deemed unfair and were boycotted by opposition parties. His son, Faure Gnassingbé, took over as president, but international pressure forced him to step down. He was, however, re-elected in 2005, 2010 and 2015. Serious challenges to the stranglehold of this family will have to await future elections.

Togo is a poor, developing country dependent on agriculture. Major food crops include cassava, maize, millet, and yams. Togo is one of the world's largest producers and exporters of phosphates. Economic growth will depend on reforms and foreign assistance.

AREA 21,925 sq mi [56,785 sq km]
POPULATION 7,757,000 **CAPITAL** Lomé
GOVERNMENT Multiparty republic **ETHNIC GROUPS** Native African 99% (largest tribes are Ewe, Mina and Kabre) **LANGUAGES** French (official), African languages **RELIGIONS** Traditional beliefs 51%, Christianity 29%, Islam 20% **CURRENCY** CFA franc = 100 centimes

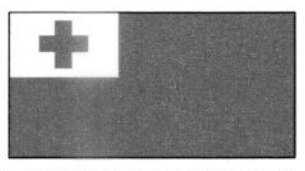
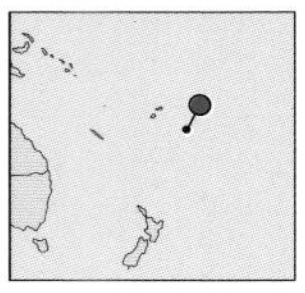

TONGA

The Kingdom of Tonga, a former British protectorate, became independent in 1970. Situated in the south Pacific Ocean, it contains more than 170 islands, 36 of which are inhabited. In 2010, Tonga held its first election for a popularly elected parliament. Agriculture is the main activity and unemployment is high.

AREA 251 sq mi [650 sq km] **POPULATION** 107,000 **CAPITAL** Nuku'alofa

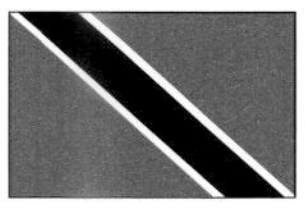
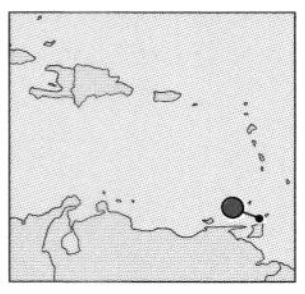

TRINIDAD AND TOBAGO

The Republic of Trinidad and Tobago became independent from Britain in 1962. These tropical islands, populated by people of African, Asian (mainly Indian) and European origin, are hilly and forested, though there are some fertile plains. Oil production is the mainstay of the economy.

AREA 1,981 sq mi [5,130 sq km]
POPULATION 1,220,000 **CAPITAL** Port of Spain

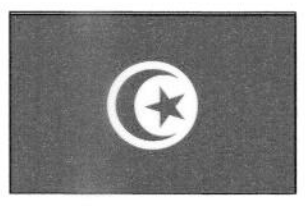
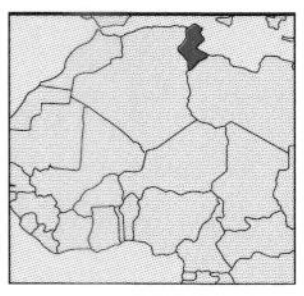

TUNISIA

GEOGRAPHY The Republic of Tunisia is the smallest country in North Africa. The mountains in the north are an eastward and comparatively low extension of the Atlas Mountains. To the north and east of the mountains lie fertile plains, especially between Sfax, Tunis, and Bizerte. In the south, low-lying regions contain the the Chott Djerid, a vast salt pan, part of the Sahara.

Northern Tunisia has a Mediterranean climate, with dry, sunny summers, and mild winters with a moderate rainfall. The average yearly rainfall decreases toward the south.

POLITICS & ECONOMY In 1881, France established a protectorate over Tunisia and ruled the country until 1956. The new parliament abolished the monarchy and declared Tunisia to be a republic in 1957, with the nationalist leader, Habib Bourguiba, as president. His government introduced many reforms, including votes for women, but there were problems including unemployment among the middle class and fears that the ideas of Western visitors might undermine Muslim values. In 1987, the prime minister, Zine el Abidine Ben Ali, removed Bourguiba, and became president. He was re-elected five times until, in 2011, anti-government demonstrations forced him to flee the country. Mohamed Béji Caid Essebsi assumed the presidency in 2014.

The World Bank classifies Tunisia as an "upper-middle-income" developing country and it is one of the more prosperous in North Africa. The main resources and chief exports are phosphates and oil. Most industries are concerned with food processing. Fishing is important. The flourishing tourism industry has been hit hard by the fallout from terrorist attacks in 2015.

AREA 63,170 sq mi [163,610 sq km] **POPULATION** 11,135,000
CAPITAL Tunis **GOVERNMENT** Multiparty republic
ETHNIC GROUPS Arab 98%, European 1% **LANGUAGES** Arabic (official), French **RELIGIONS** Islam 98%, Christianity 1%, others
CURRENCY Tunisian dinar = 1,000 millimes

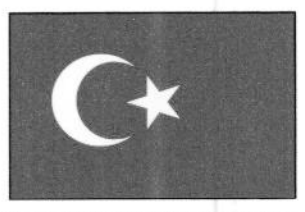
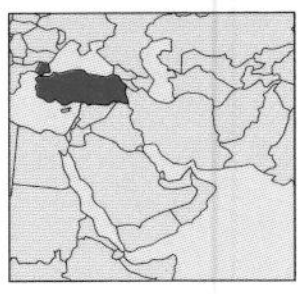

TURKEY

GEOGRAPHY The Republic of Turkey lies in two continents. European Turkey, also called Thrace, lies west of a waterway linking the Mediterranean and Black seas. Most of Asian Turkey consists of plateaux and mountains, which rise to 16,945 ft [5,165 m] at Mount Ararat, near the border with Armenia. Earthquakes are common. Central Turkey has a dry climate, with hot, sunny summers and cold winters. The west has a Mediterranean climate, but the Black Sea coast has cooler summers.

POLITICS & ECONOMY In AD 330, the Roman empire moved its capital to Byzantium, which it renamed Constantinople. Muslim Seljuk Turks from central Asia invaded Anatolia (Asian Turkey) in the 11th century. In the 14th century, another group of Turks, the Ottomans, conquered the area and, in 1453, they took Constantinople, renaming it Istanbul. The Ottomans built up a vast empire which finally collapsed during World War I (1914–18). Turkey became a republic in 1923 and its leader, Mustafa Kemal, or Atatürk ("father of the Turks"), began to modernize and secularize the country.

Since the 1940s, Turkey has sought to strengthen its ties with Western powers. It joined NATO (North Atlantic Treaty Organization) in 1951 and it applied to join the European Economic Community in 1987. But Turkey's conflict with Greece, together with its invasion of northern Cyprus in 1974, have led many Europeans to treat Turkey's aspirations to full EU membership with caution. Political instability, military coups, conflict with Kurdish nationalists in eastern Turkey, and concern about the country's record on human rights are problems still to be solved.

Turkey has enjoyed democracy since 1983. In 1999, the Muslim Virtue Party (successor to the Islamist Welfare Party) lost ground. The largest numbers of parliamentary seats were won by the ruling Democratic Left Party and the far-right National Action Party. However, in the elections in 2002, the moderate Islamic Justice and Development Party (AKP) won 362 of the 500 seats in parliament. Despite concerns about its Islamist roots, the AKP was re-elected in 2007 and 2011. In 2014, Recep Tayyip Erdogan was elected president after serving as prime minister since 2003. The conflict in Syria to the south has increased tensions along the border. A failed coup in 2016 was followed in 2017 by a referendum on giving the president more powers and extending his term in office. The result was a disputed narrow victory for Erdogan.

Turkey came close to economic collapse in 2002, but its recovery enabled it to withstand the global financial crisis in 2008, and bounce back by 2010–11. However, the economy is vulnerable to political instability in the region and investor confidence. Agriculture employs 26% of the people, with barley, cotton, fruits, nuts, maize, tobacco, and wheat being the major crops.

AREA 299,156 sq mi [774,815 sq km]
POPULATION 80,275,000 **CAPITAL** Ankara
GOVERNMENT Multiparty republic **ETHNIC GROUPS** Turkish 73%, Kurdish 18% **LANGUAGES** Turkish (official), Kurdish, Arabic
RELIGIONS Islam (mainly Sunni Muslim) 99%
CURRENCY Turkish lira = 100 kurus

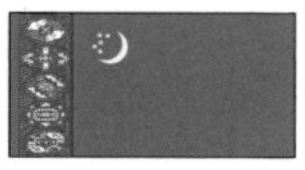

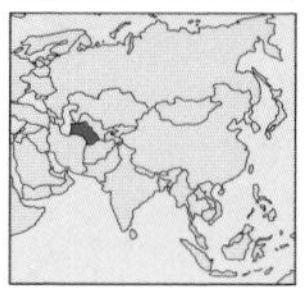

TURKMENISTAN

GEOGRAPHY The Republic of Turkmenistan is one of the five central Asian republics which once formed part of the former Soviet Union. Most of the land is low-lying, with mountains stretching along the southern and south-western borders. In the west lies the salty Caspian Sea. Most of Turkmenistan is arid and the Garagum (Kara Kum), Asia's largest sand desert, covers about 80% of the country. Turkmenistan has a continental climate, with average annual rainfall varying from 3 inches [80 mm] in the desert to 12 inches [300 mm] in the mountains. Summer months are hot, but winter temperatures drop well below freezing point.

POLITICS & ECONOMY Just over 1,000 years ago, Turkic people settled in the lands east of the Caspian Sea and the name "Turkmen" dates from this time. Mongol armies conquered the area in the 13th century and Islam was introduced in the 14th century. Russia took over the area in the 1870s and 1880s. The area came under Communist rule in 1917 and, in 1924, it became the Turkmen Soviet Socialist Republic.

In the 1980s, when the Soviet Union began to introduce reforms, the Turkmen began to demand more freedom and, in 1991, asserted that their own laws held sway over those of Soviet Russia. In late 1991, Turkmenistan became fully independent although the country maintained ties with Russia through the Commonwealth of Independent States (CIS).

In 1992, Turkmenistan adopted a new constitution, allowing for the setting up of political parties, providing that they were not ethnic or religious in character. But, effectively, Turkmenistan remained a one-party state and, in 1992, Saparmurad Niyazov, the former Communist and at that time Democratic Party leader, was the only presidential candidate. In 1999, parliament declared Niyazov president for life. Niyazov died in 2006 and was succeeded by Gurbanguly Berdymukhamedov. He was re-elected in 2012 and 2017.

Faced with many economic problems, Turkmenistan began to look south rather than to the CIS for support. As part of this policy, it joined the Economic Cooperation Organization, which had been set up in 1985 by Iran, Pakistan, and Turkey. In 1996, the completion of a rail link from Turkmenistan to the Iranian coast was an important step in the development of Central Asia. Oil and natural gas are the chief resources, and gas pipelines to China and Iran were opened in 2009 and 2010. Agriculture remains the main activity, with cotton as the most important commercial crop. Manufactures include cement, glass, petrochemicals, and textiles.

AREA 188,455 sq mi [488,100 sq km] **POPULATION** 5,291,000
CAPITAL Ashkhabad **GOVERNMENT** Single-party republic
ETHNIC GROUPS Turkmen 85%, Uzbek 5%, Russian 4%
LANGUAGES Turkmen (official), Russian, Uzbek **RELIGIONS** Islam 89%, Eastern Orthodox 9% **CURRENCY** Turkmen manat = 100 tenge

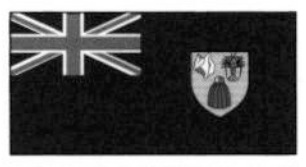

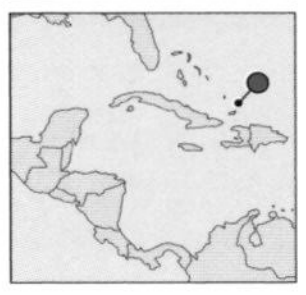

TURKS AND CAICOS ISLANDS

The Turks and Caicos Islands, a British territory in the Caribbean since 1776, are a group of about 30 islands. Fishing and tourism are the major activities.

AREA 166 sq mi [430 sq km]
POPULATION 51,000 **CAPITAL** Cockburn Town

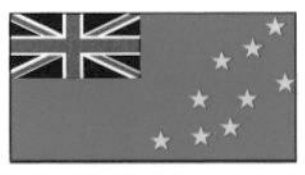

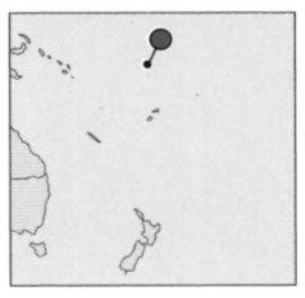

TUVALU

Tuvalu, formerly called the Ellice Islands, was a British territory from the 1890s until it became independent in 1978. It consists of nine low-lying coral atolls in the southern Pacific Ocean. Copra is the only significant export.

AREA 10 sq mi [26 sq km]
POPULATION 11,000 **CAPITAL** Fongafale

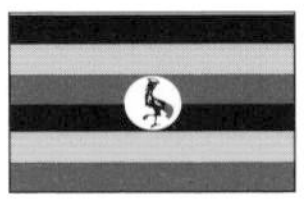

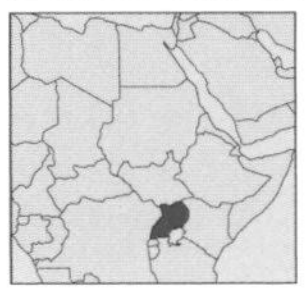

UGANDA

GEOGRAPHY The Republic of Uganda is a landlocked country on the East African plateau. It contains part of Lake Victoria, Africa's largest lake and a source of the River Nile, which occupies a shallow depression in the plateau.

The equator runs through Uganda and the country is warm throughout the year, though the high altitude moderates the temperature. The wettest regions are the lands to the north of Lake Victoria, where the capital, Kampala, is situated, and the western mountains, especially the high Ruwenzori range.

POLITICS & ECONOMY Little is known of the early history of Uganda. When Europeans first reached the area in the 19th century, many of the people were organized in kingdoms, the most powerful of which was Buganda, the home of the Baganda people. Britain took control of the country between 1894 and 1914, and administered it until independence in 1962.

In 1967, Uganda became a republic and Buganda's Kabaka (king), Sir Edward Mutesa II, was made president. But tensions between the Kabaka and the prime minister, Apollo Milton Obote, led to the dismissal of the Kabaka in 1966. Obote also abolished the traditional kingdoms, including Buganda. Obote was overthrown in 1971 by an army group led by General Idi Amin Dada. Amin ruled as a dictator; forcing most of the Asians who lived in Uganda to leave the country and had many of his opponents killed.

In 1978, a border dispute between Uganda and Tanzania led Tanzanian troops to enter Uganda. With help from Ugandan opponents of Amin, they overthrew Amin's government. In 1980, Obote led his party to victory in the elections, but following charges of fraud, Obote's opponents instigated a guerrilla war. A military group overthrew Obote in 1985, though strife continued until 1986, when Yoweri Museveni's National Resistance Movement seized power. In 1993, Museveni restored the traditional kingdoms. Elections were held in 1994, but political parties were forbidden. Museveni was re-elected five times between 1996 and 2016. In recent years, Uganda has faced the rebel Lord's Resistance Army (LRA) in the north. The LRA extended its activities into the Central African Republic, the Democratic Republic of the Congo, and Sudan. In 2010, two bombings in Kampala, killing 74 people, were carried out by a Somali Islamist group, al-Shabab.

Agriculture dominates the economy, employing over 80% of the work force. The chief export is coffee. Economic reforms and some investment in infrastructure has resulted in a strengthening of the economy. Newly discovered oil will be a valuable asset.

AREA 93,065 sq mi [241,038 sq km]
POPULATION 38,319,000 **CAPITAL** Kampala
GOVERNMENT Republic **ETHNIC GROUPS** Baganda 17%, Ankole 8%, Basogo 8%, Iteso 8%, Bakiga 7%, Langi 6%, Rwanda 6%, Bagisu 5%, Acholi 4%, Lugbara 4%, and others
LANGUAGES English and Swahili (both official), Ganda
RELIGIONS Roman Catholic 42%, Protestant 42%, Islam 12%, traditional beliefs 4%
CURRENCY Ugandan shilling = 100 cents

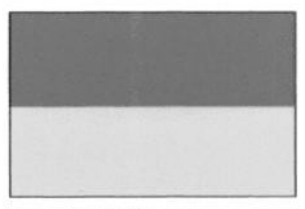

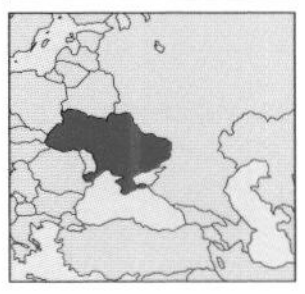

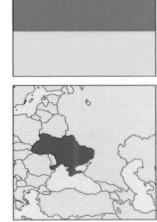

UKRAINE

GEOGRAPHY Ukraine is the second largest country in Europe after Russia. It was formerly part of the Soviet Union, which split apart in 1991. This mostly flat country faces the Black Sea in the south. The Crimean peninsula includes a highland region overlooking Yalta. Ukraine has warm summers, but the winters are cold, becoming more severe from west to east. In the summer, the east is often warmer than the west. Most rain falls in summer.

POLITICS & ECONOMY Kiev was the original capital of the early Slavic civilization known as Kievan Rus. In the 17th and 18th centuries, parts of Ukraine came under Polish and Russian rule, but, by the late 18th century, Russia had gained most of Ukraine. In 1918, Ukraine gained independence, but only until 1922 when it became part of the Soviet Union.

In the 1980s, Ukrainian people demanded more say over their affairs and regained their independence in 1991. In 2005, the pro-Western leader Viktor Yushchenko was elected president. Economic problems and political infighting led to a Russian-leaning party, led by Viktor Yanukovych, winning most seats in parliament in 2006. Yanukovych became prime minister, but an election in 2007 resulted in a pro-Western coalition government led by a former prime minister, Yulia Tymoshenko. In 2010, the pro-Russian Viktor Yanukovych was declared winner of the presidential election. Tymoshenko was later accused of exceeding her powers and was sentenced to seven years in prison.

Ukraine is being pulled in two directions: the choice is closer integration with either Russia or the EU. Mass unrest forced Yanukovych to flee the country in February 2014. In a referendum, Crimea voted to unite with Russia. This annexation has not been recognized by Ukraine or the wider world. Civil unrest continues in the eastern Donetsk and Luhansk regions.

Manufacturing is the chief economic activity including iron and steel, machinery, and vehicles. Ukraine has large coalfields. The country imports oil and natural gas (much of it from Russia), but it has its own hydroelectric and nuclear power stations. Agriculture contributes 13% of GDP and wheat and sugar are exported.

AREA 233,089 sq mi [603,700 sq km]
POPULATION 44,210,000 **CAPITAL** Kiev
GOVERNMENT Multiparty republic
ETHNIC GROUPS Ukrainian 78%, Russian 17%, Belarusian, Moldovan, Bulgarian, Hungarian, Polish
LANGUAGES Ukrainian (official), Russian
RELIGIONS Mostly Ukrainian Orthodox
CURRENCY Hryvnia = 100 kopiykas

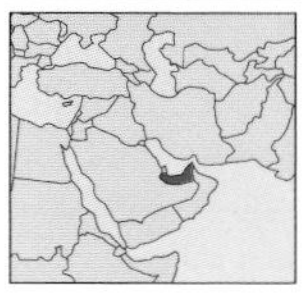

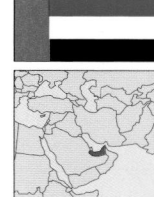

UNITED ARAB EMIRATES

The United Arab Emirates were formed in 1971 when the seven Trucial States of the Persian Gulf (Abu Dhabi, Dubai, Sharjah, Ajman, Umm al Qawayn, Ra's al Khaymah, and Al Fujayrah) opted to join together and form an independent country. The economy of this hot and dry state depends on oil production, and the resulting revenues give the United Arab Emirates one of the highest per capita GDPs in Asia.

AREA 32,278 sq mi [83,600 sq km]
POPULATION 5,927,000 **CAPITAL** Abu Dhabi

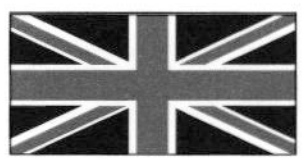

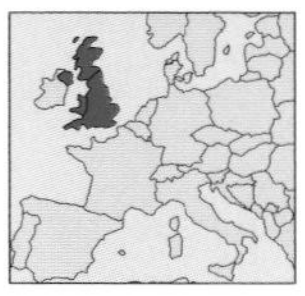

UNITED KINGDOM

GEOGRAPHY The United Kingdom (or UK) is a union of four countries. Three of them – England, Scotland, and Wales – make up Great Britain. The fourth country is Northern Ireland. The Isle of Man and the Channel Islands are not part of the UK. They are self-governing British dependencies.

The land is highly varied. Much of Scotland and Wales is mountainous, and the highest peak is Scotland's Ben Nevis at 4,411 ft [1,345 m]. England has some highland areas, including the Cumbrian Mountains (or Lake District) and the Pennine range in the north, but it also has extensive areas of fertile lowland. Northern Ireland is also a mixture of lowlands and uplands. It contains the UK's largest lake, Lough Neagh.

The UK has a mild climate, influenced by the warm North Atlantic Drift which is a continuation of the Gulf Stream originating from the Gulf of Mexico. Moist winds from the south-west bring rain, but the rainfall decreases from west to east. Winds from the east and north bring cold weather in winter.

POLITICS & ECONOMY In ancient times, Britain was invaded by many peoples, including Iberians, Celts, Romans, Angles, Saxons, Jutes, Norsemen, Danes, and the Normans, who arrived in 1066. King Edward I annexed Wales in 1282 and united it with England. Union with Scotland was achieved in 1707 and this created a country known as the United Kingdom of Great Britain.

Ireland came under Norman rule in the 11th century, and much of its later history was concerned with a struggle against English domination. In 1801, Ireland became part of the United Kingdom of Great Britain and Ireland. But in 1921, southern Ireland, where most of the people were Roman Catholics, broke away to become the Irish Free State. In Northern Ireland, where the majority of the people were Protestants, most people wanted to remain citizens of the United Kingdom. The country now became the United Kingdom of Great Britain and Northern Ireland.

The modern history of the UK began in the 18th century with the expansion of the British empire, despite the loss in 1783 of its 13 North American colonies. The other significant milestone occurred in the late 18th century, when the UK became the first country to industrialize its economy.

The British empire broke up after World War II (1939–45), though the UK still administers many small, mainly island, territories around the world. The empire was transformed into the Commonwealth of Nations, a free association of independent countries which numbered 52 in 2017.

The UK has retained an important world role. For example, in 2001, it played a prominent role in creating a broad alliance to counter international terrorism following the attacks on the United States. It was also a prominent member of the coalition force which invaded Iraq in 2003. It became a member of the European Economic Community (now the European Union) in 1973. Membership of the EU has been important to the British economy, but some have feared a loss of British sovereignty and identity. A referendum in June 2016 on the UK's future in the EU resulted in a narrow vote to leave. The process of leaving was

triggered in March 2017 and the following month, a snap general election, to be held in June, was announced.

Since the late 1990s some powers have been devolved to Scotland, Wales, and Northern Ireland. The Northern Ireland Assembly has followed a fitful path since its establishment in 1998. The National Assembly for Wales and the Scottish Parliament both opened in 1999. In a referendum on Scottish independence held in 2014, 55% of voters elected to stay within the UK.

The UK is a major industrial and trading nation. It lacks natural resources apart from coal, iron ore, oil, and natural gas, and has to import most of the materials it needs for its industries. The UK also has to import food, because it produces only about two-thirds of the food it needs. In the first half of the 20th century, Britain was a major exporter of cars, ships, steel, and textiles. But many industries have suffered from competition from other countries, with lower labor costs. From 2008, Britain's economy was hit by a global financial crisis, which led the country into recession. Severe austerity measures were introduced.

The UK is one of the world's most urbanized countries, and agriculture employs only 1% of the work force. Production is high because of the use of scientific methods and modern machinery. However, in the early 21st century, especially following the outbreak of foot-and-mouth disease in 2001, questions were raised about the future of rural industries. Major crops include barley, potatoes, sugar beet, and wheat. Sheep are the leading livestock, but beef and dairy cattle, pigs, and poultry are also important. Fishing is another major activity and the UK is one of the largest fishing countries in the EU. Important catches include cod, haddock, plaice, and mackerel.

Service industries play a major part in the UK's economy. Financial and insurance services bring in much-needed foreign exchange, while tourism has become a major earner.

AREA 93,381 sq mi [241,857 sq km]
POPULATION 64,430,000 **CAPITAL** London
GOVERNMENT Constitutional monarchy
ETHNIC GROUPS English 84%, Scottish 9%, Welsh 5%, N. Irish 3%, West Indian, Indian, Pakistani and others
LANGUAGES English (official), Welsh, Gaelic
RELIGIONS Christianity (Anglican, Roman Catholic, Presbyterian, Methodist), Islam, Sikhism, Hinduism, Judaism
CURRENCY Pound sterling = 100 pence

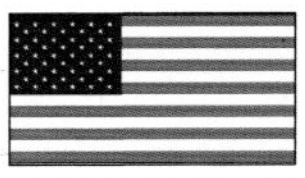
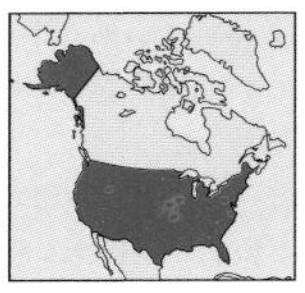

UNITED STATES OF AMERICA

GEOGRAPHY The United States of America is the world's fourth largest country in area and the third largest in population. It contains 50 states, 48 of which lie between Canada and Mexico, plus Alaska in northwestern North America, and Hawai'i, a group of volcanic islands in the north Pacific Ocean. Densely populated coastal plains lie to the east and south of the Appalachian Mountains. The central lowlands, drained by the Mississippi–Missouri rivers, stretch from the Appalachians to the Rocky Mountains in the west. The Pacific region contains fertile valleys, separated by mountain ranges.

The climate varies greatly, ranging from the Arctic cold of Alaska to the intense heat of Death Valley, a bleak desert in California. Of the 48 states between Canada and Mexico, winters are cold and snowy in the north, but mild in the south, a region which is often called the "Sun Belt."

POLITICS & ECONOMY The first people in North America, the ancestors of the Native Americans (or American Indians) arrived perhaps 40,000 years ago from Asia. Although Vikings probably reached North America 1,000 years ago, European exploration proper did not begin until the late 15th century.

The first Europeans to settle in large numbers were the British, who founded settlements on the eastern coast in the early 17th century. British rule ended in the War of Independence (1775–83). The country expanded in 1803 when a vast territory in the south and west was acquired through the Louisiana Purchase, while the border with Mexico was fixed in the mid-19th century. The Civil War (1861–5) ended slavery and the serious threat that the nation might split into two parts. In the late 19th century, the West was opened up, while immigrants flooded in from Europe and elsewhere.

During the late 19th and early 20th centuries, industrialization led to the United States becoming the world's leading economic superpower and a pioneer in science and technology. It took on the mantle of the champion of Western democracy and, following the breakup of the former Soviet Union, it became the world's only superpower. But the attacks on the country on September 11, 2001, revealed its vulnerability to terrorists and rogue states. The response was vigorous. In 2001, it attacked the Taliban government in Afghanistan, which was protecting al Qaeda terrorists. Then, in 2003, it led a coalition force to invade Iraq and overthrow Saddam Hussein.

From 2008-16, Democrat Barack Obama was president. Bitterly fought elections in 2016 resulted in a win for businessman Donald Trump, on a ticket of protectionism, removing Obama's socially progressive changes to health care and a crackdown on immigration.

The US economy has long been considered to be the world's largest, but some authorities now see it being challenged by China. Recovery from the global financial crisis of 2008 has been slow. There remains a wide disparity between rich and poor in the US and as many as 30 million Americans live below the poverty line. Although agriculture employs few people, farming is highly mechanized and scientific, and the United States leads the world in farm production. Major products include beef and dairy cattle.

Natural resources include oil, natural gas, coal, a wide range of metal ores, and timber, especially from the Pacific northwest. Manufacturing is the single most valuable activity, employing around 10% of the working population. Major products include vehicles, food products, chemicals, machinery, printed goods, metal products, and scientific instruments. California, with its high-tech electronics industries, is the top manufacturing state.

AREA 3,717,792 sq mi [9,629,091 sq km]
POPULATION 323,996,000 **CAPITAL** Washington, DC
GOVERNMENT Federal republic
ETHNIC GROUPS White 80%, African American 13%, Asian 4%, Amerindian 1%, others **LANGUAGES** English, Spanish, more than 30 others **RELIGIONS** Protestant 51%, Roman Catholic 24%, Judaism 2%, Mormon 2%, Islam 1%
CURRENCY US dollar = 100 cents

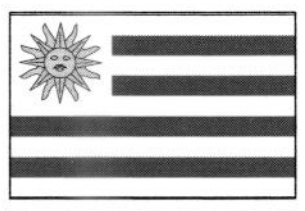
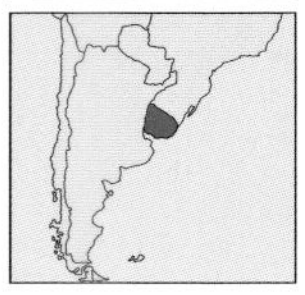

URUGUAY

GEOGRAPHY Uruguay is South America's second smallest independent country after Suriname. The land consists mainly of flat plains and hills. The River Uruguay, which forms the country's western border, flows into the Río de la Plata, a large estuary which leads into the South Atlantic Ocean.

Uruguay has a mild climate, with rain in every month, though droughts sometimes occur. Summers are pleasantly warm and winters relatively mild.

POLITICS & ECONOMY In 1726, Spanish settlers founded Montevideo in order to halt the Portuguese gaining influence in the area. By the late 18th century, Spaniards had settled in most of the country and Uruguay became part of a colony called the Viceroyalty of La Plata, which also included Argentina, Paraguay, and parts of Bolivia, Brazil, and Chile. In 1820 Brazil annexed Uruguay, ending Spanish rule. In 1825, Uruguayans, supported by Argentina, began a struggle for independence.

Finally, in 1828, Brazil and Argentina recognized Uruguay as an independent republic. Social and economic developments were slow, but, from 1903, Uruguay became stable and democratic.

From the 1950s, economic problems incited unrest from terrorist groups, notably the Tupumaros, until the army took over the government in 1973. Military rule continued until elections were held in 1984. In the early 21st century, Uruguay faced many economic problems, many of which were the result of the economic crisis in its neighboring country, Argentina. Tabaré Vázquez replaced Jose Mujica as president in March 2015. Vázquez had previously been president in 2005–10.

The World Bank now classifies Uruguay as a "high-income" economy but, although it is one of the more prosperous countries in South America, there is still a minority underclass living in poverty. Agriculture employs 13% of the work force, and farm products, notably hides and leather goods, beef, and wool, are the main exports, while many manufacturing industries process farm products. Crops include maize, potatoes, wheat, and sugar beet. Uruguay depends largely on hydroelectric power for energy. In 2008, Uruguay announced the discovery of an offshore natural gas field, which is being developed.

AREA 67,574 sq mi [175,016 sq km]
POPULATION 3,351,000 **CAPITAL** Montevideo
GOVERNMENT Multiparty republic
ETHNIC GROUPS White 88%, Mestizo 8%, Mulatto or Black 4%
LANGUAGES Spanish (official)
RELIGIONS Christianity 58% (Roman Catholic 47%), others
CURRENCY Uruguayan peso = 100 centésimos

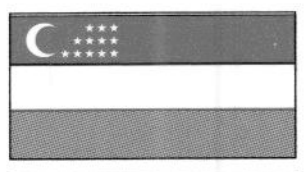
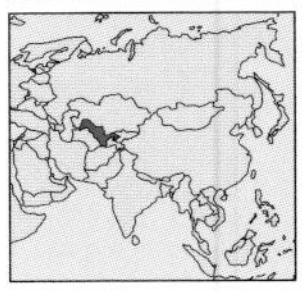

UZBEKISTAN

GEOGRAPHY The Republic of Uzbekistan is one of the five republics in Central Asia which were once part of the Soviet Union. Plains cover most of western Uzbekistan, with highlands in the east. The main rivers, the Amudarya and Syrdarya, drain into the Aral Sea. So much water has been taken from these rivers to irrigate the land to grow cotton that the Aral Sea has now shrunk to about a quarter of its size in 1960. The former lake area is now desert. Uzbekistan has cold winters and hot summers. The largely uninhabited Kyzyl Kum desert lies in central Uzbekistan.

POLITICS & ECONOMY Russia took the area in the 19th century. After the Russian Revolution of 1917, the Communists took over and, in 1924, they set up the Uzbek Soviet Socialist Republic. Under Communism, all aspects of Uzbek life were controlled and religious worship was discouraged, but education, health, housing, and transport were improved. In the late 1980s, the people demanded more autonomy, leading to independence in 1991 with the breakup of the Soviet Union.

Islam Karimov, leader of the People's Democratic Party (formerly the Communist Party), was first elected president in December 1991. Dissent is not tolerated and opposition leaders have been arrested and accused of threatening national stability. Initially, Karimov's government allowed the US to use Uzbekistan as a base for its military campaign in Afghanistan, but relations cooled in 2005 and the US was asked to remove its troops. In an about-face in 2009, ties with Russia deteriorated and those with the US improved and they were again able to transport supplies through Uzbekistan to their troops in Afghanistan. The United Nations has condemned the country's human rights record. Karimov remained in power until his death in 2016. Prime minister Shavjat Mirziyoyev was elected to replace him.

The World Bank classifies Uzbekistan as a "lower-middle-income" developing country and the government still controls most economic activity. Uzbekistan is the world's sixth largest cotton exporter. The country produces coal, copper, gold, oil, and natural gas.

AREA 172,741 sq mi [447,400 sq km]
POPULATION 29,474,000 **CAPITAL** Tashkent
GOVERNMENT Socialist republic **ETHNIC GROUPS** Uzbek 80%, Russian 5%, Tajik 5%, Kazakh 3%, Tatar 2%, Kara-Kalpak 2%
LANGUAGES Uzbek (official), Russian **RELIGIONS** Islam 88%, Eastern Orthodox 9% **CURRENCY** Uzbekistani sum = 100 tyiyn

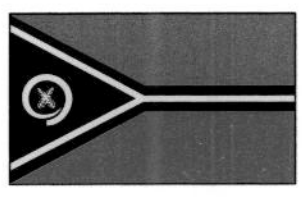
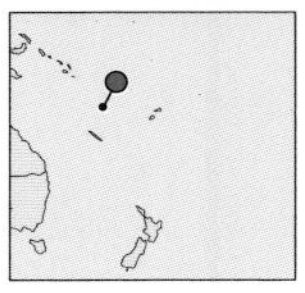

VANUATU

The Republic of Vanuatu, formerly the Anglo-French Condominium of the New Hebrides, became independent in 1980. It consists of a chain of 80 islands in the south Pacific Ocean. Its economy is based on agriculture, and it exports copra, beef and veal, timber, and cocoa.

AREA 4,706 sq mi [12,189 sq km]
POPULATION 278,000 **CAPITAL** Port-Vila

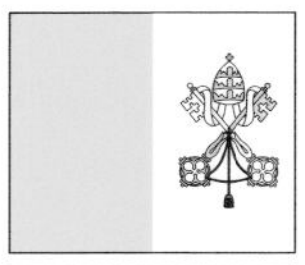
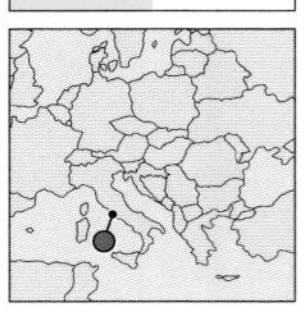

VATICAN CITY

Vatican City State, the world's smallest independent nation, is an enclave on the west bank of the River Tiber in Rome. It forms an independent base for the Holy See, the governing body of the Roman Catholic Church.

AREA 0.17 sq mi [0.44 sq km]
POPULATION 842

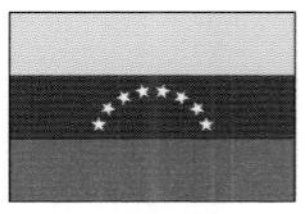
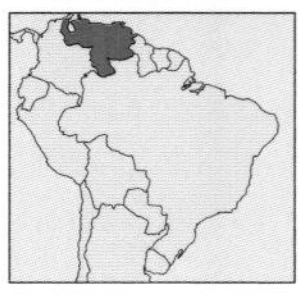

VENEZUELA

GEOGRAPHY The Bolivarian Republic of Venezuela, in northern South America, contains the Maracaibo lowlands around the oil-rich Lake Maracaibo in the west. Andean ranges enclose the lowlands and extend across most of the northern part of the country. The Orinoco river basin, containing tropical grasslands called llanos, lies between the northern highlands and the Guiana Highlands in the southeast. The Orinoco is Venezuela's longest river.

Venezuela has a tropical climate. Temperatures are high throughout the year on the lowlands, though the mountains are cooler. Rainfall is heaviest in the mountains, but much of the country has a dry season between December and April.

POLITICS & ECONOMY In the early 19th century, Venezuelans such as Simón Bolívar and Francisco de Miranda, rebeled against Spanish colonial rule leading, eventually, to full independence as a republic in 1821.

The development of Venezuela in the 19th and the first half of the 20th centuries was marred by instability, violence, and periods of harsh dictatorial rule, but it has had elected governments since 1958. The country has greatly benefited from its oil resources (first exploited in 1917) which are some of the largest in the world. In 1960, Venezuela helped to form OPEC (the Organization of Petroleum Exporting Countries) and, in 1976, the government of Venezuela took control of the country's entire oil industry. In 1999, Hugo Chavez, who had staged an unsuccessful coup in 1992, was elected president. Chavez remained in office until his death in March 2013 when he was succeeded by the socialist Nicolás Maduro. Relations with the US remain strained.

With oil accounting for about 95% of its exports, Venezuela is now classified as having a "high-income" economy by the World Bank. However, the majority of the people live in poverty and unemployment is high. Opinions are divided on whether or not Chavez's economic reforms helped or hindered the poor. Other exports include bauxite and aluminum, iron ore, and farm products. Beef cattle, dairy cattle, and poultry are raised. Crops include bananas, citrus fruits, coffee, and rice. The main industry is petroleum refining. Cement, steel, and textiles are also produced.

AREA 352,143 sq mi [912,050 sq km] **POPULATION** 30,912,000
CAPITAL Caracas **GOVERNMENT** Federal republic
ETHNIC GROUPS Spanish, Italian, Portuguese, Arab, German, African, indigenous people **LANGUAGES** Spanish (official), indigenous dialects **RELIGIONS** Roman Catholic 96%
CURRENCY Bolívar = 100 céntimos

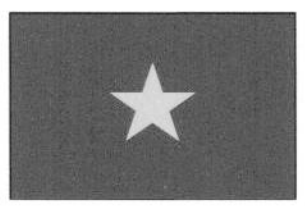

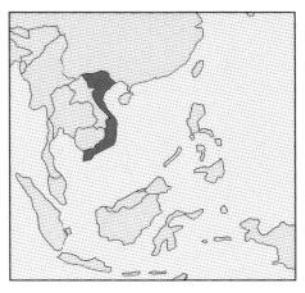

VIETNAM

GEOGRAPHY The Socialist Republic of Vietnam occupies an S-shaped strip of land facing the South China Sea in Southeast Asia. The coastal plains include two densely populated, fertile delta regions: the Red (Hong) delta facing the Gulf of Tonkin in the north and the Mekong delta in the south.

Vietnam has a tropical climate, though the driest months of January to March are a little cooler than the wet, hot summer months, when monsoon winds blow from the southwest. Typhoons (cyclones or hurricanes) sometimes hit the coast, causing extensive flooding and much damage.

POLITICS & ECONOMY China dominated Vietnam for a thousand years before AD 939, when a Vietnamese state was founded. The French took over the area between the 1850s and 1880s, and they ruled Vietnam as part of French Indochina, which also included Cambodia and Laos.

Japan conquered Vietnam during World War II (1939–45). In 1946, war broke out between the Vietminh, a nationalist group, and the French colonial government. France withdrew in 1954 and Vietnam was divided into a Communist North Vietnam, led by the Vietminh leader, Ho Chi Minh, and a non-Communist South.

In 1957, a Communist insurgency, led by the Viet Cong, rebeled against South Vietnam's government provoking a war that gradually escalated. The United States aided the South, but after it withdrew in 1975, South Vietnam surrendered. In 1976, the united Vietnam became a socialist republic. From the mid-1990s, diplomatic and trade relations were restored between the US and Vietnam, and the US is now its main trading partner. In 2007, Vietnam became a member of the World Trade Organization after 12 years of negotiations. The benefits of moves to modernize the economy have not been enjoyed by all groups in society: there is poverty in rural areas. Human rights issues remain a concern. Political power remains entirely in the hands of the ruling Communist Party.

Agriculture remains the main activity although its share of economic output is diminishing. Rice is the main crop and coffee is important. Vietnam produces chromium, tin, and phosphates.

AREA 128,065 sq mi [331,689 sq km]
POPULATION 95,261,000 **CAPITAL** Hanoi
GOVERNMENT Socialist republic
ETHNIC GROUPS Vietnamese 87%, Chinese, Hmong, Thai, Khmer, Cham, mountain groups **LANGUAGES** Vietnamese (official), English, Chinese **RELIGIONS** Buddhism, Christianity, indigenous beliefs
CURRENCY Dong = 10 hao = 100 xu

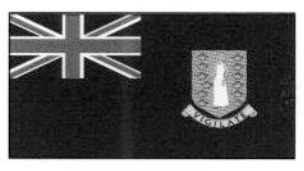

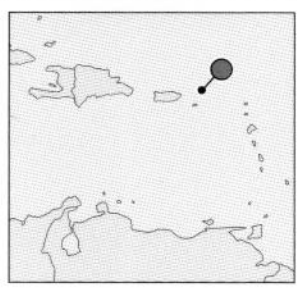

VIRGIN ISLANDS, BRITISH

The British Virgin Islands, the most northerly of the Lesser Antilles, are a British overseas territory, with a substantial measure of self-government.

AREA 58 sq mi [151 sq km]
POPULATION 28,000 **CAPITAL** Road Town

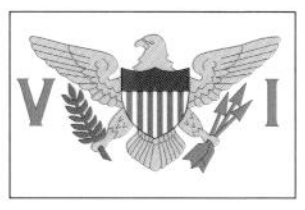

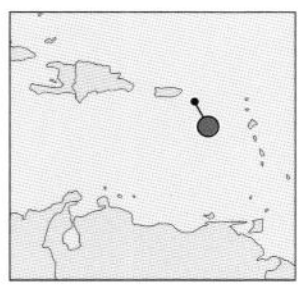

VIRGIN ISLANDS, US

The Virgin Islands of the United States, a group of three islands and 65 small islets, are a self-governing US territory, which was purchased from Denmark in 1917. Its residents are US citizens and they elect a non-voting delegate to the US House of Representatives.

AREA 134 sq mi [347 sq km]
POPULATION 103,000 **CAPITAL** Charlotte Amalie

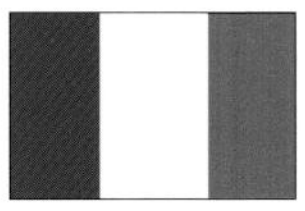

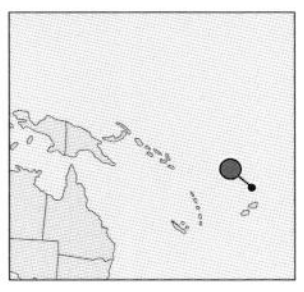

WALLIS AND FUTUNA

Wallis and Futuna, in the south Pacific Ocean, is the smallest and the poorest of France's overseas "collectivities." French aid is vital to an economy based on subsistence agriculture.

AREA 77 sq mi [200 sq km]
POPULATION 16,000 **CAPITAL** Mata-Utu

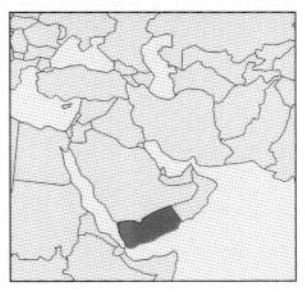

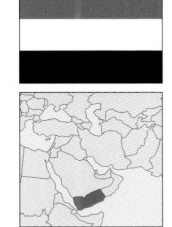

YEMEN

GEOGRAPHY The Republic of Yemen faces the Red Sea and the Gulf of Aden in the southwestern corner of the Arabian peninsula. Behind the narrow coastal plain along the Red Sea, the land rises to the mountains of the High Yemen. The climate ranges from hot and often humid conditions on the coast to the cooler highlands. Most of the country is arid. The south coasts are particularly hot and humid.

POLITICS & ECONOMY After World War I, northern Yemen, which had been ruled by Turkey, began to evolve into a separate state from the south, where Britain was in control. Britain withdrew in 1967 and a left-wing government took power in the south. In North Yemen, the monarchy was abolished in 1962 and the country became a republic.

Clashes occurred between the traditionalist Yemen Arab Republic in the north and the, formerly British, Marxist People's Democratic Republic of Yemen, but, in 1990, the two Yemens merged to form a single country. In the 2000s, the government faced conflict with Shi'ite northern rebels, called Houthis, al Qaeda supporters, and southern separatists. In 2011, protesters in the cities called on President Ali Abdullah Saleh to resign. He pledged not to run at the next election and to introduce constitutional reforms, including the introduction of a parliamentary system, but the violent protests continued. Rebel activity in the north turned into civil war in 2014, with the Houthi occupying Sana' in 2014, and declaring a new government. A Saudi-led coalition is combating the Houthi, while US drone strikes target IS and al-Qaeda bases. There is a growing refugee crisis.

Yemen is the poorest country in the Middle East. Sheep are reared and crops such as barley, fruits, wheat, and vegetables are grown. Cash crops include coffee and cotton. Since the 1980s, petroleum extraction has been important to the economy. Remittances from Yemenis abroad are a major source of revenue.

AREA 203,848 sq mi [527,968 sq km] **POPULATION** 27,393,000
CAPITAL Sana' **GOVERNMENT** Multiparty republic
ETHNIC GROUPS Predominantly Arab **LANGUAGES** Arabic (official)
RELIGIONS Islam **CURRENCY** Yemeni rial = 100 fils

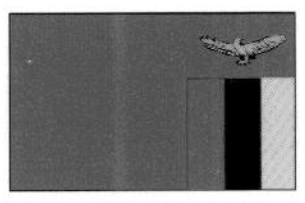

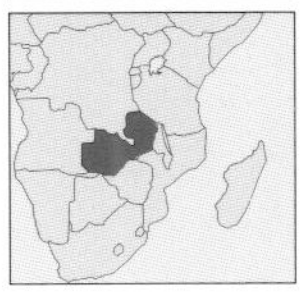

ZAMBIA

GEOGRAPHY The Republic of Zambia is a landlocked country in southern Africa. Zambia lies on the plateau that makes up most of the southern part of the continent. Much of the land is between 2,950 ft and 4,920 ft [900 m to 1,500 m] above sea level. The Muchinga Mountains in the northeast rise above this flat land. Lakes include Bangweulu, which is entirely within Zambia, together with parts of lakes Mweru and Tanganyika in the north. Zambia lies in the tropics, but temperatures are moderated by the altitude.

POLITICS & ECONOMY European contact with Zambia began in the 19th century, when the explorer David Livingstone crossed the River Zambezi. In the 1890s, the British South Africa Company, set up by Cecil Rhodes (1853–1902), the British financier and statesman, made treaties with local chiefs and gradually took over the area. In 1911, the Company named the area Northern Rhodesia and, in 1924, Britain took control of the country.

In 1953, Britain formed a federation of Northern Rhodesia, Southern Rhodesia (now Zimbabwe), and Nyasaland (now Malawi). Due to African opposition, the federation was dissolved in 1963 and Northern Rhodesia gained independence as Zambia in 1964. Kenneth Kaunda became president and one-party rule was introduced in 1972. Kaunda remained in office for 27 years until, under a new constitution, Frederick Chiluba was elected in 1996. The current president, Edgar Lungu, took office in 2015.

At 7% per annum, Zambia's economy has been growing strongly in recent years. Copper, the main resource, accounts for about 64% of the country's exports. Zambia also produces cobalt, lead, zinc, and gemstones. Agriculture employs about 85% of the people, as compared with around 6% in industry and mining. Food crops include cassava, fruits and vegetables, maize, millet, and sorghum. Cash crops include coffee, sugarcane, and tobacco.

AREA 290,586 sq mi [752,618 sq km] **POPULATION** 15,511,000
CAPITAL Lusaka **GOVERNMENT** Multiparty republic
ETHNIC GROUPS Native African (Bemba, Tonga, Maravi/Nyanja)
LANGUAGES English, Bemba, Kaonda, Nyanja and about 70 others
RELIGIONS Christianity 62%, Islam, Hinduism
CURRENCY Zambian kwacha = 100 ngwee

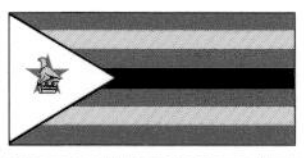

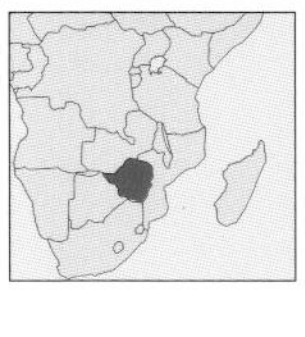

ZIMBABWE

GEOGRAPHY The Republic of Zimbabwe is a landlocked country in southern Africa. Most of the country lies on a high plateau between the Zambezi and Limpopo rivers, ranging from 2,950 ft to 4,920 ft [900 m to 1,500 m] above sea level. From October to March, the weather is hot and wet, but in the winter, daily temperatures can vary greatly.

POLITICS & ECONOMY The Shona people became dominant in the region about 1,000 years ago. The British South Africa Company, under the statesman Cecil Rhodes (1853–1902), occupied the area in the 1890s, after obtaining mineral rights from local chiefs. The area was named Rhodesia, and later Southern Rhodesia, becoming a self-governing British colony in 1923. Between 1953 and 1963, Southern and Northern Rhodesia (now Zambia) were united with Nyasaland (Malawi) in the Central African Federation.

In 1965, the European government of Southern Rhodesia (then called Rhodesia) declared their country independent, but Britain refused to accept this. Finally, after a civil war, the country became legally independent in 1980, though rivalries between the Shona and Ndebele people threatened stability. Order was restored when the Shona prime minister, Robert Mugabe, brought his Ndebele rivals into his government. In 1987, Mugabe became the country's executive president, and, in 1991, the government renounced its Marxist ideology.

From the late 1990s, Mugabe's government seized white-owned farms and landless "war veterans" began to occupy them. In elections in 2008, Mugabe's party was defeated and Mugabe lost to Morgan Tsvangirai in the presidential election. However, the intimidation of opposition supporters led Tsvangirai to withdraw from a run-off. In September 2008, a power-sharing government was set up, with Mugabe as president and Tsvangirai as prime minister, but relations between them proved difficult. The election in 2013 saw Mugabe returned as president for the seventh time. He has been picked as the ruling party's candidate for the 2018 elections.

In the 2000s, the economy collapsed. Hyperinflation occurred and many people starved, while the breakdown of public services led to a cholera epidemic. The economy now appears to be stabilizing. Zimbabwe has valuable mineral reserves and minerals are important exports. Agriculture employs 66% of the work force. Maize is the main food crop. Cash crops include cotton, sugar, and tobacco. Cattle ranching is also important.

AREA 150,871 sq mi [390,757 sq km] **POPULATION** 14,547,000
CAPITAL Harare **GOVERNMENT** Multiparty republic
ETHNIC GROUPS Shona 82%, Ndebele 14%, other African groups 2%, mixed and Asian 1% **LANGUAGES** English (official), Shona, Ndebele
RELIGIONS Christianity, traditional beliefs
CURRENCY Multiple currencies

Curved like a scimitar, the isolated island of South Georgia lies at the very ends of the Earth in the Scotia Sea in the South Atlantic Ocean. This mountainous and barren island is 100 miles (160 km) long and 20 miles (32 km) wide. Along with the South Sandwich Islands, the island is administered as a British Overseas Territory. The unforgiving, bleak Antarctic climate leaves it snow covered for most of the year. Until the 1960s, it was a base for the whaling industry and, along with whaling stations, there was a small settlement at Grytviken on the north side of the island. There is no permanent population, but a few scientists, and those catering for visitors, live there for part of the year. Sir Ernest Shackleton, the explorer, is buried there.

[Map page 151] *USGS / NPA Satellite Mapping, CGG Services (UK) Ltd*

WORLD
GEOGRAPHY

For more information:
70 Orbits of the planets
Planetary data

About 13.8 billion years ago, time and space began with the most colossal explosion in cosmic history: the so-called Big Bang that is believed to have initiated the Universe. According to current theory, in the first millionth of a second of its existence it expanded from a dimensionless point of infinite mass and density into a fireball about the size of our present Solar System – and it has been expanding ever since.

It took about 300,000 years for the primal fireball to cool enough for atoms to form. They were mostly hydrogen which is still the most abundant material in the Universe. The radiation from this era still pervades the Universe, though its subsequent expansion means that we see it at about 3° above absolute zero instead of its original 3,000°C. Observations of this faint background glow reveal slight fluctuations. It is these which appear to have become, over the next billion years or so, the large-scale structures in the present Universe. As well as the matter which we can see, there is evidence of a much greater quantity of dark matter whose nature remains unknown. Within knots of this dark matter, the first stars and galaxies formed, probably within the first billion years of the life of the Universe. Our own Galaxy was among them.

There were several generations of stars, each feeding on the wreckage of its extinct predecessors as well as the original galactic gas swirls. With each new generation, progressively larger atoms were forged in stellar furnaces, and the Galaxy's range of elements, once restricted to hydrogen and helium, grew larger. About 9 billion years after the Big Bang, a star formed on the outskirts of our Galaxy with enough matter left over to create a retinue of planets. Nearly 5 billion years after that, human beings evolved.

The Sun is one of more than 100 billion stars in the home galaxy alone. Our Galaxy, in turn, forms part of a local group consisting of approximately 50 similar structures, mostly small "dwarf" galaxies but a few large ones, and one – the Andromeda Galaxy – larger than our own. There are at least 100 billion galaxies in the Universe, many of which are members of huge galaxy clusters.

LIFE OF A STAR

For most of its existence, a star produces energy by the nuclear fusion of hydrogen into helium at its core. The duration of this hydrogen-burning period – known as the *main sequence* – depends on the star's mass; the greater the mass, the higher the core temperatures and the sooner the star's supply of hydrogen is exhausted. Dim, dwarf stars consume their hydrogen slowly, eking it out over billions of years. The Sun, like other stars of its mass, should spend about 10 billion years on the main sequence; since it was formed less than 5 billion years ago, it still has half its life left.

Once all of a star's core hydrogen has been fused into helium, nuclear activity moves outward into layers of unconsumed hydrogen. For a time, energy production increases sharply: the star grows hotter and expands enormously, turning into a so-called red giant. Its energy output will increase a thousandfold, and it will swell to a hundred times its former diameter.

After a few hundred million years, helium in the core will become sufficiently compressed to initiate a new cycle of nuclear fusion: from helium to carbon. The star will contract somewhat, before beginning its last expansion, in the Sun's case engulfing the Earth and perhaps Mars. In this bloated condition, the Sun's outer layers will break off into space, leaving a tiny inner core, mainly of carbon, that shrinks progressively under its own gravity. The white dwarf star thus formed can attain a density more than 10,000 times that of normal matter, with crushing surface gravity to match. Gradually, the nuclear fires will die down, and the Sun will reach its terminal stage: a black dwarf, emitting insignificant amounts of energy.

Black holes

However, stars more massive than the Sun may undergo a different transformation. The additional mass allows gravitational collapse to continue indefinitely: eventually, all the star's remaining matter shrinks to a point, and its density approaches infinity – a state that will not permit even subatomic structures to survive.

The star has become a *black hole*: an anomalous "singularity" in the fabric of space and time. Although vast coruscations of radiation will be emitted by any matter falling into its grasp, the singularity itself has an escape velocity that exceeds the speed of light, and nothing can ever be released from it. Within the boundaries of the black hole, the laws of physics are suspended.

GALACTIC STRUCTURES

Many of the Universe's 100 billion galaxies show clear structural patterns, originally classified by the American astronomer Edwin Hubble in 1925. Spiral galaxies like our own have a central, almost spherical bulge and a surrounding disk composed of spiral arms. Barred spirals have a central bar of stars across the nucleus, with spiral arms trailing from the ends of the bar. Elliptical galaxies have a more uniform appearance, ranging from a flattened disk to a near sphere.

▲ M51, the Whirlpool Nebula, comprises the large spiral galaxy NGC 5194 and its smaller, barred companion NGC 5195. M51 was the first astronomical object in which a spiral structure was identified, in 1845. Although smaller and less massive than our own Galaxy, M51 is much brighter, due to recent star formation.

Most galaxies, however, have no obvious structure at all. Galaxies also vary enormously in size, from dwarf galaxies only 2,000 light-years across to great assemblies of stars 80 or more times larger.

THE HOME GALAXY

The Sun and its planets are located in one of the spiral arms of the Galaxy, about 26,000 light-years from the galactic center and orbiting around it in a period of about 220 million years. The center is invisible from the Earth, masked by vast, light-absorbing clouds of interstellar dust.

The Galaxy is probably around 12 billion years old and, like other spiral galaxies, has three distinct regions. The central bulge is about 30,000 light-years in diameter. The disk in which the Sun is located is not much more than 1,000 light-years thick, but approximately 100,000 light-years from end to end. Around the Galaxy is the halo, a spherical zone 300,000 light-years across, studded with globular star clusters and sprinkled with individual suns.

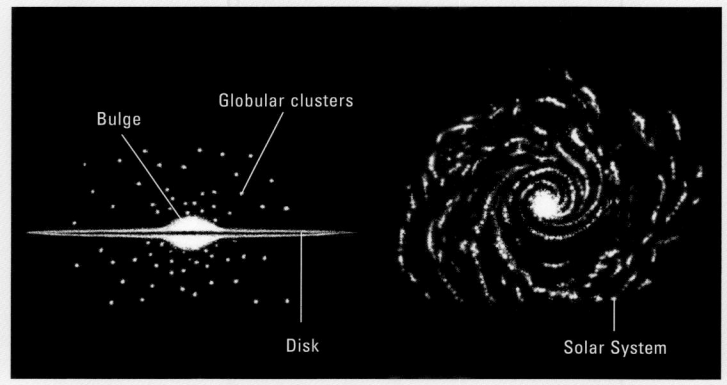

Bulge
Globular clusters
Disk
Solar System

THE END OF THE UNIVERSE

The likely fate of the Universe is disputed. According to one theory (*top of diagram, below*), the expansion begun at the time of the Big Bang will continue "indefinitely," with aging galaxies moving further and further apart in an immense, dark graveyard.

Alternatively, gravity may overcome the expansion (*bottom of diagram*). Galaxies will fall back together until everything is again concentrated at a single point, followed by a new Big Bang and a new expansion, in an endlessly repeated cycle.

Observations of distant galaxies suggest that the expansion of the Universe is accelerating. This is attributed to a hypothetical dark energy filling the Universe, so continued expansion is considered likely.

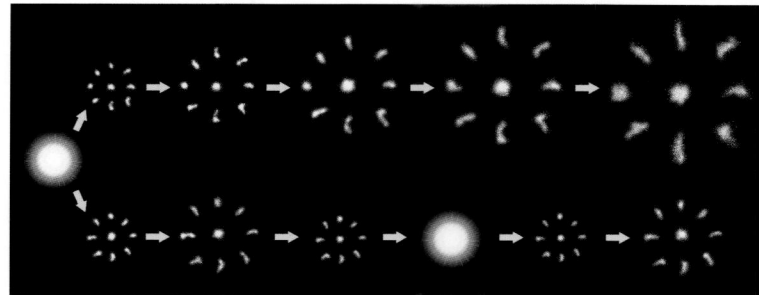

THE NEAREST STARS

The nearest stars, excluding the Sun, with their distance from Earth in light-years*

Proxima Centauri	4.2	UV Ceti A & B	8.7	61 Cygni A & B	11.4
Alpha Centauri A & B	4.4	Ross 154	9.7	Procyon A & B	11.4
Barnard's Star	6.0	Ross 248	10.3	Struve 2398 A & B	11.5
Luhman 16 A & B	6.6	Epsilon Eridani	10.5	Groombridge 34 A & B	11.6
WISE 0855-0714	7.2	HD 217987	10.7	Epsilon Indi A & B	11.8
Wolf 359	7.8	Ross 128	10.9	DX Cancri	11.8
Lalande 21185	8.3	WISE 1506+7027	11.1	* A light-year is about 5,900	
Sirius A & B	8.6	L789-6 A, B & C	11.3	billion miles [9,500 billion km]	

Many of the nearest stars, like Alpha Centauri A and B, are double stars, orbiting about their common center of gravity and to all intents and purposes equidistant from Earth. Many of them are dim objects including brown dwarfs: self-luminous objects which are intermediate in mass between planets and stars.

However, they include Sirius, the brightest star in the sky, and Procyon, the seventh brightest. Both are larger than the Sun; of the nearest stars, only Epsilon Eridani is similar in size and luminosity. Most of the other bright stars in the sky are within 500 light-years of the Sun – a small fraction of the diameter of our Galaxy.

STAR CHARTS

NORTHERN HEMISPHERE SKY

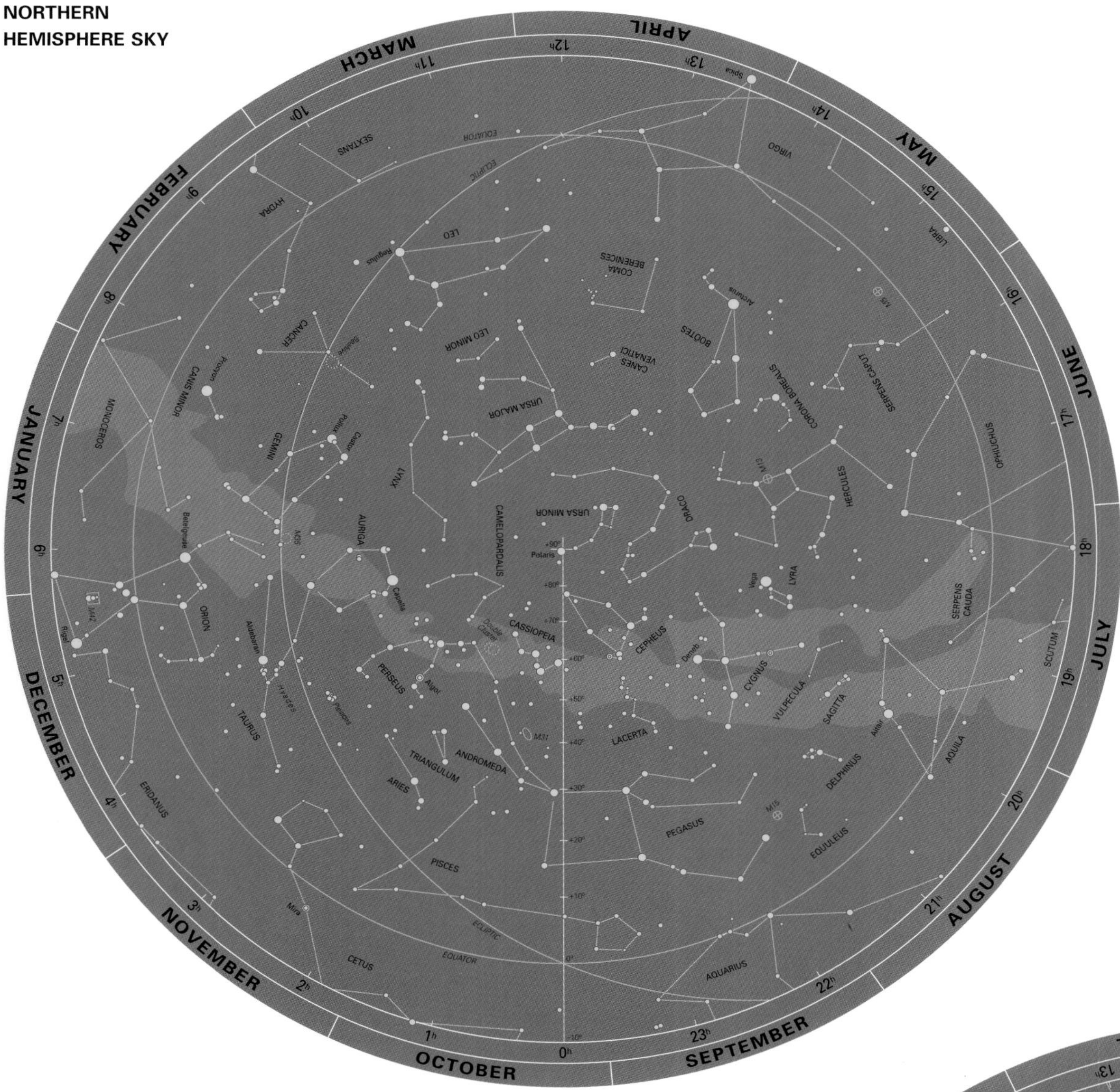

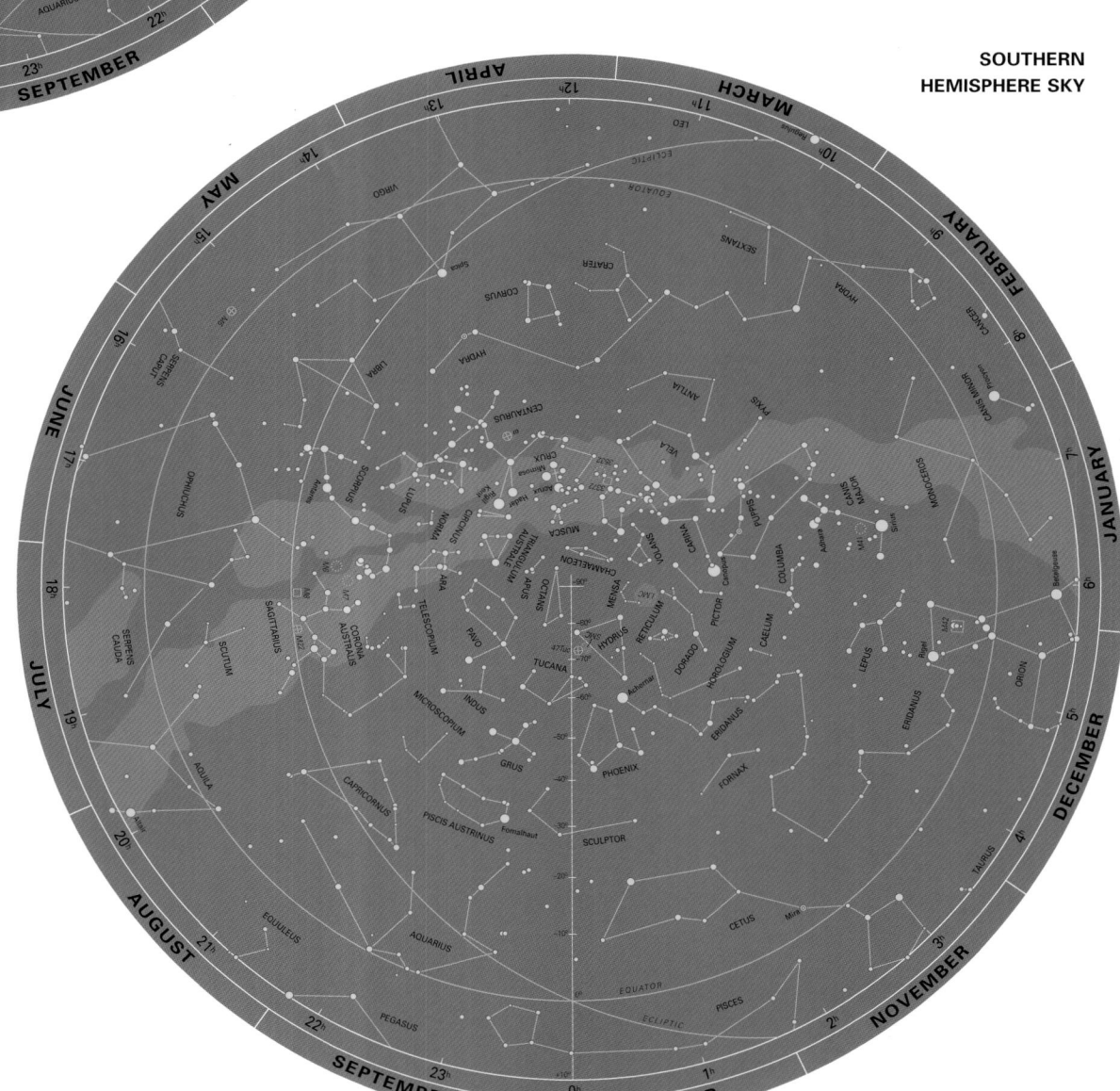

THE CONSTELLATIONS
The constellations and their English names

Andromeda	Andromeda	Lacerta	Lizard
Antlia	Air Pump	Leo	Lion
Apus	Bird of Paradise	Leo Minor	Little Lion
Aquarius	Water Carrier	Lepus	Hare
Aquila	Eagle	Libra	Scales
Ara	Altar	Lupus	Wolf
Aries	Ram	Lynx	Lynx
Auriga	Charioteer	Lyra	Lyre
Boötes	Herdsman	Mensa	Table Mountain
Caelum	Chisel	Microscopium	Microscope
Camelopardalis	Giraffe	Monoceros	Unicorn
Cancer	Crab	Musca	Fly
Canes Venatici	Hunting Dogs	Norma	Level
Canis Major	Great Dog	Octans	Octant
Canis Minor	Little Dog	Ophiuchus	Serpent Bearer
Capricornus	Sea Goat	Orion	Orion
Carina	Ship's Keel	Pavo	Peacock
Cassiopeia	Cassiopeia	Pegasus	Winged Horse
Centaurus	Centaur	Perseus	Perseus
Cepheus	Cepheus	Phoenix	Phoenix
Cetus	Whale	Pictor	Easel
Chamaeleon	Chameleon	Pisces	Fishes
Circinus	Compasses	Piscis Austrinus	Southern Fish
Columba	Dove	Puppis	Ship's Stern
Coma Berenices	Berenice's Hair	Pyxis	Mariner's Compass
Corona Australis	Southern Crown	Reticulum	Net
Corona Borealis	Northern Crown	Sagitta	Arrow
Corvus	Crow	Sagittarius	Archer
Crater	Cup	Scorpius	Scorpion
Crux	Southern Cross	Sculptor	Sculptor
Cygnus	Swan	Scutum	Shield
Delphinus	Dolphin	Serpens	Serpent
Dorado	Swordfish	Sextans	Sextant
Draco	Dragon	Taurus	Bull
Equuleus	Little Horse	Telescopium	Telescope
Eridanus	River Eridanus	Triangulum	Triangle
Fornax	Furnace	Triangulum Australe	Southern Triangle
Gemini	Twins	Tucana	Toucan
Grus	Crane	Ursa Major	Great Bear
Hercules	Hercules	Ursa Minor	Little Bear
Horologium	Clock	Vela	Ship's Sails
Hydra	Water Snake	Virgo	Virgin
Hydrus	Sea Serpent	Volans	Flying Fish
Indus	Indian	Vulpecula	Fox

The charts on this page show the entire heavens divided into northern and southern hemispheres, with 10° of overlap between them around the perimeter of each one. However, the view from any particular location on Earth will be different, and will change both hourly as the Earth turns, and throughout the year as the Earth goes around the Sun.

The Sun's annual path through the heavens is known as the "ecliptic," and is shown here by an orange line. When the Sun is in the sky its light drowns out our view of the stars, so only that part of the heavens opposite the Sun is visible at a particular time. The sky's equivalent of longitude is known as "right ascension." As the stars appear to rotate around the Earth once every 24 hours, right ascension is measured eastward in hours and minutes, and is marked around the edge of the maps. The equivalent of latitude is "declination," measured in degrees north or south of the celestial equator, and shown by the vertical line on each chart.

Using the charts

At any place and time you can see half of the whole sky, assuming a flat horizon. If you were at one of the poles your view would be shown as a circle centered on the middle of the map for the appropriate hemisphere, with the horizon marked by the celestial equator. From all other locations the center of your view (your overhead point) will be at some other point on the map whose location changes with time. The closer you are to Earth's equator, the closer the center will be to the edge of the map and more stars in the opposite hemisphere will be visible.

So first choose the appropriate chart for your hemisphere and hold it with the month at the bottom. At 11 p.m., not allowing for Daylight Saving Time (Summer Time), your overhead point will be at the same declination as your geographical latitude and stars lower on the map will be due south (or north in the southern hemisphere). From latitude 50° in mid August, for example, your overhead point will be close to the star Deneb in the constellation of Cygnus. Stars on the opposite side of the map will be below your northern horizon, while stars below Deneb will be due south.

SOUTHERN HEMISPHERE SKY

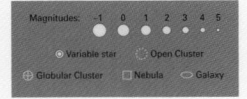

STAR MAGNITUDES
Apparent visual magnitudes

The magnitude scale of star brightnesses is developed from the system used by the Ancient Greeks in which the brightest stars were first magnitude and the faintest visible to the naked eye were sixth. Today the scale has a mathematical basis and extends, at the brightest end, through to negative magnitudes.

The Milky Way is shown in light blue on these charts.

Magnitudes: -1 0 1 2 3 4 5
- Variable star
- Open Cluster
- Globular Cluster
- Nebula
- Galaxy

For more information:
68 The Home Galaxy
72 The seasons
    Day and night
73 The Moon

Lying about halfway from the center of one of billions of galaxies that populate the observable Universe, our Solar System contains eight planets and their moons, at least five dwarf planets, innumerable asteroids, comets and other icy bodies, and a miscellany of dust and gas, all tethered by the immense gravitational field of the Sun, the star whose thermonuclear furnaces provide them all with heat and light.

The Solar System was formed about 5 billion years ago, when a spinning cloud of gas, mostly hydrogen but seeded with other heavier elements, condensed enough to ignite a nuclear reaction and create a star. The Sun still accounts for almost 99.9% of the system's total mass.

By composition as well as distance, the planetary array divides quite neatly in two: an inner system of four small, solid planets, including the Earth, and an outer system, from Jupiter to Neptune, of four much larger planets composed of lighter materials, such as gas, liquid, and ice. Lying mostly between the two groups is a scattering of rocky asteroids, numbering perhaps a million or more. They may be debris left over from the formation of the inner Solar System. In 2006, Pluto was demoted from its former status as a planet and is now regarded as a member of the Kuiper Belt of icy bodies at the fringes of the Solar System.

Much of the early history of science is the story of people trying to make sense of the wandering points of light that were all they knew of the planets. Now, men have stood on the Earth's Moon, space probes have landed on several bodies, and distant landscapes have been mapped with astonishing accuracy, transforming our knowledge of our celestial environment.

In the 1980s, the Voyager space probes skimmed all four major planets of the outer Solar System, bringing new revelations with each close approach. The Magellan (Venus), Galileo (Jupiter) and Cassini–Huygens (Saturn) missions have transformed our knowledge of those planets and the giants' moons, and a host of orbiters and landers have shown us Mars in a new light. A spacecraft also reached Pluto in 2015.

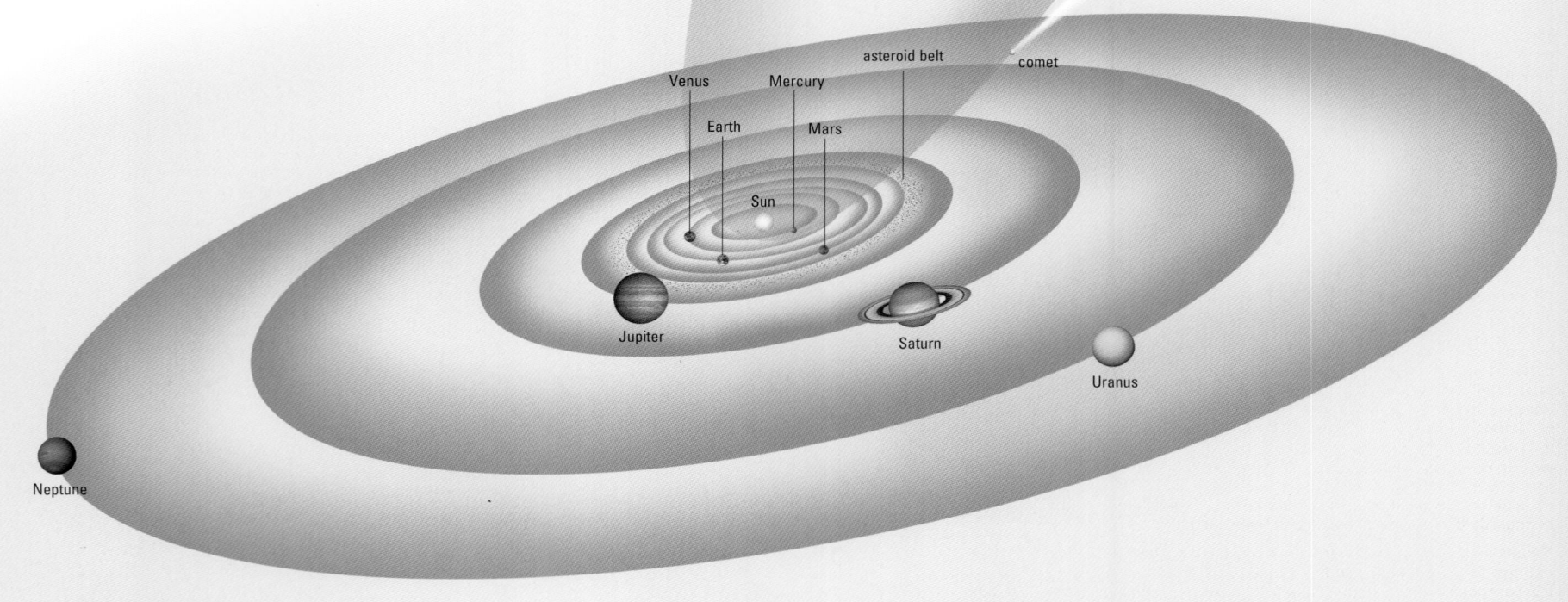

Diagram not drawn to scale

ORBITS OF THE PLANETS

The diagram above shows the Solar System as it might appear to an observer a few light-hours away in the direction of the constellation Hercules. Seen from such a position, above the plane of the ecliptic, all the planets revolve about the Sun in a counterclockwise direction. The perspective view exaggerates the elliptical form of all the planetary orbits: only Mercury follows a path that deviates noticeably from circularity.

The diagram also portrays the main asteroid belt between Mars and Jupiter, and the orbit of a comet. Comets reside in a vast spherical halo beyond the Solar System, and are occasionally diverted toward the Sun on highly elliptical orbits which may take many thousands of years to complete. Most, therefore, still await discovery, though there are a number of shorter-period comets which return regularly, such as Halley's Comet.

PLANETARY DATA

	Mean distance from Sun (million miles)	Mass (Earth = 1)	Period of orbit (Earth days/years)	Period of rotation (Earth days)	Equatorial diameter (miles)	Average density (water = 1)	Surface gravity (Earth = 1)	Number of known satellites*
Sun	–	332,946	–	25.38	865,000	1.41	27.9	–
Mercury	36.0	0.06	87.97d	58.65	3,032	5.43	0.38	0
Venus	67.2	0.82	224.7d	243.02	7,521	5.24	0.91	0
Earth	93.0	1.00	365.3d	1.00	7,926	5.51	1.00	1
Mars	141.6	0.11	687.0d	1.029	4,220	3.94	0.38	2
Jupiter	484.0	317.8	11.86y	0.411	88,848	1.33	2.36	67
Saturn	891.0	95.2	29.45y	0.428	74,900	0.69	0.91	62
Uranus	1,785.2	14.5	84.02y	0.720	31,764	1.27	0.89	27
Neptune	2,793.1	17.2	164.8y	0.673	30,776	1.64	1.13	14

Planetary days are given in sidereal days – that is, with respect to the stars rather than the Sun. The difference is caused by the movement of the planet in its orbit, so the interval between successive noons is slightly different from that between the rising of a particular star. The Earth's own sidereal day is 23h 56m in solar time. The equatorial diameters of most planets differ from their polar diameters as a consequence of their rotation, which is most marked in the case of Jupiter and Saturn, which are very noticeably flattened at the poles. Strictly speaking, the figures for surface gravity apply to the four inner planets only, as the outer planets have no solid surfaces. In their case, the figure is given for an arbitrary point in the atmosphere where the pressure is 1 bar.

* Number of known satellites at mid-2017

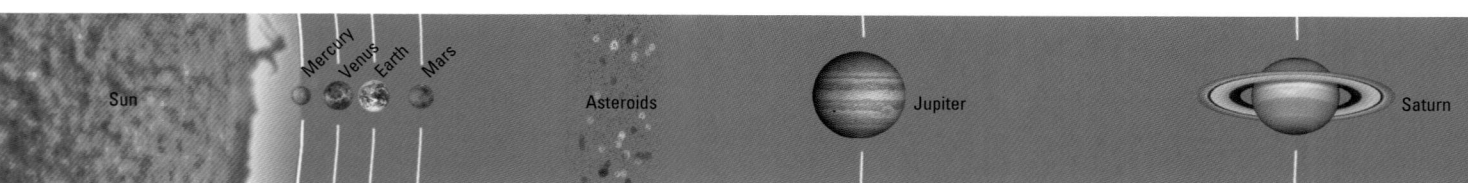

THE PLANETS

Mercury is the closest planet to the Sun and hence the fastest-moving. It is very hot, with a cratered, wrinkled surface very similar to that of Earth's Moon. It is small and has low gravity, so there is no significant atmosphere.

Venus has much the same physical dimensions as Earth. Its dense atmosphere is composed of 97% carbon dioxide resulting in a runaway greenhouse effect that makes the surface, at 890°F, the hottest of all the planets in the Solar System. Radar mapping revealed a terrain consisting of highland regions and vast, rolling plains crossed by volcanic flows and dotted with craters. Discharges from volcanic regions could explain the sulfuric-acid rain detected by spacecraft. Soft-landers last less than an hour in Venus's fierce climate.

Earth seen from space is easily the most beautiful of the inner planets; it is also, and more objectively, the largest, as well as the only known home of life. Living things are the main reason why the Earth is able to retain a substantial proportion of reactive oxygen in its atmosphere; the oxygen in turn supports the life that constantly regenerates it. The Earth's natural satellite, the Moon, is believed to have been created when an asteroid struck our planet in its infancy.

Mars, smaller and cooler than the Earth, is nevertheless the most likely planet other than Earth where life may have formed. The planet was, at some stage in the distant past, a geologically active world with water on its surface: rivers, lakes, and even an ocean. Liquid water may well exist today, but trapped beneath its dusty, boulder-strewn surface. The Martian landscape features huge extinct volcanoes, a giant canyon system, craters, and sand dunes. Its thin atmosphere is mostly carbon dioxide, and its polar caps are of frozen carbon dioxide and water ice. It has two tiny moons, probably captured asteroids.

Jupiter has about three times the mass of all the other planets combined. The planet is mostly gas, under intense pressure in the lower atmosphere above a core of fiercely compressed hydrogen and helium. The upper layers form strikingly colored rotating belts, the outward sign of the intense storms created by Jupiter's rapid rotation. The Great Red Spot is a storm feature that has persisted for at least 130 years. Jupiter has at least 67 moons. Most are very small, but the four largest – Io, Europa, Ganymede, and Callisto – are fascinating worlds in their own right. Io is the most volcanically active world known, and Europa possesses an ocean deep below its icy surface. The planet also has a system of rings, though nowhere near as prominent as Saturn's.

Saturn is structurally similar to Jupiter, rotating fast enough to produce an obvious bulge at its equator. It is composed of 89% hydrogen and 11% helium, and has wind velocities in the outer atmosphere of 1,600 ft/sec. Ever since the invention of the telescope, Saturn's rings have been the feature that has most attracted observers. The rings consist of thousands of individual ringlets, composed of icy particles ranging in size from 30 feet down to microscopic. Titan, the largest of Saturn's 62 known moons, has a dense atmosphere.

Uranus was unknown to the ancients. Although it is faintly visible to the naked eye, it was not established as a planet until 1781. In its interior is probably a rocky core surrounded by frozen methane, water, and ammonia; the atmosphere is of hydrogen, helium, and some methane, which gives the planet its greenish-blue color. There is a system of thin, dark rings and a retinue of 27 moons, all but five of which are small.

Neptune is always more than 2.5 billion miles from Earth, and despite its diameter of over 31,000 miles, it can only be seen by telescope. Its discovery in 1846 was the result of mathematical predictions by astronomers seeking to explain irregularities in the orbit of Uranus. Like Uranus, it has a ring system; recent observations have revealed a total of 14 moons.

In 2006, following an increasing number of discoveries of objects orbiting the Sun of similar size to Pluto but at a greater distance, the International Astronomical Union issued for the first time a definition of a planet. A planet is defined as "a body orbiting the Sun, which is essentially round as a consequence of its gravity, and which does not share its orbital neighborhood with similar bodies." On this definition, Pluto is no longer classified as a planet, but is instead a member of a new category of "dwarf planet," which relaxes the last criterion but excludes bodies in orbit around another one.

Mean distance from the
Sun in millions of miles

Mercury — 36.0 Mercury

Venus — 67.2 Venus

Earth — 93.0 Earth

Mars — 141.6 Mars

Jupiter — 483.7 Jupiter

Saturn — 886.6 Saturn

Uranus — 1,784.0 Uranus

Neptune — 2,795.2 Neptune

Diagrams not drawn to scale

Uranus   Neptune

For more information:

70 Orbits of the planets

76 Circulation of the air

78 Climate

84 Ocean currents

The basic units of time measurement are the day and the year. The day is one rotation of the Earth on its axis. Our present calendar is based on the solar year of 365.24 days, the time taken by the Earth to orbit the Sun. Calendars based on the movements of the Sun and Moon have been used since ancient times. The length of the year, reckoned by the Julian Calendar introduced by Julius Caesar, was about 11 minutes too long. The cumulative error was rectified in 1582 by the Gregorian Calendar, when Pope Gregory XIII decreed that the day following October 4 was October 15, and that century years did not count as leap years unless they were divisible by 400. England finally adopted the reformed calendar in 1752, when it was 11 days behind the European mainland.

The rotation of the Earth on its axis causes day and night. The Earth rotates through 360° every 24 hours, and the world is divided into 24 time zones centered on lines of longitude at 15° intervals.

The tilt of the Earth's axis, which is also called the "obliquity of the ecliptic," accounts for the seasons which are so familiar in the middle latitudes. However, geological evidence shows that, over long periods of time, climates change, and the advances and retreats of the ice during the Pleistocene Ice Age may have been caused by regular variations in the Earth's tilt, its orbit around the Sun, and changes in the season when it is closest to the Sun (perihelion).

THE SEASONS

Seasons occur because the Earth's axis is tilted at an angle of approximately 23½°. When the northern hemisphere is tilted to a maximum extent toward the Sun, on June 20 or 21, the Sun is overhead at the Tropic of Cancer (latitude 23½° North). This is midsummer, or the summer solstice, in the northern hemisphere.

On September 22 or 23, the Sun is overhead at the equator, and day and night are of equal length throughout the world. This is the autumnal equinox in the northern hemisphere.

On December 21 or 22, the Sun is overhead at the Tropic of Capricorn (23½° South), the winter solstice in the northern hemisphere. The overhead Sun then tracks north until, on March 20 or 21, it is overhead at the equator. This is the spring (vernal) equinox in the northern hemisphere.

In the southern hemisphere, the seasons are the reverse of those in the north.

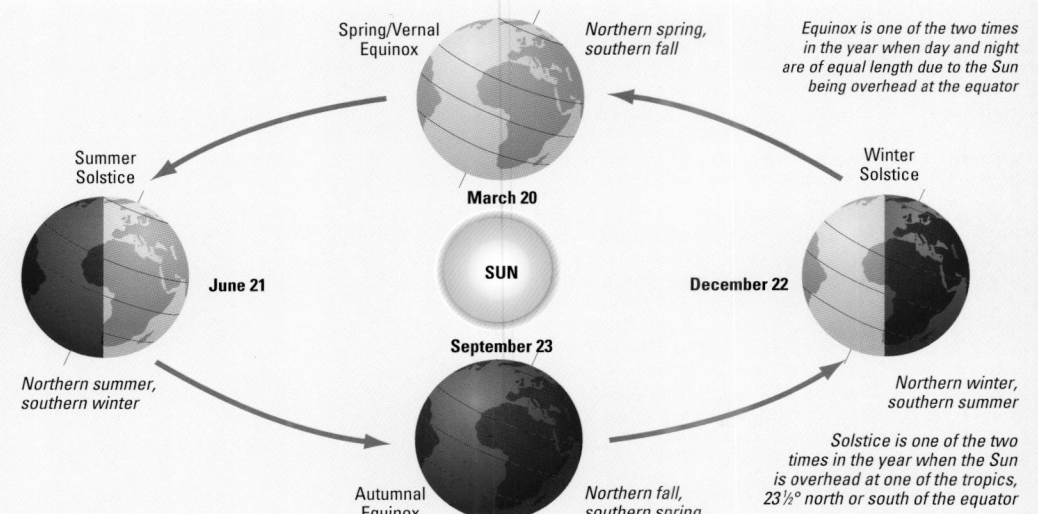

DAY AND NIGHT

The Sun appears to rise in the east, reach its highest point at noon, and then set in the west, to be followed by night. In reality, it is not the Sun that is moving but the Earth rotating from west to east. The moment when the Sun's upper limb first appears above the horizon is termed sunrise; the moment when the Sun's upper limb disappears below the horizon is sunset.

At the summer solstice in the northern hemisphere (June 21), the Arctic has total daylight and the Antarctic total darkness. The opposite occurs at the winter solstice (December 21 or 22). At the equator, the length of day and night are almost equal all year.

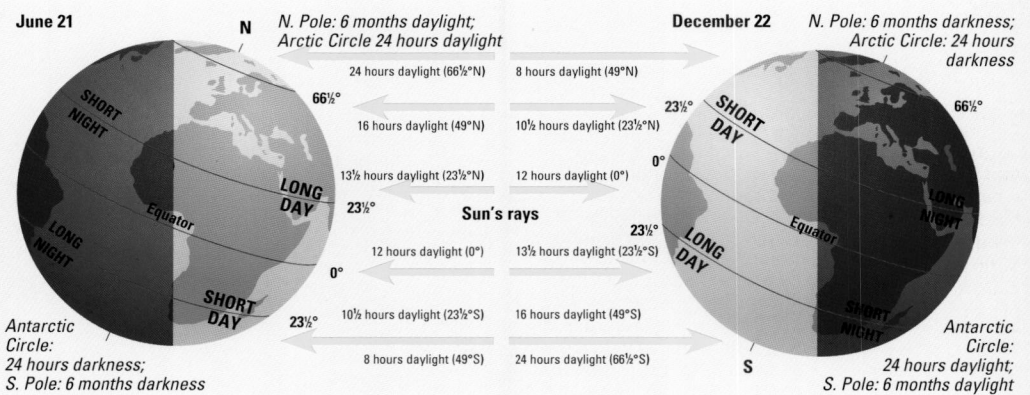

EARTH DATA

Aphelion (maximum distance from Sun):	95,000,000 miles	**Length of year:**	365 days, 5 hours, 48 minutes, 45 seconds of mean solar time	**Polar circumference:**	24,860 miles
				Equatorial diameter:	7,926 miles
Perihelion (minimum distance from Sun):	91,000,000 miles	**Superficial area:**	197,000,000 sq miles	**Polar diameter:**	7,900 miles
		Land surface:	57,500,000 sq miles (29.2%)	**Equatorial radius:**	3,963 miles
Angle of tilt (obliquity of the ecliptic):	23° 26′			**Polar radius:**	3,950 miles
Length of year – solar tropical (equinox to equinox):	365.24 days	**Water surface:**	139,500,000 sq miles (70.8%)	**Volume of the Earth:**	259,880 × 10⁶ cu miles
		Equatorial circumference:	24,901 miles	**Mass of the Earth:**	5.97 × 10²⁴ kg

SUNRISE AND SUNSET

The term "equinox" comes from the Latin for "equal night." At the spring and autumnal equinoxes, the Sun is vertically overhead at midday at the equator and all places on Earth have 12 hours of darkness and 12 hours of daylight. The graphs of sunrise and sunset show that these occasions occur on March 21 and on September 22 or 23. The graphs also show that, because the Sun remains high in the sky at the equator throughout the year, the length of day and night there remains roughly the same throughout the year, with sunrise around 6 a.m. and sunset around 6 p.m.

The further north or south one travels, the greater the difference between the number of hours of daylight and darkness. For example, the graph (*right*) shows that at latitude 60°N sunrise varies from just after 9 a.m. in midwinter (on December 22 or 23) to about 2.30 a.m. in midsummer (around the summer solstice on June 21). By contrast, the second graph (*far right*) shows that sunset at latitude 60°N occurs at about 2.45 p.m. in midwinter and 9.20 p.m. in midsummer.

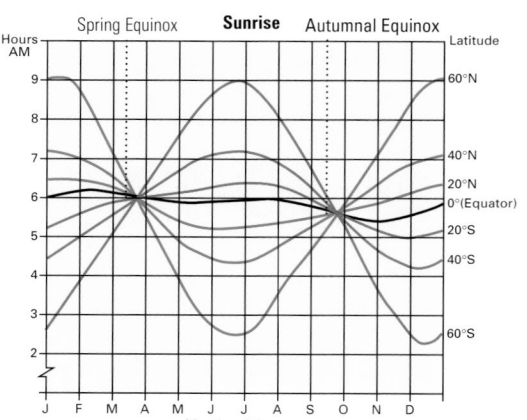

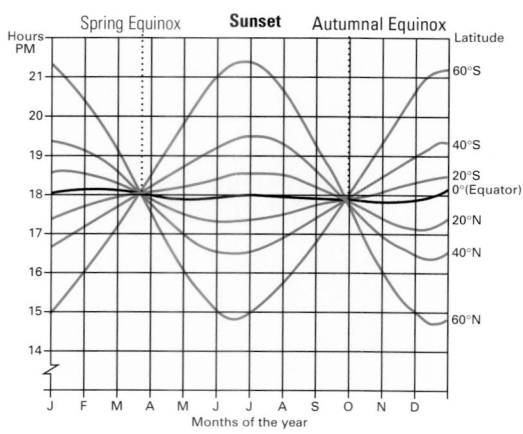

THE MOON

The Moon rotates more slowly than the Earth, taking just over 27 days to make one complete rotation on its axis. This corresponds to the Moon's orbital period around the Earth, and therefore the Moon always presents the same hemisphere toward us; some 41% of the Moon's far side is never visible from the Earth. The interval between one New Moon and the next is 29½ days – this is called a lunation, or lunar month. The Moon shines only by reflected sunlight, and emits no light of its own. During each lunation the Moon displays a complete cycle of phases, caused by the changing angle of illumination from the Sun.

PHASES OF THE MOON

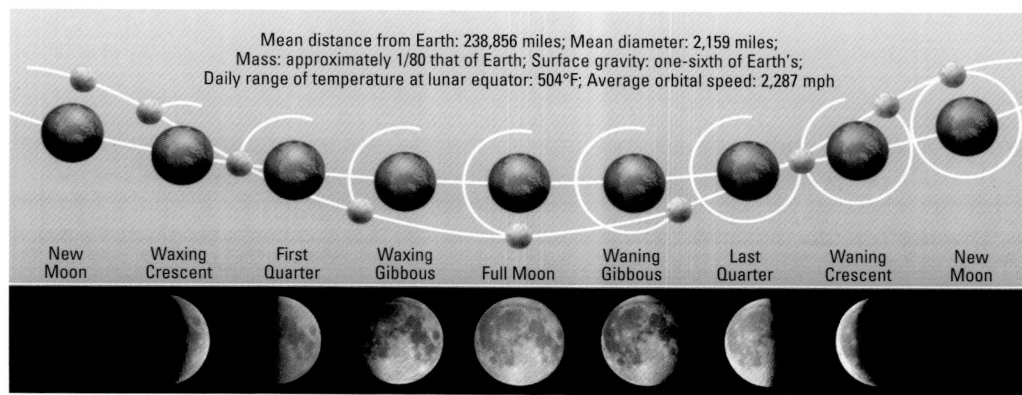

Mean distance from Earth: 238,856 miles; Mean diameter: 2,159 miles; Mass: approximately 1/80 that of Earth; Surface gravity: one-sixth of Earth's; Daily range of temperature at lunar equator: 504°F; Average orbital speed: 2,287 mph

New Moon | Waxing Crescent | First Quarter | Waxing Gibbous | Full Moon | Waning Gibbous | Last Quarter | Waning Crescent | New Moon

MOON DATA

Distance from Earth
The Moon orbits at a mean distance of 238,856 miles, at an average speed of 2,287 mph in relation to the Earth.

Size and mass
The average diameter of the Moon is 2,159 miles. It is 400 times smaller than the Sun but is about 400 times closer to the Earth, so we see them as the same size. The Moon has a mass of 7.35×10^{22} kg, with a density 3.344 times that of water.

Visibility
Only 59% of the Moon's surface is visible from the Earth over time. Sunlight reflected from the Moon takes 1.3 seconds to reach the Earth (the Sun itself is around 8½ light-minutes away).

Temperature
With the Sun overhead, the temperature on the lunar equator can reach 243°F [117°C]. At night it can sink to −261°F [−163°C].

ECLIPSES

When the Moon passes between the Sun and the Earth, the Sun becomes partially eclipsed (1). A partial eclipse becomes a total eclipse if the Moon proceeds to cover the Sun completely (2) and the dark central part of the lunar shadow touches the Earth. The broad geographical zone covered by the Moon's outer shadow (P) has only a very small central area (often less than 62 miles wide) that experiences totality. Totality can never last for more than 7½ minutes at maximum, but is usually much briefer than this. Lunar eclipses take place when the Moon moves through the shadow of the Earth, and can be partial or total. Any single location on Earth can experience a maximum of four solar and three lunar eclipses in any single year, while a total solar eclipse occurs an average of once every 360 years for any given location.

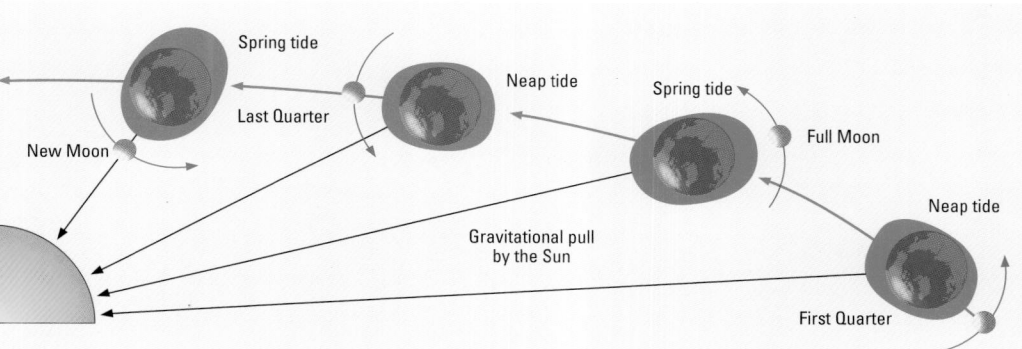

Partial eclipse (1)

P   P   P

Solar eclipse

P
P

Lunar eclipse

Total eclipse (2)

TIDES

The daily rise and fall of the ocean's tides are the result of the gravitational pull of the Moon and that of the Sun, though the effect of the latter is not as strong as that of the Moon. This effect is greatest on the hemisphere facing the Moon and causes a tidal "bulge." Spring tides occur when the Sun, Earth, and Moon are aligned; high tides are at their highest, and low tides fall to their lowest. When the Moon and Sun are farthest out of line (near the Moon's First and Last Quarters), neap tides occur, producing the smallest range between high and low tides.

Spring tide
Neap tide
Spring tide
Last Quarter
New Moon
Full Moon
Neap tide
Gravitational pull by the Sun
First Quarter

TIME ZONES

The Earth rotates through 360° in 24 hours, and so moves 15° every hour. The world is divided into 24 standard time zones, each centered on lines of longitude at 15° intervals. At the center of the first zone is the prime meridian, or Greenwich meridian. All places to the west of Greenwich are one hour behind for every 15° of longitude; places to the east are ahead by one hour for every 15°.

International Date Line
When it is 12 noon on the Greenwich meridian, 180° east it is midnight of the same day – while 180° west the day is just beginning. To overcome this, the International Date Line was established, approximately following the 180° meridian. Thus, if you were to travel eastward from Japan (140°E) to Hawai'i (160°W), you would pass from Sunday night into Sunday morning.

10   Hours behind or ahead of UT or Coordinated Universal Time

Zones using UT (GMT)

Zones behind UT (GMT)

International boundaries

Zones ahead of UT (GMT)

Half-hour zones

Time-zone boundaries

International Date Line

Actual solar time when time at Greenwich is 12:00 (noon)

Note: Some of the above time zones are affected by the incidence of Daylight Saving Time in countries where it is adopted.

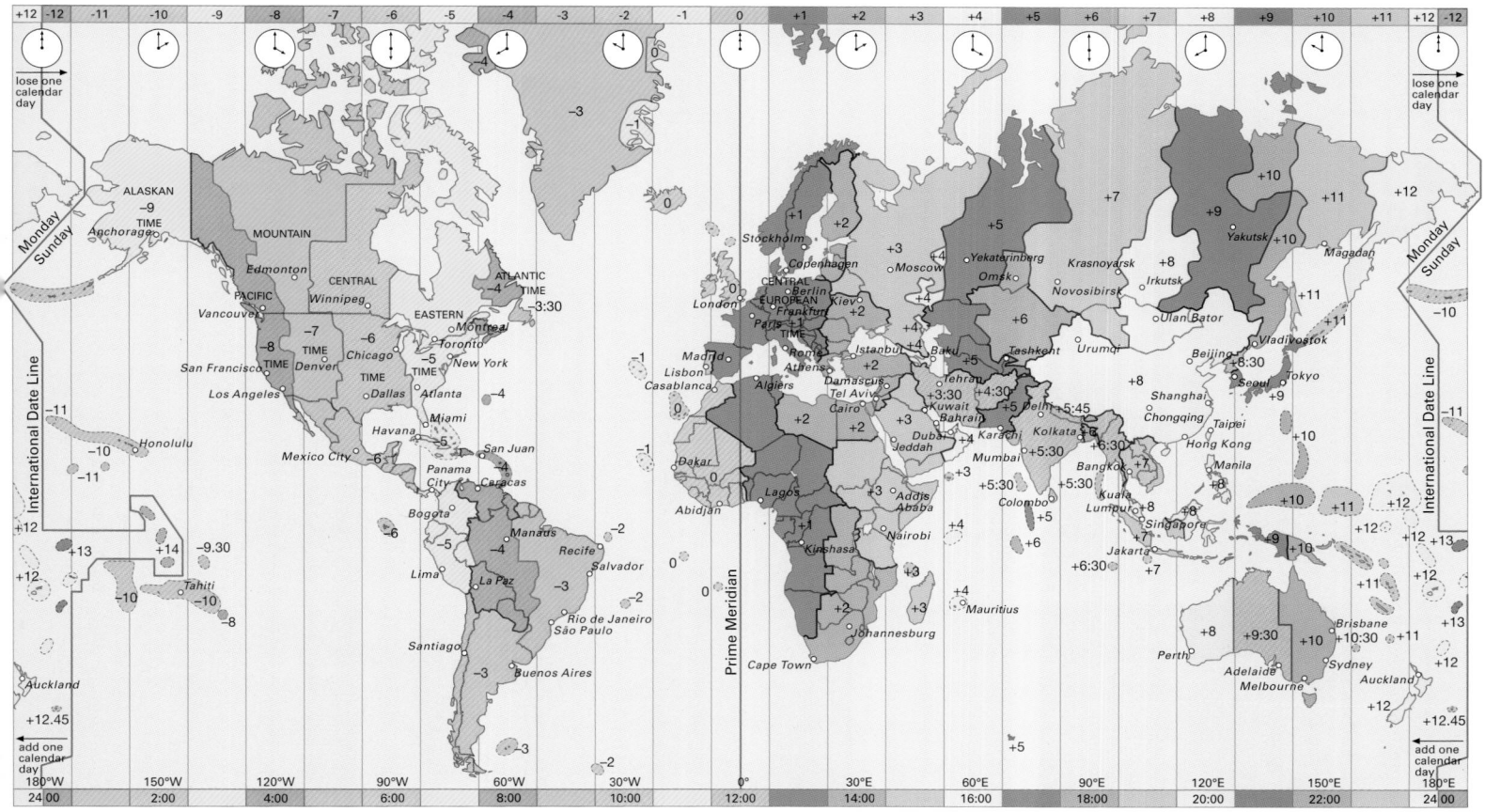

Projection: *Mercator*

For more information:
98 Minerals

Every year, earthquakes and volcanic eruptions cause much destruction throughout the world. Such phenomena were once thought to be unconnected, but since the late 1960s, scientists have understood that these events are surface manifestations of the tremendous forces operating in the Earth's interior that are slowly but constantly changing the face of our planet.

The Earth is divided into three zones. The crust, a brittle, low-density zone, overlies the dense mantle. Separating the crust from the mantle is a distinct boundary called the Mohorovičić (or Moho) discontinuity. Enclosed by the mantle is the Earth's core, which consists mainly of iron and nickel.

Temperatures inside the Earth range from about 1,600°F in the upper mantle to perhaps 9,000°F in the core. Heat creates convection currents in a semimolten part of the mantle called the asthenosphere. Above the asthenosphere is the lithosphere, a solid layer about 40 miles thick, consisting of the crust and part of the mantle. The lithosphere is divided into rigid plates, moved around by the currents in the asthenosphere, a process named plate tectonics.

The Earth was formed around 4.6 billion years ago. Lighter elements floated toward the surface, where they formed crustal rocks. The oldest rocks so far discovered are about 4 billion years old, while the oldest fossils occur in rocks formed around 3.5 billion years ago. An explosion of life occurred at the start of the Cambrian period, 570 million years ago. The fossil record since the start of the Cambrian has enabled scientists to piece together the story of life on Earth.

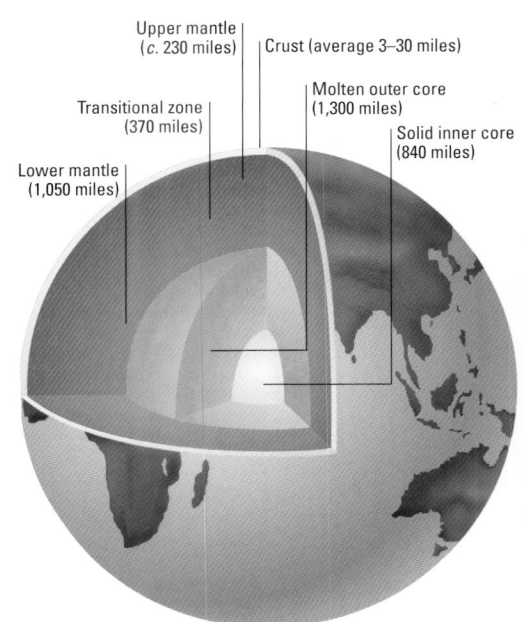

Upper mantle (c. 230 miles) | Crust (average 3–30 miles)
Transitional zone (370 miles) | Molten outer core (1,300 miles)
Lower mantle (1,050 miles) | Solid inner core (840 miles)

CONTINENTAL DRIFT

— Trench
▨ Rift
▨ New ocean floor
═ Zones of slippage

In 1915, Alfred Wegener produced a series of world maps proposing that, around 200 million years ago, the continents had been joined together in a supercontinent that he called Pangaea. This land mass started to break up about 180 million years ago and the parts drifted to their present positions. In the 1950s and 1960s, evidence from studies of the ocean floor suggested that the low-density continents rest on huge slow-moving plates. The arrows on the present-day world map (*below*) show that the continents are still on the move.

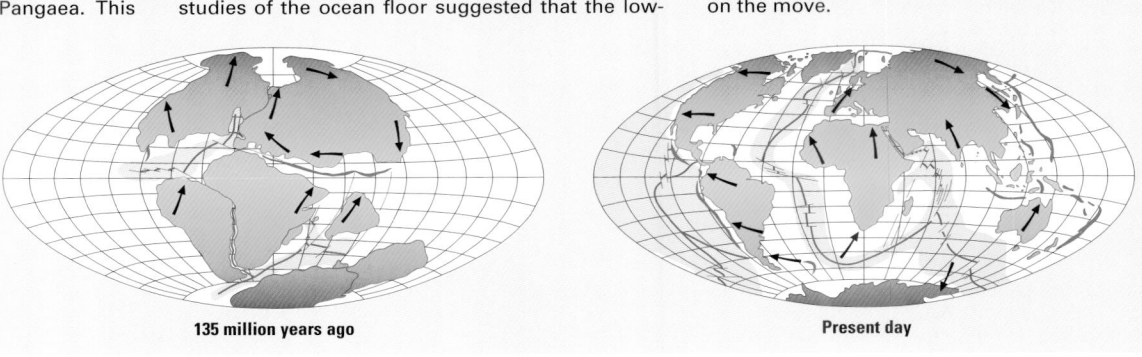

180 million years ago   **135 million years ago**   **Present day**

DISTRIBUTION OF VOLCANOES

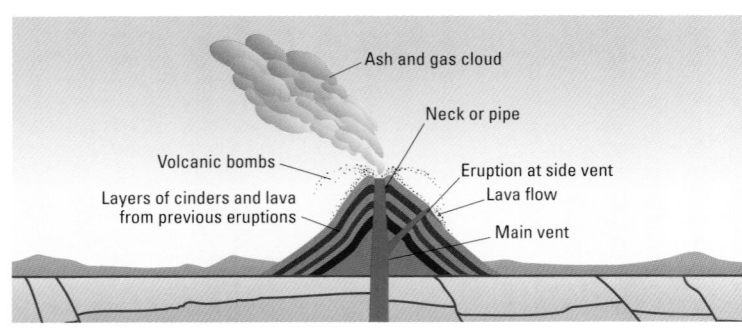

Ash and gas cloud
Neck or pipe
Volcanic bombs
Eruption at side vent
Layers of cinders and lava from previous eruptions
Lava flow
Main vent

Volcanoes occur when hot liquefied rock beneath the Earth's crust is pushed up by pressure to the surface as molten lava. There are some 550 known active volcanoes, around 20 of which are erupting at any one time.

● Submarine volcanoes
▲ Land volcanoes active since 1700
— Boundaries of tectonic plates

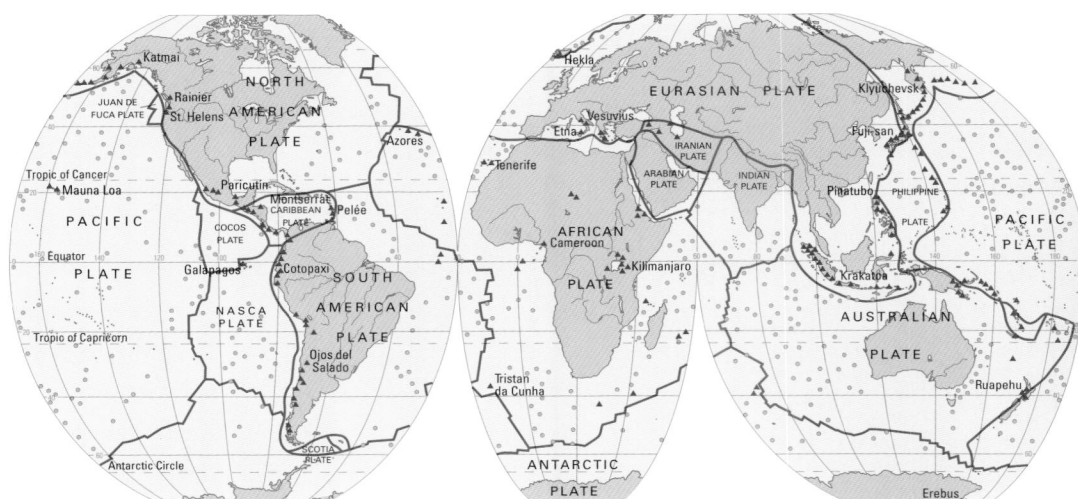

PLATE TECTONICS

The huge ridges that run through the oceans represent boundaries between plates. Here plates are diverging and molten magma from the mantle rises along a central rift valley to form new crustal rock. These ocean ridges, which are active zones where earthquakes and volcanic eruptions are common, are called constructive plate margins. Destructive plate margins, which occur when two contrasting plates converge, are marked by deep-ocean trenches as one plate is forced under the other. The descending plate is melted to produce the magma that fuels volcanoes alongside the trenches. Movements of descending plates are often sudden, triggering earthquakes in overlying continental areas.

Sea-floor spreading in the Atlantic Ocean and plate collision

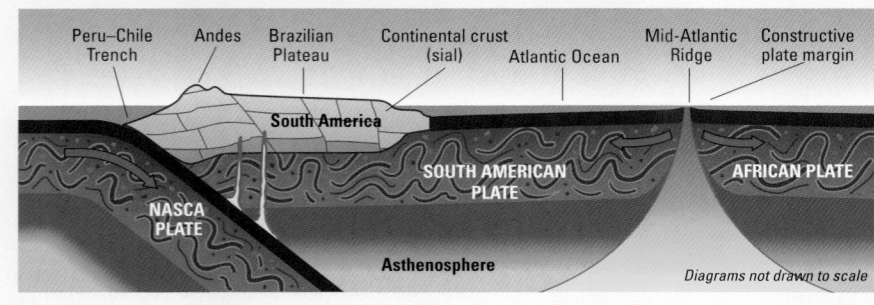

Peru–Chile Trench | Andes | Brazilian Plateau | Continental crust (sial) | Atlantic Ocean | Mid-Atlantic Ridge | Constructive plate margin
South America
SOUTH AMERICAN PLATE | AFRICAN PLATE
NASCA PLATE
Asthenosphere
Diagrams not drawn to scale

Sea-floor spreading in the Indian Ocean and continental plate collision

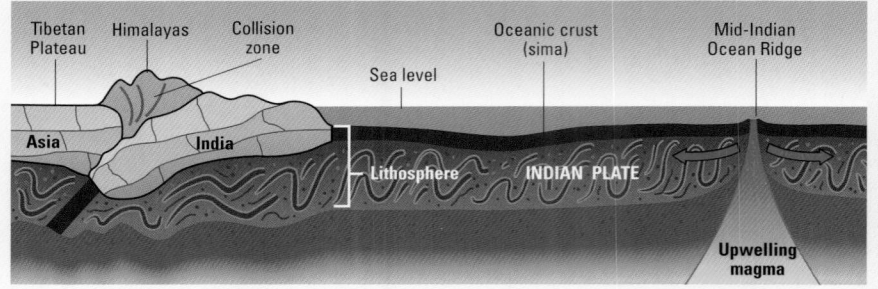

Tibetan Plateau | Himalayas | Collision zone | Oceanic crust (sima) | Mid-Indian Ocean Ridge
Sea level
Asia | India
Lithosphere | INDIAN PLATE
Upwelling magma

GEOLOGICAL TIME

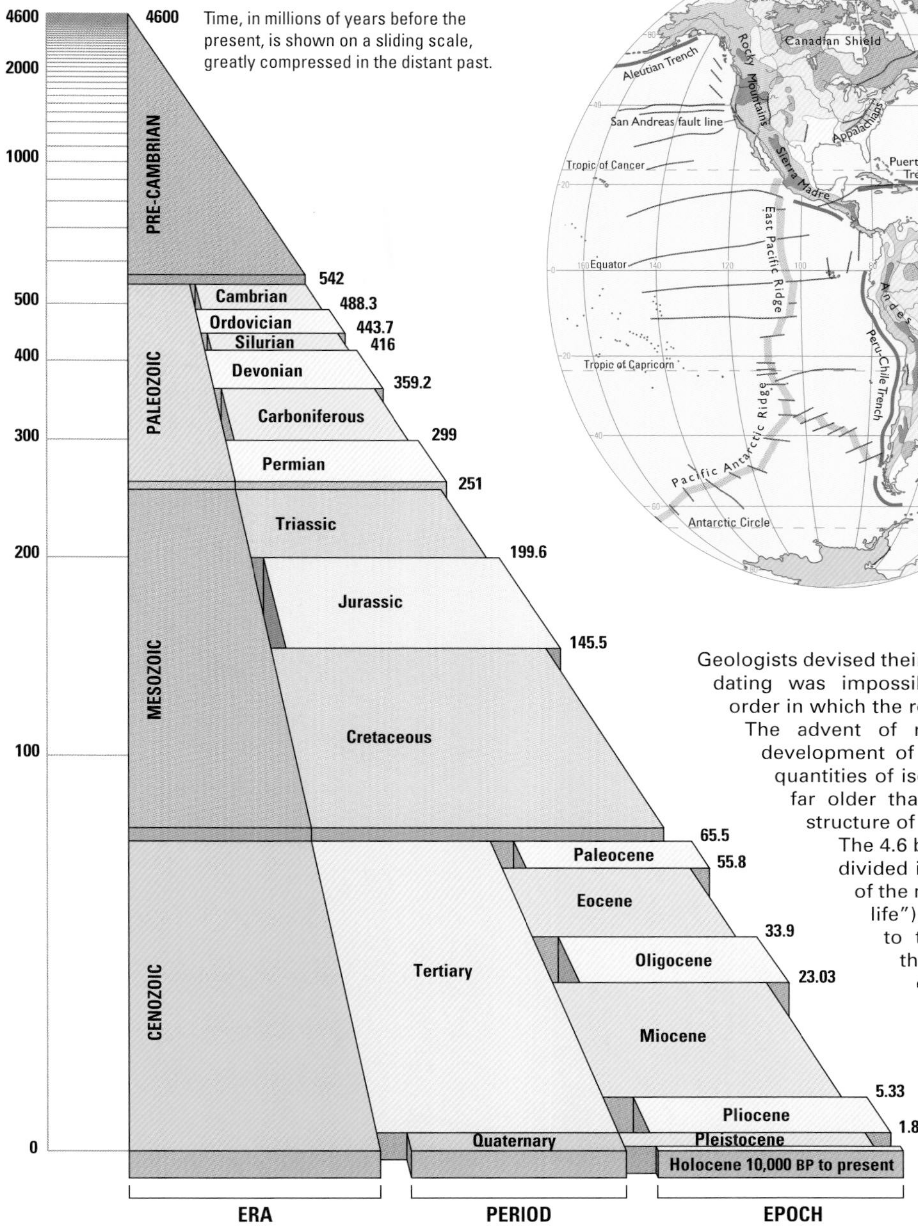

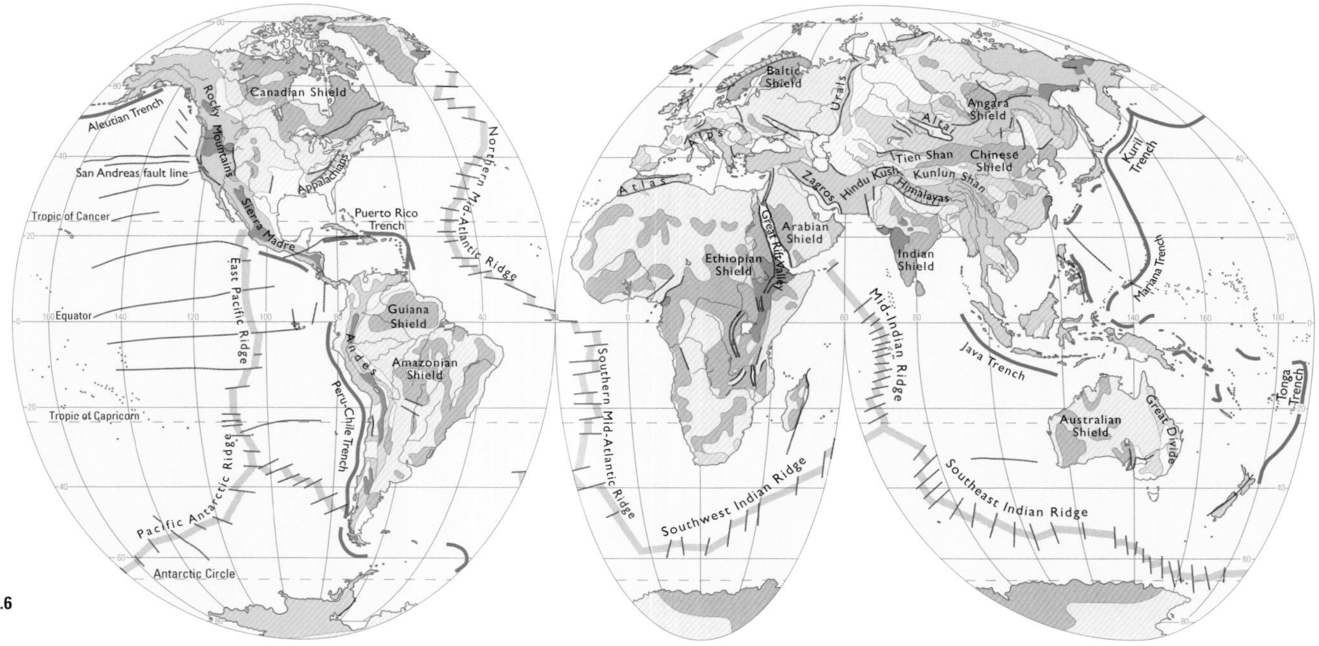

Time, in millions of years before the present, is shown on a sliding scale, greatly compressed in the distant past.

Geological Time Chart (millions of years):

ERA	PERIOD	EPOCH
PRE-CAMBRIAN		
PALEOZOIC	Cambrian 542	
	Ordovician 488.3	
	Silurian 443.7	
	Devonian 416	
	Carboniferous 359.2	
	Permian 299	
MESOZOIC	Triassic 251	
	Jurassic 199.6	
	Cretaceous 145.5	
CENOZOIC	Tertiary	Paleocene 65.5
		Eocene 55.8
		Oligocene 33.9
		Miocene 23.03
		Pliocene 5.33
	Quaternary	Pleistocene 1.81
		Holocene 10,000 BP to present

Scale markers: 4600, 2000, 1000, 500, 400, 300, 200, 100, 0

Geologists devised their timescale on the basis of relative, not calendar, ages. Accurate dating was impossible and estimates were often bitterly disputed, but the order in which the rocks were formed could be deduced from careful observation. The advent of radioactive dating – culminating in the 1950s with the development of a mass spectrometer capable of accurately measuring tiny quantities of isotopes – appears to have settled the arguments. The Earth is far older than geologists first imagined, but their painstakingly-created structure of geological time has withstood the advent of high technology.

The 4.6 billion (4,600 million) years since the formation of the Earth are divided into four great eras, further split into periods and, in the case of the most recent era, epochs. The present era is the Cenozoic ("new life"), extending backward through "middle life" and "ancient life" to the Pre-Cambrian, named after the Latin word for Wales, the location of some of the earliest known fossils. Most of the Earth's geological history is encompassed by the Pre-Cambrian: though traces of ancient life have since been found, it was largely the proliferation of fossils from the beginning of the Paleozoic era onward, some 570 million years ago, which first allowed precise subdivisions to be made.

Like the Cambrian, most are named after regions exemplifying a period's geology. Others – such as the Carboniferous ("coal-bearing") or the Cretaceous ("chalk-bearing") – are more directly descriptive.

Map legend:
- Pre-Cambrian shields
- Sedimentary cover on Pre-Cambrian shields
- Paleozoic (Caledonian and Hercynian) folding
- Sedimentary cover on Paleozoic folding
- Mesozoic folding
- Sedimentary cover on Mesozoic folding
- Cenozoic (Alpine) folding
- Sedimentary cover on Cenozoic folding
- Intensive Mesozoic and Cenozoic vulcanism
- Principal faults
- Oceanic marginal troughs
- Mid-oceanic ridges
- Overthrust faults

EARTHQUAKES

Earthquake magnitude is usually rated according to either the Richter scale or the Modified Mercalli scale, both devised by seismologists in the 1930s. The Richter scale measures absolute earthquake power with mathematical precision: each step upward represents a tenfold increase in the amplitude of the shockwave. Theoretically, there is no upper limit, but most of the largest earthquakes measured have been rated at between 8.8 and 8.9. The 12-point Mercalli scale, based on observed effects, is often more meaningful, ranging from I (earthquakes noticed only by seismographs) to XII (total destruction); intermediate points include V (people awakened at night; unstable objects overturned), VII (collapse of ordinary buildings; chimneys and monuments fall), and IX (conspicuous cracks in ground; serious damage to reservoirs).

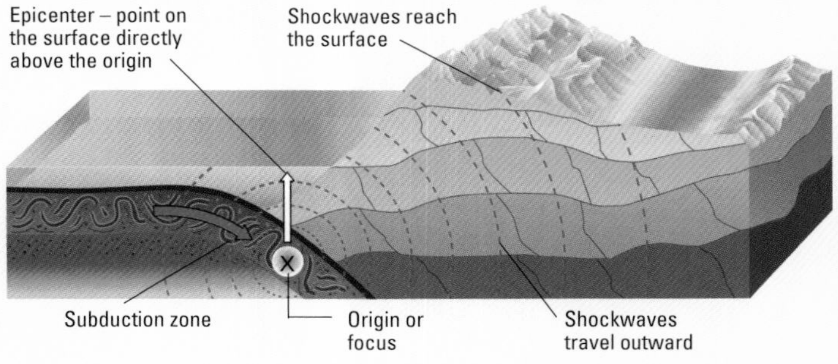

Epicenter – point on the surface directly above the origin

Shockwaves reach the surface

Subduction zone

Origin or focus

Shockwaves travel outward

Map legend:
- Mobile land areas
- Submarine zones of mobile land areas
- Stable land platforms
- Submarine extensions of land platforms
- Mid-oceanic volcanic ridges
- Oceanic platforms
- 1976 ○ Principal earthquakes and dates (since 1900)

Earthquakes are a series of rapid vibrations originating from the slipping or faulting of parts of the Earth's crust when stresses within build up to breaking point. They usually happen at depths varying from 5 to 20 miles. Severe earthquakes cause extensive damage when they take place in populated areas, destroying structures and severing communications. Most initial loss of life occurs due to secondary causes such as falling masonry, fires, and flooding.

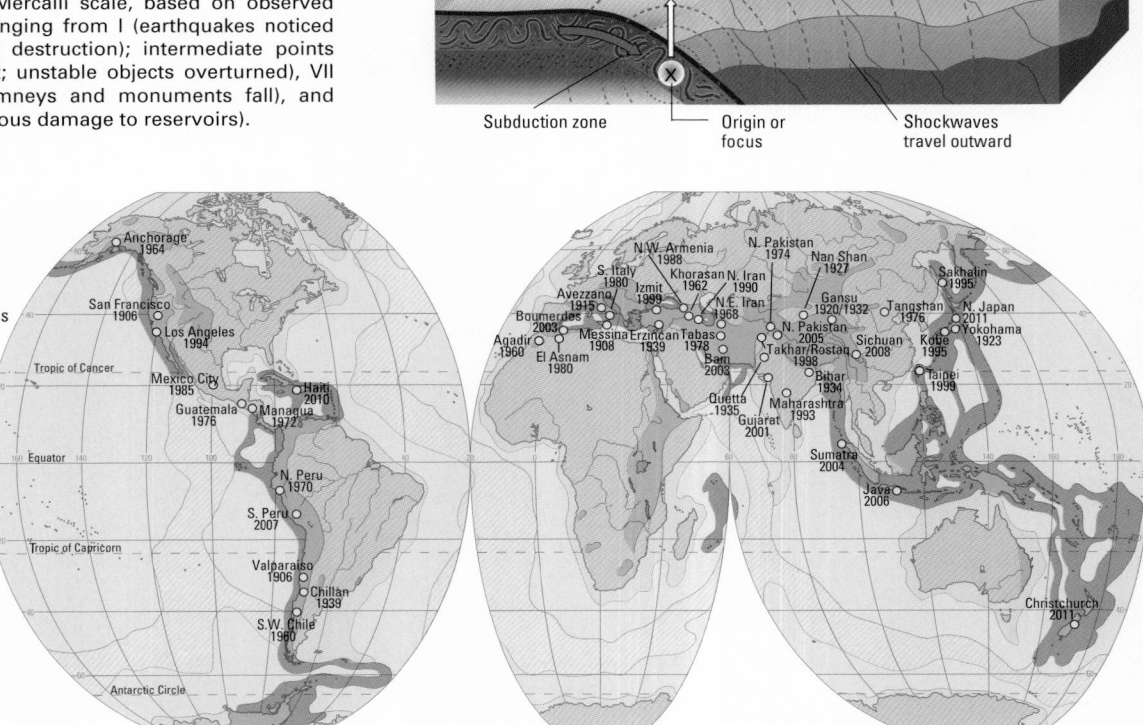

Notable Earthquakes Since 1900

Year	Location	Mag.	Deaths
1906	San Francisco, USA	8.3	3,000
1906	Valparaiso, Chile	8.6	22,000
1908	Messina, Italy	7.5	83,000
1915	Avezzano, Italy	7.5	30,000
1920	Gansu (Kansu), China	8.6	180,000
1923	Yokohama, Japan	8.3	143,000
1927	Nan Shan, China	8.3	200,000
1932	Gansu (Kansu), China	7.6	70,000
1933	Sanriku, Japan	8.9	2,990
1934	Bihar, India/Nepal	8.4	10,700
1935	Quetta, India*	7.5	60,000
1939	Chillan, Chile	8.3	28,000
1939	Erzincan, Turkey	7.9	30,000
1960	S. W. Chile	9.5	2,200
1960	Agadir, Morocco	5.8	12,000
1962	Khorasan, Iran	7.1	12,230
1964	Anchorage, USA	9.2	125
1968	N. E. Iran	7.4	12,000
1970	N. Peru	7.8	70,000
1972	Managua, Nicaragua	6.2	5,000
1974	N. Pakistan	6.3	5,200
1976	Guatemala	7.5	22,500
1976	Tangshan, China	8.2	255,000
1978	Tabas, Iran	7.7	25,000
1980	El Asnam, Algeria	7.3	20,000
1980	S. Italy	7.2	4,800
1985	Mexico City, Mexico	8.1	4,200
1988	N.W. Armenia	6.8	55,000
1990	N. Iran	7.7	36,000
1993	Maharashtra, India	6.4	30,000
1994	Los Angeles, USA	6.6	51
1995	Kobe, Japan	7.2	5,000
1995	Sakhalin, Russia	7.5	2,000
1998	Takhar, Afghanistan	6.1	4,200
1998	Rostaq, Afghanistan	7.0	5,000
1999	Izmit, Turkey	7.4	15,000
2001	Gujarat, India	7.7	14,000
2003	Bam, Iran	6.6	30,000
2004	Sumatra, Indonesia	9.0	250,000
2005	N. Pakistan	7.6	74,000
2006	Java, Indonesia	6.4	6,200
2007	S. Peru	8.0	600
2008	Sichuan, China	7.9	70,000
2010	Haiti	7.0	230,000
2011	Christchurch, NZ	6.3	182
2011	N. Japan	9.0	20,000
2013	Baluchistan, Pakistan	7.7	825
2015	Nepal	7.8	5,000

* now Pakistan

For more information:

79 Beaufort wind scale
   Monsoon
80 Climate change
   Global warming
84 Ocean currents

The atmosphere is a meteor shield, a radiation deflector, a thermal blanket, and a source of chemical energy for the Earth's diverse life forms. Five-sixths of its mass is in the lowest layer, the troposphere, which ranges in thickness from 11–6 miles between the equator and the poles. Powered by the Sun, the air is always on the move, flowing generally from high- to low-pressure areas. The troposphere is the layer where virtually all weather phenomena, including clouds, precipitation, and winds, occur. Above the troposphere is the stratosphere, which contains the important ozone layer and extends to about 30 miles above the Earth's surface. Beyond 60 miles, atmospheric density is lower than most laboratory vacuums.

STRUCTURE OF THE ATMOSPHERE

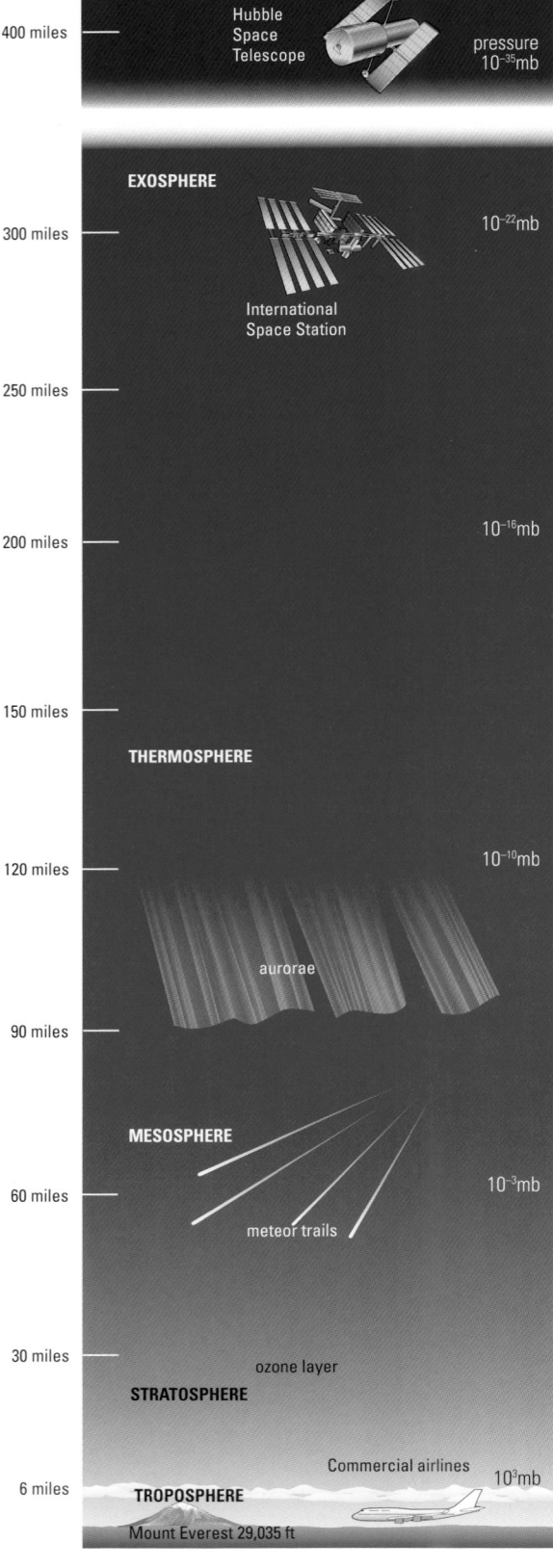

400 miles — pressure 10^{-35}mb
Hubble Space Telescope

EXOSPHERE
300 miles — 10^{-22}mb
International Space Station

250 miles —

200 miles — 10^{-16}mb

THERMOSPHERE
150 miles —

120 miles — 10^{-10}mb
aurorae

90 miles —

MESOSPHERE
60 miles — 10^{-3}mb
meteor trails

30 miles — ozone layer
STRATOSPHERE
Commercial airlines 10^3mb
6 miles — **TROPOSPHERE**
Mount Everest 29,035 ft

CIRCULATION OF THE AIR

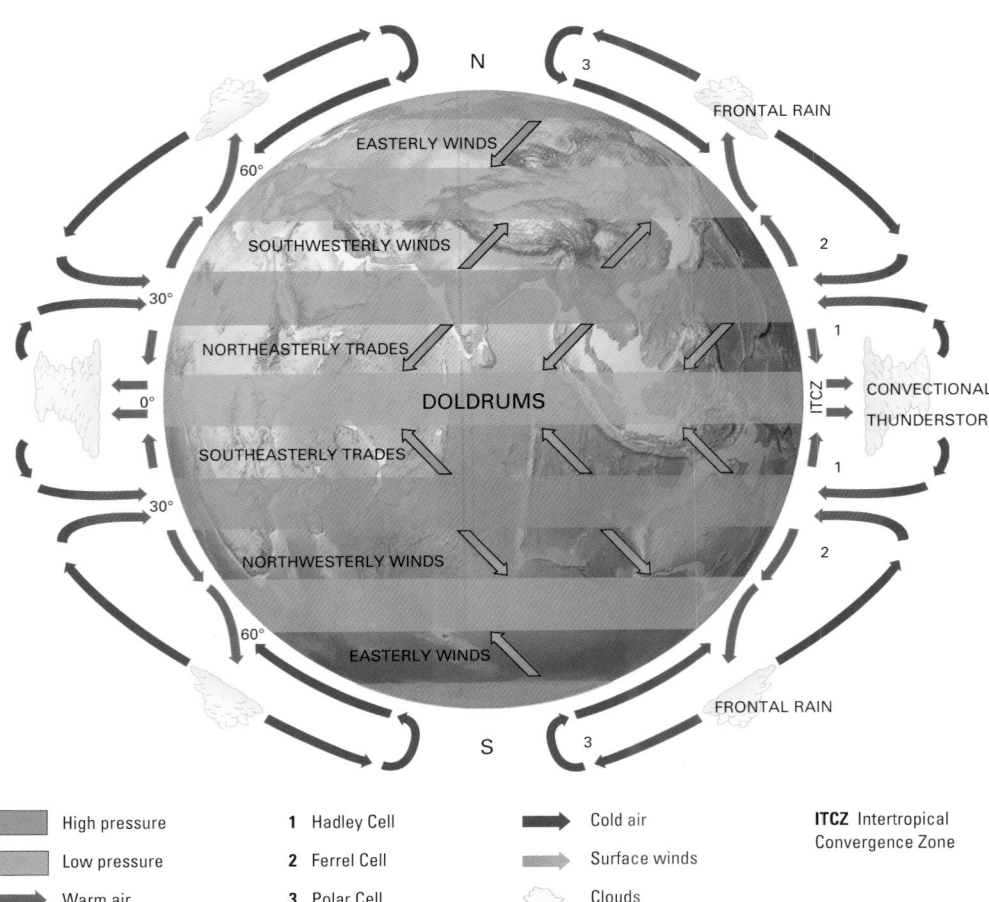

N
3
FRONTAL RAIN
60° EASTERLY WINDS
SOUTHWESTERLY WINDS
2
30° NORTHEASTERLY TRADES
1
0° DOLDRUMS
ITCZ CONVECTIONAL THUNDERSTORM
SOUTHEASTERLY TRADES
1
30° NORTHWESTERLY WINDS
2
60° EASTERLY WINDS
3
FRONTAL RAIN
S

	High pressure	**1** Hadley Cell	Cold air	**ITCZ** Intertropical Convergence Zone
	Low pressure	**2** Ferrel Cell	Surface winds	
	Warm air	**3** Polar Cell	Clouds	

FRONTAL SYSTEMS

Depressions, also known as cyclones or lows, form on the polar front where relatively cold and dry polar air flows alongside warmer, moister subtropical air. They occur when the flow high above the polar front generates a surface inward-swirling circulation that moves along the polar front as a wave.

The warm front is the leading edge of the subtropical air that glides up and over the cooler air ahead of it. This gently ascending flow produces a characteristic sequence of clouds ahead of the warm front and a band of precipitation a few hundred miles wide immediately in advance it. Conditions within the warm sector are often overcast with layer cloud and generally light rain or drizzle. The cloud sometimes breaks up downwind of hills.

Another band of precipitation often occurs just ahead of the cold front that is the leading edge of the cooler polar air. Cumulus clouds tend to occur in the air behind the cold front, producing scattered showers. The changes of temperature, wind direction, and cloud, etc, are illustrated by the diagram below.

CHEMICAL COMPOSITION

Gaseous composition of the principal atmospheric layers

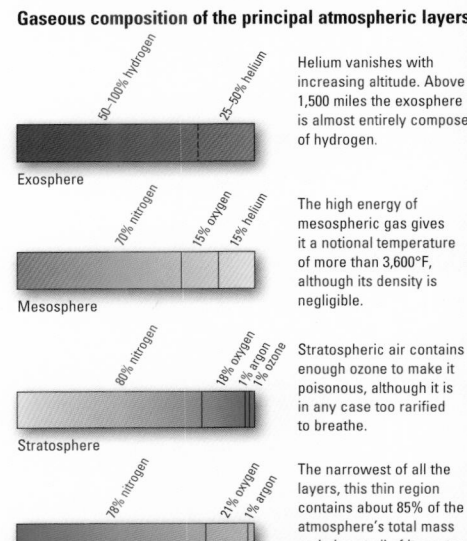

Exosphere — 50–100% hydrogen, 25–50% helium

Helium vanishes with increasing altitude. Above 1,500 miles the exosphere is almost entirely composed of hydrogen.

Mesosphere — 70% nitrogen, 15% oxygen, 15% helium

The high energy of mesospheric gas gives it a notional temperature of more than 3,600°F, although its density is negligible.

Stratosphere — 80% nitrogen, 18% oxygen, 1% argon, 1% ozone

Stratospheric air contains enough ozone to make it poisonous, although it is in any case too rarified to breathe.

Troposphere — 78% nitrogen, 21% oxygen, 1% argon

The narrowest of all the layers, this thin region contains about 85% of the atmosphere's total mass and almost all of its water vapor. It is also the realm of the Earth's weather.

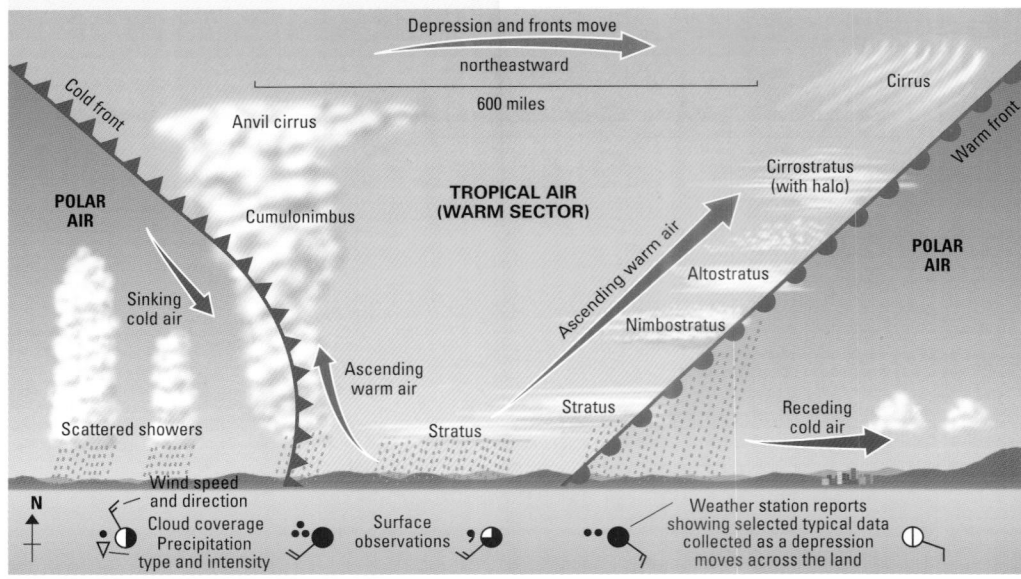

Depression and fronts move northeastward
600 miles
Cold front
Anvil cirrus
Cirrus
POLAR AIR
Cumulonimbus
TROPICAL AIR (WARM SECTOR)
Cirrostratus (with halo)
Warm front
Ascending warm air
Altostratus
POLAR AIR
Sinking cold air
Nimbostratus
Ascending warm air
Scattered showers
Stratus
Stratus
Receding cold air

N
Wind speed and direction
Cloud coverage
Precipitation type and intensity
Surface observations
Weather station reports showing selected typical data collected as a depression moves across the land

AIR MASSES

Air masses are large bodies of air where the variations of the main physical properties (that is, temperature and humidity) are relatively gentle. The term is generally applied only to the lower layers of the atmosphere, although air masses can cover areas of tens of thousands of square miles.

Air masses derive their temperature and humidity from the regions over which they lie. These regions are known as "source regions." The principal ones are:

• areas of relative calm, such as semipermanent high-pressure areas;
• areas where the surface is relatively uniform, including deserts, oceans, and ice-fields.

These are the "highs" marked on the map below.

As air masses move from their source regions, they may be changed due to the effects of the surface over which they move. These changes create "secondary air masses." For example, a warm air mass that travels over a cold surface is cooled and becomes more stable. Hence, it may form low cloud or fog, but is unlikely to produce much rain. By contrast, a cold air mass that passes over a warm surface is warmed and becomes less stable. The rising air is likely to produce more rain.

When two contrasting air masses meet, they form a "front." As warm air is lighter than cold, dense air, it begins to rise over it, condensing as it rises to form cloud and rain.

CLASSIFICATION OF CLOUDS

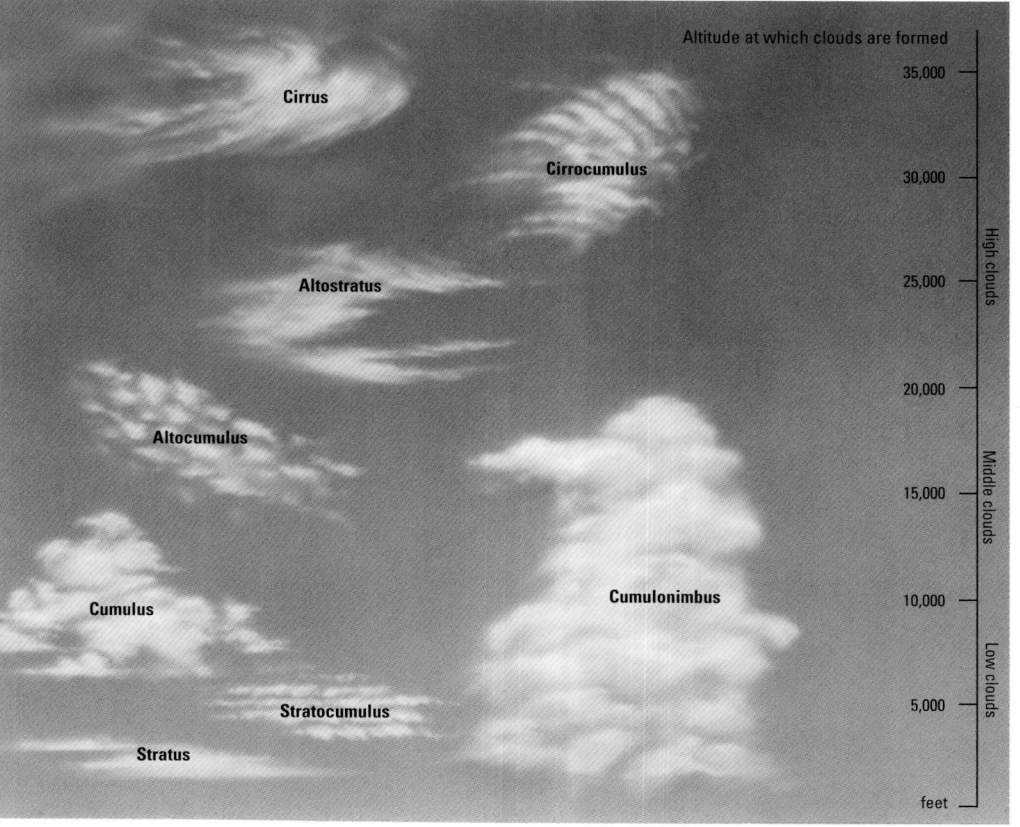

Clouds form when damp, usually rising, air is cooled. Thus they form when a wind rises to cross hills or mountains; when a mass of air rises over, or is pushed up by, another mass of denser air; or when local heating of the ground causes convection currents.

The first classification of clouds was developed by a London chemist, Luke Howard, in 1803, and it was later modified by the World Meteorological Organization. The types of clouds are classified according to altitude as high, middle, or low. The high ones, composed of ice crystals, are cirrus, cirrostratus, and cirrocumulus.

The middle clouds are altostratus – a gray or bluish striated, fibrous or uniform sheet producing light drizzle – and altocumulus, a thicker and fluffier version of cirrocumulus.

Low clouds include nimbo-stratus, a dark gray layer that brings rain or snow; cumulus, a detached heap, dark at the base; stratus, which forms dull, overcast skies at low levels; and stratocumulus, which consists of fluffy grayish-white layers. Cumulonimbus, associated with storms and rains, heavy and dense with a flat base and a high, fluffy outline, can be tall enough to occupy middle as well as low altitudes.

PRESSURE AND SURFACE WINDS

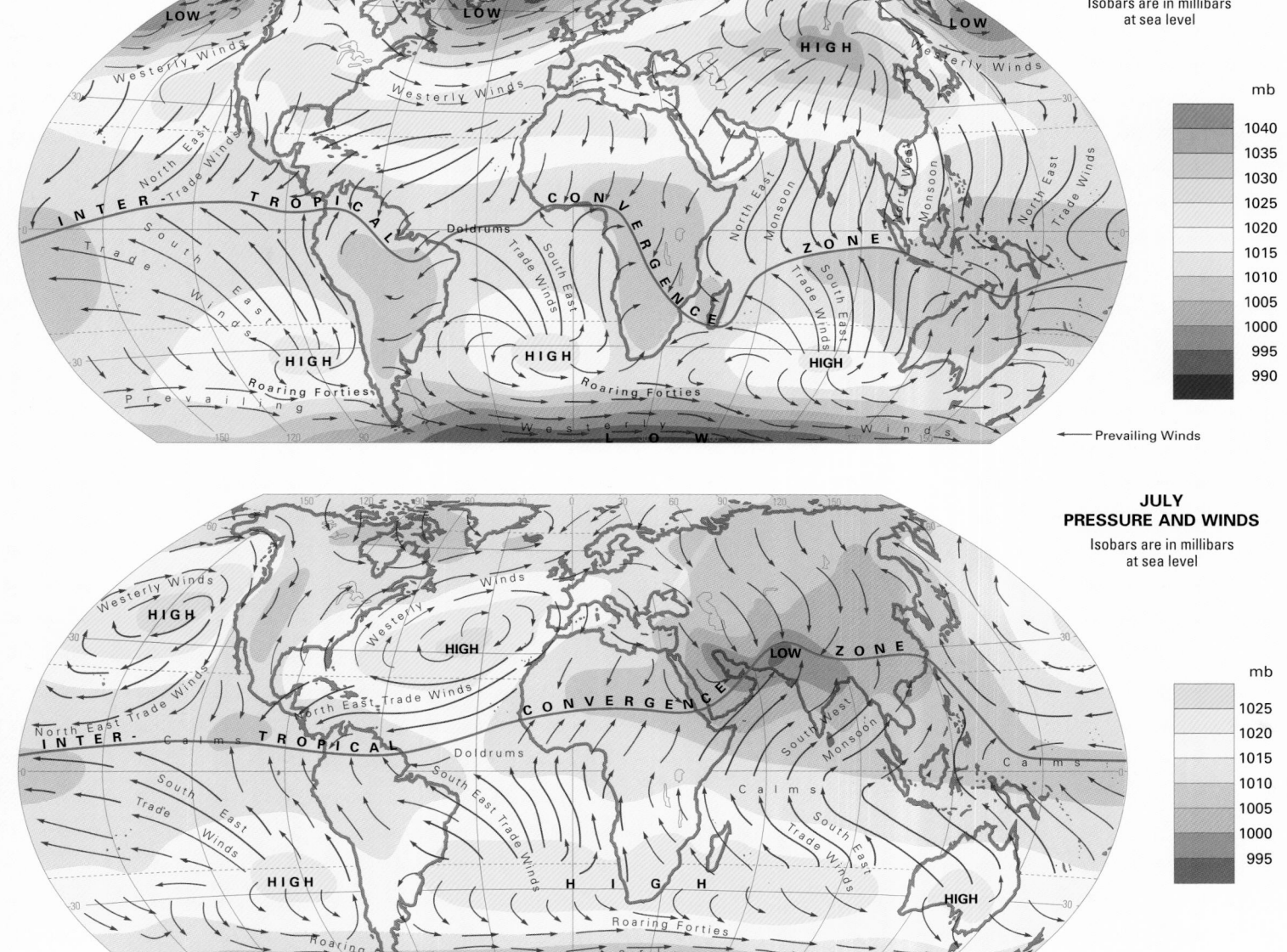

JANUARY PRESSURE AND WINDS

Isobars are in millibars at sea level

mb
1040
1035
1030
1025
1020
1015
1010
1005
1000
995
990

← Prevailing Winds

JULY PRESSURE AND WINDS

Isobars are in millibars at sea level

mb
1025
1020
1015
1010
1005
1000
995

← Prevailing Winds

WEATHER RECORDS

Pressure and winds

Highest barometric pressure:
Agata, Siberia, 1,083.8 mb at altitude 862 ft [262 m], December 31, 1968.

Lowest barometric pressure:
Typhoon Tip, 300 mi [480 km] west of Guam, Pacific Ocean, 870 mb, October 12, 1979.

Highest recorded wind speed:
Bridge Creek, Oklahoma, USA, 318 mph [512 km/h], May 3, 1999. Measured by Doppler radar monitoring a tornado.

Windiest place:
Port Martin, Antarctica, where winds of more than 40 mph [64 km/h] occur for not less than 100 days a year.

Worst recorded storm:
Bangladesh (then East Pakistan) cyclone, November 13, 1970 – over 300,000 dead or missing. The 1991 cyclone, Bangladesh's and the world's second worst in terms of loss of life, killed an estimated 138,000 people.

Worst recorded tornado:
Tri-state tornado – Missouri/Illinois/Indiana, USA, March 18, 1925 – 695 deaths, lasted 3 hours with 219 mi [352 km] path length. A suspected tornado in Bangladesh on April 26, 1989, killed approximately 1,300 people.

For more information:
76 Circulation of the air
77 Classification of clouds
   Pressure and winds
80 Climate change
   Global warming
82 Hydrological cycle
83 Natural vegetation
84 Ocean currents

Weather is the day-to-day or hour-to-hour condition of the air, while climate is weather in the long term – the seasonal pattern of hot and cold, wet and dry, averaged over a long period.

Most classifications of climate are based on a system developed in the early 19th century by Vladimir Köppen, a Russian meteorologist. Using a code based on letters and a classification centered on two main features, temperature and precipitation, he identified five main climatic types: tropical (A), dry (B), warm temperate (C), cold temperate (D), and polar (E). A highland mountain climate (H) was added later to account for the variety of altitudinal climatic zones on high mountains. Each of these main regions was then further subdivided.

Latitude is a major factor in determining climate, but other factors add to the complexity. These include the differential heating of land and sea, the distance from the sea, the effect of mountains on winds, and the influence of ocean currents. For example, New York City, Naples, and the Gobi Desert share almost the same latitude, but their climates are very different.

During the last Ice Age, the Earth underwent alternating cold periods, called glacials, separated by warm interglacials. The Milankovich theory suggests such cycles may be caused by variations in the Earth's path around the Sun, changing from almost circular to elliptical every 95,000 years, and variations in the Earth's tilt from 21.5° to 24.5° every 42,000 years. Another factor is that the Earth is now closest to the Sun in the middle of winter in the northern hemisphere and furthest away in summer. But 12,000 years ago, at the height of the last glacial period, the northern winter fell with the Sun at its most distant.

Studies of these cycles suggest that we are now in an interglacial with a new glacial period on the way. However, scientists believe that global warming, largely a result of burning fossil fuels and deforestation, may be occurring much faster than the great, slow cycles of the Solar System.

Tropical rainy climates
All mean monthly temperatures above 64°F [18°C].

Af	Rain forest climate
Am	Monsoon climate
Aw	Savanna climate

Dry climates
Low rainfall combined with a wide range of temperatures.

| BS | Steppe climate |
| BW | Desert climate |

Warm temperate rainy climates
The mean temperature is below 64°F [18°C] but above 26°F [–3°C] and that of the warmest month is over 50°F [10°C].

Cw	Dry winter climate
Cs	Dry summer climate
Cf	Climate with no dry season

Cold temperate rainy climates
The mean temperature of the coldest month is below 26°F [–3°C] but that of the warmest month is still over 50°F [10°C].

| Dw | Dry winter climate |
| Df | Climate with no dry season |

Polar climates
The mean temperature of the warmest month is below 50°F [10°C], giving permanently frozen subsoil.

| ET | Tundra climate |

The mean temperature of the warmest month is below 32°F [0°C], giving permanent ice and snow.

| EF | Polar climate |

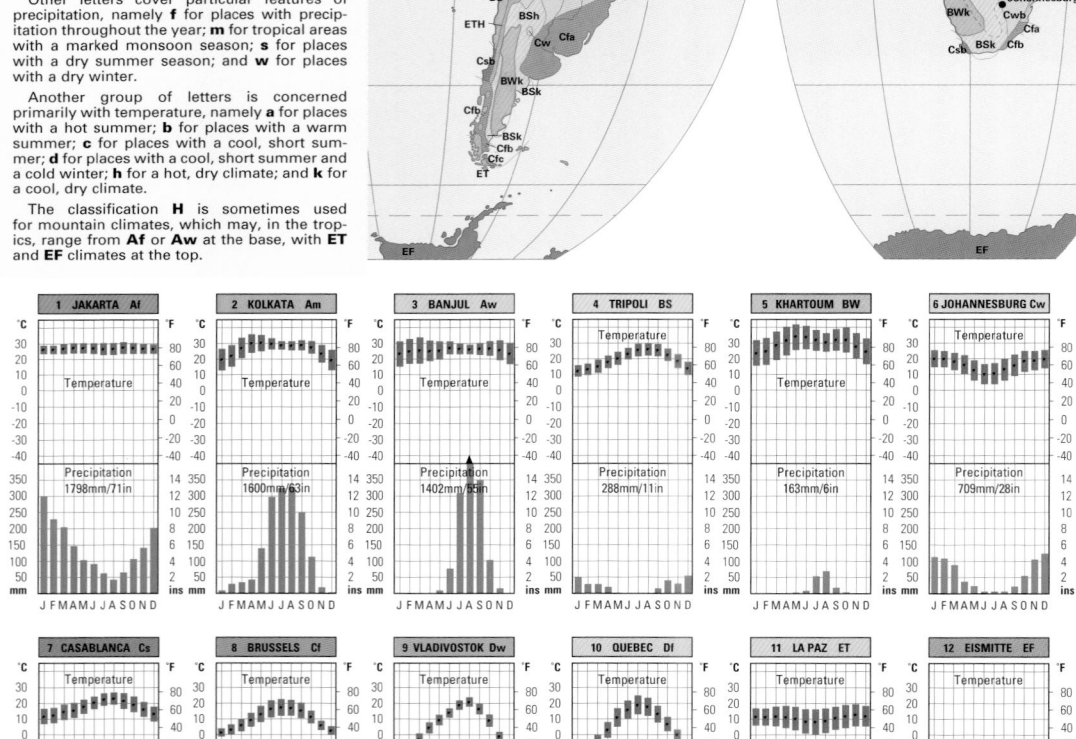

CLIMATE REGIONS

Vladimir Köppen divided the world's land areas into five main climatic regions, designated **A, B, C, D,** and **E**, which correspond broadly to the five vegetation types. Each of the five climatic regions is further subdivided using other letter codes. For example, dry climates are subdivided into deserts (**W**) and dry, semiarid steppe (**S**), while polar climates contain areas permanently covered by ice sheets and ice caps (**F**) and tundra areas (**T**).

Other letters cover particular features of precipitation, namely **f** for places with precipitation throughout the year; **m** for tropical areas with a marked monsoon season; **s** for places with a dry summer season; and **w** for places with a dry winter.

Another group of letters is concerned primarily with temperature, namely **a** for places with a hot summer; **b** for places with a warm summer; **c** for places with a cool, short summer; **d** for places with a cool, short summer and a cold winter; **h** for a hot, dry climate; and **k** for a cool, dry climate.

The classification **H** is sometimes used for mountain climates, which may, in the tropics, range from **Af** or **Aw** at the base, with **ET** and **EF** climates at the top.

CLIMATE AND WEATHER TERMS

Anticyclone: area of high pressure with light winds and generally quiet weather.
Absolute humidity: mass of water vapor contained in a given volume of air.
Cloud cover: amount of cloud in the sky; measured in oktas (from 0–9), with 0 clear, and 9 "sky obscured."
Condensation: the conversion of water vapor into liquid.
Cyclone: violent storm resulting from counterclockwise rotation of winds in the northern hemisphere and clockwise in the southern: called hurricane in North America, typhoon in the Far East.
Depression: large area of low barometric pressure, a few thousand miles across.
Dew: deposition of small water droplets on the Earth's surface by direct condensation of water vapor.
Dew point: the temperature at which air becomes saturated by cooling at constant barometric pressure and absolute humidity.
Drizzle: precipitation drops between 0.01–0.02 inches [0.2 and 0.5 mm] in diameter.
Evaporation: conversion of water from liquid into vapor or moisture in the air.
Front: the dividing line between two air masses.
Frost: the surface deposition of water vapor as minute ice crystals, when temperature reaches the frost point.

Hail: variably-sized pieces of ice that fall in downdrafts from cumulonimbus clouds.
Humidity: amount of water vapor in the air.
Isobar: line joining places with the same barometric pressure.
Isotherm: line connecting places of equal temperature.
Lightning: massive electrical discharge released in thunderstorm from cloud to cloud or cloud to ground, the result of the top becoming positively charged and the bottom negatively charged.
Precipitation: measurable rain, snow, sleet, or hail.
Prevailing wind: most common direction of wind at a given location.
Rain: precipitation of liquid particles with diameter larger than 0.02 inches [0.5 mm].
Relative humidity: observed quantity of water vapor in a mass of air over the saturation value at a given temperature (as a percentage).
Snow: flake-like coagulations of ice crystals that fall from clouds in subzero temperatures.
Thunder: sound produced by the rapid expansion of air heated by lightning.
Tornado: rapidly-rotating funnel-shaped cloud or debris column that must reach the surface and be attached to a parent cumulonimbus cloud.

BEAUFORT WIND SCALE

Named after Admiral Sir Francis Beaufort, the 19th-century British naval officer who devised it, the Beaufort Scale assesses wind speed according to its effects. It was originally designed as an aid for sailors, but has since been adapted for use on the land. It is used internationally.

Scale	Wind speed mph	Wind speed km/h	Effect
0	0–1	0–1	**Calm** Smoke rises vertically
1	1–3	1–5	**Light air** Wind direction shown only by smoke drift
2	4–7	6–11	**Light breeze** Wind felt on face; leaves rustle; vanes moved by wind
3	8–12	12–19	**Gentle breeze** Leaves and small twigs in constant motion; wind extends small flag
4	13–18	20–28	**Moderate** Raises dust and loose paper; small branches move
5	19–24	29–38	**Fresh** Small trees in leaf sway; crested wavelets on inland waters
6	25–31	39–49	**Strong** Large branches move; difficult to use umbrellas; overhead wires whistle
7	32–38	50–61	**Near gale** Whole trees in motion; difficult to walk against wind
8	39–46	62–74	**Gale** Twigs break from trees; walking very difficult
9	47–54	75–88	**Strong gale** Slight structural damage
10	55–63	89–102	**Storm** Trees uprooted; serious structural damage
11	64–72	103–117	**Violent storm** Widespread damage
12	73+	118+	**Hurricane**

▲ In the Pacific Ocean, off south-east Asia, Typhoon Haiyan developed into a Category 5 storm during November 2013. Moving westwards, wind speeds of 170 mph (275 km/h) were recorded before it hit the Philippines. This makes it the strongest typhoon to make landfall, and over 6,000 people lost their lives.

THE MONSOON

Monsoon is the term given to the seasonal reversal of wind direction, most noticeably in Southeast Asia. It results from a combination of factors: the extreme heating and cooling of large land masses in relation to the less marked changes in temperature of the adjacent seas; the northward movement of the Intertropical Convergence Zone (ITCZ); and the effect of the Himalayas on the circulation of the air.

In March, winds blow outward from the mainland. But as the Sun and the ITCZ move northward, the land is intensely heated, and a low-pressure system develops. The southeast trade winds change direction and are sucked into the interior to become southwesterlies, bringing heavy rain. By November, the Sun and the ITCZ have again moved south and the wind directions are again reversed. Cool winds blow from the Asian interior to the sea, losing any moisture on the Himalayas before descending to the coast.

TEMPERATURE

Average temperature in January

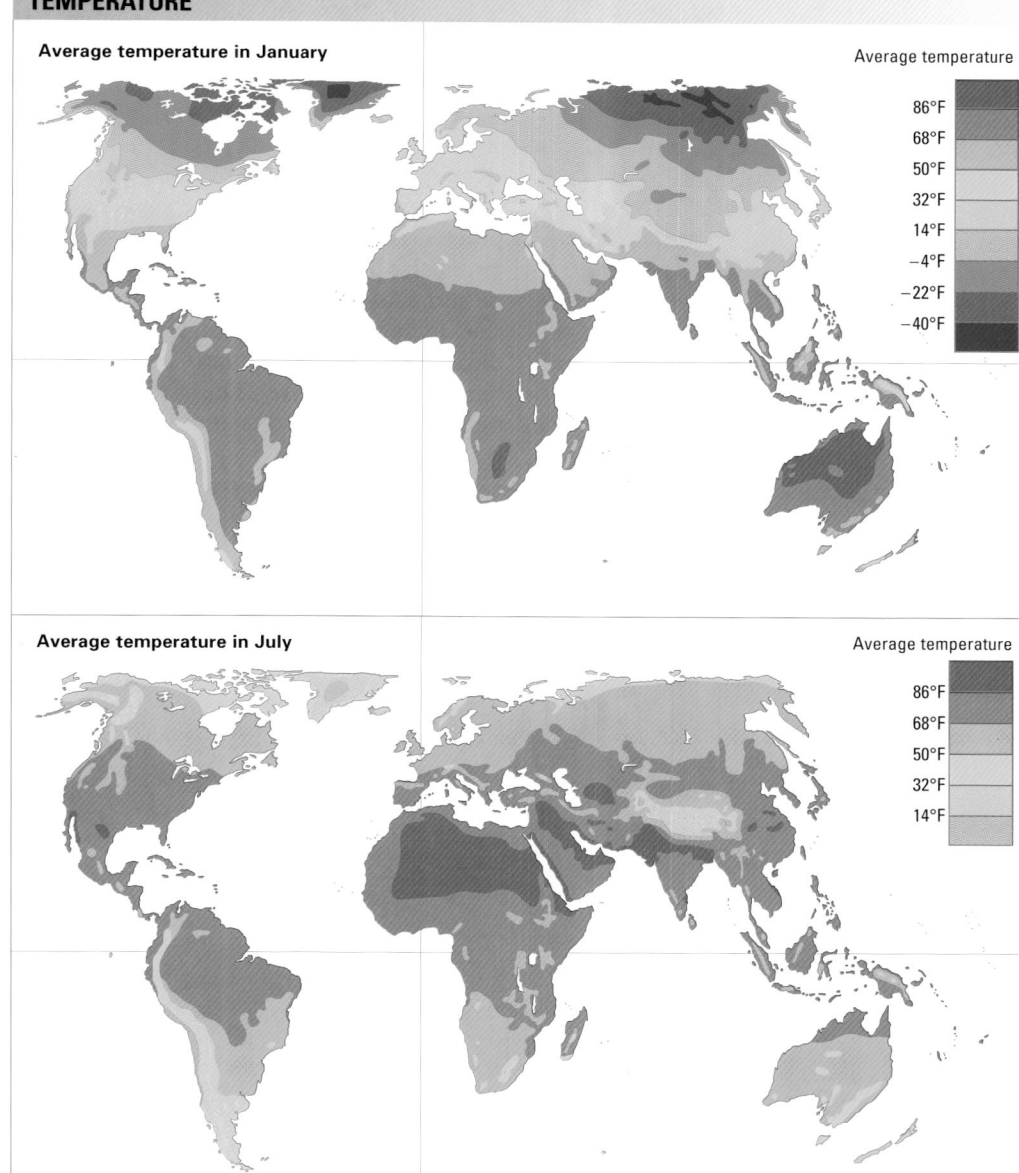

Average temperature

	86°F
	68°F
	50°F
	32°F
	14°F
	−4°F
	−22°F
	−40°F

Average temperature in July

Average temperature

	86°F
	68°F
	50°F
	32°F
	14°F

PRECIPITATION (RAINFALL AND SNOW)

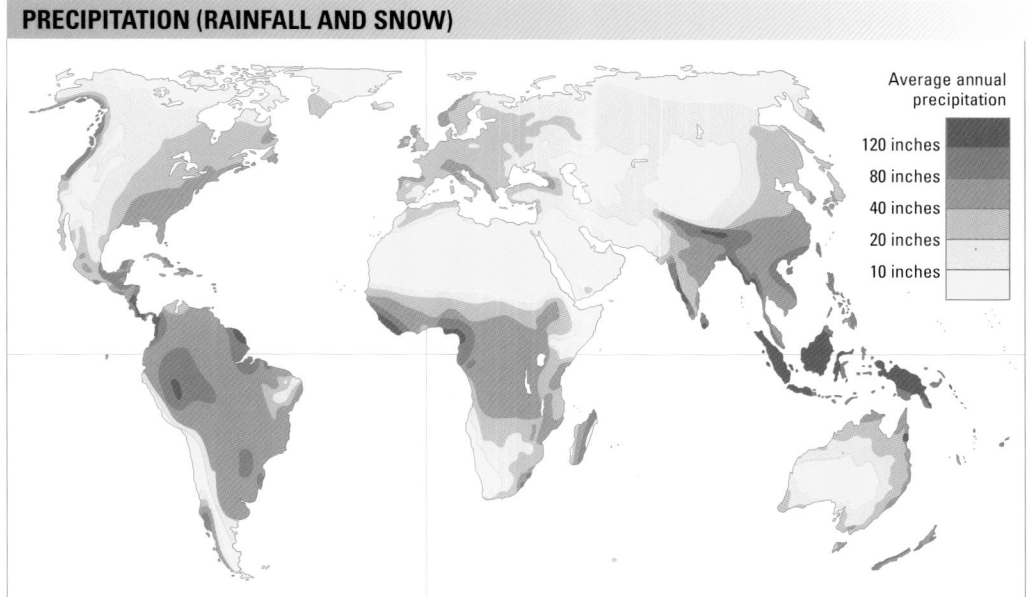

Average annual precipitation

	120 inches
	80 inches
	40 inches
	20 inches
	10 inches

CLIMATE RECORDS

TEMPERATURE

Highest recorded temperature:
Death Valley, California, USA, 134°F [56.7°C], 10 July 1913.

Highest mean annual temperature:
Dallol, Ethiopia, 94°F [34.4°C], 1960–6.

Longest heatwave:
Marble Bar, W. Australia, 162 days over 100°F [38°C], October 23, 1923, to April 7, 1924.

Lowest recorded temperature (outside poles):
Verkhoyansk, Siberia, −93.6°F [−69.8°C], February 7, 1982. Verkhoyansk also registered the greatest annual range of temperature: −90°F to 98°F [−68°C to 37°C].

Lowest mean annual temperature:
Polus Nedostupnosti, Pole of Cold, Antarctica, −72°F [−57.8°C].

PRECIPITATION

Driest place:
Quillagua, N. Chile, mean annual rainfall 0.02 inches [0.5 mm], 1964–2001.

Wettest place (average):
Mt Wai'ale'ale, Hawai'i, USA, mean annual rainfall 459.8 inches [11,680 mm].

Wettest place (12 months):
Cherrapunji, Meghalaya, N.E. India, 1,042 inches [26,461 mm], August 1860 to August 1861. Cherrapunji also holds the record for rainfall in one month: 115 inches [2,930 mm], July 1861. (*See Monsoon maps below.*)

Wettest place (24 hours):
Fac Fac, Réunion, Indian Ocean, 71.9 inches [1,825 mm], March 15–16, 1952.

Heaviest hailstones:
Gopalganj, Bangladesh, up to 2.25 lb [1.02 kg], April 14, 1986 (killed 92 people).

Heaviest snowfall (continuous):
Bessans, Savoie, France, 68 inches [1,730 mm] in 19 hours, April 5–6. 1969.

Heaviest snowfall (season/year):
Mt Baker, Washington, USA, 1,140 inches [28,956 mm], June 1998 to June 1999.

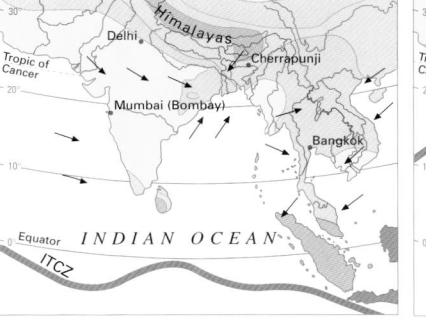

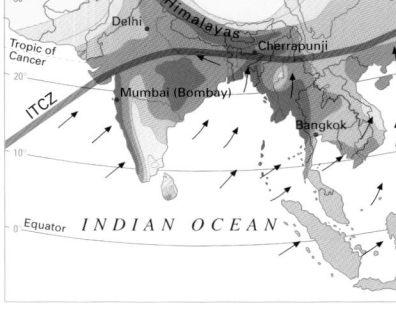

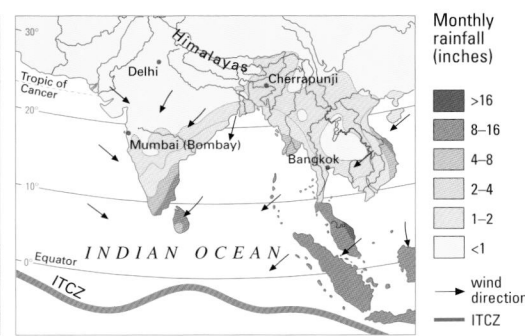

Monthly rainfall (inches)

	>16
	8–16
	4–8
	2–4
	1–2
	<1

→ wind direction
— ITCZ

March – Start of the hot, dry season. The ITCZ is over the southern Indian Ocean.

July – The rainy season. The ITCZ has migrated northward; winds blow onshore.

November – The ITCZ has returned south. The offshore winds are cool and dry.

For more information:

76 Atmosphere

78 Climate

84 Ocean currents

Ever since the Industrial Revolution began, the amount of carbon dioxide in the atmosphere has steadily increased. It is the result of burning fossil fuels, and the destruction of forests which absorb carbon dioxide. In the late 18th century, carbon dioxide made up about 280 parts per million by volume (ppmv). It has since risen from 316 ppmv to 400 ppmv in 2015.

Carbon dioxide is one of the "greenhouse gases" which also include CFCs (which also cause ozone depletion in the upper atmosphere), methane, and nitrous oxides. Another greenhouse gas is water vapor. The quantity of vapor in the atmosphere has increased during recent decades as an expression of increased evaporation. This enhances the greenhouse effect as a positive feedback.

Greenhouse gases are so-called because they absorb part of the Earth's radiation going out to space and re-radiate a proportion of it back down. This critically important natural process acts to insulate the Earth and is essential to life. Without it, our planet would be some 54°F [30°C] colder than it is. But the increase in the volume of carbon dioxide in particular has caused global temperatures to rise. These changes were detailed by the Intergovernmental Panel on Climate Change (IPCC) report in 2013. While computer projections are difficult to make, the IPCC report concluded that a rise in temperatures of between 2.7°F [1.5°C] (compared to the 1850–1900 global mean) and at least 3.6°F [2.0°C] is likely by 2100. Global warming will almost certainly alter weather patterns, causing food and water shortages in vulnerable parts of the world, massive floods, and a rise in sea levels of between 1.71 ft [0.52 m] and 3.22 ft [0.98 m].

While an international ban has been imposed on some greenhouse gases, their residence time in the atmosphere may have long-lasting consequences.

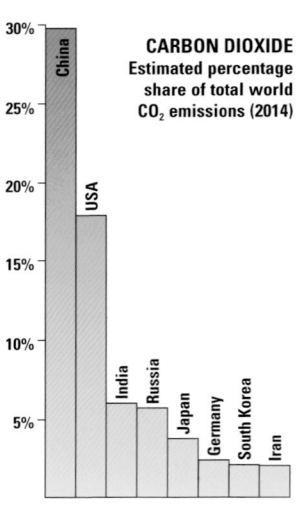

CARBON DIOXIDE
Estimated percentage share of total world CO₂ emissions (2014)

In 2010 it was estimated that China was generating almost 80% of its electricity from coal-fired power stations to support its economic boom. It has since overtaken the USA to become the world's biggest producer of carbon dioxide.

GLOBAL WARMING

High atmospheric concentrations of heat-absorbing gases are a major cause in the rise of average surface temperatures worldwide – up by 1.78°F [0.99°C] between 1880 and 2016. Global warming is also likely to bring about a rise in sea levels that may flood some of the world's densely populated coastal areas (see panel at foot of page 81).

Evidence of global warming is attributed mainly to the "greenhouse effect," caused by the emission of certain gases, notably carbon dioxide, into the atmosphere. Despite international action to control emissions of some greenhouse gases, carbon dioxide levels are still rising.

Carbon dioxide emissions in tonnes per capita (2014)

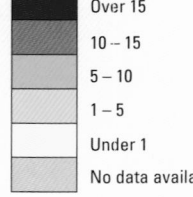

- Over 15
- 10 – 15
- 5 – 10
- 1 – 5
- Under 1
- No data available

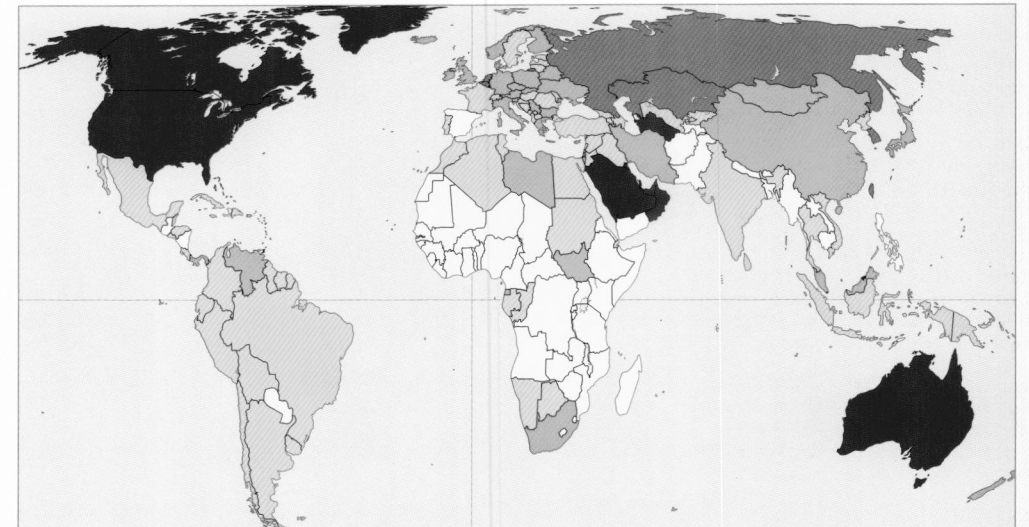

CLIMATE CHANGE

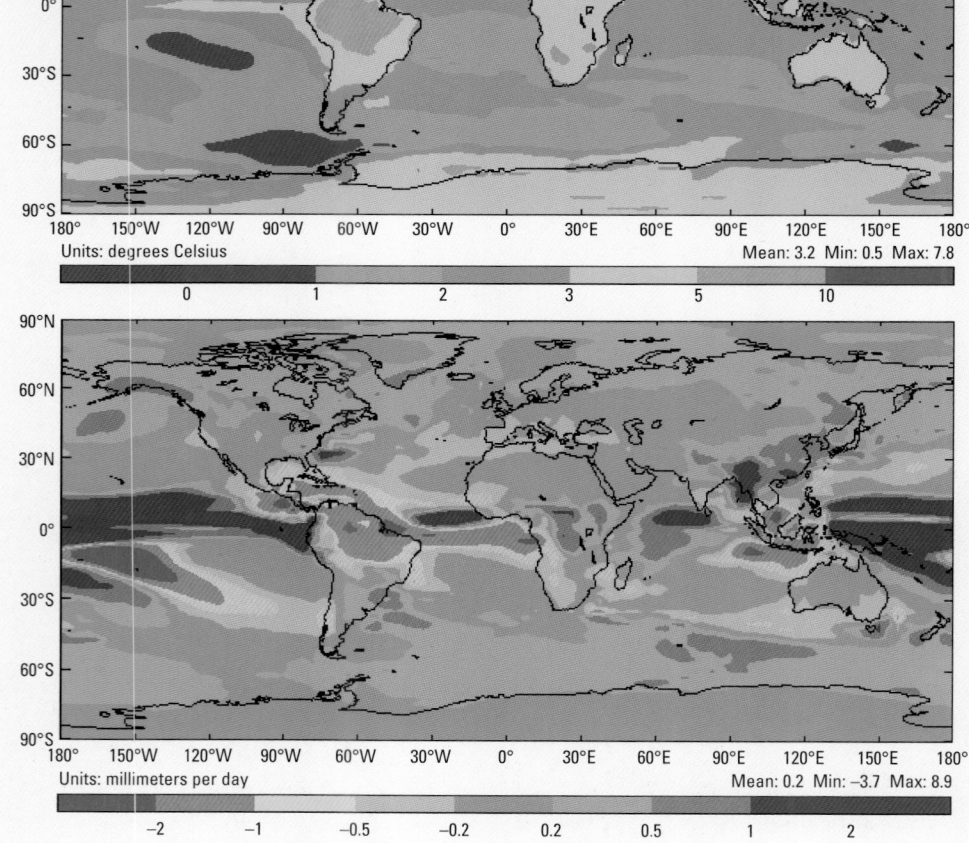

Units: degrees Celsius

Mean: 3.2 Min: 0.5 Max: 7.8

0   1   2   3   5   10

Units: millimeters per day

Mean: 0.2 Min: –3.7 Max: 8.9

–2   –1   –0.5   –0.2   0.2   0.5   1   2

Annual average surface air temperature

The map summarizes the change in long-term mean values between the predicted average for the period from 2070 to 2100, and the observed average for 1960 to 1990. The predictions are from a long-term "run" of a "coupled" atmosphere-ocean computer model that represents the complex processes in the Earth's climate system. It assumes that the atmospheric concentration of carbon dioxide will increase more than twofold during the 21st century, assuming "medium growth" of the global economy, and that no measures to combat the emission of greenhouse gases are taken. Note that the predicted increase in average surface temperature suggests a warming across Britain and Ireland of between 2°C [3.6°F] in the north and west to possibly 4°C [7.2°F] in the southeast. Very broadly, the oceans and some adjacent continental areas are likely to see the smaller increases.

Annual average precipitation

Predictions from climate models always involve some degree of uncertainty. This is because our understanding of the climate system and its complex workings are imperfect, as are the model representations of the physical system. Additionally, we are unsure quite how the world will evolve economically and politically over the coming decades – although different scenarios are used in this regard. The map of predicted precipitation change indicates broadly, for example, an increase across Britain and Ireland. The largest increases of some 0.01–0.02 inches [0.2–0.5 mm] a day are anticipated to be over northern and western areas. This equates to some 3–7 inches [75–180 mm] a year.

It should be noted that both these maps mask quite significant seasonal detail, which is also predicted by the models.

ARCTIC SEA ICE

The fact that the Arctic sea ice is disappearing has been known for decades. The underlying cause is believed by all but a handful of climatologists to be global warming, brought about by greenhouse-gas emissions. At current rates of shrinkage, this looks likely to happen some time between 2020 and 2050.

The reason is that Arctic air is warming twice as fast as the atmosphere as a whole. While some of the causes of this are understood, others are not. The darkness of land and water compared to the reflectiveness of snow and ice means that when the snow and ice melt to reveal land or water, the area exposed absorbs more heat from the Sun and reflects less of it back into space. The result is a feedback loop that accelerates local warming.

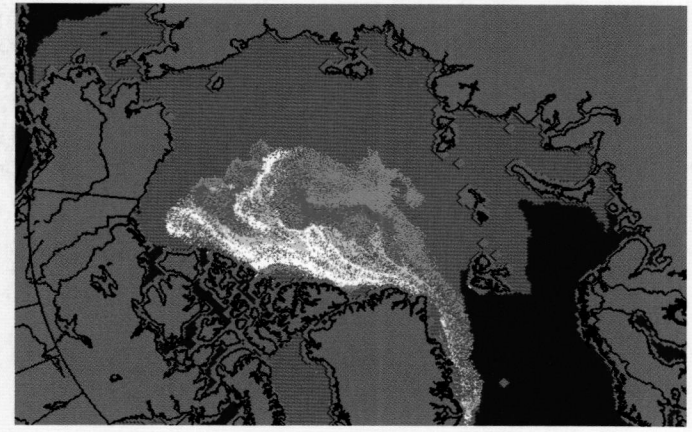

The diagram and map show that ice older than 1 year, which used to cover up to 60% of the Arctic Ocean, now covers only 30%. The oldest ice, over 4 years old, now comprises only 5% of the ice in the Arctic Ocean, whereas during the 1980s it covered roughly 25% of the region.

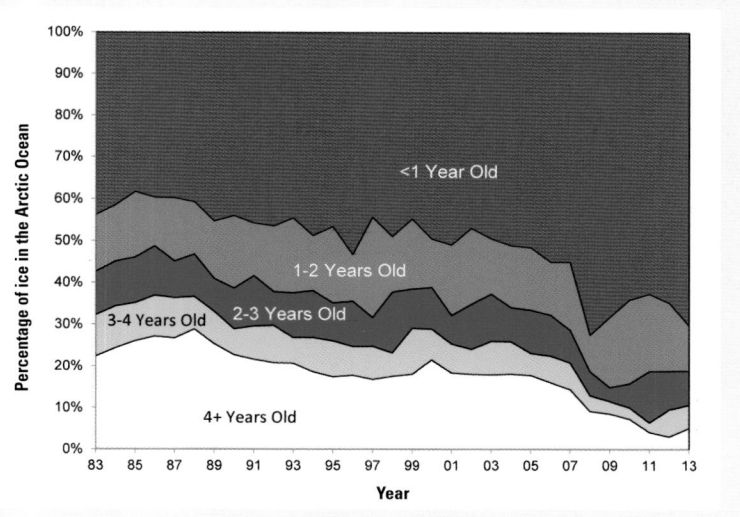

NSIDC courtesy J. Maslanik and M. Tschudi, University of Colorado

REGIONAL CLIMATE CHANGE

Climate modelers have produced simulations of global and continental surface temperature changes over the last century. This is done using only "natural forcing" by modeling the impact on atmospheric temperatures from known solar variability and volcanic eruptions. In addition, the same period of time is simulated by adding to natural forcing the impact of anthropogenic (human) influence due to measured changes in the concentration of greenhouse gases, particulate matter, etc.

The separate model "runs" are then compared with the observed temperature changes to illustrate which of the simulations matches the observations best.

This is a powerful means of verifying the relative roles of natural and human induced changes in atmospheric composition, and known solar output fluctuations on climate change.

▶ Climate model simulations for 1906 to 2009 using "natural forcings only" (blue bands) and "natural plus anthropogenic forcings" (pink bands). Regional decadal averages of observed temperature (black lines) are plotted as anomalies with respect to the 1880 to 1919 average. Blue and pink bands define the 5% to 95% range of possibilities for multiple runs for just natural forcings and natural plus anthropogenic forcings of the Coupled Model Intercomparison Project Phase 5.

Models using only natural forcings

Models using both natural and anthropogenic forcings

Observations (dashed when spatial coverage is less than 50%)

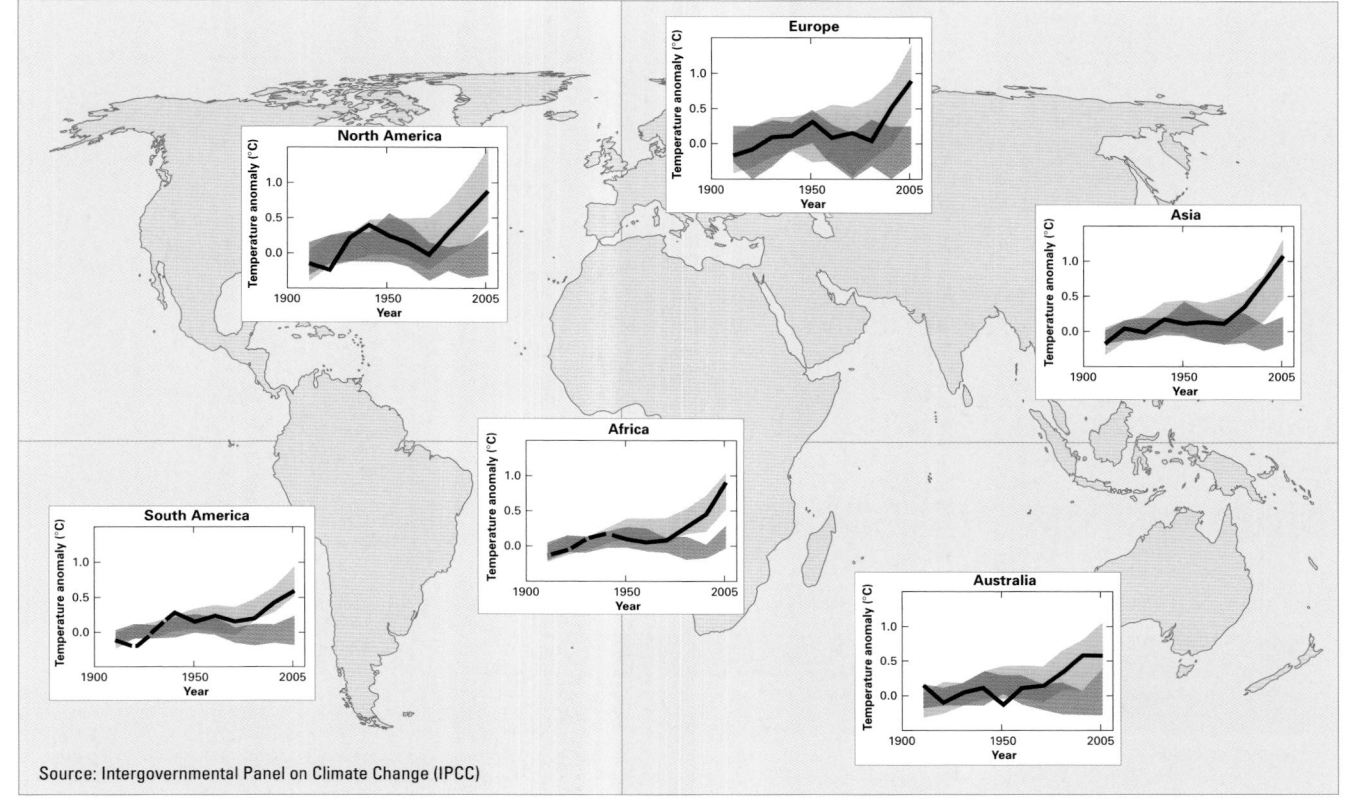

Source: Intergovernmental Panel on Climate Change (IPCC)

PROJECTED CHANGE IN GLOBAL WARMING

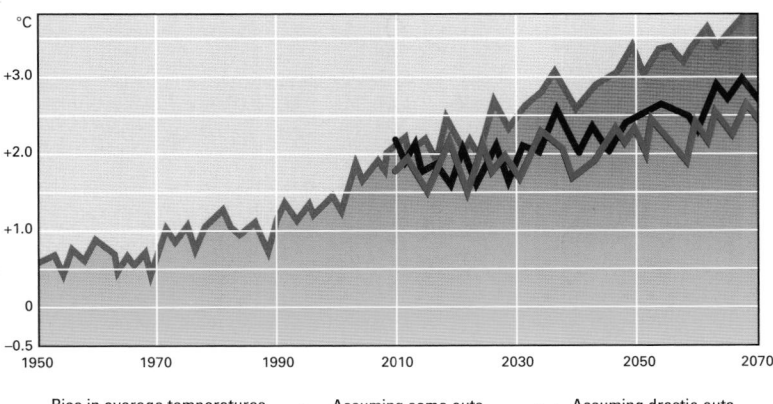

Rise in average temperatures assuming present trends in CO_2 emissions continue

Assuming some cuts are made in emissions

Assuming drastic cuts are made in emissions

Climate models are used to provide the best scientifically-based estimates of the future global climate. A typical method is to run the models for some decades ahead and then to compare the predicted average with a past 30-year period. A range of climate models are used, run with different scenarios that express the breadth of possibilities of, for example, industrial development and the degree of atmospheric pollution "clean-up" by industrial nations.

The diagram above shows global observed and predicted surface mean temperature change from 1950 to 2070 with three prediction scenarios. The first (red) assumes rapid economic growth and continued population increases. The second (blue) assumes some attempts are made to cut greenhouse gas emissions, while the green line involves the greater use of cleaner technologies, with global population peaking mid-century then declining.

REGIONAL CLIMATE CHANGE

The rate at which global sea level has increased since about the middle of the 19th century exceeds the increase estimated over the last two thousand years. The recent change is one expression of the impact of global warming through a combination of glacier melt and thermal expansion of the ocean; it is estimated that these count for 75% of the total observed rise since the 1970s. A combination of tide-gauge records and, more recently, altimeter observations from satellites, indicate that the global average increase of sea-level from 1901 to 2010 was 7.5 inches [190 mm] with an averaged global annual rise of 0.07 inches [1.7 mm] per year. This value has increased in recent periods from 0.08 inches [2.0 mm] per year (1971–2010) to 0.13 inches [3.2 mm] per year (1993–2010).

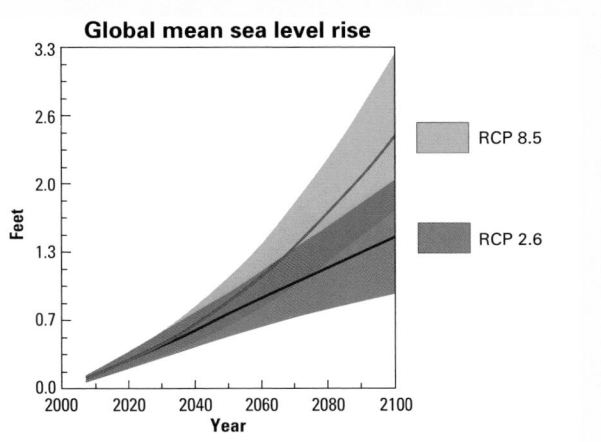

Source: Intergovernmental Panel on Climate Change (IPCC)

A combination of advanced global climate prediction models run through to 2100 produce an averaged forecast of the likely range of global mean sea level increase for two extreme CO_2, and other greenhouse gas, scenarios. The values on the graph are relative to the global mean conditions for the period 1986–2005. These "Representative Concentration Scenarios" (RCPs) vary from the lowest impact future (RCP 2.6) for which CO_2 concentration reaches 421 ppm by 2100, to the strongest

impact (RCP 8.5) for which CO_2 increases to 936 ppm by 2100.

The upper and lower boundaries of the two bands of color on the graph show the predicted upper and lower possibilities of future sea level increase. The solid colored line is the median value that has 50% of estimates above it and 50% below. The low impact future indicates a median value of a 1.31 ft [0.4 m] increase by 2100 while the highest impact future is about double that at 2.46 ft [0.75 m].

For more information:
78 Climate regions
79 Precipitation
86 Biodiversity

Without the hydrological cycle, by which water is constantly recycled between the oceans, the atmosphere and the land, the continents would be barren. Precipitation enables plants to grow and soils to form, creating the world's natural vegetation regions and the ecosystems that support animal life.

Running water also plays a major role in shaping landforms. Yet in many parts of the world, people do not have safe water to drink and suffer from diseases caused by water-borne organisms and pollution. It is estimated that 770 million people lack access to safe water and more people have a mobile phone than a toilet.

Experts argue that world demand for water is increasing at about twice the rate of population growth. It is predicted that, by 2025, half the world's population will face water shortages. This could lead to conflict and even boundary wars – 300 major rivers cross national frontiers and access to their water is likely to be disputed.

THE HYDROLOGICAL CYCLE

The world's water balance is regulated by the constant recycling of water between the oceans, the atmosphere and the land. The movement of water between these three reservoirs is known as the "hydrological cycle." The oceans play a vital role in the hydrological cycle: 74% of the total precipitation falls over the oceans and 84% of the total evaporation comes from the oceans. Water vapor in the atmosphere circulates around the planet, transporting energy as well as the water itself. When the vapor cools, it falls as rain or snow. The whole cycle is driven by the Sun.

Transfer of water vapor
10% of the balance of precipitation/
evaporation over oceans

Evaporation from oceans
84% of total
evaporation

Evapotranspiration
16% of total evaporation

Precipitation
74% of total
precipitation

Precipitation
26% of total
precipitation

Runoff
10% of the balance of
precipitation/evaporation
over land

Surface runoff

**Surface
storage**

Infiltration

Groundwater flow

WATER DISTRIBUTION

The distribution of planetary water is shown by percentage. Oceans and ice caps together account for more than 99% of the total; the breakdown of the remainder is estimated.

All water
97.4%
2.6%

Oceans
Fresh water

Fresh water
76.6%
0.5%
22.7%

Ice caps and glaciers
Groundwater
Active water

Active water
52%
36%
1.4%
7.1%
3.5%

Lakes
Soil moisture
Atmosphere
Rivers
Living things

Almost all the world's water is 3,000 million years old, and all of it cycles endlessly through the hydrosphere, though at different rates. Water vapor circulates over days, even hours; deep-ocean water circulates over millennia; and ice-cap water remains solid for millions of years.

ANNUAL SEDIMENT YIELD

tonnes/sq miles/year

0   250   500   750   1,000   1,250   1,500   1,750   2,000   2,250   2,500   2,750   3,000   3,250   3,500

Hwang Ho
Brahmaputra
Ganges
Indus
Mekong
Colorado
Amazon
Orinoco
Mississippi
Orange
Danube
Nile
Murray
Lena
Dnepr

Around 20% of all land-derived sediment is carried by three Asian rivers: the Hwang Ho (Yellow River), the Brahmaputra, and the Ganges. Together, these three rivers carry around 3,000 million tonnes of sediment each year into the oceans. Sediment yield is affected by runoff and vegetation cover, and is steadily increasing due to large-scale deforestation, most notably in South-east Asia and the Amazon basin. In these regions, deforesting the slopes allows the heavy tropical rains to wash away whatever thin and fragile soil there is, leading to severe erosion of the land.

▼ To prevent as excess of sediment building up and slowing the flow of the Hwang Ho (Yellow River), the river's mud, silt and sand is blasted downstream at an annual event at the Xiaolangdi Reservoir, near Jiyuan, in Henan province.

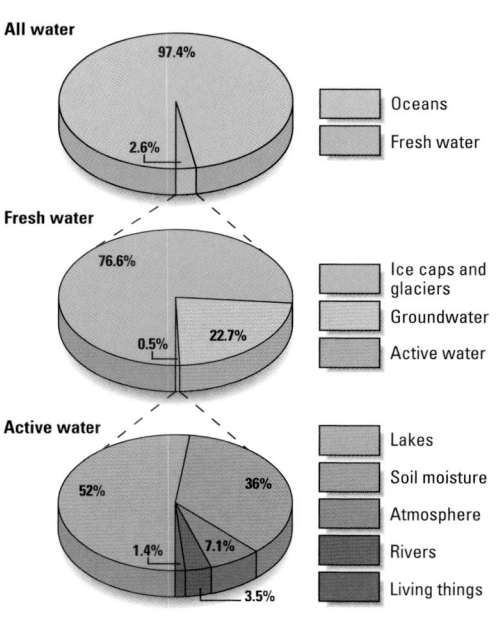

LONGEST RIVERS

		miles	km
Nile	Africa	4,160	6,695
Amazon	South America	4,010	6,450
Yangtse	Asia	3,960	6,380
Mississippi-Missouri	North America	3,710	5,971
Yenisey-Angara	Asia	3,445	5,550
Hwang Ho	Asia	3,395	5,464
Ob-Irtysh	Asia	3,360	5,410
Congo	Africa	2,900	4,670
Paraná-Plate	South America	2,796	4,500
Mekong	Asia	2,796	4,500
Amur	Asia	2,760	4,442
Lena	Asia	2,735	4,400
Irtysh	Asia	2,640	4,250
Mackenzie	North America	2,630	4,240
Niger	Africa	2,595	4,180
Yenisey	Asia	2,540	4,090
Missouri	North America	2,540	4,088
Mississippi	North America	2,350	3,782
Murray-Darling	Australia	2,330	3,750
Volga	Europe	2,300	3,700
Ob	Asia	2,285	3,680
Zambezi	Africa	2,200	3,540
Purus	South America	2,080	3,350
Madeira	South America	1,990	3,200
Yukon	North America	1,980	3,185
Indus	Asia	1,925	3,100
Darling	Australia	1,905	3,070
Rio Grande	North America	1,880	3,030
Brahmaputra	Asia	1,800	2,900
São Francisco	South America	1,800	2,900
Syrdarya	Asia	1,775	2,860
Danube	Europe	1,770	2,850
Salween	Asia	1,740	2,800
Paraná	South America	1,740	1,740
Tocantins	South America	1,710	2,750
Orinoco	South America	1,700	2,740
Euphrates	Asia	1,675	2,700
Murray	Australia	1,600	2,575
Paraguay	South America	1,580	2,550
Amudarya	Asia	1,575	2,540

WATER SCARCITY

Human populations require fresh water for many purposes – drinking, cooking, washing, farming, industry, recreation and energy production. Given population growth and rising standards of living in some areas, there will inevitably be increased pressure on this resource in certain places. Water scarcity can be physical and/or economic.

Areas with little or no water scarcity – less than 25% of water from rivers is withdrawn for agriculture, industry and domestic purposes

Areas with physical water scarcity – more than 75% of water from rivers is withdrawn for agriculture, industry and domestic purposes

Areas approaching physical water scarcity – more than 60% of water from rivers is withdrawn and scarcity is expected in the near future

Areas with economic water scarcity – less than 25% of water from rivers is withdrawn but human, institutional and financial problems limit access to water

No data available

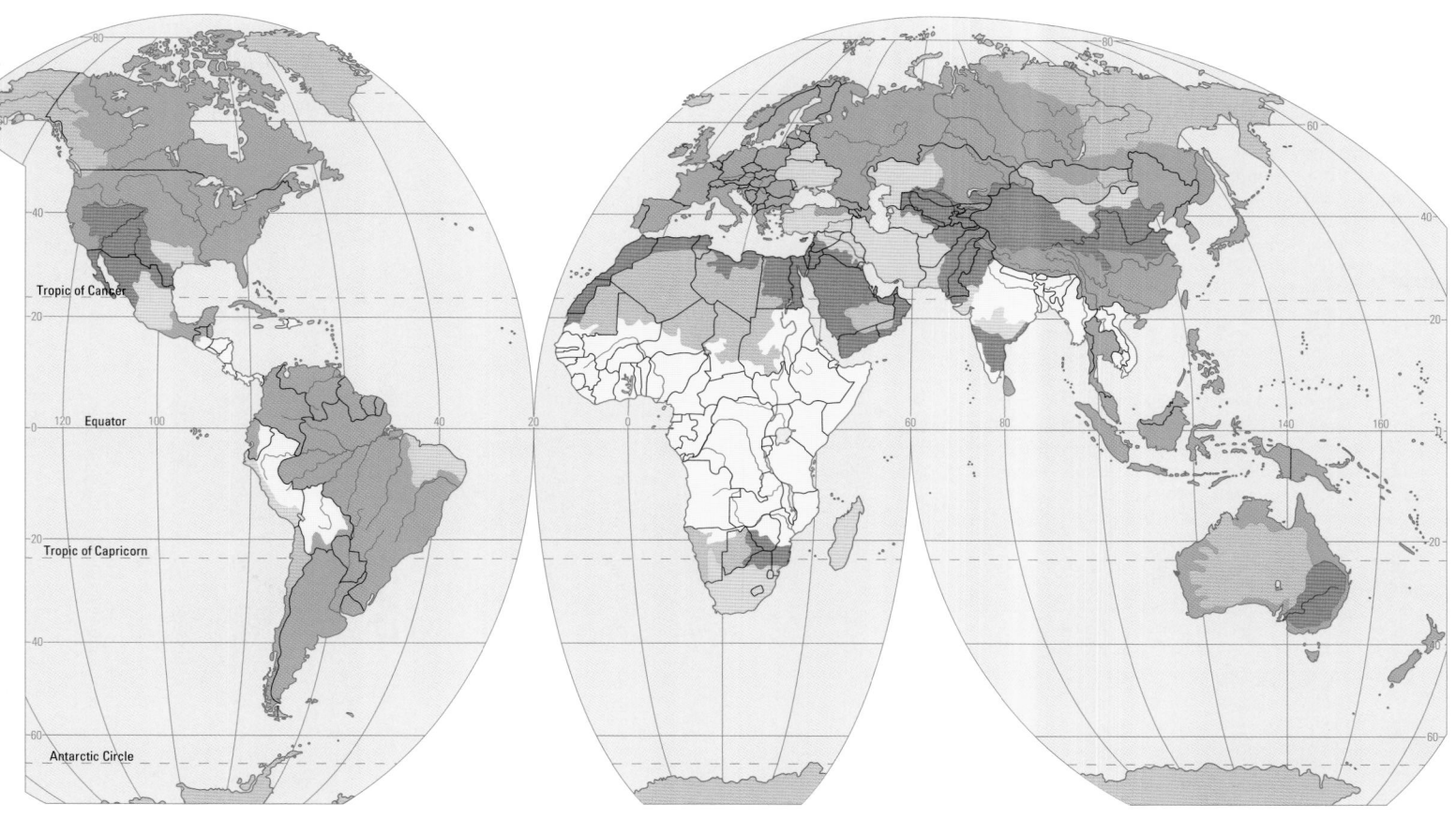

NATURAL VEGETATION

The map below illustrates the natural "climax vegetation" of a region, as dictated by its climate and topography. In most cases, human agricultural activity has drastically altered the pattern of the vegetation. The various vegetation regions support different kinds of animals and wildlife, and, in an undisturbed state, they are highly developed biological communities, or "biomes."

The blue line on the map represents the northern limit of tree growth, and the red lines indicate the northern and southern limits of palm growth. The majority of the numerous species are tropical or subtropical. Some, such as the coconut, date, sago, and oil palms, are important economically.

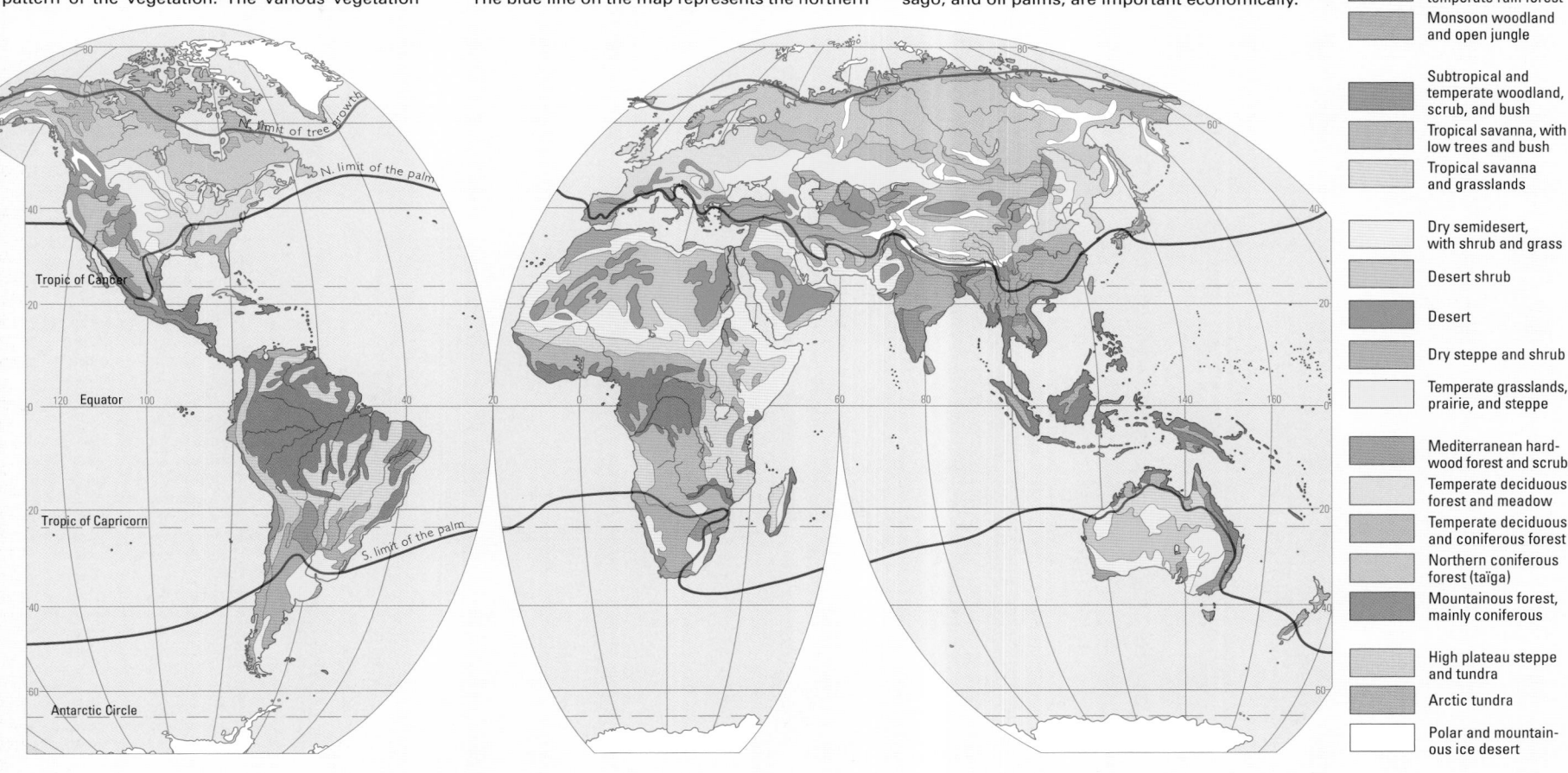

Tropical rain forest

Subtropical and temperate rain forest

Monsoon woodland and open jungle

Subtropical and temperate woodland, scrub, and bush

Tropical savanna, with low trees and bush

Tropical savanna and grasslands

Dry semidesert, with shrub and grass

Desert shrub

Desert

Dry steppe and shrub

Temperate grasslands, prairie, and steppe

Mediterranean hardwood forest and scrub

Temperate deciduous forest and meadow

Temperate deciduous and coniferous forest

Northern coniferous forest (taïga)

Mountainous forest, mainly coniferous

High plateau steppe and tundra

Arctic tundra

Polar and mountainous ice desert

For more information:

79 Temperature and precipitation
80 Climate change and global warming
82 Water distribution
86 Population
98 Minerals

Oceans cover about 70% of the Earth's surface and are of great importance to humans in a number of ways. These include regulating global climates and providing a source of economic materials, such as food resources. In addition, oceans are important for leisure and recreation. They have also been described as the "highways in the globalized world." However, anthropogenic (man-made) stresses are changing the oceans faster than at almost any time in our planet's history.

Increasingly larger fishing fleets are now catching fewer large predatory fish but greater quantities of the smaller fish that are further down the food chain. The most prized food fish, such as cod and salmon, which tend to be top-level predators, are declining in numbers, leaving smaller, less desirable fish to be caught. Not only does this affect the type of fish available for human consumption, but it could also change marine ecosystems forever.

There are a number of possible strategies for the future, but there are clearly no simple solutions to the problems associated with such a politically, economically, and environmentally sensitive global industry. Fish resources could be conserved in a number of ways – for example, the protection of juveniles as well as policies to encourage breeding and discourage the marketing of illegal catches would help boost stocks. Catches could be restricted in order to match supply with demand and to protect sensitive species.

OCEANIC CONVEYOR BELTS

Oceanic convection occurs where cold, salty water from polar regions sinks into the depths and makes its way toward the Equator. The densest water is found in the Antarctic area. This cold, dense water sweeps round Antarctica at a depth of about 2.5 miles [4 km]. It then spreads into the deep basins of the Atlantic Ocean, the Pacific Ocean, and the Indian Ocean. Surface currents bring warm water to the North Atlantic from the Indian and Pacific Oceans. These waters give up their heat to cold winds, which blow from Canada across the North Atlantic. This water then sinks and starts the reverse convection of the deep ocean current. The amount of heat given up is about a third of the energy that is received from the Sun. Because the conveyor operates in this way, the North Atlantic is warmer than the North Pacific, so there is proportionally more evaporation there. The water left behind by evaporation contains more salt and it is therefore much denser, which causes it to sink. Eventually, this water is transported into the Pacific Ocean where it picks up more warm water, and thus its salinity and therefore its density is reduced.

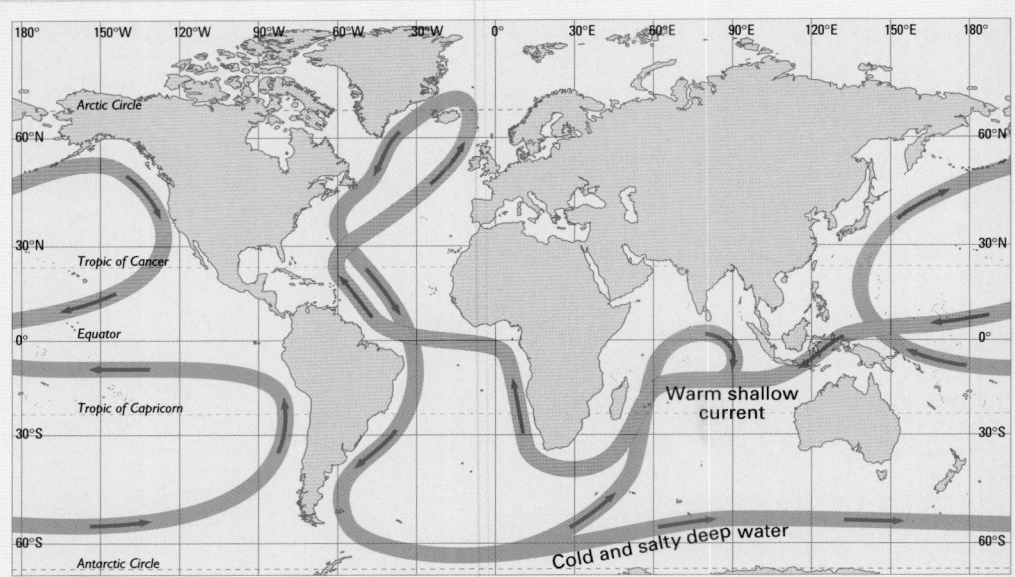

Warm shallow current

Cold and salty deep water

OCEAN CURRENTS

JANUARY CURRENTS
(Northern Hemisphere: winter)

Cold	Warm	Speed (knots)
		Less than 0.5
		0.5 – 1.0
		Over 1.0

JULY CURRENTS
(Northern Hemisphere: summer)

Cold	Warm	Speed (knots)
		Less than 0.5
		0.5 – 1.0
		Over 1.0

Moving immense quantities of energy as well as billions of tonnes of water every hour, the ocean currents are a vital part of the great heat engine that drives the Earth's climate. They themselves are produced by a twofold mechanism. At the surface, winds push huge masses of water before them; in the deep ocean below, an abrupt temperature gradient separates the churning surface waters from the still depths (*see the ocean conveyor belt diagram above*).

Coriolis effect
The pattern of circulation of the great surface currents is determined by the displacement known as the "Coriolis effect." As the Earth turns, the vast mass of ocean water is deflected to one side. The deflection is most obvious near the Equator, where the Earth's surface is spinning eastward at 1,000 mph; currents moving poleward are curved clockwise in the northern hemisphere and counterclockwise in the southern hemisphere.

Ocean currents
The result is a system of spinning circles known as "gyres." Warm currents move constantly from the Equator toward the poles, while cold water moves in the reverse direction. In this way, ocean currents act like a thermostat, helping to regulate temperatures around the world.

Depending on the annual movements of the prevailing wind belts, some currents on or near the Equator may reverse their direction in the course of the year, a variation on which Asia's monsoon rains depend and whose occasional failure has brought disaster to millions of people.

FISHING

As stocks are overfished and dwindle, it is important to manage them carefully so that there are sufficient resources for future generations. The Marine Stewardship Council (MSC) is an international, non-profit organization set up to help make the seafood market sustainable. It oversees and manages the distinctive blue labeling system that tells consumers which species of fish they can buy without destroying stocks. This system is popular with large food retailers who wish to be seen supporting sustainable fish catches. It is estimated that over 30% of shoppers worldwide recognize the MSC ecolabel. However, only 8% of the world's fisheries are MSC certified.

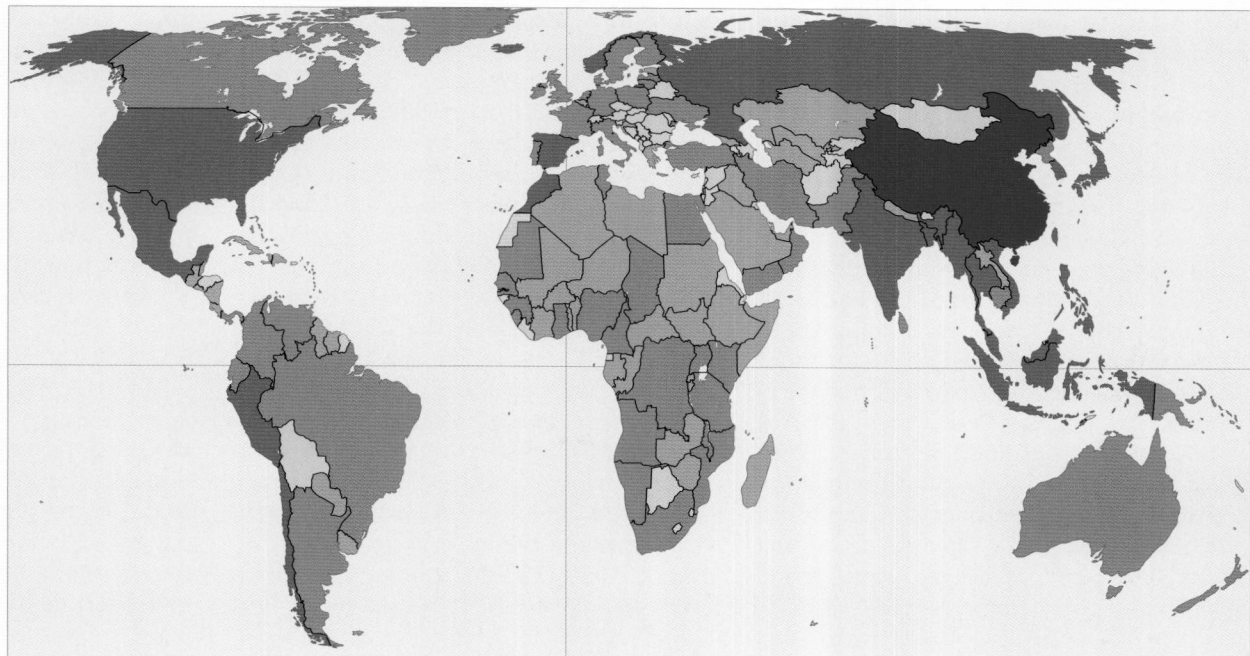
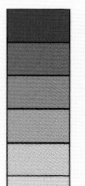

There has been a dramatic rise in world wild fish catches, from under 20 million tonnes in 1950 to an estimated 94.5 million tonnes in 2014, but this is now leveling off as the stocks become depleted and protection of fish stocks increases. During the same period, farmed fish totals rose from almost nothing in 1950 to an estimated 67 million tonnes in 2012. Currently, around 3 billion people get 20% of their animal protein from fishery products.

Total world fish catch in metric tonnes, inland and marine fishing (2014)

- Over 10 million
- 1 million – 10 million
- 100,000 – 1 million
- 10,000 – 100,000
- Under 10,000
- No data available

AQUACULTURE

▲ This aerial photo shows shrimp farms, near Mahajanga, in northwestern Madagascar. Shrimp farming is being used to stimulate the country's economy.

Aquaculture involves raising fish commercially, usually for food. In contrast, a fish hatchery releases juvenile fish into the wild for recreational fishing or to supplement a species' natural numbers. The most important fish species raised by fish farms are salmon, carp, tilapia, catfish, and cod. Salmon makes up 85% of the total sale of Norwegian fish farming. Farming was introduced when populations of wild Atlantic salmon in the North Atlantic and Baltic Sea crashed due to overfishing.

Technological costs are high, and include using drugs, such as antibiotics to keep fish healthy and steroids to improve growth. Breeding programs are also expensive. Outputs are high per hectare and per farmer, and efficiency is high also. However, environmental effects can be damaging. Salmon are carnivores and so need to be fed pellets made from other fish. It is possible that farmed salmon actually represent a net loss of protein in the global food supply, as it takes between 4–11 lbs [2–5 kg] of wild fish to grow 2 lbs [1 kg] of salmon. In contrast, most global aquaculture production (c. 85%) uses non-carnivorous fish species, such as tilapia and catfish, for domestic markets. Fish like herring, mackerel, sardine, and anchovy are used to produce the feed for farmed salmon, and so the production of salmon leads to the depletion of other fish species on a global scale.

Other environmental costs include the sea lice and disease that spread from farmed salmon into wild stocks, and pollution (created by uneaten food, faeces, and chemicals used to treat them)

contaminating surrounding waters. Organic debris of this type, with steroids and other chemical waste, can contaminate coastal waters. In addition, the accidental escape of fish can affect local wild fish gene pools, when escaped fish interbreed with wild populations, reducing their genetic diversity, and potentially introducing non-natural genetic variation. In some parts of the world, escapees of farmed fish threaten native wild fish, as salmon is an alien species (for example, the salmon farming industry in British Columbia, Canada, has inadvertently introduced a non-native species – Atlantic salmon – into the Pacific Ocean).

However, the positive environmental benefits of not removing fish from wild stocks, but of growing them in farms, are great. Wild populations are allowed to breed and maintain stocks, whilst the farmed variety provides food.

▲ These floating aquaculture pens contain northern bluefin tuna in Baja California, Mexico. Small tuna are caught off-shore and moved to large enclosures.

PLASTIC

Yet more alarming for the health of the oceans and their wildlife is the plague of plastic. The UN Environment Program estimated in 2006 that every square kilometer of sea held nearly 18,000 pieces of floating plastic. Much of it was, and is, in the central Pacific, where scientists believe as much as 100 million tonnes of plastic jetsam are suspended in two separate "gyres" of garbage over an area twice the size of the USA. This has been referred to as the Great Pacific Garbage Patch – about 90% of the plastic in the sea has been carried there by wind or water from land. It takes decades to sink or decompose.

▲ In the main, the plastic in the oceans comes from food and drink packaging. The larger pieces can be mistakenly eaten by animals such as seals, and turtles, which can choke them. Smaller pieces are swallowed by fish which can then work their way up through the food chain to humans. Harm is also caused by the chemicals contained within plastics.

RESPONSES TO THE THREATS

In the case of the oceans, a conservative estimate of the cost of climate change is that by the year 2100 it will amount to nearly US $2 trillion annually, or about 0.4% of global GDP. Economists at the Stockholm Environment Institute arrived at the figure by looking at five measures: how much fisheries and tourism stood to lose, and what the economic impact would be of rising sea levels, more storms, and less carbon being absorbed by the oceans.

If the world continues to warm at its present rate and temperatures rise by 7.2°F [4°C] by 2100, the total will come to US $1.98 trillion. However, if drastic measures are taken to cut emissions and they rise by only 4°F [2.2°C], this figure will be US $612 billion. Governments worldwide were urged by the 1972 Stockholm Convention to control the dumping of waste in their oceans by implementing new laws. The United Nations met in London after this recommendation to begin the Convention on the Prevention of Marine Pollution by Dumping of Wastes and Other Matter, which was implemented in 1975. The International Maritime Organization was given responsibility for this convention and a Protocol was finally adopted in 1996, a major step in the regulation of ocean dumping.

The United Nations Convention on the Law of the Sea, signed in 1982 but only entering into force in 1994, established a framework of law for the oceans, including rules for deep-sea mining and economic exclusion zones extending 200 nautical miles around nation states.

For more information:
78 Climate
80 Climate change
   Global warming
83 Natural vegetation

Biodiversity refers to the variety of living material. It includes the variety of species, the variety within the same species, and the variety of ecosystems within which species operate. Estimates of the number of species in the world vary from between 7 million and 80 million. The currently accepted total is about 14 million, yet only 2 million species have been formally identified.

Biodiversity is vital for human survival. It remains the basis for our food and most of our medicine. In less economically developed countries (LEDCs), over 20% of the food consumed is gathered from natural sources. At a global level, over 15% of animal protein consumed is from sea fish. More than 60% of the world's population rely on traditional medicines for their health care. In Mexico, the Popoluca Indians "farm" over 250 species of plant. Many medicines come from natural sources.

Aspirin, for example, comes from an acid taken from the bark of willow trees. The anti-cancer drug "taxol" originates from the wild Pacific yew tree. It is estimated that the pharmaceuticals industry gains US $32 billion per year in profits from traditional remedies.

However, the loss of biodiversity is increasing at an accelerating rate. Up to 27,000 species a year may be lost, and the United Nations Environment Programme (UNEP) suggests that the current rate of extinction is 50–100 times greater than "normal", and believes that up to 25% of all the world's species may be lost by 2025. The main reasons for the decline are the introduction of alien species and habitat destruction. Human impact on biodiversity has brought about more extinctions than any other single factor since the extinction of the dinosaurs (65 million years ago).

Since 1600, 39% of animal extinctions have been due to the introduction of alien species, 36% from habitat destruction, and 23% from hunting or deliberate extermination. The introduction of rats, cats and other species has led to the extinction of many flightless birds in Polynesia. Plantation crops, such as rubber, often thrive best when taken away from their natural homes, since in the new lands there may not be the pests to control them. One noted example of extinction was caused by the introduction of the Nile perch into Lake Victoria, East Africa: introduced in the 1960s, it led to the extinction of some 50 species of cichlid fish within 20 years.

In 2016, over 21,000 species out of approximately 71,000 species on the IUCN (International Union for Conservation of Nature and Natural Resources) Red List of Threatened Species, were in danger of extinction. This included one in four mammals, two in five amphibians, one in three coral and one in eight birds.

THREATENED SPECIES
Total number of threatened species for selected countries in each continent

UK
Canada
New Zealand
Russia
Papua New Guinea
South Africa
Thailand
Spain
Cameroon
Philippines
Colombia
Australia
Brazil
India
China
Tanzania
Mexico
Malaysia
Madagascar
Indonesia
USA
Ecuador

500   1000   1500   2000   2500

Source: IUCN Red List 2016

THREATENED MAMMAL SPECIES

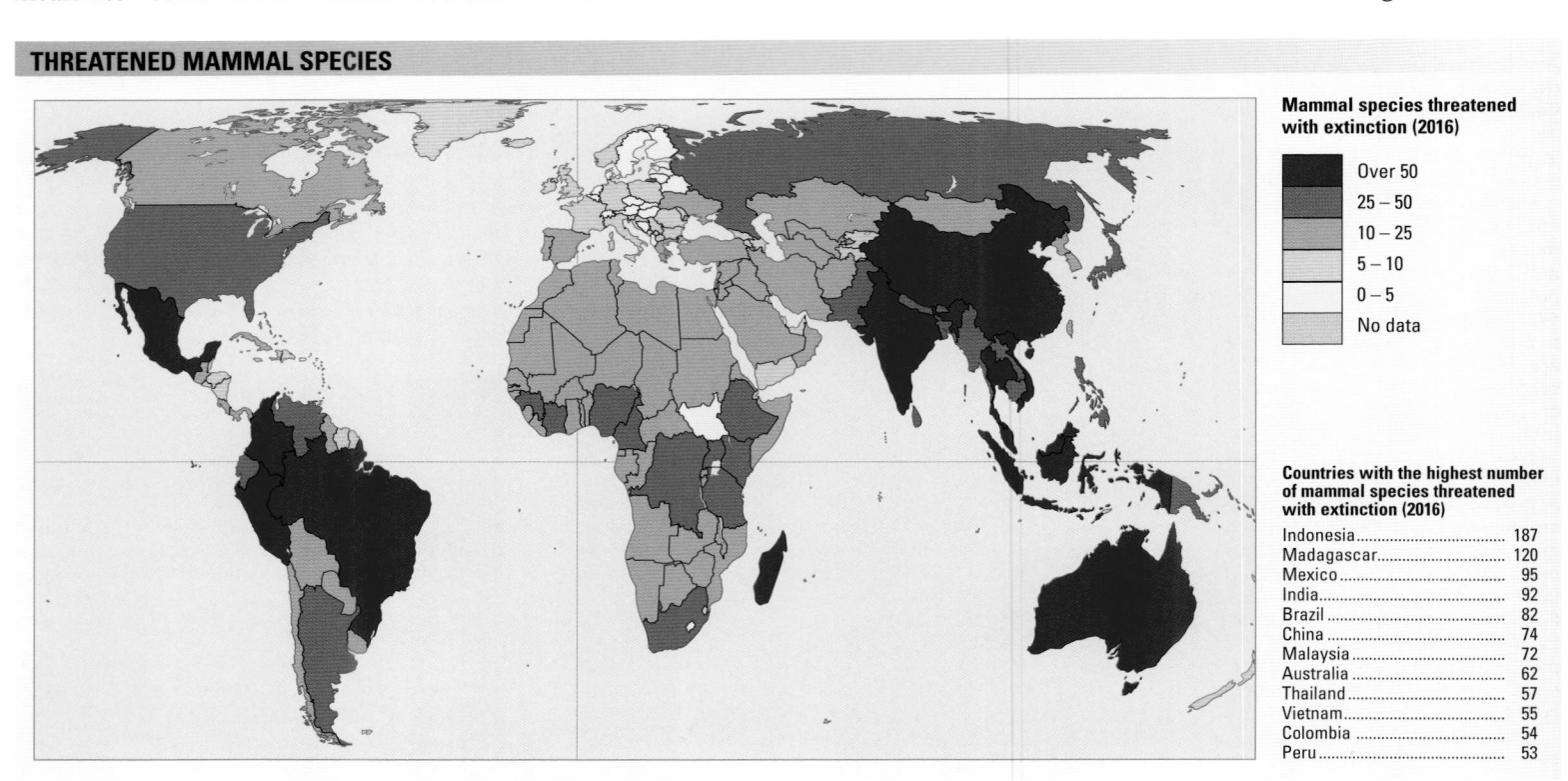

Mammal species threatened with extinction (2016)

- Over 50
- 25 – 50
- 10 – 25
- 5 – 10
- 0 – 5
- No data

Countries with the highest number of mammal species threatened with extinction (2016)

Indonesia	187
Madagascar	120
Mexico	95
India	92
Brazil	82
China	74
Malaysia	72
Australia	62
Thailand	57
Vietnam	55
Colombia	54
Peru	53

BIODIVERSITY HOTSPOTS

Up to 75% of the world's most threatened mammals, birds and amphibians live in an area covering just 2.3% of the Earth's surface, and roughly half of all flowering plant species and 42% of land-based vertebrates exist in 36 biological hotspots.

Scientists argue that, with limited financial resources, governments and conservationists should prioritize by protecting the small total land areas that account for a very high percentage of global biodiversity. In 1999, scientists identified 25 such areas, mostly in the tropics, which were the centre of global biodiversity.

The number of hotspots has risen to 36. These include the mountains of central Asia, the whole of Japan, the Horn of Africa including the Ethiopian highlands, and the Himalayas region. The hotspots once covered 15.7% of the Earth's surface, an area roughly the size of Russia and Australia combined – now they cover only 2.3% of the Earth's surface, an area slightly larger than India.

Over 70% of all mammals, 86% of all birds, and 92% of all amphibians are crammed into this small area of the world's total land mass. Madagascar and the Indian Ocean Islands hotspot was found to have very high concentrations of plant and vertebrate families that are found nowhere else on the globe.

Global warming could have a devastating effect on biodiversity hotspots such as the Amazonian and Indonesian rainforests. By 2100, between 12% and 39% of the land surface of the Earth will have a new climate. There are numerous species that will be unable to move in order to stay within their preferred climate range. These species will either have to evolve rapidly or die out.

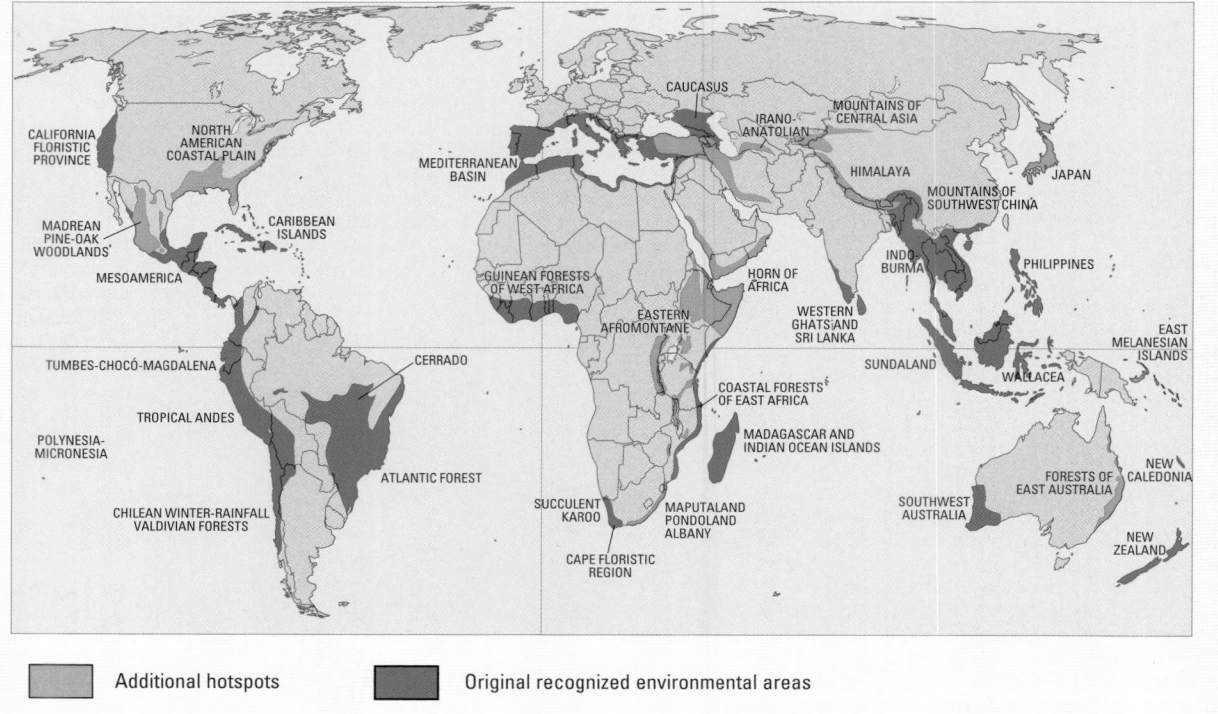

Additional hotspots   Original recognized environmental areas

AUSTRALIA'S INTRODUCED SPECIES

Australia's native plants and animals adapted to life on an isolated continent over millions of years. Since European settlement in the 18th century they have had to compete with a range of species introduced by the settlers, which impact on the native species by predation, competition for food and shelter, destroying habitat, and by spreading diseases. Introduced species typically have few predators or fatal diseases, and some have very high reproductive rates.

Management and the prevention of the introduction of new invasive species are key environmental and agricultural policy issues for the Australian federal and state governments.

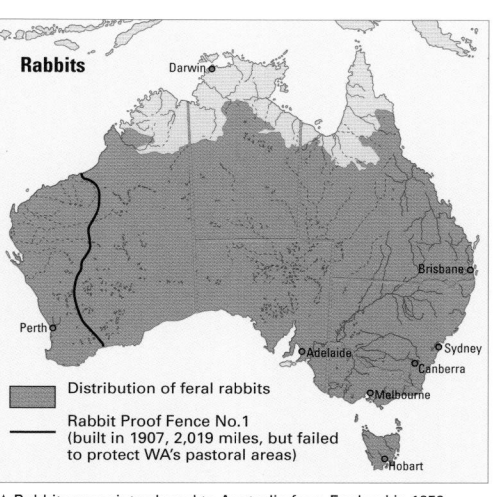

Rabbits

▨ Distribution of feral rabbits

— Rabbit Proof Fence No.1 (built in 1907, 2,019 miles, but failed to protect WA's pastoral areas)

▲ Rabbits were introduced to Australia from England in 1859 for hunting, and quickly spread throughout the country. They are one of the most destructive introduced species in Australia, competing with native wildlife, damaging vegetation, and degrading the land.

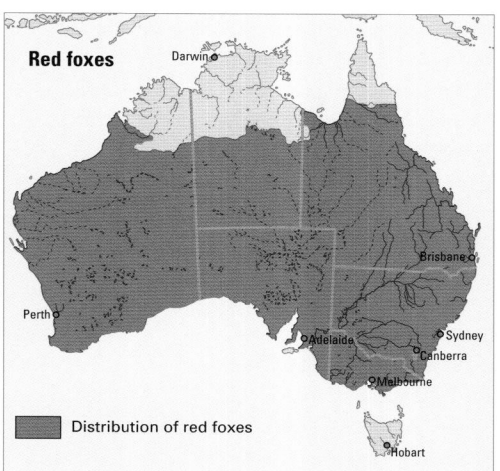

Red foxes

▨ Distribution of red foxes

▲ The red fox was introduced from Europe for recreational hunting in 1855 and populations became established in the wild within 15 years. They prey on newborn lambs and have also been responsible for the decline of a number of native species.

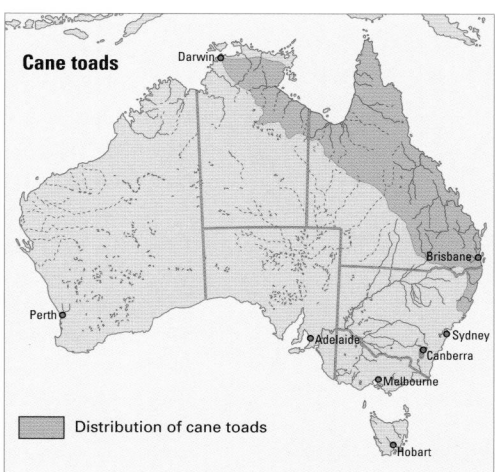

Cane toads

▨ Distribution of cane toads

▲ Cane toads were introduced in 1935 to control beetles which were threatening the sugar-cane industry. However, this failed as both the toad and the beetle are still thriving. They adapted well to the Australian environment and with no natural predators they quickly spread. They eat small native wildlife and poison any predators.

THE VALUE OF NATURE

According to the National Ecosystem Assessment (NEA), lakes, forests, parks, and wildlife are a huge financial asset. Moreover, it is claimed that the natural world is vital for human existence, not only in providing food, water, and air, but also for the cultural and spiritual benefits that it provides.

Economic benefits include food production, which utilizes insects for pollination, earthworms for mixing the soil, and soil microbes for recycling nutrients. In the UK, for example, the value of pollinating insects has been calculated to be $727 million, and the value of wetlands, which help to provide clean water, at $2.5 billion. Globally, bees are believed to provide $368 billion worth of services, or about 9.5% of the total economic value of agriculture. One third of the food the world produces is dependent on bees for pollination.

Although the natural world provides many benefits including food supply, water supply, climate regulation, and breakdown of waste products, these are under-valued. Some of the benefits are non-quantifiable but include recreation and long-term health. Moreover, the way in which ecosystems have been used has changed over the last sixty years or so. Population increase and rising standards of living have contributed to a huge growth in agricultural production. It has also, however, contributed to the decline in ecosystem services, such as air, water, and soil quality.

Although some ecosystems are delivering services well, there are others which are showing long-term decline. Those that are in decline include marine fisheries, wild species diversity, and soil quality.

Ecosystems, and ecosystems services, constantly change as a result of demographic, economic, social, and cultural factors. For example, since the 1940s there has been intensification of agriculture at the expense of many habitats, including wetlands, forests, and grasslands.

Types of ecosystem service

Provisioning services
These are the services obtained from ecosystems such as food, fibre, fuel, and water from aquifers, rivers, and lakes. Goods can come from heavily managed ecosystems (intensive farms and fish farms) or from semi-natural ones (such as by hunting and fishing). Most of these food producing ecosystems are land-based but some are water-based (aquaculture). Ecosystems also provide a variety of materials for construction and fuel including wood, charcoal, biofuels, and plant oils. They are also an important source of raw materials for the pharmaceuticals industry.

Supporting services
These are the essentials for life and include primary productivity, soil formation, and the cycling of nutrients. Ecosystems provide the conditions for growing food. Habitats provide all that an individual plant or animal needs to survive: food; water; nutrients; and shelter. Every habitat provides a variety of niches that can be essential for a species' lifecycle. For example, migratory birds depend on different habitats at different times of the year.

Ecosystems also help maintain genetic diversity (biodiversity) which is the variety of genetic materials between ecosystems, niches, and populations.

Regulating services
These are a diverse set of services and include pollination, regulation of pests and diseases, and production of goods. Other services include climate and climatic hazard regulation, and water quality regulation. For example, trees provide shade and influence water availability and, by removing air pollutants from the atmosphere, they improve air quality. Ecosystems influence global climate by storing and sequestering greenhouse gases such

as carbon dioxide. As vegetation grows, it removes carbon dioxide and locks it in its tissue.

Ecosystems moderate extreme events: they act as buffers against natural disasters. Mangrove forests can help protect a shoreline against hurricane damage, and wetlands can absorb flood waters. Vegetation can help reduce soil erosion.

Insects and the wind help pollinate plants. Around 90 out of 115 leading food crops, such as cocoa and coffee, depend upon animal pollination.

Ecosystems are also important for the control of pests and vector borne diseases. Birds, bats, wasps, frogs, and fungi are all examples of natural controls.

Cultural services
These occur when people interact with the environment and this provides cultural goods and benefits. Open spaces provide the opportunity for outdoor recreation, learning, and spiritual well-being. Recreation can lead to major improvements in physical and mental health. Also, tourism provides a major source of income to many countries.

▲ The wide variety of provisions on display in this Malaysian market are testament to the value of ecosystems for the supply of food.

▲ The destruction of large areas of vegetation can lessen the value of ecosystems. The deforested and drowned rain forest at Batang Ai, Sarawak, Malaysia, above, is the result of land being cleared for a hydroelectric power station.

The goods and services derived from mountains, moorlands, and heaths, and those from woodlands are shown in the table.

	Mountains, moorlands, and heaths	Woodlands
Provisioning	Food*	Timber*
	Fibre*	Species diversity*
	Fuel*	Fuelwood*
	Freshwater*	Freshwater*
Regulating	Climate regulation†	Climate regulation†
	Flood regulation†	Flood regulation†
	Wildfire regulation†	Erosion control†
	Water quality regulation†	Disease and pest control†
	Erosion control†	Wildfire regulation†
		Air and water quality regulation†
		Soil quality regulation†
		Noise regulation†
Cultural	Recreation and tourism*	Recreation and tourism*
	Aesthetic values*	Aesthetic values*
	Cultural heritage*	Cultural heritage*
	Spiritual values*	Employment*
	Education*	Education*
	Sense of place*	Sense of place*
	Health benefits*	Health benefits*

Key
Items marked * denote goods
Items marked † denote services

For more information:

90 Urbanization of the Earth

 Urban population

91 Largest cities

In 8000 BC, following the development of agriculture, the world had an estimated population of 8 million and by AD 1000 it was about 300 million. The onset of the Industrial Revolution in the late 18th century led to a population explosion. The 1,000 million mark was passed by 1850, it doubled by the 1920s, and doubled again to 4,000 million by 1975.

In the 1990s, demographers estimated that the world's population, which passed the 7 billion mark in 2012, would reach 9.3 billion by 2050 and only level out in 2200, at a peak of around 11 billion. However, in the early 21st century, after the rate of population growth had shown signs of decline, the Institute for Applied Systems Analysis suggested that the world's population might peak at about 9 billion in 2070. Whatever the global projections, everyone agreed that the greatest population growth would be in the developing countries.

The developing world includes what the World Bank (2017) describes as low-income economies (per capita GNI of US $1,025 or less), lower-middle-income economies (per capita GNI of US $1,026 to US $4,035), and upper-middle-income economies (per capita GNI of US $4,036 to US $12,475). Most developing countries are in Africa, Asia, and Latin America. The developed world, made up of high-income, industrialized economies (per capita GNI of US $12,736 or more), contains Australasia, most of Europe and North America, and Japan.

In developing countries, a high proportion of the population is young and so these countries face high expenditure on health and education. In developed countries, the population pyramids are becoming top-heavy, with increasingly aging populations.

LARGEST NATIONS

The world's most populous nations, in millions (2016)

1.	China	1,374
2.	India	1,267
3.	USA	324
4.	Indonesia	258
5.	Brazil	206
6.	Pakistan	202
7.	Nigeria	186
8.	Bangladesh	156
9.	Russia	142
10.	Japan	127
11.	Mexico	123
12.	Philippines	103
13.	Ethiopia	102
14.	Vietnam	95
15.	Egypt	95
16.	Iran	83
17.	Congo (Dem. Rep.)	81
18.	Germany	81
19.	Turkey	80
20.	Thailand	68
21.	France	67
22.	UK	64
23.	Italy	62
24.	Burma (Myanmar)	57
25.	South Africa	54

MOST CROWDED NATIONS

Population per square mile (2016)

1.	Monaco	39,206
2.	Singapore	22,237
3.	Bahrain	5,107
4.	Vatican City	5,000
5.	Malta	3,460
6.	Maldives	3,275
7.	Bangladesh	2,809
8.	Mauritius	1,707
9.	Barbados	1,704
10.	Taiwan	1,688

LEAST CROWDED

Population per square mile (2016)

1.	Mongolia	5.0
2.	Namibia	7.7
3.	Australia	7.7
4.	Iceland	8.4
5.	Guyana	8.9
6.	Canada	9.2
7.	Mauritania	9.3
8.	Suriname	9.3
9.	Libya	9.6
10.	Botswana	9.8

POPULATION DENSITY

The places marked on the map reflect the size of the urban agglomerations and conurbations, rather than the actual city limits. San Francisco itself, for example, has an official population of less than a million people. All cities with more than 5 million inhabitants are named on the map.

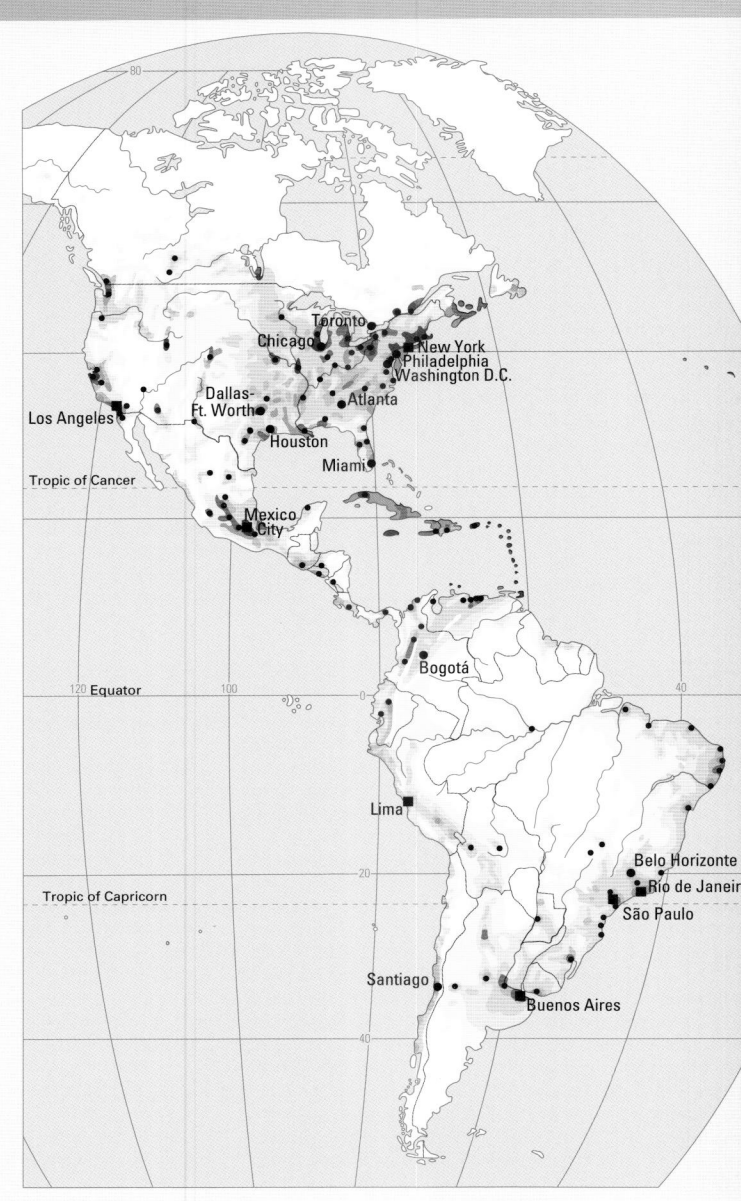

Inhabitants per square mile

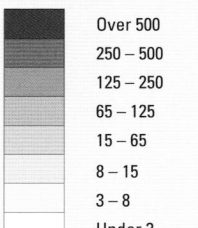

	Over 500
	250 – 500
	125 – 250
	65 – 125
	15 – 65
	8 – 15
	3 – 8
	Under 3

Urban population

■	Over 10,000,000
●	5,000,000 – 10,000,000
•	1,000,000 – 5,000,000

POPULATION CHANGE

The projected population change for the years 2004–2050

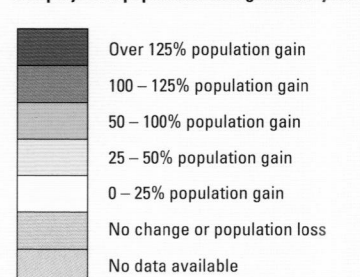

	Over 125% population gain
	100 – 125% population gain
	50 – 100% population gain
	25 – 50% population gain
	0 – 25% population gain
	No change or population loss
	No data available

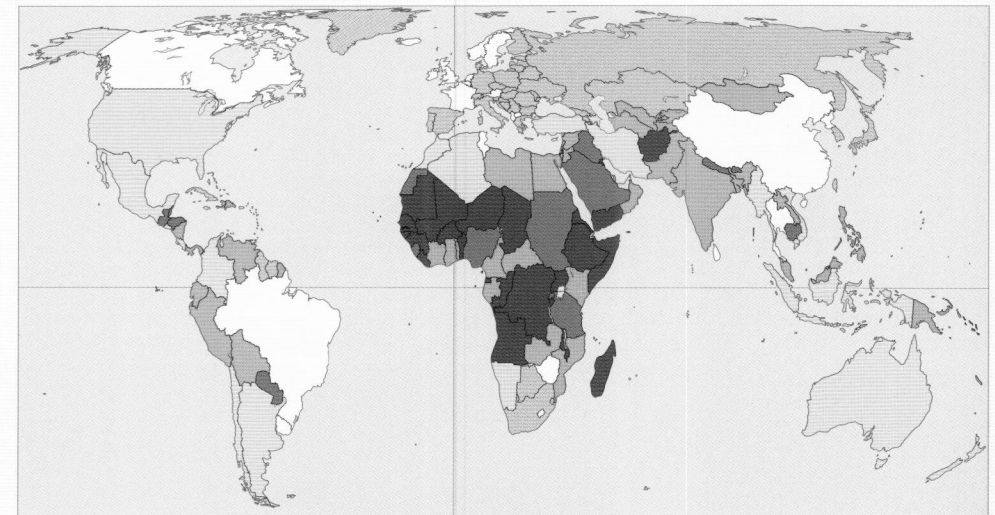

Based on estimates for the year 2050, below are listed the ten most populous nations in the world, in millions:

1.	India	1,628	6.	Pakistan	295
2.	China	1,437	7.	Bangladesh	280
3.	USA	420	8.	Brazil	221
4.	Indonesia	308	9.	Congo (Dem. Rep.)	181
5.	Nigeria	307	10.	Ethiopia	173

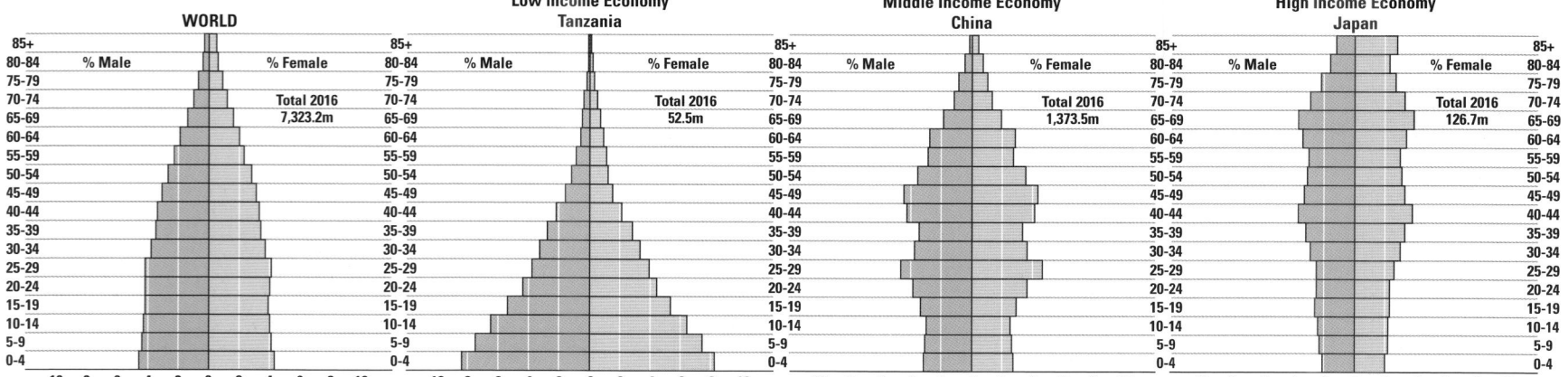

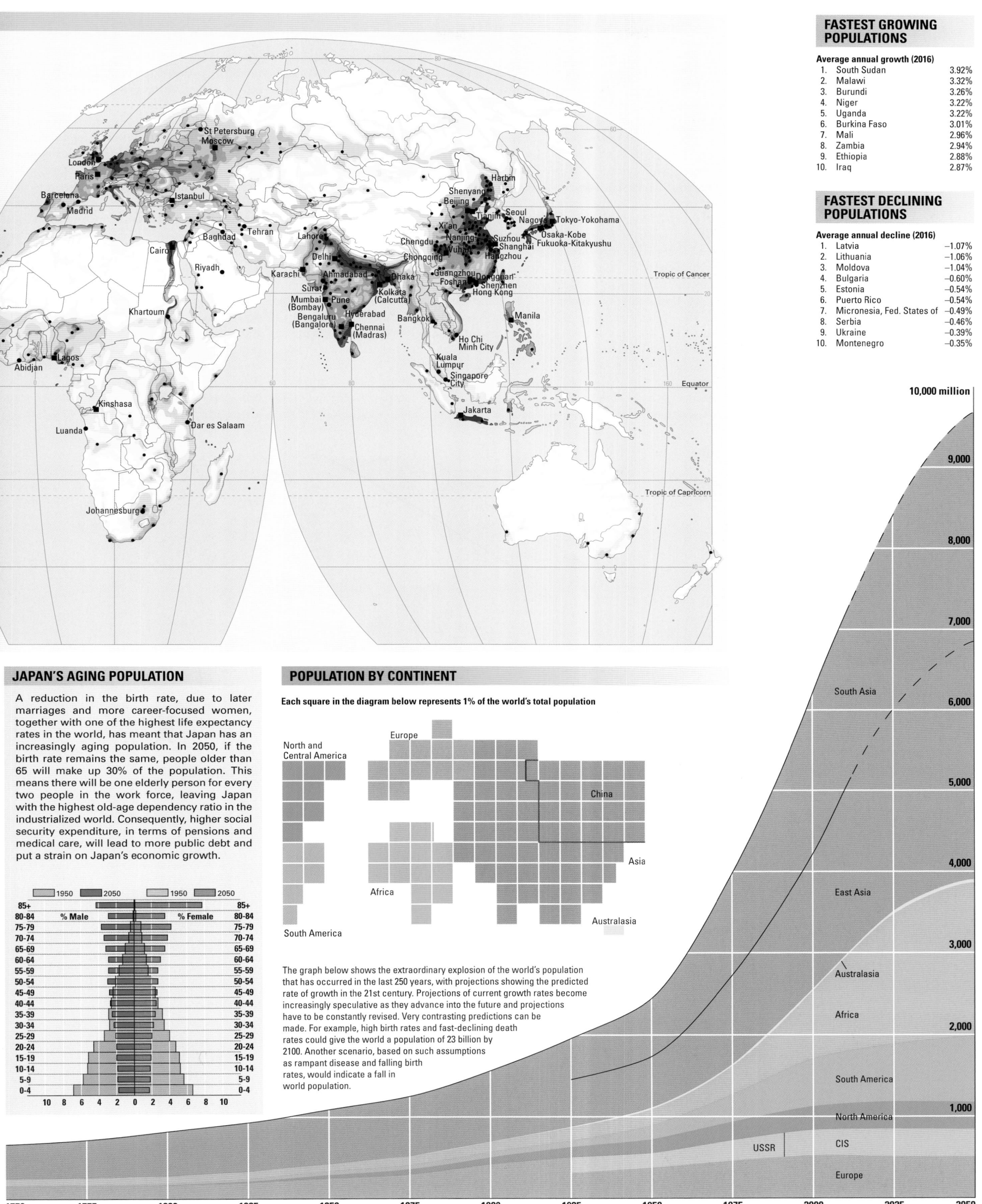

FASTEST GROWING POPULATIONS

Average annual growth (2016)

1.	South Sudan	3.92%
2.	Malawi	3.32%
3.	Burundi	3.26%
4.	Niger	3.22%
5.	Uganda	3.22%
6.	Burkina Faso	3.01%
7.	Mali	2.96%
8.	Zambia	2.94%
9.	Ethiopia	2.88%
10.	Iraq	2.87%

FASTEST DECLINING POPULATIONS

Average annual decline (2016)

1.	Latvia	−1.07%
2.	Lithuania	−1.06%
3.	Moldova	−1.04%
4.	Bulgaria	−0.60%
5.	Estonia	−0.54%
6.	Puerto Rico	−0.54%
7.	Micronesia, Fed. States of	−0.49%
8.	Serbia	−0.46%
9.	Ukraine	−0.39%
10.	Montenegro	−0.35%

JAPAN'S AGING POPULATION

A reduction in the birth rate, due to later marriages and more career-focused women, together with one of the highest life expectancy rates in the world, has meant that Japan has an increasingly aging population. In 2050, if the birth rate remains the same, people older than 65 will make up 30% of the population. This means there will be one elderly person for every two people in the work force, leaving Japan with the highest old-age dependency ratio in the industrialized world. Consequently, higher social security expenditure, in terms of pensions and medical care, will lead to more public debt and put a strain on Japan's economic growth.

POPULATION BY CONTINENT

Each square in the diagram below represents 1% of the world's total population

The graph below shows the extraordinary explosion of the world's population that has occurred in the last 250 years, with projections showing the predicted rate of growth in the 21st century. Projections of current growth rates become increasingly speculative as they advance into the future and projections have to be constantly revised. Very contrasting predictions can be made. For example, high birth rates and fast-declining death rates could give the world a population of 23 billion by 2100. Another scenario, based on such assumptions as rampant disease and falling birth rates, would indicate a fall in world population.

For more information:
80 Greenhouse gases
82 Water distribution
88 Population density
102 World trade

In 2008, for the first time in history, more than half of the world's population lived in urban areas. By 2050, it is thought that 5.3 billion people in the developing world will be living in an urban environment, with Asia having over 60% of the world's urban population and Africa almost 25%.

Urbanization is greatest in industrialized countries. For example, in 2010, 82% of the people in the US lived in urban areas; but in low-income countries, which had nearly 40% of the world's population in the early 21st century, only 31% lived in urban areas.

A typical city in a developing country contains millions of people living, often illegally, in shanty towns (or "informal settlements"), while thousands live on the streets. Yet many of these shanty towns are healthier than the industrial cities of 19th-century Europe and North America. Indeed, surveys have shown that migrants to cities in developing countries are less likely to face poverty than they are in rural areas, while benefiting from greater access to healthcare services and education.

Modern cities face many problems today, including pollution, unemployment, and crime. Yet, with competent government, they are capable of generating the wealth they need to solve them, as well as making a major contribution to the nation's economy.

Megacities are cities with a population of over 10 million people. Megacities grow as a result of economic growth, rural to urban migration, and high rates of natural increase. As the cities grow, they swallow up rural areas and nearby towns. Some of these cities have populations that are bigger than those of entire countries – Mumbai, for example, has more people than Sweden and Norway combined.

Nevertheless, megacities contain between 4% and 7% of the world's total population, and grow at relatively slow rates, perhaps 1.5% per year. The first megacity was Tokyo, which now has a population of about 38 million (larger than Canada's population). By 2017, other megacities will include Mumbai, Delhi, Mexico City, São Paulo, New York, Dhaka, Jakarta, and Lagos. Lagos has been growing at a very fast rate of 5% per annum and is expected to increase at this rate until after 2020. Usually, very large cities grow more slowly than medium-sized cities.

By 2020, all but four of the world's megacities will be in developing regions, 12 of them in Asia alone. The impact of megacities on their region is huge. For example, rapid economic growth and urbanization in China has had a negative impact on the urban environment. China contains 16 of the 20 most polluted cities in the world and is the largest producer of greenhouse gases.

Megacities are important for the generation of wealth – in more economically developed countries (MEDCs) urban areas generate over 80% of national economic output, while in less economically developed countries (LEDCs) it is over 40%. However, there are some aspects of megacities, such as crime and environmental issues, where they are less than attractive.

URBAN POPULATION

Percentage of total population living in towns and cities (2015)

Over 80%
60 – 80%
40 – 60%
20 – 40%
Under 20%
No data available

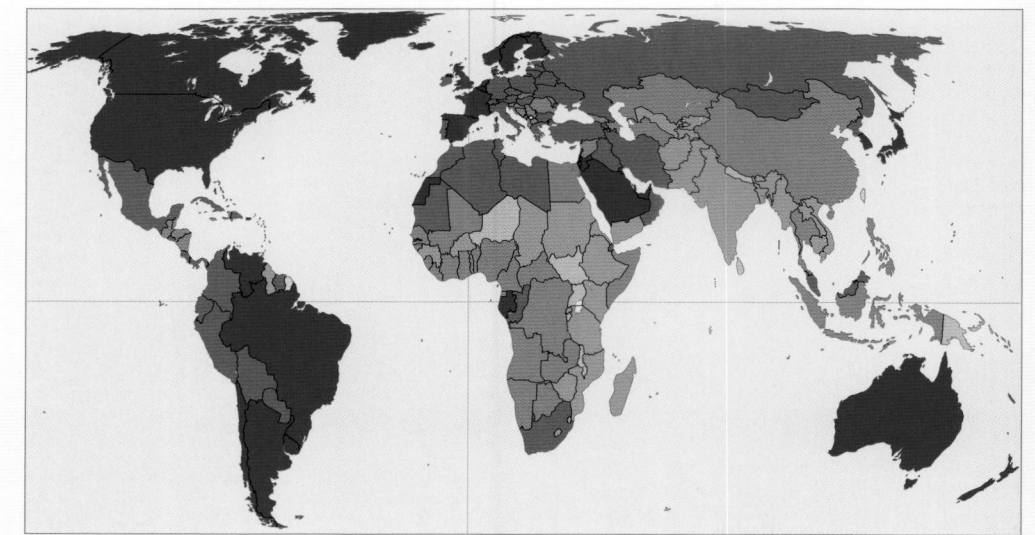

Most urbanized		Least urbanized	
Singapore	100%	Trinidad & Tobago	8%
Monaco	100%	Burundi	12%
Nauru	100%	Papua New Guinea	13%
Qatar	99%	Liechtenstein	14%
Kuwait	98%	Uganda	16%

THE URBANIZATION OF THE EARTH

City-building, 1900–2005; each white spot represents a city of at least 1 million inhabitants

1900

1950

1975

2005

URBANIZATION

The urban population of 3.7 billion people in 2012 was larger than the entire global population in 1947, 65 years earlier. Cities and urban areas are gaining an estimated 60 million people per year – over 1 million every week.

Urbanization rates vary across the world; the US and UK have far lower rates of urbanization compared to less developed countries. This is because a high proportion of their populations already live in cities. The largest percentage increases in the urban population in the next decade will be in Africa and Asia. For example, Lagos in Nigeria increased from 675,000 inhabitants in 1960 to 12,090,000 in 2013.

Rapid urban growth reflects three factors:
1. Migration to cities from rural areas.
2. Natural population increases (births minus deaths).
3. Reclassification of previously rural areas as urban as they become built up and engulfed by urban sprawl.

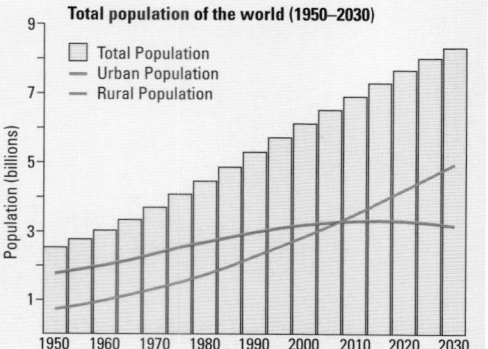

Total population of the world (1950–2030)

☐ Total Population
— Urban Population
— Rural Population

SLUM CITIES

The total number of slum dwellers in the world reached 1 billion in 2007, with one in every three city residents living in inadequate housing, with no or few basic services.

Urbanization in most developing countries has been proceeding so rapidly that local governments have been unable to provide the necessary services and housing to meet demand.

In some cities, many people make their homes in squatter settlements, or slums, which are frequently without basic services such as power, water, and sanitation. They are often on hazardous, dangerous or polluted land, and the building structures are inadequate and sometimes unsafe. Slum dwellers have limited access to credit and formal job markets due to stigmatization, discrimination, and geographical isolation.

Slums have a high concentration of poverty and social and economic deprivation, which may include broken families, unemployment, and economic, physical, and social exclusion. Yet these communities are often a dynamic part of the city's economy, keeping the wheels of the city turning in many different ways. Their inhabitants often take the initiative in setting up their own local government and self-help associations.

Some of the world's richest cities also have a homeless underclass, although calculating the numbers of people involved is problematic. Yet it is the case that homelessness and unemployment are currently affecting an increasing number of people in the developed world.

The locus of poverty is moving from the countryside to cities, in a process now recognized as the "urbanization of poverty."

Efforts to improve the living conditions of slum dwellers peaked during the 1980s. However, renewed concern about poverty has recently led governments to adopt specific targets on slums in the United Nations Millennium Declaration, which aims to improve the lives of at least 100 million slum dwellers by the year 2020.

SLUM FACTBOX

- A slum is defined by the UN as "a dilapidated area of a city characterized by substandard housing, squalor, and lacking in tenure security."
- 78% of the urban population in developing countries live in slums.
- More than 41% of Kolkata's slum households have lived there for more than 30 years.
- In most African cities between 40% and 70% of the city's population live in slums or squatter settlements.
- Slum populations in some parts of the world often include university lecturers, students, civil servants, and formal private-sector employees.
- The majority of slum households in Bangkok have a color television.
- Singapore is one of the few countries that successfully practises comprehensive public-sector housing development.
- Slums are the fastest growing human habitat in the world.

SUSTAINABLE CITIES

Large sprawling cities are often considered unsustainable because they consume huge amounts of resources and produce vast amounts of waste. The concept of "Sustainable Urban Development" is designed to meet the needs of the present generation without compromising the needs of future generations.

In the "compact" sustainable city, inputs are smaller and there is more recycling. Compact cities minimize the amount of distance traveled, use less space, require less infrastructure (pipes, cables, roads, etc), reduce urban sprawl, and the provision of public transport is easier. But if the compact city covers too large an area, it becomes congested, overcrowded, overpriced, and polluted. As a result, it then becomes unsustainable.

In order to achieve sustainability, a number of options are available:

- reducing the use of fossil fuels, e.g. by promoting public transport;
- keeping waste production to within levels that can be treated locally;
- providing sufficient green spaces;
- reusing and reclaiming land, e.g. brownfield sites;
- active involvement of the local community;
- conservation of non-renewable resources;
- using renewable resources.

CITY GROWTH

The growth of some of the world's largest cities in millions, 1950–2015
Comparisons of city populations over time are problematic due to changes in the definition of the city limits. These figures attempt to take such changes into consideration.

■ 1950   ■ 2015

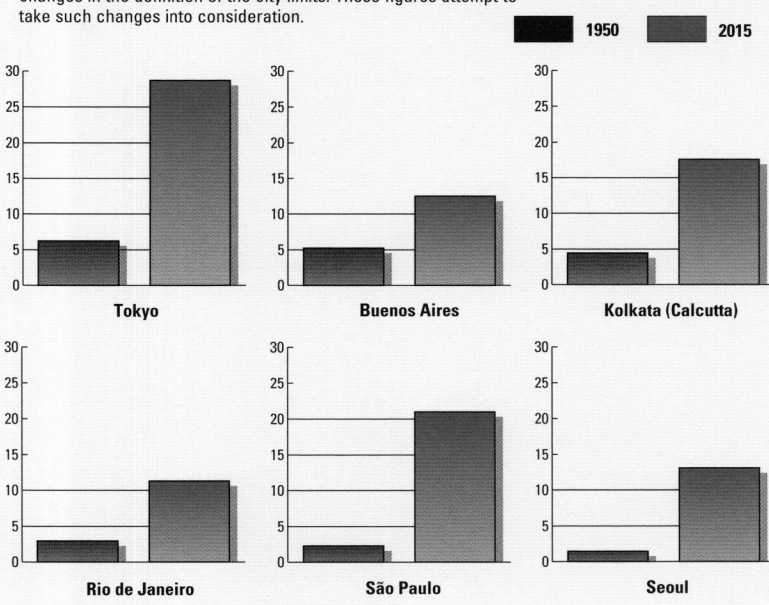

Tokyo   Buenos Aires   Kolkata (Calcutta)

Rio de Janeiro   São Paulo   Seoul

LARGEST CITIES

◄ Mt. Fuji stands sentinel over the futuristic skyline of the Shinjuku area of Tokyo, the world's most populous city. Originally a fishing village called Edo, the greater metropolitan area of Tokyo-Yokohama is now home to over 38 million people and is the capital of Japan.

In 2008, for the first time in history, the majority of the world's population lived in cities. Below is a list of the urban areas in the world with over 10 million inhabitants in 2016.

1.	Tokyo–Yokohama	39.8
2.	Delhi	27.2
3.	Shanghai	24.5
4.	Mumbai	23.6
5.	Mexico City	22.3
6.	New York	22.2
7.	São Paulo	21.9
8.	Beijing	21.2
9.	Cairo	19.1
10.	Dhaka	17.9
11.	Osaka-Kobe	17.8
12.	Karachi	17.1
13.	Kolkata	16.2
14.	Buenos Aires	16.0
15.	Istanbul	14.6
16.	Chongqing	13.7
17.	Lagos	13.7
18.	Los Angeles	13.3
19.	Manila	13.1
20.	Guangzhou	13.1
21.	Rio de Janeiro	12.7
22.	Moscow	12.3
23.	Tianjin	11.6
24.	Paris	11.3
25.	Kinshasa	10.9
26.	Bengaluru	10.8
27.	Shenzhen	10.8
28.	Jakarta	10.5
29.	Nagoya	10.5
30.	London	10.4
31.	Chennai	10.3
32.	Lima	10.1

The population figures above are based on urban agglomerations rather than legal city limits. In some cases, where two adjacent cities have merged into one concentration, such as Tokyo–Yokohama, they have been regarded as a single unit.

URBAN ADVANTAGES

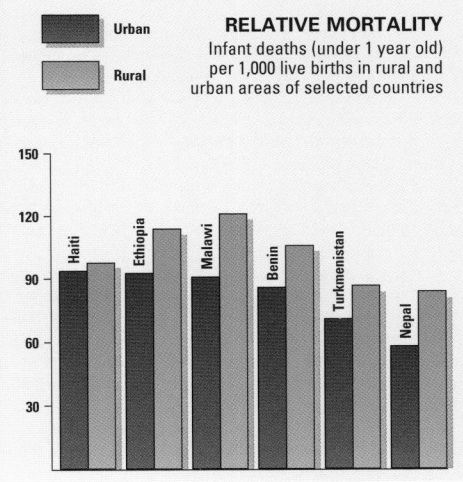

■ Urban
■ Rural

RELATIVE MORTALITY
Infant deaths (under 1 year old) per 1,000 live births in rural and urban areas of selected countries

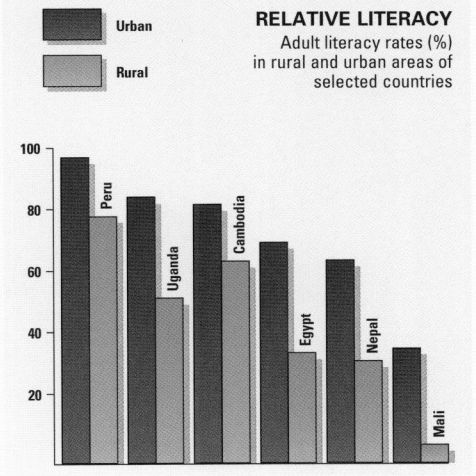

■ Urban
■ Rural

RELATIVE LITERACY
Adult literacy rates (%) in rural and urban areas of selected countries

Despite overcrowding and poor housing, living standards in the developing world's cities are almost invariably better than in the surrounding countryside. Resources – financial, material, and administrative – are concentrated in the towns, which are usually also the centers of political activity and pressure. Governments – frequently unstable, and rarely established on a solid democratic base – are usually more responsive to urban discontent than to rural misery.

In many developing countries, especially in Africa, food prices are kept artificially low, thus appeasing the underemployed urban masses at the expense of agricultural development.

This imbalance encourages further cityward migration, helping to account for the astonishing rate of post-1950 urbanization and putting great strain on the ability of many nations to provide even modest improvements for their people.

For more information:
88 Population density
94 Conflict
95 United Nations
95 International
    organizations

Migration is the permanent or semi-permanent change in residence. Migration can be voluntary or forced, international or internal, long- or short-distance. Most voluntary migrants are people moving either for work (this is especially true for young people), to retire to a small town or coastal area (this is especially true in some rich countries), or to live in a smaller urban area for a better quality of life than they had in a large urban area. Others may migrate for educational or health reasons. In contrast, forced migrations may be due to civil conflict, environmental damage, or some form of persecution.

According to the World Bank's Migration and Remittances Factbook, more than 215 million people, or 3% of the world's population, live outside their countries of birth. However, current migration flows, relative to population, are weaker than those of the last decades of the 19th century.

The top migrant destination countries are the United States, Russia, Germany, Saudi Arabia, and the United Arab Emirates. The countries with the highest proportions of immigrants in relation to the indigenous population are the United Arab Emirates, Qatar, Kuwait, and Cayman Islands.

The United States has seen the largest inflows of migrants between 2005 and 2013, despite the global financial crisis. The expansion of the European Union led to a surge of migrant flows to Spain, Italy, and the United Kingdom, with a large share from Eastern Europe. The Middle Eastern countries of Saudi Arabia, United Arab Emirates, Bahrain, Qatar, Oman, and Kuwait have also seen a significant increase in migrant flows in the last few years, mostly from South Asia and East Asia. However, immigrant stocks in all regions started to plateau in 2009–10 because of the global financial crisis.

The Mexico–United States migration corridor is the largest in the world, accounting for 13.0 million migrants in 2013. Migration corridors in the former Soviet Union (Russia–Ukraine, and Ukraine–Russia) are the next largest, followed by Bangladesh–India. In these corridors, some people have become migrants without moving when new international boundaries were drawn.

Smaller countries tend to have higher rates of skilled emigration. For example, almost all physicians trained in Grenada and Dominica have emigrated abroad. St Lucia, Cape Verde, Fiji, São Tomé and Príncipe, and Liberia are also among the countries with the highest emigration rates of physicians.

Worldwide remittance flows are estimated to have exceeded US $585 billion in 2016, of which developing countries received US $436 billion. The true size, including unrecorded flows through formal and informal channels, is believed to be significantly larger. Recorded remittances are more than twice as large as official aid and nearly two-thirds of foreign direct investment (FDI) flows to developing countries.

In 2016, the top recipient countries of recorded remittances were India, China, the Philippines, Mexico, France, and Pakistan. As a share of GDP, however, smaller countries such as Nepal (32%), Liberia (31%), Tajikistan (29%) and Kyrgyzstan (25%), were the largest recipients in 2016.

Rich countries are the main source of remittances. The United States is by far the largest, with US $134 billion in recorded outward flows in 2015. Saudi Arabia ranks as the second largest, followed by Russia and Switzerland.

WORLD MIGRATION

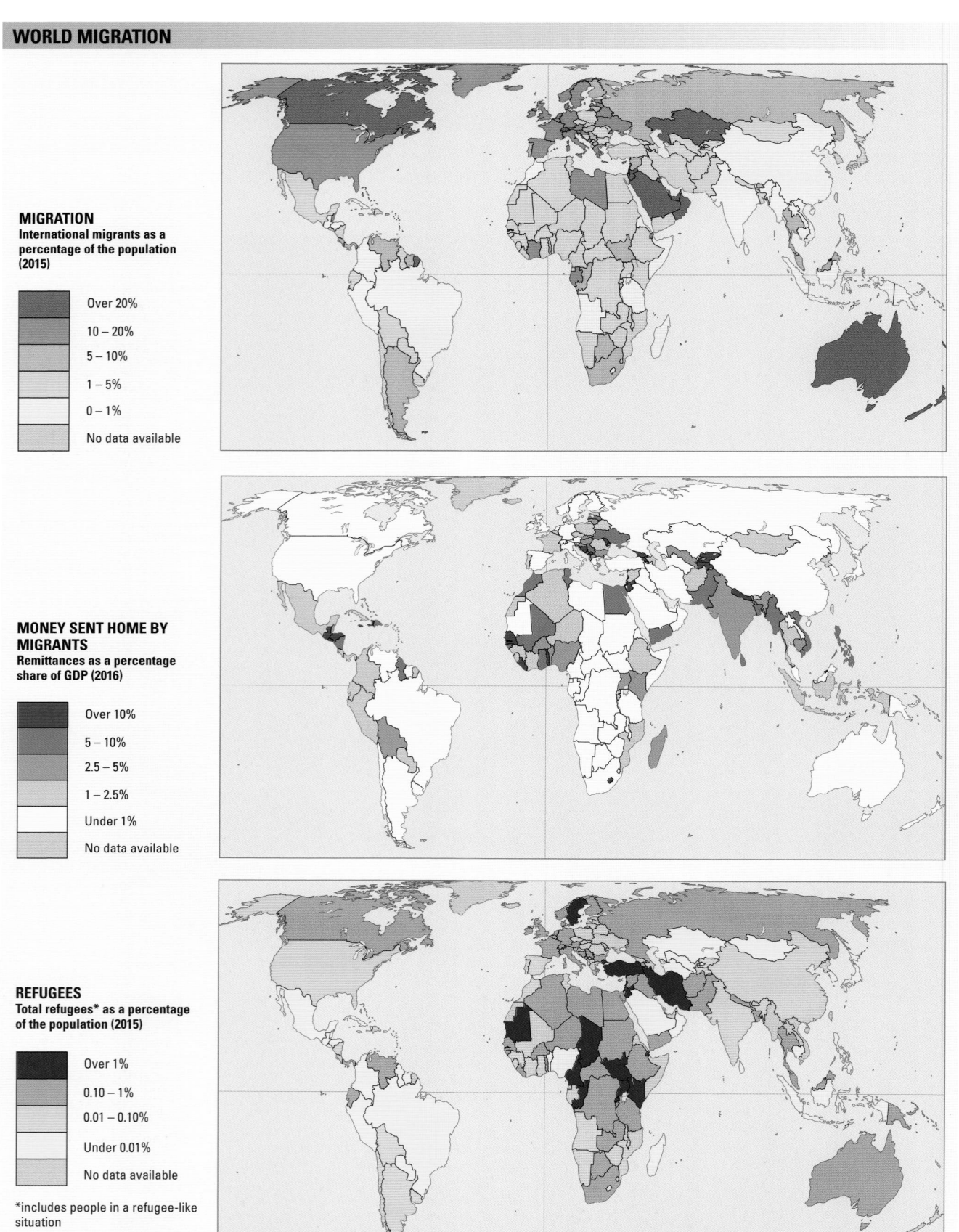

MIGRATION
International migrants as a percentage of the population (2015)

- Over 20%
- 10 – 20%
- 5 – 10%
- 1 – 5%
- 0 – 1%
- No data available

MONEY SENT HOME BY MIGRANTS
Remittances as a percentage share of GDP (2016)

- Over 10%
- 5 – 10%
- 2.5 – 5%
- 1 – 2.5%
- Under 1%
- No data available

REFUGEES
Total refugees* as a percentage of the population (2015)

- Over 1%
- 0.10 – 1%
- 0.01 – 0.10%
- Under 0.01%
- No data available

*includes people in a refugee-like situation

See also Refugees graph at the top of page 94.

According to the United Nations High Commission for Refugees (UNHCR) in 2015 there were 16.1 million refugees. However, the UNHCR definition of a refugee, "a person who has left or remains outside their own country because they have a well-founded fear of persecution, or because their safety is threatened by events seriously disturbing public order," does not include people who are in a refugee-like situation but who have not been formally recognized. In 2015, there were a further 32.3 million people who were internally displaced, and a total "population of concern" of 55 million people, worldwide.

All but a few who cross international boundaries seek asylum in neighboring countries, which are often the least equipped to deal with them. Lacking any rights or power, they frequently become an unwelcome burden to their hosts. Usually, the best any refugee can hope for is rudimentary food and shelter in temporary camps. Many Palestinians, for example, have been forced to live in camps since 1948.

In early 2016, the United Nations identified over 13 million Syrians as requiring humanitarian assistance due to the conflict in their country. Nearly 5 million are registered as refugees outside of Syria with Turkey being the largest host country.

PREDOMINANT LANGUAGES

INDO-EUROPEAN FAMILY
1 Balto-Slavic group (incl. Russian, Ukrainian)
2 Germanic group (incl. English, German)
3 Celtic group
4 Greek
5 Albanian
6 Iranian group
7 Armenian
8 Romance group (incl. Spanish, Portuguese, French, Italian)
9 Indo-Aryan group (incl. Hindi, Bengali, Urdu, Punjabi, Marathi)
10 **CAUCASIAN FAMILY**

AFRO-ASIATIC FAMILY
11 Semitic group (incl. Arabic)
12 Kushitic group
13 Berber group

14 **KHOISAN FAMILY**

15 **NIGER-CONGO FAMILY**

16 **NILO-SAHARAN FAMILY**

17 **URALIC FAMILY**

ALTAIC FAMILY
18 Turkic group (incl. Turkish)
19 Mongolian group
20 Tungus-Manchu group
21 Japanese and Korean

SINO-TIBETAN FAMILY
22 Sinitic (Chinese) languages (incl. Mandarin, Wu, Yue)
23 Tibetic-Burmic languages

24 **TAI FAMILY**

AUSTRO-ASIATIC FAMILY
25 Mon-Khmer group
26 Munda group
27 Vietnamese

DRAVIDIAN FAMILY
28 (incl. Telugu, Tamil)

AUSTRONESIAN FAMILY
29 (incl. Malay-Indonesian, Javanese)

30 **OTHER LANGUAGES**

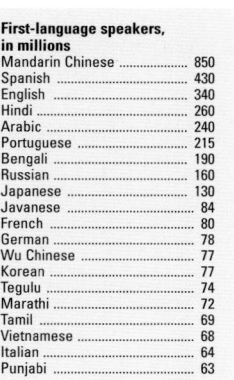

First-language speakers, in millions

Mandarin Chinese	850
Spanish	430
English	340
Hindi	260
Arabic	240
Portuguese	215
Bengali	190
Russian	160
Japanese	130
Javanese	84
French	80
German	78
Wu Chinese	77
Korean	77
Tegulu	74
Marathi	72
Tamil	69
Vietnamese	68
Italian	64
Punjabi	63

Languages form a kind of tree of development, splitting from a few ancient proto-tongues into branches that have grown apart and further divided with the passage of time. English and Hindi, for example, both belong to the great Indo-European family, although the relationship is only apparent after much analysis and comparison with non-Indo-European languages such as Chinese or Arabic. Hindi is part of the Indo-Aryan subgroup, whereas English is a member of Indo-European's Germanic branch. French, another Indo-European tongue, traces its descent through the Latin, or Romance, branch. A few languages – Basque is one example – have no apparent links with any other, living or dead. Most modern languages, of course, have acquired enormous quantities of vocabulary from each other.

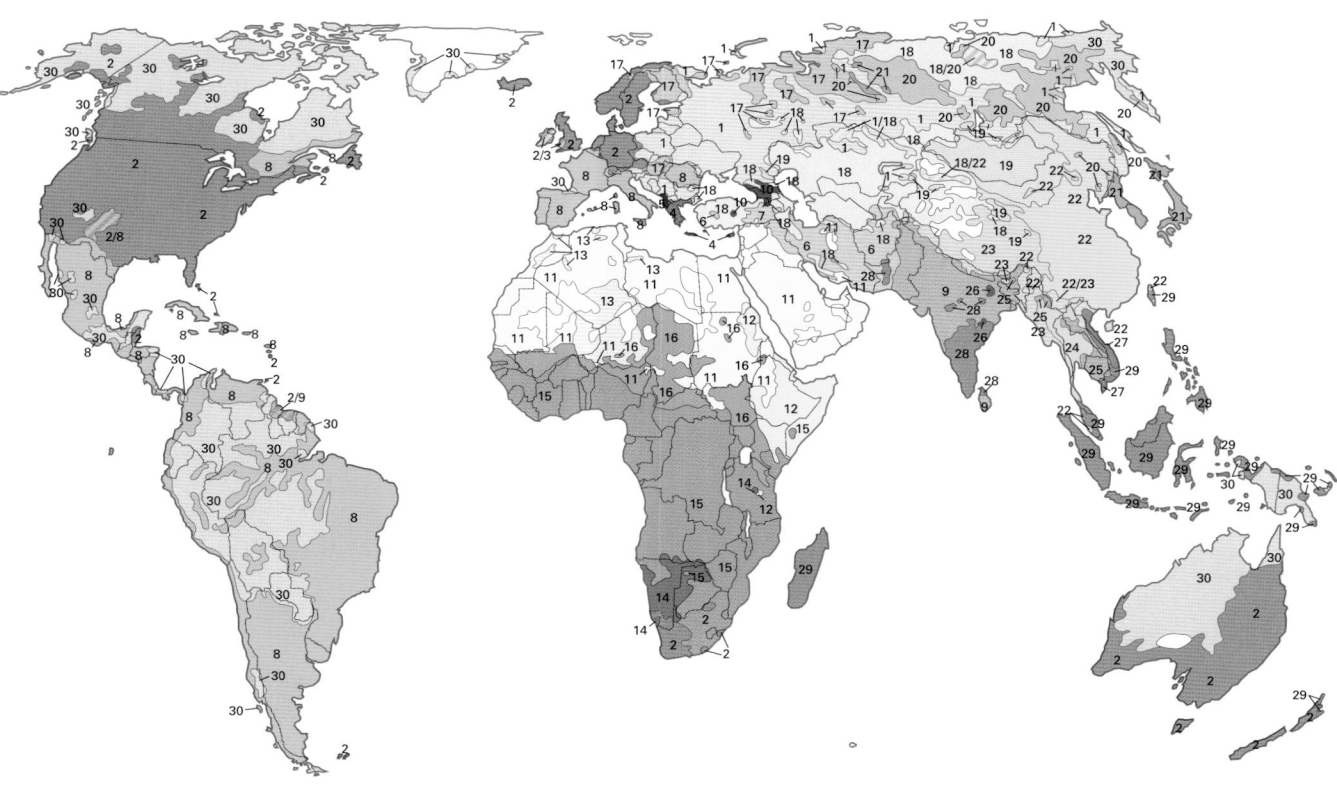

DISTRIBUTION OF LIVING LANGUAGES

The figures refer to the number of languages currently in use in the regions shown

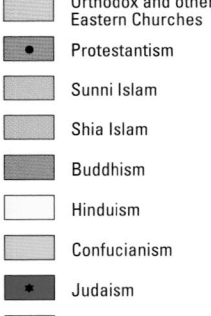

Europe 284
Americas 1,060
Asia 2,304
Pacific 1,311
Africa 2,146

PREDOMINANT RELIGIONS

- ▲ Roman Catholicism
- Orthodox and other Eastern Churches
- ● Protestantism
- Sunni Islam
- Shia Islam
- Buddhism
- Hinduism
- Confucianism
- ✶ Judaism
- Shintoism
- Tribal Religions

Religions are not as easily mapped as the physical contours of the land. Divisions are often blurred and frequently overlapping: most nations include people of many different faiths – or no faith at all. Some religions, like Islam and Christianity, have proselytes worldwide; others, like Hinduism and Confucianism, are restricted to a particular area, though modern migrations have taken some Indians and Chinese very far from their cultural origins. It is also difficult to show the degree to which religion controls daily life: Christian Western Europe, for example, is now far less dominated by its religion than are the Islamic nations of the Middle East. Similarly, figures for the major faiths' adherents make no distinction between nominal believers enrolled at birth and those for whom religion is a vital part of their existence.

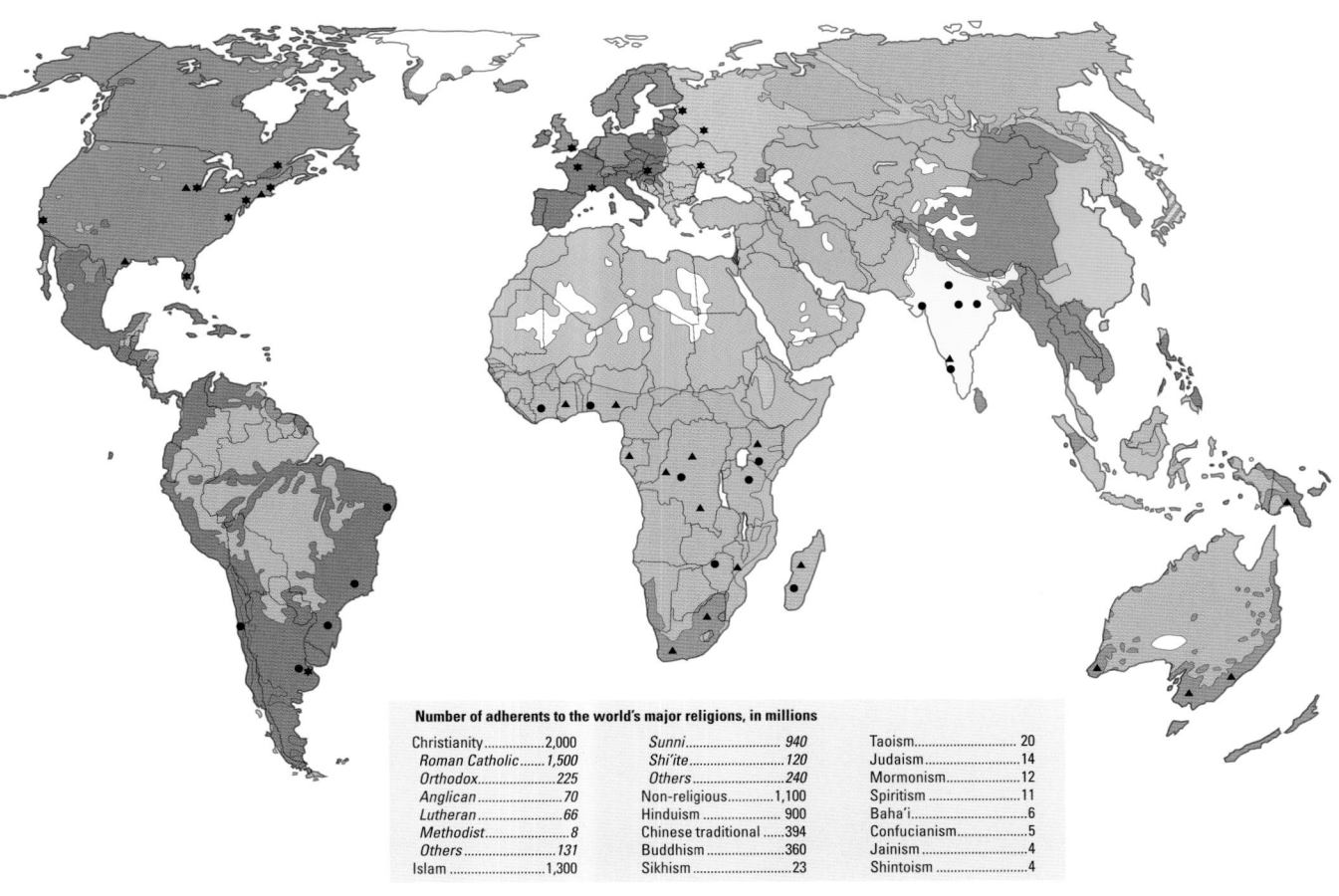

Number of adherents to the world's major religions, in millions

Christianity	2,000	Sunni	940	Taoism	20
Roman Catholic	1,500	Shi'ite	120	Judaism	14
Orthodox	225	Others	240	Mormonism	12
Anglican	70	Non-religious	1,100	Spiritism	11
Lutheran	66	Hinduism	900	Baha'i	6
Methodist	8	Chinese traditional	394	Confucianism	5
Others	131	Buddhism	360	Jainism	4
Islam	1,300	Sikhism	23	Shintoism	4

For more information:
92 Migration
93 Religion

In the late 1980s, many people hoped that the end of the Cold War, following the collapse of Communist regimes in the former Soviet Union and Eastern Europe, would herald a new era of international stability. Instead, old ethnic and religious antagonisms surfaced in many areas, leading to civil war in such places as Chechenia, in Russia, and the former Yugoslavia. Nationalist rivalries, suppressed under Communist rule, replaced ideological factors as the major cause of conflict.

Since, 2010, there has been accelerated political change, especially across North Africa and the Middle East.

Some countries are more likely to fail than others. Demographic stress is a major factor. Where there are large numbers of unemployed youths concentrated in large cities and a lack of growth, the chances of conflict escalate. Young men "out of school, out of work, and charged with hatred" are the lifeblood of deadly conflict.

The causes of state failure and civil disintegration are multiple, but certain characteristics increase vulnerability. Extreme income and gender inequality increase the risk of discord. Corrupt governments that are widely regarded as illegitimate and ineffective are "at risk." Democracy, especially with a strong parliament, lowers the risk of state failure; autocracy increases it. Population pressure, exacerbated by internally displaced people, refugees, and food scarcity, contribute to state failure and civil unrest. Governments that fail to protect human rights are especially prone to fail.

The Arab Spring, a term given to the Arab Revolution, is a wave of demonstrations, protests, and wars that began in December 2010. A number of rulers have been forced from power in Tunisia, Egypt, Libya, and Yemen. In addition, there have been civil uprisings in Bahrain, Syria, and Ukraine. However, the major oil-rich nations (Saudi Arabia, UAE, Qatar, Kuwait, and Oman) have managed to keep their ruling families in power.

The protests have shared techniques of civil resistance in sustained campaigns involving strikes, demonstrations, marches, and rallies, but were also noticeable for their use of social media to organize, communicate, and raise awareness of the situation.

Despite the words of John F. Kennedy, US President 1961–3, that "Mankind must put an end to war or war will put an end to mankind," in 2017 military conflicts are taking place around the world in countries such as Afghanistan, Somalia, Yemen, Pakistan, Mexico (the "drugs war"), South Sudan, Nigeria, Syria, Iraq, Libya, and Ukraine.

REFUGEES

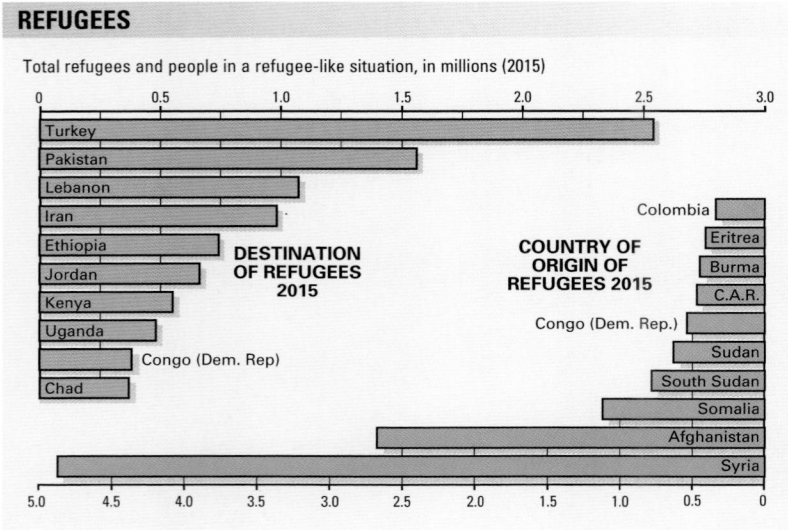

▲ Part of the extensive Badbaado refugee camp, situated outside Mogadishu in Somalia. The camp was started when famine struck the northeast of Africa, after a drought in 2011. It subsequently expanded further after the civil war intensified. There was a breakdown of law and order, and people fled there for safety. The United Nations Refugee Agency, also known as UNHCR, estimated that there were 1,188,631 people of concern in Somalia in 2015.

MILITARY SPENDING

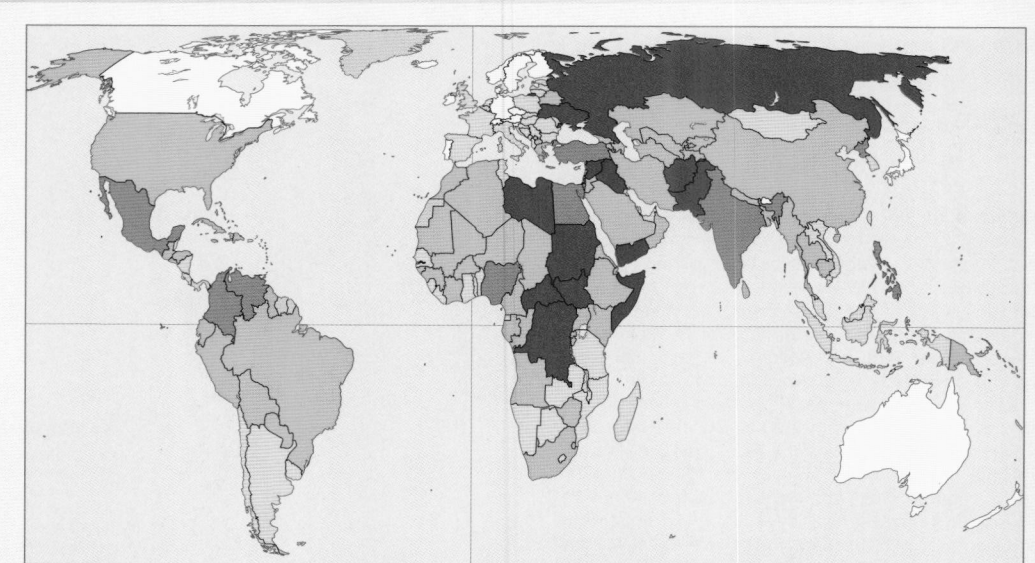

GLOBAL PEACE INDEX

The Global Peace Index (GPI) is an attempt to measure the relative position of nations' peacefulness. It quantifies: levels of security and safety; domestic and international conflict; and degree of militarization. Syria remains the least peaceful country with Libya and Ukraine showing the most deterioration.

Global Peace Index (2016)
- Under 1.500 (most peaceful)
- 1.501 – 2.000
- 2.001 – 2.500
- 2.501 – 3.000
- Over 3.001 (least peaceful)
- No data available

Five most peaceful countries		Five least peaceful countries	
Iceland	1.192	Syria	3.806
Denmark	1.246	South Sudan	3.593
Austria	1.278	Iraq	3.570
New Zealand	1.287	Afghanistan	3.538
Portugal	1.356	Somalia	3.414

INTERNATIONAL ORGANIZATIONS

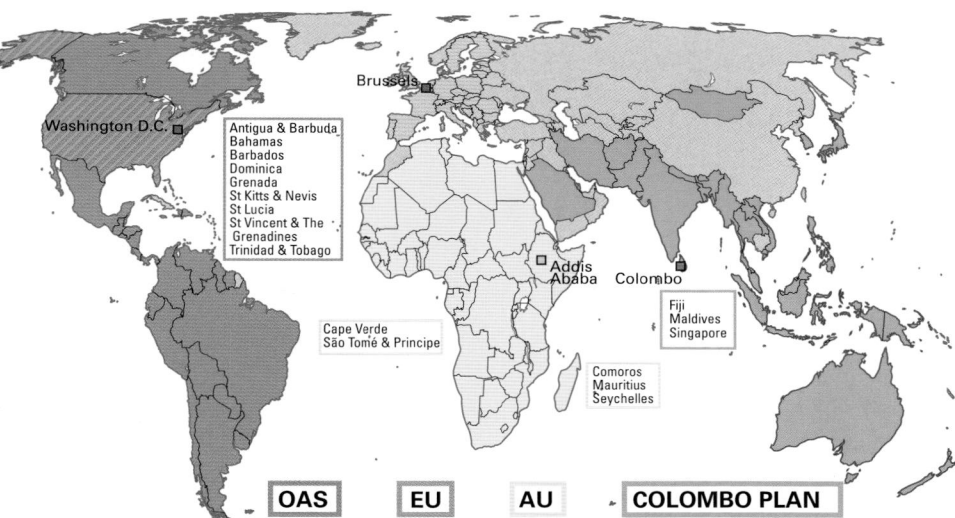

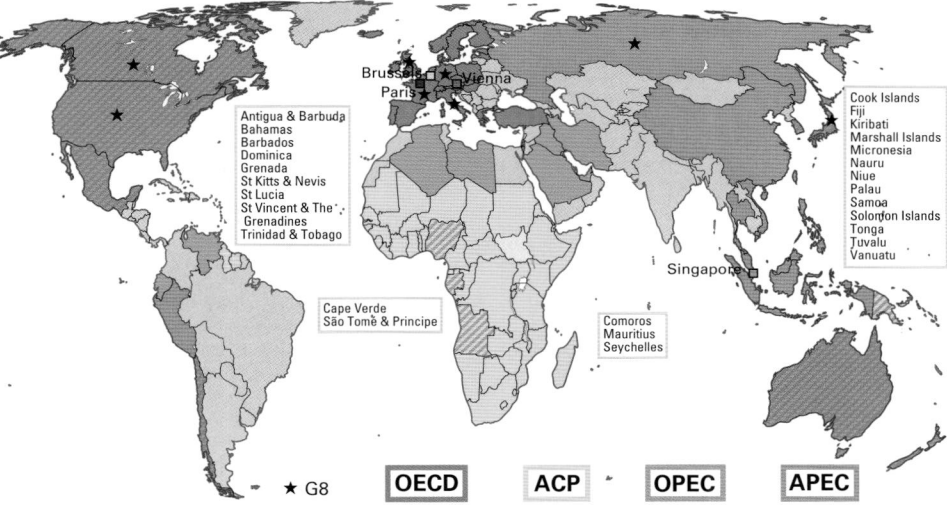

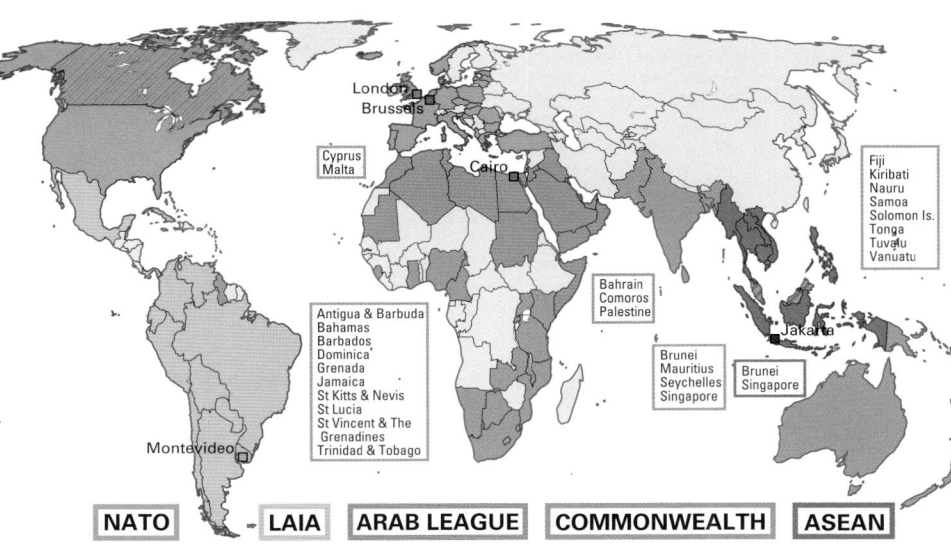

UNITED NATIONS

The creation of the United Nations in 1945 held out hope that the world's nations, tired of war, would have the means to control humanity's aggressive instincts. Although the UN lacks the power to halt conflicts, it has often helped to achieve negotiation. Economic pressures have led to another kind of cooperation, resulting in the creation of common markets and economic unions, such as ASEAN in Southeast Asia, the European Union, and NAFTA in North America.

The United Nations Organization was born as World War II drew to its conclusion. That body would replace the League of Nations, which, since its inception in 1920, had failed to curb the aggression of some of its member nations. At the United Nations Conference on International Organization held in San Francisco, the United Nations Charter was drawn up. Ratified by the Security Council and signed by the 51 original members, it came into effect on October 24, 1945.

The Charter set out the aims of the organization: to maintain peace and security, and to develop friendly relations between nations; to achieve international cooperation in solving economic, social, cultural, and humanitarian problems; to promote respect for human rights and fundamental freedoms; and to harmonize the activities of nations in order to achieve these common goals.

Membership From the original 51, membership of the UN has now grown to 193. There are only two independent states that are not members – Taiwan and the Vatican City. Official languages are Chinese, English, French, Russian, Spanish, and Arabic.

Funding The UN budget for 2016–17 was US $5.57 billion. Contributions are assessed by the members' ability to pay, with the maximum 22% of the total (the USA's share), and the minimum 0.001%. The 28-member EU pays approximately 35% of the budget.

Peacekeeping The UN has been involved in 67 peacekeeping operations worldwide since 1948.

OAS The **Organization of American States** was formed in 1948. It aims to promote social and economic cooperation between countries in the developed North America and developing Latin America.
EU The **European Union** evolved from the European Community in 1993. Cyprus, the Czech Republic, Estonia, Hungary, Latvia, Lithuania, Malta, Poland, the Slovak Republic, and Slovenia joined the EU in May 2004; Bulgaria and Romania joined in 2007; Croatia joinded in 2013. The other 15 members of the EU are Austria, Belgium, Denmark, Finland, France, Germany, Greece, Ireland, Italy, Luxembourg, Netherlands, Portugal, Spain, Sweden, and the UK. Together, the 28 members aim to integrate economies, coordinate social developments, and bring about political union. The UK will leave the EU in 2019.
AU The **African Union** was set up in 2002, taking over from the Organization of African Unity (1963). It has 54 members. The main objectives of the OAU were, *inter alia*, to rid the continent of the remaining vestiges of colonization and apartheid; to promote unity and solidarity among African states; to coordinate and intensify cooperation for development; to safeguard the sovereignty and territorial integrity of member states; and to promote international cooperation within the framework of the United Nations.
COLOMBO PLAN Formed in 1951, its 27 members aim to promote economic and social development in Asia and the Pacific. Saudi Arabia joined in 2012.

G8 Group of eight leading industrialized nations, comprising Canada, France, Germany, Italy, Japan, Russia, the UK, and the USA. Periodic meetings are held to discuss major world issues, such as world recessions. The EU is also represented at meetings. Russian membership was suspended in 2014.
OECD The **Organization for Economic Cooperation and Development** (formed in 1961) comprises 35 major free-market economies. The "G8" is its "inner group" of leading industrial nations, comprising Canada, France, Germany, Italy, Japan, Russia, the UK, and the USA. The mission of the OECD is to promote policies that will improve the economic and social well-being of people around the world.
ACP The **African, Caribbean and Pacific Group of States** was formed in 1963. Members enjoy economic ties with the EU. The ACP Group´s main objectives are sustainable development of its member states and their gradual integration into the global economy, which entails making poverty reduction a matter of priority; coordination of the activities of the ACP Group in the framework of the implementation of ACP–EU Partnership Agreements; establishment and consolidation of peace and stability in a free and democratic society.
OPEC The **Organization of Petroleum Exporting Countries** was formed in 1960. It controls about three-quarters of the world's oil supply. Its mission is to coordinate and unify the petroleum policies of its member countries, and to ensure the stabilization of oil markets in order to secure an efficient, economic, and regular supply of petroleum to consumers, a steady income to producers, and a fair return on capital for those investing in the petroleum industry. Gabon rejoined in 2016.
APEC Formed in 1989, the **Asia–Pacific Economic Cooperation** aims to enhance economic growth and prosperity for the region and to strengthen the Asia–Pacific community. APEC is the only intergovernmental grouping in the world operating on the basis of non-binding commitments, open dialog, and equal respect for the views of all participants. There are 21 member economies.

NATO The **North Atlantic Treaty Organization** (formed in 1949) continues despite the winding-up of the Warsaw Pact in 1991. Bulgaria, Estonia, Latvia, Lithuania, Romania, the Slovak Republic, and Slovenia became members in 2004, and Albania and Croatia in 2009. Its main aim is to provide peace and security to its North Atlantic members through collective defense – an attack on one country is seen as an attack on all of NATO.
LAIA The **Latin American Integration Association** (formed in 1980) superceded the Latin American Free Trade Association formed in 1961. Its aim is to promote freer regional trade.
ARAB LEAGUE Formed in 1945, the Arab League aims to promote economic, social, political, and military cooperation. There are 21 member nations. Syria's membership was suspended in 2011.
COMMONWEALTH The **Commonwealth of Nations** evolved from the British Empire. Pakistan was suspended in 1999, but reinstated in 2004. Zimbabwe was suspended in 2002 and, in response to its continued suspension, Zimbabwe left the Commonwealth in 2003. Fiji was suspended in 2006 following a military coup. Rwanda joined the Commonwealth in 2009, as the 54th member state, becoming only the second country that was not formerly a British colony to be admitted to the group. The Gambia left in 2013. Their objective is to build stronger democratic institutions and processes across the Commonwealth and to support economic growth in their member countries. There are currently 52 members.
ASEAN The **Association of Southeast Asian Nations** was formed in 1967. Cambodia joined in 1999. The aims of ASEAN include: to accelerate the economic growth, social progress, and cultural development in the region; to promote regional peace and stability; and to collaborate more effectively for the greater utilization of their agriculture and industries, the expansion of their trade, including the study of the problems of international commodity trade, the improvement of their transportation and communications facilities, and the raising of the living standards of their peoples.

For more information:
80 Global warming
   Carbon dioxide
98 Minerals

Every year, the world's energy consumption is about the equivalent of what would come from burning 12,000 million tonnes of oil (12,000 MtOe) – a 20-fold increase since 1850. Two-fifths of this total actually comes from burning oil and most of the rest comes from coal and natural gas.

The oil crises in the 1970s precipitated concern over dependence on finite fossil fuels as the primary source of energy, and growing environmental awareness has added impetus to the search for alternative energy resources. Fossil fuel combustion damages the environment through the release of gases and particulate matter, but two other major sources of energy, hydroelectricity and nuclear power, are also controversial. Hydroelectricity production involves flooding large areas to create reservoirs, while nuclear power stations generate dangerous radioactive wastes and can cause major disasters. Nuclear power has been a growing source of energy, but the 2011 Japanese earthquake, with the consequent serious damage to the Fukushima nuclear power station, has caused many countries to rethink their energy strategies.

Alternative energy resources may soon provide a much larger proportion of the world's energy consumption. Solar and wind energy may become important in such countries as China and India, while tidal, wave, and geothermal energy all have potential in appropriate areas. Experts calculate that solar power could, in theory, supply between five and ten times the present electricity supply of developing countries.

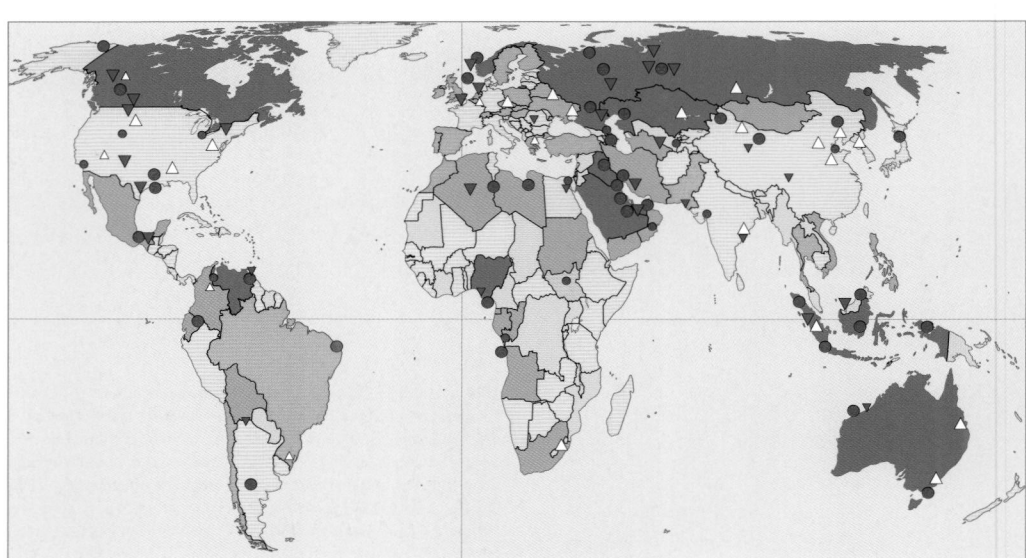

ENERGY BALANCE

Difference between energy production and consumption in millions of tonnes of oil equivalent (MtOe) (2013)

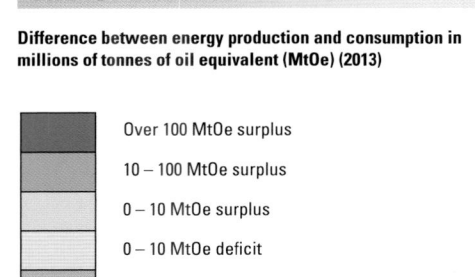

- Over 100 MtOe surplus
- 10 – 100 MtOe surplus
- 0 – 10 MtOe surplus
- 0 – 10 MtOe deficit
- 10 – 100 MtOe deficit
- Over 100 MtOe deficit
- No data available

● Principal oilfields   ● Secondary oilfields
▼ Principal gasfields   ▼ Secondary gasfields
△ Principal coalfields   △ Secondary coalfields

ENERGY CONSUMPTION

Energy consumed by world regions, measured in million tonnes of oil equivalent in 2015. Total world consumption was 13,147 MtOe. Energy from commercially traded fuels, and modern renewables used to generate electricity, are included. Excluded are biomass fuels such as wood, peat and animal waste which, though important locally in some countries, are not always reliably documented statistically.

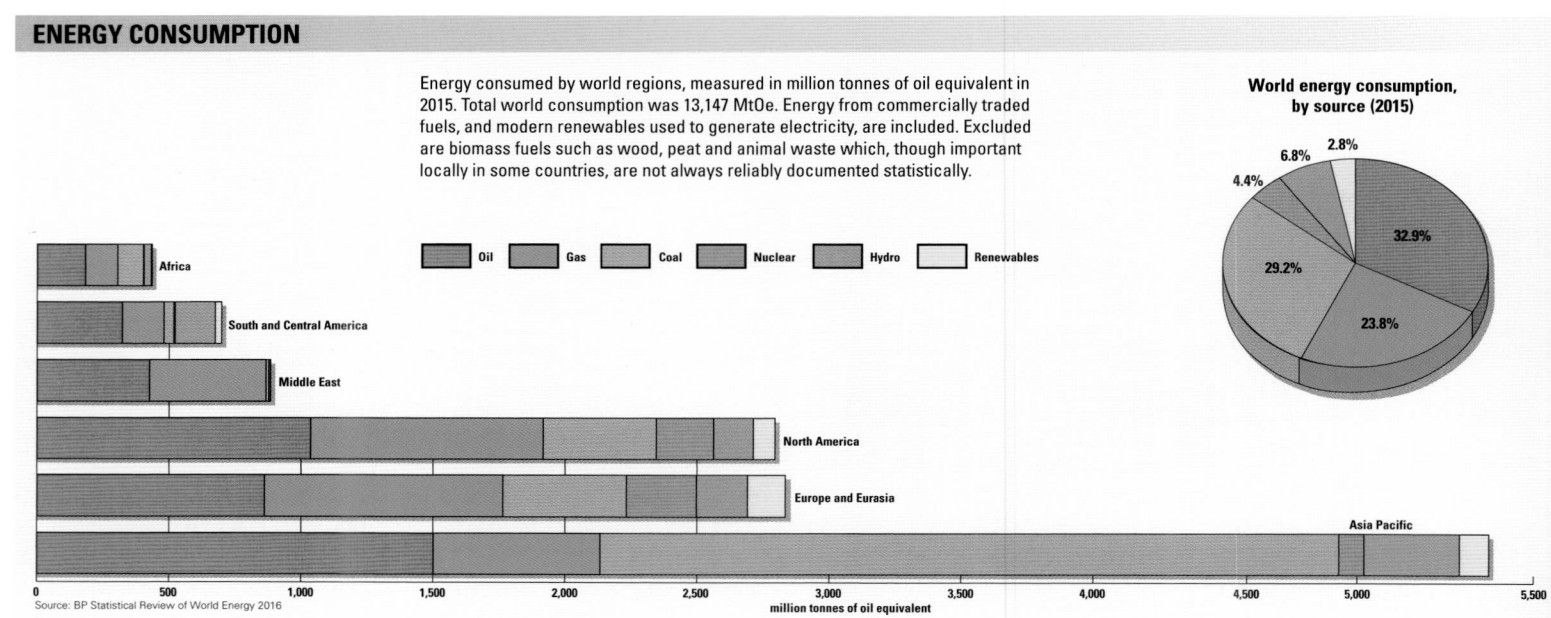

World energy consumption, by source (2015)

Oil | Gas | Coal | Nuclear | Hydro | Renewables

2.8%, 6.8%, 4.4%, 29.2%, 32.9%, 23.8%

Africa
South and Central America
Middle East
North America
Europe and Eurasia
Asia Pacific

Source: BP Statistical Review of World Energy 2016

million tonnes of oil equivalent

ENERGY PRODUCTION

Energy production in tonnes of oil equivalent per capita (2013)

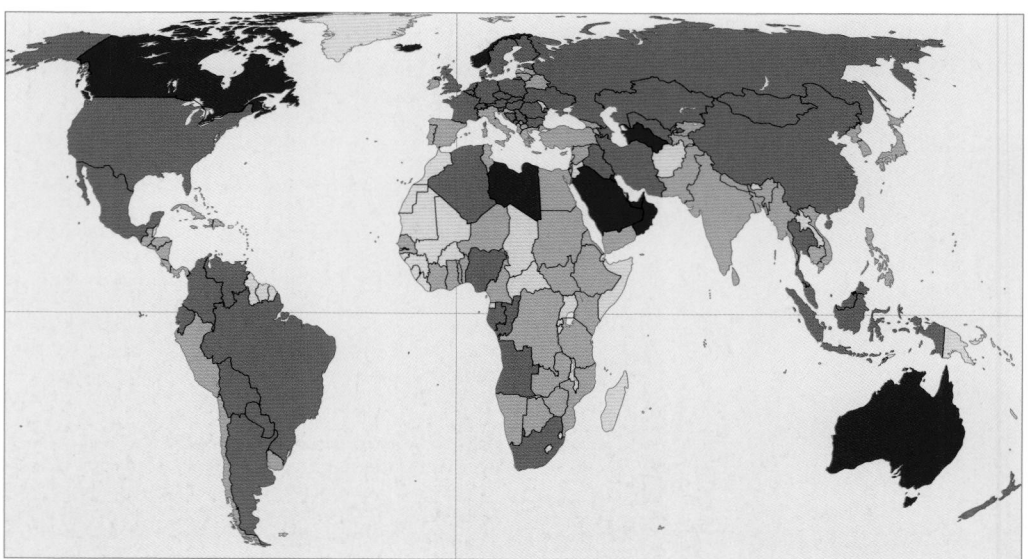

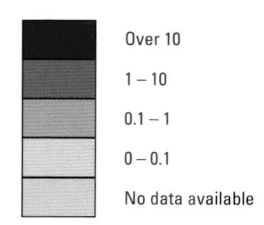

- Over 10
- 1 – 10
- 0.1 – 1
- 0 – 0.1
- No data available

Highest energy producers, tonnes of oil equivalent per capita (2013)

Qatar	109.7
Kuwait	63.3
Brunei	40.8
Norway	40.6
United Arab Emirates	36.8

OIL MOVEMENTS

Major oil exporting regions (2015)

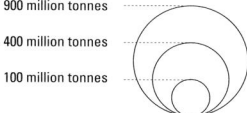

- 900 million tonnes
- 400 million tonnes
- 100 million tonnes

Major global oil movements (percentage of total world trade)

- Over 10%
- 5 – 10%
- 2 – 5%
- Under 2%

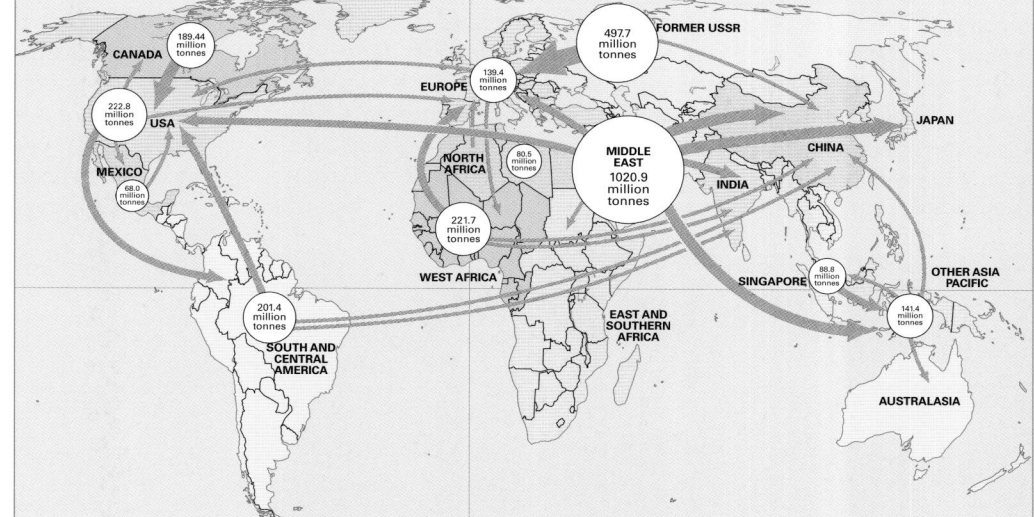

ENERGY RESERVES

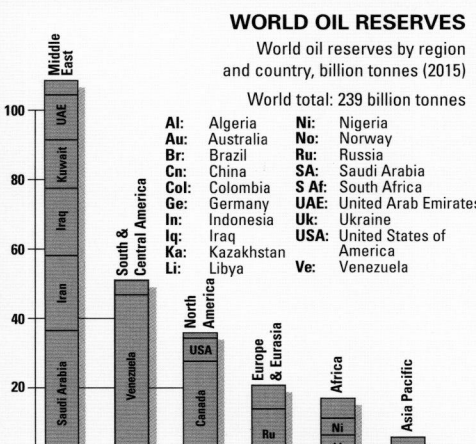

WORLD OIL RESERVES

World oil reserves by region and country, billion tonnes (2015)

World total: 239 billion tonnes

Al:	Algeria	Ni:	Nigeria
Au:	Australia	No:	Norway
Br:	Brazil	Ru:	Russia
Cn:	China	SA:	Saudi Arabia
Col:	Colombia	S Af:	South Africa
Ge:	Germany	UAE:	United Arab Emirates
In:	Indonesia	Uk:	Ukraine
Iq:	Iraq	USA:	United States of
Ka:	Kazakhstan		America
Li:	Libya	Ve:	Venezuela

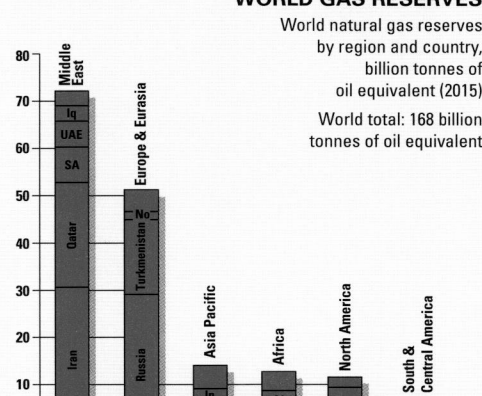

WORLD GAS RESERVES

World natural gas reserves by region and country, billion tonnes of oil equivalent (2015)

World total: 168 billion tonnes of oil equivalent

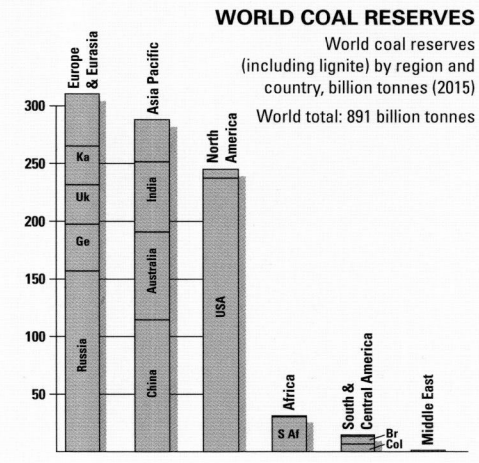

WORLD COAL RESERVES

World coal reserves (including lignite) by region and country, billion tonnes (2015)

World total: 891 billion tonnes

▲ A view over the tanks of the Liquefied Natural Gas (LNG) tanker Grand Aniva. LNG is natural gas that has been filtered and purified then cooled to -260°F (-162°C), which turns it into a liquid, 1/600th of its original volume, allowing it to be transported in special highly-insulated tanks on ships to markets around the world.

NUCLEAR POWER

Major producers by percentage of domestic electricity generation (2016)

Country	% of nuclear as proportion of domestic electricity
1. France	72.3
2. Slovakia	54.1
3. Ukraine	52.3
4. Belgium	51.7
5. Hungary	51.3
6. Sweden	40.0
7. Slovenia	35.2
8. Bulgaria	35.0
9. Switzerland	34.4
10. Finland	33.7
11. Armenia	31.4
12. South Korea	30.3
13. Czechia	29.4
14. Spain	21.4
15. UK	20.4
16. USA	19.7
17. Russia	17.1
18. Romania	17.1
19. Canada	15.6
20. Taiwan	13.7

Although the 1980s were a bad time for the nuclear power industry, the industry picked up in the early 1990s. Despite this, growth has recently been curtailed whilst countries review their energy mix, in light of the March 2011 Japanese earthquake and tsunami that seriously damaged the Fukushima nuclear power station. Germany, for example, is phasing out its nuclear power production.

PEAK OIL

"Peak oil" refers to the peak of oil production. We depend on oil for many things: we use it for fuel, transport and heating, as a raw material in the plastics industry, and for fertilizer in food production. But as oil production decreases after peak oil, so will all of these, unless we can find new materials and alternatives.

Peak oil varies by country. The peak of oil discovery occurred in the 1960s, and by the 1980s the world was using more oil than was being discovered. Since then, the gap between use and discovery has been increasing, and many countries have now passed their peak oil production.

The International Energy Agency suggests that global peak oil will occur between 2013 and 2037. In contrast, the US Geological Survey suggests it will not occur until 2059. M. King Hubbert, who popularized the theory of peak oil, predicted that it would occur in 1995. It is claimed that in 1950 the world consumed 4 billion barrels of oil per annum, while the average discovery was 30 billion barrels per annum. Now, however, research suggests the figures are reversed: new discoveries are around 4 billion barrels per year, with an annual consumption of 30 billion barrels.

FRACKING

Hydraulic fracturing, commonly known as "fracking," releases natural gas or oil that is trapped in shale rock and is unobtainable by conventional techniques. This is accomplished by boring holes into the rock and injecting a liquid mix of chemicals under pressure, thus fracturing the rock and forcing the trapped oil or gas to the surface.

Just as nuclear scientists in the 1950s and 1960s believed that nuclear energy was going to be the answer to the world's energy needs, oil and gas producers believe that gas derived from shale could provide a plentiful supply of low-cost energy. As a result, shale gas could transform the pattern of energy trade in the world. Nevertheless, fracking has its critics and there may be problems related to the extraction of shale gas.

Shale is one of the most common forms of sedimentary rock on Earth. Significant reserves have been found in China, Argentina, the USA, and South Africa, and these are therefore having a new geopolitical influence. The world's gas trade has long been dominated by Russia, Qatar, and Algeria, but shale gas development has since taken off in the USA. In 2010, the USA replaced Russia as the world's largest gas producer and a new wave of gas producers may soon emerge.

However, as with the nuclear dawn, there are potential drawbacks with fracking. It may pollute soil and ground water, release methane, produce toxic byproducts that have to be disposed of, and it may also trigger earthquakes.

HYDROELECTRICITY

Major producers by percentage of world total and by percentage of domestic electricity generation (2015)

Country	% of world total production	Country	% of hydroelectric as proportion of domestic electricity
1. China	28.4	1. Albania	100.0
2. Brazil	9.6	2. Paraguay	100.0
3. Canada	9.5	3. Nepal	99.7
4. United States	6.3	4. Tajikistan	99.7
5. Russia	4.0	5. Zambia	99.7
6. Norway	3.5	6. Congo, Dem. Rep.	99.6
7. India	3.2	7. Mozambique.	97.7
8. Japan	2.3	8. Norway	96.0
9. Venezuela	2.0	9. Ethiopia	95.6
10. Sweden	1.9	10. Namibia	95.6

Countries heavily reliant on hydroelectricity are usually small and non-industrial: a high proportion of hydroelectric power more often reflects a modest energy budget than vast hydroelectric resources. The USA, for instance, produces only 6% of its domestic power requirements from hydroelectricity; yet that 6% amounts to almost half the hydropower generated by the whole of Africa.

ALTERNATIVE ENERGY RESOURCES

Solar: Each year the Sun bestows upon the Earth almost a million times as much energy as is locked up in all the planet's oil reserves, but only an insignificant fraction is trapped and used commercially. In a few installations around the world, mirrors focus the Sun's rays on to boilers, whose steam generates electricity by spinning turbines, and the use of photovoltaic panels in sunny climates has also started to become established.

Wind: Caused by uneven heating of the Earth, winds are themselves a form of solar energy. Windmills have been long used for wind power; recent models are often arranged in banks on wind-swept high ground or situated off coastlines. Wind-power figures are given in the table (right). Wind power contributes over 30% of all electricity generated in Denmark.

Tidal: The energy from tides is potentially enormous, although only a few installations have so far been built to exploit it. In theory, at least, waves and currents could also provide almost unimaginable power, and the thermal differences in the ocean depths are another huge well of potential energy. But work on extracting it is still at the experimental stage.

Geothermal: The Earth's temperature rises by 1°F for every 50 feet descent, with much steeper temperature gradients in geologically active areas. El Salvador, for example, produces 25% of its electricity from geothermal power stations, whilst the USA is the world's leading producer. Some of the oldest and most successful applications are in Iceland, where 87% of all households are heated by geothermal energy.

Biomass: The oldest of human fuels ranges from animal dung, still burned in cooking fires in much of North Africa and elsewhere, to sugarcane plantations feeding high-technology distilleries to produce ethanol for motor-vehicle engines. In Brazil and South Africa, plant ethanol provides up to 25% of motor fuel. Throughout the developing world, most biomass energy comes from firewood: although accurate figures are impossible to obtain, it may yield as much as 10% of the world's total energy consumption.

WIND POWER

World wind energy generating capacity, in megawatts

1990	1,930
1992	2,510
1994	3,710
1996	6,115
1998	9,600
2000	17,800
2002	31,000
2003	39,300
2004	47,671
2005	58,982
2006	74,151
2007	93,927
2008	121,188
2009	157,899
2010	196,653
2011	238,035
2012	282,482
2013	318,105
2014	370,000
2015	434,856

For more information:
74   Geology
103 Globalization

The use of metals played a vital part in the evolving technologies of early peoples. Copper first came into use around 10,000 years ago, bronze about 5,000 years ago, and iron 3,300 years ago. In the early stages of the Industrial Revolution, the location of coal, iron ore, and water power usually determined the location of new industries. But due to continuing improvements in transport, including oil pipelines, industries can now be located almost anywhere.

Minerals are distributed unevenly and some industrial countries, lacking their own mineral resources, import most of the raw materials they need. Some imports come from mineral-rich countries, such as Australia, but others come from developing countries, especially in Africa and South America. Most developing countries export unprocessed ores, losing out on the higher revenues gained from exporting metals.

Most minerals come from land deposits, because undersea deposits, with the exception of oil reserves under the continental shelves, have been inaccessible. But shortages of terrestrial minerals may one day encourage exploitation of the ocean floor.

▶ Bingham Canyon Mine in Utah, USA, is one of the largest open-pit mines in the world. It measures over 2.5 miles [4 km] wide and 3,900 ft [1,200 m] deep. Copper-containing rocks are excavated from the surface downward in terraces. These terraces are 50–80 ft [15–25 m] high and provide access for equipment to work the rock face whilst maintaining stability of the sloping pit walls.

Today's copper market is booming due to global demands from construction, telecommunications, and electronics companies. Over 17 million tonnes of copper have been mined from Bingham Canyon Mine to date, as well as gold, silver and other minerals.

URANIUM

Uranium was first discovered by the German chemist Martin Klaproth in 1789. In its pure state, uranium is an immensely heavy, white metal. Its main use is as a fuel in nuclear reactors and in nuclear weaponry, although depleted uranium is employed as a projectile in anti-missile cannons, where its mass ensures a lethal punch.

Uranium is very scarce: the main source is the rare ore pitchblende, which itself contains only 0.2% uranium oxide. This blackish, lustrous ore occurs in quartz veins. Only a minute fraction of that is the radioactive U^{235} isotope, though so-called breeder reactors can transmute the more common U^{238} into highly radioactive plutonium.

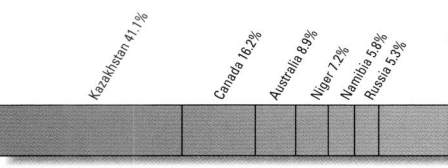

World total (2015): 56,217 tonnes

DIAMOND

Most of the world's diamond is found in kimberlite, or "blue ground," a basic igneous rock; erosion may wash the diamond from its kimberlite matrix and deposit it with sand or gravel on river beds. Only a small proportion of the world's diamond, the most flawless, is cut into gemstones – "diamonds"; most are used in industry, where the material's remarkable hardness and abrasion resistance finds a use in cutting tools, drills, and dies. In 2016, the world's major producers were Russia (31.6%), Australia (22.8%), the Democratic Republic of the Congo (19.3%), Botswana (10.5%), South Africa (7.0%), and Zimbabwe (3.5%). Natural diamonds now account for about 3% of all industrial diamond output. Synthetic diamond production in centers such as China, Ireland, Japan, Russia, and the USA far exceeds it.

BLOOD DIAMONDS

Blood Diamonds, or "Conflict Diamonds," are stones that are produced in areas controlled by rebel forces that are opposed to internationally recognized governments. The rebels sell these diamonds, using the money to purchase arms or to fund their military actions. These diamonds are often the main source of funding for the rebels – however, arms merchants, smugglers, and dishonest diamond traders facilitate their actions.

The flow of Blood Diamonds originated mainly from Sierra Leone, Angola, Democratic Republic of Congo, Liberia, and Ivory Coast. In 2003, the United Nations and other groups introduced a certification procedure known as the "Kimberley Process," to try to eradicate this practice. This procedure requires each nation to certify that all rough diamond exports are produced through legitimate mining and sales activity.

Over 80 countries participate in the agreement.

Aluminum: Produced mainly from its oxide, bauxite, which yields 25% of its weight in aluminum. The cost of refining and production is often too high for producer-countries to bear, so bauxite is largely exported. Lightweight and corrosion resistant, aluminum alloys are widely used in aircraft, vehicles, cans, and packaging.

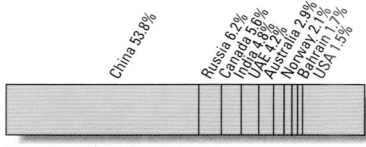

World total (2016): 57,600,000 tonnes

Lead: A soft metal, obtained mainly from galena (lead sulfide), which occurs in veins associated with iron, zinc, and silver sulfides. Its use in vehicle batteries accounts for the USA's prime consumer status; lead is also made into sheeting and piping. Its use as an additive to paints and petrol is decreasing.

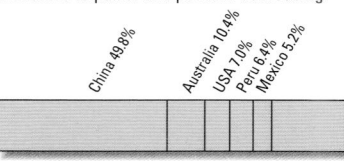

World total (2016): 4,820,000 tonnes

Tin: Soft, pliable and non-toxic, used to coat "tin" (tin-plated steel) cans, in the manufacture of foils and in alloys. The principal tin-bearing mineral is cassiterite (SnO_2), found in ore formed from molten rock.

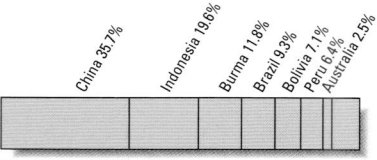

World total (2016): 280,000 tonnes

Gold: Regarded for centuries as the most valuable metal in the world and used to make coins, gold is still recognized as the monetary standard. A soft metal, it is alloyed to make jewelry; the electronics industry values its corrosion resistance and conductivity.

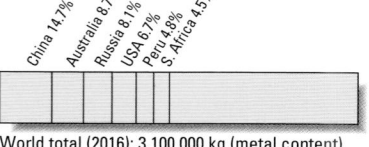

World total (2016): 3,100,000 kg (metal content)

Copper: Derived from low-yielding sulfide ores, copper is an important export for several developing countries. An excellent conductor of heat and electricity, it forms part of most electrical items, and is used in the manufacture of brass and bronze. Major importers include Japan and Germany.

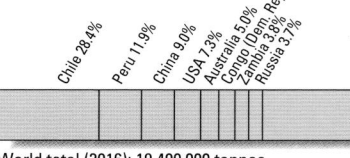

World total (2016): 19,400,000 tonnes

Mercury: The only metal that is liquid at normal temperatures, most is derived from its sulfide, cinnabar, found only in small quantities in volcanic areas. Apart from its value in thermometers and other instruments, most mercury production is used in anti-fungal and anti-fouling preparations, and to make detonators.

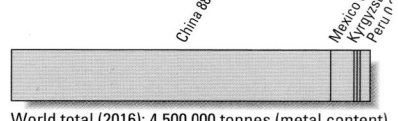

World total (2016): 4,500,000 tonnes (metal content)

Zinc: Often found in association with lead ores, zinc is highly resistant to corrosion, and about 40% of the refined metal is used to plate sheet steel, particularly vehicle bodies – a process known as galvanizing. Zinc is also used in dry batteries, paints, and dyes.

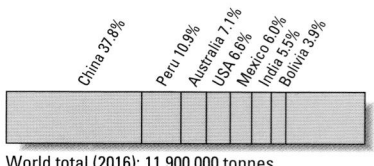

World total (2016): 11,900,000 tonnes

Silver: Most silver comes from ores mined and processed for other metals (including lead and copper). Pure or alloyed with harder metals, it is used for jewelry and ornaments. Industrial use includes dentistry, electronics, photography, and as a chemical catalyst.

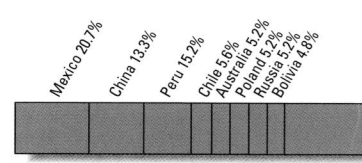

World total (2016): 27,000 tonnes (metal content)

DISTRIBUTION OF MINERALS

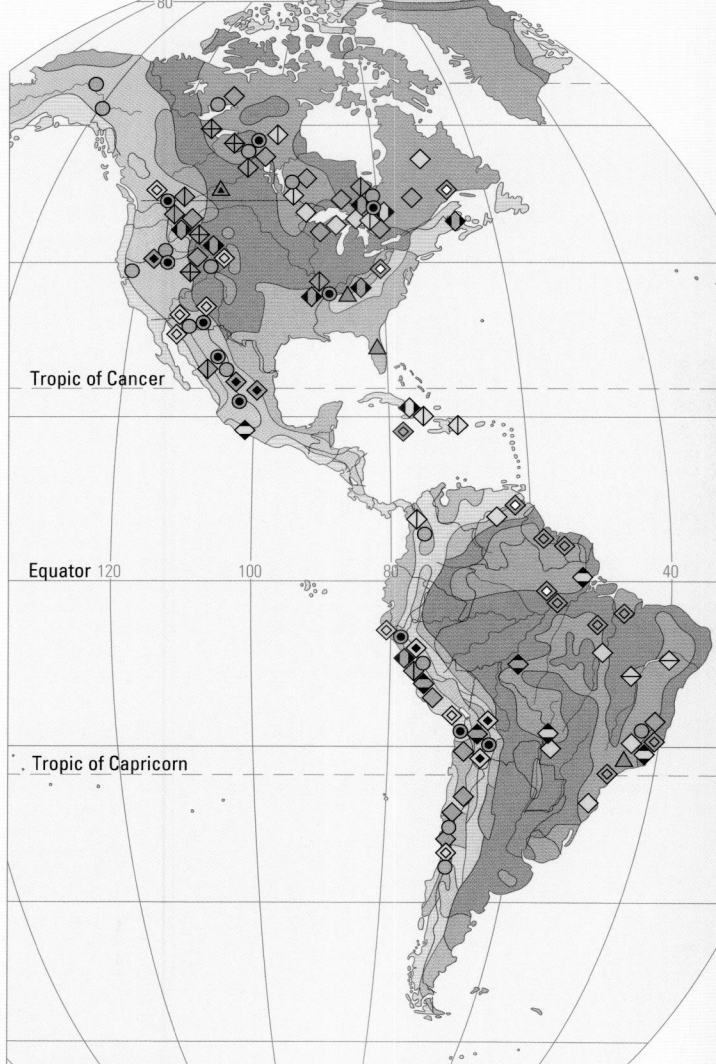

Tropic of Cancer

Equator

Tropic of Capricorn

Antarctic Circle

IRON ORE

Ever since the art of high-temperature smelting was discovered, some time in the second millennium BC, iron has been by far the most important metal known to man. The earliest iron plows transformed primitive agriculture and led to the first human population explosion, while iron weapons – or the lack of them – ensured the rise or fall of entire cultures.

Widely distributed around the world, iron ores usually contain 25–60% iron; blast furnaces process the raw product into pig-iron, which is then alloyed with carbon and other minerals to produce steels of various qualities. From the time of the Industrial Revolution, steel has been almost literally the backbone of modern civilization, the prime structural material on which all else is built.

Iron smelting usually developed close to the sources of ore and, later, to the coalfields that fueled the furnaces. Today, most ore comes from a few richly-endowed locations where large-scale mining is possible.

Iron and steel plants are generally built at coastal sites so that giant ore carriers, which account for a sizable proportion of the world's merchant fleet, can more easily discharge their cargoes.

World production of pig-iron (2015)

**Total world production:
1,180 million tonnes**

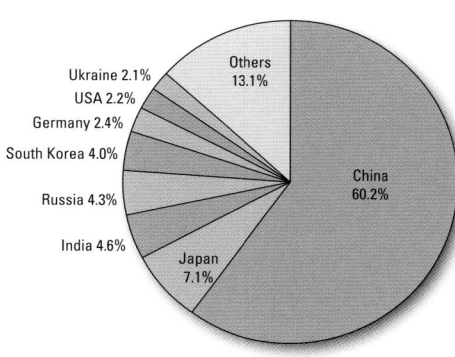

Others 13.1%
China 60.2%
Japan 7.1%
India 4.6%
Russia 4.3%
South Korea 4.0%
Germany 2.4%
USA 2.2%
Ukraine 2.1%

Iron ore

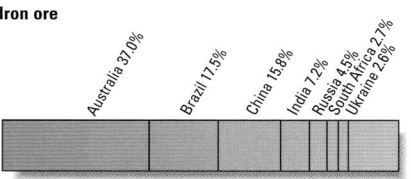

Australia 37.0%
Brazil 17.5%
China 15.8%
India 7.2%
Russia 4.5%
South Africa 2.7%
Ukraine 2.5%

World total (2016): 2,230,000 tonnes

RARE EARTHS

Rare earth elements, or rare earth metals, are a set of 17 chemical elements, specifically the 15 lanthanides plus scandium and yttrium. Despite their name, rare earth elements are relatively plentiful, but are typically dispersed and not often found concentrated in economically exploitable ore deposits.

Until 1948, most of the world's rare earths were sourced from sand deposits in India and Brazil. Between the 1960s and the 1980s, the leading producer was California, USA. Today, China produces over 90% of the world's rare earth supply, although it only has less than 23% of proven reserves. The US Geological Survey is currently actively surveying southern Afghanistan for rare earth deposits under the protection of US military forces.

New demand has recently strained supply, and there is a growing concern that the world may soon face a shortage of the rare earths. In recent years, China has reduced its export quotas and halted production in some of its mines in order to conserve scarce resources and protect the environment.

A recently developed source of rare earths is electronic waste, and other wastes have rare earth components. Advances in recycling technology have made extraction of rare earths from these materials more feasible.

Rare earths are used as follows:

- **Neodymium** To make powerful magnets in loudspeakers and computer hard drives; also used in wind turbines and hybrid cars.
- **Lanthanum** In camera and telescope lenses.
- **Cerium** In catalytic converters in cars, and in the refining of oil.
- **Praseodymium** As an alloy, to create strong metals in aircraft engines.
- **Gadolinium** For X-ray machines, MRI scanning systems, and television screens.
- **Yttrium, terbium, europium** For television and computer screens, and for visual display units.

SCRAP METAL

Scrap metal has been an important source material for the manufacturing industry in domestic markets for decades, its value fluctuating according to the state of the local economy. Recently, however, with growing concern for the global environment and the rapid development of the economies in the Far East, the industry has become far more globalized. Container loads of processed-metal scrap from time-expired machinery in the Western world are now being exported to the Far East to be recycled. Processed-steel scrap accounts for almost half of the requirements for "furnace feed" for the world's steelmakers, and 40% of the world's copper requirements are derived from scrap.

Two major advantages of using scrap rather than refining mined ore are the energy and raw material savings that can be made. If 1 tonne of steel scrap is recycled, it saves 120 lb [54 kg] of limestone, 2,500 lb [1,130 kg] of iron ore and 1,400 lb [635 kg] of coal, with a consequent 86% reduction in air pollution, 40% saving in water use, and 76% reduction in water pollution. Huge energy savings, with consequent cuts in greenhouse-gas emissions, can also be made by using scrap.

As well as bulk minerals, such as those quoted above, alloys using nickel, chromium, tungsten, molybdenum, cobalt, and titanium, which are often only available in limited supplies and are expensive to produce, can also be recycled. The techniques involved to do this work are often very sophisticated, involving X-ray spectrometry and other computer-controlled methods, in order to recover high-value but low-volume metals from devices such as computers and televisions.

With companies having to take increased responsibility for their products, from manufacturing to sale and thence to their ultimate disposal at the end of their useful life, recycling scrap metals will become a much more important method of conserving the world's raw materials and preserving the environment in the future.

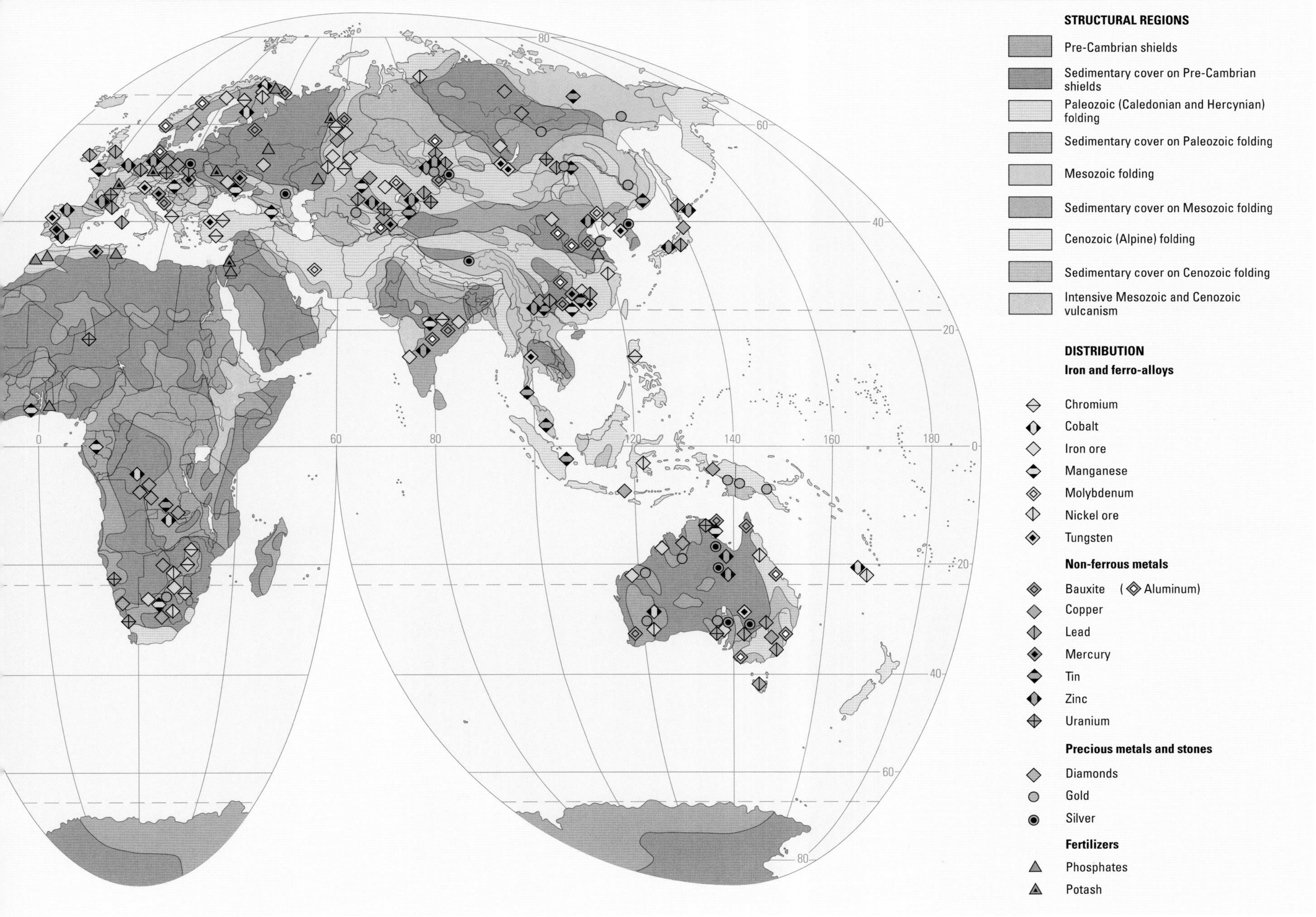

STRUCTURAL REGIONS

- Pre-Cambrian shields
- Sedimentary cover on Pre-Cambrian shields
- Paleozoic (Caledonian and Hercynian) folding
- Sedimentary cover on Paleozoic folding
- Mesozoic folding
- Sedimentary cover on Mesozoic folding
- Cenozoic (Alpine) folding
- Sedimentary cover on Cenozoic folding
- Intensive Mesozoic and Cenozoic vulcanism

DISTRIBUTION

Iron and ferro-alloys

- Chromium
- Cobalt
- Iron ore
- Manganese
- Molybdenum
- Nickel ore
- Tungsten

Non-ferrous metals

- Bauxite (Aluminum)
- Copper
- Lead
- Mercury
- Tin
- Zinc
- Uranium

Precious metals and stones

- Diamonds
- Gold
- Silver

Fertilizers

- Phosphates
- Potash

For more information:
82   Water distribution
98   Minerals
102 World trade
103 Globalization

The Industrial Revolution, which began in Britain in the late 18th century, represented a major technological advance in the evolution of human society. It enabled a group of countries to become prosperous by replacing expensive human labor with increasingly sophisticated machinery. In economic terms, manufacturing is the transformation of raw materials, energy, labor, and machines into finished goods, which have a higher value than the various elements used in production.

The economies of countries can be compared by reference to their per capita Gross Domestic Products (GDPs), namely, the total value of goods and services produced within a country in a year, divided by the population. If this is calculated using Purchasing Power Parity (PPP) exchange rates, it better reflects the real state of the economy by taking into account differences in price levels in each country. The industrialized, or developed, countries accounted for 15% of the world's population in 2015 with an average per capita GDP of over US $43,000. On the other hand, low-income developing countries, with small industrial sectors, accounted for 77% of the world's population. Their per capita GDPs can be as low as $400.

Tanzania, with its low-income economy, had a per capita GDP in 2016 of US $3,100. Agriculture employs 80% of the people, while light industry together with services employs 20%. By contrast, Germany had a per capita GDP in 2016 of $48,200. Agriculture employs only 2% of the population, with 25% in industry and 74% in services. Germany's industrial sector differs greatly from Tanzania's, with its emphasis on vehicles, machinery, chemicals, and electronics.

Since the 1970s, some former developing countries in eastern Asia achieved rapid economic growth through industrialization. Despite setbacks in the late 1990s, they demonstrated that a developing industrial sector can transform an economy, which starts off with certain advantages, such as low labor costs. But economic success also depends on such factors as education to provide skills, and regulations that attract foreign investors. China, whose economy grew by more than 10% per year between 2002 and 2012, satisfies many of these criteria, though its record on human rights leaves much to be desired.

EMPLOYMENT

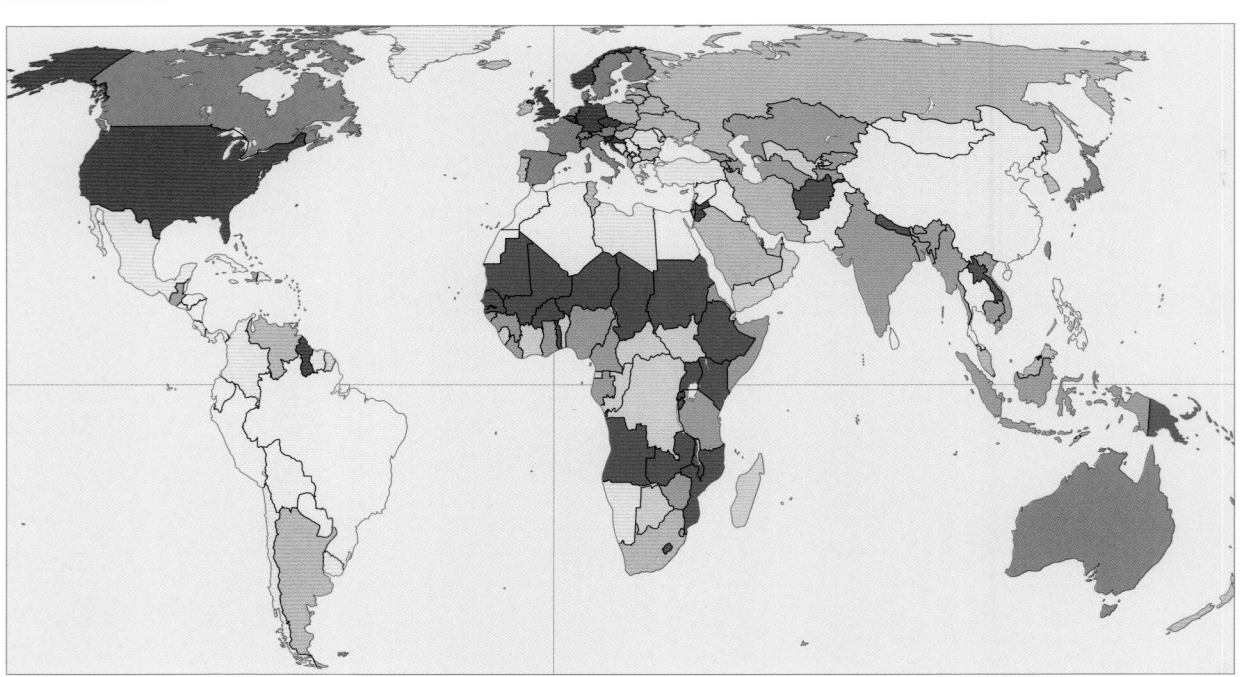

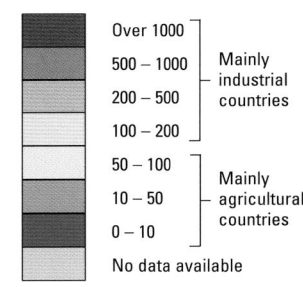

The number of workers employed in manufacturing for every 100 workers engaged in agriculture (2014)

Over 1000	
500 – 1000	Mainly industrial countries
200 – 500	
100 – 200	
50 – 100	Mainly agricultural countries
10 – 50	
0 – 10	
No data available	

Countries with the highest number of workers employed in manufacturing per 100 workers in agriculture (2014)

Bahrain	7,900
Qatar	5,400
Liechtenstein	3,900
Micronesia, Fed. States of	2,100
USA	2,000
Belgium	1,900
Guyana	1,900
Luxembourg	1,900
Slovenia	1,750
Brunei	1,575
Singapore	1,500
United Kingdom	1,500

DIVISION OF EMPLOYMENT

Distribution of workers between agriculture, industry and services, selected countries

The six countries selected illustrate the usual stages of economic development, from dependence on agriculture through industrial growth to the expansion of the service sector.

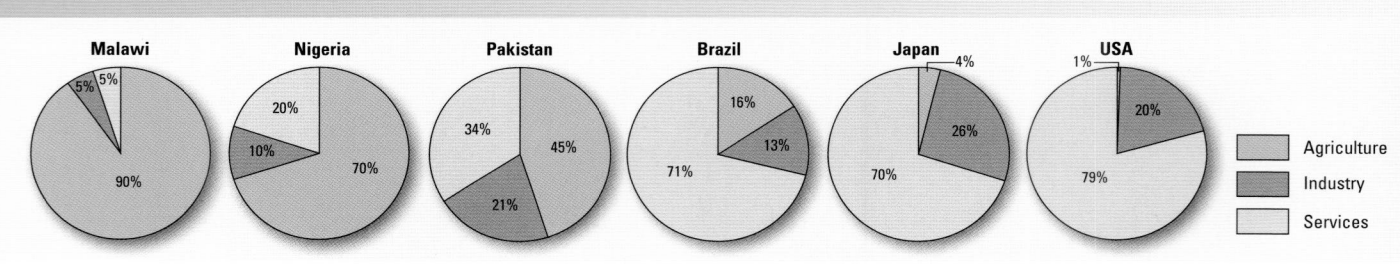

Malawi · Nigeria · Pakistan · Brazil · Japan · USA

Agriculture · Industry · Services

THE WORK FORCE

Percentages of men and women between 15 and 64 in employment (selected countries)

The figures include employees and the self-employed, who in developing countries are often subsistence farmers. People in full-time education are excluded. Because of the population age structure in developing countries, the employed population has to support a far larger number of non-workers than its industrial equivalent. For example, more than 52% of Kenya's people are under 15, an age group that makes up less than a tenth of the UK population.

Men   Women

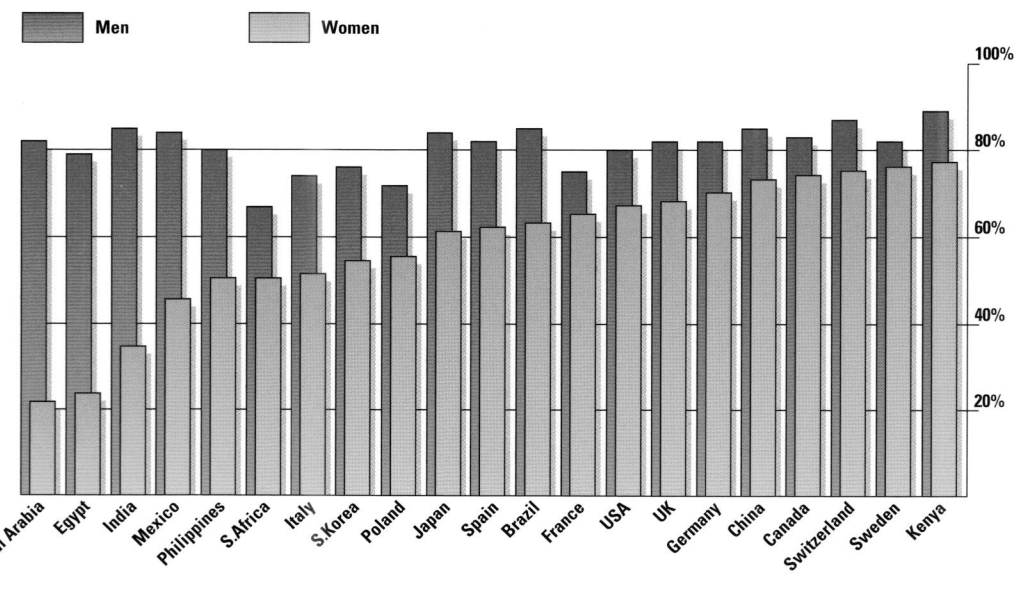

Saudi Arabia · Egypt · India · Mexico · Philippines · S.Africa · Italy · S.Korea · Poland · Japan · Spain · Brazil · France · USA · UK · Germany · China · Canada · Switzerland · Sweden · Kenya

INDUSTRIAL OUTPUT

Largest industrial output (mining, manufacturing, construction and energy), US $ billion (2014)

1.	China	4,434	21.	Norway	171
2.	USA	3,212	22.	Netherlands	168
3.	Japan	1,280	23.	Iran	159
4.	Germany	1,055	24.	Poland	159
5.	Russia	570	25.	Taiwan	149
6.	India	568	26.	Thailand	149
7.	UK	558	27.	Qatar	143
8.	Canada	506	28.	Nigeria	136
9.	France	493	29.	Malaysia	135
10.	South Korea	492	30.	Sweden	131
11.	Italy	451	31.	Argentina	130
12.	Saudi Arabia	425	32.	Colombia	125
13.	Mexico	422	33.	Egypt	122
14.	Indonesia	372	34.	Austria	109
15.	Australia	368	35.	Belgium	105
16.	Spain	282	36.	South Africa	93
17.	UAE	220	37.	Algeria	91
18.	Turkey	193	38.	Philippines	89
19.	Switzerland	178	39.	Chile	83
20.	Venezuela	172	40.	Denmark	66

INDUSTRY AND TRADE

Manufactured goods (including machinery and transport) as a percentage of total exports (2015)

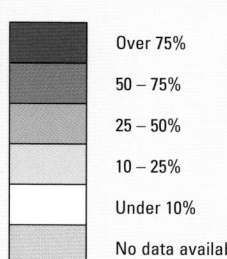

- Over 75%
- 50 – 75%
- 25 – 50%
- 10 – 25%
- Under 10%
- No data available

Countries most dependent on the export of manufactured goods (2015)

China	94%
Cambodia	93%
Switzerland	91%
Botswana	90%
South Korea	90%
Slovakia	89%

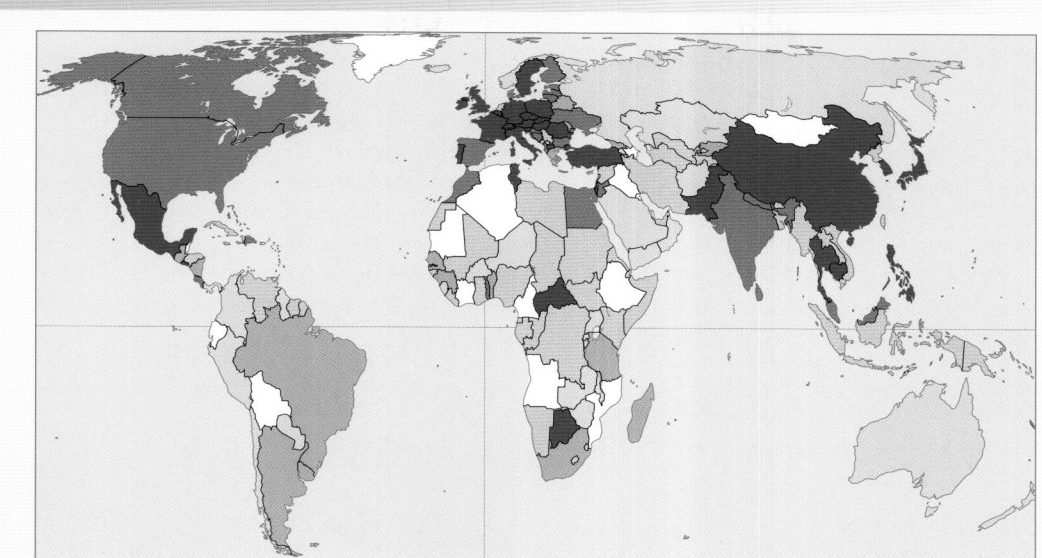

UNEMPLOYMENT

Highest rates of unemployment, percentage of the labor force (2016)

1.	Zimbabwe	95%
2.	Liberia	85%
3.	Burkina Faso	77%
4.	Djibouti	60%
5.	Congo	53%
6.	Syria	50%
7.	Senegal	48%
8.	Nepal	46%
9.	Bosnia & Herzegovina	43%
10.	Haiti	41%
11.	Kenya	40%
12.	Marshall Islands	36%
13.	Afghanistan	35%
14.	Kosovo	35%
15.	Grenada	34%
16.	Mauritania	31%
17.	Kiribati	31%
18.	Mali	30%
19.	Libya	30%
20.	Cameroon	30%

IMPORTANCE OF SERVICE SECTOR

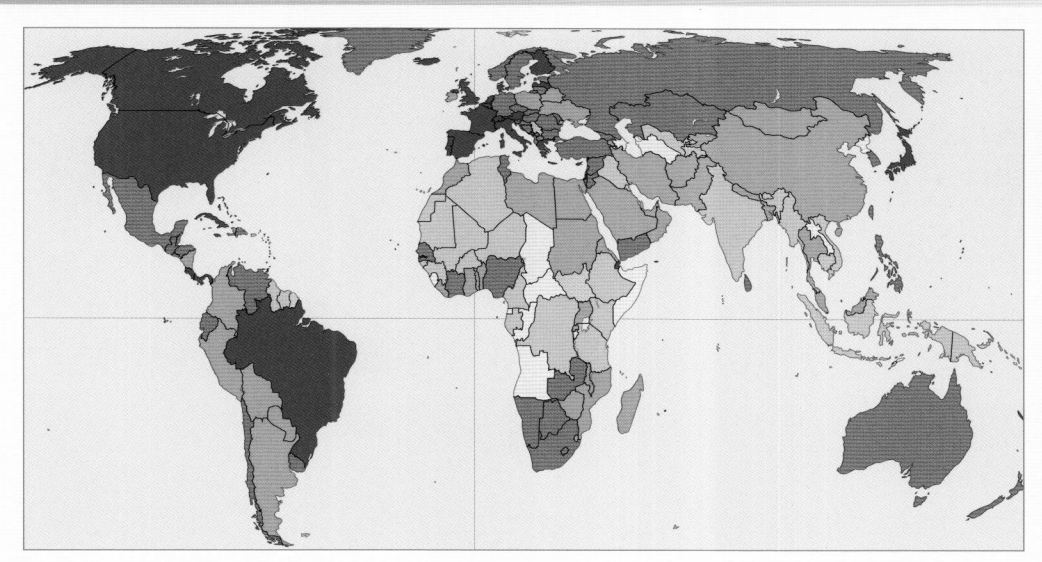

Percentage of total GDP from service sector (2016)

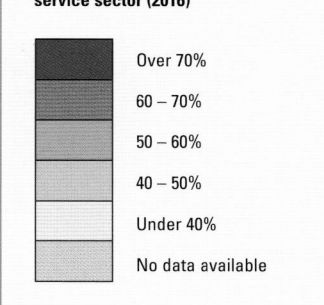

- Over 70%
- 60 – 70%
- 50 – 60%
- 40 – 50%
- Under 40%
- No data available

The service sector involves those parts of business such as accountancy, advertising, financial services, tourism, etc. No actual goods are produced, but high levels of income may be generated.

TOURISM AND TRAVEL

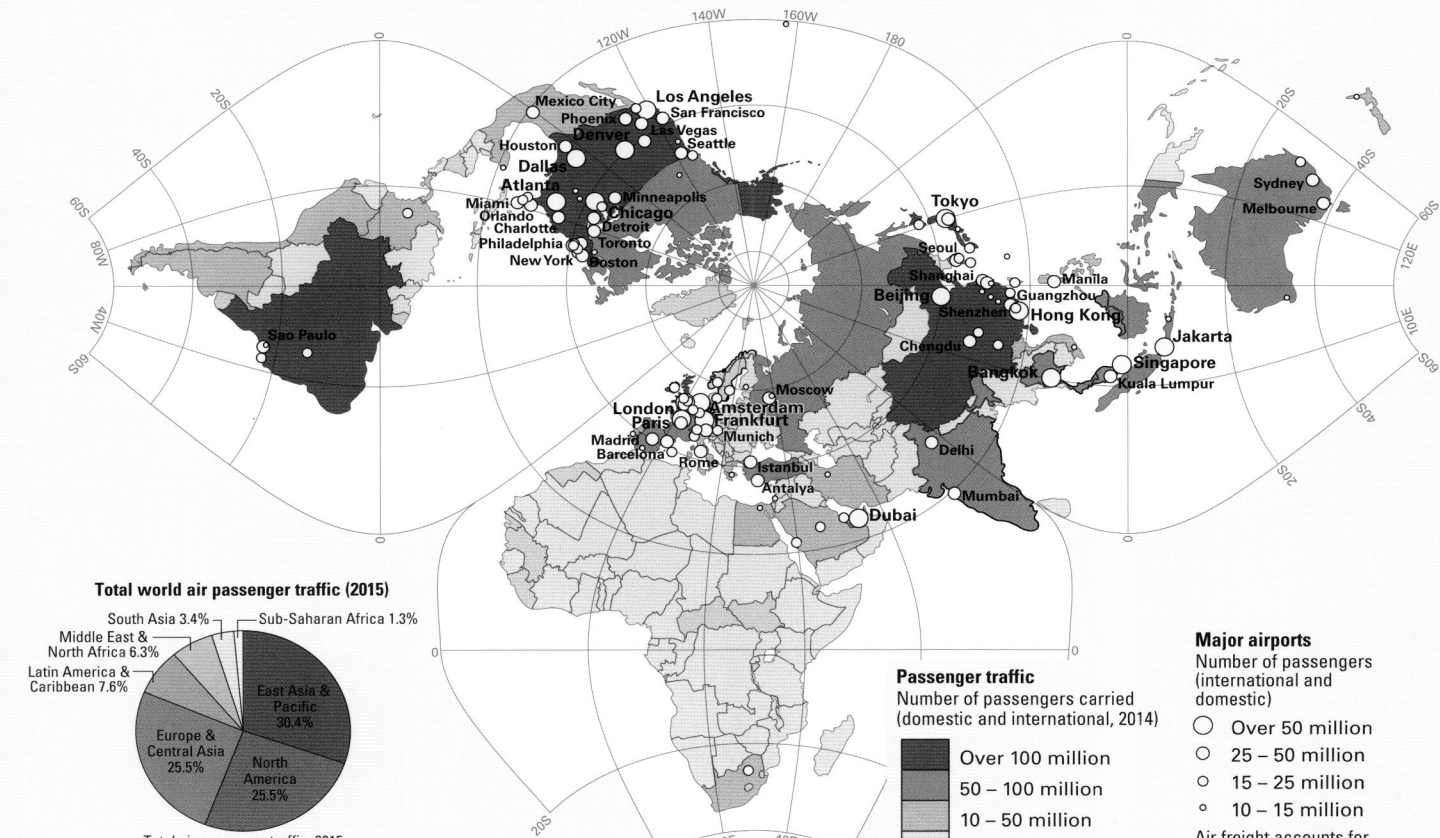

Leisure and tourism is the world's second largest industry in terms of revenue generated. Small economies in attractive areas are often completely dominated by tourism: in some Caribbean islands, for example, tourist spending provides over 90% of the total income and is the biggest foreign-exchange earner.

According to the World Bank, the United States is the world leader in earnings from tourism, taking over US $246 billion in 2015. The largest spender on international tourism is now China, which has seen an eight-fold increase in tourism spending in the 14 years from 2000. In 2015, Chinese travelers spent a record US $292 billion. The next biggest spenders are the United States, Germany, and the UK.

WORLD'S BUSIEST AIRPORTS
Total passengers in millions (2016)

1.	Atlanta Hartsfield Intl. (ATL)	104.2
2.	Beijing Capital Intl. (PEK)	94.4
6.	Dubai Intl. (DXB)	83.7
5.	Los Angeles Intl. (LAX)	80.9
4.	Tokyo Haneda (HND)	79.5
7.	Chicago O'Hare Intl. (ORD)	78.0
3.	London Heathrow (LHR)	75.7
9.	Hong Kong Intl. (HKG)	70.5
9.	Shanghai Pudong Intl. (PVG)	66.0
8.	Paris Charles de Gaulle (CDG)	66.0

Dubai International handles the most international passengers (77.5 million in 2015), followed by London's Heathrow (69.8 million).

Total world air passenger traffic (2015)

- South Asia 3.4%
- Sub-Saharan Africa 1.3%
- Middle East & North Africa 6.3%
- Latin America & Caribbean 7.6%
- East Asia & Pacific 30.4%
- Europe & Central Asia 25.5%
- North America 25.5%

Total air passenger traffic, 2015
3,440,862,893

Passenger traffic
Number of passengers carried (domestic and international, 2014)

- Over 100 million
- 50 – 100 million
- 10 – 50 million
- Under 10 million
- No data available

Major airports
Number of passengers (international and domestic)

- ◯ Over 50 million
- ◯ 25 – 50 million
- ◦ 15 – 25 million
- ∘ 10 – 15 million

Air freight accounts for 35% of all international freight handled by value.

Projection: Peirce

For more information:

95 International organizations
97 Movements of oil
98 Minerals
101 Industry and trade
Tourism and travel
107 Inflation

Trade played a vital role in the growth of early civilizations and it was later a spur to European exploration and colonization. The colonial powers grew rich by exporting cheap manufactures, such as clothing and footwear, while obtaining primary products from their colonies.

From the late 19th century to the early 1950s, as transport technology improved, primary products, especially oil in the later stages of this period, dominated world trade. However, since that time, manufactures have become the chief commodities in world trade, which is dominated by the industrialized countries. Nearly half of all world trade flows between the developed market economies of the European Union, the United States, and Japan, although a number of Asian economies, notably China, India, Malaysia, Singapore, South Korea, Taiwan, and Thailand, have dramatically increased their share since the 1990s.

China's remarkable growth means that it has rapidly overtaken countries such as Canada, Japan, and Mexico, to become the biggest exporter to the United States. China's low production costs, especially its cheap labour, were estimated to be one-twentieth of those of Japan, making its high-quality exports highly competitive in price. Growth in world trade is regarded as a sign of economic health, as is a favorable balance of trade (or trade surplus) in any country.

WORLD TRADE

Percentage share of total world exports by value (2016)

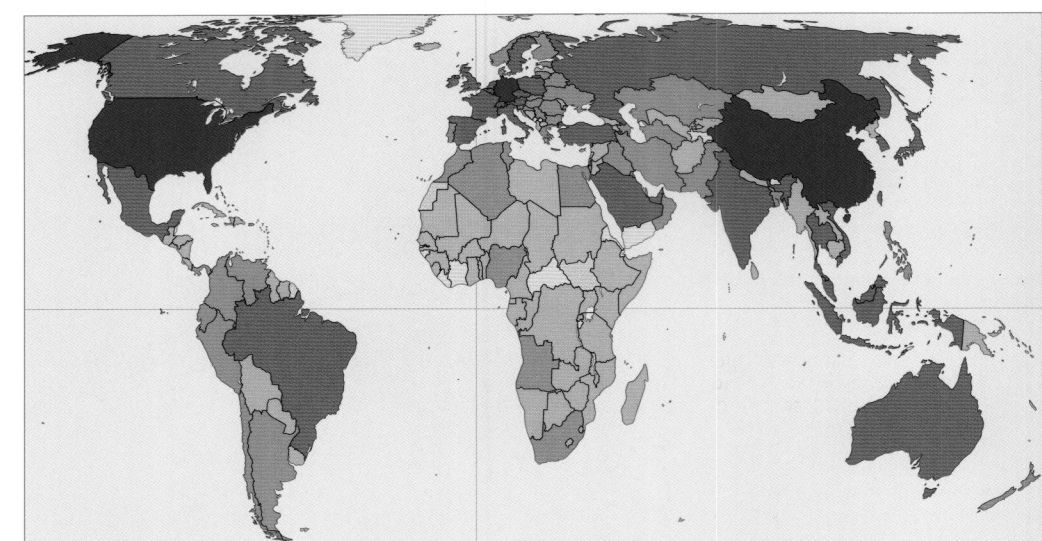

- Over 10% of world trade
- 1 – 10% of world trade
- 0.1 – 1.0% of world trade
- 0 – 0.1% of world trade
- No world trade
- No data available

International trade is dominated by a handful of powerful maritime nations: the members of "G8" (Canada, France, Germany, Italy, Japan, Russia, UK and USA) and the "BRICS" nations (Brazil, Russia, India, China, and South Africa).

DEPENDENCE ON TRADE

Exports as a percentage of GDP (2016)

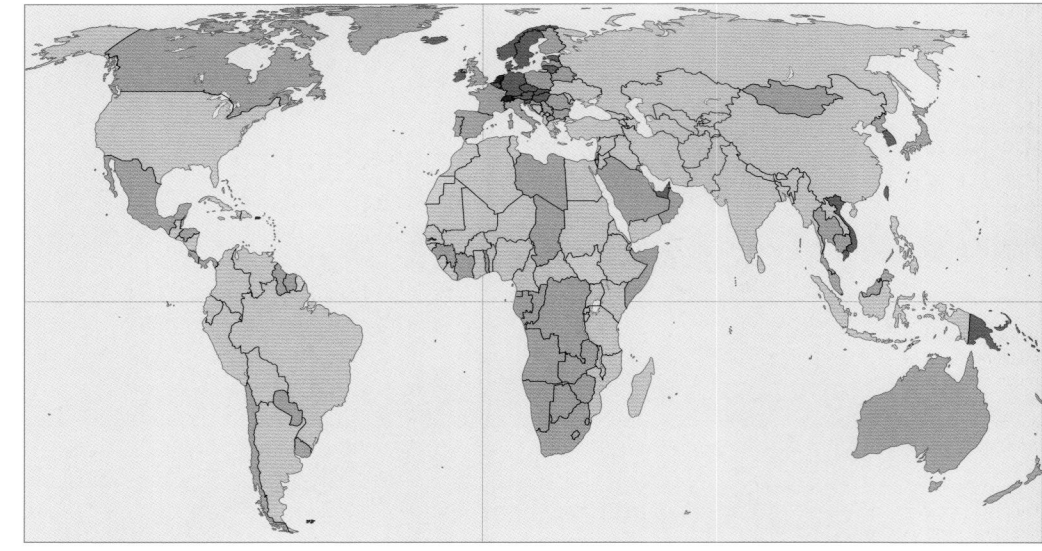

- Over 50%
- 25 – 50%
- 10 – 25%
- 0 – 10%
- No data available

The character of world trade has changed a great deal in the last 60 years or so. While many developing countries still remain heavily dependent on exporting mineral ores, fossil fuels or farm products, such as coffee or cocoa, world trade is now dominated by manufactured goods. Since the 1980s, high-tech products, such as computer equipment, telecommunications gear, and transistors, have become increasingly important.

TRADED PRODUCTS

World merchandise exports by product, percentage of total value

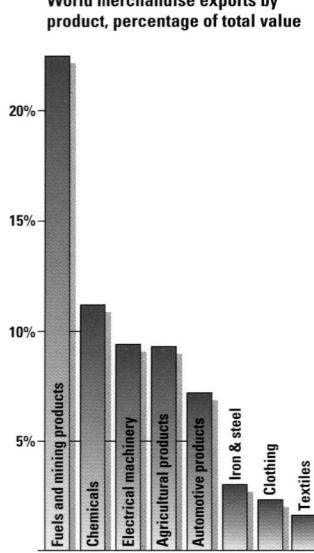

MAJOR EXPORTS

Leading manufactured items and their exporters

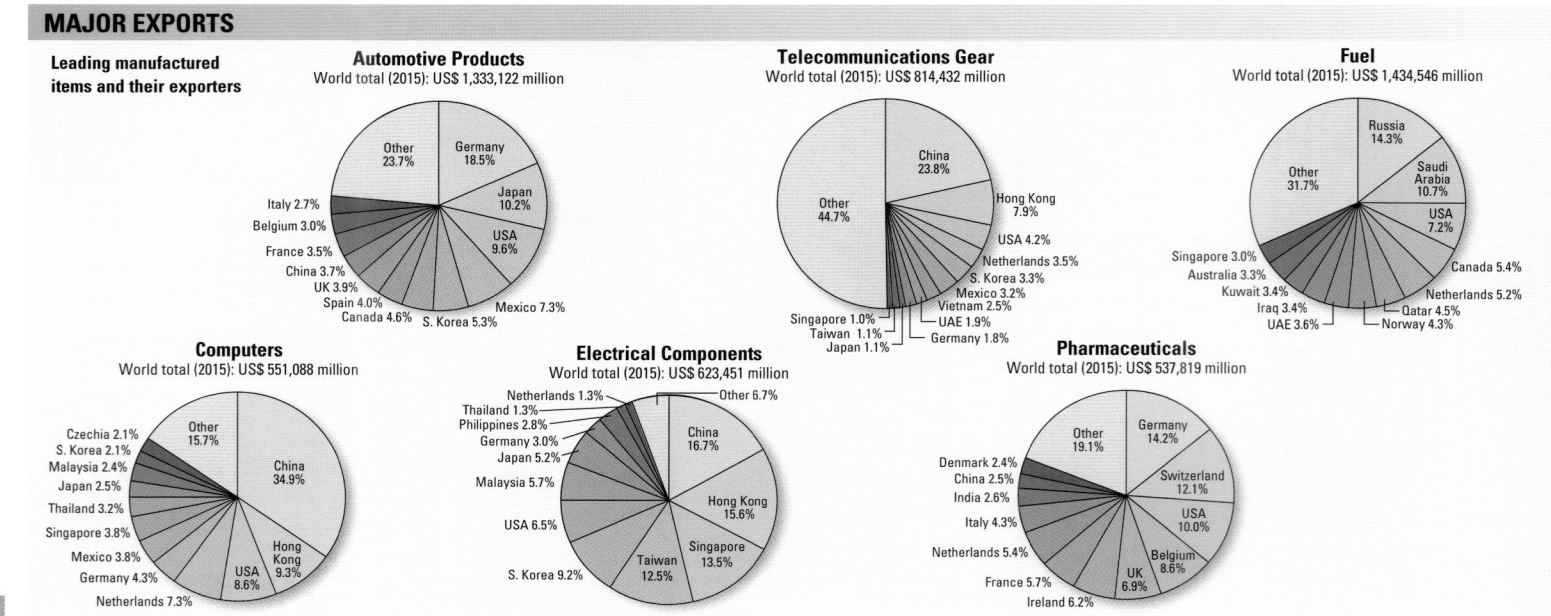

Automotive Products
World total (2015): US$ 1,333,122 million

- Germany 18.5%
- Japan 10.2%
- USA 9.6%
- Mexico 7.3%
- S. Korea 5.3%
- Canada 4.6%
- Spain 4.0%
- UK 3.9%
- China 3.7%
- France 3.5%
- Belgium 3.0%
- Italy 2.7%
- Other 23.7%

Telecommunications Gear
World total (2015): US$ 814,432 million

- China 23.8%
- Hong Kong 7.9%
- USA 4.2%
- Netherlands 3.5%
- S. Korea 3.3%
- Mexico 3.2%
- Vietnam 2.5%
- UAE 1.9%
- Germany 1.8%
- Japan 1.1%
- Taiwan 1.1%
- Singapore 1.0%
- Other 44.7%

Fuel
World total (2015): US$ 1,434,546 million

- Russia 14.3%
- Saudi Arabia 10.7%
- USA 7.2%
- Canada 5.4%
- Netherlands 5.2%
- Qatar 4.5%
- Norway 4.3%
- UAE 3.6%
- Iraq 3.4%
- Kuwait 3.4%
- Australia 3.3%
- Singapore 3.0%
- Other 31.7%

Computers
World total (2015): US$ 551,088 million

- China 34.9%
- Hong Kong 9.3%
- USA 8.6%
- Netherlands 7.3%
- Germany 4.3%
- Mexico 3.8%
- Singapore 3.8%
- Thailand 3.2%
- Japan 2.5%
- Malaysia 2.4%
- S. Korea 2.1%
- Czechia 2.1%
- Other 15.7%

Electrical Components
World total (2015): US$ 623,451 million

- China 16.7%
- Hong Kong 15.6%
- Singapore 13.5%
- Taiwan 12.5%
- S. Korea 9.2%
- USA 6.5%
- Malaysia 5.7%
- Japan 5.2%
- Germany 3.0%
- Philippines 2.8%
- Thailand 1.3%
- Netherlands 1.3%
- Other 6.7%

Pharmaceuticals
World total (2015): US$ 537,819 million

- Germany 14.2%
- Switzerland 12.1%
- USA 10.0%
- Belgium 8.6%
- UK 6.9%
- Ireland 6.2%
- France 5.7%
- Netherlands 5.4%
- Italy 4.3%
- India 2.6%
- China 2.5%
- Denmark 2.4%
- Other 19.1%

GLOBALIZATION

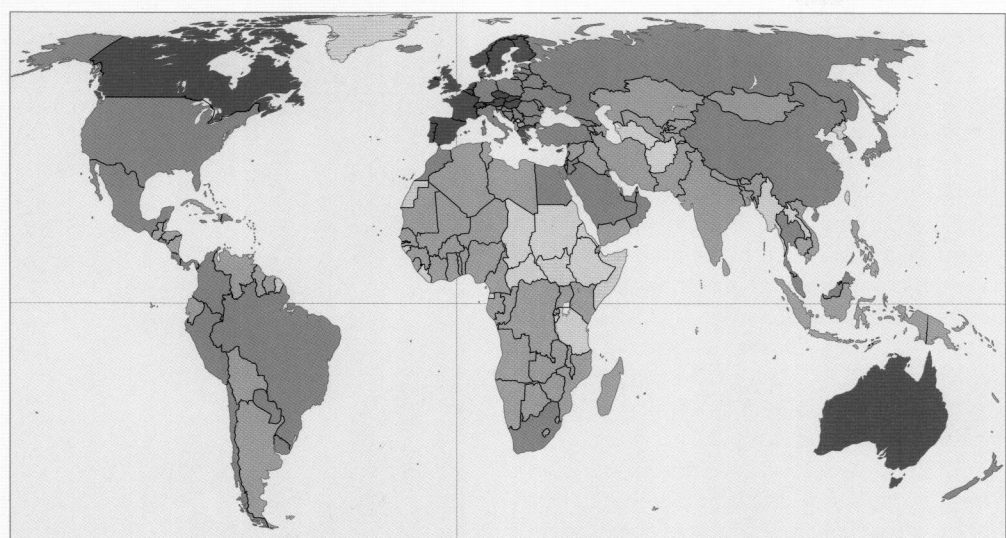

GLOBALIZATION INDEX
KOF index of globalization (2015)

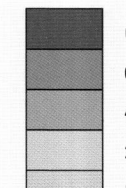

Over 80

60 – 80

40 – 60

20 – 40

No data available

The KOF index of globalization is named after the Swiss Federal Institute of Technology in Zürich, Switzerland, which devised it. Countries are scored on each of the three criteria below:

• **economic globalization**, characterized as long-distance flows of goods, capital and services, as well as information and perceptions that accompany market exchanges (this accounts for 38% of the globalization index);
• **political globalization**, characterized by a diffusion of government policies (this accounts for 23% of the globalization index);
• **social globalization**, expressed as the spread of ideas, information, images, and people (this accounts for the remaining 39% of the globalization index).

The higher values denote a greater level of globalization.

The concept of globalization developed in the 1960s after the Canadian academic Marshall McLuhan used the term "global village" to describe the breakdown of spatial barriers around the world. He argued that the similarities between places were greater than the differences between them, and that much of the world had been caught up in the same economic and social processes. He suggested that economic activities operated at a global scale and that other scales were becoming less important.

Today, globalization is defined by the International Monetary Fund (IMF) as "the growing interdependence of countries worldwide through the increasing volume and variety of cross-border transactions in goods and services and of international capital flows, and through the more rapid and widespread diffusion of technology." Essentially, it means that all countries,

with the possible exception of North Korea, are increasingly bound in a global network of migration, trade, products and services, investment, and the diffusion of ideas and culture.

Globalization has occurred as a result of many factors, such as:
• improvements in transport and ICT, leading to a "shrinking" world;
• the desire to reach new markets;
• the attempt to tap cheap sources of labor;
• the expansion of economic activity to use resources from a wide range of locations;
• the rise of free-market economies and the spread of democratic governments;
• the role of trading blocs, free trade, and the impact of the World Trade Organization;
• the importance of multinational companies.

▲ The first ship of Maersk's Triple E class of container vessels, departing Aarhus, Denmark. In 2014, this became the longest ship in service in the world and, when fully laden, it is the the world's most fuel-efficient container ship. World trade depends on transport. Containerization, introduced in the 1950s, reduced the risk of damage to cargo and cut the time and cost of loading and unloading.

TRADE IN PRIMARY EXPORTS

Primary exports as a percentage of total export value (2014)

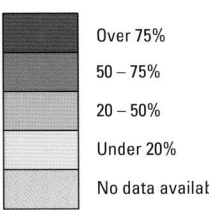

Over 75%

50 – 75%

20 – 50%

Under 20%

No data available

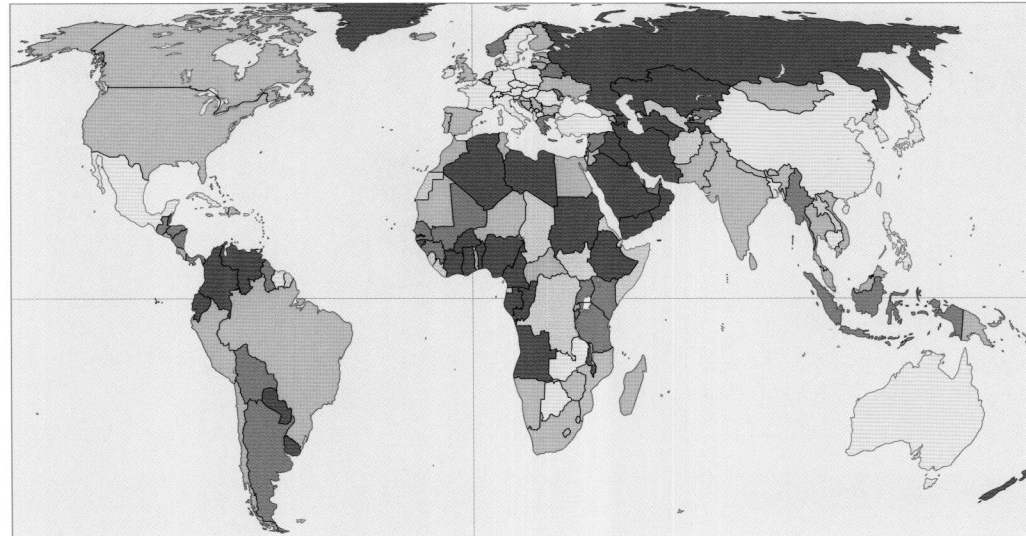

Primary exports are raw materials or partly processed products that form the basis for manufacturing. They are the necessary requirements of industries and include agricultural products, minerals, fuels, and timber, as well as many semimanufactured goods such as cotton, which has been spun but not woven, wood pulp, or flour. Many developed countries have few natural resources and rely on imports for the majority of their primary products. The countries of Southeast Asia export hardwoods to the rest of the world, while many South American countries are heavily dependent on coffee exports.

BALANCE OF TRADE

Value of exports in proportion to the value of imports (2016)

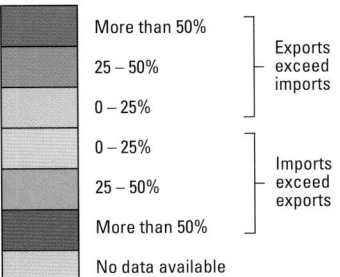

More than 50%

25 – 50%   Exports
            exceed
0 – 25%   imports

0 – 25%

25 – 50%   Imports
            exceed
More than 50% exports

No data available

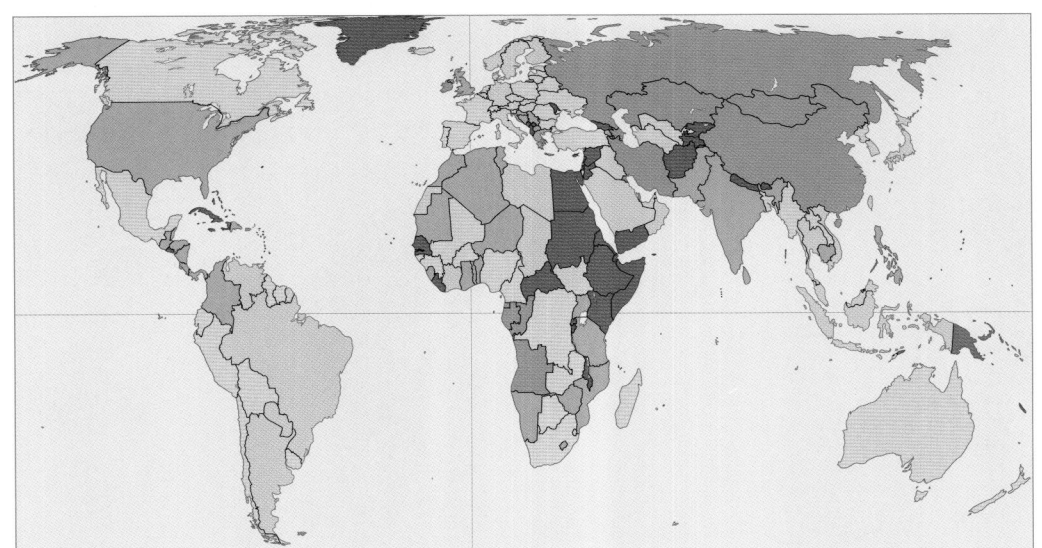

The total world trade balance should amount to zero, since exports must equal imports on a global scale. In practice, though, at least US $100 billion in exports go unrecorded, leaving the world with an apparent deficit and many countries in a better position than public accounting reveals. However, a favorable trade balance is not necessarily a sign of prosperity: many poorer countries must maintain a high surplus in order to service debts, and do so by restricting imports below the levels needed to sustain successful economies.

For more information:
82 Water distribution
91 Slum cities
    Urban advantages
109 Distribution of
    spending

Until the late 1990s, when the full extent of the AIDS crisis emerged, average life expectancies at birth were rising almost everywhere. By 2011, they ranged from 81 years in high-income economies to 56 in sub-Saharan Africa. These figures represented an enormous advance on the situation in 1880, when citizens of Berlin had an estimated life expectancy of 30 years.

The ravages of AIDS have been greatest in southern Africa. One of the worst affected countries is Swaziland, where over 25% of the adult population were thought to be infected in 2009. Life expectancy fell from 61 years in 2000, to 32 years in 2009, but recovered to 52 years in 2016. In much of the world, average life expectancies are still increasing. The rises are attributed to improvements in agriculture and, hence, nutrition, as well as health education, improved sanitation and the quality of drinking water, together with advances in medicine.

Besides AIDS, the people of the developing world are subject to another affliction – malnutrition. The map below shows that in most of Africa, Asia, and Latin America, the average daily calorie supply per person is so low as to cause malnutrition. Malnutrition is a serious condition – among pregnant women it causes high rates of child mortality.

Deficiency diseases occur when people do not have a balanced diet. Protein deficiency causes stunting and kwashiorkor, which can be fatal, especially among young children, while vitamin deficiencies cause such illnesses as beri beri, pellagra, scurvy, and rickets. Iron deficiency causes anemia, while a lack of iodine causes mental retardation.

Infectious diseases, in association with deficient diets, continue to affect people in developing countries. Around the turn of the century, a WHO report stated that infectious diseases cause over 16 million deaths a year. Most of the victims are young and otherwise fit people in developing countries. The major killers are AIDS, cholera, dysentery, malaria, measles, pneumonia, respiratory infections, tuberculosis, and typhoid.

Infectious diseases are much less important as causes of death in developed countries, where cancer and circulatory diseases, such as atherosclerosis and hypertension, which cause strokes and heart attacks, are the most common causes of fatality. Because these diseases tend to kill older people, they are relatively less important in the developing countries where people have shorter lifespans.

Harmful habits are also generally practiced more by the rich than the poor. For example, smoking is an important cause of death in developed countries, while poor diet and high alcohol consumption can badly affect health.

▲ Almost 10% of the world's population does not have access to safe water (the diagram at the bottom left-hand corner of page 105 shows how this breaks down by region). This places a huge strain on the millions of mainly women and children who have to walk, collect, and carry drinkable water in order to survive. UNICEF is dedicated to help improve this situation and to react swiftly in the case of emergencies such as civil war, as with the case of this man in Liberia.

MALNUTRITION

Prevalence of undernourishment as a percentage of the population (2015)

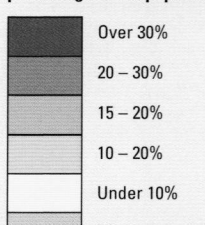

- Over 30%
- 20 – 30%
- 15 – 20%
- 10 – 20%
- Under 10%
- No data available

This map highlights the countries where, for a large part of the population, the food intake is insufficient to meet dietary energy requirements.

MATERNAL MORTALITY RATE

The number of mothers who died during pregnancy or childbirth per 100,000 live births (2015)

Countries with highest maternal mortality rate

Sierra Leone	1,360
Central African Republic	882
Chad	856
Nigeria	814
South Sudan	789
Somalia	732
Liberia	725
Burundi	712
Gambia	706
Congo, Dem. Rep.	693

The maternal mortality rate is the annual number of female deaths per 100,000 live births from any cause related to or aggravated by pregnancy or its management (excluding accidental or incidental causes).

FOOD CONSUMPTION

Average daily food intake in calories per person (2014)

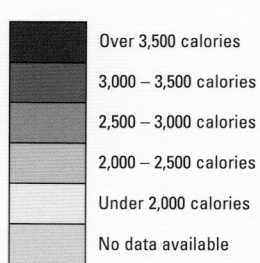

- Over 3,500 calories
- 3,000 – 3,500 calories
- 2,500 – 3,000 calories
- 2,000 – 2,500 calories
- Under 2,000 calories
- No data available

The daily food intake rated adequate by the World Health Organization is between 2,300 and 2,500 calories per day. Approximately 6 million children under the age of 5 years die of starvation each year, the vast majority in Africa. In 2013, the FAO estimated that 842 million people were undernourished, contrasting sharply with the overconsumption of food in some Western cultures.

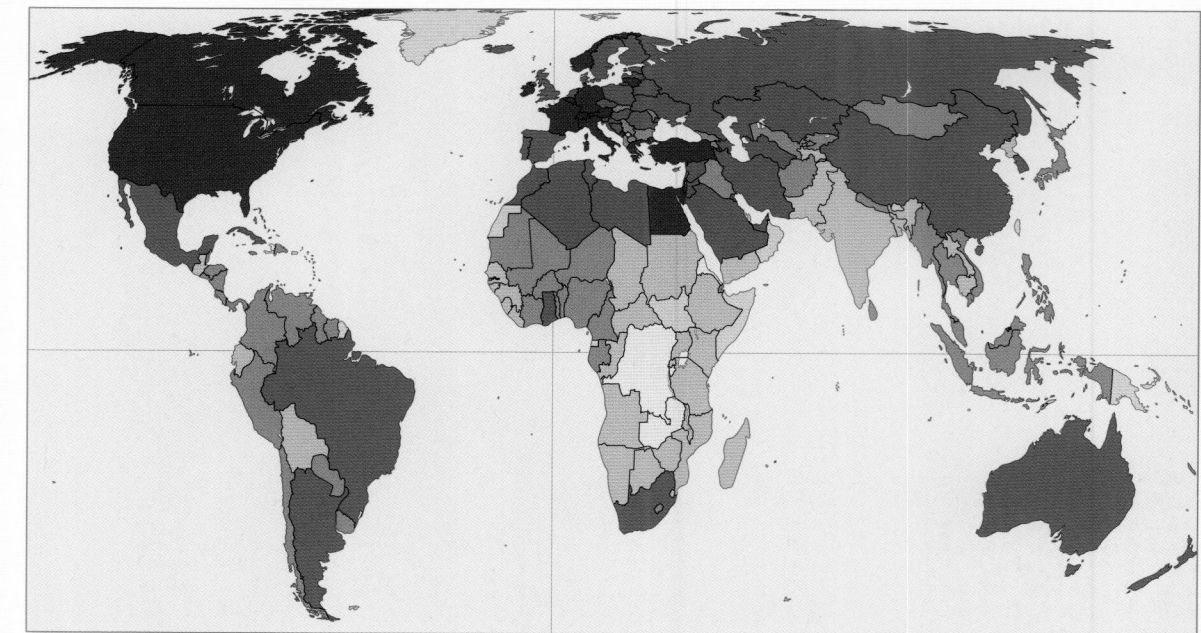

INFANT MORTALITY

Number of babies who died under the age of one, per 1,000 live births (2016)

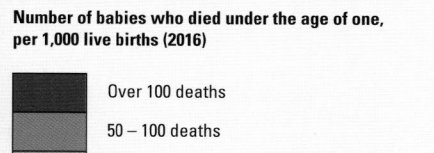

- Over 100 deaths
- 50 – 100 deaths
- 20 – 50 deaths
- 10 – 20 deaths
- Under 10 deaths
- No data available

Highest infant mortality

Afghanistan	122.8 deaths
Mali	100.0 deaths
Somalia	96.6 deaths

Lowest infant mortality

Monaco	1.8 deaths
Japan	2.0 deaths
Iceland	2.1 deaths

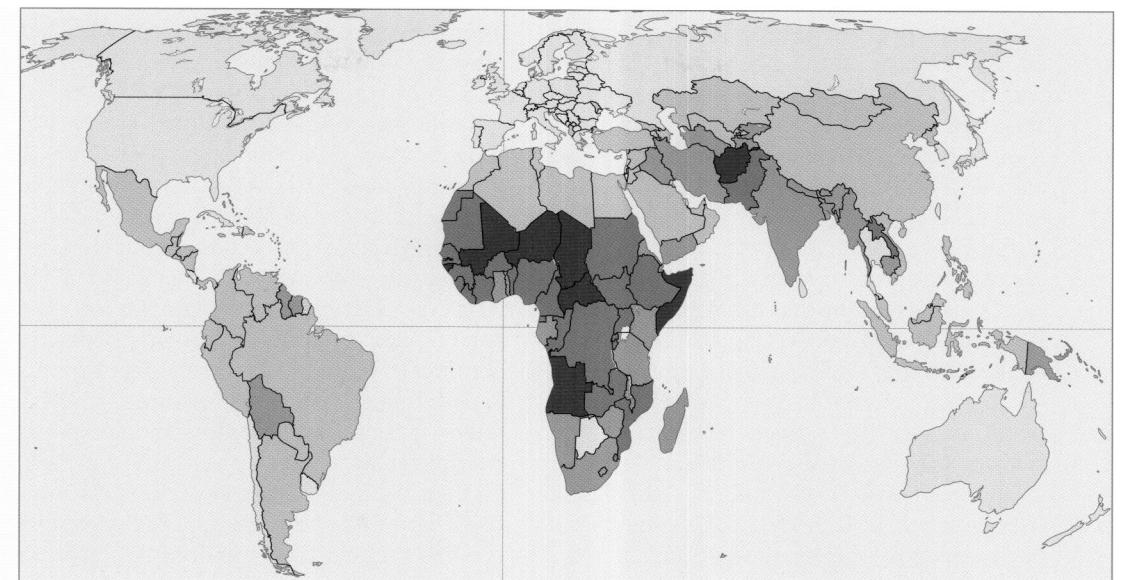

THE AIDS CRISIS

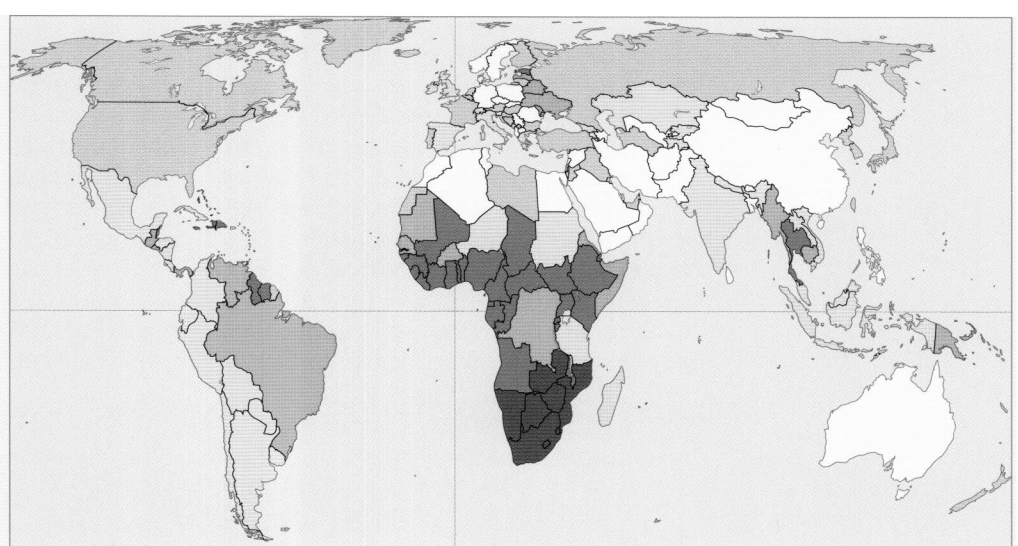

Number of children orphaned due to AIDS (2015)

Millions of children (bar chart): South Africa, Nigeria, Tanzania, Uganda, Kenya, Mozambique, Malawi, Zimbabwe, Ethiopia, Zambia

Percentage of adults living with HIV/AIDS (2015)

- Over 10 %
- 1 – 10 %
- 0.5 – 1 %
- 0.2 – 0.5 %
- Under 0.2 %
- No data available

EXPENDITURE ON HEALTH

Public health expenditure per capita, in US $ PPP

Countries with the highest spending		Countries with the lowest spending	
Luxembourg	$5,356	Burma (Myanmar)	$6
Monaco	$5,337	Eritrea	$8
Norway	$5,080	Afghanistan	$10
Netherlands	$4,298	Congo (Democratic Republic)	$12
United States	$4,126	South Sudan	$13
Denmark	$4,037	Central African Republic	$16
Austria	$3,826	Niger	$18
Switzerland	$3,739	Haiti	$19
Germany	$3,522	Ethiopia	$21
Sweden	$3,397	Bangladesh	$23

The allocation of limited funds for health care in developing countries is rarely evenly spread – for example, the quality of treatment can vary enormously from place to place within the same country. Urban dwellers tend to have much better access to health provisions than those living in rural areas.

CAUSES OF DEATH

- Accidents, poisoning, and violence
- Respiratory and digestive diseases
- Nervous and circulatory diseases
- Metabolic disorders
- Cancers
- Infectious and parasitic diseases

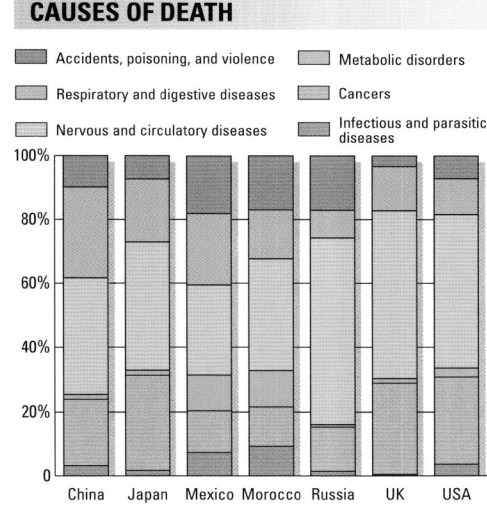

(bar chart: China, Japan, Mexico, Morocco, Russia, UK, USA; 0–100%)

MEDICAL PROVISION

Doctors per 100,000 population, selected countries (2013)

Although the ratio of people to doctors gives a good approximation of a country's health provision, it is not an absolute indicator. Raw numbers may mask inefficiency and other weaknesses. The definition of a doctor also varies from nation to nation.

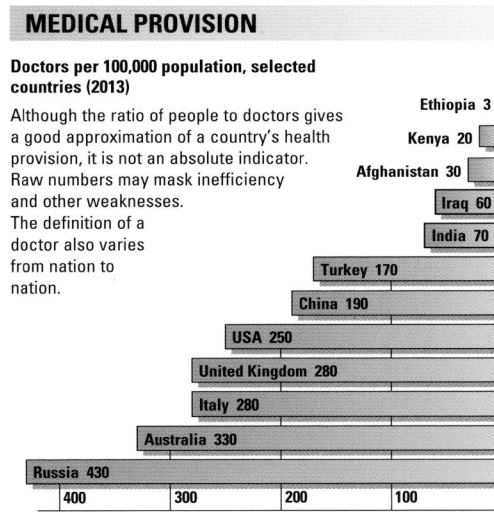

Ethiopia	3
Kenya	20
Afghanistan	30
Iraq	60
India	70
Turkey	170
China	190
USA	250
United Kingdom	280
Italy	280
Australia	330
Russia	430

ACCESS TO SAFE WATER

Percentage of urban and rural population with access to safe water, by region

- Urban
- Rural

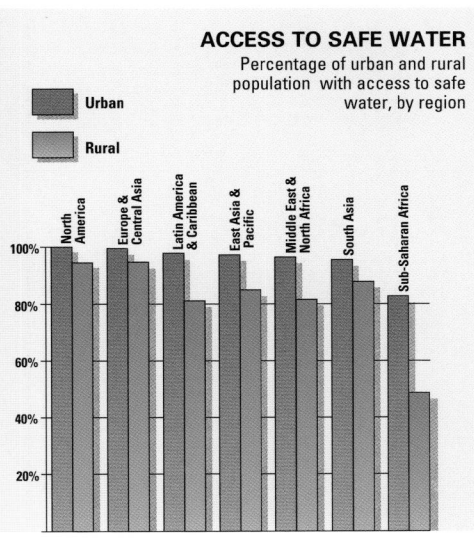

(North America, Europe & Central Asia, Latin America & Caribbean, East Asia & Pacific, Middle East & North Africa, South Asia, Sub-Saharan Africa)

SANITATION

Percentage of population with access to sanitation services, selected countries

- Urban
- Rural

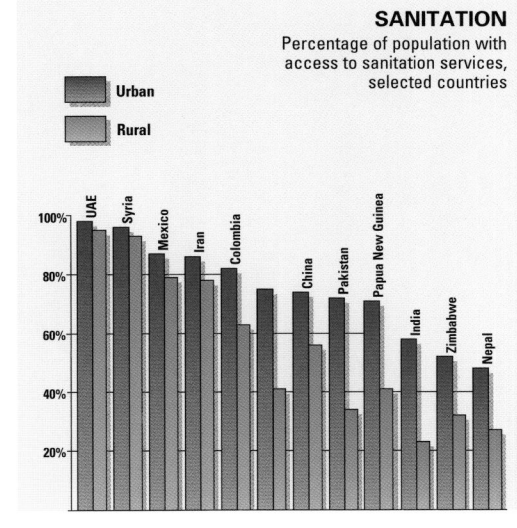

(UAE, Syria, Mexico, Iran, Colombia, China, Pakistan, Papua New Guinea, India, Zimbabwe, Nepal)

MALARIA

Cases of malaria per 100,000 people exposed to malaria-infected environments

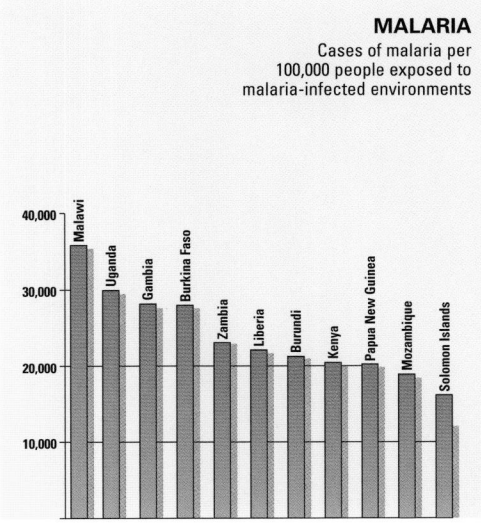

(Malawi, Uganda, Gambia, Burkina Faso, Zambia, Liberia, Burundi, Kenya, Papua New Guinea, Mozambique, Solomon Islands)

For more information:
100 Industrial output
102 World trade
      Major exports
103 Balance of trade
109 Distribution of
      spending

Perhaps the most glaring differences in the world today are those between the rich and the poor. The World Bank divides countries into three main groups based on average economic production expressed in terms of per capita GNI (Gross National Income). They are the low-income economies (most African countries and much of Asia), the middle-income economies (most of Latin America and most of the former USSR), and the high-income economies of Canada, the United States, Western Europe, Japan, and Australia.

Per capita GNIs are a measure of the total goods and services produced by a country divided by the population, and then converted into US dollars at official exchange rates. They are useful indicators of a country's prosperity, though, like all statistics, they must be treated with care. For example, the prices for goods and services in China are far cheaper than they are in the United States. China's per capita GNI in 2015 was $7,900 (as compared with $55,980 in the US), but the PPP (Purchasing Power Parity, which adjusts the figure for cost-of-living differences) estimate of China's per capita GNI was considerably higher at $13,170. Another problem with per capita GNIs is that they are averages, which often conceal wide internal variations.

The pattern of poverty varies from region to region. In Latin America, much progress has been made through industrialization, though startling inequalities still exist between rich and poor. China and other countries in eastern Asia, including South Korea and Taiwan, have followed Japan's example in pursuing export-led industrial policies. The success of China's Special Economic Zones, where foreign investment is encouraged, has led to a huge rise in China's per capita GNI.

In contrast to the dynamism of Asia, Africa lags behind as an impoverished continent. Corrupt governments, wasteful expenditures, civil wars, natural disasters, faulty national and international policy environments, high population growth, and the failure to break away from the neo-colonial trading patterns – all these contribute to keeping the majority of Africans impoverished. An initiative in some African countries has been to improve the infrastructure and develop tourism, creating employment and providing much-needed foreign currency. But the social and environmental cost of mass tourism needs to be taken seriously too.

The International Monetary Fund and the World Bank argue that real economic progress in Africa will be achieved only when African countries create market-friendly economies that encourage trade through export-led manufacturing, while at the same time strictly controlling public spending.

CONTINENTAL SHARES

Shares of population and of wealth (GNI) by continent (2015)

These generalized continental figures show the startling difference between rich and poor, but mask the successes or failures of individual countries. Japan, for example, with just over 3% of Asia's population, produces almost 19% of the continent's output. Within countries, the difference between rich and poor can also be startling. In Brazil, for example, the richest 20% of the population own 60% of the wealth.

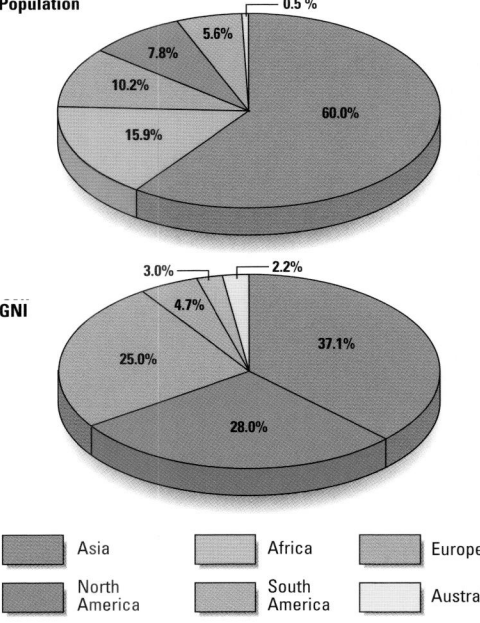

LEVELS OF INCOME

Gross National Income per capita: the value of total production divided by the population (2015)

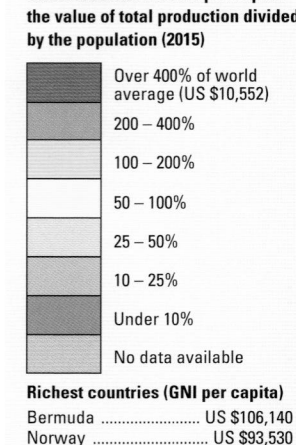

- Over 400% of world average (US $10,552)
- 200 – 400%
- 100 – 200%
- 50 – 100%
- 25 – 50%
- 10 – 25%
- Under 10%
- No data available

Richest countries (GNI per capita)
Bermuda .... US $106,140
Norway .... US $93,530
Switzerland .... US $84,550
Qatar .... US $83,990
Luxembourg .... US $77,480

Poorest countries (GNI per capita)
Malawi .... US $250
Burundi .... US $270
Central African Rep. .... US $320
Liberia .... US $370
Congo (Dem. Rep.) .... US $380

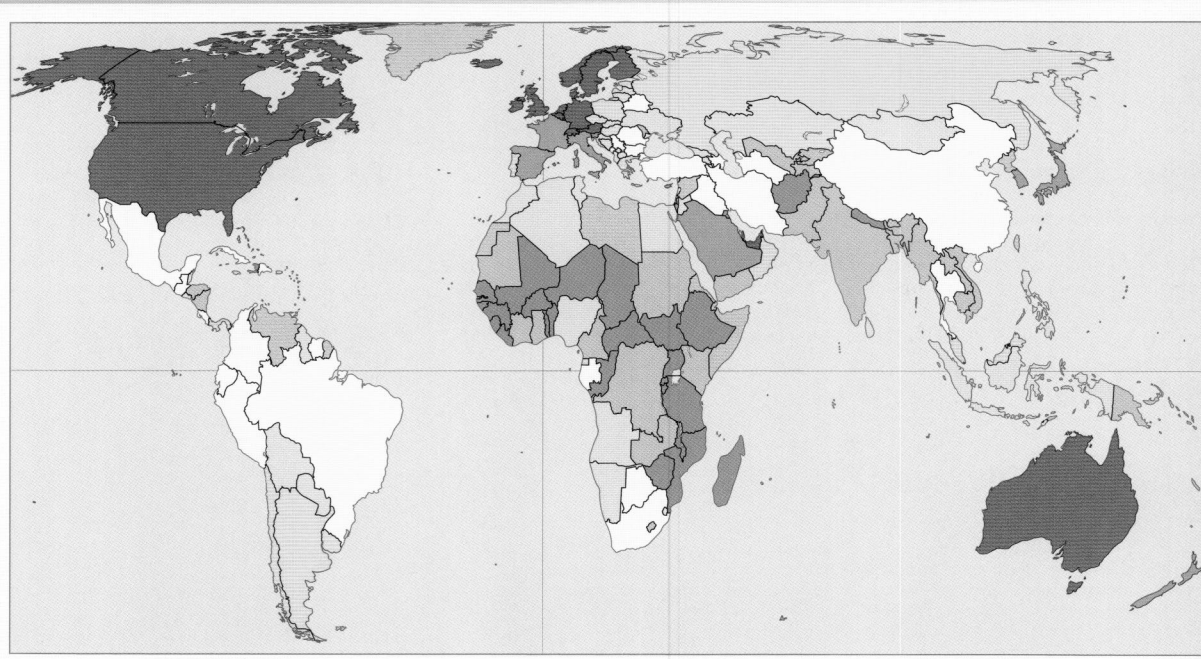

INDICATORS

The gap between the world's rich and poor is now so great that it is difficult to illustrate on a single graph. Within each income group (as defined by the World Bank), however, comparisons have some meaning. The wealth gap in many developing countries, though, is wide, with a small, rich class and a large, impoverished majority, while many high-income countries contain an underclass of unemployed and homeless people.

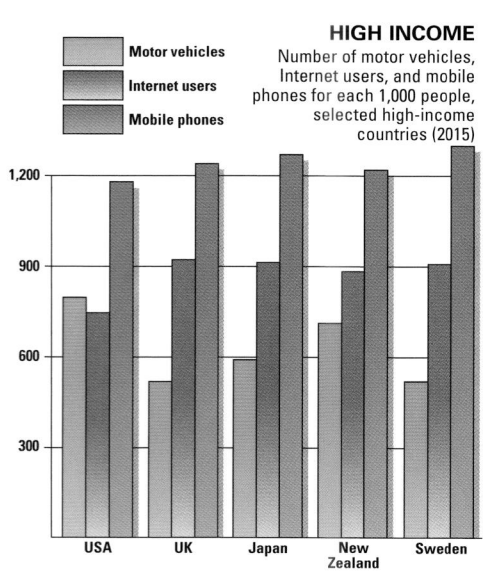

HIGH INCOME
Number of motor vehicles, Internet users, and mobile phones for each 1,000 people, selected high-income countries (2015)

- Motor vehicles
- Internet users
- Mobile phones

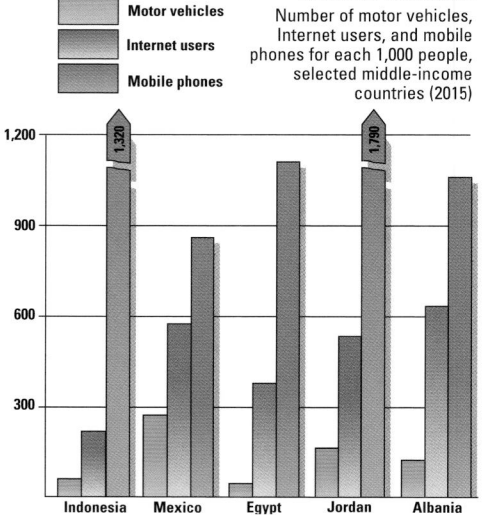

MIDDLE INCOME
Number of motor vehicles, Internet users, and mobile phones for each 1,000 people, selected middle-income countries (2015)

- Motor vehicles
- Internet users
- Mobile phones

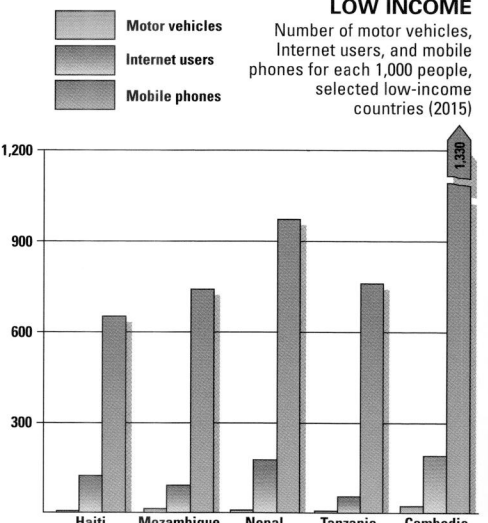

LOW INCOME
Number of motor vehicles, Internet users, and mobile phones for each 1,000 people, selected low-income countries (2015)

- Motor vehicles
- Internet users
- Mobile phones

STATE FINANCE

Inflation rates (*shown on the map, right*) are an indication of a country's financial stability and, usually, of its prosperity. Annual inflation rates above 20% are usually marked by slow or even negative growth of the GNI. Above 50%, it becomes hyperinflation and an economy is left reeling.

In the late 1980s and early 1990s, many high-income countries had to contend with annual inflation rates of 10% or more, while Japan, the growth leader, had an average inflation rate of just 1.3% between 1985 and 1994.

Market-friendly policies, including low taxes and state spending, liberal trade policies, and a warm welcome for foreign investors, are major factors in countries that have enjoyed rapid economic growth in the decades since 1980. For example, the setting-up of Special Economic Zones in eastern China has led to a spectacular rise in that country's per capita GNI. However, an effective government remains a crucial factor in economic growth in most countries.

Other successful countries include South Korea and Singapore, although an Asian market crash in 1997 temporarily halted the dramatic economic expansion of these countries.

INFLATION

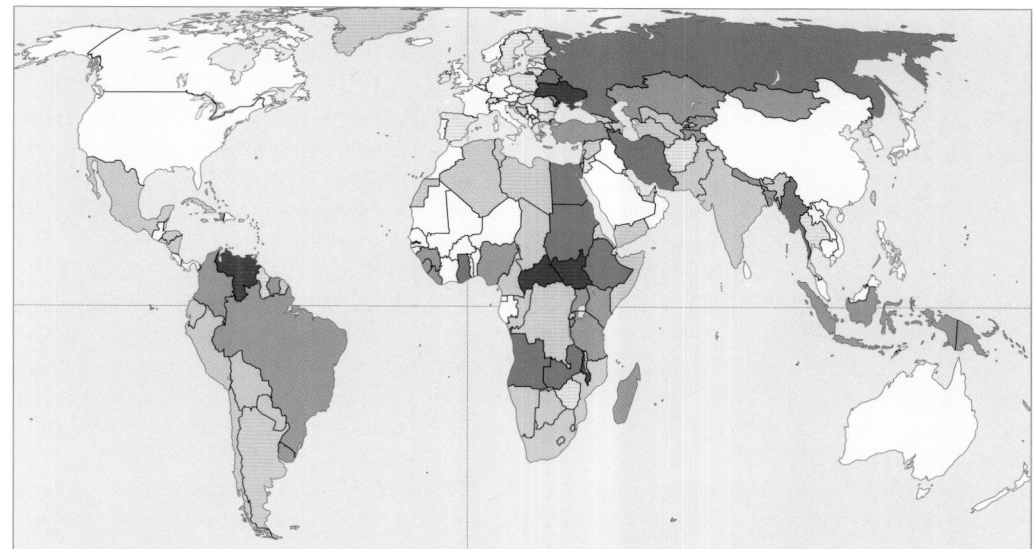

Average annual rate of inflation (2015)

- Over 20%
- 10 – 20%
- 5 – 10%
- 2.5 – 5%
- 0 – 2.5%
- Negative inflation
- No data available

Highest average inflation
Venezuela 109.7%
South Sudan 50.1%
Ukraine 48.7%

Lowest average inflation
Comoros .... -8.1%
Lebanon .... -3.7%
Zimbabwe .... -2.4%

UNITED NATIONS SUSTAINABLE DEVELOPMENT GOALS

In 2000, the United Nations set out 8 Millennium Development Goals (MDGs) that were to be achieved by 2015. The goals were:

1. To eradicate extreme poverty and hunger.
2. To achieve universal primary education.
3. To promote gender equality and empower women.
4. To reduce child mortality.
5. To improve maternal health.
6. To combat HIV/AIDS, malaria, and other diseases.
7. To ensure environmental sustainability.
8. To develop a global partnership for development.

Progress towards achieving these goals has been uneven: some countries achieved many of the goals, whereas others achieved few, if any. However, some targets have been met such as the MDG for poverty reduction. According to the 2015 MDG Report, the poverty rates and the number of people living in extreme poverty fell in every developing region – including in Sub-Saharan Africa, where rates were highest. In the developing regions, the proportion of people living on less than $1.25 a day fell from 47% in 1990 to 14% in 2015. In 2015, about 900 million fewer people than in 1990 lived in conditions of extreme poverty.

To follow on from the MDG, the Sustainable Development Goals (SDGs) were adopted by all the world's governments at the United Nations in September 2015. The aim is that they will guide global development for the 15 years until 2030. There are 17 goals - as illustrated by the official United Nations icons below. Although the SDGs are not legally binding, governments are expected to establish national frameworks in order to achieve them.

The ultimate aim is to go further than the MDGs and end all forms of poverty. It has been recognized that defeating poverty has to be coupled with strategies to encourage economic growth, and to address a range of social needs including education, health, social protection, and job opportunites, while tackling climate change and protecting the environment.

Progress will be monitored by using a set of global indicators, and annual reports will be published. There is, of course, a cost to achieving these goals. The more developed countries will have to provide development assistance to help the countries most in need.

It is acknowledged that climate change has affected public health, food and water security, migration, peace, and security. Collective action will have to be taken to mitigate the worst effects of climate change. Goal 13 (Climate Action) reflects the importance of this issue, and the hope is that it will be possible to limit the increases in global mean temperature to no more than 3.6°F [2.0°C] above pre-industrial levels.

▲ To mark the 70th anniversary of the United Nations, and ahead of the United Nations Sustainable Development Summit in September 2015, massive projections of the icons for the 17 goals are seen on the façade of the General Assembly building in New York, United States. The aim was to raise awareness of the 2030 Agenda for Sustainable Development.

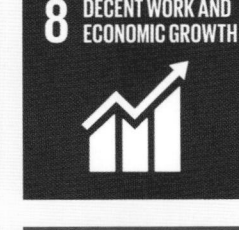

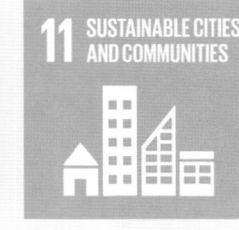

Philip's supports the Sustainable Development Goals

For more information:
82 Water supply
88 Population density
90 Urban population
91 Urban advantages
92 World's refugees
100 Employment
    The work force
105 Infant mortality
106 Wealth

Wealth is a basic factor in determining standards of living. Everywhere, the rich have more of everything, including higher average life expectancies, while the poor have to spend most of their income on basic human needs, such as food and clothing. Yet poverty and wealth are relative terms: slum dwellers living on social security in an industrial society feel their poverty acutely, but have far more resources than an average African living in a rural area.

In 1990 the United Nations Development Program published its first Human Development Index (HDI), an attempt to construct a comparative scale by which a simplified form of well-being might be measured. The HDI, expressed as a value between 0 and 0.999, combines figures for life expectancy and literacy with a wealth scale, based on Purchasing Power Parity.

The world's countries are divided into three groups: those with a high HDI (0.8 and above); those with a medium HDI (0.5 to 0.799); and those with a low HDI (below 0.5). In 2015, Norway and Switzerland were top in the world rankings and CAR was bottom. In fact, 34 of the 41 countries with a low HDI were from Africa. Besides having low per capita GNIs, the average life expectancy in these countries was 59 years, while the adult literacy rate was 36%. By comparison, the average life expectancy at birth in countries in the high HDI group was 79 years, while the literacy rate was 94%.

Comparisons between countries with similar per capita GNIs reveal the effects of government actions. For example, the World Bank classifies both India and China as low-income economies, but India's HDI at 0.624 is much lower than that of China, at 0.738. This reflects not only China's economic progress in the 1980s and 1990s, but also differences in average life expectancies (68 years in India and 76 years in China), and adult literacy rates (71% in India and 96% in China).

Disparities in standards of living exist not only between countries but also between individuals, groups, and regions within countries. For example, income distribution figures show that, in the United States, the poorest 10% of households receive less than 2% of the income.

Other contrasts exist in developing countries between rural communities, where incomes are low and basic services are often in short supply, and urban areas, where even those living in slums are generally better off than their rural neighbors. Other striking differences exist between men and women. For example, while adult literacy rates for men and women living in developed countries are more or less the same, large differences exist in many developing countries. In countries in the lowest HDI category, only 36% of women were literate, as compared with 58% of men.

Female education is a factor in population control, especially as women's fertility rates appear to fall in direct proportion to the amount of secondary education they receive. This point was acknowledged in 2004 by the UN Population Fund, which defined four main objectives relating to women and population control: the reduction of maternal, infant, and child mortality; better education, especially for girls; universal access to reproductive health services; and gender equality.

Statistical analysis presents many problems of interpretation, especially when trying to define such intangible factors as a sense of well-being. For example, education helps create wealth; but are rich countries wealthy because their people are well educated, or are they well educated because they are rich?

HUMAN DEVELOPMENT INDEX

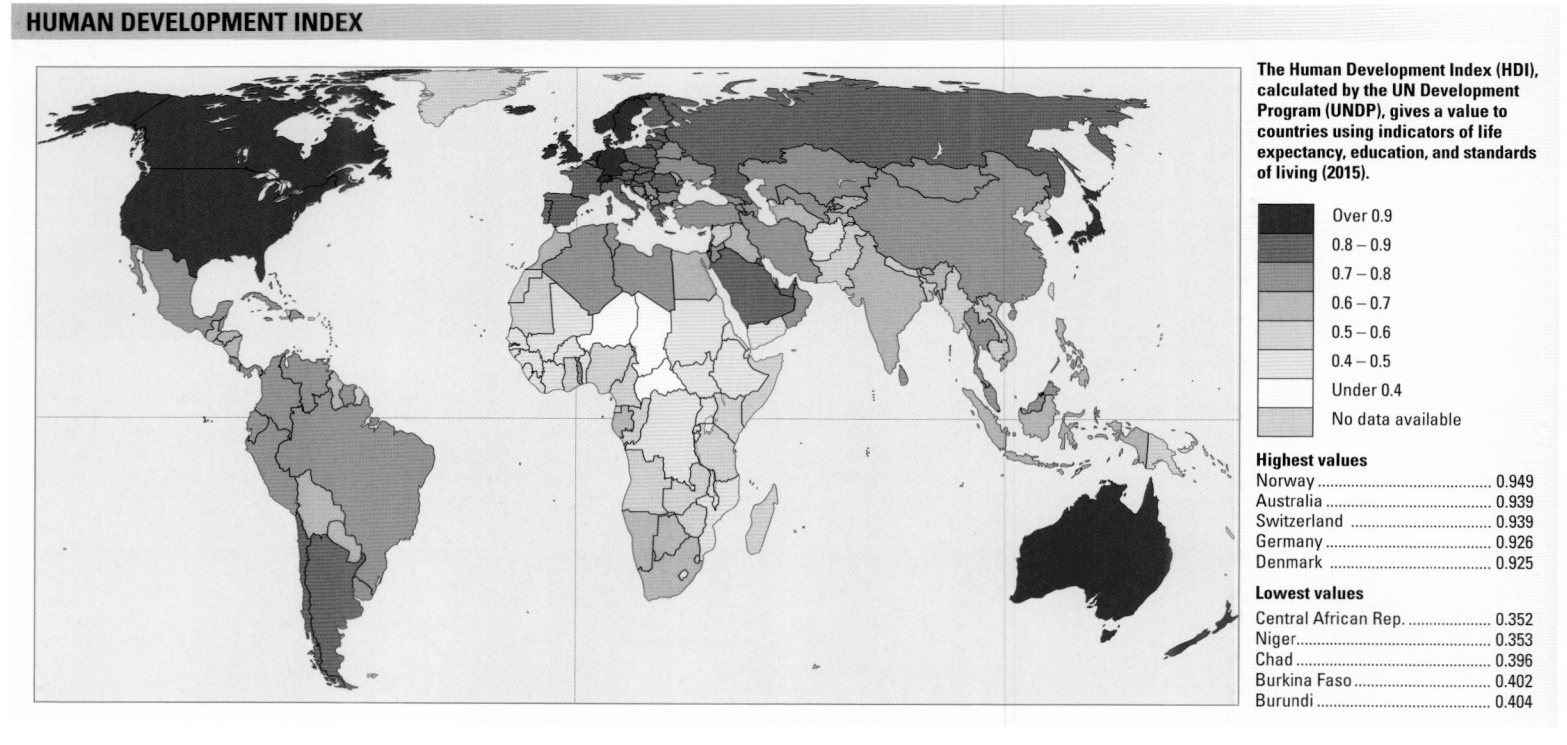

The Human Development Index (HDI), calculated by the UN Development Program (UNDP), gives a value to countries using indicators of life expectancy, education, and standards of living (2015).

Over 0.9
0.8 – 0.9
0.7 – 0.8
0.6 – 0.7
0.5 – 0.6
0.4 – 0.5
Under 0.4
No data available

Highest values
Norway 0.949
Australia 0.939
Switzerland 0.939
Germany 0.926
Denmark 0.925

Lowest values
Central African Rep. 0.352
Niger................................. 0.353
Chad 0.396
Burkina Faso 0.402
Burundi 0.404

EDUCATION

The developing countries made great efforts in the 1970s and 1980s to bring at least a basic education to their people. In all but the poorest nations, primary school enrolments rose above 60%. However, figures often include teenagers or young adults, and there are still 300 million children worldwide who receive no schooling at all. A lack of resources has restricted the development of secondary and higher education. Most primary school education is free in the poorer countries, but fees are often paid for secondary and higher education, thus heightening the differences between rich and poor.

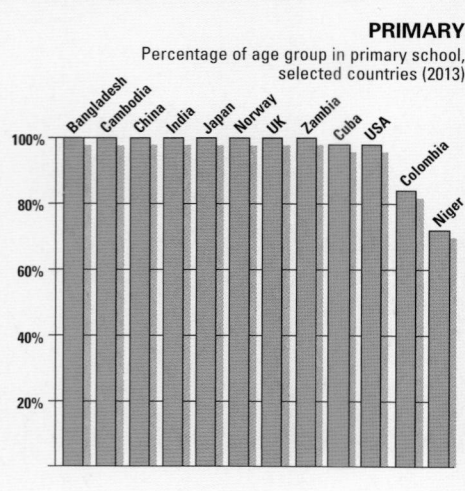

PRIMARY
Percentage of age group in primary school, selected countries (2013)

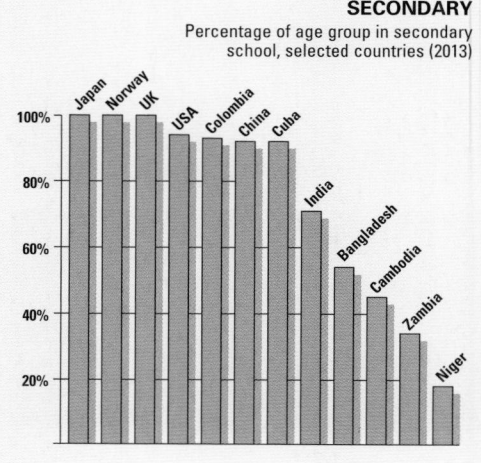

SECONDARY
Percentage of age group in secondary school, selected countries (2013)

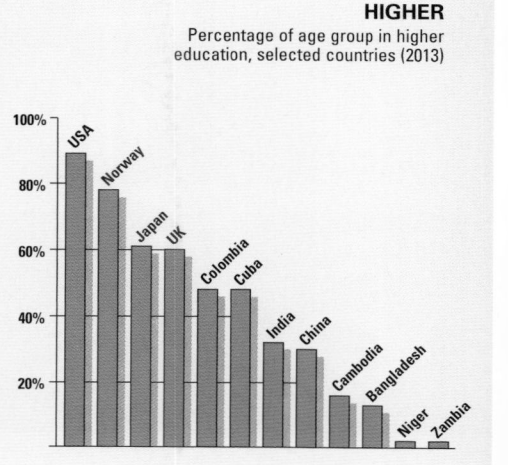

HIGHER
Percentage of age group in higher education, selected countries (2013)

DISTRIBUTION OF SPENDING

Percentage share of household spending

A high proportion of the average income of households in developing nations is spent on basic needs such as food and clothing. In most Western countries food and clothing account for less than 25% of expenditure.

Food | Clothing | Energy & Housing
Medicine & Education | Transport | Other

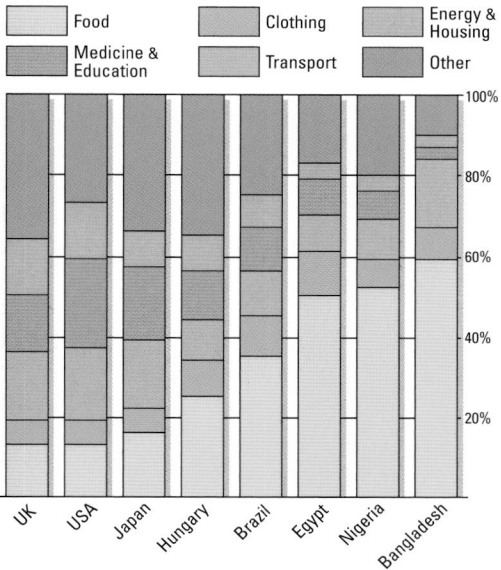

FERTILITY AND EDUCATION

Fertility rates compared with female education, selected countries

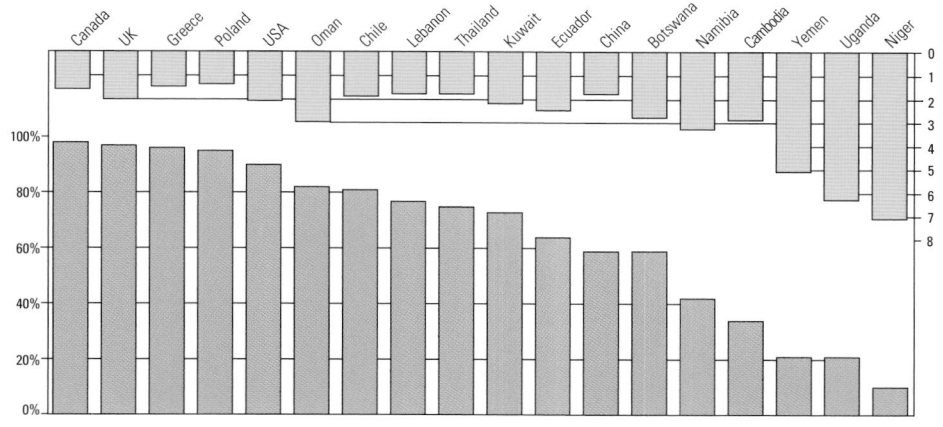

Canada, UK, Greece, Poland, USA, Oman, Chile, Lebanon, Thailand, Kuwait, Ecuador, China, Botswana, Namibia, Cambodia, Yemen, Uganda, Niger

There seems to be a strong link between access to secondary education and the fertility rate. In developed countries, young girls have a high access to education and a low fertility rate. In contrast, in many developing countries women have a high fertility rate but lack access to education. This can be for a complex mix of social, economic, and cultural reasons. Despite a few high-profile examples of female politicians in different parts of the world, all evidence points to the continuing marginalization of women from the political and economic processes of decision-making. Female wages are, on average, only two-thirds of those of men.

Fertility rate: average number of children borne per woman

Percentage of females aged 12–17 in secondary education

GENDER INEQUALITY INDEX

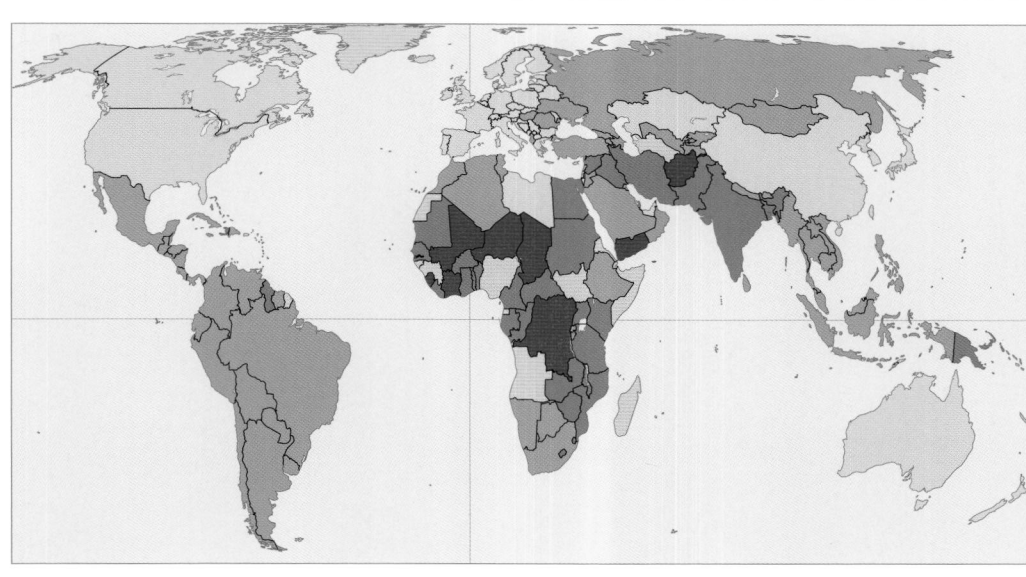
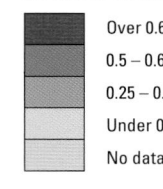

The Gender Inequality Index is a composite measure reflecting inequality in achievements between women and men in three categories: reproductive health, empowerment, and the labor market. It varies between 0, when women and men fare equally, and 1, when women or men fare poorly compared to the other in all categories (2015).

Over 0.65
0.5 – 0.65
0.25 – 0.5
Under 0.25
No data available

Most equal
Switzerland 0.040
Denmark 0.041
Netherlands 0.044

Least equal
Yemen....................................... 0.767
Niger... 0.695
Chad 0.695

GENDER EQUALITY

The UN's Millennium Development Goal 3 was to "*Eliminate gender disparity in primary and secondary education*" in all levels of education no later than 2015. According to the 2015 Millennium Development Goal Report, achieving parity in education is an important step toward equal opportunity for men and women in the social, political, and economic domains. The Gender Parity Index (GPI) shows the ratio between the enrolment rate of girls and that of boys. The GPI grew from 91% in 1999 to 98% in 2015 for the developing regions as a whole – falling within the +/– 3-point margin of 100% that is the accepted measure for parity.

While most of the developing world had reached a GPI of at least 99% at the primary level by 2015, the Index was still lagging behind in Western Asia and sub-Saharan Africa. These two regions, however, have recorded the greatest progress. Between 1999 and 2015, girls' participation in primary education increased from 72% to 96% in sub-Saharan Africa, and from 87% to 97% in Western Asia.

Girls have shown the greatest progress at the secondary level of education. The GPI for secondary education in the developing world as a whole has risen from 78% in 1990 to 98% in 2015.

It is in tertiary education where the greatest disparities are to be found. Only one developing region, Western Asia, has achieved the target. The most extreme disparities at the expense of women are in sub-Saharan Africa and Southern Asia.

In general, countries with lower levels of national wealth tend to have more men enrolled in tertiary education than women, while the opposite occurs in countries with higher average incomes.

The GPI measures the rate of girls' school enrolment as a percentage of boys' enrolment in primary, secondary and tertiary education.

GENDER PARITY INDEX (GPI)

■ 1999 □ 2015   Target for GPI is between 97% and 103%   ■ 1999 □ 2015

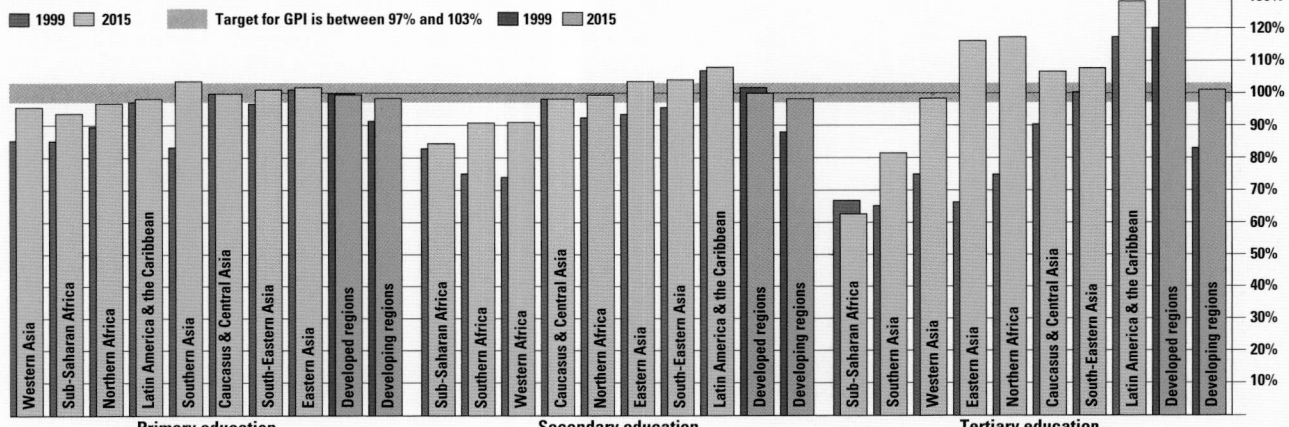

Primary education | Secondary education | Tertiary education

▲ These two images illustrate the reality of suburban life for people at either end of the economic scale. At the top is part of a huge area of "tract housing" in California, where large houses of a similar design are laid out by a developer, complete with gardens, drives, and swimming pools. Below, is a much more haphazard arrangement of home-built, rudimentary shelters, many without sanitation and most with no electricity, in Crossroads Township, outside Cape Town in South Africa.

WORLD CITIES

The urban conglomeration of Dallas–
Fort Worth in north Texas forms the
largest inland metropolitan area in the
USA. Its origins lie as a cotton-shipping
center, its rapid growth linked to the
coming of the railroads in the 1870s.
Oil interests came in the 20th century
and World War II brought an increase in
the manufacturing industries. Dallas
sums up much that is quintessentially
American with images of oil barons in
cowboy hats. But culture is taken seriously
here with the addition of the extensive
Dallas Arts District. Fort Worth, "where
the west begins", holds on to its heritage
with cattle-drives and rodeos.

[Map page 120] *Copernicus Sentinel
data 2016 / NPA Satellite Mapping,
CGG Services (UK) Ltd*

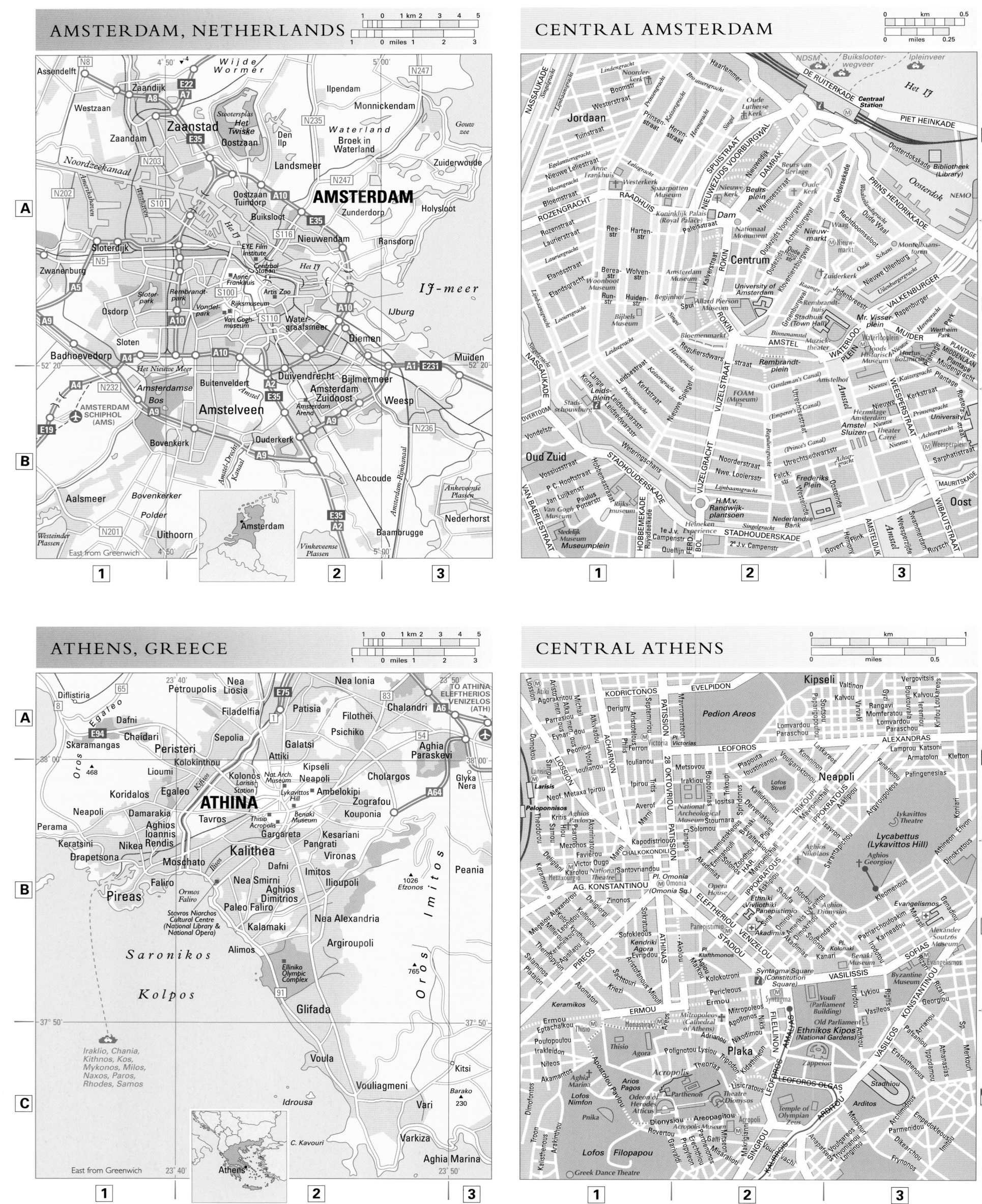

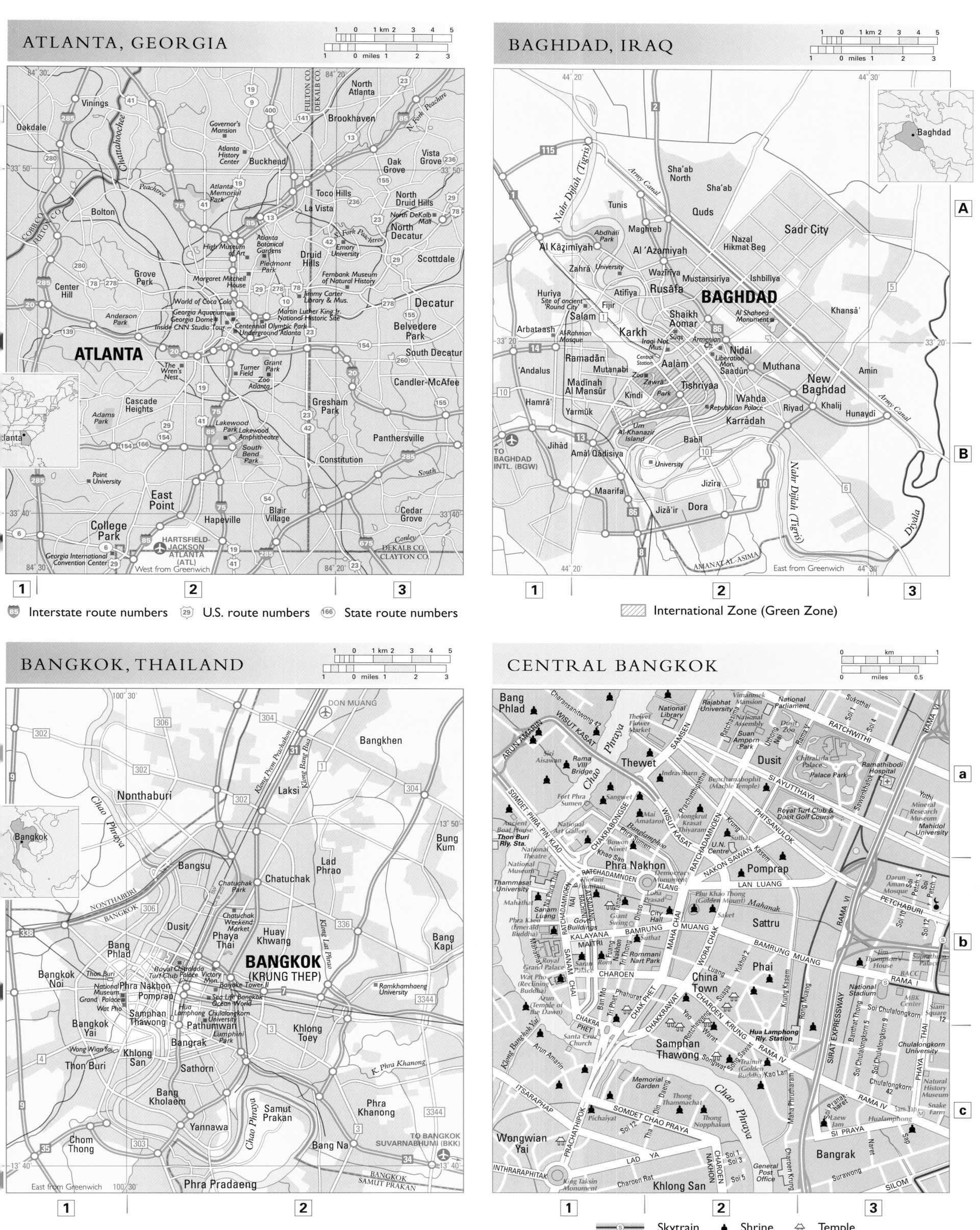

ATLANTA, GEORGIA

Vinings · Oakdale · Dunwoody · North Atlanta · Brookhaven · North Atlanta
Governor's Mansion · Buckhead · Atlanta History Center · Vista Grove · Oak Grove
Bolton · Peachtree · Atlanta Memorial Park · Toco Hills · North Druid Hills · North DeKalb Mall · North Decatur · Scottdale
Grove Park · High Museum of Art · Atlanta Botanical Gardens · Piedmont Park · Emory University · Druid Hills · Fernbank Museum of Natural History
Center Hill · Anderson Park · World of Coca Cola · Georgia Aquarium · Inside CNN Studio Tour · Martin Luther King Jr. National Historic Site · Decatur
ATLANTA · Margaret Mitchell House · Centennial Olympic Park · Underground Atlanta · Belvedere Park · South Decatur
The Wren's Nest · Turner Field · Grant Park · Zoo Atlanta · Candler-McAfee
Cascade Heights · Gresham Park · Pantersville
Adams Park · Lakewood Park · Lakewood Amphitheatre · South Bend Park
Point University · Constitution · Cedar Grove
East Point · Blair Village · Conley · DeKalb Co. Clayton Co.
College Park · Hapeville · HARTSFIELD-JACKSON ATLANTA (ATL)
Georgia International Convention Center · West from Greenwich

Interstate route numbers · U.S. route numbers · State route numbers

BAGHDAD, IRAQ

Baghdad
Tunis · Sha'ab North · Sha'ab · Quds · Sadr City
Al Kāzimīyah · Abdhali Park · Maghreb · Nazal · Hikmat Beg
Zahrā · University · Al 'Azamiyah · Mustansiriya · Ishbiliya
Hurīya · Site of ancient 'Round City' · Waziriya · **BAGHDAD**
Arbataash · Fijir · Salam · Rusafa · Khansá'
Al-Rahman Mosque · Suqs · Iraqi Nat. Mus. · Shaikh Aomar · Armenian
'Andalus · Ramadān · Madīnah Al Mansūr · Aalam · Nidāl · Liberation Mon. · Muthana · Amin
Hamrā' · Mutanabi · Zoo · Zawrā Park · Saadūn · Tishriyaa · Wahda · New Baghdad
Jihād · Yarmūk · Kindi · Babil · Karrādah · Riyad · Khalij · Hunaydi
Amāl Qādisiya · Um Al-Khanazir Island · University · Jizira
Maarifa · Jizā'ir · Dora · Nahr Dijlah (Tigris)
AMANAT AL-ASIMA · East from Greenwich

International Zone (Green Zone)

BANGKOK, THAILAND

DON MUANG
Nonthaburi · Bangkhen
Laksi · Bangsu · Lad Phrao · Bung Kum
Chatuchak Park · Chatuchak · Bang Kapi
Chatuchak Weekend Market · Dusit · Phaya Thai · Huay Khwang
Bang Phlad · Royal Chitralada Palace · Victory Mon. · Baiyoke Tower II
Bangkok Noi · National Museum · Phra Nakhon · Pomprap · Hua Lamphong · Sea Life Bangkok Ocean World · Ramkhamhaeng University
BANGKOK (KRUNG THEP)
Grand Palace · Wat Pho · Samphan Thawong · Pathumwan · Chulalongkorn University · Lumphini Park
Bangkok Yai · Bangrak · Khlong Toey
Thon Buri · Khlong San · Sathorn
Bang Kholaem · Yannawa · Samut Prakan · Phra Khanong
Chom Thong · TO BANGKOK SUVARNABHUMI (BKK)
Phra Pradaeng · BANGKOK SAMUT PRAKAN · East from Greenwich

CENTRAL BANGKOK

Bang Phlad · Thewet · Vimanmek Mansion · National Parliament
National Library · Rajabhat University · Dusit · Ratchwithi
Wisut Kasat · Dusit Zoo · Chitralada Palace · Ramathibodi Hospital
Si Ayutthaya · Royal Turf Club & Dusit Golf Course · Mahidol University
Phra Nakhon · Pomprap · Phitsanulok · U.N. Centre
Democracy Monument · Phu Khao Thong (Golden Mount) · Nakon Sawan
Sanam Luang · City Hall · Saket · Mahanak · Sattru
Grand Palace · Wat Pho · China Town · Phai · Jim Thompson's House
Samphan Thawong · Hua Lamphong Rly. Station · Trimit (Golden Buddha) · National Stadium · MBK Center · Siam Square
Memorial Garden · Chulalongkorn University · Natural History Museum
Wongwian Yai · King Taksin Monument · Khlong San · Bangrak · General Post Office · Silom

Skytrain · Shrine · Temple

COPYRIGHT PHILIP'S

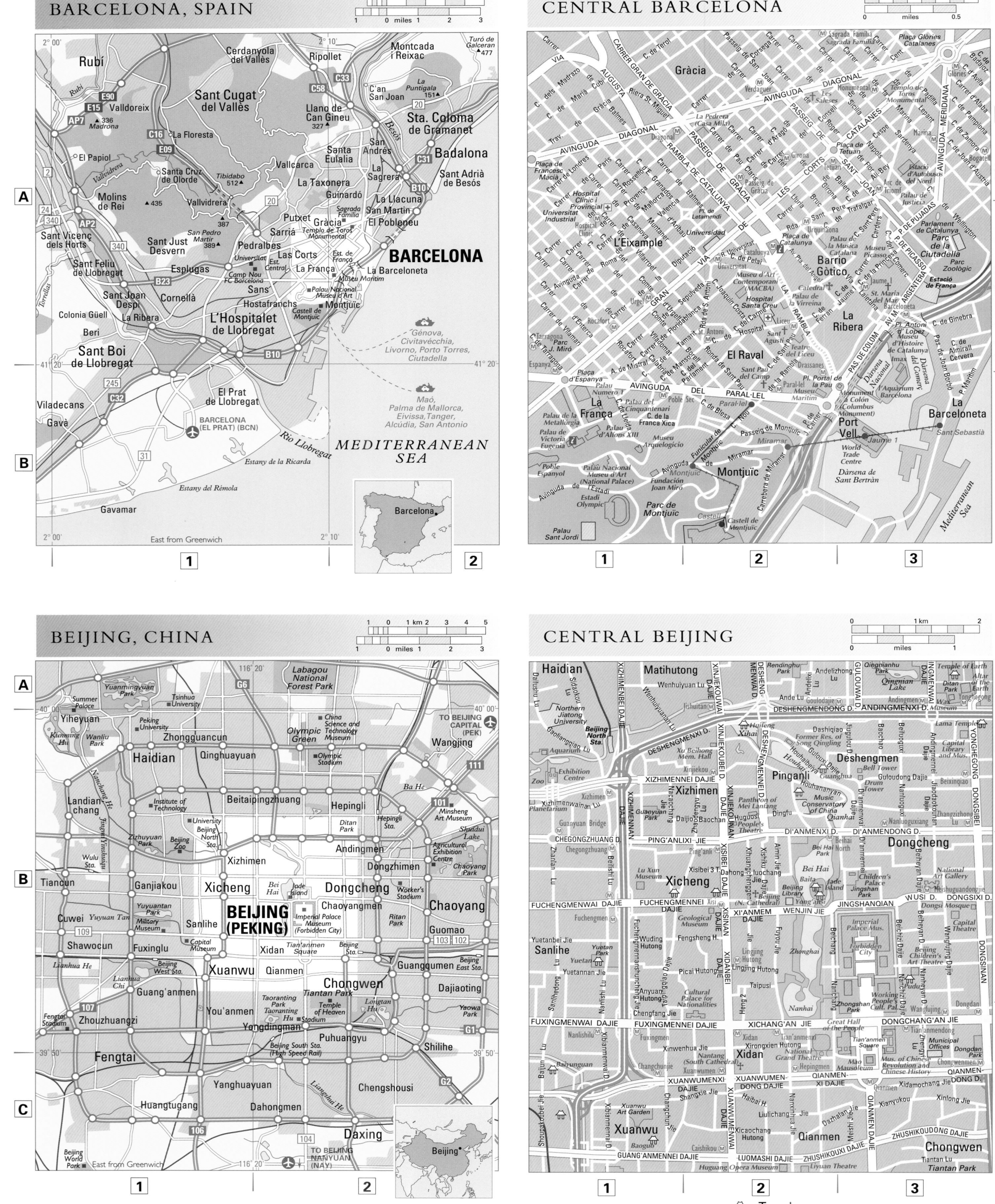

BERLIN, GERMANY

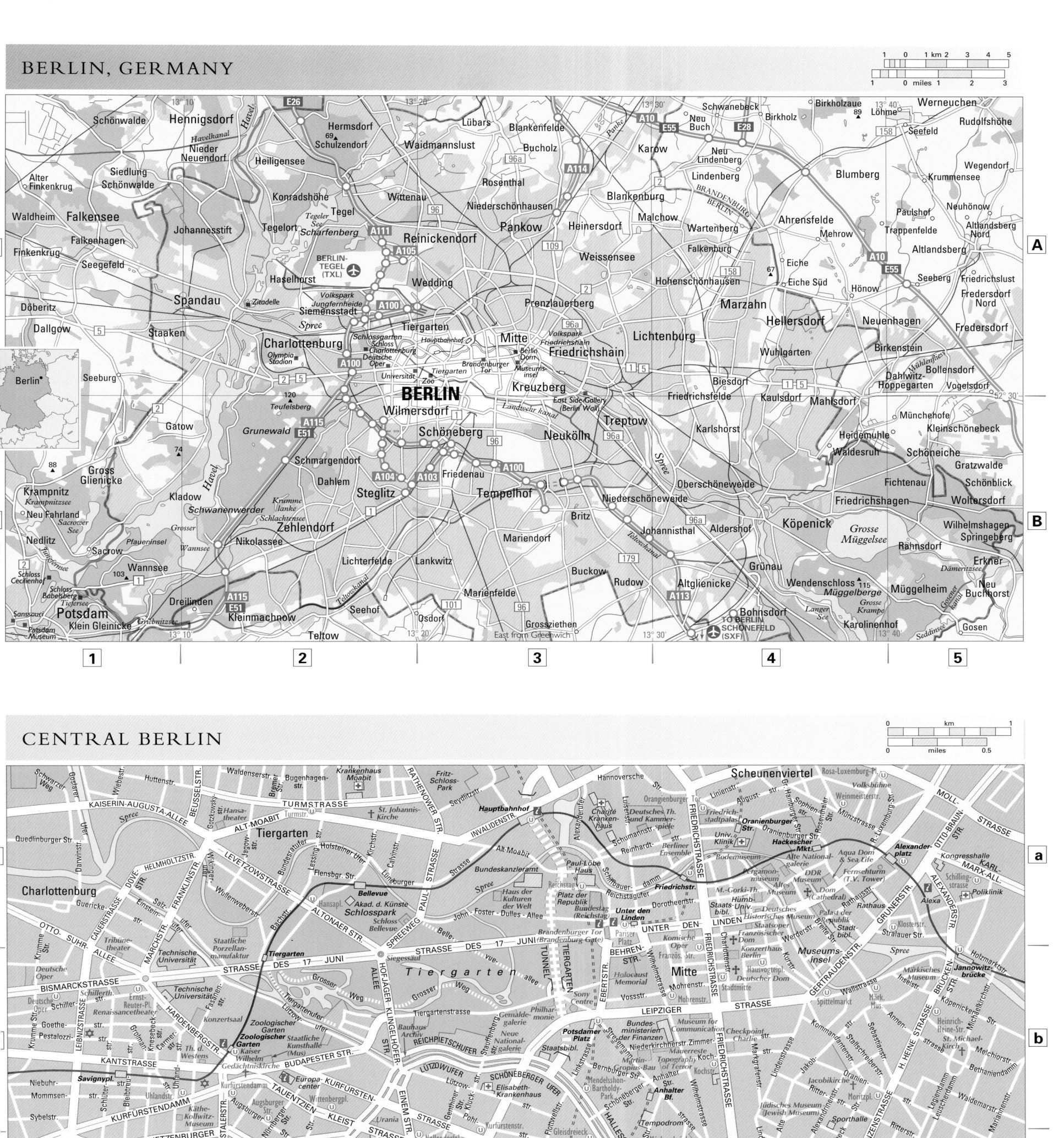

CENTRAL BERLIN

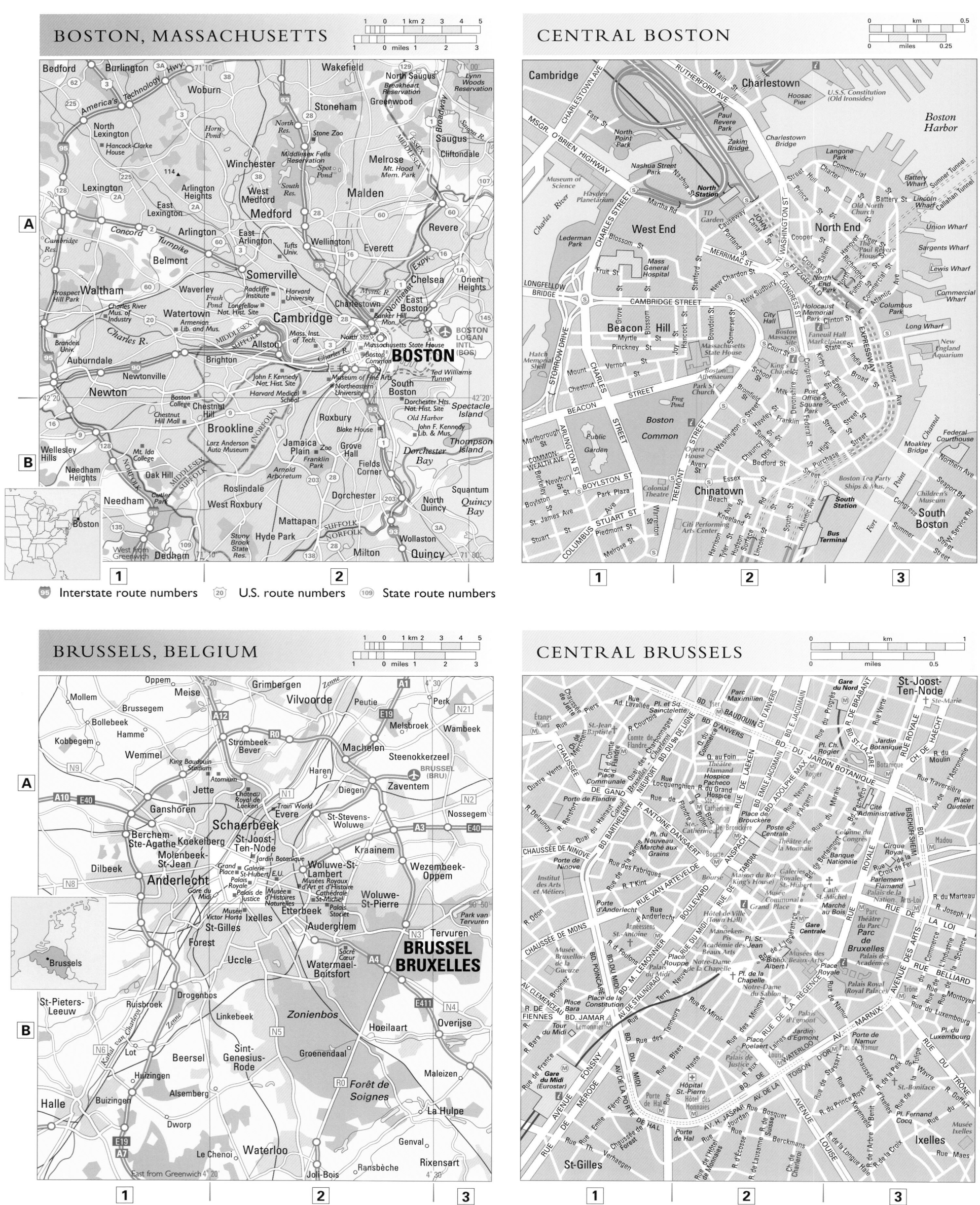

BOSTON, MASSACHUSETTS

Bedford, Burlington, Woburn, Wakefield, North Saugus, Lynn Woods Reservation, Breakheart Reservation, Greenwood, Stoneham, Stone Zoo, Saugus, Cliftondale, Melrose, Mt. Hood Mem. Park, Revere, Orient Heights, East Boston, Chelsea, Everett, Charlestown, Bunker Hill Mon., BOSTON LOGAN INTL. (BOS), Ted Williams Tunnel, South Boston, Spectacle Island, Dorchester Bay, Thompson Island, North Quincy, Squantum, Quincy Bay, Wollaston, Quincy, Milton

North Lexington, Hancock-Clarke House, Lexington, East Lexington, Arlington Heights, West Medford, Medford, Winchester, Middlesex Fells Reservation, Spot Pond, South Res., Malden, Wellington, East Arlington, Arlington, Belmont, Somerville, Waverley, Radcliffe Institute, Fresh Pond, Harvard University, Longfellow Nat. Hist. Site, Cambridge, Mass. Inst. of Tech., North Sta., Massachusetts State House, Boston Common

Prospect Hill Park, Waltham, Watertown, Charles River Mus. of Industry, Armenian Lib. and Mus., Brandeis Univ., Auburndale, Newtonville, Newton, Allston, Brighton, John F. Kennedy Nat. Hist. Site, Harvard Medical School, Northeastern University, Museum of Fine Arts

Wellesley Hills, Needham Heights, Mt. Ida College, Oak Hill, Needham, Cutler Park, Boston College, Chestnut Hill, Chestnut Hill Mall, Brookline, Larz Anderson Auto Museum, Jamaica Plain, Zoo, Franklin Park, Arnold Arboretum, Roslindale, West Roxbury, Blake House, Grove Hall, Fields Corner, Dorchester, Dorchester Hts. Nat. Hist. Site, Old Harbor, John F. Kennedy Lib. & Mus.

Needham, West from Greenwich, Dedham, Stony Brook State Res., Hyde Park, Mattapan, Milton

95 Interstate route numbers   20 U.S. route numbers   109 State route numbers

CENTRAL BOSTON

Cambridge, Charlestown, U.S.S. Constitution (Old Ironsides), Boston Harbor, Hoosac Pier, Paul Revere Park, Charlestown Bridge, Langone Park, Battery Wharf, Sumner Tunnel, Callahan Tunnel, Lincoln Wharf, Union Wharf, Sargents Wharf, Lewis Wharf, Commercial Wharf, North End, Old North Church, Paul Revere House, Long Wharf, New England Aquarium, Museum of Science, Hayden Planetarium, North Station, TD Garden, West End, Mass General Hospital, Beacon Hill, City Hall, Holocaust Memorial Park, Faneuil Hall Marketplace, Boston Massacre Site, Columbus Park, Boston Athenaeum, Boston Common, Park St. Church, Public Garden, Chinatown, Colonial Theatre, Boston Tea Party Ships & Mus., Children's Museum, South Station, Bus Terminal, Federal Courthouse, Moakley Bridge, South Boston

BRUSSELS, BELGIUM

Oppem, Meise, Grimbergen, Vilvoorde, Peutie, Perk, Strombeek-Bever, Machelen, Melsbroek, Wambeek, Steenokkerzeel, BRUSSEL (BRU), Zaventem, Nossegem, Woluwe-St-Stevens-Woluwe, Kraainem, Wezembeek-Oppem, Woluwe-St-Lambert, Woluwe-St-Pierre, Park van Tervuren, Tervuren

Mollem, Brussegem, Bollebeek, Hamme, Kobbegem, Wemmel, King Baudouin Stadium, Atomium, Jette, Château Royal de Laeken, Train World, Evere, Schaerbeek, Ganshoren, Berchem-Ste-Agathe, Koekelberg, St-Joost-Ten-Node, Molenbeek-St-Jean, Jardin Botanique, Grand Place, Galerie St-Hubert, Palais Royale, Gare du Midi, Musée de Justice, Musée Victor Horta, Dilbeek, Anderlecht, St-Gilles, Ixelles, Etterbeek, Auderghem, Musées Royaux d'Art et d'Histoire, Cathédrale St-Michel, Palais Stoclet

St-Pieters-Leeuw, Forest, Uccle, Watermael-Boitsfort, Sacré Cœur, Zonienbos, Hoeilaart, Overijse, Drogenbos, Ruisbroek, Linkebeek, Halle, Buizingen, Lot, Beersel, Sint-Genesius-Rode, Groenendaal, Maleizen, Huizingen, Dworp, Alsemberg, Forêt de Soignes, La Hulpe, Waterloo, Le Chenoi, Buizingen, Genval, Joli-Bois, Ransbèche, Rixensart

East from Greenwich

BRUSSEL BRUXELLES

CENTRAL BRUSSELS

St-Joost-Ten-Node, Ste-Marie, Gare du Nord, Parc Maximilien, Étangs Noirs, St-Jean Baptiste, Jardin Botanique, Botanique, Madou, Place Quetelet, Cité Administrative, Porte de Flandre, Ste-Catherine, Bourse, Théâtre de la Monnaie, Banque Nationale, Galeries Royales St-Hubert, Colonne du Congrès, Cirque Royal, Parlement Flamand, Palais de la Nation, Hôtel de Ville (Town Hall), Grand Place, Manneken-Pis, Gare Centrale, Parc de Bruxelles, Palais des Académies, Palais Royal (Royal Palace), Porte d'Anderlecht, Musées des Beaux-Arts, Place Royale, Notre-Dame de la Chapelle, Palais de Justice, Porte de Namur, Gare du Midi (Eurostar), Hôpital St-Pierre, Porte de Hal, St-Gilles, Ixelles

COPYRIGHT PHILIP'S

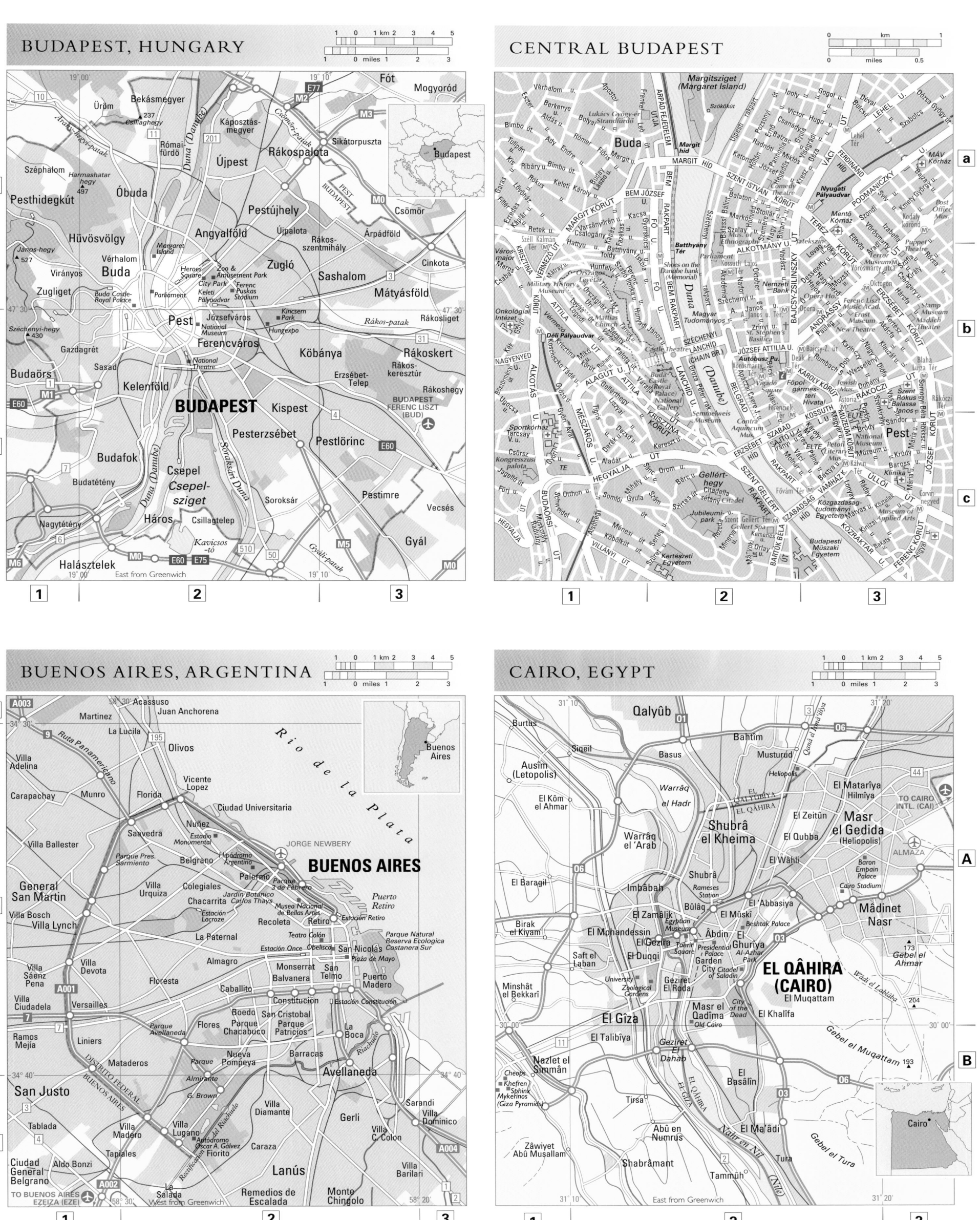

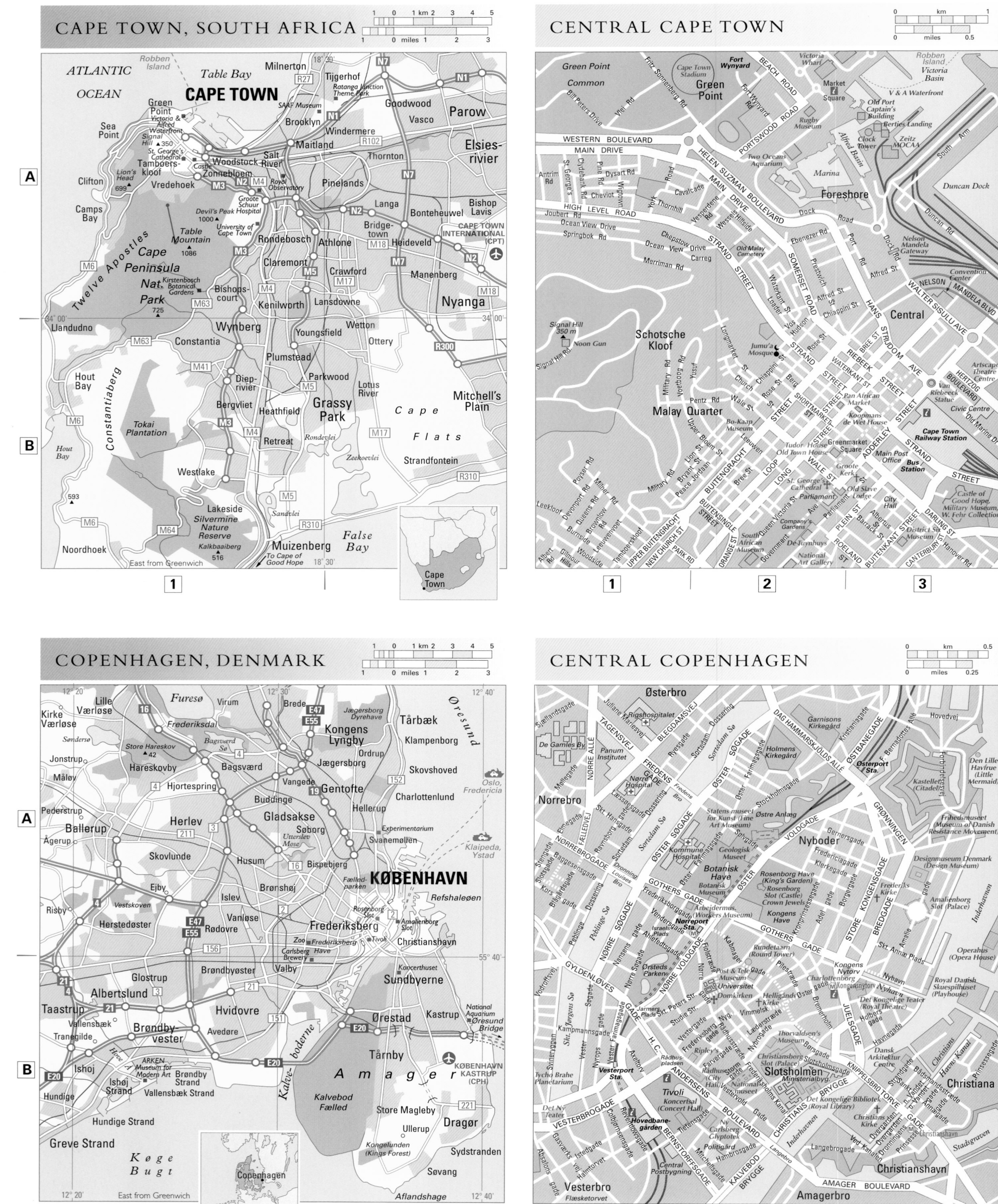

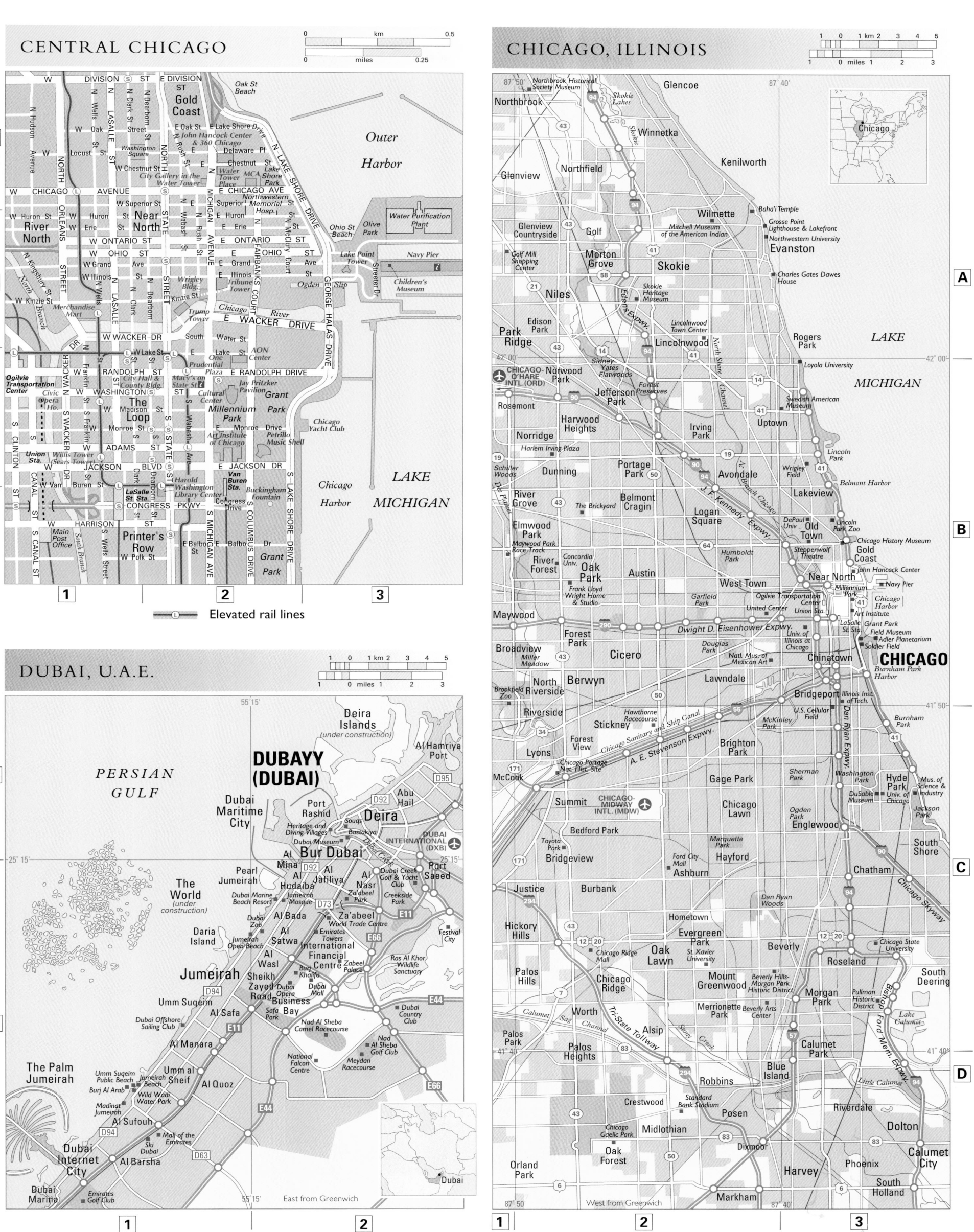

CENTRAL CHICAGO

0 km 0.5
0 miles 0.25

DIVISION ST · E DIVISION ST
Oak St Beach
Gold Coast
E Oak St · E Lake Shore Drive
John Hancock Center & 360 Chicago
Delaware Pl
Chestnut
Water Tower Place
City Gallery in the Water Tower
MCA
Lake Shore Park
W CHICAGO AVENUE · E CHICAGO AVE
Outer Harbor
Near North
River North
W Superior St
W Huron St
W Erie St
W Ontario St
W Ohio St
W Grand Ave
W Illinois St
Northwestern Memorial Hosp.
Ohio St Beach
Olive Park
Water Purification Plant
Wrigley Bldg.
Tribune Tower
Ogden Slip
Lake Point Tower
Navy Pier
Merchandise Mart
Trump Tower
Chicago River
Children's Museum
W Kinzie St
E WACKER DRIVE
Streeter Dr
South Water St
AON Center
One Prudential Plaza
W WACKER DR
W Lake St
Ogilvie Transportation Center
RANDOLPH ST · E RANDOLPH DRIVE
City Hall & County Bldg.
Jay Pritzker Pavilion
Grant Park
Civic Opera Ho.
WASHINGTON
Macy's on State St
Cultural Center
Millennium Park
The Loop
Madison St
Monroe St
Monroe St · E Monroe Drive
Art Institute of Chicago
Petrillo Music Shell
Chicago Yacht Club
W ADAMS ST
Willis Tower Sears Tower
JACKSON BLVD
LaSalle St. Sta.
Harold Washington Library Center
Van Buren Sta.
E Jackson Dr
Buckingham Fountain
LAKE MICHIGAN
Union Sta.
W Van Buren St
CONGRESS PKWY
Congress Drive
Chicago Harbor
Main Post Office
HARRISON ST
Printer's Row
W Polk St
E Balbo Ave
Grant Park
S COLUMBUS DRIVE
S LAKE SHORE DRIVE

1   2   3

⎯L⎯ Elevated rail lines

DUBAI, U.A.E.

1 0 1 km 2 3 4 5
1 0 miles 1 2 3

PERSIAN GULF

Deira Islands (under construction)
Al Hamriya Port
D95
DUBAYY (DUBAI)
Dubai Maritime City
Port Rashid
Heritage and Diving Villages
Dubai Museum
Bastakiya
Deira
Abu Hail
D92
Souqs
Al Nasr
Bur Dubai
DUBAI INTERNATIONAL (DXB)
Mina
Pearl Jumeirah
Al Hudaiba
Al Jafiliya
Za'abeel Park
Port Saeed
The World (under construction)
Jumeirah Mosque
D92
Dubai Creek Golf & Yacht Club
Creekside Park
Al Bada
World Trade Centre
D73
Daria Island
Dubai Marine Beach Resort
Jumeirah Open Beach
Emirates Towers
International Financial Centre
E11
E66
Festival City
Ras Al Khor Wildlife Sanctuary
Jumeirah
Umm Suqeim
Al Satwa
Al Wasl
Sheikh Zayed Road
Dubai Business
Dubai Opera
Safa Bay
Burj Khalifa
Za'abeel Palace
Dubai Mall
Nad Al Sheba Camel Racecourse
E44
D94
Al Safa
Safa Park
Nad Al Sheba Golf Club
Dubai Country Club
Dubai Offshore Sailing Club
Al Manara
National Falcon Centre
Meydan Racecourse
The Palm Jumeirah
Umm Suqeim Public Beach
Jumeirah Beach
Burj Al Arab
Madinat Jumeirah
Al Quoz
Wild Wadi Water Park
Umm al Sheif
E66
Al Sufouh
D94
Mall of the Emirates
Ski Dubai
Dubai Internet City
Al Barsha
D63
Dubai Marina
Emirates Golf Club

East from Greenwich
55°15'
55°15'
25°15'

Dubai

1   2

CHICAGO, ILLINOIS

1 0 1 km 2 3 4 5
1 0 miles 1 2 3

Chicago

87°50'
Northbrook Historical Society Museum
Glencoe
Skokie Lakes
Northbrook
43
Winnetka
87°40'
Glenview
Northfield
Kenilworth
Glenview Countryside
Golf
Wilmette
Baha'i Temple
43
Morton Grove
41
Mitchell Museum of the American Indian
Grosse Point Lighthouse & Lakefront
Golf Mill Shopping Center
58
Skokie
Northwestern University
Evanston
21
Niles
Skokie Heritage Museum
Charles Gates Dawes House
Edison Park
Eden's Expwy
LAKE MICHIGAN
Park Ridge
Lincolnwood Town Center
94
Rogers Park
14
42°00'
42°00'
CHICAGO-O'HARE INTL. (ORD)
Norwood Park
Sidney Yates Flatwoods
North Shore Channel
41
Loyola University
14
Rosemont
90
Jefferson Park
Forest Preserves
Swedish American Museum
19
Norridge
Harwood Heights
Harlem Irving Plaza
Irving Park
19
Uptown
Lincoln Park
41
Schiller Woods
Dunning
Portage Park
90
Avondale
Wrigley Field
Belmont Harbor
Des Plaines River
River Grove
The Brickyard
50
Belmont Cragin
94
Logan Square
J. F. Kennedy Expwy
Lakeview
DePaul Univ.
Old Town
Lincoln Park Zoo
Elmwood Park
64
Maywood Park Race Track
Humboldt Park
Steppenwolf Theatre
Chicago History Museum
Concordia Univ.
River Forest
Oak Park
Austin
West Town
Near North
Gold Coast
John Hancock Center
Frank Lloyd Wright Home & Studio
Garfield Park
Ogilvie Transportation Center
Navy Pier
Millennium Park
Chicago Harbor
Maywood
Union Sta.
Art Institute
Forest Park
290
Dwight D. Eisenhower Expwy
Univ. of Illinois at Chicago
LaSalle St. Sta.
Grant Park
Field Museum
Broadview
Douglas Park
Natl. Mus. of Mexican Art
Adler Planetarium
Soldier Field
Miller Meadow
43
Cicero
CHICAGO
Brookfield Zoo
North Riverside
Berwyn
Lawndale
Chinatown
Burnham Park Harbor
Riverside
50
Bridgeport
Illinois Inst. of Tech.
34
Hawthorne Racecourse
41°50'
41°50'
Stickney
U.S. Cellular Field
Burnham Park
Forest View
Lyons
Chicago Sanitary and Ship Canal
McKinley Park
41
McCook
171
Chicago Portage Nat. Hist. Site
A. E. Stevenson Expwy
Brighton Park
Sherman Park
Washington Park
Hyde Park
Mus. of Science & Industry
Summit
CHICAGO MIDWAY INTL. (MDW)
Gage Park
DuSable Museum
Univ. of Chicago
Jackson Park
Chicago Lawn
Ogden Park
Englewood
Toyota Park
Bedford Park
Marquette Park
Bridgeview
Ford City Mall
Hayford
South Shore
171
Ashburn
90
Justice
Burbank
Dan Ryan Woods
Chatham
Chicago Skyway
Hometown
Hickory Hills
12 20
Chicago Ridge Mall
Evergreen Park
St. Xavier University
Beverly
12 20
Chicago State University
Palos Hills
Oak Lawn
Roseland
South Deering
7
Chicago Ridge
Mount Greenwood
Beverly Hills-Morgan Park Historic District
Morgan Park
Pullman Historic District
Lake Calumet
Merrionette Park
Beverly Arts Center
Bishop Ford Mem. Expwy
Calumet
Worth
Alsip
57
Calumet Park
Sag Channel
Stony Creek
41°40'
41°40'
Palos Park
Palos Heights
83
29
Robbins
Blue Island
Little Calumet
94
Riverdale
Dolton
Crestwood
Standard Bank Stadium
Posen
Dixmoor
Calumet City
Orland Park
43
Chicago Gaelic Park
Midlothian
83
Phoenix
South Holland
Oak Forest
50
Harvey
6
Markham
87°50'
West from Greenwich
87°40'

A   B   C   D

1   2   3

🛡85 Interstate route numbers   ⬭29 U.S. route numbers   ⬡166 State route numbers

COPYRIGHT PHILIP'S

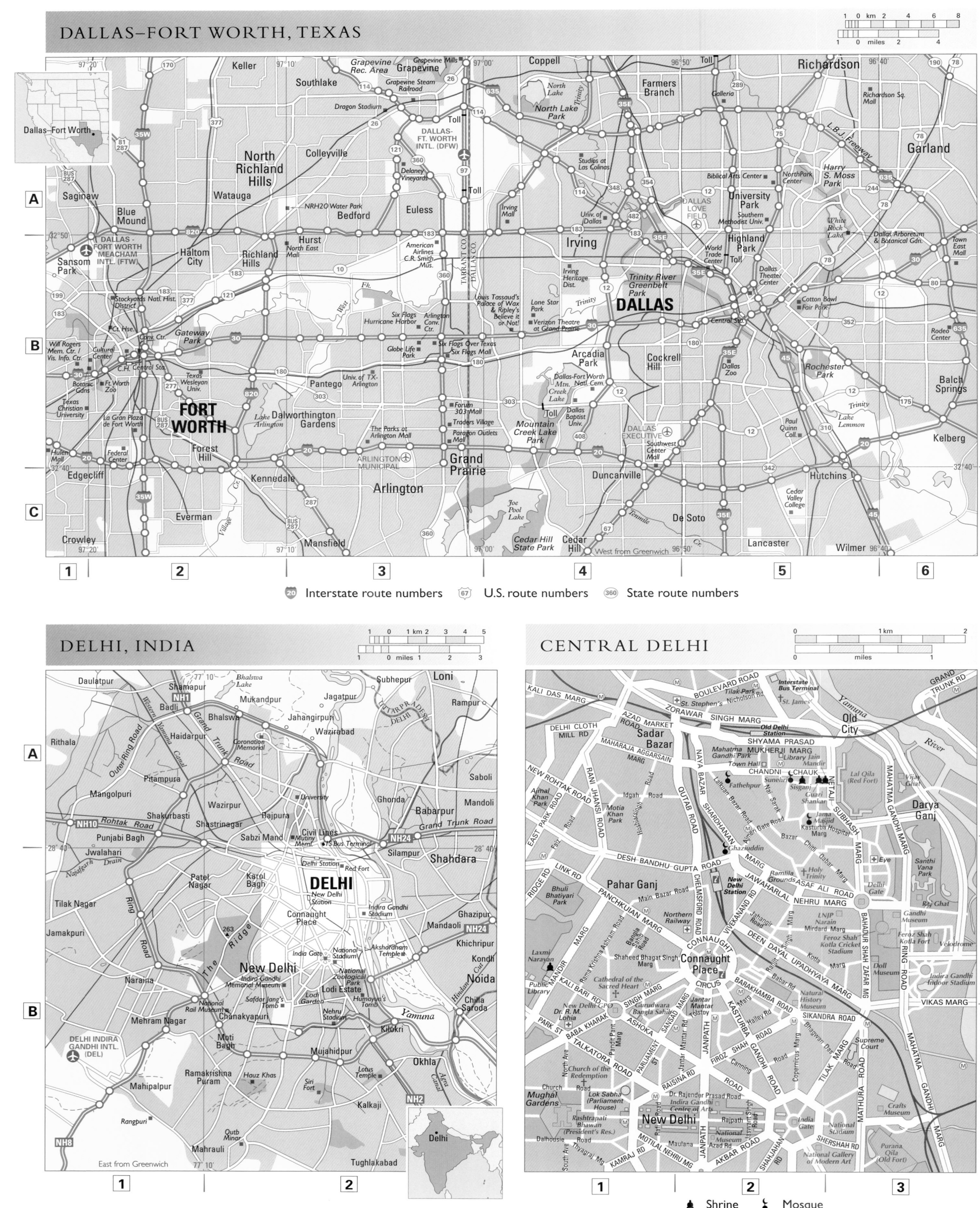

DALLAS–FORT WORTH, TEXAS

Keller
Southlake
Grapevine Rec. Area
Grapevine
Grapevine Mills
Coppell
Richardson
Richardson Sq. Mall

North Richland Hills
Colleyville
Grapevine Steam Railroad
Dragon Stadium
Farmers Branch
Galleria

Saginaw
Watauga
DALLAS-FT. WORTH INTL. (DFW)
North Lake Park
Studios at Las Colinas
NorthPark Center
Harry S. Moss Park
Garland

Blue Mound
Bedford
Delaney Vineyards
Biblical Arts Center
Univ. of Dallas
University Park
Southern Methodist Univ.

DALLAS-FORT WORTH MEACHAM INTL. (FTW)
Hurst
NRH2O Water Park
Euless
American Airlines C.R. Smith Mus.
Irving Mall
DALLAS LOVE FIELD
White Rock Lake
Dallas Arboretum & Botanical Gdn.
Town East Mall

Sansom Park
Haltom City
Richland Hills
North East Mall
Irving
Irving Heritage Dist.
Highland Park
World Trade Center
Dallas Theater Center

Will Rogers Mem. Ctr. / Vis. Info. Ctr.
Cultural Center
Gateway Park
Six Flags Hurricane Harbor
Arlington Conv. Ctr.
Louis Tussaud's Palace of Wax & Ripley's Believe it or Not!
Lone Star
Trinity River Greenbelt Park
DALLAS
Central Stn.
Cotton Bowl
Fair Park
Rodeo Center

Botanic Gdns
Ft. Worth Zoo
Texas Wesleyan Univ.
FORT WORTH
Pantego
Univ. of TX-Arlington
Globe Life Park
Six Flags Over Texas
Six Flags Mall
Verizon Theatre at Grand Prairie
Arcadia Park
Cockrell Hill
Dallas Zoo
Rochester Park
Balch Springs

Texas Christian University
La Gran Plaza de Fort Worth
Lake Dalworthington Gardens
Forum 303 Mall
Traders Village
The Parks at Arlington Mall
Paragon Outlets Mall
Dallas-Fort Worth Mtn. Creek Natl. Cem.
Mountain Creek Lake Park
Dallas Baptist Univ.
Paul Quinn Coll.
Lake Lemmon

Hulen Mall
Federal Center
Forest Hill
ARLINGTON MUNICIPAL
Grand Prairie
DALLAS EXECUTIVE
Southwest Center Mall

Edgecliff
Kennedale
Arlington
Duncanville
Cedar Valley College
Hutchins

Crowley
Everman
Joe Pool Lake
De Soto
Lancaster
Wilmer

Mansfield
Cedar Hill State Park
Cedar Hill
West from Greenwich

Interstate route numbers | **U.S. route numbers** | **State route numbers**

DELHI, INDIA

Daulatpur
Shamapur
Bhalswa Lake
Subhepur
Loni
NH1
Badli
Mukandpur
Jagatpur
Rampur

Rithala
Haidarpur
Bhalswa
Jahangirpuri
Wazirabad
Saboli

Mangolpuri
Pitampura
Coronation Memorial
University
Ghonda
Babarpur
Mandoli

NH10
Rohtak Road
Shakurbasti
Wazirpur
Rajpura
Grand Trunk Road
NH24

Punjabi Bagh
Shastrinagar
Sabzi Mand
Mutiny Meml.
TS Bus Terminal
Silampur
Shahdara

Jwalahari
Patel Nagar
Karol Bagh
Delhi Station
Red Fort

Tilak Nagar
DELHI
New Delhi Station
Indira Gandhi Stadium
Ghazipur
NH24

Jamakpuri
Naraina
Connaught Place
Akshardham Temple
Mandaoli
Khichripur
Noida

The Ridge
India Gate
National Stadium
Indira Gandhi Memorial Museum
NEW DELHI
Lodi Estate
National Zoological Park
Humayun's Tomb
Kondli
Chilla Saroda

National Rail Museum
Safdar Jang's Tomb
Lodi Garden
Nehru Stadium
Yamuna

Mehram Nagar
Chanakyapuri
Moti Bagh
Mujahidpur
Kalkaji
Kitokri

DELHI INDIRA GANDHI INTL. (DEL)
Ramakrishna Puram
Hauz Khas
Siri Fort
Lotus Temple
Agra Canal

Mahipalpur
NH8
Mahrauli
Qutb Minar
Tughlakabad
East from Greenwich

CENTRAL DELHI

Kali Das Marg
BOULEVARD ROAD
Tilak Park
Interstate Bus Terminal
St. James
GRAND TRUNK RD

ZORAWAR
St. Stephen's
Nicholson Rd.
Old Delhi Station
Old City
Yamuna River

DELHI CLOTH MILL RD
AZAD MARKET ROAD
SINGH MARG
SHYAMA PRASAD
Sadar Bazar
Vijai Ghat

NEW ROHTAK ROAD
MAHARAJA AGGARSAIN MARG
Mahatma Gandhi Park
Town Hall
Library Jain Mandir
Lal Qila (Red Fort)

Ajmal Khan Park
Idgah
Road
CHANDNI CHAUK
Sisganj
NETAJI
Darya Ganj

EAST PARK ROAD
Motia Park
Fatehpur
Jama Masjid
Kasturba Hospital
MAHATMA GANDHI MARG

Pahar Ganj
DESH BANDHU GUPTA ROAD
Ghaziuddin
Ramlila Grounds
Holy Trinity
Delhi Gate

New Delhi Station
JAWAHARLAL NEHRU MARG
ASAF ALI ROAD
Gandhi Museum

Bhuli Bhatiyari Park
Main Bazar Road
Northern Railway
LNJP Narain Mirdard Marg
Feroz Shah Kotla Cricket Stadium
Feroz Shah Kotla Fort
Velodrome

Laxmi Narayan
Shaheed Bhagat Singh Marg
CONNAUGHT
Doll Museum
RING ROAD

Cathedral of the Sacred Heart
Jantar Mantar
Connaught Place
DEEN DAYAL UPADHYAYA MARG
Indira Gandhi Indoor Stadium

Public Library
Gurudwara Bangla Sahib
CIRCUS
BARAKHAMBA ROAD
VIKAS MARG

New Delhi GPO
Dr. R.M. Lohia
KASTURBA GANDHI MARG
Natural History Museum

Church of the Redemption
TALKATORA ROAD
PARLIAMENT ST
SIKANDRA ROAD
Supreme Court

Mughal Gardens
Lok Sabha (Parliament House)
Dr. Rajender Prasad Road
Indira Gandhi Centre of Arts
India Gate
Crafts Museum

Rashtrapati Bhawan (President's Res.)
NEW DELHI
National Museum
National Gallery of Modern Art
Purana Qila (Old Fort)

Dalhousie
AKBAR ROAD
SHERSHAH RD
MATHURA

▲ Shrine | **☽ Mosque**

COPYRIGHT PHILIP'S

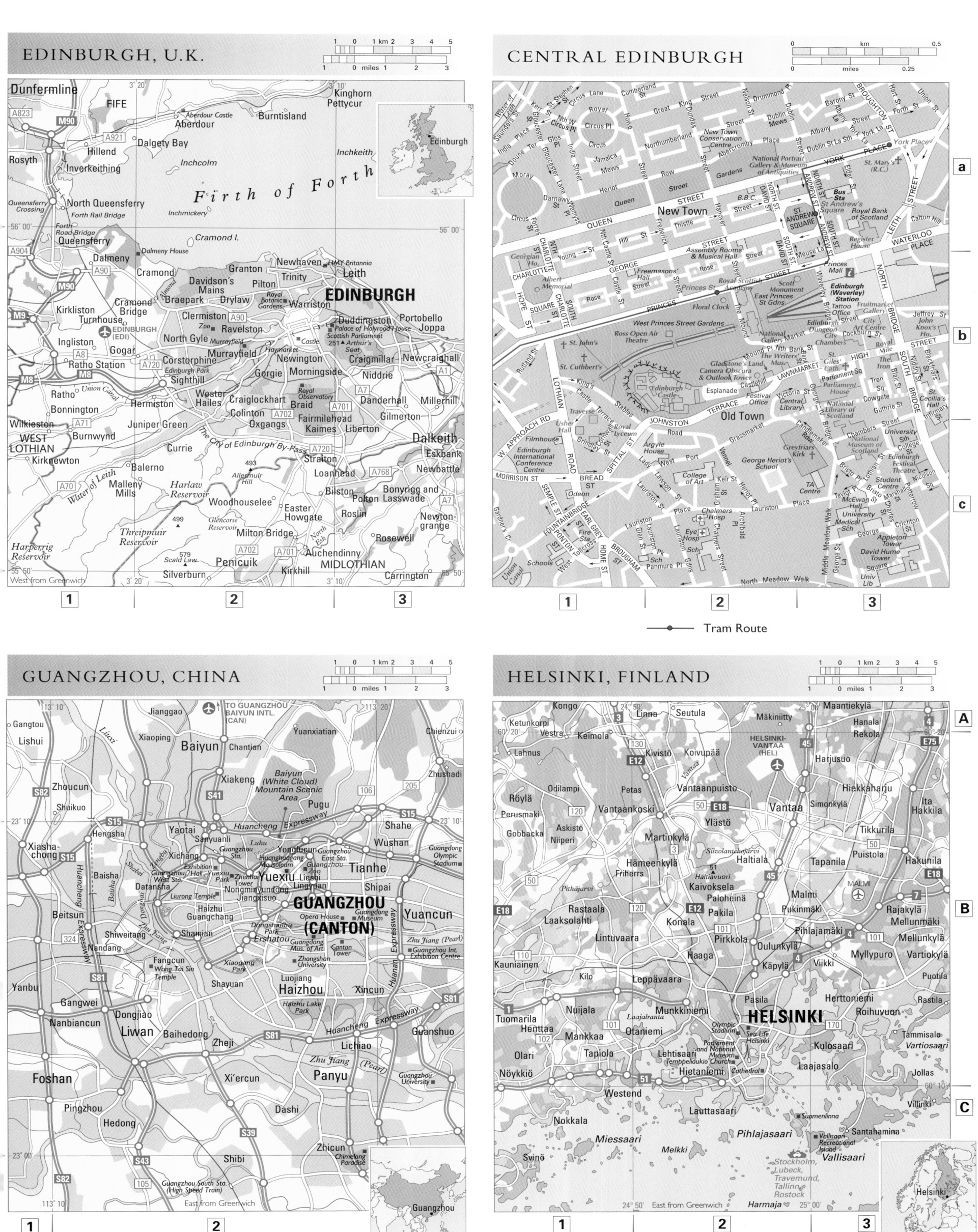

EDINBURGH, U.K.

CENTRAL EDINBURGH

Tram Route

GUANGZHOU, CHINA

HELSINKI, FINLAND

HONG KONG, CHINA

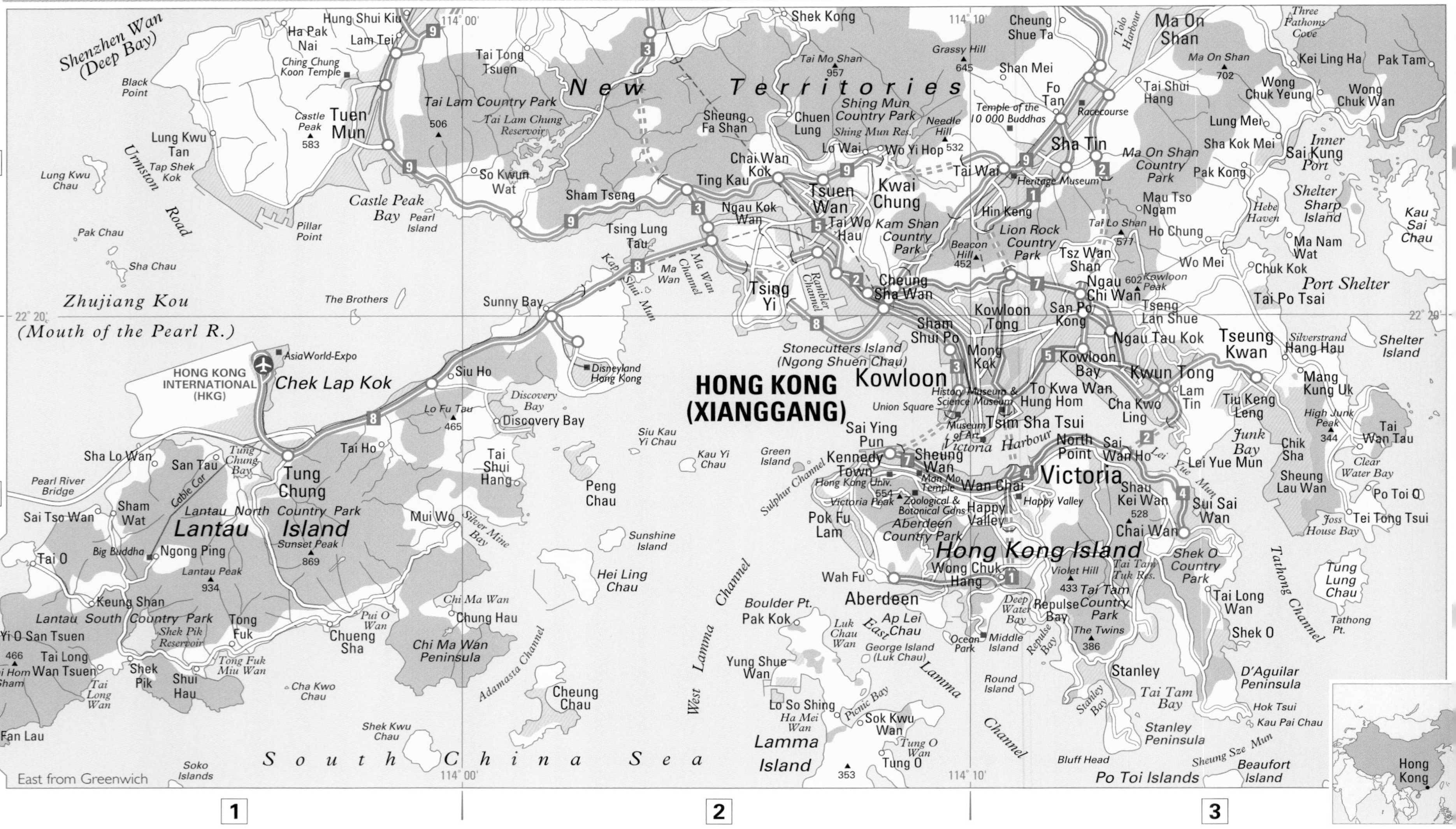

1 0 1 km 2 3 4 5
1 0 miles 1 2 3

Shenzhen Wan (Deep Bay)
Hung Shui Kiu
Ha Pak Nai
Lam Tei
Black Point
Ching Chung Koon Temple
Castle Peak 583
Tuen Mun
Tai Tong Tsuen
Tai Lam Country Park
Tai Lam Chung Reservoir 506
Shek Kong
Cheung Shue Ta
Tolo Harbour
Ma On Shan
Three Fathoms Cove
New Territories
Tai Mo Shan 957
Grassy Hill 645
Shan Mei
Ma On Shan 702
Kei Ling Ha
Pak Tam
Wong Chuk Yeung
Wong Chuk Wan

A
Lung Kwu Tan
Tap Shek Kok
Lung Kwu Chau
Pak Chau
Sha Chau
Castle Peak Bay
Pearl Island
Pillar Point
So Kwun Wat
Sham Tseng
Shing Mun Country Park
Sheung Fa Shan
Chuen Lung
Needle Hill 532
Temple of the 10 000 Buddhas
Sha Tin
Heritage Museum
Ma On Shan Country Park
Sha Kok Mei
Lung Mei
Inner Sai Kung Port
Hebe Haven
Shelter Island
Kau Sai Chau
Chai Wan Kok
Ting Kau
Tsuen Wan
Kwai Chung
Tai Wai
Lion Rock Country Park
Tsz Wan Shan
Mau Tso Ngam
Ho Chung
Ma Nam Wat

Zhujiang Kou (Mouth of the Pearl R.)
The Brothers
Sunny Bay
Tsing Lung Tau
Kap Shui Mun
Ma Wan Channel
Tsing Yi
Rambler Channel
Cheung Sha Wan
Sham Shui Po
Kowloon Tong
Ngau Chi Wan
San Po Kong
Ngau Tau Kok
Lam Tin
Tseng Lan Shue
Tseung Kwan
Silverstrand
Hang Hau
Shelter Island

B
Pearl River Bridge
Sai Tso Wan
Sha Lo Wan
San Tau
Sham Wat
Tung Chung Bay
Cable Car
Lantau North Country Park
Lantau Peak 934
Tung Chung
Ngong Ping
Big Buddha
Lo Fu Tau 465
Tai Ho
Siu Ho
Discovery Bay
Disneyland Hong Kong
Tai Shui Hang
Peng Chau
Mui Wo
Silver Mine Bay
Sunset Peak 869
Siu Kau Yi Chau
Kau Yi Chau
Sunshine Island
Green Island
Hong Kong Univ.
Kennedy Town
Sheung Wan
Victoria Peak
Sai Ying Pun
Union Square
History Museum & Science Museum
Museum of Art
Hung Hom
Tsim Sha Tsui
To Kwa Wan
Cha Kwo Ling
Kwun Tong
Tiu Keng Leng
Junk Bay
High Junk Peak 344
Chik Sha
Clear Water Bay
Po Toi O
HONG KONG (XIANGGANG)
Kowloon
Mong Kok
Kowloon Bay

Chek Lap Kok
HONG KONG INTERNATIONAL (HKG)
AsiaWorld-Expo
Stonecutters Island (Ngong Shuen Chau)
Discovery Bay

Lantau Island
Lantau South Country Park
Yi O San Tsuen 466
Tai Long
Tai Hom Wan Tsuen
Sham
Keung Shan
Shek Pik
Shek Pik Reservoir
Tai O
Fan Lau
Shui Hau
Tong Fuk
Pui O
Tong Fuk Miu Wan
Cheung Sha
Chi Ma Wan
Chung Hau
Chi Ma Wan Peninsula
Cha Kwo Chau
Adamasta Channel
Shek Kwu Chau
Soko Islands
Cheung Chau
Hei Ling Chau
West Lamma Channel
Boulder Pt.
Pak Kok
Yung Shue Wan
Lo So Shing
Ha Mei Wan
Lamma Island
353
Luk Chau Wan
George Island (Luk Chau)
Picnic Bay
Sok Kwu Wan
Tung O Wan
Tung O
Wah Fu
Pok Fu Lam
Victoria Peak
Zoological & Botanical Gdns
Victoria
Wan Chai
Happy Valley
Aberdeen Country Park
Victoria
Happy Valley
Kei Wan 528
Shau Kei Wan
Sai Wan Ho
Sui Sai Wan
Chai Wan
Sheung Sha Wan
Tei Tong Tsui
Joss House Bay
Tung Lung Chau
Wong Chuk Hang
Aberdeen
Ap Lei Chau
Ocean Park
Deep Water Bay
Middle Island
Repulse Bay
Round Island
Violet Hill 433
The Twins 386
Tai Tam Country Park
Hong Kong Island
Tai Tam Res.
Shek O Country Park
Shek O
Tai Long Wan
D'Aguilar Peninsula
Tathong Channel
Tathong Pt.
Stanley
Tai Tam Bay
Stanley Bay
Stanley Peninsula
Hok Tsui
Kau Pai Chau
Beaufort Island
Bluff Head
Sheung Sze Mun
Po Toi Islands
Lamma Island
South China Sea

East from Greenwich
114° 00'
114° 10'

Hong Kong [locator]

1 | 2 | 3

ISTANBUL, TURKEY

1 0 1 km 2 3 4 5
1 0 miles 1 2 3

A
Göktürk
Pirinçci
Bahçeköy
Sarıyer
Anadolukavağı
Kemerburgaz
Yuşa Tepesi 197
Sinop
Büyükdere
Beykoz
Alibey Barajı
Cebecci
Tarabya
Yeniköy
Paşabahçe
İstinye
Ayazağa
Istanbul Technical University
Emirgan
Boyacıköy
Çubuklu
Kanlıca
Göz Tepe 285
Türk Telekom Arena

B
Gaziosmanpaşa
E80
Levent
Rumelihisarı
Rumelian Castle
Anadoluhisarı
Elmalı Barajı
Alibeyköy
Kağithane
Mecidiyeköy
Bebek
Kandilli
Küçüksu
Vaniköy
Küçükköy
Şişli
Ortaköy
Çengelköy
İnkilap
Atışalen
Istanbul SEA LIFE Akvaryum
Beşiktaş
Yıldız Park
Beylerbeyi
Vialand
Eyüp Mosque
Taksim
Dolmabahçe Palace
Kuzguncuk
Çamlıca
Bayrampaşa
Esenler
Eyüp
Haskôy
Galata
Leander's Tower
Üsküdar
Ümraniye
Bağcılar
Fener
Topkapı
Galata Tower
Kısıklı
Güngören
Halıç (Golden Horn)
Beyoğlu
Grand Bazaar
Topkapı Palace
Esat Paşa
Bahçelievler
The Theodosian Walls
Fatih
Hagia Sophia
Selimiye
Kadıköy
TO ISTANBUL ATATÜRK (IST)
Yenikapı
Blue Mosque
Bakırköy
Sarayatı
Yedikule
İSTANBUL
Zeytinburnu
Kızıltoprak
Fenerbahçe
Erenköy
İçerenköy
TO ISTANBUL SABHA GÖKCEN (SAW)

C
Marmara Denizi (Sea of Marmara)
Bostancı
İzmir
Yalova
East from Greenwich
29° 00'
41° 10'
41° 00'

Istanbul [locator]

1 | 2

JAKARTA, INDONESIA

1 0 1 km 2 3 4 5
1 0 miles 1 2 3

Jakarta [locator]

A
JAVA SEA
Surabaya, Makassar, Jayapura, Semarang, Kupang, Bitung
Waduk Pluit
Teluk Jakarta
Koja Utara
TO JAKARTA SOEKARNO-HATTA (CGK)
Sunda Kelapa Harbour
Taman Impian Jaya Ancol (Ancol Dreamland)
Cilincing
Penjaringan
Ancol
Aquarium
Tanjung Priok
Koja

B
Kapuk
Jakarta Museum
International Trade Centre
Sunter
Kota
Koja
Cengkareng
Tambora
Taman Sari
Sawah Besar
JAKARTA
Kelapa Gading
Grogol Petamburin
Gambir
Istiqlal Mosque
Kemayoran
Kayu Putih
Kedoya
Merdeka Palace
National Monument
Cathedral
Kebon Jeruk
Tanjung Duren
Orchid Palace
National Museum
Gambir Station
Senen
Cempaka Putih
Race Course
Slipi
Kampung Bali
Welcome Monument
Menteng
Taman Ismail Marzuki
University
Pulo Gadung
Tanah Abang
Setia Budi
Matraman
Rawamangun
Joglo
Gelora Bung Karno Stadium
KidZania
Parliament House
Kebayoran Lama
Kebon Jeruk
Kuningan
Tebet
Jatinegara
Duren Sawit
Klender
Tanah Kusir
Kebayoran Baru
Kemang
Mampang Prapatan
Cipete
Pasar Minggu
Kramat Jati
Makasar
Pondok Kelapa
Bintaro Jaya
Pondok Indah
Halim
Cilandak
JAKARTA HALIM PERDANAKUSUMA (HLP)
Condet
Pondok Gede
Jatiwaringin

East from Greenwich
106° 50'
6° 10'

1 | 2

JERUSALEM, ISRAEL / W. BANK

CENTRAL JERUSALEM

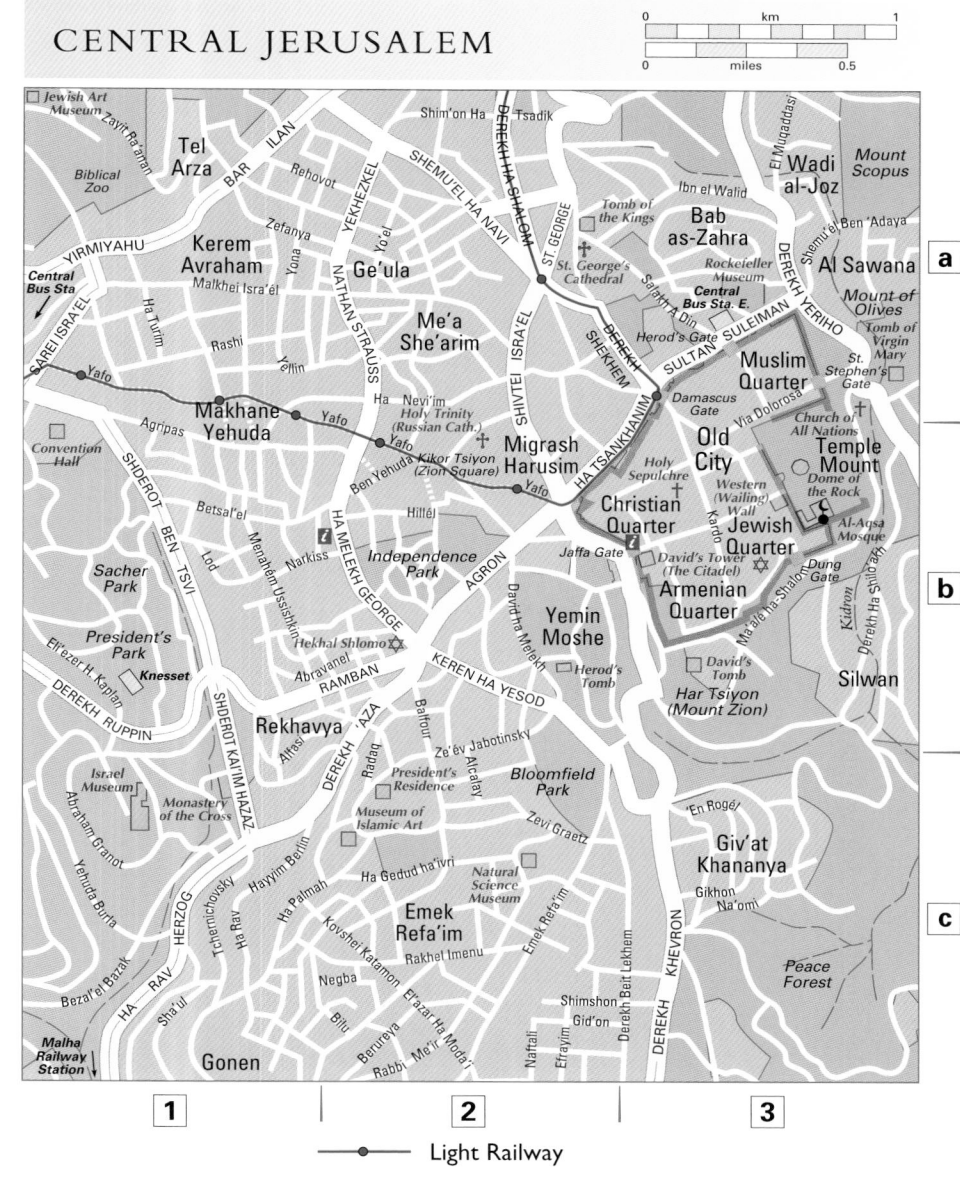

- - - 1949 Cease-fire line —— Israeli security fence

—●— Light Railway

JOHANNESBURG, S. AFRICA

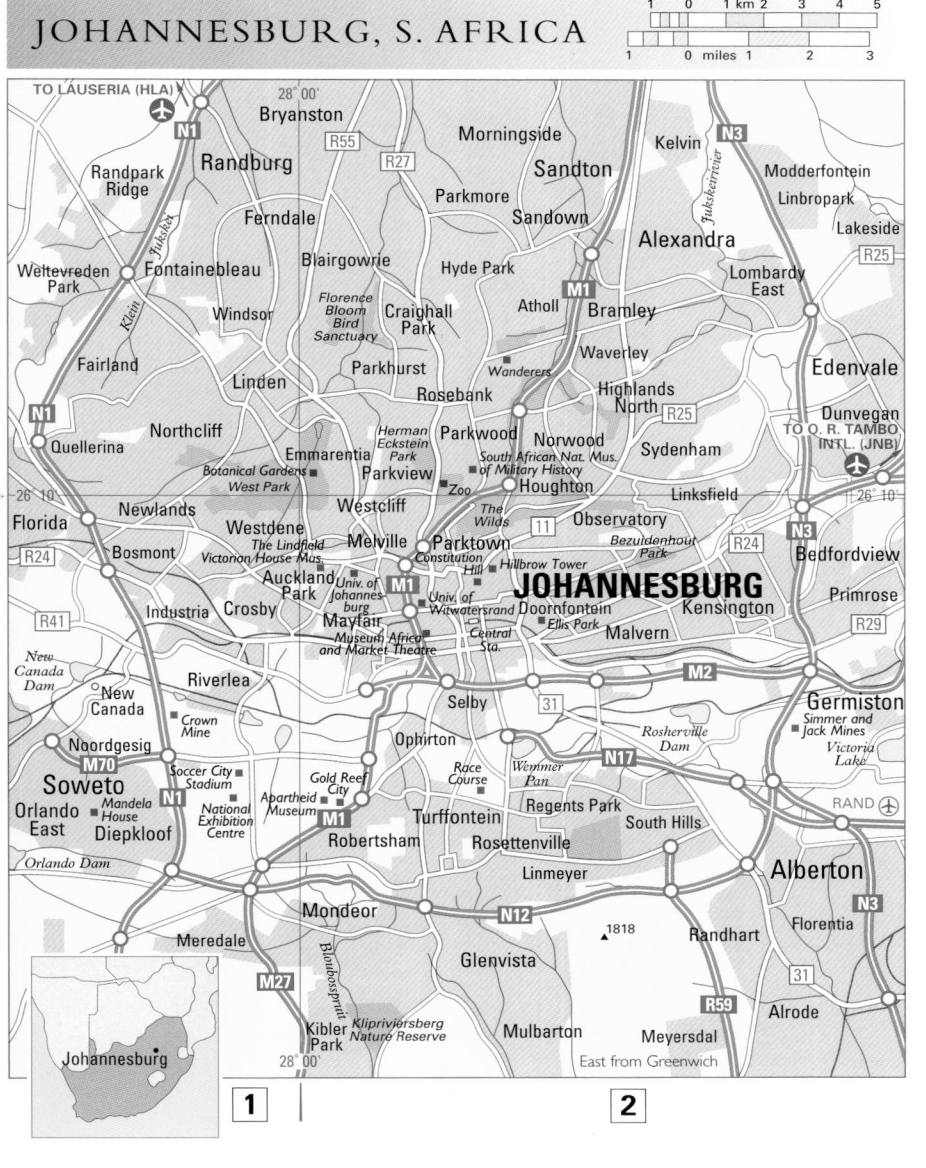

KARACHI, PAKISTAN

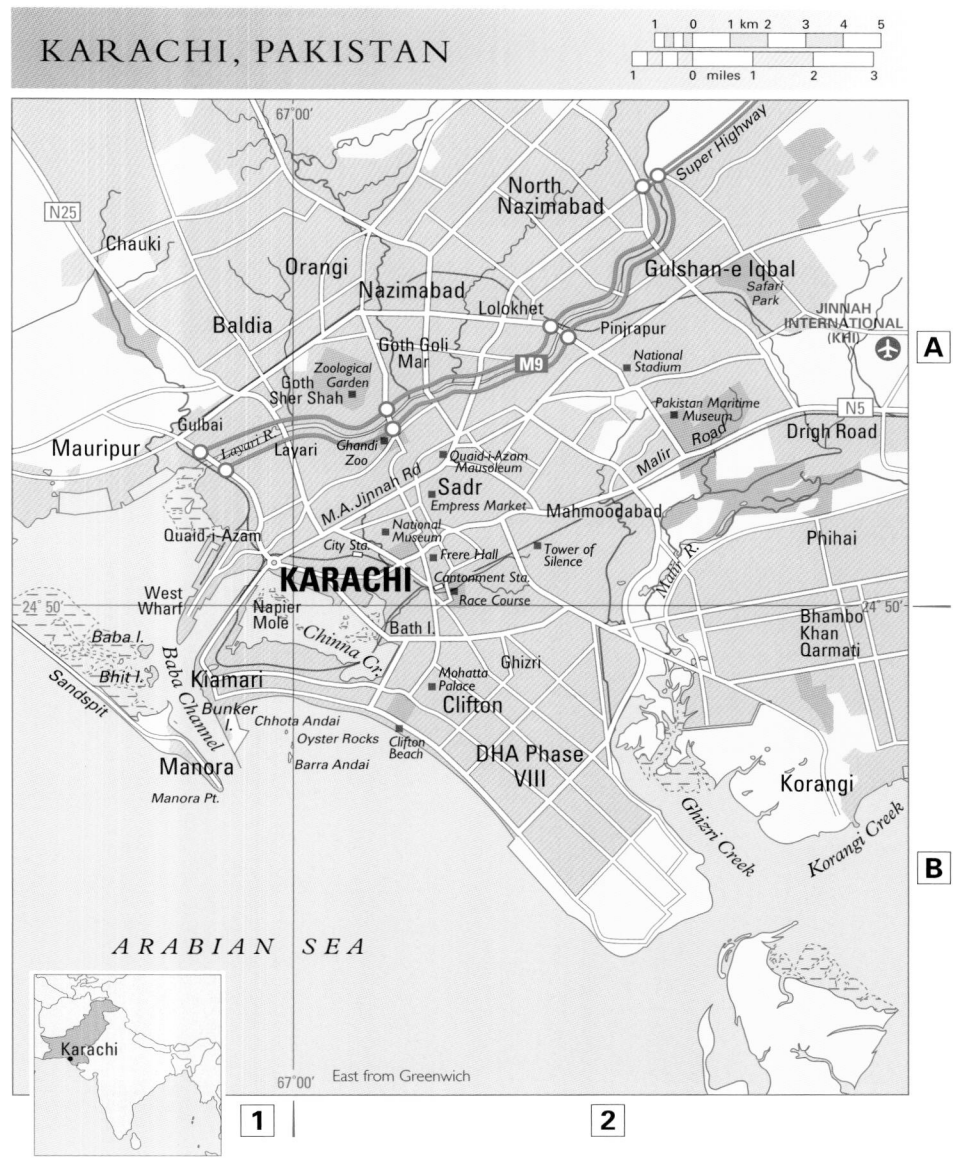

COPYRIGHT PHILIP'S

KOLKATA, INDIA

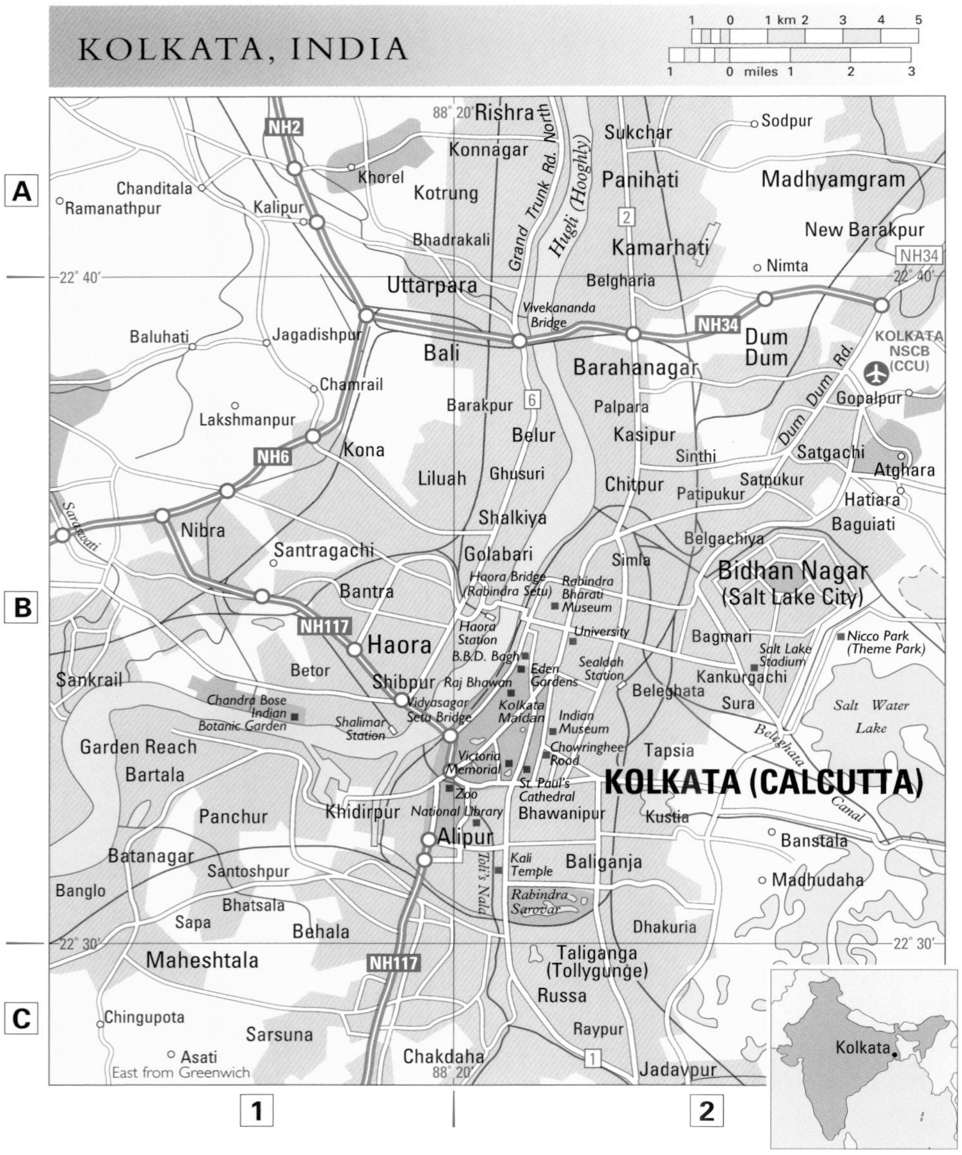

1 0 1 km 2 3 4 5
1 0 miles 1 2 3

NH2 · Rishra · Sukchar · Sodpur · Konnagar · Panihati · Madhyamgram · Khorel · Kotrung · Chanditala · Ramanathpur · Kalipur · Bhadrakali · New Barakpur · Kamarhati · Nimta · NH34 · Uttarpara · Belgharia · Vivekananda Bridge · Baluhati · Jagadishpur · Dum Dum · NH34 · Bali · Barahanagar · Palpara · KOLKATA NSCB (CCU) · Chamrail · Barakpur · Belur · Kasipur · Satgachi · Gopalpur · Lakshmanpur · Kona · Liluah · Ghusuri · Chitpur · Patipukur · Satpukur · Atghara · NH6 · Shalkiya · Sinthi · Hatiara · Baguiati · Nibra · Santragachi · Golabari · Simla · Belgachiya · Bantra · Haora Bridge (Rabindra Setu) · Rabindra Bharati Museum · University · Bidhan Nagar (Salt Lake City) · NH117 · Haora · Haora Station B.B.D. Bagh · Bagmari · Salt Lake Stadium · Nicco Park (Theme Park) · Sankrail · Betor · Shibpur · Eden Gardens · Sealdah Station · Kankurgachi · Chandra Bose Indian Botanic Garden · Vidyasagar Setu Bridge · Kolkata Maidan · Indian Museum · Sura · Beleghata · Salt Water Lake · Garden Reach · Shalimar Station · Victoria Memorial · Chowringhee · Tapsia · Belghuria Canal · Bartala · Raj Bhawan · Zoo · St. Paul's Cathedral · Bhawanipur · Kustia · Banstala · Panchur · Khidirpur · National Library · Alipur · Kali Temple · Baliganja · Madhudaha · Banglo · Batanagar · Santoshpur · Bhatsala · Sapa · Behala · Rabindra Sarovar · Dhakuria · Maheshtala · NH117 · Taliganga (Tollygunge) · Russa · Chingupota · Sarsuna · Raypur · Asati · Chakdaha · East from Greenwich · Jadavpur

Kolkata (inset)

LAGOS, NIGERIA

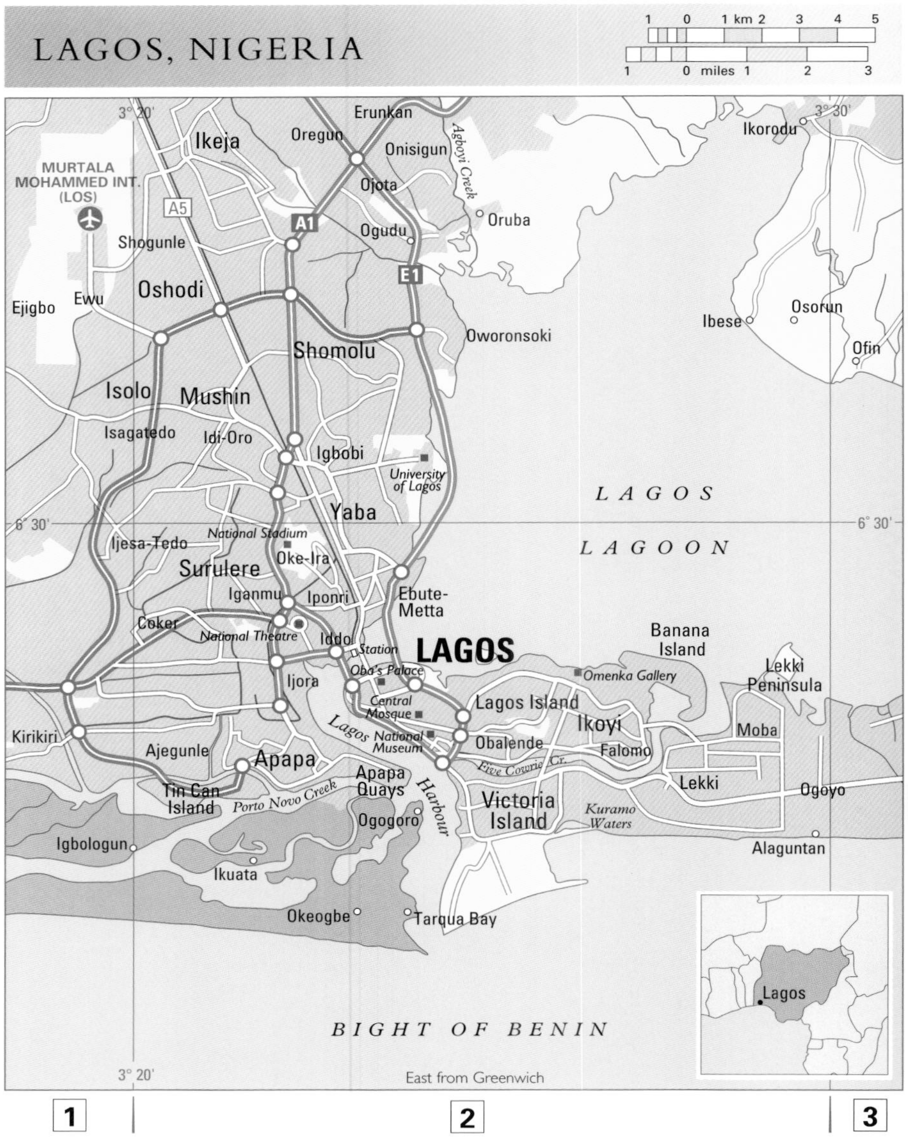

1 0 1 km 2 3 4 5
1 0 miles 1 2 3

MURTALA MOHAMMED INT. (LOS) · Ikeja · Oregun · Erunkan · Onisigun · Ikorodu · Shogunle · Ojota · Oruba · Ejigbo · Ewu · Oshodi · Oworonsoki · Ibese · Osorun · Ofin · Isolo · Mushin · Igbobi · University of Lagos · Isagatedo · Idi-Oro · Yaba · LAGOS LAGOON · Ijesa-Tedo · National Stadium · Oke-Ira · Surulere · Iganmu · Iponri · Ebute-Metta · Banana Island · Coker · National Theatre · Iddo · Station · Lekki Peninsula · Omenka Gallery · Kirikiri · Ijora · Lagos Island · Ikoyi · Falomo · Moba · Ajegunle · Oba's Palace · Central Mosque · National Museum · Obalende · Lekki · Tin Can Island · Apapa · Porto Novo Creek · Apapa Quays · Ogogoro · Victoria Island · Kuramo Waters · Ogoyo · Igbologun · Harbour · Alaguntan · Ikuata · Okeogbe · Tarqua Bay · BIGHT OF BENIN · East from Greenwich

Lagos (inset)

LAS VEGAS, NEVADA

1 0 1 km 2 3 4 5
1 0 miles 1 2 3

North Las Vegas · NELLIS AFB · NORTH LAS VEGAS (VGT) · City View Park · BUS 95 · Old Las Vegas Mormon Fort State Historic Park · Las Vegas Natural History Museum · Neon Museum · Sunrise Mountain Natural Area · Lorenzi Park · Cashman Field · Meadows Mall · Nevada State Museum & Historical Society · The Mob Museum · LAS VEGAS · Sunrise Manor · Stratosphere Tower · Circus Circus/Adventure Theme Park · Fashion Show Mall · Las Vegas Country Club · Convention Center · Boulevard Mall · Clark County Wetlands Park · Treasure Island · Wynn · The Venetian · Caesars Palace · The Mirage · Flamingo · National Atomic Testing Museum · Bellagio · Paris · University of Nevada L.V. · Monte Carlo · MGM Grand · Thomas & Mack Center · New York New York · Hooters · Spring Valley · Excalibur · Luxor · Tropicana · Paris · Whitney (East Las Vegas) · Mandalay Bay · Four Seasons · LAS VEGAS McCARRAN INTL. (LAS) · Paradise · Sam Boyd Stadium · Town Square Mall · Sunset Park · Galleria at Sunset · Las Vegas · Las Vegas South Premium Outlets · Henderson · The Strip · Enterprise · West from Greenwich

LIMA, PERU

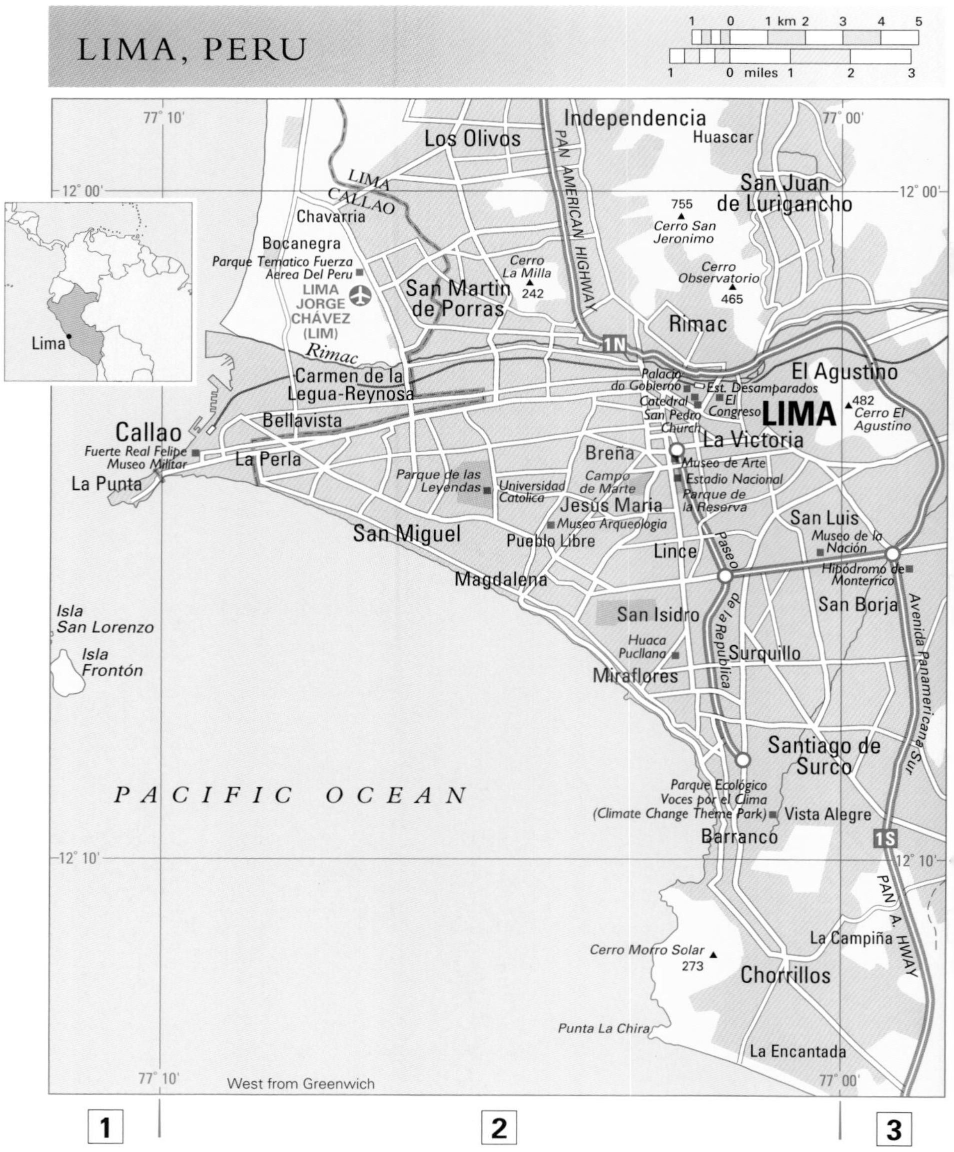

1 0 1 km 2 3 4 5
1 0 miles 1 2 3

Independencia · Los Olivos · Huascar · LIMA CALLAO · Chavarria · San Juan de Lurigancho · Bocanegra · Cerro San Jeronimo · Parque Temático Fuerza Aérea Del Peru · Cerro La Milla · Cerro Observatorio · LIMA JORGE CHÁVEZ (LIM) · San Martin de Porras · Rimac · Rimac · 1N · Palacio de Gobierno · Est. Desamparados · Carmen de la Legua-Reynosa · Catedral · El Congreso · El Agustino · Callao · Bellavista · San Pedro Church · Cerro El Agustino · Fuerte Real Felipe Museo Militar · La Perla · Breña · LIMA · La Victoria · La Punta · Museo de Arte · Parque de las Leyendas · Campo de Marte · Estadio Nacional · San Luis · Isla San Lorenzo · San Miguel · Universidad Catolica · Jesús Maria · Parque de la Reserva · Museo Arqueológico · Museo de la Nacion · Isla Frontón · Magdalena · Pueblo Libre · Lince · Hipódromo de Monterrico · San Isidro · San Borja · Huaca Pucllana · Surquillo · Miraflores · Santiago de Surco · Parque Ecológico Voces por el Clima (Climate Change Theme Park) · Vista Alegre · PACIFIC OCEAN · Barranco · Cerro Morro Solar · La Campiña · Chorrillos · Punta La Chira · La Encantada · West from Greenwich

Lima (inset)

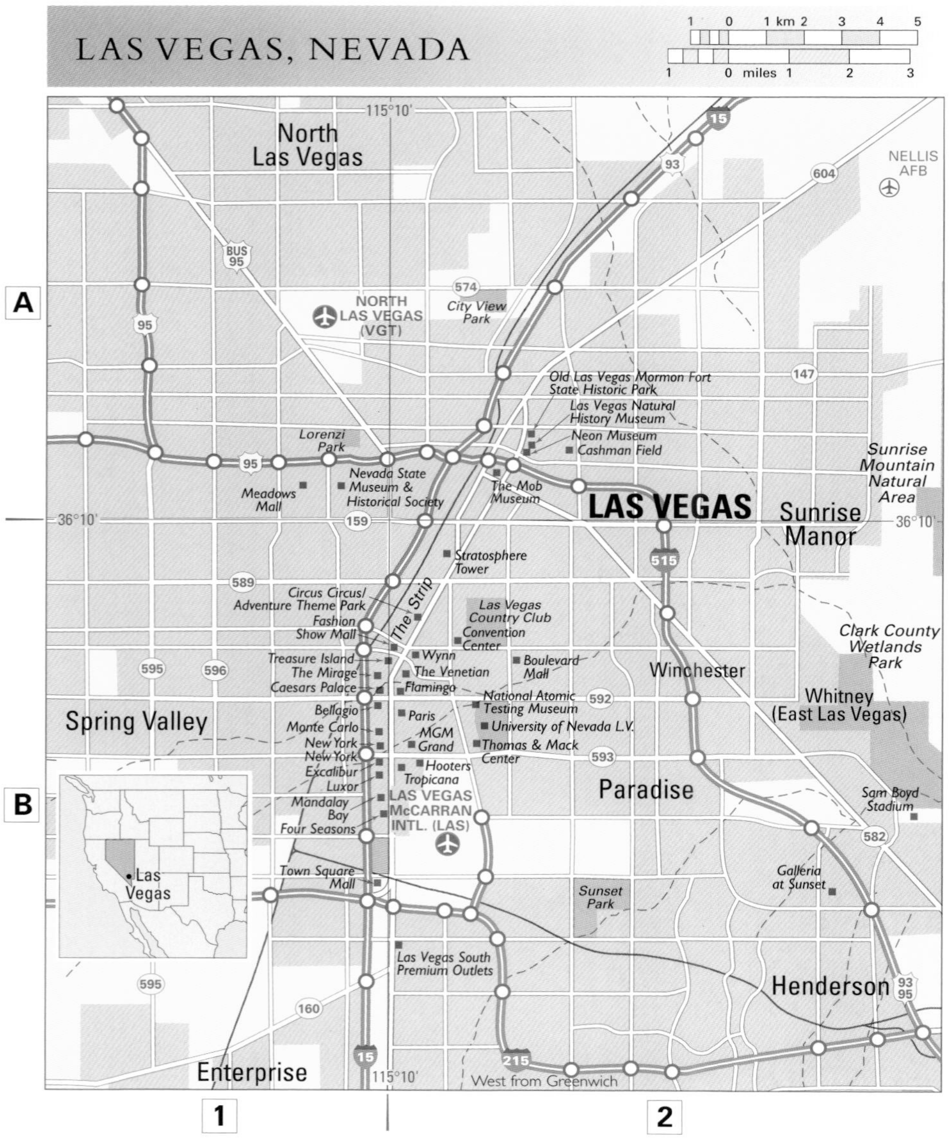

15 Interstate route numbers 95 U.S. route numbers 147 State route numbers

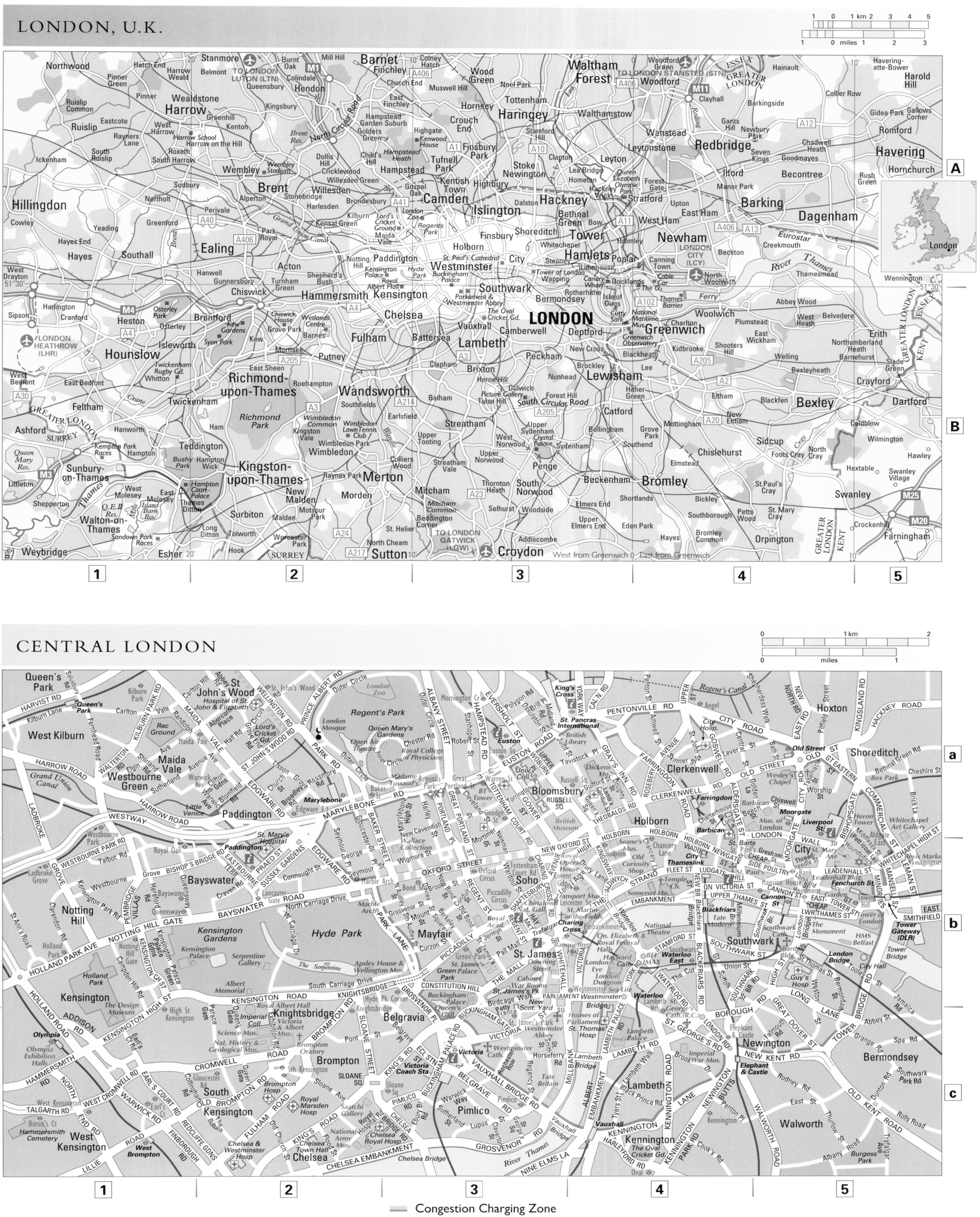

LONDON, U.K.

1 0 1 km 2 3 4 5
1 0 miles 1 2 3

Northwood
Pinner Green
Hatch End
Stanmore
Belmont
Burnt Oak
Colindale
Queensbury
Mill Hill
Colney Hatch
Barnet
Finchley
Church End
East Finchley
Wood Green
Noel Park
Waltham Forest
Woodford
Hainault
Havering-atte-Bower
Harold Hill
Collier Row
Gidea Park
Gallows Corner
Romford

TO LONDON LUTON (LTN)
TO LONDON STANSTED (STN)
GREATER LONDON

Harrow
Harrow Weald
Wealdstone
Greenhill
Kenton
Kingsbury
Hendon
Hornsey
Muswell Hill
Crouch End
Highgate
Stamford Hill
Leytonstone
Wanstead
Snaresbrook
Barkingside
Newbury Park
Seven Kings
Goodmayes
A12
Chadwell Heath

Ruislip Common
Eastcote
West Harrow
Harrow School
Harrow on the Hill
Brent Res.
North Circular Road
Hampstead Garden Suburb
Golders Green
Kenwood House
Hampstead Heath
Tufnell Park
Clapton
Leyton
Forest Gate
Manor Park
Ilford
Becontree

Ickenham
South Ruislip
Roxeth
Stonebridge
Dollis Hill
Cricklewood
Childs Hill
Finsbury Park
Stoke Newington
Homerton
Queen Elizabeth Olympic Park
Stratford
Upton
East Ham
Barking
Dagenham

Ruislip
Rayners Lane
Northolt
Perivale
Alperton
Willesden Green
Harlesden
Kilburn
Kensal Green
Maida Vale
Lord's Cricket Ground
Regents Park
London Zoo
Camden
Islington
Dalston
Bethnal Green
Bow
West Ham
LONDON CITY (LCY)
Beckton

Hillingdon
Cowley
Yeading
Greenford
Ealing
Acton
Shepherd's Bush
Notting Hill
Paddington
Holborn
Westminster
City
Whitechapel
Stepney
Limehouse
Poplar
Canning Town
North Woolwich
Thamesmead
Wennington

West Drayton
Hayes End
Hayes
Southall
Hanwell
Gunnersbury
Turnham Green
Chiswick
Kensington
Hyde Park
Buckingham Palace
St Paul's Cathedral
Parliament & Westminster Abbey
Southwark
Bermondsey
Rotherhithe
Isle of Dogs
Docklands
Canary Wharf
Cutty Sark
National Maritime Mus.
Greenwich
Woolwich
Abbey Wood
Belvedere
Erith

Harlington
Cranford
Heston
Osterley Park
Brentford
Kew Gardens
Chiswick House
Grove Park
Barnes
Fulham
Chelsea
Battersea
Vauxhall
Lambeth
Camberwell
The Oval Cricket Gd.
New Cross
Deptford
Greenwich Observatory
Blackheath
Charlton
Kidbrooke
Shooters Hill
Plumstead
East Wickham
Northumberland Heath
Barnehurst

LONDON HEATHROW (LHR)
Sipson
Hounslow
Isleworth
Syon Park
Kew
Mortlake
Putney
Clapham
Brixton
Herne Hill
Brockley
Nunhead
Peckham
Lewisham
Lee
Hither Green
Eltham
Welling
Bexleyheath

West Bedfont
East Bedfont
Twickenham Rugby Gd.
Whitton
Richmond-upon-Thames
Roehampton
East Sheen
Southfields
Wandsworth
Belham
Tooting
Streatham
Dulwich
Picture Gallery
Tulse Hill
Forest Hill
South Circular Road
Catford
Grove Park
Mottingham
New Eltham
Blackfen
Bexley
Crayford
Dartford

A30
Ashford
SURREY
GREATER LONDON
Feltham
Hanworth
Crane
Twickenham
Teddington
Richmond Park
Ham
Wimbledon Common
Kingston Vale
Wimbledon Lawn Tennis Club
Wimbledon
Streatham Vale
Upper Norwood
Crystal Palace
Sydenham
Bellingham
Southend
Chislehurst
Sidcup
Foots Cray
North Cray
Coldblow
Wilmington
Hextable
Swanley Village

Queen Mary Res.
Sunbury-on-Thames
Kempton Races
Hampton
Bushy Park
Hampton Wick
Kingston-upon-Thames
New Malden
Raynes Park
Merton
Mitcham
Mitcham Common
Beddington Corner
Thornton Heath
South Norwood
Woodside
Penge
Beckenham
Shortlands
Bickley
Bromley
St.Paul's Cray
St. Mary Cray
Petts Wood
Orpington
Swanley
M25
M20
Farningham

Littleton
Shepperton
Walton-on-Thames
Q.E. II Res.
Sandown Park Races
Island Barn Res.
Thames Ditton
Long Ditton
Surbiton
Tolworth
Hook
Worcester Park
North Cheam
Sutton
Carshalton
Wallington
Elmers End
Upper Elmers End
Eden Park
Hayes
Bromley Common
Southborough
Crockenhill
GREATER LONDON
KENT

Weybridge
Esher 20'
SURREY
A217
TO LONDON GATWICK (LGW)
Croydon
Addiscombe
West from Greenwich 0 East from Greenwich

1 2 3 4 5

CENTRAL LONDON

0 1 km 2
0 miles 1

Queen's Park
West Kilburn
Maida Vale
Westbourne Green
Paddington
Bayswater
Notting Hill
Kensington
Holland Park
West Kensington
Olympia
South Kensington
Chelsea
St John's Wood
Regent's Park
London Zoo
Marylebone
Mayfair
Knightsbridge
Belgravia
Brompton
Pimlico
Victoria
St James
Westminster
Lambeth
Kennington
Walworth
Bermondsey
Newington
Elephant & Castle
Southwark
Borough
City
Clerkenwell
Shoreditch
Hoxton
Bloomsbury
Holborn
Soho
Mayfair

Congestion Charging Zone

COPYRIGHT PHILIP'S

LISBON, PORTUGAL

Almargem do Bispo
Botica Sete
Santo Antão do Tojal
São Julião do Tojal
Santa Iria da Azóia
Sabugo
Tapada
Piedade
Montemor
Camaroes
Loures
Telhal
Caneças
Unhos
Apelação
Santa Iria da Azóia
Rio de Mouro
Amoreira
Famões
Odivelas
Camarate
Sacavém
Ponte Vasco da Gama
Venda Seca
Belas
Aguava-Cacem
Massamá
Ada Beja
Lumiar
Pontinha
Charneca
Ameixoeira
Moscavide
Parque das Nações (Park of Nations)
Cotão
Queluz
Amadora
Benfica
Estádio de Luz
Carnide
Campo Grande
University
Alvalade
Olivais
Damaia
Monsanto
Parque Florestal de Monsanto
Campo Pequeno
Gulbenkian Museum
Matinha
Barcarena
Carnaxide
Rato
Campolide
Alto do Pina
Beato
Xabregas
LISBOA
Leião
Talaide
Ajuda
Alcantara
Estação do Rossio
Castelo de S. Jorge
Estação Santa Apolónia
Linda-a-Pastora
Algés
Santo Amaro
Basílica da Estrela
Museu do Dinheiro
Terrugem
Caxias
Mosteiro dos Jerónimos
Estação Cais do Sodré
Estação do Comércio
Belém
Museum for Art, Architecture & Technology (MAAT)
Paco de Arcos
Torre de Belém
Padrão dos Descobrimentos
Ponte 25 de Abril
Cacilhas
Oeiras
Porto Brandão
Banática
Cristo Rei
Almada
Lavradio
Trafaria
Raposo
Caparica
Cova de Piedade
Rio Tejo
Bugio
OCEAN
Barreiro
Coina
Quinta de Santo António
Sobreda
Laranjeiro
Costa da Caparica
Capuchos
Corroios
Seixal
Santo André
Amora
Cruz de Pau
Palhais
Arrentela
Charneca

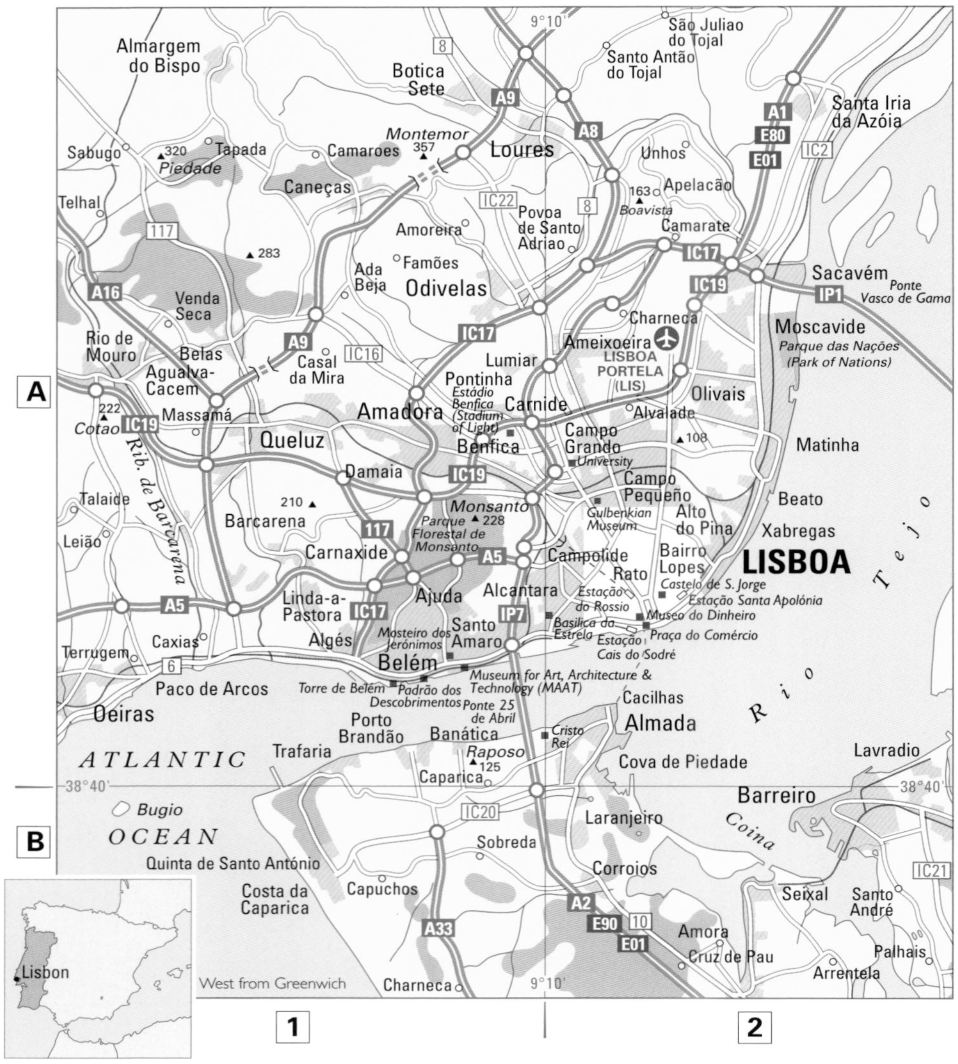

ATLANTIC

West from Greenwich

CENTRAL LISBON

Penitenciária
Palacio de Justiça
Praça Duque Saladanha
Instituto Superior Técnico
Hosp. Infantil
Maternidade
Estefânia
Amoreiros
Parque Eduardo VII
Pavilhão Carlos Lopes
Marquês de Pombal
Penha de França
Rato
Museu Nacional História Natural e de Ciência
Jardim Botânico
Anjos
Graça
Bairro Lopes
Instituto de Medicina Legal
Palácio de Assembleia Nacional
Hospital de São José
Bairro Alto
Teatro Nac. de São Carlos
Museu do Arqueologia
Praça Rossio
Estação do Rossio
Castelo de São Jorge (St. George's Castle)
Museu de Arte Decorativas
Alfama
Military Trigo Museum
Sé Catedral
Igreja Sta. Engrácia
Estação Santa Apolónia
Biblioteca Nacional
Chiado
Museu do Dinheiro
Baixa
Praça do Comércio
Dom José I
Museu de Arte Contemporânea
Praça Dom Luís I
Estação Cais do Sodré
Estação Fluvial
Terreiro do Paço
Rio Tejo (Tagus)
Seixal
Montijo, Barreiro

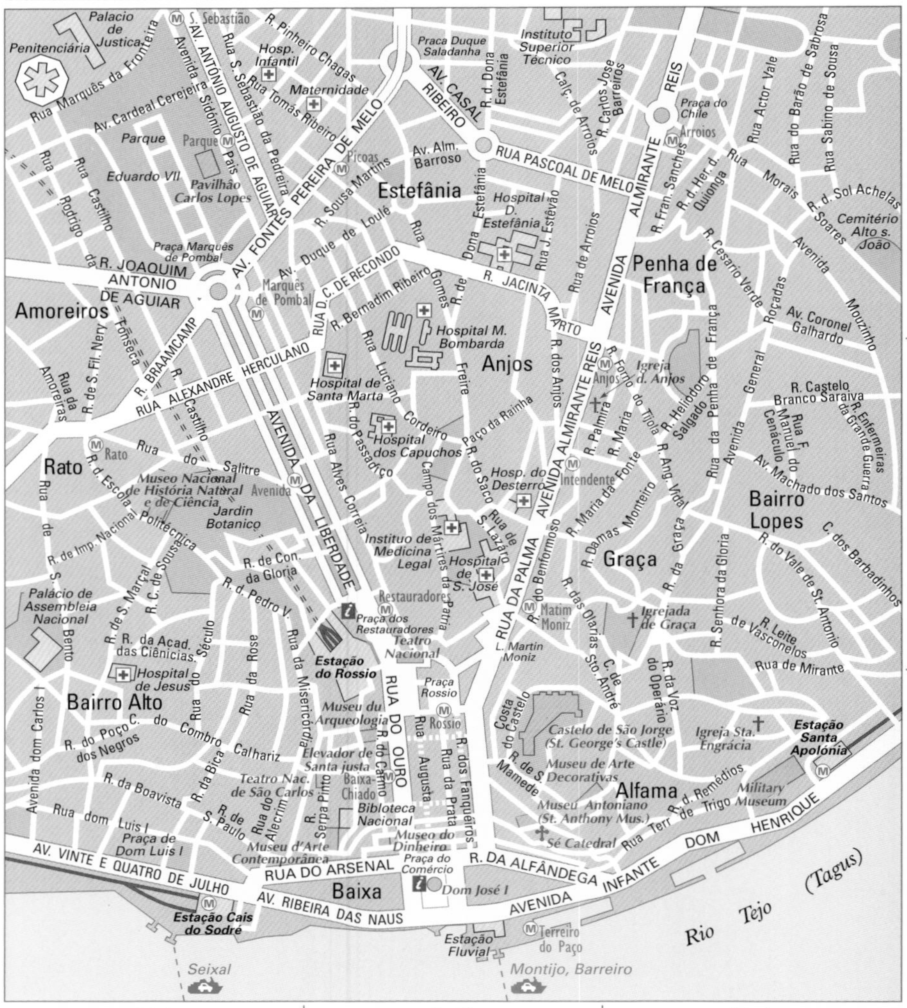

LOS ANGELES, CALIFORNIA

Tarzana
Van Nuys
Burbank
San Gabriel Mts.
Altadena
Eaton Canyon Park
Sepulveda Basin Rec. Area
San Fernando Valley
Verdugo Mts.
San Rafael Hills
Encino
Westfield Fashion Square
North Hollywood
Burbank Studios
Walt Disney Studios
Flint Peak 575
Rose Bowl
Pasadena
Sierra Madre
Monrovia
Encino Reservoir
Sherman Oaks
Studio City
CBS Studio Center
Warner Brothers Studios
Autry Museum of the American West
Zoo
Glendale
Glendale Galleria
Norton Simon Museum
USC Pacific Asia Museum
California Institute of Technology
L.A. County Arboretum
Santa Anita Park
Arcadia
Mulholland Dr.
Universal Studios
Cahuenga Peak 555
Griffith Park
Griffith Observatory
Eagle Rock
Occidental Coll.
South Pasadena
The Huntington
San Marino
Santa Anita Mall
Temple City
Santa Monica Mts.
Nat. Rec. Area
Stone Canyon Reservoir
Beverly Glen
Mount Olympus
Lake Hollywood
Hollywood
Los Feliz Blvd.
Highland Park
Garvanza
Mission San Gabriel Archangel
San Gabriel
Topanga State Park
Franklin Reservoir
TCL Chinese Theatre
Dolby Theatre
Hollywood Walk of Fame
Sunset Blvd.
L.A. Municipal Art Gallery
Silver Lake Reservoir
Southwest Museum
Monterey Hills
Alhambra
Rosemead
El Monte
The Getty Center
Bel Air
Beverly Hills
West Hollywood
Los Angeles Museum of the Holocaust
Santa Monica Blvd.
Paramount Studios
Silver Lake
Cypress Park
Heritage Square Museum
El Sereno
Brentwood
University of California Los Angeles
Westwood Village
Century City
20th Century Fox
Farmers Market
L.A. County Art Museum
La Brea Tar Pits
Petersen Automotive Museum
Beverly Blvd.
Getty Ho.
Westlake
MacArthur Park
Echo Park
Dodger Stadium
Elysian Park
Lincoln Heights
California State University
Monterey Park
San Bernardino Fwy.
South San Gabriel
South El Monte
Will Rogers State Historic Park
Brentwood Park
Sunset Blvd.
Sawtelle
Westfield Century City
Rancho Park
Cheviot Hills
Mid-City
LOS ANGELES
Civic Center
City Hall
Union Sta.
City Terrace
Boyle Heights
East Los Angeles
Montebello
Whittier Narrows Recreation Area
Pacific Palisades
Santa Monica
Museum of Art
Palms
Santa Monica Fwy.
Jefferson Park
University of Southern California
Shrine Auditorium
California Science Center
Convention Center
Vernon
Commerce
Pico Rivera Sports Arena
Puente Hills
PACIFIC OCEAN
Venice
Mar Vista
Culver City
Sony Picture Studio
Kenneth Hahn SRA
Baldwin Hills Reservoir
View Park
Exposition Park
Memorial Coliseum
Maywood
Pico Rivera
Pio Pico State Historic Park
Venice Boardwalk
Fisherman's Village
Del Rey
Westfield Culver City
Ladera Heights
Windsor Hills
Hyde Park
Vermont Knolls
Manchester Ave.
Slauson Ave.
Huntington Park
Florence
Walnut Park
Bell
Bell Gardens
Los Nietos
Marina del Rey
Westchester
Loyola Marymount University
University of West Los Angeles
The Forum
LOS ANGELES INTERNATIONAL (LAX)
Inglewood
Lennox
Watts
Cudahy
South Gate
Downey
Whittier
Whittier College
Santa Fe Springs

West from Greenwich

Interstate route numbers   U.S. route numbers   State route numbers

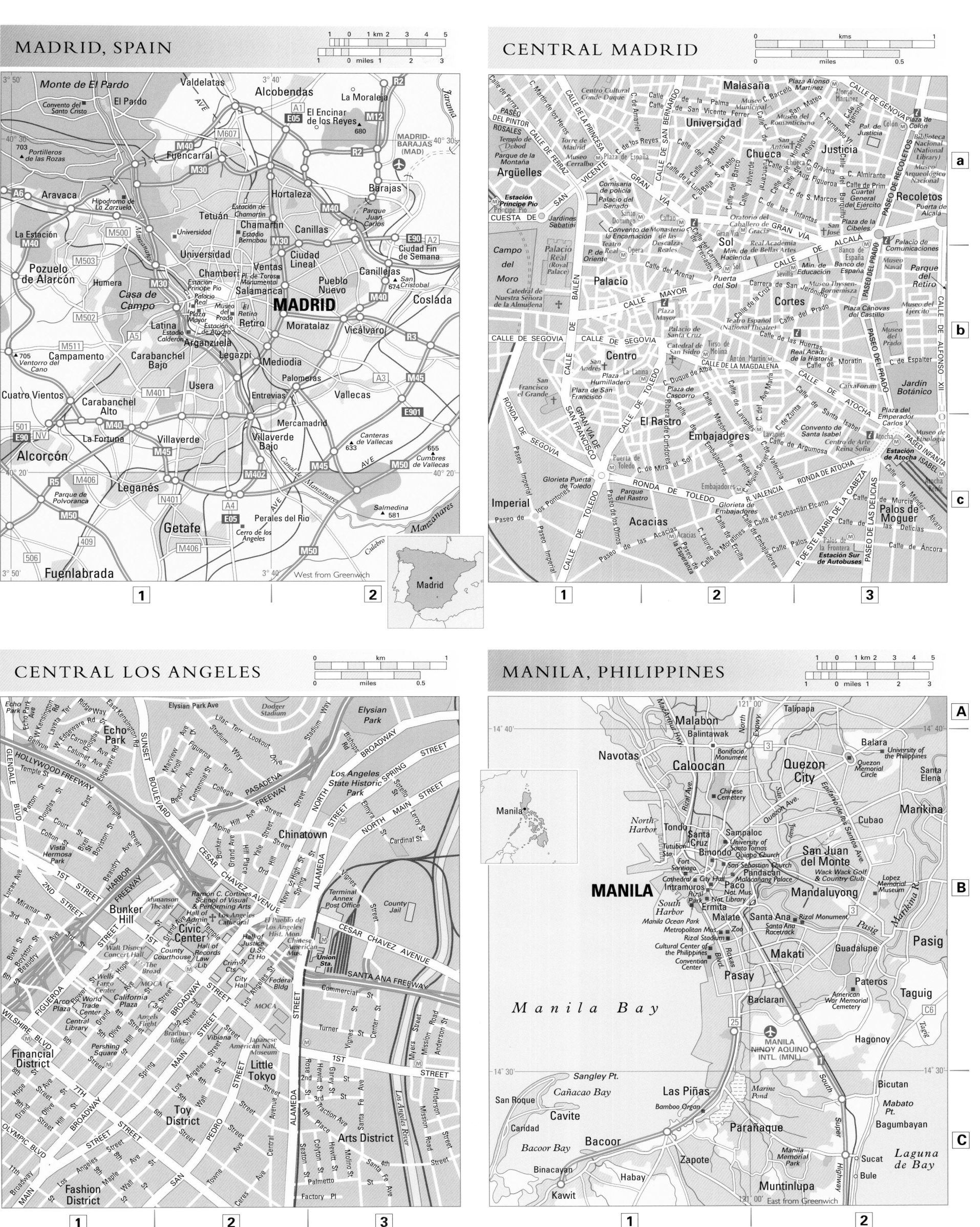

MADRID, SPAIN

Monte de El Pardo
Valdelatas
Alcobendas
La Moraleja
El Encinar
de los Reyes
Convento del
Santo Cristo
El Pardo
Portilleros
de las Rozas
Fuencarral
MADRID-
BARAJAS
(MAD)
Aravaca
Hortaleza
Barajas
Hipodromo de
La Zarzuela
Tetuán
Chamartín
Parque Juan
Carlos
La Estación
Universidad
Canillas
Ciudad Fin
de Semana
Pozuelo
de Alarcón
Chamberí
Ventas
Ciudad
Lineal
Canillejas
Humera
Salamanca
Pueblo
Nuevo
Coslada
Casa de
Campo
MADRID
Latina
El Retiro
Retiro
Moratalaz
Vicálvaro
Campamento
Arganzuela
Legazpi
Carabanchel
Bajo
Mediodía
Palomeras
Usera
Vallecas
Cuatro Vientos
Carabanchel
Alto
Entrevías
La Fortuna
Mercamadrid
Villaverde
Canteras
de Vallecas
Cumbres
de Vallecas
Alcorcón
Villaverde
Bajo
Leganés
Parque de
Polvoranca
Perales del Rio
Getafe
Cerro de los
Angeles
Fuenlabrada
West from Greenwich
Madrid

CENTRAL MADRID

Malasaña
Plaza Alonso
Martínez
Centro Cultural
Conde Duque
Universidad
Justicia
Chueca
Biblioteca
Nacional (National
Library)
Argüelles
Recoletos
Estación
Príncipe Pío
Sol
Palacio
Palacio Real
(Royal
Palace)
Campo
del
Moro
Cortes
Catedral de
Nuestra Señora
de la Almudena
Plaza
Mayor
Centro
El Rastro
Embajadores
Jardín
Botánico
Imperial
Acacias
Palos de
Moguer
Estación Sur
de Autobuses

CENTRAL LOS ANGELES

Echo Park
Dodger
Stadium
Elysian
Park
Echo
Park
Los Angeles
State Historic
Park
HOLLYWOOD FREEWAY
Chinatown
Bunker
Hill
Civic
Center
Union
Sta.
Little
Tokyo
Financial
District
CESAR CHAVEZ AVENUE
SANTA ANA FREEWAY
Toy
District
Arts District
Fashion
District

MANILA, PHILIPPINES

Malabon
Talipapa
Balintawak
Balara
Navotas
Caloocan
Quezon
City
University of
the Philippines
Quezon
Memorial
Circle
Santa
Elena
Manila
Marikina
North
Harbor
Tondo
Sampaloc
Cubao
Santa
Cruz
Binondo
San Juan
del Monte
Wack Wack Golf
& Country Club
MANILA
Intramuros
Paco
Pandacan
Malacañang Palace
Mandaluyong
Lopez
Memorial
Museum
South
Harbor
Ermita
Malate
Santa Ana
Pasig
Makati
Guadalupe
Pasay
Pateros
Taguig
Manila Bay
Baclaran
American
War Memorial
Cemetery
MANILA
NINOY AQUINO
INTL. (MNL)
Hagonoy
Sangley Pt.
Marine
Pond
Bicutan
Las Piñas
Mabato
Pt.
Cavite
Bamboo Organ
Bacoor Bay
Parañaque
Bagumbayan
Bacoor
Manila
Memorial
Park
Sucat
Binacayan
Zapote
Laguna
de Bay
Kawit
Muntinlupa
Bule
Habay
East from Greenwich

COPYRIGHT PHILIP'S

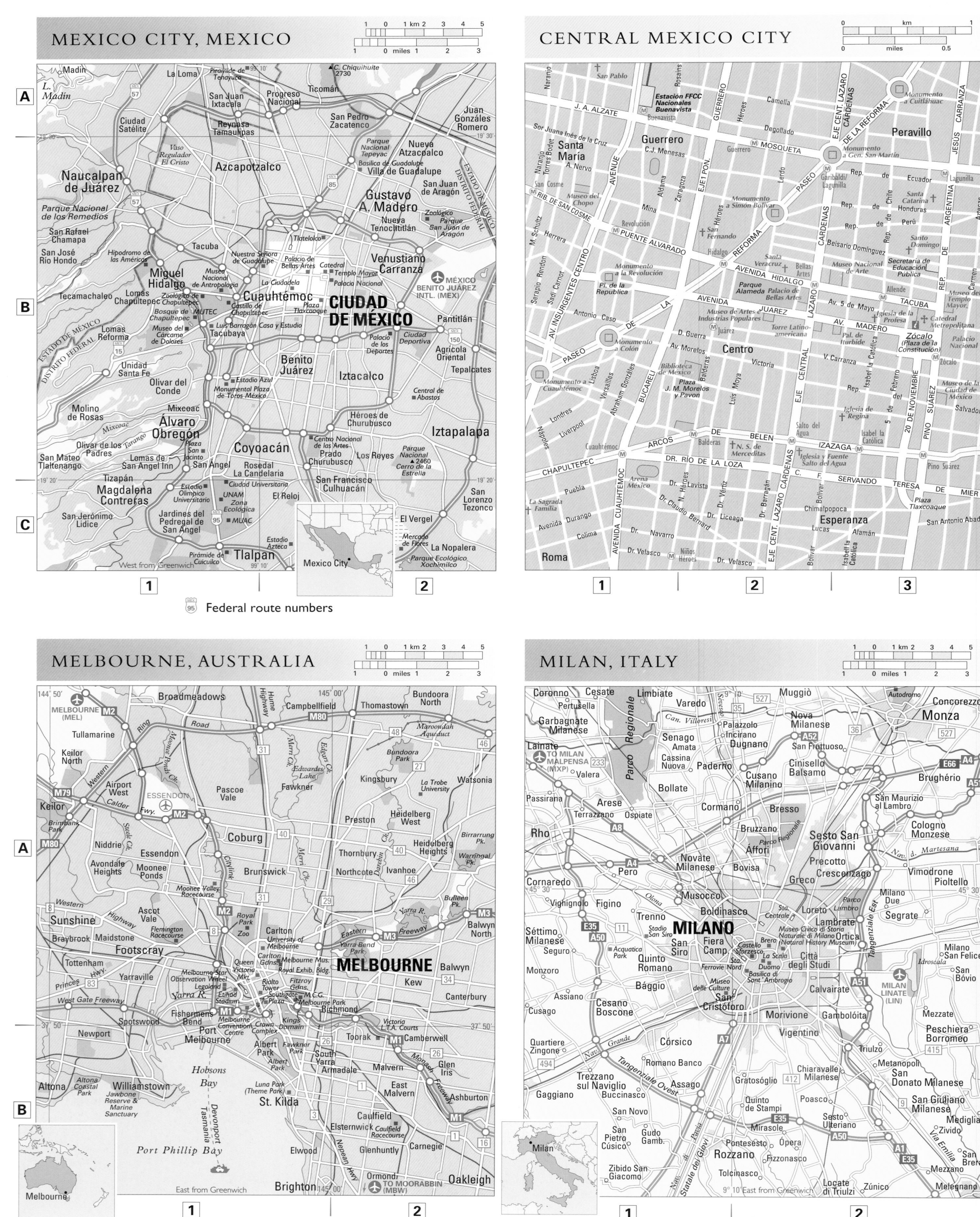

MEXICO CITY, MEXICO

CENTRAL MEXICO CITY

95 Federal route numbers

MELBOURNE, AUSTRALIA

MILAN, ITALY

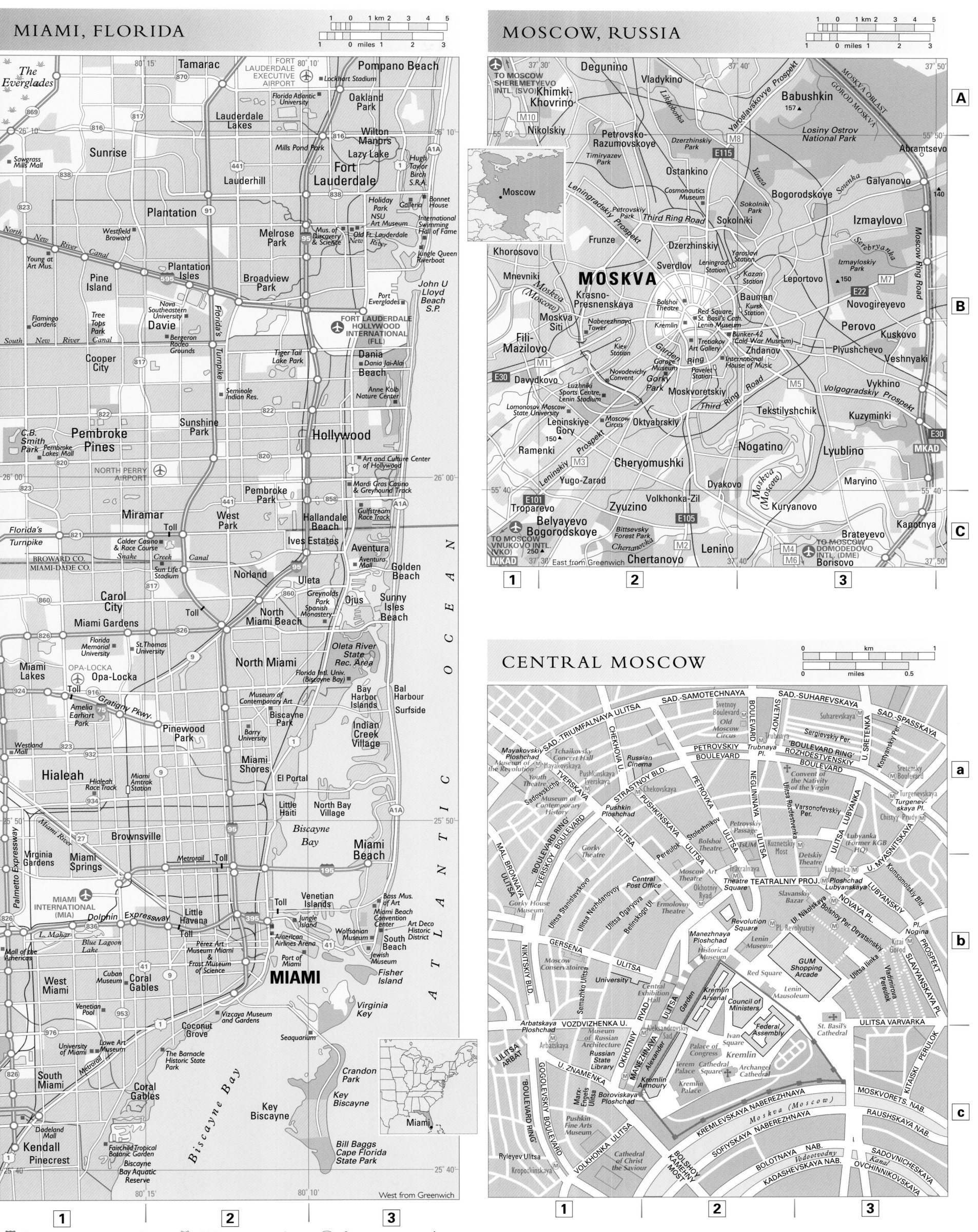

MIAMI, FLORIDA

The Everglades · Tamarac · FORT LAUDERDALE EXECUTIVE AIRPORT · Pompano Beach · Lockhart Stadium · Oakland Park · Lauderdale Lakes · Florida Atlantic University · Wilton Manors · Lazy Lake · Hugh Taylor Birch S.R.A. · Sunrise · Lauderhill · Mills Pond Park · Fort Lauderdale · Sawgrass Mills Mall · Plantation · Melrose Park · Holiday Park NSU Art Museum · Bonnet House · Old Ft. Lauderdale River · International Swimming Hall of Fame · Mus. of Discovery & Science · Westfield Broward · Nova Southeastern University · Plantation Isles · Broadview Park · Jungle Queen Riverboat · Pine Island · Tree Tops Park · Davie · Bergeron Races Grounds · Tiger Tail Lake Park · Port Everglades · John U Lloyd Beach S.P. · Flamingo Gardens · Cooper City · Seminole Indian Res. · Dania · Dania Jai-Alai Beach · FORT LAUDERDALE HOLLYWOOD INTERNATIONAL (FLL) · C.B. Smith Park · Pembroke Lakes Mall · Pembroke Pines · Sunshine Park · Anne Kolb Nature Center · NORTH PERRY AIRPORT · Hollywood · Art and Culture Center of Hollywood · Miramar · Pembroke Park · Mardi Gras Casino & Greyhound Track · West Park · Hallandale Beach · Gulfstream Race Track · Florida's Turnpike · Calder Casino & Race Course · Snake Creek Canal · Ives Estates · Aventura · Aventura Mall · BROWARD CO. MIAMI-DADE CO. · Carol City · Norland · Uleta · Golden Beach · Miami Gardens · Greynolds Park Spanish Monastery · Ojus · Sunny Isles Beach · Florida Memorial University · St. Thomas University · North Miami Beach · Oleta River State Rec. Area · Miami Lakes · OPA-LOCKA · Opa-Locka · North Miami · Museum of Contemporary Art · Bay Harbor Islands · Bal Harbour · Surfside · Amelia Earhart Park · Gratigny Pkwy. · Pinewood Park · Barry University · Biscayne Park · Indian Creek Village · Westland Mall · Florida Intl. Univ. (Biscayne Bay) · Hialeah · Hialeah Race Track · Miami Amtrak Station · Miami Shores · Little Haiti · North Bay Village · El Portal · Mall of the Americas · Miami Springs · Metrorail · Brownsville · Biscayne Bay · Miami Beach · Virginia Gardens · MIAMI INTERNATIONAL (MIA) · Dolphin Expressway · Little Havana · Venetian Islands · Bass Mus. of Art · Miami Beach Convention Center · Art Deco Historic District · L. Mahar · Blue Lagoon Lake · Pérez Art Museum Miami & Frost Museum of Science · American Airlines Arena · Jungle Island · Wolfsonian Museum · South Beach · Jewish Museum · Port of Miami · MIAMI · West Miami · Cuban Museum · Coral Gables · Fisher Island · Venetian Pool · Vizcaya Museum and Gardens · Virginia Key · University of Miami · Lowe Art Museum · Coconut Grove · Seaquarium · The Barnacle Historic State Park · Crandon Park · South Miami · Coral Gables · Key Biscayne · Dadeland Mall · Fairchild Tropical Botanic Garden · Kendall · Pinecrest · Biscayne Bay Aquatic Reserve · Bill Baggs Cape Florida State Park

West from Greenwich

Miami

MOSCOW, RUSSIA

TO MOSCOW SHEREMETYEVO INTL. (SVO) · Degunino · Vladykino · Khimki-Khovrino · Babushkin · GOROD MOSKVA · Nikolskiy · Petrovsko-Razumovskoye · Dzerzhinsky Park · Losiny Ostrov National Park · Abramtsevo · Ostankino · Timiryazev Park · Cosmonautics Museum · Sokolniki · Bogorodskoye · Galyanovo · Frunze · Petrovsky Park · Third Ring Road · Sokolniki · Izmaylovo · Khorosovo · Dzerzhinsky · Sverdlov · Yaroslav Station · Bauman · Leningrad Station · Kazan Station · Kursk Station · Leportovo · Izmayloskiy Park · Novogireyevo · MOSKVA · Bolshoi Theatre · Red Square, St. Basil's Cath. Lenin Museum · Mnevniki · Krasno-Presnenskaya · Kremlin · Bunker-42 (Cold War Museum) · Perovo · Kuskovo · Moskva Siti · Naberezhnyd Tower · Tretiakov Art Gallery · Zhdanov · Plyushchevo · Veshnyaki · Fili-Mazilovo · Kiev Station · Gorky Park · International House of Music · Davydkovo · Novodevichy Convent · Garden Ring · Pavelet Station · Moskvoretskiy · Vykhino · Volgogradskiy Prospekt · Luzhniki Sports Centre, Lenin Stadium · Third Ring Road · Tekstilyshchik · Kuzyminki · Lomonosov Moscow State University · Moscow Circus · Oktyabrskiy · Leninskie Gory · Leninskiy Prospekt · Moskva (Moscow) · Ramenki · Nogatino · Lyublino · Cheryomushki · Yugo-Zarad · Dyakovo · Maryino · Troparevo · Zyuzino · Volkhonka-Zil · Kuryanovo · Kapotnya · Belyayevo Bogorodskoye · Bittsevsky Forest Park · Lenino · Brateyevo · TO MOSCOW VNUKOVO INTL. (VKO) · Chertanovka · TO MOSCOW DOMODEDOVO INTL. (DME) · Borisovo · Chertanovo

East from Greenwich

CENTRAL MOSCOW

SAD.-TRIUMFALNAYA ULITSA · SAD.-SAMOTECHNAYA · SAD.-SUHAREVSKAYA · SAD.-SPASSKAYA · Svetnoy Boulevard · Old Moscow Circus · Mayakovski Ploshchad · Tchaikovsky Concert Hall · Mayakovskaya · Museum of the Revolution · Russian Cinema · Suharevskaya · U. SRETENKA · BOULEVARD RING · Suvorovskiy Per. · Sergievskiy Per. · Sretensky Boulevard · Youth Theatre · Pushkinskaya · Trubnaya Pl. · BOULEVARD RING ROZHDESTVENSKY · Chistiy Prudy · Turgenevskaya Pl. · MAL. BRONNAYA · TVERSKOY BOULEVARD · Sadovskaya · Pushkin Ploshchad · Chekovskaya · PETROVKA · BOULEVARD · Stolesnikov · Varsonofevskiy Per. · Turgenevskaya · Lubyanka (Former KGB HQ) · Gorky Theatre · Pushkinskaya ULITSA · NEGLINNAYA ULITSA · Petrovsky Passage · ULITSA MYASNITSKAYA · NIKITSKIY BLD. · GERSENA ULITSA · Bolshoi Theatre · TsUM · Kuznetsky Most · NOVAYA PL. · Moscow Conservatoire · University · Central Exhibition Hall · Moscow Art Theatre · Okhotnov Ryad · Theatralniy Proj. · Ploshchad Lubyanskaya · LUBYANSKY · Ermolovoy Theatre · Teatralniy Square · Slavansky Bazar · Uli. Nikolskaya · Kitai Gored · Bolshoy Per. Devyatinskiy · Pl. Nogina · Gorky House Museum · Revolution Square · Manezhnaya Ploshchad · Lenin Museum · GUM Shopping Arcade · Vladimirova Pereulok · PROSPEKT · Arbatskaya Ploshchad · Historical Museum · ULITSA VARVARKA · VOZDVIZHENKA U. · Museum of Russian Architecture · Russian State Library · Aleksandrovsky Sad · Alexander Garden · Kremlin Arsenal · Red Square · Lenin Mausoleum · St. Basil's Cathedral · ULITSA ARBAT · Terem Palace · Kremlin · Ivan Palace of Congress · Palace of Congress · Council of Ministers · Federal Assembly · KITAISKI PEREULOK · U. ZNAMENKA · Kremlin Square · Archangel Cathedral · MOSKVORETS. NAB. · GOGOLEVSKY BOULEVARD · Borovitskaya Ploshchad · Marx-Engels Ploshchad · Kremlin Armoury · Pushkin Fine Arts Museum · Ryleyev Ulitsa · VOLKHONKA ULITSA · Moskva (Moscow) · KREMLEVSKAYA NABEREZHNAYA · RAUSHSKAYA NAB. · 'BOULEVARD RING · Kropotkinskaya · Cathedral of Christ the Saviour · SOFIYSKAYA NABEREZHNAYA · NAB. · Vodootvodny · SADOVNICHESKAYA · BOLSHOY KAMENNY MOST · Bolotnaya · Kanal OVCHINNIKOVSKAYA · KADASHEVSKAYA NAB.

COPYRIGHT PHILIP'S

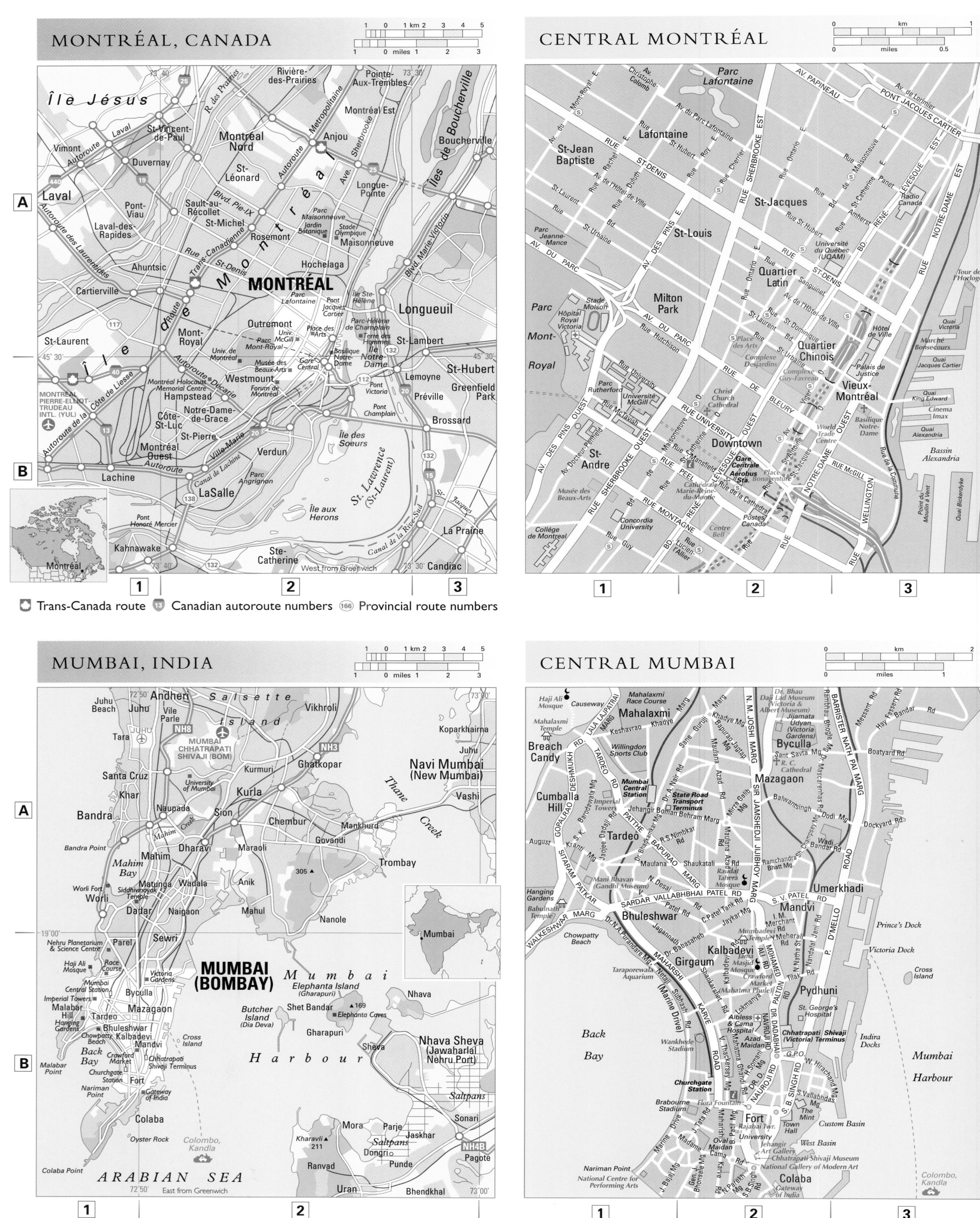

MUNICH, GERMANY

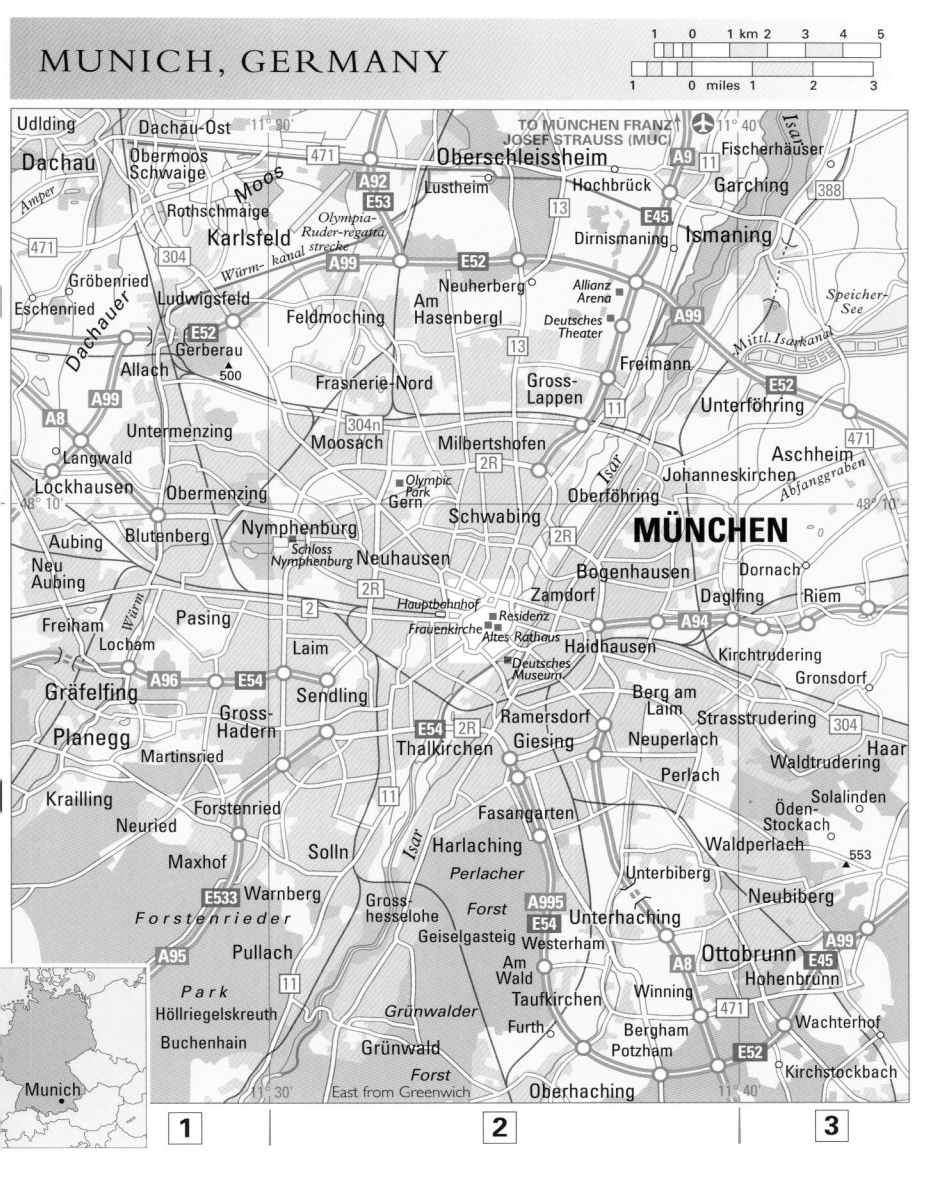

CENTRAL MUNICH

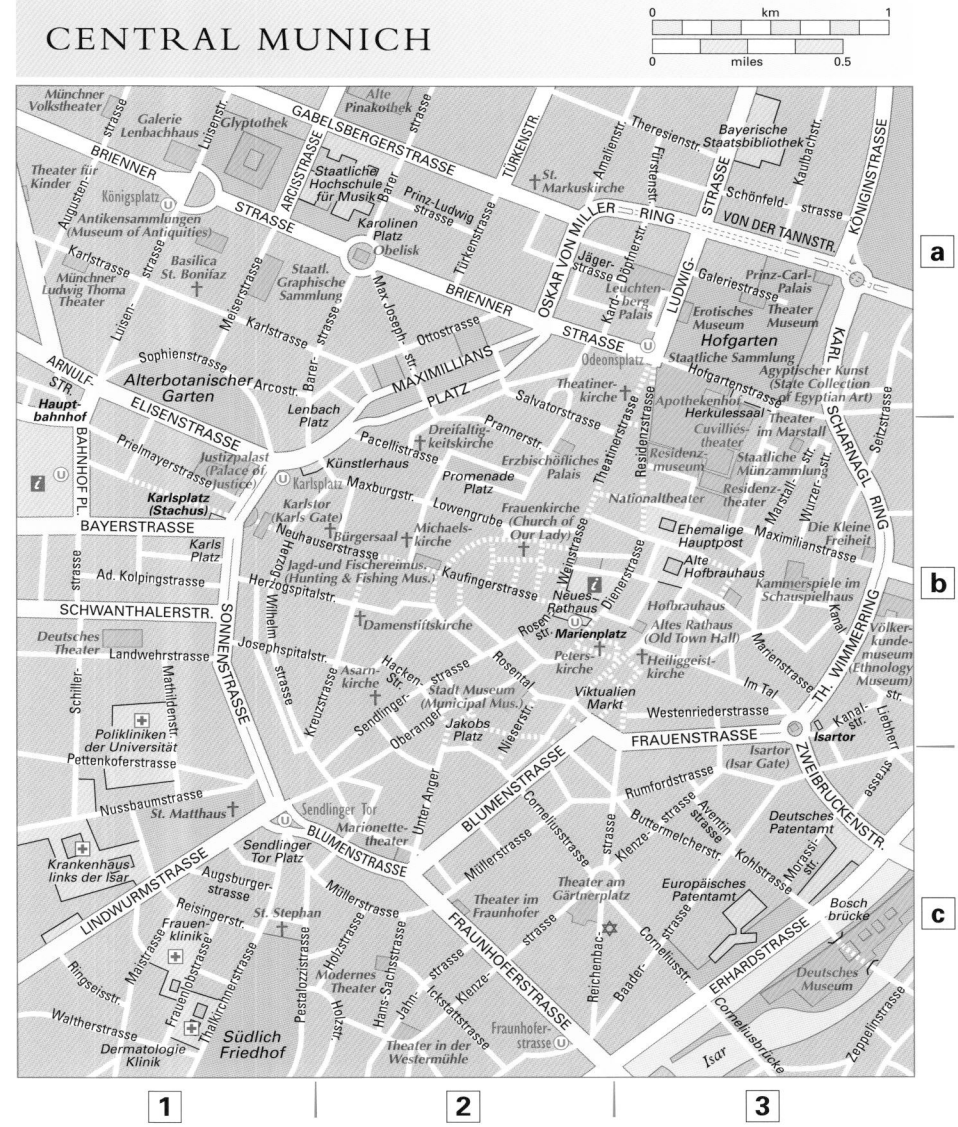

NEW ORLEANS, LOUISIANA

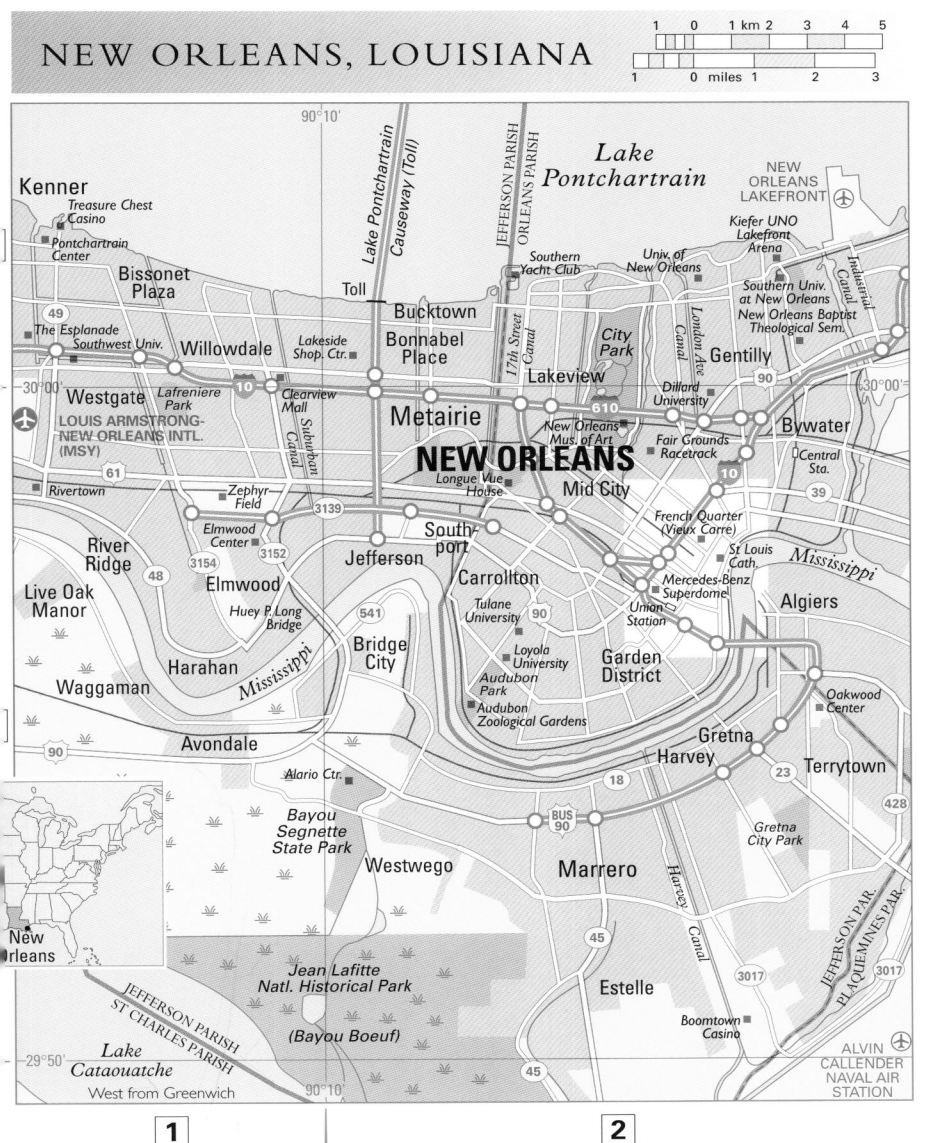

CENTRAL NEW ORLEANS

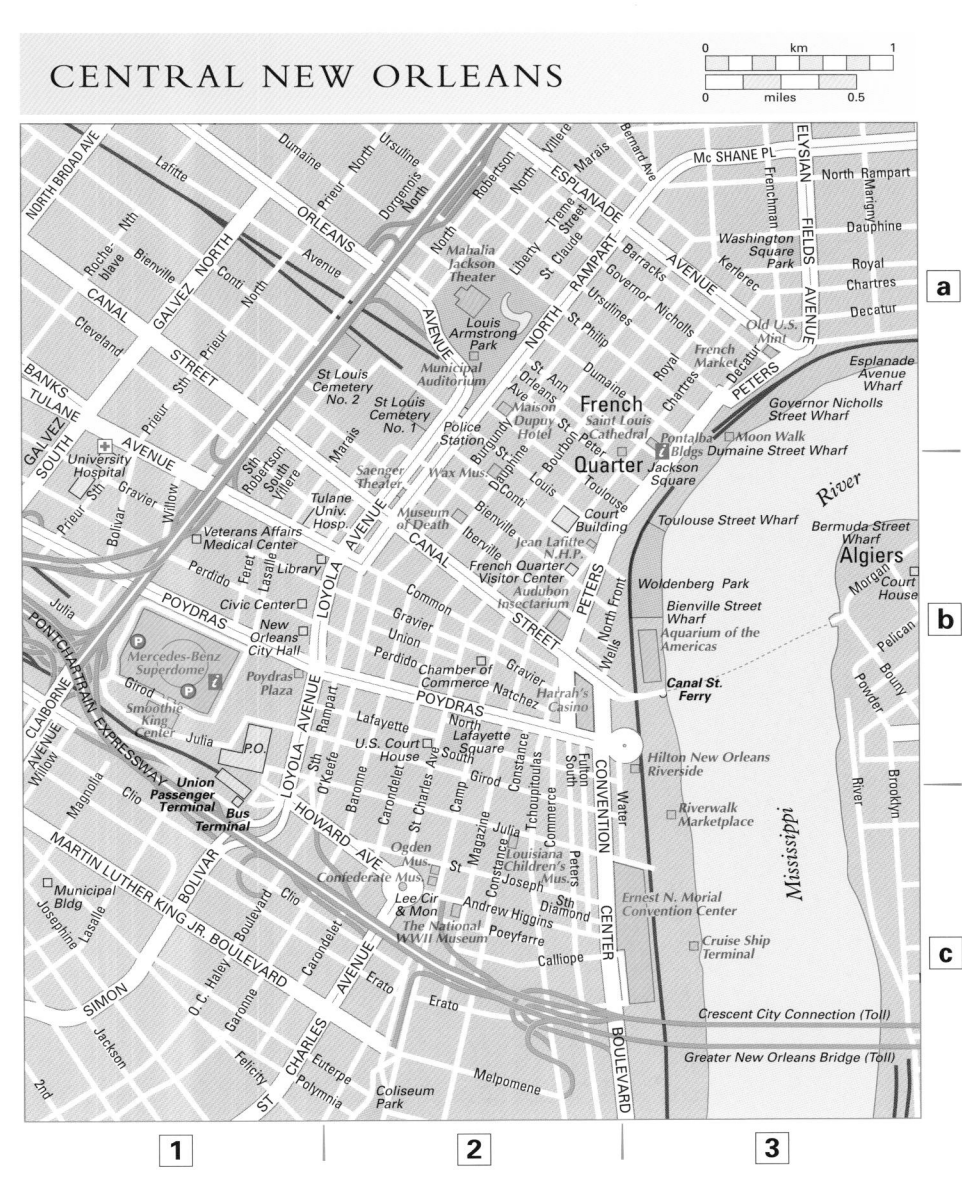

 Interstate route numbers   (17) U.S. route numbers   (417) State route numbers

COPYRIGHT PHILIP'S

NEW YORK, NEW YORK

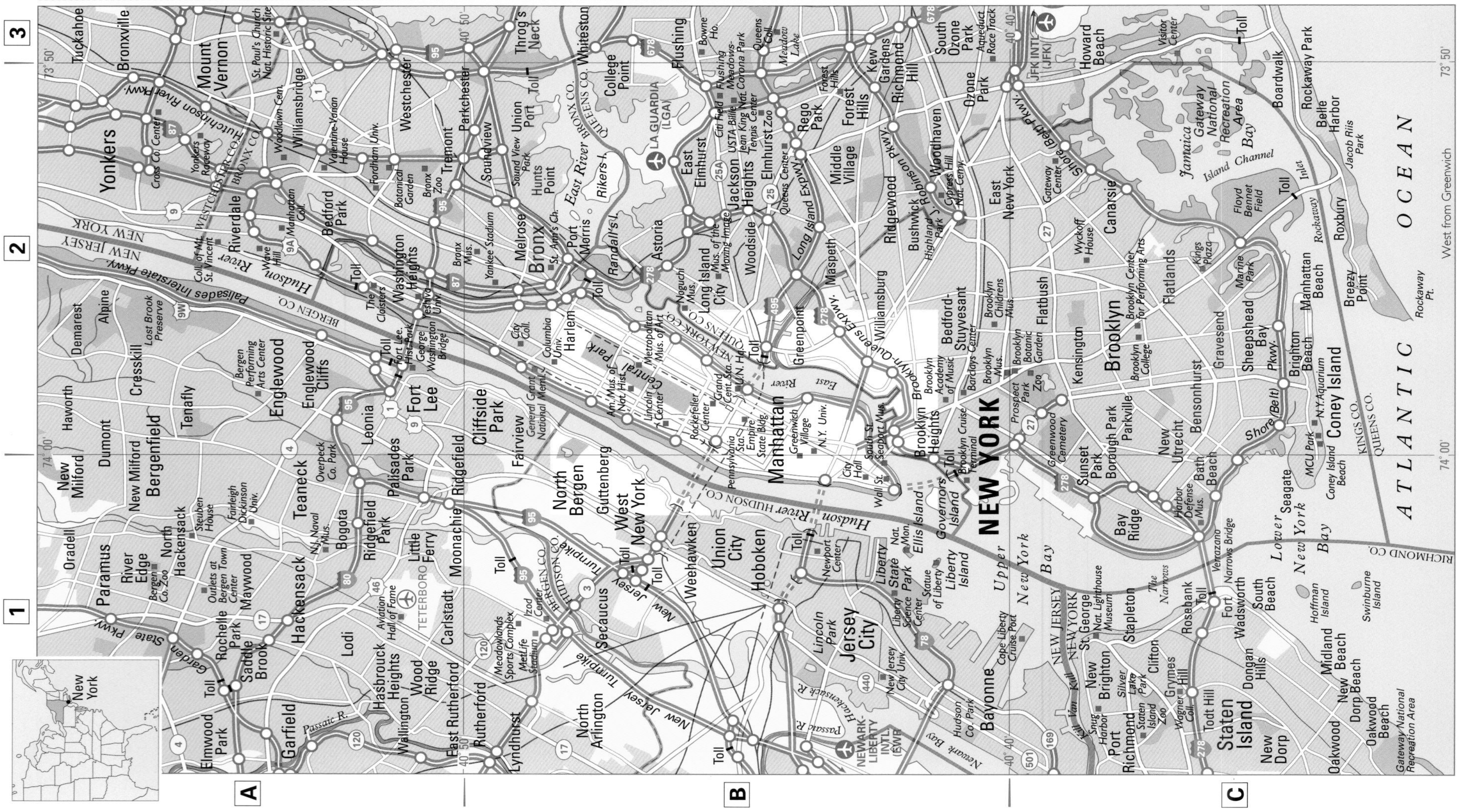

1 0 1 km 2 3 4 5
1 0 miles 1 2 3

West from Greenwich

ATLANTIC OCEAN

NEW YORK

Manhattan · Bronx · Brooklyn · Queens · Staten Island

Yonkers · Mount Vernon · Bronxville · Tuckahoe · Westchester · Paramus · Hackensack · Englewood · Fort Lee · Hoboken · Jersey City · Bayonne · Union City · Weehawken · West New York · North Bergen · Coney Island · Rego Park · Forest Hills · Flushing · Howard Beach · Rockaway Park · Gateway National Recreation Area

LA GUARDIA (LGA) · JFK INT'L (JFK) · NEWARK LIBERTY INT'L (EWR)

CENTRAL NEW YORK

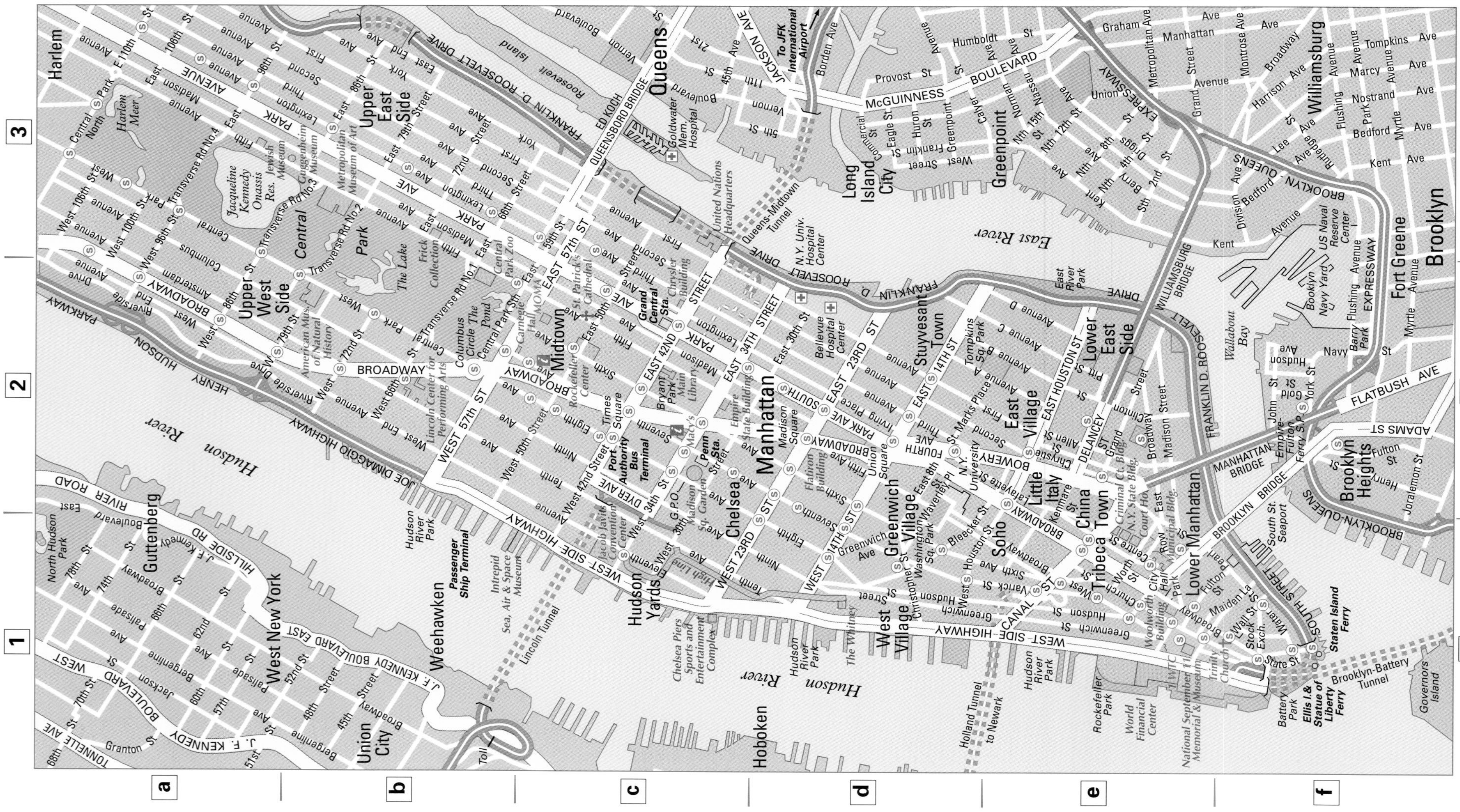

0 1 km 2
0 miles 1

Hudson River · East River

Harlem · Upper West Side · Upper East Side · Central Park · Midtown · Chelsea · Greenwich Village · East Village · Lower East Side · Soho · Little Italy · China Town · Tribeca · Lower Manhattan · Manhattan

Queens · Long Island City · Greenpoint · Williamsburg · Fort Greene · Brooklyn Heights · Brooklyn

Times Square · Broadway · Grand Central Sta. · Penn Sta. · Port Authority Bus Terminal · United Nations Headquarters · World Financial Center · National September 11 Memorial & Museum · Statue of Liberty · Ellis Island · Staten Island Ferry

ORLANDO, FLORIDA

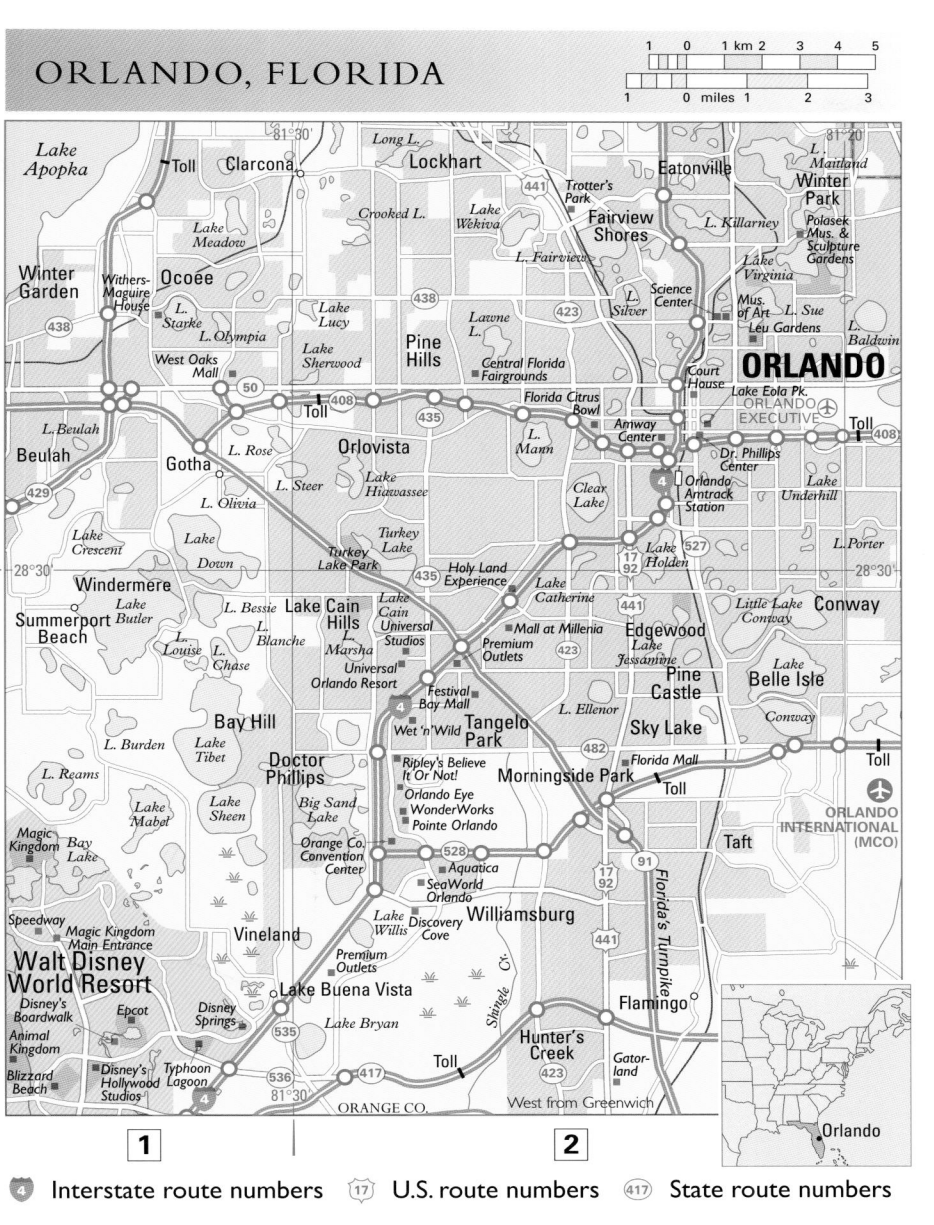

OSAKA, JAPAN

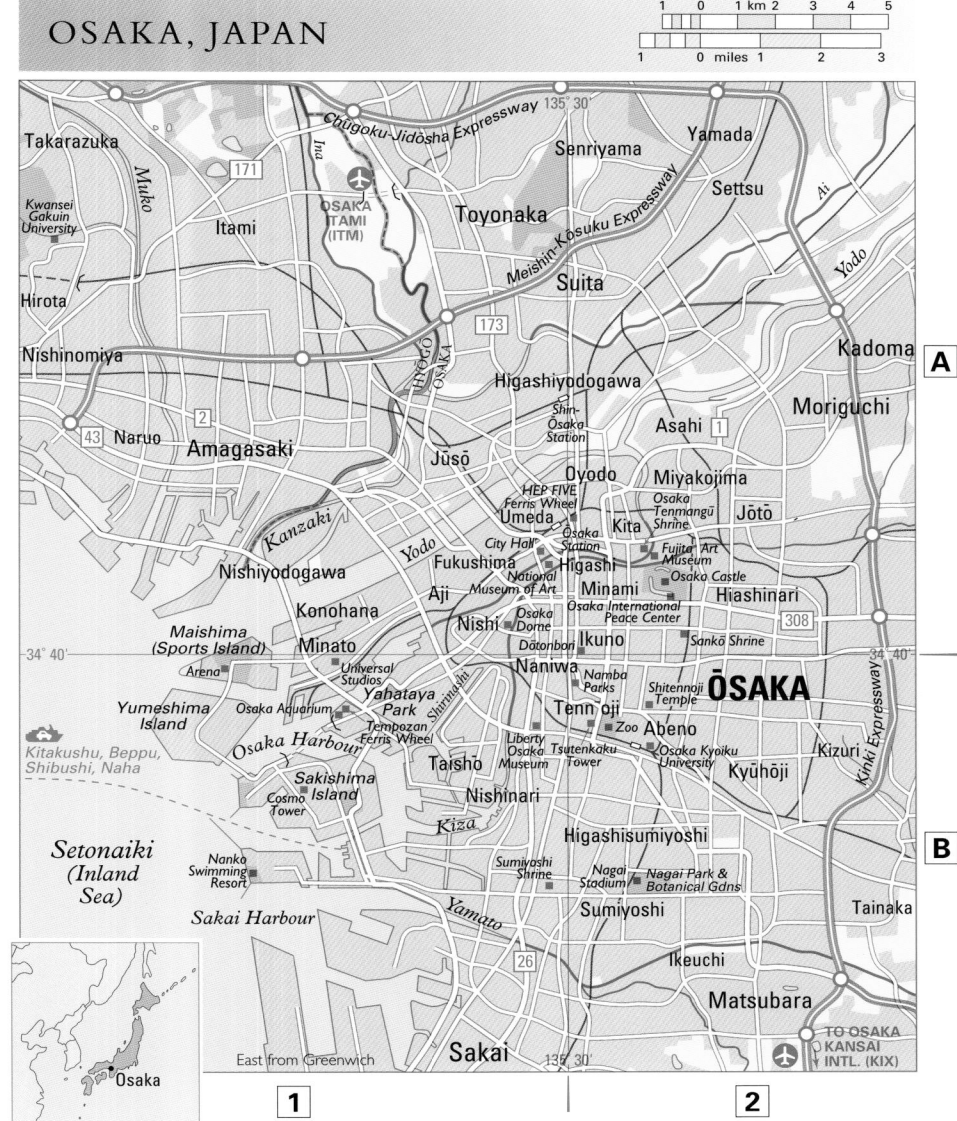

4 Interstate route numbers   **17** U.S. route numbers   **417** State route numbers

OSLO, NORWAY

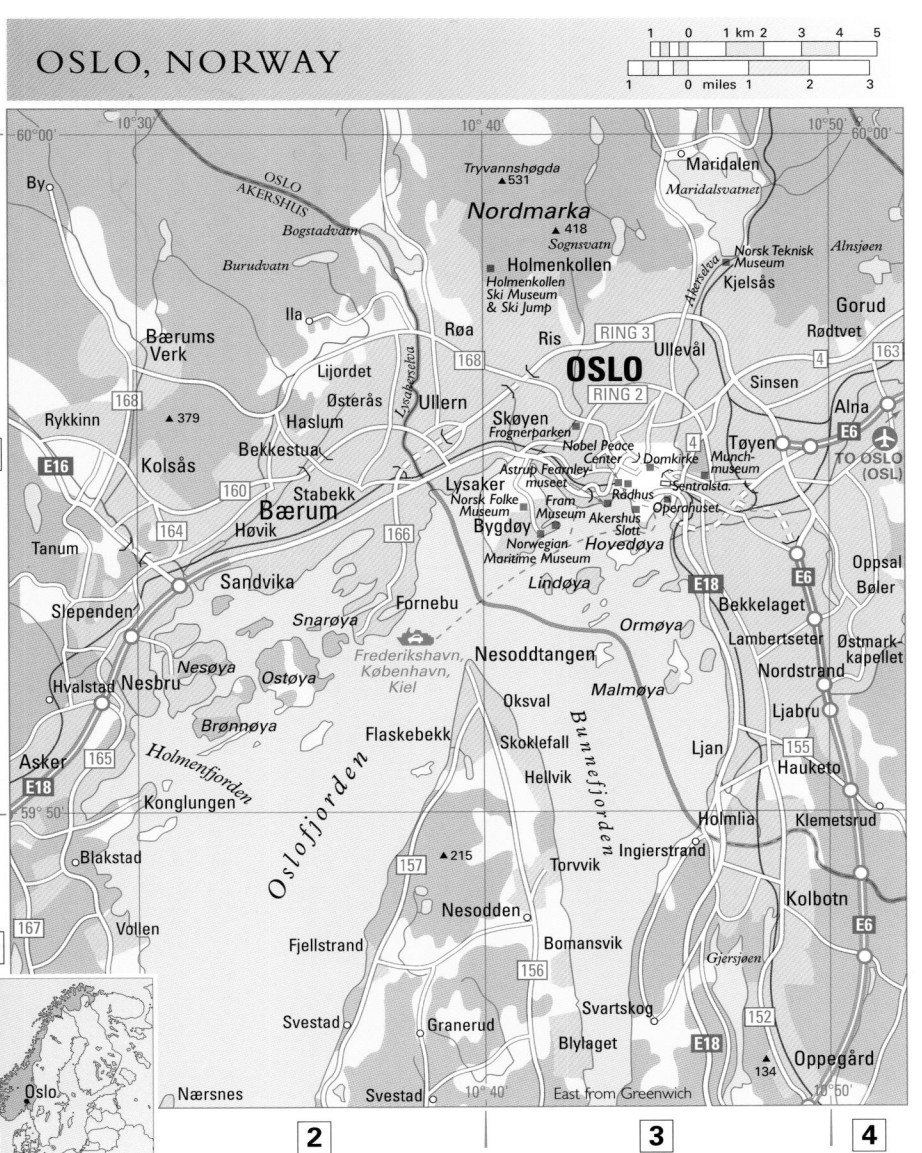

CENTRAL OSLO

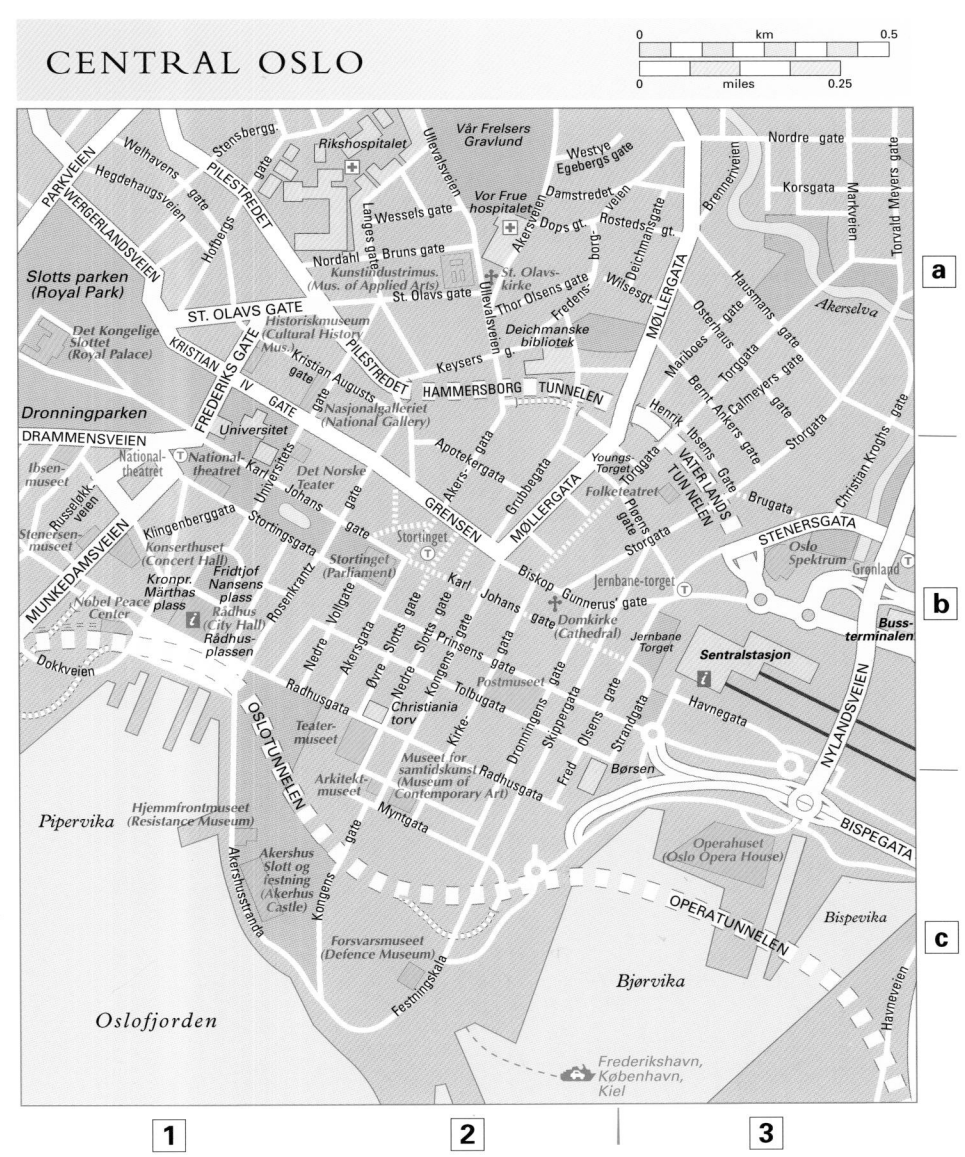

PARIS, FRANCE

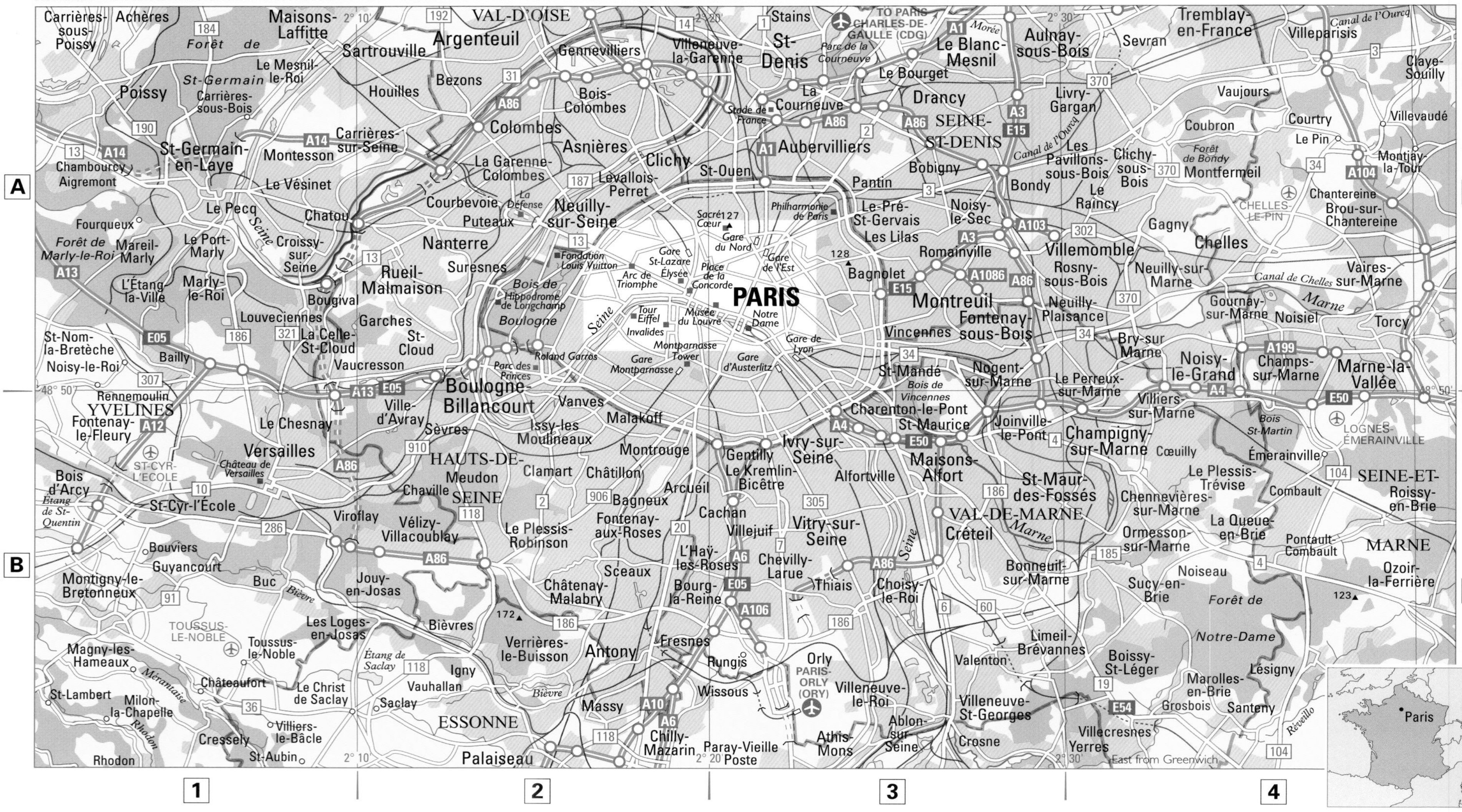

1 0 1 km 2 3 4 5
1 0 miles 1 2 3

VAL-D'OISE

Carrières-sous-Poissy · Achères · Maisons-Laffitte · Argenteuil · Gennevilliers · Villeneuve-la-Garenne · Stains · St-Denis · Aulnay-sous-Bois · Sevran · Tremblay-en-France · Villeparisis

Forêt de St-Germain · Sartrouville · Houilles · Bezons · Bois-Colombes · La Courneuve · Le Bourget · Le Blanc-Mesnil · Drancy · Livry-Gargan · Vaujours · Claye-Souilly

Poissy · Carrières-sous-Bois · Colombes · Asnières · St-Ouen · Aubervilliers · SEINE-ST-DENIS · Les Pavillons-sous-Bois · Forêt de Bondy · Coubron · Courtry

St-Germain-en-Laye · Montesson · Carrières-sur-Seine · La Garenne-Colombes · Clichy · Pantin · Bobigny · Romainville · Le Pré-St-Gervais · Le Raincy · Montfermeil · Chanterein · Brou-sur-Chantereine

Chambourcy · Aigremont · Le Pecq · Chatou · Courbevoie · Puteaux · Neuilly-sur-Seine · La Défense · Noisy-le-Sec · Villemomble · Rosny-sous-Bois · Neuilly-Plaisance · Chelles · Le Pin

Fourqueux · Mareil-Marly · Le Port-Marly · Croissy-sur-Seine · Nanterre · Suresnes · Sacré Cœur · Philharmonie de Paris · Les Lilas · Bagnolet · Montreuil · Gagny · Vaires-sur-Marne

Forêt de Marly-le-Roi · Bougival · Rueil-Malmaison · Bois de Boulogne · Gare du Nord · Gare de l'Est · Fondation Louis Vuitton · Arc de Triomphe · Place de la Concorde · **PARIS** · Notre Dame · Vincennes · Fontenay-sous-Bois · Gournay-sur-Marne · Noisiel · Torcy

L'Étang-la-Ville · Bailly · Louveciennes · Garches · St-Cloud · Hippodrome de Longchamp · Tour Eiffel · Musée du Louvre · Invalides · Gare de Lyon · St-Mandé · Bois de Vincennes · Nogent-sur-Marne · Le Perreux-sur-Marne · Noisy-le-Grand · Champs-sur-Marne · Marne-la-Vallée

St-Nom-la-Bretèche · Noisy-le-Roi · La Celle-St-Cloud · Vaucresson · Boulogne-Billancourt · Roland Garros · Parc des Princes · Montparnasse · Tour Montparnasse · Gare d'Austerlitz · Charenton-le-Pont · St-Maurice · Joinville-le-Pont · Villiers-sur-Marne · Émerainville · LOGNES EMERAINVILLE

Rennemoulin · YVELINES · Fontenay-le-Fleury · Le Chesnay · Sèvres · Ville-d'Avray · Vanves · Issy-les-Moulineaux · Malakoff · Ivry-sur-Seine · Maisons-Alfort · Champigny-sur-Marne · Le Plessis-Trévise · SEINE-ET-MARNE

Bois d'Arcy · Versailles · Château de Versailles · HAUTS-DE-SEINE · Meudon · Chaville · Clamart · Montrouge · Gentilly · Le Kremlin-Bicêtre · Alfortville · St-Maur-des-Fossés · Chennevières-sur-Marne · Combault · Roissy-en-Brie

St-Cyr-l'École · Viroflay · Vélizy-Villacoublay · Bagneux · Châtillon · Arcueil · Cachan · Vitry-sur-Seine · Créteil · VAL-DE-MARNE · Ormesson-sur-Marne · La Queue-en-Brie · Pontault-Combault

Bouviers · Guyancourt · Le Plessis-Robinson · Fontenay-aux-Roses · Villejuif · L'Haÿ-les-Roses · Chevilly-Larue · Choisy-le-Roi · Bonneuil-sur-Marne · Sucy-en-Brie · Noiseau · MARNE

Montigny-le-Bretonneux · Jouy-en-Josas · Sceaux · Châtenay-Malabry · Bourg-la-Reine · Thiais · Limeil-Brévannes · Forêt de Notre-Dame · Ozoir-la-Ferrière

Magny-les-Hameaux · Les Loges-en-Josas · Bièvres · Verrières-le-Buisson · Antony · Fresnes · Rungis · Orly · Valenton · Boissy-St-Léger · Marolles-en-Brie · Lésigny

St-Lambert · Toussus-le-Noble · Igny · Vauhallan · Saclay · Massy · Wissous · PARIS-ORLY (ORY) · Villeneuve-le-Roi · Crosne · Villecresnes · Santeny

Cresnely · St-Aubin · Le Christ de Saclay · ESSONNE · Chilly-Mazarin · Paray-Vieille-Poste · Athis-Mons · Ablon-sur-Seine · Villeneuve-St-Georges · Grosbois · Rhodon · Palaiseau

East from Greenwich

Paris

1 2 3 4
A B

CENTRAL PARIS

0 km 1
0 miles 0.5

Montmartre · Sacré Cœur · Av. de la Pte. de Champerret · Clinique Hartmann · Bois de Boulogne · Fondation Louis Vuitton (Art Gallery) · Porte Maillot · Palais des Congrès · Parc Monceau · Gare St-Lazare · Gare du Nord · Gare de l'Est · Canal St-Martin · Canal de l'Ourcq

PORTE DAUPHINE · Université Paris IX · Arc de Triomphe · Av. des Champs Elysées · Place de la Concorde · Jardin des Tuileries · Musée du Louvre (Louvre Museum) · Les Halles · Centre Pompidou (Beaubourg) · Le Marais · Place des Vosges · Place de la République

PORTE DE LA MUETTE · Musée Guimet (Guimet Mus.) · Palais de Chaillot (Chaillot Palace) · Musée du quai Branly · Grand Palais · Petit Palais · Assemblée Nationale · Musée d'Orsay (Orsay Museum) · Hôtel de Ville · Musée Picasso · Place de la Bastille

Maison de Radio France · Tour Eiffel (Eiffel Tower) · Parc du Champ de Mars · Invalides · Musée Rodin · UNESCO · École Militaire · St-Germain-des-Prés · Notre Dame · Île de la Cité · Île St-Louis · Quartier Latin · Sorbonne · Panthéon · Jardin du Luxembourg · Palais du Luxembourg · Luxembourg · Gare de Lyon

1 2 3 4 5
a b c

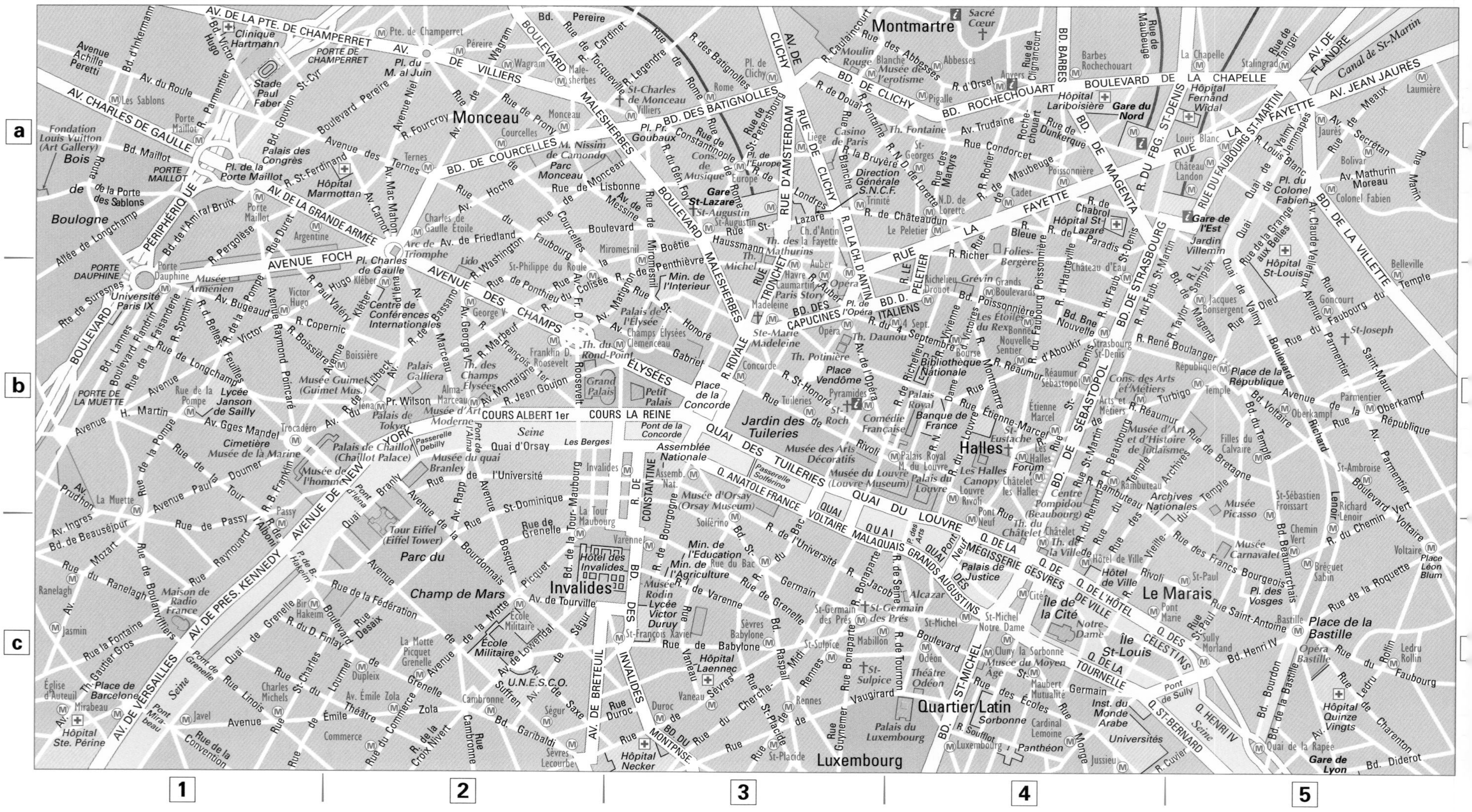

COPYRIGHT PHILIP'S

PRAGUE, CZECHIA

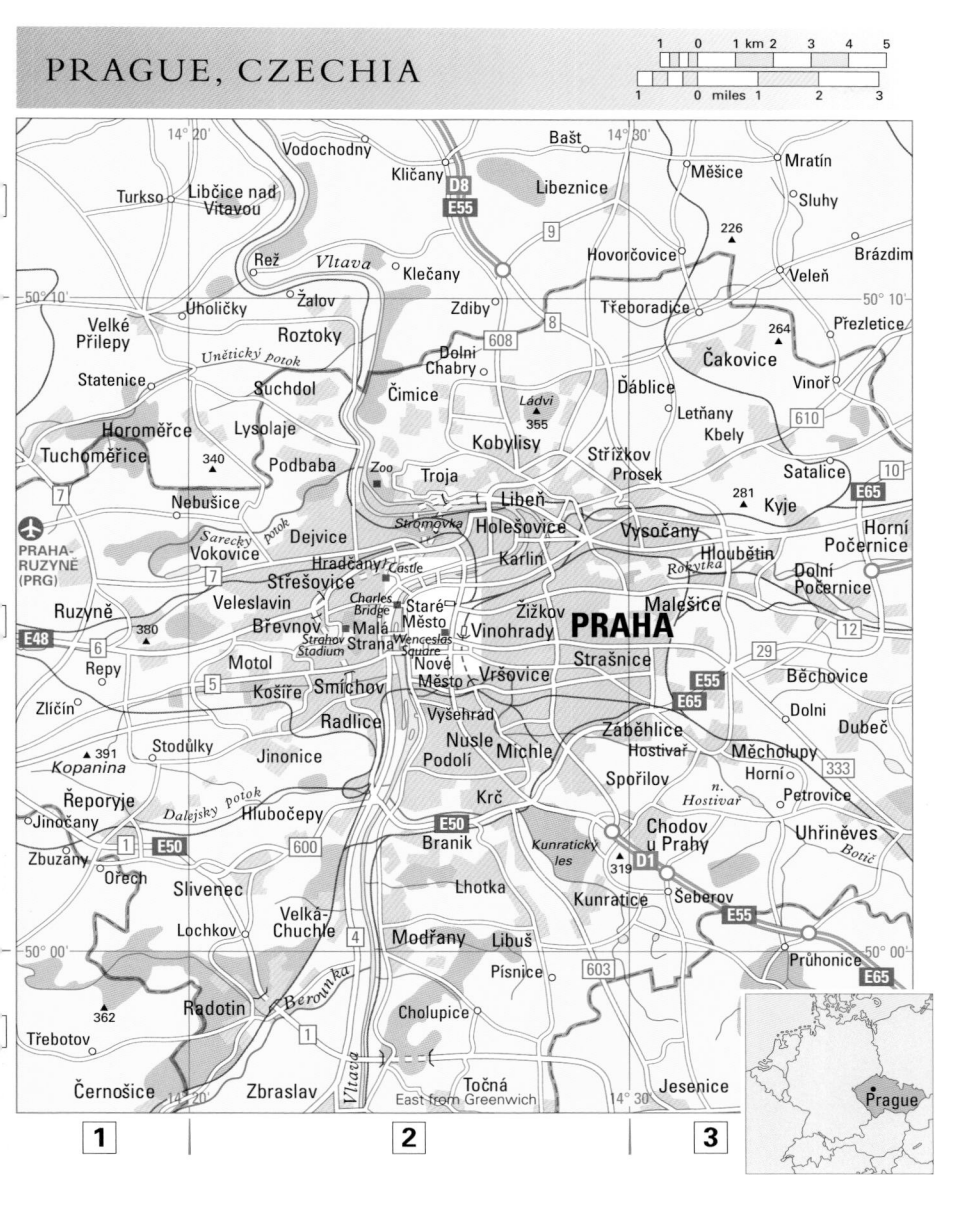

CENTRAL PRAGUE

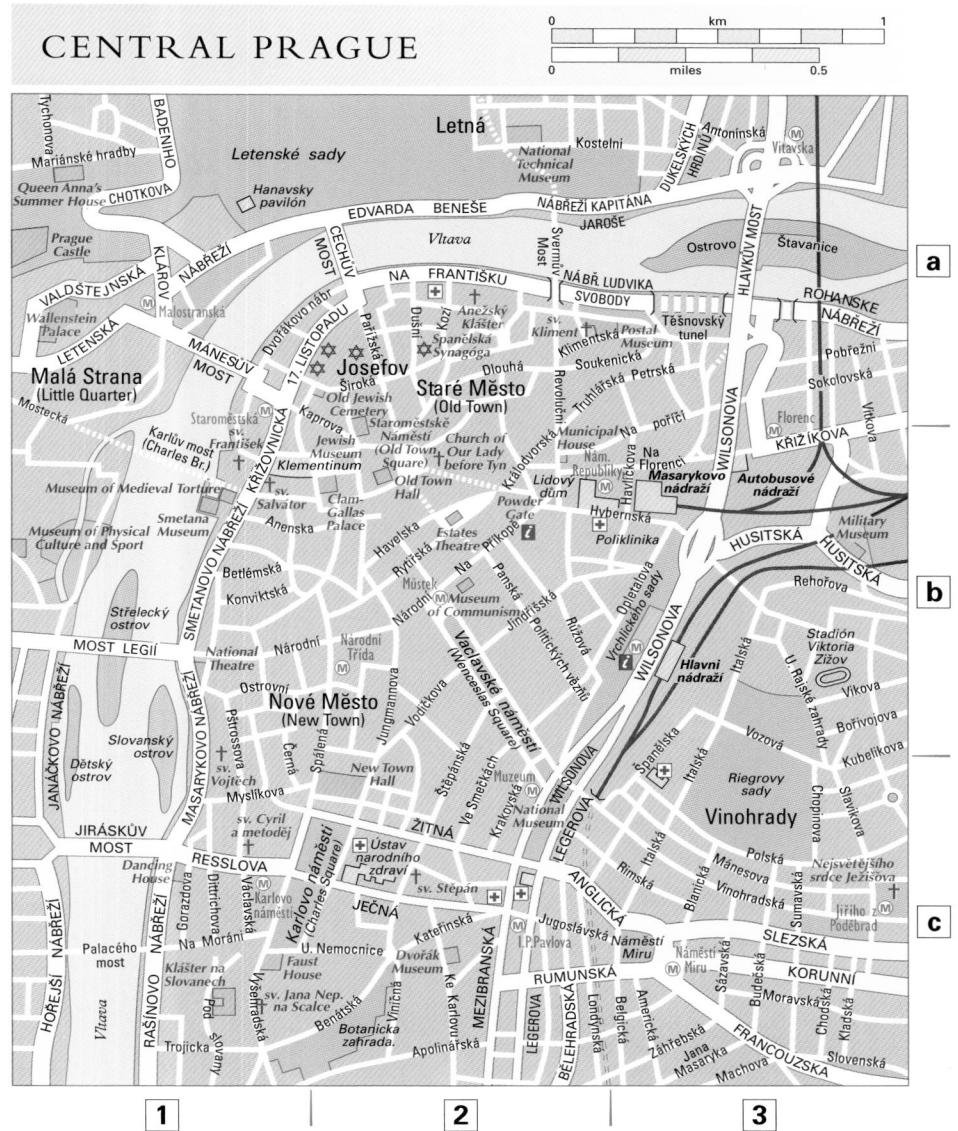

RIO DE JANEIRO, BRAZIL

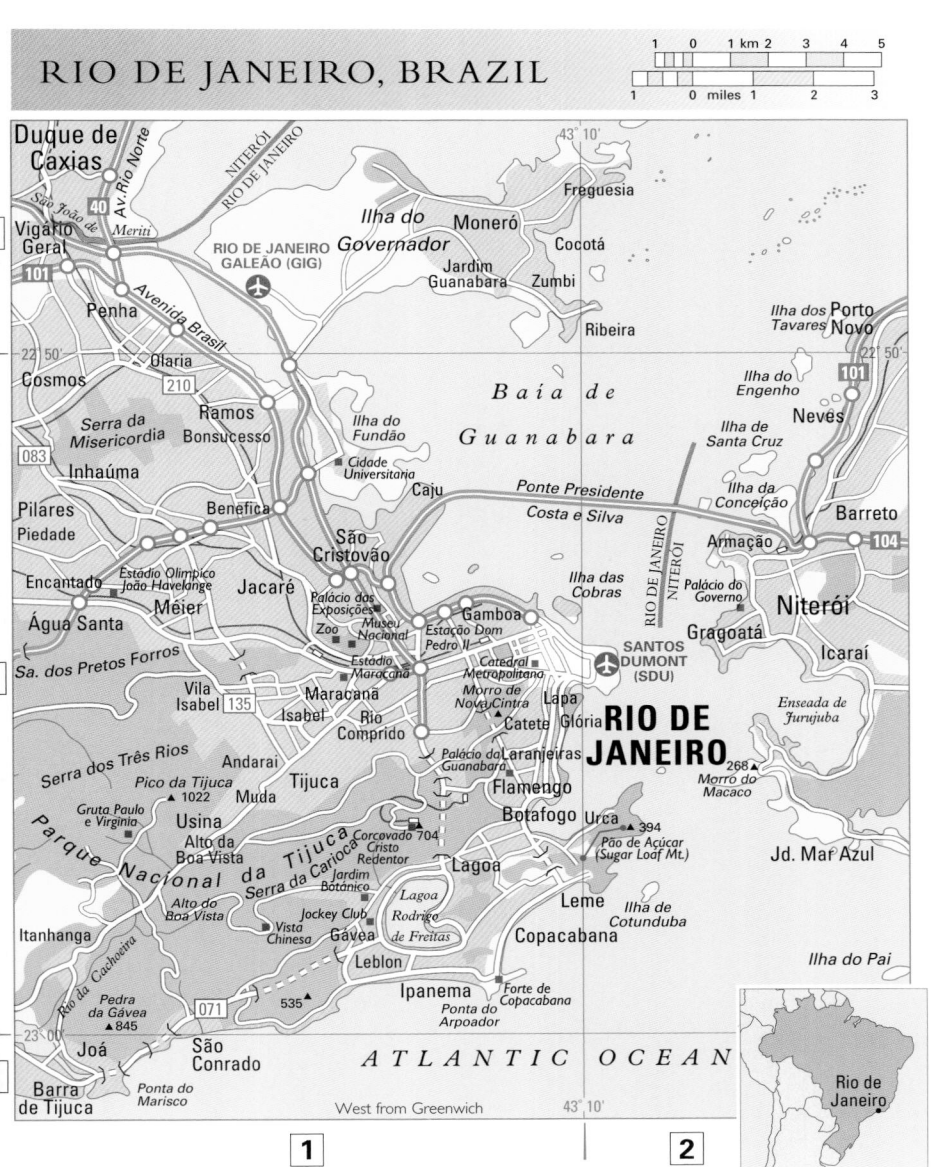

CENTRAL RIO DE JANEIRO

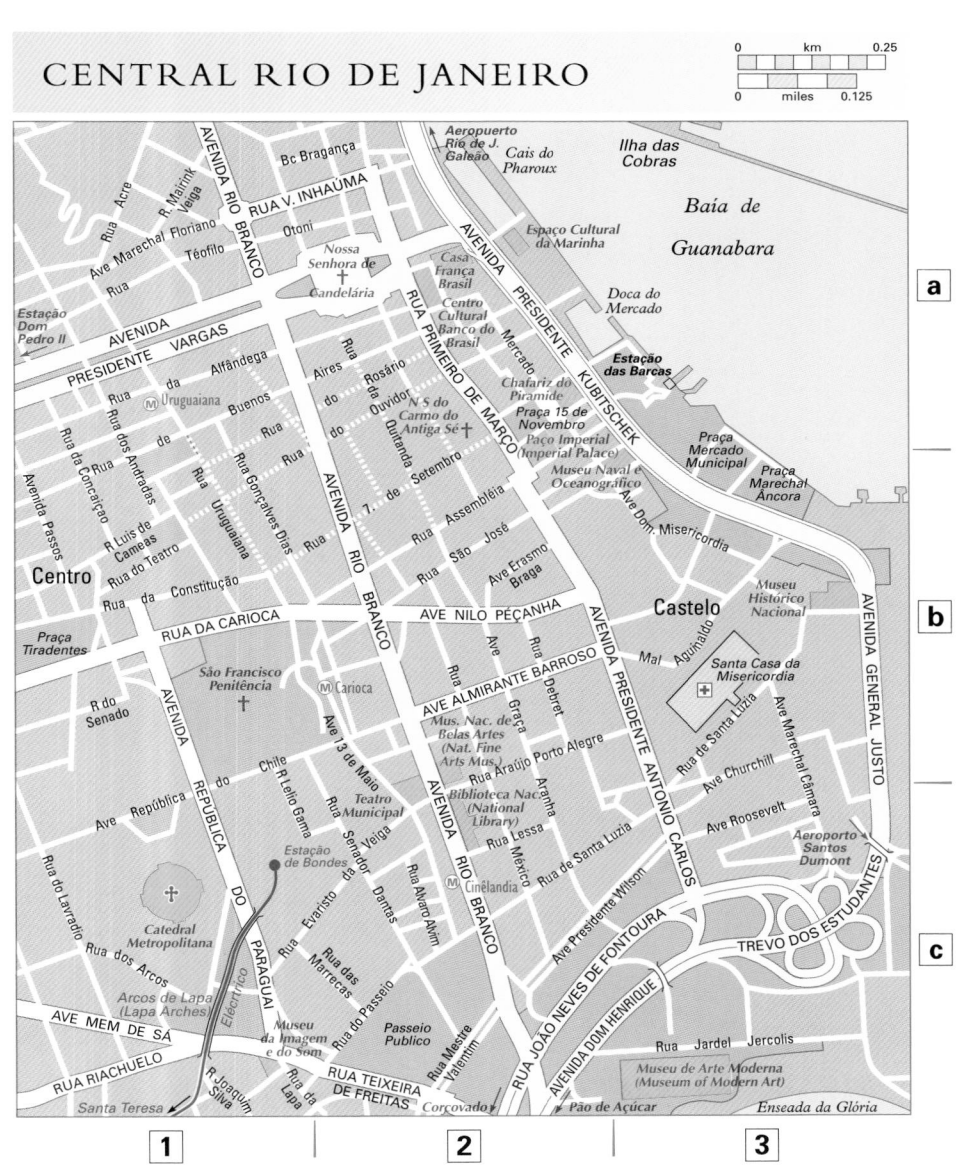

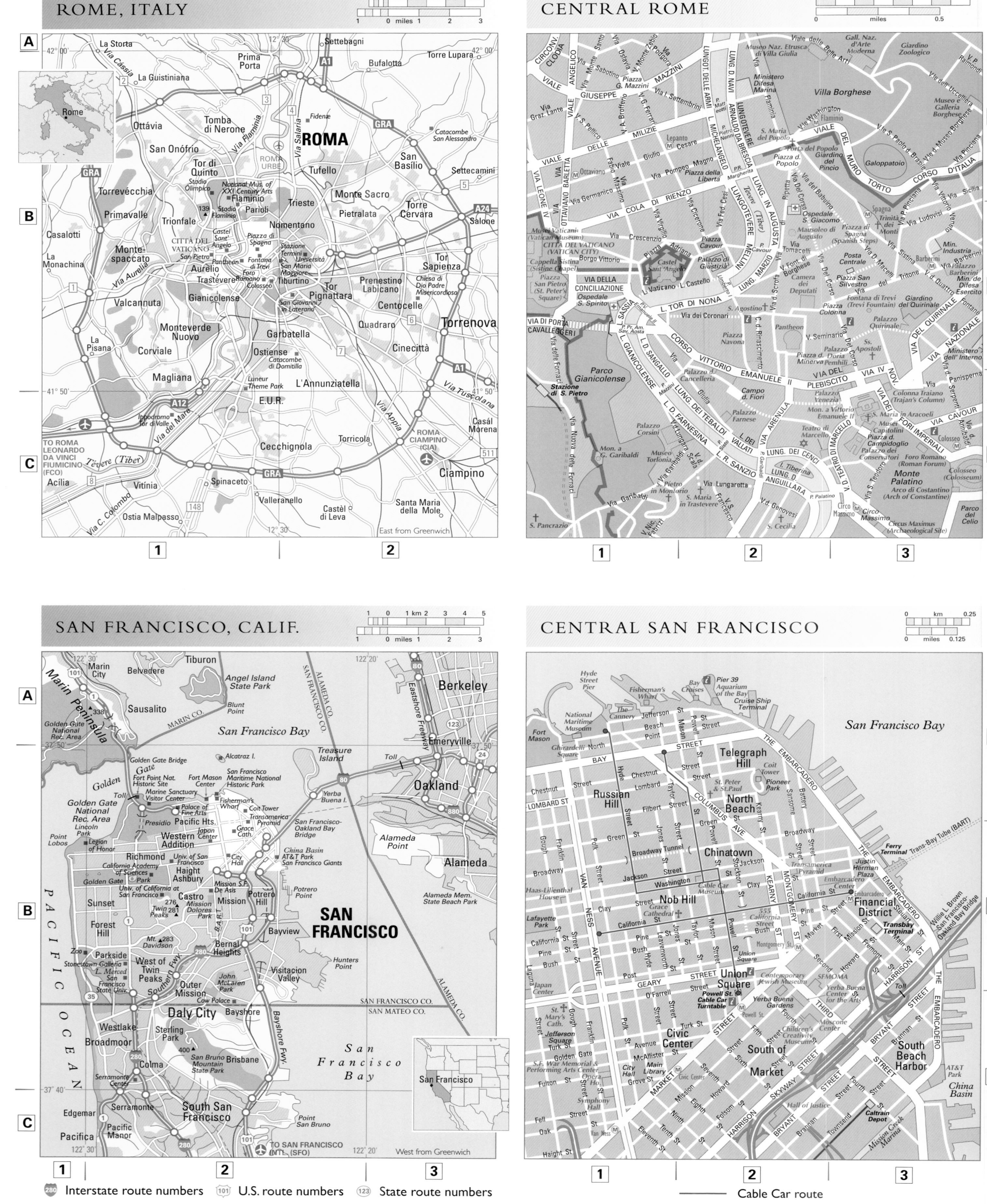

ROME, ITALY

1 0 1 km 2 3 4 5
1 0 miles 1 2 3

A 42° 00′ 12° 20′
La Storta
Prima Porta
Settebagni
Bufalotta
Torre Lupara
42° 00′ A1
Via Cassia
La Guistiniana
Fidene
Tomba di Nerone
GRA
Catacombe San Alessandro
Ottávia
San Onófrio
ROMA
San Basílio
Settecamini
Tor di Quinto
ROMA URBE
Tufello
Monte Sacro
Via Flaminia
Via Salaria
A24
Torrevécchia
National Mus of XXI Century Arts Flaminio
Stadio Olimpico
Trieste
Torre Cervara
Salone
B Primavalle
Trionfale
139 Stadio Flaminio
Parioli
Nomentano
Pietralata
Casalotti
CITTÀ DEL VATICANO
Piazza di Spagna
Stazione Termini
Prenestino Labicano
La Monachina
San Pietro
Pantheon
Universitá
Tor Sapienza
Monte-spaccato
Aurelio
Fontana di Trevi
San Maria Maggiore
Tiburtino
Via Aurelia
Trastévere
Foro Colosseo
Tor Pignattara
Chiesa di Dio Padre Misericordioso
Valcannuta
Gianicolense
San Giovanni in Laterano
Centocelle
Torrenova
La Pisana
Monteverde Nuovo
Garbatella
Quadraro
Cinecittà
Corviale
Ostiense Catacombe di Domitilla
A1
Magliana
Luneur Theme Park
L'Annunziatella
Via Tuscolana
41° 50′
A12
E.U.R.
41° 50′
Ippodromo Tor di Valle
Via del Mare
Casál Morena
C TO ROMA LEONARDO DA VINCI FIUMICINO (FCO)
Cecchignola
Torricola
ROMA CIAMPINO (CIA)
Tévere (Tiber)
GRA
Ciampino
Acilia
Vitínia
Spinaceto
148
Vallerano
Santa Maria della Mole
Via C. Colombo
Ostia Malpasso
Castél di Leva
511
East from Greenwich
12° 30′

1 **2**

CENTRAL ROME

0 km 1
0 miles 0.5

SAN FRANCISCO, CALIF.

1 0 1 km 2 3 4 5
1 0 miles 1 2 3

A 122° 30′
Marin City
Tiburon
122° 20′
80
Belvedere
Angel Island State Park
Berkeley
Marin Peninsula
101
Sausalito
SAN FRANCISCO BAY
Eastshore Freeway
338
Blunt Point
MARIN CO.
San Francisco Bay
123
37° 50′
Treasure Island
Emeryville
37° 50′
Golden Gate National Rec. Area
Alcatraz I.
Toll
24
80
Oakland
Golden Gate
Fort Point Nat. Historic Site
Fort Mason Center
San Francisco Maritime National Historic Park
Yerba Buena I.
880
Marine Sanctuary Visitor Center
Fisherman's Wharf
Coit Tower
San Francisco-Oakland Bay Bridge
Presidio
Palace of Fine Arts
Transamerica Pyramid
Pacific Hts.
Japan Center
Grace Cath.
B Richmond
Western Addition
Univ. of San Francisco
China Basin
AT&T Park
San Francisco Giants
Alameda Point
Point Lobos
Legion of Honor
Haight Ashbury
City Hall
Alameda Mem. State Beach Park
Sunset
Golden Gate Park
Mission S.F. De Asís
276
Castro
Mission Dolores Park
Potrero Hill
Alameda
California Academy of Sciences
Mt. 283 Davidson
281 Twin Peaks
Mission
Bayview
SAN FRANCISCO
Forest Hill
Parkside
Zoo
101
Bernal Heights
Hunters Point
Stonestown Galleria
280
John McLaren Park
Visitacion Valley
West of Twin Peaks
Outer Mission
Cow Palace
ALAMEDA CO.
C Westlake
Daly City
Bayshore
SAN FRANCISCO CO.
San Mateo CO.
Broadmoor
400
San Bruno Mountain State Park
Brisbane
San Francisco Bay
Colma
Serramonte Center
Sterling Park
Serramonte
Bayshore Fwy
Edgemar
Serramonte
South San Francisco
Point San Bruno
San Francisco
Pacifica
Pacific Manor
1
280
101
TO SAN FRANCISCO INTL. (SFO)
122° 30′
122° 20′
West from Greenwich

1 **2** **3**

CENTRAL SAN FRANCISCO

0 km 0.25
0 miles 0.125

---

280 Interstate route numbers   101 U.S. route numbers   123 State route numbers   — Cable Car route

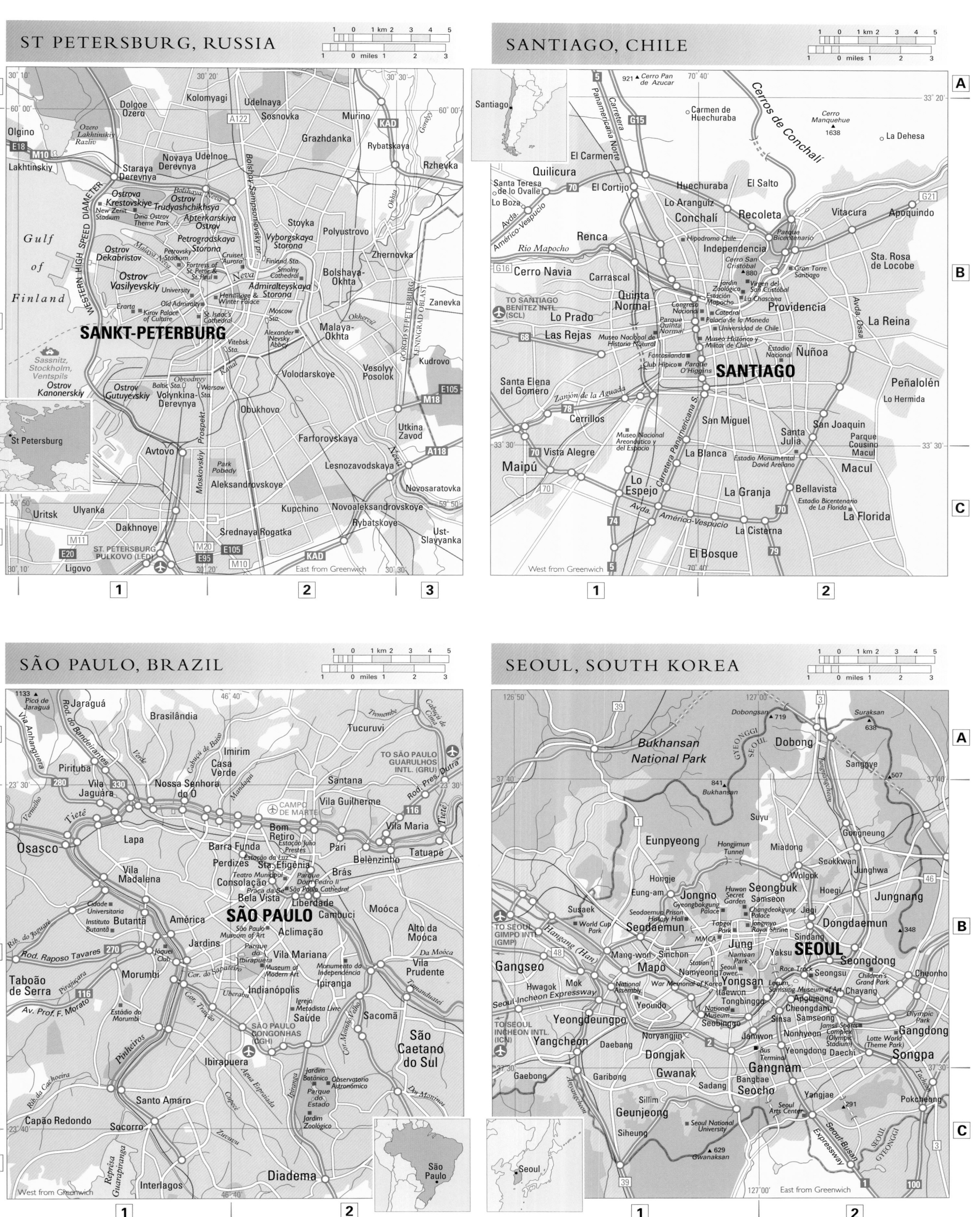

ST PETERSBURG, RUSSIA

SANTIAGO, CHILE

SÃO PAULO, BRAZIL

SEOUL, SOUTH KOREA

COPYRIGHT PHILIP'S

SHANGHAI, CHINA

1 0 1 km 2 3 4 5
1 0 miles 1 2 3

Gucun
Tangqiao
Yangjiazhuang
Baoshan
Wusong
Chang Ji (Yangtze)
Gaoqiao
A20
Yinhangzhen
Jiangwan
Gonggong Forest Park
Gaohang
Jiangwan Stadium
Wujiaochang
Dachang
Beijing
Donggou
Qingningsi
Lu Xun Park
Heping Park
Yangpu
Zhabei
Hongkou Stadium
Tomb of Lu Xun
Hongkou
Fuxing Dao
Yangpu Bridge
Zhoujiazhen
Jinqiao
Zhenru
Putuo
Shanghai West
Shanghai
Shanghai University
Nanjing Road
Tilanqiao
Yangjing
Oriental Pearl Tower
The Bund
Jade Buddha Temple
Lujiazui
Jin Mao Tower
World Financial Centre
Shanghai Tower
Jingan
Jiaodong University
Changfeng Park
Zhongshan Park
Xi Zhan
People's Park
People's Square
Huangpu
Shanghai Museum
Old City
Yuyuan Garden
SHANGHAI
Science & Technology Museum
Century Park
Shanghai International Expo Centre
Changning
Shanghai Zoo
Sun Yat Sen's Former Residence
Fuxing Park
Puxi
Luwan
Nanshi
Pudong New Area
Hongqiao
TO SHANGHAI HONGQIAO (SHA)
Xujiahui
Museum of Folk Art
Xuhui
Shanghai Stadium
Nanpu
Nanpu Bridge
Lupu Bridge
Zhoujiadu
Expo Centre
Nanshi
Beicai
TO SHANGHAI PUDONG (PVG)
Caohejing
Longhua Park
Longhua Pagoda
Shanghai South
Sanlintang
Botanical Gardens
Shanghai South
Gangkou
Sanlin
Disneyland
A20
East from Greenwich 121°30'

Shanghai

— Magnetic Levitation (Maglev) Railway

CENTRAL SINGAPORE

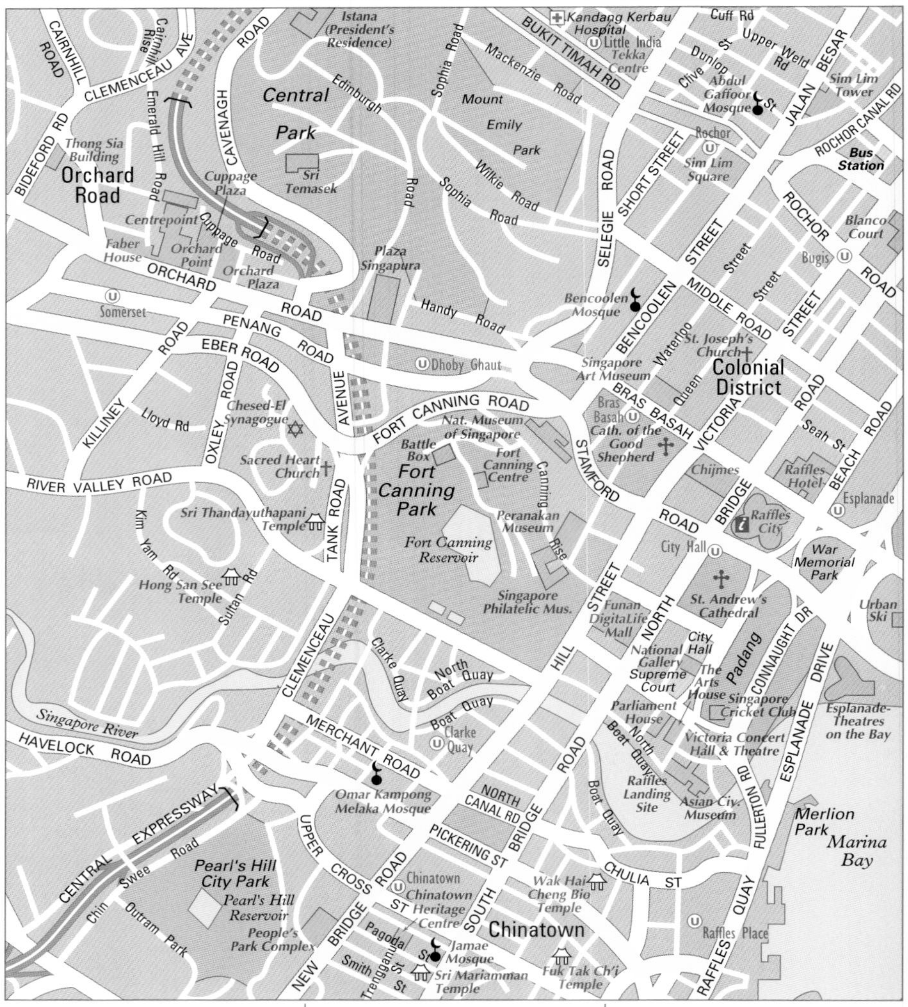

0 km 1
0 miles 0.5

CAIRNHILL ROAD
CLEMENCEAU AVE
Istana (President's Residence)
Kandang Kerbau Hospital
Cuff Rd
Upper Weld Rd
Little India
Tekka Centre
BIDEFORD RD
Emerald Hill
Edinburgh
Central Park
Cairnhill Rise
BUKIT TIMAH RD
Sophia Road
Mackenzie Road
SELEGIE ROAD
SHORT STREET
Dunlop
Clive
Abdul Gaffoor Mosque
JALAN BESAR
ROCHOR CANAL RD
Jalan Tower
Thong Sia Building
Mount Emily
Rochor
Sim Lim Tower
Sim Lim Square
Orchard Road
Cuppage Plaza
Sri Temasek
Wilkie Road
Bus Station
Faber House
Centrepoint
Orchard Point
Cuppage Road
MIDDLE ROAD
Blanco Court
ORCHARD ROAD
Orchard Plaza
Plaza Singapura
Sophia Road
Bencoolen Mosque
WATERLOO STREET
St. Joseph's Church
Bugis
Somerset
PENANG ROAD
Handy Road
BENCOOLEN STREET
Singapore Art Museum
Cath. of the Good Shepherd
Raffles Hotel
KILLINEY ROAD
EBER ROAD
Lloyd Rd
Dhoby Ghaut
FORT CANNING ROAD
BRAS BASAH ROAD
VICTORIA STREET
BEACH ROAD
Colonial District
Esplanade
RIVER VALLEY ROAD
Oxley Rd
Chesed-El Synagogue
Battle Box
Nat. Museum of Singapore
Peranakan Museum
Chijmes
Raffles City
City Hall
War Memorial Park
Sacred Heart Church
Sri Thandayuthapani Temple
TANK ROAD
Fort Canning Centre
Fort Canning Reservoir
STAMFORD ROAD
Funan DigitaLife Mall
St. Andrew's Cathedral
Urban Ski
Fort Canning Park
CLEMENCEAU
Hong San See Temple
Singapore Philatelic Mus.
HILL STREET
National Gallery
Supreme Court
City Hall
Padang
CONNAUGHT DRIVE
Clarke Quay
North Quay
Parliament House
The Arts House
Singapore Cricket Club
ESPLANADE DRIVE
Esplanade—Theatres on the Bay
Singapore River
MERCHANT ROAD
Boat Quay
Raffles Landing Site
Asian Civ. Museum
Merlion Park
HAVELOCK ROAD
UPPER CROSS ROAD
NORTH CANAL ROAD
SOUTH CANAL ROAD
Boat Quay
FULLERTON RD
Marina Bay
CENTRAL EXPRESSWAY
Omar Kampong Melaka Mosque
PICKERING ST
CHULIA ST
QUAY
Chin Swee Road
Pearl's Hill City Park
Pearl's Hill Reservoir
People's Park Complex
Chinatown
Chinatown Heritage Centre
NEW BRIDGE ROAD
SOUTH BRIDGE ROAD
Wak Hai Cheng Bio Temple
Raffles Place
Chin Swee Rd
Outram Park
Pagoda St
Smith St
Temple St
Chinatown
Jamae Mosque
Sri Mariamman Temple
Fuk Tak Ch'i Temple

SINGAPORE

1 0 1 km 2 3 4 5
1 0 miles 1 2 3

103°40'E
103°50'E
104°00'E
Johor Bahru
Senoko Ind. Est.
Sembawang
Selat Johor
Pasir Gudang
Causeway
Sungai Buloh Nature Park
WTCP
Kranji Ind. Est.
Woodlands
Chong Pang
Pulau Seletar
MALAYSIA
SINGAPORE
Lim Chu Kang
Kranji Reservoir
S. Punggol
Yishun
Sembawang
Dam
Seletar Reservoir
Punggol Point
Pulau Ubin
Pulau Tekong Kechil
Pulau Tekong
Sarimbun Res.
Sungai Kadut Ind. Est.
Singapore Turf Club
Mandai
Singapore Zoo
Seletar Reservoir
SELETAR
Jalan Kayu
Punggol
Pulau Serangoon (Coney I.)
Pulau Ketam
Selat Johor
Sarimbun Res.
85
Murai Res.
Ama Keng
Peng Siang
Nee Soon
SLE
Yio Chu Kang
Seletar
Sengkang
Serangoon
TPE
Serangoon Harbour
Pasir Ris Park
Changi
SINGAPORE CHANGI (SIN)
MALAYSIA
SINGAPORE
Tuas Second Link
Poyan Res.
Choa Chu Kang
BKE
Central Catchment Nature Reserve
Lower Peirce Reservoir
Hougang
Chia Keng
Pasir Ris
Loyang Ind. Est.
Yan Kit
The Changi Museum
Tengeh Res.
Choa Chu Kang
Bukit Panjang
132
Upper Peirce Reservoir
Ang Mo Kio
Serangoon
Bishan
Bedok Reservoir
Tampines
Changi Exhibition Centre
Raffles Golf Course & Country Club
KJE
Choa Chu Kang 88
Nanyang University
Bukit Batok
Bukit Timah Nature Reserve
164
MacRitchie Reservoir
Paya Lebar
CTE
Simei
Singapore Expo
Tanah Merah Golf Course
PIE
Boon Lay
Jurong West
Snow City
Air View Park
Raffles Park
Toa Payoh
Tai Seng
Kg Landang
PIE
Jurong Industrial Estate
Singapore Discovery Centre
Chinese & Japanese Gardens
Jurong East
Jurong Science Centre
Tang Dynasty Museum
PIE
Clementi
Maryland
Dunearn
Geylang Serai
Chai Chee
Bedok
Jurong
Jurong Bird Park
Pandan Res.
Holland Village
Victoria Park
Botanic Gardens
Little India
Katong
East Coast Park
Changi Naval Base
Pulau Jurong
Seraya
LKC Natural History Mus.
AYE
N.U.S.
Queenstown
Telok Blangah
National Stadium
Kallang Park
Singapore Indoor Stadium
Frankel
ECP
Selat Jurong
Kg Tanjong Penjuru
Pasir Panjang
Buona Vista Park
St. Andrew's Cathedral
National Museum
City Hall
Singapore Flyer and F1 track
Marina Bay Golf Course
Pasir Panjang Terminal
Mt. Faber 105
Thian Hock Keng Temple
Artscience Mus.
Gardens by the Bay
Pulau Jurong
Seraya
Sakra
Selat Pandan
Bukom Island, Semakau Island
Pulau Busing
Fort Siloso
Siloso Pt.
Harbour Front Centre
Cable Cars
Vivo City
P. Brani
Keppel Harbour
SINGAPORE
Marina Bay Sands
Imbiah Lookout
Universal Studios
Tanjong Golf Course
Straits of Singapore
Pulau Bukum
Tanjung Balai Sebana
Sentosa
East from Greenwich
104°00'E

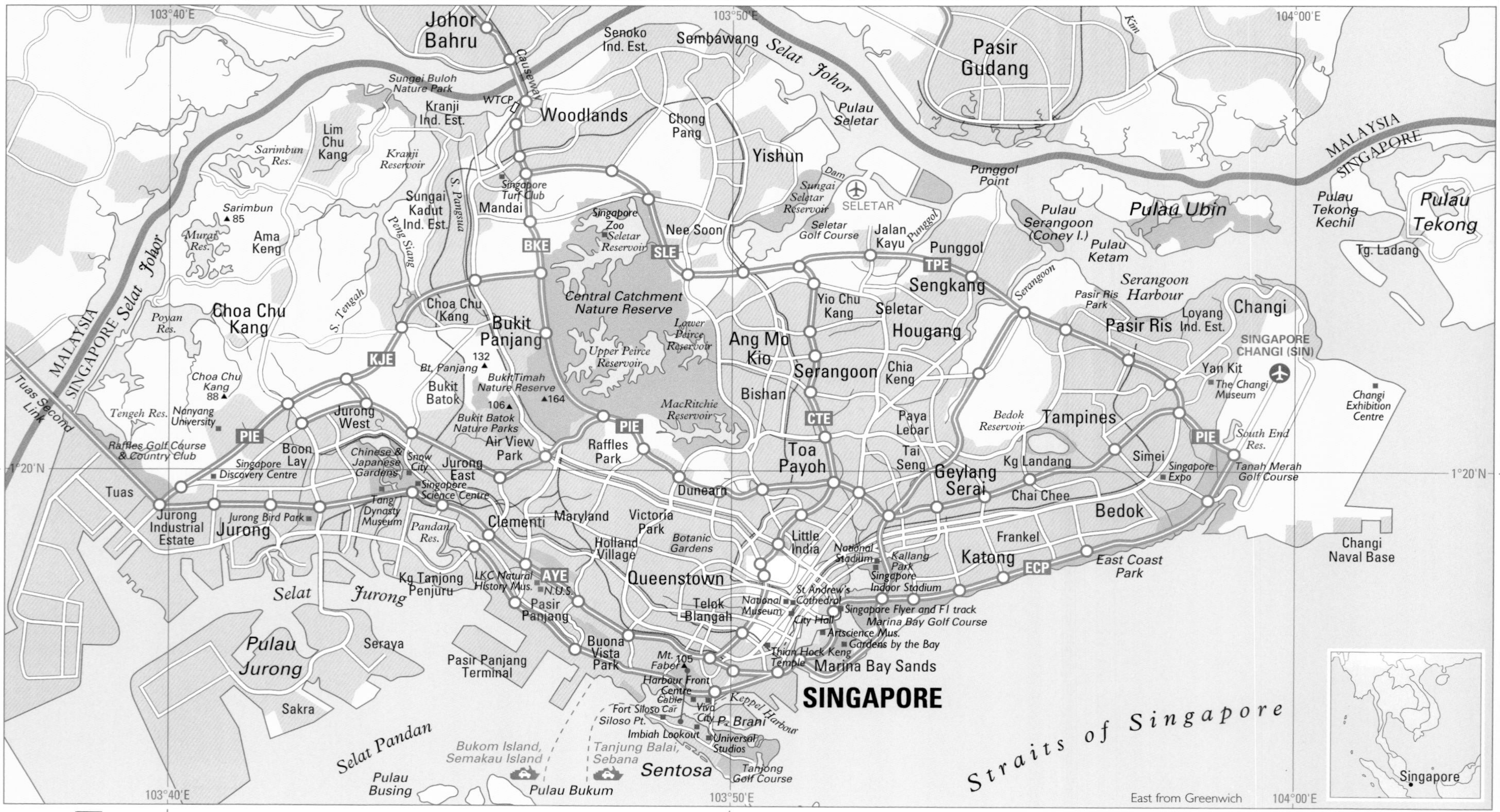

Singapore

1°20'N
1°20'N

STOCKHOLM, SWEDEN

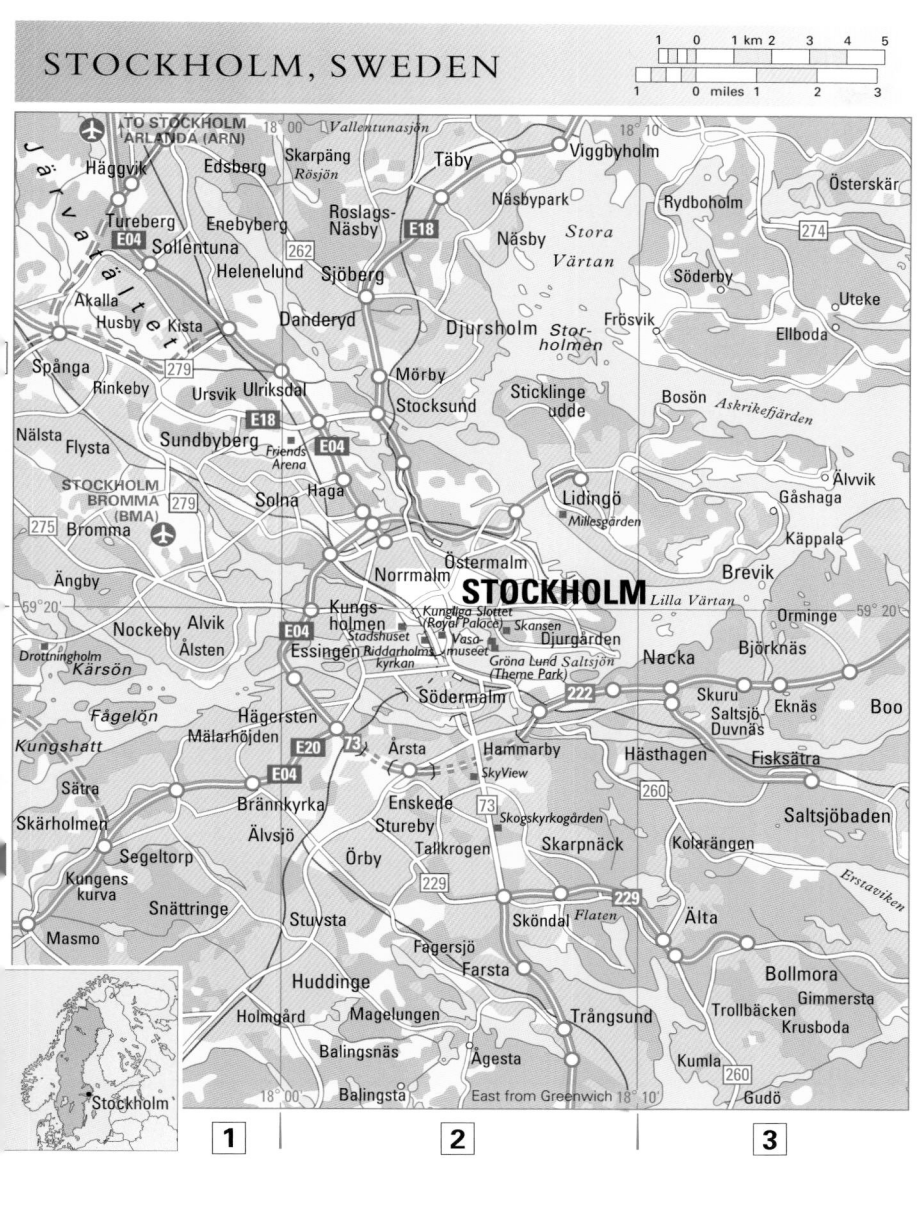

CENTRAL STOCKHOLM

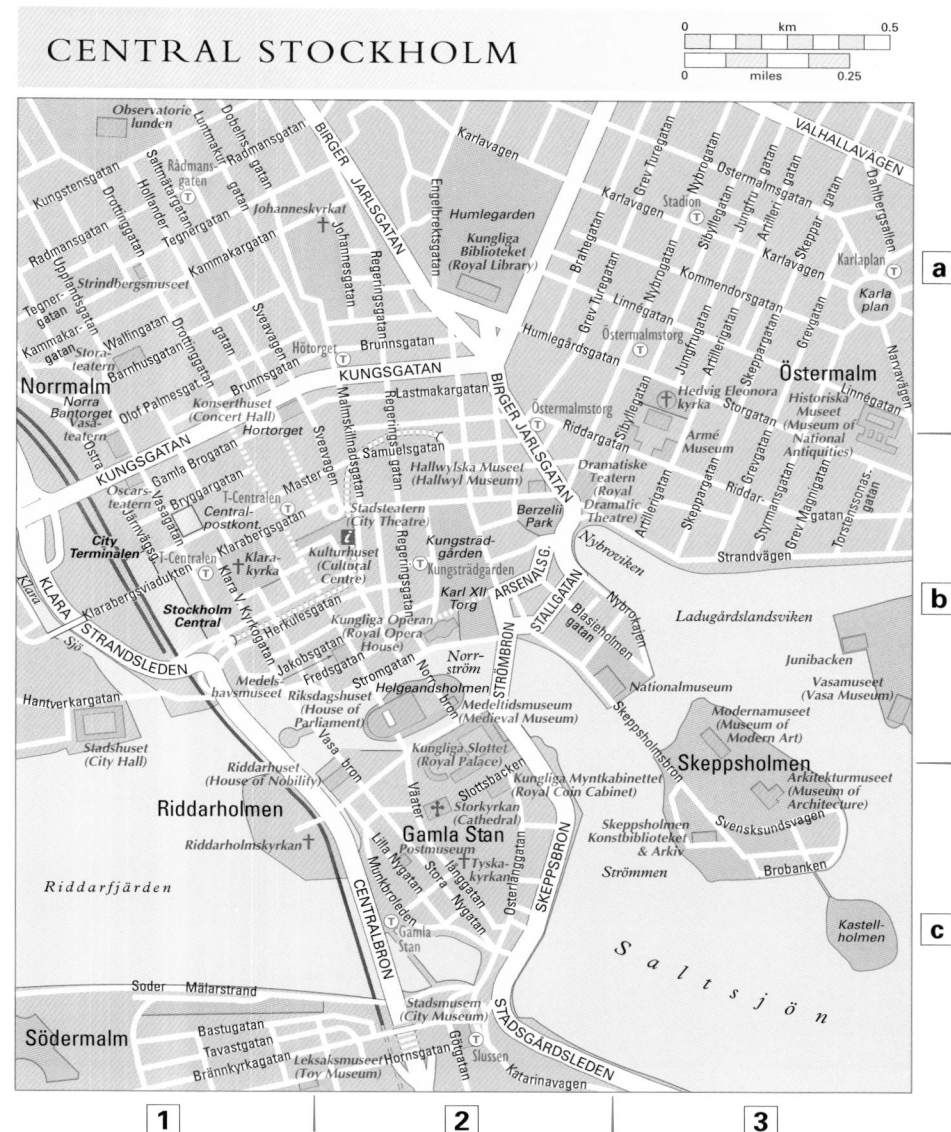

SYDNEY, AUSTRALIA

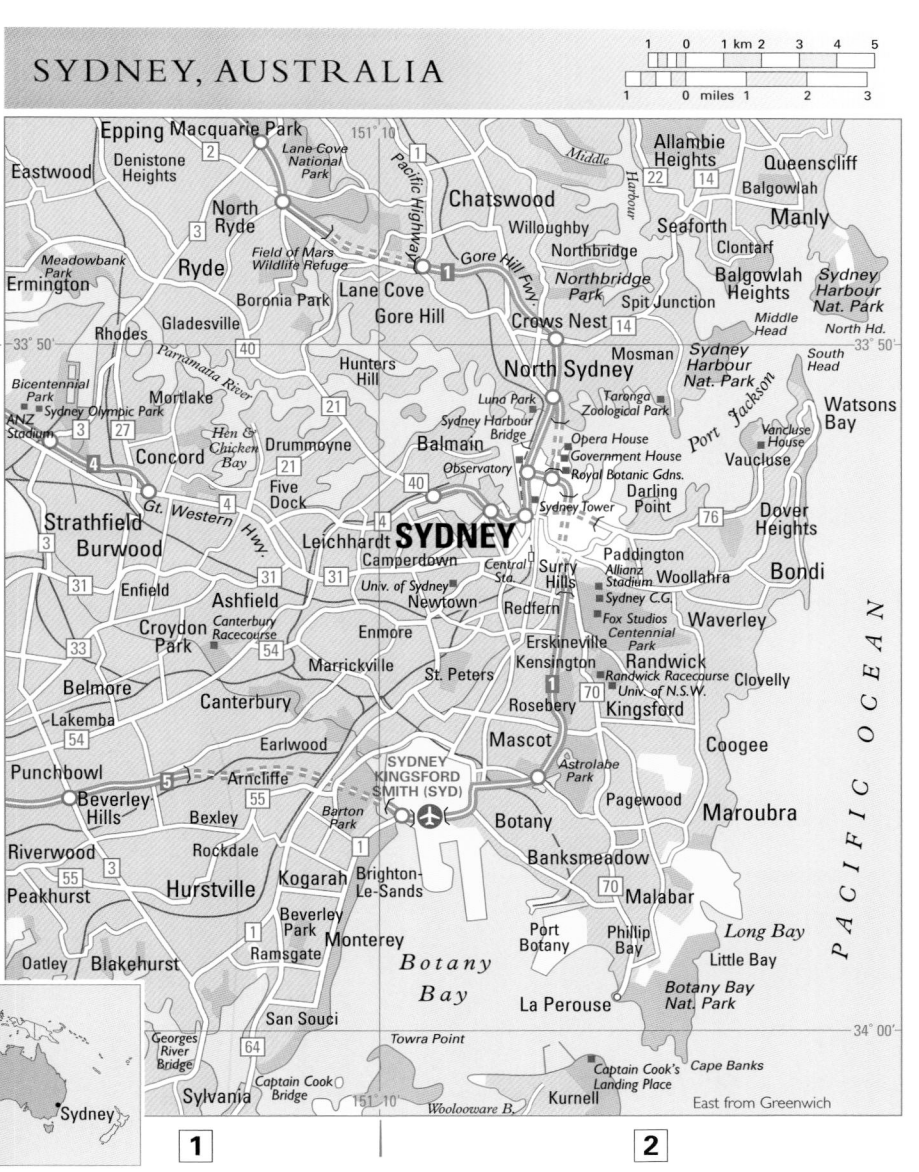

CENTRAL SYDNEY

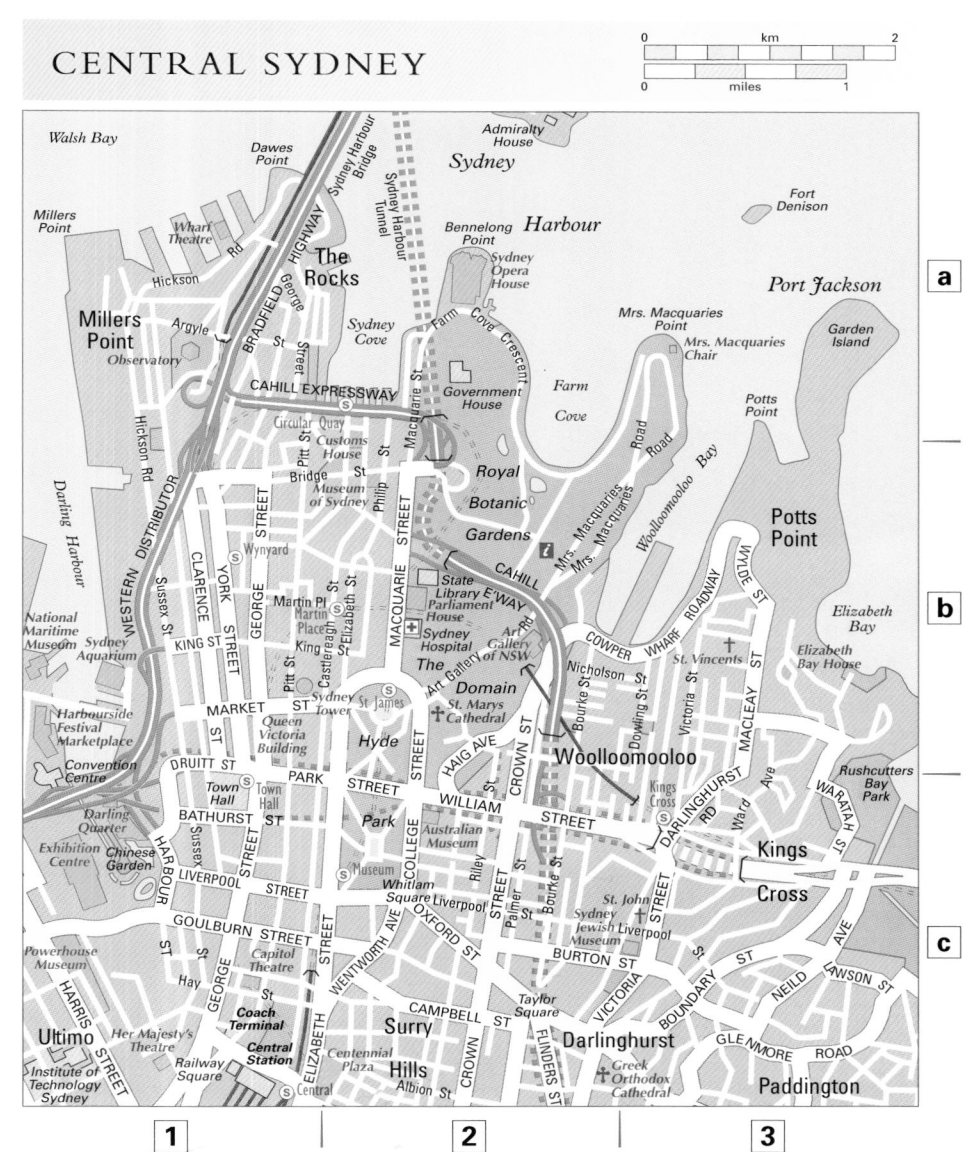

TOKYO, JAPAN

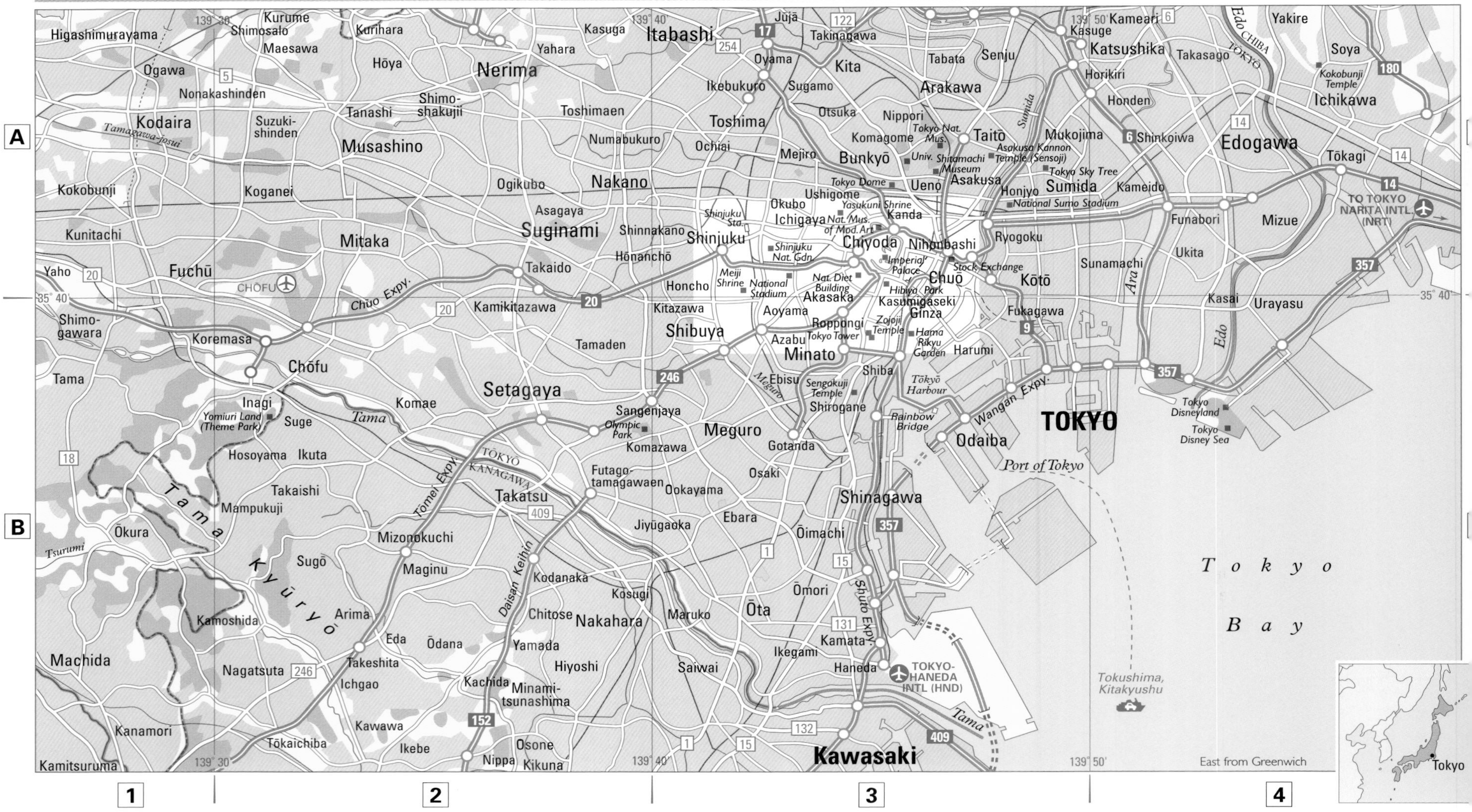

Higashimurayama · Kurume · Shimosato · Kurihara · Kasuga · Jūjō · Takinagawa · Kita · Tabata · Senju · Katsushika · Takasago · Kameari · Kasuge · Soya · Yakire

Ogawa · Shimo-shakujii · Yahara · Itabashi · Oyama · Horikiri · Honden · Kokubunji Temple · Ichikawa

Nonakashinden · Nerima · Ikebukuro · Sugamo · Otsuka · Nippori · Arakawa · Mukojima · Shinkoiwa · Edogawa

Kodaira · Hōya · Tanashi · Toshimaen · Toshima · Komagome · Tokyo Nat. Mus. · Asakusa Kannon Temple (Sensōji) · Tokyo Sky Tree · Tōkagi

Kokobunji · Musashino · Ogikubo · Nakano · Asagaya · Numabukuro · Ochiai · Mejiro · Bunkyō · Ueno · Asakusa · Honjo · Sumida · Kameido · Mizue

Kunitachi · Koganei · Mitaka · Suginami · Takaido · Shinnakano · Shinjuku · Okubo · Ichigaya · Nat. Mus. of Mod. Art · Chiyoda · Nihonbashi · Kōtō · To Tokyo Narita Intl. (NRT)

Yaho · Fuchū · Chūō Expy. · Kamikitazawa · Honchō · Meiji Shrine · National Stadium · Imperial Palace · Chūō · Stock Exchange · Funabori · Ukita

Shimo-gawara · Koremasa · Tamaden · Kitazawa · Shibuya · Aoyama · Akasaka · Roppongi · Kasumigaseki · Ginza · Koto · Kasai · Urayasu

Tama · Inagi · Chōfu · Komae · Setagaya · Meguro · Minato · Tokyo Tower · Zojoji Temple · Hama Rikyu Garden · Harumi · Shiba

Yomiuri Land (Theme Park) · Suge · Hosoyama · Ikuta · Sangenjaya · Olympic Park · Komazawa · Ebisu · Sengakuji Temple · Shirogane · Bainbow Bridge · Odaiba · TOKYO · Tokyo Disneyland · Tokyo Disney Sea

Takaishi · Mizonokuchi · Takatsu · Jiyūgaoka · Gotanda · Shinagawa · Port of Tokyo

Ōkura · Tsurumi · Kamoshida · Arima · Sugō · Maginu · Nakahara · Kodanaka · Kōsugi · Ōimachi · Ōmori · Kamata · Haneda · Tokyo-Haneda Intl. (HND)

Machida · Nagatsuta · Eda · Ōdana · Yamada · Hiyoshi · Saiwai · Ōta · Ikegami · Tokushima, Kitakyushu

Kanamori · Takeshita · Ichgao · Kachida · Minami-tsunashima · Kawawa · Ikebe · Osone · Kikuna · Nippa · Kawasaki

Kamitsuruma · Tōkaichiba

Tokyo Bay · East from Greenwich · Tokyo

CENTRAL TOKYO

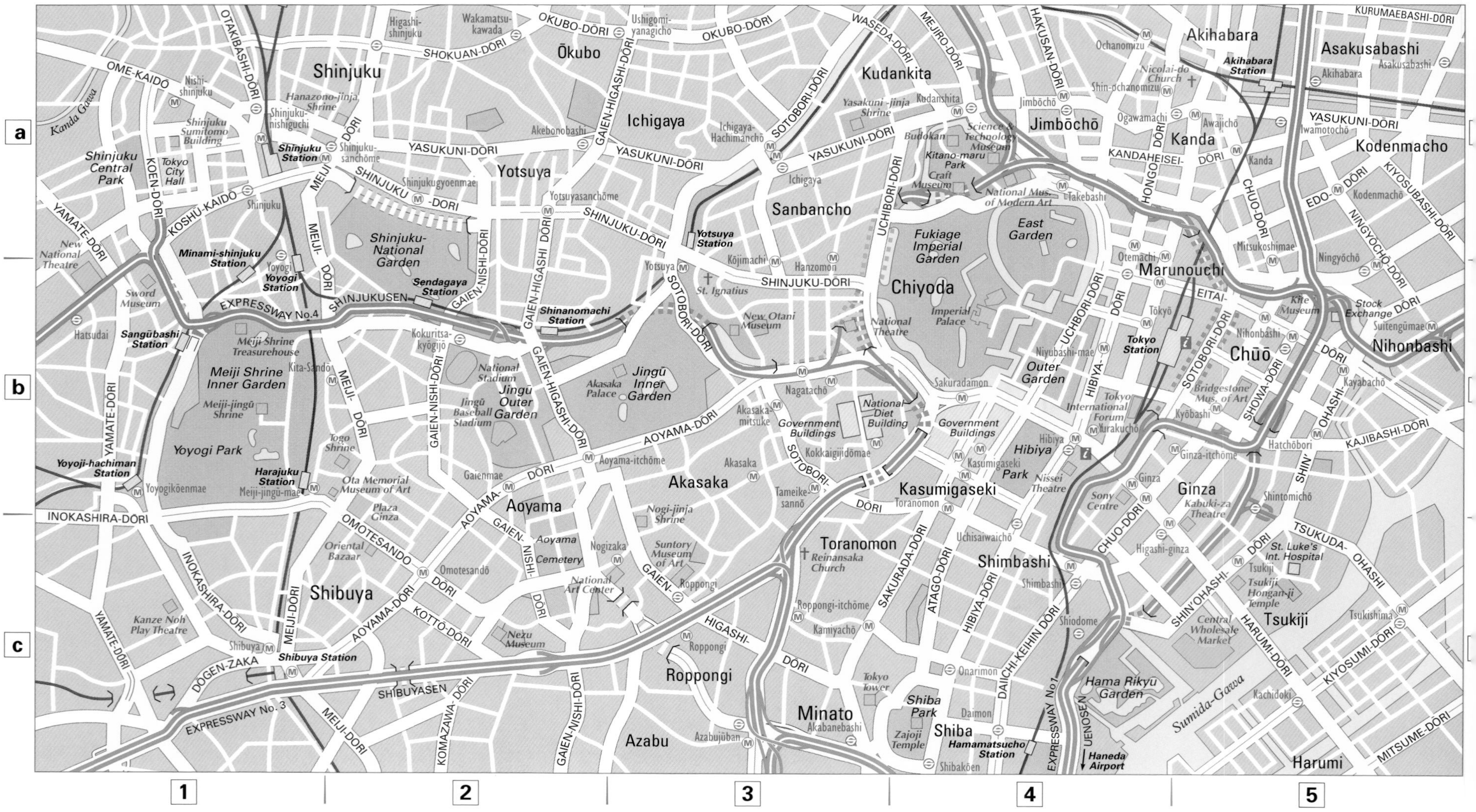

Shinjuku · Okubo · Akihabara · Asakusabashi

Nishi-shinjuku · Higashi-shinjuku · Wakamatsu-kawada · Ushigomi-yanagicho · Kudankita · Ochanomizu · Akihabara Station

Shinjuku Sumitomo Building · Hanazono-jinja Shrine · Yotsuya · Ichigaya · Sanbancho · Jimbōchō · Kanda · Kodenmacho

Shinjuku Central Park · Shinjuku City Hall · Shinjuku Station · Shinjuku-sanchōme · Science & Technology Museum · National Mus. of Modern Art

New National Theatre · Minami-shinjuku Station · Yoyogi Station · Shinjuku-National Garden · Sendagaya Station · Yotsuya Station · Fukiage Imperial Garden · East Garden · Marunouchi

Sword Museum · Meiji Shrine Treasurehouse · Sangūbashi Station · Shinanomachi Station · Kōjimachi · St. Ignatius · Chiyoda · Imperial Palace · Tokyo Station · Chūō · Nihonbashi

Meiji Shrine Inner Garden · Meiji-jingū Shrine · National Stadium · Jingū Outer Garden · Jingū Inner Garden · Akasaka Palace · National Theatre · National Diet Building · Government Buildings · Hibiya · Ginza

Yoyogi Park · Togo Shrine · Jingū Baseball Stadium · Akasaka-mitsuke · Nagatachō · Kasumigaseki · Hibiya Park · Sony Centre

Yoyoji-hachiman Station · Harajuku Station · Ota Memorial Museum of Art · Gaienmae · Aoyama-itchōme · Government Buildings · Kokkaigijidōmae · Toranomon · Nissei Theatre · Kabuki-za Theatre

Plaza Ginza · Oriental Bazaar · Omotesando · Aoyama · Nogi-jinja Shrine · Suntory Museum of Art · Shimbashi · Higashi-ginza · St. Luke's Int. Hospital · Tsukiji

Kanze Noh Play Theatre · Shibuya Station · Nezu Museum · Nogizaka · National Art Center · Roppongi-itchōme · Toranomon · Shimbashi · Tsukiji Hongan-ji Temple

Shibuya · Aoyama · Roppongi · Higashi-Roppongi · Kamiyachō · Uchisaiwaichō · Shiodome · Central Wholesale Market · Tsukishima

Dōgen-zaka · Minato · Shiba Park · Tokyo Tower · Zojoji Temple · Shiba · Daimon · Hamamatsucho Station · Hama Rikyū Garden · Harumi

Azabu · Azabujūban · Akabanebashi · Haneda Airport · Shibakōen

⊖ Toei Subway   Ⓜ Tokyo Metro

TEHRAN, IRAN

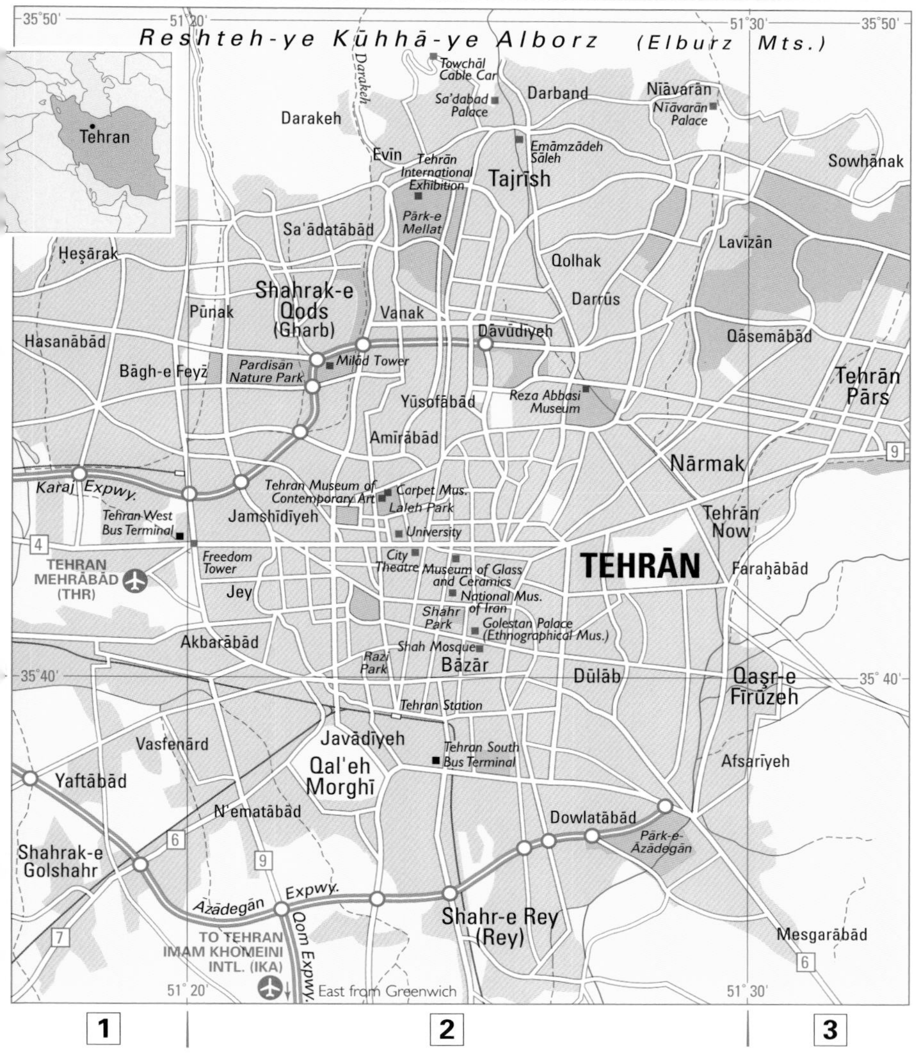

Reshteh-ye Kūhhā-ye Alborz (Elburz Mts.)

Tehran

Darakeh
Towchāl Cable Car
Sa'dabad Palace
Darband
Niāvarān Palace
Evin
Tehrān International Exhibition
Emāmzādeh Sāleh
Niāvarān
Sowhānak
Darakeh
Tajrīsh
Park-e Mellat
Heṣārak
Sa'ādatābād
Qolhak
Lavīzān
Tehrān Pārs
Shahrak-e Qods (Gharb)
Pūnak
Vanak
Darrūs
Qāsemābād
Hasanābād
Pardisan Nature Park
Mīlād Tower
Dāvūdīyeh
Bāgh-e Feyẕ
Yūsofābād
Reza Abbasi Museum
Nārmak
Amīrābād
Tehrān Museum of Contemporary Art
Carpet Mus.
Tehran Now
Karaj Expwy
Laleh Park
Tehrān Mehrābād (THR)
Jamshīdīyeh
University
Farahābād
Tehran West Bus Terminal
Freedom Tower
City Theatre
Museum of Glass and Ceramics
TEHRĀN
Jey
National Mus.
Shahr Park
Golestan Palace (Ethnographical Mus.)
Akbarābād
Razi Park
Shah Mosque
Bāzār
Dūlāb
Qaṣr-e Fīrūzeh
Tehran Station
Javādīyeh
Qal'eh Morghī
Tehran South Bus Terminal
Afsarīyeh
Vasfenārd
Yaftābād
N'ematābād
Dowlatābād
Park-e Āzādegān
Mesgarābād
Shahrak-e Golshahr
Āzādegān Expwy.
Qom Expwy
Shahr-e Rey (Rey)
TO TEHRAN IMAM KHOMEINI INTL. (IKA)

East from Greenwich

CENTRAL TORONTO

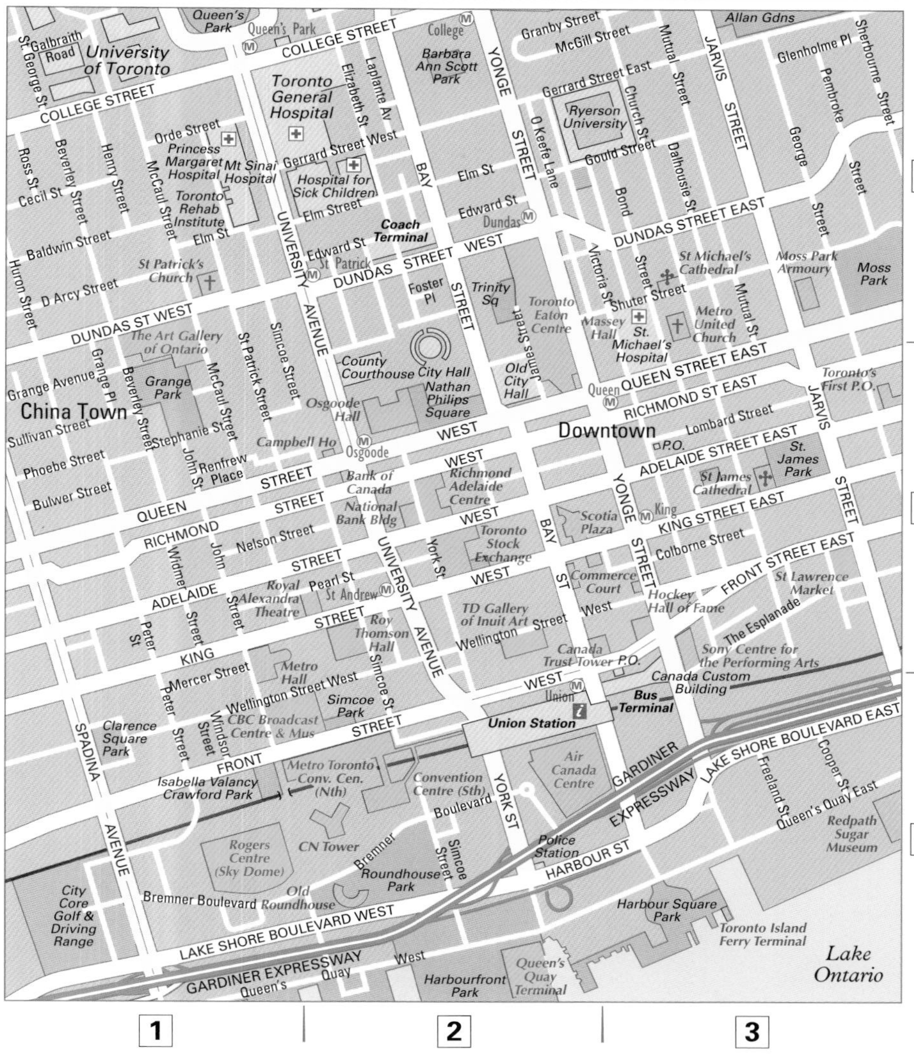

Queen's Park
University of Toronto
College Street
College
Granby Street
McGill Street
Galbraith Road
Toronto General Hospital
Orde Street
Princess Margaret Hospital
Mt Sinai Hospital
Gerrard Street West
Gerrard Street East
Ryerson University
Barbara Ann Scott Park
Hospital for Sick Children
Elm St
Edward St
Baldwin Street
Toronto Rehab Institute
Elm St
Coach Terminal
Huron Street
D'Arcy Street
St Patrick's Church
Foster Pl
DUNDAS STREET WEST
DUNDAS STREET EAST
St Michael's Cathedral
Moss Park Armoury
Moss Park
Trinity Sq
The Art Gallery of Ontario
Massey Hall
Metro United Church
China Town
Grange Avenue
St Michael's Hospital
Grange
County Courthouse
City Hall
Nathan Phillips Square
Sullivan Street
Osgoode Hall
Old City Hall
QUEEN STREET EAST
Toronto's First P.O.
Phoebe Street
Campbell Ho
Osgoode
RICHMOND ST EAST
Lombard Street
P.O.
Bulwer Street
Downtown
ADELAIDE STREET EAST
St James Park
Bank of Canada
Richmond Adelaide Centre
National Bank Bldg
St James' Cathedral
Colborne Street
Toronto Stock Exchange
Scotia Plaza
KING STREET EAST
Royal Alexandra Theatre
Commerce Court
Hockey Hall of Fame
St Lawrence Market
TD Gallery of Inuit Art
St Andrew
Roy Thomson Hall
Wellington
The Esplanade
Metro Hall
Canada Trust Tower P.O.
Canada Custom Building
Mercer Street
CBC Broadcast Centre & Mus
Union
Sony Centre for the Performing Arts
Clarence Square Park
Bus Terminal
Isabella Valancy Crawford Park
Metro Toronto Conv. Cen. (Nth)
Union Station
Air Canada Centre
Convention Centre (Sth)
Police Station
Queen's Quay East
Rogers Centre (Sky Dome)
CN Tower
Roundhouse Park
HARBOUR ST
Redpath Sugar Museum
City Core Golf & Driving Range
Bremner Boulevard Roundhouse
LAKE SHORE BOULEVARD EAST
Harbour Square Park
LAKE SHORE BOULEVARD WEST
Toronto Island Ferry Terminal
GARDINER EXPRESSWAY
Queen's Quay
Harbourfront Park
Queen's Quay Terminal
Lake Ontario

TORONTO, CANADA

Boyd Conservation Area
Markham
Toronto Zoo
Fairport
Vaughan
Thornhill
The Promenade
Brown
West Rouge
Concord
Newtonbrook
Rouge Glen Park
Port Union
Pine Grove
Edgeley
Willowdale
Fairview Mall
Highland Creek
Woodbridge
Fisherville
G. Ross Lord Park
East Don Parkland
Agincourt
Malvern
Humber Summit
Black Creek Pioneer Village
York University
Gibson House Museum
Northmount
Macdonald-Cartier Frwy
Scarborough Town Centre
Morningside Park
West Hill
Beaumonte Heights
North York
Lansing
York Mills
Victoria Village
Bendale
Woburn
Thistletown
Northwood Park
Armour Heights
Wexford
Scarborough
Eastpoint Park
Claireville Reservoir
Rowntree Mills Park
Downsview Park
Don Mills
Guildwood
Humberwood Park
Kipling Heights
Downsview
Edwards Gardens & the Toronto Botanical Garden
Cliffside
Rexdale
Humberlea
Yorkdale Shopping Centre
Lawrence Heights
York Univ Sunnybrook Health Sciences Centre
Wilket Creek Park
Ontario Science Centre
Scarborough Junction
Bluffers Park
Malton
Woodbine Racetrack
Weston
Forest Hill
Leaside
Thorncliffe
Dentonia Park
TORONTO PEARSON INTL. (YYZ)
Cedarvale Park
York
Casa Loma
East York
Birch Cliff
Humber Valley Village
Mount Dennis
Royal Ontario Museum
Riverdale Park
Kew Gardens
Scarborough Bluffs
Hanlon
Swansea
University of Toronto
Ontario Legislative Building
Ashbridge's Bay Park
Etobicoke
Mimico Creek
Lambton Mills
High Park
Old City Hall
CN Tower & Rogers Centre
Union Sta
TORONTO
Islington
Kingsway
Humber
Old Fort York
Parkdale
Gardiner Expy
Lower Don Lands
Tommy Thompson Park
Markland Wood
Exhibition Place
Billy Bishop Toronto City
Toronto Harbour
Humber Bay
Burnhamthorpe
Summerville
Ontario Place
Toronto Islands
Alderwood
Humber Bay Park
Gibraltar Point
Mimico
Dixie Mall
New Toronto
Humber College
Samuel Smith Park
Cooksville
Mississauga
Long Branch
West from Greenwich

LAKE ONTARIO

Toronto

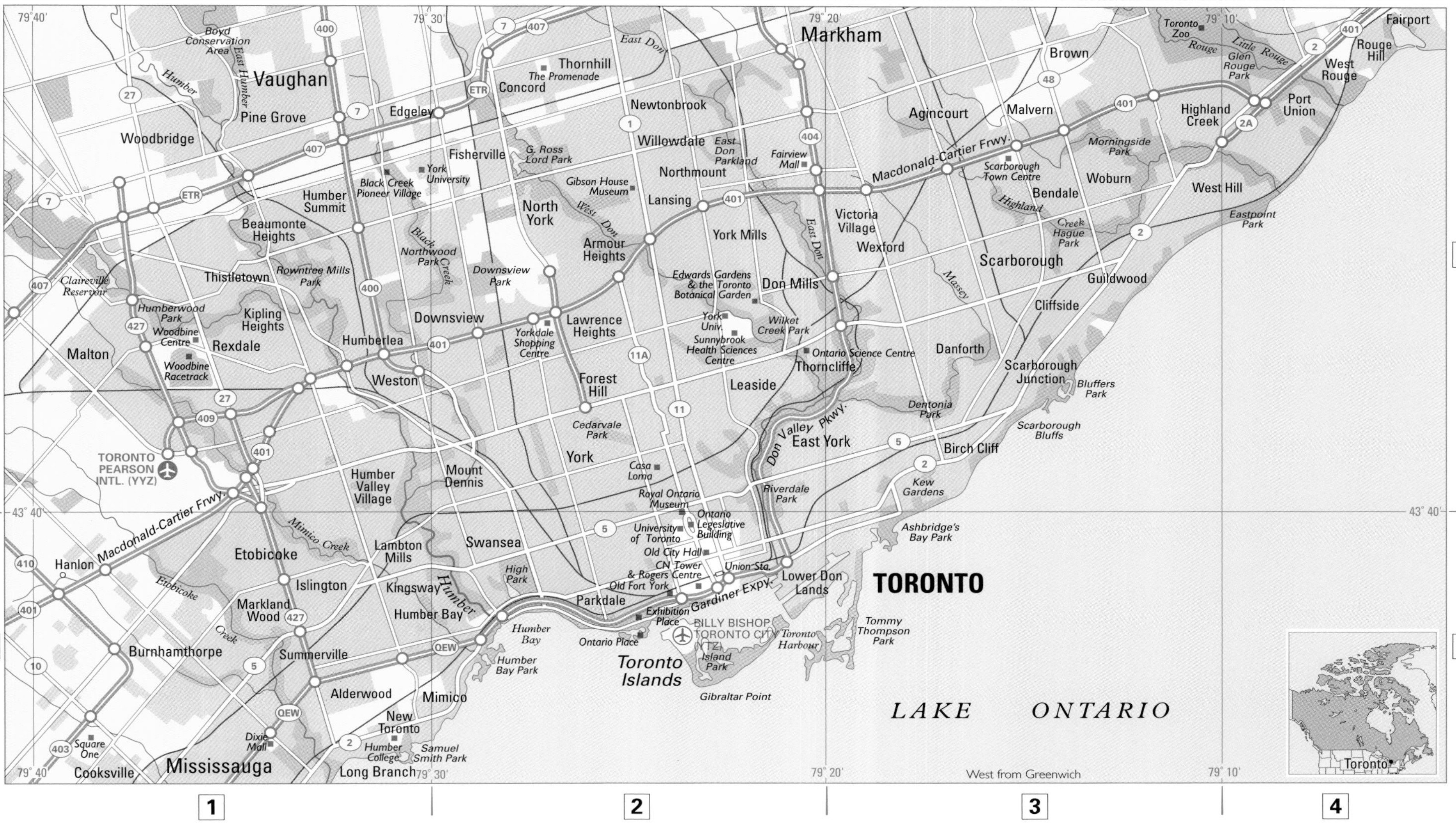

427 Provincial route numbers

COPYRIGHT PHILIP'S

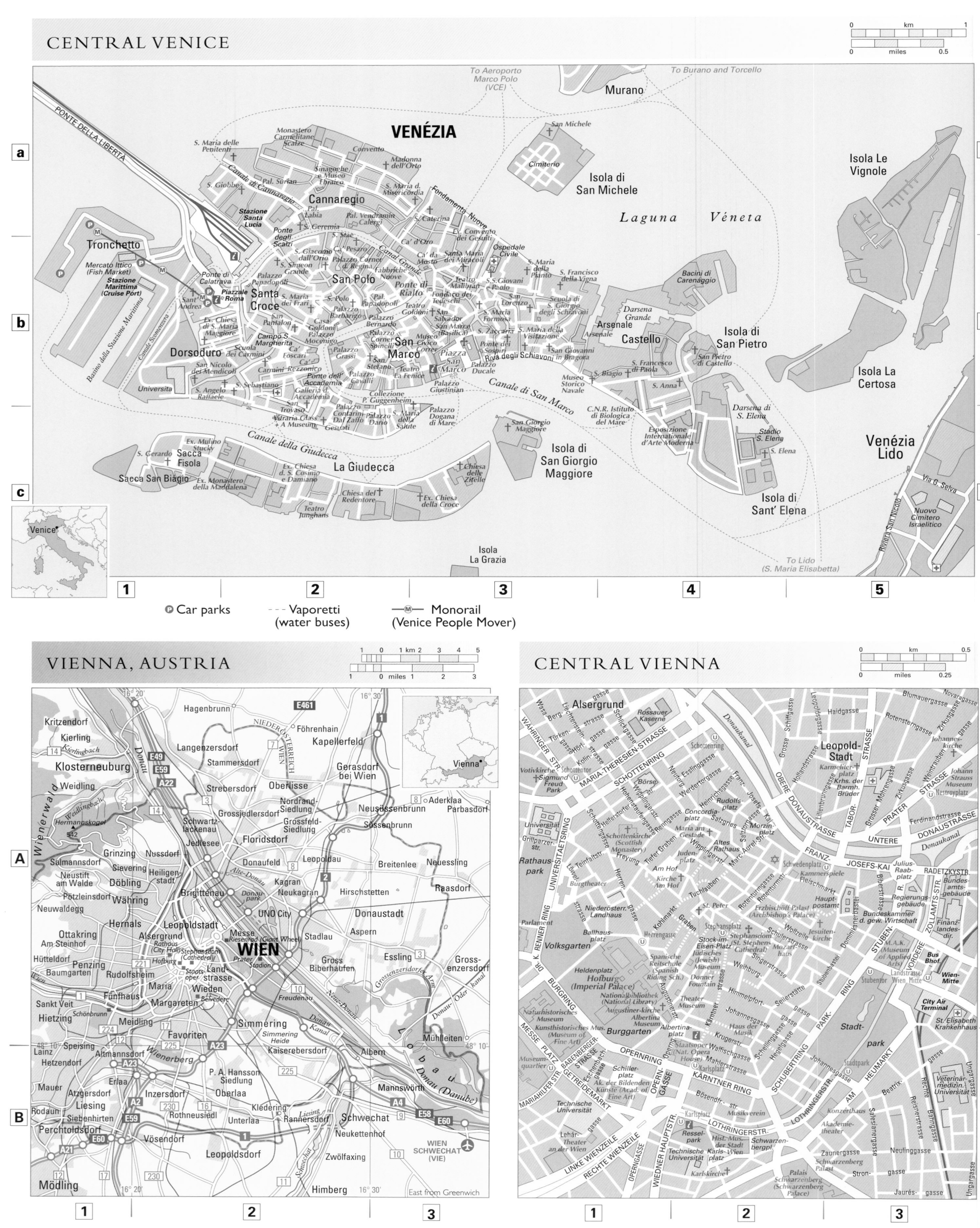

WARSAW, POLAND

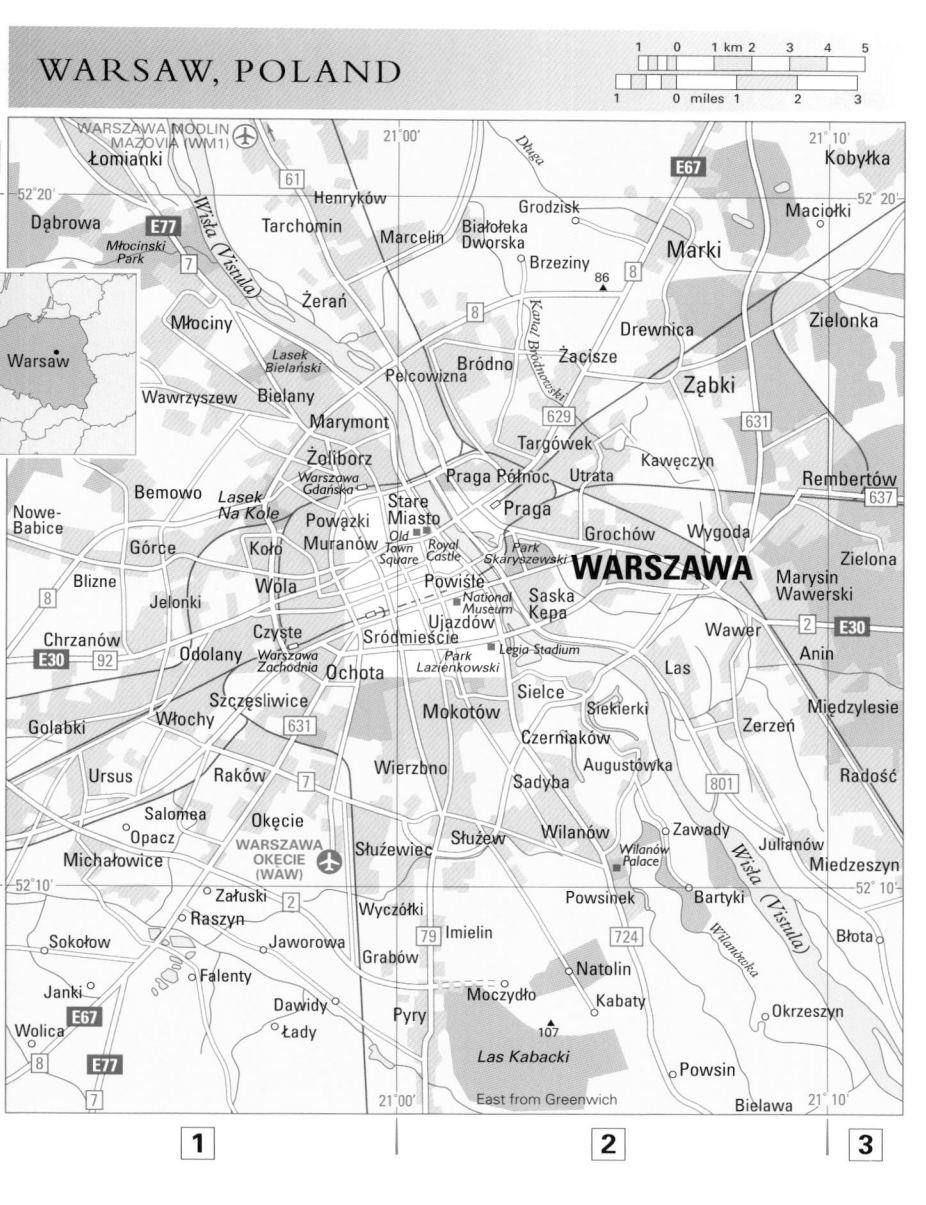

CENTRAL WARSAW

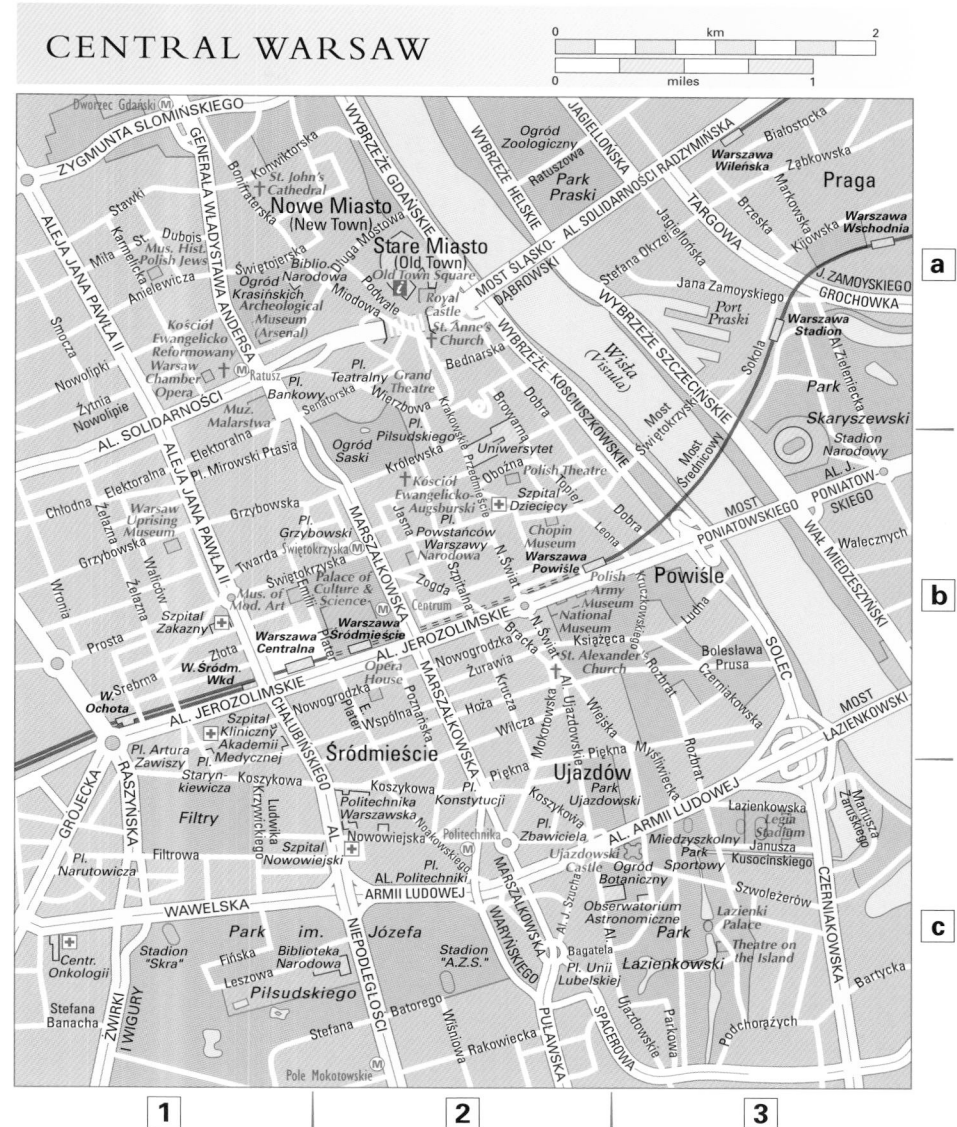

WASHINGTON D.C.

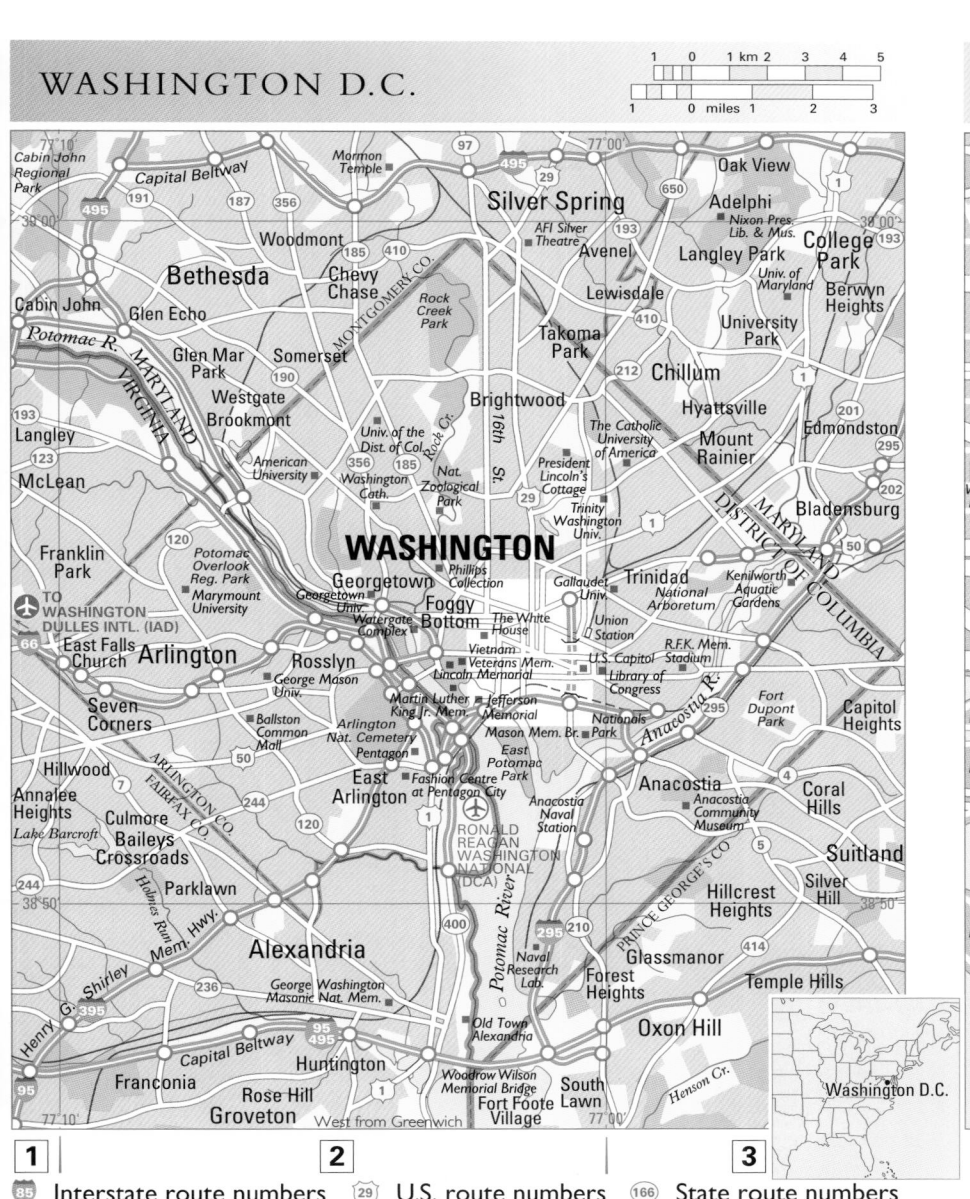

CENTRAL WASHINGTON

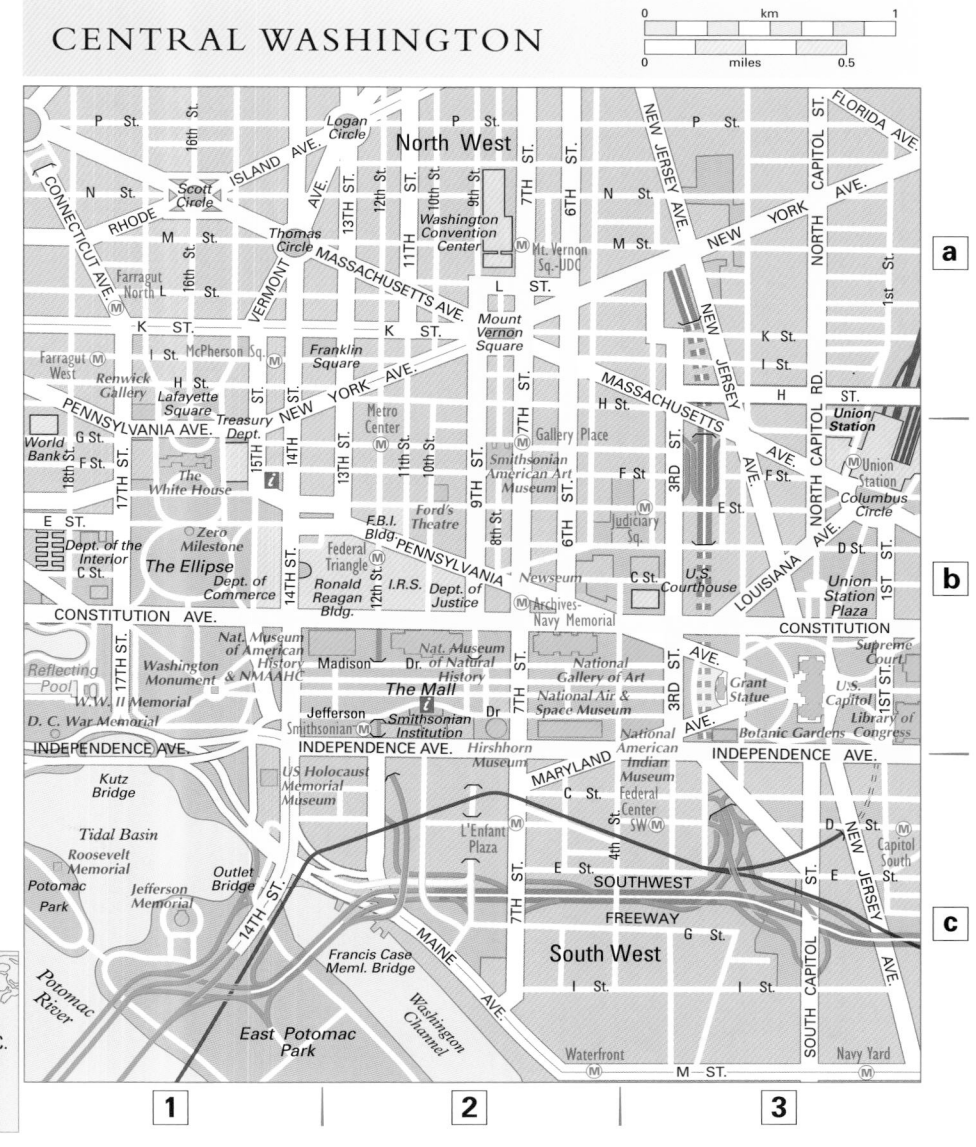

85 Interstate route numbers   29 U.S. route numbers   166 State route numbers

COPYRIGHT PHILIP'S

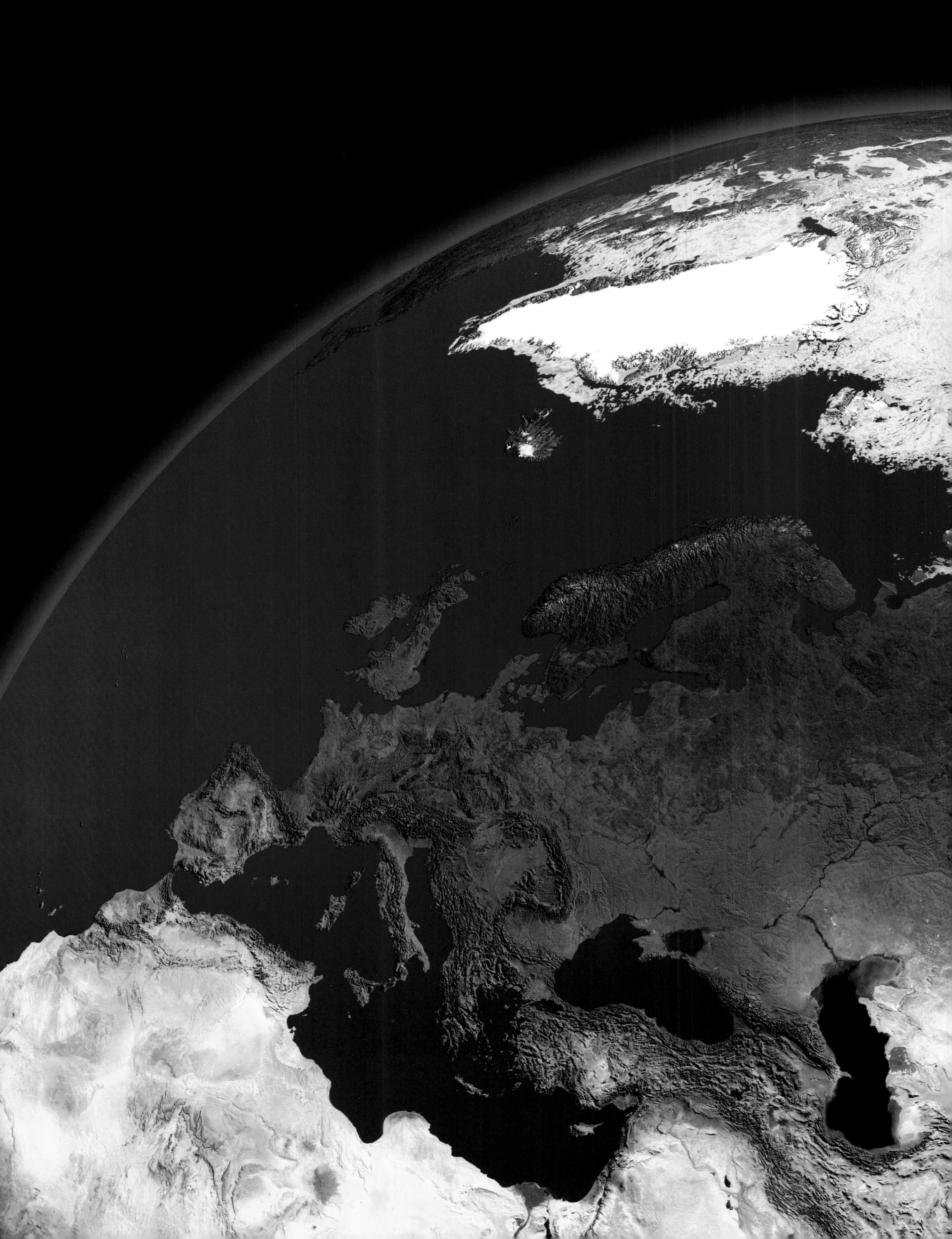

WORLD
MAPS

1 2 3 4 5 6 7 8 9

A

B

A 40

C

D

E

F

G

H

Beaufort
Sea

Pt. Barrow

A l a s k a
Yukon Denali
6190 (Mt. McKinley)

Bering
Sea

Gulf of
Alaska

Aleutian Is.

Kodiak I.

Haida Gwaii
(Queen Charlotte Is.)

Vancouver I.

C. Mendocino

Hawaiian Is.

Mauna Kea
4205

Revilla Gigedo Is.

P A C I F I C

O C E A N

Line Is.

Kiritimati

P o l y n e s i a

Marquesas Is.

Society Is.   Tuamotu Is.

Tahiti

Cook Is.

Tubuai Is.

Pitcairn I.

Easter I.

Arch. de
Juan Fernández

Magellan's Str.

Amundsen Sea

Roosevelt I.

Marie Byrd Land

Ross
Sea

Bering Str.

Sierra Nevada Mt. Elbert
4399
Mt. Whitney
4418 Death Valley

Lower
California

C. San Lucas

Galapagos
Is.

Chimborazo
6310

Marañón
6768

6425

Cerro Ojos del Salado
6863

Cerro Aconcagua
6960

4058

Banks I.

Victoria I.

Gr. Bear L.

Gr. Slave L.

Peace

Mackenzie

Nelson

North
America

Great
Plains

Rocky Mountains

Cascade Coast Mts.

Sierra Madre

Great
Basin

Colorado

Arkansas

Rio Grande

Gulf of California

Mississippi

Popocatepetl
5452

Pico de Orizaba
5610

Yucatan

4093

Central
America

Isthmus
of Panama

5775

Galapagos

L. Winnipeg

Great
Lakes

Ohio

Mt. Mitchell
2037

Appalachian Mts.

Florida

Gulf of
Mexico

Florida Str.

Bahamas

Cuba

Hispaniola

Greater
Antilles

Jamaica

Caribbean Sea

Llanos

Orinoco

Mt. Roraima
2810

2994

Parry Is.

Devon I.

Baffin Island

Hudson Str.

Hudson
Bay

Laurentian Plateau

Labrador

St. Lawrence

G. of St. Lawrence

Nova Scotia

C. Cod

C. Hatteras

Bermuda

Sargasso
Sea

3175

Milwaukee Deep
8605

Puerto
Rico

Lesser
Antilles

Trinidad

Guiana Highlands

South
America

Japurá

Negro

Amazon

Purus

Madeira

Tapajós

Xingu

Tocantins

Selvas

Queen Elizabeth
Islands

Ellesmere I.

Greenland

Arctic Circle

3693

Denmark Str.

2119
Iceland

C. Farewell

Labrador
Sea

Newfoundland

C. Race

A T L A N T I C

O C E A N

Azores

Madeira

Canary Is.   3718

C. Verde
Is.

C. Verde

Equator

Ascension

St. Helena

Trindade

Tristan da Cunha

Jan Mayen

Norwegian

Faroe Is.

British
Isles   1345

B. of
Biscay

Pic d'A

Iberian
Pen.

Str. of Gibraltar

Atlas Mts.   4165
Toubkal   Maghre

Tropic of Cancer

Se
Senegal   A

C. Palmas   i

Gulf of Guin
1752

Tropic of Capricorn

A T L A N T I C

O C E A N

South
Orkney Is.

South
Sandwich Is.

2937
S. Georgia

Chile Trench
8050

L. Titicaca

Bolivian
Plateau

Gran Chaco

Plateau of
Mato Grosso

São Francisco

Brazilian Highlands

2890

C. Frio

C. de São Roque

Paraná

Pampas

Negro

Patagonia

R. de la Plata

-40

-105

Falkland Is.

Tierra del
Fuego

C. Horn

Scotia
Sea

Drake Passage

South
Shetland Is.

Bellingshausen
Sea

Thurston I.

Ellsworth Land

Vinson Massif
4897

Alexander I.

Antarctic Peninsula

Palmer
Land

Ronne
Ice Shelf

Weddell Sea

Berkner I.

Antarctic Circle

Caird Coast

Coats Land

Projection: Winkel III

West from Greenwich

1 2 3 4 5 6 7 8 9

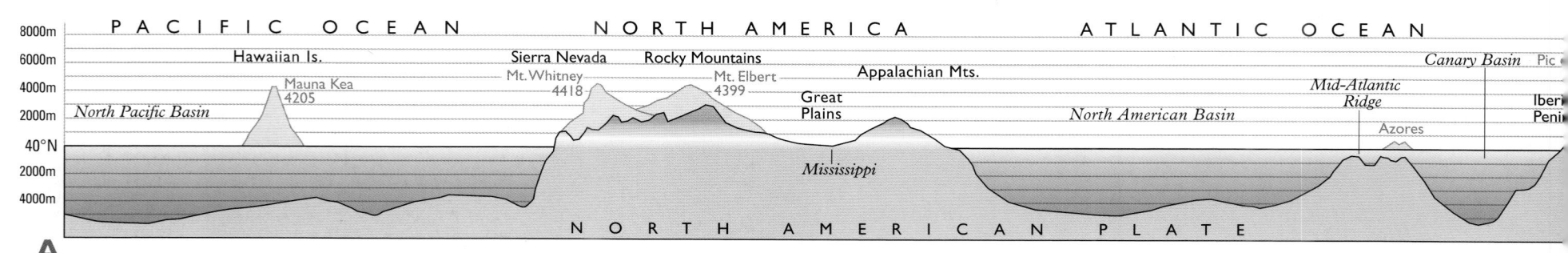

PACIFIC OCEAN   NORTH AMERICA   ATLANTIC OCEAN

8000m
6000m   Hawaiian Is.   Sierra Nevada   Rocky Mountains   Canary Basin   Pic
4000m   Mauna Kea   Mt. Whitney   Mt. Elbert   Appalachian Mts.   Mid-Atlantic
2000m   4205   4418   4399   Great   Ridge   Iber
North Pacific Basin   Plains   North American Basin   Peni
40°N   Azores
2000m   Mississippi
4000m

NORTH AMERICAN PLATE

A

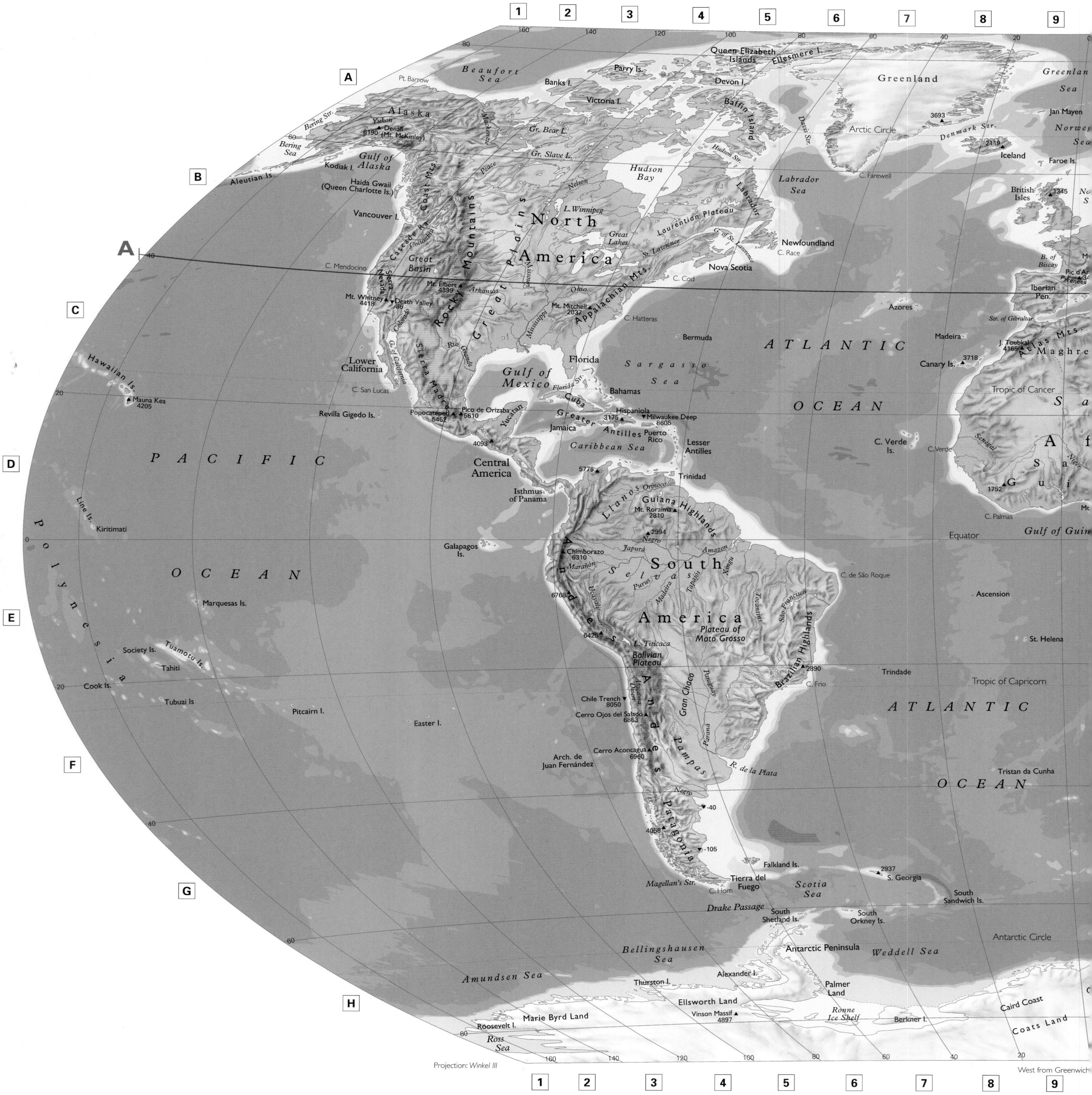

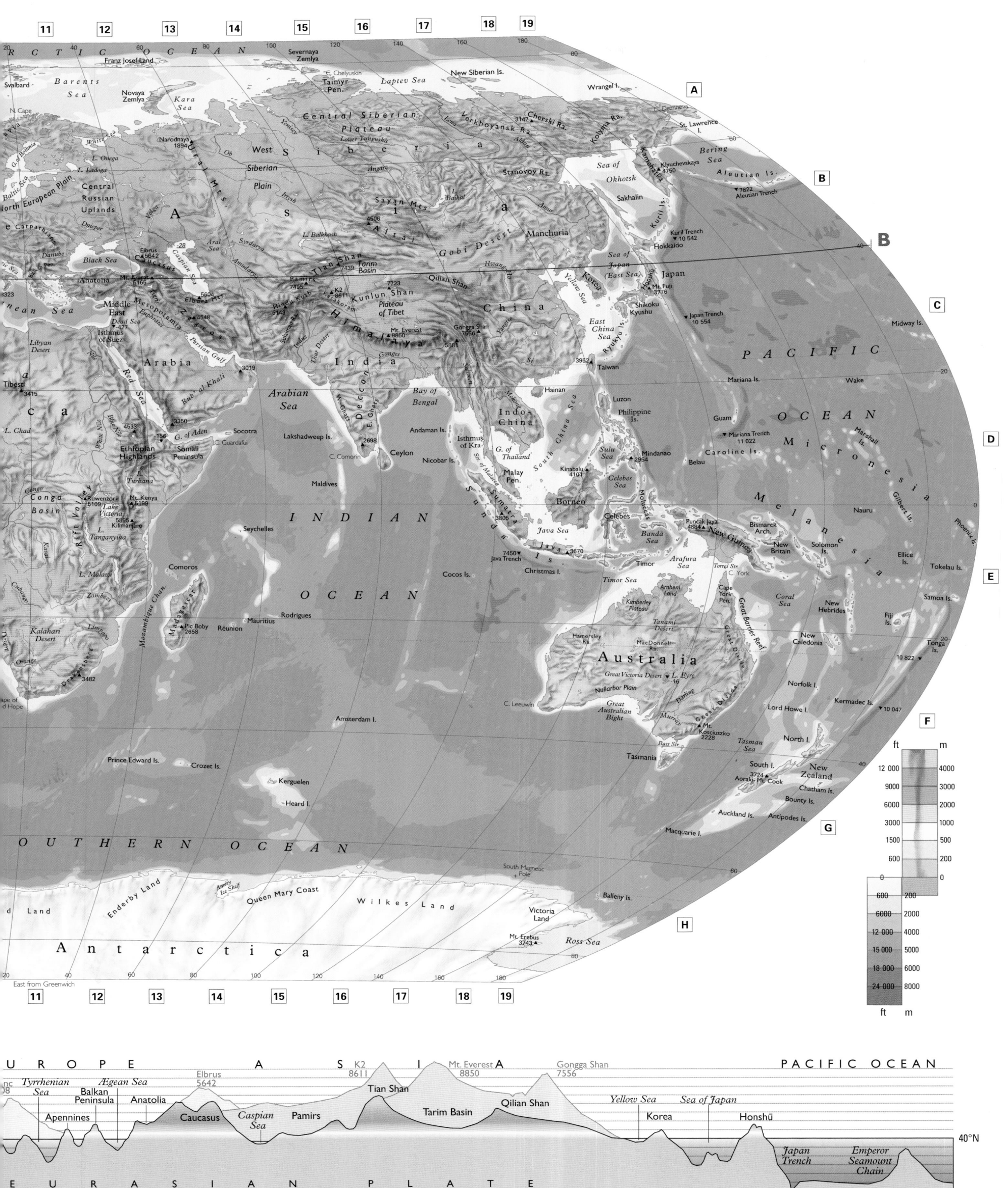

Equatorial Scale 1:76 000 000

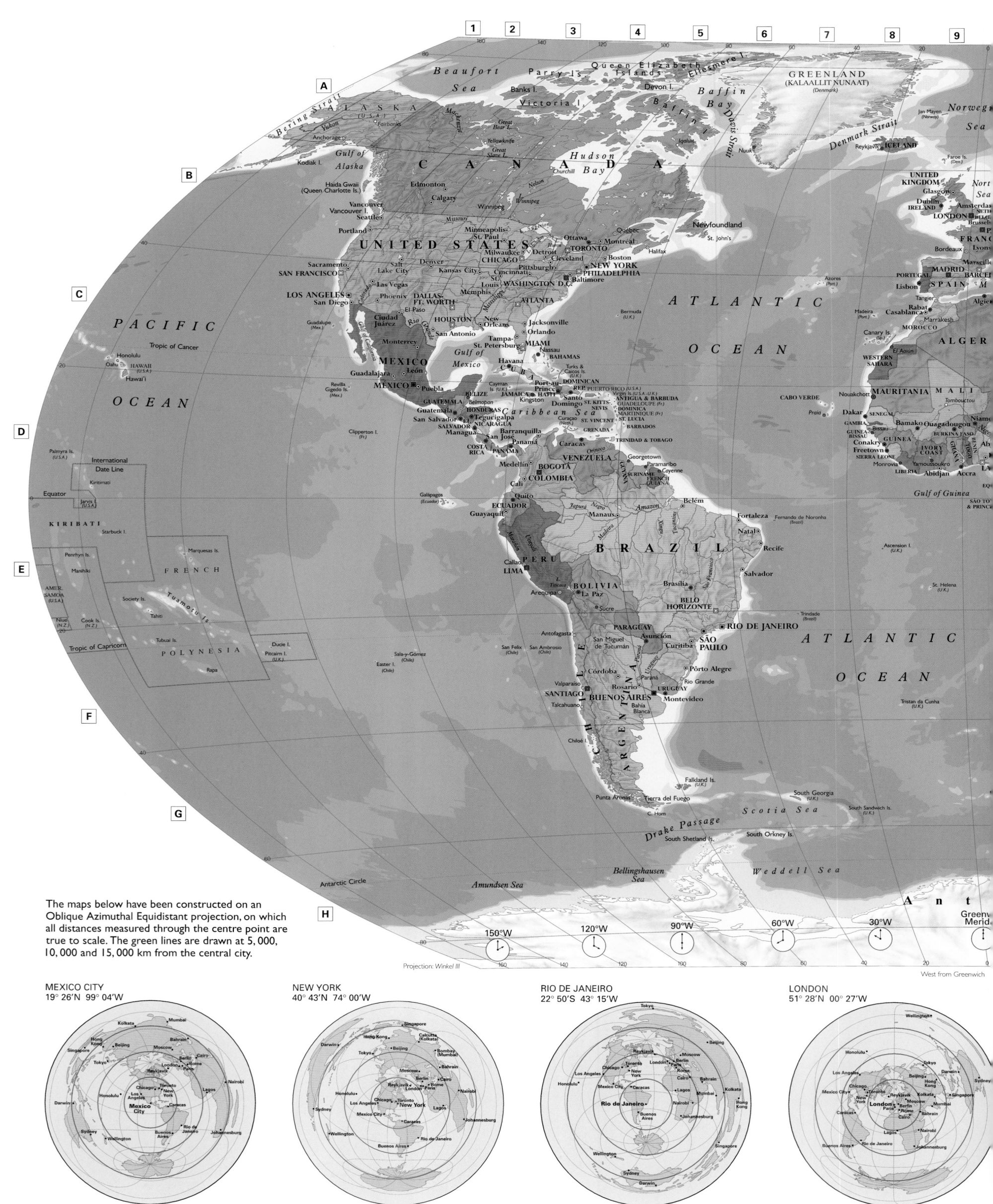

The maps below have been constructed on an Oblique Azimuthal Equidistant projection, on which all distances measured through the centre point are true to scale. The green lines are drawn at 5,000, 10,000 and 15,000 km from the central city.

Projection: Winkel III

West from Greenwich

MEXICO CITY
19° 26'N 99° 04'W

NEW YORK
40° 43'N 74° 00'W

RIO DE JANEIRO
22° 50'S 43° 15'W

LONDON
51° 28'N 00° 27'W

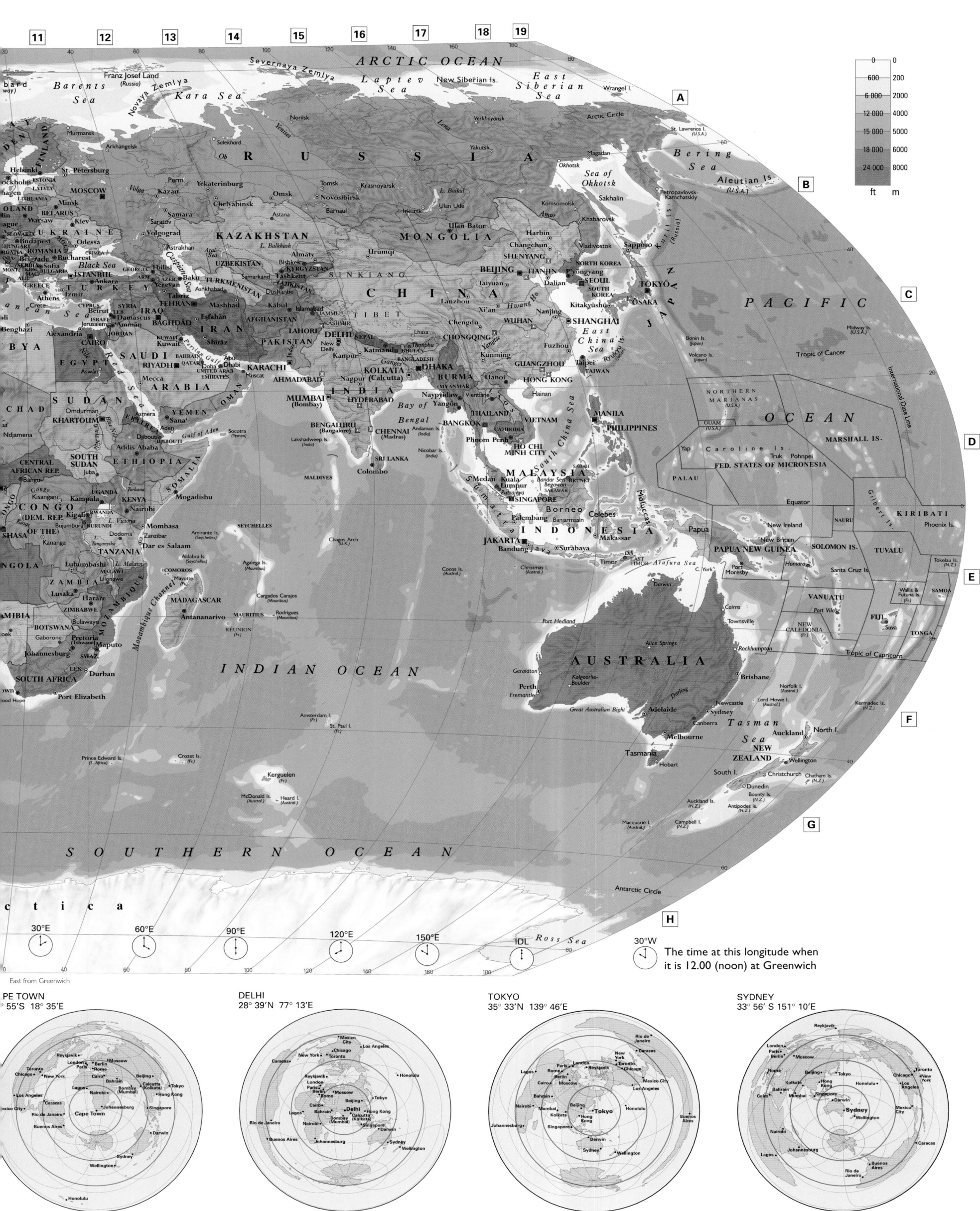

1:28 000 000

Maximum extent of sea ice

Minimum extent of sea ice

Ice caps and permanent ice shelf

Projection : Zenithal Equidistant

West from Greenwich   East from Greenwich

COPYRIGHT PHILIP'S

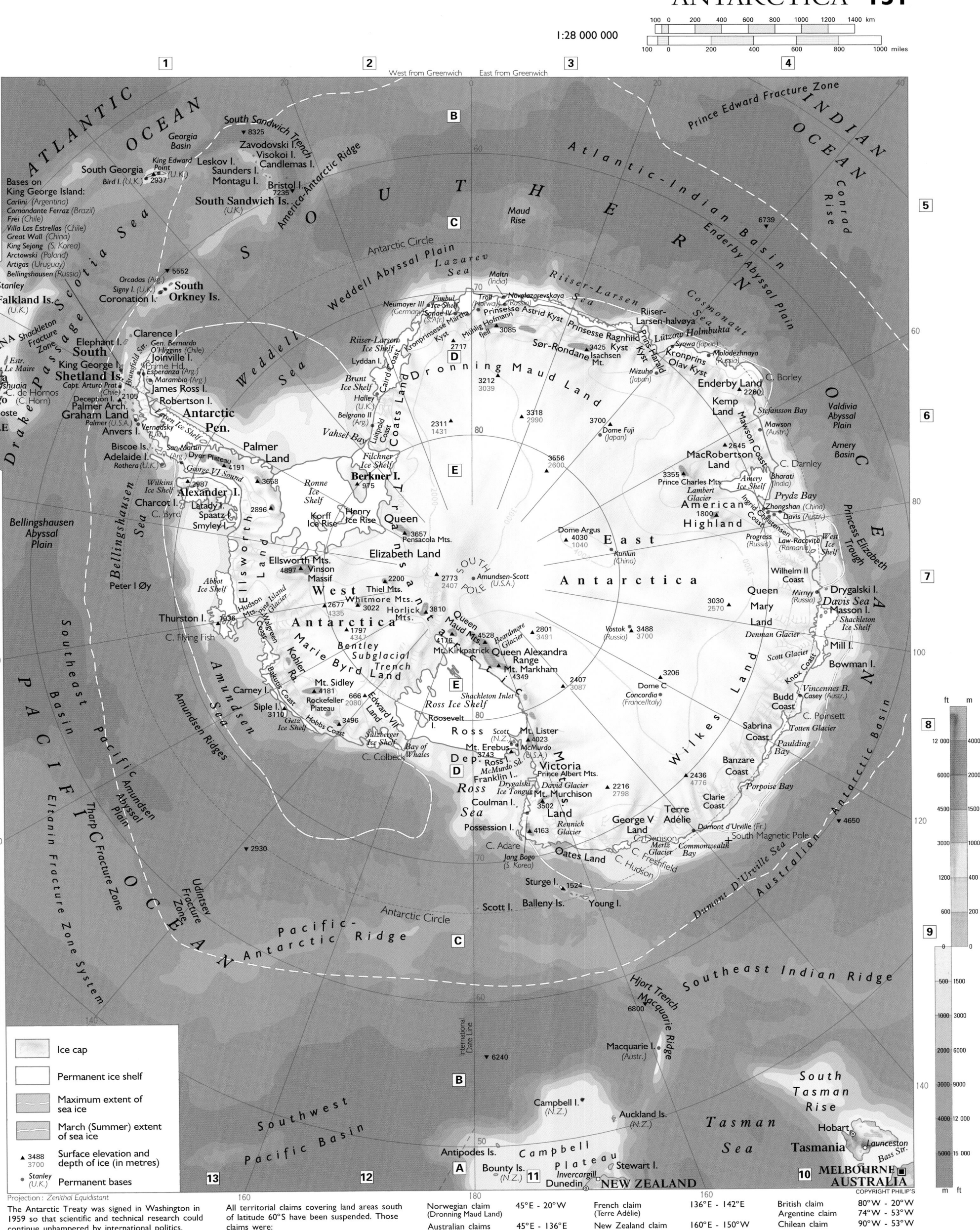

1:28 000 000

West from Greenwich   East from Greenwich

Bases on King George Island:
Carlini (Argentina)
Comandante Ferraz (Brazil)
Frei (Chile)
Villa Las Estrellas (Chile)
Great Wall (China)
King Sejong (S. Korea)
Arctowski (Poland)
Artigas (Uruguay)
Bellingshausen (Russia)

Legend:

	Ice cap
	Permanent ice shelf
	Maximum extent of sea ice
	March (Summer) extent of sea ice
▲ 3488 / 3700	Surface elevation and depth of ice (in metres)
● Stanley (U.K.)	Permanent bases

Projection : Zenithal Equidistant

The Antarctic Treaty was signed in Washington in 1959 so that scientific and technical research could continue unhampered by international politics.

All territorial claims covering land areas south of latitude 60°S have been suspended. Those claims were:

Norwegian claim (Dronning Maud Land)	45°E - 20°W
Australian claims	45°E - 136°E / 142°E - 160°E
French claim (Terre Adélie)	136°E - 142°E
New Zealand claim (Ross Dependency)	160°E - 150°W
British claim	80°W - 20°W
Argentine claim	74°W - 53°W
Chilean claim	90°W - 53°W

COPYRIGHT PHILIP'S

Equatorial Scale 1:41 000 000

CANADA

Hudson Bay
Churchill
Belcher Is.
C. Henrietta Maria
James Bay
Regina
Winnipeg
Nelson
L. Winnipeg
Moosonee
Albany
Hudson Str.
C. Chidley
Northwest Atlantic Mid-Ocean Canyon
Davis Strait
GREENLAND (Denmark)
Nuuk
Nunap Isua (K. Farvel)
Tasiilaq
Denmark Strait
Reykjanes Ridge
Reykjavík
ICELAND
Oræfajökull 2119
Norwegian Sea
Trondheim
NORWAY
Bergen
Oslo

Labrador Sea
Str. of Belle Isle
Hamilton Inlet
Charlie Gibbs Fracture Zone
Newfoundland
Flemish Cap
Rockall (U.K.)
Rockall Trough
UNITED KINGDOM
Glasgow
North Sea
DENMARK
København
Stockholm
Göteborg
Malmö
Gdańsk
POLAND

Minneapolis
St. Paul
L. Superior
Québec
Montréal
St. Lawrence
Gulf of St. Lawrence
St. John's
C. Race
Cape Breton I.
Halifax
Grand Banks of Newfoundland
Porcupine Abyssal Plain
Dublin
IRELAND
Liverpool
Amsterdam
London
NETH.
Hamburg
Berlin
GERMANY
Warszawa

Omaha
Chicago
L. Michigan
L. Huron
Toronto
L. Ontario
L. Erie
Detroit
Celtic Sea
English Channel
Le Havre
Paris
FRANCE
Brussel BELG.
CZECHIA
Wien
SLOVAKIA
AUSTRIA
HUNGARY
Milano
Zagreb
CROATIA

St. Louis
Pittsburgh
New York
Philadelphia
Baltimore
Washington D.C.
Appalachian Mts.
New England Seamounts
King's Trough
Açores-Biscay Rise
5225
Bay of Biscay
Biscay Abyssal Plain
A Coruña
C. Fisterra
Bordeaux
Mt. Blanc 4808
Marseille
Corse
Barcelona
Roma
ITALY
Adriatic Sea
BOS.H.

UNITED STATES
Atlanta
Chesapeake Bay
C. Hatteras
Corner Seamounts
Açores (Port.)
2351
Ponta Delgada
Porto
Madrid
SPAIN
Is. Baleares
Sardegna
Nápoli
Sicilia

Houston
Galveston
New Orleans
Charleston
Jacksonville
Hamilton
Bermuda (U.K.)
6028
Sohm Abyssal Plain
Bermuda Rise
Hatteras Abyssal Plain
Lisboa
PORTUGAL
C. de São Vicente
Str. of Gibraltar
Tanger
Alger
Tunis
MALTA
Mediterranean Sea

Orlando
Sargasso Sea
Funchal
Madeira (Port.)
Casablanca
Rabat
MOROCCO
Marrakech
Chott Djerid
Tarābulus

Tampico
Veracruz
G. de Campeche
Miami
Nassau
BAHAMAS
Tropic of Cancer
Florida Strait
Is. Canarias (Sp.)
3718
Las Palmas
El Aaiún
WESTERN SAHARA
Saharan Seamounts
ALGERIA
Sahara

Gulf of Mexico
Sigsbee 3504
Deep Canal de Yucatan
La Habana
CUBA
West Indies
Nares Abyssal Plain
5638
Cape Verde Abyssal Plain
Ras Nouâdhibou

MEXICO
BELIZE
G. de Honduras
Santiago de Cuba
Cayman Trough
JAMAICA
Kingston
HAITI
DOM. REP.
Milwaukee Deep 8605
PUERTO RICO (USA)
San Juan
ANTIGUA
GUADELOUPE (Fr.)
Leeward Is.
Cape Verde Plateau
Nouakchott
MAURITANIA
CABO VERDE
St-Louis
Dakar
C. Vert
SENEGAL

GUATEMALA
Guatemala
HONDURAS
EL SALVADOR
NICARAGUA
L. de Nicaragua
Santo Domingo
ST. KITTS
DOMINICA
MARTINIQUE (Fr.)
ST. LUCIA
BARBADOS
7292
2829
Praia
Kayes
MALI
GAMBIA
Banjul
GUINEA-BISSAU
Bamako
Ouagadougou
BURKINA FASO
NIGER
Kano

Caribbean Sea
Colombian Basin
Barranquilla
5779
Sierra Nevada de Santa Marta
ST. VINCENT
GRENADA
Windward Is.
Demerara Abyssal Plain
GUINEA
Conakry
Freetown
SIERRA LEONE
NIGERIA

COSTA RICA
Panama Canal
G. del Darién
Caracas
TRINIDAD & TOBAGO
Port of Spain
Sierra Leone Rise
Sierra Leone Basin
Monrovia
LIBERIA
IVORY COAST
Abidjan
GHANA
Accra
TOGO
BENIN
Lagos

PANAMA
G. de Panamá
VENEZUELA
Orinoco
Meta
Georgetown
GUYANA
Paramaribo
SURINAM
Cayenne
FRENCH GUIANA
C. Orange
Ceara Rise
Sekondi-Takoradi
Gulf of Guinea
Port Harcourt
CAM.
4870
EQUATORIAL GUINEA
Bioko
3008

Cali
Bogotá
Sierra Pacaraima
Mt. Roraima 2810
Branco
Ceara Abyssal Plain
Equator
São Pedro & São Paulo (Brazil)
7758
Guinea Basin
São TOMÉ & PRÍNCIPE
C. Lopez
Annobón (Eq. Guinea)
GAB.

COLOMBIA
Quito
ECUADOR
Cotopaxi 5897
Chimborazo 6310
Putumayo
Napo
Japurá
Negro
Amazonas
Santarém
Belém
São Luís
6537
Fernando de Noronha (Brazil)
C. de São Roque
Pointe Noire

Guayaquil
G. de Guayaquil
Pta. Parinas
Iquitos
Manaus
Madeira
Tapajós
Xingu
Tocantins
Fortaleza
Atol das Rocas
Natal
Pernambuco Abyssal Plain

Trujillo
PERU
Lima
Purus
Juruá
BRAZIL
Amazonas
Araguaia
São Francisco
Recife
Maceió
Ascension I. (U.K.) 859
Brazil Basin
Angola
Angola Basin
ANG.
5656

Nevado Ancohuma 6550
La Paz
BOLIVIA
L. Titicaca
Brasília
Góiânia
Salvador
St. Helena (U.K.) 820
Hotspur Seamount
Angola Abyssal Plain

Arica
Iquique
L. de Poopó
Pilcomayo
Belo Horizonte
Vitória Seamount
2890
Martin Vaz
Banco Abrolhos

Antofagasta
8064
Peru-Chile Trench
Nasca Ridge
PARAGUAY
Gran Chaco
Pilcomayo
São Paulo
Santos
Rio de Janeiro
C. de São Tomé
C. Frio
Trindade (Brazil)
Tropic of Capricorn
Walvis Ridge

San Miguel de Tucumán
Asunción
Paraná
Pampas
Curitiba
ATLANTIC OCEAN
Namibia Abyssal Plain
Port Nolloth

Ojos del Salado (6893)
CHILE
ARGENTINA
Córdoba
Santa Fe
Rosario
URUGUAY
Pôrto Alegre
L. dos Patos
638
Rio Grande Rise
5457
Cape Basin
Cape Town

San Ambrosio (Chile)
Arch. de Juan Fernández (Chile)
Aconcagua 6962
Valparaíso
Santiago
Montevideo
Buenos Aires
Bahía Blanca
Rio de la Plata
Colorado
Tristan da Cunha (U.K.) 2062
Inaccessible I. (U.K.)
887
C. of Good Hope

Concepción
Pampas
Puerto Montt
I. de Chiloé
G. San Matías
Pen. Valdés
Chubut
Argentine Basin
910
Gough I. (U.K.)
5704
411
Discovery Seamount
Agulhas Ridge

Arch de los Chonos
Pen. de Taitao
G. de Penas
Golfo San Jorge
Argentine Abyssal Plain
Falkland Ridge

PACIFIC OCEAN
Est. de Magallanes (Magellan Str.)
Punta Arenas
I. Santa Inés
Tierra del Fuego
C. de Hornos
705
Burdwood Bank
Falkland Is. (U.K.)
Stanley
Falkland Plateau
Shag Rocks
South Georgia (U.K.)
Mt. Paget 2937
Grytviken 8325
Georgia Basin
South Sandwich Trench
Bouvetøya (Norw.)

ft m
12000 4000
9000 3000
6000 2000
3000 1000
1500 500
600 200
0
200 600
1000 3000
2000 6000
4000 12000
6000 18000
8000 24000
m ft

West from Greenwich
Projection: Mollweide

COPYRIGHT PHILIP'S

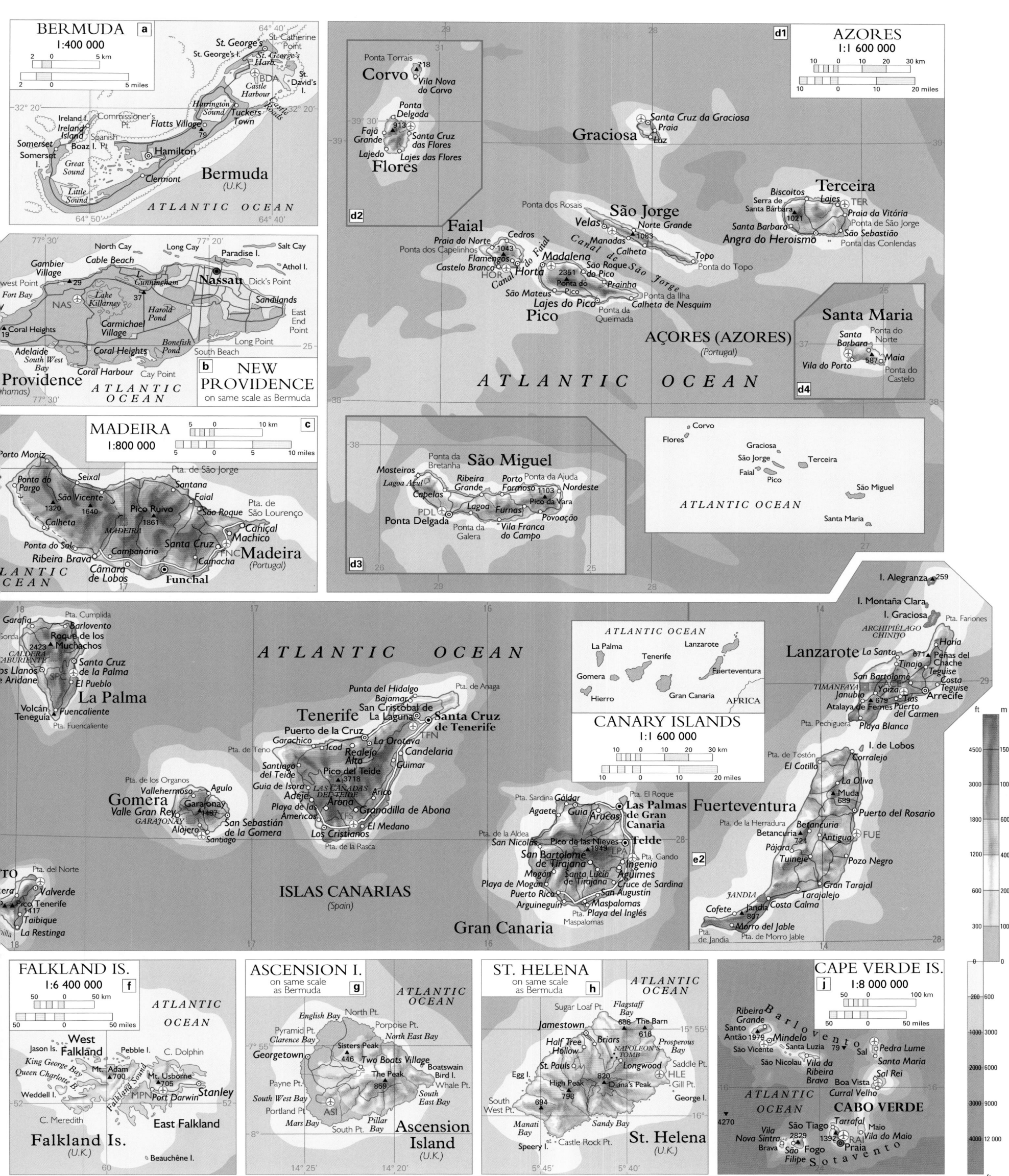

BERMUDA
1:400 000

NEW PROVIDENCE
on same scale as Bermuda

MADEIRA
1:800 000

AZORES
1:1 600 000

AÇORES (AZORES)
(Portugal)

CANARY ISLANDS
1:1 600 000

ISLAS CANARIAS
(Spain)

FALKLAND IS.
1:6 400 000

Falkland Is.
(U.K.)

ASCENSION I.
on same scale as Bermuda

Ascension Island
(U.K.)

ST. HELENA
on same scale as Bermuda

St. Helena
(U.K.)

CAPE VERDE IS.
1:8 000 000

CABO VERDE

West from Greenwich

COPYRIGHT PHILIP'S

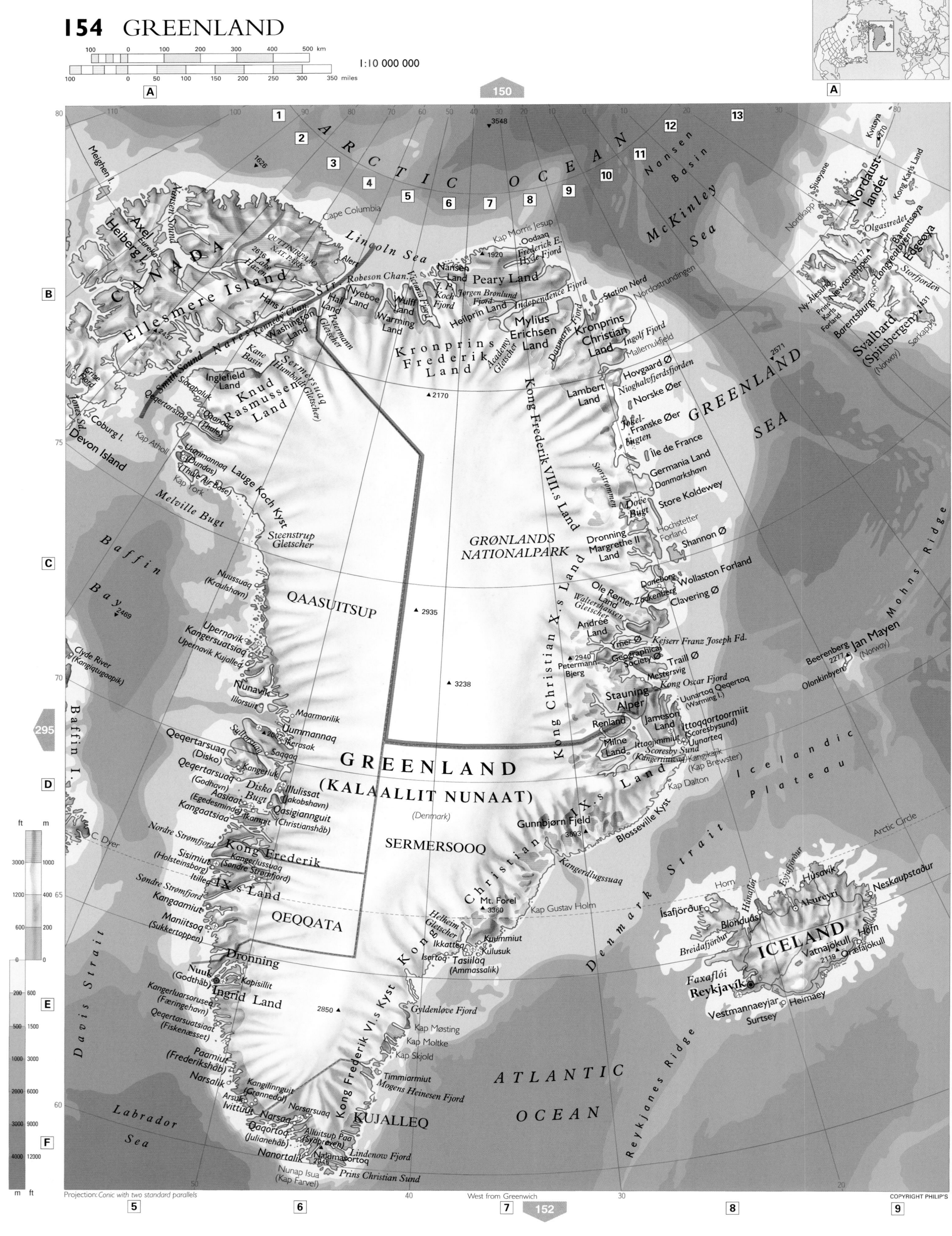

100   0   100   200   300   400   500 km
1:10 000 000
100   50   0   50   100   150   200   250   300   350 miles

Projection: Conic with two standard parallels

West from Greenwich

152

COPYRIGHT PHILIP'S

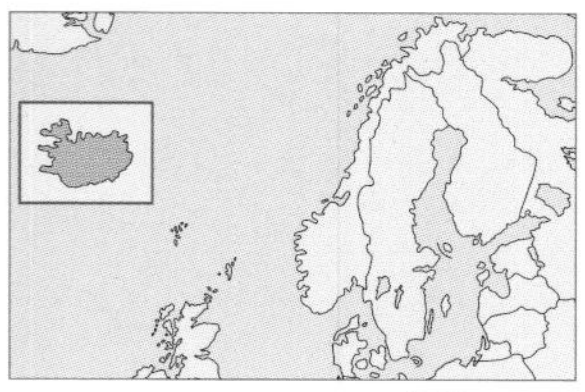

1:2 000 000

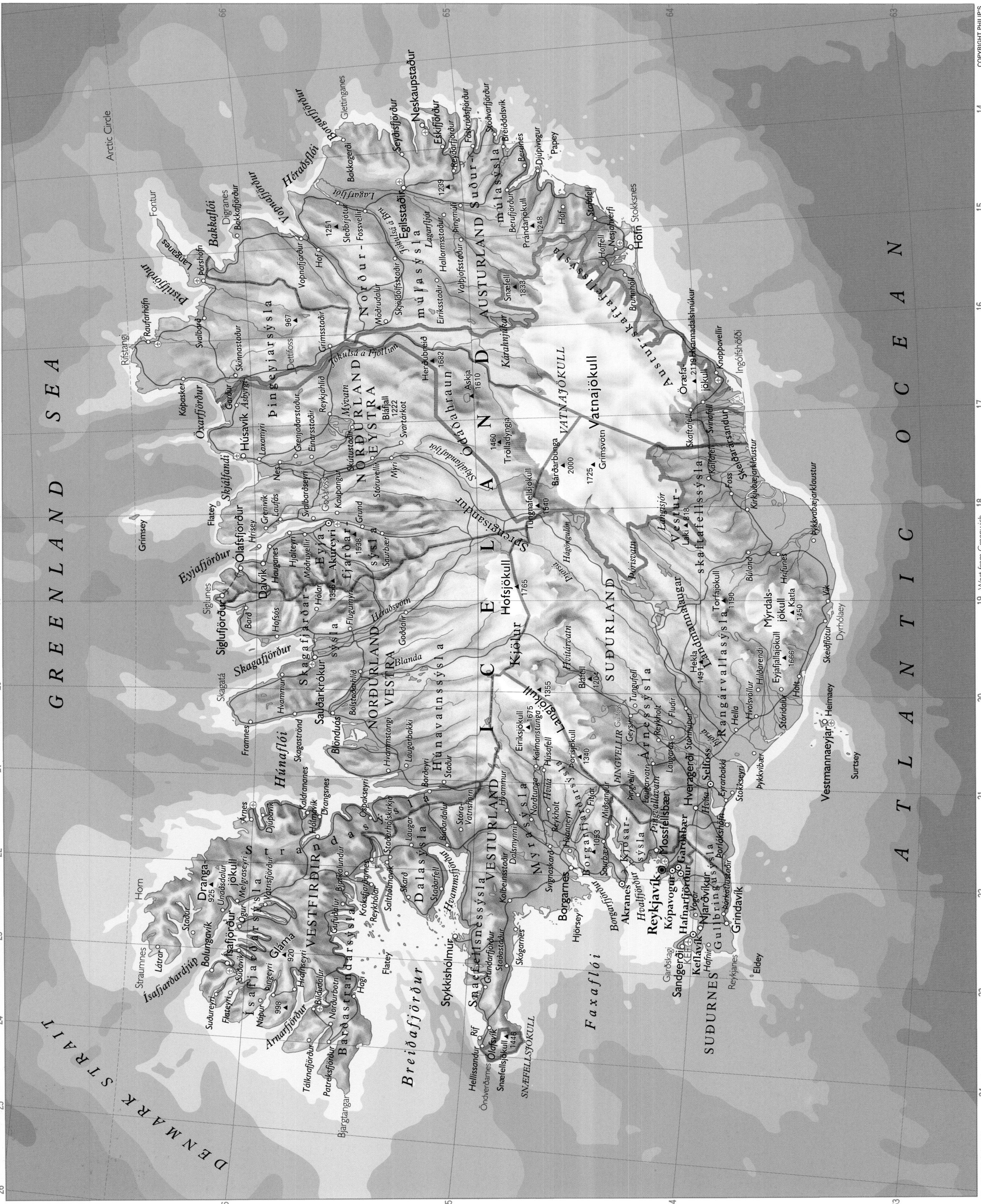

| 10 | 0 | 10 | 20 | 30 | 40 | 50 | 60 | 70 | 80 | 100 km |

| 10 | 0 | 10 | 20 | 30 | 40 | 50 | 60 miles |

Projection: Polyconic

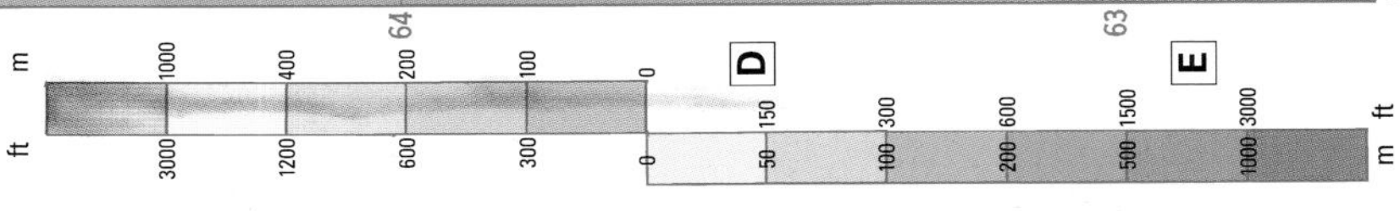

West from Greenwich

152

GREENLAND SEA

ATLANTIC OCEAN

DENMARK STRAIT

Arctic Circle

ICELAND

VESTFIRÐIR

NORÐURLAND VESTRA

NORÐURLAND EYSTRA

AUSTURLAND

VESTURLAND

SUÐURLAND

SUÐURNES

Reykjavík
Kópavogur
Hafnarfjörður
Keflavík
Grindavík
Akranes
Borgarnes
Selfoss
Vík
Höfn
Egilsstaðir
Neskaupstaður
Seyðisfjörður
Húsavík
Akureyri
Dalvík
Ólafsfjörður
Siglufjörður
Sauðárkrókur
Blönduós
Ísafjörður
Bolungavík
Stykkishólmur

VATNAJÖKULL
Hofsjökull
Langjökull
Mýrdalsjökull
Snæfellsjökull
Drangajökull
Eiríksjökull
Þórisjökull
Torfajökull
Tungnafellsjökull
Eyjafjallajökull

Hekla
Katla
Askja
Herðubreið
Bárðarbunga
Grímsvötn

Vestmannaeyjar
Surtsey
Heimaey
Grímsey
Papey

Faxaflói
Breiðafjörður
Húnaflói
Skagafjörður
Eyjafjörður
Skjálfandi
Öxarfjörður
Þistilfjörður
Bakkaflói
Héraðsflói
Vopnafjörður
Berufjörður
Faxaflói

m	ft
3000	1000
1200	400
600	200
300	100
150	50
0	0
100	50-150
200	150-300
600	300-600
1500	600-1500
3000	1000-3000

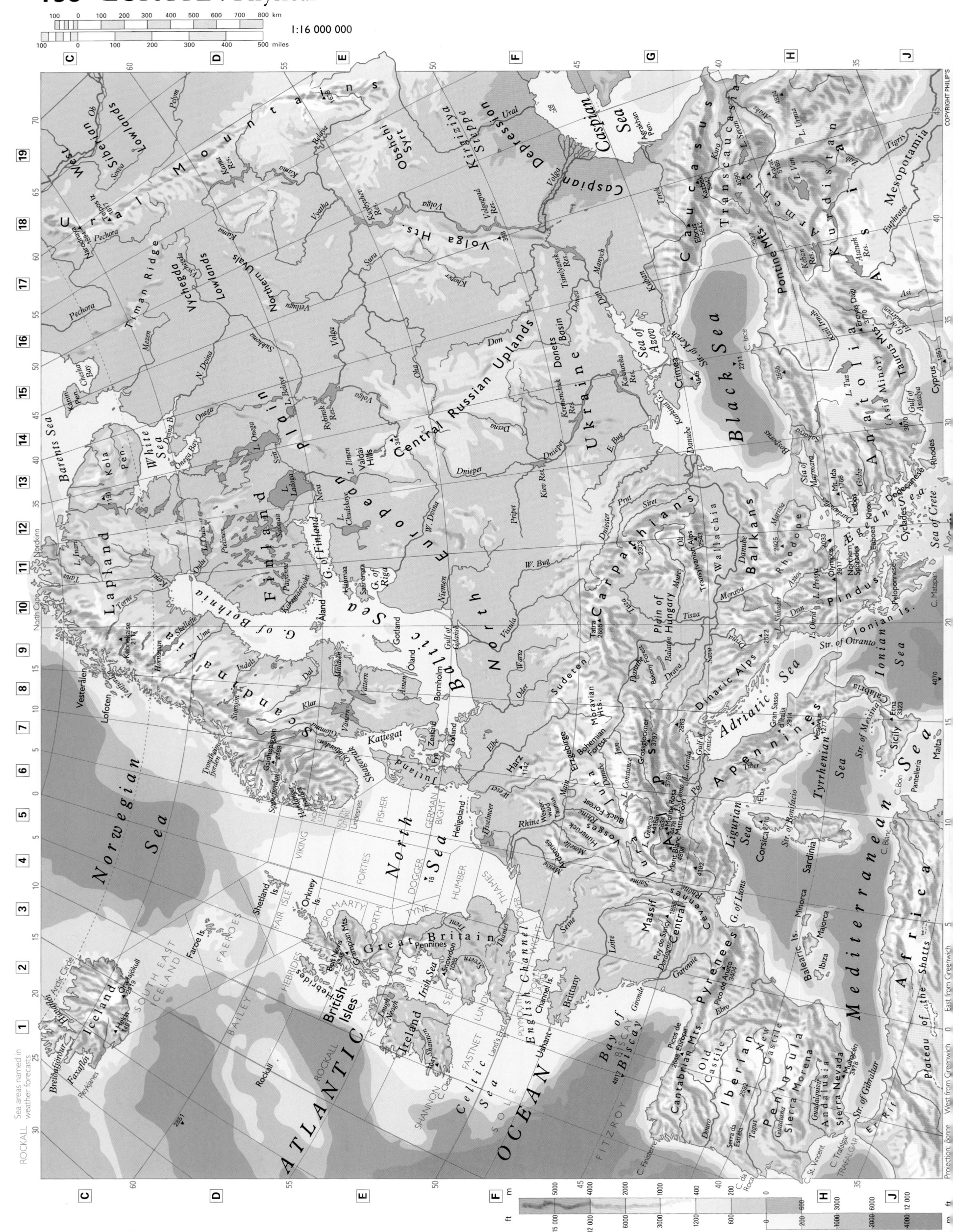

1:16 000 000

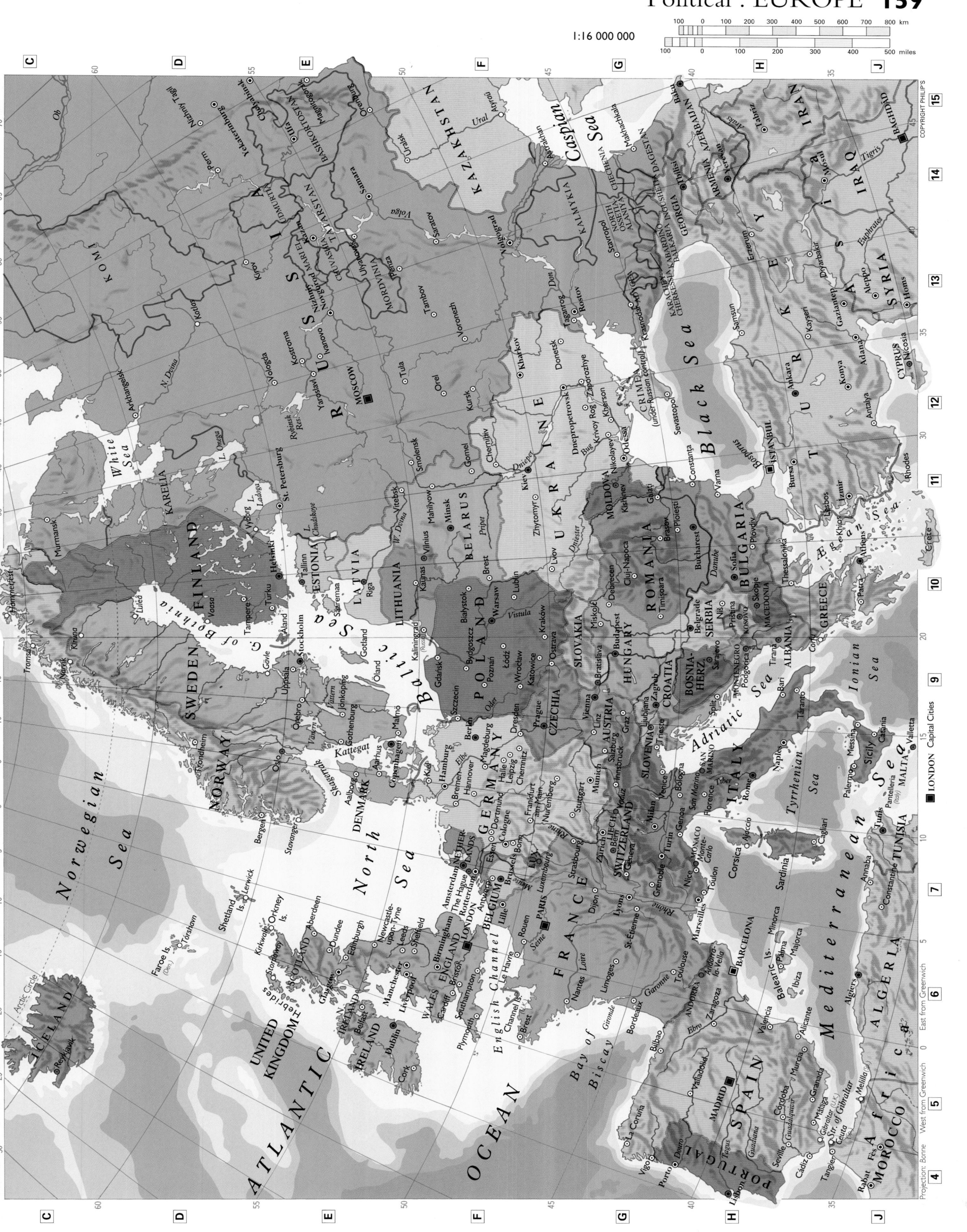

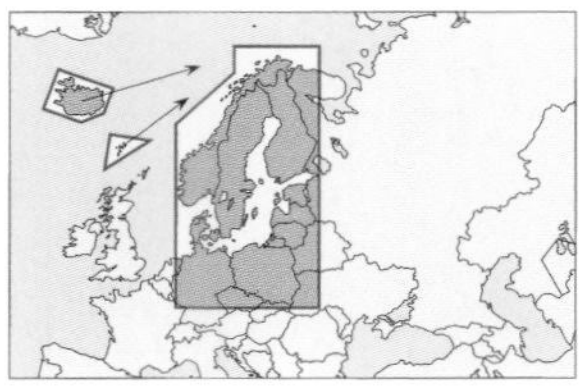

1:4 800 000

50 0 25 50 75 100 125 150 175 km
50 0 25 50 75 100 125 miles

A B C D E F

BARENTS SEA

RUSSIA

KARELIA

Kola
Murmansk
Severomorsk
Pechenga
Nikel
Kirkenes
Vadsø
Vardø
Varangerfjorden
Varanger halvøya
Tanafjorden
Nordkinn-halvøya
Nordkapp
Magerøya
Honningsvåg
Hammerfest
Sørøya
Kvaløya
Tromsø
Senja
Andøya
Narvik
Bodø
Lofoten
Vesterålen

N O R W A Y

Inari
Inarijärvi
Ivalo
Lappland
Finnmark
Kautokeino
Kiruna
Gällivare
Kebnekaise 2114

S W E D E N

F I N L A N D

Rovaniemi
Kemijärvi
Kemi
Tornio
Haparanda
Oulu
Luleå
Boden
Piteå
Skellefteå
Umeå
Örnsköldsvik
Sundsvall
Söderhamn

Gulf of Bothnia

Kokkola
Vaasa
Pori
Rauma
Tampere
Jyväskylä
Kuopio
Joensuu
Mikkeli

Trondheim
Östersund
Österdalen
Gudbrandsdalen

ATLANTIC OCEAN

N O R W E G I A N   S E A

ICELAND on same scale

Reykjavik
Vatnajökull
Keflavík
Akureyri
Húnaflói
Faxaflói
Breiðafjörður

FÆROE ISLANDS on same scale
Føroyar (Færoe Is.) (Den.)
Tórshavn
Streymoy
Suðuroy

Arctic Circle

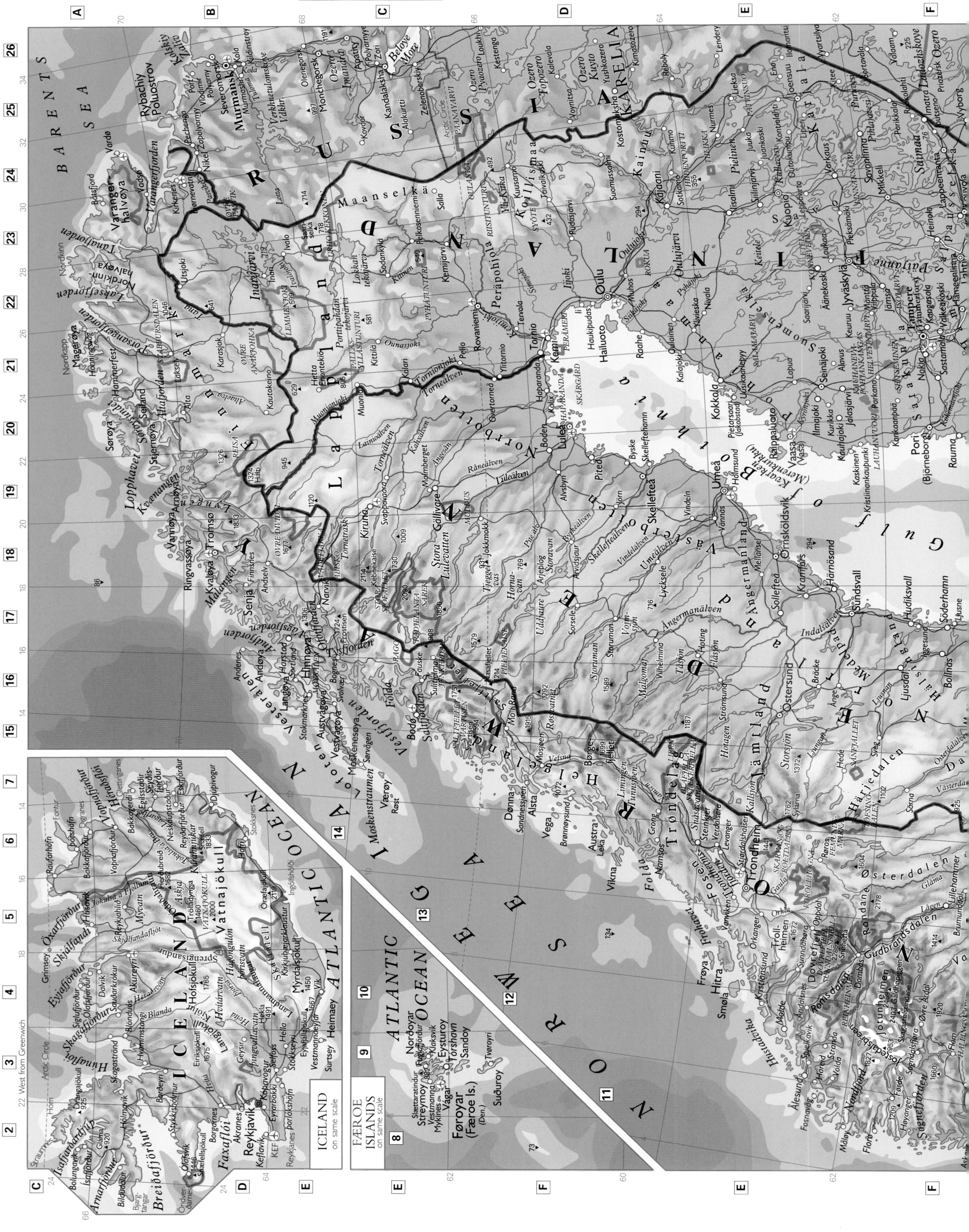

1:2 000 000

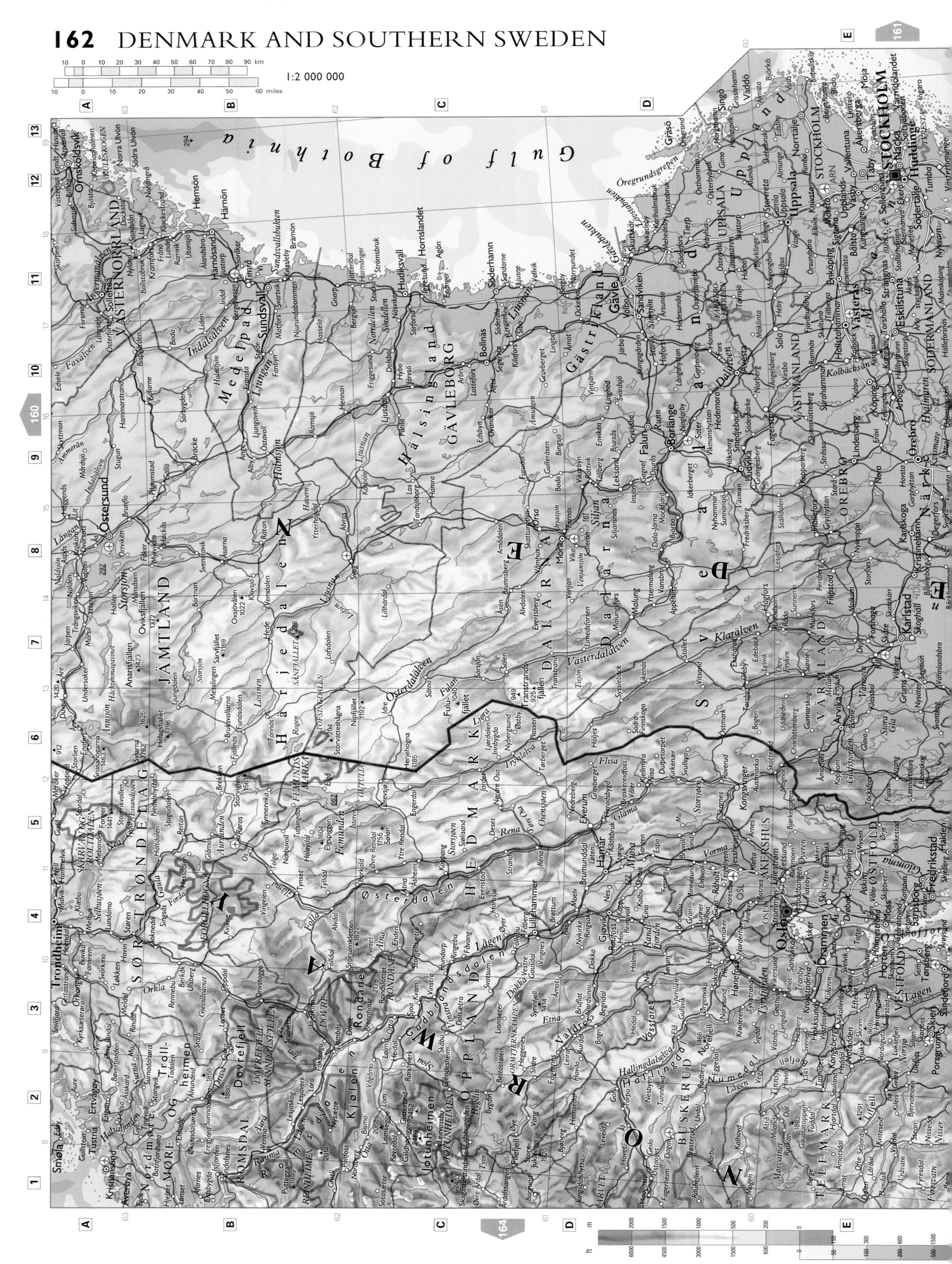

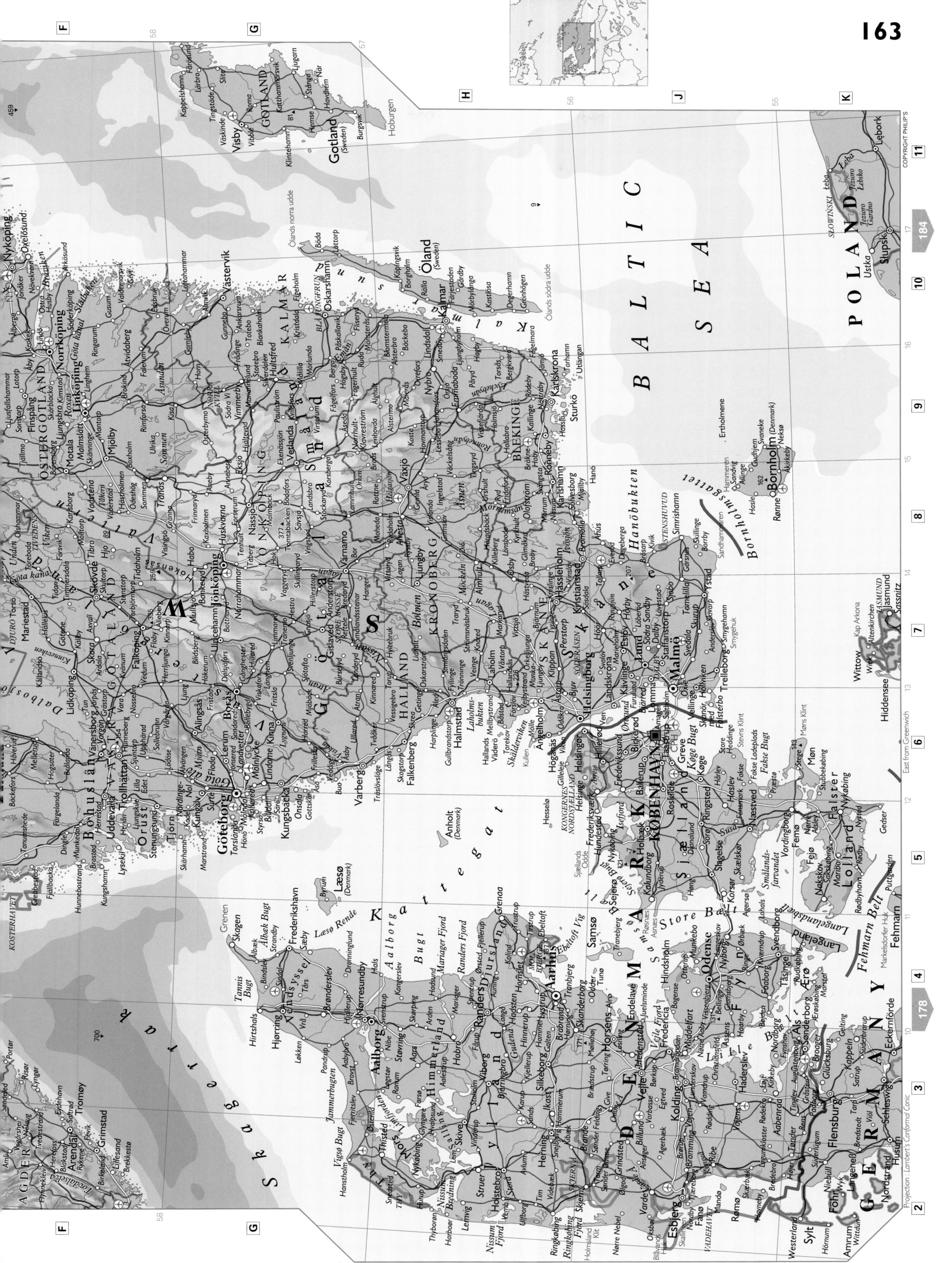

1:2 000 000

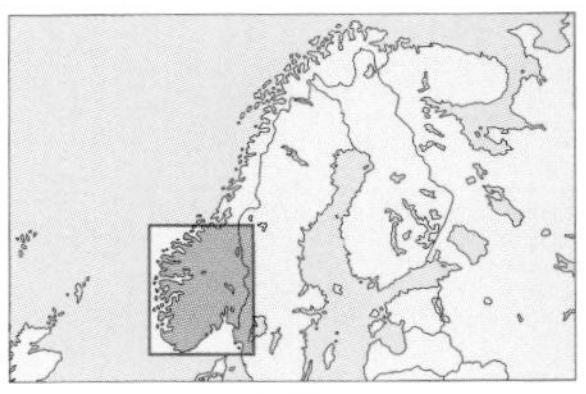

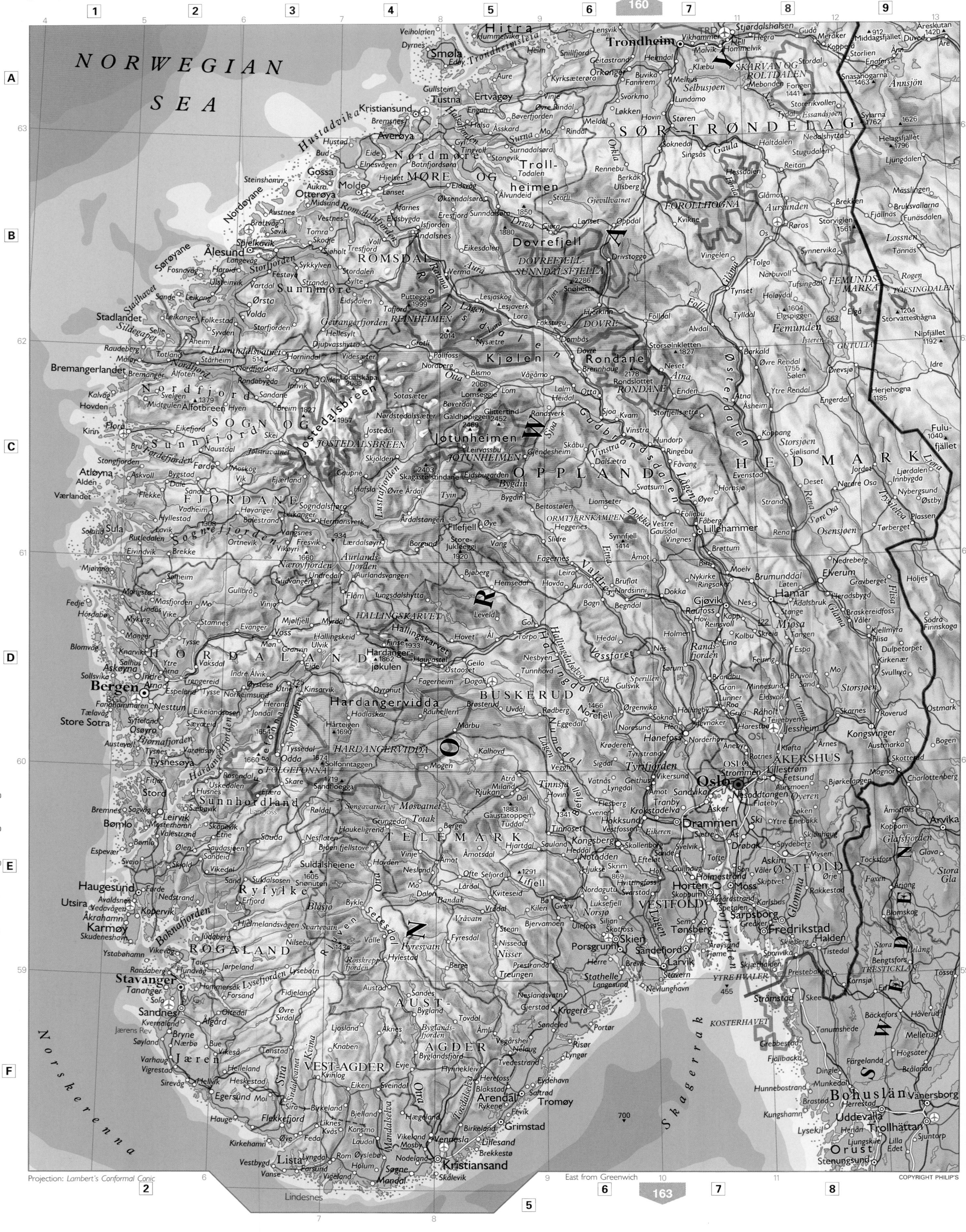

10 0 10 20 30 40 50 60 70 80 90 km

10 0 10 20 30 40 50 60 miles

NORWEGIAN SEA

NORDMØRE OG ROMSDAL — MØRE

SØR-TRØNDELAG

DOVREFJELL

DOVREFJELL-SUNNDALSFJELLA

Trondheim

Ålesund

Molde

Kristiansund

SOGN OG FJORDANE

JOSTEDALSBREEN

JOTUNHEIMEN

Galdhøpiggen 2469

RONDANE

Rondslottet 2178

HEDMARK

OPPLAND

Lillehammer

Hamar

Elverum

Mjøsa

Gjøvik

FEMUNDS-MARKA

Femunden

Røros

Bergen

HORDALAND

Hardangervidda

BUSKERUD

Hardangerjøkulen 1862

Voss

SOGNEFJORDEN

NORDFJORD

Hønefoss

Drammen

Oslo

AKERSHUS

Kongsvinger

TELEMARK

Gaustatoppen 1883

VESTFOLD

Tønsberg

Sandefjord

Larvik

ØSTFOLD

Sarpsborg

Fredrikstad

Halden

Skien

Porsgrunn

ROGALAND

RYFYLKE

Haugesund

Stavanger

Sandnes

JÆREN

Egersund

Flekkefjord

VEST-AGDER

AUST-AGDER

Arendal

Grimstad

Kristiansand

Mandal

Skagerrak

SWEDEN

BOHUSLÄN

Uddevalla

Trollhättan

Vänersborg

Arvika

Projection: Lambert's Conformal Conic

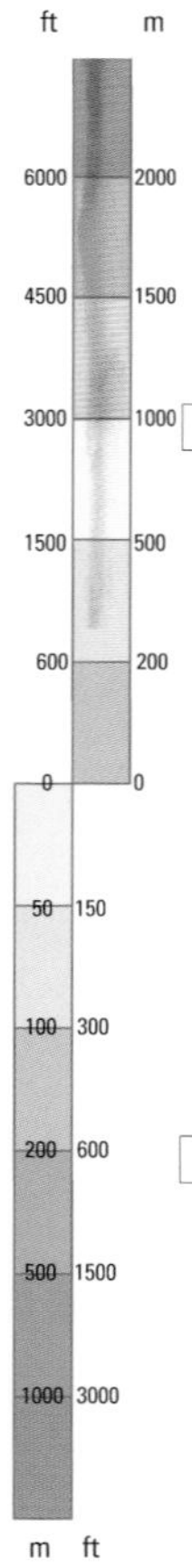

East from Greenwich

COPYRIGHT PHILIP'S

50 0 25 50 75 100 125 150 175 km

50 0 25 50 75 100 125 miles

A

NORWAY
Bergen
Osøyra
Stord
Bømlo Leirvik
Haugesund
Kopervik
Åkrahamn
Stavanger
Sandnes
Bryne
Nærbø

C

161

D

m ft

ft m

3000 1000

1500 500

600 200

50 150

100 300

200 600

500 1500

1000 3000

2000 6000

m ft

Shetland Is.
(U.K.)
Yell Unst
Fetlar
458
Foula Mainland
Lerwick

Fair Isle

A T L A N T I C   O C E A N

1224

316

North
Rona
Orkney Is.
Westray Sanday
Stronsay
Mainland Kirkwall
Hoy 481 South
Ronaldsay

P e n t l a n d   F i r t h
C. Wrath
Thurso Wick
Flannan Is.
Lewis Stornoway
Harris
St. Kilda
(U.K.)
789
North
Uist
Benbecula
South Uist
Barra
Skye
992
Rum
Eigg
Coll
Tiree
966
Mull
Iona
Colonsay
Jura
Islay

Lairg
Helmsdale
Ullapool
Golspie
1081 Tain
Invergordon
Dingwall Nairn Elgin Buckie Banff
Inverness CAIRNGORMS Fraserburgh
L. Ness Aviemore Don Huntly Peterhead
1182 Inverurie
Glen Mor 1311 Dee Aberdeen
Mallaig SCOTLAND
Fort William Ballater Stonehaven
Ben Nevis 1345 Grampian Mts.
Oban 1214 Montrose
Tobermory L. Awe Forfar Arbroath
Perth
L. Lomond & Trossachs Dundee
L. Fyne St. Andrews
973 Stirling Glenrothes
Dumbarton Kirkcaldy
Greenock GLASGOW Dunfermline Dunbar
Paisley Edinburgh
East Kilbride Hamilton Berwick-upon-Tweed
Arran Cumbernauld
Irvine Kilmarnock Galashiels
Campbeltown Ayr 840 Jedburgh Cheviot
Southern Uplands Hawick Hills 816
Girvan Dumfries NORTHUMBERLAND Alnwick
Kirkcudbright Annan Hexham
Stranraer Carlisle 893

M o r a y   F i r t h

N O R T H

S E A

Sea of the Hebrides
Inner Hebrides
Outer Hebrides
North West Highlands
North Minch
The Minch

238

16

161

Tory I.
Malin Hd.
Arranmore Buncrana Coleraine
Arranmore Letterkenny Derry/Londonderry Ballymena Larne
Donegal GLENVEAGH Lifford Omagh NORTHERN Antrim Bangor
Bundoran Lower L. Erne Enniskillen Ulster IRELAND Belfast Lisburn
Ballina Sligo Clones Armagh Newry
Lough Neagh Craigavon
Conn Leitrim Cavan Castleblaney

North Channel
Firth of Clyde
Mull of Galloway
Workington
Whitehaven
Newcastle-upon-Tyne
South Shields
Gateshead Sunderland
Durham Hartlepool
Darlington Redcar
Middlesbrough
Stockton-on-Tees N. YORK MOORS
Scarborough

D

CELTIC

SEA

Westport Castlebar Roscommon Longford
Lough Mask Lough Corrib Athlone Mullingar
Connemara IRELAND Ballinasloe Kells
Galway B. Galway Tullamore Birr
Aran Is. BURREN Ennis Nenagh Portlaoise Athy Carlow
Lough Derg Thurles Kilkenny
Limerick Tipperary 920 Clonmel Carrick-on-Suir
Listowel 1041 Carrantuohill Mallow Clonmel Waterford
Tralee MacGillycuddy's Reeks Killarney Blackwater Dungarvan Youghal
Dingle Bandon Cork Cobh
Bantry Kinsale
C. Clear

99

Lough
Ree
Mullingar DUB.
DUBLIN
Dun Laoghaire
Holyhead Bray
Wicklow Mts.
926
Carlow SNOWDONIA
Wexford
Rosslare
Fishguard

I R I S H

S E A

St. George's Channel

UNITED

KINGDOM

I. of Man
Douglas 620
852
Castletown

Cumbrian
Mts.
978 LAKE
DISTRICT
Borrowdale
Barrow-in-Furness
Lancaster
YORKSHIRE
DALES
Blackpool
Preston Keighley Leeds York
Blackburn Burnley Bradford
Southport Bolton Halifax Harrogate
Liverpool MANCHESTER Huddersfield Barnsley
Warrington Stockport Oldham 636 Doncaster
Chester Crewe Chesterfield Sheffield Rotherham
Stoke- Mansfield
on-Trent Derby Nottingham
Stafford Trent
Telford Granthham
Shrewsbury ENGLAND
Welshpool Nuneaton Leicester
Wolverhampton Coventry Corby
Worcester BIRMINGHAM Rugby Northampton
Redditch Royal Bedford
Hereford Leamington Spa Milton Keynes
Cheltenham Cotswold Hills Luton
Gloucester Oxford Harlow
High Wycombe Watford
Newport Slough LONDON
Swindon Reading
Bristol Newbury Guildford
Bath Basingstoke Crawley
Weston-super- Reigate Maidstone
Mare Salisbury Winchester SOUTH
Taunton DOWNS
Yeovil Southampton Fareham Brighton
Bournemouth Havant Worthing
Poole Portsmouth Eastbourne
Weymouth Isle of Worthing
Wight Hastings
Newport

Pennine

Bridlington
Beverley
Kingston upon Hull
Scunthorpe
Grimsby
Louth
Lincoln
Skegness
Boston The Wash
King's Lynn
THE
BROADS
Peterborough Norwich Great Yarmouth
Ely Lowestoft
Thetford
Cambridge Bury St. Edmunds Ipswich
Harwich Felixstowe
Colchester
Chelmsford
Southend-on-Sea
Chatham Margate
Canterbury Dover
Ashford Folkestone
Str. of Dover

Anglesey
Bangor
Colwyn Bay
Conwy
Wrexham
Llangollen
1085
Pwllheli
SNOWDONIA
Cardigan
Bay
WALES
Aberystwyth
Cambrian Mts.
Carmarthen
BRECON
BEACONS 886
Haverfordwest
Milford Haven
PEMBROKESHIRE
COAST
Llanelli
Swansea Neath
Port Talbot Rhondda
Barry
Merthyr Tydfil
Brecon
Cwmbran
Newport
Cardiff

Bristol Channel

Exmoor
Barnstaple
EXMOOR
Bude
Newquay
DARTMOOR
Truro
St. Austell
Penzance
Land's End
Isles of Scilly
Falmouth

618
Dartmoor
Exmouth
Plymouth
Torbay

E n g l i s h   C h a n n e l

Alderney C. de la Hague
Pte. de Barfleur
Guernsey St. Peter Port
Sark Cotentin
Channel Is.
(U.K.)
Jersey St. Helier
Cherbourg-Octeville
Valognes
Bayeux
Caen

Texel
Den Helder
NETHERLANDS
's-Gravenhage
(Den Haag)
Hoek van Holland
ROTTERDAM
Dordrecht
Zeeland
Vlissingen
Zeebrugge
Oostende
Brugge
Gent Mechelen
BELGIUM
BRUSSEL
(Bruxelles)
LILLE
Tournai

Haarlem
Alkmaar

Antwerpen

Dunkerque
Calais Gris-
Nez
Boulogne-
sur-Mer
Le Touquet-
Paris-Plage
St-Omer
Béthune
Bruay-la- Lens
Buissière
Abbeville

33
36

St-Quentin
Amiens
Cambrai

176

171

Le Tréport
Dieppe
Fécamp
Le Havre
Trouville-sur-Mer
Lisieux
Elbeuf
Rouen
Seine
Bolbec

Pays de
Caux

Picardie

Villeneuve-
d'Ascq
Valenciennes

G

FRANCE

50

52

54

56

58

60

Projection: Conical with two standard parallels

West from Greenwich

East from Greenwich
COPYRIGHT PHILIP'S

10 0 10 20 30 40 50 60 70 80 km
10 0 10 20 30 40 50 miles
1:1 600 000

SCOTLAND
Kintyre
Brodick
Arran
Campbeltown
Mull of Oa
Mull of Kintyre
Ailsa Craig
Firth of Clyde
Cairnryan Stranraer
Portpatrick
L. Ryan

ATLANTIC OCEAN

Trawbreaga B.
Malin Hd.
Inishtrahull
Sheep Haven
Tory I.
Horn Hd.
Lough Swilly
Mulroy B.
Fanad Hd.
Malin Pen.
Carndonagh
Glengad Hd.
Inishowen Pen.
Moville
Giants Causeway
Fair Hd.
Ballycastle
Cushendall
Cushendun
Garron Pt.
Bloody Foreland
Cloghaneely
Dunfanaghy
L. Foyle
Portstewart Portrush
Coleraine
Limavady
Ballymoney
554
Trostan
Carncastle
Larne
Inishfree B.
Gweedore Errigal 752
Rathmelton
Derryveagh Mts.
GLENVEAGH
L. Foyle
Derry/Londonderry
Dungiven
Ballymena
Antrim
Carrickfergus
269
Arranmore
The Rosses
Dunglow
Crohy Hd.
683
Letterkenny
DONEGAL
Lifford
Strabane
Sawel Mt. 683
Sion Mills
Newtownstewart
Magherafelt
Moneymore
Randalstown Ballyclare
ANTRIM
Belfast L.
Bangor
Donaghadee
Newtownabbey
Gweebarra B.
Dawros Hd.
Glenties
Stranorlar
Finn
TYRONE
Omagh
Cookstown
Coalisland
Dungannon
Lough Neagh
Lisburn
Belfast
Hollywood
Comber
Newtownards
Ards Pen.
Loughros More B.
Ardara
Lavagh More 676
601
Killybegs
Slieve League
St. John's Pt.
Donegal
Glencolumbkille
Rossan Pt.
806
Ballyshannon
Bundoran
Enniskillen
Dromore
Irvinestown
Ballygawley
Armagh
Portadown
Craigavon
Lurgan
Banbridge
Dromore
DOWN
Dundrum
Downpatrick
Ardglass
St. John's Pt.
Portaferry
Ballyquintin Pt.
Strangford L.
Saintfield
Ballynahinch
NORTHERN IRELAND
FERMANAGH
Monaghan
MONAGHAN
Clones
Castleblaney
Keady
Middletown
Newry
Slieve Gullion 577
Warrenpoint
Greenore
Carlingford L.
Mourne Mts.
Slieve Donard 852
Newcastle
Dundrum B.
Broad Haven
Erris Hd.
Portacloy
Downpatrick Hd.
Killala
Lenadoon Pt.
Sligo Bay
Drumcliff
Sligo
Lackagh Hills
Lower L. Erne
Upper L. Erne
Belturbet
Annalee
Cootehill
Carrickmacross
Dundalk
(Dún Dealgan)
Louth
Dundalk Bay
Clogher Hd.
Mullet Pen.
Inishkea North
Inishkea South
Blacksod Bay
Belmullet
BALLYCROY
380
Nephin Beg Range
672
Crossmolina
Ballina
L. Conn
Nephin 806
Foxford
Swinford
SLIGO
Ballymote
L. Arrow
Colooney
Boyle
L. Key
Carrick-on-Shannon
LEITRIM
Drumshanbo
L. Gara
Ballaghaderreen
Strokestown
LONGFORD
Granard
L. Sheelin
Oldcastle
Kells (Ceanannus Mor)
Blackwater
Navan
Drogheda
(Droichead Átha)
BEND OF THE BOYNE
Balbriggan
Skerries
Achill Hd.
Achill I.
Corraun Pen.
Clare I.
Clew Bay
Louisburgh
Westport
Newport
Castlebar
461
765
Croagh Patrick
Mweelrea 819
Knock
Claremorris
Ballyhaunis
Castlerea
ROSCOMMON
Roscommon
Longford
Castlepollard
Mullingar
WESTMEATH
Delvin
Athboy
Trim
Dunshaughlin
MEATH
Dunleer
Ardee
Bailieborough
Kingscourt
Castleblaney
CAVAN
Cavan
Carrickmacross
L. Gowna
L. Oughter
Inishturk
Inishbofin
Inishshark
Killary Harbour
683
Partry Mts.
Connemara
L. Carra
Ballinrobe
Lough Mask
Glennamaddy
Mount Bellew Bridge
Lough Ree
Strokestown
Athlone
Moate
Kilbeggan
Edenderry
Kinnegad
Royal Canal
Maynooth
Leixlip
Lucan
DUBLIN (Baile Átha Cliath)
Dún Laoghaire
Howth
Howth Hd.
Lambay I.
Malahide
Swords
Rush
Clifden
CONNEMARA
Roundstone
Slyne Hd.
Oughterard
Lough Corrib
Tuam
Athenry
Ballinasloe
Shannonbridge
Banagher
Ferbane
Clara
OFFALY
Tullamore
Daingean
Grand Canal
Bog of Allen
Rathangan
Kildare
Celbridge
Naas
Newbridge
KILDARE
Bertraghboy B.
Kilkieran B.
Galway Bay
Aran Is.
Inishmore
Inishmaan
Inisheer
Galway (Gaillimh)
Spiddle
Black Hd.
GALWAY
Gort
Loughrea
Portumna
Birr
Slieve Bloom
Mountmellick
Portlaoise
Portarlington
Monasterevin
Athy
LAOIS
Abbeyleix
Durrow
Castlecomer
Carlow
CARLOW
Muine Bheag (Bagenalstown)
Tullow
Rathvilly
Baltinglass
Poulaphouca Res.
WICKLOW
Wicklow Mts.
Lugnaquilla 926
Kippure 754
Bray
Greystones
Killiney
Dalkey
123
Cliffs of Moher
Hags Hd.
Liscannor Bay
Lisdoonvarna
BURREN
345
Kinvarra
Slieve Aughty
368
Gort
Feakle
Loughrea
Borrisokane
Roscrea
Mountrath
Donaghmore
Templemore
Thurles
Johnstown
Abbeyleix
Kilkenny
KILKENNY
Callan
Thomastown
Inishmore
Inishmaan
Inisheer
Loop Hd.
Kilkee
Kilrush
Mouth of the Shannon
Milltown Malbay
Mal Bay
Mutton I.
CLARE
Ennis
Ennistimon
Crusheen
Tulla
Sixmilebridge
Shannon
Limerick (Luimneach)
LIMERICK
Lough Derg
Killaloe
Nenagh
Silvermine Mts. 694
Keeper Hill
TIPPERARY
Tipperary
Golden Vale
Cashel
Cahir
Clonmel
Carrick-on-Suir
Slievenamon 722
Comeragh Mts. 792
WATERFORD
Waterford (Port Láirge)
Dungarvan
Tramore
Kerry Hd.
Tralee B.
Ballybunion
Tarbert
Foynes
Glin
Rathkeale
Adare
Newcastle West
Abbeyfeale
Charleville (Rath Luirc)
519
Kilfinnane
Galtymore 920
Galty Mts.
Mitchelstown
Knockmealdown Mts. 795
Lismore
Youghal B.
Carnsore Pt.
WEXFORD
Wexford
Rosslare
Rosslare Harbour
Rosslare Europort
Greenore Pt.
Kilmore Quay
Saltee Is.
Hook Hd.
Passage East
Dunmore East
Waterford Harbour
Enniscorthy
Blackstairs Mts. 784
Mt. Leinster 796
Bunclody
Ballycanew
Gorey
Arklow
Mizen Hd.
Wicklow Hd.
Wicklow
Wicklow Mts.
Smerwick Harbour
Great Blasket I.
Inishvickillane
Dingle Bay
Dingle Pen.
953
Brandon Mt.
Slieve Mish 853
Dingle
Slea Hd.
Castlegregory
Castleisland
Tralee
Ardfert
Listowel
Feale
Newmarket
Kanturk
Buttevant
Mallow
Fermoy
Mitchelstown
Nagles Mts. 429
Blackwater
Youghal
Midleton
Cobh
Cork Harbour
Crosshaven
Valencia I.
Puffin I.
Great Skellig
Iveragh Pen.
Cahirciveen
Ballinskelligs B.
Scariff I.
Waterville
Sneem
Kenmare River
Caha Mts. 686
707
Glengarriff
Kenmare
Killorglin
Killarney
Glenbeigh
Carrauntoohil 1041
Macgillycuddy's Reeks
KERRY
Killarney
775
Millstreet
Boggeragh Mts. 646
Blarney
Macroom
Ballincollig
CORK
Cork (Corcaigh)
Passage West
Carrigaline
Bandon
Kinsale
Old Head of Kinsale
Clonakilty
Clonakilty B.
Galley Hd.
Dursey I.
Castletown Bearhaven
Bear I.
Bantry Bay
Whiddy I.
Bantry
Ballydehob
Skibbereen
Dunmanus B.
Mizen Hd.
Long I.
Sherkin I.
Clear I.
C. Clear
Fastnet Rock
Baltimore
Skull

St. George's Channel
St. David's Hd.
St. David's
St. Brides Bay
WALES
115
IRISH SEA
North Channel

CELTIC SEA

1. DUBLIN
2. FINGAL
3. SOUTH DUBLIN
4. DÚN LAOGHAIRE-RATHDOWN

MUNSTER
CONNAUGHT
LEINSTER
ULSTER
IRELAND

West from Greenwich

Projection: Lambert's Conformal Conic

COPYRIGHT PHILIP'S

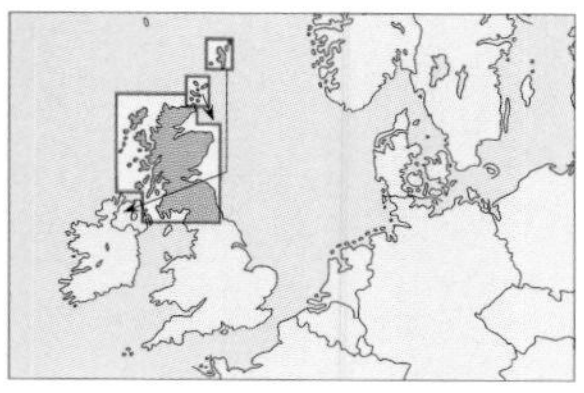

1:1 600 000

10 0 10 20 30 40 50 60 70 80 km
10 0 10 20 30 40 50 miles

Key to Scottish unitary authorities on map
1 ABERDEEN CITY
2 DUNDEE CITY
3 WEST DUNBARTONSHIRE
4 EAST DUNBARTONSHIRE
5 GLASGOW CITY
6 INVERCLYDE
7 RENFREWSHIRE
8 EAST RENFREWSHIRE
9 NORTH LANARKSHIRE
10 FALKIRK
11 CLACKMANNANSHIRE
12 WEST LOTHIAN
13 CITY OF EDINBURGH
14 MIDLOTHIAN

ORKNEY IS. on same scale
ORKNEY
North Ronaldsay
Papa Westray
Westray
Rousay
Eday
Sanday
Stronsay
Shapinsay
Kirkwall
Mainland
Stromness
Scapa Flow
St. Mary's
Burray
South Ronaldsay
Hoy
Burwick
Duncansby Head
John o' Groats
Dunnet Hd.
Stroma
Sinclair's Bay
Thurso
Pentland Firth

SHETLAND IS. on same scale
SHETLAND
Muckle Flugga
Haroldswick
Unst
Fetlar
Yell
Ulsta
Out Skerries
Esha Ness
Yell Sound
Whalsay
Sullom Voe
St. Magnus Bay
Voe
Papa Stour
Walls
Bressay
Lerwick
Scalloway
West Burra
Foula
Boddam

Scotland labels (mainland):
ATLANTIC OCEAN
NORTH SEA
Pentland Firth
Scapa Flow
Hoy
Burwick
Stroma
John o' Groats
Dunnet Hd.
Dounreay
Thurso
Strathy Pt.
Halkirk
Lybster
Sinclair's Bay
Noss Hd.
Wick
C. Wrath
Durness
L. Eriboll
Tongue
Reay Forest
Caithness
Sutherland
Ben Hope 927
Handa
Eddrachillis B.
L. Laxford
Pt. of Stoer
Ben More Assynt 998
L. Assynt
Lochinver
Enard B.
Rubha Coigeach
Ord of Caithness
Helmsdale
Brora
Golspie
Greenstone Pt.
L. Broom
Ullapool
L. Shin
Lairg
Shin
Oykel
Brora
Dornoch
Bonar Bridge
Tarbat Ness
Darnoch Firth
Tain
Invergordon
Cromarty
Moray Firth
Butt of Lewis
Flannan Is.
Gallan Hd.
Broad Bay
Stornoway
Eye Peninsula
Lewis
Scarp
North Minch
EILEAN SIAR (WESTERN ISLES)
Taransay
Toe Hd.
Harris
Clisham 799
Tarbert
L. Seaforth
Pabbay
Berneray
North Uist
Lochmaddy
Baleshare
Grimsay
Benbecula
Ardivachar Pt.
Wiay
South Uist
Ben Mhor 620
Lochboisdale
Eriskay
Barra
Castlebay
Vatersay
Sandray
Barra Hd. 268
Little Minch
Sound of Harris
Rubha Hunish
Dunvegan
Skye
Portree
Raasay
Rona
Inner Sound
L. Torridon
Gairloch
L. Maree 1053
Loch Ewe
L. Fannich 1045
Strathpeffer
Dingwall
Muir of Ord
Beauly
Inverness
Lossiemouth
Elgin
Forres
Nairn
MORAY
Burghead
Portknockie
Portsoy
Rosehearty
Kinnairds Hd.
Fraserburgh
Banff
Macduff
Cullen
Buckie
Fochabers
Keith
Aberchirder
Turriff
Rothes
Dufftown
Huntly
Peterhead
Buchan Ness
Cruden Bay
Ellon
Oldmeldrum
BUCHAN
ABERDEENSHIRE
Inverurie
Kintore
Dyce
Aberdeen
Girdle Ness
Peterculter
Banchory
Stonehaven
Inverbervie
Laurencekirk
Brechin
Montrose
ANGUS
Arbroath
Carnoustie
Monifieth
Dundee
Firth of Tay
Cuillin Hills 992
Cuillin Sound
Kyle of Lochalsh
Glenelg
Glen Affric
Loch Ness
Fort Augustus
Glen Moriston
Glen Garry
Monadhliath Mts.
Aviemore
Kingussie
Newtonmore
CAIRNGORM Mts.
Ben Macdhui 1309
CAIRNGORMS
Braemar
Ballater
Aboyne
Lochnagar 1154
Grantown-on-Spey
Tomintoul
Alford
Strath Spey
Canna
Rùm (Rhum)
Eigg
Muck
Arisaig
Mallaig
L. Morar
L. Eil
Fort William
Ben Nevis 1345
Kinlochleven
Glen Coe
Ballachulish
Rannoch Moor
L. Rannoch
Forest of Atholl
Blair Atholl
Pitlochry
Kirriemuir
Forfar
Strathmore
Alyth
Blairgowrie
Aberfeldy
Dunkeld
PERTH AND KINROSS
Crieff
Perth
Scone
Auchterarder
Tobermory
Morvern
Mull
Staffa
Ulva
Iona
Ben More 966
Kerrera
Oban
Lorn
Firth of Lorn
Lismore
Coll
Tiree
Passage of Tiree
ARGYLL AND BUTE
Loch Awe
Ben Cruachan 1126
Crianlarich
Ben More 1174
Killin
Ben Lawers 1214
Loch Tay
Aberfoyle
LOCH LOMOND AND THE TROSSACHS
Loch Katrine
Callander
Dunblane
STIRLING
Bannockburn
Stirling
Alloa
Alexandria
Helensburgh
Dumbarton
Kirkintilloch
Falkirk
Grangemouth
Bo'ness
Dunfermline
Kirkcaldy
Cowdenbeath
Glenrothes
Leven
Buckhaven
Anstruther
FIFE
Cupar
St. Andrews
Fife Ness
Leuchars
Tayport
Firth of Tay
Firth of Forth
North Berwick
Dunbar
St. Abb's Head
Eyemouth
Musselburgh
EDINBURGH
Dalkeith
Livingston
Bonnyrigg
Penicuik
Pentland Hills
Haddington
EAST LOTHIAN
Lammermuir Hills
Duns
Coldstream
Berwick-upon-Tweed
Holy I.
Greenock
Gourock
Port Glasgow
Paisley
GLASGOW
Clydebank
Cumbernauld
Airdrie
Coatbridge
Motherwell
Hamilton
East Kilbride
Wishaw
Carluke
Lanark
Biggar
Peebles
Moorfoot Hills
Galashiels
Melrose
Jedburgh
Hawick
Kelso
SCOTTISH BORDERS
Broad Law 840
Cheviot Hills
The Cheviot 816
Alnwick
Alnmouth
Amble
Morpeth
NORTHUMBERLAND
Bamburgh
Wooler
Flodden
Farne Is.
Rothesay
Bute
Largs
Saltcoats
Ardrossan
Kilwinning
Irvine
Troon
Prestwick
Ayr
NORTH AYRSHIRE
EAST AYRSHIRE
SOUTH AYRSHIRE
Kilmarnock
Strathaven
Dalry
Maybole
Cumnock
Sanquhar
Moffat
Lockerbie
Langholm
Carter Bar
Arran
Goat Fell 874
Brodick
Kintyre
Kilbrannan Sd.
Campbeltown
Mull of Kintyre
Ailsa Craig
Girvan
Merrick 844
Dalmellington
New Galloway
Loch Ryan
Stranraer
Portpatrick
Wigtown
Mull of Galloway
Burrow Hd.
Luce Bay
Whithorn
Newton Stewart
Gatehouse of Fleet
Castle Douglas
Dalbeattie
Kirkcudbright
DUMFRIES AND GALLOWAY
GALLOWAY
Dumfries
Lochmaben
Annan
Gretna
Solway Firth
Carlisle
CUMBRIA
Wigton
Aspatria
Silloth
Maryport
Workington
Cockermouth
Keswick
Whitehaven
St. Bees Hd.
Skiddaw 893
Derwent Water
Ullswater
Helvellyn 950
Penrith
Appleby-in-Westmorland
Alston
Brough
Cross Fell 893
ENGLAND
Newcastle-upon-Tyne
Blaydon
Gateshead
Consett
Stanley
Hexham
Haltwhistle
HADRIAN'S WALL
NORTHUMBERLAND
Kielder Water
Crook
Bishop Auckland
DURHAM
Barnard Castle

NORTHERN IRELAND
Belfast
Belfast L.
Carrickfergus
Larne
Bangor
Holywood
Newtownards
Donaghadee
Cushendall
Garron Pt.
North Channel

Projection: Lambert's Conformal Conic
West from Greenwich

ft m
3000 1000
1500 500
600 200
300 100
0 0
50 150
200 600
500 1500
1000 3000
m ft

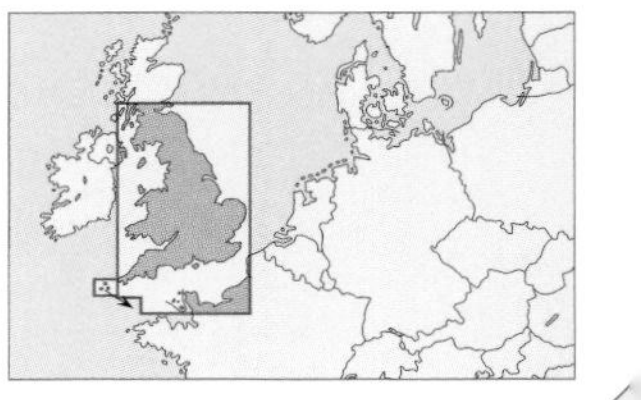

1:1 600 000

10 0 10 20 30 40 50 60 70 80 km
10 0 10 20 30 40 50 miles

Key to English unitary authorities on map
25 HARTLEPOOL
26 DARLINGTON
27 STOCKTON-ON-TEES
28 MIDDLESBROUGH
29 REDCAR AND CLEVELAND
30 BLACKPOOL
31 BLACKBURN WITH DARWEN
32 HALTON
33 WARRINGTON
34 KINGSTON UPON HULL
35 NORTH EAST LINCOLNSHIRE
36 STOKE-ON-TRENT
37 TELFORD AND WREKIN
38 DERBY CITY
39 CITY OF NOTTINGHAM
40 LEICESTER CITY
41 RUTLAND
42 PETERBOROUGH
43 MILTON KEYNES
44 LUTON
45 NORTH SOMERSET
46 CITY OF BRISTOL
47 BATH AND NORTH EAST SOMERSET
48 SWINDON
49 READING
50 WOKINGHAM
51 WINDSOR AND MAIDENHEAD
52 SLOUGH
53 BRACKNELL FOREST
54 THURROCK
55 SOUTHEND-ON-SEA
56 MEDWAY
57 PLYMOUTH
58 TORBAY
59 POOLE
60 BOURNEMOUTH
61 SOUTHAMPTON
62 PORTSMOUTH
63 BRIGHTON AND HOVE
64 BEDFORD
65 CENTRAL BEDFORDSHIRE
66 CHESHIRE WEST AND CHESTER
67 CHESHIRE EAST

Key to Welsh unitary authorities on map
15 SWANSEA
16 NEATH PORT TALBOT
17 BRIDGEND
18 RHONDDA CYNON TAFF
19 MERTHYR TYDFIL
20 CAERPHILLY
21 BLAENAU GWENT
22 TORFAEN
23 CARDIFF
24 NEWPORT

NORTH SEA

IRISH SEA

North Channel

NORTHERN IRELAND

ISLE OF MAN

SCOTLAND

ENGLAND

WALES

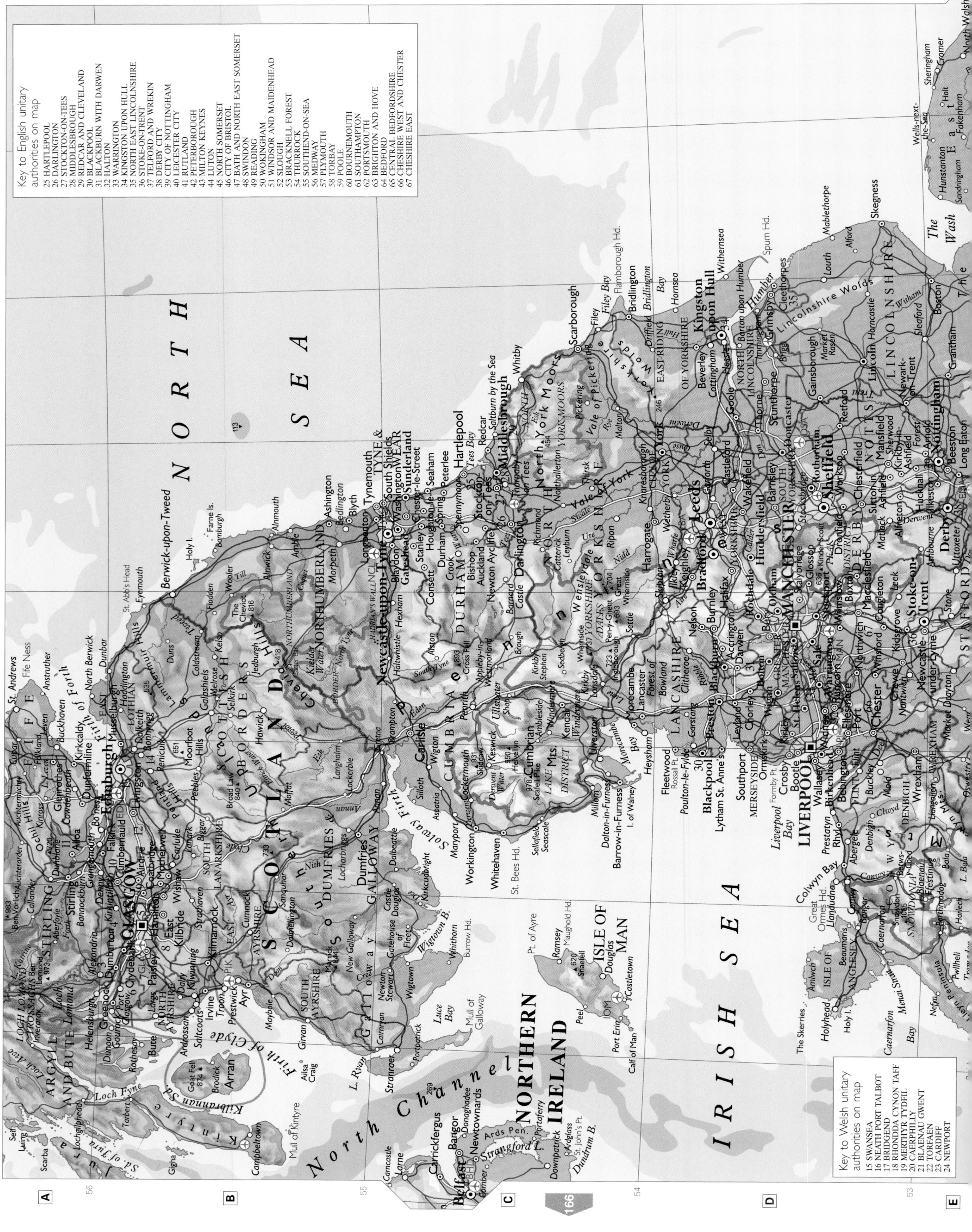

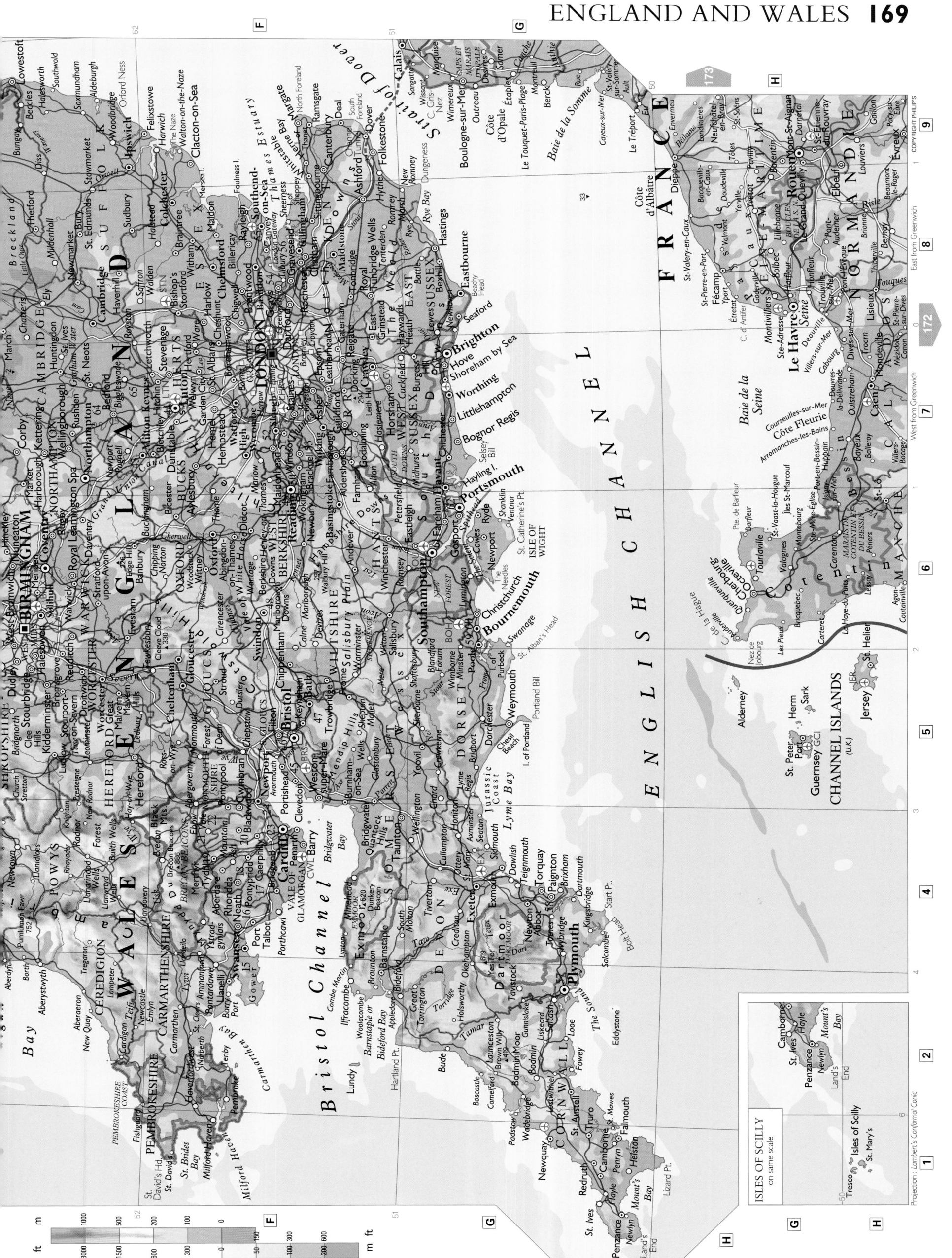

Projection : Lambert's Conformal Conic

ISLES OF SCILLY
on same scale

Tresco
Isles of Scilly
St. Mary's

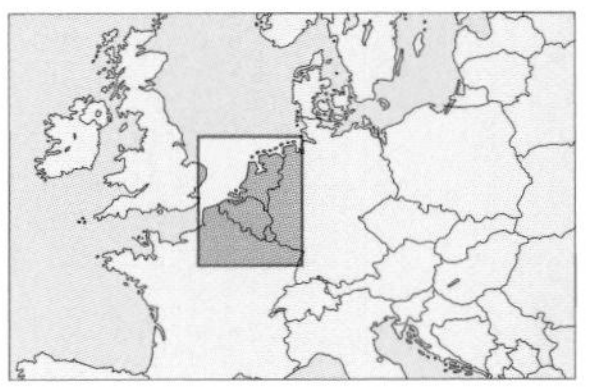

1:2 000 000

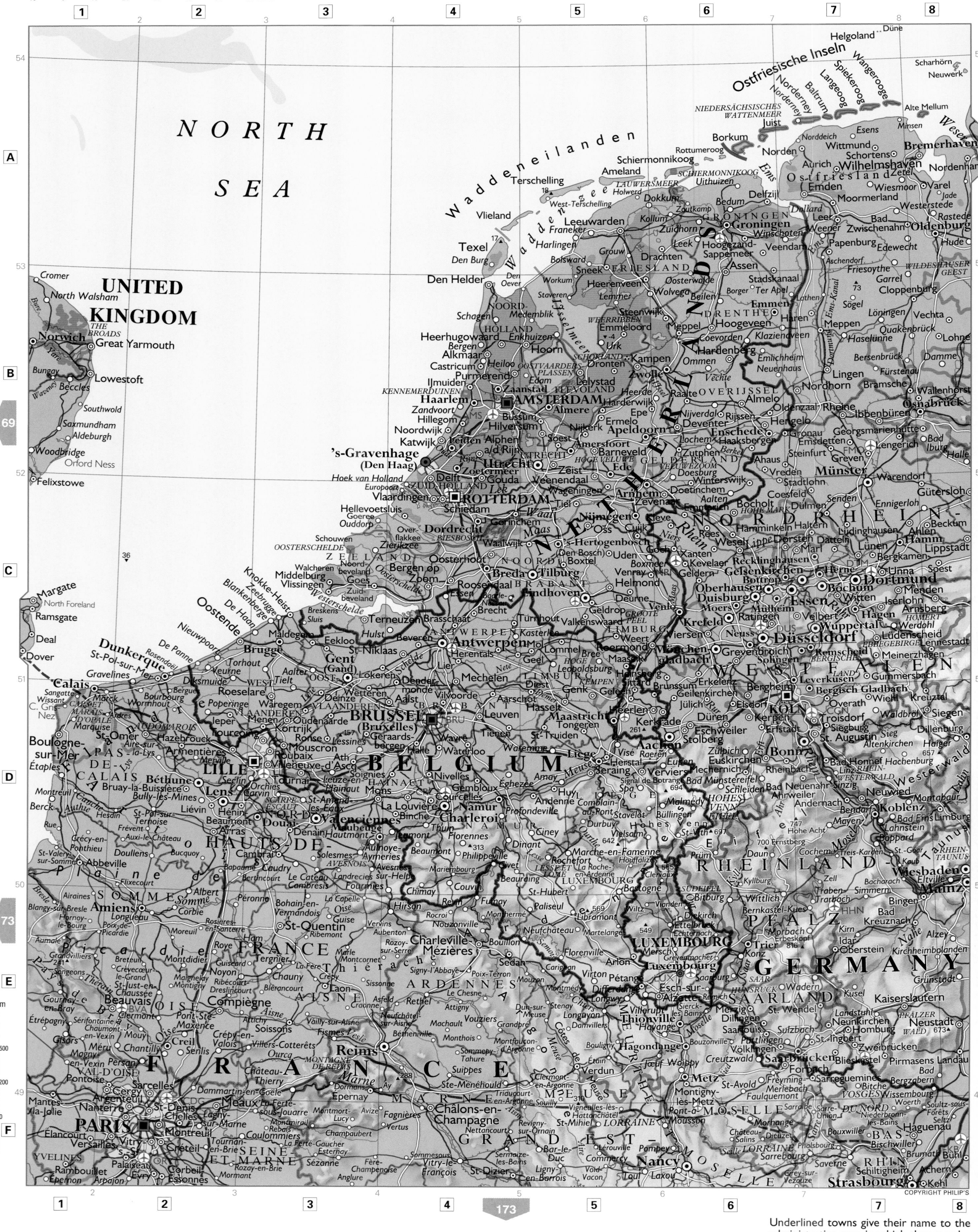

NORTH

SEA

UNITED KINGDOM

Cromer
North Walsham
Norwich
Great Yarmouth
Lowestoft
Southwold
Aldeburgh
Woodbridge
Orford Ness
Felixstowe
Margate
North Foreland
Ramsgate
Deal
Dover
Calais
Dunkerque
Oostende

Waddeneilanden

Terschelling
Vlieland
Texel
Den Helder
Den Burg
Leeuwarden
Harlingen
Franeker
Bolsward
Sneek
FRIESLAND
Heerenveen
NETHERLANDS
DRENTHE
Assen
Emmen
Hoogeveen
Meppel
Zwolle
OVERIJSSEL
Almelo
Enschede
Deventer
Apeldoorn
Amersfoort
GELDERLAND
Arnhem
Nijmegen
AMSTERDAM
Haarlem
Almere
Hilversum
Utrecht
UTRECHT
's-Gravenhage (Den Haag)
Leiden
Gouda
ROTTERDAM
Delft
Schiedam
Dordrecht
ZUID-HOLLAND
Hoek van Holland
ZEELAND
Middelburg
Vlissingen
Bergen op Zoom
Breda
Tilburg
NOORD-BRABANT
Eindhoven
Roosendaal
's-Hertogenbosch
LIMBURG
Venlo
Roermond
Maastricht

Groningen
GRONINGEN

Bremerhaven
Nordenham
Oldenburg
Emden
Leer
Papenburg
Lingen
Nordhorn
Münster
NORDRHEIN-WESTFALEN
Dortmund
Bochum
Essen
Duisburg
Düsseldorf
Mönchengladbach
Krefeld
Neuss
Köln
Bonn
Aachen
Leverkusen
Solingen
Remscheid
Wuppertal
Siegen

GERMANY
RHEINLAND-PFALZ
SAARLAND
Saarbrücken
Trier
Koblenz
Wiesbaden
Mainz
Kaiserslautern
Neustadt
Landau

BELGIUM
BRUSSEL (Bruxelles)
Antwerpen
Gent (Gand)
Brugge
Oostende
WEST-VLAANDEREN
OOST-VLAANDEREN
Mechelen
Leuven
VLAAMS-BRABANT
BRABANT WALLON
LIMBURG
Hasselt
Genk
Liège
Namur
NAMUR
HAINAUT
Mons
Charleroi
La Louvière
Tournai
LIÈGE
Verviers
LUXEMBOURG
Arlon
Bastogne

LUXEMBOURG
Luxembourg
Esch-sur-Alzette
Diekirch
Ettelbruck

FRANCE
HAUTS-DE-FRANCE
Lille
Roubaix
Tourcoing
Valenciennes
Douai
Lens
Béthune
Arras
Cambrai
Dunkerque
Boulogne-sur-Mer
Calais
St-Omer
PAS-DE-CALAIS
SOMME
Amiens
Abbeville
St-Quentin
AISNE
Laon
Soissons
Compiègne
OISE
Beauvais
Reims
Châlons-en-Champagne
Épernay
Charleville-Mézières
Sedan
ARDENNES
MARNE
Verdun
Metz
MEUSE
MOSELLE
Thionville
Nancy
GRAND-EST
LORRAINE
VOSGES
Sarreguemines
Saverne
Strasbourg
BAS-RHIN
PARIS
Versailles
Nanterre
St-Denis

High-speed rail routes

Underlined towns give their name to the administrative area in which they stand.

COPYRIGHT PHILIP'S

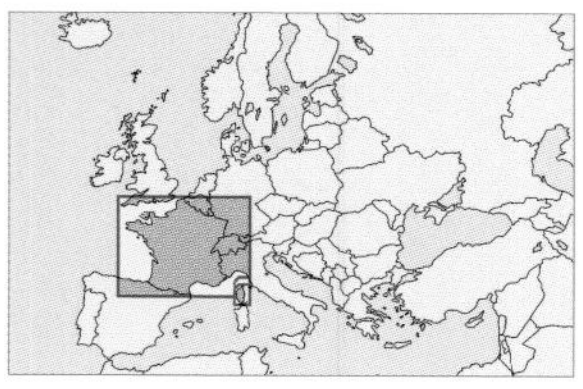

1:4 000 000

50 0 25 50 75 100 125 150 175 km
50 0 25 50 75 100 125 miles

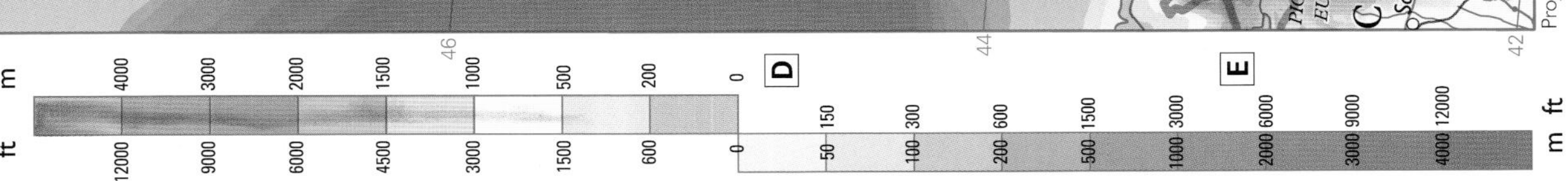

COPYRIGHT PHILIP'S

FRANCE

Corse (Corsica)

C. Corse · Bastia · L'Île-Rousse · Mte. Cinto 2710 · Corte · Aléria · Porto-Vecchio · Sagone · Ajaccio 2386 · Propriano · Bonifacio

---

GERMANY · AUSTRIA · SWITZERLAND · ITALY · LUXEMBOURG · BELGIUM · UNITED KINGDOM · ANDORRA · SPAIN

FRANCE

English Channel · Bay of Biscay · MEDITERRANEAN SEA · Golfe du Lion · Golfe de Gascogne

PARIS · MARSEILLE · LYON · ZÜRICH · MILANO · TORINO (Turin) · Bern · MONACO · Nice

Normandie · Bretagne · Île-de-France · Picardie · Lorraine · Bourgogne · Auvergne · Massif Central · Provence · Côte d'Azur · Pyrénées · Gascogne · Guyenne · Aquitaine · Limousin · Poitou · Anjou · Maine · Perche · Beauce · Sologne · Nivernais · Bourbonnais · Franche-Comté · Alsace · Ardenne · Côte d'Or

Projection: Conical with two standard parallels

East from Greenwich · West from Greenwich

176 · 192

m ft
4000 12000
3000 9000
2000 6000
1500 4500
1000 3000
500 1500
200 600
0

1:2 000 000

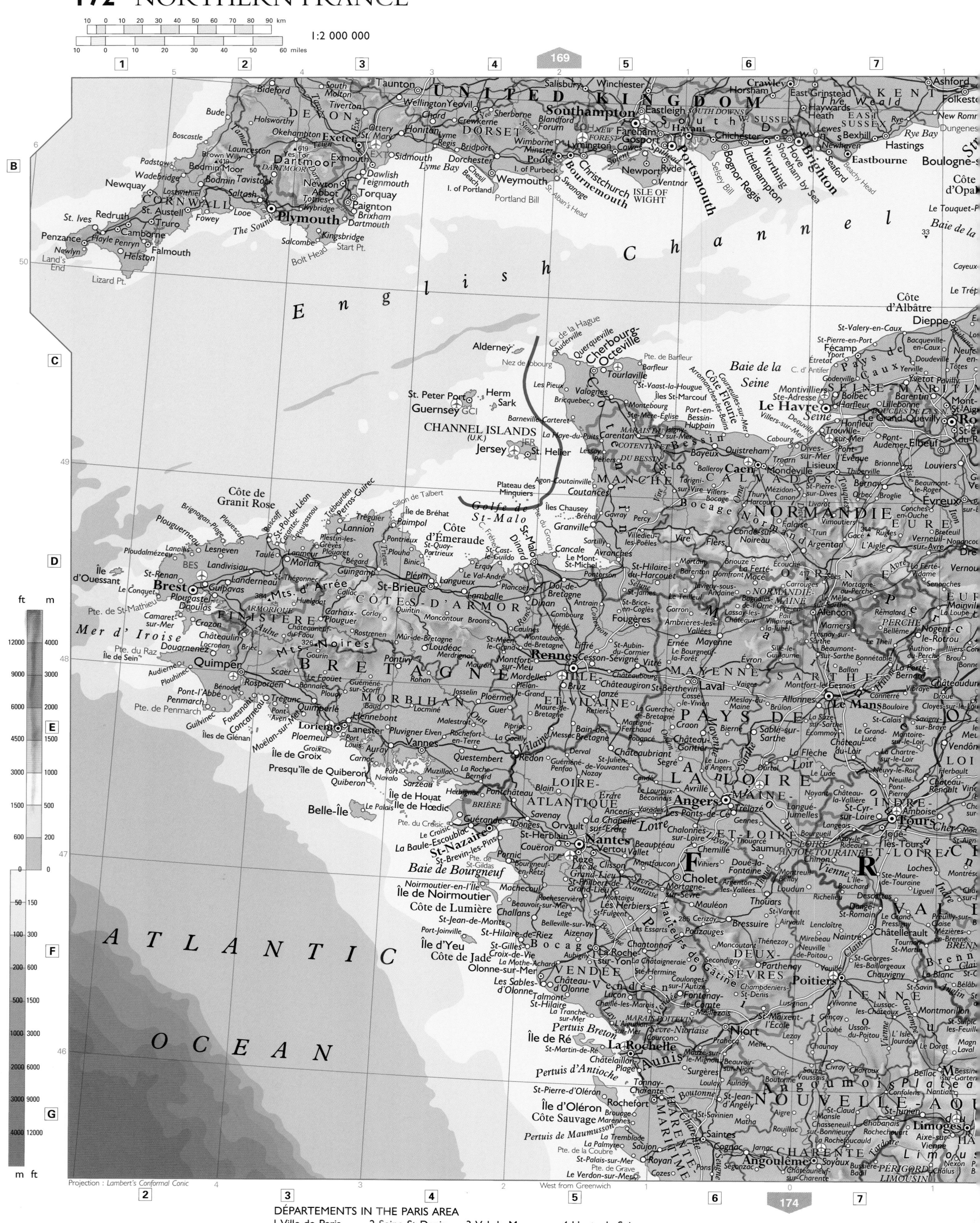

Projection : Lambert's Conformal Conic

West from Greenwich

DÉPARTEMENTS IN THE PARIS AREA
1 Ville de Paris   2 Seine-St-Denis   3 Val-de-Marne   4 Hauts-de-Seine

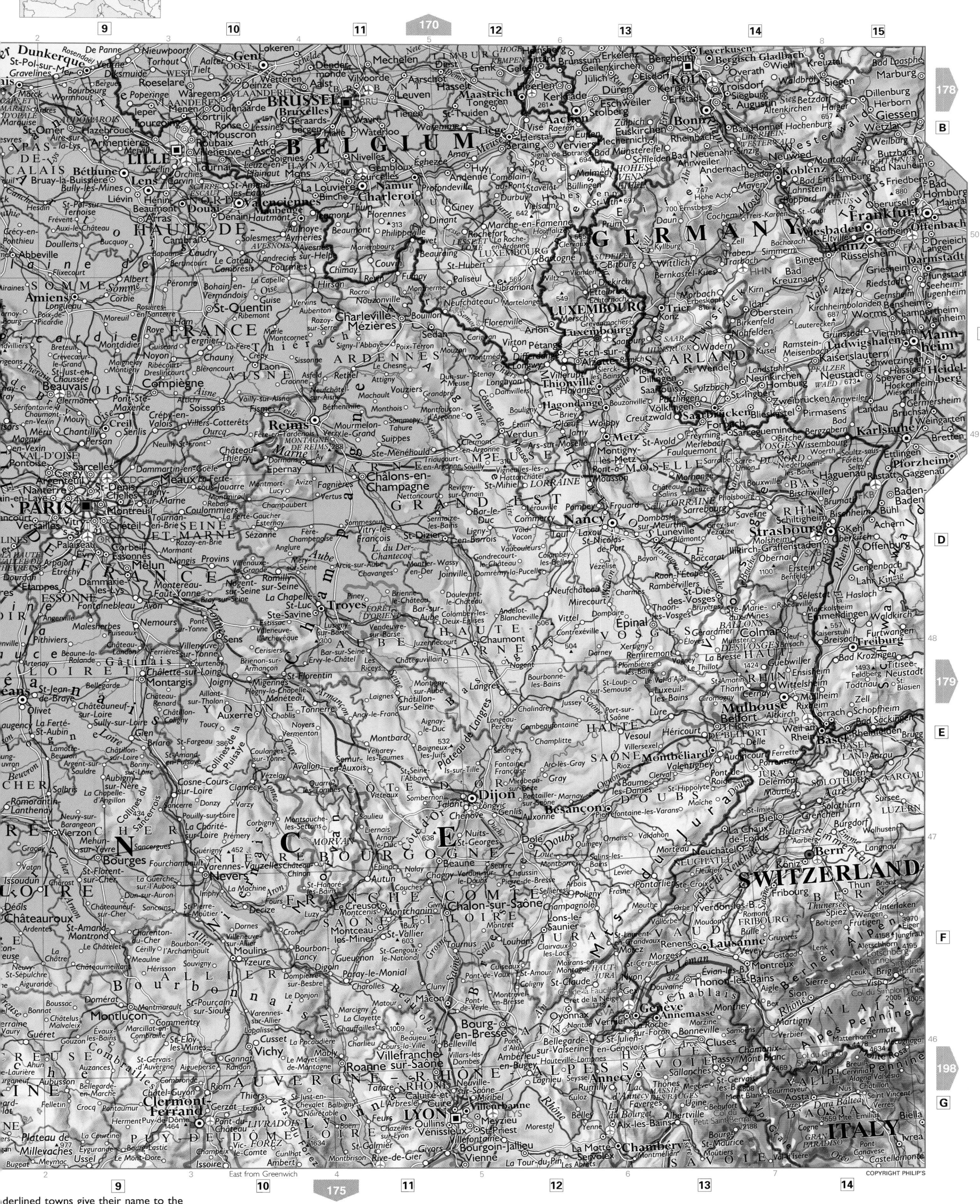

…derlined towns give their name to the
…inistrative area in which they stand.

————— High-speed rail routes

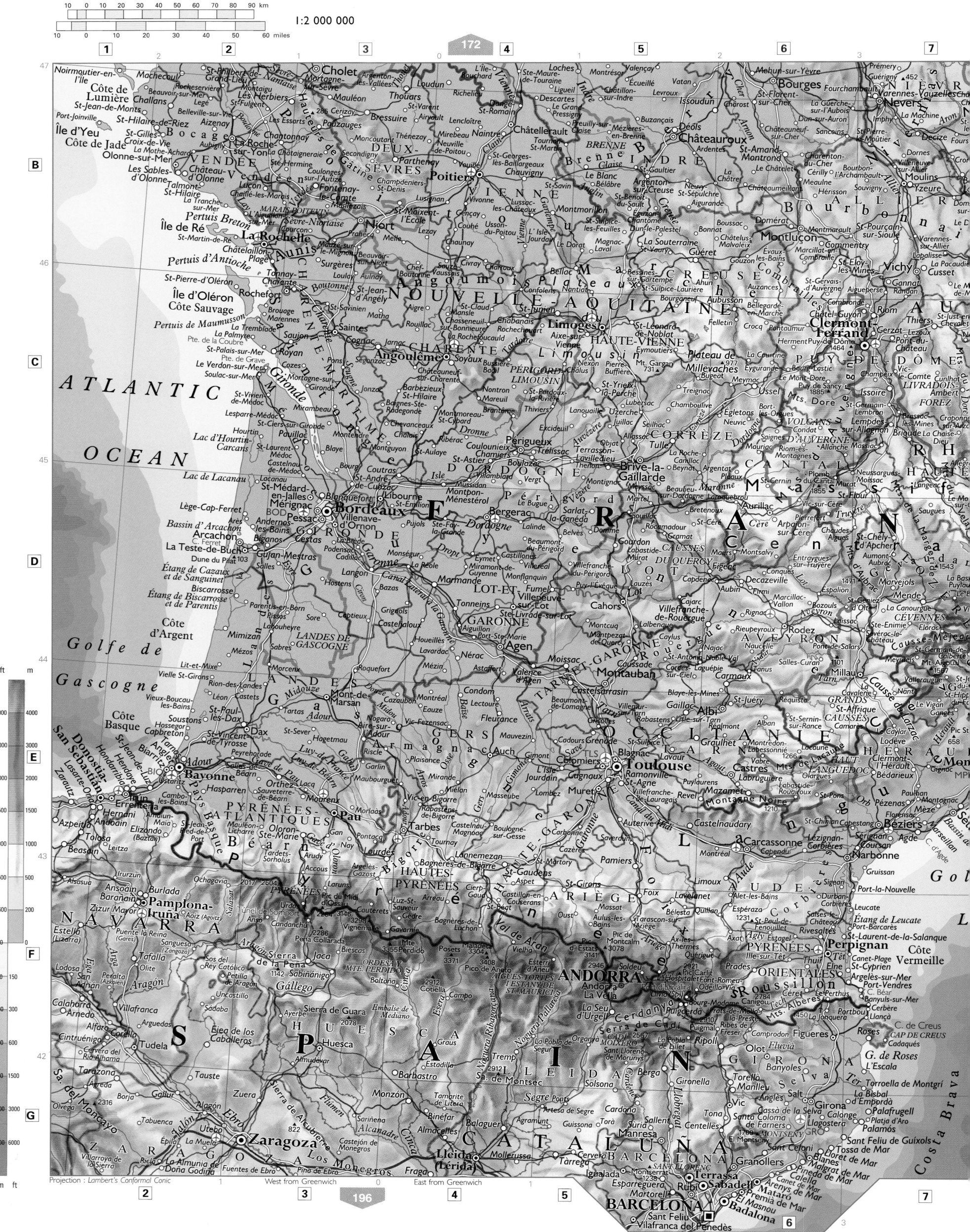

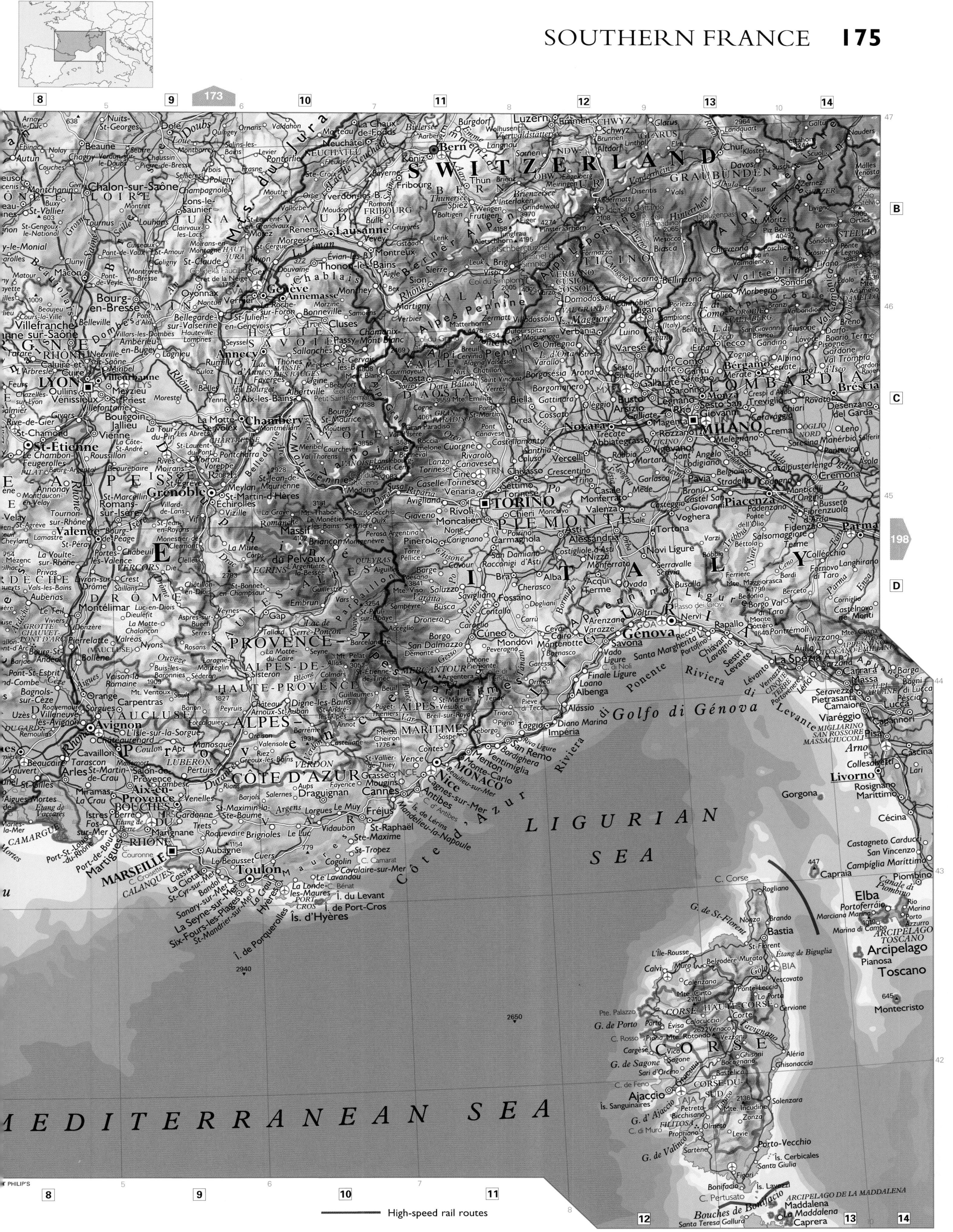

High-speed rail routes

1:4 000 000

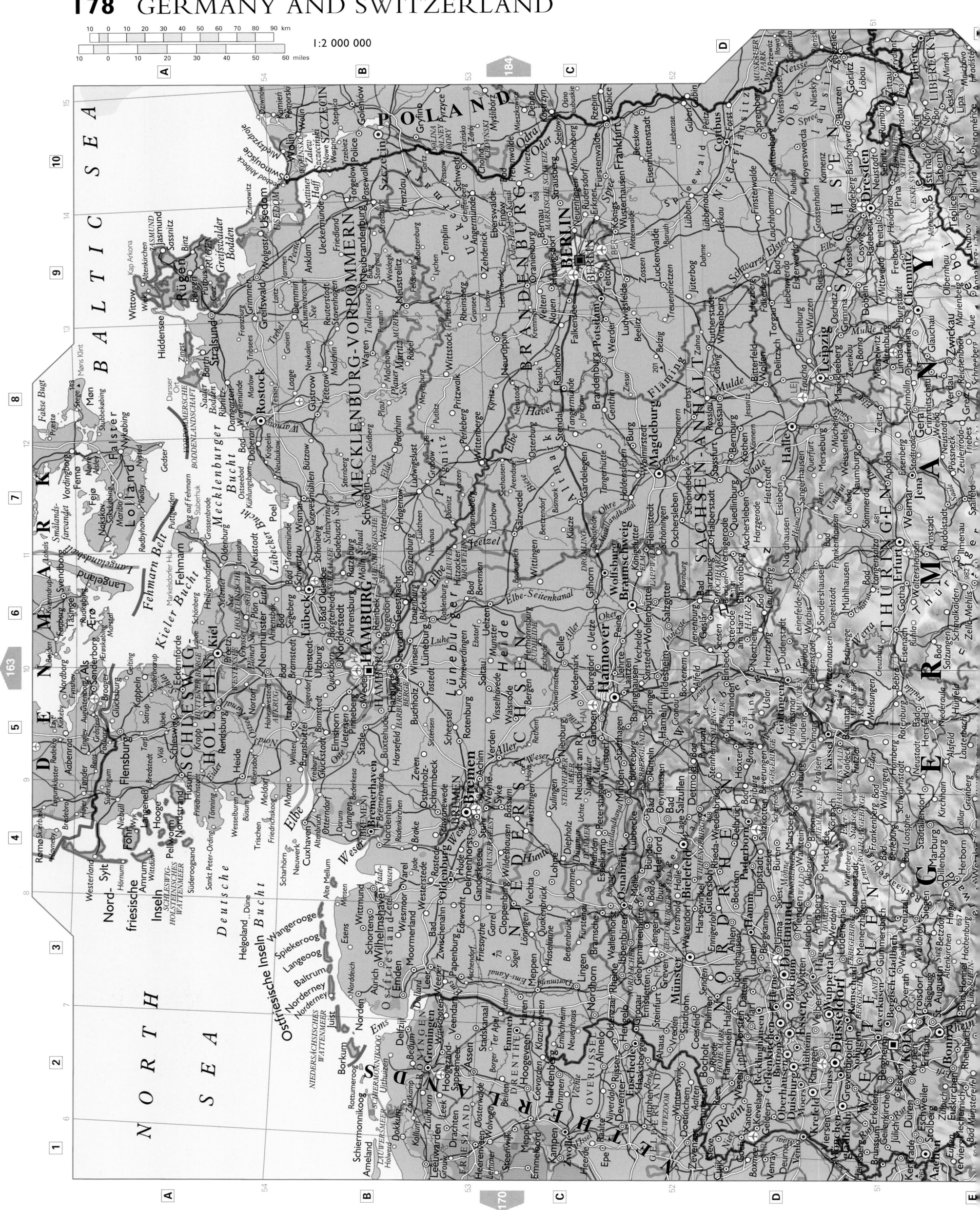

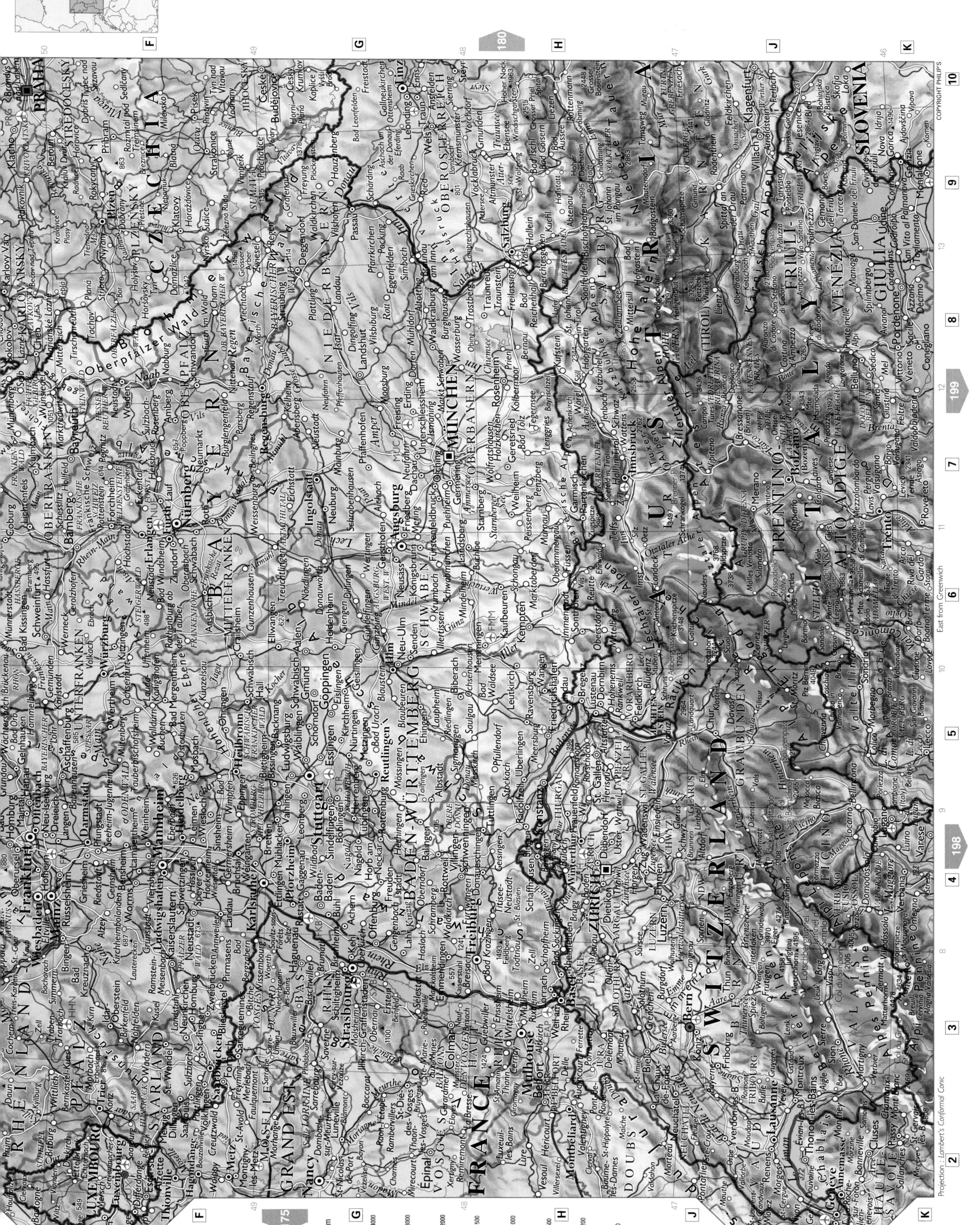

High-speed rail routes

Underlined towns give their name to the
administrative area in which they stand.

Projection : Lambert's Conformal Conic

COPYRIGHT PHILIP'S

Underlined towns give their name to the administrative area in which they stand.

Projection : Lambert's Conformal Conic

East from Greenwich

1:2 000 000

Administrative divisions in Croatia:
1 Brodsko-Posavska   4 Medimurska   6 Požeško-Slavonska
2 Koprivničko-Križevačka 5 Osječko-Baranjska   8 Virovitičko-Podravska
                                                9 Vukovarsko-Srijemska

Underlined towns give their name to the
administrative area in which they stand.

COPYRIGHT PHILIP'S

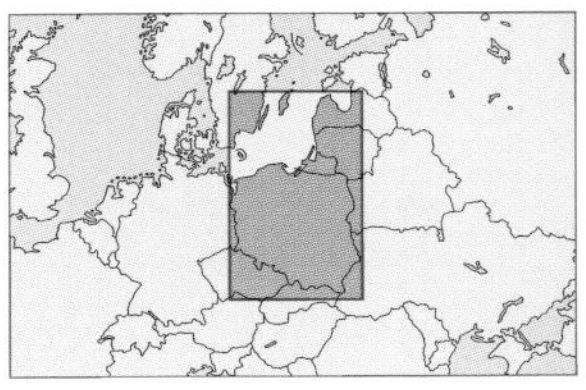

10 0 10 20 30 40 50 60 70 80 90 km
10 0 10 20 30 40 50 60 miles

1:2 000 000

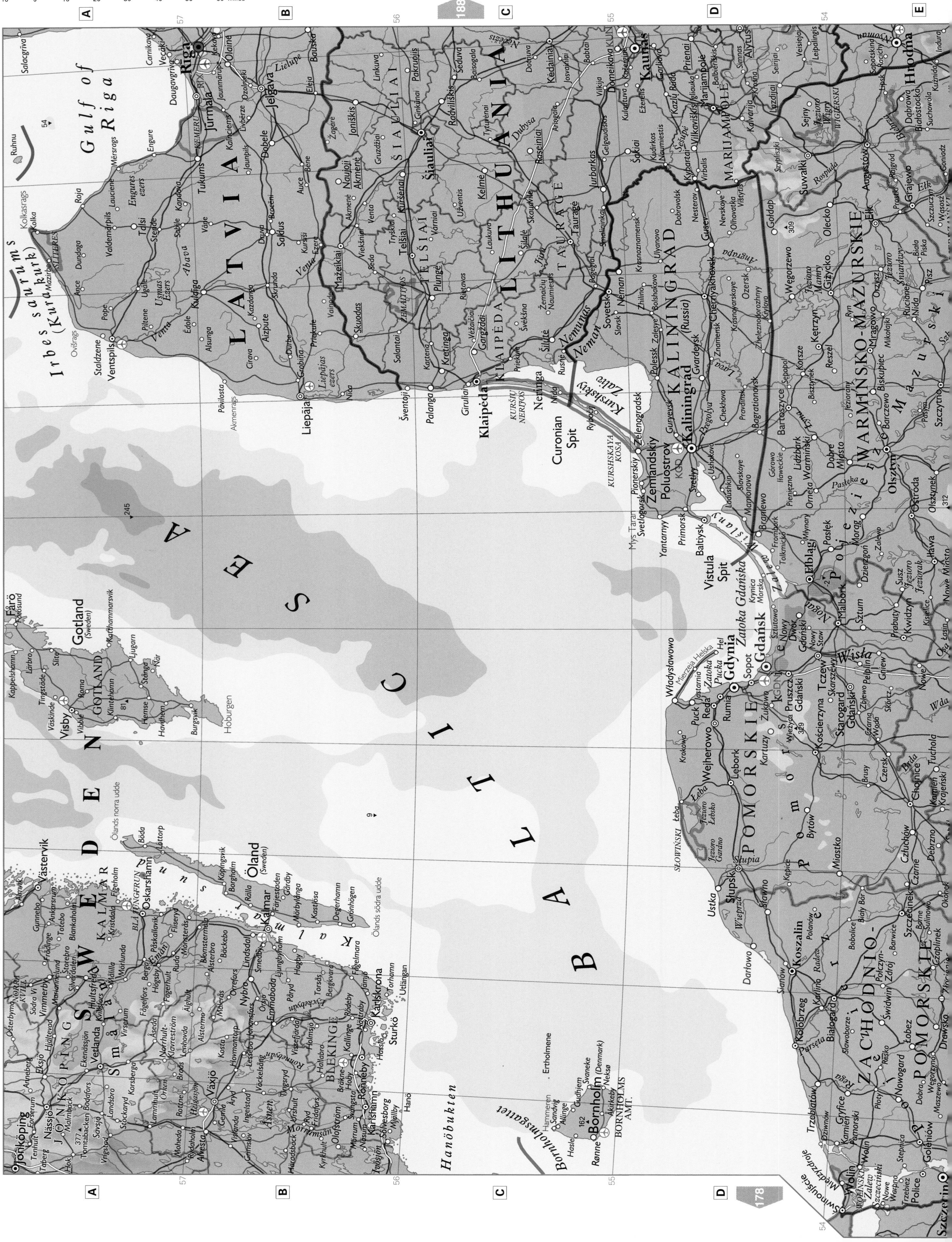

Gulf of Riga

LATVIA

LITHUANIA

KALININGRAD (Russia)

SWEDEN

Gotland (Sweden)

Öland (Sweden)

Bornholm (Denmark)

BALTIC SEA

POLAND

Riga
Jūrmala
Jelgava
Ventspils
Liepāja
Šiauliai
Telšiai
Klaipēda
Palanga
Šventoji
Curonian Spit
Kuršių Nerijos
Nemunas
Neman
Kaunas
Marijampolė
Kaliningrad
Zelenogradsk
Zemlandsky
Poluostrov
Baltiysk
Vistula Spit
Gdańsk
Gdynia
Sopot
Elbląg
Malbork
Słupsk
Koszalin
Kołobrzeg
Ustka
Darłowo

WARMIŃSKO-MAZURSKIE
POMORSKIE
ZACHODNIO-POMORSKIE
Mazury
Pojezierze

Gotland
Visby
Kalmar
Oskarshamn
Västervik
Karlskrona
Karlshamn
Ronneby
Växjö
Jönköping
Nässjö

Hanöbukten
Bornholmsgattet

Underlined towns give their name to the administrative area in which they stand.

Projection : Lambert's Conformal Conic

East from Greenwich

COPYRIGHT PHILIP'S

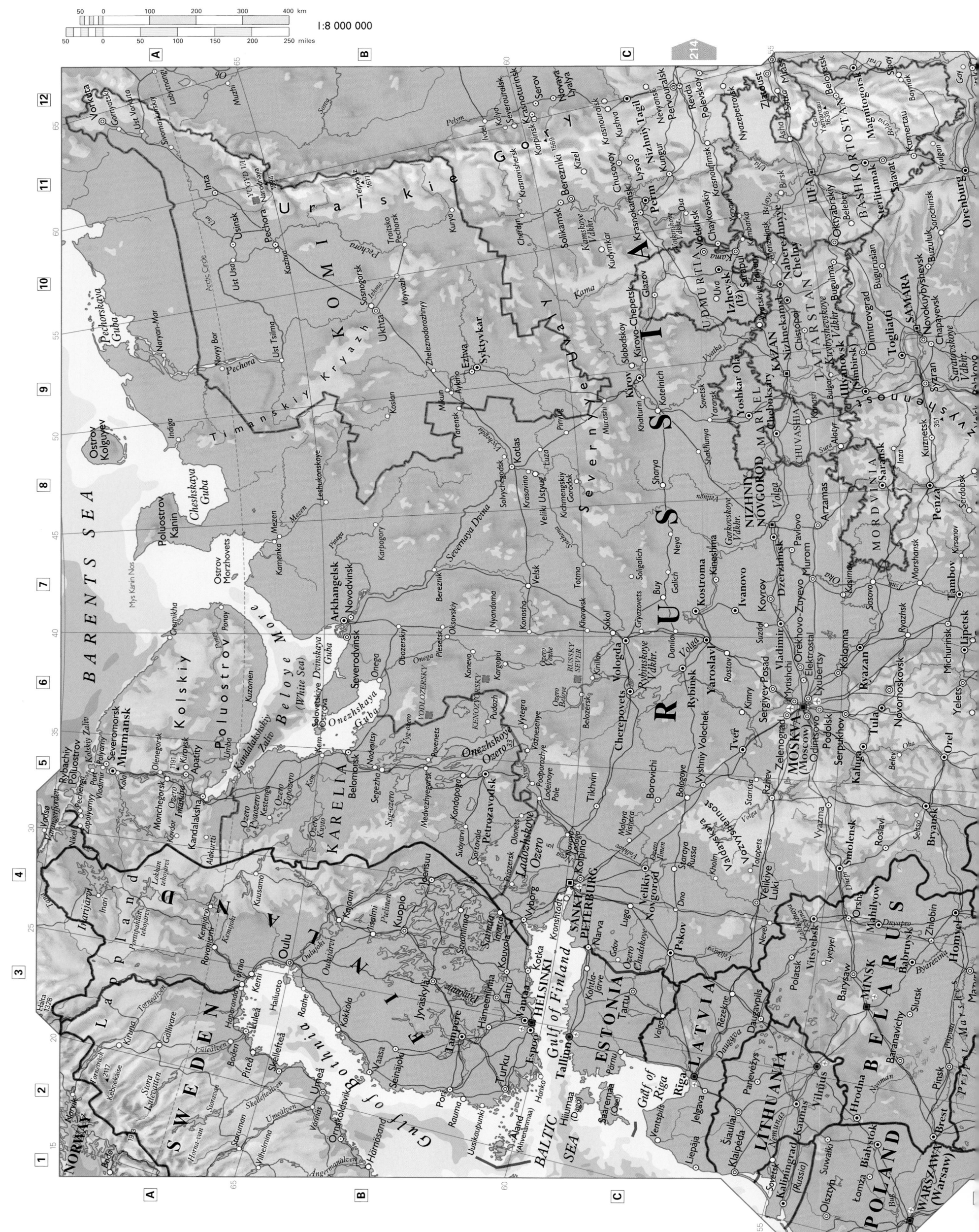

1:8 000 000

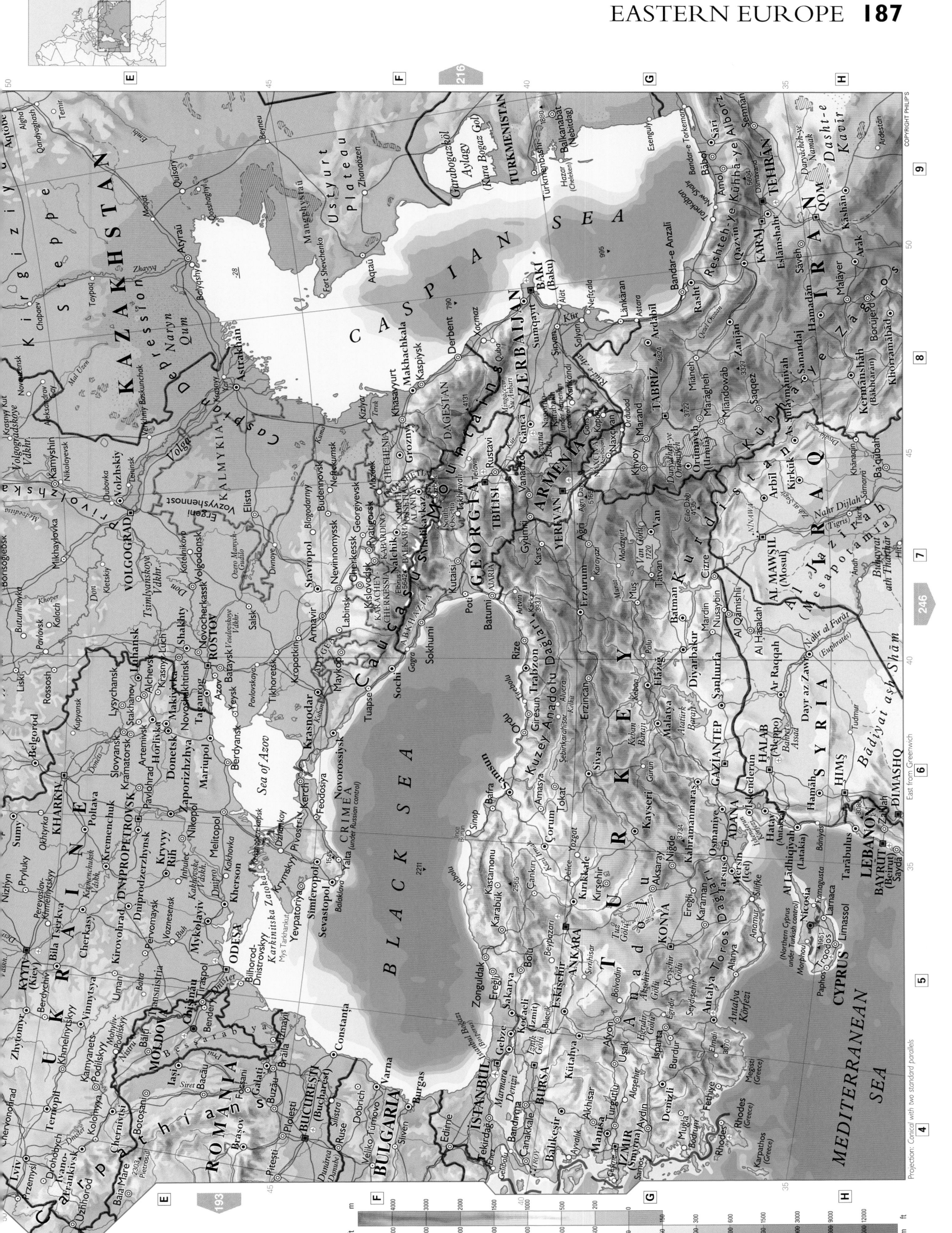

CASPIAN SEA

BLACK SEA

MEDITERRANEAN SEA

Sea of Azov

KAZAKHSTAN

Kirgiziy Steppe

TURKMENISTAN

IRAN

AZERBAIJAN

ARMENIA

GEORGIA

TURKEY

SYRIA

IRAQ

LEBANON

CYPRUS

UKRAINE

ROMANIA

BULGARIA

MOLDOVA

Caucasus Mountains

Projection: Conical with two standard parallels

East from Greenwich

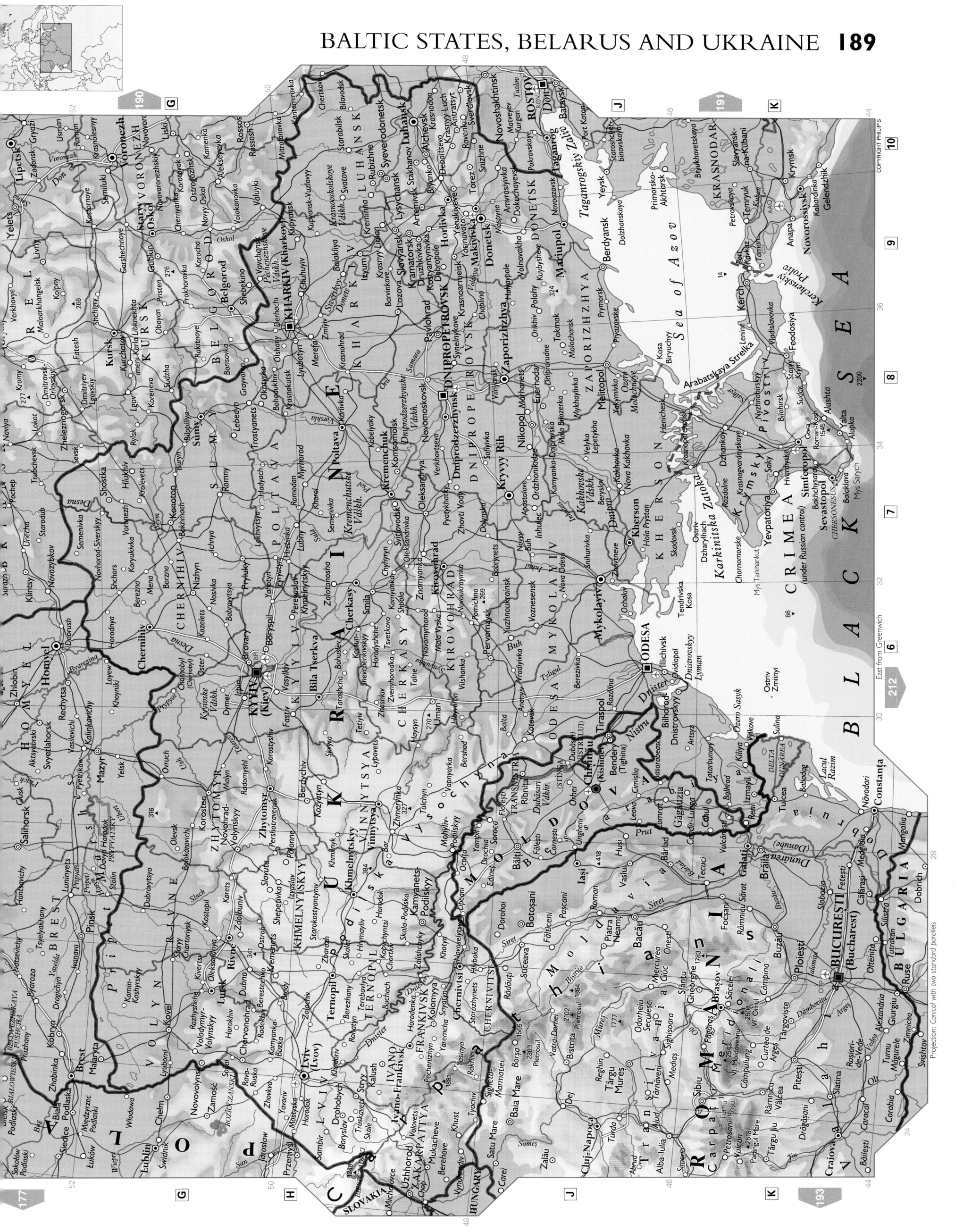

Projection: Conical with two standard parallels

East from Greenwich

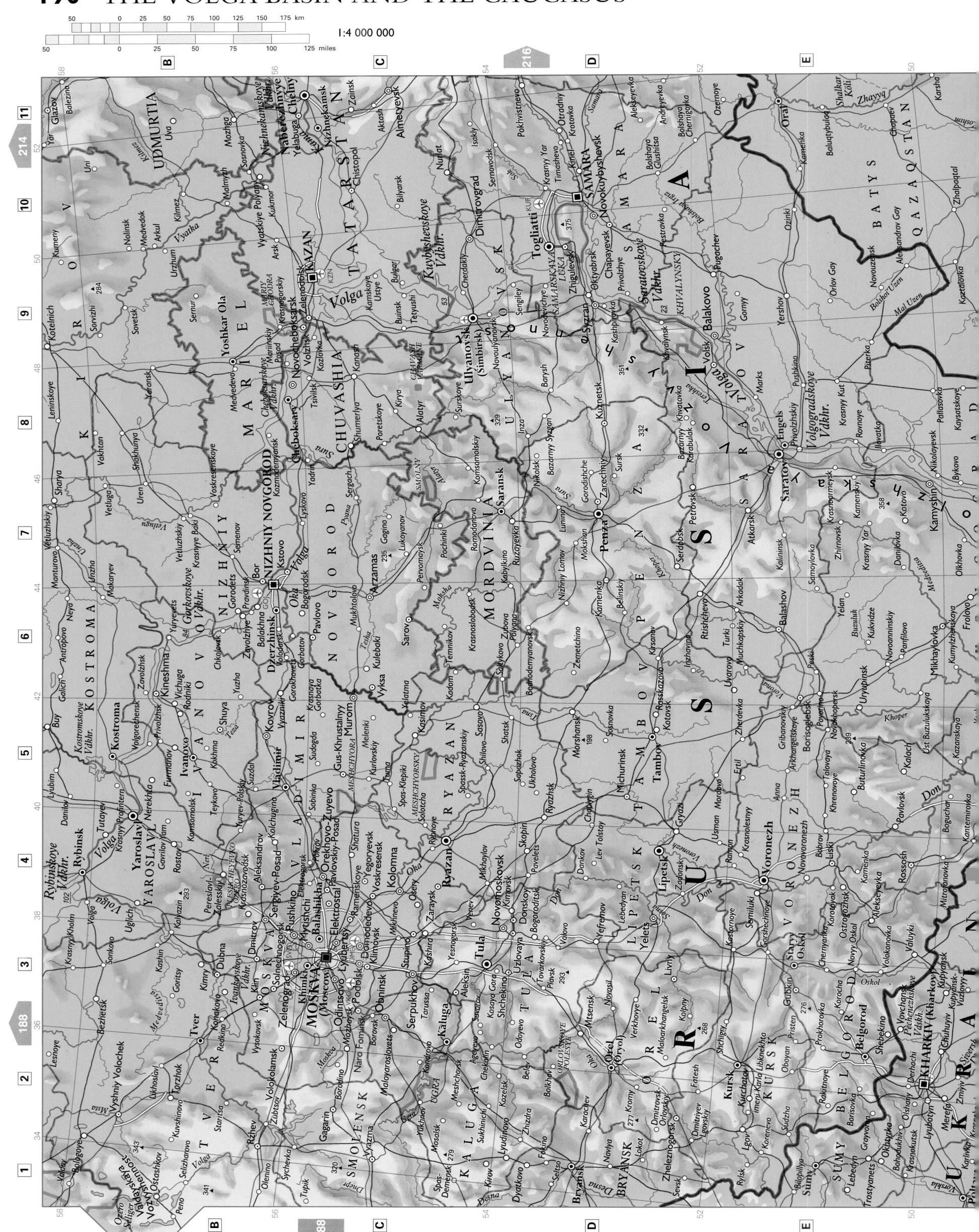

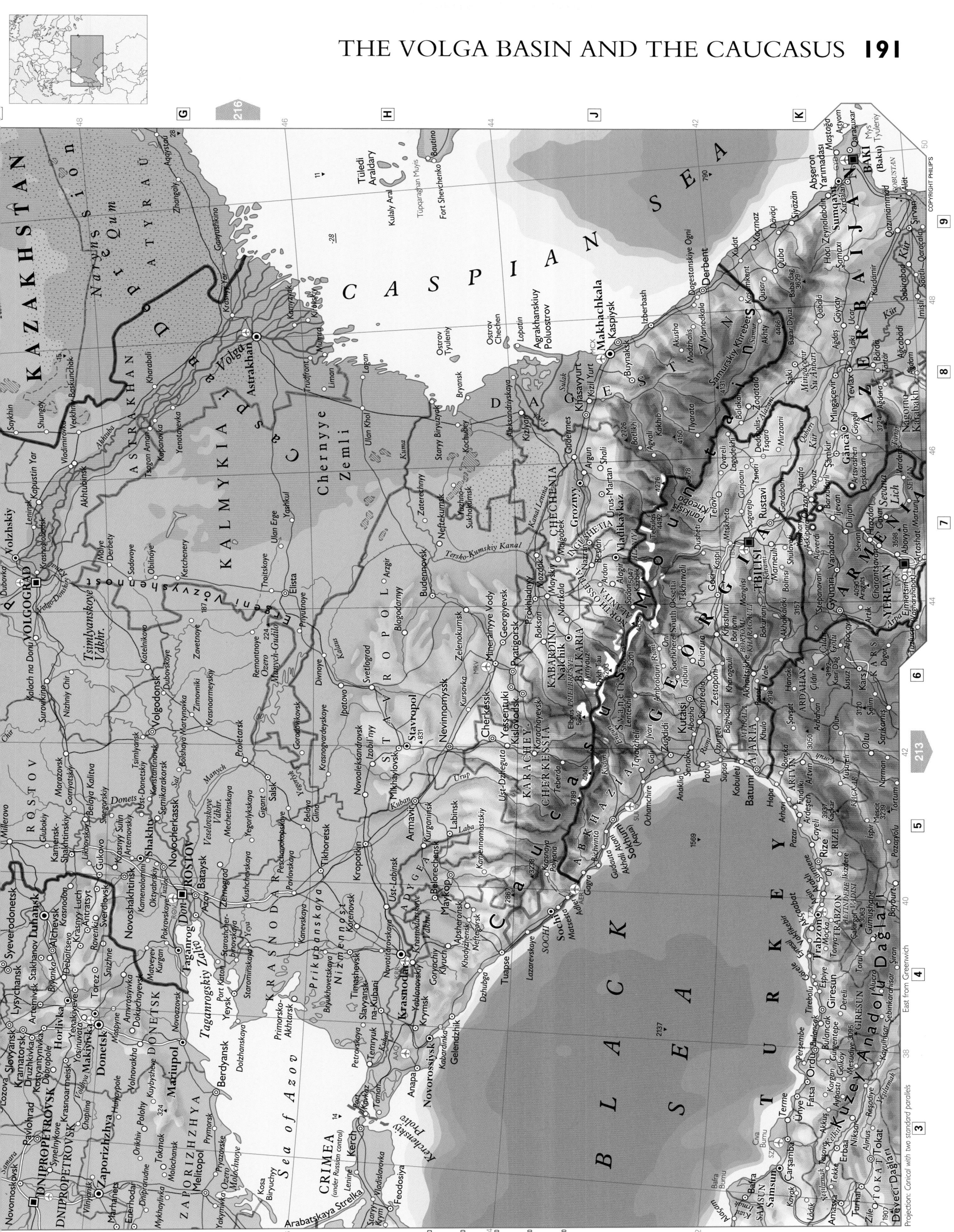

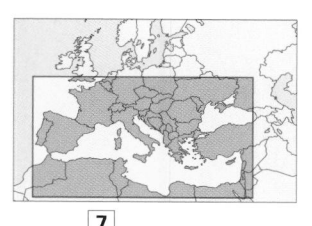

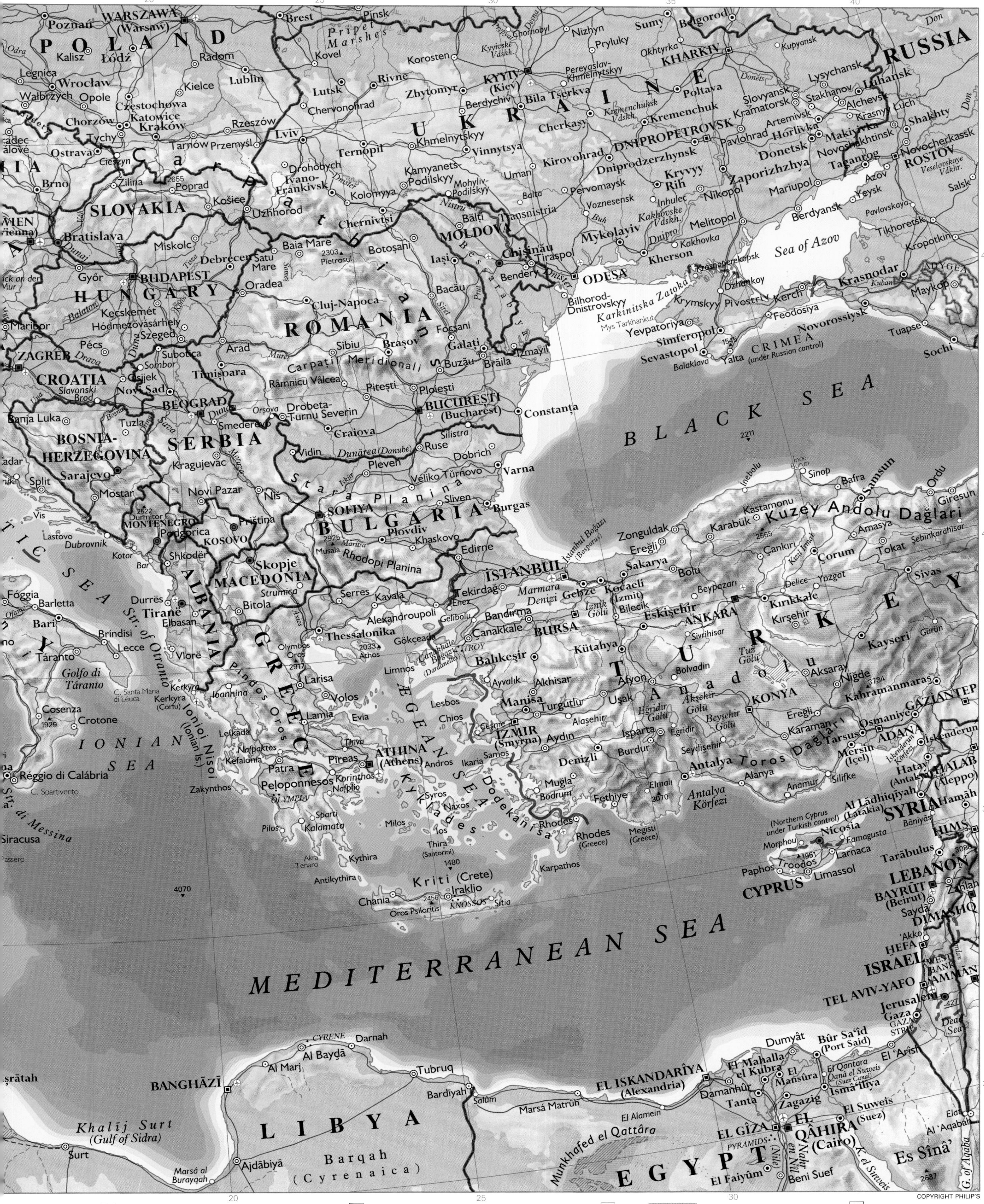

1:2 000 000

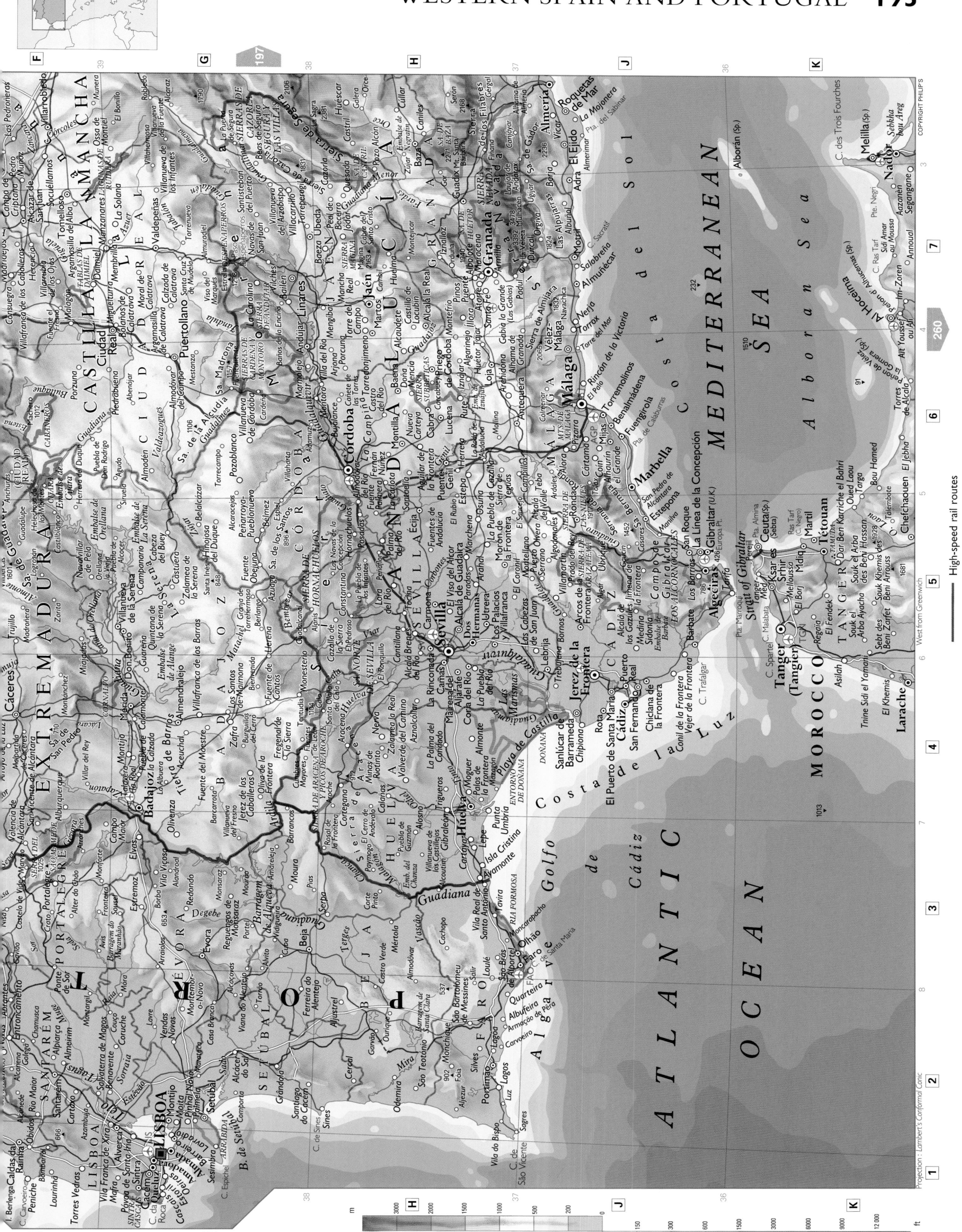

High-speed rail routes

Projection: Lambert's Conformal Conic

1:2 000 000

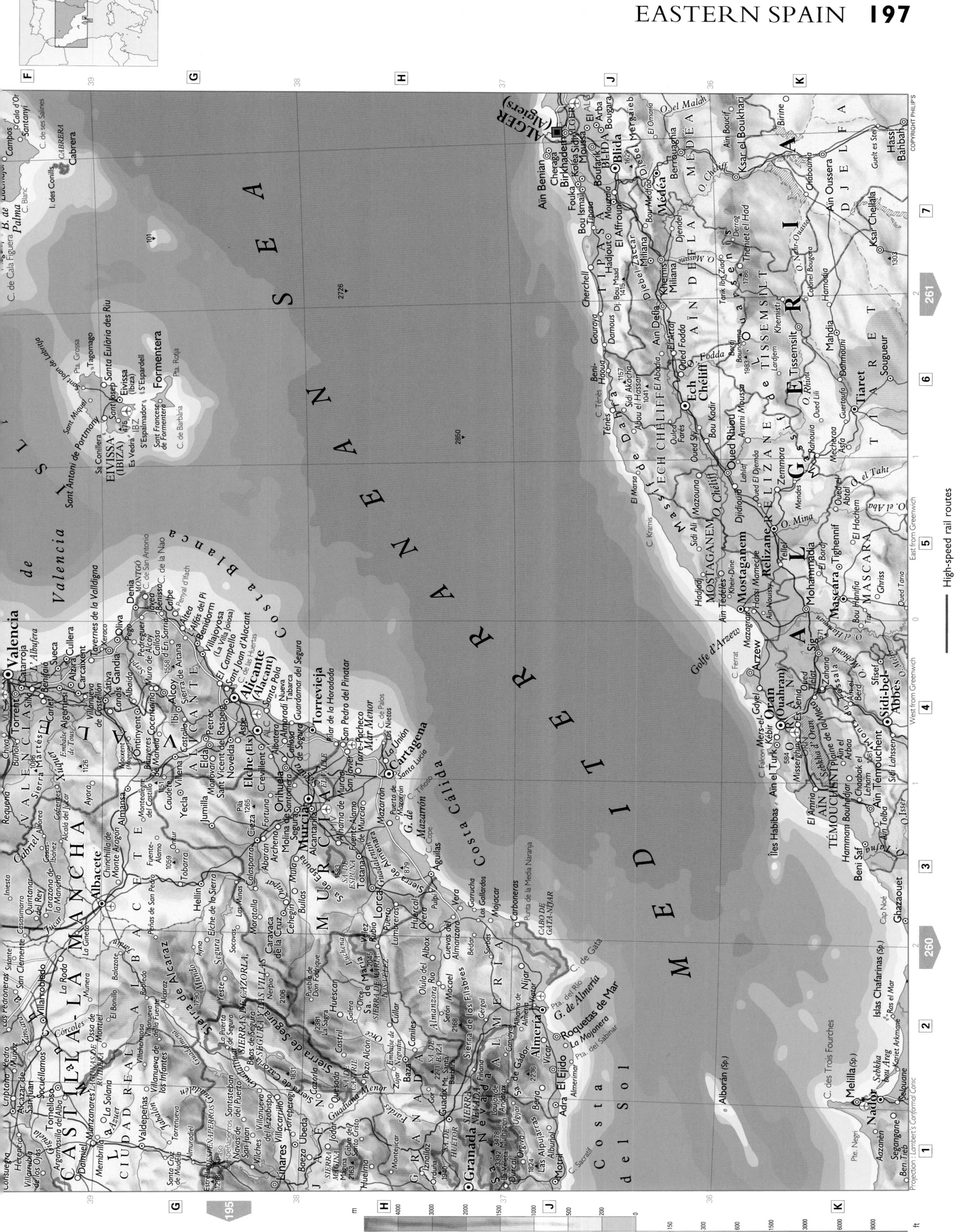

High-speed rail routes

East from Greenwich

West from Greenwich

Projection: Lambert's Conformal Conic

Administrative divisions in Croatia:

1 Bjelovarsko-Bilogorska
2 Koprivničko-Križevačka
3 Krapinsko-Zagorska
4 Medimurska
6 Požeško-Slavonska
7 Varaždinska
8 Virovitičko-Podravska
10 Zagrebačka

— High-speed rail routes

COPYRIGHT PHILIP'S

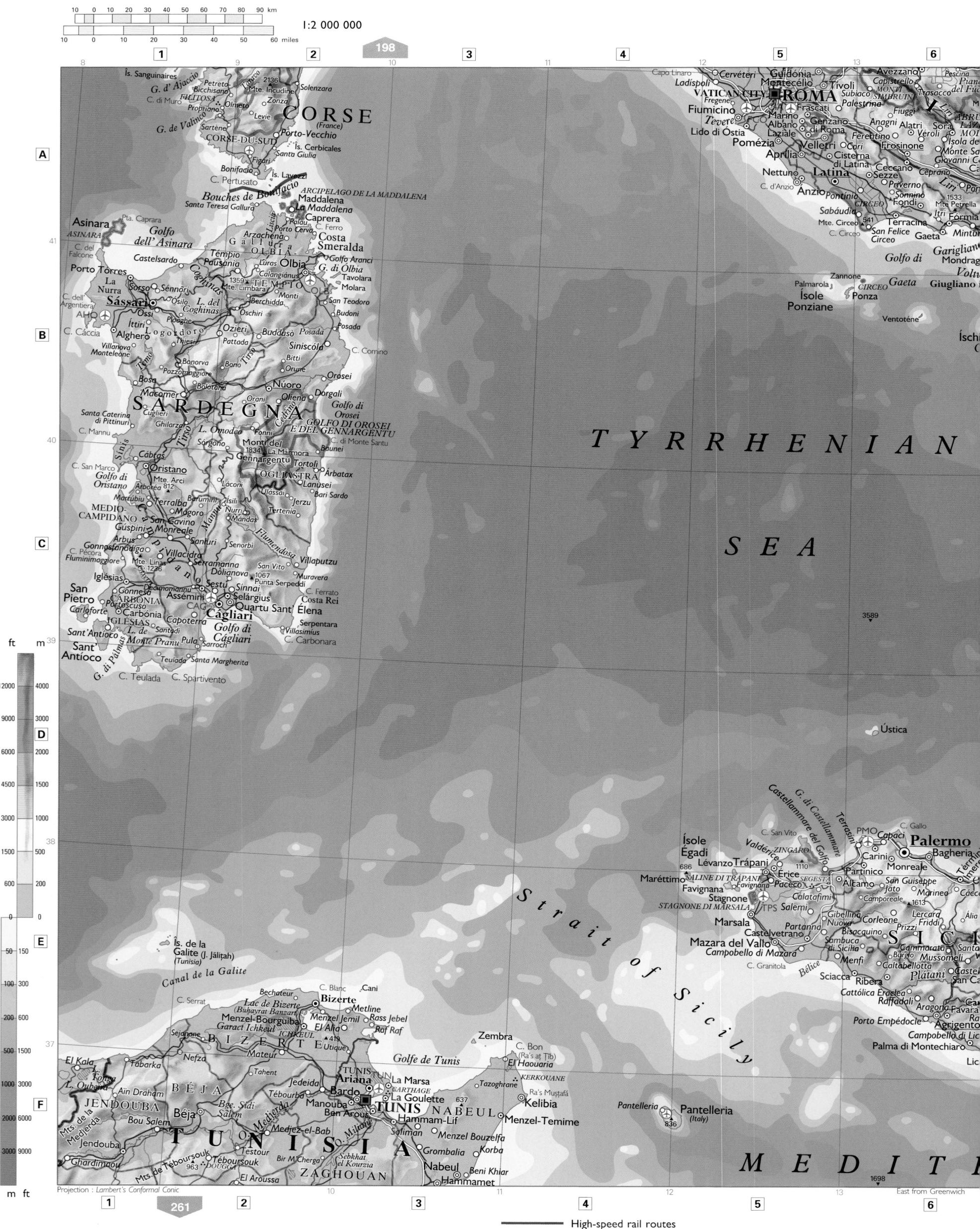

High-speed rail routes

Underlined towns give their name to the
administrative area in which they stand.

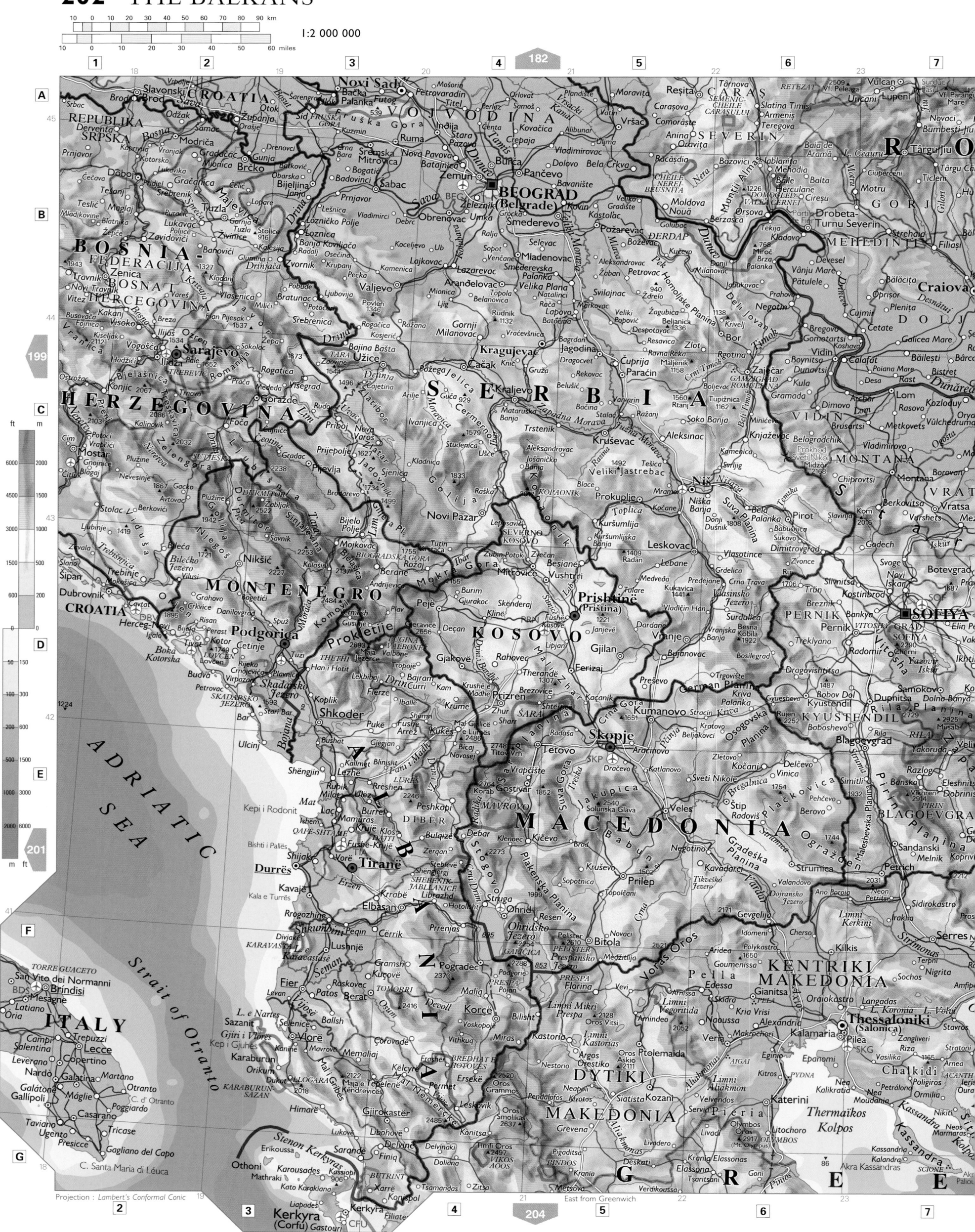

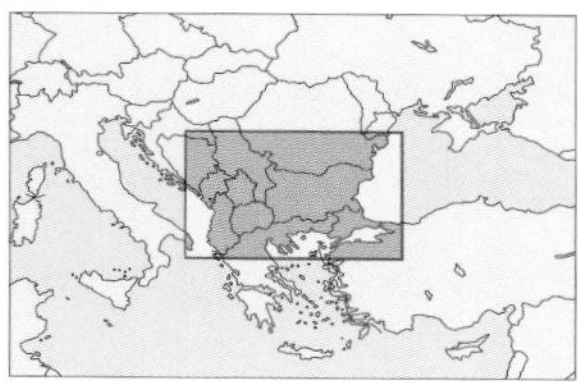

BUCUREȘTI (Bucharest)

ROMANIA

BULGARIA

TURKEY

BLACK SEA

Constanța

Varna

Burgas

Plovdiv

Ruse

Pleven

Galați

Brăila

Buzău

Ploiești

Pitești

Edirne

İSTANBUL

Kırklareli

Tekirdağ

Çorlu

BURSA

Kocaeli (İzmit)

Marmara Denizi (Sea of Marmara)

Sea of Thrace

Alexandroupoli

Komotini

Kavala

ANATOLIKI MAKEDONIA KAI THRAKI

Çanakkale

Gökçeada (İmroz)

Limnos

Thasos

Samothraki

Bozcaada

DELTA DUNĂREA

Tulcea

Mangalia

Dobrich

Shumen

Razgrad

Veliko Tŭrnovo

Gabrovo

Sliven

Stara Zagora

Yambol

Khaskovo

Kŭrdzhali

Smolyan

Istanbul Boğazı (Bosporus)

Çanakkale Boğazı (Dardanelles)

Dunăv (Danube)

Underlined towns give their name to the administrative area in which they stand.

COPYRIGHT PHILIP'S

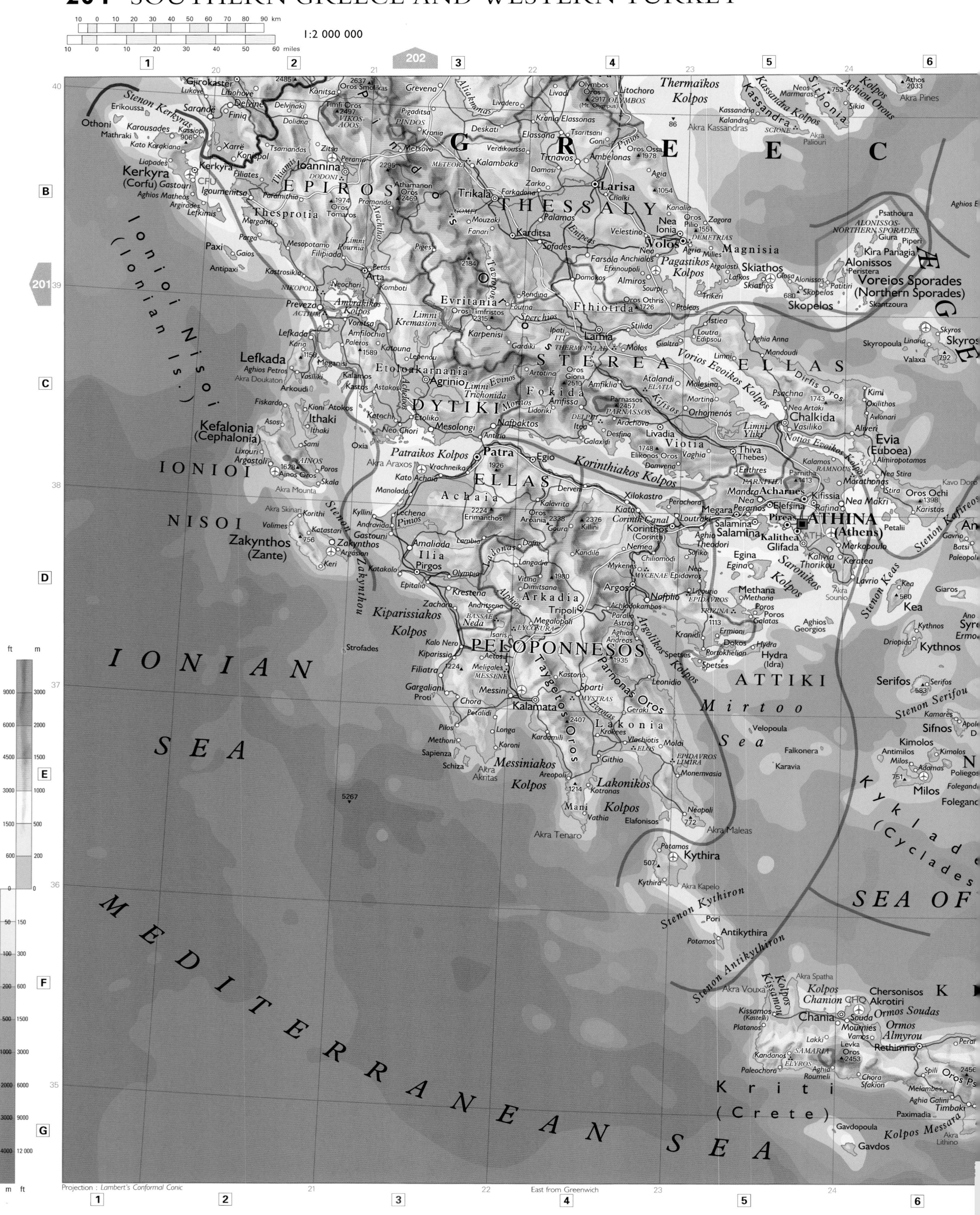

1:2 000 000

IONIAN SEA

MEDITERRANEAN SEA

Projection : Lambert's Conformal Conic

East from Greenwich

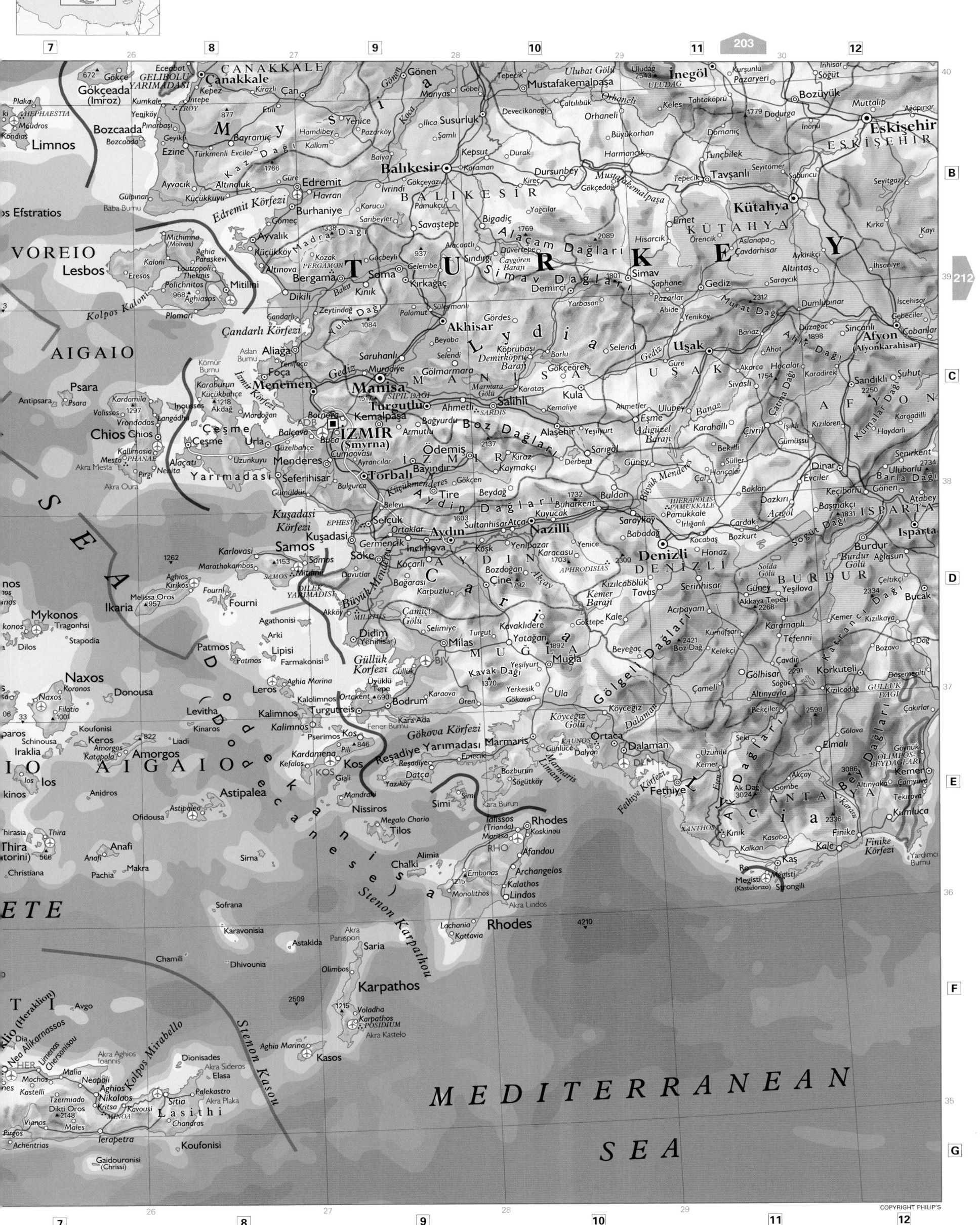

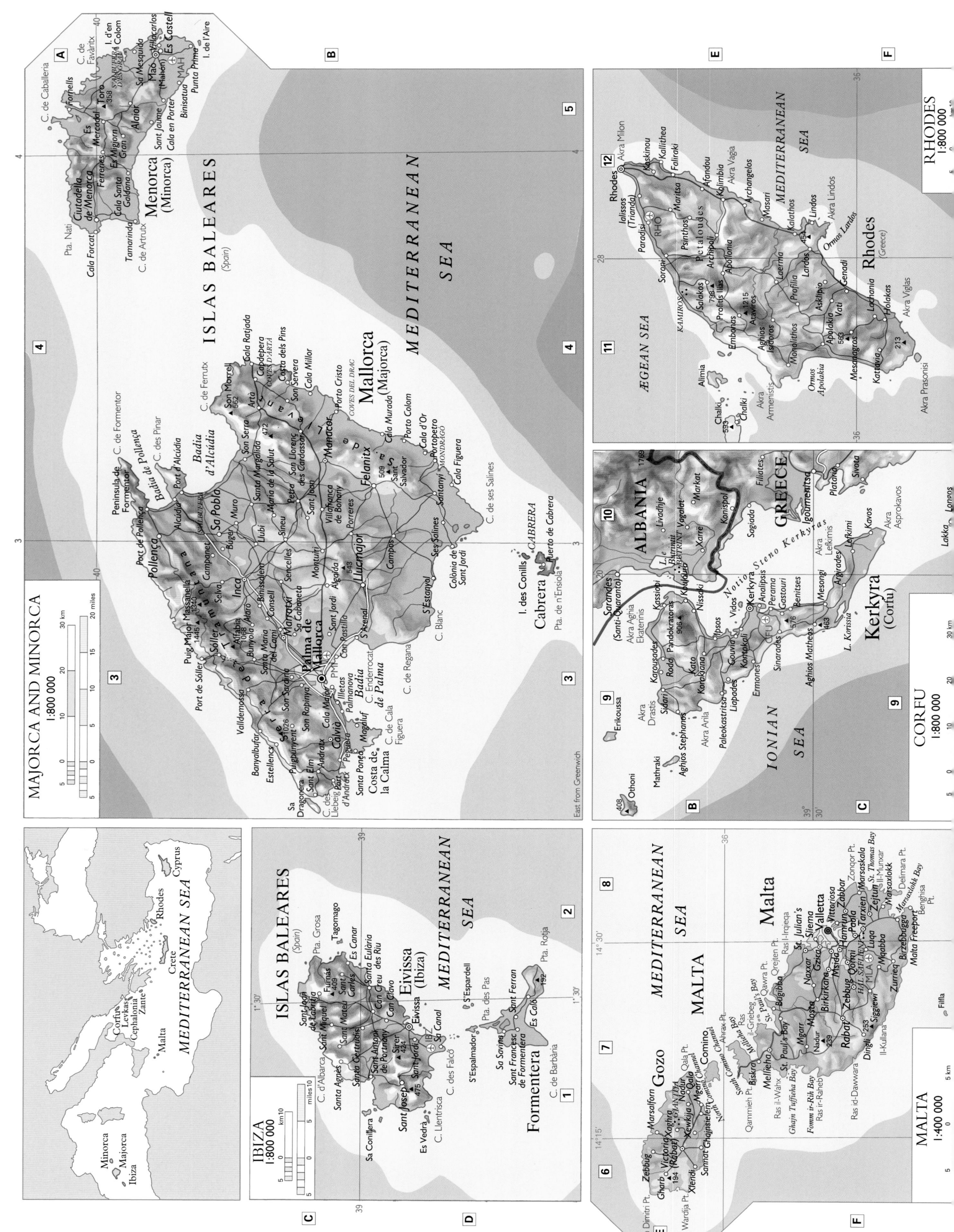

MAJORCA AND MINORCA
1:800 000

ISLAS BALEARES
(Spain)

Menorca
(Minorca)

Mallorca
(Majorca)

MEDITERRANEAN SEA

Cabrera

IBIZA
1:800 000

ISLAS BALEARES
(Spain)

Eivissa
(Ibiza)

Formentera
de Formentera

MEDITERRANEAN SEA

MEDITERRANEAN SEA

Minorca
Majorca
Ibiza

RHODES
1:800 000

MEDITERRANEAN SEA

AEGEAN SEA

Rhodes
(Greece)

CORFU
1:800 000

ALBANIA

GREECE

Kerkyra
(Corfu)

IONIAN SEA

MALTA
1:400 000

MEDITERRANEAN SEA

Gozo

Malta

MALTA

East from Greenwich

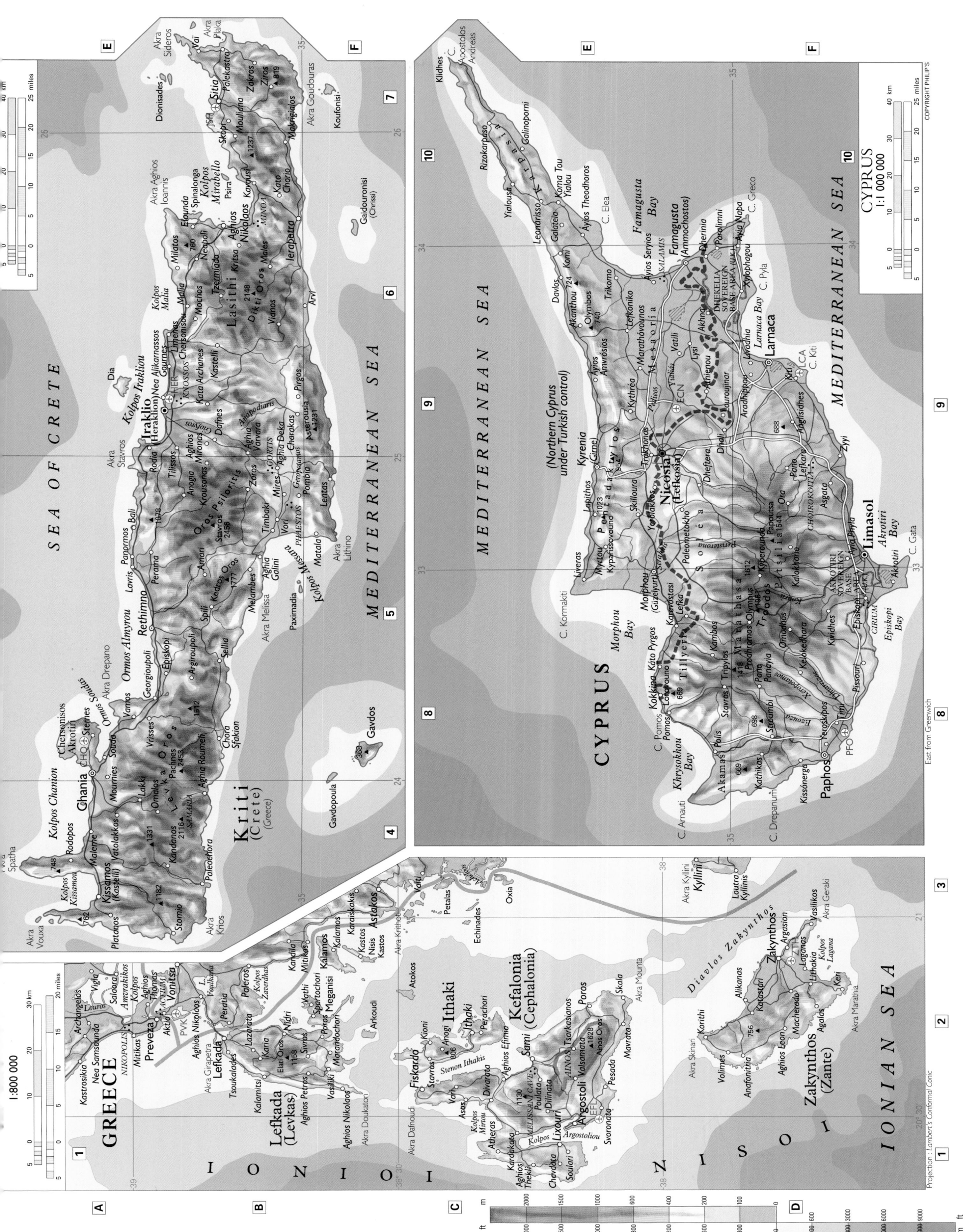

SEA OF CRETE

Kriti
(Crete)
(Greece)

MEDITERRANEAN SEA

CYPRUS

CYPRUS
1:1 000 000

(Northern Cyprus
under Turkish control)

MEDITERRANEAN SEA

East from Greenwich

GREECE

IONIOI NISOI

IONIAN SEA

1:800 000

Projection: Lambert's Conformal Conic

ASIA

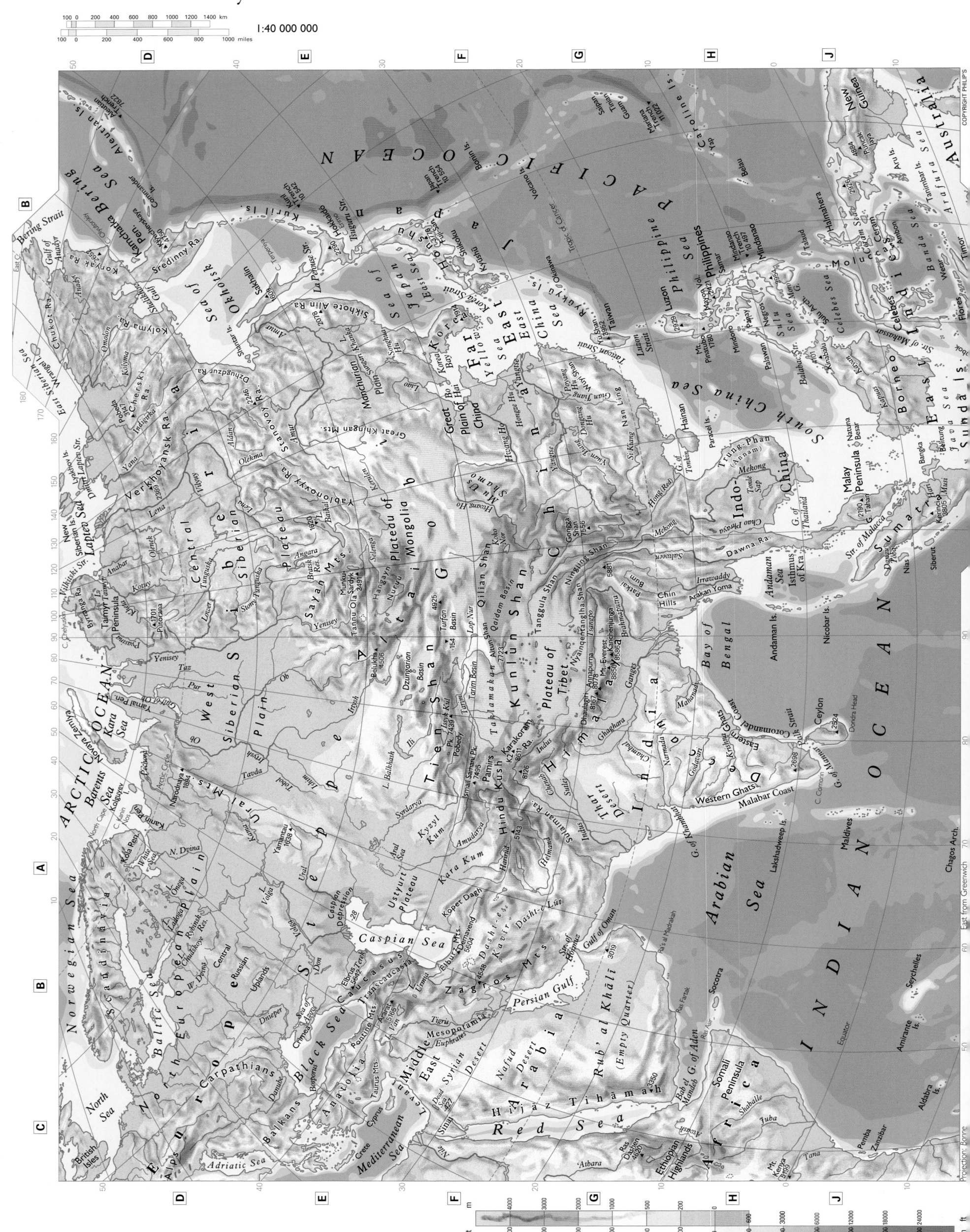

1:40 000 000

1:40 000 000

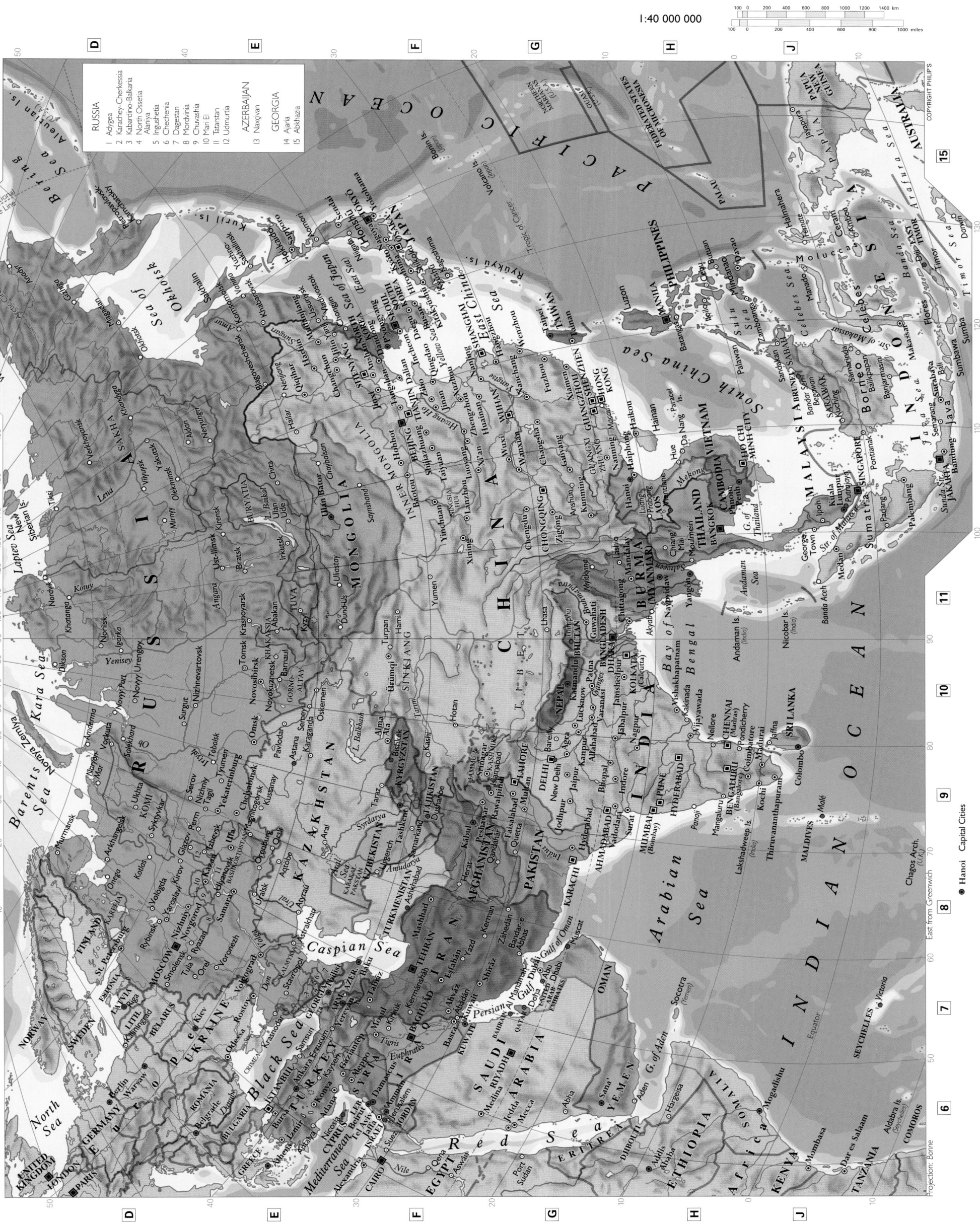

RUSSIA
1 Adygea
2 Karachey-Cherkessia
3 Kabardino-Balkaria
4 North Ossetia
5 Alaniya
6 Ingushetia
7 Chechenia
8 Dagestan
9 Mordovia
10 Chuvashia
11 Tatarstan
12 Udmurtia

AZERBAIJAN
13 Naxçivan

GEORGIA
14 Ajaria
15 Abkhazia

● Hanoi Capital Cities

Projection: Bonne

50 0 25 50 75 100 125 150 175 km
1: 4 000 000
50 0 25 50 75 100 125 miles

1 2 3 4 189 5 6 7

B L A C K   S E A

BULGARIA

Stara Zagora
Yambol
Aytos
Nos Emine
Burgas
Elkhovo
Michurin
1830
2206

Kırklareli
Edirne
Pınarhisar
İğneada
İğneada Burnu
Demirköy
1018
Arda
Orestiada
Uzunköprü
Hayrabolu
Lüleburgaz
Vize
Babaeski
Muratlı
Saray
Çatalca
Çorlu
Çerkezköy
İstanbul Boğazı (Bosporus)
Kerempe Burnu
İnce Burun
Sinop
Çatalzeytin
Erfelek
Ayancık
İnebolu
Abana
Bafra Burnu
Gerze
SINOP
Civa Burnu
Keşan
Malkara
Tekirdağ
Silivri
Büyükçekmece
İSTANBUL
Kartal
Kocaeli (İzmit)
Sakarya (Adapazarı)
Zonguldak
Çatalağzı
Kozlu
Ereğli
Devrek
Karabük
Akçakoca
Düzce
Bolu
Kurucaşile
Cide
Kilimli
Bartın
Devrekani
Küre
Kastamonu
Taşköprü
Daday
Araç
Boyabat
Durağan
SAMSUN
Altınkaya Barajı
Kavak
Çarşamba
Terme
Ünye
Fatsa
Bafra
Amasra
Amasya
Merzifon
Suluova
Havza
Vezirköprü
Ladik
Tekke
Akkuş

İpsala
Enez
Saros Körfezi
Gelibolu
Gökçeada
Çanakkale (Dardanelles)
Lapseki
Biga
Bandırma
Mudanya
Gemlik
BURSA
İznik Gölü
Yenişehir
İnegöl
Bilecik
Söğüt
Bozüyük
Eskişehir
Sakarya
Beypazarı
Ayaş
Kızılcahamam
ANKARA
Kırıkkale
Kırşehir
Çankırı
ÇANKIRI
ÇORUM
Çorum
Sungurlu
Alaca
Osmancık
İskilip
Kargı
Tosya
TOKAT
Tokat
Turhal
Zile
Almus
Niksar
Reşadiye
Deveci Dağları

Lesbos
Chios
İzmir (Smyrna)
Manisa
MANISA
KÜTAHYA
Kütahya
Afyon (Afyonkarahisar)
Eskişehir
Sivrihisar
Polatlı
Bala
Haymana
Kulu
Tuz Gölü
Aksaray
AKSARAY
NEVŞEHİR
Nevşehir
KAYSERİ
Kayseri
Talas
SİVAS
Sivas
Yozgat
YOZGAT
Şarkışla
Gemerek
Kangal

A N A D O L U   **ANATOLIA**

İZMİR
Turgutlu
Salihli
Alaşehir
Uşak
UŞAK
Eşme
Banaz
DENİZLİ
Denizli
Nazilli
Aydın
AYDIN
Söke
Çine
Muğla
MUĞLA
Milas
Bodrum
Marmaris
Fethiye
Antalya
ANTALYA
Burdur
BURDUR
Isparta
ISPARTA
Beyşehir
Beyşehir Gölü
KONYA
Konya
Ereğli
Karaman
KARAMAN
NİĞDE
Niğde
Bor
ADANA
Adana
Mersin (İçel)
Tarsus
KAHRAMAN-MARAŞ
Kahramanmaraş
GAZİANTEP
Gaziantep (Antep)
İskenderun
HATAY
Kilis

GREECE
Rhodes
Karpathos
Kasos

Dodekanisa

Antalya Körfezi
Alanya
Gazipaşa
Anamur
Anamur Burnu
Silifke
Bozyazı

M E D I T E R R A N E A N   S E A

Rizokarpaso
C. Apostolos Andreas
Al Lādhiqīyah (Latakia)
IDLIB
İskenderun Körfezi
Nicosia
Morphou
Kyrenia
Famagusta
Olympus 1951
Troodos
Larnaca
Limassol
Akrotiri
Episkopi
Paphos
Polis
CYPRUS
(Northern Cyprus under Turkish control)

HAMAH
HAMĀH
Ḥamāh
Tartūs
TARTŪS
HIMS
HIMŞ
Ḥimş (Homs)
Tarābulus (Tripoli)
LEBANON
BAYRŪT (Beirut)
Saydā
Sūr
DIMASHQ (Damascus)

2775

ISRAEL
HEFA (Haifa)
Teverya
Nazerat
Hadera
Netanya
TEL AVIV-YAFO
Rehovot
Ashdod
Ashqelon
Jerusalem
WEST BANK
Nābulus
Ramla
El Arīḥā
Irbid
AMMĀN
Az Zarqā
JORDAN

AS SUWAYDĀ'
As Suwaydā'

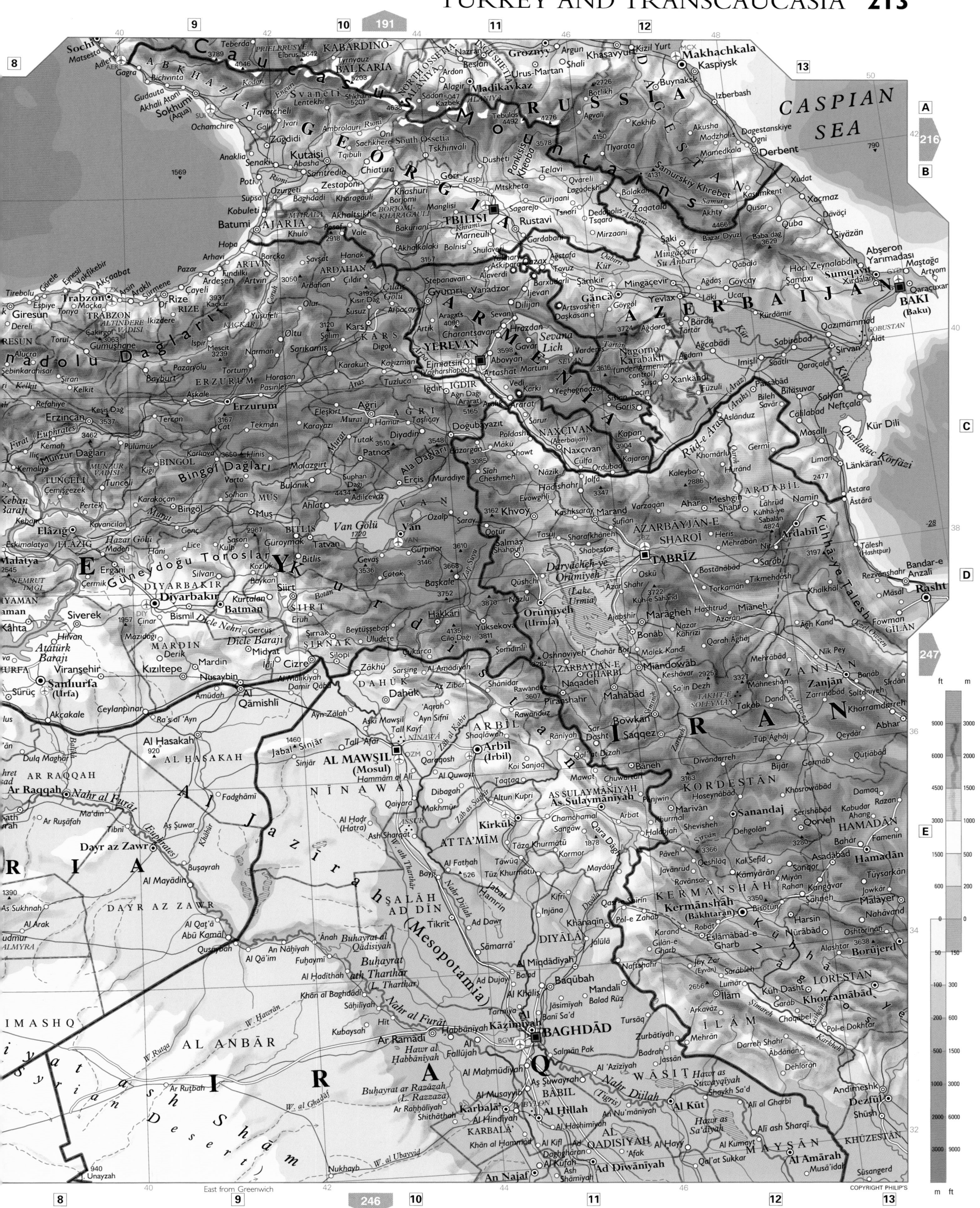

Underlined towns give their name
to the administrative area in which they stand

COPYRIGHT PHILIP'S

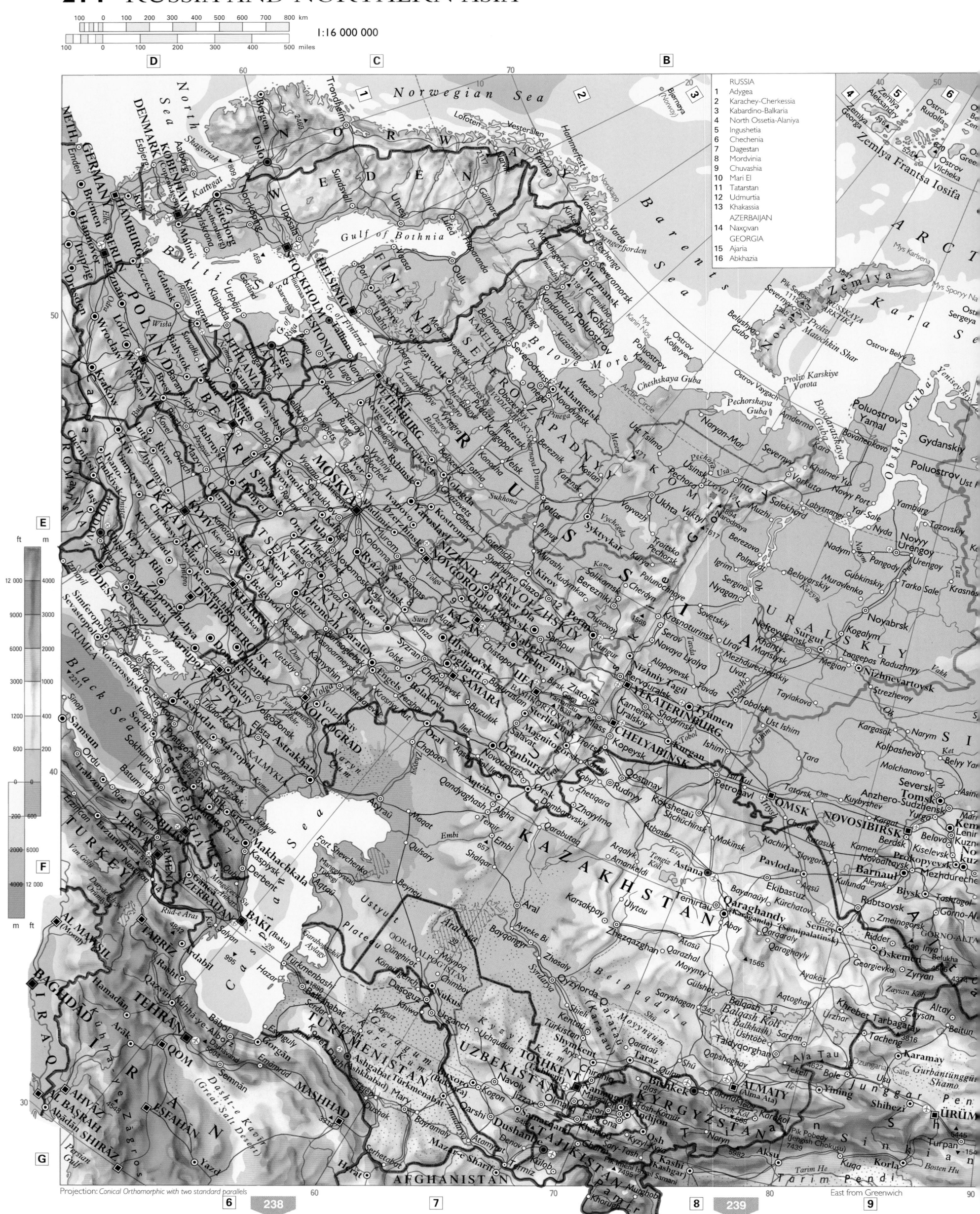

1:16 000 000

RUSSIA
1 Adygea
2 Karachey-Cherkessia
3 Kabardino-Balkaria
4 North Ossetia-Alaniya
5 Ingushetia
6 Chechenia
7 Dagestan
8 Mordvinia
9 Chuvashia
10 Mari El
11 Tatarstan
12 Udmurtia
13 Khakassia
AZERBAIJAN
14 Naxçivan
GEORGIA
15 Ajaria
16 Abkhazia

Projection: Conical Orthomorphic with two standard parallels

East from Greenwich

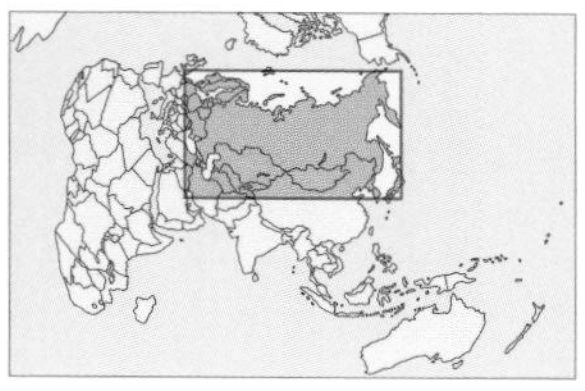

OCEAN

East Siberian Sea

Laptev Sea

Chukchi Sea

Bering Sea

Bering Str.

Mys Dezhneva (East C.)

St. Lawrence I. (USA)

International Date Line

Severnaya Zemlya

Ostrov Komsomolets

Ostrov Bolshevik

Ostrov Oktyabrskoy Revolyutsii

Ostrov Pioner

Ostrova Novosibirskiye Ostrova

Ostrov Kotelnyy

Lyakhovskiye Ostrova

Proliv Dmitriya Lapteva

Mys Arkticheskiy

Proliv Vilkitskogo

Mys Chelyuskin

Poluostrov Taymyr

Gory Byrranga

Oz. Taymyr

Nordvik

Khatanga

Tiksi

Verkhoyansk

Khrebet Cherskogo

Kolymskoye Nagorye

Koryakskoye Nagorye

Poluostrov Kamchatka

Kamchatskiy

Petropavlovsk-Kamchatskiy

Kurilskiye Ostrova

Sea of Okhotsk

Sakhalin

Yuzhno-Sakhalinsk

Khrebet Sikhote Alin

Khabarovsk

Komsomolsk-na-Amure

Blagoveshchensk

Heihe

HARBIN

QIQIHAR

DAQING

JIAMUSI

JIXI

MUDANJIANG

CHANGCHUN

JILIN

FUSHUN

SHENYANG

ANSHAN

Vladivostok

NORTH KOREA

Ch'ŏngjin

Hamhŭng

Wŏnsan

PYŎNGYANG

NAMP'O

SEOUL

INCHEON

SOUTH KOREA

DAEJEON

DAEGU

BUSAN

GWANGJU

Sea of Japan (East Sea)

Hokkaidō

SAPPORO

Hakodate

Honshū

JAPAN

KYOTO

KŌBE

OSAKA

RUSSIA

Yakutsk

Lena

Vilyuysk

Mirnyy

Olekminsk

Lensk

Bratsk

Krasnoyarsk

Irkutsk

Ulan Ude

Chita

MONGOLIA

ULAANBAATAR

Gobi

CHINA

BEIJING

HOHHOT

BAOTOU

ZHANGJIAKOU

TANGSHAN

DALIAN

Arctic Circle

COPYRIGHT PHILIP'S

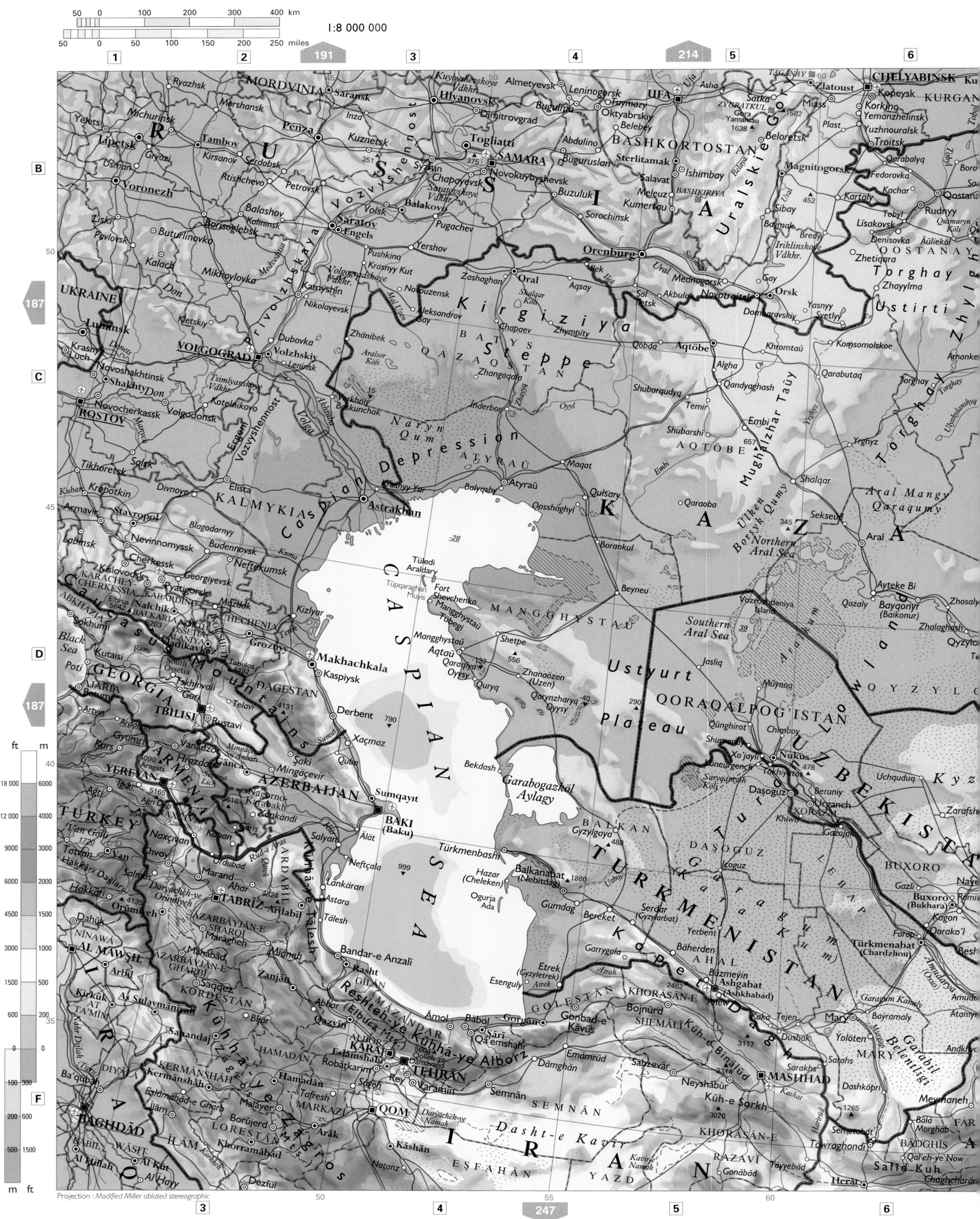

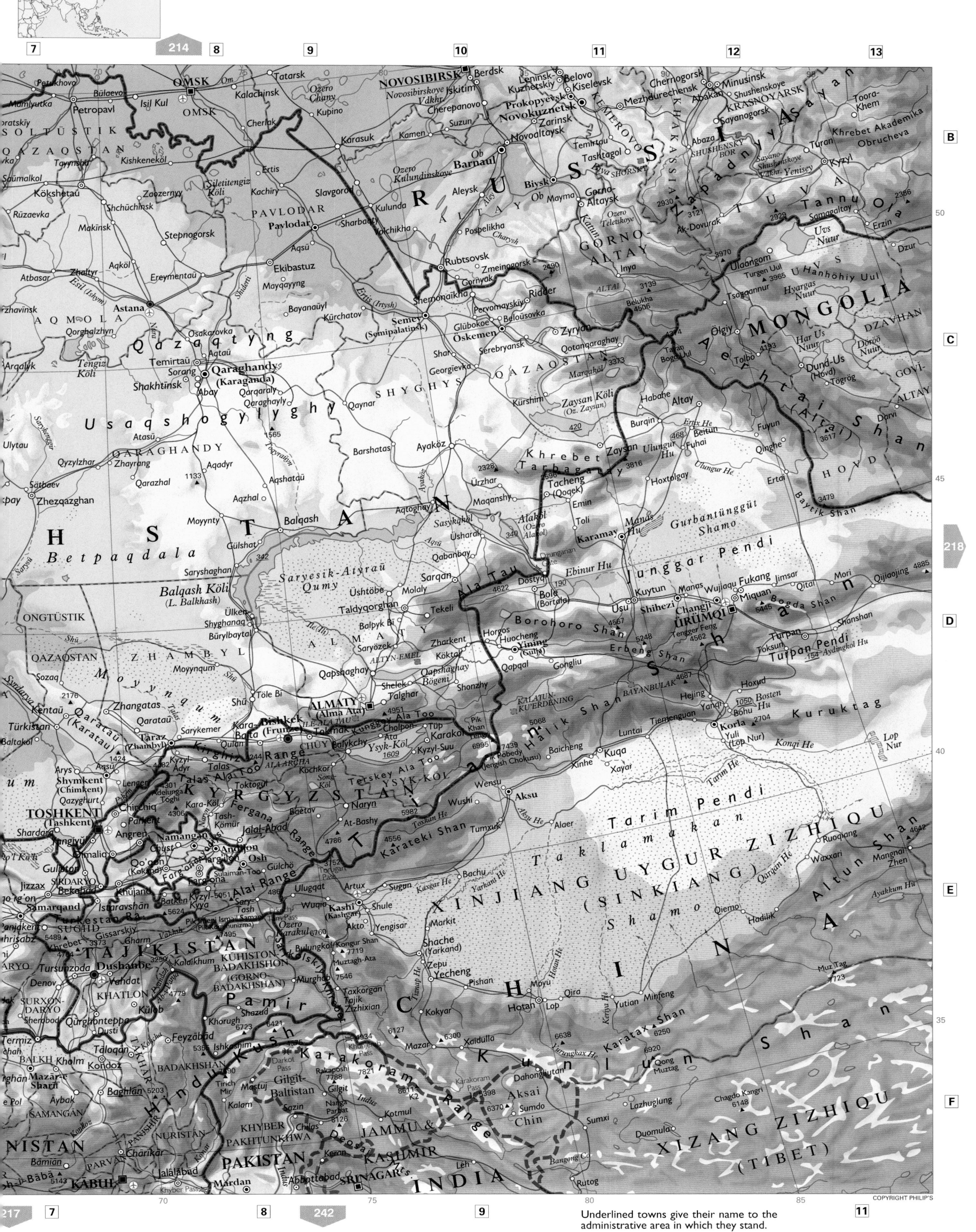

Underlined towns give their name to the
administrative area in which they stand.

COPYRIGHT PHILIP'S

Projection: Bonne

East from Greenwich

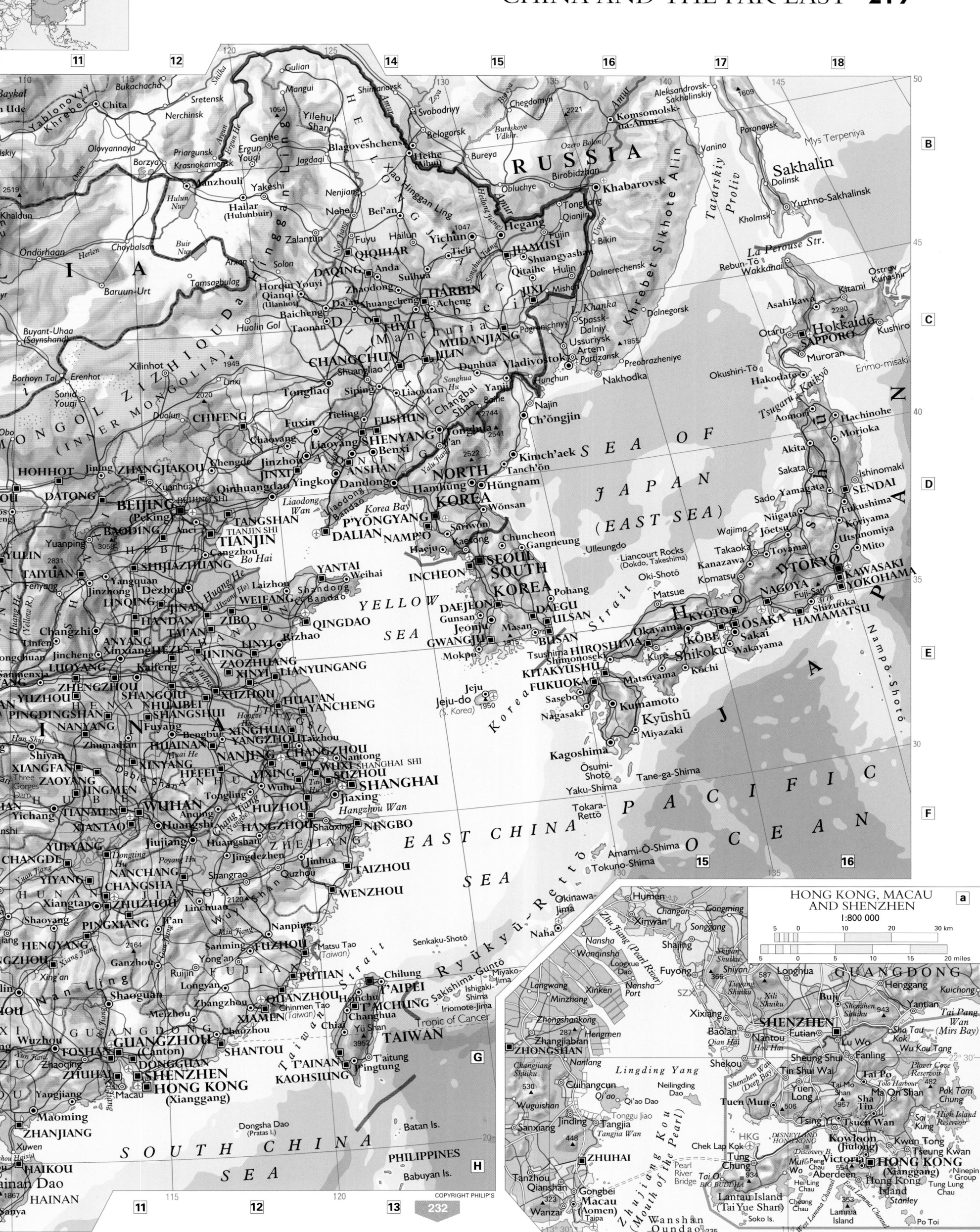

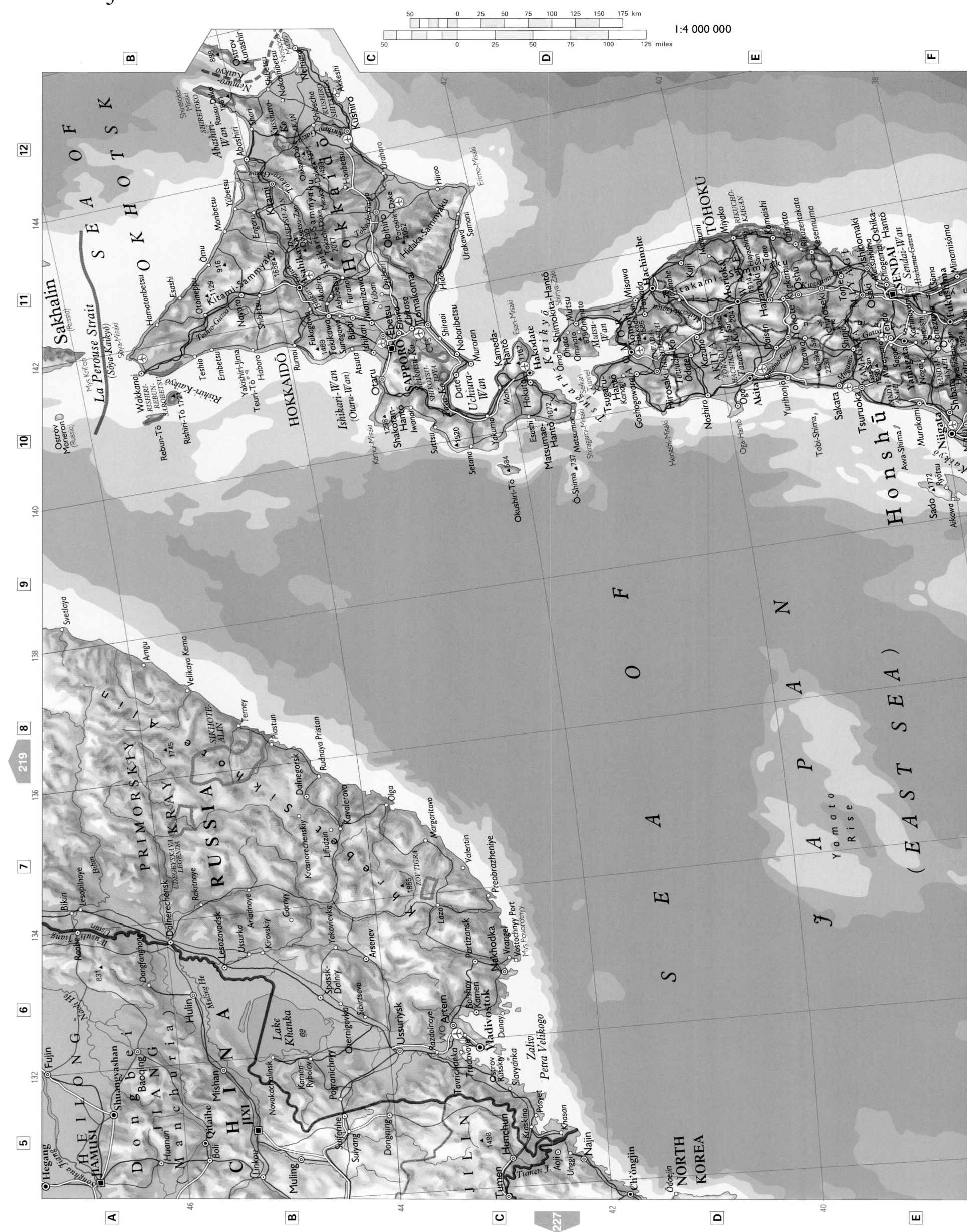

1:4 000 000

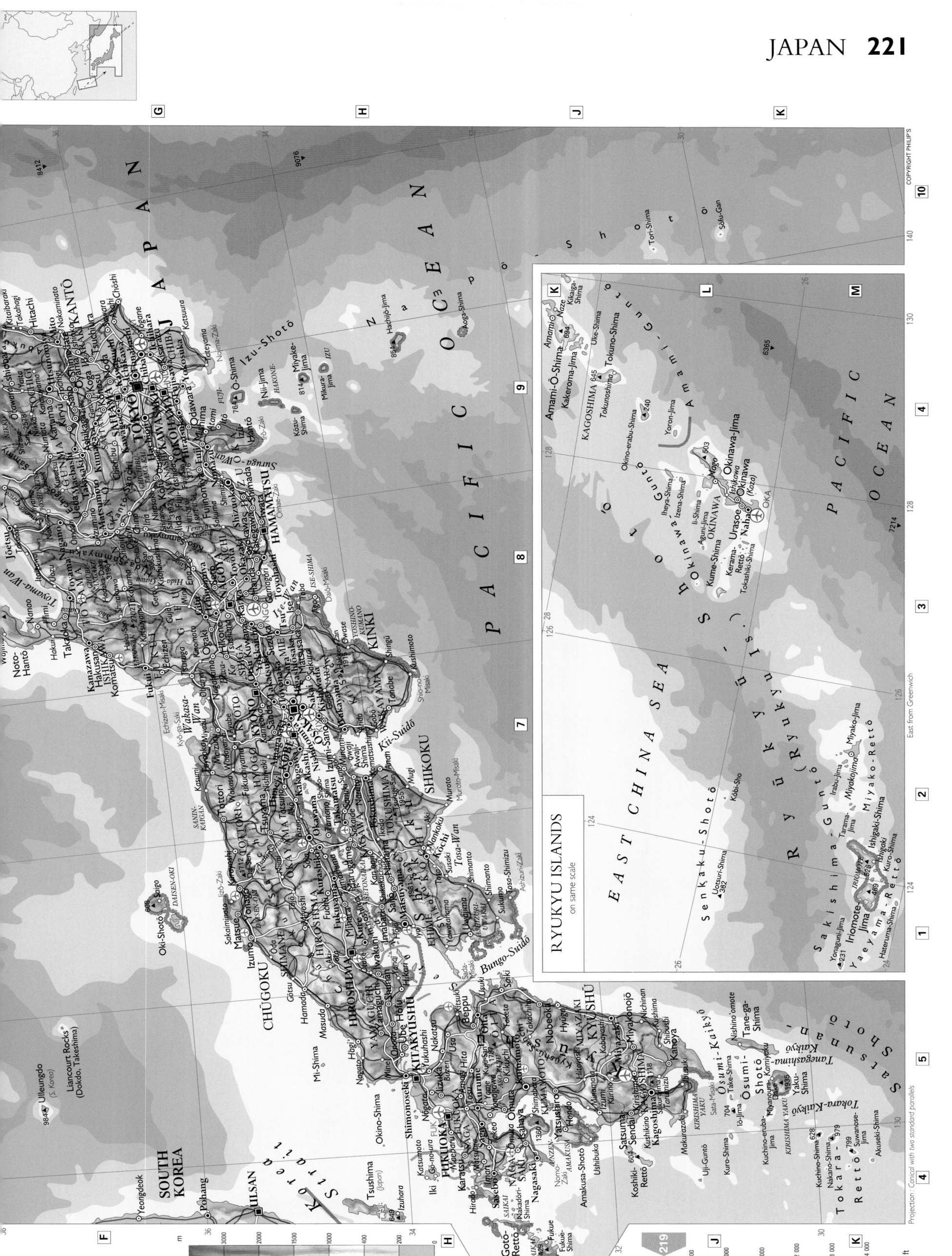

1:2 000 000

SEA OF JAPAN

(EAST SEA)

SOUTH KOREA

CHŪGOKU-DISTRICT

Korea Strait

Tsushima

HIROSHIMA

KITAKYŪSHŪ

FUKUOKA

Shikoku

SHIKOKU-DISTRICT

KUMAMOTO

Kyūshū

KYŪSHŪ-DISTRICT

KAGOSHIMA

Kagoshima

⌇⌇ Shinkansen lines

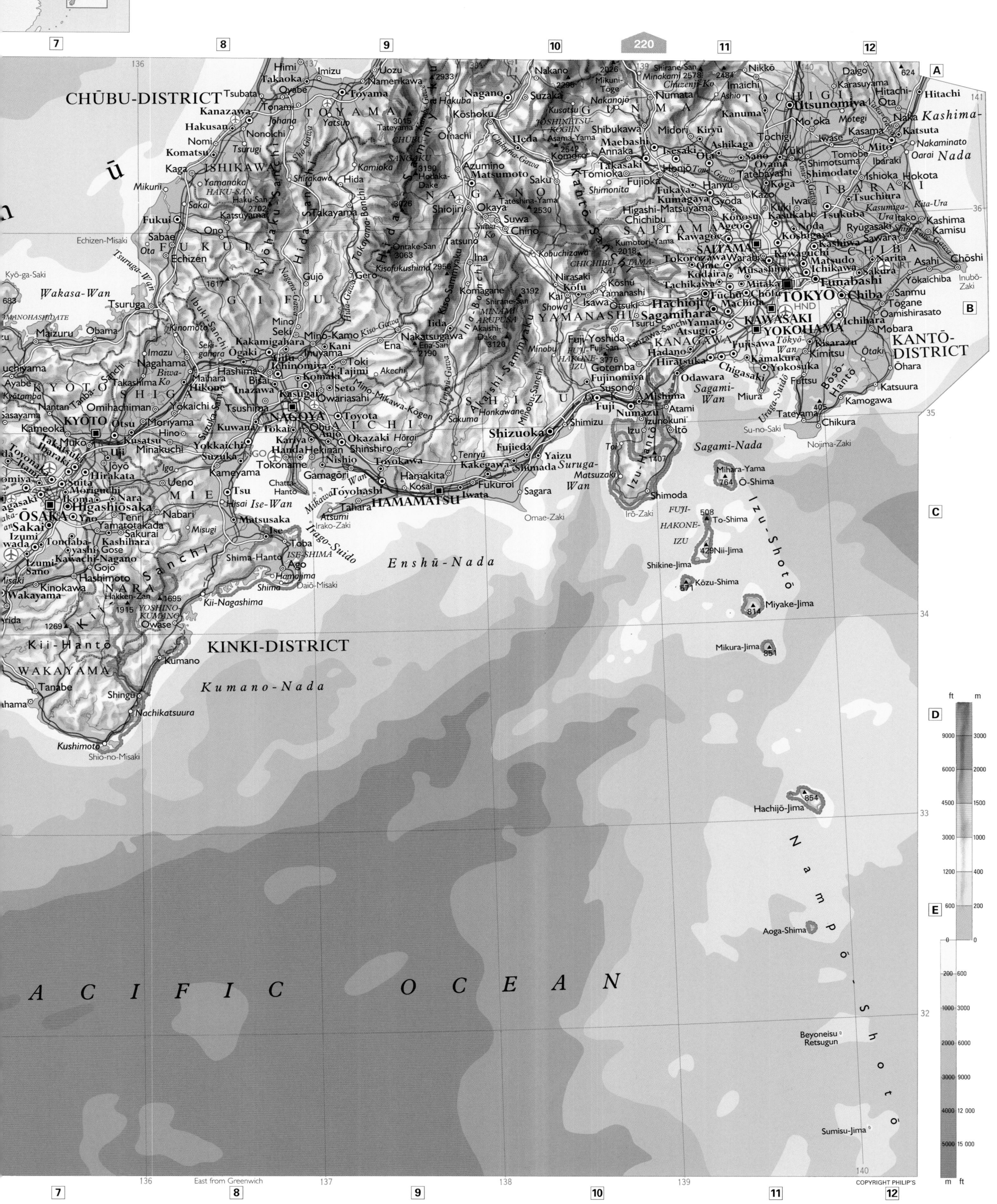

CHŪBU-DISTRICT

KANTŌ-DISTRICT

KINKI-DISTRICT

Kumano-Nada

Enshū-Nada

Sagami-Nada

Izu-Shotō

PACIFIC OCEAN

East from Greenwich

COPYRIGHT PHILIP'S

ft	m
9000	3000
6000	2000
4500	1500
3000	1000
1200	400
600	200
0	0
200	600
1000	3000
2000	6000
3000	9000
4000	12 000
5000	15 000
m	ft

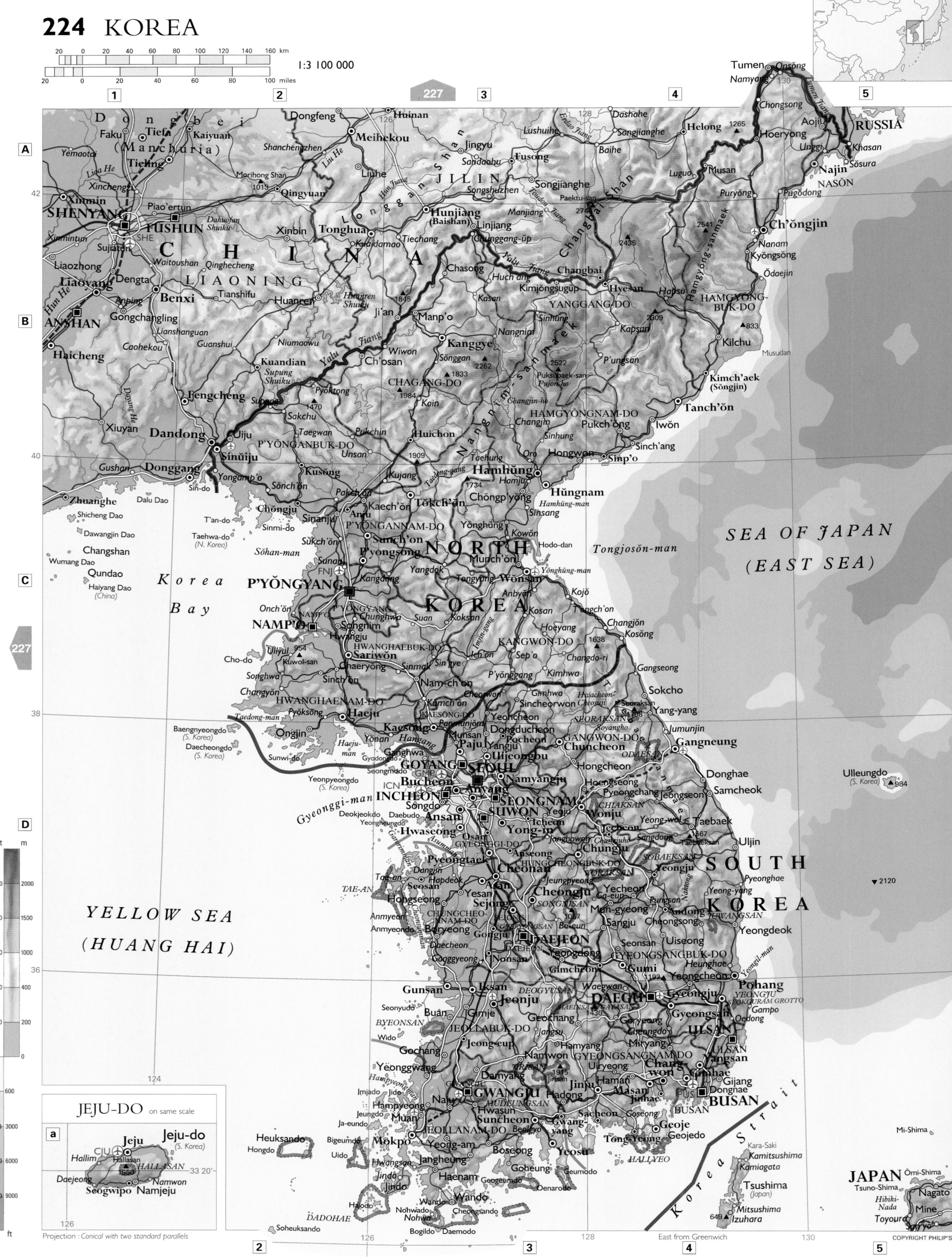

1:3 100 000

20 0 20 40 60 80 100 120 140 160 km
20 0 20 40 60 80 100 miles

SEA OF JAPAN
(EAST SEA)

YELLOW SEA
(HUANG HAI)

Korea
Bay

Projection : Conical with two standard parallels

JEJU-DO on same scale

Jeju-do
(S. Korea)

RUSSIA

CHINA

NORTH
KOREA

SOUTH
KOREA

JAPAN

COPYRIGHT PHILIP'S

——— High-speed rail routes

1:1 400 000

5 0 10 20 30 40 50 60 70 km
5 0 10 20 30 40 50 miles

CHINA FUJIAN
Jimei
Xinglin   Shijing   Jinjing
XIAMEN   Kuahao
Zhenhai   Xiamen Gang   Hsiao-chinmen Tao   Chinmen (Quemoy)   Chinmen Tao (Taiwan)

Taiwan Strait

CHINMEN
on same scale

a

CHINA FUJIAN
Huangqi
Liang Tao   Tungyin Tao
Lianjiang   Peikant'ang Tao   Tongsha Tao
Langqi *Min Jiang*   Matsu Tao (Taiwan)
Changle   Paichuan Liehtao

Taiwan Strait

MATSU
on same scale

b

229

232

A
Fukuei Chiao   Shihmen
Sanchih
NEW TAIPEI   Chinshan
Tanshui   YANGMINGSHAN   Chilung (Keelung)
Chuwei   Peitou   Wanli
Kuanyin   Tayuan   Sanch'ung   Haichih   Pitou Chiao
Niulantsun   Hsinchuang   Nankang   Santiao Chiao
TAOYUAN   Panch'iao   **T'AIPEI (Taibei)**   Kunghao
Hsinfeng   Chungli   Taoyuan   Chungho   Maoao
Yangmei   Pate   Hsintien   Santiao Chiao
Nanliao   Lungt'an   Wulai   Pinglin
Hsinchu (Xinzhu)   Chupei   Kuanhsi   Shihmen   Chiaohsi   T'ouch'eng
Hsiangshan   Chutung   Neiwan   Taman Shan   Wuchieh
Chunan   Toufen   Paleng   Sanhsing   Lotung
Houlung   Sanwan   Shihiu   Chingshui   Suao
Kungssuliao   Tsaochiao   T'uch'ang   Nanao
MIAOLI   Shihtan   Chitan   **ILAN**
Chungtungwan   Miaoli   Kungkuan   Tungshan   Nanao
T'unghsiao   Tunglo   Tungao
Yuanli   Sani   Tahu   Hualien
Taan   Jihnan   Houli
Tachia   Cholan   Kuanyin
Ch'ingshui   Tengyüan   Tungshih   Ushan   Tachoushui
Wuch'i   Shalu   Peitun   **TAROKO**
Lungching   T'antzu   Hsinche   Hoping   T'ailuko   Hsinch'eng
Shenkang   Homei   **T'AICHUNG (Taizhong)**   Taping   Tayuling   Peipu
Changhua   Wujih   Wufeng   Kuohsing   Chan   **Hualien (Hualian)**
Lukang   Hsiushui   Fenyuan   Shihkangkeng   Jenai   Nengkao Shan   Peipu
Fuhsing   **CHANGHUA**   Ts'aot'un   Puli   Shoufeng
Fangyüan   Chihu   Yüanlin   **NANT'OU**   Yüchih   Fenglin
Ernlin   Pitou   Shetou   **Nant'ou**   Choshih   Chichi
Tacheng   Hsilo   Chiehi'ou   Mingchien   Shuili   Chusheta Shan   Fengpin
Mailiao   Lunpei   Tzutung   Chichi   Wulicheng   Luyeh
Taihsi   **YUNLIN**   Linnei   Tingkan   Luku   Wanjung   Kuangfu
Santiaolun   Tuku   Tounan   Hsini   Tafu   Fengpin
K'ouhu   Yuanch'ang   Touliu   Kukleng   Juisui
Kanghsi   Talin   Meishan   Chushan   Sanhsien
Peikang   Minhsiung   Alishan   **TAIWAN**   Takangkou   Chingpu
Ch'üntou (Pescadores)   Chiai   Chuchi   Fanlu   **YÜ SHAN**   Changyuan
Tungshih   **CHIAI**   Leyeh   Yü Shan (Jade Mt.)   Ch'angpin
Putai   Ichu   Yunshui   Choch'i   Yüli

P'ENGHU
Yüweng Tao   Paisha
Hsiyu   Huhsi   P'enghu
Makung   P'enghu Tao
P'ENGHU
Hua Yü
Wangan   Pachao Yü
Ch'imei Yü   Tungchi Yü
Ch'imei

STRAIT
TAIWAN
T A I W A N   S T R A I T

Peimen   Hsinying   Tapu   Meishan   Fuhsing   Antung   Sanhsien
Hsüehchia   Liuchia   Tsengwen   Shanhu   Kuan Shan   Shajuwan
Chiangchun   Chiali   Hsinhua   Taoyuan   Wulu   Sanhsien
Matou   **T'AINAN**   Shanhua   Yuching   Ch'ihshang   Ch'engkung
Shanshang   Nanhua   Chiahsien   Peinanchu Shan   Ch'engkung
Chengkeng   Hsinshih   Shanlin   Hsinfa   Kuanshan   Hoping
T'AINAN (Tainan)   Yungk'ang   Luikuei   Kuanshan   Tungho
Jente   Kuanmiao   **KAOHSUNG**   Luyeh   Tulan
Chiehting   Hunei   Ch'ishan   Meinung   Lichia   Chialulantsun
Luchu   Alien   Kaoshu   Chianapu   Peinan
Yungan   Yenchao   Yenpu   Santi   Lachia   **T'aitung (Taidong)**
Kangshan   Likang   Changchih   Chuju   Ch'ihpen   **Lü Tao (Green I.)**
Tzukuan   Nantzu   Tashu   Pingtung (Pingdong)   Lütao
Tsoying   Fengshan   Neipu   Wanluan   Peitawu Shan   T'aimali
KAOHSIUNG (Gaoxiong)   Chienchen   Tailiao   Ch'aochou   Ch'inlun
Hsiaokang   Hsinchuang   Wantan   Hsiatahsi
Linyuan   Hsinyuan   Hsinpi   Taniao
Tungkang   Linpien   Shuitiliao   Tawu
Chiatung
Liuch'iu Yü   Fangliao   Tajen
Liuch'iu   Shouchia
Fangshan   Tanlu   Hsühaitsun
P'INGTUNG   Mutanshe
Fengkang   Kangtzu   Lan Yü (Orchid I.)
Ch'ulin   Ch'ech'eng   Lanyü
Hengch'un   Manchou   Hsiaohungt'ou Hsü
K'ENTING   Nanwan
Maopi T'ou   Oluanpi
Oluan Pi

Bashi Channel

P A C I F I C   O C E A N

Tropic of Cancer

ft   m
9000   3000
6000   2000
4500   1500
3000   1000
1200   400
600   200
0   0
200   600
1000   3000
2000   6000
3000   9000
4000   12 000
5000   15 000
m   ft

Projection: *Lambert Conformal Conic*

East from Greenwich

COPYRIGHT PHILIP'S

—— Taiwan High Speed Rail (THSR)

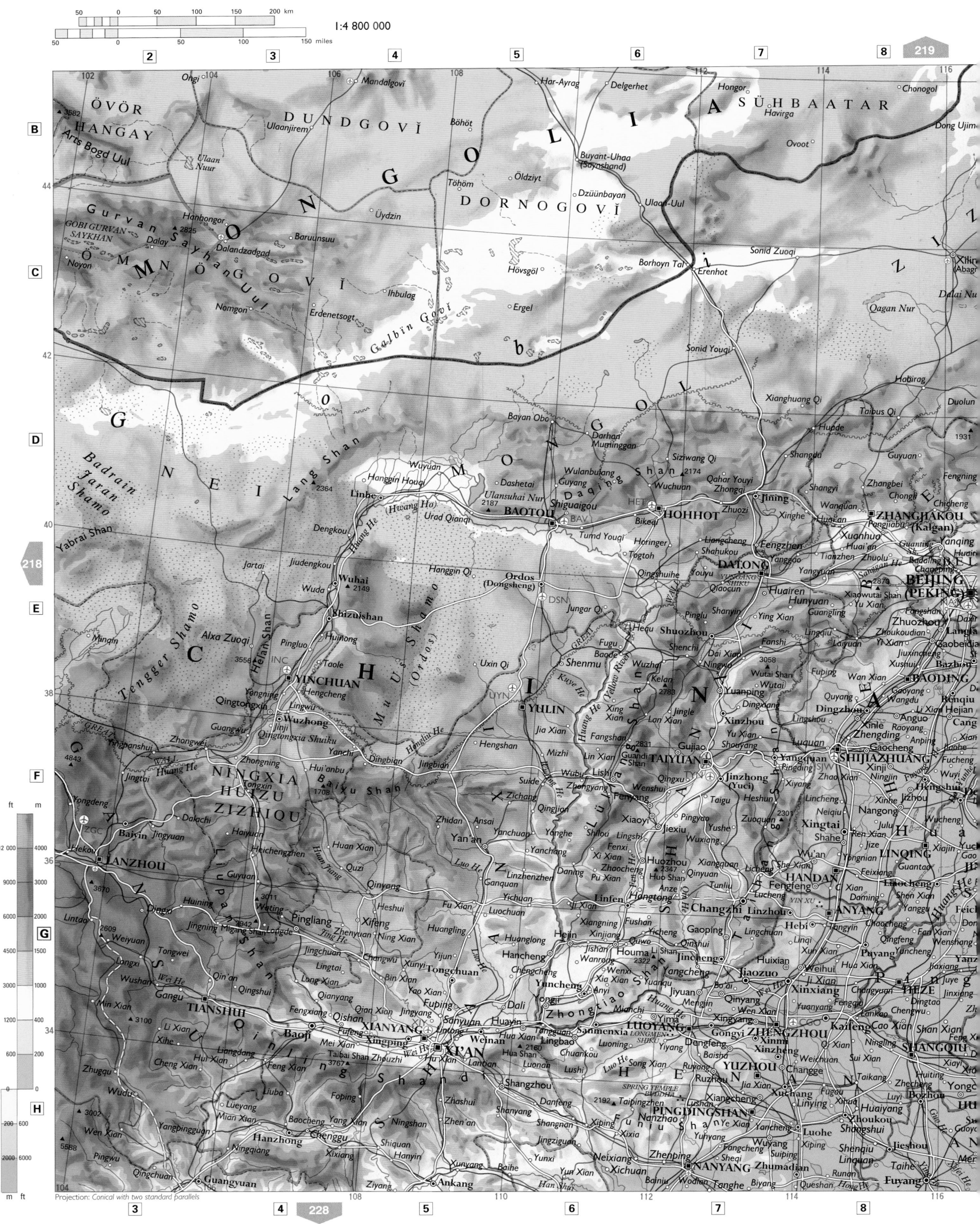

1:4 800 000

Projection: Conical with two standard parallels

East from Greenwich

COPYRIGHT PHILIP'S

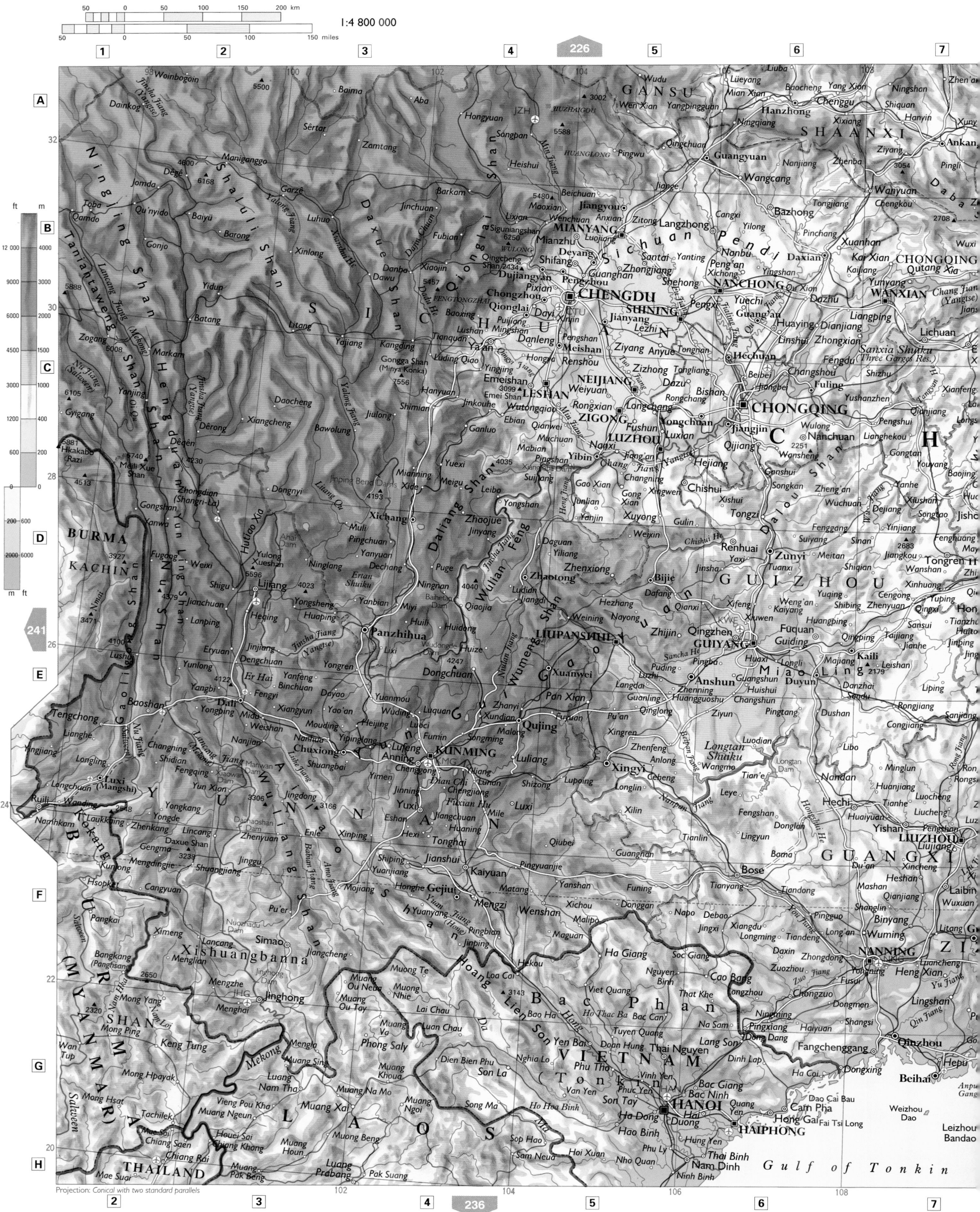

Projection: Conical with two standard parallels

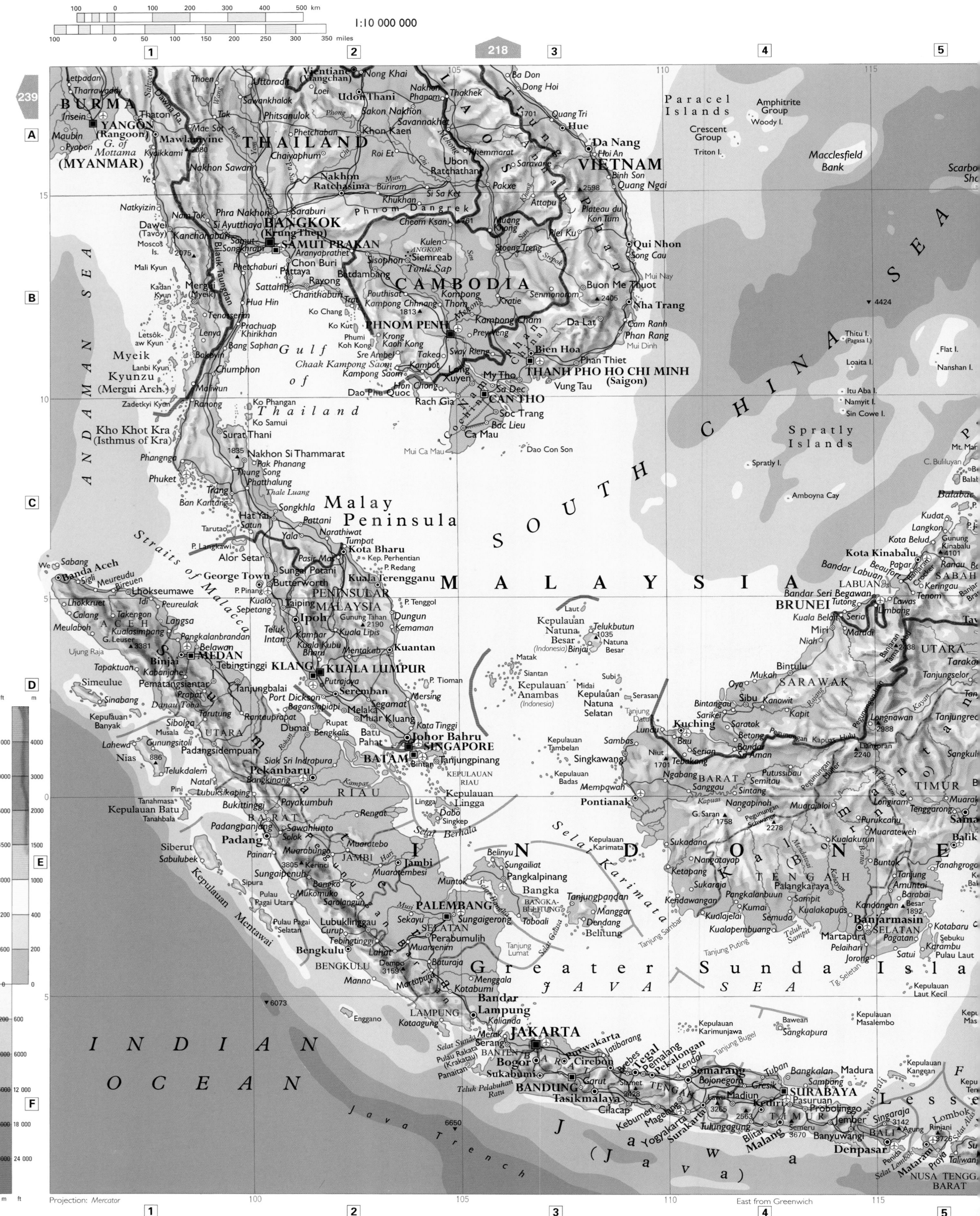

JAVA AND MADURA

1:6 000 000

```
50    0    50   100   150   200   250   300 km
50    0    50        100        150      200 miles
```

BALI

1:1 600 000

```
10    0    10    20    30 km
10         0         10         20 miles
```

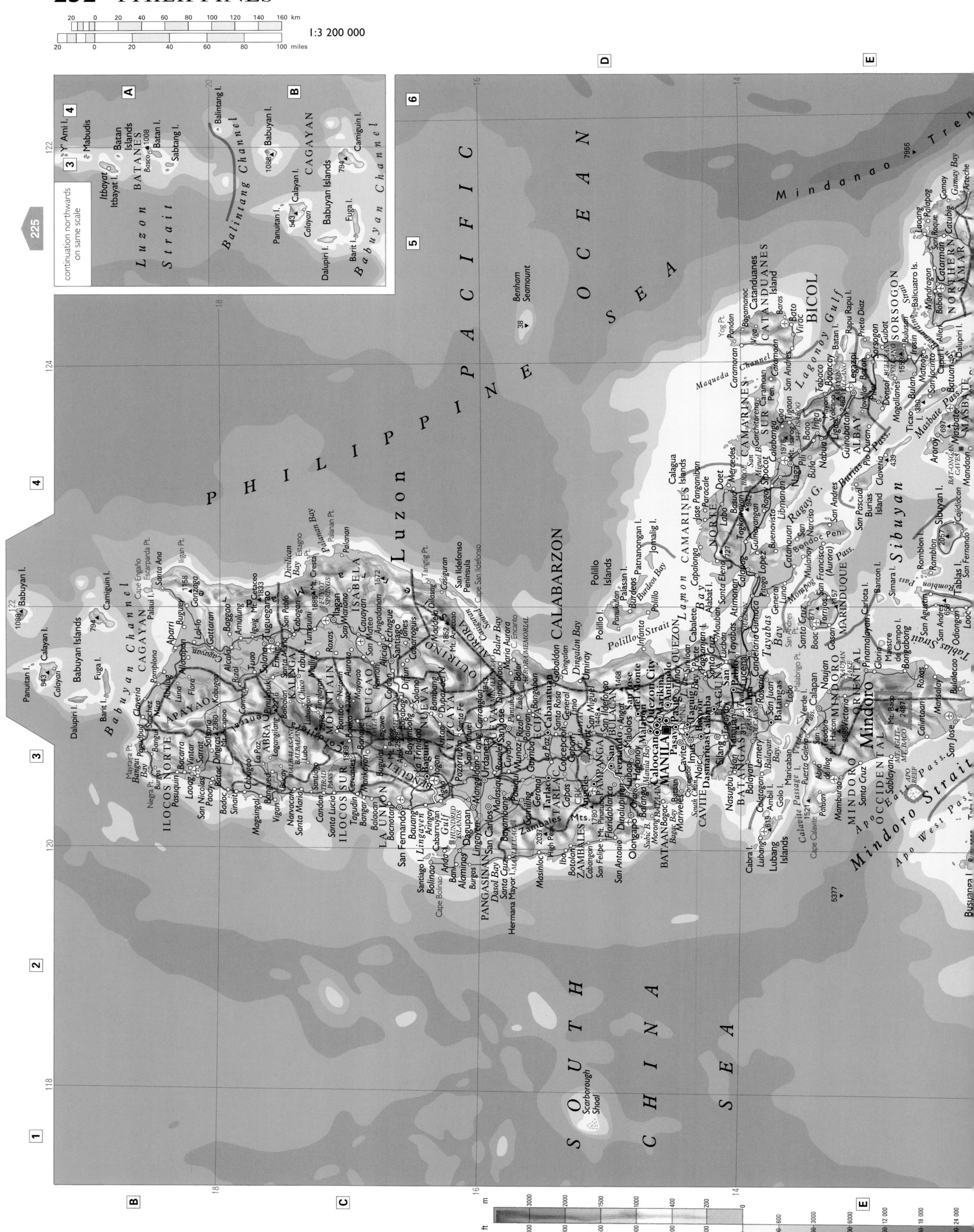

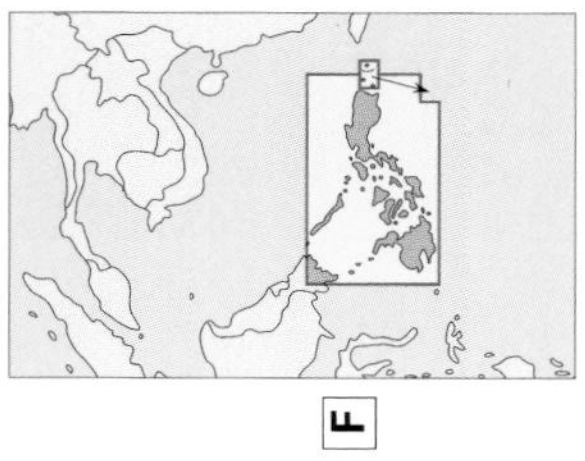

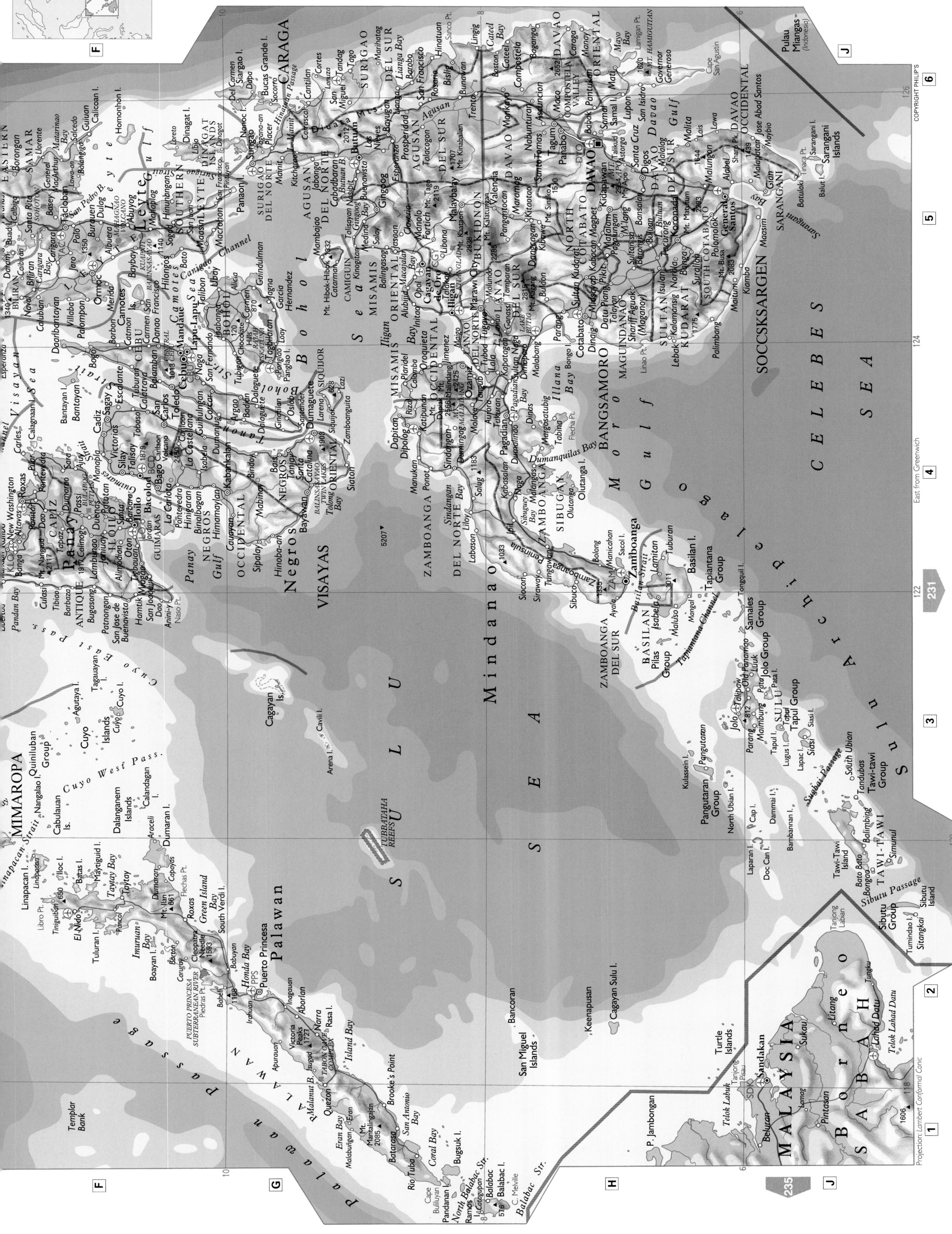

MALAYSIA

SABAH

Borneo

CELEBES SEA

SULU SEA

Sulu Archipelago

MIMAROPA

Palawan

Palawan Passage

VISAYAS

Negros

Panay

Mindanao

Zamboanga Peninsula

Moro Gulf

DAVAO ORIENTAL

DAVAO DEL SUR

BUKIDNON

SOCCSKSARGEN

BANGSAMORO

SARANGANI

Davao Gulf

CARAGA

SAMAR

Leyte

Leyte Gulf

BOHOL

CEBU

NEGROS OCCIDENTAL

NEGROS ORIENTAL

Bohol Sea

Camotes Sea

Visayan Sea

Panay Gulf

Sulu Sea

Celebes Sea

Pulau Miangas (Indonesia)

TAWI-TAWI

TAWI-TAWI Group

Sibutu Passage

Projection Lambert Conformal Conic

East from Greenwich

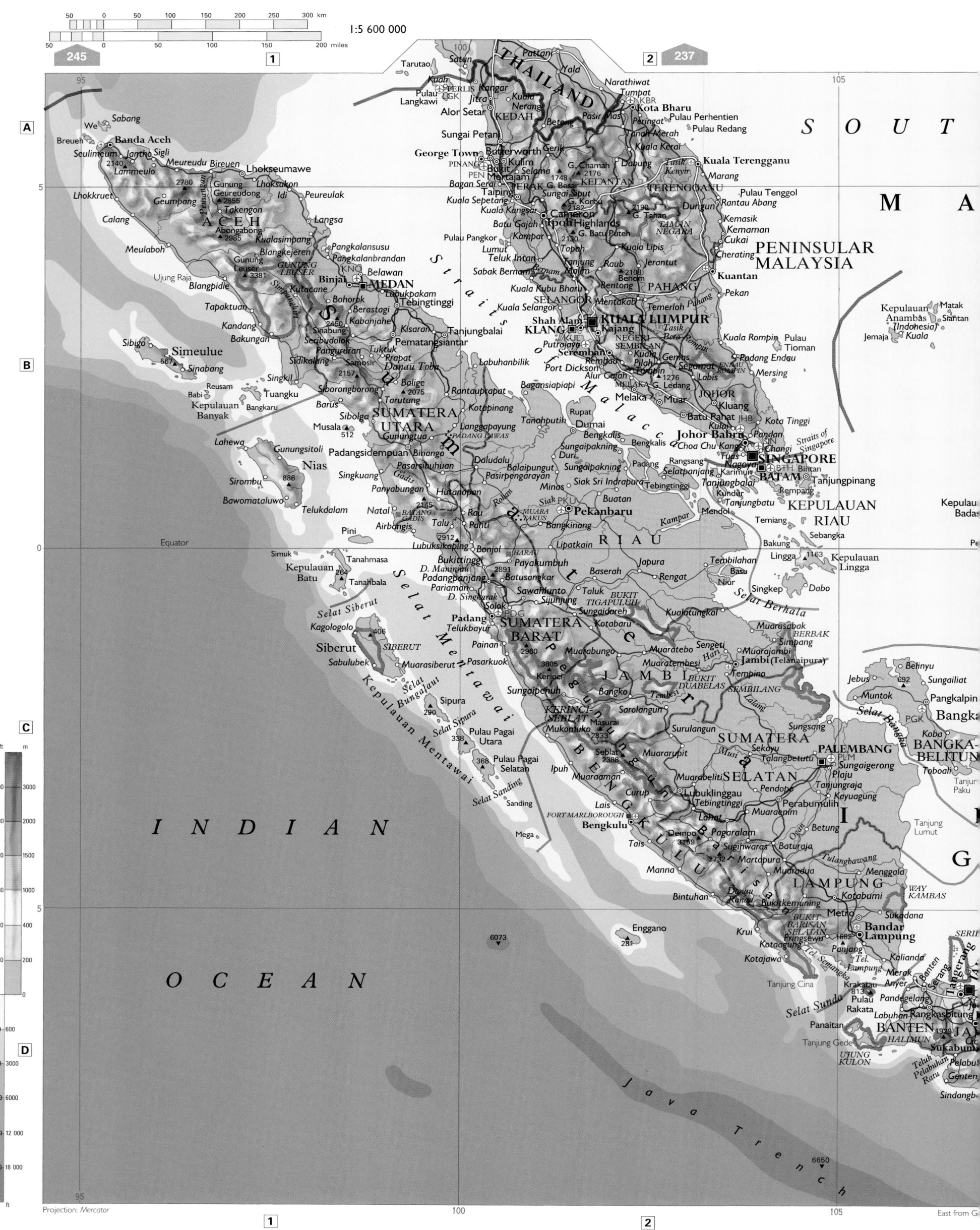

1:5 600 000

Projection: Mercator

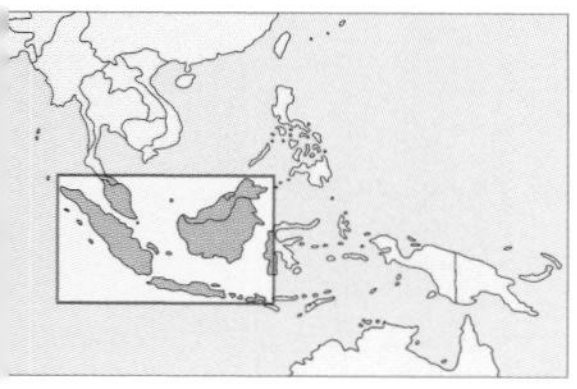

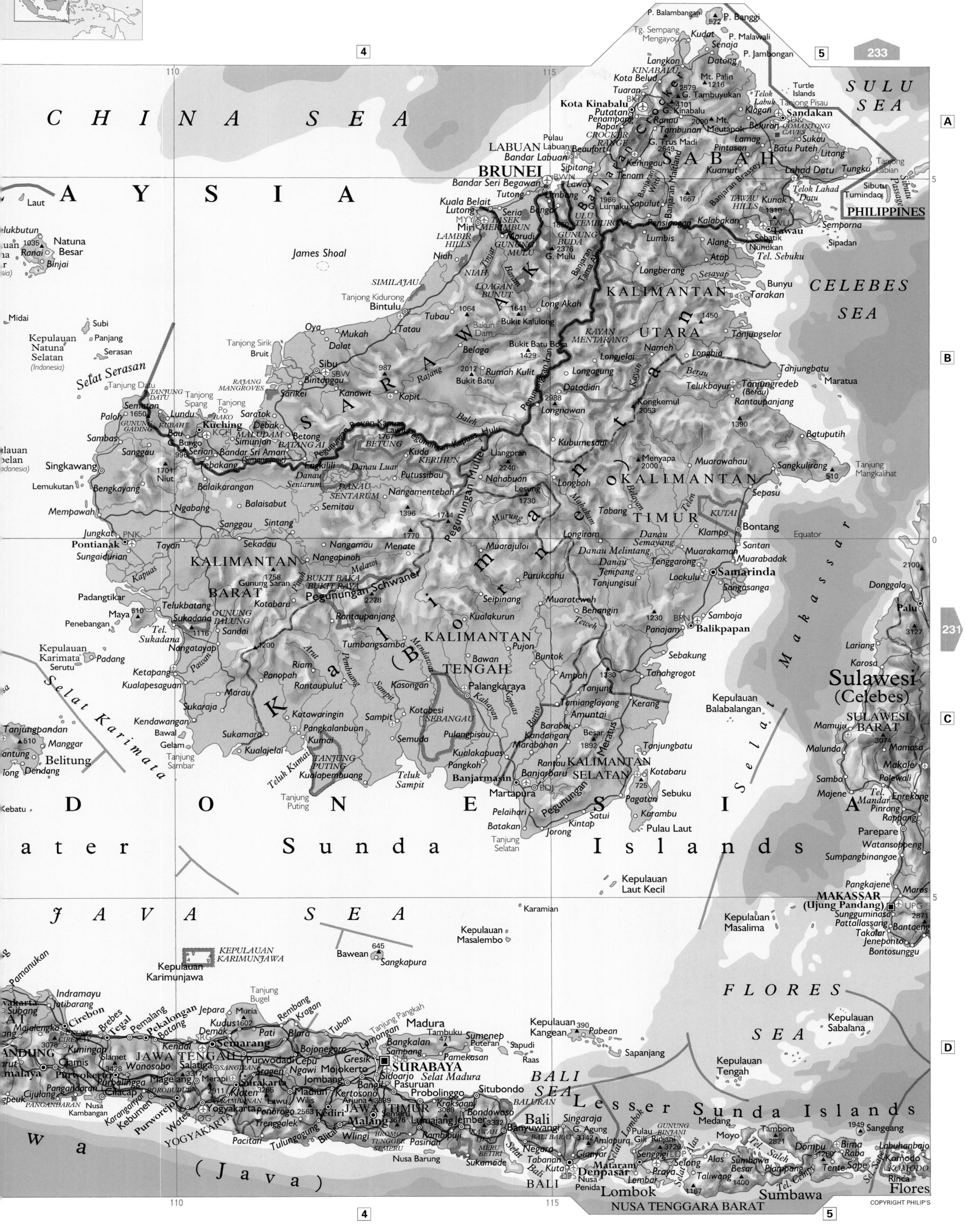

233

CHINA SEA

SULU SEA

SABAH

BRUNEI

Bandar Seri Begawan

Kuala Belait

Miri

LABUAN
Labuan
Bandar Labuan

Kota Kinabalu

PHILIPPINES

KALIMANTAN
UTARA

CELEBES SEA

S A R A W A K

Kuching

Sibu

Bintulu

Singkawang

Pontianak

KALIMANTAN
BARAT

B o r n e o   (B)

KALIMANTAN
TIMUR

Samarinda

Balikpapan

Equator

Selat Makassar

Palu

Sulawesi
(Celebes)

SULAWESI
BARAT

KALIMANTAN
TENGAH

Palangkaraya

KALIMANTAN
SELATAN

Banjarmasin

Makassar
(Ujung Pandang)

Greater   Sunda   Islands

Kepulauan
Natuna
Selatan
(Indonesia)

Belitung

Selat Karimata

J A V A   S E A

Kepulauan
Karimunjawa

FLORES SEA

Semarang

SURABAYA

Madura

JAWA TENGAH

JAWA TIMUR

Malang

YOGYAKARTA

BALI SEA

Bali

Denpasar

Lombok

Sumbawa

L e s s e r   S u n d a   I s l a n d s

NUSA TENGGARA BARAT

Flores

(Java)

231

COPYRIGHT PHILIP'S

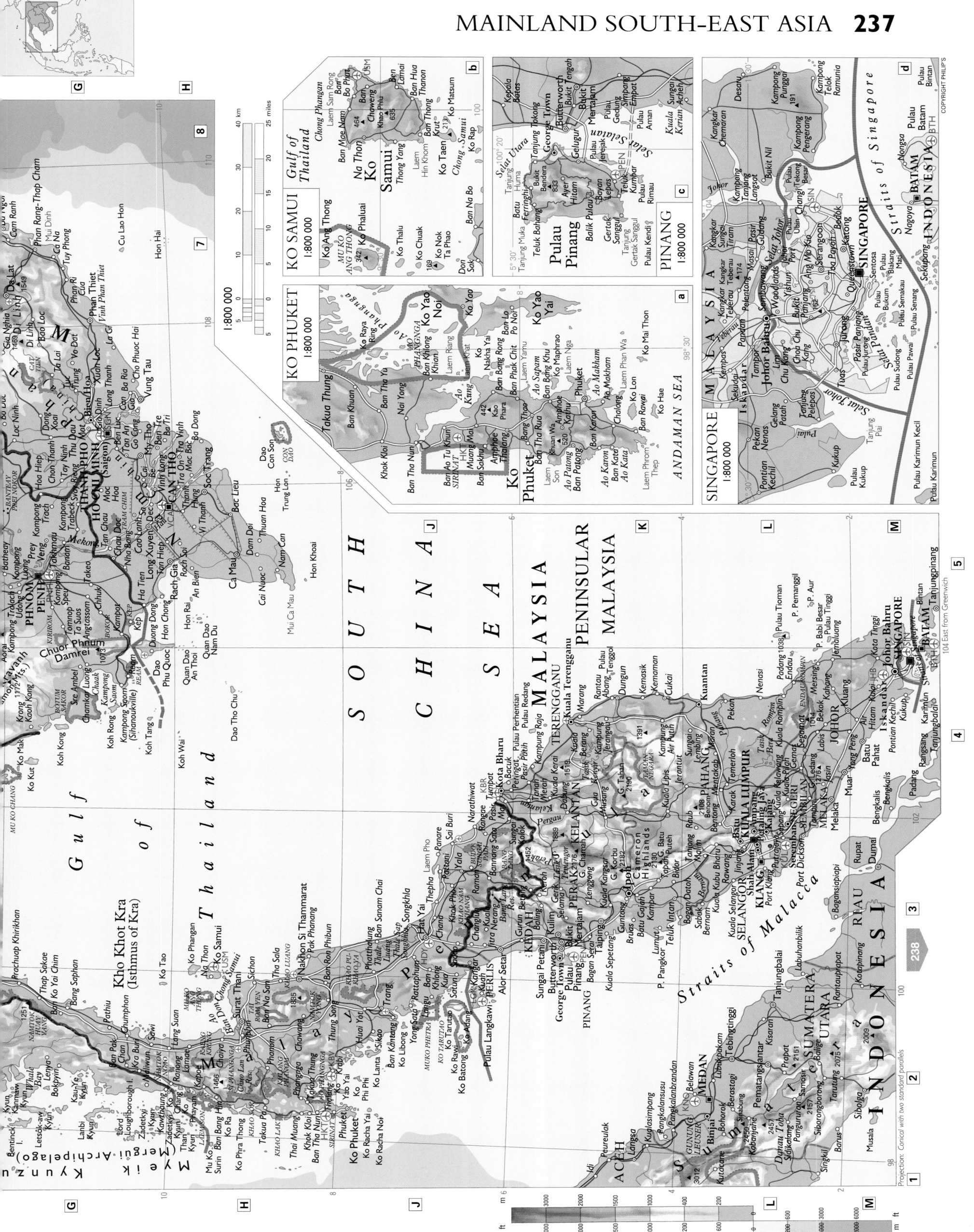

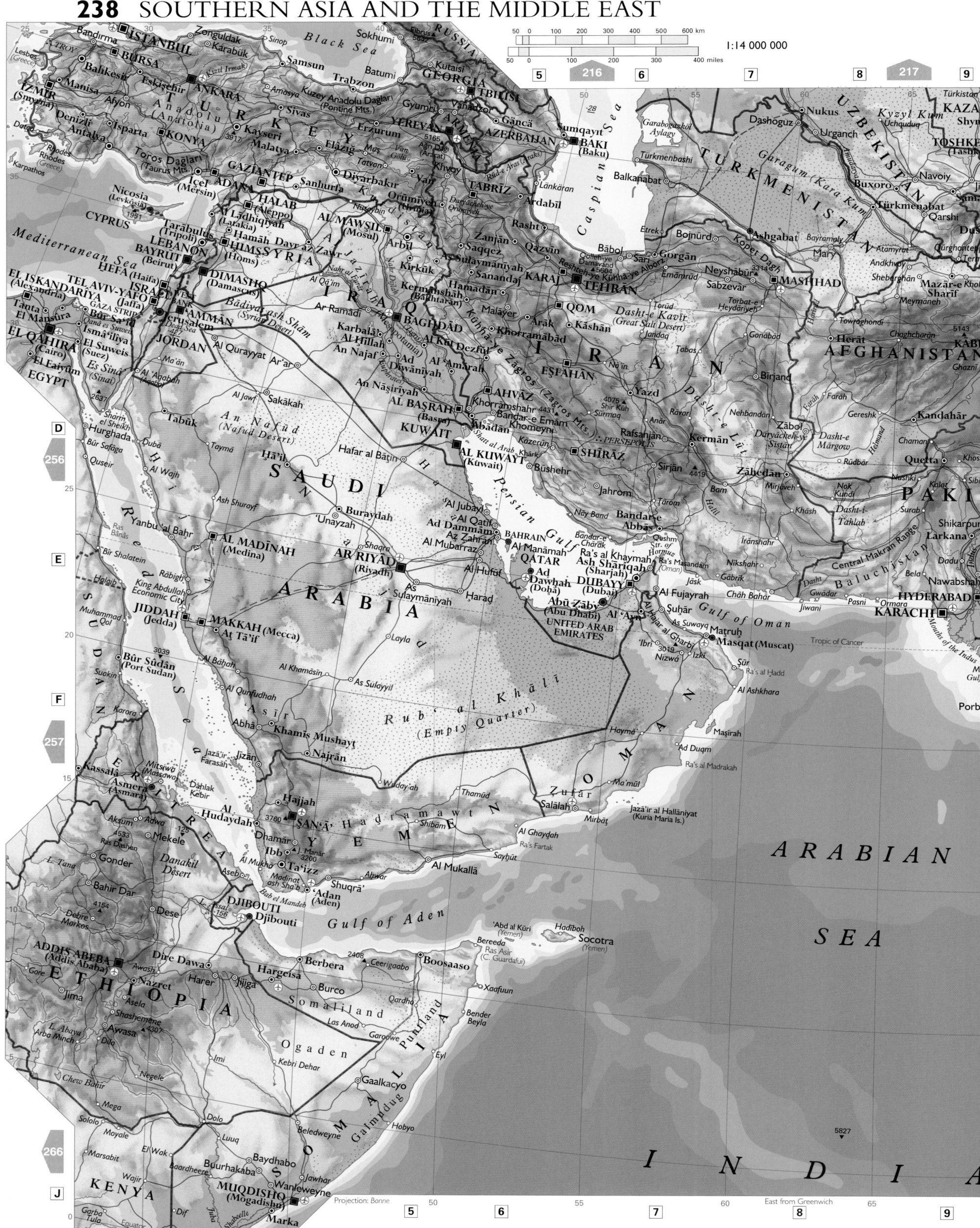

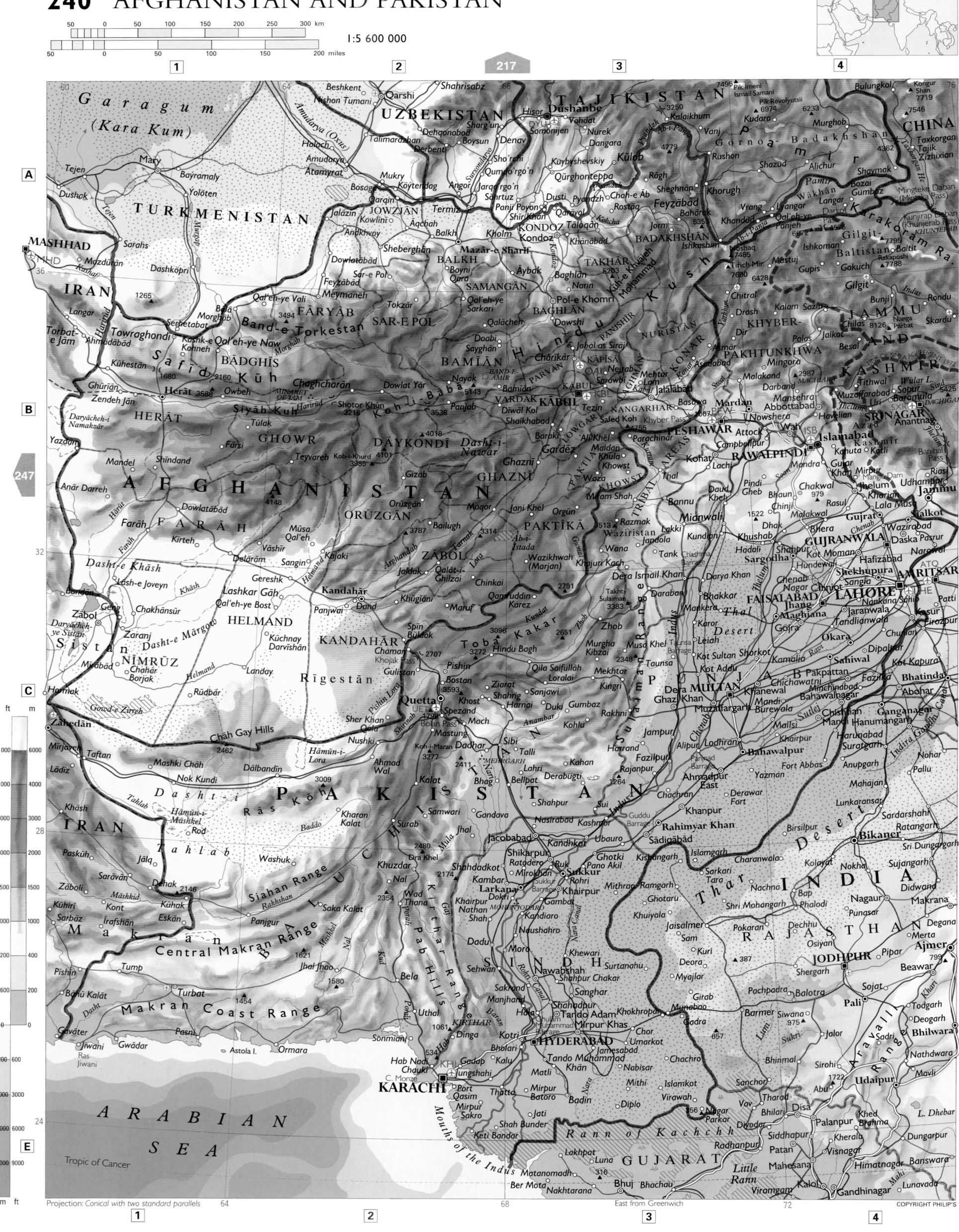

Garagum
(Kara Kum)

TURKMENISTAN

UZBEKISTAN

TAJIKISTAN

CHINA

MASHHAD

IRAN

AFGHANISTAN

HERĀT

GHOWR

DĀYKONDĪ

GHAZNĪ

BĀDGHĪS

FĀRYĀB

SAR-E POL

BALKH

SAMANGĀN

BAGHLĀN

TAKHĀR

BADAKHSHĀN

Hindu Kush

KĀBUL

NURISTĀN

KONAR

NANGARHĀR

PESHĀWAR

ISLAMABAD

RAWALPINDI

SRINAGAR

JAMMU AND KASHMIR

FARĀH

ORŪZGĀN

ZĀBOL

PAKTĪKĀ

Waziristan

TRIBAL AREAS

GUJRANWALA

LAHORE

AMRITSAR

NĪMRŪZ

HELMAND

KANDAHĀR

Rīgestān

Tobā Kakar

Quetta

FAISALABAD

MULTAN

PUNJAB

IRAN

BALUCHISTAN

PAKISTAN

Thar Desert

Bikaner

INDIA

RAJASTHAN

JODHPUR

KARACHI

SINDH

HYDERABAD

ARABIAN SEA

Tropic of Cancer

GUJARAT

Rann of Kachchh

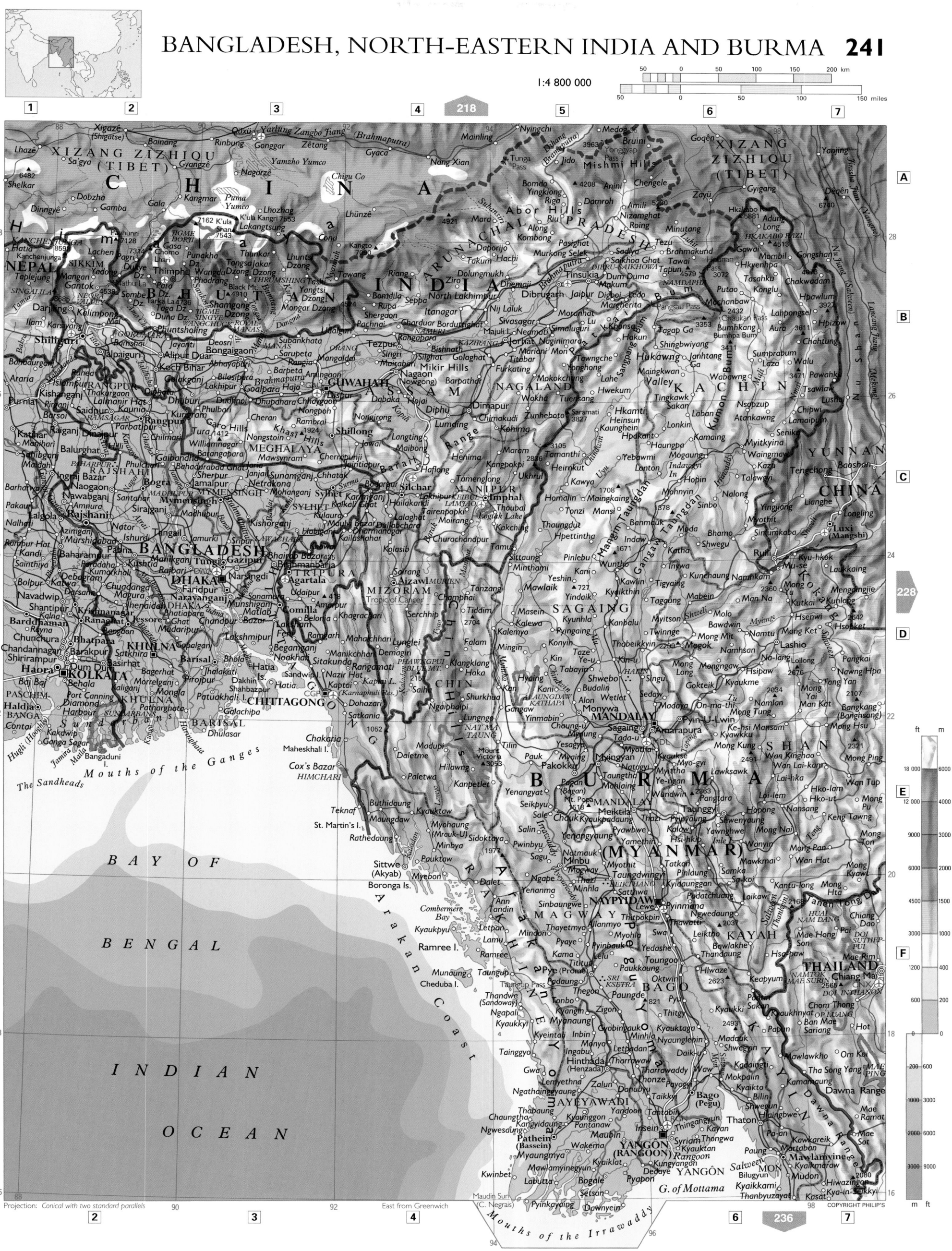

ARABIAN SEA

Projection: Conical with two standard parallels

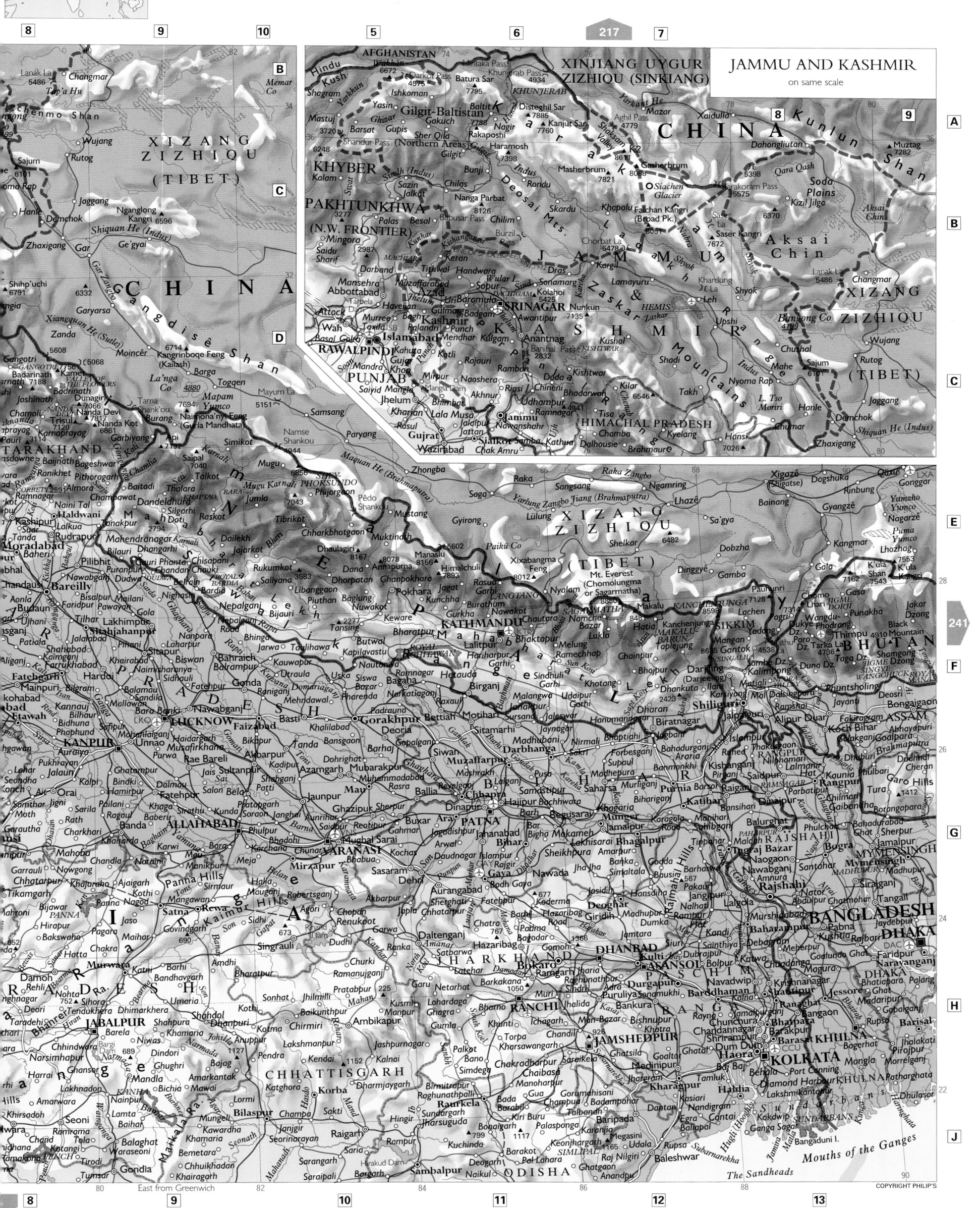

JAMMU AND KASHMIR
on same scale

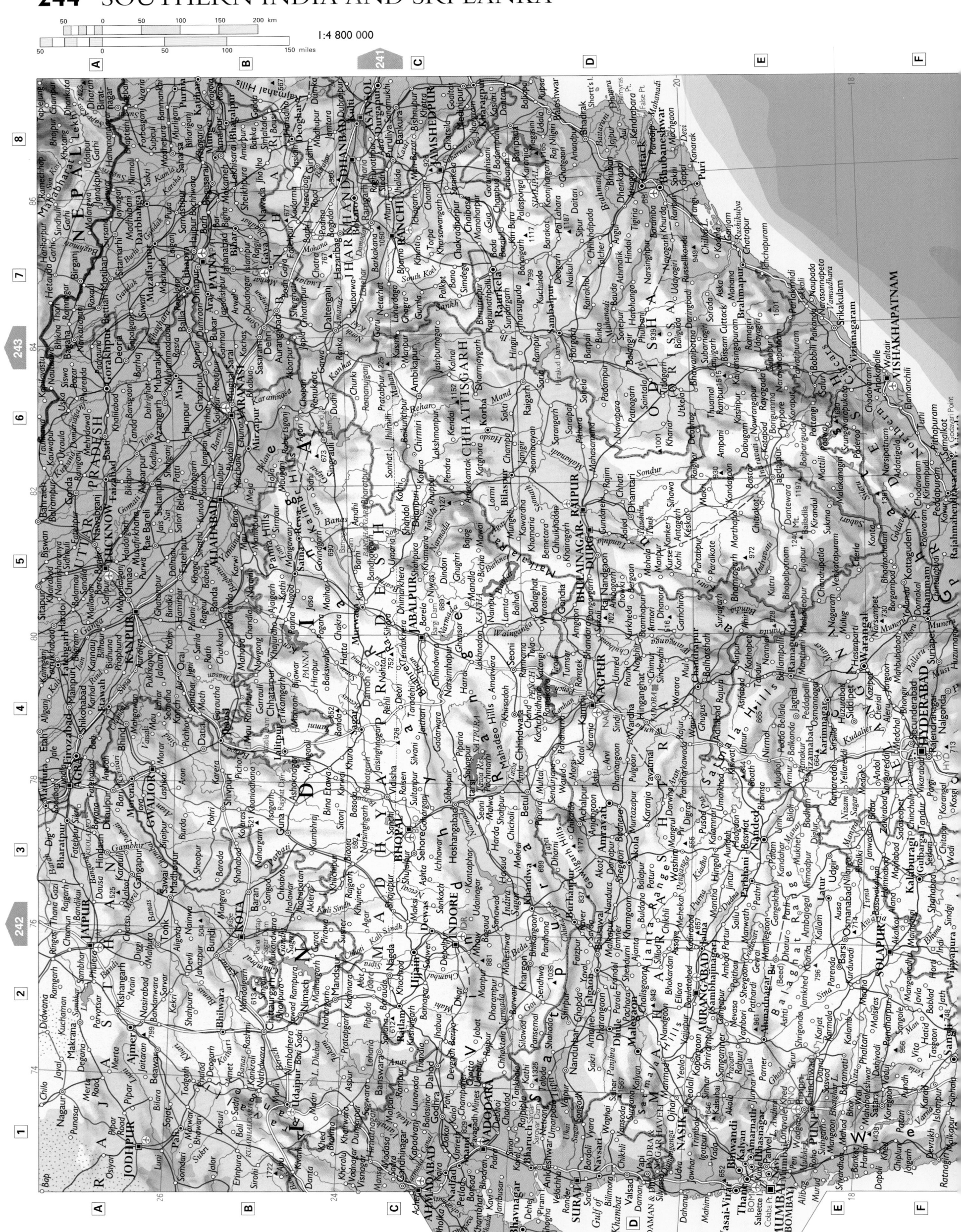

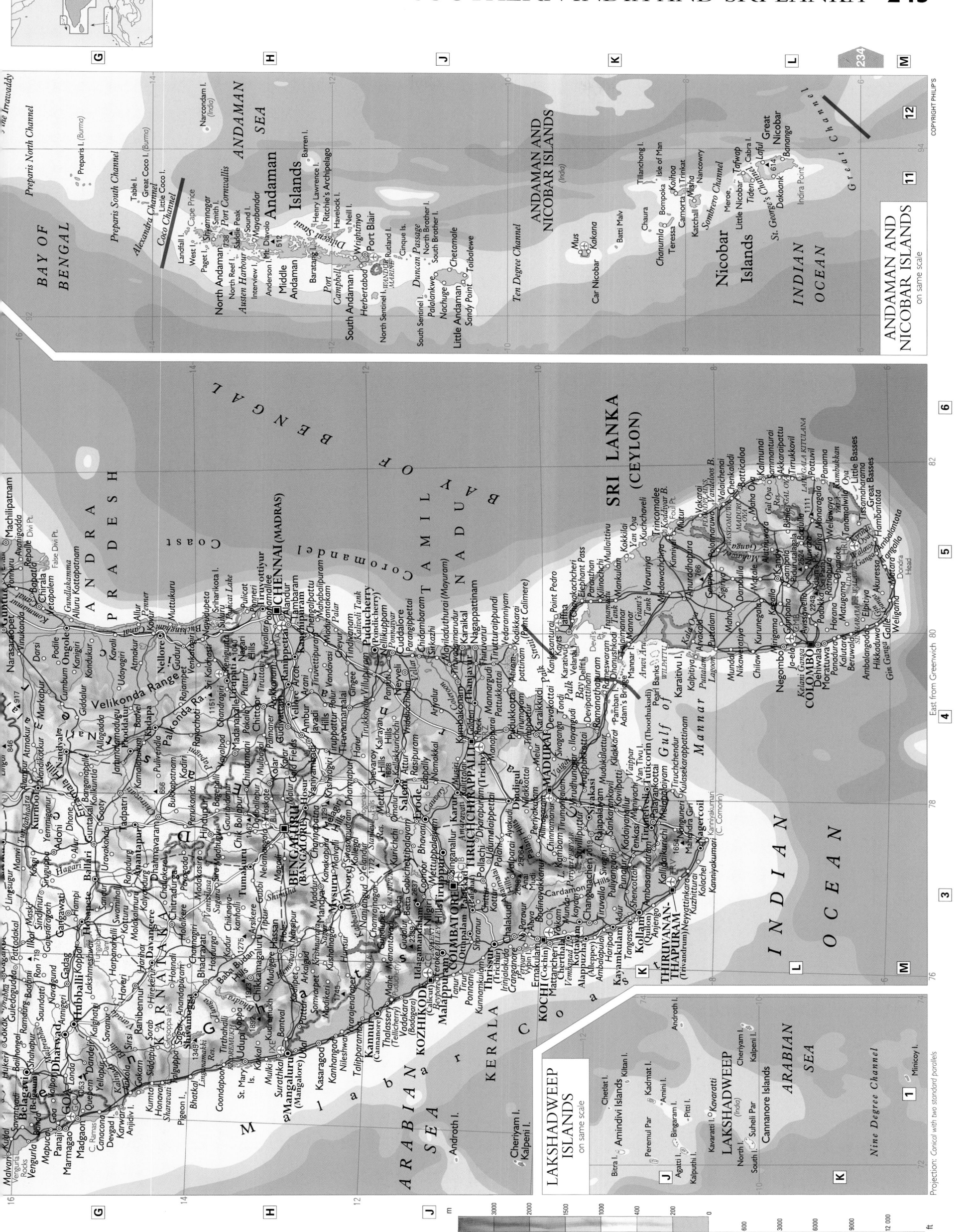

ANDAMAN AND NICOBAR ISLANDS
on same scale

LAKSHADWEEP ISLANDS
on same scale

Projection: Conical with two standard parallels

East from Greenwich

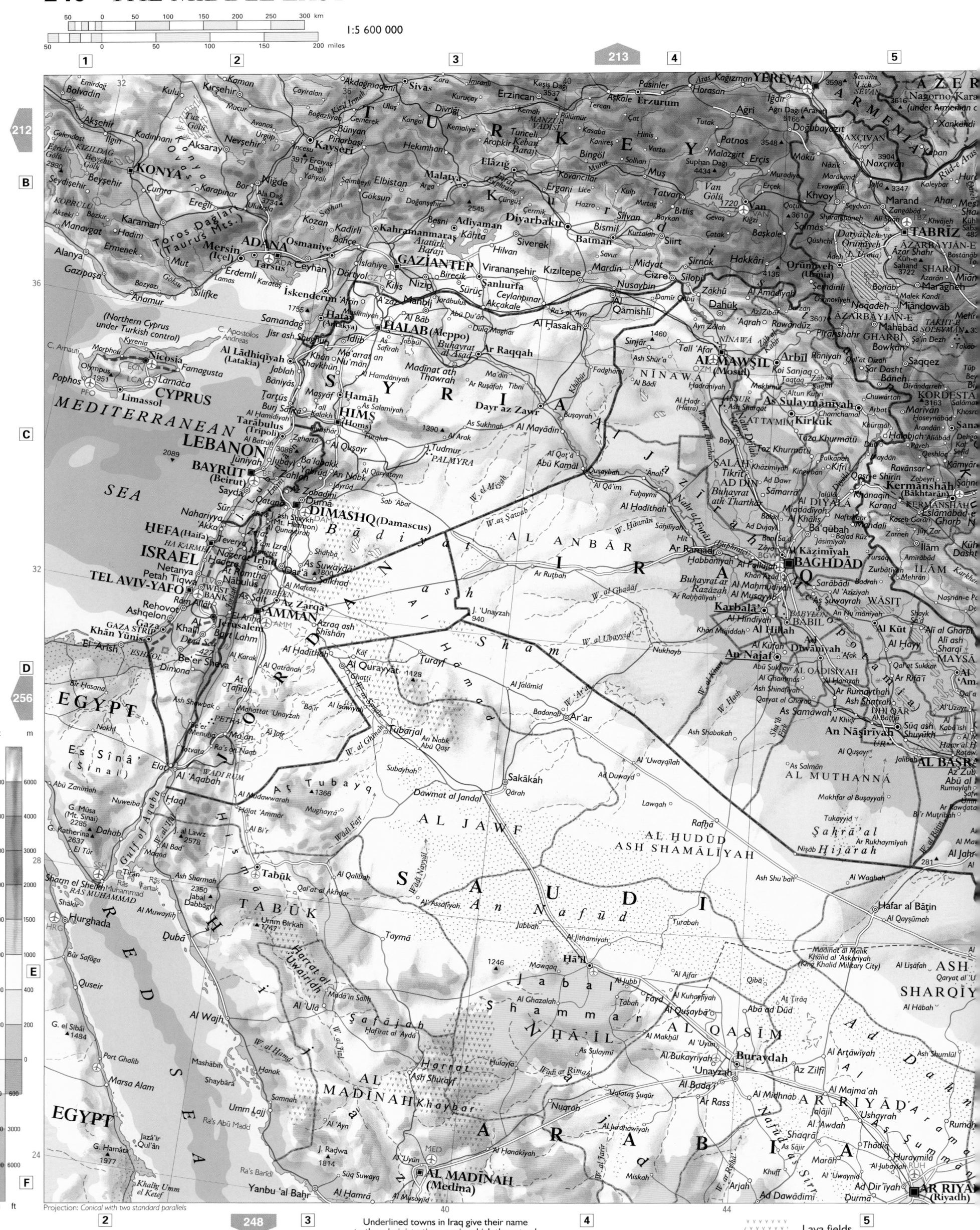

TURKMENISTAN
Garagum (Kara Kum)
Kopet Dagh
CASPIAN SEA
BAKI (Baku)
Türkmenbashi
Balkanabat (Nebitdag)
Ashgabat
Mary
Türkmenabat (Chardzhou)
Amudarya
Lankaran
Astara
Rasht
GILAN
MAZANDARAN
GOLESTAN
Gorgan
Sari
Babol
Amol
Reshteh-ye Kuhha-ye Alborz (Elburz Mts.)
QAZVIN
Qazvin
ALBORZ
KARAJ
TEHRAN
Qom
QOM
Semnan
SEMNAN
KHORASAN-E SHEMALI
Bojnurd
MASHHAD
Neyshabur
Sabzevar
KHORASAN-E RAZAVI
Torbat-e Heydariyeh
Dasht-e Kavir (Great Salt Desert)
IRAN
Kashan
ESFAHAN
Najafabad
YAZD
Yazd
Tabas
Birjand
KHORASAN-E JANUBI
Dasht-e Lut
Kerman
KERMAN
Rafsanjan
Zahedan
SISTAN VA BALUCHESTAN
Zabol
Iranshahr
Chah Bahar
AFGHANISTAN
Herat
HERAT
FARAH
Safid Kuh
NIMRUZ
Dasht-e Margow
PAKISTAN
Hamadan
MARKAZI
Arak
Borujerd
Khorramabad
Dezful
Shushtar
AHVAZ
KHUZESTAN
CHAHAR MAHALL VA BAKHTIARI
Shahr-e Kord
KOHKILUYEH VA BUYER AHMADI
Zagros Mts.
SHIRAZ
FARS
PERSEPOLIS
PASARGADAE
Bushehr
BUSHEHR
Jahrom
Lar
HORMOZGAN
Bandar-e Abbas
Qeshm
Str. of Hormuz
Kuhha-ye Bashakerd
Makran
Jask
PERSIAN GULF
Gulf of Oman
KUWAIT
KUWAYT (Kuwait)
Ad Dammam
Al Khubar
Dhahran
Al Hufuf
Al Jubayl
BAHRAIN
Al Manamah
QATAR
Ad Dawhah (Doha)
UNITED ARAB EMIRATES
DUBAYY (Dubai)
Abu Zaby (Abu Dhabi)
Ash Shariqah (Sharjah)
Ajman
Ras al Khaymah
Al Fujayrah
Al Ayn
Musandam (Oman)
OMAN
Suhar
Al Hajar al Gharbi
Al Jafurah
East from Greenwich
COPYRIGHT PHILIP'S

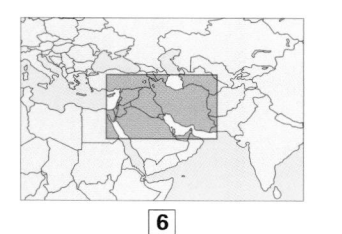

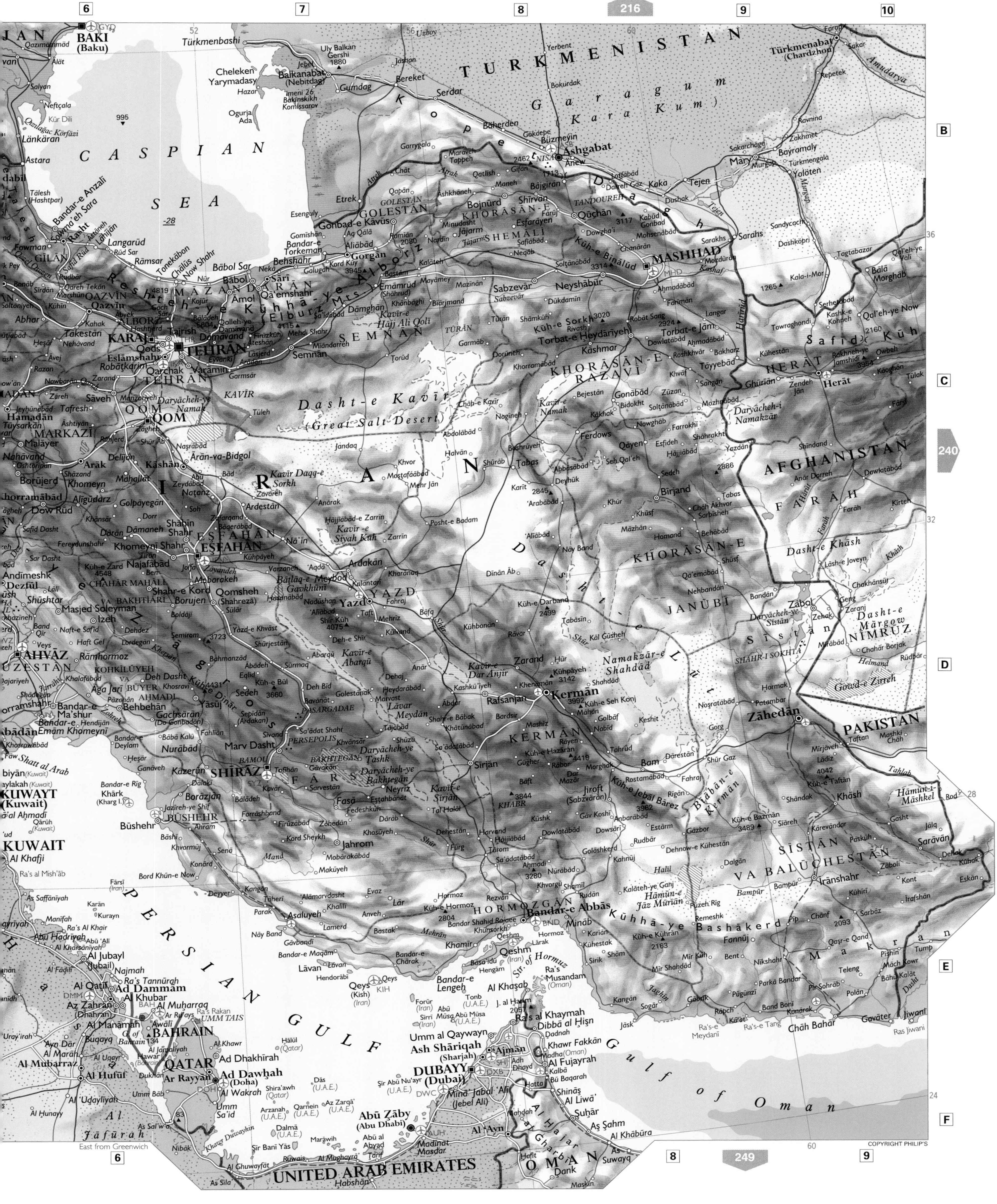

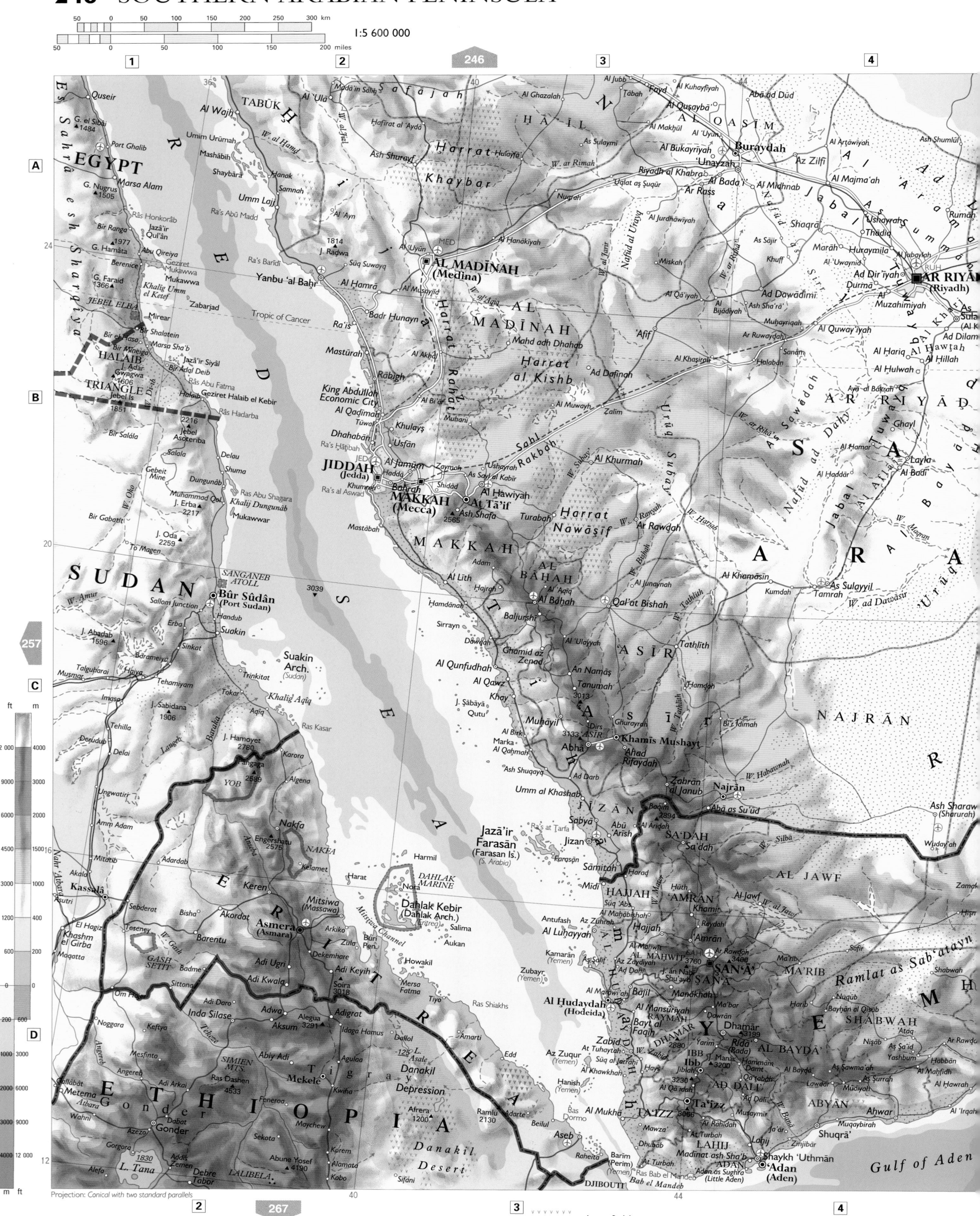

1:5 600 000

50   0   50   100   150   200   250   300 km
50   0   50   100   150   200 miles

246

257

267

Projection: Conical with two standard parallels

Lava fields

Gulf of Aden

EGYPT

SUDAN

ERITREA

ETHIOPIA

YEMEN

Tropic of Cancer

RED SEA

TABŪK

AL MADĪNAH (Medina)

JIDDAH (Jedda)

MAKKAH (Mecca)

AR RIYĀD (Riyadh)

Buraydah

ASĪR

NAJRĀN

AL BĀHAH

SAN'Ā

Al Hudaydah (Hodeida)

TA'IZZ

ADAN (Aden)

Bûr Sûdân (Port Sudan)

Kassalā

Asmera (Asmara)

Mekele

Gonder

L. Tana

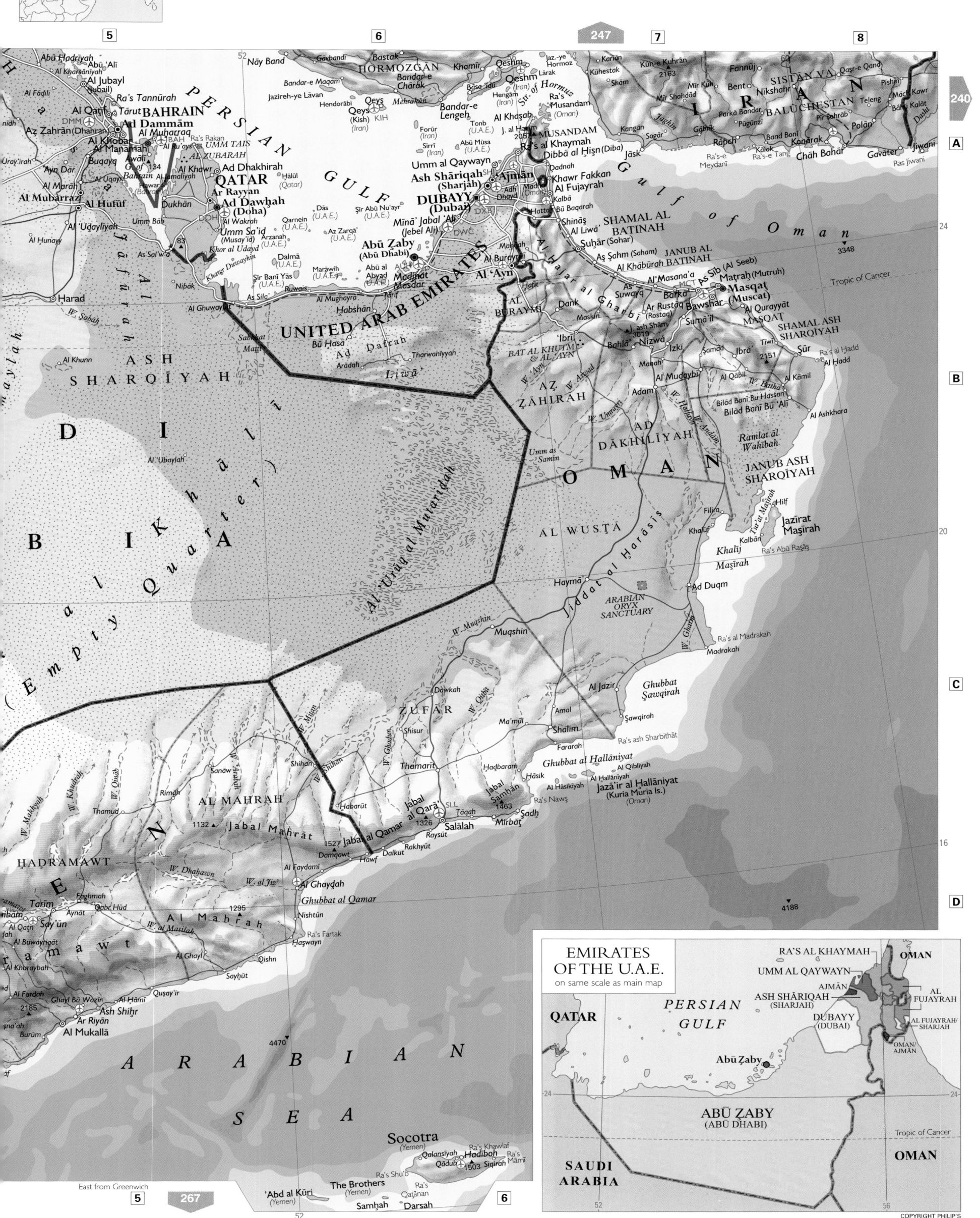

247
240
267

Abū Hadrīyah
Al Kharsānīyah
Al Fādlī
Al Jubayl (Jubail)
Az Zahrān (Dhahran)
Al Khobar
Al Manāmah
Uray'irah
Ayn Dār
Al Marāh
Al Mubarraz
Al Hufūf
Al 'Udaylīyah
Al Hunayy
Harad

BAHRAIN
Al Dammām
Al Muharraq
Ra's Tannūrah
Tārut
Al Qatīf

QATAR
Ar Rayyan
Ad Dawhah (Doha)
Dukhān
Umm Sa'id (Musay'id)
Al Wakrah

PERSIAN GULF

HORMOZGĀN
Bandar-e Chārak
Jazireh-ye Lavan
Hendorābī
Qeys (Kish)
Sirri (Iran)
Tonb (Iran)
Abū Mūsā (U.A.E.)
Dās (U.A.E.)
Qarnein (U.A.E.)
Arzanah (U.A.E.)
Şir Abū Nu'ayr (U.A.E.)
Şir Banī Yās (U.A.E.)

Bastak
Khamīr
Qeshm
Larak (Iran)
Hengam (Iran)
Bandar-e Lengeh

IRAN
SISTĀN VA
BALŪCHESTAN

Ra's al Khaymah
Dibbā al Ḥiṣn (Diba)
Dadnah
Khawr Fakkan
Al Fujayrah
Kalbā

UNITED ARAB EMIRATES
Abū Zaby (Abū Dhabi)
Madīnat Masdar
Al 'Ayn
Al Burayqī

OMAN
Masqaţ (Muscat)
SHAMAL AL BATINAH
JANUB AL BATINAH
Ṣuḥār (Sohar)
Aṣ Saḥm (Saham)
Barkā
Ar Rustāq (Rostaq)
As Sīb (Al Seeb)
Maṭrah (Mutruh)
Bawshar
AZ ZĀHIRAH
AD DĀKHILĪYAH
Nizwā
Bahlā
Izkī
Ibrā
MASQAT
SHAMAL ASH SHARQĪYAH

AL WUSTĀ
Haymā'
Arabian Oryx Sanctuary
Ad Duqm
JANUB ASH SHARQĪYAH
Ramlat āl Wahībah
Jazīrat Maşīrah
Ra's Abū Raşāş

ASH SHARQĪYAH

RUB' AL KHĀLĪ (Empty Quarter)

DI BA

ZUFĀR
Shisur
Muqshin
Dawkah
Thamarīt
Salālah
AL MAHRAH
Jabal Mahrāt
Habarūt
Ghubbat al Qamar

YEMEN
HADRAMAWT
Al Mukallā
Al Ghaydah
Tarīm
Say'ūn
Qishn

ARABIAN SEA

Socotra (Yemen)
Hadiboh
'Abd al Kūri (Yemen)
The Brothers
Samhah
Darsah

EMIRATES OF THE U.A.E.
on same scale as main map

RA'S AL KHAYMAH
UMM AL QAYWAYN
ASH SHĀRIQAH (SHARJAH)
AJMĀN
DUBAYY (DUBAI)
OMAN
AL FUJAYRAH
AL FUJAYRAH/SHARJAH
OMAN/AJMĀN
Abū Ẕaby

QATAR
PERSIAN GULF
ABŪ ẔABY (ABŪ DHABI)
SAUDI ARABIA
OMAN
Tropic of Cancer

COPYRIGHT PHILIP'S

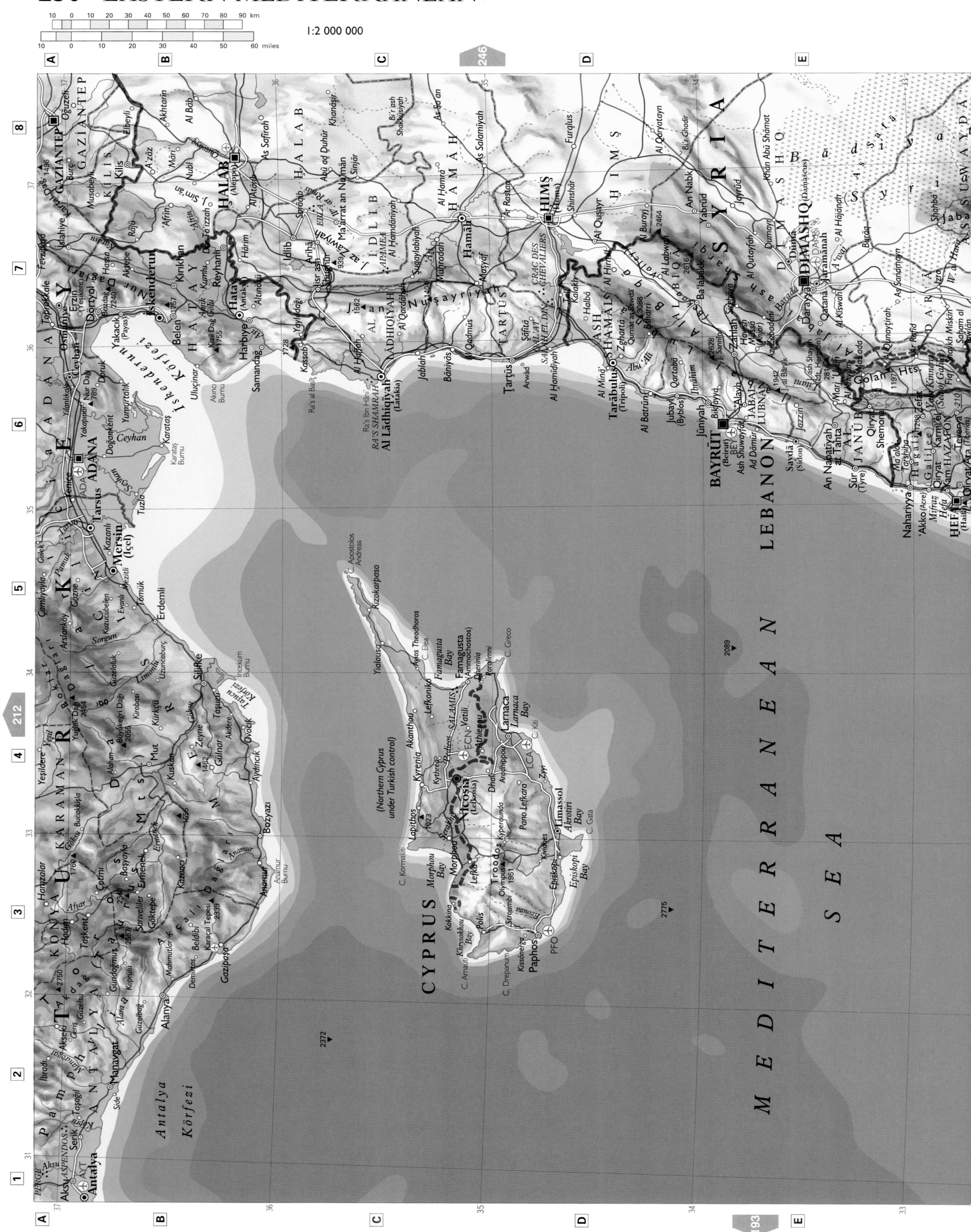

1:2 000 000

Lava fields

=== 1974 Cease Fire Lines

Projection : Polyconic

East from Greenwich

AFRICA

1:33 600 000

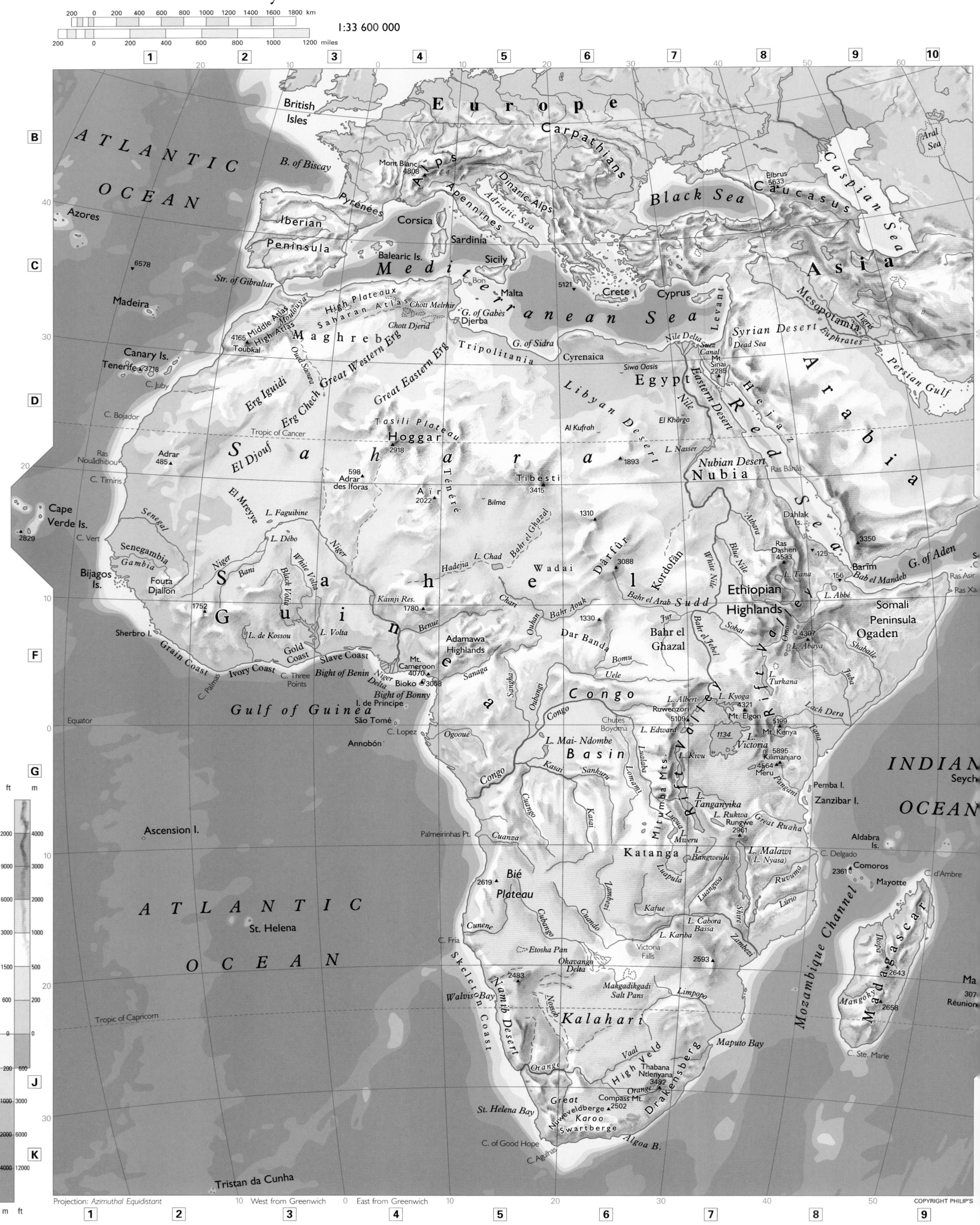

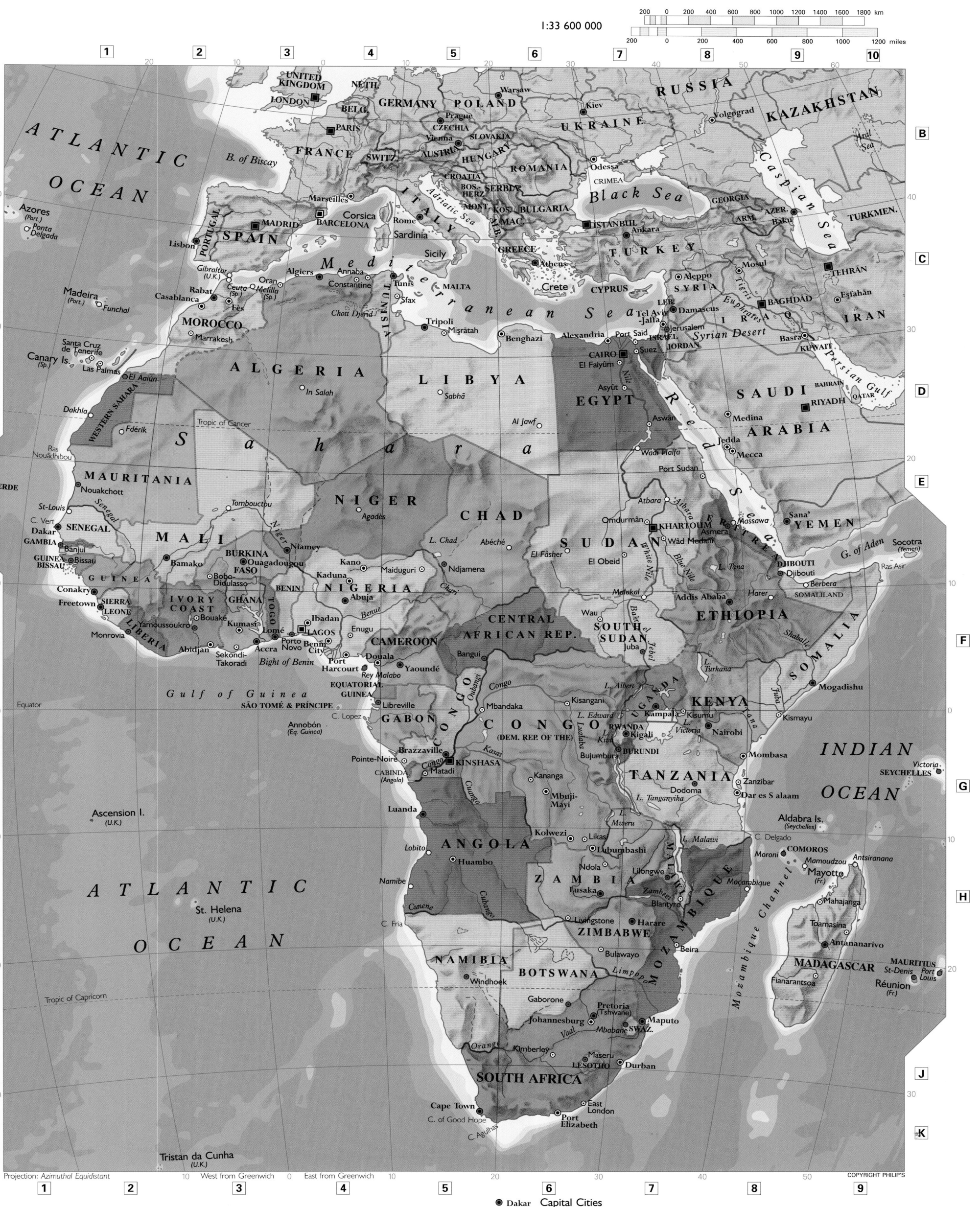

1:33 600 000

200 0 200 400 600 800 1000 1200 1400 1600 1800 km
200 0 200 400 600 800 1000 1200 miles

● Dakar Capital Cities

Projection: *Azimuthal Equidistant*   10   West from Greenwich   0   East from Greenwich   10   COPYRIGHT PHILIP'S

1:6 400 000

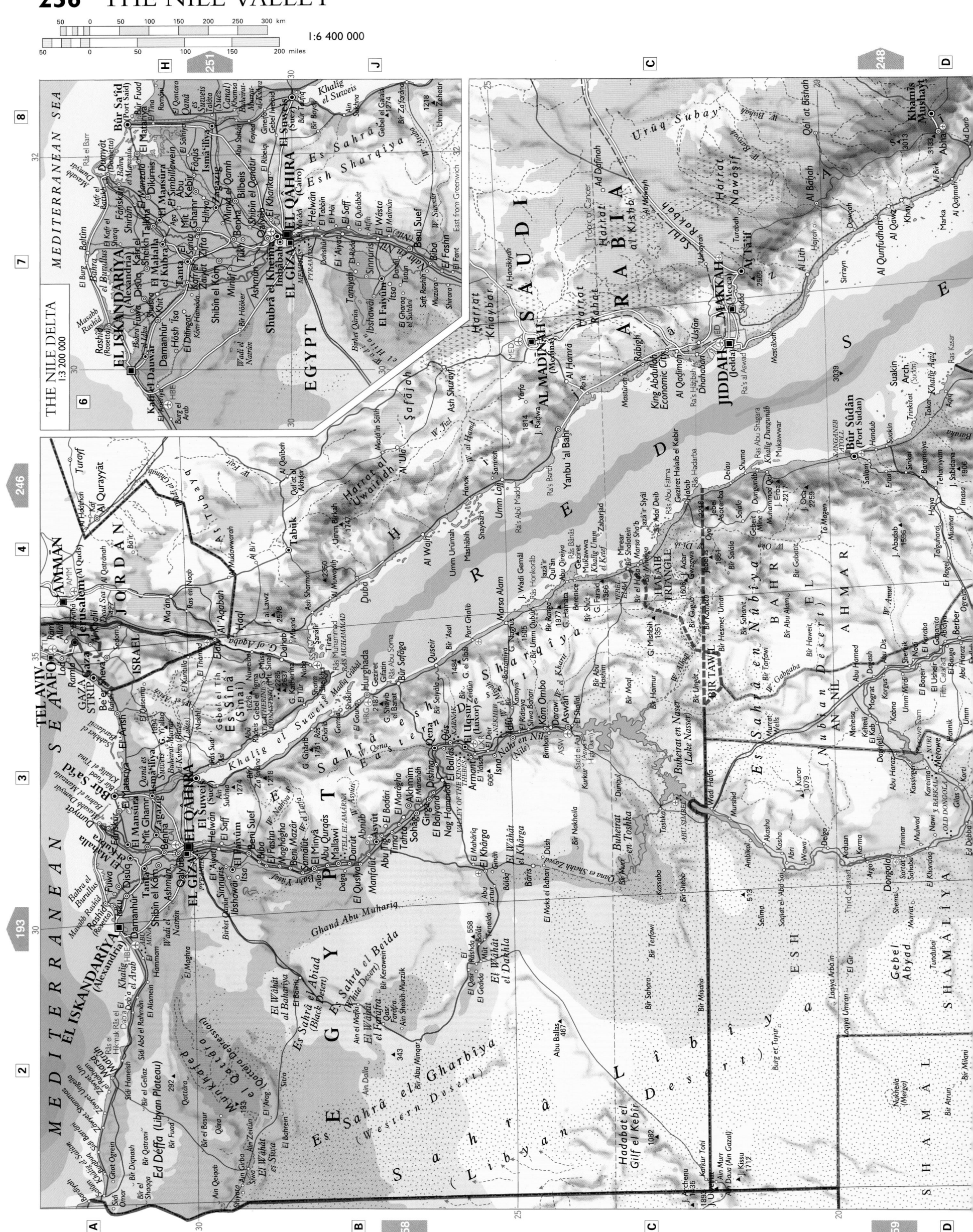

THE NILE DELTA
1:3 200 000

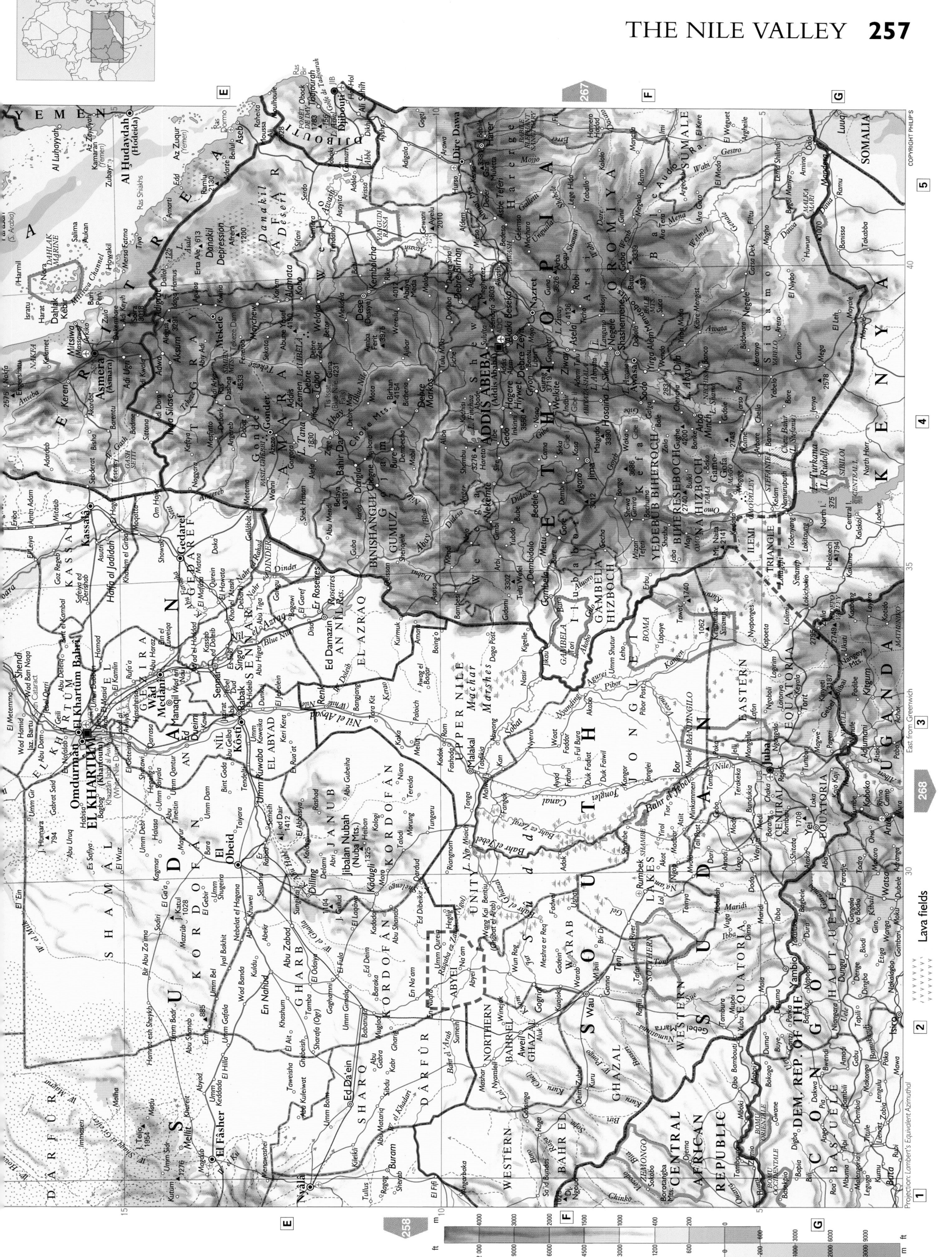

COPYRIGHT PHILIP'S

Lava fields

East from Greenwich

Projection: Lambert's Equivalent Azimuthal

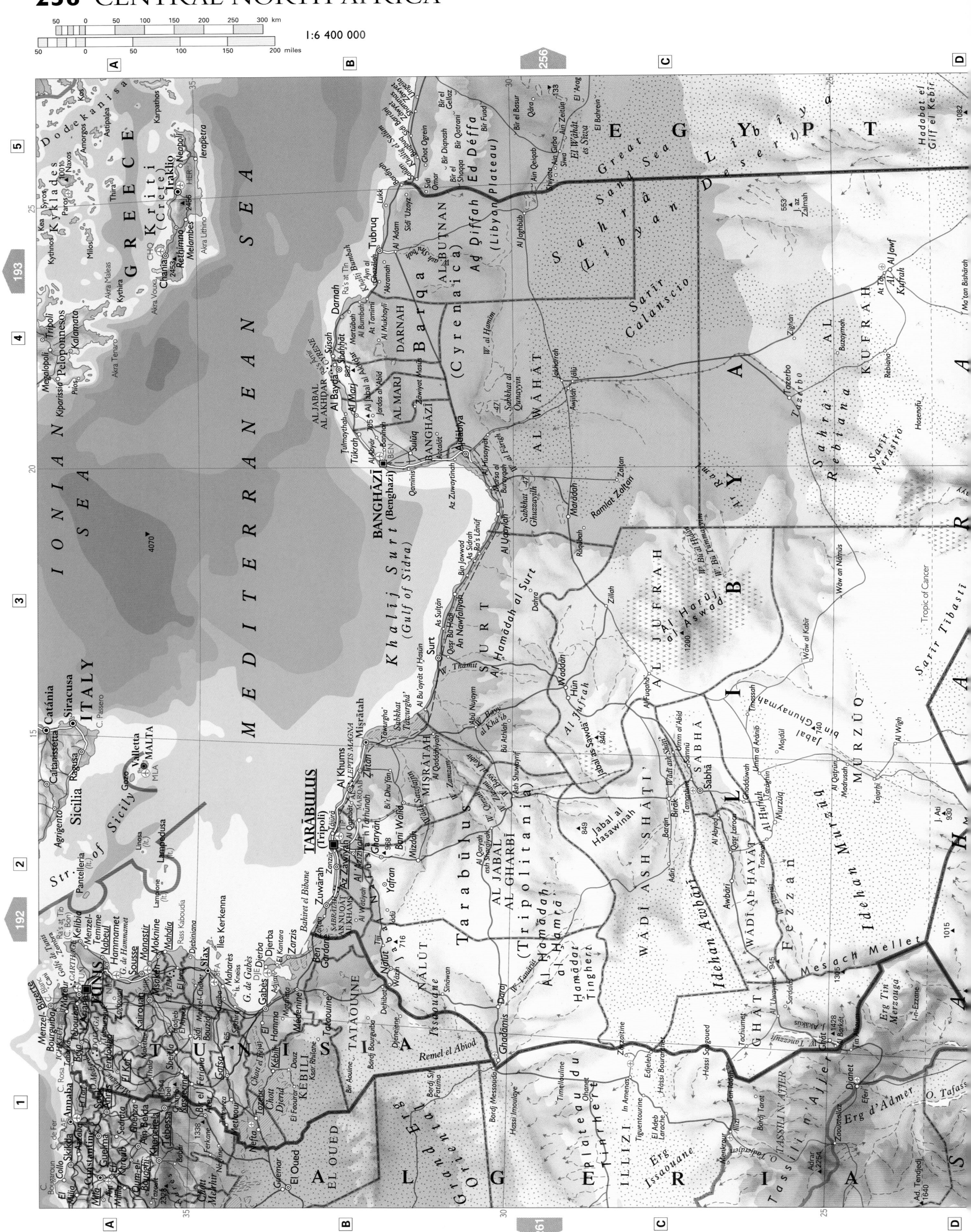

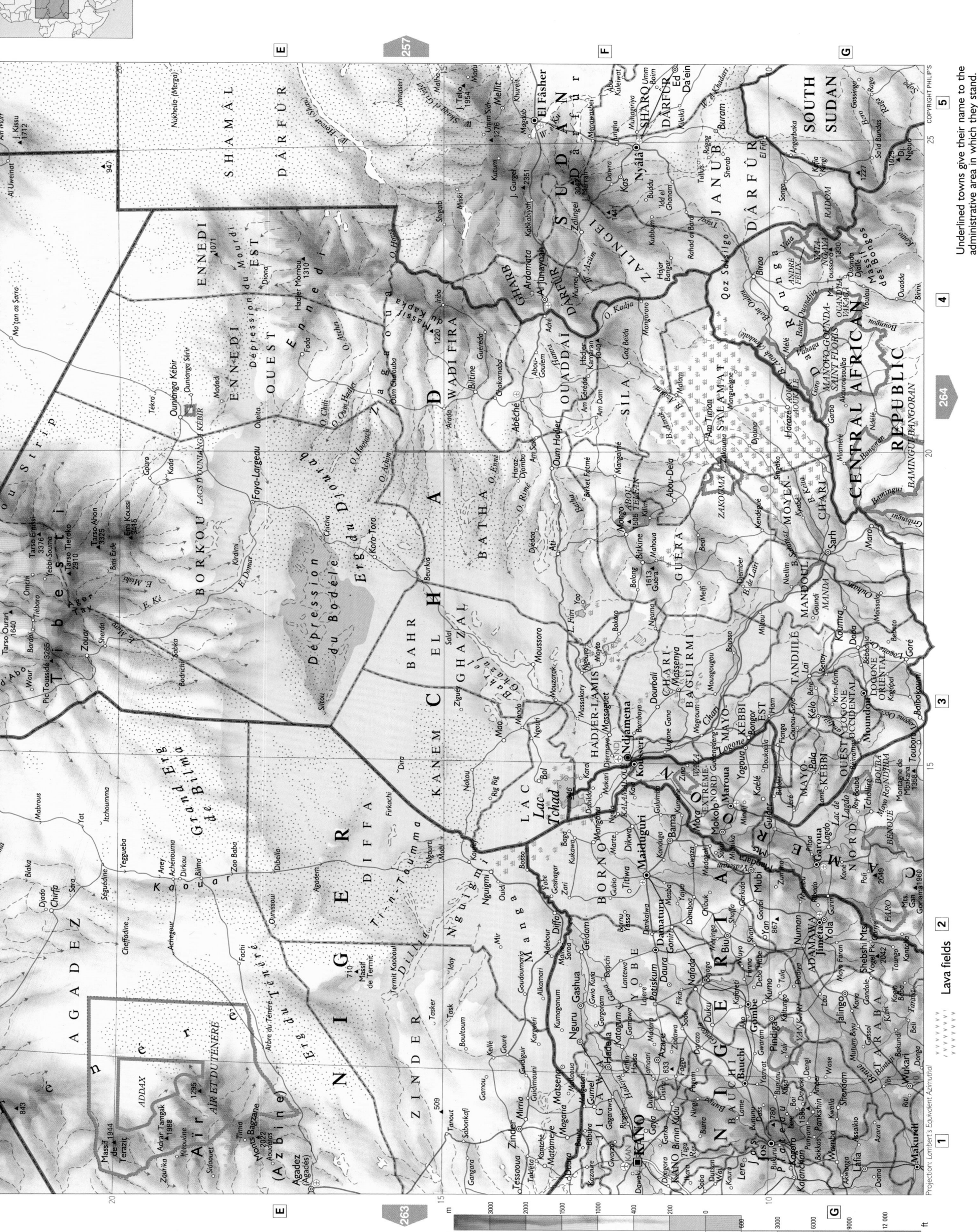

1:6 400 000

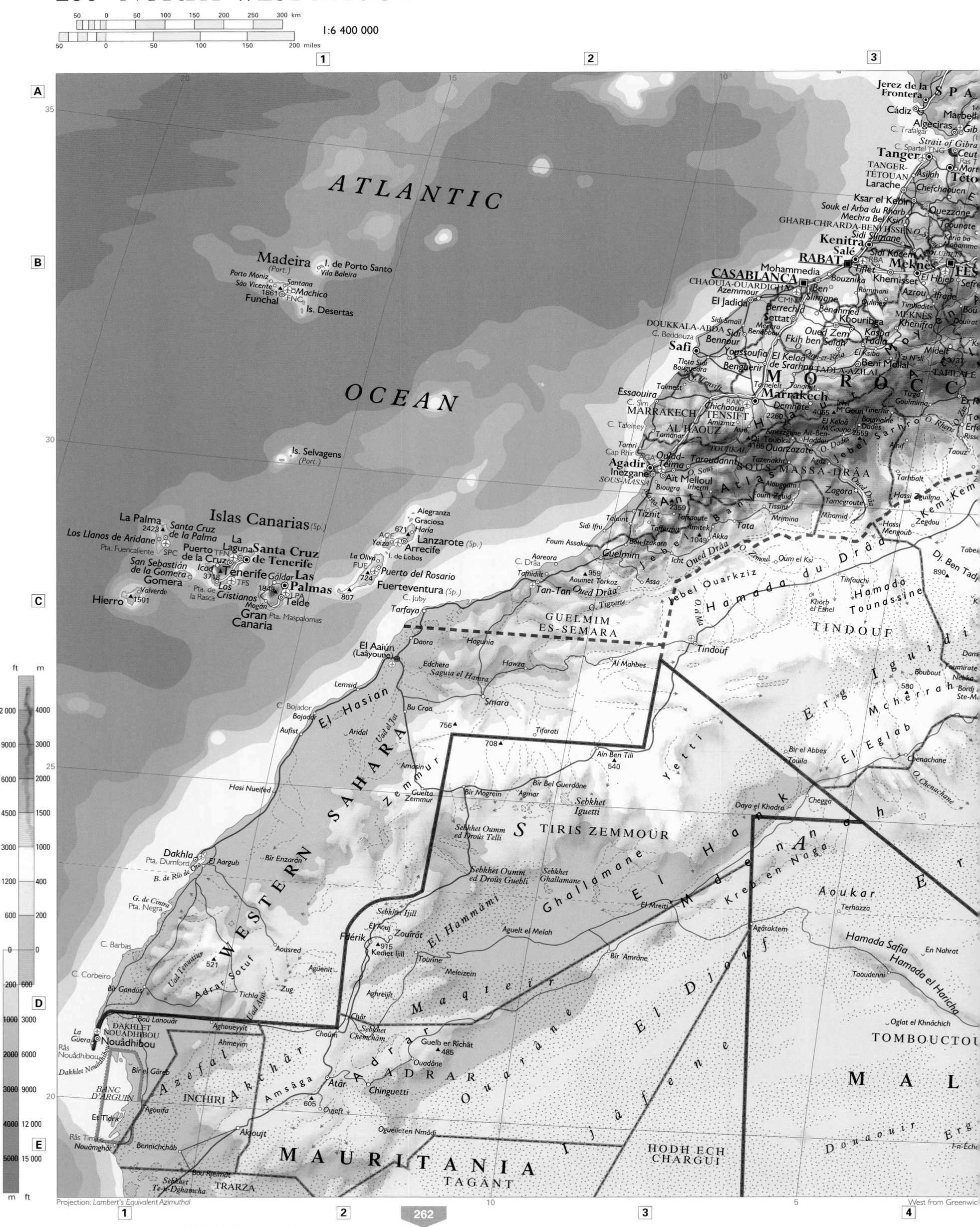

Projection: Lambert's Equivalent Azimuthal

Underlined towns give their name
to the administrative area in which they stand

West from Greenwich

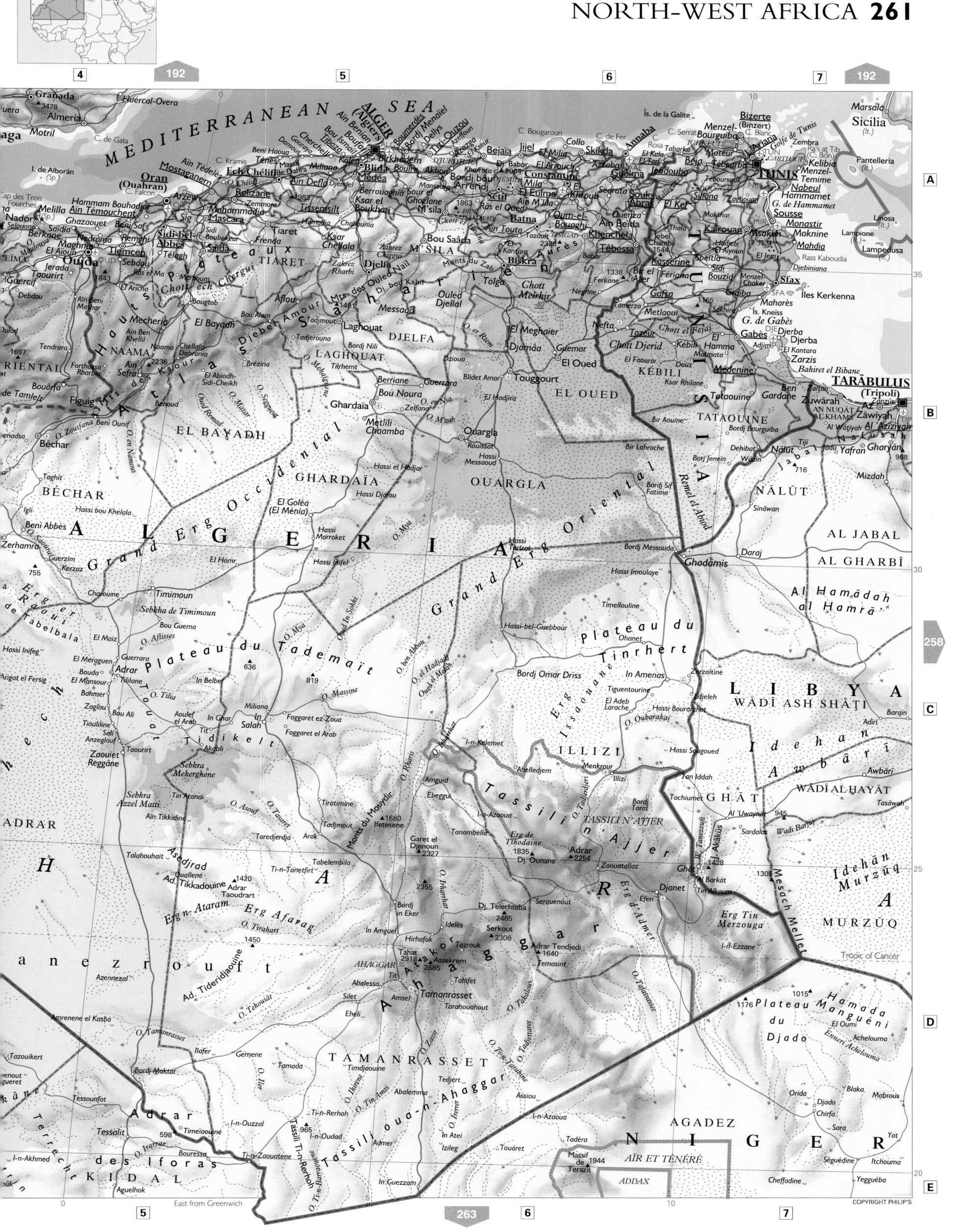

50 0 50 100 150 200 250 300 km

1:6 400 000

50 0 50 100 150 200 miles

1 | **2** | 260 | **3**

INCHIRI

Et Tidra
Râs Tinira
Nouâmghâr

Akjoujt

Oujeft

Bollé

ADRAR

Ogueileten
Nmâdi

SAHARA

Araouane

Bou-Djébé

MAURITANIA

Bennichchâb

TAGÂNT

Araouane

Az

Nouakchott NKC

TRARZA

Bou Naga

Rachid
Tidjikja 420

Gâneb

Dahr Tichît

Tichît
Akreijit

Tombouctou

Dayet en
Naharat

BRAKNA

Boutilimit

Magta Lahjar

Moudjeria

Togba

Aoukâr Depression

Aratâne

Oualâta

TOMBOUCTOU

Mederdra

Aleg

Mâl

Boûmdeïd

Tâmchekket

HODH EL GHARBI

HODH ECH CHARGUI

Néma

Koniâmbou

L. Faguibine

Rosso

Dagana

Podor

N'Dioum

Bogué

Mbagne

Kiffa

Ayoûn el 'Atroûs

Tintâne

Agjert

Timbedgha

Amourj

Fassalé

Léré

Goundam

Akka

Ngorkou

L. Korarou

Ross Béthio
St-Louis

Richard
Toll

Thillé-
Boubacar

Kaédi

Matam

Mbout

Kankossa

Kirane

Bassikounou

L. Débo

Niafounké

Sarévama

DAKAR

Thiès

Touba

Diourbel

Bakel

Kayes

BAMAKO

Mopti

SIERRA
LEONE

FREETOWN

LIBERIA

MONROVIA

ATLANTIC

OCEAN

CONAKRY

GUINEA

IVORY COAST

ABIDJAN

Underlined towns give their name to the
administrative area in which they stand.

Administrative division in Ivory Coast:
1 Sassandra-Marahoué

1 | **2** | **3** | **4**

261
259
264
4
5
6
7
A
B
C
D
E
ALGERIA
NIGER
NIGERIA
BENIN
TOGO
GHANA
CAMEROON
CHAD
EQUATORIAL GUINEA
Adrar des Iforas
KIDAL
GAO
TILLABÉRI
TAHOUA
AGADEZ
MARADI
ZINDER
DIFFA
DOSSO
Aïr (Azbine)
Talak
Ténéré
ADDAX
ÄIR ET TÉNÉRÉ
Massif de Terazit
Monts Bagzane
Agadez (Agadès)
Arlit
NIAMEY
OUAGADOUGOU
Tahoua
Zinder
Maradi
Sokoto
Katsina
KANO
KADUNA
Zaria
ABUJA
Jos
Bauchi
Maiduguri
Yola
Ilorin
OGBOMOSHO
Oshogbo
IBADAN
Abeokuta
LAGOS
Porto-Novo
Cotonou
LOMÉ
ACCRA
BENIN CITY
Onitsha
Enugu
PORT HARCOURT
Calabar
DOUALA
YAOUNDÉ
Malabo
Bioko
ZAMFARA
KEBBI
JIGAWA
YOBE
GOMBE
PLATEAU
ADAMAWA
TARABA
KOGI
BENUE
EDO
DELTA
RIVERS
Lake Volta
Kainji Lake
Lac Tchad
N.E. NIGERIA
on same scale
Slave Coast
Bight of Benin
Niger Delta
Bight of Bonny
GULF OF GUINEA
East from Greenwich
COPYRIGHT PHILIP'S

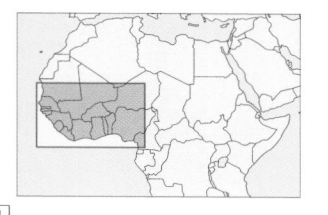

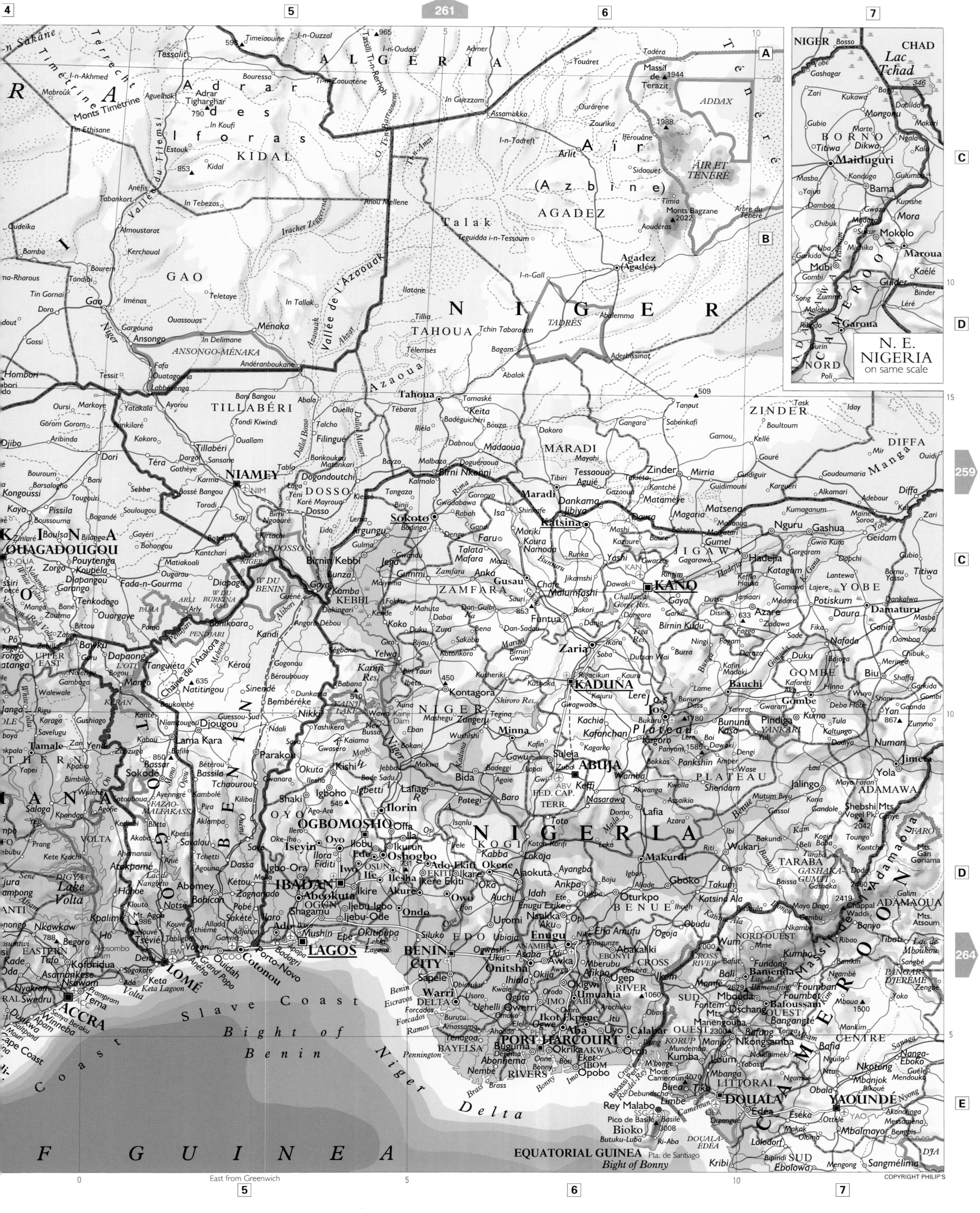

1:6 400 000

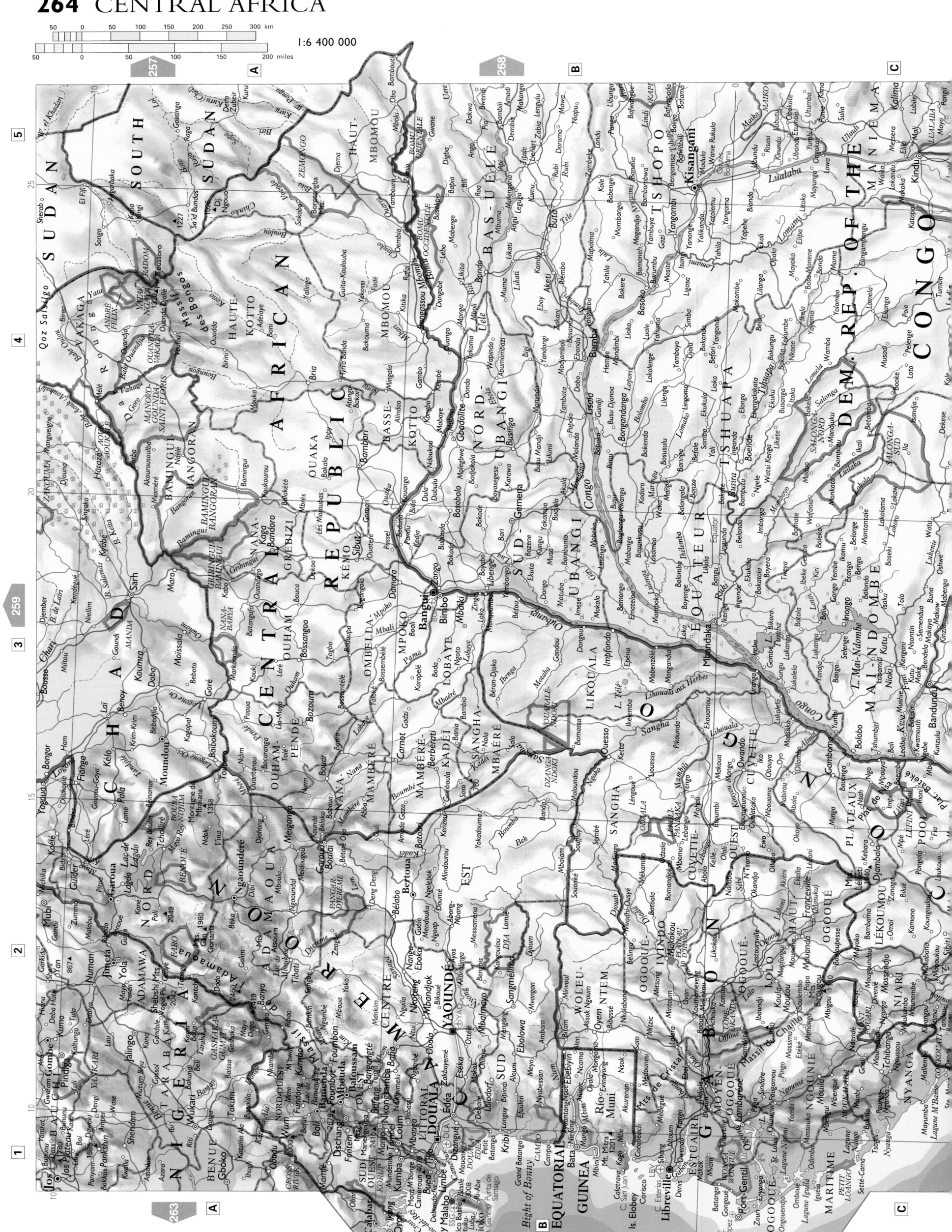

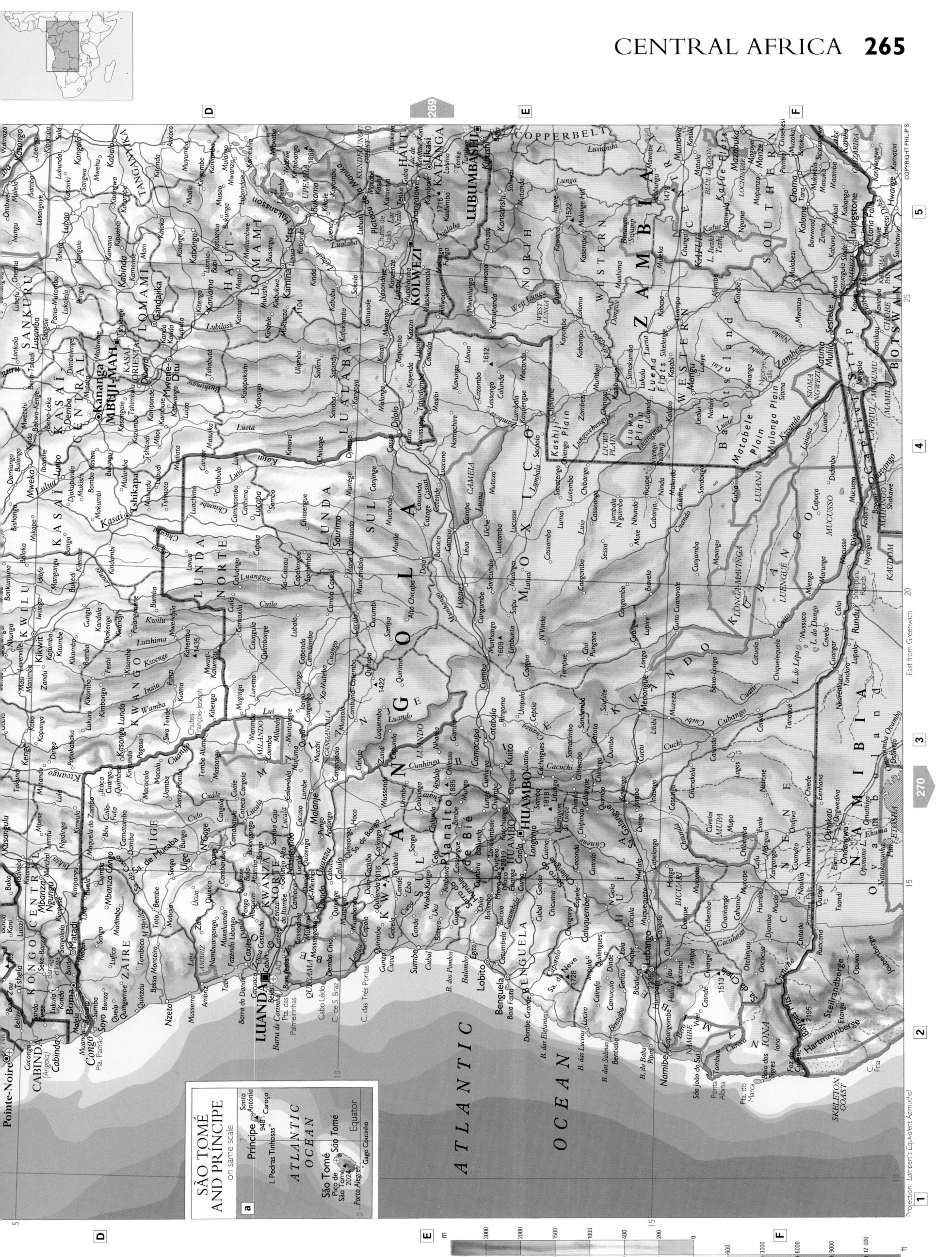

SÃO TOMÉ AND PRÍNCIPE
on same scale

Príncipe
Santo António
948 Caroço
I. Pedras Tinhosas

ATLANTIC OCEAN

São Tomé
Pico de São Tomé 2024
Porto Alegre
Gago Coutinho

Equator

Projection: Lambert's Equivalent Azimuthal

East from Greenwich

m / ft

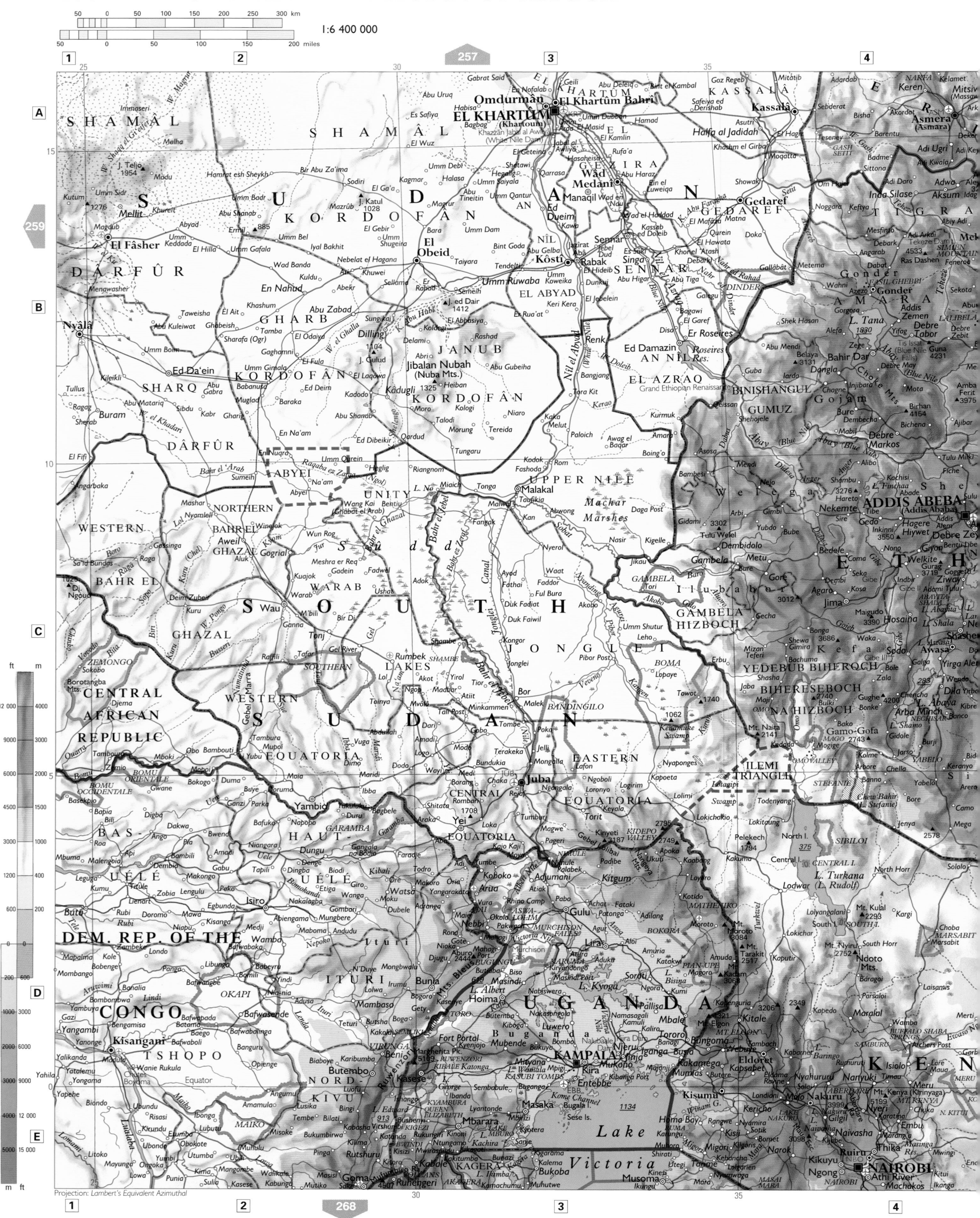

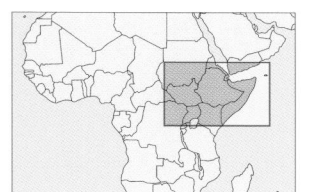

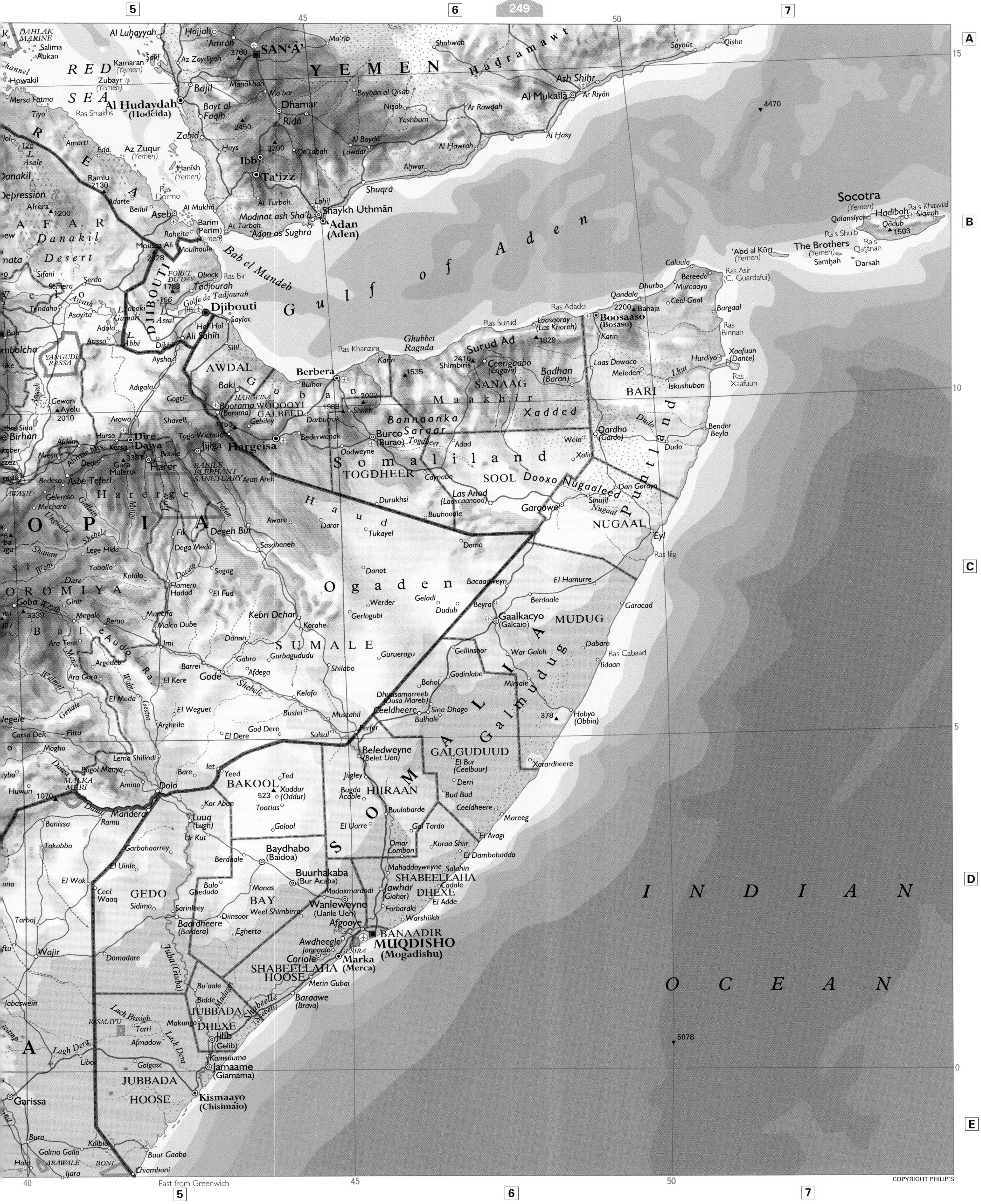

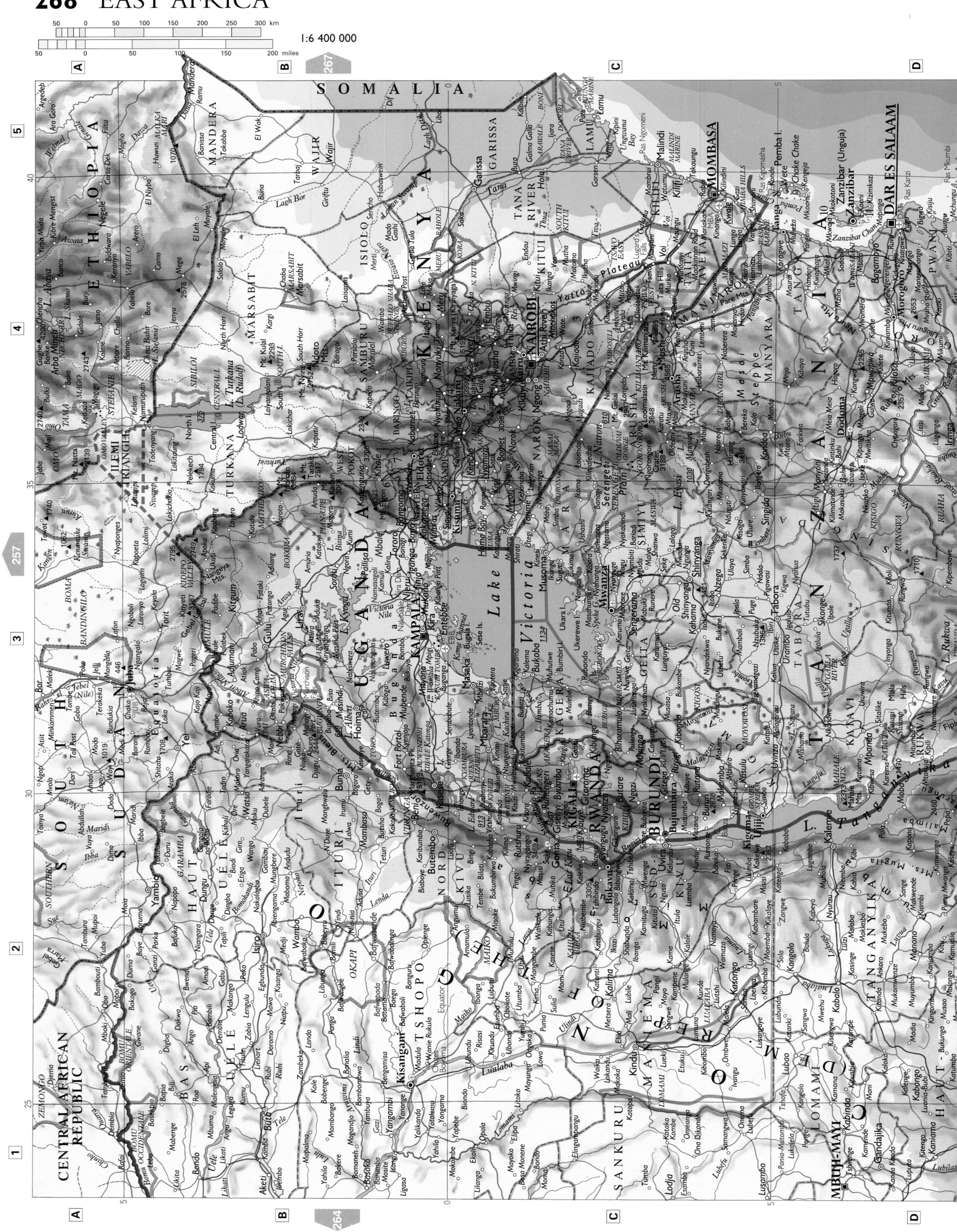

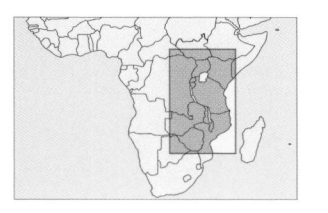

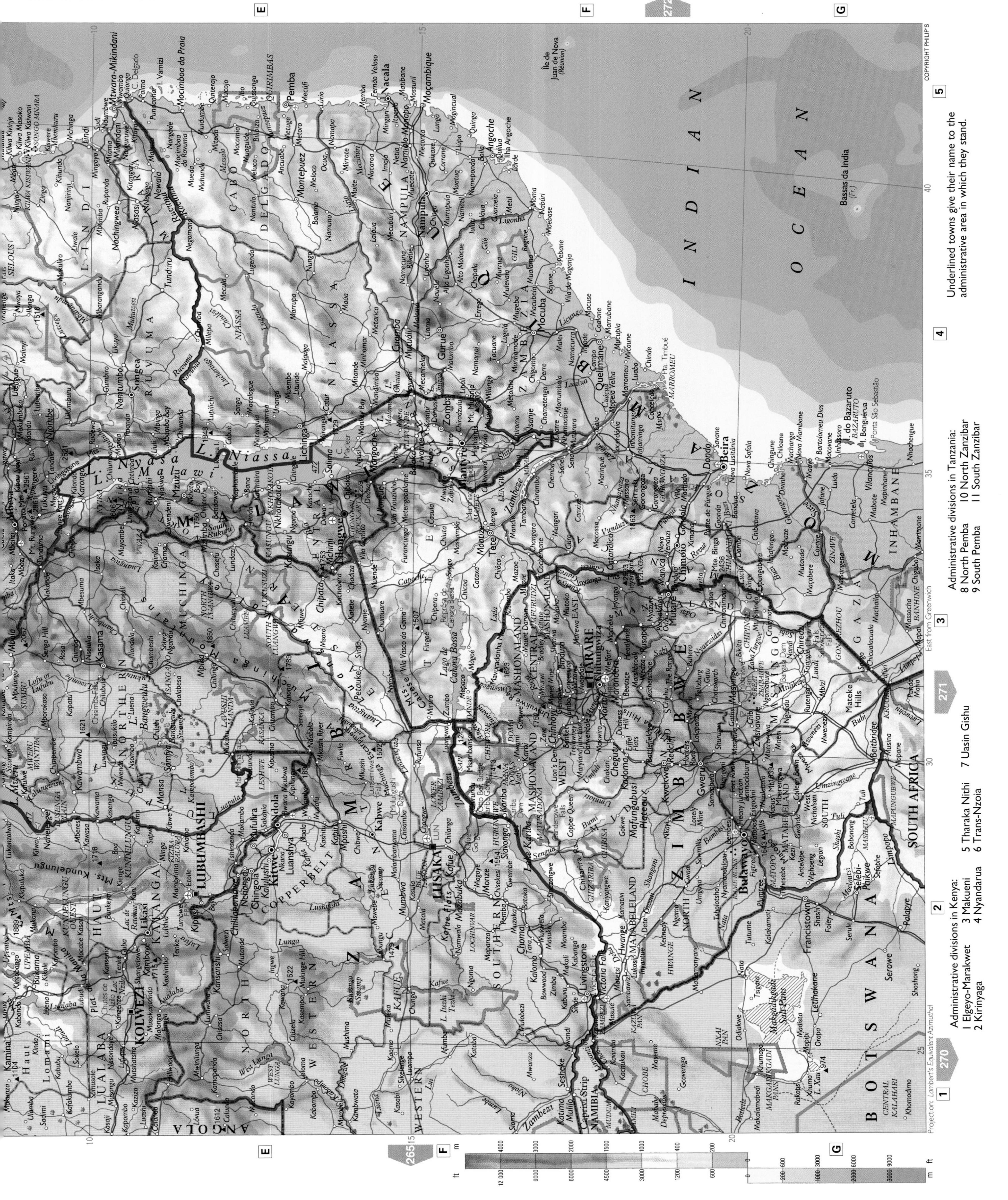

INDIAN OCEAN
ZAMBIA
ZIMBABWE
BOTSWANA
MOZAMBIQUE
MALAWI
ANGOLA
NAMIBIA
SOUTH AFRICA
LUSAKA
HARARE
Lilongwe
Administrative divisions in Kenya:
1 Elgeyo-Marakwet
2 Kirinyaga
3 Makueni
4 Nyandarua
5 Tharaka Nithi
6 Trans-Nzoia
7 Uasin Gishu
Administrative divisions in Tanzania:
8 North Pemba
9 South Pemba
10 North Zanzibar
11 South Zanzibar
Underlined towns give their name to the administrative area in which they stand.
Projection: Lambert's Equivalent Azimuthal
East from Greenwich
COPYRIGHT PHILIP'S

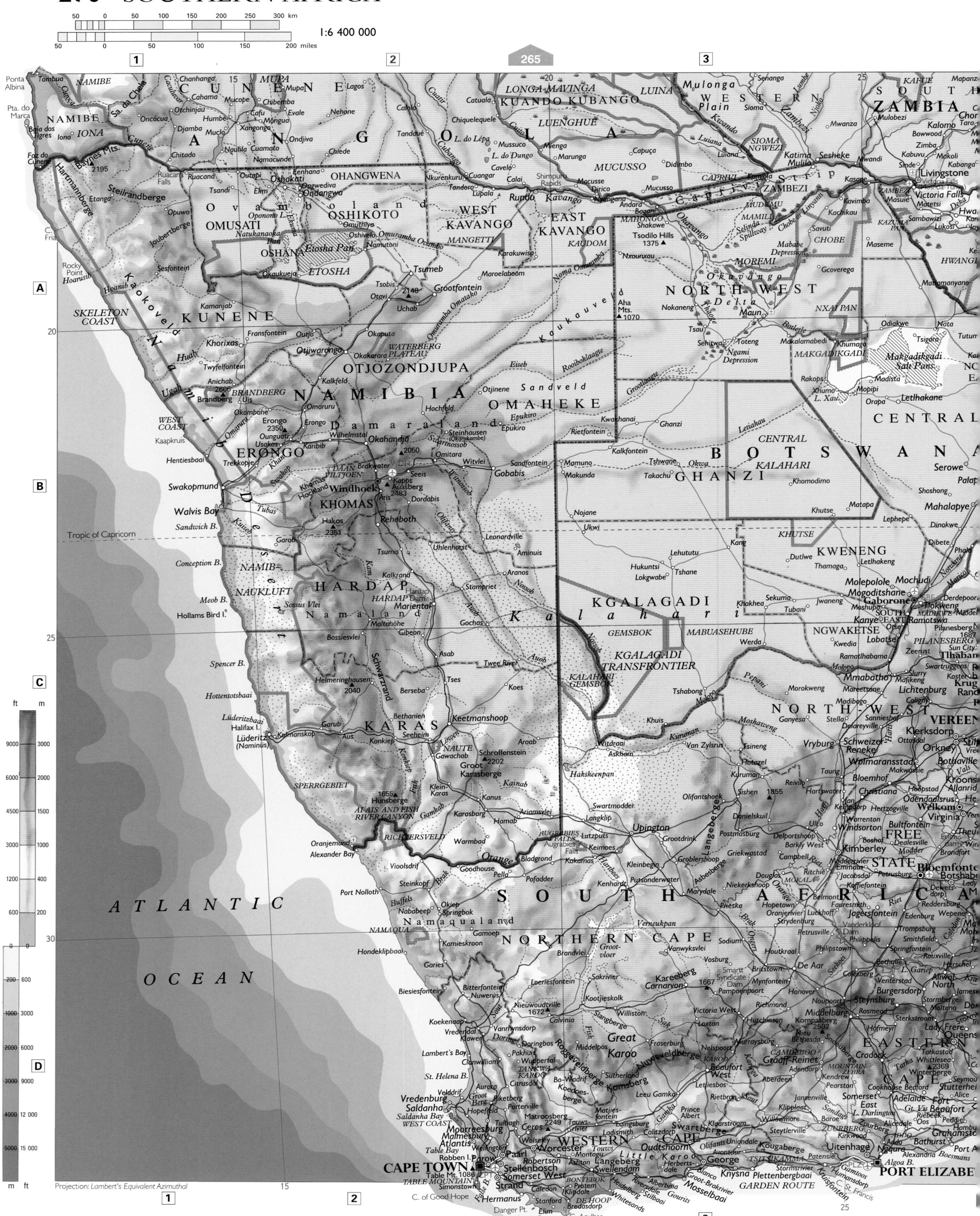

1:6 400 000

265

ATLANTIC

OCEAN

MOZAMBIQUE CHANNEL

INDIAN

OCEAN

Tropic of Capricorn

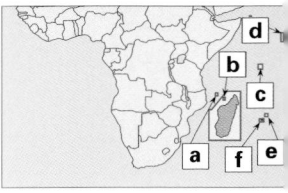

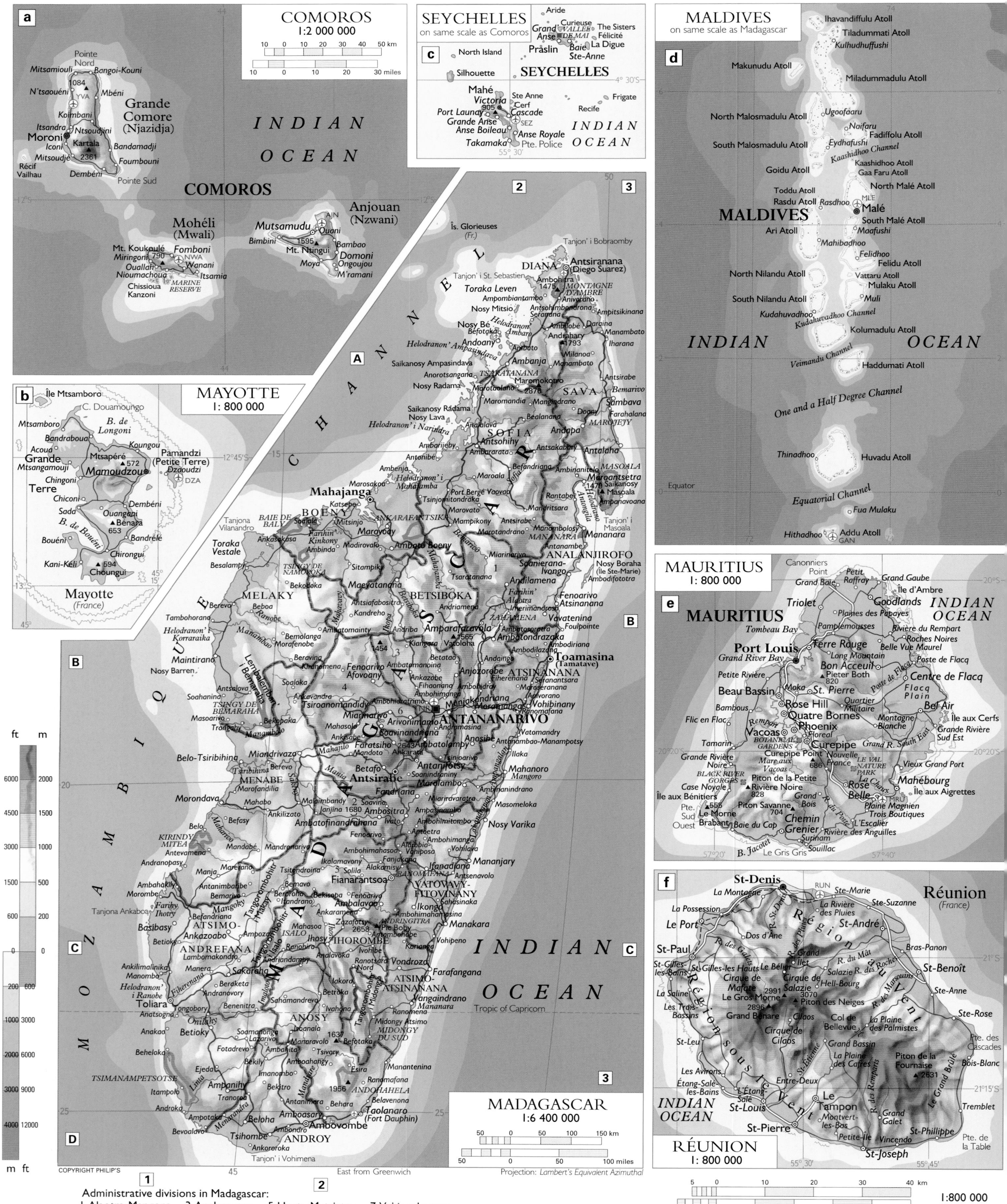

COMOROS
1:2 000 000

10 0 10 20 30 40 50 km
10 0 10 20 30 miles

SEYCHELLES
on same scale as Comoros

MALDIVES
on same scale as Madagascar

MAYOTTE
1:800 000

MAURITIUS
1:800 000

RÉUNION
1:800 000

MADAGASCAR
1:6 400 000

50 0 50 100 150 km
50 0 50 100 miles

COPYRIGHT PHILIP'S

East from Greenwich

Projection: Lambert's Equivalent Azimuthal

Administrative divisions in Madagascar:
1 Alaotra-Mangoro   3 Analamanga   5 Haute Matsiatra   7 Vakinankaratra
2 Amoron'i Mania   4 Bongolava   6 Itasy

ft m
6000 2000
4500 1500
3000 1000
1500 500
600 200
0
200 600
1000 3000
2000 6000
3000 9000
4000 12000
m ft

INDIAN OCEAN

MOZAMBIQUE CHANNEL

Tropic of Capricorn

5 0 10 20 30 40 km
5 0 5 10 15 20 25 miles
1:800 000

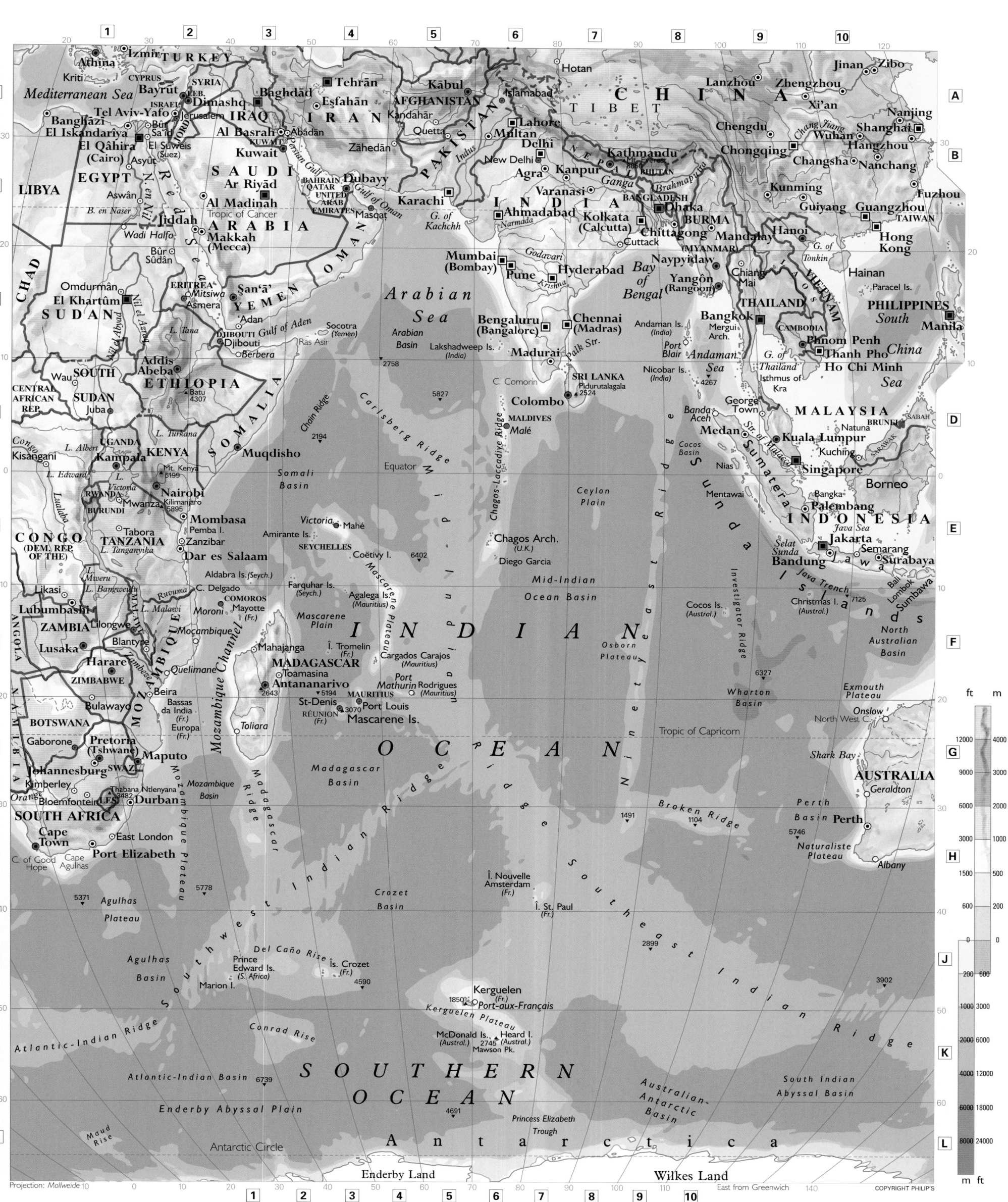

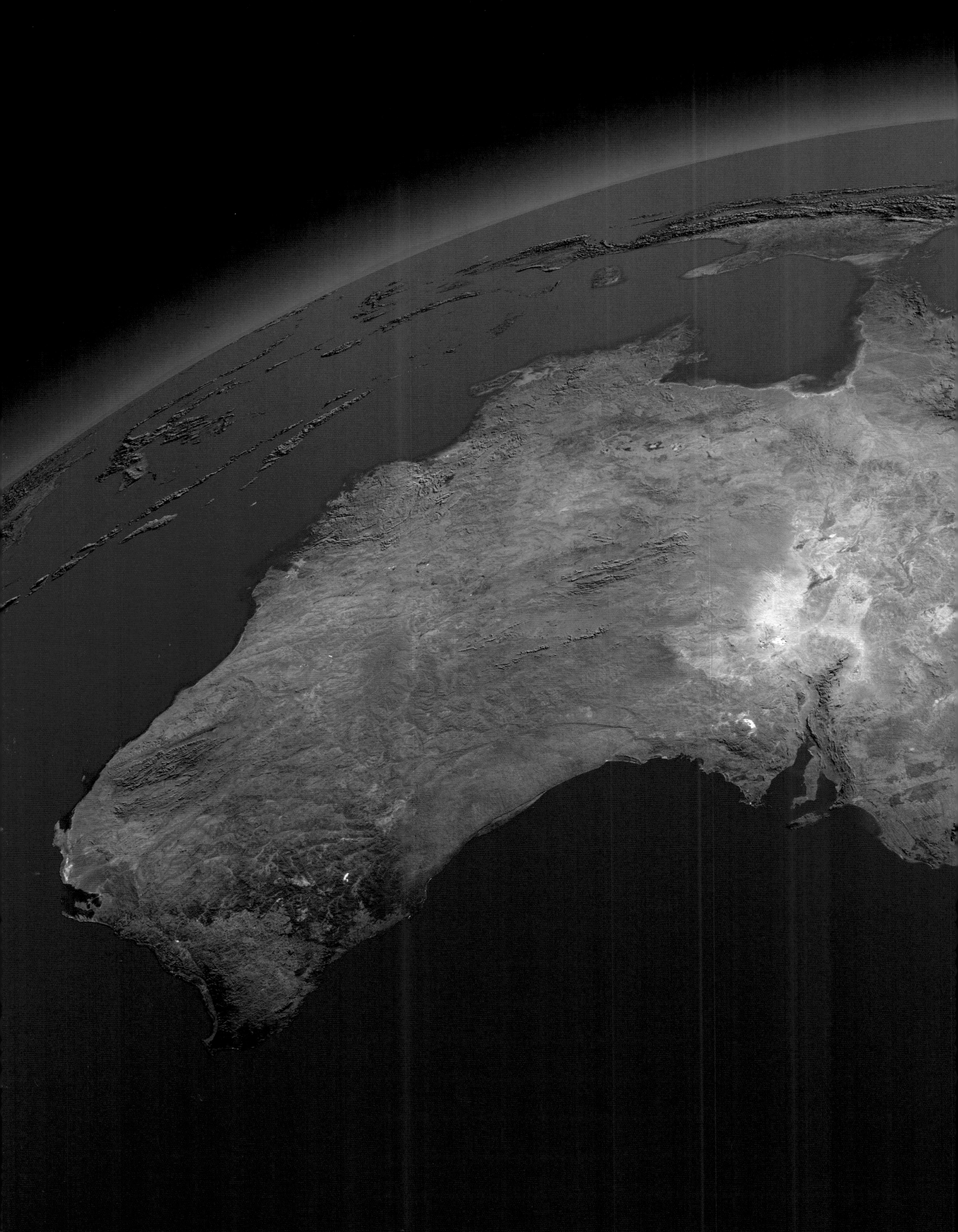

AUSTRALIA
AND
OCEANIA

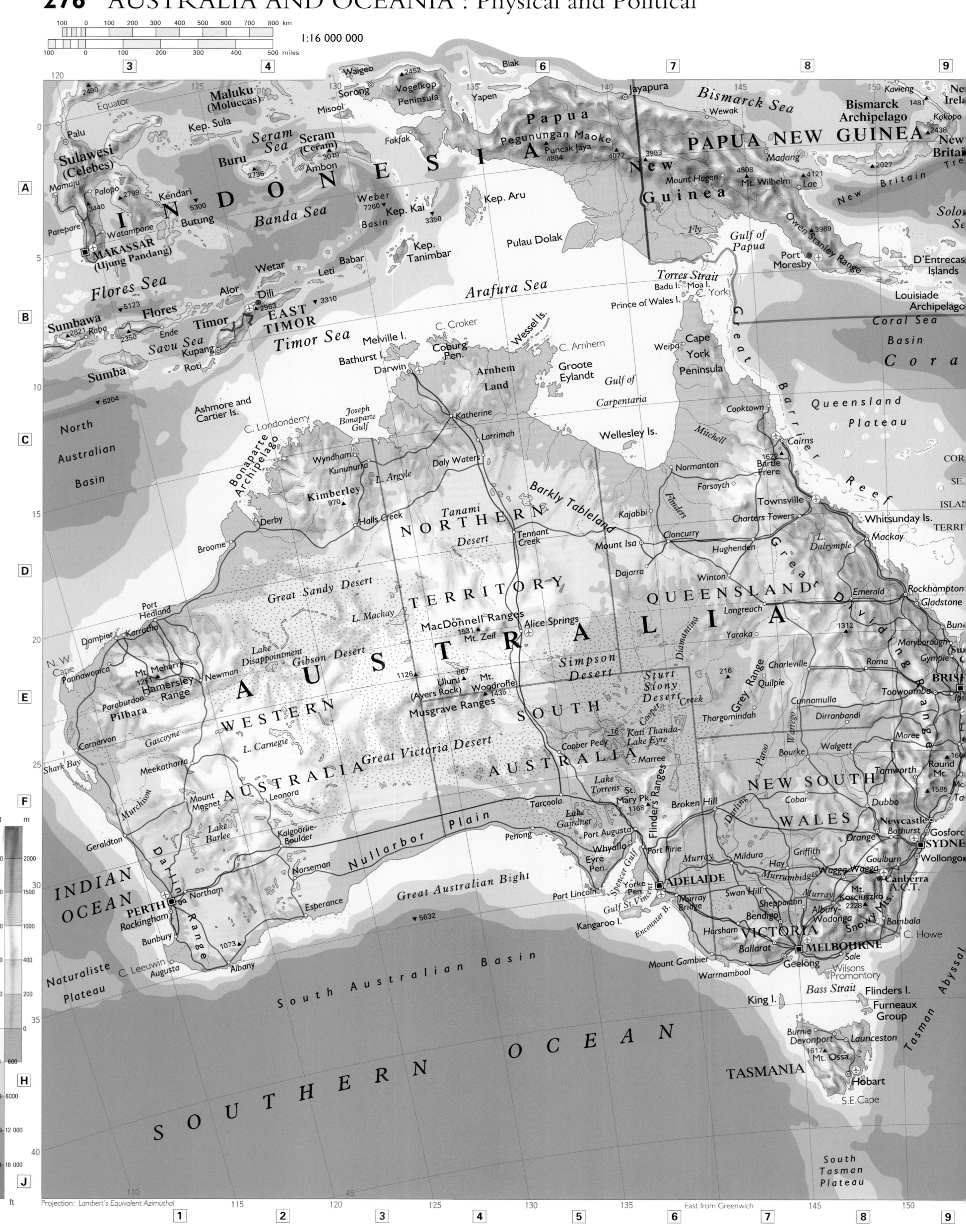

1:16 000 000

Projection: Lambert's Equivalent Azimuthal

East from Greenwich

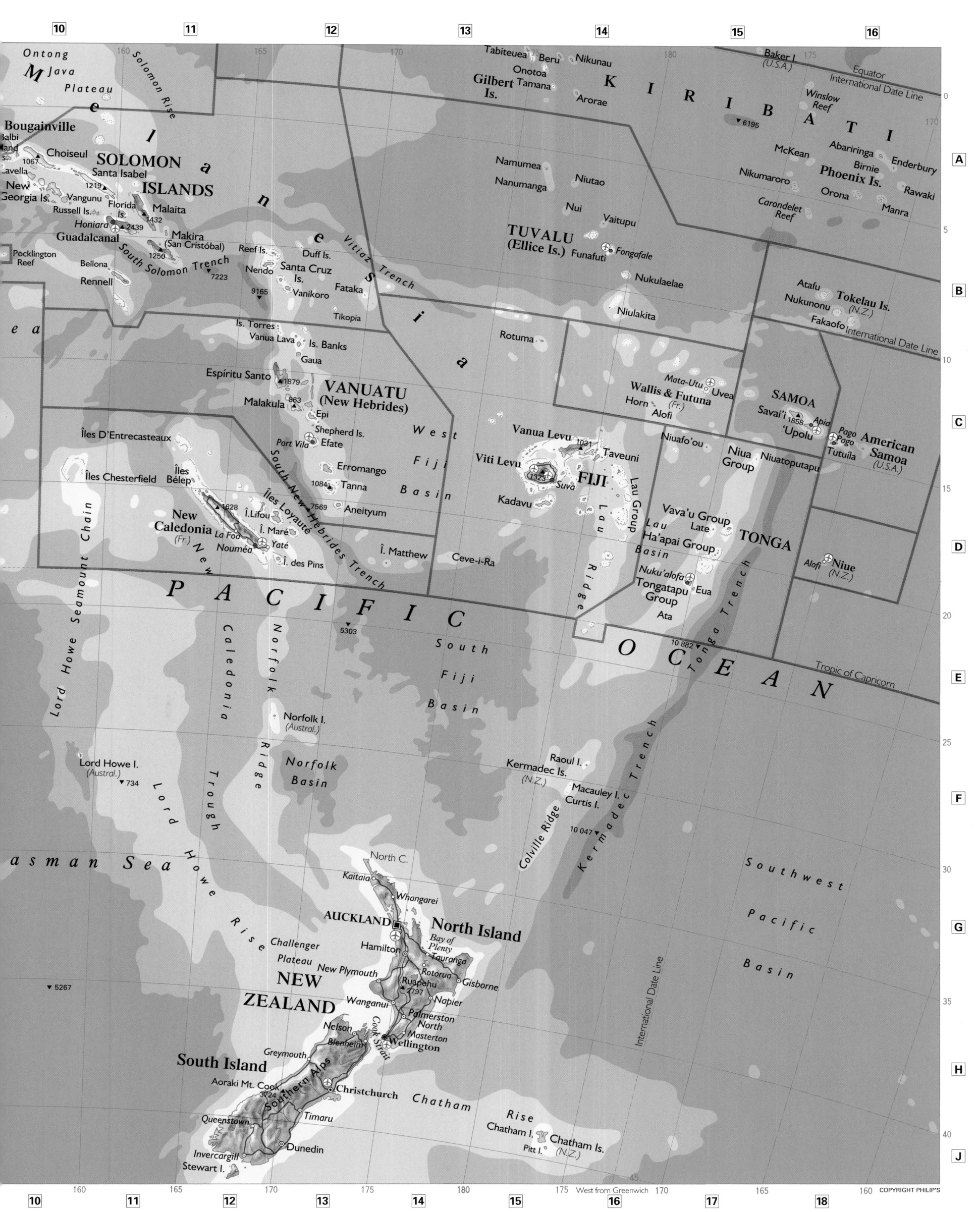

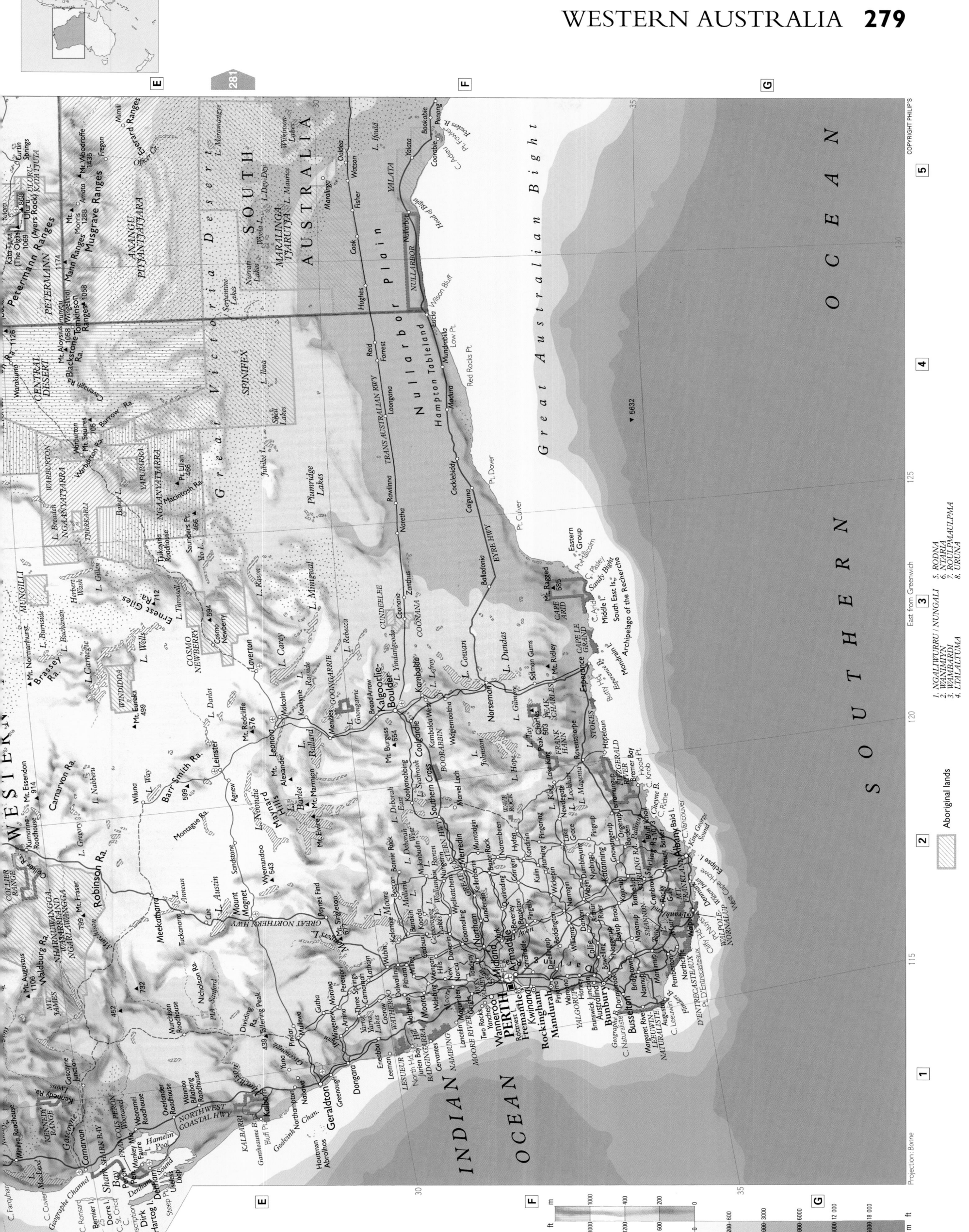

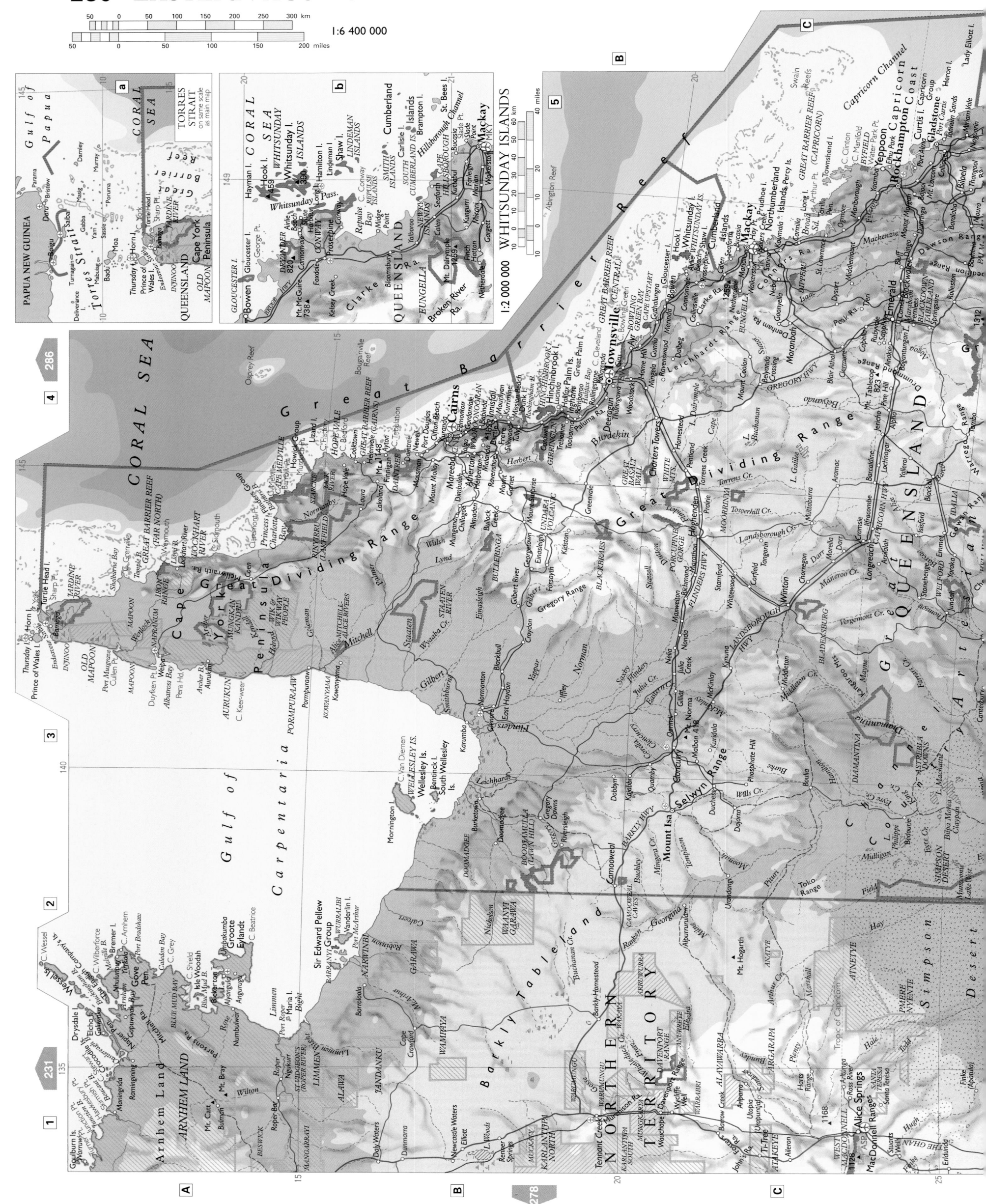

1:6 400 000

a

PAPUA NEW GUINEA

TORRES STRAIT
on same scale
as main map

QUEENSLAND
Cape York Peninsula

OLD MAPOON

b

CORAL SEA

Cumberland

WHITSUNDAY ISLANDS

QUEENSLAND

1:2 000 000

CORAL SEA

Great Barrier Reef

Gulf of Carpentaria

ARNHEM LAND

NORTHERN TERRITORY

QUEENSLAND

Great Dividing Range

Cape York Peninsula

Barkly Tableland

Simpson Desert

Townsville

Cairns

Mackay

Rockhampton

Gladstone

Mount Isa

Alice Springs

Tropic of Capricorn

TASMAN SEA

NEW SOUTH WALES

SOUTH AUSTRALIA

QUEENSLAND

VICTORIA

TASMANIA

Great Dividing Range

BRISBANE
SYDNEY
MELBOURNE
ADELAIDE
Canberra
Newcastle
Wollongong
Hobart
Launceston

Gold Coast
Sunshine Coast
Coffs Harbour
Port Macquarie
Toowoomba
Warwick
Armidale
Tamworth
Dubbo
Orange
Bathurst
Broken Hill
Wagga Wagga
Albury
Bendigo
Ballarat
Geelong
Warrnambool
Mount Gambier
Port Augusta
Whyalla
Port Pirie
Port Lincoln

Lake Eyre
Lake Torrens
Lake Gairdner
Lake Frome
Lake Blanche

Darling R.
Murray R.
Murrumbidgee R.
Cooper Cr.

Bass Strait
King Island
Flinders Island
Furneaux Group
Cape Barren I.
Kangaroo I.
Spencer Gulf
Gulf St. Vincent
Eyre Peninsula

Aboriginal lands

COPYRIGHT PHILIP'S
Projection Bonne
East from Greenwich

on same scale

m ft
1500 4500
1000 3000
400 1200
200 600
0 0
200 600
2000 6000
3000 12 000
4000
m ft

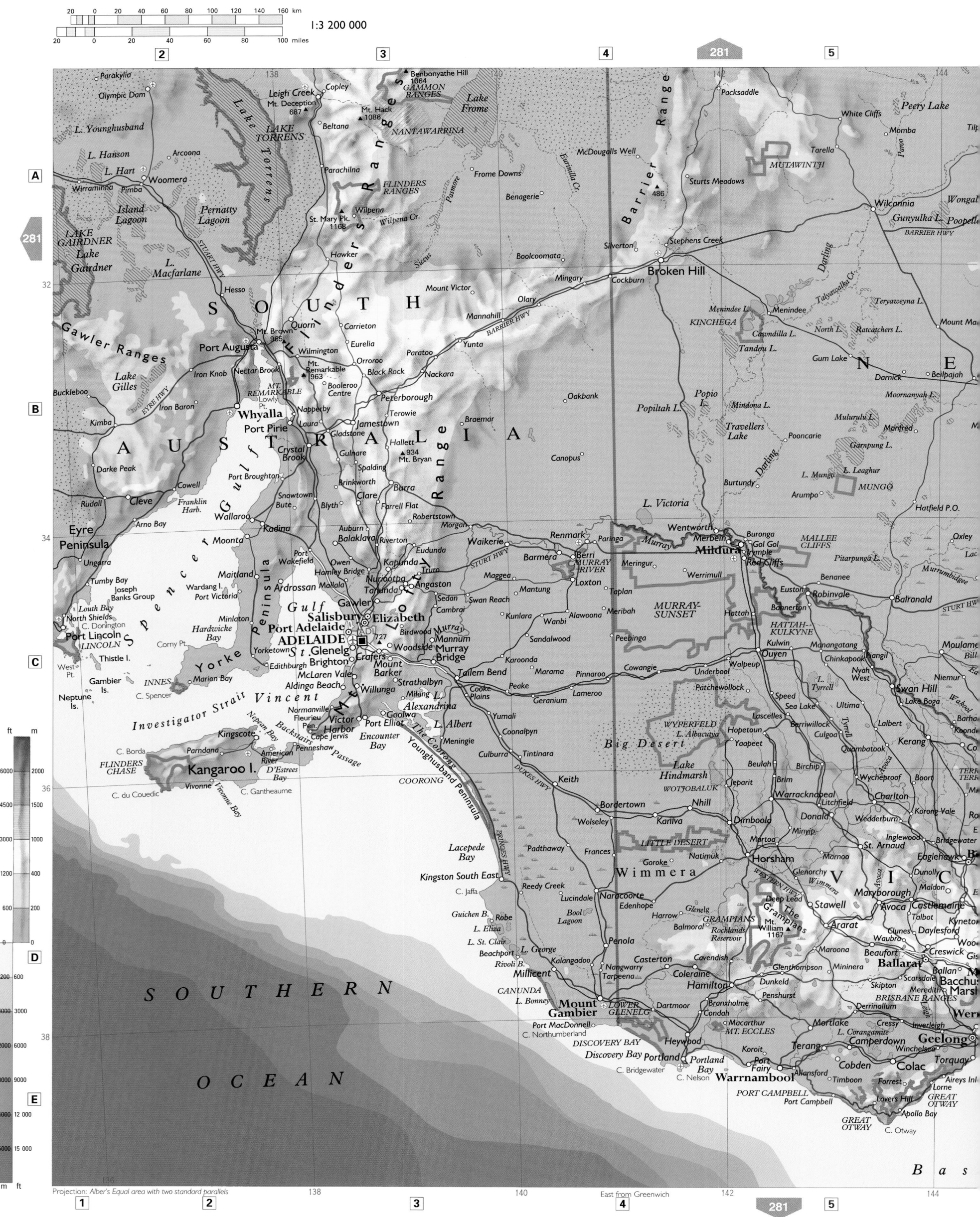

1:3 200 000

Projection: Alber's Equal area with two standard parallels

East from Greenwich

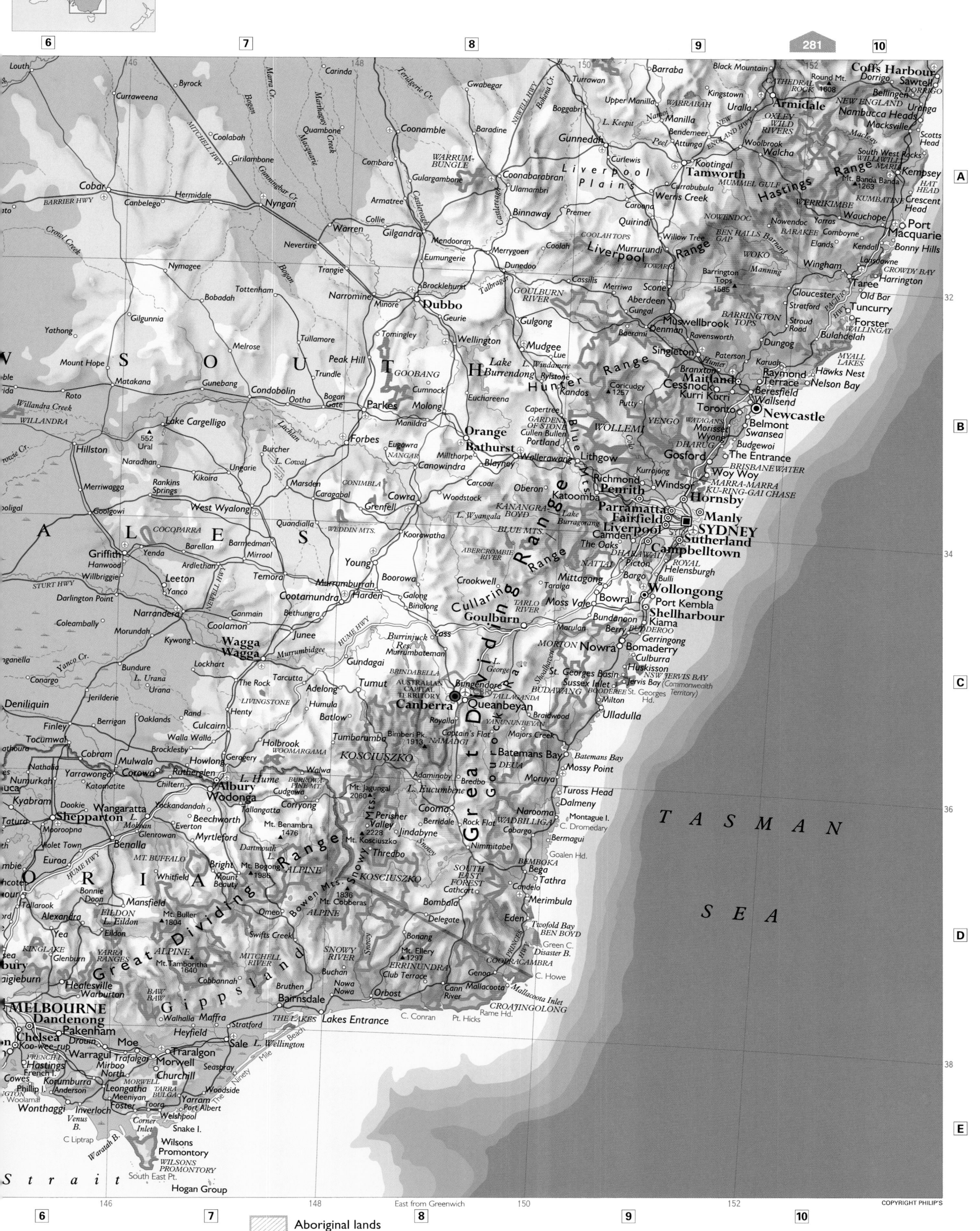

Aboriginal lands

1:2 800 000

10 0 20 40 60 80 100 120 140 km
10 0 20 40 60 80 100 miles

1 2 3 4 5 6 7 8

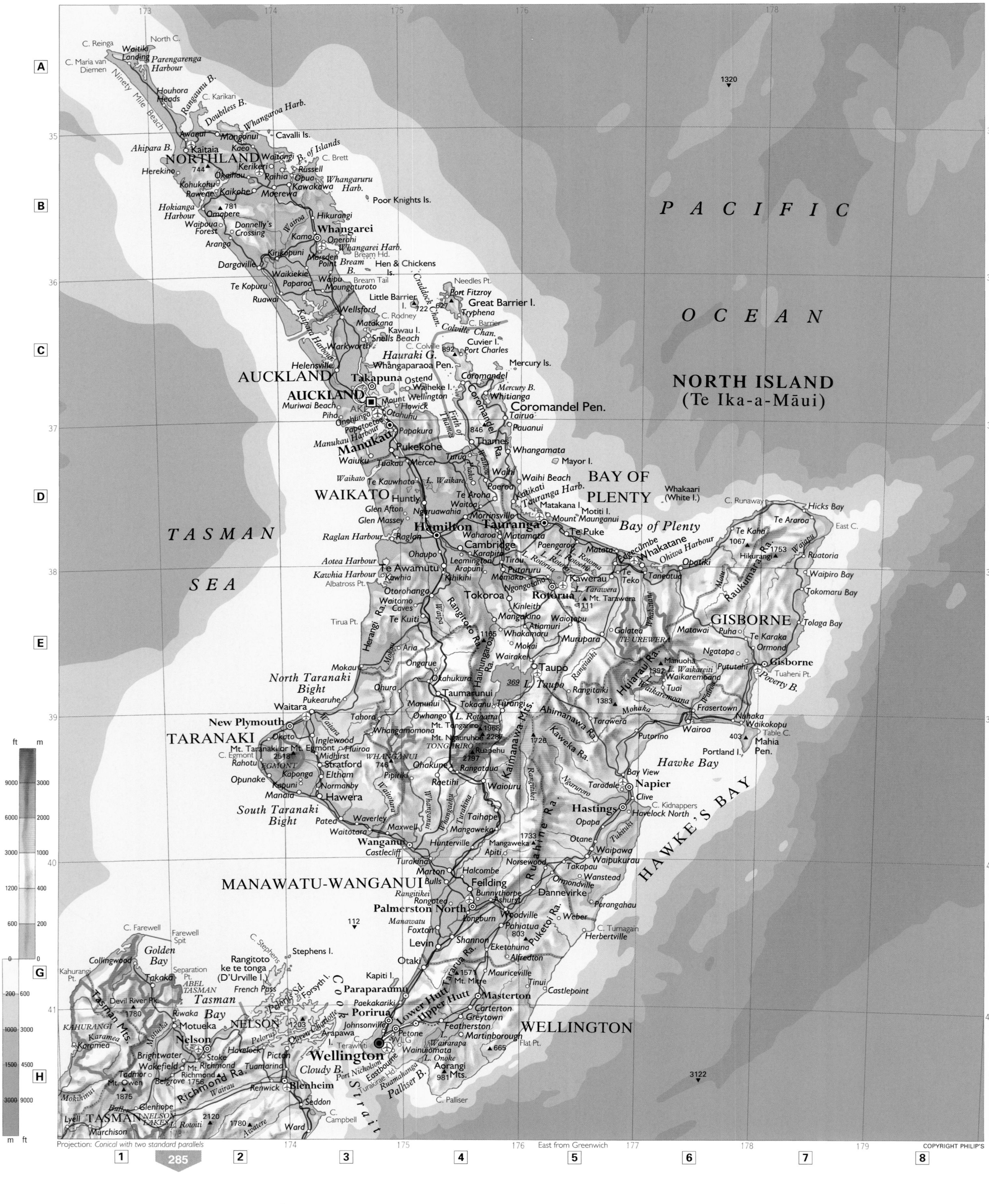

P A C I F I C

O C E A N

NORTH ISLAND
(Te Ika-a-Māui)

C. Reinga
Waitiki Landing
North C.
C. Maria van Diemen
Houhora Heads
Parengarenga Harbour
Rangaunu B.
Doubtless B.
Whangaroa Harb.
Awanui
Mangonui
Cavalli Is.
Ahipara B.
Kaitaia
Kaeo
Waitangi
B. of Islands
C. Karikari
NORTHLAND
Herekino
744
Okaihau
Kerikeri
Russell
C. Brett
Kohukohu
Raihia
Opua
Kawakawa
Rawene
Kaikohe
Moerewa
Whangaruru Harb.
Poor Knights Is.
Hokianga Harbour
781
Omapere
Hikurangi
Waipoua Forest
Donnelly's Crossing
Kamo
Whangarei
Aranga
Wairoa
Onerahi
Whangarei Harb.
Dargaville
Kirikopuni
Morsden Point
Bream Hd.
Waikiekie
Maungaturoto
Waipu
Bream Tail
Hen & Chickens
Te Kopuru
Paparoa
Bream B.
Ruawai
Needles Pt.
Little Barrier I.
722
627
Port Fitzroy
Great Barrier I.
Wellsford
C. Rodney
Tryphena
Matakana
Kawau I.
C. Barrier
Coville Chan.
Helensville
Snells Beach
Cuvier I.
Warkworth
892
Port Charles
Mercury Is.
AUCKLAND
Takapuna
Whangaparaoa Pen.
Ostend
Waiheke I.
Coromandel
Mercury B.
AUCKLAND
Mount Wellington
Whitianga
Coromandel Pen.
Muriwai Beach
Howick
Tairua
Piho
Otahuhu
Papatoetoe
Pauanui
Manukau
Papakura
846
Thames
Pukekohe
Whangamata
Waiuku
Mercer
Firth of Thames
Tuakau
L. Waikare
Waihi
Mayor I.
Waikato
Te Kauwhata
Waihi Beach
WAIKATO
Huntly
Te Aroha
Katikati
BAY OF PLENTY
Ngaruawahia
Waitoa
Tauranga Harb.
Whakaari
(White I.)
Glen Afton
Morrinsville
Matakana I.
Glen Massey
Motiti I.
Hamilton
Waharoa
Tauranga
Mount Maunganui
Bay of Plenty
C. Runaway
Hicks Bay
Raglan Harbour
Raglan
Cambridge
Matamata
Te Puke
Whakatane
Te Kaha
Te Araroa
1067
1753
East C.
Aotea Harbour
Ohaupo
Karapiro
Paengaroa
Edgecumbe
Ohiwa Harbour
Opotiki
Hikurangi
Ruatoria
Te Awamutu
Tirau
L. Rotorua
Kawerau
Te Teko
Taneatua
Waipiro Bay
Kawhia Harbour
Kihikihi
Arapuni
Putaruru
Tarawera
Tolaga Bay
Albatross Pt.
Otorohanga
Leamington
Ngongotaha
Rotorua
Matawai
GISBORNE
Waitomo Caves
Mangaka
Tokoroa
Mt. Tarawera
Puha
Te Karaka
Ormond
Tirua Pt.
Te Kuiti
Kinleith
1111
Galatea
TE UREWERA
Ngatapa
Gisborne
Mangakino
Atiamuri
Murupara
Manuoha
Pututahi
Aria
Waiotapu
1392
L. Waikareiti
Tuaheni Pt.
Ongarue
Mokai
Wairaki
Waikaremoana
Tuai
Poverty B.
Mokau
Okahukura
369
Wairakei
1383
Taupo
Taupo
North Taranaki Bight
Ohura
Taumarunui
Tokaanu
Turangi
Rangitaiki
Mohaka
Frasertown
Nahaka
New Plymouth
Pukearuhe
Monunui
Owhango
L. Rotoaira
Waikokopu
Waitara
Tahora
Whangamomona
Mt. Tongariro 1968
Putorino
403
Mahia Pen.
TARANAKI
Inglewood
Huiroa
Mt. Ngauruhoe 2287
TONGARIRO
Kaweka Ra.
Portland I.
Mt. Taranaki or Mt. Egmont 2518
Midhirst
WHANGANUI
1728
Mtable C.
C. Egmont
Rahotu
Stratford
746
Ruapehu 2797
Bay View
Hawke Bay
EGMONT
Kaponga
Eltham
Ohakune
Rangataua
Taradale
Napier
Opunake
Kapuni
Pipiriki
Raetihi
Waiouru
Clive
Manaia
Normanby
C. Kidnappers
Hawera
Taihape
Hastings
South Taranaki Bight
Waverley
Mangaweka
1733
Havelock North
Patea
Maxwell
Hunterville
Mangawera
Opapa
Waitotara
Apiti
Otane
Wanganui
Turakina
Waipawa
Castlecliff
Marton
Halcombe
Norsewood
Waipukurau
Bulls
Feilding
Ormondville
Takapau
MANAWATU-WANGANUI
Rongotea
Bunnythorpe
Wanstead
Dannevirke
Rangitikei
Ashurst
Porangahau
Palmerston North
Woodville
112
Longburn
Pahiatua
803
Foxton
Shannon
Eketahuna
Herbertville
Levin
Weber
Mauriceville
C. Turnagain
Otaki
157
Mt. Mitre
Tinui
Kapiti I.
Paraparaumu
Masterton
Castlepoint
Paekakariki
Carterton
Porirua
Lower Hutt
Greytown
Upper Hutt
Featherston
Martinborough
WELLINGTON
Petone
L. Onoke
Wainuiomata
L. Wairarapa
665
Flat Pt.
Wellington
Port Nicholson
Palliser B.
C. Palliser
3122

T A S M A N

S E A

WAIKATO (region names)

Golden Bay
C. Farewell
Farewell Spit
Collingwood
Separation Pt.
Stephens I.
Kahurangi Pt.
Takaka
French Pass
ABEL TASMAN
Rangitoto ke te tonga (D'Urville I.)
Forsyth I.
Devil River Pk.
1780
Tasman Bay
Riwaka
Queen Charlotte
Arapawa
Cook
Nelson
Pelorus Sd.
Picton
KAHURANGI MTS.
Motueka
1203
NELSON
Brightwater
Stoke
Havelock
Tuamarina
Karamea
Wakefield
Mt. Richmond 1756
Cloudy B.
Koromea
Tadmor
Belgrove
Renwick
Mt. Owen 1875
Blenheim
Seddon
Richmond Ra.
Wairau
Glenhope
Lyell
TASMAN
2120
1780
Ward
Murchison
Mokihinui
Buller
Aorangi 981 Mts.

Cook
Strait

ft m
9000 3000
6000 2000
3000 1000
1200 400
600 200
0 0
200 600
1000 3000
1500 4500
3000 9000
m ft

1:2 800 000

10   0   20   40   60   80   100   120   140 km
10   0   20   40   60   80   100 miles

284

TASMAN SEA

SOUTH ISLAND
(Te Waipounamu)

C. Farewell
Farewell Spit
Golden Bay
Collingwood
Kahurangi Pt.
Takaka
Separation Pt.
Rangitoto ke te tonga (D'Urville I.)
C. Stephens
Stephens I.
French Pass
ABEL TASMAN
Devil River Pk. 1780
Riwaka
Motueka
Tasman Bay
Pelorus Sd.
Forsyth I.
Jackson
Queen Charlotte Sd.
Arapawa I.
Picton
KAHURANGI
Karamea
Karamea
Mohua
NELSON
Pelorus
Havelock
Tuamarina
Cloudy B.
Kahurangi Pt.
Karamea Bight
Waimarie
Seddonville
Granity
Millerton
Brightwater
Wakefield
Stoke
Belgrove
Mt. Owen 1875
Matiri Ra.
Glenhope
Mt. Richmond 1756
Richmond Ra.
Renwick
Blenheim
Seddon
C. Campbell
Waimangaroa
Westport
Lyell
Buller
Murchison
TASMAN
Tadmor
MARLBOROUGH
Wairau
Ward
Wharanui
C. Foulwind
Buller Gorge
Inangahua
Mt. Travers 2337
St. Arnaud Ra.
Rotoiti 2120
Molesworth
Seaward Kaikoura Ra.
Benmore
PAPAROA
Punakaiki
Paparoa Ra.
Reefton
Grey
Mt. Franklin 2340
NELSON LAKES
Marua
Clarence
Inland Kaikoura Ra. 2885
Tapuae-o-Uenuku
Manakau 2608
Kaikoura
Ikamatua
Blackball
Runanga
Greymouth
Taramakau
L. Brunner
Kaimata
Ahaura
Maruia Springs
Lewis Pass
Hanmer Springs
Mt. Ajax 1834
1615
Waiau
Kaikoura Pen.
Hokitika
Kumara
Jacksons
Otira
ARTHUR'S PASS
Mt. Crossley 1980
L. Sumner
Culverden
Parnassus
Ross
Otira Gorge
Arthur's Pass 926
Mt. Murchison 2408
Puketeraki
Hurunui
Waikari
Waipara
Domett
Sedgill
Wanganui
Abut Hd.
Harihari
Whataroa
2650
Whitcombe Pass
Lake Coleridge
L. Coleridge
Springfield
Sheffield
Ashley
Oxford
Sefton
Rangiora
Pegasus Bay
Okarita
L. Mapourika
Franz Josef Glacier
Fox Glacier
Arrowsmith 2781
Mt. Taylor 2333
South Branch
Whitecliffs
Darfield
Kaiapoi
Belfast
New Brighton
Gillespies Pt.
WESTLAND TAI POUTINI
Bruce B. Mt. Tasman 3497
Aoraki/Mount Cook 3724
Tasman Gl.
Mount Cook
Highbank
Rolleston
Hornby
CHC
Niccarton
Christchurch
Sumner
Lyttelton
Tititira Hd.
Two Thumbs Ra. 2251
Mount Somers
Methven
Lincoln
Ellesmere
Banks Pen.
919
Little River
Jackson
Jackson Hd. B.
Okuru
Haast
Cascade Pt.
Haast Pass
Glenmark
Ben Ohau Ra. 2590
L. Tekapo
Lake Tekapo
Mackenzie Plains
Geraldine
Fairlie
Hinds
Ashburton
Tinwald
Akaroa
Southbridge
L. Ellesmere
Akaroa Harbour
MOUNT ASPINTG
Mt. Aspiring 3033
Barrier Ra.
L. Ohau
Lake Pukaki
Waitaki Plains
Kirkliston Ra. 1894
Benmore Pk.
Temuka
Winchester
Pleasant Point
Timaru
Canterbury Bight
Awarua Pt.
Awarua B.
Yates Pt.
McKerrow
Mt. Tutoko 2723
Darran Mts.
Olivine Ra.
Young Ra.
Hunter Ra.
The Hunter Ra.
St. Andrews
Hunter
Studholme
Waimate
Milford Sd.
Mitre Peak 1683
Milford Sound
Sutherland Falls
Mt. Earnslaw 2819
Richardson Mts.
Hawea Flat
L. Hawea
Mt. St. Bathan's 2087
Hakataramea
Waihao
Morven
Bligh Sound
George Sound
Humboldt Mts.
Glenorchy
Harris Mts.
Wanaka 1936
Pisa Ra.
L. Aviemore
Waitaki
Kurow
Duntroon
Ngapara
Glenavy
Caswell Sound
Charles Sound
Stuart Mts.
1810
L. Te Anau
Queenstown
Arrowtown
2319
Cromwell
Dunstan Mts.
St. Bathans
Hawkdun Ra.
Kakanui Mts.
Windsor
Pukeuri
Thompson Sd.
Secretary I.
Murchison Mts.
2022
Jane Pk. 1892
Eyre Mts.
The Remarkables
Kingston
Double Cone
Clyde
Rough Ridge
Naseby
Ranfurly
Maheno
Oamaru
Doubtful Sd.
Kepler Mts.
Te Anau
Athol
Alexandra
Roxburgh
Middlemarch
Hyde
Dunback
Hampden
Dagg Sd.
FIORDLAND
L. Manapouri
Garvie Mts.
Miller's Flat
Sutton
Waikouaiti Downs
Shag Pt.
Palmerston
Breaksea Sd.
Resolution I.
Manapouri
Heath Mts.
Cameron Mts.
Hunter Mts.
Mossburn
Lumsden
Waikaia
Edievale
Beaumont
Waikouaiti
Port Chalmers
Otago Harbour
Dusky Sd.
Monowai
Birchwood
Dipton
Waipahi
Clinton
Lawrence
Kelso
Tapanui
Warrington
Otago Pen.
Dunedin
Mosgiel
St. Saunders
C.
Providence
Chalky Inlet
Coal
L. Hauroko 1704
Caroline Pk. 4
1765
Monowai
Ohai
Nightcaps
Riversdale
L. Mahinerangi
Waikaka
L. Waihola
Allanton
Waihola
Taieri
St. Kilda
Preservation Inlet
Puysegur Pt.
Orawia
Otautau
Wairio
Tuatapere
Waikawa
Winton
Gore
Mataura
Waipahi
Stirling
Milton
Te Waewae B.
Pahia Pt.
Orepuki
Thornbury
Makarewa
Hedgehope
Edendale
Wyndham
Balclutha
Kaitangata
Centre I.
Wallacetown
Riverton
Gleham
Invercargill
South Invercargill
Fortrose
Catlins
Tahakopa
Owaka
Nugget Pt.
Solander I.
Bluff
Bluff Harbour
Toetoes B.
Waipapa Pt.
Long Pt.
Chaslands Mistake
Codfish I.
Mt. Anglem 980
Ruapuke I.
Foveaux Str.
Mason B.
Halfmoon Bay
Paterson Inlet
PACIFIC
Doughboy B.
RAKIURA
Stewart I. (Rakiura)
Port Pegasus
South West C.
OCEAN

4870

41   167   168   169   170   171   172   173   174
A   B   C   D   E

CHATHAM ISLANDS
on same scale

PACIFIC OCEAN

The Sisters
C. Young
Munning Pt.
Western Reef
Te One
Waitangi
Chatham I. (Rekohu)
The Forty Fours
Owenga
C. Fournier
Mangere
Pitt I.
Star Keys
The Horns
Pitt Strait
The Pyramid
Rangitira I.

Chatham Islands
(Wharekauri)

178   177   176
43   44   45

ft   m
9000   3000
6000   2000
3000   1000
1200   400
600   200
0   0
200   600
1000   3000
1500   4500
3000   9000
4000   12 000
m   ft

Projection: Conical with two standard parallels

West from Greenwich   East from Greenwich

50 0 50 100 150 200 km

1:5 200 000

50 0 50 100 150 miles

287

East from Greenwich

Projection: Lambert Conformal Conic

PACIFIC OCEAN

Solomon Islands

BOUGAINVILLE

NEW IRELAND

Bismarck Archipelago

St. Matthias Group

New Hanover Group

Admiralty Islands

MANUS

Bismarck Sea

NEW BRITAIN

EAST NEW BRITAIN

WEST NEW BRITAIN

Solomon Sea

MILNE BAY

Louisiade Archipelago

D'Entrecasteaux Islands

Trobriand Islands

NORTHERN

CENTRAL

Owen Stanley Range

Port Moresby

MOROBE

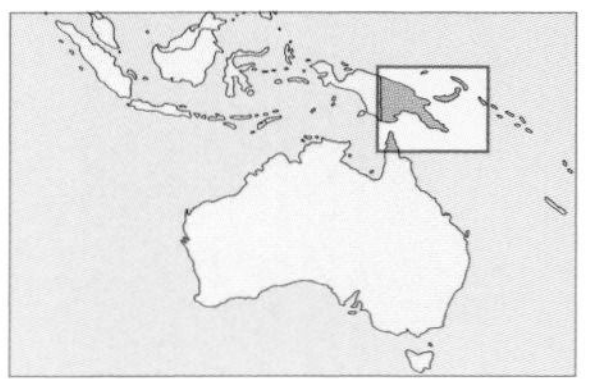

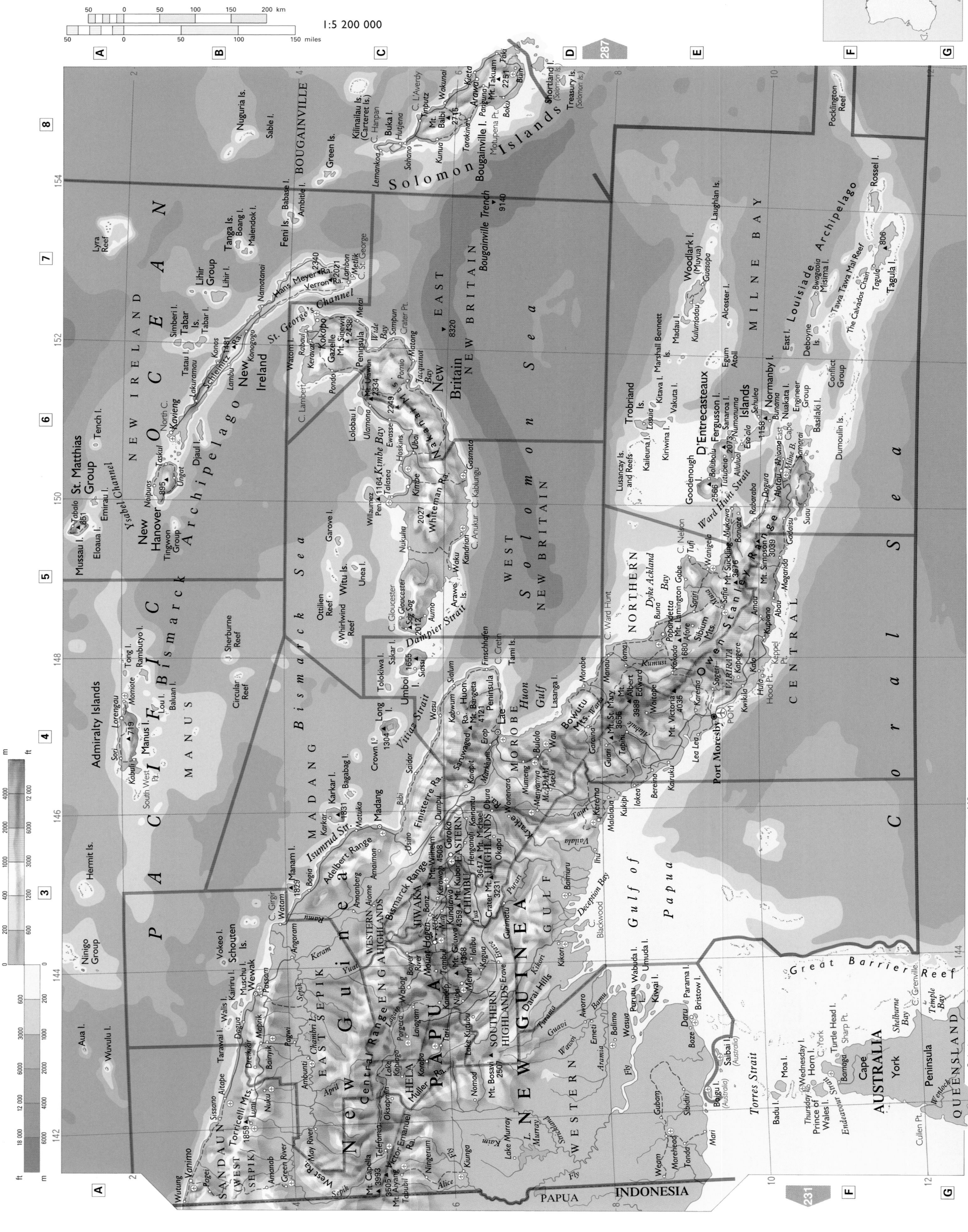

MADANG

Huon Peninsula

Huon Gulf

EASTERN HIGHLANDS

WESTERN HIGHLANDS

ENGA

CHIMBU

SOUTHERN HIGHLANDS

HELA

Bismarck Range

Central Range

EAST SEPIK

WEST SEPIK (SANDAUN)

Torricelli Mts.

NEW GUINEA

PAPUA

WESTERN

Gulf of Papua

Coral Sea

Great Barrier Reef

Torres Strait

AUSTRALIA

Cape York Peninsula

QUEENSLAND

INDONESIA

PAPUA

231

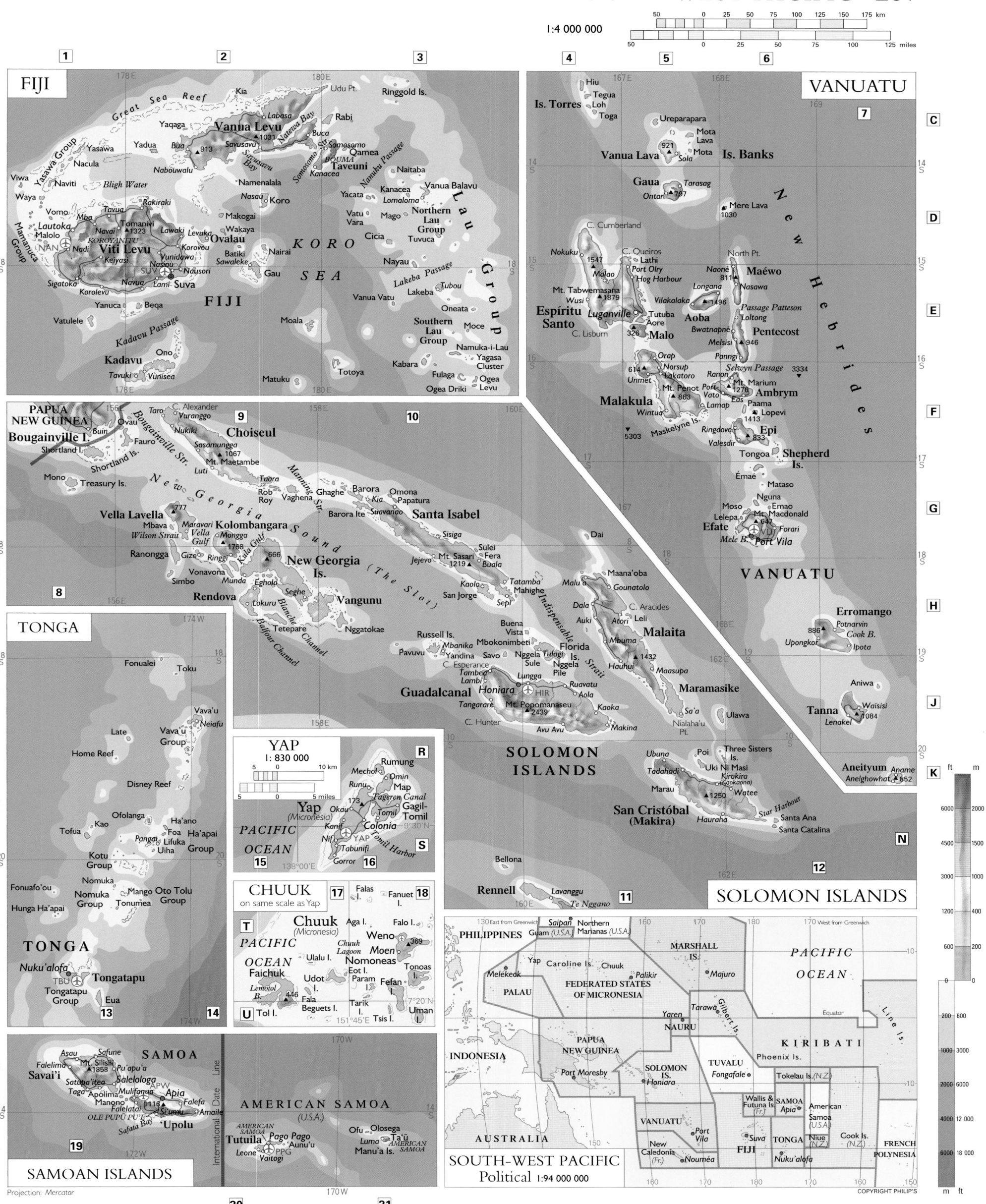

FIJI

1:4 000 000

VANUATU

Great Sea Reef
Kia
Udu Pt.
Ringgold Is.
Yaqaga
Labasa
Rabi
Vanua Levu ▲1031
Natewa Bay
Buca
Savusavu
Somosomo Str.
Yasawa Group
Yasawa
Yadua
Bua ▲913
Somosomo
Qamea
Taveuni
Nacula
Nabouwalu
BOUMA
Navai
Naitaba
Viwa
Naviti
Bligh Water
Rakiraki
Namenalala
Nasau
Kanacea
Vanua Balavu
Waya
Vomo
Tavua
Makogai
Koro
Yacata
Lomaloma
Vomo
Mba
KOROYANITU ▲1323
Lawaki
Levuka
Wakaya
Vatu
Vara
Mago
Northern Lau Group
Malolo
Lautoka
Navai ▲1323
Korovou
Ovalau
Cicia
NAN
Nadi
Viti Levu
Yunidawa
Nairai
Tuvuca
Mamanuca Group
Keiyasi
Nasinu
Nausori
KORO SEA
Nayau
Lakeba Passage
Vatulele
Sigatoka
Korolevu
Navua
Lami
Suva
SUV
Gau
Vanua Vatu
Lakeba
Tubou
Beqa
FIJI
Moala
Southern Lau Group
Oneata
Moce
Yanuca
Kadavu Passage
Ono
Namuka-i-Lau
Yagasa Cluster
Kadavu
Tavuki
Vunisea
Matuku
Totoya
Fulaga
Ogea Levu
Ogea Driki

PAPUA NEW GUINEA
Bougainville I.
Buin
Buka
Ovau
Taro
C. Alexander
Vuranggo
Nukiki
Choiseul
Shortland I.
Fauro
Shortland Is.
Sasamungga ▲1067
Luti
Mt. Maetambe
Mono
Treasury Is.
New Georgia Sound (The Slot)
Taara
Rob Roy
Ghaghe
Barora
Omona
Papatura
Vaghena
Kia
Barora Ite
Suavanao
Santa Isabel
Vella Lavella ▲777
Mbava
Maravari
Vella Gulf
Kolombangara
Mongga ▲1768
Sisiga
Vonavona
Simbo
Gizo
Ringgi
Kula Gulf
New Georgia Is. ▲666
Jejevo
Mt. Sasari ▲1219
Fera
Buala
Ranongga
Munda
Egholo
Kaola
Sulei
Rendova
Lokuru
Seghe
Vangunu
San Jorge
Sepi
Tetepare
Blanche Channel
Nggatokae
Russell Is.
Tatamba
Mahighe
Balfour Channel
Pavuvu
Mbanika
Mbokonimbeti
Ngella
Tulagi
Buena Vista
C. Esperance
Yandina
Savo
Sule
Ngella Pile
Tambea
Lambi
Lungga
Honiara
HIR
Guadalcanal
Tangarare
Mt. Popomanaseu ▲2439
Aola
Ruavatu
Kaoka
C. Hunter
Avu Avu
Makina

SOLOMON ISLANDS

Is. Torres
Hiu
Tegua
Loh
Toga
Ureparapara
Vanua Lava
Mota Lava ▲921
Mota
Is. Banks
Gaua
Ontar ▲787
Tarasag
Mere Lava ▲1030
C. Cumberland
C. Queiros
Lathi
North Pt.
Nokuku ▲1547
Port Olry
Hog Harbour
Naoné ▲811
Maéwo
Malao
Mt. Tabwemasana ▲1879
Wusi
Vilakalaka
Longana
Nasawa
Espíritu Santo
Luganville
Tutuba
Aoba
Aore
▲1496
Passage Patteson
Loltong
Malo ▲326
C. Lisburn
Bwatnapné
Pentecost
Melsisi ▲946
Panngi
Orap
Norsup ▲614
Lakatoro
Selwyn Passage
Ranon ▲3334
Unmet
Mt. Marium
Malakula
Mt. Penot ▲863
Port Vato ▲1270
Lamap
Eas
Ambrym
Wintua
Lopevi ▲1270
Paama
Maskelyne Is.
▲5303
Valesdir ▲833
Epi
Tongoa
Shepherd Is.
Émaé
Mataso
Nguna
Moso
Emao
Lelepa
Mt. Macdonald ▲647
Efate
VLI
Forari
Mele B.
Port Vila
VANUATU
Erromango
Potnarvin ▲886
Cook B.
Upongkor
Ipota
Aniwa
Tanna
Waïsisi ▲1084
Lenakel
Aneityum
Anelghowhat ▲852
Aname

TONGA
Fonualei
Toku
Vava'u
Neiafu
Late
Vava'u Group
Home Reef
Disney Reef
Tofua
Kao
Ofolanga
Ha'ano
Foa
Ha'apai
Pangai
Lifuka
Ha'apai Group
Kotu Group
Uiha
Fonuafo'ou
Nomuka
Mango
Oto Tolu Group
Nomuka Group
Tonumea
Hunga Ha'apai
TONGA
Nuku'alofa
TBU
Tongatapu
Eua
Tongatapu Group

YAP
1:830 000
Rumung
Mechol
Runu
Omin
Map
Tageren Canal
Gagil-Tomil
Yap (Micronesia)
Okau
Tomil
Kanif
Colonia
Nif
YAP
Tabunifi
Tomil Harbor
Gorror
PACIFIC OCEAN

CHUUK
on same scale as Yap
Falas
Fanuet
Chuuk (Micronesia)
Aga I.
Falo I.
Weno ▲369
Chuuk Lagoon
Moen
Nomoneas
Faichuk
Ulalu I.
Tonoas
Lemiol B.
Udot
Eot I.
Param
Fefan
Tol I. ▲446
Fala
Tarik I.
Beguets I.
Uman I.
Tsis I.
PACIFIC OCEAN

SAMOA
Asau
Safune
Falelima
Mt. Silisili ▲1858
Pu'apu'a
Savai'i
Satupa'itea
Saleloga
Taga
Apolima
Mulifanua
Apia
APW
Manono
Falelatai ▲1116
Falefa
OLE PUPU PUE
Upolu
SFU
Amaile
AMERICAN SAMOA
(U.S.A.)
Tutuila
AMERICAN SAMOA
Ofu
Olosega
Pago Pago
Aunu'u
Luma
Ta'u
Leone
Vaitogi
PPG
Manu'a Is.
SAMOAN ISLANDS

SOUTH-WEST PACIFIC
Political 1:94 000 000
PHILIPPINES
Saipan
Northern Marianas (U.S.A.)
Guam (U.S.A.)
MARSHALL IS.
Yap
Caroline Is.
Chuuk
Palikir
Melekeok
Majuro
PALAU
FEDERATED STATES OF MICRONESIA
Yaren
Tarawa
Gilbert Is.
NAURU
INDONESIA
PAPUA NEW GUINEA
Port Moresby
SOLOMON IS.
Honiara
KIRIBATI
Phoenix Is.
TUVALU
Fongafale
Tokelau Is. (N.Z.)
Line Is.
VANUATU
Port Vila
Wallis & Futuna (Fr.)
SAMOA
Apia
American Samoa (U.S.A.)
New Caledonia (Fr.)
Nouméa
FIJI
Suva
TONGA
Nuku'alofa
Niue (N.Z.)
Cook Is. (N.Z.)
FRENCH POLYNESIA
AUSTRALIA
PACIFIC OCEAN

Projection: Mercator

COPYRIGHT PHILIP'S

Equatorial Scale 1:43 200 000

OKINAWA
on same scale as Palau

a

Hedo-misaki · Hedo
Kunigami
Ie-shima · Kouri-shima · Yagaji-shima
Seseko-shima · Nakijin · 503 · Yonaha-Dake
Okinawa *(Japan)*
Minna-shima · Motobu
Arume-wan
EAST CHINA SEA
Nago-wan · **Nago**
Banno-saki
Ishikawa
Kadena · Kin-wan · Ikei-shima
Uruma
Henna · Heanza-shima
Okinawa
(Koza) · Takabanare-shima
Ginowan · Tsuken-jima
Urasoe · Nakagusuku-wan
Naha · Kudaka-shima
OKA · Shuri
Rukan-sho · Gushikami
Kyan-zaki · Itoman
128° E
26° 30′ N
24° N
PACIFIC OCEAN

IWO-JIMA
(Japan)
b
Kangoku Iwa · Kitano Hana
COAST GUARD STATION
Iwo-Jima *(Japan)* · ▲108 · Hanare Iwa
Kama Iwa
IWO JIMA AIRFIELD
Suribachi Yama 167 ▲
Fatatsu Ne
Tobiishi Hana
141° 20′ E
45′
PACIFIC OCEAN

IWO-JIMA 1:200 000
3 2 1 0 1 2 3 km
1 0 1 2 m

PALAU **c**
1:1 550 000

Ngaregur · Konrei
Ngardmau Bay
Ngardmau · 218
Babelthuap I.
Namai Bay · Melekeok
Komebail Lagoon · **Koror** · ROR · Garusuun
Malakal Harbor · Koror I. · Garreru
Aulong · Ngobasangel · Urukthapel I.
Apurashokoru · Eil Malk I. *(Mecherchar)*
Orukuizui · Shonian Harbor · Ngeregong
Barnum Bay · Ngergoi
Ngesebus · Kongauru I. · Ngardololok
· Ngardolok
Peleliu I.
Angaur I.
134° 30′ E
7° N
PACIFIC OCEAN

1:1 550 000
10 0 10 20 30 km
10 0 10 20 miles

NEW CALEDONIA
1:5 750 000
d
Îles Belep
Récif du Grand
Récif de l'Astrolabe
Île Art · Île Balabio
Poum
Quégéa · Pouébo · Mt. Panié 1628 · C. Escarpé · 7570
Koumac · Ouégoa · Hienghène
Kaala-Gomén · Voh · 3566 · Poindimié · Île Ouvéa
Koné · Ponérihouen · Fayaoué
Houailou · Chépénéhé · Wé
Nouvelle- · La Foa · Île Lifou
Calédonie · 1618 · Mou · Île Tiga
(France) · Boulouparis · C. de Flotte · La Roche
Paita · 1618 · Bourail · Tadine · Île Maré
Dumbéa · Yaté · Mont Dore
GEA · **Nouméa** · Ndoua · Île des Pins
Grand Récif Sud
CORAL SEA
20° S
22° S
164° E · 165° E · 166° E · 167° E · 168° E

NEW CALEDONIA 1:5 750 000
50 0 50 100 km
50 0 50 miles

RUSSIA
Okhotsk
Sea of Okhotsk
Poluostrov Kamchatka
Komandorskiye Ostrova *(Russia)*
Near Is.
Aleutian Basin
Be S.
Irkutsk · Chita
Oz. Baykal · Lena · Amur
Blagoveshchensk
Khabarovsk
Sakhalin
Petropavlovsk-Kamchatskiy
Andrea
Ulaanbaatar
MONGOLIA
La Pérouse Str.
Kuril'skiye Ostrova *(Russia)*
Kuril-Kamchatka Trench
7822
Aleutian Trench
Aleuti
Chinook
Ürümqi
Harbin
Changchun
Sapporo
Hokkaidō
Hakodate
Emperor Seamount Chain
CHINA
Beijing · Shenyang
Vladivostok
Sea of Japan
Northwest
Taiyuan · **Tianjin**
NORTH KOREA
Dalian · **Seoul**
Honshū
Shatsky Rise
Lanzhou
Huang He
Qingdao · SOUTH KOREA · **Nagoya** · Fuji-San 3776 · **Tokyo**
Pacific
Tamu Massif 1980
Xi'an · **Nanjing** · Yellow Sea · **Kyōto** · **Yokohama**
Kitakyūshū · **Osaka** · **JAPAN**
Midway Is. *(U.S.A.)*
Kunlun Shan · **Chengdu** · **Wuhan**
Shikoku · **Kyūshū**
10,554
Japan Trench
XIZANG
Chongqing · **Shanghai**
Lhasa · Chang J. · **Hangzhou**
East China Sea
Okinawa
Iwo-Jima *(Japan)*
Ogasawara Gunto *(Japan)*
Lisianski I. *(U.S.A.)*
Changsha
Brahmaputra
Kunming
Fuzhou
Ryūkyū-rettō *(Japan)*
Kazan-Rettō *(Japan)*
Minami-Tori-Shima *(Japan)*
Basin
Dhaka
Guangzhou
Taipei
TAIWAN
Philippine Sea
Kyushu-Palau Ridge
Shizoku-Ozima Ridge
Mid
Pacific
Steam
Mandalay
Hong Kong · Macau
C. Engano
West Mariana Basin
NORTHERN MARIANAS *(U.S.A.)*
East Mariana Basin
Wake I. *(U.S.A.)*
BURMA · LAOS · **Hanoi**
Hainan
Luzon
Philippine Basin
Tinian · Saipan
MARSHALL IS.
Yangôn · **THAILAND**
Paracel Is. · **Manila**
GUAM *(U.S.A.)*
Bikini Atoll
Bangkok
VIETNAM · CAMBODIA
South China Sea
Mindoro · **PHILIPPINES**
Challenger 11,022 Deep
Mariana Trench
Enewetak Atoll · Kwajalein
Phnom Penh
G. of Thailand
Palawan · Samar · 10,497
Yap
Caroline Is. · **Micrones**
Chuuk
Majuro
Thanh Pho Ho Chi Minh
Sulu Sea · Mindanao
Davao
Melekeok
PALAU
FED. STATES OF MICRONESIA
Pohnpei · Palikir
East Caroline Basin
Jaluit I.
SRI LANKA
Nicobar Is. *(India)*
MALAYSIA · Sea · 4101
Celebes Sea
West Caroline Basin
Eauripik Rise
Me · Solomon Rise · Melanesian Basin
Butaritari · Tarawa
Gilbert Is.
Paci
Colombo
Kuala Lumpur
PEN. MALAYSIA · BRUNEI · SABAH
SARAWAK
Halmahera
Seram
Puncak Jaya 4884 · PAPUA
PAPUA NEW GUINEA
Admiralty Is. · Bismarck Arch.
New Ireland
Banaba
Yaren · NAURU
Phoenix Is. · Abariri · Enderb
Singapore
Borneo
Sumatera
Palembang
INDONESIA
Sulawesi · Buru
Maluku
Banda Sea · 7440
New Guinea · 8940 · Kokopo
New Britain
Bougainville
SOLOMON IS.
Fongafale · **TUVALU**
Toke
KI
Jawa · **Jakarta**
Java Sea · Flores Sea
Makassar
Flores
Dili · EAST TIMOR
Arafura Sea
Lae · Port Moresby
Honiara · Guadalcanal
Santa Cruz Is. 9165
Sunda Islands · Sunda Trench *(Java Trench)* · Bali · Sumbawa · Sumba
Torres Strait · C. York
Louisiade Arch.
Rotuma
Is. Wallis & Futuna *(Fr.)*
SAM
At
Ninety east Ridge
Christmas I. *(Austral.)*
North Australian Basin
C. Arnhem
Coral Sea Basin
VANUATU
Espíritu Santo
Vanua Levu · **FIJI**
Cocos Is. *(Austral.)*
Darwin
Gulf of Carpentaria
Coral Sea
Port Vila
West Fiji Basin
Viti Levu · Suva
Nuku'alofa · T
INDIAN
Exmouth Plateau
Broome
Cairns
Îs. Chesterfield
7570 · East Fiji Basin
NEW CALEDONIA *(Fr.)*
Townsville
Mount Isa
Is. Loyauté · **Nouméa**
10,822
Wharton Basin
North West C.
AUSTRALIA
Alice Springs
Great Dividing Ra.
Rockhampton
OCEAN
Brisbane
Middleton Basin
Lord Howe Rise
South Fiji Basin
Kermadec Is. *(N.Z.)*
Broken Ridge
Geraldton
Perth Basin
Kati Thanda-L. Eyre
Darling
Lord Howe I. *(Austral.)*
Norfolk I. *(Austral.)*
10,047
Perth
Naturaliste Plateau
Great Australian Bight
Sydney
Murray · Mt. Kosciuszko 2228
Norfolk Ridge
New Caledonia Trough
New Caledonia Ridge
NEW ZEALAND
Albany
Adelaide
Canberra
Bass Str.
Melbourne
Tasman Sea
Auckland
South Australian Basin
Tasmania
Aoraki Mt. Cook 3724
Cook Strait
Wellington
Hobart
East Tasman Plateau
Chatham Rise
Christchurch · Chath
South Tasman Rise
Dunedin
Bounty Trough
Bounty Is. *(N.Z.)*
Invercargill
Antipodes Is. *(N.Z.)*
Campbell Rise
SOUTHERN OCEAN
Auckland Is. *(Austral.)*
Campbell I. *(Austral.)*
Macquarie I. *(Austral.)*
Campbell Plateau

Projection: Mollweide's Homolographic · East from Greenwich

Arctic Circle
12 150 13 140 14 130 15 16 120 17 110

ALASKA
Anchorage
3959
Gulf of Alaska
Bristol Bay (U.S.A.)
Juneau
Prince of Wales I. (U.S.A.)
Haida Gwaii (Queen Charlotte Is.) (Canada)
Prince Rupert
CANADA
ROCKY MTS
Edmonton
Calgary
B
Vancouver
Vancouver I.
Victoria
Seattle
Portland
Boise
Snake
Tufts Abyssal Plain
Mendocino Fracture Zone C. Mendocino
Sacramento
San Francisco
6741
Murray Fracture Zone
4418
Salt Lake City
Denver
Colorado
C
UNITED STATES
Oklahoma City
Memphis
Atlanta
D
Los Angeles
San Diego
Phoenix
Dallas
Mississippi
Jacksonville
Guadalupe (Mex.)
Molokai Fracture Zone
Baja California
Ciudad Juárez
Houston
San Antonio
New Orleans
Pacific
Tropic of Cancer
Basin
C. San Lucas
Sigsbee Deep 3504
Gulf of Mexico
Monterrey
Miami
BAHAMAS
E
Honolulu
O'ahu 4205
HAWAI'I (U.S.A.)
Hawai'i
Clarion Fracture Zone
Is. de Revillagigedo (Mex.)
Guadalajara
Mexico 5610
Puebla
La Habana
Canal de Yucatán
Florida Str.
CUBA
HAITI
Kingston
JAMAICA
Acapulco
Mérida
7680
GUATEMALA
BELIZE
Caribbean Sea
F
Middle America Trench
Guatemala
San Salvador
EL SALVADOR
HONDURAS
NICARAGUA
Managua
Guatemala Basin
Barranquilla
San José
Î. Clipperton (Fr.)
Clipperton Fracture Zone
COSTA RICA
PANAMA
Colón
Panamá
Medellín
G
I. del Coco (Costa Rica)
Coco Ridge
Panama Basin
Cali
COLOMBIA
Equator
Galápagos Fracture Zone
Galápagos (Ecuador)
Carnegie Ridge
I. de Malpelo (Colombia)
Quito
ECUADOR
East Pacific Rise
Guayaquil
C. Pariñas
PERU
6369
Trujillo
Lima
Cusco
L. Titicaca 6550
Nevado Ancohuma
Arequipa
6866
Peru–Chile Trench
Peru
Arica
La Paz
BOLIVIA
Iquique
Chile
PARAGUAY
Asunción
Antofagasta
8064
Nazca Ridge
San Félix (Chile)
San Ambrosio (Chile)
San Miguel de Tucumán
Chile Basin
Tropic of Capricorn
Sala-y-Gómez Ridge
Sala-y-Gómez (Chile)
I. de Pascua (Chile)
Easter Fracture Zone
Córdoba
Rosario
URUGUAY
Oeno I.
Henderson I.
Ducie I.
Pitcairn I. (U.K.)
Chile Rise
Aconcagua 6962
Valparaíso
Santiago
Buenos Aires
Montevideo
Río de la Plata
Rapa
Challenger Fracture Zone
Menard Fracture Zone
Concepción
ARGENTINA
Argentine Basin
Nemo Point (furthest point from any land)
114
Falkland Plateau
ATLANTIC OCEAN
Southeast Pacific Basin
Punta Arenas
Est. de Magallanes
C. de Hornos
Tierra del Fuego
Drake Passage
4402
Falkland Is. (U.K.)
South Georgia Ridge
Georgia Basin
South Georgia (U.K.)
6212

Pacific Antarctic Ridge

160 11 150 12 140 13 130 14 120 15 110 16 100 17 90 18 80 19 70 20 60 West from Greenwich 40
COPYRIGHT PHILIP'S

PACIFIC OCEAN

Palmyra I. (U.S.A.)
Teraina
Tabuaeran
Kiritimati
Cooper Ridge
Line Islands Ridge
International Date Line
Jarvis I. (U.S.A.)
KIRIBATI
Malden I.
Starbuck I.
Penrhyn (Tongareva)
Manihiki
Pukapuka
Manihiki Plateau
Caroline I. (Millennium I.)
Vostok I.
Flint I.
Nuku-Hiva
Îs. Marquises
Hiva Oa
Marquesas Fracture Zone
Suwarrow Is.
Îs. de la Société
Bora Bora
Huahine
Raiatea
Papeete
Tahiti
Îs. Tuamotu
Rangiroa
Tuamotu Ridge
Aitutaki
Atiu
Cook Is. (N.Z.)
Rarotonga
Mangaia
FRENCH POLYNESIA
Austral/Seamount Chain
Îs. Gambier
Mururoa
Îs. Tubuaï

TAHITI
e
Pte. Aroa B. de Matavai
Pte. Vénus
Mahina
Pabetooi
MOZ
Mt. Tohiea 1207
Popoo
Papeete
Arue
Pirae
Papenoo
Tiarei
17°30'S
Haapiti
Afareaitu
PPT
Faaa
Pte. Nuupere
Mt. Aorai 2060
Mt. Orohena 2241
Faaone
Tahiti (France)
Hitiaa
Moorea
Mt. Tetufera 1798
Faaone
Lac Vaihiria
Punaauia
Paea
Isthme de Taravao Pte.
Afaahiti
Maraa
Papara
Atimaono
Mataiea
Taravao
Tatutua
Pueu
Vairao
Tautira
PACIFIC OCEAN
17°45'S
Mt. Roonui 1332
Teahupoo
Presqu'île de Taiarapu
149°30'W 149°15'W

1:1 150 000
10 0 10 km
10 0 10 miles

FRENCH POLYNESIA
1:26 000 000
f
200 0 200 400 km
200 0 200 400 miles
Hatutu
Eiao
Îles Marquises
Nuku Hiva
Ua Huka
Ua Pu
Hiva Oa
Tahuata
Motané
4884
6513
Flint I. (Kiribati)
Îles
Îles du Roi-Georges
Tikahau
Ahé
Manihi
Rangiroa
Tikéi
Îles du Désappointement
Puka Puka
Îles Sous-le-Vent
Matahiva
Apataki
Kauehi
Takume
Fangatau
Tatakoto
Bora Bora
Îles du Vent
Maupiti
Huahine
Raiatea
Fakarava
Raraka
Makemo
Tekokota
Maupihaa
Tahiti
Anaa
Le Raeuki
Hiti
Marokau
Amanu
Puka Ruha
Moorea
Papeete
Méhétia
Hiti
Haraiki
Nengonengo
Ravahere
Paraoa
Vahitahi
Réao
Îles de la Société
Héréhérétué
4616
Ahunui
Vanavana
Vairaatea
Turéia
Groupe Actéon
Îles Maria
Rimatara
Îles du Duc-de-Gloucester
Tematagi
Mururoa
Fangataufa
Îles Gambier
Morané
Rurutu
Tropic of Capricorn
Raivavae
Récif Portland
Tubuaï
Récif Président-Thiers
Îles Tubuaï (Îles Australes)
Rapa
Récif Neilson
Îlots de Bass
PACIFIC OCEAN

NIUE
1:830 000
g
5 0 10 km
3 0 5 miles
Hikutavake
Mutalau
Namukulu
Toi
Tuapa
Makefu
Lakepa
Alofi Bay
Alofi
Liku
Halangingie Pt.
IUE
Fonuakula
Niue (N.Z.)
Avatele
Tamakautoga
Tepa Pt.
Vaiea
Hakupu
PACIFIC OCEAN
170°W

RAROTONGA
1:415 000
h
5 km 0
5 miles 0
Rarotonga (N.Z.)
RAR
Avarua Harbour
Nikao
Avatiu
Avarua
Pue
Matavera
Arorangi
509
Maungaroa
588
653
Te Manga
Ngatangiia
Motu Tapu
222
Te Kou
329
Maungatongalti
Muri
Koromiri
Taakoka
Oneroa
Taroume
Titikaveka
PACIFIC OCEAN
21°15'S 159°45'W

ft m
H
10 12 000 4000
J
9000 3000
6000 2000
20
K
3000 1000
1500 500
600 200
30
0 0
200 600
40
1000 3000
2000 6000
4000 12 000
50
6000 18 000
8000 24 000
m ft

PACIFIC
NORTHEAST Pacific Basin
OCEAN
Southwest Pacific Basin

NORTH
AMERICA

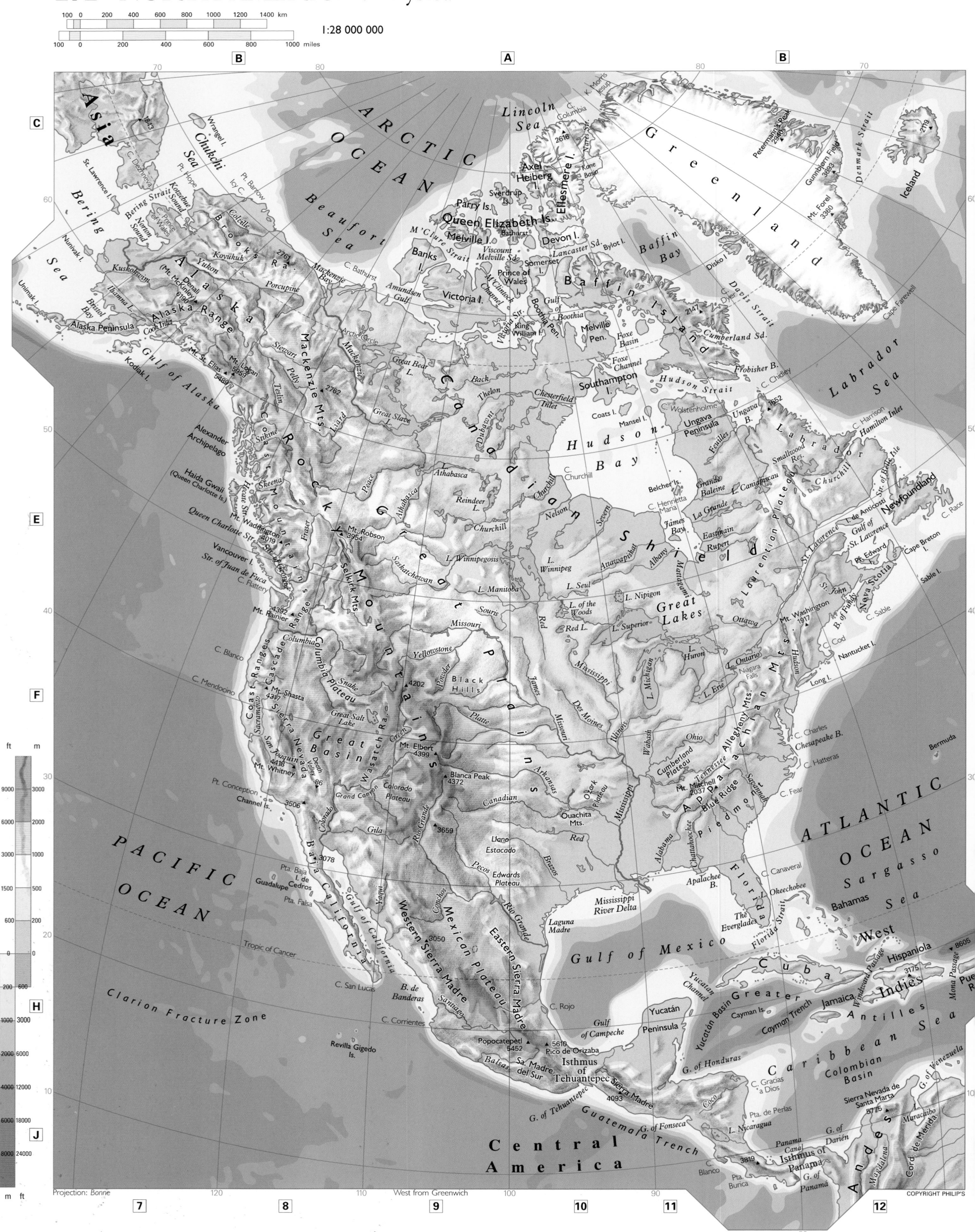

100 0   200 400 600 800 1000 1200 1400 km

100 0   200   400   600   800   1000 miles

1:28 000 000

Projection: Bonne

West from Greenwich

COPYRIGHT PHILIP'S

Projection: *Bonne*

West from Greenwich

COPYRIGHT PHILIP'S

7 ■ MÉXICO Capital Cities **8**

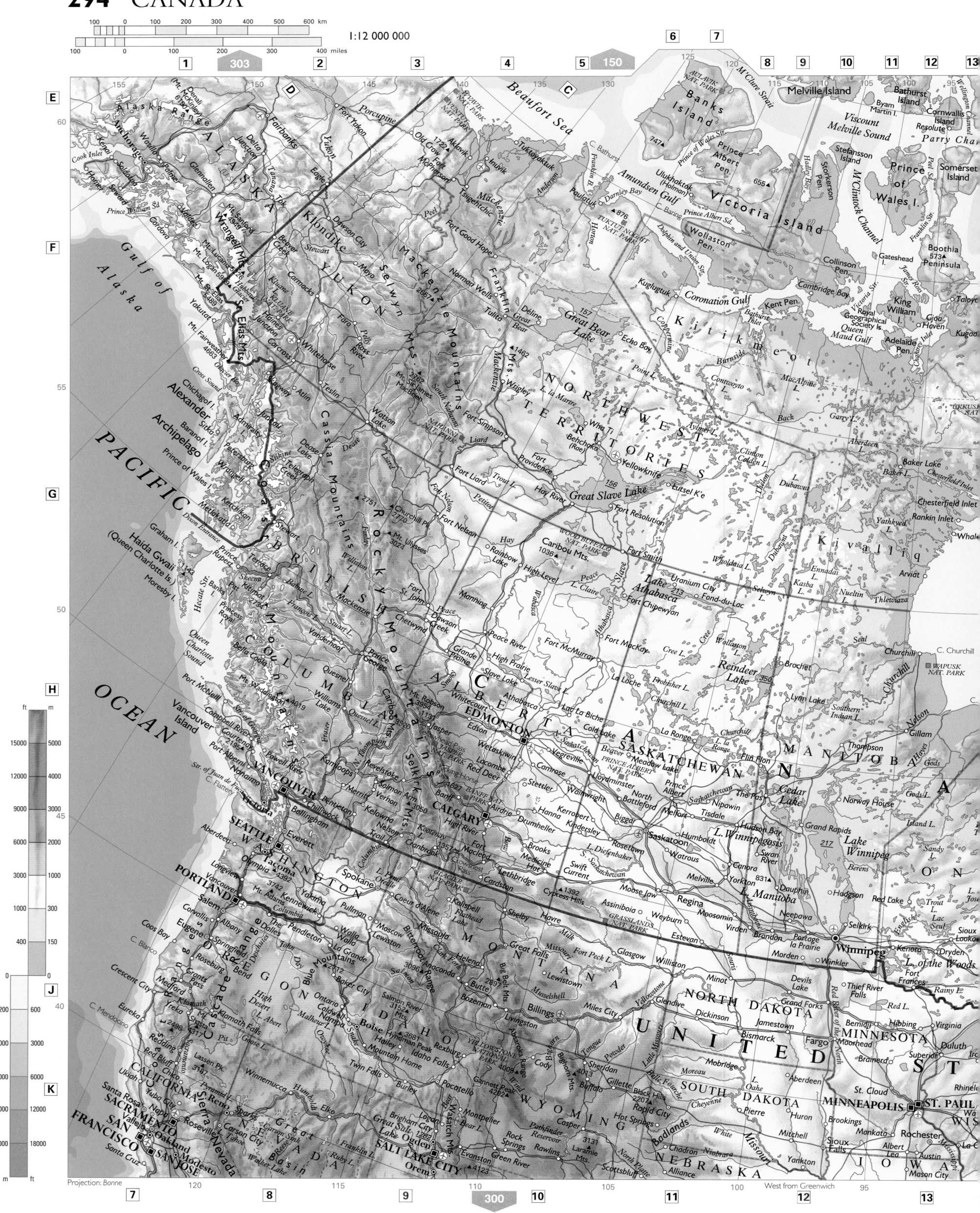

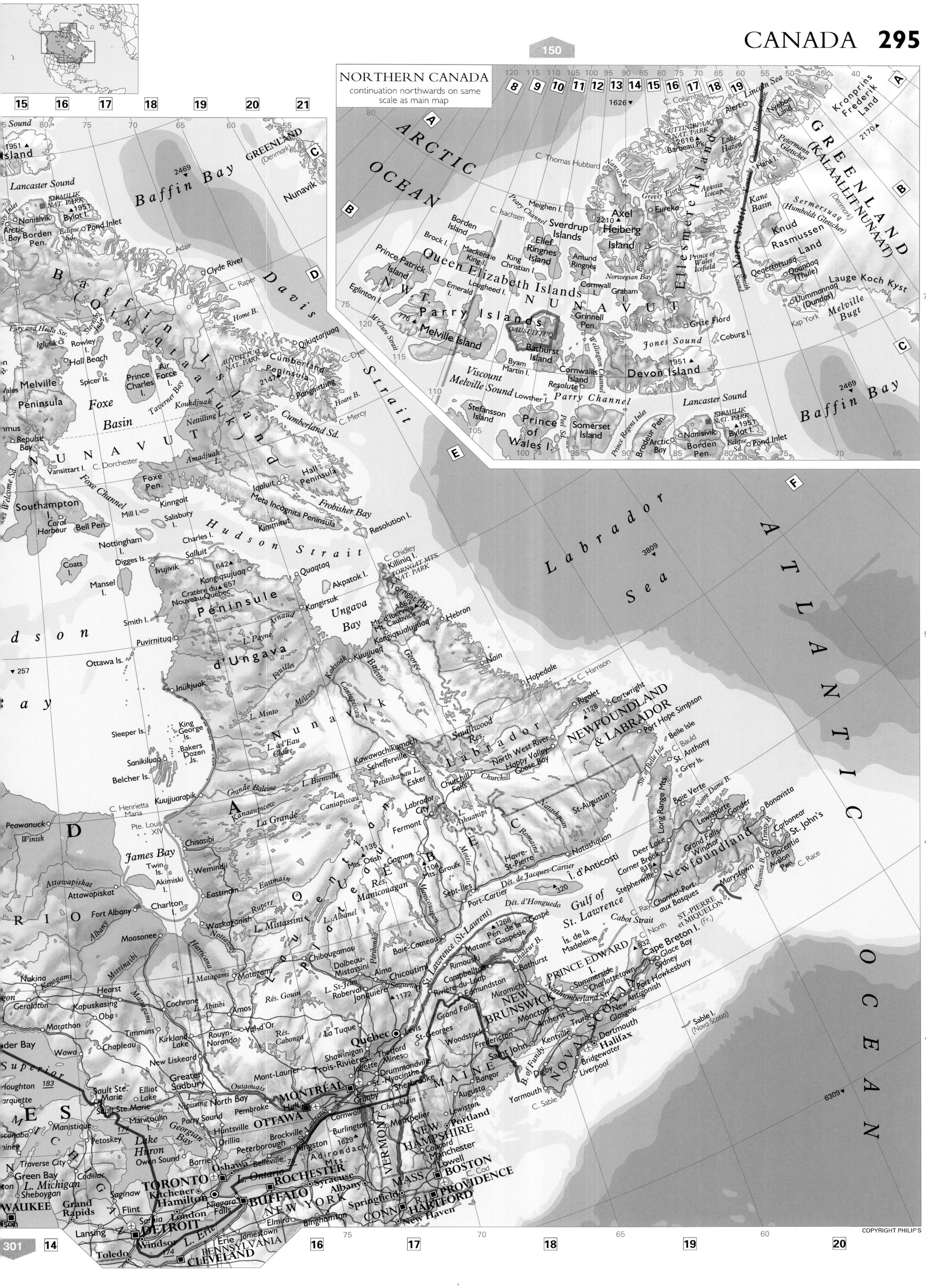

150

154

NORTHERN CANADA
continuation northwards on same
scale as main map

ARCTIC OCEAN

GREENLAND (KALAALLIT NUNAAT) (Denmark)

Kronprins Frederik Land

Lincoln Sea

Queen Elizabeth Islands

Sverdrup Islands

Axel Heiberg Island

Ellesmere Island

N W T

NUNAVUT

Parry Islands

Melville Island

Bathurst Island

Devon Island

Prince of Wales I.

Somerset Island

Parry Channel

Lancaster Sound

Baffin Bay

Viscount Melville Sound

Agassiz Icecap

Knud Rasmussen Land

Lauge Koch Kyst

Melville Bugt

GREENLAND (Denmark)

Baffin Bay

Davis Strait

Baffin (Qikirtaaluk) Island

AUYUITTUQ NAT. PARK

Cumberland Peninsula

Foxe Basin

NUNAVUT

Foxe Pen.

Hudson Strait

Southampton I.

Foxe Channel

Meta Incognita Peninsula

Frobisher Bay

Resolution I.

Iqaluit

Ungava Bay

Péninsule d'Ungava

Nunavik

James Bay

ONTARIO

Hudson Bay

QUÉBEC

Labrador

NEWFOUNDLAND & LABRADOR

Labrador Sea

ATLANTIC OCEAN

Happy Valley–Goose Bay

Churchill Falls

Labrador City

Newfoundland

St. John's

Gulf of St. Lawrence

Cabot Strait

ST-PIERRE & MIQUELON (Fr.)

PRINCE EDWARD I.

Charlottetown

Cape Breton I.

Sydney

NEW BRUNSWICK

Fredericton

NOVA SCOTIA

Halifax

Sable I. (Nova Scotia)

MAINE

QUÉBEC

MONTREAL

OTTAWA

TORONTO

Lake Ontario

L. Erie

VERMONT

NEW HAMPSHIRE

MASS.

BOSTON

NEW YORK

CONN.

HARTFORD

PROVIDENCE

Lake Huron

L. Michigan

DETROIT

CLEVELAND

BUFFALO

ROCHESTER

PENNSYLVANIA

COPYRIGHT PHILIP'S

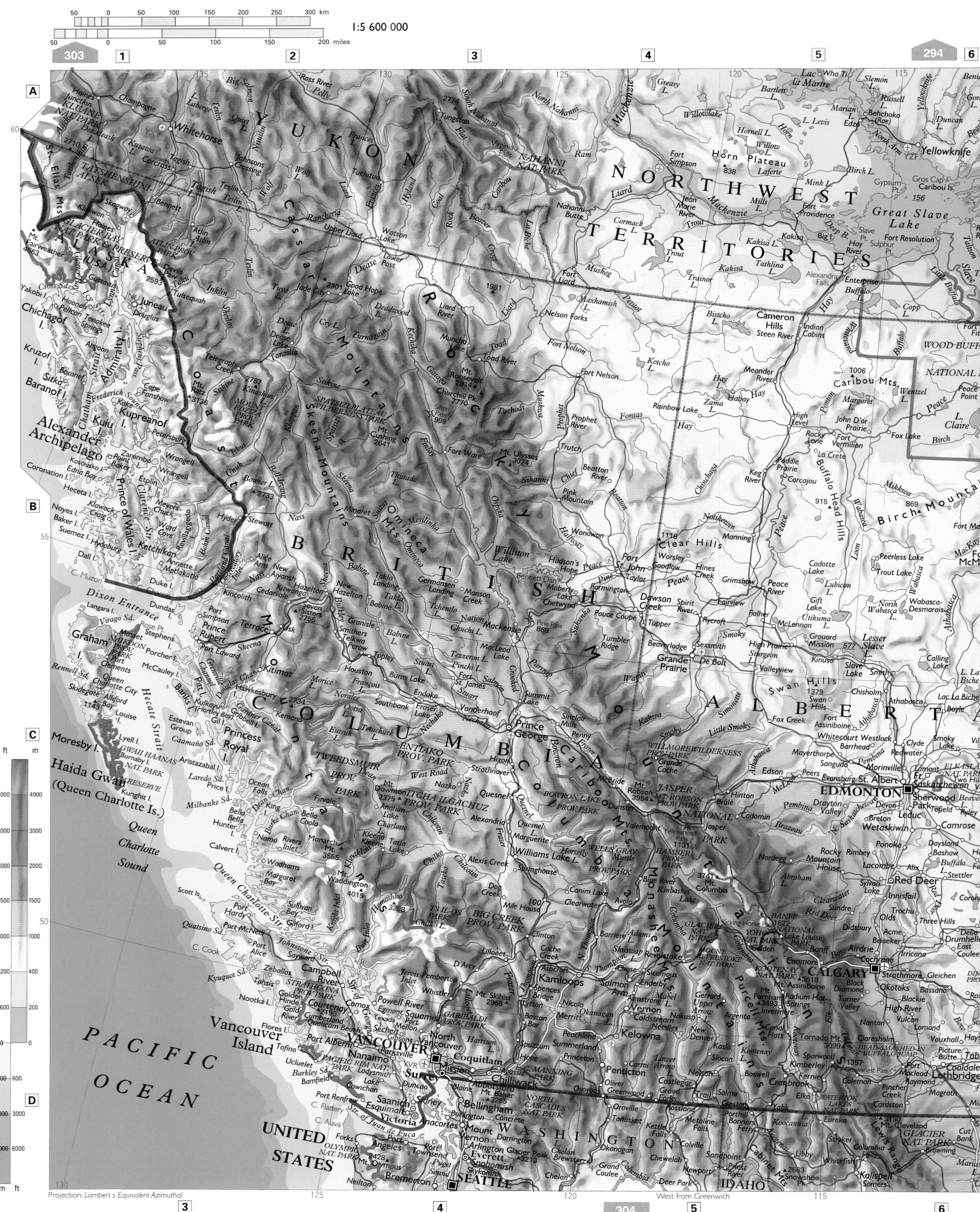

1:5 600 000

Projection: Lambert's Equivalent Azimuthal

West from Greenwich

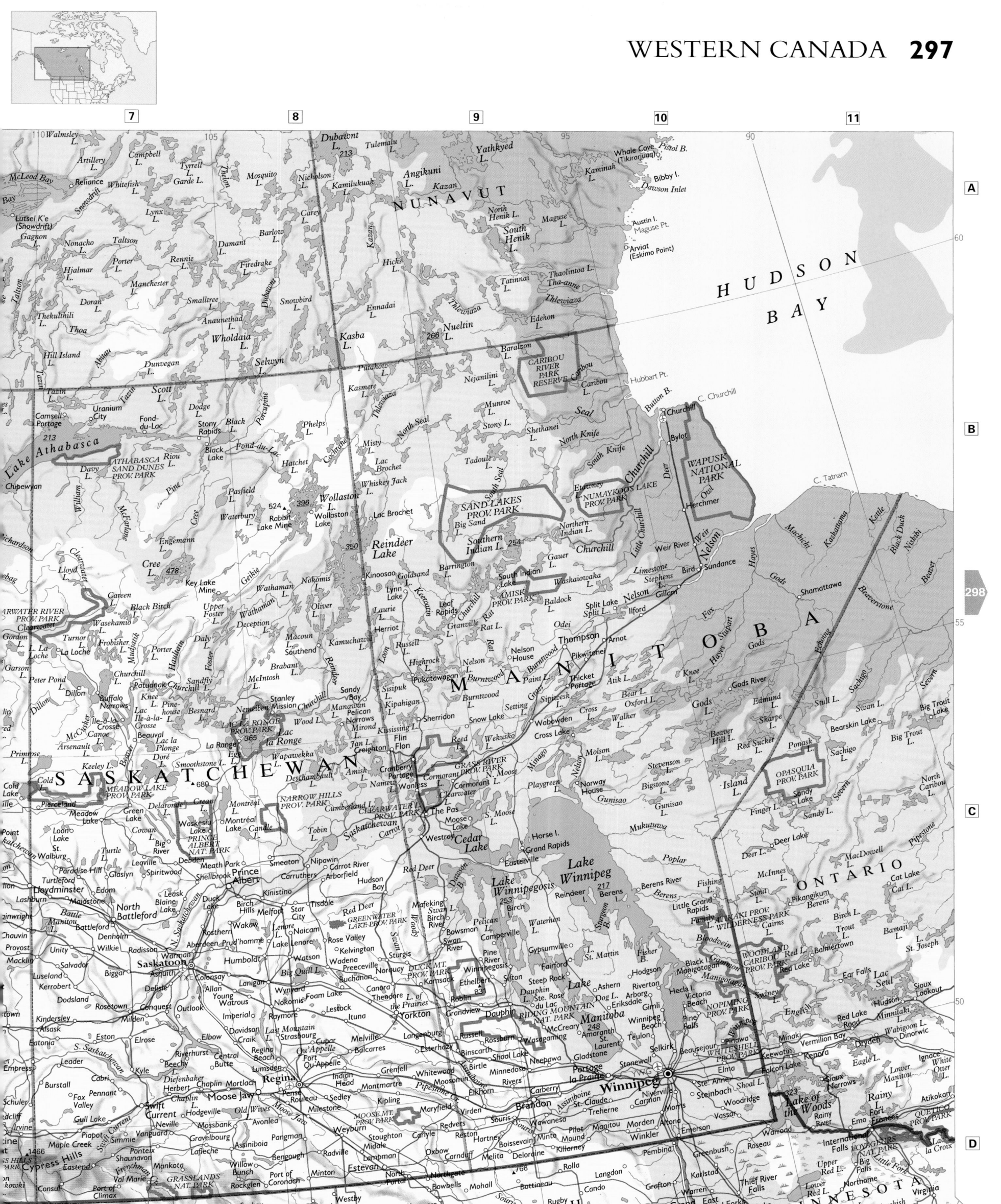

West from Greenwich

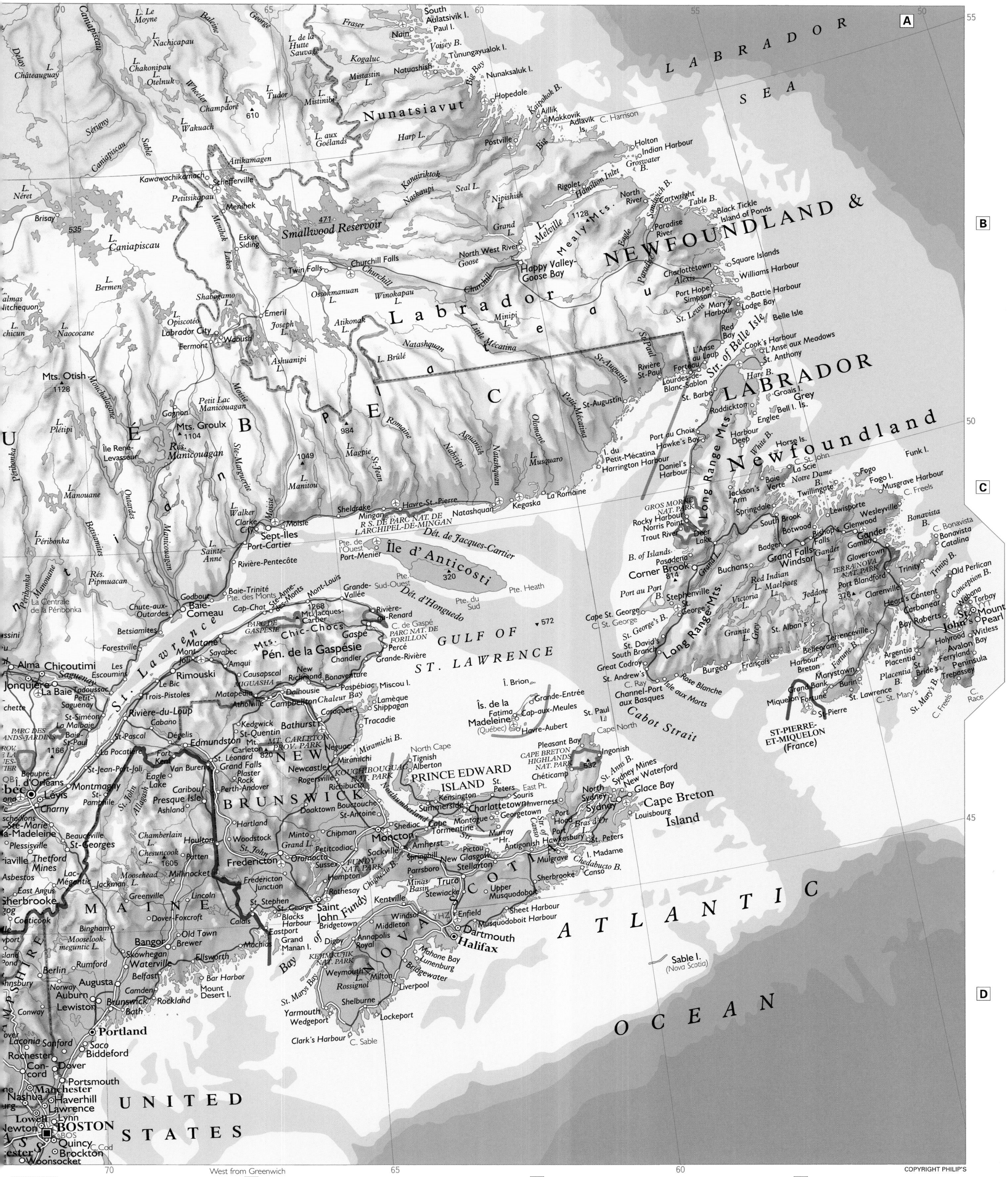

100 0 100 200 300 400 500 600 km
100 0 100 200 300 400 miles

1:12 000 000

PACIFIC OCEAN

West from Greenwich

ALASKA
on same scale

RUSSIA

ARCTIC OCEAN

CHUKCHI SEA

North Slope

Brooks Range

A L A S K A

U.S.A.

BERING SEA

Bering Strait

Seward Peninsula

Yukon Flats

Fairbanks

Nunivak I.

Yukon Delta

Kuskokwim Mountains

Anchorage

Aleutian Islands

Near Islands
Rat Islands
Andreanof Islands
Fox Islands

Alaska Peninsula

Kodiak I.

Gulf of Alaska

Projection: Albers' Equal Area with two standard parallels

West from Greenwich

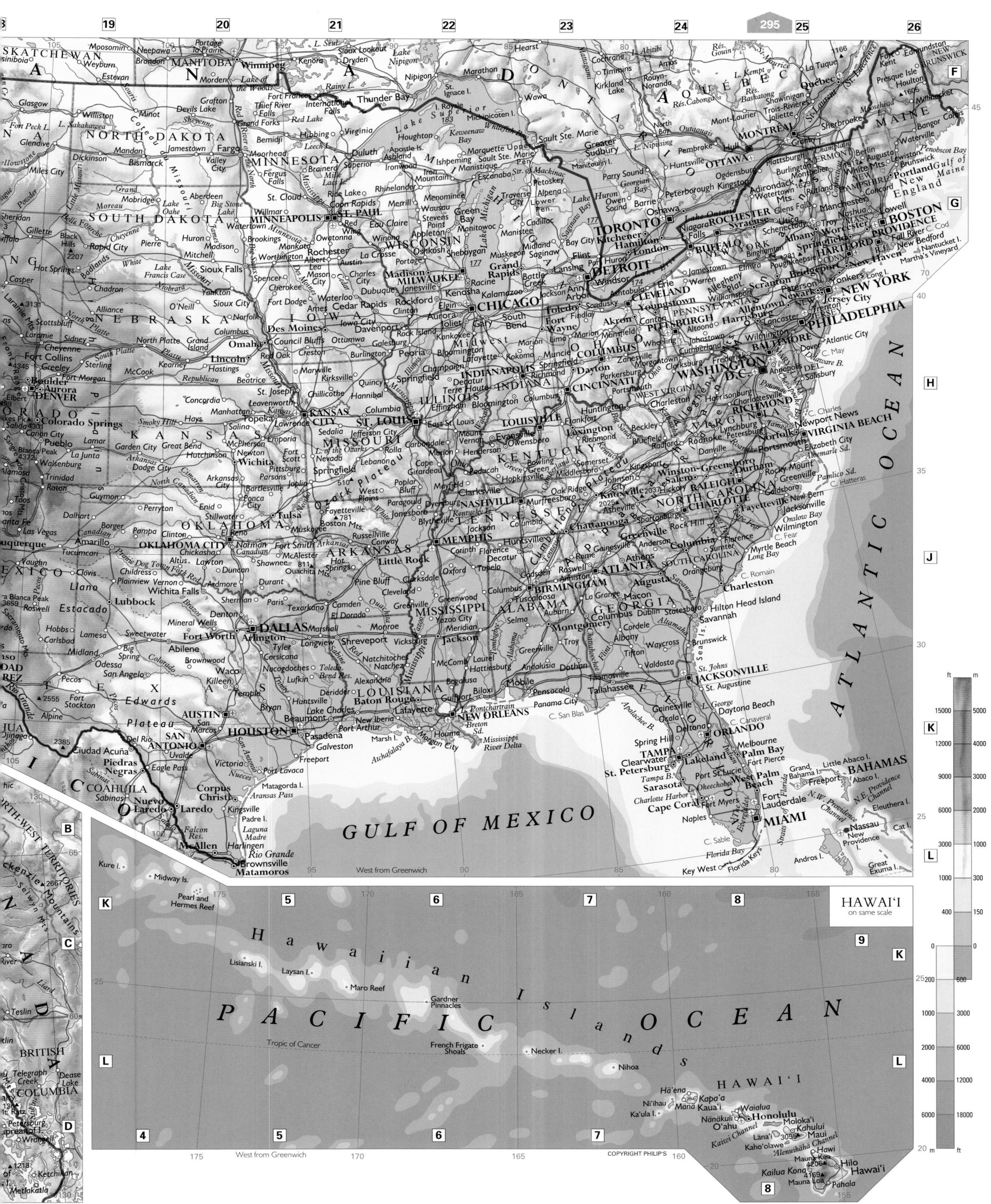

HAWAI'I
on same scale

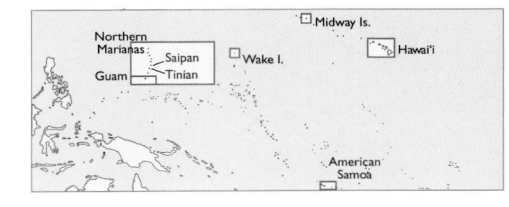

Northern Marianas
Saipan
Tinian
Guam
Midway Is.
Wake I.
Hawaiʻi
American Samoa

HAWAIʻI
1: 2 500 000
HAWAIIAN ISLANDS
1:21 000 000
Kure I.
Midway Is.
HONOLULU COUNTY
Pearl and Hermes Reef
Lisianski I.
Laysan I.
Maro Reef
Gardner Pinnacles
French Frigate Shoals
Necker I.
Nihoa
PAPAHĀNAUMOKUĀKEA MARINE NAT. MONUMENT
Tropic of Cancer
Hawaiian Islands
PACIFIC OCEAN
Kauaʻi
Niʻihau
Oʻahu
Molokaʻi
Lānaʻi
Mauí
Kahoʻolawe
Hawaiʻi
Kauai Channel
Kaiwi Channel
Pailolo Channel
Kalohi Channel
Kealaikahiki Channel
ʻAlalākeiki Channel
ʻAlenuihāhā Channel
Kaulakahi Channel
KAUAI COUNTY
KALAWAO COUNTY
MAUI COUNTY
HAWAIʻI COUNTY
Līhuʻe
Honolulu
Kahului
Hilo
Kailua Kona
Mauna Kea 4205
Mauna Loa 4169
HAWAIʻI VOLCANOES NATIONAL PARK
HALEAKALĀ NAT. PARK
KALAUPAPA NAT. HIST. PARK
Projection: Lambert's Conformal Conic
Projection: Albers Equal Area
West from Greenwich
OʻAHU
1: 500 000
Koʻolau Range
Waiʻanae Range
North Shore
Waiʻanae Coast
Pearl Harbor
Kāneʻohe Bay
Māmala Bay
Diamond Head
Koko Head
Kailua
Kāneʻohe
Pearl City
Mililani Town
Wahiawā
Haleʻiwa
Lāʻie
Waikīkī
NORTHERN MARIANAS
1: 17 500 000
Farallon de Pajaros
Maug Is.
Asuncion
Agrihan
Pagan
Alamagan
Guguan
Sarigan
Anatahan
Farallon de Medinilla
Garapan
Saipan
Tinian
Rota
Guam (U.S.A.)
Hagåtña
Mariana Islands
Mariana Trench
Northern Marianas (U.S.A.)
PACIFIC OCEAN
WAKE I.
1:200 000
Peale Island
Wilkes Island
Wake I. (U.S.A.)
Lagoon
WAKE AIRFIELD
Peacock Point
MIDWAY IS.
1:200 000
Sand Islet
Midway Islands (U.S.A.)
Sand Island
Eastern Island
Welles Harbor
MIDWAY AIRFIELD
GUAM
1: 800 000
Guam (Guåhån) (U.S.A.)
Ritidian Pt.
Hagåtña (Agana)
Apra Harbor
Orote Peninsula
Mt. Lamlam
Umatac
Merizo
Inarajan
SAIPAN & TINIAN
1: 800 000
Saipan (U.S.A.)
Tinian (U.S.A.)
Saipan Channel
Tinian Channel
San Jose
Capitol Hill
TUTUILA (AMER. SAMOA)
1: 640 000
Pago Pago
Pago Pago Harbor
Tutuila (U.S.A.)
FAGATELE BAY
MANUʻA IS. (AMER. SAMOA)
1: 640 000
Manuʻa Islands
Ofu
Olosega
Taʻū (U.S.A.)
Lata Mt.
AMERICAN SAMOA
COPYRIGHT PHILIP'S
1: 17 500 000
1: 800 000
1: 200 000
1: 640 000

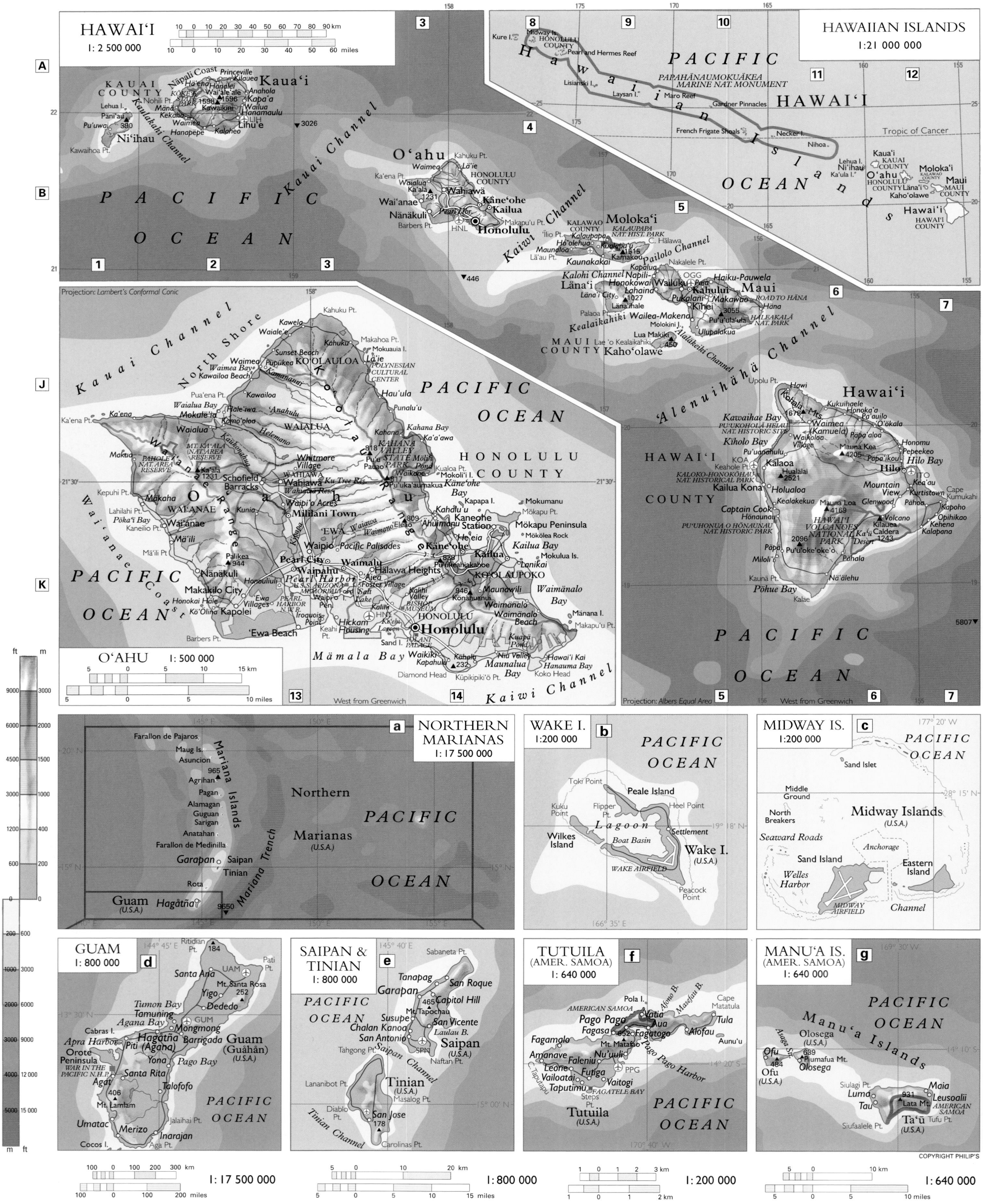

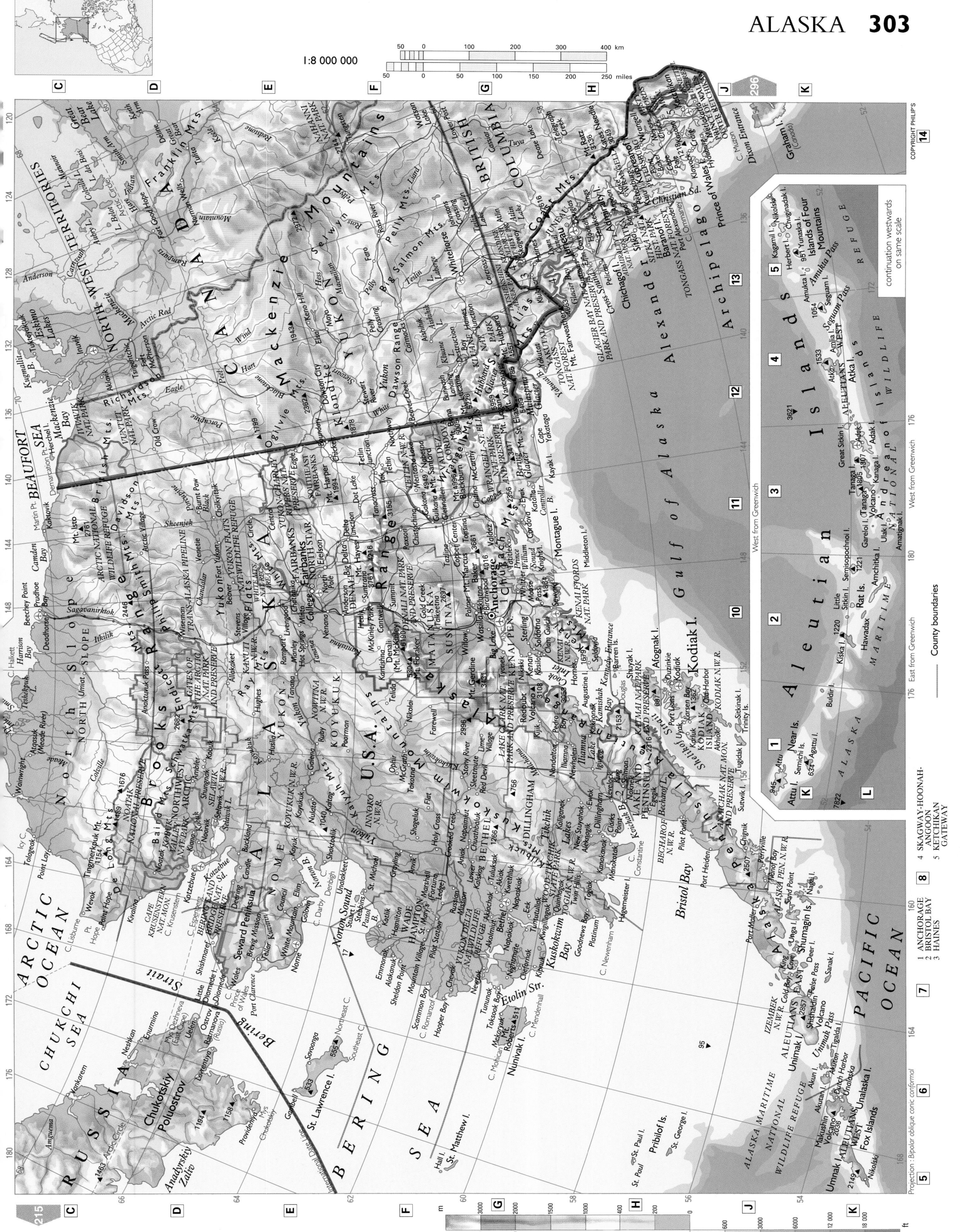

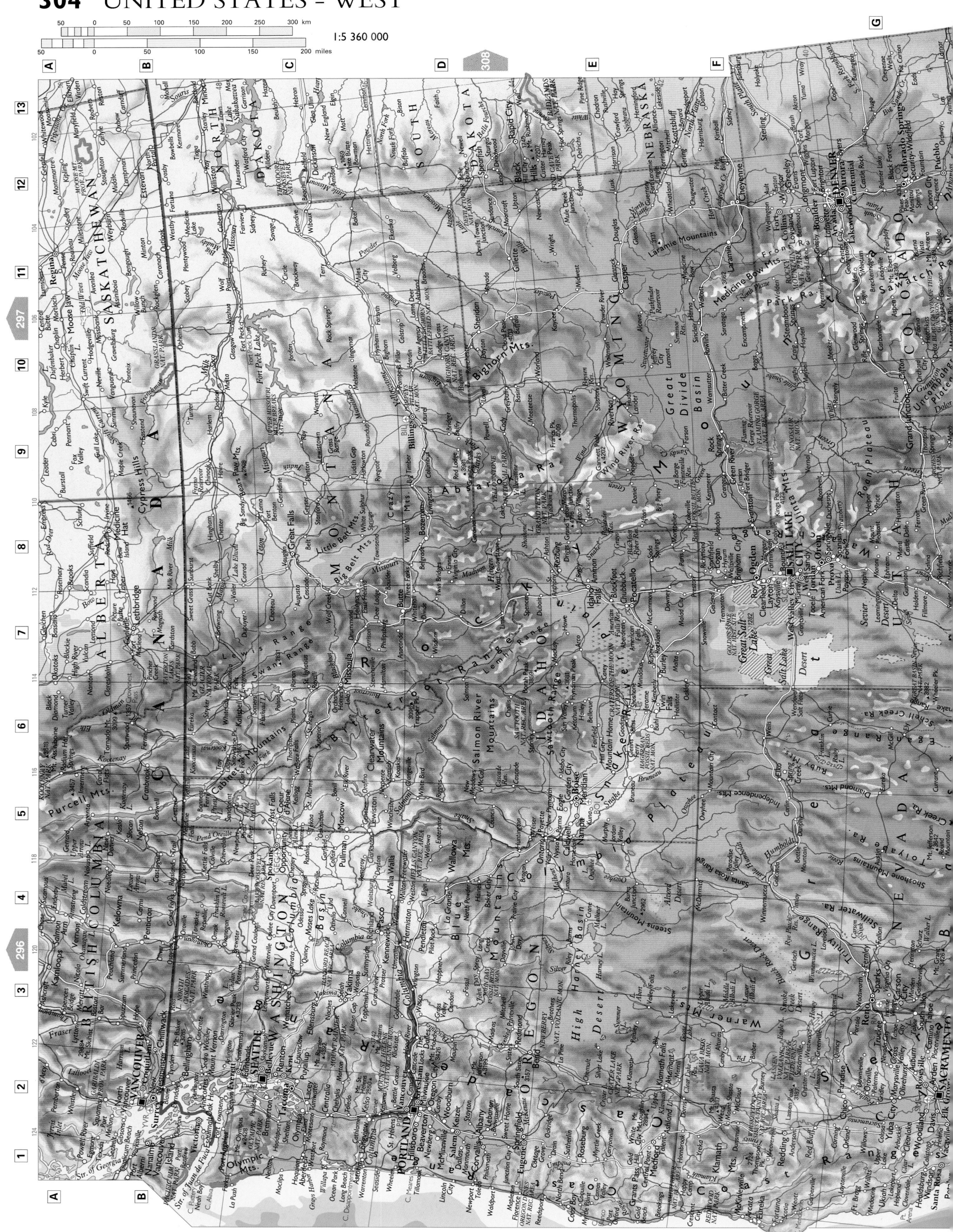

Projection: Albers' Equal Area with two standard parallels

West from Greenwich

Lava fields

1:2 000 000

WESTERN WASHINGTON
REGION
on same scale

Lava fields

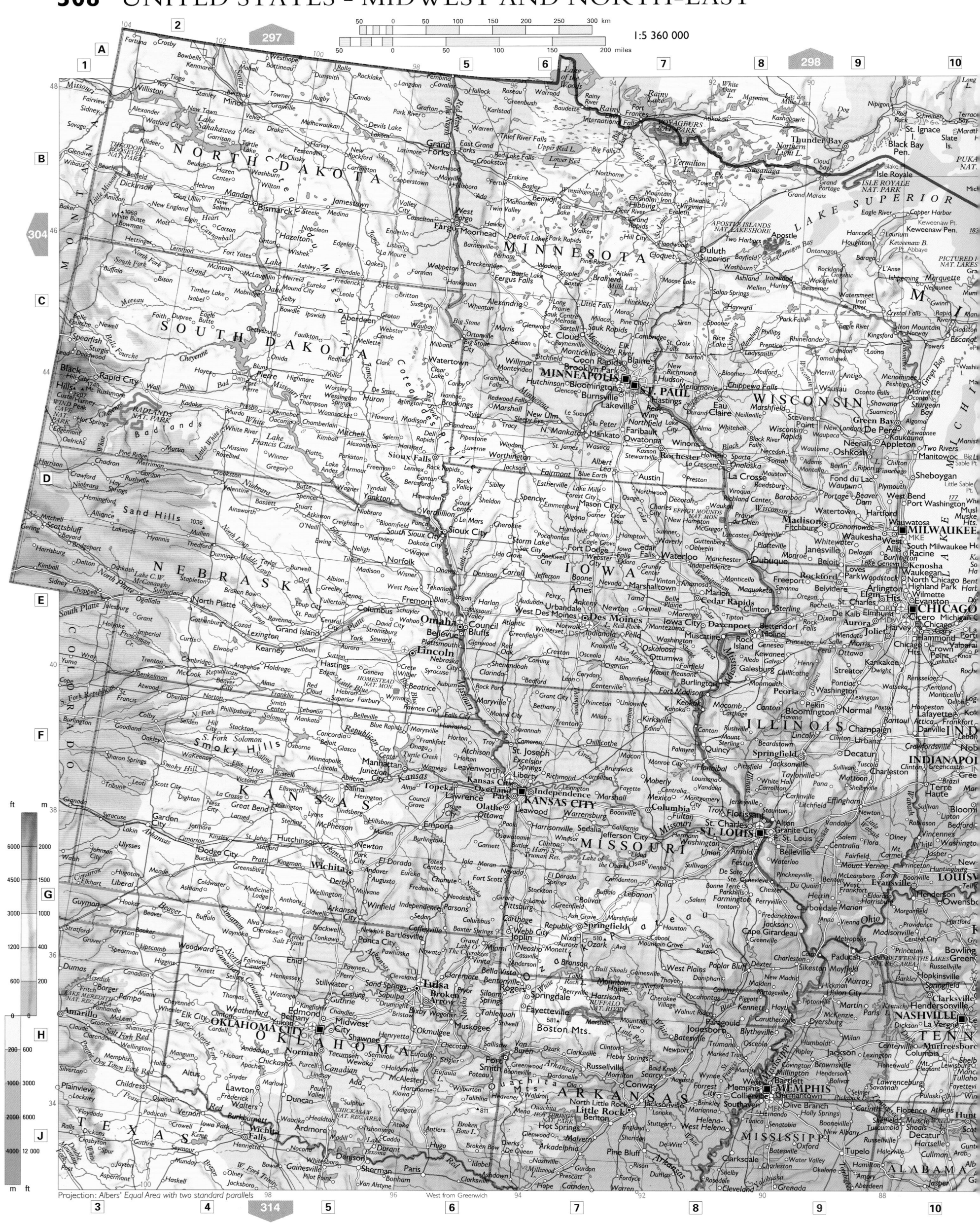

1:5 360 000

Projection: Albers' Equal Area with two standard parallels

West from Greenwich

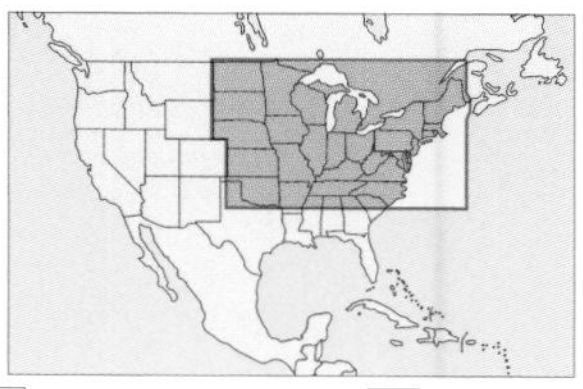

11 12 13 **298** 14 15 16 17 18 19 **299** 20

B
C
D
E
F
G
H
J

ONTARIO

QUÉBEC

NEW BRUNSWICK

MAINE

VERMONT

NEW HAMPSHIRE

NEW YORK

MASSACHUSETTS (MA.)

CONNECTICUT (CT.)

RHODE ISLAND (R.I.)

NEW JERSEY

PENNSYLVANIA

OHIO

MARYLAND

DELAWARE

WEST VIRGINIA

VIRGINIA

KENTUCKY

NORTH CAROLINA

SOUTH CAROLINA

GEORGIA

LAKE HURON

LAKE ERIE

LAKE ONTARIO

Georgian Bay

Gulf of Maine

Chesapeake Bay

Delaware Bay

Pamlico Sound

Albemarle Sd.

ATLANTIC OCEAN

Major cities: Sault Ste. Marie, Sudbury, North Bay, OTTAWA, MONTREAL, Québec, Laval, Sherbrooke, TORONTO, Hamilton, ROCHESTER, BUFFALO, Syracuse, Albany, BOSTON, PROVIDENCE, HARTFORD, Springfield, DETROIT, Windsor, Toledo, CLEVELAND, Akron, Youngstown, PITTSBURGH, COLUMBUS, CINCINNATI, Dayton, PHILADELPHIA, Harrisburg, NEW YORK CITY, Newark, Allentown, BALTIMORE, WASHINGTON D.C., Arlington, Alexandria, Annapolis, Charleston, RICHMOND, NORFOLK, VIRGINIA BEACH, RALEIGH, Durham, Greensboro, Winston-Salem, CHARLOTTE, Knoxville, Asheville, Chattanooga, ATLANTA, Columbia

11 12 13 **315** 14 15 16 17 18

84 82 80 78 76 74 72

48 46 44 42 40 38 36 34

COPYRIGHT PHILIP'S

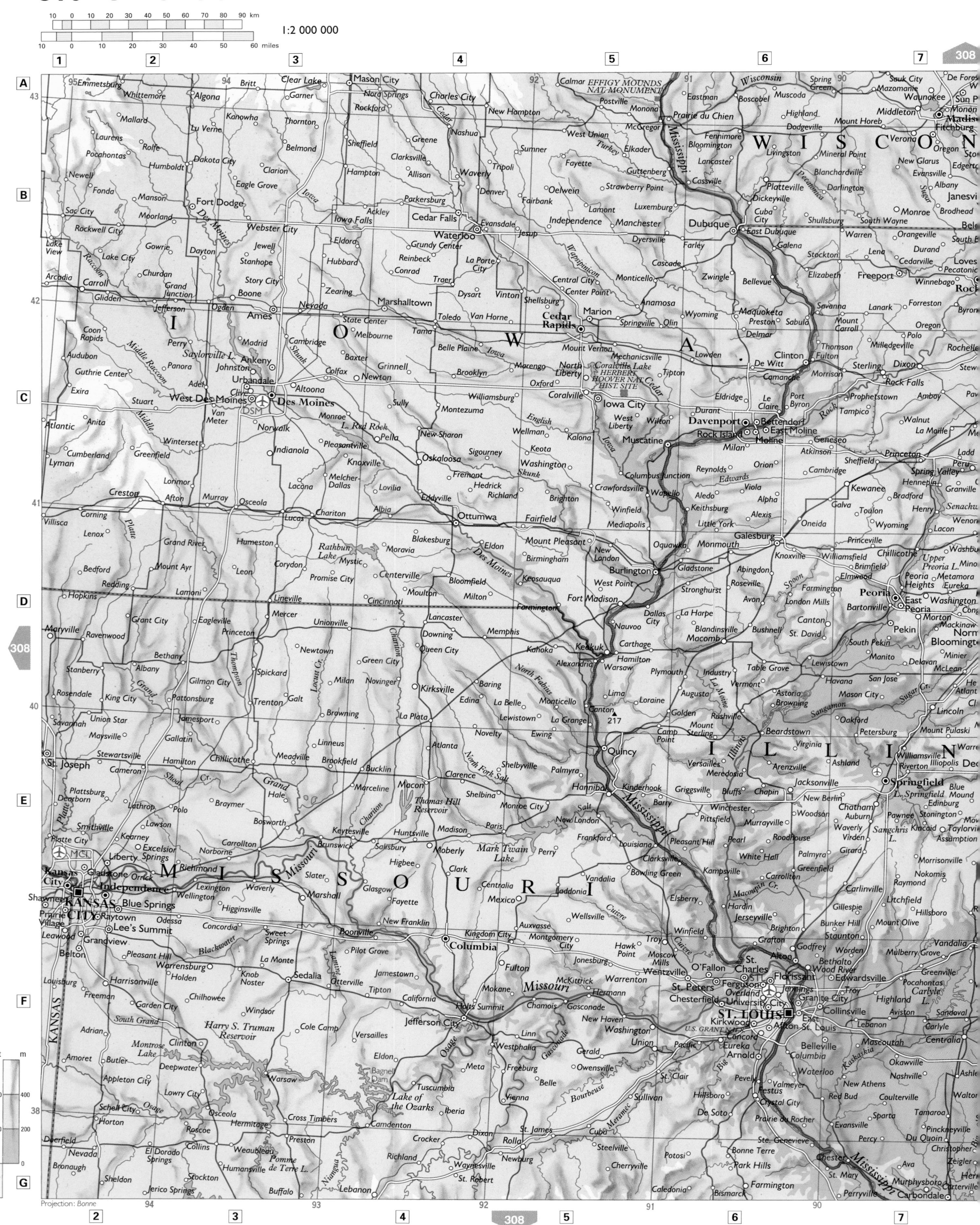

1:2 000 000

Projection: Bonne

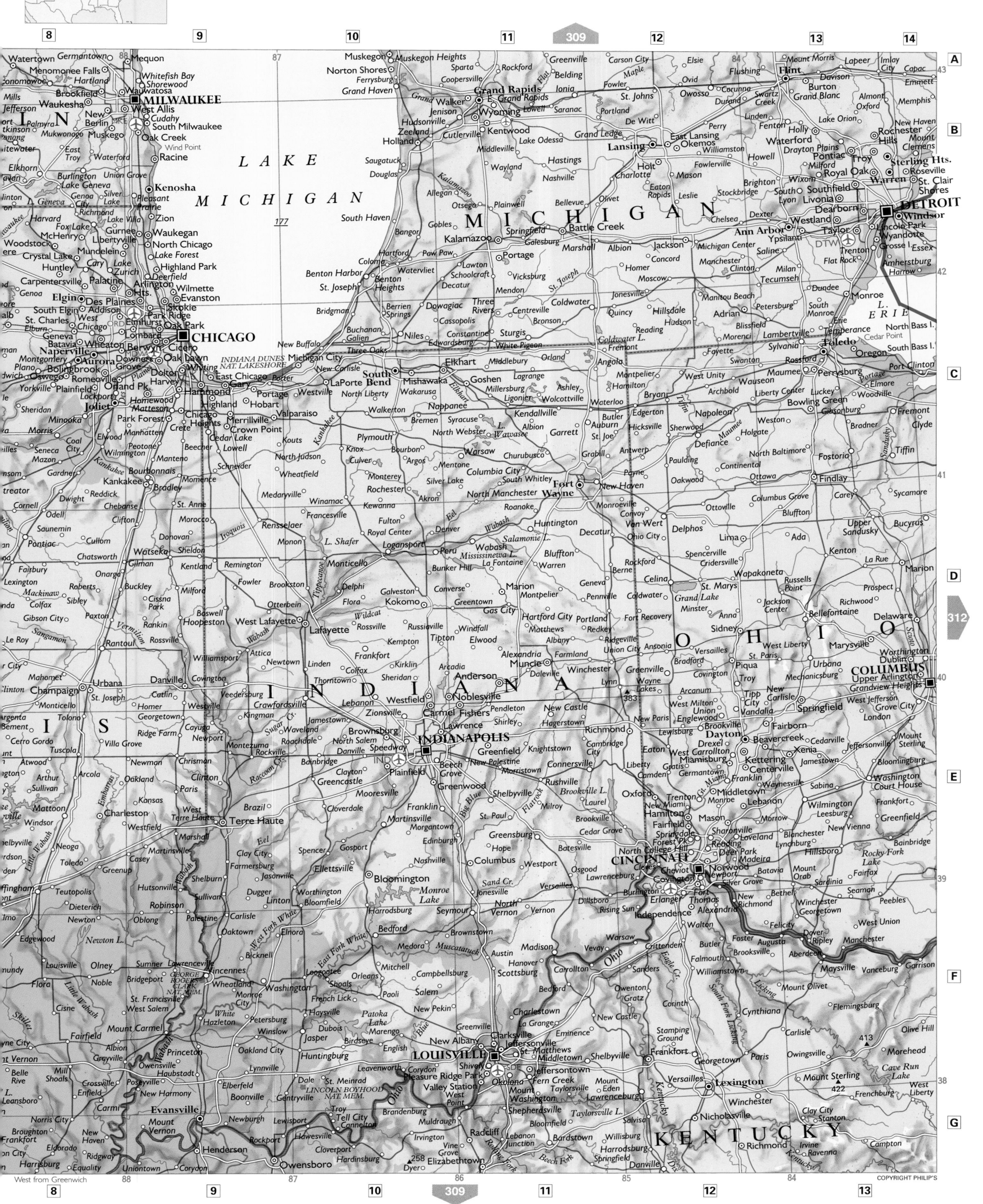

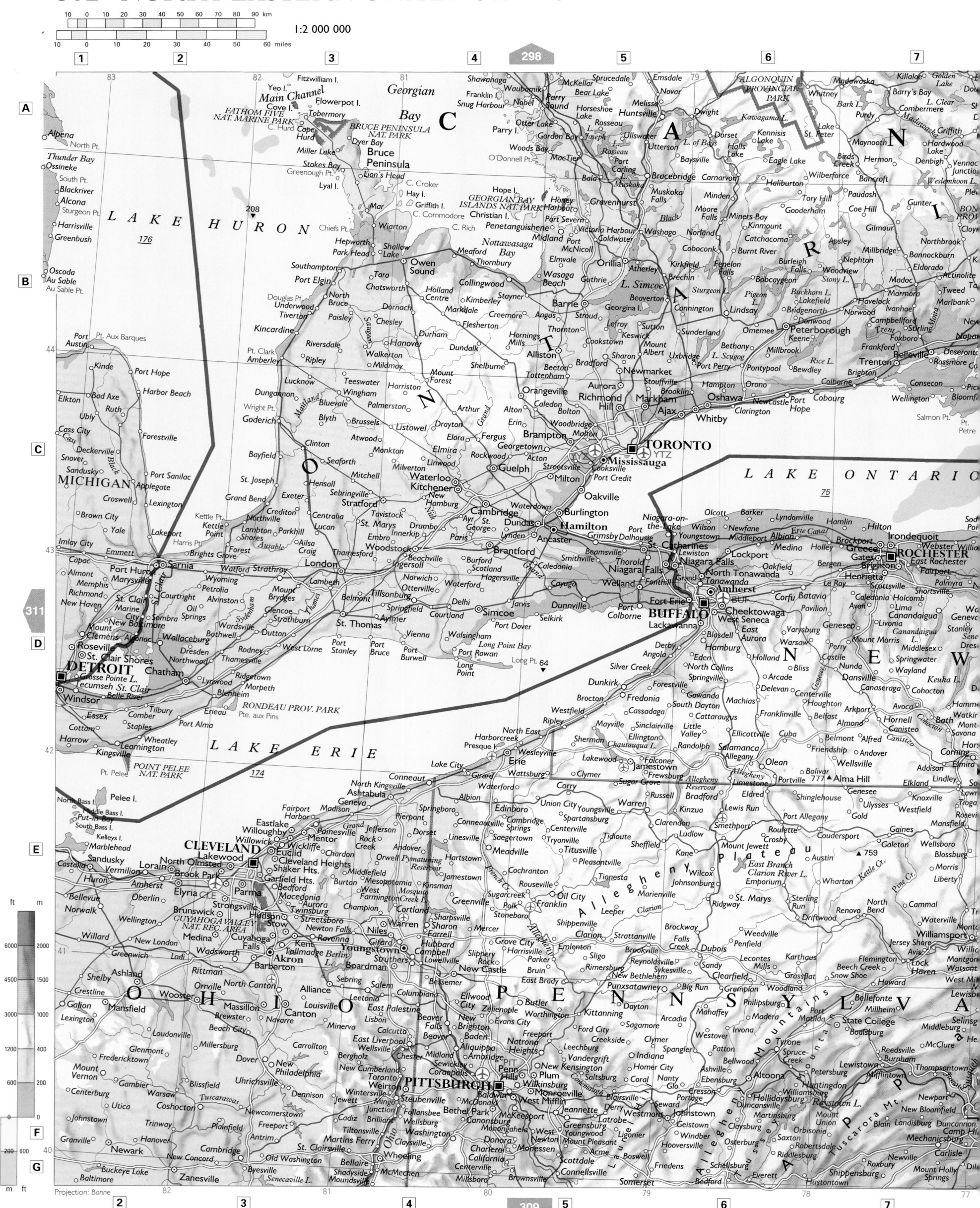

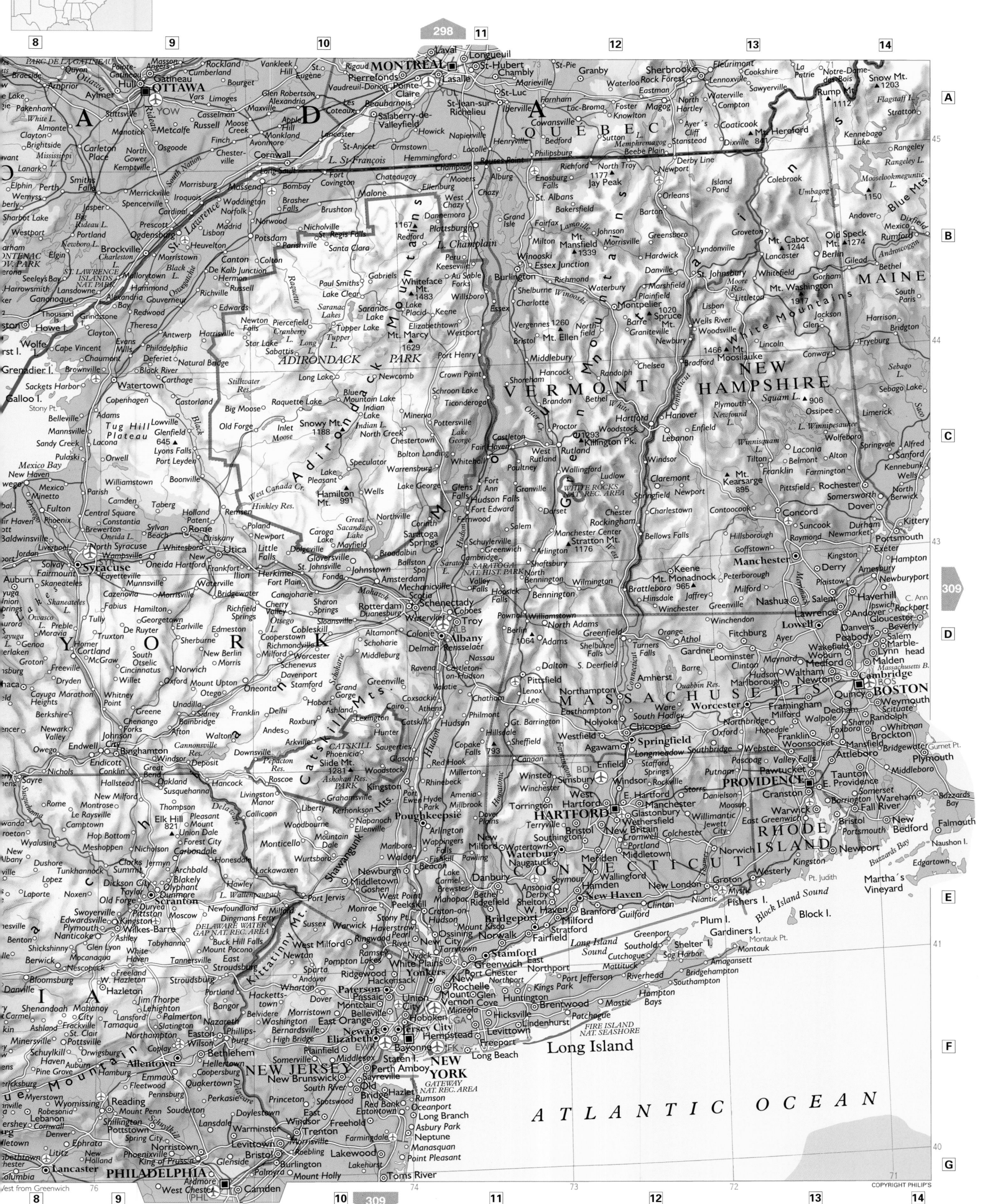

Projection: Albers' Equal Area with two standard parallels

West from Greenwich

1:5 360 000

1:2 000 000

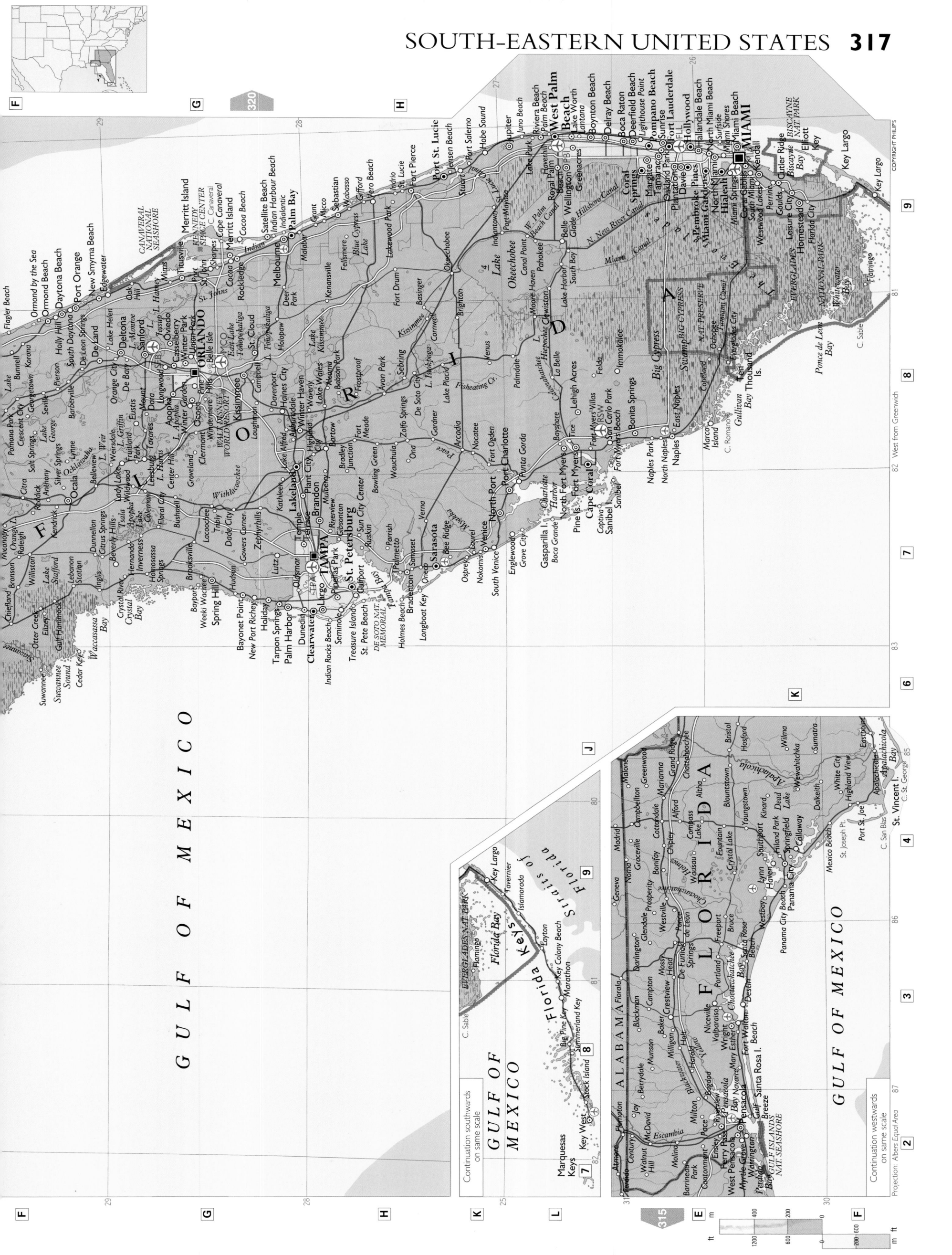

F G H

G U L F   O F   M E X I C O

F L O R I D A

CANAVERAL NATIONAL SEASHORE

KENNEDY SPACE CENTER

Orlando

WALT DISNEY WORLD RESORT

TAMPA

St. Petersburg

Clearwater

Sarasota

DE SOTO NAT. MEMORIAL

Fort Myers

Cape Coral

EVERGLADES NATIONAL PARK

BIG CYPRESS NAT. PRESERVE

West Palm Beach

Fort Lauderdale

MIAMI

Miami Beach

BISCAYNE NAT. PARK

Key Largo

COPYRIGHT PHILIP'S

82 West from Greenwich

K

J

Continuation southwards on same scale

G U L F   O F   M E X I C O

Florida Keys

Straits of Florida

Florida Bay

EVERGLADES N.P.

Key West

Marquesas Keys

GULF ISLANDS NAT. SEASHORE

A L A B A M A

F L O R I D A

Apalachicola

Panama City

GULF OF MEXICO

Pensacola

Continuation westwards on same scale

Projection: Albers Equal Area

315

L E F

Scale bar: m ft 1200 600 400 200 0 200-600 ft

9 8 7 6 K 5 4 3 2

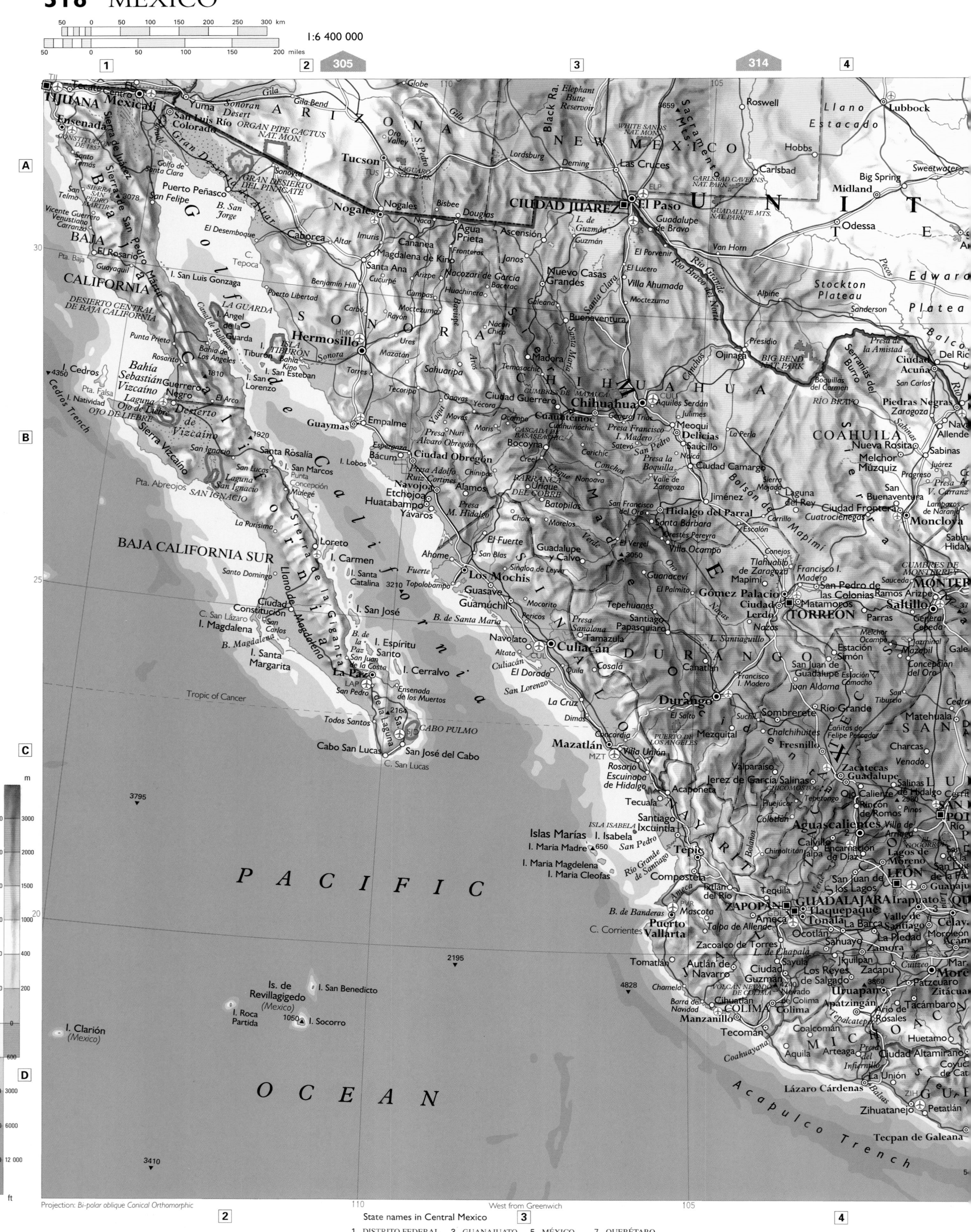

1:6 400 000

State names in Central Mexico

1 DISTRITO FEDERAL 3 GUANAJUATO 5 MÉXICO 7 QUERÉTARO
2 AGUASCALIENTES 4 HIDALGO 6 MORELOS 8 TLAXCALA

PUERTO RICO AND THE VIRGIN IS.
b 1:1 600 000

10 0 10 20 30 40 50 60 70 km
10 0 10 20 30 40 50 miles

ATLANTIC OCEAN

Ruffling Pt. · The Settlement · Anegada · East Pt.

VIRGIN ISLANDS (U.K.)

Jost Van Dyke I. · Great Camanoe · Guana I. · EIS · Beef I. · Virgin Gorda
Hans Lollik I. · Tortola · 521 · Spanish Town
Charlotte Amalie · St. Thomas I. · Road Town · Peter I.
Cruz Bay · VIRGIN IS. NAT. PARK
Dewey · Culebra · St. John I.
VIRGIN ISLANDS (U.S.A.)

Pta. Agujereada · Quebradillas · Camuy · Hatillo · Arecibo
Aguadilla · Isabela · Barceloneta · Vega Baja · Levittown · **SAN JUAN**
Pta. Higuero · Moca · Manati · Vega Alta · Cataño · SJU · Carolina · Rio Grande
Rincon · Aguada · PARQUE DE LAS CAVERNAS DEL RIO CAMUY · Florida · Ciales · **Bayamón** · Guaynabo · Trujillo Alto · Luquillo · Fajardo
San Sebastian · Lares · OBSERVATORIO DE ARECIBO · Corozal · Comerio · Sierra de Luquillo · EL YUNQUE · Ceiba
Añasco · **MAYAGÜEZ** · Maricao · Utuado · 1338 · Adjuntas · Cordillera Central · Cayey · Naguabo
Hormigueros · Cerro de Punta · Villalba · Barranquitas · Cidra · Las Piedras · Pta. Puerca
San German · Sabana Grande · Juana Diaz · Coamo · **Humacao** · Isabel Segunda
Cabo Rojo · Yauco · **Ponce** · Salinas · Yabucoa · Pta. Arenas
Parguera · Guayanilla · PSE · **Guayama** · Maunabo · Esperanza · **Vieques**
Guanica · Santa Isabel · I. Caja de Muertos · Sonda de Vieques

Virgin Passage

4983

353 · Christiansted · East Pt.
Frederiksted · Mt. Eagle · Southwest Pt. · STX · **St. Croix I. (U.S.A.)**

CARIBBEAN SEA
West from Greenwich

BAHAMAS
New Bight · Cat I. · Salvador I. · Conception I. · Rum Cay · Long I.
Clarence Town · Tropic of Cancer · Samana Cay
Albert Town · Crooked I. · Plana Cays · Snug Corner · Mayaguana I.
Acklins I. · Mira por vos Cay · Mayaguana Passage
Verde · Hogsty Reef · Little Inagua I. · Turks & Caicos Is. (U.K.)
Lake Rose · INAGUA · Providenciales · Caicos Is. · Cockburn Town
Lucrecia · Matthew Town · Great Inagua I.
Moa · Mouchoir Bank · Silver Bank
Baracoa · Pta. de Maisi · Î. de la Tortue · Monte Cristi · Navidad Bank
GUANTANAMO (U.S.A.) · Paso de los Vientos (Windward Passage) · Cap-Haïtien · Puerto Plata · **Santiago de los Caballeros** · San Francisco de Macorís · Milwaukee Deep 8605
Jean Rabel · Port-de-Paix · Fort Liberté · La Vega · Nagua · Samana
Cap-à-Foux · G. de la Gonâve · Gonaïves · Hinche · 3175 · Sanchez · Sabana de la Mar
Jérémie · St-Marc · Pico Duarte · HAITISES · **SANTO DOMINGO** · Hato Mayor · C. Engaño
HAITI · Î. de la Gonâve · **DOMINICAN REP.** · San Pedro de Macorís · Higüey · PUJ
PORT-AU-PRINCE · PAP · San Juan · L. Enriquillo · **La Romana** · Yuma
Les Cayes · Massif de la Hotte · Petit Goâve · Jacmel · 2680 · SIERRA DE BAHORUCO · San Cristóbal · B. de Saona · I. Saona
C. Carcasse · Aquin · Î. à Vache · Barahona · Pedernales · Mona Passage · Isla Mona (U.S.A.)

Hispaniola
I. Beata · C. Beata

Antilles
Beata Ridge · 5500 · Muertas Trough

4530

CARIBBEAN SEA
Colombian Basin

Venezuelan Basin
5420

Greater Antilles

Puerto Rico Trench

Bayamón · San Juan · Carolina · Virgin Gorda · Anegada · Sombrero (U.K.)
Aguadilla · Arecibo · SLU · St. Thomas · Virgin Is. (U.K.) · Tortola · Road Town · Anguilla (U.K.)
Mayagüez · 1338 · Ponce · Caguas · Fajardo · Culebra · Charlotte Amalie · Virgin Is. (U.S.A.) · SXM · St-Martin (Fr.) · St-Barthélemy (Fr.)
PUERTO RICO (U.S.A.) · Guayama · Vieques · Christiansted · St. Croix (U.S.A.) · St. Eustatius (Neth.) · Mt. Liamuiga 1156 · Saba (Neth.) · Barbuda
Frederiksted · St. Kitts · SKB · St. Martin · **ANTIGUA & BARBUDA**
Basseterre · ST. KITTS & NEVIS · St. John's
Nevis · ANU · Antigua
Redonda · Soufrière Hills
Montserrat (U.K.) · 914 · Guadeloupe Passage
Ste-Rose · Le Moule · La Désirade
Portsmouth · PTP · **GUADELOUPE (Fr.)** · 1467 · **Pointe-à-Pitre** · Marie-Galante (Fr.)
Morne · 1447 · Basse-Terre · Grand-Bourg · Dominica Passage
Roseau · MORNE TROIS PITONS · I. des Saintes (Fr.) · **DOMINICA** · DOM
Diablotin · Martinique Passage
Mt. Pelée 1397 · Ste-Marie
Fort-de-France · Le Robert · Rivière-Pilote · **MARTINIQUE (Fr.)**
FDF · St. Lucia Channel · **MARTINIQUE**
Castries · **ST. LUCIA**
Soufrière · UVF
St. Vincent Passage
Soufrière 1234 · St. Vincent · Speightstown · BGI
Kingstown · SVD · Bridgetown · **BARBADOS**
Bequia · Tobago
Canouan · **ST. VINCENT & THE GRENADINES** · The Grenadines
Carriacou · 840 · **GRENADA**
St. George's · GND

Leeward Islands · Lesser Antilles

Windward Islands · Aves Ridge · Grenada Basin · Tobago Basin

I. de Aves (Venezuela)

Lesser Antilles
ABC Islands · Oranjestad · Aruba (Neth.) · AUA · Curaçao (Neth.) · Willemstad · CUR · Bonaire (Neth.) · ARC. LOS ROQUES · I. Orchila (Ven.) · I. Blanquilla (Ven.) · Is. Los Hermanos (Ven.) · Is. Los Testigos (Ven.)
C. San Román · Is. Las Aves (Ven.) · Is. Los Roques (Ven.) · NUEVA ESPARTA · I. de Margarita (Ven.)

COLOMBIA
Santa Marta · TAYRONA · ISLA DE SALAMANCA · GUAJIRA · Pta. Gallinas · Puerto Bolívar · MACUIRA · Uribia · Pen. de la Guajira · Pta. Espada
Ríohacha · Maicao · Golfo de Venezuela · Punta Cardón · I. La Tortuga (Ven.)
Ciénaga · Sierra Nevada de Santa Marta 5775 · Pen. de Paraguaná · Punto Fijo · MEDANOS DE CORO · Puerto Cumarebo
Fundación · San Rafael · Machiques · La Concepción · Coro · La Vela · CUEVA DE LA QUEBRADA DEL TORO · Tucacas · Puerto Cabello · **MARACAY** · La Guaira · **CARACAS** · Petare · I. La Tortuga · Cumaná · Carúpano · Güiria · **Port of Spain** · Scarborough
Calamar · Agustín Codazzi · SA. NEVADA DE · San Carlos del Zulia · MENE GRANDE · Barquisimeto · San Felipe · YARACUY · HENRI PITTIER · Vargas · MIRANDA · Los Teques · Ocumare del Tuy · Higuerote · Rio Chico · Barcelona · Cariaco · Pen. de Paria · Arima · POS · **TRINIDAD & TOBAGO**
Magangué · CÉSAR · **MARACAIBO** · MAR · LARA · **VALENCIA** · Villa de Cura · San Juan de los Morros · Anaco · Maturín · DELTA · Galera Point · Trinidad · Rio Claro
El Banco · ZULIA · Lago de Maracaibo · Cabimas · Ciudad Ojeda · **BARQUISIMETO** · Yaritagua · Aragua de Barcelona · Altagracia de Orituco · MONAGAS · AMACURO
NORTE · PERIJA · TRUJILLO · Acarigua · COJEDES · El Baúl · Calabozo · El Tigre · Los Barrancos
DE · SIERRA DE PERIJA · Valera · Betijoque · PORTUGUESA · GUARICO · Santa María de Ipire · ANZOÁTEGUI · Ciudad Guayana
SANTANDER · Ocaña · MÉRIDA · SA. NEVADA · Barinas · San Fernando · GUARICO · San Fernando de Apure · **Ciudad Bolívar** · Upata
Cúcuta · TÁCHIRA · Mérida 4981 · Ciudad Bolivia · BARINAS · LIBERTAD · Bruzual · Achaguas · **VENEZUELA** · Apure · Mapire · Caicara · El Callao · Tumeremo · Guasipati · Embalse de Guri
BOLÍVAR · TÁRIPA · San Cristóbal · San Carlos

West from Greenwich

COPYRIGHT PHILIP'S

4000 3000 2000 1000 400 200 0 200 1000 2000 3000 4000 6000 8000 m
12000 9000 6000 4500 3000 1200 600 0 600 3000 6000 12000 18000 24000 ft

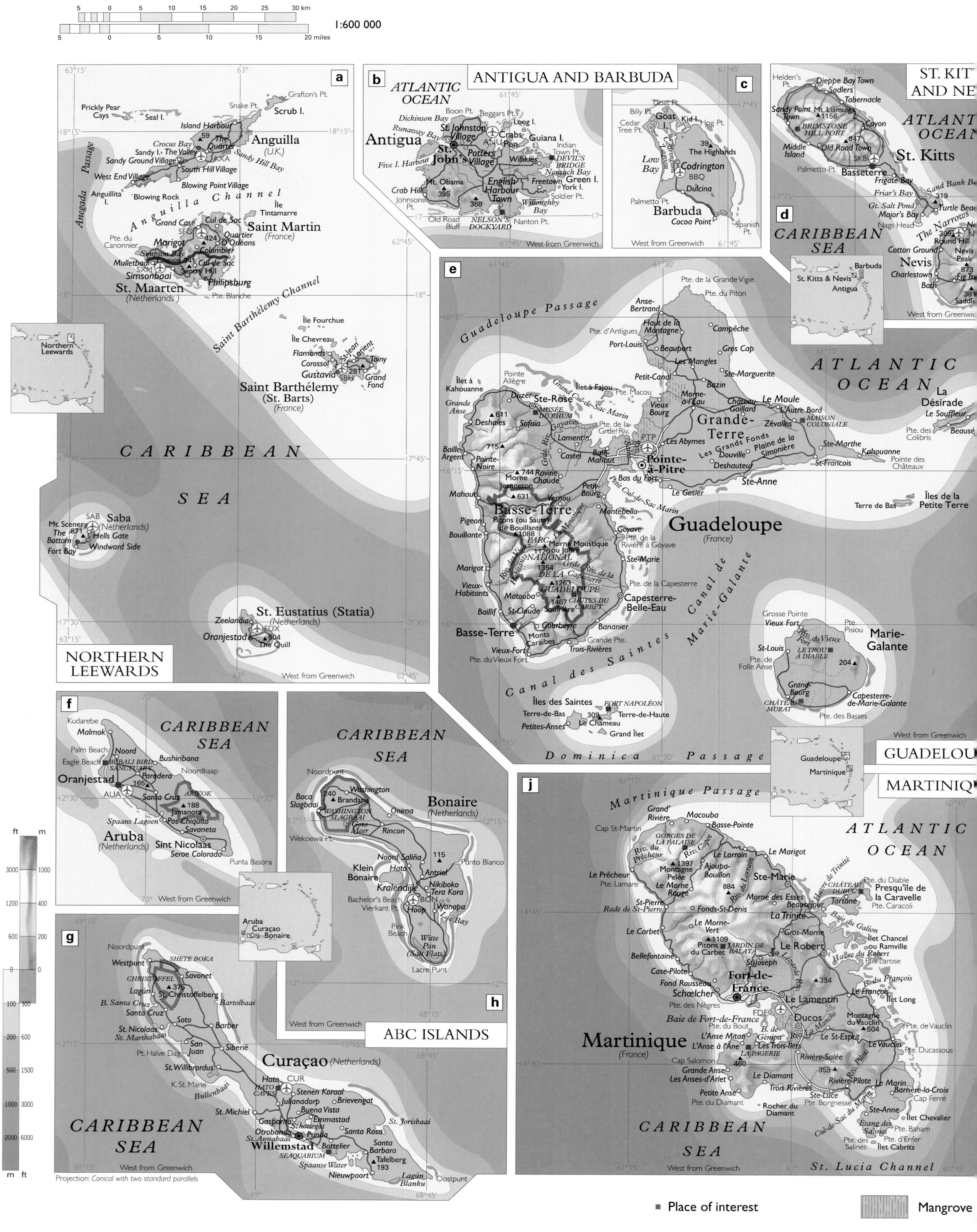

1:600 000

5 0 5 10 15 20 25 30 km
5 0 5 10 15 20 miles

a

Prickly Pear Cays
Seal I.
Snake Pt.
Grafton's Pt.
Scrub I.
Island Harbour
Crocus Bay
Sandy I.
The Quarter
59
AXA
Sandy Ground Village
The Valley
Anguilla
(U.K.)
South Hill Village
Sandy Hill Bay
West End Village
Blowing Point Village
Anguillita I.
Blowing Rock
Anguilla Channel
Île Tintamarre
Anegada Passage
Grand Case
Cul de Sac
Île Chevreau
SFG
Marigot
Quartier D'Orléans
424
Colombier
Saint Martin
(France)
Simpson Bay
Cul de Sac
SXM
Sept Hill
Mulletbaai
Simsonbaai
Philipsburg
St. Maarten
(Netherlands)
Pte. Blanche

Northern Leewards

b
ATLANTIC OCEAN
ANTIGUA AND BARBUDA
Dickinson Bay
Boon Pt.
Beggars Pt.
Long I.
Runaway Bay
St. Johnston Village
Crabs Pen
Guiana I.
Antigua
ANU
Indian Town Pt.
St. John's
Potters Village
Willikies
DEVIL'S BRIDGE
Five I. Harbour
Nonsuch Bay
Freetown
Green I.
Mt. Obama
395
York I.
Soldier Pt.
Crab Hill
English Harbour Town
Willoughby Bay
Johnsons Pt.
368
Old Road Bluff
NELSON'S DOCKYARD
Nanton Pt.
West from Greenwich

c
Billy Pt.
Goat Pt.
Goat I.
Kid I.
Hog Pt.
Cedar Tree Pt.
The Highlands
Low Bay
Codrington
BBQ
Dulcina
Palmetto Pt.
Barbuda
Cocoa Point
Spanish Pt.
West from Greenwich

d
ST. KITTS AND NE[VIS]
Helden's Pt.
Dieppe Bay Town
Sadlers
Tabernacle
Sandy Point Town
Mt. Liamuiga 1156
Cayon
BRIMSTONE HILL FORT
847
Old Road Town
Middle Island
St. Kitts
SKB
Palmetto Pt.
Basseterre
Frigate Bay
Friar's Bay
Gt. Salt Pond
319
Sand Bank Bay
Turtle Beach
Major's Bay
The Narrows
Nags Head
305
Round Hill
Cotton Ground
Nevis Peak
873
Fig Tree
Nevis
Charlestown
Bath
381 Saddle
St. Kitts & Nevis / Antigua
West from Greenwich

e
Pte. de la Grande Vigie
Pte. du Piton
Anse-Bertrand
Guadeloupe Passage
Campêche
Pte. d'Antigues
Haut de la Montagne
Gros Cap
Port-Louis
Beauport
Les Mangles
Petit-Canal
Ste-Marguerite
Pte. Macou
Bazin
Vieux Bourg
Morne-à-l'Eau
Château Gaillard
Le Moule
L'Autre Bord
Îlet à Kahouanne
Pointe Allègre
Îlet à Fajou
Zévallos
MAISON COLONIALE
Grande Anse
Deshaies
611
Ste-Rose
Duzer
Sofaia
Goyaves
Grd. Cul-de-Sac Marin
Pte. de la Grde Riv.
Grande-Terre
Les Abymes
Ste-Marthe
Kahouanne
715
Lamentin
PTP
Les Grands Fonds
Plaine de la Simonière
Pte. des Colibris
Baille-Argent
Pointe-Noire
Castel
Baie Mahaut
Douville
Deshauteur
Pointe des Châteaux
744 Ravine Chaude
Pointe-à-Pitre
Ste-Anne
St-François
Beauséjour
Morne Jeanneton
Mahaut
631
Vernou
Petit Bourg
Bas du Fort
Le Gosier
Morne Moustique
Pigeon
PARC NATIONAL DE GUADELOUPE
1088 Pitons (ou Soufre de Bouillante)
Montebello
Petit Cul-de-Sac Marin
Bouillante
1120 ou Joffre
Goyave
Grde Riv. de Goyave
Guadeloupe
(France)
Marigot
1354
Grde. Riv. de la Capesterre
Ste-Marie
Terre de Bas
Îles de la Petite Terre
Vieux-Habitants
1263
Pte. de la Capesterre
Matouba
1467 CHUTES DU CARBET
Capesterre-Belle-Eau
St-Claude
Soufrière
Baillif
Canal de Marie-Galante
Basse-Terre
Gourbeyre
Bananier
Grosse Pointe
Vieux Fort
Pte. Pisiou
Marie-Galante
Vieux-Fort
Monts Caraïbes
Trois-Rivières
St-Louis
Pte. du Vieux Fort
Pte. de Folle Anse
LE TROU À DIABLE
204
Îles des Saintes
FORT NAPOLÉON
Grand-Bourg
Capesterre-de-Marie-Galante
Terre-de-Bas
Terre-de-Haute
CHÂTEAU MURAT
Petites-Anses
309
Le Château
Pte. des Basses
Grand Îlet
West from Greenwich
Canal des Saintes
Dominica Passage

Guadeloupe / Martinique

f
Kudarebe
Malmok
CARIBBEAN SEA
Palm Beach
Noord
BUBALI BIRD SANCTUARY
Bushiribana
Eagle Beach
Noordkaap
Paradera
165
ARIKOK
Oranjestad
AUA
Santa Cruz
188
Jamanota
Spaans Lagoen
Pos Chiquito
Savaneta
Aruba
(Netherlands)
Seroe Colorado
Sint Nicolaas
Punta Basora
West from Greenwich

Aruba / Curaçao / Bonaire

h
CARIBBEAN SEA
Noordpunt
Washington
Boca Slagbaai
240
Brandaris
WASHINGTON SLAGBAAI
Onima
Goto Meer
Rincon
Bonaire
(Netherlands)
Wekoewa Pt.
115
Noord Saliña
Punto Blanco
Klein Bonaire
Hato
Antriol
BON
Nikiboko
Tera Kora
Kralendijk
Wanapo
Bachelor's Beach
Lac Bay
Vierkant Pt.
Hoop
Pink Beach
Witte Pan (Salt Flats)
Lacre Punt
West from Greenwich
ABC ISLANDS

g
Noordpunt
SHETE BOKA
Westpunt
Savonet
CHRISTOFFEL
375
Lagun
St. Christoffelberg
Bartolbaai
B. Santa Cruz
Santa Cruz
Soto
Barber
St. Nicolaas
St. Marthabaai
San Juan
Siberië
Pt. Halve Dag
St. Willibrordus
K. St. Marie
Curaçao (Netherlands)
Hato
CUR
HATO CAVES
St. Michiel
Stenen Koraal
Brievengat
Gasparito
Buena Vista
Soto
St. Jorisbaai
Otrobanda
Emmastad
Santa Rosa
Punda
Willemstad
SEAQUARIUM
Santa Barbara
Bottelier
193 Tafelberg
Spaanse Water
CARIBBEAN SEA
Lagun Blanku
Nieuwpoort
Oostpunt
Projection: Conical with two standard parallels

j
Martinique Passage
Grand' Rivière
Macouba
Basse-Pointe
Cap St-Martin
GORGES DE LA FALAISE
Le Lorrain
Le Marigot
ATLANTIC OCEAN
Riv. du Prêcheur
1397
Ajoupa-Bouillon
Le Précheur
Montagne Pelée
Le Morne Rouge
Ste-Marie
Pte. du Diable
Pte. Lamare
884
CHÂTEAU DUBUC
Presqu'île de la Caravelle
St-Pierre
Fonds-St-Denis
Morne des Esses
Tartane
Pte. Caracoli
Rade de St-Pierre
1109
La Trinité
Le Morne-Vert
Pitons du Carbet
JARDIN DE BALATA
Le Carbet
Gros-Morne
Îlet Chancel ou Ramville
Bellefontaine
St-Joseph
Le Robert
Pte. Larose
Case-Pilote
354
B. du François
Fond Rousseau
Le François
Schœlcher
Fort-de-France
Îlet Long
FDF
Le Lamentin
Martinique
(France)
Ducos
504 Montagne du Vauclin
Pte. de Vauclin
Cap Salomon
L'Anse Mitan
Génipa
Le St-Esprit
L'Anse à l'Âne
Les Trois-Îlets
Le Vauclin
LA PAGERIE
Rivière-Salée
460
Pte. Ducassous
Grande Anse
Les Anses-d'Arlet
Le Diamant
Trois Rivières
Rivière-Pilote
Le Marin
Petite Anse
359
Ste-Luce
Barrière-la-Croix
Rocher du Diamant
Pte. du Diamant
Ste-Anne
Cap Ferré
CARIBBEAN SEA
Cul-de-Sac du Marin
Étang des Salines
Îlet Chevalier
Pte. Baham
Pte. des Salines
Pte. d'Enfer
Îlet Cabrits
St. Lucia Channel

■ Place of interest   Mangrove

DOMINICA

Dominica Passage

ATLANTIC OCEAN

Capucin · Pte. Jaco
Morne aux Diables 830▲
Vieille Case · Thibaud · Hampstead
Douglas Bay · Prince Rupert Bluff Pt. · CABRITS NAT. PARK · Calibishie
Portsmouth · Belmanier
Prince Rupert Bay · Glanvillia · Bense
Wesley
Marigot · DOM
Pagua Bay
Dublanc
MORNE DIABLOTINS NAT. PARK
1419▲ Morne Diablotins
Salibia
Colihaut · Coulibistrie
Jenny Pt.
692
Castle Bruce
Morne Raquette · Macoucheri
Salisbury
St. Joseph · Layou · 704 · Morne Trois Pitons
Grand Marigot Bay
Bells · Belle Fille
Petit Soufrière Bay
Mero · 1423 · Morne Macaque
Rosalie
Mahaut · Springfield · MORNE TROIS PITONS NAT. PARK · 1220
Pont Casse · Laudat · 1225
Bout Sable Bay
Massacre · Pringles Bay · Trafalgar
Pte. Giraud
Canefield · Woodbridge Bay
Watt Mountain
La Plaine
Roseau · Charlotte Ville
Délices
CARIBBEAN SEA
Pointe Michel · Loubière
Pte. Mulâtre
Soufrière · Berekua
Soufrière Bay · 371 · Grand Bay
Petite Savane
Scotts Head · Scotts Head Village
Pte. des Fous
Martinique Passage

Dominica / St. Lucia

West from Greenwich

ST. LUCIA

St. Lucia Channel

Cap Point · Pte. Hardy
Pigeon Island · Anse Lavoutte
Gros Islet
Choc Bay · Rodney Bay
Rat Island · Q. Marquis
Castries · Girard
Grande Cul Sac Bay · 352 · 571
Marigot · Marquis
Marigot Bay · Bexon
Anse la Raye · Dennière Rouche Island
Riviere
Durandeau
FREGATE ISLAND NATURE RESERVE
Canaries · Millet
Fond d'Or Bay
Blanche I. · Mt. Gimie 950
Dennery
DIAMOND BOTANICAL GARDENS
Anse Chastanet · Praslin
Soufrière · Fond St. Jacques
Trou Gras Pt.
Petit Piton 750 · Micoud
Anse des Pitons · 620 · Vierge Pt.
Gros Piton 796
Morne Caillandre 351
Choiseul
Canelles
Laborie
Savannes Bay
Vieux Fort · UVF
Maria Islands
C. Moule à Chique

CARIBBEAN SEA

St. Vincent Passage

West from Greenwich

ATLANTIC OCEAN

ST. VINCENT AND THE GRENADINES

St. Vincent Passage
Fancy · Owia
FALLS OF BALEINE · New Sandy Bay Village
La Soufrière 1234 · Orange Hill
Richmond Beach · Richmond
Chateaubelair · 1074 Richmond Peak · Rabacca
Troumaka · Rose Bank · Georgetown
Cumberland · Spring Village
Wallilabou Bay · Colonarie
St. Vincent · Barrouallie · North Union · Sans Souci
Mount Wynne · Greiggs · Biabou
Layou · Pembroke · Mesopotamia · Peruvian Vale
Buccament Bay · Camden Park · Belair · Belmont
FORT CHARLOTTE · Vigie · Stubbs
2793▼ · **Kingstown** · Villa · Belvedere
SVD · Calliaqua
FORT DUVERNETTE

CARIBBEAN SEA
Bequia Channel
Man Pt.
55
Bequia · Spring Bay
Admiralty Bay · Port Elizabeth
Ships Stern · BQU · 270
2756▼ · Derrick · Friendship Bay
Petit Nevis · Battowia
Bednoe · Pigeon I.
Isle à Quatre · Baliceaux
The Pillories · All Awash I.
MQS · Ansecoy Bay
Britannia Bay · Lovell Village
Petit Mustique · **Mustique**
Savan Island
Savan Rock
Petit Canouan
Grand Bay · 267
Mahault Bay
Canouan
Glossy Bay · Charlestown
Catholic I. · North Mayreau
Saltwhistle Bay · Tobago Cays
Mayreau · Saline Bay · Petit Tobac
Chatham · 305 · UNI · Palm I.
Bay · Ashton · Clifton
Union Island · Frigate I.
Martinique Channel
Petit St. Vincent

West from Greenwich

The Grenadines

ATLANTIC OCEAN

MONTSERRAT

NORTHERN ZONE
N.W. Bluff · Silver Hill · 403
Little Bay · Brades · St. Johns
Montserrat (U.K.) · Cudjoehead · MNI
St. Peters · 739 · Trants Bay
Salem · Centre Hills
CARIBBEAN SEA
PLYMOUTH · EXCLUSION ZONE
Soufrière Hills 914 Volcano
754 · South · Roche's Bluff
Old Fort Point · Soufrière Hills

West from Greenwich

Montserrat
St. Vincent & The Grenadines
Grenada

GRENADA

Petit St. Vincent
Gun Pt. · Windward
Sparrow Bay · Bogles · 281 · Petit Martinique
Mabouya I. · Sandy I. · Petite Dominique
White I. · Saline I. · Hillsborough
Tyrrel Bay · Hermitage · **Carriacou**
Manchineel Bay
Large I. · Frigate I.
Bonaparte Rocks · Rose Rock

CARIBBEAN SEA

Diamond I.
Ronde Island · 46
The Sisters · Les Tantes
1668 · London Bridge · Caille I.
Tanga Langua · Sugar Loaf · Green I.
Sauteurs · LEVERA NAT. PARK · Sandy I.
St. Mark Bay · Victoria · Morne Fendue · 840
Gouyave · Mt. St. Catherine · Tivoli · Lake Antoine
Concord · Pearls · Pearls Rock
Grand Roy · GRAND ETANG NAT. PARK · Grenville
Halifax Harbour · Birch Grove · Telescope Pt.
Mt. Sinai · Marquis I.
Grand Mal Bay · 702 · Pomme · Rose
FORT GEORGE · Great Bacolet Bay
St. George's · St. David's
Grand Anse Bay · Belmont · Requin Bay
Grand Anse · Corinth
Salines · L'Anse aux Epines
GND · Hog I. · Pt. of Fort Jeudy
Glover I. · Pricky Pt. · Calivigny I.

West from Greenwich

BARBADOS

ATLANTIC OCEAN

North Point
Crab Hill · Cumberland
Boscobelle
Mile and a Quarter
Orange Hill · Belleplaine · Bathsheba
ESTONE NAT. PARK · Mt. Hillaby 340
Welchman Hall · HARRISON'S CAVE
Rock Hall · GUN HILL TOWER
Jackson · Ellerton · Brereton
Thorpes · Six Cross Roads · St. Patricks
Black Rock · The Crane
Rendezvous · Newton Terrace
Hastings · Olstins
South Point

CARIBBEAN SEA

West from Greenwich

TRINIDAD AND TOBAGO

CARIBBEAN SEA
Chupara Pt. · Grande Matelot Pt. · Grande Riviere · Sans Souci
La Filette · Blanchisseuse · Matelot · Toco
Trinidad · La Vache · Maracas Bay · Mt. Roberts 658 · Galera Pt.
La Vache Bay · Chupara Bay · PIARCO · Cumana Bay
Saut D'Eau I. · Las Cuevas · RINCON FALLS · Redhead
Corozal Pt. · Maracas · El Tucuche 936 · Mt. Aripo · Rampanalgas
Macqueripe Bay · RIVER ESTATE WATERWHEEL · 848 · Brasso Seco
Huevos I. · **Diego Martin** · 565 · AST WRIGHT NATURE CENTRE · Northern Range · Salybia
The Dragon's Mouths · Carenage · Santa Cruz · Maraval · La Veronica · ARIPO CAVES · Hollis Reservoir · Balandra Bay
Chaguaramas · Four Roads · San Juan · La Pastora · Orupuche · Saline Bay
Chacachacare I. · Monos I. · **PORT OF SPAIN** · **Morvant** · St. Joseph · Lopinot · Valencia · Matura Bay
Gaspar Grande · Pt. Gourde · San Juan · Tunapuna · Tacarigua · **Arima** · Cuare
MILITARY MUSEUM · **Port of Spain** · LAVENTILLE · St. Augustine · ARIMA · SANGRE GRANDE · Matura
CARONI BIRD SANCTUARY · Caroni · Arouca · Verdant Vale · Valencia · Cuare
Boca Grande · Caroni Swamp · Caroni · Piarco · **La Horquetta** · Guaico · Cuare
Cacandee · Cunupia · San Rafael · Cumuto · **Sangre Grande**
Settlement · Jerningham Junction · Talparo · Coryal · Cheeyou · Upper Manzanilla
Barrancones Pt. · Longdenville · Cunaripa · Lower Manzanilla
Chaguanas · Todds Road · Mundo Nuevo · Mt. Tamana 308 · Manzanilla Pt.
Waterloo · Carapichaima · Freeport · Biche · Manzanilla Bay
COUVA · TABAQUITE/TALPARO · Flanagin Town · Poole
California · Montserrat · Nariva Swamp
Point Lisas Industrial Estate · Gran Couva · Hills · RIO CLARO · Cocos Bay
Tortuga · Tabaquite · CENTRAL RANGE WILDLIFE SANCTUARY · Navet · Cuche
Claxton Bay · Mayo · Navet Reservoir · **Rio Claro**
Couva · Central Range · Busy Corner
Pointe-à-Pierre · Claxton Bay · Guatuaro Pt.
Ste. Madeleine · New Grant · Poole · Ecclesville · St. Joseph
Vistabella · Jere · Tableland · Mayaro
San Fernando · **La Romain** · Indian Walk · PRINCES TOWN · Ortoire · Mayaro Bay
SAN FERNANDO · Princes Town · DEVILS WOODFORD MUD VOLCANO
Brighton · Pitch Lake · Otaheite Bay · Hermitage · Guayaguayare Bay
Pitch Pt. · **La Brea** · St. Mary's · Monkey Town
Guapo Bay · Rousillac · Oropuche Lagoon · Debe · Preau · Trinity Hills
Point Fortin · Guapo · PENAL/DEBE · MAYARO · Rushville
POINT FORTIN · Fyzabad · DIGITY MUD VOLCANOES · Lizard
Irois Bay · Cap-de-Ville · **Siparia** · **Penal** · Guayaguayare
Cedros Pt. · SIPARIA · Oropuche · Basse Terre · Moruga
Granville · Buenos Ayres · Erin · Palo Seco · La Lune · Galeota Pt.
Cedros Bay · Islote Pt. · Erin Bay · Erin (San Franciqui) · Sadhoowa · Moruga
Los Gallos Pt. · Icacos Bay · Bonasse · Fullarton · Tarapo Pt. · Negra Pt.
Icacos Pt.

West from Greenwich

Gulf of Paria

TRINIDAD AND TOBAGO (Tobago inset)

CARIBBEAN SEA
Sisters Rocks · Man of War Bay · **Charlotteville**
Bloody Bay · Parlatuvier · Speyside
Castara Bay · 565 · ARGYLE WATERFALLS
Castara · Moriah · Main Ridge
Arnos Vale · Hillsborough · **Roxborough**
Plymouth · Mason Hall · Pembroke · Carapuse Bay
Buccoo Reef · Mason Hall Dam · Studley Park
BUCCOO · GRAFTON · **Scarborough** · **Tobago**
TAB · Canaan · Rockly Bay
Crown Pt.

West from Greenwich

Barbados
Tobago · Trinidad

Coral reef

COPYRIGHT PHILIP'S

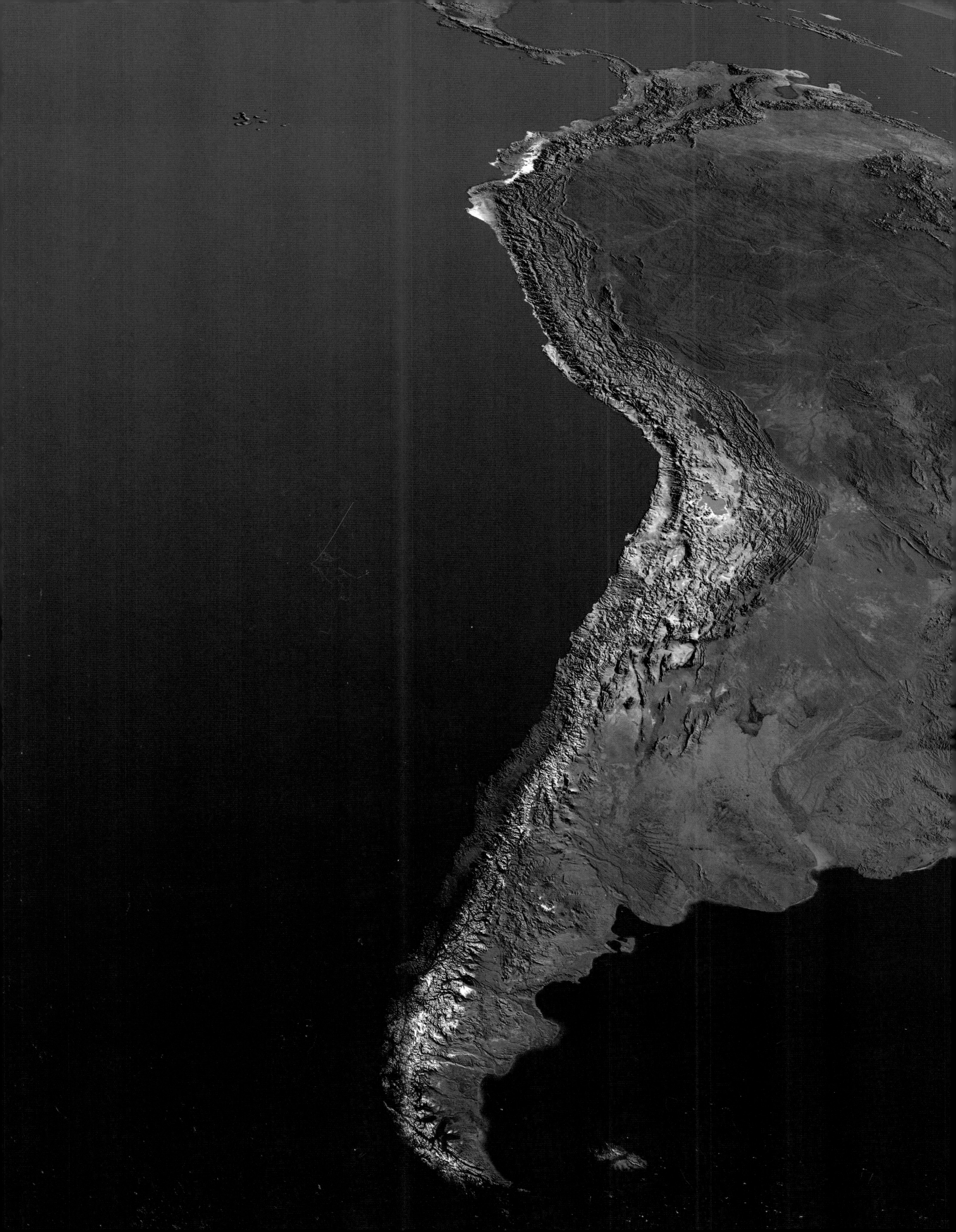

SOUTH AMERICA

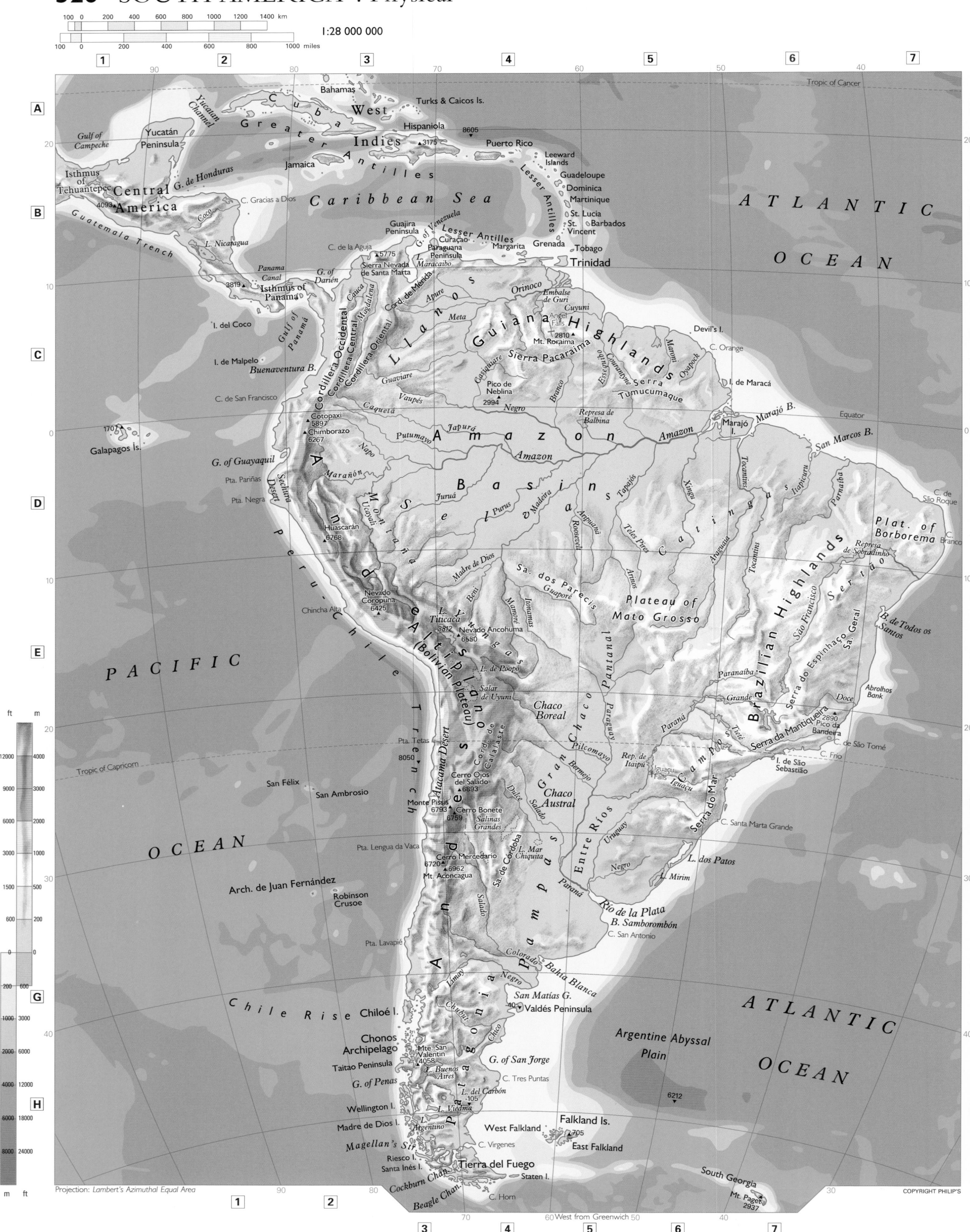

1:28 000 000

Projection: Lambert's Azimuthal Equal Area

COPYRIGHT PHILIP'S

1:28 000 000

LIMA ■ Capital Cities

Projection: *Lambert's Azimuthal Equal Area*

COPYRIGHT PHILIP'S

Projection: Lamberts Equivalent Azimuthal

MARGARITA
1 : 600 000

CARIBBEAN SEA

Isla Los Frailes
Cabo Negro
Manzanillo
Guayacán
Pedro González
El Agua
PLAYA EL AGUA
El Tirano
Puerte Fermín
700
El Cardón
480 Cerro
Guayamuri
Cerro Matasiete
La Asunción
Punta Ballena
Pampatar
Porlamar

NUEVA ESPARTA
Bahía de Juangriego
Juangriego
Altagracia
La Fuente
La Plaza
La Vecindad
Las Cabreras
529
Manzanillo
El Tunal
San Francisco de Macanao
760
San Juan Bautista
957
El Valle del Espíritu Santo
El Copey
La Asunción

Punta de Tigre
NUEVA ESPARTA
Ensenada La Guardia
La Guardia
Laguna de la Restinga
Chacachocare
El Espinal
El Tuey
San Antonio
Porlamar

Punta Relámpago
Bahía de Macanao
Boca de Pozo
Robledal
Parque Nacional Laguna de La Restinga
Boca del Río
Los Gómez
Mata Redonda
Las Bermúdez
Los Bagres
Parate Bueno
Punta Arenas
Manglillo
Guayacancito
Bahía de Mangle
Laguna de Raya
Laguna de las Marites
El Guamache
El Yaque
La Isleta
Punta Mosquito

Peninsula de Macanao
Punta Charagato
Punta de Piedras
Bahía de Guamache
Punta Mangle
Isla Cubagua
Punta La Playa
San Pedro de Coche
El Bichar
Güinima
70
El Guamache

Isla de Margarita
(Venezuela)

Isla Coche

West from Greenwich

The Grenadines
St. George's GRENADA
GND
Blanquilla (Ven.)
Is Los Hermanos (Ven.)
I. de Margarita
NUEVA ESPARTA
La Asunción
Porlamar
Is. Los Testigos (Ven.)
Tobago
Scarborough
TRINIDAD AND TOBAGO
Port of Spain
Arima
San Fernando
Trinidad
Río Claro
Guayaguayare

Coche
Carúpano
Río Caribe
Pen. de Paria
Pta. Peñas
Dragon's Mouths
Cumaná
Cariaco
El Pilar
Irapa
Güiria
SUCRE
San Juan
Golfo de Paria
La Brea
Araya
Guanta
Barcelona
Anaco
Cantaura
MONAGAS
Maturín
Caripito
ANZOÁTEGUI
San José de Guanipa
El Tigre
Temblador
Guampa
Tucupita
DELTA
AMACURO
Delta del Orinoco

ATLANTIC OCEAN

Morawhanna
Mabaruma
Port Kaituma
BARIMA-WAINI
Charity
Anna Regina
Suddie
Spring Garden
Parika
Georgetown
Mahaicony
New Amsterdam
Rose Hall
Paramaribo
Nieuw Amsterdam
Mana
Albina
St-Laurent-du-Maroni
Sinnamary
I. du Diable
Iles du Salut
Kourou
Cayenne

El Tigre
Pao
Ciudad Guayana
Pto. Ordaz
Upata
El Palmar
El Miamo
La Horqueta
Guasipati
Curiapo
I. Corocoro
Boca Grande
El Manteco
El Collao
Tumeremo
El Dorado
Matthews Ridge
Kokerite
CUYUNI-MAZARUNI
Issano
Rockstone
Linden
Corriverton
Wageningen
Groningen
Totness
Onverwacht
Lelydorp
Zanderij
Moengo
Langatabbetje
Apatou
Gare Tigre
Citron
Paul Isnard
St-Elie
Rémire
Roura
Kaw

Ciudad Bolívar
El Pao
EL A
B O L Í V A R
Serranía Turagua
1839
Embalse de Guri
King George VI Falls
Imbaimadai
GUYANA
Bartica
Kwakwani
DEMERARA-
BERBICE
Tapoeripa
Alliance
Nieuw Nickerie
Wageningen

Angel Falls
Kerepakupai-Merú
2560
Great Falls
CANAIMA
Equeipa
Luepa
La Gran Sabana
Pakaraima Mts.
Roraima
2810
MONTE RORAIMA
Kaieteur Falls
Mahdia
Kurupukari
POTARO-SIPARUNI
Owenteik
Avanavero
W. J. Van Blommestein Meer
SURINAME
Wilhelmina Geb.
Julianatop
1230
Brokopondo
Brownsweg
Pokigron
Bottopassi
FRENCH
Papaichton
ST-LAURENT-DU MARONI
GUIANA
CAYENNE
Régina

Guaina
Arabelo
Sta. Elena de Uairen
Sta. Teresa
Orinduik
Apoteri
Annai
Lethem
Bonfim
UPPER TAKUTU-
UPPER ESSEQUIBO
Isherton
Kamoa Mts.
Biloku
Serra Acarai
Kwamala-samutu
Antécume Pata
Benzdorp
Maripasoula
Saül
Bienvenue
Camopi
Oiapoque
Clevelândia do Norte
Vila Velha

Motocurunya
Catisiming
Catisimiña
SIERRA SARISARIÑAMA
TALU
SARISARIÑAMA
Sa. Pacaraima
Conceição do Maú
Uraricoera
Uricoera
Pirara
Wichabai
Dadanawa
Shea
Novo Paraíso
São João da Baliza
Uberlândia
EAST BERBICE-CORENTYNE
906
734
690

PARIMA-PIRAPECÓ
Serra Curupira
1047
2340
Serra Parima
SERRA DA MOCIDADE
R O R A I M A
Caracaraí
Boa Vista
Alto Alegre
Mucajaí
Serra do Mucajaí
Serra do Apiaú
Viruá
Anauá
San José de Anauá
Serra Tumucumaque
MONTANHAS DO TUMUCUMAQUE
AMAPÁ
Merirumã
Maloca
Serra do Navio
Pedra Branca
Porto Grande
Macapá
I. de Maracá
Sucuriju
Aporema
Araguari

Orinoco
Parima
Serra Tabatinga
Demini
Catrimani
Missão Catrimani
Branco
Novo Paraíso
Jauaperi
Santa Maria do Boiaçu
Alalaú
Anauá
Uatumã
Jatapu
Nhamundá
Trombetas
Paru do Oeste
Cuminá
Citaré
Paru
Jari
Maicuru
Equator
Arere
Laranjal do Jari
Monte Dourado
Boca do Jari
Mazagão
Afuá
Caviana
Chaves
Ilha de Marajó
Anajás
Breves
Oeiras do Para
Portel

Sta. Isabel do Rio Negro
Tapurucuará
Padauiri
Preto
Barcelos
Caurés
Moura
Carvoeiro
B R A Z I L
Represa de Balbina
Balbina
Uatumã
Brás
Porteira
Cuminá
Óbidos
Oriximiná
Faro
Alenquer
Monte Alegre
Prainha
Porto de Moz
Almeirim
Gurupá
Curuá
Amazonas
Jari
Porto de Moz

Agua Preta
Cuiuni
Unini
Pauini
JAÚ
Jaú
L. Amaná
Mucura
Novo Airão
Manacapuru
Manaquiri
Careiro da Várzea
MANAUS
MAO
Itacoatiara
Itapiranga
Silves
Urucará
Parintins
Juruti
Alter do Chão
Belterra
Santarém
Pacoval
Mojui dos Campos
Boim
Aveiro
Vitória
Senador José Porfirio
Altamira
Brasil Novo
Belo Monte
Medicilândia
Favânia
Anapu
Norte
I. de Janaucu

Tefé
L. Piorini
Coari
Lima
Andradé
Foz do Copeá
Codajás
Beruri
Anamã
Caapiranga
Santo Antônio
Arquipélago das Anavilhanas
Presidente Figueiredo
Rio Preto da Eva
Tabocal
Barreirinha
Maués
Mujá
Itaituba
Rurópolis
P A R Á
Brasília Legal
Uruará
Xingu
Tapajós

A M A Z O N A S
Purus
Itanhauá
Coari
Sales
Foz do Copeá
Autazes
Nova Olinda do Norte
Borba
Aruma
Canumã
Maués-Açu
Osório do Fonseca
Careiro do Norte
Ilha Tupinambarana
Madeira
Preto do Igapó-Açu
Hevelândia
Novo Aripuanã
Abacaxis
AMAZÔNIA
São Luís do Tapajós
Tapajós
Trairão

West from Greenwich

COPYRIGHT PHILIP'S

---

6 Administrative divisions in Guyana

1 POMEROON-SUPENAAM   3 DEMERARA-MAHAICA   5 EAST BERBICE - CORENTYNE
2 ESSEQUIBO ISLANDS - WEST DEMERARA   4 MAHAICA-BERBICE

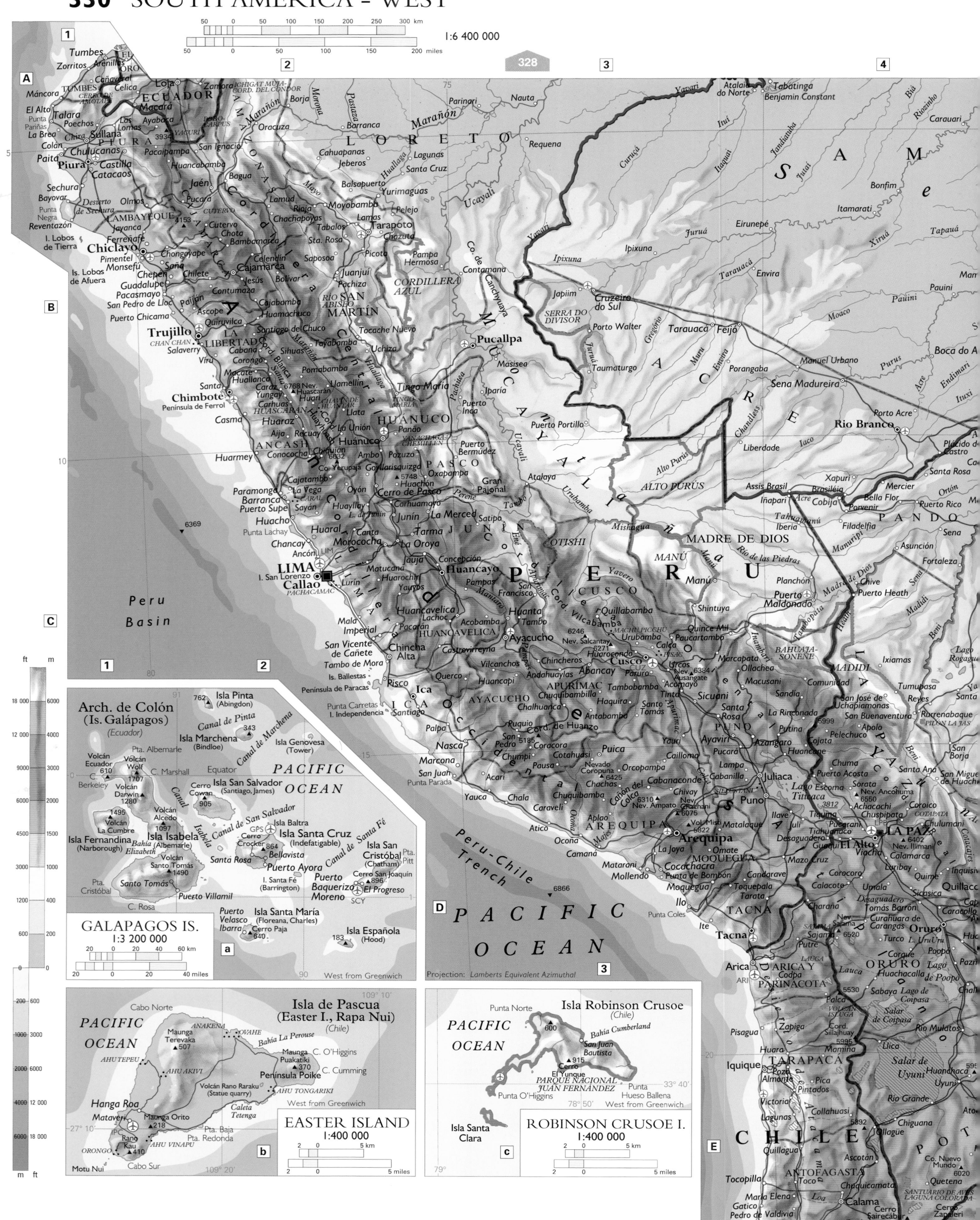

1:6 400 000

328

GALAPAGOS IS.
1:3 200 000

Arch. de Colón
(Is. Galápagos)
(Ecuador)

Isla de Pascua
(Easter I., Rapa Nui)
(Chile)

EASTER ISLAND
1:400 000

Isla Robinson Crusoe
(Chile)

ROBINSON CRUSOE I.
1:400 000

Projection: Lamberts Equivalent Azimuthal

West from Greenwich

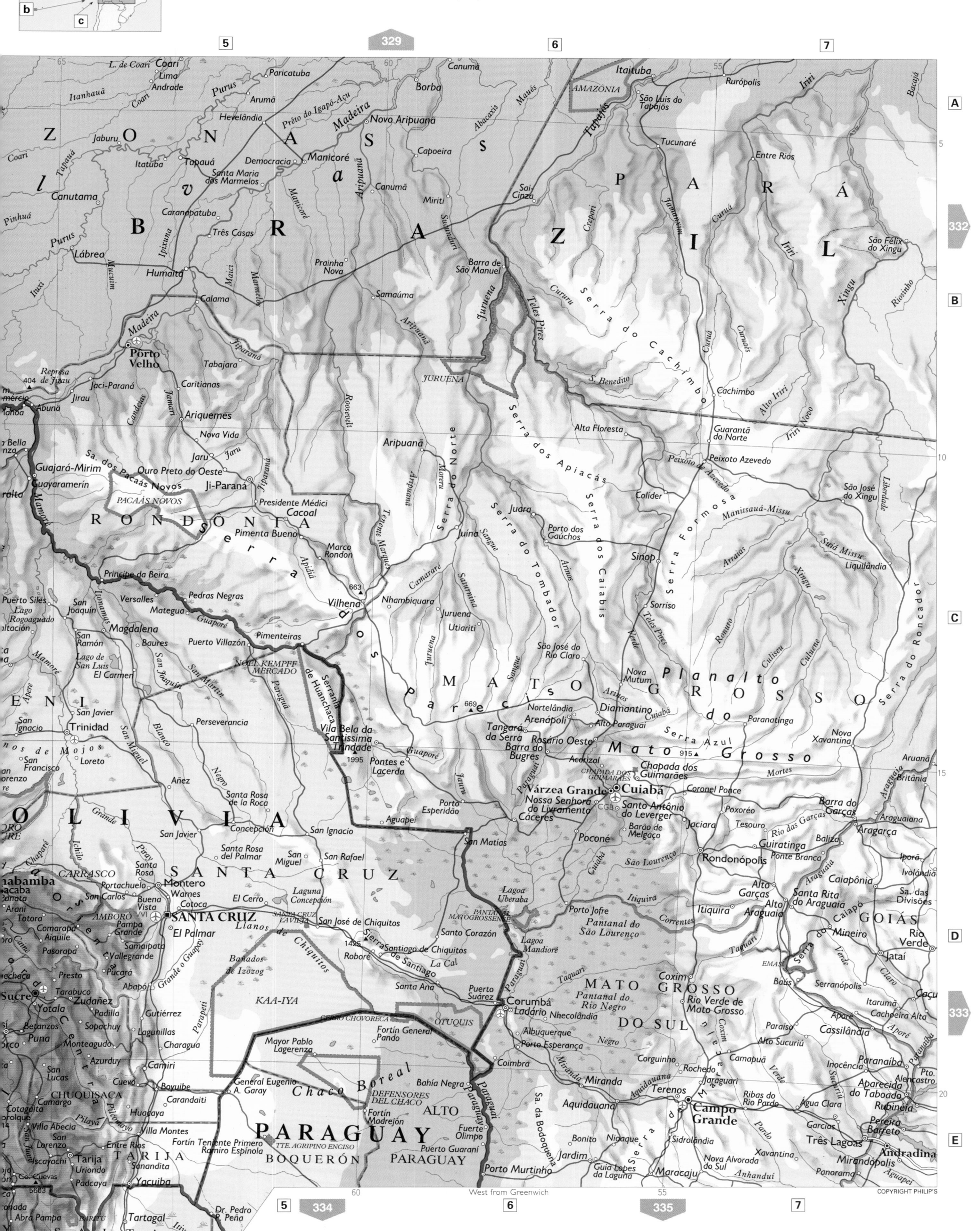

A

332

B

C

D

333

E

West from Greenwich

COPYRIGHT PHILIP'S

1:6 400 000

ATLANTIC OCEAN
BAHIA
GOIÁS
MINAS GERAIS
ESPÍRITO SANTO
SÃO PAULO
PARANÁ
RIO DE JANEIRO
DISTRITO FEDERAL
BRASÍLIA
SALVADOR (Bahia)
BELO HORIZONTE
VITÓRIA
RIO DE JANEIRO
SÃO PAULO
CAMPINAS
SANTOS
CURITIBA
GOIÂNIA
Feira de Santana
Vitória da Conquista
Montes Claros
Uberlândia
Ribeirão Preto
Londrina
Juiz de Fora
Campos
Ilhéus
Porto Seguro
Abrolhos
Banco dos Abrolhos
Hotspur Seamount
Vitória Seamount
Serra Geral de Goiás
Espinhaço
Tropic of Capricorn
West from Greenwich
Projection: Lambert's Equivalent Azimuthal
COPYRIGHT PHILIP'S
331
335

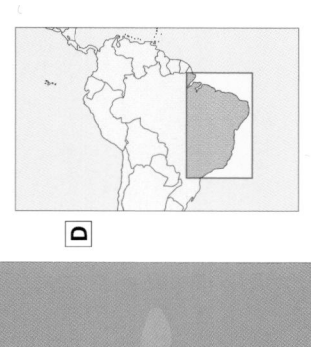

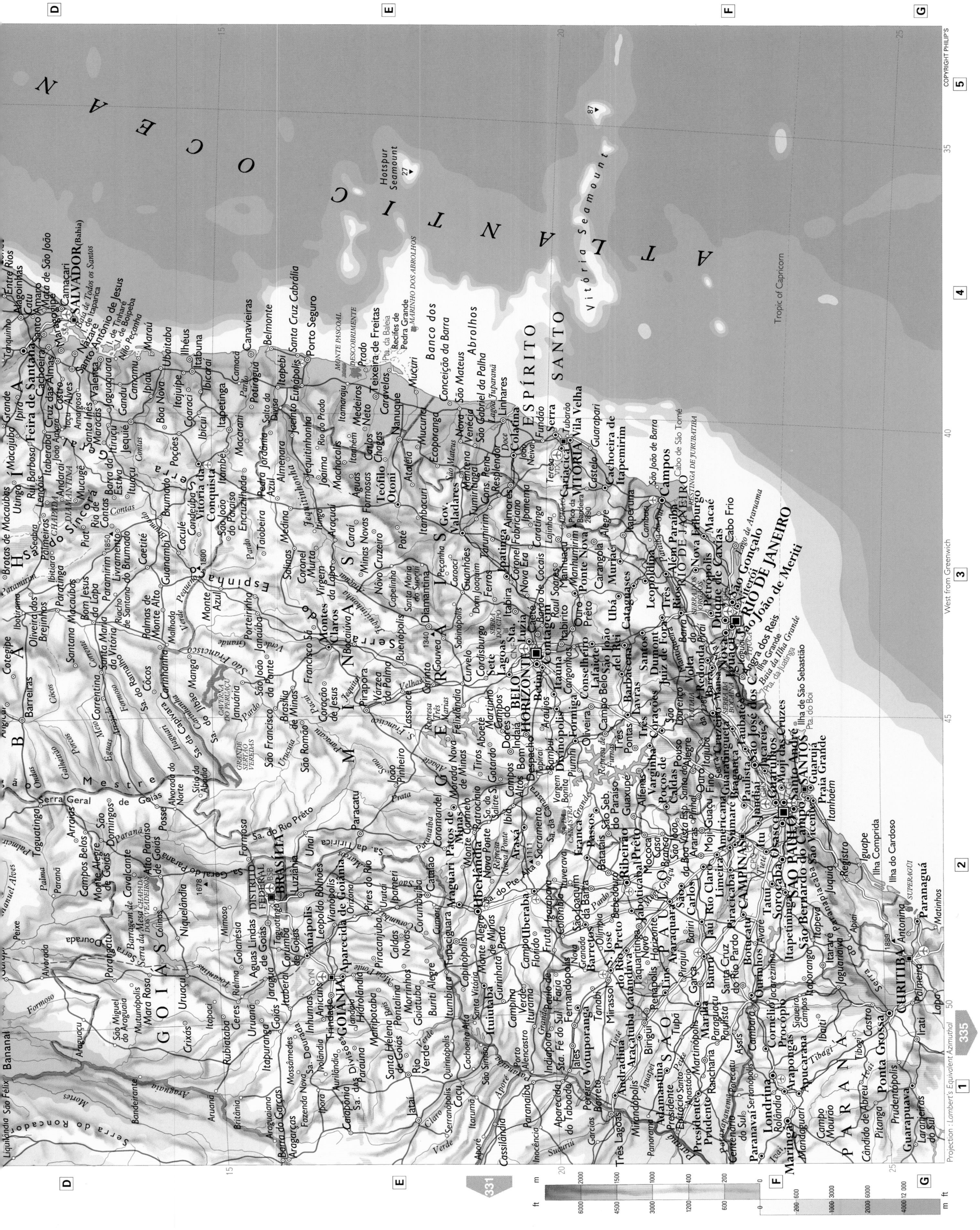

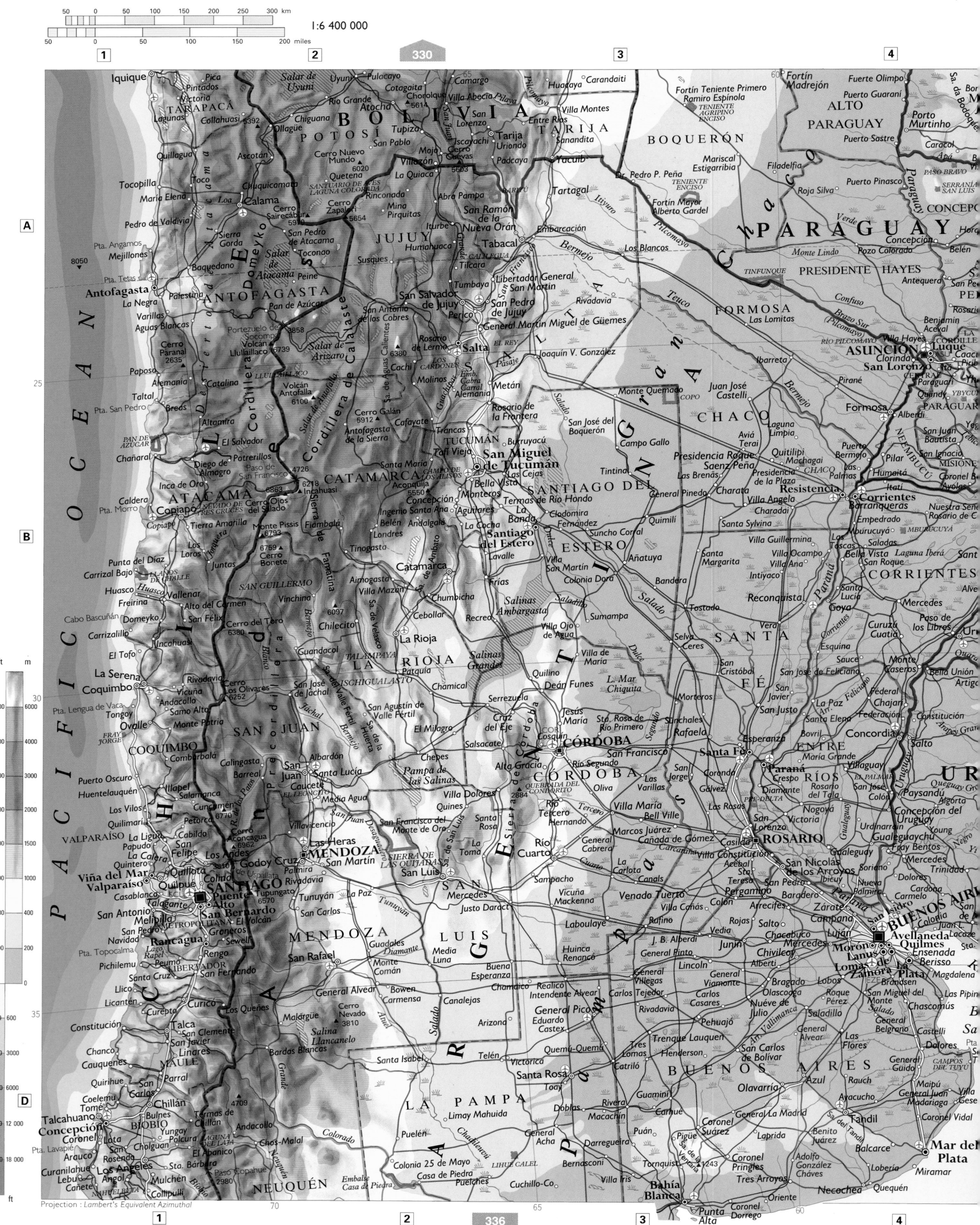

Projection : Lambert's Equivalent Azimuthal

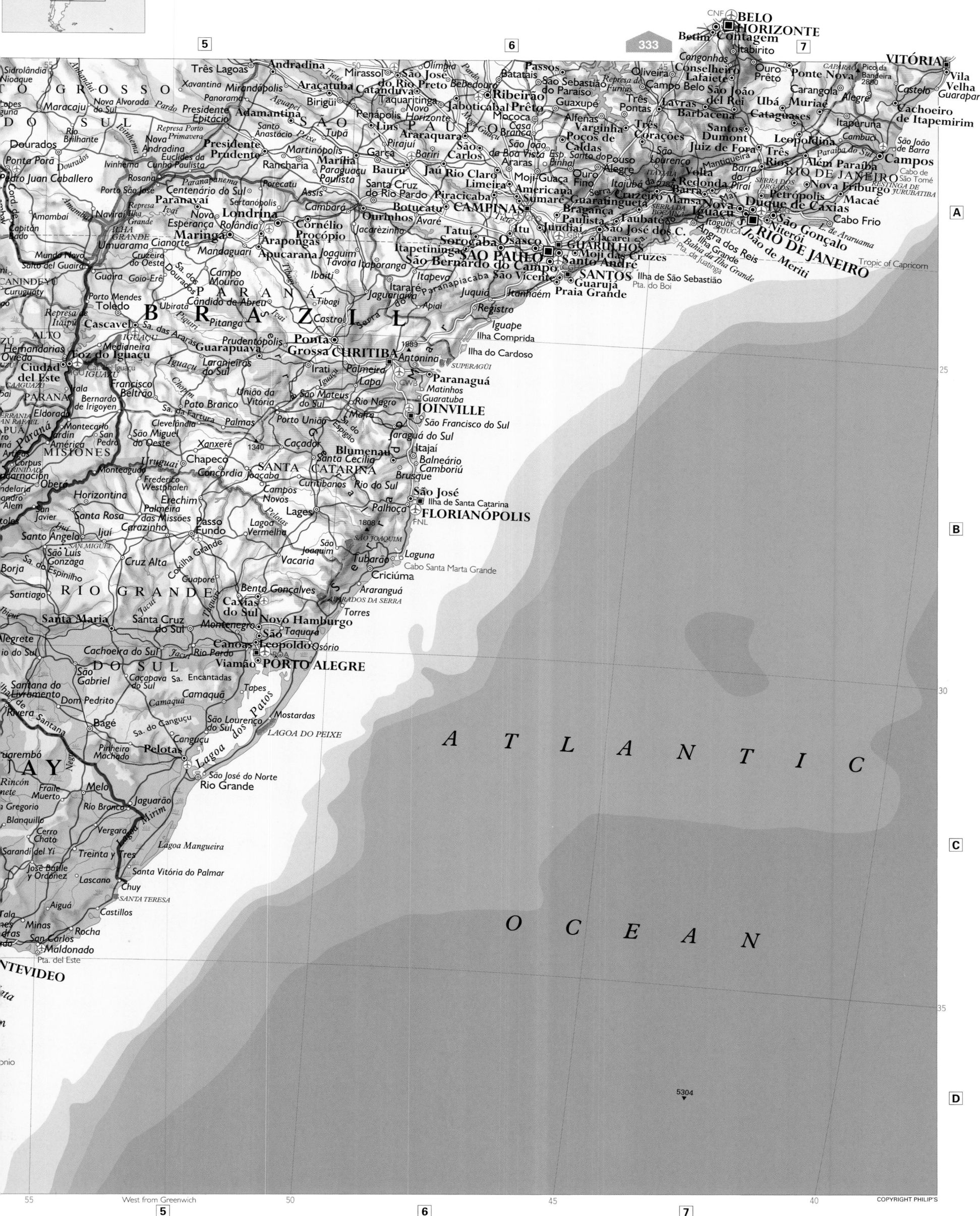

VITÓRIA

CNF BELO
HORIZONTE
Betim Contagem
Itabirito

Congonhas
Conselheiro
Lafaiete
Campo Belo
São João
del Rei

Ouro
Prêto
Ponte Nova
Pico da
Bandeira
2890

Vila
Velha
Guarapari

Passos
Batatais
São Sebastião
do Paraíso
Oliveira
Três
Pontas
Carangola
Alegre
Cachoeiro
de Itapemirim

Olímpia
São José
do Rio Preto
Ribeirão
Prêto
Guaxupé
Alfenas
Varginha
Lavras
Barbacena
Muriaé
Itaperuna

Andradina
Mirassol
Catanduva
Jaboticabal
Casa
Branca
Poços de
Caldas
Três
Corações
Santos
Dumont
Ubá
Cataguases

Três Lagoas
Aracatuba
Birigüi
Penápolis
Taquaritinga
Novo
Horizonte
Mococa
São João
da Boa Vista
Pouso
Alegre
Juiz de Fora
Leopoldina
São João
de Barra
Campos

Xavantina
Mirandópolis
Panorama
Lins
Araraquara
São
Carlos
Araras
Moji-Guaçu
Esp. Santo do
Pinhal
São
Lourenço
Volta
Redonda
Além Paraíba
Paraíba do Sul

Nova Alvorada
do Sul
Presidente
Adamantina
Tupã
Marília
Bauru
Jaú
Rio Claro
Limeira
Americana
Itajubá
da Serra
Mansa
Barra
RIO DE
JANEIRO
Macaé

Maracaju
Presidente
Epitácio
Santo
Anastácio
Pirajuí
Garça
Bariri
Piracicaba
Sumaré
Guaratinguetá
Cruzeiro
Petrópolis
Nova Friburgo

Dourados
Nova
Andradina
Euclides da
Cunha Paulista
Rancharia
Paraguaçu
Paulista
Assis
Santa Cruz
do Rio Pardo
Botucatu
CAMPINAS
Bragança
Paulista
Taubaté
Resende
Duque de Caxias
Cabo Frio

Ponta Porã
Ivinhema
Porto São José
Paranavaí
Nova
Esperança
Cambará
Ourinhos
Avaré
Itu
Jundiaí
São José dos C.
Iguaçu
Nova
Iguaçu

Pedro Juan Caballero
Rosana
Sertanópolis
Londrina
Rolândia
Cornélio
Procópio
Tatuí
Sorocaba
Osasco
GUARULHOS
Moji das Cruzes
São Gonçalo
Niterói
João
de Meriti

Amambaí
Umuarama
Cianorte
Maringá
Apucarana
Itapetininga
SÃO PAULO
Santo André
Angra dos Reis
Viterói

Salto do Guairá
Cruzeiro
do Oeste
Mandaguari
Arapongas
Joaquim
Távora
Itaporanga
Itapeva
São Bernardo
do Campo
Santos
Guarujá
Praia Grande

Amapá
Goio-Erê
Campo
Mourão
Cândido de Abreu
Ibaiti
Itararé
Apiaí
São Vicente
Itanhaém
Ilha de São Sebastião
Pta. do Boi

Ciudad
del Este
Toledo
Cascavel
Medianeira
Guarapuava
Prudentópolis
Ponta
Grossa
CURITIBA
Antonina
Registro
Iguape
Ilha Comprida

Foz do Iguaçu
Laranjeiras
do Sul
Irati
Palmeira
Lapa
Paranaguá
Matinhos
Guaratuba
Ilha do Cardoso

Hernandarias
Francisco
Beltrão
Pato Branco
União da
Vitória
São Mateus
do Sul
Rio Negro
Mafra
JOINVILLE
São Francisco do Sul

Oviedo
Bernardo
de Irigoyen
Clevelândia
Palmas
Porto União
Caçador
Jaraguá do Sul
Itajaí
Balneário
Camboriú

Montecarlo
San
Pedro
Xanxerê
Concórdia
Blumenau
Brusque

MISIONES
Chapecó
Joaçaba
Campos
Novos
Rio do Sul
São José
Ilha de Santa Catarina
FLORIANÓPOLIS

Horizontina
Frederico
Westphalen
Erechim
Palmeira
das Missões
Curitibanos
Lages
Palhoça

Santa Rosa
Carazinho
Passo
Fundo
Vacaria
São
Joaquim
Tubarão
Laguna

Ijuí
Cruz Alta
Bento Gonçalves
Criciúma
Cabo Santa Marta Grande

RIO GRANDE
Caxias
do Sul
Novo Hamburgo
Torres

Santa Maria
Santa Cruz
do Sul
Montenegro
Canoas
São
Leopoldo
Osório

Cachoeira do Sul
Rio Pardo
Viamão
PORTO ALEGRE

DO SUL
São
Gabriel
Cachoeira
do Sul
Camaquã

Bagé
Canguçu
LAGOA DO PEIXE

Pelotas
Lagoa
dos Patos
Mostardas

AY
Melo
Jaguarão
Rio Grande
São José do Norte

ATLANTIC

OCEAN

Tropic of Capricorn

1:6 400 000

50 0 50 100 150 200 250 300 km
50 0 50 100 150 200 miles

2 | **334** | **3** | **4** | **335** | **5**

Labels (selected)

Chile / Pacific side

La Araucanía · Arauco · Cañete · Angol · Mulchén · Colipulli · Victoria · Collipulli · Capitán Pastene · I. Mocha · Curacautín · Lautaro · Carahue · Temuco · Nueva Imperial · Puerto Saavedra · Pitrufquén · Toltén · Loncoche · Villarrica · Panguipulli · Valdivia · Corral · Los Ríos · La Unión · Osorno · Río Bueno · Puyehue · Puerto Varas · Puerto Montt · Los Muermos · Maullín · Ancud · Isla de Chiloé · Castro · Chonchi · Quellón · Chaitén · Achao

Los Lagos · G. de los Coronados · Canal · Hornopirén · Alerce Andino · Chiloé

Archipiélago de los Chonos · Archipiélago Guayaneco · I. Guamblin · I. Campana · I. Patricio Lynch · I. Esmeralda · Península de Taitao · C. Tres Montes · Golfo de Penas · I. Javier · I. Madre de Dios · I. Mornington · G. Trinidad · I. Duque de York · Wellington · Puerto Aisén · Coihaique · Balmaceda · Cochrane · Laguna San Rafael · Cerro Arenales · San Valentín

Magallanes y Antártica Chilena · Puerto Natales · Torres del Paine · Cerro Paine Grande · Punta Arenas · Porvenir · Pen. de Brunswick · I. Riesco · Estrecho de Magallanes · Dawson I. · Tierra del Fuego · Ushuaia · Puerto Williams · I. Navarino · Cabo de Hornos (Cape Horn) · Islas Diego Ramírez

Argentina

La Pampa · Neuquén · Río Negro · Chubut · Santa Cruz · Patagonia

Colonia 25 de Mayo · Puelches · Bernasconi · Neuquén · Cipolletti · Allen · General Roca · Cinco Saltos · Zapala · Cutral-Có · Las Lajas · Junín de los Andes · San Martín de los Andes · San Carlos de Bariloche · El Bolsón · Esquel · El Maitén · Gastre · Gan Gan · Telsen · Puerto Madryn · Trelew · Rawson · Gaimán · Península Valdés · Puerto Pirámides · Punta Delgada · Comallo · Maquinchao · Ingeniero Jacobacci · Los Menucos · Valcheta · San Antonio Oeste · Viedma · Carmen de Patagones · Golfo San Matías · Sierra Grande

Las Plumas · Paso de Indios · José de San Martín · Gran Laguna Salada · Camarones · C. Dos Bahías · B. Bustamante · Sarmiento · Comodoro Rivadavia · Golfo San Jorge · Caleta Olivia · Las Heras · Pico Truncado · Fitz Roy · Puerto Deseado · Puerto San Julián · Gobernador Gregores · Perito Moreno · Los Antiguos · Bajo Caracoles · Las Horquetas · Mt. Inés · Altiplanicie Central · Comandante Luis Piedra Buena · Puerto Santa Cruz · Bahía Grande · Puerto Coig · Río Gallegos · Río Turbio · Güer Aike · Monte Dinero · Punta Delgada · Río Grande · Tierra del Fuego · I. de los Estados (Staten I.)

Lago Buenos Aires (L. General Carrera) · Lago Posadas · El Chaltén · Cerro Fitz Roy · Lago Viedma · Lago Argentino · El Calafate · Los Glaciares · Cerro Murallón

Buenos Aires · Bahía Blanca · Tornquist · Coronel Pringles · Tres Arroyos · Necochea · Balcarce · Lobería · Benito Juárez · Aldo González Cháves

Oceans / Water bodies

PACIFIC OCEAN · ATLANTIC OCEAN · Golfo San Matías · Golfo San Jorge · Bahía Grande · Estrecho de Magallanes · Canal Beagle · Burdwood Bank

FALKLAND ISLANDS (ISLAS MALVINAS) (U.K.)
Jason Is. · Pebble I. · King George B. · Queen Charlotte B. · West Falkland · East Falkland · Weddell I. · Port Stanley · Mt. Adam 700 · Mt. Usborne 705 · C. Dolphin · C. Meredith · Beauchêne I.

Elevation scale

ft	m
9000	3000
6000	2000
4500	1500
3000	1000
1200	400
600	200
0	0
600	200
3000	1000
6000	2000
12 000	4000

m ft

Projection: Lambert's Equivalent Azimuthal

West from Greenwich

GEOGRAPHICAL GLOSSARY

This is a list of the geographical terms from various foreign languages that are found in the place names on the maps and in the index. Each is followed by the language and its English meaning.

Afr. Afrikaans
Alb. Albanian
Amh. Amharic
Ar. Arabic
Belo. Belorussian
Berb. Berber
Bulg. Bulgarian
Burm. Burmese
Cam. Cambodian
Cat. Catalan
Chin. Chinese
Czec. Czech
Dan. Danish
Dut. Dutch
Est. Estonian
Fin. Finnish
Fr. French
Gae. Gaelic
Ger. German
Gr. Greek
Heb. Hebrew
Hin. Hindi
Hung. Hungarian
I.-C. Indo-Chinese
Ice. Icelandic
It. Italian
Indo. Indonesian
Jap. Japanese
Kaz. Kazakh
Kor. Korean
Kyrg. Kyrgyz
Lapp. Lapp (Sami)
Lat. Latvian
Lith. Lithuanian
Malag. Malagasy
Mong. Mongolian
Nor. Norway
Pash. Pashto
Per. Persian
Pol. Polish
Port. Portuguese
Rom. Romanian
Russ. Russian
Sin. Sinhalese
Ser.-Cr. Serbo-Croat
Slov. Slovene
Som. Somali
Span. Spanish
Swe. Swedish
Tib. Tibetan
Turk. Turkish
Ukr. Ukrainian
Viet. Vietnamese

-á *Ice.* river
-å *Dan., Nor., Swe.* stream
-abad *Farsi, Russ.* town
Abyad *Ar.* white mountain
Ada, Adasi *Turk.* island
Addis *Amh.* new
Adrar *Ar., Berb.* mountains
Aiguille *Fr.* peak
Aïn, Aîn (A.) *Ar.* spring
Ákra *Gr.* cape, point
Akrotíri *Gr.* cape, point
Alb *Ger.* mountains
Albufera *Span.* lagoon
-ålen *Nor.* islands
Alpen *Ger.* mountain ranges
Alpes *Fr.* mountains
Alpi *It.* mountains
Alt *Ger.* old
Alta, Alto *Port.* high, upper
Altos *Span.* mountains
-älv, -älven *Swe.* stream, river
Amtskommune (Amt.) *Dan.* first-order administrative division
-ån *Swe.* river
Anse *Fr.* bay
Ao *Thai* bay
Appennino *It.* mountain range
Archipel *Fr.* archipelago
Archipiélago (Arch.) *Span.* archipelago
Arcipélago *It.* archipelago
Arquipélago (Arq.) *Port.* archipelago
Arrecife *Span.* reef
Arroyo (Arr.) *Span.* stream
-ås, -åsen *Nor., Swe.* hill
Ayios *Gr.* island
Ayn *Ar.* well, waterhole

Baai, -baai *Afr., Dut.* bay
Bāb *Ar.* gate, strait
Bäck, -bäcken *Swe.* stream
Back, -backen, *Swe.* hill
Bad, -baden *Ger.* spa
Badia *Cat.* bay
Bādiyah, Bādiyat *Ar.* desert
Bæk *Dan.* stream
Bælt *Dan.* strait
Baharu *Malay* new
Bahía (B.) *Span.* bay
Bahiret *Ar.* lagoon
Bahr *Ar.* sea, lake, river
Bahra Bahrat *Ar.* lake
Baía (B.) *Port.* bay
Baie (B.) *Fr.* bay
Baixa, Baixo *Port.* lower
Baja, Bajo *Span.* lower
Bakke *Nor.* hill
Bala *Farsi* upper
Ballon *Fr.* dome
Baltă *Rom.* marsh, lake
Ban *Lao, Thai* village
-Bana *Jap.* cape
Banc *Fr.* bank
Banco *Span.* bank
Bandao *Chin.* peninsula
Bandar *Ar., Malay* port, harbour
Bandar *Farsi* bay
Banja *Ser.-Cr.* spa, resort
Banjaran *Malay* mountain range
Baraji *Turk.* dam
Barat *Indo., Malay* western
Barrage (Barr.) *Fr.* dam
Barragem (Barr.) *Port.* dam, reservoir
Bas, basse *Fr.* lower
Bassin *Fr.* basin
-batang *Indo.* river
Baṭlaq *Farsi* marsh
Batu *Malay* mountain
Bayt *Heb.* house, village
Bazar *Hin.* market, bazaar
-beek *Afr., Dut.* river
Be'er *Heb.* well
Bei *Chin.* north, northern
Beinn, Ben *Gae.* mountain
Beit *Heb.* village
Belaya, Belo, Beloye, Belyy *Russ.* white
Belogorye *Russ.* hills, mountain range
Bender *Som.* harbour
Berg(e), -berg(e) *Afr., Ger.* mountain(s)
-berg, -en, -et *Nor., Swe.* hill, mountain, rock
Besar *Indo., Malay* big
Bet *Heb.* house, village
Bir, Bîr, Bi'r *Ar.* well
Birkat, Birket *Ar.* lake, marsh, well
Bishti *Alb.* cape
-bjerg *Dan.* hill, point
Blaenau *Welsh* upland
-bo *Chin.* lake
Boca *Port., Span.* river mouth, inlet
Bodden *Ger.* bay, inlet
Bogaz, Boğazı *Turk.* channel, strait
Bogd *Mong.* mountain range
Bois *Fr.* woods
Boka *Ser.-Cr.* gulf, inlet
Bolshoi, Bolshaya, Bolshoye (Bol.) *Russ.* great, large
Bordj (Bj.) *Ar.* fort
-borg *Dan., Nor., Swe.* castle, fort
Bory *Pol.* woods
Bosque *Span.* woods
-botn *Nor.* valley floor
Bouche(s) *Fr.* mouth(s)
Braţul *Rom.* distributary stream, branch
-bre, -breen *Nor.* glacier
Bredning *Dan.* bay
Brücke *Ger.* bridge
-brug *Dut.* bridge
-brunn *Swe.* well, spring
Bucht *Ger.* bay
Bugt *Dan.* bay
-bugten *Dan.* bay
Buheirat *Ar.* lake, reservoir
Bukit *Malay* hill
-bukt, -a *Nor.* bay
-bukten *Swe.* bay
-bulag *Mong.* spring
Bulag *Chin.* lake
Bulu *Malay* mountain
Bum *Burm.* mountain
Bûr *Ar.* port
Burg. *Ar.* fort
Burg, -burg *Ger.* castle
Burnu, Burun *Turk.* cape
Butt *Gae.* promontory
Büyük *Turk.* big
-by *Dan., Nor., Swe.* town
-byen *Nor., Swe.* town

Cabeza *Span.* peak, hill
Cabo (C.) *Port., Span.* headland, cape
Cachoeira *Port.* waterfall
Cala Cat. *It.* bay
Camp Port. *Span.* land, field
Câmpia *Rom.* plain
Campo *It., Port., Span.* plain
Campos *Span.* upland
Canal (Can.) *Fr., Port., Span.* canal, channel
Canale (Can.) *It.* channel
Canalul (Can.) *Ser.-Cr.* canal
Cao Nguyen *Thai* plateau, tableland
Cap (C.) *Cat., Fr.* cape
Capo (C) *It.* cape
Carn *Gae.* hill
Carse *Gae.* valley
Catarata *Port., Span.* cataract
Cauce *Span.* intermittent stream
Causse *Fr.* limestone plateau
Cay, Cayi, -cay, -cayi *Turk.* river
Cayo(s) *Span.* rock(s), islet(s)
Cefn *Welsh* hill
Cerro *Span.* hill, peak
Česká, Český, České *Czec.* Czech
Chaco *Span.* jungle
Chaîne(s) *Fr.* mountain range(s)
Chang *Chin.* mountain
Chapa *Span.* hills, upland
Chapada *Port.* hills, upland
Chaung *Burm.* stream, river
Chi *Chin.* small lake
-ch'ŏn *Kor.* river
-chŏsuji *Kor.* reservoir
Chott *Ar.* salt lake, depression
Chu *Tib.* river
Chute *Fr.* waterfall
Città *It.* city
Ciudad *Span.* city
Co *Tib.* lake
Cochilla (Coch.) *Port.* hills
Col *Fr., It.* pass
Colina(s) *Span.* hill(s)
Colle *It.* pass
Colline(s) *Fr.* hill(s)
Conca *It.* plain, basin
Cordillera (Cord.) *Span.* mountain range
Costa *It., Port., Span.* coast
Côte *Fr.* coast, slope, hill
Coteaux *Fr.* hills
Cuchilla *Span.* hills
Cuenca *Span.* river basin
Cu-Lao *Viet.* island

Da *Chin.* big
Da *Viet.* river
Daban *Mong.* pass
Dağ(ı) *Turk.* mountain(s)
Dāgh *Farsi* mountain
Dağları *Turk.* mountain range
-dai, -daichi *Jap.* plateau
-Dake *Jap.* mountain
-dal, -e *Dan., Swe.* valley
-dal, -en *Swe., Nor.* valley, stream
Dalay Mong. large lake
-ðalir, -ðalur *Ice.* valley
-damm, -en *Swe.* lake
Danau *Malay* lake
Dao *Chin., Viet.* island
Dar *Ar.* region
Darya *Russ.* river
Daryācheh *Farsi* marshy lake, lake
Dasht *Farsi* desert, steppe
Daung *Burm.* mountain, hill
Dayr *Ar.* monastery
Debre *Amh.* hill
Deli *Ser.-Cr.* mountain
Deniz, -i *Turk.* sea
Département (Dépt.) *Fr.* first-order administrative division
Dere *Turk.* stream
Desierto (Des.) *Span.* desert
Détroit *Fr.* strait
Dhar *Ar.* region, mountain range
Diep *Dut.* channel
Dijk *Dut.* dyke
Ding *Chin.* mountain
Dingzi *Chin.* hill, mountain
Djebel (Dj.) *Ar.* mountain
-djúp *Ice.* fjord
-djupet *Swe.* channel, sound
-Do *Jap., Kor.* island
Dolina *Russ.* valley
Dolna, Dolni *Bulg.* lower
Dolna, Dolne, Dolny *Russ.* lower
Dolní *Czec.* lower
Dolok (D.) *Malay* mountain
-dong *Kor.* village, town
Dong *Chin.* east, eastern
Donja, Donji *Ser.-Cr.* lower
-dorf *Ger.* village
-dorp *Afr.* village
-drif *Afr.* ford
-dybet *Dan.* marine channel
Dzong *Tib.* town, settlement
Dzüün *Mong.* east, eastern

-egga *Nor.* peak
-eiland, -en (eil.) *Afr., Dut.* island(s)
Eilean *Gae.* island
-elv, -a *Nor.* river
Embalse *Span.* reservoir
'Emeq *Heb.* plain, valley
Ensenada *Span.* bay
Erg *Ar.* sand desert
Estero *Span.* estuary
Estrada *Span.* bay
Estrecho *Span.* strait
Estuaire *Fr.* estuary
Estuario *Span.* estuary
Étang *Fr.* lagoon, lake
-ey, -jar *Ice.* island(s)
-ežeras *Lith.* lake
-ezers *Lat.* lake

Falaise *Fr.* cliff
-fallet *Swe.* waterfall
Farihy *Malag.* lake
Faro *Span.* lighthouse
-feld *Ger.* field
-fell *Ice.* mountain, hill
Feng *Chin.* mountain range
Fiume (F.) *It.* river
-fjäll, -en, -et *Swe.* hill(s), mountain(s), ridge
-fjärden *Swe.* fjord
Fjeld *Dan.* mountain
-fjell, -et *Nor.* mountain range
-fjord, -en *Dan., Nor., Swe.* fjord
-fjorður *Ice.* fjord, bay, inlet
Fleuve (Fl.) *Fr.* river
-flói *Ice.* bay, marshy country
Fluss (F.) *Ger.* river
Foce, Foci *It.* mouth(s)
Folyó (F.) *Hung.* river
-fonn *Nor.* glacier
-fontein *Afr.* fountain, spring
Forêt *Fr.* forest
-fors, -en *Swe.* waterfall, rapids
-foss, -en *Ice., Nor.* waterfall
Forst *Ger.* forest
Foum *Ar.* pass
Fuente *Span.* source
-furt *Ger.* ford
Fylke *Nor.* first-order administrative division

-gang *Chin.* bay, harbour
-gang *Kor.* river
Ganga *Hin., Sin.* river
Gangri *Tib.* mountain
Gaoyuan *Chin.* plateau
-gat *Dan.* sound
-Gata *Jap.* lake
-gau *Ger.* district
-Gawa *Jap.* river
Gebel (G.) *Ar.* mountain
Gebirge (Geb.) *Ger.* hills, mountains
Gezirat, Geziret *Ar.* island
Ghat *Hin.* range of hills
Ghiol *Rom.* lake
Ghubbat *Ar.* bay, inlet
Gjiri *Alb.* bay
Gjol *Alb.* lagoon, lake
Glava (Gl.) *Ser.-Cr.* mountain, peak
Glen *Gae.* valley
Gletscher (Gl.) *Ger.* glacier
Gobi *Mong.* desert
Gol *Mong.* river
Göl *Azeri, Turk.* lake
Golfe (G.) *Fr.* gulf
Golfo (G.) *It., Span.* gulf
Gölü *Turk.* lake
Gomba *Tib.* settlement
Gora, Góra *Bulg., Russ., Ser.-Cr., Pol.* mountain
Gorje *Ser.-Cr.* hills, mountains
Gorno *Russ.* mountainous
-gorod *Russ.* small town
Gory, Góry *Pol., Russ.* mountain
-grad *Bulg. Russ., Ser.-Cr.* town, city
-grada *Russ.* ridge
Gran *It., Span.* big, great
Grand, -e *Fr.* big, great
Groot (Gt.) *Afr., Dut.* big, great
Gross, -e, -en, -er *Ger.* big, great(er)
Grupo *Span.* group
Gruppo *It.* group
Guan *Chin.* pass
Guba (G.) *Russ.* bay
-Guntō *Jap.* island group
Gunong, Gunung (G.) *Indo., Malay* mountain
Gură *Rom.* passage

Hadabat *Ar.* plateau
Hadjer *Ar.* mountain
-hafen *Ger.* harbour, port
Haff *Ger.* bay, lagoon
Hai *Chin.* lake, sea
Haixia *Chin.* channel, strait
Halbinsel *Ger.* peninsula
Halvø *Dan.* peninsula
Halvøya *Nor.* peninsula
Hămad, Hamada, Hammādah, Hammādat *Ar.* stony desert, plateau
-hamn *Swe., Nor.* harbour, anchorage
Hāmūn *Farsi* marsh, lake
-Hantō *Jap.* peninsula
Har(e) *Heb.* hill(s), mountain(s)
Hassi (Hi.) *Ar.* well
-haug *Nor.* hill
Hav, Havet *Nor., Swe.* sea
-havn *Dan., Nor.* bay, harbour
Havre *Fr.* harbour
Hawd *Ar.* oasis
Hawr *Ar.* lake, marsh
He *Chin.* river
-hegység *Hung.* hills, forest
Heide *Ger.* heath, moor
Helodranon' *Malag.* bay
Higashi *Jap.* east, eastern
-ho *Kor.* lake
-hø *Nor.* peak
Hoch *Ger.* high
Hochland *Afr.* highland
Hoek, -hoek *Afr., Dut.* cape, point
-höfn *Ice.* harbour, port
-hög, -en, -högar, -högarna *Swe.* hill(s), peak, mountain
Höhe *Ger.* height
Hohen *Ger.* high, upper
-hoi *Chin.* bay
-høj, -e *Dan.* hills
-holm, -holme, -holmen *Dan., Nor., Swe.* island
Hon *Viet.* island
Hoog *Dut.* high
Hora *Czec., Ukr.* mountain
-horn *Ger.* peak
Hory *Czec.* mountains, hills
-hot *Mong.* town
-hoved *Dan.* point, headland, peninsula
-hrad *Czec.* town
Hráun *Ice.* lava
-hsi *Chin.* river
-hsia *Chin.* gorge, strait
-hsien *Chin.* district
Hu *Chin.* lake, reservoir
Huk *Dan., Ger.* cape
-huk *Swe.* cape
Huken *Nor.* cape

Idd *Ar.* well
Idehan *Ar., Berb.* sandy plain, dunes
-ike *Jap.* lake
Île(s) (I(s).) *Fr.* island(s)
Ilha(s) (I(s).) *Port.* island(s)
imeni *Russ.* 'in the name of'
Inish *Gae.* island
Insel(n) (I.) *Ger.* island(s)
Irmak *Turk.* river
'Irq *Ar.* dunes
Isla(s) (I(s).) *Span.* island(s)
Iso *Fin.* big, great
Isol, -a, -e (I.) *It.* island(s)
Isthme *Fr.* isthmus
Istmo *Span.* isthmus
-iwa *Jap.* island

Jabal *Ar.* mountain range
Järv *Est.* lake
järvi *Fin.* lake, bay, pond
-jaur, -javre *Lapp.* lake
Jazā'ir *Ar.* islands
Jazīra, jazīrat *Ar.* island
Jazireh *Farsi* island
Jebel *Ar.* mountain
Jezero *Ser.-Cr.* lake
Jezioro *Pol.* lake
Jiang *Chin.* river
Jiao *Chin.* cape
-Jima *Jap.* island
Jøkulen *Nor.* glacier, ice cap
-joki *Fin.* river
-jökull *Ice.* glacier, ice cap
Jūras Līcis *Lat.* bay, gulf

Kaap (K.) *Afr.* cape
-kai *Jap.* bay, channel, sea
-kaikyō *Jap.* strait
-kaise *Lapp.* mountain
kalnas *Lith.* hill
Kamennyy *Russ.* stony
Kampong *Cam.* village
Kampung *Malay* village
-kanaal *Dut.* canal
Kanal *Dan.* channel, gulf
Kanal *Ger., Swe.* canal
-kanal *Ser.-Cr.* channel, canal
Kanava *Fin.* canal
Kang *Kor.* river, bay
Kap (K.) *Dan., Ger.* cape, point
-kapp *Nor.* cape, point
-kaupstaður *Ice.* market town
-kaupunki *Fin.* town
Kavīr *Farsi* salt desert
Kébir *Ar.* great
Kecil *Malay* lesser, little
Kefar *Heb.* village, hamlet
-Ken *Jap.* first-order administrative division
Kep, -i (K.) *Alb.* cape
Kepulauan (Kep.) *Indo., Malay* archipelago
Keski- *Fin.* middle, central
Khalīg, Khalīj *Ar.* gulf
-khamba *Tib.* source, spring
Khawr *Ar.* bay, channel, wadi
Khlong *Thai* river
Kho Khot *Thai* isthmus
Khōr *Farsi* bay, estuary
Khrebet *Russ.* mountain range
Kita- *Jap.* north
Klein,-e, -er *Ger.* small
-klint *Dan.* cliff
Klintar *Swe.* hills
-kloof *Afr.* gorge, pass
Knude *Dan.* point
-Ko *Jap.* lake
Ko *Thai* island
-kōchi *Jap.* mountainous region
-kōgen *Jap.* plateau
Kohi *Pash.* mountains
Kol *Kaz., Kyrg.* lake
Kólpos *Gr., Turk.* gulf, bay
Kolymskoye *Russ.* mountain range
Kompong *Malay* landing place
-kop *Afr.* hill
-kopf *Ger.* hill
-köping *Swe.* market town
Körfäzi *Azeri* gulf
Körfezi *Turk.* gulf
Kosa *Russ., Ukr.* spit
-koski *Fin.* rapids
-kraal *Afr.* native village
-kraj *Czec., Pol., Ser.-Cr.* region
Krasnyy *Russ.* red
Kryazh *Russ.* ridge, hills
Kuala *Malay* bay
-kuan *Chin.* pass
Kūh(ha) *Farsi* mountain(s)
Kul *Russ.* lake
-kulle *Swe.* hill
Kum *Russ.* sandy desert
Kumpu *Fin.* hill
Kwe *Burm.* bay, gulf
-kylä *Fin.* village
Kyst, -en *Dan., Nor.* coast
Kyun(zu) *Burm.* island(s)

La *Tib.* pass
-laagte *Afr.* watercourse

Lääni *Fin.* first-order administrative division
Lac (L.) *Fr.* lake
Lacul (L.) *Rom.* lake, lagoon
Lago (L.) *It., Port., Span.* lake, lagoon
Lagoa (L.) *Port.* lagoon
Lagos *Port., Span.* lakes
Laguna (L.) *It., Span.* lagoon, lake
Lagune (L.) *Fr.* lake
-laht *Est.* bay
Lahti *Fin.* bay, gulf, cove
Lakhti *Russ.* bay, gulf
Lam *Thai* river
Lampi *Fin.* lake
Län *Swe.* first-order administrative division
Land *Ger.* first-order administrative division
-land *Dan.* region
-land *Afr., Nor.* land, province
Lande *Fr.* heath
Laut *Indo.* sea
Law *Gae.* hill, mountain
Līcis *Lat.* gulf
Lido *It.* beach, shore
Liedao *Chin.* islands
Lilla *Swe.* small
Lille *Dan., Nor.* small
Liman *Russ.* bay, gulf
Límni (L.) *Gr.* lake
Ling *Chin.* mountain range
-linna *Fin.* fort
Llano *Span.* prairie, plain
Llyn *Welsh* lake
Loch (L.) *Gae.* lake, inlet
Lough (L.) *Gae.* lake, inlet
Lum *Alb.* river
Lund *Dan.* forest
-lund, -en *Swe.* wood(s)
-luoto *Fin.* island

-maa *Est.* island
Madīnat *Ar.* town, city
Madiq *Ar.* strait
Maja *Alb.* mountains
-mäki *Fin.* hill, hillside
Mal *Alb.* mountain
Maloye, Malyy, Malyya *Russ.* little, small
Mala, Mali, Malo *Ser.-Cr.* little, small
Malaya *Belo.* small
Malé *Czec., Slovak* small
Mali *Alb.* mountain
-man *Kor.* bay
Mar *Span.* lagoon, sea
Marais *Fr.* marsh
Mare *It.* sea
Mare *Rom.* great
Marisma *Span.* marsh
-mark *Dan., Nor.* land
Marsâ *Ar.* anchorage, bay, inlet
Masabb *Ar.* river mouth, estuary
Massif *Fr.* upland, mountains
Mato *Port.* forest
Mazar *Farsi* shrine, tomb
Meer, -meer *Afr., Dut., Ger.* lake, sea
-men *Chin.* bay, gorge, channel
Mesto *Ser.-Cr., Czec.* town
Mezzo *It.* middle
Midbar *Heb.* wilderness
Mierzeja *Pol.* spit
Mifraz *Heb.* bay
Mina *Ar.* port
Minami *Jap.* south, southern
-misaki *Jap.* cape, point
Mittel *Ger.* central, middle
-mo *Nor., Swe.* heath, island
-mon *Swe.* heath
Mong *Burm.* town
Mont(s) (Mt(s).) *Fr.* hill(s), mountain(s)
Montagna (Mt.) *It.* mountain
Montagne(s) (Mt(s).) *Fr.* hill(s), mountain(s)
Montaña(s) (Mt(s).) *Span.* mountain(s)
Montanyes *Cat.* mountains
Monte(s) (Mte(s).) *It., Port., Span.* mountain(s)
Monti (Mti.) *It.* mountains
More *Russ.* sea
Mörön *Mong.* river
Moyen *Fr.* central, middle
Muang *Malay* town
Mui *Viet.* cape
Mull *Gae.* promontory
Mund, -mund *Afr.* mouth
Munkhafed *Ar.* depression
Munte (Mte.) *Rom.* mount
Munţi(i) (Mti.) *Rom.* mountain(s)
Muong *Malay* village
Myit *Burm.* river
Myitwanya *Burm.* mouths of river
Mynydd *Welsh* mountain
-myr *Nor., Swe.* swamp
-mýri *Ice.* swamp
Mys (M.) *Russ.* cape

-Nada *Jap.* bay, gulf
-næs *Dan.* point, cape
Nafūd *Ar.* sandy desert
Nagorye *Russ.* hills, mountains
Nagy *Hung.* big
Nahal (N.) *Heb.* river
Nahr (N.) *Ar.* river, stream
Najd *Ar.* plateau, pass
Nakhon *Thai* town
Nam *Kor., Viet.* river
-nam *Kor.* south
Namakzār *Per.* salt flat
Nan *Chin.* south, southern
-nao *Chin.* lake
-näs *Swe.* cape
Neder *Dut.* lower
Nedre *Nor.* lower
Nei *Chin.* inner
Nek *Afr.* pass
-nes *Ice., Nor.* cape
Ness, -ness *Gae.* promontory, cape
Nevada, Nevado *Span.* snow-capped mountain
Nez *Fr.* cape
Nieder *Ger.* lower
-niemi *Fin.* cape, point, peninsula, island
Nieuw, -e *Dut.* new
Nishi *Jap.* west, western
Nisos, Nisoi *Gr.* island(s)
Nizhneye, Nizhniy *Russ.* lower
Nizina *Belo., Pol.* lowland
Nizmennost *Russ.* plain, lowland
Nízní *Czec.* lower
Noord *Dut.* north, northern
Nord *Fr.* north, northern
Norra *Swe.* north, northern
Nørre *Dan.* north, northern
Norte *Port., Span.* north, northern
Nos *Bulg., Russ.* cape, point
Nosy *Malag.* island
Nouveau, Nouvelle *Fr.* new
Nova, Novi *Bulg., Port., Serb.-Cr.* new
Novaya, Novo, Novoye, Novyy *Russ.* new
Nové, Novy *Czec., Slovak* new
Novo *Port.* new
Nowa, Nowe, Nowy *Pol.* new
Nudo *Span.* mountain
Nueva, Nuevo *Span.* new
Nur *Chin.* lake
Nur *Tib.* peak
Nuruu *Mong.* mountain range
Nusa *Indo.* island
Nuur *Mong.* lake
Ny *Dan., Nor., Swe.* new

-ø *Dan., Nor.* island
-ö *Swe.* island,
-öar, -na *Swe.* islands
Ober *Ger., Ukr.* upper
Oblast *Russ.* administrative division
Öbor *Mong.* inner
Occidental *Fr., Span.* western
-odde *Dan., Nor.* point, peninsula, cape
Oeste *Span.* west, western
Oglat *Ar.* well
Oji *Alb.* bay
Ojo *Span.* spring
-Oki *Jap.* bay
-ön *Swe.* island
Ondör *Mong.* upper
Oost(er) *Dut.* east(ern)
Oraşu *Rom.* city
Ord *Gae.* point
Óri *Gr.* mountains
Oriental, -e *Fr., Span.* east, eastern
Órmos *Gr.* bay
Óros *Gr.* mountain(s)
Ort *Ger.* point, cape
Ost *Ger.* east
Øst(er) *Den., Nor.* east(ern)
Öst(ra) *Swe.* east(ern)
Ostriv *Ukr.* island
Ostrov(a) *Russ.* island(s)
Otok(i) *Ser.-Cr.* island(s)
Ouabi, Ouadi (O.) *Ar.* dry watercourse, wadi
Oud, -e *Dut.* old
Oued, -i (O.) *Ar.* watercourse
Ouest *Fr.* west, western
Ouzan *Farsi* river
Ova, -si *Turk.* plains, lowlands
Över- *Dan., Dut.* upper
Över-, Övre *Nor., Swe.* upper
-øy, -a *Nor.* island(s)
Oya *Hin.* point
Oya *Sin.* river
Ozero, Ozera (Oz.) *Russ., Ukr.* lake(s)

-pää *Fin.* hill(s), mountain
Pahta *Lapp.* hill
Pampa(s) *Span.* plain(s)
Pantanal *Port.* marsh
Pantano *Span.* reservoir
Pantao *Chin.* peninsula
Parbat *Urdu* mountain
Pas *Fr.* strait
Paso (P.) *Span.* pass
Passage *Fr.* channel
Passe *Fr.* channel
Passo (P.) *It.* pass
Pasul (P.) *Rom.* pass
Patam *Hin.* small village
Patna, -patnam *Hin.* small village
Pegunungan *Indo., Malay* mountain range
Pei, -pei *Chin.* north
Pélagos *Gr.* sea
Pen *Welsh* hill
Peña *Span.* rock, peak
Pendi *Chin.* basin, depression
Péninsule *Fr.* peninsula
Penisola (Pen.) *It.* peninsula
Pereval (Per.) *Russ.* pass
Pervo-, Pervyy- *Russ.* first
Pertuis *Fr.* channel, strait
Peski *Russ.* sand desert
Petit, -e *Fr.* small
Phanom *Thai* mountain
Phnum *Cam.* mountain
Phou *Lao.* mountain
Phu *Thai, Viet.* mountain
Piano *It.* plain
Pic *Cat., Fr.* peak
Pico(s) *Span.* peak(s)
-piggen *Dan.* peak
Pik *Russ.* peak
Pingyuan *Chin.* plain
Pique *Fr.* peak
Piton *Fr.* peak
Pivostriv *Ukr.* peninsula
Piz, Pizzo *It.* peak
Plage *Fr.* beach
Plaine *Fr.* plain
Planalto *Port.* plateau
Planina (Pl.) *Bulg., Ser.-Cr.* mountain range
Plato *Russ., Bulg.* plateau
Playa *Span.* beach
-po *Chin.* lake, wetland
Pointe (Pte.) *Fr.* point, cape
Pojezierze *Pol.* lakes
Polder *Dut.* reclaimed farmland
-pólis *Gr.* city, town
Poluostrov (Pov.) *Russ.* peninsula
Półwysep *Pol.* peninsula
Pont *Fr.* bridge
Ponta (Pta.) *Port.* point, cape
Ponte *Port.* bridge
Poort *Afr.* passage, gate
-poort *Dut.* port
Porta *Port.* pass
Porţile *Rom.* gate
Portillo *Span.* pass
Porto *It., Port., Span.* port
Potámi, Potamós *Gr.* river
Pradesh *Hin.* state
Praia *Port.* beach, shore
Presa *Span.* reservoir
Presqu'île *Fr.* peninsula
Prokhod *Bulg.* pass
Proliv *Russ.* strait
Promontorio *Span.* promontory
Průsmyk (Pr.) *Czec.* pass
Pueblo *Span.* village
Puerto (Pto.) *Span.* port
Puig *Cat.* peak
Pulau (P.) *Indo., Malay* island
Puna *Span.* desert plateau
Puncak *Indo.* peak
Punta (Pta.) *It., Span.* point, peak
Puy *Fr.* peak

Qal'at *Ar.* fort
Qanat *Ar.* canal
Qasr *Ar.* fort
Qiryat *Heb.* town
Qiuling *Chin.* plateau
Qolleh *Farsi* mountain
-qundao *Chin.* islands

Rach *Viet.* river
Rags *Lat.* cape
Rambla *Cat.* river
Ramlat *Ar.* sandy desert
Rão (R.) *Port.* river
Rann *Hin.* swampy region
Rao *I.-C.* river
Ras *Amh., Ar., Farsi* cape, point
Récif(s) *Fr.* reef(s)
Recife(s) *Port.* reef(s)
Reka *Bulg.* river
Repede *Rom.* rapids
Reprêsa *Port.* reservoir
Reshteh *Farsi* mountain range
-rettō *Jap.* group of islands, chain
Ria *Port., Span.* estuary, bay
Ribeirão (R.) *Port.* river
Ribera (R.) *Span.* river bank
Rijeka *Ser.-Cr.* river
Rio (R.) *Port., Span.* river
Rivier (R.) *Afr., Dut.* river
Riviera *It.* coastal plain, coast
Rivière (R.) *Fr.* river
Roca *Span.* rock
Rocca *It.* rock, peak
Roche *Fr.* rock
Rt *Ser.-Cr.* cape, point
Rubh', Rubha *Gae.* cape, point
-rück *Ger.* ridge
Rūd *Farsi* stream, river
Rudohorie *Slovak* mountains
Rzeka (R.) *Pol.* river

-saar *Est.* island
-saari *Fin.* island
Sabkhat, Sabkhet *Ar.* salt flats
Sadd *Ar.* dam
Sagar,-a *Hin., Urdu* lake
Sahrâ *Ar.* desert
-Saki *Jap.* cape, point
Salar *Span.* salt flat
Salina(s) *Span.* salt marsh(es)
-salmi *Fin.* strait, sound, lake, channel
Saltsjöbad *Swe.* resort
-Sammyaku *Jap.* mountain range
Samut *Thai* gulf
San (S.) *It., Port., Span.* saint
-San *Jap., Kor.* hill, mountain
-Sanchi *Jap.* mountain range
Sankt (St.) *Ger., Russ.* saint
-sanmaek *Kor.* mountain range
-sanmyaku *Jap.* mountain range
Santa (Sta.) *It., Port., Span.* saint
Santo (Sto.) *It. Port., Span.* saint
São (S.) *Port.* saint
Sarir *Ar.* desert
Sasso *It.* mountain
Satu *Rom.* village
Saurums *Lat.* strait
Sebkha, Sebkhet *Ar.* salt flat
See, -see *Ger.* lake
-şehir *Turk.* town
Selat *Indo., Malay* strait
Selatan *Indo.* southern
-selkä *Fin.* bay, lake, ridge, hills
Selo *Ser.-Cr., Russ.* village
Selva *Port., Span.* forest, wood
Seno *Span.* bay, sound
Serir *Ar.* stony desert
Serra (Sa.) *Cat., Port.* range of hills
Serranía *Span.* mountain ridge
Severo, Severnaya, Severnoye, Severnyy (Sev.) *Russ.* north, northern
Sfântu *Rom.* saint
Shahr, -shahr *Farsi* city, town
Shamo *Chin.* desert
Shan *Chin.* hills, mountains
Shankou *Chin.* pass
Shanmo *Chin.* mountain range
Sharm *Ar.* bay
Shatt *Ar.* river mouth, estuary
-Shima *Jap.* island
Shimāli *Ar.* northern
-Shotō *Jap.* group of islands
-shui *Chin.* river
-shuiku *Chin.* reservoir
Sierra (Sa.) *Span.* mountain range
-sjö, -sjön, -sjø *Swe., Nor.* lake
-sjøen *Dan.* sea
-sjór *Ice.* lake
-sker *Ice.* island
-skär *Swe.* island, rock, cape
-skog, -skogen *Nor., Swe.* wood(s)
-skov *Dan.* forest
Slieve *Gae.* hill, mountain
Sø *Dan., Nor.* lake
Söder, Södra *Swe.* south, southern
Sør *Nor.* south, southern
Solonchak *Russ.* salt lake, marsh
Sønder, Søndra *Dan.* south, southern
Song *Viet.* river
Souk *Ar.* market
-spitze *Ger.* peak, mountain
-spruit *Afr.* stream
Sredna, Sredno *Bulg.* middle, central
Sredne, Sredneye *Russ.* middle, central
Srednja *Ser.-Cr.* middle, central
-stad *Afr., Nor., Swe.* town
-stadt *Ger.* town
-staður *Ice.* town
Stara, Stari *Ser.-Cr.* old
Stará, Staré, Stary *Czec.* old
Staraya, Staroye, Staryy *Russ.* old
Stare, Staro, Stary *Ukr.* old
Stausee *Ger.* reservoir
Stenón *Gr.* strait, pass
Step *Russ.* steppe
Stor, -a *Swe.* big
Store *Dan.* big
-strand *Dan., Ger., Nor., Swe.* beach
-strede *Nor.* straits
Strelka *Russ.* spit
-strete *Nor.* straits
Stretto (Str.) *It.* strait
Strædet (Str.) *Dan.* strait
-ström, -strömmen *Swe.* stream(s)
-stroom *Afr.* large river
Sud *Fr.* south, southern
Süd, -er *Ger.* south, southern
Suid *Afr.* south, southern
-Suidō *Jap.* strait, channel
Sul *Port.* south, southern
Sûn *Burm.* cape
-sund, -et *Swe., Nor.* sound, estuary, inlet
Sungai *Indo., Malay* river
Sur *Span.* south, southern
Sveti *Bulg.* saint
Syd *Dan., Swe.* south, southern
Sýsla *Ice.* first-order administrative division

-tag *Uighur* mountain
Tai -tai *Chin.* tower
-Take *Jap.* mountain
Tal *Mong.* plain, steppe
-tal *Ger.* valley
Tall *Ar.* hills
Tanjona *Malag.* cape, point
Tanjung, Tanjong (Tg.) *Indo., Malay.* cape, point
Tao *Chin.* island
Tasik *Malay* lake
Tassili *Ar.* rocky plateau
Tau *Russ.* mountain range
Taung *Burm.* mountain
Taungdan. *Burm.* mountain range
Taunggya *Burm.* pass
-tekojärvi *Fin.* reservoir
Teluk *Indo., Malay* bay, gulf
Ténéré *Berb.* desert
Tengah *Indo.* middle, central
-thal *Ger.* valley
Thok *Tib.* town
Tien *Chin.* lake, marsh
Tierra *Span.* land, country
Timur *Indo.* eastern
-tind *Nor.* peak
-ting *Chin.* mountain
Tjärn, -en, -et *Swe.* lake
-Tō *Jap.* island
Tong *Kor.* village, town
Tong *Burm., Thai, Kor.* mountain range
Tonlé *Cam.* lake
Top *Dut.* peak
-topp, -en *Nor.* peak
-träsk *Swe.* lake, swamp
Tsangpo *Tib.* large river
Tso *Tib.* lake
Tsu *Jap.* entrance, bay
Tsui *Chin.* cape, point
Tulur *Ar.* hill
-tunturi *Fin.* hill(s), mountain(s), ridge

Uad *Ar.* dry watercourse, wadi
Über *Ger.* upper
-udde, -udden *Swe.* point, cape
Uebi *Som.* river
Ujung *Indo., Malay* cape
Unter- *Ger.* lower
Us *Mong.* water
Ust, Ustye *Russ.* river mouth
Utara *Indo.* north, northern
Uttar *Hin.* north, northern
Uul *Mong., Russ.* mountain range

-vaara *Fin.* hill, mountain ridge, peak
Vaart *Dut.* canal
-våg *Nor.* bay
Val *Fr., Port., Span.* valley
Valea *Rom.* valley
-vall, -en *Swe.* mountain
Valle *It., Span.* valley
Vallée *Fr.* valley
Valli *It.* lake, lagoon
-város *Hung.* town
-varre *Nor.* mountain
Väst, Västra *Swe.* west, western
-vatn *Ice., Nor.* lake
-vatnet *Nor.* lake
-vatten, vattnet *Swe.* lake
-vecchio *It.* old
Vechi *Rom.* old
-ved, -veden *Swe.* hills
Veld, -veld *Afr.* field
Velha, Velho *Port.* old
Velika, Velike, Veliki, Veliko *Ser.-Cr., Slov.* big, large
Velikaya, Velikiy *Russ.* big, large
Velká, Velké, Velký *Czec.* big, large
Verkhne, Verkhniy *Russ.* upper
-vesi *Fin.* water, lake, bay, sound, strait
Vest, Vester, Vestre *Dan., Nor.* west, western
-vidda *Nor.* plateau
Vieille, Vieux *Fr.* old
Vieja, Vejo *Span.* old
Vig *Dan.* bay, inlet, cove, lagoon, lake
-vík *Ice.* bay
-vik, -a, -en *Nor., Swe.* bay, gulf, inlet, lake
Vila *Port.* small town
Villa *Span.* town
Ville *Fr.* town
Vinh *Viet.* bay
Vîrful (Vf.) *Rom.* peak, mountain
-viz *Hung.* river
-víztároló *Hung.* reservoir
-vlei *Afr.* lake, salt pan
-vliet *Dut.* canal
-vloer *Afr.* salt pan
Vodokhranilishche (Vdkhr.) *Russ.* reservoir
Vodoskovyshche (Vdskh.) *Ukr.* reservoir
Volcán (Vol.) *Span.* volcano, mountain
Vorota *Russ.* pass, channel, strait
Vostochno, Vostochnyy *Russ.* east, eastern
-vötn *Ice.* lakes
Vozvyshennost *Russ.* heights, uplands
Vozyera *Belo.* lake
Vrata *Bulg.* gate, pass
Vrchovina *Czec.* mountainous country
Vrch(y) *Czec.* mountain (range)
Vung *Viet.* bay, gulf
-vuori *Fin.* mountain, hill
Vychodné *Slovak* east, eastern
Vysochyna *Ukr.* upland

-waard *Dut.* polder
Wadi (W.) *Ar.* dry watercourse
Wâhât *Ar.* oasis
Wald *Ger.* forest, mountains
-Wan *Chin., Jap.* bay, harbour
Wāw *Ar.* well
Webi *Amh.* river
Wes *Afr.* west, western
Wielka, Wielki, Wielko *Pol.* big, large
Woestyn *Afr.* desert
Wysoka, Wysoki *Pol.* upper
Wyżyna *Pol.* plateau

Xi *Chin.* river
Xia *Chin.* gorge, strait
Xiao *Chin.* small

Yam *Heb.* sea
-Yama *Jap.* mountain
-yan *Chin.* gorge, island
Yang *Chin.* bay, sea, sound
Yangi *Russ.* new
Yazovir *Bulg.* reservoir
Yeni *Turk.* new
Yli *Fin.* upper
Ynys *Welsh* island
Yoma *Burm.* mountain range
Ytre-, Ytter- *Nor., Swe.* outer
-yuan *Chin.* stream
Yugo- *Ser.-Cr.* south, southern
Yunhe *Chin.* canal
Yuzhni, Yuzhno *Russ.* south, southern

-Zaki *Jap.* point
Zalew *Pol.* lagoon, swamp
Zaliv *Russ.* bay, gulf
-Zan *Jap.* mountain
Zangbo *Tib.* stream, river
Zapadnaya, Zapadno, Zapadnyi (Zap.) *Russ.* west, western
Zatoka *Pol., Ukr.* bay, gulf
-zee *Dut.* lake, sea
Zemlya *Russ.* land, island(s)
Zhang *Chin.* mountain
-zhou *Chin.* island
Zhong *Chin.* middle, central
Zhou *Chin.* island
Zizhiqu *Chin.* autonomous region
Zuid, Zuider *Dut.* south, southern

INDEX TO WORLD MAPS

The index contains the names of all the principal places and features shown on the World and City Maps. Each name is followed by an additional entry in italics giving the country or region within which it is located. The alphabetical order of names composed of two or more words is governed primarily by the first word, then by the second, and then by the country or region name that follows. This is an example of the rule:

Mīr *Niger*	14°5N 11°59E	**259** F2
Mīr Kūh *Iran*	26°22N 58°55E	**247** E8
Mīr Shahdād *Iran*	26°15N 58°29E	**247** E8
Mira *Italy*	45°26N 12°8E	**199** C9

Physical features composed of a proper name (Erie) and a description (Lake) are positioned alphabetically by the proper name. The description is positioned after the proper name and is usually abbreviated:

Erie, L. *N. Amer.*	42°15N 81°0W	**312** D4

Where a description forms part of a settlement or administrative name, however, it is always written in full and put in its true alphabetical position:

Mount Olive *U.S.A.*	39°4N 89°44W	**310** E7

Names beginning with M' and Mc are indexed as if they were spelled Mac. Names beginning St. are alphabetized under Saint, but Sankt, Sint, Sant', Santa and San are all spelt in full and are alphabetized accordingly. If the same place name occurs two or more times in the index and all are in the same country, each is followed by the name of the administrative subdivision in which it is located.

The geographical co-ordinates which follow each name in the index give the latitude and longitude of each place. The first co-ordinate indicates latitude – the distance north or south of the Equator. The second co-ordinate indicates longitude – the distance east or west of the Greenwich Meridian. Both latitude and longitude are measured in degrees and minutes (there are 60 minutes in a degree). Latitude and longitude references are not used on the Central Area City Maps.

The latitude is followed by N(orth) or S(outh) and the longitude by E(ast) or W(est).

The number in bold type which follows the geographical co-ordinates refers to the number of the map page where that feature or place will be found. This is usually the largest scale at which the place or feature appears.

The letter and figure that are immediately after the page number give the grid square on the map page, within which the feature is situated. The letter represents the latitude and the figure the longitude. A lower-case letter immediately after the page number refers to an inset map on that page.

In some cases the feature itself may fall within the specified square, while the name is outside. This is usually the case only with features that are larger than a grid square.

Rivers are indexed to their mouths or confluences, and carry the symbol ➜ after their names. The following symbols are also used in the index: ■ country, ☑ overseas territory or dependency, ☐ first-order administrative area, ☆ U.S. county, △ national park, ◠ other park (provincial park, nature reserve or game reserve), ⚙ Australian aboriginal land, ▲ U.S. Indian reservation, ✈ (LHR) principal airport (and location identifier).

English-speaking people usually have no difficulty in reading and pronouncing correctly English place names. However, foreign place name pronunciations may present many problems. Such problems can be minimized by following some simple rules. However, these rules cannot be applied to all situations, and there will be many exceptions.

1. In general, stress each syllable equally, unless your experience suggests otherwise.
2. Pronounce the letter 'a' as a broad 'a' as in 'arm'.
3. Pronounce the letter 'e' as a short 'e' as in 'elm'.
4. Pronounce the letter 'i' as a cross between a short 'i' and long 'e', as the two 'i's in 'California'.
5. Pronounce the letter 'o' as an intermediate 'o' as in 'soft'.
6. Pronounce the letter 'u' as an intermediate 'u' as in 'sure'.
7. Pronounce consonants hard, except in the Romance-language areas where 'g's are likely to be pronounced softly like 'j' in 'jam'; 'j' itself may be pronounced as 'y'; and 'x's may be pronounced as 'h'.
8. For names in mainland China, pronounce 'q' like the 'ch' in 'chin', 'x' like the 'sh' in 'she', 'zh' like the 'j' in 'jam', and 'z' as if it were spelled 'dz'. In general, pronounce 'a' as in 'father', 'e' as in 'but', 'i' as in 'keep', 'o' as in 'or', and 'u' as in 'rule'.

Moreover, English has no diacritical marks (accent and pronunciation signs), although some languages do. The following is a brief and general guide to the pronunciation of those most frequently used in the principal Western European languages.

		Pronunciation as in
French	é	day and shows that the 'e' is to be pronounced; e.g. Orléans.
	è	mare
	î	used over any vowel and does not affect pronunciation; shows contraction of the name, usually omission of 's' following a vowel.
	ç	's' before 'a', 'o' and 'u'.
	ë, ï, ü	over 'e', 'i' and 'u' when they are used with another vowel and shows that each is to be pronounced.
German	ä	fate
	ö	fur
	ü	no English equivalent; like French 'tu'.
Italian	à, é	over vowels and indicates stress.
Portuguese	ã, õ	vowels pronounced nasally.
	ç	boss
	á	shows stress.
	ô	shows that a vowel has an 'i' or 'u' sound combined with it.
Spanish	ñ	canyon
	ü	pronounced as 'w' and separately from adjoining vowels.
	á	usually indicates that this is a stressed vowel.

A.C.T. – Australian Capital Territory
A.R. – Autonomous Region
Afghan. – Afghanistan
Afr. – Africa
Ala. – Alabama
Alta. – Alberta
Amer. – America(n)
Ant. – Antilles
Arch. – Archipelago
Ariz. – Arizona
Ark. – Arkansas
Atl. Oc. – Atlantic Ocean
B. – Baie, Bahía, Bay, Bucht, Bugt
B.C. – British Columbia
Bangla. – Bangladesh
Barr. – Barrage
Bos.-H. – Bosnia-Herzegovina
C. – Cabo, Cap, Cape, Coast
C.A.R. – Central African Republic
C. Prov. – Cape Province
Calif. – California
Cat. – Catarata
Cent. – Central
Chan. – Channel
Colo. – Colorado
Conn. – Connecticut
Cord. – Cordillera
Cr. – Creek
D.C. – District of Columbia
Del. – Delaware
Dem. – Democratic
Dep. – Dependency
Des. – Desert
Dét. – Détroit
Dist. – District
Dj. – Djebel
Dom. Rep. – Dominican Republic
E. – East

El Salv. – El Salvador
Eq. Guin. – Equatorial Guinea
Est. – Estrecho
Falk. Is. – Falkland Is.
Fd. – Fjord
Fla. – Florida
Fr. – French
G. – Golfe, Golfo, Gulf, Guba, Gebel
Ga. – Georgia
Gt. – Great, Greater
Guinea-Biss. – Guinea-Bissau
H.K. – Hong Kong
H.P. – Himachal Pradesh
Hants. – Hampshire
Harb. – Harbor, Harbour
Hd. – Head
Hts. – Heights
I.(s). – Île, Ilha, Insel, Isla, Island, Isle
Ill. – Illinois
Ind. – Indiana
Ind. Oc. – Indian Ocean
Ivory C. – Ivory Coast
J. – Jabal, Jebel
Jaz. – Jazīrah
Junc. – Junction
K. – Kap, Kapp
Kans. – Kansas
Kep. – Kepulauan
Ky. – Kentucky
L. – Lac, Lacul, Lago, Lagoa, Lake, Limni, Loch, Lough
La. – Louisiana
Ld. – Land
Liech. – Liechtenstein
Lux. – Luxembourg
Mad. P. – Madhya Pradesh
Madag. – Madagascar

Man. – Manitoba
Mass. – Massachusetts
Md. – Maryland
Me. – Maine
Medit. S. – Mediterranean Sea
Mich. – Michigan
Minn. – Minnesota
Miss. – Mississippi
Mo. – Missouri
Mont. – Montana
Mozam. – Mozambique
Mt.(s) – Mont, Montaña, Mountain
Mte. – Monte
Mti. – Monti
N. – Nord, Norte, North, Northern, Nouveau, Nahal, Nahr
N.B. – New Brunswick
N.C. – North Carolina
N. Cal. – New Caledonia
N. Dak. – North Dakota
N.H. – New Hampshire
N.I. – North Island
N.J. – New Jersey
N. Mex. – New Mexico
N.S. – Nova Scotia
N.S.W. – New South Wales
N.W.T. – North West Territory
N.Y. – New York
N.Z. – New Zealand
Nac. – Nacional
Nat. – National
Nebr. – Nebraska
Neths. – Netherlands
Nev. – Nevada
Nfld. & L. – Newfoundland and Labrador
Nic. – Nicaragua
O. – Oued, Ouadi
Occ. – Occidentale

Okla. – Oklahoma
Ont. – Ontario
Or. – Orientale
Oreg. – Oregon
Os. – Ostrov
Oz. – Ozero
P. – Pass, Passo, Pasul, Pulau
P.E.I. – Prince Edward Island
Pa. – Pennsylvania
Pac. Oc. – Pacific Ocean
Papua N.G. – Papua New Guinea
Pass. – Passage
Peg. – Pegunungan
Pen. – Peninsula, Péninsule
Phil. – Philippines
Pk. – Peak
Plat. – Plateau
Prov. – Province, Provincial
Pt. – Point
Pta. – Ponta, Punta
Pte. – Pointe
Qué. – Québec
Queens. – Queensland
R. – Rio, River
R.I. – Rhode Island
Ra. – Range
Raj. – Rajasthan
Recr. – Recreational, Récréatif
Reg. – Region
Rep. – Republic
Res. – Reserve, Reservoir
Rhld-Pfz. – Rheinland-Pfalz
S. – South, Southern, Sur
Si. Arabia – Saudi Arabia
S.C. – South Carolina
S. Dak. – South Dakota
S.I. – South Island
S. Leone – Sierra Leone
Sa. – Serra, Sierra

Sask. – Saskatchewan
Scot. – Scotland
Sd. – Sound
Sev. – Severnaya
Sib. – Siberia
Sprs. – Springs
St. – Saint
Sta. – Santa
Ste. – Sainte
Sto. – Santo
Str. – Strait, Stretto
Switz. – Switzerland
Tas. – Tasmania
Tenn. – Tennessee
Terr. – Territory, Territoire
Tex. – Texas
Tg. – Tanjung
Trin. & Tob. – Trinidad & Tobago
U.A.E. – United Arab Emirates
U.K. – United Kingdom
U.S.A. – United States of America
Univ. – University, Université, Universidad
Ut. P. – Uttar Pradesh
Va. – Virginia
Vdkhr. – Vodokhranilishche
Vdskh. – Vodoskhovyshche
Vf. – Vírful
Vic. – Victoria
Vol. – Volcano
Vt. – Vermont
W. – Wadi, West
W. Va. – West Virginia
Wall. & F. Is. – Wallis and Futuna Is.
Wash. – Washington
Wis. – Wisconsin
Wlkp. – Wielkopolski
Wyo. – Wyoming
Yorks. – Yorkshire

A

A ʿÁli an Nîl = Upper Nile □
  South Sudan 9°30N 33°0E **257** F3
A Baiuca Spain 43°19N 8°29W **194** B2
A Baña = San Vicenzo
  Spain 42°58N 8°46W **194** C2
A Cañiza Spain 42°13N 8°16W **194** C2
A Carballa Spain 43°13N 8°54W **194** B2
A Carreira Spain 43°21N 8°12W **194** B2
A Coruña Spain 43°20N 8°25W **194** B2
A Coruña □ Spain 43°10N 8°30W **194** B2
A Cruz do Incio Spain 42°39N 7°21W **194** C3
A Estrada Spain 42°43N 8°27W **194** C2
A Feira do Monte Spain 43°12N 7°34W **194** B3
A Fonsagrada Spain 43°8N 7°4W **194** B3
A Guarda Spain 41°56N 8°52W **194** D2
A Gudiña Spain 42°4N 7°8W **194** C3
A Pobre Spain 42°58N 7°3W **194** C3
A Ramallosa Spain 42°45N 8°30W **194** C2
A Rúa Spain 42°24N 7°6W **194** C3
A Serra de Outes Spain 42°52N 8°55W **194** C2
A Shau Vietnam 16°6N 107°22E **236** D6
A.N.R. Robinson Int. ✈ (TAB)
  Trin. & Tob. 11°9N 60°50W **323** s
A.N.Z. Stadium
  Sydney, Australia 33°51S 151°5E **139** B1
A.R.M.M. = Bangsamoro □
  Phil. 8°0N 123°0E **233** H3
Aabenraa Denmark 55°3N 9°25E **163** J3
Aabybro Denmark 57°10N 9°44E **163** G3
Aachen Germany 50°45N 6°6E **178** E2
Aalám Iraq 33°19N 44°23E **113** B2
Aalborg Denmark 57°2N 9°54E **163** G3
Aalborg Bugt Denmark 56°50N 10°35E **163** H4
Aalen Germany 48°51N 10°6E **179** G6
Aalestrup Denmark 56°42N 9°29E **163** H3
Aalsmeer Neths. 52°16N 4°46E **112** B1
Aalst Belgium 50°56N 4°2E **170** D4
Aalten Neths. 51°56N 6°35E **170** C6
Aalter Belgium 51°5N 3°28E **170** C3
Äänekoski Finland 62°36N 25°44E **160** E21
Aarau Switz. 47°23N 8°4E **179** H4
Aarberg Switz. 47°2N 7°16E **179** H3
Aare → Switz. 47°33N 8°14E **179** H4
Aargau □ Switz. 47°26N 8°10E **179** H4
Aarhus Denmark 56°8N 10°11E **163** H4
Aarlen = Arlon Belgium 49°42N 5°49E **170** E5
Aars Denmark 56°48N 9°30E **163** H3
Aarschot Belgium 50°59N 4°49E **170** D4
Aasiaat Greenland 68°43N 52°56W **154** D5
Ab-i-Istada Afghan. 32°29N 67°55E **240** B3
Ab-i-Panja = Pyandzh →
  Asia 37°6N 68°20E **240** A2
Aba Sichuan, China 32°59N 101°42E **228** A3
Aba Dem. Rep. of the Congo 3°58N 30°17E **268** B3
Aba Nigeria 5°10N 7°19E **263** D6
Ãbã, Jazãrat Sudan 13°30N 32°31E **257** D3
Abacaxis → Brazil 3°54S 58°47W **329** D6
Abaco I. Bahamas 26°25N 77°10W **320** A4
Abadab, J. Sudan 18°54N 35°56E **256** D4
Ãbãdãn Iran 30°22N 48°20E **247** D6
Ãbãdeh Ethiopia 31°8N 52°40E **247** D7
Ãbãdeh Iran 31°8N 52°40E **247** D7
Abadin Iran 43°21N 7°29W **194** B3
Abadla Algeria 31°2N 2°45W **261** B4
Abaeté Brazil 19°9S 45°27W **333** E2
Abaeté → Brazil 17°40S 45°0W **333** F2
Abaetetuba Brazil 1°40S 48°50W **332** B2
Abagnar Qi = Xilinhot
  China 43°52N 116°2E **228** C9
Abah, Tanjung Indonesia 8°46S 115°38E **231** K18
Abai Paraguay 25°58S 55°54W **335** B4
Abakaliki Nigeria 6°22N 8°2E **263** D6
Abakan Russia 53°40N 91°10E **217** D12
Abala Russia 1°17S 15°36E **264** C3
Abala Congo 14°56N 3°22E **263** C5
Abalak Niger 15°22N 6°21E **263** B6
Abalemma Algeria 20°51N 5°59E **261** D6
Abalemma Niger 16°12N 7°50E **263** B6
Abalessa Algeria 22°58N 4°47E **261** D5
Abana Turkey 41°59N 34°1E **212** B6
Abancay Peru 13°35S 72°55W **330** C3
Abang, Gunung
  Indonesia 8°16S 115°25E **231** J18
Abanga → Gabon 0°20S 10°30E **264** C2
Abano Terme Italy 45°22N 11°46E **199** C8
Abapó Bolivia 18°48S 63°25W **331** D5
Abarán Spain 38°12N 1°23W **197** G3
Abariringa Kiribati 2°50S 171°40W **277** A16
Abarqu Iran 31°10N 53°20E **247** D7
Abasha Georgia 42°11N 42°13E **191** J6
Abashiri Japan 44°0N 144°15E **220** B12
Abashiri-Wan Japan 44°0N 144°30E **220** C12
Abau Papua N. G. 10°11S 148°46E **286** F5
Abaújszántó Hungary 48°16N 21°12E **182** B6
Abava → Latvia 57°6N 21°54E **184** A8
Ābay = Nîl el Azraq →
  Sudan 15°38N 32°31E **257** D3
Abay Kazakhstan 49°38N 72°53E **217** C8
Abaya, L. Ethiopia 6°30N 37°50E **257** F4
Abaza Russia 52°39N 90°6E **217** D12
Abba C.A.R. 5°20N 15°11E **264** A3
Abbadia di Fiastra △
  Italy 43°12N 13°24E **199** E10
Abbadia San Salvatore
  Italy 42°53N 11°41E **199** F8
ʿAbbãsãbãd Iran 33°34N 58°23E **247** C8
Abbay = Nîl el Azraq →
  Sudan 15°38N 32°31E **257** D3
Abbaye, Pt. U.S.A. 46°58N 88°8W **308** B9
Abbazia = Opatija
  Croatia 45°21N 14°17E **199** C11
Abbé, L. Ethiopia 11°8N 41°47E **257** E5
Abbeville Somme, France 50°6N 1°49E **173** B8
Abbeville Ala., U.S.A. 31°34N 85°15W **316** D4
Abbeville Ga., U.S.A. 31°59N 83°18W **316** D6
Abbeville La., U.S.A. 29°58N 92°8W **314** G8
Abbeville S.C., U.S.A. 34°11N 82°23W **316** C7
Abbey Wood U.K. 51°29N 0°7E **125** B4
Abbeyfeale Ireland 52°23N 9°18W **166** D2
Abbeyleix Ireland 52°54N 7°22W **166** D4
Abbiategrasso Italy 45°24N 8°54E **198** C5
Abbot Ice Shelf Antarctica 73°0S 92°0W **151** D16
Abbotsford Canada 49°5N 122°20W **296** D4
Abbottabad Pakistan 34°10N 73°15E **242** B5
Abbou, O. ben → Algeria 28°32N 5°14E **261** C6
ABC Islands W. Indies 12°15N 69°0W **322** g
Abcoude Neths. 52°17N 4°59E **170** B5
Abd al Kûrî Yemen 12°5N 52°20E **249** D6
Ãbdãnãn Iran 32°56N 47°28E **247** C6
Abdar Iran 30°16N 55°19E **247** D7
Ãbdin Iran 30°2N 31°14E **117** A2
Abdulino Russia 53°42N 53°40E **216** D6
Abdullah South Sudan 9°30N 29°55E **257** F3
Abdurauf Bangla. 24°15N 88°59E **243** G13
Abéché Chad 13°50N 20°35E **259** F4
Abejar Spain 41°48N 2°47W **196** D2
Abekr Sudan 12°48N 28°50E **257** E2
Abel Tasman △ N.Z. 40°59S 173°8E **295** J4
Abengourou Ivory C. 6°42N 3°27W **262** D4
Abeno Japan 34°38N 135°31E **133** B2
Abenójar Spain 38°53N 4°21W **195** G6
Ãbenrã = Aabenraa
  Denmark 55°3N 9°25E **163** J3
Abensberg Germany 48°48N 11°51E **179** G7

Abeokuta Nigeria 7°3N 3°19E **263** D5
Aberaeron U.K. 52°15N 4°15W **169** E3
Aberayron = Aberaeron
  U.K. 52°15N 4°15W **169** E3
Aberchirder U.K. 57°34N 2°37W **167** D6
Abercorn = Mbala Zambia 8°46S 31°24E **269** D3
Abercorn Australia 25°12S 151°5E **281** D5
Abercrombie River △
  Australia 34°5S 149°40E **283** C8
Aberdare U.K. 51°43N 3°27W **169** F4
Aberdare △ Kenya 0°22S 36°44E **268** C4
Aberdare Ra. Kenya 0°15S 36°50E **268** C4
Aberdeen
  Hong Kong, China 22°14N 114°8E **122** B2
Aberdeen Eastern Cape,
  S. Africa 32°28S 24°2E **270** D3
Aberdeen Aberd. City, U.K. 57°9N 2°5W **167** D6
Aberdeen Idaho, U.S.A. 42°57N 112°50W **304** E7
Aberdeen Md., U.S.A. 39°31N 76°10W **309** F15
Aberdeen Miss., U.S.A. 33°49N 88°33W **315** E10
Aberdeen Ohio, U.S.A. 38°39N 83°46W **311** F13
Aberdeen S. Dak., U.S.A. 45°28N 98°29W **308** C4
Aberdeen Wash., U.S.A. 46°59N 123°50W **306** D3
Aberdeen City □ U.K. 57°10N 2°10W **167** D6
Aberdeen Country Park ◠
  Hong Kong, China 22°16N 114°9E **122** B2
Aberdeen L. Canada 64°30N 99°0W **294** E12
Aberdeenshire □ U.K. 57°17N 2°36W **167** D6
Aberdour U.K. 56°3N 3°18W **121** A2
Aberdour Castle U.K. 56°3N 3°18W **121** A2
Aberdovey = Aberdyfi U.K. 52°33N 4°3W **169** E3
Aberdyfi U.K. 52°33N 4°3W **169** E3
Aberfeldy U.K. 56°37N 3°51W **167** E5
Aberfoyle U.K. 56°11N 4°23W **167** E4
Abergavenny U.K. 51°49N 3°1W **169** F4
Abergele U.K. 53°17N 3°35W **168** D4
Abergwaun = Fishguard
  U.K. 52°0N 4°58W **169** E3
Aberhonddu = Brecon
  U.K. 51°57N 3°23W **169** F4
Abermaw = Barmouth
  U.K. 52°44N 4°4W **168** E3
Abernathy U.S.A. 33°50N 101°51W **314** E4
Aberpennar = Mountain Ash
  U.K. 51°40N 3°23W **169** F4
Aberystwyth U.K. 52°25N 4°5W **169** E3
Abfanggraben →
  Germany 48°10N 11°41E **131** A3
Abhã Si. Arabia 18°0N 42°34E **248** C3
Abhar Iran 36°9N 49°13E **213** D13
Abhayapuri India 26°24N 90°38E **241** B3
Abia □ Nigeria 5°30N 7°35E **263** D6
Abiad, Es Sahrã el Egypt 28°0N 28°0E **256** B2
Abide Turkey 38°55N 29°20E **205** C11
Abidiya Sudan 18°18N 34°3E **256** D3
Abidjan Ivory C. 5°26N 3°58W **262** D4
Abidjan □ Ivory C. 5°20N 4°0W **262** D4
Abilene Kans., U.S.A. 38°55N 97°13W **308** F5
Abilene Tex., U.S.A. 32°28N 99°43W **314** E5
Abingdon Ill., U.S.A. 40°48N 90°24W **310** D6
Abingdon Va., U.S.A. 36°43N 81°59W **309** G13
Abingdon, I. = Pinta, I.
  Ecuador 0°35N 90°44W **330** a
Abingdon-on-Thames
  U.K. 51°40N 1°17W **169** F6
Abington Reef Australia 18°0S 149°35E **280** B4
Abiod, Remel el Tunisia 34°30N 9°35E **261** B6
Abisko → Sweden 68°18N 18°44E **160** B18
Abitau → Canada 59°53N 109°3W **297** B7
Abitibi, L. Canada 51°3N 80°55W **298** D3
Abiy Adi Ethiopia 13°39N 39°3E **257** E4
Abiyata, L. Ethiopia 7°37N 38°36E **266** C4
Abkhaz Republic = Abkhazia □
  Georgia 43°12N 41°5E **191** J5
Abkhazia □ Georgia 43°12N 41°5E **191** J5
Abladion-sur-Seine France 48°43N 2°25E **134** B3
Abminga Australia 26°8S 134°51E **281** D1
Abnûb Egypt 27°18N 31°4E **256** B3
Ābo = Turku Finland 60°30N 22°19E **188** B2
Abo, Massif d' Chad 21°41N 16°8E **259** D2
Abohar India 30°10N 74°10E **242** D6
Aboisso Ivory C. 5°30N 3°5W **262** D4
Abolo Congo 0°8N 14°16E **264** B2
Abomey Benin 7°10N 2°5E **263** D5
Abong-Mbang Cameroon 4°0N 13°8E **264** B2
Abongabong Indonesia 4°15N 96°48E **234** B1
Abonnema Nigeria 4°41N 6°49E **263** E6
Abony Hungary 47°12N 20°3E **182** C5
Abor Hills India 28°25N 94°46E **241** A5
Aborlan Phil. 9°26N 118°33E **233** G2
Aboso Ghana 5°23N 1°57W **262** D4
Abou-Deïa Chad 11°20N 19°20E **259** F3
Abou-Goulem Chad 13°37N 21°38E **259** F4
Abou-Telfan ◠ Chad 11°28N 18°58E **259** F3
Abovyan Armenia 40°16N 44°37E **191** K7
Aboyne U.K. 57°4N 2°47W **167** D6
Abra □ Phil. 17°35N 120°45E **232** E3
Abra de Ilog Phil. 13°27N 120°44E **232** E3
Abra Pampa Argentina 22°43S 65°42W **334** A2
Abram U.K. 53°30N 2°30W **168** D2
Abramtsevo Russia 55°49N 37°49E **129** B3
Abrantes Portugal 39°24N 8°7W **195** F2
Abreojos, Pta. Mexico 26°50N 113°40W **318** B2
Abri Esh Shamâliya, Sudan 20°50N 30°27E **256** C3
Abri Janub Kordofân, Sudan 11°40N 30°21E **257** E3
Abrolhos, Banco dos Brazil 18°0S 38°0W **333** E4
Abrud Romania 46°19N 23°5E **182** E8
Abruzzo □ Italy 42°15N 14°0E **199** F10
Absaroka Range U.S.A. 44°45N 109°50W **304** D9
Abtenau Austria 47°33N 13°21E **180** D6
Abtsgmünd Germany 48°57N 9°57E **132** B2
Abū aḍ Ḑuhūr Syria 35°44N 37°20E **250** B2
Abū al Abyad U.A.E. 24°11N 53°50E **247** E7
Abū al Khaṣīb Iraq 30°25N 48°0E **246** D5
Abū ʿAlī Si. Arabia 27°20N 49°27E **247** E6
Abū ʿAlī → Lebanon 34°25N 35°50E **250** D6
Abū ʿArīsh Si. Arabia 16°53N 42°48E **248** C3
Abū Ballas Egypt 24°26N 27°36E **256** C2
Abū Dā, W. → Egypt 26°49N 31°0E **256** B3
Abū Gabra Sudan 11°2N 26°50E **257** E2
Abū Gelba Sudan 13°11N 31°52E **257** E3
Abū Ghraib Israel 31°48N 35°56E **123** B1
Abū Gubeiha Sudan 11°30N 31°30E **257** E3
Abū Habl, Khawr →
  Sudan 12°37N 31°0E **257** E3
Abū Ḩadrīyah Si. Arabia 27°20N 48°58E **247** E6

Acquasparta Italy 42°41N 12°33E **199** F9
Acquaviva delle Fonti
  Italy 40°54N 16°50E **201** B9
Ácqui Terme Italy 44°41N 8°28E **198** D5
Acraman, L. Australia 32°2S 135°23E **281** E2
Acre □ ʿAkko Israel 32°55N 35°4E **250** D6
Acre □ Brazil 9°1S 71°0W **330** B3
Acre → Brazil 8°45S 67°22W **330** B4
Acri Italy 39°29N 16°23E **201** C9
Acropolis Athens, Greece 112 c2
Acs Hungary 47°42N 18°2E **182** C3
Actaeon Mt. = Diana's Peak
  St. Helena 15°58S 5°42W **153** h
Actéon, Groupe
  French Polynesia 21°20S 136°30W **289** f
Actinolite Canada 44°32N 77°19W **312** B7
Actium Greece 38°57N 20°45E **207** B2
Acton Canada 43°38N 80°3W **312** C4
Acton London, U.K. 51°30N 0°16W **125** A2
Açúcar, Pão de Brazil 5°34S 36°54W **332** C4
Acul → Vidin Bulgaria 43°59N 22°50E **202** C6
Acworth U.S.A. 34°4N 84°41W **316** A5
Ad Dafrah Si. Arabia 23°18N 41°58E **248** B3
Ad Dafrah U.A.E. 23°30N 54°0E **249** B6
Ad Daghghâran Iraq 32°8N 44°55E **213** G11
Ad Ḑabī Sudan 15°13N 43°4E **248** D3
Ad Ḑahā Si. Arabia 24°30N 48°10E **249** A5
Ad Dākhilīyah □ Oman 22°30N 57°30E **249** B7
Ad Ḑalī □ Yemen 13°42N 44°44E **248** D4
Ad Ḑalī □ Yemen 13°42N 44°44E **248** D4
Ad Dammām Si. Arabia 26°20N 50°5E **247** E6
Ad Dāmūr Lebanon 33°43N 35°27E **250** E6
Ad Darb Si. Arabia 18°2N 43°7E **248** C3
Ad Dawādimī Si. Arabia 24°35N 44°15E **246** E5
Ad Dawḩah Qatar 25°15N 51°35E **247** E6
Ad Dawr Iraq 34°27N 43°47E **213** F10
Ad Dhakhīrah Qatar 25°44N 51°33E **247** E6
Ad Ḑiffah Libya 23°55N 47°10E **258** B4
Ad Dir'īyah Si. Arabia 24°44N 46°35E **246** E5
Ad Dīwānīyah Iraq 32°0N 45°0E **213** F11
Ad Dujayl Iraq 33°51N 44°14E **213** F11
Ad Duqm Oman 19°39N 57°42E **249** C7
Ad Duwayd Si. Arabia 30°15N 42°17E **246** D4
Ada Ghana 5°44N 0°40E **263** D5
Ada Serbia 45°49N 20°9E **182** E5
Ada Minn., U.S.A. 47°18N 96°31W **308** B5
Ada Ohio, U.S.A. 40°46N 83°49W **311** D13
Ada Okla., U.S.A. 34°46N 96°41W **314** D6
Ada Beja Portugal 38°47N 9°13W **126** A1
Adad Somalia 11°29N 46°49E **267** C6
Adado, Ras Somalia 11°19N 48°39E **267** B6
Adair, C. Canada 71°30N 71°34W **299** C17
Adaja → Spain 41°32N 4°52W **194** D6
Adak U.S.A. 51°45N 176°45W **303** L3
Adak I. U.S.A. 51°45N 176°45W **303** L3
Ädalsbruk Norway 60°43N 11°19E **164** D8
Adam Oman 22°15N 57°28E **249** B7
Adam, Mt. Falk. Is. 51°34S 60°4W **153** f
Adamantina Brazil 21°42S 51°4W **333** F1
Adamaoua □ Cameroon 6°30N 13°0E **263** D7
Adamaoua, Massif de l'
  Cameroon 7°20N 12°20E **263** D7
Adamasta Channel
  Hong Kong, China 22°14N 114°1E **122** B2
Adamawa □ Nigeria 9°20N 12°30E **263** D7
Adamawa Highlands = Adamaoua,
  Massif de l' Cameroon 7°20N 12°20E **263** D7
Adamello, Mte. Italy 46°9N 10°30E **198** B7
Adamello △ Italy 46°4N 10°28E **198** B7
Adami Tulu Ethiopia 7°53N 38°41E **257** F4
Adaminaby Australia 36°0S 148°45E **283** D8
Adams Mass., U.S.A. 42°38N 73°7W **313** D11
Adams N.Y., U.S.A. 43°49N 76°1W **313** C8
Adams Wis., U.S.A. 43°57N 89°49W **308** D9
Adams, Mt. U.S.A. 46°12N 121°30W **306** D5
Adam's Bridge Sri Lanka 9°15N 79°40E **245** K4
Adams L. Canada 51°10N 119°40W **296** C5
Adams Park U.S.A. 33°43N 84°27W **113** B2
Adam's Peak Sri Lanka 6°48N 80°30E **245** L5
Adamuz Spain 38°2N 4°32W **195** G6
ʿAdan Yemen 12°45N 45°0E **248** D4
Adana Turkey 37°0N 35°16E **250** B2
Adana □ Turkey 37°0N 35°0E **250** B2
Adanero Spain 40°56N 4°36W **194** E6
Adang, Ko Thailand 6°43N 99°18E **237** J2
Adapazarı = Sakarya
  Turkey 40°48N 30°25E **212** B4
Adar Gwagwa, J. Sudan 14°10N 35°20E **256** C4
Adarama Sudan 17°10N 34°52E **256** D3
Adare Ireland 52°34N 8°47W **166** D3
Adare, C. Antarctica 71°0S 171°0E **151** D11
Adaut Indonesia 8°8S 131°7E **231** F8
Adavale Australia 25°52S 144°32E **281** D3
Addatigala India 17°31N 82°3E **244** F6
Addax ◠ Niger 19°17N 9°22E **259** E1
Addis Ababa = Addis Abeba
  Ethiopia 9°2N 38°42E **257** F4
Addis Abeba Ethiopia 9°2N 38°42E **257** F4
Addis Alem Ethiopia 9°2N 38°17E **257** F4
Addis Zemen Ethiopia 12°7N 37°47E **257** E4
Addiscombe U.K. 51°22N 0°4W **125** B3
Addison Ala., U.S.A. 34°12N 87°11W **316** C5
Addison N.Y., U.S.A. 42°1N 77°14W **312** D7
Addo S. Africa 33°32S 25°45E **270** D4
Addo △ S. Africa 33°30S 25°50E **270** D4
Addu Atoll Maldives 0°38S 73°10E **272** d
Adebour Niger 13°17N 11°50E **259** F2
Ädeh Iran 37°42N 45°11E **246** B5
Adeje Canary Is. 28°7N 16°43W **153** e1
Adel Ga., U.S.A. 31°8N 83°25W **316** D6
Adel Iowa, U.S.A. 41°37N 94°1W **310** C2
Adel Bagrou Mauritania 15°29N 6°57W **262** B3
Adelaide S. Austral.,
  Australia 34°52S 138°30E **282** C2
Adelaide Eastern Cape,
  S. Africa 32°42S 26°20E **270** D4
Adelaide I. Antarctica 67°15S 68°30W **151** C17
Adelaide Pen. Canada 68°15N 97°30W **294** D12
Adelaide River Australia 13°15S 131°7E **278** B5
Adelaide Village Bahamas 25°4N 77°31W **323** B4
Adelanto U.S.A. 34°35N 117°22W **307** J9
Adelaye C.A.R. 7°7N 22°49E **264** A4
Adele I. Australia 15°32S 123°9E **278** C3
Adélie, Terre Antarctica 68°0S 140°0E **151** C10
Adelong Australia 35°16S 148°4E **283** C8
Adelphi U.S.A. 39°0N 76°58W **143** h
Adelsk Belarus 53°24N 23°47E **184** C10
Adelunga Toghi Uzbekistan 40°57N 113°13W **298** B10
Ademuz Spain 40°5N 1°13W **196** E3
Aden = ʿAdan Yemen 12°45N 45°0E **248** D4
Aden, G. of Ind. Oc. 12°30N 47°30E **267** B6
Adendorp S. Africa 32°25N 24°30E **270** D3
Adéri Libya 27°34N 22°30E **258** C5
Aderbissinat Niger 15°34N 7°54E **263** B6
Adhoi India 23°26N 70°32E **242** H4
Adhyāman Turkey 37°48N 38°30E **250** B1
Adi Indonesia 4°15S 133°30E **231** E8
Adi Arkai Ethiopia 13°24N 37°57E **257** E4
Adi Daro Eritrea 14°20N 38°14E **257** E4
Adi Keyih Eritrea 14°51N 39°22E **257** E4
Adi Kwala Eritrea 14°38N 38°48E **257** E4
Adi Ugri Eritrea 14°58N 38°48E **257** E4

Adieu, C. Australia 32°0S 132°10E **279** F5
Adieu Pt. Australia 15°14S 124°35E **278** C3
Adigala Ethiopia 10°24N 42°15E **257** E5
Adige → Italy 45°9N 12°20E **198** C9
Adigrat Ethiopia 14°20N 39°26E **257** E4
Adıgüzel Baraji Turkey 38°13N 29°14E **205** C11
Adilabad India 19°33N 78°20E **244** E4
Adilcevaz Turkey 38°47N 42°43E **213** C10
Adri Libya 27°32N 13°2E **258** C2
Adirondack □ U.S.A. 44°0N 74°20W **313** C10
Adirondack Mts. U.S.A. 44°0N 74°0W **313** C10
Adis Abeba = Addis Abeba
  Ethiopia 9°2N 38°42E **257** F4
Adiyaman Turkey 37°45N 38°16E **213** D8
Adıyaman □ Turkey 37°30N 38°10E **213** D8
Adjim Tunisia 33°47N 10°55E **261** B8
Adjohon Benin 6°41N 2°32E **263** D5
Adjud Romania 46°7N 27°10E **183** D12
Adjumani Uganda 3°20N 31°50E **268** B3
Adlavik Is. Canada 55°0N 58°40W **299** B8
Adler Russia 43°28N 39°52E **191** J4
Adler Planetarium
  Chicago, U.S.A. 41°51N 87°36W **119** B3
Admer Algeria 20°21N 5°27E **261** D6
Admer, Erg d' Algeria 24°0N 9°5E **261** D6
Admiralteyskaya Storona
  Russia 59°56N 30°20E **137** B2
Admiralty G. Australia 14°20S 125°55E **278** B4
Admiralty Gulf ○
  Australia 14°16S 125°52E **278** B4
Admiralty I. U.S.A. 57°30N 134°30W **296** B2
Admiralty Inlet Canada 72°30N 86°0W **295** C14
Admiralty Is. Papua N. G. 2°0S 147°0E **286** B4
Admiralty Island △
  U.S.A. 57°40N 134°10W **303** H14
Adnan Menderes, İzmir ✈ (ADB)
  Turkey 38°23N 27°6E **205** C9
Ado Nigeria 6°36N 2°56E **263** D5
Ado-Ekiti Nigeria 7°38N 5°12E **263** D6
Adok South Sudan 8°10N 30°20E **257** F3
Adola India 11°14N 41°44E **112** A2
Adonara Indonesia 8°15S 123°5E **231** F6
Adoni India 15°33N 77°18E **245** G3
Adony Hungary 47°6N 18°52E **182** C3
Adour → France 43°32N 1°32W **174** E2
Adra India 23°30N 86°42E **243** H12
Adra Spain 36°43N 3°3W **195** J7
Adrano Italy 37°40N 14°50E **201** E7
Adrar Algeria 27°51N 0°19W **261** C4
Adrar des Ḭforas Africa 19°40N 1°40E **261** D5
Adré Chad 13°40N 22°20E **259** F4
Ãdria Italy 45°3N 12°3E **199** C9
Adrian Mich., U.S.A. 41°54N 84°2W **311** C12
Adrian Mo., U.S.A. 38°24N 94°21W **310** F2
Adrian Tex., U.S.A. 35°16N 102°40W **314** D3
Adrianople = Edirne
  Turkey 41°40N 26°34E **203** E10
Adriatic Sea Medit. S. 43°0N 16°0E **193** C7
Adua Indonesia 1°45S 129°50E **231** E7
Adung Long Burma 28°7N 97°42E **241** A6
Adur India 9°8N 76°40E **245** K3
Adwa Ethiopia 14°15N 38°52E **257** E4
Adygeası ◇ Russia 45°0N 40°0E **191** H5
Adzhar Republic = Ajaria □
  Georgia 41°30N 42°0E **191** K6
Adzopé Ivory C. 6°7N 3°49W **262** D4
Aegae = Aigai Greece 40°28N 22°19E **202** F6
Ægean Sea Medit. S. 38°30N 25°0E **203** E7
Aerhtai Shan Mongolia 46°40N 92°45E **217** C12
Ærø Denmark 54°52N 10°25E **163** K4
Ærøskøbing Denmark 54°53N 10°24E **163** K4
Aetdia-Akarnania =
  Etoloakarnania Greece 38°45N 21°18E **204** C3
Aetos Greece 38°45N 21°50E **204** C3
Afaahiti Tahiti 17°45S 149°17W **289** e
Afabet Eritrea 16°51N 38°58E **257** E4
Afanasyevo Russia 58°52N 53°12E **216** C6
Afándou Greece 36°18N 28°12E **206** D12
ʿAfak Iraq 32°4N 45°15E **213** F11
Afandou Greece 36°18N 28°12E **206** D12
Afar □ Ethiopia 12°0N 41°0E **257** E5
Afarag, Erg Algeria 23°50N 2°47E **261** D5
Afareaitu Moorea 17°33S 149°47W **289** e
Åfarnes Norway 62°40N 7°32E **164** D4
Afdega Ethiopia 6°4N 43°3E **267** C5
Aff → France 47°38N 2°8W **172** F5
Afghanistan ■ Asia 33°0N 65°0E **242** B3
Afgooye Somalia 2°7N 44°59E **267** C5
ʿAfīf Si. Arabia 23°53N 42°56E **248** B3
Afikpo Nigeria 5°53N 7°54E **263** D6
Aflandshage Denmark 55°33N 12°35E **118** D3
Aflisses, O. → Algeria 28°40N 0°50E **261** C5
Aflou Algeria 34°7N 2°3E **261** B5
Afmadow Somalia 0°31N 42°4E **267** D5
Afogados da Ingàzeira
  Brazil 7°45S 37°39W **332** C4
Afognak I. U.S.A. 58°15N 152°30W **303** G9
Afono B. Amer. Samoa 14°15S 170°38W **302** f
Afore Papua N. G. 9°9S 148°22E **286** E5
Afragóla Italy 40°55N 14°18E **201** B7
Afram → Ghana 6°10N 0°52W **263** D4
Afrera Ethiopia 13°16N 41°5E **257** E5
Africa 10°0N 20°0E **254** F6
ʿAfrīn Syria 36°32N 36°50E **250** B7
ʿAfrīn → Syria 36°37N 37°0E **250** B7
Afşar → Turkey 37°2N 32°56E **205** D13
Afşin Turkey 38°20N 36°32E **250** B3
Afsluitdijk Neths. 53°0N 5°30E **170** B5
Afton Iowa, U.S.A. 41°2N 94°12W **310** C2
Afton N.Y., U.S.A. 42°14N 75°32W **313** D9
Afton Wyo., U.S.A. 42°44N 110°56W **304** E8
Afuá Brazil 0°15S 50°20W **329** D7
ʿAfula Israel 32°37N 35°17E **250** C6
Afyon Turkey 38°45N 30°33E **205** C13
Afyon □ Turkey 38°20N 30°30E **205** C12
Afyonkarahisar = Afyon
  Turkey 38°45N 30°33E **205** C13
Aga Egypt 30°55N 31°10E **117** A2
Aga Jari Iran 30°42N 49°50E **247** D6
Agadem Niger 16°58N 13°19E **259** F2
Agadez Niger 16°58N 7°59E **259** F1
Agadez □ Niger 18°0N 8°0E **259** E1
Agadir Morocco 30°28N 9°55W **260** B3
Agaete Canary Is. 28°6N 15°43W **153** e1
Agaie Nigeria 9°0N 6°15E **263** D6
Agalas Greece 37°43N 20°47E **207** D1
Agalega Is. Mauritius 11°0S 55°0E **54** d
Agana = Hagåtña Guam 13°28N 144°45E **302** c
Aganoa B. Guam 13°29N 144°50E **302** c
Agapa Russia 71°27N 89°15E **217** B10
Ãgapovka Russia 53°14N 59°9E **216** D6
Agar → India 21°0N 70°52E **242** J4
Agar India 23°40N 76°2E **242** H7
Agaram Mali 16°37N 3°23W **262** B4
Agaro Ethiopia 7°50N 36°38E **257** F4
Agartala India 23°50N 91°23E **241** D8
Agãş Romania 46°28N 26°15E **183** D11
Agassiz Canada 49°14N 121°46W **296** D4

Agassiz Icecap Canada 80°15N 76°0W **295** A16
Agat Guam 13°25N 144°40E **302** d
Agats Indonesia 5°33S 138°0E **231** F9
Agatti I. India 10°50N 72°12E **245** J7
Agattu I. U.S.A. 52°25N 173°35E **303** K1
Agawam U.S.A. 42°5N 72°37W **313** D12
Agbélouvé Togo 6°35N 1°14E **263** D5
Agboville Ivory C. 5°55N 4°15W **262** D4
Agboyi Cr. → Nigeria 6°33N 3°24E **124** A2
Ağcabädi Azerbaijan 40°5N 47°27E **191** K8
Ağdam Azerbaijan 40°0N 46°58E **191** K8
Ağdara Azerbaijan 40°13N 46°49E **191** K8
Ağdaş Azerbaijan 40°44N 47°22E **191** K8
Agde France 43°19N 3°28E **174** E7
Agde, C. d' France 43°16N 3°28E **174** E7
Agdz Morocco 30°47N 6°30W **260** B3
Agdzhabedi = Ağcabädi
  Azerbaijan 40°5N 47°27E **191** K8
Agen France 44°12N 0°38E **174** D4
Ageo Japan 35°58N 139°36E **223** B11
Agerbæk Denmark 55°36N 8°48E **163** J2
Agersø Denmark 55°13N 11°12E **163** J5
Ãgerup Denmark 55°43N 12°19E **118** A1
Ãgesta Sweden 59°12N 18°6E **139** B2
Ageyevo Russia 54°10N 36°27E **188** D9
Aggteleki ◠ Hungary 48°27N 20°36E **182** B5
Ãgh Kand Iran 37°15N 48°4E **213** D13
Aghathonisi Greece 37°28N 27°0E **205** D8
Aghia Anna Greece 38°52S 23°24E **204** C5
Aghia Deka Greece 35°3N 24°58E **207** E5
Aghia Ekaterinis, Akra
  Greece 39°50N 19°50E **206** B9
Aghia Galini Greece 35°6N 24°41E **207** E5
Aghia Marina Athina,
  Greece 37°48N 23°51E **112** C3
Aghia Marina Kasos,
  Greece 35°27N 26°53E **205** E8
Aghia Marina Leros,
  Greece 37°11N 26°48E **205** D8
Aghia Paraskevi Athina,
  Greece 38°1N 23°49E **112** A2
Aghia Paraskevi Voreio Aigaio,
  Greece 39°14N 26°21E **205** B8
Aghia Roumeli Greece 35°14N 23°58E **207** E4
Aghia Varvara Greece 35°8N 25°1E **207** E6
Aghiasos Greece 39°5N 26°23E **205** B8
Aghio Theodori Greece 37°55N 23°9E **204** D5
Aghion Oros = Athos
  Greece 40°9N 24°22E **203** F8
Aghion Oros □ Greece 40°25N 24°6E **203** F8
Aghios Andreas Greece 37°21N 22°45E **204** D4
Aghios Dimitrios Greece 37°40N 14°50E **112** B2
Aghios Efimia Greece 38°19N 20°29E **204** C2
Aghios Estratios Greece 39°34N 24°58E **204** B6
Aghios Georgios Greece 37°28N 23°57E **204** D5
Aghios Ioannis, Akra
  Greece 35°20N 25°40E **207** E6
Aghios Ioannis Rendis
  Greece 37°57N 23°39E **112** B1
Aghios Isidoros Greece 36°9N 27°51E **206** E11
Aghios Kirikos Greece 37°34N 26°17E **205** D8
Aghios Leon Greece 37°47N 20°43E **207** D1
Aghios Matheos Greece 39°30N 19°52E **206** B9
Aghios Mironas Greece 35°15N 25°1E **207** E6
Aghios Nikolaos Etoloakarnania,
  Greece 38°52N 20°48E **207** B2
Aghios Nikolaos Kriti,
  Greece 35°11N 25°41E **207** E6
Aghios Nikolaos Lefkada,
  Greece 38°36N 20°34E **207** B2
Aghios Petros Greece 38°40N 20°36E **207** B2
Aghios Stephanos Greece 39°46N 19°39E **206** B9
Aghios Thekli Greece 38°15N 20°27E **207** C1
Aghios Thomas Greece 38°58N 20°47E **207** B2
Aghiou Orous, Kolpos
  Greece 40°6N 24°0E **202** F7
Aghireșu Romania 46°53N 23°15E **182** D8
Aghoueyyit Mauritania 21°10N 15°56W **260** D1
Aghreijit Mauritania 21°58N 12°11W **260** D2
Agia Greece 39°43N 22°45E **204** B4
Agincourt Canada 43°47N 79°16W **141** A3
Aginskoye Russia 51°6N 114°32E **215** D12
Agjert Mauritania 16°23N 9°17W **262** B3
Ağlasun Turkey 37°39N 30°31E **205** D12
Agly → France 42°46N 3°3E **174** F7
Agmar Mauritania 25°16N 6°40W **260** C2
Agnew Australia 28°1S 120°31E **279** E3
Agnibilékrou Ivory C. 7°10N 3°11W **262** D4
Agnita Romania 45°59N 24°40E **183** E9
Agno Italy 45°33N 11°5E **199** C11
Ago Japan 34°20N 136°51E **223** G8
Ago-Are Nigeria 8°30N 3°25E **263** D5
Agofie Ghana 8°27N 0°15E **263** D5
Agogna → Italy 45°4N 8°52E **198** C5
Agogo S. Sudan 7°50N 28°45E **257** F2
Agon-Coutainville France 49°2N 1°34W **172** D5
Agoo Phil. 16°20N 120°22E **232** E4
Agora Athens, Greece 112 c1
Ãgordo Italy 46°18N 12°2E **199** B9
Agori India 24°33N 82°57E **243** G10
Agoufia Mauritania 19°57N 16°10W **260** D1
Agouna Benin 7°39N 1°47E **263** D5
Agout → France 43°47N 1°41E **174** E5
Agra India 27°17N 77°58E **242** F7
Agra Canal India 28°33N 77°17E **120** D2
Agrã Brazil 7°45S 37°39W **332** C4
Agram = Zagreb Croatia 45°50N 15°58E **199** C12
Agramunt Spain 41°48N 1°6E **196** D6
Ãgreda Spain 41°51N 1°55W **196** D3
Ağri Turkey 39°44N 43°3E **213** C10
Ağri □ Turkey 40°15N 42°30E **213** C10
Ağri Daği Turkey 39°50N 44°15E **213** C11
Ağri Karakose = Ağri
  Turkey 39°44N 43°3E **213** C10
Agria Greece 39°20N 23°1E **204** B5
Agricola Oriental Mexico 19°23N 99°4W **128** B2
Agrigento Italy 37°19N 13°34E **201** F6
Agrihan N. Marianas 18°46N 145°40E **302** a
Agrinio Greece 38°37N 21°27E **204** C3
Agrópoli Italy 40°21N 14°59E **201** B7
Ãgskarsta Azerbaijan 41°7N 45°22E **191** K7
Agua Branca Brazil 5°50S 42°40W **332** C3
Agua Caliente Mexico 32°29N 116°59W **307** N10
Agua Caliente Springs
  U.S.A. 32°56N 116°19W **307** N10
Água Clara Brazil 20°25S 52°45W **331** E7
Água Espraiada → Brazil 23°41N 112°0W **305** d
Agua Hechicera
  Mexico 32°28N 116°15W **307** N10
Água Preta → Brazil 1°41S 63°48W **329** D5
Agua Prieta Mexico 31°18N 109°34W **318** A3
Aguachica Colombia 8°19N 73°38E **328** B4
Aguada Cecilio Argentina 40°51N 65°53W **335** D3
Aguada Puerto Rico 18°23N 67°11W **323** d
Aguadas Colombia 5°40N 75°38W **328** B3
Aguadilla Puerto Rico 18°26N 67°10W **302** f
Aguadulce Panama 8°15N 80°32W **320** E3
Agualva-Cacem Portugal 38°46N 9°18W **126** A1
Aguanga U.S.A. 33°27N 116°51W **307** M10
Aguanus → Canada 50°14N 62°5W **299** B7
Aguapei → Brazil 16°15S 59°45W **331** D6
Aguapey → Argentina 29°7S 56°36W **334** B4

Aguaray Guazú →
  Paraguay 24°47S 57°19W 334 A4
Aguarico → Ecuador 0°59S 75°11W 328 D2
Aguaro-Guariquito △
  Venezuela 8°20N 66°35W 328 B4
Aguas → Spain 41°20N 0°30W 196 D4
Aguas Blancas Chile 24°15S 69°55W 334 A2
Aguas Calientes, Sierra de
  Argentina 25°26S 66°40W 334 B2
Águas Formosas Brazil 17°5S 40°57W 333 E3
Águas Lindas de Goiás
  Brazil 15°46S 48°15W 333 E2
Aguascalientes Mexico 21°53N 102°18W 318 C4
Aguascalientes □ Mexico 22°00N 102°20W 318 C4
Aguateca Guatemala 16°25N 90°11W 320 C1
Águeda Portugal 38°59N 4°52W 195 G6
Águeda → Spain 40°34N 8°27W 194 E2
Águeda → Spain 41°2N 6°56W 194 D4
Aguelhok Mali 19°29N 0°52E 261 E5
Aguelt el Melah
  Mauritania 23°3N 10°40W 260 D2
Agüenit W. Sahara 22°11N 13°8W 260 D2
Aguié Niger 13°31N 7°46E 263 C6
Aguila, Punta Puerto Rico 17°57N 67°13W 321 b
Aguilafuente Spain 41°13N 4°7W 194 D6
Aguilar de Campóo Spain 42°47N 4°15W 194 C6
Aguilar de la Frontera
  Spain 37°31N 4°40W 195 H6
Aguilares Argentina 27°26S 65°35W 334 B2
Águilas Spain 37°23N 1°35W 197 H3
Agüimes Canary Is. 27°58N 15°27W 153 e1
Aguja, C. de la Colombia 11°18N 74°12W 328 A3
Agujereada, Pta.
  Puerto Rico 18°30N 67°8W 321 b
Agulaa Ethiopia 13°40N 39°40E 257 E4
Agulhas, C. S. Africa 34°52S 20°0E 270 D3
Agulhas Ridge Atl. Oc. 42°0S 15°0E 152 L13
Agulo Canary Is. 28°11N 17°12W 153 e1
Agung, Gunung
  Indonesia 8°20S 115°28E 231 J18
Aguni-Jima Japan 26°30N 127°10E 221 L3
Agur Uganda 2°28N 32°55E 268 B3
Agurei → South Sudan 7°45N 33°0E 257 F3
Agusan → Phil. 9°0N 125°30E 233 G5
Agusan del Norte □ Phil. 9°20N 125°10E 233 G5
Agusan del Sur □ Phil. 8°30N 125°30E 233 G5
Agustín Codazzi Colombia 10°2N 73°14W 328 A3
Agutaya I. Phil. 11°9N 120°58E 233 F3
Ağva Turkey 41°8N 29°51E 205 C13
Agvali Russia 42°36N 46°8E 191 J8
Aha Mts. Botswana 19°45S 21°0E 270 A3
Ahad Rifaydah Si. Arabia 17°50N 42°55E 248 C3
Ahaggar △ Algeria 23°0N 6°30E 261 D6
Ahaggar △ Algeria 23°0N 4°50E 261 D5
Ahai Dam China 27°21N 100°30E 228 D3
Ahamansu Ghana 7°38N 0°35E 263 D5
Ahar Iran 38°35N 47°0E 213 C12
Ahat Turkey 38°39N 29°47E 205 C11
Ahaura → N.Z. 42°21S 171°34E 285 C6
Ahaus Germany 52°4N 7°0E 178 C2
Ahé French Polynesia 14°30S 146°18W 289 f
Aheim Norway 62°2N 5°13E 164 B2
Ahelledjem Algeria 26°37N 6°58E 261 C6
Ahimanawa Ra. N.Z. 39°3S 176°30E 284 F5
Ahioma Papua N. G. 10°20S 150°33E 286 F6
Ahipara B. N.Z. 35°5S 173°5E 284 B3
Ahiri India 19°30N 80°0E 244 E5
Ahlat Turkey 38°45N 42°29E 213 C10
Ahlen Germany 51°45N 7°53E 178 D3
Ahmad Wal Pakistan 29°18N 65°58E 242 E1
Ahmadabad Iran 35°3N 60°50E 247 C9
Aḥmadābād Khorāsān, Iran 35°3N 60°50E 247 C9
Aḥmadābād Khorāsān,
  Iran 35°49N 59°42E 247 C8
Aḥmadī Iran 27°56S 56°42E 247 D6
Ahmadnagar India 19°7N 74°46E 244 E2
Ahmadpur India 18°40N 76°57E 244 E3
Ahmadpur East Pakistan 29°12N 71°10E 242 E4
Ahmadpur Lamma
  Pakistan 28°19N 70°3E 242 E4
Ahmanson Theater Los Angeles, U.S.A. 127 b2
Ahmar, Mts. Ethiopia 9°20N 41°15E 257 F5
Ahmedabad = Ahmadabad
  India 23°0N 72°40E 242 H5
Ahmednagar = Ahmadnagar
  India 19°7N 74°46E 244 E2
Ahmetbey Turkey 41°26N 27°34E 203 E11
Ahmetler Turkey 38°38N 29°5E 205 C11
Ahmetli Turkey 38°32N 27°57E 205 C9
Ahmeyim Mauritania 20°51N 14°25W 260 D2
Ahoada Nigeria 5°8N 6°36E 263 D6
Ahome Mexico 25°55N 109°11W 318 B3
Ahon, Tarso Chad 20°23N 18°18E 259 D3
Ahoskie U.S.A. 36°17N 76°59W 315 C16
Ahr → Germany 50°32N 7°16E 178 E3
Ahram Iran 28°52N 51°16E 247 D6
Ahrax Pt. Malta 36°0N 14°22E 206 F7
Ahrensbök Germany 54°2N 10°33E 178 A6
Ahrensburg Germany 53°40N 10°13E 178 B6
Ahrensfelde Germany 52°34N 13°34E 115 A4
Ahu Akivi Chile 27°7S 109°24W 330 b
Ahu Tepeu Chile 27°6S 109°25W 330 b
Ahu Tongariki Chile 27°8S 109°17W 330 b
Ahu Vinapu Chile 27°10S 109°25W 330 b
Ahuachapán El Salv. 13°54N 89°52W 320 D2
'Āhuimanu U.S.A. 21°26N 157°50W 302 K14
Ahun France 46°4N 2°5E 173 F9
Ahuntsic Canada 45°32N 73°41W 130 A1
Ahunui French Polynesia 19°39S 140°25W 289 f
Åhus Sweden 55°56N 14°18E 163 d2
Ahvāz Iran 31°20N 48°40E 247 D6
Ahvenanmaa = Åland
  Finland 60°15N 20°0E 161 F19
Aḥwar Yemen 13°30N 46°40E 248 E4
Ahzar → Mali 15°30N 3°20E 263 B5
Ai → Ōsaka, Japan 34°26N 135°35E 133 A2
Ai → Ōsaka, Japan 34°46N 135°35E 133 A2
Ai-Ais Namibia 27°54S 17°59E 270 C2
Ai-Ais and Fish River Canyon △
  Namibia 24°45S 17°15E 270 B2
Aiari → Brazil 0°22N 68°36W 328 C4
Aichach Germany 48°27N 11°9E 179 G7
Aichi □ Japan 35°0N 137°15E 222 G5
'Aiea U.S.A. 21°23N 157°56W 302 K14
Aigai Greece 40°28N 22°0E 202 F6
Aigle Switz. 46°18N 6°58E 179 J1
Aignay-le-Duc France 47°40N 4°43E 173 E11
Aigoual, Mt. France 44°8N 3°5E 174 C4
Aigre France 45°54N 0°1E 174 C4
Aigremont France 48°32N 2°1E 134 A1
Aigrettes, Île aux Mauritius 20°25S 57°43E 272 e
Aiguá Uruguay 34°13S 54°46W 335 D5
Aigueperse France 46°3N 3°13E 173 F10
Aigues → France 44°7N 4°43E 175 D8
Aigues-Mortes France 43°35N 4°12E 175 E8
Aigües-Tortes i Estany de St.
  Maurici △ Spain 42°34N 0°31E 196 C6
Aiguilles France 44°47N 6°51E 175 D10
Aiguillon France 44°18N 0°21E 174 D4
Aigurande France 46°27N 1°49E 173 F8
Ailao Shan China 24°0N 101°20E 228 D3

Aileron Australia 22°39S 133°20E 280 C1
Ailey U.S.A. 32°11N 82°34W 316 C7
Ailigandi Panama 9°14N 78°1W 328 B2
Aillant-sur-Tholon France 47°52N 3°20E 173 E10
Aillik Canada 55°11N 59°18W 299 A8
Ailsa Craig Ont., Canada 43°8N 81°33W 312 C3
Ailsa Craig S. Ayrs., U.K. 55°15N 5°6W 167 F3
Ailuinal Papua N. G. 9°38S 150°35E 286 F6
Aim Russia 59°0N 133°55E 215 D14
Aimogasta Argentina 28°33S 66°50W 334 B2
Aimorés Brazil 19°30S 41°4W 333 E3
Ain → France 46°5N 5°20E 173 F12
Ain → France 45°45N 5°11E 175 C9
Aïn Beïda Algeria 35°50N 7°29E 261 A6
Aïn Ben Khellil Algeria 33°15N 0°49W 261 B4
Aïn Ben Tili Mauritania 25°59N 9°27W 260 C3
Aïn Beni Mathar Morocco 34°1N 2°0W 261 B4
Aïn Benian Algeria 36°48N 2°55E 261 A5
Aïn Dalla Egypt 27°20N 27°23E 256 B4
Aïn Defla Algeria 36°16N 1°58E 261 A5
Aïn Defla □ Algeria 36°10N 2°10E 261 A5
Aïn Girba Egypt 29°20N 25°14E 256 B2
Aïn M'lila Algeria 36°2N 6°35E 261 A6
Aïn Murr Sudan 21°50N 25°9E 256 C2
Aïn Qeiqab Egypt 29°42N 24°55E 256 B1
Aïn Salah = In Salah
  Algeria 27°10N 2°32E 261 C5
Aïn Sefra Algeria 32°47N 0°37W 261 B4
Aïn Sheikh Murzûk
  Egypt 26°47N 27°45E 256 B2
Aïn Sukhna Egypt 29°50N 33°6E 251 A4
Aïn Sukhna Egypt 29°32N 32°20E 256 J8
Aïn Tédélès Algeria 36°0N 0°21E 261 A5
Aïn Témouchent Algeria 35°16N 1°8W 261 A4
Aïn Témouchent □ Algeria 35°20N 1°5W 261 A4
Aïn Tikkidine Algeria 25°33N 1°24E 261 C5
Aïn Touta Algeria 35°26N 5°54E 261 A6
Aïn Zeïtûn Egypt 29°10N 25°48E 256 B2
Aïn Zorah Morocco 34°37N 3°32W 261 B4
Ainazi Latvia 57°50N 24°24E 188 D3
Ainos Oros Greece 38°9N 20°40E 202 E2
Ainsworth U.S.A. 42°33N 99°52W 308 D4
Aintab = Gaziantep Turkey 37°6N 37°23E 250 B8
Aioi Japan 34°48N 134°28E 222 C6
Aiome Papua N. G. 5°8S 144°44E 286 B2
Aipe Colombia 3°13N 75°15W 328 C2
Aiquile Bolivia 18°10S 65°10W 330 D4
Aïr Niger 18°30N 8°0E 259 E1
Air Canada Centre Toronto, Canada 141 c2
Aïr et Ténéré △ Niger 18°12N 9°56E 263 B6
Air Force I. Canada 67°58N 74°5W 295 D17
Air Hitam Malaysia 1°55N 103°11E 237 M4
Air View Park Singapore 1°20N 103°46E 138 d2
Aira Japan 31°43N 130°43E 222 F2
Airaines France 49°58N 1°55E 173 C8
Airão Brazil 1°56S 61°22W 329 D5
Airbangis Indonesia 0°12N 99°22E 234 S1
Airdrie Alta., Canada 51°18N 114°2W 296 C6
Airdrie N. Lanarks., U.K. 55°52N 3°57W 167 F5
Aire → Meuse, France 49°18N 4°49E 173 C11
Aire → Yorks., U.K. 53°43N 0°55W 168 D7
Aire, I. de l' Spain 39°48N 4°16E 206 B11
Aire-sur-la-Lys France 50°37N 2°22E 173 B9
Aire-sur-l'Adour France 43°42N 0°15W 174 E3
Aireys Inlet Australia 38°29S 144°5E 282 E6
Airlie Beach Australia 20°16S 148°43E 280 b
Airport West Australia 37°42S 144°52E 128 A1
Airvault France 46°50N 0°8W 172 F6
Aisch → Germany 49°49N 10°58E 179 F6
Aisne □ France 49°42N 3°40E 173 C10
Aisne → France 49°26N 2°50E 173 C9
Ait India 25°54N 79°14E 243 G8
Ait Ben Haddou Morocco 31°3N 7°7W 260 B3
Aït Melloul Morocco 30°20N 9°30W 260 B3
Aitana, Sierra de Spain 38°35N 0°24W 196 C4
Aitape Papua N. G. 3°11S 142°22E 286 B2
Aitkin U.S.A. 46°32N 93°42W 308 B7
Aitutaki Cook Is. 18°52S 159°45W 289 J12
Aiuaba Brazil 6°38S 40°7E 332 D4
Aiud Romania 46°19N 23°44E 183 D8
Aix-en-Provence France 43°32N 5°27E 175 E9
Aix-la-Chapelle = Aachen
  Germany 50°45N 6°6E 178 E2
Aix-les-Bains France 45°41N 5°53E 175 C9
Aixe-sur-Vienne France 45°47N 1°9E 174 C5
Aiyang, Mt. Papua N. G. 5°10S 141°20E 286 C1
Aiyina = Egina Greece 37°45N 23°26E 204 D5
Aizawl India 23°40N 92°44E 241 D4
Aizenay France 46°44N 1°38E 172 F5
Aizkraukle Latvia 56°36N 25°11E 188 D3
Aizpute Latvia 56°43N 21°40E 184 B8
Aizuwakamatsu Japan 37°30N 139°56E 220 F9
Ajabshīr Iran 37°28N 45°54E 213 C11
Ajaccio France 41°55N 8°40E 175 G12
Ajaccio, G. d' France 41°52N 8°40E 175 G12
Ajai → Uganda 2°52N 31°16E 268 B3
Ajaju → Colombia 0°59N 72°20W 328 C3
Ajalpan Mexico 18°22N 97°15W 319 D5
Ajanta Ra. India 20°30N 75°48E 244 D2
Ajanta Ra. India 20°28N 75°50E 244 D2
Ajari Rep. = Ajaria □
  Georgia 41°30N 42°0E 191 K6
Ajaria □ Georgia 41°30N 42°0E 191 K6
Ajax Canada 43°50N 79°1W 312 C5
Ajax, Mt. N.Z. 42°35S 172°5E 285 C7
Ajdābiyā Libya 30°54N 20°4E 258 B4
Ajdovščina Slovenia 45°54N 13°54E 199 C10
Ajegunle Nigeria 6°26N 3°20E 124 D2
Ajibar Ethiopia 10°35N 38°36E 257 E4
Ajigarh India 30°47N 76°41E 242 D7
Ajka Hungary 47°4N 17°31E 182 C2
'Ajlūn Jordan 32°18N 35°47E 251 H6
'Ajmān U.A.E. 25°25N 55°30E 247 E7
Ajmer India 26°28N 74°37E 242 F6
Ajnala India 31°50N 74°48E 242 D6
Ajo U.S.A. 32°22N 112°52W 305 K7
Ajo, C. de Spain 43°31N 3°35W 194 B7
Ajoupa-Bouillon Martinique 14°49N 61°7W 322 j
Ajuda Portugal 38°42N 9°12W 126 A1
Ajuda, Pta. da Azores 37°52N 25°19W 153 d3
Ajuy Phil. 11°10N 123°1E 233 F4
Ak Dağı Turkey 36°30N 29°32E 205 E11
Ak Dağları Turkey 39°32N 36°12E 212 C7
Ak-Dovurak Russia 51°11N 90°36E 217 B12
Ak-Mechet = Qyzylorda
  Kazakhstan 44°48N 65°28E 216 D7
Ak-Mednet = Chornomorske
  Ukraine 45°30N 32°40E 189 K7
Ak-Sheikh = Razdolnoye
  Ukraine 45°46N 33°29E 189 K7
Akaba Togo 8°10N 1°2E 263 D5
Akabira Japan 43°33N 142°5E 220 C11
Akadémia Obrucheva, Khrebet
  Russia 59°0N 96°0E 217 B13
Akagera △ Rwanda 1°31S 30°33E 268 C3
Akaishi-Dake Japan 35°27N 138°9E 223 B10
Akaishi-Sammyaku Japan 35°25N 138°10E 223 B10
Akaki Beseka Ethiopia 8°55N 38°45E 257 F4
Akákús, J. Libya 25°26N 10°48E 258 D2
Akalkot India 17°32N 76°13E 244 F3
Akalla Sweden 59°1N 17°55E 139 A1

Akamas Cyprus 35°3N 32°18E 207 E8
Akan △ Japan 43°20N 144°20E 220 C12
Akanthou Cyprus 35°22N 33°45E 207 E9
Akarca Turkey 38°35N 29°35E 205 C11
Akaroa N.Z. 43°49S 172°59E 285 D7
Akaroa Harbour N.Z. 43°50S 172°55E 285 D7
Akasaka Tokyo, Japan 140 b3
Akasha Sudan 21°10N 30°32E 256 C3
Akashi Japan 34°45N 134°58E 222 C6
Akbarābād Iran 35°40N 51°20E 141 A2
Akbarpur Bihar, India 24°39N 83°58E 243 G10
Akbarpur Ut. P., India 26°25N 82°32E 243 F10
Akbou Algeria 36°31N 4°31E 261 A5
Akbulak Russia 51°1N 55°37E 216 B5
Akçaabat Turkey 41°1N 39°34E 213 B8
Akçadağ Turkey 38°27N 37°43E 212 C7
Akçakale Turkey 36°41N 38°56E 213 D8
Akçakoca Turkey 41°5N 31°8E 212 B4
Akçaova Turkey 41°3N 29°57E 203 E13
Akçay Turkey 36°18N 33°21E 250 B4
Akçay → Turkey 36°36N 29°45E 205 E11
Akçay → Turkey 20°39N 28°15E 205 D10
Akchâr Mauritania 20°20N 14°28W 260 D2
Akchi-Karasu = Toktogul
  Kyrgyzstan 41°50N 72°50E 217 D8
Akdağ Antalya, Turkey 37°0N 32°0E 250 B3
Akdağ İzmir, Turkey 38°33N 26°30E 205 C8
Akdağmadeni Turkey 39°39N 35°53E 212 C6
Akdere Turkey 36°14N 33°46E 250 B4
Akechi Japan 35°18N 137°23E 223 B9
Akelamo Indonesia 1°35N 129°40E 231 D7
Åkernes = Åknes Norway 58°45N 7°30E 164 F2
Åkers styckebruk Sweden 59°15N 17°5E 162 G11
Åkersberga Sweden 59°29N 18°18E 162 G12
Akershus □ Norway 60°0N 11°10E 164 D8
Akershus Slott Oslo, Norway 133 c1
Akeru → India 17°25N 80°5E 244 F5
Aketi Dem. Rep. of the Congo 2°38N 23°47E 264 B4
Akhali Atoni Georgia 43°7N 40°50E 191 J5
Akhalkalaki Georgia 41°27N 43°25E 191 K6
Akhaltsikhe Georgia 41°40N 43°0E 191 K6
Akhḍar, W. al →
  Si. Arabia 28°36N 36°36E 251 K7
Akhiok U.S.A. 56°57N 154°10W 303 H9
Akhisar Turkey 38°56N 27°48E 205 C9
Akhmîm Egypt 26°31N 31°47E 256 B3
Akhna Cyprus 35°3N 33°47E 207 E9
Akhnur India 32°52N 74°45E 243 C6
Akhtarīn Syria 36°31N 37°20E 250 B8
Akhtopol Bulgaria 42°6N 27°56E 203 D11
Akhtubinsk Russia 48°13N 46°7E 191 F8
Akhty Russia 41°30N 47°45E 191 K8
Akhtyrka = Okhtyrka
  Ukraine 50°25N 35°0E 189 G8
Aki Japan 33°30N 133°54E 222 D5
Aki-Nada Japan 34°5N 132°40E 222 C4
Akiachak U.S.A. 60°55N 161°13W 303 F7
Akiak U.S.A. 60°55N 161°13W 303 F7
Akiéni Gabon 1°11S 13°53E 264 C2
Akihabara Tokyo, Japan 140 a5
Akimiski I. Canada 52°50N 81°30W 298 B3
Akıncı Burnu Turkey 36°19N 35°46E 250 B6
Akıncılar = Louroujina
  Cyprus 35°0N 33°28E 207 F9
Akiōta Japan 34°36N 132°19E 222 C4
Akirkeby Denmark 55°4N 14°55E 163 J8
Akita Japan 39°45N 140°7E 220 E10
Akita □ Japan 39°40N 140°30E 220 E10
Akjoujt Mauritania 19°45N 14°15W 262 B2
Akka Mali 15°24N 4°11W 262 B4
Akka Morocco 29°22N 8°9W 260 C3
Akkaraipattu Sri Lanka 7°13N 81°51E 245 L5
Akkaya Tepesi Turkey 37°25N 29°38E 205 D11
Akkerman = Bilhorod-
  Dnistrovskyy Ukraine 46°11N 30°23E 189 J9
Akkeshi Japan 43°2N 144°51E 220 C12
'Akko Israel 32°55N 35°4E 250 F6
Akköy Turkey 37°29N 27°15E 205 D9
Akkuş Turkey 40°47N 37°0E 212 B7
Aklampa Benin 8°15N 2°10E 263 D5
Aklan □ Phil. 11°50N 122°30E 233 F4
Aklavik Canada 68°12N 135°0W 294 C6
Aklera India 24°26N 76°32E 242 G7
Akmené Lithuania 56°15N 22°45E 184 B8
Akmenrags Latvia 56°50N 21°4E 184 B8
Akmolinsk = Astana
  Kazakhstan 51°10N 71°30E 217 B8
Akmonte = Almonte
  Spain 37°13N 6°38W 195 H4
Åknes Norway 58°45N 7°30E 164 F2
Aknoul Morocco 34°40N 3°55W 261 B4
Akō Japan 34°45N 134°24E 222 C6
Akobo → South Sudan 7°47N 33°1E 257 F3
Akobo → Ethiopia 7°48N 33°3E 257 F3
Akola Maharashtra, India 20°42N 77°2E 244 D3
Akola Maharashtra, India 19°32N 74°3E 244 E2
Akolmiut U.S.A. 60°55N 162°20W 303 F7
Akonolinga Cameroon 3°50N 12°18E 263 D7
Akor Mali 14°59N 6°58W 262 C3
Akordat Eritrea 15°30N 37°40E 257 D4
Akosombo Dam Ghana 6°20N 0°5E 263 D5
Akot India 21°10N 77°10E 244 D3
Akot South Sudan 6°31N 30°9E 257 F3
Akoupé Ivory C. 6°23N 3°54W 262 D4
Akpatok I. Canada 60°25N 68°8W 295 E18
Ákrahamn Norway 59°15N 5°10E 164 E22
'Akramah Syria 32°23N 41°4E 213 E9
Akranes Iceland 64°19N 21°58W 155 C4
Akreijit Mauritania 18°19N 9°11W 262 B3
Akritas, Akra Greece 36°43N 21°54E 204 E3
Akritas, Akra Greece 36°43N 22°4E 204 E4
Akron Colo., U.S.A. 40°10N 103°13W 304 F12
Akron Ind., U.S.A. 41°2N 86°1W 311 C10
Akron Ohio, U.S.A. 41°5N 81°31W 312 E3
Akrotiri Cyprus 34°36N 32°57E 207 F8
Akrotiri, Akra Greece 40°26N 25°27E 203 F9
Akrotiri Bay Cyprus 34°35N 33°10E 207 F9
Aksai Chin China 35°15N 79°55E 243 B8
Aksaray Turkey 38°25N 34°2E 212 C6
Aksay = Aqsay Kazakhstan 51°11N 53°0E 189 D9
Akşehir Turkey 38°18N 31°30E 212 C5
Akşehir Gölü Turkey 38°30N 31°25E 212 C5
Akseki Turkey 37°4N 31°47E 250 B3
Akstafa = Ağstafa
  Azerbaijan 41°7N 45°27E 191 K7
Aksu Xinjiang Uygur, China 41°5N 80°10E 217 D10
Aksu → China 40°26N 80°8E 217 D10
Aksu He → China 40°26N 80°6E 217 D10
Aksu Turkey 36°52N 30°57E 205 E13
Aksum Ethiopia 14°5N 38°40E 257 D4
Aktash Russia 42°14N 47°56E 191 C11
Aktepe Turkey 36°42N 36°27E 250 B6
Aktio Greece 38°55N 20°46E 202 E2
Akto China 39°5N 75°45E 217 F9
Aktogay Kazakhstan 46°57N 79°40E 217 E9
Aktsyabrski Belarus 52°38N 28°53E 177 B15
Aktyubinsk = Aqtöbe
  Kazakhstan 50°17N 57°10E 187 D10
Aku Nigeria 6°40N 7°18E 263 D6
Akula Dem. Rep. of the Congo 2°22N 20°9E 264 B3
Akun I. U.S.A. 54°11N 165°32W 303 J6
Akure Nigeria 7°15N 5°5E 263 D6
Akuressa Sri Lanka 6°5N 80°28E 245 L5
Akureyri Iceland 65°40N 18°6W 155 B8

Al Jahrah Kuwait 29°25N 47°40E 246 D5
Al Jalāmīd Si. Arabia 31°20N 40°6E 246 D3
Al Jamalīyah Qatar 25°37N 51°5E 247 E6
Al Janūb □ Lebanon 33°20N 35°20E 250 B5
Al Jawf Libya 24°10N 23°24E 258 D4
Al Jawf Si. Arabia 29°55N 39°40E 246 D3
Al Jawf □ Si. Arabia 29°30N 39°30E 246 D3
Al Jazair = Algeria ■ Africa 28°30N 2°0E 261 C5
Al Jazirah Iraq 33°30N 44°0E 213 E10
Al Jithāmīyah Si. Arabia 27°41N 41°43E 246 E4
Al Jubayl Si. Arabia 27°0N 49°50E 247 E6
Al Jubaylah Si. Arabia 24°55N 46°25E 246 E5
Al Jubb Si. Arabia 27°11N 42°17E 246 E4
Al Jufrah Libya 29°10N 16°0E 258 C3
Al Jufrah □ Libya 27°30N 16°0E 258 C3
Al Jumūm Si. Arabia 21°37N 39°42E 248 C2
Al Junaynah Sudan 13°27N 22°45E 257 E10
Al Kabā'ish Iraq 30°58N 47°0E 246 D6
Al Kāmil Oman 22°13N 59°12E 249 B7
Al Karak Jordan 31°11N 35°42E 251 G6
Al Karak □ Jordan 31°0N 36°0E 251 H7
Al Kāzimīyah Iraq 33°22N 44°18E 213 E11
Al Khābūrah Oman 23°57N 57°5E 247 F8
Al Khafjī Si. Arabia 28°24N 48°29E 247 E6
Al Khalīl West Bank 31°32N 35°6E 251 G6
Al Khāliṣ Iraq 33°49N 44°32E 213 E11
Al Khamāsīn Si. Arabia 20°0N 44°46E 248 B4
Al Kharj Si. Arabia 24°0N 47°0E 248 B4
Al Kharsānīyah Si. Arabia 27°13N 49°18E 247 E6
Al Khaṣab Oman 26°14N 56°15E 247 E8
Al Khāṣirah Si. Arabia 23°30N 43°47E 248 B3
Al Khawr Qatar 25°41N 51°30E 247 E6
Al Khiḍr Iraq 31°12N 45°33E 246 D5
Al Khiyām Lebanon 33°20N 35°36E 250 B5
Al Khubar Si. Arabia 26°17N 50°12E 247 E6
Al Khums Libya 32°40N 14°17E 258 B2
Al Khurmah Si. Arabia 21°54N 42°3E 248 B3
Al Kifl Iraq 32°13N 44°22E 213 E11
Al Kiswah Syria 33°23N 36°14E 250 B5
Al Kūfah Iraq 32°2N 44°24E 213 E11
Al Kufrah Libya 24°17N 23°15E 258 D4
Al Kuhayfiyah Si. Arabia 27°12N 43°3E 246 E4
Al Kumayt Iraq 32°36N 46°52E 213 E12
Al Kūt Iraq 32°30N 46°0E 213 E11
Al Kuwayt Kuwait 29°30N 48°0E 246 D6
Al Labwah Lebanon 34°11N 36°20E 250 D7
Al Lādhiqīyah Syria 35°30N 35°45E 250 C6
Al Lādhiqīyah □ Syria 35°45N 36°0E 250 C7
Al Līth Si. Arabia 20°9N 40°15E 248 B3
Al Liwā' Oman 24°31N 56°36E 247 E8
Al Luḥayyah Yemen 15°45N 42°40E 248 D3
Al Madīnah Iraq 30°57N 47°16E 246 D6
Al Madīnah Si. Arabia 24°35N 39°52E 246 E3
Al Mafraq Jordan 32°17N 36°14E 251 F7
Al Mafraq □ Jordan 32°17N 36°14E 251 F7
Al Maghreb = Morocco ■
  N. Afr. 32°0N 5°50W 260 B3
Al Maḥbishah Yemen 15°55N 43°24E 248 D3
Al Mahbes W. Sahara 27°10N 9°50W 260 C3
Al Mahjal Yemen 14°5N 46°55E 248 E4
Al Maḥmūdīyah Iraq 33°3N 44°21E 213 E11
Al Mahrah Yemen 16°0N 51°0E 249 D6
Al Mahrah Yemen 17°0N 52°0E 249 D6
Al Majma'ah Si. Arabia 25°57N 45°22E 246 E5
Al Makhruq, W. → Jordan 31°28N 37°0E 251 G8
Al Makhūl Si. Arabia 26°37N 42°39E 246 E4
Al Mālikīyah Syria 37°10N 42°8E 213 D10
Al Manāmah Bahrain 26°10N 50°30E 247 E6
Al Manshāh Egypt 26°28N 31°52E 256 B3
Al Maqwa' Kuwait 29°10N 47°59E 246 D6
Al Marāh Si. Arabia 25°35N 49°35E 247 E6
Al Marāwi'ah Yemen 15°30N 43°9E 248 D3
Al Marj Libya 32°25N 20°30E 258 B4
Al Marj □ Libya 32°0N 21°0E 258 B4
Al Maṣna'ah Oman 23°50N 57°38E 249 C7
Al Maṭlā Kuwait 29°24N 47°40E 246 D6
Al Mawsil Iraq 36°15N 43°5E 213 D10
Al Mayādin Syria 35°1N 40°27E 213 E9
Al Mazar Jordan 31°4N 35°41E 251 G6
Al Midhnab Si. Arabia 25°50N 44°18E 246 E5
Al Minā' Lebanon 34°24N 35°49E 250 D6
Al Mina U.A.E. 25°15N 55°19E 119 B1
Al Miqdādīyah Iraq 34°0N 45°0E 213 E11
Al Mubarraz Si. Arabia 25°30N 49°40E 247 E6
Al Mudawwarah Jordan 29°19N 36°0E 251 J7
Al Muḍayrib Oman 22°34N 58°37E 249 C7
Al Mughayrā' U.A.E. 24°5N 53°32E 247 E7
Al Muḥarraq Bahrain 26°15N 50°40E 247 E6
Al Mukallā Yemen 14°33N 49°2E 249 E4
Al Mukhā Yemen 13°18N 43°15E 248 E3
Al Mukhaylī Libya 32°30N 22°50E 258 B4
Al Musayjid Si. Arabia 24°5N 39°5E 246 E3
Al Musayyib Iraq 32°49N 44°20E 213 E11
Al Muthanná □ Iraq 30°30N 45°15E 246 D5
Al Muwayh Si. Arabia 22°45N 41°37E 248 B3
Al Muwaylih Si. Arabia 27°40N 35°30E 246 E2
Al Muẓaybimīyah
  Si. Arabia 24°29N 46°18E 248 A4
Al Nasr U.A.E. 24°23N 54°18E 119 B1
Al Owuho = Otukpa Nigeria 7°9N 7°41E 263 D6
Al Qābil Oman 22°34N 58°42E 249 C7
Al Qaddāḥīyah Libya 31°15N 15°9E 258 B3
Al Qadīmah Si. Arabia 22°20N 39°13E 248 B2
Al Qādisīyah □ Iraq 32°0N 45°0E 246 D5
Al Qahmah Si. Arabia 18°0N 41°14E 248 D3
Al Qā'im Iraq 34°21N 41°7E 213 E9
Al Qā'iyah Si. Arabia 24°33N 43°15E 248 B4
Al Qalībah Si. Arabia 28°24N 37°42E 246 E3
Al Qāmishlī Syria 37°2N 41°14E 213 D9
Al Qardāḥah Syria 35°27N 36°3E 250 C7
Al Qaryah ash Sharqīyah
  Libya 30°28N 13°40E 258 B2
Al Qaryatayn Syria 34°12N 37°13E 250 C8
Al Qaṣabāt Libya 32°39N 14°1E 258 B2
Al Qaṣīm □ Si. Arabia 26°0N 43°0E 246 E4
Al Qaṭ'ā Syria 34°40N 40°48E 213 E9
Al Qaṭīf Si. Arabia 26°35N 50°0E 247 E6
Al Qaṭrānah Jordan 31°12N 36°6E 251 G7
Al Qaṭrūn Libya 24°56N 15°3E 258 D2
Al Qawz Si. Arabia 18°58N 41°8E 248 D3
Al Qayṣūmah Si. Arabia 28°20N 46°7E 246 D5
Al Quds = Jerusalem
  Israel/West Bank 31°47N 35°10E 251 G6
Al Qunayṭirah Syria 33°5N 35°45E 250 F6
Al Qunfudhah Si. Arabia 19°3N 41°4E 248 C3
Al Quoz U.A.E. 25°8N 55°14E 119 B1
Al Qurayyāt Si. Arabia 31°20N 37°20E 246 D3
Al Qurnah Iraq 31°1N 47°25E 246 D6
Al Quṣayr Iraq 30°39N 45°50E 246 D5
Al Quṣayr Syria 34°31N 36°34E 250 D7
Al Qutayfah Syria 33°44N 36°36E 250 B6
Al Quwārah Si. Arabia 26°8N 43°28E 246 E4
Al Quwaysimah Jordan 31°55N 35°57E 251 G7
Al Safa Syria 33°12N 36°50E 250 B6
Al Satwa U.A.E. 25°13N 55°16E 119 B1
Al Seeb = As Sīb Oman 23°40N 58°10E 249 C7
Al Sufouh U.A.E. 25°5N 55°9E 119 B1
Al 'Ubaylah Si. Arabia 21°59N 50°57E 248 B5

Al 'Uḍaylīyah Si. Arabia 25°8N 49°18E 247 E6
Al 'Ulā Si. Arabia 26°35N 38°0E 246 E3
Al 'Ulayyah Si. Arabia 19°39N 41°54E 248 C3
Al Uqaylah ash Sharqīgah
  Libya 30°12N 19°10E 258 B3
Al 'Uqayr Si. Arabia 25°40N 50°15E 247 E6
Al 'Urūq al Mutaridah
  Si. Arabia 21°0N 53°30E 249 B6
Al 'Uwaynāt Libya 25°47N 10°33E 261 C7
Al 'Uwaynid Si. Arabia 24°50N 46°0E 246 E5
Al 'Uwayqilah Si. Arabia 30°30N 42°10E 246 D4
Al Uweinat Libya 21°54N 24°50E 259 D4
Al 'Uyūn Ḥijāz, Si. Arabia 24°33N 39°35E 246 E3
Al 'Uyūn Najd, Si. Arabia 26°30N 43°50E 246 E4
Al 'Uzayr Iraq 31°19N 47°25E 246 D5
Al Wāhāt □ Libya 29°0N 22°0E 258 C4
Al Wajh Si. Arabia 26°10N 36°30E 246 E3
Al Wakrah Qatar 25°10N 51°40E 247 E6
Al Walaja West Bank 31°44N 35°9E 123 B1
Al Waqbah Si. Arabia 28°48N 45°33E 246 D5
Al Wari'ah Si. Arabia 27°51N 47°25E 246 E5
Al Wasl □ U.A.E. 25°12N 55°16E 119 B2
Al Waṭīyah Libya 32°28N 11°57E 258 B2
Al Wigh Libya 24°16N 15°30E 258 D3
Al Wusṭā □ Oman 20°0N 57°0E 249 C7
Al Yaman = Yemen ■ Asia 15°0N 44°0E 248 D3
Ala Italy 45°45N 11°0E 198 C8
Ala Archa △ Kyrgyzstan 42°32N 74°28E 217 D8
Ala Dağ Turkey 37°44N 35°9E 250 B6
Ala Dağları Turkey 39°15N 43°33E 213 C10
Ala Tau Asia 45°30N 80°40E 217 C10
Ala Tau Shankou = Dzungarian
  Gate Asia 45°10N 82°0E 217 C10
Alabama □ U.S.A. 33°0N 87°0W 315 E11
Alabama → U.S.A. 31°8N 87°57W 315 F11
Alabaster U.S.A. 33°15N 86°49W 315 E11
Alabat I. Phil. 14°7N 122°3E 232 D4
Alabel Phil. 6°4N 125°16E 233 H5
Alabule → Papua N. G. 8°31S 146°56E 286 E4
Alaca Turkey 40°10N 34°51E 212 B6
Alaçaatı Turkey 39°15N 28°3E 205 B10
Alaçam Turkey 41°36N 35°36E 212 B6
Alaçam Dağları Turkey 39°18N 28°49E 205 B10
Alacant = Alicante Spain 38°23N 0°30W 197 G4
Alaçatı Turkey 38°15N 26°22E 205 C8
Alachua U.S.A. 29°47N 82°30W 316 F7
Alaejos Spain 41°18N 5°13W 194 D5
Alaer China 40°30N 81°16E 217 D10
Alagir Russia 43°3N 44°11E 191 J7
Alagna Valsésia Italy 45°51N 7°56E 198 C4
Alagoa de Baixo = Sertânia
  Brazil 8°5S 37°20W 332 C4
Alagoa Grande Brazil 7°3S 35°35W 332 C4
Alagoas □ Brazil 9°0S 36°0W 332 C4
Alagoinhas Brazil 12°7S 38°20W 333 D4
Alagón Spain 41°46N 1°12W 196 D3
Alagón → Spain 39°44N 6°53W 194 F4
Alaguntan = Aragats
  Armenia 40°30N 44°15E 191 K7
Alagyoz = Aragats
  Armenia 40°30N 44°15E 191 K7
Alahan Turkey 36°46N 33°19E 250 B4
Alahärmä Finland 63°20N 22°50E 161 E20
Alaheaieatnu = Altaelva →
  Norway 69°54N 23°17E 160 B20
Alai Range Asia 39°45N 72°0E 217 E8
Alaior Spain 39°57N 4°8E 206 B5
Alajärvi Finland 63°0N 23°48E 161 E20
Alajero Canary Is. 28°3N 17°13W 153 e1
Alajuela Costa Rica 10°2N 84°8W 320 E3
Alajuela, L. Panama 9°14N 79°34W 321 a
Alakamisy Madag. 21°19S 47°14E 272 C2
Alakanuk U.S.A. 62°41N 164°37W 303 E6
Alaknanda → India 30°8N 78°36E 243 D8
Alakol □ Kazakhstan 46°0N 81°5E 217 C10
Alakurtti Russia 66°58N 30°25E 160 C24
'Alalākeiki Channel
  U.S.A. 20°30N 156°30W 302 C5
Alalapura Suriname 2°20N 56°25W 329 C6
Alalaú → Brazil 0°30S 61°9W 329 D5
Alamagan N. Marianas 17°36N 145°50E 302 a
Alamarvdasht Iran 27°37N 52°59E 247 E7
Alamata Ethiopia 12°25N 39°33E 257 E4
Alameda Calif., U.S.A. 37°46N 122°15W 136 B3
Alameda N. Mex.,
  U.S.A. 35°11N 106°37W 305 J10
Alameda, Parque Mexico City, Mexico 128 b2
Alameda Memorial State Beach
  Park U.S.A. 37°44N 122°16W 136 B3
Alaminos Phil. 16°10N 119°59E 232 C2
Alamo Ga., U.S.A. 32°9N 82°47W 316 C7
Alamo Nev., U.S.A. 37°22N 115°10W 307 H11
Alamogordo U.S.A. 32°54N 105°57W 305 K11
Alamos Mexico 27°1N 108°56W 318 B3
Alamosa U.S.A. 37°28N 105°52W 305 H11
Alampur India 15°55N 78°9E 245 G4
Åland Finland 60°15N 20°0E 161 F19
Alandroal Portugal 38°41N 7°24W 195 G3
Ålands hav Europe 60°0N 19°30E 161 G18
Ålandsbro Sweden 62°40N 17°51E 162 B11
Alandur India 13°0N 80°15E 245 H5
Alang Indonesia 4°7N 117°0E 235 B5
Alange, Embalse d' Spain 38°45N 6°18W 195 G4
Alanís Spain 38°3N 5°43W 195 G5
Alaniya = North Ossetia-Alaniya □
  Russia 43°30N 44°30E 191 J7
Alaniya Russia 42°55N 44°30E 191 J7
Alanya Turkey 36°38N 32°0E 250 B3
Alaotra, Farihin' Madag. 17°30S 48°30E 272 B2
Alaotra-Mangoro □
  Madag. 17°50S 48°25E 272 B2
Alapaha U.S.A. 31°23N 83°13W 316 D7
Alapayevsk Russia 57°52N 61°42E 216 C7
Alappuzha India 9°30N 76°28E 245 K3
'Alāqān Si. Arabia 29°10N 35°21E 251 J6
Alar del Rey Spain 42°38N 4°20W 194 C6
Alara → Turkey 36°45N 31°24E 250 B3
Alaraz Spain 40°45N 5°17W 194 E5
Alarcón, Embalse de Spain 39°36N 2°10W 196 F2
Alaró Spain 39°42N 2°47E 206 B9
Alarobia-Vohiposa Madag. 20°59S 47°9E 272 C2
Alas Indonesia 8°29S 117°10E 235 D5
Alas, Selat Indonesia 8°38S 116°40E 235 D5
Alaşehir Turkey 38°23N 28°30E 205 C10
Alashtar Iran 33°51N 48°15E 213 E13
Alaska □ U.S.A. 64°0N 154°0W 303 D9
Alaska, G. of Pac. Oc. 58°0N 145°0W 303 F11
Alaska Maritime Nat. Wildlife
  Refuge △ U.S.A. 56°0N 159°0W 303 L4
Alaska Peninsula U.S.A. 56°0N 159°0W 303 H8
Alaska Peninsula Nat. Wildlife
  Refuge △ U.S.A. 56°0N 159°0W 303 J8
Alaska Range U.S.A. 62°50N 151°0W 303 E9
Alássio Italy 44°0N 8°10E 198 C5
Ālāt Azerbaijan 39°58N 49°25E 191 L10
Alatau Shan = Ala Tau
  Asia 45°30N 80°40E 217 C10
Alatri Italy 41°43N 13°21E 199 G10
Alatyr Russia 54°45N 46°35E 190 C8
Alatyr → Russia 54°52N 46°36E 190 C8
Alaungdaw Kathapa △
  Burma 22°30N 94°30E 241 H19
Alausi Ecuador 2°0S 78°50W 328 D2
Álava □ = Araba/Álava □
  Spain 42°48N 2°28W 194 C7
Alava, C. U.S.A. 48°10N 124°44W 306 B2
Alaverdi Armenia 41°15N 44°37E 191 K7
Alavieska Finland 64°10N 24°30E 161 D21
Alavo = Alavus Finland 62°35N 23°36E 160 E20
Alavus Finland 62°35N 23°36E 160 E20

Alawa ✪ Australia 15°42S 134°39E 280 B1
Alawoona Australia 34°45S 140°30E 282 C4
Alayawarra ✪ Australia 22°0S 134°30E 280 C1
'Alayh Lebanon 33°46N 35°33E 250 E6
Alayköy = Yerolakkos Cyprus 35°11N 33°15E 207 E9
Alazani → Azerbaijan 41°5N 46°40E 191 K8
Alba Italy 44°42N 8°2E 198 D5
Alba □ Romania 46°10N 23°30E 183 D8
Alba Adriática Italy 42°50N 13°56E 199 F10
Alba de Tormes Spain 40°50N 5°30W 194 E5
Alba-Iulia Romania 46°8N 23°39E 183 D8
Albac Romania 46°28N 22°58E 182 D7
Albacete Spain 39°0N 1°50W 197 F3
Albacete □ Spain 38°50N 2°0W 197 G3
Albacutya, L. Australia 35°45S 141°58E 282 C4
Ålbæk Denmark 57°36N 10°25E 163 G4
Ålbæk Bugt Denmark 57°35N 10°40E 163 G4
Albaida Spain 38°51N 0°31W 197 G4
Albalate de las Nogueras Spain 40°22N 2°18W 196 E2
Albalate del Arzobispo Spain 41°6N 0°31W 196 D4
Alban France 43°53N 2°28E 174 E6
Albanel, L. Canada 50°55N 73°12W 298 B5
Albania ■ Europe 41°0N 20°0E 202 E4
Albano Laziale Italy 41°44N 12°39E 199 G9
Albany W. Austral., Australia 35°1S 117°58E 279 G2
Albany Ga., U.S.A. 31°35N 84°10W 316 D5
Albany Ind., U.S.A. 40°18N 85°14W 311 D11
Albany Mo., U.S.A. 40°15N 94°20W 310 D2
Albany N.Y., U.S.A. 42°39N 73°45W 313 D11
Albany Oreg., U.S.A. 44°38N 123°6W 304 D2
Albany Tex., U.S.A. 32°44N 99°18W 314 E5
Albany Wis., U.S.A. 42°42N 89°26W 310 B7
Albany → Canada 52°17N 81°31W 298 B3
Albarca, C. d' Spain 39°4N 1°22E 206 C1
Albardón Argentina 31°20S 68°30W 334 C2
Albarracín Spain 40°25N 1°26W 196 E3
Albarracín, Sierra de Spain 40°30N 1°30W 196 E3
Albatera Spain 38°11N 0°52W 197 G4
Albâtre, Côte d' France 49°55N 0°50E 172 C7
Albatross B. Australia 12°45S 141°30E 280 A3
Albatross Pt. N.Z. 38°7S 174°44E 284 E3
Albay □ Phil. 13°13N 123°33E 232 E4
Albegna → Italy 42°30N 11°11E 199 F8
Albemarle U.S.A. 35°21N 80°12W 315 D14
Albemarle, I. = Isabela, I. Ecuador 0°30S 91°4W 330 a
Albemarle, Pta. Ecuador 0°11N 91°21W 330 a
Albemarle Sd. U.S.A. 36°5N 76°0W 315 C16
Albenga Italy 44°3N 8°13E 198 D5
Alberche → Spain 39°58N 4°46W 194 F6
Alberdi Paraguay 26°14S 58°20W 334 B4
Albères, Mts. France 42°28N 2°56E 174 F6
Ålberga Sweden 58°44N 16°35E 163 F10
Alberga → Australia 27°6S 135°33E 281 D2
Albern Austria 48°9N 16°29E 142 B2
Albersdorf Germany 54°8N 9°17E 178 A5
Albert France 50°0N 2°38E 173 C9
Albert, L. Africa 1°30N 31°0E 268 B3
Albert, L. S. Austral., Australia 35°30S 139°10E 282 C3
Albert Edward, Mt. Papua N. G. 8°20S 147°24E 286 E4
Albert Edward Ra. Australia 18°17S 127°57E 278 C4
Albert Lea U.S.A. 43°39N 93°22W 308 D7
Albert Nat. Park = Virunga △ Dem. Rep. of the Congo 0°5N 29°38E 268 B2
Albert Nile → Uganda 3°36N 32°2E 268 B3
Albert Park Australia 37°51S 144°58E 128 B1
Albert Town Bahamas 22°37N 74°33W 321 B5
Albert Town Jamaica 18°17N 77°33W 320 a
Alberta □ Canada 54°40N 115°0W 296 C6
Alberti Argentina 35°1S 60°16W 334 D3
Albertinia S. Africa 34°11S 21°34E 270 D3
Albertirsa Hungary 47°14N 19°37E 182 C4
Alberto de Agostini △ Chile 54°38S 71°37W 336 D2
Alberton P.E.I., Canada 46°50N 64°0W 299 C7
Alberton Gauteng, S. Africa 26°15S 28°7E 123 B2
Albertslund Denmark 55°39N 12°21E 118 B2
Albertville = Kalemie Dem. Rep. of the Congo 5°55S 29°9E 268 D2
Albertville Savoie, France 45°40N 6°22E 175 C10
Albertville Ala., U.S.A. 34°16N 86°13W 315 D11
Albi France 43°56N 2°9E 174 E6
Albia U.S.A. 41°2N 92°48W 310 C4
Albina Suriname 5°37N 54°15W 329 B7
Albina, Ponta Angola 15°52S 11°44E 265 F2
Albino Italy 45°46N 9°47E 198 C6
Albion Ill., U.S.A. 38°23N 88°4W 311 F8
Albion Ind., U.S.A. 41°24N 85°25W 311 C11
Albion Mich., U.S.A. 42°15N 84°45W 311 B12
Albion Nebr., U.S.A. 41°42N 98°0W 308 E4
Albion Pa., U.S.A. 41°53N 80°22W 312 E4
Albocásser Spain 40°21N 0°1E 196 E5
Albolote Spain 37°14N 3°39W 195 H7
Alborán Medit. S. 35°57N 3°0W 195 K7
Alboran Sea Medit. S. 36°0N 3°30W 195 K7
Alborea Spain 39°17N 1°24W 197 F3
Ålborg = Aalborg Denmark 57°2N 9°54E 163 G3
Ålborg Bugt = Aalborg Bugt Denmark 56°50N 10°35E 163 H4
Alborz □ Iran 36°0N 50°50E 247 B6
Alborz, Reshteh-ye Kūhhā-ye Iran 36°0N 52°0E 247 C7
Albox Spain 37°23N 2°8W 197 H2
Albstadt Germany 48°13N 9°1E 179 G5
Albuera Phil. 10°55N 124°42E 233 F5
Albufeira Portugal 37°5N 8°15W 195 H2
Albula → Switz. 46°38N 9°28E 179 J5
Albuñol Spain 36°48N 3°11W 195 J7
Albuquerque Brazil 19°23S 57°26W 331 D6
Albuquerque N. Mex., U.S.A. 35°5N 106°39W 305 J10
Albuquerque, Cayos de Caribbean 12°10N 81°50W 320 D3
Alburg U.S.A. 44°59N 73°18W 313 B11
Alburno, Mte. Italy 40°33N 15°17E 201 B8
Alburquerque Spain 39°15N 6°59W 195 F4
Albury Australia 36°3S 146°56E 283 D7
Alby Sweden 62°30N 15°28E 162 B9
Alcácer do Sal Portugal 38°22N 8°33W 195 G2
Alcáçovas Portugal 38°23N 8°9W 195 G2
Alcala Phil. 17°54N 121°39E 232 C3
Alcalá de Guadaira Spain 37°20N 5°50W 195 H5
Alcalá de Henares Spain 40°28N 3°22W 194 E7
Alcalá de los Gazules Spain 36°29N 5°43W 195 J5
Alcalá de Xivert Spain 40°19N 0°13E 196 E5
Alcalá del Júcar Spain 39°12N 1°26W 197 F3
Alcalá del Río Spain 37°31N 5°59W 195 H5
Alcalá del Valle Spain 36°54N 5°10W 195 J5
Alcalá la Real Spain 37°27N 3°57W 195 H7
Álcamo Italy 37°59N 12°55E 200 E5
Alcanadre Spain 42°24N 2°7W 196 C2
Alcanadre → Spain 41°43N 0°12W 196 D4
Alcanar Spain 40°33N 0°28E 196 E5
Alcanede Portugal 39°25N 8°49W 195 F2
Alcanena Portugal 39°27N 8°40W 195 F2
Alcañices Spain 41°41N 6°21W 194 D4
Alcañiz Spain 41°2N 0°8W 196 D4
Alcântara Brazil 2°20S 44°30W 332 B3
Alcantara Lisboa, Portugal 38°43N 9°10W 126 A1
Alcántara Spain 39°41N 6°57W 194 F4
Alcántara, Embalse de Spain 39°44N 6°50W 194 F4
Alcantarilla Spain 37°59N 1°12W 197 H3
Alcaracejos Spain 38°24N 4°58W 195 G6
Alcaraz Spain 38°40N 2°29W 197 G2
Alcaraz, Sierra de Spain 38°40N 2°20W 197 G2
Alcatraz I. U.S.A. 37°49N 122°25W 136 B2
Alcaudete Spain 37°35N 4°5W 195 H6
Alcázar de San Juan Spain 39°24N 3°12W 195 F7
Alcazarquivir = Ksar el Kebir Morocco 35°0N 6°0W 260 B3
Alcedo, Volcán Ecuador 0°24S 91°6W 330 a
Alchevsk Ukraine 48°30N 38°45E 189 H10
Alcira = Alzira Spain 39°9N 0°30W 197 F4
Alcobaça = Tucuruí Brazil 3°42S 49°44W 332 B2
Alcobaça Portugal 39°32N 8°58W 195 F2
Alcobendas Spain 40°32N 3°38W 127 A2
Alcolea del Pinar Spain 41°2N 2°28W 196 D2
Alcoma U.S.A. 27°54N 81°29W 317 H8
Alcorcón Spain 40°20N 3°48W 127 B1
Alcoutim Portugal 37°25N 7°28W 195 H3
Alcova U.S.A. 42°34N 106°43W 304 E10
Alcoy Spain 38°43N 0°30W 197 G4
Alcubierre, Sierra de Spain 41°45N 0°22W 196 D4
Alcublas Spain 39°48N 0°43W 196 F4
Alcúdia Spain 39°51N 3°7E 206 B4
Alcúdia, B. d' Spain 39°47N 3°15E 206 B4
Alcúdia, Sierra de la Spain 38°34N 4°30W 195 G6
Aldabra Is. Seychelles 9°22S 46°28E 255 G8
Aldama Mexico 22°55N 98°4W 319 C5
Aldan Russia 58°40N 125°30E 215 D13
Aldan → Russia 63°28N 129°35E 215 C13
Aldea, Pta. de la Canary Is. 28°0N 15°50W 153 e1
Aldeburgh U.K. 52°10N 1°37E 169 E9
Alden Norway 61°19N 4°45E 164 C1
Alder Pk. U.S.A. 35°53N 121°22W 306 K5
Alderney U.K. 49°42N 2°11W 169 H5
Aldershof Germany 52°26N 13°33E 115 B4
Aldershot U.K. 51°15N 0°44W 169 F7
Alderwood Canada 43°36N 79°32W 141 B1
Aldinga Beach Australia 35°17S 138°27E 282 C3
Aldo Bonzi Argentina 34°42S 58°31W 117 C1
Åled Sweden 56°44N 12°57E 163 H6
Aledo U.S.A. 41°12N 90°45W 310 C6
Alefa Ethiopia 11°55N 36°55E 257 E4
Aleg Mauritania 17°3N 13°55W 262 B2
Alegranza Canary Is. 29°23N 13°32W 260 C2
Alegranza, I. Canary Is. 29°23N 13°32W 153 e2
Alegre Brazil 20°50S 41°30W 333 F3
Alegrete Brazil 29°40S 56°0W 335 B4
Aleknagik U.S.A. 59°17N 158°36W 303 G8
Aleksandriya = Oleksandriya Kirovohrad, Ukraine 48°42N 33°3E 189 H7
Aleksandriya = Oleksandriya Rivne, Ukraine 50°37N 26°19E 177 C14
Aleksandriyskaya Russia 43°58N 47°14E 191 J8
Aleksandropol = Gyumri Armenia 40°47N 43°50E 191 K6
Aleksandrov Russia 56°23N 38°44E 188 D10
Aleksandrov Gay Russia 50°9N 48°34E 190 E9
Aleksandrovac Serbia 43°28N 21°3E 202 C5
Aleksandrovac Serbia 44°28N 21°13E 202 B5
Aleksandrovka = Oleksandrivka Ukraine 48°55N 32°20E 189 H7
Aleksandrovka = Ordzhonikidze Ukraine 47°39N 34°3E 189 J8
Aleksandrovo Bulgaria 43°14N 24°51E 203 C8
Aleksandrovsk = Belogorsk Russia 51°0N 128°20E 215 D13
Aleksandrovsk = Polyarny Russia 69°8N 33°20E 160 B25
Aleksandrovsk = Zaporizhzhya Ukraine 47°50N 35°10E 189 J8
Aleksandrovsk-Grushevsky = Shakhty Russia 47°40N 40°16E 191 G5
Aleksandrovsk-Sakhalinskiy Russia 50°50N 142°20E 219 A17
Aleksandrovskoye Russia 59°51N 30°20E 137 B2
Aleksandrów Kujawski Poland 52°53N 18°43E 185 F5
Aleksandrów Łódźki Poland 51°49N 19°17E 185 G6
Aleksandry, Zemlya Russia 80°25N 48°0E 214 A5
Alekseyevka Samara, Russia 52°35N 51°17E 190 D10
Alekseyevka Voronezh, Russia 50°43N 38°40E 189 G10
Alekseyevsk = Svobodnyy Russia 51°20N 128°0E 215 D13
Alekseyevskoye = Qazyghurt Kazakhstan 41°45N 69°23E 217 D7
Aleksin Russia 54°31N 37°9E 188 E9
Aleksinac Serbia 43°31N 21°42E 202 C5
Além Paraíba Brazil 21°52S 42°41W 333 F3
Alemania Argentina 25°40S 65°30W 334 B2
Alemania Chile 25°10S 69°55W 334 B2
Alen Eq. Guin. 1°58N 11°19E 264 B2
Alençon France 48°27N 0°4E 172 D7
'Alenuihähä Channel U.S.A. 20°30N 156°0W 302 C5
Alépé Ivory C. 5°29N 3°40W 262 D4
Aleppo = Ḥalab Syria 36°10N 37°15E 250 B8
Alerce Andino △ Chile 41°33S 72°29W 336 B2
Alerce Costero △ Chile 40°10S 73°30W 336 B2
Aléria France 42°5N 9°26E 175 F13
Alert Canada 83°2N 60°0W 295 A20
Aleru India 17°39N 79°3E 244 F4
Alès France 44°9N 4°5E 175 D8
Aleşd Romania 47°3N 22°22E 182 C7
Alessándria Italy 44°54N 8°37E 198 D5
Ålesund Norway 62°28N 6°12E 164 B3
Alet-les-Bains France 42°59N 2°14E 174 F6
Aletschhorn Switz. 46°28N 8°0E 179 J4
Aleutian Basin Pac. Oc. 57°0N 177°0E 288 B9
Aleutian Is. Pac. Oc. 52°0N 175°0W 303 K3
Aleutian Range U.S.A. 60°0N 154°0W 303 G9
Aleutian Trench Pac. Oc. 48°0N 180°0E 150 D17
Alexander Ga., U.S.A. 33°1N 81°53W 316 B8
Alexander N. Dak., U.S.A. 47°51N 103°39W 308 B2
Alexander, C. Solomon Is. 6°34S 156°32E 287 L9
Alexander, Mt. Australia 28°58S 120°16E 279 E3
Alexander Arch. U.S.A. 56°0N 136°0W 303 J14
Alexander Bay S. Africa 28°40S 16°30E 270 C2
Alexander City U.S.A. 32°56N 85°58W 316 C4
Alexander I. Antarctica 69°0S 70°0W 151 C17
Alexander Nevsky Abbey Russia 59°54N 30°23E 137 B2
Alexander Soutzos Museum Athens, Greece 112 b3
Alexandra Vic., Australia 37°8S 145°40E 283 D6
Alexandra N.Z. 45°14S 169°25E 285 F4
Alexandra Singapore, Singapore 1°17N 103°49E 138 B2
Alexandra Gauteng, S. Africa 26°6S 28°5E 123 A2
Alexandra Channel Burma 14°7N 93°13E 245 G11
Alexandra Falls Canada 60°29N 116°18W 296 A5
Alexandretta = İskenderun Turkey 36°32N 36°10E 250 B7
Alexandria = El Iskandarîya Egypt 31°13N 29°58E 256 H6
Alexandria B.C., Canada 52°35N 122°27W 296 C4
Alexandria Ont., Canada 45°19N 74°38W 313 A10
Alexandria Romania 43°57N 25°24E 183 G10
Alexandria Eastern Cape, S. Africa 33°38S 26°28E 270 D4
Alexandria W. Dunb., U.K. 55°59N 4°35W 167 F4
Alexandria Ind., U.S.A. 40°16N 85°41W 311 D11
Alexandria Ky., U.S.A. 38°58N 84°23W 311 F12
Alexandria La., U.S.A. 31°18N 92°27W 314 F8
Alexandria Minn., U.S.A. 45°53N 95°22W 308 C6
Alexandria Mo., U.S.A. 40°27N 91°28W 310 D5
Alexandria S. Dak., U.S.A. 43°39N 97°47W 308 D5
Alexandria Va., U.S.A. 38°49N 77°5W 143 C2
Alexandria Bay U.S.A. 44°20N 75°55W 313 B9
Alexandrina, L. Australia 35°25S 139°10E 282 C3
Alexandroupoli Greece 40°50N 25°54E 203 F9
Alexis U.S.A. 41°4N 90°33W 310 C6
Alexis → Canada 52°33N 56°8W 299 B8
Alexis Creek Canada 52°10N 123°20W 296 C4
Aley → Russia 52°51N 83°36E 217 B10
Aleysk Russia 52°40N 83°0E 217 B10
Alfabia Spain 39°44N 2°44E 206 B3
Alfama Lisbon, Portugal 126 c3
Alfambra Spain 40°33N 1°5W 196 E3
Alfândega da Fé Portugal 41°20N 6°59W 194 D4
Alfaro Spain 42°10N 1°50W 196 C3
Alfatar Bulgaria 43°59N 27°13E 203 C11
Alfeld Germany 51°59N 9°50E 178 D5
Alfenas Brazil 21°20S 46°10W 335 A6
Alföld Hungary 46°30N 20°0E 182 D5
Alfonsine Italy 44°30N 12°3E 199 D9
Alford Aberds., U.K. 57°14N 2°41W 167 D6
Alford Lincs., U.K. 53°15N 0°10E 168 D8
Alford Fla., U.S.A. 30°42N 85°24W 316 E4
Alfortville France 48°48N 2°24E 134 B3
Ålfotbreen Norway 61°45N 5°39E 164 C2
Ålfoten Norway 61°51N 5°41E 164 C2
Alfred Maine, U.S.A. 43°29N 70°43W 313 C14
Alfred N.Y., U.S.A. 42°16N 77°48W 312 D7
Alfredton N.Z. 40°41S 175°54E 284 G4
Alfreton U.K. 53°6N 1°24W 168 D6
Alfta Sweden 61°21N 16°4E 162 C10
Algaida Spain 39°33N 2°53E 206 B3
Algar Spain 36°40N 5°39W 195 J5
Ålgård Norway 58°46N 5°53E 164 F2
Algarinejo Spain 37°19N 4°9W 195 H6
Algarve Portugal 36°58N 8°20W 195 J2
Algeciras Spain 36°9N 5°28W 195 J5
Algemesí Spain 39°11N 0°27W 197 F4
Alger Algeria 36°42N 3°8E 261 A5
Alger □ Algeria 36°45N 3°10E 197 J8
Alger ✈ (ALG) Algeria 36°39N 3°13E 197 J8
Algeria ■ Africa 28°30N 2°0E 261 C5
Algés Portugal 38°42N 9°13W 126 A1
Algha Kazakhstan 49°53N 57°20E 187 E10
Alghero Italy 40°33N 8°19E 200 B1
Älghult Sweden 57°0N 15°35E 163 G9
Algiers = Alger Algeria 36°42N 3°8E 261 A5
Algiers U.S.A. 29°56N 90°2W 131 B2
Algoa B. S. Africa 33°50S 25°45E 270 D4
Algodonales Spain 36°54N 5°24W 195 J5
Algodones Dunes U.S.A. 32°50N 115°5W 307 N11
Algodor → Spain 39°55N 3°53W 194 F7
Algoma U.S.A. 44°36N 87°26W 308 C10
Algona U.S.A. 43°4N 94°14W 310 A2
Algonac U.S.A. 42°37N 82°32W 312 D2
Algonquin ⌓ Canada 45°50N 78°30W 298 C4
Algorta Spain 43°21N 2°59W 196 B2
Algorta Uruguay 32°25S 57°24W 334 C4
Alhama de Almería Spain 36°57N 2°34W 195 J8
Alhama de Aragón Spain 41°18N 1°54W 196 D3
Alhama de Granada Spain 37°0N 3°59W 195 H7
Alhama de Murcia Spain 37°51N 1°25W 197 H3
Alhambra U.S.A. 34°5N 118°7W 126 B4
Alhaurín el Grande Spain 36°39N 4°41W 195 J6
Alhucemas = Al Hoceïma Morocco 35°8N 3°58W 261 A4
'Alī al Gharbī Iraq 32°30N 46°45E 213 F12
'Alī ash Sharqī Iraq 32°7N 46°44E 213 F12
Äli Bayramlı = Şirvan Azerbaijan 39°59N 48°52E 191 L9
'Alī Khēl Afghan. 33°57N 69°43E 242 C3
Ali Sahîh Djibouti 11°10N 42°44E 257 E5
Alī Shāh Iran 38°9N 45°50E 246 B5
Ália Italy 37°47N 13°43E 200 E6
'Alīābād Golestān, Iran 36°40N 54°33E 247 B7
'Alīābād Khorāsān, Iran 32°30N 57°30E 247 C8
'Alīābād Kordestān, Iran 35°4N 46°58E 246 C5
'Alīābād Yazd, Iran 31°41N 53°49E 247 D7
Aliade Nigeria 7°18N 8°29E 263 D6
Aliaga Spain 40°40N 0°42W 196 E4
Aliağa Turkey 38°47N 26°59E 205 C8
Aliakmonas → Greece 40°30N 22°36E 202 F6
Alibag India 18°38N 72°56E 244 E1
Alibey → Turkey 41°3N 28°56E 122 B1
Alibey Barajı Turkey 41°8N 28°53E 122 B1
Alibeyköy Turkey 41°4N 28°56E 122 B1
Alibo Ethiopia 9°52N 37°5E 257 F4
Alibori → Benin 11°56N 3°17E 263 C5
Alibunar Serbia 45°5N 20°57E 182 E5
Alicante Spain 38°23N 0°30W 197 G4
Alicante □ Spain 38°30N 0°37W 197 G4
Alicante ✈ (ALC) Spain 38°14N 0°36W 197 G4
Alice Eastern Cape, S. Africa 32°48S 26°55E 270 D4
Alice Tex., U.S.A. 27°45N 98°5W 314 H5
Alice → Queens., Australia 24°2S 144°50E 280 C3
Alice → Queens., Australia 15°35S 142°20E 280 B3
Alice → Papua N. G. 6°10S 141°8E 286 D1
Alice, Punta Italy 39°24N 17°9E 201 C10
Alice Arm Canada 55°29N 129°31W 296 B3
Alice Springs Australia 23°40S 133°50E 280 C1
Alicedale S. Africa 33°15S 26°4E 270 D4
Aliceville U.S.A. 33°8N 88°9W 315 E10
Alicia Bohol, Phil. 9°54N 124°26E 233 G5
Alicia Isabela, Phil. 16°46N 121°42E 232 C3
Alicudi Italy 38°33N 14°20E 201 D7
Alien Taiwan 22°52N 120°19E 225 D2
Aliganj India 27°30N 79°10E 243 F8
Aligarh Raj., India 25°55N 76°15E 242 G7
Aligarh Ut. P., India 27°55N 78°10E 242 F8
Alīgūdarz Iran 33°25N 49°45E 247 C6
Alijó Portugal 41°16N 7°27W 194 D3
Alikanas Greece 37°51N 20°47E 207 D2
Alima → Congo 1°35S 16°37E 264 C3
Alimia Greece 36°16N 27°43E 206 E11
Alimodian Phil. 10°49N 122°26E 233 F4
Alimos Greece 37°52N 23°43E 112 B2
Alindao C.A.R. 5°2N 21°13E 264 A4
Alingsås Sweden 57°56N 12°31E 163 G6
Alipur Paschimbanga, India 22°43N 88°12E 124 B1
Alipur Pakistan 29°25N 70°55E 242 E4
Alipur Duar India 26°30N 89°35E 241 B2
Aliquippa U.S.A. 40°37N 80°15W 312 F4
Alishan Taiwan 23°31N 120°48E 225 C2
Aliste → Spain 41°34N 5°58W 194 D5
Alitus = Alytus Lithuania 54°24N 24°3E 188 E3
Aliveri Greece 38°24N 24°2E 204 C6
Aliwal North S. Africa 30°45S 26°45E 270 D4
Alix Canada 52°24N 113°11W 296 C6
Aljezur Portugal 37°18N 8°49W 195 H2
Aljustrel Portugal 37°55N 8°10W 195 H2
Alkamari Niger 13°27N 11°10E 259 F2
Alkhanay △ Russia 51°0N 113°30E 215 D12
Alkmaar Neths. 52°37N 4°45E 170 B4
All American Canal U.S.A. 32°45N 115°15W 307 N11
Allacapan Phil. 18°15N 121°35E 232 B3
Allach Germany 48°11N 11°27E 131 A1
Allada Benin 6°41N 2°9E 263 D5
Allagadda India 15°8N 78°30E 245 G4
Allagash → U.S.A. 47°5N 69°3W 309 B19
Allah Dad Pakistan 25°38N 67°34E 242 G2
Allahabad India 25°25N 81°58E 243 G9
Allakaket U.S.A. 66°34N 152°39W 303 C9
Allambie Heights Australia 33°46S 151°15E 139 A2
Allan Canada 51°53N 106°4W 297 C7
Allanche France 45°14N 2°57E 174 C6
Allanmyo Burma 19°30N 95°17E 241 F5
Allanridge S. Africa 27°45S 26°40E 270 C4
Allansford Australia 38°26S 142°39E 282 E5
Allanton N.Z. 45°55S 170°15E 285 F5
Allaqi, Wadi → Egypt 23°7N 32°47E 256 C3
Allariz Spain 42°11N 7°50W 194 C3
Allassac France 45°15N 1°29E 174 C5
Allatoona L. U.S.A. 34°10N 84°44W 316 A5
Ålleberg Sweden 58°8N 13°36E 163 F7
Allegan U.S.A. 42°32N 85°51W 311 B11
Allegany U.S.A. 42°6N 78°30W 312 D6
Allegheny → U.S.A. 40°27N 80°1W 312 F5
Allegheny Mts. U.S.A. 38°15N 80°10W 309 F13
Allegheny Plateau U.S.A. 41°30N 78°30W 309 E14
Allegheny Res. U.S.A. 41°50N 79°0W 312 E6
Allègre France 45°12N 3°41E 174 C7
Allègre, Pte. Guadeloupe 16°22N 61°46W 322 e
Allen Argentina 38°58S 67°50W 336 A3
Allen Phil. 12°30N 124°17E 232 E5
Allen, Bog of Ireland 53°15N 7°0W 166 C5
Allen, L. Ireland 54°8N 8°4W 166 B3
Allendale U.S.A. 33°1N 81°18W 316 B8
Allende Mexico 28°20N 100°51W 318 B4
Allenstein = Olsztyn Poland 53°48N 20°29E 184 E7
Allentown U.S.A. 40°37N 75°29W 313 F9
Allentsteig Austria 48°41N 15°20E 180 C8
Alleppey = Alappuzha India 9°30N 76°28E 245 K3
Allepuz Spain 40°29N 0°44W 196 E4
Aller → Germany 52°56N 9°12E 178 C5
Allermuir Hill U.K. 55°53N 3°14W 121 B2
Alley, The Jamaica 17°48N 77°17W 320 a
Alliance Suriname 5°50N 54°50W 329 B7
Alliance Nebr., U.S.A. 42°6N 102°52W 308 D2
Alliance Ohio, U.S.A. 40°55N 81°6W 312 F3
Allianz Arena Munich, Germany 48°13N 11°37E 131 A2
Allier □ France 46°25N 2°40E 173 F9
Allier → France 46°57N 3°4E 173 F10
Alliford Bay Canada 53°12N 131°58W 296 C2
Alligator Pond Jamaica 17°52N 77°34W 320 a
Allinagaram India 10°2N 77°30E 245 J3
Allinge Denmark 55°17N 14°50E 163 J8
Allison U.S.A. 42°45N 92°48W 310 B4
Alliston Canada 44°9N 79°52W 312 B5
Alloa U.K. 56°7N 3°47W 167 E5
Allones France 48°20N 1°40E 172 D8
Allora Australia 28°2S 152°0E 281 D5
Allos France 44°15N 6°38E 175 D10
Allston U.S.A. 42°21N 71°7W 116 A2
Alluitsup Paa Greenland 60°30N 45°35W 154 E6
Allur India 14°40N 80°4E 245 G5
Alluru Kottapatnam India 15°24N 80°7E 245 G5
Alma Qué., Canada 48°35N 71°40W 299 C5
Alma Ga., U.S.A. 31°33N 82°28W 316 D7
Alma Kans., U.S.A. 39°1N 96°17W 308 F5
Alma Mich., U.S.A. 43°23N 84°39W 309 D11
Alma Nebr., U.S.A. 40°6N 99°22W 308 E4
Alma Wis., U.S.A. 44°20N 91°55W 308 C8
Alma Ata = Almaty Kazakhstan 43°15N 76°57E 217 D9
Alma Hill U.S.A. 42°2N 78°0W 312 D7
Almacelles Spain 41°43N 0°27E 196 D5
Almada Portugal 38°41N 9°8W 126 A2
Almaden Queens., Australia 17°22S 144°40E 280 B3
Almadén Spain 38°49N 4°52W 195 G6
Almagro Argentina 34°38S 58°24W 117 B2
Almagro I. Phil. 11°55N 124°18E 233 F5
Almalyk = Olmaliq Uzbekistan 40°50N 69°35E 217 D7
Almanor, L. U.S.A. 40°14N 121°9W 304 F3
Almansa Spain 38°51N 1°5W 197 G3
Almanza Spain 42°39N 5°3W 194 C5
Almanzor, Pico Spain 40°15N 5°18W 194 E5
Almanzora → Spain 37°14N 1°46W 197 H3
Almargem do Bispo Portugal 38°49N 9°17W 126 A1
Almas Brazil 11°33S 47°9W 333 D2
Almaş, Munţii Romania 44°49N 22°12E 182 F7
Almaty Kazakhstan 43°15N 76°57E 217 D9
Almaty □ Kazakhstan 44°30N 78°0E 217 D9
Almazán Spain 41°30N 2°30W 196 D2
Almazora Spain 39°57N 0°3W 196 F4
Almeirim Brazil 1°30S 52°34W 329 D7
Almeirim Portugal 39°12N 8°37W 195 F2
Almelo Neths. 52°22N 6°42E 170 B6
Almenar de Soria Spain 41°43N 2°12W 196 D2
Almenara Brazil 16°11S 40°42W 333 E3
Almenara Spain 39°46N 0°14W 196 F4
Almenara, Sierra de Spain 37°34N 1°32W 197 H3
Almendra, Embalse de Spain 41°10N 6°5W 194 D4
Almendralejo Spain 38°41N 6°26W 195 G4
Almere Neths. 52°20N 5°15E 170 B5
Almería Spain 36°52N 2°27W 195 J8
Almería □ Spain 37°20N 2°20W 197 H2
Almería, G. de Spain 36°41N 2°28W 197 J2
Almetyevsk Russia 54°53N 52°20E 190 C11
Älmhult Sweden 56°33N 14°8E 163 H8
Almirante Panama 9°10N 82°30W 320 E3
Almirante G. Brown, Parque Argentina 34°40S 58°28W 117 C2
Almirante Montt, G. Chile 51°52S 72°50W 336 D2
Almiropotamos Greece 38°16N 24°11E 204 C6
Almiros Greece 39°11N 22°45E 204 B4
Almodôvar Portugal 37°31N 8°2W 195 H2
Almodóvar del Campo Spain 38°43N 4°10W 195 G6
Almodóvar del Río Spain 37°48N 5°1W 195 H5
Almon West Bank 31°49N 35°17E 123 B2
Almond U.S.A. 42°19N 77°44W 312 D7
Almond → U.K. 55°58N 3°18W 121 B2
Almont U.S.A. 42°55N 83°3W 312 D1
Almonte Ont., Canada 45°14N 76°12W 313 A8
Almonte Spain 37°13N 6°38W 195 H4
Almora India 29°38N 79°40E 243 E8
Almoradí Spain 38°7N 0°46W 197 G4
Almorox Spain 40°14N 4°24W 194 E6
Almoustarat Mali 17°35N 0°8E 263 B5
Älmsta Sweden 59°58N 18°50E 162 E12
Almudévar Spain 42°3N 0°35W 196 C4
Almuñécar Spain 36°43N 3°41W 195 J7
Almunge Sweden 59°53N 18°3E 162 E12
Almuradiel Spain 38°32N 3°28W 195 G7
Almus Turkey 40°22N 36°54E 212 B7
Almvik Sweden 57°49N 16°30E 163 G10
Almyrou, Ormos Greece 35°23N 24°20E 207 E5
Alna Norway 59°55N 10°50E 133 A4
Alness U.K. 57°41N 4°16W 167 D4
Alnif Morocco 31°10N 5°8W 260 B3
Alnmouth U.K. 55°24N 1°37W 168 B6
Alnsjøen Norway 59°57N 10°51E 133 A4
Alnwick U.K. 55°24N 1°42W 168 B6
Alofau Amer. Samoa 14°16S 170°36W 302 f
Alofi Niue 19°1S 169°55W 289 g
Alofi, I. Wall. & F. Is. 14°27S 178°5W 277 C15
Alofi B. Niue 19°1S 169°56W 289 g
Aloi Uganda 2°16N 33°10E 268 B3
Alon Burma 22°12N 95°5E 241 D5
Along India 28°10N 94°46E 241 A5
Alonissos Greece 39°9N 23°50E 204 B5
Alonissos-Northern Sporades △ Greece 39°15N 24°5E 204 B6
Alor Indonesia 8°15S 124°30E 231 F6
Alor Setar Malaysia 6°7N 100°22E 237 J3
Álora Spain 36°49N 4°46W 195 J6
Alosno Spain 37°33N 7°7W 195 H3
Alost = Aalst Belgium 50°56N 4°2E 170 D4
Alot India 23°56N 75°40E 242 H6
Alotau Papua N. G. 10°16S 150°30E 286 F6
Alougoum Morocco 30°17N 6°56W 260 B3
Aloum Cameroon 2°16N 10°34E 264 B2
Aloysius, Mt. Australia 26°0S 128°38E 279 E4
Alpaugh U.S.A. 35°53N 119°29W 306 K7
Alpe Apuane ⌓ Italy 44°4N 10°15E 198 D7
Alpedrinha Portugal 40°6N 7°27W 194 E3
Alpena U.S.A. 45°4N 83°27W 312 A1
Alpercatas → Brazil 6°2S 44°19W 332 C3
Alperton U.K. 51°32N 0°17W 125 A2
Alpes-de-Haute-Provence □ France 44°8N 6°10E 175 D10
Alpes-Maritimes □ France 43°55N 7°10E 175 E11
Alpha Queens., Australia 23°39S 146°37E 280 C4
Alpha Ill., U.S.A. 41°12N 90°23W 310 C6
Alpha Ridge Arctic 84°0N 118°0W 150 A2
Alpharetta U.S.A. 34°5N 84°18W 316 A5
Alphen aan den Rijn Neths. 52°7N 4°40E 170 B4
Alphios → Greece 37°40N 21°33E 204 D3
Alpiarça Portugal 39°15N 8°35W 195 F2
Alpine Ariz., U.S.A. 33°51N 109°9W 305 K9
Alpine Calif., U.S.A. 32°50N 116°46W 307 N10
Alpine N.J., U.S.A. 40°57N 73°57W 132 A2
Alpine Tex., U.S.A. 30°22N 103°40W 314 F3
Alpine △ Australia 36°56S 148°10E 283 D7
Alps Europe 46°30N 9°30E 176 E5
Alpu Turkey 39°46N 30°58E 212 C4
Alpurrurulam Australia 20°59S 137°50E 280 C2
Alqueta, Barragem do Portugal 38°20N 7°25W 195 G3
Alrø Denmark 55°52N 10°5E 163 J4
Alrode S. Africa 26°17S 28°7E 123 B2
Als Denmark 54°59N 9°55E 163 K3
Alsace France 48°15N 7°25E 171 B7
Alsask Canada 51°21N 109°59W 297 C7
Alsasua Spain 42°54N 2°10W 196 C2
Alsek → U.S.A. 59°10N 138°12W 296 B1
Alsemberg Belgium 50°44N 4°20E 116 B2
Alsergrund Austria 48°13N 16°21E 142 A2
Alsfeld Germany 50°44N 9°16E 178 E5
Alsip U.S.A. 41°40N 87°44W 119 C2
Alsta Norway 65°58N 12°40E 160 D15
Ålsten Sweden 59°19N 17°57E 139 B1
Alsterbro Sweden 56°57N 15°55E 163 H9
Alstermo Sweden 56°58N 15°38E 163 H9
Alston U.K. 54°49N 2°25W 168 C5
Alta Finnmark, Norway 69°57N 23°10E 160 B20
Älta Sweden 59°15N 18°11E 139 B3
Alta, Sierra Spain 40°31N 1°30W 196 E3
Alta Floresta Brazil 9°57S 55°58W 331 B6
Alta Gracia Argentina 31°40S 64°30W 334 C3
Alta Murgia △ Italy 40°55N 16°30E 201 B9
Alta Sierra U.S.A. 35°42N 118°33W 307 K8
Altadena U.S.A. 34°11N 118°8W 126 A4
Altaelva → Norway 69°54N 23°17E 160 B20
Altafjorden Norway 70°5N 23°5E 160 A20
Altagracia Nueva Esparta, Venezuela 11°6N 63°57W 329 a
Altagracia Zulia, Venezuela 10°45N 71°30W 328 A3
Altagracia de Orituco Venezuela 9°52N 66°23W 328 B4
Altai = Aerhtai Shan Mongolia 46°40N 92°45E 217 C12
Altai = Gorno-Altay □ Russia 51°0N 86°0E 217 B11
Altai △ Russia 50°30N 85°30E 217 B11
Altamachi → Bolivia 16°8S 66°50W 330 D4
Altamaha → U.S.A. 31°20N 81°20W 316 D8
Altamira Brazil 3°12S 52°10W 329 D7
Altamira Chile 25°47S 69°51W 334 B2
Altamira Colombia 2°3N 75°47W 328 C2
Altamira Tamaulipas, Mexico 22°24N 97°55W 319 C5
Altamira, Cuevas de Spain 43°20N 4°5W 194 B6
Altamont Ill., U.S.A. 39°4N 88°45W 311 E8
Altamont N.Y., U.S.A. 42°42N 74°2W 313 D10
Altamura Italy 40°49N 16°33E 201 B9
Altanbulag Mongolia 50°16N 106°30E 218 A10
Altar Mexico 30°43N 111°44W 318 A2
Altar, Gran Desierto de Mexico 31°50N 114°10W 318 B2
Altata Mexico 24°40N 107°55W 318 C3
Altavas Phil. 11°32N 122°29E 233 F4
Altavista U.S.A. 37°6N 79°17W 309 G14
Altay Xinjiang Uygur, China 47°48N 88°10E 217 C11
Altay Mongolia 46°22N 96°15E 218 B8
Altdorf Switz. 46°52N 8°36E 179 J4
Alte-Donau → Austria 48°14N 16°25E 142 A2
Alte Mellum Germany 53°43N 8°10E 178 B4
Altea Spain 38°38N 0°2W 197 G4
Altenberg Germany 50°45N 13°45E 178 E9
Altenbruch Germany 53°49N 8°46E 178 B4
Altenburg Germany 50°59N 12°25E 178 E8
Altenkirchen Mecklenburg-Vorpommern, Germany 54°38N 13°22E 178 A9
Altenkirchen Rhld-Pfz., Germany 50°41N 7°39E 178 E3
Altenmarkt Austria 47°43N 14°39E 180 D7
Alter do Chão Brazil 2°31S 54°57W 329 D6
Alter do Chão Portugal 39°12N 7°40W 195 F3
Alter Finkenkrug Germany 52°35N 13°3E 115 A1
Altes Rathaus Munich, Germany 131 b3
Altglienicke Germany 52°25N 13°32E 115 B4
Altha U.S.A. 30°34N 85°8W 316 E4
Altınkaya Barajı Turkey 41°18N 35°30E 212 B6
Altınoluk Turkey 39°34N 26°45E 205 B8
Altınova Turkey 39°12N 26°47E 205 B8
Altınözü Turkey 36°7N 36°14E 250 B7
Altıntaş Turkey 39°4N 30°7E 205 B12
Altınyaka Turkey 36°33N 30°20E 205 E12
Altınyayla Turkey 37°0N 29°33E 205 D11
Altiplano Bolivia 17°0S 68°0W 330 D4
Altkirch France 47°37N 7°15E 173 E14
Altlandsberg Germany 52°33N 13°43E 115 A5
Altlandsberg Nord Germany 52°34N 13°43E 115 A5
Altmannsdorf Austria 48°9N 16°18E 142 B1
Altmark Germany 52°45N 11°30E 178 C7
Altmühl → Germany 48°54N 11°52E 179 G7
Altmühltal ⌓ Germany 48°55N 11°15E 179 G7
Altmunster Austria 47°54N 13°45E 180 D6
Alto Adige = Trentino-Alto Adige □ Italy 46°30N 11°20E 199 B8
Alto Alegre Brazil 2°50N 61°20W 329 C5
Alto Araguaia Brazil 17°15S 53°20W 331 D7
Alto Chicapa Angola 10°52S 19°17E 265 E3
Alto Cuchumatanes = Cuchumatanes, Sierra de los Guatemala 15°35N 91°25W 320 C1
Alto Cuito = Tempué Angola 13°27S 18°49E 265 E3
Alto da Boa Vista Brazil 22°57S 43°16W 135 B1
Alto da Moóca Brazil 23°34S 46°33W 137 B2
Alto del Carmen Chile 28°46S 70°30W 334 B1
Alto do Pina Portugal 38°44N 9°7W 126 A2
Alto Douro Portugal 41°6N 7°47W 194 D3
Alto Garças Brazil 16°56S 53°32W 331 D7
Alto Garda Bresciano ⌓ Italy 45°42N 10°38E 198 C7
Alto Iriri → Brazil 8°50S 53°25W 331 B7
Alto Ligonha Mozam. 15°30S 38°11E 269 F4
Alto Molocue Mozam. 15°50S 37°35E 269 F4
Alto Paraguai Brazil 14°30S 56°31W 331 C6
Alto Paraguay □ Paraguay 21°0S 58°30W 334 A4
Alto Paraiso de Goiás Brazil 14°7S 47°31W 333 D2
Alto Paraná □ Paraguay 25°30S 54°50W 335 B5
Alto Parnaíba Brazil 9°6S 45°57W 332 C2
Alto Purús → Peru 9°12S 70°28W 330 B3
Alto Río Senguerr Argentina 45°2S 70°50W 336 C2
Alto Santo Brazil 5°31S 38°15W 332 C4
Alto Sucuriú Brazil 19°19S 52°47W 331 D7
Alto Tajo ⌓ Spain 40°44N 2°30W 196 E2
Alton Ont., Canada 43°54N 80°5W 312 C4
Alton Hants., U.K. 51°9N 0°59W 169 F7
Alton Ill., U.S.A. 38°53N 90°11W 310 F6
Alton N.H., U.S.A. 43°27N 71°13W 313 C13
Altona Vic., Australia 37°51S 144°49E 128 B1
Altona Man., Canada 49°6N 97°33W 297 D9
Altoona Ala., U.S.A. 34°2N 86°20W 316 A3
Altoona Iowa, U.S.A. 41°39N 93°28W 310 C3
Altoona Pa., U.S.A. 40°31N 78°24W 312 F6
Altos Brazil 5°3S 42°28W 332 C3
Altötting Germany 48°12N 12°39E 179 G8
Altsasu = Alsasua Spain 42°54N 2°10W 196 C2
Altstätten Switz. 47°22N 9°33E 179 H5
Altun Kupri Iraq 35°45N 44°9E 213 E11
Altun Shan China 38°30N 88°0E 217 E11
Alturas U.S.A. 41°29N 120°32W 304 F3
Altus U.S.A. 34°38N 99°20W 314 D5
Altyn-Emel △ Kazakhstan 44°40N 78°26E 217 D9
Alubijid Phil. 8°35N 124°29E 233 G5
Alucra Turkey 40°22N 38°47E 213 B8
Aluk South Sudan 8°25N 27°30E 257 F2
Alūksne Latvia 57°24N 27°3E 188 D4
Alunda Sweden 60°4N 18°5E 162 D12
Alunite U.S.A. 35°59N 114°55W 307 K12
Aluoro → Ethiopia 8°26N 33°24E 257 F3
Alupka Ukraine 44°23N 34°2E 189 K8
Alur India 15°24N 77°15E 245 E3
Alur Gajah Malaysia 2°23N 102°13E 234 B2
Alushta Ukraine 44°40N 34°25E 189 K8
Alusi Indonesia 7°35S 131°40E 231 F8
Alustante Spain 40°36N 1°40W 196 E3
Alutgama Sri Lanka 6°26N 79°59E 245 L4
Alutnuwara Sri Lanka 7°19N 80°59E 245 L5
Aluva India 10°8N 76°24E 245 J3
Alva U.S.A. 36°48N 98°40W 314 C5
Alvaiázere Portugal 39°49N 8°23W 194 F2
Alvalade Portugal 38°45N 9°8W 126 A2
Älvängen Sweden 57°58N 12°8E 163 G6
Alvão ⌓ Portugal 41°22N 7°48W 194 D3
Alvarado Veracruz, Mexico 18°46N 95°46W 319 D5
Alvarado Tex., U.S.A. 32°24N 97°13W 314 E6
Alvarães Brazil 3°12S 64°50W 329 D5
Alvaro Obregón, Presa Mexico 27°52N 109°52W 318 B3
Alvdal Norway 62°6N 10°37E 164 B7
Älvdalen Sweden 61°13N 14°4E 162 C8
Alvear Argentina 29°5S 56°30W 334 B4
Alverca Portugal 38°56N 9°1W 195 G1
Alvesta Sweden 56°54N 14°35E 163 H8
Alvik Sweden 59°19N 17°58E 139 B1
Alvin Callendar Naval Air Station U.S.A. 29°50N 90°1W 131 B2
Alvinston Canada 42°49N 81°52W 312 D3
Alvito Portugal 38°15N 7°58W 195 G3
Älvkarleby Sweden 60°34N 17°26E 162 D11
Alvorado Brazil 12°28S 49°6W 333 D2
Alvord Desert U.S.A. 42°30N 118°25W 304 E4
Älvros Sweden 62°3N 14°38E 162 B8
Älvsbyn Sweden 65°40N 21°0E 160 D19
Älvsjo Sweden 59°16N 18°0E 139 B2
Ålvundeid Norway 62°45N 8°33E 164 B5
Älvvik Sweden 59°21N 18°15E 139 A3
Alwar India 27°38N 76°34E 242 F7
Alwaye = Aluva India 10°8N 76°24E 245 J3
Alxa Zuoqi China 38°50N 105°40E 226 E3
Alyangula Australia 13°55S 136°30E 280 A2
Alyata = Älät Azerbaijan 39°58N 49°25E 191 L9
Alyth U.K. 56°38N 3°13W 167 E5
Alytus Lithuania 54°24N 24°3E 188 E3
Alzada U.S.A. 45°2N 104°25W 304 D11
Alzamay Russia 55°33N 98°39E 215 D10
Alzey Germany 49°45N 8°7E 179 F4
Alzira Spain 39°9N 0°30W 197 F4
Am Dam Chad 12°40N 20°35E 259 F4
Am Géréda Chad 12°53N 21°14E 259 F4
Am Hasenbergl Germany 48°12N 11°33E 131 A2
Am Sak Chad 13°39N 20°8E 259 F4
Am Steinhof Austria 48°12N 16°17E 142 A1
Am Timan Chad 11°0N 20°10E 259 F4
Am Wald Germany 48°3N 11°36E 131 B2
Ama Keng Singapore 1°23N 103°41E 138 A2
Amacayacu △ Colombia 3°21S 70°8W 328 D3
Amada Gaza C.A.R. 4°46N 15°9E 264 B3
Amådalen Sweden 61°20N 14°44E 162 C8
Amadeus, L. Australia 24°54S 131°0E 279 D5
Amadi Dem. Rep. of the Congo 3°40N 26°40E 268 B2
Amadi South Sudan 5°29N 30°25E 257 F3
Amadjuak L. Canada 65°0N 71°8W 295 E17
Amadora Portugal 38°45N 9°13W 126 A1
Amagansett U.S.A. 40°59N 72°9W 313 F12
Amagasaki Japan 34°42N 135°23E 133 A1
Amager Denmark 55°36N 12°35E 118 B3
Amagi Japan 33°25N 130°39E 222 D2
Amagunze Nigeria 6°20N 7°40E 263 D6
Amahai Indonesia 3°20S 128°55E 231 E7
Amaile Samoa 13°59S 171°22W 287 V20
Amaimon Papua N. G. 5°12S 145°30E 286 C3
Amaiun-Maia Spain 43°12N 1°29W 196 B3
Amakusa = Hondo Japan 32°27N 130°12E 222 E2
Amakusa-Nada Japan 32°35N 130°5E 222 E2
Amakusa-Shotō Japan 32°15N 130°10E 222 E2
Amal Oman 18°21N 55°39E 249 C6
Åmål Sweden 59°3N 12°42E 162 E6
Amāl Qādisiya Iraq 33°16N 44°20E 113 B2
Amalapuram India 16°35N 81°55E 245 F5
Amalfi Colombia 6°55N 75°4W 328 B2
Amalfi Italy 40°38N 14°36E 201 B7
Amaliada Greece 37°47N 21°22E 204 D3
Amalienborg Slot Copenhagen, Denmark 118 b3
Amalner India 21°5N 75°5E 244 D2
Amamapare Indonesia 4°53S 136°38E 231 E9
Amambaí Brazil 23°5S 55°13W 335 A4
Amambaí → Brazil 23°22S 53°56W 335 A5
Amambay □ Paraguay 23°0S 56°0W 335 A4
Amambay, Cordillera de S. Amer. 23°0S 55°45W 335 A4
Amami Japan 28°22N 129°27E 221 K4
Amami-Guntō Japan 27°16N 129°21E 221 L4
Amami-Ō-Shima Japan 28°16N 129°21E 221 K4
Aman, Pulau Malaysia 5°16N 100°24E 237 c
Amana → Venezuela 9°45N 62°39W 329 B5
Amaná, L. Brazil 2°35S 64°40W 329 D5
Amanab Papua N. G. 3°40S 141°14E 286 B1
Amanat → India 24°7N 84°4E 243 G11
Amanave Amer. Samoa 14°20S 170°50W 302 f
Amanda Park U.S.A. 47°28N 123°55W 306 C3
Amankeldi Kazakhstan 50°10N 65°10E 216 B7
Amanohashidate Japan 35°40N 135°15E 223 B7
Amantea Italy 39°8N 16°4E 201 C9
Amanu French Polynesia 17°48S 140°46W 289 f

Amapá Brazil 2°5N 50°50W 329 C7
Amapá □ Brazil 1°40N 52°0W 329 C7
Amapari = Ferreira Gomes
Brazil 0°48N 51°8W 329 C7
Amara Sudan 10°25N 34°10E 257 E3
Amara □ Ethiopia 12°30N 37°30E 257 E4
Amaração = Luís Correia
Brazil 3°0S 41°35W 332 B3
Amarante Brazil 6°14S 42°50W 332 C3
Amarante Portugal 41°16N 8°5W 194 D2
Amarante do Maranhão
Brazil 5°36S 46°45W 332 C2
Amaranth Canada 50°36N 98°43W 297 C9
Amarapura Burma 21°54N 96°3E 241 E6
Amaravati → India 11°0N 78°15E 245 J4
Amareleja Portugal 38°12N 7°13W 195 G3
Amargosa Brazil 13°2S 39°36W 333 D4
Amargosa → U.S.A. 36°14N 116°51W 307 J10
Amargosa Desert
U.S.A. 36°40N 116°30W 307 J10
Amargosa Range
U.S.A. 36°20N 116°45W 307 J10
Amari Greece 35°13N 24°40E 207 E5
Amarillo U.S.A. 35°13N 101°50W 314 D4
Amarkantak India 22°40N 81°45E 243 H9
'Amârna, Tell el Egypt 27°38N 30°52E 256 B3
Amarnath India 19°12N 73°22E 244 E1
Amaro, Mte. Italy 42°5N 14°5E 199 F11
Amarpur Bihar, India 25°5N 87°0E 243 G12
Amarpur Tripura, India 23°31N 91°39E 241 D3
Amarti Eritrea 14°17N 41°6E 257 E5
Amarwara India 22°18N 79°10E 243 H8
Amasin W. Sahara 25°45N 13°20W 260 C2
Amasra Turkey 41°45N 32°23E 212 B5
Amassama Nigeria 5°1N 6°2E 263 D6
Amasya Turkey 40°40N 35°50E 212 B6
Amasya □ Turkey 40°40N 35°50E 212 B6
Amata S. Austral., Australia 26°9S 131°9E 279 E5
Amata Piemonte, Italy 45°34N 9°8E 128 A1
Amataurá Brazil 3°29S 68°6W 328 D4
Amatignak I. U.S.A. 51°16N 179°6W 303 L3
Amatikulu S. Africa 29°3S 31°33E 271 C5
Amatitlán Guatemala 14°29N 90°38W 320 D1
Amatrice Italy 42°38N 13°17E 199 F10
Amau Papua N. G. 10°2S 148°34E 286 F5
Amay Belgium 50°33N 5°19E 170 D5
Amazon = Amazonas →
S. Amer. 0°5S 50°0W 329 D8
Amazonas □ Brazil 5°0S 65°0W 331 B5
Amazonas □ Peru 5°0S 78°0W 330 B2
Amazonas □ Venezuela 3°30N 66°0W 328 C4
Amazonas → S. Amer. 0°5S 50°0W 329 D8
Amba Ferit Ethiopia 10°55N 38°50E 257 E4
Ambad India 19°38N 75°50E 244 E2
Ambae = Aoba Vanuatu 15°25S 167°50E 287 E5
Ambagarh Chowki India 20°47N 80°43E 244 D5
Ambah India 26°43N 78°13E 242 F8
Ambahakily Madag. 21°36S 43°41E 272 C1
Ambahita Madag. 24°1S 45°16E 272 C2
Ambajogal India 18°44N 76°23E 244 E3
Ambala India 30°23N 76°56E 242 D7
Ambalangoda Sri Lanka 6°15N 80°5E 245 L5
Ambalantota Sri Lanka 6°7N 81°1E 245 L5
Ambalapulai India 9°25N 76°25E 245 K3
Ambalavao Madag. 21°50S 46°56E 272 C2
Ambam Cameroon 2°20N 11°15E 264 B2
Ambanja Madag. 13°40S 48°27E 272 A2
Ambararata Madag. 15°3S 48°33E 272 B2
Ambarchik Russia 69°40N 162°20E 215 C17
Ambarijeby Madag. 14°56S 47°41E 272 A2
Ambarlı Turkey 40°58N 28°40E 203 E12
Ambaro, Helodranon'
Madag. 13°23S 48°38E 272 A2
Ambasamudram India 8°43N 77°25E 245 K3
Ambato Ecuador 1°5S 78°42W 328 D2
Ambato Madag. 13°24S 48°29E 272 A2
Ambato, Sierra de
Argentina 28°25S 66°10W 334 B2
Ambato Boeny Madag. 16°28S 46°43E 272 B2
Ambatofinandrahana
Madag. 20°33S 46°48E 272 C2
Ambatolampy Madag. 19°20S 47°35E 272 B2
Ambatomainty Madag. 17°41S 45°40E 272 B2
Ambatomanoina Madag. 18°18S 47°37E 272 B2
Ambatondrazaka Madag. 17°55S 48°28E 272 B2
Ambatosoratra Madag. 17°37S 48°31E 272 B2
Ambelokipi Greece 37°58N 23°47E 112 B2
Ambelonas Greece 39°45N 22°22E 204 B4
Ambenja Madag. 15°17S 46°58E 272 B2
Amberg Germany 49°26N 11°52E 179 F7
Ambergris Cay Belize 18°0N 87°55W 320 C2
Ambérieu-en-Bugey
France 45°57N 5°20E 175 C9
Amberley Ont., Canada 44°2N 81°42W 312 B3
Amberley N.Z. 43°9S 172°44E 285 D7
Ambert France 45°33N 3°44E 174 C7
Ambidédi Mali 14°35N 11°47W 262 C2
Ambikapur India 23°15N 83°15E 243 H10
Ambikol Sudan 21°20N 30°50E 256 C3
Ambil I. Phil. 13°48N 120°18E 232 E3
Ambilobé Madag. 13°10S 49°3E 272 A2
Ambinanindrano Madag. 20°5S 48°23E 272 C2
Ambinanitelo Madag. 15°21S 49°35E 272 B2
Ambinda Madag. 16°25S 45°52E 272 B2
Ambitle I. Papua N. G. 4°5S 153°37E 286 C7
Amble U.K. 55°20N 1°36W 168 B6
Ambler U.S.A. 67°5N 157°52W 303 C8
Ambleside U.K. 54°26N 2°58W 168 C5
Ambo Peru 10°5S 76°10W 330 C2
Amboahangy Madag. 24°15S 46°22E 272 C2
Amboasary Madag. 25°1S 46°45E 272 D2
Ambodifototra Madag. 16°59S 49°52E 272 B2
Ambodilazana Madag. 18°6S 49°10E 272 B2
Ambodiriana Madag. 17°55S 49°18E 272 B2
Ambohidratrimo Madag. 18°50S 47°26E 272 B2
Ambohidray Madag. 18°36S 48°18E 272 B2
Ambohimahamasina
Madag. 21°56S 47°11E 272 C2
Ambohimahasoa Madag. 21°7S 47°13E 272 C2
Ambohimanga Analamanga,
Madag. 18°45S 47°33E 272 B2
Ambohimanga Vatovavy-Fitovinany,
Madag. 20°52S 47°36E 272 C2
Ambohimitombo Madag. 20°43S 47°26E 272 C2
Ambohitra Madag. 12°30S 49°10E 272 A2
Amboise France 47°24N 1°2E 172 E8
Amboiva Angola 11°33S 14°43E 265 E2
Ambon Indonesia 3°43S 128°12E 231 E7
Ambondro Madag. 25°13S 45°44E 272 D2
Amboró △ Bolivia 17°39S 64°3W 331 D5
Amboseli, L. Kenya 2°40S 37°10E 268 C4
Amboseli △ Kenya 2°37S 37°13E 268 C4
Ambositra Madag. 20°31S 47°25E 272 C2
Ambovombe Madag. 25°11S 46°5E 272 D2
Amboy Calif., U.S.A. 34°33N 115°45W 307 L11
Amboy Ill., U.S.A. 41°44N 89°20W 310 C7
Amboyna Cay S. China Sea 7°50N 112°50E 230 C4
Ambre, Île d' Mauritius 20°2S 57°41E 272 e
Ambridge U.S.A. 40°36N 80°14W 312 F4
Ambriz Angola 7°48S 13°8E 265 D2
Ambriz ⌓ Angola 7°56S 10°27E 265 D2
Ambrolauri Georgia 42°31N 43°9E 213 A10
Ambrym Vanuatu 16°15S 168°10E 287 F6
Ambulong I. Phil. 12°13N 121°1E 232 E3
Ambunti Papua N. G. 4°13S 142°52E 286 C2
Ambur India 12°48N 78°43E 245 H4
Amchitka I. U.S.A. 51°32N 179°0E 303 L2
Amderma Russia 69°45N 61°30E 214 C7
Amdhi India 23°51N 81°27E 243 H9
Amdo China 32°20N 91°40E 218 E7
Ameca Mexico 20°33N 104°2W 318 C4
Ameca → Mexico 20°41N 105°18W 318 C3
Amecameca de Juárez
Mexico 19°8N 98°46W 319 D5
Amed Indonesia 8°19S 115°39E 231 J18
Ameixoeira Portugal 38°46N 9°8W 126 A2
Ameland Neths. 53°27N 5°45E 170 A5
Amélia Italy 42°33N 12°25E 199 F9
Amelia City U.S.A. 30°35N 81°28W 316 E8
Amelia Earhart Park
U.S.A. 25°53N 80°16W 129 C1
Amelia I. U.S.A. 30°40N 81°25W 316 E8
Amendolara Italy 39°57N 16°35E 201 C9
Amenia U.S.A. 41°51N 73°33W 313 E11
América Brazil 23°35S 46°41W 137 B1
America-Antarctica Ridge
S. Ocean 59°0S 16°0W 151 B2
American Falls U.S.A. 42°47N 112°51W 304 E7
American Falls Res.
U.S.A. 42°47N 112°52W 304 E7
American Fork U.S.A. 40°23N 111°48W 304 F8
American Highland
Antarctica 73°0S 75°0E 151 D6
American Indian Museum
Washington, D.C., U.S.A. 143 b3
American Museum of Natural
History New York, U.S.A. 132 b2
American River Australia 35°47S 137°46E 282 C2
American Samoa ☑
Pac. Oc. 14°20S 170°0W 302 f
American Samoa △
Amer. Samoa 14°15S 170°28W 302 g
American Univ. U.S.A. 38°56N 77°5W 143 B2
Americana Brazil 22°45S 47°20W 335 A6
Americus U.S.A. 32°4N 84°14W 316 C5
Amerigo Vespucci, Firenze ✈ (FLR)
Italy 43°49N 11°13E 199 E8
Amerika = Nakhodka
Russia 42°53N 132°54E 220 C6
Amersfoort Neths. 52°9N 5°23E 170 B5
Amersfoort Mpumalanga,
S. Africa 26°59S 29°53E 271 C4
Amery Basin S. Ocean 68°15S 74°30E 151 C6
Amery Ice Shelf Antarctica 69°30S 72°0E 151 C6
Amerzgane Morocco 31°4N 7°14W 260 B3
Ames = Bertamirans
Spain 42°54N 8°38W 194 C2
Ames U.S.A. 42°2N 93°37W 310 C3
Amesbury U.S.A. 42°51N 70°56W 313 D14
Amet India 25°18N 73°56E 242 G5
Amfiklia Greece 38°38N 22°35E 204 C4
Amfilochia Greece 38°52N 21°9E 204 C3
Amfipoli Greece 40°48N 23°52E 202 F7
Amfissa Greece 38°32N 22°22E 204 C4
Amga Russia 60°50N 132°0E 215 C14
Amga → Russia 62°38N 134°32E 215 C14
Amgaon India 21°22N 80°22E 244 D5
Amgu Russia 45°45N 137°15E 220 B8
Amguid Algeria 26°26N 5°22E 261 C6
Amgun → Russia 52°56N 139°38E 215 D14
Amherst = Kyaikkami
Burma 16°4N 97°34E 241 G6
Amherst N.S., Canada 45°48N 64°8W 299 C7
Amherst Mass., U.S.A. 42°23N 72°31W 313 D12
Amherst N.Y., U.S.A. 42°59N 78°48W 312 D6
Amherst Ohio, U.S.A. 41°24N 82°14W 312 E2
Amherst I. Canada 44°8N 76°43W 313 B8
Amherstburg Canada 42°6N 83°6W 311 B13
Amiata, Mte. Italy 42°53N 11°37E 199 F8
Amidon U.S.A. 46°29N 103°19W 308 B2
Amiens France 49°54N 2°16E 173 C9
Amik Gölü Turkey 36°22N 36°17E 250 B7
Amili India 28°25N 95°52E 241 A5
Amin Iraq 33°19N 44°29E 113 B2
Aminadav Israel 31°45N 35°8E 123 B1
Amindeo Greece 40°42N 21°42E 202 F5
Amindivi Is. India 11°23N 72°23E 245 J1
Amingaon India 26°11N 91°40E 241 B3
Amini I. India 11°6N 72°45E 245 J1
Amino Ethiopia 4°25N 41°52E 257 G5
Aminuis Namibia 23°43S 19°21E 270 B2
Āmir, Ra's Libya 32°57N 21°43E 258 B4
Amīrābād Īlām, Iran 33°20N 46°16E 246 C5
Amīrābād Tehrān, Iran 35°43N 51°24E 141 A2
Amirante Is. Seychelles 6°0S 53°0E 210 J7
Amisk ⌓ Canada 56°43N 98°0W 297 B9
Amisk L. Canada 54°35N 102°15W 297 C8
Amistad, Presa de la
Mexico 29°26N 101°3W 318 B4
Amistad ⌓ U.S.A. 29°32N 101°12W 314 G4
Amite U.S.A. 30°44N 90°30W 315 F9
Amizmiz Morocco 31°12N 8°15W 260 B3
Amla India 21°56N 78°7E 242 J8
Amlapura Indonesia 8°27S 115°37E 231 J18
Åmli Norway 58°45N 8°32E 164 F5
Amlia I. U.S.A. 52°4N 173°30W 303 K4
Amlwch U.K. 53°24N 4°20W 168 D3
Amm Adam Sudan 16°20N 36°1E 257 D4
'Ammān Jordan 31°57N 35°52E 251 G6
Ammanford U.K. 51°48N 3°59W 169 F4
Ammassalik = Tasiilaq
Greenland 65°40N 37°20W 154 D7
Ammerån → Sweden 63°9N 16°13E 162 A10
Ammersee Germany 48°0N 11°7E 179 G7
Ammochostos = Famagusta
Cyprus 35°8N 33°55E 207 E9
Ammon U.S.A. 43°28N 111°58W 304 E8
Amnat Charoen Thailand 15°51N 104°38E 236 E5
Amnura Bangla. 24°37N 88°25E 243 G13
Amo Jiang → China 23°0N 101°50E 228 F3
Āmol Iran 36°23N 52°20E 247 B7
Amora Portugal 38°37N 9°6W 126 B2
Amoreira Portugal 38°48N 9°11W 126 A1
Amoret U.S.A. 38°15N 94°35W 310 F2
Amorgos Greece 36°50N 25°57E 205 E7
Amoron'i Mania □ Madag. 20°0S 46°0E 272 C2
Amory U.S.A. 33°59N 88°29W 315 E10
Amos Canada 48°35N 78°5W 298 C4
Åmot Buskerud, Norway 59°57N 9°54E 164 E6
Åmot Oppland, Norway 61°0N 10°2E 164 D7
Åmot Telemark, Norway 59°34N 8°0E 164 E5
Åmot Sweden 60°58N 16°27E 162 D10
Åmotfors Sweden 59°47N 12°22E 162 E6
Amotsdal Norway 59°37N 8°26E 164 E5
Amour, Djebel Algeria 33°42N 1°37E 261 B5
Amoy = Xiamen China 24°25N 118°4E 229 E12
Ampah Indonesia 1°46S 115°7E 235 C5
Ampanavoana Madag. 15°41S 50°22E 272 B3
Ampang Malaysia 3°8N 101°45E 139 A2
Ampangalana, Lakandranon'
Madag. 22°48S 47°50E 272 C2
Ampani India 19°35N 82°38E 244 E6
Ampanihy Madag. 24°40S 44°45E 272 C1
Amparafaravola Madag. 17°35S 48°13E 272 B2
Ampasinambo Madag. 20°31S 48°0E 272 C2
Ampasindava, Helodranon'
Madag. 13°40S 48°15E 272 A2
Ampasindava, Saikanosy
Madag. 13°42S 47°55E 272 A2
Ampato, Nevado Peru 15°40S 71°56W 330 D3
Ampenan Indonesia 8°34S 116°4E 231 K18
Amper Nigeria 9°25N 9°40E 263 D6
Amper → Bayern,
Germany 48°29N 11°55E 179 G7
Amper → Oberbayern,
Germany 48°14N 11°25E 131 A1
Ampezzo Italy 46°25N 12°48E 199 B9
Amphitrite Group
S. China Sea 16°50N 112°20E 230 A4
Amphoe Kathu Thailand 7°55N 98°21E 237 a
Amphoe Thalang Thailand 8°1N 98°20E 237 a
Ampitsikinana Madag. 12°57S 49°49E 272 A2
Ampombiantambo
Madag. 12°42S 48°57E 272 A2
Amposta Spain 40°43N 0°34E 196 E5
Ampotaka Madag. 25°3S 44°41E 272 D1
Ampoza Madag. 22°20S 44°44E 272 C1
Amqui Canada 48°28N 67°27W 299 C6
Amrabad India 16°23N 78°50E 245 F4
'Amrān Yemen 15°41N 43°55E 248 D3
'Amrān □ Yemen 15°41N 43°55E 248 D3
Amraoti = Amravati
India 20°55N 77°45E 244 D3
Amravati India 20°55N 77°45E 244 D3
Amreli India 21°35N 71°17E 242 J4
Amrenene el Kasba Algeria 22°10N 0°30E 261 D5
Amritsar India 31°35N 74°57E 242 D6
Amroha India 28°53N 78°30E 243 E8
Amrum Germany 54°38N 8°22E 178 A4
Amsâga Mauritania 20°7N 14°10W 260 D2
Amsel Algeria 22°47N 5°29E 261 D6
Amstel Amsterdam, Neths. 112 b2
Amstel → Amsterdam, Neths. 112 b3
Amstel-Drecht-Kanaal
Neths. 52°18N 4°54E 112 B2
Amstelveen Neths. 52°18N 4°51E 112 B2
Amsterdam Neths. 52°23N 4°54E 112 A2
Amsterdam N.Y., U.S.A. 42°56N 74°11W 313 D10
Amsterdam ✈ (AMS)
Neths. 52°18N 4°45E 112 B1
Amsterdam Arena Neths. 52°19N 4°56E 112 B2
Amsterdam I. = Nouvelle
Amsterdam, Î. Ind. Oc. 38°30S 77°30E 273 H6
Amsterdam-Rijnkanaal
Neths. 52°17N 5°1E 112 B3
Amsterdam Zuidoost
Neths. 52°18N 4°58E 112 B2
Amsterdamse Bos Neths. 52°19N 4°50E 112 B1
Amstetten Austria 48°7N 14°51E 180 C7
'Amūdah Syria 37°6N 40°55E 213 D9
Amudarya Turkmenistan 37°53N 65°15E 216 E7
Amudarya → Uzbekistan 43°58N 59°34E 216 D5
Amukta I. U.S.A. 52°30N 171°16W 303 K5
Amukta Pass U.S.A. 52°0N 171°0W 303 K5
Amulung Phil. 17°50N 121°43E 232 C3
Amund Ringnes I.
Canada 78°20N 96°25W 295 B12
Amundsen Abyssal Plain
S. Ocean 65°0S 125°0W 151 C14
Amundsen Basin Arctic 87°30N 80°0E 150 A4
Amundsen Gulf Canada 71°0N 124°0W 294 C7
Amundsen Ridges
S. Ocean 69°15S 123°0W 151 C14
Amundsen-Scott Antarctica 90°0S 166°0E 151 E
Amundsen Sea Antarctica 72°0S 115°0W 151 D15
Amungen Sweden 61°10N 15°40E 162 C9
Amuntai Indonesia 2°28S 115°25E 235 C5
Amur → Russia 52°56N 141°10E 215 D15
Amur, W. → Sudan 18°56N 33°34E 256 D3
Amurang Indonesia 1°5N 124°40E 231 D6
Amurrio Spain 43°3N 3°0W 196 B1
Amursk Russia 50°14N 136°54E 215 D14
Amusco Spain 42°10N 4°28W 194 C6
Amvrakikos Kolpos Greece 39°0N 20°55E 204 C2
Amvrosiyivka Ukraine 47°43N 38°30E 189 J10
Amyderya = Amudarya →
Uzbekistan 43°58N 59°34E 216 D5
An Bang, Dao = Amboyna Cay
S. China Sea 7°50N 112°50E 230 C4
An Bien Vietnam 9°45N 105°0E 237 H5
An Hoa Vietnam 15°40N 108°5E 236 E7
An Khe Vietnam 13°57N 108°51E 236 F7
An Nabatīyah at Tahta
Lebanon 33°23N 35°27E 250 E6
An Nabk Syria 34°2N 36°44E 250 D7
An Nafūd Si. Arabia 28°15N 41°0E 246 D4
An Nāḥiyah Iraq 34°26N 41°33E 213 E9
An Najaf Iraq 32°3N 44°15E 213 G11
An Namāṣ Si. Arabia 19°7N 42°8E 248 C3
An Nāṣirīyah Iraq 31°0N 46°15E 246 D5
An Nawfalīyah Libya 30°54N 17°58E 258 B3
An Nhon = Binh Dinh
Vietnam 13°55N 109°7E 236 F7
An Nîl □ Sudan 19°30N 33°0E 256 D3
An Nîl el Abyad □ Sudan 14°0N 32°15E 257 E3
An Nîl el Azraq □ Sudan 11°30N 34°30E 257 E3
An Nu'ayrīyah Si. Arabia 27°30N 48°30E 247 E6
An Nu'mānīyah Iraq 32°32N 45°25E 213 F11
An Nuqat al Khams □
Libya 32°42N 11°57E 258 B2
An Ros = Rush Ireland 53°31N 6°6W 166 C5
An Thoi, Quan Dao
Vietnam 9°58N 104°0E 237 H5
Åna-Sira Norway 58°17N 6°25E 164 F3
Anaa French Polynesia 17°25S 145°30W 289 f
Anabar → Russia 73°8N 113°36E 215 B12
Anaco Venezuela 9°27N 64°28W 329 B5
Anaconda U.S.A. 46°8N 112°57W 304 C7
Anacortes U.S.A. 48°30N 122°37W 306 B4
Anacostia U.S.A. 38°51N 76°59W 143 B3
Anacostia → U.S.A. 38°52N 77°1W 143 B3
Anacuao, Mt. Phil. 16°16N 121°53E 232 C3
Anadarko U.S.A. 35°4N 98°15W 314 D5
Anadia Brazil 9°42S 36°18W 332 C4
Anadia Portugal 40°26N 8°27W 194 E2
Anadolu Turkey 39°0N 30°0E 212 C5
Anadoluhisarı Turkey 41°4N 29°3E 122 B2
Anadolukavağı Turkey 41°10N 29°7E 122 A2
Anadyr Russia 64°35N 177°20E 215 C18
Anadyr → Russia 64°55N 176°5E 215 C18
Anadyrskiy Zaliv Russia 64°0N 180°0E 215 C19
Anafi Greece 36°22N 25°48E 205 E7
Anafonitria Greece 37°51N 20°39E 207 D2
Anaga, Pta. de Canary Is. 28°34N 16°9W 153 e1
Anagni Italy 41°44N 13°9E 199 G10
'Ānah Iraq 34°25N 42°0E 213 E10
Anaheim U.S.A. 33°50N 117°55W 307 M9
Anahim Lake Canada 52°28N 125°18W 296 C3
Anahola U.S.A. 22°9N 159°19W 302 A2
'Anahulu → U.S.A. 21°37N 158°6W 302 J13
Anai Mudi India 10°12N 77°4E 245 J3
Anaichak ⌓ U.S.A. 56°50N 158°15W 303 H8
Anaimalai Hills India 10°20N 76°40E 245 J3
Anajás Brazil 0°59S 49°57W 332 B2
Anajatuba Brazil 3°16S 44°37W 332 B3
Anakao Madag. 23°40S 43°39E 272 C1
Anakapalle India 17°42N 83°6E 244 F6
Anakie Australia 23°32S 147°45E 280 C4
Anaklia Georgia 42°22N 41°35E 191 J5
Anaktuvuk Pass U.S.A. 68°8N 151°45W 303 B10
Analalava Madag. 14°35S 48°0E 272 A2
Analamanga □ Madag. 18°0S 47°30E 272 B2
Analanjirofo □ Madag. 16°30S 49°30E 272 B2
Analavoka Madag. 22°23S 46°30E 272 C2
Analipsis Greece 39°36N 19°55E 206 B9
Anamã Brazil 3°35S 61°22W 329 D5
Anambar → Pakistan 30°15N 68°50E 242 D3
Anambas, Kepulauan
Indonesia 3°20N 106°30E 234 B3
Anambas Is. = Anambas,
Kepulauan Indonesia 3°20N 106°30E 234 B3
Anambra □ Nigeria 6°20N 7°0E 263 D6
Anamé Vanuatu 20°8S 169°47E 287 K7
Anamosa U.S.A. 42°7N 91°17W 310 B5
Anamur Turkey 36°8N 32°58E 250 B3
Anamur → Turkey 36°5N 32°53E 250 B3
Anamur Burnu Turkey 36°2N 32°47E 250 B3
Anan Japan 33°54N 134°40E 222 D6
Anand India 22°32N 72°59E 242 H5
Anandapuram India 14°5N 75°12E 245 G2
Anandpur India 21°16N 86°13E 244 D8
Anánes Greece 36°33N 24°9E 204 E6
Anangu Pitjantjatjara ☼
Australia 27°0S 132°0E 279 E5
Ananindeua Brazil 1°22S 48°22W 332 B2
Anantapur India 14°39N 77°42E 245 G3
Anantnag India 33°45N 75°10E 243 C6
Ananyiv Ukraine 47°44N 29°58E 183 C14
Anapa Russia 44°55N 37°25E 189 K9
Anapodiaris → Greece 34°59N 25°20E 207 F6
Anápolis = Simão Dias
Brazil 10°44S 37°49W 332 D4
Anápolis Brazil 16°15S 48°50W 333 E2
Anapu → Brazil 1°53S 50°53W 329 D7
Anār Iran 30°55N 55°13E 247 D7
Anār Darreh Afghan. 32°46N 61°39E 240 B1
Anārak Iran 33°25N 53°40E 247 C7
Anarisfjällen Sweden 63°6N 13°10E 162 A7
Anas → India 23°26N 74°0E 242 H5
Añasco Puerto Rico 18°17N 67°8W 321 b
Anata West Bank 31°49N 35°16E 123 B2
Anatahan N. Marianas 16°21N 145°40E 302 a
Anatolia = Anadolu Turkey 39°0N 30°0E 212 C5
Anatoliki Makedonia kai Thraki □
Greece 41°10N 24°30E 203 E8
Anatsogno Madag. 23°33S 43°46E 272 C1
Añatuya Argentina 28°20S 62°50W 334 B3
Anatye ☼ Australia 22°29S 137°3E 280 C2
Anauá → Brazil 0°58N 61°21W 329 C5
Anaunethad L. Canada 60°55N 104°25W 297 A8
Anavilhanas, Arquipélago das
Brazil 2°42S 60°45W 329 D5
Anbyŏn N. Korea 39°1N 127°35E 224 C3
Ancares, Sierra dos Spain 42°51N 6°52W 194 C4
Ancares ⌓ Spain 42°50N 6°40W 194 C4
Ancash □ Peru 9°30S 77°45W 330 B2
Ancaster Canada 43°13N 79°59W 312 C5
Ancenis France 47°21N 1°10W 172 E5
Anchieta = Piatã Brazil 13°9S 41°48W 333 D3
Anch'ing = Anqing
China 30°30N 117°3E 229 B11
Ancho, Canal Chile 50°0S 74°20W 336 D2
Anchor Bay U.S.A. 38°48N 123°34W 306 G3
Anchorage U.S.A. 61°13N 149°54W 303 F10
Anchorage ✈ (ANC)
U.S.A. 61°10N 150°0W 303 F10
Anchuras Spain 39°29N 4°50W 195 F6
Anchuthengu India 8°40N 76°46E 245 K3
Anci China 39°20N 116°40E 226 E9
Ancohuma, Nevado
Bolivia 16°0S 68°50W 330 D4
Ancol Indonesia 6°7S 106°49E 122 A1
Ancón Peru 11°50S 77°10W 330 C2
Ancona Italy 43°38N 13°30E 199 E10
Ancud Chile 42°0S 73°50W 336 B2
Ancud, G. de Chile 42°0S 73°0W 336 B2
Ancy-le-Franc France 47°46N 4°10E 173 E11
Anda Heilongjiang, China 46°24N 125°19E 219 B14
Anda Phil. 16°17N 119°57E 232 C2
Andacollo Argentina 37°10S 70°42W 334 D1
Andacollo Chile 30°14S 71°6W 334 C1
Andahuaylas Peru 13°40S 73°25W 330 C3
Andaingo Madag. 18°12S 48°17E 272 B2
Andalgalá Argentina 27°40S 66°30W 334 B2
Åndalsnes Norway 62°35N 7°43E 164 B4
Andalucía □ Spain 37°35N 5°0W 195 H6
'Andalus Iraq 33°19N 44°18E 113 B1
Andalusia = Andalucía □
Spain 37°35N 5°0W 195 H6
Andalusia U.S.A. 31°18N 86°29W 315 F11
Andaman & Nicobar Is. □
India 10°0N 93°0E 245 K11
Andaman Is. Ind. Oc. 12°30N 92°45E 245 H11
Andaman Sea Ind. Oc. 13°0N 96°0E 230 B1
Andamooka Australia 30°27S 137°9E 281 E2
Andapa Madag. 14°39S 49°39E 272 A2
Andara Namibia 18°2S 21°9E 270 A3
Andaraí Bahia, Brazil 12°48S 41°20W 333 D3
Andaraí Rio de J., Brazil 22°56S 43°14W 135 B1
Andelot-Blancheville
France 48°15N 5°18E 173 D12
Andenes Norway 69°19N 16°18E 160 B17
Andenne Belgium 50°28N 5°5E 170 D5
Andéranboukane Mali 15°26N 3°2E 263 B5
Anderlecht Belgium 50°50N 4°19E 116 A1
Andermatt Switz. 46°38N 8°35E 179 J4
Andernach Germany 50°26N 7°24E 178 E3
Andernos-les-Bains France 44°44N 1°6W 174 D2
Andersen Air Force Base ✈ (UAM)
Guam 13°35N 144°55E 302 d
Anderslöv Sweden 55°26N 13°19E 163 J7
Anderson Vic., Australia 38°31S 145°26E 283 E6
Anderson Alaska,
U.S.A. 64°25N 149°15W 303 D10
Anderson Calif., U.S.A. 40°27N 122°18W 304 F2
Anderson Ind., U.S.A. 40°10N 85°41W 311 D11
Anderson Mo., U.S.A. 36°39N 94°27W 308 G6
Anderson S.C., U.S.A. 34°31N 82°39W 315 D13
Anderson → Canada 69°42N 129°0W 294 D6
Anderson I. India 12°46N 92°43E 245 H11
Anderson Park U.S.A. 33°45N 84°27W 113 B2
Andersonville U.S.A. 32°12N 84°9W 316 C5
Andersonville ⌓ U.S.A. 32°12N 84°1W 316 C5
Anderstorp Sweden 57°19N 13°39E 163 G7
Andes Colombia 5°39N 75°54W 328 B2
Andes N.Y., U.S.A. 42°12N 74°47W 313 D10
Andes, Cord. de los S. Amer. 20°0S 68°0W 330 E4
Andfjorden Norway 69°10N 16°20E 160 B17
Andhra, L. India 18°54N 73°32E 244 E1
Andhra Pradesh □ India 18°0N 79°0E 244 F4
Andijon Uzbekistan 41°10N 72°15E 217 D8
Andijon □ Uzbekistan 40°45N 72°20E 217 D8
Andikithira = Antikythira
Greece 35°52N 23°15E 204 F5
Andilamena Madag. 17°1S 48°35E 272 B2
Andīmeshk Iran 32°27N 48°21E 213 F13
Andímilos = Antimilos
Greece 36°47N 24°12E 204 E6
Anding = Anting Taiwan 23°7N 120°14E 225 C2
Andingmen China 39°55N 116°23E 114 B2
Andiparos = Antiparos
Greece 37°0N 25°3E 205 D7
Andipaxoi = Antipaxi
Greece 39°9N 20°13E 204 B2
Andipsara = Antipsara
Greece 38°30N 25°29E 205 C7
Andizhan = Andijon
Uzbekistan 41°10N 72°15E 217 D8
Andkhvoy Afghan. 36°52N 65°8E 240 A2
Andoain Spain 43°13N 2°1W 196 B2
Andoany Madag. 13°25S 48°16E 272 A2
Andoas Peru 2°55S 76°25W 328 D2
Andohahela ⌓ Madag. 24°4S 46°44E 272 C2
Andol India 17°51N 78°4E 244 F4
Andola India 16°57N 76°50E 244 F3
Andong S. Korea 36°40N 128°43E 224 D4
Andorra Spain 40°59N 0°28W 196 E4
Andorra ■ Europe 42°30N 1°30E 174 F5
Andorra La Vella Andorra 42°31N 1°32E 174 F5
Andover Hants., U.K. 51°12N 1°29W 169 F6
Andover Kans., U.S.A. 37°43N 97°7W 308 G5
Andover Maine, U.S.A. 44°38N 70°45W 313 B14
Andover Mass., U.S.A. 42°40N 71°8W 313 D13
Andover N.J., U.S.A. 40°59N 74°45W 313 F10
Andover N.Y., U.S.A. 42°10N 77°48W 312 D7
Andover Ohio, U.S.A. 41°36N 80°34W 312 E4
Andøya Norway 69°10N 15°50E 160 B16
Andrade Brazil 4°40S 63°49W 329 D5
Andradina Brazil 20°54S 51°23W 333 F1
Andrahary Madag. 13°37S 49°17E 272 A2
Andramasina Madag. 19°11S 47°35E 272 B2
Andranopasy Madag. 21°17S 43°44E 272 C1
Andranovory Madag. 23°8S 44°10E 272 C1
Andratx Spain 39°39N 2°25E 206 B3
Andravida Greece 37°54N 21°16E 204 D3
André Félix △ C.A.R. 9°29N 23°18E 264 A4
Andreanof Is. U.S.A. 51°30N 176°0W 303 L4
Andreapol Russia 56°40N 32°17E 188 D7
Andrée Land Greenland 73°40N 26°0W 154 C8
Andrews S.C., U.S.A. 33°27N 79°34W 315 E15
Andrews Tex., U.S.A. 32°19N 102°33W 314 E3
Andreyev = Jędrzejów
Poland 50°35N 20°15E 185 H7
Andreyevka Russia 52°19N 51°55E 190 D10
Ándria Italy 41°13N 16°17E 201 A9
Andriamena Madag. 17°26S 47°30E 272 B2
Andriandampy Madag. 22°45S 45°41E 272 C2
Andriba Madag. 17°30S 46°58E 272 B2
Andrijevica Montenegro 42°45N 19°48E 202 D3
Andringitra ⌓ Madag. 22°13S 46°55E 272 C2
Andritsena Greece 37°29N 21°52E 204 D3
Androka Madag. 24°58S 44°2E 272 C1
Andropov = Rybinsk
Russia 58°5N 38°50E 188 C10
Andros Greece 37°50N 24°57E 204 D6
Andros I. Bahamas 24°30N 78°0W 320 B4
Andros Town Bahamas 24°43N 77°47W 320 B4
Androth I. India 10°50N 73°41E 245 J1
Androy □ Madag. 25°10S 46°10E 272 D3
Andrychów Poland 49°51N 19°18E 185 J6
Andselv Norway 69°4N 18°34E 160 B18
Andújar Spain 38°3N 4°5W 195 G6
Andulo Angola 11°25S 16°45E 265 E3
Åneby Akershus, Norway 60°5N 10°51E 164 D7
Aneby Sweden 57°48N 14°49E 163 G8
Anéfis Mali 18°2N 0°36E 263 B5
Anegada Br. Virgin Is. 18°45N 64°20W 321 C7
Anegada, B. Argentina 40°20S 62°20W 336 B4
Anegada Passage
W. Indies 18°15N 63°45W 321 C7
Aného Togo 6°12N 1°34E 263 D5
Aneityum Vanuatu 20°12S 169°45E 287 K7
Anelghowhat Vanuatu 20°19S 169°53E 287 K7
Añelo Argentina 38°20S 68°45W 336 A3
Anenii-Noi Moldova 46°53N 29°15E 183 D14
Aneto, Pico de Spain 42°37N 0°40E 196 C5
Änew Turkmenistan 37°52N 58°31E 216 E5
Aney Niger 19°15N 12°50E 259 E2
Añez Bolivia 15°40S 63°10W 331 D5
Anfu China 27°21N 114°40E 229 D10
Ang Mo Kio Singapore 1°23N 103°50E 138 A3
Ang Thong Thailand 14°35N 100°31E 236 E3
Ang Thong, Ko Thailand 9°37N 99°41E 237 b
Ang Thong, Mu Ko △
Thailand 9°40N 99°43E 237 b
Angadanan Phil. 16°45N 121°45E 232 C3
Angamos, Punta Chile 23°1S 70°32W 334 A1
Angara → Russia 58°5N 94°20E 215 D10
Angara-Débou Benin 11°19N 3°3E 263 C5
Angarbaka South Sudan 9°44N 24°44E 257 F1
Angarsk Russia 52°30N 104°0E 218 A9
Angas Hills Australia 23°0S 127°50E 278 D4
Angaston Australia 34°30S 139°8E 282 C3
Angat Phil. 14°56N 121°2E 232 D3
Angaur I. Palau 6°54N 134°9E 288 c
Ånge Sweden 62°31N 15°35E 162 B9
Ángel, Salto = Angel Falls
Venezuela 5°57N 62°30W 329 B5
Ángel de la Guarda, I.
Mexico 29°20N 113°25W 318 B2
Angel Falls Venezuela 5°57N 62°30W 329 B5
Angel I. U.S.A. 37°52N 122°25W 136 A2
Angel Island State Park ⌓
U.S.A. 37°52N 122°25W 136 A2
Angeles Phil. 15°9N 120°33E 232 D3
Ängelholm Sweden 56°15N 12°50E 163 H6
Angels Camp U.S.A. 38°4N 120°32W 306 G6
Ängelsberg Sweden 59°58N 16°0E 162 E10
Anger → Ethiopia 9°37N 36°6E 257 F4
Angerburg = Węgorzewo
Poland 54°13N 21°43E 184 D8
Angereb Ethiopia 13°11N 37°7E 257 E4
Angereb → Ethiopia 13°45N 36°40E 257 E4
Ångermanälven →
Sweden 63°0N 17°20E 162 A11
Ångermanland Sweden 63°36N 17°45E 160 E17
Angermünde Germany 53°0N 14°0E 178 D9
Angers Qué., Canada 45°31N 75°29W 313 A9
Angers Maine-et-Loire,
France 47°30N 0°35W 172 E6
Angerville France 48°19N 2°0E 173 D9
Ångesån → Sweden 66°16N 22°47E 160 C20
Angical Brazil 12°0S 44°42W 333 D3
Angikuni L. Canada 62°12N 99°59W 297 A9
Angke, Kali → Indonesia 6°6S 106°46E 122 A1
Angkor Cambodia 13°22N 103°50E 236 F4
Angledool Australia 29°5S 147°55E 281 D4
Anglem, Mt. N.Z. 46°45S 167°53E 285 G2
Anglès Spain 41°57N 2°38E 196 D7
Anglesey U.K. 53°17N 4°20W 168 D3
Anglesey, Isle of □ U.K. 53°16N 4°18W 168 D3
Anglet France 43°29N 1°31W 174 E2
Angleton U.S.A. 29°10N 95°26W 314 G7
Anglin → France 46°42N 0°52E 174 B4
Anglisidhes Cyprus 34°51N 33°27E 207 F9
Anglure France 48°35N 3°50E 173 D10
Angmagssalik = Tasiilaq
Greenland 65°40N 37°20W 154 D7
Ango Dem. Rep. of the Congo 4°10N 26°5E 268 B2
Angoche Mozam. 16°8S 39°55E 269 F4
Angoche, I. Mozam. 16°20S 39°50E 269 F4
Angol Chile 37°56S 72°45W 334 D1
Angola Ind., U.S.A. 41°38N 85°0W 311 C12
Angola N.Y., U.S.A. 42°38N 79°2W 312 D5
Angola ■ Africa 12°0S 18°0E 265 E3
Angola Abyssal Plain
Atl. Oc. 15°0S 2°0E 152 H12
Angola Basin Atl. Oc. 15°0S 3°0E 152 H12
Angoon U.S.A. 57°30N 134°35W 303 H14
Angora = Ankara Turkey 39°57N 32°54E 212 C5
Angoram Papua N. G. 4°4S 144°4E 286 C3
Angoulême France 45°39N 0°10E 174 C4
Angoumois France 45°50N 0°25E 174 C4
Angra do Heroismo
Azores 38°39N 27°13W 153 d1
Angra dos Reis Brazil 23°0S 44°10W 335 A7
Angren Uzbekistan 41°1N 70°12E 217 D8
Angtassom Cambodia 11°1N 104°41E 237 G5
Anguang China 45°15N 123°45E 227 B12
Anguilla ☑ W. Indies 18°14N 63°5W 322 a
Anguillita I. Anguilla 18°9N 63°11W 322 a
Angul India 20°51N 85°6E 244 D7
Anguo China 38°28N 115°15E 226 E8
Angurugu Australia 14°0S 136°25E 280 A2
Angus Canada 44°19N 79°53W 312 B5
Angus □ U.K. 56°46N 2°56W 167 E6
Angwa → Zimbabwe 16°0S 30°23E 271 A5
Angyalföld Hungary 47°32N 19°4E 130 B2
Anhanduí → Brazil 21°46S 52°9W 335 A5
Anholt Denmark 56°42N 11°33E 163 H5
Anhua China 28°23N 111°12E 229 C8
Anhui □ China 32°0N 117°0E 229 B11
Anhwei = Anhui □ China 32°0N 117°0E 229 B11
Aniak U.S.A. 61°35N 159°32W 303 F8
Anichab Namibia 21°0S 14°46E 270 B1
Anicuns Brazil 16°28S 49°58W 333 E2
Anidros Greece 36°38N 25°43E 205 E7
Anié Togo 7°42N 1°8E 263 D5
Anik India 19°1N 72°53E 130 A2
Anil Brazil 2°32S 44°14W 332 B3
Animas → U.S.A. 36°43N 108°13W 305 H9
Anin Burma 15°36N 97°50E 236 E1
Anin Warszawa, Poland 52°13N 21°9E 143 B2
Anina Romania 45°6N 21°51E 182 E6
Anini India 28°47N 95°53E 241 A5
Anini-y Phil. 10°25N 121°55E 233 F3
Aninoasa Romania 44°47N 24°10E 183 F9
Añisoc Eq. Guin. 1°51N 10°46E 264 B2
Anita U.S.A. 41°27N 94°46W 310 C2
Anivorano Atsinanana,
Madag. 18°44S 48°58E 272 B2
Anivorano Diana, Madag. 12°44S 49°14E 272 A2
Aniwa Vanuatu 19°17S 169°35E 287 J7
Anjalankoski Finland 60°45N 26°51E 188 B4
Anjangaon India 21°10N 77°20E 244 D3
Anjar = Hawsh Mūssá
Lebanon 33°45N 35°55E 250 E6
Anjar India 23°6N 70°10E 242 H4
Anjengo = Anchuthengu
India 8°40N 76°46E 245 K3
Anji China 30°46N 119°40E 229 B12
Anjidiv I. India 14°40N 74°10E 245 G2
Anjō Japan 34°57N 137°5E 223 C9
Anjou Qué., Canada 45°36N 73°33W 130 A2
Anjou Maine-et-Loire,
France 47°20N 0°15W 172 E6
Anjouan Comoros Is. 12°15S 44°20E 272 a
Anjouan ✈ (AJN)
Comoros Is. 12°9S 44°26E 272 a
Anjozorobe Madag. 18°22S 47°52E 272 B2
Anju N. Korea 39°36N 125°40E 224 C2
Anka Nigeria 12°13N 5°58E 263 C6
Ankaboa, Tanjona
Madag. 21°58S 43°20E 272 C1
Ankang China 32°40N 109°1E 226 H5
Ankara Turkey 39°57N 32°54E 212 C5
Ankara □ Turkey 39°55N 32°50E 212 C5
Ankarafantsika ⌓ Madag. 16°8S 47°5E 272 B2
Ankaramena Madag. 21°57S 46°39E 272 C2
Ankarata Madag. 19°20S 47°30E 272 B2
Ankarsrum Sweden 57°41N 16°20E 163 G10
Ankasakasa Madag. 16°21S 44°52E 272 B1
Ankavandra Madag. 18°46S 45°18E 272 B2
Ankazoabo Madag. 22°18S 44°31E 272 C1
Ankazobe Madag. 18°20S 47°10E 272 B2
Ankeny U.S.A. 41°44N 93°36W 310 C3
Ankhialo = Pomorie
Bulgaria 42°32N 27°41E 203 D11
Ankilimalinika Madag. 22°58S 43°45E 272 C1
Ankilizato Madag. 20°25S 45°1E 272 C2
Anking = Anqing China 30°30N 117°3E 229 B11
Ankisabe Madag. 19°17S 46°29E 272 B2
Anklam Germany 53°51N 13°41E 178 B9
Ankleshwar India 21°38N 73°3E 244 D1
Ankober Ethiopia 9°35N 39°40E 257 F4
Ankola India 14°40N 74°18E 245 G2
Ankoro
Dem. Rep. of the Congo 6°45S 26°55E 268 D2
Ankororoka Madag. 25°30S 45°11E 272 D2
Ankpa Nigeria 7°22N 7°38E 263 D6
Anlong China 25°2N 105°27E 228 E5
Anlong Veng Cambodia 14°14N 104°5E 236 E5
Anlu China 31°15N 113°45E 229 B9
Anmyeondo S. Korea 36°25N 126°25E 224 D3
Ann Burma 19°48N 94°0E 241 F5
Ånn Sweden 63°19N 12°33E 162 A6
Ann, C. U.S.A. 42°38N 70°35W 313 D14
Ann Arbor U.S.A. 42°17N 83°45W 311 B13
Anna Russia 51°28N 40°23E 190 E5
Anna Ill., U.S.A. 37°28N 89°15W 308 G9
Anna Ohio, U.S.A. 40°24N 84°11W 311 D12
Anna Regina Guyana 7°10N 58°30W 329 B6
Annaba Algeria 36°50N 7°46E 261 A6
Annaba □ Algeria 36°12N 7°45E 261 A6
Annaberg-Buchholz
Germany 50°34N 13°0E 178 E9
Annai Guyana 3°57N 59°8W 329 C6
Annaka Japan 36°19N 138°54E 223 A10
Annalee → Ireland 54°2N 7°24W 166 B4
Annalee Heights U.S.A. 38°51N 77°10W 143 B1
Annam = Trung Phan
Vietnam 17°0N 109°0E 236 D6
Annamitique, Chaîne
Asia 17°0N 106°0E 236 D6
Annan U.K. 54°59N 3°16W 167 G5
Annan → U.K. 54°58N 3°16W 167 G5
Annanberg Papua N. G. 4°52S 144°42E 286 C3
Annapolis U.S.A. 38°59N 76°30W 309 F15
Annapolis Royal Canada 44°44N 65°32W 299 D6
Annapurna Nepal 28°34N 83°50E 243 E10
Anne Frankhuis Amsterdam, Neths. 112 a1
Annean, L. Australia 26°54S 118°14E 279 E2
Anneberg Sweden 57°44N 14°49E 163 G8
Annecy France 45°55N 6°8E 175 C10
Annecy, Lac d' France 45°52N 6°11E 175 C10
Annemasse France 46°12N 6°16E 173 F13
Annenfeld = Şämkir
Azerbaijan 40°50N 46°0E 191 K8
Annensky Most Russia 60°45N 37°10E 188 B9
Annette I. U.S.A. 55°9N 131°28W 296 B2
Annette Island ▲ U.S.A. 55°9N 131°28W 303 J15
Annigeri India 15°26N 75°26E 245 G2
Anning China 24°55N 102°26E 228 E4
Anniston U.S.A. 33°39N 85°50W 316 B4
Annobón Atl. Oc. 1°25S 5°36E 255 G4
Annonay France 45°15N 4°40E 175 C8
Annot France 43°58N 6°38E 175 E10
Annotto B. Jamaica 18°17N 76°45W 320 a
Annotto Bay Jamaica 18°16N 76°47W 320 a
Ånnsjön Sweden 63°19N 12°34E 162 A6
Annville U.S.A. 40°20N 76°31W 313 F8
Annweiler Germany 49°12N 7°57E 179 F3
Ano Poroia Greece 41°17N 23°2E 202 E7
Ano Siros Greece 37°29N 24°56E 204 D6
Anogi Greece 38°25N 20°40E 207 C2
Anogia Greece 35°16N 24°52E 207 E6
Anorotsangana Madag. 13°56S 47°55E 272 A2
Anosibe Madag. 19°26S 48°13E 272 B2
Anosy □ Madag. 24°0S 46°0E 272 C2
Anou Mellene Mali 17°29N 0°33E 263 B5
Anoumaba Ivory C. 6°23N 4°38W 262 D4
Anping Hebei, China 38°15N 115°30E 226 E8
Anping Liaoning, China 41°5N 123°30E 224 B1
Anpu Gang China 21°25N 109°50E 228 G7
Anqing China 30°30N 117°3E 229 B11
Anqiu China 36°25N 119°10E 227 F10
Anren China 26°43N 113°18E 229 D9
Ansager Denmark 55°43N 8°45E 163 J2
Ansai China 36°50N 109°20E 226 F5
Ansan S. Korea 37°21N 126°52E 224 D3
Ansbach Germany 49°28N 10°34E 179 F6
Anse-Bertrand Guadeloupe 16°28N 61°32W 322 e
Anse Boileau Seychelles 4°43S 55°29E 272 c
Anse la Raye St. Lucia 13°55N 61°3W 323 m
Anse Royale Seychelles 4°44S 55°31E 272 c
Anseba → Eritrea 16°0N 38°30E 257 D4
Anseong S. Korea 37°0N 127°16E 224 D3
Anserma Colombia 5°13N 75°48W 328 B2
Ansfelden Austria 48°12N 14°17E 180 C7

Anshan *China* 41°5N 122°58E **224** B1
Anshun *China* 26°18N 105°57E **228** D5
Ansião *Portugal* 39°56N 8°27W **194** F2
Ansley *U.S.A.* 41°18N 99°23W **308** E4
Ansó *Spain* 42°51N 0°48W **196** C4
Ansoáin *Spain* 42°50N 1°38W **196** C3
Anson *U.S.A.* 32°45N 99°54W **314** E5
Anson B. *Australia* 13°20S 130°6E **278** B5
Ansongo *Mali* 15°25N 0°35E **263** B5
Ansongo-Ménaka △ *Mali* 15°3N 1°37E **263** B5
Ansonia *Conn., U.S.A.* 41°21N 73°5W **313** E11
Ansonia *Ohio, U.S.A.* 40°13N 84°38W **311** D12
Anstruther *U.K.* 56°14N 2°41W **167** E6
Ansudu *Indonesia* 2°11S 139°22E **231** E9
Antabamba *Peru* 14°40S 73°0W **330** C3
Antagarh *India* 20°6N 81°9E **244** D5
Antakya = Hatay *Turkey* 36°14N 36°10E **250** B7
Antalaha *Madag.* 14°57S 50°20E **272** A3
Antalät *Libya* 31°8N 20°42E **258** B4
Antalya *Turkey* 36°52N 30°45E **250** B1
Antalya □ *Turkey* 36°50N 30°45E **250** B1
Antalya ✈ (AYT) *Turkey* 36°54N 30°47E **212** D4
Antalya Körfezi *Turkey* 36°15N 31°30E **250** B2
Antambohobe *Madag.* 22°20S 46°47E **272** C2
Antanambao-Manampotsy
    Madag. 19°29S 48°34E **272** B2
Antanambe *Madag.* 16°26S 49°52E **272** B2
Antananarivo *Madag.* 18°55S 47°31E **272** B2
Antananarivo □ *Madag.* 19°0S 47°0E **272** B2
Antanifotsy *Madag.* 19°39S 47°19E **272** B2
Antanimbaribe *Madag.* 21°30S 44°48E **272** C1
Antanimora *Madag.* 24°49S 45°40E **272** C2
Antarctic Pen. *Antarctica* 67°0S 60°0W **151** C18
Antarctica 90°0S 0°0 **151** E3
Antécume Pata *Fr. Guiana* 3°17N 54°4W **329** C7
Antelope = Zimbabwe 21°2S 28°31E **269** G2
Antelope *U.S.A.* 37°6N 37°23E **250** A8
Antequera *Paraguay* 24°8S 57°7W **334** A4
Antequera *Spain* 37°5N 4°33W **195** H6
Antero, Mt. *U.S.A.* 38°41N 106°15W **304** G10
Antevamena *Madag.* 21°2S 44°8E **272** C1
Anthony *Fla., U.S.A.* 29°18N 82°7W **317** F7
Anthony *Kans., U.S.A.* 37°9N 98°2W **308** G4
Anthony *N. Mex., U.S.A.* 32°0N 106°36W **305** K10
Anti Atlas *Morocco* 30°0N 8°30W **260** C3
Anti-Lebanon = Sharqi, Al Jabal ash
    Lebanon 33°40N 36°10E **250** B5
Antibes *France* 43°34N 7°6E **175** E11
Antibes, C. d' *France* 43°31N 7°7E **175** E11
Anticosti, Î. d' *Canada* 49°30N 63°0W **299** C7
Antifer, C. d' *France* 49°41N 0°10E **172** C7
Antigo *U.S.A.* 45°9N 89°9W **308** C9
Antigonish *Canada* 45°38N 61°58W **299** C7
Antigua *Canary Is.* 28°24N 14°1W **153** e2
Antigua *Guatemala* 14°34N 90°41W **320** D1
Antigua *W. Indies* 17°0N 61°50W **322** b
Antigua & Barbuda ■
    W. Indies 17°20N 61°48W **322** b
Antigua & B. 17°8N 61°47W **322** b
Antigua Int. ✈ (ANU)
    Antigua & B. 17°8N 61°47W **322** b
Antigues, Pte. d'
    Guadeloupe 16°26N 61°32W **322** e
Antikythira *Greece* 35°52N 23°15E **204** F5
Antilla *Cuba* 20°40N 75°50W **320** B4
Antilles = West Indies
    Cent. Amer. 15°0N 65°0W **321** D7
Antimilos *Greece* 36°47N 24°12E **204** E6
Anting *Taiwan* 23°7N 120°14E **225** C2
Antioch = Hatay *Turkey* 36°14N 36°10E **250** B7
Antioch *U.S.A.* 38°1N 121°48W **306** G5
Antioche, Pertuis d' *France* 46°6N 1°20W **174** B2
Antioquia *Colombia* 6°40N 75°55W **328** B2
Antioquia □ *Colombia* 7°0N 75°30W **328** B2
Antiparos *Greece* 37°0N 25°3E **205** D7
Antipaxi *Greece* 39°9N 20°13E **204** B2
Antipodes Is. *Pac. Oc.* 49°45S 178°40E **288** M9
Antipolo *Phil.* 14°35N 121°10E **232** D3
Antipsara *Greece* 38°30N 25°46E **205** F8
Antique □ *Phil.* 11°10N 122°5E **233** F4
Antirio *Greece* 38°20N 21°46E **204** C3
Antlers *U.S.A.* 34°14N 95°37W **314** D7
Antoetra *Madag.* 20°46S 47°20E **272** C2
Antofagasta *Chile* 23°50S 70°30W **334** A1
Antofagasta □ *Chile* 24°0S 69°0W **334** A2
Antofagasta de la Sierra
    Argentina 26°5S 67°20W **334** B2
Antofalla *Argentina* 25°30S 68°5W **334** B2
Antofalla, Salar de
    Argentina 25°40S 67°45W **334** B2
Antoine, L. *Grenada* 12°11N 61°36W **323** q
Anton *U.S.A.* 33°49N 102°10W **314** E3
Antongila, Helodrano
    Madag. 15°30S 49°50E **272** B2
Antonibé *Madag.* 15°7S 47°24E **272** B2
Antonina *Brazil* 25°26S 48°42E **335** B6
Antônio B. Won Pat Int. ✈ (GUM)
    Guam 13°29N 144°48E **302** a
Antonio Carlos Jobim Int. ✈ (GIG)
    Brazil 22°49S 43°15W **135** A1
António Enes = Angoche
    Mozam. 16°8S 39°55E **269** F4
Antony *France* 48°44N 2°17E **134** B2
Antrain *France* 48°28N 1°30W **172** D5
Antratsyt *Ukraine* 48°7N 39°5E **189** H10
Antrim *Antrim, U.K.* 54°43N 6°14W **166** B5
Antrim *Ohio, U.S.A.* 40°7N 81°21W **312** F3
Antrim □ *U.K.* 54°56N 6°25W **166** B5
Antrim, Mts. of *U.K.* 55°3N 6°14W **166** A5
Antrim Plateau *Australia* 18°8S 128°20E **278** C4
Antriol *Bonaire* 12°12N 68°16W **322** h
Antrodoco *Italy* 42°25N 13°5E **199** F10
Antropovo *Russia* 58°24N 43°6E **190** A6
Antsalova *Madag.* 18°40S 44°37E **272** B1
Antsenavolo *Madag.* 21°24S 48°3E **272** C2
Antsiafabositra *Madag.* 17°18S 46°57E **272** B2
Antsirabe *Sofia, Madag.* 15°57S 48°58E **272** B2
Antsirabe *Vakinankaratra,
    Madag.* 19°55S 47°2E **272** B2
Antsiranana *Madag.* 12°25S 49°20E **272** A2
Antsohihy *Madag.* 14°50S 47°59E **272** A2
Antsohimbondrona Seranana
    Madag. 13°7S 48°48E **272** A2
Antu *China* 42°30N 128°20E **227** C15
Antufash *Yemen* 15°22N 42°25E **248** D3
Antung *Taiwan* 23°18N 121°20E **225** C3
Antwerp = Antwerpen
    Belgium 51°13N 4°25E **170** C4
Antwerp *N.Y., U.S.A.* 44°12N 75°37W **313** B9
Antwerp *Ohio, U.S.A.* 41°11N 84°45W **311** C12
Antwerpen *Belgium* 51°13N 4°25E **170** C4
Antwerpen □ *Belgium* 51°15N 4°40E **170** C4
Anukur, C. *Papua N. G.* 5°30S 149°37E **286** D5
Anupgarh *India* 29°10N 73°10E **242** E5
Anuppur *India* 23°6N 81°41E **243** H9
Anuradhapura *Sri Lanka* 8°22N 80°28E **245** K5
Anurrete ○ *Australia* 20°50S 135°38E **280** C2
Anveh *Iran* 27°23N 54°11E **247** E7
Anvers = Antwerpen
    Belgium 51°13N 4°25E **170** C4
Anvers I. *Antarctica* 64°30S 63°40W **151** C17
Anvik *U.S.A.* 62°39N 160°13W **303** E7
Anxi *Fujian, China* 25°2N 118°12E **229** E12
Anxi *Gansu, China* 40°30N 95°43E **218** C3
Anxian *China* 31°40N 104°25E **228** B5
Anxiang *China* 29°22N 112°20E **229** C9
Anxious B. *Australia* 33°24S 134°45E **281** E1
Anyama *Ivory C.* 5°30N 4°3W **262** D4

Anyang *Henan, China* 36°5N 114°21E **226** F8
Anyang *S. Korea* 37°23N 126°55E **227** F14
Anyer *Indonesia* 6°4S 105°53E **234** D3
Anyi *Jiangxi, China* 28°49N 115°25E **229** C10
Anyi *Shanxi, China* 35°2N 111°2E **226** G6
Anyuan *China* 25°9N 115°21E **229** E10
Anyue *China* 30°9N 105°50E **228** B5
Anze *China* 36°10N 112°12E **226** F7
Anzegloufd △ *Algeria* 26°50N 0°1E **261** C6
Anzhenzo-Sudzhensk
    Russia 56°10N 86°0E **214** D9
Ánzio *Italy* 41°27N 12°37E **200** D5
Anzoátegui □ *Venezuela* 9°0N 64°30W **329** B5
Ao Makham *Thailand* 7°50N 98°24E **237** a
Ao Phangnga △ *Thailand* 8°10N 98°32E **237** a
Aoba *Vanuatu* 15°25S 167°50E **287** E5
Aoga-Shima *Japan* 32°28N 139°46E **223** E11
Aohan Qi *China* 43°18N 119°43E **227** C10
Aoiz *Spain* 42°46N 1°22W **196** C3
Aoji *N. Korea* 42°31N 130°23E **224** A5
Aola *Solomon Is.* 9°30S 160°30E **287** M11
Aomen = Macau *China* 22°12N 113°33E **229** F9
Aomori *Japan* 40°45N 140°45E **220** D10
Aomori □ *Japan* 40°45N 140°40E **220** D10
AON Center *Chicago, U.S.A.* **119** b2
t'Aonach, An = Nenagh
    Ireland 52°52N 8°11W **166** D3
Aonla *India* 28°16N 79°11E **243** E8
Aono-Yama *Japan* 34°20N 131°48E **222** C3
Aorai, Mt. *Tahiti* 17°34S 149°30W **289** e
Aoraki Mount Cook *N.Z.* 43°36S 170°9E **285** K3
Aoral, Phnum *Cambodia* 12°0N 104°15E **237** G5
Aorangi Ra. *N.Z.* 41°28S 175°22E **284** H4
Aoreora *Morocco* 28°51N 10°53W **260** C2
Aosta *Italy* 45°45N 7°20E **198** C4
Aotea Harbour *N.Z.* 38°0S 174°50E **284** E5
Aotearoa = New Zealand ■
    Oceania 40°0S 176°0E **284** G5
Aoudéras *Niger* 17°45N 8°20E **259** E1
Aouinet Torkoz *Morocco* 28°31N 9°46E **260** C3
Aouk, Bahr △ *Africa* 8°51N 18°53E **259** G3
Aouk-Aoukalé △ *C.A.R.* 9°52N 21°25E **264** A4
Aoukâr *Mauritania* 17°40N 10°0W **262** B3
Aoulef el Arab *Algeria* 26°55N 1°2E **261** C5
Aousred *W. Sahara* 22°32N 14°17W **260** D2
Aoya *Japan* 35°29N 134°10E **220** F4
Aozou, Couloir d' *Chad* 22°0N 19°0E **259** D3
Ap Lei Chau
    Hong Kong, China 22°14N 114°9E **122** B2
Apá → *S. Amer.* 22°6S 58°2W **334** A4
Apache *U.S.A.* 34°54N 98°22W **314** D5
Apache Junction *U.S.A.* 33°25N 111°33W **305** K8
Apalachee B. *U.S.A.* 30°0N 84°0W **317** F6
Apalachicola *U.S.A.* 29°43N 84°59W **316** F5
Apalachicola → *U.S.A.* 29°43N 84°58W **316** F5
Apalachicola B. *U.S.A.* 29°40N 85°0W **316** F5
Apam *Ghana* 5°19N 0°42W **263** D4
Apamea *Syria* 35°31N 36°28E **250** C7
Apapa *Nigeria* 6°26N 3°21E **124** B2
Apapa Quays *Nigeria* 6°26N 3°22E **124** B2
Apaporis → *Colombia* 1°23S 69°25W **328** D4
Aparados da Serra △
    Brazil 29°10S 50°8W **335** B5
Aparecida = Bertolinia
    Brazil 7°38S 43°57W **332** C3
Aparecida de Goiânia
    Brazil 16°45S 49°16W **333** E2
Aparecida do Taboado
    Brazil 20°5S 51°5W **333** F1
Aparri *Phil.* 18°22N 121°38E **232** A3
Apaturén *Venezuela* 5°6N 62°8W **329** B5
Apataki French Polynesia* 15°26S 146°20W **289** f
Apateu *Romania* 46°36N 21°47E **182** D6
Apatin *Serbia* 45°40N 19°0E **182** E4
Apatity *Russia* 67°34N 33°22E **160** C25
Apatou *Fr. Guiana* 5°10N 54°20W **329** C7
Apatula = Finke
    Australia 25°34S 134°35E **280** D1
Apatzingán *Mexico* 19°5N 102°21W **318** D4
Apayao □ *Phil.* 18°10N 121°10E **232** A3
Apeldoorn *Netherlands* 52°13N 5°57E **170** B5
Apelação *Portugal* 38°48N 9°7W **126** A2
Apen *Germany* 53°13N 7°48E **178** B3
Apennines = Appennini
    Italy 44°30N 10°0E **198** D7
Apenrade = Aabenraa
    Denmark 55°3N 9°25E **163** J3
Apere → *Bolivia* 13°44S 65°18W **331** C4
Apgujeong *S. Korea* 37°32N 127°2E **128** b
Aphrodisias *Turkey* 37°42N 28°46E **205** D10
Api *Nepal* 30°0N 80°57E **218** F5
Apia *Samoa* 13°50S 171°50W **287** V20
Apiacás, Serra dos *Brazil* 9°50S 57°0W **331** B6
Apiaí *Brazil* 24°31S 48°50W **333** F2
Apiaú → *Brazil* 2°39N 61°12W **329** C5
Apiaú, Serra de *Brazil* 2°30N 62°0W **329** C5
Apidiá → *Brazil* 11°39S 61°11W **331** C5
Apies → *S. Africa* 25°15S 28°8E **271** C4
Apinajé *Brazil* 11°31S 48°18W **333** D2
Apiti *N.Z.* 39°58S 175°54E **284** F4
Apizaco *Mexico* 19°25N 98°8W **319** D5
Aplao *Peru* 16°0S 72°40W **330** D3
Apo, Mt. *Phil.* 6°53N 125°14E **233** H5
Apo East Pass. *Phil.* 12°40N 120°42E **232** E2
Apo Reef △ *Phil.* 12°50N 120°22E **232** E2
Apo West Pass. *Phil.* 12°31N 120°22E **232** E2
Apodi *Brazil* 5°39S 37°48W **332** C4
Apoera *Suriname* 5°12N 57°10W **329** B6
Apokia *Greece* 36°5N 27°48E **206** E11
Apolakkia *Greece* 36°5N 27°45E **206** E11
Apolakkia, Ormos *Greece* 36°5N 27°45E **206** E11
Apolda *Germany* 51°2N 11°32E **178** D7
Apolima *Samoa* 13°49S 172°9W **287** V19
Apollo Bay *Australia* 38°45S 143°40E **282** E5
Apollonia = Süsah *Libya* 32°52N 21°59E **258** B4
Apollonia *Greece* 36°15N 27°58E **206** E11
Apolo *Bolivia* 14°30S 68°30W **330** C4
Apónguao → *Venezuela* 4°48N 61°36W **329** B5
Apopa *El Salv.* 13°48N 89°10W **320** D2
Apopka *U.S.A.* 28°40N 81°31W **317** G8
Apopka, L. *U.S.A.* 28°37N 81°37W **317** G8
Apoquindo *Chile* 33°24S 70°32W **137** B2
Aporé *Brazil* 18°58S 52°1W **333** E1
Aporé → *Brazil* 19°27S 50°57W **333** E1
Aporema *Brazil* 1°14N 50°49W **333** B1
Aporé Is. *U.S.A.* 47°0N 90°40W **308** B8
Aposentos *Argentina* 46°55S 91°0W **308** B8
Apóstoles *Argentina* 28°0S 56°0W **335** B4
Apostol Andreas, C.
    Cyprus 35°42N 34°35E **207** E10
Apostolove *Ukraine* 47°39N 33°39E **189** J7
Apoteri *Guyana* 4°2N 58°32W **329** C6
Appalachian Mts. *U.S.A.* 38°0N 80°0W **309** G14
Appalachian *Sweden* 60°29N 14°10E **162** D8
Appennino Lucano-Val d'Agri-
    Lagonegrese *Italy* 40°16N 16°10E **201** B9
Appennino Tosco-Emiliano □
    Italy 44°10N 10°0E **198** D7
Appenzell *Switz.* 47°20N 9°25E **179** H5
Appenzell-Ausser Rhoden □
    Switz. 47°23N 9°23E **179** H5
Appenzell-Inner Rhoden □
    Switz. 47°20N 9°25E **179** H5
Appiano *Italy* 46°28N 11°15E **199** B8

Apple Hill *Canada* 45°13N 74°46W **313** A10
Apple Valley *U.S.A.* 34°32N 117°14W **307** L9
Appleby-in-Westmorland
    U.K. 54°35N 2°29W **168** C5
Appledore *U.K.* 51°3N 4°13W **169** F3
Appleton *U.S.A.* 44°16N 88°25W **308** C9
Appleton City *U.S.A.* 38°11N 94°2W **310** F7
Appleton Rum Distillery
    Jamaica 18°10N 77°44W **320** a
Appling *U.S.A.* 33°33N 82°19W **316** F7
Apra Harbor *Guam* 13°26N 144°40E **302** d
Apricena *Italy* 41°47N 15°27E **199** G12
April → *Papua N. G.* 4°18S 142°26E **286** C2
Aprília *Italy* 41°36N 12°39E **200** A5
Apsheronsk *Russia* 44°28N 39°42E **191** H4
Apsley *Canada* 44°45N 78°6W **312** B6
Apt *France* 43°53N 5°24E **175** E9
Apterskarskiy Ostrov
    Russia 59°57N 30°20E **137** B2
Apuane, Alpi *Italy* 44°7N 10°14E **198** D7
Apuaú *Brazil* 2°25S 60°53W **329** D5
Apucarana *Brazil* 23°55S 51°33W **335** A5
Apulia = Púglia □ *Italy* 41°15N 16°15E **201** A9
Apurashokoru *Palau* 7°16N 134°17E **288** c
Apurauan *Phil.* 9°35N 118°20E **233** G2
Apure □ *Venezuela* 7°10N 68°50W **328** B4
Apure → *Venezuela* 7°37N 66°25W **328** B4
Apurímac □ *Peru* 14°0S 73°0W **330** C3
Apurímac → *Peru* 12°17S 73°56W **330** C3
Apuseni, Munţii *Romania* 46°30N 22°45E **182** D7
Āq Qālā *Iran* 37°10N 54°30E **247** B7
'Aqaba = Al 'Aqabah *Jordan* 29°31N 35°0E **251** J6
Aqaba, G. of *Red Sea* 29°0N 34°40E **251** K5
'Aqabah, Khalīj al = Aqaba, G. of
    Red Sea 29°0N 34°40E **251** K5
Aqadyr *Kazakhstan* 48°17N 74°50E **217** C8
Āqcheh *Afghan.* 36°56N 66°11E **240** A2
'Aqdā *Iran* 32°26N 53°37E **247** C7
Aqiq *Sudan* 18°14N 38°12E **256** D4
Aqiq, Khalig *Sudan* 18°20N 38°10E **256** D4
'Aqīq, W. al → *Si. Arabia* 20°16N 41°40E **248** B3
Aqköl *Kazakhstan* 51°59N 70°56E **217** B8
Aqmola = Astana
    Kazakhstan 51°10N 71°30E **217** B8
Aqmola □ *Kazakhstan* 51°30N 70°0E **217** B8
'Aqrah *Iraq* 36°46N 43°45E **213** D10
Aqsay *Kazakhstan* 51°11N 53°0E **187** D9
Aqshataū *Kazakhstan* 47°59N 74°3E **217** C8
Aqsū *Ongtüstik Qazaqstan,
    Kazakhstan* 42°25N 69°50E **217** D7
Aqsū *Pavlodar, Kazakhstan* 52°2N 76°55E **217** B9
Aqsūgek *Kazakhstan* 44°37N 74°30E **217** D8
Aqtaū *Mangghystaū,
    Kazakhstan* 43°39N 51°12E **187** F9
Aqtaū *Qaraghandy,
    Kazakhstan* 50°14N 73°3E **217** B8
Aqtoghay *Kazakhstan* 46°57N 79°40E **217** D9
Aqtöbe *Kazakhstan* 50°17N 57°10E **187** D10
Aqtoghay *Kazakhstan* 47°0N 84°0E **217** E10
Aqua = Sokhumi *Georgia* 43°0N 41°0E **191** J5
Aquarium of the Americas
    New Orleans, U.S.A. **131** b3
Aquidauana *Brazil* 20°30S 55°50W **331** E6
Aquidauana → *Brazil* 19°44S 56°50W **331** D6
Aquila *Mexico* 18°36N 103°30W **318** D4
Aquileia *Italy* 45°46N 13°22E **199** C10
Aquiles Serdán *Mexico* 28°36N 105°53W **318** B3
Aquin *Haiti* 18°16N 73°24W **321** C5
Aquitain, Bassin *France* 44°0N 0°30W **171** D3
Ar Horqin Qi *China* 43°45N 120°0E **227** C11
Ar Kazimiyah *Iraq* 33°22N 44°20E **113** B1
Ar Rafid *Syria* 32°57N 35°52E **250** F6
Ar Rahḥālīyah *Iraq* 32°44N 43°23E **213** F10
Ar Rāhidah *Yemen* 13°23N 44°19E **248** D4
Ar Ram *West Bank* 31°51N 35°15E **123** A2
Ar Ramādi *Iraq* 33°25N 43°20E **213** F10
Ar Raml *Libya* 26°45N 19°40E **258** C3
Ar Ramthah *Jordan* 32°34N 36°0E **251** F7
Ar Raqqah *Syria* 35°59N 39°8E **213** E8
Ar Raqqah □ *Syria* 36°20N 39°0E **213** D8
Ar Rashidiya = Er Rachidia
    Morocco 31°58N 4°20W **260** B4
Ar Rass *Si. Arabia* 25°50N 43°40E **246** E4
Ar Rastan *Syria* 34°55N 36°43E **250** D7
Ar Rawdah *Si. Arabia* 21°16N 42°50E **248** C3
Ar Rawdah *San'ā', Yemen* 15°26N 44°13E **248** D4
Ar Rawdah *Shabwah,
    Yemen* 14°28N 47°17E **248** D4
Ar Rayyan *Qatar* 25°17N 51°25E **247** E6
Ar Rifā'ī *Iraq* 31°50N 46°10E **246** D5
Ar Riyād *Si. Arabia* 24°41N 46°42E **246** E5
Ar Riyād □ *Si. Arabia* 23°0N 45°50E **248** B4
Ar Riyān *Yemen* 14°33N 49°19E **249** D5
Ar Ru'ays *Qatar* 26°8N 51°12E **247** E6
Ar Rukhaymiyah *Iraq* 29°22N 45°38E **246** D5
Ar Rumaythah *Iraq* 31°31N 45°12E **246** D5
Ar Ruṣāfah *Syria* 35°45N 38°49E **213** E8
Ar Ruṣayfah *Jordan* 32°1N 36°3E **251** F7
Ar Rustāq *Oman* 23°23N 57°26E **249** F8
Ar Ruṭbah *Iraq* 33°0N 40°15E **213** F9
Ar Ruwaydah *Si. Arabia* 23°40N 44°40E **246** E5
Ara *India* 25°35N 84°32E **243** G11
Ara → *Japan* 35°41N 139°50E **140** A4
Ara Goro *Ethiopia* 5°48N 41°18E **257** F5
Ara Tera *Ethiopia* 6°40N 71°10W **328** B3
Arab *U.S.A.* 34°19N 86°30W **315** D11
'Arab, Bahr el →
    South Sudan 9°0N 29°30E **257** F2
Arab, Khalig el *Egypt* 30°55N 29°0E **256** A2
Arab, Shatt al → *Asia* 29°57N 48°34E **247** D6
'Araba, W. → *Egypt* 28°19N 33°31E **256** J8
'Arabābād *Iran* 33°2N 57°41E **247** C8
'Araban *Turkey* 37°28N 37°44E **212** D7
Araban *Turkey* 37°28N 37°44E **212** D7
Arabatskaya Strelka
    Ukraine 45°40N 35°0E **189** K8
Araba/Álava □ *Spain* 42°48N 2°28W **196** C2
Arabba *Italy* 46°30N 11°52E **199** B8
Arabelo *Venezuela* 4°40N 64°30W **329** B5
Arabi *Italy* 31°50N 83°44W **316** D6
Arabia *Asia* 25°0N 45°0E **210** F6
Arabian Basin *Ind. Oc.* 11°30N 65°0E **273** C5
Arabian Desert = Sharqiya, Es
    Sahrâ esh *Egypt* 27°30N 32°30E **256** B3
Arabian Gulf = Persian Gulf
    Asia 27°0N 50°0E **247** E6
Arabian Sea *Ind. Oc.* 16°0N 65°0E **238** F9
Arabistan = Khūzestān □
    Iran 31°0N 49°0E **247** D6
Araç *Turkey* 41°15N 33°21E **212** B5
Aracaju *Brazil* 10°55S 37°4W **332** D4
Aracataca *Colombia* 10°38N 74°9W **328** A3
Aracati *Brazil* 4°30S 37°44W **332** C4
Araçatuba *Brazil* 21°10S 50°30W **335** A5
Araceli *Phil.* 10°33N 119°59E **233** F2
Aracena *Spain* 37°53N 6°38W **195** H4
Aracena, Sierra de *Spain* 37°50N 6°50W **195** H4
Araçuaí *Brazil* 16°52S 42°4W **333** E3
Araçuaí → *Brazil* 16°45S 42°23W **333** E3
'Arad *Israel* 31°15N 35°12E **251** G6
Arad *Romania* 46°10N 21°20E **182** D6
Arad □ *Romania* 46°20N 22°0E **182** D7
Arada *Chad* 15°0N 20°20E **259** F4
Arādān *Iran* 35°21N 52°30E **247** C7
Aradhippou *Cyprus* 34°57N 33°36E **207** E12

Arafura Sea *E. Indies* 9°0S 135°0E **288** H5
Aragarças *Brazil* 15°55S 52°15W **331** D7
Aragón □ *Spain* 41°25N 0°40W **196** B5
Aragón *Spain* 34°2N 85°3W **316** A4
Aragón □ *Spain* 42°13N 1°44W **196** C3
Aragón → *Spain* 42°13N 1°44W **196** C3
Aragua □ *Venezuela* 10°0N 67°10W **328** A4
Aragua de Barcelona
    Venezuela 9°28N 64°49W **329** B5
Araguacema *Brazil* 8°50S 49°20W **332** D2
Araguaçu = Paraguaçu Paulista
    Brazil 22°50S 50°35W **335** A5
Araguaçu *Brazil* 12°49S 49°51W **333** D2
Araguaia → *Brazil* 5°21S 48°41W **332** C2
Araguaia □ *Brazil* 10°30S 50°0W **332** D2
Araguaiana *Brazil* 15°43S 51°51W **331** D7
Araguari *Brazil* 18°38S 48°11W **333** E2
Araguari → *Brazil* 1°15N 49°55W **332** C8
Araguatins *Brazil* 5°38S 48°7W **332** C2
Arahal *India* 26°27N 75°2E **242** F6
Araioses *Brazil* 2°53S 41°55W **332** B3
Arak *Algeria* 25°20N 3°45E **261** C5
Arāk *Iran* 34°0N 49°40E **247** C6
Araka *South Sudan* 4°20N 30°23E **257** G3
Arakan = Rakhine □
    Burma 19°0N 94°15E **241** F5
Arakan Coast *Burma* 19°0N 94°0E **241** F4
Arakan Yoma *Burma* 20°0N 94°40E **241** F5
Arakawa *Japan* 38°10N 139°32E **220** E9
Arakkonam *India* 13°7N 79°43E **245** N4
Araklı *Turkey* 41°6N 40°2E **213** B9
Araks = Aras, Rūd-e →
    Asia 40°5N 48°29E **213** B13
Araks → *Iran* 39°10N 47°10E **216** E3
Aral *Kazakhstan* 46°41N 61°45E **216** C6
Aral *India* 13°7N 79°43E **245** N4
Aral Mangy Qaraqumy
    Kazakhstan 46°50N 60°20E **216** C6
Aral Sea *Asia* 45°0N 58°20E **216** C5
Aral Tengizi = Aral Sea
    Asia 45°0N 58°20E **216** C5
Aralık *Turkey* 39°52N 44°31E **213** D11
Aralkum *Asia* 45°0N 60°0E **216** D6
Aralsk = Aral *Kazakhstan* 46°41N 61°45E **216** C6
Aralskoye More = Aral Sea
    Asia 45°0N 58°20E **216** C5
Aralsor, Ozero = Aralsor Köli
    Kazakhstan 49°5N 48°12E **191** F9
Aralsor Köli *Kazakhstan* 49°5N 48°12E **191** F9
Aramac *Australia* 22°58S 145°14E **280** C4
Aramia → *Papua N. G.* 7°55S 143°22E **286** D3
Aran → *India* 19°55N 78°12E **244** E4
Aran, Val de *Spain* 42°50N 0°55E **196** C5
Arana, Sa. *Venezuela* 9°2N 43°54E **257** F5
Aran Areh *Ethiopia* 9°2N 43°54E **257** F5
Aran I. = Arranmore
    Ireland 55°0N 8°30W **166** A3
Aran Is. *Ireland* 53°6N 9°38W **166** C2
Aranda de Duero *Spain* 41°39N 3°42W **194** D7
Arandān *Iran* 35°23N 46°55E **246** C5
Arandelovac *Serbia* 44°18N 20°34E **202** B4
Aranga *N.Z.* 35°44S 173°40E **284** C4
Arani *Bolivia* 17°34S 65°46W **330** D4
Arani *India* 12°43N 79°19E **245** N4
Aranjuez *Spain* 40°1N 3°40W **194** E7
Aranos *Namibia* 24°9S 19°7E **270** C2
Aransas Pass *U.S.A.* 27°55N 97°9W **314** H6
Arany-hegyi-patak →
    Hungary 47°34N 19°4E **117** A2
Aranyaprathet *Thailand* 13°41N 102°30E **236** F4
Arao *Japan* 32°59N 130°25E **222** D2
Araouane *Mali* 18°55N 3°30W **262** B4
Arapahoe *U.S.A.* 40°18N 99°54W **308** E4
Arapari *Brazil* 5°34S 49°15W **332** C2
Arapawa I. *N.Z.* 41°11S 174°17E **285** J5
Arapey Grande →
    Uruguay 30°55S 57°49W **334** C4
Arapgir *Turkey* 39°5N 38°30E **213** C8
Arapiraca *Brazil* 9°45S 36°39W **332** D4
Arapis, Akra *Greece* 40°27N 24°0E **203** F8
Arapongas *Brazil* 23°29S 51°28W **335** A5
Arapuni *N.Z.* 38°4S 175°39E **284** E4
Ar'ar *Si. Arabia* 30°59N 41°2E **246** D4
Araracuara *Colombia* 0°24S 72°17W **328** D3
Araranguá *Brazil* 29°0S 49°30W **335** B6
Araraquara *Brazil* 21°50S 48°0W **333** F2
Ararás, Serra das *Brazil* 25°0S 53°10W **335** B5
Ararat *Australia* 37°16S 142°58E **282** D5
Ararat, Mt. = Ağrı Dağı
    Turkey 39°50N 44°15E **213** C11
Arari *Brazil* 3°28S 44°47W **332** B3
Araria *India* 26°9N 87°33E **243** F12
Araripe, Chapada do *Brazil* 7°20S 40°0W **332** D4
Araripina *Brazil* 7°33S 40°34W **332** D4
Araruama *Brazil* 22°53S 42°12W **333** F3
Araruama, L. de *Brazil* 22°53S 42°0W **333** F3
Araruna *Brazil* 6°52S 35°44W **332** C4
Aratānē *Mauritania* 18°24N 8°32W **262** B2
Araticu = Oeiras do Para
    Brazil 1°58S 49°51W **329** D8
Arauca *Colombia* 7°0N 70°40W **328** B4
Arauca □ *Colombia* 6°40N 71°0W **328** B3
Arauca → *Venezuela* 7°24N 66°35W **328** B4
Arauco *Chile* 37°16S 73°25W **334** D1
Araújos *Brazil* 19°56S 45°14W **333** E2
Arauquita *Colombia* 7°2N 71°25W **328** B3
Araure *Venezuela* 9°34N 69°13W **328** B4
Aravaca *Spain* 40°27N 3°47W **127** B1
Aravalli Range *India* 25°0N 73°30E **242** G5
Arawa *Ethiopia* 9°57N 41°58E **257** F5
Arawale → *Kenya* 1°24S 40°9E **268** C5
Arawe Is. *Papua N. G.* 6°6S 149°0E **286** D5
Arawhata → *N.Z.* 44°0S 168°40E **285** F2
Araxá *Brazil* 19°35S 46°55W **333** E2
Araxos, Akra *Greece* 38°13N 21°20E **204** C3
Araya, Pen. de *Venezuela* 10°40N 64°0W **329** A5
Arayat *Phil.* 15°10N 120°46E **232** D3
Arba Gugu *Ethiopia* 8°40N 40°15E **257** F5
Arba Minch *Ethiopia* 6°0N 37°30E **257** F4
Arbat *Iraq* 35°25N 45°35E **213** F11
Arbataash *Iraq* 33°20N 44°11E **113** A1
Ārbatax *Italy* 39°56N 9°42E **200** C2
Arbi *Ethiopia* 9°4N 35°7E **257** F4
Arbil *Iraq* 36°15N 44°5E **213** D11
Arbil □ *Iraq* 36°20N 44°18E **213** D11
Arboga *Sweden* 59°24N 15°52E **163** F9
Arbois *France* 46°55N 5°46E **173** F12
Arbolotes *Colombia* 8°51N 76°26W **328** B2
Arbore *Ethiopia* 5°0N 36°50E **257** F4
Arborea *Italy* 39°46N 8°35E **200** C1
Arborfield *Canada* 53°6N 103°39W **297** C8
Arborg *Canada* 50°54N 97°13W **297** C9
Arbroath *U.K.* 56°34N 2°35W **167** E6
Arbuckle *U.S.A.* 39°1N 122°3W **306** F4
Arbuckle, L. *U.S.A.* 27°38N 81°2W **317** H7
Arc → *France* 45°34N 6°12E **175** C10
Arc de Triomphe *Paris, France* **134** a2
Arc-lès-Gray *France* 47°27N 5°34E **172** E12
Arcachon *France* 44°40N 1°10W **174** D2
Arcachon, Bassin d'
    France 44°42N 1°10W **174** D2
Arcade *U.S.A.* 42°32N 78°25W **312** D6
Arcadia = Arkadia *Greece* 37°30N 22°0E **204** D4
Arcadia *Calif., U.S.A.* 34°7N 118°1W **126** B4
Arcadia *Fla., U.S.A.* 27°13N 81°52W **317** H7

Argamasilla de Calatrava
    Spain 38°44N 4°4W **195** G6
Arganda del Rey *Spain* 40°19N 3°26W **194** E7
Arganil *Portugal* 40°13N 8°3W **194** E2
Arganzuela *Spain* 40°23N 3°42W **127** B1
Argao *Phil.* 9°52N 123°36E **233** G4
Argarapa ○ *Australia* 22°20S 134°58E **280** C1
Argasi *Greece* 37°45N 20°54E **204** D2
Argedeb *Ethiopia* 6°11N 41°13E **257** F5
Argelès-Gazost *France* 43°0N 0°6W **174** E3
Argelès-sur-Mer *France* 42°34N 3°1E **174** F7
Argens → *France* 43°24N 6°44E **175** E10
Argent, Côte d' *France* 44°15N 1°30W **174** D2
Argent-sur-Sauldre *France* 47°33N 2°25E **173** E9
Argenta = North Little Rock
    U.S.A. 34°45N 92°16W **314** D8
Argenta *B.C., Canada* 50°11N 116°56W **296** C5
Argenta *Italy* 44°37N 11°50W **198** D8
Argenta *Ill., U.S.A.* 39°59N 88°49W **311** E8
Argentan *France* 48°45N 0°1W **172** D6
Argentário, Mte. *Italy* 42°24N 11°9E **199** F8
Argentat *France* 45°6N 1°56E **174** D5
Argentera *Italy* 44°12N 7°5E **198** D4
Argenteuil *France* 48°56N 2°15E **134** A2
Argentia *Canada* 47°18N 53°58W **299** C9
Argentière, C. dell' *Italy* 40°44N 8°22E **200** B1
Argentina ■, *S. Amer.* 35°0S 66°0W **327** G4
Argentine Abyssal Plain
    Atl. Oc. 46°0S 52°0W **152** L4
Argentine Basin *Atl. Oc.* 45°0S 50°0W **152** L7
Argentino, L. *Argentina* 50°10S 73°0W **338** D2
Argenton-les-Vallées
    France 46°59N 0°27W **172** F6
Argenton-sur-Creuse
    France 46°36N 1°30E **173** F8
Argeş □ *Romania* 45°0N 24°45E **183** F9
Argeş → *Romania* 44°5N 26°38E **183** F11
Arghandab → *Afghan.* 31°30N 64°15E **242** D1
Argheile *Ethiopia* 5°19N 42°4E **257** F5
Argirades *Greece* 39°27N 19°58E **206** C9
Argiroupoli Athina, *Greece* 37°52N 23°44E **112** B2
Argiroupoli *Kriti, Greece* 35°17N 24°20E **207** E5
Argo *Sudan* 19°28N 30°30E **256** D3
Argolikos Kolpos *Greece* 37°20N 22°52E **204** D4
Argonne *France* 49°10N 5°0E **173** C12
Argos *Greece* 37°40N 22°43E **204** D4
Argos Ind., *U.S.A.* 41°14N 86°15W **311** C10
Argos Orestiko *Greece* 40°27N 21°18E **202** F5
Argostoli *Greece* 38°11N 20°29E **204** C2
Argostoliou, Kolpos
    Greece 38°10N 20°27E **207** C1
Arguello, Pt. *U.S.A.* 34°35N 120°39W **307** L6
Arguineguín *Canary Is.* 27°46N 15°41W **153** d
Argun *Russia* 43°18N 45°52E **191** J7
Argun → *Russia* 53°20N 121°28E **219** A13
Argungu *Nigeria* 12°40N 4°31E **263** C5
Argus Pk. *U.S.A.* 35°52N 117°26W **307** K9
Argyle, L. *Australia* 16°20S 128°40E **278** C4
Argyle Waterfalls
    Trin. & Tob. 11°15N 60°35W **323** K
Argyll & Bute □ *U.K.* 56°13N 5°28W **167** E3
Arhavi *Turkey* 41°21N 41°15E **213** B9
Århus = Aarhus *Denmark* 56°8N 10°11E **163** H4
Ari Atoll *Maldives* 3°53N 72°50E **272** d
Aria *N.Z.* 38°33S 175°0E **284** F4
Ariadnoye *Russia* 45°8N 134°25E **222** B7
Ariamsvlei *Namibia* 28°9S 19°51E **270** C2
Ariana, L' □ *Tunisia* 36°52N 10°12E **258** A2
Ariana, L' □ *Tunisia* 41°9N 15°50E **201** A8
Ariano Irpino *Italy* 41°9N 15°50E **201** A8
Ariari → *Colombia* 2°35N 72°47W **328** C3
Aribinda *Burkina Faso* 14°17N 0°52E **263** C4
Arica *Chile* 18°32S 70°20W **330** D3
Arica *Colombia* 1°54S 67°45W **328** D4
Arica y Parinacota □
    Chile 18°45S 69°50W **330** D4
Arid, C. *Australia* 34°1S 123°10E **279** F3
Arida *Japan* 34°5N 135°8E **223** G7
Aridal, W. *Sahara* 25°59N 13°54W **260** D2
Aride *Seychelles* 4°13S 55°40E **272** c
Aridea *Greece* 40°58N 22°3E **203** D4
Ariège □ *France* 42°56N 1°30E **174** F5
Ariège → *France* 43°30N 1°25E **174** E5
Ariel → *Romania* 46°24N 23°20E **183** E8
Arima *Japan* 34°48N 135°15E **128** b
Arima *Trin. & Tob.* 10°38N 61°17W **323** l
Arinagur → *Brazil* 10°25S 58°20W **331** D8
Ario de Rosales *Mexico* 19°12N 101°43W **318** D4
Ariogola *Lithuania* 55°16N 23°28E **184** C10
Aríos Pagos *Athens, Greece* **112** c1
Aripo *Trin. & Tob.* 10°35N 61°14W **323** l
Aripo, Mt. *Trin. & Tob.* 10°45N 61°15W **323** l
Aripo Caves *Trin. & Tob.* 10°43N 61°14W **323** l
Aripuanã *Brazil* 9°25S 60°30W **331** B5
Aripuanã → *Brazil* 5°7S 60°25W **331** B5
Ariquemes *Brazil* 9°55S 63°6W **331** B5
Arisaig *U.K.* 56°55N 5°51W **167** E3
Arish, W. el → *Egypt* 31°9N 33°49E **256** B3
Arissa *Ethiopia* 11°10N 41°35E **257** E5
Aristazabal I. *Canada* 52°40N 129°10W **296** C3
Arita *Japan* 33°11N 129°54E **222** D1
Aritao *Phil.* 16°18N 121°2E **232** D3
Ariton *U.S.A.* 31°36N 85°43W **316** F4
Arivonimamo *Madag.* 19°1S 47°11E **272** B2
Ariyalur *India* 11°8N 79°8E **245** J4
Ariza *Spain* 41°19N 2°3W **196** D2
Arizaro, Salar de
    Argentina 24°40S 67°50W **334** A2
Arizona *Argentina* 35°45S 65°25W **334** D2
Arizona □ *U.S.A.* 34°0N 112°0W **305** J8
Arizpe *Mexico* 30°20N 110°10W **318** A2
'Arjah *Si. Arabia* 24°43N 44°17E **246** E5
Ārjäng *Sweden* 59°24N 12°8E **162** F6
Arjeplog *Sweden* 66°3N 17°54E **160** C17
Arjeplouvee = Arjeplog
    Sweden 66°3N 17°54E **160** C17
Arjona *Colombia* 10°14N 75°22W **328** A3
Arjuna *Indonesia* 7°49S 112°34E **235** G15
Arka *Russia* 60°15N 142°0E **215** C15
Arkadak *Russia* 51°58N 43°30E **190** E6
Arkadelphia *U.S.A.* 34°7N 93°4W **314** D8
Arkadia *Greece* 37°30N 22°0E **204** D4
Arkaig, L. *U.S.A.* 56°59N 5°10W **167** E3
Arkalgud *India* 12°46N 76°3E **245** H3
Arkalyk = Arqalyk
    Kazakhstan 50°13N 66°50E **217** B7
Arkansas □ *U.S.A.* 35°0N 92°30W **314** D8
Arkansas → *U.S.A.* 33°47N 91°4W **314** D8
Arkansas City *U.S.A.* 37°4N 97°2W **314** A6
Arkaroola *Australia* 30°12S 139°12E **282** A3
Arkavidae *Iran* **213** F12
Arken *Denmark* 55°36N 12°33E **131** B5
Arkhangelsk *Russia* 64°38N 40°36E **190** B6
Arkhangelskoye *Russia* 51°32N 40°58E **190** D5
Arki *Greece* 37°22N 26°45E **205** D9
Arki *India* 31°9N 76°58E **242** D7
Arkiko *Eritrea* 15°33N 39°30E **257** D4

Arklow *Ireland* 52°48N 6°10W **166** D5
Arkona, Kap *Germany* 54°41N 13°26E **178** A9
Arkösund *Sweden* 58°29N 16°56E **163** F10
Arkoudi *Greece* 38°33N 20°43E **207** B2
Arkport *U.S.A.* 42°24N 77°42W **312** D7
Arkticheskiy, Mys *Russia* 81°10N 95°0E **215** A10
Arkul *Russia* 57°17N 50°3E **190** B10
Arkville *U.S.A.* 42°9N 74°37W **313** D10
Ärla *Sweden* 59°17N 16°40E **162** F10
Arlanda, Stockholm ✈ (ARN)
  Sweden 59°41N 17°56E **139** A1
Arlanza → *Spain* 42°6N 4°9W **194** C6
Arlanzón → *Spain* 42°3N 4°17W **194** C6
Arlbergpass *Austria* 47°9N 10°12E **180** D3
Arlbergtunnel *Austria* 47°9N 10°12E **180** D3
Arles *France* 43°41N 4°40E **175** E8
Arli *Burkina Faso* 11°35N 1°28E **263** C5
Arli → *Burkina Faso* 11°35N 1°28E **263** C5
Arlington *Free State,*
  S. Africa 28°1S 27°53E **271** C4
Arlington *Ga., U.S.A.* 31°26N 84°44W **316** D5
Arlington *Mass., U.S.A.* 42°24N 71°10W **116** A1
Arlington *N.Y., U.S.A.* 41°42N 73°54W **313** E11
Arlington *Oreg., U.S.A.* 45°43N 120°12W **304** D3
Arlington *S. Dak., U.S.A.* 44°22N 97°8W **308** C5
Arlington *Tex., U.S.A.* 32°44N 97°6W **124** B3
Arlington *Va., U.S.A.* 38°53N 77°7W **143** B2
Arlington *Vt., U.S.A.* 43°5N 73°9W **313** C11
Arlington *Wash., U.S.A.* 48°12N 122°8W **306** B4
Arlington, L. *U.S.A.* 32°40N 97°10W **124** B3
Arlington Heights *Ill.,*
  U.S.A. 42°5N 87°59W **311** B9
Arlington Heights *Mass.,*
  U.S.A. 42°25N 71°10W **116** A1
Arlington Municipal ✈ (JLH)
  U.S.A. 38°52N 77°4W **143** B2
Arlington Nat. Cemetery
  U.S.A. 38°52N 77°4W **143** B2
Arlon *Belgium* 49°42N 5°49E **170** E5
Arlparra *Australia* 22°11S 134°30E **280** C1
Arltunga *Australia* 23°26S 134°41E **280** C1
Armação *Brazil* 22°52S 43°6W **135** E2
Armação de Pêra *Portugal* 37°6N 8°22W **195** H2
Armadale *Australia* 32°15S 116°0E **279** F2
Armadale *W. Austral.,*
  Australia 32°9S 116°0E **279** F2
Armagh *U.K.* 54°21N 6°39W **166** B5
Armagh □ *U.K.* 54°18N 6°37W **166** B5
Armagnac *France* 43°50N 0°10E **174** E4
Armançon → *France* 47°59N 3°30E **173** E10
Armant *Russia* 40°28N 50°20E **191** K10
Armant *Russia* 43°22N 132°13E **220** C6
Armavir *Ukraine* 48°35N 38°0E **189** H9
Armenia *Colombia* 4°35N 75°45W **328** C3
Armenia ■ *Asia* 40°20N 45°0E **191** K7
Armenian Quarter *Jerusalem* **123** b3
Armenis *Romania* 45°13N 22°17E **182** E7
Armenistis, Akra *Greece* 36°8N 27°42E **206** E11
Armentières *France* 50°40N 2°50E **173** B9
Armero *Colombia* 4°58N 74°54W **328** C3
Armidale *Australia* 30°30S 151°40E **283** A8
Armilla *Spain* 37°9N 3°37W **195** H7
Armori *India* 20°28N 79°59E **244** D4
Armorique △ *France* 48°22N 3°55W **172** D3
Armour *U.S.A.* 43°19N 98°21W **308** D4
Armour Heights *Canada* 43°45N 79°25W **141** A2
Armstrong *B.C., Canada* 50°25N 119°10W **296** C5
Armstrong *Ont., Canada* 50°18N 89°4W **298** B2
Armur *India* 18°48N 78°16E **244** E4
Armutlu *Bursa, Turkey* 40°31N 28°50E **203** F12
Armutlu *İzmir, Turkey* 38°24N 27°34E **205** C9
Arnarfjörður *Iceland* 65°48N 23°40W **155** D3
Arnaud → *Canada* 59°59N 69°46W **295** F18
Arnauti, C. *Cyprus* 35°6N 32°17E **207** E8
Arnay-le-Duc *France* 47°10N 4°27E **173** E11
Arncliffe *Australia* 33°56S 151°8E **139** B1
Arnea *Greece* 40°30N 23°38E **202** F7
Arnedillo *Spain* 42°13N 2°14W **196** C2
Arnedo *Spain* 42°12N 2°5W **196** C2
Ärnes *Iceland* 66°1N 21°31W **155** A5
Årnes *Akershus, Norway* 60°7N 11°28E **164** D8
Árnessýsla *Iceland* 64°15N 20°30W **155** C6
Arnett *U.S.A.* 36°8N 99°46W **314** C5
Arnhem *Neths.* 51°58N 5°55E **170** C5
Arnhem, C. *Australia* 12°20S 137°30E **280** A2
Arnhem B. *Australia* 12°20S 136°10E **280** A2
Arnhem Land *Australia* 13°10S 134°30E **280** A1
Arnhem Land ○
  Australia 12°50S 134°50E **280** A1
Arnissa *Greece* 40°47N 21°49E **202** F5
Arno → *Italy* 43°41N 10°17E **198** E7
Arno Bay *Australia* 33°54S 136°34E **282** D2
Arnold *Notts., U.K.* 53°1N 1°7W **166** D6
Arnold *Calif., U.S.A.* 38°15N 120°20W **306** G6
Arnold *Mo., U.S.A.* 38°26N 90°23W **310** F8
Arnold Arboretum *U.S.A.* 42°18N 71°8W **116** B2
Arnoldstein *Austria* 46°33N 13°43E **180** E8
Arnon → *France* 47°13N 2°1E **173** E9
Arnos Vale *Trin. & Tob.* 11°13N 60°45W **323** s
Arnot *Canada* 55°56N 96°41W **297** B9
Arnøya *Norway* 70°9N 20°40E **160** A19
Arnprior *Canada* 45°26N 76°21W **313** A8
Arnsberg *Germany* 51°24N 8°5E **178** D4
Arnsberger Wald △
  Germany 51°22N 8°1E **178** D4
Arnstadt *Germany* 50°50N 10°56E **178** E6
Arnswalde = Choszczno
  Poland 53°7N 15°25E **185** E2
Aro → *Venezuela* 9°38N 64°25W **329** c
Aroa, Pte. *Moorea* 17°28S 149°46W **289** e
Aroab *Namibia* 26°41S 19°39E **270** C2
Aroania Oros *Greece* 37°56N 22°12E **204** D4
Aroche *Spain* 37°56N 6°57W **195** H4
Arochuku *Nigeria* 5°21N 7°54E **263** D6
Aroeiras *Brazil* 7°31S 35°41W **332** C4
Arolsen *Germany* 51°23N 9°2E **178** D5
Aron *India* 25°57N 77°56E **242** G6
Aron → *France* 46°50N 3°28E **173** F10
Arona *Canary Is.* 28°6N 16°40W **153** e1
Arona *Italy* 45°46N 8°34E **198** C5
Arorae *Kiribati* 2°38S 176°49E **277** A14
Arorangi *Cook Is.* 21°13S 159°49W **289** h
Aroroy *Phil.* 12°31N 123°24E **233** F6
Aros → *Mexico* 29°9N 107°57W **318** B3
Arouca *Trin. & Tob.* 10°38N 61°20W **323** t
Arousa, Ría de → *Spain* 42°28N 8°57W **194** C2
Arøysund *Norway* 59°10N 10°27E **164** D8
Arpa → *Asia* 39°28N 44°56E **213** C11
Arpaçay *Turkey* 40°50N 43°19E **213** D11
Árpádföld *Hungary* 47°32N 19°8E **117** A3
Arpajon *France* 48°36N 2°15E **173** D9
Arpajon-sur-Cère *France* 44°53N 2°28E **174** D6
Arpaşu de Jos *Romania* 45°47N 24°37E **182** D9
Arqalyk *Kazakhstan* 50°13N 66°50E **217** B7
Arque *Bolivia* 17°48S 66°33W **334** G5
Arrah = Ara *India* 25°35N 84°32E **243** G11
Arrah *Ivory C.* 6°40N 3°58E **262** D4
Arraias *Brazil* 12°56S 46°57W **333** D2
Arraias → *Mato Grosso,*
  Brazil 11°10S 53°35W **331** C2
Arraias → *Pará, Brazil* 7°30S 49°20W **332** C2
Arraiján *Panama* 8°56N 79°36W **320** c
Arraiolos *Portugal* 38°44N 7°59W **195** G3
Arran *U.K.* 55°34N 5°12W **167** F3
Arras *France* 50°17N 2°46E **173** B9
Arrasate *Spain* 43°4N 2°30W **196** B2

Arrats → *France* 44°6N 0°52E **174** D4
Arreau *France* 42°54N 0°22E **174** F4
Arrecife *Canary Is.* 28°57N 13°37W **153** e2
Arrecifes *Argentina* 34°6S 60°9W **334** C3
Arée, Mts. d' *France* 48°26N 3°55W **172** D3
Arrentela *Portugal* 38°37N 9°9E **196** D2
Arreso *Denmark* 55°58N 12°6E **163** J6
Arriaga *Mexico* 16°14N 93°54W **319** D6
Arrilalah *Australia* 23°43S 143°54E **280** C3
Arrino *Australia* 29°30S 115°40E **279** E2
Arriondas *Spain* 43°23N 5°11W **194** B5
Arrojado → *Brazil* 13°24S 44°20W **333** D3
Arromanches-les-Bains
  France 49°20N 0°38W **172** C6
Arronches *Portugal* 39°8N 7°16W **195** F3
Arros → *France* 43°40N 0°2W **174** E3
Arrow, L. *Ireland* 54°3N 8°19W **166** B3
Arrowsmith, Mt. *N.Z.* 43°20S 170°55E **285** D5
Arrowtown *N.Z.* 44°57S 168°50E **285** D3
Arroyo de la Luz *Spain* 39°30N 6°38W **195** F4
Arroyo del Puerco = Arroyo de la
  Luz *Spain* 39°30N 6°38W **195** F4
Arroyo Grande *U.S.A.* 35°7N 120°35W **307** K6
Arroyo Seco Park *U.S.A.* 34°6N 118°11W **126** B3
Ars *Iran* 37°9N 47°46E **246** B5
Ars-sur-Moselle *France* 49°5N 6°4E **173** C13
Arsenale *Venice, Italy* **142** b4
Arsenault L. *Canada* 55°6N 108°32W **297** B7
Arsenev *Russia* 44°10N 133°15E **220** B6
Arsi *Ethiopia* 7°45N 39°0E **257** F4
Arsiero *Italy* 45°48N 11°21E **199** C8
Arsikere *India* 13°15N 76°15E **245** H3
Arsin *Turkey* 41°8N 39°55E **213** D8
Arsk *Russia* 56°10N 49°50E **190** B9
Arslanköy *Turkey* 37°0N 34°17E **250** B5
Ärsunda *Sweden* 60°31N 16°45E **162** D10
Art, Î. *N. Cal.* 19°43S 163°38E **288** d
Arta *Greece* 39°8N 21°2E **206** B3
Artà *Spain* 39°41N 3°21E **206** B4
Artà, Coves d' *Spain* 39°40N 3°24E **206** B4
Artashat *Armenia* 40°0N 44°35E **213** F11
Arteaga *Mexico* 18°28N 102°25W **318** D4
Arteche *Phil.* 12°17N 125°22E **233** F7
Arteixo = A Baiuca *Spain* 43°19N 8°29W **194** B2
Artem *Azerbaijan* 40°28N 50°20E **191** K10
Artëm *Russia* 43°22N 132°13E **220** C6
Artemivsk *Ukraine* 48°35N 38°0E **189** H9
Artemovsk *Russia* 54°45N 93°35E **215** D10
Artemovskiy *Russia* 47°45N 40°16E **191** G5
Artenay *France* 48°5N 1°50E **173** D9
Artern *Germany* 51°22N 11°18E **178** D7
Artesa de Segre *Spain* 41°54N 1°3E **196** D6
Artesia = Mosamane
  Botswana 24°2S 26°19E **270** B4
Artesia *U.S.A.* 32°51N 104°24W **305** K11
Artesia *Highlands U.S.A.* 6°35N 10°45W **262** D2
Arthur *Ont., Canada* 43°50N 80°32W **312** C4
Arthur *Ill., U.S.A.* 39°43N 88°28W **311** E8
Arthur → *Australia* 41°2S 144°40E **281** G3
Arthur Cr. → *Australia* 22°30S 136°25E **280** C2
Arthur Pt. *Australia* 22°7S 150°3E **280** C5
Arthur River *Australia* 33°20S 117°2E **279** F2
Arthur's Pass *N.Z.* 42°54S 171°35E **285** D5
Arthur's Pass △ *N.Z.* 42°53S 171°42E **285** C6
Arthur's Seat *U.K.* 55°57N 3°11W **123** b2
Arthur's Town *Bahamas* 24°38N 75°42W **321** B4
Artigas = Rio Branco
  Uruguay 32°40S 53°40W **335** C5
Artigas *Antarctica* 62°30S 58°0W **151** C18
Artigas *Uruguay* 30°20S 56°30W **334** C4
Artik *Armenia* 40°38N 43°58E **191** K6
Artillery L. *Canada* 63°9N 107°52W **297** A7
Artois *France* 50°20N 2°30E **173** B9
Artotina *Greece* 38°42N 22°2E **204** C4
Artrutx, C. de *Spain* 39°55N 3°49E **206** B4
Arts, Place des *Montréal, Canada* **130** b2
Arts Bogd Uul *Mongolia* 44°40N 102°20E **226** B2
Artsvashen *Armenia* 40°38N 45°30E **213** B11
Artsyz *Ukraine* 46°4N 29°26E **183** D14
Artux *China* 39°40N 76°10E **217** F9
Artvin *Turkey* 41°14N 41°44E **213** B9
Artvin □ *Turkey* 41°10N 41°50E **213** B9
Artyk *Russia* 64°12N 145°6E **215** C15
Artyom *Azerbaijan* 40°28N 50°20E **191** K10
Aru, Kepulauan *Indonesia* 6°0S 134°30E **231** F8
Aru Is. = Aru, Kepulauan
  Indonesia 6°0S 134°30E **231** F8
Arua *Uganda* 3°1N 30°58E **268** B3
Aruanã *Brazil* 14°54S 51°10W **333** D1
Aruba ☐ *W. Indies* 12°30N 70°0W **322** f
Arudy *France* 43°7N 0°28W **174** E3
Aruf *Tahiti* 17°31S 149°30W **289** e
Arumã *Brazil* 4°44S 62°8W **329** D5
Arume-wan *Japan* 26°35N 128°8E **288** a
Arumpo *Australia* 33°48S 142°55E **282** C3
Arun → *Nepal* 26°55N 87°10E **243** F12
Arun → *W. Susx., U.K.* 50°49N 0°33W **167** G7
Arunachal Pradesh ☐ *India* 28°0N 95°0E **241** B5
Aruppukkottai *India* 9°31N 78°8E **245** K4
Arusha *Tanzania* 3°20S 36°30E **268** C4
Arusha □ *Tanzania* 3°16S 36°47E **268** C4
Arusha Chini *Tanzania* 3°32S 37°20E **268** C4
Arut → *Indonesia* 2°42S 111°34E **235** C4
Aruwimi →
  Dem. Rep. of the Congo 1°13N 23°36E **264** B4
Arvada *Colo., U.S.A.* 39°48N 105°5W **304** G11
Arvada *Wyo., U.S.A.* 44°39N 106°8W **304** D10
Arvayheer *Mongolia* 46°15N 102°48E **218** B9
Arvi *Kriti, Greece* 34°59N 25°28E **207** F6
Arvi *India* 20°59N 78°16E **244** D4
Arviat *Canada* 61°6N 93°59W **297** A10
Arvidsjaur *Sweden* 65°35N 19°10E **160** D18
Arvika *Sweden* 59°40N 12°36E **162** F6
Arvin *U.S.A.* 35°12N 118°50W **307** K8
Arwad *Syria* 34°51N 35°51E **250** D6
Arwal *India* 25°15N 84°41E **243** G11
Arxan *China* 47°11N 119°57E **218** B2
Arys *Kazakhstan* 42°26N 68°48E **217** D7
Arzachena *Italy* 41°5N 9°23E **200** A2
Arzgir *Russia* 45°18N 44°23W **191** H7
Arzew *Algeria* 35°50N 0°23W **261** A4
Arzgir *Russia* 45°18N 44°23W **191** H7
Arzúa *Spain* 42°56N 8°9W **194** C2
Aš *Czechia* 50°13N 12°12E **178** E7
Aš *Akershus, Norway* 59°40N 10°48E **164** C7
As Sa'an *Syria* 35°16N 37°22E **250** C4
As Safā *Syria* 33°10N 37°0E **250** C8
As Saffānīyah *Si. Arabia* 27°55N 48°50E **247** E6
As Safīrah *Syria* 36°5N 37°21E **250** B8
As Sahm *Oman* 24°10N 56°53E **247** E8
As Sājir *Si. Arabia* 25°11N 44°36E **246** E5
As Salamīyah *Syria* 35°1N 37°2E **250** C8

Aş Şalif *Yemen* 15°18N 42°41E **248** D3
Aş Salmān *Iraq* 30°30N 44°32E **246** D5
As Salṭ *Jordan* 32°2N 35°43E **251** F6
As Sal'wa *Qatar* 24°23N 50°50E **247** E6
As Samāwah *Iraq* 31°15N 45°15E **246** D5
As Sanamayn *Syria* 33°3N 36°10E **250** E7
As Sawādah *Si. Arabia* 22°24N 44°28E **248** B4
Aş Şawma'ah *Yemen* 14°5N 45°48E **248** D4
As Sayl al Kabīr *Si. Arabia* 21°38N 40°25E **248** B3
As Shawawra *West Bank* 31°41N 35°15E **123** B2
As Sib *Oman* 23°41N 58°11E **249** B7
As Sila' *U.A.E.* 24°4N 51°54E **247** E6
As Sukhnah *Syria* 34°52N 38°52E **213** E8
Aş Sulaymānīyah *Iraq* 35°35N 45°29E **213** E11
As Sulaymānīyah
  Si. Arabia 24°9N 47°18E **248** B4
As Sulaymī *Si. Arabia* 26°17N 41°21E **246** E4
As Sulayyil *Si. Arabia* 20°27N 45°34E **248** B4
As Sulṭān *Libya* 31°4N 17°8E **258** B3
As Summān *Si. Arabia* 25°0N 47°0E **246** E5
Aş Şurrah *Yemen* 13°57N 46°14E **248** D4
As Suwaydā' *Syria* 32°40N 36°30E **250** F7
As Suwaydā' ☐ *Syria* 32°45N 36°45E **250** F7
As Suwayq *Oman* 23°51N 57°26E **247** F8
Aş Şuwayrah *Iraq* 32°55N 45°0E **213** F11
Āsa *Sweden* 57°21N 12°8E **163** G6
Asab *Namibia* 25°30S 18°0E **270** C2
Asaba *Nigeria* 6°12N 6°38E **263** D6
Asad, Buhayrat al *Syria* 36°0N 38°15E **213** D8
Asadābād *Iran* 34°47N 48°7E **213** C13
Asafo *Ghana* 6°20N 2°40W **262** D4
Asaga Str. *Amer. Samoa* 14°10S 169°37W **302** g
Asahi, Chiba, *Japan* 35°41N 139°38E **224** B2
Asahi *Toyama, Japan* 36°51N 137°33E **223** B12
Asahi-Ōsaka, *Japan* 34°43N 135°31E **133** A2
Asahi-Gawa → *Japan* 34°36N 133°58E **222** C5
Asahigawa = Asahikawa
  Japan 43°46N 142°22E **220** C11
Asahikawa *Japan* 43°46N 142°22E **220** C11
Asakusa *Japan* 32°54N 139°47E **140** a3
Asakusabashi *Tokyo, Japan* **140** a5
Asale, L. *Ethiopia* 14°0N 40°20E **257** E5
Asaluyeh *Iran* 27°29N 52°37E **247** E7
Asama-Yama *Japan* 36°24N 138°31E **223** A10
Asamankese *Ghana* 5°50N 0°40W **263** D4
Asan → *India* 26°37N 78°24E **243** F8
Asansol *India* 23°40N 87°1E **243** H12
Āsārna *Sweden* 62°39N 14°22E **162** B8
Asati *India* 22°28N 88°15E **144** C2
Asau *Samoa* 13°27S 172°33W **287** V19
Asayita *Ethiopia* 11°34N 41°5E **257** E5
Asba Littoria = Asbe Teferi
  Ethiopia 9°4N 40°49E **257** F5
Asbe Teferi *Ethiopia* 9°4N 40°49E **257** F5
Asbesberg *S. Africa* 29°0S 23°0E **270** C3
Asbestos *Canada* 45°47N 71°58W **299** C5
Asbury Park *U.S.A.* 40°13N 74°1W **313** F10
Åsbyrgi *Iceland* 66°0N 16°30W **155** A11
Ascea *Italy* 40°8N 15°11E **201** B8
Ascensión *Mexico* 31°6N 107°59W **318** A3
Ascensión, B. de la
  Mexico 19°40N 87°30W **319** D7
Ascension I. *Atl. Oc.* 7°57S 14°23W **153** s
Ascension I. ✈ (ASI)
  Ascension I. 7°58S 14°23W **153** s
Aschach an der Donau
  Austria 48°22N 14°2E **180** C7
Aschaffenburg *Germany* 49°58N 9°6E **179** F5
Aschendorf *Germany* 53°3N 7°19E **178** B3
Aschersleben *Germany* 51°45N 11°29E **178** D7
Aschheim *Germany* 48°10N 11°42E **131** A3
Asciano *Italy* 43°14N 11°33E **199** E8
Áscoli Piceno *Italy* 42°51N 13°34E **199** F10
Áscoli Satriano *Italy* 41°11N 15°32E **201** A8
Ascope *Peru* 7°46S 79°8W **330** B2
Ascot Vale *Australia* 37°46S 144°53E **128** A1
Ascotán *Chile* 21°45S 68°17W **334** A2
Ascunción *Phil.* 7°35N 125°45E **233** H5
Aseb = Assab *Eritrea* 13°0N 42°40E **257** E5
Åseda *Sweden* 57°10N 15°20E **163** G9
Asedjrad *Algeria* 24°51N 1°29E **261** D5
Aseki *Papua N. G.* 7°21S 146°12E **286** D4
Āsela *Ethiopia* 8°0N 39°0E **257** F4
Åsen *Sweden* 61°17N 13°50E **162** C7
Asenovgrad *Bulgaria* 42°1N 24°51E **203** D8
Asfeld *France* 49°27N 4°5E **173** C11
Asfūn el Matā'na *Egypt* 25°26N 32°30E **256** B3
Aşgabat = Ashgabat
  Turkmenistan 37°58N 58°24E **247** B8
Åsgårdstrand *Norway* 59°22N 10°27E **164** E7
Ásgata *Cyprus* 34°46N 33°15E **207** F9
Ash Fork *U.S.A.* 35°13N 112°29W **305** J7
Ash Grove *U.S.A.* 37°19N 93°35W **308** G7
Ash Shabakah *Iraq* 30°49N 43°39E **246** D4
Ash Shafā *Si. Arabia* 21°27N 39°49E **248** B2
Ash Shamāl ☐ *Lebanon* 34°25N 36°0E **250** D7
Ash Shāmīyah *Iraq* 31°55N 44°35E **213** G11
Ash Sha'rā' *Si. Arabia* 25°55N 44°11E **248** A4
Ash Shāriqah *U.A.E.* 25°23N 55°26E **247** E7
Ash Sharmah *Si. Arabia* 28°1N 35°16E **251** K6
Ash Sharqāt *Iraq* 35°27N 43°16E **213** E10
Ash Sharqīyah ☐ *Si. Arabia* 23°0N 50°0E **249** B6
Ash Shaṭrah *Iraq* 31°30N 46°10E **246** D5
Ash Shawbak *Jordan* 30°32N 35°34E **246** D2
Ash Shiḥḥ Ḥumayd
  Si. Arabia 28°6N 34°33E **251** K5
Ash Shiḥr *Yemen* 14°45N 49°36E **248** D5
Ash Shiḥr *Yemen* 14°45N 49°36E **248** D5
Ash Shināfīyah *Iraq* 31°35N 44°39E **246** D5
Ash Shu'bah *Si. Arabia* 28°54N 44°44E **246** D5
Ash Shumlūl *Si. Arabia* 26°31N 47°20E **246** E5
Ash Shuqayq *Si. Arabia* 17°44N 42°11E **248** D3
Ash Shūr'ā *Iraq* 35°58N 43°13E **246** C4
Ash Shurayf *Si. Arabia* 25°43N 39°14E **246** E4
Ash Shuwayfāt *Lebanon* 33°45N 35°30E **250** B6
Ash Shuwayrif *Libya* 29°59N 14°16E **258** C2
Asha *Russia* 55°0N 57°16E **186** D10
Ashanti ☐ *Ghana* 7°30N 1°30W **263** D4
Ashbourne *U.K.* 53°2N 1°43W **168** D6
Ashbridge's Bay Park
  Canada 43°40N 79°18W **141** B3
Ashburn *Ga., U.S.A.* 31°43N 83°39W **316** D6
Ashburn *Ill., U.S.A.* 41°45N 87°43W **119** C2
Ashburton *Vic., Australia* 37°51S 145°4E **128** B2
Ashburton *N.Z.* 43°53S 171°48E **285** D6
Ashburton → *Australia* 21°40S 114°56E **278** D1
Ashburton, North Branch →
  N.Z. 43°54S 171°44E **285** D6
Ashburton, South Branch →
  N.Z. 43°54S 171°44E **285** D6
Ashcroft *Canada* 50°40N 121°20W **296** C4
Ashdod *Israel* 31°49N 34°35E **251** G5
Ashdown *U.S.A.* 33°40N 94°8W **314** E7
Asheboro *U.S.A.* 35°43N 79°49W **315** D15
Åsheim *Norway* 61°42N 11°11E **164** C8
Ashern *Canada* 51°11N 98°21W **297** C9
Asherton *U.S.A.* 28°27N 99°46W **314** G5
Asheville *U.S.A.* 35°36N 82°33W **315** D13
Asheweig → *Canada* 54°17N 87°12W **298** B2
Ashfield *N.S.W., Australia* 33°53S 151°7E **139** B1
Ashford *Kent, U.K.* 51°8N 0°53E **169** F8

Ashford *Surrey, U.K.* 51°25N 0°26W **125** B1
Ashford *Ala., U.S.A.* 31°11N 85°14W **316** D4
Ashgabat *Turkmenistan* 37°58N 58°24E **247** B8
Ashhurst *N.Z.* 40°16S 175°45E **284** C4
Ashibetsu *Japan* 43°31N 142°11E **220** C11
Ashikaga *Japan* 36°28N 139°29E **223** A11
Ashington *U.K.* 55°11N 1°33W **168** B6
Ashio *Japan* 36°38N 139°27E **223** A11
Ashizuri-Uwakai △
  Japan 32°56N 132°32E **222** E4
Ashizuri-Zaki *Japan* 32°44N 133°0E **222** E5
Ashkarkot *Afghan.* 33°3N 67°58E **242** C2
Ashkhabad = Ashgabat
  Turkmenistan 37°58N 58°24E **247** B8
Ashkhāneh *Iran* 37°26N 56°55E **247** B8
Ashland *Kans., U.S.A.* 33°16N 85°50W **316** B4
Ashland *Ill., U.S.A.* 39°53N 90°1W **310** F7
Ashland *Kans., U.S.A.* 37°11N 99°46W **308** G4
Ashland *Ky., U.S.A.* 38°28N 82°38W **309** F12
Ashland *Maine, U.S.A.* 46°38N 68°24W **301** B19
Ashland *Mont., U.S.A.* 45°36N 106°16W **304** D10
Ashland *Ohio, U.S.A.* 40°52N 82°19W **312** F2
Ashland *Oreg., U.S.A.* 42°12N 122°43W **304** E2
Ashland *Pa., U.S.A.* 40°45N 76°22W **313** F8
Ashland *Va., U.S.A.* 37°46N 77°29W **309** G15
Ashland *Wis., U.S.A.* 46°35N 90°53W **308** B8
Ashley *Ill., U.S.A.* 38°20N 89°11W **310** F7
Ashley *Ind., U.S.A.* 41°32N 85°4W **311** C11
Ashley *N. Dak., U.S.A.* 46°2N 99°22W **308** B4
Ashley → *N.Z.* 43°17S 172°44E **285** D7
Ashmore and Cartier Is.
  Ind. Oc. 12°15S 123°0E **278** B3
Ashmore Reef *Australia* 12°14S 123°5E **278** B3
Ashmūn *Egypt* 30°18N 30°58E **251** H1
Ashmyany *Belarus* 54°26N 25°52E **177** A13
Ashokan Res. *U.S.A.* 41°56N 74°13W **313** E10
Ashoknagar *India* 24°34N 77°43E **244** B3
Asheqlon *Israel* 31°42N 34°35E **251** G5
Ashraf = Behshahr *Iran* 36°45N 53°50E **247** B7
Ashta *India* 23°1N 76°43E **242** H7
Ashtabula *U.S.A.* 41°52N 80°47W **312** E4
Ashti *Maharashtra, India* 21°12N 78°11E **244** D4
Ashti *Maharashtra, India* 18°50N 75°15E **244** E2
Ashton *Western Cape,*
  S. Africa 33°50S 20°5E **270** D3
Ashton *Idaho, U.S.A.* 44°4N 111°27W **304** D8
Ashuanipi, L. *Canada* 52°45N 66°15W **299** B6
Ashuapmushuan →
  Canada 48°37N 72°20W **298** C5
Ashur = Assur *Iraq* 35°27N 43°15E **213** E10
Ashville *Ala., U.S.A.* 33°50N 86°15W **316** B3
Ashville *Pa., U.S.A.* 40°34N 78°33W **312** F6
At Ţafilah *Jordan* 30°45N 35°30E **251** H6
At Ţafilah ☐ *Jordan* 30°45N 35°30E **251** H6
At Ţā'if *Si. Arabia* 21°5N 40°27E **248** B3
At Tāj *Libya* 24°13N 23°18E **258** D4
At Ta'mīm ☐ *Iraq* 35°30N 44°30E **213** E11
At Tamīmī *Libya* 32°20N 23°4E **258** B4
At Ţiraq *Si. Arabia* 27°19N 44°33E **246** E4
At Ṭubayq *Si. Arabia* 29°30N 37°0E **251** J8
At Tuhaytah *Yemen* 14°18N 43°15E **248** D3
At Ṭunayb *Jordan* 31°48N 35°57E **251** G6
At Turbah *Lahij, Yemen* 12°42N 44°23E **248** E3
At Turbah *Ta'izz, Yemen* 13°13N 44°7E **248** E3
Atabey *Turkey* 37°57N 30°39E **205** D12
Atacama ☐ *Chile* 27°30S 70°0W **334** B2
Atacama, Desierto de
  Chile 24°0S 69°20W **334** A2
Atacama, Salar de *Chile* 23°30S 68°20W **334** A2
Ataco *Colombia* 3°35N 75°23W **328** C3
Atafu *Pac. Oc.* 8°32S 172°31W **277** B16
Atakeye ◇ *Australia* 22°30S 133°45E **278** D5
Atakor *Algeria* 23°27N 5°31E **261** D6
Atakpamé *Togo* 7°31N 1°13E **263** D5
Atalaia do Norte *Brazil* 4°20S 70°12W **328** D3
Ataléia *Brazil* 18°3S 41°6W **333** E3
Atami *Japan* 35°5N 139°4E **223** B11
Atamyrat *Turkmenistan* 37°50N 65°12E **217** F7
Atankawng *Burma* 25°50N 97°47E **241** C6
Atapupu *Indonesia* 9°0S 124°51E **231** F6
'Ataq *Yemen* 14°33N 46°47E **248** D4
Atâr *Mauritania* 20°30N 13°5W **260** D2
Atarfe *Spain* 37°13N 3°40W **195** H7
Atari *Pakistan* 30°48N 74°2E **242** D6
Atascadero *U.S.A.* 35°29N 120°40W **306** K6
Atasū *Kazakhstan* 48°30N 71°0E **217** D8
Atatürk, İstanbul ✈ (IST)
  Turkey 40°59N 28°49E **203** F12
Atatürk Baraji *Turkey* 37°28N 38°30E **213** D8
Atauro E. *Timor* 8°10S 125°30E **231** F7
Ataviros *Greece* 36°12N 27°50E **206** E11
'Atbara, Nahr → *Sudan* 17°40N 33°56E **257** D3
Atbasar *Kazakhstan* 51°48N 68°20E **217** B7
Atbashi = At-Bashy
  Kyrgyzstan 41°10N 75°48E **217** D9
Atça *Turkey* 37°53N 28°13E **205** D10
Atchafalaya B. *U.S.A.* 29°25N 91°25W **314** H9
Atchison *U.S.A.* 39°34N 95°7W **308** F6
Ateca *Spain* 41°20N 1°49W **196** D3
Aterno → *Italy* 42°11N 13°51E **199** F10
Ateshān *Iran* 35°35N 52°37E **247** C7
Atesine, Alpi *Italy* 46°55N 11°30E **199** B8
Atessa *Italy* 42°4N 14°27E **199** F11
Atfih *Egypt* 29°25N 31°15E **251** J1
Athabasca *Canada* 54°45N 113°20W **296** C6
Athabasca → *Canada* 58°40N 110°50W **297** B6
Athabasca, L. *Canada* 59°15N 109°15W **297** B7
Athabasca Sand Dunes ◇
  Canada 59°4N 108°43W **297** B7
Athagarh *India* 20°45N 85°35E **245** A8
Athboy *Ireland* 53°37N 6°55W **166** C5
Athena *U.S.A.* 45°49N 118°30W **304** D4
Atheni *Greece* 40°30N 19°47W **166** B3
Athenry *Ireland* 53°18N 8°44W **166** C3
Athens = Athína *Greece* 37°58N 23°43E **204** D5
Athens *Ala., U.S.A.* 34°48N 86°58W **315** D11
Athens *Ga., U.S.A.* 33°57N 83°23W **316** B6
Athens *N.Y., U.S.A.* 42°16N 73°49W **313** D11
Athens *Ohio, U.S.A.* 39°20N 82°6W **312** G3
Athens *Pa., U.S.A.* 41°57N 76°31W **313** E8
Athens *Tenn., U.S.A.* 35°27N 84°36W **315** D12
Athens *Tex., U.S.A.* 32°12N 95°51W **314** E6
Atherley *Canada* 44°37N 79°20W **141** A3
Atherton *Australia* 17°17S 145°30E **280** B4
Athína *Greece* 37°58N 23°43E **204** D5
Athína ✈ (ATH) *Greece* 37°57N 23°43E **204** D5
Athína = Athína *Greece* 37°58N 23°43E **204** D5
Athinai = Athína *Greece* 37°58N 23°43E **204** D5
Athis-Mons *France* 48°43N 2°23E **173** B9
Athlone *Ireland* 53°25N 7°56W **166** C4
Athlone *Westmeath, Ireland* 53°25N 7°56W **166** C4
Athlone *Western Cape,*
  S. Africa 33°57S 18°31E **118** A2
Athmallik *India* 20°43N 84°32E **245** A8
Athni *India* 16°44N 75°6E **244** F2
Athol *N.Z.* 45°30S 168°35E **285** F3

Assur *Iraq* 35°27N 43°15E **213** E10
Assynt, L. *U.K.* 58°10N 5°3W **167** C3
Astaffort *France* 44°4N 0°40E **174** D4
Astakida *Greece* 35°53N 26°50E **205** F8
Astakos *Greece* 38°32N 21°5E **207** B3
Astana *Kazakhstan* 51°10N 71°30E **217** B8
Āstāneh *Iran* 37°17N 49°59E **247** B6
Astara *Azerbaijan* 38°30N 48°50E **213** C13
Āstārā *Iran* 38°20N 48°52E **213** C13
Astarabad = Gorgān *Iran* 36°55N 54°30E **247** B7
Asterousia *Greece* 34°59N 25°3E **207** F6
Asti *Italy* 44°54N 8°12E **198** D5
Astipalea *Greece* 36°32N 26°22E **205** E8
Astola I. *Pakistan* 25°1N 63°51E **240** D1
Astorga *Davao del S., Phil.* 6°54N 125°27E **233** H5
Astorga *Spain* 42°29N 6°8W **194** C4
Astoria *Ill., U.S.A.* 40°14N 90°21W **310** D6
Astoria *N.Y., U.S.A.* 40°46N 73°55W **132** B2
Astoria *Oreg., U.S.A.* 46°11N 123°50W **306** D3
Åstorp *Sweden* 56°6N 12°55E **163** H6
Astrakhan *Russia* 46°25N 48°5E **191** G9
Astrakhan *Russia* 47°45N 46°20E **191** G8
Astrebla Downs *Australia* 24°12S 140°34E **280** C3
Astrolabe, Récifs de l'
  N. Cal. 19°48S 165°37E **288** d
Astrolabe Park *Australia* 33°57S 151°12E **139** B2
Astudillo *Spain* 42°12N 4°22W **194** C6
Asturias ☐ *Spain* 43°15N 6°0W **194** B5
Asturias ✈ (OVD) *Spain* 43°33N 6°3W **194** B4
Asumman *S. Korea* 37°4N 126°40E **224** D3
Asunción *Bolivia* 11°46S 67°50W **330** C4
Asunción N. Marianas *Asunción* 19°40N 145°24E **302** a
Asunción *Paraguay* 25°10S 57°30W **334** B4
Asunción Nochixtlán
  Mexico 17°28N 97°14W **319** D5
Āsunden *Sweden* 58°0N 15°51E **163** F9
Asutri *Sudan* 15°25N 35°45E **257** D3
Aswa → *Uganda* 3°43N 31°55E **268** B3
Aswa-Lolim ◇ *Uganda* 2°43N 31°35E **268** B3
Aswad, Ra's al *Si. Arabia* 21°20N 39°0E **248** B2
Aswān *Egypt* 24°4N 32°57E **256** C3
Aswân High Dam = Sadd el Aali
  Egypt 23°54N 32°54E **256** C3
Asyût *Egypt* 27°11N 31°4E **256** B3
Asyûti, Wadi → *Egypt* 27°11N 31°16E **256** B3
Aszód *Hungary* 47°39N 19°28E **182** C4
At-Bashy *Kyrgyzstan* 41°10N 75°48E **217** D9
Atal *Chad* 13°13N 18°20E **258** F3
Atalaia do Norte *Brazil* 4°20S 70°12W **328** D3

Auburn S. Austral., Australia 34°1S 138°42E 282 C3
Auburn Ala., U.S.A. 32°36N 85°29W 316 C4
Auburn Calif., U.S.A. 38°54N 121°4W 306 G5
Auburn Ill., U.S.A. 39°36N 89°45W 310 E7
Auburn Ind., U.S.A. 41°22N 85°4W 311 C11
Auburn Maine, U.S.A. 44°6N 70°14W 309 C18
Auburn N.Y., U.S.A. 42°56N 76°34W 313 D8
Auburn Nebr., U.S.A. 40°23N 95°51W 308 E6
Auburn Pa., U.S.A. 40°36N 76°6W 313 F8
Auburn Wash., U.S.A. 47°18N 122°14W 306 C4
Auburn Ra. Australia 25°15S 150°30E 281 D5
Auburndale Fla., U.S.A. 28°4N 81°48W 317 G8
Auburndale Mass., U.S.A. 42°20N 71°14W 116 A1
Aubusson France 45°57N 2°11E 174 C6
Auce Latvia 56°28N 22°53E 184 B9
Auch France 43°39N 0°36E 174 E4
Auchendinny U.K. 55°51N 3°11W 121 B2
Auchi Nigeria 7°6N 6°13E 263 D6
Auchterarder U.K. 56°18N 3°41W 167 E5
Auchtermuchty U.K. 56°18N 3°13W 167 E5
Auckland N.Z. 36°52S 174°46E 284 C3
Auckland ☐ N.Z. 36°50S 175°0E 284 C3
Auckland Int. ✈ (AKL) N.Z. 37°0S 174°50E 284 C3
Auckland Is. Pac. Oc. 50°40S 166°5E 288 N8
Auckland Park S. Africa 26°11S 28°0E 123 B2
Aude ☐ France 43°8N 2°28E 174 E6
Aude ➔ France 43°13N 3°14E 174 E7
Auden Canada 50°14N 87°53W 298 B2
Auderghem Belgium 50°49N 4°26E 116 B2
Auderville France 49°43N 1°57W 172 C5
Audierne France 48°1N 4°34W 172 D2
Audincourt France 47°30N 6°50E 173 E13
Audo Ra. Ethiopia 6°20N 41°50E 257 F5
Audomarois ⌓ France 50°50N 2°30E 173 B9
Audubon U.S.A. 41°43N 94°56W 310 C2
Audubon Park U.S.A. 29°55N 90°8W 131 B2
Aue Germany 50°35N 12°41E 178 E8
Auerbach Germany 50°30N 12°24E 178 E8
Aufist W. Sahara 25°44N 14°39W 260 C2
Augathella Australia 25°48S 146°35E 281 D4
Aughnacloy U.K. 54°25N 6°59W 166 B5
Aughrim Ireland 53°18N 8°19W 166 C3
Augrabies Falls S. Africa 28°35S 20°20E 270 C3
Augrabies Falls △ S. Africa 28°40S 20°22E 270 C3
Augsburg Germany 48°25N 10°52E 179 G6
Augsburg-Westliche Wälder ⌓ Germany 48°22N 10°40E 179 G6
August Town Jamaica 17°59N 76°44W 320 a
Augusta W. Austral., Australia 34°19S 115°9E 279 F2
Augusta Italy 37°13N 15°13E 201 E8
Augusta Ark., U.S.A. 35°17N 91°22W 314 D9
Augusta Ga., U.S.A. 33°28N 81°58W 316 B8
Augusta Ill., U.S.A. 40°14N 90°57W 310 D6
Augusta Kans., U.S.A. 37°41N 96°59W 308 G5
Augusta Ky., U.S.A. 38°47N 84°0W 311 F12
Augusta Maine, U.S.A. 44°19N 69°47W 309 C19
Augusta Mont., U.S.A. 47°30N 112°24W 304 C7
Augusta, Mausoleo di Rome, Italy 136 b2
Augustenborg Denmark 54°57N 9°53E 163 K3
Augustine I. U.S.A. 59°22N 153°26W 303 G9
Augusto Cardosa = Metangula Mozam. 12°40S 34°50E 269 E3
Augustów Poland 53°51N 23°0E 184 E9
Augustówka Poland 52°11N 21°5E 143 B2
Augustus, Mt. Australia 24°20S 116°50E 279 D2
Augustus I. Australia 15°20S 124°30E 278 C3
Aujuittuq = Grise Fiord Canada 76°25N 82°57W 295 B15
Aukan Eritrea 15°29N 40°50E 257 D5
Auki Solomon Is. 8°45S 160°42E 287 M11
Aukra Norway 62°47N 6°55E 164 B3
Aukrug ⌓ Germany 54°5N 9°45E 178 A5
Aukštaitija △ Lithuania 55°15N 26°0E 161 J22
Aukum U.S.A. 38°34N 120°43W 306 G6
Aul India 20°41N 86°39E 244 D8
Aulavik △ Canada 73°42N 119°55W 294 C8
Auld, L. Australia 22°25S 123°50E 278 D3
Äūlīeköl Kazakhstan 52°32N 62°45E 216 B6
Aulifeltet Norway 60°30N 11°21E 162 D5
Auliye-Ata = Taraz Kazakhstan 42°54N 71°22E 217 D8
Aulla Italy 44°12N 9°58E 198 D6
Aulnay France 46°2N 0°22W 174 B3
Aulnay-sous-Bois France 48°56N 2°29E 134 A3
Aulne ➔ France 48°17N 4°16W 172 D2
Aulnoye-Aymeries France 50°12N 3°50E 173 B10
Aulong Palau 7°16N 134°17E 288 c
Ault Somme, France 50°8N 1°26E 172 B8
Ault Colo., U.S.A. 40°35N 104°44W 304 F11
Aulus-les-Bains France 42°49N 1°19E 174 F5
Aumale = Sour el Ghozlane Algeria 36°10N 3°45E 261 A5
Aumale France 49°46N 1°46E 173 C8
Aumo Papua N. G. 5°44S 148°30E 286 C5
Aumont-Aubrac France 44°43N 3°17E 174 D7
Auna Nigeria 10°9N 4°42E 263 C5
Aundah India 19°32N 77°3E 244 E3
Aundh India 17°33N 74°23E 244 F2
Auning Denmark 56°26N 10°22E 163 H4
Aunis France 46°5N 0°50W 174 B3
Aunu'u Amer. Samoa 14°20S 170°31W 302 f
Auponhia Indonesia 1°58S 125°27E 231 E7
Aups France 43°37N 6°15E 175 E10
Aur, Pulau Malaysia 2°35N 104°10E 237 L5
Aura Burma 26°59N 97°57E 241 B6
Auraiya India 26°28N 79°33E 243 F8
Aurangabad Bihar, India 24°45N 84°18E 243 G11
Aurangabad Maharashtra, India 19°50N 75°23E 244 E2
Auray France 47°40N 2°59W 172 E4
Aurdal Norway 60°55N 9°26E 164 D6
Aure Norway 63°16N 8°33E 164 A5
Aurelio Italy 41°54N 12°26E 136 B1
Aurès Algeria 35°8N 6°30E 261 A6
Aurich Germany 53°28N 7°28E 178 B3
Aurilândia Brazil 16°44S 50°28W 333 E1
Aurillac France 44°55N 2°26E 174 D6
Aurlandsfjorden Norway 61°3N 7°1E 164 C4
Aurlandsvangen Norway 60°55N 7°12E 164 D4
Auronzo di Cadore Italy 46°33N 12°26E 199 B9
Aurora = Maéwo Vanuatu 15°10S 168°10E 287 E6
Aurora = San Francisco Phil. 13°21N 122°31E 232 E4
Aurora Ont., Canada 44°0N 79°28W 312 C5
Aurora Isabela, Phil. 16°59N 121°38E 232 C3
Aurora Zamboanga del S., Phil. 7°57N 123°36E 233 H4
Aurora Western Cape, S. Africa 32°40S 18°29E 270 D2
Aurora Colo., U.S.A. 39°43N 104°49W 304 G11
Aurora Ill., U.S.A. 41°45N 88°19W 311 C8
Aurora Mo., U.S.A. 36°58N 93°43W 308 G7
Aurora N.Y., U.S.A. 42°45N 76°42W 313 D8
Aurora Nebr., U.S.A. 40°52N 98°0W 308 E5
Aurora Ohio, U.S.A. 41°21N 81°20W 312 E3
Aurora ☐ Phil. 15°30N 121°30E 232 D3
Aurora Memorial △ Phil. 15°40N 121°20E 232 D3
Aursmoen Norway 59°55N 11°26E 164 E8
Aursunden Norway 62°40N 11°40E 164 B8
Aurukun Australia 13°20S 141°45E 280 A3
Aurukun ✪ Australia 13°36S 141°48E 280 A3
Aus Namibia 26°35S 16°12E 270 C2
Ausa India 18°15N 76°30E 244 E3
Ausable ➔ Canada 43°19N 81°46W 312 C3
Auschwitz = Oświęcim Poland 50°2N 19°11E 185 H6
Ausîm Egypt 30°7N 31°8E 117 A1
Auski Roadhouse Australia 22°22S 118°41E 278 D2
Auspitz = Hustopeče Czechia 48°57N 16°43E 181 C9
Aussig = Ústí nad Labem Czechia 50°41N 14°3E 180 A7
Aust-Agder ☐ Norway 58°45N 8°0E 164 F4
Austad Norway 58°58N 7°37E 164 F4
Austen Harbour India 12°55N 92°45E 245 H11
Austerlitz = Slavkov u Brna Czechia 49°10N 16°52E 181 B9
Austerlitz, Gare d' Paris, France 48°50N 2°22E 134 A3
Austevoll Norway 60°5N 5°13E 164 D2
Austin Ill., U.S.A. 41°53N 87°45W 119 B2
Austin Ind., U.S.A. 38°45N 85°49W 311 F11
Austin Minn., U.S.A. 43°40N 92°58W 308 D7
Austin Nev., U.S.A. 39°30N 117°4W 304 G5
Austin Pa., U.S.A. 41°38N 78°6W 312 E6
Austin Tex., U.S.A. 30°17N 97°45W 314 F6
Austin, L. Australia 27°40S 118°0E 279 E2
Austin I. Canada 61°10N 94°0W 297 A10
Austmarka Norway 60°6N 12°21E 164 D9
Austnes Norway 62°38N 6°16E 164 B3
Austra Norway 65°8N 11°55E 160 D14
Austral Is. = Tubuaï, Îs. French Polynesia 25°0S 150°0W 289 f
Austral Seamount Chain Pac. Oc. 24°0S 150°0W 289 K13
Australia ■ Oceania 23°0S 135°0E 276 E3
Australian-Antarctic Basin S. Ocean 60°0S 120°0E 151 C9
Australian Capital Territory ☐ Australia 35°30S 149°0E 283 C8
Australind Australia 33°17S 115°42E 279 F2
Austria ■ Europe 47°0N 14°0E 180 E7
Austur-skaftafellssýsla Iceland 64°15N 16°0W 155 C10
Austurland ☐ Iceland 64°55N 15°30W 155 C11
Austvågøya Norway 68°20N 14°40E 160 B16
Autazes Brazil 3°35S 59°8W 329 D6
Auterive France 43°21N 1°29E 174 E5
Authie ➔ France 50°22N 1°38E 173 B8
Authon-du-Perche France 48°12N 0°54E 172 D7
Autlán de Navarro Mexico 19°46N 104°22W 318 D4
Autry Museum of the American West U.S.A. 34°9N 118°17W 126 B3
Autun France 46°58N 4°17E 173 F11
Auvergne France 45°20N 3°15E 171 D5
Auvergne, Mts. d' France 45°20N 2°55E 174 C6
Auvergne -Rhône-Alpes ☐ France 45°30N 5°0E 175 C8
Auvézère ➔ France 45°12N 0°50E 174 C4
Auxerre France 47°48N 3°32E 173 E10
Auxi-le-Château France 50°15N 2°8E 173 B9
Auxonne France 47°10N 5°20E 173 E12
Auxvasse U.S.A. 39°1N 91°54W 310 E5
Auyuittuq △ Canada 67°30N 66°0W 295 D18
Auzances France 46°2N 2°30E 173 F9
Auzangate, Nevado Peru 13°47S 71°13W 330 C3
Av-Dovurak Russia 51°17N 91°35E 215 D10
Ava Ill., U.S.A. 37°53N 89°30W 310 G7
Ava Mo., U.S.A. 36°57N 92°40W 308 G7
Avachinskaya Sopka Russia 53°15N 158°50E 215 D16
Avaldsnes Norway 59°21N 5°20E 164 E2
Avallon France 47°30N 3°53E 173 E10
Avalon U.S.A. 33°21N 118°20W 307 M8
Avalon Pen. Canada 47°30N 53°20W 299 C9
Avana ➔ Cook Is. 21°14S 159°43W 289 h
Avanavero Suriname 4°51N 57°22W 329 C6
Avanigadda India 16°0N 80°56E 245 G5
Avanos Turkey 38°43N 34°51E 212 C6
Avantas Greece 40°57N 25°56E 203 F9
Avaré Brazil 23°4S 48°58W 335 A6
Avarua Cook Is. 21°12S 159°46W 289 h
Avarua Harb. Cook Is. 21°12S 159°46W 289 h
Avatele Cook Is. 19°6S 169°55W 289 g
Avatiu Cook Is. 21°12S 159°47W 289 h
Avawatz Mts. U.S.A. 35°40N 116°30W 307 K10
Avdan Dağı Turkey 40°23N 29°46E 203 F13
Avedøre Denmark 55°37N 12°27E 118 B2
Aveiro Brazil 3°10S 55°5W 329 D6
Aveiro Portugal 40°37N 8°38W 194 E2
Aveiro ☐ Portugal 40°40N 8°35W 194 E2
Āvej Iran 35°40N 49°15E 247 C6
Avellaneda Argentina 34°40S 58°22W 117 C2
Avellino Italy 40°54N 14°47E 201 B7
Avenal U.S.A. 36°0N 120°8W 306 K6
Avenel U.S.A. 38°59N 76°59W 143 B3
Aventura U.S.A. 25°57N 80°8W 129 C3
Averøya Norway 63°0N 7°35E 164 A4
Aversa Italy 40°58N 14°12E 201 B7
Avery U.S.A. 47°15N 115°49W 304 C6
Aves, I. de W. Indies 15°45N 63°55W 321 C7
Aves, Is. las Venezuela 12°0N 67°30W 321 D6
Aves Laguna Colorada, Santuario de ⌓ Bolivia 22°30S 67°30W 330 E4
Aves Ridge W. Indies 14°0N 63°30W 321 D7
Avesnes-sur-Helpe France 50°8N 3°55E 173 B10
Avesnois ⌓ France 50°10N 3°45E 173 B10
Avesta Sweden 60°9N 16°10E 162 D10
Aveyron ☐ France 44°22N 2°45E 174 D6
Aveyron ➔ France 44°5N 1°16E 174 D5
Avezzano Italy 42°2N 13°25E 199 F10
Avgo Greece 35°33N 25°37E 205 F7
Aviá Terai Argentina 26°45S 60°50W 334 B3
Aviano Italy 46°4N 12°36E 199 B9
Aviatu ➔ Cook Is. 21°12S 159°49W 289 h
Aviemore U.K. 57°12N 3°50W 167 D5
Aviemore, L. N.Z. 44°37S 170°18E 285 E5
Avigliana Italy 45°5N 7°23E 198 C4
Avigliano Italy 40°44N 15°43E 201 B8
Avignon France 43°57N 4°50E 175 E8
Ávila Spain 40°39N 4°43W 194 E6
Ávila ☐ Spain 40°30N 5°0W 194 E6
Ávila, Sierra de Spain 40°40N 5°15W 194 E5
Avila Beach U.S.A. 35°11N 120°44W 307 K6
Avilés Spain 43°35N 5°57W 194 B5
Aviño Spain 43°36N 8°8W 194 B2
Avintes Portugal 41°7N 8°33W 194 D2
Avis Portugal 39°4N 7°53W 195 F3
Avis Pa., U.S.A. 41°11N 77°19W 312 E7
Avísio ➔ Italy 46°7N 11°5E 198 B8
Avissawella Sri Lanka 6°56N 80°11E 245 L5
Aviston U.S.A. 38°36N 89°36W 310 F7
Aviz = Avis Portugal 39°4N 7°53W 195 F3
Avize France 48°59N 4°1E 173 D11
Avlona = Vlorë Albania 40°32N 19°28E 202 F3
Avlonari Greece 38°31N 24°8E 204 C6
Avlum Denmark 56°16N 8°47E 163 H2
Avoca Vic., Australia 37°5S 143°26E 282 D5
Avoca N.Y., U.S.A. 42°25N 77°25W 312 D7
Avoca ➔ Vic., Australia 35°40S 143°43E 282 C5
Avoca ➔ Wicklow, Ireland 52°48N 6°10W 166 D5
Avola B.C., Canada 51°45N 119°19W 296 C5
Avola Italy 36°56N 15°7E 201 F8
Avon Ill., U.S.A. 40°40N 90°26W 310 D6
Avon N.Y., U.S.A. 42°55N 77°45W 312 D7
Avon ➔ W. Austral., Australia 31°40S 116°7E 279 F2
Avon ➔ Bristol, U.K. 51°29N 2°41W 169 F5
Avon ➔ Dorset, U.K. 50°44N 1°46W 169 G6
Avon ➔ Warks., U.K. 52°0N 2°8W 169 E5
Avon Park U.S.A. 27°36N 81°31W 317 H8
Avondale Ill., U.S.A. 41°56N 87°41W 119 B2
Avondale La., U.S.A. 29°54N 90°12W 131 B1
Avondale Zimbabwe 17°43S 30°58E 269 F3
Avondale Heights Australia 37°45S 144°52E 128 A1
Avonlea Canada 50°0N 105°0W 297 D8
Avonmore Canada 45°10N 74°58W 313 A10
Avonmouth U.K. 51°30N 2°42W 169 F5
Avramov Bulgaria 42°45N 26°38E 203 D10
Avranches France 48°40N 1°20W 172 D5
Avre ➔ France 48°47N 1°22E 172 D8
Avrig Romania 45°43N 24°21E 183 E9
Avrillé France 47°30N 0°35W 172 E6
Avtovac Bos.-H. 43°9N 18°35E 202 C2
Avtovo Russia 59°51N 30°16E 137 B1
Avu Avu Solomon Is. 9°50S 160°22E 287 M11
Awa-Shima Japan 38°27N 139°14E 220 E9
Awag el Baqar South Sudan 10°10N 33°10E 257 E3
A'waj ➔ Syria 33°23N 36°20E 250 E7
Awaji Japan 34°28N 134°56E 222 C6
Awaji-Shima Japan 34°30N 134°50E 222 C6
'Awālī Bahrain 26°0N 50°30E 247 E6
Awantipur India 33°55N 75°3E 243 C6
Awanui N.Z. 35°4S 173°17E 284 B2
Aware Ethiopia 8°16N 44°9E 267 C5
Awarja ➔ India 17°5N 76°15E 244 F3
Awarua B. N.Z. 44°28S 168°4E 285 E3
Awarua Pt. N.Z. 44°15S 168°5E 285 E3
Awasa Ethiopia 7°2N 38°28E 257 F4
Awasa, L. Ethiopia 7°0N 38°30E 257 F4
Awash Ethiopia 9°1N 40°10E 257 F5
Awash ➔ Ethiopia 11°45N 41°5E 257 E5
Awash △ Ethiopia 9°8N 40°0E 257 F5
Awaso Ghana 6°15N 2°22W 262 D4
Awat China 40°35N 80°24E 217 D10
Awatere ➔ N.Z. 41°37S 174°10E 285 B9
Awbārī Libya 26°46N 12°57E 258 C2
Awbārī, Idehan Libya 27°10N 11°30E 258 C2
Awdal ☐ Somalia 10°30N 43°30E 267 B5
Awdheegle Somalia 1°59N 44°50E 267 D5
Awe, L. U.K. 56°17N 5°16W 167 E3
Aweil South Sudan 8°42N 27°20E 257 F2
Awgu Nigeria 6°4N 7°24E 263 D6
Awjilah Libya 29°8N 21°7E 258 C4
Awka Nigeria 6°12N 7°5E 263 D6
Aworro Papua N. G. 7°43S 143°11E 286 D2
Awsard Mauritania 22°37N 14°22W 260 D2
Ax-les-Thermes France 42°44N 1°50E 174 F5
Axat France 42°48N 2°13E 174 F6
Axe ➔ U.K. 50°42N 3°4W 169 F5
Axel Heiberg I. Canada 80°0N 90°0W 295 B14
Axim Ghana 4°51N 2°15W 262 E4
Axinim Brazil 4°2S 59°22W 329 D6
Axintele Romania 44°37N 26°47E 183 F11
Axioma Brazil 6°45S 64°31W 331 B5
Axios ➔ Greece 40°57N 22°35E 202 F6
Axminster U.K. 50°46N 3°0W 169 G4
Axson U.S.A. 31°17N 82°44W 316 D7
Axvall Sweden 58°23N 13°34E 163 F7
Ay France 49°3N 4°1E 173 C11
Ayaantang Eq. Guin. 1°58N 10°24E 264 B2
Ayabaca Peru 4°40S 79°53W 330 A2
Ayabe Japan 35°20N 135°20E 223 B7
Ayacucho Argentina 37°5S 58°20W 334 D4
Ayacucho Peru 13°0S 74°0W 330 C3
Ayacucho ☐ Peru 14°0S 74°0W 330 C3
Ayaguz = Ayaköz Kazakhstan 48°10N 80°10E 217 C10
Ayakkum Hu China 37°30N 89°20E 217 E11
Ayaköz Kazakhstan 48°10N 80°10E 217 C10
Ayaköz ➔ Kazakhstan 46°40N 79°14E 217 C9
Ayakudi India 10°28N 77°56E 245 J3
Ayala Phil. 6°57N 121°57E 233 H3
Ayamé Ivory C. 5°35N 3°9W 262 D4
Ayamonte Spain 37°12N 7°24W 195 H3
Ayan Russia 56°30N 138°16E 215 D14
Ayancık Turkey 41°57N 34°35E 212 B6
Ayangba Nigeria 7°31N 7°8E 263 D6
Ayapel Colombia 8°19N 75°9W 328 B2
Ayas Turkey 40°2N 32°21E 212 B5
Ayaviri Peru 14°50S 70°35W 330 C3
Ayazağa Turkey 41°6N 28°59E 122 B1
Āybak Afghan. 36°15N 68°5E 240 A3
Aybastı Turkey 40°41N 37°23E 212 B7
Aydarko'l Ko'li Uzbekistan 40°50N 67°10E 217 D7
Aydın Turkey 37°51N 27°51E 212 D2
Aydin ☐ Turkey 37°50N 28°0E 205 D9
Aydin Dağları Turkey 38°0N 28°0E 205 D10
Aydıncık Turkey 36°9N 33°21E 250 B4
Aydingkol Hu China 42°40N 89°15E 217 D11
Ayelu Ethiopia 10°5N 40°42E 257 E5
Ayenngré Togo 8°40N 1°1E 263 D5
Ayer U.S.A. 42°34N 71°35W 313 D13
Ayer Chawan, Pulau Singapore 1°16N 103°41E 138 B2
Ayer Hitam Malaysia 5°24N 100°16E 237 c
Ayer Merbau, Pulau Singapore 1°16N 103°42E 138 B2
Ayerbe Spain 42°17N 0°41W 196 C4
Ayer's Cliff Canada 45°10N 72°3W 313 A12
Ayers Rock = Uluru Australia 25°23S 131°5E 279 E5
Ayeyarwady = Ayeyawadi ➔ Burma 15°50N 95°6E 241 G5
Ayeyawadi ➔ Burma 15°50N 95°6E 241 G5
Áyia Napa Cyprus 34°59N 34°0E 207 F10
Áyia Phyla Cyprus 34°43N 33°1E 207 F9
Áyios Amvrósios Cyprus 35°20N 33°35E 207 E9
Áyios Seryios Cyprus 35°12N 33°53E 207 E9
Áyios Theodhoros Cyprus 35°22N 34°1E 207 E10
Áyios Yeóryios = Aghios Georgios Greece 37°28N 23°57E 204 D5
Aykhal Russia 66°0N 111°30E 215 C12
Aykino Russia 62°15N 49°56E 186 B8
Aykirikçi Turkey 39°8N 30°9E 205 B12
Aylesbury U.K. 51°49N 0°49W 169 F7
Aylmer Canada 42°46N 80°59W 312 D4
Aylmer, L. Canada 64°5N 108°30W 294 E10
'Ayn al Ghazālah Libya 32°10N 23°20E 258 B4
Ayn Dār Si. Arabia 25°55N 49°10E 247 E7
Ayn Sifnī Iraq 36°41N 43°20E 213 D10
Ayn Zālah Iraq 36°45N 42°35E 213 D10
Ayna Spain 38°34N 2°3W 197 G2
Aynāt Yemen 16°4N 49°9E 249 C5
'Aynūnah Si. Arabia 28°5N 35°8E 251 K6
Ayod South Sudan 8°7N 31°26E 257 F3
Ayolas Paraguay 27°10S 56°59W 334 B4
Ayon, Ostrov Russia 69°50N 169°0E 215 C17
Ayora Spain 39°3N 1°3W 197 F3
Ayorou Niger 14°53N 1°0E 263 C5
Ayos Cameroon 3°53N 12°31E 264 B2
'Ayoûn el 'Atroûs Mauritania 16°38N 9°37W 262 B3
Ayr Queens., Australia 19°35S 147°25E 280 B4
Ayr Ont., Canada 43°17N 80°27W 312 C4
Ayr S. Ayrs., U.K. 55°28N 4°38W 167 F4
Ayr ➔ U.K. 55°28N 4°38W 167 F4
Ayrancı Turkey 37°21N 33°41E 212 D5
Ayrancılar Turkey 38°15N 27°18E 205 C9
Ayre, Pt. of I. of Man 54°25N 4°21W 168 C3
Ayribaba Turkmenistan 37°50N 66°34E 217 E7
Aysén ☐ Chile 46°30S 73°0W 336 C2
Aysha Ethiopia 10°50N 42°23E 257 E5
Ayteke Bi Kazakhstan 45°48N 62°6E 216 C6
Ayton Australia 15°56S 145°22E 280 B4
Aytos Bulgaria 42°42N 27°16E 203 D11
Aytoska Planina Bulgaria 42°45N 27°30E 203 D11
Ayu, Kepulauan Indonesia 0°35N 131°5E 231 D8
Ayutla Guatemala 14°40N 92°10W 320 D1
Ayutla de los Libres Mexico 16°54N 99°13W 319 D5
Ayutthaya = Phra Nakhon Si Ayutthaya Thailand 14°25N 100°30E 236 E3
Ayvacık Turkey 39°36N 26°24E 212 C2
Ayvalık Turkey 39°20N 26°46E 205 B8
Az Zabadānī Syria 33°43N 36°5E 250 E7
Aẓ Ẓāhirāh ☐ Oman 22°40N 56°0E 249 B7
Aẓ Ẓāhirīyah West Bank 31°25N 34°58E 251 G5
Aẓ Ẓahrān Si. Arabia 26°10N 50°7E 247 E6
Az Zarqā Jordan 32°5N 36°4E 251 F7
Az Zarqā' U.A.E. 24°53N 53°4E 247 E7
Az Zāwiyah Libya 32°52N 12°56E 258 B2
Az Zāwiyah ☐ Libya 32°44N 12°43E 261 B7
Az Zaydīyah Yemen 15°20N 43°1E 248 D3
Az Zībār Iraq 36°52N 44°4E 213 D11
Az Zilfī Si. Arabia 26°12N 44°52E 246 E5
Az Zubayr Iraq 30°26N 47°40E 246 D5
Az Zuhrah Yemen 15°44N 43°0E 248 D3
Az Zuqur Yemen 14°0N 42°45E 248 D3
Az Zuwaytīnah Libya 30°58N 20°7E 258 B4
Azabu Tokyo, Japan 140 c3
Azad Kashmir ☐ Pakistan 33°50N 73°50E 243 C5
Azahar, Costa del Spain 40°0N 0°5E 196 F5
Azambuja Portugal 39°4N 8°51W 195 F2
Azamgarh India 26°5N 83°13E 243 F10
Azangaro Peru 14°55S 70°13W 330 C3
Azaoua Niger 15°50N 4°0E 263 B5
Azaouad Mali 19°0N 3°0W 262 B4
Azaouak ➔ Mali 15°30N 3°18E 263 B5
Azaouak, Vallée de l' Mali 15°50N 3°20E 263 B5
Āzār Shahr Iran 37°45N 45°59E 213 D11
Azara Nigeria 8°22N 9°12E 263 D6
Azarān Iran 37°25N 47°16E 213 D12
Azärbayjan = Azerbaijan ■ Asia 40°20N 48°0E 191 K9
Āzarbāyjān-e Gharbī ☐ Iran 37°0N 44°30E 246 B5
Āzarbāyjān-e Sharqī ☐ Iran 37°20N 47°0E 246 B5
Azare Nigeria 11°55N 10°10E 263 C7
Azay-le-Rideau France 47°16N 0°30E 172 E7
A'zāz Syria 36°36N 37°4E 250 B8
Azazga Algeria 36°48N 4°22E 261 A5
Azbine = Aïr Niger 18°30N 8°0E 259 E1
Azcapotzalco Mexico 19°28N 99°10W 128 B1
Azefal Mauritania 21°0N 14°45W 260 D2
Azeffoun Algeria 36°51N 4°26E 261 A5
Azemmour Morocco 33°20N 9°20W 260 B3
Azennezal Algeria 22°58N 0°43E 261 D5
Azerbaijan ■ Asia 40°20N 48°0E 191 K9
Azezo Ethiopia 12°28N 37°15E 257 E4
Azkoien = Peralta Spain 42°20N 1°48W 196 C3
Aznalcóllar Spain 37°32N 6°17W 195 H4
Azogues Ecuador 2°35S 78°0W 328 D2
Azores = Açores, Is. dos Atl. Oc. 38°0N 27°0W 153 d1
Azores-Biscay Rise Atl. Oc. 42°0N 20°0W 152 B9
Azoum, B. ➔ Chad 10°53N 20°15E 259 F4
Azov Russia 47°3N 39°25E 191 G4
Azov, Sea of Europe 46°0N 36°30E 189 J9
Azovskoye More = Azov, Sea of Europe 46°0N 36°30E 189 J9
Azpeitia Spain 43°12N 2°19W 196 B2
Azrak, B. ➔ Chad 10°52N 20°35E 259 F4
Azraq ash Shīshān Jordan 31°50N 36°49E 251 G7
Azrou Morocco 33°28N 5°19W 260 B3
Aztec U.S.A. 36°49N 107°59W 305 H10
Azteca, Estadia Mexico 19°19N 99°9W 128 C2
Azua de Compostela Dom. Rep. 18°25N 70°44W 321 C5
Azuaga Spain 38°16N 5°39W 195 G5
Azuara Spain 41°15N 0°53W 196 D4
Azuay ☐ Ecuador 2°55S 79°0W 328 D2
Azucar, Cerro Pan de Chile 33°19S 70°41W 137 A1
Azuer ➔ Spain 39°8N 3°36W 195 F7
Azuero, Pen. de Panama 7°30N 80°30W 320 E3
Azuga Romania 45°27N 25°33E 183 E10
Azul Argentina 36°42S 59°43W 334 D4
Azul, Lagoa Azores 37°52N 25°47W 153 d3
Azul, Serra Brazil 14°50S 54°50W 331 C7
Azumino Japan 36°20N 137°50E 223 A9
Azur, Côte d' France 43°25N 7°10E 175 E11
Azurduy Bolivia 19°59S 64°29W 331 D5
Azusa U.S.A. 34°8N 117°52W 307 L9
Azzaba Algeria 36°48N 7°6E 261 A6
Azzano Décimo Italy 45°52N 12°56E 199 C9
Azzel Matti, Sebkra Algeria 26°10N 0°43E 261 C5

B

Ba Be △ Vietnam 22°25N 105°37E 236 A5
Ba Don Vietnam 17°45N 106°26E 236 D6
Ba Dong Vietnam 9°40N 106°33E 237 H6
Ba Ngoi Vietnam 11°54N 109°10E 237 G7
Ba Ria Vietnam 10°30N 107°10E 237 G6
Ba Tri Vietnam 10°2N 106°36E 237 G6
Ba Vi △ Vietnam 21°1N 105°22E 236 B5
Ba Xian = Bazhou China 39°8N 116°22E 226 E9
Baa Indonesia 10°50S 123°0E 278 B3
Baalbek = Ba'labakk Lebanon 34°0N 36°10E 250 E7
Baambrugge Neths. 52°15N 4°59E 112 B2
Baamonde Spain 43°7N 7°44W 194 B3
Baao Phil. 13°27N 123°22E 232 E4
Baardheere Somalia 2°20N 42°27E 267 D5
Baarle-Nassau Belgium 51°27N 4°56E 170 C4
Bab el Mandeb Red Sea 12°35N 43°25E 248 D3
Baba Bulgaria 42°44N 23°59E 202 D7
Baba, B. do Angola 14°50S 12°14E 265 E2
Bābā, Koh-i- Afghan. 34°30N 67°0E 240 B2
Baba Budan Hills India 13°30N 75°44E 245 H2
Baba Burnu Turkey 39°29N 26°2E 205 B8
Baba Channel Pakistan 24°48N 66°58E 123 B1
Baba dag Azerbaijan 41°0N 48°19E 191 K9
Baba I. Pakistan 24°49N 66°57E 123 B1
Bābā Kalū Iran 30°7N 50°49E 247 D6
Babaçulândia Brazil 7°13S 47°46W 332 C2
Babadag Romania 44°53N 28°44E 183 F13
Babadağ Turkey 37°49N 28°52E 205 D10
Babaeski Turkey 41°26N 27°6E 203 E11
Babahoyo Ecuador 1°40S 79°30W 328 D2
Babai = Sarju ➔ India 27°21N 81°23E 243 F9
Babai ➔ Nepal 28°10N 82°21E 243 E10
Babak Phil. 7°8N 125°41E 233 H5
Babana Nigeria 10°31N 3°46E 263 C5
Babanusa Sudan 11°20N 27°48E 257 E2
Babar Algeria 35°10N 7°6E 261 A6
Babar Indonesia 8°0S 129°30E 231 F7
Babar Pakistan 31°7N 69°32E 242 D3
Babarkach Pakistan 29°45N 68°0E 242 E3
Babarpur India 28°41N 77°16E 120 A2
Babase I. Papua N. G. 4°0S 153°42E 286 B7
Babayevo Russia 59°24N 35°55E 188 C8
Babb U.S.A. 48°51N 113°27W 304 B7
Babelthuap Palau 7°30N 134°30E 288 c
Babenhausen Germany 49°57N 8°57E 179 F4
Băbeni Romania 44°59N 24°11E 183 F9
Baberu India 25°33N 80°43E 243 G9
Babi Indonesia 2°5N 96°39E 234 B1
Babi Besar, Pulau Malaysia 2°25N 103°59E 237 L4
Babia Gora Europe 49°38N 19°38E 185 J6
Babian Jiang ➔ China 22°55N 101°47E 228 F3
Bābil ☐ Iraq 32°30N 44°30E 246 C5
Babile Ethiopia 9°16N 42°11E 257 F5
Babile ⌓ Ethiopia 8°45N 42°20E 267 C5
Babimost Poland 52°10N 15°49E 185 F2
Babinda Australia 17°20S 145°56E 280 B4
Babine Canada 55°22N 126°37W 296 B3
Babine ➔ Canada 55°45N 127°44W 296 B3
Babine L. Canada 54°48N 126°0W 296 C3
Babiogórski △ Poland 49°38N 19°39E 185 J6
Babo Indonesia 2°30S 133°30E 231 E8
Babócsa Hungary 46°2N 17°21E 182 D2
Bābol Iran 36°40N 52°50E 247 B7
Bābol Sar Iran 36°45N 52°45E 247 B7
Babor, Dj. Algeria 36°31N 5°25E 261 A6
Baborów Poland 50°7N 18°1E 185 H5
Baboua C.A.R. 5°49N 14°58E 264 A2
Babruysk Belarus 53°10N 29°15E 177 B15
Babson Park U.S.A. 27°49N 81°32W 317 H8
Babuhri India 26°49N 69°43E 242 F3
Babuna Macedonia 41°30N 21°40E 202 E5
Babura Nigeria 12°51N 8°59E 263 C6
Babusar Pass Pakistan 35°12N 73°59E 243 B5
Babushkin Russia 55°51N 37°42E 129 A3
Babušnica Serbia 43°7N 22°27E 202 C6
Babuyan Phil. 10°0N 118°54E 233 F2
Babuyan Chan. Phil. 18°40N 121°30E 232 B3
Babuyan I. Phil. 19°32N 121°57E 232 B3
Babuyan Is. Phil. 19°10N 121°40E 232 B3
Babylon Iraq 32°34N 44°22E 213 F11
Bač Serbia 45°29N 19°17E 182 E4
Bâc ➔ Moldova 46°55N 29°26E 183 D14
Bac Can Vietnam 22°8N 105°49E 228 F5
Bac Giang Vietnam 21°16N 106°11E 228 G6
Bac Lieu Vietnam 9°17N 105°43E 237 H5
Bac Ninh Vietnam 21°13N 106°4E 228 G6
Bac Phan Vietnam 22°0N 105°0E 228 G5
Bacaadweyn Somalia 7°15N 47°40E 267 C6
Bacabal Brazil 4°15S 44°45W 332 B3
Bacacay Phil. 13°18N 123°47E 232 E4
Bacajá ➔ Brazil 3°25S 51°50W 329 D7
Bacalar Mexico 18°43N 88°27W 319 D7
Bacan, Kepulauan Indonesia 0°35S 127°30E 231 E7
Bacarra Phil. 18°15N 120°37E 232 B3
Bacău Romania 46°35N 26°55E 183 D11
Bacău ☐ Romania 46°30N 26°45E 183 D11
Baccarat France 48°28N 6°42E 173 D13
Bacchus Marsh Australia 37°43S 144°27E 282 D6
Bacerac Mexico 30°18N 108°50W 318 A3
Băceşti Romania 46°50N 27°11E 183 D12
Bach Long Vi, Dao Vietnam 20°10N 107°40E 236 B6
Bach Ma △ Vietnam 16°11N 107°49E 236 D6
Bachaquero Venezuela 9°56N 71°8W 328 B3
Bacharach Germany 50°3N 7°44E 179 E3
Bachelor's Beach Bonaire 12°11N 68°18W 322 h
Bachhwara India 25°35N 85°54E 243 G11
Bachu China 39°46N 78°34E 217 E9
Bachuma Ethiopia 6°48N 35°53E 257 F4
Bačina Serbia 43°42N 21°23E 202 C5
Back ➔ Canada 65°10N 104°0W 294 D11
Back B. India 18°56N 72°48E 130 B1
Bačka Palanka Serbia 45°17N 19°27E 182 E4
Bačka Topola Serbia 45°49N 19°39E 182 E4
Bäckebo Sweden 56°53N 16°4E 163 H10
Bäckefors Sweden 58°48N 12°9E 163 F6
Bäckhammar Sweden 59°10N 14°11E 162 E8
Bački Petrovac Serbia 45°29N 19°32E 182 E4
Backnang Germany 48°56N 9°26E 179 G5
Backstairs Passage Australia 35°40S 138°5E 282 C3
Baclaran Phil. 14°31N 121°0E 127 B2
Bacnotan Phil. 16°43N 120°21E 232 C3
Baco, Mt. Phil. 12°49N 121°10E 232 E3
Bacolod Phil. 10°40N 122°57E 233 F4
Bacon Phil. 13°3N 124°3E 232 E5
Baconton U.S.A. 31°23N 84°10W 316 D5
Bacoor Phil. 14°27N 120°56E 127 C1
Bacoor B. Phil. 14°27N 120°54E 127 C1
Bacqueville-en-Caux France 49°47N 1°0E 172 C8
Bács-Kiskun ☐ Hungary 46°43N 19°30E 182 D4
Bácsalmás Hungary 46°8N 19°17E 182 D4
Bacuag = Placer Phil. 9°36N 125°38E 233 G5
Bacuit = El Nido Phil. 11°10N 119°25E 233 F2
Bacuk Malaysia 6°4N 102°25E 237 J4
Bácum Mexico 27°33N 110°5W 318 B2
Bād Iran 33°41N 52°1E 247 C7
Bad ➔ U.S.A. 44°21N 100°22W 308 C3
Bad Aussee Austria 47°43N 13°45E 180 D6
Bad Axe U.S.A. 43°48N 83°0W 312 C2
Bad Bergzabern Germany 49°6N 7°59E 179 F3
Bad Berleburg Germany 51°2N 8°26E 178 D4
Bad Bevensen Germany 53°5N 10°35E 178 B6
Bad Bramstedt Germany 53°55N 9°53E 178 B5
Bad Brückenau Germany 50°18N 9°47E 179 E5
Bad Doberan Germany 54°6N 11°53E 178 A7
Bad Driburg Germany 51°43N 9°1E 178 D5
Bad Ems Germany 50°20N 7°43E 179 E3
Bad Frankenhausen Germany 51°21N 11°5E 178 D7
Bad Freienwalde Germany 52°46N 14°1E 178 C10
Bad Goisern Austria 47°38N 13°38E 180 D6
Bad Harzburg Germany 51°52N 10°34E 178 D6
Bad Hersfeld Germany 50°52N 9°42E 178 E5
Bad Hofgastein Austria 47°17N 13°6E 180 D6
Bad Homburg Germany 50°13N 8°38E 179 E4
Bad Honnef Germany 50°38N 7°13E 178 E3
Bad Iburg Germany 52°10N 8°3E 178 C4
Bad Ischl Austria 47°44N 13°38E 180 D6
Bad Kissingen Germany 50°11N 10°4E 179 E6
Bad Königshofen Germany 50°17N 10°28E 179 E6
Bad Kreuznach Germany 49°50N 7°51E 179 F3
Bad Krozingen Germany 47°54N 7°42E 179 H3
Bad Kudowa = Kudowa-Zdrój Poland 50°27N 16°15E 185 H3
Bad Laasphe Germany 50°56N 8°25E 178 E4
Bad Landeck = Lądek-Zdrój Poland 50°21N 16°53E 185 H3
Bad Langensalza Germany 51°5N 10°38E 178 D6
Bad Lauterberg Germany 51°38N 10°28E 178 D6
Bad Leonfelden Austria 48°31N 14°18E 180 C7
Bad Liebenwerda Germany 51°31N 13°24E 178 D9
Bad Mergentheim Germany 49°28N 9°42E 179 F5
Bad Münstereifel Germany 50°33N 6°46E 178 E2
Bad Nauheim Germany 50°21N 8°43E 179 E4
Bad Neuenahr-Ahrweiler Germany 50°32N 7°5E 178 E3
Bad Neustadt Germany 50°18N 10°13E 179 E6
Bad Oeynhausen Germany 52°12N 8°46E 178 C4
Bad Oldesloe Germany 53°48N 10°22E 178 B6
Bad Orb Germany 50°12N 9°22E 179 E5
Bad Polzin = Polanica-Zdrój Poland 50°24N 16°32E 185 H3
Bad Pyrmont Germany 51°59N 9°16E 178 D5
Bad Reichenhall Germany 47°43N 12°54E 179 H8
Bad Reinerz = Duszniki-Zdrój Poland 50°24N 16°24E 185 H3
Bad Säckingen Germany 47°33N 7°56E 179 H3
Bad Salzuflen Germany 52°5N 8°45E 178 C4
Bad Salzungen Germany 50°48N 10°14E 178 E6
Bad Sankt Leonhard Austria 46°58N 14°47E 180 E7
Bad Schönfliess = Trzcińsko Zdrój Poland 52°58N 14°35E 185 F1
Bad Schwartau Germany 53°55N 10°41E 178 B6
Bad Segeberg Germany 53°56N 10°17E 178 B6
Bad Tölz Germany 47°45N 11°34E 179 H7
Bad Urach Germany 48°29N 9°23E 179 G5
Bad Vöslau Austria 47°58N 16°12E 181 D9
Bad Waldsee Germany 47°55N 9°45E 179 H5
Bad Wildungen Germany 51°6N 9°7E 178 D5
Bad Wimpfen Germany 49°13N 9°11E 179 F5
Bad Windsheim Germany 49°36N 10°25E 179 F6
Bad Zwischenahn Germany 53°12N 8°1E 178 B4
Bada Barabil India 22°7N 85°24E 243 H11
Badagara = Vadakara India 11°35N 75°40E 245 J2
Badagri Nigeria 6°25N 2°55E 263 D5
Badain Jaran Shamo China 40°23N 102°0E 218 C9
Badajós, L. Brazil 3°15S 62°50W 329 D5
Badajoz Spain 38°50N 6°59W 195 G4
Badajoz ☐ Spain 38°40N 6°30W 195 G4
Badakhshān ☐ Afghan. 36°30N 71°0E 240 A3
Badaling China 40°20N 116°0E 226 D9
Badalona Spain 41°26N 2°15E 114 A2
Badalzai Afghan. 29°50N 65°35E 242 E1
Badami India 15°55N 75°41E 245 G2
Badampahar India 22°10N 86°10E 244 C8
Badanah Si. Arabia 30°58N 41°30E 246 D4
Badarinath India 30°45N 79°30E 243 D8
Badarpur India 24°54N 92°36E 241 C4
Badas, Kepulauan Indonesia 0°45N 107°5E 234 B3
Baddo ➔ Pakistan 28°0N 64°20E 240 D2
Bade = Pate Taiwan 24°56N 121°17E 225 B3
Bade Indonesia 7°10S 139°35E 231 F9
Badeggi Nigeria 9°1N 6°8E 263 D6
Badéguichéri Niger 14°30N 5°22E 263 C6
Baden Austria 48°1N 16°13E 181 C9
Baden Switz. 47°28N 8°18E 179 H4
Baden Pa., U.S.A. 40°38N 80°14W 312 F4
Baden-Baden Germany 48°44N 8°13E 179 G4
Baden-Württemberg ☐ Germany 48°20N 8°40E 179 G4
Badgam India 34°1N 74°45E 243 B6
Badgastein Austria 47°7N 13°9E 180 D6
Badger Nfld. & L., Canada 49°0N 56°4W 299 C8
Badger Calif., U.S.A. 36°38N 119°1W 306 J7
Bādghīs ☐ Afghan. 35°0N 63°0E 240 B1
Badgingarra △ Australia 30°23S 115°22E 279 F2
Badhan = Buraan Somalia 10°14N 48°44E 267 B6
Badhoevedorp Neths. 52°20N 4°47E 112 A1
Badia Polésine Italy 45°5N 11°29E 199 C8
Badian Phil. 9°55N 123°24E 233 G4
Badiar △ Guinea 13°37N 13°11W 262 C2
Badin Pakistan 24°38N 68°54E 242 G3
Badinka ⌓ Mali 13°31N 9°28W 262 C3
Badjokola Dem. Rep. of the Congo 3°54N 20°17E 264 B4
Badlands U.S.A. 43°55N 102°30W 308 D2
Badlands △ U.S.A. 43°38N 102°56W 308 D2
Badli India 28°44N 77°8E 120 A1
Badme Africa 14°43N 37°48E 248 D2
Badnera India 20°48N 77°44E 244 D3
Badoc Phil. 17°56N 120°28E 232 C3
Badogo Mali 11°2N 8°13W 262 C3
Badoumbé Mali 13°42N 10°15W 262 C2
Badr Ḥunayn Si. Arabia 23°44N 38°46E 248 B2
Badrah Iraq 33°6N 45°58E 213 F11
Badrain Jaran Shamo China 40°40N 103°20E 226 D2
Badrinath India 30°44N 79°29E 243 D8
Badu Australia 10°7S 142°11E 280 a
Badulla Sri Lanka 7°1N 81°7E 245 L5
Badung, Bukit Indonesia 8°49S 115°10E 231 K18
Badung, Selat Indonesia 8°40S 115°22E 231 K18
Badvel India 14°45N 79°3E 245 G4
Baena Spain 37°37N 4°20W 195 H6
Baengnyeongdo S. Korea 37°57N 124°40E 224 D2
Baerami Australia 32°27S 150°27E 283 B9
Bærum Norway 59°54N 10°36E 133 A2
Baetov Kyrgyzstan 41°13N 74°54E 217 D8
Baeza Ecuador 0°25S 77°53W 328 D2
Baeza Spain 37°57N 3°25W 195 H7
Bafang Cameroon 5°9N 10°11E 263 D7
Bafatá Guinea-Biss. 12°8N 14°40W 262 C2
Baffin B. N. Amer. 72°0N 64°0W 292 B13
Baffin I. Canada 68°0N 75°0W 295 D17
Bafia Cameroon 4°40N 11°10E 263 E7
Bafilo Togo 9°22N 1°22E 263 D5
Bafing ➔ Mali 13°49N 10°50W 262 C2
Bafing △ Mali 12°38N 10°28W 262 C2
Bafliyūn Syria 36°37N 36°59E 246 B3
Bafoulabé Mali 13°50N 10°55W 262 C2
Bafoussam Cameroon 5°28N 10°25E 263 D7
Bāfq Iran 31°40N 55°25E 247 D7
Bafra Turkey 41°34N 35°54E 212 B6
Bafra Burnu Turkey 41°45N 36°2E 212 B7
Bāft Iran 29°15N 56°38E 247 D8
Bafut Cameroon 6°6N 10°2E 263 D7
Bafwasende Dem. Rep. of the Congo 1°3N 27°5E 268 B2
Bagabag Phil. 16°30N 121°15E 232 C3
Bagabag I. Papua N. G. 4°48S 146°14E 286 C4
Bagac Phil. 14°36N 120°23E 232 D3
Bagac B. Phil. 14°36N 120°20E 232 D3
Bagaha India 27°6N 84°5E 244 A7
Bagalkot India 16°10N 75°40E 245 F2
Bagam Niger 15°43N 6°35E 263 B6
Bagamanoc Phil. 13°57N 124°17E 232 E5
Bagamoyo Tanzania 6°28S 38°55E 268 D4
Bagan = Pagan Burma 21°10N 94°52E 241 E5
Bagan Datoh Malaysia 3°59N 100°47E 237 L3
Bagan Serai Malaysia 5°1N 100°32E 237 K3
Baganga Phil. 7°34N 126°33E 233 H6
Bagani Namibia 18°7S 21°41E 270 A3
Bagansiapiapi Indonesia 2°12N 100°50E 234 B2
Bagasra India 21°30N 71°0E 242 J4
Bagata Dem. Rep. of the Congo 3°44S 17°57E 264 C3
Bagaud India 22°19N 75°53E 242 H6
Bagawi Sudan 12°20N 34°18E 257 E3
Bagbag Sudan 15°23N 31°30E 257 D3
Bağcılar Turkey 41°2N 28°49E 122 B1
Bagdad Calif., U.S.A. 34°35N 115°53W 307 L11
Bagdad Fla., U.S.A. 30°36N 87°2W 317 E2
Bagdarin Russia 54°26N 113°36E 215 D12
Bagé Brazil 31°20S 54°15W 335 C5
Bagenalstown Ireland 52°42N 6°58W 166 D5
Bagepalli India 13°47N 77°47E 245 H3
Bagerhat Bangla. 22°40N 89°47E 241 D2
Bageshwar India 29°51N 79°46E 243 E8
Bagevadi India 16°35N 75°58E 244 F2
Baggao Phil. 17°56N 121°46E 232 C3
Bággio Italy 45°27N 9°6E 128 B1
Baggs U.S.A. 41°2N 107°39W 304 F10
Bagh Pakistan 33°59N 73°45E 243 C5
Bāgh-e-Feyz Iran 35°44N 51°19E 141 A1
Baghain ➔ India 25°32N 81°1E 243 G9
Baghdād Iraq 33°20N 44°23E 113 A2
Baghdad Int. ✈ (BGW) Iraq 33°15N 44°14E 113 B1
Baghdadi Georgia 42°5N 42°49E 213 A10
Bagheria Italy 38°5N 13°30E 200 D6
Baghlān Afghan. 32°12N 68°46E 240 A3
Baghlān ☐ Afghan. 36°0N 68°30E 240 B3
Bagley U.S.A. 47°32N 95°24W 308 B6
Baglung Nepal 28°16N 83°36E 243 E10
Bagmari India 22°34N 88°23E 124 B2
Bagn Norway 60°49N 9°34E 164 D6
Bagnara Cálabra Italy 38°17N 15°48E 201 D8
Bagnasco Italy 44°18N 8°2E 198 D5
Bagnell Dam U.S.A. 38°14N 92°36W 310 F4
Bagnères-de-Bigorre France 43°5N 0°9E 174 E4

Bagnères-de-Luchon France 42°47N 0°38E 174 F4
Bagneux France 48°47N 2°18E 134 B2
Bagni di Lucca Italy 44°1N 10°35E 198 D7
Bagno di Romagna Italy 43°50N 11°57E 199 E8
Bagnoles-de-l'Orne France 48°32N 0°25W 172 D6
Bagnolet France 48°52N 2°25E 134 A3
Bagnols-sur-Cèze France 44°10N 4°36E 175 D8
Bagnorea = Bagnorégio Italy 42°37N 12°5E 199 F9
Bagnorégio Italy 42°37N 12°5E 199 F9
Bago Burma 17°20N 96°29E 241 G6
Bago Phil. 10°32N 122°50E 233 F4
Bago □ Burma 17°30N 96°30E 241 G6
Bagodar India 24°5N 85°52E 243 G11
Bagram ✈ (OAI) Afghan. 34°57N 69°16E 240 B3
Bagrationovsk Russia 54°23N 20°39E 184 D7
Bagrdan Serbia 44°5N 21°11E 202 B5
Bagsværd Denmark 55°45N 12°27E 118 A2
Bagsværd Sø Denmark 55°46N 12°28E 118 A2
Bagua Peru 5°35S 78°22W 330 B2
Baguiati India 22°36N 88°25E 124 B2
Baguio Phil. 16°26N 120°34E 232 C3
Bagumbayan Phil. 14°28N 121°3E 127 C2
Bağyurdu Turkey 38°25N 27°41E 205 C9
Bagzane, Monts Niger 17°43N 8°45E 259 E1
Bahabón de Esgueva Spain 41°52N 3°43W 194 D7
Bahadurabad Ghat Bangla. 25°11N 89°44E 241 C2
Bahadurganj India 26°16N 87°49E 243 F12
Bahadurgarh India 28°40N 76°57E 242 E7
Baha'i Temple U.S.A. 42°4N 87°41W 119 A2
Bahaja Somalia 11°16N 49°50E 267 B6
Baham, Pte. Martinique 14°24N 60°50W 322 j
Bahama, Canal Viejo de W. Indies 22°10N 77°30W 320 B4
Bahamas ■ N. Amer. 24°0N 75°0W 321 B5
Bahār Iran 34°54N 48°26E 213 E13
Baharak Afghan. 37°0N 70°53E 240 A3
Baharampur India 24°2N 88°27E 243 G13
Baharîya, El Wâhât al Egypt 28°0N 28°50E 256 B2
Baharu Pandan = Pandan Malaysia 1°32N 103°46E 237 d
Bahawalnagar Pakistan 30°0N 73°15E 242 E5
Bahawalpur Pakistan 29°24N 71°40E 242 E4
Bahçe Turkey 37°13N 36°34E 212 D7
Bahçecik Turkey 40°41N 29°44E 203 F13
Bahçeköy Turkey 41°10N 28°59E 122 A1
Bahçelievler Turkey 41°0N 28°50E 122 B1
Baheli Phil. 10°0N 118°47E 233 F2
Bäherden Turkmenistan 38°25N 57°26E 247 B8
Baheri India 28°45N 79°34E 243 E8
Bahgul → India 27°45N 79°36E 243 F8
Bahi Tanzania 5°58S 35°21E 268 D4
Bahi Swamp Tanzania 6°10S 35°0E 268 D4
Bahia = Salvador Brazil 13°0S 38°30W 333 D4
Bahia □ Brazil 12°0S 42°0W 333 D3
Bahía, Is. de la Honduras 16°45N 86°15W 320 C2
Bahía Blanca Argentina 38°35S 62°13W 334 D3
Bahía de Caráquez Ecuador 0°40S 80°27W 328 D1
Bahía de Los Angeles Mexico 28°56N 113°34W 318 B2
Bahía Honda Cuba 22°54N 83°10W 320 B3
Bahía Kino Mexico 28°47N 111°58W 318 B2
Bahía Laura Argentina 48°10S 66°30W 336 C3
Bahía Mansa Chile 40°33S 73°46W 336 B2
Bahía Negra Paraguay 20°5S 58°5W 331 E6
Bahía Solano Colombia 6°14N 77°25W 328 B2
Bahir Dar Ethiopia 11°37N 37°10E 257 E4
Bahlā' Oman 22°58N 57°18E 249 B7
Bahmanzād Iran 31°15N 51°47E 247 D6
Bahmer Algeria 27°32N 0°10W 261 C4
Bahr el Ahmar □ Sudan 20°0N 35°0E 256 D4
Bahr el Ghazal = Kanem □ Chad 15°0N 15°0E 259 F3
Bahr el Jebel = Central Equatoria □ South Sudan 4°0N 31°0E 257 G3
Bahraich India 27°38N 81°37E 243 F9
Bahrain ■ Asia 26°0N 50°35E 247 E6
Bahror India 27°51N 76°20E 242 F7
Bahtīm Egypt 30°8N 31°16E 117 A2
Bāhū Kalāt Iran 25°43N 61°25E 247 E9
Bai Mali 13°35N 3°28W 262 C4
Bai Bung, Mui = Ca Mau, Mui Vietnam 8°38N 104°44E 237 H5
Bai Thuong Vietnam 19°54N 105°23E 236 C5
Baia de Aramā Romania 45°0N 22°50E 182 E7
Baía dos Tigres Angola 16°40S 11°47E 265 F2
Baía Farta Angola 12°40S 13°11E 265 E2
Baia Mare Romania 47°40N 23°35E 183 C8
Baia-Sprie Romania 47°41N 23°43E 183 C8
Baião Brazil 2°40S 49°40W 332 B2
Baïbokoum Chad 7°46N 15°43E 259 G3
Baicheng Jilin, China 45°38N 122°42E 227 B12
Baicheng Xinjiang Uygur, China 41°46N 81°52E 217 D10
Băicoi Romania 45°3N 25°52E 183 E10
Baidoa = Baydhabo Somalia 3°8N 43°30E 267 D5
Baie-Comeau Canada 49°12N 68°10W 299 C6
Baie de Baly △ Madag. 16°2S 45°15E 272 B2
Baie du Cap Mauritius 20°29S 57°22E 272 e
Baie-Mahault Guadeloupe 16°16N 61°35W 322 e
Baie-St-Paul Canada 47°28N 70°32W 299 C5
Baie Ste-Anne Seychelles 4°18S 55°45E 272 c
Baie-Trinité Canada 49°25N 67°20W 299 C6
Baie Verte Canada 49°55N 56°12W 299 C8
Baignes-Ste-Radegonde France 45°23N 0°25W 174 C3
Baigneux-les-Juifs France 47°31N 4°39E 173 E11
Baihar India 22°6N 80°33E 243 H9
Baihe = Paiho Taiwan 23°21N 120°25E 225 C2
Baihe Hubei, China 32°50N 110°5E 229 A8
Baihe Jilin, China 42°27N 128°9E 227 C15
Baihedong China 23°4N 113°14E 121 B2
Baihetan Dam China 27°11N 102°54E 228 D4
Ba'ījī Iraq 35°0N 43°30E 213 E10
Baijnath India 29°55N 79°37E 243 E8
Baikal, L. = Baykal, Oz. Russia 53°0N 108°0E 215 D11
Baikonur = Bayqonyr Kazakhstan 45°40N 63°20E 216 C6
Baikunthpur India 23°15N 82°33E 243 H10
Bailadila, Mt. India 18°43N 81°15E 244 E5
Baile Átha Cliath = Dublin Ireland 53°21N 6°15W 166 C5
Baile Átha Fhirdhia = Ardee Ireland 53°52N 6°33W 166 C5
Baile Átha Í = Athy Ireland 53°0N 7°0W 166 C5
Baile Átha Luain = Athlone Ireland 53°25N 7°56W 166 C4
Baile Átha Troim = Trim Ireland 53°33N 6°48W 166 C5
Baile Brigín = Balbriggan Ireland 53°37N 6°11W 166 C5
Băile Govora Romania 45°5N 24°11E 183 E9
Băile Herculane Romania 44°53N 22°26E 182 F7
Băile Olăneşti Romania 45°12N 24°14E 183 E9
Baile Sear = Baleshare U.K. 57°31N 7°22W 167 D1
Băile Tuşnad Romania 46°9N 25°51E 183 D10
Bailén Spain 38°8N 3°48W 195 G7
Băileşti Romania 44°1N 23°20E 183 F8
Baileys Crossroads U.S.A. 38°50N 77°6W 143 B2
Bailhongal India 15°55N 74°53E 245 G2
Bailieborough Ireland 53°56N 6°59W 166 C5
Bailique, Ilha Brazil 1°2N 49°58W 332 A2
Baille-Argent Guadeloupe 16°15N 61°48W 322 e
Baillif Guadeloupe 16°1N 61°44W 322 e
Bailly France 48°50N 2°4E 134 A1
Bailugh Afghan. 32°40N 66°47E 240 B2
Bailundo = Luau Angola 10°40S 22°10E 265 E4
Bailundo Angola 12°10S 15°50E 265 E3
Baima China 33°0N 100°26E 228 A3
Baimuru Papua N. G. 7°35S 144°51E 286 D3
Bain-de-Bretagne France 47°50N 1°40W 172 E5
Bainbridge Ga., U.S.A. 30°55N 84°35W 316 E5
Bainbridge Ind., U.S.A. 39°46N 86°49W 311 E10
Bainbridge N.Y., U.S.A. 42°18N 75°29W 313 D9
Bainbridge Ohio, U.S.A. 39°14N 83°16W 311 E13
Bainbridge Island U.S.A. 47°38N 122°32W 306 C4
Baine China 42°0N 128°0E 219 C14
Baing Indonesia 10°14S 120°34E 231 F6
Bainiu China 32°50N 112°15E 229 A9
Bainyik Papua N. G. 3°40S 143°4E 286 B2
Baiona Spain 42°6N 8°52W 194 C2
Bā'ir Jordan 30°45N 36°55E 251 H7
Bā'ir, W. → Jordan 30°59N 37°24E 251 H8
Baird Mts. U.S.A. 67°0N 160°0W 303 C7
Bairiki = Tarawa Kiribati 1°30N 173°0E 288 G9
Bairin Youqi China 43°30N 118°35E 227 C10
Bairin Zuoqi China 43°58N 119°15E 227 C10
Bairnsdale Australia 37°48S 147°36E 283 D7
Bairro Alto Lisbon, Portugal 126 c1
Bairro Lopes Lisbon, Portugal 126 b3
Bais Phil. 9°35N 123°7E 233 G4
Baisha Guangdong, China 23°8N 113°11E 121 B2
Baisha Henan, China 34°20N 112°32E 226 G7
Baisha Li China 19°12N 109°20E 229 a
Baishan = Hunjiang China 41°54N 126°26E 224 B3
Baishan China 42°43N 127°14E 227 C14
Baissa Nigeria 7°14N 10°38E 263 D7
Baitadi Nepal 29°35N 80°25E 243 E9
Baitarani → India 20°45N 86°48E 244 D8
Baixa Lisbon, Portugal 126 c2
Baixa Grande Brazil 11°57S 40°11W 333 D3
Baixa Limia-Sierra do Xurés ⌓ Spain 41°59N 8°2W 194 D2
Baixo-Longa Angola 15°41S 18°45E 265 F3
Baiyer River Papua N. G. 5°32S 144°9E 286 C3
Baiyin China 36°45N 104°14E 226 F3
Baiyü China 31°16N 98°50E 228 B2
Baiyu Shan China 37°15N 107°30E 226 F4
Baiyuda Sudan 17°35N 32°7E 256 D3
Baiyun China 23°11N 113°16E 121 A2
Baiyun Mountain Scenic Area ⌓ China 23°11N 113°17E 121 A2
Baj Baj India 22°30N 88°5E 243 H13
Baja Hungary 46°12N 18°59E 182 D3
Baja, Pta. Easter I., Chile 27°10S 109°22W 330 b
Baja, Pta. Baja Calif., Mexico 29°58N 115°49W 318 B1
Baja California Mexico 31°10N 115°12W 318 A1
Baja California □ Mexico 30°0N 115°0W 318 B2
Baja California Sur □ Mexico 25°50N 111°50W 318 B2
Bajag India 22°40N 81°21E 243 H9
Bajamar Canary Is. 28°33N 16°20W 153 e1
Bajana India 23°7N 71°49E 242 H4
Bajatrejo Indonesia 8°29S 114°19E 231 J17
Bajawa Indonesia 8°47S 120°59E 231 F6
Bajera Indonesia 8°31S 115°2E 231 J18
Bājgīrān Iran 37°36N 58°24E 247 B8
Bājil Yemen 15°4N 43°17E 248 D3
Bajimba, Mt. Australia 29°17S 152°6E 281 D5
Bajina Bašta Serbia 43°58N 19°35E 202 C3
Bajmok Serbia 45°57N 19°24E 182 E4
Bajo Boquete Panama 8°46N 82°27W 320 E3
Bajo Caracoles Argentina 47°27S 70°56W 336 C2
Bajo Nuevo Caribbean 15°40N 78°50W 320 C4
Bajoga Nigeria 10°57N 11°20E 263 C7
Bajool Australia 23°40S 150°35E 280 C5
Bak Hungary 46°43N 16°51E 182 D1
Bakala C.A.R. 6°15N 20°20E 264 A4
Bakar Croatia 45°18N 14°32E 199 C11
Bakassi Pen. Cameroon 4°42N 8°20E 263 E6
Bakel Senegal 14°56N 12°20W 262 C2
Baker Calif., U.S.A. 35°16N 116°4W 307 K10
Baker Fla., U.S.A. 30°48N 86°41W 317 E3
Baker Mont., U.S.A. 46°22N 104°17W 304 C11
Baker, Canal Chile 47°45S 74°45W 336 C2
Baker, L. Canada 64°0N 96°0W 294 E12
Baker, Mt. U.S.A. 48°50N 121°49W 304 B3
Baker City U.S.A. 44°47N 117°50W 304 D5
Baker I. Pac. Oc. 0°10N 176°35W 277 A15
Baker I. Alaska, U.S.A. 55°20N 133°40W 296 B2
Baker L. Australia 26°54S 126°5E 279 E4
Baker Lake Canada 64°20N 96°3W 294 E12
Bakere Dem. Rep. of the Congo 1°36N 23°50E 264 B4
Bakerhill U.S.A. 31°47N 85°18W 316 D4
Bakers Creek Australia 21°13S 149°7E 280 C4
Bakers Dozen Is. Canada 56°45N 78°45W 298 A4
Bakersfield Calif., U.S.A. 35°23N 119°1W 307 K8
Bakersfield Vt., U.S.A. 44°45N 72°48W 313 B12
Bākharden = Bäherden Turkmenistan 38°25N 57°26E 247 B8
Bakhchysaray Ukraine 44°40N 33°45E 189 K7
Bakhmach Ukraine 51°10N 32°45E 189 G7
Bakhmut = Artemivsk Ukraine 48°35N 38°0E 189 H9
Bākhtarān = Kermānshāh Iran 34°23N 47°0E 213 E12
Bākhtarān = Kermānshāh □ Iran 34°0N 46°30E 246 C5
Bakhtegān, Daryācheh-ye Iran 29°40N 53°50E 247 D7
Bakhtegān △ Iran 29°51N 53°40E 247 D7
Baki = Krasnyye Baki Russia 57°8N 45°10E 190 B7
Bakı Azerbaijan 40°29N 49°56E 191 K9
Baki Somalia 10°30N 43°8E 267 B5
Bakır → Turkey 38°55N 27°0E 205 C9
Bakırdağı Turkey 38°13N 35°46E 212 C6
Bakırköy Turkey 40°58N 28°52E 122 C1
Bakkafjörður Iceland 66°2N 14°48W 155 A12
Bakkaflói Iceland 66°10N 14°45W 155 A12
Bakkagerði Iceland 65°31N 13°49W 155 B13
Baklan Turkey 38°0N 29°36E 205 C11
Bako Ethiopia 5°51N 36°23E 257 F4
Bako Ivory C. 9°8N 7°40W 262 D3
Bako △ Malaysia 1°43N 110°28E 235 D4
Bakony Hungary 47°10N 17°30E 182 C2
Bakony Forest = Bakony Hungary 47°10N 17°30E 182 C2
Bakool □ Somalia 4°0N 44°0E 267 D5
Bakori Nigeria 11°34N 7°25E 263 C6
Bakouma C.A.R. 5°40N 22°56E 264 A4
Baksan Russia 43°42N 43°32E 191 J6
Bakswaho India 24°15N 79°18E 243 G8
Baku = Bakı Azerbaijan 40°29N 49°56E 191 K9
Bakun Dam Malaysia 2°50N 113°50E 235 B4
Bakundi Nigeria 8°2N 10°45E 263 D7
Bakung Indonesia 0°5N 104°26E 234 B2
Bakungan Indonesia 2°55N 97°28E 234 B1
Bakuriani Georgia 41°44N 43°32E 213 B10
Bakutis Coast Antarctica 74°0S 120°0W 151 D15
Bakwa-Kenge Dem. Rep. of the Congo 4°51S 22°4E 265 C4
Bakwanga = Mbuji-Mayi Dem. Rep. of the Congo 6°9S 23°40E 265 D4
Baky = Bakı Azerbaijan 40°29N 49°56E 191 K9
Bal Harbor U.S.A. 25°53N 80°7W 129 C3
Bala Ont., Canada 45°1N 79°37W 312 A5
Bala Senegal 14°1N 13°8W 262 C2
Balâ Turkey 39°32N 33°6E 212 C5
Bala U.K. 52°54N 3°36W 168 E4
Bala, L. U.K. 52°53N 3°37W 168 E4
Bālā Morghāb Afghan. 35°35N 63°20E 240 B1
Balabac Phil. 7°59N 117°4E 233 H1
Balabac I. Phil. 8°0N 117°0E 233 H1
Balabac Str. E. Indies 7°53N 117°5E 230 C5
Balabagh Afghan. 34°25N 70°12E 242 B4
Ba'labakk Lebanon 34°0N 36°10E 250 E7
Balabalangan, Kepulauan Indonesia 2°20S 117°30E 235 C5
Bālādeh, Ī. N. Cal. 20°7S 164°11E 288 d
Bălăciţa Romania 44°23N 23°8E 183 F8
Balad Iraq 34°0N 44°9E 213 F11
Balad Rūz Iraq 33°42N 45°5E 213 F11
Bālādeh Fārs, Iran 29°17N 51°56E 247 D6
Bālādeh Māzandaran, Iran 36°12N 51°48E 247 B6
Balaghat India 21°49N 80°12E 244 D5
Balaghat Ra. India 18°50N 76°30E 244 E3
Balaguer Spain 41°50N 0°50E 196 D5
Balaikarangan Indonesia 0°49N 110°25E 235 B4
Balaipungut Indonesia 1°3N 101°17E 234 B2
Balaisabut Indonesia 0°28N 110°49E 235 B4
Balaka Dem. Rep. of the Congo 4°52S 19°57E 265 C3
Balakān Azerbaijan 41°43N 46°24E 191 K8
Balakété C.A.R. 6°56N 19°54E 264 A3
Balakhna Russia 56°25N 43°32E 190 B6
Balaklava S. Austral., Australia 34°7S 138°22E 282 C3
Balaklava Ukraine 44°30N 33°30E 189 K7
Balakliya Ukraine 49°28N 36°55E 189 H9
Balakovo Russia 52°4N 47°55E 190 D8
Balamau India 27°10N 80°21E 243 F9
Balamban Phil. 10°30N 123°43E 233 F4
Balambangan, Pulau Malaysia 7°17N 116°55E 235 A5
Balan Romania 46°39N 25°49E 183 D10
Balancán Mexico 17°48N 91°32W 319 D6
Balanda = Kalininsk Russia 51°30N 44°40E 190 E7
Balandra B. Trin. & Tob. 10°42N 61°0W 323 t
Balanga Phil. 14°41N 120°32E 232 D3
Balangala Dem. Rep. of the Congo 0°30N 19°56E 264 B3
Balangiga Phil. 11°7N 125°23E 233 F5
Balangir India 20°43N 83°35E 244 D6
Balaoan Phil. 16°49N 120°24E 232 C3
Balapur India 20°40N 76°45E 244 D3
Balara Phil. 14°39N 121°3E 127 B2
Balashikha Russia 55°48N 37°58E 188 E9
Balashov Russia 51°30N 43°10E 190 E6
Balasinor India 22°57N 73°23E 242 H5
Balasore = Baleshwar India 21°35N 87°3E 244 D8
Balassagyarmat Hungary 48°4N 19°15E 182 B4
Balât Egypt 25°36N 29°19E 256 B2
Balaton Hungary 46°50N 17°40E 182 D2
Balaton-Felvidéki △ Hungary 46°52N 17°30E 182 D2
Balatonboglár Hungary 46°46N 17°40E 182 D2
Balatonfüred Hungary 46°58N 17°54E 182 D2
Balatonszentgyörgy Hungary 46°41N 17°19E 182 D2
Balayan Phil. 13°57N 120°44E 232 E3
Balayan B. Phil. 13°51N 120°48E 232 E3
Balazote Spain 38°54N 2°9W 197 G2
Balbalan Phil. 17°27N 121°12E 232 C3
Balbalasang-Balbalan △ Phil. 17°23N 121°1E 232 C3
Balbi, Mt. Papua N. G. 5°55S 154°58E 286 C8
Balbieriškis Lithuania 54°32N 23°53E 184 D10
Balbigny France 45°49N 4°11E 175 C8
Balbina Brazil 1°58S 59°29W 329 D6
Balbina, Represa de Brazil 2°0S 59°30W 329 D6
Balboa Panama 8°57N 79°34W 320 c
Balbriggan Ireland 53°37N 6°11W 166 C5
Balcarce Argentina 38°0S 58°10W 334 D4
Balcarres Canada 50°50N 103°35W 297 C8
Bălceşti Romania 44°37N 23°57E 183 F8
Balch Springs U.S.A. 32°43N 96°37W 120 B6
Balchik Bulgaria 43°28N 28°11E 203 C12
Balclutha N.Z. 46°15S 169°45E 285 G4
Balcones Escarpment U.S.A. 29°30N 99°15W 314 G5
Balçova Turkey 38°22N 27°4E 205 C9
Bald I. Australia 34°57S 118°27E 279 F2
Bald Knob U.S.A. 35°19N 91°34W 314 D9
Baldenburg = Biały Bór Poland 53°53N 16°51E 184 E3
Baldia Pakistan 24°54N 66°58E 123 A1
Baldock L. Canada 56°33N 97°57W 297 B9
Baldwin Fla., U.S.A. 30°18N 81°59W 316 E8
Baldwin Mich., U.S.A. 43°54N 85°51W 309 D11
Baldwin Pa., U.S.A. 40°21N 79°58W 312 F5
Baldwin, L. U.S.A. 28°34N 81°19W 133 A3
Baldwin Hills U.S.A. 34°0N 118°21W 126 B2
Baldwin Hills Res. U.S.A. 34°0N 118°21W 126 B2
Baldwinsville U.S.A. 43°10N 76°20W 313 C8
Baldy Peak U.S.A. 33°54N 109°34W 305 K9
Bale Croatia 45°4N 13°46E 199 C10
Bale Oromiya, Ethiopia 6°57N 40°8E 257 F5
Bale Oromiya, Ethiopia 6°20N 41°30E 257 F5
Bale Mts. △ Ethiopia 6°59N 39°52E 257 F4
Baleares, Is. Spain 39°30N 3°0E 206 B4
Balearic Is. = Baleares, Is. Spain 39°30N 3°0E 206 B4
Baleh → Malaysia 2°1N 113°1E 235 B4
Baleia, Pta. da Brazil 17°40S 39°7W 333 E4
Baleine → Canada 58°15N 67°40W 299 A6
Baleine, Petite R. de la → Canada 56°0N 76°45W 298 A4
Băleni Romania 45°48N 27°51E 183 E12
Baler Phil. 15°46N 121°34E 232 D3
Baler B. Phil. 15°50N 121°35E 232 D3
Baleshare U.K. 57°31N 7°22W 167 D1
Baleshwar India 21°35N 87°3E 244 D8
Balestrand Norway 61°11N 6°31E 164 C3
Baley Russia 51°36N 116°37E 215 D12
Balezino Russia 58°2N 53°6E 190 B11
Balfate Honduras 15°48N 86°25W 320 C2
Balfour Channel Solomon Is. 8°43S 157°27E 287 M9
Balgo Australia 20°9S 127°58E 278 D4
Balgowlah Australia 33°47S 151°16E 139 A2
Balgowlah Heights Australia 33°48S 151°16E 139 A2
Balham U.K. 51°26N 0°8W 125 B3
Balharshah India 19°50N 79°23E 244 E4
Bali Cameroon 5°54N 10°0E 263 D7
Bali Dem. Rep. of the Congo 0°52N 25°12E 264 C3
Bali Kriti, Greece 35°25N 24°47E 207 E5
Bali Paschimbanga, India 22°39N 88°20E 124 B1
Bali Raj., India 25°11N 73°17E 242 G5
Bali Indonesia 8°20S 115°0E 231 J18
Bali □ Indonesia 8°20S 115°0E 231 J17
Bali, Selat Indonesia 8°18S 114°25E 231 J17
Bali Barat △ Indonesia 8°12S 114°35E 231 J17
Bali Sea Indonesia 8°0S 115°0E 231 J17
Balla S. Leone 9°22N 11°1W 262 D2
Baliapal India 21°40N 87°17E 243 J12
Baliceaux St. Vincent 12°57N 61°8W 323 n
Balicuatro Is. Phil. 12°39N 124°24E 232 E5
Baliganja India 22°31N 88°22E 124 B2
Balige Indonesia 2°14N 99°7E 234 B1
Baligród Poland 49°20N 22°17E 185 J9
Baliguda India 20°12N 83°55E 244 D6
Balik Pulau Malaysia 5°21N 100°14E 237 c
Balıkeşir Turkey 39°39N 27°53E 205 B9
Balıkeşir □ Turkey 39°45N 28°0E 205 B9
Balīkh → Syria 35°52N 39°12E 213 E8
Balıkçeşme Turkey 40°18N 27°56E 203 F11
Balikpapan Indonesia 1°10S 116°55E 235 C5
Balimbing Phil. 5°5N 119°58E 233 J2
Balimo Papua N. G. 8°6S 142°57E 286 E2
Baling Malaysia 5°41N 100°55E 237 K3
Balingasag Phil. 8°45N 124°47E 233 G5
Balinge Sweden 59°57N 17°33E 162 E11
Balingen Germany 48°16N 8°51E 179 G4
Balingsnäs Sweden 59°13N 18°0E 139 B2
Balingsta Sweden 59°12N 18°3E 139 B2
Balinsasayao Twin Lakes △ Phil. 9°21N 123°9E 233 G4
Balinţ Romania 45°48N 21°54E 182 E6
Balintang Channel Phil. 19°49N 121°40E 232 B3
Balintang I. Phil. 19°58N 122°9E 232 B4
Balintawak Phil. 14°39N 120°59E 127 B1
Baliza Brazil 16°0S 52°20W 331 D7
Baljurashī Si. Arabia 19°51N 41°33E 248 C3
Balkan □ Turkmenistan 40°0N 54°30E 216 D5
Balkan Mts. = Stara Planina Bulgaria 43°15N 23°0E 202 C7
Balkanabat Turkmenistan 39°30N 54°22E 247 B7
Balkh Afghan. 36°44N 66°47E 217 E7
Balkh □ Afghan. 36°50N 67°0E 240 A2
Balkhash = Balqash Kazakhstan 46°50N 74°50E 214 E8
Balkhash, Ozero = Balqash Köli Kazakhstan 46°0N 74°50E 217 C8
Balkonda India 18°52N 78°21E 244 E4
Ballachulish U.K. 56°41N 5°8W 167 E3
Balladonia Australia 32°27S 123°51E 279 F3
Ballaghaderreen Ireland 53°55N 8°34W 166 C3
Ballan Australia 37°35S 144°13E 282 D6
Ballarat Australia 37°33S 143°50E 282 D5
Ballard, L. Australia 29°20S 120°40E 279 E3
Ballari India 15°10N 76°56E 245 G3
Ballater U.K. 57°3N 3°3W 167 D5
Ballé Mali 15°18N 8°33W 262 B3
Ballena, Pta. Venezuela 11°11N 63°47W 329 a
Ballenas, Canal de Mexico 29°10N 113°29W 318 B2
Balleny Is. Antarctica 66°30S 163°0E 151 C11
Balleroy France 49°11N 0°50W 172 C6
Ballerup Denmark 55°43N 12°21E 118 A2
Ballestas, Is. Peru 13°44S 76°25W 330 C2
Ballı Turkey 40°50N 27°3E 203 F11
Ballia India 25°46N 84°12E 243 G11
Ballina N.S.W., Australia 28°50S 153°31E 281 D5
Ballina Mayo, Ireland 54°7N 9°9W 166 B2
Ballinasloe Ireland 53°20N 8°13W 166 C3
Ballincollig Ireland 51°53N 8°33W 166 E3
Ballinger U.S.A. 31°45N 99°57W 314 F5
Ballinrobe Ireland 53°38N 9°13W 166 C2
Ballinskelligs B. Ireland 51°48N 10°13W 166 E1
Ballon France 48°10N 0°14E 172 D7
Ballons des Vosges ⌓ France 48°0N 7°0E 173 E14
Ballsh Albania 40°36N 19°44E 202 F3
Ballston Spa U.S.A. 43°0N 73°51W 313 D11
Ballyboghil Ireland 53°32N 6°16W 166 C5
Ballybunion Ireland 52°31N 9°40W 166 D2
Ballycanew Ireland 52°37N 6°19W 166 D5
Ballycastle U.K. 55°12N 6°15W 166 A5
Ballyclare U.K. 54°46N 6°0W 166 B5
Ballycroy △ Ireland 54°5N 9°50W 166 B2
Ballydehob Ireland 51°34N 9°28W 166 E2
Ballygawley U.K. 54°27N 7°2W 166 B4
Ballyhaunis Ireland 53°46N 8°46W 166 C3
Ballyheigue Ireland 52°23N 9°49W 166 D2
Ballymena U.K. 54°52N 6°17W 166 B5
Ballymoney U.K. 55°5N 6°31W 166 A5
Ballymote Ireland 54°5N 8°31W 166 B3
Ballynahinch U.K. 54°24N 5°54W 166 B6
Ballyporeen Ireland 52°16N 8°6W 166 D3
Ballyquintin Pt. U.K. 54°20N 5°30W 166 B6
Ballyshannon Ireland 54°30N 8°11W 166 B3
Balmaceda Chile 46°0S 71°50W 336 C2
Balmain Australia 33°51S 151°11E 139 B2
Balmaseda Spain 43°11N 3°12W 196 B1
Balmazújváros Hungary 47°37N 21°21E 182 C6
Balmertown Canada 51°4N 93°41W 297 C10
Balmoral Australia 37°15S 141°48E 282 D4
Balmorhea U.S.A. 30°59N 103°45W 314 F3
Balneário Camboriú Brazil 26°59S 48°38W 335 B6
Balochistan = Baluchistan □ Pakistan 27°30N 65°0E 240 D2
Balod India 20°44N 81°13E 244 D5
Balombo Angola 12°21S 14°46E 265 E2
Balombo → Angola 11°57S 13°46E 265 E2
Balonne → Australia 28°47S 147°56E 281 D4
Balotra India 25°50N 72°14E 242 G5
Balpyq Bī Kazakhstan 44°52N 78°12E 217 D9
Balqash Kazakhstan 46°50N 74°50E 214 E8
Balqash Köli Kazakhstan 46°0N 74°50E 217 C8
Balrampur India 27°30N 82°20E 243 F10
Balranald Australia 34°38S 143°33E 282 C5
Balş Romania 44°22N 24°5E 183 F9
Balsapuerto Peru 5°48S 76°33W 330 B2
Balsas → Maranhão, Brazil 7°15S 44°35W 332 C3
Balsas → Tocantins, Brazil 9°58S 47°52W 332 C2
Balsas → Michoacan, Mexico 17°55N 102°10W 318 D4
Balsas del Norte Mexico 18°0N 99°46W 319 D5
Bålsta Sweden 59°35N 17°30E 162 E11
Balta Romania 44°54N 22°38E 182 F7
Balta Ukraine 47°56N 29°45E 183 C14
Balta Ialomiţei Romania 44°20N 27°55E 183 F12
Baltaköl Kazakhstan 43°7N 67°46E 217 D7
Baltanás Spain 41°56N 4°15W 194 D6
Bălţi Moldova 47°48N 27°58E 183 C12
Baltic Sea Europe 57°0N 19°0E 161 H18
Baltîm Egypt 31°35N 31°10E 256 H7
Baltimore Cork, Ireland 51°29N 9°22W 166 E2
Baltimore Md., U.S.A. 39°17N 76°36W 309 F15
Baltimore Ohio, U.S.A. 39°51N 82°36W 312 G2
Baltimore-Washington Int. ✈ (BWI) U.S.A. 39°10N 76°40W 309 F15
Baltinglass Ireland 52°56N 6°43W 166 D5
Baltit Pakistan 36°15N 74°40E 243 A6
Baltiysk Russia 54°41N 19°58E 184 D6
Baltiyskiy = Paldiski Estonia 59°23N 24°9E 188 C3
Baltra, I. Ecuador 0°26S 90°16W 330 a
Baltrum Germany 53°43N 7°24E 178 B3
Baluan I. Papua N. G. 2°33S 147°17E 286 B4
Baluchistan □ Pakistan 27°30N 65°0E 240 D2
Balud Phil. 12°2N 123°12E 232 E4
Baluhati India 22°39N 88°15E 124 B1
Baluqtybulaq Kazakhstan 50°51N 51°8E 190 E10
Baluran △ Indonesia 7°50S 114°23E 235 D4
Balurghat India 25°15N 88°44E 243 G13
Balut I. Phil. 5°24N 125°23E 233 J5
Balvanera Argentina 34°37S 58°23W 138 B2
Balvi Latvia 57°8N 27°15E 188 D4
Balwyn Australia 37°48S 145°4E 128 A2
Balwyn North Australia 37°47S 145°4E 128 A2
Balya Turkey 39°44N 27°35E 205 B9
Balykchy Kyrgyzstan 42°26N 76°12E 217 D9
Balyqshy Kazakhstan 47°4N 51°52E 191 G10
Balzar Ecuador 2°2S 79°54W 328 D2
Bam Iran 29°7N 58°14E 247 D8
Bama Guangxi Zhuangzu, China 24°8N 107°12E 228 E6
Bama Nigeria 11°33N 13°41E 263 C7
Bamaga Australia 10°50S 142°25E 280 A3
Bamaji L. Canada 51°9N 91°25W 298 B1
Bamako Mali 12°34N 7°55W 262 C3
Bamba Dem. Rep. of the Congo 5°45S 18°23E 265 D3
Bamba Mali 17°5N 1°24W 263 B4
Bambama Congo 2°32S 13°32E 264 C2
Bambamarca Peru 6°36S 78°32W 330 B2
Bambang Phil. 16°23N 121°6E 232 C3
Bambannan I. Phil. 5°37N 120°17E 233 J3
Bambao Comoros Is. 12°11S 44°31E 272 a
Bambara Maoundé Mali 15°26N 4°3W 262 B4
Bambari C.A.R. 5°40N 20°35E 264 A4
Bambaroo Australia 18°50S 146°10E 280 B4
Bambaya Guinea 10°55N 13°38W 262 D2
Bamberg Bayern, Germany 49°54N 10°54E 179 F6
Bamberg S.C., U.S.A. 33°18N 81°2W 316 B8
Bambesi Ethiopia 9°45N 34°40E 257 F3
Bambey Senegal 14°42N 16°28W 262 C1
Bambili Dem. Rep. of the Congo 3°40N 26°0E 268 B2
Bambinga Dem. Rep. of the Congo 3°43S 18°53E 264 C3
Bambio C.A.R. 3°55N 16°57E 264 B3
Bamboi Ghana 8°13N 2°1W 262 D4
Bamboo Avenue Jamaica 18°6N 77°47W 320 a
Bambous Mauritius 20°15S 57°24E 272 e
Bambouti C.A.R. 5°24N 27°12E 264 A5
Bambuí Brazil 20°1S 45°58W 333 F2
Bamburgh U.K. 55°37N 1°43W 168 B6
Bamenda Cameroon 5°57N 10°11E 263 D7
Bamendjing, L. de Cameroon 5°50N 10°30E 263 D7
Bamfield Canada 48°45N 125°10W 296 D3
Bāmīān Afghan. 34°49N 67°49E 240 B2
Bāmīān □ Afghan. 35°0N 67°0E 240 B2
Bamiancheng China 43°15N 124°2E 227 C13
Bamingui C.A.R. 7°34N 20°11E 264 A4
Bamingui → C.A.R. 8°33N 19°5E 264 A3
Bamingui-Bangoran □ C.A.R. 8°30N 20°0E 264 A4
Bamingui-Bangoran △ C.A.R. 8°30N 19°46E 264 A3
Bamkin Cameroon 6°3N 11°27E 263 D7
Bamou △ Iran 29°45N 52°35E 247 D7
Bampūr Iran 27°15N 60°21E 247 E9
Bampūr → Iran 27°24N 59°0E 247 E8
Bamu → Papua N. G. 8°1S 143°33E 286 E2
Ban Burkina Faso 14°5N 2°27W 262 C4
Ban Ao Tu Khun Thailand 8°9N 98°20E 237 a
Ban Ban Laos 19°31N 103°30E 236 C4
Ban Bang Hin Thailand 9°32N 98°35E 237 H2
Ban Bang Khu Thailand 7°57N 98°23E 237 a
Ban Bang Rong Thailand 8°3N 98°25E 237 a
Ban Bo Phut Thailand 9°33N 100°2E 237 b
Ban Chaweng Thailand 9°32N 100°3E 237 b
Ban Chiang Thailand 17°30N 103°10E 236 D4
Ban Chiang Klang Thailand 19°25N 100°55E 236 C3
Ban Choho Thailand 15°2N 102°9E 236 E4
Ban Dan Lan Hoi Thailand 17°0N 99°35E 236 D2
Ban Don = Surat Thani Thailand 9°6N 99°20E 237 H2
Ban Don Vietnam 12°53N 107°48E 236 F6
Ban Don, Ao → Thailand 9°20N 99°25E 237 H2
Ban Dong Thailand 19°30N 100°59E 236 C3
Ban Hong Thailand 18°18N 98°50E 236 C2
Ban Hua Thanon Thailand 9°26N 100°1E 237 b
Ban Kantang Thailand 7°25N 99°31E 237 J2
Ban Karon Thailand 7°51N 98°18E 237 a
Ban Kata Thailand 7°50N 98°18E 237 a
Ban Keun Laos 18°22N 102°35E 236 C4
Ban Khai Thailand 12°46N 101°18E 236 F3
Ban Kheun Laos 20°13N 101°7E 236 B3
Ban Khlong Khian Thailand 8°10N 98°26E 237 a
Ban Khlong Kua Thailand 6°57N 100°8E 237 J3
Ban Khuan Thailand 8°20N 98°25E 237 a
Ban Ko Yai Chim Thailand 11°17N 99°26E 237 G2
Ban Laem Thailand 13°13N 99°59E 236 F2
Ban Lamai Thailand 9°28N 100°3E 237 b
Ban Lao Ngam Laos 15°28N 106°10E 236 E6
Ban Le Kathe Thailand 15°49N 98°53E 236 E2
Ban Lo Po Noi Thailand 8°1N 98°34E 237 a
Ban Mae Chedi Thailand 19°11N 99°31E 236 C2
Ban Mae Nam Thailand 9°34N 100°0E 237 b
Ban Mae Sariang Thailand 18°10N 97°56E 236 C1
Ban Mê Thuôt = Buon Ma Thuot Vietnam 12°40N 108°3E 236 F7
Ban Mi Thailand 15°3N 100°32E 236 E3
Ban Muang Mo Laos 19°4N 103°58E 236 C4
Ban Na Bo Thailand 9°19N 99°41E 237 b
Ban Na San Thailand 8°53N 99°52E 237 H2
Ban Na Tong Laos 20°56N 101°47E 236 B3
Ban Nam Bac Laos 20°38N 102°20E 236 B4
Ban Nammi Laos 17°7N 105°40E 236 D5
Ban Nong Bok Laos 17°5N 104°48E 236 D5
Ban Nong Pling Thailand 15°40N 100°10E 236 E3
Ban Pak Chan Thailand 10°32N 98°51E 237 G2
Ban Patong Thailand 7°54N 98°18E 237 a
Ban Phai Thailand 16°4N 102°44E 236 D4
Ban Phak Chit Thailand 8°0N 98°24E 237 a
Ban Pong Thailand 13°50N 99°55E 236 F2
Ban Rawai Thailand 7°47N 98°20E 237 a
Ban Ron Phibun Thailand 8°9N 99°51E 237 H2
Ban Sakhu Thailand 8°4N 98°18E 237 a
Ban Sanam Chai Thailand 7°33N 100°25E 237 J3
Ban Tak Thailand 17°2N 99°4E 236 D2
Ban Tako Thailand 14°5N 102°40E 236 E4
Ban Tha Nun Thailand 8°12N 98°18E 237 a
Ban Tha Rua Thailand 7°59N 98°22E 237 a
Ban Tha Yu Thailand 8°17N 98°22E 237 a
Ban Thong Krut Thailand 9°25N 99°57E 237 b
Ban Xien Kok Laos 20°54N 100°39E 236 B3
Ban Yen Nhan Vietnam 20°57N 106°2E 236 B6
Banā, W. → Yemen 13°3N 45°24E 248 D4
Banaadir □ Somalia 2°7N 45°24E 267 D6
Banaba Kiribati 0°45S 169°50E 288 H8
Banagher Ireland 53°11N 7°59W 166 C3
Banalia Dem. Rep. of the Congo 1°32N 25°5E 268 B2
Banam Cambodia 11°20N 105°17E 237 G5
Banamba Mali 13°29N 7°22W 262 C3
Banana Dem. Rep. of the Congo 6°1S 12°25E 265 D2
Banana Is. S. Leone 8°7N 13°15W 262 D2
Banana Island Nigeria 6°28N 3°27E 124 B2
Bananal, I. do Brazil 11°30S 50°30W 333 D1
Banangan India 6°57N 93°54E 245 L11
Bananier Guadeloupe 16°0N 61°36W 322 e
Banaras = Varanasi India 25°22N 83°0E 243 G10
Banas → Gujarat, India 23°45N 71°25E 242 H4
Banas → Mad. P., India 24°15N 81°30E 243 G9
Bânâs, Ras Egypt 23°57N 35°59E 256 C4
Banática Portugal 38°40N 9°11W 126 A1
Banaue Phil. 16°55N 121°4E 232 C3
Banaz Turkey 38°46N 29°46E 205 C11
Banaz → Turkey 38°12N 29°14E 205 C11
Banbridge U.K. 54°22N 6°16W 166 B5
Banbury U.K. 52°4N 1°20W 169 E6
Banc d'Arguin △ Mauritania 20°10N 16°20W 260 D1
Banchory U.K. 57°3N 2°29W 167 D6
Banco Ethiopia 6°12N 38°13E 257 F4
Banco do Brazil, Centro Cultural Rio de J., Brazil 135 a2
Bancoran Phil. 7°45N 118°30E 233 H2
Bancroft = Chililabombwe Zambia 12°18S 27°43E 269 E2
Bancroft Canada 45°3N 77°51W 312 A7
Band Romania 46°30N 24°25E 183 D9
Band Bonī Iran 25°30N 59°33E 247 E8
Band-e-Amīr Afghan. 34°50N 67°10E 240 B2
Band-e Torkestan Afghan. 35°30N 64°0E 240 B2
Band Qīr Iran 31°39N 48°53E 247 D6
Banda Cameroon 3°58N 14°32E 264 B2
Banda Mad. P., India 24°3N 78°57E 243 G8
Banda Maharashtra, India 15°49N 73°52E 245 G1
Banda Ut. P., India 25°30N 80°26E 243 G9
Banda, Kepulauan Indonesia 4°37S 129°50E 231 E7
Banda Aceh Indonesia 5°35N 95°20E 234 A1
Banda Banda, Mt. Australia 31°10S 152°28E 283 A10
Banda Elat Indonesia 5°40S 133°5E 231 F8
Banda Is. = Banda, Kepulauan Indonesia 4°37S 129°50E 231 E7
Banda Kani Dem. Rep. of the Congo 4°48S 13°52E 265 C2
Banda Sea Indonesia 6°0S 130°0E 231 F8
Bandai-Asahi △ Japan 37°38N 140°5E 220 F10
Bandai-San Japan 37°36N 140°4E 220 F10
Bandak Norway 59°23N 8°29E 164 E5
Bandama → Ivory C. 6°32N 4°30W 262 D3
Bandama Blanc → Ivory C. 6°55N 5°30W 262 D4
Bandama Rouge → Ivory C. 6°55N 5°10W 262 D4
Bandamadji Comoros Is. 11°47S 43°26E 272 a
Bandān Iran 31°23N 60°44E 247 D9
Bandanaira Indonesia 4°32S 129°54E 231 E7
Bandanwara India 26°9N 74°38E 242 F6
Bandar = Machilipatnam India 16°12N 81°8E 245 F5
Bandar-e Abbās Iran 27°15N 56°15E 247 E8
Bandar-e Anzalī Iran 37°30N 49°30E 213 D13
Bandar-e Bushehr = Būshehr Iran 28°55N 50°55E 247 D6
Bandar-e Chārak Iran 26°45N 54°20E 247 E7
Bandar-e Deylam Iran 30°5N 50°10E 247 D6
Bandar-e Emām Khomeynī Iran 30°30N 49°5E 247 D6
Bandar-e Lengeh Iran 26°35N 54°58E 247 E7
Bandar-e Maqām Iran 26°56N 53°29E 247 E7
Bandar-e Ma'shur Iran 30°35N 49°10E 247 D6
Bandar-e Rīg Iran 29°29N 50°38E 247 D6
Bandar-e Torkeman Iran 37°0N 54°10E 247 B7
Bandar Labuan Malaysia 5°20N 115°14E 235 A5
Bandar Lampung Indonesia 5°20S 105°10E 234 D3
Bandar Maharani = Muar Malaysia 2°3N 102°34E 237 L4
Bandar Penggaram = Batu Pahat Malaysia 1°50N 102°56E 237 M4
Bandar Seri Begawan Brunei 4°52N 115°0E 235 B4
Bandar Shahid Rajaee Iran 27°7N 56°4E 247 E8
Bandar Sri Aman Malaysia 1°15N 111°32E 235 B4
Bandawe Malawi 11°58S 34°5E 269 E3
Bande Spain 42°3N 7°58W 194 C3
Bandeira, Pico da Brazil 20°26S 41°47W 333 F3
Bandeirante Brazil 13°41S 50°48W 333 D1
Bandera Argentina 28°55S 62°20W 334 B3
Banderas, B. de Mexico 20°40N 105°25W 318 C3
Bandhavgarh India 23°40N 81°2E 243 H9
Bandhavgarh △ India 23°45N 81°10E 244 C5
Bandi → India 26°12N 75°47E 242 F6
Bandia → India 19°2N 80°28E 244 E5
Bandiagara Mali 14°12N 3°29W 262 C4
Bandiagara, Falaise de Mali 14°14N 3°29W 262 D4
Bandikui India 27°3N 76°34E 242 F7
Bandingilo △ South Sudan 5°26N 32°17E 257 F3
Bandipur △ India 11°45N 76°30E 245 J3
Bandırma Turkey 40°20N 28°0E 203 F11
Bandjarmasin = Banjarmasin Indonesia 3°20S 114°35E 235 C4
Bandol France 43°8N 5°46E 175 E9
Bandon Ireland 51°44N 8°44W 166 E3
Bandon → Ireland 51°43N 8°37W 166 E3
Bandra India 19°3N 72°49E 130 A1
Bandra Pt. India 19°2N 72°49E 130 A1
Bandraboua Mayotte 12°42S 45°8E 272 b
Bandrélé Mayotte 12°54S 45°11E 272 b
Bandula Mozam. 19°0S 33°7E 269 F3
Bandundu Dem. Rep. of the Congo 3°15S 17°22E 264 C3
Bandung Indonesia 6°54S 107°36E 235 D3
Bané Burkina Faso 11°42N 0°15W 263 C4
Băneasa Romania 45°56N 27°55E 183 E12
Bāneh Iran 35°59N 45°53E 213 E11
Banes Cuba 21°0N 75°42W 320 B4
Banff Alta., Canada 51°10N 115°34W 296 C5
Banff Aberds., U.K. 57°40N 2°33W 167 D6
Banff △ Canada 51°30N 116°15W 296 C5
Banfora Burkina Faso 10°40N 4°40W 262 C4
Bang Fai → Laos 16°57N 104°45E 236 D5
Bang Hieng → Laos 16°10N 105°10E 236 D5
Bang Kapi Thailand 13°45N 100°38E 113 B2
Bang Krathum Thailand 16°34N 100°18E 236 D3
Bang Lang △ Thailand 5°58N 101°19E 237 K3
Bang Lang Res. Thailand 6°6N 101°17E 237 J3
Bang Mun Nak Thailand 16°2N 100°23E 236 D3
Bang Na Thailand 13°40N 100°36E 113 B2
Bang Pa In Thailand 14°14N 100°35E 236 E3
Bang Phlad Bangkok, Thailand 113 a1
Bang Rakam Thailand 16°45N 100°7E 236 D3
Bang Saphan Thailand 11°14N 99°28E 237 G2
Bang Thao Thailand 7°59N 98°18E 237 a
Banga Angola 8°43S 15°13E 265 D3
Banga Dem. Rep. of the Congo 5°25S 20°28E 265 D4
Banga S. Cotabato, Phil. 6°21N 124°47E 233 H5
Bangaduni I. India 21°34N 88°52E 243 J13
Bangala Dam Zimbabwe 21°7S 31°25E 269 G3
Bangalore = Bengaluru India 12°59N 77°40E 245 H3
Banganapalle India 15°19N 78°14E 245 G4
Banganga → India 27°6N 77°25E 242 F6
Bangangté Cameroon 5°8N 10°32E 263 D7
Bangaon India 23°0N 88°47E 243 H13
Bangar Brunei 4°43N 115°4E 235 B4
Bangar La Union, Phil. 16°54N 120°25E 232 C3
Bangassou C.A.R. 4°55N 23°7E 264 B4
Bangbae S. Korea 37°29N 126°59E 137 C1
Bangeta, Mt. Papua N. G. 6°21S 147°3E 286 D4
Banggai Indonesia 1°34S 123°30E 231 E6
Banggai, Kepulauan Indonesia 1°40S 123°30E 231 E6
Banggai Arch. = Banggai, Kepulauan Indonesia 1°40S 123°30E 231 E6
Banggi, Pulau Malaysia 7°17N 117°12E 235 A5
Banghāzī Libya 32°11N 20°3E 258 B4
Banghāzī □ Libya 32°0N 20°0E 258 B4
Bangil Indonesia 7°36S 112°50E 235 D4
Bangjang South Sudan 11°23N 32°41E 257 E3
Bangka Sulawesi, Indonesia 1°50N 125°5E 231 D7
Bangka Sumatera, Indonesia 2°0S 105°50E 234 C3
Bangka, Selat Indonesia 2°30S 105°30E 234 C3
Bangka-Belitung □ Indonesia 2°30S 107°0E 234 C3
Bangkalan Indonesia 7°2S 112°46E 235 D4
Bangkang Burma 22°4N 99°1E 228 F2
Bangkaru Indonesia 2°4N 97°7E 234 B1
Bangkhen Thailand 13°52N 100°36E 113 A2
Bangkinang Indonesia 0°18N 101°5E 234 B2
Bangko Indonesia 2°5S 102°9E 234 C2
Bangkok Thailand 13°45N 100°35E 113 B2
Bangkok, Bight of Thailand 12°55N 100°30E 236 F3
Bangkok Don Muang Int. ✈ (BKK) Thailand 13°53N 100°36E 113 A2

Bangkok Noi *Thailand* 13°45N 100°29E **113** B1
Bangkok Yai *Thailand* 13°43N 100°29E **113** B1
Bangla = Paschimbanga □ *India* 23°0N 88°0E **243** H13
Bangladesh ■ *Asia* 24°0N 90°0E **241** D3
Bangli *Indonesia* 8°27S 115°21E **231** J18
Banglo *India* 22°31N 88°14E **124** B1
Bangoi-Kouni *Comoros Is.* 11°22S 43°21E **272** a
Bangolo *Ivory C.* 7°1N 7°29W **262** D3
Bangong Co *China* 33°45N 78°43E **243** C8
Bangor *Down, U.K.* 54°40N 5°40W **166** B6
Bangor *Gwynedd, U.K.* 53°14N 4°8W **168** D3
Bangor *Maine, U.S.A.* 44°48N 68°46W **309** C19
Bangor *Mich., U.S.A.* 42°18N 86°7W **311** B10
Bangor *Pa., U.S.A.* 40°52N 75°13W **313** F9
Bangoran → *C.A.R.* 8°42N 19°6E **264** A3
Bangrak *Thailand* 13°43N 100°31E **113** B2
Bangsamoro □ *Phil.* 8°0N 123°0E **233** H3
Bangsu *Thailand* 13°49N 100°31E **113** B2
Bangu *Dem. Rep. of the Congo* 0°3S 19°12E **264** C3
Bangued *Phil.* 17°40N 120°37E **232** C3
Bangui *C.A.R.* 4°23N 18°35E **264** B3
Bangui *Phil.* 18°32N 120°46E **232** B3
Bangui B. *Phil.* 18°33N 120°43E **232** B3
Banguru *Dem. Rep. of the Congo* 0°30N 27°10E **268** B2
Bangweulu, L. *Zambia* 11°0S 30°0E **269** E3
Bangweulu Swamp *Zambia* 11°20S 30°15E **269** E3
Banhine △ *Mozam.* 22°49S 32°55E **271** B5
Bani *Burkina Faso* 13°43N 0°10W **263** C4
Bani *C.A.R.* 7°6N 22°50E **264** A4
Bani *Dom. Rep.* 18°16N 70°22W **321** C5
Bani *Phil.* 16°11N 119°52E **232** C2
Bani → *Mali* 14°30N 4°12W **262** C4
Bani, Jebel *Morocco* 29°16N 8°0W **260** C3
Bani Bangou *Niger* 15°3N 2°42E **263** B5
Banī Sa'd *Iraq* 33°34N 44°32E **213** F11
Banī Walīd *Libya* 31°36N 13°53E **258** B2
Bania *C.A.R.* 4°1N 16°7E **264** B3
Bania *Ivory C.* 9°4N 3°6W **262** D4
Baniara *Papua N. G.* 9°44S 149°54E **286** E5
Banihal Pass *India* 33°30N 75°12E **243** C6
Banikoara *Benin* 11°18N 2°26E **263** C5
Banīnah *Libya* 32°0N 20°12E **258** B4
Banissa *Kenya* 3°55N 40°19E **268** B5
Bāniyās *Syria* 35°10N 36°0E **250** C7
Banja Luka *Bos.-H.* 44°49N 17°11E **182** F2
Banjar *India* 31°38N 77°21E **242** D7
Banjar → *India* 22°36N 80°22E **243** H9
Banjarbaru *Indonesia* 3°25S 114°49E **235** C4
Banjarmasin *Indonesia* 3°20S 114°35E **235** C4
Banjul *Gambia* 13°28N 16°40W **262** C1
Bank *London, U.K.* **125** b5
Banka *India* 24°53N 86°55E **243** G12
Bankas *Mali* 14°4N 3°31W **262** C4
Bankeryd *Sweden* 57°53N 14°6E **163** G8
Banket *Zimbabwe* 17°27S 30°19E **269** F3
Bankilaré *Niger* 14°35N 0°44E **263** C5
Bankot *India* 17°58N 73°2E **244** F1
Banks *U.S.A.* 31°49N 85°51W **316** D4
Banks, C. *Australia* 34°0S 151°16E **139** C2
Banks I. = Moa *Australia* 10°11S 142°16E **280** a
Banks I. *B.C., Canada* 53°20N 130°0W **296** C3
Banks I. *N.W.T., Canada* 73°15N 121°30W **294** C7
Banks Is. *Vanuatu* 13°50S 167°30E **287** C5
Banks L. *U.S.A.* 31°2N 83°6W **316** D6
Banks Pen. *N.Z.* 43°45S 173°15E **285** D8
Banks Str. *Australia* 40°40S 148°10E **281** G4
Banksmeadow *Australia* 33°57S 151°12E **139** B2
Bankumuna *Dem. Rep. of the Congo* 4°28S 19°57E **265** C3
Bankura *India* 23°11N 87°18E **243** H12
Bankya *Bulgaria* 42°43N 23°8E **202** D7
Banmankhi *India* 25°53N 87°11E **243** G12
Banmauk *Burma* 24°24N 95°51E **241** C5
Bann → *Armagh, U.K.* 54°30N 6°31W **166** B5
Bann → *L'derry., U.K.* 55°8N 6°41W **166** A5
Bannaanka Saraar *Somalia* 9°25N 46°17E **267** C6
Bannalec *France* 47°57N 3°42W **172** E3
Bannang Sata *Thailand* 6°16N 101°16E **237** J3
Bannerton *Australia* 34°42S 142°47E **282** C5
Banning *U.S.A.* 33°56N 116°53W **307** M10
Banningville = Bandundu *Dem. Rep. of the Congo* 3°15S 17°22E **264** C3
Banno *Ethiopia* 4°51N 37°24E **257** G4
Banno-saki *Japan* 26°33N 128°8E **288** a
Bannockburn *Ont., Canada* 44°39N 77°33W **312** B7
Bannockburn *Stirling, U.K.* 56°5N 3°55W **167** E5
Bannockburn *Zimbabwe* 20°17S 29°48E **269** G2
Bannu *Pakistan* 33°0N 70°18E **242** C4
Bano *India* 22°40N 84°55E **243** H11
Bañolas = Banyoles *Spain* 42°16N 2°44E **196** C7
Banon *France* 44°2N 5°38E **175** D9
Baños de la Encina *Spain* 38°10N 3°46W **195** G7
Baños de Molgas *Spain* 42°15N 7°40W **194** C3
Bánovce nad Bebravou *Slovakia* 48°44N 18°16E **181** C11
Banovići *Bos.-H.* 44°25N 18°32E **182** F3
Banqiao = Panch'iao *Taiwan* 25°1N 121°27E **225** A3
Bansagar Dam *India* 24°11N 81°17E **244** B5
Bansalan *Phil.* 6°55N 125°13E **233** H5
Bansgaon *India* 26°33N 83°21E **243** F10
Banská Bystrica *Slovakia* 48°46N 19°14E **181** C12
Banská Štiavnica *Slovakia* 48°25N 18°55E **181** C11
Bansko *Bulgaria* 41°52N 23°28E **202** E7
Banskobystrický □ *Slovakia* 48°20N 19°0E **181** C12
Banstala *India* 22°31N 88°24E **124** B2
Banswara *India* 23°32N 74°24E **242** H6
Bantaeng *Indonesia* 5°32S 119°56E **235** D5
Bantaji → *Nigeria* 8°6N 10°5E **263** D7
Bantayan *Phil.* 11°10N 123°43E **233** F4
Bantayan I. *Phil.* 11°13N 123°44E **233** F4
Banteay Prei Nokor *Cambodia* 11°56N 105°40E **237** G5
Banten *Indonesia* 6°5S 106°8E **234** D3
Banten □ *Indonesia* 6°30S 106°0E **234** D3
Banton I. *Phil.* 12°56N 122°4E **232** E4
Bantra *India* 22°35N 88°18E **124** B1
Bantry *Ireland* 51°41N 9°27W **166** E2
Bantry B. *Ireland* 51°37N 9°44W **166** E2
Bantva *India* 21°29N 70°12E **242** J4
Bantval *India* 12°55N 75°0E **245** H2
Banya *Bulgaria* 42°33N 24°50E **203** D8
Banya, Pta. de la *Spain* 40°33N 0°36E **196** E5
Banyak, Kepulauan *Indonesia* 2°10N 97°10E **234** B1
Banyalbufar *Spain* 39°42N 2°31E **206** B3
Banyeres de Mariola *Spain* 38°44N 0°38W **197** G4
Banyo *Cameroon* 6°52N 11°45E **263** D7
Banyoles *Spain* 42°16N 2°44E **196** C7
Banyuls-sur-Mer *France* 42°28N 3°8E **174** F7
Banyuwangi *Indonesia* 8°13S 114°21E **231** J17
Banz *Papua N. G.* 5°47S 144°37E **286** C3
Banza *Dem. Rep. of the Congo* 0°28N 20°10E **264** B4
Banzare Coast *Antarctica* 68°0S 125°0E **151** C9
Banzyville = Mobayi *Dem. Rep. of the Congo* 4°15N 21°8E **264** B4
Bao Ha *Vietnam* 22°11N 104°21E **228** F5
Bao Lac *Vietnam* 22°57N 105°40E **236** A5
Bao Loc *Vietnam* 11°32N 107°48E **237** G6
Bao'an *China* 22°34N 113°52E **219** a
Baocheng *China* 33°12N 106°56E **228** A6
Baode *China* 39°1N 111°5E **226** E6
Baodi *China* 39°38N 117°20E **227** E9
Baoding *China* 38°50N 115°28E **226** E8
Baoji *China* 34°20N 107°5E **226** G4
Baojing *China* 28°45N 109°41E **228** C7
Baokang *China* 31°54N 111°12E **229** B8
Baoro *C.A.R.* 5°40N 15°58E **264** A3
Baoshan *Shanghai, China* 31°24N 121°28E **138** A1
Baoshan *Yunnan, China* 25°10N 99°5E **228** E2
Baotou *China* 40°32N 110°2E **226** D6
Baotow = Baotou *China* 40°32N 110°2E **226** D6
Baoulé → *Mali* 12°36N 9°45W **262** C3
Baoxing *China* 30°24N 102°50E **228** B4
Baoying *China* 33°17N 119°20E **227** H10
Baoyou = Ledong *China* 18°41N 109°5E **229** a
Bap *India* 27°23N 72°18E **242** F5
Bapatla *India* 15°55N 80°30E **245** G5
Bapaume *France* 50°7N 2°50E **173** B9
Baqar, Bahr el → *Egypt* 31°7N 32°6E **251** G3
Bāqerābād *Iran* 33°2N 51°58E **247** C6
Ba'qūbah *Iraq* 33°45N 44°50E **213** F11
Baquedano *Chile* 23°20S 69°52W **334** A2
Bar *Montenegro* 42°8N 19°6E **202** D3
Bar *Ukraine* 49°4N 27°40E **177** D14
Bar Bigha *India* 25°21N 85°47E **243** G11
Bar Giyora *Israel* 31°45N 35°5E **123** B1
Bar Harbor *U.S.A.* 44°23N 68°13W **309** C19
Bar-le-Duc *France* 48°47N 5°10E **173** D12
Bar-sur-Aube *France* 48°14N 4°40E **173** D11
Bar-sur-Seine *France* 48°7N 4°20E **173** D11
Bara *India* 25°16N 81°43E **243** G9
Bâra *Romania* 47°2N 27°3E **183** C12
Bara *Sudan* 13°42N 30°22E **266** B3
Bara Banki *India* 26°55N 81°12E **243** F9
Baraawe *Somalia* 1°20N 44°8E **267** D5
Barabai *Indonesia* 2°32S 115°34E **235** C5
Baraboo *U.S.A.* 43°28N 89°45W **308** D9
Baracoa *Cuba* 20°20N 74°30W **321** B5
Baradā → *Syria* 33°33N 36°34E **250** E7
Baradero *Argentina* 33°52S 59°29W **334** C4
Baradine *Australia* 30°56S 149°4E **283** A8
Baraga *U.S.A.* 46°47N 88°30W **308** B9
Bărăganul *Romania* 44°49N 27°31E **183** F12
Baragoi *Kenya* 1°47N 36°47E **268** B4
Barah → *India* 27°42N 77°5E **242** F6
Barahanagar *India* 22°39N 88°22E **124** B2
Barahona *Dom. Rep.* 18°13N 71°7W **321** C5
Barail Range *India* 25°15N 93°20E **241** C4
Barajas *Spain* 40°28N 3°34W **127** B2
Barajas, Madrid ✕ (MAD) *Spain* 40°26N 3°34W **127** B2
Barak → *India* 24°52N 92°30E **241** C4
Baraka *Sudan* 10°59N 27°59E **257** E2
Baraka → *Sudan* 18°13N 37°35E **256** D4
Barakaldo *Spain* 43°18N 2°59W **196** B2
Barakar → *India* 24°7N 86°14E **243** G12
Barakee △ *Australia* 31°37S 151°53E **283** A9
Barakī *Afghan.* 33°56N 68°55E **240** B3
Barakot *India* 21°33N 84°59E **243** J11
Barakpur *India* 22°47N 88°21E **124** A2
Baralaba *Australia* 24°13S 149°50E **280** C4
Baralla *Spain* 42°53N 7°15W **194** C3
Baralzon L. *Canada* 60°0N 98°3W **297** B9
Baram → *Malaysia* 4°35N 113°58E **235** B4
Baramati *India* 18°11N 74°33E **244** E2
Baramba *India* 20°25N 85°23E **244** D7
Barameiya *Sudan* 18°32N 36°38E **256** D4
Baramula *India* 34°15N 74°20E **243** B6
Baran *India* 25°9N 76°40E **242** G7
Baran → *Pakistan* 25°13N 68°17E **242** G3
Barañain *Spain* 42°48N 1°40W **196** C3
Baranavichy *Belarus* 53°10N 26°0E **177** B14
Barani *Burkina Faso* 13°9N 3°51W **262** C4
Baranoa *Colombia* 10°48N 74°55W **328** A3
Baranof *U.S.A.* 57°5N 134°50W **296** B2
Baranof I. *U.S.A.* 57°0N 135°0W **303** H14
Baranów Sandomierski *Poland* 50°29N 21°30E **185** H8
Baranowicze = Baranavichy *Belarus* 53°10N 26°0E **177** B14
Baranya □ *Hungary* 46°0N 18°15E **182** E3
Barão de Cocais *Brazil* 19°56S 43°28W **333** E3
Barão de Grajaú *Brazil* 6°45S 43°1W **332** C3
Barão de Melgaço *Mato Grosso, Brazil* 16°14S 55°52W **331** D6
Barão de Melgaço *Rondônia, Brazil* 11°50S 60°45W **331** C5
Baraolt *Romania* 46°5N 25°34E **183** D10
Baraona *Spain* 41°17N 2°39W **196** D2
Barapasi *Indonesia* 2°15S 137°5E **231** E9
Barapina = Panguna *Papua N. G.* 6°21S 155°25E **286** D8
Baras *Phil.* 13°40N 124°22E **232** E5
Barasat *India* 22°46N 88°31E **243** H13
Barat Daya, Kepulauan *Indonesia* 7°30S 128°0E **231** F7
Baratang I. *India* 12°13N 92°45E **245** H11
Barataria B. *U.S.A.* 29°20N 89°55W **315** G10
Barauda *India* 23°33N 75°15E **242** H6
Baraut *India* 29°13N 77°7E **242** E7
Baraya *Colombia* 3°10N 75°4W **328** C2
Barbacan = Roxas *Phil.* 10°20N 119°21E **233** F2
Barbacena *Brazil* 21°15S 43°56W **333** F3
Barbacoas *Colombia* 1°45N 78°0W **328** C2
Barbados ■ *W. Indies* 13°10N 59°30W **323** r
Barbalha *Brazil* 7°19S 39°17W **332** C4
Barban *Croatia* 45°5N 14°2E **199** C11
Barbària, C. de *Spain* 38°39N 1°24E **206** D1
Barbarigo, Palazzo *Venice, Italy* **142** b2
Barbaros *Turkey* 40°54N 27°27E **203** F11
Barbas, C. *W. Sahara* 22°20N 16°42W **260** D1
Barbastro *Spain* 42°2N 0°5E **196** C5
Barbate *Spain* 36°13N 5°56W **195** J5
Barbaza *Phil.* 11°12N 122°2E **233** F4
Barbeau Pk. *Canada* 81°54N 75°1W **295** A16
Barber *Curaçao* 12°17N 69°4W **322** g
Barberini, Palazzo *Rome, Italy* **136** b3
Barberino di Mugello *Italy* 44°0N 11°15E **199** E8
Barbers Pt. *U.S.A.* 21°18N 158°7W **302** K13
Barberton *Mpumalanga, S. Africa* 25°42S 31°2E **271** C5
Barberton *Ohio, U.S.A.* 41°1N 81°39W **312** E3
Barberville *U.S.A.* 29°11N 81°26W **317** F8
Barbezieux-St-Hilaire *France* 45°28N 0°9W **174** C3
Barbican *London, U.K.* **125** a4
Barbosa *Colombia* 5°57N 73°37W **328** B3
Barbourville *U.S.A.* 36°52N 83°53W **309** G12
Barbuda *W. Indies* 17°30N 61°40W **322** c
Bârca *Romania* 43°59N 23°36E **183** G8
Barcaldine *Australia* 23°43S 145°6E **280** C4
Barcarena *Brazil* 1°30S 48°40W **332** B2
Barcarena *Lisboa, Portugal* 38°43N 9°16W **126** A1
Barcarena, Rib. de → *Portugal* 38°41N 9°16W **126** A1
Barcarrota *Spain* 38°31N 6°51W **195** G4
Barce = Al Marj *Libya* 32°25N 20°30E **258** B4
Barcellona Pozzo di Gotto *Italy* 38°9N 15°13E **201** D8
Barcelona *Spain* 41°22N 2°10E **114** A2
Barcelona *Venezuela* 10°10N 64°40W **329** A5
Barcelona □ *Spain* 41°30N 2°0E **196** D7
Barcelona, El Prat ✕ (BCN) *Spain* 41°18N 2°5E **114** B1
Barceloneta *Puerto Rico* 18°27N 66°32W **321** b
Barcelonette *France* 44°23N 6°40E **175** D10
Barcelos *Brazil* 1°0S 63°0W **329** D5
Barcin *Poland* 52°52N 17°55E **185** F4
Barclayville *Liberia* 4°48N 8°10W **262** E3
Barcoo → *Australia* 25°30S 142°50E **280** D3
Barcroft, L. *U.S.A.* 38°52N 77°9W **143** B2
Barcs *Hungary* 45°58N 17°28E **182** E2
Barczewo *Poland* 53°50N 20°42E **184** E7
Bärdä *Azerbaijan* 40°25N 47°10E **191** K8
Barda del Medio *Argentina* 38°45S 68°11W **336** A3
Bardaï *Chad* 21°25N 17°0E **259** D3
Bardas Blancas *Argentina* 35°49S 69°45W **334** D2
Bardawīl, Sabkhet el *Egypt* 31°10N 33°15E **251** G4
Barddhaman *India* 23°14N 87°39E **243** H12
Bardejov *Slovakia* 49°18N 21°15E **181** B14
Bardera = Baardheere *Somalia* 2°20N 42°27E **267** D5
Bardi *Italy* 44°38N 9°44E **198** D6
Bardīyah *Libya* 31°45N 25°5E **258** B5
Bardoli *India* 21°12N 73°5E **244** D1
Bardolino *Italy* 45°33N 10°43E **198** C7
Bardonécchia *Italy* 45°5N 6°42E **198** C3
Bardsey I. *U.K.* 52°45N 4°47W **168** E3
Bardstown *U.S.A.* 37°49N 85°28W **311** G11
Bare *Ethiopia* 4°37N 42°43E **267** D5
Bareilly *India* 28°22N 79°27E **243** E8
Barela *India* 23°6N 80°3E **243** H9
Barellan *Australia* 34°16S 146°24E **283** C7
Barentin *France* 49°33N 0°58E **172** C7
Barenton *France* 48°38N 0°50W **172** D6
Barents Sea *Arctic* 73°0N 39°0E **150** B9
Barentsøya *Svalbard* 78°25N 21°20E **154** B13
Barentu *Eritrea* 15°2N 37°35E **257** D4
Barfleur *France* 49°40N 1°17W **172** C5
Barfleur, Pte. de *France* 49°42N 1°16W **172** C5
Barfrush = Bābol *Iran* 36°40N 52°50E **247** B7
Barga *Italy* 44°4N 10°29E **198** D7
Bargal *Somalia* 11°25N 51°0E **267** B7
Bargara *Australia* 24°50S 152°25E **280** C5
Bargarh *India* 21°20N 83°37E **244** D6
Bargas *Spain* 39°56N 4°3W **194** F6
Barge *Italy* 44°43N 7°20E **198** D4
Bargi Dam *India* 22°59N 80°0E **244** C5
Bargo *Australia* 34°18S 150°35E **283** C9
Bargteheide *Germany* 53°44N 10°14E **178** B6
Barguzin *Russia* 53°37N 109°37E **215** D11
Barh *India* 25°29N 85°46E **243** G11
Barhaj *India* 26°18N 83°44E **243** F10
Barham *Australia* 35°36S 144°8E **282** C6
Barharwa *India* 24°52N 87°47E **243** G12
Barhi *India* 24°15N 85°25E **243** G11
Bari *Dem. Rep. of the Congo* 3°20N 19°25E **264** B3
Bari *India* 26°39N 77°39E **242** F7
Bari *Italy* 41°8N 16°51E **201** A9
Bari □ *Somalia* 10°0N 50°0E **267** B6
Bari Doab *Pakistan* 30°20N 73°0E **242** D5
Bari Sadri *India* 24°28N 74°30E **242** G6
Bari Sardo *Italy* 39°50N 9°38E **200** C2
Bariadi *Tanzania* 2°48S 34°0E **268** C3
Barīdī, Ra's *Si. Arabia* 24°17N 37°31E **246** E3
Barīm *Yemen* 12°39N 43°25E **248** D3
Barima → *Guyana* 8°33N 60°25W **329** B5
Barima-Waini □ *Guyana* 7°34N 59°40W **329** B6
Barinas *Venezuela* 8°36N 70°15W **328** B3
Barinas □ *Venezuela* 8°10N 69°50W **328** B4
Baring *U.S.A.* 40°15N 92°12W **310** D4
Baring, C. *Canada* 70°0N 117°30W **294** D8
Baringa *Dem. Rep. of the Congo* 0°45N 20°52E **264** B4
Baringo *Kenya* 0°38N 36°16E **266** D4
Baringo □ *Kenya* 0°40N 36°0E **268** B4
Baringo, L. *Kenya* 0°47N 36°16E **268** B4
Barinitas *Venezuela* 8°45N 70°25W **328** B3
Baripada *India* 21°57N 86°45E **244** D8
Bariri *Brazil* 22°4S 48°44W **333** F2
Bârîs *Egypt* 24°42N 30°31E **256** C3
Barisal *Bangla.* 22°45N 90°20E **241** D3
Barisal □ *Bangla.* 22°45N 90°20E **241** D3
Barisan, Pegunungan *Indonesia* 3°30S 102°15E **234** C2
Barit I. *Phil.* 18°51N 121°15E **232** B3
Barito → *Indonesia* 4°0S 114°50E **235** C4
Baritú △ *Argentina* 23°43S 64°40W **334** A3
Barjac *France* 44°20N 4°22E **175** D8
Barjols *France* 43°34N 6°2E **175** E10
Barjūj, Wadi → *Libya* 25°26N 12°12E **258** C2
Bark L. *Canada* 45°27N 77°51W **312** A7
Barka = Baraka → *Sudan* 18°13N 37°35E **256** D4
Barkā' *Oman* 23°40N 58°0E **249** B7
Barkakana *India* 23°37N 85°29E **243** H11
Barkal, J. *Sudan* 18°32N 31°50E **256** D3
Barkald *Norway* 61°59N 10°53E **164** C7
Barkam *China* 31°51N 102°28E **228** B4
Barker *U.S.A.* 43°20N 78°33W **312** C6
Barking *U.K.* 51°32N 0°5E **125** A4
Barkingside *U.K.* 51°35N 0°4E **125** A4
Barkley, L. *U.S.A.* 37°1N 88°14W **315** C10
Barkley Sound *Canada* 48°50N 125°10W **296** D3
Barkly East *S. Africa* 30°58S 27°33E **270** D4
Barkly Homestead *Australia* 19°52S 135°50E **280** B2
Barkly Tableland *Australia* 17°50S 136°40E **280** B2
Barkly West *S. Africa* 28°5S 24°31E **270** C3
Barkol Kazak Zizhixian *China* 43°37N 93°2E **218** C7
Barla Dağı *Turkey* 38°5N 30°40E **205** C12
Bârlad *Romania* 46°15N 27°38E **183** D12
Bârlad → *Romania* 45°38N 27°32E **183** E12
Barlee, L. *Australia* 29°15S 119°30E **279** E2
Barlee, Mt. *Australia* 24°38S 128°13E **279** D4
Barletta *Italy* 41°19N 16°17E **201** A9
Barlinek *Poland* 53°0N 15°15E **185** F2
Barlovento *Canary Is.* 28°48N 17°48W **153** e1
Barlovento *C. Verde Is.* 17°0N 25°0W **153** j
Barlow L. *Canada* 62°0N 103°0W **297** A8
Barmedman *Australia* 34°9S 147°21E **283** C7
Barmer *India* 25°45N 71°20E **242** G4
Barmera *Australia* 34°15S 140°28E **282** C4
Barmouth *U.K.* 52°44N 4°4W **168** E3
Barmstedt *Germany* 53°47N 9°46E **178** B5
Barn, The *St. Helena* 15°55S 5°40W **153** h
Barna → *India* 25°21N 83°3E **243** G10
Barnagar *India* 23°7N 75°19E **242** H6
Barnard Castle *U.K.* 54°33N 1°55W **168** C6
Barnaul *Russia* 53°20N 83°40E **217** B10
Barnes *N.S.W., Australia* 36°2S 144°49E **282** D6
Barnes *London, U.K.* 51°28N 0°14W **125** B2
Barnesville *Ga., U.S.A.* 33°3N 84°9W **316** B5
Barnesville *Minn., U.S.A.* 46°43N 96°28W **308** B5
Barnet *U.K.* 51°39N 0°11W **125** A2
Barnet □ *U.K.* 51°38N 0°9W **169** F7
Barneveld *Neths.* 52°7N 5°36E **178** D5
Barneville-Cartevert *France* 49°23N 1°46W **172** C5
Barnhart *U.S.A.* 31°8N 101°10W **314** F4
Barnsley *U.K.* 53°34N 1°27W **168** D6
Barnstable *U.S.A.* 41°42N 70°18W **309** E18
Barnstaple *U.K.* 51°5N 4°4W **169** F3
Barnstaple Bay = Bideford Bay *U.K.* 51°5N 4°20W **169** F3
Barnum B. *Palau* 7°6N 134°15E **288** c
Barnwell *U.S.A.* 33°15N 81°23W **316** B8
Baro *Nigeria* 8°35N 6°18E **263** D6
Baro → *Ethiopia* 8°26N 33°13E **257** F3
Barobo *Phil.* 8°33N 126°7E **233** G6
Baroda = Vadodara *India* 22°20N 73°10E **242** H5
Baroda *India* 25°29N 76°35E **242** G7
Baroe *S. Africa* 33°13S 24°33E **270** D3
Baron Empain Palace *Egypt* 30°5N 31°20E **117** A2
Baron Ra. *Australia* 23°30S 127°45E **278** D4
Barong *China* 31°3N 99°20E **228** B2
Barora *Solomon Is.* 7°30S 158°20E **287** L10
Barora Ite *Solomon Is.* 7°36S 158°24E **287** L10
Barotse = Western □ *Zambia* 15°0S 24°4E **265** F4
Barotseland *Zambia* 15°0S 24°0E **265** F4
Barouéli *Mali* 13°4N 6°50W **262** C3
Barpali *India* 21°11N 83°35E **244** D6
Barpathar *India* 26°17N 93°53E **241** B4
Barpeta *India* 26°20N 91°10E **241** B3
Barqa *Libya* 27°0N 23°0E **258** B4
Barqin *Libya* 27°33N 13°34E **258** C2
Barques, Pt. Aux *U.S.A.* 44°4N 82°58W **312** B2
Barquísimeto *Venezuela* 10°4N 69°19W **328** A4
Barr, Ras el *Egypt* 31°32N 31°50E **256** H7
Barr Smith Range *Australia* 27°4S 120°20E **279** E3
Barra *Brazil* 11°5S 43°10W **332** D3
Barra *Gambia* 13°28N 16°32W **262** C1
Barra *W. Isles, U.K.* 57°0N 7°29W **167** E1
Barra, Pta. *Mozam.* 23°48S 35°32E **271** B6
Barra, Sd. of *U.K.* 57°4N 7°25W **167** D1
Barra Andai *Pakistan* 24°47N 66°59E **123** B2
Barra Bonita = Ibaiti *Brazil* 23°50S 50°10W **333** F1
Barra da Estiva *Brazil* 13°38S 41°19W **333** D3
Barra de Navidad *Mexico* 19°12N 104°41W **318** D4
Barra de São Manuel *Brazil* 7°19S 58°5W **331** B6
Barra do Bugres *Brazil* 15°0S 57°11W **331** D6
Barra do Corda *Brazil* 5°30S 45°10W **332** C2
Barra do Dande *Angola* 8°28S 13°22E **265** D2
Barra do Garças *Brazil* 15°54S 52°16W **331** D7
Barra do Mendes *Brazil* 11°43S 42°4W **333** D3
Barra do Piraí *Brazil* 22°30S 43°50W **333** F3
Barra Falsa, Pta. da *Mozam.* 22°58S 35°37E **271** B6
Barra Funda *Brazil* 23°31S 46°39W **137** B2
Barra Hd. *U.K.* 56°47N 7°40W **167** E1
Barra Mansa *Brazil* 22°35S 44°12W **333** F3
Barraba *Australia* 30°21S 150°35E **283** A9
Barracão do Barreto *Brazil* 8°48S 58°24W **331** B6
Barracas *Argentina* 34°39S 58°24W **117** B2
Barracas al Sur = Avellaneda *Argentina* 34°40S 58°22W **117** C2
Barrackpur = Barakpur *India* 22°47N 88°21E **124** A2
Barrafranca *Italy* 37°22N 14°12E **201** E7
Barrage de Petit-Saut *Fr. Guiana* 5°3N 53°3W **329** B7
Barrāmīya *Egypt* 25°4N 33°47E **256** B3
Barranca *Lima, Peru* 10°45S 77°50W **330** C2
Barranca *Loreto, Peru* 4°50S 76°50W **328** D2
Barranca del Cobre ⌓ *Mexico* 27°18N 107°40W **318** B3
Barrancabermeja *Colombia* 7°0N 73°50W **328** B3
Barrancas *Colombia* 10°57N 72°50W **328** A3
Barrancas *Venezuela* 8°55N 62°5W **329** B5
Barranco *Peru* 12°9S 77°2W **124** B2
Barrancones Pt. *Trin. & Tob.* 10°31N 61°28W **323** t
Barrancos *Portugal* 38°10N 6°58W **195** G4
Barranqueras *Argentina* 27°30S 59°0W **334** B4
Barranquilla *Colombia* 11°0N 74°50W **328** A3
Barranquitas *Puerto Rico* 18°11N 66°19W **321** b
Barras *Brazil* 4°15S 42°18W **332** B3
Barras *Colombia* 1°45S 73°13W **328** D3
Barraute *Canada* 48°26N 77°38W **298** C4
Barre *Mass., U.S.A.* 42°25N 72°6W **313** D12
Barre *Vt., U.S.A.* 44°12N 72°30W **313** B12
Barre de L'Isle Ridge *St. Lucia* 13°55N 60°58W **323** m
Barreal *Argentina* 31°33S 69°28W **334** C2
Barrei *Ethiopia* 6°10N 42°49E **267** C5
Barreiras *Brazil* 12°8S 45°0W **333** D3
Barreirinha *Brazil* 2°47S 57°3W **329** D6
Barreirinhas *Brazil* 2°30S 42°50W **332** B3
Barreiro *Portugal* 38°39N 9°5W **126** B2
Barreiros *Brazil* 8°49S 35°12W **332** C4
Barrême *France* 43°57N 6°23E **175** E10
Barren, Nosy *Madag.* 18°25S 43°40E **272** B1
Barren I. *India* 12°16N 93°51E **245** H11
Barren Is. *U.S.A.* 58°55N 152°15W **303** G9
Barreto *Brazil* 22°50S 43°5W **135** B2
Barretos *Brazil* 20°30S 48°35W **333** F2
Barrhead *Canada* 54°10N 114°24W **296** C6
Barrie *Canada* 44°24N 79°40W **312** B5
Barrier, C. *N.Z.* 36°25S 175°32E **284** C4
Barrier Ra. *N.S.W., Australia* 31°0S 141°30E **282** A4
Barrier Ra. *Otago, N.Z.* 44°15S 169°32E **285** E4
Barrier Ra. *W. Coast, N.Z.* 44°30S 168°30E **285** E3
Barrière *Canada* 51°12N 120°7W **296** C4
Barrière-la-Croix *Martinique* 14°27N 60°51W **322** j
Barrigada *Guam* 13°28N 144°48E **302** d
Barrineau Park *U.S.A.* 30°42N 87°26W **317** E2
Barrington *U.S.A.* 41°44N 71°18W **313** E13
Barrington, I. = Santa Fé, I. *Ecuador* 0°49S 90°5W **330** a
Barrington L. *Canada* 56°55N 100°15W **297** B8
Barrington Tops *Australia* 32°6S 151°28E **283** B9
Barrington Tops △ *Australia* 32°4S 151°25E **283** B9
Barringun *Australia* 29°1S 145°41E **281** D4
Barrit-Luluno = Luba *Phil.* 17°19N 120°42E **232** C3
Barron *U.S.A.* 45°24N 91°51W **308** C8
Barrouallie *St. Vincent* 13°14N 61°17W **323** n
Barroui = Salisbury *Dominica* 15°26N 61°27W **323** k
Barrow *U.S.A.* 71°18N 156°47W **303** A8
Barrow → *Ireland* 52°25N 6°58W **166** D5
Barrow, Pt. *U.S.A.* 71°23N 156°29W **303** A8
Barrow Creek *Australia* 21°30S 133°55E **280** C1
Barrow I. *Australia* 20°45S 115°20E **278** D2
Barrow-in-Furness *U.K.* 54°7N 3°14W **168** C4
Barrow Pt. *Australia* 14°20S 144°40E **280** A3
Barrow Ra. *Australia* 26°0S 127°40E **279** E4
Barrow Str. *Canada* 74°20N 95°0W **295** C13
Barruecopardo *Spain* 41°4N 6°40W **194** D4
Barruelo de Santullán *Spain* 42°54N 4°17W **194** C6
Barry *V. of Glam., U.K.* 51°24N 3°16W **169** F4
Barry *Ill., U.S.A.* 39°42N 91°2W **310** E5
Barry's Bay *Canada* 45°29N 77°41W **312** A7
Barsalogho *Burkina Faso* 13°25N 1°3W **263** C4
Barsat *Pakistan* 36°10N 72°45E **243** A5
Barsham *Syria* 35°21N 40°33E **213** E9
Barshatas *Kazakhstan* 48°10N 78°39E **217** C9
Barsi *India* 18°10N 75°50E **244** E2
Barsinghausen *Germany* 52°18N 9°28E **178** C5
Barsoi *India* 25°48N 87°57E **241** C1
Barstow *U.S.A.* 34°54N 117°1W **307** L9
Bartala *India* 22°32N 88°15E **124** B1
Bartenstein = Bartoszyce *Poland* 54°15N 20°55E **184** D7
Bartfeld = Bardejov *Slovakia* 49°18N 21°15E **181** B14
Barth *Germany* 54°22N 12°42E **178** A8
Bartica *Guyana* 6°25N 58°40W **329** B6
Bartin *Turkey* 41°38N 32°21E **212** B5
Bartle Frere *Australia* 17°27S 145°50E **280** B4
Bartlesville *U.S.A.* 36°45N 95°59W **314** C7
Bartlett *Calif., U.S.A.* 36°29N 118°2W **306** J8
Bartlett *Tenn., U.S.A.* 35°12N 89°52W **315** D10
Bartlett, L. *Canada* 63°5N 118°20W **296** A5
Bartolbaai *Curaçao* 12°20N 69°2W **322** g
Bartolo = Betanzos *Bolivia* 19°34S 65°27W **331** D4
Bartolomeu Dias *Mozam.* 21°10S 35°8E **269** G4
Barton *Phil.* 10°24N 119°8E **233** F2
Barton *Vt., U.S.A.* 44°45N 72°11W **313** B12
Barton Park *Australia* 33°56S 151°9E **139** B1
Barton-upon-Humber *U.K.* 53°41N 0°25W **168** D7
Bartonville *U.S.A.* 40°39N 89°39W **310** D7
Bartoszyce *Poland* 54°15N 20°55E **184** D7
Bartow *Fla., U.S.A.* 27°54N 81°50W **317** H8
Bartow *Ga., U.S.A.* 32°53N 82°29W **316** C7
Bartyki *Poland* 52°10N 21°6E **143** C2
Barú, I. de *Colombia* 10°15N 75°35W **328** A2
Barú, Volcan *Panama* 8°55N 82°35W **320** E3
Barumba *Dem. Rep. of the Congo* 1°3N 23°37E **268** B1
Barumbu *Dem. Rep. of the Congo* 1°14N 23°31E **264** B4
Barúmini *Italy* 39°42N 8°59E **200** C1
Barung, Nusa *Indonesia* 8°30S 113°30E **235** D4
Barus *Indonesia* 2°0N 98°24E **234** B1
Baruth *Germany* 52°4N 13°30E **178** C9
Baruun Urt *Mongolia* 46°46N 113°15E **219** B11
Baruunsuu *Mongolia* 43°43N 105°35E **226** C3
Barvinkove *Ukraine* 48°57N 37°0E **189** H9
Bärwalde = Barwice *Poland* 53°44N 16°21E **184** E3
Barwani *India* 22°2N 74°57E **242** H6
Barwice *Poland* 53°44N 16°21E **184** E3
Barwick *U.S.A.* 30°54N 83°44W **316** E6
Barxudarlı *Azerbaijan* 41°0N 45°14E **213** B11
Barycz → *Poland* 51°42N 16°15E **185** G3
Barysaw *Belarus* 54°17N 28°28E **177** A15
Barysh *Russia* 53°39N 47°8E **190** D8
Barzān *Iraq* 36°55N 44°3E **246** B5
Bârzava *Romania* 46°7N 21°59E **182** D6
Bas du Fort *Guadeloupe* 16°13N 61°30W **322** e
Bas-Kouilou *Congo* 4°28S 11°42E **265** C2
Bas-Rhin □ *France* 48°40N 7°30E **173** D14
Bas-Sassandra □ *Ivory C.* 5°30N 7°0W **262** D3
Bas-Uélé □ *Dem. Rep. of the Congo* 3°30N 25°0E **264** B4
Bašaid *Serbia* 45°38N 20°25E **182** E5
Bāsa'idū *Iran* 26°35N 55°20E **247** E7
Basal *Pakistan* 33°33N 72°13E **242** C5
Basankusu *Dem. Rep. of the Congo* 1°5N 19°50E **264** B3
Basarabeasca *Moldova* 46°21N 28°58E **183** D13
Basarabi *Romania* 44°10N 28°26E **183** F13
Basarabia = Bessarabiya *Moldova* 47°0N 28°10E **177** E15
Basauri *Spain* 43°13N 2°53W **196** B2
Basavakalyan *India* 17°52N 76°57E **244** F3
Basawa *Afghan.* 34°15N 70°50E **242** B4
Basco *Phil.* 20°27N 121°58E **232** A3
Bascuñán, C. *Chile* 28°52S 71°35W **334** B1
Basekpio *Dem. Rep. of the Congo* 4°43N 24°36E **264** B4
Basel *Switz.* 47°35N 7°35E **179** H3
Basel-Landschaft □ *Switz.* 47°26N 7°45E **179** H3
Basento → *Italy* 40°20N 16°49E **201** B9
Baserah *Indonesia* 0°25S 101°43E **234** C2
Basey *Phil.* 11°17N 125°4E **233** F5
Bashākerd, Kūhhā-ye *Iran* 26°42N 58°35E **247** E8
Bashanta = Gorodovikovsk *Russia* 46°8N 41°58E **191** G5
Bashaw *Canada* 52°35N 112°58W **296** C6
Bāshī *Iran* 28°41N 51°4E **247** D6
Bashi Channel *Asia* 21°25N 121°30E **225** E2
Bashkand = Artsvashen *Armenia* 40°38N 45°30E **213** B11
Bashkir Republic = Bashkortostan □ *Russia* 54°0N 57°0E **186** D10
Bashkiriya △ *Russia* 52°58N 56°30E **216** B5
Bashkortostan □ *Russia* 54°0N 57°0E **186** D10
Bashtanivka *Ukraine* 45°46N 29°29E **183** E14
Basibasy *Madag.* 22°10S 43°40E **272** C1
Basilaki I. *Papua N. G.* 10°35S 151°0E **286** F6
Basilan □ *Phil.* 6°33N 122°4E **233** H3
Basilan I. *Phil.* 6°35N 122°0E **233** H4
Basilan Str. *Phil.* 6°50N 122°0E **233** H4
Basildon *U.K.* 51°34N 0°28E **169** F8
Basilé *Eq. Guin.* 3°42N 8°48E **263** E6
Basilé, Pico de *Eq. Guin.* 3°36N 8°49E **263** E6
Basilicata □ *Italy* 40°30N 16°30E **201** B9
Basim = Washim *India* 20°3N 77°0E **244** D3
Basin *U.S.A.* 44°23N 108°2W **304** D9
Basinger *U.S.A.* 27°23N 81°2W **317** H8
Basingstoke *U.K.* 51°15N 1°5W **169** F6
Basirhat *Bangla.* 22°40N 88°54E **241** D2
Basīţ, Ra's al *Syria* 35°51N 35°48E **250** C6
Baška *Croatia* 44°58N 14°45E **199** D11
Başkale *Turkey* 38°2N 43°59E **213** C10
Baskatong, Rés. *Canada* 46°46N 75°50W **298** C4
Basle = Basel *Switz.* 47°35N 7°35E **179** H3
Basle Euroairport ✕ (EAP) *France* 47°36N 7°33E **173** E14
Başmakçı *Turkey* 37°54N 30°1E **205** D12
Basmat *India* 19°15N 77°12E **244** E3
Basoda *India* 23°52N 77°54E **242** H7
Basoko *Dem. Rep. of the Congo* 1°16N 23°40E **264** B4
Basongo *Dem. Rep. of the Congo* 4°15S 20°20E **265** C4
Basora, Pta. *Aruba* 12°25N 69°51W **322** f
Basque, Côte *France* 43°50N 2°0W **174** E2
Basque, Pays *France* 43°15N 1°20W **174** E2
Basque Provinces = País Vasco □ *Spain* 42°50N 2°45W **196** C2
Basra = Al Başrah *Iraq* 30°30N 47°50E **246** D5
Bass, Îs. de *French Polynesia* 27°55S 143°26W **289** f
Bass Str. *Australia* 39°15S 146°30E **281** F4
Bassae *Greece* 37°26N 21°53E **204** D3
Bassano *Canada* 50°48N 112°20W **296** C6
Bassano del Grappa *Italy* 45°46N 11°44E **199** C8
Bassar *Togo* 9°19N 0°57E **263** D5
Bassas da India *Ind. Oc.* 22°0S 39°0E **269** G4
Basse-Kotto □ *C.A.R.* 5°0N 21°30E **264** A4
Basse-Pointe *Martinique* 14°52N 61°8W **322** j
Basse Santa-Su *Gambia* 13°13N 14°15W **262** C2
Basse-Terre *Guadeloupe* 16°0N 61°44W **322** e
Basse Terre *Trin. & Tob.* 10°7N 61°19W **323** t
Bassein = Pathein *Burma* 16°45N 94°30E **241** G5
Basses, Pte. des *Guadeloupe* 15°52N 61°17W **322** e
Basses-Alpes = Alpes-de-Haute-Provence □ *France* 44°8N 6°10E **175** D10
Basses-Pyrénées = Pyrénées-Atlantiques □ *France* 43°10N 0°50W **174** E3
Basseterre *St. Kitts & Nevis* 17°17N 62°43W **322** d
Bassett *U.S.A.* 42°35N 99°32W **308** D4
Bassi *India* 30°44N 76°21E **242** D7
Bassigny *France* 48°0N 5°30E **173** E12
Bassikounou *Mauritania* 15°55N 6°1W **262** B3
Bassila *Benin* 9°1N 1°46E **263** D5
Bassum *Germany* 52°50N 8°40E **178** C4
Båstad *Sweden* 56°25N 12°51E **163** H6
Bastak *Iran* 27°15N 54°25E **247** E7
Baştām *Iran* 36°29N 55°4E **247** B7
Bastar *India* 19°15N 81°40E **244** E5
Bastelica *France* 42°1N 9°3E **175** F13
Basti *India* 26°52N 82°55E **243** F10
Bastia *France* 42°40N 9°30E **175** F13
Bastille, Place de la *Paris, France* **134** c5
Bastogne *Belgium* 50°1N 5°43E **170** D5
Bastrop *La., U.S.A.* 32°47N 91°55W **314** E9
Bastrop *Tex., U.S.A.* 30°7N 97°19W **314** F6
Basu *Indonesia* 0°18S 103°36E **234** C2
Basud *Phil.* 14°4N 122°58E **232** D4
Basuo = Dongfang *China* 18°50N 108°33E **229** a
Basus *Egypt* 30°7N 31°12E **117** A2
Basutoland = Lesotho ■ *Africa* 29°40S 28°0E **271** C4
Başyayla *Turkey* 36°45N 32°40E **250** B3
Bat al Khutm & Al 'Ayn *Oman* 23°16N 56°44E **249** B7
Bat-ongan Caves *Phil.* 12°20N 123°15E **232** E4
Bat Yam *Israel* 32°2N 34°44E **251** F5
Bata *Eq. Guin.* 1°57N 9°50E **264** B1
Bata *Romania* 46°1N 22°4E **182** D7
Bataan □ *Phil.* 14°40N 120°25E **232** D3
Bataan △ *Phil.* 14°45N 120°27E **232** D3
Batabanó *Cuba* 22°41N 82°18W **320** B3
Batabanó, G. de *Cuba* 22°30N 82°30W **320** B3
Batac *Phil.* 18°3N 120°34E **232** B3
Batagai *Russia* 67°38N 134°38E **215** C14
Batajnica *Serbia* 44°54N 20°17E **202** B4
Batak *Bulgaria* 41°57N 24°12E **203** E8
Batakan *Indonesia* 4°4S 114°37E **235** C4
Batala *India* 31°48N 75°12E **242** D6
Batalha *Portugal* 39°40N 8°50W **194** F2
Batalpashinsk = Cherkessk *Russia* 44°15N 42°5E **191** H6
Batam *Indonesia* 1°10N 104°2E **237** d
Batama *Dem. Rep. of the Congo* 0°58N 26°33E **268** B2
Batamay *Russia* 63°30N 129°15E **215** C13
Batan I. *Albay, Phil.* 13°15N 124°0E **232** E4
Batan I. *Batanes, Phil.* 20°26N 121°58E **232** A3
Batan Is. *Phil.* 20°30N 122°0E **232** A3
Batanagar *India* 22°31N 88°15E **124** B1
Batanes □ *Phil.* 20°40N 121°55E **232** A3
Batang *Sichuan, China* 30°1N 99°0E **228** B2
Batang *Indonesia* 6°55S 109°45E **235** D3
Batang Ai △ *Malaysia* 1°32N 112°2E **235** B4
Batang Gadis △ *Indonesia* 0°28N 99°12E **234** B1
Batanga *Gabon* 0°21S 9°18E **264** C1
Batangafo *C.A.R.* 7°25N 18°20E **264** A3
Batangas *Phil.* 13°35N 121°10E **232** E3
Batangas □ *Phil.* 13°40N 121°5E **232** E3
Batanta *Indonesia* 0°55S 130°40E **231** E8
Batarasa *Phil.* 8°40N 117°37E **233** G1
Batas I. *Phil.* 11°10N 119°36E **233** F2
Batatais *Brazil* 20°54S 47°37W **335** A6
Batavia = Jakarta *Indonesia* 6°9S 106°52E **122** A2
Batavia *Ill., U.S.A.* 41°51N 88°19W **311** C8
Batavia *N.Y., U.S.A.* 43°0N 78°11W **312** D6
Batavia *Ohio, U.S.A.* 39°5N 84°11W **311** E12
Bataysk *Russia* 47°3N 39°45E **189** J10
Batbakara = Amankeldi *Kazakhstan* 50°10N 65°10E **216** B7
Batchelor *Australia* 13°4S 131°1E **278** B5
Batdambang *Cambodia* 13°7N 103°12E **236** F4
Batéké, Plateau *Congo* 3°30S 15°45E **264** C3
Batemans B. *Australia* 35°40S 150°12E **283** C9
Batemans Bay *Australia* 35°44S 150°11E **283** C9
Batesburg-Leesville *U.S.A.* 33°54N 81°33W **316** B8
Batesville *Ark., U.S.A.* 35°46N 91°39W **314** D9
Batesville *Ind., U.S.A.* 39°18N 85°13W **311** E11
Batesville *Miss., U.S.A.* 34°19N 89°57W **315** D10
Batesville *Tex., U.S.A.* 28°58N 99°37W **314** G5
Bath *Ont., Canada* 44°11N 76°47W **313** B8
Bath *St. Kitts & Nevis* 17°8N 62°37W **322** d
Bath *Bath & N.E. Somerset, U.K.* 51°23N 2°22W **169** F5
Bath *Maine, U.S.A.* 43°55N 69°49W **309** D19
Bath *N.Y., U.S.A.* 42°20N 77°19W **312** D7
Bath & North East Somerset □ *U.K.* 51°21N 2°27W **169** F5
Bath Beach *U.S.A.* 40°36N 74°0W **132** C1
Bath I. *Pakistan* 24°49N 67°1E **123** B2
Batha □ *Chad* 14°0N 19°0E **259** F3
Batha → *Chad* 12°47N 17°34E **259** F3
Batheay *Cambodia* 11°59N 104°57E **237** G5
Bathsheba *Barbados* 13°13N 59°32W **323** r
Bathurst = Banjul *Gambia* 13°28N 16°40W **262** C1
Bathurst *N.S.W., Australia* 33°25S 149°31E **283** B8
Bathurst *N.B., Canada* 47°37N 65°43W **299** C6
Bathurst *Eastern Cape, S. Africa* 33°30S 26°50E **270** D4
Bathurst, C. *Canada* 70°34N 128°0W **294** C6
Bathurst B. *Australia* 14°16S 144°25E **280** A3
Bathurst Harb. *Australia* 43°15S 146°10E **281** G4
Bathurst I. *N. Terr., Australia* 11°30S 130°10E **278** B5
Bathurst I. *Nunavut, Canada* 76°0N 100°30W **295** B11
Bathurst Inlet *Canada* 66°50N 108°1W **294** D10
Bati *Ethiopia* 11°10N 40°0E **257** E5
Batie *Burkina Faso* 9°53N 2°53W **262** D4
Batiki *Fiji* 17°48S 179°10E **287** A2
Batir *West Bank* 31°43N 35°8E **123** B1
Batken *Kyrgyzstan* 40°3N 70°50E **217** D8
Batken □ *Kyrgyzstan* 39°50N 71°0E **217** E8
Batlow *Australia* 35°31S 148°9E **283** C8
Batman *Turkey* 37°55N 41°5E **213** D9
Baţn al Ghūl *Jordan* 29°36N 35°56E **251** J6
Batna *Algeria* 35°34N 6°15E **261** A6
Batna □ *Algeria* 35°30N 5°55E **261** A6
Batnfjordsøra *Norway* 62°53N 7°42E **164** B4
Bato *Catanduanes, Phil.* 13°36N 124°18E **232** E5
Bato *Leyte, Phil.* 10°13N 124°48E **233** F5
Bato Bato *Phil.* 5°6N 119°49E **233** J2
Batoala *Gabon* 0°48N 13°27E **264** B2
Batobato = San Isidro *Phil.* 6°50N 126°5E **233** H6
Batočina *Serbia* 44°7N 21°5E **202** B5
Batok, Bukit *Singapore* 1°21N 103°46E **138** A2
Batoka *Zambia* 16°45S 27°15E **269** F2
Baton Rouge *U.S.A.* 30°27N 91°11W **314** F9
Batong, Ko *Thailand* 6°32N 99°12E **237** J2
Bátonyterenye *Hungary* 47°59N 19°50E **182** C4
Batopilas *Mexico* 27°1N 107°44W **318** B3
Batouri *Cameroon* 4°30N 14°25E **264** B2
Batovany = Partizánske *Slovakia* 48°38N 18°23E **181** C11
Båtsfjord *Norway* 70°38N 29°39E **160** A23
Batsi *Greece* 37°52N 24°47E **204** D6
Battambang = Batdambang *Cambodia* 13°7N 103°12E **236** F4
Battersea *U.K.* 51°28N 0°9W **125** B3
Battery Park *New York, U.S.A.* **132** f1
Batti Malv *India* 8°50N 92°51E **245** K11
Batticaloa *Sri Lanka* 7°43N 81°45E **245** L5
Battipáglia *Italy* 40°37N 14°58E **201** B7
Battle *U.K.* 50°55N 0°30E **169** G8
Battle → *Canada* 52°43N 108°15W **297** C7
Battle Creek *U.S.A.* 42°19N 85°11W **311** B11
Battle Ground *U.S.A.* 45°47N 122°32W **306** E4
Battle Harbour *Canada* 52°16N 55°35W **299** B8
Battle Lake *U.S.A.* 46°17N 95°43W **308** B6
Battle Mountain *U.S.A.* 40°38N 116°56W **304** F5
Battlefields *Zimbabwe* 18°37S 29°47E **269** F2
Battleford *Canada* 52°45N 108°15W **297** C7
Battonya *Hungary* 46°16N 21°3E **182** D6
Batu *Ethiopia* 6°55N 39°45E **257** F4
Batu *Malaysia* 3°15N 101°40E **237** L3
Batu, Bukit *Malaysia* 2°16N 113°43E **235** B4
Batu, Kepulauan *Indonesia* 0°30S 98°25E **234** C1

Batu Bora, Bukit *Malaysia* 2°43N 114°43E **235** B4
Batu Ferringhi *Malaysia* 5°28N 100°15E **237** c
Batu Gajah *Malaysia* 4°28N 101°3E **237** K3
Batu Is. = Batu, Kepulauan
Indonesia 0°30S 98°25E **234** C1
Batu Pahat *Malaysia* 1°50N 102°56E **237** M4
Batu Puteh *Malaysia* 5°25N 117°55E **235** A5
Batu Puteh, Gunung
Malaysia 4°15N 101°31E **237** K3
Batuan *Phil.* 12°25N 123°46E **232** E4
Batuata *Indonesia* 6°12S 122°42E **231** F6
Batugondang, Tanjung
Indonesia 8°6S 114°29E **231** J17
Batukaru, Gunung
Indonesia 8°20S 115°5E **231** J18
Batulaki *Phil.* 5°34N 125°19E **233** J5
Batuli = San Isidro *Phil.* 6°50N 126°5E **233** H6
Batumi *Georgia* 41°39N 41°44E **191** K5
Batuputih *Indonesia* 1°24N 118°28E **235** B5
Batur, Gunung *Indonesia* 8°14S 115°23E **231** J18
Batura Sar *Pakistan* 36°30N 74°31E **243** A6
Baturaja *Indonesia* 4°11S 104°15E **234** C2
Baturité *Brazil* 4°28S 38°45W **332** B4
Baturiti *Indonesia* 8°19S 115°11E **231** J18
Batusangkar *Indonesia* 0°27S 100°35E **234** C2
Batys Qazaqstan □
Kazakhstan 50°0N 50°0E **216** C3
Bau *Malaysia* 1°25N 110°9E **235** B4
Bauang *Phil.* 16°31N 120°20E **232** C3
Baubau *Indonesia* 5°25S 122°38E **231** F6
Baucau *E. Timor* 8°27S 126°27E **231** F7
Bauchi *Nigeria* 10°22N 9°48E **263** C6
Bauchi □ *Nigeria* 10°30N 10°0E **263** C7
Baud *France* 47°52N 3°1W **172** E3
Bauda *India* 20°50N 84°25E **244** D7
Baudette *U.S.A.* 48°43N 94°36W **308** A6
Bauer, C. *Australia* 32°44S 134°4E **281** E1
Bauerwitz = Baborów
Poland 50°7N 18°1E **185** H5
Bauguen = Salcedo *Phil.* 11°9N 125°40E **233** F5
Bauhinia *Australia* 24°35S 149°18E **280** C4
Baukau = Baucau
E. Timor 8°27S 126°27E **231** F7
Bauko *Phil.* 17°0N 120°52E **232** C3
Baulai ➔ *Bangla.* 24°22N 91°1E **241** C3
Bauld, C. *Canada* 51°38N 55°26W **295** G20
Bauman *Russia* 55°45N 37°40E **189** D3
Baume-les-Dames *France* 47°22N 6°22E **173** E13
Baumgarten *Austria* 48°12N 16°17E **142** A1
Baunatal *Germany* 51°14N 9°24E **178** D5
Baunei *Italy* 40°2N 9°40E **200** B2
Baure *Nigeria* 12°52N 8°50E **263** C6
Baures *Bolivia* 13°35S 63°35W **331** C5
Bauru *Brazil* 22°10S 49°0W **335** A6
Baús *Brazil* 18°22S 52°47W **331** D7
Bausi *India* 24°48N 87°1E **243** G12
Bauska *Latvia* 56°24N 24°15E **184** B11
Bautino *Kazakhstan* 44°35N 50°14E **191** H10
Bautzen *Germany* 51°10N 14°26E **178** D10
Bauya *S. Leone* 8°12N 12°38W **262** D2
Bavānāt *Iran* 30°28N 53°27E **247** D7
Bavanište *Serbia* 44°49N 20°55E **182** F5
Bavaria = Bayern □
Germany 48°50N 12°0E **179** G7
Båven *Sweden* 59°0N 16°56E **162** E10
Bavispe ➔ *Mexico* 29°15N 109°11W **318** B3
Baw Baw △ *Australia* 37°50S 146°17E **283** D7
Bawal *Indonesia* 7°52S 111°13E **235** D4
Bawan *Indonesia* 1°42S 113°55E **235** C4
Bawdwin *Burma* 23°5N 97°20E **241** D6
Bawean *Indonesia* 5°46S 112°35E **235** D4
Bawku *Ghana* 11°3N 0°19W **263** C4
Bawlakhe *Burma* 19°11N 97°21E **241** F6
Bawolung *China* 28°50N 101°16E **228** C3
Bawomataluwo *Indonesia* 0°38N 97°44E **234** B1
Baxley *U.S.A.* 31°47N 82°21W **316** D7
Baxter *Iowa, U.S.A.* 41°49N 93°9W **310** C3
Baxter *Minn., U.S.A.* 46°21N 94°17W **308** B6
Baxter Springs *U.S.A.* 37°2N 94°44W **308** G6
Baxter State ⌂ *U.S.A.* 46°5N 68°57W **309** B19
Bay □ *Somalia* 2°30N 43°30E **267** D5
Bay, L. *U.S.A.* 28°25N 81°34W **133** A2
Bay, Laguna de *Phil.* 14°20N 121°11E **232** D3
Bay City *Mich., U.S.A.* 43°36N 83°54W **309** D12
Bay City *Tex., U.S.A.* 28°59N 95°58W **314** G7
Bay Harbor Islands *U.S.A.* 25°53N 80°7W **129** C3
Bay Hill *U.S.A.* 28°28N 81°30W **133** B1
Bay Is. = Bahía, Is. de la
Honduras 16°45N 86°15W **320** C2
Bay Minette *U.S.A.* 30°53N 87°46W **315** F11
Bay of Plenty □ *N.Z.* 38°0S 177°0E **284** D5
Bay Ridge *U.S.A.* 40°37N 74°1W **132** C1
Bay Roberts *Canada* 47°36N 53°16W **299** C9
Bay St. Louis *U.S.A.* 30°19N 89°20W **315** F10
Bay Springs *U.S.A.* 31°59N 89°17W **315** F10
Bay View *N.Z.* 39°25S 176°50E **284** F5
Baya *Dem. Rep. of the Congo* 11°53S 27°25E **269** E2
Bayambang *Phil.* 15°49N 120°27E **232** D3
Bayamo *Cuba* 20°20N 76°40W **320** B4
Bayamón *Puerto Rico* 18°24N 66°9W **321** C6
Bayan Har Shan *China* 34°0N 98°0E **218** E8
Bayan Hot = Alxa Zuoqi
China 38°50N 105°40E **226** E3
Bayan Lepas *Malaysia* 5°17N 100°16E **237** c
Bayan Obo *China* 41°52N 109°59E **226** D5
Bayan-Ovoo = Erdenetsogt
Mongolia 42°55N 106°5E **226** C4
Bayan-Tumen = Choybalsan
Mongolia 48°4N 114°30E **219** B11
Bayana *India* 26°55N 77°18E **242** F7
Bayanaūyl *Kazakhstan* 50°45N 75°45E **217** B9
Bayanbulak ⌂ *China* 42°20N 84°0E **217** D10
Bayanhongor *Mongolia* 46°8N 102°43E **218** B9
Bayard *N. Mex., U.S.A.* 32°46N 108°8W **305** K9
Bayard *Nebr., U.S.A.* 41°45N 103°20W **308** E2
Bayawan *Phil.* 9°46N 122°45E **233** G4
Baybay *Phil.* 10°40N 124°55E **233** F5
Bayburt *Turkey* 40°15N 40°20E **213** B9
Bayburt □ *Turkey* 40°35N 39°25E **213** B8
Baydaratskaya Guba
Russia 69°0N 67°30E **214** C7
Baydhabo *Somalia* 3°8N 43°30E **267** D5
Bayelsa □ *Nigeria* 4°30N 6°0E **263** E6
Bayerische Alpen
Germany 47°35N 11°30E **179** H7
Bayerische Rhön ⌂
Germany 50°15N 10°5E **179** E6
Bayerischer Spessart ⌂
Germany 49°58N 10°15E **179** F6
Bayerischer Wald
Germany 48°56N 12°50E **179** G8
Bayern □ *Germany* 48°50N 12°0E **179** G7
Bayeux *France* 49°17N 0°42W **172** C6
Bayfield *Ont., Canada* 43°34N 81°42W **312** C3
Bayfield *Wis., U.S.A.* 46°49N 90°49W **308** B8
Bayḩān al Qiṣāb *Yemen* 15°48N 45°44E **248** D4
Bayındır *Turkey* 38°13N 27°39E **205** C9
Bayit Va-Gan *Israel* 31°46N 35°11E **123** B2
Baykal, Oz. *Russia* 53°0N 108°0E **215** D11
Baykan *Turkey* 38°7N 41°44E **213** C9
Baymak *Russia* 52°36N 58°19E **186** D10
Baynes Mts. *Namibia* 17°15S 13°0E **270** A1
Bayombong *Phil.* 16°30N 121°10E **232** C3
Bayon *France* 48°30N 6°20E **173** D13
Bayona = Baiona *Spain* 42°6N 8°52W **194** C2
Bayonet Point *U.S.A.* 28°20N 82°41W **317** G7
Bayonne *Pyrénées-Atlantiques,*
France 43°30N 1°28W **174** E2
Bayonne *N.J., U.S.A.* 40°40N 74°6W **132** B1
Bayou Boeuf *U.S.A.* 29°50N 90°10W **131** B1
Bayou Segnette State Park ⌂
U.S.A. 29°53N 90°10W **131** B2
Bayovar *Peru* 5°50S 81°0W **330** B1
Bayport *U.S.A.* 28°32N 82°39W **317** G7
Bayqonyr *Kazakhstan* 45°40N 63°20E **216** C6
Bayram-Ali = Baýramaly
Turkmenistan 37°37N 62°10E **247** B9
Baýramaly *Turkmenistan* 37°37N 62°10E **247** B9
Bayramiç *Turkey* 39°48N 26°36E **205** B8
Bayrampaşa *Turkey* 41°1N 28°56E **122** B1
Bayreuth *Germany* 49°56N 11°35E **179** F7
Bayrischzell *Germany* 47°41N 12°0E **179** H8
Bayrūt *Lebanon* 33°53N 35°31E **250** E6
Bays, L. of *Canada* 45°15N 79°4W **312** A5
Bayshore *Calif., U.S.A.* 37°42N 122°24W **136** B2
Bayshore *Fla., U.S.A.* 26°43N 81°50W **317** J8
Baysville *Canada* 45°9N 79°7W **312** A5
Bayswater *London, U.K.* **125** b2
Bayt al Faqīh *Yemen* 14°31N 43°19E **248** D3
Bayt Lahm *West Bank* 31°43N 35°12E **123** B2
Baytik Shan *China* 45°15N 90°50E **217** C12
Baytown *U.S.A.* 29°43N 94°59W **314** G7
Bayugan *Phil.* 8°43N 125°42E **233** G5
Bayuquan *China* 40°16N 122°8E **227** D12
Bayview *U.S.A.* 37°44N 122°23W **136** B2
Bayville = Kirkwood
S. Africa 33°22S 25°15E **270** D4
Bayy al Kabīr, W. *Libya* 31°10N 15°53E **258** B3
Bayy al Khā'ib, Wādī ➔
Libya 30°55N 15°29E **258** B3
Bayzo *Niger* 13°52N 4°35E **263** C5
Baza *Spain* 37°30N 2°47W **195** H8
Bāzār Iran *Iran* 35°40N 51°25E **141** A2
Bazar Dyuzi *Russia* 41°12N 47°50E **191** K8
Bazardüzü = Bazar Dyuzi
Russia 41°12N 47°50E **191** K8
Bāzargān *Iran* 39°22N 44°26E **213** C11
Bazargic = Dobrich
Bulgaria 43°37N 27°49E **203** C11
Bazarny Karabulak
Russia 52°20N 46°29E **190** D8
Bazarnyy Syzgan *Russia* 53°45N 46°40E **190** D8
Bazaruto, I. do *Mozam.* 21°40S 35°28E **271** B6
Bazaruto △ *Mozam.* 21°42S 35°26E **271** B6
Bazas *France* 44°27N 0°13W **174** D3
Bazhong *China* 31°52N 106°46E **228** B6
Bazhou *China* 39°8N 116°22E **226** E9
Bazin *Guadeloupe* 16°22N 61°26W **322** e
Bazmān, Kūh-e *Iran* 28°4N 60°1E **247** D9
Baztan = Elizondo *Spain* 43°12N 1°30W **196** B3
Bé, Nosy *Madag.* 13°25S 48°15E **272** A2
Beach *U.S.A.* 46°58N 104°0W **308** B2
Beach City *U.S.A.* 40°39N 81°35W **312** F3
Beachport *Australia* 37°29S 140°0E **282** D4
Beachville *Canada* 43°5N 80°49W **312** C4
Beachy Hd. *U.K.* 50°44N 0°15E **169** G8
Beacon *W. Austral.,*
Australia 30°26S 117°52E **279** F2
Beacon *N.Y., U.S.A.* 41°30N 73°58W **313** E11
Beacon Hill
Hong Kong, China 22°21N 114°10E **122** A3
Beacon Hill *Boston, U.S.A.* **116** b1
Beaconsfield *Australia* 41°11S 146°48E **281** G4
Beagle, Canal *S. Amer.* 55°0S 68°30W **336** E3
Beagle Bay *Australia* 16°58S 122°40E **278** C3
Beagle Bay ✪ *Australia* 16°53S 122°40E **278** C3
Beagle G. *Australia* 12°15S 130°25E **278** B5
Béal an Átha = Ballina
Ireland 54°7N 9°9W **166** B2
Béal Átha na Sluaighe = Ballinasloe
Ireland 53°20N 8°13W **166** C3
Bealanana *Madag.* 14°33S 48°44E **272** A2
Beals Cr. ➔ *U.S.A.* 32°10N 100°51W **314** E4
Beamsville *Canada* 43°12N 79°28W **312** C5
Bear ➔ *Calif., U.S.A.* 38°56N 121°36W **306** G5
Bear ➔ *Utah, U.S.A.* 41°30N 112°8W **300** G17
Béar, C. *France* 42°31N 3°8E **174** F7
Bear I. = Bjørnøya *Arctic* 74°30N 19°0E **150** B8
Bear I. *Ireland* 51°38N 9°50W **166** E2
Bear L. *Man., Canada* 55°8N 96°0W **297** B9
Bear L. *Utah, U.S.A.* 41°59N 111°21W **304** F8
Bear Lake *Canada* 45°27N 79°35W **312** A5
Beardmore *Canada* 49°36N 87°57W **298** C2
Beardmore Glacier
Antarctica 84°30S 170°0E **151** E11
Beardstown *U.S.A.* 40°1N 90°26W **310** E6
Bearma ➔ *India* 24°20N 79°51E **243** G8
Béarn *France* 43°20N 0°30W **174** E3
Bearpaw Mts. *U.S.A.* 48°12N 109°30W **304** B9
Bearskin Lake *Canada* 53°58N 91°2W **298** B1
Beas ➔ *India* 31°10N 74°59E **242** D6
Beas de Segura *Spain* 38°15N 2°53W **195** G8
Beasain *Spain* 43°3N 2°11W **196** B2
Beata, C. *Dom. Rep.* 17°40N 71°30W **321** C5
Beata, I. *Dom. Rep.* 17°34N 71°31W **321** C5
Beato Ridge *W. Indies* 16°0N 72°30W **321** C5
Beato *Portugal* 38°44N 9°5W **126** A2
Beatrice *Nebr., U.S.A.* 40°16N 96°45W **308** E5
Beatrice *Zimbabwe* 18°15S 30°55E **269** F3
Beatrice, C. *Australia* 14°20S 136°55E **280** A2
Beatton ➔ *Canada* 56°15N 120°45W **296** B4
Beatton River *Canada* 57°26N 121°20W **296** B4
Beatty *U.S.A.* 36°54N 116°46W **306** J10
Beau Bassin *Mauritius* 20°13S 57°27E **272** d
Beauharnois = Pittsworth
Australia 27°41S 151°37E **281** D5
Beaucaire *France* 43°48N 4°39E **175** E8
Beauce, Plaine de la *France* 48°10N 1°45E **173** D8
Beauceville *Canada* 46°13N 70°46W **299** C5
Beauchêne, I. *Falk. Is.* 52°55S 59°15W **153** f
Beaudesert *Australia* 27°59S 153°0E **281** D5
Beaufort *Vic., Australia* 37°25S 143°25E **282** D5
Beaufort *Savoie, France* 45°44N 6°34E **175** C10
Beaufort *Malaysia* 5°30N 115°40E **235** A5
Beaufort *N.C., U.S.A.* 34°43N 76°40W **315** D16
Beaufort *S.C., U.S.A.* 32°26N 80°40W **316** C9
Beaufort Sea *Arctic* 72°0N 140°0W **292** B5
Beaufort West *S. Africa* 32°18S 22°36E **270** D3
Beaugency *France* 47°47N 1°38E **173** E8
Beauharnois *Canada* 45°20N 73°52W **313** A11
Beaujeu *France* 46°10N 4°35E **173** F11
Beaujolais *France* 46°0N 4°22E **173** F11
Beaulieu ➔ *Canada* 62°3N 113°11W **296** A6
Beaulieu-sur-Dordogne
France 44°58N 1°50E **174** D5
Beaulieu-sur-Mer *France* 43°42N 7°20E **175** E11
Beauly *U.K.* 57°30N 4°28W **167** D4
Beauly ➔ *U.K.* 57°29N 4°27W **167** D4
Beaumaris *U.K.* 53°16N 4°6W **168** D3
Beaumont *Belgium* 50°15N 4°14E **170** D4
Beaumont *N.Z.* 45°50S 169°33E **285** F4
Beaumont *Calif., U.S.A.* 33°57N 116°59W **307** M9
Beaumont *Tex., U.S.A.* 30°5N 94°6W **314** F7
Beaumont-de-Lomagne
France 43°53N 1°0E **174** E5
Beaumont-du-Périgord
France 44°45N 0°46E **174** D4
Beaumont-le-Roger *France* 49°4N 0°47E **172** C7
Beaumont-sur-Sarthe
France 48°13N 0°8E **172** D7
Beaumonte Heights
Canada 43°45N 79°34W **141** A1
Beaune *France* 47°2N 4°50E **173** E11
Beaune-la-Rolande *France* 48°4N 2°25E **173** D9
Beauport *Guadeloupe* 16°25N 61°30W **322** e
Beaupré *Canada* 47°3N 70°54W **299** C5
Beaupréau *France* 47°12N 1°0W **172** E6
Beauraing *Belgium* 50°7N 4°57E **170** D4
Beaurepaire *France* 45°22N 5°1E **175** C9
Beausejour *Man., Canada* 50°5N 96°35W **297** C9
Beauséjour *Guadeloupe* 16°18N 61°4W **322** e
Beauséjour *Martinique* 14°44N 60°57W **322** j
Beauvais *France* 49°25N 2°8E **173** C9
Beauval *Canada* 55°9N 107°37W **297** B7
Beauvoir-sur-Mer *France* 46°55N 2°2W **172** F4
Beauvoir-sur-Niort *France* 46°12N 0°30W **174** B3
Beaver *Alaska, U.S.A.* 66°22N 147°24W **303** C11
Beaver *Okla., U.S.A.* 36°49N 100°31W **314** C4
Beaver *Pa., U.S.A.* 40°42N 80°19W **312** F4
Beaver *Utah, U.S.A.* 38°17N 112°38W **304** G7
Beaver ➔ *B.C., Canada* 59°52N 124°20W **296** B4
Beaver ➔ *Ont., Canada* 55°55N 87°48W **298** A2
Beaver ➔ *Sask., Canada* 55°26N 107°45W **297** B7
Beaver ➔ *Okla., U.S.A.* 36°35N 99°30W **314** C5
Beaver City *U.S.A.* 40°8N 99°50W **308** E4
Beaver Creek *Canada* 63°0N 141°0W **294** E3
Beaver Dam *U.S.A.* 43°28N 88°50W **308** D9
Beaver Falls *U.S.A.* 40°46N 80°20W **312** F4
Beaver Hill L. *Canada* 54°5N 94°50W **297** C10
Beaver I. *U.S.A.* 45°40N 85°33W **309** C11
Beavercreek *U.S.A.* 39°43N 84°11W **311** E12
Beaverhill L. *Canada* 53°27N 112°32W **296** C6
Beaverlodge *Canada* 55°11N 119°29W **296** B5
Beaverstone ➔ *Canada* 54°59N 89°25W **298** B2
Beaverton *Ont., Canada* 44°26N 79°9W **312** B5
Beaverton *Oreg., U.S.A.* 45°29N 122°48W **306** E4
Beawar *India* 26°3N 74°18E **242** F6
Bebedouro *Brazil* 21°0S 48°25W **335** A6
Bebek *Turkey* 41°4N 29°2E **122** B2
Bebera, Tanjung
Indonesia 8°44S 115°51E **231** K18
Bebington *U.K.* 53°22N 3°0W **168** D4
Beboa *Madag.* 17°22S 44°33E **272** B1
Beboto *Chad* 8°16N 16°56E **259** G3
Bebra *Germany* 50°58N 9°48E **178** E5
Becán *Mexico* 18°34N 89°31W **319** D7
Bécancour *Canada* 46°20N 72°26W **309** B17
Beccles *U.K.* 52°27N 1°35E **169** E9
Bečej *Serbia* 45°36N 20°3E **182** E5
Beceni *Romania* 45°23N 26°48E **183** E11
Becerreá *Spain* 42°51N 7°10W **194** C3
Béchar *Algeria* 31°38N 2°18W **261** B4
Béchar □ *Algeria* 30°15N 3°5E **261** B5
Becharof L. *U.S.A.* 57°56N 156°23W **303** H8
Becharof Nat. Wildlife Refuge ⌂
U.S.A. 58°0N 156°15W **303** H8
Becharre = Bsharri
Lebanon 34°15N 36°0E **250** D7
Běchovice *Czechia* 50°4N 14°36E **135** B3
Bechuanaland = Botswana ■
Africa 22°0S 24°0E **270** B3
Bechyně *Czechia* 49°17N 14°29E **180** B7
Beckenham *U.K.* 51°24N 0°1W **125** B3
Beckerek = Zrenjanin
Serbia 45°22N 20°23E **182** E5
Beckley *U.S.A.* 37°47N 81°11W **309** G13
Beckton *U.K.* 51°30N 0°4E **125** A4
Beckum *Germany* 51°45N 8°3E **178** D4
Beclean *Romania* 47°11N 24°11E **183** C9
Becontree *U.K.* 51°33N 0°7E **125** A4
Bečov nad Teplou *Czechia* 50°5N 12°49E **180** A5
Bečva ➔ *Czechia* 49°31N 17°20E **181** B10
Bédar *Spain* 37°11N 1°59W **197** H3
Bédarieux *France* 43°37N 3°10E **174** E7
Beddington Corner *U.K.* 51°23N 0°9W **125** B3
Beddouza, C. *Morocco* 32°33N 9°9W **260** B3
Bedeau = Râs el Ma
Algeria 34°26N 0°50W **261** B4
Bedele *Ethiopia* 8°31N 36°23E **257** F4
Bederkesa *Germany* 53°37N 8°50E **178** B4
Bederwanak *Somalia* 9°34N 44°23E **267** C5
Bedeso *Ethiopia* 9°58N 40°52E **257** F5
Bedford *Qué., Canada* 45°7N 72°59W **313** A12
Bedford *Eastern Cape,*
S. Africa 32°40S 26°10E **270** D4
Bedford *Beds., U.K.* 52°8N 0°28W **169** E7
Bedford *Ind., U.S.A.* 38°52N 86°29W **311** F10
Bedford *Iowa, U.S.A.* 40°40N 94°44W **310** D2
Bedford *Ky., U.S.A.* 38°36N 85°19W **311** F11
Bedford *Mass., U.S.A.* 42°27N 71°15W **116** A1
Bedford *Ohio, U.S.A.* 41°23N 81°32W **312** E3
Bedford *Pa., U.S.A.* 40°1N 78°30W **312** F6
Bedford *Tex., U.S.A.* 32°50N 97°8W **120** A3
Bedford *Va., U.S.A.* 37°20N 79°31W **309** G14
Bedford □ *U.K.* 52°4N 0°28W **169** E7
Bedford, C. *Australia* 15°14S 145°21E **280** B4
Bedford Park *Ill., U.S.A.* 41°46N 87°46W **119** C2
Bedford Park *N.Y., U.S.A.* 40°52N 73°52W **132** A2
Bedford Stuyvesant
U.S.A. 40°41N 73°56W **132** B2
Bedford View *S. Africa* 26°10S 28°7E **123** B2
Bedi *Chad* 11°6N 18°33E **259** F3
Będków *Poland* 51°36N 19°44E **185** G6
Bednja ➔ *Croatia* 46°20N 16°52E **199** B13
Bednodemyanovsk
Russia 53°55N 43°15E **190** D6
Bedok *Singapore* 1°19N 103°56E **138** B3
Bedok, Res. *Singapore* 1°20N 103°56E **138** A3
Bedónia *Italy* 44°30N 9°38E **198** D6
Bedourie *Australia* 24°30S 139°30E **280** C2
Bedti ➔ *India* 14°50N 74°44E **245** G2
Bedugul *Indonesia* 8°17S 115°10E **231** J18
Bedum *Neths.* 53°18N 6°36E **170** A6
Będzin *Poland* 50°19N 19°7E **185** H6
Bee Ridge *U.S.A.* 27°17N 82°29W **317** H7
Beebe Plain *Canada* 45°1N 72°9W **313** A12
Beech Creek *U.S.A.* 41°5N 77°36W **312** E7
Beech Fork ➔ *U.S.A.* 37°46N 85°41W **311** G11
Beech Grove *U.S.A.* 39°43N 86°5W **311** E10
Beecher *U.S.A.* 41°21N 87°38W **311** C9
Beechey Point *U.S.A.* 70°29N 149°9W **303** A10
Beechworth *Australia* 36°22S 146°43E **283** D7
Beechy *Canada* 50°53N 107°24W **297** C7
Beed = Bir *India* 19°4N 75°46E **244** E2
Beef I. *Br. Virgin Is.* 18°26N 64°30W **321** b
Beelitz *Germany* 52°14N 12°58E **178** C8
Beenleigh *Australia* 27°43S 153°10E **281** D5
Be'er Menuḥa *Israel* 30°19N 35°8E **251** H6
Be'er Sheva *Israel* 31°15N 34°48E **251** G5
Beerenberg *Norway* 71°0N 8°20W **154** C10
Beersel *Belgium* 50°46N 4°18E **116** B1
Beersheba = Be'er Sheva
Israel 31°15N 34°48E **251** G5
Beeskow *Germany* 52°10N 14°15E **178** C10
Beestekraal *S. Africa* 25°23S 27°38E **271** C4
Beeston *U.K.* 52°56N 1°14W **168** E6
Beeton *Canada* 44°5N 79°47W **312** B5
Beetzendorf *Germany* 52°42N 11°6E **178** C7
Beeville *U.S.A.* 28°24N 97°45W **314** G6
Befale *Dem. Rep. of the Congo* 0°25N 20°45E **264** B4
Befandriana *Atsimo-Andrefana,*
Madag. 21°55S 44°0E **272** C1
Befandriana *Sofia, Madag.* 15°16S 48°32E **272** B2
Befasy *Madag.* 20°33S 44°23E **272** C1
Befori *Dem. Rep. of the Congo* 0°8N 22°22E **264** B4
Befotaka *Atsimo-Atsinanana,*
Madag. 23°49S 47°0E **272** C2
Befotaka *Diana, Madag.* 13°15S 48°16E **272** A2
Bega *Australia* 36°41S 149°51E **283** D8
Bega, Canalul *Romania* 45°37N 20°46E **182** E5
Begamganj *Bangla.* 22°56N 91°6E **241** D3
Bégard *France* 48°38N 3°18W **172** D3
Begendik *Turkey* 40°55N 26°34E **203** F10
Beggars Pt. *Antigua & B.* 17°10N 61°48W **322** b
Begndal *Norway* 60°49N 9°46E **164** D6
Begoro *Ghana* 6°23N 0°23W **263** D4
Begusarai *India* 25°24N 86°9E **243** G12
Behābād *Iran* 32°24N 59°47E **247** C8
Behala *India* 22°30N 88°18E **124** B1
Behara *Madag.* 24°55S 46°20E **272** C2
Behbehān *Iran* 30°30N 50°15E **247** D6
Behchoko *Canada* 62°50N 116°3W **296** A5
Beheloka *Madag.* 23°54S 43°40E **272** C1
Behm Canal *U.S.A.* 55°10N 131°0W **296** B2
Behshahr *Iran* 36°45N 53°35E **247** B7
Bei Hai *Beijing, China* **114** b2
Bei Hai Park *Beijing, China* **114** b2
Bei Jiang ➔ *China* 23°2N 112°58E **229** F9
Bei Shan *China* 41°30N 96°0E **218** C8
Bei'an *China* 48°10N 126°20E **219** B14
Beibei *China* 29°47N 106°22E **228** C6
Beicai *China* 31°11N 121°32E **138** B2
Beichuan *China* 31°55N 104°39E **228** B5
Beida, Es Sahrâ al *Egypt* 27°50N 28°45E **256** B2
Beigang = Peikang
Taiwan 23°34N 120°18E **225** C2
Beihai *China* 21°28N 109°6E **228** G7
Beijing *China* 39°53N 116°21E **114** B1
Beijing Capital Int. ✈ (PEK)
China 40°5N 116°35E **226** D9
Beijing Shi □ *China* 39°55N 116°20E **226** E9
Beijing Zoo *Beijing, China* **114** a1
Beikthano *Burma* 20°0N 95°23E **241** F5
Beilau = Pilawa *Poland* 51°57N 21°32E **185** G8
Beilen *Neths.* 52°52N 6°27E **170** B6
Beiliu *China* 22°41N 110°21E **229** F8
Beilngries *Germany* 49°2N 11°28E **179** F7
Beilpajah *Australia* 32°54S 143°52E **282** B5
Beilul *Eritrea* 13°2N 42°20E **257** E5
Béinamar *Chad* 8°40N 15°23E **259** G3
Beinan = Peinan *Taiwan* 22°47N 121°7E **225** D3
Beinn na Faoghla = Benbecula
U.K. 57°26N 7°21W **167** D1
Beipan Jiang ➔ *China* 24°55N 106°5E **228** E6
Beipiao *China* 41°52N 120°32E **227** D11
Beira *Mozam.* 19°50S 34°52E **269** F3
Beirut = Bayrūt *Lebanon* 33°53N 35°31E **250** E6
Beiseker *Canada* 51°23N 113°32W **296** C6
Beit Duqu *West Bank* 31°51N 35°6E **123** A1
Beit Ghur at-Taht
West Bank 31°54N 35°5E **123** A1
Beit Ghur el-Fawqa
West Bank 31°53N 35°5E **123** A1
Beit Hanina *West Bank* 31°50N 35°12E **123** B2
Beit Ij'za *West Bank* 31°51N 35°9E **123** A1
Beit Iksa *West Bank* 31°49N 35°11E **123** B2
Beit I'nan *West Bank* 31°51N 35°7E **123** A1
Beit Jala *West Bank* 31°43N 35°11E **123** B2
Beit Lāhiyā *Gaza Strip* 31°33N 34°30E **251** G5
Beit Lahm = Bayt Lahm
West Bank 31°43N 35°12E **123** B2
Beit Liqya *West Bank* 31°52N 35°4E **123** A1
Beit Nekofa *Israel* 31°49N 35°7E **123** B1
Beit Sahur *West Bank* 31°42N 35°13E **123** B2
Beit Sofafa *West Bank* 31°45N 35°12E **123** B2
Beit Surik *West Bank* 31°50N 35°9E **123** B1
Beit Ur al-Fawqa
West Bank 31°53N 35°7E **123** A1
Beit Zayit *Israel* 31°47N 35°9E **123** B1
Beitaipingzhuan *China* 39°57N 116°20E **114** B1
Beitaolaizhao *China* 44°58N 125°58E **227** B13
Beitar Ilit *West Bank* 31°42N 35°7E **123** B1
Beitbridge *Zimbabwe* 22°12S 30°0E **269** G3
Beitin *West Bank* 31°56N 35°14E **123** A2
Beitou = Peitou *Taiwan* 25°11N 121°27E **225** A3
Beitsun *China* 23°7N 113°10E **121** B2
Beitun *China* 47°22N 87°4E **217** D11
Beitunya *West Bank* 31°53N 35°10E **123** A2
Beiuş *Romania* 46°40N 22°21E **182** D7
Beixing Jing Park *China* 31°14N 121°21E **138** B1
Beizhen = Binzhou *China* 37°20N 118°2E **227** F10
Beizhen *China* 41°38N 121°54E **227** D11
Beizhengzhen *China* 44°31N 123°30E **227** B12
Beja *Portugal* 38°2N 7°53W **195** G3
Béja *Tunisia* 36°43N 9°12E **258** A1
Beja □ *Portugal* 37°55N 7°55W **195** H3
Béja □ *Tunisia* 36°40N 9°29E **261** A6
Bejaïa *Algeria* 36°42N 5°2E **261** A6
Bejaïa □ *Algeria* 36°40N 4°55E **261** A5
Béjar *Spain* 40°23N 5°46W **194** E5
Bejestān *Iran* 34°30N 58°5E **247** C8
Bek-Budi = Qarshi
Uzbekistan 38°53N 65°48E **217** E7
Bekaa Valley = Al Biqā
Lebanon 34°10N 36°10E **250** D7
Bekasi *Indonesia* 6°14S 106°59E **234** D3
Békásmegyer *Hungary* 47°35N 19°3E **117** A2
Bekçiler *Turkey* 36°56N 29°44E **205** E11
Bekdash *Turkmenistan* 41°34N 52°32E **216** D4
Békés *Hungary* 46°47N 21°9E **182** D6
Békés □ *Hungary* 46°45N 21°0E **182** D6
Békéscsaba *Hungary* 46°40N 21°5E **182** D6
Bekilli *Turkey* 38°17N 29°27E **205** C11
Bekily *Madag.* 24°13S 45°19E **272** C2
Bekisopa *Madag.* 21°40S 45°54E **272** C2
Bekitro *Madag.* 24°33S 45°18E **272** C2
Bekkelaget *Norway* 59°53N 10°47E **133** A2
Bekkestua *Norway* 59°55N 10°35E **133** A2
Bekodoka *Madag.* 16°58S 45°7E **272** B2
Bekoji *Ethiopia* 7°40N 39°17E **257** F4
Bekok *Malaysia* 2°20N 103°7E **237** L4
Bekopaka *Madag.* 19°9S 44°48E **272** B1
Bekwai *Ghana* 6°30N 1°34W **263** D4
Bel Air *Mauritius* 20°15S 57°44E **272** e
Bel Air *Calif., U.S.A.* 34°4N 118°27W **126** B2
Bela *India* 25°50N 82°0E **243** G10
Bela *Pakistan* 26°12N 66°20E **242** F2
Bela Aliança = Rio do Sul
Brazil 27°13S 49°37W **335** B6
Bela Bela *S. Africa* 24°51S 28°19E **271** B4
Bela Crkva *Serbia* 44°55N 21°27E **182** F6
Bela Palanka *Serbia* 43°13N 22°17E **202** C6
Bela Vista *Mato Grosso do Sul,*
Brazil 22°12S 56°20W **334** A4
Bela Vista *São Paulo,*
Brazil 23°33S 46°38W **137** B2
Bela Vista *Mozam.* 26°10S 32°44E **271** C5
Bélabo *Cameroon* 4°56N 13°18E **264** B2
Bélâbre *France* 46°34N 1°8E **174** B5
Belaga *Malaysia* 2°42N 113°47E **235** B4
Belalcázar *Spain* 38°35N 5°10W **195** G5
Belan ➔ *India* 24°2N 81°45E **243** G9
Bélanger *Canada* 45°35N 73°42W **130** A1
Belanovica *Serbia* 44°15N 20°23E **202** B4
Belarus ■ *Europe* 53°30N 27°0E **177** B14
Belas *Angola* 8°55S 13°9E **265** D2
Belas *Lisboa, Portugal* 38°46N 9°17W **126** A1
Belau = Palau ■ *Palau* 7°30N 134°30E **288** c
Belavenona *Madag.* 24°50S 47°4E **272** C2
Belawan *Indonesia* 3°33N 98°32E **234** B1
Belaya *Ethiopia* 11°25N 36°8E **257** E4
Belaya ➔ *Russia* 54°40N 56°0E **186** C9
Belaya Glina *Russia* 46°5N 40°48E **191** G5
Belaya Kalitva *Russia* 48°13N 40°50E **191** F5
Belaya Tserkov = Bila Tserkva
Ukraine 49°45N 30°10E **177** D16
Belaya Zemlya, Ostrova
Russia 81°36N 62°18E **214** A7
Belayan ➔ *Indonesia* 0°14S 116°36E **235** C5
Belceşti *Romania* 47°19N 27°7E **183** C12
Bełchatów *Poland* 51°21N 19°22E **185** G6
Belcher Is. *Canada* 56°15N 78°45W **298** A3
Belchite *Spain* 41°18N 0°43W **196** D4
Belden *U.S.A.* 40°2N 121°17W **306** E5
Beldibi *Turkey* 36°25N 32°26E **250** B3
Belding *U.S.A.* 43°6N 85°14W **311** A11
Belebey *Russia* 54°7N 54°7E **186** D9
Beledweyne *Somalia* 4°30N 45°5E **267** D6
Beleghata *India* 22°33N 88°22E **124** B2
Belém = Palmeirais *Brazil* 6°0S 43°0W **332** C3
Belém *Brazil* 1°20S 48°30W **332** B2
Belém *Lisboa, Portugal* 38°41N 9°12W **126** A1
Belém, Torre de *Portugal* 38°41N 9°12W **126** A1
Belém de São Francisco
Brazil 8°46S 38°58W **332** C4
Belén *Argentina* 27°40S 67°5W **334** B2
Belén *Colombia* 1°26N 75°56W **328** C2
Belén *Paraguay* 23°30S 57°6W **334** A4
Belen *Turkey* 36°31N 36°10E **250** B7
Belen *N. Mex., U.S.A.* 34°40N 106°46W **305** J10
Belene *Bulgaria* 43°39N 25°10E **203** C9
Belénzinho *Brazil* 23°32S 46°34W **137** B2
Belep, Îs. *N. Cal.* 19°45S 163°40E **288** d
Belesta *France* 42°55N 1°56E **174** F5
Belet Uen = Beledweyne
Somalia 4°30N 45°5E **267** D6
Belev *Russia* 53°50N 36°5E **188** F9
Belevi *Turkey* 38°0N 27°28E **205** C9
Belfair *U.S.A.* 47°27N 122°50W **306** C4
Belfast = eMakhazeni
S. Africa 25°42S 30°2E **271** C5
Belfast *N.Z.* 43°27S 172°39E **285** D7
Belfast *Antrim, U.K.* 54°37N 5°56W **166** B6
Belfast *Maine, U.S.A.* 44°26N 69°1W **309** C19
Belfast *N.Y., U.S.A.* 42°21N 78°7W **312** D6
Belfast L. *U.K.* 54°40N 5°50W **166** B6
Belfield *U.S.A.* 46°53N 103°12W **308** B2
Belfort *France* 47°38N 6°50E **173** E13
Belfort, Territoire de □
France 47°40N 6°55E **173** E13
Belfry *U.S.A.* 45°9N 109°1W **304** D9
Belgachiya *India* 22°36N 88°23E **124** B2
Belgard = Białogard *Poland* 54°2N 15°58E **184** D2
Belgaum = Belgavi *India* 15°55N 74°35E **245** G2
Belgavi *India* 15°55N 74°35E **245** G2
Belgharia *India* 22°39N 88°22E **124** B2
Belgian Congo = Congo, Dem. Rep.
of the ■ *Africa* 3°0S 23°0E **265** C4
Belgioioso *Italy* 45°10N 9°19E **198** C6
Belgium ■ *Europe* 50°30N 5°0E **170** D4
Belgodère *France* 42°35N 9°1E **175** F13
Belgorod *Russia* 50°35N 36°35E **189** G9
Belgorod □ *Russia* 50°45N 36°45E **189** G9
Belgorod-Dnestrovskiy = Bilhorod-
Dnistrovskyy *Ukraine* 46°11N 30°23E **189** J6
Belgrade = Beograd *Serbia* 44°50N 20°37E **202** B4
Belgrade *U.S.A.* 45°47N 111°11W **304** D8
Belgrano *Argentina* 34°33S 58°27W **117** B2
Belgrano II *Antarctica* 77°52S 34°37W **151** D1
Belgravia *London, U.K.* **125** c3
Belgrove *N.Z.* 41°27S 172°59E **285** B7
Belhaven *U.S.A.* 35°33N 76°37W **315** D16
Béli *Guinea-Biss.* 11°51N 13°56W **262** C2
Beli *Nigeria* 7°52N 10°58E **263** D7
Beli Drim ➔ *Europe* 42°6N 20°25E **202** D4
Beli Manastir *Croatia* 45°45N 18°36E **182** E3
Beli Timok ➔ *Serbia* 43°53N 22°14E **202** C6
Bélice ➔ *Italy* 37°35N 12°55E **200** E5
Belimbing *Indonesia* 8°24S 115°2E **231** J18
Bélinga *Gabon* 1°10N 13°2E **264** B2
Belinskiy *Russia* 53°0N 43°25E **190** D6
Belinyu *Indonesia* 1°35S 105°50E **234** C3
Beliton Is. = Belitung
Indonesia 3°10S 107°50E **235** C3
Belitung *Indonesia* 3°10S 107°50E **235** C3
Beliu *Romania* 46°30N 22°0E **182** D7
Belize *Angola* 4°39S 12°46E **265** C2
Belize ■ *Cent. Amer.* 17°0N 88°30W **320** C2
Belize Barrier Reef *Belize* 17°9N 88°3W **319** D7
Belize City *Belize* 17°25N 88°10W **320** C2
Beljakovci *Macedonia* 42°6N 21°59E **202** D5
Beljanica *Serbia* 44°8N 21°43E **202** B5
Belkovskiy, Ostrov
Russia 75°32N 135°44E **215** B14
Bell *Calif., U.S.A.* 33°58N 118°11W **126** C3
Bell *Fla., U.S.A.* 29°45N 82°52W **316** F7
Bell ➔ *Canada* 49°48N 77°38W **298** C4
Bell Gardens *U.S.A.* 33°58N 118°9W **126** C4
Bell I. *Canada* 50°46N 55°35W **299** B8
Bell-Irving ➔ *Canada* 56°12N 129°5W **296** B3
Bell Peninsula *Canada* 63°50N 82°0W **295** E15
Bell Tower *Beijing, China* **114** a3
Bell Ville *Argentina* 32°40S 62°40W **334** C3
Bella *Italy* 40°45N 15°32E **201** B8
Bella Bella *Canada* 52°10N 128°10W **296** C3
Bella Coola *Canada* 52°25N 126°40W **296** C3
Bella Flor *Bolivia* 11°9S 67°49W **330** C4
Bella Unión *Uruguay* 30°15S 57°40W **334** C4
Bella Vista *Corrientes,*
Argentina 28°33S 59°0W **334** B4
Bella Vista *Tucuman,*
Argentina 27°10S 65°25W **334** B2
Bella Vista *Ark., U.S.A.* 36°28N 94°16W **308** G6
Bellac *France* 46°7N 1°3E **174** B5
Bellágio *Italy* 45°59N 9°15E **198** C6
Bellaire *U.S.A.* 40°1N 80°45W **312** F4
Bellária *Italy* 44°9N 12°28E **199** D9
Bellata *Australia* 29°53S 149°46E **281** D4
Bellavista *Santiago, Chile* 33°31S 70°35W **137** C2
Bellavista *Galápagos Is.,*
Ecuador 0°41S 90°18W **330** a
Bellavista *Lima, Peru* 12°4S 77°8W **124** B2
Belle *U.S.A.* 38°17N 91°43W **310** F5
Belle ➔ *Trin. & Tob.* 11°14N 60°37W **323** s
Belle Fille ➔ *Dominica* 15°25N 61°16W **323** k
Belle Fourche *U.S.A.* 44°40N 103°51W **308** C2
Belle Fourche ➔ *U.S.A.* 44°26N 102°18W **308** C2
Belle Glade *U.S.A.* 26°41N 80°40W **317** J9
Belle Harbor *U.S.A.* 40°34N 73°51W **132** C2
Belle-Île *France* 47°20N 3°10W **172** E3
Belle Isle *Nfld. & L.,*
Canada 51°57N 55°25W **299** B8
Belle Isle *Fla., U.S.A.* 28°27N 81°12W **317** G8
Belle Isle, Str. of *Canada* 51°30N 56°30W **299** B8
Belle Plaine *U.S.A.* 41°54N 92°17W **310** C4
Belle Rive *U.S.A.* 38°14N 88°45W **311** F8
Belle River *Canada* 42°18N 82°43W **312** D2
Belle Vue Maurel *Mauritius* 20°7S 57°39E **272** e
Belle Yella *Liberia* 7°24N 10°0W **262** D3
Belledonne *France* 45°20N 6°10E **175** C10
Bellefontaine *Martinique* 14°39N 61°10W **322** j
Bellefontaine *Ohio,*
U.S.A. 40°22N 83°46W **311** D13
Bellefonte *U.S.A.* 40°55N 77°47W **312** F7
Bellegarde *France* 47°59N 2°26E **173** E9
Bellegarde-en-Marche
France 45°59N 2°18E **174** C6
Bellegarde-sur-Valserine
France 46°4N 5°50E **173** F12
Bellême *France* 48°22N 0°34E **172** D7
Belleoram *Canada* 47°31N 55°25W **299** C8
Belleplaine *Barbados* 13°15N 59°34W **323** r
Belleview *U.S.A.* 29°4N 82°3W **317** F7
Belleville *Ont., Canada* 44°10N 77°23W **312** B7
Belleville *Rhône, France* 46°7N 4°45E **173** F11
Belleville *Ill., U.S.A.* 38°31N 89°59W **310** F7
Belleville *Kans., U.S.A.* 39°50N 97°38W **308** F5
Belleville *N.J., U.S.A.* 40°47N 74°9W **313** F10
Belleville *N.Y., U.S.A.* 43°46N 76°10W **313** C8
Belleville-sur-Vie *France* 46°46N 1°25W **172** F5
Bellevue *Idaho, U.S.A.* 43°28N 114°16W **304** E6
Bellevue *Iowa, U.S.A.* 42°16N 90°26W **310** B6
Bellevue *Mich., U.S.A.* 42°27N 85°1W **311** B11
Bellevue *Nebr., U.S.A.* 41°9N 95°54W **308** E6
Bellevue *Ohio, U.S.A.* 41°17N 82°51W **312** E2
Bellevue *Wash., U.S.A.* 47°37N 122°12W **306** C4
Bellevue, Col de *Réunion* 21°9S 55°36E **272** f
Bellevue, Schloss *Berlin, Germany* **115** a2
Belley *France* 45°46N 5°41E **175** C9
Bellin = Kangirsuk *Canada* 60°0N 70°0W **295** F18
Bellinge *Denmark* 55°20N 10°20E **163** J4
Bellingen *Australia* 30°25S 152°50E **283** A10
Bellingham *London, U.K.* 51°25N 0°1W **125** B3
Bellingham *Wash.,*
U.S.A. 48°46N 122°29W **306** B4
Bellingshausen Abyssal Plain
S. Ocean 64°0S 90°0W **151** C16
Bellingshausen Sea
Antarctica 66°0S 80°0W **151** C17
Bellinzona *Switz.* 46°11N 9°1E **179** J5
Bello *Colombia* 6°20N 75°33W **328** B2
Bellona *Solomon Is.* 11°17S 159°47E **287** N10
Bellows Falls *U.S.A.* 43°8N 72°27W **313** C12
Bellpat *Pakistan* 29°0N 68°5E **242** E3
Bellpuig *Spain* 41°37N 1°1E **196** D6
Bells *Dominica* 15°25N 61°21W **323** k
Belluno *Italy* 46°9N 12°13E **199** B9
Bellville *U.S.A.* 32°9N 81°59W **316** C8
Bellwood *U.S.A.* 40°36N 78°20W **312** F6
Belmanier *Dominica* 15°35N 61°24W **323** k
Bélmez *Spain* 38°17N 5°17W **195** G5
Belmond *U.S.A.* 42°51N 93°37W **310** B3
Belmont *N.S.W., Australia* 33°4S 151°42E **283** B9
Belmont *Ont., Canada* 42°53N 81°5W **312** D3
Belmont *Grenada* 12°2N 61°45W **323** q
Belmont *Northern Cape,*
S. Africa 29°28S 24°22E **270** C3
Belmont *London, U.K.* 51°36N 0°18W **125** A2
Belmont *Mass., U.S.A.* 42°23N 71°10W **116** A1
Belmont *N.Y., U.S.A.* 42°14N 78°2W **312** D6
Belmont Cragin *U.S.A.* 41°55N 87°45W **119** B2
Belmont Harbor *U.S.A.* 41°56N 87°38W **119** B3
Belmonte *Brazil* 16°0S 39°0W **333** E4
Belmonte *Portugal* 40°21N 7°20W **194** E3
Belmonte *Spain* 39°34N 2°43W **197** F2
Belmopan *Belize* 17°18N 88°30W **320** C2
Belmore *Australia* 33°55S 151°5E **139** B1
Belmullet *Ireland* 54°14N 9°58W **166** B2
Belo *Dem. Rep. of the Congo* 0°32S 23°13E **264** C4
Belo *Madag.* 20°44S 44°0E **272** C1
Belo Horizonte *Brazil* 19°55S 43°56W **333** E3
Belo Jardim *Brazil* 8°20S 36°26W **332** C4
Belo Monte *Brazil* 3°5S 51°46W **329** D7
Belo-Tsiribihina *Madag.* 19°40S 44°30E **272** B1
Belogorsk = Bilohirsk
Ukraine 45°3N 34°35E **189** K8
Belogorsk *Russia* 51°0N 128°20E **215** D13
Belogradchik *Bulgaria* 43°53N 22°42E **202** C6
Belogradets *Bulgaria* 43°22N 27°18E **203** C11
Beloha *Madag.* 25°10S 45°3E **272** D2
Beloit *Kans., U.S.A.* 39°28N 98°6W **308** F4
Beloit *Wis., U.S.A.* 42°31N 89°2W **310** B7
Belokalitvenskaya = Belaya Kalitva
Russia 48°13N 40°50E **191** F5
Belokorovichi *Ukraine* 51°7N 28°2E **177** C15
Belomorsk *Russia* 64°35N 34°54E **186** B5
Belondo
Dem. Rep. of the Congo 0°19S 19°31E **264** C3
Belonge
Dem. Rep. of the Congo 2°7S 19°33E **264** C3
Belonia *India* 23°15N 91°30E **241** D3
Belopolye = Bilopillya
Ukraine 51°14N 34°20E **189** G8
Belorechensk *Russia* 44°46N 39°52E **191** H4
Beloretsk *Russia* 53°58N 58°24E **186** D10
Belorussia = Belarus ■
Europe 53°30N 27°0E **177** B14
Beloshchelye = Naryan-Mar
Russia 67°42N 53°12E **186** A9
Beloslav *Bulgaria* 43°11N 27°42E **203** C11
Belotsarsk = Kyzyl
Russia 51°50N 94°30E **217** B12
Belousovka *Kazakhstan* 50°8N 82°31E **217** B10
Belovezhskaya Pushcha =
Białowieski △ *Poland* 52°43N 23°50E **185** F10
Belovo *Bulgaria* 42°13N 24°1E **203** D8
Belovo *Russia* 54°30N 86°0E **217** B11
Beloyarskiy *Russia* 63°42N 66°40E **214** C7
Beloye, Ozero *Russia* 60°10N 37°35E **188** B9
Beloye More *Russia* 66°30N 38°0E **186** A6
Belozem *Bulgaria* 42°12N 25°2E **203** D9
Belozersk *Russia* 60°1N 37°45E **188** B9
Belpasso *Italy* 37°35N 14°58E **201** E7
Belpre *U.S.A.* 39°17N 81°34W **309** F13
Belrain *India* 28°23N 80°55E **243** E9
Belt *U.S.A.* 47°23N 110°55W **304** C8
Beltana *Australia* 30°48S 138°25E **282** A3
Belterra *Brazil* 2°45S 55°0W **329** D7
Beltinci *Slovenia* 46°37N 16°20E **199** B13
Belton *Mo., U.S.A.* 38°49N 94°32W **310** F2
Belton *Tex., U.S.A.* 31°3N 97°28W **314** F6
Belton L. *U.S.A.* 31°6N 97°28W **314** F6
Beltsy = Bălţi *Moldova* 47°48N 27°58E **183** C12
Belturbet *Ireland* 54°6N 7°26W **166** B4
Belukha *Russia* 49°50N 86°50E **217** C11
Belur *India* 22°37N 88°21E **124** B2
Beluran *Malaysia* 5°48N 117°35E **235** A5
Beluša *Slovakia* 49°5N 18°17E **181** B11
Belushya Guba *Russia* 71°32N 52°19E **214** B6
Belušić *Serbia* 43°50N 21°10E **202** C5
Belvedere *St. Vincent* 13°8N 61°11W **323** n
Belvedere *London, U.K.* 51°29N 0°9E **125** B4
Belvedere *Calif., U.S.A.* 37°52N 122°27W **136** A2
Belvedere Maríttimo *Italy* 39°37N 15°52E **201** C8
Belvedere Park *U.S.A.* 33°45N 84°16W **113** B3
Belvès *France* 44°46N 1°0E **174** D5
Belvidere *Ill., U.S.A.* 42°15N 88°50W **311** B8
Belvidere *N.J., U.S.A.* 40°50N 75°5W **313** F9
Belvis de la Jara *Spain* 39°45N 4°57W **194** F6
Bely Bychek = Chagoda
Russia 59°10N 35°15E **188** C8
Belyando ➔ *Australia* 21°38S 146°50E **280** C4
Belyando Crossing
Australia 21°32S 146°51E **280** C4
Belyayevo Bogorodskoye
Russia 55°39N 37°31E **129** C2
Belyuen *Australia* 12°34S 130°42E **278** B5
Belyy *Russia* 55°49N 33°3E **188** E7
Belyy, Ostrov *Russia* 73°30N 71°0E **214** B8
Belyy Yar *Russia* 58°26N 84°39E **214** D9
Belyye Vody = Aqsū
Kazakhstan 42°25N 69°50E **217** D7
Belz *Ukraine* 50°23N 24°1E **185** H11
Bełżec *Poland* 50°23N 23°26E **185** H10
Belzig *Germany* 52°8N 12°35E **178** C8
Belzoni *U.S.A.* 33°11N 90°29W **315** E9
Bełżyce *Poland* 51°11N 22°17E **185** G9
Bemaraha, Lembalemban' i
Madag. 18°40S 44°45E **272** B1
Bemarivo *Madag.* 21°45S 44°45E **272** C1
Bemarivo ➔ *Sava, Madag.* 14°9S 50°9E **272** A3
Bemarivo ➔ *Sofia, Madag.* 15°27S 47°40E **272** B2
Bemavo *Madag.* 21°33S 45°25E **272** C2
Bembe *Angola* 7°3S 14°25E **265** D2
Bembéréke *Benin* 10°11N 2°43E **263** C5
Bembesi *Zimbabwe* 20°0S 28°58E **269** G2
Bembesi ➔ *Zimbabwe* 18°57S 27°47E **269** F2
Bembézar ➔ *Spain* 37°45N 5°13W **195** H5
Bembibre *Spain* 42°37N 6°25W **194** C4
Bemboka △ *Australia* 36°35S 149°41E **283** D8
Bement *U.S.A.* 39°55N 88°34W **311** E8
Bemetara *India* 21°42N 81°32E **243** J9
Bemidji *U.S.A.* 47°28N 94°53W **308** B6
Bemolanga *Madag.* 17°44S 45°6E **272** B2

Biggar Sask., Canada 52°4N 108°0W 297 C7
Biggar S. Lanarks., U.K. 55°38N 3°32W 167 F5
Bigge I. Australia 14°35S 125°10E 278 B4
Biggenden Australia 25°31S 152°4E 281 D5
Biggleswade U.K. 52°5N 0°14W 169 E7
Biggs U.S.A. 39°25N 121°43W 306 F5
Bighorn U.S.A. 46°10N 107°27W 304 C10
Bighorn → U.S.A. 46°10N 107°28W 304 C10
Bighorn Canyon ⌓ U.S.A. 45°10N 108°0W 304 D10
Bighorn L. U.S.A. 44°55N 108°15W 304 D9
Bighorn Mts. U.S.A. 44°25N 107°0W 304 D10
Bigi Dem. Rep. of the Congo 3°2N 22°25E 264 B4
Bignona Senegal 12°52N 16°14W 262 C1
Bigorre France 43°10N 0°5E 174 E4
Bigstone L. Canada 53°42N 95°44W 297 C9
Biguglia, Étang de France 42°36N 9°29E 175 F13
Bigwa Tanzania 7°10S 39°10E 268 D4
Bihać Bos.-H. 44°49N 15°57E 199 D12
Bihar India 25°5N 85°40E 243 G11
Bihar □ India 25°0N 86°0E 243 G12
Biharamulo Tanzania 2°25S 31°25E 268 C3
Biharamulo ⌓ Tanzania 2°24S 31°26E 268 C3
Bihariganj India 25°44N 86°59E 243 G12
Biharkeresztes Hungary 47°8N 21°44E 182 C6
Bihor □ Romania 47°0N 22°10E 182 D7
Bihor, Munţii Romania 46°29N 22°47E 182 D7
Bijagós, Arquipélago dos Guinea-Biss. 11°15N 16°10W 262 C1
Bijaipur India 26°2N 77°20E 242 F7
Bijapur = Vijayapura India 16°50N 75°55E 244 F2
Bijapur India 18°50N 80°50E 244 E5
Bījār Iran 35°52N 47°35E 213 E12
Bijauri Nepal 28°6N 82°20E 243 E10
Bijawar India 24°38N 79°30E 243 G8
Bijbels Museum Amsterdam, Neths. 112 b1
Bijela Montenegro 42°28N 18°39E 202 D2
Bijeljina Bos.-H. 44°46N 19°14E 182 F4
Bijelo Polje Montenegro 43°1N 19°45E 202 C3
Bijie China 27°20N 105°16E 228 D5
Bijlmermeer Neths. 52°19N 4°59E 112 B2
Bijnor India 29°27N 78°11E 242 E8
Bikaner India 28°2N 73°18E 242 E5
Bikapur India 26°30N 82°7E 243 F10
Bikeqi China 40°43N 111°20E 226 D6
Bikfayyā Lebanon 33°55N 35°41E 250 E6
Bikié Congo 3°7S 13°52E 264 C2
Bikin Russia 46°50N 134°20E 220 A7
Bikin → Russia 46°51N 134°2E 220 A7
Bikini Atoll Marshall Is. 12°0N 167°30E 288 F8
Bikita Zimbabwe 20°6S 31°41E 271 B5
Bīkkū Bīttī Libya 22°0N 19°12E 259 D3
Bikoro Dem. Rep. of the Congo 0°48S 18°15E 264 C3
Bikoué Cameroon 3°55N 11°50E 263 E7
Bila Tserkva Ukraine 49°45N 30°10E 177 D16
Bilād Banī Bū 'Alī Oman 22°1N 59°19E 249 B7
Bīlād Banī Bu Hassan Oman 22°5N 59°17E 249 B7
Bilanga Burkina Faso 12°40N 0°1W 263 C4
Bilara India 26°14N 73°53E 242 F5
Bilasipara India 26°13N 90°14E 241 B3
Bilaspur Chhattisgarh, India 22°2N 82°15E 243 H10
Bilaspur Punjab, India 31°19N 76°50E 242 D7
Biläsuvar Azerbaijan 39°27N 48°32E 213 C13
Bilauk Taungdan Thailand 13°0N 99°0E 236 F2
Bilauri Nepal 28°41N 80°21E 243 E9
Bilbao Spain 43°16N 2°56W 196 B2
Bilbao ✈ (BIO) Spain 43°18N 2°57W 196 B2
Bilbeis Egypt 30°25N 31°34E 256 H7
Bilbo = Bilbao Spain 43°16N 2°56W 196 B2
Bilbor Romania 47°6N 25°30E 183 C10
Bilche-Zolote Ukraine 48°47N 25°53E 183 B10
Bilciureşti Romania 44°44N 25°48E 183 F10
Bíldudalur Iceland 65°41N 23°36W 155 B3
Bílé Karpaty Europe 49°5N 18°0E 181 B11
Bileća Bos.-H. 42°53N 18°27E 202 D2
Bilecik Turkey 40°5N 30°5E 212 B4
Bilecik □ Turkey 40°0N 30°0E 212 B3
Bilećko Jezero Bos.-H. 42°48N 18°28E 202 D2
Bileh Savār Iran 39°21N 48°21E 213 C13
Biłgoraj Poland 50°33N 22°42E 185 H9
Bilgram India 27°11N 80°2E 243 F9
Bilhaur India 26°51N 80°5E 243 F9
Bilhorod-Dnistrovskyy Ukraine 46°11N 30°23E 189 J6
Bili → Dem. Rep. of the Congo 4°9N 22°29E 264 B4
Bilibino Russia 68°3N 166°20E 215 C17
Bilibiza Mozam. 12°30S 40°20E 269 E5
Bilimora India 20°45N 72°57E 244 D1
Bilin Burma 17°14N 97°15E 241 G6
Biliran Phil. 11°28N 124°28E 233 F5
Biliran □ Phil. 11°35N 124°28E 233 F5
Bilisht Albania 40°37N 21°2E 202 F5
Bill Baggs Cape Florida State Recr. Area ⌓ U.S.A. 25°40N 80°9W 129 D3
Billabong Cr. → Australia 35°5S 144°2E 282 C6
Billdal Sweden 57°35N 11°57E 163 G5
Billiluna Australia 19°37S 127°41E 278 C4
Billings U.S.A. 45°47N 108°30W 304 D9
Billiton Is. = Belitung Indonesia 3°10S 107°50E 235 C3
Billsta Sweden 63°20N 18°28E 162 A12
Billund Denmark 55°44N 9°6E 163 J3
Billy Pt. Antigua & B. 17°44N 61°52W 322 c
Bilma Niger 18°50N 13°30E 259 E2
Bilma, Grand Erg de Niger 18°30N 14°0E 259 E2
Bilo Gora Croatia 45°53N 17°15E 182 E2
Biloela Australia 24°24S 150°31E 280 C5
Bilohirsk Ukraine 45°3N 34°35E 189 K8
Biloku Guyana 1°50N 58°25W 329 C6
Biloli India 18°46N 77°44E 244 E3
Bilopillya Ukraine 51°14N 34°20E 189 G8
Bilovodsk Ukraine 49°13N 39°36E 189 H10
Biloxi U.S.A. 30°24N 88°53W 315 F10
Bilpa Morea Claypan Australia 25°0S 140°0E 280 D3
Bilqâs Qism Auwal Egypt 31°12N 31°21E 251 G2
Bilston U.K. 55°52N 3°10W 121 B2
Biltine Chad 14°40N 20°50E 259 F4
Bilugyun Burma 16°24N 97°32E 241 G6
Bilyarsk Russia 54°58N 50°22E 190 C10
Bim Son Vietnam 20°4N 105°51E 236 B5
Bima Indonesia 8°22S 118°49E 235 D5
Bimban Egypt 24°24N 32°54E 256 C3
Bimbe Angola 11°50S 15°50E 265 E3
Bimberi Pk. Australia 35°44S 148°51E 283 C8
Bimbila Ghana 8°54N 0°5E 263 D5
Bimbini Comoros Is. 12°11S 44°14E 272 a
Bimbo C.A.R. 4°15N 18°33E 264 B3
Bimini Is. Bahamas 25°42N 79°25W 320 A4
Bin Ghunaymah, Jabal Libya 25°0N 15°30E 258 D3
Bin Jawwād Libya 30°47N 18°4E 258 B3
Bin Xian Heilongjiang, China 45°42N 127°32E 227 B14
Bin Xian Shaanxi, China 35°2N 108°4E 226 G5
Bin Yauri Nigeria 10°46N 4°45E 263 C5
Bina-Etawah India 24°13N 78°14E 242 G8
Binacayan Phil. 14°27N 120°55E 127 C1
Binalbagan Phil. 10°12N 122°50E 233 F4
Binalong Australia 34°40S 148°39E 283 C8
Bīnālūd, Kūh-e Iran 36°30N 58°30E 247 B8
Binanga Indonesia 1°24N 99°46E 234 B1
Binangonan de Lampon = Infanta Phil. 14°45N 121°39E 232 D3
Binatang = Bintangau Malaysia 2°10N 111°40E 235 B4
Binche Belgium 50°26N 4°10E 170 D4
Binchuan China 25°42N 100°38E 228 E3
Binda Dem. Rep. of the Congo 5°52S 13°14E 265 D2
Binder Chad 9°56N 14°27E 259 G2
Bindki India 26°2N 80°36E 243 F9
Bindloe, I. = Marchena, I. Ecuador 0°19N 90°29W 330 a
Bindoy Phil. 9°48N 123°5E 233 G4
Bindslev Denmark 57°33N 10°11E 163 G4
Bindura Zimbabwe 17°18S 31°18E 269 F3
Binéfar Spain 41°51N 0°18E 196 D5
Bingara Australia 29°52S 150°36E 281 D5
Bingaram I. India 10°56N 72°17E 245 J1
Bingen Germany 49°57N 7°55E 179 F3
Bingerau = Węgrów Poland 52°24N 22°0E 185 F9
Bingerville Ivory C. 5°18N 3°49W 262 D4
Bingham U.S.A. 45°3N 69°53W 309 C19
Binghamton U.S.A. 42°6N 75°55W 313 D9
Bingo-Ochiai Japan 34°59N 133°8E 222 C4
Bingöl Turkey 38°53N 40°29E 213 C9
Bingöl □ Turkey 38°55N 40°30E 213 C9
Bingöl Dağları Turkey 39°16N 41°9E 213 C9
Bingsjö Sweden 61°1N 15°39E 162 C9
Binh Dinh Vietnam 13°55N 109°7E 236 F7
Binh Son Vietnam 15°20N 108°40E 236 E7
Binhai China 34°2N 119°49E 227 G10
Bini Erde Chad 20°6N 18°1E 259 D3
Binic France 48°46N 2°50W 172 D4
Binisatua Spain 39°50N 4°11E 206 B5
Binishangul Gumuz □ Ethiopia 11°0N 35°30E 257 E4
Binissalem Spain 39°41N 2°50E 206 B3
Binjai Kepulauan Riau, Indonesia 3°48N 108°13E 235 B3
Binjai Sumatera Utara, Indonesia 3°20N 98°30E 234 B1
Binji Nigeria 13°10N 4°55E 263 C5
Binka India 21°2N 83°48E 244 D6
Binnah, Ras Somalia 11°9N 51°10E 267 B7
Binnaway Australia 31°28S 149°24E 283 A8
Binondo Phil. 14°36N 120°58E 127 B1
Binongko Indonesia 5°57S 124°2E 231 F6
Binscarth Canada 50°37N 101°17W 297 C8
Bint Goda Sudan 13°17N 31°33E 257 E3
Bintan Indonesia 1°0N 104°0E 234 B2
Bintangau Malaysia 2°10N 111°40E 235 B4
Bintaro Jaya Indonesia 6°16S 106°44E 122 B1
Bintuhan Indonesia 4°48S 103°22E 234 C2
Bintulu Malaysia 3°10N 113°0E 235 B4
Bintuni Indonesia 2°7S 133°32E 231 E8
Binyang China 23°12N 108°47E 228 F7
Binz Germany 54°24N 13°35E 178 A9
Binza Dem. Rep. of the Congo 4°21S 15°14E 265 C3
Binzert = Bizerte Tunisia 37°15N 9°50E 258 A1
Binzhou China 37°20N 118°2E 227 F10
Bíobío □ Chile 37°35S 72°0W 334 D1
Bíobío → Chile 36°49S 73°10W 334 D1
Biograd na Moru Croatia 43°56N 15°29E 199 E12
Biogradska Gora △ Montenegro 42°55N 19°40E 202 D3
Bioko Eq. Guin. 3°30N 8°40E 263 E6
Biokovo Croatia 43°23N 17°0E 199 E14
Biougra Morocco 30°15N 9°14W 260 B3
Bipindi Cameroon 3°6N 10°30E 263 E7
Bir India 19°4N 75°46E 244 E2
Bir, Ras Djibouti 12°0N 43°20E 257 E5
Bîr Abu Hashim Egypt 23°42N 34°6E 256 C3
Bîr Abu Minqar Egypt 26°33N 27°33E 256 B2
Bîr Abu Muḥammad Egypt 29°44N 34°14E 251 J5
Bîr Abu Sandûq Egypt 29°24N 32°30E 251 J3
Bîr Adal Deib Sudan 22°35N 36°10E 256 C4
Bi'r al Butayyihāt Jordan 29°47N 35°20E 251 J6
Bi'r al Ḥamḍah Si. Arabia 28°30N 34°55E 251 K5
Bi'r al Mārī Jordan 30°4N 35°33E 251 H6
Bi'r al Musallam Si. Arabia 28°56N 35°38E 251 K6
Bi'r al Qattār Jordan 29°47N 35°32E 251 J6
Bir 'Ali Yemen 14°1N 48°20E 249 D5
Bîr 'Amrâne Mauritania 22°45N 8°39W 260 D3
Bir Aouine Tunisia 32°25N 9°18E 258 B1
Bîr 'Asal Egypt 25°55N 34°20E 256 B3
Bi'r ash Shakkūsīyah Syria 35°23N 37°26E 250 C8
Bîr Atrun Sudan 18°15N 26°40E 256 D2
Bîr Beiḍa Egypt 30°25N 34°29E 251 H5
Bîr Bel Guerdâne Mauritania 25°24N 10°31W 260 C2
Bîr Bireida Egypt 29°8N 32°7E 251 J3
Bîr Buerât Egypt 28°59N 32°11E 251 K3
Bi'r Dhu'fān Libya 31°59N 14°32E 258 B2
Bir Di South Sudan 7°34N 28°49E 257 F2
Bîr Diqnash Egypt 31°3N 25°23E 256 A2
Bir el Abbes Algeria 26°7N 6°9W 260 C3
Bîr el 'Abd Egypt 31°2N 33°0E 251 G4
Bîr el 'Agramîya Egypt 29°38N 31°50E 251 J2
Bir el Ater Algeria 34°46N 8°3E 261 B6
Bîr el Basur Egypt 29°51N 25°49E 256 B2
Bîr el Biarât Egypt 29°30N 34°43E 251 J5
Bîr el Dakhal Egypt 28°39N 32°23E 251 K3
Bîr el Duweidar Egypt 30°56N 32°32E 251 H3
Bîr el Garârât Egypt 31°3N 33°34E 251 G4
Bîr el Gâreb Mauritania 20°33N 16°12W 260 D1
Bîr el Gellaz Egypt 30°50N 26°40E 256 A2
Bîr el Ghamr Egypt 28°43N 31°20E 251 K2
Bîr el Heisi Egypt 29°22N 34°36E 251 J5
Bîr el Jafir Egypt 30°50N 32°41E 251 H3
Bîr el Mâlḥi Egypt 30°38N 33°19E 251 H4
Bîr el Manâyif Egypt 30°31N 32°12E 251 H3
Bîr el-Naṣb Egypt 29°3N 33°2E 251 J4
Bîr el Ṣafra Egypt 28°45N 34°21E 251 K5
Bîr el-Saura Egypt 29°9N 34°30E 251 J5
Bîr el Shaqqa Egypt 30°54N 25°1E 256 A2
Bîr el Thamâda Egypt 30°12N 33°27E 251 H4
Bîr Enzarán W. Sahara 23°53N 14°32W 260 D2
Bîr Fuad Egypt 30°35N 26°28E 256 A2
Bîr Gandús W. Sahara 21°36N 16°30W 260 D1
Bîr Gebeil Ḥiṣn Egypt 30°2N 33°18E 251 H4
Bi'r Ghadīr Syria 34°6N 37°3E 250 D8
Bîr Ghalla Egypt 28°23N 32°19E 251 K3
Bi'r Gharr Si. Arabia 28°7N 35°32E 251 K6
Bîr Gindali Egypt 29°55N 31°40E 251 J2
Bîr Haimur Egypt 22°45N 33°40E 256 C3
Bîr Ḥasana Egypt 30°29N 33°46E 251 H4
Bîr Hōōker Egypt 30°22N 30°21E 256 H7
Bi'r Īdimah Si. Arabia 18°31N 44°12E 248 C4
Bi'r Jadīd Si. Arabia 29°10N 35°6E 251 J6
Bîr Kanayis Egypt 24°59N 33°15E 256 C3
Bîr Kaseiba Egypt 31°0N 33°17E 251 H4
Bîr Kerawein Egypt 27°10N 28°25E 256 B2
Bîr Lahfân Egypt 31°0N 33°51E 251 H4
Bir Lahrache Algeria 32°1N 8°12E 261 B6
Bîr Madkûr Egypt 30°44N 32°33E 251 H3
Bîr Maql Egypt 23°7N 33°40E 256 C3
Bîr Mîneiga Sudan 22°47N 35°12E 256 C4
Bîr Misaha Egypt 22°13N 27°59E 256 C2
Bîr Mogreïn Mauritania 25°10N 11°25W 260 C2
Bîr Mureir Egypt 28°25N 31°15E 251 K2
Bîr Murr Egypt 23°28N 30°10E 256 C3
Bi'r Muṭribah Kuwait 29°54N 47°17E 246 D5
Bir Nabala West Bank 31°51N 35°12E 123 A2
Bîr Nakheila Egypt 24°1N 30°50E 256 C3
Bîr Nakhul Egypt 29°5N 33°16E 251 J4
Bîr Qaṭia Egypt 30°58N 32°45E 251 H3
Bîr Qatrani Egypt 30°55N 26°10E 256 A2
Bîr Ranga Egypt 24°25N 35°15E 256 C4
Bîr Sahara Egypt 22°54N 28°40E 256 C2
Bîr Sa'îd Egypt 29°38N 31°24E 251 J2
Bîr Seiyâla Egypt 26°10N 33°50E 256 B3
Bîr Shalatein Egypt 23°5N 35°25E 256 C4
Bîr Shebb Egypt 22°25N 29°40E 256 C2
Bîr Shût Egypt 23°50N 35°15E 256 C4
Bîr Sidri Egypt 28°53N 33°28E 251 K4
Bîr Tâba Egypt 29°29N 34°53E 251 J5
Bîr Terfawi Egypt 22°57N 28°55E 256 C2
Bîr Umm Qubûr Egypt 24°35N 34°2E 256 C3
Bîr Ungât Egypt 22°8N 33°48E 256 C3
Bîr Wuseit Egypt 29°14N 33°1E 251 J4
Bîr Za'farâna Egypt 29°10N 32°40E 256 J8
Bîr Zeidûn Egypt 25°45N 33°40E 256 B3
Birāk Libya 27°31N 14°20E 258 C2
Birak el Kiyam Egypt 30°2N 31°9E 117 A1
Biramféro Guinea 11°40N 9°10W 262 C3
Birao C.A.R. 10°20N 22°47E 264 A4
Biratnagar Nepal 26°27N 87°17E 243 F12
Birawa Dem. Rep. of the Congo 2°20S 28°48E 268 C2
Birch → Canada 58°28N 112°17W 296 B6
Birch Cliff Canada 43°41N 79°16W 141 A3
Birch Grove Grenada 12°6N 61°40W 323 q
Birch Hills Canada 52°59N 105°25W 297 C7
Birch I. Canada 52°26N 99°54W 297 C9
Birch L. N.W.T., Canada 62°4N 116°33W 296 A5
Birch L. Ont., Canada 51°23N 92°18W 298 B1
Birch Mts. Canada 57°30N 113°10W 296 B6
Birch River Canada 52°24N 101°6W 297 C8
Birchip Australia 35°56S 142°55E 282 C5
Birchiş Romania 45°58N 22°9E 182 E7
Birchwood N.Z. 45°55S 167°53E 285 F2
Birchwood Alaska, U.S.A. 61°24N 149°28W 303 F10
Bird Canada 56°30N 94°13W 297 B10
Bird I. = Aves, I. de W. Indies 15°45N 63°55W 321 C7
Bird I. S. Georgia 54°0S 38°3W 151 B1
Birds Creek Canada 45°6N 77°52W 312 A7
Birdseye U.S.A. 38°19N 86°42W 311 F10
Birdsville Australia 25°51S 139°20E 280 D2
Birdum Cr. → Australia 15°14S 133°0E 278 C5
Birdwood Australia 34°51S 138°58E 282 C3
Birecik Turkey 37°2N 38°0E 213 D8
Birein Israel 30°50N 34°28E 251 H5
Bireuen Indonesia 5°14N 96°39E 234 A1
Birganj Nepal 27°1N 84°52E 243 F11
Birgu = Vittoriosa Malta 35°54N 14°31E 206 F8
Birhan Ethiopia 10°45N 38°4E 266 B4
Biri Norway 60°58N 10°35E 164 D7
Biri → South Sudan 7°56N 26°33E 257 F2
Birifo Gambia 13°30N 14°0W 262 C2
Birigüi Brazil 21°18S 50°16W 335 A5
Birini C.A.R. 7°51N 22°24E 264 A4
Bīrjand Iran 32°53N 59°13E 247 C8
Birka Sweden 59°20N 17°32E 162 E11
Birkeland Norway 58°24N 7°12E 164 F4
Birkenfeld Germany 49°38N 7°9E 179 F3
Birkenhead U.K. 53°23N 3°2W 168 D4
Birkenstein Germany 52°31N 13°40E 115 A5
Birkerød Denmark 55°50N 12°25E 163 J6
Birket Fatmé Chad 12°55N 19°7E 259 F3
Birket Qârûn Egypt 29°30N 30°40E 256 J7
Birkfeld Austria 47°21N 15°45E 180 D8
Birkhadem Algeria 36°43N 3°3E 261 A5
Birkholz Germany 52°37N 13°34E 115 A4
Birkholzaue Germany 52°38N 13°36E 115 A4
Birkirkara Malta 35°54N 14°28E 206 F7
Bîrlad = Bârlad Romania 46°15N 27°38E 183 D12
Birmingham W. Mids., U.K. 52°29N 1°52W 169 E6
Birmingham Ala., U.S.A. 33°31N 86°48W 315 E11
Birmingham Iowa, U.S.A. 40°53N 91°57W 310 D5
Birmingham Int. ✈ (BHX) U.K. 52°26N 1°45W 169 E6
Birmitrapur India 22°24N 84°46E 244 C7
Birni Ngaouré Niger 13°5N 2°51E 263 C5
Birni Nkonni Niger 13°55N 5°15E 263 C6
Birnie Kiribati 3°35S 171°31W 277 A16
Birnin Gwari Nigeria 11°0N 6°45E 263 C6
Birnin Kebbi Nigeria 12°32N 4°12E 263 C5
Birnin Kudu Nigeria 11°30N 9°29E 263 C6
Birobidzhan Russia 48°50N 132°50E 219 B15
Birougou, Mts. Gabon 1°51S 12°20E 264 C2
Birr Ireland 53°6N 7°54W 166 C4
Birrarrung Park Australia 37°45S 145°4E 128 A2
Birrie → Australia 29°43S 146°37E 281 D4
Birsilpur India 28°11N 72°15E 242 E5
Birsk Russia 55°25N 55°30E 186 C10
Birtle Canada 50°30N 101°5W 297 C8
Biryuchiy Ukraine 46°10N 35°0E 189 J8
Biržai Lithuania 56°11N 24°45E 188 D3
Birzebbugga Malta 35°50N 14°32E 206 F8
Birzhi = Madona Latvia 56°53N 26°5E 188 D4
Birzula = Kotovsk Ukraine 47°45N 29°35E 177 E15
Bisa Indonesia 1°15S 127°28E 231 E7
Bisáccia Italy 41°1N 15°22E 201 A8
Bisacquino Italy 37°42N 13°15E 200 E6
Bisai Japan 35°16N 136°44E 223 B8
Bisalpur India 28°14N 79°48E 243 E8
Bisbee U.S.A. 31°27N 109°55W 305 L9
Biscarrosse France 44°22N 1°20W 174 D2
Biscarrosse et de Parentis, Étang de France 44°21N 1°10W 174 D2
Biscay, B. of Atl. Oc. 45°0N 2°0W 171 D1
Biscay Abyssal Plain Atl. Oc. 45°0N 8°0W 152 B11
Biscayne △ U.S.A. 25°25N 80°12W 317 K9
Biscayne B. U.S.A. 25°40N 80°12W 317 K9
Biscayne Bay Aquatic Reserve U.S.A. 25°40N 80°16W 129 E2
Biscayne Park U.S.A. 25°52N 80°10W 129 C2
Biscéglie Italy 41°14N 16°30E 201 A9
Bischheim France 48°37N 7°46E 173 D14
Bischoflack = Škofja Loka Slovenia 46°9N 14°19E 199 B11
Bischofsburg = Biskupiec Poland 53°53N 20°58E 184 E7
Bischofshofen Austria 47°26N 13°14E 180 D6
Bischofstal = Ujazd Poland 50°23N 18°21E 185 H5
Bischofstein = Bisztynek Poland 54°8N 20°53E 184 D7
Bischofswerda Germany 51°7N 14°10E 178 D10
Bischwiller France 48°46N 7°50E 173 D14
Biscoe Is. Antarctica 66°0S 67°0W 151 C17
Biscoitos Azores 38°47N 27°15W 153 d1
Biscostasing Canada 47°18N 82°9W 298 C3
Biševo Croatia 42°57N 16°3E 199 F13
Bisha Eritrea 15°30N 37°31E 257 D4
Bishah, W. → Si. Arabia 21°24N 43°26E 248 B3
Bishan China 29°33N 106°12E 228 C6
Bishanga Dem. Rep. of the Congo 4°31S 21°2E 265 C4
Bishkek Kyrgyzstan 42°54N 74°46E 217 D8
Bishnath India 26°40N 93°10E 241 B4
Bishnupur India 23°8N 87°20E 243 H12
Bisho = Bhisho S. Africa 32°50S 27°23E 270 D4
Bishoftu = Debre Zeyit Ethiopia 8°50N 39°0E 257 F4
Bishop Calif., U.S.A. 37°22N 118°24W 306 H8
Bishop Ga., U.S.A. 33°49N 83°26W 316 B6
Bishop Tex., U.S.A. 27°35N 97°48W 314 H6
Bishop Auckland U.K. 54°39N 1°40W 168 C6
Bishop Lavis S. Africa 33°56S 18°35E 118 A2
Bishop Museum U.S.A. 21°20N 157°52W 302 K14
Bishop's Falls Canada 49°2N 55°30W 299 C8
Bishop's Stortford U.K. 51°52N 0°10E 169 F8
Bishopscourt S. Africa 33°59S 18°27E 118 A1
Bisignano Italy 39°31N 16°17E 201 C9
Bisina, L. Uganda 1°38N 33°56E 268 B3
Biskra Algeria 34°50N 5°44E 261 B6
Biskra Malta 35°58N 14°21E 206 F7
Biskra □ Algeria 34°40N 5°25E 261 B6
Biskupiec Poland 53°53N 20°58E 184 E7
Bislig Phil. 8°12N 126°18E 233 G6
Bismarck Mo., U.S.A. 37°46N 90°38W 310 G6
Bismarck N. Dak., U.S.A. 46°48N 100°47W 308 B3
Bismarck Arch. Papua N. G. 2°30S 150°0E 286 B6
Bismarck Ra. Papua N. G. 5°35S 145°0E 286 C3
Bismarck Sea Papua N. G. 4°10S 146°50E 286 C4
Bismarckburg = Kasanga Tanzania 8°30S 31°10E 269 D3
Bismark Germany 52°40N 11°33E 178 C7
Bismil Turkey 37°51N 40°40E 213 D9
Bismo Norway 61°54N 8°15E 164 C5
Biso Uganda 1°44N 31°26E 268 B3
Bison U.S.A. 45°31N 102°28W 308 C2
Bīsotūn Iran 34°23N 47°26E 213 E12
Bispebjerg Denmark 55°42N 12°31E 118 A3
Bispgården Sweden 63°2N 16°40E 162 A10
Bissagos = Bijagós, Arquipélago dos Guinea-Biss. 11°15N 16°10W 262 C1
Bissam Cuttack India 19°31N 83°31E 244 E6
Bissau Guinea-Biss. 11°45N 15°45W 262 C1
Bissaula Nigeria 7°0N 10°27E 263 D7
Bissigh, Lach → Somalia 0°45N 41°33E 267 D5
Bissikrima Guinea 10°50N 10°58W 262 C2
Bissonet Plaza U.S.A. 30°1N 90°13W 131 A1
Bissorã Guinea-Biss. 12°16N 15°35W 262 C1
Bistcho L. Canada 59°45N 118°50W 296 B5
Bistreţ Romania 43°54N 23°23E 183 G8
Bistrica = Ilirska-Bistrica Slovenia 45°34N 14°14E 199 C11
Bistriţa Romania 47°9N 24°35E 183 C9
Bistriţa → Romania 46°30N 26°57E 183 D11
Bistriţa Năsăud □ Romania 47°15N 24°30E 183 C9
Bistriţei, Munţii Romania 47°15N 25°40E 183 C10
Biswan India 27°29N 81°2E 243 F9
Bisztynek Poland 54°8N 20°53E 184 D7
Bita → C.A.R. 6°26N 24°43E 264 A4
Bitam Gabon 2°5N 11°25E 264 B2
Bitburg Germany 49°58N 6°31E 179 F2
Bitche France 49°2N 7°25E 173 C14
Bithynia Turkey 40°40N 31°0E 212 B4
Bitkine Chad 11°59N 18°13E 259 F3
Bitlis Turkey 38°20N 42°3E 213 C10
Bitlis □ Turkey 38°20N 42°10E 213 C10
Bitola Macedonia 41°1N 21°20E 202 E5
Bitolj = Bitola Macedonia 41°1N 21°20E 202 E5
Bitonto Italy 41°6N 16°41E 201 A9
Bitra I. India 11°33N 72°9E 245 J1
Bitter Creek U.S.A. 41°33N 108°33W 304 F9
Bitter L. = Buheirat-Murrat-el-Kubra Egypt 30°18N 32°26E 256 H8
Bitterfeld-Wolfen Germany 51°37N 12°20E 178 D8
Bitterfontein S. Africa 31°1S 18°32E 270 D2
Bitterroot → U.S.A. 46°52N 114°7W 304 C6
Bitterroot Range U.S.A. 46°0N 114°20W 304 C6
Bitterwater U.S.A. 36°23N 121°0W 306 J6
Bitti Italy 40°29N 9°23E 200 B2
Bittou Burkina Faso 11°17N 0°18W 263 C4
Bittsevsky Forest Park Russia 55°38N 37°35E 129 C2
Biu Nigeria 10°40N 12°3E 263 C7
Bivolari Romania 47°31N 27°27E 183 C12
Bivolu, Vf. Romania 47°16N 25°58E 183 C10
Biwa-Ko Japan 35°15N 136°10E 223 B8
Biwabik U.S.A. 47°32N 92°21W 308 B7
Bixad Romania 47°56N 23°28E 183 C8
Bixby U.S.A. 35°57N 95°53W 314 D7
Biya → Russia 52°25N 85°0E 217 B11
Biyala Egypt 31°10N 31°13E 251 G2
Biyang China 32°38N 113°21E 229 A9
Biysk Russia 52°40N 85°0E 217 B11
Bizana S. Africa 30°50S 29°52E 271 D4
Bizen Japan 34°43N 134°8E 222 C6
Bizerte Tunisia 37°15N 9°50E 258 A1
Bizerte □ Tunisia 37°5N 9°35E 261 A6
Bizkaia □ Spain 43°15N 2°45W 196 B2
Bjåen fjellstove Norway 59°37N 7°26E 164 E4
Bjargtangar Iceland 65°30N 24°30W 155 B2
Bjarkalundur Iceland 65°33N 22°9W 155 B4
Bjärnum Sweden 56°17N 13°43E 163 H7
Bjästa Sweden 63°12N 18°29E 162 A12
Bjelasica Montenegro 42°50N 19°40E 202 D3
Bjelašnica Bos.-H. 43°43N 18°9E 182 G3
Bjelland Norway 58°23N 7°32E 164 F4
Bjelovar Croatia 45°56N 16°49E 199 C13
Bjerringbro Denmark 56°23N 9°39E 163 H3
Bjervamoen Norway 59°17N 9°5E 164 E6
Bjøberg Norway 60°56N 8°13E 164 D5
Björbo Sweden 60°27N 14°44E 162 D8
Bjørkelangen Norway 59°53N 11°34E 164 E8
Björklinge Sweden 60°2N 17°33E 162 D11
Björknas Sweden 59°19N 18°12E 139 B3
Björkö Sweden 59°52N 19°2E 162 E13
Bjørnafjorden Norway 60°7N 5°28E 164 D2
Björneborg = Pori Finland 61°29N 21°48E 188 B1
Björneborg Sweden 59°14N 14°16E 162 E8
Bjørnevatn Norway 69°40N 30°0E 160 B24
Bjørnøya Arctic 74°30N 19°0E 150 B8
Bjursås Sweden 60°44N 15°25E 162 D9
Bjuv Sweden 56°5N 12°55E 163 H6
Bla Mali 12°56N 5°47W 262 C3
Blå Jungfrun △ Sweden 57°16N 16°47E 163 G10
Blace Serbia 43°18N 21°17E 202 C5
Blachownia Poland 50°49N 18°56E 185 H5
Black = Da → Vietnam 21°15N 105°20E 228 G5
Black → Ont., Canada 44°42N 79°19W 312 B5
Black → Alaska, U.S.A. 66°42N 144°42W 303 C11
Black → Ariz., U.S.A. 33°44N 110°13W 305 K8
Black → Ark., U.S.A. 35°38N 91°20W 314 D9
Black → La., U.S.A. 31°16N 91°50W 314 F9
Black → Mich., U.S.A. 42°59N 82°27W 312 D2
Black → N.Y., U.S.A. 43°59N 76°4W 313 C8
Black → Wis., U.S.A. 43°57N 91°22W 308 D8
Black Bay Pen. Canada 48°38N 88°21W 298 C2
Black Birch L. Canada 56°53N 107°45W 297 B7
Black Canyon of the Gunnison ⌓ U.S.A. 38°40N 107°35W 304 G10
Black Cr. → Canada 43°40N 79°30W 141 A2
Black Creek Pioneer Village Canada 43°46N 79°30W 141 A1
Black Desert = Abiad, Es Sahrâ el Egypt 28°0N 28°0E 256 B2
Black Diamond = Pittsburg U.S.A. 38°2N 121°53W 306 G5
Black Diamond Canada 50°45N 114°14W 296 C6
Black Duck → Canada 56°51N 89°2W 298 A2
Black Forest = Schwarzwald Germany 48°30N 8°20E 179 G4
Black Forest U.S.A. 39°0N 104°43W 304 G11
Black Hd. Ireland 53°9N 9°16W 166 C2
Black Hills U.S.A. 44°0N 103°45W 308 D2
Black I. Canada 51°12N 96°30W 297 C9
Black L. Sask., Canada 59°12N 105°15W 297 B7
Black L. Mich., U.S.A. 45°28N 84°16W 309 C11
Black L. N.Y., U.S.A. 44°31N 75°36W 313 B9
Black Lake Canada 59°11N 105°20W 297 B7
Black Mesa U.S.A. 36°58N 102°58W 314 C3
Black Mountain Australia 30°18S 151°39E 283 A9
Black Mt. = Mynydd Du U.K. 51°52N 3°50W 169 F4
Black Mt. Bhutan 27°20N 90°25E 241 B3
Black Mts. U.K. 51°55N 3°7W 169 F4
Black Range U.S.A. 33°15N 107°50W 305 K10
Black River Jamaica 18°0N 77°50W 320 a
Black River N.Y., U.S.A. 44°0N 75°47W 313 C9
Black River B. Jamaica 18°0N 77°51W 320 a
Black River Falls U.S.A. 44°18N 90°51W 308 C8
Black River Gorges Mauritius 20°24S 57°25E 272 e
Black Rock S. Austral., Australia 32°50S 138°44E 282 B3
Black Rock Barbados 13°7N 59°37W 323 r
Black Rock Desert U.S.A. 41°10N 118°50W 304 F4
Black Sea Eurasia 43°30N 35°0E 187 F6
Black Tickle Canada 53°28N 55°45W 299 B8
Black Volta → Africa 8°41N 1°33W 262 D4
Black Warrior → U.S.A. 32°32N 87°51W 315 E11
Blackall Australia 24°25S 145°45E 280 C4
Blackball N.Z. 42°22S 171°26E 285 C6
Blackbraes △ Australia 19°10S 144°10E 280 B3
Blackbull Australia 17°55S 141°45E 280 B3
Blackburn U.K. 53°45N 2°29W 168 D5
Blackburn, Mt. U.S.A. 61°44N 143°26W 303 F12
Blackburn with Darwen □ U.K. 53°45N 2°29W 168 D5
Blackdown Tableland △ Australia 23°52S 149°8E 280 C4
Blackfen U.K. 51°26N 0°6E 125 B4
Blackfoot U.S.A. 43°11N 112°21W 304 E7
Blackfoot → U.S.A. 46°52N 113°53W 304 C7
Blackfoot Res. U.S.A. 42°55N 111°39W 304 E8
Blackheath U.K. 51°28N 0°0 125 B4
Blackman U.S.A. 30°56N 86°38W 317 E3
Blackpool U.K. 53°49N 3°3W 168 D4
Blackpool □ U.K. 53°49N 3°3W 168 D4
Blackriver U.S.A. 44°46N 83°17W 312 B1
Blacks Harbour Canada 45°3N 66°49W 299 C6
Blacksburg U.S.A. 37°14N 80°25W 309 G13
Blackshear U.S.A. 31°18N 82°14W 316 D7
Blackshear, L. U.S.A. 31°51N 83°56W 316 D6
Blacksod B. Ireland 54°6N 10°0W 166 B1
Blackstairs Mt. Ireland 52°33N 6°48W 166 D5
Blackstone U.S.A. 37°5N 78°0W 309 G14
Blackstone Ra. Australia 26°0S 128°30E 279 E4
Blackville U.S.A. 33°22N 81°16W 316 B8
Blackwater = West Road → Canada 53°18N 122°53W 296 C4
Blackwater Australia 23°35S 148°53E 280 C4
Blackwater → Meath, Ireland 53°39N 6°41W 166 C4
Blackwater → Waterford, Ireland 52°4N 7°52W 166 D4
Blackwater → Armagh, U.K. 54°31N 6°35W 166 B5
Blackwater → Fla., U.S.A. 30°36N 87°2W 317 E2
Blackwater → Mo., U.S.A. 38°56N 92°57W 310 F4
Blackwell U.S.A. 36°48N 97°17W 314 C6
Blackwells Corner U.S.A. 35°37N 119°47W 307 K7
Blackwood U.K. 51°39N 3°12W 169 F4
Blackwood, C. Papua N. G. 7°49S 144°31E 286 D3
Bladensburg U.S.A. 38°55N 76°55W 143 B3
Bladensburg △ Australia 22°30S 142°59E 280 C3
Blaenau Ffestiniog U.K. 53°0N 3°56W 168 E4
Blaenau Gwent □ U.K. 51°48N 3°12W 169 F4
Bláfell Iceland 64°30N 19°51W 155 C7
Bláfjall Iceland 65°26N 16°50W 155 B10
Blåfjella-Skjækerfjella △ Norway 64°15N 13°8E 160 D15
Blagaj Bos.-H. 43°16N 17°55E 202 C1
Blagnac France 43°37N 1°23E 174 E5
Blagnac, Toulouse ✈ (TLS) France 43°37N 1°22E 174 E5
Blagodarnyy Russia 45°7N 43°37E 191 H6
Blagoevgrad Bulgaria 42°2N 23°5E 202 D7
Blagoevgrad □ Bulgaria 42°2N 23°5E 202 D7
Blagoveshchensk Russia 50°20N 127°30E 219 A14
Blahkiuh Indonesia 8°31S 115°12E 231 J18
Blain Loire-Atlantique, France 47°29N 1°45W 172 E5
Blain Pa., U.S.A. 40°20N 77°31W 312 F7
Blaine Minn., U.S.A. 45°10N 93°13W 308 C7
Blaine Wash., U.S.A. 48°59N 122°45W 306 B4
Blaine Lake Canada 52°51N 106°52W 297 C7
Blair U.S.A. 41°33N 96°8W 308 E5
Blair Athol Australia 22°42S 147°31E 280 C4
Blair Atholl U.K. 56°46N 3°50W 167 E5
Blair Village U.S.A. 33°40N 84°23W 113 C2
Blairgowrie Gauteng, S. Africa 26°6S 28°0E 123 A2
Blairgowrie Perth & Kinr., U.K. 56°35N 3°21W 167 E5
Blairsden U.S.A. 39°47N 120°37W 306 F6
Blairsville U.S.A. 40°26N 79°16W 312 F5
Blaj Romania 46°10N 23°57E 183 D8
Blaka Niger 21°21N 12°47E 259 D2
Blakang Mati, Pulau Singapore 1°15N 103°50E 237 d
Blake House U.S.A. 42°19N 71°3W 116 B2
Blake Pt. U.S.A. 48°11N 88°25W 308 A9
Blakehurst Australia 33°59S 151°6E 139 B1
Blakely Ga., U.S.A. 31°23N 84°56W 316 D5
Blakely Pa., U.S.A. 41°28N 75°37W 313 E9
Blakesburg U.S.A. 40°58N 92°38W 310 D4
Blakstad Akershus, Norway 59°49N 10°28E 138 B1
Blakstad Aust-Agder, Norway 58°30N 8°39E 164 F5
Blambangan, Semenanjung Indonesia 8°42S 114°29E 231 K17
Blâmont France 48°35N 6°50E 173 D13
Blanc, C. Spain 39°21N 2°51E 206 B3
Blanc, C. Tunisia 37°15N 9°56E 258 A1
Blanc, Mont Europe 45°48N 6°50E 175 C10
Blanca, B. Argentina 39°10S 61°30W 336 A4
Blanca, Costa Spain 38°25N 0°10W 197 G4
Blanca Peak U.S.A. 37°35N 105°29W 305 H11
Blanchardville U.S.A. 42°49N 89°52W 310 B7
Blanche, C. Australia 33°1S 134°9E 281 E1
Blanche, L. S. Austral., Australia 29°15S 139°40E 281 D2
Blanche, L. W. Austral., Australia 22°25S 123°17E 278 D3
Blanche, L. Fla., U.S.A. 28°28N 81°30W 133 B1
Blanche, Pte. St. Lucia 13°53N 61°5W 323 m
Blanche, Pte. St.-Maarten 18°0N 63°2W 322 a
Blanche Channel Solomon Is. 8°30S 157°30E 287 M9
Blanchester U.S.A. 39°17N 83°59W 311 E13
Blanchisseuse Trin. & Tob. 10°48N 61°18W 323 t
Blanco Western Cape, S. Africa 33°55S 22°23E 270 D3
Blanco Tex., U.S.A. 30°6N 98°25W 314 F5
Blanco → Argentina 30°20S 68°42W 334 C2
Blanco → Bolivia 12°30S 64°18W 331 C5
Blanco, C. Costa Rica 9°34N 85°8W 320 E2
Blanco, C. Oreg., U.S.A. 42°51N 124°34W 304 E1
Blanco, Pta. Bonaire 12°13N 68°14W 322 h
Blanda → Iceland 65°37N 20°9W 155 B6
Blandford Forum U.K. 50°51N 2°9W 169 G5
Blanding U.S.A. 37°37N 109°29W 305 H9
Blandinsville U.S.A. 40°33N 90°52W 310 D6
Blanes Spain 41°40N 2°48E 196 D7
Blangkejeren Indonesia 3°59N 97°20E 234 B1
Blangpidie Indonesia 3°44N 96°49E 234 B1
Blangy-sur-Bresle France 49°55N 1°37E 173 C8
Blanice → Czechia 49°10N 14°5E 180 B7
Blankaholm Sweden 57°36N 16°31E 163 G10
Blankenberge Belgium 51°20N 3°9E 170 C3
Blankenburg Berlin, Germany 52°35N 13°27E 115 A3
Blankenburg Sachsen-Anhalt, Germany 51°47N 10°57E 178 D6
Blankenfelde Germany 52°37N 13°23E 115 A3
Blanku, L. Curaçao 12°2N 68°47W 322 g
Blanquefort France 44°55N 0°38W 174 D3
Blanquilla, I. Venezuela 11°51N 64°37W 321 D7
Blanquillo Uruguay 32°53S 55°37W 335 C4
Blansko Czechia 49°22N 16°40E 181 B9
Blantyre Malawi 15°45S 35°0E 269 F4
Blarney Ireland 51°56N 8°33W 166 E3
Blasdell U.S.A. 42°48N 78°50W 312 D6
Blåsjø Norway 59°20N 6°50E 164 E3
Błaszki Poland 51°38N 18°30E 185 G5
Blatná Czechia 49°25N 13°52E 180 B6
Blato Croatia 42°56N 16°48E 199 F13
Blaubeuren Germany 48°24N 9°46E 179 G5
Blaustein Germany 48°25N 9°53E 179 G5
Blåvands Huk Denmark 55°33N 8°4E 163 J2
Blaydon U.K. 54°58N 1°42W 168 C6
Blaye France 45°8N 0°40W 174 C3
Blaye-les-Mines France 44°1N 2°8E 174 D6
Blayney Australia 33°32S 149°14E 283 B8
Blaze, Pt. Australia 12°56S 130°11E 278 B5
Błażowa Poland 49°53N 22°7E 185 J9
Blechhammer = Blachownia Poland 50°49N 18°56E 185 H5
Bleckede Germany 53°17N 10°43E 178 B6
Bled Slovenia 46°27N 14°7E 199 B11
Blefjell Norway 59°48N 9°10E 164 E6
Bleiburg Austria 46°35N 14°49E 180 E7
Blejeşti Romania 44°19N 25°27E 183 F10
Blekinge Sweden 56°25N 15°20E 161 H16
Blekinge □ Sweden 56°20N 15°20E 163 H9
Blenheim Ont., Canada 42°20N 82°0W 312 D3
Blenheim N.Z. 41°38S 173°57E 285 B8
Bléone → France 44°5N 6°0E 175 D10
Blérancourt France 49°31N 3°9E 173 C10
Bletchley U.K. 51°59N 0°44W 169 F7
Bleus, Monts Dem. Rep. of the Congo 1°30N 30°30E 268 B3
Blida Algeria 36°30N 2°49E 261 A5
Blida □ Algeria 36°35N 3°0E 261 A5
Blidet Amor Algeria 32°59N 5°58E 261 B6
Blidö Sweden 59°37N 18°53E 162 E12
Blidsberg Sweden 57°56N 13°30E 163 G7
Blieskastel Germany 49°14N 7°12E 179 F3
Bligh Sound N.Z. 44°47S 167°32E 285 E2
Bligh Water Fiji 17°0S 178°0E 287 A2
Blind River Canada 46°10N 82°58W 298 C3
Blinisht Albania 41°52N 19°59E 202 E3
Bliss Idaho, U.S.A. 42°56N 114°57W 304 E6
Bliss N.Y., U.S.A. 42°34N 78°15W 312 D6
Blissfield Mich., U.S.A. 41°50N 83°52W 311 C13
Blissfield Ohio, U.S.A. 40°24N 81°58W 312 F3
Blitar Indonesia 8°5S 112°11E 235 D4
Blitchton U.S.A. 32°12N 81°26W 316 C8
Blitta Togo 8°23N 1°6E 263 D5
Blizne Poland 52°14N 20°52E 143 B1
Block I. U.S.A. 41°11N 71°35W 313 E13
Block Island Sd. U.S.A. 41°15N 71°40W 313 E13
Bloemenmarkt Amsterdam, Neths. 112 b2
Bloemfontein S. Africa 29°6S 26°7E 270 C4
Bloemhof S. Africa 27°38S 25°32E 270 C4
Blois France 47°35N 1°20E 172 E8
Blomskog Sweden 59°16N 12°2E 162 E6
Blomstermåla Sweden 56°59N 16°21E 163 H10
Blomvåg Norway 60°32N 4°50E 164 D1
Blönduós Iceland 65°40N 20°12W 155 B6
Blongas Indonesia 8°53S 116°2E 231 K19
Błonie Poland 52°12N 20°37E 185 F7
Bloodvein → Canada 51°47N 96°43W 297 C9
Bloody B. Trin. & Tob. 11°18N 60°38W 323 s
Bloody Foreland Ireland 55°10N 8°17W 166 A3
Bloom = Chicago Heights U.S.A. 41°30N 87°38W 311 C9
Bloomer U.S.A. 45°6N 91°29W 308 C8
Bloomfield Ont., Canada 43°59N 77°14W 312 C7
Bloomfield Ind., U.S.A. 39°1N 86°57W 311 E10
Bloomfield Iowa, U.S.A. 40°45N 92°25W 310 D4
Bloomfield Ky., U.S.A. 37°55N 85°19W 311 G11
Bloomfield N. Mex., U.S.A. 36°43N 107°59W 305 H10
Bloomfield Nebr., U.S.A. 42°36N 97°39W 308 D5
Bloomingburg U.S.A. 39°36N 83°24W 311 E13
Bloomington Ill., U.S.A. 40°28N 89°0W 310 D8
Bloomington Ind., U.S.A. 39°10N 86°32W 310 E10
Bloomington Minn., U.S.A. 44°50N 93°17W 308 C7
Bloomington Wis., U.S.A. 42°53N 90°55W 310 B6
Bloomsburg U.S.A. 41°0N 76°27W 313 F8
Bloomsbury Australia 20°48S 148°38E 280 b
Bloomsbury London, U.K. 125 a3
Blora Indonesia 6°57S 111°25E 235 D4
Blossburg U.S.A. 41°41N 77°4W 312 E7
Blosseville Kyst Greenland 68°50N 26°30W 154 D8
Błota Poland 52°9N 21°11E 143 C3
Blouberg S. Africa 23°8S 28°59E 271 B4
Blountstown U.S.A. 30°27N 85°3W 316 E4
Blowing Point Village Anguilla 18°11N 63°6W 322 a
Blowing Rock Anguilla 18°9N 63°10W 322 a
Bludenz Austria 47°10N 9°50E 180 D2
Blue → U.S.A. 38°11N 86°19W 311 F10
Blue Cypress L. U.S.A. 27°44N 80°45W 317 H9
Blue Earth U.S.A. 43°38N 94°6W 308 D6
Blue Hole Jamaica 18°10N 76°24W 320 a
Blue Hole △ Belize 17°9N 88°40W 320 C2
Blue Island U.S.A. 41°40N 87°40W 119 D2
Blue Lagoon △ Zambia 15°28S 27°26E 269 F2
Blue Lagoon I. U.S.A. 25°46N 80°17W 129 D1
Blue Mesa Res. U.S.A. 38°28N 107°20W 304 G10
Blue Mosque = Sultanahme Camil Turkey 41°0N 28°58E 122 B1
Blue Mound Ill., U.S.A. 39°42N 89°7W 310 E7
Blue Mound Tex., U.S.A. 32°51N 97°20W 120 A2
Blue Mountain Lake U.S.A. 43°51N 74°27W 313 C10
Blue Mountain Pk. Jamaica 18°3N 76°36W 320 a
Blue Mountains and John Crow Mountains △ Jamaica 18°5N 76°34W 320 a
Blue Mt. U.S.A. 40°30N 76°30W 313 F8
Blue Mts. N.S.W., Australia 33°40S 150°15E 283 B9
Blue Mts. Jamaica 18°3N 76°36W 320 a
Blue Mts. Maine, U.S.A. 44°50N 70°35W 313 B14
Blue Mts. Oreg., U.S.A. 45°0N 118°20W 304 D4
Blue Mts. △ Australia 34°2S 150°15E 283 C9
Blue Mud B. Australia 13°30S 136°0E 280 A2
Blue Mud Bay ☼ Australia 13°25S 136°2E 280 A2
Blue Nile = Nîl el Azraq → Sudan 15°38N 32°31E 257 D3
Blue Nile Falls = Tis Issat Ethiopia 11°25N 37°45E 257 E4
Blue Rapids U.S.A. 39°41N 96°39W 308 F5
Blue Ridge U.S.A. 36°40N 80°50W 309 G13
Blue River Canada 52°6N 119°18W 296 C5
Blue Springs U.S.A. 39°1N 94°17W 310 E2
Bluefield U.S.A. 37°15N 81°17W 309 G13
Bluefields Nic. 12°20N 83°50W 320 D3
Bluevale Canada 43°51N 81°15W 312 C3
Bluff Queens., Australia 23°35S 149°4E 280 C4
Bluff N.Z. 46°37S 168°20E 285 G3
Bluff Utah, U.S.A. 37°17N 109°33W 305 H9
Bluff Harbour N.Z. 46°36S 168°21E 285 G3
Bluff Hd. Hong Kong, China 22°11N 114°12E 122 B3
Bluff Knoll Australia 34°24S 118°15E 279 F2

Bluff Pt. Australia 27°50S 114°5E 279 E1
Bluffers Park Canada 43°43N 79°14W 141 A3
Bluffs U.S.A. 39°45N 90°32W 310 E6
Bluffton Ga., U.S.A. 31°31N 84°52W 316 D5
Bluffton Ind., U.S.A. 40°44N 85°11W 311 D11
Bluffton Ohio, U.S.A. 40°54N 83°54W 311 D13
Bluffton S.C., U.S.A. 32°14N 80°52W 316 C9
Blumberg Germany 52°36N 13°39E 115 A4
Blumenau = Stettler Canada 52°19N 112°40W 296 C6
Blumenau Brazil 27°0S 49°0W 335 B6
Blunt U.S.A. 44°31N 99°59W 308 C4
Blunt Pt. U.S.A. 37°51N 122°25W 136 A2
Blutenberg Germany 48°9N 11°27E 131 B1
Bly U.S.A. 42°24N 121°3W 304 E3
Blyde River Canyon ⌓ S. Africa 24°37S 31°2E 271 B5
Blylaget Norway 59°46N 10°41E 133 B3
Blyth S. Austral., Australia 33°49S 138°28E 282 B3
Blyth Ont., Canada 43°44N 81°26W 312 C3
Blyth Northumberland, U.K. 55°8N 1°31W 168 B6
Blythe Calif., U.S.A. 33°37N 114°36W 307 M12
Blythe Ga., U.S.A. 33°17N 82°12W 316 B7
Blytheville U.S.A. 35°56N 89°55W 315 D10
Bø Telemark, Norway 59°25N 9°3E 164 E6
Bo S. Leone 7°55N 11°50W 262 D2
Bo Duc Vietnam 11°58N 106°50E 237 G6
Bo-eun S. Korea 36°29N 127°43E 224 D3
Bo Hai China 39°0N 119°0E 227 E10
Bo Hai Haixia Asia 38°25N 121°10E 227 E11
Bo-Kaap Museum Cape Town, S. Africa 118 c2
Bō-no-Misaki Japan 31°15N 130°13E 222 F2
Bo Xian = Bozhou China 33°55N 115°41E 226 H8
Boa Esperança Brazil 3°21N 61°23W 329 C5
Boa Esperança, Represa Brazil 6°50S 43°50W 332 C3
Boa Nova Brazil 14°22S 40°10W 333 D3
Boa Viagem Brazil 5°7S 39°44W 332 C4
Boa Vista = Tocantinópolis Brazil 6°20S 47°25W 332 C2
Boa Vista Brazil 2°48N 60°30W 329 C5
Boa Vista C. Verde Is. 16°0N 22°49W 153 j
Boa Vista, Alto do Brazil 22°58S 43°16W 135 B1
Boa Vista do Erechim = Erechim Brazil 27°35S 52°15W 335 B5
Boac Phil. 13°27N 121°50E 232 E3
Boaco Nic. 12°29N 85°35W 320 D2
Bo'ai China 35°10N 113°3E 226 G7
Boal Spain 43°25N 6°49W 194 B4
Boali C.A.R. 4°48N 18°7E 264 B3
Boalsburg U.S.A. 40°47N 77°49W 312 F7
Boane Mozam. 26°6S 32°19E 271 C5
Boang I. Papua N. G. 3°23S 153°18E 286 B7
Boao China 19°8N 110°34E 229 a
Boardman U.S.A. 41°2N 80°40W 312 E4
Boardwalk U.S.A. 40°34N 73°49W 132 C3
Boath India 19°20N 78°20E 244 E4
Boatswain Bird I. Ascension I. 7°56S 14°18W 153 g
Boavista Portugal 38°48N 9°8W 126 A2
Boayan I. Phil. 10°34N 119°9E 233 F2
Boaz I. Bermuda 32°18N 64°51W 153 a
Bob Marley Mausoleum Jamaica 18°18N 77°18W 320 a
Bobadah Australia 32°19S 146°41E 283 B7
Bobai China 22°17N 109°59E 228 F7
Bobbili India 18°35N 83°30E 244 E6
Bòbbio Italy 44°46N 9°23E 198 D6
Bobcaygeon Canada 44°33N 78°33W 312 B6
Bobigny France 48°54N 2°26E 134 A3
Boblad India 17°13N 75°26E 244 F2
Böblingen Germany 48°40N 9°1E 179 G5
Bobo-Dioulasso Burkina Faso 11°8N 4°13W 262 C4
Bobolice Poland 53°58N 16°37E 184 E3
Bobon Phil. 12°32N 124°34E 232 E5
Bobonaza → Ecuador 2°36S 76°38W 328 D2
Bobonong Botswana 21°58S 28°20E 271 B4
Boboshevo Bulgaria 42°9N 23°0E 202 D7
Bobov Dol Bulgaria 42°20N 23°0E 202 D6
Bóbr → Poland 52°4N 15°4E 185 F2
Bobraomby, Tanjon' i Madag. 12°40S 49°10E 272 A2
Bobrov Russia 51°5N 40°2E 190 E5
Bobrovytsya Ukraine 50°45N 31°23E 189 G6
Bobruysk = Babruysk Belarus 53°10N 29°15E 177 B15
Bobrynets Ukraine 48°4N 32°5E 189 H7
Bobures Venezuela 9°15N 71°11W 328 B3
Boby, Pic Madag. 22°12S 46°55E 272 C2
Boca de Pozo Venezuela 11°0N 64°23W 329 a
Boca del Rio Veracruz, Mexico 19°5N 96°4W 319 D5
Boca del Río Venezuela 10°58N 64°11W 329 a
Boca do Acre Brazil 8°50S 67°27W 330 B4
Boca do Jari Brazil 1°7S 51°58W 329 D7
Boca Grande Fla., U.S.A. 26°45N 82°16W 317 J7
Boca Grande Venezuela 8°40N 60°40W 329 B5
Boca Raton U.S.A. 26°21N 80°5W 317 J9
Boca Slagbaai Bonaire 12°16N 68°24W 322 h
Bocaiúva Brazil 17°7S 43°49W 333 E3
Bocanda Ivory C. 7°5N 4°31W 262 D4
Bocanegra Peru 12°1S 77°7W 124 B2
Bocaranga C.A.R. 7°0N 15°35E 264 A3
Bocas del Dragon = Dragon's Mouths Trin. & Tob. 11°0N 61°50W 323 t
Bocas del Toro Panama 9°15N 82°20W 320 E3
Boceguillas Spain 41°20N 3°39W 194 D7
Bochkarevo = Belogorsk Russia 51°0N 128°20E 215 D13
Bochmanivka Ukraine 47°40N 29°34E 183 C14
Bochnia Poland 49°58N 20°27E 185 J7
Bocholt Germany 51°50N 6°36E 178 D2
Bochum = Senwabarana S. Africa 23°17S 29°7E 271 B4
Bochum Germany 51°28N 7°13E 178 D3
Bockenem Germany 52°1N 10°8E 178 C6
Boćki Poland 52°39N 23°3E 185 F10
Bocognano France 42°5N 9°4E 175 F13
Bocoio Angola 12°28S 14°10E 265 E2
Boconó Venezuela 9°15N 70°16W 328 B3
Boconó → Venezuela 8°43N 69°34W 328 B4
Bocoyna Mexico 27°52N 107°35W 318 B3
Bocşa Romania 45°21N 21°47E 182 E6
Boda C.A.R. 4°19N 17°26E 264 B3
Boda Dalarna, Sweden 61°1N 15°13E 162 C9
Böda Kalmar, Sweden 57°15N 17°3E 163 G11
Boda Västernorrland, Sweden 62°52N 16°39E 162 B10
Bodafors Sweden 57°48N 14°23E 163 G8
Bodaybo Russia 57°50N 114°0E 215 D12
Boddam U.K. 59°56N 1°17W 167 B7
Boddington Australia 32°50S 116°30E 279 F2
Bode Sadu Nigeria 9°0N 4°47E 263 D5
Bodega Bay U.S.A. 38°20N 123°3W 306 G3
Boden Sweden 65°50N 21°42E 160 D19
Bodensee Europe 47°35N 9°25E 179 H5
Bodenteich Germany 52°50N 10°42E 178 C6
Bodh Gaya India 24°41N 84°59E 243 G11
Bodhan India 18°40N 77°44E 244 E3
Bodinayakkanur India 10°2N 77°10E 245 J3
Bodinga Nigeria 12°58N 5°10E 263 C6
Bodmin U.K. 50°28N 4°43W 169 G3
Bodmin Moor U.K. 50°33N 4°36W 169 G3
Bodø Norway 67°17N 14°24E 160 C16
Bodoquena, Serra da Brazil 21°0S 56°50W 331 E6
Bodoupa C.A.R. 5°43N 17°36E 264 A3
Bodrichi Chad 19°11N 15°54E 259 E3
Bodrog → Hungary 48°11N 21°22E 182 B6
Bodrum Turkey 37°3N 27°30E 205 D9
Boduna Dem. Rep. of the Congo 5°5N 19°44E 264 A3
Bódva → Hungary 48°19N 20°45E 182 B5
Boedo Argentina 34°38S 58°25W 117 B2
Boembé Congo 2°54S 15°39E 264 C3
Boën France 45°44N 4°1E 175 C8
Boende Dem. Rep. of the Congo 0°24S 21°12E 264 C4
Boeny □ Madag. 15°45S 46°20E 272 B2
Boeotia = Viotia Greece 38°20N 23°0E 204 C5
Boerne U.S.A. 29°47N 98°44W 314 G5
Boesmans → S. Africa 33°42S 26°39E 270 D4
Boffa Guinea 10°16N 14°3W 262 C2
Bog Walk Jamaica 18°6N 77°1W 320 a
Bogal, Lagh → Kenya 0°41N 40°57E 267 D5
Bogale Burma 16°17N 95°24E 241 G5
Bogalusa U.S.A. 30°47N 89°52W 315 F10
Bogan → Australia 30°20S 146°55E 283 A7
Bogan Gate Australia 33°7S 147°49E 283 B7
Bogandé Burkina Faso 13°2N 0°8W 263 C4
Bogangolo C.A.R. 5°34N 18°15E 264 A3
Bogantungan Australia 23°41S 147°17E 280 C4
Bogata U.S.A. 33°28N 95°13W 314 E7
Bogatić Serbia 44°51N 19°30E 202 B3
Boğazkale Turkey 40°2N 34°37E 212 B6
Boğazlıyan Turkey 39°11N 35°14E 212 C6
Bogbonga Dem. Rep. of the Congo 1°36N 19°24E 264 B3
Bogda Shan China 43°35N 89°40E 217 D11
Bogen Sweden 60°4N 12°33E 162 D6
Bogenhausen Germany 48°8N 11°36E 131 B2
Bogense Denmark 55°34N 10°5E 163 J4
Bogetići Montenegro 42°41N 18°58E 202 D2
Boggabilla Australia 28°36S 150°24E 281 D5
Boggabri Australia 30°45S 150°5E 283 A9
Boggeragh Mts. Ireland 52°2N 8°55W 166 D3
Boghari = Ksar el Boukhari Algeria 35°51N 2°52E 261 A5
Bogia Papua N. G. 4°9S 145°0E 286 C3
Bogildo S. Korea 34°9N 126°32E 224 E3
Boglan = Solhan Turkey 38°57N 41°3E 213 C9
Bogles Grenada 12°30N 61°26W 323 q
Bognes Norway 68°13N 16°5E 160 B17
Bognor Regis U.K. 50°47N 0°40W 169 G7
Bogo Phil. 11°3N 124°0E 233 F4
Bogodukhov = Bohodukhiv Ukraine 50°9N 35°33E 189 G8
Bogol Manya Ethiopia 4°34N 41°29E 267 C5
Bogong, Mt. Australia 36°47S 147°17E 283 D7
Bogor Indonesia 6°36S 106°48E 234 D3
Bogoroditsk Russia 53°47N 38°8E 188 F10
Bogorodsk Russia 56°4N 43°30E 190 B6
Bogorodskoye = Kamskoye Ustye Russia 55°10N 49°20E 190 C9
Bogorodskoye = Leninskoye Russia 58°23N 47°3E 190 A8
Bogorodskoye Russia 55°48N 37°42E 129 B3
Bogoslovsky = Karpinsk Russia 59°45N 60°1E 186 C11
Bogoso Ghana 5°38N 2°3W 262 D4
Bogotá Colombia 4°34N 74°0W 328 C3
Bogota N.J., U.S.A. 40°52N 74°2W 132 A1
Bogotol Russia 56°15N 89°50E 214 D9
Bogou Togo 10°40N 0°12E 263 C5
Bogra Bangla. 24°51N 89°22E 241 C2
Bogstadvatnet Norway 59°58N 10°37E 133 A2
Boguchanskoye Vdkhr. Russia 58°42N 99°9E 215 D10
Boguchany Russia 58°40N 97°30E 215 D10
Boguchar Russia 49°55N 40°32E 190 F5
Bogué Mauritania 16°45N 14°10W 262 B2
Boguszów-Gorce Poland 50°45N 16°12E 185 H3
Bohain-en-Vermandois France 49°59N 3°28E 173 C10
Bohdan Ukraine 48°2N 24°22E 183 B9
Bohemian Forest = Böhmerwald Germany 49°8N 13°14E 179 F9
Bohena Cr. → Australia 30°17S 149°42E 283 A8
Bohinjska Bistrica Slovenia 46°17N 14°1E 199 B11
Böhmerwald Germany 49°8N 13°14E 179 F9
Böhmisch-Brod = Český Brod Czechia 50°4N 14°52E 180 A7
Böhmisch-Leipa = Česká Lípa Czechia 50°45N 14°30E 180 A7
Böhmisch-Trübau = Česká Třebová Czechia 49°54N 16°27E 181 B9
Bohmte Germany 52°22N 8°19E 178 C4
Bohnsdorf Germany 52°23N 13°34E 115 B4
Bohodukhiv Ukraine 50°9N 35°33E 189 G8
Bohol Somalia 5°45N 46°9E 267 C6
Bohol □ Phil. 9°50N 124°10E 233 G5
Bohol Sea Phil. 9°0N 124°0E 233 G5
Bohol Str. Phil. 9°45N 123°40E 233 G4
Bohongou Burkina Faso 12°30N 0°40E 263 C5
Bőhönye Hungary 46°25N 17°28E 182 D2
Bohorodchany Ukraine 48°48N 24°32E 183 B9
Bohorok Indonesia 3°30N 98°12E 237 L2
Böhöt Mongolia 45°13N 108°16E 226 B5
Bohu China 41°58N 86°37E 217 D11
Bohuslän Sweden 58°25N 12°0E 163 F5
Bohuslev Ukraine 49°33N 30°56E 189 H6
Boi Nigeria 9°35N 9°27E 263 D6
Boi, Pta. do Brazil 23°55S 45°15W 335 A6
Boiaçu Brazil 0°27S 61°46W 329 D5
Boigu Australia 9°16S 142°13E 280 a
Boigu I. Australia 9°15S 142°14E 286 E2
Boileau, C. Australia 17°40S 122°7E 278 C3
Boim Brazil 2°49S 55°10W 329 D6
Boing'o South Sudan 9°58N 33°44E 257 F3
Boipariguda India 18°46N 82°26E 244 E6
Boipeba, I. de Brazil 13°39S 38°55W 333 D4
Boiro Spain 42°39N 8°54W 194 C2
Bois → Brazil 18°35S 50°2W 333 E1
Bois-Blanc Réunion 21°11S 55°49E 272 f
Bois-Colombes France 48°55N 2°16E 134 A2
Bois-d'Arcy France 48°48N 2°1E 134 B1
Boise U.S.A. 43°37N 116°13W 304 E5
Boise City U.S.A. 36°44N 102°31W 314 C3
Boissevain Canada 49°15N 100°5W 297 D8
Bois-St-Léger France 48°44N 2°31E 134 B4
Bóite → Italy 46°5N 12°5E 199 B9
Boitzenburg Germany 53°16N 13°35E 178 B9
Boizenburg Germany 53°23N 10°43E 178 B6
Bojador C. W. Sahara 26°0N 14°30W 260 C2
Bojador, C. W. Sahara 26°0N 14°30W 260 C2
Bojana → Albania 41°52N 19°22E 202 E3
Bojano Italy 41°29N 14°29E 201 A7
Bojanowo Poland 51°43N 16°42E 185 G3
Bøjden Denmark 55°6N 10°7E 163 J4
Bojnūrd Iran 37°30N 57°20E 247 B8
Bojonegoro Indonesia 7°11S 111°54E 235 D4
Boju Nigeria 7°22N 7°55E 263 D6
Boka Serbia 45°22N 20°52E 182 E5
Boka Kotorska Montenegro 42°23N 18°32E 202 D2
Bokada Dem. Rep. of the Congo 4°8N 19°23E 264 B3
Bokala Dem. Rep. of the Congo 3°13S 17°4E 264 C3
Bokala Ivory C. 8°31N 4°33W 262 D4
Bokani Nigeria 9°28N 5°10E 263 D6
Bokaro India 23°46N 85°55E 243 H11
Bokatola Dem. Rep. of the Congo 0°38S 18°46E 264 C3
Boké Guinea 10°56N 14°17W 262 C2
Bokela Dem. Rep. of the Congo 1°10S 21°59E 264 C4
Bokenda Dem. Rep. of the Congo 1°16N 21°21E 264 B4
Bokhara → Australia 29°55S 146°42E 281 D4
Bokkos Nigeria 9°17N 9°1E 263 D6
Boklar Dağları Turkey 37°5N 33°55E 250 A4
Boknafjorden Norway 59°14N 5°40E 164 E2
Boko Congo 4°46S 14°36E 265 C2
Bokode Dem. Rep. of the Congo 3°55N 19°30E 264 B3
Bokolo Gabon 2°40S 10°10E 264 C2
Bokondo Dem. Rep. of the Congo 0°15N 22°32E 264 B4
Bokor △ Cambodia 10°50N 104°1E 237 G5
Bokora ⌓ Uganda 2°12N 31°32E 268 B3
Bokoro Chad 12°25N 17°14E 259 F3
Bokota Dem. Rep. of the Congo 0°56S 22°24E 264 C4
Bokote Dem. Rep. of the Congo 0°12S 21°8E 264 C4
Bokpyin Burma 11°18N 98°42E 237 G2
Boksitogorsk Russia 59°22N 33°50E 188 C7
Boku Papua N. G. 6°34S 155°21E 286 D8
Bokungu Dem. Rep. of the Congo 0°35S 22°50E 264 C4
Bol Chad 13°30N 14°40E 259 F2
Bol Croatia 43°18N 16°38E 199 E13
Bolama Guinea-Biss. 11°30N 15°30W 262 C1
Bolan → Pakistan 28°38N 67°42E 242 E2
Bolan Pass Pakistan 29°50N 67°20E 240 C2
Bolaños → Mexico 21°12N 104°5W 318 C4
Bolaños de Calatrava Spain 38°54N 3°40W 195 G7
Bolayır Turkey 40°31N 26°45E 203 F10
Bolbec France 49°30N 0°30E 172 C7
Boldājī Iran 31°56N 51°3E 247 D6
Boldeşti-Scăeni Romania 45°3N 26°2E 183 E11
Boldinasco Italy 45°29N 9°8E 128 B1
Bole Xinjiang Uygur, China 44°55N 81°37E 217 C10
Bole Ethiopia 6°36N 37°20E 257 F4
Bole Ghana 9°3N 2°23W 262 D4
Bolekhiv Ukraine 49°0N 23°57E 177 D12
Boleko Dem. Rep. of the Congo 1°35S 19°50E 264 C3
Bøler Norway 59°53N 10°50E 133 A4
Bolesławiec Poland 51°17N 15°37E 185 G2
Bolgatanga Ghana 10°44N 0°53W 263 C4
Bolgrad = Bolhrad Ukraine 45°40N 28°32E 183 E13
Bolhrad Ukraine 45°40N 28°32E 183 E13
Bolia Dem. Rep. of the Congo 1°36S 18°22E 264 C3
Bolinao Phil. 16°23N 119°54E 232 C2
Bolinao, C. Phil. 16°23N 119°55E 232 C2
Bolingbroke U.S.A. 32°57N 83°48W 316 C6
Bolingbrook U.S.A. 41°42N 88°4W 311 C8
Bolingo Dem. Rep. of the Congo 3°31S 21°43E 264 C4
Bolintin-Vale Romania 44°27N 25°46E 183 F10
Bolívar Antioquia, Colombia 5°50N 76°1W 328 B2
Bolívar Cauca, Colombia 2°0N 77°0W 328 C2
Bolívar Peru 7°18S 77°48W 330 B2
Bolivar Mo., U.S.A. 37°37N 93°25W 308 G7
Bolivar N.Y., U.S.A. 42°4N 78°10W 312 D6
Bolivar Tenn., U.S.A. 35°12N 89°0W 315 D10
Bolívar □ Colombia 9°0N 74°40W 328 B3
Bolívar □ Ecuador 1°15S 79°5W 328 D2
Bolívar □ Venezuela 6°20N 63°30W 329 B5
Bolivia ■ S. Amer. 17°6S 64°0W 331 D5
Bolivian Plateau = Altiplano Bolivia 17°0S 68°0W 330 D4
Boljevac Serbia 43°51N 21°58E 202 C5
Bolkhov Russia 53°25N 36°0E 188 F9
Bolków Poland 50°55N 16°6E 185 H3
Bollate Italy 45°32N 9°7E 128 A1
Bollebeek Belgium 50°55N 4°14E 116 A1
Bollebygd Sweden 57°40N 12°35E 163 G6
Bollène France 44°18N 4°45E 175 D8
Bollensdorf Germany 52°30N 13°42E 115 A5
Bollmora Sweden 59°14N 18°14E 139 B3
Bollnäs Sweden 61°21N 16°24E 162 C10
Bollon Australia 28°2S 147°29E 281 D4
Bollstabruk Sweden 62°59N 17°40E 162 B11
Bolmen Sweden 56°55N 13°40E 163 H7
Bolnisi Georgia 41°26N 44°32E 191 K7
Bolobo Dem. Rep. of the Congo 2°6S 16°20E 264 C3
Bologna Italy 44°29N 11°20E 199 D8
Bologna ✕ (BLQ) Italy 44°34N 11°16E 199 D8
Bologoye Russia 57°55N 34°5E 188 D8
Bolomba Dem. Rep. of the Congo 0°35N 19°0E 264 B3
Bolombo → Dem. Rep. of the Congo 1°32N 21°14E 264 B4
Bolonchén Mexico 20°1N 89°45W 319 D7
Bolondo Dem. Rep. of the Congo 2°12S 18°42E 264 C3
Bolong Chad 12°3N 17°45E 259 F3
Bolong Phil. 7°6N 122°14E 233 H4
Bolongongo Angola 8°28S 15°16E 265 D3
Bolótana Italy 40°20N 8°52E 200 B1
Boloven, Cao Nguyen Laos 15°10N 106°30E 236 E6
Bolpur India 23°40N 87°45E 243 H12
Bolsena Italy 42°39N 11°59E 199 F8
Bolsena, L. di Italy 42°36N 11°56E 199 F8
Bolshakovo Russia 54°53N 21°40E 184 D8
Bolshaya Chernigovka Russia 52°6N 50°52E 190 D10
Bolshaya Garmanda = Evensk Russia 62°12N 159°30E 215 C16
Bolshaya Glushitsa Russia 52°28N 50°30E 190 D10
Bolshaya Martynovka Russia 47°19N 41°37E 191 G5
Bolshaya Okhta Russia 59°56N 30°26E 137 B2
Bolshaya Tsaryovshchina = Volzhskiy Russia 48°56N 44°46E 191 F7
Bolshaya Vradiyevka Ukraine 47°50N 30°40E 189 J6
Bolshevik, Ostrov Russia 78°30N 102°0E 215 B11
Bolshoi Theatre Russia 129 b2
Bolshoy Anyuy → Russia 68°30N 160°49E 215 C17
Bolshoy Begichev, Ostrov Russia 74°20N 112°30E 215 B12
Bolshoy Kamen Russia 43°7N 132°19E 220 C6
Bolshoy Kavkas = Caucasus Mountains Eurasia 42°50N 44°0E 191 J7
Bolshoy Lyakhovskiy, Ostrov Russia 73°35N 142°0E 215 B15
Bolshoy Tokmak = Tokmak Kyrgyzstan 42°49N 75°15E 217 D9
Bolshoy Tyuters, Ostrov Russia 59°51N 27°13E 188 C4
Bólstaðarhlíð Iceland 65°31N 19°49W 155 B7
Bolsward Neths. 53°3N 5°32E 170 A5
Bolt Head U.K. 50°12N 3°48W 169 G4
Boltaña Spain 42°28N 0°4E 196 C5
Boltigen Switz. 46°38N 7°24E 179 J3
Bolton Ont., Canada 43°54N 79°45W 312 C5
Bolton Gt. Man., U.K. 53°35N 2°26W 168 D5
Bolton Georgia, U.S.A. 33°48N 84°28W 113 B2
Bolton Landing U.S.A. 43°32N 73°35W 313 C11
Bolu Turkey 40°45N 31°35E 212 B4
Bolu □ Turkey 40°40N 31°30E 212 B4
Bolubolu Papua N. G. 9°21S 150°20E 286 E6
Bolungavík Iceland 66°9N 23°15W 155 A3
Boluo China 23°3N 114°21E 229 F10
Bolvadin Turkey 38°45N 31°4E 212 C4
Bolzano Italy 46°31N 11°22E 199 B8
Bom Comércio Brazil 9°45S 65°54W 331 B4
Bom Conselho Brazil 9°10S 36°41W 332 C4
Bom Despacho Brazil 19°43S 45°15W 333 E2
Bom Jesus Angola 9°11S 13°34E 265 D2
Bom Jesus Brazil 9°4S 44°22W 332 C3
Bom Jesus da Gurguéia, Serra Brazil 9°0S 43°0W 332 C3
Bom Jesus da Lapa Brazil 13°15S 43°25W 333 D3
Bom Retiro Brazil 23°31S 46°38W 137 B2
Boma Dem. Rep. of the Congo 5°50S 13°4E 265 D2
Boma △ South Sudan 7°0N 34°0E 257 F3
Bomaderry Australia 34°52S 150°37E 283 C9
Bomandjokou Congo 0°34N 14°23E 264 B2
Bomaneh Dem. Rep. of the Congo 1°18N 23°47E 264 B4
Bomassa Congo 2°12N 16°12E 264 B3
Bomate Dem. Rep. of the Congo 2°14N 25°15E 264 C3
Bombala Australia 36°56S 149°15E 283 D8
Bombarral Portugal 39°15N 9°9W 195 F1
Bombay = Mumbai India 18°56N 72°50E 130 B2
Bombay U.S.A. 44°56N 74°34W 313 B10
Bombedor, Pta. Venezuela 9°53N 61°37W 329 B5
Bomberai, Semenanjung Indonesia 3°0S 133°0E 231 E8
Bombo Kasani Dem. Rep. of the Congo 5°51S 21°54E 265 D4
Bomboma Dem. Rep. of the Congo 2°25N 18°55E 264 B3
Bombombwa Dem. Rep. of the Congo 1°40N 25°40E 268 B2
Bomboyo Chad 12°1N 15°28E 259 F3
Bomdila India 27°18N 92°22E 241 B4
Bomdo India 28°44N 94°54E 241 A5
Bomet Kenya 0°47S 35°21E 266 E4
Bomi China 29°50N 95°45E 218 F8
Bomi Liberia 7°1N 10°38W 262 D2
Bomili Dem. Rep. of the Congo 1°45N 27°5E 268 B2
Bømlo Norway 59°37N 5°13E 164 E2
Bomokandi → Dem. Rep. of the Congo 3°39N 26°8E 268 B2
Bomongo Dem. Rep. of the Congo 1°27N 18°21E 264 B3
Bompoka India 8°15N 93°13E 245 K11
Bomputu Dem. Rep. of the Congo 0°23S 20°6E 264 C4
Bomst = Babimost Poland 52°10N 15°49E 185 F2
Bomu → C.A.R. 4°40N 22°30E 264 B4
Bomu Occidentale ⌓ Dem. Rep. of the Congo 4°48N 24°17E 264 B4
Bomu Orientale ⌓ Dem. Rep. of the Congo 5°0N 25°50E 264 B2
Bon, C. = Ra's aṭ Ṭib Tunisia 37°1N 11°2E 258 A2
Bon Acceuil Mauritius 20°10S 57°39E 272 e
Bon Echo ⌓ Canada 44°55N 77°16W 312 B7
Bon Sar Pa Vietnam 12°24N 107°35E 236 F6
Bona, Mt. U.S.A. 61°23N 141°45W 303 F12
Bonāb Āzarbājān-e Sharqī, Iran 37°20N 46°4E 213 D12
Bonāb Zanjān, Iran 36°35N 48°41E 213 D13
Bonaigarh India 21°50N 84°57E 243 J11
Bonaire Ga., U.S.A. 32°33N 83°36W 316 C6
Bonaire W. Indies 12°10N 68°15W 322 h
Bonampak Mexico 16°44N 91°5W 319 D6
Bonang Australia 37°11S 148°41E 283 D8
Bonanza Nic. 13°54N 84°35W 320 D3
Bonaparte Arch. Australia 14°0S 124°30E 278 B3
Bonaparte Rocks Grenada 12°24N 61°30W 323 q
Boñar Spain 42°52N 5°19W 194 C5
Bonar Bridge U.K. 57°54N 4°20W 167 D4
Bonasse Trin. & Tob. 10°5N 61°54W 323 t
Bonaventure Canada 48°5N 65°32W 299 C6
Bonaventure, Place Montréal, Canada 130 c2
Bonavista Canada 48°40N 53°5W 299 C9
Bonavista, C. Canada 48°42N 53°5W 299 C9
Bonavista B. Canada 48°45N 53°25W 299 C9
Bondeno Italy 44°53N 11°25E 199 D8
Bondi Australia 33°53S 151°16E 139 B2
Bondo Équateur, Dem. Rep. of the Congo 1°22S 23°54E 264 C4
Bondo Orientale, Dem. Rep. of the Congo 3°55N 23°53E 264 B4
Bondoc Pen. Phil. 13°26N 122°33E 232 E4
Bondokodi Indonesia 9°33S 119°0E 278 A2
Bondoukou Ivory C. 8°2N 2°47W 262 D4
Bondowoso Indonesia 7°55S 113°49E 235 D4
Bondy France 48°54N 2°28E 134 A3
Bondy, Forêt de France 48°54N 2°33E 134 A4
Bône = Annaba Algeria 36°50N 7°46E 261 A6
Bone, Teluk Indonesia 4°10S 120°50E 231 E6
Bonefish Pond Bahamas 24°59N 77°23W 153 b
Bonerate Indonesia 7°25S 121°5E 231 F6
Bonerate, Kepulauan Indonesia 6°30S 121°10E 231 F6
Bo'ness U.K. 56°1N 3°37W 167 E5
Bonete, Cerro Argentina 27°55S 68°40W 334 B2
Bonfim = Senhor-do-Bonfim Brazil 10°30S 40°10W 332 D3
Bonfim Brazil 3°33N 59°25W 329 C6
Bong Son = Hoai Nhon Vietnam 14°28N 109°1E 236 E7
Bonga Ethiopia 7°15N 36°14E 257 F4
Bongabon Phil. 15°38N 121°8E 232 D3
Bongabong Phil. 12°45N 121°29E 232 E3
Bongaigaon India 26°28N 90°34E 241 B3
Bongandanga Dem. Rep. of the Congo 1°24N 21°3E 264 B4
Bongao Phil. 5°2N 119°46E 233 J2
Bongo Dem. Rep. of the Congo 1°47S 17°41E 264 C3
Bongo, Sa. de Angola 10°3S 15°15E 265 E3
Bongo I. Phil. 7°20N 124°3E 233 H5
Bongolava □ Madag. 18°45S 46°0E 272 B2
Bongor Chad 10°35N 15°20E 259 F3
Bongos, Massif des C.A.R. 8°40N 22°25E 264 A4
Bongouanou Ivory C. 6°42N 4°15W 262 D4
Bonham U.S.A. 33°35N 96°11W 314 E6
Boni Mali 15°3N 2°10W 262 B4
Boni ⌓ Kenya 1°35S 41°18E 268 C5
Bonifacio France 41°24N 9°10E 175 G13
Bonifacio, Bouches de Medit. S. 41°12N 9°15E 200 A2
Bonifacio Monument Phil. 14°38N 120°58E 127 B1
Bonifay U.S.A. 30°47N 85°41W 316 E4
Bonin Is. = Ogasawara Gunto Pac. Oc. 27°0N 142°0E 288 E6
Bonita Springs U.S.A. 26°21N 81°47W 317 J8
Bonito Brazil 21°8S 56°28W 331 E6
Bonjol Indonesia 0°1S 100°13E 234 C2
Bonke Ethiopia 6°5N 37°16E 257 F4
Bonkoukou Niger 14°0N 3°15E 263 C5
Bonn Germany 50°46N 7°6E 178 E3
Bonnabel Place U.S.A. 30°0N 90°8W 131 A2
Bonnat France 46°20N 1°54E 173 F8
Bonne Terre U.S.A. 37°55N 90°33W 310 G6
Bonneau U.S.A. 33°16N 79°58W 316 B10
Bonners Ferry U.S.A. 48°42N 116°19W 304 B5
Bonnétable France 48°11N 0°25E 172 D7
Bonneuil-sur-Marne France 48°46N 2°30E 134 B4
Bonneval France 45°22N 7°3E 175 C11
Bonneval-sur-Arc France 48°11N 1°24E 172 D8
Bonneville France 46°4N 6°24E 173 F13
Bonney, L. Australia 37°50S 140°20E 282 D4
Bonnie Doon Australia 37°2S 145°53E 283 D6
Bonnie Rock Australia 30°29S 118°22E 279 F2
Bonnington U.K. 55°54N 3°25W 121 B1
Bonny Nigeria 4°25N 7°13E 263 E6
Bonny → Nigeria 4°20N 7°10E 263 E6
Bonny, Bight of Africa 3°30N 9°20E 263 E6
Bonny Hills Australia 31°36S 152°51E 283 A10
Bonny-sur-Loire France 47°33N 2°50E 173 E9
Bonnyrigg U.K. 55°53N 3°6W 167 F5
Bonnyrigg and Lasswade U.K. 55°52N 3°6W 121 B3
Bonnyville Canada 54°20N 110°45W 297 C6
Bono Italy 40°25N 8°46E 200 B1
Bonoi Indonesia 1°45S 137°41E 231 E9
Bonorva Italy 40°25N 8°46E 200 B1
Bonsall U.S.A. 33°16N 117°14W 307 M9
Bonsucesso Brazil 22°51S 43°15W 135 B1
Bontang Indonesia 0°10N 117°30E 235 B5
Bontebok △ S. Africa 34°5S 20°28E 270 D3
Bonteheuwel S. Africa 33°57S 18°33E 118 A2
Bonthe S. Leone 7°30N 12°33W 262 D2
Bontoc Phil. 17°7N 120°58E 232 C3
Bontosunggu Indonesia 5°41S 119°42E 235 D5
Bonyeri Ghana 5°1N 2°46W 262 D4
Bonyhád Hungary 46°18N 18°32E 182 D3
Bonython Ra. Australia 23°40S 128°45E 278 D4
Boo Sweden 59°20N 18°16E 139 A3
Booderee △ Australia 35°12S 150°42E 283 C9
Boodjamulla △ Australia 18°15S 138°6E 280 B2
Bookabie Australia 31°50S 132°41E 279 F5
Booke Dem. Rep. of the Congo 2°34S 22°3E 264 C4
Booker U.S.A. 36°27N 100°32W 314 C4
Bool Lagoon Australia 37°7S 140°40E 282 D4
Boola Guinea 8°22N 8°41W 262 D3
Boolcoomata Australia 31°57S 140°33E 282 A4
Booleroo Centre Australia 32°53S 138°21E 282 B3
Booligal Australia 33°58S 144°53E 283 B6
Boon Pt. Antigua & B. 17°10N 61°50W 322 b
Böön Tsagaan Nuur Mongolia 45°35N 99°9E 218 B8
Boonah Australia 27°58S 152°41E 281 D5
Boone Iowa, U.S.A. 42°4N 93°53W 310 B3
Boone N.C., U.S.A. 36°13N 81°41W 315 C14
Booneville Ark., U.S.A. 35°8N 93°55W 314 D8
Booneville Miss., U.S.A. 34°39N 88°34W 315 D10
Boonville Calif., U.S.A. 39°1N 123°22W 306 F3
Boonville Ind., U.S.A. 38°3N 87°16W 311 F9
Boonville Mo., U.S.A. 38°58N 92°44W 310 F4
Boonville N.Y., U.S.A. 43°29N 75°20W 313 C9
Boorabbin △ Australia 31°30S 120°10E 279 F3
Boorama Somalia 9°55N 43°7E 267 C5
Boorindal Australia 30°22S 146°11E 281 E4
Boorowa Australia 34°28S 148°44E 283 C8
Boort Australia 36°7S 143°46E 282 D5
Boosaaso Somalia 11°12N 49°18E 267 B6
Boothia, Gulf of Canada 71°0N 90°0W 294 C14
Boothia Pen. Canada 71°0N 94°0W 294 C13
Bootle U.K. 53°28N 3°1W 168 D4
Booué Gabon 0°5S 11°55E 264 C2
Bopako Dem. Rep. of the Congo 1°53N 21°13E 264 B4
Bopolu Liberia 7°4N 10°29W 262 D2
Boppard Germany 50°13N 7°35E 179 E3
Boquerón □ Paraguay 23°0S 60°0W 331 E6
Boquilla, Presa de la Mexico 27°31N 105°30W 318 B3
Boquillas del Carmen Mexico 29°11N 102°58W 318 B4
Bor Czechia 49°41N 12°45E 180 B5
Bor Russia 56°28N 43°59E 190 B7
Bor Serbia 44°5N 22°7E 202 B6
Bor South Sudan 6°10N 31°40E 257 F3
Bor Sweden 57°9N 14°10E 163 G8
Bor Turkey 37°54N 34°32E 212 D6
Bor, Lagh → Kenya 0°18N 40°40E 267 D5
Bor Mashash Israel 31°7N 34°50E 251 G5
Bor u Ceske Lipy = Nový Bor Czechia 50°46N 14°35E 180 A7
Bora Bora French Polynesia 16°30S 151°45W 289 f
Borah Peak U.S.A. 44°8N 113°47W 304 D7
Boraha, Nosy Madag. 16°50S 49°55E 272 B2
Borang South Sudan 4°50N 30°59E 257 G3
Borangapara India 25°14N 90°14E 241 C3
Borankul Kazakhstan 46°11N 54°25E 216 C4
Borås Sweden 57°43N 12°56E 163 G6
Borāzjān Iran 29°22N 51°10E 247 D6
Borba Brazil 4°12S 59°34W 329 D6
Borba Portugal 38°50N 7°26W 195 G3
Borbon Phil. 10°50N 124°2E 233 F5
Borborema, Planalto da Brazil 7°0S 37°0W 332 C4
Borča Serbia 44°52N 20°28E 202 B4
Borcea Romania 44°20N 27°45E 183 F12
Borchalo = Marneuli Georgia 41°30N 44°48E 191 K7
Borçka Turkey 41°25N 41°41E 213 B9
Bord Khūn-e Now Iran 28°3N 51°28E 247 D6
Borda, C. Australia 35°45S 136°34E 282 C2
Bordeaux France 44°50N 0°36W 174 D3
Bordeaux ✕ (BOD) France 44°50N 0°35W 174 D3
Borden Australia 34°3S 118°12E 279 F2
Borden-Carleton Canada 46°18N 63°47W 299 C7
Borden I. Canada 78°30N 111°30W 295 B9
Borden Pen. Canada 73°0N 83°0W 295 C15
Borden Springs U.S.A. 33°56N 85°28W 316 B4
Border Ranges △ Australia 28°24S 152°56E 281 D5
Borders = Scottish Borders □ U.K. 55°35N 2°50W 167 F6
Bordertown Australia 36°19S 140°45E 282 D4
Borðeyri Iceland 65°12N 21°6W 155 B5
Bordighera Italy 43°46N 7°39E 198 E4
Bordj bou Arreridj Algeria 36°4N 4°45E 261 A5
Bordj Bourguiba Tunisia 32°12N 10°2E 258 B2
Bordj Flye Ste-Marie Algeria 27°19N 2°32W 260 C4
Bordj in Eker Algeria 24°9N 5°3E 261 D6
Bordj Menaïel Algeria 36°46N 3°43E 261 A5
Bordj Messouda Algeria 30°12N 9°25E 261 B6
Bordj Mokhtar Algeria 21°20N 0°56E 261 D5
Bordj Nili Algeria 33°28N 3°2E 261 B5
Bordj Omar Driss Algeria 28°10N 6°40E 261 C6
Bordj Sif Fatima Algeria 31°6N 8°41E 261 B6
Bordj Tarat Algeria 25°55N 9°3E 261 C6
Borduttighat India 26°57N 93°58E 241 B4
Bore Ethiopia 4°39N 37°39E 257 G4
Borehamwood U.K. 51°40N 0°15W 169 F7
Borek Wielkopolski Poland 51°54N 17°11E 185 G4
Borensberg Sweden 58°34N 15°17E 163 F9
Borgå = Porvoo Finland 60°24N 25°40E 188 B3
Borgampad India 17°39N 80°52E 244 F5
Borgarfjarðarsýsla Iceland 64°30N 21°30W 155 C5
Borgarfjörður Austurland Iceland 65°33N 13°47W 155 B13
Borgarfjörður Vesturland Iceland 64°30N 22°0W 155 C4
Borgarnes Iceland 64°32N 21°55W 155 C5
Børgefjellet Norway 65°20N 13°45E 160 D15
Borger Neths. 52°54N 6°44E 170 B6
Borger Tex., U.S.A. 35°39N 101°24W 314 D4
Borgholm Sweden 56°52N 16°39E 163 H10
Bòrgia Italy 38°49N 16°30E 201 D9
Borgnesse, Pte. Martinique 14°26N 60°54W 322 j
Borgo San Dalmazzo Italy 44°20N 7°30E 198 D4
Borgo San Donnino = Fidenza Italy 44°52N 10°3E 198 D7
Borgo San Lorenzo Italy 43°57N 11°23E 199 E8
Borgo Val di Taro Italy 44°29N 9°46E 198 D6
Borgo Valsugana Italy 46°3N 11°27E 199 B8
Borgomanero Italy 45°42N 8°28E 198 C5
Borgorose Italy 42°11N 13°13E 199 F10
Borgosèsia Italy 45°43N 8°16E 198 C5
Borgotaro = Borgo Val di Taro Italy 44°29N 9°46E 198 D6
Borgund Norway 61°3N 7°48E 164 C4
Borhoyn Tal Mongolia 43°50N 111°58E 226 C6
Bori Nigeria 4°42N 7°21E 263 E6
Borigumma India 19°3N 82°33E 244 E6
Borikhane Laos 18°33N 103°43E 236 C4
Borisoglebsk Russia 51°27N 42°5E 190 E6
Borisov = Barysaw Belarus 54°17N 28°28E 177 A15
Borisovgrad = Pŭrvomay Bulgaria 42°8N 25°17E 203 D9
Borisovka Russia 50°36N 36°1E 189 G9
Borisovo Russia 55°38N 37°44E 129 C3
Borj Jenein Tunisia 31°45N 10°9E 258 B2
Borja Peru 4°20S 77°40W 328 D2
Borja Spain 41°48N 1°34W 196 D3
Borjas Blancas = Les Borges Blanques Spain 41°31N 0°52E 196 D5
Borjomi Georgia 41°48N 43°28E 191 K6
Børkop Denmark 55°39N 9°39E 163 J3
Borkou Chad 18°15N 18°50E 259 E3
Borkou □ Chad 18°0N 18°0E 259 E3
Borkum Germany 53°34N 6°40E 178 B2
Borlänge Sweden 60°29N 15°26E 162 D9
Borle India 19°2N 72°54E 130 A2
Borley, C. Antarctica 66°15S 52°30E 151 C5
Borlu Turkey 38°44N 28°27E 205 C10
Bormida → Italy 44°23N 8°13E 198 D5
Bórmio Italy 46°28N 10°22E 198 B7
Borna Germany 51°7N 12°29E 178 D8
Borne Sulinowo Poland 53°32N 16°36E 184 E3
Borneo E. Indies 1°0N 115°0E 235 B4
Bornholm Denmark 55°10N 15°0E 163 J8
Bornholmsgattet Europe 55°15N 14°20E 163 J8
Borno □ Nigeria 11°30N 13°0E 263 C7
Bornos Spain 36°48N 5°42W 195 J5
Bornova Turkey 38°27N 27°14E 205 C9
Bornu Yassa Nigeria 12°14N 12°25E 263 C7
Boro → South Sudan 8°52N 26°11E 257 F2
Borobudur △ Indonesia 7°36S 110°12E 231 G14
Borobudur Indonesia 7°40S 110°11E 235 D4
Borocay I. Phil. 11°58N 121°55E 233 F3
Borodino Russia 55°31N 35°40E 188 E8
Borodino Ukraine 46°18N 29°15E 183 D14
Borogontsy Russia 62°42N 131°8E 215 C14
Borohoro Shan China 44°6N 83°10E 217 D10
Boromo Burkina Faso 11°45N 2°58W 262 C4
Boron U.S.A. 35°0N 117°39W 307 L9
Borong Indonesia 8°36S 120°3E 235 D6
Borongan Phil. 11°37N 125°26E 233 F5
Borotangba Mts. C.A.R. 6°30N 25°0E 257 F2
Borotou Ivory C. 8°46N 7°30W 262 D3
Borovan Bulgaria 43°27N 23°45E 202 C7
Borovichi Russia 58°25N 33°55E 188 C7
Borovsk Russia 55°12N 36°24E 188 E9
Borovskoy Kazakhstan 53°48N 64°9E 216 B6
Borrby Sweden 55°27N 14°10E 163 J8
Borrego Springs U.S.A. 33°15N 116°23W 307 M10
Borriol Spain 40°4N 0°4W 196 E4
Borrisokane Ireland 53°0N 8°7W 166 D3
Borroloola Australia 16°4S 136°17E 280 B2
Borşa Cluj, Romania 46°56N 23°40E 183 D8
Borşa Maramureş, Romania 47°41N 24°50E 183 C9
Borsad India 22°25N 72°54E 242 H5
Borsec Romania 46°57N 25°34E 183 D10
Borshchiv Ukraine 48°48N 26°3E 183 B11
Borsod-Abaúj-Zemplén □ Hungary 48°20N 21°0E 182 B6
Bort-les-Orgues France 45°24N 2°29E 174 C6
Bortala = Bole China 44°55N 81°37E 217 C10
Borth U.K. 52°29N 4°2W 169 E3
Börtnan Sweden 62°45N 13°50E 162 B7
Borūjerd Iran 33°55N 48°50E 213 F13
Boryeong S. Korea 36°21N 126°36E 224 D3
Borynya Ukraine 49°4N 23°0E 185 J10
Boryslav Ukraine 49°18N 23°28E 185 J10
Boryspil Ukraine 50°21N 30°59E 189 G6
Borzhomi = Borjomi Georgia 41°48N 43°28E 191 K6
Borzna Ukraine 51°18N 32°26E 189 G7
Borzya Russia 50°24N 116°31E 219 A12
Bosa Italy 40°18N 8°30E 200 B1
Bosa Monene Dem. Rep. of the Congo 1°16S 23°40E 264 C4
Bosaga Turkmenistan 37°33N 65°41E 240 A2
Bosambi Dem. Rep. of the Congo 2°24N 22°39E 264 B4
Bosanska Dubica = Dubica Bos.-H. 45°10N 16°50E 199 C13
Bosanska Gradiška = Gradiška Bos.-H. 45°10N 17°15E 182 E2
Bosanska Kostajnica = Kostajnica Bos.-H. 45°11N 16°33E 199 C13
Bosanska Krupa Bos.-H. 44°53N 16°10E 199 D13
Bosanski Brod = Brod Bos.-H. 45°10N 18°0E 182 E2
Bosanski Novi = Novi Grad Bos.-H. 45°2N 16°22E 199 C13
Bosanski Petrovac Bos.-H. 44°35N 16°21E 199 D13
Bosanski Šamac = Šamac Bos.-H. 45°3N 18°29E 182 E3
Bosansko Grahovo Bos.-H. 44°12N 16°26E 199 D13
Bosavi, Mt. Papua N. G. 6°30S 142°49E 286 D2
Boscastle U.K. 50°41N 4°42W 169 G3
Boscobel U.S.A. 43°8N 90°42W 310 A6
Boscobelle Barbados 13°17N 59°35W 323 r
Bose China 23°53N 106°35E 228 F6
Boseki Dem. Rep. of the Congo 2°34S 19°38E 264 C3
Boseong S. Korea 34°46N 127°5E 224 E3
Boshan China 36°28N 117°49E 227 F9
Boshof S. Africa 28°31S 25°13E 270 C4
Boshrūyeh Iran 33°50N 57°30E 247 C8
Bosilegrad Serbia 42°30N 22°27E 202 D6
Boskovice Czechia 49°29N 16°40E 181 B9
Bosmont S. Africa 26°10S 27°57E 123 B1
Bosna → Bos.-H. 45°4N 18°29E 182 E3
Bosna i Hercegovina = Bosnia-Herzegovina ■ Europe 44°0N 18°0E 182 G2
Bosnia-Herzegovina ■ Europe 44°0N 18°0E 182 G2
Bosnik Indonesia 1°5S 136°10E 231 E9
Bōsō-Hantō Japan 35°20N 140°20E 223 B12
Bosobolo Dem. Rep. of the Congo 4°15N 19°50E 264 B3
Bosön Sweden 59°22N 18°11E 139 A3
Bosporus = İstanbul Boğazı Turkey 41°5N 29°3E 122 B2
Bosque Farms U.S.A. 35°51N 106°42W 305 J10
Bosra = Buşra ash Shām Syria 32°30N 36°25E 251 F7
Bossangoa C.A.R. 6°35N 17°30E 264 A3
Bossé Bangou Niger 13°20N 1°18E 263 C5
Bossembélé C.A.R. 5°25N 17°40E 264 A3
Bossemtélé C.A.R. 5°41N 16°38E 264 A3
Bossier City U.S.A. 32°31N 93°44W 314 E8
Bossiesvlei Namibia 25°1S 16°44E 270 C2
Bosso Niger 13°43N 13°19E 259 F2
Bosso, Dallol → Niger 12°25N 2°50E 263 C5
Bostan Pakistan 30°26N 67°2E 242 D2
Bostānābād Iran 37°50N 46°50E 213 D12
Bostancı Turkey 40°57N 29°5E 122 C2
Bosten Hu China 41°55N 87°40E 217 D11
Boston Phil. 7°52N 126°22E 233 H6
Boston Lincs., U.K. 52°59N 0°2W 168 E7
Boston Ga., U.S.A. 30°47N 83°47W 316 E6
Boston Mass., U.S.A. 42°22N 71°3W 116 A2
Boston Bar Canada 49°52N 121°30W 296 D4

Boston Bay *Jamaica* 18°9N 76°22W **320** a
Boston Common *Boston, U.S.A.* **116** c1
Boston Logan Int. ✈ **(BOS)** *U.S.A.* 42°22N 71°1W **116** A2
Boston Mts. *U.S.A.* 35°42N 93°15W **314** D8
Boston Tea Party Ship & Museum *Boston, U.S.A.* **116** c3
Bostwick *U.S.A.* 29°46N 81°38W **316** F8
Bosumtwi, L. *Ghana* 6°30N 1°25W **263** D4
Bosusulu *Dem. Rep. of the Congo* 0°50N 20°45E **264** B4
Bosut → *Croatia* 45°20N 18°45E **182** E3
Boswell *B.C., Canada* 49°28N 116°45W **296** D5
Boswell *Ind., U.S.A.* 40°31N 87°23W **311** D9
Boswell *Pa., U.S.A.* 40°10N 79°2W **312** F5
Bosworth *U.S.A.* 39°28N 93°20W **310** E3
Botad *India* 22°15N 71°40E **242** H4
Botafogo *Brazil* 22°56S 43°10W **135** B1
Botan → *Turkey* 37°57N 42°2E **213** D10
Botanic Gardens *Washington, D.C., U.S.A.* **143** b3
Botanisk Have *Copenhagen, Denmark* **118** b2
Botany *Australia* 33°56S 151°12E **139** B2
Botany B. *Australia* 33°58S 151°11E **139** B2
Botany Bay △ *Australia* 34°0S 151°14E **139** B2
Botene *Laos* 17°35N 101°12E **236** D3
Botera *Angola* 11°37S 14°16E **265** E2
Botev *Bulgaria* 42°44N 24°52E **203** D8
Botevgrad *Bulgaria* 42°55N 23°47E **202** D7
Bothaville *S. Africa* 27°23S 26°34E **270** C4
Bothnia, G. of *Europe* 62°0N 20°0E **160** F19
Bothwell *Tas., Australia* 42°20S 147°1E **281** G4
Bothwell *Ont., Canada* 42°38N 81°52W **312** D3
Botič → *Czechia* 50°4N 14°26E **135** B3
Botica Sete *Portugal* 38°49N 9°10W **126** A1
Boticas *Portugal* 41°41N 7°40W **194** D3
Botletle → *Botswana* 20°10S 23°15E **270** B3
Botlikh *Russia* 42°39N 46°11E **191** J8
Botna → *Moldova* 46°45N 29°34E **183** D14
Botola *Dem. Rep. of the Congo* 1°17S 18°13E **264** C3
Botolan *Phil.* 15°17N 120°1E **232** D3
Botoroaga *Romania* 44°8N 25°32E **183** F10
Botoşani *Romania* 47°42N 26°41E **183** C11
Botoşani □ *Romania* 47°50N 26°50E **183** C11
Botou *Burkina Faso* 12°42N 1°59E **263** C5
Botou *China* 38°4N 116°34E **226** E9
Botricello *Italy* 38°56N 16°51E **201** D9
Botro *Ivory C.* 7°51N 5°19W **262** D3
Botshabelo *S. Africa* 29°14S 26°44E **270** C4
Botswana ■ *Africa* 22°0S 24°0E **270** B3
Bottelier *Curaçao* 12°6N 68°54W **322** g
Bottineau *U.S.A.* 48°50N 100°27W **308** A3
Bottnaryd *Sweden* 57°47N 13°50E **163** G7
Bottom, The *Saba* 17°38N 63°15W **322** a
Bottopassi *Suriname* 4°14N 55°27W **329** C6
Bottrop *Germany* 51°31N 6°58E **178** D2
Botucatu *Brazil* 22°55S 48°30W **335** A6
Botum Sakor △ *Cambodia* 11°5N 103°15E **237** G4
Botwood *Canada* 49°6N 55°23W **299** C8
Bou Alam *Algeria* 33°50N 1°26E **261** B5
Bou Ali *Algeria* 27°11N 0°4W **261** C4
Bou Djébéha *Mali* 18°25N 2°45W **262** B4
Bou Guema *Algeria* 28°49N 0°19E **261** C5
Bou Ismaïl *Algeria* 36°38N 2°42E **261** A5
Bou Izakarn *Morocco* 29°12N 9°46W **260** C3
Boû Lanouâr *Mauritania* 21°12N 16°34W **260** D1
Boû Naga *Mauritania* 18°49N 13°20W **262** B2
Bou Noura *Algeria* 32°29N 3°43E **261** B5
Boû Rjeïmât *Mauritania* 19°4N 15°3W **262** B1
Bou Saâda *Algeria* 35°11N 4°9E **261** A5
Bou Salem *Tunisia* 36°45N 9°2E **258** A1
Bouaflé *Ivory C.* 7°1N 5°47W **262** D3
Bouaké *Ivory C.* 7°40N 5°2W **262** D3
Bouanga *Congo* 2°7S 16°8E **264** C3
Bouar *C.A.R.* 6°0N 15°40E **264** A3
Bouârfa *Morocco* 32°32N 1°58W **261** B4
Bouba Ndjida △ *Cameroon* 8°50N 14°45E **264** A2
Boubout *Algeria* 27°26N 4°30W **260** C4
Bouca *C.A.R.* 6°45N 18°25E **264** A3
Boucaut B. *Australia* 12°0S 134°25E **280** A1
Boucherville *Canada* 45°36N 73°28W **130** A3
Boucherville, Îs. de *Canada* 45°36N 73°28W **130** A3
Bouches-du-Rhône □ *France* 43°37N 5°2E **175** E9
Boucle de Baoulé △ *Mali* 13°53N 9°0W **262** C3
Boucles de la Seine Normande ⌓ *France* 49°32N 0°35E **172** C7
Bouctouche *Canada* 46°30N 64°45W **299** C7
Bouda *Algeria* 27°50N 0°27W **261** C4
Boudenib *Morocco* 31°59N 3°31W **260** B4
Bouéni *Mayotte* 12°54S 45°4E **272** b
Bouéni, B. de *Mayotte* 12°55S 45°7E **272** b
Bouenza □ *Congo* 4°30S 13°0E **264** C2
Boufarik *Algeria* 36°34N 2°58E **261** A5
Bougainville □ *Papua N. G.* 4°0S 155°0E **286** B8
Bougainville, C. *Australia* 13°57S 126°4E **278** B4
Bougainville I. *Papua N. G.* 6°0S 155°0E **277** B10
Bougainville Reef *Australia* 15°30S 147°5E **280** B4
Bougainville Str. *Solomon Is.* 6°40S 156°10E **287** L9
Bougaroun, C. *Algeria* 37°6N 6°30E **261** A6
Bougie = Bejaïa *Algeria* 36°42N 5°2E **261** A6
Bougival *France* 48°51N 2°8E **134** A1
Bougouni *Mali* 11°30N 7°20W **262** C3
Bougtob *Algeria* 34°2N 0°5E **261** B5
Bouillante *Guadeloupe* 16°8N 61°46W **322** e
Bouillante, Pitons de *Guadeloupe* 16°8N 61°43W **322** e
Bouillon *Belgium* 49°44N 5°3E **170** E5
Bouïra *Algeria* 36°20N 3°59E **261** A5
Bouïra □ *Algeria* 36°15N 3°55E **261** A5
Boukombé *Benin* 10°13N 1°9E **263** C5
Boulal *Mali* 15°8N 8°21W **262** B3
Boulazac *France* 45°10N 0°47E **174** C4
Boulder *Colo., U.S.A.* 40°1N 105°17W **304** F11
Boulder *Mont., U.S.A.* 46°14N 112°7W **304** C7
Boulder City *U.S.A.* 35°58N 114°49W **307** K12
Boulder Creek *U.S.A.* 37°7N 122°7W **306** H4
Boulder Dam = Hoover Dam *U.S.A.* 36°1N 114°44W **307** K12
Boulder Pt. *Hong Kong, China* 22°14N 114°6E **122** B2
Boulembo *Gabon* 1°26S 12°0E **264** C2
Bouli *Mauritania* 15°17N 12°18W **262** B2
Boulia *Australia* 22°52S 139°51E **280** C2
Bouligny *France* 49°17N 5°45E **173** C12
Boulogne → *France* 47°12N 1°47W **172** E5
Boulogne, Bois de *France* 48°51N 2°14E **134** A2
Boulogne-Billancourt *France* 48°50N 2°14E **134** A2
Boulogne-sur-Gesse *France* 43°18N 0°38E **174** E4
Boulogne-sur-Mer *France* 50°42N 1°36E **173** B8
Bouloire *France* 47°59N 0°45E **172** E7
Boulou → *C.A.R.* 6°45N 24°16E **264** A4
Boulouli *Mali* 15°30N 9°25W **262** B3
Bouloupari *N. Cal.* 21°52S 166°4E **288** d
Bouloupesse *Congo* 1°58S 12°40E **264** C2
Boulsa *Burkina Faso* 12°39N 0°34W **263** C4
Boultoum *Niger* 14°45N 10°25E **259** F2
Bouma △ *Fiji* 16°50S 179°52W **287** A2
Boumalne Dadès *Morocco* 31°25N 6°0W **260** B3
Boumba → *Cameroon* 2°2N 15°12E **264** B2
Boumbé → *C.A.R.* 4°4N 15°23E **264** B3
Boûmdeïd *Mauritania* 17°25N 11°50W **262** B2
Boumerdès *Algeria* 36°46N 3°28E **261** A5
Boumerdès □ *Algeria* 36°45N 3°40E **261** A5
Boun Neua *Laos* 21°38N 101°54E **236** B3
Boun Tai *Laos* 21°23N 101°58E **236** B3
Bouna *Ivory C.* 9°10N 3°0W **262** D4
Boundary *U.S.A.* 64°5N 141°1W **303** D12
Boundary Peak *U.S.A.* 37°51N 118°21W **306** H8
Boundiali *Ivory C.* 9°30N 6°20W **262** D3
Boungou → *C.A.R.* 8°21N 23°48E **264** A4
Bountiful *U.S.A.* 40°53N 111°52W **304** F8
Bounty Is. *Pac. Oc.* 48°0S 178°30E **288** M9
Bounty Trough *Pac. Oc.* 46°0S 178°0E **288** M9
Boura *Mali* 12°25N 4°33W **262** C4
Bourail *N. Cal.* 21°34S 165°30E **288** d
Bourbeuse → *U.S.A.* 38°24N 90°53W **310** F6
Bourbon *U.S.A.* 41°18N 86°7W **311** C10
Bourbon-Lancy *France* 46°37N 3°45E **173** F10
Bourbon-l'Archambault *France* 46°36N 3°4E **173** F10
Bourbon Street *New Orleans, U.S.A.* **131** b2
Bourbonnais *Allier, France* 46°28N 3°0E **173** F10
Bourbonnais *Ill., U.S.A.* 41°9N 87°52W **311** C9
Bourbonne-les-Bains *France* 47°54N 5°45E **173** E12
Bourbourg *France* 50°56N 2°12E **173** B9
Bourdel L. *Canada* 56°43N 74°10W **298** A5
Bourem *Mali* 17°0N 0°24W **263** B4
Bouressa *Mali* 20°0N 2°15E **261** E5
Bourg *France* 45°3N 0°34W **174** C3
Bourg-Argental *France* 45°18N 4°32E **175** C8
Bourg-de-Péage *France* 45°2N 5°3E **175** C9
Bourg-en-Bresse *France* 46°13N 5°12E **173** F12
Bourg-la-Reine *France* 48°46N 2°19E **134** B2
Bourg-Lastic *France* 45°39N 2°35E **174** C6
Bourg-Madame *France* 42°26N 1°55E **174** F5
Bourg-St-Andéol *France* 44°23N 4°39E **175** D8
Bourg-St-Maurice *France* 45°35N 6°46E **175** C10
Bourganeuf *France* 45°57N 1°45E **174** C5
Bourgas = Burgas *Bulgaria* 42°33N 27°29E **203** D11
Bourges *France* 47°9N 2°25E **173** E9
Bourget *Canada* 45°26N 75°9W **313** A9
Bourget, Lac du *France* 45°44N 5°52E **175** C9
Bourgneuf, B. de *France* 47°3N 2°10W **172** E4
Bourgneuf-en-Retz *France* 47°2N 1°58W **172** E5
Bourgogne *France* 47°0N 4°50E **171** C6
Bourgogne -Franche-Comté □ *France* 47°0N 5°0E **173** E11
Bourgoin-Jallieu *France* 45°36N 5°17E **175** C9
Bourgueil *France* 47°17N 0°10E **172** E7
Bourke *Australia* 30°8S 145°55E **281** E4
Bourne *U.K.* 52°47N 0°22W **168** E7
Bournemouth *U.K.* 50°43N 1°52W **169** G6
Bournemouth □ *U.K.* 50°43N 1°52W **169** G6
Bouroum *Burkina Faso* 13°37N 0°39W **263** C4
Bouse *U.S.A.* 33°56N 114°0W **307** M13
Boussac *France* 46°22N 2°13E **173** F9
Boussé *Burkina Faso* 12°39N 1°53W **263** C4
Bousso *Chad* 10°34N 16°52E **259** F3
Boussouma *Burkina Faso* 12°52N 1°13W **263** C4
Bout, Pte. du *Martinique* 14°33N 61°3W **322** j
Bout Stable Bay *Dominica* 15°21N 61°15W **323** k
Boutilimit *Mauritania* 17°45N 14°40W **262** B2
Boutonne → *France* 45°54N 0°50W **174** C3
Bouvet I. = Bouvetøya *Antarctica* 54°26S 3°24E **152** M12
Bouvetøya *Antarctica* 54°26S 3°24E **152** M12
Bouviers *France* 48°46N 2°4E **134** B1
Bouxwiller *France* 48°49N 7°27E **173** D14
Bouza *Niger* 14°29N 6°2E **263** C6
Bouznika *Morocco* 33°46N 7°6W **260** B3
Bouzonville *France* 49°17N 6°32E **173** C13
Bova Marina *Italy* 37°56N 15°55E **201** E8
Bovalino *Italy* 38°10N 16°10E **201** D9
Bovanenkovo *Russia* 70°22N 68°40E **214** B7
Bovec *Slovenia* 46°20N 13°33E **199** B10
Boven Kapuas, Pegunungan *Malaysia* 1°25N 113°15E **235** B4
Bovenkerk *Neths.* 52°18N 4°51E **112** B2
Bovenkerker Polder *Neths.* 52°16N 4°52E **112** B2
Bøverdal *Norway* 61°44N 8°20E **164** C5
Bøverfjorden *Norway* 63°1N 8°32E **164** A5
Bovill *U.S.A.* 46°51N 116°24W **304** C5
Bovino *Italy* 41°15N 15°20E **201** A8
Bovisa *Italy* 45°30N 9°10E **128** A2
Bovril *Argentina* 31°21S 59°26W **334** C4
Bow *U.K.* 51°31N 0°1W **125** A3
Bow → *Canada* 49°57N 111°41W **296** C6
Bow Island *Canada* 49°50N 111°23W **304** B8
Bowbells *U.S.A.* 48°48N 102°15W **308** A2
Bowdle *U.S.A.* 45°27N 99°39W **308** C4
Bowdon *U.S.A.* 33°32N 85°15W **316** B4
Bowdon Junction *U.S.A.* 33°40N 85°9W **316** B4
Bowelling *Australia* 33°25S 116°30E **279** F2
Bowen *Argentina* 35°0S 67°31W **334** D2
Bowen *Queens., Australia* 20°0S 148°16E **280** J6
Bowen Mts. *Australia* 37°0S 147°50E **283** D7
Bowers Basin *Pac. Oc.* 53°45N 176°0E **150** D16
Bowers Ridge *Pac. Oc.* 54°0N 180°0E **150** D17
Bowery *New York, U.S.A.* **132** e2
Bowie *Ariz., U.S.A.* 32°19N 109°29W **305** K9
Bowie *Tex., U.S.A.* 33°34N 97°51W **314** E6
Bowkān *Iran* 36°31N 46°12E **213** D12
Bowland, Forest of *U.K.* 54°0N 2°30W **168** D5
Bowling Green *Fla., U.S.A.* 27°38N 81°50W **317** H8
Bowling Green *Ky., U.S.A.* 36°59N 86°27W **308** G10
Bowling Green *Mo., U.S.A.* 39°21N 91°12W **310** E5
Bowling Green *Ohio, U.S.A.* 41°23N 83°39W **311** C13
Bowling Green, C. *Australia* 19°19S 147°25E **280** B4
Bowling Green Bay △ *Australia* 19°26S 146°57E **280** B4
Bowman *N. Dak., U.S.A.* 46°11N 103°24W **308** B2
Bowman *S.C., U.S.A.* 33°21N 80°41W **316** B9
Bowman I. *Antarctica* 65°0S 104°0E **151** C8
Bowmanville = Clarington *Canada* 43°55N 78°41W **312** C6
Bowmore *U.K.* 55°45N 6°17W **167** F2
Bowral *Australia* 34°26S 150°27E **283** C9
Bowraville *Australia* 30°37S 152°52E **281** E5
Bowron → *Canada* 54°3N 121°50W **296** C4
Bowron Lake ⌓ *Canada* 53°10N 121°5W **296** C4
Bowser L. *Canada* 56°30N 129°30W **296** B3
Bowsman *Canada* 52°14N 101°12W **297** C8
Bowutu Mts. *Papua N. G.* 7°45S 147°10E **286** D4
Bowwood *Zambia* 17°5S 26°20E **269** F2
Box Cr. → *Australia* 34°10S 143°50E **281** E3
Boxholm *Sweden* 58°12N 15°3E **163** F9
Boxmeer *Neths.* 51°38N 5°56E **170** C5
Boxtel *Neths.* 51°36N 5°20E **170** C5
Boyabat *Turkey* 41°28N 34°47E **212** B6
Boyabo *Dem. Rep. of the Congo* 3°43N 18°46E **264** B3
Boyacá □ *Colombia* 5°30N 73°20W **328** B3
Boyacıköy *Turkey* 41°5N 29°2E **122** B2
Boyalıca *Turkey* 40°29N 29°33E **203** F13
Boyang *China* 29°0N 116°38E **229** C11
Boyany *Ukraine* 48°17N 26°8E **183** B11
Boyasegese *Dem. Rep. of the Congo* 3°29N 20°33E **264** B4
Boyce *U.S.A.* 31°23N 92°40W **314** F8
Boyd *U.S.A.* 30°11N 83°37W **316** E6
Boyd Conservation Area *Canada* 43°49N 79°35W **141** A1
Boyd L. *Canada* 52°46N 76°42W **298** B4
Boyenge *Dem. Rep. of the Congo* 0°14N 18°55E **264** B3
Boyer, C. *N. Cal.* 21°37S 168°6E **288** d
Boyera *Dem. Rep. of the Congo* 0°40S 19°23E **264** C3
Boyle *Alta., Canada* 54°35N 112°49W **296** C6
Boyle *Roscommon, Ireland* 53°59N 8°18W **166** C3
Boyle Heights *U.S.A.* 34°1N 118°12W **126** B3
Boyne → *Ireland* 53°43N 6°15W **166** C5
Boyne, Bend of the *Ireland* 53°41N 6°27W **166** C5
Boyne City *U.S.A.* 45°13N 85°1W **309** C11
Boyni Qara *Afghan.* 36°20N 67°0E **240** A2
Boynitsa *Bulgaria* 43°58N 22°32E **202** C6
Boynton Beach *U.S.A.* 26°32N 80°4W **317** J9
Boyoma, Chutes *Dem. Rep. of the Congo* 0°35N 25°23E **264** B5
Boysen Res. *U.S.A.* 43°25N 108°11W **304** E9
Boysun *Uzbekistan* 38°12N 67°12E **240** A2
Boyup Brook *Australia* 33°50S 116°23E **279** F2
Boz Burun *Turkey* 40°32N 28°46E **203** F12
Boz Dağ *Turkey* 37°18N 29°11E **205** D11
Boz Dağları *Turkey* 38°20N 28°0E **205** C10
Bozai Gumbaz *Afghan.* 37°8N 74°0E **240** A4
Bozburun *Turkey* 36°43N 28°4E **205** E10
Bozcaada *Turkey* 39°49N 26°3E **212** C2
Bozdağ *Turkey* 36°50N 36°22E **250** B7
Bozdoğan *Turkey* 37°40N 28°17E **205** D10
Boze *Papua N. G.* 9°3S 143°3E **286** E2
Bozeman *U.S.A.* 45°41N 111°2W **304** D8
Bozen = Bolzano *Italy* 46°31N 11°22E **199** B8
Bozene *Dem. Rep. of the Congo* 2°56N 19°12E **264** B3
Boževac *Serbia* 44°32N 21°24E **202** B5
Bozhou *China* 33°55N 115°41E **226** H8
Bozkır *Turkey* 37°11N 32°14E **212** D5
Bozkurt *Turkey* 37°50N 29°37E **205** D11
Bozouls *France* 44°28N 2°43E **174** D6
Bozoum *C.A.R.* 6°25N 16°35E **264** A3
Bozova *Antalya, Turkey* 37°13N 30°18E **205** D12
Bozova *Sanliurfa, Turkey* 37°21N 38°32E **213** D8
Bozovici *Romania* 44°56N 22°0E **182** F7
Bozüyük *Turkey* 39°54N 30°3E **205** B12
Bozyazı *Turkey* 36°6N 33°0E **250** B4
Bra *Italy* 44°42N 7°51E **198** D4
Braås *Sweden* 57°4N 15°3E **163** G9
Brabant □ *Belgium* 50°46N 4°30E **170** D4
Brabant L. *Canada* 55°58N 103°43W **297** B8
Brabrand *Denmark* 56°9N 10°7E **163** H4
Brač *Croatia* 43°20N 16°40E **199** E13
Bracadale, L. *U.K.* 57°20N 6°30W **167** D2
Bracciano *Italy* 42°6N 12°10E **199** F9
Bracciano, L. di *Italy* 42°7N 12°14E **199** F9
Bracebridge *Canada* 45°2N 79°19W **312** A5
Bracieux *France* 47°30N 1°30E **172** E8
Bräcke *Sweden* 62°45N 15°26E **162** B9
Brackettville *U.S.A.* 29°19N 100°25W **314** G4
Brački Kanal *Croatia* 43°24N 16°40E **199** E13
Bracknell *U.K.* 51°25N 0°43W **169** F7
Bracknell Forest □ *U.K.* 51°25N 0°44W **169** F7
Brad *Romania* 46°10N 22°50E **182** D7
Brádano → *Italy* 40°23N 16°51E **201** B9
Bradbury Building *Los Angeles, U.S.A.* **127** b2
Bradenton *U.S.A.* 27°30N 82°34W **317** H7
Brades *Montserrat* 16°47N 62°13W **323** p
Bradford *Ont., Canada* 44°7N 79°34W **312** B5
Bradford *W. Yorks., U.K.* 53°47N 1°45W **168** D6
Bradford *Ill., U.S.A.* 41°11N 89°39W **310** C7
Bradford *Ohio, U.S.A.* 40°8N 84°27W **311** D12
Bradford *Pa., U.S.A.* 41°58N 78°38W **312** E6
Bradford *Vt., U.S.A.* 43°59N 72°9W **313** C12
Bradley *Ark., U.S.A.* 33°6N 93°39W **314** E8
Bradley *Calif., U.S.A.* 35°52N 120°48W **306** K6
Bradley *Ill., U.S.A.* 41°9N 87°52W **311** C9
Bradley Institute *Zimbabwe* 17°7S 31°25E **269** F3
Bradley Junction *U.S.A.* 27°48N 81°59W **317** H8
Bradner *U.S.A.* 41°20N 83°26W **311** C13
Brady *U.S.A.* 31°9N 99°20W **314** F5
Brædstrup *Denmark* 55°58N 9°37E **163** J3
Braemar *Australia* 33°12S 139°35E **282** B3
Braepark *U.K.* 55°58N 3°18W **121** B2
Braeside *Canada* 45°28N 76°24W **313** A8
Braeton *Jamaica* 17°57N 76°53W **320** a
Braga *Portugal* 41°35N 8°25W **194** D2
Braga □ *Portugal* 41°30N 8°30W **194** D2
Bragadiru *Romania* 43°46N 25°31E **183** G10
Bragado *Argentina* 35°2S 60°27W **334** D3
Bragança *Brazil* 1°0S 47°2W **332** B2
Bragança *Portugal* 41°48N 6°50W **194** D4
Bragança □ *Portugal* 41°30N 6°45W **194** D4
Bragança Paulista *Brazil* 22°55S 46°32W **335** A6
Bragg's Spur = West Memphis *U.S.A.* 35°8N 90°10W **315** D9
Brahestad = Raahe *Finland* 64°40N 24°28E **160** D21
Brahmakund *India* 27°52N 96°22E **241** B6
Brahmanbaria *Bangla.* 23°58N 91°15E **241** D3
Brahmani → *India* 20°39N 86°46E **244** D8
Brahmapur *India* 19°15N 84°54E **244** E7
Brahmaputra → *Asia* 23°40N 90°35E **241** D3
Braich-y-pwll *U.K.* 52°47N 4°46W **168** E3
Braid *U.K.* 55°55N 3°11W **121** B2
Braidwood *Australia* 35°27S 149°49E **283** C8
Brăila *Romania* 45°19N 27°59E **183** E12
Brăila □ *Romania* 45°5N 27°30E **183** E12
Brainerd *U.S.A.* 46°22N 94°12W **308** B6
Braintree *Essex, U.K.* 51°53N 0°34E **169** F8
Braintree *Mass., U.S.A.* 42°13N 71°0W **313** D14
Brak → *S. Africa* 29°35S 22°55E **270** C3
Brake *Germany* 53°20N 8°28E **178** B4
Brakel *Germany* 51°42N 9°11E **178** D5
Brakna □ *Mauritania* 17°0N 13°20W **262** B2
Bräkne-Hoby *Sweden* 56°14N 15°6E **163** H9
Brakwater *Namibia* 22°28S 17°3E **270** B2
Brålanda *Sweden* 58°34N 12°21E **163** F6
Bramberg *Germany* 50°6N 10°40E **179** E6
Bramdrupdam *Denmark* 55°31N 9°28E **163** J3
Bramhapuri *India* 20°36N 79°52E **244** D4
Bramley *S. Africa* 26°7S 28°4E **123** A2
Bramming *Denmark* 55°28N 8°42E **163** J2
Brämön *Sweden* 62°14N 17°40E **162** B11
Brampton *Ont., Canada* 43°45N 79°45W **312** C5
Brampton *Cumb., U.K.* 54°57N 2°44W **168** C5
Brampton I. *Australia* 20°49S 149°16E **280** b
Bramsche *Germany* 52°24N 7°59E **178** C3
Branchville *U.S.A.* 33°15N 80°49W **316** B9
Branco → *Brazil* 1°20S 61°50W **329** D5
Branco, C. *Brazil* 7°9S 34°47W **332** C5
Brandaris *Bonaire* 12°16N 68°23W **322** h
Brandberg *Namibia* 21°10S 14°33E **270** B1
Brandberg ⌓ *Namibia* 21°10S 14°30E **270** B1
Brandbu *Norway* 60°26N 10°28E **164** D7
Brande *Denmark* 55°57N 9°8E **163** J3
Brandeis Univ. *U.S.A.* 42°21N 71°17W **116** A1
Brandenburg = Neubrandenburg *Germany* 53°33N 13°15E **178** B9
Brandenburg *Brandenburg, Germany* 52°25N 12°33E **178** C8
Brandenburg *Ky., U.S.A.* 38°0N 86°10W **311** G10
Brandenburg □ *Germany* 52°50N 13°0E **178** C9
Brandenburger Tor *Germany* 52°30N 13°21E **115** A3
Brandfort *S. Africa* 28°40S 26°30E **270** C4
Brando *France* 42°47N 9°27E **175** F13
Brandon *Man., Canada* 49°50N 99°57W **297** D9
Brandon *Fla., U.S.A.* 27°56N 82°17W **317** H7
Brandon *Vt., U.S.A.* 43°48N 73°6W **313** C11
Brandon B. *Ireland* 52°17N 10°8W **166** D1
Brandon Mt. *Ireland* 52°15N 10°15W **166** D1
Brandsen *Argentina* 35°10S 58°15W **334** D4
Brandvlei *S. Africa* 30°25S 20°30E **270** D3
Brandýs nad Labem *Czechia* 50°10N 14°40E **180** A7
Branford *Conn., U.S.A.* 41°17N 72°49W **313** E12
Branford *Fla., U.S.A.* 29°58N 82°56W **316** F7
Brani, Pulau *Singapore* 1°15N 103°50E **138** B3
Braniewo *Poland* 54°25N 19°50E **184** D6
Branik *Czechia* 50°1N 14°25E **135** B2
Brännkyrka *Sweden* 59°17N 18°0E **139** B2
Bransfield Str. *Antarctica* 63°0S 59°0W **151** C18
Brańsk *Poland* 52°45N 22°50E **185** F9
Branson *U.S.A.* 36°39N 93°13W **308** G7
Brantford *Canada* 43°10N 80°15W **312** C4
Brantley *U.S.A.* 31°35N 86°16W **316** D3
Brantôme *France* 45°22N 0°39E **174** C4
Branxholme *Australia* 37°52S 141°49E **282** D4
Branxton *Australia* 32°38S 151°21E **283** B9
Branzi *Italy* 46°1N 9°46E **198** B6
Brás *Amazonas, Brazil* 2°5S 58°10W **329** D6
Brás *São Paulo, Brazil* 23°32S 46°36W **137** B2
Bras d'Or L. *Canada* 45°50N 60°50W **299** C7
Bras-Panon *Réunion* 20°59S 55°41E **272** f
Brasher Falls *U.S.A.* 44°49N 74°47W **313** B10
Brasil = Brazil ■ *S. Amer.* 12°0S 50°0W **327** E6
Brasil, Planalto *Brazil* 18°0S 46°30W **326** E6
Brasil Novo *Brazil* 3°19S 52°38W **329** D7
Brasilândia *Brazil* 23°28S 46°42W **137** A1
Brasiléia *Brazil* 11°0S 68°45W **330** C4
Brasília *Distrito Federal, Brazil* 15°47S 47°55W **333** E2
Brasília *Minas Gerais, Brazil* 16°12S 44°26W **333** E3
Brasília △ *Brazil* 15°41S 48°8W **333** E2
Brasília Int. ✈ **(BSB)** *Brazil* 15°52S 47°55W **333** E2
Brasília Legal *Brazil* 3°49S 55°36W **329** D6
Braskereidfoss *Norway* 60°44N 11°46E **164** D8
Braslaw *Belarus* 55°38N 27°0E **188** E4
Braslawskiya Azyory △ *Belarus* 55°36N 27°3E **188** E4
Braslovče *Slovenia* 46°21N 15°3E **199** B12
Braşov *Romania* 45°38N 25°35E **183** E10
Braşov □ *Romania* 45°45N 25°15E **183** E10
Brass *Nigeria* 4°35N 6°14E **263** E6
Brass → *Nigeria* 4°15N 6°13E **263** E6
Brassac-les-Mines *France* 45°24N 3°20E **174** C7
Brasschaat *Belgium* 51°19N 4°27E **170** C4
Brassey, Banjaran *Malaysia* 5°0N 117°15E **235** B5
Brassey Ra. *Australia* 25°8S 122°15E **279** E3
Brasso Seco *Trin. & Tob.* 10°45N 61°16W **323** t
Brasstown Bald *U.S.A.* 34°53N 83°49W **315** D13
Brastad *Sweden* 58°23N 11°30E **163** F5
Brastavăţu *Romania* 43°55N 24°24E **183** G9
Bratan = Morozov *Bulgaria* 42°30N 25°10E **203** D9
Brateş *Romania* 45°50N 26°4E **183** E11
Brateyevo *Russia* 55°39N 37°45E **129** C3
Bratislava *Slovakia* 48°10N 17°7E **181** C10
Bratislava M.R. Štefánik ✈ **(BTS)** *Slovakia* 48°11N 17°9E **181** C10
Bratislavský □ *Slovakia* 48°15N 17°20E **181** C10
Bratsberg = Telemark □ *Norway* 59°25N 8°30E **164** E5
Bratsigovo *Bulgaria* 42°1N 24°22E **203** D8
Bratsk *Russia* 56°10N 101°30E **215** D11
Bratskoye Vdkhr. *Russia* 56°0N 101°40E **215** D11
Brattleboro *U.S.A.* 42°51N 72°34W **313** D12
Brattvåg *Norway* 62°37N 6°25E **164** B3
Bratunac *Bos.-H.* 44°13N 19°21E **182** F4
Braunau am Inn *Austria* 48°15N 13°3E **180** C6
Braunsberg = Braniewo *Poland* 54°25N 19°50E **184** D6
Braunschweig *Germany* 52°15N 10°31E **178** C6
Braunton *U.K.* 51°7N 4°10W **169** F3
Brava = Baraawe *Somalia* 1°20N 44°8E **267** D5
Brava *C. Verde Is.* 15°0N 24°40W **153** j
Brava, Costa *Spain* 41°30N 3°0E **196** D8
Bravicea *Moldova* 47°22N 28°27E **183** C13
Bråviken *Sweden* 58°38N 16°32E **163** F10
Bravo del Norte, Rio = Grande, Rio → *N. Amer.* 25°58N 97°9W **314** J6
Brawley *U.S.A.* 32°59N 115°31W **307** N11
Bray *Ireland* 53°13N 6°7W **166** C5
Bray, Mt. *Australia* 14°0S 134°30E **280** A1
Bray, Pays de *France* 49°46N 1°26E **173** C8
Bray-sur-Seine *France* 48°25N 3°14E **173** D10
Braybrook *Australia* 37°46S 144°51E **128** A1
Braymer *U.S.A.* 39°35N 93°48W **310** E3
Brázdim *Czechia* 50°10N 14°35E **135** A3
Brazeau → *Canada* 52°55N 115°14W **296** C5
Brazil *U.S.A.* 39°32N 87°8W **311** E9
Brazil ■ *S. Amer.* 12°0S 50°0W **327** E6
Brazil Basin *Atl. Oc.* 15°0S 25°0W **152** H9
Brazilian Highlands = Brasil, Planalto *Brazil* 18°0S 46°30W **326** E6
Brazo Sur → *S. Amer.* 25°21S 57°42W **334** B4
Brazos → *U.S.A.* 28°53N 95°23W **314** G7
Brazzaville *Congo* 4°9S 15°12E **265** C3
Brčko *Bos.-H.* 44°54N 18°46E **182** F3
Brda → *Poland* 53°8N 18°8E **185** E5
Brdy *Czechia* 49°43N 13°55E **180** B6
Bré = Bray *Ireland* 53°13N 6°7W **166** C5
Breach Candy *Mumbai, India* **130** a1
Breaden, L. *Australia* 25°51S 125°28E **279** E4
Breakheart Reservation *U.S.A.* 42°28N 71°1W **116** A2
Breaksea Sd. *N.Z.* 45°35S 166°35E **285** F1
Bream B. *N.Z.* 35°56S 174°28E **284** B3
Bream Hd. *N.Z.* 35°51S 174°36E **284** B3
Bream Tail *N.Z.* 36°3S 174°36E **284** C3
Breas *Chile* 25°29S 70°24W **334** B1
Breaza *Romania* 45°11N 25°40E **183** E10
Brebes *Indonesia* 6°52S 109°3E **235** D3
Brechin *Ont., Canada* 44°32N 79°10W **312** B5
Brechin *Angus, U.K.* 56°44N 2°39W **167** E6
Brecht *Belgium* 51°21N 4°38E **170** C4
Breckenridge *Colo., U.S.A.* 39°29N 106°3W **304** G10
Breckenridge *Minn., U.S.A.* 46°16N 96°35W **308** B5
Breckenridge *Tex., U.S.A.* 32°45N 98°54W **314** E5
Breckland *U.K.* 52°30N 0°40E **169** E8
Brecknock, Pen. *Chile* 54°35S 71°30W **336** D2
Břeclav *Czechia* 48°46N 16°53E **181** C9
Brecon *U.K.* 51°57N 3°23W **169** F4
Brecon Beacons *U.K.* 51°53N 3°26W **169** F4
Brecon Beacons △ *U.K.* 51°50N 3°30W **169** F4
Breda *Neths.* 51°35N 4°45E **170** C4
Bredaryd *Sweden* 57°10N 13°45E **163** G7
Bredasdorp *S. Africa* 34°33S 20°2E **270** D3
Bredbo *Australia* 35°58S 149°10E **283** C8
Brede *Denmark* 55°47N 12°30E **118** A3
Bredebro *Denmark* 55°4N 8°50E **163** J2
Bredhat e Hotovës △ *Albania* 40°18N 20°25E **202** F4
Bredstedt *Germany* 54°37N 8°55E **178** A4
Bredy *Russia* 52°26N 60°21E **216** B6
Bree *Belgium* 51°8N 5°35E **170** C5
Breezy Point *U.S.A.* 40°33N 73°56W **132** C2
Brega = Marsa al Burayqah *Libya* 30°24N 19°37E **258** B3
Bregalnica → *Macedonia* 41°43N 22°9E **202** E6
Bregenz *Austria* 47°30N 9°45E **180** D2
Bregovo *Bulgaria* 44°9N 22°39E **202** B6
Bréhal *France* 48°53N 1°30W **172** D5
Bréhat, Î. de *France* 48°51N 3°0W **172** D4
Breiðafjörður *Iceland* 65°15N 23°15W **155** B3
Breiðdalsvík *Iceland* 64°44N 14°0W **155** C13
Breil-sur-Roya *France* 43°56N 7°31E **175** E11
Breim *Norway* 61°44N 6°25E **164** C3
Breisach *Germany* 48°1N 7°36E **179** G3
Breitenlee *Austria* 48°15N 16°30E **142** A3
Brejinho de Nazaré *Brazil* 11°1S 48°34W **332** D2
Brejo *Brazil* 3°41S 42°47W **332** B3
Brekke *Norway* 61°1N 5°26E **164** C2
Brekken *Norway* 62°40N 11°51E **164** B8
Brekkestø *Norway* 58°11N 8°22E **164** F5
Bremanger *Norway* 61°51N 4°58E **164** C1
Bremangerlandet *Norway* 61°51N 5°0E **164** C1
Bremen *Bremen, Germany* 53°4N 8°47E **178** B4
Bremen *Ga., U.S.A.* 33°43N 85°9W **316** B4
Bremen *Ind., U.S.A.* 41°27N 86°9W **311** C10
Bremen □ *Germany* 53°4N 8°50E **178** B4
Bremer Bay *Australia* 34°21S 119°20E **279** F2
Bremer I. *Australia* 12°5S 136°45E **280** A2
Bremerhaven *Germany* 53°33N 8°36E **178** B4
Bremersdorp = Manzini *Swaziland* 26°30S 31°25E **271** C5
Bremerton *U.S.A.* 47°34N 122°37W **306** C4
Bremervörde *Germany* 53°29N 9°8E **178** B5
Bremnes *Norway* 59°47N 5°8E **164** E2
Bremsnes *Norway* 63°6N 7°40E **164** A4
Breña *Peru* 12°3S 77°3W **124** B2
Brenes *Spain* 37°32N 5°54W **195** H5
Brenham *U.S.A.* 30°10N 96°24W **314** F6
Brenne *France* 46°44N 1°14E **174** B5
Brenne ⌓ *France* 46°40N 1°15E **174** B5
Brennerpass *Austria* 47°2N 11°30E **180** D4
Brennhaug *Norway* 61°54N 9°21E **164** C6
Breno *Italy* 45°57N 10°18E **198** C7
Brent *U.S.A.* 32°56N 87°10W **315** E11
Brent □ *U.K.* 51°33N 0°16W **125** A2
Brent Res. *U.K.* 51°34N 0°14W **125** A2
Brenta → *Italy* 45°11N 12°18E **199** C9
Brentford *U.K.* 51°28N 0°18W **125** B2
Brentwood *Essex, U.K.* 51°37N 0°19E **169** F8
Brentwood *Calif., U.S.A.* 34°3N 118°28W **126** B2
Brentwood *Calif., U.S.A.* 37°56N 121°42W **306** H5
Brentwood *N.Y., U.S.A.* 40°47N 73°15W **313** F11
Brentwood Park *U.S.A.* 34°3N 118°29W **126** B2
Brera *Italy* 45°28N 9°11E **128** B2
Brereton *Barbados* 13°7N 59°30W **323** r
Bréscia *Italy* 45°33N 10°15E **198** C7
Breskens *Neths.* 51°23N 3°33E **170** C3
Breslau = Wrocław *Poland* 51°5N 17°5E **185** G4
Bresle → *France* 50°4N 1°22E **172** B8
Bressanone *Italy* 46°43N 11°39E **199** B8
Bressay *U.K.* 60°9N 1°6W **167** A7
Bresse *France* 46°50N 5°10E **173** F12
Bresso *Italy* 45°32N 9°11E **128** A2
Bressuire *France* 46°51N 0°30W **172** F6
Brest *Belarus* 52°10N 23°40E **177** B12
Brest *Finistère, France* 48°24N 4°31W **172** D2
Brest □ *Belarus* 52°30N 26°10E **177** B13
Brest-Litovsk = Brest *Belarus* 52°10N 23°40E **177** B12
Bretagne □ *France* 48°10N 3°0W **172** D3
Bretanha, Pta. da *Azores* 37°54N 25°47W **153** d3
Bretçu *Romania* 46°7N 26°18E **183** D11
Bretenoux *France* 44°54N 1°51E **174** D5
Breteuil *Eure, France* 48°50N 0°57E **172** D7
Breteuil *Oise, France* 49°38N 2°18E **173** C9
Breton *Canada* 53°7N 114°28W **296** C6
Breton, Pertuis *France* 46°17N 1°25W **174** B2
Breton Sd. *U.S.A.* 29°35N 89°15W **315** G10
Brett, C. *N.Z.* 35°10S 174°20E **284** B3
Bretten *Germany* 49°2N 8°42E **179** F4
Breueh *Indonesia* 5°44N 95°3E **234** A1
Breuil-Cervínia *Italy* 45°56N 7°38E **198** C4
Brevard *U.S.A.* 35°14N 82°44W **315** D13
Breves *Brazil* 1°40S 50°29W **332** B1
Brevig Mission *U.S.A.* 65°20N 166°29W **303** D6
Brevik *Telemark, Norway* 59°4N 9°42E **164** E6
Brevik *Stockholm, Sweden* 59°20N 18°12E **139** A3
Břevnov *Czechia* 50°4N 14°22E **135** B2
Brewarrina *Australia* 30°0S 146°51E **281** E4
Brewer *U.S.A.* 44°48N 68°46W **309** C19
Brewer, Mt. *U.S.A.* 36°44N 118°28W **306** J8
Brewerville *Liberia* 6°26N 10°47W **262** D2
Brewster *N.Y., U.S.A.* 41°24N 73°36W **313** E11
Brewster *Ohio, U.S.A.* 40°43N 81°36W **312** F3
Brewster *Wash., U.S.A.* 48°6N 119°47W **304** B4
Brewster, Kap = Kangikajik *Greenland* 70°7N 22°0W **154** C8
Brewton *U.S.A.* 31°7N 87°4W **315** F11
Breyten *S. Africa* 26°16S 30°0E **271** C5
Breza *Bos.-H.* 44°2N 18°16E **182** F3
Brežice *Slovenia* 45°54N 15°35E **199** C12
Brézina *Algeria* 33°4N 1°14E **261** B5
Březnice *Czechia* 49°32N 13°57E **180** B6
Breznik *Bulgaria* 42°44N 22°55E **202** D6
Brezno *Slovakia* 48°50N 19°40E **181** C12
Brezoi *Romania* 45°21N 24°15E **183** E9
Brezovicë *Kosovo* 42°15N 21°3E **202** D5
Brezovo *Bulgaria* 42°21N 25°5E **203** D9
Bria *C.A.R.* 6°30N 21°58E **264** A4
Briançon *France* 44°54N 6°39E **175** D10
Briare *France* 47°38N 2°45E **173** E9
Briars *St. Helena* 15°56S 5°43W **153** h
Briático *Italy* 38°43N 16°2E **201** D9
Bribie I. *Australia* 27°0S 153°10E **281** D5
Bribri *Costa Rica* 9°38N 82°50W **320** E3
Briceni *Moldova* 48°22N 27°6E **183** B12
Brickyard, The *U.S.A.* 41°55N 87°47W **119** B2
Bricquebec *France* 49°28N 1°38W **172** C5
Bridge City *U.S.A.* 29°55N 90°9W **131** B2
Bridge of Sighs = Sospiri, Ponte dei *Venice, Italy* **142** b3
Bridgehampton *U.S.A.* 40°56N 72°19W **313** F12
Bridgend *U.K.* 51°30N 3°34W **169** F4
Bridgend □ *U.K.* 51°36N 3°36W **169** F4
Bridgenorth *Canada* 44°23N 78°23W **312** B6
Bridgeport *Calif., U.S.A.* 38°15N 119°14W **306** G7
Bridgeport *Conn., U.S.A.* 41°11N 73°12W **313** E11
Bridgeport *Ill., U.S.A.* 41°50N 87°38W **119** B3
Bridgeport *Ill., U.S.A.* 38°43N 87°46W **311** F9
Bridgeport *N.Y., U.S.A.* 43°9N 75°58W **313** C9
Bridgeport *Nebr., U.S.A.* 41°40N 103°6W **308** E2
Bridgeport *Tex., U.S.A.* 33°13N 97°45W **314** E6
Bridger *U.S.A.* 45°18N 108°55W **304** D9
Bridgeton *U.S.A.* 39°26N 75°14W **309** F16
Bridgetown *W. Austral., Australia* 33°58S 116°7E **279** F2
Bridgetown *Barbados* 13°6N 59°37W **323** r
Bridgetown *N.S., Canada* 44°55N 65°18W **299** D6
Bridgetown *Western Cape, S. Africa* 33°58S 18°33E **118** A2
Bridgeview *U.S.A.* 41°45N 87°48W **119** C2
Bridgewater *Tas., Australia* 42°44S 147°14E **281** G4
Bridgewater *Vic., Australia* 36°36S 143°59E **282** D5
Bridgewater *N.S., Canada* 44°25N 64°31W **299** D7
Bridgewater *Mass., U.S.A.* 41°59N 70°58W **313** E14
Bridgewater *N.Y., U.S.A.* 42°53N 75°15W **313** D9
Bridgewater, C. *Australia* 38°23S 141°23E **282** E4
Bridgman *U.S.A.* 41°57N 86°33W **311** C10
Bridgnorth *U.K.* 52°32N 2°25W **169** E5
Bridgton *U.S.A.* 44°3N 70°42W **313** B14
Bridgwater *U.K.* 51°8N 2°59W **169** F5
Bridgwater B. *U.K.* 51°15N 3°15W **169** F4
Bridlington *U.K.* 54°5N 0°12W **168** C7
Bridlington B. *U.K.* 54°4N 0°10W **168** C7
Bridport *Tas., Australia* 40°59S 147°23E **281** G4
Bridport *Dorset, U.K.* 50°44N 2°45W **169** G5
Briec *France* 48°6N 4°0W **172** D2
Brieg = Brzeg *Poland* 50°52N 17°30E **185** H4
Brienne-le-Château *France* 48°24N 4°30E **173** D11
Brienon-sur-Armançon *France* 47°59N 3°38E **173** E10
Brienz *Switz.* 46°46N 8°2E **179** J4
Brienzersee *Switz.* 46°44N 7°53E **179** J3
Brier Cr. → *U.S.A.* 32°44N 81°26W **316** C8
Brière ⌓ *France* 47°22N 2°13W **172** E4
Brievengat *Curaçao* 12°9N 68°54W **322** g
Brig *Switz.* 46°18N 7°59E **179** J3
Brigg *U.K.* 53°34N 0°28W **168** D7
Brigham City *U.S.A.* 41°31N 112°1W **304** F7
Bright *Australia* 36°42S 146°56E **283** D7
Brighton *S. Austral., Australia* 35°5S 138°30E **282** C3
Brighton *Vic., Australia* 37°55S 144°59E **128** B1
Brighton *Ont., Canada* 44°2N 77°44W **312** B7
Brighton *Trin. & Tob.* 10°15N 61°39W **323** t
Brighton *Brighton & Hove, U.K.* 50°49N 0°7W **169** G7
Brighton *Fla., U.S.A.* 27°14N 81°6W **317** H8
Brighton *Ill., U.S.A.* 39°2N 90°8W **310** E6
Brighton *Iowa, U.S.A.* 41°10N 91°49W **310** C5
Brighton *Mass., U.S.A.* 42°21N 71°9W **116** A2
Brighton *Mich., U.S.A.* 42°32N 83°47W **311** B13
Brighton *N.Y., U.S.A.* 43°8N 77°34W **312** C7
Brighton Beach *U.S.A.* 40°34N 73°57W **132** C2
Brighton-Le-Sands *Australia* 33°57S 151°9E **139** B1
Brighton Park *U.S.A.* 41°48N 87°41W **119** C2
Brightside *Canada* 45°7N 76°29W **313** A8
Brightwater *N.Z.* 41°22S 173°9E **285** B8
Brightwood *U.S.A.* 38°57N 77°1W **143** B2
Brigittenau *Austria* 48°14N 16°22E **142** A2
Brignogan-Plage *France* 48°40N 4°20W **172** D2
Brignoles *France* 43°25N 6°5E **175** E10
Brihuega *Spain* 40°45N 2°52W **196** E2
Brikama *Gambia* 13°15N 16°45W **262** C1
Brilliant *U.S.A.* 40°15N 80°39W **312** F4
Brilon *Germany* 51°23N 8°35E **178** D4
Brim *Australia* 36°3S 142°27E **282** D5
Brimbank Park *Australia* 37°43S 144°50E **128** A1
Brimfield *U.S.A.* 40°50N 89°53W **310** D7
Brimstone Hill Fort *St. Kitts & Nevis* 17°20N 62°50W **322** d
Brindabella △ *Australia* 35°14S 148°5E **283** C8
Bríndisi *Italy* 40°39N 17°55E **201** B10
Brinje *Croatia* 44°59N 15°9E **199** D12
Brinkley *U.S.A.* 34°53N 91°12W **314** D9
Brinkworth *Australia* 33°42S 138°26E **282** B3
Brinnon *U.S.A.* 47°41N 122°54W **306** C4
Brinson *U.S.A.* 30°59N 84°44W **316** E5
Brion, Î. *Canada* 47°46N 61°26W **299** C7
Brionne *France* 49°11N 0°43E **172** C7
Brionski *Croatia* 44°55N 13°45E **199** D10
Brioude *France* 45°18N 3°24E **174** C7
Briouze *France* 48°42N 0°23W **172** D6
Brisay *Canada* 54°26N 70°31W **299** B5
Brisbane *Queens., Australia* 27°25S 153°2E **281** D5
Brisbane *Calif., U.S.A.* 37°40N 122°23W **136** B2
Brisbane → *Australia* 27°24S 153°9E **281** D5
Brisbane ✈ **(BNE)** *Australia* 27°35S 153°7E **281** D5
Brisbane Ranges △ *Australia* 37°47S 144°16E **282** D6
Brisbane Water △ *Australia* 33°26S 151°13E **283** B9
Brisighella *Italy* 44°13N 11°46E **199** D8
Bristol *Bristol, U.K.* 51°26N 2°35W **169** F5
Bristol *Conn., U.S.A.* 41°40N 72°57W **313** E12
Bristol *Fla., U.S.A.* 30°26N 84°59W **316** E5
Bristol *Pa., U.S.A.* 40°6N 74°51W **313** F10
Bristol *R.I., U.S.A.* 41°40N 71°16W **313** E13
Bristol *Tenn., U.S.A.* 36°36N 82°11W **315** C13
Bristol *Vt., U.S.A.* 44°8N 73°4W **313** B11
Bristol, City of □ *U.K.* 51°27N 2°36W **169** F5
Bristol B. *U.S.A.* 58°0N 160°0W **303** H8
Bristol Channel *U.K.* 51°18N 4°30W **169** F3
Bristol I. *Antarctica* 58°45S 28°0W **151** B1
Bristol L. *U.S.A.* 34°28N 115°41W **307** L11
Bristow *U.S.A.* 35°50N 96°23W **314** D6
Bristow I. *Papua N. G.* 9°8S 143°14E **286** E2
Britain = Great Britain *Europe* 54°0N 2°15W **158** E5
Britânia *Brazil* 15°14S 51°9W **331** D7
British Central Africa = Malawi ■ *Africa* 11°55S 34°0E **269** E3
British Columbia □ *Canada* 55°0N 125°15W **296** C3
British East Africa = Kenya ■ *Africa* 1°0N 38°0E **268** B4
British Guiana = Guyana ■ *S. Amer.* 5°0N 59°0W **329** C6
British Honduras = Belize ■ *Cent. Amer.* 17°0N 88°30W **320** C2
British Indian Ocean Terr. = Chagos Arch. ☒ *Ind. Oc.* 6°0S 72°0E **273** E6
British Isles *Europe* 54°0N 4°0W **165** D5
British Mts. *N. Amer.* 68°50N 140°0W **300** B12
British Museum *London, U.K.* **125** a3
British Virgin Is. ☒ *W. Indies* 18°30N 64°30W **321** C7
Brits *S. Africa* 25°37S 27°48E **271** C4
Britstown *S. Africa* 30°37S 23°30E **270** D3
Britt *Ont., Canada* 45°46N 80°34W **298** C3
Britt *Iowa, U.S.A.* 43°6N 93°48W **310** A3
Brittany = Bretagne □ *France* 48°10N 3°0W **172** D3
Britton *U.S.A.* 45°48N 97°45W **308** C5
Britz *Germany* 52°26N 13°27E **115** B3
Brive-la-Gaillarde *France* 45°10N 1°32E **174** C5
Briviesca *Spain* 42°32N 3°19W **194** C7
Brixen = Bressanone *Italy* 46°43N 11°39E **199** B8
Brixham *U.K.* 50°23N 3°31W **169** G4
Brixton *U.K.* 51°27N 0°8W **125** B3
Brnaze *Croatia* 43°41N 16°40E **199** E13
Brnenský = Jihomoravský □ *Czechia* 49°5N 16°30E **181** B9
Brno *Czechia* 49°10N 16°35E **181** B9
Broach = Bharuch *India* 21°47N 73°0E **244** D1
Broad → *Ga., U.S.A.* 33°59N 82°39W **316** B7
Broad → *S.C., U.S.A.* 34°1N 81°4W **315** D14
Broad Arrow *Australia* 30°23S 121°15E **279** F3
Broad B. *U.K.* 58°14N 6°18W **167** C2
Broad Haven *Ireland* 54°20N 9°55W **166** B2
Broad Law *U.K.* 55°30N 3°21W **167** F5
Broad Pk. = Faichan Kangri *India* 35°48N 76°34E **243** B7
Broad Sd. *Australia* 22°0S 149°45E **280** C4
Broadalbin *U.S.A.* 43°4N 74°12W **313** C10
Broadback → *Canada* 51°21N 78°52W **298** B4
Broadford *Australia* 37°14S 145°4E **283** D6
Broadhurst Ra. *Australia* 22°30S 122°30E **278** D3
Broadmeadows *Australia* 37°40S 144°55E **128** A1
Broadmoor *U.S.A.* 37°41N 122°29W **136** B2
Broads, The *U.K.* 52°45N 1°30E **168** E9
Broadus *U.S.A.* 45°27N 105°25W **304** D11
Broadview *U.S.A.* 41°51N 87°52W **119** B1
Broadview Park *U.S.A.* 26°5N 80°12W **129** B2
Broadway *New York, U.S.A.* **132** d2
Broager *Denmark* 54°53N 9°40E **163** K3
Broby *Sweden* 56°15N 14°4E **163** H8
Brocēni *Latvia* 56°42N 22°32E **184** B9
Brochet *Canada* 57°53N 101°40W **297** B8
Brochet, L. *Canada* 58°36N 101°35W **297** B8
Brock I. *Canada* 77°52N 114°19W **295** B9
Brocken *Germany* 51°47N 10°37E **178** D6
Brocklehurst *Australia* 32°9S 148°38E **283** B8
Brocklesby *Australia* 35°48S 146°40E **283** C7
Brockley *U.K.* 51°27N 0°2W **125** B3
Brockport *U.S.A.* 43°13N 77°56W **312** C7

Brockton U.S.A. 42°5N 71°1W 313 D13
Brockville Canada 44°35N 75°41W 313 B9
Brockway Mont., U.S.A. 47°18N 105°45W 304 C11
Brockway Pa., U.S.A. 41°15N 78°47W 312 E6
Brocton U.S.A. 42°23N 79°26W 312 D5
Brod Bos.-H. 45°10N 18°0E 182 E7
Brod Macedonia 41°32N 21°17E 202 E5
Brodarevo Serbia 43°14N 19°44E 202 C3
Brodeur Pen. Canada 72°30N 88°10W 295 C14
Brodhead U.S.A. 42°37N 89°22W 310 B7
Brodick U.K. 55°35N 5°9W 167 F3
Brodnica Poland 53°15N 19°25E 185 E6
Bródno Poland 52°17N 21°1E 143 B2
Bródnowski, Kanal Poland 52°17N 21°3E 143 B2
Brody Ukraine 50°5N 25°10E 177 C13
Broek Neths. 52°26N 5°0E 112 A2
Brogan U.S.A. 44°15N 117°31W 304 D5
Broglie France 49°2N 0°30E 172 C7
Brok Poland 52°43N 21°52E 185 F8
Broken Arrow U.S.A. 36°3N 95°48W 314 C7
Broken Bow Nebr., U.S.A. 41°24N 99°38W 308 E4
Broken Bow Okla., U.S.A. 34°2N 94°44W 314 D7
Broken Bow Lake U.S.A. 34°9N 94°40W 314 D7
Broken Hill = Kabwe Zambia 14°30S 28°29E 269 E2
Broken Hill Australia 31°58S 141°29E 282 A4
Broken River Ra. Australia 21°0S 148°22E 280 b
Brokind Sweden 58°13N 15°42E 163 F19
Brokopondo Suriname 5°5N 55°0W 329 B7
Bromberg = Bydgoszcz Poland 53°10N 18°0E 185 E5
Bromley □ U.K. 51°24N 0°2E 125 B4
Bromley Common U.K. 51°22N 0°2E 125 B4
Bromma Sweden 59°21N 17°55E 139 A1
Bromma ✈ (BMA) Sweden 59°21N 17°56E 139 A1
Bromo, Gunung Indonesia 7°56N 112°57E 231 H15
Bromo Tengger Semeru △ Indonesia 7°56S 112°57E 235 D4
Bromölla Sweden 56°5N 14°28E 163 H8
Brompton London, U.K. 125 c2
Bromsgrove U.K. 52°21N 2°2W 169 E5
Bronaugh U.S.A. 37°41N 94°28W 310 G2
Brøndby Strand Denmark 55°36N 12°25E 118 B2
Brøndbyøster Denmark 55°39N 12°26E 118 B2
Brøndbyvester Denmark 55°37N 12°23E 118 B2
Brønderslev Denmark 57°16N 9°57E 163 G3
Brondesbury U.K. 51°33N 0°12W 125 A2
Brong-Ahafo □ Ghana 7°50N 2°0W 262 D4
Broni Italy 45°4N 9°16E 198 C6
Bronkhorstspruit S. Africa 25°46S 28°45E 271 C4
Brønnøya Norway 59°51N 10°32E 133 A2
Brønnøysund Norway 65°28N 12°14E 160 D15
Brønshøj Denmark 55°41N 12°29E 118 A2
Bronson Fla., U.S.A. 29°27N 82°39W 317 F7
Bronson Mich., U.S.A. 41°52N 85°12W 311 C11
Bronte Italy 37°47N 14°50E 201 E7
Bronwood U.S.A. 31°50N 84°22W 316 D5
Bronxville U.S.A. 40°56N 73°49W 132 C2
Brook Park U.S.A. 41°23N 81°48W 312 E4
Brooke's Point Phil. 8°47N 117°50E 233 G1
Brookfield Mo., U.S.A. 39°47N 93°4W 310 E3
Brookfield Wis., U.S.A. 43°4N 88°9W 311 A8
Brookfield Zoo U.S.A. 41°50N 87°50W 119 B1
Brookhaven Georgia, U.S.A. 33°52N 84°19W 113 A2
Brookhaven Miss., U.S.A. 31°35N 90°26W 315 F9
Brookings Oreg., U.S.A. 42°3N 124°17W 304 E1
Brookings S. Dak., U.S.A. 44°19N 96°48W 308 C5
Brookland = West Columbia U.S.A. 33°59N 81°4W 316 B8
Brooklandville U.S.A. 32°23N 81°40W 316 D8
Brooklin Canada 43°55N 78°55W 312 C6
Brookline U.S.A. 42°19N 71°8W 116 B2
Brooklyn Western Cape, S. Africa 33°54S 18°29E 118 A1
Brooklyn Iowa, U.S.A. 41°44N 92°27W 310 E4
Brooklyn N.Y., U.S.A. 40°37N 73°57W 132 C2
Brooklyn-Battery Tunnel New York, U.S.A. 132 f1
Brooklyn Bridge New York, U.S.A. 132 f2
Brooklyn Heights New York, U.S.A. 132 f2
Brooklyn Park U.S.A. 45°6N 93°23W 308 C7
Brookmont U.S.A. 38°57N 77°7W 143 B2
Brooks Canada 50°35N 111°55W 296 C5
Brooks Range U.S.A. 68°0N 152°0W 303 C9
Brookston U.S.A. 40°36N 86°52W 311 D10
Brooksville Fla., U.S.A. 28°33N 82°23W 317 G7
Brooksville Ky., U.S.A. 38°41N 84°4W 311 F12
Brookton Australia 32°22S 117°0E 279 F2
Brookville Ind., U.S.A. 39°25N 85°1W 311 E12
Brookville Ohio, U.S.A. 39°50N 84°24W 311 E12
Brookville Pa., U.S.A. 41°10N 79°5W 312 E5
Brookville L. U.S.A. 39°29N 85°0W 311 E11
Broom, L. U.K. 57°55N 5°15W 167 D3
Broome Australia 18°0S 122°15E 278 C3
Broons France 48°20N 2°16W 172 D4
Brora U.K. 58°0N 3°52W 167 C5
Brora → U.K. 58°0N 3°51W 167 C5
Brørup Denmark 55°29N 9°1E 163 J3
Brösarp Sweden 55°43N 14°6E 163 J8
Brosna → Ireland 53°14N 7°58W 164 D2
Brossard Canada 45°27N 73°28W 130 B3
Broșteni Mehedinți, Romania 44°45N 22°59E 182 F7
Broșteni Suceava, Romania 47°14N 25°43E 183 C10
Brøstrud Norway 60°18N 8°34E 164 D5
Brotas de Macaúbas Brazil 12°0S 42°38W 333 D3
Brothers, The Hong Kong, China 22°20N 113°58E 122 A1
Brothers, The Yemen 12°8N 53°10E 249 D6
Brøttum Norway 61°2N 10°34E 164 C7
Brou France 48°13N 1°11E 172 D8
Brou-sur-Chantereine France 48°53N 2°37E 124 B4
Brouage France 45°52N 1°4W 174 C2
Brough U.K. 54°32N 2°18W 168 C5
Brough Hd. U.K. 59°8N 3°20W 167 B5
Broughton U.S.A. 37°56N 88°27W 311 G8
Broughton Island = Qikiqtarjuaq Canada 67°33N 63°0W 295 D19
Broumov Czechia 50°35N 16°20E 181 A9
Brovary Ukraine 50°34N 30°48E 189 G6
Brovst Denmark 57°6N 9°31E 163 G3
Brown Canada 43°48N 79°14W 141 A3
Brown, L. Australia 31°5S 118°15E 279 F2
Brown, Mt. Australia 32°30S 138°0E 282 B2
Brown, Pt. Australia 32°33S 133°50E 281 E1
Brown Willy U.K. 50°35N 4°37W 169 G3
Brownfield U.S.A. 33°11N 102°17W 314 E2
Browning Ill., U.S.A. 40°8N 90°22W 310 D6
Browning Mo., U.S.A. 40°3N 93°12W 310 D3
Browning Mont., U.S.A. 48°34N 113°1W 304 B7
Brown's Town Jamaica 18°24N 77°22W 320 a
Brownsburg U.S.A. 39°51N 86°24W 311 E10
Brownstown U.S.A. 38°53N 86°3W 311 F10
Brownsville Oreg., U.S.A. 44°24N 122°59W 304 D2
Brownsville Tenn., U.S.A. 35°36N 89°16W 315 D10
Brownsville Tex., U.S.A. 25°54N 97°30W 314 J6
Brownsweg Suriname 5°1N 55°15W 329 B6
Brownville U.S.A. 44°0N 75°59W 313 C9
Brownwood U.S.A. 31°43N 98°59W 314 F5

Browse I. Australia 14°7S 123°33E 278 B3
Broxton U.S.A. 31°38N 82°53W 316 D6
Bru Norway 61°32N 5°11E 164 C2
Bruas Malaysia 4°30N 100°47E 237 K3
Bruay-la-Buissière France 50°29N 2°33E 173 B9
Bruce U.S.A. 30°28N 85°58W 316 D4
Bruce, Mt. Australia 22°37S 118°8E 278 D2
Bruce B. N.Z. 43°35S 169°42E 285 D4
Bruce Pen. Canada 45°0N 81°30W 312 B3
Bruce Peninsula △ Canada 45°14N 81°36W 312 A3
Bruce Rock Australia 31°52S 118°8E 279 F2
Bruche → France 48°34N 7°43E 173 D14
Bruchsal Germany 49°7N 8°35E 179 F4
Bruck an der Leitha Austria 48°1N 16°47E 181 C9
Bruck an der Mur Austria 47°24N 15°16E 180 D8
Brue → U.K. 51°13N 2°59W 169 F5
Bruflat Norway 60°53N 9°37E 164 D6
Brugg Switz. 47°29N 8°11E 179 H4
Brugge Belgium 51°13N 3°13E 170 C3
Brughério Italy 45°33N 9°17E 128 A2
Bruin U.S.A. 41°3N 79°43E 312 E5
Bruit, Pulau Malaysia 2°35N 111°20E 235 B4
Brûk, W. el → Egypt 30°15N 33°50E 251 H4
Bruksvallarna Sweden 62°38N 12°27E 162 B6
Brûlé Canada 53°15N 117°58W 296 C5
Brûlé, L. Canada 53°35N 64°4W 299 B7
Brûlon France 47°58N 0°15W 172 E6
Brumado Brazil 14°14S 41°40W 333 D3
Brumado → Brazil 14°13S 41°40W 333 D3
Brumath France 48°43N 7°40E 173 D14
Brumunddal Norway 60°53N 10°56E 164 D7
Brundidge U.S.A. 31°43N 85°49W 316 D4
Bruneau U.S.A. 42°53N 115°48W 304 E6
Bruneau → U.S.A. 42°56N 115°57W 304 E6
Bruneck = Brunico Italy 46°48N 11°56E 199 B8
Brunei = Bandar Seri Begawan Brunei 4°50N 115°0E 235 B4
Brunei ■ Asia 4°50N 115°0E 235 B4
Brunflo Sweden 63°5N 14°50E 162 A8
Brunico Italy 46°48N 11°56E 199 B8
Brunnen Switz. 46°59N 8°37E 179 J4
Brunner, L. N.Z. 42°37S 171°27E 285 C6
Brunnhöll Iceland 64°17N 15°26W 155 C11
Brunnsberg Sweden 61°17N 13°56E 162 C8
Brunsbüttel Germany 53°53N 9°6E 178 B5
Brunssum Neths. 50°57N 5°59E 170 D5
Brunswick = Braunschweig Germany 52°15N 10°31E 178 C6
Brunswick Vic., Australia 37°45S 144°57E 128 A1
Brunswick Ga., U.S.A. 31°10N 81°30W 316 D8
Brunswick Maine, U.S.A. 43°55N 69°58W 309 D19
Brunswick Md., U.S.A. 39°19N 77°38W 309 F15
Brunswick Mo., U.S.A. 39°26N 93°8W 310 E3
Brunswick Ohio, U.S.A. 41°14N 81°51W 312 E3
Brunswick, Pen. de Chile 53°30S 71°30W 336 D2
Brunswick B. Australia 15°15S 124°50E 278 C3
Brunswick Junction Australia 33°15S 115°50E 279 F2
Brunt Ice Shelf Antarctica 75°30S 25°0W 151 D2
Brúntal Czechia 49°59N 17°27E 181 B10
Brus Laguna Honduras 15°47N 84°35W 320 C3
Brusa = Bursa Turkey 40°15N 29°5E 203 F13
Brusartsi Bulgaria 43°40N 23°5E 202 C7
Brush U.S.A. 40°15N 103°37W 304 F12
Brushton U.S.A. 44°50N 74°31W 313 B10
Brusio Switz. 46°14N 10°8E 179 J6
Brusque Brazil 27°5S 49°0W 335 B6
Brussegem Belgium 50°56N 4°16E 116 A1
Brussel Belgium 50°51N 4°21E 116 A2
Brussel ✈ (BRU) Belgium 50°54N 4°29E 116 A2
Brussels = Brussel Belgium 50°51N 4°21E 116 A2
Brussels Canada 43°44N 81°15W 312 C3
Brusy Poland 53°53N 17°43E 184 E4
Bruthen Australia 37°42S 147°50E 283 D7
Brutvoll Norway 60°27N 11°29E 164 D8
Bruxelles = Brussel Belgium 50°51N 4°21E 116 A2
Bruyères France 48°10N 6°40E 173 D13
Bruz France 48°1N 1°46W 172 D5
Bruzzano Italy 45°31N 9°10E 128 A2
Brwinów Poland 52°9N 20°40E 185 F7
Bry-sur-Marne France 48°50N 2°32E 134 A4
Bryagovo Bulgaria 41°58N 25°8E 203 F9
Bryan Ohio, U.S.A. 41°28N 84°33W 311 C12
Bryan Tex., U.S.A. 30°40N 96°22W 314 F6
Bryan, L. U.S.A. 28°22N 81°29W 133 B2
Bryan, Mt. Australia 33°30S 139°5E 282 B3
Bryanka Ukraine 48°32N 38°45E 189 H10
Bryansk Bryansk, Russia 53°13N 34°25E 189 F8
Bryansk Dagestan, Russia 44°20N 46°53E 205 E8
Bryanston S. Africa 53°10N 33°10E 189 F7
Bryant Park New York, U.S.A. 132 c2
Bryce Canyon △ U.S.A. 37°30N 112°10W 305 H7
Bryne Norway 58°44N 5°38E 164 F2
Bryson City U.S.A. 35°26N 83°27W 315 D13
Bryukhovetskaya Russia 45°48N 39°0E 189 K10
Brza Palanka Serbia 44°28N 22°27E 202 B6
Brzeg Poland 50°52N 17°30E 185 H4
Brzeg Dolny Poland 51°16N 16°41E 185 G3
Brześć Kujawski Poland 52°36N 18°55E 185 F5
Brześć nad Bugiem = Brest Belarus 52°10N 23°40E 177 B12
Brzesko Poland 49°59N 20°34E 185 J7
Brzeziny Łódzkie, Poland 51°49N 19°42E 185 G6
Brzeziny Warszawa, Poland 52°19N 21°2E 143 B2
Brzozów Poland 49°41N 22°3E 185 J9
Bsharri Lebanon 34°15N 36°0E 250 D7
Bū al Ḩidān, W. → Libya 27°25N 19°22E 256 D7
Bü Athlah Libya 30°9N 15°39E 258 B3
Bü Baqarah U.A.E. 25°35N 56°25E 247 E8
Bu Craa W. Sahara 26°45N 12°50W 260 C2
Bü Ḩasā U.A.E. 23°30N 53°0E 247 F7
Bü Tummayyim, W. → Libya 26°56N 19°13E 258 C3
Bua Fiji 16°48S 178°37E 287 A2
Bua Sweden 57°14N 12°7E 163 G6
Bua → Malawi 12°45S 34°16E 269 E3
Bu'aale Somalia 1°5N 42°35E 267 G3
Buad I. Phil. 11°40N 124°51E 233 F5
Buala Solomon Is. 8°10S 159°35E 287 M10
Buan S. Korea 35°44N 126°44E 224 G3
Buapinang Indonesia 4°40S 121°30E 233 E6
Buatan Indonesia 0°44N 101°49E 234 B2
Buaya → Phil. 6°5N 125°14E 233 H5
Bubali Bird Sanctuary Aruba 12°33N 70°2W 322 f
Bubanza Burundi 3°6S 29°23E 268 C2
Bubaque Guinea-Biss. 11°16N 15°51W 262 C1
Bube Ethiopia 8°46N 35°48E 257 F4
Bubeneč Czechia 50°6N 14°24E 185 B2
Bubi → Zimbabwe 22°20N 31°7E 271 B5
Bübiyän Kuwait 29°45N 48°15E 247 D6
Buc France 48°46N 2°7E 134 B1
Buca Fiji 16°38S 179°52E 287 A2
Buca Turkey 38°22N 27°11E 205 C9
Bucaco Angola 11°26S 20°10E 268 F4
Bucak Turkey 37°28N 30°36E 205 D12
Bucakkışla Turkey 36°57N 33°1E 250 B4

Bucaramanga Colombia 7°0N 73°0W 328 B3
Bucas Grande I. Phil. 9°40N 125°57E 233 G5
Bucasia Australia 21°2S 149°10E 280 b
Bucay Phil. 17°32N 120°43E 232 C2
Buccaneer Arch. Australia 16°7S 123°20E 278 C3
Buccino Italy 40°38N 15°22E 201 B8
Buccoo Reef Trin. & Tob. 11°10N 60°51W 323 s
Bucecea Romania 47°47N 26°28E 183 C11
Bucegi △ Romania 45°25N 25°25E 183 E10
Buchach Ukraine 49°5N 25°25E 177 D13
Buchan Vic., Australia 37°30S 148°12E 283 D8
Buchan Aberds., U.K. 57°32N 2°21W 167 D6
Buchan Ness, U.K. 57°29N 1°46W 167 D7
Buchans Sask., Canada 51°40N 102°45W 297 C8
Buchanan Liberia 5°57N 10°2W 262 D2
Buchanan Ga., U.S.A. 33°48N 85°11W 316 C4
Buchanan Mich., U.S.A. 41°50N 86°22W 311 C10
Buchanan, L. Queens., Australia 21°35S 145°52E 280 C4
Buchanan, L. W. Austral., Australia 25°33S 123°2E 279 E3
Buchanan, L. Tex., U.S.A. 30°45N 98°25W 314 F5
Buchanan Cr. → Australia 19°13S 136°33E 280 B2
Buchans Canada 48°50N 56°52W 299 C8
Bucharest = București Romania 44°27N 26°10E 183 F11
Buchen Germany 49°31N 9°20E 179 F5
Buchenhain Germany 48°1N 11°31E 131 B1
Bucheon S. Korea 37°28N 126°45E 224 D3
Buchholz Berlin, Germany 52°36N 13°25E 115 A3
Buchholz Niedersachsen, Germany 53°19N 9°52E 178 B5
Buchloe Germany 48°1N 10°44E 179 G6
Buchon, Pt. U.S.A. 35°15N 120°54W 306 K6
Buciumi Romania 47°2N 23°5E 182 C8
Buck Hill Falls U.S.A. 41°11N 75°16W 313 E9
Bückeburg Germany 52°16N 9°7E 178 C5
Buckeye Lake U.S.A. 39°55N 82°29W 312 G2
Buckhannon U.S.A. 39°0N 80°8W 309 F13
Buckhaven U.K. 56°11N 3°3W 167 E5
Buckhead U.S.A. 33°50N 84°23W 113 A2
Buckhorn L. Canada 44°29N 78°23W 312 B6
Buckie U.K. 57°41N 2°58W 167 D6
Buckingham Qué., Canada 45°37N 75°24W 298 C4
Buckingham Bucks., U.K. 51°59N 0°57W 169 F7
Buckingham B. Australia 12°10S 135°40E 280 A2
Buckingham Canal India 14°0N 80°5E 245 H5
Buckingham Fountain Chicago, U.S.A. 119 d2
Buckingham Palace London, U.K. 125 b3
Buckinghamshire □ U.K. 51°53N 0°55W 169 F7
Buckland U.K. 51°53N 0°32W 169 F7
Buckle Hd. Australia 14°26S 127°52E 278 B4
Buckleboo Australia 32°54S 136°12E 282 B2
Buckley Flints., U.K. 53°10N 3°5W 168 D4
Buckley Ill., U.S.A. 40°36N 88°2W 311 D8
Buckley → Australia 20°10S 138°49E 280 C2
Bucklin Kans., U.S.A. 37°33N 99°38W 308 G4
Bucklin Mo., U.S.A. 39°47N 92°53W 310 E4
Buckow Germany 52°45N 14°4E 115 B5
Bucktown U.S.A. 30°1N 90°8W 131 A2
Bucks L. U.S.A. 39°54N 121°12W 306 F5
Buco Zau Angola 4°46S 12°33E 265 C2
Bucquoy France 50°9N 2°43E 173 B9
București Romania 44°27N 26°10E 183 F11
București Otopeni ✈ (OTP) Romania 44°36N 26°11E 183 F11
Bucyrus U.S.A. 40°48N 82°59W 311 D14
Bud Norway 62°55N 6°56E 164 B3
Bud Somalia 4°11N 46°28E 267 D6
Buda Hungary 47°30N 19°2E 117 A2
Buda Castle = Budavári palota Budapest, Hungary 117 b2
Budacu, Vf. Romania 47°7N 25°41E 183 C10
Budafok Hungary 47°27N 19°2E 117 B2
Budai = Putai Taiwan 23°23N 120°9E 225 C2
Budalin Burma 22°20N 95°10E 241 D5
Budapest Hungary 47°29N 19°5E 117 B2
Budapest □ Hungary 47°29N 19°5E 117 B2
Budapest Ferihegy ✈ (BUD) Hungary 47°26N 19°14E 117 B2
Budatétény Hungary 47°25N 19°1E 117 B2
Budaun India 28°5N 79°10E 243 E8
Budavári palota Budapest, Hungary 117 b2
Budawang △ Australia 35°10S 150°12E 283 C9
Budd Coast Antarctica 68°0S 112°0E 151 C8
Buddenbrock = Brodnica Poland 53°15N 19°25E 185 E6
Budderoo △ Australia 35°40S 150°41E 283 C9
Buddusò Italy 40°35N 9°15E 200 B2
Bude U.K. 50°49N 4°34W 169 G3
Budennovsk Russia 44°50N 44°10E 191 H7
Budești Romania 44°13N 26°30E 183 F11
Budeyi Ukraine 48°41N 28°43E 183 B14
Budge Budge = Baj Baj India 22°30N 88°5E 243 H13
Budgewoi Australia 33°13S 151°34E 283 B9
Buðardalur Iceland 65°7N 21°46W 155 B5
Budia Spain 40°38N 2°46W 196 E2
Büdingen Germany 50°17N 9°7E 179 E5
Budja → Dem. Rep. of the Congo 2°50N 19°40E 264 B3
Budo-Sungai Padi △ Thailand 6°19N 101°42E 237 J3
Budokan Tokyo, Japan 140 a4
Budoni Italy 40°40N 9°45E 200 B2
Búðrio Italy 44°32N 11°32E 199 D8
Büdszentmihály = Tiszavasvári Hungary 47°58N 21°18E 182 C6
Budva Montenegro 42°17N 18°50E 202 D2
Budweis = České Budějovice Czechia 48°55N 14°25E 180 C7
Budyonnovka = Novoazovsk Ukraine 47°15N 38°4E 189 J10
Budzyń Poland 52°54N 16°59E 185 F3
Bue Norway 58°40N 5°58E 164 F2
Buea Cameroon 4°10N 9°9E 263 E6
Buela Angola 5°54S 14°40E 268 F2
Buellton U.S.A. 34°37N 120°12W 307 L6
Buena Esperanza Argentina 34°45S 65°15W 334 C2
Buena Park U.S.A. 33°52N 117°59W 307 M9
Buena Vista Bolivia 17°27S 63°40W 331 D5
Buena Vista Colo., U.S.A. 38°51N 106°8W 304 G10
Buena Vista Va., U.S.A. 37°44N 79°21W 309 G14
Buena Vista Solomon Is. 8°52S 160°3E 287 M11
Buena Vista Lake Bed U.S.A. 35°12N 119°18W 307 K7
Buenaventura Colombia 3°53N 77°4W 328 C2
Buenaventura Chihuahua, Mexico 29°51N 107°29W 318 B3
Buenaventura, B. de Colombia 3°48N 77°17W 328 C2
Buenavista Agusan del N., Phil. 8°59N 125°24E 233 G5
Buenavista Quezon, Phil. 13°35N 122°34E 232 E4
Buendía, Embalse de Spain 40°25N 2°43W 196 E2
Buenópolis Brazil 17°54S 44°11W 333 E3
Buenos Aires Argentina 34°36S 58°22W 117 B2
Buenos Aires Colombia 1°36S 69°58W 328 D3
Buenos Aires Costa Rica 9°10N 83°20W 320 E3
Buenos Aires □ Argentina 36°30S 60°0W 334 D3
Buenos Aires, L. = General Carrera, L. S. Amer. 46°35S 72°0W 336 C2

Bukki Ethiopia 6°11N 36°31E 257 F4
Bulkley → Canada 55°15N 127°40W 296 B3
Burcher Australia 33°30S 147°16E 283 B8
Burco Somalia 9°32N 45°32E 267 C6
Burda India 25°50N 77°35E 242 G7
Burdekin → Australia 19°38S 147°25E 280 B4
Burden, L. U.S.A. 28°27N 81°33W 133 B1
Burdeos Phil. 14°50N 121°52E 232 D3
Burdeos B. Phil. 14°44N 122°52E 232 D4
Burdur Turkey 37°45N 30°17E 205 D12
Burdur □ Turkey 37°45N 30°0E 205 D12
Burdur Gölü Turkey 37°44N 30°10E 205 D12
Burdwan = Barddhaman India 23°14N 87°39E 243 H12
Bure Gojam, Ethiopia 10°40N 37°4E 257 E4
Bure Ilubabor, Ethiopia 8°15N 35°7E 257 F4
Bure → U.K. 52°38N 1°43E 168 E9
Burela Spain 43°39N 7°24W 194 A3
Büren Germany 51°33N 8°35E 178 D4
Bureskoye Vdkhr. Russia 50°16N 130°20E 215 D14
Bureya → Russia 49°27N 129°30E 215 E13
Burford Canada 43°7N 80°27W 312 C4
Burg Germany 52°16N 11°51E 178 C7
Burg auf Fehmarn Germany 54°28N 11°9E 178 A7
Burg el Arab Egypt 30°54N 29°32E 256 H6
Burg et Tuyur Sudan 20°55N 27°56E 256 D4
Burg Stargard Germany 53°29N 13°18E 178 B9
Burgas Bulgaria 42°33N 27°29E 203 D11
Burgas □ Bulgaria 42°45N 27°0E 203 D11
Burgaski Zaliv Bulgaria 42°30N 27°18E 203 D11
Burgdorf Niedersachsen, Germany 52°27N 10°1E 178 C6
Burgdorf Switz. 47°3N 7°37E 179 H3
Burgenland □ Austria 47°20N 16°20E 181 D9
Burgeo Canada 47°37N 57°38W 299 C8
Burgersdorp S. Africa 30°0S 26°20E 270 D4
Burgess, Mt. Australia 30°50S 121°5E 279 F3
Burghausen Germany 48°9N 12°49E 179 G8
Burghead U.K. 57°43N 3°30W 167 D5
Búrgio Italy 37°36N 13°17E 200 E6
Burglengenfeld Germany 49°12N 12°2E 179 F8
Burgohondo Spain 40°26N 4°47W 194 E6
Burgos Ilocos N., Phil. 18°31N 120°38E 232 B3
Burgos Pangasinan, Phil. 16°4N 119°52E 232 C3
Burgos Spain 42°21N 3°41W 194 C7
Burgos □ Spain 42°21N 3°42W 194 C7
Burgstädt Germany 50°54N 12°49E 178 E8
Burgsvik Sweden 57°3N 18°19E 163 G12
Burguillos del Cerro Spain 38°23N 6°35W 195 G4
Burgundy = Bourgogne France 47°0N 4°50E 171 C6
Burhaniye Turkey 39°30N 26°58E 203 E11
Burhanpur India 21°18N 76°14E 244 D3
Burhi Gandak → India 25°20N 86°37E 243 G11
Burhner → India 22°43N 80°31E 243 H9
Buri Pen. Eritrea 15°25N 39°55E 257 D4
Burias I. Phil. 12°55N 123°5E 232 E4
Burias Pass. Phil. 13°0N 123°15E 232 E4
Burica, Pta. Costa Rica 8°3N 82°51W 320 E3
Burien U.S.A. 47°28N 122°20W 306 C4
Burigi, L. Tanzania 2°2S 31°22E 268 C3
Burigi □ Tanzania 2°0S 31°20E 268 C3
Burim Kosovo 42°45N 20°24E 202 D2
Burin Canada 47°1N 55°14W 299 C8
Buriram Thailand 15°0N 103°0E 236 E4
Buritama Brazil 21°0S 50°8W 333 H8
Buriti Alegre Brazil 18°9S 49°3W 333 E2
Buriti Bravo Brazil 5°50S 43°50W 332 D3
Buriti dos Lopes Brazil 3°10S 41°52W 332 C4
Burj Al Arab U.A.E. 25°8N 55°11E 119 B1
Burj Khalifa Dubai, U.A.E. 25°12N 55°16E 119 B2
Burji Ethiopia 5°29N 37°51E 257 F4
Burkburnett U.S.A. 34°6N 98°34W 314 D5
Burke → Australia 23°12S 139°33E 280 C2
Burke Chan. Canada 52°10N 127°30W 296 C3
Burketown Australia 17°45S 139°33E 280 B2
Burkhan Khaldun Mongolia 48°45N 108°40E 219 B10
Burkina Faso ■ Africa 12°0N 1°0W 262 C4
Burk's Falls Canada 45°37N 79°24W 298 C4
Burlada Spain 42°42N 1°36W 196 C2
Burleigh Falls Canada 44°33N 78°12W 312 B6
Burley U.S.A. 42°32N 113°48W 304 E7
Burlingame U.S.A. 37°35N 122°21W 306 H4
Burlington Ont., Canada 43°18N 79°45W 312 C5
Burlington Colo., U.S.A. 39°18N 102°16W 304 G12
Burlington Iowa, U.S.A. 40°49N 91°14W 310 E6
Burlington Kans., U.S.A. 38°12N 95°45W 308 F6
Burlington Ky., U.S.A. 39°2N 84°43W 311 F12
Burlington Mass., U.S.A. 42°30N 71°12W 116 A1
Burlington N.C., U.S.A. 36°6N 79°26W 315 C15
Burlington N.J., U.S.A. 40°4N 74°51W 313 F10
Burlington Vt., U.S.A. 44°29N 73°12W 313 B11
Burlington Wash., U.S.A. 48°28N 122°20W 306 B4
Burlington Wis., U.S.A. 42°41N 88°17W 311 B8
Burma ■ Asia 21°0N 96°30E 241 E6
Burnaby I. Canada 52°25N 131°19W 296 C2
Burnet U.S.A. 30°45N 98°14W 314 F5
Burnham U.S.A. 40°38N 77°34W 312 F7
Burnham-on-Sea U.K. 51°14N 3°0W 169 F5
Burnham Park U.S.A. 41°49N 87°35W 119 C3
Burnham Park Harbor U.S.A. 41°51N 87°36W 119 B3
Burnhamthorpe Canada 43°37N 79°35W 141 B1
Burnie Australia 41°4S 145°56E 281 D4
Burnley U.K. 53°47N 2°14W 168 D5
Burns U.S.A. 43°35N 119°3W 304 E4
Burns Junction U.S.A. 42°47N 117°51W 304 E4
Burns Lake Canada 54°14N 125°45W 296 C3
Burnside → Canada 66°51N 108°4W 294 D10
Burnside, L. Australia 25°22S 123°0E 279 E3
Burnt Oak U.K. 51°36N 0°15W 125 A2
Burnt River Canada 44°41N 78°42W 312 B6
Burntisland U.K. 56°4N 3°13W 121 A2
Burntwood → Canada 56°8N 96°34W 297 B9
Burntwood L. Canada 55°22N 100°26W 297 B8
Burnwynd U.K. 55°54N 3°23W 121 B1
Buronga Australia 34°9S 142°15E 283 B3
Burqa West Bank 32°18N 35°15E 253 C4
Burqah Kuwait 29°0N 47°57E 247 D6
Burqin China 47°43N 87°0E 217 C11
Burra S. Austral., Australia 33°40S 138°55E 282 B2
Burragorang, L. Australia 33°52S 150°37E 283 B9
Burray U.K. 58°51N 2°54W 167 C6
Burren Albania 41°36N 20°1E 202 E4
Burren → Ireland 53°9N 9°5W 166 C2
Burren Junction Australia 30°7S 148°59E 283 E8
Burrendong, L. Australia 32°45S 149°10E 283 B8
Burriana Spain 39°50N 0°4W 196 F4
Burrinjuck, L. Australia 35°0S 148°36E 283 C8
Burro, Serranías del Mexico 28°56N 102°5W 318 B4
Burrow-Pine Mountain △ Australia 36°56S 147°45E 283 D7
Burrum Coast △ Australia 25°13S 152°38E 281 D5
Burruyacú Argentina 26°30S 64°40W 334 B3
Burry Port U.K. 51°41N 4°15W 169 F3
Bursa Turkey 40°15N 29°5E 203 F13
Bursa □ Turkey 40°15N 29°5E 212 B3

Burseryd *Sweden* 57°12N 13°17E **163** G7
Burstall *Canada* 50°39N 109°54W **297** C7
Burton *Mich., U.S.A.* 43°0N 83°40W **311** B13
Burton *Ohio, U.S.A.* 41°28N 81°8W **312** E3
Burton *S.C., U.S.A.* 32°26N 80°43W **316** C9
Burton, L. *Canada* 54°45N 78°20W **298** B4
Burton upon Trent *U.K.* 52°48N 1°38W **168** E6
Burtundy *Australia* 33°45S 142°15E **282** B5
Burtus *Egypt* 30°8N 31°8E **117** A1
Buru *Indonesia* 3°30S 126°30E **231** E7
Buruanga *Phil.* 11°51N 121°53E **233** F3
Burudvatn *Norway* 59°58N 10°35E **133** A2
Burullus, Bahra el *Egypt* 31°25N 31°0E **256** H7
Burūm *Yemen* 14°22N 48°59E **249** D5
Burûn, Râs *Egypt* 31°14N 33°7E **251** G4
Burundi ■ *Africa* 3°15S 30°0E **268** C3
Burunny = Tsagan Aman
Russia 47°34N 46°43E **191** G8
Bururi *Burundi* 3°57S 29°37E **268** C2
Burutu *Nigeria* 5°20N 5°29E **263** D6
Burwell *U.S.A.* 41°47N 99°8W **308** E4
Burwick *U.K.* 58°45N 2°58W **167** C5
Burwood *Australia* 33°52S 151°5E **139** B1
Bury *U.K.* 53°35N 2°17W **168** D5
Bury St. Edmunds *U.K.* 52°15N 0°43E **169** E8
Buryatia □ *Russia* 53°0N 110°0E **215** D12
Būrylbaytal *Kazakhstan* 44°56N 74°0E **217** D8
Buryn *Ukraine* 51°13N 33°50E **189** G7
Burzenin *Poland* 51°28N 18°47E **185** G5
Busa, Mt. *Phil.* 6°8N 124°39E **233** H5
Busalla *Italy* 44°34N 8°57E **198** D5
Busan *S. Korea* 35°5N 129°0E **224** E4
Busanga
Dem. Rep. of the Congo 0°53S 22°7E **264** C4
Busango Swamp *Zambia* 14°15S 25°45E **269** E2
Busaso = Boosaaso
Somalia 11°12N 49°18E **267** B6
Buşayrah *Syria* 35°9N 40°26E **213** E9
Busca *Italy* 44°31N 7°29E **198** D4
Bûsh *Egypt* 29°9N 31°8E **251** J2
Bushat *Albania* 41°58N 19°34E **202** E3
Būshehr *Iran* 28°55N 50°55E **247** D6
Būshehr □ *Iran* 28°20N 51°45E **247** D6
Bushenyi *Uganda* 0°35S 30°10E **268** C3
Bushimaie →
Dem. Rep. of the Congo 6°2S 23°45E **265** D4
Bushire = Būshehr *Iran* 28°55N 50°55E **247** D6
Bushiribana *Aruba* 12°33N 69°58W **322** f
Bushnell *Fla., U.S.A.* 28°40N 82°7W **317** G7
Bushnell *Ill., U.S.A.* 40°33N 90°31W **310** D6
Bushtyna *Ukraine* 48°3N 23°28E **183** B8
Bushwick *U.S.A.* 40°41N 73°54W **132** B2
Bushy Park *U.K.* 51°24N 0°20W **125** B1
Busie *Ghana* 10°29N 2°22W **262** C4
Business Bay *U.A.E.* 25°11N 55°16E **119** B2
Businga
Dem. Rep. of the Congo 3°16N 20°59E **264** B4
Büsingen *Germany* 47°42N 8°41E **179** H4
Busira = Tshuapa →
Dem. Rep. of the Congo 0°14S 20°42E **264** C4
Buskerud □ *Norway* 60°20N 9°0E **164** D5
Busko-Zdrój *Poland* 50°28N 20°42E **185** H7
Buslei *Ethiopia* 5°28N 44°25E **267** C5
Busovača *Bos.-H.* 44°6N 17°53E **182** F2
Buşra ash Shām *Syria* 32°30N 36°25E **251** F7
Busselton *Australia* 33°42S 115°15E **279** F2
Busseri → *South Sudan* 7°41N 28°3E **257** F2
Busseto *Italy* 44°59N 10°2E **198** D7
Bussière-Badil *France* 45°39N 0°36E **174** C4
Bussol, Proliv *Russia* 46°30N 151°0E **215** E16
Bussolengo *Italy* 45°28N 10°51E **198** C7
Bussum *Neths.* 52°16N 5°10E **170** B5
Bustamante, B. *Argentina* 45°5S 66°18W **336** C3
Buşteni *Romania* 45°24N 25°32E **183** E10
Busto, C. *Spain* 43°34N 6°28W **194** B4
Busto Arsizio *Italy* 45°37N 8°51E **198** C5
Busu Djanoa
Dem. Rep. of the Congo 1°43N 21°23E **264** B4
Busu Kwanga
Dem. Rep. of the Congo 1°48N 20°21E **264** B4
Busu Mandji
Dem. Rep. of the Congo 2°52N 21°14E **264** B4
Busuanga *Phil.* 12°14N 119°52E **232** E2
Busuanga I. *Phil.* 12°10N 120°0E **232** E2
Büsum *Germany* 54°7N 8°51E **178** A4
Busungbiu *Indonesia* 8°16S 114°58E **231** J17
Busy Corner *Trin. & Tob.* 10°18N 61°17W **323** t
Buta *Dem. Rep. of the Congo* 2°50N 24°53E **264** B4
Butantã *Brazil* 23°34S 46°42W **137** B1
Butare *Rwanda* 2°31S 29°52E **268** C2
Butaritari *Kiribati* 3°30N 174°0E **288** G9
Butcher I. *India* 18°57N 72°53E **130** B2
Bute *S. Austral., Australia* 33°51S 138°0E **282** B3
Bute *Scotland, U.K.* 55°48N 5°2W **167** F3
Bute Inlet *Canada* 50°40N 124°53W **296** C4
Butemba *Uganda* 1°9N 31°37E **268** B3
Butembo
Dem. Rep. of the Congo 0°9N 29°18E **268** B2
Buteni *Romania* 46°19N 22°7E **182** D7
Butera *Italy* 37°11N 14°11E **201** E7
Butere *Kenya* 0°13N 34°30E **268** B3
Butha-Buthe *Lesotho* 28°47S 28°14E **271** C4
Buthidaung *Burma* 20°52N 92°32E **241** E4
Butiaba *Uganda* 1°50N 31°20E **268** B3
Butler *Ga., U.S.A.* 32°33N 84°14W **316** C5
Butler *Ind., U.S.A.* 41°26N 84°52W **311** C12
Butler *Ky., U.S.A.* 38°47N 84°22W **311** F12
Butler *Mo., U.S.A.* 38°16N 94°20W **310** F2
Butler *Pa., U.S.A.* 40°52N 79°54W **312** F5
Butler, L. *U.S.A.* 28°29N 81°33W **133** B1
Buton *Indonesia* 5°0S 122°45E **231** E6
Bütow = Bytów *Poland* 54°10N 17°30E **184** D4
Butrint *Albania* 39°45N 20°1E **206** B10
Butrint △ *Albania* 39°45N 20°1E **202** G4
Butrintit, L. e *Albania* 39°43N 20°5E **206** B10
Butte *Mont., U.S.A.* 46°0N 112°32W **304** C7
Butte *Nebr., U.S.A.* 42°58N 98°51W **308** D4
Butte Creek → *U.S.A.* 39°12N 121°56W **306** F5
Butterworth = Gcuwa
S. Africa 32°20S 28°11E **271** D4
Butterworth *Malaysia* 5°24N 100°23E **237** c
Buttevant *Ireland* 52°14N 8°40W **166** D3
Buttfield, Mt. *Australia* 24°45S 128°9E **279** D4
Button B. *Canada* 58°45N 94°23W **297** B10
Buttonwillow *U.S.A.* 35°24N 119°28W **307** K7
Butty Hd. *Australia* 33°54S 121°39E **279** F3
Butuan *Phil.* 8°57N 125°33E **233** G5
Butuan B. *Phil.* 9°4N 125°21E **233** G5
Butuku-Luba *Eq. Guin.* 3°29N 8°33E **263** E6
Butung = Buton *Indonesia* 5°0S 122°45E **231** E6
Buturlinovka *Russia* 50°50N 40°35E **190** E5
Butwal *Nepal* 27°33N 83°31E **243** F10
Butzbach *Germany* 50°25N 8°40E **179** E4
Bützow *Germany* 53°50N 11°58E **178** B7
Buuhoodle *Somalia* 8°20N 46°25E **267** C6
Buulobarde *Somalia* 3°50N 45°33E **267** D6
Buur Gaabo *Somalia* 1°13S 41°51E **267** E5
Buurhakaba *Somalia* 3°12N 44°20E **267** D5
Buvika *Norway* 63°18N 10°11E **164** A4
Buxa Duar *India* 27°45N 89°35E **243** F13
Buxar *India* 25°34N 83°58E **243** G10
Buxoro *Uzbekistan* 39°48N 64°25E **216** E6
Buxtehude *Germany* 53°28N 9°39E **178** B5
Buxton *U.K.* 53°16N 1°54W **168** D6
Buxy *France* 46°44N 4°40E **173** F11
Buy *Russia* 58°28N 41°28E **190** A5
Buyant-Uhaa *Mongolia* 44°55N 110°11E **226** B6
Buynaksk *Russia* 42°48N 47°7E **191** J8
Buyo *Ivory C.* 6°21N 7°5W **262** D3
Buyo, L. de *Ivory C.* 6°16N 7°10W **262** D3
Büyük Menderes →
Turkey 37°28N 27°11E **205** D9
Büyükçekmece *Turkey* 41°2N 28°35E **203** E12
Büyükdere *Turkey* 41°9N 29°2E **122** B2
Büyükeğri Dağı *Turkey* 36°45N 33°33E **250** B4
Büyükkariştiran *Turkey* 41°18N 27°33E **203** E11
Büyükkemikli Burnu
Turkey 40°18N 26°14E **203** F10
Büyükkonuk = Komi
Cyprus 35°24N 34°0E **207** E9
Büyükorhan *Turkey* 39°46N 28°56E **205** B10
Büyükyoncalı *Turkey* 41°20N 27°55E **203** E11
Buyun Shan *China* 40°4N 122°43E **227** D12
Buzançais *France* 46°54N 1°25E **172** F8
Buzău *Romania* 45°10N 26°50E **183** E11
Buzău □ *Romania* 45°20N 26°30E **183** E11
Buzău → *Romania* 45°26N 27°44E **183** E12
Buzău, Pasul *Romania* 45°35N 26°12E **183** E11
Buzaymah *Libya* 24°55N 22°2E **258** D4
Buzen *Japan* 33°35N 131°5E **222** D3
Buzet *Croatia* 45°24N 13°58E **199** C10
Buzi → *Mozam.* 19°50S 34°43E **269** F3
Buziaş *Romania* 45°38N 21°36E **182** E6
Büzmeýin *Turkmenistan* 38°3N 58°12E **247** B8
Buzuluk *Russia* 52°48N 52°12E **186** D9
Buzuluk → *Russia* 50°15N 42°7E **190** E6
Buzzards Bay *U.S.A.* 41°45N 70°37W **313** E14
Bwagaoia *Papua N. G.* 10°40S 152°52E **286** F7
Bwana Mkubwa *Zambia* 13°8S 28°38E **269** E2
Bwasa *Dem. Rep. of the Congo* 3°55S 18°24E **264** C3
Bwatnapné *Vanuatu* 15°41S 168°9E **287** E6
Bwindi △ *Uganda* 1°2S 29°42E **268** C2
Byakar Dzong = Jakar Dzong
Bhutan 27°33N 90°43E **241** B3
Byala *Ruse, Bulgaria* 43°28N 25°44E **203** C9
Byala *Varna, Bulgaria* 42°53N 27°55E **203** D11
Byala Slatina *Bulgaria* 43°26N 23°58E **202** C7
Byam Martin I. *Canada* 75°15N 104°15W **295** B11
Byarezina → *Belarus* 52°33N 30°14E **177** B16
Byaroza *Belarus* 52°31N 24°51E **177** B13
Byblos = Jubayl *Lebanon* 34°5N 35°39E **250** D6
Bychawa *Poland* 51°1N 22°36E **185** G9
Byculla *India* 18°58N 72°50E **130** B2
Byczyna *Poland* 51°7N 18°12E **185** G5
Bydgoszcz *Poland* 53°10N 18°0E **185** E5
Byelorussia = Belarus ■
Europe 53°30N 27°0E **177** B14
Byeonsan △ *S. Korea* 35°40N 126°30E **224** E3
Byers *U.S.A.* 39°43N 104°14W **304** G11
Byesville *U.S.A.* 39°58N 81°32W **312** G3
Byfield △ *Australia* 22°52S 150°45E **280** C5
Bygdin *Norway* 61°21N 8°32E **164** C5
Bygdøy *Norway* 59°54N 10°40E **133** A3
Bygland *Norway* 58°50N 7°48E **164** F4
Byglandsfjorden *Norway* 58°44N 7°50E **164** F4
Bygstad *Norway* 61°23N 5°40E **164** C2
Bykhaw *Belarus* 53°31N 30°14E **177** B16
Bykhov = Bykhaw
Belarus 53°31N 30°14E **177** B16
Bykle *Norway* 59°20N 7°22E **164** E4
Bykovo *Russia* 49°50N 45°25E **190** F7
Bylas *U.S.A.* 33°8N 110°7W **305** K8
Bylot *Canada* 58°25N 94°8W **297** B10
Bylot I. *Canada* 73°13N 78°34W **295** C16
Byram *U.S.A.* 32°11N 90°15W **315** E9
Byrd, C. *Antarctica* 69°38S 76°7W **151** C17
Byrock *Australia* 30°40S 146°27E **283** A7
Byron *Ga., U.S.A.* 32°39N 83°46W **316** C6
Byron *Ill., U.S.A.* 42°8N 89°15W **310** B7
Byron, C. *Australia* 28°43S 153°38E **281** D5
Byron Bay *Australia* 28°43S 153°37E **281** D5
Byrranga, Gory *Russia* 75°0N 100°0E **215** B11
Byrranga Mts. = Byrranga, Gory
Russia 75°0N 100°0E **215** B11
Byrum *Denmark* 57°16N 11°0E **163** G5
Byske *Sweden* 64°57N 21°11E **160** D19
Byskeälven → *Sweden* 64°57N 21°13E **160** D19
Bystrytsya *Ukraine* 48°27N 24°14E **183** B9
Bystrzyca → *Dolnośląskie, Poland* 51°12N 16°55E **185** G3
Bystrzyca → *Lubelskie, Poland* 51°21N 22°46E **185** G9
Bystrzyca Kłodzka *Poland* 50°19N 16°39E **185** H3
Bytča *Slovakia* 49°13N 18°34E **181** B11
Bytkiv *Ukraine* 48°38N 24°28E **183** B9
Bytom *Poland* 50°25N 18°54E **185** H5
Bytom Odrzański *Poland* 51°44N 15°48E **185** G2
Bytów *Poland* 54°10N 17°30E **184** D4
Byumba *Rwanda* 1°35S 30°4E **268** C3
Byvatter *U.S.A.* 29°58N 90°2W **131** B2
Byzantine Museum = Vizandino, Moussio *Athens, Greece* **112** b3
Bzenec *Czechia* 48°58N 17°18E **181** C10
Bzura → *Poland* 52°25N 20°15E **185** F7

C

C.B.S. Fox Studios *U.S.A.* 34°9N 118°24W **126** B2
C.N. Tower *Toronto, Canada* **141** c1
C.W. McConaughy, L.
U.S.A. 41°14N 101°40W **308** E3
Ca → *Vietnam* 18°45N 105°45E **236** C5
Ca' da Mosto *Venice, Italy* **142** b3
Ca' d'Oro *Venice, Italy* **142** b2
Ca' Foscari *Venice, Italy* **142** b2
Ca Mau *Vietnam* 9°7N 105°8E **237** H5
Ca Mau, Mui *Vietnam* 8°38N 104°44E **237** H5
Ca Na *Vietnam* 11°20N 108°54E **237** G7
Ca' Pesaro *Venice, Italy* **142** b2
Ca' Rezzonico *Venice, Italy* **142** b2
Caacupé *Paraguay* 25°23S 57°5W **334** B4
Caaguazú △ *Paraguay* 26°5S 55°31W **335** B4
Caála *Angola* 12°46S 15°30E **265** E3
Caamaño Sd. *Canada* 52°55N 129°25W **296** C3
Caapiranga *Brazil* 3°18S 61°13W **329** D5
Caazapá *Paraguay* 26°8S 56°19W **334** B4
Caazapá □ *Paraguay* 26°10S 56°0W **335** B4
Cabaad, Ras *Somalia* 6°18N 49°4E **267** C6
Cabadbaran *Phil.* 9°10N 125°38E **233** G5
Cabagan *Phil.* 17°26N 121°46E **232** C3
Cabalete I. *Phil.* 14°16N 121°49E **232** D3
Cabalian = San Juan
Phil. 10°16N 125°10E **233** F5
Caballito *Argentina* 34°37S 58°25W **117** B2
Cabana *Peru* 8°25S 78°5W **330** B2
Cabana de Bergantiños = A Carballa
Spain 43°13N 8°54W **194** B2
Cabanaconde *Peru* 15°38S 71°58W **330** D3
Cabañaquinta *Spain* 43°10N 5°38W **194** B5
Cabanatuan *Phil.* 15°30N 120°58E **232** D3
Cabañeros △ *Spain* 39°18N 4°35W **195** F6
Cabanes *Spain* 40°9N 0°2E **196** E5
Cabangon *Phil.* 15°10N 120°3E **232** D3
Cabanilla *Peru* 15°36S 70°28W **330** D3
Cabano *Canada* 47°40N 68°56W **299** C6
Čabar *Croatia* 45°36N 14°39E **199** C11
Cabarroguis *Phil.* 16°30N 121°30E **232** C3
Cabarruyan I. *Phil.* 16°18N 119°59E **232** C2
Cabazon *U.S.A.* 33°55N 116°47W **307** M10
Cabedelo *Brazil* 7°0S 34°50W **332** C5
Cabeza del Buey *Spain* 38°44N 5°13W **195** G5
Cabezón de la Sal *Spain* 43°18N 4°14W **194** B6
Cabhán, An = Cavan
Ireland 54°0N 7°22W **166** B4
Cabildo *Chile* 32°30S 71°5W **334** C1
Cabimas *Venezuela* 10°23N 71°25W **328** A3
Cabin John *U.S.A.* 38°58N 77°10W **143** B1
Cabin John Regional Park ⌂
U.S.A. 39°0N 77°10W **143** A1
Cabinda *Angola* 5°33S 12°11E **265** D2
Cabinda □ *Angola* 5°0S 12°30E **265** D2
Cabinet Mts. *U.S.A.* 48°10N 115°50W **304** B6
Cabiri *Angola* 8°52S 13°39E **265** D2
Cable Beach *Bahamas* 25°4N 77°24W **153** b
Cabo Blanco *Argentina* 47°15S 65°47W **336** C3
Cabo de Gata-Níjar △ *Spain* 36°51N 2°6W **197** J2
Cabo de Hornos △ *Chile* 55°42S 67°20W **336** E3
Cabo de Santo Agostinho
Brazil 8°20S 34°55W **332** C5
Cabo Frio *Brazil* 22°51S 42°3W **333** F3
Cabo Pantoja *Peru* 1°0S 75°10W **328** D2
Cabo Pulmo △ *Mexico* 23°20N 109°28W **318** C3
Cabo Raso *Argentina* 44°20S 65°15W **336** B3
Cabo Rojo *Puerto Rico* 18°5N 67°9W **321** b
Cabo San Lucas *Mexico* 22°53N 109°54W **318** C3
Cabo Verde ■ *Atl. Oc.* 16°0N 24°0W **153** j
Cabo Yubi = Tarfaya
Morocco 27°55N 12°55W **260** C2
Cabonga, Réservoir
Canada 47°20N 76°40W **298** C4
Cabool *U.S.A.* 37°7N 92°6W **308** G7
Caboolture *Australia* 27°5S 152°58E **281** D5
Cabora Bassa Dam = Cahora Bassa, Lago de *Mozam.* 15°20S 32°50E **269** F3
Caborca *Mexico* 30°37N 112°6W **318** A2
Cabot, Mt. *U.S.A.* 44°30N 71°25W **313** B13
Cabot Hd. *Canada* 45°14N 81°17W **312** A3
Cabot Str. *Canada* 47°15N 59°40W **299** C8
Cabourg *France* 49°17N 0°7W **172** C6
Cabra *Spain* 37°30N 4°28W **195** H6
Cabra del Santo Cristo
Spain 37°42N 3°16W **195** H7
Cabra I. *India* 7°18N 93°50E **245** L11
Cabra I. *Phil.* 13°53N 120°2E **232** E3
Cábras *Italy* 39°56N 8°32E **200** C1
Cabras I. *Guam* 13°27N 144°44E **302** d
Cabrera *Spain* 39°8N 2°57E **206** B3
Cabrera, Sierra de la *Spain* 42°12N 6°40W **194** C4
Cabrera △ *Spain* 39°13N 2°53E **197** F7
Cabri *Canada* 50°35N 108°25W **297** C7
Cabriel → *Spain* 39°14N 1°3W **197** F3
Cabrits, Î. *Martinique* 14°23N 60°52W **322** j
Cabrits △ *Dominica* 15°35N 61°26W **323** k
Cabruta *Venezuela* 7°50N 66°10W **328** B4
Cabuçú de Baixo →
Brazil 23°30S 46°40W **137** A1
Cabuçú de Cima →
Brazil 23°30S 46°33W **137** A2
Cabugao *Phil.* 17°48N 120°27E **232** C3
Cabulauan Is. *Phil.* 11°25N 120°8E **233** F3
Cabulo *Angola* 10°18S 16°22E **265** E3
Caburan = Jose Abad Santos
Phil. 5°55N 125°39E **233** J5
Cabuta *Angola* 9°48S 14°58E **265** D2
Cabuyaro *Colombia* 4°18N 72°49W **328** C3
Cacabelos *Spain* 42°36N 6°44W **194** C4
Caçador *Brazil* 26°47S 51°0W **335** B5
Čačak *Serbia* 43°54N 20°20E **202** C4
Cacandee Settlement
Trin. & Tob. 10°33N 61°26W **323** t
Cacao *Fr. Guiana* 4°33N 52°26W **329** C7
Caçapava do Sul *Brazil* 30°30S 53°30W **335** C5
Cáccamo *Italy* 37°56N 13°40E **200** E6
Cacém *Portugal* 38°46N 9°18W **195** G1
Cáceres *Brazil* 16°5S 57°40W **331** D6
Cáceres *Colombia* 7°35N 75°20W **328** B2
Cáceres *Spain* 39°26N 6°23W **195** F4
Cáceres □ *Spain* 39°45N 6°0W **194** F5
Cachan *France* 48°47N 2°19E **134** B2
Cache Bay *Canada* 46°22N 80°0W **298** C4
Cache Cr. → *U.S.A.* 38°42N 121°42W **306** G5
Cache Creek *Canada* 50°48N 121°19W **296** C4
Cacheu *Guinea-Biss.* 12°14N 16°8W **262** C1
Cachi *Argentina* 25°5S 66°10W **334** B2
Cachimbo *Brazil* 8°57S 54°54W **331** B7
Cachimbo, Serra do *Brazil* 9°30S 55°30W **331** B6
Cachimo *Angola* 8°21S 21°24E **265** D4
Cachinal de la Sierra
Chile 24°58S 69°32W **334** A2
Cachingues *Angola* 13°5S 16°45E **265** E3
Cachoeira = Solonópole
Brazil 5°44S 39°1W **332** C4
Cachoeira *Brazil* 12°30S 39°0W **333** D4
Cachoeira, Rib. da →
Brazil 23°38S 46°43W **137** B1
Cachoeira Alta *Brazil* 18°48S 50°58W **333** E1
Cachoeira do Sul *Brazil* 30°3S 52°53W **335** C5
Cachoeiro de Itapemirim
Brazil 20°51S 41°7W **333** F3
Cachoeiro do Arari *Brazil* 1°1S 48°58W **332** B2
Cachopo *Portugal* 37°20N 7°49W **195** H3
Cachuela Esperanza
Bolivia 10°32S 65°38W **331** C4
Cacilhas *Portugal* 38°41N 9°8W **126** A2
Cacine *Guinea-Biss.* 11°8N 14°57W **262** C1
Cacoal *Brazil* 11°32S 61°18W **331** C5
Cacólo *Angola* 10°9S 19°21E **265** E3
Caconda *Angola* 13°48S 15°8E **265** E3
Cacongo *Angola* 5°11S 12°5E **265** D2
Caçu *Brazil* 18°37S 51°4W **333** E1
Cacuaco *Angola* 8°47S 13°21E **265** D2
Cacuchi → *Angola* 14°26S 16°46E **265** E3
Cacula *Angola* 14°29S 14°10E **265** E2
Caculé *Brazil* 14°30S 42°13W **333** D3
Caculuvar → *Angola* 16°47S 14°56E **265** F2
Cacuso *Angola* 9°25S 15°45E **265** D3
Cadale *Somalia* 2°45N 46°19E **267** D6
Cadaqués *Spain* 42°17N 3°17E **196** C8
Čadca *Slovakia* 49°26N 18°45E **181** B11
Caddo *U.S.A.* 34°7N 96°16W **314** D6
Cader Idris *U.K.* 52°42N 3°53W **169** E4
Cadereyta de Jiménez
Mexico 25°36N 100°0W **318** B5
Cades *U.S.A.* 33°47N 79°47W **316** B10
Cadí, Serra del *Spain* 42°17N 1°42E **196** C6
Cadí-Moixeró △ *Spain* 42°17N 1°44W **196** C3
Cadibarrawirracanna, L.
Australia 28°52S 135°27E **281** D2
Cadillac *Gironde, France* 44°38N 0°20W **174** D3
Cadillac *Mich., U.S.A.* 44°15N 85°24W **309** C11
Cadiz *Phil.* 10°57N 123°15E **233** F4
Cádiz *Spain* 36°30N 6°20W **195** J4
Cadiz *Calif., U.S.A.* 34°30N 115°28W **307** L11
Cadiz *Ohio, U.S.A.* 40°22N 81°0W **312** F4
Cádiz □ *Spain* 36°36N 5°45W **195** J5
Cádiz, G. de *Spain* 36°40N 7°0W **195** J3
Cadiz L. *U.S.A.* 34°18N 115°24W **307** L11
Cadley *U.S.A.* 33°32N 82°40W **316** B7
Cadney Park *Australia* 27°55S 134°3E **281** D1
Cadomin *Canada* 53°2N 117°20W **296** C5
Cadotte Lake *Canada* 56°26N 116°23W **296** B5
Cadours *France* 43°44N 1°2E **174** E5
Cadoux *Australia* 30°46S 117°7E **279** F2
Cadwell *U.S.A.* 32°20N 83°3W **316** C6
Caen *France* 49°10N 0°22W **172** C6
Caerdydd = Cardiff *U.K.* 51°29N 3°10W **169** F4
Caerfyrddin = Carmarthen
U.K. 51°52N 4°19W **169** F3
Caergybi = Holyhead *U.K.* 53°18N 4°38W **168** D3
Caernarfon *U.K.* 53°8N 4°16W **168** D3
Caernarfon B. *U.K.* 53°4N 4°40W **168** D3
Caernarvon = Caernarfon
U.K. 53°8N 4°16W **168** D3
Caerphilly *U.K.* 51°35N 3°13W **169** F4
Caerphilly □ *U.K.* 51°37N 3°12W **169** F4
Caesarea *Israel* 32°30N 34°53E **251** F5
Caeté *Brazil* 19°55S 43°40W **333** E3
Caetité *Brazil* 13°50S 42°32W **333** D3
Cafayate *Argentina* 26°2S 66°0W **334** B2
Cafu *Angola* 16°30S 15°8E **265** F3
Cagayan □ *Phil.* 18°0N 121°50E **232** C3
Cagayan → *Phil.* 18°25N 121°42E **232** B3
Cagayan de Oro *Phil.* 8°30N 124°40E **233** G5
Cagayan Is. *Phil.* 9°40N 121°16E **233** G3
Cagayan Sulu I. *Phil.* 7°1N 118°30E **233** H2
Cagli *Italy* 43°33N 12°39E **199** E9
Cágliari *Italy* 39°13N 9°7E **200** C2
Cágliari, G. di *Italy* 39°8N 9°11E **200** C2
Cagnano Varano *Italy* 41°49N 15°47E **199** G12
Cagnes-sur-Mer *France* 43°40N 7°9E **175** E11
Caguán → *Colombia* 0°8S 74°18W **328** D3
Caguas *Puerto Rico* 18°14N 66°2W **321** C6
Caha Mts. *Ireland* 51°45N 9°40W **166** E2
Cahama *Angola* 16°17S 14°19E **265** F2
Caherciveen *Ireland* 51°56N 10°14W **166** E1
Cahir *Ireland* 52°22N 7°56W **166** D4
Cahora Bassa, Lago de
Mozam. 15°20S 32°50E **269** F3
Cahore Pt. *Ireland* 52°33N 6°12W **166** D5
Cahors *France* 44°27N 1°27E **174** D5
Cahuapanas *Peru* 5°15S 77°0W **330** B2
Cahuenga Pk. *U.S.A.* 34°8N 118°19W **126** B3
Cahuinari → *Colombia* 1°21S 70°44W **328** D3
Cahuinari △ *Colombia* 1°20S 71°10W **328** D3
Cahul *Moldova* 45°50N 28°15E **183** E13
Cai Bau, Dao *Vietnam* 21°10N 107°27E **228** G6
Cai Be *Vietnam* 10°20N 106°2E **237** G6
Cai Nuoc *Vietnam* 8°56N 105°1E **237** H5
Caia *Mozam.* 17°51S 35°24E **269** F4
Caiabis, Serra dos *Brazil* 11°30S 56°30W **331** C6
Caianda *Angola* 11°2S 23°31E **265** E4
Caiapó, Serra do *Brazil* 17°0S 52°0W **331** D7
Caiapônia *Brazil* 16°57S 51°49W **331** D7
Caibarién *Cuba* 22°30N 79°30W **320** B4
Caibiran *Phil.* 11°34N 124°35E **233** F5
Caiçara = Alvarães *Brazil* 3°12S 64°50W **329** D5
Caicara *Bolívar, Venezuela* 7°38N 66°10W **328** B4
Caicara *Monagas, Venezuela* 9°52N 63°38W **329** B5
Caicó *Brazil* 6°20S 37°0W **332** C4
Caicos Is. *Turks & Caicos* 21°40N 71°40W **321** B5
Caicos Passage *W. Indies* 22°45N 72°45W **321** B5
Caidian *China* 30°35N 114°2E **229** B10
Caiguna *Australia* 32°16S 125°29E **279** F4
Caillandre, Morne
St. Lucia 13°46N 60°57W **323** m
Caille I. *Grenada* 12°16N 61°34W **323** q
Cailloma *Peru* 15°9S 71°45W **330** D3
Cain, L. *U.S.A.* 28°28N 81°28W **133** B2
Căinari *Moldova* 46°41N 29°3E **183** D14
Cainde *Angola* 15°29S 13°24E **265** F2
Caine → *Bolivia* 18°23S 65°21W **331** D4
Caird Coast *Antarctica* 75°0S 25°0W **151** D1
Cairn Gorm *U.K.* 57°7N 3°39W **167** D5
Cairngorm Mts. *U.K.* 57°6N 3°42W **167** D5
Cairngorms △ *U.K.* 57°10N 3°50W **167** D5
Cairnryan *U.K.* 54°59N 5°1W **167** G3
Cairns *Australia* 16°57S 145°45E **280** B4
Cairns L. *Canada* 51°42N 94°30W **297** C10
Cairo = El Qâhira *Egypt* 30°2N 31°13E **117** A2
Cairo *Ga., U.S.A.* 30°52N 84°13W **316** E5
Cairo *Ill., U.S.A.* 37°0N 89°11W **308** G9
Cairo *N.Y., U.S.A.* 42°18N 74°0W **313** D10
Cairo Int. ✕ (CAI) *Egypt* 30°7N 31°24E **117** A3
Cairo Montenotte *Italy* 44°23N 8°16E **198** D5
Cairofa *Angola* 14°3S 12°54E **265** E2
Caiseal = Cashel *Ireland* 52°30N 7°53W **166** D4
Caisleán an Bharraigh = Castlebar
Ireland 53°52N 9°18W **166** C2
Caithness *U.K.* 58°25N 3°35W **167** C5
Caithness, Ord of *U.K.* 58°8N 3°36W **167** C5
Caitou *Angola* 14°28S 13°7E **265** E2
Caiuás = Rio Brilhante
Brazil 21°48S 54°33W **335** A5
Caiundo *Angola* 15°50S 17°28E **265** F3
Caiza *Bolivia* 20°2S 65°40W **331** E4
Caja de Muertos, I.
Puerto Rico 17°54N 66°32W **321** b
Cajabamba *Peru* 7°38S 78°4W **330** B2
Cajamarca *Peru* 7°5S 78°28W **330** B2
Cajamarca □ *Peru* 6°15S 78°50W **330** B2
Cajamarquilla = Bolivar
Peru 7°18S 77°48W **330** B2
Cajapió *Brazil* 2°58S 44°48W **332** B3
Cajarc *France* 44°29N 1°50E **174** D5
Cajas △ *Ecuador* 2°48S 79°15W **328** D2
Cajatambo *Peru* 10°30S 77°2W **330** C2
Cajazeiras *Brazil* 6°52S 38°30W **332** C4
Čajetina *Serbia* 43°47N 19°42E **202** C3
Cajidiocan *Phil.* 12°22N 122°41E **232** E4
Caju *Brazil* 22°52S 43°12W **135** B1
Çakirgol *Turkey* 40°33N 39°40E **213** B8
Çakırlar *Turkey* 36°52N 30°33E **205** E12
Čakovec *Croatia* 46°23N 16°26E **199** B13
Čakovice *Czechia* 50°9N 14°31E **135** B3
Çal *Turkey* 38°4N 29°23E **205** C11
Cala *Spain* 37°59N 6°21W **195** H4
Cala → *Spain* 37°38N 6°5W **195** H4
Cala Cadolar, Punta de = Rotja, Pta.
Spain 38°38N 1°35E **206** D2
Cala d'Or *Spain* 39°23N 3°14E **206** B4
Cala en Porter *Spain* 39°52N 4°8E **206** B5
Cala Figuera *Spain* 39°20N 3°10E **206** B4
Cala Figuera, C. de *Spain* 39°27N 2°31E **206** B3
Cala Forcat *Spain* 40°0N 3°47E **206** B4
Cala Major *Spain* 39°33N 2°37E **206** B3
Cala Mezquida = Sa Mesquida
Spain 39°55N 4°16E **206** B5
Cala Millor *Spain* 39°35N 3°22E **206** B4
Cala Murada *Spain* 39°25N 3°17E **206** B4
Cala Ratjada *Spain* 39°43N 3°27E **206** B4
Cala Santa Galdana *Spain* 39°56N 3°58E **206** B4
Calabanga *Phil.* 13°42N 123°17E **232** E4
Calabar *Nigeria* 4°57N 8°20E **263** E6
Calabarzon □ *Phil.* 15°30N 121°0E **232** D3
Calabogie *Canada* 45°18N 76°43W **313** A8
Calabozo *Venezuela* 9°0N 67°28W **328** B4
Calábria □ *Italy* 39°0N 16°30E **201** C9
Calábria △ *Italy* 39°6N 16°35E **201** C9
Calaburras, Pta. de *Spain* 36°30N 4°38W **195** J6
Calaceite *Spain* 41°1N 0°11E **196** D5
Calacoto *Bolivia* 17°16S 68°38W **330** D4
Calacuccia *France* 42°21N 9°1E **175** F13
Calafat *Romania* 43°58N 22°59E **182** G7
Calafell *Spain* 41°11N 1°34E **196** D6
Calagnaan I. *Phil.* 11°29N 123°12E **233** F4
Calagua Is. *Phil.* 14°30N 122°55E **232** D4
Calahorra *Spain* 42°18N 1°59W **196** C3
Calai *Angola* 17°47S 19°41E **265** F3
Calais *Pas-de-Calais, France* 50°57N 1°56E **173** B8
Calais *Maine, U.S.A.* 45°11N 67°17W **309** C20
Calakmul △ *Mexico* 18°14N 89°48W **319** D7
Calalaste, Cord. de
Argentina 25°0S 67°0W **334** B2
Calama *Brazil* 8°0S 62°50W **331** B5
Calama *Chile* 22°30S 68°55W **334** A2
Calamar *Bolívar, Colombia* 10°15N 74°55W **328** A3
Calamar *Vaupés, Colombia* 1°58N 72°32W **328** C3
Calamarca *Bolivia* 16°55S 68°9W **330** D4
Calamba *Cavite, Phil.* 14°13N 121°10E **232** D3
Calamba *Mis. Occ., Phil.* 8°35N 123°39E **233** G4
Calamian Group *Phil.* 11°50N 119°55E **233** F2
Calamocha *Spain* 40°50N 1°17W **196** E3
Calamonte *Spain* 38°53N 6°23W **195** G4
Călan *Romania* 45°44N 22°59E **182** E7
Calañas *Spain* 37°40N 6°53W **195** H4
Calanda *Spain* 40°56N 0°15W **196** E4
Calandagan I. *Phil.* 10°39N 120°15E **233** F3
Calandula *Angola* 9°6S 15°57E **265** D3
Calang *Indonesia* 4°37N 95°37E **234** B1
Calangiánus *Italy* 40°56N 9°11E **200** B2
Calanques △ *France* 43°14N 5°30E **175** E9
Calanscio, Sarir *Libya* 27°30N 22°30E **258** C4
Calapan *Phil.* 13°25N 121°7E **232** E3
Călăraşi *Moldova* 47°16N 28°19E **183** C13
Călăraşi *Romania* 44°12N 27°20E **183** F12
Călăraşi □ *Romania* 44°10N 27°0E **183** F12
Calasparra *Spain* 38°14N 1°41W **197** G3
Calatafimi *Italy* 37°55N 12°52E **200** E5
Calatagan *Phil.* 13°50N 120°38E **232** E3
Calatayud *Spain* 41°20N 1°40W **196** D3
Călăţele *Romania* 46°46N 23°1E **182** D8
Calato = Kalathos *Greece* 36°9N 28°8E **206** E12
Calatrava *Eq. Guin.* 1°6N 9°25E **264** B1
Calatrava *Phil.* 10°35N 123°28E **233** F4
Calatrava, Ponte di *Venice, Italy* **142** b1
Calauag *Phil.* 13°55N 122°15E **232** E4
Calavà, C. *Italy* 38°11N 14°55E **201** D7
Calavite, C. *Phil.* 13°26N 120°20E **232** E3
Calavite Pass. *Phil.* 13°36N 120°25E **232** E3
Calayan *Phil.* 19°16N 121°28E **232** B3
Calayan I. *Phil.* 19°20N 121°27E **232** B3
Calbayog *Phil.* 12°4N 124°38E **232** E5
Calbiga *Phil.* 11°38N 125°0E **233** F5
Calca *Peru* 13°22S 72°0W **330** C3
Calcasieu L. *U.S.A.* 29°55N 93°18W **314** G8
Calcium *U.S.A.* 44°1N 75°50W **313** B9
Calcutta = Kolkata *India* 22°34N 88°21E **124** B2
Calcutta *U.S.A.* 40°40N 80°34W **312** F4
Caldaro *Italy* 46°25N 11°14E **199** B8
Caldas □ *Colombia* 5°15N 75°30W **328** B2
Caldas da Rainha *Portugal* 39°24N 9°8W **195** F1
Caldas de Reis *Spain* 42°36N 8°39W **194** C2
Caldas Novas *Brazil* 17°45S 48°38W **333** E2
Calder → *U.K.* 53°44N 1°22W **168** D6
Caldera *Chile* 27°5S 70°55W **334** B1
Caldera de Taburiente △
Canary Is. 28°43N 17°52W **153** e1
Caldwell *Idaho, U.S.A.* 43°40N 116°41W **304** E5
Caldwell *Kans., U.S.A.* 37°2N 97°37W **308** G5
Caldwell *Tex., U.S.A.* 30°32N 96°42W **314** F6
Caledon *Ont., Canada* 43°51N 79°51W **312** C5
Caledon *Western Cape, S. Africa* 34°14S 19°26E **270** D2
Caledon → *S. Africa* 30°31S 26°5E **270** D4
Caledon B. *Australia* 12°45S 137°0E **280** A2
Caledonia *Ont., Canada* 43°7N 79°58W **312** C5
Caledonia *Mo., U.S.A.* 37°45N 90°46W **310** G6
Caledonia *N.Y., U.S.A.* 42°58N 77°51W **312** D7
Calella *Spain* 41°37N 2°40E **196** D7
Calemba *Angola* 16°0S 15°44E **270** A2
Calen *Australia* 20°56S 148°48E **280** b
Calenzana *France* 42°31N 8°51E **175** F12
Caleta Olivia *Argentina* 46°25S 67°25W **336** C3
Caletones *Chile* 34°6S 70°27W **334** C1
Calexico *U.S.A.* 32°40N 115°30W **307** N11
Calf of Man *I. of Man* 54°3N 4°48W **168** C3
Calgary *Canada* 51°0N 114°10W **296** C6
Calheta *Azores* 38°36N 28°1W **153** d1
Calheta *Madeira* 32°44N 17°11W **153** c
Calheta de Nesquim
Azores 38°24N 28°5W **153** d1
Calhoun *U.S.A.* 34°30N 84°57W **315** D12
Calhoun Falls *U.S.A.* 34°6N 82°36W **316** A7
Cali *Colombia* 3°25N 76°35W **328** C2
Calibishie *Dominica* 15°35N 61°21W **323** k
Calicoan I. *Phil.* 10°59N 125°48E **233** F5
Calicut = Kozhikode *India* 11°15N 75°43E **245** J2
Cálida, Costa *Spain* 37°30N 1°30W **197** H3
Caliente *U.S.A.* 37°37N 114°31W **305** H6
California *Trin. & Tob.* 10°24N 61°28W **323** t
California *Mo., U.S.A.* 38°38N 92°34W **310** F4
California *Pa., U.S.A.* 40°4N 79°54W **312** F5
California □ *U.S.A.* 37°30N 119°30W **306** H7
California, Baja, T.N. = Baja California □ *Mexico* 30°0N 115°0W **318** B2
California, Baja, T.S. = Baja California Sur □
Mexico 25°50N 111°50W **318** B2
California, G. de *Mexico* 27°0N 111°0W **318** B2
California City *U.S.A.* 35°10N 117°55W **307** K9
California Hot Springs
U.S.A. 35°51N 118°41W **307** K8
California Institute of Technology
Los Angeles, U.S.A. 34°8N 118°8W **126** B4
California Los Angeles, Univ. of
U.S.A. 34°4N 118°27W **126** B2
California Plaza *Los Angeles, U.S.A.* **127** b1
California State Univ.
U.S.A. 34°4N 118°10W **126** B3
Cälilabad *Azerbaijan* 39°12N 48°29E **213** C13
Calilegua △ *Argentina* 25°36S 64°50W **334** B3
Călimăneşti *Romania* 45°14N 24°20E **183** E9
Călimani, Munţii *Romania* 47°12N 25°0E **183** C10
Călimani △ *Romania* 47°7N 25°10E **183** C10
Calingasta *Argentina* 31°15S 69°30W **334** C2
Calinog *Phil.* 11°7N 122°32E **233** F4
Calintaan *Phil.* 12°35N 120°57E **232** E3
Calipatria *U.S.A.* 33°8N 115°31W **307** M11
Calistoga *U.S.A.* 38°35N 122°35W **306** G4
Calitri *Italy* 40°54N 15°26E **201** B8
Calitzdorp *S. Africa* 33°33S 21°42E **270** D3
Calivigny I. *Grenada* 12°0N 61°43W **323** q
Callabonna, L. *Australia* 29°40S 140°5E **281** D3
Callac *France* 48°25N 3°27W **172** D3
Callahan *U.S.A.* 30°34N 81°50W **316** E8
Callahan Tunnel *Boston, U.S.A.* **116** a3
Callan *Ireland* 52°32N 7°24W **166** D4
Callander *U.K.* 56°15N 4°13W **167** E4
Callang = San Manuel
Phil. 16°4N 120°40E **232** C3
Callao *Peru* 12°3S 77°8W **124** B2
Callaway *U.S.A.* 30°8N 85°36W **316** E4
Calliaqua *St. Vincent* 13°8N 61°12W **323** n
Callicoon *U.S.A.* 41°46N 75°3W **313** E9
Calling Lake *Canada* 55°15N 113°12W **296** B6
Calliope *Australia* 24°0S 151°16E **280** C5
Callosa de Segura *Spain* 38°7N 0°53W **197** G4
Callosa d'En Sarrià *Spain* 38°40N 0°8W **197** G4
Calma, Costa de la *Spain* 39°28N 2°26E **206** B3
Calmar *U.S.A.* 43°11N 91°52W **310** A5
Calne *U.K.* 51°26N 2°0W **169** F6
Calola *Angola* 16°25S 17°48E **265** F3
Calolbon = San Andres
Phil. 13°36N 124°6E **232** E5
Calonge *Spain* 41°52N 3°5E **196** D8
Caloocan *Phil.* 14°39N 120°58E **232** D3
Caloosahatchee → *U.S.A.* 26°31N 82°1W **317** J7
Calore → *Italy* 41°11N 14°28E **201** A7
Caloundra *Australia* 26°45S 153°10E **281** D5
Calpe *Spain* 38°39N 0°3E **197** G5
Calpella *U.S.A.* 39°14N 123°12W **306** F3
Calpine *U.S.A.* 39°40N 120°27W **306** F6
Calstock *Canada* 49°47N 84°9W **298** C3
Caltabellotta *Italy* 37°34N 13°13E **200** E6
Caltagirone *Italy* 37°14N 14°31E **201** E7
Caltanissetta *Italy* 37°29N 14°4E **201** E7
Çaltılıbük *Turkey* 39°57N 28°36E **203** G12
Caluango *Angola* 8°20S 19°39E **265** D3
Calubian *Phil.* 11°27N 124°26E **233** F5
Calucinga *Angola* 11°18S 16°12E **265** E3
Caluire-et-Cuire *France* 45°48N 4°52E **173** G11
Calulo *Angola* 10°1S 14°56E **265** E2
Calumet, L. *U.S.A.* 41°41N 87°35W **119** C3
Calumet City *U.S.A.* 41°37N 87°32W **119** D3
Calumet Park *U.S.A.* 41°40N 87°39W **119** C3
Calumet Sag Channel →
U.S.A. 41°40N 87°47W **119** C2
Calunda *Angola* 12°7S 23°36E **265** E4
Caluquembe *Angola* 13°47S 14°44E **265** E2
Caluso *Italy* 45°18N 7°53E **198** C4
Caluula *Somalia* 11°50N 50°45E **267** B7
Caluya I. *Phil.* 11°55N 121°34E **233** F3
Calvados □ *France* 49°5N 0°15W **172** C6
Calvados Chain, The
Papua N. G. 11°10S 152°45E **286** F7
Calvairate *Italy* 45°27N 9°13E **128** B2
Calvert → *Australia* 16°17S 137°44E **280** B2
Calvert I. *Canada* 51°30N 128°0W **296** C3
Calvert Ra. *Australia* 24°0S 122°30E **278** D3
Calvi *France* 42°34N 8°45E **175** F12
Calvià *Spain* 39°34N 2°31E **206** B3
Calvillo *Mexico* 21°51N 102°43W **318** C4
Calvinia *S. Africa* 31°28S 19°45E **270** D2
Calvo, Mte. *Italy* 41°44N 15°46E **199** G12
Calwa *U.S.A.* 36°42N 119°46W **306** J7
Calzada Almuradiel = Almuradiel
Spain 38°32N 3°28W **195** G7
Calzada de Calatrava
Spain 38°42N 3°46W **195** G7
Cam → *U.K.* 52°21N 0°16E **169** E8
Cam Lam = Ba Ngoi
Vietnam 11°54N 109°10E **237** G7
Cam Pha *Vietnam* 21°7N 107°18E **228** G6
Cam Ranh *Vietnam* 11°54N 109°12E **237** G7
Cam Xuyen *Vietnam* 18°15N 106°0E **236** C6
Camabatela *Angola* 8°20S 15°26E **265** D3
Camacã *Brazil* 15°24S 39°30W **333** E4
Camaçari *Brazil* 12°41S 38°18W **333** D4
Camacha *Madeira* 32°41N 16°49W **153** c
Camacupa *Angola* 11°58S 17°22E **265** E3
Camaguán *Venezuela* 8°6N 67°36W **328** B4
Camagüey *Cuba* 21°20N 77°55W **320** B4
Camagüey, Arch. de *Cuba* 22°18N 78°0W **320** B4
Camaiore *Italy* 43°56N 10°18E **198** E7
Camamu *Brazil* 13°57S 39°7W **333** D4
Camaná *Peru* 16°30S 72°50W **330** D3
Camanche *U.S.A.* 41°47N 90°15W **310** C6
Camanche Res. *U.S.A.* 38°14N 121°1W **306** G6
Camaquã *Brazil* 30°51S 51°49W **335** C5
Camaquã → *Brazil* 31°17S 51°47W **335** C5
Câmara de Lobos *Madeira* 32°39N 16°59W **153** c
Camaragibe *Brazil* 19°30S 54°5W **331** D7
Camaraté → *Brazil* 12°15S 58°55W **331** C6
Camarat, C. *France* 43°12N 6°41E **175** E10
Camarate *Portugal* 38°48N 9°7W **126** A2
Çamardı *Turkey* 37°49N 34°58E **212** D6
Camarès *France* 43°49N 2°53E **174** E6
Camaret-sur-Mer *France* 48°16N 4°37W **172** D2
Camargo *Bolivia* 20°38S 65°15W **331** E4
Camargo *Tamaulipas, Mexico* 26°19N 98°50W **319** B5
Camargue *France* 43°34N 4°34E **175** E8
Camargue △ *France* 43°30N 4°30E **175** E8
Camarillo *U.S.A.* 34°13N 119°2W **307** L7
Camariñas *Spain* 43°8N 9°12W **194** B1
Camarines Norte □ *Phil.* 14°10N 122°45E **232** D4
Camarines Sur □ *Phil.* 13°40N 123°20E **232** E4
Camaroes *Portugal* 38°49N 9°14W **126** A1
Camarón, C. *Honduras* 16°0N 85°5W **320** C2
Camarones *Argentina* 44°50S 65°40W **336** B3
Camarones, B. *Argentina* 44°45S 65°35W **336** B3
Camas *Spain* 37°24N 6°2W **195** H4
Camas *Wash., U.S.A.* 45°35N 122°24W **306** E4
Camas Valley *U.S.A.* 43°2N 123°40W **304** E2
Camatambo *Angola* 6°31S 15°21E **265** D3
Camataquí = Villa Abecia
Bolivia 21°0S 68°18W **334** A2
Camaxilo *Angola* 8°21S 18°56E **265** D3
Camba Cassai *Angola* 9°47S 19°9E **265** D3
Camballin *Australia* 17°59S 124°12E **278** C3
Cambambe *Angola* 8°53S 14°44E **265** D2
Cambará *Brazil* 23°2S 50°5W **335** A5
Cambay = Khambhat
India 22°23N 72°33E **242** H5
Cambay, G. of = Khambhat, G. of
India 20°45N 72°30E **239** E10
Camberwell *Vic., Australia* 37°50S 145°5E **128** B2
Camberwell *London, U.K.* 51°28N 0°5W **125** B3
Cambil *Spain* 37°40N 3°33W **195** H7
Cambo *Angola* 10°55S 20°6E **265** D3
Cambo-les-Bains *France* 43°22N 1°23W **174** E2
Cambodia ■ *Asia* 12°15N 105°0E **236** F5
Camborne *U.K.* 50°12N 5°19W **169** G2
Cambrai *S. Austral., Australia* 34°40S 139°16E **282** C3
Cambrai *Nord, France* 50°11N 3°14E **173** B10
Cambre *Spain* 43°17N 8°20W **194** B2
Cambria *U.S.A.* 35°34N 121°5W **306** K5
Cambrian Mts. *U.K.* 52°3N 3°57W **169** E4
Cambridge *Ont., Canada* 43°23N 80°15W **312** C4
Cambridge *Jamaica* 18°18N 77°54W **320** a
Cambridge *N.Z.* 37°54S 175°29E **284** D4
Cambridge *Cambs., U.K.* 52°12N 0°8E **169** E8
Cambridge *Ill., U.S.A.* 41°18N 90°12W **310** C6
Cambridge *Iowa, U.S.A.* 41°54N 93°32W **310** C3
Cambridge *Mass., U.S.A.* 42°23N 71°7W **116** A2
Cambridge *Minn., U.S.A.* 45°34N 93°13W **308** C7
Cambridge *N.Y., U.S.A.* 43°2N 73°22W **313** C11
Cambridge *Nebr., U.S.A.* 40°17N 100°10W **308** E3
Cambridge *Ohio, U.S.A.* 40°2N 81°35W **312** F3
Cambridge Bay *Canada* 69°10N 105°0W **294** D11
Cambridge City *U.S.A.* 39°49N 85°10W **311** E11
Cambridge G. *Australia* 14°55S 128°15E **278** B4
Cambridge Springs *U.S.A.* 41°48N 80°4W **312** E4
Cambridgeshire □ *U.K.* 52°25N 0°7W **169** E7
Cambrils *Spain* 41°8N 1°3E **196** D6
Cambuci *Rio de J., Brazil* 21°35S 41°55W **333** F3
Cambuci *São Paulo, Brazil* 23°33S 46°47W **137** B2
Cambulo *Angola* 7°49S 21°15E **265** D4
Cambundi-Catembo
Angola 10°10S 17°35E **265** E3
Camdeboo △ *S. Africa* 32°28S 24°25E **270** D3
Camden *N.S.W., Australia* 34°1S 150°43E **283** C9
Camden *Ala., U.S.A.* 31°59N 87°17W **315** F11
Camden *Ark., U.S.A.* 33°35N 92°50W **314** E8
Camden *Maine, U.S.A.* 44°13N 69°4W **309** C19
Camden *N.J., U.S.A.* 39°55N 75°7W **313** G9
Camden *N.Y., U.S.A.* 43°20N 75°45W **313** C9
Camden *Ohio, U.S.A.* 39°38N 84°39W **311** E12
Camden *S.C., U.S.A.* 34°16N 80°36W **315** D14
Camden □ *U.K.* 51°32N 0°8W **125** B3
Camden Bay *U.S.A.* 70°10N 145°15W **303** A11
Camden Sd. *Australia* 15°27S 124°25E **278** C3
Camdenton *U.S.A.* 38°1N 92°45W **310** F4
Cameia △ *Angola* 12°5S 21°40E **265** E4
Camelford *U.K.* 50°37N 4°42W **169** G3
Çameli *Turkey* 37°5N 29°24E **205** D11
Camenca *Moldova* 48°3N 28°42E **183** B13
Camerino *Italy* 43°8N 13°4E **199** E10
Cameron *Chile* 53°38S 69°39W **336** D3
Cameron *Ariz., U.S.A.* 35°53N 111°25W **305** J8
Cameron *La., U.S.A.* 29°48N 93°20W **314** G8
Cameron *Mo., U.S.A.* 39°44N 94°14W **310** E2
Cameron *S.C., U.S.A.* 33°34N 80°43W **316** B9
Cameron *Tex., U.S.A.* 30°51N 96°59W **314** F6
Cameron Highlands
Malaysia 4°27N 101°22E **237** K3
Cameron Hills *Canada* 59°48N 118°0W **296** B5
Cameron Mts. *N.Z.* 46°1S 167°0E **285** G2
Cameroon ■ *Africa* 6°0N 12°30E **264** A2
Camerota *Italy* 40°2N 15°22E **201** B8
Cameroun → *Cameroon* 4°0N 9°35E **263** E6
Cameroun, Mt. *Cameroon* 4°13N 9°10E **263** E6

Cametá Brazil 2°12S 49°30W 332 B2
Çamiçi Gölü Turkey 37°29N 27°28E 205 D9
Camiguin ☐ Phil. 9°11N 124°42E 233 G5
Camiguin I. Phil. 18°56N 121°55E 232 B3
Camiling Phil. 15°42N 120°24E 232 D3
Camilla U.S.A. 31°14N 84°12W 316 D5
Caminha Portugal 41°50N 8°50W 194 D2
Camino U.S.A. 38°44N 120°41W 306 G6
Camiranga Brazil 1°48S 46°17W 332 B2
Camiri Bolivia 20°3S 63°31W 331 E5
Camissombo Angola 8°7S 20°38E 265 D4
Camlıbel = Myrtou Cyprus 35°18N 33°4E 207 E9
Çamlıca Turkey 41°1N 29°3E 122 B2
Çamlıyayla Turkey 37°10N 34°36E 250 A5
Cammal U.S.A. 41°24N 77°28W 312 E7
Cammarata Italy 37°38N 13°38E 200 E6
Cammin = Kamień Pomorski Poland 53°57N 14°43E 184 E1
Camo Ethiopia 4°29N 38°24E 266 D4
Camocim Brazil 2°55S 40°50W 332 B3
Camonica, Val Italy 46°0N 10°20E 198 B7
Camooweal Australia 19°56S 138°7E 280 B2
Camooweal Caves △ Australia 20°1S 138°11E 280 C2
Camopi Fr. Guiana 3°12N 52°17W 329 C7
Camopi → Fr. Guiana 3°10N 52°20W 329 C7
Camorta India 8°8N 93°30E 245 K11
Camotes Is. Phil. 10°40N 124°24E 233 F5
Camotes Sea Phil. 10°30N 124°15E 233 F5
Camp Coulter = Powell U.S.A. 44°45N 108°46W 304 D9
Camp Hill Ala., U.S.A. 32°48N 85°39W 316 C4
Camp Hill Pa., U.S.A. 40°14N 76°55W 312 F8
Camp Nelson U.S.A. 36°8N 118°39W 307 J8
Camp Nou F.C. Barcelona Spain 41°22N 2°7E 114 A1
Camp Pendleton U.S.A. 33°13N 117°24W 307 M9
Camp Point U.S.A. 40°3N 91°4W 310 D5
Camp Springs U.S.A. 38°48N 76°55W 143 C3
Camp Verde U.S.A. 34°34N 111°51W 305 J8
Camp Wood U.S.A. 29°40N 100°1W 314 G4
Campagna Italy 40°40N 15°6E 201 B8
Campamento Spain 40°23N 3°46W 127 B1
Campana Argentina 34°10S 58°55W 334 C4
Campana, I. Chile 48°20S 75°20W 336 C1
Campanário Madeira 32°39N 17°2W 153 c
Campanario Spain 38°52N 5°36W 195 G5
Campanet Spain 39°46N 2°58E 206 B3
Campánia ☐ Italy 41°0N 14°30E 201 B7
Campas del Tuyú △ Argentina 36°17S 56°50W 334 D4
Campbell Northern Cape, S. Africa 28°48S 23°44E 270 C3
Campbell Calif., U.S.A. 37°17N 121°57W 306 H5
Campbell Fla., U.S.A. 28°16N 81°27W 317 G8
Campbell Ohio, U.S.A. 41°5N 80°37W 312 E4
Campbell, C. N.Z. 41°47S 174°18E 285 B9
Campbell I. Pac. Oc. 52°30S 169°0E 288 N8
Campbell L. Canada 63°14N 106°55W 297 A7
Campbell Plateau S. Ocean 50°0S 170°0E 151 A11
Campbell River Canada 50°5N 125°20W 296 C3
Campbellfield Australia 37°41S 144°57E 128 A1
Campbellford Canada 44°18N 77°48W 312 B7
Campbellpur Pakistan 33°46N 72°26E 242 C5
Campbellsburg U.S.A. 38°39N 86°16W 311 F10
Campbellsville U.S.A. 37°21N 85°20W 309 G11
Campbellton N.B., Canada 47°57N 66°43W 299 C6
Campbellton Fla., U.S.A. 30°57N 85°24W 316 E4
Campbelltown = Bluff N.Z. 46°37S 168°20E 285 G3
Campbelltown Australia 34°4S 150°49E 283 C9
Campbeltown U.K. 55°26N 5°36W 167 F3
Campêche Guadeloupe 16°26N 61°26W 322 e
Campeche Campeche, Mexico 19°51N 90°32W 319 D6
Campeche ☐ Mexico 19°0N 90°30W 319 D6
Campeche, Banco Mexico 22°30N 88°0W 319 C7
Campeche, Golfo de Mexico 19°30N 93°0W 319 D6
Câmpeni Romania 46°22N 23°3E 182 D8
Camperdown N.S.W., Australia 33°53S 151°11E 139 B2
Camperdown Vic., Australia 38°14S 143°9E 282 E5
Camperville Canada 51°59N 100°9W 297 C8
Campi Salentina Italy 40°24N 18°1E 201 B11
Câmpia Turzii Romania 46°34N 23°53E 183 D8
Campidano Italy 39°30N 8°47E 200 C1
Campidoglio, Piazza de Rome, Italy 136 c3
Campíglia Maríttima Italy 43°4N 10°37E 198 E7
Campillo de Altobuey Spain 39°36N 1°49W 197 F3
Campillos Spain 37°4N 4°51W 195 H6
Câmpina Romania 45°10N 25°45E 183 E10
Campina Grande Brazil 7°20S 35°47W 332 C4
Campina Verde Brazil 19°31S 49°28W 333 E2
Campinas Brazil 22°50S 47°0W 335 A6
Campione Italy 45°58N 8°58E 175 C12
Campli Italy 42°43N 13°41E 199 F10
Campo = Ntem → Cameroon 2°21N 9°49E 264 B2
Campo Cameroon 2°22N 9°50E 264 B1
Campo Spain 42°25N 0°24E 196 C5
Campo, Casa de Spain 40°25N 3°45W 127 B1
Campo △ Cameroon 2°23N 10°5E 264 B2
Campo Belo Brazil 20°52S 45°16W 333 F2
Campo de Criptana Spain 39°24N 3°7W 195 F7
Campo de Diauarum Brazil 11°12S 53°14W 331 C7
Campo de Gibraltar Spain 36°15N 5°25W 195 J5
Campo de los Alisos △ Argentina 27°15S 66°0W 334 B2
Campo Florido Brazil 19°47S 48°35W 333 E2
Campo Formoso = Campo Florido Brazil 19°47S 48°35W 333 E2
Campo Formoso Brazil 10°30S 40°20W 332 D3
Campo Grande Brazil 20°25S 54°40W 331 E7
Campo Grando Portugal 38°45N 9°9W 126 A2
Campo Maior Brazil 4°50S 42°12W 332 B3
Campo Maior Portugal 39°2N 7°7W 195 F3
Campo Mourão Brazil 24°3S 52°22W 335 A5
Campo Pequeño Portugal 38°44N 9°8W 126 A2
Campo Santa Margherita Venice, Italy 142 b2
Campo Túres Italy 46°53N 11°55E 199 B8
Campoalegre Colombia 2°41N 75°20W 328 C2
Campobasso Italy 41°34N 14°39E 201 A7
Campobello di Licata Italy 37°15N 13°55E 200 E6
Campobello di Mazara Italy 37°38N 12°45E 200 E5
Campofelice di Roccella Italy 37°59N 13°53E 200 E6
Campolide Portugal 38°43N 9°9W 126 A2
Campomarino Italy 41°57N 15°2E 199 G12
Camporeale Italy 37°54N 13°6E 200 E6
Camporrobles Spain 39°39N 1°24W 196 F3
Campos Brazil 21°50S 41°20W 333 F3
Campos Spain 39°26N 3°1E 206 B4
Campos Altos Brazil 19°47S 46°10W 333 E2
Campos Belos Brazil 13°10S 47°3W 333 D2
Campos del Paraíso = Carrascosa del Campo Spain 40°2N 2°45W 196 E2
Campos Novos Brazil 27°21S 51°50W 335 B5
Campos Sales Brazil 7°4S 40°23W 332 C3
Camprodon Spain 42°19N 2°23E 196 C7
Camps Bay S. Africa 33°57S 18°23E 118 A1
Campton Fla., U.S.A. 30°53N 86°31W 317 E3
Campton Ga., U.S.A. 33°52N 83°43W 316 B6
Campton Ky., U.S.A. 37°44N 83°33W 311 G13
Camptonville U.S.A. 39°27N 121°3W 306 F5
Camptown U.S.A. 41°44N 76°14W 313 E8
Câmpulung Romania 45°17N 25°3E 183 E10
Câmpulung Moldovenesc Romania 47°32N 25°30E 183 C10
Câmpuri Romania 46°0N 26°50E 183 D11
Campuya → Peru 1°40S 73°30W 328 D3
Campville U.S.A. 29°40N 82°7W 316 F7
Camrose Canada 53°0N 112°50W 296 C6
Camsell Portage Canada 59°37N 109°15W 297 B7
Camucuio Angola 14°7S 13°15E 265 E2
Camuy Puerto Rico 18°29N 66°51W 321 b
Çamyuva Turkey 36°30N 30°30E 205 E12
Çan Turkey 40°2N 27°3E 203 F11
Can Clavo Spain 38°57N 1°27E 206 D1
Can Creu Spain 38°58N 1°28E 206 D1
Can Gio Vietnam 10°25N 106°58E 237 G6
Can Pastilla Spain 39°32N 2°42E 206 B3
C'an San Joan Spain 41°28N 2°11E 114 A2
Can Tho Vietnam 10°2N 105°46E 237 G5
Canaan Trin. & Tob. 11°9N 60°49W 323 s
Canaan Conn., U.S.A. 42°2N 73°20W 313 D11
Canaan Hill Jamaica 18°23N 77°14W 320 a
Cañacao B. Phil. 14°29N 120°54E 127 C1
Canacona India 15°1N 74°4E 245 G2
Canada ■ N. Amer. 60°0N 100°0W 294 G11
Canada Abyssal Plain Arctic 80°0N 140°0W 150 B18
Canada Basin Arctic 75°0N 145°0W 150 B18
Cañada de Gómez Argentina 32°40S 61°30W 334 C3
Canadian U.S.A. 35°55N 100°23W 314 D4
Canadian → U.S.A. 35°28N 95°3W 314 D7
Canadian Shield Canada 53°0N 75°0W 292 D12
Canadys U.S.A. 33°3N 80°37W 316 B9
Canajoharie U.S.A. 42°54N 74°35W 313 D10
Çanakkale Turkey 40°8N 26°24E 203 F10
Çanakkale ☐ Turkey 40°10N 26°25E 203 F10
Çanakkale Boğazı Turkey 40°17N 26°32E 203 F10
Canal Flats Canada 50°10N 115°48W 296 C5
Canal Grande Venice, Italy 142 b2
Canal Point U.S.A. 26°52N 80°38W 317 J9
Canal Street New Orleans, U.S.A. 131 b2
Canala N. Cal. 21°32S 165°57E 288 d
Canalejas Argentina 35°15S 66°34W 334 D2
Canals Argentina 33°35S 62°53W 334 C3
Canals Spain 38°58N 0°35W 197 G4
Canandaigua U.S.A. 42°54N 77°17W 312 D7
Canandaigua L. U.S.A. 42°47N 77°19W 312 D7
Cananea Mexico 31°0N 110°18W 318 A2
Cañar Ecuador 2°33S 78°56W 328 D2
Cañar ☐ Ecuador 2°30S 79°0W 328 D2
Canarias, Is. Atl. Oc. 28°30N 16°0W 153 e1
Canaries St. Lucia 13°55N 61°4W 323 m
Canarreos, Arch. de los Cuba 21°35N 81°40W 320 B3
Canarsie U.S.A. 40°38N 73°53W 132 C2
Canary Is. = Canarias, Is. Atl. Oc. 28°30N 16°0W 153 e1
Canary Wharf U.K. 51°30N 0°1W 125 A3
Canaseraga U.S.A. 42°27N 77°45W 312 D7
Canastra, Serra da Brazil 20°0S 46°20W 333 F2
Canatlán Mexico 24°31N 104°47W 318 C4
Cañaveral Peru 3°56S 80°39W 328 D1
Canaveral, C. U.S.A. 28°27N 80°32W 317 G9
Canaveral △ U.S.A. 28°28N 80°34W 317 G9
Cañaveruelas Spain 40°24N 2°38W 196 E2
Canavieiras Brazil 15°39S 39°0W 333 E4
Canbelego Australia 31°32S 146°18E 283 A7
Canberra Australia 35°15S 149°8E 283 C8
Canby Calif., U.S.A. 41°27N 120°52W 304 F3
Canby Minn., U.S.A. 44°43N 96°16W 308 C5
Canby Oreg., U.S.A. 45°16N 122°42W 306 E4
Cancale France 48°40N 1°50W 172 D5
Cancellería, Palazzo dei Rome, Italy 136 c2
Canche → France 50°31N 1°39E 173 B8
Canchungo = Teixeira Pinto Guinea-Biss. 12°3N 16°0W 262 C1
Canchungo Guinea-Biss. 12°26N 16°5W 262 C1
Canchyuaya, Cordillera de Peru 7°30S 74°0W 330 B3
Cancún Mexico 21°8N 86°44W 319 C7
Candanchú Spain 42°47N 0°32W 196 C4
Candarave Peru 17°15S 70°13W 330 D3
Çandarlı Turkey 38°56N 26°56E 205 C8
Çandarlı Körfezi Turkey 38°52N 26°55E 205 C8
Candás Spain 43°35N 5°45W 194 B5
Candé France 47°34N 1°2W 172 E5
Candeias → Brazil 8°39S 63°31W 331 B5
Candela Italy 41°8N 15°31E 201 A8
Candelaria Argentina 27°29S 55°44W 335 B4
Candelaria Canary Is. 28°22N 16°22W 153 e1
Candelaria Phil. 13°56N 121°25E 232 E3
Candelario △ Spain 40°20N 5°46W 194 E5
Candeleda Spain 40°10N 5°14W 194 E5
Candelo Australia 36°47S 149°43E 283 D8
Candi Dasa Indonesia 8°30S 115°34E 231 J18
Candia = Iraklio Greece 35°20N 25°12E 207 E6
Candia, Sea of = Crete, Sea of Greece 36°0N 25°0E 205 E7
Candiac Canada 45°23N 73°29W 130 B3
Cândido de Abreu Brazil 24°35S 51°20W 333 F1
Cândido Mendes Brazil 1°27S 45°43W 332 B2
Candle U.S.A. 65°55N 161°56W 303 D7
Candle L. Canada 53°50N 105°18W 297 C7
Candlemas I. Antarctica 57°3S 26°40W 151 B1
Candler-McAfee U.S.A. 33°44N 84°16W 113 B3
Cando U.S.A. 48°32N 99°12W 308 A4
Candon Phil. 17°12N 120°27E 232 C3
Canea = Chania Greece 35°30N 24°4E 207 E5
Caneças Portugal 38°48N 9°13W 126 A1
Canefield Dominica 15°20N 61°24W 323 k
Canela Brazil 10°15S 48°25W 332 D2
Canelles → St. Lucia 13°47N 60°55W 323 m
Canelli Italy 44°43N 8°17E 198 D5
Canelones Uruguay 34°32S 56°17W 335 C4
Canet de Mar Spain 41°35N 2°35E 196 D7
Canet-Plage France 42°41N 3°2E 174 F7
Cañete Chile 37°50S 73°30W 334 D1
Cañete Spain 40°3N 1°54W 196 E3
Cañete de las Torres Spain 37°53N 4°19W 195 H6
Cangamba Angola 13°40S 19°54E 265 E3
Cangandala Angola 9°45S 16°33E 265 D3
Cangandala △ Angola 9°53S 16°42E 265 D3
Cangas Spain 42°16N 8°47W 194 C2
Cangas de Onís Spain 43°21N 5°8W 194 B5
Cangas de Tineo = Cangas del Narcea Spain 43°10N 6°32W 194 B4
Cangas del Narcea Spain 43°10N 6°32W 194 B4
Cangnan China 27°30N 120°23E 229 D13
Cangoa Angola 13°8S 18°30E 265 E3
Cangola Angola 7°58S 15°53E 265 D3
Cangolo Angola 15°0S 13°52E 265 E2
Cangombe Angola 14°24S 19°59E 265 E3
Cangongo Angola 9°24S 17°30E 265 D3
Cangshan China 34°50N 118°2E 227 G10
Canguaretama Brazil 6°20S 35°5W 332 C4
Canguçu Brazil 31°22S 52°43W 335 C5
Canguçu, Serra do Brazil 31°20S 52°40W 335 C5
Cangumbe Angola 11°58S 19°12E 265 E3
Cangxi China 31°47N 105°59E 228 B5
Cangyuan China 23°12N 99°14E 228 F2
Cangzhou China 38°19N 116°52E 226 E9
Canhoca Angola 9°15S 14°41E 265 D2
Cani, I. Tunisia 36°21N 10°5E 258 A2
Caniapiscau → Canada 56°40N 69°30W 299 A6
Caniapiscau, L. Canada 54°10N 69°55W 299 B6
Caniçal Madeira 32°44N 16°44W 153 c
Canicattì Italy 37°21N 13°51E 200 E6
Canicattini Bagni Italy 37°2N 15°4E 201 E8
Canigao Channel Phil. 10°15N 124°42E 233 F5
Canigou France 42°31N 2°27E 174 F6
Caniles Spain 37°26N 2°43W 195 H8
Canillas Spain 40°27N 3°38W 127 B2
Canillejas Spain 40°26N 3°36W 127 B2
Canim Lake Canada 51°47N 120°54W 296 C4
Canindé Brazil 4°22S 39°19W 332 B4
Canindé → Brazil 6°15S 42°52W 332 C3
Canindeyu ☐ Paraguay 24°10S 55°0W 335 A5
Canino Italy 42°28N 11°45E 199 F8
Canisteo U.S.A. 42°16N 77°36W 312 D7
Canisteo → U.S.A. 42°7N 77°8W 312 D7
Cañitas de Felipe Pescador Mexico 23°36N 102°43W 318 C4
Cañizal Spain 41°12N 5°22W 194 D5
Canjáyar Spain 37°1N 2°44W 195 H8
Canjinge Angola 10°12S 21°17E 265 E4
Çankırı Turkey 40°40N 33°37E 212 B5
Çankırı ☐ Turkey 40°40N 33°30E 212 B5
Cankuzo Burundi 3°10S 30°31E 268 C3
Canlaon Phil. 10°22N 123°12E 233 F4
Canlaon Volcano Phil. 10°25N 123°8E 233 F4
Canmore Canada 51°7N 115°18W 296 C5
Cann River Australia 37°35S 149°7E 283 D8
Canna U.K. 57°3N 6°33W 167 D2
Cannanore = Kannur India 11°53N 75°27E 245 J2
Cannanore Is. India 10°30N 72°30E 245 J1
Cannaregio Venice, Italy 142 a2
Cannaregio, Canale di Venice, Italy 142 a1
Cannelton U.S.A. 37°55N 86°45W 311 G10
Cannery, The San Francisco, U.S.A. 136 a1
Cannes France 43°32N 7°1E 175 E11
Canning Town = Port Canning India 22°23N 88°40E 243 H13
Canning Town U.K. 51°30N 0°1E 125 A4
Cannington Canada 44°20N 79°2W 312 B5
Cannóbio Italy 46°4N 8°42E 198 B5
Cannock U.K. 52°41N 2°1W 169 E5
Cannonball → U.S.A. 46°26N 100°35W 308 B3
Cannondale Mt. Australia 25°13S 148°57E 280 D4
Cannonsville Res. U.S.A. 42°4N 75°22W 313 D9
Cannonvale Australia 20°17S 148°43E 280 b
Caño Colorado Colombia 2°18N 68°22W 328 C4
Canoas Brazil 29°56S 51°11W 335 B5
Canoe L. Canada 55°10N 108°15W 297 B7
Cañon City U.S.A. 38°27N 105°14W 304 G11
Cañón del Río Blanco △ Mexico 18°43N 97°15W 319 D5
Cañón del Río Lobos △ Spain 41°46N 3°28W 194 D7
Canonnier, Pte. du St.-Martin 18°4N 63°7W 322 a
Canonniers Pt. Mauritius 20°2S 57°32E 272 e
Canoochee → U.S.A. 31°59N 81°19W 316 D8
Canopus Australia 33°29S 140°42E 282 B4
Canora Canada 51°40N 102°30W 297 C8
Canosa di Púglia Italy 41°13N 16°4E 201 A9
Canouan St. Vincent 12°43N 61°20W 323 n
Canowindra Australia 33°35S 148°38E 283 B8
Canso Canada 45°20N 61°0W 299 C7
Canso, Str. of Canada 45°37N 61°22W 299 C7
Canta Peru 11°29S 76°37W 330 C2
Cantabria ☐ Spain 43°10N 4°0W 194 B7
Cantabria, Sierra de Spain 42°40N 2°30W 196 C2
Cantabrian Mts. = Cantábrica, Cordillera Spain 43°0N 5°10W 194 C5
Cantábrica, Cordillera Spain 43°0N 5°10W 194 C5
Cantal ☐ France 45°5N 2°45E 174 C6
Cantal, Plomb du France 45°3N 2°45E 174 C6
Cantanhede Portugal 40°20N 8°36W 194 E2
Cantaura Venezuela 9°19N 64°21W 329 B5
Cantavieja Spain 40°31N 0°25W 196 E4
Čantavir Serbia 45°55N 19°46E 182 E4
Cantemir Moldova 46°17N 28°14E 183 D13
Canteras de Vallecas Spain 40°20N 3°37W 127 B2
Canterbury = Invermere Canada 50°30N 116°2W 296 C5
Canterbury N.S.W., Australia 33°55S 151°7E 139 B1
Canterbury Queens., Australia 25°23S 141°53E 280 D3
Canterbury Vic., Australia 37°49S 145°4E 128 A2
Canterbury Kent, U.K. 51°16N 1°6E 169 F9
Canterbury ☐ N.Z. 43°45S 171°19E 285 D6
Canterbury Bight N.Z. 44°16S 171°55E 285 E6
Canterbury Plains N.Z. 43°55S 171°22E 285 D6
Cantil U.S.A. 35°18N 117°58W 307 K9
Cantilan Phil. 9°20N 125°58E 233 G5
Cantillana Spain 37°36N 5°50W 195 H5
Canto do Buriti Brazil 8°7S 42°58W 332 C3
Canton = Guangzhou China 23°6N 113°13E 121 B2
Canton Ga., U.S.A. 34°14N 84°29W 315 D12
Canton Ill., U.S.A. 40°33N 90°2W 310 D6
Canton Miss., U.S.A. 32°37N 90°2W 315 E9
Canton Mo., U.S.A. 40°8N 91°32W 310 D5
Canton N.Y., U.S.A. 44°36N 75°10W 313 B9
Canton Ohio, U.S.A. 40°48N 81°23W 312 F3
Canton Pa., U.S.A. 41°39N 76°51W 312 E8
Canton S. Dak., U.S.A. 43°18N 96°35W 308 D5
Canton L. U.S.A. 36°6N 98°35W 314 C5
Canton Tower China 23°6N 113°19E 121 B2
Cantonment U.S.A. 30°37N 87°20W 317 E2
Cantù Italy 45°44N 9°8E 198 C6
Cantwell U.S.A. 63°24N 148°57W 303 E10
Canudos Brazil 7°13S 58°5W 331 B6
Canumã Amazonas, Brazil 4°2S 59°4W 329 D6
Canumã Amazonas, Brazil 6°8S 60°10W 331 B5
Canumã → Brazil 3°55S 59°10W 331 A6
Canunda △ Australia 37°42S 140°16E 282 D4
Canutama Brazil 6°30S 64°20W 331 B5
Canutillo U.S.A. 31°55N 106°36W 314 F1
Canvey Island U.K. 51°31N 0°37E 169 F8
Canyon U.S.A. 34°59N 101°55W 314 D4
Canyon De Chelly △ U.S.A. 36°10N 109°20W 305 H9
Canyonlands △ U.S.A. 38°15N 110°0W 305 G9
Canyons of the Ancients △ U.S.A. 37°30N 108°55W 305 H9
Canyonville U.S.A. 42°56N 123°17W 304 E2
Canzar Angola 7°35S 21°34E 265 D4
Cao Bang Vietnam 22°40N 106°15E 228 F6
Cao He → China 40°10N 124°32E 227 D13
Cao Lanh Vietnam 10°27N 105°38E 237 G5
Cao Xian China 34°50N 115°35E 226 G8
Caofeidian China 38°56N 118°32E 227 E10
Caoheijing China 25°15N 103°12E 138 B1
Caombo Angola 8°42S 16°33E 265 D3
Cáorle Italy 45°36N 12°53E 199 C9
Cap-aux-Meules Canada 47°23N 61°52W 299 C7
Cap-Chat Canada 49°6N 66°40W 299 C6
Cap-de-la-Madeleine Canada 46°22N 72°31W 298 C5
Cap-de-Ville Trin. & Tob. 10°9N 61°42W 323 t
Cap-Haïtien Haiti 19°40N 72°20W 321 C5
Cap I. Phil. 5°57N 120°56E 233 J3
Cap Pt. St. Lucia 14°7N 60°57W 323 m
Capac U.S.A. 43°1N 82°56W 312 C2
Capáccio Italy 40°25N 15°5E 201 B8
Capaci Italy 38°10N 13°14E 200 D6
Capaia Angola 8°27S 20°13E 265 D4
Capalonga Phil. 14°20N 122°30E 232 D4
Capanaparo → Venezuela 7°1N 67°7W 328 B4
Capanema Brazil 1°12S 47°11W 332 B2
Capangombe Angola 15°6S 13°8E 265 F2
Capànnori Italy 43°50N 10°34E 198 E7
Capão Redondo Brazil 23°39S 46°45W 137 B1
Caparaó △ Brazil 20°25S 41°46W 333 F3
Caparica Portugal 38°40N 9°9W 126 A2
Caparica, Costa da Portugal 38°38N 9°15W 126 B1
Caparo → Trin. & Tob. 10°31N 61°28W 323 t
Capas Phil. 15°38N 120°28E 232 D3
Capatárida Venezuela 11°11N 70°37W 328 A3
Capayas Phil. 10°28N 119°39E 233 F2
Capbreton France 43°39N 1°26W 174 E2
Capdenac France 44°34N 2°5E 174 D6
Capdepera Spain 39°42N 3°26E 206 B4
Cape → Australia 20°59S 146°51E 280 C4
Cape Arid △ Australia 33°58S 123°13E 279 F3
Cape Barren I. Australia 40°25S 148°15E 281 G4
Cape Basin Atl. Oc. 34°0S 7°0W 152 K12
Cape Breton Highlands △ Canada 46°50N 60°40W 299 C7
Cape Breton I. Canada 46°0N 60°30W 299 C7
Cape Canaveral U.S.A. 28°24N 80°36W 317 G9
Cape Charles U.S.A. 37°16N 76°1W 309 G15
Cape Coast Ghana 5°5N 1°15W 263 D4
Cape Cod △ U.S.A. 41°56N 70°6W 309 E18
Cape Coral U.S.A. 26°33N 81°57W 317 J8
Cape Crawford Australia 16°41S 135°43E 280 B2
Cape Dorset = Kinngait Canada 64°14N 76°32W 295 E16
Cape Fear → U.S.A. 33°53N 78°1W 315 E15
Cape Flats S. Africa 34°3S 18°33E 118 B2
Cape Girardeau U.S.A. 37°19N 89°32W 308 G9
Cape Hatteras △ U.S.A. 35°30N 75°28W 315 D17
Cape Hillsborough △ Australia 20°54S 149°2E 280 b
Cape Jervis Australia 35°40S 138°5E 282 C3
Cape Krusenstern △ U.S.A. 67°30N 163°30W 303 C7
Cape Lambert Australia 20°36S 117°11E 278 D2
Cape Le Grand △ Australia 33°54S 122°26E 279 F3
Cape Lisburne = Wevok U.S.A. 68°53N 166°13W 303 B6
Cape Lookout △ U.S.A. 35°45N 76°25W 315 D16
Cape May U.S.A. 38°56N 74°56W 309 F16
Cape May Point U.S.A. 38°56N 74°58W 309 F16
Cape Melville △ Australia 14°26S 144°28E 280 A3
Cape Mount △ Liberia 6°44N 11°24W 262 D2
Cape Pole U.S.A. 55°58N 133°48W 303 J14
Cape Range △ Australia 22°3S 114°0E 278 D1
Cape St. George Canada 48°28N 59°14W 299 C8
Cape Tormentine Canada 46°8N 63°47W 299 C7
Cape Town S. Africa 33°55S 18°22E 118 A1
Cape Town Int. ✕ (CPT) S. Africa 33°58S 18°35E 118 A2
Cape Upstart △ Australia 19°45S 147°48E 280 B4
Cape Verde Abyssal Plain Atl. Oc. 23°0N 26°0W 152 D9
Cape Verde Is. = Cabo Verde ■ Atl. Oc. 16°0N 24°0W 153 j
Cape Verde Is. Atl. Oc. 16°0N 24°0W 153 j
Cape Verde Plateau Atl. Oc. 18°0N 20°0W 152 E10
Cape Vincent U.S.A. 44°8N 76°20W 313 B8
Cape Yakataga U.S.A. 60°4N 142°26W 303 F12
Cape York Peninsula Australia 12°0S 142°30E 286 F2
Capela Brazil 10°30S 37°0W 332 D4
Capelas Azores 37°50N 25°41W 153 d3
Capele Angola 13°39S 14°53E 265 E2
Capelengue Angola 8°53S 19°42E 265 D3
Capelinha Brazil 17°42S 42°31W 333 E3
Capelinhos, Pta. dos Azores 38°36N 28°50W 153 d1
Capella Australia 23°2S 148°1E 280 C4
Capella, Mt. Papua N. G. 5°4S 141°8E 286 C1
Capelongo Angola 14°54S 15°8E 265 E3
Capenda Camulemba Angola 9°24S 18°27E 265 D3
Capendu France 43°11N 2°31E 174 E6
Capertree Australia 33°6S 149°58E 283 B8
Capestang France 43°20N 3°2E 174 E7
Capesterre, Grande Rivière de la → Guadeloupe 16°3N 61°33W 322 e
Capesterre, Pte. de la Guadeloupe 16°3N 61°33W 322 e
Capesterre-Belle-Eau Guadeloupe 16°4N 61°36W 322 e
Capesterre-de-Marie-Galante Guadeloupe 15°53N 61°14W 322 e
Capim → Brazil 1°40S 47°47W 332 B2
Capinópolis Brazil 18°41S 49°35W 333 E2
Capinota Bolivia 17°43S 66°14W 330 D4
Capira Panama 8°45N 79°53W 328 B2
Capistrello Italy 41°57N 13°23E 199 G10
Capitan U.S.A. 33°35N 105°35W 305 K11
Capitán Aracena, I. Chile 54°10S 71°20W 336 D2
Capitán Arturo Prat Antarctica 63°0S 61°0W 151 C17
Capitán Pastene Chile 38°13S 73°1W 336 A2
Capitão de Campos Brazil 4°40S 41°55W 332 B3
Capitol Heights U.S.A. 38°52N 76°55W 143 B3
Capitol Hill N. Marianas 15°13N 145°45E 302 e
Capitol Reef △ U.S.A. 38°15N 111°10W 305 G8
Capitola U.S.A. 36°59N 121°57W 306 J5
Capitolini, Musei Rome, Italy 136 c3
Capivara, Serra da Brazil 14°35S 45°0W 333 D3
Capiz ☐ Phil. 11°35N 122°30E 233 F4
Capizzi Italy 37°51N 14°29E 201 E7
Capoche → Mozam. 15°35S 33°0E 269 F3
Capodichino, Nápoli ✕ (NAP) Italy 40°53N 14°16E 201 B7
Capodistria = Koper Slovenia 45°31N 13°44E 199 C10
Capoeira Brazil 5°37S 59°33W 331 B6
Capolo Angola 10°22S 14°7E 265 E2
Caporetto = Kobarid Slovenia 46°15N 13°30E 199 B10
Caporolo → Angola 12°56S 12°58E 265 E2
Capot → Martinique 14°50N 61°5W 322 j
Capoterra Italy 39°11N 8°58E 200 C1
Cappadocia Turkey 39°0N 35°0E 212 C6
Capps U.S.A. 30°24N 83°54W 316 E6
Capraia Italy 43°2N 9°50E 198 E6
Caprara, Pta. Italy 41°7N 8°19E 200 A1
Caprarola Italy 42°19N 12°14E 199 F9
Caprera Italy 41°12N 9°28E 200 A2
Capri Italy 40°33N 14°14E 201 B7
Capricorn Coast Australia 23°16S 150°49E 280 C5
Capricorn Group Australia 23°30S 151°55E 280 C5
Capricorn Ra. Australia 23°20S 116°50E 278 D2
Caprino Veronese Italy 45°36N 10°47E 198 C7
Caprivi △ Namibia 17°55S 22°37E 270 A3
Caprivi Strip Namibia 18°0S 23°0E 270 A3
Caps et Marais d'Opale △ France 50°40N 2°0E 173 B9
Captain Cook U.S.A. 19°30N 155°55W 302 D6
Captain Cook Bridge Australia 34°0S 151°7E 139 C1
Captain Cook Landing Place Park Australia 34°1S 151°14E 139 C2
Captains Flat Australia 35°35S 149°27E 283 C8
Captieux France 44°18N 0°16W 174 D3
Captiva U.S.A. 26°31N 82°11W 317 J7
Capuça Angola 17°22S 21°18E 265 F4
Capuchos Portugal 38°38N 9°16W 126 B1
Capucin Dominica 15°38N 61°28W 323 k
Capul I. Phil. 12°26N 124°10E 232 E5
Capulin Volcano △ U.S.A. 36°47N 103°58W 314 C3
Capunda Angola 10°41S 17°23E 265 E3
Caquetá ☐ Colombia 1°0N 74°0W 328 C3
Caquetá → Colombia 1°15S 69°15W 328 D4
Car Nicobar India 9°10N 92°47E 245 K11
Cara-Paraná → Colombia 1°45S 73°13W 328 D3
Carabanchel Alto Spain 40°22N 3°44W 127 B1
Carabanchel Bajo Spain 40°23N 3°44W 127 B1
Carabao I. Phil. 12°4N 121°56E 232 E3
Carabobo ☐ Venezuela 10°10N 68°5W 328 A4
Caracal Romania 44°8N 24°22E 183 F9
Caracaraí Brazil 1°50N 61°8W 329 C5
Caracas Venezuela 10°30N 66°55W 328 A4
Caracol Belize 16°45N 89°6W 320 C2
Caracol Mato Grosso do Sul, Brazil 22°18S 57°1W 334 A4
Caracol Piauí, Brazil 9°15S 43°22W 332 C3
Caracoli, Pte. Martinique 14°45N 60°52W 322 j
Caracollo Bolivia 17°39S 67°10W 330 D4
Caraga Phil. 7°20N 126°34E 233 H6
Caraga ☐ Phil. 9°40N 125°50E 233 G6
Caragabal Australia 33°49S 147°45E 283 B7
Caráglio Italy 44°25N 7°26E 198 D4
Carahue Chile 38°43S 73°12W 336 A2
Caraí Brazil 17°12S 41°42W 333 E3
Caraïbes, Mts. Guadeloupe 15°58N 61°41W 322 e
Carajás Brazil 2°57S 51°22W 332 C1
Carajás, Serra dos Brazil 6°0S 51°30W 332 C1
Caral Peru 10°53S 77°31W 330 C2
Caramoan Phil. 13°46N 123°52E 232 E4
Caramoan Pen. Phil. 13°47N 123°44E 232 E4
Caramoran Phil. 14°0N 124°8E 232 D5
Caranapatuba Brazil 6°38S 62°34W 331 B5
Carandaití Bolivia 20°45S 63°4W 331 E5
Carangola Brazil 20°44S 42°5W 333 F3
Caransebeş Romania 45°28N 22°18E 182 E7
Carantec France 48°40N 3°55W 172 D3
Carapachay Argentina 34°31S 58°32W 117 B1
Carapichaima Trin. & Tob. 10°28N 61°27W 323 t
Carapo → Barinas, Venezuela 7°46N 70°23W 328 B3
Carapo → Bolivar, Venezuela 7°30N 64°0W 329 B5
Carapuse B. Trin. & Tob. 11°14N 60°35W 323 s
Caraquet Canada 47°48N 64°57W 299 C6
Caraş Severin ☐ Romania 45°10N 22°10E 182 E7
Caraşova Romania 45°11N 21°51E 182 E6
Caratasca, L. de Honduras 15°20N 83°40W 320 C3
Caratinga Brazil 19°50S 42°10W 333 E3
Carauari Brazil 4°52S 66°54W 328 D4
Caraúbas Brazil 5°43S 37°33W 332 C4
Caravaca de la Cruz Spain 38°8N 1°52W 197 G3
Caravággio Italy 45°30N 9°38E 198 C6
Caravela Guinea-Biss. 11°30N 16°30W 262 C1
Caravelas Brazil 17°45S 39°15W 333 E4
Caraveli Peru 15°45S 73°25W 330 D3
Caravelle, Presqu'île de la Martinique 14°46N 60°48W 322 j
Caraz Peru 9°3S 77°47W 330 B2
Caraza Argentina 34°41S 58°25W 117 C2
Carazinho Brazil 28°16S 52°46W 335 B5
Carbalia Moldova 45°52N 28°27E 183 E13
Carballino = O Carballiño Spain 42°26N 8°5W 194 C2
Carballo Spain 43°13N 8°41W 194 B2
Carberry Canada 49°50N 99°25W 297 D9
Carbet, Chutes du Guadeloupe 16°2N 61°38W 322 e
Carbet, Pitons du Martinique 14°42N 61°7W 322 j
Carbó Mexico 29°42N 110°58W 318 B2
Carbón, L. del Argentina 49°35S 68°21W 336 C3
Carbonara, C. Italy 39°6N 9°31E 200 C2
Carbondale Colo., U.S.A. 39°24N 107°13W 304 G10
Carbondale Ill., U.S.A. 37°44N 89°13W 310 G7
Carbondale Pa., U.S.A. 41°35N 75°30W 313 E9
Carbonear Canada 47°42N 53°13W 299 C9
Carboneras Spain 36°59N 1°53W 197 J3
Carboneras de Guadazón Spain 39°54N 1°50W 196 F3
Carbónia Italy 39°10N 8°30E 200 C1
Carbonne France 43°18N 1°11E 174 E5
Carcabuey Spain 37°27N 4°17W 195 H6
Carcagente = Carcaixent Spain 39°8N 0°28W 197 F4
Carcaixent Spain 39°8N 0°28W 197 F4
Carcajou Canada 57°47N 117°6W 296 B5
Carcar Phil. 10°6N 123°38E 233 F4
Carcarana → Argentina 32°27S 60°48W 334 C3
Carcasse, C. Haiti 18°30N 74°28W 321 C5
Carcassonne France 43°13N 2°20E 174 E6
Carchi ☐ Ecuador 0°45N 78°0W 328 C2
Carcoar Australia 33°36S 149°8E 283 B8
Carcross Canada 60°13N 134°45W 296 A2
Çardak Çanakkale, Turkey 40°22N 26°43E 203 F10
Çardak Denizli, Turkey 37°49N 29°39E 205 D11
Cardamon Hills India 9°30N 77°15E 245 K3
Cardamon Mts. = Kravanh, Chuor Phnum Cambodia 12°0N 103°32E 237 G4
Cardeña Spain 38°16N 4°20W 195 G6
Cárdenas Cuba 23°0N 81°30W 320 B3
Cárdenas San Luis Potosí, Mexico 22°0N 99°38W 319 C5
Cárdenas Tabasco, Mexico 17°59N 93°22W 319 D6
Cardener → Spain 41°41N 1°51E 196 D6
Cardenete Spain 39°46N 1°41W 196 F3
Cardiel, L. Argentina 48°55S 71°10W 336 C2
Cardiff U.K. 51°29N 3°10W 169 F4
Cardiff ☐ U.K. 51°31N 3°12W 169 F4
Cardiff-by-the-Sea U.S.A. 33°1N 117°17W 307 M9
Cardigan U.K. 52°5N 4°40W 169 E3
Cardigan B. U.K. 52°30N 4°30W 169 E3
Cardinal Canada 44°47N 75°23W 313 B9
Cardón, Punta Venezuela 11°37N 70°14W 328 A3
Cardona Spain 41°56N 1°40E 196 D6
Cardona Uruguay 33°53S 57°18W 334 C4
Cardoso, Ilha do Brazil 25°8S 47°58W 335 A6
Cardston Canada 49°15N 113°20W 296 D6
Cardwell Australia 18°14S 146°2E 280 B4
Careen L. Canada 57°0N 108°11W 297 B7
Carei Romania 47°40N 22°29E 182 C7
Careiro Brazil 3°12S 59°45W 329 D6
Carenage Trin. & Tob. 10°41N 61°36W 323 t
Carentan France 49°19N 1°15W 172 C5
Carey Idaho, U.S.A. 43°19N 113°57W 304 E7
Carey Ohio, U.S.A. 40°57N 83°23W 311 D13
Carey, L. Australia 29°0S 122°15E 279 E3
Carey L. Canada 62°12N 102°55W 297 A8
Careysburg Liberia 6°34N 10°30W 262 D2
Cargados Carajos Ind. Oc. 17°0S 59°0E 273 F4
Cargèse France 42°7N 8°35E 175 F12
Carhaix-Plouguer France 48°18N 3°36W 172 D3
Carhuamayo Peru 10°51S 76°4W 330 C2
Carhuas Peru 9°15S 77°39W 330 B2
Carhué Argentina 37°10S 62°50W 334 D3
Caria Turkey 37°20N 28°10E 205 D10
Cariacica Brazil 20°16S 40°25W 333 F3
Cariaco Venezuela 10°29N 63°33W 329 A5
Cariango Angola 10°37S 15°20E 265 E3
Cariati Italy 39°30N 16°57E 201 C9
Caribbean Sea W. Indies 15°0N 75°0W 320 C4
Cariboo Mts. Canada 53°0N 121°0W 296 C4
Caribou U.S.A. 46°52N 68°1W 309 B19
Caribou → Man., Canada 59°20N 94°44W 297 B10
Caribou → N.W.T., Canada 61°27N 125°45W 296 A3
Caribou I. Canada 47°22N 85°49W 298 C2
Caribou Is. Canada 61°55N 113°15W 296 A6
Caribou L. Man., Canada 59°21N 96°10W 297 B9
Caribou L. Ont., Canada 50°25N 89°5W 298 B2
Caribou Mts. Canada 59°12N 115°40W 296 B5
Caribou River △ Canada 59°35N 96°35W 297 B9
Caribrod = Dimitrovgrad Serbia 43°2N 22°48E 202 C6
Carichic Mexico 27°56N 107°3W 318 B3
Caridad Phil. 14°28N 120°53E 127 C1
Carigara Phil. 11°18N 124°41E 233 F5
Carigara B. Phil. 11°22N 124°37E 233 F5
Carignan France 49°38N 5°10E 173 C12
Carignano Italy 44°55N 7°40E 198 D4
Carinda Australia 30°28S 147°41E 283 A7
Cariñena Spain 41°20N 1°13W 196 D3
Carinhanha Brazil 14°15S 44°46W 333 D3
Carinhanha → Brazil 14°20S 43°47W 333 D3
Carini Italy 38°8N 13°11E 200 D6
Cariño Spain 43°45N 7°52W 194 B3
Carínola Italy 41°11N 13°58E 200 A6
Carinthia = Kärnten ☐ Austria 46°52N 13°30E 180 E6
Carioca, Sa. da Brazil 22°57S 43°13W 135 B1
Caripito Venezuela 10°8N 63°6W 329 A5
Cariré Brazil 3°57S 40°27W 332 B3
Caritianas Brazil 9°20S 63°6W 331 B5
Carles Phil. 11°34N 123°8E 233 F4
Carlet Spain 39°14N 0°31W 197 F4
Carleton, Mt. Canada 47°23N 66°53W 299 C6
Carleton Place Canada 45°8N 76°9W 313 A8
Carletonville S. Africa 26°23S 27°22E 270 C4
Cârlibaba Romania 47°35N 25°8E 183 C10
Carlin U.S.A. 40°43N 116°7W 304 F5
Carlingford L. U.K. 54°3N 6°9W 166 B5
Carlini Base Antarctica 62°30S 58°0W 151 C18
Carlinville U.S.A. 39°17N 89°53W 310 E7
Carlisle Cumb., U.K. 54°54N 2°56W 168 C5
Carlisle Ind., U.S.A. 38°58N 87°24W 311 F9
Carlisle Ky., U.S.A. 38°19N 84°1W 311 F12
Carlisle Pa., U.S.A. 40°12N 77°12W 312 F7
Carlisle I. Australia 20°49S 149°18E 280 b
Carlit, Pic France 42°35N 1°55E 174 F5
Carloforte Italy 39°8N 8°18E 200 C1
Carlos Casares Argentina 35°32S 61°20W 334 D3
Carlos Chagas Brazil 17°43S 40°45W 333 E3
Carlos Tejedor Argentina 35°25S 62°25W 334 D3
Carlota I. Phil. 13°1N 121°53E 232 E3
Carlow Ireland 52°50N 6°56W 166 D5
Carlow ☐ Ireland 52°43N 6°50W 166 D5
Carlsbad = Karlovy Vary Czechia 50°13N 12°51E 180 A5
Carlsbad Calif., U.S.A. 33°10N 117°21W 307 M9
Carlsbad N. Mex., U.S.A. 32°25N 104°14W 305 K11
Carlsbad Caverns △ U.S.A. 32°10N 104°35W 305 K11
Carlsberg Ridge Ind. Oc. 1°0N 66°0E 273 D5
Carlstadt U.S.A. 40°50N 74°6W 132 A1
Carlton Australia 37°47S 144°57E 128 A1
Carlton Gardens Australia 37°48S 144°58E 128 A1
Carluke U.K. 55°45N 3°50W 167 F5
Carlyle Sask., Canada 49°40N 102°20W 297 D8
Carlyle Ill., U.S.A. 38°37N 89°22W 310 F7
Carlyle L. U.S.A. 38°37N 89°21W 310 F7
Carmacks Canada 62°5N 136°16W 294 E4
Carmagnola Italy 44°51N 7°43E 198 D4
Carman Canada 49°30N 98°0W 297 D9
Carmarthen U.K. 51°52N 4°19W 169 F3
Carmarthen B. U.K. 51°40N 4°30W 169 F3
Carmarthenshire ☐ U.K. 51°55N 4°13W 169 F3
Carmaux France 44°3N 2°10E 174 D6
Carmel Ind., U.S.A. 39°58N 86°7W 311 E10
Carmel N.Y., U.S.A. 41°26N 73°41W 313 E11
Carmel, Mt. = Ha Karmel, Har Israel 32°44N 35°3E 250 F5
Carmel-by-the-Sea U.S.A. 36°33N 121°55W 306 J5
Carmel Valley U.S.A. 36°29N 121°43W 306 J5
Carmelitane Scalze, Monastero Venice, Italy 142 a2
Carmelo Uruguay 34°0S 58°20W 334 C4
Carmen Bolivia 11°40S 67°51W 330 C4
Carmen Paraguay 27°13S 56°12W 335 B4
Carmen Bohol, Phil. 9°50N 124°12E 233 G5
Carmen Cebu, Phil. 10°35N 124°1E 233 F5
Carmen N. Cotabato, Phil. 7°13N 124°45E 233 H5
Carmen Venezuela 1°16N 66°52W 328 C4
Carmen, I. Mexico 25°57N 111°12W 318 B2
Carmen de Huechuraba Chile 33°20S 70°40W 137 B1
Carmen de la Legua -Reynosa Peru 12°3S 77°7W 124 B2
Carmen de Patagones Argentina 40°50S 63°0W 336 B4
Cármenes Spain 42°58N 5°34W 194 C5
Carmensa Argentina 35°15S 67°40W 334 D2
Carmi B.C., Canada 49°36N 119°8W 296 D5
Carmi Ill., U.S.A. 38°5N 88°10W 311 F8
Carmichael Village Bahamas 25°0N 77°26W 153 b
Carmila Australia 21°55S 149°24E 280 C4
Carmini, Scuola dei Venice, Italy 142 b2
Carmona Costa Rica 10°0N 85°15W 320 E2
Carmona Spain 37°28N 5°42W 195 H5
Carn Ban U.K. 57°7N 4°15W 167 D4
Carn Eige U.K. 57°17N 5°8W 167 D3
Carnac France 47°35N 3°6W 172 E3
Carnamah Australia 29°41S 115°53E 279 E2
Carnarvon W. Austral., Australia 24°51S 113°42E 279 D1
Carnarvon Ont., Canada 45°3N 78°41W 312 A6
Carnarvon Northern Cape, S. Africa 30°56S 22°8E 270 D3
Carnarvon △ Australia 24°54S 148°2E 280 C4
Carnarvon Ra. Queens., Australia 25°15S 148°30E 280 D4
Carnarvon Ra. W. Austral., Australia 25°20S 120°45E 279 E3
Carnatic India 9°40N 77°50E 245 K3
Carnation U.S.A. 47°39N 121°55W 306 C5
Carnaxide Portugal 38°43N 9°14W 126 A1
Carncastle U.K. 54°54N 5°53W 166 B6
Carndonagh Ireland 55°16N 7°15W 166 A4
Carnduff Canada 49°10N 101°50W 297 D8
Carnegie Vic., Australia 37°53S 145°3E 128 B2
Carnegie U.S.A. 40°24N 80°5W 312 F4
Carnegie, L. Australia 26°5S 122°30E 279 E3
Carnegie Hall New York, U.S.A. 132 c2
Carnegie Ridge Pac. Oc. 1°0S 87°0W 289 H19
Carney I. Antarctica 74°0S 121°0W 151 D14
Carnic Alps = Karnische Alpen Europe 46°36N 13°0E 180 E6
Carniche Alpi = Karnische Alpen Europe 46°36N 13°0E 180 E6
Carnide Portugal 38°45N 9°10W 126 A1
Carnot C.A.R. 4°59N 15°56E 264 B3
Carnot, C. Australia 34°57S 135°38E 281 E2
Carnot B. Australia 17°20S 122°15E 278 C3
Carnoustie U.K. 56°30N 2°42W 167 E6
Carnsore Pt. Ireland 52°10N 6°22W 166 D5
Caro U.S.A. 43°29N 83°24W 309 D12
Caroço São Tomé & Príncipe 1°32N 7°27E 265 a
Caroga Lake U.S.A. 43°8N 74°28W 313 C10
Carol City U.S.A. 25°56N 80°14W 129 C1
Carolina Brazil 7°10S 47°30W 332 C2
Carolina Puerto Rico 18°23N 65°58W 321 C6
Carolina Mpumalanga, S. Africa 26°5S 30°6E 271 C5
Carolinas Pt. N. Marianas 14°55N 145°38E 302 e
Caroline I. Kiribati 9°58S 150°13W 289 H12
Caroline Is. Micronesia 8°0N 150°0E 288 G6
Caroline Pk. N.Z. 45°57S 167°15E 285 F2

Carollton U.S.A. 29°57N 90°8W 131 B2
Carondelet Reef Kiribati 5°33S 173°50E 277 B16
Caroni Trin. & Tob. 10°34N 61°23W 323 t
Caroni → Trin. & Tob. 10°37N 61°30W 323 t
Caroní → Venezuela 8°21N 62°43W 329 B5
Caroni Arena Res. Trin. & Tob. 10°33N 61°15W 323 t
Caroni Bird Sanctuary Trin. & Tob. 10°36N 61°28W 323 t
Caroni Swamp Trin. & Tob. 10°36N 61°27W 323 t
Caronie = Nébrodi, Monti Italy 37°54N 14°35E 201 E7
Caroona Australia 31°24S 150°26E 283 A9
Carora Venezuela 10°11N 70°5W 328 A3
Carpathians Europe 49°30N 21°0E 177 D11
Carpații Meridionali Romania 45°30N 25°0E 183 E9
Carpentaria, G. of Australia 14°0S 139°0E 280 A2
Carpentersville U.S.A. 42°6N 88°17W 311 B8
Carpentras France 44°3N 5°2E 175 D9
Carpi Italy 44°47N 10°53E 198 D7
Carpina Brazil 7°51S 35°15W 332 C4
Cărpineni Moldova 46°46N 28°22E 183 D13
Carpinteria U.S.A. 34°24N 119°31W 307 L7
Carpio Spain 41°13N 5°7W 194 D5
Carr Boyd Ra. Australia 16°15S 128°35E 278 C4
Carra, L. Ireland 53°41N 9°14W 166 C2
Carrabelle U.S.A. 29°51N 84°40W 316 F5
Carraig Mhachaire Rois = Carrickmacross Ireland 53°59N 6°43W 166 C5
Carraig na Siúire = Carrick-on-Suir Ireland 52°21N 7°24W 166 D4
Carral Spain 43°14N 8°21W 194 B2
Carranglan Phil. 15°58N 121°4E 232 D3
Carranya ✪ Australia 19°13S 127°46E 278 C4
Carrara Italy 44°5N 10°6E 198 D7
Carrascal Santiago, Chile 33°25S 70°42W 137 B1
Carrascal Phil. 9°22N 125°56E 233 G5
Carrasco △ Bolivia 17°23S 64°59W 331 D5
Carrascosa del Campo Spain 40°2N 2°45W 196 E2
Carrauntoohill Ireland 52°0N 9°45W 166 D2
Carretas, Punta Peru 14°12S 76°17W 330 C2
Carriacou Grenada 12°29N 61°26W 323 q
Carrick-on-Shannon Ireland 53°57N 8°7W 166 C3
Carrick-on-Suir Ireland 52°21N 7°24W 166 D4
Carrickfergus U.K. 54°43N 5°49W 166 B6
Carrickmacross Ireland 53°59N 6°43W 166 C5
Carrières-sous-Bois France 48°55N 2°6E 134 A1
Carrières-sous-Poissy France 48°56N 2°2E 134 A1
Carrières-sur-Seine France 48°55N 2°11E 134 A2
Carrieton Australia 32°25S 138°31E 282 B3
Carrigaline Ireland 51°48N 8°23W 166 E3
Carrillo Mexico 26°54N 103°55W 318 B4
Carrington U.S.A. 47°27N 99°8W 308 B4
Carrión → Spain 41°53N 4°32W 194 D6
Carrión de los Condes Spain 42°20N 4°37W 194 C6
Carrizal Bajo Chile 28°5S 71°20W 334 B1
Carrizalillo Chile 29°5S 71°30W 334 B1
Carrizo Cr. → U.S.A. 36°55N 103°55W 305 H12
Carrizo Plain ⌓ U.S.A. 35°11N 119°47W 306 K7
Carrizo Springs U.S.A. 28°31N 99°52W 314 G5
Carrizozo U.S.A. 33°38N 105°53W 305 K11
Carroll U.S.A. 42°4N 94°52W 310 B2
Carrollton Ga., U.S.A. 33°35N 85°5W 316 B4
Carrollton Ill., U.S.A. 39°18N 90°24W 310 E6
Carrollton Ky., U.S.A. 38°41N 85°11W 311 F11
Carrollton Mo., U.S.A. 39°22N 93°30W 310 E3
Carrollton Ohio, U.S.A. 40°34N 81°5W 312 F3
Carron → U.K. 57°53N 4°22W 167 D4
Carron, L. U.K. 57°22N 5°35W 167 D3
Carrot → Canada 53°50N 101°17W 297 C8
Carrot River Canada 53°17N 103°35W 297 C8
Carrouges France 48°34N 0°10W 172 D6
Carrù Italy 44°29N 7°52E 198 D4
Carruthers Canada 52°52N 109°16W 297 C7
Carsa Dek Ethiopia 5°13N 39°50E 257 F4
Çarşamba Turkey 41°11N 36°44E 212 B7
Carsóli Italy 42°6N 13°5E 199 F10
Carson Calif., U.S.A. 33°49N 118°16W 307 M8
Carson N. Dak., U.S.A. 46°25N 101°34W 308 B3
Carson → U.S.A. 39°45N 118°40W 306 F8
Carson City Mich., U.S.A. 43°11N 84°51W 311 A12
Carson City Nev., U.S.A. 39°10N 119°46W 306 F7
Carson Sink U.S.A. 39°50N 118°25W 304 G4
Carstensz Pyramid = Jaya, Puncak Indonesia 3°57S 137°17E 231 E9
Cartagena Colombia 10°25N 75°33W 328 A2
Cartagena Spain 37°38N 0°59W 197 H4
Cartago Colombia 4°45N 75°55W 328 C2
Cartago Costa Rica 9°50N 83°55W 320 E3
Cártama Spain 36°43N 4°39W 195 J6
Cartaxo Portugal 39°10N 8°47W 195 F2
Cartaya Spain 37°16N 7°9W 195 H3
Carter Bar U.K. 55°21N 2°29W 167 F6
Carteret Is. = Kilinailau Is. Papua N. G. 4°45S 155°20E 286 C8
Cartersville U.S.A. 34°10N 84°48W 316 A5
Carterton N.Z. 41°2S 175°31E 284 H4
Carterville U.S.A. 37°46N 89°5W 310 G7
Carthage Tunisia 36°52N 10°20E 200 F3
Carthage Ill., U.S.A. 40°25N 91°8W 310 D5
Carthage Mo., U.S.A. 37°11N 94°19W 308 G6
Carthage N.Y., U.S.A. 43°59N 75°37W 313 C9
Carthage Tex., U.S.A. 32°9N 94°20W 314 E7
Cartier I. Australia 12°31S 123°29E 278 B3
Cartierville Canada 45°31N 73°42W 130 A1
Cartwright Canada 53°41N 56°58W 299 B8
Caruaru Brazil 8°15S 35°55W 332 C4
Carúpano Venezuela 10°39N 63°15W 329 A5
Caruray Phil. 10°20N 119°0E 233 F2
Carutapera Brazil 1°13S 46°1W 332 B2
Caruthersville U.S.A. 36°11N 89°39W 308 G9
Carvalho Brazil 2°16S 51°29W 329 D7
Carvin France 50°30N 2°57E 173 B9
Carvoeiro Brazil 1°30S 61°59W 329 D5
Carvoeiro, C. Portugal 39°21N 9°24W 195 F1
Cary Ill., U.S.A. 42°13N 88°14W 311 B8
Cary N.C., U.S.A. 35°47N 78°46W 315 D15
Cas-gwent = Chepstow U.K. 51°38N 2°41W 169 F5
Casa, Pas de la = Envalira, Port d' Europe 42°33N 1°43E 196 C6
Casa Branca Brazil 21°46S 47°4W 333 F2
Casa Branca Portugal 38°29N 8°12W 195 G2
Casa de Piedra Argentina 38°5S 67°28W 334 D2
Casa de Piedra, Embalse Argentina 38°5S 67°32W 334 D2
Casa Grande U.S.A. 32°53N 111°45W 305 K8
Casa Loma Canada 43°41N 79°24W 141 A2
Casa Nova Brazil 9°25S 41°5W 332 C3
Casa Verde Brazil 23°29S 46°40W 137 A1
Casablanca Chile 33°20S 71°25W 334 C1
Casablanca Morocco 33°36N 7°36W 260 B3
Casablanca □ Morocco 33°38N 7°30W 260 B3
Casacalenda Italy 41°44N 14°51E 199 G11
Casal da Mira Portugal 38°47N 9°14W 126 A1
Casál Morena Italy 41°49N 12°37E 136 C2
Casalbordino Italy 42°9N 14°35E 199 F11
Casale Monferrato Italy 45°8N 8°27E 198 C5
Casalmaggiore Italy 44°59N 10°26E 198 D7
Casalotti Italy 41°54N 12°22E 136 B1
Casalpusterlengo Italy 45°11N 9°39E 198 C6
Casamance Senegal 13°0N 15°30W 262 C1
Casamance → Senegal 12°33N 16°46W 262 C1
Casanare □ Colombia 5°30N 72°0W 328 B3
Casanare → Colombia 6°2N 69°51W 328 B4
Casarano Italy 40°0N 18°10E 201 B11
Casares Spain 36°27N 5°16W 195 J5
Casas Ibáñez Spain 39°17N 1°30W 197 F3
Casasimarro Spain 39°22N 2°3W 197 F2
Casatejada Spain 39°54N 5°40W 194 F5
Casavieja Spain 40°17N 4°46W 194 E6
Cascada de Basaseachic △ Mexico 28°9N 108°15W 318 B3
Cascade Seychelles 4°39S 55°29E 272 c
Cascade Idaho, U.S.A. 44°31N 116°2W 304 D5
Cascade Iowa, U.S.A. 42°18N 91°0W 310 B6
Cascade Mont., U.S.A. 47°16N 111°42W 304 C8
Cascade Heights U.S.A. 33°43N 84°26W 113 B2
Cascade Locks U.S.A. 45°40N 121°54W 306 E5
Cascade Pt. N.Z. 44°1S 168°20E 285 E3
Cascade Ra. U.S.A. 47°0N 121°30W 306 D5
Cascade Res. U.S.A. 44°32N 116°3W 304 D5
Cascades, Pte. des Réunion 21°9S 55°51E 272 f
Cascais Portugal 38°41N 9°25W 195 G1
Cascavel Ceará, Brazil 4°7S 38°14W 332 B4
Cascavel Paraná, Brazil 24°57S 53°28W 335 A5
Cáscina Italy 43°41N 10°33E 198 E7
Casco B. U.S.A. 43°45N 70°0W 309 D19
Case Noyale Mauritius 20°23S 57°22E 272 e
Case-Pilote Martinique 14°38N 61°9W 322 j
Caselle Torinese Italy 45°10N 7°39E 198 C4
Caserta Italy 41°4N 14°20E 201 A7
Casey Antarctica 66°0S 76°0E 151 C8
Casey Ill., U.S.A. 39°18N 87°59W 311 E9
Caseyr, Raas = Asir, Ras Somalia 11°55N 51°10E 267 B7
Cashel Ireland 52°30N 7°53W 166 D4
Casibare → Colombia 3°48N 72°18W 328 C3
Casiguran Phil. 16°22N 122°7E 232 C4
Casiguran Sound Phil. 16°6N 121°58E 232 C3
Casilda Argentina 33°10S 61°10W 334 C3
Casim = General Toshevo Bulgaria 43°42N 28°6E 203 C12
Casimcea Romania 44°45N 28°23E 183 F13
Casino Australia 28°52S 153°3E 281 D5
Casiquiare → Venezuela 2°1N 67°7W 328 C4
Casitas Peru 3°54S 80°39W 330 A1
Čáslav Czechia 49°54N 15°22E 180 B8
Casma Peru 9°30S 78°20W 330 B2
Casmalia U.S.A. 34°50N 120°32W 307 L6
Casnewydd = Newport U.K. 51°35N 3°0W 169 F5
Cásola Valsénio Italy 44°12N 11°40E 199 D8
Cásoli Italy 42°7N 14°18E 199 F11
Caspe Spain 41°14N 0°1W 196 D4
Casper U.S.A. 42°51N 106°19W 304 E10
Caspian Depression Eurasia 47°0N 48°0E 191 G9
Caspian Sea Eurasia 43°0N 50°0E 187 F9
Cass City U.S.A. 43°36N 83°10W 312 C1
Cass Lake U.S.A. 47°23N 94°37W 308 B6
Cassà de la Selva Spain 41°53N 2°52E 196 D7
Cassadaga U.S.A. 42°20N 79°19W 312 D5
Cassai Angola 10°33S 21°59E 265 E4
Cassai → Angola 3°2S 16°57E 265 E4
Cassamba Angola 13°6S 20°18E 265 E4
Cassano allo Iónio Italy 39°47N 16°20E 201 C9
Casselberry U.S.A. 28°41N 81°20W 317 G8
Casselman Canada 45°19N 75°5W 313 A9
Casselton U.S.A. 46°54N 97°13W 308 B5
Cassiar Mts. Canada 59°30N 130°30W 296 B2
Cassilândia Brazil 19°9S 51°45W 331 D7
Cassilis Australia 32°3S 149°58E 283 B8
Cassinga Angola 15°5S 16°4E 265 F3
Cassino Italy 41°30N 13°49E 200 A6
Cassis France 43°14N 5°32E 175 E9
Cassoalala Angola 9°30S 14°22E 265 D2
Cassoango Angola 13°42S 20°56E 265 E4
Cassongue Angola 11°53S 15°2E 265 E3
Cassopolis U.S.A. 41°55N 86°1W 311 C10
Cassunda Angola 10°57S 21°3E 265 E4
Cassville Mo., U.S.A. 36°41N 93°52W 308 G7
Cassville Wis., U.S.A. 42°43N 90°59W 310 B6
Castagneto Carducci Italy 43°9N 10°36E 198 E7
Castaic U.S.A. 34°30N 118°38W 307 L8
Castalia U.S.A. 41°24N 82°49W 312 E2
Castanhal Brazil 1°18S 47°55W 332 B2
Castara Trin. & Tob. 11°17N 60°42W 323 s
Castara B. Trin. & Tob. 11°17N 60°42W 323 s
Casteddu = Cágliari Italy 39°13N 9°7E 200 C2
Castéggio Italy 45°0N 9°7E 198 C6
Castejón de Monegros Spain 41°37N 0°15W 196 D4
Castel Guadeloupe 16°15N 61°35W 322 e
Castèl del Monte Italy 41°5N 16°16E 201 A9
Castèl di Leva Italy 41°46N 12°33E 136 C2
Castèl di Sangro Italy 41°47N 14°6E 199 G11
Castèl San Giovanni Italy 45°4N 9°26E 198 C6
Castèl San Pietro Terme Italy 44°24N 11°35E 199 D8
Castèl Sant' Angelo Rome, Italy 136 b1
Castelbuono Italy 37°56N 14°5E 201 E7
Castelfidardo Italy 43°28N 13°33E 199 E10
Castelfiorentino Italy 43°36N 10°58E 198 E7
Castelfranco Véneto Italy 45°40N 11°55E 199 C8
Casteljaloux France 44°19N 0°6E 174 D4
Castell-Nedd = Neath U.K. 51°39N 3°48W 169 F4
Castellabate Italy 40°17N 14°57E 201 B7
Castellammare, G. di Italy 38°8N 12°54E 200 D5
Castellammare del Golfo Italy 38°1N 12°53E 200 D5
Castellammare di Stábia Italy 40°42N 14°29E 201 B7
Castellamonte Italy 45°23N 7°42E 198 C4
Castellane France 43°50N 6°31E 175 E10
Castellaneta Italy 40°38N 16°56E 201 B9
Castelli Argentina 36°7S 57°47W 334 D4
Castello Venice, Italy 142 b4
Castelló de la Plana Spain 39°58N 0°3W 196 F4
Castellón de la Plana □ Spain 40°15N 0°5W 196 E4
Castellote Spain 40°48N 0°15W 196 E4
Castelmáuro Italy 41°50N 14°43E 199 G11
Castelnau-de-Médoc France 45°2N 0°48W 174 C3
Castelnau-Magnoac France 43°17N 0°31E 174 E4
Castelnaudary France 43°20N 1°58E 174 E5
Castelnovo ne' Monti Italy 44°26N 10°24E 198 D7
Castelnuovo di Val di Cécina Italy 43°12N 10°59E 198 E7
Castelo = Manuel Urbano Brazil 8°53S 69°18W 330 B4
Castelo Brazil 20°33S 41°14W 333 F3
Castelo, Pta. do Azores 36°56N 25°1W 153 d4
Castelo Branco Azores 38°31N 28°44W 153 d1
Castelo Branco Portugal 39°50N 7°31W 194 F3
Castelo Branco □ Portugal 39°52N 7°45W 194 F3
Castelo de Paiva Portugal 41°2N 8°16W 194 D2
Castelo de Vide Portugal 39°25N 7°27W 195 F3
Castelo do Piauí Brazil 5°20S 41°33W 332 C3
Castelrosso = Megisti Greece 36°8N 29°34E 205 E11
Castelsardo Italy 40°55N 8°43E 200 B1
Castelsarrasin France 44°2N 1°7E 174 D5
Casteltérmini Italy 37°32N 13°39E 200 E6
Castelvetrano Italy 37°41N 12°47E 200 E5
Castendo Angola 8°39S 14°10E 265 D2
Casterton Australia 37°30S 141°30E 282 D4
Castets France 43°52N 1°6W 174 E2
Castiglion Fiorentino Italy 43°20N 11°55E 199 E8
Castiglione = Bou Ismaïl Algeria 36°38N 2°42E 261 A5
Castiglione del Lago Italy 43°7N 12°3E 199 E9
Castiglione della Pescáia Italy 42°46N 10°53E 198 F7
Castiglione delle Stiviere Italy 45°23N 10°29E 198 C7
Castilblanco Spain 39°17N 5°5W 195 F5
Castile U.S.A. 42°38N 78°3W 312 D6
Castilla Peru 5°12S 80°38W 330 B1
Castilla, Playa de Spain 37°0N 6°33W 195 J4
Castilla-La Mancha □ Spain 39°30N 3°30W 195 F7
Castilla y Leon □ Spain 42°0N 5°0W 194 D6
Castillo de Locubín Spain 37°32N 3°56W 195 H7
Castillo de San Marcos ⌓ U.S.A. 29°54N 81°19W 316 F8
Castillon-en-Couserans France 42°56N 1°1E 174 F5
Castillonès France 44°39N 0°37E 174 D4
Castillos Uruguay 34°12S 53°52W 335 C5
Castle Bruce Dominica 15°26N 61°16W 323 k
Castle Dale U.S.A. 39°13N 111°1W 304 G8
Castle Douglas U.K. 54°56N 3°56W 167 G5
Castle Harbour Bermuda 32°21N 64°40W 153 a
Castle Mt. Jamaica 18°8N 76°22W 320 a
Castle of Good Hope Cape Town, S. Africa 118 c3
Castle Peak B. Hong Kong, China 22°23N 113°58E 122 A1
Castle Pk. Hong Kong, China 22°23N 113°57E 122 A1
Castle Roads Bermuda 32°20N 64°40W 153 a
Castle Rock Colo., U.S.A. 39°22N 104°51W 304 G11
Castle Rock Wash., U.S.A. 46°17N 122°54W 306 D4
Castle Rock Pt. St. Helena 16°1S 5°45W 153 h
Castlebar Ireland 53°52N 9°18W 166 C2
Castlebay U.K. 56°57N 7°31W 167 E1
Castleblayney Ireland 54°7N 6°44W 166 B5
Castlecliff N.Z. 39°57S 175°5E 284 F4
Castlecomer Ireland 52°48N 7°14W 166 D4
Castlederg U.K. 54°42N 7°36W 166 B4
Castleford U.K. 53°43N 1°21W 168 D6
Castlegar Canada 49°20N 117°40W 296 D5
Castleisland Ireland 52°14N 9°28W 166 D2
Castlemaine Vic., Australia 37°2S 144°12E 282 D6
Castlemaine Kerry, Ireland 52°10N 9°42W 166 D2
Castlepoint N.Z. 40°54S 176°15E 284 G5
Castlepollard Ireland 53°41N 7°19W 166 C4
Castlerea Ireland 53°46N 8°29W 166 C3
Castlereagh → Australia 30°12S 147°32E 283 A7
Castlereagh B. Australia 12°10S 135°10E 280 A2
Castleton U.S.A. 43°37N 73°11W 313 C11
Castleton Corners U.S.A. 40°36N 74°8W 132 C1
Castleton-on-Hudson U.S.A. 42°31N 73°45W 313 D11
Castletown I. of Man 54°5N 4°38W 168 C3
Castletown Bearhaven Ireland 51°39N 9°55W 166 E2
Castor Canada 52°15N 111°50W 296 C6
Castor → Canada 53°24N 78°58W 298 B4
Castorland U.S.A. 43°53N 75°31W 313 C9
Castres France 43°37N 2°13E 174 E6
Castricum Neths. 52°33N 4°40E 170 B4
Castries St. Lucia 14°2N 60°58W 323 m
Castril Spain 37°48N 2°46W 195 H8
Castro Brazil 24°45S 50°0W 335 A6
Castro Chile 42°30S 73°50W 336 B2
Castro Alves Brazil 12°46S 39°33W 333 D4
Castro del Río Spain 37°41N 4°29W 195 H6
Castro-Urdiales Spain 43°23N 3°11W 194 B7
Castro Valley U.S.A. 37°41N 122°5W 306 H4
Castro Verde Portugal 37°41N 8°4W 195 H2
Castrogiovanni = Enna Italy 37°34N 14°16E 201 E7
Castrojeriz Spain 42°17N 4°9W 194 C6
Castropol Spain 43°32N 7°0W 194 B4
Castroreale Italy 38°6N 15°12E 201 D8
Castrovíllari Italy 39°49N 16°12E 201 C9
Castroville U.S.A. 36°46N 121°45W 306 J5
Castrovirreyna Peru 13°20S 75°18W 330 C2
Castuera Spain 38°43N 5°37W 195 G5
Caswell Sound N.Z. 44°59S 167°8E 285 E2
Çat Turkey 39°40N 41°3E 213 C9
Cat Ba, Dao Vietnam 20°50N 107°0E 236 B6
Cat Ba △ Vietnam 20°47N 107°3E 236 B6
Cat I. Bahamas 24°30N 75°30W 321 B4
Cat L. Canada 51°40N 91°50W 298 B1
Cat Lake Canada 51°40N 91°50W 298 B1
Cat Tien △ Vietnam 11°25N 107°17E 237 G6
Čata Slovakia 47°58N 18°38E 181 D11
Catabola Angola 12°9S 17°16E 265 E3
Catacamas Honduras 14°54N 85°56W 320 D2
Catacaos Peru 5°20S 80°45W 330 B1
Cataguases Brazil 21°23S 42°39W 333 F3
Catagupan Phil. 8°1N 116°58E 233 G1
Cataingan Phil. 12°0N 124°0E 232 E4
Çatak Turkey 38°1N 43°8E 213 C10
Çatalağzı Turkey 41°30N 31°59E 212 B4
Catalão Brazil 18°10S 47°57W 333 E2
Çatalca Turkey 41°8N 28°27E 203 E12
Catalina Nfld. & L., Canada 48°31N 53°4W 299 C9
Catalina Chile 25°13S 69°43W 334 B2
Catalina Ariz., U.S.A. 32°30N 110°50W 305 K8
Catalonia = Cataluña □ Spain 41°40N 1°15E 196 D6
Cataluña □ Spain 41°40N 1°15E 196 D6
Çatalzeytin Turkey 41°57N 34°12E 212 B6
Catamarca Argentina 28°30S 65°50W 334 B2
Catamarca □ Argentina 27°0S 65°50W 334 B2
Catanauan Phil. 13°36N 122°19E 232 E4
Catanduanes □ Phil. 13°50N 124°20E 232 E5
Catanduva Brazil 21°5S 48°58W 335 A6
Catánia Italy 37°30N 15°6E 201 E8
Catánia, G. di Italy 37°24N 15°9E 201 E8
Cataño Puerto Rico 18°27N 66°7W 321 b
Catanzaro Italy 38°54N 16°35E 201 D9
Cataouatche, L. U.S.A. 29°50N 90°14W 131 B1
Catarman Camiguin, Phil. 9°8N 124°40E 233 G5
Catarman N. Samar, Phil. 12°28N 124°35E 232 E5
Catatumbo → Venezuela 9°21N 71°45W 328 B3
Cataula U.S.A. 32°39N 84°52W 316 C5
Catbalogan Phil. 11°46N 124°53E 233 F5
Catchacoma Canada 44°44N 78°19W 312 B6
Cateco Cangola Angola 8°28S 15°51E 265 D3
Cateel Phil. 7°47N 126°24E 233 H6
Cateel B. Phil. 7°54N 126°25E 233 H6
Catembe Mozam. 26°0S 32°33E 271 C5
Catende Angola 11°14S 21°30E 265 E4
Catende Brazil 8°40S 35°43W 332 C4
Caterham U.K. 51°15N 0°4W 169 F7
Catete Angola 9°6S 13°43E 265 D2
Catete Rio de J., Brazil 22°54S 43°10W 135 B1
Catford U.K. 51°26N 0°1W 125 B3
Cathair na Mart = Westport Ireland 53°48N 9°31W 166 C2
Cathcart N.S.W., Australia 36°52S 149°24E 283 D8
Cathcart Eastern Cape, S. Africa 32°18S 27°10E 270 D4
Cathedral City U.S.A. 33°47N 116°28W 307 M10
Cathedral Rock △ Australia 30°24S 152°15E 283 A10
Catherine, L. U.S.A. 28°30N 81°24W 133 B2
Cathlamet U.S.A. 46°12N 123°23W 306 D3
Catió Guinea-Biss. 11°17N 15°15W 262 C1
Catismiña Venezuela 4°5N 63°40W 329 C5
Catita Brazil 9°31S 43°1W 332 C3
Cativa Panama 9°21N 79°49W 320 c
Catlettsburg U.S.A. 38°25N 82°36W 309 F12
Catlin U.S.A. 40°4N 87°42W 311 D9
Catlins N.Z. 46°22S 169°17E 285 G4
Çatma Dağı Turkey 38°25N 29°50E 205 C11
Catmon Phil. 10°43N 124°1E 233 F5
Catoche, C. Mexico 21°35N 87°5W 319 C7
Catolé do Rocha Brazil 6°21S 37°45W 332 C4
Catota Angola 13°57S 17°30E 265 E3
Cátria, Mte. Italy 43°28N 12°42E 199 E9
Catriló Argentina 36°26S 63°24W 334 D3
Catrimani Brazil 0°27N 61°41W 329 C5
Catrimani → Brazil 0°28N 61°44W 329 C5
Catskill U.S.A. 42°14N 73°52W 313 D11
Catskill ⌓ U.S.A. 42°8N 74°39W 313 D10
Catskill Mts. U.S.A. 42°10N 74°25W 313 D10
Catt, Mt. Australia 13°49S 134°23E 280 A1
Cattaraugus U.S.A. 42°20N 78°52W 312 D6
Cattaro = Kotor Montenegro 42°25N 18°47E 202 D2
Catterick U.K. 54°23N 1°37W 168 C6
Cattólica Italy 43°58N 12°44E 199 E9
Cattólica Eraclea Italy 37°26N 13°24E 200 E6
Catu Brazil 12°21S 38°23W 333 D4
Catuala Angola 16°25S 19°2E 265 F3
Catuane Mozam. 26°48S 32°18E 271 C5
Catubig Phil. 12°24N 125°3E 232 E5
Catumbela Angola 12°25S 13°34E 265 E2
Catumbela → Angola 12°29S 13°28E 265 E2
Catur Mozam. 13°45S 35°30E 269 E4
Catwick Is. = Hon Hai Vietnam 10°0N 109°0E 237 H7
Cauayan Isabela, Phil. 16°56N 121°46E 232 C3
Cauayan Neg. Occ., Phil. 9°58N 122°37E 233 G4
Caubvick, Mt. = Iberville, Mt. d' Canada 58°50N 63°50W 295 F19
Cauca □ Colombia 2°30N 76°50W 328 C2
Cauca → Colombia 8°54N 74°28W 328 B3
Caucaia Brazil 3°40S 38°35W 332 B4
Caucasia Colombia 8°0N 75°12W 328 B2
Caucasus Mountains Eurasia 42°50N 44°0E 191 J7
Caucete Argentina 31°38S 68°20W 334 C2
Caudete Spain 38°42N 1°2W 197 G3
Caudry France 50°7N 3°22E 173 B10
Cauese Mts. Mozam. 15°14S 30°33E 269 F3
Caulfield Australia 37°52S 145°1E 128 B2
Caulnes France 48°18N 2°10W 172 D4
Caulónia Italy 38°23N 16°24E 201 D9
Caungula Angola 8°26S 18°38E 265 D3
Cauquenes Chile 36°0S 72°22W 334 D1
Caura → Venezuela 7°38N 64°53W 329 B5
Caurés → Brazil 1°21S 62°20W 329 D5
Cauresi → Mozam. 17°8S 33°0E 269 F3
Căuşani Moldova 46°38N 29°25E 183 D14
Causapscal Canada 48°19N 67°12W 299 C6
Caussade France 44°10N 1°33E 174 D5
Causse-Méjean France 44°18N 3°42E 174 D7
Causses du Quercy ⌓ France 44°35N 1°35E 174 D5
Cauterets France 42°52N 0°8W 174 F3
Cauvery → India 11°9N 78°52E 245 J4
Caux, Pays de France 49°38N 0°35E 172 C7
Cava de' Tirreni Italy 40°42N 14°42E 201 B7
Cávado → Portugal 41°32N 8°48W 194 D2
Cavagrande del Cassibile ⌓ Italy 36°58N 15°6E 201 F8
Cavaillon France 43°50N 5°2E 175 E9
Cavalaire-sur-Mer France 43°10N 6°33E 175 E10
Cavalcante Brazil 13°48S 47°30W 333 D2
Cavalese Italy 46°17N 11°27E 199 B8
Cavalier U.S.A. 48°48N 97°37W 308 A5
Cavalla = Cavally → Africa 4°22N 7°32W 262 E3
Cavalla △ Liberia 5°8N 7°20W 262 D3
Cavalli, Palazzo Venice, Italy 142 b2
Cavalli Is. N.Z. 35°0S 173°58E 284 B2
Cavally → Africa 4°22N 7°32W 262 E3
Cavan Ireland 54°0N 7°22W 166 B4
Cavan □ Ireland 54°1N 7°16W 166 C4
Cavárzere Italy 45°8N 12°5E 199 C9
Cavazuccherina = Jésolo Italy 45°32N 12°38E 199 C9
Çavdarhisar Turkey 39°12N 29°37E 205 B11
Çavdır Turkey 37°10N 29°42E 205 D11
Cave Creek U.S.A. 33°50N 111°57W 305 K8
Cave Run L. U.S.A. 38°5N 83°25W 311 F13
Cave Spring U.S.A. 34°6N 85°20W 316 A4
Cavelleria, C. de Spain 40°5N 4°5E 206 A5
Cavenagh Ra. Australia 26°12S 127°55E 279 E4
Cavendish Australia 37°31S 142°2E 282 D5
Caverna do Peruaçu △ Brazil 15°0S 44°35W 333 E3
Caviana, I. Brazil 0°10N 50°10W 329 C7
Cavili I. Phil. 9°16N 120°49E 233 G3
Cavite Phil. 14°29N 120°54E 127 C1
Cavite □ Phil. 14°15N 120°50E 232 D3
Caviúna = Rolândia Brazil 23°18S 51°23W 335 A5
Cavnic Romania 47°40N 23°52E 183 C8
Cavour Italy 44°47N 7°22E 198 D4
Cavtat Croatia 42°35N 18°13E 202 D2
Cawayan Phil. 11°56N 123°46E 233 F4
Cawayanon = Vintar Phil. 18°14N 120°39E 232 B3
Cawndilla L. Australia 32°30S 142°15E 282 B5
Cawnpore = Kanpur India 26°28N 80°20E 243 F9
Caxias Brazil 4°55S 43°20W 332 B3
Caxias Lisboa, Portugal 38°42N 9°16W 126 A1
Caxias do Sul Brazil 29°10S 51°10W 335 B5
Caxito Angola 8°30S 13°30E 265 D2
Caxopa Angola 11°52S 20°52E 265 E4
Çay Turkey 38°35N 31°1E 212 C4
Cay Pt. Bahamas 24°59N 77°25W 153 b
Cay Sal Bank Bahamas 23°45N 80°0W 320 B4
Cayambe Napo, Ecuador 0°2N 77°59W 328 C2
Cayambe Quito, Ecuador 0°3N 78°8W 328 C2
Cayce U.S.A. 33°58N 81°4W 316 B8
Çaycuma Turkey 41°25N 32°4E 212 B5
Çayeli Turkey 41°5N 40°45E 213 B9
Cayenne Fr. Guiana 5°5N 52°18W 329 B7
Cayenne □ Fr. Guiana 3°52N 52°37W 329 C7
Cayey Puerto Rico 18°7N 66°10W 321 b
Caygören Barajı Turkey 39°15N 28°12E 205 B10
Cayiralan Turkey 39°17N 35°38E 212 C6
Cayırova = Áyios Theodhoros Cyprus 35°22N 34°1E 207 E10
Caylus France 44°15N 1°47E 174 D5
Cayman Brac Cayman Is. 19°43N 79°49W 320 C4
Cayman Is. ☒ W. Indies 19°40N 80°30W 320 C3
Cayman Trench Caribbean 17°0N 83°0W 320 C3
Caynabo Somalia 9°0N 46°25E 267 C6
Cayo Coco Cuba 22°32N 78°22W 320 B4
Cayon St. Kitts & Nevis 17°21N 62°52W 322 d
Cayres France 44°55N 3°48E 174 D7
Cayuga Ont., Canada 42°59N 79°50W 312 D5
Cayuga Ind., U.S.A. 39°57N 87°28W 311 E9
Cayuga N.Y., U.S.A. 42°54N 76°44W 313 D8
Cayuga Heights U.S.A. 42°27N 76°29W 313 D8
Cayuga L. U.S.A. 42°41N 76°41W 313 D8
Cazage Angola 11°2S 20°45E 265 E4
Cazalla de la Sierra Spain 37°56N 5°45W 195 H5
Căzăneşti Romania 44°36N 27°3E 183 F12
Cazaubon France 43°56N 0°3W 174 E3
Cazaux et de Sanguinet, Étang de France 44°29N 1°10W 174 D2
Cazenovia U.S.A. 42°56N 75°51W 313 D9
Cazères France 43°13N 1°5E 174 E5
Cazin Bos.-H. 44°57N 15°57E 199 D12
Čazma Croatia 45°45N 16°39E 199 C13
Cazombo Angola 11°54S 22°56E 265 E4
Cazorla Spain 37°55N 3°2W 195 H7
Cazorla, Sierra de Spain 38°5N 2°55W 195 G8
Cea → Spain 42°0N 5°36W 194 C5
Ceadîr-Lunga Moldova 46°3N 28°51E 183 D13
Ceahlău △ Romania 46°58N 25°55E 183 D10
Ceamurlia de Jos Romania 44°43N 28°47E 183 F13
Ceanannus Mor = Kells Ireland 53°44N 6°53W 166 C5
Ceará = Fortaleza Brazil 3°45S 38°35W 332 B4
Ceará □ Brazil 5°0S 40°0W 332 B4
Ceara Abyssal Plain Atl. Oc. 0°0 36°30W 332 B4
Ceará-Mirim Brazil 5°38S 35°25W 332 C4
Ceara Rise Atl. Oc. 4°30N 43°30W 152 F7
Ceatharlach = Carlow Ireland 52°50N 6°56W 166 D5
Ceauru, L. Romania 44°58N 23°11E 183 F8
Cébaco, I. de Panama 7°33N 81°9W 320 E3
Cebeccı Turkey 41°7N 28°52E 122 B1
Cebollar Argentina 29°10S 66°35W 334 B2
Cebollera, Sierra Spain 42°0N 2°30W 196 D2
Cebreros Spain 40°27N 4°28W 194 E6
Cebu Phil. 10°18N 123°54E 233 F4
Cebu □ Phil. 10°20N 123°40E 233 F4
Čečava Bos.-H. 44°42N 17°44E 182 F2
Ceccano Italy 41°34N 13°20E 200 A6
Cecchignola Italy 41°48N 12°29E 136 C2
Cece Hungary 46°46N 18°39E 182 D3
Cechi Ivory C. 6°15N 4°25W 262 D4
Cecil Plains Australia 27°30S 151°11E 281 D5
Cecilienhof, Schloss Germany 52°35N 13°5E 115 B1
Cécina Italy 43°19N 10°31E 198 E7
Cécina → Italy 43°18N 10°29E 198 E7
Ceclavín Spain 39°50N 6°45W 194 F4
Cedar → U.S.A. 41°17N 91°21W 310 C5
Cedar City U.S.A. 37°41N 113°4W 305 H7
Cedar Creek Res. U.S.A. 32°11N 96°4W 314 E6
Cedar Falls Iowa, U.S.A. 42°32N 92°27W 310 B4
Cedar Falls Wash., U.S.A. 47°25N 121°45W 306 C5
Cedar Grove Georgia, U.S.A. 33°40N 84°16W 113 C3
Cedar Grove Ind., U.S.A. 39°22N 84°56W 311 E12
Cedar Hill U.S.A. 32°35N 96°57W 120 C4
Cedar Hill State Park ⌓ U.S.A. 32°36N 96°59W 120 C4
Cedar Key U.S.A. 29°8N 83°2W 317 F6
Cedar L. Canada 53°10N 100°0W 297 C9
Cedar Lake U.S.A. 41°22N 87°26W 311 C9
Cedar Park U.S.A. 30°30N 97°49W 314 F6
Cedar Point U.S.A. 41°44N 83°21W 311 C13
Cedar Rapids U.S.A. 41°59N 91°40W 310 C5
Cedar Tree Pt. Antigua & B. 17°42N 61°53W 322 c
Cedartown U.S.A. 34°1N 85°15W 316 A4
Cedarvale Canada 55°1N 128°22W 296 B3
Cedarvale Park Canada 43°42N 79°36W 141 A2
Cedarville KwaZulu Natal, S. Africa 30°23S 29°3E 271 D4
Cedarville Ill., U.S.A. 42°23N 89°38W 310 B7
Cedarville Ohio, U.S.A. 39°44N 83°49W 311 E13
Cedeira Spain 43°39N 8°2W 194 B2
Cedral Mexico 23°50N 100°45W 318 C4
Cedrino → Italy 40°11N 9°24E 200 B2
Cedro Brazil 6°34S 39°3W 332 C4
Cedros Azores 38°38N 28°42W 153 d1
Cedros, I. Mexico 28°12N 115°15W 318 B1
Cedros B. Trin. & Tob. 10°16N 61°54W 323 t
Cedros Pt. Trin. & Tob. 10°7N 61°49W 323 t
Ceduna Australia 32°7S 133°46E 281 E1
Cedynia Poland 52°53N 14°12E 185 F1
Cée Spain 42°57N 9°10W 194 C1
Ceel Gaal Somalia 10°58N 50°20E 267 B7
Ceel Waaq Kenya 2°49N 40°56E 267 D5
Ceelbuur = El Bur Somalia 4°40N 46°37E 267 D6
Ceeldheere Galguduud, Somalia 3°50N 47°8E 267 D6
Ceeldheere Galguduud, Somalia 5°22N 46°11E 267 C6
Ceerigaabo Somalia 10°35N 47°20E 267 B6
Cefalù Italy 38°2N 14°1E 201 D7
Cega → Spain 41°33N 4°46W 194 D6
Cegléd Hungary 47°11N 19°47E 182 C4
Céglie Messápica Italy 40°39N 17°31E 201 B10
Cehegín Spain 38°6N 1°48W 197 G3
Ceheng China 24°58N 105°48E 228 E5
Cehu-Silvaniei Romania 47°24N 23°9E 183 C8
Ceiba Puerto Rico 18°16N 65°39W 321 b
Ceica Romania 46°53N 22°10E 182 D7
Ceira → Portugal 40°13N 8°16W 194 E2
Çekerek Turkey 40°4N 35°29E 212 B6
Cekik Indonesia 8°12S 114°27E 231 J17
Cela Angola 11°25S 15°7E 265 E3
Čelákovice Czechia 50°10N 14°46E 180 A7
Celano Italy 42°5N 13°33E 199 F10
Celanova Spain 42°9N 7°58W 194 C3
Celaque △ Honduras 14°30N 88°43W 320 D2
Celaya Mexico 20°31N 100°37W 318 C4
Celbridge Ireland 53°20N 6°32W 166 C5
Celebes = Sulawesi Indonesia 2°0S 120°0E 235 C5
Celebes Sea Indonesia 3°0N 123°0E 231 D6
Celendín Peru 6°52S 78°10W 330 B2
Celestial Mts. = Tian Shan Asia 40°30N 76°0E 217 D9
Čelić Bos.-H. 44°43N 18°49E 182 F3
Celica Ecuador 4°7S 79°59W 328 D2
Celina U.S.A. 40°33N 84°35W 311 D12
Celinac Bos.-H. 44°44N 17°22E 182 F2
Celje Slovenia 46°16N 15°18E 199 B12
Celldömölk Hungary 47°16N 17°10E 182 C2
Celle Germany 52°37N 10°4E 178 C6
Celorico da Beira Portugal 40°38N 7°24W 194 E3
Celtic Sea Atl. Oc. 50°9N 9°34W 165 F2
Çeltikçi Turkey 37°32N 30°29E 205 D12
Çemişgezek Turkey 39°3N 38°56E 213 C8
Cempaka Putih Indonesia 6°10S 106°51E 122 B2
Cempi, Teluk Indonesia 8°44S 118°22E 235 D5
Cenderawasih, Teluk Indonesia 3°0S 135°20E 231 E9
Cenepa → Peru 4°40S 78°10W 328 D2
Çengelköy Turkey 41°2N 29°3E 122 B2
Cengkareng Indonesia 6°9S 106°45E 122 A1
Cengong China 27°13N 108°44E 228 D7
Ceno → Italy 44°43N 10°5E 198 D7
Centallo Italy 44°30N 7°35E 198 D4
Centelles Spain 41°50N 2°14E 196 D7
Centenário do Sul Brazil 22°48S 51°36W 333 F1
Centennial U.S.A. 39°34N 104°52W 304 G11
Centennial Olympic Park Atlanta, U.S.A. 33°46N 84°23W 113 B2
Centennial Park Sydney, Australia 33°53S 151°14E 139 B2
Center N. Dak., U.S.A. 47°7N 101°18W 308 B3
Center Tex., U.S.A. 31°48N 94°11W 314 F7
Center Hill Fla., U.S.A. 28°38N 82°3W 317 G7
Center Hill Georgia, U.S.A. 33°46N 84°29W 113 B2
Center Point U.S.A. 42°12N 91°46W 310 B5
Centerburg U.S.A. 40°18N 82°42W 312 F2
Centerville Calif., U.S.A. 36°44N 119°30W 306 J7
Centerville Iowa, U.S.A. 40°44N 92°52W 310 D4
Centerville Ohio, U.S.A. 39°38N 84°8W 311 E12
Centerville Pa., U.S.A. 40°3N 79°59W 312 F5
Centerville Tenn., U.S.A. 35°47N 87°28W 315 D11
Centerville Tex., U.S.A. 31°16N 95°59W 314 F7
Cento Italy 44°43N 11°17E 199 D8
Centocelle Italy 41°52N 12°34E 136 B2
Centraal Station Amsterdam, Neths. 112 a3
Central = Tsentralnyy □ Russia 52°0N 40°0E 214 D4
Central Brazil 11°8S 42°8W 332 D3
Central Alaska, U.S.A. 65°35N 144°48W 303 D11
Central □ Botswana 22°0S 26°30E 270 B4
Central □ Ghana 5°30N 1°0W 263 D4
Central □ Malawi 13°30S 33°30E 269 E3
Central □ Papua N. G. 10°0S 148°0E 286 F5
Central □ Zambia 14°25S 28°50E 269 E2
Central, Cordillera Bolivia 18°30S 64°55W 331 D5
Central, Cordillera Colombia 5°0N 75°0W 328 C3
Central, Cordillera Costa Rica 10°10N 84°5W 320 D3
Central, Cordillera Dom. Rep. 19°15N 71°0W 321 C5
Central, Cordillera Peru 7°0S 77°30W 330 B2
Central, Cordillera Phil. 17°20N 120°57E 232 C3
Central, Cordillera Puerto Rico 18°8N 66°35W 321 b
Central, Gare Montréal, Canada 130 c2
Central African Empire = Central African Rep. ■ Africa 7°0N 20°0E 264 A4
Central African Rep. ■ Africa 7°0N 20°0E 264 A4
Central America America 12°0N 85°0W 292 H11
Central Australia ✪ Australia 22°30S 128°30E 278 D4
Central Bedfordshire □ U.K. 52°5N 0°20W 169 E7
Central Butte Canada 50°48N 106°31W 297 C7
Central City Colo., U.S.A. 39°48N 105°31W 304 G11
Central City Iowa, U.S.A. 42°12N 91°32W 310 B5
Central City Ky., U.S.A. 37°18N 87°7W 308 G10
Central City Nebr., U.S.A. 41°7N 98°0W 308 E4
Central Desert ✪ Australia 19°56S 130°46E 278 C5
Central Equatoria □ South Sudan 4°0N 31°0E 257 G3
Central I. Kenya 3°30N 36°0E 268 B4
Central Island △ Kenya 2°33N 36°1E 268 B4
Central Japan Int. ✈ (NGO) Japan 34°53N 136°45E 223 C8
Central Kalahari ⌓ Botswana 22°36S 23°58E 270 B3
Central Makran Range Pakistan 26°30N 64°15E 240 D2
Central Pacific Basin Pac. Oc. 8°0N 175°0W 288 G10
Central Park New York, U.S.A. 132 a3
Central Park Zoo New York, U.S.A. 132 b2
Central Patricia Canada 51°30N 90°9W 298 B1
Central Point U.S.A. 42°23N 122°55W 304 E2
Central Provinces = Madhya Pradesh □ India 22°50N 78°0E 242 J8
Central Ra. Papua N. G. 5°0S 143°0E 286 C2
Central Ra. Trin. & Tob. 10°25N 61°15W 323 t
Central Range Wildlife Sanctuary △ Trin. & Tob. 10°27N 61°14W 323 t
Central Russian Uplands Europe 54°0N 36°0E 158 E13
Central Siberian Plateau Russia 65°0N 105°0E 210 B12
Central Square U.S.A. 43°17N 76°9W 313 C8
Central Village Jamaica 17°59N 76°55W 320 a
Centralia Ont., Canada 43°17N 81°28W 312 C3
Centralia Ill., U.S.A. 38°32N 89°8W 310 F7
Centralia Mo., U.S.A. 39°13N 92°8W 310 E4
Centralia Wash., U.S.A. 46°43N 122°58W 306 D4
Centre U.S.A. 34°9N 85°41W 316 A4
Centre □ Cameroon 4°45N 12°0E 263 E7
Centre de Flacq Mauritius 20°12S 57°43E 272 e
Centre -Val de Loire □ France 47°30N 1°30E 172 E8
Centreville Mich., U.S.A. 41°55N 85°32W 311 C11
Centreville N.Y., U.S.A. 42°28N 78°14W 312 D6
Centreville Pa., U.S.A. 41°44N 79°45W 312 E5
Century U.S.A. 30°58N 87°16W 317 E2
Century City U.S.A. 34°3N 118°25W 126 B2
Cenxi China 22°57N 110°57E 229 F8
Čeotina → Bos.-H. 43°36N 18°50E 202 C2
Cephalonia = Kefalonia Greece 38°15N 20°30E 207 C2
Čepin Croatia 45°32N 18°34E 182 E3
Ceprano Italy 41°33N 13°31E 200 A6
Ceptia Angola 12°56S 17°35E 265 E3
Ceptura Romania 45°1N 26°21E 183 E11
Cepu Indonesia 7°9S 111°35E 235 D4
Ceram = Seram Indonesia 3°10S 129°0E 231 E7
Ceram Sea = Seram Sea Indonesia 2°30S 128°30E 231 E7
Cerbère France 42°26N 3°10E 174 F7
Cerbicales, Îs. France 41°33N 9°22E 175 G13
Cercal Portugal 37°48N 8°40W 195 H2
Cerdanya Spain 42°22N 1°35E 196 C6
Cerdanyola del Vallès Spain 41°27N 2°8W 114 A1
Cère → France 44°55N 1°49E 174 D5
Cerea Italy 45°12N 11°13E 199 C8
Ceredigion □ U.K. 52°16N 4°15W 169 E3
Ceres Argentina 29°55S 61°55W 334 B3
Ceres Brazil 15°17S 49°35W 333 E2
Ceres Western Cape, S. Africa 33°21S 19°18E 270 D2
Ceres Calif., U.S.A. 37°35N 120°57W 306 H6
Cerésio, L. di = Lugano, L. di Switz. 46°0N 9°0E 198 C6
Céret France 42°30N 2°42E 174 F6
Cereté Colombia 8°53N 75°48W 328 B2
Cerf Seychelles 4°38S 55°40E 272 c
Cerfs, Îs. aux Mauritius 20°16S 57°47E 272 e
Cergy France 49°2N 2°4E 173 C9
Cerignola Italy 41°17N 15°53E 201 A8
Cerigo = Kythira Greece 36°8N 23°0E 204 E5
Cerillos Chile 33°29S 70°42W 137 B1
Cérilly France 46°37N 2°50E 173 F9
Cerisiers France 48°8N 3°30E 173 D10
Cerizay France 46°50N 0°40W 172 F6
Çerkeş Turkey 40°49N 32°52E 212 B5
Çerkezköy Turkey 41°17N 28°0E 203 E12
Cerknica Slovenia 45°48N 14°21E 199 C11
Cerkovica Bulgaria 43°41N 24°50E 203 C8
Cermerno Serbia 43°35N 20°25E 202 C4
Çermik Turkey 38°8N 39°26E 213 C8
Cerna Romania 45°4N 28°17E 183 E13
Cerna → Romania 44°38N 23°58E 183 F8
Cernauti = Chernivtsi Ukraine 48°15N 25°52E 183 B10
Cernavodă Romania 44°22N 28°3E 183 F13
Cernay France 47°44N 7°10E 173 E14
Cernik Croatia 45°17N 17°22E 182 E2
Cerralvo, I. Mexico 24°15N 109°55W 318 C3
Cërrik Albania 41°2N 19°58E 202 E3
Cerritos Mexico 22°25N 100°16W 318 C4
Cerro Chato Uruguay 33°6S 55°8W 335 C4
Cerro Chovoreca △ Paraguay 19°19S 59°7W 331 D6
Cerro Cofre de Perote △ Mexico 19°29N 97°8W 319 D5
Cerro Corá △ Paraguay 22°35S 56°2W 335 A4
Cerro de la Estrella △ Mexico 19°23N 99°5W 128 B2
Cerro de los Angeles Spain 40°18N 3°41W 127 C1
Cerro de Pasco Peru 10°45S 76°10W 330 C2
Cerro El Copey △ Venezuela 11°11N 63°54W 329 a
Cerro Gordo U.S.A. 39°53N 88°44W 311 E8
Cerro Hoya △ Panama 7°17N 80°45W 320 E3
Cerro Navia Chile 33°25S 70°42W 137 B1
Cerro Saroche △ Venezuela 10°8N 69°38W 328 A4
Cerro Sombrero Chile 52°45S 69°15W 336 D3
Cerros Colorados, Embalse Argentina 38°30S 68°50W 336 A3
Certaldo Italy 43°33N 11°2E 198 E8

Cervantes Phil. 17°0N 120°44E 232 C3
Cervaro → Italy 41°30N 15°52E 201 A8
Cervati, Monte Italy 40°17N 15°29E 201 B8
Cerventes Australia 30°31S 115°3E 279 F2
Cervera Spain 41°40N 1°16E 196 D6
Cervera de Pisuerga Spain 42°51N 4°30W 194 C6
Cervera del Río Alhama Spain 42°2N 1°58W 196 C3
Cervéteri Italy 42°0N 12°6E 199 F9
Cérvia Italy 44°15N 12°22E 199 D9
Cervignano del Friuli Italy 45°49N 13°20E 199 C10
Cervinara Italy 41°1N 14°37E 201 A7
Cervione France 42°20N 9°29E 175 F13
Cervo Spain 43°40N 7°24W 194 B3
Cesano Boscone Italy 45°26N 9°5E 128 B1
César □ Colombia 9°0N 73°30W 328 B3
Cesarò Italy 37°50N 14°38E 201 E7
Cesate Italy 45°35N 9°4E 128 A1
Cesena Italy 44°8N 12°15E 199 D9
Cesenático Italy 44°12N 12°24E 199 D9
Cēsis Latvia 57°18N 25°15E 188 D3
Česká Lípa Czechia 50°45N 14°30E 180 A7
Česká Rep. = Czechia ■ Europe 50°0N 15°0E 180 B8
Česká Třebová Czechia 49°54N 16°27E 181 B9
České Budějovice Czechia 48°55N 14°25E 180 C7
České Švýcarsko △ Czechia 50°50N 14°15E 180 A7
České Velenice Czechia 48°45N 14°57E 180 C7
Českobudějovický = Jihočeský □ Czechia 49°8N 14°35E 180 B7
Českomoravská Vrchovina Czechia 49°30N 15°40E 180 B8
Český Brod Czechia 50°4N 14°52E 180 A7
Český Krumlov Czechia 48°43N 14°21E 180 C7
Český Těšín Czechia 49°45N 18°39E 181 B11
Česma → Croatia 45°35N 16°29E 199 C13
Çeşme Turkey 38°20N 26°23E 205 C8
Çeşme Yarımadası Turkey 38°20N 26°30E 205 C8
Cessnock Australia 32°50S 151°21E 283 B9
Cesson-Sévigné France 48°7N 1°36W 172 D5
Cestas France 44°44N 0°41W 174 D3
Cestos → Liberia 5°40N 9°10W 262 D3
Cestos Sehnkwehn △ Liberia 5°40N 9°10W 262 D3
Cetaceo, Mt. Phil. 17°42N 122°3E 232 C4
Cetate Romania 44°7N 23°2E 182 F8
Cetatea-Albă = Bilhorod-Dnistrovskyy Ukraine 46°11N 30°23E 189 J6
Cetin Grad Croatia 45°9N 15°45E 199 C12
Cetina → Croatia 43°26N 16°42E 199 E13
Cetinje Montenegro 42°23N 18°59E 202 D2
Çetmi Turkey 36°52N 32°38E 250 B3
Cetraro Italy 39°31N 15°55E 201 C8
Ceuta N. Afr. 35°52N 5°18W 260 A3
Ceva Italy 44°23N 8°2E 198 D5
Ceve-i-Ra Fiji 21°46S 174°31E 277 E13
Cévennes France 44°10N 3°50E 174 D7
Cévennes △ France 44°15N 3°45E 174 D7
Ceyhan Turkey 37°4N 35°47E 250 A6
Ceyhan → Turkey 36°38N 35°40E 250 B6
Ceylanpınar Turkey 36°50N 40°2E 213 D9
Ceylon = Sri Lanka ■ Asia 7°30N 80°50E 245 L5
Ceylon Plain Ind. Oc. 4°0S 82°0E 273 E7
Cèze → France 44°6N 4°43E 175 D8
Cha-am Thailand 12°48N 99°58E 236 F2
Cha Kwo Ling Hong Kong, China 22°18N 114°13E 122 B3
Chá Pungana Angola 13°44S 18°39E 265 E3
Chabanais France 45°52N 0°48E 174 C4
Chabeuil France 44°54N 5°3E 175 D9
Chablais France 46°20N 6°36E 173 F13
Chablis France 47°47N 3°48E 173 E10
Chabounia Algeria 35°30N 2°38E 261 A5
Chacabuco Argentina 34°40S 60°27W 334 C3
Chacachacare Venezuela 10°58N 64°9W 329 a
Chacachacare I. Trin. & Tob. 10°41N 61°45W 323 t
Chacao, Canal Chile 41°47S 73°42W 336 B2
Chacarrita Argentina 34°35S 58°27W 117 B2
Chachani, Nevado Peru 16°11S 71°31W 330 D3
Chachapoyas Peru 6°15S 77°50W 330 B2
Chachasp Peru 15°30S 72°15W 330 D3
Chachoengsao Thailand 13°42N 101°5E 236 F3
Chachran Pakistan 28°55N 70°30E 242 E4
Chachro Pakistan 25°5N 70°15E 242 G4
Chaco □ Argentina 26°30S 61°0W 334 B3
Chaco □ Paraguay 26°0S 60°0W 334 B4
Chaco → U.S.A. 36°46N 108°39W 305 H9
Chaco △ Argentina 27°0S 59°30W 334 B4
Chaco Culture ⌂ U.S.A. 36°3N 107°58W 305 H10
Chacon, C. U.S.A. 54°42N 132°0W 296 C2
Chad ■ Africa 15°0N 17°15E 259 F3
Chad, L. = Tchad, L. Chad 13°30N 14°30E 259 F2
Chadileuvú → Argentina 37°46S 66°0W 334 D2
Chadiza Zambia 14°45S 32°27E 269 E3
Chadron U.S.A. 42°50N 103°0W 308 D2
Chadwell Heath U.K. 51°34N 0°8E 125 A4
Chadyr-Lunga = Ceadîr-Lunga Moldova 46°3N 28°51E 183 D13
Chae Hom Thailand 18°43N 99°35E 236 C2
Chae Son △ Thailand 18°42N 99°20E 236 C2
Chaem → Thailand 18°11N 98°38E 236 C2
Chaeryŏng N. Korea 38°24N 125°36E 224 C2
Chafe Nigeria 11°59N 6°50E 263 C6
Chagai Hills = Chāh Gay Hills Afghan. 29°30N 64°0E 240 C2
Chagang-do □ N. Korea 40°50N 126°30E 224 B3
Chagda Russia 58°45N 130°38E 215 D14
Chagdo Kangri China 34°15N 84°10E 217 F10
Chaghcharān Afghan. 34°31N 65°15E 240 B2
Chagne Ethiopia 10°57N 36°30E 266 B4
Chagny France 46°57N 4°45E 173 F11
Chagoda Russia 59°10N 35°15E 188 C8
Chagos Arch. ☒ Ind. Oc. 6°0S 72°0E 273 E6
Chagos-Laccadive Ridge Ind. Oc. 3°0N 73°0E 273 D6
Chagres → Panama 9°10N 79°40W 320 c
Chagres △ Panama 9°33N 79°37W 320 c
Chaguanas Trin. & Tob. 10°30N 61°26W 323 t
Chaguaramas Trin. & Tob. 10°41N 61°38W 323 t
Chāh Ākhvor Iran 32°41N 59°40E 247 C8
Chāh Bahar Iran 25°20N 60°40E 247 E9
Chāh-e Āb Afghan. 37°23N 69°48E 240 A3
Chāh-e Kavīr Iran 34°29N 56°52E 247 C8
Chāh Gay Hills Afghan. 29°30N 64°0E 240 C2
Chahār Borj Iran 37°6N 45°59E 213 D11
Chahār Borjak Afghan. 30°17N 62°3E 240 C1
Chahār Mahāll va Bakhtīarī □ Iran 32°0N 49°0E 247 C6
Chahtung Burma 26°41N 98°10E 241 B7
Chai Badan Thailand 15°12N 101°8E 236 E3
Chai Chee Singapore 1°19N 103°46E 138 B3
Chai Wan Hong Kong, China 22°16N 114°14E 122 B3
Chai Wan Kok Hong Kong, China 22°22N 114°6E 122 A2
Chaibasa India 22°42N 85°49E 243 H11
Chaidari Greece 38°2N 23°38E 112 A1
Chaillé-les-Marais France 46°25N 1°2W 174 B2
Chaillot, Palais de Paris, France 134 b2
Chaillu, Massif du Gabon 2°32S 11°10E 264 C2
Chain Ridge Ind. Oc. 6°0N 54°0E 273 D4
Chainat Thailand 15°11N 100°8E 236 E3
Chainpur Nepal 27°17N 87°19E 243 F12
Chaires U.S.A. 30°26N 84°7W 316 E5
Chaitén Chile 42°55S 72°43W 336 B2
Chaiya Thailand 9°23N 99°14E 237 H2
Chaiyaphum Thailand 15°48N 102°2E 236 E4
Chaj Doab Pakistan 32°15N 73°0E 242 C5
Chajari Argentina 30°42S 58°0W 334 C4
Chak Amru Pakistan 32°22N 75°11E 242 C6
Chaka South Sudan 4°49N 31°14E 257 G3
Chakar → Pakistan 29°29N 68°2E 242 E3
Chakari Zimbabwe 18°5S 29°51E 271 A4
Chakaria Bangla. 21°45N 92°5E 241 E4
Chakarnaba Chad 14°13N 20°51E 259 F4
Chakdaha India 22°28N 88°19E 124 C1
Chake Chake Tanzania 5°15S 39°45E 268 D4
Chakhānsūr Afghan. 31°10N 62°0E 240 C1
Chakonipau, L. Canada 56°18N 68°30W 299 A6
Chakradharpur India 22°45N 85°40E 243 H11
Chakrata India 30°42N 77°51E 242 D7
Chakwadam Burma 27°29N 98°31E 241 B7
Chakwal Pakistan 32°56N 72°53E 242 C5
Chala Peru 15°48S 74°20W 330 D3
Chalais France 45°16N 0°3E 174 C4
Chalakudi India 10°18N 76°20E 245 J3
Chalan Kanoa N. Marianas 15°9N 145°42E 302 e
Chalandri Greece 38°3N 23°48E 112 A2
Chalchihuites Mexico 23°29N 103°53W 318 C4
Chalcis = Chalkida Greece 38°27N 23°42E 204 C5
Châlette-sur-Loing France 48°1N 2°44E 173 D9
Chaleur B. Canada 47°55N 65°30W 299 C6
Chalfant U.S.A. 37°32N 118°21W 306 H8
Chalhuanca Peru 14°15S 73°15W 330 C3
Chalindrey France 47°43N 5°26E 173 E12
Chaling China 26°58N 113°30E 229 D9
Chalisgaon India 20°30N 75°10E 244 D2
Chalk River Canada 46°1N 77°27W 298 C4
Chalkar, Ozero = Shalkar Köli Kazakhstan 50°35N 51°47E 190 E10
Chalki Dodekanisa, Greece 36°17N 27°35E 205 E9
Chalki Thessaly, Greece 39°36N 22°30E 204 B4
Chalkida Greece 38°27N 23°42E 204 C5
Chalkidiki Greece 40°25N 23°20E 202 F7
Chalky Inlet N.Z. 46°3S 166°31E 285 G1
Chalkyitsik U.S.A. 66°39N 143°43W 303 C12
Challakere India 14°19N 76°39E 245 G3
Challans France 46°50N 1°52W 172 F5
Challapata Bolivia 18°53S 66°50W 330 D4
Challawa Gorge Res. Nigeria 11°54N 8°25E 263 C6
Challenger Deep Pac. Oc. 11°30N 142°0E 288 F6
Challenger Fracture Zone Pac. Oc. 35°0S 105°0W 289 L17
Challis U.S.A. 44°30N 114°14W 304 D6
Chalmette U.S.A. 29°56N 89°57W 315 G10
Chaloem Rattanakosin △ Thailand 14°40N 99°17E 236 E2
Chalon-sur-Saône France 46°48N 4°50E 173 F11
Chalong Thailand 7°50N 98°22E 237 a
Chalonnes-sur-Loire France 47°20N 0°45W 172 E6
Châlons-en-Champagne France 48°58N 4°20E 173 D11
Chálten, Cerro = Fitz Roy, Cerro Argentina 49°17S 73°5W 336 C2
Châlus Haute-Vienne, France 45°39N 0°58E 174 C4
Chālūs Iran 36°38N 51°26E 247 B6
Cham Germany 49°13N 12°39E 179 F8
Cham, Cu Lao Vietnam 15°57N 108°30E 236 E7
Chama U.S.A. 36°54N 106°35W 305 H10
Chamah, Gunung Malaysia 5°13N 101°35E 234 A2
Chamaicó Argentina 35°3S 64°58W 334 D3
Chaman Pakistan 30°58N 66°25E 240 C2
Chamartin Spain 40°27N 3°40W 127 B1
Chamba India 32°35N 76°10E 242 C7
Chamba Tanzania 11°37S 37°0E 269 E4
Chambal → India 26°29N 79°15E 243 F8
Chamberi Spain 40°26N 3°42W 127 B1
Chamberlain U.S.A. 43°49N 99°20W 308 D4
Chamberlain → Australia 15°30S 127°54E 278 C4
Chamberlain L. U.S.A. 46°14N 69°19W 309 B19
Chambers U.S.A. 35°11N 109°26W 305 J9
Chambersburg U.S.A. 39°56N 77°40W 309 F15
Chambéry France 45°34N 5°55E 175 C9
Chambi, Jebel Tunisia 35°11N 8°39E 261 A6
Chamblee U.S.A. 33°53N 84°18W 316 B5
Chambly Canada 45°27N 73°17W 313 A11
Chambord Canada 48°25N 72°6W 299 C5
Chamboulive France 45°26N 1°42E 174 C5
Chambourcy France 48°54N 2°2E 134 A1
Chambri L. Papua N. G. 4°15S 143°10E 286 C2
Chamchamal Iraq 35°32N 44°50E 213 E11
Chamela Mexico 19°32N 105°5W 318 D3
Chamical Argentina 30°22S 66°27W 334 C2
Chamili Greece 35°50N 26°15E 205 F8
Chamkar Luong Cambodia 11°0N 103°45E 237 G4
Chamois U.S.A. 38°41N 91°46W 310 F5
Chamoli India 30°24N 79°21E 243 D8
Chamonix-Mont Blanc France 45°55N 6°51E 175 C10
Chamouchuane = Ashuapmushuan → Canada 48°37N 72°20W 298 C5
Champ de Mars, Parc du Paris, France 134 c2
Champa India 22°2N 82°43E 243 H10
Champagne Canada 60°49N 136°30W 296 A1
Champagne France 48°40N 4°20E 173 D11
Champagnole France 46°45N 5°55E 173 F12
Champaign U.S.A. 40°7N 88°15W 311 D8
Champaner India 22°29N 73°32E 242 H5
Champassak Laos 14°53N 105°52E 236 E5
Champaubert France 48°50N 3°45E 173 D10
Champawat India 29°20N 80°6E 243 E9
Champdeniers-St-Denis France 46°29N 0°25W 174 B3
Champdoré, L. Canada 55°55N 65°49W 299 A6
Champeix France 45°37N 3°8E 174 C7
Champhai India 23°28N 93°20E 241 D4
Champigny-sur-Marne France 48°49N 2°30E 134 B4
Champion U.S.A. 41°19N 80°51W 312 E4
Champlain U.S.A. 44°59N 73°27W 313 B11
Champlain, L. U.S.A. 44°40N 73°20W 313 B11
Champlain, Pont Canada 45°28N 73°31W 130 B2
Champlitte France 47°37N 5°31E 173 E12
Champotón Mexico 19°21N 90°43W 319 D6
Champs Elysées, Avenue des Paris, France 134 b2
Champs-sur-Marne France 48°50N 2°34E 134 A4
Champua India 22°5N 85°40E 243 H11
Chamrail India 22°38N 88°17E 124 B1
Chamrajnagar India 11°52N 76°52E 245 J3
Chamusca Portugal 39°21N 8°29W 195 F2
Chan Chan Peru 8°7S 79°0W 330 B2
Chana Thailand 6°55N 100°44E 237 J3
Chanakyapuri India 28°35N 77°11E 120 B2
Chañaral Chile 26°23S 70°40W 334 B1
Chanārān Iran 36°39N 59°6E 247 B8
Chanasma India 23°44N 72°5E 242 H5
Chancay Peru 11°32S 77°25W 330 C2
Chancel, Î. Martinique 14°41N 60°53W 322 j
Chanching = Zhanjiang China 21°15N 110°20E 229 G8
Chanco Chile 35°44S 72°32W 334 D1
Chand India 21°57N 79°7E 243 J8
Chandalar → U.S.A. 66°37N 146°0W 303 C11
Chandan Chauki India 28°33N 80°47E 243 E9
Chandannagar India 22°52N 88°24E 243 H13
Chandausi India 28°27N 78°49E 243 E8
Chandeleur Is. U.S.A. 29°55N 88°57W 315 G10
Chandeleur Sd. U.S.A. 29°55N 89°0W 315 G10
Chandigarh India 30°43N 76°47E 242 D7
Chandil India 22°58N 86°3E 243 H12
Chanditala India 22°41N 88°15E 124 A1
Chandler S. Austral., Australia 27°0S 133°19E 281 D1
Chandler Qué., Canada 48°18N 64°46W 299 C7
Chandler Ariz., U.S.A. 33°18N 111°50W 305 K8
Chandler Okla., U.S.A. 35°42N 96°53W 314 D6
Chandless → Brazil 9°8S 69°51W 330 B4
Chandod India 21°59N 73°28E 242 J5
Chandpur Bangla. 23°8N 90°45E 241 D3
Chandra Greece 35°3N 26°8E 205 F8
Chandragiri India 13°35N 79°19E 245 H4
Chandrapur India 19°57N 79°25E 244 E4
Chandrupatla India 18°33N 80°24E 244 E5
Chānf Iran 26°38N 60°29E 247 E9
Chang Pakistan 26°59N 68°30E 242 F3
Chang, Ko Thailand 12°0N 102°23E 237 G4
Chang, Ko Thailand 9°50N 98°27E 237 H2
Ch'ang Chiang = Chang Jiang → China 31°48N 121°10E 229 B13
Chang Jiang → China 31°48N 121°10E 229 B13
Chang-won S. Korea 35°16N 128°37E 224 E4
Changan = Xi'an China 34°15N 109°0E 226 G5
Changan China 22°48N 113°48E 219 a
Changanacheri India 9°25N 76°31E 245 K3
Changanassery = Changanacheri India 9°25N 76°31E 245 K3
Changane → Mozam. 24°30S 33°30E 271 B5
Changbai China 41°25N 128°5E 224 B4
Changbai Shan China 42°20N 129°0E 224 A4
Changchiak'ou = Zhangjiakou China 40°48N 114°55E 226 D8
Ch'angchih = Changzhi China 36°10N 113°6E 226 F7
Changchih Taiwan 22°41N 120°32E 225 D2
Ch'angchou = Changzhou China 31°47N 119°58E 229 B12
Changchow = Changzhou China 31°47N 119°58E 229 B12
Changchun China 43°57N 125°17E 227 C13
Changchunling China 45°18N 125°27E 227 B13
Changde China 29°4N 111°35E 229 C8
Changdo-ri N. Korea 38°30N 127°40E 224 C3
Changfeng China 32°28N 117°10E 229 A11
Changfeng Park China 31°14N 121°24E 138 B1
Changge China 34°13N 113°46E 226 G7
Changhai = Shanghai China 31°15N 121°26E 138 B2
Changhua Zhejiang, China 30°12N 119°12E 229 B12
Changhua Taiwan 24°2N 120°30E 225 B2
Changhua □ Taiwan 24°15N 120°55E 225 B2
Changhŭngni N. Korea 40°24N 128°19E 224 B4
Changi Singapore 1°23N 103°59E 138 A3
Changi, Singapore ✕ (SIN) Singapore 1°23N 103°59E 138 A3
Changji China 44°1N 87°19E 217 D11
Changjiang China 19°20N 108°55E 229 a
Changjiang Shuiku China 22°29N 113°27E 219 a
Changjin N. Korea 40°23N 127°15E 224 B3
Changjin-ho N. Korea 40°30N 127°15E 224 B3
Changle China 25°59N 119°27E 229 E12
Changli China 39°40N 119°13E 227 E10
Changling China 44°20N 123°58E 227 B12
Changlun Malaysia 6°25N 100°26E 237 J3
Changming Hunan, China 26°28N 112°22E 229 D9
Changning Shanghai, China 31°13N 121°24E 138 B1
Changning Sichuan, China 28°40N 104°56E 228 C5
Changning Yunnan, China 24°45N 99°30E 228 E2
Ch'angpin Taiwan 23°19N 121°27E 225 C3
Changping China 40°14N 116°12E 226 D9
Changsha China 28°12N 113°0E 229 C9
Changshan China 28°55N 118°27E 229 C12
Changshan Qundao China 39°11N 122°32E 227 E12
Changshou China 29°50N 107°4E 228 C6
Changshu China 31°38N 120°43E 229 B13
Changshun China 26°3N 106°25E 228 D6
Changtai China 24°35N 117°42E 229 E11
Changt'e = Chongde China 30°32N 120°26E 229 B13
Changting China 25°50N 116°22E 229 E11
Changtu China 42°46N 124°6E 227 C13
Changuinola Panama 9°26N 82°31W 320 E3
Changwu Guangxi Zhuangzu, China 23°25N 111°17E 229 F8
Changwu Shaanxi, China 35°10N 107°45E 226 G4
Changxing China 31°0N 119°55E 229 B12
Changyang China 30°30N 111°10E 229 B8
Changyi China 36°40N 119°30E 227 F10
Changyŏn N. Korea 38°15N 125°6E 224 C2
Changyuan Henan, China 35°15N 114°42E 226 G8
Changyuan Taiwan 23°25N 121°29E 225 C3
Changzhi = Changchih Taiwan 22°41N 120°32E 225 D2
Changzhi China 36°10N 113°6E 226 F7
Changzhou China 31°47N 119°58E 229 B12
Chanhanga Angola 16°0S 14°8E 265 F2
Chania Greece 35°30N 24°4E 207 E5
Chania ✕ (CHQ) Greece 35°30N 24°6E 207 E5
Chanion, Kolpos Greece 35°33N 23°55E 207 E4
Chanlar = Goygöl Azerbaijan 40°37N 46°12E 191 K8
Channagiri India 14°2N 75°56E 245 G2
Channapatna India 12°40N 77°15E 245 H3
Channel Is. U.K. 49°19N 2°24W 169 H5
Channel Is. Calif., U.S.A. 33°40N 119°15W 307 M7
Channel Islands △ U.S.A. 34°0N 119°24W 307 L7
Channel-Port aux Basques Canada 47°30N 59°9W 299 C8
Channel Tunnel Europe 51°0N 1°30E 169 F9
Channing U.S.A. 35°41N 102°20W 314 D3
Chantada Spain 42°36N 7°46W 194 C3
Chantereine France 48°53N 2°37E 134 A4
Chanthaburi Thailand 12°38N 102°12E 236 F4
Chantian China 23°12N 113°16E 121 A2
Chantilly France 49°12N 2°29E 173 C9
Chantonnay France 46°40N 1°3W 172 F5
Chantrey Inlet Canada 67°48N 96°20W 294 D12
Chanumla India 8°19N 93°5E 245 K11
Chanute U.S.A. 37°41N 95°27W 308 G6
Chanza → Spain 37°32N 7°30W 195 H3
Chany, Ozero Russia 54°49N 77°29E 217 B9
Chao Hu China 31°30N 117°30E 229 B11
Chao Phraya → Thailand 13°40N 100°31E 236 F3
Chao Phraya Lowlands Thailand 15°30N 100°0E 236 E3
Chaocheng China 36°4N 115°37E 226 F8
Ch'aochou Taiwan 22°33N 120°32E 225 D2
Chaohu China 31°38N 117°50E 229 B11
Chaouia-Ouardigha □ Morocco 33°0N 7°30W 260 B3
Chaoyang Beijing, China 39°53N 116°26E 114 B2
Chaoyang Guangdong, China 23°17N 116°30E 229 F11
Chaoyang Liaoning, China 41°35N 120°22E 227 D11
Chaoyangmen China 39°54N 116°23E 114 B2
Chaozhou = Ch'aochou Taiwan 22°33N 120°32E 225 D2
Chaozhou China 23°42N 116°32E 229 F11
Chapada Diamantina △ Brazil 12°52S 41°30W 333 D3
Chapada dos Guimarães Brazil 15°26S 55°45W 331 D6
Chapada dos Guimarães △ Brazil 15°18S 55°54W 331 D6
Chapada dos Veadeiros △ Brazil 14°0S 47°30W 333 D2
Chapaev Kazakhstan 50°25N 51°10E 190 E10
Chapais Canada 49°47N 74°51W 298 C5
Chapala Mozam. 15°50S 37°35E 269 F4
Chapala, L. de Mexico 20°15N 103°0W 318 C4
Chaparé → Bolivia 15°58S 64°42W 331 D5
Chaparmukh India 26°12N 92°31E 241 B4
Chaparral Colombia 3°43N 75°28W 328 C2
Chapayevsk Russia 53°0N 49°40E 190 D9
Chapecó Brazil 27°14S 52°41W 335 B5
Chapel Hill U.S.A. 35°55N 79°4W 315 D15
Chapelton Jamaica 18°5N 77°16W 320 a
Chapin = Edinburg U.S.A. 26°18N 98°10W 314 H5
Chapin U.S.A. 39°46N 90°24W 310 E6
Chapleau Canada 47°50N 83°24W 298 C3
Chaplin Canada 50°28N 106°40W 297 C7
Chaplin L. Canada 50°22N 106°36W 297 C7
Chaplino Ukraine 48°8N 36°15E 189 H9
Chaplygin Russia 53°15N 40°0E 188 F11
Chappell U.S.A. 41°6N 102°28W 308 E2
Chappells U.S.A. 34°11N 81°52W 316 A8
Chapra = Chhapra India 25°48N 84°44E 243 G11
Chapultepec, Bosque de Mexico 19°25N 99°11W 128 B1
Chapultepec, Castillo de Mexico 19°25N 99°10W 128 B1
Chaqābel Iran 33°16N 47°30E 213 F12
Châr Mauritania 21°32N 12°45W 260 D2
Chara Russia 56°54N 118°20E 215 D12
Charadai Argentina 27°35S 59°55W 334 B4
Charagato, Pta. Venezuela 10°50N 64°9W 329 a
Charagua Bolivia 19°45S 63°10W 331 D5
Charakas Greece 35°1N 25°7E 207 E6
Charalá Colombia 6°17N 73°10W 328 B3
Charambirá, Punta Colombia 4°16N 77°32W 328 C2
Charaña Bolivia 17°30S 69°25W 330 D4
Charantsavan Armenia 40°35N 44°41E 191 K7
Charanwala India 27°51N 72°10E 242 F5
Charapita Colombia 0°37S 74°21W 328 D3
Charata Argentina 27°13S 61°14W 334 B3
Charcas Mexico 23°8N 101°7W 318 C4
Charcot I. Antarctica 70°0S 70°0W 151 C17
Chard U.K. 50°52N 2°58W 169 G5
Chardon U.S.A. 41°35N 81°12W 312 E3
Charduar India 26°51N 92°46E 241 B4
Chardzhou = Türkmenabat Turkmenistan 39°6N 63°34E 247 B9
Charente □ France 45°50N 0°16E 174 C4
Charente → France 45°57N 1°5W 174 C2
Charente-Inférieure = Charente-Maritime □ France 45°45N 0°45W 174 C3
Charente-Maritime □ France 45°45N 0°45W 174 C3
Charenton-du-Cher France 46°44N 2°39E 173 F9
Charenton-le-Pont France 48°49N 2°25E 134 B3
Chari → Chad 12°58N 14°31E 259 F2
Chari-Baguirmi □ Chad 11°0N 17°0E 259 F3
Chārīkār Afghan. 35°0N 69°10E 240 B3
Charing U.S.A. 32°28N 84°22W 316 C5
Charing Cross London, U.K. 125 b4
Chariton U.S.A. 41°1N 93°19W 310 C3
Chariton → U.S.A. 39°19N 92°58W 310 E4
Charity Guyana 7°24N 58°36W 329 B6
Chärjew = Türkmenabat Turkmenistan 39°6N 63°34E 247 B9
Charkhari India 25°24N 79°45E 243 G8
Charkhi Dadri India 28°37N 76°17E 242 E7
Charleroi Belgium 50°24N 4°27E 170 D4
Charleroi Pa., U.S.A. 40°9N 79°57W 312 F5
Charleroi, Kanal de → Belgium 50°51N 4°19E 116 B1
Charles, C. U.S.A. 37°7N 75°58W 309 G16
Charles, I. = Santa María, I. Ecuador 1°17S 90°26W 330 a
Charles, Peak Australia 32°52S 121°11E 279 F3
Charles Bridge = Karlův most Prague, Czechia 135 b1
Charles City U.S.A. 43°4N 92°41W 310 A4
Charles de Gaulle, Paris ✕ (CDG) France 49°0N 2°32E 173 D9
Charles Gates Dawes House U.S.A. 42°2N 87°40W 119 A2
Charles I. Canada 62°39N 74°15W 295 E17
Charles L. Canada 59°50N 110°33W 297 B6
Charles Sound N.Z. 45°2S 167°4E 285 F2
Charles Square = Karlovo náměstí Prague, Czechia 135 c1
Charles Town U.S.A. 39°17N 77°52W 309 F15
Charlesbourg Canada 46°51N 71°16W 309 B18
Charleston Ill., U.S.A. 39°30N 88°10W 311 E8
Charleston Miss., U.S.A. 34°1N 90°4W 315 D9
Charleston Mo., U.S.A. 36°55N 89°21W 308 G9
Charleston S.C., U.S.A. 32°46N 79°56W 316 C10
Charleston W. Va., U.S.A. 38°21N 81°38W 309 F13
Charleston L. Canada 44°32N 76°0W 313 B9
Charleston Peak U.S.A. 36°16N 115°42W 307 J11
Charlestown Mayo, Ireland 53°58N 8°48W 166 C3
Charlestown St. Kitts & Nevis 17°8N 62°37W 322 d
Charlestown KwaZulu Natal, S. Africa 27°26S 29°53E 271 C4
Charlestown Ind., U.S.A. 38°27N 85°40W 311 F11
Charlestown Mass., U.S.A. 42°22N 71°4W 116 A2
Charlestown N.H., U.S.A. 43°14N 72°25W 313 C12
Charlestown Bridge Boston, U.S.A. 116 a2
Charlestown of Aberlour U.K. 57°28N 3°14W 167 D5
Charleville Queens., Australia 26°24S 146°15E 281 D4
Charleville Cork, Ireland 52°21N 8°40W 166 D3
Charleville-Mézières France 49°44N 4°40E 173 C11
Charlevoix U.S.A. 45°19N 85°16W 309 C11
Charlie Gibbs Fracture Zone Atl. Oc. 52°45N 35°30W 152 A8
Charlieu France 46°10N 4°10E 173 F11
Charlotte Mich., U.S.A. 42°34N 84°50W 311 B12
Charlotte N.C., U.S.A. 35°13N 80°50W 315 D14
Charlotte Vt., U.S.A. 44°19N 73°16W 313 B11
Charlotte Amalie U.S. Virgin Is. 18°21N 64°56W 321 C7
Charlotte-Douglas Int. ✕ (CLT) U.S.A. 35°12N 80°56W 315 D14
Charlotte Harbor U.S.A. 26°57N 82°4W 317 J7
Charlotte L. Canada 52°12N 125°19W 296 C3
Charlotte Ville Dominica 15°17N 61°24W 323 k
Charlottenberg Sweden 59°54N 12°17E 162 E6
Charlottenburg Germany 52°31N 13°15E 115 A2
Charlottenburg, Schloss Germany 52°31N 13°18E 115 A2
Charlottenlund Denmark 55°44N 12°35E 118 A3
Charlottesville U.S.A. 38°2N 78°30W 309 F14
Charlottetown Nfld. & L., Canada 52°46N 56°7W 299 B8
Charlottetown P.E.I., Canada 46°14N 63°8W 299 C7
Charlotteville Trin. & Tob. 11°20N 60°33W 323 s
Charlton Vic., Australia 36°16S 143°24E 282 D5
Charlton London, U.K. 51°29N 0°1E 125 B4
Charlton I. Canada 52°0N 79°20W 298 B4
Charmes France 48°22N 6°17E 173 D13
Charneca Lisboa, Portugal 38°47N 9°8W 126 A2
Charneca Setúbal, Portugal 38°37N 9°12W 126 B1
Charny Canada 46°43N 71°15W 299 C5
Charnyany Belarus 51°59N 24°12E 185 G11
Charolles France 46°27N 4°16E 173 F11
Chârost France 47°0N 2°7E 173 F9
Charouine Algeria 29°0N 0°15W 261 C4
Charre Mozam. 17°13S 35°10E 269 F4
Charroux France 46°9N 0°25E 174 B4
Charsadda Pakistan 34°7N 71°45E 242 B4
Charshanga = Köýtendag Turkmenistan 37°30N 66°1E 240 A2
Charters Towers Australia 20°5S 146°13E 280 C4
Chartres France 48°29N 1°30E 172 D8
Chartreuse ⌂ France 45°22N 5°42E 175 C9
Charuma Trin. & Tob. 10°24N 61°9W 323 t
Charysh → Russia 52°22N 83°45E 217 B10
Chascomús Argentina 35°30S 58°0W 334 D4
Chase Canada 50°50N 119°41W 296 C5
Chase, L. U.S.A. 28°28N 81°31W 133 B1
Chasefu Zambia 11°55S 33°8E 269 E3
Chashma Barrage Pakistan 32°27N 71°20E 242 C4
Chaslands Mistake N.Z. 46°38S 169°22E 285 G4
Chasong N. Korea 41°27N 126°38E 224 B3
Chasseneuil-sur-Bonnieure France 45°52N 0°29E 174 C4
Chastanet, Anse St. Lucia 13°52N 61°5W 323 m
Chāt Iran 37°59N 55°16E 247 B7
Chatal Balkan = Udvoy Balkan Bulgaria 42°50N 26°50E 203 D10
Chatanika U.S.A. 65°7N 147°28W 303 D11
Château-Arnoux-St-Auban France 44°6N 6°0E 175 D10
Château-Chinon France 47°4N 3°56E 173 E10
Château-d'Olonne France 46°30N 1°44W 174 B2
Château-du-Loir France 47°40N 0°25E 172 E7
Château Dubug Martinique 14°46N 60°55W 322 j
Château Gaillard Guadeloupe 16°18N 61°23W 322 e
Château-Gontier France 47°50N 0°48W 172 E6
Château-la-Vallière France 47°30N 0°20E 172 E7
Château-Landon France 48°8N 2°40E 173 D9
Château Murat Guadeloupe 15°52N 61°17W 322 e
Château-Renard France 47°56N 2°55E 173 E9
Château-Renault France 47°36N 0°56E 172 E7
Château-Salins France 48°50N 6°30E 173 D13
Château-Thierry France 49°3N 3°20E 173 C10
Chateaubelair St. Vincent 13°17N 61°15W 323 n
Châteaubourg France 48°7N 1°25W 172 D5
Châteaubriant France 47°43N 1°23W 172 E5
Châteaudun France 48°3N 1°20E 172 D8
Châteaufort France 48°44N 2°5E 134 B1
Chateaugay U.S.A. 44°56N 74°5W 313 B10
Châteaugiron France 48°3N 1°30W 172 D5
Châteauguay, L. Canada 56°26N 70°3W 299 A5
Châteaulin France 48°11N 4°8W 172 D2
Châteaumeillant France 46°35N 2°12E 173 F9
Châteauneuf-du-Faou France 48°11N 3°50W 172 D3
Châteauneuf-sur-Charente France 45°36N 0°3W 174 C3
Châteauneuf-sur-Cher France 46°52N 2°18E 173 F9
Châteauneuf-sur-Loire France 47°52N 2°13E 173 E9
Châteaurenard France 43°53N 4°51E 175 E8
Châteauroux France 46°50N 1°40E 173 F8
Châteauvillain France 48°2N 4°55E 173 D11
Châteaux, Pte. des Guadeloupe 16°15N 61°10W 322 e
Châtel-Guyon France 45°55N 3°4E 174 C7
Châtelaillon-Plage France 46°5N 1°5W 174 B2
Châtellerault France 46°50N 0°30E 172 F7
Châtelus-Malvaleix France 46°18N 2°1E 173 F9
Châtenay-Malabry France 48°46N 2°16E 134 B2
Chatham = Miramichi Canada 47°2N 65°28W 299 C6
Chatham Ont., Canada 42°24N 82°11W 312 D2
Chatham Medway, U.K. 51°22N 0°32E 169 F8
Chatham Ill., U.S.A. 41°45N 87°36W 119 C3
Chatham Ill., U.S.A. 39°40N 89°42W 310 E7
Chatham N.Y., U.S.A. 42°21N 73°36W 313 D11
Chatham, I. = San Cristóbal, I. Ecuador 0°50S 89°26W 330 a
Chatham, I. Chile 50°40S 74°25W 336 D2
Chatham I. N.Z. 43°50S 176°20W 285 a
Chatham Is. Pac. Oc. 44°0S 176°40W 285 a
Chatham Rise Pac. Oc. 43°30S 180°0E 288 M10
Châtillon Hauts-de-Seine, France 48°48N 2°17E 134 B2
Châtillon Italy 45°45N 7°37E 198 C4
Châtillon-Coligny France 47°50N 2°51E 173 E9
Châtillon-en-Diois France 44°41N 5°29E 175 D9
Châtillon-sur-Indre France 46°59N 1°10E 172 F8
Châtillon-sur-Loire France 47°35N 2°44E 173 E9
Châtillon-sur-Seine France 47°50N 4°33E 173 E11
Chatmohar Bangla. 24°15N 89°15E 243 G13
Chatou France 48°53N 2°9E 134 A1
Chatpur India 22°36N 88°22E 124 B2
Chatra India 24°12N 84°56E 243 G11
Chatrapur India 19°22N 85°2E 244 E7
Chats, L. des Canada 45°30N 76°20W 313 A8
Chatsu India 26°36N 75°57E 242 F6
Chatswood Australia 33°47S 151°11E 139 A2
Chatsworth Ont., Canada 44°27N 80°54W 312 B4
Chatsworth Ill., U.S.A. 40°45N 88°18W 311 D8
Chatsworth Zimbabwe 19°38S 31°13E 269 F3
Chatta-Hantō Japan 34°45N 136°55E 223 C8
Châttagâm = Chittagong Bangla. 22°19N 91°48E 241 D3
Chattahoochee U.S.A. 30°42N 84°51W 316 E5
Chattahoochee → U.S.A. 30°54N 84°57W 316 E5
Chattanooga U.S.A. 35°3N 85°19W 315 D12
Chatteris U.K. 52°28N 0°2E 169 E8
Chatturat Thailand 15°40N 101°51E 236 E3
Chatuchak Thailand 13°48N 100°33E 138 B2
Chatuchak Park Thailand 13°48N 100°32E 138 B2
Chau Doc Vietnam 10°42N 105°7E 237 G5
Chaubourg, Mt. St. Lucia 14°2N 60°57W 323 m
Chaudes-Aigues France 44°51N 3°1E 174 D7
Chauffailles France 46°13N 4°20E 173 F11
Chauk Burma 20°53N 94°49E 241 E5
Chaukan Pass Burma 27°8N 97°10E 241 B6
Chauki Pakistan 24°55N 66°56E 123 A1
Chaumont Haute-Marne, France 48°7N 5°8E 173 D12
Chaumont N.Y., U.S.A. 44°4N 76°8W 313 B8
Chaumont-en-Vexin France 49°16N 1°53E 173 C8
Chaumont-sur-Loire France 47°29N 1°11E 172 E8
Chaunay France 46°13N 0°9E 174 B4
Chaung-u Burma 21°57N 95°16E 241 E5
Chaungtha Burma 16°58N 94°27E 241 G5
Chaunskaya G. Russia 69°0N 169°0E 215 C17
Chauny France 49°37N 3°12E 173 C10
Chaura India 8°27N 93°2E 245 K11
Chausey, Îs. France 48°52N 1°49W 172 D5
Chaussin France 46°59N 5°22E 173 F12
Chautara Nepal 27°46N 85°42E 243 F11
Chautauqua L. U.S.A. 42°10N 79°24W 312 D5
Chauvigny France 46°34N 0°39E 172 F7
Chauvin Canada 52°45N 110°10W 297 C6
Chavakachcheri Sri Lanka 9°39N 80°9E 245 K5
Chavanges France 48°30N 4°35E 173 D11
Chavantina Brazil 14°40S 52°21W 331 C7
Chavarria Peru 12°0S 77°7W 124 B2
Chavash Varmane △ Russia 54°50N 47°10E 190 C8
Chavdata Greece 38°12N 20°23E 207 C1
Chaves Brazil 0°15S 49°55W 332 B2
Chaves Portugal 41°45N 7°32W 194 D3
Chaville France 48°48N 2°11E 134 B2
Chavín de Huantar Peru 9°35S 77°10W 330 B2
Chavuma Zambia 13°4S 22°40E 265 E4
Chawang Thailand 8°25N 99°30E 237 H2
Chayang S. Korea 37°32N 127°3E 137 B2
Chaykovskiy Russia 56°47N 54°9E 186 C9
Chazelles-sur-Lyon France 45°39N 4°22E 175 C8
Chazuta Peru 6°30S 76°0W 330 B2
Chazy U.S.A. 44°53N 73°26W 313 B11
Cheaha Mt. U.S.A. 33°29N 85°49W 316 B4
Cheb Czechia 50°9N 12°28E 180 A5
Chebanse U.S.A. 41°0N 87°54W 311 D9
Chebbi, Erg Africa 31°12N 3°58W 260 B4
Cheboksarskoye Vdkhr. Russia 56°13N 46°58E 190 B8
Cheboksary Russia 56°8N 47°12E 190 B8
Cheboygan U.S.A. 45°39N 84°29W 309 C11
Chebsara Russia 59°10N 38°59E 188 C10
Chech, Erg Africa 25°0N 2°15W 260 D4
Chechelnyk Ukraine 48°13N 29°22E 183 B14
Chechen, Ostrov Russia 43°59N 47°40E 191 H8
Ch'ech'eng Taiwan 22°55N 120°42E 225 D2
Chechenia □ Russia 43°30N 45°29E 191 J7
Checheno-Ingush Republic = Chechenia □ Russia 43°30N 45°29E 191 J7
Chechnya = Chechenia □ Russia 43°30N 45°29E 191 J7
Chęciny Poland 50°46N 20°28E 185 H7
Checotah U.S.A. 35°28N 95°31W 314 D7
Chedabucto B. Canada 45°25N 61°8W 299 C7
Cheduba I. Burma 18°45N 93°40E 241 F4
Cheektowaga U.S.A. 42°54N 78°45W 312 D6
Cheepie Australia 26°33S 145°0E 281 D4
Cheeyou Trin. & Tob. 10°33N 61°8W 323 t
Chef-Boutonne France 46°7N 0°4W 174 B3
Chefchaouen Morocco 35°9N 5°15W 260 A3
Cheffadine Niger 19°57N 12°11E 259 D2
Chefoo = Yantai China 37°34N 121°22E 227 F11
Chefornak U.S.A. 60°13N 164°12W 303 F6
Chegdomyn Russia 51°7N 133°1E 215 D14
Chegga Mauritania 25°27N 5°40W 260 C3
Chegutu Zimbabwe 18°10S 30°14E 269 F3
Chehalis U.S.A. 46°40N 122°58W 306 D4
Chehalis → U.S.A. 46°57N 123°50W 306 D3
Cheile Bicazului-Hășmaș △ Romania 46°55N 25°50E 183 D10
Cheile Nerei-Beusnita △ Romania 44°56N 21°52E 182 F6
Cheiron, Mt. du France 43°49N 6°58E 175 E10
Cheju = Jeju S. Korea 33°31N 126°32E 224 a
Cheju-do = Jeju-do S. Korea 33°29N 126°34E 224 a
Cheju Str. = Jeju Haehyop S. Korea 33°50N 126°30E 227 H14
Chek Lap Kok Hong Kong, China 22°18N 113°56E 122 B1
Chek Lap Kok ✕ (HKG) Hong Kong, China 22°19N 113°57E 122 B1
Chekalin Russia 54°10N 36°10E 188 E9
Chekhovo Russia 54°33N 20°43E 184 D7
Chekiang = Zhejiang □ China 29°0N 120°0E 229 C13
Chel = Kuru, Bahr el → South Sudan 8°10N 26°50E 257 F2
Chela, Sa. da Angola 16°20S 13°20E 265 F2
Chelan U.S.A. 47°51N 120°1W 304 C3
Chelan, L. U.S.A. 48°11N 120°30W 304 B3
Cheleken = Hazar Turkmenistan 39°34N 53°16E 187 G9
Cheleken Yarymadasy Turkmenistan 39°30N 53°15E 247 B7
Chelforó Argentina 39°0S 66°33W 336 A3
Chéliff, O. → Algeria 36°0N 0°8E 261 A5
Chelkar = Shalqar Kazakhstan 47°48N 59°39E 216 C5
Chella Ethiopia 5°0N 37°26E 257 F4
Chellala Dahrania Algeria 33°2N 0°1E 261 B5
Chelles France 48°52N 2°35E 134 A4
Chelles, Canal de France 48°51N 2°35E 134 A4
Chelles-le-Pin ✕ France 48°53N 2°36E 134 A4
Chelm Poland 51°8N 23°30E 185 G10
Chełmno Poland 53°20N 18°30E 185 E5
Chelmsford U.K. 51°44N 0°29E 169 F8
Chelmża Poland 53°10N 18°39E 185 E5
Chelny = Naberezhnyye Chelny Russia 55°42N 52°19E 190 C11
Chelsea Vic., Australia 38°5S 145°8E 283 E6
Chelsea London, U.K. 51°29N 0°10W 125 B2
Chelsea Mass., U.S.A. 42°23N 71°1W 116 A2
Chelsea Mich., U.S.A. 42°19N 84°1W 311 B12
Chelsea New York, U.S.A. 132 c1
Chelsea Vt., U.S.A. 43°59N 72°27W 313 C12
Cheltenham U.K. 51°54N 2°4W 169 F5
Chelva Spain 39°45N 1°0W 196 F4
Chelyabinsk Russia 55°10N 61°24E 216 A6
Chelyakobi = Kopeysk Russia 55°7N 61°37E 216 A6
Chelyuskin, C. = Chelyuskin, Mys Russia 77°30N 103°0E 215 B11
Chelyuskin, Mys Russia 77°30N 103°0E 215 B11
Chemainus Canada 48°55N 123°42W 306 B3
Chembar = Belinskiy Russia 53°0N 43°25E 190 D6
Chembur India 19°3N 72°53E 130 A2
Chemchâm, Sebkhet Mauritania 21°2N 12°4W 260 D2
Chemillé France 47°14N 0°45W 172 E6
Chemin Grenier Mauritius 20°29S 57°28E 272 e
Chemnitz Germany 50°51N 12°54E 178 E8
Chemulpho = Incheon S. Korea 37°27N 126°40E 224 D3
Chemult U.S.A. 43°14N 121°47W 304 E3
Chen, Gora Russia 65°16N 141°50E 215 C15
Chenab → Pakistan 30°23N 71°2E 242 D4
Chenab Nagar Pakistan 31°45N 72°55E 242 D5
Chenachane Algeria 26°0N 4°15W 260 C4
Chenachane, O. → Algeria 25°20N 3°20W 260 C4
Chenango Forks U.S.A. 42°15N 75°51W 313 D9
Chencha Ethiopia 6°15N 37°32E 257 F4
Chenchiang = Zhenjiang China 32°11N 119°26E 229 A12
Cheney U.S.A. 47°30N 117°35W 304 C5
Cheng Xian China 33°43N 105°42E 226 H3
Chengalpattu India 12°42N 79°58E 245 H4
Chengbu China 26°18N 110°16E 229 D8
Chengcheng China 35°8N 109°56E 226 G5
Chengchou = Zhengzhou China 34°45N 113°34E 226 G7
Chengde China 40°59N 117°58E 227 D9
Chengdong Hu China 32°15N 116°20E 229 A11
Chengdu China 30°38N 104°2E 228 B5
Chengdu Shuangliu Int. ✕ (CTU) China 30°35N 103°57E 228 B4
Chengele India 28°47N 96°16E 241 A6
Chenggong = Ch'engkung Taiwan 23°6N 121°22E 225 C3
Chenggong China 24°52N 102°56E 228 E4
Chenggu China 33°10N 107°21E 228 A6
Chenghai China 23°30N 116°42E 229 F11
Chengjiang China 24°39N 103°0E 228 E4
Chengkou China 31°54N 108°31E 228 B7
Ch'engkung Taiwan 23°6N 121°22E 225 C3
Chengmai China 19°50N 109°58E 229 a
Chengnan Taiwan 23°3N 120°7E 225 C2
Chengshan Jiao China 37°25N 122°44E 227 F12

Chengshousi China 39°49N 116°24E 114 C2
Chengteh = Chengde
China 40°59N 117°58E 227 D9
Ch'engtu = Chengdu
China 30°38N 104°2E 228 B5
Chengwu China 34°58N 115°50E 226 G8
Chengxi Hu China 32°15N 116°10E 229 A11
Chengyang China 36°18N 120°21E 227 F11
Chenjiagang China 34°23N 119°47E 227 G10
Chenkaladi Sri Lanka 7°47N 81°35E 245 L5
Chennai India 13°8N 80°19E 245 H5
Chennevières-sur-Marne
France 48°47N 2°31E 134 B4
Chenoa U.S.A. 40°45N 88°43W 311 D8
Chenôve France 47°16N 5°1E 173 E12
Chenxi China 28°2N 110°12E 229 C8
Chenzhou China 25°47N 113°1E 229 E9
Cheò, Eilean a' = Skye
U.K. 57°15N 6°10W 167 D2
Cheo Reo Vietnam 13°20N 108°25E 236 F7
Cheom Ksan Cambodia 14°13N 104°56E 236 E5
Cheonan S. Korea 36°48N 127°9E 224 D3
Cheongdam S. Korea 37°31N 127°2E 137 B2
Cheongdo S. Korea 35°38N 128°42E 224 E4
Cheongju S. Korea 36°39N 127°27E 224 D3
Cheongsando S. Korea 34°11N 126°53E 224 E3
Cheongsong S. Korea 36°25N 129°3E 224 D4
Cheonho S. Korea 37°32N 127°6E 137 B2
Cheonsumman S. Korea 36°33N 126°25E 224 D3
Cheops Egypt 29°58N 31°8E 117 B1
Cheorwon S. Korea 38°15N 127°10E 224 C3
Chepelare Bulgaria 41°44N 24°40E 203 E8
Chepelarska → Bulgaria 42°9N 24°54E 203 D8
Chepén Peru 7°15S 79°23W 330 B2
Chépénéhé N. Cal. 20°47S 167°9E 288 d
Chepes Argentina 31°20S 66°35W 334 C2
Chepo Panama 9°10N 79°6W 320 E4
Chepstow U.K. 51°38N 2°41W 169 F5
Chequamegon B. U.S.A. 46°39N 90°51W 308 B8
Cher □ France 47°10N 2°30E 173 E9
Cher → France 47°21N 0°29E 172 E7
Chéradi Italy 40°27N 17°10E 201 B10
Cheran India 25°45N 90°44E 241 C3
Cherasco Italy 44°39N 7°51E 198 D4
Cherating Malaysia 3°35N 103°5E 234 B2
Cheraw U.S.A. 34°42N 79°53W 315 D15
Cherbourg-Octeville
France 49°39N 1°40W 172 C5
Cherchell Algeria 36°35N 2°12E 261 A5
Cherdakly Russia 54°25N 48°50E 190 C9
Cherdyn Russia 60°24N 56°29E 186 B10
Cheremkhovo Russia 53°8N 103°1E 218 A9
Cherepanovo Russia 54°15N 83°30E 217 B10
Cherepovets Russia 59°5N 37°55E 188 C9
Chergui, Chott ech Algeria 34°21N 0°25E 261 B5
Chergui, Zahrez Algeria 35°11N 3°31E 261 A5
Cherial India 17°55N 78°59E 244 F4
Cheribon = Cirebon
Indonesia 6°45S 108°32E 235 D3
Cherikov = Cherykaw
Belarus 53°32N 31°20E 177 B16
Cheriyam I. India 10°9N 73°40E 245 J1
Cherkasy Ukraine 49°27N 32°4E 189 H7
Cherkasy □ Ukraine 48°55N 30°50E 189 H6
Cherkessk Russia 44°15N 42°5E 191 H6
Cherla India 18°5N 80°49E 244 E5
Cherlak Russia 54°15N 74°55E 217 B8
Chernaya Russia 70°30N 89°10E 215 B9
Chernelytsya Ukraine 48°49N 25°26E 183 B10
Cherni Bulgaria 42°35N 23°18E 202 D7
Chernigov = Chernihiv
Ukraine 51°28N 31°20E 189 G6
Chernigovka Russia 44°19N 132°34E 220 B6
Chernihiv Ukraine 51°28N 31°20E 189 G6
Chernihiv □ Ukraine 51°10N 32°5E 189 G7
Chernivtsi Chernivtsi, Ukraine 48°15N 25°52E 183 B10
Chernivtsi Vinnyts'ka, Ukraine 48°32N 28°9E 183 B13
Chernivtsi □ Ukraine 48°5N 25°30E 183 B10
Chernobyl = Chornobyl
Ukraine 51°20N 30°15E 177 C16
Chernogorsk Russia 53°49N 91°18E 217 B12
Chernomorskoye = Chornomorske
Ukraine 45°31N 32°40E 189 K7
Chernorechye = Dzerzhinsk
Russia 56°14N 43°30E 190 B6
Chernovtsy = Chernivtsi
Ukraine 48°15N 25°52E 183 B10
Chernyakhovsk Russia 54°36N 21°48E 184 D8
Chernyanka Russia 50°56N 37°49E 189 G9
Chernysheyskiy Russia 63°0N 112°30E 215 C12
Chernyye Zemli Russia 46°10N 46°0E 191 H8
Cherokee Iowa, U.S.A. 42°45N 95°33W 308 D6
Cherokee Okla., U.S.A. 36°45N 98°21W 314 C5
Cherokee Village U.S.A. 36°18N 91°31W 314 C9
Cherokees, Grand Lake O' The
U.S.A. 36°28N 94°55W 314 C7
Cherquenco Chile 38°35S 72°0W 336 A2
Cherrapunji India 25°17N 91°47E 241 C3
Cherry Valley U.S.A. 42°48N 74°45W 313 D10
Cherryville U.S.A. 37°51N 91°16W 310 G5
Cherskiy Russia 68°45N 161°18E 215 C17
Cherskogo Khrebet
Russia 65°0N 143°0E 215 C15
Cherso Greece 41°5N 22°47E 202 E6
Chersonesus Ukraine 44°37N 33°30E 189 K7
Chersonisos Akrotiri
Greece 35°30N 24°10E 207 E5
Chertanovka → Russia 55°38N 37°48E 129 C2
Chertanovo Russia 55°38N 37°36E 129 C2
Cherthala India 9°42N 76°20E 245 K3
Chertkov = Chortkiv
Ukraine 49°2N 25°46E 177 D13
Chertkovo Russia 49°25N 40°19E 189 H11
Cherven Belarus 53°45N 28°28E 177 B15
Cherven-Bryag Bulgaria 43°17N 24°7E 203 C8
Chervonoarmiyske
Ukraine 45°47N 28°44E 183 E13
Chervonohrad Ukraine 50°25N 24°10E 177 C13
Cherwell → U.K. 51°44N 1°14W 169 F6
Cherykaw Belarus 53°32N 31°20E 177 B16
Cheryomushki Russia 55°40N 37°35E 129 B2
Chesapeake U.S.A. 36°49N 76°16W 309 G15
Chesapeake B. U.S.A. 38°0N 76°10W 309 F14
Cheshire East □ U.K. 53°15N 2°15W 168 D5
Cheshire West and Chester □
U.K. 53°15N 2°40W 168 D5
Cheshskaya Guba Russia 67°20N 47°0E 186 A8
Cheshunt U.K. 51°43N 0°1W 169 F7
Chesil Beach U.K. 50°37N 2°33W 169 G5
Chesley Canada 44°17N 81°5W 312 B3
Chesnokovka = Novoaltaysk
Russia 53°30N 84°0E 217 B10
Cheste Spain 39°30N 0°41W 197 F4
Chester Ches., U.K. 53°12N 2°53W 168 D5
Chester Calif., U.S.A. 40°19N 121°14W 304 F3
Chester Ga., U.S.A. 32°24N 83°9W 316 C6
Chester Ill., U.S.A. 37°55N 89°49W 310 G7
Chester Mont., U.S.A. 48°31N 110°58W 304 B8
Chester Pa., U.S.A. 39°51N 75°22W 309 F16
Chester S.C., U.S.A. 34°43N 81°12W 315 D14
Chester Vt., U.S.A. 43°16N 72°36W 313 C12
Chester W. Va., U.S.A. 40°37N 80°34W 312 F4
Chester-le-Street U.K. 54°51N 1°34W 168 C6
Chesterfield Derby, U.K. 53°15N 1°25W 168 D6
Chesterfield Va., U.S.A. 38°40N 90°35W 310 F6
Chesterfield, Îs. N. Cal. 19°52S 158°15E 277 D10
Chesterfield Inlet Canada 63°30N 90°45W 294 E13
Chesterton Ra. Australia 25°30S 147°27E 281 D4
Chesterton Range △
Australia 26°16S 147°22E 281 D4
Chestertown U.S.A. 43°40N 73°48W 313 C11
Chesterville Canada 45°6N 75°14W 313 A9
Chestnut Hill U.S.A. 42°19N 71°10W 116 B1
Chesuncook L. U.S.A. 46°0N 69°21W 309 C19
Chetamale India 10°43N 92°33E 245 J11
Chéticamp Canada 46°37N 60°59W 302 C7
Chetlat I. India 11°42N 72°42E 245 J1
Chetrosu Moldova 48°5N 27°54E 183 B12
Chetumal Mexico 18°30N 88°20W 319 D7
Chetumal, B. de
Cent. Amer. 18°40N 88°10W 319 D7
Chetwynd Canada 55°45N 121°36W 296 B4
Cheung Chau
Hong Kong, China 22°13N 114°1E 122 B2
Cheung Sha
Hong Kong, China 22°14N 113°57E 122 B1
Cheung Sha Wan
Hong Kong, China 22°20N 114°8E 122 B1
Cheung Shue Tan
Hong Kong, China 22°26N 114°11E 122 A3
Chevak U.S.A. 61°32N 165°35W 303 F6
Chevalier, Î. de Martinique 14°25N 60°50W 322 j
Chevanceaux France 45°18N 0°14W 174 C3
Cheverly U.S.A. 38°55N 76°54W 143 B3
Chevilly-Larue France 48°46N 2°21E 134 B3
Cheviot U.S.A. 39°9N 84°36W 311 E12
Cheviot, The U.K. 55°29N 2°9W 168 B5
Cheviot Hills Northumberland, U.K. 55°20N 2°30W 168 B5
Cheviot Hills Calif., U.S.A. 34°2N 118°24W 126 B2
Cheviot Ra. Australia 25°20S 143°45E 280 D3
Chevreau, Île St. Barts 17°56N 62°51W 322 a
Chevy Chase U.S.A. 38°59N 77°4W 143 B2
Chew Bahir Ethiopia 4°40N 36°50E 257 G4
Chewelah U.S.A. 48°17N 117°43W 304 B5
Chewore ⌂ Zimbabwe 16°0S 29°52E 269 F2
Cheyenne Okla., U.S.A. 35°37N 99°40W 314 D5
Cheyenne Wyo., U.S.A. 41°8N 104°49W 304 F11
Cheyenne → U.S.A. 44°41N 101°18W 308 C3
Cheyenne Wells U.S.A. 38°49N 102°21W 304 G12
Cheyne B. Australia 34°35S 118°50E 279 F2
Cheyur India 12°21N 80°0E 245 H5
Chhabra India 24°40N 76°54E 242 G7
Chhaktala India 22°6N 74°11E 242 H6
Chhapra India 25°48N 84°44E 243 G11
Chhata India 27°42N 77°30E 242 F7
Chhatak Bangla. 25°5N 91°37E 241 C3
Chhatarpur Jharkhand, India 24°23N 84°11E 243 G11
Chhatarpur Mad. P., India 24°55N 79°35E 243 G8
Chhati India 20°47N 81°40E 244 D5
Chhatrapati Shivaji Int., Mumbai ✕ (BOM) India 19°5N 72°51E 130 A2
Chhatrapati Shivaji Terminus
India 18°56N 72°50E 130 B2
Chhattisgarh □ India 22°0N 82°0E 243 J10
Chhaygaon India 26°3N 91°24E 241 B3
Chhep Cambodia 13°45N 105°24E 236 F5
Chhindwara Mad. P., India 23°3N 79°29E 243 H8
Chhindwara Mad. P., India 22°2N 78°59E 243 H8
Chhinhdipada India 21°6N 84°52E 244 D7
Chhlong Cambodia 12°15N 105°58E 237 F5
Chhota Tawa → India 22°14N 76°36E 242 H7
Chhoti Kali Sindh → India 24°2N 75°31E 242 G6
Chhuikhadan India 21°32N 80°59E 243 J9
Chhuk Cambodia 10°46N 104°28E 237 G5
Chi → Thailand 15°11N 104°43E 236 E5
Chi Ma Wan Pen.
Hong Kong, China 22°14N 114°0E 122 B1
Chi Thanh Vietnam 13°17N 109°16E 236 F7
Chia Keng Singapore 1°21N 103°52E 138 A3
Chiahsien Taiwan 23°5N 120°35E 225 D2
Chiai Taiwan 23°29N 120°25E 225 C2
Chiai □ Taiwan 23°30N 120°30E 225 C2
Chiaksan △ S. Korea 37°15N 128°0E 224 D4
Chiali Taiwan 23°9N 120°10E 225 D2
Chialulantsun Taiwan 22°49N 121°11E 225 D3
Chiamboni Somalia 1°39S 41°35E 267 E5
Chiamussu = Jiamusi
China 46°40N 130°26E 219 B15
Chian Taiwan 23°59N 121°33E 225 C3
Chianapu Taiwan 22°47N 120°36E 225 D2
Chianciano Terme Italy 43°2N 11°49E 199 E8
Chiang Dao Thailand 19°22N 98°58E 236 C2
Chiang Dao, Doi Thailand 19°23N 98°54E 236 C2
Chiang Kham Thailand 19°32N 100°18E 236 C3
Chiang Khan Thailand 17°52N 101°36E 236 D3
Chiang Khong Thailand 20°17N 100°24E 228 G3
Chiang Mai Thailand 18°47N 98°59E 236 C2
Chiang Rai Thailand 19°52N 99°50E 228 H2
Chiang Saen Thailand 20°16N 100°5E 228 G3
Chiangchun Taiwan 23°12N 120°9E 225 C2
Chiange Angola 15°35S 13°40E 265 F2
Chianti Italy 43°32N 11°25E 199 E8
Chiaohsi Taiwan 24°49N 121°46E 225 B3
Chiaotou Taiwan 22°45N 120°18E 225 D2
Chiapa de Corzo Mexico 16°42N 93°0W 319 D6
Chiapas □ Mexico 16°30N 92°30W 319 D6
Chiapas, Sa. Madre de
Mexico 15°40N 93°0W 319 D6
Chiaramonte Gulfi Italy 37°2N 14°42E 201 E7
Chiaravalle Italy 43°36N 13°19E 199 E10
Chiaravalle Centrale Italy 38°41N 16°25E 201 D9
Chiaravalle Milanese Italy 45°24N 9°16E 128 B2
Chiari Italy 45°32N 9°56E 198 C6
Chiatung Taiwan 22°25N 120°32E 225 D2
Chiatura Georgia 42°15N 43°17E 191 J6
Chiautla de Tapia Mexico 18°18N 98°36W 319 D5
Chiávari Italy 44°19N 9°19E 198 D6
Chiavenna Italy 46°19N 9°24E 198 B6
Chiayi = Chiai Taiwan 23°29N 120°25E 225 C2
Chiba Japan 35°30N 140°7E 223 B12
Chiba □ Japan 35°30N 140°20E 223 B12
Chibabava Mozam. 20°17S 33°35E 271 B5
Chibango Angola 13°38S 21°56E 265 E4
Chibemba Cunene, Angola 15°48S 14°8E 265 F2
Chibemba Huila, Angola 16°20S 15°20E 265 F3
Chibi Zimbabwe 20°18S 30°25E 271 B5
Chibia Angola 15°10S 13°42E 265 F2
Chibizovka = Zherdevka
Russia 51°56N 41°29E 190 E5
Chibougamau Canada 49°56N 74°24W 298 C5
Chibougamau, L. Canada 49°50N 74°20W 298 C5
Chibuk Nigeria 10°52N 12°50E 263 C7
Chibuto Mozam. 24°40S 33°33E 271 B5
Chibyu = Ukhta Russia 63°34N 53°41E 186 B9
Chic-Chocs, Mts. Canada 48°55N 66°0W 299 C6
Chicacole = Srikakulam
India 18°14N 83°58E 244 E6
Chicago U.S.A. 41°52N 87°38W 119 B3
Chicago, Univ. of U.S.A. 41°47N 87°35W 119 C3
Chicago Harbor Chicago, U.S.A. 119 d3
Chicago Heights U.S.A. 41°30N 87°38W 311 C9
Chicago Lawn U.S.A. 41°47N 87°40W 119 C2
Chicago-Midway ✕ (MDW)
U.S.A. 41°47N 87°45W 311 C9
Chicago O'Hare Int. ✕ (ORD)
U.S.A. 41°59N 87°54W 311 C9
Chicago Ridge U.S.A. 41°41N 87°46W 119 C2
Chicago River → Chicago, U.S.A. 119 b2
Chicago River, North Branch →
U.S.A. 41°53N 87°42W 119 B2
Chicago Sanitary and Ship Canal
U.S.A. 41°49N 87°45W 119 C2
Chicago State Univ.
U.S.A. 41°43N 87°36W 119 C3
Chicapa →
Dem. Rep. of the Congo 6°25S 20°48E 265 D4
Chicha Chad 16°57N 18°34E 259 E3
Chichagof I. U.S.A. 57°30N 135°30W 303 H14
Chichaoua Morocco 31°32N 8°44W 260 B3
Chichawatni Pakistan 30°32N 72°42E 242 D5
Chichén-Itzá Mexico 20°37N 88°35W 319 C7
Chicheng China 40°55N 115°55E 226 D8
Chichester U.K. 50°50N 0°47W 169 G7
Chichester Ra. Australia 22°12S 119°15E 278 D2
Chichi Hualien, Taiwan 23°44N 121°33E 225 C3
Chichi Nant'ou, Taiwan 23°49N 120°47E 225 C2
Chichibu Japan 35°59N 139°10E 223 A11
Chichibu-Tama-Kai △
Japan 35°52N 138°42E 223 B10
Ch'ich'ihaerh = Qiqihar
China 47°26N 124°0E 219 B13
Chicholi India 22°1N 77°40E 242 H8
Ch'ich'ou Taiwan 23°45N 120°33E 225 C2
Chickasaw ⌂ U.S.A. 34°26N 97°0W 314 D6
Chickasha U.S.A. 35°3N 97°58W 314 D6
Chicken U.S.A. 64°5N 141°56W 303 D12
Chiclana de la Frontera
Spain 36°26N 6°9W 195 J4
Chiclayo Peru 6°42S 79°50W 330 B2
Chico U.S.A. 39°44N 121°50W 306 F5
Chico → Chubut, Argentina 44°0S 67°0W 336 B3
Chico → Santa Cruz,
Argentina 50°0S 68°30W 336 D3
Chico → Phil. 17°57N 121°36E 232 C3
Chicoa Mozam. 15°36S 32°20E 269 F3
Chicomba Angola 14°10S 14°52E 265 E2
Chicomo Mozam. 24°31S 34°6E 271 B5
Chicomostoc Mexico 22°28N 102°46W 318 C4
Chiconi Mayotte 12°50S 45°7E 272 b
Chicontepec Mexico 20°58N 98°10W 319 C5
Chicopee U.S.A. 42°9N 72°37W 313 D12
Chicoutimi Canada 48°28N 71°5W 299 C5
Chicualacuala Mozam. 22°6S 31°42E 271 B5
Chicuma Angola 13°26S 14°50E 265 E2
Chidambaram India 11°20N 79°45E 245 J4
Chidenguele Mozam. 24°55S 34°11E 271 B5
Chidley, C. Canada 60°23N 64°26W 295 E19
Chiducuane Mozam. 24°35S 34°25E 271 B5
Chiede Angola 17°15S 16°22E 265 F3
Chiefland U.S.A. 29°29N 82°52W 317 F7
Chiefs Pt. Canada 44°41N 81°18W 312 B3
Chiehting Taiwan 22°54N 120°11E 225 D2
Chiem Hoa Vietnam 22°12N 105°17E 236 A5
Chiemsee Germany 47°53N 12°28E 179 H8
Chienchen Taiwan 22°35N 120°18E 225 D2
Chiengi Zambia 8°45S 29°10E 269 D2
Chiengmai = Chiang Mai
Thailand 18°47N 98°59E 236 C2
Chiengo Angola 13°20S 21°55E 265 E4
Chienti → Italy 43°18N 13°45E 199 E10
Chienzui China 23°12N 113°22E 121 A3
Chieri Italy 45°1N 7°49E 198 C4
Chiers → France 49°39N 4°59E 173 C11
Chiesa in Valmalenco Italy 46°16N 9°51E 198 B6
Chiese → Italy 45°8N 10°25E 198 C7
Chieti Italy 42°21N 14°10E 199 F11
Chifeng China 42°18N 118°58E 227 C10
Chigasaki Japan 35°19N 139°24E 223 B11
Chigirin Ukraine 49°4N 32°38E 189 H7
Chignecto B. Canada 45°30N 64°40W 299 C7
Chignik U.S.A. 56°18N 158°24W 303 H8
Chigorodó Colombia 7°41N 76°42W 328 B2
Chiguana Bolivia 21°0S 67°58W 334 A2
Chigwell U.K. 51°37N 0°6E 169 F8
Chihli, G. of = Bo Hai
China 39°0N 119°0E 227 E10
Ch'ihpen Taiwan 22°42N 121°2E 225 D3
Ch'ihshang Taiwan 23°7N 121°12E 225 C3
Chihsi = Jixi China 45°20N 130°50E 227 B16
Chihu Taiwan 23°54N 120°24E 225 C2
Chihuahua Mexico 28°38N 106°5W 318 B3
Chihuahua □ Mexico 28°30N 106°0W 318 B3
Chiili = Shīeli Kazakhstan 44°20N 66°15E 217 D7
Chik Bollapur India 13°25N 77°45E 245 H3
Chik Sha
Hong Kong, China 22°17N 114°16E 122 B3
Chikalda India 21°24N 77°19E 244 D3
Chikhli Ahmadabad, India 20°45N 73°4E 244 D1
Chikhli Maharashtra, India 20°20N 76°18E 244 D3
Chikkamagaluru India 13°15N 75°45E 245 H2
Chiknayakanhalli India 13°26N 76°37E 245 H3
Chikodi India 16°26N 74°38E 245 F2
Chiku Taiwan 23°8N 120°7E 225 C2
Chikugo Japan 33°14N 130°28E 222 D2
Chikuma-Gawa →
Japan 36°59N 138°35E 223 A10
Chikura Japan 34°55N 139°57E 223 C11
Chikushino Japan 33°30N 130°30E 222 D2
Chikwawa Malawi 16°2S 34°50E 269 F3
Chila Angola 12°3S 14°29E 265 E2
Ch'ilaichu Shan Taiwan 24°5N 121°20E 225 C3
Chilanga Zambia 15°33S 28°16E 269 F2
Chilapa Mexico 17°36N 99°10W 319 D5
Chilas Pakistan 35°25N 74°5E 243 B6
Chilaw Sri Lanka 7°30N 79°50E 245 L4
Chilcotin → Canada 51°44N 122°23W 296 C4
Childers Australia 25°15S 152°17E 281 D5
Childersburg U.S.A. 33°16N 86°21W 316 B3
Children's Museum Boston, U.S.A. 116 c3
Children's Palace Beijing, China 114 b2
Childress U.S.A. 34°25N 100°13W 314 D4
Child's Hill U.K. 51°33N 0°12W 125 A2
Chile ■ S. Amer. 35°0S 72°0W 327 G3
Chile, Univ. de Chile 33°26S 70°39W 137 B2
Chile Chico Chile 46°33S 71°44W 336 C2
Chile Rise Pac. Oc. 38°0S 92°0W 289 L18
Chilecito Argentina 29°10S 67°30W 334 B2
Chilengue, Serra do
Angola 13°18S 15°22E 265 E2
Chilesso Angola 11°35S 16°34E 265 E3
Chilete Peru 7°10S 78°50W 330 B2
Chilhowee U.S.A. 38°36N 93°51W 310 F3
Chilia, Braţul →
Romania 45°14N 29°42E 183 E14
Chilibre Panama 9°9N 79°37W 320 c
Chilik = Shelek
Kazakhstan 43°33N 78°17E 217 D9
Chililabombwe Zambia 12°18S 27°43E 269 E2
Chilim Pakistan 35°5N 75°5E 243 B6
Chilin = Jilin China 43°44N 126°30E 227 C14
Chiliomodi Greece 37°48N 22°51E 204 D4
Chilka L. India 19°40N 85°25E 244 E7
Chilko → Canada 52°0N 123°40W 296 C4
Chilko L. Canada 51°20N 124°10W 296 C4
Chilla Saroda India 28°35N 77°18E 120 B2
Chillagoe Australia 17°7S 144°33E 280 B3
Chillán Chile 36°40S 72°10W 334 D1
Chillicothe Ill., U.S.A. 40°55N 89°29W 310 D7
Chillicothe Mo., U.S.A. 39°48N 93°33W 310 E3
Chillicothe Ohio, U.S.A. 39°20N 82°59W 309 F12
Chilliwack Canada 49°10N 121°54W 296 D4
Chillum U.S.A. 38°56N 76°58W 143 B3
Chilly-Mazarin France 48°42N 2°17E 134 B2
Chilmari Bangla. 25°33N 89°43E 241 C2
Chilo India 27°25N 73°32E 242 F5
Chiloane, I. Mozam. 20°40S 34°55E 271 B5
Chiloé, I. de Chile 42°30S 73°50W 336 B2
Chiloé △ Chile 42°11S 73°59W 336 B2
Chilonda Angola 11°19S 16°12E 265 E3
Chilongo Angola 13°55S 16°35E 265 E3
Chilpancingo Mexico 17°33N 99°30W 319 D5
Chiltern Australia 36°10S 146°36E 283 D7
Chiltern Hills U.K. 51°40N 0°53W 169 F7
Chilton U.S.A. 44°2N 88°10W 308 C9
Chiluage Angola 9°30S 21°50E 265 D4
Chilubi Zambia 11°5S 29°58E 269 E2
Chilubula Zambia 10°14S 30°51E 269 E3
Chilumba Malawi 10°28S 34°12E 269 E3
Chilung Taiwan 25°3N 121°45E 225 A3
Chilwa, L. Malawi 15°15S 35°40E 269 F4
Chimakela Angola 15°24S 16°58E 265 F3
Chimakudi India 25°47N 93°48E 241 C4
Chimaltitán Mexico 21°35N 103°50W 318 C4
Chimán Panama 8°45N 78°40W 320 E4
Chimanimani Zimbabwe 19°48S 32°52E 271 A5
Chimanimani △ Zimbabwe 19°48S 33°0E 271 A5
Chimay Belgium 50°3N 4°20E 170 D4
Chimayo U.S.A. 36°0N 105°56W 305 J11
Chimba Zambia 9°54S 31°28E 269 D3
Chimborazo Ecuador 1°29S 78°55W 328 D2
Chimborazo □ Ecuador 1°0S 78°40W 328 D2
Chimbote Peru 9°0S 78°35W 330 B2
Chimboy Uzbekistan 42°57N 59°47E 216 D5
Chimbu □ Papua N. G. 6°15S 144°50E 286 D3
Ch'imei Taiwan 23°12N 119°25E 225 C1
Ch'imei Yü Taiwan 23°13N 119°26E 225 C1
Chimichagua Colombia 9°15N 73°49W 328 B3
Chimkent = Shymkent
Kazakhstan 42°18N 69°36E 217 D7
Chimoio Mozam. 19°4S 33°30E 269 F3
Chimpembe Zambia 9°31S 29°33E 269 D2
Chimur India 20°30N 79°23E 244 D4
Chin □ Burma 22°0N 93°0E 241 E4
Chin Hills Burma 22°30N 93°30E 241 D4
Chin Ling Shan = Qinling Shandi
China 33°50N 108°10E 226 H5
China Mexico 25°42N 99°14W 319 B5
China ■ Asia 30°0N 110°0E 219 E11
China, Great Plain of Asia 35°0N 115°0E 210 E13
China Basin San Francisco, U.S.A. 136 c3
China Lake U.S.A. 35°44N 117°37W 307 K9
China Town Toronto, Canada 141 b1
Chinacota Colombia 7°37N 72°36W 328 B3
Chinan = Jinan China 36°38N 117°1E 226 F9
Chinandega Nic. 12°35N 87°12W 320 D2
Chinati Peak U.S.A. 29°57N 104°29W 314 G2
Chinatown Singapore 138 c2
Chinatown Boston, U.S.A. 116 c2
Chinatown Los Angeles, U.S.A. 127 a3
Chinatown New York, U.S.A. 132 e2
Chinatown San Francisco, U.S.A. 136 b2
Chincha Alta Peru 13°25S 76°7W 330 C2
Chinchaga → Canada 58°53N 118°20W 296 B5
Chincheros Peru 13°30S 73°44W 330 C3
Chinchilla Australia 26°45S 150°38E 281 D5
Chinchilla de Monte Aragón
Spain 38°53N 1°40W 197 G3
Chincholi India 17°28N 77°26E 244 E3
Chinchorro, Banco
Mexico 18°35N 87°22W 319 D7
Chinchou = Jinzhou
China 41°5N 121°3E 227 D11
Chinchoua Gabon 0°1N 9°48E 264 B1
Chincoteague U.S.A. 37°56N 75°23W 309 G16
Chinde Mozam. 18°35S 36°30E 269 F4
Chindwin → Burma 21°26N 95°15E 241 E5
Chineni India 33°2N 75°15E 243 C6
Chinese Theatre
Los Angeles, U.S.A. 34°6N 118°20W 126 B2
Chinga Mozam. 15°13S 38°35E 269 F4
Chingaza △ Colombia 4°30N 73°40W 328 C3
Chingola Zambia 12°31S 27°53E 269 E2
Chingole Malawi 13°4S 34°17E 269 E3
Chingoni Mayotte 12°48S 45°8E 272 b
Chingpu Taiwan 23°28N 121°29E 225 C3
Ch'ingshui Changhua, Taiwan 24°16N 120°34E 225 B2
Chingshui Hualien, Taiwan 24°13N 121°41E 225 B3
Chingshui Ilan, Taiwan 24°39N 121°35E 225 B3
Ch'ingtao = Qingdao
China 36°5N 120°20E 227 F11
Chinguar Angola 12°25S 16°45E 265 E3
Chinguetti Mauritania 20°25N 12°24W 260 D2
Chingune Mozam. 20°33S 34°58E 271 B5
Chingupota India 22°29N 88°14E 124 C1
Chinhanguanine Mozam. 25°21S 32°30E 271 C5
Chinhoyi Zimbabwe 17°20S 30°8E 269 F3
Chinhsien = Jinxian
China 28°26N 116°17E 229 C11
Chiniot Pakistan 31°45N 73°0E 242 D5
Chinipas Mexico 27°23N 108°32W 318 B3
Chinji Pakistan 32°42N 72°22E 242 C5
Chinju = Jinju S. Korea 35°12N 128°2E 224 E4
Chinkai Afghan. 31°57N 67°26E 242 D2
Chinkapook Australia 35°11S 142°57E 282 C5
Chinkiang = Zhenjiang
China 32°11N 119°26E 229 A12
Chinko → C.A.R. 4°50N 23°53E 264 B4
Chinle U.S.A. 36°9N 109°33W 305 H9
Ch'inlun Taiwan 22°32N 120°57E 225 D2
Chinmen Taiwan 24°26N 118°19E 225 a
Chinmen Tao Taiwan 24°26N 118°22E 225 a
Chinna Cr. → Pakistan 24°50N 67°0E 123 B2
Chinnamanur India 9°50N 77°24E 245 K3
Chinnampo = Namp'o
N. Korea 38°52N 125°10E 224 C2
Chino Japan 35°59N 138°9E 223 B10
Chino Calif., U.S.A. 34°1N 117°41W 307 L9
Chino Valley U.S.A. 34°45N 112°27W 305 J7
Chinois, Quartier Montréal, Canada 130 b2
Chinon France 47°10N 0°15E 172 E7
Chinook U.S.A. 48°35N 109°14W 304 B9
Chinook Trough Pac. Oc. 44°0N 175°0W 288 C10
Chinoya Zambia 13°55S 23°16E 265 E4
Chinsali Zambia 10°30S 32°2E 269 E3
Chinshan Taiwan 25°13N 121°38E 225 A3
Chinsura = Chunchura
India 22°53N 88°27E 243 H13
Chintalapudi India 17°4N 80°59E 244 F5
Chintamani India 13°26N 78°3E 245 H4
Chinwangtao = Qinhuangdao
China 39°56N 119°30E 227 E10
Chióggia Italy 45°13N 12°17E 199 C9
Chíos Greece 38°27N 26°9E 205 C8
Chipata Zambia 13°38S 32°28E 269 E3
Chipei Tao Taiwan 23°45N 119°37E 225 C1
Chiperceni Moldova 47°31N 28°50E 183 C13
Chipindo Angola 13°49S 15°48E 265 E3
Chipinge Zimbabwe 20°13S 32°28E 269 G3
Chipinge △ Zimbabwe 20°14S 33°0E 269 G3
Chipiona Spain 36°44N 6°26W 195 J4
Chipley U.S.A. 30°47N 85°32W 316 E4
Chiplun India 17°31N 73°34E 244 F1
Chipman Canada 46°6N 65°53W 299 C6
Chipoka Malawi 13°57S 34°28E 269 E3
Chippenham U.K. 51°27N 2°6W 169 F5
Chippewa → U.S.A. 44°25N 92°5W 308 C7
Chippewa Falls U.S.A. 44°56N 91°24W 308 C8
Chipping Norton U.K. 51°56N 1°32W 169 F6
Chiprovtsi Bulgaria 43°24N 22°52E 202 C6
Chiputneticook Lakes
N. Amer. 45°35N 67°35W 309 C20
Chiputo = Vila Vasco da Gama
Mozam. 14°54S 32°14E 269 E3
Chipwi Burma 25°53N 98°8E 241 C7
Chiquelquele Angola 16°44S 19°5E 265 F3
Chiquián Peru 10°10S 77°0W 330 C2
Chiquibul △ Belize 16°49N 88°52W 320 C2
Chiquihuite, Cerro Mexico 19°32N 99°8W 128 A2
Chiquimula Guatemala 14°51N 89°37W 320 D2
Chiquinquira Colombia 5°37N 73°50W 328 B3
Chiquitos, Llanos de
Bolivia 18°0S 61°30W 331 D5
Chir → Russia 48°30N 43°0E 191 F6
Chira → Peru 4°54S 81°8W 328 D1
Chirala India 15°50N 80°26E 245 G5
Chiramba Mozam. 16°55S 34°39E 269 F3
Chirawa India 28°14N 75°42E 242 E6
Chirchiq Uzbekistan 41°29N 69°35E 217 D7
Chiredzi Zimbabwe 21°0S 31°38E 271 B5
Chirfa Niger 20°55N 12°22E 259 D2
Chirgua → Venezuela 8°54N 67°58W 328 B4
Chiribiquete △ Colombia 0°31N 72°50W 328 C3
Chiricahua ⌂ U.S.A. 32°0N 109°20W 305 K9
Chiricahua Peak U.S.A. 31°51N 109°18W 305 L9
Chirikof I. U.S.A. 55°50N 155°40W 300 D8
Chiriquí, G. de Panama 8°0N 82°10W 320 E3
Chiriquí, L. de Panama 9°10N 82°0W 320 E3
Chirisa ⌂ Zimbabwe 17°53S 28°15E 269 F2
Chirivira Falls Zimbabwe 21°10S 32°12E 269 G3
Chirmiri India 23°15N 82°20E 243 H10
Chirnogi Romania 44°7N 26°32E 183 F11
Chirongui Mayotte 12°55S 45°9E 272 b
Chirpan Bulgaria 42°10N 25°19E 203 D9
Chirripó Grande, Cerro
Costa Rica 9°29N 83°29W 320 E3
Chirundu Zimbabwe 16°3S 28°50E 271 A4
Chisamba Zambia 14°55S 28°20E 269 E2
Chisapani Nepal 28°37N 81°16E 243 E9
Chisasa Zambia 12°6S 25°30E 265 E5
Chisasibi Canada 53°50N 79°0W 298 B4
Ch'ishan Taiwan 22°44N 120°31E 225 D2
Ch'ishan Hsi → Taiwan 22°51N 120°28E 225 C2
Chisholm Alta., Canada 54°55N 114°10W 296 C6
Chisholm Minn., U.S.A. 47°29N 92°53W 308 B7
Chishtian Mandi Pakistan 29°50N 72°55E 242 E5
Chishui China 28°30N 105°42E 228 C5
Chishui He → China 28°49N 105°50E 228 C5
Chisimaio = Kismaayo
Somalia 0°22S 42°32E 267 E5
Chisimba Falls Zambia 10°12S 30°56E 269 E3
Chişinău Moldova 47°2N 28°50E 183 C13
Chişinău ✕ (KIV) Moldova 47°3N 28°46E 183 C13
Chişineu Criş Romania 46°32N 21°37E 182 D6
Chislehurst U.K. 51°24N 0°6E 125 B4
Chisone → Italy 44°49N 7°25E 198 D4
Chisos Mts. U.S.A. 29°5N 103°15W 314 G3
Chissenque Angola 9°13S 20°34E 265 D4
Chissilo Angola 13°48S 16°31E 265 E3
Chistochina U.S.A. 62°34N 144°40W 303 E11
Chistopol Russia 55°25N 50°38E 190 C10
Chiswick U.K. 51°29N 0°16W 125 B2
Chiswick House U.K. 51°28N 0°15W 125 B2
Chita Colombia 6°11N 72°28W 328 B3
Chita Russia 52°0N 113°35E 219 A11
Chitado Angola 17°10S 14°8E 265 F2
Chitaldrug = Chitradurga
India 14°14N 76°24E 245 G3
Chitan Taiwan 24°35N 121°29E 225 B3
Chitato → Angola 16°1S 15°12E 265 F3
Chitapur India 17°10N 77°5E 244 F3
Chitembo Angola 13°30S 16°50E 265 E3
Chitina U.S.A. 61°31N 144°26W 303 F11
Chitipa Malawi 9°41S 33°19E 269 D3
Chitose Hokkaidō, Japan 42°49N 141°39E 220 C10
Chitose Kanagawa, Japan 35°33N 139°37E 140 B2
Chitradurga India 14°14N 76°24E 245 G3
Chitrakot India 19°10N 81°40E 244 E5
Chitral Pakistan 35°50N 71°56E 240 B3
Chitralada Palace
Thailand 13°45N 100°31E 113 B2
Chitravati → India 14°45N 78°15E 245 G4
Chitré Panama 7°59N 80°27W 320 E3
Chittagong Bangla. 22°19N 91°48E 241 D3
Chittagong □ Bangla. 24°5N 91°0E 241 C3
Chittaurgarh India 24°52N 74°38E 242 G6
Chittoor India 13°15N 79°5E 245 H4
Chittur India 10°40N 76°45E 245 J3
Chitungwiza Zimbabwe 18°0S 31°6E 269 F3
Chiuju Taiwan 22°44N 120°29E 225 D2
Chiumbe →
Dem. Rep. of the Congo 6°59S 21°12E 265 D4
Chiumbo Angola 12°29S 16°8E 265 E3
Chiume Angola 15°3S 21°14E 265 F4
Chiusi Italy 43°1N 11°57E 199 E8
Chiva Spain 39°27N 0°41W 197 F4
Chivacoa Venezuela 10°10N 68°54W 328 A4
Chivasso Italy 45°11N 7°53E 198 C4
Chivay Peru 15°40S 71°35W 330 D3
Chive Bolivia 12°23S 68°35W 330 C4
Chivhu Zimbabwe 19°2S 30°52E 269 F3
Chivilcoy Argentina 34°55S 60°0W 334 C4
Chiwanda Tanzania 11°23S 34°55E 269 E3
Chixi China 22°0N 112°58E 229 G9
Chiyoda Tokyo, Japan 140 b2
Chizarira ⌂ Zimbabwe 17°44S 27°52E 269 F2
Chizarira Ra. Zimbabwe 17°36S 27°45E 269 F2
Chizela Zambia 13°8S 25°0E 265 E4
Chizu Japan 35°16N 134°14E 222 B6
Chkalov = Orenburg
Russia 51°45N 55°6E 186 D10
Chkolovsk Russia 56°50N 43°10E 190 B6
Chloride U.S.A. 35°25N 114°12W 307 K12
Chlumec nad Cidlinou
Czechia 50°9N 15°29E 180 A8
Chmielnik Poland 50°37N 20°43E 185 H7
Cho-do N. Korea 38°30N 124°40E 224 C2
Cho Phuoc Hai Vietnam 10°26N 107°18E 237 G6
Choa Chu Kang Singapore 1°22N 103°41E 138 A2
Choba Kenya 2°30N 38°5E 266 D4
Chobe △ Botswana 18°37S 24°23E 270 A4
Choc B. St. Lucia 14°3N 60°59W 323 m
Choch'i Taiwan 23°20N 121°16E 225 C3
Chocianów Poland 51°27N 15°55E 185 G2
Chociwel Poland 53°29N 15°21E 184 E2
Chocó □ Colombia 6°0N 77°0W 328 B2
Chocolate Hills Phil. 9°55N 124°10E 233 G5
Chocolate Mts. U.S.A. 33°15N 115°15W 307 M11
Chocontá Colombia 5°9N 73°41W 328 B3
Choctawhatchee →
U.S.A. 30°25N 86°8W 316 E3
Choctawhatchee B.
U.S.A. 30°20N 86°20W 317 E3
Chodavaram Andhra Pradesh,
India 17°50N 82°57E 244 F6
Chodavaram Andhra Pradesh,
India 17°27N 81°46E 244 F5
Chodecz Poland 52°24N 19°2E 185 F6
Chodov Czechia 50°15N 12°45E 180 A5
Chodov u Prahy Czechia 50°1N 14°30E 135 B3
Chodziez Poland 52°58N 16°58E 185 F3
Choele Choel Argentina 39°11S 65°40W 336 A3
Chōfu Japan 35°38N 139°32E 140 B2
Choghā Zanbīl Iran 32°1N 48°32E 247 C6
Choirokoitia Cyprus 34°47N 33°20E 207 F9
Choiseul St. Lucia 13°47N 61°3W 323 m
Choiseul Solomon Is. 7°0S 156°40E 287 L9
Choisy-le-Roi France 48°46N 2°24E 134 B3
Choix Mexico 26°43N 108°17W 318 B3
Chojna Poland 52°58N 14°25E 185 F1
Chojnice Poland 53°42N 17°32E 184 E4
Chojnów Poland 51°18N 15°58E 185 G2
Chok Chai Thailand 14°44N 102°10E 236 E4
Chōkai-San Japan 39°6N 140°3E 220 E10
Choke Canyon Res.
U.S.A. 28°30N 98°20W 314 G5
Choke Mts. Ethiopia 11°18N 37°15E 257 E4
Chokurdakh Russia 70°38N 147°55E 215 B15
Chokwé Mozam. 24°32S 32°59E 271 B5
Cholame U.S.A. 35°44N 120°18W 306 K6
Cholan Taiwan 24°18N 120°49E 225 B2
Cholargos Greece 37°59N 23°48E 112 B2
Cholet France 47°4N 0°52W 172 E6
Cholguan Chile 37°10S 72°3W 334 D1
Choloma Honduras 15°37N 87°57W 320 C2
Cholpon-Ata Kyrgyzstan 42°40N 77°6E 217 D9
Cholupice Czechia 49°59N 14°27E 135 C2
Choluteca Honduras 13°20N 87°14W 320 D2
Choluteca → Honduras 13°0N 87°20W 320 D2
Chom Bung Thailand 13°37N 99°36E 236 F2
Chom Thong Bangkok,
Thailand 13°41N 100°29E 113 B1
Chom Thong Chiang Mai,
Thailand 18°25N 98°41E 236 C2
Choma Zambia 16°48S 26°59E 269 F2
Chomo Lhari Asia 27°49N 89°16E 241 B2
Chomolungma = Everest, Mt.
Nepal 28°5N 86°58E 243 E12
Chomun India 27°15N 75°40E 242 F6
Chomutov Czechia 50°28N 13°23E 180 A6
Chon Buri Thailand 13°21N 101°1E 236 F3
Chon Thanh Vietnam 11°24N 106°36E 237 G6
Chone Ecuador 0°40S 80°0W 328 D2
Chong Kai Cambodia 13°57N 103°35E 236 F4
Chong Mek Thailand 15°10N 105°27E 236 E5
Chong Pang Singapore 1°26N 103°49E 138 A2
Chong Phangan Thailand 9°39N 100°0E 237 b
Chong Samui Thailand 9°21N 99°50E 237 b
Chongde China 30°32N 120°26E 229 B13
Ch'ŏngjin N. Korea 41°47N 129°50E 224 B4
Chŏngju N. Korea 39°40N 125°5E 224 C2
Chongli China 40°58N 115°15E 226 D8
Chongming China 31°38N 121°23E 229 B13
Chongming Dao China 31°40N 121°30E 229 B13
Chongoni Rock Art
Malawi 14°17S 34°16E 269 E3
Chongoroi Angola 13°37S 14°1E 265 E2
Chongoyape Peru 6°35S 79°25W 330 B2
Chŏngp'yŏng N. Korea 39°47N 127°23E 224 C3
Chongqing Chongqing,
China 29°35N 106°25E 228 C6
Chongqing Sichuan,
China 30°38N 103°40E 228 B4
Chongqing Jiangbei Int. ✕ (CKG)
China 29°43N 106°38E 228 C6
Chongqing Shi □ China 30°0N 108°0E 228 C6
Chongren China 27°46N 116°3E 229 D11
Chonguene Mozam. 25°3S 33°49E 271 C5
Chongwe Zambia 15°21S 28°42E 269 F2
Chongwen Beijing, China 114 c2
Chongyi China 25°45N 114°29E 229 E10
Chongzuo China 22°23N 107°20E 228 F6
Chonogol Mongolia 45°54N 115°22E 226 B8
Chonos, Arch. de los Chile 45°0S 75°0W 336 C2
Chop Ukraine 48°26N 22°12E 182 B7
Chopda India 21°20N 75°15E 244 D2
Chopim → Brazil 25°35S 53°5W 335 B5
Chopin Museum Warsaw, Poland 143 b2
Chor Pakistan 25°31N 69°46E 242 G3
Chora Greece 37°3N 21°42E 204 D3
Chora Sfakion Greece 35°15N 24°9E 207 E5
Chorbat La India 34°42N 76°37E 243 B7
Chorley U.K. 53°39N 2°38W 168 D5
Chorna Ukraine 47°36N 29°20E 183 C14
Chornobyl Ukraine 51°20N 30°15E 177 C16
Chornomorske Ukraine 45°31N 32°40E 189 K7
Chorolque, Cerro Bolivia 20°59S 66°5W 334 A2
Choroszcz Poland 53°10N 22°59E 185 E9
Chorregon Australia 22°40S 143°32E 280 C3
Chorrillos Peru 12°10S 77°1W 124 C2
Chortkiv Ukraine 49°2N 25°46E 177 D13
Chorzele Poland 53°15N 20°55E 185 E7
Chorzów Poland 50°18N 18°57E 185 H5
Chos-Malal Argentina 37°20S 70°15W 334 D1
Ch'osan N. Korea 40°50N 125°47E 224 B2
Chosheta Shan Taiwan 23°50N 121°6E 225 C3
Chōshi Japan 35°45N 140°51E 223 B12
Choshui Hsi → Taiwan 23°50N 120°15E 225 C2
Choszczno Poland 53°7N 15°25E 185 E2
Chota Peru 6°33S 78°39W 330 B2
Choteau U.S.A. 47°49N 112°11W 304 C7
Chotěboř Czechia 49°43N 15°40E 180 B8
Chotila India 22°23N 71°15E 242 H4
Chotta Udepur India 22°19N 74°1E 242 H6
Choûm Mauritania 21°11N 13°30W 260 D2
Choungui Mayotte 12°57S 45°8E 272 b
Chowchilla U.S.A. 37°7N 120°16W 306 H6
Chowpatty Beach Mumbai, India 130 b1
Choybalsan Mongolia 48°4N 114°30E 219 B11
Choyr Mongolia 46°24N 108°30E 219 B10
Chrisman U.S.A. 39°48N 87°41W 311 E9
Chrisoupoli Greece 40°58N 24°42E 203 F8
Chrissi = Gaidouronisi
Greece 34°53N 25°41E 207 F6
Christ Church Cathedral
Montréal, Canada 130 c2
Christburg = Dzierzgoń
Poland 53°58N 19°20E 184 E6
Christchurch N.Z. 43°33S 172°47E 285 D7
Christchurch Dorset, U.K. 50°44N 1°47W 169 G6
Christian I. Canada 44°50N 80°12W 312 B4
Christian Quarter Jerusalem 123 b3
Christian Sd. U.S.A. 55°56N 134°40W 303 J14
Christiana Greece 36°14N 25°13E 205 E7
Christiana Jamaica 18°10N 77°29W 320 a
Christiana North West,
S. Africa 27°52S 25°8E 270 C4
Christiansborg Slot
Copenhagen, Denmark 118 c2
Christiansfeld Denmark 55°21N 9°29E 163 J3
Christianshåb = Qasigiannguit
Greenland 68°50N 51°18W 154 D5
Christianshavn Denmark 55°40N 12°35E 118 A3
Christiansted
U.S. Virgin Is. 17°45N 64°42W 321 C7
Christie B. Canada 62°32N 111°10W 297 A6
Christina → Canada 56°40N 111°3W 297 B6
Christmas Cr. →
Australia 18°29S 125°23E 278 C4
Christmas I. = Kiritimati
Kiribati 1°58N 157°27W 289 G12
Christmas I. Ind. Oc. 10°30S 105°40E 273 F9
Christoffel △ Curaçao 12°21N 69°8W 322 g
Christopher U.S.A. 37°59N 89°3W 310 G7
Christopher, L. Australia 24°49S 127°42E 279 D4
Christyakovo = Thorez
Ukraine 48°4N 38°34E 189 H10
Chrudim Czechia 49°58N 15°43E 180 B8
Chrysler Building New York, U.S.A. 132 c2
Chrzanów Małopolskie,
Poland 50°10N 19°21E 185 H6
Chrzanów Warszawa,
Poland 52°13N 20°53E 143 B1
Chtimba Malawi 10°35S 34°13E 269 E3
Chū = Shū Kazakhstan 43°36N 73°42E 217 D8
Chū = Shū → Kazakhstan 45°0N 67°44E 217 D7
Chu → Vietnam 19°53N 105°45E 236 C5
Chu Lai Vietnam 15°28N 108°45E 236 E7
Chu Mom Ray △
Vietnam 14°29N 107°38E 236 E6
Chu Se Vietnam 13°40N 108°8E 236 F7
Chuadanga Bangla. 23°38N 88°51E 241 D2
Chuak, Ko Thailand 9°28N 99°41E 237 b
Ch'uanchou = Quanzhou
China 24°55N 118°34E 229 E12
Chüanchow = Quanzhou
China 24°55N 118°34E 229 E12
Chuangwei Taiwan 24°45N 121°47E 225 B3

Chuankou *China* 34°20N 110°59E **226** G6
Chuathbaluk *U.S.A.* 61°40N 159°15W **303** F8
Chubarovka = Pology *Ukraine* 47°29N 36°15E **189** J9
Chubbuck *U.S.A.* 42°55N 112°28W **304** E7
Chūbu □ *Japan* 36°45N 137°30E **223** A9
Chūbu-Sangaku △ *Japan* 36°30N 137°40E **223** A9
Chubut □ *Argentina* 43°30S 69°00W **336** B3
Chubut → *Argentina* 43°20S 65°5W **336** B3
Chuçand = Khŭjand *Tajikistan* 40°17N 69°37E **217** D7
Chuch'i *Taiwan* 23°31N 120°33E **225** C2
Chuchi L. *Canada* 55°12N 124°30W **296** B4
Chuchow = Zhuzhou *China* 27°49N 113°12E **229** D9
Chuda *India* 22°29N 71°41E **242** H4
Chudovo *Russia* 59°10N 31°41E **188** C6
Chudskoye, Ozero *Russia* 58°13N 27°30E **188** C4
Chuen Lung *Hong Kong, China* 22°23N 114°6E **122** A2
Chugach Mts. *U.S.A.* 60°45N 147°0W **303** F11
Chuginadak I. *U.S.A.* 52°50N 169°45W **303** K5
Chūgoku □ *Japan* 35°0N 133°0E **222** C5
Chūgoku-Sanchi *Japan* 35°0N 133°0E **222** B5
Chuguyev = Chuhuyiv *Ukraine* 49°55N 36°45E **189** H9
Chugwater *U.S.A.* 41°46N 104°50W **304** F11
Chuhuyiv *Ukraine* 49°55N 36°45E **189** H9
Chuk Kok *Hong Kong, China* 22°20N 114°15E **122** A3
Chuka *Kenya* 0°20S 37°39E **268** C4
Chukchi Plateau *Arctic* 78°0N 165°0W **150** B17
Chukchi Sea *Russia* 68°0N 175°0W **215** C19
Chukotskiy, Mys *Russia* 64°14N 173°8W **300** C5
Chukotskiy Poluostrov *Russia* 66°0N 174°0W **300** B5
Chukotskoye Nagorye *Russia* 68°0N 175°0E **215** C18
Chula *U.S.A.* 31°33N 83°32W **316** D6
Chula Vista *U.S.A.* 32°38N 117°5W **307** N9
Chulalongkorn Univ. *Thailand* 13°44N 100°31E **113** B2
Chulband → *India* 20°40N 79°54E **244** D4
Ch'ulin *Taiwan* 22°8N 120°42E **225** D2
Chulucanas *Peru* 5°8S 80°10W **330** B1
Chulumani *Bolivia* 16°24S 67°31W **330** D4
Chulym → *Russia* 57°43N 83°51E **214** D9
Chum Phae *Thailand* 16°40N 102°6E **236** D4
Chum Saeng *Thailand* 15°55N 100°15E **236** E3
Chuma *Bolivia* 15°24S 68°56W **330** D4
Chumar *India* 32°40N 78°35E **243** C8
Chumbicha *Argentina* 29°0S 66°10W **334** B2
Chumerna *Bulgaria* 42°45N 25°55E **203** D9
Chumikan *Russia* 54°40N 135°10E **215** D14
Chumphon *Thailand* 10°35N 99°14E **237** G2
Chumpi *Peru* 15°4S 73°46W **330** D3
Chumuare *Mozam.* 14°31S 31°50E **269** E3
Chuna → *Russia* 57°47N 94°37E **215** D10
Chun'an *Zhejiang, China* 29°35N 119°3E **229** C12
Chunan *Taiwan* 24°41N 120°52E **225** B2
Chuncheon *S. Korea* 37°58N 127°44E **224** D3
Chunchura *India* 22°53N 88°27E **243** H13
Chung Hau *Hong Kong, China* 22°14N 114°0E **122** B2
Chunga *Zambia* 15°0S 26°2E **269** F2
Chungcheongbuk-do □ *S. Korea* 36°45N 128°0E **224** D4
Chungcheongnam-do □ *S. Korea* 36°30N 127°0E **224** D3
Ch'ungch'ing = Chongqing *China* 29°35N 106°25E **228** C6
Chunggang-ŭp *N. Korea* 41°48N 126°48E **224** B3
Chungho *Taiwan* 25°0N 121°28E **225** A3
Chunghwa *N. Korea* 38°52N 125°47E **224** C2
Chungju *S. Korea* 36°58N 127°58E **224** D3
Chungjuho *S. Korea* 36°57N 128°3E **224** D4
Chungking = Chongqing *China* 29°35N 106°25E **228** C6
Chungli *Taiwan* 24°57N 121°13E **225** B3
Chungpu *Taiwan* 23°26N 120°31E **225** C2
Chungt'iaoshan = Zhongtiao Shan *China* 35°0N 111°10E **226** G6
Chungtungwan *Taiwan* 24°31N 120°40E **225** B2
Chungyang Shanmo *Taiwan* 23°10N 121°0E **225** C3
Chunian *Pakistan* 30°57N 74°0E **242** D6
Chunya *Tanzania* 8°30S 33°27E **269** D3
Chunyang *China* 43°38N 129°23E **227** C15
Chuō *Tokyo, Japan* **140** b5
Chupara B. *Trin. & Tob.* 10°48N 61°22W **323** t
Chupara Pt. *Trin. & Tob.* 10°49N 61°22W **323** t
Chupei *Taiwan* 24°50N 121°0E **225** B3
Chuquibamba *Peru* 15°47S 72°44W **330** D3
Chuquibambilla *Peru* 14°7S 72°41W **330** C3
Chuquicamata *Chile* 22°15S 69°0W **334** A2
Chuquisaca □ *Bolivia* 20°30S 63°30W **331** E5
Chur *Switz.* 46°52N 9°32E **179** J5
Churachandpur *India* 24°20N 93°40E **241** C4
Church End *U.K.* 51°35N 0°11W **125** A2
Church of our Lady = Frauenkirche *Munich, Germany* **131** b2
Church Stretton *U.K.* 52°32N 2°48W **169** E5
Churchill *Vic., Australia* 38°19S 146°25E **283** E7
Churchill *Man., Canada* 58°47N 94°11W **297** B10
Churchill → *Man., Canada* 58°47N 94°12W **297** B10
Churchill → *Nfld. & L., Canada* 53°19N 60°10W **299** B7
Churchill, C. *Canada* 58°46N 93°12W **297** B10
Churchill Falls *Canada* 53°36N 64°19W **299** B7
Churchill L. *Canada* 55°55N 108°20W **297** B7
Churchill Pk. *Canada* 58°10N 125°10W **296** B3
Churdan *U.S.A.* 42°9N 94°29W **310** B2
Churki *India* 23°50N 83°12E **243** H10
Churu *India* 28°20N 74°50E **242** E6
Churubusco *U.S.A.* 41°14N 85°19W **311** C11
Churún Merú = Angel Falls *Venezuela* 5°57N 62°30W **329** B5
Chushal *India* 33°40N 78°40E **243** C8
Chushan *Taiwan* 23°45N 120°40E **225** C2
Chuska Mts. *U.S.A.* 36°15N 108°50W **305** H9
Chusovoy *Russia* 58°22N 57°50E **186** C10
Chusovskoy Zavod = Chusovoy *Russia* 58°22N 57°50E **186** C10
Chuspipata *Bolivia* 16°18S 67°48W **330** D4
Chust = Khust *Ukraine* 48°10N 23°18E **183** B8
Chust *Uzbekistan* 41°0N 71°13E **217** D8
Chute-aux-Outardes *Canada* 49°7N 68°24W **299** C6
Chutung *Taiwan* 24°44N 121°5E **225** B3
Chuuk = Truk *Micronesia* 7°25N 151°46E **287** T17
Chuuk Lagoon *Micronesia* 7°24N 151°45E **287** T18
Chuvash Republic = Chuvashia □ *Russia* 55°30N 47°0E **190** C8
Chuvashia □ *Russia* 55°30N 47°0E **190** C8
Chuwārtah *Iraq* 35°43N 45°34E **213** E11
Chuwei *Taiwan* 25°6N 121°14E **225** A3
Chuxiong *China* 25°2N 101°28E **228** E3
Chūy *Kyrgyzstan* 42°55N 75°15E **217** D9
Chuy *Uruguay* 33°41S 53°27W **335** C5
Chūy □ *Kyrgyzstan* 42°25N 75°16E **217** D9
Chuzenji-Ko *Japan* 36°44N 139°27E **223** A11
Chuzhou *China* 32°19N 118°20E **229** A12
Chynadiyeve *Ukraine* 48°29N 22°50E **182** B7
Chyulu Hills *Kenya* 2°35S 37°50E **268** C4
Ci Xian *China* 36°20N 114°25E **226** F8
Ciacova *Romania* 45°35N 21°10E **182** E6
Ciales *Puerto Rico* 18°20N 66°28W **321** b
Ciamis *Indonesia* 7°20S 108°21E **235** D3
Ciampino *Italy* 41°47N 12°36E **136** C2
Ciampino ✈ (CIA) *Italy* 41°47N 12°35E **136** C2
Cianjur *Indonesia* 6°49S 107°8E **234** D3
Cianorte *Brazil* 23°37S 52°37W **335** A5
Cibola *U.S.A.* 33°17N 114°42W **307** M12
Çiçekdağı *Turkey* 39°36N 34°24E **212** C6
Cicero *U.S.A.* 41°51N 87°44W **119** B2
Cicero Dantas *Brazil* 10°36S 38°23W **332** D4
Ciceron *St. Lucia* 13°59N 61°1W **323** m
Cicia *Fiji* 17°45S 179°18W **287** A3
Cicilia *Turkey* 36°30N 34°0E **212** D5
Cidacos → *Spain* 42°21N 1°38W **196** C3
Cidade de Minas = Belo Horizonte *Brazil* 19°55S 43°56W **333** E3
Cide *Turkey* 41°53N 33°1E **212** B5
Cidra *Puerto Rico* 18°11N 66°10W **321** b
Ciechanów *Poland* 52°52N 20°38E **185** F7
Ciechanowiec *Poland* 52°40N 22°31E **185** F9
Ciechocinek *Poland* 52°53N 18°45E **185** F5
Ciego de Ávila *Cuba* 21°50N 78°50W **320** B4
Ciénaga *Colombia* 11°1N 74°15W **328** A3
Ciénaga de Oro *Colombia* 8°53N 75°37W **328** B2
Ciénagas del Catatumbo △ *Venezuela* 9°26N 72°8W **328** B3
Cienfuegos *Cuba* 22°10N 80°30W **320** B3
Cierp-Gaud *France* 42°55N 0°40E **174** F4
Cíes, Is. *Spain* 42°12N 8°55W **194** C2
Cieszanów *Poland* 50°14N 23°8E **185** H10
Cieszyn *Poland* 49°45N 18°35E **185** J5
Cieza *Spain* 38°17N 1°23W **197** G3
Çifteler *Turkey* 39°22N 31°2E **212** C4
Cifuentes *Spain* 40°47N 2°37W **196** E2
Cihanbeyli *Turkey* 38°40N 32°55E **212** C5
Cihuatlán *Mexico* 19°14N 104°35W **318** D4
Cijara, Embalse de *Spain* 39°18N 4°52W **195** F6
Cijara △ *Spain* 39°18N 4°35W **195** F6
Cijulang *Indonesia* 7°42S 108°27E **235** D3
Cilacap *Indonesia* 7°43S 109°0E **235** D3
Cilandak *Indonesia* 6°17S 106°47E **122** B1
Cilao, Cirque de *Réunion* 21°7S 55°28E **272** f
Cilaos *Réunion* 21°8S 55°27E **272** f
Çıldır *Turkey* 41°7N 43°8E **213** B10
Çıldır Gölü *Turkey* 41°5N 43°15E **213** B10
Cilento e Vallo di Diano △ *Italy* 40°15N 15°20E **201** B8
Cili *China* 29°30N 111°8E **229** C8
Cilibia *Romania* 45°4N 27°4E **183** E12
Cilicia *Turkey* 36°30N 35°0E **250** B5
Cilincing *Indonesia* 6°6S 106°54E **122** A2
Ciliwung → *Indonesia* 6°6S 106°47E **122** B2
Cill Airne = Killarney *Ireland* 52°4N 9°30W **166** D2
Cill Chainnigh = Kilkenny *Ireland* 52°39N 7°15W **166** D4
Cill Dara = Kildare *Ireland* 53°9N 6°55W **166** C5
Cill Droichid = Celbridge *Ireland* 53°20N 6°32W **166** C5
Cill Mhantáin = Wicklow *Ireland* 52°59N 6°3W **166** D5
Cilo Dağı *Turkey* 37°28N 43°55E **213** D10
Cima *U.S.A.* 35°14N 115°30W **307** K11
Cimarron *Kans., U.S.A.* 37°48N 100°21W **308** G3
Cimarron *N. Mex., U.S.A.* 36°31N 104°55W **305** H11
Cimarron → *U.S.A.* 36°10N 96°16W **314** C6
Čimice *Czechia* 50°8N 14°25E **135** B2
Cimişlia *Moldova* 46°34N 28°44E **183** D13
Cimone, Mte. *Italy* 44°12N 10°42E **198** D7
Cina, Tanjung *Indonesia* 5°55S 104°45E **234** D2
Çinar *Turkey* 37°46N 40°19E **213** D9
Çinarcik *Turkey* 40°38N 29°5E **203** F13
Cinaruco-Capanaparo △ *Venezuela* 6°51N 67°32W **328** B4
Cinca → *Spain* 41°26N 0°21E **196** D5
Cincar *Bos.-H.* 43°55N 17°5E **182** G2
Cincinnati *Iowa, U.S.A.* 40°38N 92°56W **310** D4
Cincinnati *Ohio, U.S.A.* 39°6N 84°27W **311** E12
Cincinnati-Northern Kentucky Int. ✈ (CVG) *U.S.A.* 39°3N 84°40W **311** E12
Cincinnatus *U.S.A.* 42°33N 75°54W **313** D9
Çine *Turkey* 37°37N 28°2E **205** D10
Cinecittà *Italy* 41°51N 12°34E **136** B2
Ciney *Belgium* 50°18N 5°5E **170** D5
Cingoli *Italy* 43°23N 13°10E **199** E10
Cinigiano *Italy* 42°53N 11°24E **199** F8
Cinisello Bálsamo *Italy* 45°33N 9°13E **128** A2
Cinkota *Hungary* 47°31N 19°14E **117** A3
Cinque I. *India* 11°16N 92°42E **245** J11
Cinque Terre △ *Italy* 44°10N 9°45E **198** D6
Cinto, Mte. *France* 42°24N 8°54E **175** F12
Cintra, G. de *W. Sahara* 23°0N 16°15W **260** D1
Cintruénigo *Spain* 42°5N 1°49W **196** C3
Ciocile *Romania* 44°49N 27°14E **183** F12
Ciolănești din Deal *Romania* 44°19N 25°5E **183** F10
Ciorani *Romania* 44°45N 26°25E **183** F11
Čiovo *Croatia* 43°30N 16°17E **199** E13
Cipete *Indonesia* 6°15S 106°47E **122** B1
Cipó *Brazil* 11°6S 38°31W **332** D4
Cipolletti *Argentina* 38°56S 67°59W **336** A3
Circeo, Mte. *Italy* 41°14N 13°3E **200** A6
Çirçir *Turkey* 40°3N 36°47E **212** C7
Circle *Alaska, U.S.A.* 65°50N 144°4W **303** D11
Circle *Mont., U.S.A.* 47°25N 105°35W **304** C11
Circleville *U.S.A.* 39°36N 82°57W **309** F12
Circular Reef *Papua N. G.* 3°25S 147°47E **286** B4
Cirebon *Indonesia* 6°45S 108°32E **235** D3
Cirencester *U.K.* 51°43N 1°57W **169** F6
Cireşu *Romania* 44°47N 22°31E **182** F7
Cirey-sur-Vezouze *France* 48°35N 6°57E **173** D13
Ciriè *Italy* 45°14N 7°36E **198** C4
Cirium *Cyprus* 34°40N 32°53E **207** F8
Cirò *Italy* 39°23N 17°4E **201** C10
Cirò Marina *Italy* 39°22N 17°8E **201** C10
Ciron → *France* 44°36N 0°18W **174** D3
Cisco *U.S.A.* 32°23N 98°59W **314** E5
Cislău *Romania* 45°14N 26°20E **183** E11
Cisna *Poland* 49°12N 22°20E **185** J9
Cisnădie *Romania* 45°42N 24°9E **183** E9
Cisne *U.S.A.* 38°31N 88°26W **311** F8
Cisneros *Colombia* 6°33N 75°4W **328** B2
Cissna Park *U.S.A.* 40°34N 87°54W **311** D9
Cisterna di Latina *Italy* 41°35N 12°49E **200** A5
Cisternino *Italy* 40°44N 17°25E **201** B10
Cistierna *Spain* 42°48N 5°7W **194** C5
Citadel = Kastellet *Copenhagen, Denmark* **118** a3
Citadel *Budapest, Hungary* **117** c2
Citaré → *Brazil* 1°11N 54°41W **329** C7
Citeli-Ckaro = Dedopolis Tsqaro *Georgia* 41°33N 46°0E **191** K8
Citi Performing Arts Center *Boston, U.S.A.* **116** c2
Citlaltépetl = Orizaba, Pico de *Mexico* 18°58N 97°15W **319** D5
Citra *U.S.A.* 29°25N 82°7W **317** F7
Citron *Fr. Guiana* 4°44N 53°57W **329** C7
Citrus Heights *U.S.A.* 38°42N 121°17W **306** G5
Citrus Springs *U.S.A.* 29°2N 82°27W **317** F7
Citrusdal *S. Africa* 32°35S 19°0E **270** D2
Città degli Studi *Italy* 45°28N 9°13E **128** B2
Città del Vaticano = Vatican City ■ *Europe* 41°54N 12°27E **136** B1
Città della Pieve *Italy* 42°57N 12°1E **199** F9
Città di Castello *Italy* 43°27N 12°14E **199** E9
Città Sant' Angelo *Italy* 42°32N 14°5E **199** F11
Cittadella *Italy* 45°39N 11°47E **199** C8
Cittaducale *Italy* 42°23N 12°57E **199** F9
Cittanova *Italy* 38°21N 16°5E **201** D9
City, The *U.K.* 51°30N 0°6W **125** A3
City Hall = Rådhus *Oslo, Norway* **133** b1
City Hall = Stadshuset *Stockholm, Sweden* **139** b1
City of the Dead *Egypt* 30°0N 31°15E **117** A2
City Park *U.S.A.* 30°0N 90°5W **131** A2
City Terrace *U.S.A.* 34°3N 118°11W **126** B3
Ciuc, Munţii *Romania* 46°25N 26°5E **183** D11
Ciucaş, Vf. *Romania* 45°31N 25°56E **183** E10
Ciucea *Romania* 46°57N 22°49E **182** D7
Ciuciulea *Moldova* 47°40N 27°29E **183** C12
Ciuciuleni *Moldova* 47°2N 28°25E **183** C13
Ciudad Acuña *Mexico* 29°18N 100°55W **318** B4
Ciudad Altamirano *Mexico* 18°20N 100°40W **318** D4
Ciudad Anáhuac *Mexico* 27°14N 100°7W **318** B4
Ciudad Bolívar *Venezuela* 8°5N 63°36W **329** B5
Ciudad Bolivia *Venezuela* 8°21N 70°34W **328** B3
Ciudad Camargo *Mexico* 27°40N 105°10W **318** B3
Ciudad Cortés *Costa Rica* 8°55N 84°0W **320** E3
Ciudad de México *Mexico* 19°24N 99°9W **128** B2
Ciudad de Nutrias *Venezuela* 8°5N 69°18W **328** B4
Ciudad del Carmen *Mexico* 18°38N 91°50W **319** D6
Ciudad del Este *Paraguay* 25°30S 54°50W **335** B5
Ciudad Delicias = Delicias *Mexico* 28°13N 105°28W **318** B3
Ciudad Deportiva *Mexico* 19°24N 99°5W **128** B2
Ciudad Fin de Semana *Spain* 40°26N 3°34W **127** B2
Ciudad Frontera *Mexico* 26°56N 101°27W **318** B4
Ciudad General Belgrano *Argentina* 34°43S 58°33W **117** C1
Ciudad Guayana *Venezuela* 8°0N 62°30W **329** B5
Ciudad Guerrero *Mexico* 28°33N 107°30W **318** B3
Ciudad Guzmán *Mexico* 19°41N 103°29W **318** D4
Ciudad Juárez *Mexico* 31°44N 106°29W **318** A3
Ciudad Lerdo *Mexico* 25°32N 103°32W **318** B4
Ciudad Lineál *Spain* 40°26N 3°38W **127** B2
Ciudad Madero *Mexico* 22°19N 97°50W **319** C5
Ciudad Mante *Mexico* 22°44N 98°59W **319** C5
Ciudad Obregón *Mexico* 27°29N 109°56W **318** B3
Ciudad Ojeda *Venezuela* 10°12N 71°19W **328** A3
Ciudad Piar *Venezuela* 7°27N 63°19W **329** B5
Ciudad Porfirio Díaz = Piedras Negras *Mexico* 28°42N 100°31W **318** B4
Ciudad Real *Spain* 38°59N 3°55W **195** G7
Ciudad Real □ *Spain* 38°50N 4°0W **195** G7
Ciudad Rodrigo *Spain* 40°35N 6°32W **194** E4
Ciudad Satélite *Mexico* 19°30N 99°13W **128** A1
Ciudad Trujillo = Santo Domingo *Dom. Rep.* 18°30N 69°59W **321** C6
Ciudad Universitaria *B. Aires, Argentina* 34°33S 58°27W **117** B2
Ciudad Universitaria *México, Mexico* 19°20N 99°11W **128** C1
Ciudad Valles *Mexico* 21°59N 99°1W **319** C5
Ciudad Victoria *Mexico* 23°44N 99°8W **319** C5
Ciudadela *Spain* 40°0N 3°50E **206** B4
Ciulnița *Romania* 44°26N 27°22E **183** F12
Ciumeghiu *Romania* 46°44N 21°35E **182** D6
Ciuperceni *Romania* 44°54N 23°4E **182** F8
Ciutadella, Parc de la *Barcelona, Spain* **114** b3
Civa Burnu *Turkey* 41°21N 36°38E **212** B7
Civic Center *Los Angeles, U.S.A.* **127** b2
Civico Correr, Museo *Venice, Italy* **142** b3
Cividale del Friuli *Italy* 46°6N 13°25E **199** B10
Civita Castellana *Italy* 42°18N 12°24E **199** F9
Civitanova Marche *Italy* 43°18N 13°44E **199** E10
Civitavécchia *Italy* 42°6N 11°48E **199** F8
Civray *France* 46°10N 0°17E **174** B4
Çivril *Turkey* 38°20N 29°43E **205** C11
Cixerri → *Italy* 39°17N 8°59E **200** C1
Cixi *China* 30°17N 121°9E **229** B13
Cizre *Turkey* 37°19N 42°10E **213** D10
Clackmannanshire □ *U.K.* 56°10N 3°43W **167** E5
Clacton-on-Sea *U.K.* 51°47N 1°11E **169** F9
Clain → *France* 46°47N 0°33E **172** F7
Claire, L. *Canada* 58°35N 112°5W **296** B6
Claireville Res. *Canada* 43°45N 79°39W **141** A1
Clairton *U.S.A.* 40°18N 79°53W **312** F5
Clairvaux-les-Lacs *France* 46°35N 5°45E **173** F12
Claise → *France* 46°56N 0°42E **174** B5
Clallam Bay *U.S.A.* 48°15N 124°16W **306** B2
Clam Gulch *U.S.A.* 60°15N 151°23W **303** F10
Clamart *France* 48°48N 2°15E **134** B2
Clamecy *France* 47°28N 3°30E **173** E10
Clanton *U.S.A.* 32°51N 86°38W **315** E11
Clanwilliam *S. Africa* 32°11S 18°52E **270** D2
Clapham *U.K.* 51°27N 0°8W **125** B3
Clapton *U.K.* 51°33N 0°3W **125** A3
Clara *Ireland* 53°21N 7°37W **166** C4
Claraville *U.S.A.* 35°24N 118°20W **307** K8
Clare *S. Austral., Australia* 33°50S 138°37E **282** B3
Clare *Mich., U.S.A.* 43°49N 84°46W **309** D11
Clare □ *Ireland* 52°45N 9°0W **166** D3
Clare → *Ireland* 53°20N 9°2W **166** C2
Clare I. *Ireland* 53°47N 10°0W **166** C1
Claremont *Jamaica* 18°19N 77°11W **320** a
Claremont *Western Cape, S. Africa* 34°8S 18°28E **118** A1
Claremont *Calif., U.S.A.* 34°6N 117°43W **307** L9
Claremont *N.H., U.S.A.* 43°23N 72°20W **313** C12
Claremont Pt. *Australia* 14°1S 143°41E **280** A3
Claremore *U.S.A.* 36°19N 95°36W **314** C7
Claremorris *Ireland* 53°45N 9°0W **166** C3
Clarence *N.Z.* 42°10S 173°56E **285** C8
Clarence → *Australia* 29°25S 153°22E **281** D5
Clarence → *N.Z.* 42°10S 173°56E **285** C8
Clarence, I. *Chile* 54°0S 72°0W **336** D2
Clarence, Port *U.S.A.* 65°15N 166°40W **303** D6
Clarence B. *Ascension I.* 7°55S 14°25W **153** g
Clarence I. *Antarctica* 61°10S 54°0W **151** C18
Clarence Str. *Australia* 12°0S 131°0E **278** B5
Clarence Town *Bahamas* 23°6N 74°59W **321** B5
Clarendon *Pa., U.S.A.* 41°47N 79°6W **312** E5
Clarendon *Tex., U.S.A.* 34°56N 100°53W **314** D4
Clarenville *Canada* 48°10N 54°1W **299** C9
Claresholm *Canada* 50°2N 113°33W **296** D6
Clarie Coast *Antarctica* 68°0S 135°0E **151** C9
Clarinda *U.S.A.* 40°44N 95°2W **308** E6
Clarington *Canada* 43°55N 78°41W **312** C6
Clarion *Iowa, U.S.A.* 42°44N 93°44W **310** B3
Clarion *Pa., U.S.A.* 41°13N 79°23W **312** E5
Clarion → *U.S.A.* 41°7N 79°41W **312** E5
Clarion Fracture Zone *Pac. Oc.* 20°0N 120°0W **292** H7
Clark *Mo., U.S.A.* 39°17N 92°21W **310** E4
Clark *S. Dak., U.S.A.* 44°53N 97°44W **308** C5
Clark, Pt. *Canada* 44°4N 81°45W **312** B3
Clark Fork *U.S.A.* 48°9N 116°11W **304** B5
Clark Fork → *U.S.A.* 48°9N 116°15W **304** B5
Clarkdale *U.S.A.* 34°46N 112°3W **305** J7
Clarke City *Canada* 50°12N 66°38W **299** B6
Clarke I. *Australia* 40°32S 148°10E **281** G4
Clarke Ra. *Australia* 20°40S 148°30E **280** b
Clarks Fork Yellowstone → *U.S.A.* 45°32N 108°50W **304** D9
Clark's Harbour *Canada* 43°25N 65°38W **299** D6
Clarks Hill L. = J. Strom Thurmond L. *U.S.A.* 33°40N 82°12W **316** B7
Clarks Point *U.S.A.* 58°51N 158°33W **303** G8
Clarks Summit *U.S.A.* 41°30N 75°42W **313** E9
Clark's Town *Jamaica* 18°25N 77°33W **320** a
Clarksburg *U.S.A.* 39°17N 80°30W **309** F13
Clarksdale *U.S.A.* 34°12N 90°35W **315** D9
Clarkston *U.S.A.* 46°25N 117°3W **304** C5
Clarksville *Ark., U.S.A.* 35°28N 93°28W **314** D8
Clarksville *Ind., U.S.A.* 38°17N 85°45W **311** F11
Clarksville *Iowa, U.S.A.* 42°47N 92°40W **310** B4
Clarksville *Mo., U.S.A.* 39°22N 90°54W **310** E6
Clarksville *Tenn., U.S.A.* 36°32N 87°21W **315** C11
Clarksville *Tex., U.S.A.* 33°37N 95°3W **314** E7
Claro → *Brazil* 19°8S 50°40W **333** E1
Clatskanie *U.S.A.* 46°6N 123°12W **306** D3
Claude *U.S.A.* 35°7N 101°22W **314** D4
Claveria *Cagayan, Phil.* 18°37N 121°4E **232** B3
Claveria *Masbate, Phil.* 12°54N 123°15E **232** E4
Claveria *Mis. Or., Phil.* 8°38N 124°55E **233** G5
Clavering Ø *Greenland* 74°15N 21°0W **154** C8
Claxton *U.S.A.* 32°10N 81°55W **316** C8
Claxton B. *Trin. & Tob.* 10°21N 61°28W **323** t
Claxton Bay *Trin. & Tob.* 10°21N 61°28W **323** t
Clay *U.S.A.* 38°17N 121°10W **306** G5
Clay Center *U.S.A.* 39°23N 97°8W **308** F5
Clay City *Ind., U.S.A.* 39°17N 87°7W **311** E9
Clay City *Ky., U.S.A.* 37°52N 83°55W **311** G13
Clayhall *U.K.* 51°35N 0°3E **125** A4
Claypool *U.S.A.* 33°25N 110°51W **305** K8
Claysburg *U.S.A.* 40°17N 78°27W **312** F6
Claysville *U.S.A.* 40°7N 80°25W **312** F4
Clayton *Ont., Canada* 45°11N 76°19W **313** A8
Clayton *Ala., U.S.A.* 31°53N 85°27W **316** D4
Clayton *Ind., U.S.A.* 39°41N 86°31W **311** E10
Clayton *N. Mex., U.S.A.* 36°27N 103°11W **305** H12
Clayton *N.Y., U.S.A.* 44°14N 76°5W **313** B8
Clear, C. *Ireland* 51°25N 9°32W **166** E2
Clear, L. *Ont., Canada* 45°26N 77°12W **312** A7
Clear, L. *Fla., U.S.A.* 28°31N 81°24W **133** A2
Clear Hills *Canada* 56°40N 119°30W **296** B5
Clear I. *Ireland* 51°26N 9°30W **166** E2
Clear L. *U.S.A.* 39°2N 122°47W **306** G4
Clear Lake *Iowa, U.S.A.* 43°8N 93°23W **310** A3
Clear Lake *S. Dak., U.S.A.* 44°45N 96°41W **308** C5
Clear Lake Res. *U.S.A.* 41°56N 121°5W **304** F3
Clear Water B. *Hong Kong, China* 22°17N 114°18E **122** B3
Clearfield *Pa., U.S.A.* 41°2N 78°27W **312** E6
Clearfield *Utah, U.S.A.* 41°7N 112°2W **304** F7
Clearlake *U.S.A.* 38°57N 122°38W **306** G4
Clearwater *B.C., Canada* 51°38N 120°2W **296** C4
Clearwater *Fla., U.S.A.* 27°59N 82°48W **317** H7
Clearwater → *Alta., Canada* 52°22N 114°57W **296** C6
Clearwater → *Alta., Canada* 56°44N 111°23W **297** B6
Clearwater L. *Canada* 53°34N 99°49W **297** C9
Clearwater Lake △ *Canada* 54°0N 101°0W **297** C8
Clearwater Mts. *U.S.A.* 46°5N 115°20W **304** C6
Clearwater River △ *Canada* 56°55N 109°10W **297** B7
Cleburne *U.S.A.* 32°21N 97°23W **314** E6
Clee Hills *U.K.* 52°26N 2°35W **169** E5
Cleethorpes *U.K.* 53°33N 0°3W **168** D7
Cleeve Cloud *U.K.* 51°56N 2°0W **169** F6
Clelles *France* 44°50N 5°38E **175** D9
Clemson *U.S.A.* 34°41N 82°50W **315** D13
Cleopatra Needle *Phil.* 10°7N 118°58E **233** F2
Clerke Reef *Australia* 17°22S 119°20E **278** C2
Clerkenwell *London, U.K.* **125** a4
Clermiston *U.K.* 55°57N 3°17W **121** B2
Clermont *Queens., Australia* 22°49S 147°39E **280** C4
Clermont *Oise, France* 49°23N 2°24E **173** C9
Clermont *Fla., U.S.A.* 28°33N 81°46W **317** G8
Clermont-en-Argonne *France* 49°5N 5°4E **173** C12
Clermont-Ferrand *France* 45°46N 3°4E **174** C7
Clermont-l'Hérault *France* 43°38N 3°26E **174** E7
Clerval *France* 47°25N 6°30E **173** E13
Clervaux *Lux.* 50°4N 6°2E **170** D6
Cles *Italy* 46°22N 11°2E **198** B8
Cleve *Australia* 33°43S 136°30E **282** B2
Clevedon *U.K.* 51°26N 2°52W **169** F5
Cleveland *Miss., U.S.A.* 33°45N 90°43W **315** E9
Cleveland *Ohio, U.S.A.* 41°29N 81°41W **312** E3
Cleveland *Okla., U.S.A.* 36°19N 96°28W **314** C6
Cleveland *Tenn., U.S.A.* 35°10N 84°53W **315** D12
Cleveland *Tex., U.S.A.* 30°21N 95°5W **314** F7
Cleveland, C. *Australia* 19°11S 147°1E **280** B4
Cleveland, Mt. *U.S.A.* 48°56N 113°51W **304** B7
Cleveland Heights *U.S.A.* 41°31N 81°33W **312** E3
Clevelândia *Brazil* 26°24S 52°23W **335** B5
Clevelândia do Norte *Brazil* 3°49N 51°52W **329** C7
Cleves *U.S.A.* 39°10N 84°45W **311** E11
Clew B. *Ireland* 53°50N 9°49W **166** C2
Clewiston *U.S.A.* 26°45N 80°56W **317** J9
Clichy *France* 48°54N 2°18E **134** A2
Clichy-sous-Bois *France* 48°54N 2°32E **134** A4
Clifden *Galway, Ireland* 53°29N 10°1W **166** C1
Clifden *N.Z.* 46°1S 167°42E **285** G2
Cliffdell *U.S.A.* 46°56N 121°5W **306** D5
Cliffside *Canada* 43°44N 79°14W **141** A3
Cliffside Park *U.S.A.* 40°49N 73°59W **132** B2
Cliffy Hd. *Australia* 35°1S 116°29E **279** G2
Clifton *Queens., Australia* 27°59S 151°53E **281** D5
Clifton *Sindh, Pakistan* 24°48N 67°1E **123** B2
Clifton *Western Cape, S. Africa* 33°56S 18°22E **118** A1
Clifton *Ariz., U.S.A.* 33°3N 109°18W **305** K9
Clifton *Colo., U.S.A.* 39°7N 108°25W **304** G9
Clifton *Ill., U.S.A.* 40°56N 87°56W **311** D9
Clifton *N.Y., U.S.A.* 40°37N 74°4W **132** C1
Clifton *Tex., U.S.A.* 31°47N 97°35W **314** F6
Clifton Beach *Queens., Australia* 16°46S 145°39E **280** B4
Clifton Beach *Sindh, Pakistan* 24°48N 67°2E **123** B2
Clifton Pt. *Bahamas* 25°1N 77°34W **153** b
Cliftondale *U.S.A.* 42°26N 71°0W **116** A2
Climax *U.S.A.* 30°53N 84°26W **316** E5
Clinch → *U.S.A.* 35°53N 84°29W **315** D12
Clingmans Dome *U.S.A.* 35°34N 83°30W **315** D13
Clint *U.S.A.* 31°35N 106°14W **314** F1
Clinton *B.C., Canada* 51°6N 121°35W **296** C4
Clinton *Ont., Canada* 43°37N 81°32W **312** C3
Clinton *N.Z.* 46°12S 169°23E **285** G4
Clinton *Ark., U.S.A.* 35°36N 92°28W **314** D8
Clinton *Conn., U.S.A.* 41°17N 72°32W **313** E12
Clinton *Ill., U.S.A.* 40°9N 88°57W **310** D8
Clinton *Ind., U.S.A.* 39°40N 87°24W **311** E9
Clinton *Iowa, U.S.A.* 41°51N 90°12W **310** C6
Clinton *Mass., U.S.A.* 42°25N 71°41W **313** D13
Clinton *Mich., U.S.A.* 42°4N 83°58W **311** B13
Clinton *Miss., U.S.A.* 32°20N 90°20W **315** E9
Clinton *Mo., U.S.A.* 38°22N 93°46W **310** F3
Clinton *N.C., U.S.A.* 35°0N 78°22W **315** D15
Clinton *Okla., U.S.A.* 35°31N 98°58W **314** D5
Clinton *S.C., U.S.A.* 34°29N 81°53W **315** D14
Clinton *Tenn., U.S.A.* 36°6N 84°8W **315** C12
Clinton *Wash., U.S.A.* 47°59N 122°21W **306** C4
Clinton *Wis., U.S.A.* 42°34N 88°52W **311** B8
Clinton, C. *Australia* 22°30S 150°45E **280** C5
Clinton, L. *U.S.A.* 40°15N 88°45W **311** D8
Clinton Colden L. *Canada* 63°58N 107°27W **294** E10
Clio *U.S.A.* 31°43N 85°37W **316** D4
Clipperton, Î. *Pac. Oc.* 10°18N 109°13W **289** F17
Clipperton Fracture Zone *Pac. Oc.* 19°0N 122°0W **289** G16
Clisham *U.K.* 57°58N 6°49W **167** D2
Clisson *France* 47°5N 1°16W **172** E5
Clitheroe *U.K.* 53°53N 2°22W **168** D5
Clive *N.Z.* 39°36S 176°58E **284** F5
Clive *Iowa, U.S.A.* 41°36N 93°43W **310** C3
Cliza *Bolivia* 17°36S 65°56W **331** D4
Clo-oose *Canada* 48°39N 124°49W **306** B2
Cloates, Pt. *Australia* 22°43S 113°40E **278** D1
Clocolan *S. Africa* 28°55S 27°34E **271** C4
Clodomira *Argentina* 27°35S 64°14W **334** B3
Cloghaneely *Ireland* 55°8N 8°5W **166** A3
Clogher Hd. *Ireland* 53°48N 6°14W **166** C5
Clonakilty *Ireland* 51°37N 8°53W **166** E3
Clonakilty B. *Ireland* 51°35N 8°51W **166** E3
Cloncurry *Queens., Australia* 20°40S 140°28E **280** C3
Cloncurry *Kildare, Ireland* 53°25N 6°48W **166** C5
Cloncurry → *Australia* 18°37S 140°40E **280** B3
Clondalkin *Ireland* 53°19N 6°25W **166** C5
Clones *Ireland* 54°11N 7°15W **166** B4
Clonmel *Ireland* 52°21N 7°42W **166** D4
Clontarf *Australia* 33°48S 151°16E **139** A2
Cloppenburg *Germany* 52°51N 8°1E **178** C4
Cloquet *U.S.A.* 46°43N 92°28W **308** B7
Clorinda *Argentina* 25°16S 57°45W **334** B4
Cloud Peak *U.S.A.* 44°23N 107°11W **304** D10
Cloudcroft *U.S.A.* 32°58N 105°45W **305** K11
Cloudy B. *N.Z.* 41°25S 174°10E **285** B9
Clovelly *Australia* 33°54S 151°15E **139** B2
Cloverdale *Calif., U.S.A.* 38°48N 123°1W **306** G4
Cloverdale *Ind., U.S.A.* 39°31N 86°48W **311** E10
Cloverport *U.S.A.* 37°50N 86°38W **311** G10
Clovis *Calif., U.S.A.* 36°49N 119°42W **306** J7
Clovis *N. Mex., U.S.A.* 34°24N 103°12W **305** J12
Cloyes-sur-le-Loir *France* 48°0N 1°14E **172** E8
Cloyne *Canada* 44°49N 77°11W **312** B7
Cluain Meala = Clonmel *Ireland* 52°21N 7°42W **166** D4
Club Terrace *Australia* 37°35S 148°58E **283** D8
Cluj □ *Romania* 46°45N 23°30E **183** D8
Cluj-Napoca *Romania* 46°47N 23°38E **183** D8
Clunes *Australia* 37°20S 143°45E **282** D5
Cluny *France* 46°26N 4°38E **173** F11
Cluses *France* 46°5N 6°35E **173** F13
Clusone *Italy* 45°53N 9°57E **198** C6
Clutha → *N.Z.* 46°20S 169°49E **285** G4
Clwyd → *U.K.* 53°19N 3°31W **168** D4
Clyattville *U.S.A.* 30°42N 83°19W **316** E6
Clyde *Alta., Canada* 54°9N 113°39W **296** C6
Clyde *N.Z.* 45°12S 169°20E **285** F4
Clyde *N.Y., U.S.A.* 43°5N 76°52W **312** C8
Clyde *Ohio, U.S.A.* 41°18N 82°59W **311** C14
Clyde → *U.K.* 55°55N 4°30W **167** F4
Clyde, Firth of *U.K.* 55°22N 5°1W **167** F3
Clyde River *Canada* 70°30N 68°30W **295** C18
Clydebank *U.K.* 55°54N 4°23W **167** F4
Clymer *N.Y., U.S.A.* 42°1N 79°37W **312** D5
Clymer *Pa., U.S.A.* 40°40N 79°1W **312** D5
Clyo *U.S.A.* 32°29N 81°16W **316** C8
Ćmielów *Poland* 50°53N 21°31E **185** H8
CNN Center *U.S.A.* 33°45N 84°23W **113** B2
Côa → *Portugal* 41°5N 7°6W **194** D3
Coachella *U.S.A.* 33°41N 116°10W **307** M10
Coachella Canal *U.S.A.* 32°43N 114°57W **307** N12
Coahoma *U.S.A.* 32°18N 101°18W **314** E4
Coahuayana → *Mexico* 18°41N 103°45W **318** D4
Coahuila □ *Mexico* 27°20N 102°0W **318** B4
Coal → *Canada* 59°39N 126°57W **296** B3
Coal City *U.S.A.* 41°17N 88°17W **311** C8
Coal I. *N.Z.* 46°8S 166°40E **285** G1
Coalane *Mozam.* 17°48S 37°2E **269** F4
Coalcomán *Mexico* 18°47N 103°9W **318** D4
Coaldale *Canada* 49°45N 112°35W **296** D6
Coalgate *U.S.A.* 34°32N 96°13W **314** D6
Coalinga *U.S.A.* 36°9N 120°21W **306** J6
Coalisland *U.K.* 54°33N 6°42W **166** B5
Coalville *Leics., U.K.* 52°44N 1°23W **168** E6
Coalville *Utah, U.S.A.* 40°55N 111°24W **304** F8
Coamo *Puerto Rico* 18°5N 66°22W **321** b
Coari *Brazil* 4°8S 63°7W **329** D5
Coari → *Brazil* 4°30S 63°33W **329** D5
Coari, L. *Brazil* 4°15S 63°22W **329** D5
Coast Mts. *Canada* 55°0N 129°20W **296** C3
Coast Ranges *U.S.A.* 39°0N 123°0W **306** G4
Coatbridge *U.K.* 55°52N 4°6W **167** F4
Coatepec *Mexico* 19°27N 96°58W **319** D5
Coatepeque *Guatemala* 14°46N 91°55W **320** D1
Coatesville *U.S.A.* 39°59N 75°50W **309** F16
Coaticook *Canada* 45°10N 71°46W **313** A13
Coats I. *Canada* 62°30N 83°0W **295** E15
Coats Land *Antarctica* 77°0S 25°0W **151** D1
Coatzacoalcos *Mexico* 18°7N 94°25W **319** D6
Cobá *Mexico* 20°31N 87°45W **319** C7
Cobadin *Romania* 44°5N 28°13E **183** F13
Cobalt *Canada* 47°25N 79°42W **298** C4
Cobán *Guatemala* 15°30N 90°21W **320** C1
Çobanlar *Turkey* 38°41N 30°47E **205** C12
Cobar *Australia* 31°27S 145°48E **283** A6
Cobargo *Australia* 36°20S 149°55E **283** D8
Cobbannah *Australia* 37°37S 147°13E **283** D7
Cobberas, Mt. *Australia* 36°53S 148°12E **283** D8
Cobden *Australia* 38°20S 143°3E **282** E5
Cobh *Ireland* 51°51N 8°17W **166** E3
Cóbh, An = Cobh *Ireland* 51°51N 8°17W **166** E3
Cobija *Bolivia* 11°0S 68°50W **330** C4
Cobleskill *U.S.A.* 42°41N 74°29W **313** D10
Coboconk *Canada* 44°39N 78°48W **312** B6
Cobourg *Canada* 43°58N 78°10W **312** C6
Cobourg Pen. *Australia* 11°20S 132°15E **278** B5
Cobram *Australia* 35°54S 145°40E **283** C6
Cobras, I. das *Brazil* 22°53S 43°9W **118** B2
Cóbué *Mozam.* 12°0S 34°58E **269** E3
Coburg *Vic., Australia* 37°44S 144°56E **128** A1
Coburg *Bayern, Germany* 50°15N 10°58E **179** E6
Coburg I. *Canada* 75°57N 79°26W **295** B16
Coca *Spain* 41°13N 4°32W **194** D6
Coca → *Ecuador* 0°29S 76°58W **328** D2
Cocachacra *Peru* 17°5S 71°45W **330** D3
Cocal *Brazil* 3°28S 41°34W **332** B3
Cocanada = Kakinada *India* 16°57N 82°11E **244** F6
Cocentaina *Spain* 38°45N 0°27W **197** G4
Cochabamba *Bolivia* 17°26S 66°10W **331** D4
Coche, I. *Venezuela* 10°47N 63°56W **329** a
Cochem *Germany* 50°9N 7°9E **179** E3
Cochemane *Mozam.* 17°0S 32°54E **269** F3
Cochin *India* 9°58N 76°20E **245** K3
Cochin China = Nam Phan *Vietnam* 10°30N 106°0E **237** G6
Cochran *U.S.A.* 32°23N 83°21W **316** C6
Cochrane *Alta., Canada* 51°11N 114°30W **296** C6
Cochrane *Ont., Canada* 49°0N 81°0W **298** C3
Cochrane *Chile* 47°15S 72°33W **336** C2
Cochrane → *Canada* 59°0N 103°40W **297** B8
Cochrane, L. *Chile* 47°10S 72°0W **336** C2
Cochranton *U.S.A.* 41°31N 80°3W **312** E4
Cockburn *Australia* 32°5S 141°0E **282** B4
Cockburn, Canal *Chile* 54°30S 72°0W **336** D2
Cockburn I. *Canada* 45°55N 83°22W **298** C3
Cockburn Ra. *Australia* 15°46S 128°0E **278** C4
Cockermouth *U.K.* 54°40N 3°22W **168** C4
Cocklebiddy *Australia* 32°0S 126°3E **279** F4
Cockpit *Jamaica* 18°16N 77°39W **320** a
Cockpit Country, The *Jamaica* 18°15N 77°45W **320** a
Cockrell Hill *U.S.A.* 32°44N 96°53W **120** B4
Côco → *Brazil* 9°27S 50°2W **332** C2
Coco → *Cent. Amer.* 15°0N 83°8W **320** D3
Coco, Cayo *Cuba* 22°29N 78°34W **320** B4
Coco, I. del *Pac. Oc.* 5°25N 87°55W **289** G19
Coco, Pta. *Colombia* 2°58N 77°43W **328** C2
Coco Channel *Asia* 13°45N 93°10E **245** H11
Cocoa *U.S.A.* 28°21N 80°44W **317** G9
Cocoa Beach *U.S.A.* 28°19N 80°37W **317** G9
Cocoa Point *Antigua & B.* 17°33N 61°46W **322** c
Cocobeach *Gabon* 0°59N 9°34E **264** B1
Coconut Grove *U.S.A.* 25°42N 80°15W **129** D2
Cocoparra △ *Australia* 34°10S 146°12E **283** C7
Cocora *Romania* 44°45N 27°3E **183** F12
Côcos *Brazil* 14°10S 44°33W **333** D3
Côcos → *Brazil* 12°44S 44°48W **333** D3
Cocos B. *Trin. & Tob.* 10°24N 61°2W **323** t
Cocos Basin *Ind. Oc.* 1°0N 94°0E **273** D8
Cocos I. = Coco, I. del *Pac. Oc.* 5°25N 87°55W **289** G19
Cocos I. *Guam* 13°14N 144°39E **302** d
Cocos Is. *Ind. Oc.* 12°10S 96°55E **273** F8
Cocos Ridge *Pac. Oc.* 4°0N 88°0W **289** G19
Cocotá *Brazil* 22°48S 43°11W **135** A1
Cod, C. *U.S.A.* 42°5N 70°10W **309** D18
Codajás *Brazil* 3°55S 62°0W **329** D5
Codera, C. *Venezuela* 10°35N 66°4W **328** A4
Codfish I. *N.Z.* 46°47S 167°38E **285** G2
Codigoro *Italy* 44°49N 12°8E **199** D9
Codlea *Romania* 45°42N 25°27E **183** E10
Codó *Brazil* 4°30S 43°55W **332** B3
Codogno *Italy* 45°9N 9°42E **198** C6
Codpa *Chile* 18°50S 69°44W **330** D4
Codrington *Antigua & B.* 17°38N 61°50W **322** c
Codrington Lagoon *Antigua & B.* 17°39N 61°50W **322** c
Codróipo *Italy* 45°58N 13°0E **199** C10
Codru, Munţii *Romania* 46°30N 22°15E **182** D7
Cody *U.S.A.* 44°32N 109°3W **304** D9
Coe Hill *Canada* 44°52N 77°50W **312** B7
Coelemu *Chile* 36°30S 72°48W **334** D1
Coelho Neto *Brazil* 4°15S 43°0W **332** B3
Coen *Australia* 13°52S 143°12E **280** A3
Coeroeni *Suriname* 3°22N 57°21W **329** C6
Coeroeni → *Suriname* 3°21N 57°31W **329** C6
Coesfeld *Germany* 51°56N 7°10E **178** D3
Coetivy I. *Seychelles* 7°8S 56°16E **273** E4
Cœuilly *France* 48°48N 2°32E **134** B4
Coeur d'Alene *U.S.A.* 47°41N 116°46W **304** C5
Coeur d'Alene L. *U.S.A.* 47°32N 116°49W **304** C5
Coevorden *Neths.* 52°40N 6°44E **170** B6
Cofete *Canary Is.* 28°6N 14°23W **153** e2
Coffeyville *U.S.A.* 37°2N 95°37W **308** G6
Coffin B. *Australia* 34°38S 135°28E **281** E2
Coffin Bay *Australia* 34°37S 135°29E **281** E2
Coffin Bay △ *Australia* 34°34S 135°19E **281** E2
Coffin Bay Peninsula *Australia* 34°32S 135°15E **281** E2
Coffs Harbour *Australia* 30°16S 153°5E **283** A10
Cofrentes *Spain* 39°13N 1°5W **197** F3
Cogalnic = Kohylnyk → *Ukraine* 45°49N 29°40E **183** E14
Cogealac *Romania* 44°36N 28°36E **183** F13
Coghinas → *Italy* 40°55N 8°48E **200** B1
Coghinas, L. del *Italy* 40°46N 9°3E **200** B2
Cognac *France* 45°41N 0°20W **174** C3
Cogne *Italy* 45°37N 7°21E **198** C4
Cogolin *France* 43°15N 6°32E **175** E10
Cogolludo *Spain* 40°59N 3°10W **196** E1
Cohocton *U.S.A.* 42°30N 77°30W **312** D7
Cohocton → *U.S.A.* 42°9N 77°6W **312** D7
Cohoes *U.S.A.* 42°46N 73°42W **313** D11
Cohuna *Australia* 35°45S 144°15E **282** C6
Coiba, I. de *Panama* 7°30N 81°40W **320** E3
Coig → *Argentina* 51°0S 69°10W **336** D3
Coigeach, Rubha *U.K.* 58°6N 5°26W **167** C3
Coihaique *Chile* 45°30S 71°45W **336** C2
Coimbatore *India* 11°2N 76°59E **245** J3
Coimbra *Mato Grosso, Brazil* 19°55S 57°48W **331** D6
Coimbra *Portugal* 40°15N 8°27W **194** E2
Coimbra □ *Portugal* 40°12N 8°25W **194** E2
Coín *Spain* 36°40N 4°48W **195** J6
Coina *Portugal* 38°39N 9°2W **126** B2
Coipasa, L. de *Bolivia* 19°12S 68°7W **330** D4
Coipasa, Salar de *Bolivia* 19°26S 68°9W **330** D4
Coit Tower *San Francisco, U.S.A.* **136** a2
Cojata *Peru* 15°2S 69°25W **330** D4
Cojedes □ *Venezuela* 9°20N 68°20W **328** B4
Cojedes → *Venezuela* 8°34N 68°5W **328** B4
Cojimies *Ecuador* 0°20N 80°0W **328** C1
Cojocna *Romania* 46°45N 23°50E **183** D8
Cojutepequé *El Salv.* 13°41N 88°54W **320** D2
Čoka *Serbia* 45°57N 20°12E **182** E5
Coker *Nigeria* 6°28N 3°20E **124** B2
Cokeville *U.S.A.* 42°5N 110°57W **304** E8
Colaba *India* 18°53N 72°48E **130** B1
Colaba Pt. *India* 18°53N 72°48E **130** B1
Colac *Australia* 38°21S 143°35E **282** E5
Colachel = Kolachel *India* 8°10N 77°15E **245** K3
Colán *Peru* 5°0S 81°0W **330** B1
Colatina *Brazil* 19°32S 40°37W **333** E3
Colbeck, C. *Antarctica* 77°6S 157°48W **151** D13
Colbert *U.S.A.* 34°2N 83°13W **316** A6
Colborne *Canada* 44°0N 77°53W **312** C7
Colby *U.S.A.* 39°24N 101°3W **308** F3
Colca = Majes → *Peru* 16°40S 72°44W **330** D3
Colca, Cañón del *Peru* 15°50S 72°20W **330** D3
Colchester *Essex, U.K.* 51°54N 0°55E **169** F8
Colchester *Conn., U.S.A.* 41°35N 72°20W **313** E12
Cold Bay *U.S.A.* 55°12N 162°42W **303** J7
Cold L. *Canada* 54°33N 110°5W **297** C7
Cold Lake *Canada* 54°27N 110°10W **297** C6
Coldstream *B.C., Canada* 50°13N 119°11W **296** C5
Coldstream *Borders, U.K.* 55°39N 2°15W **167** F6
Coldwater *Ont., Canada* 44°42N 79°40W **312** B5
Coldwater *Kans., U.S.A.* 37°16N 99°20W **308** G4
Coldwater *Mich., U.S.A.* 41°57N 85°0W **311** C11
Coldwater *Ohio, U.S.A.* 40°29N 84°38W **311** D12
Coldwater, L. *U.S.A.* 41°48N 84°59W **311** C12
Cole Camp *U.S.A.* 38°28N 93°12W **310** F3
Coleambally *Australia* 34°49S 145°52E **283** C6
Colebrook *U.S.A.* 44°54N 71°30W **313** B13
Colegiales *Argentina* 34°34S 58°27W **117** B2
Coleman *Alta., Canada* 49°40N 114°30W **296** D6
Coleman *Fla., U.S.A.* 28°48N 82°4W **317** G7
Coleman *Tex., U.S.A.* 31°50N 99°26W **314** F5
Coleman → *Australia* 15°6S 141°38E **280** B3
Colenso *S. Africa* 28°44S 29°50E **271** C4
Coleraine *Vic., Australia* 37°36S 141°40E **282** D4
Coleraine *L'derry., U.K.* 55°8N 6°41W **166** A5
Coleridge, L. *N.Z.* 43°17S 171°30E **285** D6
Coleroon → *India* 11°25N 79°50E **245** J4
Colesberg *S. Africa* 30°45S 25°5E **270** D4
Coleville *U.S.A.* 38°34N 119°30W **306** G7
Colfax *Calif., U.S.A.* 39°6N 120°57W **306** F6
Colfax *Ill., U.S.A.* 40°34N 88°37W **311** D8
Colfax *Ind., U.S.A.* 40°12N 86°40W **311** D10
Colfax *Iowa, U.S.A.* 41°41N 93°14W **310** C3
Colfax *La., U.S.A.* 31°31N 92°42W **314** F8
Colfax *Wash., U.S.A.* 46°53N 117°22W **304** C5
Colhué Huapi, L. *Argentina* 45°30S 69°0W **336** C3
Colibaşi = Mioveni *Romania* 44°56N 24°54E **183** F9
Colibaşi *Moldova* 45°43N 28°11E **183** E13
Colibris, Pte. des *Guadeloupe* 16°17N 61°5W **322** e
Cólico *Italy* 46°8N 9°22E **198** B6
Colíder *Brazil* 10°45S 55°29W **331** C6
Coligny *Ain, France* 46°23N 5°21E **173** F12
Coligny *North West, S. Africa* 26°17S 26°15E **271** C4
Colihaut *Dominica* 15°29N 61°29W **323** k
Colima *Mexico* 19°14N 103°43W **318** D4
Colima □ *Mexico* 19°10N 104°0W **318** D4

Colima, Nevado de Mexico 19°33N 103°38W 318 D4
Colina Chile 33°13S 70°45W 334 C1
Colina do Norte Guinea-Biss. 12°28N 15°0W 262 C2
Colinas Goiás, Brazil 14°15S 48°2W 333 D2
Colinas Maranhão, Brazil 6°0S 44°10W 332 C3
Colindale U.K. 51°35N 0°15W 125 A2
Colindres Spain 43°24N 3°27W 194 B7
Colinton U.K. 55°55N 3°14W 121 B2
Coll U.K. 56°39N 6°34W 167 E2
Collahuasi Chile 21°5S 68°45W 334 A2
Collarada, Peña Spain 42°43N 0°29W 196 C4
Collarenebri Australia 29°33S 148°34E 281 D4
Colle di Val d'Elsa Italy 43°25N 11°7E 198 E8
Collécchio Italy 44°45N 10°13E 198 D7
Colleen Bawn Zimbabwe 21°0S 29°12E 269 G2
College U.S.A. 64°52N 147°49W 303 D11
College Park Ga., U.S.A. 33°39N 84°27W 113 C2
College Park Md., U.S.A. 38°59N 76°55W 143 B3
College Point U.S.A. 40°47N 73°50W 132 B2
College Station U.S.A. 30°37N 96°21W 314 F6
Collégien France 48°50N 2°41E 134 A4
Collesalvetti Italy 43°34N 10°27E 198 E7
Colleyville U.S.A. 32°52N 97°9W 120 A3
Colli Euganei ⌓ Italy 45°18N 11°43E 199 C8
Collie N.S.W., Australia 31°41S 148°18E 283 A8
Collie W. Austral., Australia 33°22S 116°8E 279 F2
Collier B. Australia 16°10S 124°15E 278 C3
Collier Ra. Australia 24°45S 119°10E 279 D2
Collier Range △ Australia 24°39S 119°7E 279 D2
Collier Row U.K. 51°35N 0°9E 125 A4
Colliers Wood U.K. 51°24N 0°10W 125 B2
Collierville U.S.A. 35°3N 89°40W 315 D10
Collina, Passo di Italy 44°2N 10°56E 198 D7
Collingwood Ont., Canada 44°29N 80°13W 312 B4
Collingwood N.Z. 40°41S 172°40E 285 A7
Collins Ont., Canada 50°17N 89°27W 298 B2
Collins Ga., U.S.A. 32°11N 82°7W 316 C7
Collins Mo., U.S.A. 37°54N 93°37W 310 G3
Collins Bay Canada 44°14N 76°36W 313 B8
Collinson Pen. Canada 69°58N 101°24W 294 D11
Collinsville Queens., Australia 20°30S 147°56E 280 C4
Collinsville Ill., U.S.A. 38°40N 89°59W 310 F7
Collipulli Chile 37°55S 72°30W 334 D1
Collo Algeria 36°58N 6°37E 261 A6
Collooney Ireland 54°11N 8°29W 166 B3
Colma U.S.A. 37°40N 122°27W 136 B2
Colmar France 48°5N 7°20E 173 D14
Colmars France 44°11N 6°39E 175 D10
Colmenar Spain 36°54N 4°20W 195 J6
Colmenar de Oreja Spain 40°6N 3°25W 194 E7
Colmenar Viejo Spain 40°39N 3°47W 194 E7
Colney Hatch U.K. 51°36N 0°9W 125 A3
Colo → Australia 33°25S 150°52E 283 B9
Cologne = Köln Germany 50°56N 6°57E 178 E2
Cologno Monzese Italy 45°31N 9°16E 128 A2
Coloma Calif., U.S.A. 38°48N 120°53W 306 G6
Coloma Mich., U.S.A. 42°11N 86°19W 311 B10
Colomb-Béchar = Béchar Algeria 31°38N 2°18W 261 B4
Colombes France 48°55N 2°15E 134 A2
Colombey-les-Belles France 48°32N 5°54E 173 D12
Colombey-les-Deux-Églises France 48°13N 4°50E 173 D11
Colômbia Brazil 20°10S 48°40W 333 F2
Colombia ■ S. Amer. 3°45N 73°0W 328 C3
Colombian Basin Caribbean 14°0N 76°0W 321 D5
Colombier St.-Martin 18°5N 63°4W 322 a
Colombo Sri Lanka 6°56N 79°58E 245 L4
Colomiers France 43°36N 1°21E 174 E5
Colón B. Aires, Argentina 33°53S 61°7W 334 C3
Colón Entre Ríos, Argentina 32°12S 58°10W 334 C4
Colón Cuba 22°42N 80°54W 320 B3
Colón Panama 9°20N 79°54W 320 c
Colón, Arch. de Ecuador 0°0 91°0W 330 a
Colón, Monumento a Barcelona, Spain 114 c3
Colón, Plaza de Madrid, Spain 127 a3
Colonarie St. Vincent 13°14N 61°8W 323 n
Colonia Micronesia 9°30N 138°10E 287 R16
Colonia 25 de Mayo Argentina 37°48S 67°41W 336 A3
Colònia de Sant Jordi Spain 39°19N 2°59E 206 B3
Colonia del Sacramento Uruguay 34°25S 57°50W 334 C4
Colonia Dora Argentina 28°34S 62°59W 334 B3
Colonia Güell Spain 41°21N 2°2E 114 A1
Colonial Beach U.S.A. 38°15N 76°58W 309 F15
Colonie U.S.A. 42°43N 73°50W 313 D11
Colonna, C. Italy 39°2N 17°12E 201 C10
Colonsay Sask., Canada 51°59N 105°52W 297 C7
Colonsay Argyll & Bute, U.K. 56°5N 6°12W 167 E2
Colorado □ U.S.A. 39°30N 105°30W 304 G11
Colorado → Argentina 39°50S 62°8W 336 A4
Colorado → N. Amer. 31°45N 114°40W 305 L6
Colorado → Tex., U.S.A. 28°36N 95°59W 314 G7
Colorado City U.S.A. 32°24N 100°52W 314 E4
Colorado Plateau U.S.A. 37°0N 111°0W 305 H8
Colorado River Aqueduct U.S.A. 33°50N 117°23W 307 L12
Colorado Springs U.S.A. 38°50N 104°49W 304 G11
Colorno Italy 44°56N 10°23E 198 D7
Colosseo Rome, Italy 136 c3
Colosseum = Colosseo Rome, Italy 136 c3
Colotlán Mexico 22°6N 103°16W 318 C4
Colquechaca Bolivia 18°40S 66°1W 331 D4
Colquitt U.S.A. 31°10N 84°44W 316 D5
Colstrip U.S.A. 45°53N 106°38W 304 D10
Colton U.S.A. 44°33N 74°56W 313 B10
Columbia Ala., U.S.A. 31°18N 85°7W 316 D4
Columbia Ill., U.S.A. 38°27N 90°12W 310 F6
Columbia Ky., U.S.A. 37°6N 85°18W 309 G11
Columbia La., U.S.A. 32°6N 92°5W 314 E8
Columbia Miss., U.S.A. 31°15N 89°50W 315 F10
Columbia Mo., U.S.A. 38°57N 92°20W 310 F4
Columbia Pa., U.S.A. 40°2N 76°30W 313 F8
Columbia S.C., U.S.A. 34°0N 81°2W 316 A8
Columbia Tenn., U.S.A. 35°37N 87°2W 315 D11
Columbia → N. Amer. 46°15N 124°5W 306 D2
Columbia, C. Canada 83°6N 69°57W 295 A18
Columbia, District of □ U.S.A. 38°55N 77°0W 309 F15
Columbia, Mt. Canada 52°8N 117°20W 296 C5
Columbia Basin U.S.A. 46°45N 119°5W 304 C4
Columbia City U.S.A. 41°10N 85°29W 311 C11
Columbia Falls U.S.A. 48°23N 114°11W 304 B6
Columbia Mts. Canada 52°0N 119°0W 296 C5
Columbia Plateau U.S.A. 44°0N 117°30W 304 E5
Columbiana U.S.A. 40°53N 80°42W 312 F4
Columbretes, Is. Spain 39°50N 0°50E 196 F5
Columbus Ga., U.S.A. 32°28N 84°59W 316 C5
Columbus Ind., U.S.A. 39°13N 85°55W 311 E11
Columbus Kans., U.S.A. 37°10N 94°50W 308 G6
Columbus Miss., U.S.A. 33°30N 88°25W 315 E10
Columbus Mont., U.S.A. 45°38N 109°15W 304 D9
Columbus N. Mex., U.S.A. 31°50N 107°38W 305 L10
Columbus Nebr., U.S.A. 41°26N 97°22W 308 E5
Columbus Ohio, U.S.A. 39°58N 83°0W 311 E13
Columbus Tex., U.S.A. 29°42N 96°33W 314 G6
Columbus Circle New York, U.S.A. 132 b2
Columbus Circle Washington, D.C., U.S.A. 143 b3
Columbus Grove U.S.A. 40°55N 84°4W 311 D12
Columbus Junction U.S.A. 41°17N 91°22W 310 C5
Columbus Monument = Colón, Monumento a Barcelona, Spain 114 c3
Columbus Park Jamaica 18°28N 77°25W 320 a
Columbus Park Boston, U.S.A. 116 b3
Colunga Spain 43°29N 5°16W 194 B5
Colusa U.S.A. 39°13N 122°1W 306 F4
Colville U.S.A. 48°33N 117°54W 304 B5
Colville → U.S.A. 70°25N 150°30W 303 A10
Colville, C. N.Z. 36°29S 175°21E 284 C4
Colville Channel N.Z. 36°25S 175°27E 284 C4
Colville Ridge Pac. Oc. 30°0S 180°0E 277 G15
Colwood Canada 48°26N 123°29W 306 B3
Colwyn Bay U.K. 53°18N 3°44W 168 D4
Coma Ethiopia 8°29N 36°53E 257 F4
Comácchio Italy 44°42N 12°11E 199 D9
Comalcalco Mexico 18°16N 93°13W 319 D6
Comallo Argentina 41°0S 70°5W 336 B2
Comana Romania 44°10N 26°10E 183 F11
Comanche U.S.A. 31°54N 98°36W 314 F5
Comandante Arbues = Mirandópolis Brazil 21°9S 51°6W 335 A5
Comandante Ferraz Antarctica 62°30S 58°0W 151 C18
Comandante Luis Piedrabuena Argentina 49°59S 68°54W 336 C3
Comănești Romania 46°25N 26°26E 183 D11
Comarapa Bolivia 17°54S 64°29W 331 D5
Comarnic Romania 45°15N 25°38E 183 E10
Comayagua Honduras 14°25N 87°37W 320 D2
Combahee → U.S.A. 32°31N 80°31W 316 C9
Combara Australia 31°10S 148°22E 283 A8
Combarbalá Chile 31°11S 71°2W 334 C1
Combault France 48°48N 2°37E 134 B4
Combe Martin U.K. 51°12N 4°3W 169 F3
Combeaufontaine France 47°38N 5°54E 173 E12
Comber Ont., Canada 42°14N 82°33W 312 D2
Comber Down, U.K. 54°33N 5°45W 166 B6
Combermere Canada 45°22N 77°37W 312 A7
Combermere Bay Burma 19°37N 93°34E 241 F4
Comblain-au-Pont Belgium 50°29N 5°35E 170 D5
Combourg France 48°25N 1°46W 172 D5
Comboyne Australia 31°34S 152°27E 283 A10
Combrailles France 46°8N 2°8E 173 F9
Combronde France 45°58N 3°5E 174 C7
Comer Ala., U.S.A. 32°2N 85°23W 316 C4
Comer Ga., U.S.A. 34°4N 83°8W 316 A6
Comeragh Mts. Ireland 52°18N 7°34W 166 D4
Comércio, Praça do Portugal 38°41N 9°9W 126 A2
Comerío Puerto Rico 18°12N 66°12W 321 b
Comet Australia 23°36S 148°38E 280 C4
Comilla Bangla. 23°28N 91°10E 241 D3
Comino Malta 36°1N 14°20E 206 E7
Comino, C. Italy 40°32N 9°49E 200 B2
Cómiso Italy 36°56N 14°36E 201 F7
Comitán de Domínguez Mexico 16°15N 92°8W 319 D6
Commentry France 46°20N 2°46E 173 F9
Commerce Calif., U.S.A. 34°0N 118°9W 126 B4
Commerce Ga., U.S.A. 34°12N 83°28W 316 A6
Commerce Tex., U.S.A. 33°15N 95°54W 314 E7
Commercy France 48°43N 5°34E 173 D12
Commissioner's Pt. Bermuda 32°19N 64°49W 153 a
Committee B. Canada 68°30N 86°30W 295 D14
Commodore, C. Canada 44°47N 80°54W 312 B4
Commonwealth B. Antarctica 67°0S 144°0E 151 C10
Commoron Cr. → Australia 28°22S 150°8E 281 D5
Communism Pk. = imeni Ismail Samani, Pik Tajikistan 39°0N 72°2E 217 E8
Como Italy 45°47N 9°5E 198 C6
Como, L. di Italy 46°0N 9°11E 198 B6
Comodoro Rivadavia Argentina 45°50S 67°40W 336 C3
Comoé □ Ivory C. 6°48N 3°30W 262 D4
Comoé → Ivory C. 5°12N 3°44W 262 D4
Comoé △ Ivory C. 9°0N 3°35W 262 D4
Comorâște Romania 45°10N 21°35E 182 E6
Comorin, C. = Kannyakumari India 8°3N 77°40E 245 K3
Comoros ■ Ind. Oc. 12°10S 44°15E 272 a
Comox Canada 49°42N 124°55W 296 D4
Company's Gardens Cape Town, S. Africa 118 c2
Compass Lake U.S.A. 30°36N 85°24W 316 E4
Compiègne France 49°24N 2°50E 173 C9
Comporta Portugal 38°22N 8°46W 195 G2
Compostela Nayarit, Mexico 21°14N 104°55W 318 C4
Compostela Phil. 7°40N 126°2E 233 H6
Compostela Valley □ Phil. 7°50N 126°0E 233 H5
Comprida, I. Brazil 24°50S 47°42W 335 A6
Compton Qué., Canada 45°14N 71°49W 313 A13
Compton Calif., U.S.A. 33°53N 118°13W 307 M8
Comrat Moldova 46°18N 28°40E 183 D13
Comunidad Peru 13°59S 69°20W 330 C4
Con Cuong Vietnam 19°2N 104°54E 236 C5
Con Dao △ Vietnam 8°42N 106°35E 237 H6
Con Son, Dao Vietnam 8°41N 106°37E 237 H6
Cona Niyeu Argentina 41°58S 67°0W 336 B3
Conakry Guinea 9°29N 13°49W 262 D2
Conara Australia 41°50S 147°26E 281 G4
Conargo Australia 35°16S 145°10E 283 C6
Concarneau France 47°52N 3°56W 172 E3
Conceição Paraíba, Brazil 7°33S 38°31W 332 C4
Conceição Mozam. 18°47S 36°7E 269 F4
Conceição, I. da Brazil 22°52S 43°6W 135 B2
Conceição da Barra Brazil 18°35S 39°45W 333 E4
Conceição do Araguaia Brazil 8°0S 49°2W 332 C2
Conceição do Canindé Brazil 7°54S 41°34W 332 C3
Conceição do Maú Brazil 3°35N 59°53W 329 C6
Conceição do Paraiba = Capela Brazil 10°30S 37°0W 332 D4
Concepción Argentina 27°20S 65°35W 334 B2
Concepción Bolivia 16°15S 62°8W 331 D5
Concepción Chile 36°50S 73°0W 334 D1
Concepción Paraguay 23°22S 57°26W 334 A4
Concepción Peru 11°54S 75°19W 330 C2
Concepción Tarlac, Phil. 15°27N 120°47E 232 D3
Concepción □ Chile 37°0S 72°30W 334 D1
Concepción, Est. de Chile 50°30S 74°55W 336 D1
Concepción, L. Bolivia 17°20S 61°20W 331 D5
Concepción, Pta. Mexico 26°53N 111°50W 318 B2
Concepción del Oro Mexico 24°38N 101°25W 318 C4
Concepción del Uruguay Argentina 32°35S 58°20W 334 C4
Conception, Pt. U.S.A. 34°27N 120°28W 307 L6
Conception B. Nfld. & L., Canada 47°45N 53°0W 299 C9
Conception B. Namibia 23°55S 14°22E 270 B1
Conception I. Bahamas 23°52N 75°9W 321 B4
Concession Zimbabwe 17°27S 30°56E 269 F3
Conchali Chile 33°22S 70°39W 137 B2
Conchas Dam U.S.A. 35°22N 104°11W 305 J11
Conches-en-Ouche France 48°58N 0°56E 172 D7
Concho U.S.A. 34°28N 109°36W 305 J9
Concho → U.S.A. 31°34N 99°43W 314 F5
Conchos → Chihuahua, Mexico 29°35N 104°25W 318 B4
Conchos → Tamaulipas, Mexico 24°55N 97°38W 319 B5
Concord N.S.W., Australia 33°52S 151°6E 139 B1
Concord Ont., Canada 43°48N 79°29W 141 A2
Concord Grenada 12°7N 61°44W 323 q
Concord Calif., U.S.A. 37°59N 122°2W 306 H4
Concord Ga., U.S.A. 33°5N 84°27W 316 B5
Concord Mich., U.S.A. 42°11N 84°38W 311 B12
Concord Mo., U.S.A. 38°32N 90°23W 310 F6
Concord N.C., U.S.A. 35°25N 80°35W 315 D14
Concord N.H., U.S.A. 43°12N 71°32W 313 C13
Concorde, Place de la Paris, France 134 b3
Concordia Antarctica 75°6S 123°23E 151 D9
Concordia Argentina 31°20S 58°2W 334 C4
Concórdia Amazonas, Brazil 4°36S 66°36W 328 D4
Concórdia Sta. Catarina, Brazil 27°14S 52°1W 335 B5
Concordia Sinaloa, Mexico 23°17N 106°4W 318 C3
Concordia Kans., U.S.A. 39°34N 97°40W 308 F5
Concordia Mo., U.S.A. 38°59N 93°34W 310 F3
Concordia Univ. Montréal, Canada 130 c1
Concorezzo Italy 45°35N 9°19E 128 A2
Concrete U.S.A. 48°32N 121°45W 304 B3
Conda Angola 11°9S 14°20E 265 E2
Condah Australia 37°57S 141°44E 282 D4
Condamine Australia 26°56S 150°9E 281 D5
Condat France 45°21N 2°46E 174 C6
Condé Angola 10°50S 14°37E 265 E2
Conde Brazil 11°49S 37°37W 333 D4
Conde S. Dak., U.S.A. 45°9N 98°6W 308 C4
Condé-sur-Noireau France 48°51N 0°33W 172 D6
Condet Indonesia 6°17S 106°51E 122 A2
Condeúba Brazil 14°52S 42°0W 333 D3
Condobolin Australia 33°4S 147°6E 283 B7
Condom France 43°57N 0°22E 174 E4
Condon U.S.A. 45°14N 120°11W 304 D3
Conegliano Italy 45°53N 12°18E 199 C9
Conejera, I. = Conills, I. des Spain 39°11N 2°58E 206 B3
Conejos Mexico 26°14N 103°53W 318 B4
Conemaugh → U.S.A. 40°28N 79°19W 312 F5
Conero ⌓ Italy 43°32N 13°35E 199 E10
Coney I. = Serangoon, Pulau Singapore 1°23N 103°55E 138 A3
Coney Island U.S.A. 40°34N 74°0W 132 C2
Conflict Group Papua N. G. 10°47S 151°45E 286 F6
Confolens France 46°2N 0°40E 174 B4
Confuso → Paraguay 25°9S 57°34W 334 B4
Congaree → U.S.A. 33°44N 80°38W 316 B9
Congaree △ U.S.A. 33°47N 80°47W 316 B9
Congaz Moldova 46°7N 28°36E 183 D13
Congerville U.S.A. 40°38N 89°11W 310 D7
Conghua China 23°36N 113°31E 229 F9
Congjiang China 25°43N 108°52E 228 E7
Congleton U.K. 53°10N 2°13W 168 D5
Congo Brazil 7°48S 36°40W 332 C4
Congo (Brazzaville) = Congo ■ Africa 1°0S 16°0E 264 C3
Congo (Kinshasa) = Congo, Dem. Rep. of the ■ Africa 3°0S 23°0E 265 C4
Congo ■ Africa 1°0S 16°0E 264 C3
Congo → Africa 6°4S 12°24E 265 D2
Congo, Dem. Rep. of the ■ Africa 3°0S 23°0E 265 C4
Congo Basin Africa 0°10S 24°30E 254 G6
Congo Free State = Congo, Dem. Rep. of the ■ Africa 3°0S 23°0E 265 C4
Congonhas Brazil 20°30S 43°52W 333 F3
Congonhas, São Paulo ✈ (CGH) Brazil 23°38S 46°39W 137 B2
Congress U.S.A. 34°9N 112°51W 305 J7
Conguillio △ Chile 38°40S 71°42W 336 A2
Conil de la Frontera Spain 36°17N 6°10W 195 J4
Conills, I. des Spain 39°11N 2°58E 206 B3
Conimbla △ Australia 33°45S 148°28E 283 B8
Coniston Canada 46°29N 80°51W 298 C3
Conjeeveram = Kanchipuram India 12°52N 79°45E 245 H4
Conklin Alta., Canada 55°38N 111°5W 297 B6
Conklin N.Y., U.S.A. 42°2N 75°49W 313 D9
Conkouati ⌓ Congo 3°50S 11°28E 264 C2
Conlendas, Pta. das Azores 38°38N 27°14W 153 d1
Conley → U.S.A. 33°40N 84°17W 113 C3
Conn, L. Ireland 54°3N 9°15W 166 B2
Connaught □ Ireland 53°43N 9°12W 166 C2
Connaught Place Delhi, India 120 b2
Conneaut U.S.A. 41°57N 80°34W 312 E4
Conneautville U.S.A. 41°45N 80°22W 312 E4
Connecticut □ U.S.A. 41°30N 72°45W 313 E12
Connecticut → U.S.A. 41°16N 72°20W 313 E12
Connell U.S.A. 46°40N 118°52W 304 C4
Connellsville U.S.A. 40°1N 79°35W 312 F5
Connemara Ireland 53°29N 9°45W 166 C2
Connemara △ Ireland 53°32N 9°52W 166 C2
Conner Phil. 17°48N 121°19E 232 C3
Connerré France 48°3N 0°30E 172 D7
Connersville U.S.A. 39°39N 85°8W 311 E11
Connors Ra. Australia 21°40S 149°10E 280 C4
Conoble Australia 32°55S 144°33E 283 B6
Conococha Peru 10°7S 77°18W 330 C2
Cononaco → Ecuador 1°32S 75°35W 328 D2
Conques France 44°36N 2°23E 174 D6
Conquest Canada 51°32N 107°14W 297 C7
Conquista = Vitória da Conquista Brazil 14°51S 40°51W 333 D3
Conrad Iowa, U.S.A. 42°14N 92°52W 310 B4
Conrad Mont., U.S.A. 48°10N 111°57W 304 B8
Conrad Rise S. Ocean 53°0S 41°0E 151 B5
Conran, C. Australia 37°49S 148°44E 283 D8
Conroe U.S.A. 30°19N 95°27W 314 F7
Consecon Canada 44°0N 77°31W 312 C7
Conselheiro Lafaiete Brazil 20°40S 43°48W 333 F3
Conselheiro Pena Brazil 19°10S 41°30W 333 E3
Consell Spain 39°40N 2°49E 206 B3
Conselve Italy 45°14N 11°52E 199 C8
Conservatori, Palazzo dei Rome, Italy 136 c3
Consett U.K. 54°51N 1°50W 168 C6
Consolação Brazil 23°32S 46°38W 137 B2
Consort Canada 52°1N 110°46W 297 C6
Constance = Konstanz Germany 47°40N 9°10E 179 H5
Constance, L. = Bodensee Europe 47°35N 9°25E 179 H5
Constanța Romania 44°14N 28°38E 183 F13
Constanța □ Romania 44°15N 28°15E 183 F13
Constantia S. Africa 34°2S 18°26E 118 B1
Constantina Spain 37°51N 5°40W 195 H5
Constantine Algeria 36°25N 6°42E 261 A6
Constantine Mich., U.S.A. 41°50N 85°40W 311 C11
Constantine □ Algeria 36°30N 6°40E 261 A6
Constantine, Arch of = Costantino, Arco di Rome, Italy 136 c3
Constantine, C. U.S.A. 58°24N 158°54W 303 G8
Constantinople = İstanbul Turkey 41°0N 28°58E 122 C1
Constitución B. Aires, Argentina 34°38S 58°23W 117 B2
Constitución Chile 35°20S 72°30W 334 D1
Constitución Uruguay 31°0S 57°50W 334 C4
Constitución de 1857 △ Mexico 32°4N 115°55W 318 A1
Constitution U.S.A. 33°42N 84°20W 113 B2
Constitution Avenue Washington, D.C., U.S.A. 143 b2
Constitution Square = Syntagma Square Athens, Greece 112 b2
Consuegra Spain 39°28N 3°36W 195 F7
Consul Canada 49°20N 109°30W 297 D7
Contact U.S.A. 41°46N 114°45W 304 F6
Contagem Brazil 19°55S 44°6W 333 E3
Contai India 21°54N 87°46E 243 J12
Contamana Peru 7°19S 74°55W 330 B3
Contarini Dal Zaffo, Palazzo Venice, Italy 142 c2
Contas → Brazil 14°17S 39°1W 333 D4
Contes France 43°49N 7°19E 175 E11
Continental U.S.A. 41°6N 84°16W 311 C12
Contoocook U.S.A. 43°13N 71°45W 313 C13
Contra Costa Mozam. 25°9S 33°30E 271 C5
Contres France 47°24N 1°26E 172 E8
Contrexéville France 48°10N 5°53E 173 D12
Controller B. U.S.A. 60°7N 144°15W 303 F11
Contumaza Peru 7°23S 78°57W 330 B2
Contwoyto L. Canada 65°42N 110°50W 294 D9
Convención Colombia 8°28N 73°21W 328 B3
Conversano Italy 40°58N 17°7E 201 B10
Converse U.S.A. 40°35N 85°52W 311 D11
Convoy U.S.A. 40°55N 84°43W 311 D12
Conway = Conwy U.K. 53°17N 3°50W 168 D4
Conway = Conwy → U.K. 53°17N 3°50W 168 D4
Conway Australia 20°24S 148°41E 280 b
Conway Ont., Canada 44°6N 76°54W 312 B8
Conway Ark., U.S.A. 35°5N 92°26W 314 D8
Conway Fla., U.S.A. 28°30N 81°19W 133 B2
Conway N.H., U.S.A. 43°59N 71°7W 313 C13
Conway S.C., U.S.A. 33°51N 79°3W 315 E15
Conway, C. Australia 20°34S 148°46E 280 b
Conway, L. S. Austral., Australia 28°17S 135°35E 281 D2
Conway, L. Fla., U.S.A. 28°28N 81°21W 133 B2
Conwy U.K. 53°17N 3°50W 168 D4
Conwy □ U.K. 53°10N 3°44W 168 D4
Conwy → U.K. 53°17N 3°50W 168 D4
Conyers U.S.A. 33°40N 84°1W 316 B5
Coober Pedy Australia 29°1S 134°43E 281 D1
Cooch Behar = Koch Bihar India 26°22N 89°29E 241 B2
Coogee Australia 33°55S 151°16E 139 B2
Cooinda Australia 13°15S 130°5E 278 B5
Cook S. Austral., Australia 30°37S 130°25E 279 F5
Cook Minn., U.S.A. 47°51N 92°41W 308 B7
Cook, B. Chile 55°10S 70°0W 336 E3
Cook, C. Canada 50°8N 127°55W 296 C3
Cook, Mt. = Aoraki Mount Cook N.Z. 43°36S 170°9E 285 D5
Cook, Récif de N. Cal. 19°25S 163°50E 288 d
Cook B. Vanuatu 18°46S 169°15E 287 H7
Cook Inlet U.S.A. 60°0N 152°0W 303 G10
Cook Is. ⧄ Pac. Oc. 17°0S 160°0W 289 J12
Cook Strait N.Z. 41°15S 174°29E 284 H3
Cooke Plains Australia 35°23S 139°34E 282 C3
Cookeville U.S.A. 36°10N 85°30W 315 C12
Cookhouse S. Africa 32°44S 25°47E 270 D4
Cooks Hammock U.S.A. 29°56N 83°17W 316 F6
Cooks Harbour Canada 51°36N 55°52W 299 B8
Cookshire Canada 45°25N 71°38W 313 A13
Cookstown Ont., Canada 44°11N 79°42W 312 B5
Cookstown Tyrone, U.K. 54°38N 6°45W 166 B5
Cooksville Canada 43°35N 79°38W 141 B1
Cooktown Australia 15°30S 145°16E 280 B4
Coolabah Australia 31°1S 146°43E 283 A7
Cooladdi Australia 26°37S 145°23E 281 D4
Coolah Australia 31°48S 149°41E 283 A8
Coolah Tops △ Australia 31°52S 150°0E 283 A9
Coolamon Australia 34°46S 147°8E 283 C7
Coolgardie Australia 30°55S 121°8E 279 F3
Coolidge Ariz., U.S.A. 32°59N 111°31W 305 K8
Coolidge Ga., U.S.A. 31°1N 83°52W 316 D6
Coolidge Dam U.S.A. 33°10N 110°32W 305 K8
Cooma Australia 36°12S 149°8E 283 D8
Coon Rapids Iowa, U.S.A. 41°53N 94°41W 310 C2
Coon Rapids Minn., U.S.A. 45°9N 93°19W 308 C7
Coonabarabran Australia 31°14S 149°18E 283 A8
Coonalpyn Australia 35°43S 139°52E 282 C3
Coonamble Australia 30°56S 148°27E 283 A8
Coonana Australia 31°0S 123°0E 279 F3
Coonana ✪ Australia 30°51S 122°53E 279 F3
Coondapoor India 13°42N 74°40E 245 H2
Cooninnie, L. Australia 26°4S 139°59E 281 D2
Coonoor India 11°21N 76°45E 245 J3
Cooper U.S.A. 33°23N 95°42W 314 E7
Cooper → U.S.A. 32°50N 79°56W 316 C10
Cooper City U.S.A. 26°3N 80°16W 129 B1
Cooper Cr. → Australia 28°29S 137°46E 281 D2
Cooper Ridge Pac. Oc. 10°0N 150°30W 289 G12
Cooper's Hill Jamaica 18°4N 76°51W 320 a
Cooperstown N. Dak., U.S.A. 47°27N 98°8W 308 B4
Cooperstown N.Y., U.S.A. 42°42N 74°56W 313 D10
Coopersville U.S.A. 43°4N 85°57W 311 A11
Coopracambra △ Australia 37°20S 149°20E 283 D8
Coora → Trin. & Tob. 10°10N 61°28W 323 t
Coorabie Australia 31°54S 132°18E 279 F5
Coorong, The Australia 35°50S 139°20E 282 C3
Coorong △ Australia 36°0S 139°29E 282 D3
Coorow Australia 29°53S 116°2E 279 E2
Cooroy Australia 26°22S 152°54E 281 D5
Coos Bay U.S.A. 43°22N 124°13W 304 E1
Coosa → U.S.A. 32°30N 86°16W 315 E11
Cootamundra Australia 34°36S 148°1E 283 C8
Cootehill Ireland 54°4N 7°5W 166 B4
Copacabana Brazil 22°58S 43°11W 135 B1
Copahue Paso Argentina 37°49S 71°8W 334 D1
Copainalá Mexico 17°4N 93°18W 319 D6
Copake U.S.A. 42°7N 73°33W 313 D11
Copalnic Mănăştur Romania 47°30N 23°41E 183 C8
Copán Honduras 14°50N 89°9W 320 D2
Copatana Brazil 2°48S 67°4W 328 D4
Copceac Moldova 45°51N 28°42E 183 E13
Cope Colo., U.S.A. 39°40N 102°51W 304 G12
Cope S.C., U.S.A. 33°23N 81°0W 316 B8
Cope, C. Spain 37°26N 1°28W 197 H3
Copeland U.S.A. 25°57N 81°22W 317 K8
Copenhagen = København Denmark 55°40N 12°26E 118 A2
Copenhagen U.S.A. 43°54N 75°41W 313 C9
Copertino Italy 40°16N 18°3E 201 B11
Copiapó Chile 27°30S 70°20W 334 B1
Copiapó → Chile 27°19S 70°56W 334 B1
Coplay U.S.A. 40°44N 75°29W 313 F9
Copley Australia 30°36S 138°26E 282 A3
Copo △ Argentina 25°53S 61°57W 334 B3
Copp L. Canada 60°14N 114°40W 296 A6
Copparo Italy 44°54N 11°49E 199 D8
Coppell U.S.A. 32°57N 96°59W 120 A4
Coppename → Suriname 5°48N 55°55W 329 B6
Copper → U.S.A. 60°18N 145°3W 303 F11
Copper Canyon = Barranca del Cobre △ Mexico 27°18N 107°40W 318 B3
Copper Center U.S.A. 61°58N 145°18W 303 F11
Copper City = Invermere Canada 50°30N 116°2W 296 C5
Copper Harbor U.S.A. 47°28N 87°53W 308 B10
Copper Queen Zimbabwe 17°29S 29°18E 269 F2
Copperas Cove U.S.A. 31°8N 97°54W 314 F6
Copperbelt □ Zambia 13°15S 27°30E 269 E2
Coppermine = Kugluktuk Canada 67°50N 115°5W 294 D8
Coppermine → Canada 67°49N 116°4W 294 D8
Copperopolis U.S.A. 37°58N 120°38W 306 H6
Copșa Mică Romania 46°7N 24°15E 183 D9
Coquet → U.K. 55°20N 1°32W 168 B6
Coquilhatville = Mbandaka Dem. Rep. of the Congo 0°1N 18°18E 264 B3
Coquille U.S.A. 43°11N 124°11W 304 E1
Coquimbo Chile 30°0S 71°20W 334 C1
Coquimbo □ Chile 31°0S 71°0W 334 C1
Coquitlam Canada 49°17N 122°45W 296 D4
Corabia Romania 43°48N 24°30E 183 G9
Coração de Jesus Brazil 16°43S 44°22W 333 E3
Coracora Peru 15°5S 73°45W 330 D3
Coraki Australia 28°59S 153°17E 281 D5
Coral U.S.A. 40°29N 79°10W 312 F5
Coral B. Phil. 8°25N 117°20E 233 G1
Coral Bay Australia 23°8S 113°46E 278 D1
Coral Gables U.S.A. 25°43N 80°16W 129 D1
Coral Harbour Bahamas 24°58N 77°28W 153 b
Coral Harbour Nunavut, Canada 64°8N 83°10W 295 E15
Coral Heights Bahamas 25°0N 77°27W 153 b
Coral Hills U.S.A. 38°51N 76°55W 143 B3
Coral Sea Pac. Oc. 15°0S 150°0E 276 C9
Coral Sea Basin Pac. Oc. 14°0S 152°0E 288 J7
Coral Sea Islands Terr. □ Australia 20°0S 155°0E 276 D9
Coral Springs U.S.A. 26°16N 80°16W 317 J9
Corales del Rosario △ Colombia 10°8N 75°46W 328 A2
Coralville U.S.A. 41°40N 91°35W 310 C5
Coralville L. U.S.A. 41°42N 91°33W 310 C5
Corangamite, L. Australia 38°5S 143°30E 282 E5
Corantijn = Courantyne → S. Amer. 5°50N 57°8W 329 B6
Coraopolis U.S.A. 40°31N 80°10W 312 F4
Corato Italy 41°9N 16°25E 201 A9
Corbeil-Essonnes France 48°36N 2°26E 173 D9
Corbeiro, C. W. Sahara 21°50N 17°0W 260 D1
Corbett △ India 29°20N 79°0E 243 E8
Corbie France 49°54N 2°30E 173 C9
Corbières France 42°55N 2°35E 174 F6
Corbigny France 47°16N 3°40E 173 E10
Corbin U.S.A. 36°57N 84°6W 309 G11
Corbones → Spain 37°36N 5°39W 195 H5
Corbu Romania 44°25N 28°39E 183 F13
Corby U.K. 52°30N 0°41W 169 E7
Corcaigh = Cork Ireland 51°54N 8°29W 166 E3
Corcoran U.S.A. 36°6N 119°33W 306 J7
Corcovado, Cristo Redentor Brazil 22°57S 43°12W 135 B1
Corcovado △ Chile 43°25S 72°45W 336 B2
Corcovado △ Costa Rica 8°33N 83°35W 320 E3
Cordele U.S.A. 31°58N 83°47W 316 D6
Cordell U.S.A. 35°17N 98°59W 314 D5
Cordenòns Italy 45°59N 12°42E 199 C9
Cordes-sur-Ciel France 44°5N 1°57E 174 D5
Cordillera Azul △ Peru 7°30S 76°30W 330 B2
Cordillera de los Picachos △ Colombia 2°39N 74°30W 328 C3
Cordisburgo Brazil 19°7S 44°21W 333 E3
Córdoba Argentina 31°20S 64°10W 334 C3
Córdoba Veracruz, Mexico 18°53N 96°56W 319 D5
Córdoba Spain 37°50N 4°50W 195 H6
Córdoba □ Argentina 31°22S 64°15W 334 C3
Córdoba □ Colombia 8°20N 75°40W 328 B2
Córdoba □ Spain 38°5N 5°0W 195 G6
Córdoba, Sierra de Argentina 31°10S 64°25W 334 C3
Cordon Phil. 16°42N 121°32E 232 C3
Cordova U.S.A. 60°33N 145°45W 303 F11
Corella Spain 42°7N 1°48W 196 C3
Corella → Australia 19°34S 140°47E 280 B3
Coremas Brazil 7°1S 37°58W 332 C4
Corentyne = Courantyne → S. Amer. 5°50N 57°8W 329 B6
Corfield Australia 21°40S 143°21E 280 C3
Corfu = Kerkyra Greece 39°38N 19°50E 206 B9
Corfu U.S.A. 42°57N 78°24W 312 D6
Corfu ✈ (CFU) Greece 39°35N 19°54E 204 B1
Corfu, Str. of = Kerkyras, Notio Steno Greece 39°34N 20°0E 206 B10
Corgo = O Corgo Spain 42°56N 7°25W 194 C3
Corguinho Brazil 19°53S 54°52W 331 D7
Cori Italy 41°39N 12°55E 200 A5
Coria Spain 39°58N 6°33W 194 F4
Coria del Río Spain 37°16N 6°3W 195 H4
Coricudgy Australia 32°51S 150°24E 283 B9
Corigliano Cálabro Italy 39°36N 16°31E 201 C9
Corimba, Barra de Angola 8°52S 13°9E 265 D2
Coringa Is. Australia 16°58S 149°58E 280 B4
Corinth = Korinthos Greece 37°56N 22°55E 204 D4
Corinth Grenada 12°2N 61°40W 323 q
Corinth Ky., U.S.A. 38°30N 84°34W 311 F12
Corinth Miss., U.S.A. 34°56N 88°31W 315 D10
Corinth N.Y., U.S.A. 43°15N 73°49W 313 C11
Corinth, G. of = Korinthiakos Kolpos Greece 38°16N 22°30E 204 C4
Corinth Canal Greece 37°58N 23°0E 204 D4
Corinto Brazil 18°20S 44°30W 333 E3
Corinto Nic. 12°30N 87°10W 320 D2
Coriole Somalia 1°47N 44°32E 257 G5
Corisco Eq. Guin. 0°55N 9°18E 264 B1
Cork Ireland 51°54N 8°29W 166 E3
Cork □ Ireland 51°57N 8°40W 166 E3
Cork Harbour Ireland 51°47N 8°16W 166 E3
Corlay France 48°20N 3°5W 172 D3
Corleone Italy 37°49N 13°18E 200 E6
Corleto Perticara Italy 40°23N 16°2E 201 B9
Çorlu Turkey 41°11N 27°49E 203 E11
Cormack L. Canada 60°56N 121°37W 296 A4
Cormano Italy 45°32N 9°10E 128 A2
Cormòns Italy 45°58N 13°28E 199 C10
Cormorant Canada 54°14N 100°35W 297 C8
Cormorant L. Canada 54°15N 100°50W 297 C8
Corn Is. = Maíz, Is. del Nic. 12°15N 83°4W 320 D3
Cornalvo ⌓ Spain 39°1N 6°13W 195 F4
Cornaredo Italy 45°30N 9°1E 128 A1
Cornélio Procópio Brazil 23°7S 50°40W 335 A5
Cornell U.S.A. 41°0N 88°44W 311 D8
Corner Brook Canada 48°57N 57°58W 299 C8
Corner della Regina, Palazzo Venice, Italy 142 b2
Corner Inlet Australia 38°45S 146°20E 283 E7
Corner Seamounts Atl. Oc. 35°0N 52°0W 152 C6
Corner Spinelli, Palazzo Venice, Italy 142 b2
Cornești Moldova 47°21N 28°1E 183 C13
Corneto = Tarquinia Italy 42°15N 11°45E 199 F8
Corníglio Italy 44°29N 10°5E 198 D7
Corning Ark., U.S.A. 36°25N 90°35W 315 C9
Corning Calif., U.S.A. 39°56N 122°11W 304 G2
Corning Iowa, U.S.A. 40°59N 94°44W 310 D2
Corning N.Y., U.S.A. 42°9N 77°3W 312 D7
Corno Grande Italy 42°28N 13°34E 199 F10
Cornwall Ont., Canada 45°2N 74°44W 313 A10
Cornwall Pa., U.S.A. 40°17N 76°25W 313 F8
Cornwall □ Jamaica 18°15N 77°54W 320 a
Cornwall □ U.K. 50°26N 4°40W 169 G3
Cornwall I. Canada 77°37N 94°38W 295 B13
Cornwallis I. Canada 75°8N 95°0W 295 B13
Cornwell U.S.A. 27°23N 81°6W 317 H8
Corny Pt. Australia 34°55S 137°0E 282 C2
Coro Venezuela 11°25N 69°41W 328 A4
Coroaci Brazil 18°35S 42°17W 333 E3
Coroatá Brazil 4°8S 44°0W 332 B3
Corocoro Bolivia 17°15S 68°28W 330 D4
Corocoro, I. Venezuela 8°30N 60°10W 329 B5
Coroico Bolivia 16°0S 67°50W 330 D4
Coromandel Brazil 18°28S 47°13W 333 E2
Coromandel N.Z. 36°45S 175°31E 284 C4
Coromandel Coast India 12°30N 81°0E 245 H5
Coromandel Pen. N.Z. 37°0S 175°45E 284 D4
Coromandel Ra. N.Z. 37°0S 175°40E 284 D4
Coron Phil. 12°1N 120°12E 232 E3
Coron B. Phil. 11°54N 120°8E 233 F3
Coron I. Phil. 11°55N 120°14E 233 F3
Corona Calif., U.S.A. 33°53N 117°34W 307 M9
Corona N. Mex., U.S.A. 34°15N 105°36W 305 J11
Coronado U.S.A. 32°41N 117°10W 307 N9
Coronado, B. de Costa Rica 9°0N 83°40W 320 E3
Coronados, G. de los Chile 41°40S 74°0W 336 B2
Coronados, Is. Los Mexico 32°26N 117°19W 307 N9
Coronation Canada 52°5N 111°27W 296 C6
Coronation Gulf Canada 68°25N 110°0W 294 D10
Coronation I. Antarctica 60°45S 46°0W 151 C18
Coronation Is. Australia 14°57S 124°55E 278 B3
Coronda Argentina 31°58S 60°56W 334 C3
Coronel Chile 37°0S 73°10W 334 D1
Coronel Bogado Paraguay 27°11S 56°18W 334 B4
Coronel Dorrego Argentina 38°40S 61°10W 334 D3
Coronel Fabriciano Brazil 19°31S 42°38W 333 E3
Coronel Murta Brazil 16°37S 42°11W 333 E3
Coronel Oviedo Paraguay 25°24S 56°30W 334 B4
Coronel Ponce Brazil 15°34S 55°1W 331 D6
Coronel Pringles Argentina 38°0S 61°30W 334 D3
Coronel Suárez Argentina 37°30S 61°52W 334 D3
Coronel Vidal Argentina 37°28S 57°45W 334 D4
Corongo Peru 8°30S 77°53W 330 B2
Coropuna, Nevado Peru 15°30S 72°41W 330 D3
Corossol St. Barts 17°54N 62°51W 322 a
Çorovodë Albania 40°31N 20°14E 202 F4
Corowa Australia 35°58S 146°21E 283 C7
Corozal Colombia 9°19N 75°18W 328 B2
Corozal □ Belize 18°23N 88°23W 319 D7
Corozal Pt. Trin. & Tob. 10°45N 61°37W 323 t
Corps France 44°50N 5°56E 175 D9
Corpus Argentina 27°10S 55°30W 335 B4
Corpus Christi U.S.A. 27°47N 97°24W 314 H6
Corpus Christi, L. U.S.A. 28°2N 97°52W 314 G6
Corque Bolivia 18°20S 67°41W 330 D4
Corral Chile 39°52S 73°26W 336 A2
Corral de Almaguer Spain 39°45N 3°10W 194 F7
Corralejo Canary Is. 28°43N 13°53W 153 e2
Corraun Pen. Ireland 53°54N 9°54W 166 C2
Corrèggio Italy 44°46N 10°47E 198 D7
Corregidor Phil. 14°23N 120°35E 232 D3
Corrente Brazil 10°27S 45°10W 332 D2
Corrente → Brazil 13°8S 43°28W 333 D3
Correntes → Brazil 17°38S 55°8W 331 D6
Correntes, C. das Mozam. 24°6S 35°34E 271 B6
Correntina Brazil 13°20S 44°39W 333 D3
Corrèze □ France 45°20N 1°45E 174 C5
Corrèze → France 45°10N 1°28E 174 C5
Corrib, L. Ireland 53°27N 9°16W 166 C2
Corridônia Italy 43°15N 13°30E 199 E10
Corrientes Argentina 27°30S 58°45W 334 B4
Corrientes □ Argentina 28°0S 57°0W 334 B4
Corrientes → Argentina 30°42S 59°38W 334 C4
Corrientes → Peru 3°43S 74°35W 328 D3
Corrientes, C. Colombia 5°30N 77°34W 328 B2
Corrientes, C. Cuba 21°43N 84°30W 320 B3
Corrientes, C. Jalisco, Mexico 20°25N 105°42W 318 C3
Corrigan U.S.A. 31°0N 94°52W 314 F7
Corrigin Australia 32°20S 117°53E 279 F2
Corriverton Guyana 5°55N 57°20W 329 B6
Corry U.S.A. 41°55N 79°39W 312 E5
Corryong Australia 36°12S 147°53E 283 D7
Corse □ France 42°0N 9°0E 175 G13
Corse, C. France 43°1N 9°25E 175 E13
Corse ⌓ France 42°14N 9°10E 175 F13
Corse-du-Sud □ France 41°45N 9°0E 175 G13
Corsica = Corse □ France 42°0N 9°0E 175 G13
Corsicana U.S.A. 32°6N 96°28W 314 E6
Córsico Italy 45°25N 9°6E 128 B1
Corsini, Palazzo Rome, Italy 136 c1
Corstorphine U.K. 55°56N 3°17W 121 B2
Corte France 42°19N 9°11E 175 F13
Corte Pinto Portugal 37°42N 7°29W 195 H3
Cortegana Spain 37°52N 6°49W 195 H4
Cortes Phil. 9°17N 126°11E 233 G6
Cortés, Mar de = California, G. de Mexico 27°0N 111°0W 318 B2
Cortez U.S.A. 37°21N 108°35W 305 H9
Córthaidh, Inis = Enniscorthy Ireland 52°30N 6°34W 166 D5
Cortina d'Ampezzo Italy 46°32N 12°8E 199 B9
Cortland N.Y., U.S.A. 42°36N 76°11W 313 D8
Cortland Ohio, U.S.A. 41°20N 80°44W 312 E4
Cortona Italy 43°16N 11°59E 199 E8
Corubal → Guinea-Biss. 11°57N 15°5W 262 C2
Coruche Portugal 38°57N 8°30W 195 G2
Çoruh → Turkey 41°38N 41°38E 191 K5
Çorum Turkey 40°30N 34°57E 212 B6
Çorum □ Turkey 40°40N 35°0E 212 B6
Corumbá Brazil 19°0S 57°30W 331 D6
Corumbá → Brazil 18°19S 48°55W 333 E2
Corumbá de Goiás Brazil 16°0S 48°50W 333 E2
Corumbaiba Brazil 18°9S 48°34W 333 E2
Corund Romania 46°30N 25°13E 183 D10
Corunna = A Coruña Spain 43°20N 8°25W 194 B2
Corunna U.S.A. 42°59N 84°7W 311 B12
Corvallis U.S.A. 44°34N 123°16W 304 D2
Corvette, L. de la Canada 53°25N 74°3W 298 B5
Corviale Italy 41°51N 12°25E 136 B1
Corvo Azores 39°42N 31°6W 153 d2
Coryal Trin. & Tob. 10°30N 61°11W 323 t
Corydon Ind., U.S.A. 38°13N 86°7W 311 F10
Corydon Iowa, U.S.A. 40°46N 93°19W 310 D3
Corydon Ky., U.S.A. 37°44N 87°43W 311 G9
Cosalá Mexico 24°23N 106°41W 318 C3
Cosamaloapan de Carpio Mexico 18°22N 95°48W 319 D5
Cosenza Italy 39°18N 16°15E 201 C9
Coșereni Romania 44°38N 26°35E 183 F11
Coshocton U.S.A. 40°16N 81°51W 312 F3
Coslada Spain 40°25N 3°35W 127 B2
Cosmo Newberry Australia 28°0S 122°54E 279 E3
Cosmo Newberry ✪ Australia 27°59S 122°53E 279 E3
Cosmonaut Sea S. Ocean 66°30S 40°0E 151 C5
Cosmonautics Museum Russia 55°49N 37°38E 129 B2
Cosne-Cours-sur-Loire France 47°24N 2°54E 173 E9
Coso Junction U.S.A. 36°3N 117°57W 307 J9
Coso Pk. U.S.A. 36°13N 117°44W 307 J9
Cospeito = A Feira do Monte Spain 43°12N 7°34W 194 B3
Cosquín Argentina 31°15S 64°30W 334 C3
Cossato Italy 45°34N 8°10E 198 C5
Cossé-le-Vivien France 47°57N 0°54W 172 E6
Cossigny France 48°43N 2°40E 134 B4
Cosson → France 47°30N 1°15E 172 E8
Costa Calma Canary Is. 28°8N 14°16W 153 e2
Costa dels Pins Spain 39°38N 3°26E 206 B4
Costa Mesa U.S.A. 33°38N 117°55W 307 M9
Costa Rica ■ Cent. Amer. 10°0N 84°0W 320 E3
Costa Teguise Canary Is. 29°0N 13°31W 153 e2
Costantino, Arco di Rome, Italy 136 c3
Costermansville = Bukavu Dem. Rep. of the Congo 2°20S 28°52E 268 C2
Costești Romania 44°40N 24°53E 183 F9
Costigliole d'Asti Italy 44°47N 8°11E 198 D5
Cosumnes → U.S.A. 38°16N 121°26W 306 G5
Coswig Sachsen, Germany 51°7N 13°34E 178 D9

Coswig Sachsen-Anhalt, Germany 51°53N 12°27E 178 D8
Cotabato Phil. 7°14N 124°15E 233 H5
Cotacajes → Bolivia 16°0S 67°1W 330 D4
Cotagaita Bolivia 20°45S 65°40W 334 A2
Cotahuasi Peru 15°12S 72°50W 330 D3
Cotao Portugal 38°45N 9°17W 126 A1
Côte-d'Ivoire = Ivory Coast ■ Africa 7°30N 5°0W 262 D4
Côte-d'Or □ France 47°30N 4°50E 173 E11
Côte-St-Luc Canada 45°28N 73°39W 130 B2
Coteau des Prairies U.S.A. 45°20N 97°50W 308 C5
Coteau du Missouri U.S.A. 47°0N 100°0W 308 B4
Cotegipe Brazil 12°2S 44°15W 333 D3
Cotentin France 49°15N 1°30W 172 C5
Côtes-d'Armor □ France 48°25N 2°40W 172 D4
Côtes de Meuse France 49°15N 5°22E 173 C12
Côtes-du-Nord = Côtes-d'Armor □ France 48°25N 2°40W 172 D4
Cotiella Spain 42°31N 0°19E 196 C5
Cotiujeni Moldova 47°51N 28°33E 183 C13
Cotoca Bolivia 17°49S 63°3W 331 D5
Cotonou Benin 6°20N 2°25E 263 D5
Cotopaxi Ecuador 0°40S 78°30W 328 D2
Cotopaxi □ Ecuador 0°5S 78°55W 328 D2
Cotopaxi △ Ecuador 0°39S 78°24W 328 D2
Cotronei Italy 39°9N 16°47E 201 C9
Cotswold Hills U.K. 51°42N 2°10W 169 F5
Cottage Grove U.S.A. 43°48N 123°3W 304 E2
Cottageville U.S.A. 32°56N 80°29W 316 C9
Cottam Canada 42°8N 82°45W 312 D2
Cottbus Germany 51°45N 14°20E 178 D10
Cottingham U.K. 53°48N 0°25W 168 D7
Cotton Ground St. Kitts & Nevis 17°11N 62°36W 322 d
Cottondale U.S.A. 30°48N 85°23W 316 E4
Cottonwood Ala., U.S.A. 31°3N 85°18W 316 D4
Cottonwood Ariz., U.S.A. 34°45N 112°1W 305 J7
Cotulla U.S.A. 28°26N 99°14W 314 G5
Cotunduba, I. de Brazil 22°57S 43°8W 135 B2
Coubre, Pte. de la France 45°42N 1°15W 174 C2
Coubron France 48°54N 2°34E 134 A4
Couches France 46°53N 4°30E 173 F11
Couço Portugal 38°59N 8°17W 195 G2
Coudersport U.S.A. 41°46N 78°1W 312 E6
Couedic, C. du Australia 36°5S 136°40E 282 D2
Couëron France 47°13N 1°44W 172 E5
Couesnon → France 48°38N 1°32W 172 D5
Couhé France 46°17N 0°11E 174 B4
Coulanges-sur-Yonne France 47°31N 3°33E 173 E10
Coulee City U.S.A. 47°37N 119°17W 304 C4
Coulee Dam Nat. Recr. Area = Lake Roosevelt ⌂ U.S.A. 48°5N 118°14W 304 B4
Coulibistrie Dominica 15°27N 61°28W 323 k
Coulman I. Antarctica 73°35S 170°0E 151 D11
Coulommiers France 48°50N 3°3E 173 D10
Coulon → France 43°51N 5°6E 175 E9
Coulonge → Canada 45°52N 76°46W 298 C4
Coulonges-sur-l'Autize France 46°29N 0°36W 174 B3
Coulounieix-Chamiers France 45°11N 0°42E 174 C4
Coulterville Calif., U.S.A. 37°43N 120°12W 306 H6
Coulterville Ill., U.S.A. 38°11N 89°36W 310 F7
Council Alaska, U.S.A. 64°53N 163°41W 303 D7
Council Ga., U.S.A. 30°37N 82°31W 316 E7
Council Idaho, U.S.A. 44°44N 116°26W 304 D5
Council Bluffs U.S.A. 41°16N 95°52W 308 E6
Council Grove U.S.A. 38°40N 96°29W 308 F5
Coupeville U.S.A. 48°13N 122°41W 306 B4
Courantyne → S. Amer. 5°50N 57°8W 329 B6
Courbevoie France 48°53N 2°14E 134 A2
Courcelles Belgium 50°28N 4°22E 170 D4
Courchevel France 45°25N 6°36E 175 C10
Courçon France 46°15N 0°50W 174 B3
Courland → Trin. & Tob. 11°13N 60°47W 323 s
Courmayeur Italy 45°47N 6°58E 198 C3
Couronne, C. France 43°19N 5°3E 175 E9
Cours-la-Ville France 46°7N 4°19E 173 F11
Coursan France 43°14N 3°4E 174 E7
Courseulles-sur-Mer France 49°20N 0°29W 172 C6
Courtenay B.C., Canada 49°45N 125°0W 296 D4
Courtenay Loiret, France 48°2N 3°3E 173 D10
Courtland Ont., Canada 42°51N 80°38W 312 D4
Courtland Calif., U.S.A. 38°20N 121°34W 306 G5
Courtrai = Kortrijk Belgium 50°50N 3°17E 170 D3
Courtright Canada 42°49N 82°28W 312 D2
Courtry France 48°55N 2°35E 134 A4
Coushatta U.S.A. 32°1N 93°21W 314 E8
Coutances France 49°3N 1°28W 172 C5
Coutras France 45°3N 0°8W 174 C3
Coutts Crossing Australia 29°49S 152°55E 281 D5
Couva Trin. & Tob. 10°25N 61°27W 323 t
Couva □ Trin. & Tob. 10°25N 61°27W 323 t
Couvin Belgium 50°3N 4°29E 170 D4
Covarrubias Spain 42°4N 3°31W 194 C7
Covasna Romania 45°50N 26°10E 183 E11
Covasna □ Romania 45°50N 26°0E 183 E10
Cove I. Canada 45°17N 81°44W 312 A3
Coveñas Colombia 9°24N 75°44W 328 B2
Covent Garden London, U.K. 125 b4
Coventry U.K. 52°25N 1°28W 169 E6
Coverdale U.S.A. 31°38N 83°58W 316 D6
Covilhã Portugal 40°17N 7°31W 194 E3
Covington Ga., U.S.A. 33°36N 83°51W 316 B6
Covington Ind., U.S.A. 40°9N 87°24W 311 D9
Covington Ky., U.S.A. 39°5N 84°30W 311 E12
Covington Ohio, U.S.A. 40°7N 84°21W 311 D12
Covington Tenn., U.S.A. 35°34N 89°39W 315 D10
Covington Va., U.S.A. 37°47N 79°59W 309 G14
Cowal, L. Australia 33°40S 147°25E 283 B7
Cowan, Cerro Ecuador 0°12S 90°48W 330 a
Cowan, L. Australia 31°45S 121°45E 279 F3
Cowan L. Canada 54°0N 107°15W 297 C7
Cowangie Australia 35°12S 141°26E 282 C4
Cowansville Canada 45°14N 72°46W 313 A12
Coward Springs Australia 29°24S 136°49E 281 D2
Cowcowing Lakes Australia 30°55S 117°20E 279 F2
Cowden U.S.A. 39°15N 88°52W 311 E8
Cowdenbeath U.K. 56°7N 3°21W 167 E5
Cowell Australia 33°39S 136°56E 282 B2
Cowes Vic., Australia 38°28S 145°14E 283 E6
Cowes I. of W., U.K. 50°45N 1°18W 169 G6
Cowgate Edinburgh, U.K. 121 b3
Cowichan L. Canada 48°53N 124°17W 306 B2
Cowley U.K. 51°31N 0°28W 125 A1
Cowlitz → U.S.A. 46°6N 122°55W 306 D4
Cowra Australia 33°49S 148°42E 283 B8
Cox Spain 38°8N 0°53W 197 G4
Coxilha Grande Brazil 28°18S 51°30W 335 B5
Coxim Brazil 18°30S 54°55W 331 D7
Coxim → Brazil 18°34S 54°46W 331 D7
Cox's Bazar Bangla. 21°26N 91°59E 241 E3
Coyah Guinea 9°42N 13°22W 262 D2
Coyoacán Mexico 19°21N 99°9W 128 B2
Coyote Wells U.S.A. 32°44N 115°58W 307 N11
Coyuca de Benítez Mexico 17°2N 100°4W 319 D4
Coyuca de Catalán Mexico 18°20N 100°39W 318 D4
Cozad U.S.A. 40°52N 99°59W 308 E4
Cozes France 45°34N 0°49W 174 C3
Cozia △ Romania 45°25N 24°16E 183 E9
Cozumel Mexico 20°31N 86°55W 319 C7
Cozumel, Isla Mexico 20°30N 86°40W 319 C7
Crab Hill Antigua & B. 17°2N 61°53W 322 b
Crab Hill Barbados 13°19N 59°38W 323 r
Crabs Pen. Antigua & B. 17°7N 61°45W 322 b
Crac des Chevaliers Syria 34°47N 36°18E 250 D7
Cracow = Kraków Poland 50°4N 19°57E 185 H6
Cracow Australia 25°17S 150°17E 281 D5
Craddock Channel N.Z. 36°10S 175°13E 284 C4
Cradle Mt.-Lake St. Clair △ Australia 41°49S 147°56E 281 G4
Cradock S. Austral., Australia 32°6S 138°31E 281 E2
Cradock Eastern Cape, S. Africa 32°8S 25°36E 270 D4
Crafers Australia 35°0S 138°42E 282 C3
Craig Alaska, U.S.A. 55°29N 133°9W 303 J14
Craig Colo., U.S.A. 40°31N 107°33W 304 F10
Craigavon U.K. 54°27N 6°23W 166 B5
Craighall Park S. Africa 26°7S 28°1E 123 A2
Craigieburn Australia 37°36S 144°56E 283 D6
Craiglockhart U.K. 55°55N 3°14W 121 B2
Craigmillar U.K. 55°56N 3°9W 121 B3
Craigmore Zimbabwe 20°28S 32°50E 269 G3
Craik Canada 51°3N 105°49W 297 C7
Crailsheim Germany 49°8N 10°5E 179 F6
Craiova Romania 44°21N 23°48E 183 F8
Cramond U.K. 55°58N 3°18W 121 B2
Cramond Bridge U.K. 55°57N 3°19W 121 B1
Cramond I. U.K. 55°59N 3°17W 121 B1
Cramsie Australia 23°20S 144°15E 280 C3
Cranberry L. U.S.A. 44°11N 74°50W 313 B10
Cranberry Portage Canada 54°35N 101°23W 297 C8
Cranbrook W. Austral., Australia 34°18S 117°33E 279 F2
Cranbrook B.C., Canada 49°30N 115°46W 296 D5
Crandon U.S.A. 45°34N 88°54W 308 C9
Crandon Park U.S.A. 25°42N 80°9W 129 D3
Crane Oreg., U.S.A. 43°25N 118°35W 304 E4
Crane Tex., U.S.A. 31°24N 102°21W 314 F3
Crane, The Barbados 13°6N 59°27W 323 r
Cranford U.K. 51°29N 0°25W 125 B1
Cranganore India 10°13N 76°13E 245 J3
Cranston U.S.A. 41°47N 71°26W 313 E13
Craon France 47°50N 0°58W 172 E6
Craonne France 49°27N 3°46E 173 C10
Craponne-sur-Arzon France 45°19N 3°51E 174 C7
Crasna Romania 46°32N 27°51E 183 D12
Crasna → Romania 47°44N 22°35E 182 C7
Crasnei, Munții Romania 47°0N 23°20E 183 C8
Crater L. U.S.A. 42°56N 122°6W 304 E2
Crater Lake △ U.S.A. 42°55N 122°10W 304 E2
Crater Mt. Papua N. G. 6°37S 145°7E 286 D3
Crater Pt. Papua N. G. 5°25S 152°9E 286 C7
Craters of the Moon ⌂ U.S.A. 43°25N 113°30W 304 E7
Crateús Brazil 5°10S 40°39W 332 C3
Crati → Italy 39°43N 16°31E 201 C9
Crato Brazil 7°10S 39°25W 332 C4
Crato Portugal 39°16N 7°39W 195 F3
Craven, L. Canada 54°20N 76°56W 298 B4
Cravo Norte Colombia 6°18N 70°12W 328 B3
Cravo Norte → Colombia 6°18N 70°12W 328 B3
Crawford Western Cape, S. Africa 33°59S 18°30E 118 A2
Crawford Ala., U.S.A. 32°27N 85°11W 316 C4
Crawford Nebr., U.S.A. 42°41N 103°25W 308 D2
Crawfordsville Ind., U.S.A. 40°2N 86°54W 311 D10
Crawfordsville Iowa, U.S.A. 41°12N 91°32W 310 C5
Crawfordville Fla., U.S.A. 30°11N 84°23W 316 E5
Crawfordville Ga., U.S.A. 33°33N 82°54W 316 B7
Crawley U.K. 51°7N 0°11W 169 F7
Crayford U.K. 51°27N 0°11E 125 B5
Crazy Mts. U.S.A. 46°12N 110°20W 304 C8
Crean L. Canada 54°5N 106°9W 297 C7
Crécy-en-Ponthieu France 50°15N 1°53E 173 B8
Crediton Ont., Canada 43°17N 81°33W 312 C3
Crediton Devon, U.K. 50°47N 3°40W 169 G4
Cree → Sask., Canada 58°57N 105°47W 297 B7
Cree → Dumf. & Gall., U.K. 54°55N 4°25W 167 G4
Cree L. Canada 57°30N 106°30W 297 B7
Creede U.S.A. 37°51N 106°56W 305 H10
Creekmouth U.K. 51°30N 0°6E 125 A4
Creekside U.S.A. 40°40N 79°11W 312 F5
Creel Mexico 27°45N 107°38W 318 B3
Creemore Canada 44°19N 80°6W 312 B4
Creighton Sask., Canada 54°45N 101°54W 297 C8
Creighton Nebr., U.S.A. 42°28N 97°54W 308 D5
Creil France 49°15N 2°29E 173 C9
Crema Italy 45°22N 9°41E 198 C6
Cremona Italy 45°7N 10°2E 198 C7
Crepaja Serbia 45°1N 20°38E 182 E5
Crepori → Brazil 5°42S 57°8W 331 B6
Crépy France 49°35N 3°32E 173 C10
Crépy-en-Valois France 49°14N 2°54E 173 C9
Cres Croatia 44°58N 14°25E 199 D11
Crescent L. U.S.A. 28°30N 81°33W 133 A1
Crescent Beach U.S.A. 29°46N 81°15W 316 F8
Crescent City Calif., U.S.A. 41°45N 124°12W 304 F1
Crescent City Fla., U.S.A. 29°26N 81°31W 317 F8
Crescent Group S. China Sea 16°30N 111°40E 230 A4
Crescent Hd. Australia 31°11S 152°59E 283 A10
Crescent L. U.S.A. 29°28N 81°30W 317 F8
Crescentino Italy 45°11N 8°6E 198 C5
Crescenzago Italy 45°30N 9°14E 128 A2
Crespi d'Adda Italy 45°35N 9°32E 198 C6
Crespo Argentina 32°2S 60°19W 334 C3
Cressely France 48°44N 2°6E 134 B1
Cresskill U.S.A. 40°56N 73°57W 132 A2
Cresson U.S.A. 40°28N 78°36W 312 F6
Cressy Australia 38°2S 143°40E 282 E5
Crest France 44°44N 5°2E 175 D9
Cresta, Mt. Phil. 17°17N 122°6E 233 C4
Crestline Calif., U.S.A. 34°14N 117°18W 307 L9
Crestline Ohio, U.S.A. 40°47N 82°44W 312 F2
Creston B.C., Canada 49°10N 116°31W 296 D5
Creston Calif., U.S.A. 35°32N 120°33W 306 K6
Creston Iowa, U.S.A. 41°4N 94°22W 310 C2
Crestview Calif., U.S.A. 37°46N 118°58W 306 H8
Crestview Fla., U.S.A. 30°46N 86°34W 317 E3
Crestwood U.S.A. 41°38N 87°46W 119 D2
Creswick Australia 37°25S 143°58E 282 D5
Crêt de la Neige France 46°16N 5°58E 173 F12
Crete = Kriti Greece 35°15N 25°0E 207 E6
Crete Ill., U.S.A. 41°27N 87°38W 311 C9
Crete Nebr., U.S.A. 40°38N 96°58W 308 E5
Crete, Sea of Greece 36°0N 25°0E 205 E7
Créteil France 48°47N 2°27E 134 B3
Cretin, C. Papua N. G. 6°40S 147°53E 286 D4
Creus, C. de Spain 42°20N 3°19E 196 C8
Creuse □ France 46°10N 2°0E 173 F9
Creuse → France 47°0N 0°34E 174 B4
Creutzwald France 49°12N 6°42E 173 C13
Creuzburg Germany 51°3N 10°14E 178 D6
Crèvecœur-le-Grand France 49°37N 2°5E 173 C9
Crevillent Spain 38°12N 0°48W 197 G4
Crewe U.K. 53°6N 2°26W 168 D5
Crewkerne U.K. 50°53N 2°48W 169 G5
Crianlarich U.K. 56°24N 4°37W 167 E4
Criciúma Brazil 28°40S 49°23W 335 B6
Cricklewood U.K. 51°33N 0°13W 125 A2
Cricova Moldova 47°8N 28°52E 183 C13
Cridersville U.S.A. 40°39N 84°9W 311 D12
Crieff U.K. 56°22N 3°50W 167 E5
Crikvenica Croatia 45°11N 14°40E 199 C11
Crimea □ Ukraine 45°30N 33°10E 189 K8
Crimean Pen. = Krymskyy Pivostriv Ukraine 45°0N 34°0E 189 K8
Crimmitschau Germany 50°48N 12°24E 178 E8
Cristal, Mts. de Gabon 0°30N 10°30E 264 B2
Cristalândia Brazil 10°36S 49°11W 332 D2
Cristino Castro Brazil 8°49S 44°13W 332 C3
Cristo Redentor, Corcovado Brazil 22°56S 43°12W 135 B1
Cristóbal Panama 9°19N 79°54W 320 c
Cristóbal, Pta. Ecuador 0°54S 91°31W 330 a
Cristuru Secuiesc Romania 46°17N 25°2E 183 D10
Crişul Alb → Romania 46°42N 21°17E 182 D6
Crişul Negru → Romania 46°42N 21°16E 182 D6
Crişul Repede → Romania 46°55N 20°59E 182 D5
Crittenden U.S.A. 38°47N 84°36W 311 F12
Criuleni Moldova 47°13N 29°10E 183 C14
Crivitz Germany 53°34N 11°39E 178 B7
Crixás Brazil 14°27S 49°58W 333 D2
Crkvice Montenegro 42°34N 18°38E 202 D2
Crna → Macedonia 41°33N 21°59E 202 E5
Crna Gora = Montenegro ■ Europe 42°40N 19°20E 202 D3
Crna Gora Macedonia 42°10N 21°30E 202 D5
Crna Reka = Crna → Macedonia 41°33N 21°59E 202 E5
Crna Trava Serbia 42°49N 22°19E 202 D6
Crni Drim → Macedonia 41°17N 20°40E 202 E4
Crni Timok → Serbia 43°53N 22°15E 202 C6
Crnoljeva Planina = Zhar, Mali Kosovo 42°20N 21°0E 202 D5
Črnomelj Slovenia 45°33N 15°10E 199 C12
Croagh Patrick Ireland 53°46N 9°40W 166 C2
Croajingolong △ Australia 37°45S 149°26E 283 D8
Croatia ■ Europe 45°20N 16°0E 199 C13
Croce, Ex Chiesa della Venice, Italy 142 c3
Crockenhill U.K. 51°22N 0°9E 125 B4
Crocker U.S.A. 37°57N 92°16W 310 G4
Crocker, Banjaran Malaysia 5°40N 116°30E 235 A5
Crocker, Cerro Ecuador 0°36S 90°21W 330 a
Crocker Range △ Malaysia 5°33N 116°8E 235 A5
Crockett U.S.A. 31°19N 95°27W 314 F7
Crocodile = Umgwenya → Mozam. 25°14S 32°18E 271 C5
Crocodile → S. Africa 24°12S 26°53E 270 B4
Crocodile Is. Australia 12°3S 134°58E 280 A1
Crocq France 45°52N 2°21E 174 C6
Crocus B. Anguilla 18°13N 63°5W 322 a
Crohy Hd. Ireland 54°55N 8°26W 166 B3
Croisette, C. France 43°14N 5°22E 175 E9
Croisic, Pte. du France 47°19N 2°31W 172 E4
Croissy-Beaubourg France 48°49N 2°39E 134 B4
Croissy-sur-Seine France 48°52N 2°8E 134 A1
Croix, L. la Canada 48°20N 92°15W 298 C1
Croker, C. N. Terr., Australia 10°58S 132°35E 278 B5
Croker, C. Ont., Canada 44°58N 80°59W 312 B4
Croker, I. Australia 11°12S 132°32E 278 B5
Croker Islands Seas ✪ Australia 11°20S 132°30E 278 B5
Cromarty U.K. 57°40N 4°2W 167 D4
Cromer U.K. 52°56N 1°17E 168 E9
Crompton Pt. Dominica 15°35N 61°19W 323 k
Cromwell N.Z. 45°3S 169°14E 285 F4
Cromwell Conn., U.S.A. 41°36N 72°39W 313 E12
Cronat France 46°43N 3°40E 173 F10
Crook U.K. 54°43N 1°45W 168 C6
Crooked → B.C., Canada 54°50N 122°54W 296 C4
Crooked → Oreg., U.S.A. 44°32N 121°16W 304 D3
Crooked Creek U.S.A. 61°52N 158°7W 303 F8
Crooked I. Bahamas 22°50N 74°10W 321 B5
Crooked Island Passage Bahamas 22°55N 74°35W 321 B5
Crookston Minn., U.S.A. 47°47N 96°37W 308 B5
Crookston Nebr., U.S.A. 42°56N 100°45W 308 D3
Crookwell Australia 34°28S 149°24E 283 C8
Cropane-Micone ⌂ Italy 38°31N 16°18E 201 D9
Crosby Gauteng, S. Africa 26°11S 27°59E 123 B1
Crosby Mersey., U.K. 53°30N 3°3W 168 D4
Crosby N. Dak., U.S.A. 48°55N 103°18W 308 A2
Crosby Pa., U.S.A. 41°45N 78°23W 312 E6
Crosbyton U.S.A. 33°40N 101°14W 314 E4
Crosía Italy 39°35N 16°45E 201 C9
Crosne France 48°43N 2°27E 134 B3
Cross → Nigeria 4°42N 8°21E 263 E6
Cross City U.S.A. 29°38N 83°7W 317 F6
Cross Fell U.K. 54°43N 2°28W 168 C5
Cross I. India 18°56N 72°51E 130 B2
Cross L. Canada 54°45N 97°30W 297 C9
Cross Lake Canada 54°37N 97°47W 297 C9
Cross River □ Nigeria 6°0N 8°0E 263 D6
Cross River △ Nigeria 5°50N 9°50E 263 D6
Cross Sound U.S.A. 58°0N 135°0W 303 G14
Cross Timbers U.S.A. 38°1N 93°14W 310 F3
Crossen = Krosno Odrzańskie Poland 52°3N 15°7E 185 F2
Crossett U.S.A. 33°8N 91°58W 314 E9
Crosshaven Ireland 51°47N 8°17W 166 E3
Crossley, Mt. N.Z. 42°50S 172°5E 285 C7
Crossmaglen U.K. 54°5N 6°36W 166 B5
Crossmolina Ireland 54°6N 9°20W 166 B2
Crossville Ill., U.S.A. 38°10N 88°4W 311 F8
Crossville Tenn., U.S.A. 35°57N 85°2W 315 D12
Croswell U.S.A. 43°16N 82°37W 312 C2
Croton-on-Hudson U.S.A. 41°12N 73°55W 313 E11
Crotone Italy 39°5N 17°8E 201 C10
Crouch End U.K. 51°34N 0°7W 125 A3
Crow → Canada 59°41N 124°20W 296 B4
Crow Agency U.S.A. 45°36N 107°28W 304 D10
Crow Hd. Ireland 51°35N 10°9W 166 E1
Crowdy Bay △ Australia 31°45S 152°45E 283 A10
Crowell U.S.A. 33°59N 99°43W 314 E5
Crowl Cr. → Australia 32°0S 145°30E 283 B6
Crowley La., U.S.A. 30°13N 92°22W 314 F8
Crowley Tex., U.S.A. 32°34N 97°21W 120 C1
Crowley, L. U.S.A. 37°35N 118°42W 306 H8
Crown I. Papua N. G. 5°7S 146°58E 286 C4
Crown Mine S. Africa 26°12S 27°57E 123 B1
Crown Point Ind., U.S.A. 41°25N 87°22W 311 C9
Crown Point N.Y., U.S.A. 43°57N 73°26W 313 C11
Crown Pt. Trin. & Tob. 11°18N 60°51W 323 s
Crownpoint U.S.A. 35°41N 108°9W 305 J9
Crows Landing U.S.A. 37°23N 121°6W 306 H5
Crows Nest N.S.W., Australia 33°49S 151°12E 139 A2
Crows Nest Queens., Australia 27°16S 152°4E 281 D5
Crowsnest Pass Canada 49°40N 114°40W 296 D6
Croydon Queens., Australia 18°13S 142°14E 280 B3
Croydon London, U.K. 51°22N 0°5W 125 B3
Croydon □ U.K. 51°22N 0°5W 169 F7
Croydon Park Australia 33°55S 151°7E 139 B1
Crozet, Îs. Ind. Oc. 46°27S 52°0E 277 J4
Crozet Basin Ind. Oc. 39°0S 60°0E 273 H5
Crozon France 48°15N 4°30W 172 D2
Cruce de Sardina Canary Is. 27°52N 15°22W 153 e1
Cruces, Punta Colombia 6°39N 77°32W 328 B2
Crusheen Ireland 52°57N 8°53W 166 D3
Cruz, C. Cuba 19°50N 77°50W 320 C4
Cruz Alta Brazil 28°45S 53°40W 335 B5
Cruz Bay U.S. Virgin Is. 18°20N 64°48W 321 b
Cruz das Almas Brazil 12°0S 39°6W 333 D4
Cruz de Pau Portugal 38°37N 9°7W 126 B2
Cruz del Eje Argentina 30°45S 64°50W 334 C3
Cruzeiro Brazil 22°33S 45°0W 333 F3
Cruzeiro do Oeste Brazil 23°46S 53°4W 335 A5
Cruzeiro do Sul = Joaçaba Brazil 27°5S 51°31W 335 B5
Cruzeiro do Sul Brazil 7°35S 72°35W 330 B3
Cry L. Canada 58°45N 129°0W 296 B3
Crystal B. U.S.A. 28°50N 82°45W 317 G7
Crystal Bay U.S.A. 39°15N 120°0W 306 F7
Crystal Brook Australia 33°21S 138°12E 282 B3
Crystal City Mo., U.S.A. 38°13N 90°23W 310 F6
Crystal City Tex., U.S.A. 28°41N 99°50W 314 G5
Crystal Falls U.S.A. 46°5N 88°20W 308 B9
Crystal Lake Fla., U.S.A. 30°26N 85°42W 316 E4
Crystal Lake Ill., U.S.A. 42°14N 88°19W 311 B8
Crystal Palace U.K. 51°25N 0°4W 125 B3
Crystal River U.S.A. 28°54N 82°35W 317 G7
Crystal Springs U.S.A. 31°59N 90°21W 315 F9
Csenger Hungary 47°50N 22°41E 182 C7
Csepel Hungary 47°25N 19°4E 117 B2
Csepelsziget Hungary 47°25N 19°4E 117 B2
Csillaghegy Hungary 47°35N 19°2E 117 A2
Csillagtelep Hungary 47°24N 19°5E 117 B2
Csömör Hungary 47°33N 19°14E 117 A3
Csömöri-patak → Hungary 47°35N 19°5E 117 A3
Csongrád Hungary 46°43N 20°12E 182 D5
Csongrád □ Hungary 46°32N 20°15E 182 D5
Csorna Hungary 47°38N 17°18E 182 C2
Csurgo Hungary 46°16N 17°9E 182 D2
Cu Lao Hon Vietnam 10°54N 108°18E 237 G7
Cua Rao Vietnam 19°16N 104°27E 236 C5
Cuácua → Mozam. 17°54S 37°0E 269 F4
Cuale Angola 8°22S 16°10E 265 D3
Cuále → Angola 8°29S 15°1E 265 D3
Cuamato Angola 17°2S 15°7E 265 F3
Cuamba Mozam. 14°45S 36°22E 269 E4
Cuando Angola 14°34S 19°1E 265 E3
Cuando → Angola 17°30S 23°15E 265 F4
Cuando Cubango □ Angola 16°25S 20°0E 265 F3
Cuangar Angola 17°36S 18°39E 265 F3
Cuango = Kwango → Dem. Rep. of the Congo 3°14S 17°22E 264 C3
Cuango Lunda Norte, Angola 9°8S 18°3E 265 D3
Cuango Moxico, Angola 14°30S 19°0E 265 D3
Cuango Uíge, Angola 6°15S 16°42E 265 D3
Cuanza → Angola 9°21S 13°9E 265 D2
Cuao → Venezuela 4°55N 67°40W 328 C4
Cuare → Trin. & Tob. 10°36N 61°6W 323 t
Cuarto → Argentina 33°25S 63°2W 334 C3
Cuatir → Angola 17°1S 18°9E 265 F3
Cuatro Vientos Spain 40°22N 3°47W 127 B1
Cuatrociénegas Mexico 26°59N 102°5W 318 B4
Cuauhtémoc Chihuahua, Mexico 28°25N 106°52W 318 B3
Cuauhtémoc México, Mexico 19°25N 99°9W 128 B2
Cuba Portugal 38°10N 7°54W 195 G3
Cuba Mo., U.S.A. 38°4N 91°24W 310 F5
Cuba N. Mex., U.S.A. 36°1N 107°4W 305 H10
Cuba N.Y., U.S.A. 42°13N 78°17W 312 D6
Cuba ■ W. Indies 22°0N 79°0W 320 B4
Cuba City U.S.A. 42°36N 90°26W 310 B6
Cubagua, I. Venezuela 10°49N 64°11W 329 a
Cubal Angola 12°26S 14°3E 265 E2
Cubal → Angola 15°9S 12°9E 265 F2
Cuban Museum U.S.A. 25°45N 80°13W 129 D1
Cubango → Africa 18°50S 22°25E 265 F4
Cubanja Angola 14°49S 21°20E 265 E4
Cubao Phil. 14°37N 121°3E 127 B2
Cubia Angola 15°58S 21°42E 265 F4
Çubuk Turkey 40°14N 33°3E 212 B5
Çubuklu Turkey 41°5N 29°4E 122 B2
Cuc Phuong △ Vietnam 20°17N 105°38E 236 B5
Cuche Trin. & Tob. 10°22N 61°10W 323 t
Cuchi Angola 14°37S 16°58E 265 E3
Cuchi → Angola 15°13S 17°26E 265 F3
Cuchillo-Có Argentina 38°20S 64°37W 336 A4
Cuchivero → Venezuela 7°40N 65°57W 328 B4
Cuchumatanes, Sierra de los Guatemala 15°35N 91°25W 320 C1
Cuckfield U.K. 51°1N 0°8W 169 F7
Cucuí Brazil 1°12N 66°50W 328 C4
Cucumbi Angola 10°17S 19°5E 265 E3
Cucurpé Mexico 30°20N 110°43W 318 A2
Cucurrupí Colombia 4°23N 76°56W 328 C2
Cúcuta Colombia 7°54N 72°31W 328 B3
Cudahy Calif., U.S.A. 33°57N 118°11W 126 C3
Cudahy Wis., U.S.A. 42°57N 87°51W 311 B9
Cudalbi Romania 45°46N 27°41E 183 E12
Cudarebe = Kudarebe Aruba 12°37N 70°4W 322 f
Cuddalore India 11°46N 79°45E 245 J4
Cuddapah = Kadapa India 14°30N 78°47E 245 G4
Cuddapan, L. Australia 25°45S 141°26E 280 D3
Cudgewa Australia 36°10S 147°42E 283 D7
Cudillero Spain 43°33N 6°9W 194 B4
Cudjoehead Montserrat 16°47N 62°12W 323 p
Cue Australia 27°25S 117°54E 279 E2
Cuebe → Angola 15°46S 17°42E 265 F3
Cuéllar Spain 41°23N 4°21W 194 D6
Cuemba Angola 11°50S 17°42E 265 E3
Cuenca Ecuador 2°50S 79°9W 328 D2
Cuenca Spain 40°5N 2°10W 196 E2
Cuenca □ Spain 40°0N 2°0W 196 F3
Cuenca, Serranía de Spain 39°55N 1°50W 196 F3
Cuenca Alta del Manzanares ⌂ Spain 40°40N 3°55W 194 E7
Cuerda del Pozo, Embalse de la Spain 41°51N 2°44W 196 D2
Cuernavaca Mexico 18°55N 99°15W 319 D5
Cuero U.S.A. 29°6N 97°17W 314 G6
Cuers France 43°14N 6°5E 175 E10
Cueva de la Quebrada del Toro △ Venezuela 10°46N 69°3W 328 A4
Cueva de los Guácharos △ Colombia 1°35N 76°1W 328 C2
Cuevas, Cerro Bolivia 22°0S 65°12W 331 E4
Cuevas de Vera = Cuevas del Almanzora Spain 37°18N 1°58W 197 H3
Cuevas del Almanzora Spain 37°18N 1°58W 197 H3
Cuevo Bolivia 20°15S 63°30W 331 E5
Cugir Romania 45°48N 23°25E 183 E8
Cuglieri Italy 40°11N 8°34E 200 B1
Cugnaux France 43°32N 1°20E 174 E5
Cuhai-Bakony → Hungary 47°35N 17°54E 182 C2
Cuiabá Brazil 15°30S 56°0W 331 D6
Cuiabá → Brazil 17°5S 56°36W 331 D6
Cuicuilco, Pirámide de Mexico 19°18N 99°11W 128 C1
Cuihangcun China 22°27N 113°32E 219 a
Cuijk Neths. 51°44N 5°50E 170 C5
Cuilco Guatemala 15°24N 91°58W 320 C1
Cuillin Hills U.K. 57°13N 6°15W 167 D2
Cuillin Sd. U.K. 57°4N 6°20W 167 D2
Cuilo = Kwilu → Dem. Rep. of the Congo 3°22S 17°22E 265 C3
Cuilo Angola 8°12S 19°28E 265 D3
Cuilo-Futa Angola 6°28S 15°51E 265 D3
Cuima Angola 13°25S 15°45E 265 E3
Cuimba Angola 6°10S 14°41E 265 D2
Cuiseaux France 46°30N 5°22E 173 F12
Cuité Brazil 6°29S 36°9W 332 C4
Cuito → Angola 18°1S 20°48E 265 F4
Cuito Cuanavale Angola 15°10S 19°10E 265 F3
Cuitzeo, L. de Mexico 19°55N 101°5W 318 D4
Cuiuni → Brazil 0°45S 63°7W 329 D5
Cuivre → U.S.A. 38°56N 90°41W 310 F6
Cujmir Romania 44°13N 22°57E 182 F7
Cukai Malaysia 4°13N 103°25E 237 K4
Çukurca Turkey 37°14N 43°36E 213 D10
Çukurova = Cilicia Turkey 36°30N 34°0E 212 D5
Cul-de-Sac St.-Maarten 18°2N 63°4W 322 a
Cul de Sac St.-Martin 18°6N 63°2W 322 a
Culasi Phil. 11°26N 122°3E 233 F4
Culbertson U.S.A. 48°9N 104°31W 304 B11
Culburra N.S.W., Australia 34°56S 150°46E 283 C9
Culburra S. Austral., Australia 35°50S 139°58E 282 C3
Culcairn Australia 35°41S 147°3E 283 C7
Culebra Puerto Rico 18°19N 65°18W 321 b
Culebra, Sierra de la Spain 41°55N 6°20W 194 D4
Culfa Azerbaijan 38°57N 45°38E 213 C11
Culgoa Australia 35°44S 143°6E 282 C5
Culgoa → Australia 29°56S 146°20E 281 D4
Culgoa Flood Plain △ Australia 28°58S 147°5E 281 D4
Culiacán Mexico 24°50N 107°23W 318 C3
Culiacán → Mexico 24°30N 107°42W 318 C3
Culik Indonesia 8°21S 115°37E 231 J18
Culion Phil. 11°54N 119°58E 233 F3
Culion I. Phil. 11°50N 120°0E 233 F2
Culiseu → Brazil 12°14S 53°17W 331 C7
Cúllar Spain 37°35N 2°34W 195 H8
Cullarin Ra. Australia 34°30S 149°30E 283 C8
Cullen U.K. 57°42N 2°49W 167 D6
Cullen Bullen Australia 33°18S 150°2E 283 B9
Cullen Pt. Australia 11°57S 141°54E 286 F1
Cullera Spain 39°9N 0°17W 197 F4
Cullman U.S.A. 34°11N 86°51W 315 D11
Culloden U.S.A. 32°52N 84°6W 316 C5
Cullom U.S.A. 40°53N 88°16W 311 D8
Cullompton U.K. 50°51N 3°24W 169 G4
Culmore U.S.A. 38°51N 77°8W 143 B2
Culo → Angola 6°13S 15°34E 265 D3
Culoz France 45°47N 5°46E 175 C9
Culpeper U.S.A. 38°30N 78°0W 309 F14
Culuene → Brazil 12°56S 52°51W 331 C7
Culver U.S.A. 41°13N 86°25W 311 C10
Culver, Pt. Australia 32°54S 124°43E 279 F3
Culver City U.S.A. 34°1N 118°24W 126 B2
Culverden N.Z. 42°47S 172°49E 285 C7
Culverton U.S.A. 33°19N 82°54W 316 B7
Cuma Angola 12°52S 15°5E 265 E3
Cumaná Venezuela 10°30N 64°5W 329 A5
Cumana B. Trin. & Tob. 10°48N 60°56W 323 t
Cumaovası Turkey 38°15N 27°9E 205 C9
Cumari Brazil 18°16S 48°11W 333 E2
Cumballa Hill Mumbai, India 130 a1
Cumbe = Euclides da Cunha Brazil 10°31S 39°1W 332 D4
Cumberland B.C., Canada 49°40N 125°0W 296 D4
Cumberland Ont., Canada 45°29N 75°24W 313 A9
Cumberland St. Vincent 13°16N 61°16W 323 n
Cumberland Iowa, U.S.A. 41°16N 94°52W 310 C2
Cumberland Md., U.S.A. 39°39N 78°46W 309 F14
Cumberland → U.S.A. 37°9N 88°25W 308 G9
Cumberland, B. Chile 33°37S 78°49W 330 c
Cumberland, C. Vanuatu 14°39S 166°37E 287 D4
Cumberland, L. U.S.A. 36°52N 85°9W 309 G11
Cumberland Gap ⌂ U.S.A. 36°36N 83°40W 309 G12
Cumberland I. U.S.A. 30°50N 81°25W 316 E8
Cumberland Is. Australia 20°35S 149°10E 280 b
Cumberland Island ⌂ U.S.A. 30°12N 81°24W 316 E8
Cumberland L. Canada 54°3N 102°18W 297 C8
Cumberland Pen. Canada 67°0N 64°0W 295 D19
Cumberland Plateau U.S.A. 36°0N 85°0W 315 D12
Cumberland Sd. Canada 65°30N 66°0W 295 D18
Cumbernauld U.K. 55°57N 3°58W 167 F5
Cumbira Angola 12°11S 15°8E 265 E3
Cumborah Australia 29°40S 147°45E 281 D4
Cumbres de Majalca △ Mexico 28°48N 106°30W 318 B3
Cumbres de Monterrey △ Mexico 25°26N 100°25W 318 B4
Cumbres Mayores Spain 38°4N 6°39W 195 G4
Cumbria □ U.K. 54°42N 2°52W 168 C5
Cumbrian Mts. U.K. 54°30N 3°0W 168 C5
Cumbum India 15°40N 79°10E 245 G4
Cuminá Brazil 1°57S 56°2W 329 D6
Cuminá → Brazil 1°30S 56°0W 329 D6
Cuminapanema → Brazil 1°9S 54°54W 329 D7
Cumming, C. Chile 27°6S 109°14W 330 b
Cummings Mt. U.S.A. 35°2N 118°34W 307 K8
Cummins Australia 34°16S 135°43E 281 E2
Cumnock N.S.W., Australia 32°59S 148°46E 283 B8
Cumnock E. Ayrs., U.K. 55°28N 4°17W 167 F4
Cumpas Mexico 30°2N 109°48W 318 B3
Cumplida, Pta. Canary Is. 28°50N 17°48W 153 e1
Çumra Turkey 37°34N 32°45E 212 D5
Cumuto Trin. & Tob. 10°35N 61°12W 323 t
Cunapo → Trin. & Tob. 10°35N 61°8W 323 t
Cuñare Colombia 0°49N 72°32W 328 C3
Cunaripa Trin. & Tob. 10°33N 61°1W 323 t
Cuncumén Chile 31°53S 70°38W 334 C1
Cundeelee ✪ Australia 30°43S 123°25E 279 F3
Cunderdin Australia 31°37S 117°12E 279 F2
Cundinamarca □ Colombia 5°0N 74°0W 328 C3
Cunene □ Angola 16°30S 15°0E 265 F3
Cunene → Angola 17°20S 11°50E 265 F2
Cúneo Italy 44°23N 7°32E 198 D4
Cung Son Vietnam 13°2N 108°58E 236 F7
Çüngüş Turkey 38°13N 39°17E 213 C8
Cunhinga Angola 12°11S 16°47E 265 E3
Cunhinga → Angola 10°42S 16°41E 265 E3
Cunillera, I. = Sa Conillera Spain 38°59N 1°13E 206 D1
Cunjamba Angola 15°27S 20°10E 265 F4
Cunlhat France 45°38N 3°32E 174 C7
Cunnamulla Australia 28°2S 145°38E 281 D4
Cunningham Bahamas 25°5N 77°26W 153 b
Cunupia Trin. & Tob. 10°32N 61°22W 323 t
Cuorgnè Italy 45°23N 7°39E 198 C4
Cupar Sask., Canada 50°57N 104°10W 297 C8
Cupar Fife, U.K. 56°19N 3°1W 167 E5
Cupcini Moldova 48°6N 27°23E 183 B12
Cupecé → Brazil 23°39S 46°40W 137 B1
Cupertino U.S.A. 37°19N 122°2W 306 H4
Cupica, G. de Colombia 6°25N 77°30W 328 B2
Ćuprija Serbia 43°57N 21°26E 202 C5
Curaçá Brazil 8°59S 39°54W 332 C4
Curaçao W. Indies 12°10N 69°0W 322 g
Curaçao Int. ✈ (CUR) Curaçao 12°11N 68°57W 322 g
Curacautín Chile 38°26S 71°53W 336 A2
Curador = Presidente Dutra Brazil 5°15S 44°30W 332 C3
Curahuara de Carangas Bolivia 17°52S 68°26W 330 D4
Curalhinho = Coelho Neto Brazil 4°15S 43°0W 332 B3
Curamata → Trin. & Tob. 10°11N 61°28W 323 t
Curanilahue Chile 37°29S 73°28W 334 D1
Curaray → Peru 2°20S 74°5W 328 D3
Curatabaca Venezuela 6°19N 62°51W 329 B5
Cure → France 47°40N 3°41E 173 E10
Curepipe Mauritius 20°19S 57°31E 272 d
Curepipe Point Mauritius 20°21S 57°31E 272 e
Curepto Chile 35°8S 72°1W 334 D1
Curia Portugal 40°22N 8°29W 194 E2
Curiapo Venezuela 8°33N 61°5W 329 B5
Curicó Chile 34°55S 71°20W 334 C1
Curicuriari → Brazil 0°14S 66°48W 328 D4
Curieuse Seychelles 4°15S 55°44E 272 c
Curimatá Brazil 10°2S 44°17W 332 D3
Curinga Italy 38°49N 16°19E 201 D9
Curiplaya Colombia 0°16N 74°52W 328 C3
Curitiba Brazil 25°20S 49°10W 335 B6
Curitibanos Brazil 27°18S 50°36W 335 B5
Curlewis Australia 31°7S 150°16E 283 A9
Curoca → Angola 15°43S 11°55E 265 F2
Curonian Lagoon = Kurshskiy Zaliv Russia 55°9N 21°6E 184 C8
Curonian Spit Europe 55°20N 20°55E 184 C7
Currabubula Australia 31°16S 150°44E 283 A9
Currais Novos Brazil 6°13S 36°30W 332 C4
Curral Velho C. Verde Is. 16°8N 22°48W 153 j
Curralinho Brazil 1°45S 49°46W 332 B2
Currane, L. Ireland 51°49N 10°4W 166 E1
Currant U.S.A. 38°44N 115°28W 304 G6
Curraweena Australia 30°47S 145°54E 283 A6
Currawinya △ Australia 28°55S 144°27E 281 D3
Current → U.S.A. 36°15N 90°55W 314 C9
Currie Tas., Australia 39°56S 143°53E 281 F3
Currie Edinburgh, U.K. 55°54N 3°17W 121 B2
Currie, Mt. Nev., U.S.A. 40°16N 114°45W 304 F6
Curt-Bunar = Tervel Bulgaria 43°45N 27°28E 203 C11
Curtea de Argeş Romania 45°12N 24°42E 183 E9
Curtici Romania 46°21N 21°18E 182 D6
Curtin Springs Australia 25°20S 131°45E 279 E5
Curtis U.S.A. 40°38N 100°31W 308 E3
Curtis Group Australia 39°30S 146°37E 281 F4
Curtis I. Queens., Australia 23°35S 151°10E 280 C5
Curtis I. Pac. Oc. 30°30S 178°34W 277 G15
Curuá → Pará, Brazil 2°24S 54°5W 329 D7
Curuá → Pará, Brazil 5°23S 54°22W 331 B7
Curuá, I. Brazil 0°48N 50°10W 332 A1
Curuaés → Brazil 7°30S 54°45W 331 B7
Curuaí Brazil 2°17S 55°29W 329 D6
Curuápanema → Brazil 2°25S 55°2W 329 D6
Curuçá Brazil 0°43S 47°50W 332 B2
Curuçá → Brazil 4°27S 71°23W 330 A3
Curuguaty Paraguay 24°31S 55°42W 335 A4
Çürüksu Çayi = Büyük Menderes → Turkey 37°28N 27°11E 205 D9
Curup Indonesia 3°26S 102°13E 234 C2
Curupira, Serra S. Amer. 1°25N 64°30W 329 C5
Cururu → Brazil 7°12S 58°3W 331 B6
Cururupu Brazil 1°50S 44°50W 332 B3
Curuzú Cuatiá Argentina 29°50S 58°5W 334 B4
Curvelo Brazil 18°45S 44°27W 333 E3
Cusago Italy 45°26N 9°1E 128 B1
Cusano Milanino Italy 45°33N 9°11E 128 A2
Cusco Peru 13°32S 72°0W 330 C3
Cusco □ Peru 13°31S 71°59W 330 C3
Cushendall U.K. 55°5N 6°4W 166 A5
Cushing U.S.A. 35°59N 96°46W 314 D6
Cushing, Mt. Canada 57°35N 126°57W 296 B3
Cusihuiriáchic Mexico 28°14N 106°50W 318 B3
Cusna, Mte. Italy 44°17N 10°23E 198 D7
Cussabat = Al Qaşabāt Libya 32°39N 14°1E 258 B2
Cusset France 46°8N 3°28E 173 F10
Cusseta U.S.A. 32°18N 84°47W 316 C5
Cusso, Sa. do Angola 6°30S 14°58E 265 D2
Custer U.S.A. 43°46N 103°36W 308 D2
Cut Bank U.S.A. 48°38N 112°20W 304 B7
Cutchogue U.S.A. 41°1N 72°30W 313 E12
Cutervo Peru 6°25S 78°55W 330 B2
Cuthbert U.S.A. 31°46N 84°48W 316 D5
Cutler U.S.A. 36°31N 119°17W 306 J7
Cutler Park U.S.A. 42°17N 71°12W 116 B1
Cutler Ridge U.S.A. 25°35N 80°20W 317 K9
Cutlerville U.S.A. 42°50N 85°40W 311 B11
Cutral-Có Argentina 38°58S 69°15W 336 A3
Cutro Italy 39°2N 16°59E 201 C9
Cuttaburra → Australia 29°43S 144°22E 281 D3
Cuttack India 20°25N 85°57E 244 D7
Cuva → Angola 11°42S 14°52E 265 E2
Cuvelai Angola 15°44S 15°50E 265 F3
Cuvette □ Congo 0°30S 16°0E 264 C3
Cuvette-Ouest □ Congo 0°10N 14°30E 264 B2
Cuvier, C. Australia 23°14S 113°22E 279 D1
Cuvier I. N.Z. 36°27S 175°50E 284 C4
Çuvuşabaşı → Turkey 40°58N 28°51E 122 B1
Cuwei China 39°54N 116°15E 114 B1
Cuxhaven Germany 53°51N 8°41E 178 B4
Cuyabeno Ecuador 0°16S 75°53W 328 D2
Cuyahoga Falls U.S.A. 41°8N 81°29W 312 E3
Cuyahoga Valley △ U.S.A. 41°24N 81°33W 312 E3
Cuyapo Phil. 15°46N 120°40E 232 D3
Cuyo Phil. 10°51N 121°2E 233 F3
Cuyo East Pass. Phil. 11°0N 121°28E 233 F3
Cuyo Islands Phil. 11°4N 120°57E 233 F3
Cuyo West Pass. Phil. 11°0N 120°30E 233 F3
Cuyuni → Guyana 6°23N 58°41W 329 B6
Cuyuni-Mazaruni □ Guyana 6°5N 59°46W 329 B5
Cuzco = Cusco Peru 13°32S 72°0W 330 C3
Cuzco Bolivia 20°0S 66°50W 330 E4
Čvrsnica Bos.-H. 43°36N 17°35E 182 G2
Cwmbran U.K. 51°39N 3°2W 169 F4
Cyangugu Rwanda 2°29S 28°54E 268 C2
Cybinka Poland 52°12N 14°46E 185 F1
Cyclades = Kyklades Greece 37°0N 24°30E 204 E6
Cygnet Australia 43°8S 147°1E 281 G4
Cynthiana U.S.A. 38°23N 84°18W 311 F12
Cypress Hills Sask., Canada 49°40N 109°30W 297 D7
Cypress Hills N.Y., U.S.A. 40°41N 73°53W 132 B2
Cypress Hills ⌂ Canada 49°40N 109°30W 297 D7
Cypress Park U.S.A. 34°6N 118°13W 126 B3
Cyprus ■ Asia 35°0N 33°0E 207 F9
Cyrenaica = Barqa Libya 27°0N 23°0E 258 B4
Cyrene Libya 32°53N 21°52E 258 B4
Czaplinek Poland 53°34N 16°14E 184 E3
Czar Canada 52°27N 110°50W 297 C6
Czarna → Łódzkie, Poland 51°18N 19°55E 185 G6
Czarna → Świętokrzyskie, Poland 50°28N 21°21E 185 H8
Czarna Białostocka Poland 53°18N 23°17E 185 E10
Czarna Woda Poland 53°51N 18°6E 184 E5
Czarne Poland 53°42N 16°58E 184 E3
Czarnków Poland 52°55N 16°38E 185 F3
Czaslau = Čáslav Czechia 49°54N 15°22E 180 B8
Czech Rep. = Czechia ■ Europe 50°0N 15°0E 180 B8
Czechia ■ Europe 50°0N 15°0E 180 B8
Czechowice-Dziedzice Poland 49°54N 18°59E 185 J5
Czempiń Poland 52°9N 16°43E 185 F3
Czeremcha Poland 52°31N 23°21E 185 F10
Czerniejewo Poland 52°26N 17°30E 185 F4
Czernowitz = Chernivtsi Ukraine 48°15N 25°52E 183 B10
Czerniaków Poland 52°11N 21°3E 143 B2
Czersk Poland 53°46N 17°58E 184 E4
Czerwieńsk Poland 52°1N 15°23E 185 F2
Czerwionka-Leszczyny Poland 50°7N 18°37E 185 H5
Częstochowa Poland 50°49N 19°7E 185 H6
Człopa Poland 53°6N 16°6E 185 E3
Człuchów Poland 53°41N 17°22E 184 E4
Czortów = Chortkiv Ukraine 49°2N 25°46E 177 D13
Czyste Poland 52°13N 20°57E 143 B1
Czyżew-Osada Poland 52°48N 22°19E 185 F9

D

D.C. War Memorial Washington, D.C., U.S.A. 143 b1
D.H.A. Phase VIII Pakistan 24°47N 67°2E 123 B2
Da → Vietnam 21°15N 105°20E 228 G5
Da Hinggan Ling China 48°0N 121°0E 219 B13
Da Moóca → Brazil 23°35S 46°35W 137 B2
Da Nang Vietnam 16°4N 108°13E 236 D7
Da Qaidam China 37°50N 95°15E 218 D8
Da Yunhe → Hopei, China 39°10N 117°10E 227 E9
Da Yunhe → Jiangsu, China 34°25N 120°5E 227 H10
Da'an China 45°30N 124°7E 227 B13
Daan Viljoen ⌂ Namibia 22°2S 16°45E 270 B2
Daanbantayan Phil. 11°17N 124°2E 233 F5
Dab'a, Ras el Egypt 31°3N 28°31E 256 H6
Daba Shan China 32°0N 109°0E 228 B7
Dabai Nigeria 11°25N 5°15E 263 C6
Dabajuro Venezuela 11°2N 70°40W 328 A3
Dabakala Ivory C. 8°15N 4°20W 262 D4
Dabaka India 26°7N 92°52E 241 B4
Dabaro Somalia 6°21N 48°43E 267 C6
Dabas Hungary 47°11N 19°19E 182 C4
Dabat Ethiopia 12°58N 37°41E 257 E4
Dabbagh, Jabal Si. Arabia 27°52N 35°45E 246 E2
Dabeiba Colombia 7°1N 76°16W 328 B2
Daber = Dobra Poland 53°34N 15°20E 184 E2
Dabhoi India 22°10N 73°20E 242 H5
Dąbie Poland 52°5N 18°50E 185 F5
Dabie Shan China 31°20N 115°20E 229 B10
Dabilda Cameroon 12°45N 14°35E 259 F2
Dabl, W. → Si. Arabia 29°5N 36°16E 251 J7
Ďáblice Czechia 50°8N 14°29E 135 B2
Dabnou Niger 14°10N 5°22E 263 C6
Dabo Indonesia 0°30S 104°33E 234 C2
Dabola Guinea 10°50N 11°5W 262 C2
Dabou Ivory C. 5°20N 4°23W 262 D4
Daboya Ghana 9°30N 1°20W 263 D4
Dabravolya Belarus 52°55N 23°59E 185 F10
Dąbrowa Poland 52°19N 20°52E 143 B1
Dąbrowa Białostocka Poland 53°40N 23°21E 184 E10
Dąbrowa Górnicza Poland 50°15N 19°10E 185 H6
Dąbrowa Tarnowska Poland 50°10N 20°59E 185 H7
Dabu China 24°22N 116°41E 229 E11
Dabugam India 19°27N 82°26E 244 E6
Dabung Malaysia 5°23N 102°1E 237 K4
Dabus → Ethiopia 10°48N 35°10E 257 E4
Dacato → Ethiopia 7°25N 42°40E 257 F5
Dacca = Dhaka Bangla. 23°43N 90°26E 241 D3
Dachang Jiangsu, China 32°13N 118°45E 229 A12
Dachang Shanghai, China 31°17N 121°24E 138 B1
Dachang ✈ China 31°18N 121°25E 138 B1
Dachaoshan Dam China 24°1N 100°22E 228 E3
Dachau Germany 48°15N 11°26E 131 A1
Dachau-Ost Germany 48°15N 11°27E 131 A1
Dachauer Moos Germany 48°13N 11°27E 131 A1
Dacheng = Tacheng Taiwan 23°51N 120°19E 225 C2
Dachigam △ India 34°10N 75°0E 242 B6
Dachstein, Hoher Austria 47°28N 13°35E 180 D6
Dačice Czechia 49°5N 15°26E 180 B8
Dacre Canada 45°22N 76°57W 312 A8
Dacula U.S.A. 33°59N 83°54W 316 B6
Dadanawa Guyana 2°50N 59°30W 329 C6
Dadar India 19°0N 72°49E 130 A1
Daday Turkey 41°28N 33°27E 212 B5
Dade City U.S.A. 28°22N 82°11W 317 G7
Dadès, Oued → Morocco 30°58N 6°44W 260 B3
Dadeville U.S.A. 32°50N 85°46W 316 C4
Dadhar Pakistan 29°28N 67°39E 242 E2
Dadiya Nigeria 9°35N 11°24E 263 D7
Ḑadnah U.A.E. 25°32N 56°22E 247 E8
Dadohae ⌂ S. Korea 34°0N 126°0E 224 E3
Dadra = Achalpur India 21°22N 77°32E 244 D3
Dadra & Nagar Haveli □ India 20°5N 73°0E 244 D1
Dadri = Charkhi Dadri India 28°37N 76°17E 242 E7
Dadu Pakistan 26°45N 67°45E 242 F2
Dadu He → China 29°31N 103°46E 228 C4
Daebang S. Korea 37°30N 126°55E 137 B1
Daebudo S. Korea 37°14N 126°35E 224 D3
Daecheongdo S. Korea 37°49N 124°42E 224 D2
Daechi S. Korea 37°30N 127°4E 137 B2
Daegu S. Korea 35°50N 128°37E 224 E4
Daejeon S. Korea 36°20N 127°28E 224 D3
Daejeon □ S. Korea 36°20N 127°25E 224 D3
Daejeong S. Korea 33°8N 126°17E 224 a
Daemodo S. Korea 34°11N 126°45E 224 E3
Daet Phil. 14°2N 122°55E 232 D4
Daeyeonpyeong = Yeonpyeongdo S. Korea 37°40N 125°45E 224 D2
Dafang China 27°9N 105°39E 228 D5
Dafdaf, J. Si. Arabia 28°16N 35°35E 251 K6
Dafeng China 33°3N 120°45E 227 H11
Dafnes Greece 35°13N 25°3E 207 E6
Dafni Athina, Greece 37°55N 23°44E 112 B2
Dafni Peloponnese, Greece 37°48N 22°1E 204 D4
Dafnoudi, Akra Greece 38°28N 20°32E 207 C2
Dağ Turkey 37°12N 30°31E 205 D12
Daga Post South Sudan 9°13N 33°58E 266 C3
Dagali Norway 60°25N 8°28E 164 D5
Dagana Senegal 16°30N 15°35W 262 B1
Dagash Sudan 19°19N 33°25E 256 D3
Dagenham U.K. 51°32N 0°8E 125 A4
Dagestan □ Russia 42°30N 47°0E 191 J8
Dagestanskiye Ogni Russia 42°6N 48°12E 191 J9
Dagg Sd. N.Z. 45°23S 166°45E 285 F1
Daggett U.S.A. 34°52N 116°52W 307 L10
Daghestan Republic = Dagestan □ Russia 42°30N 47°0E 191 J8
Daghfeli Sudan 19°18N 32°40E 256 D3
Dagling Germany 48°8N 11°39E 131 B2
Dağlıq Qarabağ = Nagorno-Karabakh □ Azerbaijan 39°55N 46°45E 213 C12
Dagö = Hiiumaa Estonia 58°50N 22°45E 188 C2
Dagu China 38°59N 117°40E 227 E9
Dagua Papua N. G. 3°27S 143°20E 286 B2
Daguan China 27°43N 103°56E 228 D4
D'Aguilar Pen. Hong Kong, China 22°13N 114°5E 122 B2
Dagupan Phil. 16°3N 120°20E 232 C3
Daguragu Australia 17°33S 130°30E 278 C5
Daguragu ⊙ Australia 17°24S 130°48E 278 C5
Dahab Egypt 28°31N 34°31E 251 K5
Dahab, Gezîret el Egypt 29°59N 31°13E 117 B2
Dahanu India 19°58N 72°44E 244 E1
Daheisha West Bank 31°42N 35°11E 123 B2
Dahivadi India 17°43N 74°33E 244 F2
Dahlak Kebir Eritrea 15°50N 40°10E 257 D5
Dahlak Marine ⌂ Eritrea 15°35N 40°1E 257 D5
Dahlem Germany 52°27N 13°16E 115 B2
Dahlenburg Germany 53°11N 10°44E 178 B6
Dahlonega U.S.A. 34°32N 83°59W 315 D13
Dahlwitz-Hoppegarten Germany 52°30N 13°41E 115 A5
Dahme Germany 51°52N 13°25E 178 D9
Dahod India 22°50N 74°15E 242 H6
Dahomey = Benin ■ Africa 10°0N 2°0E 263 D5
Dahong Shan China 31°25N 113°0E 229 B9
Dahongliutan China 35°45N 79°20E 243 B8
Dahongmen China 39°48N 116°21E 114 C2
Dahra Libya 29°30N 17°50E 258 C3
Dahra Senegal 15°22N 15°30W 262 B1
Dahra, Massif de Algeria 36°7N 1°21E 261 A5
Dahshûr Egypt 29°45N 31°14E 256 J7
Dahu = Tahu Taiwan 24°26N 120°52E 225 B2
Dahūk Iraq 36°50N 43°1E 213 D10
Dahūk □ Iraq 36°50N 42°50E 213 D10
Dahuofan Shuiku China 41°52N 124°12E 224 B2
Dahy, Nafūd ad Si. Arabia 22°0N 45°25E 248 B4
Dai Solomon Is. 7°54S 160°40E 287 L11
Dai Hao Vietnam 18°1N 106°25E 236 C6
Dai-Sen Japan 35°22N 133°32E 222 B5
Dai Shan China 30°25N 122°10E 229 B14
Dai Xian China 39°4N 112°58E 226 E7
Daiba = Odaiba Japan 35°38N 139°47E 140 B3
Daicheng China 38°42N 116°38E 226 E9
Daigo Japan 36°46N 140°21E 223 A12
Daik-u Burma 17°47N 96°40E 241 G6
Daikondi = Dāykondī □ Afghan. 34°0N 66°0E 240 B2
Dailekh Nepal 28°50N 81°44E 243 E9
Daimanji-San Japan 36°14N 133°20E 222 A5
Daimiel Spain 39°5N 3°35W 195 F7
Daingean Ireland 53°18N 7°17W 166 C4
Daingean, An = Dingle Ireland 52°9N 10°17W 166 D1
Dainkog China 32°30N 97°58E 228 A1
Daintree Australia 16°20S 145°20E 280 B4
Daintree △ Australia 16°8S 145°2E 280 B4
Daiō-Misaki Japan 34°15N 136°45E 223 C8
Dair, J. ed Sudan 12°27N 30°42E 257 E3
Dairen = Dalian China 38°50N 121°40E 227 E11
Dairût Egypt 27°34N 30°43E 256 B3
Daisen Japan 39°27N 140°29E 220 E10
Daisen-Oki △ Japan 35°23N 133°34E 222 B5
Daisetsu-Zan Japan 43°30N 142°57E 220 C11
Daisetsu-Zan △ Japan 43°30N 142°55E 220 C11
Daitari India 21°10N 85°46E 244 D7
Daitō Japan 35°19N 132°58E 222 B4
Daiyun Shan China 25°50N 118°15E 229 E12
Dajarra Australia 21°42S 139°30E 280 C2
Dajia = Tachia Taiwan 24°25N 120°28E 225 B2
Dajiaoting China 39°51N 116°27E 114 B2
Dajiawa China 37°9N 119°0E 227 F10
Dajin Chuan → China 31°16N 101°59E 228 B3
Dajti △ Albania 41°22N 19°56E 202 E3
Dak Dam Cambodia 12°20N 107°21E 236 F6
Dak Nhe Vietnam 15°28N 107°48E 236 E6
Dak Pek Vietnam 15°4N 107°44E 236 E6
Dak Song Vietnam 12°19N 107°35E 237 F6
Dak Sui Vietnam 14°55N 107°43E 236 E6
Dakar Senegal 14°34N 17°29W 262 C1
Dakar □ Senegal 14°45N 17°20W 262 C1
Dakhal, W. el → Egypt 28°48N 32°47E 251 K3
Dakhin Bangla. 22°30N 90°45E 241 D3
Dakhla W. Sahara 23°50N 15°53W 260 D1
Dakhla, El Wâhât el Egypt 25°30N 28°50E 256 B2
Dakhnoye Russia 59°49N 30°15E 137 C1
Dakingari Nigeria 11°37N 4°1E 263 C5
Dakoank India 7°2N 93°43E 245 L11
Dakor India 22°45N 73°11E 242 H5
Dakoro Niger 14°31N 6°46E 263 C6
Dakota City Iowa, U.S.A. 42°43N 94°12W 310 B2
Dakota City Nebr., U.S.A. 42°25N 96°25W 308 D5
Đakovica = Gjakovë Kosovo 42°22N 20°26E 202 D4
Đakovo Croatia 45°19N 18°24E 182 E3
Dal Norway 59°53N 8°40E 164 E5
Dala Lunda Sul, Angola 11°3S 20°17E 265 E4
Dala Uige, Angola 8°5S 15°49E 265 D3
Dala Solomon Is. 8°30S 160°41E 287 M11
Dala-Cachibo Angola 10°30S 14°41E 265 E2
Dala-Järna Sweden 60°33N 14°26E 162 D8
Dalaba Guinea 10°47N 12°12W 262 C2
Dalachi China 36°48N 105°0E 226 F3
Dalagan = San Antonio Phil. 14°57N 120°5E 232 D3
Dalaguete Phil. 9°46N 123°32E 233 G4
Dalai Nur China 43°20N 116°45E 226 C9
Dālakī Iran 29°26N 51°17E 247 D6
Dalälven → Sweden 60°12N 16°43E 162 D10
Dalaman Turkey 36°48N 28°47E 205 E10
Dalaman → Turkey 36°41N 28°43E 205 E10
Dalandzadgad Mongolia 43°27N 104°30E 226 C3
Dalanganem Is. Phil. 10°40N 120°17E 233 F3
Dalap-Uliga-Darrit = Majuro Marshall Is. 7°9N 171°12E 288 G9
Dalarna Sweden 61°0N 14°0E 162 D8
Dalarna □ Sweden 61°0N 14°15E 162 C8
Dalasýsla Iceland 65°15N 22°0W 155 B4
Dalat Malaysia 2°44N 111°56E 235 B4
Dalay Mongolia 43°28N 103°30E 226 C2
Dālbandīn Pakistan 29°0N 64°23E 240 C2
Dalbeattie U.K. 54°56N 3°50W 167 G5
Dalbeg Australia 20°16S 147°18E 280 C4
Dalbosjön Sweden 58°40N 12°45E 163 F6
Dalby Queens., Australia 27°10S 151°17E 281 D5
Dalby Skåne, Sweden 55°40N 13°22E 163 J7
Dalby Söderskog △ Sweden 55°41N 13°21E 163 J7
Dale Sogn og Fjordane, Norway 61°22N 5°23E 164 C2
Dale Ind., U.S.A. 38°10N 86°59W 311 F10
Dale City U.S.A. 38°38N 77°19W 309 F15
Dale Hollow L. U.S.A. 36°32N 85°27W 315 C12
Dalejský potok → Czechia 50°2N 14°24E 135 B2
Dalen Norway 59°26N 8°0E 164 E4
Dalet Burma 19°59N 93°51E 241 F4
Daletme Burma 21°36N 92°46E 241 E4
Daleville Ala., U.S.A. 31°19N 85°43W 316 D4
Daleville Ind., U.S.A. 40°7N 85°33W 311 D11
Dalga Egypt 27°39N 30°41E 256 B3
Dalgān Iran 27°31N 59°19E 247 E8
Dalgety Bay U.K. 56°2N 3°20W 121 A1
Dalhart U.S.A. 36°4N 102°31W 314 C3
Dalhousie N.B., Canada 48°5N 66°26W 299 C6
Dalhousie India 32°38N 75°58E 242 C6
Dali Shaanxi, China 34°48N 109°58E 226 G5
Dali Yunnan, China 25°40N 100°10E 228 E3
Dalian China 38°50N 121°40E 227 E11
Daliang Shan China 28°0N 102°45E 228 D4
Daliao = Taliao Taiwan 22°36N 120°23E 225 D2
Dalin = Talin Taiwan 23°36N 120°27E 225 C2
Daling He → China 40°55N 121°40E 227 D11
Dalj Croatia 45°29N 18°59E 182 E3
Dalkeith Midloth., U.K. 55°54N 3°4W 121 B3
Dalkeith Fla., U.S.A. 30°0N 85°9W 316 E4
Dalkey Ireland 53°16N 6°6W 166 C5
Dallas Ga., U.S.A. 33°55N 84°51W 316 B5
Dallas Oreg., U.S.A. 44°55N 123°19W 304 D3
Dallas Tex., U.S.A. 32°47N 96°48W 120 B4
Dallas City U.S.A. 40°38N 91°10W 310 D5
Dallas-Fort Worth Int. ✈ (DFW) U.S.A. 32°54N 97°2W 314 E6
Dallas-Fort Worth Int. ✈ (DFW) Tex., U.S.A. 32°53N 97°2W 120 A3
Dallas-Fort Worth Meacham Int. ✈ (FTW) U.S.A. 32°49N 97°21W 120 B2
Dalle = Yirga Alem Ethiopia 6°48N 38°22E 257 F4
Dalles, The U.S.A. 45°36N 121°10W 304 D3
Dallgow Germany 52°32N 13°5E 115 A1
Dallol Ethiopia 14°14N 40°17E 257 E5
Dalmā U.A.E. 24°30N 52°20E 247 E7
Dalmacija Croatia 43°20N 17°0E 199 E13
Dalmas, L. Canada 53°30N 71°50W 299 B5
Dalmatia = Dalmacija Croatia 43°20N 17°0E 199 E13
Dalmau India 26°4N 81°2E 243 F9
Dalmellington U.K. 55°19N 4°23W 167 F4
Dalmeny N.S.W., Australia 36°10S 150°8E 283 D9
Dalmeny Edinburgh, U.K. 55°59N 3°22W 121 B1
Dalnegorsk Russia 44°32N 135°33E 220 B7
Dalnerechensk Russia 45°50N 133°40E 220 B6
Dalnevostochnyy □ Russia 67°0N 140°0E 215 C14
Dalny = Dalian China 38°50N 121°40E 227 E11
Daloa Ivory C. 7°0N 6°30W 262 D3
Dalou Shan China 28°15N 107°0E 228 C6
Dalry U.K. 55°42N 4°43W 167 F4
Dalrymple, L. Australia 20°40S 147°0E 280 C4
Dalrymple, Mt. Australia 21°1S 148°39E 280 b
Dals Långed Sweden 58°56N 12°18E 163 F6
Dalsætra Norway 61°28N 9°26E 164 C6
Dalsjöfors Sweden 57°46N 13°5E 163 G7
Dalsland Sweden 58°50N 12°15E 163 F6
Dalsmynni Iceland 64°48N 21°29W 155 C5
Dalston U.K. 51°32N 0°4W 125 A3
Daltenganj India 24°0N 84°4E 243 H11
Dalton Ga., U.S.A. 34°46N 84°58W 315 D12
Dalton Mass., U.S.A. 42°28N 73°11W 313 D11
Dalton Nebr., U.S.A. 41°25N 102°58W 308 E2
Dalton, Kap Greenland 69°25N 24°3W 154 D8
Dalton-in-Furness U.K. 54°10N 3°11W 168 C4
Daludalu Indonesia 1°4N 100°15E 234 B2
Dalupiri I. Cagayan, Phil. 19°5N 121°12E 232 B3
Dalupiri I. N. Samar, Phil. 12°25N 124°16E 232 E5
Dalvík Iceland 65°58N 18°32W 155 B8
Dálvvadis = Jokkmokk Sweden 66°35N 19°50E 160 C18
Dalwallinu Australia 30°17S 116°40E 279 F2
Dalworthington Gardens U.S.A. 32°42N 97°9W 120 B3
Daly → Australia 13°35S 130°19E 278 B5
Daly City U.S.A. 37°42N 122°27W 136 B2
Daly L. Canada 56°32N 105°39W 297 B7
Daly River Australia 13°46S 130°42E 278 B5
Daly River-Port Keats ⊙ Australia 14°13S 129°36E 278 B4
Daly Waters Australia 16°15S 133°24E 280 B1
Dalyan Turkey 36°50N 28°39E 205 E10
Dam Amsterdam, Neths. 112 a2
Dam Doi Vietnam 8°50N 105°12E 237 H5
Dam Ha Vietnam 21°21N 107°36E 236 B6
Damachova Belarus 51°45N 23°36E 185 G10
Damaia Portugal 38°44N 9°12W 126 A1
Daman India 20°25N 72°57E 244 D1
Daman & Diu □ India 20°25N 72°58E 244 D1
Dāmaneh Iran 33°1N 50°29E 247 C6
Damanganga → India 20°25N 72°56E 244 D1
Damanhûr Egypt 31°0N 30°30E 256 H7
Damant L. Canada 61°45N 105°5W 297 A7
Damaq Iran 35°25N 48°49E 213 E13
Damar Indonesia 7°7S 128°40E 231 F7
Damara C.A.R. 4°58N 18°42E 264 B3
Damarakia Greece 37°58N 23°39E 112 B1
Damaraland Namibia 20°0S 15°0E 270 B2
Damascus = Dimashq Syria 33°30N 36°18E 250 E7
Damascus U.S.A. 31°18N 84°43W 316 D5
Damasi Greece 39°43N 22°11E 204 B4
Damaturu Nigeria 11°45N 11°55E 263 C7
Damavand = Damāvand, Qolleh-ye Iran 35°57N 52°7E 247 C7
Damāvand Iran 35°57N 52°7E 247 C7
Damāvand, Qolleh-ye Iran 35°57N 52°7E 247 C7
Damba Angola 6°44S 15°20E 265 D3
Damboa Nigeria 11°15N 12°55E 259 F2
Dâmboviţa □ Romania 45°0N 25°30E 183 F10
Dâmboviţa → Romania 44°12N 26°26E 183 F11
Dâmbovnic → Romania 44°28N 25°18E 183 F10
Dambrowica = Dubrovytsya Ukraine 51°31N 26°35E 177 C14
Dambulla Sri Lanka 7°51N 80°39E 245 L5
Dame Marie Haiti 18°34N 74°26W 321 C5
Dämeritzsee Germany 52°34N 13°43E 115 B5
Dāmghān Iran 36°10N 54°17E 247 B7
Dămienesti Romania 46°44N 26°59E 183 D11
Damietta = Dumyât Egypt 31°24N 31°48E 251 G2
Daming China 36°15N 115°6E 226 F8
Damîr Qābū Syria 36°58N 41°51E 246 B4
Dammai I. Phil. 5°47N 120°25E 233 J3
Dammam = Ad Dammām Si. Arabia 26°20N 50°5E 247 E6
Dammarie-les-Lys France 48°31N 2°39E 173 D9
Dammartin-en-Goële France 49°3N 2°41E 173 C9
Damme Germany 52°32N 8°11E 178 C4
Damodar → India 23°17N 87°35E 243 H12
Damoh India 23°50N 79°28E 243 H8
Damous Algeria 36°31N 1°42E 261 A5
Dampier Australia 20°41S 116°42E 278 D2
Dampier, Selat Indonesia 0°40S 131°0E 231 E8
Dampier Arch. Australia 20°38S 116°32E 278 D2
Dampier Str. Papua N. G. 5°50S 148°0E 286 C5
Damqawt Yemen 16°34N 52°50E 249 C6
Damrak Amsterdam, Neths. 112 a2
Damrani Algeria 27°45N 2°56W 260 C4
Damrei, Chuor Phnum Cambodia 11°30N 103°0E 237 G4
Damroh India 28°26N 95°14E 241 A5
Damvillers France 49°20N 5°21E 173 C12
Damyang S. Korea 35°19N 126°59E 224 E3
Dan Gorayo Somalia 8°43N 49°20E 267 C6
Dan-Gulbi Nigeria 11°40N 6°15E 263 C6
Dan Ryan Woods U.S.A. 41°44N 87°40W 119 C2
Dan-Sadau Nigeria 11°17N 6°29E 263 C6
Dana Indonesia 11°0S 121°15E 231 F6
Dana Jordan 30°41N 35°37E 251 H6
Dana Nepal 28°32N 83°37E 243 E10
Dana, L. Canada 50°53N 77°20W 298 B4
Dana, Mt. U.S.A. 37°54N 119°12W 306 H7
Danakil Depression Ethiopia 13°0N 41°0E 267 B5
Danakil Desert Ethiopia 12°45N 41°0E 257 E5
Danan Ethiopia 6°31N 43°30E 267 C5
Danané Ivory C. 7°16N 8°9W 262 D3
Danao Phil. 10°31N 124°1E 233 F5
Danau Sentarum △ Indonesia 0°51N 112°6E 235 B4
Danba China 30°54N 101°48E 228 B3
Danbury U.S.A. 41°24N 73°28W 313 E11
Danby L. U.S.A. 34°13N 115°5W 307 L11
Dand Afghan. 31°28N 65°32E 242 D1
Dande → Angola 8°28S 13°21E 265 D2
Dande ⌂ Zimbabwe 15°56S 30°16E 269 F3
Dandeldhura Nepal 29°20N 80°35E 243 E9
Dandeli India 15°5N 74°30E 245 G2
Dandenong Australia 38°0S 145°15E 283 E6
Danderhall U.K. 55°55N 3°7W 121 B3
Danderyd Sweden 59°24N 18°1E 139 A2
Dandī Iran 36°32N 47°37E 213 D12
Dandîl Egypt 29°10N 31°2E 256 J7
Dandong China 40°10N 124°20E 224 B2
Daneborg Greenland 74°18N 20°14W 154 C8
Danfeng China 33°45N 110°25E 226 H6
Danforth Canada 43°43N 79°16W 141 A3
Dangan Liedao China 22°2N 114°8E 229 F10
Dangcagan Phil. 7°36N 125°0E 233 H5
Dange Angola 7°56S 15°3E 265 D3
Dangé-St-Romain France 46°56N 0°36E 174 B4
Dângeni Romania 47°51N 26°58E 183 C11
Danger Is. = Pukapuka Cook Is. 10°53S 165°49W 289 J11
Danger Pt. S. Africa 34°40S 19°17E 270 D2
Dangjin S. Korea 36°53N 126°37E 224 D3
Dangla Ethiopia 11°18N 36°56E 257 E4
Dangla Shan = Tanggula Shan China 32°40N 92°10E 218 E7
Dangora Nigeria 11°30N 8°7E 263 C6
Dangouadougou Burkina Faso 10°9N 4°56W 262 D4
Dangrek, Mts. = Dangrek, Phnom Thailand 14°20N 104°0E 236 E5
Dangrek, Phnom Thailand 14°20N 104°0E 236 E5
Dangriga Belize 17°0N 88°13W 320 C2
Dangshan China 34°27N 116°22E 226 G9
Dangtu China 31°32N 118°25E 229 B12
Dangyang China 30°52N 111°44E 229 B8
Dania Beach U.S.A. 26°3N 80°8W 129 B3
Daniel U.S.A. 42°52N 110°4W 304 E8
Daniel's Harbour Canada 50°13N 57°35W 299 B8
Danielskuil S. Africa 28°11S 23°33E 270 C3
Danielson U.S.A. 41°48N 71°53W 313 E13
Danielsville U.S.A. 34°8N 83°13W 316 A6
Danilov Russia 58°16N 40°13E 188 C11
Danilovgrad Montenegro 42°38N 19°4E 202 D3
Danilovka Russia 50°25N 44°12E 190 E7
Daning China 36°28N 110°45E 226 F6
Danish West Indies = Virgin Is. (U.S.) ☒ W. Indies 18°20N 65°0W 321 C7
Danissa Kenya 3°17N 40°59E 267 D5
Danja Nigeria 11°21N 7°30E 263 C6
Danje-la-Menha Angola 9°32S 14°39E 265 D2
Danjiangkou China 32°31N 111°30E 229 A8
Danjiangkou Shuiku China 32°37N 111°30E 229 A8
Ḑank Oman 23°33N 56°16E 247 F8
Dankalwa Nigeria 11°52N 12°12E 263 C7
Dankama Nigeria 13°20N 7°44E 263 C6
Dankhar Gompa India 32°10N 78°10E 242 C8
Dankov Russia 53°20N 39°5E 188 F10
Danleng China 30°1N 103°31E 228 B4
Danlí Honduras 14°4N 86°35W 320 D2
Danmark = Denmark ■ Europe 55°45N 10°0E 163 J3
Danmark Fjord Greenland 81°30N 22°0W 154 A8
Danmarkshavn Greenland 76°45N 18°50W 154 B9
Dannemora U.S.A. 44°43N 73°44W 313 B11
Dannenberg Germany 53°6N 11°5E 178 B7
Dannevirke N.Z. 40°12S 176°8E 284 G5
Dannhauser S. Africa 28°0S 30°3E 271 C5
Danot Ethiopia 7°33N 45°17E 267 C6
Dansalan = Marawi City Phil. 8°0N 124°21E 233 G5
Danshuei = Tanshui Taiwan 25°10N 121°28E 225 A3
Dansville U.S.A. 42°34N 77°42W 312 D7
Danta India 24°11N 72°46E 242 G5
Dantan India 21°57N 87°20E 243 J12
Dante = Xaafuun Somalia 10°25N 51°16E 267 B7
Dantewara India 18°54N 81°21E 244 E5
Danube = Dunărea → Europe 45°20N 29°40E 183 E14
Danubyu Burma 17°15N 95°35E 241 G5
Danvers U.S.A. 42°34N 70°56W 313 D14
Danville Ga., U.S.A. 32°37N 83°15W 316 C6
Danville Ill., U.S.A. 40°8N 87°37W 311 D9
Danville Ind., U.S.A. 39°46N 86°32W 311 E10
Danville Ky., U.S.A. 37°39N 84°46W 311 G12
Danville Pa., U.S.A. 40°58N 76°37W 313 F8
Danville Va., U.S.A. 36°36N 79°23W 309 G14
Danville Vt., U.S.A. 44°25N 72°9W 313 B12
Danyang China 32°0N 119°31E 229 B12
Danzhai China 26°11N 107°48E 228 D6
Danzhou China 19°31N 109°33E 229 a
Danzig = Gdańsk Poland 54°22N 18°40E 184 D5
Dao Antique, Phil. 10°30N 121°57E 233 F3
Dao Capiz, Phil. 11°24N 122°41E 233 F4
Dão → Portugal 40°20N 8°11W 194 E2
Dao Xian China 25°36N 111°31E 229 E8
Daocheng China 29°0N 100°10E 228 C3
Daora W. Sahara 27°5N 12°59W 260 C2
Daoud = Aïn Beïda Algeria 35°50N 7°29E 261 A6
Daoukro Ivory C. 7°10N 3°58W 262 D4
Dapa Phil. 9°46N 126°3E 233 G6
Dapaong Togo 10°55N 0°16E 263 C5
Dapchi Nigeria 12°32N 11°31E 263 C7
Dapiak, Mt. Phil. 8°15N 123°28E 233 G4
Dapitan Phil. 8°39N 123°25E 233 G4
Dapoli India 17°46N 73°11E 244 F1
Daporijo India 27°59N 94°13E 241 B5
Daqahlîya □ Egypt 30°55N 31°30E 251 H2
Daqing China 46°35N 125°0E 219 B13
Daqing Shan China 40°40N 111°0E 226 D6
Daqq-e Sorkh, Kavīr Iran 33°45N 52°50E 247 C7
Daqu Shan China 30°25N 122°20E 229 B14
Dar Banda Africa 8°0N 23°0E 254 F6
Dar el Beida = Casablanca Morocco 33°36N 7°36W 260 B3
Dar es Salaam Tanzania 6°50S 39°12E 268 D4
Dar Mazār Iran 29°14N 57°20E 247 D8
Dar Rounga C.A.R. 0°45N 22°20E 264 A4
Dār Ta'izzah Syria 36°20N 36°52E 250 B7
Dar'ā Syria 32°36N 36°7E 250 F7
Dar'ā □ Syria 32°55N 36°10E 250 F7
Dara Dere = Zlatograd Bulgaria 41°22N 25°7E 203 E9
Dārāb Iran 28°50N 54°30E 247 D7
Daraban Pakistan 31°44N 70°20E 242 D4
Darabani Romania 48°10N 26°39E 183 B11
Darai Hills Papua N. G. 7°8S 143°33E 286 D2
Daraina Madag. 13°12S 49°40E 272 A2
Daraj Libya 30°10N 10°28E 258 B2
Darakeh Iran 35°49N 51°22E 141 A2
Daram Phil. 11°38N 124°48E 233 F5
Dārān Iran 32°59N 50°24E 247 C6
Daravica = Gjeravicë Kosovo 42°32N 20°8E 202 D4
Daraw Egypt 24°22N 32°51E 256 C3
Dārayyā Syria 33°28N 36°15E 250 E7
Darazo Nigeria 11°1N 10°24E 263 C7
Darband Tehrān, Iran 35°49N 51°27E 141 A2
Darband Pakistan 34°20N 72°50E 242 B5
Darband, Kūh-e Iran 31°34N 57°8E 247 D8
Darbhanga India 26°15N 85°55E 243 F11
Darburruk Somalia 9°44N 44°31E 267 C5
Darby, C. U.S.A. 64°19N 162°47W 303 D7
D'Arcy Canada 50°33N 122°29W 296 C4
Darda Croatia 45°40N 18°41E 182 E3
Dardanë Kosovo 42°35N 21°35E 202 D5
Dardanelle Ark., U.S.A. 35°13N 93°9W 314 D8
Dardanelle Calif., U.S.A. 38°20N 119°50W 306 G7
Dardanelles = Çanakkale Boğazı Turkey 40°17N 26°32E 203 F10
Dare → Ethiopia 7°20N 42°11E 257 F5
Darende Turkey 38°31N 37°30E 212 C7
Dārestān Iran 29°9N 58°42E 247 D8
Darfield N.Z. 43°29S 172°7E 285 D7
Darfo-Boario Terme Italy 45°53N 10°11E 198 C7
Dārfūr Sudan 13°40N 24°0E 259 F4
Dargai Pakistan 34°25N 71°55E 242 B4
Dargaville N.Z. 35°57S 173°52E 284 B2
Dargol Niger 13°54N 1°22E 263 C5
Darhan Mongolia 49°37N 106°21E 218 B10
Darhan Muminggan China 41°40N 110°28E 226 D6
Dari South Sudan 5°48N 30°26E 257 F3
Darica Turkey 40°45N 29°23E 212 B3
Darien U.S.A. 31°23N 81°26W 316 D8
Darién, G. del Caribbean 9°0N 77°0W 320 E4
Darién, Serranía del Cent. Amer. 8°30N 77°30W 320 E4
Darién △ Panama 7°36N 77°57W 320 E4
Dariganga = Ovoot Mongolia 45°21N 113°45E 226 B7
Daringbadi India 19°54N 84°8E 244 E7
Dario, Palazzo Venice, Italy 142 c2
Darjeeling = Darjiling India 27°3N 88°18E 241 B2
Darjiling India 27°3N 88°18E 241 B2
Darkan Australia 33°20S 116°43E 279 F2
Darke Peak Australia 33°27S 136°12E 282 B2
Darkhana Pakistan 30°39N 72°11E 242 D5
Darkhazīneh Iran 31°54N 48°39E 247 D6
Darkot Pass Pakistan 36°45N 73°26E 243 A5
Darling → Australia 34°4S 141°54E 282 C4
Darling Downs Australia 27°30S 150°30E 281 D5
Darling Harbour Sydney, Australia 139 b1
Darling Point Australia 33°52S 151°15E 139 B2
Darling Ra. Australia 32°30S 116°20E 279 F2
Darlington Durham, U.K. 54°32N 1°33W 168 C6
Darlington Fla., U.S.A. 30°57N 86°3W 316 E3
Darlington S.C., U.S.A. 34°18N 79°52W 315 D15
Darlington Wis., U.S.A. 42°41N 90°7W 310 B6
Darlington □ U.K. 54°32N 1°33W 168 C6
Darlington, L. S. Africa 33°10S 25°9E 270 D4
Darlington Point Australia 34°37S 146°1E 283 C7
Darlot, L. Australia 27°48S 121°35E 279 E3
Darlowo Poland 54°25N 16°25E 184 D3
Dărmăneşti Bacău, Romania 46°21N 26°33E 183 D11
Dărmăneşti Suceava, Romania 47°44N 26°9E 183 C11
Darmstadt Germany 49°51N 8°39E 179 F4
Darnah Libya 32°45N 22°45E 258 B4
Darnah □ Libya 31°0N 23°40E 258 B4
Darnall S. Africa 29°23S 31°18E 271 C5
Darney France 48°5N 6°2E 173 D13
Darnick Australia 32°48S 143°38E 282 B5
Darnley Australia 9°35S 143°46E 280 a
Darnley, C. Antarctica 68°0S 69°0E 151 C6
Darnley B. Canada 69°30N 123°30W 294 D7
Daroca Spain 41°9N 1°25W 196 D3
Darror Ethiopia 8°14N 44°42E 267 C5
Darou-Mousti Senegal 15°3N 16°3W 262 B1
Darr → Australia 23°39S 143°50E 280 C3
Darra Pezu Pakistan 32°19N 70°44E 242 C4
Darran Mts. N.Z. 44°37S 167°59E 285 E2
Darreh Shahr Iran 33°7N 47°22E 213 F12
Darrequeira Argentina 37°42S 63°10W 334 D3
Darrington U.S.A. 48°15N 121°36W 304 B3
Darrūs Iran 35°46N 51°27E 141 A2
Darsah Yemen 12°6N 53°16E 249 D6
Darsana Bangla. 23°35N 88°48E 241 D2
Darsi India 15°46N 79°44E 245 G4
Darsser Ort Germany 54°28N 12°32E 178 A8
Dart → U.K. 50°24N 3°39W 169 G4
Dartford U.K. 51°26N 0°13E 125 B5
Dartmoor Vic., Australia 37°56S 141°19E 282 D4
Dartmoor Devon, U.K. 50°38N 3°57W 169 G4
Dartmoor △ U.K. 50°37N 3°59W 169 G4
Dartmouth N.S., Canada 44°40N 63°30W 299 D7
Dartmouth Devon, U.K. 50°21N 3°36W 169 G4
Dartmouth, L. Queens., Australia 26°4S 145°18E 281 D4
Dartmouth, L. Vic., Australia 36°34S 147°32E 283 D7
Dartuch, C. = Artrutx, C. de Spain 39°55N 3°49E 206 B4
Daru Papua N. G. 9°3S 143°13E 286 E2
Daruvar Croatia 45°35N 17°14E 182 E2
Darvaza = Içoguz Turkmenistan 40°11N 58°24E 216 D5
Darvel, Teluk = Lahad Datu, Telok Malaysia 4°50N 118°20E 235 B5
Darvi Mongolia 46°27N 94°7E 217 C12
Darwen U.K. 53°42N 2°29W 168 D5
Darwendale Zimbabwe 17°41S 30°33E 271 A5
Darwha India 20°15N 77°45E 244 D3
Darwin N. Terr., Australia 12°25S 130°51E 278 B5
Darwin Calif., U.S.A. 36°15N 117°35W 307 J9
Darwin, Mt. Chile 54°47S 69°55W 336 D3
Darwin, Volcán Ecuador 0°10S 91°18W 330 a
Darya Ganj Delhi, India 120 a3
Darya Khan Pakistan 31°48N 71°6E 242 D4
Daryapur India 20°55N 77°20E 244 D3
Daryoi Amu = Amudarya → Uzbekistan 43°58N 59°34E 216 D5
Dās U.A.E. 25°20N 53°30E 247 E7
Dashahe China 42°44N 128°10E 224 A4
Dashen, Ras Ethiopia 13°8N 38°26E 257 E4
Dasher U.S.A. 30°45N 83°13W 316 E6
Dashetai China 41°0N 109°5E 226 D5
Dashi China 23°1N 113°17E 121 B2
Dashiqiao China 40°38N 122°30E 227 D12
Dashkesan = Daşkäsän Azerbaijan 40°25N 46°0E 191 K7
Dashköpri Turkmenistan 36°16N 62°8E 247 B9
Dasht → Pakistan 25°10N 61°40E 240 D1
Dasht-i-Tahlab Pakistan 28°40N 62°25E 240 C1
Dashu = Tashu Taiwan 22°41N 120°25E 225 D2
Daska Pakistan 32°20N 74°20E 242 C6
Daşkäsän Azerbaijan 40°25N 46°0E 191 K7
Dasmariñas Phil. 14°20N 120°56E 232 D3
Daşoguz Turkmenistan 41°49N 59°58E 216 D5
Dasol B. Phil. 15°52N 119°50E 232 D2
Dassa Benin 7°46N 2°14E 263 D5
Dasuya India 31°49N 75°38E 242 D6
Datadian Indonesia 2°1N 115°13E 235 B5
Datansha China 23°8N 113°12E 121 B2
Datça Turkey 36°46N 27°40E 205 E9
Date Japan 42°28N 140°52E 220 C10
Datia India 25°39N 78°27E 243 G8
Datian China 25°40N 117°50E 229 E11
Datong Anhui, China 30°48N 117°44E 229 B11
Datong Qinghai, China 36°20N 102°50E 218 D9
Datong Shanxi, China 40°6N 113°18E 226 D7
Dattakhel Pakistan 32°54N 69°46E 242 C3
Dattapur = Dhamangaon India 20°48N 78°9E 244 D4
Datteln Germany 51°39N 7°21E 178 D3
Datu, Tanjung Indonesia 2°5N 109°39E 235 B3
Datu Piang Phil. 7°2N 124°30E 233 H5
Datuk, Tanjong = Datu, Tanjung Indonesia 2°5N 109°39E 235 B3
Datun China 40°0N 116°23E 114 B2
Daua = Dawa → Africa 4°11N 42°6E 257 G5
Daud Khel Pakistan 32°53N 71°34E 242 C4
Daudnagar India 25°2N 84°24E 243 G11
Daugava → Latvia 57°4N 24°3E 188 D3
Daugavpils Latvia 55°53N 26°32E 188 E4
Daulatabad India 19°57N 75°15E 244 E2
Daulatpur India 28°44N 77°6E 120 A1
Daule Ecuador 1°56S 79°56W 328 D2
Daule → Ecuador 2°10S 79°52W 328 D2
Daule-Peripa, Presa Ecuador 1°0S 79°35W 328 D2
Daulpur India 26°45N 77°59E 242 F7
Daun Germany 50°11N 6°49E 179 E2
Daund India 18°26N 74°40E 244 E2
Daung Kyun Burma 12°13N 98°4E 237 F1
Dauphin Man., Canada 51°9N 100°5W 297 C8
Dauphin Pa., U.S.A. 40°22N 76°56W 312 F8
Dauphin L. Canada 51°20N 99°45W 297 C9
Dauphiné France 45°15N 5°25E 175 C9
Daura Borno, Nigeria 11°31N 11°24E 263 C7
Daura Katsina, Nigeria 13°2N 8°21E 263 C6
Daurada, Costa Spain 41°12N 1°15E 196 D6
Dausa India 26°52N 76°20E 242 F7
Däväçi Azerbaijan 41°15N 48°57E 191 K9
Davangere India 14°25N 75°55E 245 G2
Davao Phil. 7°0N 125°40E 233 H5
Davao □ Phil. 7°50N 125°55E 233 H5
Davao del Sur □ Phil. 7°0N 125°30E 233 H5
Davao G. Phil. 6°30N 125°48E 233 H5
Davao Occidental □ Phil. 6°0N 125°30E 233 H5
Davao Oriental □ Phil. 7°10N 126°30E 233 H6
Dāvar Panāh = Sarāvān Iran 27°25N 62°15E 247 E9
Davenport Calif., U.S.A. 37°1N 122°12W 306 H4
Davenport Fla., U.S.A. 28°10N 81°36W 317 G8
Davenport Iowa, U.S.A. 41°32N 90°35W 310 C6
Davenport Wash., U.S.A. 47°39N 118°9W 304 C4
Davenport Ra. Australia 20°28S 134°0E 280 C1
Davenport Range △ Australia 20°36S 134°22E 280 C1
Daventry U.K. 52°16N 1°10W 169 E6
David Panama 8°30N 82°30W 320 E3
David City U.S.A. 41°15N 97°8W 308 E5
David Glacier Antarctica 75°20S 162°0E 151 D11
David Gorodok = Davyd Haradok Belarus 52°4N 27°8E 177 B14
David's Citadel Jerusalem 123 b3
David's Tomb Jerusalem 123 b3
Davidson Canada 51°16N 105°59W 297 C7
Davidson, Mt. U.S.A. 37°44N 122°27W 136 B2
Davidson Mts. U.S.A. 68°41N 142°22W 303 B12
Davidson's Mains U.K. 55°58N 3°16W 121 B2
Davie U.S.A. 26°3N 80°14W 129 B2
Davis Antarctica 68°34S 77°55E 151 C6
Davis Calif., U.S.A. 38°33N 121°44W 306 G5
Davis Dam U.S.A. 35°12N 114°34W 307 K12
Davis Mts. U.S.A. 30°50N 103°55W 314 F3
Davis Sea Antarctica 66°0S 92°0E 151 C7
Davis Str. N. Amer. 65°0N 58°0W 295 D19
Davisboro U.S.A. 32°59N 82°36W 316 C7
Davison U.S.A. 43°2N 83°31W 311 A13
Davlos Cyprus 35°25N 33°54E 207 E9
Davo → Ivory C. 5°0N 6°10W 262 D3
Davos Switz. 46°48N 9°49E 179 J5
Dāvūdiyeh Iran 35°45N 51°25E 141 A2
Davutlar Turkey 37°43N 27°17E 205 D9
Davy L. Canada 58°53N 108°18W 297 B7
Davyd Haradok Belarus 52°4N 27°8E 177 B14
Davydkovo Russia 55°43N 37°29E 129 B1
Dawa → Africa 4°11N 42°6E 257 G5
Dawaki Bauchi, Nigeria 9°25N 9°33E 263 D6
Dawaki Kano, Nigeria 12°5N 8°23E 263 C6
Dawei Burma 14°2N 98°12E 236 E2
Dawes Ra. Australia 24°40S 150°40E 280 C5
Dawidy Poland 52°8N 20°58E 143 C1
Dawkah Oman 18°39N 54°5E 249 C6
Dawley = Telford U.K. 52°40N 2°27W 169 E5
Dawlish U.K. 50°35N 3°28W 169 G4
Dawmat al Jandal Si. Arabia 29°55N 39°40E 246 D3
Dawna Ra. Burma 16°30N 98°30E 236 D2
Dawnyein Burma 15°54N 95°36E 241 G5
Dawqah Si. Arabia 19°36N 40°54E 248 C3
Dawrān Yemen 14°45N 44°12E 248 D4
Dawros Hd. Ireland 54°50N 8°33W 166 B3
Dawson Ga., U.S.A. 31°46N 84°27W 316 D5
Dawson, I. Chile 53°50S 70°50W 336 D2
Dawson B. Canada 52°53N 100°49W 297 C8
Dawson City Canada 64°10N 139°30W 294 E4
Dawson Creek Canada 55°45N 120°15W 296 B4
Dawson Inlet Canada 61°50N 93°25W 297 A10
Dawson Ra. Australia 24°30S 149°48E 280 C4
Dawu Hubei, China 31°34N 114°7E 229 B10
Dawu Sichuan, China 30°55N 101°10E 228 B3
Dawwah Oman 20°33N 58°48E 249 B7
Dawwara, Ras id- Malta 35°52N 14°21E 206 F7
Dax France 43°44N 1°3W 174 E2
Daxi = Tach'i Taiwan 24°53N 121°17E 225 B3
Daxian China 31°15N 107°23E 228 B6
Daxin China 22°50N 107°11E 228 F6
Daxindian China 37°30N 120°50E 227 F11
Daxing China 39°47N 116°24E 114 C2
Daxinggou China 43°25N 129°40E 227 C15
Daxue Shan Sichuan, China 30°30N 101°30E 228 B3
Daxue Shan Yunnan, China 23°42N 99°48E 228 F2
Day U.S.A. 30°12N 83°17W 316 E6
Daya el Khadra Mauritania 25°14N 6°2W 260 C3
Dayang He → China 39°51N 123°38E 224 C1
Dayao China 25°43N 101°20E 228 E3
Daye China 30°6N 114°58E 229 B10
Dayet en Naharat Mali 17°39N 3°10W 262 B4
Dayi China 30°41N 103°29E 228 B4
Dāykondī □ Afghan. 34°0N 66°0E 240 B2
Daylesford Australia 37°21S 144°9E 282 D6
Dayong = Zhangjiajie China 29°11N 110°30E 229 C8
Dayr az Zawr Syria 35°20N 40°5E 213 E9
Dayr az Zawr □ Syria 34°50N 40°10E 213 E9
Daysland Canada 52°50N 112°20W 296 C6
Dayton Iowa, U.S.A. 42°16N 94°4W 310 B2
Dayton Nev., U.S.A. 39°14N 119°36W 306 F7
Dayton Ohio, U.S.A. 39°45N 84°12W 311 E12
Dayton Pa., U.S.A. 40°53N 79°15W 312 F5
Dayton Tenn., U.S.A. 35°30N 85°1W 315 D12
Dayton Wash., U.S.A. 46°19N 117°59W 304 C5
Dayton Wyo., U.S.A. 44°53N 107°16W 304 D10
Daytona Beach U.S.A. 29°13N 81°1W 317 F8
Dayu China 25°24N 114°22E 229 E10
Dayuan = Tayuan Taiwan 25°3N 121°11E 225 A3
Dayville U.S.A. 44°28N 119°32W 304 D4
Dazaifu Japan 33°32N 130°32E 222 D2
Dazhu China 30°41N 107°15E 228 B6
Dazkırı Turkey 37°57N 29°52E 205 D11
Dazu China 29°40N 105°42E 228 C5
De Aar S. Africa 30°39S 24°0E 270 D3
De Armanville U.S.A. 33°38N 85°45W 316 B4
De Bary U.S.A. 28°54N 81°18W 317 G8
De Forest U.S.A. 43°15N 89°20W 310 A7
De Funiak Springs U.S.A. 30°43N 86°7W 316 E3
De Grey → Australia 20°12S 119°13E 278 D2
De Haan Belgium 51°16N 3°2E 170 C3
De Hoop ⌂ S. Africa 34°30S 20°28E 270 D3
De Kalb Junction U.S.A. 44°30N 75°16W 313 B9
De Land U.S.A. 29°2N 81°18W 317 F8
De Leon U.S.A. 32°7N 98°32W 314 E5
De Leon Springs U.S.A. 29°7N 81°21W 317 F8
De Long Mts. U.S.A. 68°10N 163°30W 303 B7
De Panne Belgium 51°6N 2°34E 170 C2
De Pere U.S.A. 44°27N 88°4W 308 C9
De Queen U.S.A. 34°2N 94°21W 314 D7
De Quincy U.S.A. 30°27N 93°26W 314 F8
De Ruyters U.S.A. 42°45N 75°53W 313 D9
De Smet U.S.A. 44°23N 97°33W 308 C5
De Soto Mo., U.S.A. 38°8N 90°34W 310 F6
De Soto Tex., U.S.A. 32°35N 96°51W 120 C5
De Soto City U.S.A. 27°27N 81°24W 317 H8
De Tour Village U.S.A. 46°0N 83°56W 309 B12
De Witt Ark., U.S.A. 34°18N 91°20W 314 D9
De Witt Iowa, U.S.A. 41°49N 90°33W 310 C6
De Witt Mich., U.S.A. 42°51N 84°34W 311 B12
Dead L. U.S.A. 30°10N 85°10W 316 E4
Dead Sea Asia 31°30N 35°30E 251 G6
Deadhorse U.S.A. 70°11N 148°27W 303 A10
Deadman B. U.S.A. 29°30N 83°30W 317 F6
Deadwood U.S.A. 44°23N 103°44W 308 C2
Deadwood L. Canada 59°10N 128°30W 296 B3
Deal U.K. 51°13N 1°25E 169 F9
Deal I. Australia 39°30S 147°20E 281 F4
Dealesville S. Africa 28°41S 25°44E 270 C4
De'an China 29°22N 115°46E 229 C10
Dean → Canada 52°49N 126°58W 296 C3
Dean, Forest of U.K. 51°45N 2°33W 169 F5

Dean Chan. Canada 52°30N 127°15W 296 C3
Deán Funes Argentina 30°20S 64°20W 334 C3
Dearborn Mich., U.S.A. 42°19N 83°10W 311 B13
Dearborn Mo., U.S.A. 39°32N 94°46W 310 E2
Dease ➜ Canada 59°56N 128°32W 296 B3
Dease Inlet U.S.A. 71°2N 155°26W 303 A9
Dease L. Canada 58°40N 130°5W 296 B2
Dease Lake Canada 58°25N 130°6W 296 B2
Death Valley U.S.A. 36°15N 116°50W 307 J10
Death Valley △ U.S.A. 36°29N 117°6W 307 J9
Death Valley Junction U.S.A. 36°20N 116°25W 307 J10
Deatnu = Tana ➜ Norway 70°30N 28°14E 160 A23
Deauville France 49°23N 0°2E 172 C7
Deba Spain 43°18N 2°21W 196 B2
Deba Habe Nigeria 10°14N 11°20E 263 C7
Debagram India 23°41N 88°18E 243 H13
Debak Malaysia 1°34N 111°25E 235 B4
Debaltsevo Ukraine 48°22N 38°26E 189 H10
Debao China 23°21N 106°46E 228 F6
Debar Macedonia 41°31N 20°30E 202 E4
Debark Ethiopia 13°1N 37°48E 257 E4
Debden Canada 53°30N 106°50W 297 C7
Debdou Morocco 33°59N 3°0W 261 B4
Debe Trin. & Tob. 10°12N 61°27W 323 t
Dębica Poland 50°2N 21°25E 185 H8
Dęblin Poland 51°34N 21°50E 185 G8
Dębno Poland 52°44N 14°41E 185 F1
Débo, L. Mali 15°14N 4°15W 262 B4
DeBolt Canada 55°12N 118°1W 296 B5
Deborah East, L. Australia 30°45S 119°30E 279 F2
Deborah West, L. Australia 30°45S 119°5E 279 F2
Deboyne Is. Papua N. G. 10°43S 152°22E 286 F7
Debrc Serbia 44°38N 19°53E 202 B3
Debre Birhan Ethiopia 9°41N 39°31E 257 F4
Debre Markos Ethiopia 10°20N 37°40E 257 E4
Debre May Ethiopia 11°20N 37°25E 257 E4
Debre Sina Ethiopia 9°51N 39°50E 257 F4
Debre Tabor Ethiopia 11°50N 38°26E 257 E4
Debre Zebit Ethiopia 11°48N 38°30E 257 E4
Debre Zeyit Ethiopia 8°50N 39°0E 257 F4
Debrecen Hungary 47°33N 21°42E 182 C6
Debrzno Poland 53°31N 17°14E 184 E4
Debundscha Cameroon 4°7N 8°59E 263 E6
Deçan Kosovo 42°30N 20°18E 202 D4
Decatur Ala., U.S.A. 34°36N 86°59W 315 D11
Decatur Ga., U.S.A. 33°46N 84°16W 113 B3
Decatur Ill., U.S.A. 39°51N 88°57W 310 E8
Decatur Ind., U.S.A. 40°50N 84°56W 311 D12
Decatur Mich., U.S.A. 42°7N 85°58W 311 B11
Decatur Tex., U.S.A. 33°14N 97°35W 314 E6
Decazeville France 44°34N 2°15E 174 D6
Deccan India 18°0N 79°0E 244 F4
Deception, Mt. Australia 30°42S 138°16E 282 A3
Deception B. Papua N. G. 7°45S 144°40E 286 D3
Deception Bay Australia 27°10S 153°5E 281 D5
Deception I. Antarctica 63°0S 60°15W 151 C17
Deception L. Canada 56°33N 104°13W 297 B8
Dechang China 27°25N 102°11E 228 D4
Dechhu India 26°46N 72°20E 242 F5
Decimomannu Italy 39°19N 8°58E 200 C1
Děčín Czechia 50°47N 14°12E 180 A7
Decize France 46°50N 3°28E 173 F10
Deckerville U.S.A. 43°32N 82°44W 312 C2
Decollatura Italy 39°3N 16°21E 201 C9
Decorah U.S.A. 43°18N 91°48W 308 D8
Deda Romania 46°56N 24°50E 183 D9
Dedaye Burma 16°24N 95°53E 241 G5
Dedéagach = Alexandroupoli Greece 40°50N 25°54E 203 F9
Dededo Guam 13°31N 144°50E 302 d
Deder Ethiopia 9°19N 41°27E 257 F5
Dedham U.S.A. 42°15N 71°10W 116 B1
Dedopolis Tsqaro Georgia 41°33N 46°0E 191 K8
Dédougou Burkina Faso 12°30N 3°25W 262 C4
Dedovichi Russia 57°32N 29°56E 188 D5
Dedza Malawi 14°20S 34°20E 269 E3
Dee ➜ Aberds., U.K. 57°9N 2°5W 167 D6
Dee ➜ Dumf. & Gall., U.K. 54°51N 4°3W 167 G4
Dee ➜ Wales, U.K. 53°22N 3°17W 168 D4
Deep B. Canada 61°15N 116°35W 296 A5
Deep Bay = Chilumba Malawi 10°28S 34°12E 269 E3
Deep Bay = Shenzhen Wan China 22°27N 113°55E 219 a
Deep Lead Australia 37°0S 142°43E 282 D5
Deep Water B. Hong Kong, China 22°14N 114°11E 122 B3
Deepwater N.S.W., Australia 29°25S 151°51E 281 D5
Deepwater Mo., U.S.A. 38°16N 93°47W 310 F3
Deer ➜ Canada 58°23N 94°13W 297 B10
Deer I. U.S.A. 54°55N 162°18W 303 J7
Deer L. Canada 52°40N 94°20W 297 C10
Deer Lake Nfld. & L., Canada 49°11N 57°27W 299 C8
Deer Lake Ont., Canada 52°36N 94°20W 297 C10
Deer Lodge U.S.A. 46°24N 112°44W 304 C7
Deer Park Fla., U.S.A. 28°6N 80°54W 317 G9
Deer Park Ohio, U.S.A. 39°12N 84°23W 311 E12
Deer Park Wash., U.S.A. 47°57N 117°28W 304 C5
Deer River U.S.A. 47°20N 93°48W 308 B7
Deeragun Australia 19°16S 146°33E 280 B4
Deerfield Ill., U.S.A. 42°10N 87°51W 311 B9
Deerfield Mo., U.S.A. 37°50N 94°30W 310 G2
Deerfield Beach U.S.A. 26°19N 80°6W 317 J9
Deering U.S.A. 66°4N 162°42W 303 C7
Defensores del Chaco △ Paraguay 20°13S 60°27W 331 E5
Defiance U.S.A. 41°17N 84°22W 311 C12
Dega Medo Ethiopia 7°59N 43°1E 267 C5
Degana India 26°50N 74°20E 242 F6
Dêgê China 31°44N 98°39E 228 B2
Degebe ➜ Portugal 38°13N 7°29W 195 G3
Degeberga Sweden 55°51N 14°5E 163 J8
Degeh Bur Ethiopia 8°11N 43°31E 267 C5
Dégelis Canada 47°30N 68°35W 299 C6
Degema Nigeria 4°50N 6°48E 263 E6
Degerfors Sweden 59°15N 14°27E 162 E8
Degerhamn Sweden 56°20N 16°24E 163 H10
Deggendorf Germany 48°50N 12°57E 179 G8
Degh ➜ Pakistan 31°3N 73°21E 242 D5
Değirmendere Turkey 40°42N 29°47E 203 F13
Degirmenlik = Kythréa Cyprus 35°15N 33°29E 207 E9
Degunino Russia 55°52N 37°33E 129 A2
Deh Bīd Iran 30°39N 53°11E 247 D7
Deh Dasht Iran 30°47N 50°33E 247 D6
Deh-e Shīr Iran 31°29N 53°45E 247 D7
Deh Nugaled = Nugaaleed, Dooxo Somalia 8°35N 48°35E 267 C6
Dehaj Iran 30°42N 54°53E 247 D7
Dehak Iran 27°11N 62°37E 240 D1
Déhane Cameroon 3°30N 10°5E 264 B2
Dehdez Iran 31°43N 50°17E 247 D6
Dehej India 21°44N 72°40E 242 J5
Dehestān Iran 28°30N 55°35E 247 D7
Dehgolān Iran 35°17N 47°25E 213 E12
Dehibat Tunisia 32°0N 10°47E 258 B2
Dehiwala Sri Lanka 6°50N 79°51E 245 L4
Dehlorān Iran 32°41N 47°16E 213 F12
Dehnow-e Kūhestān Iran 27°58N 58°32E 247 E8
Dehqonobod Uzbekistan 38°21N 66°30E 240 A2
Dehra Dun India 30°20N 78°4E 242 D8
Dehri India 24°50N 84°15E 243 G11
Dehua China 25°26N 118°14E 229 E12
Dehui China 44°30N 125°40E 227 B13
Deim Zubeir South Sudan 7°49N 26°16E 257 F2
Deinze Belgium 50°59N 3°32E 170 D3
Deir al Balah Gaza Strip 31°25N 34°21E 251 G5
Deir Dibwan West Bank 31°55N 35°16E 123 A2
Deir Ibzi'e West Bank 31°55N 35°7E 123 A1
Deira U.A.E. 25°16N 55°18E 119 A2
Dej Romania 47°10N 23°52E 183 C8
Deje Sweden 59°35N 13°29E 162 E7
Dejiang China 28°18N 108°7E 228 C7
Dejvice Czechia 50°6N 14°23E 135 B2
Deka ➜ Zimbabwe 18°4S 26°42E 270 A4
Dekabristov, Ostrov Russia 59°56N 30°15E 137 B1
DeKalb U.S.A. 41°56N 88°46W 311 C8
Dekemhare Eritrea 15°6N 39°0E 257 D4
Dekese Dem. Rep. of the Congo 3°24S 21°24E 264 C4
Dekoa C.A.R. 6°19N 19°4E 264 A3
Del Caño Rise Ind. Oc. 45°15S 44°15E 273 J3
Del Carmen Phil. 9°50N 126°0E 233 G6
Del Mar U.S.A. 32°58N 117°16W 307 N9
Del Norte U.S.A. 37°41N 106°21W 305 H10
Del Rey U.S.A. 33°59N 118°25W 126 C2
Del Rio U.S.A. 29°22N 100°54W 314 G4
Delai Sudan 17°21N 36°6E 256 D4
Delambre I. Australia 20°26S 117°5E 278 D2
Delami Sudan 11°38N 30°23E 257 E3
Delano U.S.A. 35°46N 119°15W 307 K7
Delano Peak U.S.A. 38°22N 112°22W 304 G7
Delārām Afghan. 32°9N 63°25E 240 B1
Delareyville S. Africa 26°41S 25°26E 270 C4
Delaronde L. Canada 54°3N 107°3W 297 C7
Delavan Ill., U.S.A. 40°22N 89°33W 310 D7
Delavan Wis., U.S.A. 42°38N 88°39W 311 B8
Delaware U.S.A. 40°18N 83°4W 311 D13
Delaware □ U.S.A. 39°0N 75°20W 309 F16
Delaware B. U.S.A. 39°0N 75°10W 309 F16
Delaware Water Gap ◠ U.S.A. 41°10N 74°55W 313 E10
Delay ➜ Canada 56°56N 71°28W 299 A5
Delbrück Germany 51°46N 8°34E 178 D4
Delčevo Macedonia 41°58N 22°46E 202 E6
Delegate Australia 37°4S 148°56E 283 D8
Delémont Switz. 47°22N 7°20E 179 H3
Delevan U.S.A. 42°29N 78°29W 312 D6
Delft Neths. 52°1N 4°22E 170 B4
Delft I. Sri Lanka 9°30N 79°40E 245 K4
Delfzijl Neths. 53°20N 6°55E 170 A6
Delgada, Punta Chile 52°28S 69°32W 336 D3
Delgado, C. Mozam. 10°45S 40°40E 269 E5
Delgerhet Mongolia 45°50N 110°30E 226 B6
Delgo Sudan 20°6N 30°40E 256 C3
Delhi Ont., Canada 42°51N 80°30W 312 D4
Delhi India 28°39N 77°13E 120 B2
Delhi La., U.S.A. 32°28N 91°30W 314 E9
Delhi N.Y., U.S.A. 42°17N 74°55W 313 D10
Delhi Gate Delhi, India 120 b3
Delhi Indira Gandhi Int. ✈ (DEL) India 28°34N 77°5E 120 B1
Deli Jovan Serbia 44°13N 22°9E 202 B6
Delia Canada 51°38N 112°23W 296 C6
Delice Turkey 39°54N 34°2E 212 C6
Delice ➜ Turkey 40°45N 34°15E 212 B6
Délices Dominica 15°17N 61°17W 323 k
Delicias Mexico 28°13N 105°28W 318 B3
Delījān Iran 33°59N 50°40E 247 C6
Delimara Point Malta 35°49N 14°34E 206 F8
Déline Canada 65°11N 123°25W 294 D7
Delingha China 37°23N 97°23E 218 D8
Delisle Canada 51°55N 107°8W 297 C7
Delitzsch Germany 51°31N 12°20E 178 D8
Deliverance I. Australia 9°31S 141°34E 280 a
Dell City U.S.A. 31°56N 105°12W 314 F2
Dell Rapids U.S.A. 43°50N 96°43W 308 D5
Delle France 47°30N 7°2E 173 E14
Dellys Algeria 36°57N 3°57E 261 A5
Delmar Iowa, U.S.A. 42°0N 90°37W 310 C6
Delmar N.Y., U.S.A. 42°37N 73°47W 313 D11
Delmenhorst Germany 53°3N 8°37E 178 B4
Delmiro Gouveia Brazil 9°24S 38°6W 332 C4
Delnice Croatia 45°23N 14°50E 199 C11
Delonga, Ostrova Russia 76°40N 149°20E 215 B15
Deloraine Tas., Australia 41°30S 146°40E 281 G4
Deloraine Man., Canada 49°15N 100°29W 297 D8
Delos = Dilos Greece 37°23N 25°15E 205 D7
Delphi Greece 38°28N 22°30E 204 C4
Delphi Ind., U.S.A. 40°36N 86°41W 311 D10
Delphos U.S.A. 40°51N 84°21W 311 D12
Delportshoop S. Africa 28°22S 24°20E 270 C3
Delray Beach U.S.A. 26°28N 80°4W 317 J9
Delsbo Sweden 61°48N 16°32E 162 C10
Delta Ala., U.S.A. 33°26N 85°42W 316 B4
Delta Colo., U.S.A. 38°44N 108°4W 304 G9
Delta Utah, U.S.A. 39°21N 112°35W 304 G7
Delta □ Nigeria 5°30N 6°0E 263 D6
Delta Amacuro □ Venezuela 8°30N 61°30W 329 B5
Delta del Ebre ◠ Spain 40°43N 0°43E 196 E5
Delta del Po ◠ Italy 44°50N 12°15E 199 D9
Delta du Saloum △ Senegal 13°42N 16°43W 262 C1
Delta Dunărea ◠ Romania 45°15N 29°25E 183 E14
Delta Junction U.S.A. 64°2N 145°44W 303 D11
Deltebre Spain 40°43N 0°43E 196 E5
Deltona U.S.A. 28°54N 81°16W 317 G8
Delungra Australia 29°39S 150°51E 281 D5
Delvada India 20°46N 71°2E 242 J4
Delvinaki Greece 39°57N 20°32E 204 B2
Delvinë Albania 39°59N 20°6E 202 G4
Delyatyn Ukraine 48°32N 24°38E 183 B9
Demagiri India 22°55N 92°28E 241 D4
Demak Indonesia 6°53S 110°38E 235 D4
Demanda, Sierra de la Spain 42°15N 3°0W 196 C2
Demarcation Pt. U.S.A. 69°41N 141°18W 303 B12
Demarest U.S.A. 40°57N 73°57W 132 A2
Demavend = Damāvand, Qolleh-ye Iran 35°57N 52°7E 247 C7
Demba Dem. Rep. of the Congo 5°28S 22°15E 265 D4
Demba Chio Angola 9°41S 13°41E 265 D2
Dembecha Ethiopia 10°32N 37°30E 257 E4
Dembéni Comoros Is. 11°52S 43°23E 272 a
Dembéni Mayotte 12°50S 45°11E 272 b
Dembi Ethiopia 8°5N 36°25E 257 F4
Dembia C.A.R. 4°56N 23°53E 264 B4
Dembia Dem. Rep. of the Congo 3°33N 25°48E 268 B2
Dembica = Dębica Poland 50°2N 21°25E 185 H8
Dembidolo Ethiopia 8°34N 34°50E 257 F3
Demchok India 32°42N 79°29E 243 C8
Demer ➜ Belgium 50°57N 4°42E 170 D4
Demerara Abyssal Plain Atl. Oc. 10°0N 48°0W 152 F7
Demerara-Mahaica □ Guyana 6°30N 58°8W 329 B6
Demetrias Greece 39°22N 23°1E 204 B5
Demidov Russia 55°16N 31°30E 188 E6
Deming N. Mex., U.S.A. 32°16N 107°46W 305 K10
Deming Wash., U.S.A. 48°50N 122°13W 306 B4
Demini ➜ Brazil 0°46S 62°56W 329 D5
Demirci Turkey 39°2N 28°38E 205 B10
Demirköprü Barajı Turkey 38°42N 28°25E 205 C10
Demirköy Turkey 41°49N 27°45E 203 E11
Demirtas Turkey 36°25N 32°11E 250 B3
Demmin Germany 53°54N 13°2E 178 B9
Demnate Morocco 31°44N 6°59W 260 B3
Democracia Brazil 5°48S 61°26W 331 B5
Demonte Italy 44°19N 7°17E 198 D4
Demopolis U.S.A. 32°31N 87°50W 315 E11
Dempo Indonesia 4°2S 103°15E 234 C2
Demyansk Russia 57°40N 32°27E 188 D7
Den Bosch = 's-Hertogenbosch Neths. 51°42N 5°17E 170 C5
Den Burg Neths. 53°3N 4°47E 170 A4
Den Chai Thailand 17°59N 100°4E 236 D3
Den Haag = 's-Gravenhage Neths. 52°7N 4°17E 170 B4
Den Helder Neths. 52°57N 4°45E 170 B4
Den Ilp Neths. 52°27N 4°55E 112 A2
Den Lille Havfrue Copenhagen, Denmark 118 a3
Den Oever Neths. 52°56N 5°2E 170 B5
Denain France 50°20N 3°22E 173 B10
Denair U.S.A. 37°32N 120°48W 306 H6
Denali U.S.A. 63°4N 151°0W 303 E10
Denali △ U.S.A. 63°30N 152°0W 303 E10
Denau = Denov Uzbekistan 38°16N 67°54E 217 E7
Denbigh Ont., Canada 45°8N 77°15W 312 A7
Denbigh Denbs., U.K. 53°12N 3°25W 168 D4
Denbigh, C. U.S.A. 64°23N 161°32W 303 D7
Denbighshire □ U.K. 53°8N 3°22W 168 D4
Dendang Indonesia 3°7S 107°56E 235 C3
Dendé = Ndindi Gabon 3°46S 11°9E 264 C2
Dendermonde Belgium 51°2N 4°5E 170 C4
Deneba Ethiopia 9°47N 39°10E 257 F4
Deng Deng Cameroon 5°12N 13°31E 264 A2
Dengchuan China 25°59N 100°3E 228 E3
Denge Nigeria 12°52N 5°21E 263 C6
Dengfeng China 34°25N 113°2E 226 G7
Dengi Nigeria 9°25N 9°55E 263 D6
Dengkou China 40°18N 106°55E 226 D4
Denguélé □ Ivory C. 9°45N 7°30W 262 D3
Dengzhou China 32°34N 112°4E 229 A9
Denham Australia 25°56S 113°31E 279 E1
Denham, Mt. Jamaica 18°13N 77°32W 320 a
Denham Ra. Australia 21°55S 147°46E 280 C4
Denham Sd. Australia 25°45S 113°15E 279 E1
Denholm Canada 52°39N 108°1W 297 C7
Denia Spain 38°49N 0°8E 197 G5
Denial B. Australia 32°14S 133°32E 281 E1
Deniliquin Australia 35°30S 144°58E 283 C6
Denimoo = Fort Resolution Canada 61°10N 113°40W 296 A6
Denis Gabon 0°19N 9°22E 264 B1
Denison Iowa, U.S.A. 42°1N 95°21W 308 D6
Denison Tex., U.S.A. 33°45N 96°33W 314 E6
Denison, C. Antarctica 67°0S 142°40E 151 C10
Denison Plains Australia 18°35S 128°0E 278 C4
Denīsovka Kazakhstan 52°27N 61°39E 216 B6
Denistone Heights Australia 33°48S 151°8E 139 A1
Deniyaya Sri Lanka 6°21N 80°33E 245 L5
Denizli Turkey 37°42N 29°2E 205 D11
Denizli □ Turkey 37°45N 29°5E 205 D11
Denman Australia 32°24S 150°42E 283 B9
Denman Glacier Antarctica 66°45S 100°0E 151 C8
Denmark W. Austral., Australia 34°59S 117°25E 279 F2
Denmark S.C., U.S.A. 33°19N 81°9W 316 B8
Denmark ■ Europe 55°45N 10°0E 163 J3
Denmark Str. Atl. Oc. 66°0N 30°0W 154 D8
Dennery St. Lucia 13°55N 60°54W 323 m
Dennison U.S.A. 40°24N 81°19W 312 F3
Denny U.K. 56°1N 3°55W 167 E5
Denov Uzbekistan 38°16N 67°54E 217 E7
Denpasar Indonesia 8°39S 115°13E 231 K18
Denpasar ✈ (DPS) Indonesia 8°44S 115°10E 231 K18
Denton Ga., U.S.A. 31°44N 82°42W 316 D7
Denton Mont., U.S.A. 47°19N 109°57W 304 C9
Denton Tex., U.S.A. 33°13N 97°8W 314 E6
Dentonia Park Canada 43°42N 79°17W 141 A3
D'Entrecasteaux, Îs. N. Cal. 18°0S 163°0E 277 D11
D'Entrecasteaux, Pt. Australia 34°50S 115°57E 279 F2
D'Entrecasteaux △ Australia 34°20S 115°33E 279 F2
D'Entrecasteaux Is. Papua N. G. 9°0S 151°0E 286 E6
Dentsville U.S.A. 34°4N 80°58W 316 A9
Denu Ghana 6°4N 1°8E 263 D5
Denver Colo., U.S.A. 39°42N 104°59W 304 G11
Denver Ind., U.S.A. 40°52N 86°5W 311 D10
Denver Iowa, U.S.A. 42°40N 92°20W 310 B4
Denver Pa., U.S.A. 40°14N 76°8W 313 F8
Denver City U.S.A. 32°58N 102°50W 314 E3
Denver Int. ✈ (DEN) U.S.A. 39°52N 104°40W 304 G11
Denwood = Wainwright Canada 52°50N 110°50W 297 C6
Deoband India 29°42N 77°43E 242 E7
Deobhog India 19°53N 82°44E 244 E6
Deodrug India 16°26N 76°55E 245 F3
Deogarh Odisha, India 21°32N 84°45E 244 D7
Deogarh Raj., India 25°32N 73°54E 242 G5
Deoghar India 24°30N 86°42E 243 G12
Deogyusan △ S. Korea 35°45N 127°40E 224 E3
Deokjeokdo S. Korea 37°13N 126°7E 224 D3
Deolali India 19°58N 73°50E 244 E1
Deoli = Devli India 25°50N 75°20E 242 G6
Déols France 46°50N 1°43E 173 F8
Deora India 26°22N 70°55E 242 F4
Deorha = Jubbal India 31°5N 77°40E 242 D7
Deori India 23°24N 79°1E 243 H8
Deoria India 26°31N 83°48E 243 F10
Deosai Mts. Pakistan 35°40N 75°0E 243 B6
Deosri India 26°46N 90°29E 241 B3
Depalpur India 22°51N 75°33E 242 H6
DePaul Univ. U.S.A. 41°55N 87°39W 119 B3
Deposit U.S.A. 42°4N 75°25W 313 D9
Deptford U.K. 51°28N 0°1W 125 B3
Depuch I. Australia 20°37S 117°44E 278 D2
Deputati, Camera dei Rome, Italy 136 b2
Deputatskiy Russia 69°18N 139°54E 215 C14
Dêqên China 28°34N 98°51E 228 C2
Deqing China 23°8N 111°42E 229 F8
Der-Chantecoq, L. du France 48°35N 4°40E 173 D11
Dera, Lach ➜ Somalia 0°15N 42°17E 267 D5
Dera Ghazi Khan Pakistan 30°5N 70°43E 242 D4
Dera Ismail Khan Pakistan 31°50N 70°50E 242 D4
Derabugti Pakistan 29°2N 69°9E 242 E3
Derawar Fort Pakistan 28°46N 71°20E 242 E4
Derbent Russia 42°5N 48°15E 191 J9
Derbent Turkey 38°11N 28°33E 205 C10
Derby W. Austral., Australia 17°18S 123°38E 278 C3
Derby Derby City, U.K. 52°56N 1°28W 168 E6
Derby Conn., U.S.A. 41°19N 73°5W 313 E11
Derby Kans., U.S.A. 37°33N 97°16W 308 G5
Derby N.Y., U.S.A. 42°41N 78°58W 312 D6
Derby City □ U.K. 52°56N 1°28W 168 E6
Derby Line U.S.A. 45°0N 72°6W 313 B12
Derbyshire □ U.K. 53°11N 1°38W 168 D6
Đerdap △ Serbia 44°40N 22°23E 202 B6
Derdepoort S. Africa 24°38S 26°24E 270 B4
Derecske Hungary 47°20N 21°33E 182 C6
Dereham U.K. 52°41N 0°57E 169 E8
Dereköy Turkey 41°55N 27°21E 203 E11
Dereli Turkey 40°44N 38°26E 213 B8
Derg ➜ U.K. 54°44N 7°26W 166 B4
Derg, L. Ireland 53°0N 8°20W 166 D3
Dergachi = Derhaci Ukraine 50°9N 36°11E 189 G9
Derhaci Ukraine 50°9N 36°11E 189 G9
Deridder U.S.A. 30°51N 93°17W 314 F8
Derik Turkey 37°21N 40°18E 213 D9
Derinkuyu Turkey 38°22N 34°45E 212 C6
Dermantsi Bulgaria 43°8N 24°17E 203 C8
Dermott U.S.A. 33°32N 91°26W 314 E9
Dernière Rivière St. Lucia 13°57N 60°55W 323 m
Dêrong China 28°44N 99°9E 228 C2
Derri Somalia 4°20N 46°37E 267 D6
Derrinallum Australia 37°57S 143°15E 282 D5
Derry = Londonderry U.K. 55°0N 7°20W 166 B4
Derry = Londonderry □ U.K. 55°0N 7°20W 166 B4
Derry N.H., U.S.A. 42°53N 71°19W 313 D13
Derry Pa., U.S.A. 40°20N 79°18W 312 F5
Derryveagh Mts. Ireland 54°56N 8°11W 166 B3
Derudub Sudan 17°31N 36°7E 256 D4
Derval France 47°40N 1°41W 172 E5
Derveni Greece 38°8N 22°25E 204 C4
Derventa Bos.-H. 44°59N 17°55E 182 F2
Derwent ➜ Cumb., U.K. 54°39N 3°33W 168 C4
Derwent ➜ Derby, U.K. 52°57N 1°28W 168 E6
Derwent ➜ N. Yorks., U.K. 53°45N 0°58W 168 D7
Derwent Water U.K. 54°35N 3°9W 168 C4
Derzhavīnsk Kazakhstan 51°6N 66°19E 217 B7
Des Moines Iowa, U.S.A. 41°35N 93°37W 310 C3
Des Moines N. Mex., U.S.A. 36°46N 103°50W 305 H12
Des Moines Wash., U.S.A. 47°24N 122°19W 306 C4
Des Moines ➜ U.S.A. 40°23N 91°25W 310 D5
Des Moines ✈ (DSM) U.S.A. 41°32N 93°40W 310 C3
Des Plaines U.S.A. 42°2N 87°54W 311 B9
Des Plaines ➜ U.S.A. 41°23N 88°15W 311 C8
Desa Romania 43°52N 23°2E 182 G8
Desaguadero Peru 16°34S 69°3W 330 D4
Desaguadero ➜ Argentina 34°30S 66°46W 334 C2
Desaguadero ➜ Bolivia 16°35S 69°5W 330 D4
Desantne Ukraine 45°34N 29°32E 183 E14
Désappointement, Is. du French Polynesia 14°10S 141°20W 289 f
Desaru Malaysia 1°31N 104°17E 237 d
Descanso, Pta. Mexico 32°21N 117°3W 307 N9
Descartes France 46°59N 0°42E 174 B4
Deschaillons-sur-St-Laurent Canada 46°32N 72°7W 299 C5
Deschambault L. Canada 54°50N 103°30W 297 C8
Deschutes ➜ U.S.A. 45°38N 120°55W 304 D3
Descobrimente △ Brazil 16°53S 39°21W 333 E4
Dese Ethiopia 11°5N 39°40E 257 E4
Deseado, C. Chile 52°45S 74°42W 336 D2
Desenzano del Garda Italy 45°28N 10°32E 198 C7
Deseronto Canada 44°12N 77°3W 312 B7
Desert Center U.S.A. 33°43N 115°24W 307 M11
Desert Hot Springs U.S.A. 33°58N 116°30W 307 M10
Desert Wetlands Park U.S.A. 36°7N 115°2W 124 B2
Desertas, Ilhas Madeira 32°30N 16°30W 260 B1
Deset Norway 61°20N 11°26E 164 C8
Desfina Greece 38°25N 22°31E 204 C4
Deshaies Guadeloupe 16°18N 61°47W 322 e
Deshauteur Guadeloupe 16°15N 61°25W 322 e
Deshnok India 27°48N 73°21E 242 F5
Desierto Central de Baja California ◠ Mexico 29°40N 114°50W 318 B2
Desjardins, Complexe Montréal, Canada 130 b2
Deskati Greece 39°55N 21°49E 202 G5
Desna ➜ Ukraine 50°33N 30°32E 177 C16
Desnătui ➜ Romania 43°53N 23°35E 183 G8
Desnogorsk Russia 54°9N 33°17E 188 E7
Desolación, I. Chile 53°0S 74°0W 336 D2
Despeñaperros, Paso Spain 38°24N 3°30W 195 G7
Despeñaperros ◠ Spain 38°23N 3°32W 195 G7
Despotiko Greece 36°57N 24°58E 204 E6
Despotovac Serbia 44°6N 21°30E 202 B5
Dessau Germany 51°51N 12°14E 178 D8
Dessye = Dese Ethiopia 11°5N 39°40E 257 E4
Destin U.S.A. 30°24N 86°30W 317 E3
D'Estrees B. Australia 35°55S 137°45E 282 C2
Desuri India 25°18N 73°35E 242 G5
Desvres France 50°40N 1°48E 173 B8
Det Udom Thailand 14°54N 105°5E 236 E5
Deta Romania 45°24N 21°13E 182 E6
Dete Zimbabwe 18°38S 26°50E 270 A4
Đetinja ➜ Serbia 43°51N 20°5E 202 C4
Detmold Germany 51°56N 8°52E 178 D4
Detour, Pt. U.S.A. 45°40N 86°40W 308 C10
Detroit U.S.A. 42°19N 83°12W 312 D1
Detroit Lakes U.S.A. 46°49N 95°51W 308 B6
Detroit Metropolitan Wayne County ✈ (DTW) U.S.A. 42°13N 83°21W 311 B13
Detskoye Selo = Pushkin Russia 59°45N 30°25E 188 C6
Dettifoss Iceland 65°48N 16°24W 155 B10
Detva Slovakia 48°34N 19°25E 181 C12
Deua △ Australia 35°32S 149°46E 283 C8
Deurne Neths. 51°27N 5°49E 170 C5
Deutsch = Przemyśl Poland 49°50N 22°45E 185 J9
Deutsch Brod = Havlíčkův Brod Czechia 49°36N 15°33E 180 B8
Deutsch-Eylau = Iława Poland 53°36N 19°34E 184 E6
Deutsch Krone = Wałcz Poland 53°17N 16°27E 185 E3
Deutsch-Luxemburgischer ◠ Germany 49°58N 6°12E 179 F2
Deutsche Bucht Germany 54°15N 8°0E 178 A4
Deutsche Oper Germany 52°30N 13°19E 115 A2
Deutsches Museum Germany 48°7N 11°35E 131 B2
Deutschland = Germany ■ Europe 51°0N 10°0E 178 E6
Deutschlandsberg Austria 46°49N 15°14E 180 E8
Deux-Sèvres □ France 46°35N 0°20W 172 F6
Deva Romania 45°53N 22°55E 182 E7
Devakottai India 9°55N 78°45E 245 K4
Devaprayag India 30°13N 78°35E 243 D8
Devarkonda India 16°42N 78°56E 244 F4
Dévaványa Hungary 47°2N 20°59E 182 C5
Deveci Dağları Turkey 40°6N 36°15E 212 B7
Devecikonağı Turkey 39°55N 28°34E 203 G12
Devecser Hungary 47°6N 17°26E 182 C2
Develi Turkey 38°23N 35°29E 212 C6
Deventer Neths. 52°15N 6°10E 170 B6
Devereux U.S.A. 33°13N 83°5W 316 B6
Deveron ➜ U.K. 57°41N 2°32W 167 D6
Devesel Romania 44°28N 22°41E 182 F7
Devgad I. India 14°48N 74°5E 245 G2
Devgadh Bariya India 22°40N 73°55E 242 H5
Devgarh India 16°23N 73°23E 245 F1
Devi ➜ India 19°59N 86°24E 244 E8
Devikot India 26°42N 71°12E 242 F4
Devil River Pk. N.Z. 40°56S 172°37E 285 A7
Devil's Bridge Antigua & B. 17°6N 61°41W 322 b
Devils Den U.S.A. 35°46N 119°58W 306 K7
Devils Hole = Death Valley △ U.S.A. 36°29N 117°6W 307 J9
Devils Island, I. = Diable, Île du Fr. Guiana 5°16N 52°34W 329 B7
Devils Lake U.S.A. 48°7N 98°52W 308 A4
Devils Paw Canada 58°47N 134°0W 296 B2
Devil's Peak S. Africa 33°57S 18°27E 118 A1
Devils Postpile ◠ U.S.A. 37°37N 119°5W 306 H7
Devil's Pt. Sri Lanka 9°26N 80°6E 245 K5
Devils Tower U.S.A. 44°35N 104°42W 304 D11
Devils Tower △ U.S.A. 44°48N 104°55W 304 D11
Devil's Woodyard Mud Volcano Trin. & Tob. 10°16N 61°22W 323 t
Devin Bulgaria 41°44N 24°24E 203 E8
Devine U.S.A. 29°8N 98°54W 314 G5
Devipattinam India 9°29N 78°54E 245 K4
Devizes U.K. 51°22N 1°58W 169 F6
Devli India 25°50N 75°20E 242 G6
Devnya Bulgaria 43°13N 27°33E 203 C11
Devoll ➜ Albania 40°57N 20°15E 202 F4
Devon Canada 53°24N 113°44W 296 C6
Devon □ U.K. 50°50N 3°40W 169 G4
Devon I. Canada 75°10N 85°0W 295 B15
Devonport Australia 41°10S 146°22E 281 G4
Devrek Turkey 41°13N 31°57E 212 B4
Devrekâni Turkey 41°36N 33°50E 212 B5
Devrez ➜ Turkey 41°6N 34°25E 212 B6
Devrukh India 17°3N 73°37E 244 F1
Dewas India 22°59N 76°3E 242 H7
Dewetsdorp S. Africa 29°33S 26°39E 270 C4
Dewey Puerto Rico 18°18N 65°18W 321 b
Dexing China 28°46N 117°30E 229 C11
Dexter Maine, U.S.A. 45°1N 69°18W 309 C19
Dexter Mich., U.S.A. 42°20N 83°53W 311 B13
Dexter Mo., U.S.A. 36°48N 89°57W 308 G9
Dexter N. Mex., U.S.A. 33°12N 104°22W 305 K11
Dey-Dey, L. Australia 29°12S 131°4E 279 E5
Deyang China 31°3N 104°27E 228 B5
Deyhūk Iran 33°15N 57°30E 247 C8
Deyyer Iran 27°55N 51°55E 247 E6
Dez ➜ Iran 31°39N 48°52E 213 F13
Dezadeash L. Canada 60°28N 136°58W 296 A1
Dezfūl Iran 32°20N 48°30E 213 F13
Dezhneva, Mys Russia 66°5N 169°40W 215 C19
Dezhou China 37°26N 116°18E 226 F9
Dhadhar ➜ India 24°56N 85°24E 243 G11
Dhahabān Si. Arabia 21°58N 39°3E 248 B2
Dhahiriya = Az̧ Z̧āhirīyah West Bank 31°25N 34°58E 251 G5
Dhahran = Az̧ Z̧ahrān Si. Arabia 26°10N 50°7E 247 E6
Dhak Pakistan 32°25N 72°33E 242 C5
Dhaka Bangla. 23°43N 90°26E 241 D3
Dhaka □ Bangla. 23°30N 90°0E 241 D2
Dhakuria India 22°30N 88°22E 124 B2
Dhali Cyprus 35°1N 33°25E 207 E9
Dhamangaon India 20°48N 78°9E 244 D4
Dhamār Yemen 14°30N 44°20E 248 D4
Dhamār □ Yemen 14°30N 44°20E 248 D4
Dhampur India 29°19N 78°33E 243 E8
Dhamra ➜ India 20°47N 86°58E 244 D8
Dhamtari India 20°42N 81°35E 244 D5
Dhanbad India 23°50N 86°30E 243 H12
Dhangarhi Nepal 28°55N 80°40E 243 E9
Dhankuta Nepal 26°55N 87°40E 243 F12
Dhanora India 20°20N 80°22E 244 D5
Dhanpuri India 23°13N 81°30E 244 C5
Dhanushkodi India 9°11N 79°24E 245 K4
Dhar India 22°35N 75°26E 242 H6
Dharampur India 22°13N 75°18E 242 H6
Dharamsala = Dharmsala India 32°16N 76°23E 242 C7
Dharan Nepal 26°49N 87°17E 243 F12
Dharangaon India 21°1N 75°16E 244 D2
Dharapuram India 10°45N 77°34E 245 J3
Dharavi India 19°1N 72°51E 130 A2
Dharawal △ Australia 34°12S 150°52E 283 C9
Dhariwal India 31°57N 75°19E 242 D6
Dharla ➜ Bangla. 25°46N 89°42E 243 G13
Dharmanagar India 24°22N 92°10E 241 C4
Dharmapuri India 12°10N 78°10E 245 H4
Dharmavaram India 14°29N 77°44E 245 G3
Dharmjaygarh India 22°28N 83°13E 243 H10
Dharmsala India 32°16N 76°23E 242 C7
Dharni India 21°33N 76°53E 242 J7
Dharug △ Australia 33°20S 151°2E 283 B9
Dharur India 18°3N 76°8E 244 E3
Dharwad India 15°30N 75°4E 245 G2
Dhasan ➜ India 25°48N 79°24E 243 G8
Dhaulagiri Nepal 28°39N 83°28E 243 E10
Dhebar, L. India 24°10N 74°0E 242 G6
Dheftera Cyprus 35°5N 33°16E 207 E9
Dhemaji India 27°29N 94°35E 241 B5
Dhenkanal India 20°45N 85°35E 244 D7
Dherinia Cyprus 35°3N 33°57E 207 E9
Dheskáti = Deskati Greece 39°55N 21°49E 202 G5
Dhī Qār □ Iraq 31°0N 46°15E 246 D5
Dhiarrizos ➜ Cyprus 34°41N 32°34E 207 F8
Dhībān Jordan 31°30N 35°46E 251 G6
Dhilwan India 31°31N 75°21E 242 D6
Dhimarkhera India 23°28N 80°22E 243 H9
Dholka India 22°44N 72°29E 242 H5
Dhomokós = Domokos Greece 39°10N 22°18E 204 B4
Dhond = Daund India 18°26N 74°40E 244 E2
Dhone India 15°25N 77°53E 245 E3
Dhoraji India 21°45N 70°37E 242 J4
Dhorpatan Nepal 28°29N 83°4E 243 E10
Dhragonísi = Tragonhsi Greece 37°27N 25°29E 205 D7
Dhrangadhra India 22°59N 71°31E 242 H4
Dhrol India 22°33N 70°25E 242 H4
Dhubāb Yemen 12°56N 43°25E 248 D3
Dhuburi India 26°2N 89°59E 241 B2
Dhulasar Bangla. 21°52N 90°14E 241 E3
Dhule India 20°58N 74°50E 244 D2
Dhupdhara India 26°10N 91°4E 241 B3
Dhurbo Somalia 11°37N 50°20E 267 B7
Dhuusamarreeb Somalia 5°30N 46°15E 267 C6
Di-ib, W. ➜ Sudan 22°38N 36°6E 256 C4
Di Linh Vietnam 11°35N 108°4E 237 G7
Di Linh, Cao Nguyen Vietnam 11°30N 108°0E 237 G7
Dia Greece 35°28N 25°14E 207 E6
Dia Deva = Butcher I. India 18°57N 72°53E 130 B2
Diabakania Guinea 10°38N 10°58W 262 C2
Diable, Île du Fr. Guiana 5°16N 52°34W 329 B7
Diable, Pte. du Martinique 14°46N 60°53W 322 j
Diables, Morne aux Dominica 15°37N 61°27W 323 k
Diablo Pt. N. Marianas 15°0N 145°35E 302 e
Diablo Range U.S.A. 37°20N 121°25W 306 J5
Diablotins, Morne Dominica 15°30N 61°24W 323 k
Diadema Brazil 23°41S 46°37W 137 C2
Diafarabé Mali 14°9N 4°57W 262 C4
Diala Mali 14°10N 9°58W 262 C3
Dialakoro Mali 12°18N 7°54W 262 C3
Dialakoto Senegal 13°21N 13°19W 262 C2
Diallassagou Mali 13°47N 3°41W 262 C4
Diamant, Pte. du Martinique 14°27N 61°3W 322 j
Diamant, Rocher du Martinique 14°27N 61°2W 322 j
Diamante Argentina 32°5S 60°40W 334 C3
Diamante Italy 39°41N 15°49E 201 C8
Diamante ➜ Argentina 34°30S 66°46W 334 C2
Diamantina Brazil 18°17S 43°40W 333 E3
Diamantina ➜ Australia 26°45S 139°10E 281 D2
Diamantina △ Australia 23°33S 141°23E 280 C3
Diamantino Brazil 14°30S 56°30W 331 C6
Diamond Bar U.S.A. 34°1N 117°48W 307 L9
Diamond Harbour India 22°11N 88°14E 243 H13
Diamond Head U.S.A. 21°16N 157°49W 302 K14
Diamond I. Grenada 12°20N 61°35W 323 q
Diamond Is. Australia 17°25S 151°5E 280 B5
Diamond Mts. U.S.A. 39°40N 115°50W 304 G6
Diamond Springs U.S.A. 38°42N 120°49W 306 G6
Diamou Mali 14°5N 11°16W 262 C2
Dian Chi China 24°50N 102°43E 228 E4
Diana □ Madag. 12°15S 49°15E 272 A2
Dianalund Denmark 55°32N 11°30E 163 J5
Diana's Peak St. Helena 15°58S 5°42W 153 h
Dianbai China 21°33N 111°0E 229 G8
Diancheng China 21°30N 111°4E 229 G8
Dianjiang China 30°24N 107°20E 228 B6
Diano Marina Italy 43°54N 8°5E 198 E5
Dianópolis Brazil 11°38S 46°50W 333 D2
Dianra Ivory C. 8°45N 6°14W 262 D3
Diaoyu Dao = Senkaku-Shotō E. China Sea 25°45N 123°30E 221 M1
Diaoyu Tai = Senkaku-Shotō E. China Sea 25°45N 123°30E 221 M1
Diapaga Burkina Faso 12°5N 1°46E 263 C5
Diapangou Burkina Faso 12°5N 0°10E 263 C5
Diariguila Guinea 10°35N 10°2W 262 C2
Diavolo, Mt. India 12°40N 92°56E 245 H11
Diba = Dibbā al Ḩişn U.A.E. 25°45N 56°16E 247 E8
Dibagah Iraq 35°52N 43°48E 213 E10
Dibai India 28°13N 78°15E 242 E8
Dibaya Dem. Rep. of the Congo 6°30S 22°57E 265 D4
Dibaya-Lubue Dem. Rep. of the Congo 4°12S 19°54E 265 C3
Dibbā al Ḩişn U.A.E. 25°45N 56°16E 247 E8
Dibbeen △ Jordan 32°20N 35°45E 251 F6
Dibella Niger 17°32N 13°6E 259 E2
Dibër □ Albania 41°30N 20°20E 202 E4
D'Iberville, Lac Canada 55°55N 73°15W 298 A5
Dibete Botswana 23°45S 26°32E 270 B4
Dibi Cameroon 7°8N 13°43E 264 A2
Dibru-Saikhowa △ India 27°40N 95°25E 241 B5
Dibrugarh India 27°29N 94°55E 241 B5
Diciosânmartin = Târnăveni Romania 46°19N 24°13E 183 D9
Dickens U.S.A. 33°37N 100°50W 314 E4
Dickenson B. Antigua & B. 17°10N 61°51W 322 b
Dickeyville U.S.A. 42°38N 90°36W 310 B6
Dickinson U.S.A. 46°53N 102°47W 308 B2
Dick's Pt. Bahamas 25°4N 77°18W 153 b
Dickson = Dikson Russia 73°40N 80°5E 214 B9
Dickson U.S.A. 36°5N 87°23W 315 C11
Dickson City U.S.A. 41°28N 75°36W 313 E9
Dicle Barajı Turkey 38°20N 40°11E 213 C9
Dicle Nehri ➜ Turkey 37°44N 41°10E 213 D9
Dicomano Italy 43°53N 11°31E 199 E8
Didesa, W. ➜ Ethiopia 10°2N 35°32E 257 E4
Didiéni Mali 13°53N 8°6W 262 C3
Didim Turkey 37°22N 27°16E 205 D9
Didimbo Angola 17°30S 21°45E 265 F4
Didimoticho Greece 41°22N 26°29E 203 E10
Didsbury Canada 51°35N 114°10W 296 C6
Didwana India 27°23N 74°36E 242 F6
Die France 44°47N 5°22E 175 D9
Diébougou Burkina Faso 11°0N 3°15W 262 C4
Diecke Guinea 7°27N 8°54W 262 D3
Diedenhofen = Thionville France 49°20N 6°10E 173 C13
Diefenbaker, L. Canada 51°0N 106°55W 297 C7
Diegen Belgium 50°53N 4°26E 116 A2
Diego de Almagro Chile 26°22S 70°3W 334 B1
Diego Garcia Ind. Oc. 7°50S 72°50E 273 E6
Diego Martin Trin. & Tob. 10°43N 61°34W 323 t
Diego Ramírez, Islas Chile 56°30S 68°44W 336 E3
Diego Suarez = Antsiranana Madag. 12°25S 49°20E 272 A2
Diekirch Lux. 49°52N 6°10E 170 E6
Diéma Mali 14°32N 9°12W 262 C3
Diembéring Senegal 12°29N 16°47W 262 C1
Diemelsee ◠ Germany 51°20N 8°40E 178 D4
Diemen Neths. 52°21N 4°58E 112 A2
Dien Ban Vietnam 15°53N 108°16E 236 E7
Dien Bien Phu Vietnam 21°20N 103°0E 228 G4
Dien Chau, Vinh Vietnam 19°0N 105°55E 236 C5
Dien Khanh Vietnam 12°15N 109°6E 237 F7
Diepholz Germany 52°37N 8°22E 178 C4
Diepkloof S. Africa 26°14S 27°57E 123 B1
Dieppe France 49°54N 1°4E 172 C8
Dieppe Bay Town St. Kitts & Nevis 17°25N 62°48W 322 d
Dieprivier S. Africa 34°2S 18°27E 118 B1
Dierks U.S.A. 34°7N 94°1W 314 D7
Diest Belgium 50°58N 5°4E 170 D5
Dieterich U.S.A. 39°4N 88°23W 311 E8
Dietikon Switz. 47°24N 8°24E 179 H4
Dieulefit France 44°32N 5°4E 175 D9
Dieuze France 48°49N 6°43E 173 D13
Dievenow = Dziwnów Poland 54°2N 14°45E 184 D1
Dif Somalia 0°59N 40°58E 267 D5
Diffa Niger 13°18N 12°36E 263 C7
Diffa □ Niger 14°0N 12°30E 263 C7
Differdange Lux. 49°31N 5°54E 170 E5
Diffun Phil. 16°36N 121°33E 232 C3
Dig India 27°28N 77°20E 242 F7
Digba Dem. Rep. of the Congo 4°25N 25°48E 268 B2
Digboi India 27°23N 95°38E 241 B5
Digby Canada 44°38N 65°50W 299 D6
Digges Is. Canada 62°40N 77°50W 295 E16
Diggi India 26°22N 75°26E 242 F6
Dighinala Bangla. 23°15N 92°5E 241 D4
Dighton U.S.A. 38°29N 100°28W 308 F3
Digity Mud Volcanoes Trin. & Tob. 10°12N 61°25W 323 t
Diglur India 18°34N 77°33E 244 E3
Digna Mali 14°48N 8°10W 262 C3
Digne-les-Bains France 44°5N 6°12E 175 D10
Digoin France 46°29N 4°1E 173 F11
Digor Turkey 40°22N 43°25E 213 B10
Digos Phil. 6°45N 125°20E 233 H5
Digranes Iceland 66°4N 14°44W 155 A12
Digras India 20°6N 77°45E 244 D3
Digul ➜ Indonesia 7°7S 138°42E 231 F9
Digya △ Ghana 7°15N 0°5E 263 D5
Dihang = Brahmaputra ➜ Asia 23°40N 90°35E 241 D3
Diinsoor Somalia 2°24N 42°59E 267 D5
Dijlah, Nahr ➜ Asia 31°0N 47°25E 246 D5
Dijon France 47°20N 5°3E 173 E12
Dikhil Djibouti 11°8N 42°20E 257 E5
Dikili Turkey 39°4N 26°53E 205 B8
Dikirnis Egypt 31°6N 31°35E 256 H7
Dikodougou Ivory C. 9°4N 5°45W 262 D3
Diksmuide Belgium 51°2N 2°52E 170 C2
Dikson Russia 73°40N 80°5E 214 B9
Dikti Oros Greece 35°8N 25°30E 207 E6
Dikwa Nigeria 12°4N 13°30E 263 C7
Dila Ethiopia 6°21N 38°22E 257 F4
Dilasag Phil. 16°25N 122°11E 232 C4
Dilbeek Belgium 50°51N 4°17E 116 A1
Dilek Yarimadisi △ Turkey 37°40N 27°10E 205 D9
Dili E. Timor 8°39S 125°34E 231 F7
Diligent Strait India 12°11N 92°57E 245 H11
Dilijan Armenia 40°46N 44°57E 191 K7
Dilinata Greece 38°13N 20°31E 207 C2
Dilj Croatia 45°29N 18°1E 182 E3
Dillenburg Germany 50°43N 8°17E 178 E4

Dilley U.S.A. 28°40N 99°10W 314 G5
Dilli = Delhi India 28°39N 77°13E 120 B2
Dilli Mali 15°1N 7°40W 262 C3
Dillia → Niger 14°9N 12°50E 259 F2
Dilling Sudan 12°3N 29°35E 257 E2
Dillingen Bayern, Germany 48°36N 10°30E 179 G6
Dillingen Saarland, Germany 49°22N 6°43E 179 F2
Dillingham U.S.A. 59°3N 158°28W 303 G8
Dillon Sask., Canada 55°56N 108°35W 297 B7
Dillon Mont., U.S.A. 45°13N 112°38W 304 D7
Dillon S.C., U.S.A. 34°25N 79°22W 315 D15
Dillon → Canada 55°56N 108°56W 297 B7
Dillsboro U.S.A. 39°1N 85°4W 311 E11
Dillsburg U.S.A. 40°7N 77°2W 312 F7
Dilolo
Dem. Rep. of the Congo 10°28S 22°18E 265 E4
Dilos Greece 37°23N 25°15E 205 D7
Dilove Ukraine 47°56N 24°11E 183 C9
Dimapur India 25°54N 93°45E 241 C4
Dimas Mexico 23°43N 106°47W 318 C3
Dimasalang Phil. 12°12N 123°51E 232 E4
Dimashq Syria 33°30N 36°18E 250 E7
Dimashq □ Syria 33°30N 36°30E 250 E7
Dimbaza S. Africa 32°50S 27°14E 271 D4
Dimbelenge
Dem. Rep. of the Congo 5°33S 23°7E 265 D4
Dimbokro Ivory C. 6°45N 4°46W 262 D4
Dimboola Australia 36°28S 142°7E 282 D5
Dîmbovița = Dâmbovița →
Romania 44°12N 26°26E 183 F11
Dimbulah Australia 17°8S 145°4E 280 B4
Dimitrovgrad Bulgaria 42°5N 25°35E 203 D9
Dimitrovgrad Russia 54°14N 49°39E 190 C9
Dimitrovgrad Serbia 43°2N 22°48E 202 C6
Dimitrovo = Pernik
Bulgaria 42°35N 23°2E 202 D7
Dimitsana Greece 37°36N 22°3E 204 D4
Dimmitt U.S.A. 34°33N 102°19W 314 D3
Dimo South Sudan 5°19N 29°10E 257 F2
Dimona Israel 31°2N 35°1E 251 G6
Dimonika ⌓ Congo 4°13S 12°21E 264 C2
Dimovo Bulgaria 43°43N 22°50E 202 C6
Dinagat I. Phil. 10°10N 125°40E 233 F5
Dinagat Islands □ Phil. 10°0N 125°35E 233 F5
Dinaig Phil. 7°11N 124°10E 233 H5
Dinajpur Bangla. 25°33N 88°43E 241 C2
Dinalupihan Phil. 14°52N 120°28E 232 D3
Dinan France 48°28N 2°2W 172 D4
Dīnān Āb Iran 32°4N 56°49E 247 C8
Dinant Belgium 50°16N 4°55E 170 D4
Dinapur India 25°38N 85°5E 243 G11
Dinar Turkey 38°5N 30°10E 205 C12
Dīnār, Kūh-e Iran 30°42N 51°46E 247 D6
Dinara Planina Croatia 44°0N 16°30E 199 D13
Dinard France 48°38N 2°6W 172 D4
Dinaric Alps = Dinara Planina
Croatia 44°0N 16°30E 199 D13
Dinas Phil. 7°38N 123°20E 233 H4
Dinbych-y-Pysgod = Tenby
U.K. 51°40N 4°42W 169 F3
Dindanko Mali 14°8N 9°30W 262 C3
Dinde Angola 14°17S 13°42E 265 E2
Dinder, Nahr ed → Sudan 14°6N 33°40E 257 E3
Dinder △ Sudan 12°30N 35°10E 257 E4
Dindi → India 16°24N 78°15E 245 F4
Dindigul India 10°25N 78°0E 245 J4
Dindori India 22°57N 81°5E 243 H9
Ding Xian = Dingzhou
China 38°30N 114°59E 226 E8
Dinga Dem. Rep. of the Congo 5°17S 16°42E 265 D3
Dinga Pakistan 25°26N 67°10E 242 G2
Dingalan Phil. 15°18N 121°25E 232 D3
Dingalan B. Phil. 15°18N 121°25E 232 D3
Ding'an China 19°42N 110°19E 229 a
Dingbian China 37°35N 107°32E 226 F4
Dingelstädt Germany 51°18N 10°19E 178 D6
Dingle Kerry, Ireland 52°9N 10°17W 166 D1
Dingle Sweden 58°32N 11°35E 163 F5
Dingle B. Ireland 52°3N 10°20W 166 D1
Dingle Pen. Ireland 52°12N 10°5W 166 D1
Dingli Malta 35°52N 14°23E 206 F7
Dingmans Ferry U.S.A. 41°13N 74°55W 313 E10
Dingnan China 24°45N 115°0E 229 E10
Dingo Australia 23°38S 149°19E 280 C4
Dingolfing Germany 48°37N 12°30E 179 G8
Dingras Phil. 18°6N 120°42E 232 B3
Dingtao China 35°5N 115°35E 226 G8
Dinguiraye Guinea 11°18N 10°49W 262 C2
Dingwall U.K. 57°36N 4°26W 167 D4
Dingxi China 35°30N 104°33E 226 G3
Dingxiang China 38°30N 112°58E 226 E7
Dingyuan China 32°32N 117°41E 229 A11
Dingzhou China 38°30N 114°59E 226 E8
Dinh, Mui Vietnam 11°22N 109°1E 237 G7
Dinh Lap Vietnam 21°33N 107°6E 228 G6
Dinhata India 26°8N 89°27E 241 B2
Dinin → Ireland 52°43N 7°18W 166 D4
Dinira △ Venezuela 9°57N 70°6W 328 B3
Dinokwe Botswana 23°29S 26°37E 270 B4
Dinorwic Canada 49°41N 92°30W 297 D10
Dinosaur ⌓ Alta.,
Canada 50°47N 111°30W 296 C6
Dinosaur ⌓ Colo., U.S.A. 40°30N 108°45W 304 F9
Dinuba U.S.A. 36°32N 119°23W 306 J7
Diö Sweden 56°37N 14°15E 163 H8
Dioïla Mali 12°23N 6°50W 262 C3
Dioka Mali 14°57N 10°4W 262 C2
Diomede U.S.A. 65°47N 169°0W 303 D5
Diona Chad 17°51N 22°36E 259 E4
Diongoï Mali 14°38N 8°34W 262 C3
Dionisades Greece 35°20N 26°10E 207 E7
Dionysos, Theatro Athens, Greece 112 c2
Diósgyör Hungary 48°7N 20°43E 182 B5
Diosig Romania 47°18N 22°2E 182 C7
Diougani Mali 14°19N 2°44W 262 C4
Dioulouolou Senegal 13°5N 16°38W 262 C1
Dioura Mali 14°59N 5°12W 262 C3
Diourbel Senegal 14°39N 16°12W 262 C1
Diourbel □ Senegal 14°45N 16°15W 262 C1
Dipaculao Phil. 15°51N 121°32E 232 D3
Dipalpur Pakistan 30°40N 73°39E 242 D5
Diphu India 25°50N 93°26E 241 C4
Dipkarpaz = Rizokarpaso
Cyprus 35°36N 34°23E 207 E10
Diplo Pakistan 24°35N 69°35E 242 G3
Dipolog Phil. 8°36N 123°20E 233 G4
Dipperu △ Australia 21°56S 148°42E 280 C4
Dipton N.Z. 45°54S 168°22E 285 F3
Dir Pakistan 35°8N 71°59E 240 B3
Diré Mali 16°20N 3°25W 262 B4
Dire Dawa Ethiopia 9°35N 41°45E 257 F5
Dirfis Oros Greece 38°40N 23°54E 204 C5
Diriamba Nic. 11°51N 86°19W 320 D2
Dirico Angola 17°50S 20°42E 265 F4
Dirk Hartog I. Australia 25°50S 113°5E 279 E1
Dirkou Niger 19°1N 12°53E 259 E2
Dirnismaning Germany 48°13N 11°38E 131 A2
Dirranbandi Australia 28°33S 148°17E 281 D4
Dirs Si. Arabia 18°32N 42°5E 248 C3
Dirschau = Tczew Poland 54°8N 18°50E 184 D5
Disa India 24°18N 72°10E 242 G5
Disa Sudan 12°5N 34°15E 257 E3
Disappointment, C.
U.S.A. 46°18N 124°5W 306 D2
Disappointment, L.
Australia 23°20S 122°40E 278 D3
Disaster B. Australia 37°15S 149°58E 283 D8
Discovery B. Vic.,
Australia 38°10S 140°40E 282 E4
Discovery B.
Hong Kong, China 22°18N 114°1E 122 B2
Discovery Bay △ Australia 38°9S 141°16E 282 E4
Discovery Seamount
Atl. Oc. 42°0S 0°10E 152 L12
Disentis Muster Switz. 46°42N 8°50E 179 J4
Dishna Egypt 26°9N 32°32E 256 B3
Disina Nigeria 11°35N 9°50E 263 C6
Disko = Qeqertarsuaq
Greenland 69°45N 53°30W 154 D5
Disko Bugt Greenland 69°10N 52°0W 154 D5
Disna = Dzisna →
Belarus 55°34N 28°12E 188 E5
Disney-M.G.M. Studios
U.S.A. 28°21N 81°33W 133 B1
Disney Reef Tonga 19°17S 174°7W 287 P13
Disney Studios U.S.A. 34°9N 118°19W 126 B3
Disneyland Hong Kong
China 22°19N 114°2E 122 B2
Disneyland Tōkyō
Tokyo, Japan 35°37N 139°53E 140 B4
Dispur India 26°3N 91°52E 241 B3
Diss U.K. 52°23N 1°7E 169 E9
Disteghil Sar Pakistan 36°20N 75°12E 243 A6
District of Columbia □
U.S.A. 38°55N 77°0W 309 F15
Distrito Federal □ Brazil 15°45S 47°45W 333 E2
Distrito Federal □ Mexico 19°15N 99°10W 319 D5
Distrito Federal □
Venezuela 10°30N 66°55W 328 A4
Disûq Egypt 31°8N 30°35E 256 H7
Ditan Park Beijing, China 114 a2
Diu India 20°45N 70°58E 242 J4
Diuata Mts. Phil. 9°0N 125°50E 233 G5
Dīvāndarreh Iran 35°55N 47°2E 213 E12
Divarata Greece 38°20N 20°33E 207 C2
Divenié Congo 2°43S 12°1E 264 C2
Dives → France 49°18N 0°7W 172 C6
Dives-sur-Mer France 49°18N 0°8W 172 C6
Divi Pt. India 15°59N 81°9E 245 G5
Divichi = Däväçi
Azerbaijan 41°15N 48°57E 191 K9
Divide U.S.A. 45°45N 112°45W 304 D7
Dividing Ra. Australia 27°45S 116°0E 279 E2
Divilican B. Phil. 17°21N 122°19E 232 C4
Divinópolis Brazil 20°10S 44°54W 333 F3
Divisões, Serra dos Brazil 17°0S 51°0W 333 E1
Divjake Albania 41°0N 19°32E 202 F3
Divnoye Russia 45°55N 43°21E 191 H6
Divo Ivory C. 5°48N 5°15W 262 D3
Divriği Turkey 39°22N 38°7E 213 C8
Dīwāl Kol Afghan. 34°23N 67°52E 242 B2
Dix → U.S.A. 37°49N 84°43W 311 G12
Dixie Mt. U.S.A. 39°55N 120°16W 306 F6
Dixie Union U.S.A. 31°20N 82°28W 316 D7
Dixmoor U.S.A. 41°37N 87°41W 119 D2
Dixon Calif., U.S.A. 38°27N 121°49W 306 G5
Dixon Ill., U.S.A. 41°50N 89°29W 310 C7
Dixon Mo., U.S.A. 37°59N 92°6W 310 G4
Dixon Entrance U.S.A. 54°30N 132°0W 303 J14
Dixville Canada 45°4N 71°46W 313 A13
Diyadin Turkey 39°33N 43°40E 213 C10
Diyālá □ Iraq 33°45N 44°50E 246 C5
Diyālá → Iraq 33°13N 44°30E 213 F11
Diyarb Nigm Egypt 30°45N 31°26E 251 H2
Diyarbakır Turkey 37°55N 40°18E 213 D9
Diyarbakır □ Turkey 38°0N 40°10E 213 D9
Diyodar India 24°8N 71°50E 242 G4
Dizangué Cameroon 3°46N 9°59E 264 B1
Dja ⌓ Cameroon 3°10N 12°58E 264 B2
Djadié → Gabon 0°46N 12°58E 264 B2
Djado Niger 21°4N 12°14E 259 D2
Djado, Plateau du Niger 21°29N 12°21E 259 D2
Djakarta = Jakarta
Indonesia 6°9S 106°52E 122 A2
Djalma Dutra = Miguel Calmon
Brazil 11°26S 40°36W 332 D3
Djalma Dutra = Poções
Brazil 14°31S 40°21W 333 D3
Djamâa Algeria 33°32N 5°59E 261 B6
Djamba Angola 16°45S 13°58E 265 F2
Djambala Congo 2°32S 14°30E 264 C2
Djanet Algeria 24°35N 9°32E 261 D6
Djaul I. Papua N. G. 2°58S 150°57E 286 B6
Djawa = Jawa Indonesia 7°0S 110°0E 235 D4
Djebel Tazzeka △ Morocco 34°6N 4°11W 260 B4
Djebiniana Tunisia 35°1N 11°0E 258 A2
Djédaa Chad 13°31N 18°34E 259 F3
Djelfa Algeria 34°40N 3°15E 261 B5
Djelfa □ Algeria 34°20N 3°40E 261 B5
Djema C.A.R. 6°3N 25°15E 264 A5
Djember Chad 10°25N 17°50E 259 F3
Djembo
Dem. Rep. of the Congo 9°54S 22°18E 265 D4
Djémila Algeria 36°19N 5°44E 261 A6
Djendel Algeria 36°15N 2°25E 261 A5
Djenné Mali 14°0N 4°30W 262 C4
Djenoun, Garet el Algeria 25°4N 5°31E 261 C6
Djerba Tunisia 33°48N 10°54E 258 B2
Djerba, Î. de Tunisia 33°50N 10°48E 258 B2
Djeréme → Cameroon 5°20N 13°24E 264 A2
Djerid, Chott Tunisia 33°42N 8°30E 258 B1
Djermaya Chad 12°24N 15°3E 259 F3
Djibo Burkina Faso 14°9N 1°35W 263 C4
Djibouti Djibouti 11°30N 43°5E 257 E5
Djibouti ■ Africa 12°0N 43°0E 257 E5
Djohong Cameroon 6°47N 14°20E 264 A2
Djolu Dem. Rep. of the Congo 0°35N 22°5E 264 B4
Djouab → Gabon 1°13N 13°12E 264 B2
Djoudj △ Senegal 16°24N 16°14W 262 B1
Djougou Benin 9°40N 1°45E 263 D5
Djoum Cameroon 2°41N 12°35E 264 B2
Djouna Chad 10°27N 20°4E 259 F4
Djugu Dem. Rep. of the Congo 1°55N 30°35E 268 B3
Djukbinj △ Australia 12°11S 131°2E 278 B5
Djúpavík Iceland 65°57N 21°34W 155 B5
Djúpivogur Iceland 64°39N 14°17W 155 C12
Djupvasshytta Norway 62°2N 7°16E 164 B4
Djurås Sweden 60°34N 15°8E 162 D9
Djurdjura △ Algeria 36°20N 4°15E 261 A5
Djurö △ Sweden 58°52N 13°28E 163 F7
Djursholm Sweden 59°24N 18°5E 139 A2
Djursland Denmark 56°27N 10°45E 163 H4
Dmitriya Lapteva, Proliv
Russia 73°0N 140°0E 215 B15
Dmitriyev Lgovskiy Russia 52°10N 35°0E 189 F8
Dmitriyevsk = Makiyivka
Ukraine 48°0N 38°0E 189 H9
Dmitriyevskoye = Talas
Kyrgyzstan 42°30N 72°13E 217 D8
Dmitrov Russia 56°25N 37°32E 188 D9
Dmitrovsk-Orlovskiy
Russia 52°29N 35°10E 189 F8
Dnepr = Dnipro →
Ukraine 46°30N 32°18E 189 J7
Dneprodzerzhinsk =
Dniprodzerzhynsk
Ukraine 48°32N 34°37E 189 H8
Dneprodzerzhinskoye Vdkhr. =
Dniprodzerzhynske Vdskh.
Ukraine 48°49N 34°8E 189 H8
Dnepropetrovsk = Dnipropetrovsk
Ukraine 48°30N 35°0E 189 H8
Dneprorudnoye = Dniprorudne
Ukraine 47°21N 34°58E 189 J8
Dnestr = Dnister →
Europe 46°18N 30°17E 177 E16
Dnestrovski = Belgorod
Russia 50°35N 36°35E 189 G9
Dnieper = Dnipro →
Ukraine 46°30N 32°18E 189 J7
Dniester = Dnister →
Europe 46°18N 30°17E 177 E16
Dnipro → Ukraine 46°30N 32°18E 189 J7
Dniprodzerzhynsk
Ukraine 48°32N 34°37E 189 H8
Dniprodzerzhynske Vdskh.
Ukraine 48°49N 34°8E 189 H8
Dnipropetrovsk Ukraine 48°30N 35°0E 189 H8
Dnipropetrovsk □
Ukraine 48°15N 34°50E 189 H8
Dniprorudne Ukraine 47°21N 34°58E 189 J8
Dnister → Europe 46°18N 30°17E 177 E16
Dnistrovskyy Lyman
Ukraine 46°15N 30°17E 189 J6
Dno Russia 57°50N 29°58E 188 D5
Dnyapro = Dnipro →
Ukraine 46°30N 32°18E 189 J7
Do Gonbadān = Gachsārān
Iran 30°15N 50°45E 247 D6
Doabi Afghan. 36°1N 69°32E 240 A3
Doaktown Canada 46°33N 66°8W 299 C6
Doan Hung Vietnam 21°30N 105°10E 228 G5
Doany Madag. 14°21S 49°30E 272 A2
Doba Chad 8°40N 16°50E 259 G3
Dobandi Pakistan 31°13N 66°50E 242 D2
Dobbiaco Italy 46°44N 12°14E 199 B9
Dobbyn Australia 19°44S 140°2E 280 B3
Dobczyce Poland 49°52N 20°5E 185 J7
Dobele Latvia 56°37N 23°16E 184 B10
Döbeln Germany 51°6N 13°7E 178 D9
Doberai, Jazirah Indonesia 1°25S 133°0E 231 E8
Döberitz Germany 52°32N 13°3E 115 A1
Dobiegniew Poland 52°59N 15°45E 185 F2
Doblas Argentina 37°5S 64°0W 334 D3
Döbling Austria 48°14N 16°20E 142 A2
Dobo Dem. Rep. of the Congo 2°20N 22°11E 264 B4
Dobo Indonesia 5°45S 134°15E 231 F8
Doboj Bos.-H. 44°46N 18°4E 182 F3
Dobong S. Korea 37°39N 127°2E 137 B2
Dobongsan S. Korea 37°40N 127°0E 137 A2
Dobra Wielkopolskie, Poland 51°55N 18°37E 185 G5
Dobra Zachodnio-Pomorskie,
Poland 53°34N 15°20E 184 E2
Dobra Dâmbovita,
Romania 44°52N 25°40E 183 F10
Dobra Hunedoara, Romania 45°54N 22°36E 182 E7
Dobre Miasto Poland 53°58N 20°26E 184 E7
Dobrești Romania 46°51N 22°18E 182 D7
Dobrich Bulgaria 43°37N 27°49E 203 C11
Dobrich □ Bulgaria 43°37N 27°49E 203 C11
Dobrinishte Bulgaria 41°49N 23°34E 202 E7
Dobříš Czechia 49°46N 14°10E 180 B7
Dobrodzień Poland 50°45N 18°25E 185 H5
Dobromyl Ukraine 49°34N 22°46E 185 J9
Dobron Ukraine 48°25N 22°23E 182 B7
Dobropole Ukraine 48°25N 37°2E 189 H9
Dobrovolsk Russia 54°46N 22°31E 184 D9
Dobruja Europe 44°30N 28°15E 183 F13
Dobrush Belarus 52°25N 31°22E 177 B16
Dobrzany Poland 53°22N 15°25E 184 E2
Dobrzyń nad Wisłą Poland 52°39N 19°22E 185 F6
Doc, Mui Vietnam 17°58N 106°30E 236 D6
Doc Can I. Phil. 5°55N 119°56E 233 J2
Doce → Brazil 19°37S 39°49W 333 E4
Docker River = Kaltukatjara
Australia 24°52S 129°5E 279 D4
Docklands U.K. 51°30N 0°1W 125 A3
Docksta Sweden 63°3N 18°18E 162 A12
Doctor Arroyo Mexico 23°40N 100°11W 318 C4
Doctor Pedro P. Peña
Paraguay 22°27S 62°21W 331 E5
Doctor Phillips U.S.A. 28°26N 81°29W 133 B2
Doctors Inlet U.S.A. 30°6N 81°47W 316 E8
Doda India 33°10N 75°34E 243 C6
Doda, L. Canada 49°25N 75°13W 298 C4
Doda Betta India 11°24N 76°44E 245 J3
Dodballapur India 13°18N 77°32E 245 H3
Dodecanese = Dodekanisa
Greece 36°35N 27°0E 205 E8
Dodekanisa Greece 36°35N 27°0E 205 E8
Dodge City U.S.A. 37°45N 100°1W 308 G3
Dodge L. Canada 59°50N 105°36W 297 B7
Dodger Stadium
Los Angeles, U.S.A. 34°4N 118°14W 126 B3
Dodgeville U.S.A. 42°58N 90°8W 310 B6
Dodo Cameroon 7°30N 12°3E 263 D7
Dodo South Sudan 5°10N 29°57E 257 F2
Dodola Ethiopia 6°59N 39°11E 257 F4
Dodoma Tanzania 6°8S 35°45E 268 D4
Dodoma □ Tanzania 6°0S 36°0E 268 D4
Dodoni Greece 39°40N 20°46E 204 B2
Dodori ⌓ Kenya 1°55S 41°7E 268 C5
Dodsland Canada 51°50N 108°45W 297 C7
Dodson U.S.A. 48°24N 108°15W 304 B9
Dodurga Turkey 39°49N 29°57E 205 B11
Doerun U.S.A. 31°19N 83°55W 316 D6
Doesburg Neths. 52°1N 6°9E 170 B6
Doetinchem Neths. 51°59N 6°18E 170 C6
Dog Creek Canada 51°35N 122°14W 296 C4
Dog I. U.S.A. 29°48N 84°36W 316 F5
Dog L. Man., Canada 51°2N 98°31W 297 C9
Dog L. Ont., Canada 48°48N 89°30W 298 C2
Dogana di Mare, Palazzo Venice, Italy 142 c3
Doğankent Turkey 36°52N 35°18E 250 B6
Doğanşehir Turkey 38°5N 37°53E 212 C7
Dogliani Italy 44°32N 7°56E 198 D4
Dōgo Japan 36°15N 133°16E 222 A5
Dōgo-San Japan 35°2N 133°13E 222 B5
Dogondoutchi Niger 13°38N 4°2E 263 C5
Dogons, Land of the = Bandiagara,
Falaise de Mali 14°14N 3°29W 262 D4
Dogran Pakistan 31°48N 73°35E 242 D5
Dogs, Isle of U.K. 51°29N 0°1W 125 B3
Doğubayazıt Turkey 39°31N 44°5E 213 C11
Doguéraoua Niger 14°0N 5°31E 263 C6
Dogura Papua N. G. 10°6S 150°5E 286 F6
Doha = Ad Dawḩah
Qatar 25°15N 51°35E 247 E6
Doha Int. ✈ (DOH) Qatar 25°16N 51°34E 247 E6
Dohazari Bangla. 22°10N 92°5E 241 D4
Dohinog = Manukan
Phil. 8°32N 123°12E 233 G4
Dohrighat India 26°16N 83°31E 243 F10
Doi Indonesia 2°14N 127°49E 231 D7
Doi Inthanon Thailand 18°35N 98°29E 236 C2
Doi Inthanon △ Thailand 18°33N 98°34E 236 C2
Doi Khuntan △ Thailand 18°33N 99°14E 236 C2
Doi Luang Thailand 18°30N 101°0E 236 C3
Doi Luang △ Thailand 19°22N 99°35E 236 C2
Doi Phukha △ Thailand 19°8N 101°9E 236 C3
Doi Saket Thailand 18°52N 99°9E 236 C2
Doi Suthep Pui △ Thailand 18°49N 98°53E 236 C2
Doi Toa Thailand 17°55N 98°30E 236 D2
Dois Irmãos, Sa. Brazil 9°0S 42°30W 332 C3
Dojransko Jezero
Macedonia 41°13N 22°44E 202 E6
Doka Sudan 13°31N 35°46E 257 E4
Dokdo = Liancourt Rocks
Asia 37°15N 131°52E 221 F5
Dokka Norway 60°49N 10°7E 164 D7
Dokka → Norway 60°49N 10°7E 164 D7
Dokkum Neths. 53°20N 5°59E 170 A5
Dokos Greece 37°20N 23°20E 204 D5
Dokri Pakistan 27°25N 68°7E 242 F3
Dokshukino = Nartkala
Russia 43°33N 43°51E 191 J6
Dokuchayevsk Ukraine 47°44N 37°40E 189 J9
Dol-de-Bretagne France 48°34N 1°47W 172 D5
Dolak, Pulau Indonesia 8°0S 138°30E 231 F9
Dolban = Liman Russia 45°45N 47°12E 191 H8
Dolbeau-Mistassini
Canada 48°53N 72°14W 299 C5
Dole France 47°7N 5°31E 173 E12
Doleib, Wadi → Sudan 12°10N 33°15E 257 E3
Dolenji Logatec = Logatec
Slovenia 45°56N 14°15E 199 C11
Dolgellau U.K. 52°45N 3°53W 168 E4
Dolgelley = Dolgellau
U.K. 52°45N 3°53W 168 E4
Dolgoe Ozero Russia 60°0N 30°15E 137 A1
Dolhasca Romania 47°26N 26°36E 183 C11
Doliana Greece 39°54N 20°32E 204 B2
Dolianova Italy 39°22N 9°10E 200 C2
Dolinsk Russia 47°21N 142°48E 215 E15
Dolinskaya = Dolynska
Ukraine 48°6N 32°46E 189 H7
Dolj □ Romania 44°10N 23°30E 183 F8
Doll Museum Delhi, India 120 b3
Dollard Neths. 53°20N 7°10E 170 A7
Dollis Hill U.K. 51°33N 0°13W 125 A2
Dolna Banya Bulgaria 42°18N 23°44E 202 D7
Dolni Czechia 50°3N 14°33E 135 B3
Dolni Chabry Czechia 50°8N 14°26E 135 B2
Dolni Chiflik Bulgaria 42°59N 27°43E 203 D11
Dolni Dŭbnik Bulgaria 43°24N 24°26E 203 C8
Dolni Počernice Czechia 50°5N 14°34E 135 B3
Dolnośląskie □ Poland 51°10N 16°30E 185 G3
Dolný Kubín Slovakia 49°12N 19°18E 181 B12
Dolo Ethiopia 4°11N 42°3E 257 G5
Dolo Italy 45°25N 12°5E 199 C9
Dolomites = Dolomiti
Italy 46°23N 11°51E 199 B8
Dolomiti Italy 46°23N 11°51E 199 B8
Dolomiti Bellunesi △ Italy 46°10N 12°5E 199 B9
Dolores Argentina 36°20S 57°40W 334 D4
Dolores Phil. 12°2N 125°29E 232 E5
Dolores Uruguay 33°34S 58°15W 334 C4
Dolores Colo., U.S.A. 37°28N 108°30W 305 H9
Dolores → U.S.A. 38°49N 109°17W 304 G9
Dolovo Serbia 44°55N 20°52E 182 F5
Dolphin, C. Falk. Is. 51°10S 59°0W 153 f
Dolphin and Union Str.
Canada 69°5N 114°45W 294 D9
Dolphin Head Jamaica 18°22N 78°10W 320 a
Dolphin I. Jamaica 17°48N 77°10W 320 a
Dolsk Poland 51°59N 17°3E 185 G4
Dolton U.S.A. 41°38N 87°36W 119 D3
Dolungmukh India 27°30N 94°18E 241 B5
Dolyna Ukraine 48°58N 24°1E 183 B9
Dolynska Ukraine 48°6N 32°46E 189 H7
Dolynske Ukraine 47°32N 29°55E 183 C14
Dolzhanskaya Russia 46°37N 37°48E 189 J9
Dom Joaquim Brazil 18°57S 43°16W 333 E3
Dom Pedrito Brazil 31°0S 54°40W 335 C5
Dom Pedro Brazil 4°59S 44°27W 332 B3
Dom Pedro II, Parque
Brazil 23°33S 46°36W 137 B2
Doma = Gombe Nigeria 10°19N 11°2E 263 C7
Doma Nigeria 8°25N 8°18E 263 D6
Doma ⌓ Zimbabwe 16°28S 30°12E 269 F3
Domadare Somalia 1°52N 41°15E 267 D5
Domain, The Sydney, Australia 139 b2
Domaniç Turkey 39°48N 29°36E 205 B11
Domar, Enneri → Chad 18°11N 18°4E 259 E3
Domariaganj → India 26°17N 83°44E 243 F10
Domasi Malawi 15°15S 35°22E 269 F4
Domažlice Czechia 49°28N 12°58E 180 B5
Dombarovka = Dombarovskiy
Russia 50°46N 59°32E 214 D6
Dombarovskiy Russia 50°46N 59°32E 214 D6
Dombås Norway 62°4N 9°8E 164 B6
Dombasle-sur-Meurthe
France 48°38N 6°21E 173 D13
Dombe Grande Angola 12°57S 13°6E 265 E2
Dombes France 45°58N 5°0E 175 C9
Dombóvár Hungary 46°21N 18°9E 182 D3
Dombrád Hungary 48°13N 21°54E 182 B6
Dombrova = Dąbrowa Górnicza
Poland 50°15N 19°10E 185 H6
Dombrowitsa = Dubrovytsya
Ukraine 51°31N 26°35E 177 C14
Dome Argus Antarctica 80°50S 76°30E 151 E6
Dome C. Antarctica 75°12S 123°37E 151 D9
Dome Fuji Antarctica 77°20S 39°45E 151 D5
Dome of the Rock Jerusalem 123 b3
Domel I. = Letsôk-aw Kyun
Burma 11°30N 98°25E 237 G2
Domérat France 46°21N 2°32E 173 F9
Domett N.Z. 42°53S 173°12E 285 C8
Domeyko Chile 29°0S 71°0W 334 B1
Domeyko, Cordillera Chile 24°30S 69°0W 334 A2
Domfront France 48°37N 0°40W 172 D6
Dominador Chile 24°21S 69°20W 334 A2
Dominica ■ W. Indies 15°20N 61°20W 323 k
Dominica Passage
W. Indies 15°10N 61°20W 321 C7
Dominican Rep. ■
W. Indies 19°0N 70°30W 321 C5
Dominion Centre Toronto, Canada 141 b2
Domiongo
Dem. Rep. of the Congo 4°37S 21°15E 265 C4
Dömitz Germany 53°8N 11°15E 178 B7
Domme France 44°48N 1°12E 174 D5
Domnești Romania 45°12N 24°50E 183 E9
Domo Ethiopia 7°50N 47°10E 267 C6
Domodedovo Russia 55°26N 37°46E 188 E9
Domodedovo Int., Moscow ✈
(DME) Russia 55°24N 37°54E 188 E9
Domodóssola Italy 46°7N 8°17E 198 B5
Domogled-Valea Cernei △
Romania 44°52N 22°27E 182 F7
Domokos Greece 39°10N 22°18E 204 B4
Domoni Comoros Is. 12°15S 44°32E 272 a
Dompaire France 48°14N 6°14E 173 D13
Dompierre-sur-Besbre
France 46°31N 3°41E 173 F10
Dompim Ghana 5°10N 2°5W 262 D4
Dompu Indonesia 8°32S 118°28E 235 D5
Domrémy-la-Pucelle
France 48°26N 5°40E 173 D12
Domvena Greece 38°15N 22°59E 204 C4
Domville, Mt. Australia 28°1S 151°15E 281 D5
Domžale Slovenia 46°9N 14°35E 199 B11
Don → India 16°20N 76°15E 245 F3
Don → Russia 47°4N 39°18E 189 J10
Don → Aberds., U.K. 57°11N 2°5W 167 D6
Don → S. Yorks., U.K. 53°41N 0°52W 168 D7
Don, C. Australia 11°18S 131°46E 278 B5
Don Benito Spain 38°53N 5°51W 195 G5
Don Figuereroa Mts.
Jamaica 18°5N 77°36W 320 a
Don Mills Canada 43°44N 79°21W 141 A2
Don Muang Int. ✈ (BKK)
Thailand 13°53N 100°36E 113 A2
Don Sak Thailand 9°18N 99°41E 237 b
Dona Ana = Nhamaabué
Mozam. 17°25S 35°5E 269 F4
Doña Mencía Spain 37°33N 4°21W 195 H6
Donaghadee U.K. 54°39N 5°33W 166 B6
Donaghmore Ireland 52°52N 7°36W 166 D4
Donald Australia 36°23S 143°0E 282 D5
Donaldsonville U.S.A. 30°6N 90°59W 314 F9
Donalsonville U.S.A. 31°3N 84°53W 316 D5
Doñana △ Spain 36°59N 6°23W 195 J4
Donau = Dunărea →
Europe 45°20N 29°40E 183 E14
Donau → Austria 48°10N 17°0E 181 C10
Donau Auen △ Austria 48°8N 16°44E 181 C9
Donau-Oder Kanal
Austria 48°12N 16°32E 142 A3
Donaueschingen Germany 47°56N 8°29E 179 H4
Donaufeld Austria 48°15N 16°24E 142 A2
Donaupark Austria 48°14N 16°24E 142 A2
Donaustadt Austria 48°13N 16°29E 142 A2
Donauwörth Germany 48°43N 10°47E 179 G6
Doncaster U.K. 53°32N 1°6W 168 D6
Dondo Angola 9°45S 14°25E 265 D2
Dondo
Dem. Rep. of the Congo 4°11N 21°39E 264 B4
Dondo Mozam. 19°33S 34°46E 269 F3
Dondo, Teluk Indonesia 0°50N 120°30E 231 D6
Dondra Head Sri Lanka 5°55N 80°40E 245 M5
Dondușeni Moldova 48°14N 27°36E 183 B12
Donegal Ireland 54°39N 8°5W 166 B3
Donegal □ Ireland 54°53N 8°0W 166 B4
Donegal B. Ireland 54°31N 8°49W 166 B3
Donets → Russia 47°33N 40°55E 191 G5
Donets Basin Ukraine 49°0N 38°0E 158 F13
Donetsk Ukraine 48°0N 37°45E 189 J9
Donetsk □ Ukraine 47°30N 37°50E 189 J9
Dong Ba Thin Vietnam 12°8N 109°13E 237 F7
Dong Dang Vietnam 21°54N 106°42E 228 G6
Dong Giam Vietnam 19°25N 105°31E 236 C5
Dong Ha Vietnam 16°55N 107°8E 236 D6
Dong Hene Laos 16°40N 105°18E 236 D5
Dong Hoi Vietnam 17°29N 106°36E 236 D6
Dong Jiang → China 23°6N 114°0E 229 F10
Dong Khe Vietnam 22°26N 106°27E 236 A6
Dong Phayayen Thailand 14°20N 101°22E 236 E3
Dong Ujimqin Qi China 45°32N 116°55E 226 B9
Dong Van Vietnam 23°16N 105°22E 236 A5
Dong Xoai Vietnam 11°32N 106°55E 237 G6
Donga Nigeria 7°45N 10°2E 263 D7
Donga → Nigeria 8°20N 9°58E 263 D7
Dong'an China 26°23N 111°12E 229 D8
Dongan Hills U.S.A. 40°35N 74°5W 132 C1
Dongara Australia 29°14S 114°57E 279 E1
Dongargarh India 21°10N 80°40E 244 D5
Dongbei China 45°0N 125°0E 227 D13
Dongcheng Beijing, China 114 b2
Dongchuan China 26°8N 103°1E 228 D4
Dongdaemung S. Korea 37°34N 127°2E 137 B2
Dongducheon S. Korea 37°54N 127°3E 224 D3
Donges France 47°18N 2°4W 172 E4
Dongfang China 18°50N 108°33E 229 a
Dongfeng China 42°40N 125°34E 224 A2
Donggala Indonesia 0°30S 119°40E 235 C5
Donggan China 23°22N 105°9E 228 F5
Donggang = Tungkang
Taiwan 22°27N 120°26E 225 D2
Donggang China 39°52N 124°10E 224 C2
Donggou China 31°17N 121°33E 138 B2
Dongguan China 22°58N 113°44E 229 F9
Dongguang China 37°50N 116°30E 226 F9
Donghae S. Korea 37°29N 129°7E 224 D4
Donghai Dao China 21°0N 110°15E 229 G8
Dongjak S. Korea 37°30N 126°56E 137 B1
Dongjiao China 23°5N 113°12E 121 B2
Dongjingcheng China 44°5N 129°10E 227 B15
Dongkou China 27°6N 110°35E 229 D8
Donglan China 24°30N 107°21E 228 E6
Dongliao He → China 42°58N 123°32E 227 C12
Dongliu China 30°13N 116°55E 229 B11
Dongmen China 22°20N 107°48E 228 F6
Dongnae S. Korea 35°12N 129°5E 224 E4
Dongning China 44°2N 131°5E 227 B16
Dongnyi China 28°3N 100°15E 228 C3
Dongo Angola 14°36S 15°48E 265 E3
Dongobe
Dem. Rep. of the Congo 4°35N 23°13E 264 B4
Dongola Sudan 19°9N 30°22E 256 D3
Dongou Congo 2°0N 18°5E 264 B3
Dongping China 35°55N 116°20E 226 G9
Dongri India 18°53N 72°57E 130 B2
Dongsha Dao
S. China Sea 20°45N 116°43E 219 G12
Dongshan = Tungshan
Taiwan 24°38N 121°47E 225 B3
Dongshan China 23°43N 117°30E 229 F11
Dongshanhu Park China 23°7N 113°17E 121 B2
Dongsheng = Ordos
China 39°50N 110°0E 226 E6
Dongshi = Tungshih Changhua,
Taiwan 24°12N 120°43E 225 B2
Dongshi = Tungshih Chiai,
Taiwan 23°27N 120°8E 225 C2
Dongsi Mosque Beijing, China 114 b2
Dongtai China 32°51N 120°21E 229 A13
Dongting Hu China 29°18N 112°45E 229 C9
Dongtou China 27°51N 121°10E 229 D13
Dongwe → Zambia 13°59S 23°53E 265 E4
Dongxiang China 28°11N 116°34E 229 C11
Dongxing China 21°34N 108°0E 228 G7
Dongyang China 29°13N 120°15E 229 C13
Dongying China 37°37N 118°37E 227 F10
Dongyinggang China 37°55N 118°58E 227 F10
Dongzhi China 30°9N 117°0E 229 B11
Dongzhimen China 39°55N 116°24E 114 B2
Donington, C. Australia 34°45S 136°0E 282 C2
Doniphan U.S.A. 36°37N 90°50W 308 G8
Donja Stubica Croatia 45°59N 15°59E 199 C12
Donji Dušnik Serbia 43°12N 22°5E 202 C6
Donji Miholjac Croatia 45°45N 18°10E 182 E3
Donji Milanovac Serbia 44°28N 22°6E 202 B6
Donji Vakuf Bos.-H. 44°8N 17°24E 182 F2
Dønna Nordland, Norway 66°6N 12°30E 160 C15
Donna Tex., U.S.A. 26°9N 98°4W 314 H5
Donnacona Canada 46°41N 71°41W 299 C5
Donnelly's Crossing N.Z. 35°42S 173°38E 284 B2
Donner Pass U.S.A. 39°19N 120°20W 306 F6
Donnybrook W. Austral.,
Australia 33°34S 115°48E 279 F2
Donnybrook KwaZulu Natal,
S. Africa 29°59S 29°48E 271 C4
Donora U.S.A. 40°11N 79°52W 312 F5
Donostia = Donostia-San Sebastián
Spain 43°17N 1°58W 196 B3
Donostia-San Sebastián
Spain 43°17N 1°58W 196 B3
Donousa Greece 37°8N 25°48E 205 D7
Donovan U.S.A. 40°53N 87°37W 311 D9
Donque Angola 15°28S 14°6E 265 F2
Donskoy Russia 53°55N 38°15E 188 F10
Donsol Phil. 12°54N 123°36E 232 E4
Donwood Canada 44°19N 78°16W 312 B6
Donzère France 44°28N 4°43E 175 D8
Donzy France 47°20N 3°6E 173 E10
Dookie Australia 36°20S 145°41E 283 D6
Doomadgee Australia 17°56S 138°49E 280 B2
Doomadgee ✪ Australia 17°56S 138°49E 280 B2
Doon → U.K. 55°27N 4°39W 167 F4
Doon Doon ✪ Australia 16°18S 128°14E 278 C4
Doornfontein S. Africa 26°11S 28°3E 123 B2
Doornik = Tournai
Belgium 50°35N 3°25E 170 D3
Dora Iraq 33°15N 44°23E 113 A2
Dora, L. Australia 22°0S 123°0E 278 D3
Dora Báltea → Italy 45°11N 8°3E 198 C5
Dora Ripária → Italy 45°5N 7°44E 198 C4
Doran L. Canada 61°13N 108°6W 297 A7
Doraville U.S.A. 33°54N 84°17W 316 B5
Dorchester Dorset, U.K. 50°42N 2°27W 169 G5
Dorchester Mass., U.S.A. 42°17N 71°4W 116 B2
Dorchester, C. Canada 65°27N 77°27W 295 D16
Dorchester B. U.S.A. 42°18N 71°1W 116 B2
Dorchester Heights Nat. Historical
Site ⌓ U.S.A. 42°20N 71°2W 116 B2
Dordabis Namibia 22°52S 17°38E 270 B2
Dordogne □ France 45°5N 0°40E 174 C4
Dordogne → France 45°2N 0°36W 174 C3
Dordrecht Neths. 51°48N 4°39E 170 C4
Dordrecht Eastern Cape,
S. Africa 31°20S 27°3E 270 D4
Dore → France 45°50N 3°35E 174 C7
Dore, Mts. France 45°32N 2°50E 174 C6
Doré L. Canada 54°46N 107°17W 297 C7
Dorée → St. Lucia 13°46N 61°3W 323 m
Dores da Boa Esperança = Boa
Esperança Brazil 3°21N 61°23W 329 C5
Dores do Indaiá Brazil 19°27S 45°36W 333 E2
Dorfen Germany 48°15N 12°8E 179 G8
Dorgali Italy 40°17N 9°35E 200 B2
Dori Burkina Faso 14°3N 0°2W 263 C4
Doring → S. Africa 31°54S 18°39E 270 D2
Doringbos S. Africa 31°59S 19°16E 270 D2
Dorking U.K. 51°14N 0°19W 169 F7
Dormaa-Ahenkro Ghana 7°15N 2°52W 262 D4
Dormans France 49°4N 3°38E 173 C10
Dormo, Ras Eritrea 13°14N 42°35E 257 E5
Dornach Germany 48°9N 11°41E 131 B3
Dornakal India 17°27N 80°10E 244 F5
Dornbirn Austria 47°25N 9°45E 180 D2
Dornes France 46°48N 3°18E 173 F10
Dornești Romania 47°52N 26°1E 183 C11
Dornie U.K. 57°17N 5°31W 167 D3
Dornoch Ont., Canada 44°18N 80°51W 312 B4
Dornoch Highl., U.K. 57°53N 4°2W 167 D4
Dornoch Firth U.K. 57°51N 4°4W 167 D4
Dornogovĭ □ Mongolia 44°0N 110°0E 226 C6
Doro Mali 16°9N 0°51W 263 B4
Doro, Kavo Greece 38°9N 24°38E 204 C6
Dorog Hungary 47°42N 18°45E 182 C3
Dorogobuzh Russia 54°50N 33°18E 188 E7
Dorohoi Romania 47°56N 26°23E 183 C11
Döröö Nuur Mongolia 48°0N 93°0E 217 C12
Dorpat = Tartu Estonia 58°20N 26°44E 188 C4
Dorr Iran 33°17N 50°38E 247 C6
Dorre I. Australia 25°13S 113°12E 279 E1
Dorrigo Australia 30°20S 152°44E 283 A10
Dorrigo △ Australia 30°22S 152°47E 283 A10
Dorris U.S.A. 41°58N 121°55W 304 F3
Dorset Ont., Canada 45°14N 78°54W 312 A6
Dorset Ohio, U.S.A. 41°40N 80°40W 312 E4
Dorset Vt., U.S.A. 43°15N 73°5W 313 C11
Dorset □ U.K. 50°45N 2°26W 169 G5
Dorsoduro Venice, Italy 142 b1
Dorsten Germany 51°40N 6°58E 178 D2
Dortmund Germany 51°30N 7°28E 178 D3
Dortmund-Ems-Kanal →
Germany 51°50N 7°26E 178 D3
Dörtyol Turkey 36°50N 36°13E 250 B7
Doruk Turkey 36°53N 35°45E 250 B6
Dorum Germany 53°41N 8°34E 178 B4
Doruma
Dem. Rep. of the Congo 4°42N 27°33E 268 B2
Dorūneh Iran 35°10N 57°18E 247 C8
Dorval Int., Montréal ✈ (YUL)
Canada 45°28N 73°44W 130 B1
Dos Bahías, C. Argentina 44°58S 65°32W 336 B3
Dos d'Âne Réunion 20°58S 55°23E 272 f
Dos Hermanas Spain 37°16N 5°55W 195 H5
Dos Moninos → Brazil 23°40S 46°33W 137 B2
Dos Palos U.S.A. 36°59N 120°37W 306 J6
Döşemealtı Turkey 37°4N 30°36E 205 D12
Dosso Niger 13°0N 3°13E 263 C5
Dosso □ Niger 13°30N 3°30E 263 C5
Dosso ⌓ Niger 12°36N 2°36E 263 C5
Dostyq Kazakhstan 45°15N 82°29E 217 C10
Dot Lake U.S.A. 63°40N 144°4W 303 E11
Dothan U.S.A. 31°13N 85°24W 316 D4
Doty U.S.A. 46°38N 123°17W 306 D3
Douai France 50°21N 3°4E 173 B10
Douako Guinea 9°45N 10°8W 262 D2
Douala Cameroon 4°0N 9°45E 263 E6
Douala-Édéa ⌓ Cameroon 3°20N 9°41E 264 B1
Douamoungo, C. Mayotte 12°38S 45°8E 272 b
Douaouir Mali 20°45N 3°0W 260 D4
Douarnenez France 48°6N 4°21W 172 D2
Doubabougou Mali 14°13N 7°59W 262 C3
Double Cone N.Z. 45°4S 168°49E 285 F3
Double Island Pt.
Australia 25°56S 153°11E 281 D5
Double Mountain Fork →
U.S.A. 33°16N 100°0W 314 E4
Doubrava → Czechia 50°2N 15°20E 180 A8
Doubs □ France 47°10N 6°20E 173 E13
Doubs → France 46°53N 5°1E 173 F12
Doubtful Sd. N.Z. 45°20S 166°49E 285 F1
Doubtless B. N.Z. 34°55S 173°26E 284 A2
Doudeville France 49°43N 0°47E 172 C7
Doué-la-Fontaine France 47°11N 0°16W 172 E6
Douentza Mali 14°58N 2°48W 262 C4
Douentza ⌓ Mali 15°40N 2°25W 262 B4
Dougga Tunisia 36°25N 9°13E 258 A1
Doughboy B. N.Z. 47°2S 167°40E 285 H2
Douglas Ont., Canada 45°31N 76°56W 312 A8
Douglas I. of Man 54°10N 4°28W 168 C3
Douglas Northern Cape,
S. Africa 29°4S 23°46E 270 C3
Douglas Alaska, U.S.A. 58°17N 134°24W 303 G14
Douglas Ariz., U.S.A. 31°21N 109°33W 305 L9
Douglas Ga., U.S.A. 31°31N 82°51W 316 D7
Douglas Mich., U.S.A. 42°39N 86°14W 311 B10
Douglas Wyo., U.S.A. 42°45N 105°24W 304 E11
Douglas Apsley △
Australia 41°45S 148°11E 281 G4
Douglas B. Dominica 15°36N 61°29W 323 k
Douglas C. U.S.A. 58°51N 153°15W 303 G9
Douglas Chan. Canada 53°40N 129°20W 296 C3
Douglas Park U.S.A. 41°51N 87°42W 119 B2
Douglas Pt. Canada 44°19N 81°37W 312 B3
Douglasville U.S.A. 33°45N 84°45W 316 B5
Douirat Morocco 33°2N 4°11W 260 B4
Doukaton, Akra Greece 38°34N 20°33E 207 B2
Doukkala-Abda □
Morocco 32°10N 8°50W 260 B3
Doukoula Cameroon 10°10N 15°0E 259 F2
Doulevant-le-Château
France 48°23N 4°55E 173 D11
Douliou = Touliu Taiwan 23°42N 120°31E 225 C2
Doullens France 50°10N 2°20E 173 B9
Doumé Cameroon 4°15N 13°25E 264 B2
Doumen China 22°10N 113°18E 229 F9
Douna Mali 13°13N 6°0W 262 C3
Dounan = Tounan
Taiwan 23°41N 120°28E 225 C2
Dounreay U.K. 58°35N 3°44W 167 C5
Dourada, Serra Brazil 13°10S 48°45W 333 D2
Dourados Brazil 22°9S 54°50W 335 A5
Dourados → Brazil 21°58S 54°18W 335 A5
Dourados, Serra dos
Brazil 23°30S 53°30W 335 A5
Dourbali Chad 11°49N 15°52E 259 F3
Dourdan France 48°30N 2°1E 173 D9
Douro → Europe 41°8N 8°40W 194 D2
Douvaine France 46°19N 6°16E 173 F13
Douville Guadeloupe 16°15N 61°22W 322 e
Douz Tunisia 33°25N 9°0E 258 B1
Douze → France 43°54N 0°30W 174 E3
Dove → U.K. 52°51N 1°36W 168 E6
Dove Creek U.S.A. 37°46N 108°54W 305 H9
Dover Tas., Australia 43°18S 147°2E 281 G4
Dover Kent, U.K. 51°7N 1°19E 169 F9
Dover Del., U.S.A. 39°10N 75°32W 309 F16

Dover Ky., U.S.A. 38°43N 83°52W 311 F13
Dover N.H., U.S.A. 43°12N 70°56W 313 C14
Dover N.J., U.S.A. 40°53N 74°34W 313 F10
Dover Ohio, U.S.A. 40°32N 81°29W 312 F3
Dover, Pt. Australia 32°32S 125°32E 279 F4
Dover, Str. of Europe 51°0N 1°30E 169 G9
Dover-Foxcroft U.S.A. 45°11N 69°13W 309 C19
Dover Heights Australia 33°52S 151°16E 139 B2
Dover Plains U.S.A. 41°43N 73°35W 313 E11
Dovey = Dyfi → U.K. 52°32N 4°3W 169 E3
Dovhe Ukraine 48°22N 23°17E 183 B8
Dovlen = Devin Bulgaria 41°44N 24°24E 203 E8
Dovre Norway 61°58N 9°15E 164 C6
Dovre △ Norway 62°10N 9°30E 164 B6
Dovrefjell Norway 62°15N 9°33E 164 B6
Dovrefjell-Sunndalsfjella △ Norway 62°23N 9°11E 164 B6
Dow Rūd Iran 33°28N 49°4E 247 C6
Dowa Malawi 13°38S 33°58E 269 E3
Dowagiac U.S.A. 41°59N 86°6W 311 C10
Dowerin Australia 31°12S 117°2E 279 F2
Dowgha'i Iran 36°54N 58°32E 247 B8
Dowlat Yār Afghan. 34°30N 65°45E 240 B2
Dowlatābād Farāh, Afghan. 32°47N 62°40E 240 B1
Dowlatābād Fāryāb, Afghan. 36°26N 64°55E 240 A2
Dowlatābād Kermān, Iran 28°20N 56°40E 247 D8
Dowlatābād Khorāsān, Iran 35°16N 59°29E 247 C8
Dowlatābād Tehrān, Iran 35°38N 51°27E 141 B2
Dowling Park U.S.A. 30°15N 83°15W 316 E6
Down □ U.K. 54°23N 6°2W 166 B5
Down, L. U.S.A. 28°30N 81°31W 133 A1
Downers Grove U.S.A. 41°48N 88°1W 311 C8
Downey Calif., U.S.A. 33°56N 118°9W 126 C4
Downey Idaho, U.S.A. 42°26N 112°7W 304 E7
Downham Market U.K. 52°37N 0°23E 169 E8
Downieville U.S.A. 39°34N 120°50W 306 F6
Downing U.S.A. 40°29N 92°22W 310 D4
Downpatrick U.K. 54°20N 5°43W 166 B6
Downpatrick Hd. Ireland 54°20N 9°21W 166 B2
Downsview Canada 43°43N 79°30W 141 A2
Downsview Park Canada 43°45N 79°29W 141 A2
Downsville U.S.A. 42°5N 75°0W 313 D10
Downton, Mt. Canada 52°42N 124°52W 296 C4
Dowsārī Iran 28°25N 57°59E 247 D8
Dowshī Afghan. 35°35N 68°43E 240 B3
Doxato Greece 41°9N 24°16E 203 E8
Doyle U.S.A. 40°2N 120°6W 306 E6
Doylestown U.S.A. 40°21N 75°10W 313 F9
Dōzen Japan 36°5N 133°5E 222 A5
Dozois, Rés. Canada 47°30N 77°5W 298 C4
Dra Khel Pakistan 27°58N 66°45E 242 F2
Drâa, C. Morocco 28°47N 11°0W 260 C2
Drâa, Hamada du Algeria 28°0N 7°0W 260 C3
Drâa, Oued → Morocco 28°40N 11°10W 260 C2
Drac → France 45°12N 5°42E 175 C9
Drac, Coves del Spain 39°31N 3°19E 206 B4
Dračevo Macedonia 41°56N 21°31E 202 E5
Drachten Neths. 53°7N 6°5E 170 A6
Drăgănești Moldova 47°43N 28°15E 183 C13
Drăgănești-Olt Romania 44°9N 24°32E 183 F9
Drăgănești-Vlașca Romania 44°5N 25°33E 183 F10
Dragaš = Sharr Kosovo 42°5N 20°41E 202 D4
Drăgășani Romania 44°39N 24°17E 183 F9
Dragichyn Belarus 52°15N 25°8E 177 B13
Dragocvet Serbia 43°58N 21°15E 202 C5
Dragon's Mouths Trin. & Tob. 11°0N 61°50W 323 t
Dragør Denmark 55°35N 12°38E 118 B3
Dragovishtitsa Bulgaria 42°22N 22°39E 202 D6
Draguignan France 43°32N 6°27E 175 E10
Drahove Ukraine 48°14N 23°33E 183 B8
Drain U.S.A. 43°40N 123°19W 304 E2
Drake U.S.A. 47°55N 100°23W 308 B3
Drake Passage S. Ocean 58°0S 68°0W 151 B17
Drakensberg S. Africa 31°0S 28°0E 271 D4
Drama Greece 41°9N 24°10E 203 E8
Dramburg = Drawsko Pomorskie Poland 53°35N 15°50E 184 E2
Drammen Norway 59°42N 10°12E 164 E7
Drancy France 48°55N 2°26E 134 A3
Drangajökull Iceland 66°9N 22°15W 155 A4
Drangedal Norway 59°6N 9°3E 164 E6
Drangsnes Iceland 65°41N 21°27W 155 B5
Dranov, Ostrovul Romania 44°55N 29°30E 183 F14
Drapetsona Greece 37°56N 23°37E 112 B1
Dras India 34°25N 75°48E 243 B6
Drastis, Akra Greece 39°48N 19°40E 206 B9
Drau = Drava → Croatia 45°33N 18°55E 182 E3
Drava → Croatia 45°33N 18°55E 182 E3
Dravograd Slovenia 46°36N 15°5E 199 B12
Drawa → Poland 52°52N 15°59E 185 F2
Drawieński △ Poland 53°6N 15°58E 185 E2
Drawno Poland 53°13N 15°46E 185 E2
Drawsko Pomorskie Poland 53°35N 15°50E 184 E2
Drayton Canada 43°46N 80°40W 312 C4
Drayton Plains U.S.A. 42°41N 83°23W 311 B13
Drayton Valley Canada 53°12N 114°58W 296 C6
Dreieich Germany 50°1N 8°41E 179 E4
Dreikikir Papua N. G. 3°35S 142°46E 286 B2
Dreilinden Germany 52°24N 13°10E 115 B2
Drenthe □ Neths. 52°52N 6°40E 170 B6
Drepano, Akra Greece 35°28N 24°14E 207 E5
Drepanum, C. Cyprus 34°54N 32°19E 207 F8
Dresden Ont., Canada 42°35N 82°11W 312 D2
Dresden Sachsen, Germany 51°3N 13°44E 178 D9
Dresden N.Y., U.S.A. 42°41N 76°57W 312 D8
Dreux France 48°44N 1°23E 172 D8
Drevsjø Norway 61°53N 12°1E 164 C9
Drewnica Poland 52°18N 21°6E 143 B2
Drexel U.S.A. 39°45N 84°18W 311 E12
Drezdenko Poland 52°50N 15°49E 185 F2
Driesen = Drezdenko Poland 52°50N 15°49E 185 F2
Driffield U.K. 54°0N 0°26W 168 C7
Driftwood U.S.A. 41°20N 78°8W 312 E6
Driggs U.S.A. 43°44N 111°6W 304 E8
Drigh Road Pakistan 24°52N 67°7E 123 A2
Drin → Albania 42°1N 19°38E 202 D3
Drin i Zi → Albania 41°37N 20°28E 202 E4
Drina → Bos.-H. 44°53N 19°21E 202 B3
Drincea → Romania 44°20N 22°55E 182 F7
Drinjača → Bos.-H. 44°15N 19°8E 182 F4
Driopida Greece 37°25N 24°26E 204 D6
Drissa = Vyerkhnyadzvinsk Belarus 55°45N 27°58E 188 E4
Driva → Norway 62°41N 9°31E 164 B6
Drivstoggo Norway 62°26N 9°47E 164 B6
Drniš Croatia 43°51N 16°10E 199 E13
Drøbak Norway 59°39N 10°39E 164 E7
Drobeta-Turnu Severin Romania 44°39N 22°41E 182 F7
Drobin Poland 52°42N 19°58E 185 F6
Drochia Moldova 48°2N 27°48E 183 B12
Drogenbos Belgium 50°47N 4°19E 116 B1
Drogheda Ireland 53°43N 6°22W 166 C5
Drogichin = Dragichyn Belarus 52°15N 25°8E 177 B13
Drogobych = Drohobych Ukraine 49°20N 23°30E 185 J10
Drohiczyn Poland 52°24N 22°39E 185 F9
Drohobych Ukraine 49°20N 23°30E 185 J10
Droichead Átha = Drogheda Ireland 53°43N 6°22W 166 C5
Droichead na Bandan = Bandon Ireland 51°44N 8°44W 166 E3
Droichead Nua = Newbridge Ireland 53°11N 6°48W 166 C5
Droitwich U.K. 52°16N 2°8W 169 E5
Drôme □ France 44°38N 5°15E 175 D9
Drôme → France 44°46N 4°46E 175 D8
Dromedary, C. Australia 36°17S 150°10E 283 D9
Drömling △ Germany 52°29N 11°5E 178 C7
Dromore Down, U.K. 54°25N 6°9W 166 B5
Dromore Tyrone, U.K. 54°31N 7°28W 166 B4
Dromore West Ireland 54°15N 8°52W 166 B3
Dronero Italy 44°28N 7°22E 198 D4
Dronfield U.K. 53°19N 1°27W 168 D6
Dronne → France 45°2N 0°9W 174 C3
Dronning Ingrid Land Greenland 64°25N 52°5W 154 E5
Dronning Maud Land Antarctica 72°30S 12°0E 151 D3
Dronninglund Denmark 57°10N 10°19E 163 G4
Dronten Neths. 52°32N 5°43E 170 B5
Dropt → France 44°35N 0°6W 174 D3
Drosendorf Austria 48°52N 15°37E 180 C8
Drosh Pakistan 35°33N 71°48E 240 B4
Drottningholm Sweden 59°19N 17°53E 139 B1
Droué France 48°3N 1°6E 172 D8
Drouin Australia 38°10S 145°53E 283 E6
Druid Hills U.S.A. 33°47N 84°21W 113 B2
Druk Yul = Bhutan ■ Asia 27°25N 90°30E 241 B3
Drum Tower Beijing, China 114 a3
Drumbo Canada 43°16N 80°35W 312 C4
Drumcliff Ireland 54°20N 8°29W 166 B3
Drumheller Canada 51°25N 112°40W 296 C6
Drummond U.S.A. 46°40N 113°9W 304 C7
Drummond I. U.S.A. 46°1N 83°39W 309 B12
Drummond Pt. Australia 34°9S 135°16E 281 E2
Drummond Ra. Australia 23°45S 147°10E 280 C4
Drummondville Canada 45°55N 72°25W 298 C5
Drummoyne Australia 33°51S 151°8E 139 B1
Drumright U.S.A. 35°59N 96°36W 314 D6
Druskeniki = Druskininkai Lithuania 54°3N 23°58E 188 E2
Druskininkai Lithuania 54°3N 23°58E 188 E2
Drut → Belarus 53°8N 30°5E 177 B16
Druya Belarus 55°45N 27°28E 188 E4
Druzhba Bulgaria 43°15N 28°1E 203 C12
Druzhina Russia 68°14N 145°18E 215 C15
Druzhkivka Ukraine 48°38N 37°32E 189 H9
Drvar Bos.-H. 44°21N 16°23E 199 D13
Drvenik Croatia 43°27N 16°3E 199 E13
Drwęca → Poland 53°0N 18°42E 185 E5
Dry Harbour Mts. Jamaica 18°19N 77°24W 320 a
Dry Tortugas U.S.A. 24°38N 82°55W 315 J13
Dryander △ Australia 20°13S 148°34E 280 b
Dryanovo Bulgaria 42°59N 25°28E 203 D9
Dryden Ont., Canada 49°47N 92°50W 297 D10
Dryden N.Y., U.S.A. 42°30N 76°18W 313 D8
Drygalski I. Antarctica 66°0S 92°0E 151 C7
Drygalski Ice Tongue Antarctica 75°24S 163°30E 151 D11
Drylaw U.K. 55°58N 3°15W 121 B2
Drysdale → Australia 13°59S 126°51E 278 B4
Drysdale I. Australia 11°41S 136°0E 280 A2
Drysdale River △ Australia 14°56S 127°2E 278 B4
Drzewica Poland 51°27N 20°29E 185 G7
Drzewiczka → Poland 51°36N 20°36E 185 G7
Dschang Cameroon 5°32N 10°3E 263 D7
Du Gué → Canada 57°21N 70°45W 298 A5
Du He → China 32°48N 110°40E 229 A8
Du Quoin U.S.A. 38°1N 89°14W 310 G7
Du'an China 23°59N 108°3E 228 F7
Duanesburg U.S.A. 42°45N 74°11W 313 D10
Duaringa Australia 23°42S 149°42E 280 C4
Duarte, Pico Dom. Rep. 19°2N 70°59W 321 C5
Dubai = Dubayy U.A.E. 25°18N 55°20E 119 A2
Dubai Creek U.A.E. 25°15N 55°19E 119 A2
Dubai Int. ✈ (DXB) U.A.E. 25°15N 55°21E 119 A2
Dubai Int. Financial Centre U.A.E. 25°12N 55°17E 119 B2
Dubai Internet City U.A.E. 25°11N 55°10E 119 B1
Dubai Marina U.A.E. 25°11N 55°10E 119 B1
Dubai Maritime City U.A.E. 25°16N 55°16E 119 A2
Dubăsari Moldova 47°15N 29°10E 183 C14
Dubăsari Vdkhr. Moldova 47°30N 29°0E 183 C13
Dubawnt → Canada 64°33N 100°6W 297 A8
Dubawnt L. Canada 63°8N 101°28W 297 A8
Dubayy U.A.E. 25°18N 55°20E 119 A2
Dubbo Australia 32°11S 148°35E 283 B8
Dube → Liberia 5°16N 7°29W 262 D3
Dubeč Czechia 50°3N 14°35E 135 B3
Dubele Dem. Rep. of the Congo 2°56N 29°35E 268 B2
Dübendorf Switz. 47°24N 8°37E 179 H4
Dubica Bos.-H. 45°10N 16°50E 199 C13
Dubica Croatia 45°11N 16°48E 199 C13
Dublanc Dominica 15°31N 61°28W 323 k
Dublin Dublin, Ireland 53°21N 6°15W 166 C5
Dublin Ga., U.S.A. 32°32N 82°54W 316 C7
Dublin Ohio, U.S.A. 40°5N 83°7W 311 D13
Dublin Tex., U.S.A. 32°5N 98°21W 314 E5
Dublin □ Ireland 53°24N 6°20W 166 C5
Dublin ✈ (DUB) Ireland 53°26N 6°15W 166 C5
Dubna Russia 56°44N 37°10E 188 D9
Dubnica nad Váhom Slovakia 48°58N 18°11E 181 C11
Dubno Ukraine 50°25N 25°45E 177 D13
Dubois Idaho, U.S.A. 44°10N 112°14W 304 D7
Dubois Ind., U.S.A. 38°27N 86°48W 311 F10
DuBois Pa., U.S.A. 41°7N 78°46W 312 E6
Dubossary = Dubăsari Moldova 47°15N 29°10E 183 C14
Dubove Ukraine 48°10N 23°53E 183 B8
Dubovka Russia 49°5N 44°50E 191 F7
Dubovskoye Russia 47°28N 42°46E 191 G6
Dubrajpur India 23°48N 87°25E 243 H12
Dubréka Guinea 9°46N 13°31W 262 D2
Dubrovitsa = Dubrovytsya Ukraine 51°31N 26°35E 177 C14
Dubrovnik Croatia 42°39N 18°6E 202 D2
Dubrovytsya Ukraine 51°31N 26°35E 177 C14
Dubulu Dem. Rep. of the Congo 4°18N 20°16E 264 B4
Dubuque U.S.A. 42°30N 90°41W 310 B6
Dubysa → Lithuania 55°5N 23°26E 184 C10
Duc de Gloucester, Îs. French Polynesia 20°38S 143°20W 289 f
Duc Tho Vietnam 18°32N 105°35E 236 C5
Ducale, Palazzo Venice, Italy 142 b3
Ducassous, Pte. Martinique 14°32N 60°50W 322 j
Duchang China 29°18N 116°12E 229 C11
Duchesne U.S.A. 40°10N 110°24W 304 F8
Duchess Australia 21°20S 139°50E 280 C2
Ducie I. Pac. Oc. 24°40S 124°48W 289 K15
Duck → U.S.A. 36°2N 87°52W 315 C11
Duck Cr. → Australia 22°37S 116°53E 278 D2
Duck Lake Canada 52°50N 106°16W 297 C7
Duck Mountain △ Canada 51°45N 101°0W 297 C8
Duckwall, Mt. U.S.A. 37°58N 120°7W 306 H6
Ducos Martinique 14°33N 60°59W 322 j
Duda → Colombia 2°34N 74°3W 328 C3
Duddington U.K. 55°56N 3°8W 121 B3
Duderstadt Germany 51°31N 10°15E 178 D6
Dudhi India 24°15N 83°10E 243 G10
Dudhnoi India 25°59N 90°47E 241 C3
Dudinka Russia 69°30N 86°13E 215 C9
Dudley W. Mids., U.K. 52°31N 2°5W 169 E5
Dudley Ga., U.S.A. 32°32N 83°5W 316 C6
Dudna → India 19°17N 76°54E 244 E3
Dudo Somalia 9°20N 50°12E 267 C7
Dudo, W. → Somalia 9°14N 50°40E 267 C7
Dudub Ethiopia 6°55N 46°43E 267 D6
Dudwa India 28°30N 80°41E 243 E9
Dudwa △ India 28°30N 80°40E 243 E9
Duékoué Ivory C. 6°40N 7°15W 262 D3
Duenas Phil. 11°4N 122°37E 233 F4
Dueñas Spain 41°52N 4°33W 194 D6
Duerê Brazil 11°20S 49°17W 333 D2
Duero = Douro → Europe 41°8N 8°40W 194 D2
Duff Is. Pac. Oc. 9°50S 167°10E 277 B12
Dufftown U.K. 57°27N 3°8W 167 D5
Dufourspitz Switz. 45°56N 7°52E 179 K3
Dugger U.S.A. 39°4N 87°18W 311 E9
Dugi Otok Croatia 44°0N 15°3E 199 D11
Dugiuma Somalia 1°15N 42°34E 267 D5
Dugnano Italy 45°33N 9°11E 128 A2
Dugo Selo Croatia 45°51N 16°18E 199 C13
Duida-Marahuaca △ Venezuela 3°33N 65°33W 328 C4
Duisburg Germany 51°26N 6°45E 178 D2
Duitama Colombia 5°50N 73°2W 328 B3
Duivendrecht Neths. 52°20N 4°55E 112 B2
Duiwelskloof = Modjadjiskloof S. Africa 23°42S 30°10E 271 B5
Dujiangyan China 31°2N 103°38E 228 B4
Duk Fadiat South Sudan 7°45N 31°25E 257 F3
Duk Faiwil South Sudan 7°30N 31°29E 257 F3
Dukat Albania 40°16N 19°32E 202 F3
Dūkdamīn Iran 35°59N 57°43E 247 C8
Dukelský Průsmyk Slovakia 49°25N 21°42E 181 B14
Dukhān Qatar 25°25N 50°50E 247 E6
Dukhovshchina Russia 55°15N 32°27E 188 E7
Duki Pakistan 30°14N 68°25E 240 C3
Dukla Poland 49°30N 21°35E 185 J8
Duku Bauchi, Nigeria 10°43N 10°43E 263 C7
Duku Sokoto, Nigeria 11°11N 4°55E 263 C5
Dukuza = Stanger S. Africa 29°27S 31°14E 271 C5
Dula Dem. Rep. of the Congo 4°40N 20°21E 264 B4
Dūlāb Iran 35°39N 51°27E 141 B2
Dulag Phil. 10°57N 125°2E 233 F5
Dulan China 36°0N 97°11E 218 D8
Dulawan = Datu Piang Phil. 7°2N 124°30E 233 H5
Dulce U.S.A. 36°56N 107°0W 305 H10
Dulce → Argentina 30°32S 62°33W 334 C3
Dulce, G. Costa Rica 8°40N 83°20W 320 E3
Dulcina Antigua & B. 17°35N 61°49W 322 c
Dulf Iraq 35°7N 45°51E 246 C5
Dŭlgopol Bulgaria 43°3N 27°22E 203 C11
Duliu China 39°2N 116°55E 226 E9
Dullabchara India 24°30N 92°26E 241 C4
Dulles Int. ✈ (IAD) U.S.A. 38°57N 77°27W 309 F15
Dullewala Pakistan 31°50N 71°25E 242 D4
Dullstroom S. Africa 25°27S 30°7E 271 C5
Dülmen Germany 51°49N 7°17E 178 D3
Dulovo Bulgaria 43°48N 27°9E 203 C11
Dulpetorpet Norway 60°34N 12°19E 164 D9
Dulq Maghār Syria 36°22N 38°39E 213 D8
Duluth Ga., U.S.A. 34°0N 84°9W 316 A5
Duluth Minn., U.S.A. 46°47N 92°6W 308 B7
Dulwich U.K. 51°27N 0°5W 125 B3
Dum Dum India 22°39N 88°26E 124 B2
Dum Duma India 27°40N 95°40E 241 B5
Dūmā Syria 33°34N 36°24E 250 E7
Dumaguete Phil. 9°17N 123°15E 233 G4
Dumai Indonesia 1°35N 101°28E 234 B2
Dumalinao Phil. 7°49N 123°23E 233 H4
Dumanjug Phil. 10°4N 123°26E 233 F4
Dumanquilas B. Phil. 7°34N 123°4E 233 H4
Dumaran Phil. 10°33N 119°51E 233 F2
Dumaran I. Phil. 10°33N 119°51E 233 F2
Dumarao Phil. 11°16N 122°41E 233 F4
Dumas Ark., U.S.A. 33°53N 91°29W 314 E9
Dumas Tex., U.S.A. 35°52N 101°58W 314 D4
Dumayr Syria 33°39N 36°42E 250 E7
Dumbarton U.K. 55°57N 4°33W 167 F4
Dumbéa N. Cal. 22°10S 166°27E 288 d
Ďumbier Slovakia 48°56N 19°38E 181 C12
Dumbleyung Australia 33°17S 117°42E 279 F2
Dumbo Angola 14°6S 17°24E 265 E3
Dumbrăveni Romania 46°14N 24°34E 183 D9
Dumfries U.K. 55°4N 3°37W 167 F5
Dumfries & Galloway □ U.K. 55°9N 3°58W 167 F5
Dumingag Phil. 8°20N 123°20E 233 G4
Dumitrești Romania 45°33N 26°55E 183 E11
Dumka India 24°12N 87°15E 243 G12
Dumlupınar Turkey 38°53N 30°0E 205 C12
Dümmer Germany 52°31N 8°20E 178 C4
Dümmer △ Germany 52°31N 8°21E 178 C4
Dumoine → Canada 46°13N 77°51W 298 C4
Dumoine, L. Canada 46°55N 77°55W 298 C4
Dumont U.S.A. 40°56N 73°59W 132 A2
Dumont d'Urville Antarctica 66°40S 140°0E 151 C10
Dumont d'Urville Sea S. Ocean 63°30S 138°0E 151 C9
Dumoulin Is. Papua N. G. 10°54S 150°46E 286 F6
Dumpu Papua N. G. 5°53S 145°44E 286 C3
Dumyât Egypt 31°24N 31°48E 251 G2
Dumyât, Far → Egypt 31°32N 31°51E 251 G2
Dumyât, Masabb Egypt 31°28N 31°51E 251 G2
Dún Dealgan = Dundalk Ireland 54°1N 6°24W 166 B5
Dún Garbhán = Dungarvan Ireland 52°5N 7°37W 166 D4
Dún Laoghaire Ireland 53°17N 6°8W 166 C5
Dún Laoghaire-Rathdown □ Ireland 53°14N 6°11W 166 C5
Dun-le-Palestel France 46°18N 1°39E 173 F8
Dun-sur-Auron France 46°53N 2°33E 173 F9
Dun-sur-Meuse France 49°23N 5°11E 173 C12
Duna = Dunărea → Europe 45°20N 29°40E 183 E14
Duna-Drava △ Hungary 46°15N 18°50E 182 D3
Duna Dzong Bhutan 27°29N 89°24E 241 B2
Duna-völgyi-főcsatorna Hungary 46°40N 19°14E 182 D4
Dünaburg = Daugavpils Latvia 55°53N 26°32E 188 E4
Dunaföldvár Hungary 46°50N 18°57E 182 D3
Dunagiri India 30°31N 79°52E 243 D8
Dunaj = Dunărea → Europe 45°20N 29°40E 183 E14
Dunajec → Poland 50°15N 20°44E 185 H7
Dunajská Streda Slovakia 48°0N 17°37E 181 D10
Dunakeszi Hungary 47°37N 19°8E 182 C4
Dunapataj Hungary 46°39N 19°4E 182 D4
Dunărea → Europe 45°20N 29°40E 183 E14
Dunaszekcső Hungary 46°6N 18°45E 182 D3
Dunaújváros Hungary 46°58N 18°57E 182 D3
Dunav = Dunărea → Europe 45°20N 29°40E 183 E14
Dunavațu de Jos Romania 44°59N 29°13E 183 F14
Dunavtsi Bulgaria 43°57N 22°53E 202 C6
Dunay Russia 42°52N 132°22E 220 C6
Dunayivtsi Ukraine 48°54N 26°50E 183 B11
Dunback N.Z. 45°23S 170°36E 285 F5
Dunbar U.K. 56°0N 2°31W 167 E6
Dunblane U.K. 56°11N 3°58W 167 E5
Duncan B.C., Canada 48°45N 123°40W 306 B3
Duncan Ariz., U.S.A. 32°43N 109°6W 305 K9
Duncan Okla., U.S.A. 34°30N 97°57W 314 D6
Duncan, L. Canada 53°29N 77°58W 298 B4
Duncan Dock Cape Town, S. Africa 118 a3
Duncan L. Canada 62°51N 113°58W 296 A6
Duncan Passage India 11°0N 92°0E 245 J11
Duncan Town Bahamas 22°15N 75°45W 320 B4
Duncannon U.S.A. 40°23N 77°2W 312 F7
Duncans Jamaica 18°27N 77°32W 320 a
Duncansby Head U.K. 58°38N 3°1W 167 C5
Duncansville U.S.A. 40°25N 78°26W 312 F6
Duncanville U.S.A. 32°39N 96°54W 120 C4
Dund-Us Mongolia 48°1N 91°38E 217 C12
Dundaga Latvia 57°31N 22°21E 184 A9
Dundalk Ont., Canada 44°10N 80°24W 312 B4
Dundalk Louth, Ireland 54°1N 6°24W 166 B5
Dundalk Md., U.S.A. 39°15N 76°31W 309 F15
Dundalk Bay Ireland 53°55N 6°15W 166 C5
Dundas = Uummannaq Greenland 77°33N 68°52W 154 B4
Dundas Canada 43°17N 79°59W 312 C5
Dundas, L. Australia 32°35S 121°50E 279 F3
Dundas I. Canada 54°30N 130°50W 296 C2
Dundas Str. Australia 11°15S 131°35E 278 B5
Dundee KwaZulu Natal, S. Africa 28°11S 30°15E 271 C5
Dundee Dundee C., U.K. 56°28N 2°59W 167 E6
Dundee Mich., U.S.A. 41°57N 83°40W 311 C13
Dundee N.Y., U.S.A. 42°32N 76°59W 312 D8
Dundee City □ U.K. 56°30N 2°58W 167 E6
Dundgovi □ Mongolia 45°10N 106°0E 226 B4
Dundrum U.K. 54°16N 5°52W 166 B6
Dundrum B. U.K. 54°13N 5°47W 166 B6
Dunearn Singapore 1°19N 103°49E 138 B2
Dunedin N.Z. 45°50S 170°33E 285 F5
Dunedin Fla., U.S.A. 28°1N 82°46W 317 G7
Dunedoo Australia 32°0S 149°25E 283 A8
Dunfanaghy Ireland 55°11N 7°58W 166 A4
Dunfermline U.K. 56°5N 3°27W 167 E5
Dungannon Ont., Canada 43°51N 81°36W 312 C3
Dungannon Tyrone, U.K. 54°31N 6°46W 166 B5
Dungarpur India 23°52N 73°45E 242 H5
Dungarvan Ireland 52°5N 7°37W 166 D4
Dungarvan Harbour Ireland 52°4N 7°35W 166 D4
Dungeness U.K. 50°54N 0°59E 169 G8
Dungiven U.K. 54°56N 6°56W 166 B5
Dungloe Ireland 54°57N 8°21W 166 B3
Dungo, L. do Angola 17°15S 19°0E 265 F3
Dungog Australia 32°22S 151°46E 283 B9
Dungu Dem. Rep. of the Congo 3°40N 28°32E 268 B2
Dungun Malaysia 4°45N 103°25E 237 K4
Dungunâb Sudan 21°10N 37°9E 256 C4
Dungunâb, Khalîg Sudan 21°5N 37°12E 256 C4
Dunhua China 43°20N 128°14E 227 C15
Dunhuang China 40°8N 94°36E 218 C7
Dunk I. Australia 17°59S 146°29E 280 B4
Dunkassa Benin 10°21N 3°10E 263 C5
Dunkeld Queens., Australia 33°25S 149°29E 281 E4
Dunkeld Vic., Australia 37°40S 142°22E 282 D5
Dunkeld Perth & Kinr., U.K. 56°34N 3°35W 167 E5
Dunkerque France 51°2N 2°20E 173 A9
Dunkery Beacon U.K. 51°9N 3°36W 169 F4
Dunkirk = Dunkerque France 51°2N 2°20E 173 A9
Dunkirk U.S.A. 42°29N 79°20W 312 D5
Dunkuj Sudan 12°50N 32°49E 257 E3
Dunkwa Central, Ghana 6°0N 1°47W 262 D4
Dunkwa Central, Ghana 5°30N 1°0W 263 D4
Dunleary = Dún Laoghaire Ireland 53°17N 6°8W 166 C5
Dunleer Ireland 53°50N 6°24W 166 C5
Dunmanus B. Ireland 51°31N 9°50W 166 E2
Dunmanway Ireland 51°43N 9°6W 166 E2
Dunmarra Australia 16°42S 133°25E 280 B1
Dunmore U.S.A. 41°25N 75°38W 313 E9
Dunmore East Ireland 52°9N 7°0W 166 D5
Dunmore Town Bahamas 25°30N 76°39W 320 A4
Dunn U.S.A. 35°19N 78°37W 315 D15
Dunnellon U.S.A. 29°3N 82°28W 317 F7
Dunnet Hd. U.K. 58°40N 3°21W 167 C5
Dunning Ill., U.S.A. 41°56N 87°48W 119 B2
Dunning Nebr., U.S.A. 41°50N 100°6W 308 E3
Dunn's River Falls Jamaica 18°25N 77°8W 320 a
Dunnville Canada 42°54N 79°36W 312 D5
Dunolly Australia 36°51S 143°44E 282 D5
Dunoon U.K. 55°57N 4°56W 167 F4
Dunqul Egypt 23°26N 31°37E 256 C3
Duns U.K. 55°47N 2°20W 167 F6
Dunseith U.S.A. 48°50N 100°3W 308 A3
Dunshaughlin Ireland 53°31N 6°33W 166 C5
Dunsmuir U.S.A. 41°13N 122°16W 304 F2
Dunstable U.K. 51°53N 0°32W 169 F7
Dunstan Mts. N.Z. 44°53S 169°35E 285 E4
Dunster Canada 53°8N 119°50W 296 C5
Duntroon N.Z. 44°51S 170°40E 285 E5
Dunvegan Gauteng, S. Africa 26°9S 28°8E 123 A2
Dunvegan Highl., U.K. 57°27N 6°35W 167 D2
Dunvegan L. Canada 60°8N 107°10W 297 A7
Duolun China 42°12N 116°28E 226 C9
Duomo Italy 45°28N 9°11E 128 B2
Duomula China 34°8N 82°29E 217 F10
Duong Dong Vietnam 10°13N 103°58E 237 G4
Dupax del Norte Phil. 16°17N 121°5E 232 C3
Dupree U.S.A. 45°4N 101°35W 308 C3
Dupuyer U.S.A. 48°13N 112°30W 304 B7
Duque de Caxias Brazil 22°46S 43°18W 135 A1
Duque de York, I. Chile 50°37S 75°25W 336 D1
Durack → Australia 15°33S 127°52E 278 C4
Durack Ra. Australia 16°50S 127°40E 278 C4
Durack River Australia 15°32S 127°39E 278 C4
Durağan Turkey 41°25N 35°3E 212 B6
Durak Turkey 39°42N 28°17E 205 B10
Durakovac = Gjurakoc Kosovo 42°43N 20°29E 202 D4
Durance → France 43°55N 4°45E 175 E8
Durand Ga., U.S.A. 32°55N 84°46W 316 C5
Durand Ill., U.S.A. 42°26N 89°20W 310 B7
Durand Mich., U.S.A. 42°55N 83°59W 311 B13
Durand Wis., U.S.A. 44°38N 91°58W 308 C8
Durandeau St. Lucia 13°56N 60°59W 323 m
Durango Mexico 24°3N 104°39W 318 C4
Durango Colo., U.S.A. 37°16N 107°53W 305 H10
Durango □ Mexico 24°50N 105°20W 318 C4
Duranillin Australia 33°30S 116°45E 279 F2
Durankulak Bulgaria 43°41N 28°32E 203 C12
Durant Iowa, U.S.A. 41°36N 90°54W 310 C6
Durant Miss., U.S.A. 33°4N 89°51W 315 E10
Durant Okla., U.S.A. 33°59N 96°25W 314 E6
Duratón → Spain 41°37N 4°7W 194 D6
Durazno Uruguay 33°25S 56°31W 334 C4
Durazzo = Durrës Albania 41°19N 19°28E 202 E3
Durban Aude, France 42°59N 2°49E 174 F6
Durban KwaZulu Natal, S. Africa 29°49S 31°1E 271 C5
Durban ✈ (DUR) S. Africa 29°37S 31°7E 271 C5
Durbuy Belgium 50°21N 5°28E 170 D5
Dúrcal Spain 36°59N 3°34W 195 J7
Đurđevac Croatia 46°2N 17°3E 182 D2
Düren Germany 50°48N 6°29E 178 E2
Duren Sawit Indonesia 6°13N 106°54E 122 B2
Durg = Bhilainagar-Durg India 21°13N 81°26E 244 D5
Durgapur India 23°30N 87°20E 243 H12
Durham Ont., Canada 44°10N 80°49W 312 B4
Durham Darlington, U.K. 54°47N 1°34W 168 C6
Durham Calif., U.S.A. 39°39N 121°48W 306 F5
Durham N.C., U.S.A. 35°59N 78°54W 315 D15
Durham N.H., U.S.A. 43°8N 70°56W 313 C14
Durham □ U.K. 54°42N 1°45W 168 C6
Duri Indonesia 1°27N 101°15E 234 B2
Durlas = Thurles Ireland 52°41N 7°49W 166 D4
Durlești Moldova 47°1N 28°46E 183 C13
Ḑurmā Si. Arabia 24°37N 46°8E 246 E5
Durmitor Montenegro 43°10N 19°0E 202 C2
Durmitor △ Montenegro 43°15N 19°5E 202 C3
Durness U.K. 58°34N 4°45W 167 C4
Durnford, Pta. W. Sahara 23°37N 16°0W 260 D1
Durrës Albania 41°19N 19°28E 202 E3
Durrow Ireland 52°51N 7°24W 166 D4
Dursey I. Ireland 51°36N 10°12W 166 E1
Dursley U.K. 51°40N 2°21W 169 F5
Dursunbey Turkey 39°35N 28°37E 205 B10
Durtal France 47°40N 0°18W 172 E6
Duru Dem. Rep. of the Congo 4°14N 28°50E 268 B2
Duru Gölü Turkey 41°20N 28°35E 203 E12
Durukhsi Ethiopia 8°31N 45°28E 267 C6
Durusu Turkey 41°17N 28°41E 203 E12
Durūz, Jabal ad Jordan 32°35N 36°40E 250 F7
D'Urville, Tanjung Indonesia 1°28S 137°54E 231 E9
D'Urville I. N.Z. 40°50S 173°55E 285 A8
Duryea U.S.A. 41°20N 75°45W 313 E9
Dusa Mareb = Dhuusamarreeb Somalia 5°30N 46°15E 267 C6
Dûsh Egypt 24°35N 30°41E 256 C3
Dushak Turkmenistan 37°13N 60°1E 247 B9
Dushan China 25°48N 107°30E 228 E6
Dushanbe Tajikistan 38°33N 68°48E 217 E7
Dusheti Georgia 42°10N 44°42E 191 J7
Dushore U.S.A. 41°31N 76°24W 313 E8
Dusit Bangkok, Thailand 113 a2
Dusit Zoo Bangkok, Thailand 113 a2
Dusky Sd. N.Z. 45°47S 166°30E 285 F1
Dussejour, C. Australia 14°45S 128°13E 278 B4
Düsseldorf Germany 51°14N 6°47E 178 D2
Düsseldorf Rhein-Ruhr ✈ (DUS) Germany 51°17N 6°46E 178 D2
Dusti Tajikistan 37°20N 68°40E 217 E7
Duszniki-Zdrój Poland 50°24N 16°24E 185 H3
Dutch East Indies = Indonesia ■ Asia 5°0S 115°0E 235 C4
Dutch Guiana = Suriname ■ S. Amer. 4°0N 56°0W 329 C6
Dutch Harbor U.S.A. 53°53N 166°32W 303 K6
Dutlwe Botswana 23°58S 23°46E 270 B3
Dutsan Wai Nigeria 10°50N 8°10E 263 C6
Dutse Nigeria 11°46N 9°20E 263 C6
Dutton Canada 42°39N 81°30W 312 D3
Dutton → Australia 20°44S 143°10E 280 C3
Dutywa S. Africa 32°8S 28°18E 271 D4
Duved Sweden 63°23N 12°55E 162 A6
Düvertepe Turkey 39°14N 28°27E 205 B10
Dúvida = Roosevelt → Brazil 7°35S 60°20W 331 B5
Duwayhin, Khawr U.A.E. 24°20N 51°25E 247 E6
Duyfken Pt. Australia 12°33S 141°38E 280 A3
Duyun China 26°18N 107°29E 228 D6
Düzağac Turkey 38°48N 30°10E 205 C12
Düzce = Akhna Cyprus 35°3N 33°47E 207 E9
Düzce Turkey 40°50N 31°10E 212 B4
Düzce □ Turkey 40°50N 31°10E 212 B4
Duzdab = Zāhedān Iran 29°30N 60°50E 247 D9
Duzer Guadeloupe 16°20N 61°44W 322 e
Düziçi Turkey 37°15N 36°28E 212 D7
Dve Mogili Bulgaria 43°35N 25°55E 203 C9
Dvigatelstroy = Kaspiysk Russia 42°52N 47°40E 191 J8
Dvina, Severnaya → Russia 64°32N 40°30E 186 B7
Dvinsk = Daugavpils Latvia 55°53N 26°32E 188 E4
Dvinskaya Guba Russia 65°0N 39°0E 186 B6
Dvor Croatia 45°4N 16°22E 199 C13
Dvůr Králové nad Labem Czechia 50°27N 15°50E 180 A8
Dwarka India 22°18N 69°8E 242 H3
Dwellingup Australia 32°43S 116°4E 279 F2
Dwight Ont., Canada 45°20N 79°1W 312 A5
Dwight Ill., U.S.A. 41°5N 88°26W 310 C8
Dworp Belgium 50°44N 4°18E 116 B1
Dyakove Ukraine 48°1N 23°0E 182 B7
Dyakovo Russia 55°40N 37°39E 129 B2
Dyatkovo Russia 53°40N 34°27E 188 F8
Dyatlovo = Dzyatlava Belarus 53°28N 25°28E 177 B13
Dyce U.K. 57°13N 2°12W 167 D6
Dyer, C. Canada 66°37N 61°16W 295 D19
Dyer Bay Canada 45°10N 81°20W 312 A3
Dyer Plateau Antarctica 70°45S 65°30W 151 D17
Dyersburg U.S.A. 36°3N 89°23W 315 C10
Dyersville U.S.A. 42°29N 91°8W 310 B5
Dyfi → U.K. 52°32N 4°3W 169 E3
Dyhernfurth = Brzeg Dolny Poland 51°16N 16°41E 185 G3
Dyje → Czechia 48°37N 16°56E 181 C9
Dyke Ackland B. Papua N. G. 9°0S 148°45E 286 E5
Dyker Beach Park U.S.A. 40°36N 74°1W 132 C1
Dykh Tau Russia 43°3N 43°8E 191 J6
Dymer Ukraine 50°47N 30°18E 177 C16
Dynów Poland 49°50N 22°11E 185 J9
Dyranut Norway 60°22N 7°31E 164 D4
Dyrhólaey Iceland 63°24N 19°8W 155 D7
Dyrnes Norway 63°25N 7°52E 164 A4
Dysart Queens., Australia 22°32S 148°23E 280 C4
Dysart Iowa, U.S.A. 42°10N 92°18W 310 B4
Dytiki Ellas □ Greece 38°20N 21°30E 204 C3
Dyushambe = Dushanbe Tajikistan 38°33N 68°48E 217 E7
Dyviziya Ukraine 45°55N 29°59E 183 E14
Dzamin Üüd = Borhoyn Tal Mongolia 43°50N 111°58E 226 C6
Dzaoudzi Mayotte 12°47S 45°16E 272 b
Dzaoudzi ✈ (DZA) Mayotte 12°48S 45°18E 272 b
Dzaudzhikau = Vladikavkaz Russia 43°0N 44°35E 191 J7
Dzavhan □ Mongolia 48°0N 96°0E 217 C13
Dzavhan Gol → Mongolia 48°54N 93°23E 218 B7
Dzerzhinsk Russia 56°14N 43°30E 190 B6
Dzerzhinskiy Russia 55°47N 37°37E 129 B2
Dzerzhinskiy Park Russia 55°47N 37°37E 129 B2
Dzhalal-Abad = Jalal-Abad Kyrgyzstan 40°56N 73°0E 217 D8
Dzhalal-Ogly = Stepanavan Armenia 41°1N 44°23E 191 K7
Dzhalinda Russia 53°26N 124°0E 215 D13
Dzhambeyty = Zhympity Kazakhstan 50°16N 52°35E 216 B4
Dzhambul = Taraz Kazakhstan 42°54N 71°22E 217 D8
Dzhankoy Ukraine 45°40N 34°20E 189 K8
Dzhanybek = Zhänibek Kazakhstan 49°25N 46°50E 190 F8
Dzhargalantu = Hovd □ Mongolia 48°2N 91°37E 217 C12
Dzharkent = Zharkent Kazakhstan 44°10N 80°0E 217 D10
Dzharkurgan = Jarqo'rg'on Uzbekistan 37°31N 67°25E 240 A2
Dzharylhach, Ostriv Ukraine 46°2N 32°55E 189 J7
Dzhezkazgan = Zhezqazghan Kazakhstan 47°44N 67°40E 217 C7
Dzhibkhalantu = Uliastay Mongolia 47°56N 97°28E 218 B8
Dzhizak = Jizzax Uzbekistan 40°6N 67°50E 217 D7
Dzhugba Russia 44°19N 38°48E 191 H4
Dzhugdzur, Khrebet Russia 57°30N 138°0E 215 D14
Dzhulynk Ukraine 48°26N 29°45E 183 B14
Dzhumgoltau, Khrebet Kyrgyzstan 42°15N 74°30E 217 D8
Dzhungarskiye Vorota = Dzungarian Gate Asia 45°10N 82°0E 217 C10
Dzhuryn Ukraine 48°41N 28°18E 183 B13
Dzhvari = Jvari Georgia 42°42N 42°4E 191 J6
Działdowo Poland 53°15N 20°15E 185 E7
Działoszyce Poland 50°22N 20°20E 185 H7
Działoszyn Poland 51°6N 18°50E 185 G5
Dzibilchaltún Mexico 21°10N 89°35W 319 C7
Dzierzgoń Poland 53°58N 19°20E 184 E6
Dzierżoniów Poland 50°45N 16°39E 185 H3
Dzilam de Bravo Mexico 21°24N 88°53W 319 C7
Dzioua Algeria 33°14N 5°14E 261 B6
Dzisna Belarus 55°34N 28°12E 188 E5
Dzisna → Belarus 55°34N 28°12E 188 E5
Dziwnów Poland 54°2N 14°45E 184 D1
Dzūkija △ Lithuania 54°10N 24°30E 161 J21
Dzungarian Basin = Junggar Pendi China 44°30N 86°0E 217 D11
Dzungarian Gate Asia 45°10N 82°0E 217 C10
Dzur Mongolia 49°39N 95°46E 217 C13
Dzüünbayan Mongolia 44°29N 110°2E 226 B6
Dzüünharaa Mongolia 48°52N 106°28E 218 B10
Dzüünmod Mongolia 47°45N 106°58E 218 B10
Dzyarzhynsk Belarus 53°40N 27°1E 177 B14
Dzyatlava Belarus 53°28N 25°28E 177 B13

E

E.C. Manning △ Canada 49°5N 120°45W 296 D4
E.T. Joshua ✈ (SVD) St. Vincent 13°8N 61°13W 323 n
E.U.R. = Esposizione Universale di Roma Italy 41°49N 12°28E 136 C1
Eabamet L. Canada 51°30N 87°46W 298 B2
Eabametoong Canada 51°30N 88°0W 298 B2
Éadan Doire = Edenderry Ireland 53°21N 7°4W 166 C4
Eads U.S.A. 38°29N 102°47W 304 G12
Eagar U.S.A. 34°6N 109°17W 305 J9
Eagle Alaska, U.S.A. 64°47N 141°12W 303 D12
Eagle Colo., U.S.A. 39°39N 106°50W 304 G10
Eagle → Canada 53°36N 57°26W 299 B8
Eagle, Mt. U.S. Virgin Is. 17°46N 64°49W 321 b
Eagle Beach Aruba 12°32N 70°3W 322 f
Eagle Butte U.S.A. 45°0N 101°10W 308 C3
Eagle Cr. → U.S.A. 38°36N 85°4W 311 F11
Eagle Grove U.S.A. 42°40N 93°54W 310 B3
Eagle L. Ont., Canada 49°42N 93°13W 297 D10
Eagle L. Calif., U.S.A. 40°39N 120°45W 304 F3
Eagle L. Maine, U.S.A. 46°20N 69°22W 309 B19
Eagle Lake Ont., Canada 45°8N 78°29W 312 A6
Eagle Lake Maine, U.S.A. 47°3N 68°36W 309 B19
Eagle Lake Tex., U.S.A. 29°35N 96°20W 314 G6
Eagle Mountain U.S.A. 33°49N 115°27W 307 M11
Eagle Nest U.S.A. 36°33N 105°16W 305 H11
Eagle Pass U.S.A. 28°43N 100°30W 314 G4
Eagle Pk. U.S.A. 38°10N 119°25W 306 G7
Eagle Pt. Australia 16°11S 124°23E 278 C3
Eagle River Mich., U.S.A. 47°25N 88°18W 308 B9
Eagle River Wis., U.S.A. 45°55N 89°15W 308 C9
Eagle Rock U.S.A. 34°8N 118°12W 126 B3
Eaglehawk Australia 36°44S 144°15E 282 D6
Eagles Mere U.S.A. 41°25N 76°33W 313 E8
Eagleville U.S.A. 40°28N 93°59W 310 D3
Ealing □ U.K. 51°31N 0°20W 125 A2
Ear Falls Canada 50°38N 93°13W 297 C10
Earlimart U.S.A. 35°53N 119°16W 307 K7
Earl's Court London, U.K. 125 c1
Earlsfield U.K. 51°26N 0°10W 125 B2
Earlville Ill., U.S.A. 41°35N 88°55W 311 C8
Earlville N.Y., U.S.A. 42°44N 75°32W 313 D9
Earlwood Australia 33°55S 151°8E 139 B1
Early Branch U.S.A. 32°45N 80°55W 316 C9
Earn → U.K. 56°21N 3°18W 167 E5
Earn, L. U.K. 56°23N 4°13W 167 E4
Earnslaw, Mt. N.Z. 44°32S 168°27E 285 E3
Earth U.S.A. 34°14N 102°24W 314 D3
Eas Vanuatu 16°20S 168°15E 287 F6
Easley U.S.A. 34°50N 82°36W 315 D13
East Anglia U.K. 52°50N 1°0E 168 E9
East Angus Canada 45°30N 71°40W 299 C5
East Antarctica Antarctica 80°0S 90°0E 151 D7
East Arlington Mass., U.S.A. 42°24N 71°8W 116 A2
East Arlington Va., U.S.A. 38°51N 77°4W 143 B2
East Aurora U.S.A. 42°46N 78°37W 312 D6
East Ayrshire □ U.K. 55°26N 4°11W 167 F4
East Bedfont U.K. 51°26N 0°28W 125 B1
East Berbice-Corentyne □ Guyana 4°11N 58°11W 329 C6
East Beskids = Vychodné Beskydy Europe 49°20N 22°0E 181 B15
East Boston U.S.A. 42°22N 71°1W 116 A2
East Brady U.S.A. 40°59N 79°37W 312 F5
East Branch Clarion River L. U.S.A. 41°35N 78°35W 312 E6
East C. = Dezhneva, Mys Russia 66°5N 169°40W 215 C19
East C. N.Z. 37°42S 178°35E 284 D7
East C. Papua N. G. 10°13S 150°53E 286 F6
East Caroline Basin Pac. Oc. 4°0N 146°45E 288 G6
East Chicago U.S.A. 41°38N 87°27W 311 C9
East China Sea Asia 30°0N 126°0E 219 F14
East Coulee Canada 51°23N 112°27W 296 C6
East Dereham = Dereham U.K. 52°41N 0°57E 169 E8
East Don → Canada 43°48N 79°25W 141 A2
East Don Parkland Canada 43°47N 79°22W 141 A2
East Dublin U.S.A. 32°32N 82°52W 316 C7
East Dubuque U.S.A. 42°29N 90°39W 310 B6
East Dunbartonshire □ U.K. 55°57N 4°13W 167 F4
East Elmhurst U.S.A. 40°45N 73°52W 132 B2
East End Pt. Bahamas 25°3N 77°16W 153 b
East Falkland Falk. Is. 51°30S 58°30W 153 f
East Falls Church U.S.A. 38°53N 77°9W 143 B2
East Finchley U.K. 51°35N 0°10W 125 A2
East Flatbush U.S.A. 40°38N 73°56W 132 C2
East Fork White → U.S.A. 38°33N 87°14W 311 F9
East Grand Forks U.S.A. 47°56N 97°1W 308 B5
East Grand Rapids U.S.A. 42°58N 85°37W 311 B11
East Greenwich U.S.A. 41°40N 71°27W 313 E13
East Grinstead U.K. 51°7N 0°0 169 F8
East Ham U.K. 51°32N 0°3E 125 A4
East Hartford U.S.A. 41°46N 72°39W 313 E12
East Haydon Australia 18°0S 141°30E 280 B3
East Helena U.S.A. 46°35N 111°56W 304 C8
East Humber → Canada 43°47N 79°35W 141 A1
East Indies Asia 0°0 120°0E 210 J14
East Kavango □ Namibia 18°0S 20°15E 270 A3
East Kilbride U.K. 55°47N 4°11W 167 F4
East Lamma Channel Hong Kong, China 22°14N 114°9E 122 B2
East Lansing U.S.A. 42°44N 84°29W 311 B12

INDEX
Élancourt 367

East Las Vegas = Whitney U.S.A. 36°4N 115°5W 124 B2
East Lexington U.S.A. 42°25N 71°12W 116 A1
East Livermore = Livermore Falls U.S.A. 44°29N 70°11W 309 C18
East Liverpool U.S.A. 40°37N 80°35W 312 F4
East London S. Africa 33°0S 27°55E 271 D4
East Los Angeles U.S.A. 34°1N 118°10W 126 B3
East Lothian □ U.K. 55°58N 2°44W 167 F6
East Main = Eastmain Canada 52°10N 78°30W 298 B4
East Mariana Basin Pac. Oc. 12°0N 153°0E 288 F7
East Milwaukee = Shorewood U.S.A. 43°5N 87°53W 311 A9
East Molesey U.K. 51°24N 0°21W 125 B1
East Moline U.S.A. 41°32N 90°26W 310 C6
East Naples U.S.A. 26°8N 81°46W 317 J8
East New Britain □ Papua N. G. 6°30S 152°30E 286 D7
East New York U.S.A. 40°40N 73°53W 132 B2
East Northport U.S.A. 40°53N 73°19W 313 F11
East Orange U.S.A. 40°46N 74°12W 313 F10
East Pacific Rise Pac. Oc. 15°0S 110°0W 289 J17
East Pakistan = Bangladesh ■ Asia 24°0N 90°0E 241 D3
East Palatka U.S.A. 29°39N 81°36W 316 F8
East Palestine U.S.A. 40°50N 80°33W 312 F4
East Peoria U.S.A. 40°40N 89°34W 310 D7
East Pine Canada 55°48N 120°12W 296 B4
East Pines U.S.A. 38°57N 76°54W 143 B3
East Point U.S.A. 33°41N 84°25W 113 B2
East Potomac Park Washington, D.C., U.S.A. 143 c1
East Providence U.S.A. 41°49N 71°23W 313 E13
East Pt. Br. Virgin Is. 18°40N 64°18W 321 b
East Pt. N.S., Canada 46°27N 61°58W 299 C7
East Pt. U.S. Virgin Is. 17°45N 64°34W 321 b
East Renfrewshire □ U.K. 55°46N 4°21W 167 F4
East Retford = Retford U.K. 53°19N 0°56W 168 D7
East Riding of Yorkshire □ U.K. 53°55N 0°30W 168 D7
East River ➔ New York, U.S.A. 132 e3
East Rochester U.S.A. 43°7N 77°29W 312 C7
East Rutherford U.S.A. 40°50N 74°5W 132 A1
East St. Louis U.S.A. 38°37N 90°9W 310 F6
East Schelde = Oosterschelde ➔ Neths. 51°33N 4°0E 170 C4
East Sea = Japan, Sea of Asia 40°0N 135°0E 220 E7
East Sepik □ Papua N. G. 4°0S 143°45E 286 C2
East Sheen U.K. 51°27N 0°16W 125 B2
East Siberian Sea Russia 73°0N 160°0E 215 B17
East Stroudsburg U.S.A. 41°1N 75°11W 313 E9
East Sussex □ U.K. 50°56N 0°19E 169 G8
East Talpiyot West Bank 31°45N 35°13E 123 B2
East Tasman Plateau Pac. Oc. 43°30S 152°0E 288 M7
East Tawas U.S.A. 44°17N 83°29W 309 C12
East Timor ■ Asia 8°50S 126°0E 231 F7
East Toorale Australia 30°27S 145°28E 281 E4
East Troy U.S.A. 42°47N 88°24W 311 B8
East Village New York, U.S.A. 132 e2
East Walker ➔ U.S.A. 38°52N 119°10W 306 G7
East Wickham U.K. 51°28N 0°5E 125 B4
East Windsor U.S.A. 40°17N 74°34W 313 F10
East York Canada 43°40N 79°22W 141 A2
East Youngstown = Campbell U.S.A. 41°5N 80°37W 312 E4
Eastbourne N.Z. 41°19S 174°55E 284 H3
Eastbourne E. Sussex, U.K. 50°46N 0°18E 169 G8
Eastcote U.K. 51°34N 0°23W 125 A1
Eastend Canada 49°32N 108°50W 297 D7
Easter Fracture Zone Pac. Oc. 25°0S 115°0W 289 K16
Easter Howgate U.K. 55°52N 3°12W 121 B2
Easter I. = Pascua, I. de Chile 27°7S 109°23W 330 b
Eastern □ Ghana 6°30N 0°30W 263 D4
Eastern □ S. Leone 8°15N 11°0W 262 D2
Eastern Cape □ S. Africa 32°0S 26°0E 270 D4
Eastern Cr. ➔ Australia 20°40S 141°35E 280 C3
Eastern Desert = Sharqîya, Es Sahrâ esh Egypt 27°30N 32°30E 256 B3
Eastern Equatoria □ South Sudan 5°0N 33°0E 257 G3
Eastern Ghats India 14°0N 78°50E 245 H4
Eastern Group = Lau Group Fiji 17°0S 178°30W 287 A3
Eastern Group Australia 33°30S 124°30E 279 F3
Eastern Guruma ◎ Australia 22°0S 117°30E 278 D2
Eastern Highlands □ Papua N. G. 6°30S 145°35E 286 D3
Eastern I. Midway Is. 28°12N 177°19W 302 c
Eastern Samar □ Phil. 11°40N 125°40E 233 F5
Eastern Transvaal = Mpumalanga □ S. Africa 26°0S 30°0E 271 C5
Easterville Canada 53°8N 99°49W 297 C9
Easthampton U.S.A. 42°16N 72°40W 313 D12
Eastlake U.S.A. 41°40N 81°26W 312 E3
Eastland U.S.A. 32°24N 98°49W 314 E5
Eastleigh U.K. 50°58N 1°21W 169 G6
Eastmain Canada 52°10N 78°30W 298 B4
Eastmain ➔ Canada 52°27N 78°26W 298 B4
Eastman Qué., Canada 45°18N 72°19W 313 A12
Eastman Ga., U.S.A. 32°12N 83°11W 316 C6
Eastman Wis., U.S.A. 43°10N 91°1W 310 A5
Easton Md., U.S.A. 38°47N 76°5W 309 F15
Easton Pa., U.S.A. 40°41N 75°13W 313 F9
Easton Wash., U.S.A. 47°14N 121°11W 306 C5
Eastover U.S.A. 33°52N 80°41W 316 B9
Eastpoint U.S.A. 29°44N 84°53W 316 F5
Eastpoint Park Canada 43°46N 79°10W 141 A4
Eastport U.S.A. 44°56N 67°0W 309 C20
Eastsound U.S.A. 48°42N 122°55W 306 B4
Eastwood Australia 33°47S 151°4E 139 A1
Eaton Colo., U.S.A. 40°32N 104°42W 304 F11
Eaton Ohio, U.S.A. 39°45N 84°38W 311 E12
Eaton Canyon Park U.S.A. 34°10N 118°7W 126 A4
Eaton Centre Toronto, Canada 141 a2
Eaton Rapids U.S.A. 42°31N 84°39W 311 B12
Eatonia Canada 51°13N 109°25W 297 C7
Eatonton U.S.A. 33°20N 83°23W 316 B6
Eatontown U.S.A. 40°19N 74°4W 313 F10
Eatonville U.S.A. 46°52N 122°16W 306 D4
Eau Claire U.S.A. 44°49N 91°30W 308 C8
Eau Claire, L. à l' Canada 56°10N 74°25W 298 A5
Eauripik Rise Pac. Oc. 2°0N 142°0E 288 G6
Eauze France 43°53N 0°7E 174 E4
Eban Nigeria 9°40N 4°50E 263 D5
Ebanga Angola 12°45S 14°45E 265 E2
Ebangalakata Dem. Rep. of the Congo 0°29S 21°29E 264 C4
Ebano Mexico 22°13N 98°24W 319 C5
Ebara Japan 35°35N 139°42E 140 B3
Ebbegebirge ⌂ Germany 51°10N 7°55E 178 D3
Ebbw Vale U.K. 51°46N 3°12W 169 F4
Ebebiyín Eq. Guin. 2°9N 11°20E 264 B2
Ebel Gabon 0°7N 11°5E 264 B2
Ebeltoft Denmark 56°12N 10°41E 163 H4
Ebeltoft Vig Denmark 56°10N 10°35E 163 H4
Ebensburg U.S.A. 40°29N 78°44W 312 F6
Ebensee Austria 47°48N 13°46E 180 D6
Eber Gölü Turkey 38°38N 31°11E 212 C4
Eberbach Germany 49°28N 8°59E 179 F4
Eberswalde-Finow Germany 52°50N 13°49E 178 C9
Ebetsu Japan 43°7N 141°34E 220 C10
Ebey's Landing ⌂ U.S.A. 48°12N 122°41W 306 B4
Ebian China 29°11N 103°13E 228 C4
Ebingen = Albstadt Germany 48°13N 9°1E 179 G5
Ebino Japan 32°2N 130°48E 222 E2
Ebinur Hu China 44°55N 82°55E 217 D10
Ebisu Japan 35°38N 139°42E 140 B3
Ebla Syria 35°50N 36°48E 250 C7
Ebo Angola 11°40S 14°40E 265 E2
Ebola ➔ Dem. Rep. of the Congo 3°20N 20°57E 264 B4
Éboli Italy 40°39N 15°2E 201 B8
Ebolowa Cameroon 2°55N 11°10E 263 E7
Ebonda Dem. Rep. of the Congo 2°12N 22°21E 264 B4
Ebonyi □ Nigeria 6°20N 8°0E 263 D6
Eboy Dem. Rep. of the Congo 2°50N 23°11E 264 B4
Ebrach Germany 49°51N 10°29E 179 F6
Ebre = Ebro ➔ Spain 40°43N 0°54E 196 E5
Ébrié, Lagune Ivory C. 5°12N 4°26W 262 D4
Ebro ➔ Spain 40°43N 0°54E 196 E5
Ebro, Embalse del Spain 43°0N 3°58W 194 C7
Ebstorf Germany 53°2N 10°24E 178 B6
Ebute-Metta Nigeria 6°28N 3°23E 124 B2
Ecatepec de Morelos Mexico 19°36N 99°3W 319 D5
Ecbatana = Hamadān Iran 34°52N 48°32E 213 E13
Ecclesville Trin. & Tob. 10°19N 61°8W 323 t
Eceabat Turkey 40°11N 26°21E 203 F10
Ech Chéliff Algeria 36°10N 1°20E 261 A5
Ech Chéliff □ Algeria 36°15N 1°30E 261 A5
Echague Phil. 16°42N 121°38E 232 C3
Echechonnee ➔ U.S.A. 32°39N 83°36W 316 C6
Echigo-Sammyaku Japan 36°50N 139°50E 221 F9
Echinades Greece 38°25N 21°2E 207 C3
Echinos Greece 41°16N 25°1E 203 E9
Échirolles France 45°8N 5°44E 175 C9
Echizen Japan 35°50N 136°10E 223 B8
Echizen-Misaki Japan 35°59N 135°57E 223 B7
Echmiadzin = Ejmiatsin Armenia 40°12N 44°19E 191 K7
Echo U.S.A. 31°29N 85°28W 316 D4
Echo Bay N.W.T., Canada 66°5N 117°55W 294 D8
Echo Bay Ont., Canada 46°29N 84°4W 298 C3
Echo Park Los Angeles, U.S.A. 127 a1
Echoing ➔ Canada 55°51N 92°5W 298 B1
Echterdingen, Stuttgart ✕ (STR) Germany 48°42N 9°11E 179 G5
Echternach Lux. 49°49N 6°25E 170 E6
Echuca Australia 36°10S 144°45E 283 D6
Écija Spain 37°30N 5°10W 195 H5
Eckental Germany 49°35N 11°12E 179 F7
Eckernförde Germany 54°28N 9°50E 178 A5
Eclectic U.S.A. 32°38N 86°2W 316 C3
Eclipse I. Australia 35°5S 117°58E 279 G2
Eclipse Is. Australia 13°54S 126°19E 278 B4
Eclipse Sd. Canada 72°38N 79°0W 295 C16
Écommoy France 47°50N 0°17E 172 E7
Economy = Ambridge U.S.A. 40°36N 80°14W 312 F4
Ecoporanga Brazil 18°23S 40°50W 333 E3
Écouché France 48°42N 0°10W 172 D6
Ecrins △ France 44°54N 6°18E 175 D10
Ecuador ■ S. Amer. 2°0S 78°0W 328 D2
Ecuador, Volcán Ecuador 1°1S 91°32W 330 a
Écueillé France 47°5N 1°21E 172 E8
Ed Sweden 58°55N 11°55E 163 F5
Ed Dabbura Sudan 17°40N 34°15E 256 D3
Ed Da'ein Sudan 11°26N 26°9E 257 E2
Ed Damazin Sudan 11°46N 34°21E 266 B3
Ed Dâmer Sudan 17°27N 34°0E 256 D3
Ed Dar el Beida = Casablanca Morocco 33°36N 7°36W 260 B3
Ed Debba Sudan 18°0N 30°51E 256 D3
Ed Déffa Egypt 30°40N 26°30E 256 A2
Ed Deim Sudan 10°10N 28°20E 257 E2
Ed Dibeikir Sudan 10°23N 29°9E 266 B2
Ed Dueim Sudan 14°0N 32°10E 257 E3
Eda Japan 35°33N 139°33E 140 B2
Edam Sask., Canada 53°11N 108°46W 297 C7
Edam Neths. 52°31N 5°3E 170 B5
Edane Sweden 59°38N 12°49E 162 E6
Edapally India 11°19N 78°3E 245 J4
Eday U.K. 59°11N 2°47W 167 B6
Edchera W. Sahara 27°2N 13°4W 260 C2
Edd Eritrea 14°0N 41°38E 257 E5
Eddrachillis B. U.K. 58°17N 5°14W 167 C3
Eddystone U.K. 50°11N 4°16W 169 G3
Eddystone Pt. Australia 40°59S 148°20E 281 G4
Eddyville U.S.A. 41°9N 92°38W 310 C4
Ede Neths. 52°4N 5°40E 170 B5
Ede Nigeria 7°45N 4°29E 263 D5
Edéa Cameroon 3°51N 10°9E 263 E7
Edebäck Sweden 60°4N 13°32E 162 D7
Edehon L. Canada 60°25N 97°15W 297 A9
Edelény Hungary 48°18N 20°44E 182 B5
Eden = Bar Harbor U.S.A. 44°23N 68°13W 309 C19
Eden N.S.W., Australia 37°3S 149°55E 283 D8
Eden N.C., U.S.A. 36°29N 79°53W 315 C15
Eden N.Y., U.S.A. 42°39N 78°55W 312 D6
Eden Tex., U.S.A. 31°13N 99°51W 314 F5
Eden ➔ U.K. 54°57N 3°1W 168 C4
Eden Gardens Kolkata, India 22°34N 88°20E 124 B2
Edenburg S. Africa 29°43S 25°58E 270 C4
Edendale N.Z. 46°19S 168°48E 285 G3
Edendale Gauteng, S. Africa 26°8S 28°9E 123 A2
Edendale KwaZulu Natal, S. Africa 29°39S 30°18E 271 C5
Edenderry Ireland 53°21N 7°4W 166 C4
Edenhope Australia 37°4S 141°19E 282 D4
Edenton U.S.A. 36°4N 76°39W 315 C16
Edenville S. Africa 27°37S 27°34E 271 C4
Eder ➔ Germany 51°12N 9°28E 178 D5
Eder-Stausee Germany 51°10N 8°57E 178 D4
Edessa Greece 40°48N 22°5E 202 F6
Edewecht Germany 53°8N 7°58E 178 B3
Edfu = Idfû Egypt 24°55N 32°49E 256 C3
Edgar U.S.A. 40°22N 97°58W 308 E5
Edgars Cr. ➔ Australia 37°43S 144°58E 128 A1
Edgartown U.S.A. 41°23N 70°31W 313 E14
Edge Hill U.K. 52°8N 1°26W 169 E6
Edgecliff U.S.A. 32°39N 97°20W 120 C1
Edgecumbe N.Z. 37°59S 176°47E 284 D5
Edgefield U.S.A. 33°47N 81°56W 316 B8
Edgeley Ont., Canada 43°47N 79°31W 141 A1
Edgeley N. Dak., U.S.A. 46°22N 98°43W 308 B4
Edgemar U.S.A. 37°39N 122°29W 136 C2
Edgemont U.S.A. 43°18N 103°50W 308 D2
Edgeøya Svalbard 77°45N 22°30E 150 B9
Edgerton Ohio, U.S.A. 41°27N 84°45W 311 C12
Edgerton Wis., U.S.A. 42°50N 89°4W 310 B7
Edgewater Fla., U.S.A. 28°59N 80°54W 317 G9
Edgewater N.J., U.S.A. 40°49N 73°58W 132 B2
Edgewood Fla., U.S.A. 28°29N 81°22W 133 B2
Edgewood Ill., U.S.A. 38°55N 88°40W 311 F8
Édhessa = Edessa Greece 40°48N 22°5E 202 F6
Edievale N.Z. 45°49S 169°22E 285 F4
Edina Liberia 6°0N 10°10W 262 D2
Edina Mo., U.S.A. 40°10N 92°11W 310 D4
Edinboro U.S.A. 41°52N 80°8W 312 E4
Edinburg Ill., U.S.A. 39°39N 89°23W 310 E7
Edinburg Tex., U.S.A. 26°18N 98°10W 314 H5
Edinburgh U.K. 55°57N 3°13W 121 B2
Edinburgh Ind., U.S.A. 39°21N 85°58W 311 E11
Edinburgh ✕ (EDI) U.K. 55°54N 3°22W 121 B1
Edinburgh, City of □ U.K. 55°57N 3°17W 167 F5
Edinburgh Castle Edinburgh, U.K. 121 b2
Edineţ Moldova 48°9N 27°18E 183 B12
Edirne Turkey 41°40N 26°34E 203 E10
Edirne □ Turkey 41°12N 26°30E 203 E10
Edison Ga., U.S.A. 31°34N 84°44W 316 D5
Edison Wash., U.S.A. 48°33N 122°27W 306 B4
Edison Park U.S.A. 42°1N 87°48W 119 A2
Edisto ➔ U.S.A. 32°29N 80°21W 316 C9
Edisto Beach U.S.A. 32°29N 80°20W 316 C9
Edisto I. U.S.A. 32°35N 80°20W 316 C9
Edithburgh Australia 35°5S 137°43E 282 C2
Edjeleh Algeria 28°38N 9°50E 261 C6
Edmeston U.S.A. 42°42N 75°15W 313 D9
Edmond U.S.A. 35°39N 97°29W 314 D6
Edmonds U.S.A. 47°48N 122°22W 306 C4
Edmondston U.S.A. 38°56N 76°54W 143 B3
Edmonton Queens., Australia 17°2S 145°46E 280 B4
Edmonton Alta., Canada 53°30N 113°30W 296 C6
Edmund L. Canada 54°45N 93°17W 298 B1
Edmundston Canada 47°23N 68°20W 299 C6
Edna U.S.A. 28°59N 96°39W 314 G6
Edo □ Nigeria 6°30N 6°0E 263 D6
Edo ➔ Japan 35°38N 139°52E 140 B4
Edogawa Japan 35°43N 139°52E 140 A4
Edolo Italy 46°10N 10°21E 198 B7
Edøya Norway 63°18N 8°10E 164 A5
Edremit Turkey 39°34N 27°0E 205 B9
Edremit Körfezi Turkey 39°30N 26°45E 205 B8
Edsberg Sweden 59°26N 17°57E 139 A1
Edsbro Sweden 59°54N 18°29E 162 E12
Edsbruk Sweden 58°1N 16°29E 163 F10
Edsbyn Sweden 61°23N 15°49E 162 C9
Edson Canada 53°35N 116°28W 296 C5
Eduardo Castex Argentina 35°50S 64°18W 334 D3
Eduardo Frei Montalva = Frei Antarctica 62°30S 58°0W 151 C18
Edward ➔ Australia 35°5S 143°30E 282 C5
Edward, L. Africa 0°25S 29°40E 268 C2
Edward VII Land Antarctica 80°0S 150°0W 151 E13
Edwardesabad = Bannu Pakistan 33°0N 70°18E 240 B3
Edwards Calif., U.S.A. 34°50N 117°40W 307 L9
Edwards N.Y., U.S.A. 44°20N 75°15W 313 B9
Edwards ➔ U.S.A. 41°9N 90°59W 310 C6
Edwards L. Australia 37°42S 144°59E 128 A1
Edwards Plateau U.S.A. 30°45N 101°20W 314 F4
Edwardsburg U.S.A. 41°48N 86°6W 311 C10
Edwardsville Ill., U.S.A. 38°49N 89°58W 310 F7
Edwardsville Pa., U.S.A. 41°15N 75°56W 313 E9
Edzná Mexico 19°39N 90°19W 319 D6
Edzo = Behchoko Canada 62°50N 116°3W 296 A5
Eek U.S.A. 60°14N 162°2W 303 F7
Eeklo Belgium 51°11N 3°33E 170 C3
Eel ➔ Ind., U.S.A. 39°7N 86°57W 311 E10
Eel ➔ Ind., U.S.A. 40°45N 86°22W 311 D10
Eenhana Namibia 17°30S 16°23E 270 A2
Eesti = Estonia ■ Europe 58°30N 25°30E 188 C3
Efate, I. Vanuatu 17°40S 168°25E 287 G6
Eferding Austria 48°18N 14°1E 180 C7
Effigy Mounds ⌂ U.S.A. 43°5N 91°11W 310 A5
Effingham U.S.A. 39°7N 88°33W 311 E8
Eforie Romania 44°1N 28°37E 183 F13
Efoulen Cameroon 2°46N 10°43E 264 B2
Efteløt Norway 59°33N 9°49E 164 E6
Efxinoupoli Greece 39°12N 22°42E 204 B4
Efzonos Greece 37°55N 23°49E 112 B2
Ega ➔ Spain 42°19N 1°55W 196 C3
Égadi, Ísole Italy 37°55N 12°16E 200 E5
Egaleo Greece 37°59N 23°40E 112 B2
Egaleo, Oros Greece 38°0N 23°36E 112 B1
Egan Range U.S.A. 39°35N 114°55W 304 G6
Eganville Canada 45°32N 77°5W 312 A7
Egedesminde = Aasiaat Greenland 68°43N 52°56W 154 D5
Egegik U.S.A. 58°13N 157°22W 303 G8
Eger = Cheb Czechia 50°9N 12°28E 180 A5
Eger Hungary 47°53N 20°27E 182 C5
Eger ➔ Hungary 47°38N 20°50E 182 C5
Egersund Norway 58°26N 6°1E 164 F3
Egg I. St. Helena 15°58S 5°47W 153 h
Egg L. Canada 55°5N 105°30W 297 B7
Eggedal Norway 60°14N 9°22E 164 D6
Eggegebirge Südlicher Teutoburger Wald ⌂ Germany 51°40N 8°59E 178 D4
Eggenburg Austria 48°38N 15°50E 180 C8
Eggenfelden Germany 48°23N 12°46E 179 G8
Egherta Somalia 2°4N 43°11E 267 D5
Éghezée Belgium 50°35N 4°55E 170 D4
Egholo Solomon Is. 8°25S 157°25E 287 M9
Egilsstaðir Iceland 65°16N 14°25W 155 B12
Egina Greece 37°45N 23°26E 204 D5
Eginio Greece 40°28N 22°28E 202 F6
Egio Greece 38°15N 22°5E 204 C4
Egito Angola 12°4S 13°58E 265 E2
Égletons France 45°24N 2°3E 174 C6
Eglinton I. Canada 75°48N 118°30W 295 B8
Egmont Canada 49°45N 123°56W 296 D4
Egmont, C. N.Z. 39°16S 173°45E 284 F2
Egmont, Mt. = Taranaki, Mt. N.Z. 39°17S 174°5E 284 F3
Egmont △ N.Z. 39°17S 174°4E 284 F3
Egra India 21°54N 87°32E 243 J12
Eğridir Turkey 37°52N 30°51E 212 D4
Eğridir Gölü Turkey 37°53N 30°50E 212 D4
Egtved Denmark 55°38N 9°18E 163 J3
Éguas ➔ Brazil 13°26S 44°14W 333 D3
Egum Atoll Papua N. G. 9°25S 152°0E 286 E7
Éguzon-Chantôme France 46°27N 1°33E 173 F8
Egvekinot Russia 66°19N 179°50W 215 C19
Egyek Hungary 47°39N 20°52E 182 C5
Egypt ■ Africa 28°0N 31°0E 256 B3
Eha Amufu Nigeria 6°30N 7°46E 263 D6
Eheli Algeria 22°26N 4°40E 261 D5
Ehime □ Japan 33°30N 132°40E 222 D4
Ehingen Germany 48°16N 9°43E 179 G5
Ehrenberg U.S.A. 33°36N 114°31W 307 M12
Ehrhardt U.S.A. 33°6N 81°1W 316 B8
Ehrwald Austria 47°24N 10°56E 180 D3
Eiao French Polynesia 8°0S 140°40W 289 f
Eibar Spain 43°11N 2°28W 196 B2
Eibenschitz = Ivančice Czechia 49°6N 16°23E 181 B9
Eiche Germany 52°33N 13°35E 115 A4
Eiche Süd Germany 52°33N 13°35E 115 A4
Eichstätt Germany 48°54N 11°11E 179 G7
Eide Hordaland, Norway 60°31N 6°44E 164 D3
Eide Møre og Romsdal, Norway 62°55N 7°27E 164 B4
Eider ➔ Germany 54°19N 8°57E 178 A4
Eidsbugarden Norway 61°23N 8°16E 164 C5
Eidsbygda Norway 62°36N 7°30E 164 B4
Eidsdalen Norway 62°16N 7°10E 164 B4
Eidsvåg Norway 62°46N 8°2E 164 B5
Eidsvold Australia 25°25S 151°12E 281 D5
Eidsvoll Norway 60°19N 11°14E 164 D8
Eielson U.S.A. 64°40N 147°4W 303 D11
Eifel Germany 50°15N 6°50E 179 E2
Eiffel, Tour Paris, France 134 c2
Eiffel Flats Zimbabwe 18°20S 30°0E 269 F3
Eiger Switz. 46°34N 8°1E 198 B5
Eigg U.K. 56°54N 6°10W 167 E2
Eighty Mile Beach Australia 19°30S 120°40E 278 C3
Eikefjord Norway 61°35N 5°27E 164 C2
Eikelandsosen Norway 60°15N 5°43E 164 D2
Eiken Norway 58°29N 7°14E 164 F4
Eikeren Norway 59°38N 9°58E 164 E6
Eikesdalen Norway 62°28N 8°12E 164 B5
Eil, L. U.K. 56°51N 5°16W 167 E3
Eil Malk Palau 7°10N 134°23E 288 c
Eilat = Elat Israel 29°30N 34°56E 251 J5
Eildon Australia 37°14S 145°55E 283 D6
Eildon, L. Australia 37°10S 146°0E 283 D7
Eilean Siar □ U.K. 57°30N 7°10W 167 D1
Eilenburg Germany 51°27N 12°36E 178 D8
Ein Arik West Bank 31°54N 35°8E 123 A1
Ein el Luweiqa Sudan 14°5N 33°50E 257 E3
Ein Naquba Israel 31°47N 35°7E 123 B1
Ein Rafa Israel 31°47N 35°7E 123 B1
Eina Norway 60°38N 10°35E 164 D7
Einarsstaðir Iceland 65°44N 17°24W 155 B9
Einasleigh Australia 18°32S 144°5E 280 B3
Einasleigh ➔ Australia 17°30S 142°17E 280 B3
Einbeck Germany 51°49N 9°53E 178 D5
Eindhoven Neths. 51°26N 5°28E 170 C5
Einsiedeln Switz. 47°7N 8°46E 179 H4
Eire = Ireland ■ Europe 53°50N 7°52W 166 C4
Eiríksjökull Iceland 64°46N 20°24W 155 C6
Eiríksstaðir Iceland 65°7N 15°25W 155 B11
Eiriosgaigh = Eriskay U.K. 57°4N 7°18W 167 D1
Eirunepé Brazil 6°35S 69°53W 330 B4
Eiseb ➔ Namibia 20°33S 20°59E 270 B2
Eisenach Germany 50°58N 10°19E 178 E6
Eisenberg Germany 50°58N 11°54E 178 E7
Eisenerz Austria 47°32N 14°54E 180 D7
Eisenhüttenstadt Germany 52°9N 14°38E 178 C10
Eisenkappel Austria 46°29N 14°36E 180 E7
Eisenstadt Austria 47°51N 16°31E 181 D9
Eisenstein = Železná Ruda Czechia 49°8N 13°15E 180 B6
Eisleben Germany 51°32N 11°32E 178 D7
Eislingen Germany 48°41N 9°42E 179 G5
Eivindvik Norway 60°59N 5°5E 164 D2
Eivissa Spain 38°54N 1°26E 206 D1
Eixe, Serra do Spain 42°24N 6°54W 194 C4
Eizariya West Bank 31°46N 35°16E 123 B2
Ejby Denmark 55°41N 12°24E 118 A2
Ejea de los Caballeros Spain 42°7N 1°9W 196 C3
Ejeda Madag. 24°20S 44°31E 272 C1
Ejigbo Nigeria 6°33N 3°18E 124 A1
Ejmiatsin Armenia 40°12N 44°19E 191 K7
Ejura Ghana 7°23N 1°15W 263 D4
Ejutla Mexico 16°34N 96°44W 319 D5
Ekalaka U.S.A. 45°53N 104°33W 304 D11
Ekalla Gabon 1°27S 14°0E 264 C2
Ekanga Dem. Rep. of the Congo 2°23S 23°14E 264 C4
Ekaterinburg = Yekaterinburg Russia 56°50N 60°30E 214 D7
Ekeberg Norway 59°53N 10°46E 133 A3
Ekenäs = Raasepori Finland 60°0N 23°26E 188 B2
Ekenässjön Sweden 57°28N 15°1E 163 G9
Ekerö Sweden 59°16N 17°45E 162 E11
Eket Nigeria 4°38N 7°56E 263 E6
Eketahuna N.Z. 40°38S 175°43E 284 G4
Ekibastuz Kazakhstan 51°50N 75°10E 217 B9
Ekiti □ Nigeria 7°25N 5°20E 263 D6
Eklutna U.S.A. 61°27N 149°22W 303 F10
Eknäs Sweden 59°18N 18°13E 139 B3
Ekoli Dem. Rep. of the Congo 0°23S 24°13E 264 C4
Ekoln Sweden 59°45N 17°37E 162 E11
Ekouamou Congo 0°8N 16°31E 264 B3
Ekoungounou Congo 1°10S 15°52E 264 C3
Ekshärad Sweden 60°10N 13°30E 162 D7
Eksjö Sweden 57°40N 14°58E 163 G8
Ekukola Dem. Rep. of the Congo 0°31S 18°56E 264 C3
Ekuku Dem. Rep. of the Congo 0°41S 21°42E 264 C4
Ekukula Dem. Rep. of the Congo 0°15N 21°30E 264 B4
Ekuma ➔ Namibia 18°40S 16°2E 270 A2
Ekuta Dem. Rep. of the Congo 3°0N 18°50E 264 B3
Ekwan ➔ Canada 53°12N 82°15W 298 B3
Ekwan Pt. Canada 53°16N 82°7W 298 B3
Ekwok U.S.A. 59°22N 157°30W 303 G8
El Aaiún W. Sahara 27°9N 13°12W 260 C2
El Aargub Mauritania 23°37N 15°52W 260 D1
El Abanico Chile 37°20S 71°31W 334 D1
El 'Abbasiya El Qâhira, Egypt 30°3N 31°16E 117 A2
El Abbasiya Sudan 12°10N 31°18E 257 E3
El Abiodh-Sidi-Cheikh Algeria 32°53N 0°31E 261 B5
El Adde Somalia 2°35N 46°9E 267 D6
El Adeb Larache Algeria 27°22N 8°52E 261 C6
El 'Agrûd Egypt 30°14N 34°24E 251 H5
El Agua Venezuela 11°8N 63°52W 329 a
El Agustino Peru 12°2S 77°0W 124 B2
El Agustino, Cerro Peru 12°3S 76°59W 124 B3
El Aïoun Morocco 34°33N 2°30W 261 B4
El Ait Sudan 12°22N 27°27E 257 E2
El 'Aiyat Egypt 29°36N 31°15E 256 J7
El Alamein Egypt 30°48N 28°58E 256 A2
El Alto La Paz, Bolivia 16°30S 68°10W 330 D4
El Alto Peru 4°15S 81°14W 330 A1
El Aouj Mauritania 22°53N 12°49W 260 D2
El 'Aqaba, W. ➔ Egypt 30°7N 33°54E 251 H4
El 'Arag Egypt 28°40N 26°20E 256 B2
El Aricha Algeria 34°13N 1°10W 261 B4
El Arīḥā West Bank 31°52N 35°27E 251 G6
El 'Arîsh Egypt 31°8N 33°50E 251 G4
El 'Arîsh, W. ➔ Egypt 31°8N 33°47E 251 G4
El Arrouch Algeria 36°37N 6°53E 261 A6
El Asnam = Ech Chéliff Algeria 36°10N 1°20E 261 A5
El Astillero Spain 43°24N 3°49W 194 B7
El Avagi Somalia 3°36N 46°57E 267 D6
El Badâri Egypt 27°4N 31°25E 256 B3
El Badrshein Egypt 29°51N 31°16E 251 J2
El Bagur Egypt 30°25N 31°2E 251 H2
El Bahr el Ahmar □ Egypt 28°15N 32°50E 251 K3
El Bahrein Egypt 28°30N 26°25E 256 B2
El Ballâs Egypt 26°2N 32°43E 256 B3
El Balyana Egypt 26°10N 32°3E 256 B3
El Banco Colombia 9°0N 73°58W 328 B3
El Baqeir Sudan 18°40N 33°40E 256 D3
El Baragil Egypt 30°4N 31°9E 117 A1
El Barco de Ávila Spain 40°21N 5°31W 194 E5
El Barco de Valdeorras = O Barco Spain 42°23N 6°58W 194 C4
El Basâlîn Egypt 29°58N 31°16E 117 B2
El Bauga Sudan 18°18N 33°52E 256 D3
El Baúl Venezuela 8°57N 68°17W 328 B4
El Bawiti Egypt 28°25N 28°45E 256 B2
El Bayadh Algeria 33°40N 1°1E 261 B5
El Bayadh □ Algeria 32°30N 1°10E 261 B5
El Bichar Venezuela 10°46N 63°58W 329 a
El Bierzo Spain 42°45N 6°30W 194 C4
El Bira West Bank 31°54N 35°13E 123 A2
El Bluff Nic. 11°59N 83°40W 320 D3
El Bolsón Argentina 41°55S 71°30W 336 B2
El Bonillo Spain 38°57N 2°35W 197 G2
El Bosque Chile 33°32S 70°40W 137 C2
El Buheirat = Lakes □ South Sudan 7°0N 30°0E 257 F3
El Bur Somalia 4°40N 46°37E 267 D6
El Burgo de Osma Spain 41°35N 3°4W 196 D1
El Caín Argentina 41°38S 68°19W 336 B3
El Cajon U.S.A. 32°48N 116°58W 307 N10
El Calafate Argentina 50°19S 72°15W 336 D2
El Callao Venezuela 7°18N 61°50W 329 B5
El Campello Spain 38°26N 0°24W 197 G4
El Campo U.S.A. 29°12N 96°16W 314 G6
El Capitan U.S.A. 37°44N 119°38W 306 H7
El Carbón Honduras 15°25N 85°32W 320 C2
El Cardón Venezuela 11°6N 63°51W 329 a
El Carmen Bolivia 13°40S 63°55W 331 C5
El Carmen Santiago, Chile 33°22S 70°43W 137 B1
El Carmen Colombia 9°43N 75°8W 328 B2
El Centro U.S.A. 32°48N 115°34W 307 N11
El Cerro Bolivia 17°30S 61°40W 331 D5
El Cerro de Andévalo Spain 37°45N 6°57W 195 H4
El Chaltén Argentina 49°19S 72°56W 336 C2
El Cocuy Colombia 6°25N 72°27W 328 B3
El Cocuy △ Colombia 6°33N 72°5W 328 B3
El Compadre Mexico 32°20N 116°14W 307 N10
El Copey, Cerro Venezuela 11°11N 63°55W 329 a
El Corcovado Argentina 43°25S 71°35W 336 B2
El Coronil Spain 37°5N 5°38W 195 H5
El Cortijo Chile 33°22S 70°42W 137 B1
El Cotillo Canary Is. 28°41N 14°1W 153 e2
El Cristo, Vaso Regulador Mexico 19°30N 99°5W 128 B1
El Cuy Argentina 39°55S 68°25W 336 A3
El Cuyo Mexico 21°31N 87°41W 319 C7
El Dab'a Egypt 31°0N 28°27E 256 H6
El Daheir Egypt 31°13N 34°10E 251 G5
El Dambahaddo Somalia 3°17N 46°40E 267 D6
El Deir Egypt 25°25N 32°20E 256 B3
El Dere = Ceeldheere Somalia 5°22N 46°11E 267 C6
El Dere Ethiopia 5°6N 43°5E 267 C5
El Descanso Mexico 32°12N 116°58W 307 N10
El Desemboque Mexico 30°33N 113°1W 318 A2
El Dilingat Egypt 30°50N 30°31E 256 H7
El Diviso Colombia 1°22N 78°14W 328 C2
El Djouf Mauritania 21°25N 6°40W 260 D3
El Dorado Sinaloa, Mexico 24°17N 107°21W 318 C3
El Dorado Ark., U.S.A. 33°12N 92°40W 314 E8
El Dorado Kans., U.S.A. 37°49N 96°52W 308 G5
El Dorado Venezuela 6°55N 61°37W 329 B5
El Dorado Int. ✕ (BOG) Colombia 4°42N 74°9W 328 C3
El Dorado Springs U.S.A. 37°52N 94°1W 310 G2
El Duqqi Egypt 30°1N 31°12E 117 A2
El Eglab Algeria 26°20N 4°30W 260 C4
El 'Ein Sudan 16°35N 29°22E 257 D2
El Ejido Spain 36°47N 2°49W 195 J8
El Encinar de los Reyes Spain 40°30N 3°39W 127 A2
El Escorial Spain 40°35N 4°7W 194 E6
El Espinal Venezuela 10°58N 63°59W 329 a
El Espinar Spain 41°43N 4°15W 194 D6
El Eulma Algeria 36°9N 5°42E 261 A6
El Faiyûm Egypt 29°19N 30°50E 256 J7
El Faourar Tunisia 33°22N 8°45E 258 B1
El Fâsher Sudan 13°33N 25°26E 257 E2
El Fashn Egypt 28°50N 30°54E 256 J7
El Ferrol = Ferrol Spain 43°29N 8°15W 194 B2
El Fifi Sudan 10°4N 25°0E 257 E2
El Fud Ethiopia 7°15N 42°52E 267 C5
El Fuerte Mexico 26°25N 108°39W 318 B3
El Ga'a Sudan 14°16N 29°59E 257 E2
El Gamâlîya Egypt 31°10N 31°52E 251 G2
El Garef Sudan 12°3N 34°19E 257 E3
El Gebir Sudan 13°40N 29°40E 257 E2
El Gedida Egypt 25°40N 28°30E 256 B2
El Geneina = Al Junaynah Sudan 13°27N 22°45E 259 F4
El Geteina Sudan 14°50N 32°27E 257 E3
El Gezira Egypt 30°2N 31°13E 117 A2
El Gezira □ Sudan 15°0N 33°0E 257 E3
El Gharbîya □ Egypt 30°50N 31°0E 251 H2
El Ghurîya Egypt 30°2N 31°15E 117 A2
El Gir Sudan 19°50N 28°18E 256 D2
El Gîza Egypt 30°0N 31°12E 117 A2
El Gogorrón △ Mexico 21°49N 100°57W 318 C4
El Goléa Algeria 30°30N 2°50E 261 B5
El Gouna Egypt 27°5N 33°47E 256 B3
El Guamache Nueva Esparta, Venezuela 10°44N 63°54W 329 a
El Guamache Nueva Esparta, Venezuela 10°54N 64°3W 329 a
El Hadjira Algeria 32°36N 5°30E 261 B6
El Hagiz Sudan 15°15N 35°50E 257 D4
El Hâi Egypt 29°39N 31°18E 256 J7
El Hajeb Morocco 33°43N 5°13W 260 B3
El Hamma Tunisia 33°54N 9°48E 258 B1
El Hammam Egypt 30°52N 29°25E 256 A2
El Hammâmi Mauritania 23°3N 11°30W 260 D2
El Hâmûl Egypt 31°18N 31°9E 251 G2
El Hamurre Somalia 7°13N 48°54E 267 C6
El Hank Mauritania 24°30N 7°0W 260 D3
El Hasian W. Sahara 26°20N 14°0W 260 C2
El Hawata Sudan 13°25N 34°42E 257 E3
El Hideib Sudan 13°0N 32°50E 257 E3
El Hilla Sudan 13°24N 27°2E 257 E2
El Homr Algeria 29°43N 1°45E 261 C5
El 'Idisât Egypt 25°30N 32°35E 256 B3
El Iskandarîya Egypt 31°13N 29°58E 256 H6
El Jadida Morocco 33°11N 8°17W 260 B3
El Jardal Honduras 14°54N 88°50W 320 D2
El Jebelein Sudan 12°40N 32°55E 257 E3
El Jebha Morocco 35°11N 4°43W 260 A4
El Jem Tunisia 35°19N 10°41E 258 A2
El Kab Sudan 19°27N 32°46E 256 D3
El Kafr el Sharqi Egypt 31°16N 31°10E 256 H7
El Kala Algeria 36°53N 8°26E 261 A6
El Kamlin Sudan 15°3N 33°11E 257 D3
El Kantara Algeria 35°14N 5°45E 261 A6
El Kantara Tunisia 33°45N 10°58E 258 B2
El Karaba Sudan 18°32N 33°41E 256 D3
El Kef Tunisia 36°12N 8°47E 258 A1
El Kef □ Tunisia 36°0N 9°0E 261 A6
El Kelaâ de Srahna Morocco 32°4N 7°27W 260 B3
El Kelaâ M'Gouna Morocco 31°14N 6°7W 260 B3
El Kere Ethiopia 5°50N 42°5E 257 F5
El Khadr West Bank 31°42N 35°10E 123 B1
El Khalîfa Egypt 30°0N 31°15E 117 A2
El Khandaq Sudan 18°30N 30°30E 256 D3
El Khanka Egypt 30°13N 31°21E 251 H2
El Khârga Egypt 25°30N 30°33E 256 B3
El Khartûm Sudan 15°31N 32°35E 257 D3
El Khartûm □ Sudan 16°0N 33°0E 257 D3
El Khartûm Bahrî Sudan 15°40N 32°31E 257 D3
El Khroub Algeria 36°10N 6°55E 261 A6
El Kôm el Ahmar Egypt 30°6N 31°10E 117 A2
El Kseur Algeria 36°46N 4°49E 261 A5
El Ksiba Morocco 32°45N 6°1W 260 B3
El Kuntilla Egypt 30°1N 34°45E 251 H5
El Laqâwa Sudan 11°25N 29°1E 257 E2
El Leh Ethiopia 3°46N 39°13E 257 G4
El Leiya Sudan 16°15N 35°28E 257 D4
El Leoncito △ Argentina 31°58S 69°10W 334 C2
El Limón Panama 9°15N 79°49W 320 c
El Lucero Mexico 30°37N 106°31W 318 A3
El Ma'âdi Egypt 29°57N 31°15E 117 B2
El Maestrazgo Spain 40°30N 0°25W 196 E4
El Mafâza Sudan 13°38N 34°30E 257 E3
El Maghra Egypt 30°15N 28°55E 256 A2
El Mahalla el Kubra Egypt 31°0N 31°0E 256 H7
El Mahârîq Egypt 25°35N 30°35E 256 B3
El Maîmûn Egypt 29°14N 31°12E 256 J7
El Maitén Argentina 42°3S 71°10W 336 B2
El Maiz Algeria 28°19N 0°9W 261 C4
El Maks el Bahari Egypt 24°30N 30°40E 256 C3
El Malpais ⌂ U.S.A. 34°53N 108°0W 305 J10
El Manshâh Egypt 26°26N 31°50E 256 B3
El Mansour Algeria 27°47N 0°14W 261 C4
El Mansûra Egypt 31°0N 31°19E 256 H7
El Manteco Venezuela 7°38N 62°45W 329 B5
El Manzala Egypt 31°10N 31°50E 256 H7
El Marâgha Egypt 26°35N 31°10E 256 B3
El Masid Sudan 15°15N 33°0E 257 D3
El Masnou Spain 41°28N 2°20E 196 D7
El Matarîya El Mansûra, Egypt 31°15N 32°0E 256 H8
El Matarîya El Qâhira, Egypt 30°7N 31°18E 117 A2
El Meda Ethiopia 5°39N 41°47E 257 F5
El Medano Canary Is. 28°3N 16°32W 153 e1
El Meghaier Algeria 33°55N 5°58E 261 B6
El Ménia = El Goléa Algeria 30°30N 2°50E 261 B5
El Meraguen Algeria 28°0N 0°7W 261 C4
El Metemma Sudan 16°50N 33°10E 257 D3
El Miamo Venezuela 7°39N 61°46W 329 B5
El Milagro Argentina 30°59S 65°59W 334 C2
El Milia Algeria 36°51N 6°13E 261 A6
El Minufîya □ Egypt 30°30N 31°0E 251 H2
El Minyâ Egypt 28°7N 30°33E 256 B3
El Mohandessin Egypt 30°2N 31°11E 117 A2
El Monte U.S.A. 34°4N 118°1W 126 B4
El Montseny Spain 41°55N 2°25E 196 D7
El Mreiti Mauritania 23°29N 7°51W 260 D3
El Mreyye Mauritania 18°0N 6°0W 262 B3
El Muqattam Egypt 30°1N 31°17E 117 A2
El Mûskî Egypt 30°3N 31°15E 117 A2
El Nido Phil. 11°10N 119°25E 233 F2
El Niybo Ethiopia 4°40N 39°55E 257 G4
El Obeid Sudan 13°8N 30°10E 257 E3
El Odaiya Sudan 12°8N 28°12E 257 E2
El Oro Mexico 19°51N 100°7W 319 D4
El Oro □ Ecuador 3°30S 79°50W 328 D2
El Oued Algeria 33°20N 6°58E 261 B6
El Oued □ Algeria 33°10N 7°15E 261 B6
El Palmar Bolivia 17°50S 63°9W 331 D5
El Palmar Venezuela 7°58N 61°53W 329 B5
El Palmar △ Argentina 32°10S 58°31W 334 C4
El Pardo Spain 40°30N 3°46W 127 A1
El Paso = Derby U.S.A. 37°33N 97°16W 308 G5
El Paso Ill., U.S.A. 40°44N 89°1W 310 D7
El Paso Tex., U.S.A. 31°45N 106°29W 314 F1
El Paso de Robles = Paso Robles U.S.A. 35°38N 120°41W 306 K6
El Pedernoso Spain 39°29N 2°45W 197 F2
El Pedroso Spain 37°51N 5°45W 195 H5
El Pilar Venezuela 10°32N 63°9W 329 A5
El Pinacate y Gran Desierto de Altar = Gran Desierto del Pinacate ⌂ Mexico 31°51N 113°32W 318 A2
El Pobleneu Spain 41°23N 2°11E 114 A2
El Pobo de Dueñas Spain 40°46N 1°39W 196 E3
El Portal Calif., U.S.A. 37°41N 119°47W 306 H7
El Portal Fla., U.S.A. 25°51N 80°11W 129 C2
El Porvenir Mexico 31°15N 105°51W 318 A3
El Prat Barcelona ✕ (BCN) Spain 41°18N 2°5E 114 B1
El Prat de Llobregat Spain 41°19N 2°5E 114 B1
El Progreso Galápagos Is., Ecuador 0°54S 89°33W 330 a
El Progreso Honduras 15°26N 87°51W 320 C2
El Pueblo Canary Is. 28°36N 17°47W 153 e1
El Pueblo Historic Park ⌂ Los Angeles, U.S.A. 127 b2
El Puente del Arzobispo Spain 39°48N 5°10W 194 F5
El Puerto de Santa María Spain 36°36N 6°13W 195 J4
El Qâhira Egypt 30°2N 31°13E 117 A2
El Qâhira □ Egypt 29°30N 31°30E 251 J2
El Qanâyat Egypt 30°37N 31°27E 251 H2
El Qantara Egypt 30°51N 32°20E 251 H3
El Qasr Egypt 25°44N 28°42E 256 B2
El Qassâsîn Egypt 30°33N 31°55E 251 H2
El Qubâbât Egypt 29°28N 31°16E 256 J7
El Qubba Egypt 30°4N 31°16E 117 A2
El Quseima Egypt 30°40N 34°15E 251 H5
El Qusîya Egypt 27°29N 30°44E 256 B3
El Râshda Egypt 25°36N 28°57E 256 B2
El Reloj Mexico 19°19N 99°9W 128 C2
El Reno U.S.A. 35°32N 97°57W 301 H20
El Retiro Spain 40°25N 3°41W 127 B1
El Rey △ Argentina 24°40S 64°34W 334 A3
El Rîdisiya Egypt 24°56N 32°51E 256 C3
El Rio U.S.A. 34°14N 119°10W 307 L7
El Ronquillo Spain 37°44N 6°10W 195 H4
El Roque, Pta. Canary Is. 28°10N 15°25W 153 e1
El Rosario Mexico 30°1N 115°45W 318 A1
El Rubio Spain 37°22N 5°0W 195 H5
El Saff Egypt 29°34N 31°16E 256 J7
El Salto Santiago, Chile 33°22S 70°38W 137 B2
El Salto Durango, Mexico 23°47N 105°22W 318 C3
El Salvador ■ Cent. Amer. 13°50N 89°0W 320 D2
El Sauce Nic. 13°0N 86°40W 320 D2
El Saucejo Spain 37°4N 5°6W 195 H5
El Sereno U.S.A. 34°4N 118°10W 126 B3
El Shallal Egypt 24°0N 32°53E 256 C3
El Sharqîya □ Egypt 30°48N 31°48E 251 H2
El Simbillawein Egypt 30°48N 31°13E 256 H7
El Sombrero Venezuela 9°23N 67°3W 328 B4
El Suweis Egypt 29°58N 32°31E 256 B3
El Suweis □ Egypt 29°30N 32°15E 251 J3
El Tabbîn Egypt 29°47N 31°18E 256 J7
El Talibîya Egypt 29°59N 31°10E 117 B2
El Tamá △ S. Amer. 7°25N 72°25W 328 B3
El Tamarâni, W. ➔ Egypt 30°7N 34°43E 251 H5
El Tarf Algeria 36°46N 8°19E 261 A6
El Tarf □ Algeria 36°45N 8°10E 261 A6
El Thamad Egypt 29°40N 34°28E 251 J5
El Tigre Venezuela 8°44N 64°15W 329 B5
El Tîh, Gebel Egypt 29°40N 33°50E 251 J4
El Tîna Egypt 31°3N 32°22E 256 H8
El Tirano Puerte Fermín Venezuela 11°7N 63°51W 329 a
El Tocuyo Venezuela 9°47N 69°48W 328 B4
El Tofo Chile 29°22S 71°18W 334 B1
El Tránsito Chile 28°52S 70°17W 334 B1
El Tucuche Trin. & Tob. 10°43N 61°25W 323 t
El Tuey Venezuela 11°1N 63°57W 329 a
El Tunal Venezuela 11°4N 64°18W 329 a
El Tuparro △ Colombia 5°19N 68°28W 328 B4
El Tûr Egypt 28°14N 33°36E 251 K4
El Turbio Argentina 51°45S 72°5W 336 D2
El Uarre Somalia 3°4N 45°20E 267 D6
El Uqsur Egypt 25°41N 32°38E 256 B3
El Valle ⌂ Spain 37°56N 1°6W 197 H3
El Valle del Espíritu Santo Venezuela 10°49N 63°53W 329 a
El Vendrell Spain 41°10N 1°30E 196 D6
El Vergel Chihuahua, Mexico 26°28N 106°22W 318 B3
El Vergel Distrito Federal, Mexico 19°18N 99°5W 128 C2
El Vigía Venezuela 8°38N 71°39W 328 B3
El Viso del Alcor Spain 37°23N 5°43W 195 H5
El Wabeira Egypt 29°34N 33°6E 251 J4
El Wâhli Egypt 30°3N 31°16E 117 A2
El Wak Somalia 2°44N 41°1E 267 D5
El Weguet Ethiopia 5°28N 42°17E 257 F5
El Wuz Sudan 15°5N 30°7E 257 D3
El Yaque Venezuela 10°54N 63°57W 329 a
El Yunque, Cerro Chile 33°39S 78°50W 330 c
El Yunque Puerto Rico 18°19N 65°48W 321 b
El Zamâlik Egypt 30°3N 31°12E 117 A2
El Zeitûn Egypt 30°6N 31°18E 117 A2
Elafonisos Greece 36°29N 22°56E 204 E4
Elamanchili India 17°33N 82°50E 244 F6
Élancourt France 48°47N 1°58E 173 D8

Elands Australia 31°37S 152°20E 283 A10
Elandsfontein Junc. = Germiston
  S. Africa 26°13S 28°10E 123 B3
Elasa Greece 35°18N 26°21E 205 F8
Elassona Greece 39°53N 22°12E 204 B4
Elat Israel 29°30N 34°56E 251 J5
Elati Oros Greece 38°30N 20°39E 207 B2
Elatia Greece 38°37N 22°46E 204 C4
Elâzığ Turkey 38°37N 39°14E 213 C8
Elâzığ □ Turkey 38°37N 39°14E 213 C8
Elba Italy 42°46N 10°17E 198 F7
Elba, Ala., U.S.A. 31°25N 86°4W 316 K3
Elbe → Europe 53°50N 9°0E 178 B4
Elbe-Seitenkanal Germany 52°45N 10°32E 178 C6
Elberfeld U.S.A. 38°10N 87°27W 311 F9
Elbert, Mt. U.S.A. 39°7N 106°27W 304 G10
Elberton U.S.A. 34°7N 82°52W 316 A7
Elbeuf France 49°17N 1°2E 172 C8
Elbeyli Turkey 36°40N 37°27E 250 B8
Elbing = Elbląg Poland 54°10N 19°25E 184 D6
Elbistan Turkey 38°13N 37°15E 212 C7
Elbląg Poland 54°10N 19°25E 184 D6
Elbow Canada 51°7N 106°35W 297 C7
Elbrus Russia 43°21N 42°30E 191 J6
Elbufer-Drawehn △
  Germany 53°8N 10°58E 178 B6
Elburn U.S.A. 41°54N 88°28W 311 C8
Elburz Mts. = Alborz, Reshteh-ye
  Kūhhā-ye Iran 36°0N 52°0E 247 C7
Elche Spain 38°15N 0°42W 197 G4
Elche de la Sierra Spain 38°27N 2°3W 197 G2
Elcho I. Australia 11°55S 135°45E 280 A2
Elda Spain 38°29N 0°47W 197 G4
Eldama Ravine Kenya 0°3N 35°43E 268 B4
Elde → Germany 53°7N 11°15E 178 B7
Eldey Iceland 63°45N 22°55W 155 D4
Eldon Iowa, U.S.A. 40°55N 92°13W 310 D4
Eldon Mo., U.S.A. 38°21N 92°35W 310 F4
Eldon Wash., U.S.A. 47°33N 123°3W 306 C3
Eldora U.S.A. 42°22N 93°5W 310 B3
Eldorado = Echo Bay
  Canada 66°5N 117°55W 294 D8
Eldorado Argentina 26°28S 54°43W 335 B5
Eldorado Ont., Canada 44°35N 77°31W 312 B7
Eldorado Ill., U.S.A. 37°49N 88°26W 311 G8
Eldorado Tex., U.S.A. 30°52N 100°36W 314 F4
Eldorendo U.S.A. 31°3N 84°39W 316 F5
Eldoret Kenya 0°30N 35°17E 268 B4
Eldred U.S.A. 41°58N 78°23W 312 E6
Eldridge U.S.A. 41°39N 90°35W 310 E8
Elea, C. Cyprus 35°19N 34°4E 207 E10
Eleanora, Pk. Australia 32°57S 121°9E 279 F3
Eleao U.S.A. 21°27N 157°52W 302 K14
Elefantes → Africa 24°10S 32°40E 271 B5
Elefantes, B. das Angola 13°13S 12°44E 265 F2
Elefantes, G. Chile 46°28S 73°49W 336 F1
Elefsina Greece 38°4N 23°26E 204 C5
Eleftherios Venizelos ✈ (ATH)
  Greece 37°56N 23°56E 112 A3
Elektrogorsk Russia 55°56N 38°50E 188 E10
Elektroperedacha = Elektrogorsk
  Russia 55°56N 38°50E 188 E10
Elektrostal Russia 55°41N 38°32E 188 E10
Elektrovoz = Stupino
  Russia 54°57N 38°2E 188 E10
Elele Nigeria 5°5N 6°50E 263 D6
Elemi Triangle = Ilemi Triangle
  Africa 5°0N 35°20E 257 H7
Elena Bulgaria 42°55N 25°53E 203 D9
Elephant Butte Res.
  U.S.A. 33°9N 107°11W 305 K10
Elephant I. Antarctica 61°0S 55°0W 151 C18
Elephant Pass Sri Lanka 9°35N 80°25E 245 K5
Elephanta Caves India 18°57N 72°57E 130 B2
Elephanta I. India 18°57N 72°56E 130 B2
Elesbão Veloso Brazil 6°13S 42°8W 332 C5
Eleshnitsa Bulgaria 42°52N 23°36E 202 E7
Eleşkirt Turkey 39°50N 42°50E 213 C10
Eleuthera I. Bahamas 25°0N 76°20W 320 B4
Eleutheroupoli Greece 40°52N 24°20E 203 F8
Elfin Cove U.S.A. 58°12N 136°22W 303 G13
Elgå Norway 62°10N 11°56E 164 B8
Elgeyo-Marakwet □ Kenya 0°50N 35°35E 268 B4
Elgin Ont., Canada 44°36N 76°13W 313 B8
Elgin Moray, U.K. 57°39N 3°19W 167 D5
Elgin Ill., U.S.A. 42°2N 88°17W 311 B8
Elgin N. Dak., U.S.A. 46°24N 101°51W 308 B3
Elgin Oreg., U.S.A. 45°34N 117°55W 304 D5
Elgin S.C., U.S.A. 34°10N 80°48W 316 A4
Elgin Tex., U.S.A. 30°21N 97°22W 314 F6
Elgoibar Spain 43°13N 2°24W 196 B2
Elgon, Mt. Africa 1°10N 34°30E 268 B3
Elgspiggen Norway 62°10N 11°21E 164 B8
Eliase Indonesia 8°21S 130°48E 275 D8
Elikonas Oros Greece 38°18N 22°45E 204 C4
Elim Namibia 17°48S 15°31E 270 A2
Elim Western Cape, S. Africa 34°35S 19°45E 270 D2
Elim Alaska, U.S.A. 64°37N 162°15W 303 D7
Elin Pelin Bulgaria 42°40N 23°36E 202 D7
Elingampangu
  Dem. Rep. of the Congo 2°0S 24°4E 264 C4
Elipa Dem. Rep. of the Congo 1°3S 24°20E 264 C4
Elis = Ilia Greece 37°45N 21°35E 204 D3
Eliseu Martins Brazil 8°13S 43°42W 332 C5
Elista Russia 46°16N 44°14E 191 G7
Eliza, L. Australia 37°15S 139°50E 282 D3
Elizabeth S. Austral.,
  Australia 34°42S 138°41E 282 C3
Elizabeth Ill., U.S.A. 42°19N 90°13W 310 A6
Elizabeth N.J., U.S.A. 40°39N 74°12W 313 F10
Elizabeth, B. Ecuador 0°36S 91°12W 330 a
Elizabeth City U.S.A. 36°18N 76°14W 315 C16
Elizabethton U.S.A. 36°21N 82°13W 315 C13
Elizabethtown Ky.,
  U.S.A. 37°42N 85°52W 311 G11
Elizabethtown N.Y.,
  U.S.A. 44°13N 73°36W 313 B11
Elizabethtown Pa., U.S.A. 40°9N 76°36W 313 F8
Elizabethville = Lubumbashi
  Dem. Rep. of the Congo 11°40S 27°28E 269 E2
Elizondo Spain 43°12N 1°30W 196 B3
Elk Poland 53°50N 22°21E 184 E9
Elk → Ala., U.S.A. 34°46N 87°16W 315 D11
Elk → Poland 53°41N 22°28E 184 E9
Elk → Ala., U.S.A. 34°46N 87°16W 315 D11
Elk City U.S.A. 35°25N 99°25W 314 H5
Elk Creek U.S.A. 39°36N 122°32W 306 F4
Elk Grove U.S.A. 38°25N 121°22W 306 G5
Elk Island Canada 49°20N 57°40W 298 C4
Elk Lake Canada 47°40N 80°25W 298 C3
Elk Point Canada 53°54N 110°55W 297 C6
Elk River Idaho, U.S.A. 46°47N 116°11W 304 C5
Elk River Minn., U.S.A. 45°18N 93°35W 310 C7
Elkader U.S.A. 42°51N 91°24W 310 B5
Elkedra → Australia 21°8S 136°22E 280 C2
Elkhart Ind., U.S.A. 41°41N 85°58W 311 C11
Elkhart Kans., U.S.A. 37°0N 101°54W 314 G3
Elkhart → U.S.A. 41°41N 85°58W 311 C11
Elkhorn Man., Canada 49°59N 101°14W 297 D8
Elkhorn → U.S.A. 41°8N 96°19W 308 E6
Elkhorn Wis., U.S.A. 42°40N 88°33W 311 B8
Elkhovo Bulgaria 42°10N 26°35E 203 D10
Elkin U.S.A. 36°15N 80°51W 316 B6
Elkins U.S.A. 38°55N 79°51W 309 F14
Elkland U.S.A. 41°59N 77°19W 312 E7
Elko B.C., Canada 49°20N 115°10W 296 D5
Elko Nev., U.S.A. 40°50N 115°46W 304 F6

Elkton U.S.A. 43°49N 83°11W 312 C11
Ellas = Greece ■ Europe 40°0N 23°0E 204 B3
Ellaville Fla., U.S.A. 30°23N 83°10W 316 E6
Ellaville Ga., U.S.A. 32°14N 84°19W 316 E5
Ellef Ringnes I. Canada 78°30N 102°2W 295 B11
Ellen, Mt. U.S.A. 44°9N 72°56W 313 B12
Ellenburg U.S.A. 44°54N 73°48W 313 A11
Ellendale U.S.A. 46°0N 98°32W 308 B4
Ellenor, L. U.S.A. 28°28N 81°25W 317 G9
Ellensburg U.S.A. 46°59N 120°34W 304 C3
Ellenville U.S.A. 41°43N 74°24W 313 E10
Ellerton Barbados 13°7N 59°33W 323 r
Ellery, Mt. Australia 37°28S 148°47E 283 F8
Ellesmere = Scottsdale
  Australia 41°9S 147°31E 281 G4
Ellesmere, L. N.Z. 43°47S 172°28E 285 F4
Ellesmere I. Canada 79°30N 80°0W 295 B16
Ellesmere Port U.K. 53°17N 2°54W 168 D5
Ellettsville U.S.A. 39°14N 86°38W 311 F10
Ellice Is. = Tuvalu ■
  Pac. Oc. 8°0S 178°0E 277 E14
Ellicottville U.S.A. 42°17N 78°40W 312 D6
Ellington U.S.A. 42°13N 79°6W 312 D5
Elliniko Olympic Complex
  Greece 37°50N 23°45E 112 B2
Elliot N. Terr., Australia 17°33S 133°32E 280 B1
Elliot Eastern Cape, S. Africa 31°22S 27°48E 271 D4
Elliot Lake Canada 46°25N 82°35W 298 C3
Elliotdale = Xhora
  S. Africa 31°55S 28°38E 271 D4
Elliott Australia 17°33S 133°32E 280 B1
Elliott U.S.A. 34°6N 80°10W 316 A4
Elliott Key U.S.A. 25°27N 80°12W 317 K9
Ellipse, The Washington, D.C., U.S.A. 143 b1
Ellis I. U.S.A. 38°56N 99°34W 308 F4
Ellis I. U.S.A. 40°41N 74°2W 132 B1
Elliston Australia 33°39S 134°53E 281 E1
Ellisville U.S.A. 31°36N 89°12W 315 F10
Ellon U.K. 57°22N 2°4W 167 D6
Ellora India 20°1N 75°10E 244 D2
Ellore = Eluru India 16°48N 81°8E 244 F5
Elloree U.S.A. 33°32N 80°34W 316 B4
Ellsworth Kans., U.S.A. 38°44N 98°14W 308 F4
Ellsworth Maine, U.S.A. 44°33N 68°25W 309 C19
Ellsworth Land Antarctica 76°0S 89°0W 151 D16
Ellsworth Mts. Antarctica 78°30S 85°0W 151 D16
Ellwangen Germany 48°58N 10°6E 179 G6
Ellwood City U.S.A. 40°52N 80°17W 312 F4
Ellzey U.S.A. 29°19N 82°48W 317 F7
Elm Switz. 46°54N 9°10E 179 J5
Elm-Lappwald △ Germany 52°15N 10°50E 178 C6
Elma Man., Canada 49°52N 95°55W 297 D9
Elma Wash., U.S.A. 47°0N 123°25W 306 D3
Elmadağ Turkey 39°55N 33°14E 212 C5
Elmalı Turkey 36°44N 29°56E 205 E11
Elmers End U.K. 51°23N 0°2W 125 B3
Elmhurst Ill., U.S.A. 41°53N 87°56W 311 C9
Elmhurst N.Y., U.S.A. 40°44N 73°53W 132 B2
Elmina Ghana 5°5N 1°21W 263 D4
Elmira Ont., Canada 43°36N 80°33W 312 C4
Elmira N.Y., U.S.A. 42°6N 76°48W 312 D8
Elmira Heights U.S.A. 42°8N 76°50W 312 D8
Elmodel U.S.A. 31°21N 84°29W 316 D5
Elmore Vic., Australia 36°30S 144°37E 282 D6
Elmore Ala., U.S.A. 32°32N 86°19W 316 E4
Elmore Ohio, U.S.A. 41°29N 83°18W 311 C13
Elmshorn Germany 53°43N 9°40E 178 B5
Elmstead U.K. 51°24N 0°2E 125 B4
Elmvale Canada 44°35N 79°52W 312 B5
Elmwood Ill., U.S.A. 40°47N 89°58W 310 D7
Elmwood La., U.S.A. 29°57N 90°11W 131 B1
Elmwood Park Ill., U.S.A. 41°55N 87°49W 132 A1
Elmwood Park N.J., U.S.A. 40°54N 74°7W 132 A1
Elne France 42°36N 2°58E 174 F6
Elnesvågen Norway 62°52N 7°10E 164 B4
Elora Canada 43°41N 80°26W 312 C4
Elora U.S.A. 38°53N 87°5N 179 F9
Eloaua I. Papua N. G. 1°38S 149°40E 286 A5
Elobey, Is. Eq. Guin. 1°0N 9°35E 263 D4
Elongo
  Dem. Rep. of the Congo 0°19S 21°39E 264 C4
Elora Canada 43°41N 80°26W 312 C4
Elorza Venezuela 7°3N 69°31W 328 B4
Elos Greece 36°46N 22°43E 204 D4
Elounda Greece 35°16N 25°42E 207 E6
Éloyes France 48°6N 6°36E 173 D13
Elphin Canada 44°55N 76°37W 313 B8
Elpitiya Sri Lanka 6°17N 80°10E 245 L5
Elrose Canada 51°12N 108°0W 297 C7
Elsberry U.S.A. 39°10N 90°47W 310 F6
Elsby △ Australia 14°55S 133°10E 278 B5
Elsdorf Germany 50°55N 6°34E 178 E2
Elsie Mich., U.S.A. 43°5N 84°23W 311 D12
Elsie Oreg., U.S.A. 45°52N 123°36W 306 E3
Elsiesrivier S. Africa 33°55S 18°35E 118 A2
Elsinore = Helsingør
  Denmark 56°2N 12°35E 163 H6
Elster → Germany 51°25N 11°57E 178 D7
Elsterwerda Australia 37°52S 145°0E 285 B4
Elsterwerda Germany 51°27N 13°31E 178 D9
Eltanin Fracture Zone System
  S. Ocean 54°0S 130°0W 151 B14
Eltham N.Z. 39°26S 174°19E 284 F3
Eltham London, U.K. 51°27N 0°3E 125 B4
Elton Russia 49°5N 46°52E 191 F8
Elton, Ozero Russia 49°5N 46°42E 191 F8
Eltville Germany 50°2N 8°7E 179 F4
Eluanbi = Oluanpi
  Taiwan 21°54N 120°51E 225 E2
Eluru India 16°48N 81°8E 244 F5
Elvas Portugal 38°50N 7°10W 195 C2
Elven France 47°44N 2°36W 172 E4
Elverum Norway 60°53N 11°34E 164 E6
Elvire → Australia 17°51S 128°11E 278 C4
Elvire, Mt. Australia 29°22S 119°36E 279 E2
Elvo → Italy 45°23N 8°21E 198 C5
Elwell, L. = Tiber Res.
  U.S.A. 48°19N 111°6W 304 B8
Elwood Vic., Australia 37°53S 144°59E 128 B1
Elwood Ill., U.S.A. 41°24N 88°7W 311 C8
Elwood Ind., U.S.A. 40°17N 85°50W 311 D11
Elwood Nebr., U.S.A. 40°36N 99°52W 308 E4
Elx = Elche Spain 38°15N 0°42W 197 G4
Ely U.K. 52°24N 0°16E 169 E8
Ely Minn., U.S.A. 47°55N 91°51W 308 B8
Ely Nev., U.S.A. 39°15N 114°54W 304 G6
Elyria U.S.A. 41°22N 82°7W 312 E2
Elyros Greece 35°15N 23°45E 204 F5
Élysée France 48°52N 2°19E 134 A2
Elysian Park Los Angeles, U.S.A. 127 A3
Émaé Vanuatu 17°4S 168°24E 287 G6
Émaé Vanuatu 17°4S 168°24E 287 G6
Emajõgi → Estonia 58°30N 25°43E 158 H12
eMakhazeni S. Africa 25°42S 30°2E 271 C5
eMalahleni S. Africa 25°51S 29°14E 271 C4
Emāmrūd Iran 36°30N 55°0E 247 B7
Emāmzādeh Sāleh Iran 35°46N 51°26E 141 A2
Emån → Sweden 57°8N 16°30E 163 H10
Emas △ Brazil 18°2S 52°50W 331 D7
Emba
  Dem. Rep. of the Congo 1°16N 18°42E 264 B3
Embarcación Argentina 23°10S 64°0W 334 A3
Embarcadero, The San Francisco, U.S.A. 136 b3
Embarras → U.S.A. 38°39N 87°37W 311 F9
Embetsu Japan 44°44N 141°47E 220 B10
Embi Kazakhstan 48°50N 58°8E 216 C5

Embi → Kazakhstan 46°55N 53°28E 187 E9
Embonas Greece 36°13N 27°51E 206 E11
Embro Canada 43°9N 80°54W 312 C4
Embrun France 44°34N 6°30E 175 D10
Embu Kenya 0°32S 37°38E 268 C4
Emden Germany 53°21N 7°12E 178 B3
Emecik Turkey 36°46N 27°49E 205 E9
Emei Shan China 29°31N 103°46E 228 C4
Emeishan China 29°31N 103°23E 228 C4
Emek Refa'im Jerusalem 123 c2
Émerainville France 48°48N 2°37E 134 B4
Émeraude, Côte d' France 48°45N 2°40W 172 C4
Emerald Qld., Australia 23°32S 148°10E 280 C4
Emerald Vic., Australia 37°56S 145°29E 276 E8
Emerald Buddha = Phra Kaeo
  Bangkok, Thailand 113 b1
Emerald I. Canada 76°48N 114°10W 295 B9
Emerson Man., Canada 49°0N 97°10W 297 D9
Emerson Ga., U.S.A. 34°8N 84°45W 316 A5
Emeryville U.S.A. 37°49N 122°17W 136 A3
Emet Turkey 39°20N 29°15E 205 B11
Emeti Papua N. G. 7°53S 143°15E 286 D2
Emgwenya S. Africa 25°40S 30°9E 271 C5
Emi Koussi Chad 19°45N 18°55E 259 E3
Emilia-Romagna □ Italy 44°45N 11°0E 198 D8
Emilius, Mte. Italy 45°47N 7°23E 198 C4
Emin China 46°34N 83°36E 217 C10
Eminabad Pakistan 32°2N 74°8E 242 C6
Emine, Nos Bulgaria 42°40N 27°56E 203 D11
Eminence U.S.A. 38°22N 85°11W 311 F11
Eminönü Turkey 41°0N 28°57E 122 B1
Emirates, Mall of the
  Dubai, U.A.E. 25°7N 55°12E 119 B1
Emirau I. Papua N. G. 1°40S 150°0E 286 A6
Emirdağ Turkey 39°2N 31°8E 212 C4
Emirgan Turkey 41°6N 29°2E 122 B2
Emissi, Tarso Chad 21°27N 18°36E 259 D3
eMkhondo = Piet Retief
  S. Africa 27°1S 30°50E 271 C5
Emlenton U.S.A. 41°11N 79°43W 312 E5
Emlichheim Germany 52°37N 6°51E 178 C2
Emmaboda Sweden 56°37N 15°32E 163 H9
Emmalane S. Africa 32°46N 82°0W 316 C7
Emmaus S. Africa 26°9S 25°15E 270 C4
Emmaus Pa., U.S.A. 40°32N 75°30W 313 F9
Emme → Switz. 47°14N 7°32E 179 H3
Emmeloord Neths. 52°44N 5°46E 170 B5
Emmen Neths. 52°48N 6°57E 170 B6
Emmen Switz. 47°5N 8°16E 179 H4
Emmendingen Germany 48°6N 7°51E 179 G3
Emmenbrücke Switz. 47°5N 8°16E 179 H4
Emmerich Germany 51°50N 6°12E 178 D2
Emmet Australia 24°45S 144°30E 280 C3
Emmetsburg U.S.A. 43°7N 94°41W 310 A2
Emmett Idaho, U.S.A. 43°52N 116°30W 304 E5
Emmett Mich., U.S.A. 42°59N 82°46W 312 D2
Emmiganuru = Yemmiganur
  India 15°44N 77°29E 245 G3
Emmonak U.S.A. 62°47N 164°31W 303 E6
Emo Canada 48°38N 93°50W 297 D10
Emőd Hungary 47°57N 20°47E 182 C5
Emona Bulgaria 42°43N 27°53E 203 D11
Emory Peak U.S.A. 29°15N 103°18E 314 G3
Empalme Mexico 27°58N 110°51W 318 B2
Empangeni S. Africa 28°50S 31°52E 271 C5
Empedrado Argentina 28°0S 58°46W 334 B4
Emperor Seamount Chain
  Pac. Oc. 40°0N 170°0E 288 D9
Emperor Trough Pac. Oc. 43°0N 172°0E 288 D9
Empingham Res. = Rutland Water
  U.K. 52°39N 0°38W 169 E7
Empire U.S.A. 39°21N 83°18W 316 C6
Empire State Building New York, U.S.A. 132 c2
Empoli Italy 43°43N 10°57E 198 E7
Emporia Kans., U.S.A. 38°25N 96°11W 308 F5
Emporia Va., U.S.A. 36°42N 77°32W 309 G15
Emporium U.S.A. 41°31N 78°14W 312 E6
Empress Canada 50°57N 110°0W 297 C7
Empty Quarter = Rub' al Khālī
  Si. Arabia 19°0N 48°0E 249 C5
Ems → Germany 53°20N 7°12E 178 B3
Emsdale Canada 45°32N 79°19W 312 A5
Emsdetten Germany 52°10N 7°32E 178 C3
Emu China 43°40N 128°6E 227 C14
Emu Park Australia 23°13S 150°50E 280 C5
eMuziwezinto S. Africa 30°15S 30°45E 271 D5
'En 'Avrona Israel 29°43N 35°0E 251 J6
'En Boqeq Israel 31°12N 35°21E 251 G6
'En Gannim = Ramat Gan
  Israel 32°4N 34°48E 251 F5
'En Gedi Israel 31°28N 35°25E 251 G6
En Na'am Sudan 10°21N 27°58E 266 B2
En Nahrat Mali 22°55N 3°36W 260 D4
En Nahud Sudan 12°45N 28°25E 257 E2
En Nofalab Sudan 15°52N 32°32E 257 D3
En Nuqra Sudan 10°4N 28°10E 266 B2
Ena Japan 35°25N 137°25E 223 B9
Ena-San Japan 35°26N 137°36E 223 B9
Enambú Colombia 1°1N 70°17W 328 C3
Enard B. U.K. 58°5N 5°20W 167 C3
Enare träsk = Inarijärvi
  Finland 69°0N 28°0E 160 B23
Enarotali Indonesia 3°55S 136°21E 283 F8
Encampment U.S.A. 41°12N 106°47W 304 F10
Encantadas, Serra Brazil 30°40S 53°0W 335 C5
Encantado Brazil 22°53S 43°19W 135 B1
Encarnación Paraguay 27°15S 55°50W 335 B4
Encarnación de Díaz
  Mexico 21°31N 102°14W 318 C4
Enchi Ghana 5°53N 2°48W 262 D4
Encinitas U.S.A. 33°3N 117°17W 307 M9
Encino Calif., U.S.A. 34°9N 118°28W 127 A1
Encino N. Mex., U.S.A. 34°39N 105°28W 305 J11
Encino Res. U.S.A. 34°9N 118°30W 127 A1
Encontrados Venezuela 9°3N 72°14W 328 B3
Encounter B. Australia 35°45S 138°45E 282 C2
Encruzilhada Brazil 15°31S 40°54W 333 E10
Encs Hungary 48°20N 21°8E 182 B6
Endako Canada 54°6N 125°2W 296 C3
Endau Kenya 1°18S 38°31E 268 C4
Endau Rompin △
  Malaysia 2°27N 103°45E 237 L4
Ende Indonesia 8°45S 121°40E 231 F6
Endeavour Str. Australia 10°45S 142°0E 286 F2
Endelave Denmark 55°46N 10°18E 163 J4
Enderby Canada 50°35N 119°10W 296 C5
Enderby I. Australia 20°35S 116°30E 278 D2
Enderby Land Antarctica 66°0S 53°0E 151 C5
Enderlin U.S.A. 46°38N 97°36W 308 B5
Endicott U.S.A. 42°6N 76°4W 313 D8
Endicott Mts. U.S.A. 68°0N 152°0W 303 C9
Endimari → Brazil 8°56S 66°7W 330 B4
Endwell U.S.A. 42°6N 76°1W 313 D8
Endyalgout I. Australia 11°40S 132°35E 278 A5
Ene → Peru 11°10S 74°18W 330 C3
Eneabba Australia 29°49S 115°16E 279 E2
Enebyberg Sweden 59°26N 18°11E 139 A1
Enerhodar Ukraine 47°30N 34°28E 189 K8
Enewetak Atoll
  Marshall Is. 11°30N 162°15E 288 G8
Enez Turkey 40°45N 26°5E 203 F10
Enfer, Pte. d' Martinique 14°22N 60°54W 322 j

Enfield N.S.W., Australia 33°53S 151°6E 139 B1
Enfield N.S., Canada 44°56N 63°32W 299 D7
Enfield Conn., U.S.A. 41°58N 72°36W 313 E12
Enfield Ill., U.S.A. 38°6N 88°20W 311 F8
Enfield N.C., U.S.A. 36°11N 77°41W 315 C16
Enfield N.H., U.S.A. 43°39N 72°9W 313 C12
Enga □ Papua N. G. 5°30S 143°30E 286 C2
Engadin Switz. 46°45N 10°10E 179 J6
Engan Norway 63°8N 8°31E 164 A5
Engaño, C. Dom. Rep. 18°30N 68°20E 321 C6
Engaño, C. Phil. 18°35N 122°23E 232 B4
Engaru Japan 44°3N 143°31E 220 B11
Engcobo = Ngcobo
  S. Africa 31°37S 28°0E 271 D4
Engelberg Switz. 46°48N 8°26E 179 J4
Engels Russia 51°28N 46°6E 191 D8
Engelsberg = Ängelsberg
  Sweden 59°58N 16°0E 162 E10
Engemann L. Canada 58°0N 106°55W 297 B7
Engenho, I. do Brazil 22°50S 43°6W 135 B2
Engerdal Norway 61°45N 11°58E 164 C8
Engershatu Eritrea 16°7N 38°34E 257 D4
Enggano Indonesia 5°20S 102°40E 234 D2
Engineer Group
  Papua N. G. 10°35S 151°20E 286 F6
Engkilili Malaysia 1°3N 111°42E 235 B4
England □ U.K. 53°0N 2°0W 169 D6
England □ U.K. 53°0N 2°0W 169 D6
Englee Canada 50°45N 56°5W 299 B8
Englehart Canada 47°49N 79°52W 298 C4
Englewood Fla., U.S.A. 26°58N 82°21W 317 J7
Englewood Ill., U.S.A. 41°46N 87°38W 132 C2
Englewood Ohio, U.S.A. 39°53N 84°18W 311 F12
Englewood N.J., U.S.A. 40°54N 73°58W 132 A2
Englewood Cliffs U.S.A. 40°53N 73°57W 132 A2
English → Ont., Canada 50°35N 93°30W 297 C10
English → Iowa, U.S.A. 41°18N 91°51W 310 E6
English, L. Ascension I. 7°54S 14°23W 153 g
English Bazar = Ingraj Bazar
  India 24°58N 88°10E 243 G13
English Channel Europe 50°0N 2°0W 169 G6
English Company's Is., The
  Australia 11°50S 136°32E 280 A2
English Harbour Town
  Antigua & B. 17°1N 61°46W 322 b
English River Canada 49°14N 91°0W 298 C1
Engures ezers Latvia 57°15N 23°8E 158 H3
Enguri → Georgia 42°27N 41°38E 191 J5
Enid U.S.A. 36°24N 97°53W 314 G6
Eniwa Japan 42°56N 141°36E 220 C10
Enkhuizen Neths. 52°42N 5°17E 170 B5
Enköping Sweden 59°37N 17°4E 162 E11
Enle China 23°9N 101°6E 228 F3
Enmore S. Africa 33°54S 151°10E 139 B2
Enna Italy 37°34N 14°16E 201 F6
Ennadai L. Canada 60°58N 101°20W 297 A8
Enner, O. → Chad 14°24N 18°45E 259 F4
Ennedi Chad 17°15N 22°0E 259 E4
Ennedi Est □ Chad 18°5N 23°20E 259 E4
Ennedi Ouest □ Chad 18°0N 21°56E 259 E3
Enneri Achelouma →
  Niger 21°55N 13°35E 261 D7
Enngonia Australia 29°21S 145°50E 281 D4
Ennigerloh Germany 51°50N 8°2E 178 D4
Ennis Clare, Ireland 52°51N 8°59W 166 D3
Ennis Mont., U.S.A. 45°21N 111°44W 304 D8
Ennis Tex., U.S.A. 32°20N 96°38W 314 E6
Enniscorthy Ireland 52°30N 6°34W 166 D5
Enniskillen U.K. 54°21N 7°39W 166 B4
Ennistymon Ireland 52°57N 9°17W 166 D2
Enns → Austria 48°14N 14°32E 180 C7
Eno Finland 62°47N 30°10E 160 E6
Enns → Austria 48°14N 14°32E 180 C7
Enontekiö Finland 68°23N 23°37E 160 B20
Enoshima Japan 35°18N 139°29E 141 B6
Enping China 22°16N 112°21E 229 F9
Enrekang Indonesia 3°34S 119°47E 235 C5
Enrile Phil. 17°24N 121°47E 232 B3
Enriquillo, L. Dom. Rep. 18°20N 71°40W 321 C5
Enschede Neths. 52°13N 6°53E 170 B6
Ensenada Argentina 34°55S 57°55W 334 C4
Ensenada Chile 41°12S 72°33W 336 B2
Ensenada Baja Calif.,
  Mexico 31°52N 116°37W 318 A1
Ensenada de los Muertos
  Mexico 23°59N 109°51W 318 C2
Ensenada La Guardia
  Venezuela 11°2N 64°5W 329 a
Enshi China 30°18N 109°29E 228 B7
Enshū-Nada Japan 34°27N 137°38E 223 C9
Ensiola, Pta. de n' Spain 39°7N 2°55E 206 B9
Ensisheim France 47°50N 7°20E 173 E14
Enskede Sweden 59°17N 18°4E 139 B2
Ensley U.S.A. 30°31N 87°16W 317 g3
Entebbe Uganda 0°4N 32°28E 268 B3
Enterprise N.W.T.,
  Canada 60°47N 115°45W 296 A5
Enterprise Ala., U.S.A. 31°19N 85°51W 316 F4
Enterprise Nev., U.S.A. 36°1N 115°14W 124 B1
Enterprise Oreg., U.S.A. 45°25N 117°17W 304 D5
Entiako △ Canada 53°15N 125°26W 296 C3
Entorno de Doñana =
  Spain 37°0N 6°26W 195 D2
Entrance, The Australia 33°21S 151°30E 283 B9
Entraygues-sur-Truyère
  France 44°38N 2°35E 174 D6
Entre-Deux Réunion 21°14S 55°28E 272 f
Entre Rios = Rio Brilhante
  Brazil 21°48S 54°33W 335 A5
Entre Rios □ Argentina 30°30S 58°30W 334 C4
Entre Rios Bahia, Brazil 11°56S 38°5W 333 D11
Entre Rios Pará, Brazil 5°24S 54°31W 331 B7
Entre Rios □ Argentina 30°30S 58°30W 334 C4
Entrepeñas, Embalse de
  Spain 40°34N 2°42W 196 E2
Entrevias Spain 40°22N 3°40W 127 B1
Entroncamento Portugal 39°28N 8°28W 195 C2
Enugu Nigeria 6°30N 7°30E 263 D6
Enugu □ Nigeria 6°20N 7°30E 263 D6
Enugu Ezike Nigeria 7°0N 7°29E 263 C6
Enumclaw U.S.A. 47°12N 121°59W 306 C5
Envalira, Port d' Europe 42°33N 1°43E 196 C6
Envermeu France 49°53N 1°15E 172 C8
Envigado Colombia 6°10N 75°35W 328 B3
Enviken Sweden 60°49N 15°46E 162 D9
Envira Brazil 7°20S 70°15W 330 B3
Envira → Brazil 7°30S 70°30W 330 B3
Enyamba Hungary 46°56N 18°15E 182 D3
Enyonga Gabon 0°59S 9°22E 264 C1
Enza → Italy 20°53N 116°30E 278 D2
Enzan = Kōshū Japan 35°42N 138°44E 223 B9
Eochaill = Youghal Ireland 51°56N 7°52W 166 E4
Éolie, Ís. Italy 38°30N 14°57E 201 D7
Eot I. Micronesia 7°23N 151°44E 287 T13
Epanomi Greece 40°25N 22°59E 202 F6
Epcot U.S.A. 28°21N 81°33E 317 G8
Epe Neths. 52°21N 5°59E 170 B5
Epe Nigeria 6°36N 3°59E 263 D5
Epéna Congo 1°26N 17°29E 264 B3
Épernay France 49°3N 3°56E 172 C10
Épernon France 48°35N 1°40E 172 D8
Ephesus Turkey 37°55N 27°22E 205 E9
Ephraim U.S.A. 39°22N 111°35W 304 G8
Ephrata Pa., U.S.A. 40°11N 76°11W 313 F8
Ephrata Wash., U.S.A. 47°19N 119°33W 304 C4
Epi Vanuatu 16°43S 168°15E 287 F6

Ermones Greece 39°37N 19°46E 206 B9
Ermoupoli Greece 37°28N 24°57E 204 D6
Ernakulam India 9°59N 76°22E 245 K3
Erne → Ireland 54°30N 8°16W 166 B2
Erne, Lower L. U.K. 54°28N 7°47W 166 B4
Erne, Upper L. U.K. 54°14N 7°32W 166 B4
Ernée France 48°18N 0°56W 172 D6
Ernest Giles Ra. Australia 27°0S 123°45E 279 E3
Ernest N. Morial Convention Center
  New Orleans, U.S.A. 131 c3
Ernstberg Germany 50°13N 6°47E 179 E2
Erode India 11°24N 77°45E 245 J3
Eromanga Australia 26°40S 143°11E 281 D3
Erongo Namibia 21°39S 15°58E 270 B2
Erongo □ Namibia 22°20S 15°0E 270 B2
Erquy France 48°38N 2°29W 172 D4
Erramala Hills India 15°30N 78°15E 245 G4
Errer → Ethiopia 9°32N 42°35E 257 F5
Errigal Ireland 55°2N 8°6W 166 A3
Errinundra △ Australia 37°24N 148°47E 283 D8
Erris Hd. Ireland 54°17N 10°0W 166 B1
Erromango Vanuatu 18°45S 169°5E 287 H7
Ersekë Albania 40°22N 20°40E 202 F4
Érsekújvár = Nové Zámky
  Slovakia 48°2N 18°8E 181 C11
Er Hai China 23°6N 113°18E 121 B2
Er Rachidia Morocco 31°58N 4°20W 260 B4
Er Rahad Sudan 12°45N 30°32E 257 E3
Er Rif Morocco 35°1N 4°1W 261 A4
Er Roseires Sudan 11°55N 34°30E 257 E3
Er Rua'at Sudan 12°21N 32°17E 257 E3
Eraclea Italy 45°35N 12°40E 199 C9
Eran Phil. 9°4N 117°42E 233 G1
Eran B. Phil. 9°5N 117°43E 233 G1
Erandol India 20°56N 75°20E 244 D2
Eranga
  Dem. Rep. of the Congo 1°52S 18°56E 264 C3
Erap Papua N. G. 6°37S 146°51E 286 D4
Eravadi Myit = Ayeyawady →
  Burma 15°50N 95°6E 241 G5
Erāwadi Myit = Irrawaddy,
  Mouths of the Burma 15°30N 95°0E 241 H5
Erawan △ Thailand 45°48N 9°15E 198 C6
Erba Italy 19°5N 36°51E 256 C4
Erba, J. Sudan 20°48N 36°47E 256 C4
Erbaa Turkey 40°42N 36°36E 212 B7
Erbeng Shan China 42°55N 84°59E 217 D10
Erbeskopf Germany 49°44N 7°2E 179 E3
Erbia Ethiopia 6°44N 34°53E 257 E3
Ercan, Nicosia ✈ (ECN)
  Cyprus 35°10N 33°30E 207 E9
Erçek Turkey 38°39N 43°36E 246 B4
Erciş Turkey 39°2N 43°21E 213 C10
Erciyaş Dağı Turkey 38°30N 35°30E 246 B2
Érd Hungary 47°22N 18°56E 182 C3
Erdao Jiang → China 42°37N 128°0E 224 A3
Erdek Turkey 40°23N 27°47E 203 F11
Erdély = Transilvania
  Romania 46°30N 24°0E 183 B9
Erdemli Turkey 36°36N 34°19E 250 B5
Erdene = Ulaan-Uul
  Mongolia 46°4N 100°49E 218 B9
Erdenet Mongolia 49°2N 104°5E 218 B9
Erdenetsogt Mongolia 42°55N 106°5E 226 C4
Erding Germany 48°18N 11°54E 179 G7
Erdre → France 47°13N 1°32W 172 E5
Erebato → Venezuela 5°54N 64°16W 329 B5
Erebus, Mt. Antarctica 77°35S 167°0E 151 D11
Erechim Brazil 27°35S 52°15W 335 B5
Ereğli Konya, Turkey 37°31N 34°4E 212 D6
Ereğli Zonguldak, Turkey 41°15N 31°24E 212 B4
Erei, Monti Italy 37°20N 14°20E 201 F7
Ereikoussa Greece 39°53N 19°34E 206 A9
Erenhot China 43°48N 112°2E 226 C7
Erd → Germany 50°37N 8°0E 179 E4
Eresma → Spain 41°26N 4°45W 196 D3
Eresos Greece 39°11N 25°57E 205 B7
Ereymentaū Kazakhstan 51°37N 73°6E 217 D8
Erfelek Turkey 41°53N 34°55E 212 B6
Erfenisdam S. Africa 28°30S 26°50E 270 C4
Erfjord Norway 59°30N 6°23E 164 E2
Erftstadt Germany 50°48N 6°46E 178 E2
Erfurt Germany 50°58N 11°2E 178 E6
Ergani Turkey 38°17N 39°49E 213 C8
Ergel Mongolia 43°8N 109°5E 226 C5
Ergene → Turkey 41°1N 26°22E 203 F10
Ergeni Vozvyshennost
  Russia 47°0N 44°0E 191 G7
Ergli Latvia 56°54N 25°38E 158 H5
Ergun He = Argun →
  Russia 53°20N 121°28E 219 A13
Ergun Youqi China 50°15N 120°11E 219 A13
Ergun Zuoqi China 50°47N 121°23E 219 A13
Erhlin Taiwan 23°54N 120°22E 225 C2
Erhlung Taiwan 23°45N 120°37E 225 C2
Eria → Spain 42°3N 5°44W 194 C5
Eriba Sudan 16°40N 36°10E 257 D4
Eric L. U.K. 58°30N 4°42W 167 C4
Erica, U.K. 58°31N 4°42W 167 C4
Erickson Canada 50°52N 99°55W 297 C9
Eridu Iraq 31°10N 45°59E 246 D5
Erie U.S.A. 40°15N 105°4W 308 E1
Erie Mich., U.S.A. 41°47N 83°31W 311 C13
Erie Pa., U.S.A. 42°8N 80°5W 312 D4
Erie, L. N. Amer. 42°15N 81°0W 312 D4
Erie Canal U.S.A. 43°5N 78°43W 312 D7
Erieau Canada 42°16N 81°57W 312 D3
Erigavo = Ceerigaabo
  Somalia 10°35N 47°20E 257 E5
Erikoussa Greece 39°53N 19°34E 206 B9
Eriksdale Canada 50°52N 98°6W 297 C9
Erimanthos Greece 37°57N 21°50E 204 D3
Erimo-Misaki Japan 41°50N 143°15E 220 D11
Erin Trin. & Tob. 10°3N 61°39W 323 d
Erin Pt. Trin. & Tob. 10°4N 61°43W 323 d
Erinpura India 25°9N 73°3E 242 G5
Eriskay U.K. 57°4N 7°18W 167 D1
Erith U.K. 51°29N 0°10E 125 B4
Erithres Greece 38°13N 23°20E 204 C5
Eritrea ■ Africa 14°0N 38°30E 257 D3
Erjas → Portugal 39°40N 7°1W 194 C3
Erkech-Tam Pass Asia 39°40N 73°58E 217 F8
Erkelenz Germany 51°4N 6°19E 178 D2
Erkner Germany 52°26N 13°45E 178 C9
Erlangen Germany 49°36N 11°0E 179 F6
Erlanger U.S.A. 39°1N 84°36W 311 F12
Erldunda Australia 25°14S 133°12E 280 D1
Ermelo Neths. 52°18N 5°35E 170 B5
Ermelo S. Africa 26°31S 29°59E 271 C5
Ermenek Turkey 36°38N 33°0E 212 D5
Ermenek → Turkey 36°38N 33°0E 250 B4
Ermil Sudan 13°33N 27°44E 257 E2
Ermióni Greece 37°23N 23°15E 204 D5
Ermoúpolis Greece 37°28N 24°57E 204 D6

Espada, Pta. *Colombia* 12°5N 71°7W **328** A3
Espalion *France* 44°32N 2°47E **174** D6
España = Spain ■ *Europe* 39°0N 4°0W **192** D3
Espanola *Ont., Canada* 46°15N 81°46W **298** C3
Espanola *N. Mex., U.S.A.* 35°59N 106°5W **305** J10
Española, I. *Ecuador* 1°23S 89°39W **330** a
Espanya, Plaça d' *Barcelona, Spain* **114** c1
Esparreguera *Spain* 41°33N 1°52E **196** D6
Esparza *Costa Rica* 9°59N 84°40W **320** E3
Espeland *Norway* 60°23N 5°28E **164** D2
Espelkamp *Germany* 52°24N 8°36E **178** C4
Espenberg, C. *U.S.A.* 66°33N 163°36W **303** C7
Esperança *Amazonas, Brazil* 4°24S 69°52W **328** D4
Esperança *Paraíba, Brazil* 7°1S 35°51W **332** C4
Esperance *Australia* 33°45S 121°55E **279** F3
Esperance, C. *Solomon Is.* 9°15S 159°43E **287** M10
Esperance B. *Australia* 33°48S 121°55E **279** F3
Esperantinópolis *Brazil* 4°53S 44°53W **332** B3
Esperanza *Antarctica* 65°0S 55°0W **151** C18
Esperanza *Santa Cruz, Argentina* 51°1S 70°49W **336** D2
Esperanza *Santa Fe, Argentina* 31°29S 61°3W **334** C3
Esperanza *Mexico City, Mexico* **128** c3
Esperanza *Agusan del S., Phil.* 8°43N 125°36E **233** G5
Esperanza *Masbate, Phil.* 11°45N 124°3E **233** F5
Esperanza *Puerto Rico* 18°6N 65°28W **321** b
Espéraza *France* 42°56N 2°14E **174** F6
Espevær *Norway* 59°35N 5°7E **164** E2
Espichel, C. *Portugal* 38°22N 9°16W **195** G1
Espiel *Spain* 38°11N 5°1W **195** G5
Espigão, Serra do *Brazil* 26°35S 50°30W **335** B5
Espinal *Colombia* 4°9N 74°53W **328** C3
Espinar *Peru* 14°51S 71°24W **330** C3
Espinazo, Sierra del = Espinhaço, Serra do *Brazil* 17°30S 43°30W **333** E3
Espinhaço, Serra do *Brazil* 17°30S 43°30W **333** E3
Espinho *Portugal* 41°1N 8°38W **194** D2
Espinilho, Serra do *Brazil* 28°30S 55°0W **335** B5
Espinosa de los Monteros *Spain* 43°5N 3°34W **194** B7
Espírito Santo □ *Brazil* 20°0S 40°45W **333** F3
Espírito Santo do Pinhal *Brazil* 22°10S 46°46W **335** A6
Espíritu Santo *Vanuatu* 15°15S 166°50E **287** E4
Espíritu Santo, B. del *Mexico* 19°20N 87°35W **319** D7
Espíritu Santo, I. *Mexico* 24°30N 110°22W **318** C2
Espita *Mexico* 21°1N 88°19W **319** C7
Espiye *Turkey* 40°56N 38°43E **213** B8
Esplanada *Brazil* 11°47S 37°57W **333** D4
Esplanade *Singapore* **138** c3
Esplugas *Spain* 41°22N 2°5E **114** A1
Espoo *Finland* 60°12N 24°40E **188** B3
Esposizione Universale di Roma *Italy* 41°49N 12°28E **136** C1
Espuña, Sierra de *Spain* 37°51N 1°35W **197** H3
Espungabera *Mozam.* 20°29S 32°45E **271** B5
Esquel *Argentina* 42°55S 71°20W **336** B2
Esquimalt *Canada* 48°26N 123°25W **306** B3
Esquina *Argentina* 30°0S 59°30W **334** C4
Essandsjøen *Norway* 63°0N 12°0E **164** A8
Essaouira *Morocco* 31°32N 9°42W **260** B3
Essen *Belgium* 51°28N 4°28E **170** C4
Essen *Nordrhein-Westfalen, Germany* 51°28N 7°2E **178** D3
Essendon *Australia* 37°44S 144°55E **128** A1
Essendon ✈ (MEB) *Australia* 37°43S 144°54E **128** A1
Essendon, Mt. *Australia* 25°0S 120°29E **279** E3
Essequibo → *Guyana* 6°50N 58°30W **329** B6
Essequibo Islands-West Demerara □ *Guyana* 6°33N 58°29W **329** B6
Essex *Ont., Canada* 42°10N 82°49W **312** D2
Essex *Calif., U.S.A.* 34°44N 115°15W **307** L11
Essex *N.Y., U.S.A.* 44°19N 73°21W **313** B11
Essex □ *U.K.* 51°54N 0°27E **169** F8
Essex Junction *U.S.A.* 44°29N 73°7W **313** B11
Essingen *Sweden* 59°19N 17°59E **139** B1
Essling *Austria* 48°12N 16°30E **142** A3
Esslingen *Germany* 48°44N 9°18E **179** G5
Essonne □ *France* 48°30N 2°20E **173** D9
Est, Gare de l' *Paris, France* **134** a5
Estaca de Bares, C. de *Spain* 43°46N 7°42W **194** B3
Estación Camacho *Mexico* 24°25N 102°18W **318** C4
Estación Simón *Mexico* 24°42N 102°35W **318** C4
Estadilla *Spain* 42°4N 0°16E **196** C5
Estado, Parque do *Brazil* 23°38S 46°38W **137** B2
Estados, I. de Los *Argentina* 54°40S 64°30W **336** D4
Estagel *France* 42°47N 2°40E **174** F6
Estagno Pt. *Phil.* 17°20N 122°24E **232** C4
Eşţahbānāt *Iran* 29°8N 54°4E **247** D7
Estância *Brazil* 11°16S 37°26W **332** D4
Estancia *N. Mex., U.S.A.* 34°46N 106°4W **305** J10
Estancia Monte León *Argentina* 50°14S 68°55W **336** D3
Estārm *Iran* 28°21N 58°21E **247** D8
Estarreja *Portugal* 40°45N 8°35W **194** E2
Estats, Pic d' *Spain* 42°40N 1°24E **196** C6
Estcourt *S. Africa* 29°0S 29°53E **271** C4
Este *Italy* 45°14N 11°39E **199** C8
Este △ *Dom. Rep.* 18°14N 68°42W **321** C6
Estefânia *Lisbon, Portugal* **126** a2
Estelí *Nic.* 13°9N 86°22W **320** D2
Estella *Spain* 42°40N 2°2W **196** C2
Estelle *U.S.A.* 29°50N 90°6W **131** B2
Estellencs *Spain* 39°39N 2°29E **206** B3
Estena → *Spain* 39°23N 4°44W **195** F6
Estepa *Spain* 37°17N 4°52W **195** H6
Estepona *Spain* 36°24N 5°7W **195** J5
Esterhazy *Canada* 50°37N 102°5W **297** C8
Esterias, C. *Gabon* 0°40N 9°20E **264** B1
Esternay *France* 48°44N 3°33E **173** D10
Esterri d'Aneu *Spain* 42°38N 1°5E **196** C6
Estevan *Canada* 49°10N 102°59W **297** D8
Estevan Group *Canada* 53°3N 129°38W **296** C3
Estherville *U.S.A.* 43°24N 94°50W **308** D6
Estill *U.S.A.* 32°45N 81°15W **316** C8
Estissac *France* 48°16N 3°48E **173** D10
Eston *Canada* 51°8N 108°40W **297** C7
Estonia ■ *Europe* 58°30N 25°30E **188** C3
Estoril *Portugal* 38°42N 9°23W **195** G1
Estouk *Mali* 18°14N 1°2E **263** B5
Estreito *Brazil* 6°34S 47°27W **332** C2
Estrela, Basílica da *Portugal* 38°42N 9°9W **126** A2
Estrela, Serra da *Portugal* 40°10N 7°45W **194** E3
Estrella *Spain* 38°25N 3°35W **195** G7
Estremoz *Portugal* 38°51N 7°39W **195** G3
Estrondo, Serra do *Brazil* 7°20S 48°0W **332** C2
Estuaire □ *Gabon* 0°30N 9°30E **264** B1
Esutoru = Uglegorsk *Russia* 49°5N 142°2E **215** E15
Esztergom *Hungary* 47°47N 18°44E **182** C3
Et Tîdra *Mauritania* 19°45N 16°20W **262** B1
Etah *India* 27°35N 78°40E **243** F8
Étain *France* 49°13N 5°38E **173** C12
Étampes *France* 48°26N 2°10E **173** D9
Étang-Salé-les-Bains *Réunion* 21°15S 55°20E **272** f
Etanga *Namibia* 17°55S 13°0E **270** A1
Étaples *France* 50°30N 1°39E **173** B8
Etawah *India* 26°48N 79°6E **243** F8
Etawney L. *Canada* 57°50N 96°50W **297** B9
Etchojoa *Mexico* 26°55N 109°38W **318** B3
Ete *Nigeria* 7°2N 7°28E **263** D6
Etéké *Gabon* 1°29S 11°35E **264** C2
Etelä-Konneveden △ *Finland* 62°34N 26°39E **160** E22
eThekwini = Durban *S. Africa* 29°49S 31°1E **271** C5
Ethel *U.S.A.* 46°32N 122°46W **306** D4
Ethelbert *Canada* 51°32N 100°25W **297** C8
Ethiopia ■ *Africa* 8°0N 40°0E **267** C4
Ethiopian Highlands *Ethiopia* 10°0N 37°0E **254** E7
Etili *Turkey* 39°59N 26°54E **203** G10
Etive, L. *U.K.* 56°29N 5°10W **167** E3
Etna *Italy* 37°50N 14°55E **201** E7
Etna → *Norway* 60°49N 10°7E **164** C6
Etne *Norway* 59°40N 5°58E **164** E2
Etobicoke *Canada* 43°39N 79°34W **141** B1
Etobicoke Cr. → *Canada* 43°35N 79°32W **141** B1
Etoile *Dem. Rep. of the Congo* 11°33S 27°30E **269** E2
Etoliko *Greece* 38°26N 21°21E **204** C3
Etolin Strait *U.S.A.* 60°20N 165°15W **303** F6
Etoloakarnania *Greece* 38°45N 21°18E **204** C3
Etosha △ *Namibia* 19°0S 16°0E **270** A2
Etosha Pan *Namibia* 18°40S 16°30E **270** A2
Etoumbi *Congo* 0°1S 14°57E **264** C2
Etowah *U.S.A.* 35°20N 84°32W **315** D12
Étréchy *France* 48°30N 2°12E **173** D9
Etrek *Turkmenistan* 37°36N 54°46E **247** B7
Étrépagny *France* 49°18N 1°36E **173** C8
Étretat *France* 49°42N 0°12E **172** C7
Etropole *Bulgaria* 42°50N 24°0E **203** D8
Ettelbruck *Lux.* 49°51N 6°5E **170** E6
Etterbeek *Belgium* 50°50N 4°23E **116** B2
Ettlingen *Germany* 48°56N 8°25E **179** G4
Ettrick Water → *U.K.* 55°31N 2°55W **167** F6
Etuku *Dem. Rep. of the Congo* 3°42S 25°45E **264** C5
Etulia *Moldova* 45°32N 28°27E **183** E13
Etzná-Tixmucuy = Edzná *Mexico* 19°39N 90°19W **319** D6
Eu *France* 50°3N 1°26E **172** B8
Eua *Tonga* 21°22S 174°56W **287** Q13
Euboea = Evia *Greece* 38°30N 24°0E **204** C6
Eucaliptus = Tomás Barrón *Bolivia* 17°35S 67°31W **330** D4
Euchareena *Australia* 32°57S 149°6E **283** B8
Eucla *Australia* 31°41S 128°52E **279** F4
Euclid *U.S.A.* 41°34N 81°32W **312** E3
Euclides da Cunha *Brazil* 10°31S 39°1W **332** D4
Eucumbene, L. *Australia* 36°2S 148°40E **283** D8
Eudora *U.S.A.* 33°7N 91°16W **314** E9
Eudunda *Australia* 34°12S 139°7E **282** C3
Eufaula *Ala., U.S.A.* 31°54N 85°9W **316** D4
Eufaula *Okla., U.S.A.* 35°17N 95°35W **314** D7
Eufaula L. *U.S.A.* 35°18N 95°21W **314** D7
Eugene *U.S.A.* 44°5N 123°4W **304** D2
Eugowra *Australia* 33°22S 148°24E **283** B8
Euless *U.S.A.* 32°50N 97°4W **120** A3
Eulo *Australia* 28°10S 145°3E **281** D4
Eulonia *U.S.A.* 31°32N 81°26W **316** D8
Eumungerie *Australia* 31°56S 148°36E **283** A8
Eung-am *S. Korea* 37°34N 126°55E **137** B1
Eungella △ *Australia* 20°57S 148°40E **280** b
Eunice *La., U.S.A.* 30°30N 92°25W **314** F8
Eunice *N. Mex., U.S.A.* 32°26N 103°10W **305** K12
Eunpyeong *S. Korea* 37°36N 126°56E **137** B1
Eupen *Belgium* 50°37N 6°3E **170** D6
Euphrates = Furāt, Nahr al → *Asia* 31°0N 47°25E **246** D5
Eure □ *France* 49°10N 1°0E **172** C8
Eure → *France* 49°18N 1°12E **172** C8
Eure-et-Loir □ *France* 48°22N 1°30E **172** D8
Eureka *Nunavut, Canada* 80°0N 85°56W **295** B14
Eureka *Calif., U.S.A.* 40°47N 124°9W **304** F1
Eureka *Ill., U.S.A.* 40°43N 89°16W **310** D7
Eureka *Kans., U.S.A.* 37°49N 96°17W **308** G5
Eureka *Mo., U.S.A.* 38°30N 90°38W **310** F6
Eureka *Mont., U.S.A.* 48°53N 115°3W **304** B6
Eureka *Nev., U.S.A.* 39°31N 115°58W **304** G6
Eureka *S.C., U.S.A.* 33°42N 81°46W **316** B8
Eureka *S. Dak., U.S.A.* 45°46N 99°38W **308** C4
Eureka, Mt. *Australia* 26°35S 121°35E **279** E3
Eureka Sd. *Canada* 79°0N 85°0W **295** B15
Eurelia *Australia* 32°33S 138°35E **282** B3
Eurinilla Cr. → *Australia* 30°53S 140°11E **282** A4
Euroa *Australia* 36°44S 145°35E **283** D6
Euroairport, Basle ✈ (EAP) *France* 47°36N 7°33E **173** E14
Europa, Île *Ind. Oc.* 22°20S 40°22E **271** B7
Europa, Picos de *Spain* 43°10N 4°49W **194** B6
Europa, Pt. *Gib.* 36°3N 5°21W **195** J5
Europe 50°0N 20°0E **158** E10
Europoort *Neths.* 51°57N 4°10E **170** C4
Euskadi = País Vasco □ *Spain* 42°50N 2°45W **196** C2
Euskirchen *Germany* 50°39N 6°48E **178** E2
Eustis *U.S.A.* 28°51N 81°41W **317** G8
Euston *N.S.W., Australia* 34°30S 142°46E **282** C5
Euston *London, U.K.* **125** a3
Eutawville *U.S.A.* 33°24N 80°21W **316** B9
Eutin *Germany* 54°8N 10°36E **178** A6
Eutsuk L. *Canada* 53°20N 126°45W **296** C3
Eva Perón = La Pampa □ *Argentina* 36°50S 66°0W **334** D2
Eva Perón = La Plata *Argentina* 35°0S 57°55W **334** D4
Evale *Angola* 16°33S 15°44E **265** F3
Evanger *Norway* 60°39N 6°7E **164** D3
Evanlı *Turkey* 36°46N 34°26E **250** B5
Evans *U.S.A.* 40°23N 104°41W **304** F11
Evans, L. *Canada* 50°50N 77°0W **298** B4
Evans City *U.S.A.* 40°46N 80°4W **312** F4
Evans Head *Australia* 29°7S 153°27E **281** D5
Evansburg *Canada* 53°36N 114°59W **296** C5
Evansdale *U.S.A.* 42°30N 92°17W **310** B4
Evanston *Ill., U.S.A.* 42°3N 87°40W **119** A2
Evanston *Wyo., U.S.A.* 41°16N 110°58W **304** F8
Evansville *Ill., U.S.A.* 38°5N 89°56W **310** F7
Evansville *Ind., U.S.A.* 37°58N 87°35W **310** G8
Evansville *Wis., U.S.A.* 42°47N 89°18W **310** B7
Évaux-les-Bains *France* 46°12N 2°29E **173** F9
Evaz *Iran* 27°46N 53°59E **247** E7
Evciler *Afyon, Turkey* 38°4N 29°54E **205** C11
Evciler *Çanakkale, Turkey* 39°47N 26°44E **205** B8
Eveleth *U.S.A.* 47°28N 92°32W **308** B7
Even Sapir *Israel* 31°46N 35°8E **123** B1
Evensk *Russia* 62°12N 159°30E **215** C16
Evenstad *Norway* 61°25N 11°7E **164** C8
Everard, L. *Australia* 31°30S 135°0E **281** E2
Everard Ranges *Australia* 27°5S 132°28E **279** E5
Evere *Belgium* 50°52N 4°25E **116** A2
Everest, Mt. *Nepal* 28°5N 86°58E **243** E12
Everett *Ga., U.S.A.* 31°24N 81°38W **316** D8
Everett *Mass., U.S.A.* 42°24N 71°3W **116** A2
Everett *Pa., U.S.A.* 40°1N 78°23W **312** F6
Everett *Wash., U.S.A.* 47°59N 122°12W **306** C4
Everglades, The *U.S.A.* 25°50N 81°0W **317** K9
Everglades △ *U.S.A.* 25°30N 81°0W **317** K9
Everglades City *U.S.A.* 25°52N 81°23W **317** K8
Evergreen *Ala., U.S.A.* 31°26N 86°57W **315** F11
Evergreen *Mont., U.S.A.* 48°14N 114°17W **304** B6
Evergreen Park *U.S.A.* 41°43N 87°42W **119** C2
Everman *U.S.A.* 32°37N 97°17W **120** C2
Everöd *Sweden* 55°53N 14°5E **163** J8
Everton *Australia* 36°25S 146°33E **283** D7
Evertsberg *Sweden* 61°8N 13°58E **162** C7
Evesham *U.K.* 52°6N 1°56W **169** E6
Évia *Greece* 38°30N 24°0E **204** C6
Évian-les-Bains *France* 46°24N 6°35E **173** F13
Evin *Iran* 35°47N 51°23E **141** A2
Evinayong *Eq. Guin.* 1°26N 10°35E **264** B2
Evinos → *Greece* 38°27N 21°40E **204** C3
Évisa *France* 42°15N 8°48E **175** F12
Evje *Norway* 58°36N 7°51E **164** F4
Évora *Portugal* 38°33N 7°57W **195** G3
Évora □ *Portugal* 38°33N 7°50W **195** G3
Evowghlī *Iran* 38°43N 45°13E **213** C11
Évreux *France* 49°3N 1°8E **172** C8
Evritania *Greece* 39°5N 21°30E **204** B3
Évron *France* 48°10N 0°24W **172** D6
Evros → *Greece* 41°40N 26°34E **203** F10
Evrotas → *Greece* 36°50N 22°40E **204** E4
Évry *France* 48°38N 2°27E **173** D9
Évvoia = Evia *Greece* 38°30N 24°0E **204** C6
'Ewa Beach *U.S.A.* 21°19N 158°1W **302** K13
'Ewa District *U.S.A.* 21°25N 158°0W **302** K14
'Ewa Villages *U.S.A.* 21°20N 158°3W **302** K13
Ewarton *Jamaica* 18°11N 77°6W **320** a
Ewasse *Papua N. G.* 5°19S 151°1E **286** C6
Ewe, L. *U.K.* 57°49N 5°38W **167** D3
Ewing *Mo., U.S.A.* 40°6N 91°43W **310** E5
Ewing *Nebr., U.S.A.* 42°16N 98°21W **308** D4
Ewo *Congo* 0°48S 14°45E **264** C2
Ewu *Nigeria* 6°33N 3°19E **124** A1
Exaltación *Bolivia* 13°10S 65°20W **331** C4
Excelsior Springs *U.S.A.* 39°20N 94°13W **310** E2
Excideuil *France* 45°20N 1°4E **174** C5
Exe → *U.K.* 50°41N 3°29W **169** G4
Exeter *Ont., Canada* 43°21N 81°29W **312** C3
Exeter *Devon, U.K.* 50°43N 3°31W **169** G4
Exeter *Calif., U.S.A.* 36°18N 119°9W **306** J7
Exeter *N.H., U.S.A.* 42°59N 70°57W **313** D14
Exhibition Place *Canada* 43°38N 79°25W **141** B2
Exira *U.S.A.* 41°35N 94°52W **310** C2
Exmoor *U.K.* 51°12N 3°45W **169** F4
Exmoor △ *U.K.* 51°8N 3°42W **169** F4
Exmouth *W. Austral., Australia* 21°54S 114°10E **278** D1
Exmouth *Devon, U.K.* 50°37N 3°25W **169** G4
Exmouth G. *Australia* 22°15S 114°15E **278** D1
Exmouth Plateau *Ind. Oc.* 19°0S 114°0E **288** J3
Expedition △ *Australia* 25°41S 149°7E **281** D4
Expedition Ra. *Australia* 24°30S 149°12E **280** C4
Experiment = Highland Mills *U.S.A.* 33°17N 84°17W **316** B5
Experimentarium *Denmark* 58°43N 12°35E **118** A3
Expo Centre *Shanghai, China* 31°11N 121°29E **138** B1
Exposições, Palácio das *Brazil* 22°53S 43°13W **135** B1
Extremadura □ *Spain* 39°30N 6°5W **195** F4
Extrême-Nord □ *Cameroon* 11°0N 14°30E **259** F2
Exuma Sound *Bahamas* 24°30N 76°20W **320** B4
Eyak *U.S.A.* 60°32N 145°36W **303** F11
Eyasi, L. *Tanzania* 3°30S 35°0E **268** C4
Eydehavn *Norway* 58°30N 8°53E **164** F5
Eydhafushi *Maldives* 5°7N 73°2E **272** d
Eye Pen. *U.K.* 58°13N 6°10W **167** C2
Eyemouth *U.K.* 55°52N 2°5W **167** F6
Eygues = Aigues → *France* 44°7N 4°43E **175** D8
Eygurande *France* 45°40N 2°26E **173** G9
Eyjafjallajökull *Iceland* 63°38N 19°36W **155** D7
Eyjafjarðarsýsla *Iceland* 65°30N 18°30W **155** B8
Eyjafjörður *Iceland* 66°15N 18°30W **155** A8
Eyl *Somalia* 8°0N 49°50E **267** C6
Eymet *France* 44°40N 0°25E **174** D4
Eymoutiers *France* 45°40N 1°45E **174** C5
Eynesil *Turkey* 41°4N 39°9E **213** B8
Eyrarbakki *Iceland* 63°52N 21°9W **155** D5
Eyre → *France* 44°39N 1°1W **174** D2
Eyre, L. = Kati Thanda-Lake Eyre *Australia* 29°30S 137°26E **276** F6
Eyre Mts. *N.Z.* 45°25S 168°25E **285** F3
Eyre Pen. *Australia* 33°30S 136°17E **282** C1
Eysturoy *Færoe Is.* 62°13N 6°54W **160** E9
Eyüp *Turkey* 41°2N 28°55E **122** B1
Eyvān = Jūy Zar *Iran* 33°50N 46°18E **213** F12
Eyvānkī *Iran* 35°24N 51°56E **247** C6
Ez Zeidab *Sudan* 17°25N 33°55E **256** D3
Ezcaray *Spain* 42°19N 3°0W **196** C1
Ezeiza ✈ (EZE) *Argentina* 34°49S 58°32W **117** C1
Ežerėlis *Lithuania* 54°53N 23°37E **184** D10
Ezhou *China* 30°23N 114°50E **229** B10
Ezhva *Russia* 61°48N 50°35E **186** B9
Ezine *Turkey* 39°48N 26°20E **205** B8
Ezouza → *Cyprus* 34°44N 32°27E **207** F8

F

F.Y.R.O.M. = Macedonia ■ *Europe* 41°53N 21°40E **202** E5
Faaa *Tahiti* 17°34S 149°35W **289** e
Faaborg *Denmark* 55°6N 10°15E **163** J4
Faaone *Tahiti* 17°40S 149°21W **289** e
Fabala *Guinea* 9°44N 9°5W **262** D3
Fabbriche Nuove *Venice, Italy* **142** b2
Fabens *U.S.A.* 31°30N 106°10W **314** F1
Faber, Mt. *Singapore* 1°16N 103°49E **138** B2
Fåberg *Norway* 61°10N 10°25E **164** C7
Fabero *Spain* 42°46N 6°37W **194** C4
Fabius *U.S.A.* 42°50N 75°59W **313** D9
Fabriano *Italy* 43°20N 12°54E **199** E9
Făcăeni *Romania* 44°32N 27°53E **183** F12
Facatativá *Colombia* 4°49N 74°22W **328** C3
Faceville *U.S.A.* 30°45N 84°38W **316** E5
Fachi *Niger* 18°6N 11°34E **259** E2
Facundo *Argentina* 45°18S 69°58W **336** C3
Fada *Chad* 17°13N 21°34E **259** E4
Fada-n-Gourma *Burkina Faso* 12°10N 0°30E **263** C5
Fadd *Hungary* 46°28N 18°49E **182** D3
Faddeyevskiy, Ostrov *Russia* 76°0N 144°0E **215** B15
Faddor *South Sudan* 8°7N 32°17E **257** F3
Fadghāmī *Syria* 35°53N 40°52E **213** E9
Fadiffolu Atoll *Maldives* 5°23N 73°29E **272** d
Fadlab *Sudan* 17°42N 34°2E **256** D3
Fadwel *South Sudan* 8°11N 29°20E **266** C2
Fælledparken *Denmark* 55°42N 12°34E **118** A3
Faenza *Italy* 44°17N 11°53E **199** D8
Færingehavn = Kangerluarsoruseq *Greenland* 63°45N 51°27W **154** E5
Færoe Is. = Føroyar ⊠ *Atl. Oc.* 62°0N 7°0W **160** F9
Fafa *Mali* 15°22N 0°48E **263** B5
Fafe *Portugal* 41°27N 8°11W **194** D2
Fafen → *Ethiopia* 5°59N 44°25E **267** C5
Fagam *Nigeria* 11°1N 10°1E **263** C7
Fagamalo *Amer. Samoa* 14°18S 170°48W **302** f
Făgăraş *Romania* 45°48N 24°58E **183** E9
Făgăraş, Munţii *Romania* 45°40N 24°40E **183** E9
Fagasa *Amer. Samoa* 14°17S 170°43W **302** f
Fagatele Bay △ *Amer. Samoa* 14°22S 170°46W **302** f
Fagatogo *Amer. Samoa* 14°16S 170°41W **302** f
Fågelfors *Sweden* 57°12N 15°51E **163** H9
Fågelmara *Sweden* 56°16N 15°58E **163** H9
Fågelön *Sweden* 59°18N 17°55E **139** B1
Fagerheim *Norway* 60°26N 7°46E **164** D4
Fagerhult *Sweden* 57°8N 15°40E **163** G9
Fagernes *Norway* 60°59N 9°14E **164** D6
Fagersjö *Sweden* 59°14N 18°4E **139** B2
Fagersta *Sweden* 60°1N 15°46E **162** D9
Făget *Romania* 45°52N 22°10E **182** E7
Făget, Munţii *Romania* 47°40N 23°10E **183** C8
Faggo *Nigeria* 11°21N 9°57E **263** C6
Faghmah *Yemen* 16°9N 49°26E **249** C5
Fagnano, L. *Argentina* 54°30S 68°0W **336** D3
Fagnières *France* 48°58N 4°20E **173** D11
Faguibine, L. *Mali* 16°45N 4°0W **262** B4
Fahlīān *Iran* 30°11N 51°28E **247** D6
Fahraj *Kermān, Iran* 29°0N 59°0E **247** D8
Fahraj *Yazd, Iran* 31°46N 54°36E **247** D7
Fai Tsi Long *Vietnam* 21°0N 107°30E **228** G6
Faial *Azores* 38°34N 28°42W **153** d1
Faial *Madeira* 32°47N 16°53W **153** c
Faial, Canal do *Azores* 38°33N 28°35W **153** d1
Faichan Kangri *India* 35°48N 76°34E **243** B7
Faichuk *Micronesia* 7°21N 151°38E **287** T17
Fair Haven *N.Y., U.S.A.* 43°18N 76°42W **313** C8
Fair Haven *Vt., U.S.A.* 43°36N 73°16W **313** C11
Fair Hd. *U.K.* 55°14N 6°9W **166** A5
Fair Isle *U.K.* 59°32N 1°38W **165** B6
Fair Oaks *U.S.A.* 38°39N 121°16W **306** G5
Fairbank *U.S.A.* 42°38N 92°3W **310** B4
Fairbanks *Alaska, U.S.A.* 64°51N 147°43W **303** D11
Fairbanks *Fla., U.S.A.* 29°44N 82°16W **316** F7
Fairborn *U.S.A.* 39°49N 84°2W **311** E12
Fairburn *U.S.A.* 33°34N 84°35W **316** B5
Fairbury *Ill., U.S.A.* 40°45N 88°31W **311** D8
Fairbury *Nebr., U.S.A.* 40°8N 97°11W **308** E5
Fairfax *Ohio, U.S.A.* 39°5N 83°37W **311** E13
Fairfax *S.C., U.S.A.* 32°59N 81°15W **316** C8
Fairfax *Vt., U.S.A.* 44°40N 73°1W **313** B11
Fairfield *N.S.W., Australia* 33°53S 150°57E **283** B9
Fairfield *Calif., U.S.A.* 38°15N 122°3W **306** G4
Fairfield *Conn., U.S.A.* 41°9N 73°16W **313** E11
Fairfield *Idaho, U.S.A.* 43°21N 114°44W **304** E6
Fairfield *Ill., U.S.A.* 38°23N 88°22W **311** F8
Fairfield *Iowa, U.S.A.* 40°56N 91°57W **310** D5
Fairfield *Ohio, U.S.A.* 39°20N 84°34W **311** E12
Fairfield *Tex., U.S.A.* 31°44N 96°10W **314** F6
Fairford *Canada* 51°37N 98°38W **297** C9
Fairhope *U.S.A.* 30°31N 87°54W **315** F11
Fairland *S. Africa* 26°8S 27°57E **123** A1
Fairlie *N.Z.* 44°5S 170°49E **285** E5
Fairmead *U.S.A.* 37°5N 120°10W **306** H6
Fairmilehead *U.K.* 55°54N 3°11W **121** B2
Fairmont *Minn., U.S.A.* 43°39N 94°28W **308** D6
Fairmont *W. Va., U.S.A.* 39°29N 80°9W **309** F13
Fairmount *Calif., U.S.A.* 34°45N 118°26W **307** L8
Fairmount *N.Y., U.S.A.* 43°5N 76°12W **313** C8
Fairplay *U.S.A.* 39°15N 106°2W **304** G10
Fairport *Ont., Canada* 43°49N 79°4W **141** A4
Fairport *N.Y., U.S.A.* 43°6N 77°27W **312** C7
Fairport Harbor *U.S.A.* 41°45N 81°17W **312** E3
Fairview *Alta., Canada* 56°5N 118°25W **296** B5
Fairview *Mont., U.S.A.* 47°51N 104°3W **304** C11
Fairview *N.J., U.S.A.* 40°48N 73°59W **132** B2
Fairview *Okla., U.S.A.* 36°16N 98°29W **314** C5
Fairview, L. *U.S.A.* 28°35N 81°24W **133** A2
Fairweather, Mt. *U.S.A.* 58°55N 137°32W **296** B1
Faisalabad *Pakistan* 31°30N 73°5E **242** D5
Faith *U.S.A.* 45°2N 102°2W **308** C2
Faizabad *India* 26°45N 82°10E **243** F10
Faizpur *India* 21°14N 75°49E **244** D2
Fajã Grande *Azores* 39°27N 31°16W **153** d2
Fajardo *Puerto Rico* 18°20N 65°39W **321** d
Fajou, Îlet à *Guadeloupe* 16°21N 61°35W **322** e
Fajr, W. → *Si. Arabia* 29°10N 38°10E **246** D3
Fakaofo *Pac. Oc.* 9°23S 171°15W **277** B16
Fakarava *French Polynesia* 16°20S 145°37W **289** f
Fakenham *U.K.* 52°51N 0°51E **168** E8
Fåker *Sweden* 63°0N 14°34E **162** A8
Fakfak *Indonesia* 2°55S 132°18E **231** E8
Fakiya *Bulgaria* 42°10N 27°6E **203** D11
Fakobli *Ivory C.* 7°23N 7°23W **262** D3
Fakse *Denmark* 55°15N 12°8E **163** J6
Fakse Bugt *Denmark* 55°11N 12°15E **163** J6
Fakse Ladeplads *Denmark* 55°11N 12°9E **163** J6
Faku *China* 42°32N 123°21E **224** A1
Fala Beguets I. *Micronesia* 7°21N 151°41E **287** U17
Falaba *S. Leone* 9°54N 11°22W **262** D2
Falaise *France* 48°54N 0°12W **172** D6
Falakro Oros *Greece* 41°15N 23°58E **202** E7
Falam *Burma* 23°0N 93°45E **241** D4
Falas I. *Micronesia* 7°31N 151°44E **287** T18
Fălciu *Romania* 46°17N 28°7E **183** D13
Falcó, C. des *Spain* 38°50N 1°23E **206** D1
Falcón □ *Venezuela* 11°0N 69°50W **328** A4
Falcon, C. *Algeria* 35°50N 0°50W **261** A4
Falcon, Presa *Mexico* 26°35N 99°10W **319** B5
Falcon Lake *Canada* 49°42N 95°15W **297** D9
Falcon Res. *U.S.A.* 26°34N 99°10W **314** H5
Falconara Marittima *Italy* 43°37N 13°24E **199** E10
Falcone, C. del *Italy* 40°58N 8°12E **200** B1
Falconer *U.S.A.* 42°7N 79°12W **312** D5
Faléa *Mali* 12°16N 11°17W **262** C2
Falefa *Samoa* 13°54S 171°31W **287** V20
Falelatai *Samoa* 13°55S 171°59W **287** V20
Falelima *Samoa* 13°32S 172°41W **287** V19
Falémé → *Senegal* 14°46N 12°14W **262** C2
Faleniu *Amer. Samoa* 14°20S 170°44W **302** f
Falenty *Poland* 52°8N 20°55E **143** C1
Falerum *Sweden* 58°8N 16°13E **163** F10
Faleshty = Făleşti *Moldova* 47°32N 27°44E **183** C12
Făleşti *Moldova* 47°32N 27°44E **183** C12
Falfurrias *U.S.A.* 27°14N 98°9W **314** H5
Falher *Canada* 55°44N 117°15W **296** B5
Faliraki *Greece* 36°22N 28°12E **206** E12
Faliro *Greece* 37°55N 23°39E **112** B1
Faliro, Ormos *Greece* 37°54N 23°40E **112** B2
Falkenberg *Brandenburg, Germany* 51°35N 13°14E **178** D9
Falkenberg *Sweden* 56°54N 12°30E **163** H6
Falkenburg = Niemodlin *Poland* 50°38N 17°38E **185** H4
Falkenburg *Germany* 52°34N 13°32E **115** A4
Falkenhagen *Germany* 52°34N 13°5E **115** A1
Falkensee *Germany* 52°34N 13°4E **115** A1
Falkirk *U.K.* 56°0N 3°47W **167** F5
Falkirk □ *U.K.* 55°58N 3°49W **167** F5
Falkland *U.K.* 56°16N 3°12W **167** E5
Falkland, East, I. *Falk. Is.* 51°40S 58°30W **336** D5
Falkland, West, I. *Falk. Is.* 51°40S 60°0W **336** D5
Falkland Is. ⊠ *Atl. Oc.* 51°30S 59°0W **153** f
Falkland Plateau *Atl. Oc.* 51°0S 50°0W **152** M7
Falkland Ridge *Atl. Oc.* 49°20S 40°0W **152** L8
Falkland Sd. *Falk. Is.* 52°0S 60°0W **153** f
Falknov nad Ohří = Sokolov *Czechia* 50°12N 12°40E **180** A5
Falkonera *Greece* 36°50N 23°52E **204** E5
Falköping *Sweden* 58°12N 13°33E **163** F7
Fall River *U.S.A.* 41°43N 71°10W **313** E13
Fallbrook *U.S.A.* 33°23N 117°15W **307** M9
Fallon *U.S.A.* 39°28N 118°47W **304** G4
Falls City *U.S.A.* 40°3N 95°36W **308** E6
Falls Creek *U.S.A.* 41°9N 78°48W **312** E6
Falmouth *Jamaica* 18°30N 77°40W **320** a
Falmouth *Corn., U.K.* 50°9N 5°5W **169** G2
Falmouth *Ky., U.S.A.* 38°41N 84°20W **311** F12
Falmouth *Mass., U.S.A.* 41°33N 70°37W **313** E14
Falo I. *Micronesia* 7°28N 151°52E **287** T18
Falomo *Nigeria* 6°26N 3°26E **124** B2
Falsa, Pta. *Mexico* 27°51N 115°3W **318** B1
False B. *S. Africa* 34°15S 18°40E **270** D2
False Bay *S. Africa* 34°6S 18°33E **123** B1
False Divi Pt. *India* 15°43N 80°50E **245** G5
False Pass *U.S.A.* 54°51N 163°25W **303** J7
False Pt. *India* 20°18N 86°48E **244** D8
Falso, C. *Honduras* 15°12N 83°21W **320** C3
Falster *Denmark* 54°45N 11°55E **163** K5
Fălticeni *Romania* 47°21N 26°20E **183** C11
Falun *Sweden* 60°37N 15°37E **162** D9
Famagusta *Cyprus* 35°8N 33°55E **207** E9
Famagusta Bay *Cyprus* 35°15N 34°0E **207** D10
Famatina, Sierra de *Argentina* 27°30S 68°0W **334** B2
Famenin *Iran* 35°5N 48°58E **213** E13
Family L. *Canada* 51°54N 95°27W **297** C9
Famões *Portugal* 38°47N 9°13W **126** A1
Famoso *U.S.A.* 35°37N 119°12W **307** K7
Fan Lau *Hong Kong, China* 22°12N 113°51E **122** B1
Fan Xian *China* 35°55N 115°38E **226** G8
Fana *Mali* 13°0N 6°56W **262** C3
Fanad Hd. *Ireland* 55°17N 7°38W **166** A4
Fanahammaren *Norway* 60°16N 5°20E **164** D2
Fanari *Greece* 39°24N 21°47E **204** B3
Fandriana *Madag.* 20°14S 47°21E **272** C2
Fánes-Sénnes-Braies ⌓ *Italy* 46°38N 12°4E **199** B9
Faneuil Hall Marketplace *Boston, U.S.A.* **116** b3
Fang *Thailand* 19°55N 99°13E **236** C2
Fang Xian *China* 32°3N 110°40E **229** A8
Fangaga *Sudan* 17°40N 37°50E **256** D4
Fangak *South Sudan* 9°4N 30°53E **257** F3
Fangatau *French Polynesia* 15°22S 138°45W **289** f
Fangataufa *French Polynesia* 15°50S 140°52W **289** f
Fangchang *China* 31°5N 118°4E **229** B12
Fangcheng *China* 33°18N 112°59E **226** H7
Fangchenggang *China* 21°42N 108°21E **228** G7
Fangcun *China* 23°6N 113°13E **121** B2
Fangliao *Taiwan* 22°22N 120°38E **225** D2
Fangshan *Beijing, China* 39°41N 116°0E **226** E9
Fangshan *Shanxi, China* 38°3N 111°25E **226** E6
Fangshan *Taiwan* 22°15N 120°39E **225** D2
Fangyüan *Taiwan* 23°56N 120°19E **225** C2
Fangzi *China* 36°33N 119°10E **227** F10
Fani i Madh → *Albania* 41°56N 20°16E **202** E4
Fanjakana *Madag.* 21°10S 46°53E **272** C2
Fanjiatun *China* 43°40N 125°15E **227** C13
Fanling *China* 22°30N 114°8E **219** a
Fannich, L. *U.K.* 57°38N 4°59W **167** D4
Fannrem *Norway* 63°16N 9°50E **164** A6
Fannūj *Iran* 26°35N 59°38E **247** E8
Fanø *Denmark* 55°25N 8°25E **163** J2
Fano *Italy* 43°50N 13°1E **199** E10
Fanshi *China* 39°12N 113°20E **226** E7
Fantzuliao Hsi → *Taiwan* 22°42N 120°28E **225** D2
Fanuet I. *Micronesia* 7°32N 151°48E **287** T18
Fao = Al Fāw *Iraq* 30°0N 48°30E **247** D6
Faqirwali *Pakistan* 29°27N 73°0E **242** E5
Fâqûs *Egypt* 30°44N 31°47E **256** H7
Far East = Dalnevostochnyy □ *Russia* 67°0N 140°0E **215** C14
Far East *Asia* 40°0N 130°0E **210** E14
Fara in Sabina *Italy* 42°12N 12°43E **199** F9
Faradje *Dem. Rep. of the Congo* 3°50N 29°45E **268** B2
Farafangana *Madag.* 22°49S 47°50E **272** C2
Farafenni *Gambia* 13°34N 15°36W **262** C1
Farâfra, El Wâhât el *Egypt* 27°15N 28°20E **256** B2
Farāh *Afghan.* 32°20N 62°7E **240** B1
Farāh □ *Afghan.* 32°25N 62°10E **240** B1
Farāh → *Afghan.* 31°27N 61°28E **240** C1
Faraḥābād *Iran* 35°41N 51°30E **141** A2
Farahalana *Madag.* 14°26S 50°10E **272** A3
Faraid, Gebel *Egypt* 23°33N 35°19E **256** C4
Farako *Ivory C.* 10°45N 6°50W **262** D4
Farallon de Medinilla *N. Marianas* 16°1N 146°4E **302** a
Farallon de Pajaros *N. Marianas* 20°32N 144°54E **302** a
Farallones de Cali △ *Colombia* 3°13N 76°46W **328** C2
Faramana *Burkina Faso* 11°56N 4°45W **262** C4
Faranah *Guinea* 10°3N 10°45W **262** C2
Farap *Turkmenistan* 39°10N 63°36E **216** E6
Fararah *Oman* 17°55N 55°38E **249** C6
Farasān, Jazā'ir *Si. Arabia* 16°45N 41°55E **248** C3
Farasan Is. = Farasān, Jazā'ir *Si. Arabia* 16°45N 41°55E **248** C3
Faratsiho *Madag.* 19°24S 46°57E **272** B2
Farbaraki *Somalia* 2°30N 45°30E **267** D6
Fardes → *Spain* 37°35N 3°0W **195** H7
Fareham *U.K.* 50°51N 1°11W **169** G6
Farewell *U.S.A.* 62°31N 153°54W **303** E9
Farewell, C. = Nunap Isua *Greenland* 59°48N 43°55W **154** F6
Farewell, C. *N.Z.* 40°29S 172°43E **285** A7
Farewell Spit *N.Z.* 40°35S 173°0E **285** A8
Farforovskaya *Russia* 59°52N 30°27E **137** B2
Färgelanda *Sweden* 58°34N 12°0E **163** F6
Fargo *Ga., U.S.A.* 30°41N 82°34W **316** E7
Fargo *N. Dak., U.S.A.* 46°53N 96°48W **308** B5
Farg'ona *Uzbekistan* 40°23N 71°19E **217** D8
Farg'ona □ *Uzbekistan* 40°30N 71°15E **217** D8
Farg'ona vodiysi *Asia* 40°46N 71°30E **217** D8
Fār'iah, W. al → *West Bank* 32°12N 35°27E **251** F6
Faribault *U.S.A.* 44°18N 93°16W **308** C7
Faridabad *India* 28°26N 77°19E **242** E6
Faridkot *India* 30°44N 74°45E **242** D6
Faridpur *Bangla.* 23°15N 89°55E **241** D2
Faridpur *India* 28°13N 79°33E **243** E8
Fārigh, W. al → *Libya* 30°28N 20°44E **258** B3
Färila *Sweden* 61°48N 15°50E **162** C9
Farim *Guinea-Biss.* 12°27N 15°9W **262** C1
Farīmān *Iran* 35°40N 59°49E **247** C8
Farinha → *Brazil* 6°51S 47°30W **332** C2
Fariones, Pta. *Canary Is.* 29°13N 13°28W **153** e2
Fâriskûr *Egypt* 31°20N 31°43E **256** H7
Färjestaden *Sweden* 56°39N 16°27E **163** H10
Farkadona *Greece* 39°36N 22°4E **204** B4
Farleigh *Australia* 21°4S 149°8E **280** b
Farley *U.S.A.* 42°27N 91°0W **310** B6
Farmakonisi *Greece* 37°17N 27°5E **205** D9
Farmer City *U.S.A.* 40°15N 88°39W **311** D8
Farmers Branch *U.S.A.* 32°55N 96°53W **120** A4
Farmersburg *U.S.A.* 39°15N 87°23W **311** E9
Farmerville *U.S.A.* 32°47N 92°24W **314** E8
Farmingdale *U.S.A.* 40°12N 74°10W **313** F10
Farmington *B.C., Canada* 55°54N 120°30W **296** B4
Farmington *Calif., U.S.A.* 37°55N 120°59W **306** H6
Farmington *Ga., U.S.A.* 33°47N 83°26W **316** B6
Farmington *Ill., U.S.A.* 40°42N 90°0W **310** D7
Farmington *Iowa, U.S.A.* 40°38N 91°44W **310** D5
Farmington *Maine, U.S.A.* 44°40N 70°9W **309** C18
Farmington *Mo., U.S.A.* 37°47N 90°25W **310** G6
Farmington *N.H., U.S.A.* 43°24N 71°4W **313** C13
Farmington *N. Mex., U.S.A.* 36°44N 108°12W **305** H9
Farmington *Utah, U.S.A.* 40°59N 111°53W **304** F8
Farmington → *U.S.A.* 41°51N 72°38W **313** E12
Farmland *U.S.A.* 40°15N 85°7W **311** D11
Farmville *U.S.A.* 37°18N 78°24W **309** G14
Färnäs *Sweden* 61°0N 14°39E **162** D8
Farne Is. *U.K.* 55°38N 1°37W **168** B6
Färnebofjärden △ *Sweden* 60°10N 16°48E **162** D10
Farnham *Canada* 45°17N 72°59W **313** A12
Farnham, Mt. *Canada* 50°29N 116°30W **296** C5
Farningham *U.K.* 51°23N 0°12E **125** B5
Faro *Brazil* 2°10S 56°39W **329** D6
Faro *Yukon, Canada* 62°11N 133°22W **294** E5
Faro *Portugal* 37°2N 7°55W **195** H3
Fårö *Gotland, Sweden* 57°55N 19°5E **163** G13
Faro □ *Portugal* 37°12N 8°10W **195** H2
Faro ✈ (FAO) *Portugal* 37°2N 7°57W **195** H3
Faro △ *Cameroon* 8°15N 12°37E **264** A2
Fårösund *Sweden* 57°52N 19°2E **163** G13
Farquhar, C. *Australia* 23°50S 113°36E **279** D1
Farquhar Is. *Seychelles* 11°0S 52°0E **273** F4
Farrars Cr. → *Australia* 25°35S 140°43E **280** D3
Farrāshband *Iran* 28°57N 52°5E **247** D7
Farrell *U.S.A.* 41°13N 80°30W **312** E4
Farrell Flat *Australia* 33°48S 138°48E **282** B3
Farrokhī *Iran* 33°50N 59°31E **247** C8
Farruch, C. = Ferrutx, C. de *Spain* 39°47N 3°21E **206** B4
Farrukhabad *India* 27°24N 79°34E **244** A4
Fārs □ *Iran* 29°30N 55°0E **247** D7
Farsala *Greece* 39°17N 22°23E **204** B4
Fārsī *Afghan.* 33°47N 63°15E **240** B1
Fārsī *Iran* 27°58N 50°11E **247** E6
Farsø *Denmark* 56°46N 9°19E **163** H3
Farson *U.S.A.* 42°7N 109°26W **304** E9
Farsta *Sweden* 59°14N 18°5E **139** B2
Farsund *Norway* 58°5N 6°55E **164** F3
Fartak, Râs *Si. Arabia* 28°5N 34°34E **246** D2
Fartak, Ra's *Yemen* 15°38N 52°15E **249** D6
Fârţăneşti *Romania* 45°49N 27°59E **183** E12
Fartura, Serra da *Brazil* 26°21S 52°52W **335** B5
Faru *Nigeria* 12°48N 6°12E **263** C6
Fārūj *Iran* 37°14N 58°14E **247** B8
Fårup *Denmark* 56°33N 9°51E **163** H3
Farvel, Kap = Nunap Isua *Greenland* 59°48N 43°55W **154** F6
Farwell *U.S.A.* 34°23N 103°2W **314** D3
Fāryāb □ *Afghan.* 36°0N 65°0E **240** B2
Fasā *Iran* 29°0N 53°39E **247** D7
Fasanerie-Nord *Germany* 48°11N 11°32E **131** A2
Fasangarten *Germany* 48°5N 11°36E **131** B2
Fasano *Italy* 40°50N 17°22E **201** B10
Fashoda *South Sudan* 9°50N 32°2E **257** F3
Fasil Ghebbi *Ethiopia* 12°36N 37°28E **266** B4
Fáskrúðsfjörður *Iceland* 64°56N 14°1W **155** C12
Fassa *Mali* 13°26N 8°15W **262** C3
Fassalé *Mauritania* 15°33N 5°31W **262** B3
Fastiv *Ukraine* 50°7N 29°57E **177** C15
Fastnet Rock *Ireland* 51°22N 9°37W **166** E2
Fastov = Fastiv *Ukraine* 50°7N 29°57E **177** C15
Fatagartuting, Tanjung *Indonesia* 2°46S 131°57E **231** E8
Fataka *Solomon Is.* 11°55S 170°12E **277** C12
Fatatsu Ne *Iwo Jima* 24°45N 141°18E **288** b
Fatehabad *Haryana, India* 29°31N 75°27E **242** E6
Fatehabad *Ut. P., India* 27°1N 78°19E **242** F8
Fatehgarh *India* 27°25N 79°35E **243** F8
Fatehpur *Bihar, India* 24°38N 85°14E **243** G11
Fatehpur *Raj., India* 28°0N 74°40E **242** F6
Fatehpur *Ut. P., India* 25°56N 81°13E **243** G9
Fatehpur *Ut. P., India* 27°10N 81°13E **243** F9
Fatehpur Sikri *India* 27°6N 77°40E **242** F6
Fatesh *Russia* 52°8N 35°57E **189** F8
Fathai *South Sudan* 8°5N 31°48E **257** F3
Fathom Five ⌓ *Canada* 45°17N 81°40W **312** A3
Fatick *Senegal* 14°19N 16°27W **262** C1
Fatick □ *Senegal* 14°15N 16°30W **262** C1
Fatih *Turkey* 41°0N 28°56E **122** B1
Fatima *Qué., Canada* 47°24N 61°53W **299** C7
Fátima *Portugal* 39°37N 8°39W **195** F2
Fatoya *Guinea* 11°37N 9°10W **262** C3
Fatsa *Turkey* 41°2N 37°31E **212** B7
Fatshan = Foshan *China* 23°3N 113°9E **121** B1
Faucille, Col de la *France* 46°22N 6°2E **173** F13
Faulkton *U.S.A.* 45°2N 99°8W **308** C4
Faulquemont *France* 49°3N 6°36E **173** C13
Faure I. *Australia* 25°52S 113°50E **279** E1
Făurei *Romania* 45°6N 27°19E **183** E12
Fauresmith *S. Africa* 29°44S 25°17E **270** C4
Fauro *Solomon Is.* 6°55S 156°7E **287** L9
Fauske *Norway* 67°17N 15°25E **160** C16
Fåvang *Norway* 61°27N 10°11E **164** C7
Favânia *Brazil* 3°7S 51°48W **329** D7
Favara *Italy* 37°19N 13°39E **200** E6
Faváritx, C. de *Spain* 40°0N 4°15E **206** B5
Faverges *France* 45°45N 6°17E **175** C10
Favignana *Italy* 37°56N 12°20E **200** E5
Favignana, I. *Italy* 37°56N 12°19E **200** E5
Favoriten *Austria* 48°10N 16°23E **142** B2
Fawcett, Pt. *Australia* 11°46S 130°2E **278** B5
Fawkner *Australia* 37°42S 144°58E **128** A1
Fawkner Park *Australia* 37°50S 144°58E **128** B1
Fawn → *Canada* 55°20N 87°35W **298** A2
Fawnskin *U.S.A.* 34°16N 116°56W **307** L10
Faxaflói *Iceland* 64°29N 23°0W **155** C3
Faxälven → *Sweden* 63°13N 17°13E **162** A10
Faya-Largeau *Chad* 17°58N 19°6E **259** E3
Fayaoué *N. Cal.* 20°38S 166°33E **288** d
Fayd *Si. Arabia* 27°1N 42°52E **246** E4
Fayence *France* 43°38N 6°42E **175** E10
Fayette *Ala., U.S.A.* 33°41N 87°50W **315** E11
Fayette *Iowa, U.S.A.* 42°51N 91°48W **310** B5
Fayette *Mo., U.S.A.* 39°9N 92°41W **310** E4
Fayette *N.Y., U.S.A.* 42°48N 76°48W **313** D8
Fayette *Ohio, U.S.A.* 41°40N 84°20W **311** C12
Fayetteville *Ark., U.S.A.* 36°4N 94°10W **314** C7
Fayetteville *Ga., U.S.A.* 33°27N 84°27W **316** B5
Fayetteville *N.C., U.S.A.* 35°3N 78°53W **315** D15
Fayetteville *N.Y., U.S.A.* 43°1N 76°0W **313** C9
Fayetteville *Tenn., U.S.A.* 35°9N 86°34W **315** D11
Fayied *Egypt* 30°18N 32°16E **256** H8
Faylakah *Kuwait* 29°27N 48°20E **247** D6
Fayón *Spain* 41°15N 0°20E **196** D5
Fazao-Malfakassa △ *Togo* 8°45N 0°50E **263** D5
Fazenda Libongo *Angola* 8°24S 13°24E **265** D2
Fazenda Nova *Brazil* 16°11S 50°48W **333** E1
Fazilka *India* 30°27N 74°2E **242** D6
Fazilpur *Pakistan* 29°18N 70°29E **242** E4
Fdérik *Mauritania* 22°40N 12°45W **260** D2
Feakle *Ireland* 52°56N 8°40W **166** D3
Feale → *Ireland* 52°27N 9°37W **166** D2
Fear, C. *U.S.A.* 33°50N 77°58W **315** E16
Feather → *U.S.A.* 38°47N 121°36W **306** G5
Feather Falls *U.S.A.* 39°36N 121°16W **306** F5
Featherston *N.Z.* 41°6S 175°20E **284** H4
Featherstone *Zimbabwe* 18°42S 30°55E **269** F3
Fécamp *France* 49°45N 0°22E **172** C7
Feda *Norway* 58°17N 6°50E **164** F3
Fedala = Mohammedia *Morocco* 33°44N 7°21W **260** B3
Federación *Argentina* 31°0S 57°55W **334** C4
Féderal *Argentina* 30°57S 58°48W **334** C4
Federal Capital Terr. □ *Nigeria* 9°0N 7°10E **263** D6
Federal Way *U.S.A.* 47°18N 122°19W **306** C4
Fedeshkūh *Iran* 28°49N 53°50E **247** D7
Fedje *Norway* 60°47N 4°43E **164** D1
Fedorovka *Kazakhstan* 53°37N 62°42E **216** B6
Fefan I. *Pac. Oc.* 7°21N 151°51E **287** T18
Fehérgyarmat *Hungary* 47°58N 22°30E **182** C7
Fehmarn *Germany* 54°27N 11°7E **178** A7
Fehmarn Bælt *Europe* 54°35N 11°20E **163** K5
Fehmarn Belt = Fehmarn Bælt *Europe* 54°35N 11°20E **163** K5
Fei Xian *China* 35°18N 117°59E **227** G9
Feicheng *China* 36°14N 116°45E **226** F9
Feidong *China* 32°0N 117°35E **229** B11
Feijó *Brazil* 8°9S 70°21W **330** B3
Feilding *N.Z.* 40°13S 175°35E **284** G4
Feira de Santana *Brazil* 12°15S 38°57W **333** D4
Feirân, W. → *Egypt* 28°39N 33°12E **251** K4
Feirâni, G. *Egypt* 28°42N 33°21E **251** K5
Feiring *Norway* 60°30N 11°10E **164** D8
Feixi *China* 31°43N 117°59E **229** B11

370 Feixiang

INDEX

Feixiang China 36°30N 114°45E 226 F8
Fejaj, Chott el Tunisia 33°52N 9°14E 258 B1
Fejér ☐ Hungary 47°9N 18°30E 182 C3
Fejø Denmark 54°55N 11°30E 163 K5
Feke Turkey 37°48N 35°56E 212 D6
Fekete → Hungary 45°47N 18°15E 182 E3
Felanitx Spain 39°28N 3°9E 206 B4
Felda U.S.A. 26°34N 81°26W 317 J8
Feldbach Austria 46°57N 15°52E 180 E8
Feldberg Baden-W., Germany 47°52N 8°0E 179 H3
Feldberg Mecklenburg-Vorpommern, Germany 53°20N 13°25E 178 B9
Feldkirch Austria 47°15N 9°37E 180 D2
Feldkirchen Austria 46°44N 14°6E 180 E7
Feldkirchen Oberbayern, Germany 48°8N 11°43E 131 B3
Feldmoching Germany 48°14N 11°32E 131 A2
Félicité Seychelles 4°19S 55°52E 272 c
Felicity U.S.A. 38°51N 84°6W 311 F12
Felidhoo Maldives 3°29N 73°32E 272 d
Felidu Atoll Maldives 3°29N 73°29E 272 d
Felipe Carrillo Puerto Mexico 19°38N 88°3W 319 D7
Felixburg Zimbabwe 19°29S 30°51E 271 A5
Felixlândia Brazil 18°47S 44°55W 333 E3
Felixstowe U.K. 51°58N 1°23E 169 F9
Felletin France 45°53N 2°11E 174 C6
Fellingsbro Sweden 59°26N 15°37E 162 E9
Fellsmere U.S.A. 27°46N 80°36W 317 H9
Felshtin = Gvardeyskoye Ukraine 45°7N 34°1E 189 K8
Felsögalla = Tatabánya Hungary 47°32N 18°25E 182 C3
Feltham U.K. 51°26N 0°24W 125 B1
Felton U.S.A. 37°3N 122°4W 306 H4
Feltre Italy 46°1N 11°54E 199 B8
Femer Bælt = Fehmarn Bælt Europe 54°35N 11°20E 163 K5
Femø Denmark 54°58N 11°35E 163 K5
Femunden Norway 62°10N 11°53E 164 B8
Femundsmarka △ Norway 62°18N 12°6E 164 B9
Fen He → China 35°36N 110°42E 226 G6
Fenchih Taiwan 23°30N 120°40E 225 C2
Fene Spain 43°27N 8°9W 194 B2
Fenelon Falls Canada 44°32N 78°45W 312 B6
Fener Turkey 41°1N 28°56E 122 B1
Fener Burnu Turkey 36°58N 27°18E 205 E9
Fenerbahçe Turkey 40°58N 29°2E 122 C2
Feneroa Ethiopia 13°5N 39°3E 257 E4
Feng Xian Jiangsu, China 34°43N 116°35E 226 G9
Feng Xian Shaanxi, China 33°54N 106°40E 226 H4
Fengari Greece 40°25N 25°32E 203 F9
Fengcheng Jiangxi, China 28°12N 115°48E 229 C10
Fengcheng Liaoning, China 40°28N 124°5E 224 B2
Fengdu China 29°55N 107°48E 228 C6
Fengfeng China 36°28N 114°8E 226 F8
Fenggang China 27°57N 107°47E 228 D6
Fenghua China 29°40N 121°25E 229 C13
Fenghuang China 27°57N 109°29E 228 D7
Fengjie China 31°3N 109°31E 228 B7
Fengkai China 23°24N 111°30E 229 F8
Fengkang Taiwan 22°12N 120°41E 225 D2
Fengle China 31°29N 112°29E 229 B9
Fenglin Taiwan 23°45N 121°26E 225 C3
Fengning China 41°10N 116°33E 226 D9
Fengpin Taiwan 23°36N 121°31E 225 C3
Fengqing China 24°38N 99°55E 228 E2
Fengqiu China 35°2N 114°25E 226 G8
Fengrun China 39°48N 118°8E 227 E10
Fengshan Guangxi Zhuangzu, China 24°39N 109°15E 228 E7
Fengshan Guangxi Zhuangzu, China 24°31N 107°3E 228 E6
Fengshan Taiwan 22°38N 120°21E 225 D2
Fengshun China 23°46N 116°10E 229 F11
Fengtai Anhui, China 32°50N 116°40E 229 A11
Fengtai Beijing, China 39°49N 116°14E 114 C1
Fengtai Stadium China 39°51N 116°15E 114 B1
Fengtongzhai △ China 30°32N 102°54E 228 B4
Fengxiang China 34°29N 107°25E 226 G4
Fengxin China 28°41N 115°18E 229 C10
Fengyang China 32°51N 117°29E 229 A11
Fengyi China 25°37N 100°20E 228 E3
Fengyüan Taiwan 24°15N 120°35E 225 B2
Fengzhen China 40°25N 113°2E 226 D7
Feni Bangla. 22°55N 91°32E 241 D3
Feni Is. Papua N. G. 4°0S 153°40E 286 C7
Fennimore U.S.A. 42°59N 90°39W 310 B6
Feno, C. de France 41°58N 8°33E 175 G12
Fenoarivo Amoron'i Mania, Madag. 20°52S 46°53E 272 C2
Fenoarivo Haute Matsiatra, Madag. 21°43S 46°24E 272 C2
Fenoarivo Afovoany Madag. 18°26S 46°34E 272 B2
Fenoarivo Atsinanana Madag. 17°22S 49°25E 272 B2
Fens, The U.K. 52°38N 0°2W 168 E7
Fensmark Denmark 55°17N 11°48E 163 J5
Fenton U.S.A. 42°48N 83°42W 311 B13
Fenxi China 36°40N 111°31E 226 F6
Fenyang China 37°18N 111°48E 226 F6
Fenyi China 27°45N 114°47E 229 D10
Fenyuan Taiwan 24°1N 120°37E 225 B2
Feodosiya Ukraine 45°2N 35°16E 189 K8
Fer, C. de Algeria 37°3N 7°10E 261 A6
Fera Solomon Is. 8°6S 159°37E 287 M10
Ferbane Ireland 53°16N 7°50W 166 C4
Ferdows Iran 33°58N 58°2E 247 C8
Fère-Champenoise France 48°45N 3°59E 173 D10
Fère-en-Tardenois France 49°10N 3°30E 173 C10
Ferencváros Hungary 47°29N 19°5E 117 B2
Ferentino Italy 41°42N 13°15E 199 G10
Feres Greece 40°53N 26°10E 203 F10
Ferfer Somalia 5°4N 45°9E 267 C6
Fergana = Farg'ona Uzbekistan 40°23N 71°19E 217 D8
Fergana Range Asia 41°0N 73°50E 217 D8
Fergus Canada 43°43N 80°24W 312 C4
Fergus Falls U.S.A. 46°17N 96°4W 308 B5
Ferguson U.S.A. 38°44N 90°18W 310 F6
Fergusson I. Papua N. G. 9°30S 150°45E 286 E6
Fériana Tunisia 34°59N 8°33E 258 B1
Feričanci Croatia 45°32N 18°0E 182 E2
Ferihegy, Budapest ✕ (BUD) Hungary 47°26N 19°14E 117 B3
Ferizaj Kosovo 42°23N 21°10E 202 D5
Ferkane Algeria 34°37N 7°26E 261 B6
Ferkéssédougou Ivory C. 9°35N 5°6W 262 D3
Ferlach Austria 46°32N 14°18E 180 E7
Ferland Canada 50°19N 88°27W 298 B2
Ferlo, Vallée du Senegal 15°15N 14°15W 262 B2
Ferlo-Nord △ Senegal 15°43N 14°40W 262 B2
Ferlo-Sud △ Senegal 15°43N 14°0W 262 B2
Fermanagh ☐ U.K. 54°21N 7°40W 166 B4
Fermo Italy 43°9N 13°43E 199 E10
Fermont Canada 52°47N 67°5W 299 B6
Fermoselle Spain 41°19N 6°27W 194 D4
Fermoy Ireland 52°9N 8°16W 166 D3
Fern Creek U.S.A. 38°9N 85°36W 311 G11
Fern Gully Jamaica 18°22N 77°5W 320 a
Fernán Núñez Spain 37°40N 4°44W 195 H6
Fernández Argentina 27°55S 63°50W 334 B3
Fernandina, I. Ecuador 0°25S 91°30W 330 a
Fernandina Beach U.S.A. 30°40N 81°27W 316 E8
Fernando de Noronha Brazil 4°0S 33°10W 152 G8
Fernando Póo = Bioko Eq. Guin. 3°30N 8°40E 263 E6
Fernandópolis Brazil 20°16S 50°14W 333 F1
Ferndale Ont., Canada 44°58N 81°17W 312 B3
Ferndale Gauteng, S. Africa 26°5S 28°0E 123 A2
Ferndale Wash., U.S.A. 48°51N 122°36W 306 B4
Fernie Canada 49°30N 115°5W 296 D5
Fernlees Australia 23°51S 148°7E 280 C4
Fernley U.S.A. 39°36N 119°15W 304 G4
Fernwood U.S.A. 43°16N 73°38W 313 C11
Feroke India 11°9N 75°46E 245 J2
Feroz Shah Kotla Cricket Stadium Delhi, India 120 b3
Ferozepore = Firozpur India 30°55N 74°40E 242 D6
Ferrandina Italy 40°29N 16°27E 201 B9
Ferrara Italy 44°50N 11°35E 199 D8
Ferrato, C. Italy 39°18N 9°38E 200 C2
Ferré, C. Martinique 14°27N 60°49W 322 j
Ferreira do Alentejo Portugal 38°4N 8°6W 195 G2
Ferreira Gomes Brazil 0°48N 51°8W 329 C7
Ferreñafe Peru 6°42S 79°50W 330 B2
Ferrerías Spain 39°59N 4°1E 206 B5
Ferret, C. France 44°38N 1°15W 174 D2
Ferrette France 47°30N 7°20E 173 E14
Ferriday U.S.A. 31°38N 91°33W 314 F9
Ferriere Italy 44°40N 9°30E 198 D6
Ferrières France 48°5N 2°48E 173 D9
Ferro, Capo Italy 41°9N 9°31E 200 A2
Ferrol Spain 43°29N 8°15W 194 B2
Ferrol, Pen. de Peru 9°10S 78°35W 330 B2
Ferron U.S.A. 39°5N 111°8W 304 G8
Ferros Brazil 19°14S 43°2W 333 E3
Ferrutx, C. de Spain 39°47N 3°21E 206 B4
Ferry Pass U.S.A. 30°31N 87°13W 317 E2
Ferryland Canada 47°2N 52°53W 299 C9
Ferrysburg U.S.A. 43°5N 86°13W 311 A10
Ferryville = Menzel-Bourguiba Tunisia 37°9N 9°49E 258 A1
Fertile U.S.A. 47°32N 96°17W 308 B5
Fertő-Hanság △ Hungary 47°25N 16°50E 182 C1
Fertőszentmiklós Hungary 47°35N 16°53E 182 C1
Fès Morocco 34°0N 5°0W 260 B4
Fès ☐ Morocco 34°1N 5°0W 260 B4
Feshi Dem. Rep. of the Congo 6°8S 18°10E 265 D3
Fessenden U.S.A. 47°39N 99°38W 308 B4
Festenberg = Twardogóra Poland 51°23N 17°28E 185 G4
Festøya Norway 62°22N 6°19E 164 B3
Festus U.S.A. 38°13N 90°24W 310 F6
Feté Bowé Senegal 14°56N 13°30W 262 C2
Fetești Romania 44°22N 27°51E 183 F12
Fethiye Turkey 36°36N 29°6E 205 E11
Fethiye Körfezi Turkey 36°40N 28°50E 205 E10
Fetlar U.K. 60°36N 0°52W 167 A8
Fetsund Norway 59°56N 11°10E 164 E8
Feuilles → Canada 58°47N 70°4W 295 F17
Feurs France 45°45N 4°13E 175 C8
Fevik Norway 58°22N 8°39E 164 F5
Fevzipaşa Turkey 37°6N 36°37E 250 A7
Feyzābād Badākhshān, Afghan. 37°7N 70°33E 240 A3
Feyzābād Fāryāb, Afghan. 36°17N 64°52E 240 A2
Fez = Fès Morocco 34°0N 5°0W 260 B4
Fezzan Libya 27°0N 13°0E 258 C2
Fia Congo 3°25S 14°49E 264 C2
Fiambalá Argentina 27°45S 67°37W 334 B2
Fianarantsoa Madag. 21°26S 47°5E 272 C2
Fianga Cameroon 9°55N 15°9E 259 G3
Fiche Ethiopia 9°50N 38°46E 257 F4
Fichtelgebirge Germany 50°2N 11°55E 179 E7
Fichtelgebirge △ Germany 50°8N 12°0E 179 E8
Fichtenau Germany 52°27N 13°42E 115 B5
Ficksburg S. Africa 28°51S 27°53E 271 C4
Fidenza Italy 44°52N 10°3E 198 D7
Fiditi Nigeria 7°45N 3°53E 263 D5
Fidjeland Norway 58°57N 6°56E 164 F3
Field → Australia 23°48S 138°0E 280 C2
Field I. Australia 12°5S 132°23E 278 B5
Field Museum of Natural History Chicago, U.S.A. 41°51N 87°37W 119 B3
Fields Corner U.S.A. 42°18N 71°3W 116 B2
Fieni Romania 45°8N 25°25E 183 E10
Fier Albania 40°43N 19°33E 202 F3
Fiera Camp Italy 45°28N 9°9E 128 B1
Fierzë Albania 42°15N 20°1E 202 D4
Fife ☐ U.K. 56°16N 3°1W 167 E5
Fife Ness U.K. 56°17N 2°35W 167 E6
Fifth Cataract Sudan 18°22N 33°50E 256 D3
Fig Tree St. Kitts & Nevis 17°8N 62°35W 322 d
Figari France 41°29N 9°7E 175 G13
Figeac France 44°37N 2°2E 174 D6
Figeholm Sweden 57°22N 16°33E 163 G10
Figino Italy 45°29N 9°4E 128 B1
Figline Valdarno Italy 43°37N 11°28E 199 E8
Figtree Zimbabwe 20°22S 28°20E 269 G2
Figueira = Governador Valadares Brazil 18°15S 41°57W 333 E3
Figueira Castelo Rodrigo Portugal 40°57N 6°58W 194 E4
Figueira da Foz Portugal 40°7N 8°54W 194 E2
Figueiró dos Vinhos Portugal 39°55N 8°16W 194 F2
Figueres Spain 42°18N 2°58E 196 C7
Figuig Morocco 32°5N 1°11W 261 B4
Fihaonana Madag. 18°36S 47°12E 272 B2
Fiherenana Madag. 18°29S 48°24E 272 B2
Fiherenana → Madag. 23°19S 43°37E 272 C1
Fiji ■ Pac. Oc. 17°20S 179°0E 287 a2
Fijir Iraq 33°21N 44°21E 113 A2
Fik Ethiopia 8°10N 42°19E 257 F5
Fika Nigeria 11°15N 11°13E 263 C7
Filabres, Sierra de los Spain 37°13N 2°20W 195 H8
Filabusi Zimbabwe 20°34S 29°20E 271 B4
Filadelfia Bolivia 11°20S 68°46W 330 C4
Filadélfia Brazil 7°21S 47°30W 332 C2
Filadelfia Athina, Greece 38°2N 23°43E 112 A2
Filadelfia Italy 38°47N 16°17E 201 D9
Filadelfia Paraguay 22°21S 60°2W 334 A3
Fil'akovo Slovakia 48°17N 19°50E 181 C12
Filchner Ice Shelf Antarctica 79°0S 40°0W 151 D1
Filefjell Norway 61°8N 8°10E 164 C5
Filey U.K. 54°12N 0°18W 168 C7
Filey B. U.K. 54°12N 0°15W 168 C7
Filfla Malta 35°47N 14°24E 206 F7
Fili-Mazilovo Russia 55°44N 37°29E 129 B1
Filiaşi Romania 44°32N 23°31E 183 F8
Filiates Greece 39°38N 20°16E 206 B10
Filiatra Greece 37°9N 21°35E 204 D3
Filicudi Italy 38°35N 14°33E 201 D7
Filim Oman 20°37N 58°12E 249 B7
Filingué Niger 14°21N 3°22E 263 C5
Filiouri = Lissos → Greece 41°15N 25°40E 203 E9
Filipiada Greece 39°12N 20°53E 204 B2
Filipstad Sweden 59°43N 14°9E 162 E8
Filisur Switz. 46°41N 9°40E 179 J5
Filitosa France 41°45N 8°52E 175 G12
Fillmore Calif., U.S.A. 34°24N 118°55W 307 L8
Fillmore Utah, U.S.A. 38°58N 112°20W 304 G7
Filothei Greece 38°2N 23°46E 112 A2
Filotio Greece 37°3N 25°30E 205 D7
Filottrano Italy 43°26N 13°21E 199 E10
Filtu Ethiopia 5°8N 40°35E 257 F5
Filyos Çayı → Turkey 41°35N 32°10E 212 B5
Fimbul Ice Shelf S. Ocean 69°30S 1°0W 151 C2
Fimi → Dem. Rep. of the Congo 3°1S 16°58E 264 C3
Fina △ Mali 13°15N 8°46W 262 C3
Finale Emilia Italy 44°50N 11°18E 199 D8
Finale Lígure Italy 44°10N 8°20E 198 D5
Finalmarina = Finale Lígure Italy 44°10N 8°20E 198 D5
Fiñana Spain 37°10N 2°50W 195 H8
Financial District San Francisco, U.S.A. 136 b3
Finch Canada 45°11N 75°7W 313 A9
Finch Hatton Australia 20°25S 148°39E 280 b
Finchaa, L. Ethiopia 9°35N 37°20E 266 C4
Finchley U.K. 51°36N 0°11W 125 A2
Findhorn → U.K. 57°38N 3°38W 167 D5
Fındıklı Turkey 41°16N 41°9E 213 B9
Findlay U.S.A. 41°2N 83°39W 311 C13
Fine U.S.A. 44°14N 75°8W 313 B9
Fine Art, Museum of = Kunsthistorischesmuseum Vienna, Austria 142 b1
Fine Arts, Museum of Boston, U.S.A. 42°20N 71°5W 116 A2
Fingal ☐ Ireland 53°29N 6°14W 166 C5
Finger L. Canada 53°33N 93°30W 298 B1
Finger Lakes U.S.A. 42°40N 76°30W 313 D8
Fingoè Mozam. 15°55S 31°50E 269 F3
Finike Turkey 36°21N 30°10E 205 E12
Finike Körfezi Turkey 36°17N 30°16E 205 E12
Finiq Albania 39°54N 20°3E 202 G4
Finistère ☐ France 48°20N 4°0W 172 D3
Finisterre = Fisterra Spain 42°54N 9°16W 194 C1
Finisterre, C. = Fisterra, C. Spain 42°50N 9°19W 194 C1
Finisterre Ra. Papua N. G. 6°0S 146°30E 286 D4
Finke Australia 25°34S 134°35E 280 D1
Finke Gorge △ Australia 24°8S 132°49E 278 D5
Finland ■ Europe 63°0N 27°0E 160 E22
Finland, G. of Europe 60°0N 26°0E 188 C3
Finlay → Canada 57°0N 125°10W 296 B3
Finley N.S.W., Australia 35°38S 145°35E 283 C6
Finley N. Dak., U.S.A. 47°31N 97°50W 308 B5
Finn → Ireland 54°51N 7°28W 166 B4
Finnerödja Sweden 58°57N 14°24E 163 F8
Finnigan, Mt. Australia 15°49S 145°17E 280 B4
Finniss, C. Australia 33°8S 134°51E 281 E1
Finnmark Norway 69°37N 23°57E 160 B20
Finnsnes Norway 69°14N 18°0E 160 B18
Finsbury U.K. 51°31N 0°6W 125 A3
Finsbury Park U.K. 51°34N 0°6W 125 A3
Finschhafen Papua N. G. 6°33S 147°50E 286 D4
Finse Norway 60°36N 7°30E 164 D4
Finspång Sweden 58°43N 15°47E 163 F9
Finsteraarhorn Switz. 46°31N 8°10E 179 J4
Finsterwalde Germany 51°37N 13°42E 178 D9
Fiora → Italy 42°20N 11°34E 199 F8
Fiordland △ N.Z. 45°46S 167°0E 285 F2
Fiorenzuola d'Arda Italy 44°56N 9°55E 198 D6
Fiorito Argentina 34°42S 58°26W 117 C2
Fiq Syria 32°46N 35°41E 250 F6
Firat = Furāt, Nahr al → Asia 31°0N 47°25E 246 D5
Fire Island △ U.S.A. 40°38N 73°8W 313 F11
Firebag → Canada 57°45N 111°21W 297 B6
Firebaugh U.S.A. 36°52N 120°27W 306 J6
Firedrake L. Canada 61°25N 104°30W 297 A8
Firenze Italy 43°46N 11°15E 199 E8
Firenze Amerigo Vespucci ✕ (FLR) Italy 43°49N 11°13E 199 E8
Firenze Pisa ✕ (PSA) Italy 43°40N 10°22E 198 E7
Firenzuola Italy 44°7N 11°23E 199 D8
Firk, Sha'ib → Iraq 30°59N 44°34E 246 D5
Firkachi Niger 15°40N 14°20E 259 E2
Firmi France 44°33N 2°19E 174 D6
Firminy France 45°23N 4°18E 175 C8
Firozabad India 27°10N 78°25E 243 F8
Firozpur India 30°55N 74°40E 242 D6
Firozpur-Jhirka India 27°48N 76°57E 242 F7
Fīrūzābād Iran 28°52N 52°35E 247 D7
Fīrūzkūh Iran 35°50N 52°50E 247 C7
Firvale Canada 52°27N 126°13W 296 C3
Fischerhäuser Germany 48°14N 11°41E 131 A3
Fish → Namibia 28°7S 17°10E 270 C2
Fish → Northern Cape, S. Africa 31°30S 20°16E 270 D3
Fish River Canyon Namibia 27°40S 17°35E 270 C2
Fisheating Cr. → U.S.A. 26°57N 81°7W 317 J8
Fisher B. Canada 51°35N 97°13W 297 C9
Fisher I. U.S.A. 25°45N 80°8W 129 D3
Fishermans Bend Australia 37°49S 144°55E 128 A1
Fisherman's Village U.S.A. 33°58N 118°27W 126 C2
Fisherman's Wharf San Francisco, U.S.A. 136 a1
Fishers U.S.A. 39°57N 86°0W 311 E11
Fishers I. U.S.A. 41°15N 72°0W 313 E13
Fisherville Canada 43°46N 79°28W 141 A2
Fishguard U.K. 52°0N 4°58W 169 E3
Fishing L. Canada 52°10N 95°24W 297 C9
Fishkill U.S.A. 41°32N 73°54W 313 E11
Fiskardo Greece 38°28N 20°35E 207 C2
Fiskenæsset = Qeqertarsuatsiaat Greenland 63°5N 50°45W 154 E5
Fisksätra Sweden 59°17N 18°13E 139 B3
Fismes France 49°20N 3°40E 173 C10
Fisterra Spain 42°54N 9°16W 194 C1
Fisterra, C. Spain 42°50N 9°19W 194 C1
Fitchburg Mass., U.S.A. 42°35N 71°48W 313 D13
Fitchburg Wis., U.S.A. 42°58N 89°28W 310 B7
Fitjar Iceland 64°28N 21°18W 155 C5
Fitjar Hordaland, Norway 59°55N 5°17E 164 E2
Fitri, L. Chad 12°50N 17°28E 259 F3
Fitz Roy Argentina 47°0S 67°0W 336 C3
Fitz Roy, Cerro Argentina 49°17S 73°5W 336 C2
Fitzgerald Alta., Canada 59°51N 111°36W 296 B6
Fitzgerald Ga., U.S.A. 31°43N 83°15W 316 D6
Fitzgerald River △ Australia 33°53S 119°55E 279 F3
Fitzmaurice → Australia 14°45S 130°5E 278 B5
Fitzroy → Queens., Australia 23°32S 150°52E 280 C5
Fitzroy → W. Austral., Australia 17°31S 123°35E 278 C3
Fitzroy Crossing Australia 18°9S 125°38E 278 C4
Fitzroy Gardens Australia 37°48S 144°58E 128 A1
Fitzwilliam I. Canada 45°30N 81°45W 312 A3
Fiuggi Italy 41°48N 13°13E 199 G10
Fiume = Rijeka Croatia 45°20N 14°21E 199 C11
Fiumicino Italy 41°46N 12°14E 200 A5
Fiumicino, Roma ✕ (FCO) Italy 41°48N 12°15E 199 G9
Five Cowrie Cr. → Nigeria 6°26N 3°24E 124 B2
Five Dock Australia 33°52S 151°8E 139 B1
Five Island Harbour Antigua & B. 17°6N 61°54W 322 b
Five Points U.S.A. 36°26N 120°6W 306 J6
Fivizzano Italy 44°14N 10°8E 198 D7
Fizi Dem. Rep. of the Congo 4°17S 28°55E 268 C2
Fjæra Norway 59°52N 6°22E 164 E3
Fjærland Norway 61°24N 6°43E 164 C3
Fjærlandsfjorden Norway 61°17N 6°40E 164 C3
Fjällbacka Sweden 58°36N 11°17E 163 F5
Fjällnäs Sweden 62°36N 12°11E 162 B6
Fjärdhundra Sweden 59°47N 16°56E 162 E10
Fjellerup Denmark 56°29N 10°34E 163 H4
Fjellstrand Norway 59°47N 10°36E 133 B2
Fjerritslev Denmark 57°5N 9°15E 163 G3
Fjugesta Sweden 59°11N 14°52E 162 E8
Fkih ben Salah Morocco 32°32N 6°45W 260 B3
Flå Norway 60°25N 9°28E 164 D6
Flacq Plain Mauritius 20°13S 57°43E 272 e
Flagler Beach U.S.A. 29°29N 81°8W 317 F8
Flagstaff U.S.A. 35°12N 111°39W 305 J8
Flagstaff B. St. Helena 15°54S 5°41W 153 h
Flagstaff L. U.S.A. 45°12N 70°18W 313 A14
Flaherty I. Canada 56°15N 79°15W 298 A4
Flåm Norway 60°50N 7°7E 164 D4
Flamands St. Barts 17°55N 62°51W 322 a
Flambeau → U.S.A. 45°18N 91°14W 308 C8
Flamborough Hd. U.K. 54°7N 0°5W 168 C7
Flamengo Brazil 22°56S 43°10W 135 B1
Flamengos Azores 38°33N 28°39W 153 d1
Fläming Germany 52°6N 12°23E 178 C8
Flaming Gorge △ U.S.A. 41°10N 109°25W 304 F9
Flaming Gorge Res. U.S.A. 41°10N 109°25W 304 F9
Flamingo Fla., U.S.A. 28°22N 81°22W 133 B2
Flamingo Fla., U.S.A. 25°8N 80°57W 317 K9
Flamingo, Teluk Indonesia 5°30S 138°0E 231 F9
Flaminio Italy 41°55N 12°28E 136 B1
Flanagan U.S.A. 40°53N 88°52W 311 D8
Flanagin Town Trin. & Tob. 10°25N 61°19W 323 t
Flanders = Flandre Europe 50°50N 2°30E 173 B9
Flandre Europe 50°50N 2°30E 173 B9
Flandre-Occidentale = West-Vlaanderen ☐ Belgium 51°0N 3°0E 170 D2
Flandre-Orientale = Oost-Vlaanderen ☐ Belgium 51°5N 3°50E 170 C3
Flandreau U.S.A. 44°3N 96°36W 308 C5
Flanigan U.S.A. 40°10N 119°53W 306 E7
Flannan Is. U.K. 58°17N 7°36W 167 C1
Flåsjön Sweden 64°5N 15°40E 160 D16
Flaskebekk Norway 59°51N 10°39E 133 A2
Flat U.S.A. 62°28N 158°1W 303 E8
Flat → N.W.T., Canada 61°33N 125°18W 296 A3
Flat → Mich., U.S.A. 42°56N 85°20W 311 B11
Flat I. S. China Sea 10°49N 115°49E 230 B5
Flat Pt. N.Z. 41°14S 175°57E 284 H4
Flat Rock U.S.A. 42°6N 83°17W 311 B13
Flatbush U.S.A. 40°39N 73°56W 132 C2
Flateby Norway 59°50N 11°10E 133 B3
Flaten Sweden 59°15N 18°9E 139 B2
Flatey Iceland 66°10N 17°52W 155 A9
Flateyri Iceland 66°3N 23°31W 155 A3
Flathead L. U.S.A. 47°51N 114°8W 304 C6
Flatiron Building New York, U.S.A. 132 d2
Flatlands U.S.A. 40°37N 73°56W 132 C2
Flatow = Złotów Poland 53°22N 17°2E 184 E4
Flatrock → U.S.A. 39°12N 85°56W 311 F10
Flattery, C. Queens., Australia 14°58S 145°21E 280 A4
Flattery, C. Wash., U.S.A. 48°23N 124°29W 306 B2
Flatts Village Bermuda 32°18N 64°43W 153 a
Flatwoods U.S.A. 38°31N 82°43W 309 F12
Flecha Pt. Phil. 7°22N 123°24E 233 H4
Flechas Pt. Phil. 10°22N 119°34E 232 F2
Fleetwood Lancs., U.K. 53°55N 3°1W 168 D4
Fleetwood Pa., U.S.A. 40°27N 75°49W 313 F9
Flekke Norway 61°19N 5°20E 164 C2
Flekkefjord Norway 58°18N 6°39E 164 F3
Flemingsburg U.S.A. 38°25N 83°45W 311 F13
Flemington U.S.A. 41°7N 77°28W 312 E7
Flemington Racecourse Australia 37°47S 144°54E 128 A1
Flemish Cap Atl. Oc. 47°0N 45°0W 152 B7
Flen Sweden 59°4N 16°35E 162 E10
Flensburg Germany 54°47N 9°27E 178 A5
Flers France 48°47N 0°33W 172 D6
Flesberg Norway 59°51N 9°22E 164 E6
Flesherton Canada 44°16N 80°33W 312 B4
Flesko, Tanjung Indonesia 0°29N 124°30E 231 D6
Fletcher = Aurora U.S.A. 39°43N 104°49W 304 G11
Fleurance France 43°52N 0°40E 174 E4
Fleurie, Côte France 49°25N 0°40W 172 C6
Fleurier Switz. 46°54N 6°35E 179 J2
Fleurieu Pen. Australia 35°40S 138°5E 282 C3
Flevoland ☐ Neths. 52°30N 5°30E 170 B5
Flic en Flac Mauritius 20°17S 57°22E 272 e
Flin Flon Canada 54°46N 101°53W 297 C8
Flinders → Australia 17°36S 140°36E 280 B3
Flinders B. Australia 34°19S 115°19E 279 F2
Flinders Chase △ Australia 35°50S 136°42E 282 C2
Flinders Group Australia 14°11S 144°15E 280 A3
Flinders I. S. Austral., Australia 33°44S 134°41E 281 E1
Flinders I. Tas., Australia 40°0S 148°0E 281 G4
Flinders Ranges Australia 31°30S 138°30E 282 A3
Flinders Ranges △ Australia 31°30S 138°40E 282 A3
Flinders Reefs Australia 17°37S 148°31E 280 B4
Flint Flints., U.K. 53°15N 3°8W 168 D4
Flint Mich., U.S.A. 43°1N 83°41W 311 A13
Flint → U.S.A. 30°57N 84°34W 316 E5
Flint I. Kiribati 11°26S 151°48W 289 f
Flint Pk. U.S.A. 34°9N 118°11W 126 B3
Flintshire ☐ U.K. 53°17N 3°17W 168 D4
Flipper Pt. Wake I. 19°18N 166°37E 302 b
Flisa Norway 60°37N 12°0E 164 D9
Flisa → Norway 60°37N 12°0E 164 D9
Flisery d Sweden 57°6N 16°15E 163 G10
Flix Spain 41°14N 0°32E 196 D5
Flixecourt France 50°1N 2°5E 173 B9
Floby Sweden 58°8N 13°20E 163 F7
Floda Sweden 57°49N 12°22E 163 G6
Flodden U.K. 55°37N 2°8W 168 B5
Flogny-la-Chapelle France 47°57N 3°57E 173 E10
Floodplains △ Sri Lanka 8°10N 81°10E 245 K5
Floodwood U.S.A. 46°56N 92°55W 308 B7
Flora Apayao, Phil. 18°14N 121°5E 232 B3
Flora Ill., U.S.A. 38°40N 88°29W 311 F8
Flora Ind., U.S.A. 40°33N 86°31W 311 D10
Florac France 44°20N 3°37E 174 D7
Florahome U.S.A. 29°44N 81°54W 316 F8
Floral City U.S.A. 28°45N 82°17W 317 G7
Florala U.S.A. 31°0N 86°20W 315 F11
Florânia Brazil 6°8S 36°49W 332 C4
Floreal Mauritius 20°19S 57°30E 272 e
Floreana, I. = Santa María, I. Ecuador 1°17S 90°26W 330 a
Florence = Firenze Italy 43°46N 11°15E 199 E8
Florence Ala., U.S.A. 34°48N 87°41W 315 D11
Florence Ariz., U.S.A. 33°2N 111°23W 305 K8
Florence Calif., U.S.A. 33°57N 118°13W 126 C3
Florence Colo., U.S.A. 38°23N 105°8W 304 G11
Florence Oreg., U.S.A. 43°58N 124°7W 304 D1
Florence S.C., U.S.A. 34°12N 79°46W 315 D15
Florence, L. Australia 28°53S 138°9E 281 D2
Florence Bay = Chtimba Malawi 10°35S 34°13E 269 E3
Florence Bloom Bird Sanctuary △ S. Africa 26°7S 28°0E 123 A2
Florencia Colombia 1°36N 75°36W 328 C2
Florennes Belgium 50°15N 4°35E 170 D4
Florensac France 43°23N 3°28E 174 E7
Florentia S. Africa 26°16S 28°8E 123 B2
Florenville Belgium 49°40N 5°19E 170 E5
Flores Brazil 7°51S 37°59W 332 C4
Flores Guatemala 16°59N 89°50W 320 C2
Flores Indonesia 8°35S 121°0E 231 F6
Flores = Florânia Brazil 6°8S 36°49W 332 C4
Flores = Timon Brazil 5°8S 42°52W 332 C3
Flores B. Aires, Argentina 34°37S 58°27W 117 B2
Flores Azores 39°26N 31°13W 153 d2
Flores, Mercado de Mexico 19°19N 99°55W 128 C2
Flores I. Canada 49°20N 126°10W 296 D3
Flores Sea Indonesia 6°30S 120°0E 231 F6
Floresta B. Aires, Argentina 34°37S 58°27W 117 B2
Floresta Brazil 8°40S 37°26W 332 C4
Florești Moldova 47°53N 28°17E 183 C13
Floresville U.S.A. 29°8N 98°10W 314 G5
Floriano Brazil 6°50S 43°0W 332 C3
Florianópolis Brazil 27°30S 48°30W 335 B6
Florida B. Aires, Argentina 34°31S 58°28W 117 B2
Florida Cuba 21°32N 78°14W 320 B4
Florida Puerto Rico 18°22N 66°34W 321 b
Florida Gauteng, S. Africa 26°10S 27°55E 123 B1
Florida Uruguay 34°7S 56°10W 335 C4
Florida ☐ U.S.A. 28°0N 82°0W 317 H8
Florida, Straits of U.S.A. 25°0N 80°0W 320 B4
Florida B. U.S.A. 25°0N 80°45W 320 B3
Florida City U.S.A. 25°27N 80°29W 317 K9
Florida I. Solomon Is. 9°55S 160°15E 287 M11
Florida Keys U.S.A. 24°40N 81°0W 317 L8
Floridablanca Phil. 14°59N 120°31E 232 D3
Florídia Italy 37°5N 15°9E 201 E8
Floridsdorf Austria 48°15N 16°26E 142 A2
Florin U.S.A. 38°30N 121°24W 306 G5
Florina Greece 40°48N 21°26E 202 F5
Florissant U.S.A. 38°47N 90°19W 310 F6
Florø Norway 61°35N 5°1E 164 C2
Flotte, C. de N. Cal. 21°10S 167°25E 288 d
Flower Station Canada 45°10N 76°41W 313 A8
Flowerpot I. Canada 45°18N 81°38W 312 A3
Floydada U.S.A. 33°59N 101°20W 314 E4
Fludir Iceland 64°7N 20°6W 155 C6
Flugumyri Iceland 65°34N 19°19W 155 B7
Fluk Indonesia 1°42S 127°44E 231 E7
Flúmen → Spain 41°43N 0°9W 196 D4
Flumendosa → Italy 39°26N 9°37E 200 C2
Fluminimaggiore Italy 39°26N 8°30E 200 C1
Flushing = Vlissingen Neths. 51°26N 3°34E 170 C3
Flushing Mich., U.S.A. 43°4N 83°51W 311 A13
Flushing N.Y., U.S.A. 40°45N 73°49W 132 B3
Flushing Meadows Corona Park U.S.A. 40°44N 73°50W 132 B2
Fluviá → Spain 42°12N 3°7E 196 C8
Fly → Papua N. G. 8°25S 143°0E 286 E2
Flying Fish, C. Antarctica 72°6S 102°29W 151 D15
Flysta Sweden 59°22N 17°54E 139 A1
Fo Tan Hong Kong, China 22°23N 114°11E 122 A3
Foa Tonga 19°45S 174°18W 287 P13
Foam Lake Canada 51°40N 103°32W 297 C8
Foča Bos.-H. 43°31N 18°47E 202 C2
Foça Turkey 38°39N 26°46E 205 C8
Fochabers U.K. 57°37N 3°6W 167 D5
Focșani Romania 45°41N 27°15E 183 E12
Fodé C.A.R. 5°29N 23°18E 264 A4
Fodécontéa Guinea 10°50N 14°22W 262 C2
Fogang China 23°52N 113°30E 229 F9
Foggaret el Arab Algeria 27°13N 2°49E 261 C5
Foggaret ez Zoua Algeria 27°20N 2°53E 261 C5
Fóggia Italy 41°27N 15°34E 201 A8
Foggy Bottom U.S.A. 38°54N 77°3W 143 B2
Foglia → Italy 43°55N 12°54E 199 E9
Fogo Nfld. & L., Canada 49°43N 54°17W 299 C9
Fogo C. Verde Is. 15°5N 24°20W 153 j
Fogo I. Canada 49°40N 54°5W 299 C9
Fohnsdorf Austria 47°12N 14°40E 180 D7
Föhr Germany 54°43N 8°30E 178 A4
Föhrenhain Austria 48°19N 16°26E 142 A2
Fóia Portugal 37°19N 8°37W 195 H2
Foix France 42°58N 1°38E 174 F5
Fojnica Bos.-H. 43°59N 17°51E 182 G2
Fokida Greece 38°30N 22°15E 204 C4
Fokino Russia 53°30N 34°22E 188 F8
Fokku Nigeria 11°36N 4°32E 263 C5
Fokstugu Norway 62°7N 9°17E 164 B6
Folda Nord-Trøndelag, Norway 64°32N 10°30E 160 D14
Folda Nordland, Norway 67°38N 14°50E 160 C16
Földeák Hungary 46°19N 20°30E 182 D5
Folegandros Greece 36°40N 24°55E 204 E6
Foley Botswana 21°34S 27°21E 270 B4
Foley Ala., U.S.A. 30°24N 87°41W 315 F11
Foley Fla., U.S.A. 30°4N 83°32W 316 E6
Foleyet Canada 48°15N 82°25W 298 C3
Folgefonna Norway 60°3N 6°23E 164 D3
Folgefonna △ Norway 60°5N 6°15E 164 D3
Foligno Italy 42°57N 12°42E 199 F9
Folkestad Norway 62°7N 6°1E 164 B3
Folkestone U.K. 51°5N 1°12E 169 F9
Folkestone Marine Park △ Barbados 13°11N 59°38W 323 r
Folkston U.S.A. 30°50N 82°0W 316 E7
Folla → Norway 62°7N 10°37E 164 B7
Follansbee U.S.A. 40°19N 80°35W 312 F4
Folldal Norway 62°8N 10°0E 164 B6
Folle Anse, Pte. de Guadeloupe 15°56N 61°19W 322 e
Follebu Norway 61°13N 10°16E 164 C7
Follónica Italy 42°55N 10°45E 198 F7
Follónica, G. di Italy 42°54N 10°43E 198 F7
Folsom U.S.A. 38°40N 121°9W 306 G5
Folsom L. U.S.A. 38°42N 121°9W 306 G5
Folteşti Romania 45°45N 28°3E 183 E13
Fomboni Comoros Is. 12°18S 43°46E 272 a
Fomm ir-Rih Bay Malta 35°54N 14°20E 206 F7
Fond-du-Lac Sask., Canada 59°19N 107°12W 297 B7
Fond du Lac Wis., U.S.A. 43°47N 88°27W 308 D9
Fond-du-Lac → Canada 59°17N 106°0W 297 B7
Fond Rousseau Martinique 14°38N 61°6W 322 j
Fond St. Jacques St. Lucia 13°50N 61°1W 323 m
Fonda Iowa, U.S.A. 42°35N 94°51W 310 B2
Fonda N.Y., U.S.A. 42°57N 74°22W 313 D10
Fondamenta Nuove Venice, Italy 142 a3
Fondi Italy 41°21N 13°25E 200 A6
Fonds-St-Denis Martinique 14°44N 61°8W 322 j
Fonfría Spain 41°37N 6°9W 194 D4
Fongafale Tuvalu 8°31S 179°13E 287 L14
Fongen Norway 63°11N 11°38E 164 A8
Fongshan = Fengshan Taiwan 22°38N 120°21E 225 D2
Fongyuan = Fengyüan Taiwan 24°15N 120°35E 225 B2
Fonni Italy 40°7N 9°15E 200 B2
Fonsagrada = A Fonsagrada Spain 43°8N 7°4W 194 B3
Fonseca, G. de Cent. Amer. 13°10N 87°40W 320 D2
Font-Romeu-Odeillo-Via France 42°31N 2°3E 174 F5
Fontaine-Française France 47°32N 5°21E 173 E12
Fontainebleau Seine-et-Marne, France 48°24N 2°40E 173 D9
Fontainebleau Gauteng, S. Africa 26°6S 27°57E 123 A1
Fontana U.S.A. 34°6N 117°26W 307 L9
Fontana, L. Argentina 44°55S 71°30W 336 B2
Fontas → Canada 58°14N 121°48W 296 B4
Fonte Boa Brazil 2°33S 66°0W 328 D4
Fontem Cameroon 5°32N 9°52E 263 D6
Fontenay-aux-Roses France 48°47N 2°17E 134 B2
Fontenay-le-Comte France 46°28N 0°48W 174 B3
Fontenay-le-Fleury France 48°48N 2°2E 134 B1
Fontenay-sous-Bois France 48°50N 2°28E 134 A3
Fontenelle Res. U.S.A. 42°1N 110°3W 304 E8
Fontur Iceland 66°23N 14°32W 155 A12
Fonuafo'ou Tonga 20°19S 175°25W 287 Q13
Fonuakula Cook Is. 19°2S 169°55W 289 g
Fonualei Tonga 18°1S 174°19W 287 P13
Fonyód Hungary 46°44N 17°33E 182 D2
Foochow = Fuzhou China 26°5N 119°16E 229 D12
Foots Cray U.K. 51°24N 0°7E 125 B4
Footscray Australia 37°48S 144°56E 128 A1
Foping China 33°41N 108°0E 226 H5
Foraker, Mt. U.S.A. 62°58N 151°24W 303 E10
Forari Vanuatu 17°40S 168°31E 287 G6
Forbach France 49°10N 6°52E 173 C13
Forbes Australia 33°22S 148°5E 283 B8
Forbesganj India 26°17N 87°18E 243 F12
Forbidden City = Imperial Palace Museum Beijing, China 114 b3
Forcados Nigeria 5°26N 5°26E 263 D6
Forcados → Nigeria 5°25N 5°19E 263 D6
Forcalquier France 43°58N 5°47E 175 E9
Forchheim Germany 49°43N 11°4E 179 F7
Ford City Calif., U.S.A. 35°9N 119°27W 307 K7
Ford City Pa., U.S.A. 40°46N 79°32W 312 F5
Ford d'Or B. St. Lucia 13°56N 60°54W 323 m
Ford I. U.S.A. 21°22N 157°58W 302 K14
Forda → Norway 62°57N 10°40E 164 B7
Førde Rogaland, Norway 59°26N 5°23E 164 E2
Førde Sogn og Fjordane, Norway 61°27N 5°53E 164 C2
Førdefjorden Norway 61°29N 5°18E 164 C2
Fords Bridge Australia 29°41S 145°29E 281 D4
Ford's Theater Washington, D.C., U.S.A. 143 b2
Fordyce U.S.A. 33°49N 92°25W 314 E8
Forécariah Guinea 9°28N 13°10W 262 D2
Forel, Mt. Greenland 66°52N 36°55W 154 D7
Foremost Canada 49°26N 111°34W 296 D6
Foreshore Cape Town, S. Africa 118 a3
Forest Belgium 50°49N 4°20E 116 B1
Forest Ont., Canada 43°6N 82°0W 312 C3
Forest Miss., U.S.A. 32°22N 89°29W 315 E10
Forest Acres U.S.A. 34°1N 80°58W 316 A9
Forest City Iowa, U.S.A. 43°16N 93°39W 308 D7
Forest City N.C., U.S.A. 35°20N 81°52W 315 D14
Forest City Pa., U.S.A. 41°39N 75°28W 313 E9
Forest Gate U.K. 51°32N 0°1E 125 A4
Forest Grove U.S.A. 45°31N 123°7W 306 E3
Forest Heights U.S.A. 38°48N 77°0W 143 C2
Forest Hill Ont., Canada 43°41N 79°25W 141 A2
Forest Hill London, U.K. 51°26N 0°2W 125 B3
Forest Hill Tex., U.S.A. 32°40N 97°16W 120 B2
Forest Hills U.S.A. 40°42N 73°51W 132 B2
Forest Park Ga., U.S.A. 33°37N 84°22W 316 B5
Forest Park Ill., U.S.A. 41°51N 87°47W 119 B2
Forest Park N.Y., U.S.A. 40°42N 73°51W 132 B2
Forest Park Ohio, U.S.A. 39°17N 84°30W 311 E12
Forest View U.S.A. 41°48N 87°47W 119 C2
Forestburg Canada 52°35N 112°1W 296 C6
Foreste Casentinesi-Monte Falterona-Campigna △ Italy 43°50N 11°48E 199 E8
Foresthill U.S.A. 39°1N 120°49W 306 F6
Forestier Pen. Australia 43°0S 148°0E 281 G4
Forestville Qué., Canada 48°48N 69°2W 299 C6
Forestville Calif., U.S.A. 38°28N 122°54W 306 G4
Forestville N.Y., U.S.A. 42°28N 79°10W 312 D5
Forêt d'Orient △ France 48°16N 4°25E 173 D11
Forêt du Day △ Djibouti 11°56N 42°40E 267 B5
Forez, Mts. du France 45°40N 3°50E 174 C7
Forfar U.K. 56°39N 2°53W 167 E6
Forillon △ Canada 48°46N 64°12W 299 C7
Forks U.S.A. 47°57N 124°23W 306 C2
Forks, The = Merritt Canada 50°10N 120°45W 296 C4
Forksville U.S.A. 41°29N 76°35W 313 E8
Forlì Italy 44°13N 12°3E 199 D9
Forlì-Cesena ☐ Italy 44°10N 12°0E 199 D9
Forman U.S.A. 46°7N 97°38W 308 B5
Formazza Italy 46°22N 8°26E 198 B5
Formby Pt. U.K. 53°33N 3°6W 168 D4
Formentera Spain 38°43N 1°27E 206 D1
Formentor, C. de Spain 39°58N 3°13E 206 B4
Formentor, Pen. de Spain 39°56N 3°11E 206 B4
Former Yugoslav Republic of Macedonia = Macedonia ■ Europe 41°53N 21°40E 202 E5
Fórmia Italy 41°15N 13°37E 200 A6
Formiga Brazil 20°27S 45°25W 333 F2
Formigine Italy 44°37N 10°51E 198 D7
Formosa = Taiwan ■ Asia 23°30N 121°0E 225 C3
Formosa Argentina 26°15S 58°10W 334 B4
Formosa Brazil 15°32S 47°20W 333 E2
Formosa ☐ Argentina 25°0S 60°0W 334 B4
Formosa, Serra Brazil 12°0S 55°0W 331 C7
Formosa B. = Ungwana B. Kenya 2°45S 40°20E 268 C5
Formosa do Rio Prêto Brazil 11°2S 45°3W 332 D2
Formosa Strait = Taiwan Strait Asia 24°40N 120°0E 229 E12
Formoso → Brazil 10°34S 49°56W 333 D2
Fornebu Norway 59°53N 10°36E 133 A2
Fornells Spain 40°3N 4°7E 206 A5
Fornos de Algodres Portugal 40°38N 7°32W 194 E3
Fornovo di Taro Italy 44°42N 10°6E 198 D7
Foro Romano Rome, Italy 136 c3
Forollhogna △ Norway 62°39N 10°41E 164 B7
Føroyar ☑ Atl. Oc. 62°0N 7°0W 160 F9
Forres U.K. 57°37N 3°37W 167 D5
Forrest Vic., Australia 38°33S 143°47E 282 E5
Forrest W. Austral., Australia 30°51S 128°6E 279 F4
Forrest, Mt. Australia 24°48S 127°45E 279 D4
Forrest City U.S.A. 35°1N 90°47W 315 D9
Forreston U.S.A. 42°8N 89°35W 310 B7
Fors Sweden 60°14N 16°20E 162 D10
Forsand Norway 58°54N 6°5E 164 F3
Forsayth Australia 18°33S 143°34E 280 B3
Forserum Sweden 57°42N 14°30E 163 G8
Forshaga Sweden 59°33N 13°29E 162 E7
Förslöv Sweden 56°21N 12°48E 163 H6
Forsmo Sweden 63°16N 17°11E 162 A11
Forssa Finland 60°49N 23°38E 188 B2
Forst Germany 51°45N 14°37E 178 D10
Forstenried Germany 48°5N 11°29E 131 B1
Forstenrieder Park Germany 48°3N 11°27E 131 B1
Forster Australia 32°12S 152°31E 283 B10
Forsvik Sweden 58°35N 14°26E 163 F8
Forsyth Ga., U.S.A. 33°2N 83°56W 316 B6
Forsyth Mont., U.S.A. 46°16N 106°41W 304 C10
Forsyth I. N.Z. 40°58S 174°5E 285 A9
Fort Mumbai, India 130 c2
Fort Abbas Pakistan 29°12N 72°52E 242 E5
Fort Albany Canada 52°15N 81°35W 298 B3
Fort-Aleksandrovsky = Fort Shevchenko Kazakhstan 44°35N 50°23E 191 H10
Fort Archambault = Sarh Chad 9°5N 18°23E 259 G3
Fort Assiniboine Canada 54°20N 114°45W 296 C6
Fort Atkinson U.S.A. 42°56N 88°50W 311 B8
Fort Augustus U.K. 57°9N 4°42W 167 D4
Fort Bay Saba 17°37N 63°15W 322 a
Fort Bayard = Zhanjiang China 21°15N 110°20E 229 G8
Fort Beaufort S. Africa 32°46S 26°40E 270 D4
Fort Benton U.S.A. 47°49N 110°40W 304 C8
Fort Bragg U.S.A. 39°26N 123°48W 306 F3
Fort Bridger U.S.A. 41°19N 110°23W 304 F8
Fort Canning Park Singapore 138 b2
Fort Caroline △ U.S.A. 30°23N 81°30W 316 E8
Fort Charles Jamaica 17°55N 76°50W 320 a

Fort Charlotte St. Lucia 13°59N 61°0W 323 m
Fort Chipewyan Canada 58°42N 111°8W 297 B6
Fort Clatsop = Lewis and Clark ⌓ U.S.A. 46°8N 123°53W 306 D3
Fort Collins U.S.A. 40°35N 105°5W 304 F11
Fort-Coulonge Canada 45°50N 76°45W 298 C4
Fort Covington U.S.A. 44°59N 74°29W 313 B10
Fort Dauphin = Taolanaro Madag. 25°2S 47°0E 272 D2
Fort Davis Ala., U.S.A. 32°15N 85°43W 316 C4
Fort Davis Tex., U.S.A. 30°35N 103°54W 314 F3
Fort-de-France Martinique 14°36N 61°5W 322 j
Fort-de-France, B. de Martinique 14°34N 61°4W 322 j
Fort de Kock = Bukittinggi Indonesia 0°20S 100°20E 234 C2
Fort de Polignac = Illizi Algeria 26°31N 8°32E 261 C6
Fort de Possel = Possel C.A.R. 5°5N 19°10E 264 A3
Fort Defiance U.S.A. 35°45N 109°5W 305 J9
Fort Dodge U.S.A. 42°30N 94°11W 310 B2
Fort Drum U.S.A. 27°32N 80°48W 317 H9
Fort Dupont Park U.S.A. 38°52N 76°56W 143 B3
Fort Edward U.S.A. 43°16N 73°35W 313 C11
Fort Erie Canada 42°54N 78°56W 312 D6
Fort Fairfield U.S.A. 46°46N 67°50W 309 B20
Fort Flatters = Bordj Omar Driss Algeria 28°10N 6°40E 261 C6
Fort Foote Village U.S.A. 38°46N 77°1W 143 C2
Fort Foureau = Kousseri Cameroon 12°0N 14°55E 259 F2
Fort Frances Canada 48°36N 93°24W 297 D10
Fort Franklin = Déline Canada 65°11N 123°25W 294 D7
Fort Frederica ⌓ U.S.A. 31°13N 81°23W 316 D8
Fort Gaines U.S.A. 31°36N 85°3W 316 D4
Fort Garland U.S.A. 37°26N 105°26W 305 H11
Fort George = Chisasibi Canada 53°50N 79°0W 298 B4
Fort George = Prince George Canada 53°55N 122°50W 296 C4
Fort George Grenada 12°3N 61°45W 323 q
Fort Good Hope Canada 66°14N 128°40W 294 D6
Fort Gouraud = Fdérik Mauritania 22°40N 12°45W 260 D2
Fort Hancock U.S.A. 31°18N 105°51W 314 F2
Fort Hertz = Putao Burma 27°28N 97°30E 241 B6
Fort Hill = Chitipa Malawi 9°41S 33°19E 269 D3
Fort Hope = Eabametoong Canada 51°30N 88°0W 298 B2
Fort Irwin U.S.A. 35°16N 116°41W 307 K10
Fort Jameson = Chipata Zambia 13°38S 32°28E 269 E3
Fort Jeudy, Pt. of Grenada 11°59N 61°42W 323 q
Fort Johnston = Mangoche Malawi 14°25S 35°16E 269 E4
Fort Kent U.S.A. 47°15N 68°36W 309 B19
Fort Klamath U.S.A. 42°42N 122°0W 304 D3
Fort Lamy = Ndjamena Chad 12°10N 15°0E 259 F3
Fort Laperrine = Tamanrasset Algeria 22°50N 5°30E 261 D6
Fort Laramie U.S.A. 42°13N 104°31W 304 E11
Fort Lauderdale U.S.A. 26°7N 80°8W 129 B3
Fort Lauderdale Executive ✈ (FXE) U.S.A. 26°11N 80°10W 129 A2
Fort Lauderdale-Hollywood Int. ✈ (FLL) U.S.A. 26°4N 80°10W 129 B3
Fort Lee U.S.A. 40°50N 73°58W 132 A2
Fort Liard Canada 60°14N 123°30W 296 A4
Fort Liberté Haiti 19°42N 71°51W 321 C5
Fort Lupton U.S.A. 40°5N 104°49W 304 F11
Fort MacKay Canada 57°12N 111°41W 296 B6
Fort Macleod Canada 49°45N 113°30W 296 D6
Fort MacMahon = El Homr Algeria 29°43N 1°45E 261 C5
Fort McMurray Canada 56°44N 111°7W 296 B6
Fort McPherson Canada 67°30N 134°55W 294 D5
Fort Madison U.S.A. 40°38N 91°27W 310 D5
Fort Manning = Mchinji Malawi 13°47S 32°58E 269 E3
Fort Marlborough Indonesia 3°48S 102°15E 234 C2
Fort Mason Center San Francisco, U.S.A. 136 a1
Fort Matanzas ⌓ U.S.A. 29°43N 81°14W 316 F8
Fort Meade U.S.A. 27°45N 81°48W 317 H8
Fort Mitchell U.S.A. 32°20N 85°1W 316 C4
Fort Morgan U.S.A. 40°15N 103°48W 304 F12
Fort Myers U.S.A. 26°39N 81°52W 317 J8
Fort Myers Beach U.S.A. 26°26N 81°57W 317 J8
Fort Myers Villas U.S.A. 26°33N 81°52W 317 J8
Fort Napoléon Guadeloupe 15°52N 61°35W 322 e
Fort Nelson Canada 58°50N 122°44W 296 B4
Fort Nelson → Canada 59°32N 124°0W 296 B4
Fort Norman = Tulita Canada 64°57N 125°30W 294 E6
Fort Ogden U.S.A. 27°5N 81°57W 317 H8
Fort Payne U.S.A. 34°26N 85°43W 315 D12
Fort Peck U.S.A. 48°1N 106°27W 304 B10
Fort Peck Dam U.S.A. 48°0N 106°26W 304 C10
Fort Peck L. U.S.A. 48°0N 106°26W 304 C10
Fort Pierce U.S.A. 27°27N 80°20W 317 H9
Fort Pierre U.S.A. 44°21N 100°22W 308 C3
Fort Pierre Bordes = Ti-n-Zaouatene Algeria 19°55N 2°55E 261 E5
Fort Plain U.S.A. 42°56N 74°37W 313 D10
Fort Portal Uganda 0°40N 30°20E 268 B3
Fort Providence Canada 61°3N 117°40W 296 A5
Fort Pulaski ⌓ U.S.A. 32°2N 80°56W 316 C9
Fort Qu'Appelle Canada 50°45N 103°50W 297 C8
Fort Recovery U.S.A. 40°25N 84°47W 311 D12
Fort Resolution Canada 61°10N 113°40W 296 A6
Fort Rixon Zimbabwe 20°2S 29°17E 269 G2
Fort Rosebery = Mansa Zambia 11°13S 28°55E 269 E2
Fort Ross U.S.A. 38°32N 123°13W 306 G3
Fort-Rousset = Owando Congo 0°29S 15°55E 264 C3
Fort Rupert = Waskaganish Canada 51°30N 78°40W 298 B4
Fort St. James Canada 54°30N 124°10W 296 C4
Fort St. John Canada 56°15N 120°50W 296 B4
Fort Sandeman = Zhob Pakistan 31°20N 69°31E 242 D3
Fort Saskatchewan Canada 53°40N 113°15W 296 C6
Fort Scott U.S.A. 37°50N 94°42W 308 G6
Fort Severn Canada 56°0N 87°40W 298 A2
Fort Shevchenko Kazakhstan 44°35N 50°23E 191 H10
Fort Simpson Canada 61°45N 121°15W 296 A4
Fort Smith Alta., Canada 60°0N 111°51W 296 B6
Fort Smith Ark., U.S.A. 35°23N 94°25W 314 D7
Fort Stockton U.S.A. 30°53N 102°53W 314 F3
Fort Sumner U.S.A. 34°28N 104°15W 305 J11
Fort Thomas U.S.A. 39°4N 84°26W 311 E12
Fort Thompson U.S.A. 44°3N 99°26W 308 C4
Fort Trinquet = Bîr Mogreïn Mauritania 25°10N 11°25W 260 C2
Fort Union ⌓ U.S.A. 35°54N 105°1W 305 J11
Fort Uritskogo = Fort Shevchenko Kazakhstan 44°35N 50°23E 191 H10
Fort Valley U.S.A. 32°33N 83°53W 316 C6
Fort Vermilion Canada 58°24N 116°0W 296 B5
Fort Walton Beach U.S.A. 30°25N 86°36W 317 E3
Fort Ware Canada 57°26N 125°41W 296 B3
Fort Wayne U.S.A. 41°4N 85°9W 311 C11
Fort White U.S.A. 29°55N 82°43W 316 F7
Fort William U.K. 56°49N 5°7W 167 E3
Fort Worth U.S.A. 32°43N 97°19W 120 B2
Fort Yates U.S.A. 46°5N 100°38W 308 B3
Fort Yukon U.S.A. 66°34N 145°16W 303 C11
Fortaleza = Pedra Azul Brazil 16°2S 41°17W 333 E3
Fortaleza Bolivia 12°6S 66°49W 330 C4
Fortaleza Brazil 3°45S 38°35W 332 B4
Forteau Canada 51°28N 56°58W 299 B8
Fortescue → Australia 21°0S 116°4E 278 D2
Fortescue River Roadhouse Australia 21°17S 116°8E 278 D2
Forth → U.K. 56°9N 3°50W 167 E5
Forth, Firth of U.K. 56°5N 2°55W 121 A3
Forth Rail Bridge U.K. 56°0N 3°23W 121 A1
Forth Road Bridge U.K. 56°0N 3°24W 121 A1
Forthassa Rharbia Algeria 32°52N 1°18W 261 B4
Fortín General Pando Paraguay 19°45S 59°47W 331 D6
Fortín Madrejón Paraguay 20°45S 59°52W 331 E6
Fortín Teniente Primero Ramiro Espínola Paraguay 21°27S 61°30W 331 E5
Fortín Uno Argentina 38°50S 65°18W 336 A3
Fortore → Italy 41°55N 15°17E 199 G12
Fortrose N.Z. 46°38S 168°45E 285 G3
Fortrose Highl., U.K. 57°35N 4°9W 167 D4
Fortuna Spain 38°11N 1°7W 197 G3
Fortuna Calif., U.S.A. 40°36N 124°9W 304 F1
Fortuna N. Dak., U.S.A. 48°55N 103°47W 308 A2
Fortune Ledge = Marshall U.S.A. 61°53N 162°5W 303 F7
Fortune Canada 47°4N 55°50W 299 C8
Fortune B. Canada 47°30N 55°22W 299 C8
Forum, The Los Angeles, U.S.A. 33°57N 118°20W 126 C2
Forūr Iran 26°17N 54°32E 247 E7
Fos-sur-Mer France 43°26N 4°56E 175 E8
Fosen Norway 63°50N 10°20E 160 E14
Foshan China 23°3N 113°9E 121 B1
Fosnavåg Norway 62°22N 5°38E 164 B2
Foso Ghana 5°43N 1°15W 263 D4
Foss Iceland 63°51N 17°52W 155 D9
Fossano Italy 44°33N 7°43E 198 D4
Fossil U.S.A. 45°0N 120°9W 304 D3
Fossil Butte ⌓ U.S.A. 41°50N 110°27W 304 F8
Fossombrone Italy 43°41N 12°48E 199 E9
Fossvellir Iceland 65°27N 14°37W 155 B12
Foster Vic., Australia 38°40S 146°15E 283 E7
Foster Qué., Canada 45°17N 72°30W 313 A12
Foster Ky., U.S.A. 38°48N 84°13W 311 F12
Foster → Canada 55°47N 105°49W 297 B7
Foster Village U.S.A. 21°21N 157°55W 302 K14
Fosters Ra. Australia 21°35S 133°48E 280 C1
Fostoria U.S.A. 41°10N 83°25W 311 C13
Fót Hungary 47°35N 19°11E 117 A3
Fotadrevo Madag. 24°3S 45°1E 272 C2
Fouesnant France 47°53N 4°1W 172 E2
Fougamou Gabon 1°16S 10°30E 264 C2
Fougères France 48°21N 1°14W 172 D5
Foul Pt. Sri Lanka 8°35N 81°18E 245 K5
Foula U.K. 60°10N 2°5W 167 A6
Foulalaba Mali 10°40N 7°20W 262 C3
Foulness I. U.K. 51°36N 0°55E 169 F8
Foulpointe Madag. 17°41S 49°31E 272 B2
Foulwind, C. N.Z. 41°45S 171°28E 285 D6
Foum Assaka Morocco 29°8N 10°24W 260 C2
Foum Zguid Morocco 30°2N 6°59W 260 B3
Foumban Cameroon 5°45N 10°50E 263 D7
Foumbot Cameroon 5°31N 10°28E 263 D7
Foumbouni Comoros Is. 11°51S 43°29E 272 a
Foumirate Algeria 27°30N 3°12W 260 C4
Foundiougne Senegal 14°5N 16°32W 262 C1
Fountain Colo., U.S.A. 38°41N 104°42W 304 G11
Fountain Fla., U.S.A. 30°29N 85°25W 316 E4
Fountain Hills U.S.A. 33°37N 111°43W 305 K8
Fountain Springs U.S.A. 35°54N 118°51W 307 K8
Four Mountains, Is. of U.S.A. 53°0N 170°0W 303 K5
Four Roads Trin. & Tob. 10°41N 61°33W 323 t
Fourchambault France 47°2N 3°3E 173 E10
Fourchue, Île St. Barts 17°58N 62°54W 322 a
Fouriesburg S. Africa 28°38S 28°14E 271 C4
Fourmies France 50°1N 4°2E 173 B11
Fourna Greece 39°3N 21°52E 204 B3
Fournaise, Piton de la Réunion 21°14S 55°43E 272 f
Fourni Greece 37°36N 26°32E 205 D8
Fourqueux France 48°53N 2°3E 134 A1
Fours France 46°50N 3°42E 173 F10
Fous, Pte. des Dominica 15°12N 61°20W 323 k
Fousinshin = Fuxin China 42°5N 121°48E 227 C11
Fouta Djallon Guinea 11°20N 12°10W 262 C2
Foux, Cap-à- Haiti 19°43N 73°27W 321 C5
Foveaux Str. N.Z. 46°42S 168°10E 285 G3
Fowey U.K. 50°20N 4°39W 169 G3
Fowler Calif., U.S.A. 36°38N 119°41W 306 J7
Fowler Colo., U.S.A. 38°8N 104°2W 304 G11
Fowler Ind., U.S.A. 40°37N 87°19W 311 D9
Fowler Mich., U.S.A. 43°0N 84°45W 311 B12
Fowlers B. Australia 32°2S 132°3E 279 F5
Fowlers Bay Australia 31°59S 132°34E 279 F5
Fowlerville U.S.A. 42°40N 84°4W 311 B12
Fowman Iran 37°13N 49°19E 213 D13
Fox → Canada 56°3N 93°18W 297 B10
Fox Creek Canada 54°24N 116°48W 296 C5
Fox Is. U.S.A. 53°0N 168°0W 303 K6
Fox Lake Alta., Canada 58°28N 114°31W 296 B6
Fox Lake Ill., U.S.A. 42°24N 88°11W 311 B8
Fox Studios Australia 33°55S 151°13E 139 B2
Fox Valley Canada 50°30N 109°25W 297 C7
Foxboro Ont., Canada 44°14N 77°26W 312 B7
Foxboro Mass., U.S.A. 42°4N 71°16W 313 D13
Foxdale Australia 20°22S 148°35E 280 b
Foxe Basin Canada 66°0N 77°0W 295 D16
Foxe Chan. Canada 65°0N 80°0W 295 E16
Foxe Pen. Canada 65°0N 76°0W 295 E16
Foxen Sweden 59°25N 11°55E 162 E5
Foxford Ireland 53°59N 9°7W 166 C2
Foxton N.Z. 40°29S 175°18E 284 G4
Foyle, Lough U.K. 55°7N 7°4W 166 A4
Foynes Ireland 52°37N 9°7W 166 D2
Foz Spain 43°33N 7°20W 194 B3
Foz do Copeá Brazil 3°52S 63°19W 329 D5
Foz do Cunene Angola 17°15S 11°48E 265 F2
Foz do Gregório Brazil 6°47S 70°44W 330 B3
Foz do Iguaçu Brazil 25°30S 54°30W 335 B5
Foz do Mamoriá Brazil 2°27S 66°32W 328 D4
Frackville U.S.A. 40°47N 76°14W 313 F8
Fraga Spain 41°32N 0°21E 196 D5
Fraile Muerto Uruguay 32°31S 54°32W 335 C5
Fram Museum Norway 59°54N 10°42E 133 A3
Framingham U.S.A. 42°18N 71°24W 313 D13
Framnes Iceland 66°1N 20°26W 155 A6
Frampol Poland 50°41N 22°40E 185 H9
Franca Brazil 20°33S 47°30W 333 F2
Francavilla al Mare Italy 42°25N 14°17E 199 F11
Francavilla Fontana Italy 40°32N 17°35E 201 B10
France ■ Europe 47°0N 3°0E 171 C5
Frances Australia 36°41S 140°55E 282 D4
Frances → Canada 60°16N 129°10W 296 A3
Frances L. Canada 61°23N 129°30W 296 A3
Francesville U.S.A. 40°59N 86°53W 311 D10
Franceville Gabon 1°40S 13°32E 264 C2
Franche-Comté France 46°50N 5°55E 171 C6
Francis Case, L. U.S.A. 43°4N 98°34W 308 D4
Francisco Beltrão Brazil 26°5S 53°4W 335 B5
Francisco de Orellana Ecuador 0°28S 76°58W 328 D2
Francisco Ignacio Madero Coahuila, Mexico 25°48N 103°18W 318 B4
Francisco Ignacio Madero Durango, Mexico 24°26N 104°18W 318 C4
Francisco Ignacio Madero, Presa Mexico 28°10N 105°37W 318 B3
Francisco Sá Brazil 16°28S 43°30W 333 E3
Francistown Botswana 21°7S 27°33E 271 B4
Francofonte Italy 37°14N 14°53E 201 E7
François Canada 47°35N 56°45W 299 C8
François, B. du Martinique 14°38N 60°54W 322 j
François-Joseph, Chutes Dem. Rep. of the Congo 7°37S 17°17E 265 D3
François L. Canada 54°0N 125°30W 296 C3
François Peron △ Australia 25°42S 113°33E 279 E1
Franconia U.S.A. 38°47N 77°7W 143 C2
Francs Pk. U.S.A. 43°58N 109°20W 304 E9
Franeker Neths. 53°12N 5°33E 170 A5
Frank Hann △ Australia 32°52S 120°19E 279 F3
Frank Lloyd Wright Home Chicago, U.S.A. 41°53N 87°47W 119 B2
Frankel Singapore 1°18N 103°55E 138 B3
Frankenberg Germany 51°3N 8°48E 178 D4
Frankenhöhe ⌓ Germany 49°20N 10°25E 179 F6
Frankenstein = Ząbkowice Śląskie Poland 50°35N 16°50E 185 H3
Frankenwald Germany 50°20N 11°30E 179 E7
Frankenwald ⌓ Germany 50°15N 11°30E 179 E7
Frankfield Jamaica 18°8N 77°22W 320 a
Frankford Ont., Canada 44°12N 77°36W 312 B7
Frankford Mo., U.S.A. 39°29N 91°19W 310 E5
Frankfort Free State, S. Africa 27°17S 28°30E 271 C4
Frankfort Ind., U.S.A. 40°17N 86°31W 311 D10
Frankfort Kans., U.S.A. 39°42N 96°25W 308 F5
Frankfort Ky., U.S.A. 38°12N 84°52W 311 F12
Frankfort N.Y., U.S.A. 43°2N 75°4W 313 C9
Frankfort Ohio, U.S.A. 39°24N 83°11W 311 E13
Frankfurt Brandenburg, Germany 52°20N 14°32E 178 C10
Frankfurt Hessen, Germany 50°7N 8°41E 179 E4
Frankfurt ✈ (FRA) Germany 50°1N 8°34E 179 E4
Fränkische Alb Germany 49°10N 11°23E 179 F7
Fränkische Rezat → Germany 49°11N 11°1E 179 F7
Fränkische Saale → Germany 50°3N 9°42E 179 E5
Fränkische Schweiz Germany 49°50N 11°16E 179 F7
Fränkische Schweiz-Veldensteiner Forst ⌓ Germany 49°45N 11°22E 179 F7
Frankland → Australia 35°0S 116°48E 279 G2
Franklin Ga., U.S.A. 33°17N 85°6W 316 B4
Franklin Ind., U.S.A. 39°29N 86°3W 311 E10
Franklin Ky., U.S.A. 36°43N 86°35W 308 G10
Franklin La., U.S.A. 29°48N 91°30W 314 G9
Franklin Mass., U.S.A. 42°5N 71°24W 313 D13
Franklin N.H., U.S.A. 43°27N 71°39W 313 C13
Franklin N.Y., U.S.A. 42°20N 75°9W 313 D9
Franklin Nebr., U.S.A. 40°6N 98°57W 308 E4
Franklin Ohio, U.S.A. 39°34N 84°18W 311 E12
Franklin Pa., U.S.A. 41°24N 79°50W 312 E5
Franklin Va., U.S.A. 36°41N 76°56W 309 G15
Franklin W. Va., U.S.A. 38°39N 79°20W 309 F14
Franklin, Pt. U.S.A. 70°55N 158°48W 303 A8
Franklin B. Canada 69°45N 126°0W 294 D6
Franklin D. Roosevelt L. U.S.A. 48°18N 118°9W 304 B4
Franklin-Gordon Wild Rivers △ Australia 42°19S 145°51E 281 G4
Franklin Harb. Australia 33°43S 136°55E 282 B2
Franklin I. Antarctica 76°10S 168°30E 151 D11
Franklin I. Ont., Canada 45°24N 80°20W 312 A4
Franklin L. U.S.A. 40°25N 115°22W 304 F6
Franklin Mts. N.W.T., Canada 65°0N 125°0W 294 D6
Franklin Mts. N.Z. 44°55S 167°45E 285 E2
Franklin Park Mass., U.S.A. 42°18N 71°5W 116 B2
Franklin Park Va., U.S.A. 38°55N 77°9W 143 B2
Franklin Res. U.S.A. 34°5N 118°24W 126 B2
Franklin Str. Canada 72°0N 96°0W 294 C12
Franklinton U.S.A. 30°51N 90°9W 315 F9
Franklinville U.S.A. 42°20N 78°27W 312 D6
Franklyn Mt. N.Z. 42°4S 172°42E 285 C7
Frankston Australia 38°8S 145°8E 283 E6
Frånö Sweden 62°55N 17°50E 162 B11
Fransfontein Namibia 20°12S 15°1E 270 B2
Frånsta Sweden 62°30N 16°11E 162 B10
Frantsa Iosifa, Zemlya Arctic 82°0N 55°0E 214 A6
Franz Canada 48°25N 84°30W 298 C3
Franz Josef Land = Frantsa Iosifa, Zemlya Arctic 82°0N 55°0E 214 A6
Franz Josef Strauss ✈ (MUC) Germany 48°21N 11°47E 131 A2
Franzburg Germany 54°11N 12°51E 178 A8
Frascati Italy 41°48N 12°41E 199 G9
Fraser U.S.A. 42°32N 82°57W 312 D2
Fraser → B.C., Canada 49°7N 123°11W 306 A3
Fraser → Nfld. & L., Canada 56°39N 62°10W 299 A7
Fraser, Mt. Australia 25°35S 118°20E 279 E2
Fraser I. Australia 25°15S 153°10E 281 D5
Fraser Lake Canada 54°0N 124°50W 296 C4
Fraserburg S. Africa 31°55S 21°30E 270 D3
Fraserburg Road = Leeu Gamka S. Africa 32°47S 21°59E 270 D3
Fraserburgh U.K. 57°42N 2°1W 167 D6
Fraserdale Canada 49°55N 81°37W 298 C3
Fraserpet = Kushalnagar India 12°14N 75°57E 245 H2
Frasertown N.Z. 38°58S 177°28E 284 E6
Fraserville = Rivière-du-Loup Canada 47°50N 69°30W 299 C6
Frashër Albania 40°23N 20°30E 202 F4
Frasne France 46°50N 6°10E 173 F13
Frătești Romania 43°58N 25°58E 183 G10
Frauenfeld Switz. 47°34N 8°54E 179 H4
Frauenkirche Munich, Germany 131 b2
Frauenstadt = Wadowice Poland 49°52N 19°30E 185 J6
Fraustadt = Wschowa Poland 51°48N 16°20E 185 G3
Fray Bentos Uruguay 33°10S 58°15W 334 C4
Fray Jorge △ Chile 30°42S 71°40W 334 C1
Frazier Downs ☼ Australia 18°48S 121°42E 278 C3
Frechilla Spain 42°8N 4°50W 194 C6
Fredericia Denmark 55°34N 9°45E 163 J3
Frederick Md., U.S.A. 39°25N 77°25W 309 F15
Frederick Okla., U.S.A. 34°23N 99°1W 314 D5
Frederick S. Dak., U.S.A. 45°50N 98°31W 308 C4
Frederick E. Hyde Fjord Greenland 83°25N 29°10W 154 A8
Fredericksburg Pa., U.S.A. 40°27N 76°26W 313 F8
Fredericksburg Tex., U.S.A. 30°16N 98°52W 314 F5
Fredericksburg Va., U.S.A. 38°18N 77°28W 309 F15
Fredericktown Mo., U.S.A. 37°34N 90°18W 308 G8
Fredericktown Ohio, U.S.A. 40°29N 82°33W 312 F2
Frederico Westphalen Brazil 27°22S 53°24W 335 B5
Fredericton Canada 45°57N 66°40W 299 C6
Fredericton Junction Canada 45°41N 66°40W 299 C6
Frederiksberg Denmark 55°40N 12°33E 118 A3
Frederiksdal Denmark 55°46N 12°25E 118 A2
Frederikshåb = Paamiut Greenland 62°0N 49°43W 154 E6
Frederikshald = Halden Norway 59°9N 11°23E 164 E8
Frederikshamn = Hamina Finland 60°34N 27°12E 188 B4
Frederikshavn Denmark 57°28N 10°31E 163 G4
Frederikssund Denmark 55°50N 12°3E 163 J6
Frederiksted U.S. Virgin Is. 17°43N 64°53W 321 C7
Frederiksværk Denmark 55°58N 12°4E 163 J6
Fredersdorf Germany 52°31N 13°45E 115 A5
Fredonia Ariz., U.S.A. 36°57N 112°32W 305 H7
Fredonia Kans., U.S.A. 37°32N 95°49W 308 G6
Fredonia N.Y., U.S.A. 42°26N 79°20W 312 D5
Fredriksberg Sweden 60°8N 14°23E 162 D8
Fredrikstad Norway 59°13N 10°57E 164 E7
Fredriksvern = Stavern Norway 59°0N 10°1E 164 F7
Free State □ S. Africa 28°30S 27°0E 270 C4
Freeburg U.S.A. 38°19N 91°56W 310 F5
Freehold U.S.A. 40°16N 74°17W 313 F10
Freeland U.S.A. 41°1N 75°54W 313 E9
Freels, C. Nfld. & L., Canada 49°15N 53°30W 299 C9
Freels, C. Nfld. & L., Canada 46°37N 53°32W 299 C9
Freeman Calif., U.S.A. 35°35N 117°53W 307 K9
Freeman Mo., U.S.A. 38°37N 94°30W 310 F2
Freeman S. Dak., U.S.A. 43°21N 97°26W 308 D5
Freeport Bahamas 26°30N 78°47W 320 A4
Freeport Trin. & Tob. 10°27N 61°25W 323 t
Freeport Fla., U.S.A. 30°30N 86°8W 316 E3
Freeport Ill., U.S.A. 42°17N 89°36W 310 B7
Freeport N.Y., U.S.A. 40°39N 73°35W 313 F11
Freeport Ohio, U.S.A. 40°12N 81°15W 312 F3
Freeport Pa., U.S.A. 40°41N 79°41W 312 F5
Freeport Tex., U.S.A. 28°57N 95°21W 314 G7
Freetown Antigua & B. 17°3N 61°42W 322 b
Freetown S. Leone 8°30N 13°17W 262 D2
Freeville U.S.A. 42°30N 76°20W 313 D8
Frégate, L. de la Canada 53°15N 74°45W 298 B5
Fregate Island Nature Reserve St. Lucia 13°52N 60°53W 323 m
Fregenal de la Sierra Spain 38°10N 6°39W 195 G4
Fregene Italy 41°51N 12°12E 199 G9
Fregon Australia 26°45S 132°1E 279 E5
Freguesia Brazil 22°48S 43°10W 135 A1
Fréhel, C. France 48°40N 2°20W 172 D4
Frei Antarctica 62°30S 58°0W 151 C18
Freiberg Germany 50°55N 13°20E 178 E9
Freibourg = Fribourg Switz. 46°49N 7°9E 179 J3
Freiburg Baden-W., Germany 47°59N 7°51E 179 H3
Freiburg Niedersachsen, Germany 53°49N 9°16E 178 B5
Freiburg in Schlesien = Świebodzice Poland 50°51N 16°20E 185 H3
Freidrichshain, Volkspark Germany 52°31N 13°25E 115 A3
Freienwalde = Chociwel Poland 53°29N 15°21E 184 E2
Freiham Germany 48°8N 11°25E 131 B1
Freilassing Germany 47°50N 12°58E 179 H8
Freimann Germany 48°11N 11°37E 131 A2
Freire Chile 38°54S 72°38W 336 A2
Freirina Chile 28°30S 71°10W 334 B1
Freising Germany 48°24N 11°45E 179 G7
Freistadt Austria 48°30N 14°30E 180 C7
Freital Germany 51°0N 13°39E 178 D9
Freiwaldau = Jeseník Czechia 50°14N 17°8E 181 A10
Fréjus France 43°25N 6°44E 175 E10
Fremantle Australia 32°7S 115°47E 279 F2
Fremont Calif., U.S.A. 37°32N 121°57W 306 H4
Fremont Ind., U.S.A. 41°44N 84°56W 311 C12
Fremont Iowa, U.S.A. 41°13N 92°26W 310 C4
Fremont Mich., U.S.A. 43°28N 85°57W 309 D11
Fremont Nebr., U.S.A. 41°26N 96°30W 308 E5
Fremont Ohio, U.S.A. 41°21N 83°7W 311 C13
Fremont → U.S.A. 38°24N 110°42W 304 G8
French Camp U.S.A. 37°53N 121°16W 306 H5
French Cays = Plana Cays Bahamas 22°38N 73°30W 321 B5
French Creek → U.S.A. 41°24N 79°50W 312 E5
French Frigate Shoals U.S.A. 23°45N 166°10W 302 G10
French Guiana ☑ S. Amer. 4°0N 53°0W 329 C7
French Guinea = Guinea ■ W. Afr. 10°20N 11°30W 262 C2
French I. Australia 38°20S 145°22E 283 E6
French Island △ Australia 38°20S 145°22E 283 E6
French Lick U.S.A. 38°33N 86°37W 311 F10
French Market New Orleans, U.S.A. 131 a3
French Pass N.Z. 40°55S 173°55E 285 A8
French Polynesia ☑ Pac. Oc. 20°0S 145°0W 289 f
French Quarter New Orleans, U.S.A. 131 a2
French Riviera = Azur, Côte d' France 43°25N 7°10E 175 E11
French Sudan = Mali ■ Africa 17°0N 3°0W 262 B4
French Territory of the Afars and Issas = Djibouti ■ Africa 12°0N 43°0E 257 E5
French Togoland = Togo ■ W. Afr. 8°30N 1°35E 263 D5
Frenchburg U.S.A. 37°57N 83°38W 311 G13
Frenchman Cr. → N. Amer. 48°31N 107°10W 304 B10
Frenchman Cr. → Nebr., U.S.A. 40°14N 100°50W 308 E3
Frenda Algeria 35°2N 1°1E 261 A5
Frenštát pod Radhoštěm Czechia 49°33N 18°13E 181 B11
Fresco Ivory C. 5°3N 5°31W 262 D3
Fresco → Brazil 7°15S 51°30W 331 B7
Fresh Pond U.S.A. 42°22N 71°8W 116 A2
Freshfield, C. Antarctica 68°25S 151°10E 151 C10
Fresnay-sur-Sarthe France 48°17N 0°1E 172 D7
Fresnes France 48°45N 2°18E 134 B2
Fresnillo Mexico 23°10N 102°53W 318 C4
Fresno U.S.A. 36°44N 119°47W 306 J7
Fresno Alhándiga Spain 40°42N 5°37W 194 E5
Fresno Res. U.S.A. 48°36N 109°57W 304 B9
Fresvik Norway 61°4N 6°55E 164 C3
Freudenau Austria 48°11N 16°25E 142 A2
Freudenstadt Germany 48°27N 8°24E 179 G4
Freudenthal = Bruntál Czechia 49°59N 17°27E 181 B10
Frévent France 50°15N 2°17E 173 B9
Frew → Australia 20°0S 135°38E 280 C2
Frewsburg U.S.A. 42°3N 79°10W 312 D5
Freycinet △ Australia 42°11S 148°19E 281 G4
Freycinet Pen. Australia 42°10S 148°25E 281 G4
Freyming-Merlebach France 49°8N 6°48E 173 C13
Freystadt = Kisielice Poland 53°36N 19°16E 184 E6
Freystadt = Kożuchów Poland 51°45N 15°31E 185 G2
Freyung Germany 48°48N 13°31E 179 G9
Fria Guinea 10°27N 13°38W 262 C2
Fria, C. Namibia 18°0S 12°0E 270 A1
Friant U.S.A. 36°59N 119°43W 306 J7
Friar's B. St. Kitts & Nevis 17°16N 62°40W 322 d
Frías Argentina 28°40S 65°5W 334 B2
Fribourg Switz. 46°49N 7°9E 179 J3
Fribourg □ Switz. 46°40N 7°0E 179 J3
Frick Collection New York, U.S.A. 132 b3
Fridafors Sweden 56°25N 14°39E 163 H8
Friday Harbor U.S.A. 48°32N 123°1W 306 B3
Friedberg Bayern, Germany 48°21N 10°59E 179 G6
Friedberg Hessen, Germany 50°19N 8°45E 179 E4
Friedeberg = Mirsk Poland 50°58N 15°23E 185 H2
Friedeberg in Neumark = Strzelce Krajeńskie Poland 52°52N 15°33E 185 F2
Friedenau Germany 52°28N 13°22E 115 B3
Friedens U.S.A. 40°3N 78°59W 312 F6
Friedland = Mieroszów Poland 50°40N 16°11E 185 H3
Friedland = Pravdinsk Russia 56°29N 43°28E 190 B6
Friedland Germany 53°40N 13°33E 178 B9
Friedrichsfelde Germany 52°29N 13°33E 115 B4
Friedrichshafen Germany 47°39N 9°30E 179 H5
Friedrichshagen Germany 52°27N 13°37E 115 B4
Friedrichshain Germany 52°31N 13°25E 115 A3
Friedrichskoog Germany 54°1N 8°53E 178 A4
Friedrichslust Germany 52°33N 13°43E 115 A5
Friedrichstadt Germany 54°23N 9°6E 178 A5
Friendly Is. = Tonga ■ Pac. Oc. 19°50S 174°30W 287 P13
Friends Arena Stockholm, Sweden 59°53N 18°0E 139 A2
Friendship U.S.A. 42°12N 78°8W 312 D6
Friesach Austria 46°57N 14°24E 180 E7
Friesack Germany 52°44N 12°34E 178 C8
Friesland □ Neths. 53°5N 5°50E 170 A5
Friesoythe Germany 53°1N 7°51E 178 B3
Frigate Seychelles 4°35S 55°56E 272 c
Frigate Bay St. Kitts & Nevis 17°16N 62°41W 322 d
Frigate I. Grenada 12°25N 61°29W 323 q
Friggesund Sweden 61°54N 16°33E 162 C10
Friherrs Finland 60°16N 24°49E 121 B1
Frillesås Sweden 57°20N 12°12E 163 G6
Frilufts Museum Finland 60°11N 24°52E 121 B2
Frinnaryd Sweden 57°55N 14°50E 163 G8
Frio → U.S.A. 28°26N 98°11W 314 G5
Frio, C. Brazil 22°50S 41°50W 326 F6
Friol Spain 43°2N 7°47W 194 B3
Friona U.S.A. 34°38N 102°43W 314 D3
Frisches Haff = Wiślany, Zalew Poland 54°20N 19°50E 184 D6
Frisco U.S.A. 33°8N 96°49W 314 E6
Fristad Sweden 57°50N 13°0E 163 G6
Fritch U.S.A. 35°38N 101°36W 314 D4
Fritsla Sweden 57°33N 12°47E 163 G6
Fritzlar Germany 51°7N 9°16E 178 D5
Friuli-Venézia Giulia □ Italy 46°0N 13°0E 199 B9
Friza, Proliv Russia 45°30N 149°0E 215 E15
Frobisher B. Canada 62°30N 66°0W 295 E18
Frobisher Bay = Iqaluit Canada 63°44N 68°31W 295 E18
Frobisher L. Canada 56°20N 108°15W 297 B7
Frohavet Norway 64°0N 9°30E 160 E13
Frohenbruck = Veselí nad Lužnicí Czechia 49°12N 14°43E 180 B7
Frohnleiten Austria 47°16N 15°19E 180 D8
Frolovo Russia 49°45N 43°40E 190 F6
Frombork Poland 54°21N 19°41E 184 D6
Frome U.K. 51°14N 2°19W 169 F5
Frome → U.K. 50°41N 2°6W 169 G5
Frome, L. Australia 30°45S 139°45E 282 A3
Frome Downs Australia 31°13S 139°45E 282 A3
Frómista Spain 42°16N 4°25W 194 C6
Front Range U.S.A. 40°25N 105°45W 304 F11
Front Royal U.S.A. 38°55N 78°12W 309 F14
Fronteira Portugal 39°3N 7°39W 195 F3
Fronteiras Brazil 7°5S 40°37W 332 C3
Frontenac ⌓ Canada 44°32N 76°30W 313 B8
Frontera Canary Is. 27°47N 17°59W 153 e1
Frontera Tabasco, Mexico 18°32N 92°38W 319 D6
Fronteras Mexico 30°56N 109°31W 318 A3
Frontignan France 43°27N 3°45E 174 E7
Frontón, I. Peru 12°7S 77°11W 124 B1
Frosinone Italy 41°38N 13°19E 200 A6
Frostburg U.S.A. 39°39N 78°56W 309 F14
Frostisen Norway 68°14N 17°10E 160 B17
Frostproof U.S.A. 27°45N 81°32W 317 H8
Frouard France 48°47N 6°8E 173 D13
Fröví Sweden 59°28N 15°24E 162 E9
Frøya Norway 63°43N 8°40E 160 E13
Fruita U.S.A. 39°9N 108°44W 304 G9
Fruithurst U.S.A. 33°44N 85°26W 316 B4
Fruitland Park U.S.A. 28°51N 81°54W 317 G8
Frumoasa Romania 46°28N 25°48E 183 D10
Frunze = Bishkek Kyrgyzstan 42°54N 74°46E 217 D8
Frunze Russia 55°47N 37°33E 129 B2
Frunzivka Ukraine 47°20N 29°45E 183 C14
Fruška Gora Serbia 45°7N 19°30E 182 E4
Fruška Gora △ Serbia 45°10N 19°40E 202 A3
Frutal Brazil 20°0S 49°0W 333 F2
Frutigen Switz. 46°35N 7°38E 179 J3
Frýdek-Místek Czechia 49°40N 18°20E 181 B11
Frýdlant Czechia 50°56N 15°9E 180 A8
Fryeburg U.S.A. 44°1N 70°59W 313 B14
Fryvaldov = Jeseník Czechia 50°14N 17°8E 181 A10
Fthiotida Greece 38°50N 22°25E 204 C4
Fu Jiang → China 30°0N 106°16E 228 C6
Fu Xian = Wafangdian China 39°38N 121°58E 227 E11
Fu Xian China 36°0N 109°20E 226 G5
Fua Mulaku Maldives 0°17S 73°26E 272 d
Fu'an China 27°11N 119°36E 229 D12
Fubian China 31°17N 102°22E 228 B4
Fucécchio Italy 43°44N 10°48E 198 E7
Fucheng China 37°50N 116°10E 226 F9
Fuchou = Fuzhou China 26°5N 119°16E 229 D12
Fuchū Hiroshima, Japan 34°34N 133°14E 222 C5
Fuchū Tōkyō, Japan 35°40N 139°29E 140 A1
Fuchuan China 24°50N 111°5E 229 E8
Fuchun Jiang → China 30°5N 120°5E 229 B13
Fúcino, Piana del Italy 42°1N 13°31E 199 F10
Fuding China 27°20N 120°12E 229 D13
Fuencaliente Canary Is. 28°28N 17°50W 153 e1
Fuencaliente Spain 38°25N 4°18W 195 G6
Fuencaliente, Pta. Canary Is. 28°27N 17°51W 153 e1
Fuencarral Spain 40°29N 3°42W 127 B1
Fuengirola Spain 36°32N 4°41W 195 J6
Fuenlabrada Spain 40°17N 3°48W 127 C1
Fuensalida Spain 40°3N 4°12W 194 E6
Fuente-Álamo Spain 38°44N 1°24W 197 G3
Fuente Álamo de Murcia Spain 37°42N 1°6W 197 H3
Fuente de Cantos Spain 38°15N 6°18W 195 G4
Fuente del Maestre Spain 38°31N 6°28W 195 G4
Fuente el Fresno Spain 39°14N 3°46W 195 F7
Fuente Obejuna Spain 38°15N 5°25W 195 G5
Fuente Palmera Spain 37°42N 5°6W 195 H5
Fuentes de Andalucía Spain 37°28N 5°20W 195 H5
Fuentes de Ebro Spain 41°31N 0°38W 196 D4
Fuentes de León Spain 38°5N 6°32W 195 G4
Fuentes de Oñoro Spain 40°33N 6°52W 194 E4
Fuentesaúco Spain 41°15N 5°30W 194 D5
Fuerte → Mexico 25°54N 109°22W 318 B3
Fuerte Olimpo Paraguay 21°0S 57°51W 334 A4
Fuerteventura Canary Is. 28°30N 14°0W 153 e2
Fuerteventura ✈ (FUE) Canary Is. 28°24N 13°52W 153 e2
Fufeng China 34°22N 108°0E 226 G5
Fuga I. Phil. 18°52N 121°20E 232 B3
Fugong China 27°5N 98°47E 228 D2
Fugou China 34°3N 114°25E 226 G8
Fugu China 39°2N 111°3E 226 E6
Fuhai China 47°2N 87°25E 217 C11
Fuḩaymī Iraq 34°16N 42°10E 213 E10
Fuhlsbüttel, Hamburg ✈ (HAM) Germany 53°35N 9°59E 178 B5
Fuhsien = Fu Xian China 36°0N 109°20E 226 G5
Fuhsing Changhua, Taiwan 24°3N 120°25E 225 B2
Fuhsing Kaohsiung, Taiwan 23°13N 120°48E 225 C2
Fuhsing Taoyüan, Taiwan 24°49N 121°21E 225 B3
Fuidhaigh = Wiay U.K. 57°24N 7°13W 167 D1
Fuji Japan 35°9N 138°39E 223 B10
Fuji-Hakone-Izu △ Japan 35°15N 138°45E 223 B10
Fuji-San Japan 35°22N 138°44E 223 B10
Fuji-Yoshida Japan 35°30N 138°46E 223 B10
Fujian □ China 26°0N 118°0E 229 E12
Fujieda Japan 34°52N 138°16E 223 C10
Fujin China 47°16N 132°1E 219 B15
Fujinomiya Japan 35°10N 138°40E 223 B10
Fujioka Japan 36°15N 139°3E 223 A11
Fujisawa Japan 35°22N 139°29E 223 B11
Fujiyama, Mt. = Fuji-San Japan 35°22N 138°44E 223 B10
Fukagawa Hokkaidō, Japan 43°43N 142°2E 220 C11
Fukagawa Tōkyō, Japan 35°39N 139°48E 140 B3
Fukang China 44°10N 87°59E 217 D11
Fukaya Japan 36°12N 139°12E 223 A11
Fukiage Japan 31°27N 130°17E 222 F2
Fukiage Imperial Garden Tokyo, Japan 140 a4
Fukien = Fujian □ China 26°0N 118°0E 229 E12
Fukuchiyama Japan 35°19N 135°9E 223 B7
Fukue Japan 32°41N 128°51E 221 H4
Fukue-Shima Japan 32°40N 128°45E 221 H4
Fukuei Chiao Taiwan 25°17N 121°32E 225 A3
Fukui Japan 36°5N 136°10E 223 A8
Fukui □ Japan 36°0N 136°12E 223 B8
Fukuma Japan 33°46N 130°28E 222 D2
Fukuoka Japan 33°39N 130°21E 222 D2
Fukuoka □ Japan 33°30N 131°0E 222 D3
Fukuoka Int. ✈ (FUK) Japan 33°34N 130°28E 222 D2
Fukuroi Japan 34°45N 137°55E 223 C9
Fukushima Fukushima, Japan 37°44N 140°28E 220 F10
Fukushima Ōsaka, Japan 34°41N 135°28E 133 A1
Fukushima □ Japan 37°30N 140°15E 220 F10
Fukuyama Japan 34°35N 133°20E 222 C5
Ful Bura South Sudan 7°50N 31°50E 257 F3
Fulacunda Guinea-Biss. 11°44N 15°3W 262 C1
Fulaga Fiji 19°8S 178°33W 287 B3
Fulan → Sweden 61°18N 13°4E 162 C7
Fulda Germany 50°32N 9°40E 178 E5
Fulda → Germany 51°25N 9°39E 178 D5
Fulford = North Miami Beach U.S.A. 25°55N 80°9W 129 C2
Fulford Harbour Canada 48°47N 123°27W 306 B3
Fulham U.K. 51°28N 0°12W 125 B2
Fuli Taiwan 23°11N 121°14E 225 C3
Fuliang China 29°23N 117°14E 229 C11
Fuling China 29°39N 107°17E 228 C6
Fullarton Trin. & Tob. 10°5N 61°54W 323 t
Fullerton Calif., U.S.A. 33°53N 117°56W 307 M9
Fullerton Nebr., U.S.A. 41°22N 97°58W 308 E5
Fulongquan China 44°20N 124°42E 227 B13
Fülöpszállás Hungary 46°49N 19°15E 182 D4
Fulton Ill., U.S.A. 41°52N 90°11W 310 C6
Fulton Ind., U.S.A. 40°57N 86°16W 311 D10
Fulton Mo., U.S.A. 38°52N 91°57W 310 F5
Fulton N.Y., U.S.A. 43°19N 76°25W 313 C8
Fulufjället Sweden 61°32N 12°41E 162 C6
Fumay France 49°58N 4°40E 173 C11
Fumel France 44°30N 0°58E 174 D4
Fumin China 25°10N 102°20E 228 E4
Funabashi Japan 35°45N 140°0E 223 B12
Funabori Japan 35°41N 139°52E 140 A4
Funafuti Pac. Oc. 8°31S 179°13E 277 B14
Funan China 32°39N 115°42E 229 A10
Funäsdalen Sweden 62°33N 12°32E 162 B6
Funchal Madeira 32°38N 16°54W 153 c
Funchal ✈ (FNC) Madeira 32°42N 16°45W 153 c
Fundación Colombia 10°31N 74°11W 328 A3
Fundão Brazil 19°55S 40°24W 333 E3
Fundão Portugal 40°8N 7°30W 194 E3
Fundão, I. do Brazil 22°51S 43°13W 135 B1
Fundong Cameroon 6°15N 10°16E 264 A2
Fundu Moldovei Romania 47°32N 25°24E 183 C10
Fundulea Romania 44°28N 26°31E 183 F11
Fundy, B. of Canada 45°0N 66°0W 299 D6
Fundy △ Canada 45°35N 65°10W 299 C6
Fünfhaus Austria 48°11N 16°20E 142 A2
Fünfkirchen = Pécs Hungary 46°5N 18°15E 182 D3
Funhalouro Mozam. 23°3S 34°25E 271 B5
Funing Hebei, China 39°53N 119°12E 227 E10
Funing Jiangsu, China 33°45N 119°50E 227 H10
Funing Yunnan, China 23°35N 105°45E 228 F5
Funiu Shan China 33°30N 112°20E 226 H7
Funsi Ghana 10°21N 1°54W 262 C4
Funtua Nigeria 11°30N 7°18E 263 C6
Fuping Hebei, China 38°48N 114°12E 226 E8
Fuping Shaanxi, China 34°42N 109°10E 226 G5
Fuqing China 25°41N 119°21E 229 E12
Fuquan China 26°40N 107°27E 228 D6
Furano Japan 43°21N 142°23E 220 C11
Furāt, Nahr al → Asia 31°0N 47°25E 246 D5
Furesø Denmark 55°47N 12°25E 118 A2
Fūrg Iran 28°18N 55°13E 247 D7
Furkating India 26°28N 93°59E 241 B4
Furman U.S.A. 32°41N 81°11W 316 C8
Furmanov Russia 57°10N 41°9E 190 B5
Furnas Azores 37°46N 25°19W 153 d3
Furnás Spain 39°3N 1°32E 206 B8
Furnas, Represa de Brazil 20°50S 45°30W 333 F2
Furneaux Group Australia 40°10S 147°50E 281 G4
Furqlus Syria 34°36N 37°8E 250 D8
Fürstenau Germany 52°31N 7°40E 178 C3
Fürstenberg = Eisenhüttenstadt Germany 52°9N 14°38E 178 C10
Fürstenberg Germany 53°10N 13°8E 178 B9
Fürstenfeld Austria 47°3N 16°3E 180 D9
Fürstenfeldbruck Germany 48°11N 11°15E 179 G7
Fürstenwalde Germany 52°22N 14°3E 178 C10
Fürth Mittelfranken, Germany 49°28N 10°59E 179 F6
Fürth Oberbayern, Germany 48°12N 11°35E 131 B2
Fürth im Wald Germany 49°18N 12°50E 179 F8
Furtwangen Germany 48°2N 8°12E 179 G4
Furudal Sweden 61°10N 15°11E 162 C9
Furukawa = Hida Japan 36°14N 137°11E 223 A9
Furukawa = Ōsaki Japan 38°34N 140°58E 220 E10
Furulund Sweden 55°46N 13°6E 163 J7
Furuvik Sweden 61°38N 17°20E 162 D11
Fury and Hecla Str. Canada 69°56N 84°0W 295 D15

Fusagasugá *Colombia* 4°21N 74°22W 328 C3
Fuscaldo *Italy* 39°25N 16°2E 201 C9
Fushan *Shandong, China* 37°30N 121°15E 227 F11
Fushan *Shanxi, China* 35°58N 111°51E 226 G6
Fushë Arrëz *Albania* 42°4N 20°2E 202 D4
Fushë Kosovë *Kosovo* 42°40N 21°5E 202 D5
Fushë Krujë *Albania* 41°29N 19°43E 202 E3
Fushun *Liaoning, China* 41°50N 123°56E 224 B1
Fushun *Sichuan, China* 29°13N 104°52E 228 C5
Fusong *China* 42°20N 127°15E 224 A3
Füssen *Germany* 47°34N 10°42E 179 H6
Fusui *China* 22°40N 107°56E 228 F6
Futago-tamagawaen *Japan* 35°36N 139°39E 140 B2
Futago-Yama *Japan* 33°35N 131°36E 222 D3
Futian *China* 22°32N 114°4E 219 a
Futiga *Amer. Samoa* 14°21S 170°45W 302 f
Futog *Serbia* 45°15N 19°42E 182 E4
Futrono *Chile* 40°8S 72°24W 336 B2
Futtsu *Japan* 35°13N 139°49E 223 B11
Fuwa *Egypt* 31°12N 30°33E 256 H7
Fuxian Hu *China* 24°30N 102°53E 228 E4
Fuxin *China* 42°5N 121°48E 227 C11
Fuxing Dao *China* 31°16N 121°33E 138 B2
Fuxing Park *China* 31°13N 121°27E 138 B1
Fuxinglu *China* 39°52N 116°16E 114 B1
Fuyang *Anhui, China* 33°0N 115°48E 229 A10
Fuyang *Zhejiang, China* 30°5N 119°57E 229 B12
Fuyang He ➜ *China* 38°12N 117°0E 226 E9
Fuying Dao *China* 26°34N 120°9E 229 D13
Fuyong *China* 22°40N 113°49E 219 a
Fuyot Springs △ *Phil.* 17°1N 121°58E 232 C3
Fuyu *Heilongjiang, China* 47°49N 124°27E 219 B13
Fuyu *Jilin, China* 45°12N 124°43E 227 B13
Fuyuan *China* 25°40N 104°16E 228 E5
Fuyun *China* 47°0N 89°28E 217 C11
Füzesgyarmat *Hungary* 47°6N 21°14E 182 C6
Fuzhou = Linchuan *China* 27°57N 116°15E 229 D11
Fuzhou *China* 26°5N 119°16E 229 D12
Füzuli *Azerbaijan* 39°36N 47°8E 213 C12
Fyn *Denmark* 55°20N 10°30E 163 J4
Fyne, L. *U.K.* 55°59N 5°23W 167 F3
Fynshav *Denmark* 54°59N 9°59E 163 K3
Fyresdal *Norway* 59°11N 8°5E 164 E5
Fyresvatn *Norway* 59°6N 8°10E 164 E5
Fyzabad = Faizabad *India* 26°45N 82°10E 243 F10
Fyzabad *Trin. & Tob.* 10°12N 61°33W 323 t

G

G. Ross Lord Park *Canada* 43°47N 79°28W 141 A2
Ga *Ghana* 9°47N 2°30W 262 D4
Ga-eun *S. Korea* 36°38N 128°5E 224 D4
Gaa Faru Atoll *Maldives* 4°45N 73°26E 272 d
Gaalkacyo *Somalia* 6°30N 47°30E 267 C6
Gaanda *Nigeria* 10°10N 12°27E 263 C7
Gabaldon *Phil.* 15°37N 121°20E 232 D3
Gabas ➜ *France* 43°46N 0°42W 174 E3
Gabba *Australia* 9°45S 142°38E 280 a
Gabela *Angola* 11°0S 14°24E 265 E2
Gaberones = Gaborone *Botswana* 24°45S 25°57E 270 B4
Gabès *Tunisia* 33°53N 10°2E 258 B2
Gabès □ *Tunisia* 33°35N 9°30E 261 B6
Gabès, G. de *Tunisia* 34°0N 10°30E 258 B2
Gabgaba, W. ➜ *Egypt* 22°10N 33°5E 256 C3
Gabia *Dem. Rep. of the Congo* 4°37S 17°14E 265 C3
Gabia la Grande *Spain* 37°8N 3°40W 195 H7
Gąbin *Poland* 52°23N 19°41E 185 F6
Gablonz = Jablonec nad Nisou *Czechia* 50°43N 15°10E 180 A8
Gabon ■ *Africa* 0°10S 10°0E 264 C2
Gabon ➜ *Gabon* 0°25N 9°20E 264 B1
Gaborone *Botswana* 24°45S 25°57E 270 B4
Gabrat Sai'd *Sudan* 16°6N 31°50E 266 A3
Gabriels *U.S.A.* 44°26N 74°12W 313 B10
Gābrīk *Iran* 25°44N 58°28E 247 E8
Gabro *Ethiopia* 6°18N 43°16E 267 C5
Gabrovo *Bulgaria* 42°52N 25°19E 203 D9
Gabú = Nova Lamego *Guinea-Biss.* 12°19N 14°11W 262 C2
Gacé *France* 48°49N 0°20E 172 D7
Gāch Sār *Iran* 36°7N 51°19E 247 B6
Gachsārān *Iran* 30°15N 50°45E 247 D6
Gacko *Bos.-H.* 43°10N 18°33E 202 C2
Gad Hinglaj *India* 16°14N 74°21E 245 F2
Gadag *India* 15°30N 75°45E 245 G2
Gadaisu *Papua N. G.* 10°22S 149°46E 286 F5
Gadamai *Sudan* 17°11N 36°10E 257 D4
Gadap *Pakistan* 25°5N 67°28E 242 G2
Gadarwara *India* 22°50N 78°50E 243 H8
Gadebusch *Germany* 53°42N 11°7E 178 B7
Gadein *South Sudan* 8°10N 28°45E 257 F2
Gadhada *India* 22°0N 71°35E 242 J4
Gadis ➜ *Indonesia* 1°2N 98°55E 234 B1
Gádor, Sierra de *Spain* 36°57N 2°45W 195 J8
Gadra *Pakistan* 25°40N 70°38E 242 G4
Gadsden *Ala., U.S.A.* 34°1N 86°1W 316 A3
Gadsden *S.C., U.S.A.* 33°51N 80°46W 316 B9
Gadwal *India* 16°10N 77°50E 245 F3
Gadyach = Hadyach *Ukraine* 50°21N 34°0E 189 G8
Gadzi *C.A.R.* 4°47N 16°42E 264 B3
Gaebong *S. Korea* 37°29N 126°52E 137 C1
Găeşti *Romania* 44°48N 25°19E 183 F10
Gaeta *Italy* 41°12N 13°35E 200 A6
Gaeta, G. di *Italy* 41°6N 13°30E 200 A6
Gaffney *U.S.A.* 35°5N 81°39W 315 D14
Gafsa *Tunisia* 34°24N 8°43E 258 B1
Gafsa □ *Tunisia* 34°30N 8°48E 261 B6
Gagarawa *Nigeria* 12°25N 9°32E 263 C6
Gagaria *India* 25°43N 70°46E 242 G4
Gagarin *Russia* 55°38N 35°0E 188 E8
Găgăuzia □ *Moldova* 46°10N 28°40E 183 D13
Gage Park *U.S.A.* 41°47N 87°42W 119 C2
Gaggenau *Germany* 48°48N 8°18E 179 G4
Gaghamni *Sudan* 11°41N 28°19E 257 E2
Gagil-Tomil, I. *Pac. Oc.* 9°31N 138°12E 287 R16
Gagino *Russia* 55°15N 45°1E 190 C7
Gagliano del Capo *Italy* 39°50N 18°22E 201 C11
Gagnef *Sweden* 60°36N 15°5E 162 D9
Gagnoa *Ivory C.* 6°56N 6°16W 262 D3
Gagnon *Canada* 51°50N 68°5W 299 B6
Gagnon, L. *Canada* 62°3N 110°27W 297 A6
Gagny *France* 48°53N 2°32E 134 A4
Gago Coutinho *São Tomé & Príncipe* 0°1S 6°32E 265 a
Gagra *Georgia* 43°20N 40°10E 191 J5
Gahini *Rwanda* 1°50S 30°30E 268 C3
Gahmar *India* 25°27N 83°49E 243 G10
Gahnpa = Ganta *Liberia* 7°15N 8°59W 262 D3
Gai Xian = Gaizhou *China* 40°22N 122°20E 224 B1
Gaibandha *Bangla.* 25°20N 89°36E 241 C2
Gaidouronisi *Greece* 34°53N 25°41E 207 F6
Gail *U.S.A.* 32°46N 101°27W 314 E4
Gail ➜ *Austria* 46°36N 13°53E 180 E6
Gaillac *France* 43°54N 1°54E 174 E5
Gaillard Cut *Panama* 9°3N 79°40W 320 c
Gaillimh = Galway *Ireland* 53°17N 9°3W 166 C2
Gaillon *France* 49°10N 1°20E 172 C8
Gaimán *Argentina* 43°10S 65°25W 336 B3
Gaines *U.S.A.* 41°46N 77°35W 312 E7
Gainesville *Fla., U.S.A.* 29°40N 82°20W 317 F7
Gainesville *Ga., U.S.A.* 34°18N 83°50W 315 D13
Gainesville *Mo., U.S.A.* 36°36N 92°26W 308 G7
Gainesville *Tex., U.S.A.* 33°38N 97°8W 314 E6
Gainsborough *U.K.* 53°24N 0°46W 168 D7
Gairdner, L. *Australia* 31°30S 136°0E 282 A2
Gairloch *U.K.* 57°43N 5°41W 167 D3
Gairloch, L. *U.K.* 57°43N 5°45W 167 D3
Gaizhou *China* 40°22N 122°20E 224 B1
Gaj *Croatia* 45°28N 17°3E 182 E2
Gaj ➜ *Pakistan* 26°26N 67°21E 242 F2
Gajendragarh *India* 15°44N 75°59E 245 G2
Gakona *U.S.A.* 62°18N 145°18W 303 E11
Gakuch *Pakistan* 36°7N 73°45E 243 A5
Gal Oya △ *Sri Lanka* 7°0N 81°20E 245 L5
Gal Oya Res. *Sri Lanka* 7°5N 81°30E 245 L5
Gal Tardo *Somalia* 3°34N 45°58E 267 D6
Galachipa *Bangla.* 22°8N 90°26E 241 D3
Galâla, Gebel el *Egypt* 29°21N 32°22E 256 J8
Galâla el Baharîya, G. el *Egypt* 29°22N 32°23E 251 J3
Galâla el Qiblîya, G. el *Egypt* 28°42N 32°23E 251 K3
Galán, Cerro *Argentina* 25°55S 66°52W 334 B2
Galana ➜ *Kenya* 3°9S 40°8E 268 C5
Galangue *Angola* 13°42S 16°9E 265 E3
Galangue, Serra *Angola* 14°18S 15°52E 265 E3
Galanta *Slovakia* 48°11N 17°45E 181 C10
Galapagar *Spain* 40°36N 3°58W 194 E7
Galápagos = Colón, Arch. de *Ecuador* 0°0 91°0W 330 a
Galapagos Fracture Zone *Pac. Oc.* 3°0N 110°0W 289 G17
Galapagos Rise *Pac. Oc.* 15°0S 95°0W 289 J18
Galashiels *U.K.* 55°37N 2°49W 167 F6
Galata *Turkey* 41°1N 28°58E 122 B1
Galata Tower *Turkey* 41°1N 28°59E 122 B1
Galatas *Greece* 37°30N 23°26E 204 D5
Galatea *N.Z.* 38°24S 176°45E 284 E5
Galateia *Cyprus* 35°25N 34°4E 207 E10
Galaţi *Romania* 45°27N 28°2E 183 E13
Galaţi □ *Romania* 45°45N 27°30E 183 E12
Galatia *Turkey* 39°30N 33°0E 212 C5
Galatina *Italy* 40°10N 18°10E 201 B11
Galátone *Italy* 40°9N 18°4E 201 B11
Galatsi *Greece* 38°1N 23°45E 112 A2
Galax *U.S.A.* 36°40N 80°56W 309 G13
Galaxidi *Greece* 38°22N 22°23E 204 C4
Galbīn Govĭ *Mongolia* 43°0N 107°0E 226 C4
Galcaio = Gaalkacyo *Somalia* 6°30N 47°30E 267 C6
Gäldar *Canary Is.* 28°9N 15°39W 153 e1
Galdhøpiggen *Norway* 61°38N 8°18E 164 C5
Galeana *Chihuahua, Mexico* 30°7N 107°38W 318 A3
Galeana *Nuevo León, Mexico* 24°50N 100°4W 318 A3
Galeão Int. ✈ (GIG) *Brazil* 22°49S 43°15W 135 A1
Galegu *Sudan* 12°36N 35°2E 257 E4
Galela *Indonesia* 1°50N 127°49E 231 D7
Galena *Alaska, U.S.A.* 64°44N 156°56W 303 D8
Galena *Ill., U.S.A.* 42°25N 90°26W 310 B6
Galeota Pt. *Trin. & Tob.* 10°8N 60°59W 323 t
Galera *Spain* 37°45N 2°33W 197 H2
Galera, Pta. *Chile* 39°59S 73°43W 336 A2
Galera, Pta. da *Azores* 37°42N 25°30W 153 d3
Galera Pt. *Trin. & Tob.* 10°49N 60°54W 323 t
Galeras *Colombia* 1°13N 77°20W 328 C2
Galesburg *Ill., U.S.A.* 40°57N 90°22W 310 D6
Galesburg *Mich., U.S.A.* 42°17N 85°26W 311 B11
Galestan △ *Iran* 37°30N 56°0E 247 B8
Galeton *U.S.A.* 41°44N 77°39W 312 E7
Galets ➜ *Réunion* 20°56S 55°17E 272 f
Galga *Ethiopia* 6°39N 37°47E 257 F4
Galgasc *Somalia* 0°11N 41°38E 267 D5
Galguduud □ *Somalia* 5°0N 47°0E 267 D6
Galheirão ➜ *Brazil* 12°23S 45°5W 333 D2
Gali *Georgia* 42°37N 41°46E 191 J5
Galicea Mare *Romania* 44°4N 23°19E 183 F8
Galich *Russia* 58°22N 42°24E 190 A6
Galiche *Bulgaria* 43°34N 23°53E 202 C7
Galicia □ *Spain* 42°43N 7°45W 194 C3
Galičica △ *Macedonia* 40°56N 20°50E 202 E4
Galien *U.S.A.* 41°48N 86°30W 311 C10
Galilee = Hagalil *Israel* 32°53N 35°18E 250 D6
Galilee, L. *Australia* 22°20S 145°50E 280 C4
Galilee, Sea of = Yam Kinneret *Israel* 32°45N 35°35E 250 D6
Galim *Cameroon* 7°6N 12°25E 263 D7
Galina Pt. *Jamaica* 18°24N 76°58W 320 a
Galinoporni *Cyprus* 35°31N 34°18E 207 E10
Galion *U.S.A.* 40°44N 82°47W 312 F2
Galion, B. du *Martinique* 14°44N 60°56W 322 j
Galite, Îs. de la *Tunisia* 37°30N 8°59E 261 A6
Galiuro Mts. *U.S.A.* 32°30N 110°20W 305 K8
Galiwinku *Australia* 12°2S 135°34E 280 A2
Gallabat *Sudan* 12°58N 36°11E 257 E4
Gallan Hd. *U.K.* 58°15N 7°2W 167 C1
Gallarate *Italy* 45°40N 8°48E 198 C5
Gallatin *Mo., U.S.A.* 39°55N 93°58W 310 E3
Gallatin *Tenn., U.S.A.* 36°24N 86°27W 315 C11
Galle *Sri Lanka* 6°5N 80°10E 245 L5
Gállego ➜ *Spain* 41°39N 0°51W 196 D4
Gallegos ➜ *Argentina* 51°35S 69°0W 336 D3
Gallery of Inuit Art = Dominion Centre *Toronto, Canada* 141 b2
Galletti ➜ *Ethiopia* 8°46N 41°10E 257 F5
Galley Hd. *Ireland* 51°32N 8°55W 166 E3
Galliate *Italy* 45°29N 8°42E 198 C5
Gallinas, Pta. *Colombia* 12°28N 71°40W 328 A3
Gallipoli = Gelibolu *Turkey* 40°28N 26°43E 203 F10
Gallipoli *Italy* 40°3N 17°58E 201 B10
Gallipolis *U.S.A.* 38°49N 82°12W 309 F12
Gällivare *Sweden* 67°9N 20°40E 160 C19
Gallneukirchen *Austria* 48°21N 14°25E 180 C7
Gällö *Sweden* 62°55N 15°13E 162 B9
Gallo, C. *Italy* 38°13N 13°19E 200 D6
Gallocanta, L. de *Spain* 40°58N 1°30W 196 E3
Galloo I. *U.S.A.* 43°55N 76°25W 313 C8
Galloway *U.K.* 55°1N 4°29W 167 F4
Galloway △ *U.K.* 54°39N 4°52W 167 G4
Galloway, Mull of *U.K.* 54°39N 4°52W 167 G4
Gallup *U.S.A.* 35°32N 108°45W 305 J9
Gallur *Spain* 41°52N 1°19W 196 D3
Galma Galla *Kenya* 1°11S 40°47E 267 E5
Galmudug *Somalia* 6°30N 48°0E 267 D6
Galong *Australia* 34°37S 148°34E 283 C8
Galool *Somalia* 3°38N 43°49E 267 D5
Galoya *Sri Lanka* 8°10N 80°55E 245 K5
Galt *Calif., U.S.A.* 38°15N 121°18W 306 G5
Galt *Mo., U.S.A.* 40°8N 93°23W 310 D3
Galten *Denmark* 56°9N 9°54E 163 H3
Galtür *Austria* 46°58N 10°11E 180 E3
Galty Mts. *Ireland* 52°22N 8°10W 166 D3
Galtymore *Ireland* 52°21N 8°11W 166 D3
Galugāh *Iran* 36°43N 53°48E 247 B7
Galva *U.S.A.* 41°10N 90°3W 310 C6
Galvarino *Chile* 38°24S 72°47W 336 A2
Galve de Sorbe *Spain* 41°13N 3°10W 196 D1
Galveston *Ind., U.S.A.* 40°35N 86°11W 311 D10
Galveston *Tex., U.S.A.* 29°18N 94°48W 314 G7
Galveston B. *U.S.A.* 29°36N 94°50W 314 G7
Gálvez *Argentina* 32°0S 61°14W 334 C3
Galway *Ireland* 53°17N 9°3W 166 C2
Galway □ *Ireland* 53°22N 9°1W 166 C2
Galway B. *Ireland* 53°13N 9°10W 166 C2
Galyanovo *Russia* 55°48N 37°47E 129 B3
Gam ➜ *Vietnam* 21°55N 105°12E 236 B5
Gamagōri *Japan* 34°50N 137°14E 223 G8
Gamari, L. *Ethiopia* 11°32N 41°40E 257 E5
Gamawa *Nigeria* 12°10N 10°31E 263 C7
Gamay *Phil.* 12°23N 125°18E 232 E5
Gamay B. *Phil.* 12°21N 125°21E 232 E5
Gamba *Angola* 11°42S 17°14E 265 E3
Gambaga *Ghana* 10°30N 0°28W 263 C4
Gambat *Pakistan* 27°17N 68°26E 242 F3
Gambela *Ethiopia* 8°14N 34°38E 257 F3
Gambela △ *Ethiopia* 8°0N 34°0E 257 F3
Gambela Hizboch □ *Ethiopia* 8°0N 34°0E 257 F3
Gambell *U.S.A.* 63°47N 171°45W 303 E5
Gambhir ➜ *India* 26°58N 77°27E 242 F6
Gambia ■ *W. Afr.* 13°25N 16°0W 262 C1
Gambia ➜ *W. Afr.* 13°28N 16°34W 262 C1
Gambier *U.S.A.* 40°22N 82°23W 312 F2
Gambier, C. *Australia* 11°56S 130°57E 278 B5
Gambier, Îs. *French Polynesia* 23°8S 134°58W 289 f
Gambier Is. *Australia* 35°3S 136°30E 282 C2
Gambier Village *Bahamas* 25°4N 77°30W 153 b
Gambir *Indonesia* 6°9S 106°48E 122 A1
Gambo *C.A.R.* 4°39N 22°16E 264 B4
Gambo *Canada* 48°47N 54°13W 299 C9
Gamboa *Rio de J., Brazil* 22°53S 43°11W 135 B1
Gamboa *Panama* 9°7N 79°42W 320 c
Gamboli *Pakistan* 29°53N 68°24E 242 E3
Gambolòita *Italy* 45°26N 9°13E 128 B2
Gamboma *Congo* 1°55S 15°52E 264 C3
Gamboula *C.A.R.* 4°8N 15°9E 264 B3
Gamka ➜ *S. Africa* 33°18S 21°39E 270 D3
Gamkab ➜ *Namibia* 28°4S 17°54E 270 C2
Gamla Stan *Stockholm, Sweden* 139 c2
Gamla Uppsala *Sweden* 59°54N 17°40E 162 E11
Gamlakarleby = Kokkola *Finland* 63°50N 23°8E 160 E20
Gamleby *Sweden* 57°54N 16°24E 163 G10
Gamlebyen *Norway* 59°54N 10°46E 133 A3
Gammon ➜ *Canada* 51°24N 95°44W 297 C9
Gammon Ranges △ *Australia* 30°38S 139°8E 281 E2
Gamo-Gofa *Ethiopia* 5°40N 36°40E 257 F4
Gamoda-Saki *Japan* 33°50N 134°45E 222 D6
Gamou *Niger* 14°20N 9°55E 259 F1
Gampaha *Sri Lanka* 7°5N 79°59E 245 L4
Gampo *S. Korea* 35°48N 129°31E 224 E4
Gampola *Sri Lanka* 7°10N 80°34E 245 L5
Gamtoos ➜ *S. Africa* 33°58S 25°1E 270 D4
Gamzigrad-Romuliana *Serbia* 43°53N 22°11E 202 C6
Gan *France* 43°12N 0°27W 174 E3
Gan Gan *Argentina* 42°30S 68°10W 336 B3
Gan Goriama, Mts. *Cameroon* 7°44N 12°45E 263 D7
Gan Int. ✈ (GAN) *Maldives* 0°41S 73°1E 272 d
Gan Jiang ➜ *China* 29°15N 116°0E 229 C11
Ganado *U.S.A.* 35°43N 109°33W 305 J9
Gananita *Sudan* 18°22N 33°50E 256 D3
Gananoque *Canada* 44°20N 76°10W 313 B8
Ganassi *Phil.* 7°49N 124°6E 233 H5
Ganāveh *Iran* 29°35N 50°35E 247 D6
Gäncä *Azerbaijan* 40°45N 46°20E 191 K8
Gancheng *China* 18°51N 108°37E 229 a
Gand = Gent *Belgium* 51°2N 3°42E 170 C3
Ganda *Angola* 13°3S 14°35E 265 E2
Gandajika *Dem. Rep. of the Congo* 6°46S 23°58E 265 D4
Gandak ➜ *India* 25°39N 85°13E 243 G11
Gandara *Phil.* 12°1N 124°49E 232 E5
Gandava *Pakistan* 28°32N 67°32E 242 E2
Gander *Canada* 48°58N 54°35W 299 C9
Gander L. *Canada* 48°58N 54°35W 299 C9
Ganderkesee *Germany* 53°2N 8°32E 178 B4
Ganderowe Falls *Zimbabwe* 17°20S 29°10E 269 F2
Gandesa *Spain* 41°3N 0°26E 196 D5
Gandhi Sagar *India* 24°40N 75°40E 242 G6
Gandhinagar *India* 23°15N 72°45E 242 H5
Gandi *Nigeria* 12°55N 5°49E 263 C6
Gandia *Spain* 38°58N 0°9W 197 G4
Gandino *Italy* 45°49N 9°54E 198 C6
Gando, Pta. *Canary Is.* 27°55N 15°22W 153 e1
Gandole *Nigeria* 8°28N 11°35E 263 D7
Gandou *Congo* 2°25N 17°25E 264 B3
Gandu *Brazil* 13°45S 39°30W 333 D4
Gâneb *Mauritania* 18°29N 10°8W 262 B2
Ganedidalem = Gani *Indonesia* 0°48S 128°14E 231 E7
Ganga ➜ *India* 23°20N 90°30E 243 H14
Ganga Sagar *India* 21°38N 88°5E 243 J13
Gangafani *Mali* 14°20N 2°20W 262 C4
Gangakher *India* 18°57N 76°45E 244 E3
Gangalar *India* 28°38N 78°58E 243 E8
Gangan ➜ *India* 28°38N 78°58E 243 E8
Ganganagar *India* 29°56N 73°56E 242 E5
Gangapur *Maharashtra, India* 19°41N 75°1E 244 E2
Gangapur *Raj., India* 26°32N 76°49E 242 F7
Gangara *Niger* 14°35N 8°29E 259 F1
Gangaw *Burma* 22°5N 94°5E 241 D5
Gangaw Taungdan *Burma* 24°55N 96°35E 241 C6
Gangawati *India* 15°30N 76°36E 245 G3
Gangdisê Shan *China* 31°20N 81°0E 243 D9
Gangdong *S. Korea* 37°30N 127°5E 137 B2
Ganges = Ganga ➜ *India* 23°20N 90°30E 243 H14
Ganges *Canada* 48°51N 123°31W 296 D4
Ganges *Hérault, France* 43°56N 3°42E 174 E7
Ganges, Mouths of the *India* 21°30N 90°0E 241 E3
Ganggyeong *S. Korea* 36°10N 127°0E 224 D3
Gånghester *Sweden* 57°42N 13°1E 163 G7
Ganghwa *S. Korea* 37°45N 126°30E 224 D3
Gangi *Italy* 37°48N 14°12E 201 E7
Gângiova *Romania* 43°54N 23°50E 183 G8
Gangnam *S. Korea* 37°30N 126°59E 137 B1
Gangneung *S. Korea* 37°45N 128°54E 224 D4
Gangoh *India* 29°46N 77°18E 242 E7
Gangotri *India* 30°50N 79°10E 243 D8
Gangotri △ *India* 30°50N 79°10E 243 D8
Gangseo *S. Korea* 37°32N 126°51E 137 B1
Gangseong *S. Korea* 38°24N 128°30E 224 C4
Gangshan = Kangshan *Taiwan* 22°48N 120°17E 225 D2
Gangtok *India* 27°20N 88°37E 241 B2
Gangtou *China* 23°12N 113°8E 121 A1
Gangu *China* 34°40N 105°15E 226 G3
Gangwa *Dem. Rep. of the Congo* 3°30S 20°54E 264 C4
Gangwei *China* 23°4N 113°11E 121 B2
Gangwon-do □ *S. Korea* 37°45N 128°15E 224 D4
Gangyao *China* 44°12N 126°37E 227 B14
Gani *Indonesia* 0°48S 128°14E 231 E7
Ganj *India* 27°45N 78°57E 243 F8
Ganjam *India* 19°23N 85°4E 244 E7
Ganjiakou *China* 39°54N 116°16E 114 B1
Ganluo *China* 28°58N 102°59E 228 C4
Ganmain *Australia* 34°47S 147°1E 283 C7
Ganna *South Sudan* 7°30N 28°0E 266 C2
Gannat *France* 46°7N 3°11E 173 F10
Gannett Peak *U.S.A.* 43°11N 109°39W 304 E9
Ganquan *China* 36°20N 109°20E 226 F5
Gänserdorf *Austria* 48°20N 16°43E 181 C9
Ganshoren *Belgium* 50°52N 4°18E 116 A1
Ganshui *China* 28°40N 106°40E 228 C6
Gansu □ *China* 36°0N 104°0E 226 G3
Ganta *Liberia* 7°15N 8°59W 262 D3
Gantheaume, C. *Australia* 36°4S 137°32E 282 D2
Gantheaume B. *Australia* 27°40S 114°10E 279 E1
Gants Hill *U.K.* 51°34N 0°4E 125 A4
Gantsevichi = Hantsavichy *Belarus* 52°49N 26°30E 177 B14
Gantung *Indonesia* 2°58S 108°9E 235 C3
Ganvie *Benin* 6°28N 2°25E 263 D5
Ganye *Nigeria* 8°25N 12°4E 263 D7
Ganyem = Genyem *Indonesia* 2°46S 140°12E 231 E10
Ganyu *China* 34°50N 119°8E 227 G10
Ganyushkino *Kazakhstan* 46°35N 49°20E 191 G9
Ganzhou *China* 25°51N 114°56E 229 E10
Gao *Mali* 16°15N 0°5W 263 B4
Gao Xian *China* 28°21N 104°32E 228 C5
Gao'an *China* 28°26N 115°17E 229 C10
Gaobeidian *China* 39°19N 115°51E 226 E8
Gaocheng *China* 38°2N 114°49E 226 E8
Gaochun *China* 31°20N 118°49E 229 B12
Gaohang *China* 31°20N 121°36E 138 B2
Gaohebu *China* 30°43N 116°49E 229 B11
Gaokeng *China* 27°40N 113°58E 229 D9
Gaolan Dao *China* 21°55N 113°10E 229 G9
Gaoligong Shan *China* 24°45N 98°45E 228 E2
Gaomi *China* 36°20N 119°42E 227 F10
Gaoping *China* 35°45N 112°55E 226 G7
Gaoqiao *China* 31°21N 121°34E 138 A2
Gaoshu = Kaoshu *Taiwan* 22°49N 120°36E 225 D2
Gaotang *China* 36°50N 116°15E 226 F9
Gaoua *Burkina Faso* 10°20N 3°8W 262 C4
Gaoual *Guinea* 11°45N 13°25W 262 C2
Gaoxiong = Kaohsiung *Taiwan* 22°35N 120°16E 225 D2
Gaoyang *China* 38°40N 115°45E 226 E8
Gaoyao *China* 23°3N 112°27E 229 F9
Gaoyou *China* 32°47N 119°26E 229 A12
Gaoyou Hu *China* 32°45N 119°20E 229 A12
Gaoyuan *China* 37°8N 117°58E 227 F9
Gaozhou *China* 21°58N 110°50E 229 G8
Gap *France* 44°33N 6°5E 175 D10
Gapan *Phil.* 15°19N 120°57E 232 D3
Gapat ➜ *India* 24°30N 82°28E 243 G10
Gapuwiyak *Australia* 12°25S 135°43E 280 A2
Gar *China* 32°10N 79°58E 218 E4
Gara, L. *Ireland* 53°57N 8°26W 166 C3
Garāb *Iran* 33°27N 47°16E 213 F12
Garabogazköl Aylagy *Turkmenistan* 41°0N 53°30E 187 F9
Garacad *Somalia* 6°57N 49°24E 267 C6
Garachico *Canary Is.* 28°22N 16°46W 153 e1
Garachiné *Panama* 8°0N 78°12W 320 E4
Garafia *Canary Is.* 28°48N 17°57W 153 e1
Garagum *Turkmenistan* 39°30N 60°0E 247 B8
Garah *Australia* 29°5S 149°38E 281 D4
Garaina *Papua N. G.* 7°53S 147°8E 286 D4
Garajonay *Canary Is.* 28°7N 17°14W 153 e1
Garajonay △ *Canary Is.* 28°7N 17°14W 153 e1
Garamba △ *Dem. Rep. of the Congo* 4°10N 29°40E 268 B2
Garango *Burkina Faso* 11°48N 0°34W 263 C4
Garanhuns *Brazil* 8°50S 36°30W 332 C4
Garapan *N. Marianas* 15°12N 145°43E 302 e
Garautha *India* 25°34N 79°18E 243 G8
Garawa ✪ *Australia* 16°43S 136°51E 280 B2
Garawe *Liberia* 4°35N 8°0W 262 E3
Garba Harre = Garbahaarrey *Somalia* 3°19N 42°13E 267 D5
Garba Tula *Kenya* 0°30N 38°32E 268 B4
Garbagnate Milanese *Italy* 45°34N 9°4E 128 A1
Garbagududu *Ethiopia* 6°12N 43°50E 267 C5
Garbahaarrey *Somalia* 3°19N 42°13E 267 D5
Garbatella *Italy* 41°51N 12°30E 136 B2
Garberville *U.S.A.* 40°6N 123°48W 304 F2
Garbiyang *India* 30°8N 80°52E 243 D9
Garbsen *Germany* 52°26N 9°31E 178 C5
Garça *Brazil* 22°14S 49°37W 333 F2
Garças ➜ *Mato Grosso, Brazil* 15°54S 52°16W 331 D7
Garças ➜ *Pernambuco, Brazil* 8°43S 39°41W 332 C4
Garches *France* 48°50N 2°11E 134 A2
Garching *Germany* 48°14N 11°39E 131 A3
Garchitorena *Phil.* 13°52N 123°40E 232 E4
Garcia Hernandez *Phil.* 9°37N 124°18E 233 G5
Garcias *Brazil* 20°34S 52°13W 331 E7
Gard □ *France* 44°2N 4°10E 175 D8
Gard ➜ *France* 43°51N 4°37E 175 E8
Garda, L. di *Italy* 45°40N 10°41E 198 C7
Gardabani *Georgia* 41°27N 45°5E 191 K7
Gardanne *France* 43°27N 5°27E 175 E9
Gårdby *Sweden* 56°36N 16°38E 163 H10
Garde L. *Canada* 62°50N 106°13W 297 A7
Gardelegen *Germany* 52°32N 11°24E 178 C7
Garden City = El Qâhira, Garden City *Egypt* 30°2N 31°14E 117 A2
Garden City *Ga., U.S.A.* 32°6N 81°9W 316 C8
Garden City *Kans., U.S.A.* 37°58N 100°53W 308 G3
Garden City *Mo., U.S.A.* 38°34N 94°12W 310 F2
Garden City *Tex., U.S.A.* 31°52N 101°29W 314 F4
Garden District *U.S.A.* 29°56N 90°5W 131 B2
Garden Grove *U.S.A.* 33°47N 117°55W 307 M9
Garden Reach *India* 22°33N 88°15E 124 B1
Gardens of Stone △ *Australia* 33°14S 150°11E 283 B9
Garder *Norway* 59°45N 10°38E 133 B2
Gardēz *Afghan.* 33°37N 69°9E 242 C3
Garðabær *Iceland* 64°5N 21°55W 155 C4
Garðskagi *Iceland* 64°5N 22°43W 155 C4
Garður *Iceland* 66°4N 16°46W 155 A10
Gardiki *Greece* 38°50N 21°55E 204 C3
Gardiner *Maine, U.S.A.* 44°14N 69°47W 309 C19
Gardiner *Mont., U.S.A.* 45°2N 110°22W 304 D8
Gardiners I. *U.S.A.* 41°6N 72°6W 313 E12
Gardner *Fla., U.S.A.* 27°21N 81°48W 317 H8
Gardner *Ill., U.S.A.* 41°12N 88°17W 311 C8
Gardner *Mass., U.S.A.* 42°34N 71°59W 313 D13
Gardner Canal *Canada* 53°27N 128°8W 296 C3
Gardner Pinnacles *U.S.A.* 25°0N 167°55W 302 F10
Gardnerville *U.S.A.* 38°56N 119°45W 306 G7
Gardno, Jezioro *Poland* 54°40N 17°7E 184 D4
Gardo = Qardho *Somalia* 9°30N 49°6E 267 C6
Gardone Riviera *Italy* 45°37N 10°34E 198 C7
Gardone Val Trómpia *Italy* 45°41N 10°11E 198 C7
Gárdony *Hungary* 47°12N 18°39E 182 C3
Gare Tigre *Fr. Guiana* 4°58N 53°9W 329 C7
Gareloi I. *U.S.A.* 51°48N 178°48W 303 L3
Gares = Puente la Reina *Spain* 42°40N 1°49W 196 C3
Garešnica *Croatia* 45°36N 16°56E 199 C13
Garéssio *Italy* 44°12N 8°2E 198 D5
Garey *U.S.A.* 34°53N 120°19W 307 L6
Garfield *N.J., U.S.A.* 40°52N 74°7W 132 A1
Garfield *Wash., U.S.A.* 47°1N 117°9W 304 C5
Garfield Park *U.S.A.* 41°52N 87°42W 119 B2
Garforth *U.K.* 53°47N 1°24W 168 D6
Gargaliani *Greece* 37°4N 21°38E 204 D3
Gargan, Mt. *France* 45°37N 1°39E 174 C5
Gargano △ *Italy* 41°43N 15°52E 199 G12
Gargantua, C. *Canada* 47°36N 85°2W 309 B11
Gargareta *Greece* 37°57N 23°43E 112 B2
Gargett *Australia* 21°9S 148°46E 280 b
Gargouna *Mali* 15°56N 0°13E 263 B5
Gargždai *Lithuania* 55°43N 21°24E 184 C8
Garhchiroli *India* 20°10N 80°0E 244 D5
Garibaldi △ *Canada* 49°50N 122°40W 296 D4
Garibong *S. Korea* 37°29N 126°54E 137 C1
Gariep, L. *S. Africa* 30°40S 25°40E 270 D4
Garies *S. Africa* 30°32S 17°59E 270 D2
Garig Gunak Barlu △ *Australia* 11°26S 131°58E 278 B5
Garigliano ➜ *Italy* 41°13N 13°45E 200 A6
Garissa *Kenya* 0°25S 39°40E 268 C4
Garissa □ *Kenya* 0°20S 40°10E 268 C5
Garkida *Nigeria* 10°27N 12°36E 263 C7
Garko *Nigeria* 11°45N 8°35E 263 C6
Garland *Tex., U.S.A.* 32°54N 96°38W 120 A6
Garland *Utah, U.S.A.* 41°45N 112°10W 304 F7
Garlasco *Italy* 45°12N 8°55E 198 C5
Garliava *Lithuania* 54°49N 23°52E 184 D10
Garlin *France* 43°33N 0°16W 174 E3
Garmāb *Semnān, Iran* 35°25N 56°45E 247 C8
Garmāb *Zanjān, Iran* 35°50N 48°11E 213 E13
Garmisch-Partenkirchen *Germany* 47°30N 11°6E 179 H7
Garmo, Qullai = imeni Ismail Samani, Pik *Tajikistan* 39°0N 72°2E 217 E8
Garmsār *Iran* 35°20N 52°25E 247 C7
Garner *U.S.A.* 43°6N 93°36W 310 A3
Garnett *U.S.A.* 38°17N 95°14W 308 F6
Garnpung L. *Australia* 33°25S 143°10E 282 B5
Garo Hills *India* 25°30N 90°30E 241 C3
Garoe = Garoowe *Somalia* 8°25N 48°33E 267 C6
Garonne ➜ *France* 45°2N 0°36W 174 C3
Garonne, Canal Latéral à la *France* 44°15N 0°18E 174 D4
Garoowe *Somalia* 8°25N 48°33E 267 C6
Garorimman *S. Korea* 36°54N 126°21E 224 D3
Garot *India* 24°19N 75°41E 242 G6
Garou, L. *Mali* 16°2N 2°45W 262 B4
Garoua *Cameroon* 9°19N 13°21E 263 D7
Garoua Boulaï *Cameroon* 5°53N 14°33E 264 A2
Garove I. *Papua N. G.* 4°42S 149°30E 286 C5
Garpenberg *Sweden* 60°19N 16°12E 162 D10
Garphyttan *Sweden* 59°18N 14°56E 162 E8
Garrauli *India* 25°5N 79°22E 243 G8
Garrel *Germany* 52°57N 8°1E 178 C4
Garreru *Palau* 7°19N 134°32E 288 c
Garrett *U.S.A.* 41°21N 85°8W 311 C11
Garrison *Ky., U.S.A.* 38°36N 83°10W 311 F13
Garrison *Mont., U.S.A.* 46°31N 112°49W 304 C7
Garrison *N. Dak., U.S.A.* 47°40N 101°25W 308 B3
Garrison Res. = Sakakawea, L. *U.S.A.* 47°30N 101°25W 308 B3
Garron Pt. *U.K.* 55°3N 5°59W 166 A6
Garrovillas de Alconétar *Spain* 39°40N 6°33W 195 F4
Garrucha *Spain* 37°11N 1°49W 197 H3
Garry ➜ *U.K.* 56°44N 3°47W 167 E5
Garry, L. *Canada* 65°58N 100°18W 294 D11
Garrygala *Turkmenistan* 38°31N 56°29E 247 B8
Garsen *Kenya* 2°20S 40°5E 268 C5
Gärsnäs *Sweden* 55°32N 14°10E 163 J8
Garson L. *Canada* 56°19N 110°2W 297 B6
Garstang *U.K.* 53°55N 2°46W 168 D5
Gartempe ➜ *France* 46°47N 0°49E 174 B4
Gartz *Germany* 53°13N 14°22E 178 B10
Garu *Ghana* 10°55N 0°11W 263 C4
Garu *India* 23°40N 84°14E 243 H11
Garub *Namibia* 26°37S 16°0E 270 C2
Garusuun *Palau* 7°21N 134°31E 288 c
Garut *Indonesia* 7°14S 107°53E 235 D3
Garvanza *U.S.A.* 34°6N 118°11W 126 B3
Garvão *Portugal* 37°42N 8°21W 195 H2
Garvie Mts. *N.Z.* 45°30S 168°50E 285 F3
Garwa = Garoua *Cameroon* 9°19N 13°21E 263 D7
Garwa *India* 24°11N 83°47E 243 G10
Garwolin *Poland* 51°55N 21°38E 185 G8
Gary *U.S.A.* 41°36N 87°20W 311 C9
Garz *Germany* 54°19N 13°22E 178 A9
Garzê *China* 31°38N 100°1E 228 B3
Garzón *Colombia* 2°10N 75°40W 328 C2
Gas City *U.S.A.* 40°29N 85°37W 311 D11
Gas-San *Japan* 38°32N 140°1E 220 E10
Gasa *Bhutan* 27°55N 89°40E 241 B2
Gasan *Phil.* 13°19N 121°51E 232 E3
Gasan Kuli = Esenguly *Turkmenistan* 37°37N 53°59E 216 E4
Gascogne *France* 43°45N 0°20E 174 E4
Gascogne, G. de *Europe* 44°0N 2°0W 174 E2
Gasconade *U.S.A.* 38°40N 91°33W 310 F5
Gasconade ➜ *U.S.A.* 38°41N 91°33W 310 F5
Gascony = Gascogne *France* 43°45N 0°20E 174 E4
Gascoyne ➜ *Australia* 24°52S 113°37E 279 D1
Gascoyne Junction *Australia* 25°2S 115°17E 279 E2
Gascueña *Spain* 40°18N 2°31W 196 E2
Gash, Wadi ➜ *Ethiopia* 16°48N 35°51E 257 D4
Gash Setit ⌂ *Eritrea* 15°12N 36°58E 257 D4
Gåshaga *Sweden* 59°21N 18°13E 139 A3
Gashagar *Nigeria* 13°22N 12°47E 263 C7
Gashaka *Nigeria* 7°20N 11°29E 263 D7
Gashaka-Gumti △ *Nigeria* 7°23N 11°34E 263 D7
Gasherbrum *Pakistan* 35°40N 76°40E 243 B7
Gashua *Nigeria* 12°54N 11°0E 263 C7
Gasmata *Papua N. G.* 6°17S 150°20E 286 D6
Gaspar Grande *Trin. & Tob.* 10°40N 61°39W 323 t
Gaspar Str. = Gelasa, Selat *Indonesia* 2°50S 107°0E 235 C3
Gasparilla I. *U.S.A.* 26°46N 82°16W 317 J7
Gasparillo *Trin. & Tob.* 10°18N 61°26W 323 t
Gaspé *Curaçao* 12°8N 68°56W 322 g
Gaspé *Canada* 48°52N 64°30W 299 C7
Gaspé, C. de *Canada* 48°48N 64°7W 299 C7
Gaspé Pen. = Gaspésie, Pén. de la *Canada* 48°45N 65°40W 299 C6
Gaspésie, Pén. de la *Canada* 48°45N 65°40W 299 C6
Gaspésie ⌂ *Canada* 48°55N 66°10W 299 C6
Gassan *Burkina Faso* 12°49N 3°12W 262 C4
Gassen = Jasień *Poland* 51°46N 15°0E 185 G2
Gassol *Nigeria* 8°34N 10°25E 263 D7
Gasteiz = Vitoria-Gasteiz *Spain* 42°50N 2°41W 196 C2
Gaston *U.S.A.* 33°49N 81°5W 316 B8
Gastonia *U.S.A.* 35°16N 81°11W 315 D14
Gastouni *Greece* 37°51N 21°15E 204 D3
Gastouri *Greece* 39°34N 19°54E 206 B9
Gastre *Argentina* 42°20S 69°15W 336 B3
Gästrikland *Sweden* 60°45N 16°40E 162 D10
Gata, C. *Cyprus* 34°34N 33°2E 207 F9
Gata, C. de *Spain* 36°41N 2°13W 197 J2
Gata, Sierra de *Spain* 40°20N 6°45W 194 E4
Gataga ➜ *Canada* 58°35N 126°59W 296 B3
Gătaia *Romania* 45°26N 21°30E 182 E6
Gatchina *Russia* 59°35N 30°9E 188 C6
Gatehouse of Fleet *U.K.* 54°53N 4°12W 167 G4
Gates *U.S.A.* 43°9N 77°42W 312 C7
Gates of the Arctic ⌂ *U.S.A.* 67°45N 153°15W 303 C9
Gateshead *U.K.* 54°57N 1°35W 168 C6
Gateshead I. *Canada* 70°36N 100°26W 294 C11
Gatesville *U.S.A.* 31°26N 97°45W 314 F6
Gateway ➜ *U.S.A.* 40°38N 73°51W 132 C2
Gateway of India *India* 18°55N 72°50E 130 B2
Gateway Park *U.S.A.* 32°43N 96°42W 120 B2
Gaths *Zimbabwe* 20°2S 30°32E 269 G3
Gâtinais *France* 48°5N 2°40E 173 D9
Gâtine, Hauteurs de *France* 46°35N 0°45W 174 B3
Gatineau *Canada* 45°29N 75°39W 313 A9
Gatineau ➜ *Canada* 45°27N 75°42W 298 C4
Gatineau △ *Canada* 45°40N 76°0W 298 C4
Gatow *Germany* 52°29N 13°11E 115 B1
Gattaran *Phil.* 18°4N 121°38E 232 B3
Gattinara *Italy* 45°37N 8°22E 198 C5
Gatton *Australia* 27°32S 152°17E 281 D5
Gatún, L. *Panama* 9°7N 79°56W 320 c
Gatún Dam *Panama* 9°16N 79°55W 320 c
Gatún Locks *Panama* 9°16N 79°55W 320 c
Gatwick, London ✈ (LGW) *U.K.* 51°10N 0°11W 169 F7
Gatyana *S. Africa* 32°16S 28°31E 271 D4
Gau *Fiji* 18°2S 179°18E 287 B2
Gaua *Vanuatu* 14°15S 167°30E 287 D5
Gaucín *Spain* 36°31N 5°19W 195 J5
Gauer L. *Canada* 57°0N 97°50W 297 B9
Gauhati = Guwahati *India* 26°10N 91°45E 241 B3
Gauja ➜ *Latvia* 57°10N 24°16E 188 D3
Gaujas △ *Latvia* 57°10N 24°50E 161 H21
Gaula ➜ *Norway* 63°21N 10°14E 164 A7
Gaupne *Norway* 61°25N 7°18E 164 C4
Gaurdak = Gowurdak *Turkmenistan* 37°50N 66°4E 217 E7
Gauri Phanta *India* 28°41N 80°36E 243 E9
Gauribidanur *India* 13°37N 77°32E 245 H3
Gaustatoppen *Norway* 59°48N 8°40E 164 E5
Gauteng □ *S. Africa* 26°0S 28°0E 271 C4
Gāv Koshī *Iran* 28°38N 57°12E 247 D8
Gavà *Spain* 41°18N 2°1E 114 B1
Gāvakān *Iran* 29°37N 53°10E 247 D7
Gavamar *Spain* 41°15N 2°1E 114 B1
Gavar *Armenia* 40°21N 45°7E 191 K7
Gavarnie *France* 42°44N 0°1W 174 F3
Gavāter *Iran* 25°10N 61°31E 247 E9
Gāvbandī *Iran* 27°12N 53°4E 247 E7
Gavdopoula *Greece* 34°56N 24°0E 207 F5
Gavdos *Greece* 34°50N 24°5E 207 F5
Gávea *Brazil* 22°58S 43°13W 135 B1
Gávea, Pedra da *Brazil* 22°59S 43°18W 135 B1
Gavi *Italy* 44°41N 8°49E 198 D5
Gavião *Portugal* 39°28N 7°56W 195 F3
Gaviota *U.S.A.* 34°29N 120°13W 307 L6
Gāvkhūnī, Bāţlāq-e *Iran* 32°6N 52°52E 247 C7
Gävle *Sweden* 60°40N 17°9E 162 D11
Gävleborg □ *Sweden* 61°30N 16°15E 162 C10
Gävlebukten *Sweden* 60°40N 17°20E 162 D11
Gavorrano *Italy* 42°55N 10°54E 198 F7
Gavray *France* 48°55N 1°20W 172 D5
Gavrilov Yam *Russia* 57°18N 39°49E 188 D10
Gavrio *Greece* 37°54N 24°44E 204 D6
Gawachab *Namibia* 27°4S 17°55E 270 C2
Gawai *Burma* 27°56N 97°30E 241 B6
Gawilgarh Hills *India* 21°15N 76°45E 244 D3
Gawler *Australia* 34°30S 138°42E 282 C3
Gawler Ranges *Australia* 32°30S 135°45E 282 B2
Gawu *Nigeria* 9°14N 6°52E 263 D6
Gaxun Nur *China* 42°22N 100°30E 218 C9
Gay *Russia* 51°27N 58°27E 186 D10
Gay *Ga., U.S.A.* 33°6N 84°35W 316 B5
Gaya *India* 24°47N 85°4E 243 G11
Gaya *Niger* 11°52N 3°28E 263 C5
Gaya *Nigeria* 11°57N 9°0E 263 C6
Gayasan △ *S. Korea* 35°45N 128°10E 224 E4
Gayéri *Burkina Faso* 12°39N 0°29E 263 C5
Gaylord *U.S.A.* 45°2N 84°41W 309 C11
Gayndah *Australia* 25°35S 151°32E 281 D5
Gaysin = Haysyn *Ukraine* 48°57N 29°25E 183 B14
Gayvoron = Hayvoron *Ukraine* 48°22N 29°52E 183 B14
Gaza *Gaza Strip* 31°30N 34°28E 251 G5
Gaza □ *Mozam.* 23°10S 32°45E 271 B5
Gaza Strip □ *Asia* 31°29N 34°25E 251 G5
Gazanjyk = Bereket *Turkmenistan* 39°16N 55°32E 247 B7
Gazaoua *Niger* 13°32N 7°55E 263 C6
Gāzbor *Iran* 28°5N 58°51E 247 D8
Gazdagrét *Hungary* 47°29N 19°0E 117 B1
Gazelle Pen. *Papua N. G.* 4°40S 152°0E 286 C7
Gazi *Dem. Rep. of the Congo* 1°3N 24°30E 264 B4
Gaziantep *Turkey* 37°6N 37°23E 250 A8
Gaziantep □ *Turkey* 37°0N 37°0E 250 B8
Gazimağusa = Famagusta *Cyprus* 35°8N 33°55E 207 E9
Gaziosmanpaşa *Turkey* 41°5N 28°50E 122 B1
Gazipaşa *Turkey* 36°16N 32°18E 250 B3
Gazipur *Bangla.* 23°48N 90°39E 241 D3
Gazli *Uzbekistan* 40°8N 63°27E 216 D6
Gazojak *Turkmenistan* 41°11N 61°24E 216 D6
Gbadolite *Dem. Rep. of the Congo* 4°17N 21°1E 264 B4
Gbarnga *Liberia* 7°19N 9°13W 262 D3
Gboko *Nigeria* 7°17N 9°4E 263 D6
Gcoverega *Botswana* 19°8S 24°18E 270 A3
Gcuwa *S. Africa* 32°20S 28°11E 271 D4
Gdańsk *Poland* 54°22N 18°40E 184 D5
Gdańsk ✈ (GDN) *Poland* 54°22N 18°30E 184 D5
Gdansk B. = Gdańska, Zatoka *Poland* 54°30N 19°20E 184 D6
Gdańska, Zatoka *Poland* 54°30N 19°20E 184 D6
Gdingen = Gdynia *Poland* 54°35N 18°33E 184 D5
Gdov *Russia* 58°48N 27°55E 188 C4
Gdynia *Poland* 54°35N 18°33E 184 D5
Geba ➜ *Guinea-Biss.* 11°46N 15°36W 262 C1
Gebe *Indonesia* 0°5N 129°25E 231 D7
Gebeciler *Turkey* 38°46N 30°46E 205 C12
Gebeit Mine *Sudan* 21°3N 36°29E 256 C4
Gebel Abyad *Sudan* 19°0N 28°0E 256 D2
Gebel el Ahmar *Egypt* 30°2N 31°21E 117 A3
Gebel el Muqattam *Egypt* 30°1N 31°17E 117 A2
Gebel el Tura *Egypt* 29°56N 31°15E 117 B2
Gebel Iweibid *Egypt* 30°8N 32°13E 256 H8
Gebiley *Somalia* 9°42N 43°37E 267 C5
Gebze *Turkey* 40°47N 29°25E 203 F13
Gecha *Ethiopia* 7°30N 35°18E 257 F4
Geçitkale = Lefkoniko *Cyprus* 35°18N 33°44E 207 E9
Gedaref *Sudan* 14°2N 35°28E 257 E4
Gedaref □ *Sudan* 14°0N 35°0E 257 E4
Gede, Tanjung *Indonesia* 6°46S 105°12E 234 D3
Gediz *Turkey* 39°1N 29°24E 205 B11
Gediz ➜ *Turkey* 38°35N 26°48E 205 C8
Gedo *Ethiopia* 9°2N 37°25E 257 F4
Gedo □ *Somalia* 2°15N 42°10E 267 D5
Gèdre *France* 42°47N 0°2E 174 F4
Gedser *Denmark* 54°35N 11°55E 163 K5
Gedung, Pulau *Malaysia* 5°17N 100°23E 237 c
Geegully Cr. ➜ *Australia* 18°32S 123°41E 278 C3
Geel *Belgium* 51°10N 4°59E 170 C4
Geelong *Australia* 38°10S 144°22E 282 E6
Geelvink B. = Cenderawasih, Teluk *Indonesia* 3°0S 135°20E 231 E9
Geelvink Chan. *Australia* 28°30S 114°0E 279 E1
Geesthacht *Germany* 53°26N 10°22E 178 B6
Geidam *Nigeria* 12°57N 11°57E 263 C7
Geikie ➜ *Canada* 57°45N 103°52W 297 B8
Geikie Gorge △ *Australia* 18°3S 125°41E 278 C4
Geilenkirchen *Germany* 50°57N 6°8E 178 E2
Geili *Sudan* 16°1N 32°37E 257 D3
Geilo *Norway* 60°32N 8°14E 164 D5
Geirangerfjorden *Norway* 62°7N 7°10E 164 B4
Geiselgasteig *Germany* 48°3N 11°33E 131 B2
Geisingen *Germany* 47°54N 8°39E 179 H4
Geislingen *Germany* 48°37N 9°50E 179 G5
Geistown *U.S.A.* 40°18N 78°52W 312 F6
Geita *Tanzania* 2°48S 32°12E 268 C3
Geita □ *Tanzania* 2°50S 32°10E 268 C3
Geitastrand *Norway* 63°22N 9°56E 164 A6
Geithus *Norway* 59°57N 9°58E 164 E6
Geju *China* 23°20N 103°10E 228 F4
Gel ➜ *South Sudan* 7°5N 29°10E 257 F2
Gel, Meydān-e *Iran* 29°4N 54°50E 247 D7
Gel River *South Sudan* 7°5N 29°10E 257 F2
Gela *Italy* 37°4N 14°15E 201 E7
Gela, G. di *Italy* 37°0N 14°20E 201 F7
Geladi *Ethiopia* 6°59N 46°30E 267 C6
Gelahun *Liberia* 7°55N 10°28W 262 D2

Gelam Indonesia 2°54S 110°11E 235 C4
Gelang Patah Malaysia 1°27N 103°35E 237 d
Gelasa, Selat Indonesia 2°50S 107°0E 235 C3
Gelderland □ Neths. 52°5N 6°10E 170 B6
Geldern Germany 51°31N 6°20E 178 D2
Geldrop Neths. 51°25N 5°32E 170 C5
Geleen Neths. 50°57N 5°49E 170 D5
Gelehun S. Leone 8°20N 11°40W 262 D2
Gelembe Turkey 39°10N 27°50E 205 B9
Gelemso Ethiopia 8°49N 40°31E 257 F5
Gelendost Turkey 38°7N 31°1E 212 C4
Gelendzhik Russia 44°33N 38°10E 189 K10
Gelib = Jilib Somalia 0°29N 42°46E 267 D5
Gelibolu Turkey 40°28N 26°43E 203 F10
Gelibolu Yarımadası Turkey 40°20N 26°30E 203 F10
Gelidonya Burnu Turkey 36°12N 30°24E 212 D4
Gellinsoor Somalia 6°28N 46°39E 267 C6
Gelnhausen Germany 50°11N 9°11E 179 E5
Gelnica Slovakia 48°51N 20°55E 181 C13
Gelora Bung Karno Stadium Jakarta, Indonesia 6°13S 106°47E 122 B1
Gelsenkirchen Germany 51°32N 7°6E 178 D3
Gelting Germany 54°45N 9°53E 178 A5
Gelugur Malaysia 5°22N 100°18E 237 c
Gemas Malaysia 2°37N 102°36E 237 L4
Gembloux Belgium 50°34N 4°43E 170 D4
Gembu Nigeria 6°42N 11°10E 263 D7
Gemena Dem. Rep. of the Congo 3°13N 19°48E 264 B3
Gemerek Turkey 39°15N 36°10E 212 C7
Gemikonagı = Karavostasi Cyprus 35°8N 32°50E 207 E8
Gemla Sweden 56°52N 14°39E 163 H8
Gemlik Turkey 40°26N 29°9E 203 F13
Gemlik Körfezi Turkey 40°25N 28°55E 203 F12
Gemona del Friuli Italy 46°16N 13°9E 199 B10
Gemsa Egypt 27°39N 33°35E 256 B3
Gemsbok △ Botswana 25°5S 21°1E 270 C3
Gemünden Germany 50°3N 9°42E 179 E5
Genadi Greece 36°2N 27°56E 206 E11
Genale → Ethiopia 6°2N 39°1E 257 F4
Genç Turkey 38°44N 40°34E 213 C9
Gençay France 46°23N 0°23E 174 B4
General Acha Argentina 37°20S 64°38W 334 D3
General Alvear B. Aires, Argentina 36°0S 60°0W 334 D4
General Alvear Mendoza, Argentina 35°0S 67°40W 334 D2
General Artigas Paraguay 26°52S 56°16W 334 B4
General Belgrano Argentina 36°35S 58°47W 334 D4
General Bernardo O'Higgins Antarctica 63°0S 58°3W 151 C18
General Cabrera Argentina 32°53S 63°52W 334 C3
General Carrera, L. S. Amer. 46°35S 72°0W 336 C2
General Cepeda Mexico 25°21N 101°22W 318 B4
General Conesa Argentina 40°6S 64°25W 336 B4
General Eugenio A. Garay Paraguay 20°31S 62°8W 331 E5
General Germán Busch = Villa Abecia Bolivia 21°0S 68°18W 334 A2
General Guido Argentina 36°40S 57°50W 334 D4
General Juan Madariaga Argentina 37°0S 57°0W 334 D4
General La Madrid Argentina 37°17S 61°20W 334 D3
General Lorenzo Vintter Argentina 40°45S 64°26W 336 B4
General Luna Phil. 13°41N 122°10E 232 E4
General MacArthur Phil. 11°18N 125°28E 233 F5
General Martin Miguel de Güemes Argentina 24°50S 65°0W 334 A3
General Pico Argentina 35°45S 63°50W 334 D3
General Pinedo Argentina 27°15S 61°20W 334 B3
General Pinto Argentina 34°45S 61°50W 334 C3
General Roca Argentina 39°2S 67°35W 336 A3
General Sampaio Brazil 4°2S 39°29W 332 B4
General San Martin Argentina 34°35S 58°32W 117 B1
General Santos Phil. 6°5N 125°14E 233 H5
General Tinio Phil. 15°39N 121°10E 232 D3
General Toshevo Bulgaria 43°42N 28°6E 203 C12
General Treviño Mexico 26°14N 99°29W 319 B5
General Trías Mexico 28°21N 106°22W 318 B3
General Uriburu = Zárate Argentina 34°7S 59°0W 334 C4
General Viamonte Argentina 35°1S 61°3W 334 D3
General Villegas Argentina 35°5S 63°0W 334 D3
General Vintter, L. Argentina 43°55S 71°40W 336 B2
Generoso Ponce = Jaci-Paraná Brazil 9°15S 64°23W 331 B5
Genesee Idaho, U.S.A. 46°33N 116°56W 304 C5
Genesee Pa., U.S.A. 41°59N 77°54W 312 E7
Genesee → U.S.A. 43°16N 77°36W 312 C7
Geneseo Ill., U.S.A. 41°27N 90°9W 310 C6
Geneseo N.Y., U.S.A. 42°48N 77°49W 312 D7
Geneva = Genève Switz. 46°12N 6°9E 179 J2
Geneva Ala., U.S.A. 31°2N 85°52W 316 D4
Geneva Ga., U.S.A. 32°35N 84°33W 316 C5
Geneva Ill., U.S.A. 41°53N 88°18W 311 C8
Geneva Ind., U.S.A. 40°36N 84°58W 311 D12
Geneva N.Y., U.S.A. 42°52N 76°59W 312 D8
Geneva Nebr., U.S.A. 40°32N 97°36W 308 E5
Geneva Ohio, U.S.A. 41°48N 80°57W 312 E4
Geneva, L. = Léman, L. Europe 46°26N 6°30E 173 F13
Geneva, L. U.S.A. 42°38N 88°30W 311 B8
Genève Switz. 46°12N 6°9E 179 J2
Geng Afghan. 31°22N 61°28E 240 C1
Gengenbach Germany 48°24N 8°1E 179 G4
Gengma China 23°32N 99°20E 228 F2
Genhe China 50°47N 121°31E 219 A13
Genichesk = Henichesk Ukraine 46°12N 34°50E 189 J8
Genil → Spain 37°42N 5°19W 195 H5
Génipa, B. de Martinique 14°33N 61°0W 322 j
Genisea Greece 41°1N 24°57E 203 E8
Genk Belgium 50°58N 5°32E 170 D5
Genkai-Nada Japan 34°0N 130°0E 222 D2
Genlis France 47°11N 5°12E 173 E12
Gennargentu, Mti. del Italy 40°1N 9°19E 200 B2
Gennes France 47°20N 0°17W 172 E6
Gennevilliers France 48°56N 2°17E 134 A2
Genoa = Génova Italy 44°25N 8°57E 198 D5
Genoa Vic., Australia 37°29S 149°35E 283 D8
Genoa Ill., U.S.A. 42°6N 88°42W 311 B8
Genoa N.Y., U.S.A. 42°40N 76°32W 313 D8
Genoa Nebr., U.S.A. 41°27N 97°44W 308 E5
Genoa Nev., U.S.A. 39°2N 119°50W 306 F7
Genoa → Argentina 44°55S 70°5W 336 B2
Genoa City U.S.A. 42°30N 88°20W 311 B8
Génova Italy 44°25N 8°57E 198 D5
Génova ✕ (GOA) Italy 44°25N 8°56E 198 D5
Génova, G. di Italy 44°0N 9°0E 198 E6
Genovesa, I. Ecuador 0°20N 89°58W 330 a
Genriyetty, Ostrov Russia 77°6N 156°30E 215 B16
Gent Belgium 51°2N 3°42E 170 C3
Genteng Jawa Barat, Indonesia 7°22S 106°24E 234 D3
Genteng Jawa Timur, Indonesia 8°22S 114°9E 231 J17
Genthin Germany 52°25N 12°9E 178 C8
Gentilly Val-de-Marne, France 48°48N 2°21E 134 B3
Gentilly La., U.S.A. 30°0N 90°2W 131 A2
Gentio do Ouro Brazil 11°25S 42°30W 332 D3
Gentofte Denmark 55°44N 12°32E 118 A3
Gentryville U.S.A. 38°6N 87°2W 311 F9
Genval Belgium 50°43N 4°29E 116 B2
Genyem Indonesia 2°46S 140°12E 231 E10
Genzano di Lucánia Italy 40°51N 16°2E 201 B9
Genzano di Roma Italy 41°42N 12°41E 199 G9
Geoagiu Romania 45°55N 23°12E 183 E8
Geochang S. Korea 35°41N 127°55E 224 E3
Geogeumdo S. Korea 34°27N 127°10E 224 E3
Geographe B. Australia 33°30S 115°15E 279 F2
Geographe Chan. Australia 24°30S 113°0E 279 D1
Geographical Society Ø Greenland 72°57N 23°15W 154 C8
Geoje S. Korea 34°51N 128°35E 224 E4
Geojedo S. Korea 34°51N 128°38E 224 E4
Geokchay = Göyçay Azerbaijan 40°42N 47°43E 191 K8
Georga, Zemlya Russia 80°30N 49°0E 214 A5
George S. Africa 33°58S 22°29E 270 D3
George → Canada 58°49N 66°10W 299 A6
George, L. N.S.W., Australia 35°10S 149°25E 283 C8
George, L. S. Austral., Australia 37°25S 140°0E 282 D4
George, L. W. Austral., Australia 22°45S 123°40E 278 D3
George, L. Uganda 0°5N 30°10E 268 B3
George, L. Fla., U.S.A. 29°17N 81°36W 317 F8
George, L. N.Y., U.S.A. 43°37N 73°33W 313 C11
George Bush Intercontinental, Houston ✕ (IAH) U.S.A. 29°59N 95°20W 314 G7
George Gill Ra. Australia 24°22S 131°45E 278 D5
George I. Hong Kong, China 22°13N 114°7E 122 B2
George I. St. Helena 15°58S 5°38W 153 h
George Pt. Australia 20°6S 148°36E 280 b
George River = Kangiqsualujjuaq Canada 58°30N 65°59W 295 F18
George Rogers Clark Nat. Memorial ⌓ U.S.A. 38°41N 87°32W 311 F9
George Sound N.Z. 44°52S 167°25E 285 E2
George Town Tas., Australia 41°6S 146°49E 281 G4
George Town Bahamas 23°33N 75°47W 320 B4
George Town Cayman Is. 19°20N 81°24W 320 C3
George Town Malaysia 5°25N 100°20E 237 c
George V Land Antarctica 69°0S 148°0E 151 C10
George VI Sound Antarctica 71°0S 68°0W 151 D17
George West U.S.A. 28°20N 98°7W 314 G5
Georges River Bridge Australia 34°0S 151°6E 139 C1
Georgetown = Janjanbureh Gambia 13°30N 14°47W 262 C2
Georgetown Ascension I. 7°56S 14°25W 153 g
Georgetown Queens., Australia 18°17S 143°33E 280 B3
Georgetown Ont., Canada 43°40N 79°56W 312 C5
Georgetown P.E.I., Canada 46°13N 62°24W 299 C7
Georgetown Guyana 6°50N 58°12W 329 B6
Georgetown St. Vincent 13°16N 61°7W 323 n
Georgetown Calif., U.S.A. 38°54N 120°50W 306 G6
Georgetown Colo., U.S.A. 39°42N 105°42W 304 G11
Georgetown D.C., U.S.A. 38°54N 77°3W 143 B2
Georgetown Fla., U.S.A. 29°23N 81°38W 317 F8
Georgetown Ga., U.S.A. 31°53N 85°6W 316 D4
Georgetown Ill., U.S.A. 39°59N 87°38W 311 E9
Georgetown Ky., U.S.A. 38°13N 84°33W 311 F12
Georgetown N.Y., U.S.A. 42°46N 75°44W 313 D9
Georgetown Ohio, U.S.A. 38°52N 83°54W 311 F13
Georgetown S.C., U.S.A. 33°23N 79°17W 315 E15
Georgetown Tex., U.S.A. 30°38N 97°41W 314 F6
Georgia □ U.S.A. 32°50N 83°15W 316 C6
Georgia ■ Asia 42°0N 43°0E 191 J6
Georgia, Str. of N. Amer. 49°25N 124°0W 306 A3
Georgia Aquarium Atlanta, U.S.A. 33°46N 84°23W 113 B2
Georgia Basin S. Ocean 50°45S 35°30W 151 B1
Georgia Dome Atlanta, U.S.A. 33°45N 84°23W 113 B2
Georgian B. Canada 45°15N 81°0W 312 A4
Georgian Bay Islands △ Canada 44°53N 79°52W 312 B5
Georgīevka Kazakhstan 49°19N 84°34E 217 C10
Georgina → Australia 23°30S 139°47E 280 C2
Georgina I. Canada 44°22N 79°17W 312 B5
Georgioupoli Greece 35°20N 24°15E 207 E5
Georgiu-Dezh = Liski Russia 51°3N 39°30E 189 G10
Georgiyevsk Russia 44°12N 43°28E 191 H6
Georgsmarienhütte Germany 52°13N 8°3E 178 C4
Gera Germany 50°53N 12°4E 178 E8
Geraardsbergen Belgium 50°45N 3°53E 170 D3
Geraki Greece 37°0N 22°42E 204 D4
Geraki, Akra Greece 37°42N 20°59E 207 D2
Geral, Serra Bahia, Brazil 14°0S 41°0W 333 D3
Geral, Serra Goiás, Brazil 11°15S 46°30W 332 D2
Geral, Serra Sta. Catarina, Brazil 26°25S 50°0W 335 B6
Geral de Goiás, Serra Brazil 12°0S 46°0W 333 D2
Geral do Paranã, Serra Brazil 15°0S 47°30W 333 E2
Gerald U.S.A. 38°24N 91°20W 310 F5
Geraldine N.Z. 44°5S 171°15E 285 E6
Geraldine Mont., U.S.A. 47°36N 110°16W 304 C8
Geraldton = Innisfail Australia 17°33S 146°5E 280 B4
Geraldton W. Austral., Australia 28°48S 114°32E 279 E1
Geraldton Ont., Canada 49°44N 87°10W 298 C2
Geranium Australia 35°23S 140°11E 282 C4
Gérardmer France 48°3N 6°50E 173 D13
Gerasdorf bei Wien Austria 48°17N 16°28E 142 A2
Gerberau Germany 48°12N 11°27E 131 A1
Gercüş Turkey 37°34N 41°23E 213 D9
Gerdine, Mt. U.S.A. 61°35N 152°27W 303 F9
Gerede Turkey 40°45N 32°10E 212 B5
Gerês, Sierra do Portugal 41°48N 8°0W 194 D3
Gereshk Afghan. 31°47N 64°35E 240 C2
Geretsried Germany 47°51N 11°28E 179 H7
Gérgal Spain 37°7N 2°31W 197 H2
Gerik Malaysia 5°50N 101°15E 237 K3
Gering U.S.A. 41°50N 103°40W 308 E2
Geriş Turkey 36°57N 31°43E 250 B2
Gerlach U.S.A. 40°39N 119°21W 304 F4
Gerlachovský štit Slovakia 49°11N 20°7E 181 B13
Gerli Argentina 34°41S 58°22W 117 C2
Gerlogubi Ethiopia 6°53N 45°3E 267 C6
German Bight = Deutsche Bucht Germany 54°15N 8°0E 178 A4
German East Africa = Tanzania ■ Africa 6°0S 34°0E 268 D3
German Planina Macedonia 42°20N 22°0E 202 D6
German South West Africa = Namibia ■ Africa 22°0S 18°9E 270 B2
Germania Land Greenland 77°5N 19°30W 154 B9
Germansen Landing Canada 55°43N 124°40W 296 B4
Germantown Ohio, U.S.A. 39°38N 84°22W 311 E12
Germantown Tenn., U.S.A. 35°5N 89°49W 315 D10
Germantown Wis., U.S.A. 43°14N 88°6W 311 A8
Germany ■ Europe 51°0N 10°0E 178 E6
Germencik Turkey 37°52N 27°37E 205 D9
Germering Germany 48°8N 11°22E 179 G7
Germersheim Germany 49°12N 8°22E 179 F4
Germī Iran 39°1N 48°3E 213 C13
Germiston S. Africa 26°13S 28°10E 123 B2
Gern Germany 48°10N 11°32E 131 B2
Gernene Algeria 21°40N 2°24E 261 D5
Gernika-Lumo Spain 43°19N 2°40W 196 B2
Gernsheim Germany 49°45N 8°30E 179 F4
Gero Japan 35°48N 137°14E 223 B9
Gerogery Australia 35°50S 147°1E 283 C7
Gerokgak Indonesia 8°11S 114°27E 231 J17
Gerolzhofen Germany 49°54N 10°21E 179 F6
Gerona = Girona Spain 41°58N 2°46E 196 D7
Gerona Phil. 15°36N 120°36E 232 D3
Geropotamos → Greece 35°3N 24°50E 207 E5
Gerrard Canada 50°30N 117°17W 296 C5
Gerringong Australia 34°46S 150°47E 283 C9
Gers □ France 43°35N 0°30E 174 E4
Gers → France 44°9N 0°39E 174 D4
Gersfeld Germany 50°27N 9°56E 178 E5
Gersoppa Falls India 14°12N 74°46E 245 G2
Gersthofen Germany 48°25N 10°53E 179 G6
Gertak Sanggul Malaysia 5°17N 100°12E 237 c
Gertak Sanggul, Tanjung Malaysia 5°16N 100°11E 237 c
Gerung Indonesia 8°43S 116°7E 231 K19
Géryville = El Bayadh Algeria 33°40N 1°1E 261 B5
Gerzat France 45°48N 3°8E 174 C7
Gerze Turkey 41°48N 35°12E 212 B6
Geseke Germany 51°38N 8°31E 178 D4
Geser Indonesia 3°50S 130°54E 231 E8
Gesira △ Somalia 1°58N 44°59E 267 D5
Gesso → Italy 44°24N 7°33E 198 D4
Gestro, Wabi → Ethiopia 4°12N 42°2E 257 G5
Gesuit, Ex Convento dei Venice, Italy 142 a3
Getafe Spain 40°18N 3°43W 127 C1
Getinge Sweden 56°49N 12°44E 163 H6
Getty Center, The U.S.A. 34°4N 118°29W 126 B2
Gettysburg Pa., U.S.A. 39°50N 77°14W 309 F15
Gettysburg S. Dak., U.S.A. 45°1N 99°57W 308 C4
Getxo = Algorta Spain 43°21N 2°59W 196 B2
Getz Ice Shelf Antarctica 75°0S 130°0W 151 D14
Geumodo S. Korea 34°31N 127°45E 224 E3
Geumpang Indonesia 4°52N 96°6E 234 B1
Geunjeong S. Korea 37°28N 126°54E 137 C1
Geureudong, Gunung Indonesia 4°13N 96°42E 234 B1
Geurie Australia 32°22S 148°50E 283 B8
Geva Binyamin West Bank 31°51N 35°17E 123 A2
Gevaş Turkey 38°15N 43°6E 213 C10
Gévaudan France 44°40N 3°40E 174 D7
Gevgelija Macedonia 41°9N 22°30E 202 E6
Gévora → Spain 38°53N 6°57W 195 G4
Gevrai India 19°16N 75°45E 244 E2
Gewani Ethiopia 10°12N 40°40E 257 E5
Gex France 46°21N 6°3E 173 F13
Geyikli Turkey 39°48N 26°12E 205 B8
Geylang Serai Singapore 1°19N 103°53E 138 B3
Geyser U.S.A. 47°16N 110°30W 304 C8
Geyserville U.S.A. 38°42N 122°54W 306 G4
Geysir Iceland 64°19N 20°18W 155 C6
Geyve Turkey 40°30N 30°18E 212 B4
Gezhouba Dam China 30°40N 111°20E 229 B8
Ghâbat el Arab = Wang Kai South Sudan 9°3N 29°23E 257 F2
Ghabeish Sudan 12°9N 27°21E 257 E2
Ghadāf, W. al → Iraq 32°56N 43°30E 213 F10
Ghadāmis Libya 30°11N 9°29E 258 B1
Ghaddūwah Libya 26°26N 14°19E 258 C2
Ghaggar → India 29°30N 74°53E 242 E6
Ghaghara → India 25°45N 84°40E 243 G11
Ghaghat → Bangla. 25°19N 89°38E 241 C2
Ghaghe Solomon Is. 7°24S 158°15E 287 L10
Ghagra India 23°17N 84°33E 243 H11
Ghajn Tuffieha Bay Malta 35°56N 14°21E 206 F7
Ghajnsielem Malta 36°2N 14°17E 206 E7
Ghalla, Wadi el → Sudan 10°25N 27°32E 257 E2
Ghallamane Mauritania 23°15N 10°0W 260 D3
Ghallamane, Sebkhet Mauritania 23°41N 9°50W 260 D3
Ghamid az Zenad Si. Arabia 19°35N 41°24E 248 C3
Ghana ■ W. Afr. 8°0N 1°0W 263 D4
Ghanpokhara Nepal 28°17N 84°14E 243 E11
Ghansor India 22°39N 80°1E 243 H9
Ghanzi Botswana 21°50S 21°34E 270 B3
Ghanzi □ Botswana 22°30S 22°30E 270 B3
Gharapuri = Elephanta I. India 18°57N 72°56E 130 B2
Gharb = Shahrak-e Qods Iran 35°47N 51°22E 141 A2
Gharb Malta 36°4N 14°13E 206 E6
Gharb Bahr el Ghazâl = Western Bahr el Ghazal □ South Sudan 7°30N 25°30E 257 F2
Gharb-Chrarda-Beni Hssen □ Morocco 35°35N 6°0W 260 A3
Gharb Dârfûr □ Sudan 13°0N 23°0E 259 F4
Gharb el Istiwa'iya = Western Equatoria □ South Sudan 5°0N 30°0E 257 G3
Gharb Kordofân □ Sudan 12°0N 28°0E 257 E2
Gharbîya, Es Sahrâ el Egypt 27°40N 26°30E 256 B2
Ghardaïa Algeria 32°20N 3°37E 261 B5
Ghardaïa □ Algeria 31°5N 3°10E 261 B5
Ghârib, G. Egypt 28°6N 32°54E 256 B3
Gharig Sudan 10°47N 27°33E 257 E2
Gharm Tajikistan 39°0N 70°20E 214 F8
Gharm, W. → Oman 19°57N 57°38E 249 C7
Gharyān Libya 32°10N 13°0E 258 B2
Ghāt Libya 24°59N 10°11E 258 D2
Ghāt □ Libya 25°35N 10°15E 258 C2
Ghatal India 22°40N 87°46E 243 H12
Ghatampur India 26°8N 80°13E 243 F9
Ghatgaon India 21°24N 85°53E 244 D7
Ghatkopar India 19°4N 72°54E 130 A2
Ghatprabha → India 16°15N 75°20E 245 F2
Ghats, Eastern India 14°0N 78°50E 245 H4
Ghats, Western India 14°0N 75°0E 245 H2
Ghatsila India 22°36N 86°29E 243 H12
Ghaţţī Si. Arabia 31°16N 37°31E 246 D3
Ghawdex = Gozo Malta 36°3N 14°15E 206 E7
Ghayl Si. Arabia 21°40N 46°20E 248 B4
Ghayl Bā Wazīr Yemen 14°46N 49°22E 249 D5
Ghazal, Bahr el → Chad 13°0N 15°47E 259 F3
Ghazal, Bahr el → South Sudan 9°31N 30°25E 257 F3
Ghazaouet Algeria 35°8N 1°50W 261 A4
Ghaziabad India 28°42N 77°26E 242 E7
Ghazipur Delhi, India 28°37N 77°19E 120 B2
Ghazipur Ut. P., India 25°38N 83°35E 243 G10
Ghaznī Afghan. 33°30N 68°28E 242 C3
Ghaznī □ Afghan. 32°10N 68°20E 240 B3
Ghedi Italy 45°24N 10°16E 198 C7
Ghelari Romania 45°38N 22°45E 182 E7
Ghent = Gent Belgium 51°2N 3°42E 170 C3
Gheorghe Gheorghiu-Dej = Oneşti Romania 46°17N 26°47E 183 D11
Gheorgheni Romania 46°43N 25°41E 183 D10
Gherla Romania 47°2N 23°57E 183 C8
Ghidigeni Romania 46°3N 27°30E 183 D12
Ghilarza Italy 40°7N 8°50E 200 B1
Ghimeş-Făget Romania 46°35N 26°2E 183 D11
Ghīnah, Wādī al → Si. Arabia 30°27N 38°14E 246 D3
Ghirān, W. → Si. Arabia 20°52N 47°10E 248 B4
Ghirardelli Square San Francisco, U.S.A. 136 a1
Ghisonaccia France 42°1N 9°26E 175 F13
Ghisoni France 42°7N 9°12E 175 F13
Ghizar → Pakistan 36°15N 73°43E 243 A5
Ghizri Pakistan 24°49N 67°2E 123 B2
Ghizri Cr. → Pakistan 24°47N 67°5E 123 B2
Ghod → India 18°30N 74°35E 244 E2
Ghogha India 21°40N 72°20E 244 D1
Ghonda India 28°41N 77°16E 120 A2
Ghot Ogrein Egypt 31°10N 25°20E 256 A2
Ghotaru India 27°20N 70°1E 242 F4
Ghotki Pakistan 28°5N 69°21E 242 E3
Ghowr □ Afghan. 34°0N 64°20E 240 B2
Ghubbet el Bûs Egypt 29°35N 32°21E 251 J3
Ghughri India 22°39N 80°41E 243 H9
Ghugus India 19°58N 79°12E 244 E4
Ghulam Mohammad Barrage Pakistan 25°30N 68°20E 242 G3
Ghurayrah Si. Arabia 18°37N 42°41E 248 C3
Ghūrīān Afghan. 34°17N 61°25E 240 B1
Ghusuri India 22°37N 88°21E 124 B2
Ghuzzayil, Sabkhat Libya 29°30N 19°30E 258 C3
Gia Dinh Vietnam 10°49N 106°42E 237 G6
Gia Lai = Plei Ku Vietnam 13°57N 108°0E 236 F7
Gia Nghia Vietnam 11°58N 107°42E 237 G6
Gia Ngoc Vietnam 14°50N 108°58E 236 E7
Gia Vuc Vietnam 14°42N 108°34E 236 E7
Giali Greece 36°41N 27°11E 205 E9
Gialtra Greece 38°51N 22°59E 204 C4
Giamama = Jamaame Somalia 0°4N 42°44E 267 D5
Gian Phil. 5°49N 125°12E 233 J5
Gianicolense Italy 41°53N 12°28E 136 B1
Gianicolense, Parco Italy 136 c1
Gianitsa Greece 40°46N 22°24E 202 F6
Giannutri Italy 42°15N 11°6E 198 F8
Giant Forest U.S.A. 36°36N 118°43W 306 J8
Giant Mts. = Krkonoše Czechia 50°50N 15°35E 180 A8
Giant Sequoia ⌓ U.S.A. 36°10N 118°35W 306 K8
Giant Wheel = Riesenrad Austria 48°14N 16°23E 142 A2
Giant's Causeway U.K. 55°16N 6°29W 166 A5
Giant's Tank Sri Lanka 8°51N 80°2E 245 K5
Gianyar Indonesia 8°32S 115°20E 231 K18
Giarabub = Al Jaghbūb Libya 29°42N 24°38E 258 C4
Giaros Greece 37°32N 24°40E 204 D6
Giarre Italy 37°43N 15°11E 201 E8
Giaveno Italy 45°2N 7°21E 198 C4
Gibara Cuba 21°9N 76°11W 320 B4
Gibbon U.S.A. 40°45N 98°51W 308 E4
Gibe → Ethiopia 7°20N 37°36E 257 F4
Gibe I Ethiopia 8°7N 37°0E 257 F4
Gibe II Ethiopia 8°0N 37°30E 257 F4
Gibe III Ethiopia 7°0N 37°30E 257 F4
Gibellina Nuova Italy 37°47N 12°58E 200 E5
Gibeon Namibia 25°9S 17°43E 270 C2
Gibraleón Spain 37°23N 6°58W 195 H4
Gibraltar ☑ Europe 36°7N 5°22W 195 J5
Gibraltar, Str. of Medit. S. 35°55N 5°40W 195 K5
Gibraltar Pt. Canada 43°36N 79°23W 141 B2
Gibraltar Range △ Australia 29°31S 152°19E 281 D5
Gibson U.S.A. 33°14N 82°36W 316 B7
Gibson City U.S.A. 40°28N 88°22W 311 D8
Gibson Desert Australia 24°0S 126°0E 278 D4
Gibsonburg U.S.A. 41°23N 83°19W 311 C13
Gibsons Canada 49°24N 123°32W 296 D4
Gibsonton U.S.A. 27°51N 82°23W 317 H7
Gibsonville U.S.A. 39°46N 120°54W 306 F6
Gidami Ethiopia 8°59N 34°37E 266 C3
Giddalur India 15°20N 78°57E 245 G4
Giddings U.S.A. 30°11N 96°56W 314 F6
Gidea Park U.K. 51°35N 0°11E 125 A5
Gidole Ethiopia 5°40N 37°25E 257 F4
Giebnegáisi = Kebnekaise Sweden 67°53N 18°33E 160 C18
Gien France 47°40N 2°36E 173 E9
Giengen Germany 48°37N 10°14E 179 G6
Giesing Germany 48°6N 11°35E 131 B2
Giessen Germany 50°34N 8°41E 178 E4
Gīfān Iran 37°54N 57°28E 247 B8
Gifatin, Geziret Egypt 27°10N 33°50E 256 B3
Gifford U.S.A. 27°40N 80°25W 317 H9
Gifhorn Germany 52°30N 10°33E 178 C6
Gift Lake Canada 55°53N 115°49W 296 B5
Gifu Japan 35°30N 136°45E 223 B8
Gifu □ Japan 35°40N 137°0E 223 B9
Gigant Russia 46°28N 41°20E 191 G5
Giganta, Sa. de la Mexico 26°0N 111°39W 318 B2
Gigen Bulgaria 43°40N 24°28E 203 C8
Gigha U.K. 55°42N 5°44W 167 F3
Gíglio Italy 42°20N 10°52E 198 F7
Gignac France 43°39N 3°32E 174 E7
Gigüela → Spain 39°8N 3°44W 195 F7
Gijang S. Korea 35°14N 129°12E 224 E4
Gijón Spain 43°32N 5°42W 194 B5
Gikongoro Rwanda 2°28S 29°34E 268 C2
Gil I. Canada 53°12N 129°15W 296 C3
Gila → U.S.A. 32°43N 114°33W 305 K6
Gila Bend U.S.A. 32°57N 112°43W 305 K7
Gila Bend Mts. U.S.A. 33°10N 113°0W 305 K7
Gila Cliff Dwellings ⌓ U.S.A. 33°12N 108°16W 305 K9
Gīlān □ Iran 37°0N 50°0E 247 B6
Gīlān-e Gharb Iran 34°8N 45°55E 213 E11
Gilău Romania 46°45N 23°23E 183 D8
Gilbert → Australia 16°35S 141°15E 280 B3
Gilbert Is. Kiribati 1°0N 172°0E 277 A14
Gilbert River Australia 18°9S 142°52E 280 B3
Gilbert Seamounts Pac. Oc. 52°50N 150°10W 150 D18
Gilbués Brazil 9°50S 45°21W 332 C2
Gilead U.S.A. 44°24N 70°59W 313 B14
Gilf el Kebîr, Hadabat el Egypt 23°50N 25°50E 256 C2
Gilford I. Canada 50°40N 126°30W 296 C3
Gilgandra Australia 31°43S 148°39E 283 A8
Gilgil Kenya 0°30S 36°20E 268 C4
Gilgit India 35°50N 74°15E 243 B6
Gilgit → Pakistan 35°44N 74°37E 243 B6
Gilgit-Baltistan □ Pakistan 36°30N 73°0E 243 A5
Gilgunnia Australia 32°26S 146°2E 283 B7
Gili, Pulau 10°0S 115°0E 235 D5
Gili ⌓ Mozam. 16°39S 38°27E 269 F4
Gilimanuk Indonesia 8°10S 114°26E 231 J17
Giljeva Planina Europe 43°9N 20°0E 202 C3
Gill Pt. St. Helena 15°58S 5°38W 153 h
Gillam Canada 56°20N 94°40W 297 B10
Gilleleje Denmark 56°8N 12°19E 163 H6
Gillen, L. Australia 26°11S 124°38E 279 E3
Gilles, L. Australia 32°50S 136°45E 282 B2
Gillespie U.S.A. 39°8N 89°49W 310 E7
Gillespies Pt. N.Z. 43°24S 169°49E 285 D4
Gillette U.S.A. 44°18N 105°30W 304 D11
Gilliat Australia 20°40S 141°28E 280 C3
Gillingham U.K. 51°23N 0°33E 169 F8
Gilman U.S.A. 40°46N 88°0W 311 D9
Gilman City U.S.A. 40°8N 93°53W 310 D3
Gilmer U.S.A. 32°44N 94°57W 314 E7
Gilmerton U.K. 55°54N 3°7W 121 B3
Gilmore, L. Australia 32°29S 121°37E 279 F3
Gilmour Canada 44°48N 77°37W 312 B7
Gilo West Bank 31°44N 35°11E 123 B2
Gilo → Ethiopia 8°10N 33°15E 257 F3
Gilort → Romania 44°38N 23°32E 183 F8
Gilroy U.S.A. 37°1N 121°34W 306 H5
Giluwe, Mt. Papua N. G. 6°8S 143°52E 286 D2
Gimbi Ethiopia 9°3N 35°42E 257 F4
Gimcheon S. Korea 36°11N 128°4E 224 D4
Gimhae S. Korea 35°14N 128°53E 224 E4
Gimhwa S. Korea 38°17N 127°28E 224 C3
Gimie, Mt. St. Lucia 13°54N 61°0W 323 m
Gimje S. Korea 35°48N 126°45E 224 E3
Gimli Canada 50°40N 97°0W 297 C9
Gimmersta Sweden 59°14N 18°14E 139 B3
Gimo Sweden 60°11N 18°12E 162 D12
Gimone → France 44°0N 1°6E 174 E5
Gimont France 43°38N 0°52E 174 E4
Gimpo Int. ✕ (GMP) S. Korea 37°33N 126°47E 224 D3
Gin → Sri Lanka 6°5N 80°7E 245 L5
Gin Gin Australia 25°0S 151°58E 281 D5
Ginâh Egypt 25°21N 30°30E 256 B3
Ginatilan Phil. 9°34N 123°19E 233 G4
Gineifa Egypt 30°12N 32°25E 256 H8
Gingee India 12°15N 79°25E 245 H4
Gingin Australia 31°22S 115°54E 279 F2
Gingindlovu S. Africa 29°2S 31°30E 271 C5
Gingoog Phil. 8°50N 125°7E 233 G5
Gingoog B. Phil. 8°54N 125°7E 233 G5
Ginir Ethiopia 7°6N 40°40E 257 F5
Ginosa Italy 40°35N 16°45E 201 B9
Ginowan Japan 26°15N 127°45E 288 a
Ginza Tokyo, Japan 140 b5
Ginzo de Limia = Xinzo de Limia Spain 42°3N 7°47W 194 C3
Giofyros → Greece 35°20N 25°6E 207 E6
Giohar = Jawhar Somalia 2°48N 45°30E 267 D6
Gióia, G. di Italy 38°30N 15°45E 201 D8
Gióia del Colle Italy 40°48N 16°55E 201 B9
Gióia Táuro Italy 38°25N 15°54E 201 D8
Gioiosa Iónica Italy 38°20N 16°18E 201 D9
Gioiosa Marea Italy 38°10N 14°54E 201 D7
Giona, Oros Greece 38°38N 22°14E 204 C4
Giovi, Passo dei Italy 44°33N 8°57E 198 D5
Giovinazzo Italy 41°11N 16°40E 201 A9
Gippsland Australia 37°52S 147°0E 283 D7
Gipuzkoa □ Spain 43°12N 2°15W 196 B2
Gir △ India 21°0N 71°0E 242 J4
Gir Hills India 21°0N 71°0E 242 J4
Girab India 26°2N 70°38E 242 F4
Girâfi, W. → Egypt 29°58N 34°39E 251 J5
Giraltovce Slovakia 49°7N 21°32E 181 B14
Girapetra, Akra Greece 38°51N 20°41E 207 B2
Girard St. Lucia 13°59N 60°57W 323 m
Girard Ga., U.S.A. 33°3N 81°43W 316 B8
Girard Ill., U.S.A. 39°27N 89°47W 310 E7
Girard Kans., U.S.A. 37°31N 94°51W 308 G6
Girard Ohio, U.S.A. 41°9N 80°42W 312 E4
Girard Pa., U.S.A. 42°0N 80°19W 312 E4
Girardot Colombia 4°18N 74°48W 328 C3
Giraud, Pte. Dominica 15°20N 61°15W 323 k
Girdle Ness U.K. 57°9N 2°3W 167 D6
Giresun Turkey 40°55N 38°30E 213 B8
Giresun □ Turkey 40°30N 38°30E 213 B8
Girga Egypt 26°17N 31°55E 256 B3
Girgaum Mumbai, India 130 b2
Girgenti = Agrigento Italy 37°19N 13°34E 200 E6
Girgir, C. Papua N. G. 3°50S 144°35E 286 B3
Giri → Dem. Rep. of the Congo 0°28N 17°59E 264 B3
Giri → India 30°28N 77°41E 242 D7
Giridih India 24°10N 86°21E 243 G12
Girifalco Italy 38°49N 16°25E 201 D9
Giriftu Kenya 1°59N 39°46E 268 B4
Girilambone Australia 31°16S 146°57E 283 A7
Girne = Kyrenia Cyprus 35°20N 33°20E 207 E9
Giro Nigeria 11°7N 4°42E 263 C5
Giromagny France 47°45N 6°50E 173 E13
Giron = Kiruna Sweden 67°52N 20°15E 160 C19
Girona Spain 41°58N 2°46E 196 D7
Girona □ Spain 42°11N 2°30E 196 C7
Gironde □ France 44°45N 0°30W 174 D3
Gironde → France 45°32N 1°7W 174 C2
Gironella Spain 42°2N 1°53E 196 C6
Girraween △ Australia 28°46S 151°54E 281 D5
Girringun △ Australia 18°15S 145°32E 280 B4
Giru Australia 19°30S 147°5E 280 B4
Girvan U.K. 55°14N 4°51W 167 F4
Gisborne Vic., Australia 37°29S 144°36E 282 D6
Gisborne N.Z. 38°39S 178°5E 284 E7
Gisborne □ N.Z. 38°30S 178°0E 284 E7
Gisenyi Rwanda 1°41S 29°15E 268 C2
Gislaved Sweden 57°19N 13°32E 163 G7
Gisors France 49°15N 1°47E 173 C8
Gitarama Rwanda 2°4S 29°45E 268 C2
Gitega Burundi 3°26S 29°56E 268 C2
Githio Greece 36°46N 22°34E 204 E4
Gitschin = Jičín Czechia 50°25N 15°28E 180 A8
Giuba = Juba → Somalia 1°30N 42°35E 267 D5
Giudecca, Canale della Venice, Italy 142 c2
Giugliano in Campania Italy 40°56N 14°12E 201 B7
Giulianova Italy 42°45N 13°57E 199 F10
Giura Greece 39°23N 24°10E 204 B6
Giurgeni Romania 44°45N 27°48E 183 F12
Giurgiu Romania 43°52N 25°57E 183 G10
Giurgiu □ Romania 44°20N 26°0E 183 F10
Giurgiuleşti Moldova 45°29N 28°12E 183 E13
Giustinian, Palazzo Venice, Italy 142 b3
Giv'at Ram Israel 31°47N 35°12E 123 B2
Giv'at Ye'arim Israel 31°47N 35°5E 123 B1
Giv'at Ze'ev West Bank 31°52N 35°10E 123 A2
Give Denmark 55°51N 9°13E 163 J3
Givet France 50°8N 4°49E 173 B11
Giv'on West Bank 31°51N 35°10E 123 A1
Givors France 45°35N 4°45E 175 C8
Givry France 46°41N 4°46E 173 F11
Giyani S. Africa 23°19S 30°43E 271 B5
Giyon Ethiopia 8°33N 38°1E 257 F4
Giza = El Gîza Egypt 30°0N 31°12E 117 A2
Giza Pyramids Egypt 29°58N 31°9E 117 B1
Gizab Afghan. 33°22N 66°17E 242 C1
Gizhiga Russia 62°3N 160°30E 215 C17
Gizhiginskaya Guba Russia 61°0N 158°0E 215 C16
Gizo Solomon Is. 8°7S 156°50E 287 M9
Giżycko Poland 54°2N 21°48E 184 D8
Gizzeria Italy 38°59N 16°12E 201 D9
Gjakovë Kosovo 42°22N 20°26E 202 D4
Gjalicë e Lumës, Mal. Albania 42°2N 20°25E 202 D4
Gjantija Malta 36°2N 14°16E 206 E7
Gjegjan Albania 41°58N 20°3E 202 E4
Gjendesheim Norway 61°30N 8°48E 164 C5
Gjeravicë Kosovo 42°32N 20°8E 202 D4
Gjermundshamn Norway 60°40N 5°55E 164 D2
Gjersjøen Norway 59°47N 10°47E 133 B3
Gjerstad Norway 58°54N 9°1E 164 F6
Gjevillvatnet Norway 62°43N 9°23E 164 B6
Gjilan Kosovo 42°28N 21°29E 202 D5
Gjirokastër Albania 40°7N 20°10E 202 F4
Gjoa Haven Canada 68°38N 95°53W 294 D12
Gjøra Norway 62°33N 9°4E 164 B6
Gjøvik Norway 60°47N 10°43E 164 D7
Gjuhës, Kep i Albania 40°28N 19°15E 202 F3
Gjurakoc Kosovo 42°43N 20°29E 202 D4
Glace Bay Canada 46°11N 59°58W 299 C8
Glacier △ B.C., Canada 51°15N 117°30W 296 C5
Glacier △ Mont., U.S.A. 48°42N 113°48W 304 B7
Glacier Bay U.S.A. 58°40N 136°0W 303 G14
Glacier Bay ⌓ U.S.A. 58°45N 136°30W 296 B1
Glacier Peak U.S.A. 48°7N 121°7W 304 B3
Gladesville Australia 33°50S 151°8E 139 B1
Gladewater U.S.A. 32°33N 94°56W 314 E7
Gladsakse Denmark 55°45N 12°25E 118 A2
Gladstone Queens., Australia 23°52S 151°16E 280 C5
Gladstone S. Austral., Australia 33°15S 138°22E 282 B3
Gladstone Man., Canada 50°13N 98°57W 297 C9
Gladstone Ill., U.S.A. 40°52N 90°57W 310 D6
Gladstone Mich., U.S.A. 45°51N 87°1W 308 C10
Gladstone Mo., U.S.A. 39°13N 94°35W 310 E2
Gladwin U.S.A. 43°59N 84°29W 309 D11
Glafsfjorden Sweden 59°30N 12°37E 162 E6
Glagah Indonesia 8°13S 114°18E 231 J17
Głagów Małapolski Poland 50°10N 21°56E 185 H8
Glåma = Glomma → Norway 59°12N 10°57E 164 E7
Gláma Iceland 65°48N 23°0W 155 B4
Glamis U.S.A. 32°55N 115°5W 307 N11
Glamoč Bos.-H. 44°3N 16°51E 199 D13
Glamorgan, Vale of □ U.K. 51°28N 3°25W 169 F4
Glåmos Norway 62°41N 11°25E 164 B8
Glamsbjerg Denmark 55°17N 10°6E 163 J4
Glanvillia Dominica 15°34N 61°28W 323 k
Glarus Switz. 47°3N 9°4E 179 H5
Glarus □ Switz. 47°0N 9°5E 179 J5
Glasco Kans., U.S.A. 39°22N 97°50W 308 F5
Glasco N.Y., U.S.A. 42°3N 73°57W 313 D11
Glasgow Glasg. City, U.K. 55°51N 4°15W 167 F4
Glasgow Ky., U.S.A. 37°0N 85°55W 309 G11
Glasgow Mo., U.S.A. 39°14N 92°51W 310 E4
Glasgow Mont., U.S.A. 48°12N 106°38W 304 B10
Glasgow City □ U.K. 55°51N 4°12W 167 F4
Glasgow Int. ✕ (GLA) U.K. 55°51N 4°21W 167 F4
Glaslyn Canada 53°22N 108°21W 297 C7
Glassmanor U.S.A. 38°49N 77°0W 143 C3
Glastonbury Somst., U.K. 51°9N 2°43W 169 F5
Glastonbury Conn., U.S.A. 41°43N 72°37W 313 E12
Glatz = Kłodzko Poland 50°28N 16°38E 185 H3
Glauchau Germany 50°49N 12°31E 178 E8
Glava Sweden 59°33N 12°35E 162 E6
Glavice Croatia 43°43N 16°41E 199 E13
Glazov Russia 58°9N 52°40E 190 A11
Gleichen Canada 50°52N 113°3W 296 C6
Gleisdorf Austria 47°6N 15°44E 180 D8
Gleiwitz = Gliwice Poland 50°22N 18°41E 185 H5
Glen U.S.A. 44°7N 71°11W 313 B13
Glen Affric U.K. 57°17N 5°1W 167 D3
Glen Afton N.Z. 37°37S 175°4E 284 D4
Glen Canyon U.S.A. 37°30N 110°40W 305 H8
Glen Canyon ⌓ U.S.A. 37°15N 111°0W 305 H8
Glen Canyon Dam U.S.A. 36°57N 111°29W 305 H8
Glen Coe U.K. 56°40N 5°0W 167 E3
Glen Cove U.S.A. 40°52N 73°38W 313 F11
Glen Garry U.K. 57°3N 5°7W 167 D3
Glen Innes Australia 29°44S 151°44E 281 D5
Glen Iris Australia 37°51S 145°3E 128 B2
Glen Lyon U.S.A. 41°10N 76°5W 313 E8
Glen Mar Park U.S.A. 38°57N 77°7W 143 B2
Glen Massey N.Z. 37°38S 175°2E 284 D4
Glen Mor U.K. 57°9N 4°37W 167 D4
Glen Moriston U.K. 57°11N 4°52W 167 D4
Glen Robertson Canada 45°22N 74°30W 313 A10
Glen Rouge Park Canada 43°49N 79°10W 141 A4
Glen Spean U.K. 56°53N 4°40W 167 E4
Glen Ullin U.S.A. 46°49N 101°50W 308 B3
Glenamaddy Ireland 53°37N 8°33W 166 C3
Glénan, Îs. de France 47°42N 4°0W 172 E3
Glenavy N.Z. 44°54S 171°7E 285 E6
Glenbeigh Ireland 52°3N 9°58W 166 D2
Glenburn Australia 37°27S 145°26E 283 D6
Glencoe Ont., Canada 42°45N 81°43W 312 D3
Glencoe KwaZulu Natal, S. Africa 28°11S 30°11E 271 C5
Glencoe Ala., U.S.A. 33°57N 85°56W 316 B4
Glencoe Ill., U.S.A. 42°8N 87°45W 119 A2
Glencoe Minn., U.S.A. 44°46N 94°9W 308 C6
Glencolumbkille Ireland 54°43N 8°42W 166 B3
Glencorse Res. U.K. 55°51N 3°15W 121 B2
Glendale Ariz., U.S.A. 33°32N 112°11W 305 K7
Glendale Calif., U.S.A. 34°9N 118°15W 126 B3
Glendale Fla., U.S.A. 30°52N 86°7W 316 E3
Glendale Zimbabwe 17°22S 31°5E 269 F3
Glendive U.S.A. 47°7N 104°43W 304 C11
Glendo U.S.A. 42°30N 105°2W 304 E11
Glenelg Australia 34°58S 138°31E 282 C3
Glenelg → Australia 38°4S 140°59E 282 E4
Glenfield U.S.A. 43°43N 75°24W 313 C9
Glengad Hd. Ireland 55°20N 7°10W 166 A4
Glengarriff Ireland 51°45N 9°34W 166 E2
Glengoffe Jamaica 18°10N 76°53W 320 a
Glenham N.Z. 46°26S 168°52E 285 G3
Glenhope N.Z. 41°40S 172°39E 285 B7
Glenhuntly Australia 37°52S 145°1E 128 B2
Glenmary, Mt. N.Z. 43°55S 169°55E 285 D4
Glenmont U.S.A. 40°31N 82°6W 312 F2
Glenmorgan Australia 27°14S 149°42E 281 D4
Glenn U.S.A. 39°31N 122°1W 306 F4
Glennallen U.S.A. 62°7N 145°33W 303 E11
Glenns Ferry U.S.A. 42°57N 115°18W 304 E6
Glennville U.S.A. 31°56N 81°56W 316 D8
Glenora Canada 44°2N 77°3W 312 B7
Glenorchy Tas., Australia 42°49S 147°18E 281 G4
Glenorchy Vic., Australia 36°55S 142°41E 282 D5
Glenorchy N.Z. 44°51S 168°24E 285 E3
Glenore Australia 17°50S 141°12E 280 B3
Glenreagh Australia 30°2S 153°1E 281 E5
Glenrock U.S.A. 42°52N 105°52W 304 E11
Glenrothes U.K. 56°12N 3°10W 167 E5
Glenrowan Australia 36°29S 146°13E 283 D7
Glens Falls U.S.A. 43°19N 73°39W 313 C11
Glenside U.S.A. 40°6N 75°9W 313 F9
Glenthompson Australia 37°38S 142°38E 282 D5
Glenties Ireland 54°48N 8°17W 166 B3
Glenveagh △ Ireland 55°3N 8°1W 166 A3
Glenview U.S.A. 42°3N 87°48W 119 A2
Glenview Countryside U.S.A. 42°3N 87°49W 119 A2
Glenville U.S.A. 38°56N 80°50W 309 F13
Glenvista S. Africa 26°17S 28°3E 123 B2
Glenwood Nfld. & L., Canada 49°0N 54°58W 299 C9
Glenwood Ark., U.S.A. 34°20N 93°33W 314 D8
Glenwood Ga., U.S.A. 32°11N 82°40W 316 C7
Glenwood Hawai'i, U.S.A. 19°29N 155°9W 302 D6
Glenwood Iowa, U.S.A. 41°3N 95°45W 308 E6
Glenwood Minn., U.S.A. 45°39N 95°23W 308 C6
Glenwood Wash., U.S.A. 46°1N 121°17W 306 D5
Glenwood Springs U.S.A. 39°33N 107°19W 304 G10
Glettinganes Iceland 65°30N 13°37W 155 B13
Glidden U.S.A. 42°4N 94°44W 310 B2
Glifada Athens, Greece 37°52N 23°45E 112 B2
Glimåkra Sweden 56°19N 14°7E 163 H8
Glin Ireland 52°34N 9°17W 166 D2
Glina Croatia 45°20N 16°6E 199 C13
Glinojeck Poland 52°49N 20°21E 185 F7
Glittertind Norway 61°40N 8°32E 164 C5
Gliwice Poland 50°22N 18°41E 185 H5
Globe U.S.A. 33°24N 110°47W 305 K8
Glodeanu Siliştea Romania 44°50N 26°48E 183 F11

Glodeni Moldova 47°45N 27°31E 183 C12
Glödnitz Austria 46°53N 14°7E 180 E7
Glogau = Głogów Poland 51°37N 16°5E 185 G3
Gloggnitz Austria 47°41N 15°56E 180 D8
Głogów Poland 51°37N 16°5E 185 G3
Głogówek Poland 50°21N 17°53E 185 H4
Glomma → Norway 59°12N 10°57E 164 E7
Gloria Phil. 12°59N 121°30E 232 E3
Glorieuses, Îs. Ind. Oc. 11°30S 47°20E 272 A2
Glosa Greece 39°10N 23°45E 204 B5
Glossop U.K. 53°27N 1°56W 168 D6
Glostrup Denmark 55°39N 12°23E 118 B2
Gloucester N.S.W., Australia 32°0S 151°59E 283 B9
Gloucester Papua N. G. 5°31S 148°31E 286 C5
Gloucester Glouc., U.K. 51°53N 2°15W 169 F5
Gloucester Mass., U.S.A. 42°37N 70°40W 313 D14
Gloucester, C. Papua N. G. 5°26S 148°21E 286 C5
Gloucester I. Australia 20°0S 148°30E 280 b
Gloucester Island △ Australia 20°2S 148°30E 280 b
Gloucester Point U.S.A. 37°15N 76°30W 309 G15
Gloucestershire □ U.K. 51°46N 2°15W 169 F5
Glover I. Grenada 11°59N 61°47W 323 q
Gloversville U.S.A. 43°3N 74°21W 313 C10
Glovertown Canada 48°40N 54°3W 299 C9
Gloverville = Warrenville U.S.A. 33°33N 81°48W 316 B8
Glowno Poland 51°59N 19°42E 185 G6
Głubczyce Poland 50°13N 17°52E 185 H4
Glubokiy Russia 48°35N 40°25E 191 F5
Glūbokoe Kazakhstan 50°8N 82°18E 217 B10
Glubokoye = Hlybokaye Belarus 55°10N 27°45E 188 E4
Głuchołazy Poland 50°19N 17°24E 185 H4
Glücksburg Germany 54°50N 9°33E 178 A5
Glückstadt Germany 53°45N 9°25E 178 B5
Glukhov = Hlukhiv Ukraine 51°40N 33°58E 189 G7
Glusk Belarus 52°53N 28°41E 177 B15
Głuszyca Poland 50°41N 16°23E 185 H3
Glyfada = Glifada Athens, Greece 37°52N 23°45E 112 B2
Glyn Ebwy = Ebbw Vale U.K. 51°46N 3°12W 169 F4
Glyngøre Denmark 56°46N 8°52E 163 H2
Gmünd Kärnten, Austria 46°54N 13°31E 180 E6
Gmünd Niederösterreich, Austria 48°45N 15°0E 180 C8
Gmunden Austria 47°55N 13°48E 180 D6
Gnali Gabon 2°34S 11°18E 264 C2
Gnarp Sweden 62°3N 17°16E 162 B11
Gnesen = Gniezno Poland 52°30N 17°35E 185 F4
Gnesta Sweden 59°3N 17°17E 162 E11
Gniew Poland 53°50N 18°50E 184 E5
Gniewkowo Poland 52°54N 18°25E 185 F5
Gniezno Poland 52°30N 17°35E 185 F4
Gnjilane = Gjilan Kosovo 42°28N 21°29E 202 D5
Gnoien Germany 53°58N 12°41E 178 B8
Gnosjö Sweden 57°22N 13°43E 163 G7
Gnowangerup Australia 33°58S 117°59E 279 F2
Go Cong Vietnam 10°22N 106°40E 237 G6
Gō-Gawa → Japan 35°2N 132°13E 222 B4
Gō-no-ura Japan 33°44N 129°40E 222 D1
Goa India 15°33N 73°59E 245 G1
Goa Phil. 13°42N 123°29E 232 E4
Goa □ India 15°33N 73°59E 245 G1
Goalen Hd. Australia 36°33S 150°4E 283 D9
Goalpara India 26°10N 90°40E 241 B3
Goaltor India 22°43N 87°10E 243 H12
Goalundo Ghat Bangla. 23°50N 89°47E 243 H13
Goaso Ghana 6°48N 2°30W 262 D4
Goat Fell U.K. 55°38N 5°11W 167 F3
Goat I. Antigua & B. 17°43N 61°51W 322 c
Goat Pt. Antigua & B. 17°44N 61°51W 322 c
Goba Ethiopia 7°1N 39°59E 257 F4
Goba Mozam. 26°15S 32°13E 271 C5
Gobabis Namibia 22°30S 19°0E 270 B2
Gobe Papua N. G. 9°4S 149°0E 286 E5
Göbel Turkey 40°0N 28°9E 203 F12
Gobernador Gregores Argentina 48°46S 70°15W 336 C2
Gobi Asia 44°0N 110°0E 226 C6
Gobi Gurvan Saykhan △ Mongolia 43°24N 101°24E 226 C2
Gobichettipalayam India 11°31N 77°21E 245 J3
Gobles U.S.A. 42°22N 85°53W 311 B11
Gobō Japan 33°53N 135°10E 223 D7
Gobo South Sudan 5°40N 31°10E 257 F3
Gobustan Azerbaijan 40°7N 49°22E 213 B13
Göçbeyli Turkey 39°13N 27°25E 205 B9
Goch Germany 51°41N 6°9E 178 D2
Gochang S. Korea 35°26N 126°42E 224 E3
Gochas Namibia 24°59S 18°55E 270 B2
God Dere Ethiopia 5°12N 44°1E 267 C5
Godalming U.K. 51°11N 0°36W 169 F7
Godavari → India 16°25N 82°18E 244 F6
Godavari Pt. India 17°0N 82°20E 244 F6
Godbout Canada 49°20N 67°38W 299 C6
Godda India 24°50N 87°13E 243 G12
Gode Ethiopia 5°53N 43°35E 267 C5
Godech Bulgaria 43°1N 23°4E 202 C7
Goderich Canada 43°45N 81°41W 312 C3
Goderville France 49°38N 0°22E 172 C7
Godfrey U.S.A. 38°58N 90°11W 310 F6
Godfrey Ra. Australia 24°0S 117°0E 279 D2
Godhavn = Qeqertarsuaq Greenland 69°15N 53°38W 154 D5
Godhra India 22°49N 73°40E 242 H5
Godinlabe Somalia 5°54N 46°38E 267 C6
Gödöllő Hungary 47°38N 19°25E 182 C4
Godoy Cruz Argentina 32°56S 68°52W 334 C2
Gods → Canada 56°22N 92°51W 298 A1
Gods L. Canada 54°40N 94°15W 298 B1
Gods River Canada 54°50N 94°5W 297 C10
Godthåb = Nuuk Greenland 64°10N 51°35W 154 E5
Godwin Austen = K2 Pakistan 35°58N 76°32E 243 B7
Goeie Hoop, Kaap die = Good Hope, C. of S. Africa 34°24S 18°30E 270 D2
Goéland, L. au Canada 49°50N 76°48W 298 C4
Goélands, L. aux Canada 55°27N 64°17W 299 A7
Goeree Neths. 51°50N 4°0E 170 C3
Goes Neths. 51°30N 3°55E 170 C3
Gofca → Somalia 1°10N 43°43E 267 D5
Goffstown U.S.A. 43°1N 71°36W 313 C13
Gogama Canada 47°35N 81°43W 298 C3
Gogar U.K. 55°56N 3°20W 121 B2
Gogebic, L. U.S.A. 46°30N 89°35W 308 B9
Goggetti Ethiopia 8°11N 38°35E 257 F4
Gogolin Poland 50°30N 18°0E 185 H5
Gogonou Benin 10°50N 2°50E 263 C5
Gogra = Ghaghara → India 25°45N 84°40E 243 G11
Gogrial South Sudan 8°30N 28°8E 257 F2
Gogti Ethiopia 10°7N 42°51E 257 E5
Gogui Mali 15°32N 9°25W 262 B3
Gôh-Djiboua □ Ivory C. 6°2N 5°33W 262 D3
Gohana India 29°8N 76°42E 242 E7
Goharganj India 23°1N 77°41E 242 H7
Goheung S. Korea 34°36N 127°17E 224 E3
Goi → India 22°4N 74°46E 242 H6
Goiana Brazil 7°33S 34°59W 332 C5
Goianésia Brazil 15°18S 49°7W 333 E2
Goiânia Brazil 16°43S 49°20W 333 E2
Goiás Brazil 15°55S 50°10W 333 E1
Goiás □ Brazil 12°10S 48°0W 332 D2
Goiatins Brazil 7°42S 47°10W 332 C2
Goiatuba Brazil 18°1S 49°23W 333 E2
Goidu Atoll Maldives 4°53N 72°54E 272 d
Goio-Erê Brazil 24°12S 53°1W 335 A5
Góis Portugal 40°10N 8°6W 194 E2
Gojam Ethiopia 10°55N 36°30E 257 E4
Gojeb, Wabi → Ethiopia 7°12N 36°40E 257 F4
Gojō Japan 34°21N 135°42E 223 C7
Gojra Pakistan 31°10N 72°40E 242 D5
Gokak India 16°11N 74°52E 245 F2
Gokarn India 14°33N 74°17E 245 G2
Gökçe = Sevana Lich Armenia 40°30N 45°20E 191 K7
Gökçe Turkey 40°10N 25°55E 203 F9
Gökçeada Turkey 40°10N 25°50E 203 F9
Gökçedağ Turkey 39°33N 28°56E 205 B10
Gökçen Turkey 38°7N 27°53E 205 C9
Gökçeören Turkey 38°37N 28°35E 205 C10
Gökçeyazı Turkey 39°40N 27°40E 205 B9
Gökırmak → Turkey 41°25N 35°8E 212 B6
Gökova Turkey 37°1N 28°17E 205 D10
Gökova Körfezi Turkey 36°55N 27°50E 205 E9
Göksu → Turkey 36°19N 34°5E 250 B2
Göksun Turkey 38°2N 36°30E 212 C7
Gokteik Burma 22°26N 97°0E 241 D6
Göktepe Karaman, Turkey 36°37N 32°37E 250 B3
Göktepe Muğla, Turkey 37°25N 28°34E 205 D10
Göktürk Turkey 41°10N 28°53E 122 A1
Gokurt Pakistan 29°40N 67°26E 242 E2
Gokwe Zimbabwe 18°7S 28°58E 271 A4
Gol Norway 60°42N 8°55E 164 D5
Gol Gol Australia 34°12S 142°14E 282 C5
Gola India 28°3N 80°32E 243 E9
Golabari India 22°35N 88°20E 124 B2
Golabki Poland 52°12N 20°52E 143 B1
Golaghat India 26°30N 94°0E 241 B5
Golakganj India 26°8N 89°52E 241 B2
Golan Heights = Hagolan Syria 33°0N 35°45E 250 F6
Gołańcz Poland 52°57N 17°18E 185 F4
Golāshkerd Iran 27°59N 57°16E 247 E8
Golaya Pristen = Hola Prystan Ukraine 46°29N 32°32E 189 J7
Gölbaşı Adiyaman, Turkey 37°43N 37°25E 212 D7
Gölbaşı Ankara, Turkey 39°47N 32°49E 212 C5
Golconda India 17°24N 78°23E 244 F4
Golconda Nev., U.S.A. 40°58N 117°30W 304 F5
Gölcük Kocaeli, Turkey 40°42N 29°48E 203 F13
Gölcük Niğde, Turkey 38°14N 34°47E 212 C6
Gold U.S.A. 41°52N 77°50W 312 E7
Gold Beach U.S.A. 42°25N 124°25W 304 E1
Gold Coast = Ghana ■ W. Afr. 8°0N 1°0W 263 D4
Gold Coast Queens., Australia 28°0S 153°25E 276 F9
Gold Coast Chicago, U.S.A. 119 a2
Gold Coast W. Afr. 4°0N 1°40W 263 E4
Gold Creek U.S.A. 62°46N 149°41W 303 E10
Gold Hill U.S.A. 42°26N 123°3W 304 E2
Gold River Canada 49°46N 126°3W 296 D3
Gołdap Poland 54°19N 22°18E 184 D9
Goldberg = Złotoryja Poland 51°8N 15°55E 185 G2
Goldberg Germany 53°35N 12°4E 178 B8
Golden B.C., Canada 51°20N 116°59W 296 C5
Golden Ill., U.S.A. 40°7N 91°1W 310 D5
Golden B. N.Z. 40°40S 172°50E 285 A7
Golden Beach U.S.A. 25°57N 80°7W 129 C3
Golden Buddha = Traimit Bangkok, Thailand 113 c2
Golden Gate U.S.A. 37°48N 122°29W 136 B2
Golden Gate △ U.S.A. 37°49N 122°31W 136 A2
Golden Gate Bridge U.S.A. 37°49N 122°28W 136 B2
Golden Gate Highlands △ S. Africa 28°40S 28°40E 271 C4
Golden Gate Park U.S.A. 37°46N 122°28W 136 B2
Golden Grove Middlesex, Jamaica 18°19N 77°9W 320 a
Golden Grove Surrey, Jamaica 17°55N 76°16W 320 a
Golden Hinde Canada 49°40N 125°44W 296 D3
Golden Horn = Haliç Turkey 41°1N 28°57E 122 B1
Golden Lake Canada 45°34N 77°21W 312 A7
Golden Rock India 10°45N 78°48E 245 J4
Golden Spike △ U.S.A. 41°37N 112°33W 304 F7
Golden Vale Ireland 52°33N 8°17W 166 D3
Goldendale U.S.A. 45°49N 120°50W 304 D3
Golders Green U.K. 51°34N 0°11W 125 A2
Goldfield U.S.A. 37°42N 117°14W 305 H5
Goldingen = Kuldīga Latvia 56°58N 21°59E 184 B8
Goldoni, Casa Venice, Italy 142 b2
Goldoni, Teatro Venice, Italy 142 b3
Goldsand L. Canada 57°2N 101°8W 297 B8
Goldsboro U.S.A. 35°23N 77°59W 315 D16
Goldsmith U.S.A. 31°59N 102°37W 314 F3
Goldthwaite U.S.A. 31°27N 98°34W 314 F5
Golegã Portugal 39°24N 8°29W 195 F2
Goleniów Poland 53°35N 14°50E 184 E1
Golestān □ Iran 37°20N 55°25E 247 B7
Golestan Palace Iran 35°41N 51°25E 141 A2
Golestānak Iran 30°36N 54°14E 247 D7
Goleta U.S.A. 34°27N 119°50W 307 L7
Golfito Costa Rica 8°41N 83°5W 320 E3
Golfo Aranci Italy 40°59N 9°38E 200 B2
Golfo de Santa Clara Mexico 31°42N 114°30W 318 A2
Golfo di Orosei e del Gennargentu △ Italy 40°15N 9°15E 200 B2
Gölgeli Dağları Turkey 37°10N 28°55E 205 D10
Gölhisar Turkey 37°8N 29°31E 205 D11
Goliad U.S.A. 28°40N 97°23W 314 G6
Golija Montenegro 43°5N 18°45E 202 C2
Golija Serbia 43°22N 20°15E 202 C4
Golina Poland 52°15N 18°4E 185 F5
Gölköy Turkey 40°41N 37°37E 212 B7
Gollel = Lavumisa Swaziland 27°20S 31°55E 271 C5
Göllersdorf Austria 48°29N 16°7E 180 C9
Gollnow = Goleniów Poland 53°35N 14°50E 184 E1
Gölmarmara Turkey 38°42N 27°55E 205 C9
Golmud China 36°25N 94°53E 218 D7
Golo → France 42°31N 9°32E 175 F13
Golo I. Phil. 13°39N 120°22E 232 E3
Gölova Turkey 36°48N 30°5E 205 E12
Golovin U.S.A. 64°33N 163°2W 303 D7
Golpāyegān Iran 33°27N 50°18E 247 C6
Gölpazarı Turkey 40°16N 30°18E 212 B4
Golra Pakistan 33°37N 72°56E 242 C5
Golspie U.K. 57°58N 3°59W 167 D5
Golub-Dobrzyń Poland 53°7N 19°2E 185 E6
Golubac Serbia 44°38N 21°38E 202 B5
Golungo Alto Angola 9°8S 14°46E 265 D2
Golyam Bratan = Morozov Bulgaria 42°30N 25°10E 203 D9
Golyam Perelik Bulgaria 41°36N 24°33E 203 E8
Golyama Kamchiya → Bulgaria 43°10N 27°55E 203 C11
Golyshi = Vetluzhskiy Russia 58°23N 45°26E 190 A7
Goma Dem. Rep. of the Congo 1°37S 29°10E 268 C2
Gomal Pass Pakistan 31°56N 69°20E 242 D3
Gomantong Caves Malaysia 5°40N 118°6E 235 A5
Gomati → India 25°32N 83°11E 243 G10
Gombari Dem. Rep. of the Congo 2°45N 29°3E 268 B2
Gombe Dem. Rep. of the Congo 0°45S 17°36E 264 C3
Gombe Nigeria 10°19N 11°2E 263 C7
Gömbe Turkey 36°33N 29°38E 205 E11
Gombe □ Nigeria 10°0N 11°0E 263 C7
Gombe → Tanzania 4°38S 31°40E 268 C3
Gombe Stream △ Tanzania 4°42S 29°37E 268 C2
Gombi Nigeria 10°12N 12°30E 263 C7
Gomel = Homyel Belarus 52°28N 31°0E 177 B16
Gomera Canary Is. 28°7N 17°14W 153 e1
Gómez Palacio Mexico 25°34N 103°30W 318 B4
Gomfi Greece 39°26N 21°36E 204 B3
Gomīshān Iran 37°4N 54°6E 247 B7
Gommern Germany 52°4N 11°50E 178 C7
Gomogomo Indonesia 6°39S 134°43E 231 F8
Gomoh India 23°52N 86°10E 243 H12
Gomotartsi Bulgaria 44°6N 22°57E 202 B6
Gompa = Ganta Liberia 7°15N 8°59W 262 D3
Gonābād Iran 34°15N 58°45E 247 C8
Gonaïves Haiti 19°20N 72°42W 321 C5
Gonarezhou △ Zimbabwe 21°32S 31°55E 269 G3
Gonâve, G. de la Haiti 19°29N 72°42W 321 C5
Gonâve, Île de la Haiti 18°51N 73°3W 321 C5
Gonbad-e Kāvūs Iran 37°20N 55°25E 247 B7
Gönc Hungary 48°28N 21°14E 182 B6
Gonda India 27°9N 81°58E 243 F9
Gondal India 21°58N 70°52E 242 J4
Gonder Ethiopia 12°39N 37°30E 257 E4
Gondia India 21°23N 80°10E 244 D5
Gondola Mozam. 19°10S 33°37E 269 F3
Gondomar Portugal 41°10N 8°35W 194 D2
Gondrecourt-le-Château France 48°31N 5°30E 173 D12
Gonen Israel 31°46N 35°13E 123 B2
Gönen Balıkesir, Turkey 40°6N 27°39E 203 F11
Gönen Isparta, Turkey 37°57N 30°31E 205 D12
Gönen → Turkey 40°6N 27°39E 203 F11
Gong Xian China 28°23N 104°47E 228 C5
Gong'an China 30°7N 112°12E 229 B9
Gongbei China 22°12N 113°32E 219 a
Gongchangling China 41°7N 123°27E 224 B1
Gongcheng China 24°50N 110°49E 229 E8
Gongga Shan China 29°40N 101°55E 228 C3
Gonggar China 29°23N 91°7E 218 F7
Gongguan = Kungkuan Taiwan 24°35N 120°44E 225 B2
Gongguan China 21°48N 109°36E 228 G7
Gonghe China 36°18N 100°32E 218 D9
Gongju S. Korea 36°27N 127°7E 224 D3
Gongliu China 43°28N 82°8E 217 D10
Gongming China 22°47N 113°53E 219 a
Gongneung S. Korea 37°36N 127°3E 137 B2
Gongo Yembe Dem. Rep. of the Congo 1°58S 18°40E 264 C3
Gongola → Nigeria 9°30N 12°4E 263 D7
Gongolgon Australia 30°21S 146°54E 281 E4
Gongoué Gabon 0°31S 9°13E 264 C1
Gongshan China 27°43N 98°29E 228 D2
Gongtan China 28°55N 108°20E 228 C7
Gongyi China 34°45N 112°58E 226 G7
Gongzhuling China 43°30N 124°40E 227 C13
Goni Greece 39°52N 22°29E 204 B4
Goniadz Poland 53°30N 22°44E 184 E9
Goniri Nigeria 11°30N 12°15E 263 C7
Gonjo China 30°52N 98°17E 228 B2
Gonnesa Italy 39°16N 8°28E 200 C1
Gonnosfanàdiga Italy 39°29N 8°39E 200 C1
Gonzaga Phil. 18°16N 122°0E 232 B4
Gonzales Calif., U.S.A. 36°30N 121°26W 306 J5
Gonzales Tex., U.S.A. 29°30N 97°27W 314 G6
González Mexico 22°48N 98°25W 319 C5
Goobang △ Australia 33°0S 148°32E 283 B8
Good Hope, C. of S. Africa 34°24S 18°30E 270 D2
Good Hope Lake Canada 59°16N 129°18W 296 B3
Good Hope Plantation Jamaica 18°25N 77°41W 320 a
Goodenough I. Papua N. G. 9°20S 150°15E 286 E6
Gooderham Canada 44°54N 78°21W 312 B6
Goodhouse S. Africa 28°57S 18°13E 270 C2
Gooding U.S.A. 42°56N 114°43W 304 E6
Goodland U.S.A. 39°21N 101°43W 308 F3
Goodlands Mauritius 20°2S 57°39E 272 e
Goodlow Canada 56°20N 120°8W 296 B4
Goodmayes U.K. 51°33N 0°6E 125 A4
Goodnews Bay U.S.A. 59°7N 161°35W 303 G7
Goodooga Australia 29°3S 147°28E 281 D4
Goodsprings U.S.A. 35°49N 115°27W 307 K11
Goodwater U.S.A. 33°4N 86°3W 316 B3
Goodwood S. Africa 33°55S 18°32E 118 A2
Goole U.K. 53°42N 0°53W 168 D7
Goolgowi Australia 33°58S 145°41E 283 B6
Goolwa Australia 35°30S 138°47E 282 C3
Goomalling Australia 31°15S 116°49E 279 F2
Goomeri Australia 26°12S 152°6E 281 D5
Goonda Mozam. 19°48S 33°57E 269 F3
Goondiwindi Australia 28°30S 150°21E 281 D5
Goongarrie, L. Australia 30°3S 121°9E 279 F3
Goongarrie △ Australia 30°7S 121°30E 279 F3
Goonyella Australia 21°47S 147°58E 280 C4
Goose → Canada 53°20N 60°35W 299 B7
Goose Creek U.S.A. 32°59N 80°2W 316 C9
Goose L. Calif., U.S.A. 41°56N 120°26W 304 F3
Goose L. Ill., U.S.A. 40°55N 89°27W 310 D7
Gooty India 15°7N 77°41E 245 G3
Gop India 22°5N 69°50E 242 H3
Gopalganj Bangla. 23°1N 89°50E 241 D2
Gopalganj India 26°28N 84°30E 243 F11
Gopalpur India 22°38N 88°26E 124 B2
Göppingen Germany 48°42N 9°39E 179 G5
Goqên China 29°7N 97°14E 241 A6
Gor Spain 37°23N 2°58W 195 H8
Góra Dolnośląskie, Poland 51°40N 16°31E 185 G3
Góra Mazowieckie, Poland 52°39N 20°6E 185 F7
Góra Kalwaria Poland 51°59N 21°14E 185 G8
Gorakhpur India 26°47N 83°23E 243 F10
Goražde Bos.-H. 43°38N 18°58E 182 G3
Gorbatov Russia 56°12N 43°2E 190 B6
Gorbea Spain 43°1N 2°50W 196 B2
Górce Poland 52°15N 20°55E 143 B1
Gorczański △ Poland 49°30N 20°10E 185 J7
Gorda, Banco Caribbean 15°40N 80°27W 320 C3
Gorda, Pta. Canary Is. 28°45N 18°0W 153 e1
Gorda, Pta. Nic. 14°20N 83°10W 320 D3
Gordan B. Australia 11°35S 130°10E 278 B5
Gördes Turkey 38°54N 28°17E 205 C10
Gordon Ga., U.S.A. 32°54N 83°20W 316 C6
Gordon Nebr., U.S.A. 42°48N 102°12W 308 D2
Gordon → Australia 42°27S 145°30E 281 G4
Gordon, I. Chile 54°55S 69°30W 336 D3
Gordon Bay Canada 45°12N 79°47W 312 A5
Gordon L. Alta., Canada 56°30N 110°25W 297 B6
Gordon L. N.W.T., Canada 63°5N 113°11W 296 A6
Gordonvale Australia 17°5S 145°50E 280 B4
Goré Chad 7°59N 16°31E 259 G3
Gore Ethiopia 8°12N 35°32E 257 F4
Gore N.Z. 46°5S 168°58E 285 G3
Gore Bay Canada 45°57N 82°28W 298 C3
Gore Hill Australia 33°49S 151°10E 139 A2
Gorée, Île de Senegal 14°40N 17°23W 262 C1
Görele Turkey 41°2N 39°0E 213 B8
Gorelyy → Russia 60°1N 30°30E 137 A3
Göreme Turkey 38°35N 34°52E 212 C6
Gorey Ireland 52°41N 6°18W 166 D5
Gorg Iran 29°29N 59°43E 247 D8
Gorgān Iran 36°55N 54°30E 247 B7
Gorgie U.K. 55°56N 3°14W 121 B2
Gorgol □ Mauritania 15°45N 13°0W 262 B2
Gorgona Italy 43°26N 9°54E 198 E6
Gorgora Ethiopia 12°15N 37°17E 257 E4
Gorgoram Nigeria 12°40N 10°45E 263 C7
Gorham U.S.A. 44°23N 71°10W 313 B13
Gori Georgia 42°0N 44°7E 191 J7
Goribidnur = Gauribidanur India 13°37N 77°32E 245 H3
Goriganga → India 29°45N 80°23E 243 E9
Gorinchem Neths. 51°50N 4°59E 170 C4
Goris Armenia 39°31N 46°22E 213 C12
Goritsy Russia 57°4N 36°43E 188 D9
Gorizia Italy 45°56N 13°37E 199 C10
Gorj □ Romania 45°5N 23°25E 183 E8
Gorki = Horki Belarus 54°17N 30°59E 188 E6
Gorkiy = Nizhniy Novgorod Russia 56°20N 44°0E 190 B7
Gorkovskoye Vdkhr. Russia 57°2N 43°4E 190 B6
Gorky Park Russia 55°43N 37°36E 129 B2
Gorleston-on-Sea U.K. 52°35N 1°44E 169 E9
Gorlice Poland 49°35N 21°11E 185 J8
Görlitz Germany 51°9N 14°58E 178 D10
Gorlovka = Horlivka Ukraine 48°19N 38°5E 189 H10
Gorman U.S.A. 34°47N 118°51W 307 L8
Gorna Djumaya = Blagoevgrad Bulgaria 42°2N 23°5E 202 D7
Gorna Dzhumayo = Blagoevgrad Bulgaria 42°2N 23°5E 202 D7
Gorna Oryakhovitsa Bulgaria 43°7N 25°40E 203 C9
Gornja Radgona Slovenia 46°40N 16°2E 199 B13
Gornja Tuzla Bos.-H. 44°35N 18°46E 182 F3
Gornji Grad Slovenia 46°20N 14°52E 199 B11
Gornji Milanovac Serbia 44°3N 20°29E 202 B4
Gornji Vakuf Bos.-H. 43°57N 17°34E 182 G2
Gorno Ablanovo Bulgaria 43°37N 25°43E 203 C9
Gorno-Altay □ Russia 51°0N 86°0E 217 B11
Gorno-Altaysk Russia 51°50N 86°5E 217 B11
Gorno-Badakhshan = Kŭhiston-Badakhshon □ Tajikistan 38°30N 73°0E 217 E8
Gornozavodsk Russia 46°33N 141°50E 215 E15
Gornyak Russia 50°59N 81°27E 217 B10
Gornyatski Russia 67°32N 64°3E 186 A11
Gornyatskiy Russia 48°18N 40°56E 191 F5
Gornyy Primorsk, Russia 44°57N 133°59E 220 B6
Gornyy Saratov, Russia 51°50N 48°30E 190 E9
Goro → C.A.R. 9°14N 21°16E 264 A4
Gorodenka = Horodenka Ukraine 48°41N 25°29E 183 B10
Gorodets Russia 56°38N 43°28E 190 B6
Gorodishche = Horodyshche Ukraine 49°17N 31°27E 189 H6
Gorodishche Russia 53°13N 45°40E 190 D7
Gorodnya = Horodnya Ukraine 51°55N 31°33E 189 G6
Gorodok = Haradok Belarus 55°30N 30°3E 188 E6
Gorodok = Horodok Ukraine 49°46N 23°32E 177 D12
Gorodok = Zakamensk Russia 50°23N 103°17E 215 D11
Gorodovikovsk Russia 46°8N 41°58E 191 G5
Goroka Papua N. G. 6°7S 145°25E 286 D3
Goroke Australia 36°43S 141°29E 282 D4
Gorokhov = Horokhiv Ukraine 50°30N 24°45E 177 C13
Gorokhovets Russia 56°13N 42°39E 190 B6
Gorom Gorom Burkina Faso 14°26N 0°14W 263 C4
Goromonzi Zimbabwe 17°52S 31°22E 269 F3
Gorong, Kepulauan Indonesia 3°59S 131°25E 231 E8
Gorongose → Mozam. 20°30S 34°40E 271 B5
Gorongoza Mozam. 18°44S 34°2E 269 F3
Gorongoza, Sa. da Mozam. 18°27S 34°2E 269 F3
Gorongoza △ Mozam. 18°50S 34°29E 271 A5
Gorontalo Indonesia 0°35N 123°5E 231 D6
Gorontalo □ Indonesia 0°50N 122°20E 231 D6
Goronyo Nigeria 13°29N 5°39E 263 C6
Górowo Iławeckie Poland 54°17N 20°30E 184 D7
Gorron France 48°25N 0°50W 172 D6
Gorror Micronesia 9°26N 138°4E 287 S16
Gorshechnoye Russia 51°31N 38°2E 189 G10
Gort Ireland 53°3N 8°49W 166 C3
Gortis Greece 35°4N 24°58E 207 E5
Gorumahisani India 22°20N 86°24E 244 C8
Gorumara △ India 26°42N 88°55E 241 B2
Góry Bystrzyckie Poland 50°16N 16°33E 185 H3
Goryachiy Klyuch Russia 44°38N 39°8E 191 H4
Goryeong S. Korea 35°44N 128°15E 224 E4
Gorzkowice Poland 51°13N 19°36E 185 G6
Górzno Poland 53°12N 19°38E 185 E6
Gorzów Śląski Poland 51°3N 18°22E 185 G5
Gorzów Wielkopolski Poland 52°43N 15°15E 185 F2
Gose Japan 34°27N 135°44E 223 C7
Gosen Germany 52°23N 13°43E 115 B5
Gosener kanal Germany 52°24N 13°42E 115 B5
Goseong S. Korea 34°58N 128°19E 224 E4
Gosford Australia 33°23S 151°18E 283 B9
Goshen Calif., U.S.A. 36°21N 119°25W 306 J7
Goshen Ind., U.S.A. 41°35N 85°50W 311 C11
Goshen N.Y., U.S.A. 41°24N 74°20W 313 E10
Goshogawara Japan 40°48N 140°27E 220 D10
Goskopi = Kopeysk Russia 55°7N 61°37E 216 A6
Goslar Germany 51°54N 10°25E 178 D6
Gospel Oak U.K. 51°32N 0°9W 125 A3
Gospić Croatia 44°35N 15°23E 199 D12
Gosport Hants., U.K. 50°48N 1°9W 169 G6
Gosport Ind., U.S.A. 39°21N 86°40W 311 E10
Gossa Norway 62°52N 6°50E 164 B3
Gossas Senegal 14°28N 16°0W 262 C1
Gosse → Australia 19°32S 134°37E 280 B1
Gossi Mali 15°48N 1°20W 263 B4
Gossinga South Sudan 8°36N 25°59E 257 F2
Gostingen = Gostyń Poland 51°50N 17°3E 185 G4
Gostinopolye = Volkhov Russia 59°55N 32°15E 188 C7
Gostivar Macedonia 41°48N 20°57E 202 E4
Gostyń Poland 51°50N 17°3E 185 G4
Gostynin Poland 52°26N 19°29E 185 F6
Göta älv → Sweden 57°42N 11°54E 163 G5
Göta kanal Sweden 58°30N 15°58E 163 F10
Götaland Sweden 57°30N 14°30E 163 G8
Gotanda Japan 35°37N 139°43E 140 B3
Göteborg Sweden 57°43N 11°59E 163 G5
Gotemba Japan 35°18N 138°56E 223 B10
Götene Sweden 58°32N 13°30E 163 F7
Gotenhafen = Gdynia Poland 54°35N 18°33E 184 D5
Gotești Moldova 46°9N 28°10E 183 D13
Goth Goli Mar Pakistan 24°53N 67°1E 123 A2
Goth Sher Shah Pakistan 24°53N 66°59E 123 A1
Gotha Thüringen, Germany 50°56N 10°42E 178 E6
Gotha Fla., U.S.A. 28°31N 81°31W 133 A1
Gothenburg = Göteborg Sweden 57°43N 11°59E 163 G5
Gothenburg U.S.A. 40°56N 100°10W 308 E3
Gothèye Niger 13°52N 1°34E 263 C5
Gotland Sweden 57°30N 18°33E 163 G12
Gotland □ Sweden 57°15N 18°30E 163 G12
Gotō = Fukue Japan 32°41N 128°51E 221 H4
Goto Meer Bonaire 12°14N 68°22W 322 h
Gotō-Rettō Japan 32°55N 129°5E 221 H4
Gotse Delchev Bulgaria 41°36N 23°46E 202 E7
Gotska Sandön Sweden 58°24N 19°15E 163 F13
Götsu Japan 35°0N 132°14E 222 C4
Göttero, Monte Italy 44°22N 9°42E 198 D6
Gottesberg = Boguszów-Gorce Poland 50°45N 16°12E 185 H3
Göttingen Germany 51°31N 9°55E 178 D5
Gottschee = Kočevje Slovenia 45°39N 14°50E 199 C11
Gottskär Sweden 57°25N 12°2E 163 G6
Gottwald = Zmiyev Ukraine 49°39N 36°27E 189 H9
Gottwaldov = Zlín Czechia 49°14N 17°40E 181 B10
Goubangzi China 41°20N 121°52E 227 D11
Gouda Neths. 52°1N 4°42E 170 B4
Goudiri Senegal 14°15N 12°45W 262 C2
Goudoumaria Niger 13°40N 11°10E 259 F2
Goudouras, Akra Greece 34°59N 26°6E 207 F7
Gouéké Guinea 8°2N 8°43W 262 D3
Gough I. Atl. Oc. 40°10S 9°45W 152 L11
Gouin, Rés. Canada 48°35N 74°40W 298 C5
Goulafla Ivory C. 7°30N 5°53W 262 D3
Goulburn Australia 34°44S 149°44E 283 C8
Goulburn Is. Australia 11°40S 133°20E 280 A1
Goulburn River △ Australia 32°19S 150°10E 283 B9
Goulds U.S.A. 25°33N 80°23W 317 K9
Goulia Ivory C. 10°1N 7°11W 262 C3
Goulimima Morocco 31°41N 4°57W 260 B4
Goumbou Mali 15°2N 7°25W 262 B3
Goumenissa Greece 40°56N 22°37E 202 F6
Gounatolo Solomon Is. 8°25S 160°52E 287 M11
Goundam Mali 16°27N 3°40W 262 B4
Goundi Chad 9°22N 17°21E 259 G3
Gounou-Gaya Chad 9°38N 15°31E 259 G3
Goura Greece 37°56N 22°20E 204 D4
Gouraya Algeria 36°31N 1°56E 261 A5
Gourbassi Mali 13°24N 11°38W 262 C2
Gourbeyre Guadeloupe 16°0N 61°41W 322 e
Gourde, Pt. Trin. & Tob. 10°40N 61°38W 323 t
Gourdon France 44°44N 1°23E 174 D5
Gouré Niger 14°0N 10°10E 259 F2
Gouri Chad 18°50N 16°49E 259 E3
Gourin France 48°8N 3°37W 172 D3
Gourits → S. Africa 34°21S 21°52E 270 D3
Gourma-Rharous Mali 16°55N 1°50W 263 B4
Gournay-en-Bray France 49°29N 1°44E 173 C8
Gournay-sur-Marne France 48°51N 2°34E 134 A4
Gournes Greece 35°19N 25°16E 207 E6
Gouro Chad 19°36N 19°36E 259 E3
Gourock U.K. 55°57N 4°49W 167 F4
Gourock Ra. Australia 36°0S 149°25E 283 D8
Goursi Burkina Faso 12°42N 2°37W 262 C4
Gouvea Brazil 18°27S 43°44W 333 E3
Gouverneur U.S.A. 44°20N 75°28W 313 B9
Gouvia Greece 39°39N 19°50E 206 B9
Gouyave Grenada 12°10N 61°44W 323 q
Gouzon France 46°12N 2°14E 173 F9
Gove, Barragem do Angola 13°26S 15°53E 265 E3
Gove Peninsula Australia 12°17S 136°49E 280 A2
Governador, I. do Brazil 22°48S 43°13W 135 A1
Governador Valadares Brazil 18°15S 41°57W 333 E3
Governor Generoso Phil. 6°39N 126°5E 233 H6
Governor's Harbour Bahamas 25°10N 76°14W 320 A4
Governors I. New York, U.S.A. 132 f1
Govĭaltay □ Mongolia 45°30N 96°0E 217 C13
Govindgarh India 24°23N 81°18E 243 G9
Gowan Ra. Australia 25°0S 145°0E 280 D4
Gowanda U.S.A. 42°28N 78°56W 312 D6
Gower U.K. 51°35N 4°10W 169 F3
Gowers Corner U.S.A. 28°20N 82°30W 317 G7
Gowna, L. Ireland 53°51N 7°34W 166 C4
Gowrie U.S.A. 42°17N 94°17W 310 B2
Gowurdak Turkmenistan 37°50N 66°4E 217 E7
Goya Argentina 29°10S 59°10W 334 B4
Goyang S. Korea 37°39N 126°50E 224 D3
Goyave Guadeloupe 16°8N 61°34W 322 e
Goyaves, Grande Rivière → Guadeloupe 16°18N 61°36W 322 e
Göyçay Azerbaijan 40°42N 47°43E 191 K8
Goyder Lagoon Australia 27°3S 138°58E 281 D2
Goygöl Azerbaijan 40°37N 46°12E 191 K8
Goyllarisquizga Peru 10°31S 76°24W 330 C2
Göynük Antalya, Turkey 36°41N 30°33E 205 E12
Göynük Bolu, Turkey 40°24N 30°48E 212 B4
Goz Beïda Chad 12°10N 21°20E 259 F4
Goz Regeb Sudan 16°3N 35°33E 257 D4
Gozdnica Poland 51°28N 15°4E 185 G2
Gözneköy Turkey 36°58N 34°33E 250 B5
Gozo Malta 36°3N 14°15E 206 E7
Graaff-Reinet S. Africa 32°13S 24°32E 270 D3
Graben Vienna, Austria 142 b2
Grabill U.S.A. 41°13N 84°57W 311 C12
Grabo Ivory C. 4°57N 7°30W 262 D3
Grabow Mecklenburg-Vorpommern, Germany 53°17N 11°34E 178 B7
Grabów Warszawa, Poland 52°8N 20°59E 143 C1
Grabów nad Prosną Poland 51°31N 18°7E 185 G5
Graça Lisbon, Portugal 126 b3
Gračac Croatia 44°18N 15°57E 199 D12
Gračanica Bos.-H. 44°43N 18°18E 182 F3
Graçay France 47°10N 1°50E 173 E8
Grace Cathedral San Francisco, U.S.A. 136 b2
Graceville U.S.A. 30°58N 85°31W 316 E4
Gracewood U.S.A. 33°22N 82°2W 316 B7
Gracia Spain 41°24N 2°10E 114 A2
Gracias a Dios, C. Honduras 15°0N 83°10W 320 D3
Graciosa Azores 39°4N 28°0W 153 d1
Graciosa, I. Canary Is. 29°15N 13°32W 153 e2
Grad Sofiya □ Bulgaria 42°35N 23°20E 202 D7
Gradac Montenegro 43°23N 19°9E 202 C3
Gradačac Bos.-H. 44°52N 18°26E 182 F3
Gradaús Brazil 7°43S 50°44W 332 C1
Gradaús, Serra dos Brazil 8°0S 50°45W 332 C1
Gradeška Planina Macedonia 41°30N 22°15E 202 E6
Gradets Bulgaria 42°46N 26°30E 203 D10
Gradišče Slovenia 46°37N 15°50E 199 B12
Gradiška Bos.-H. 45°10N 17°15E 182 E2
Grădiştea de Munte Romania 45°37N 23°13E 183 E8
Grado Italy 45°40N 13°23E 199 C10
Grado Spain 43°23N 6°4W 194 B4
Grady U.S.A. 34°49N 103°19W 305 J12
Graeca, Lacul Romania 44°5N 26°10E 183 F11
Grafarnes Iceland 64°55N 23°16W 155 C3
Gräfelfing Germany 48°7N 11°25E 131 B1
Grafenau Germany 48°51N 13°22E 179 G9
Gräfenberg Germany 49°39N 11°14E 179 F7
Grafham Water U.K. 52°19N 0°18W 169 E7
Grafton N.S.W., Australia 29°38S 152°58E 281 D5
Grafton Ill., U.S.A. 38°58N 90°26W 310 F6
Grafton N. Dak., U.S.A. 48°25N 97°25W 308 A5
Grafton W. Va., U.S.A. 39°21N 80°2W 309 F13
Grafton Caledonia Wildlife Estate Trin. & Tob. 11°11N 60°47W 323 s
Grafton Pt. Anguilla 18°20N 62°54W 322 a
Gragoatá Brazil 22°53S 43°8W 135 B2
Graham Ont., Canada 49°20N 90°30W 298 C1
Graham Ga., U.S.A. 31°50N 82°30W 316 D7
Graham Tex., U.S.A. 33°6N 98°35W 314 E5
Graham, Mt. U.S.A. 32°42N 109°52W 305 K9
Graham Bell, Ostrov = Greem-Bell, Ostrov Russia 81°0N 62°0E 214 A7
Graham I. B.C., Canada 53°40N 132°30W 296 C2
Graham I. Nunavut, Canada 77°25N 90°30W 295 B13
Graham Land Antarctica 65°0S 64°0W 151 C17
Grahamstown S. Africa 33°19S 26°31E 270 D4
Grahamsville U.S.A. 41°51N 74°33W 313 E10
Grahovo Montenegro 42°40N 18°40E 202 D2
Graïba Tunisia 34°30N 10°13E 258 B2
Graie, Alpi Europe 45°30N 7°10E 175 C11
Grain Coast W. Afr. 4°20N 10°0W 262 E3
Grajagan Indonesia 8°35S 114°13E 231 K17
Grajaú Brazil 5°50S 46°4W 332 C2
Grajaú → Brazil 3°41S 44°48W 332 B3
Grajewo Poland 53°39N 22°30E 184 E9
Gramada Bulgaria 43°49N 22°39E 202 C6
Gramat France 44°48N 1°43E 174 D5
Grammichele Italy 37°13N 14°38E 201 E7
Grámmos, Óros Greece 40°18N 20°47E 202 F4
Grampian U.S.A. 40°58N 78°37W 312 F6
Grampian Highlands = Grampian Mts. U.K. 56°50N 4°0W 167 E5
Grampian Mts. U.K. 56°50N 4°0W 167 E5
Grampians, The Australia 37°15S 142°20E 282 D5
Grampians △ Australia 37°15S 142°28E 282 D5
Gramsh Albania 40°52N 20°12E 202 F4
Gran Norway 60°23N 10°31E 164 D7
Gran → Suriname 4°1N 55°30W 329 C6
Gran Altiplanicie Central Argentina 49°0S 69°30W 336 C3
Gran Canaria Canary Is. 27°55N 15°35W 153 e1
Gran Chaco S. Amer. 25°0S 61°0W 334 B3
Gran Couva Trin. & Tob. 10°24N 61°22W 323 t
Gran Desierto del Pinacate △ Mexico 31°51N 113°32W 318 A2
Gran Laguna Salada Argentina 44°24S 67°23W 336 B3
Gran Pajonal Peru 10°45S 74°30W 330 C3
Gran Paradiso Italy 45°33N 7°17E 198 C4
Gran Sasso d'Itália Italy 42°27N 13°42E 199 F10
Gran Sasso e Monti Della Laga △ Italy 42°32N 13°22E 199 F10
Gran Tarajal Canary Is. 28°13N 14°1W 153 e2
Granada Nic. 11°58N 86°0W 320 D2
Granada Spain 37°10N 3°35W 195 H7
Granada Colo., U.S.A. 38°4N 102°19W 304 G12
Granada □ Spain 37°18N 3°0W 195 H7
Granadilla de Abona Canary Is. 28°7N 16°33W 153 e1
Granard Ireland 53°47N 7°30W 166 C4
Granbury U.S.A. 32°27N 97°47W 314 E6
Granby Qué., Canada 45°25N 72°45W 313 A12
Granby Colo., U.S.A. 40°5N 105°56W 304 F11
Grand → Ont., Canada 42°51N 79°34W 312 D5
Grand → Mich., U.S.A. 43°4N 86°15W 311 A10
Grand → Mo., U.S.A. 39°23N 93°7W 310 E3
Grand → S. Dak., U.S.A. 45°40N 100°45W 308 C3
Grand Abaque, Pte.du Guadeloupe 16°21N 61°0W 322 e
Grand-Anse = Portsmouth Dominica 15°34N 61°27W 323 k
Grand Anse Grenada 12°1N 61°45W 323 q
Grand Anse B. Grenada 12°2N 61°45W 323 q
Grand B. Dominica 15°14N 61°18W 323 k
Grand Bahama I. Bahamas 26°40N 78°30W 320 A4
Grand Baie Mauritius 20°0S 57°35E 272 e
Grand Bank Canada 47°6N 55°48W 299 C8
Grand Banks Atl. Oc. 45°0N 52°0W 152 B6
Grand Bassam Ivory C. 5°10N 3°49W 262 D4
Grand Bassin Réunion 21°10S 55°32E 272 f
Grand Batanga Cameroon 2°50N 9°55E 264 B1
Grand Bazaar = Kapali Carsi Turkey 41°1N 28°58E 122 B1
Grand Bénare Réunion 21°6S 55°25E 272 f
Grand Bend Canada 43°18N 81°45W 312 C3
Grand Béréby Ivory C. 4°38N 6°55W 262 E3
Grand Blanc U.S.A. 42°56N 83°38W 311 B13
Grand Bois Mauritius 20°25S 57°32E 272 e
Grand-Bourg Guadeloupe 15°53N 61°19W 322 e
Grand Canal = Canal Grande Venice, Italy 142 b2
Grand Canal = Da Yunhe → China 34°25N 120°5E 227 H10
Grand Canyon U.S.A. 36°3N 112°9W 305 H7
Grand Canyon △ U.S.A. 36°15N 112°30W 305 H7
Grand Canyon-Parashant △ U.S.A. 36°30N 113°45W 305 H7
Grand Case St.-Martin 18°6N 63°4W 322 a
Grand Cayman Cayman Is. 19°20N 81°20W 320 C3
Grand Central Station New York, U.S.A. 132 c2
Grand Cess Liberia 4°40N 8°12W 262 E3
Grand Coulee U.S.A. 47°57N 119°0W 304 C4
Grand Coulee Dam U.S.A. 47°57N 118°59W 304 C4
Grand Cul-de-Sac Marin Guadeloupe 16°20N 61°35W 322 e
Grand Est □ France 48°30N 5°0E 173 D12
Grand Étang △ Grenada 12°5N 61°42W 323 q
Grand Falls Canada 47°3N 67°44W 299 C6
Grand Falls-Windsor Canada 48°56N 55°40W 299 C8
Grand Fond St. Barts 17°53N 62°48W 322 a
Grand Forks B.C., Canada 49°0N 118°30W 296 D5
Grand Forks N. Dak., U.S.A. 47°55N 97°3W 308 B5
Grand Galet Réunion 21°17S 55°38E 272 f
Grand Gaube Mauritius 20°0S 57°39E 272 e
Grand Gorge U.S.A. 42°21N 74°29W 313 D10
Grand Haven U.S.A. 43°4N 86°13W 311 A10
Grand I. Mich., U.S.A. 46°31N 86°40W 308 B10
Grand I. N.Y., U.S.A. 43°0N 78°58W 312 D6
Grand Îlet Guadeloupe 15°50N 61°35W 322 e
Grand Îlet Réunion 21°1S 55°29E 272 f
Grand Island U.S.A. 40°55N 98°21W 308 E4
Grand Isle La., U.S.A. 29°14N 90°0W 315 G9
Grand Isle Vt., U.S.A. 44°43N 73°18W 313 B11
Grand Junction Colo., U.S.A. 39°4N 108°33W 304 G9
Grand Junction Iowa, U.S.A. 42°2N 94°14W 310 B2
Grand L. N.B., Canada 45°57N 66°7W 299 C6
Grand L. Nfld. & L., Canada 49°0N 57°30W 299 C8
Grand L. Nfld. & L., Canada 53°40N 60°30W 299 B7
Grand L. La., U.S.A. 29°55N 92°47W 314 G8
Grand L. Ohio, U.S.A. 40°32N 84°25W 311 D12
Grand Lahou Ivory C. 5°10N 5°5W 262 D3
Grand Lake U.S.A. 40°15N 105°49W 304 F11
Grand Ledge U.S.A. 42°45N 84°45W 311 B12
Grand-Lieu, L. de France 47°6N 1°40W 172 E5
Grand Mal B. Grenada 12°5N 61°46W 323 q
Grand Manan I. Canada 44°45N 66°52W 299 D6
Grand Marais Mich., U.S.A. 46°40N 85°59W 309 B11
Grand Marais Minn., U.S.A. 47°45N 90°25W 298 C1
Grand Marigot B. Dominica 15°25N 61°16W 323 k
Grand-Mère Canada 46°36N 72°40W 298 C5
Grand Palace Bangkok, Thailand 113 b1
Grand Place Belgium 50°50N 4°21E 116 A2
Grand Popo Benin 6°15N 1°57E 263 D5
Grand Portage U.S.A. 47°58N 89°41W 308 B9
Grand Prairie U.S.A. 32°44N 96°59W 120 B3
Grand Rapids = Wisconsin Rapids U.S.A. 44°23N 89°49W 308 C9
Grand Rapids Man., Canada 53°12N 99°19W 297 C9

Grand Rapids Mich., U.S.A. 42°58N 85°40W 311 B10
Grand Rapids Minn., U.S.A. 47°14N 93°31W 308 B7
Grand Rapids ✕ (GRR) U.S.A. 42°53N 85°31W 311 B11
Grand Récif Sud N. Cal. 22°47S 166°55E 288 d
Grand Ridge U.S.A. 30°43N 85°1W 316 E4
Grand River U.S.A. 40°49N 93°58W 310 D3
Grand River Bay Mauritius 20°9S 57°27E 272 e
Grand River South East → Mauritius 20°17S 57°46E 272 e
Grand' Rivière Martinique 14°52N 61°11W 322 j
Grand Roy Grenada 12°8N 61°45W 323 q
Grand St-Bernard, Col du Europe 45°50N 7°10E 179 K3
Grand Santi Fr. Guiana 4°20N 54°24W 329 C7
Grand Staircase-Escalante △ U.S.A. 37°25N 111°33W 305 H8
Grand Teton U.S.A. 43°54N 110°50W 304 E8
Grand Teton △ U.S.A. 43°50N 110°50W 304 E8
Grand Union Canal U.K. 52°7N 0°53W 169 E7
Grandas Spain 43°13N 6°53W 194 B4
Grande → Jujuy, Argentina 24°20S 65°2W 334 A2
Grande → Mendoza, Argentina 36°52S 69°45W 334 D2
Grande → Bolivia 15°51S 64°39W 331 D5
Grande → Bahia, Brazil 11°30S 44°30W 332 D3
Grande → Minas Gerais, Brazil 20°6S 51°4W 333 F1
Grande → Venezuela 8°36N 61°39W 329 B5
Grande, B. Argentina 50°30S 68°20W 336 D3
Grande, Darsena Venice, Italy 142 b4
Grande, I. Brazil 23°9S 44°14W 333 F3
Grande, Rio → N. Amer. 25°58N 97°9W 314 J6
Grande, Serra Piauí, Brazil 8°0S 45°10W 332 C2
Grande, Serra Tocantins, Brazil 11°15S 46°30W 332 D2
Grande Anse = Beauséjour Guadeloupe 16°18N 61°4W 322 e
Grande Anse Guadeloupe 16°19N 61°47W 322 e
Grande Anse Martinique 14°30N 61°5W 322 j
Grande Anse St. Lucia 14°1N 60°54W 323 m
Grande Anse Seychelles 4°18S 55°45E 272 c
Grande Baleine → Canada 55°16N 77°47W 298 A4
Grande Cache Canada 53°53N 119°8W 296 C5
Grande Casse, Pte. de la France 45°24N 6°49E 175 C10
Grande Comore Comoros Is. 11°35S 43°20E 272 a
Grande Cul de Sac B St. Lucia 13°59N 61°2W 323 m
Grande-Entrée Canada 47°30N 61°40W 299 C7
Grande Matelot Pt. Trin. & Tob. 10°49N 61°9W 323 t
Grande Place Brussels, Belgium 116 b2
Grande Prairie Canada 55°10N 118°50W 296 B5
Grande Pte. Guadeloupe 15°58N 61°37W 322 e
Grande-Rivière Qué., Canada 48°26N 64°30W 299 C7
Grande Riviere Trin. & Tob. 10°50N 61°3W 323 t
Grande Rivière, Pte. de la Guadeloupe 16°18N 61°36W 322 e
Grande Rivière Noire Mauritius 20°21S 57°21E 272 e
Grande Rivière Sud Est Mauritius 20°17S 57°46E 272 e
Grande Sertão Veredas △ Brazil 15°10S 45°40W 333 E2
Grande-Terre Guadeloupe 16°20N 61°25W 322 e
Grande Terre Mayotte 12°46S 45°7E 272 b
Grande-Vallée Canada 49°14N 65°8W 299 C6
Grande Vigie, Pte. de la Guadeloupe 16°32N 61°27W 322 e
Grandfalls U.S.A. 31°20N 102°51W 314 F3
Grândola Portugal 38°12N 8°35W 195 G2
Grandpré France 49°20N 4°50E 173 C11
Grands Causses △ France 44°5N 2°58E 174 D6
Grands-Jardins △ Canada 47°41N 70°51W 299 C5
Grandview Man., Canada 51°10N 100°42W 297 C8
Grandview Mo., U.S.A. 38°53N 94°32W 310 F2
Grandview Wash., U.S.A. 46°15N 119°54W 304 C4
Grandview Heights U.S.A. 39°58N 83°2W 311 E13
Grandvilliers France 49°40N 1°57E 173 C8
Graneros Chile 34°5S 70°45W 334 C1
Grange Hill Jamaica 18°18N 78°11W 320 a
Grangemouth U.K. 56°1N 3°42W 167 E5
Granger U.S.A. 41°35N 109°58W 304 F9
Grängesberg Sweden 60°6N 15°1E 162 D9
Grangeville U.S.A. 45°56N 116°7W 304 D5
Granisle Canada 54°53N 126°13W 296 C3
Granit Rose, Côte France 48°50N 4°10W 172 D2
Granite City U.S.A. 38°42N 90°8W 310 F6
Granite Falls U.S.A. 44°49N 95°33W 308 C6
Granite L. Canada 48°8N 57°5W 299 C8
Granite Mt. U.S.A. 33°5N 116°28W 307 M10
Granite Pk. U.S.A. 45°10N 109°48W 304 D9
Graniteville S.C., U.S.A. 33°34N 81°49W 316 B8
Graniteville Vt., U.S.A. 44°8N 72°29W 313 B12
Granitola, C. Italy 37°34N 12°39E 200 E5
Granity N.Z. 41°39S 171°51E 285 B6
Granja Brazil 3°7S 40°50W 332 B3
Granja de Moreruela Spain 41°48N 5°44W 194 D5
Granja de Torrehermosa Spain 38°19N 5°35W 195 G5
Grankulla = Kauniainen Finland 60°13N 24°44E 121 B1
Gränna Sweden 58°1N 14°28E 163 F8
Granollers Spain 41°39N 2°18E 196 D7
Gransee Germany 53°1N 13°8E 178 B9
Grant Fla., U.S.A. 27°56N 80°32W 317 H9
Grant Nebr., U.S.A. 40°50N 101°43W 308 E3
Grant, Mt. U.S.A. 38°34N 118°48W 304 G4
Grant City U.S.A. 40°29N 94°25W 310 D2
Grant I. Australia 11°10S 132°52E 278 B5
Grant Park Chicago, U.S.A. 119 c2
Grant Range U.S.A. 38°30N 115°25W 304 G6
Grantham U.K. 52°55N 0°38W 168 E7
Grantley Adams Int. ✕ (BGI) Barbados 13°4N 59°29W 323 r
Granton U.K. 55°58N 3°14W 121 B2
Grantown-on-Spey U.K. 57°20N 3°36W 167 D5
Grants U.S.A. 35°9N 107°52W 305 J10
Grants Pass U.S.A. 42°26N 123°19W 304 E2
Grantsville U.S.A. 40°36N 112°28W 304 F7
Grantville U.S.A. 33°14N 84°50W 316 B5
Granville Manche, France 48°50N 1°35W 172 D5
Granville Trin. & Tob. 10°7N 61°48W 323 t
Granville Ill., U.S.A. 41°16N 89°14W 310 C7
Granville N. Dak., U.S.A. 48°16N 100°47W 308 A3
Granville N.Y., U.S.A. 43°24N 73°16W 313 C11
Granville Ohio, U.S.A. 40°4N 82°31W 312 F2
Granville L. Canada 56°18N 100°30W 297 B8
Granvin Norway 60°33N 6°45E 164 D3
Grapevine U.S.A. 32°56N 97°4W 120 A3
Grapevine Recr. Area U.S.A. 32°58N 97°3W 120 A3
Graskop S. Africa 24°56S 30°49E 271 B5
Gräsö Sweden 60°28N 18°35E 162 D12
Grass → Canada 56°3N 96°33W 297 B9
Grass Range U.S.A. 47°2N 108°48W 304 C9
Grass River △ Canada 54°40N 100°50W 297 C8
Grass Valley Calif., U.S.A. 39°13N 121°4W 306 F6
Grass Valley Oreg., U.S.A. 45°22N 120°47W 304 D3
Grassano Italy 40°38N 16°17E 201 B9
Grasse France 43°38N 6°56E 175 E10
Grassflat U.S.A. 41°0N 78°6W 312 E6
Grassi, Palazzo Venice, Italy 142 b2
Grasslands △ Canada 49°11N 107°38W 297 D7
Grassy Australia 40°3S 144°5E 281 G3
Grassy Park S. Africa 34°3S 18°30E 118 B2
Gråsten Denmark 54°55N 9°35E 163 K3
Grästorp Sweden 58°20N 12°40E 163 F6
Gratis U.S.A. 39°38N 84°32W 311 E12
Gratkorn Austria 47°8N 15°21E 180 D8
Gratosóglio Italy 45°24N 9°11E 128 B2
Gratz U.S.A. 38°28N 84°57W 311 F12
Gratzwalde Germany 52°28N 13°42E 115 B5
Graubünden ☐ Switz. 46°45N 9°30E 179 J5
Graudenz = Grudziądz Poland 53°30N 18°47E 184 E5
Graulhet France 43°45N 1°59E 174 E5
Graus Spain 42°11N 0°20E 196 C5
Gravberget Norway 60°53N 12°14E 164 D9
Grave, Pte. de France 45°34N 1°4W 174 C2
Gravelbourg Canada 49°50N 106°35W 297 D7
Gravelines France 51°1N 2°10E 173 A9
's-Gravenhage Neths. 52°7N 4°17E 170 B4
Gravenhurst Canada 44°52N 79°20W 312 B5
Gravesend N.S.W., Australia 29°35S 150°20E 281 D5
Gravesend Kent, U.K. 51°26N 0°22E 169 F8
Gravesend N.Y., U.S.A. 40°36N 73°56W 132 C2
Gravina in Púglia Italy 40°49N 16°25E 201 B9
Gravois, Pointe-à- Haiti 18°2N 73°56W 321 C5
Gravona → France 41°58N 8°45E 175 G12
Gray Haute-Saône, France 47°22N 5°35E 173 E12
Gray Ga., U.S.A. 33°1N 83°32W 316 B6
Grayling Alaska, U.S.A. 62°57N 160°3W 303 E7
Grayling Mich., U.S.A. 44°40N 84°43W 309 C11
Grays U.K. 51°28N 0°21E 169 F8
Grays Harbor U.S.A. 46°59N 124°1W 306 D2
Grays L. U.S.A. 43°4N 111°26W 304 E8
Grays River U.S.A. 46°21N 123°37W 306 D3
Grayville U.S.A. 38°16N 88°0W 311 F9
Grayvoron Russia 50°29N 35°41E 189 G8
Graz Austria 47°4N 15°27E 180 D8
Grazhdanka Russia 59°59N 30°24E 137 B2
Grdelica Serbia 42°55N 22°3E 202 D6
Greåker Norway 59°16N 11°2E 164 E8
Greasy L. Canada 62°55N 122°12W 296 A4
Great Abaco I. = Abaco I. Bahamas 26°25N 77°10W 320 A4
Great Artesian Basin Australia 23°0S 144°0E 280 C3
Great Australian Bight Australia 33°30S 130°0E 279 F5
Great Bacolet Bay Grenada 12°4N 61°37W 323 q
Great Bahama Bank Bahamas 23°15N 78°0W 320 B4
Great Barrier I. N.Z. 36°11S 175°25E 284 C4
Great Barrier Reef Australia 18°0S 146°50E 280 B4
Great Barrier Reef △ Australia 20°0S 150°0E 280 B4
Great Barrington U.S.A. 42°12N 73°22W 313 D11
Great Basalt Wall △ Australia 19°52S 145°43E 280 B4
Great Basin U.S.A. 40°0N 117°0W 304 G5
Great Basin △ U.S.A. 38°56N 114°15W 304 G6
Great Basses Sri Lanka 6°11N 81°29E 245 L5
Great Bear → Canada 65°0N 126°0W 294 E7
Great Bear L. Canada 65°30N 120°0W 294 D8
Great Belt = Store Bælt Denmark 55°20N 11°0E 163 J4
Great Bend Kans., U.S.A. 38°22N 98°46W 308 F4
Great Bend Pa., U.S.A. 41°58N 75°45W 313 E9
Great Blasket I. Ireland 52°6N 10°32W 166 D1
Great Britain Europe 54°0N 2°15W 158 E5
Great Camanoe Br. Virgin Is. 18°30N 64°35W 321 b
Great Channel Asia 6°0N 94°0E 245 L11
Great Coco I. = Koko Kyunzu Burma 14°7N 93°22E 245 G11
Great Codroy Canada 47°51N 59°16W 299 C8
Great Divide, The = Great Dividing Ra. Australia 23°0S 146°0E 280 C4
Great Divide Basin U.S.A. 42°0N 108°0W 304 E9
Great Dividing Ra. Australia 23°0S 146°0E 280 C4
Great Driffield = Driffield U.K. 54°0N 0°26W 168 C7
Great Exuma I. Bahamas 23°30N 75°50W 320 B4
Great Falls Guyana 5°35N 61°0W 329 B5
Great Falls Mont., U.S.A. 47°30N 111°17W 304 C8
Great Fish = Groot-Vis → S. Africa 33°28S 27°5E 270 D4
Great Goat I. Jamaica 17°52N 77°3W 320 a
Great Guana Cay Bahamas 24°0N 76°20W 320 B4
Great Hall of the People Beijing, China 114 c3
Great Himalayan △ India 31°30N 77°30E 242 D7
Great Inagua I. Bahamas 21°0N 73°20W 321 B5
Great Indian Desert = Thar Desert India 28°0N 72°0E 242 F5
Great Karoo S. Africa 31°55S 21°0E 270 D3
Great Khingan Mts. = Da Hinggan Ling China 48°0N 121°0E 219 B13
Great Lake Australia 41°50S 146°40E 281 G4
Great Lakes N. Amer. 46°0N 84°0W 292 E11
Great Limpopo Transfrontier △ Africa 23°0S 31°45E 271 B5
Great Malvern U.K. 52°7N 2°18W 169 E5
Great Miami → U.S.A. 39°7N 84°49W 311 E12
Great Nicobar India 7°0N 93°50E 245 L11
Great Ormes Head U.K. 53°20N 3°52W 168 D4
Great Otway △ Australia 38°50S 143°50E 282 E5
Great Ouse → U.K. 52°48N 0°21E 168 E8
Great Palm I. Australia 18°45S 146°40E 280 B4
Great Pedro Bluff Jamaica 17°51N 77°44W 320 a
Great Pee Dee → U.S.A. 33°21N 79°10W 315 E15
Great Plains N. Amer. 47°0N 105°0W 292 E9
Great Ruaha → Tanzania 7°56S 37°52E 268 D4
Great Sacandaga L. U.S.A. 43°6N 74°16W 313 C10
Great Saint Bernard Pass = Grand St-Bernard, Col du Europe 45°50N 7°10E 179 K3
Great Salt Desert = Kavīr, Dasht-e Iran 34°30N 55°0E 247 C7
Great Salt L. U.S.A. 41°15N 112°40W 304 F7
Great Salt Lake Desert U.S.A. 40°50N 113°30W 304 F7
Great Salt Plains L. U.S.A. 36°45N 98°8W 314 C5
Great Salt Pond St. Kitts & Nevis 17°14N 62°40W 322 d
Great Sand Dunes △ U.S.A. 37°48N 105°45W 305 H11
Great Sand Sea N. Afr. 29°0N 24°0E 258 C4
Great Sandy △ Australia 26°13S 153°2E 281 D5
Great Sandy Desert Australia 21°0S 124°0E 278 D3
Great Sangi = Sangihe, Pulau Indonesia 3°35N 125°30E 231 D7
Great Scarcies → S. Leone 9°0N 13°0W 262 D2
Great Sd. Bermuda 32°17N 64°51W 153 a
Great Sea Reef Fiji 16°15S 179°0E 287 A2
Great Sitkin I. U.S.A. 52°3N 176°6W 303 K3
Great Skellig Ireland 51°47N 10°33W 166 E1
Great Slave L. Canada 61°23N 115°38W 296 A5
Great Smoky Mts. △ U.S.A. 35°40N 83°40W 315 D13
Great Stour = Stour → U.K. 51°18N 1°22E 169 F9
Great Victoria Desert Australia 29°30S 126°30E 279 E4
Great Wall Antarctica 62°30S 58°0W 151 C18
Great Wall China 38°30N 109°30E 226 E5
Great Whale River = Kuujjuarapik Canada 55°20N 77°35W 298 A4
Great Whernside U.K. 54°10N 1°58W 168 C6
Great Yarmouth U.K. 52°37N 1°44E 169 E9
Great Zab = Zāb al Kabīr → Iraq 36°1N 43°24E 213 D10
Great Zimbabwe Zimbabwe 20°16S 30°54E 269 G3
Greater Antilles W. Indies 17°40N 74°0W 321 C5
Greater London ☐ U.K. 51°31N 0°6W 169 F7
Greater Manchester ☐ U.K. 53°30N 2°15W 168 D5
Greater Sudbury Canada 46°30N 81°0W 298 C3
Greater Sunda Is. Indonesia 7°0S 112°0E 230 F4
Grebbestad Sweden 58°42N 11°15E 163 F5
Grebenka = Hrebenka Ukraine 50°9N 32°22E 189 G7
Greco Italy 45°30N 9°12E 128 A2
Greco, C. Cyprus 34°57N 34°5E 207 F10
Greco, Mte. Italy 41°48N 13°58E 199 G10
Gredos, Sierra de Spain 40°20N 5°0W 194 E6
Greece U.S.A. 43°13N 77°41W 312 C7
Greece ■ Europe 40°0N 23°0E 204 B3
Greeley Colo., U.S.A. 40°25N 104°42W 304 F11
Greeley Nebr., U.S.A. 41°33N 98°32W 308 E4
Greeleyville U.S.A. 33°40N 79°59W 316 B10
Greely Fd. Canada 80°30N 85°0W 295 A15
Greem-Bell, Ostrov Russia 81°0N 62°0E 214 A7
Green → Ky., U.S.A. 37°54N 87°30W 308 G10
Green → Utah, U.S.A. 38°11N 109°53W 304 G9
Green B. U.S.A. 45°0N 87°30W 308 C10
Green Bay U.S.A. 44°31N 88°0W 308 C9
Green C. Australia 37°13S 150°1E 283 D9
Green City U.S.A. 40°16N 92°57W 310 D4
Green Cove Springs U.S.A. 29°59N 81°42W 316 F8
Green I. = Lütao Taiwan 22°40N 121°30E 225 D3
Green I. Antigua & B. 17°2N 61°40W 322 b
Green I. Hong Kong, China 22°17N 114°6E 122 B2
Green I. Grenada 12°13N 61°35W 323 q
Green Is. Papua N. G. 4°35S 154°10E 286 C8
Green Island Jamaica 18°23N 78°17W 320 a
Green Island B. Phil. 10°12N 119°22E 233 F2
Green Lake Canada 54°17N 107°47W 297 C7
Green Mt. = Peak, The Ascension I. 7°57S 14°20W 153 g
Green Mts. U.S.A. 43°45N 72°45W 313 C12
Green Point S. Africa 33°54S 18°25E 118 A1
Green Pond U.S.A. 32°44N 80°37W 316 C9
Green River Papua N. G. 3°54S 141°11E 286 B1
Green River Utah, U.S.A. 38°59N 110°10W 304 G8
Green River Wyo., U.S.A. 41°32N 109°28W 304 F9
Green Valley U.S.A. 31°52N 110°56W 305 L8
Greenacres U.S.A. 26°38N 80°7W 317 J9
Greenbank U.S.A. 48°6N 122°34W 306 B4
Greenbush Mich., U.S.A. 44°35N 83°19W 312 B1
Greenbush Minn., U.S.A. 48°42N 96°11W 308 A5
Greencastle U.S.A. 39°38N 86°52W 311 E10
Greene Iowa, U.S.A. 42°54N 92°48W 310 B4
Greene N.Y., U.S.A. 42°20N 75°46W 313 D9
Greeneville U.S.A. 36°10N 82°50W 315 C13
Greenfield Calif., U.S.A. 36°19N 121°15W 306 J5
Greenfield Calif., U.S.A. 35°15N 119°0W 307 K8
Greenfield Ill., U.S.A. 39°21N 90°12W 310 E6
Greenfield Ind., U.S.A. 39°47N 85°46W 311 E11
Greenfield Iowa, U.S.A. 41°18N 94°28W 310 C2
Greenfield Mass., U.S.A. 42°35N 72°36W 313 D12
Greenfield Mo., U.S.A. 37°25N 93°51W 308 G7
Greenfield Ohio, U.S.A. 39°21N 83°23W 311 E13
Greenfield Park Canada 45°29N 73°28W 130 B3
Greenford U.K. 51°31N 0°21W 125 A1
Greenhill U.K. 51°34N 0°18W 125 A2
Greenland ☑ N. Amer. 66°0N 45°0W 154 D6
Greenland Sea Arctic 73°0N 10°0W 154 B10
Greenmarket Square Cape Town, S. Africa 118 c2
Greenock U.K. 55°57N 4°46W 167 F4
Greenore Ireland 54°1N 6°9W 166 B5
Greenore Pt. Ireland 52°14N 6°19W 166 D5
Greenough Australia 28°58S 114°43E 279 E1
Greenough → Australia 28°51S 114°38E 279 E1
Greenough Pt. Canada 44°58N 81°26W 312 B3
Greenpoint New York, U.S.A. 132 e3
Greenport U.S.A. 41°6N 72°22W 313 E12
Greensboro Fla., U.S.A. 30°34N 84°45W 316 E5
Greensboro Ga., U.S.A. 33°35N 83°11W 316 B6
Greensboro N.C., U.S.A. 36°4N 79°48W 315 C15
Greensboro Vt., U.S.A. 44°36N 72°18W 313 B12
Greensburg Ind., U.S.A. 39°20N 85°29W 311 E11
Greensburg Kans., U.S.A. 37°36N 99°18W 308 G4
Greensburg Pa., U.S.A. 40°18N 79°33W 312 F5
Greenstone = Geraldton Canada 49°44N 87°10W 298 C2
Greenstone Pt. U.K. 57°55N 5°37W 167 D3
Greentown U.S.A. 40°29N 85°58W 311 D11
Greenup U.S.A. 39°15N 88°10W 311 E8
Greenvale Australia 18°59S 145°7E 280 B4
Greenville Liberia 5°1N 9°6W 262 D3
Greenville Ala., U.S.A. 31°50N 86°38W 315 F11
Greenville Calif., U.S.A. 40°8N 120°57W 306 E6
Greenville Fla., U.S.A. 30°28N 83°38W 316 E6
Greenville Ga., U.S.A. 33°2N 84°43W 316 B5
Greenville Ill., U.S.A. 38°53N 89°25W 310 F7
Greenville Ind., U.S.A. 38°22N 85°59W 311 F11
Greenville Maine, U.S.A. 45°28N 69°35W 309 C19
Greenville Mich., U.S.A. 43°11N 85°15W 311 A11
Greenville Miss., U.S.A. 33°24N 91°4W 315 E9
Greenville Mo., U.S.A. 37°8N 90°27W 308 G8
Greenville N.C., U.S.A. 35°37N 77°23W 315 D16
Greenville N.H., U.S.A. 42°46N 71°49W 313 D13
Greenville N.Y., U.S.A. 42°25N 74°1W 313 D10
Greenville Ohio, U.S.A. 40°6N 84°38W 311 D12
Greenville Pa., U.S.A. 41°24N 80°23W 312 E4
Greenville S.C., U.S.A. 34°51N 82°24W 315 D13
Greenville Tex., U.S.A. 33°8N 96°7W 314 E6
Greenwater Lake △ Canada 52°32N 103°30W 297 C8
Greenwich Conn., U.S.A. 41°2N 73°38W 313 E11
Greenwich N.Y., U.S.A. 43°5N 73°30W 313 C11
Greenwich Ohio, U.S.A. 41°2N 82°31W 312 E2
Greenwich ☐ U.K. 51°29N 0°1E 125 B3
Greenwich Observatory U.K. 51°28N 0°0 125 B3
Greenwich Village New York, U.S.A. 132 d1
Greenwood B.C., Canada 49°10N 118°40W 296 D5
Greenwood Ark., U.S.A. 35°13N 94°16W 314 D7
Greenwood Fla., U.S.A. 30°52N 85°10W 316 E4
Greenwood Ind., U.S.A. 39°37N 86°7W 311 E10
Greenwood Mass., U.S.A. 42°29N 71°2W 116 A2
Greenwood Miss., U.S.A. 33°31N 90°11W 315 E9
Greenwood S.C., U.S.A. 34°12N 82°10W 316 A7
Greenwood, Mt. Australia 13°48S 130°4E 278 B5
Greenwood Great House Jamaica 18°29N 77°44W 320 a
Grefsen Norway 59°56N 10°47E 133 A3
Gregbe Ivory C. 6°48N 6°43W 262 D3
Gregório → Brazil 6°50S 70°46W 330 B3
Gregory U.S.A. 43°14N 99°26W 308 D4
Gregory → Australia 17°53S 139°17E 280 B2
Gregory, L. S. Austral., Australia 28°55S 139°0E 281 D2
Gregory, L. W. Austral., Australia 20°0S 127°40E 278 D4
Gregory, L. W. Austral., Australia 25°38S 119°58E 279 E2
Gregory △ Australia 15°38S 131°15E 278 C5
Gregory Downs Australia 18°35S 138°45E 280 B2
Gregory Ra. Queens., Australia 19°30S 143°40E 280 B3
Gregory Ra. W. Austral., Australia 21°20S 121°12E 278 D3
Greifenberg = Gryfice Poland 53°55N 15°13E 184 E2
Greifenhagen = Gryfino Poland 53°16N 14°29E 185 E1
Greiffenberg = Gryfów Śląski Poland 51°2N 15°24E 185 G2
Greiffenberg Germany 53°5N 13°57E 178 B9
Greifswald Germany 54°5N 13°23E 178 A9
Greifswalder Bodden Germany 54°12N 13°35E 178 A9
Grein Austria 48°14N 14°51E 180 C7
Greiz Germany 50°39N 12°10E 178 E8
Gremikha Russia 67°59N 39°47E 186 A6
Grenaa Denmark 56°25N 10°53E 163 H4
Grenada U.S.A. 33°47N 89°49W 315 E10
Grenada ■ W. Indies 12°10N 61°40W 323 q
Grenade France 43°47N 1°17E 174 E5
Grenadier I. U.S.A. 44°3N 76°22W 313 B8
Grenadines, The St. Vincent 12°40N 61°20W 323 n
Grenchen Switz. 47°12N 7°24E 179 H3
Grenen Denmark 57°44N 10°40E 163 G4
Grenfell N.S.W., Australia 33°52S 148°8E 283 B8
Grenfell Sask., Canada 50°30N 102°56W 297 C8
Grenivík Iceland 65°57N 18°11W 155 B8
Grenjaðarstaður Iceland 65°49N 17°21W 155 B9
Grenoble France 45°12N 5°42E 175 C9
Grenville Grenada 12°7N 61°37W 323 q
Grenville, C. Australia 12°0S 143°13E 286 F2
Grenville Chan. Canada 53°40N 129°46W 296 C3
Gréoux-les-Bains France 43°45N 5°52E 175 E9
Gresham U.S.A. 45°30N 122°25W 306 E4
Gresham Park U.S.A. 33°43N 84°20W 113 B2
Gresik Indonesia 7°13S 112°38E 235 D4
Gretna Dumf. & Gall., U.K. 55°0N 3°3W 167 F5
Gretna Fla., U.S.A. 30°37N 84°40W 316 E5
Gretna La., U.S.A. 29°54N 90°3W 131 B2
Gretna City Park U.S.A. 29°54N 90°3W 131 B2
Greve Strand Denmark 55°34N 12°18E 118 B1
Greven Germany 52°6N 7°36E 178 C3
Grevena Greece 40°4N 21°25E 202 F5
Grevenbroich Germany 51°5N 6°35E 178 D2
Grevenmacher Lux. 49°41N 6°26E 170 E6
Grevesmühlen Germany 53°52N 11°12E 178 B7
Grey → Nfld. & L., Canada 47°34N 57°6W 299 C8
Grey → N.Z. 42°27S 171°12E 285 C6
Grey, C. Australia 13°0S 136°35E 280 A2
Grey Is. Canada 50°50N 55°35W 295 G20
Grey Ra. Australia 27°0S 143°30E 281 D3
Greybull U.S.A. 44°30N 108°3W 304 D9
Greyfriars Kirk Edinburgh, U.K. 121 c3
Greymouth N.Z. 42°29S 171°13E 285 C6
Greynolds Park U.S.A. 25°56N 80°9W 129 C3
Greystones Ireland 53°9N 6°5W 166 C5
Greytown N.Z. 41°5S 175°29E 284 H4
Greytown KwaZulu Natal, S. Africa 29°1S 30°36E 271 C5
Gribanovskiy Russia 51°28N 41°50E 190 E5
Gribbell I. Canada 53°23N 129°0W 296 C3
Gribës, Mal i Albania 40°17N 19°45E 202 F3
Gribingui → C.A.R. 8°33N 19°5E 264 A3
Gribingui-Bamingui △ C.A.R. 7°45N 19°17E 264 A3
Gridley U.S.A. 39°22N 121°42W 306 F5
Griebeg, Ras il- Malta 35°58N 14°23E 206 F7
Griebnitzsee Germany 52°23N 13°8E 115 B1
Griekwastad S. Africa 28°49S 23°15E 270 C3
Griesheim Germany 49°51N 8°33E 179 F4
Grieskirchen Austria 48°16N 13°48E 180 C6
Griffin U.S.A. 33°15N 84°16W 316 B5
Griffin, L. U.S.A. 28°52N 81°51W 317 G8
Griffith N.S.W., Australia 34°18S 146°2E 283 C7
Griffith Ont., Canada 45°15N 77°10W 312 A7
Griffith I. Canada 44°50N 80°55W 312 B4
Griffith Park U.S.A. 34°8N 118°17W 126 B3
Griggsville U.S.A. 39°43N 90°43W 310 E6
Grignols France 44°23N 0°2W 174 D3
Grigoriopol Moldova 47°9N 29°18E 183 C14
Grimari C.A.R. 5°43N 20°6E 264 A4
Grimaylov = Hrymayliv Ukraine 49°20N 26°5E 177 D14
Grimbergen Belgium 50°56N 4°22E 116 A2
Grimes U.S.A. 39°4N 121°54W 306 F5
Grimm = Kamenskiy Russia 50°48N 45°25E 190 E7
Grimma Germany 51°14N 12°43E 178 D8
Grimmen Germany 54°7N 13°3E 178 A9
Grimsay U.K. 57°29N 7°14W 167 D1
Grimsby Ont., Canada 43°12N 79°34W 312 C5
Grimsby N.E. Lincs., U.K. 53°34N 0°5W 168 D7
Grimsey Iceland 66°33N 17°58W 155 A9
Grimshaw Canada 56°10N 117°40W 296 B5
Grimslöv Sweden 56°44N 14°34E 163 H8
Grímsstaðir Iceland 65°39N 16°7W 155 B10
Grimstad Norway 58°20N 8°35E 164 F5
Grímsvötn Iceland 64°26N 17°22W 155 C9
Grindavík Iceland 63°50N 22°26W 155 D4
Grindelwald Switz. 46°38N 8°2E 179 J4
Grindsted Denmark 55°46N 8°55E 163 J2
Grindstone I. U.S.A. 44°17N 76°27W 313 B8
Grindu Romania 44°44N 26°50E 183 F11
Grinnell U.S.A. 41°45N 92°43W 310 C4
Grinnell Pen. Canada 76°40N 95°0W 295 B13
Grintavec Slovenia 46°22N 14°32E 199 B11
Grinzing Austria 48°15N 16°20E 142 A2
Griomasaigh = Grimsay U.K. 57°29N 7°14W 167 D1
Gris-Nez, C. France 50°52N 1°35E 173 B8
Grise Fiord Canada 76°25N 82°57W 295 B15
Grishino = Krasnoarmeisk Ukraine 48°18N 37°11E 189 H9
Grisolles France 43°49N 1°19E 174 E5
Grisons = Graubünden ☐ Switz. 46°45N 9°30E 179 J5
Grisslehamn Sweden 60°5N 18°49E 162 D12
Grmeč Planina Bos.-H. 44°43N 16°16E 199 D13
Groais I. Canada 50°55N 55°35W 299 B8
Gröbenried Germany 48°14N 11°25E 131 A1
Grobiņa Latvia 56°33N 21°10E 184 B8
Groblersdal S. Africa 25°15S 29°25E 271 C4
Grobming Austria 47°27N 13°54E 180 D6
Grochów Poland 52°15N 21°5E 143 B2
Grocka Serbia 44°40N 20°42E 202 B4
Gródek Poland 53°6N 23°40E 185 E10
Gródek Tagielloński = Horodok Ukraine 49°46N 23°32E 177 D12
Grodekovo = Pogranichnyy Russia 44°25N 131°24E 220 B5
Grodków Poland 50°43N 17°21E 185 H4
Grodno = Hrodna Belarus 53°42N 23°52E 184 E10
Grodzisk Poland 52°19N 21°4E 143 B2
Grodzisk Mazowiecki Poland 52°7N 20°37E 185 F7
Grodzisk Wielkopolski Poland 52°15N 16°22E 185 F3
Grodzyanka = Hrodzyanka Belarus 53°31N 28°42E 177 B15
Groenendaal Belgium 50°46N 4°26E 116 B2
Groesbeck U.S.A. 31°31N 96°32W 314 F6
Grogol Petamburin Indonesia 6°9S 106°46E 122 A1
Groix France 47°38N 3°29W 172 E3
Groix, Î. de France 47°38N 3°28W 172 E3
Grójec Poland 51°50N 20°58E 185 G7
Gronau Niedersachsen, Germany 52°5N 9°47E 178 C5
Gronau Nordrhein-Westfalen, Germany 52°12N 7°2E 178 C3
Grong Norway 64°25N 12°8E 160 D15
Grönhögen Sweden 56°16N 16°24E 163 H10
Groningen Neths. 53°15N 6°35E 170 A6
Groningen Suriname 5°48N 55°28W 329 B6
Groningen ☐ Neths. 53°16N 6°40E 170 A6
Gronlands △ Greenland 75°0N 35°0W 154 C7
Grønnedal = Kangilinnguit Greenland 61°20N 47°57W 154 E6
Gronsdorf Germany 48°7N 11°42E 131 B3
Groom U.S.A. 35°12N 101°6W 314 D4
Groot → S. Africa 33°45S 24°36E 270 D3
Groot-Berg → S. Africa 32°47S 18°8E 270 D2
Groot-Brakrivier S. Africa 34°2S 22°18E 270 D3
Groot Karasberge Namibia 27°20S 18°40E 270 C2
Groot-Kei → S. Africa 32°41S 28°22E 271 D4
Groot-Vis → S. Africa 33°28S 27°5E 270 D4
Grootdrink S. Africa 28°33S 21°42E 270 C3
Groote Eylandt Australia 14°0S 136°40E 280 A2
Groote Peel △ Neths. 51°22N 5°49E 170 C5
Grootfontein Namibia 19°31S 18°6E 270 A2
Grootlaagte → Africa 20°55S 21°27E 270 B3
Grootvloer → S. Africa 30°0S 20°40E 270 D3
Grorud Norway 59°57N 10°53E 133 A4
Gros C. Canada 61°59N 113°32W 296 A6
Gros Cap Guadeloupe 16°24N 61°25W 322 e
Gros Islet St. Lucia 14°5N 60°58W 323 m
Gros-Morne Martinique 14°43N 61°2W 322 j
Gros Morne △ Canada 49°40N 57°50W 299 C8
Gros Piton St. Lucia 13°49N 61°5W 323 m
Grósio Italy 46°18N 10°16E 198 B7
Grosne → France 46°42N 4°56E 173 F11
Gross Glienicke Berlin, Germany 52°28N 13°6E 115 B1
Gross-Hadern Germany 48°6N 11°29E 131 B1
Gross-Lappen Germany 48°11N 11°35E 131 A2
Gross-Meseritsch = Velké Meziříčí Czechia 49°21N 16°1E 180 B9
Gross-Strehlitz = Strzelce Opolskie Poland 50°31N 18°18E 185 H5
Gross Wartenberg = Syców Poland 51°19N 17°40E 185 G4
Grossa, Pta. Spain 39°6N 1°36E 206 C2
Grosse I. U.S.A. 42°8N 83°9W 311 B13
Grosse Krampe Germany 52°23N 13°40E 115 B5
Grosse Müggelsee Germany 52°26N 13°38E 115 B4
Grosse Point U.S.A. 42°23N 82°54W 312 D2
Grosse Point Lighthouse U.S.A. 42°2N 87°41W 119 A2
Grosse Pte. Guadeloupe 16°1N 61°17W 322 e
Grossenbrode Germany 54°21N 11°4E 178 A7
Grossenhain Germany 51°17N 13°32E 178 D9
Grossenzersdorf Austria 48°12N 16°33E 142 A3
Grossenzersdorfer Arm → Austria 48°12N 16°31E 142 A3
Grosser Arber Germany 49°6N 13°8E 179 F9
Grosser Biberhaufen Austria 48°12N 16°28E 142 A2
Grosser Plöner See Germany 54°10N 10°22E 178 A6
Grosser Wannsee Germany 52°25N 13°10E 115 B2
Grosseto Italy 42°46N 11°8E 199 F8
Grossfeld-Siedlung Austria 48°16N 16°26E 142 A2
Grossgerungs Austria 48°34N 14°57E 180 C7
Grossglockner Austria 47°5N 12°40E 180 D5
Grosshesselohe Germany 48°4N 11°32E 131 B2
Grossjedlersdorf Austria 48°16N 16°23E 142 A2
Grosswardein = Oradea Romania 47°2N 21°58E 182 C6
Grossziethen Germany 52°23N 13°26E 115 B3
Groswater B. Canada 54°20N 57°40W 299 B8
Grotli Norway 62°2N 7°42E 164 B4
Groton Conn., U.S.A. 41°21N 72°5W 313 E12
Groton N.Y., U.S.A. 42°36N 76°22W 313 D8
Groton S. Dak., U.S.A. 45°27N 98°6W 308 C4
Grottáglie Italy 40°32N 17°26E 201 B10
Grottaminarda Italy 41°4N 15°2E 201 A8
Grottammare Italy 42°59N 13°52E 199 F10
Grotte Chauvet-Pont d'Arc France 44°23N 4°25E 175 D8
Grottkau = Grodków Poland 50°43N 17°21E 185 H4
Grouard Mission Canada 55°33N 116°9W 296 B5
Grouin, Pte. du France 48°43N 1°51W 172 D5
Groulx, Mts. Canada 51°27N 68°41W 299 B6
Ground Zero = National September 11 Memorial and Museum New York, U.S.A. 132 e1
Groundhog → Canada 48°45N 82°58W 298 C3
Grouw Neths. 53°5N 5°51E 170 A5
Grove City Fla., U.S.A. 26°56N 82°19W 317 J7
Grove City Ohio, U.S.A. 39°53N 83°6W 311 E13
Grove City Pa., U.S.A. 41°10N 80°5W 312 E4
Grove Hall U.S.A. 42°18N 71°4W 116 B2
Grove Hill U.S.A. 31°42N 87°47W 315 F11
Grove Park Hounslow, U.K. 51°28N 0°15W 125 B1
Grove Park Lewisham, U.K. 51°25N 0°1E 125 B4
Grove Park Georgia, U.S.A. 33°46N 84°26W 113 B2
Groveland Calif., U.S.A. 37°50N 120°14W 306 H6
Groveland Fla., U.S.A. 28°34N 81°51W 317 G8
Grover = Tiltonsville U.S.A. 40°10N 80°41W 312 F4
Grover Beach U.S.A. 35°7N 120°37W 307 K6
Groves U.S.A. 29°57N 93°54W 314 G8
Groveton N.H., U.S.A. 44°36N 71°31W 313 B13
Groveton Va., U.S.A. 38°46N 77°6W 143 C2
Grovetown U.S.A. 33°27N 82°12W 316 B7
Grožnjan Croatia 45°22N 13°43E 199 C10
Groznyy Russia 43°20N 45°45E 191 J7
Grua Norway 60°16N 10°40E 164 D7
Grubišno Polje Croatia 45°44N 17°12E 182 E2
Grudovo Bulgaria 42°21N 27°10E 203 D11
Grudusk Poland 53°3N 20°38E 185 E7
Grudziądz Poland 53°30N 18°47E 184 E5
Gruinard B. U.K. 57°56N 5°35W 167 D3
Gruissan France 43°8N 3°7E 174 E7
Grumo Áppula Italy 41°1N 16°42E 201 A9
Grums Sweden 59°22N 13°5E 162 E7
Grünau Germany 52°25N 13°34E 115 B4
Grünberg Germany 50°35N 8°58E 178 E4
Grünberg in Schlesien = Zielona Góra Poland 51°57N 15°31E 185 G2
Grund Iceland 65°31N 18°9W 155 B8
Gründau Germany 50°10N 9°9E 179 E5
Grundy Center U.S.A. 42°22N 92°47W 310 B4
Grunewald Germany 52°28N 13°16E 115 B2
Grünstadt Germany 49°34N 8°9E 179 F4
Grünwald Germany 48°2N 11°31E 131 B2
Grünwalder Forst Germany 48°2N 11°33E 131 B2
Gruppo di Tessa △ Italy 46°47N 11°0E 198 B8
Gruvberget Sweden 61°6N 16°10E 162 C10
Gruver U.S.A. 36°16N 101°24W 314 C4
Gruyères Switz. 46°35N 7°4E 179 J3
Gruža Serbia 43°54N 20°46E 202 C4
Gryazi Russia 52°30N 39°58E 189 F10
Gryazliv = Borovichi Russia 58°25N 33°55E 188 C7
Gryazovets Russia 58°50N 40°10E 188 C11
Grybów Poland 49°36N 20°55E 185 J7
Gryckbo Sweden 60°40N 15°29E 162 D9
Gryfice Poland 53°55N 15°13E 184 E2
Gryfino Poland 53°16N 14°29E 185 E1
Gryfów Śląski Poland 51°2N 15°24E 185 G2
Grymes Hill U.S.A. 40°36N 74°6W 132 C1
Gryt Sweden 58°12N 16°48E 163 F10
Grythyttan Sweden 59°41N 14°32E 162 E8
Grytviken S. Georgia 54°19S 36°33W 152 M8
Gstaad Switz. 46°28N 7°18E 179 J3
Gua India 22°18N 85°20E 243 H11
Gua Musang Malaysia 4°53N 101°58E 237 K3
Guabún, Pta. Chile 41°48S 74°2W 336 B2
Guacanayabo, G. de Cuba 20°40N 77°20W 320 B4
Guacara Venezuela 10°14N 67°53W 328 A4
Guachípas → Argentina 25°40S 65°30W 334 B2
Guadajoz → Spain 37°50N 4°51W 195 H6
Guadalajara Jalisco, Mexico 20°40N 103°20W 318 C4
Guadalajara Spain 40°37N 3°12W 196 E1
Guadalajara ☐ Spain 40°47N 2°30W 196 E2
Guadalaviar = Turia → Spain 39°27N 0°19W 197 F4
Guadalcanal Solomon Is. 9°32S 160°12E 287 M11
Guadalcanal Spain 38°5N 5°52W 195 G5
Guadalén → Spain 38°5N 3°32W 195 G7
Guadales Argentina 34°30S 67°55W 334 C2
Guadalete → Spain 36°35N 6°13W 195 J4
Guadalimar → Spain 38°5N 3°28W 195 G7
Guadalmena → Spain 38°19N 2°56W 195 G8
Guadalmez → Spain 38°46N 5°4W 195 G5
Guadalope → Spain 41°15N 0°3W 196 D4
Guadalquivir → Spain 36°47N 6°22W 195 J4
Guadalupe = Guadeloupe ☑ W. Indies 16°15N 61°40W 322 e
Guadalupe Brazil 6°44S 43°47W 332 C3
Guadalupe Zacatecas, Mexico 22°45N 102°31W 318 C4
Guadalupe Manila, Phil. 14°34N 121°2E 127 B2
Guadalupe Spain 39°27N 5°17W 195 F5
Guadalupe Calif., U.S.A. 34°58N 120°34W 307 L6
Guadalupe → U.S.A. 28°27N 96°47W 314 G6
Guadalupe, Basilica de Mexico 19°29N 99°7W 128 B2
Guadalupe, Sierra de Spain 39°28N 5°30W 195 F5
Guadalupe de Bravo Mexico 31°23N 106°7W 318 A3
Guadalupe I. Pac. Oc. 29°0N 118°50W 292 G8
Guadalupe Mts. △ U.S.A. 31°40N 104°30W 314 F2
Guadalupe Peak U.S.A. 31°50N 104°52W 314 F2
Guadalupe y Calvo Mexico 26°6N 106°58W 318 B3
Guadarrama, Sierra de Spain 41°0N 4°0W 194 E7
Guadeloupe ☑ W. Indies 16°15N 61°40W 322 e
Guadeloupe △ Guadeloupe 16°10N 61°40W 322 e
Guadeloupe Passage W. Indies 16°50N 62°15W 322 e
Guadelupe Peru 7°15S 79°29W 330 B2
Guadiamar → Spain 36°55N 6°24W 195 J4
Guadiana → Portugal 37°14N 7°22W 195 H3
Guadiana Menor → Spain 37°56N 3°15W 195 H7
Guadiaro → Spain 36°17N 5°17W 195 J5
Guadiato → Spain 37°48N 5°5W 195 H5
Guadiela → Spain 40°22N 2°49W 196 E2
Guadix Spain 37°18N 3°11W 195 H7
Guafo, Boca del Chile 43°35S 74°0W 336 B2
Guafo, I. Chile 43°35S 74°50W 336 B2
Guåhån = Guam ☑ Pac. Oc. 13°27N 144°45E 302 d
Guaico Trin. & Tob. 10°35N 61°9W 323 t
Guainía ☐ Colombia 2°30N 69°0W 328 C4
Guainía → Colombia 2°1N 67°7W 328 C4
Guaíra Brazil 24°5S 54°10W 335 A5
Guaíra ☐ Paraguay 25°45S 56°30W 334 B4
Guaire = Gorey Ireland 52°41N 6°18W 166 D5
Guaitecas, Is. Chile 44°0S 74°30W 336 B2
Guajará-Mirim Brazil 10°50S 65°20W 331 C4
Guajira ☐ Colombia 11°30N 72°30W 328 A3
Guajira, Pen. de la Colombia 12°0N 72°0W 328 A3
Gualaceo Ecuador 2°54S 78°47W 328 D2
Gualán Guatemala 15°8N 89°22W 320 C2
Gualdo Tadino Italy 43°14N 12°47E 199 E9
Gualeguay Argentina 33°10S 59°14W 334 C4
Gualeguaychú Argentina 33°3S 59°31W 334 C4
Gualequay → Argentina 33°19S 59°39W 334 C4
Gualicho, Salina Argentina 40°25S 65°20W 336 B3
Gualjaina Argentina 42°45S 70°30W 336 B2
Guam ☑ Pac. Oc. 13°27N 144°45E 302 d
Guamache, B. de Venezuela 10°53N 64°5W 329 a
Guamblin, I. Chile 44°50S 75°0W 336 B2
Guamini Argentina 37°1S 62°28W 334 D3
Guamote Ecuador 1°56S 78°43W 328 D2
Guampí, Sierra de Venezuela 6°0N 65°35W 329 B4
Guamúchil Mexico 25°28N 108°6W 318 B3
Guana I. Br. Virgin Is. 18°30N 64°30W 321 b
Guanabacoa Cuba 23°8N 82°18W 320 B3
Guanabara, B. de Brazil 22°52S 43°10W 135 B1
Guanabara, Jardim Brazil 22°48S 43°11W 135 A1
Guanabara, Palácio da Brazil 22°56S 43°11W 135 B1
Guanacaste Costa Rica 10°30N 85°30W 320 D2
Guanacaste, Cordillera de Costa Rica 10°40N 85°4W 320 D2
Guanacaste △ Costa Rica 10°57N 85°30W 320 D2
Guanaceví Mexico 25°56N 105°57W 318 B3
Guanahani = San Salvador I. Bahamas 24°0N 74°30W 321 B5
Guanaja Honduras 16°30N 85°55W 320 C2
Guanajay Cuba 22°56N 82°42W 320 B3
Guanajuato Mexico 21°1N 101°15W 318 C4
Guanajuato ☐ Mexico 21°0N 101°0W 318 C4
Guanambi Brazil 14°13S 42°47W 333 D3
Guanapo Trin. & Tob. 10°36N 61°15W 323 t
Guanare Venezuela 8°42N 69°12W 328 B4
Guanare → Venezuela 8°13N 67°46W 328 B4
Guandacol Argentina 29°30S 68°40W 334 B2
Guandi Shan China 37°53N 111°29E 226 F6
Guane Cuba 22°10N 84°7W 320 B3
Guang'an China 30°28N 106°35E 228 B6
Guang'anmen China 39°51N 116°18E 114 B1
Guangchang China 26°50N 116°21E 229 D11
Guangde China 30°54N 119°25E 229 B12
Guangdong ☐ China 23°0N 113°0E 229 F9
Guangdong Olympic Stadium Guangzhou, China 23°9N 113°22E 121 B3
Guangfeng China 28°20N 118°15E 229 C12
Guangfu = Kuangfu Taiwan 23°40N 121°25E 225 C3
Guanghan China 30°58N 104°17E 228 B5
Guangling China 39°47N 114°22E 226 E8
Guangnan China 24°5N 105°4E 228 E5
Guangning China 23°40N 112°22E 229 F9
Guangqumen China 39°52N 116°25E 114 B2
Guangrao China 37°5N 118°25E 227 F10
Guangshui China 31°37N 114°0E 229 B10
Guangshun China 26°8N 106°21E 228 D6
Guangwu China 37°48N 105°57E 226 F3
Guangxi Zhuangzu Zizhiqu ☐ China 24°0N 109°0E 228 F7
Guangyuan China 32°26N 105°51E 228 A5
Guangze China 27°30N 117°12E 229 D11
Guangzhou China 23°6N 113°13E 229 F9
Guangzhou Baiyun Int. ✕ (CAN) China 23°24N 113°18E 229 F9
Guanhães Brazil 18°47S 42°57W 333 E3
Guanica Puerto Rico 17°58N 66°55W 321 b
Guanipa → Venezuela 9°56N 62°26W 329 B4
Guanling China 25°56N 105°35E 228 E5

Guanmiao = Kuanmiao Taiwan 22°58N 120°19E 225 D2
Guannan China 34°8N 119°21E 227 G10
Guanshuo China 23°4N 113°22E 121 B3
Guanta Venezuela 10°14N 64°36W 329 A5
Guantánamo Cuba 20°10N 75°14W 321 B4
Guantánamo B. Cuba 19°59N 75°10W 321 C4
Guantao China 36°42N 115°25E 226 F8
Guanting Shuiku China 40°14N 115°35E 226 D8
Guanxi = Kuanhsi Taiwan 24°48N 121°10E 225 B3
Guanyang China 25°30N 111°8E 229 E8
Guanyin = Kuanyin Taiwan 25°2N 121°4E 225 A3
Guanyun China 34°20N 119°18E 227 G10
Guapay = Grande ➜ Bolivia 15°51S 64°39W 331 D5
Guapí Colombia 2°36N 77°54W 328 C2
Guápiles Costa Rica 10°10N 83°46W 320 D3
Guapo ➜ Trin. & Tob. 10°11N 61°40W 323 t
Guapo B. Trin. & Tob. 10°12N 61°41W 323 t
Guaporé = Rondônia Brazil 10°52S 61°57W 331 C5
Guaporé Brazil 28°51S 51°54W 335 B5
Guaporé ➜ Brazil 11°55S 65°4W 331 C4
Guaqui Bolivia 16°41S 68°54W 330 D4
Guara, Sierra de Spain 42°19N 0°15W 196 C4
Guarabira Brazil 6°51S 35°29W 332 C4
Guaracara ➜ Trin. & Tob. 10°18N 61°28W 323 t
Guarachirá ➜ Colombia 5°27N 70°36W 328 B3
Guaranda Ecuador 1°36S 79°0W 328 D2
Guarani = Pacajus Brazil 4°10S 38°31W 332 B4
Guarapari Brazil 20°40S 40°30W 333 F3
Guarapuava Brazil 25°20S 51°30W 333 G1
Guaratinguetá Brazil 22°49S 45°9W 335 A6
Guaratuba Brazil 25°53S 48°38W 335 B6
Guarda Portugal 40°32N 7°20W 194 E3
Guarda □ Portugal 40°40N 7°20W 194 E3
Guardafui, C. = Asir, Ras Somalia 11°55N 51°10E 267 B7
Guardamar del Segura Spain 38°5N 0°39W 197 G4
Guardavalle Italy 38°30N 16°30E 201 D9
Guárdia Sanframondi Italy 41°15N 14°36E 201 A7
Guardiagrele Italy 42°11N 14°13E 199 F11
Guardo Spain 42°47N 4°50W 194 C6
Guareña Spain 38°51N 6°6W 195 G4
Guareña ➜ Spain 41°29N 5°23W 194 D5
Guari Papua N. G. 8°3S 146°52E 286 E4
Guárico □ Venezuela 8°40N 66°35W 328 B4
Guarrojo ➜ Colombia 4°6N 70°42W 328 C3
Guarujá Brazil 24°2S 46°25W 335 A6
Guarulhos Brazil 23°29S 46°33W 335 A6
Guarulhos Int., São Paulo ✈ (GRU) Brazil 23°26S 46°28W 333 F2
Guasave Mexico 25°34N 108°27W 318 B3
Guascama, Pta. Colombia 2°32N 78°24W 328 C2
Guasdualito Venezuela 7°15N 70°44W 328 B3
Guasipati Venezuela 7°28N 61°54W 329 B5
Guasopa Papua N. G. 9°12S 152°56E 286 E7
Guastalla Italy 44°55N 10°39E 198 D7
Guatemala Guatemala 14°40N 90°22W 320 D1
Guatemala ■ Cent. Amer. 15°40N 90°30W 320 C1
Guatemala Basin Pac. Oc. 11°0N 95°0W 289 F18
Guatemala Trench Pac. Oc. 14°0N 95°0W 292 H10
Guatire Venezuela 10°28N 66°32W 328 A4
Guatopo △ Venezuela 10°5N 66°30W 328 A4
Guatuaro Pt. Trin. & Tob. 10°19N 60°59W 323 t
Guavi ➜ Papua N. G. 7°48S 143°16E 286 D2
Guaviare □ Colombia 2°0N 72°30W 328 C3
Guaviare ➜ Colombia 4°3N 67°44W 328 C4
Guaxupé Brazil 21°10S 47°5W 335 A6
Guayabero ➜ Colombia 2°36N 72°47W 328 C3
Guayacán Venezuela 11°8N 63°55W 329 a
Guayacancito Venezuela 10°56N 64°13W 329 a
Guayaguayare Trin. & Tob. 10°8N 61°2W 323 t
Guayaguayare B. Trin. & Tob. 10°7N 61°2W 323 t
Guayama Puerto Rico 17°59N 66°7W 321 C6
Guayamuri, Cerro Venezuela 11°4N 63°51W 329 a
Guayaneco, Arch. Chile 47°45S 75°10W 336 C1
Guayanilla Puerto Rico 18°1N 66°47W 321 b
Guayaquil Ecuador 2°15S 79°52W 328 D2
Guayaquil Baja Calif., Mexico 29°59N 115°4W 318 B1
Guayaquil, G. de Ecuador 3°10S 81°0W 328 D1
Guayaramerín Bolivia 10°48S 65°23W 331 C4
Guayas ➜ Ecuador 2°36S 79°52W 328 D2
Guaymas Mexico 27°56N 110°54W 318 B2
Guaynabo Puerto Rico 18°22N 66°7W 321 b
Guba Dem. Rep. of the Congo 10°38S 26°27E 269 E2
Guba Ethiopia 11°17N 35°20E 257 E4
Gûbâl, Madîq Egypt 27°30N 34°0E 251 L4
Gubam Papua N. G. 8°39S 141°53E 286 E1
Guban Somalia 10°30N 44°0E 267 B5
Gubat Phil. 12°55N 124°7E 232 E5
Gubbi India 13°19N 76°56E 245 H3
Gúbbio Italy 43°21N 12°35E 199 E9
Guben Germany 51°57N 14°42E 178 D10
Gubin Poland 51°57N 14°43E 185 G1
Gubio Nigeria 12°30N 12°42E 263 C7
Gubkin Russia 51°17N 37°32E 189 G9
Gubkinskiy Russia 64°27N 76°36E 214 C8
Guča Serbia 43°46N 20°15E 202 C4
Gucheng China 32°20N 111°30E 229 A8
Gucun China 31°21N 121°22E 138 A1
Gudå Norway 63°27N 11°36E 164 A8
Gudalur India 11°30N 76°29E 245 J3
Gudauta Georgia 43°7N 40°32E 191 J5
Gudbrandsdalen Norway 61°33N 10°10E 164 C7
Guddu Barrage Pakistan 28°30N 69°50E 242 E3
Gudenå ➜ Denmark 56°29N 10°13E 163 H4
Gudermes Russia 43°24N 46°5E 191 J8
Gudhjem Denmark 55°12N 14°58E 163 J8
Gudivada India 16°30N 81°3E 245 F5
Gudiyattam India 12°57N 78°55E 245 H4
Gudö Sweden 59°12N 18°12E 139 B3
Gudur India 14°12N 79°55E 245 G4
Gudvangen Norway 60°52N 6°49E 164 D3
Guebwiller France 47°55N 7°12E 173 E14
Guecho = Algorta Spain 43°21N 2°59W 196 B2
Guékédou Guinea 8°40N 10°5W 262 D2
Guelb er Rîchât Mauritania 21°7N 11°24W 260 D2
Guéle Mendouka Cameroon 4°23N 12°55E 263 E7
Guélengdeng Chad 10°55N 15°31E 259 F3
Güell, Parque de Spain 41°24N 2°10E 114 A2
Guelma Algeria 36°25N 7°29E 261 A6
Guelma □ Algeria 36°25N 7°25E 261 A6
Guelmim Morocco 28°56N 10°0W 260 C3
Guelmim-Es-Semara □ Morocco 28°0N 11°0W 260 C3
Guelph Canada 43°35N 80°20W 312 C4
Guelta Zemmur W. Sahara 25°8N 12°22W 260 C2
Guemar Algeria 33°30N 6°49E 261 B6
Guéméné-Penfao France 47°38N 1°50W 172 E5
Guéméné-sur-Scorff France 48°4N 3°13W 172 D3
Guéné Benin 11°44N 3°16E 263 C5
Güeppí Peru 0°7S 75°15W 328 D2
Guer France 47°54N 2°8W 172 E4
Güer Aike Argentina 51°39S 69°35W 336 D3
Guera Chad 11°55N 18°12E 259 F3
Guéra □ Chad 11°30N 18°30E 259 F3
Guérande France 47°20N 2°26W 172 E4
Guercif Morocco 34°14N 3°21W 261 B4
Guéréda Chad 14°31N 22°5E 259 F4
Guéret France 46°11N 1°51E 173 F8
Guérigny France 47°6N 3°10E 173 E10
Guerneville U.S.A. 38°30N 123°0W 306 G4
Guernica = Gernika-Lumo Spain 43°19N 2°40W 196 B2
Guernsey Chan. Is., U.K. 49°26N 2°35W 169 H5
Guernsey Wyo., U.S.A. 42°16N 104°45W 304 E11
Guerrara Oasis, Algeria 32°51N 4°22E 261 B5
Guerrara Saoura, Algeria 28°5N 0°8W 261 C4
Guerrero Mexico City, Mexico 128 a1
Guerrero □ Mexico 17°40N 100°0W 319 D5
Guerzim Algeria 29°39N 1°40W 261 C4
Guessou-Sud Benin 10°3N 2°38E 263 C5
Gueugnon France 46°36N 4°4E 173 F11
Guéyo Ivory C. 5°25N 6°5W 262 D3
Gufuðalur Iceland 65°34N 22°25W 155 B4
Guggenheim Museum New York, U.S.A. 132 b3
Gughe Ethiopia 6°12N 37°30E 257 F4
Gūgher Iran 29°28N 56°27E 247 D8
Guglionesi Italy 41°55N 14°55E 199 G11
Guguan N. Marianas 17°18N 145°51E 302 a
Guhrau = Góra Poland 51°40N 16°31E 185 G3
Gui Jiang ➜ China 23°30N 111°15E 229 F8
Guia Canary Is. 28°8N 15°38W 153 e1
Guia de Isora Canary Is. 28°12N 16°46W 153 e1
Guia Lopes da Laguna Brazil 21°26S 56°7W 335 A4
Guiana Venezuela 5°9N 63°36W 329 B5
Guiana Highlands S. Amer. 5°10N 60°40W 326 C4
Guiana I. Antigua & B. 17°6N 61°44W 322 b
Guibéroua Ivory C. 6°14N 6°10W 262 D3
Guichen B. Australia 37°10S 139°45E 282 D3
Guichi China 30°39N 117°27E 229 B11
Guider Cameroon 9°56N 13°57E 263 D7
Guidiguir Niger 13°40N 9°50E 259 F1
Guidimaka □ Mauritania 15°20N 12°0W 262 B2
Guidimouni Niger 13°42N 9°31E 259 F1
Guiding China 26°34N 107°11E 228 D6
Guidong China 26°7N 113°57E 229 D9
Guidónia-Montecélio Italy 42°1N 12°45E 199 F9
Guiers, L. de Senegal 16°10N 15°50W 262 B1
Guigang China 23°8N 109°35E 228 F7
Guiglo Ivory C. 6°45N 7°30W 262 D3
Guihulngan Phil. 10°7N 123°16E 233 F4
Guijá Mozam. 24°27S 33°0E 271 B5
Guijuelo Spain 40°33N 5°40W 194 E5
Guildford U.K. 51°14N 0°34W 169 F7
Guildwood Canada 43°45N 79°13W 141 A3
Guilford U.S.A. 41°17N 72°41W 313 E12
Guilin China 25°18N 110°15E 229 E8
Guillaume-Delisle, L. Canada 56°15N 76°17W 298 A4
Guillaumes France 44°5N 6°52E 175 D10
Guillestre France 44°39N 6°40E 175 D10
Guilvinec France 47°48N 4°17W 172 E2
Güimar Canary Is. 28°18N 16°24W 153 e1
Guimarães Brazil 2°9S 44°42W 332 B3
Guimarães Portugal 41°28N 8°24W 194 D2
Guimaras □ Phil. 10°35N 122°37E 233 F4
Guimaras Str. Phil. 10°38N 122°48E 233 F4
Guimba Phil. 15°40N 120°46E 232 D3
Guinardó Spain 41°24N 2°10E 114 A2
Guinayangan Phil. 13°54N 122°27E 232 E4
Guinda U.S.A. 38°50N 122°12W 306 G4
Guindulman Phil. 9°46N 124°29E 233 G5
Guinea Africa 8°0N 8°0E 254 F4
Guinea ■ W. Afr. 10°20N 11°30W 262 C2
Guinea, Gulf of Atl. Oc. 3°0N 2°30E 263 E5
Guinea Basin Atl. Oc. 0°0 5°0W 152 G11
Guinea-Bissau ■ Africa 12°0N 15°0W 262 C2
Güines Cuba 22°50N 82°0W 320 B3
Guingamp France 48°34N 3°10W 172 D3
Guinguinéo Senegal 14°20N 15°57W 262 C1
Güinima Venezuela 10°44N 63°55W 329 a
Guinobatan Phil. 13°11N 123°36E 232 E4
Guipavas France 48°26N 4°29W 172 D2
Guiping China 23°21N 110°2E 229 F8
Guir Mali 18°52N 2°52W 262 B4
Guir, O. ➜ Algeria 31°29N 2°17W 261 B4
Guiratinga Brazil 16°21S 53°45W 331 D7
Guirel Mauritania 15°30N 7°3W 262 B3
Güiria Venezuela 10°32N 62°18W 329 F8
Guiscard France 49°40N 3°1E 173 C10
Guise France 49°52N 3°35E 173 C10
Guishan Dao = Kueishan Tao Taiwan 24°51N 121°57E 225 B3
Guissona Spain 41°47N 1°17E 196 D6
Guita-Koulouba C.A.R. 5°58N 23°21E 264 A4
Guitiriz Spain 43°11N 7°50W 194 B3
Guitri Ivory C. 5°30N 5°14W 262 D3
Guiuan Phil. 11°5N 125°55E 233 F5
Guixi China 28°16N 117°15E 229 C11
Guiyang Guizhou, China 26°32N 106°40E 228 D6
Guiyang Hunan, China 25°46N 112°42E 229 E9
Guizhou □ China 27°0N 107°0E 228 D6
Gujan-Mestras France 44°38N 1°4W 174 D2
Gujar Khan Pakistan 33°16N 73°19E 242 C5
Gujarat □ India 23°20N 71°0E 242 H4
Gujiang China 27°11N 114°47E 229 D10
Gujiao China 37°54N 112°8E 226 F7
Gujō Japan 35°45N 136°57E 223 B8
Gujranwala Pakistan 32°10N 74°12E 242 C6
Gujrat Pakistan 32°40N 74°2E 242 C6
Gukovo Russia 48°1N 39°58E 191 F5
Gulargambone Australia 31°20S 148°30E 283 A8
Gulbai Pakistan 24°52N 66°58E 123 A1
Gulbarga = Kalaburagi India 17°20N 76°50E 244 F3
Gulbene Latvia 57°8N 26°52E 188 D4
Gülchö Kyrgyzstan 40°19N 73°26E 217 D8
Guledagudda India 16°3N 75°48E 245 F2
Gülek Turkey 37°12N 34°48E 250 A5
Gulf □ Papua N. G. 8°0S 145°0E 286 D3
Gulf, The = Persian Gulf Asia 27°0N 50°0E 247 E6
Gulf Breeze U.S.A. 30°21N 87°9W 317 E2
Gulf Hammock U.S.A. 29°15N 82°43W 317 F7
Gulf Islands ⌂ U.S.A. 30°10N 87°10W 317 K2
Gulfport Fla., U.S.A. 27°44N 82°42W 317 H7
Gulfport Miss., U.S.A. 30°22N 89°6W 315 F10
Gulgong Australia 32°20S 149°49E 283 B8
Gulian China 52°56N 122°21E 219 A13
Gulin China 28°1N 105°50E 228 C5
Gulistan Pakistan 30°30N 66°35E 242 D2
Guliston Uzbekistan 40°29N 68°46E 217 D7
Gulja = Yining China 43°58N 81°10E 217 D10
Gulkana U.S.A. 62°16N 145°23W 303 E11
Gull Lake Canada 50°10N 108°29W 297 C7
Gullbrå Norway 60°50N 6°17E 164 D3
Gullbrandstorp Sweden 56°42N 12°43E 163 H6
Gullbringusýsla Iceland 64°0N 22°0W 155 D4
Gullfoss Iceland 64°20N 20°8W 155 C6
Gullhaug Norway 59°30N 10°15E 164 E7
Gullivan B. U.S.A. 25°45N 81°40W 317 K8
Gullspång Sweden 58°59N 14°6E 163 F8
Gullstein Norway 63°13N 8°9E 164 A5
Güllük Turkey 37°14N 27°35E 205 D9
Güllük Dağı △ Turkey 37°0N 30°30E 205 E12
Güllük Korfezi Turkey 37°12N 27°30E 205 D9
Gulma Nigeria 12°40N 4°23E 263 C5
Gulmarg India 34°3N 74°25E 243 B6
Gülnar Turkey 36°19N 33°24E 250 B4
Gulnare Australia 33°27S 138°27E 282 B3
Gülpınar Turkey 39°32N 26°7E 205 B8
Gülşehir Turkey 38°44N 34°37E 212 C6
Gulshan-e Iqbal Pakistan 24°54N 67°5E 123 A2
Gülshat Kazakhstan 46°38N 74°21E 217 C8
Gulsvik Norway 60°24N 9°38E 164 D6
Gulu Uganda 2°48N 32°17E 268 B3
Gŭlŭbovo Bulgaria 42°8N 25°55E 203 D9
Gulud, J. Sudan 11°41N 29°31E 257 E2
Gulwe Tanzania 6°30S 36°25E 268 D4
Gulyaypole = Hulyaypole Ukraine 47°45N 36°21E 189 J9
Gum Lake Australia 32°42S 143°9E 282 B5
Gumaca Phil. 13°55N 122°6E 232 E4
Gumal ➜ Pakistan 31°40N 71°50E 242 D4
Gumbaz Pakistan 30°2N 69°0E 242 D3
Gumbinnen = Gusev Russia 54°35N 22°10E 184 D9
Gumdag Turkmenistan 39°9N 54°56E 216 E4
Gumel Nigeria 12°39N 9°22E 263 C6
Gumi S. Korea 36°10N 128°12E 224 D4
Gumiel de Izán Spain 41°46N 3°41W 194 D7
Gumla India 23°3N 84°33E 243 H11
Gumlu Australia 19°53S 147°41E 280 B4
Gummersbach Germany 51°1N 7°34E 178 D3
Gummi Nigeria 12°4N 5°9E 263 C6
Gümüldür Turkey 38°6N 27°0E 205 C9
Gumuljina = Komotini Greece 41°9N 25°26E 203 E9
Gümüşçay Turkey 40°16N 27°17E 203 F11
Gümüşhacıköy Turkey 40°50N 35°18E 212 B6
Gümüşhane Turkey 40°30N 39°30E 213 B8
Gümüşsu Turkey 38°14N 30°1E 205 C12
Gumzai Indonesia 5°28S 134°42E 231 F8
Gun Hill Tower Barbados 13°8N 59°33W 323 r
Gun Pt. Grenada 12°32N 61°37W 323 q
Guna Amara, Ethiopia 11°43N 38°14E 266 B4
Guna Oromiya, Ethiopia 8°18N 39°52E 257 F4
Guna India 24°40N 77°19E 242 G7
Gunbalanya Australia 12°20S 133°4E 278 B5
Gundabooka △ Australia 30°30S 145°20E 281 E4
Gundagai Australia 35°3S 148°6E 283 C8
Gundarehi India 20°57N 81°17E 244 D5
Gundelfingen Germany 48°34N 10°22E 179 G6
Gundji Dem. Rep. of the Congo 2°5N 21°27E 264 B4
Gundlakamma ➜ India 15°30N 80°15E 245 G5
Gundlupet India 11°48N 76°41E 245 J3
Gündoğmuş Turkey 36°48N 32°0E 250 B3
Gunebang Australia 33°1S 146°38E 283 B7
Güney Burdur, Turkey 37°29N 29°34E 205 D11
Güney Denizli, Turkey 38°9N 29°4E 205 C11
Güneydoğu Toroslar Turkey 38°20N 40°30E 213 C9
Gungal Australia 32°17S 150°32E 283 B9
Gungo Angola 10°58S 15°30E 265 E2
Güngören Turkey 41°1N 28°52E 122 B1
Gungu Dem. Rep. of the Congo 5°43S 19°20E 265 D3
Gunisao ➜ Canada 53°56N 97°53W 297 C9
Gunisao L. Canada 53°33N 96°15W 297 C9
Gunjur Gambia 13°12N 16°44W 262 C1
Gunjyal Pakistan 32°20N 71°55E 242 C4
Günlüce Turkey 36°50N 28°20E 205 E10
Gunma □ Japan 36°30N 138°20E 223 A10
Gunnarskog Sweden 59°49N 12°34E 162 E6
Gunnbjørn Fjeld Greenland 68°55N 29°47W 154 D8
Gunnebo Sweden 57°44N 16°32E 163 G10
Gunnedah Australia 30°59S 150°15E 283 A9
Gunnersbury U.K. 51°29N 0°17W 125 B2
Gunnewin Australia 25°59S 148°33E 281 D4
Gunningbar Cr. ➜ Australia 31°14S 147°6E 283 A7
Gunnison Colo., U.S.A. 38°33N 106°56W 304 G10
Gunnison Utah, U.S.A. 39°9N 111°49W 304 G8
Gunnison ➜ U.S.A. 39°4N 108°35W 304 G9
Gunsan S. Korea 35°59N 126°45E 224 E3
Guntakal India 15°11N 77°27E 245 G3
Gunter Canada 44°52N 77°32W 312 B7
Guntersville U.S.A. 34°21N 86°18W 315 D11
Guntong Malaysia 4°36N 101°3E 237 K3
Guntur India 16°23N 80°30E 245 F5
Gunung Buda △ Malaysia 4°12N 114°57E 235 B4
Gunung Ciremay △ Indonesia 6°53S 108°24E 235 D3
Gunung Gading △ Malaysia 2°2N 109°52E 235 B3
Gunung Leuser △ Indonesia 3°39N 97°32E 234 B1
Gunung Mulu △ Malaysia 4°6N 114°53E 235 B4
Gunung Palung △ Indonesia 1°9S 110°13E 235 C4
Gunungapi Indonesia 6°45S 126°30E 231 F7
Gunungsitoli Indonesia 1°15N 97°30E 234 B1
Gunungtua Indonesia 1°30N 99°37E 234 B1
Gunupur India 19°5N 83°50E 244 E6
Günz ➜ Germany 48°27N 10°16E 179 G6
Gunza Angola 10°50S 13°50E 265 E2
Günzburg Germany 48°26N 10°17E 179 G6
Gunzenhausen Germany 49°7N 10°44E 179 F6
Guo He ➜ China 32°59N 117°10E 229 A11
Guomao China 39°54N 116°26E 114 B2
Guoxing = Kuohsing Taiwan 24°2N 120°51E 225 B2
Guoyang China 33°32N 116°12E 226 H9
Gupis Pakistan 36°15N 73°20E 243 A5
Gura Humorului Romania 47°35N 25°53E 183 C10
Gura-Teghii Romania 45°30N 26°25E 183 E11
Gurabo Puerto Rico 18°16N 65°58W 321 b
Gurag Ethiopia 8°20N 38°20E 257 F4
Gurahonț Romania 46°16N 22°21E 182 D7
Gurbantünggüt Shamo China 45°8N 87°20E 217 C11
Gurdaspur India 32°5N 75°31E 242 C6
Gurdon U.S.A. 33°55N 93°9W 314 E8
Güre Balıkesir, Turkey 39°36N 26°54E 205 B8
Güre Uşak, Turkey 38°39N 29°10E 205 C11
Gurgaon = Gurugram India 28°27N 77°1E 242 E7
Gürgentepe Turkey 40°51N 37°50E 212 B7
Gurghiu, Munții Romania 46°41N 25°15E 183 D10
Gurgueia ➜ Brazil 6°50S 43°24W 332 C3
Gurha India 25°12N 71°39E 242 G4
Guri, Embalse de Venezuela 7°50N 62°52W 329 B5
Gurimatu Papua N. G. 6°45S 144°45E 286 D3
Gurin Nigeria 9°5N 12°54E 263 D7
Gurinhatã Brazil 19°14S 49°48W 333 E2
Gurjaani Georgia 41°43N 45°52E 191 K7
Gurk ➜ Austria 46°35N 14°31E 180 E7
Gurkfeld = Krško Slovenia 45°57N 15°30E 199 C12
Gurkha Nepal 28°5N 84°40E 243 E11
Gurla Mandhata = Naimona'nyi Feng China 30°26N 81°18E 243 D9
Gurley Australia 29°45S 149°48E 281 D4
Gurnee U.S.A. 42°22N 87°55W 311 B9
Gurnet Point U.S.A. 42°1N 70°34W 313 D14
Guro Mozam. 17°26S 32°30E 269 F3
Güroymak Turkey 38°35N 42°1E 213 C10
Gürpınar İstanbul, Turkey 40°59N 28°37E 203 F12
Gürpınar Van, Turkey 38°18N 43°25E 213 C10
Gürsu Turkey 40°13N 29°11E 203 F13
Gurué Mozam. 15°25S 36°58E 269 F4
Gurueragu Ethiopia 6°23N 45°31E 267 C6
Gurugram India 28°27N 77°1E 242 E7
Gurun Malaysia 5°49N 100°27E 237 K3
Gürün Turkey 38°43N 37°15E 212 C7
Gurupá Brazil 1°25S 51°35W 329 D7
Gurupá, I. Grande de Brazil 1°25S 51°45W 329 D7
Gurupi Brazil 11°43S 49°4W 333 D2
Gurupi ➜ Brazil 1°13S 46°6W 332 B2
Gurupi, Serra do Brazil 5°0S 47°50W 332 C2
Guruwe Zimbabwe 16°40S 30°42E 271 A5
Gurvan Sayhan Uul Mongolia 43°50N 104°0E 226 C3
Guryev = Atyraū Kazakhstan 47°5N 52°0E 187 E9
Guryevsk Russia 54°47N 20°38E 184 D7
Gus-Khrustalnyy Russia 55°42N 40°44E 190 C5
Gusau Nigeria 12°12N 6°40E 263 C6
Gusev Russia 54°35N 22°10E 184 D9
Gushan China 39°50N 123°35E 224 C1
Gushgy = Serhetabat Turkmenistan 35°20N 62°18E 247 C9
Gushi China 32°11N 115°41E 229 A10
Gushiago Ghana 9°55N 0°15W 263 D4
Gushikami Japan 26°7N 127°44E 288 a
Gushikawa = Uruma Japan 26°21N 127°52E 288 a
Gusinje Montenegro 42°35N 19°50E 202 D3
Gusinoozersk Russia 51°16N 106°27E 215 D11
Gúspini Italy 39°32N 8°37E 200 C1
Güssing Austria 47°3N 16°20E 181 D9
Gustav Holm, Kap Greenland 66°36N 34°15W 154 D7
Gustavia St. Barts 17°53N 62°51W 322 a
Gustavo A. Madero Mexico 19°29N 99°8W 128 B2
Gustavus U.S.A. 58°25N 135°44W 296 B1
Gustine U.S.A. 37°16N 121°0W 306 H6
Güstrow Germany 53°47N 12°10E 178 B8
Gusum Sweden 58°16N 16°30E 163 F10
Guta = Kolárovo Slovakia 47°54N 18°0E 181 D10
Gütersloh Germany 51°54N 8°24E 178 D4
Gutha Australia 28°58S 115°55E 279 E2
Guthalungra Australia 19°52S 147°50E 280 B4
Guthrie Ont., Canada 44°28N 79°32W 312 B5
Guthrie Okla., U.S.A. 35°53N 97°25W 314 D6
Guthrie Tex., U.S.A. 33°37N 100°19W 314 E4
Guthrie Center U.S.A. 41°41N 94°30W 310 C2
Gutian China 26°32N 118°43E 229 D12
Gutiérrez Bolivia 19°25S 63°34W 331 D5
Guttenberg Iowa, U.S.A. 42°47N 91°6W 310 B5
Guttenberg New York, U.S.A. 132 a1
Guttentag = Dobrodzień Poland 50°45N 18°25E 185 H5
Guttstadt = Dobre Miasto Poland 53°58N 20°26E 184 E7
Gutu Zimbabwe 19°41S 31°9E 271 A5
Gutulia △ Norway 62°2N 12°11E 164 B9
Gutuyevskiy, Ostrov Russia 59°53N 30°15E 137 B1
Guwahati India 26°10N 91°45E 241 B3
Guy Fawkes River △ Australia 30°0S 152°20E 281 D5
Guy-Fayreau, Complexe Montréal, Canada 130 b2
Guyana ■ S. Amer. 5°0N 59°0W 329 C6
Guyancourt France 48°46N 2°4E 134 B1
Guyane française = French Guiana ☒ S. Amer. 4°0N 53°0W 329 C7
Guyang China 41°0N 110°5E 226 D6
Guyenne France 44°30N 0°40E 174 D4
Guymon U.S.A. 36°41N 101°29W 314 C4
Guyotville = Aïn Benian Algeria 36°48N 2°55E 261 A5
Guyra Australia 30°15S 151°40E 281 E5
Guyton U.S.A. 32°20N 81°24W 316 C8
Guyuan Hebei, China 41°37N 115°40E 226 D8
Guyuan Ningxia Huizu, China 36°0N 106°20E 226 F4
Güzelbağ Turkey 36°44N 31°53E 250 B2
Güzelbahçe Turkey 38°21N 26°54E 205 C8
Güzeloluk Turkey 36°47N 34°4E 250 B5
Güzelsu Turkey 36°53N 31°51E 250 B2
Güzelyurt = Morphou Cyprus 35°12N 32°59E 207 E8
Guzhang China 28°42N 109°58E 228 C7
Guzhen China 33°22N 117°18E 227 H9
Guzmán, L. de Mexico 31°20N 107°30W 318 A3
G'uzor Uzbekistan 38°36N 66°15E 217 E7
Gvardeysk Russia 54°39N 21°5E 184 D8
Gvardeyskoye Ukraine 45°7N 34°1E 189 K8
Gvarv Norway 59°23N 9°9E 164 E6
Gwa Burma 17°36N 94°34E 241 G5
Gwaai Zimbabwe 19°15S 27°45E 269 F2
Gwaai ➜ Zimbabwe 17°59S 26°52E 269 F2
Gwabegar Australia 30°37S 148°59E 283 A8
Gwadabawa Nigeria 13°28N 5°15E 263 C6
Gwādar Pakistan 25°10N 62°18E 240 D1
Gwagwada Nigeria 10°15N 7°15E 263 C6
Gwaii Haanas △ Canada 52°21N 131°26W 296 C2
Gwalior India 26°12N 78°10E 242 F8
Gwanak S. Korea 37°29N 126°57E 137 C1
Gwanaksan S. Korea 37°27N 126°58E 137 C1
Gwanara Nigeria 8°55N 3°9E 263 D5
Gwanda Zimbabwe 20°55S 29°0E 269 G2
Gwandu Nigeria 12°30N 4°41E 263 C5
Gwane Dem. Rep. of the Congo 4°45N 25°48E 268 B2
Gwang-yang S. Korea 34°58N 127°35E 224 E3
Gwangju S. Korea 35°9N 126°54E 224 E3
Gwangju □ S. Korea 35°10N 126°45E 224 E3
Gwangyang S. Korea 34°56N 127°41E 222 E3
Gwanju = Gwangju S. Korea 35°9N 126°54E 224 E3
Gwaram Nigeria 10°15N 10°25E 263 C7
Gwarzo Nigeria 12°20N 8°55E 263 C6
Gwasero Nigeria 9°29N 3°30E 263 D5
Gwda ➜ Poland 53°3N 16°44E 185 E3
Gweebarra B. Ireland 54°51N 8°23W 166 B3
Gweedore Ireland 55°3N 8°14W 166 A3
Gweru Zimbabwe 19°28S 29°45E 269 F2
Gwi Nigeria 9°0N 7°10E 263 D6
Gwinn U.S.A. 46°19N 87°27W 308 B10
Gwio Kura Nigeria 12°40N 11°2E 263 C7
Gwoza Nigeria 11°5N 13°40E 263 C7
Gwydir ➜ Australia 29°27S 149°48E 281 D4
Gwynedd □ U.K. 52°52N 4°10W 168 E3
Gyál Hungary 47°23N 19°13E 117 B3
Gyáli-patak ➜ Hungary 47°23N 19°7E 117 B2
Gyandzha = Gäncä Azerbaijan 40°45N 46°20E 191 K8
Gyangzê China 29°5N 89°47E 218 F6
Gyaring Hu China 34°50N 97°40E 218 E8
Gydanskiy Poluostrov Russia 70°0N 78°0E 214 C8
Gyeonggi-do □ S. Korea 36°37N 127°15E 224 D3
Gyeonggi-man S. Korea 37°0N 125°30E 224 D2
Gyeongju S. Korea 35°51N 129°14E 224 E4
Gyeongsan S. Korea 35°49N 128°44E 224 E4
Gyeongsangbuk-do □ S. Korea 36°20N 128°45E 224 D4
Gyeongsangnam-do □ S. Korea 35°15N 128°15E 224 E4
Gyeryongsan △ S. Korea 36°20N 127°15E 224 D3
Gyigang China 28°40N 97°31E 241 A6
Gyl Norway 62°57N 8°7E 164 B5
Gyldenløve Fjord Greenland 64°15N 40°30W 154 E6
Gympie Australia 26°11S 152°38E 281 D5
Gyobingauk Burma 18°13N 95°39E 241 F5
Gyōda Japan 36°10N 139°30E 223 A11
Gyodongdo S. Korea 37°47N 126°15E 224 D3
Gyomaendrőd Hungary 46°56N 20°50E 182 D5
Gyöngyös Hungary 47°48N 19°56E 182 C4
Győr Hungary 47°41N 17°40E 182 C2
Győr-Moson-Sopron □ Hungary 47°40N 17°20E 182 C2
Gypsum Pt. Canada 61°53N 114°35W 296 A6
Gypsumville Canada 51°45N 98°40W 297 C9
Gyueshevo Bulgaria 42°14N 22°28E 202 D6
Gyula Hungary 46°38N 21°17E 182 D6
Gyumri Armenia 40°47N 43°50E 191 K6
Gyzylarbat = Serdar Turkmenistan 39°4N 56°23E 247 B8
Gyzyletrek = Etrek Turkmenistan 37°36N 54°46E 247 B7
Gyzylgaya Turkmenistan 40°40N 55°30E 216 D5
Gzhatsk = Gagarin Russia 55°38N 35°0E 188 E8
Gzira Malta 35°54N 14°29E 206 F7

H

H. Neely Henry L. U.S.A. 33°55N 86°2W 316 B3
Ha 'Arava ➜ Israel 30°50N 35°20E 251 H6
Ha Coi Vietnam 21°26N 107°46E 228 G6
Ha Dong Vietnam 20°58N 105°46E 228 G5
Ha Giang Vietnam 22°50N 104°59E 228 F5
Ha Karmel, Har Israel 32°44N 35°3E 250 F5
Ha Karmel △ Israel 32°45N 35°5E 250 F6
Ha Long = Hong Gai Vietnam 20°57N 107°5E 228 G6
Ha Long, Vinh Vietnam 20°56N 107°3E 236 B6
Ha Tien Vietnam 10°23N 104°29E 237 G5
Ha Tinh Vietnam 18°20N 105°54E 236 C5
Ha Trung Vietnam 19°58N 105°50E 236 C5
Haaga Finland 60°13N 24°53E 121 B2
Haakon VII Topp = Beerenberg Norway 71°0N 8°20W 154 C10
Haaksbergen Neths. 52°9N 6°45E 170 B6
Ha'ano Tonga 19°41S 174°18W 287 P13
Ha'apai Group Tonga 19°47S 174°27W 287 P13
Haapiti Moorea 17°34S 149°52W 289 e
Haapsalu Estonia 58°56N 23°30E 188 C2
Haar Germany 48°6N 11°43E 131 B3
Haarby Denmark 55°13N 10°7E 163 J4
Haarlem Neths. 52°23N 4°39E 170 B4
Haas-Lilienthal House San Francisco, U.S.A. 136 b1
Haast N.Z. 43°51S 169°1E 285 D4
Haast ➜ N.Z. 43°50S 169°2E 285 D4
Haast Pass N.Z. 44°6S 169°21E 285 E4
Haasts Bluff Australia 23°22S 132°0E 278 D5
Haasts Bluff ❂ Australia 23°39S 130°34E 278 D5
Hab ➜ Pakistan 24°53N 66°41E 242 G3
Hab Nadi Chauki Pakistan 25°0N 66°50E 242 G2
Habahe China 48°3N 86°23E 217 C11
Ḥabarūt Yemen 17°18N 52°44E 249 C6
Habaswein Kenya 1°2N 39°30E 268 B4
Ḥabawnah, W. ➜ Si. Arabia 17°57N 44°58E 248 C4
Habay Alta., Canada 58°50N 118°44W 296 B5
Habay Manila, Phil. 14°27N 120°56E 127 C1
Ḥabbān Yemen 14°21N 47°5E 248 D4
Ḥabbānīyah Iraq 33°17N 43°29E 213 F10
Ḥabbānīyah, Hawr al Iraq 33°17N 43°29E 213 F10
Habelschwerdt = Bystrzyca Kłodzka Poland 50°19N 16°39E 185 H3
Habibas, Îles Algeria 35°44N 1°8W 197 K3
Habichtswald ⌂ Germany 51°15N 9°15E 178 D5
Habiganj Bangla. 24°24N 91°30E 241 C3
Habirag China 42°17N 115°42E 226 C8
Habisa Sudan 15°38N 31°18E 266 A3
Habo Sweden 57°55N 14°6E 163 G8
Haboro Japan 44°22N 141°42E 220 B10
Ḥabshān U.A.E. 23°50N 53°37E 247 F7
Hachenburg Germany 50°40N 7°49E 178 E3
Hachi India 27°48N 94°2E 241 B5
Hachijō-Jima Japan 33°5N 139°45E 223 D11
Hachiman = Gujō Japan 35°45N 136°57E 223 B8
Hachinohe Japan 40°30N 141°29E 220 D10
Hachiōji Japan 35°40N 139°20E 223 B11
Hacı Zeynalabdin Azerbaijan 40°37N 49°33E 191 K9
Hacıbektaş Turkey 38°56N 34°33E 212 C6
Hacılar Turkey 38°38N 35°26E 212 C6
Hack, Mt. Australia 30°45S 138°55E 282 A3
Hackås Sweden 62°56N 14°30E 162 B8
Hackbridge U.K. 51°23N 0°9W 125 B3
Hackensack U.S.A. 40°52N 74°4W 132 A1
Hackensack ➜ U.S.A. 40°42N 74°7W 132 B1
Hackettstown U.S.A. 40°51N 74°50W 313 F10
Hackney □ U.K. 51°33N 0°3W 125 A3
Hackney Wick U.K. 51°32N 0°1W 125 A3
Håckrenmagasinet Sweden 63°15N 13°30E 162 C7
Haco Angola 10°15S 15°44E 265 E3
Hadali Pakistan 32°16N 72°11E 242 C5
Hadano Japan 35°22N 139°14E 223 B11
Hadarba, Ras Sudan 22°4N 36°51E 256 C4
Hadarom □ Israel 31°0N 35°0E 251 H6
Ḥaḑbaram Oman 17°27N 55°15E 249 C6
Ḥadd, Ra's al Oman 22°35N 59°50E 249 B7
Ḥaddā Si. Arabia 21°27N 39°34E 248 B2
Haddington U.K. 55°57N 2°47W 167 F6
Haddock U.S.A. 33°2N 83°26W 316 B6
Haddummati Atoll Maldives 2°0N 73°30E 272 d
Hadejia Nigeria 12°30N 10°5E 263 C7
Hadejia ➜ Nigeria 12°50N 10°51E 263 C7
Ḫadera Israel 32°27N 34°55E 251 F5
Hadersleben = Haderslev Denmark 55°15N 9°30E 163 J3
Haderslev Denmark 55°15N 9°30E 163 J3
Hadgaon India 19°30N 77°40E 244 E3
Hadhramaut = Ḥaḑramawt □ Yemen 15°30N 49°30E 249 D5
Hadīboh Yemen 12°39N 54°2E 249 D6
Hadilik China 37°56N 86°6E 217 E11
Hadım Turkey 36°58N 32°26E 250 B3
Hādīshahr Iran 38°51N 45°40E 213 C11
Hadithah Si. Arabia 31°27N 37°9E 251 G8
Hadjadj, O. el ➜ Algeria 28°18N 5°20E 261 C6
Hadjeb el Aïoun Tunisia 35°21N 9°32E 258 A1
Hadjer Kamaran Chad 12°41N 21°46E 259 F4
Hadjer-Lamis □ Chad 12°55N 16°0E 259 F3
Hadjer Mornou Chad 17°12N 23°8E 259 E4
Hadlaskar Norway 60°15N 7°9E 164 D4
Hadley B. Canada 72°31N 108°12W 294 C10
Hadong S. Korea 35°5N 127°44E 224 E3
Hadr, Warrâq el Egypt 30°5N 31°12E 117 A2
Ḥaḑramawt □ Yemen 15°30N 49°30E 249 D5
Ḥaḑramawt, W. ➜ Yemen 15°10N 51°8E 249 D5
Ḥadrānīyah Iraq 35°38N 43°14E 246 C4
Hadrian's Wall U.K. 55°0N 2°30W 168 B5
Hadsten Denmark 56°19N 10°3E 163 H4
Hadsund Denmark 56°44N 10°8E 163 H4
Hadyach Ukraine 50°21N 34°0E 189 G8
Hae, Ko Thailand 7°44N 98°22E 237 a
Hægeland Norway 58°22N 7°45E 164 F4
Haeinsa △ S. Korea 35°47N 128°5E 224 E4
Haeju N. Korea 38°3N 125°45E 224 C2
Haeju-man N. Korea 37°54N 125°45E 224 D2
Hä'ena U.S.A. 22°14N 159°34W 302 A2
Haenam S. Korea 34°34N 126°35E 224 E3
Haenertsburg S. Africa 24°0S 29°50E 271 B4
Haerhpin = Harbin China 45°48N 126°40E 227 B14
Hafar al Bāṭin Si. Arabia 28°32N 45°52E 246 D5
Hafik Turkey 39°51N 37°23E 212 C7
Ḥafīrat al 'Aydā Si. Arabia 26°26N 39°12E 246 E3
Ḥafit Oman 23°59N 55°49E 247 F7
Hafizabad Pakistan 32°5N 73°40E 242 C5
Haflong India 25°10N 93°5E 241 C4
Hafnarfjörður Iceland 64°4N 21°57W 155 C5
Hafnir Iceland 63°56N 22°41W 155 D4
Hafslo Norway 61°19N 7°10E 164 C4
Haft Gel Iran 31°30N 49°32E 247 D6
Haga Sweden 59°21N 18°1E 139 A2
Hagalil Israel 32°53N 35°18E 250 F6
Hagari ➜ India 15°40N 77°0E 245 G3
Hagåtña Guam 13°28N 144°45E 302 d
Hagby Sweden 56°34N 16°11E 163 H10
Hagemeister I. U.S.A. 58°39N 160°54W 303 G7
Hagen Germany 51°21N 7°27E 178 D3
Hagenbrunn Austria 48°19N 16°27E 142 A2
Hagenow Germany 53°26N 11°12E 178 B7
Hagere Hiywet Ethiopia 8°59N 37°51E 266 C4
Hagerman U.S.A. 33°7N 104°20W 305 K11
Hagerman Fossil Beds ⌂ U.S.A. 42°48N 114°57W 304 E6
Hägersten Sweden 59°18N 17°59E 139 B1
Hagerstown Ind., U.S.A. 39°55N 85°10W 311 E11
Hagerstown Md., U.S.A. 39°39N 77°43W 309 F15
Hagersville Canada 42°58N 80°3W 312 D4
Hagetmau France 43°39N 0°37W 174 E3
Hagfors Sweden 60°3N 13°45E 162 D7
Häggvik Sweden 59°26N 17°56E 139 A1
Hagi Iceland 65°28N 23°25W 155 B3
Hagi Japan 34°30N 131°22E 222 C3
Hagolan Syria 33°0N 35°45E 250 F6
Hagondange France 49°16N 6°11E 173 C13
Hágöngulón Iceland 64°35N 18°8W 155 C8
Hagonoy Bulacan, Phil. 14°50N 120°44E 232 D3
Hagonoy Manila, Phil. 14°31N 121°3E 127 B2
Hags Hd. Ireland 52°57N 9°28W 166 D2
Hague, C. de la France 49°44N 1°56W 172 C5
Hague, The = 's-Gravenhage Neths. 52°7N 4°17E 170 B4
Hague Park Canada 43°45N 79°14W 141 A3
Haguenau France 48°49N 7°47E 173 D14
Hagunía W. Sahara 27°26N 12°24W 260 C2
Hahira U.S.A. 30°59N 83°22W 316 E6
Hai Duong Vietnam 20°56N 106°19E 228 G6
Hai'an Guangdong, China 20°18N 110°11E 229 a
Hai'an Jiangsu, China 32°37N 120°27E 229 A13
Haian Shanmo Taiwan 23°25N 121°25E 225 C3
Haicheng China 40°50N 122°45E 224 B1
Haida Gwaii Canada 53°20N 132°10W 296 C2
Haidar Khel Afghan. 33°58N 68°38E 242 C3
Haidarâbâd = Hyderabad India 17°22N 78°29E 244 F4
Haidargarh India 26°37N 81°22E 243 F9
Haidari = Chaidari Greece 38°2N 23°38E 112 A1
Haidarpur India 28°43N 77°8E 120 A1
Haidhausen Germany 48°7N 11°36E 131 B2
Haidian China 39°59N 116°16E 114 B1
Haifa = Ḥefa Israel 32°46N 35°0E 250 F6
Haifeng China 22°58N 115°10E 229 F10
Haiger Germany 50°43N 8°12E 178 E4
Haight-Ashbury U.S.A. 37°46N 122°26W 136 B2
Haikou China 20°1N 110°16E 229 a
Haiku-Pauwela U.S.A. 20°56N 156°19W 302 C5
Ḥā'il Si. Arabia 27°28N 41°45E 246 E4
Ḥā'il □ Si. Arabia 26°40N 41°40E 246 E4
Hailakandi India 24°42N 92°34E 241 C4
Hailar China 49°10N 119°38E 219 B12
Hailey U.S.A. 43°31N 114°19W 304 E6
Haileybury Canada 47°30N 79°38W 298 C4
Hailin China 44°37N 129°30E 227 B15
Hailing Dao China 21°35N 111°47E 229 G8
Hailun China 47°28N 126°50E 219 B14
Hailuoto Finland 65°3N 24°45E 160 D21
Haimen Guangdong, China 23°15N 116°38E 229 F11
Haimen Jiangsu, China 31°52N 121°10E 229 B13
Hainan □ China 19°0N 109°30E 229 a
Hainan Dao China 19°0N 109°30E 229 a
Hainan Str. = Qiongzhou Haixia China 20°10N 110°15E 229 a
Hainault U.K. 51°36N 0°6E 125 A4
Hainaut □ Belgium 50°30N 4°0E 170 D4
Hainburg Austria 48°9N 16°56E 181 C9
Haines Alaska, U.S.A. 59°14N 135°26W 296 B1
Haines Oreg., U.S.A. 44°55N 117°56W 304 D5
Haines City U.S.A. 28°7N 81°38W 317 G8
Haines Junction Canada 60°45N 137°30W 296 A1
Hainfeld Austria 48°3N 15°48E 180 C8
Haining China 30°28N 120°40E 229 B13
Haiphong Vietnam 20°47N 106°41E 228 G6
Haitan Dao China 25°30N 119°45E 229 E12
Haiti ■ W. Indies 19°0N 72°30W 321 C5
Haiya Sudan 18°20N 36°21E 256 D4
Haiyan Qinghai, China 36°53N 100°59E 218 D9
Haiyan Zhejiang, China 30°28N 120°58E 229 B13
Haiyang China 36°47N 121°9E 227 F11
Haiyang Dao China 39°2N 123°10E 224 C1
Haiyuan Guangxi Zhuangzu, China 22°8N 107°35E 228 F6
Haiyuan Ningxia Huizu, China 36°35N 105°52E 226 F3
Haizhou Guangdong, China 23°5N 113°18E 121 B2
Haizhou Jiangsu, China 34°37N 119°7E 227 G10
Haizhou Wan China 34°50N 119°20E 227 G10
Haizhu Guangchang China 23°6N 113°14E 121 B2
Hajar Bangar Sudan 10°40N 22°45E 259 F4
Hajdú-Bihar □ Hungary 47°30N 21°30E 182 C6
Hajdúböszörmény Hungary 47°40N 21°30E 182 C6
Hajdúdorog Hungary 47°48N 21°30E 182 C6
Hajdúhadház Hungary 47°40N 21°40E 182 C6
Hajdúnánás Hungary 47°50N 21°26E 182 C6
Hajdúsámson Hungary 47°37N 21°42E 182 C6
Hajdúszoboszló Hungary 47°27N 21°22E 182 C6
Haji Ibrahim Iraq 36°40N 44°30E 213 D11
Hajipur India 25°45N 85°13E 243 G11
Ḥājj Ali Qolī, Kavīr-e Iran 35°55N 54°50E 247 C7
Ḥajjah Yemen 15°42N 43°36E 248 D3
Ḥajjah □ Yemen 15°42N 43°36E 248 D3
Ḥājjīābād Hormozgān, Iran 28°19N 55°55E 247 D7
Ḥājjīābād Khorāsān, Iran 33°37N 60°0E 247 C9
Ḥājjīābād-e Zarrīn Iran 33°9N 54°51E 247 C7
Hajnówka Poland 52°47N 23°35E 185 F10
Hajo India 26°15N 91°32E 241 B3
Hajodo S. Korea 34°17N 126°3E 224 E3
Ḥajrah Si. Arabia 20°14N 41°3E 248 B3
Haka Burma 22°39N 93°37E 241 D4
Hakansson, Mts. Dem. Rep. of the Congo 8°40S 25°45E 265 D5
Hakataramea N.Z. 44°43S 170°30E 285 E5
Hakkâri Turkey 37°34N 43°44E 213 D10
Hakkâri □ Turkey 37°30N 44°0E 213 D10
Hakkâri Dağları Turkey 38°2N 42°58E 213 C10
Hakken-Zan Japan 34°10N 135°54E 223 C7
Hakkōda San Japan 40°50N 141°0E 220 D10
Hakodate Japan 41°45N 140°44E 220 D10
Hakos Namibia 23°13S 16°21E 270 B2
Hakota Japan 36°5N 140°30E 223 A12
Håksberg Sweden 60°11N 15°12E 162 D9
Hakskeenpan S. Africa 26°48S 20°13E 270 C3
Haku-San Japan 36°9N 136°46E 223 A8
Haku-San △ Japan 36°15N 136°45E 223 A8
Hakuba Japan 36°42N 137°51E 223 A9
Hakui Japan 36°53N 136°47E 221 F8
Hakun Burma 26°46N 95°42E 241 B5
Hakunila Finland 60°16N 25°6E 121 B3
Hakupu Cook Is. 19°6S 169°50W 289 g
Hakusan Japan 36°31N 136°34E 223 A8
Hal Saflieni Malta 35°52N 14°30E 206 F8
Hala Pakistan 25°43N 68°20E 240 D3
Ḥalab Syria 36°10N 37°15E 250 B8
Ḥalab □ Syria 36°10N 37°10E 250 B8
Ḥalaban Si. Arabia 23°29N 44°23E 248 B4
Ḥalabjah Iraq 35°10N 45°58E 213 E11
Halaib Sudan 22°12N 36°30E 256 C4
Halaib Triangle Africa 22°30N 35°20E 256 C4
Halandri = Chalandri Greece 38°3N 23°48E 112 A2

Hawera N.Z. 39°35S 174°19E 284 F3
Hawesville U.S.A. 37°54N 86°45W 311 G10
Ḥawf Yemen 16°38N 53°2E 249 C6
Hawi U.S.A. 20°14N 155°50W 302 C6
Hawick U.K. 55°26N 2°47W 167 F6
Hawk Junction Canada 48°5N 84°38W 298 C3
Hawk Point U.S.A. 38°58N 91°8W 310 F5
Hawkdun Ra. N.Z. 44°53S 170°5E 285 E5
Hawke B. N.Z. 39°25S 177°20E 284 F6
Hawker Australia 31°59S 138°22E 282 A3
Hawke's Bay Canada 50°36N 57°10W 299 B8
Hawke's Bay □ N.Z. 39°45S 176°35E 284 F5
Hawkesbury Canada 45°37N 74°37W 298 C5
Hawkesbury I. Canada 53°37N 129°3W 296 C3
Hawkesbury Pt. Australia 11°55S 134°5E 280 A1
Hawkinsville U.S.A. 32°17N 83°28W 316 C6
Hawks Nest Australia 32°41S 152°11E 283 B10
Hawley Minn., U.S.A. 46°53N 96°19W 308 B5
Hawley Pa., U.S.A. 41°28N 75°11W 313 E9
Haworth U.S.A. 40°57N 73°59W 132 A2
Ḥawrā' Yemen 15°42N 48°16E 249 D5
Ḥawrān, W. → Iraq 33°58N 42°34E 213 F10
Hawsh Mūssá Lebanon 33°45N 35°55E 250 E6
Hawthorne Fla., U.S.A. 29°36N 82°5W 317 F7
Hawthorne Nev., U.S.A. 38°32N 118°38W 304 G4
Hawthorne Racecourse U.S.A. 41°49N 87°44W 119 C2
Hay Australia 34°30S 144°51E 283 C6
Hay → N. Terr., Australia 24°50S 138°0E 280 C2
Hay → Alta., Canada 60°50N 116°26W 296 A5
Hay, C. Australia 14°5S 129°29E 278 B4
Hay I. Canada 44°53N 80°58W 312 B4
Hay L. Canada 58°50N 118°50W 296 B5
Hay-on-Wye U.K. 52°5N 3°8W 169 E4
Hay Point Australia 21°18S 149°17E 280 C4
Hay River Canada 60°51N 115°44W 296 A5
Hay Springs U.S.A. 42°41N 102°41W 308 D2
Hayachine-San Japan 39°34N 141°29E 220 E10
Hayange France 49°20N 6°2E 173 C13
Hayastan = Armenia ■ Asia 40°20N 45°0E 191 K7
Hayato Japan 31°40N 130°43E 222 F2
Haydān, W. al → Jordan 31°29N 35°34E 251 G6
Haydarlı Turkey 38°16N 30°23E 205 C12
Hayden U.S.A. 40°30N 107°16W 304 F10
Hayes Jamaica 17°52N 77°14W 320 a
Hayes Kent, U.K. 51°22N 0°0 125 B4
Hayes Middlesex, U.K. 51°30N 0°25W 125 A1
Hayes S. Dak., U.S.A. 44°23N 101°1W 308 C3
Hayes → Canada 57°3N 92°12W 298 A1
Hayes, Mt. U.S.A. 63°37N 146°43W 303 E11
Hayes Creek Australia 13°43S 131°22E 278 B5
Hayes End U.K. 51°31N 0°25W 125 A1
Hayford U.S.A. 41°45N 87°42W 119 C2
Hayle U.K. 50°11N 5°26W 169 G2
Hayling I. U.K. 50°48N 0°59W 169 G7
Haymā' Oman 19°56N 56°19E 249 C7
Hayman I. Australia 20°4S 148°53E 280 b
Haymana Turkey 39°26N 32°31E 212 C5
Haynan Yemen 15°50N 48°18E 249 D5
Haynau = Chojnów Poland 51°18N 15°58E 185 G2
Hayneville U.S.A. 32°23N 83°37W 316 C6
Hayrabolu Turkey 41°12N 27°5E 203 E11
Hays Alta., Canada 50°6N 111°48W 296 C6
Hays Kans., U.S.A. 38°53N 99°20W 308 F4
Ḥays Yemen 13°56N 43°29E 248 D3
Haysville U.S.A. 38°28N 86°55W 311 F10
Haysyn Ukraine 48°57N 29°25E 183 B14
Hayvoron Ukraine 48°22N 29°52E 183 B14
Hayward Calif., U.S.A. 37°40N 122°4W 306 H4
Hayward Wis., U.S.A. 46°1N 91°29W 308 B8
Haywards Heath U.K. 51°0N 0°5W 169 G7
Haẓafon □ Israel 32°40N 35°20E 250 F6
Hazar Turkmenistan 39°34N 53°16E 187 G9
Hazārān, Kūh-e Iran 29°35N 57°20E 247 D8
Hazard U.S.A. 37°15N 83°12W 309 G12
Hazaribag India 23°58N 85°26E 243 H11
Hazaribag Road India 24°12N 85°57E 243 G11
Hazebrouck France 50°42N 2°31E 173 B9
Hazelton B.C., Canada 55°20N 127°42W 296 B3
Hazelton N. Dak., U.S.A. 46°29N 100°17W 308 B3
Hazen U.S.A. 47°18N 101°38W 308 B3
Hazen, L. Canada 81°47N 71°1W 154 A3
Hazlehurst Ga., U.S.A. 31°52N 82°36W 316 D7
Hazlehurst Miss., U.S.A. 31°52N 90°24W 315 F9
Hazlet U.S.A. 40°25N 74°12W 313 F10
Hazleton Ind., U.S.A. 38°29N 87°33W 311 F9
Hazleton Pa., U.S.A. 40°57N 75°59W 313 F9
Hazlett, L. Australia 21°30S 128°48E 278 D4
Hazro Turkey 38°15N 40°47E 246 B4
He Xian = Hezhou China 24°27N 111°30E 229 E8
He Xian China 31°45N 118°20E 229 B12
Head of Bight Australia 31°30S 131°25E 279 F5
Head-Smashed-In Buffalo Jump Canada 49°44N 113°37W 296 D6
Headland U.S.A. 31°21N 85°21W 316 D4
Headlands Zimbabwe 18°15S 32°2E 269 F3
Healdsburg U.S.A. 38°37N 122°52W 306 G4
Healdton U.S.A. 34°14N 97°29W 314 D6
Healesville Australia 37°35S 145°30E 283 D6
Healy U.S.A. 63°52N 148°58W 303 E10
Heany Junction Zimbabwe 20°6S 28°54E 271 B4
Heanza-shima Japan 26°20N 127°57E 288 a
Heard I. Ind. Oc. 53°6S 72°36E 273 K6
Hearne U.S.A. 30°53N 96°36W 314 F6
Hearst Canada 49°40N 83°41W 298 C3
Heart → U.S.A. 46°46N 100°50W 308 B3
Heart's Content Canada 47°54N 53°27W 299 C9
Heath → Bolivia 12°31S 68°38W 330 C4
Heath, Pte. Canada 49°8N 61°40W 299 C7
Heath Mts. N.Z. 45°39S 167°9E 285 F2
Heathcote Australia 36°56S 144°45E 283 D6
Heatherwood = Edson Canada 53°35N 116°28W 296 C5
Heathfield S. Africa 34°3S 18°27E 118 B1
Heathrow, London ✈ (LHR) U.K. 51°28N 0°27W 125 B1
Heavener U.S.A. 34°53N 94°36W 314 D7
Hebbronville U.S.A. 27°18N 98°41W 314 H5
Hebe Haven Hong Kong, China 22°21N 114°15E 122 A3
Hebei □ China 39°0N 116°0E 226 E9
Hebel Australia 28°58S 147°47E 281 D4
Heber U.S.A. 32°44N 115°32W 307 N11
Heber Springs U.S.A. 35°30N 92°2W 314 D8
Hebgen L. U.S.A. 44°52N 111°20W 304 D8
Hebi China 35°57N 114°7E 226 G8
Hebrides U.K. 57°30N 7°0W 158 D4
Hebrides, Sea of the U.K. 57°5N 7°0W 167 D2
Hebron = Al Khalīl West Bank 31°32N 35°6E 251 G6
Hebron Nfld. & L., Canada 58°5N 62°30W 295 F19
Hebron N. Dak., U.S.A. 46°54N 102°3W 308 B2
Hebron Nebr., U.S.A. 40°10N 97°35W 308 E5
Heby Sweden 59°56N 16°53E 162 E10
Hecate Str. Canada 53°10N 130°30W 296 C2
Heceta I. U.S.A. 55°46N 133°40W 296 B2
Hechi China 24°40N 108°2E 228 E7
Hechingen Germany 48°21N 8°57E 179 G4
Hechuan China 30°2N 106°12E 228 B6
Hecla U.S.A. 45°53N 98°9W 308 C4
Hecla I. Canada 51°10N 96°43W 297 C9
Hedal Norway 60°37N 9°41E 162 D3
Heddal Norway 59°36N 9°9E 164 E6
Hédé Ille-et-Vilaine, France 48°18N 1°49W 172 D5
Hede Jämtland, Sweden 62°23N 13°30E 162 B7
Hedemora Sweden 60°18N 15°58E 162 D9
Hedensted Denmark 55°46N 9°42E 163 J3
Hedesunda Sweden 60°24N 17°0E 162 D10
Hedgehope N.Z. 46°12S 168°34E 285 G3
Hedmark □ Norway 61°17N 11°40E 164 C8
Hedo Japan 26°52N 128°15E 288 a
Hedo-misaki Japan 26°52N 128°15E 288 a
Hedong China 42°40N 129°0E 224 A4
Hedong China 23°5N 113°14E 121 B2
Hedrick U.S.A. 41°11N 92°19W 310 C4
He'eia U.S.A. 21°25N 157°48W 302 K14
Heel Pt. Wake I. 19°18N 166°38E 302 b
Heerde Neths. 52°24N 6°2E 170 B6
Heerenveen Neths. 52°57N 5°55E 170 B5
Heerhugowaard Neths. 52°40N 4°51E 170 B4
Heerlen Neths. 50°55N 5°58E 170 D5
Heerwegen = Polkowice Poland 51°29N 16°3E 185 G3
Ḥefa Israel 32°46N 35°0E 250 F6
Ḥefa □ Israel 32°40N 35°0E 250 F6
Hefei China 31°52N 117°18E 229 B11
Hefeng China 29°55N 109°52E 228 C7
Heflin U.S.A. 33°39N 85°35W 316 B4
Hegalig Sudan 14°36N 31°54E 257 E3
Hegang China 47°20N 130°19E 219 B15
Heggenes Norway 61°9N 9°4E 164 C6
Heglig Sudan 10°0N 29°24E 257 F2
Hegra Norway 63°27N 11°8E 164 A8
Hei Ling Chau Hong Kong, China 22°15N 114°2E 122 B2
Heiban Sudan 11°13N 30°31E 257 E3
Heichengzhen China 36°24N 106°3E 226 F4
Heidal Norway 61°45N 9°19E 164 C6
Heide Germany 54°11N 9°6E 178 A5
Heidelberg Baden-W., Germany 49°24N 8°42E 179 F4
Heidelberg Western Cape, S. Africa 34°6S 20°59E 270 D3
Heidelberg Heights Australia 37°45S 145°4E 128 A2
Heidelberg West Australia 37°43S 145°2E 128 A2
Heidelburg S. Africa 26°30S 28°21E 271 C4
Heidemühle Germany 52°29N 13°40E 115 B5
Heidenau Germany 50°57N 13°52E 178 E9
Heidenheim Germany 48°41N 10°9E 179 G6
Heideveld S. Africa 33°58S 18°32E 118 A2
Heigun-Tō Japan 33°47N 132°14E 222 D4
Heihe China 50°10N 127°30E 219 A14
Heijing China 25°22N 101°44E 228 E3
Heijo = P'yŏngyang N. Korea 39°0N 125°30E 224 C2
Heilbad Heiligenstadt Germany 51°22N 10°8E 178 D6
Heilbron S. Africa 27°16S 27°59E 271 C4
Heilbronn Germany 49°9N 9°13E 179 F5
Heiligenblut Austria 47°2N 12°51E 180 D5
Heiligenhafen Germany 54°22N 10°59E 178 A6
Heiligensee Germany 52°36N 13°13E 115 A2
Heiligenstadt Austria 48°14N 16°21E 142 A2
Heilongjiang □ China 48°0N 126°0E 219 B14
Heiloo Neths. 52°36N 4°42E 170 B4
Heilprin Land Greenland 82°5N 33°0W 154 A7
Heilsberg = Lidzbark Warmiński Poland 54°7N 20°34E 184 D7
Heilunkiang = Heilongjiang □ China 48°0N 126°0E 219 B14
Heim Norway 63°26N 9°5E 164 A6
Heimaey Iceland 63°26N 20°17W 155 D6
Heimdal Norway 63°21N 10°22E 164 A7
Heineken Experience Amsterdam, Neths. 112 c2
Heinersdorf Germany 52°34N 13°26E 115 A3
Heinola Finland 61°13N 26°2E 188 B4
Heinsberg Germany 51°3N 6°5E 178 D2
Heinsun Burma 25°52N 95°35E 241 C5
Heinze Chaung Burma 14°42N 97°52E 236 E1
Heinze Kyun Burma 14°25N 97°45E 236 E1
Heirnkut Burma 25°14N 94°44E 241 C5
Heishan China 41°40N 122°5E 227 D12
Heishui Liaoning, China 42°8N 119°30E 227 C10
Heishui Sichuan, China 32°4N 103°2E 228 A4
Hejaz = Ḥijāz Si. Arabia 24°0N 40°0E 246 E3
Hejian China 38°25N 116°5E 226 E9
Hejiang China 28°43N 105°46E 228 C5
Hejin China 35°35N 110°42E 226 G6
Hejing China 42°18N 86°22E 217 C11
Hekımhan Turkey 38°50N 37°55E 212 C7
Hekinan Japan 34°52N 137°0E 223 C9
Hekla Iceland 63°56N 19°35W 155 D7
Hekou Gansu, China 36°10N 103°26E 226 F2
Hekou Guangdong, China 23°13N 112°45E 229 F9
Hekou Yunnan, China 22°30N 103°59E 228 F4
Hel Poland 54°37N 18°47E 184 D5
Hela □ Papua N. G. 5°30S 142°30E 286 C2
Helagsfjället Sweden 62°54N 12°25E 162 B6
Helan Shan China 38°30N 105°55E 226 E3
Helendorplatz Vienna, Austria 142 b1
Helden's Pt. St. Kitts & Nevis 17°25N 62°51W 322 d
Helechosa de los Montes Spain 39°22N 4°53W 195 F6
Helemano → U.S.A. 21°35N 158°7W 302 J13
Helen Atoll Palau 2°40N 132°0E 231 D8
Helena Ga., U.S.A. 32°5N 82°55W 316 C7
Helena Mont., U.S.A. 46°36N 112°2W 304 C7
Helena -West Helena U.S.A. 34°32N 90°36W 315 D9
Helendale U.S.A. 34°44N 117°19W 307 L9
Hélène de Champlain, Parc ⌂ Canada 45°31N 73°32W 130 A2
Helenelund Sweden 59°24N 17°58E 139 A1
Helensburgh N.S.W., Australia 34°11S 151°1E 283 C9
Helensburgh Argyll & Bute, U.K. 56°1N 4°43W 167 E4
Helensville N.Z. 36°41S 174°29E 284 C3
Helenvale Australia 15°43S 145°14E 280 B4
Helgasjön Sweden 56°55N 14°50E 163 H8
Helgeland Norway 66°7N 13°29E 160 C15
Helgoland Germany 54°10N 7°53E 178 A3
Heligoland = Helgoland Germany 54°10N 7°53E 178 A3
Heligoland B. = Deutsche Bucht Germany 54°15N 8°0E 178 A4
Heliopolis = Masr el Gedida Egypt 30°5N 31°21E 117 A2
Hell Norway 63°26N 10°54E 164 A7
Hell-Bourg Réunion 21°3S 55°32E 272 f
Hell Hole Gorge △ Australia 25°31S 144°12E 280 D3
Hella Iceland 63°50N 20°24W 155 D6
Hellas = Greece ■ Europe 40°0N 23°0E 204 B3
Helleland Norway 58°33N 6°7E 164 F3
Hellersdorf Germany 52°32N 13°35E 115 A4
Hellertown U.S.A. 40°35N 75°21W 313 F9
Hellerup Denmark 55°44N 12°33E 118 A3
Hellespont = Çanakkale Boğazı Turkey 40°17N 26°32E 203 F10
Hellesylt Norway 62°6N 6°51E 164 B3
Hellevoetsluis Neths. 51°50N 4°8E 170 C4
Hellín Spain 38°31N 1°40W 197 G3
Hellissandur Iceland 64°55N 23°54W 155 C6
Hells Canyon ⌂ U.S.A. 45°30N 117°45W 304 D5
Hells Gate Saba 17°39N 63°14W 322 a
Hell's Gate ⌂ Kenya 0°54S 36°19E 268 C4
Hellvik Norway 58°29N 5°52E 164 F2
Helmand □ Afghan. 31°20N 64°0E 240 C2
Helmand → Afghan. 31°12N 61°34E 240 D1
Helme → Germany 51°20N 11°21E 178 D7
Helmeringhausen Namibia 25°54S 16°57E 270 C2
Helmond Neths. 51°29N 5°41E 170 C5
Helmsdale U.K. 58°7N 3°39W 167 C5
Helmsdale → U.K. 58°8N 3°43W 167 C5
Helmstedt Germany 52°12N 11°0E 178 C7
Helong China 42°40N 129°0E 224 A4
Helper U.S.A. 39°41N 110°51W 304 G8
Helsingborg Sweden 56°3N 12°42E 163 H6
Helsinge Denmark 56°2N 12°12E 163 H6
Helsingfors = Helsinki Finland 60°10N 24°55E 121 B2
Helsingør Denmark 56°2N 12°35E 163 H6
Helsinki Finland 60°10N 24°55E 121 B2
Helsinki-Vantaa ✈ (HEL) Finland 60°18N 24°58E 121 B2
Helska, Mierzeja Poland 54°45N 18°40E 184 D5
Helston U.K. 50°6N 5°17W 169 G2
Helvellyn U.K. 54°32N 3°1W 168 C4
Helvetinjärvi △ Finland 62°5N 23°47E 160 E20
Helwân Egypt 29°50N 31°20E 256 J7
Hemavati → India 12°30N 76°20E 245 H3
Hemei = Homei Taiwan 24°7N 120°29E 225 B2
Hemel Hempstead U.K. 51°44N 0°28W 169 F7
Hemet U.S.A. 33°45N 116°58W 307 M10
Hemingford U.S.A. 42°19N 103°4W 308 D2
Hemis △ India 34°10N 77°15E 242 B7
Hemmingford Canada 45°3N 73°35W 313 A11
Hempe Dem. Rep. of the Congo 1°54N 22°42E 264 B4
Hempstead N.Y., U.S.A. 40°42N 73°37W 313 F11
Hempstead Tex., U.S.A. 30°6N 96°5W 314 F6
Hemse Sweden 57°15N 18°22E 163 G12
Hemsedal Norway 60°53N 8°30E 164 D5
Hemsön Sweden 62°42N 18°5E 162 B12
Hen Norway 60°13N 10°14E 164 D7
Hen and Chicken B. Australia 33°50S 151°7E 139 B1
Hen and Chickens Is. N.Z. 35°58S 174°45E 284 B3
Henån Sweden 58°14N 11°40E 163 F5
Henan □ China 34°0N 114°0E 226 H8
Henares → Spain 40°24N 3°30W 194 E7
Henashi-Misaki Japan 40°37N 139°51E 220 D9
Hendaye France 43°23N 1°47W 174 E2
Hendek Turkey 40°48N 30°44E 212 B4
Henderson Argentina 36°18S 61°43W 334 D3
Henderson Ga., U.S.A. 32°21N 83°47W 316 C6
Henderson Ky., U.S.A. 37°50N 87°35W 311 G9
Henderson N.C., U.S.A. 36°20N 78°25W 315 C15
Henderson N.Y., U.S.A. 43°50N 76°10W 313 C8
Henderson Nev., U.S.A. 36°2N 114°58W 124 B2
Henderson Tenn., U.S.A. 35°26N 88°38W 315 D10
Henderson Tex., U.S.A. 32°9N 94°48W 314 E7
Henderson I. Pac. Oc. 24°22S 128°19W 289 K15
Hendersonville N.C., U.S.A. 35°19N 82°28W 315 D13
Hendersonville Tenn., U.S.A. 36°18N 86°37W 315 C11
Hendījān Iran 30°14N 49°43E 247 D6
Hendon U.K. 51°35N 0°14W 125 A2
Hendorābī Iran 26°40N 53°37E 247 E7
Heng Jiang → China 28°40N 104°25E 228 C5
Heng Xian China 22°40N 109°17E 228 F7
Hengām Iran 26°38N 55°53E 247 E7
Henganofi Papua N. G. 6°15S 145°38E 286 D3
Hengcheng China 38°18N 106°28E 226 E4
Hëngch'un Taiwan 22°0N 120°44E 225 D2
Hengdaohezi China 44°52N 129°0E 227 B15
Hengduan Shan China 28°30N 98°50E 228 C2
Hengelo Neths. 52°16N 6°48E 170 B6
Henggang China 22°39N 114°12E 219 a
Hengmen China 22°33N 113°35E 219 a
Hengsha China 23°9N 113°12E 121 B2
Hengshan Hunan, China 27°16N 112°45E 229 D9
Hengshan Shaanxi, China 37°58N 109°5E 226 F5
Hengshui China 37°41N 115°40E 226 F8
Hengyang China 26°59N 112°22E 229 D9
Henichesk Ukraine 46°12N 34°50E 189 J8
Henima India 25°22N 93°36E 241 C4
Hénin-Beaumont France 50°25N 2°58E 173 B9
Hénin-Liétard = Hénin-Beaumont France 50°25N 2°58E 173 B9
Henley-on-Thames U.K. 51°32N 0°54W 169 F7
Henlopen, C. U.S.A. 38°48N 75°6W 309 F16
Henna Japan 26°19N 127°53E 288 a
Hennan Sweden 62°2N 15°54E 162 B9
Hennebont France 47°49N 3°19W 172 E3
Hennenman S. Africa 27°59S 27°1E 270 C4
Hennepin U.S.A. 41°15N 89°21W 310 C7
Hennessey U.S.A. 36°6N 97°54W 314 C6
Hennigsdorf Germany 52°38N 13°12E 115 A2
Henrietta N.Y., U.S.A. 43°4N 77°37W 312 C7
Henrietta Tex., U.S.A. 33°49N 98°12W 314 E5
Henrietta, Ostrov = Genriyetty, Ostrov Russia 77°6N 156°30E 215 B16
Henrietta Maria, C. Canada 55°9N 82°20W 298 A3
Henry U.S.A. 41°7N 89°22W 310 C7
Henry Ice Rise Antarctica 80°35S 62°0W 151 E17
Henry Lawrence I. India 12°9N 93°5E 245 H11
Henryetta U.S.A. 35°27N 95°59W 314 D7
Henryków Poland 52°19N 20°58E 143 B1
Henryville Canada 45°8N 73°11W 313 A11
Hensall Canada 43°26N 81°30W 312 C3
Henson Cr. → U.S.A. 38°47N 76°58W 143 C3
Henstedt-Ulzburg Germany 53°47N 10°0E 178 B6
Hentiesbaai Namibia 22°8S 14°18E 270 B1
Hentiyn Nuruu Mongolia 48°30N 108°30E 219 B10
Henttaa Finland 60°11N 24°45E 121 B1
Henty Australia 35°30S 147°3E 283 C7
Henzada = Hinthada Burma 17°38N 95°26E 241 G5
Hephaestia Greece 39°55N 25°14E 205 B7
Hepharba U.S.A. 33°19N 82°6W 316 B7
Heping China 24°29N 115°0E 229 E10
Heping Park China 31°16N 121°30E 138 B2
Hepingli China 39°57N 116°23E 114 B2
Heppner U.S.A. 45°21N 119°33W 304 D4
Hepu China 21°40N 109°12E 228 G7
Hepworth Canada 44°37N 81°9W 312 B3
Heqing China 26°37N 100°11E 228 D3
Hequ China 39°20N 111°15E 226 E6
Héraðsflói Iceland 65°42N 14°12W 155 B12
Héraðsvötn → Iceland 65°45N 19°25W 155 B7
Heradsbygd Norway 60°49N 11°39E 164 D8
Heraklion = Iraklio Greece 35°20N 25°12E 207 E6
Heraklion Int. ✈ (HER) Greece 35°20N 25°15E 207 E6
Herald Cays Australia 16°58S 149°9E 280 B4
Herand Norway 60°20N 6°22E 164 D3
Herangi Ra. N.Z. 38°33S 174°48E 284 E3
Herāt Afghan. 34°20N 62°7E 240 B1
Herāt □ Afghan. 35°0N 62°0E 240 B1
Hérault □ France 43°34N 3°15E 174 E7
Hérault → France 43°17N 3°26E 174 E7
Herbault France 47°36N 1°8E 172 E8
Herbert Canada 50°30N 107°10W 297 C7
Herbert → Australia 18°31S 146°17E 280 B4
Herbert Hoover Nat. Historic Site ⌂ U.S.A. 41°40N 91°21W 310 C5
Herbert I. U.S.A. 52°45N 170°7W 303 K5
Herbertabad India 11°43N 92°37E 245 J11
Herberton Australia 17°20S 145°25E 280 B4
Herbertsdale S. Africa 34°1S 21°46E 270 D3
Herbertville N.Z. 40°30S 176°33E 284 G5
Herbignac France 47°27N 2°18W 172 E4
Herborn Germany 50°40N 8°18E 178 E4
Herby Poland 50°45N 18°50E 185 H5
Herceg-Novi Montenegro 42°30N 18°33E 202 D2
Hercegfalva = Mezőfalva Hungary 46°55N 18°49E 182 D3
Herchmer Canada 57°22N 94°10W 297 B10
Herculânia = Coxim Brazil 18°30S 54°55W 331 D7
Herðubreið Iceland 65°11N 16°21W 155 B10
Hereford Hereford, U.K. 52°4N 2°43W 169 E5
Hereford Tex., U.S.A. 34°49N 102°24W 314 D3
Herefordshire □ U.K. 52°8N 2°40W 169 E5
Herefoss Norway 58°32N 8°23E 164 F5
Héréhérétué French Polynesia 19°45S 144°58W 289 f
Herehogna Sweden 61°44N 12°8E 164 C9
Herekino N.Z. 35°18S 173°11E 284 B2
Herencia Spain 39°21N 3°22W 195 F7
Herentals Belgium 51°12N 4°51E 170 C4
Herford Germany 52°7N 8°39E 178 C4
Héricourt France 47°32N 6°45E 173 E13
Herington U.S.A. 38°40N 96°57W 308 F5
Herīs Iran 38°14N 47°6E 213 C12
Herisau Switz. 47°22N 9°17E 179 H5
Hérisson France 46°32N 2°42E 173 F9
Herkimer U.S.A. 43°2N 74°59W 313 D10
Herlen → Asia 48°48N 117°0E 219 B12
Herlev Denmark 55°43N 12°27E 118 A2
Herlong U.S.A. 40°8N 120°8W 306 E6
Herm U.K. 49°30N 2°28W 169 H5
Hermakivka Ukraine 48°42N 26°11E 183 B11
Herman Eckstein Park S. Africa 26°9S 28°1E 123 A2
Hermana Mayor I. Phil. 15°47N 119°47E 232 D2
Hermann U.S.A. 38°42N 91°27W 310 F5
Hermannsbad = Ciechocinek Poland 52°53N 18°45E 185 F5
Hermannsburg N. Terr., Australia 23°57S 132°45E 278 D5
Hermannsburg Niedersachsen, Germany 52°50N 10°5E 178 C6
Hermannskogel Austria 48°16N 16°17E 142 A1
Hermannstadt = Sibiu Romania 45°45N 24°9E 183 E9
Hermansverk Norway 61°11N 6°52E 164 C3
Hermanus S. Africa 34°27S 19°12E 270 D2
Herment France 45°45N 2°24E 174 C6
Hermidale Australia 31°30S 146°42E 283 A7
Hermiston Edinburgh, U.K. 55°55N 3°19W 121 B2
Hermiston Oreg., U.S.A. 45°51N 119°17W 304 D4
Hermit Is. Papua N. G. 1°32S 145°5E 286 A3
Hermitage Grenada 12°27N 61°28W 323 q
Hermitage Mo., U.S.A. 37°56N 93°19W 310 G3
Hermitage and Winter Palace Russia 59°55N 30°19E 137 B2
Hermon Ont., Canada 45°6N 77°37W 312 A7
Hermon N.Y., U.S.A. 44°28N 75°14W 313 B9
Hermon, Mt. = Shaykh, J. ash Lebanon 33°25N 35°50E 250 E6
Hermosillo Mexico 29°10N 111°0W 318 B2
Hermsdorf Germany 52°37N 13°18E 115 A2
Hernád → Hungary 47°56N 21°8E 182 C6
Hernals Austria 48°13N 16°20E 142 A2
Hernandarias Paraguay 25°20S 54°40W 335 B5
Hernandez U.S.A. 36°24N 120°46W 306 J6
Hernando Argentina 32°28S 63°40W 334 C3
Hernando Fla., U.S.A. 28°54N 82°23W 317 G7
Hernando Miss., U.S.A. 34°50N 90°0W 315 D10
Hernando de Magallanes △ Chile 54°0S 72°40W 336 D2
Hernani Spain 43°16N 1°58W 196 B3
Herndon U.S.A. 40°43N 76°51W 312 F8
Herne Germany 51°32N 7°14E 178 D3
Herne Bay U.K. 51°21N 1°8E 169 F9
Herne Hill U.K. 51°27N 0°6W 125 B3
Herning Denmark 56°8N 8°58E 163 H2
Herod U.S.A. 31°42N 84°26W 316 D5
Héroes de Churubusco Mexico 19°21N 99°6W 128 B2
Heroica Caborca = Caborca Mexico 30°37N 112°6W 318 A2
Heroica Nogales = Nogales Mexico 31°19N 110°56W 318 A2
Heron Bay Canada 48°40N 86°25W 298 C2
Heron I. Australia 23°27S 151°55E 280 C5
Herons, Î. aux Canada 45°25N 73°34W 130 B2
Herradura, Pta. de la Canary Is. 28°26N 14°8W 153 e2
Herre Norway 59°6N 9°34E 164 E6
Herreid U.S.A. 45°50N 100°4W 308 C3
Herrenberg Germany 48°35N 8°52E 179 G4
Herrera Spain 37°26N 4°55W 195 H6
Herrera de Alcántara Spain 39°39N 7°25W 195 F3
Herrera de Pisuerga Spain 42°35N 4°20W 194 C6
Herrera del Duque Spain 39°10N 5°3W 195 F5
Herrestad Sweden 58°21N 11°50E 163 F5
Herrin U.S.A. 37°48N 89°2W 310 G7
Herriot Canada 56°22N 101°16W 297 B8
Herrljunga Sweden 58°5N 13°1E 163 F7
Hersbruck Germany 49°30N 11°26E 179 F7
Herschel I. Canada 69°35N 139°5W 150 C1
Hershey U.S.A. 40°17N 76°39W 313 F8
Herso = Cherso Greece 41°5N 22°47E 202 E6
Herstal Belgium 50°40N 5°38E 170 D5
Herstedøster Denmark 55°40N 12°22E 118 A2
Hertford U.K. 51°48N 0°4W 169 F7
Hertfordshire □ U.K. 51°51N 0°5W 169 F7
's-Hertogenbosch Neths. 51°42N 5°17E 170 C5
Hertsa Ukraine 48°9N 26°15E 183 B11
Herttoniemi Finland 60°12N 25°2E 121 B3
Hertzogville S. Africa 28°9S 25°30E 270 C4
Hervás Spain 40°16N 5°52W 194 E5
Hervey B. Australia 25°0S 152°52E 280 C5
Herzberg Brandenburg, Germany 51°41N 13°14E 178 D9
Herzberg Niedersachsen, Germany 51°38N 10°20E 178 D6
Herzliyya Israel 32°10N 34°50E 251 F5
Herzogenburg Austria 48°17N 15°41E 180 C8
Ḥesār Fārs, Iran 29°52N 50°16E 247 D6
Ḥeşār Markazī, Iran 35°50N 49°12E 247 C6
Ḥeşārak Iran 35°47N 51°18E 141 A1
Hesdin France 50°21N 2°2E 173 B9
Heshan Guangdong, China 22°34N 113°4E 229 F9
Heshan Guangxi Zhuangzu, China 23°50N 108°53E 228 F7
Heshui China 35°48N 108°0E 226 G5
Heshun China 37°22N 113°32E 226 F7
Heskestad Norway 58°28N 6°22E 164 F3
Hesperia U.S.A. 34°25N 117°18W 307 L9
Hessdalen Norway 62°48N 11°10E 164 B8
Hesse = Hessen □ Germany 50°30N 9°0E 178 E4
Hessen □ Germany 50°30N 9°0E 178 E4
Hessenreuther und Manteler Wald ⌂ Germany 49°45N 12°1E 179 F8
Hessle U.K. 53°44N 0°24W 168 D7
Hesso Australia 32°8S 137°58E 282 B2
Hesteyri Iceland 66°20N 22°53W 155 A4
Heston U.K. 51°28N 0°22W 125 B1
Hestra Sweden 57°26N 13°35E 163 G7
Hetauda Nepal 27°25N 85°2E 243 F11
Hetch Hetchy Aqueduct U.S.A. 37°29N 122°19W 306 H5
Hetta Enontekiö Finland 68°23N 23°37E 160 B20
Hettinger U.S.A. 46°0N 102°42W 308 B2
Hettstedt Germany 51°39N 11°31E 178 D7
Hetzendorf Austria 48°9N 16°17E 142 B1
Heuksando S. Korea 34°40N 125°30E 224 E2
Heunghae S. Korea 36°12N 129°21E 224 D4
Heuvelton U.S.A. 44°37N 75°25W 313 B9
Hevelândia Brazil 5°12S 61°50W 329 E5
Heves Hungary 47°36N 20°17E 182 C5
Heves □ Hungary 47°50N 20°0E 182 C5
Hewitt U.S.A. 31°28N 97°12W 314 F6
Hexham U.K. 54°58N 2°4W 168 C5
Hexi Yunnan, China 24°9N 102°38E 228 E4
Hexi Zhejiang, China 27°58N 119°38E 229 D12
Hexigten Qi China 43°18N 117°30E 227 C9
Hextable U.K. 51°24N 0°10E 125 B5
Ḥeydarābād Iran 30°33N 55°38E 247 D7
Heydebreck = Kędzierzyn-Koźle Poland 50°20N 18°12E 185 H5
Heyfield Australia 37°59S 146°47E 283 D7
Heysham U.K. 54°3N 2°53W 168 C5
Heyuan China 23°39N 114°40E 229 F10
Heywood Australia 38°8S 141°37E 282 E4
Heyworth U.S.A. 40°19N 88°59W 310 D8
Heze China 35°14N 115°20E 226 G8
Hezhang China 27°8N 104°41E 228 D5
Hezhou China 24°27N 111°30E 229 E8
Hi-no-Misaki Japan 35°26N 132°38E 222 B4
Hi Vista U.S.A. 34°45N 117°46W 307 L9
Hialeah U.S.A. 25°51N 80°16W 129 C1
Hialeah Race Track U.S.A. 25°51N 80°16W 129 C1
Hiawassa, L. U.S.A. 28°33N 81°28W 133 A2
Hiawatha U.S.A. 39°51N 95°32W 308 F6
Hibbing U.S.A. 47°25N 92°56W 308 B7
Hibernia Reef Australia 12°0S 123°23E 278 B3
Hibiki-Nada Japan 34°0N 130°0E 222 D2
Hibok-Hibok, Mt. Phil. 9°12N 124°40E 233 G5
Hickam Housing U.S.A. 21°21N 157°57W 302 K14
Hickman U.S.A. 36°34N 89°11W 308 G9
Hickory U.S.A. 35°44N 81°21W 315 D14
Hickory Hills U.S.A. 41°43N 87°49W 119 C2
Hicks, Pt. Australia 37°49S 149°17E 283 D8
Hicks Bay N.Z. 37°34S 178°21E 284 D7
Hicks L. Canada 61°25N 100°0W 297 A9
Hicksville N.Y., U.S.A. 40°46N 73°32W 313 F11
Hicksville Ohio, U.S.A. 41°18N 84°46W 311 C12
Hicpochee, L. U.S.A. 26°48N 81°9W 317 J8
Hida Gifu, Japan 36°14N 137°11E 223 A9
Hida Romania 47°10N 23°19E 183 C8
Hida-Gawa → Japan 35°26N 137°3E 223 B9
Hida-Sammyaku Japan 36°30N 137°40E 223 A9
Hida-Sanchi Japan 36°10N 137°0E 223 A9
Hidaka Hokkaidō, Japan 42°30N 142°10E 220 C11
Hidaka Hyōgo, Japan 35°30N 134°44E 222 B6
Hidaka-Sammyaku Japan 42°35N 142°45E 220 C11
Hidalgo □ Mexico 20°30N 99°0W 319 C5
Hidalgo del Parral Mexico 26°56N 105°40W 318 B3
Hiddensee Germany 54°32N 13°6E 178 A9
Hidrolândia Brazil 17°0S 49°15W 333 E2
Hieflau Austria 47°36N 14°46E 180 D7
Hiekkaharju Finland 60°18N 25°2E 121 B3
Hiendelaencina Spain 41°5N 3°0W 196 D2
Hienghène N. Cal. 20°41S 164°56E 288 d
Hierapolis-Pamukkale Turkey 37°55N 29°7E 205 D11
Hierro Canary Is. 27°44N 18°0W 153 e1
Hietaniemi Finland 60°10N 24°54E 121 B2
Hietzing Austria 48°10N 16°17E 142 A1
Higashi Japan 34°41N 135°30E 133 A2
Higashi-Hiroshima Japan 34°25N 132°45E 222 C4
Higashi-Matsuyama Japan 36°2N 139°25E 223 A11
Higashi-Suidō Japan 34°0N 129°30E 222 D1
Higashiajima-San Japan 37°40N 140°10E 220 F10
Higashikagawa Japan 34°13N 134°24E 222 C6
Higashimurayama Japan 35°45N 139°26E 140 A1
Higashinari Japan 34°40N 135°32E 133 A2
Higashiōsaka Japan 34°39N 135°37E 223 C7
Higashisumiyoshi Japan 34°37N 135°31E 133 B2
Higashiyodogawa Japan 34°44N 135°28E 133 A1
Higbee U.S.A. 39°19N 92°31W 310 E4
Higgins U.S.A. 36°7N 100°2W 314 C4
Higgins Corner U.S.A. 39°2N 121°5W 306 F5
Higginsville U.S.A. 39°4N 93°43W 310 E3
High Bridge U.S.A. 40°40N 74°54W 313 F10
High Desert U.S.A. 43°40N 120°20W 304 E3
High Island Res. China 22°22N 114°21E 219 a
High Junk Pk. Hong Kong, China 22°18N 114°17E 122 B3
High Level Canada 58°31N 117°8W 296 B5
High Park Canada 43°38N 79°27W 141 B2
High Peak Phil. 15°29N 120°7E 232 D3
High Pk. St. Helena 15°58S 5°44W 153 h
High Point U.S.A. 35°57N 80°0W 315 D15
High Prairie Canada 55°30N 116°30W 296 B5
High River Canada 50°30N 113°50W 296 C6
High Springs U.S.A. 29°50N 82°36W 316 F7
High Tatra = Tatry Slovakia 49°20N 20°0E 181 B13
High Veld Africa 27°0S 27°0E 254 J6
High Wycombe U.K. 51°37N 0°45W 169 F7
Highbank N.Z. 43°37S 171°45E 285 D6
Highbury U.K. 51°33N 0°6W 125 A3
Highgate Jamaica 18°16N 76°57W 320 a
Highgate London, U.K. 51°34N 0°8W 125 A3
Highland Ill., U.S.A. 38°44N 89°41W 310 F7
Highland Ind., U.S.A. 41°33N 87°28W 311 C9
Highland Wis., U.S.A. 43°5N 90°22W 310 A6
Highland □ U.K. 57°17N 4°21W 167 D4
Highland City U.S.A. 27°58N 81°53W 317 H8
Highland Cr. → Canada 43°45N 79°13W 141 A3
Highland Creek Canada 43°46N 79°8W 141 A3
Highland Home U.S.A. 31°57N 86°19W 316 D3
Highland Mills U.S.A. 33°17N 84°17W 316 B5
Highland Park Calif., U.S.A. 34°7N 118°13W 126 B3
Highland Park Ill., U.S.A. 42°11N 87°48W 311 B9
Highland Park Tex., U.S.A. 32°50N 96°47W 120 B5
Highland View U.S.A. 29°50N 85°19W 316 F4
Highlands = Fort Thomas U.S.A. 39°4N 84°26W 311 E12
Highlands, The Antigua & B. 17°38N 61°47W 322 c
Highlands North S. Africa 26°8S 28°5E 123 A2
Highmore U.S.A. 44°31N 99°27W 308 C4
Highrock L. Canada 55°45N 100°30W 297 B8
Higuero, Pta. Puerto Rico 18°22N 67°16W 321 b
Higüey Dom. Rep. 18°37N 68°42W 321 D6
Hihya Egypt 30°40N 31°36E 256 H7
Hiidenportti △ Finland 63°53N 29°10E 160 E23
Hiiraan □ Somalia 4°0N 45°30E 267 D6
Hiiumaa Estonia 58°50N 22°45E 188 C2
Hijar Spain 41°10N 0°27W 196 D4
Ḥijārah, Ṣaḥrā' al Iraq 30°25N 44°30E 246 D5
Ḥijāz Si. Arabia 24°0N 40°0E 246 E3
Hiji Japan 33°22N 131°32E 222 D3
Hijo = Tagum Phil. 7°33N 125°53E 233 H5
Hikari Japan 33°58N 131°58E 222 D3
Hiketa = Higashikagawa Japan 34°13N 134°24E 222 C6
Hikkaduwa Sri Lanka 6°8N 80°6E 245 L5
Hikmak, Ras el Egypt 31°15N 27°51E 256 A2
Hiko U.S.A. 37°32N 115°14W 306 H11
Hikone Japan 35°15N 136°10E 223 B8
Hikurangi Gisborne, N.Z. 37°55S 178°4E 284 D7
Hikurangi Northland, N.Z. 35°36S 174°17E 284 B3
Hikutavake Niue 18°56S 169°53W 289 g
Hiland Park U.S.A. 30°12N 85°33W 316 E4
Hilary Burma 21°23N 93°48E 241 J4
Hildburghausen Germany 50°25N 10°42E 178 E6
Hildesheim Germany 52°9N 9°56E 178 C5
Hildarendi Iceland 63°44N 19°57W 155 D7
Hill → Australia 30°23S 115°3E 279 F2
Hill City Idaho, U.S.A. 43°18N 115°3W 304 E6
Hill City Kans., U.S.A. 39°22N 99°51W 308 F4
Hill City Minn., U.S.A. 46°59N 93°36W 308 B7
Hill City S. Dak., U.S.A. 43°56N 103°35W 308 D2
Hill Island L. Canada 60°30N 109°50W 297 A7
Hillaby, Mt. Barbados 13°12N 59°35W 323 r
Hillared Sweden 57°37N 13°10E 163 G7
Hillbrow Tower Johannesburg, S. Africa 26°11S 28°3E 123 B2
Hillcrest Heights U.S.A. 38°49N 76°57W 143 C3
Hillegom Neths. 52°18N 4°35E 170 B4
Hillend U.K. 56°2N 3°22W 121 A1
Hillerød Denmark 55°56N 12°19E 163 J6
Hillerstorp Sweden 57°20N 13°52E 163 G7
Hilli Bangla. 25°17N 89°1E 241 C2
Hilliard U.S.A. 30°41N 81°55W 316 E8
Hillingdon □ U.K. 51°32N 0°27W 125 A1
Hillsboro = Deerfield Beach U.S.A. 26°19N 80°6W 317 J9
Hillsboro Ga., U.S.A. 33°11N 83°38W 316 B6
Hillsboro Ill., U.S.A. 39°9N 89°29W 310 E7
Hillsboro Kans., U.S.A. 38°21N 97°12W 308 F5
Hillsboro Mo., U.S.A. 38°14N 90°34W 310 F6
Hillsboro N. Dak., U.S.A. 47°26N 97°3W 308 B5
Hillsboro Ohio, U.S.A. 39°12N 83°37W 311 E13
Hillsboro Oreg., U.S.A. 45°31N 122°59W 306 E4
Hillsboro Tex., U.S.A. 32°1N 97°8W 314 E6
Hillsboro Canal U.S.A. 26°30N 80°15W 317 J9
Hillsborough Grenada 12°28N 61°28W 323 q
Hillsborough N.H., U.S.A. 43°7N 71°54W 313 C13
Hillsborough Channel Australia 20°56S 149°15E 280 b
Hillsborough Dam Trin. & Tob. 11°13N 60°40W 323 s
Hillsborough Land = Belle Glade U.S.A. 26°41N 80°40W 317 J9
Hillsdale Mich., U.S.A. 41°56N 84°38W 311 C12
Hillsdale N.Y., U.S.A. 42°11N 73°32W 313 D11
Hillsport Canada 49°27N 85°34W 298 C2
Hillston Australia 33°30S 145°31E 283 B6
Hilltonia U.S.A. 32°53N 81°40W 316 C8
Hillwood U.S.A. 38°52N 77°9W 143 B2
Hilmīya Egypt 30°6N 31°19E 117 A2
Hilo U.S.A. 19°44N 155°5W 302 D6
Hilo ✈ (ITO) U.S.A. 19°43N 155°2W 302 D6
Hilo B. U.S.A. 19°45N 155°5W 302 D6
Hilongos Phil. 10°22N 124°44E 233 F5
Hilton U.S.A. 43°17N 77°48W 312 C7
Hilton Head Island U.S.A. 32°13N 80°45W 316 C9
Hilvan Turkey 37°34N 38°58E 213 D8
Hilversum Neths. 52°14N 5°10E 170 B5
Himachal Pradesh □ India 31°30N 77°0E 242 D7
Himalaya Asia 29°0N 84°0E 243 E11
Himalchuli Nepal 28°27N 84°38E 243 E11
Himamaylan Phil. 10°6N 122°52E 233 F4
Himarë Albania 40°8N 19°43E 202 F3
Himatnagar India 23°37N 72°57E 242 H5
Himchari △ Bangla. 21°28N 92°5E 241 E4
Hime-Jima Japan 33°43N 131°40E 222 D3
Himeji Japan 34°50N 134°40E 222 C6
Himi Japan 36°50N 136°55E 223 A8
Himmerland Denmark 56°45N 9°30E 163 H3
Ḥimş Syria 34°40N 36°45E 250 D7
Ḥimş □ Syria 34°30N 37°0E 250 D8
Hin Keng Hong Kong, China 22°22N 114°10E 122 A3
Hin Khom, Laem Thailand 9°25N 99°56E 237 b
Hinatuan Phil. 8°23N 126°20E 233 G6
Hinatuan Passage Phil. 9°45N 125°47E 233 G5
Hinche Haiti 19°9N 72°1W 321 C5
Hinchinbrook I. Australia 18°20S 146°15E 280 B4
Hinchinbrook Island △ Australia 18°14S 146°6E 280 B4
Hinckley Leics., U.K. 52°33N 1°22W 169 E6
Hinckley Minn., U.S.A. 46°1N 92°56W 308 B7
Hindaun India 26°44N 77°5E 242 F7
Hindenburg = Zabrze Poland 50°18N 18°50E 185 H5
Hindmarsh, L. Australia 36°5S 141°55E 282 D4
Hindol India 20°40N 85°10E 244 D7
Hinds N.Z. 43°59S 171°36E 285 D6
Hindsholm Denmark 55°30N 10°40E 163 J4
Hindu Bagh Pakistan 30°56N 67°50E 242 D2
Hindu Kush Asia 36°0N 71°0E 240 B3
Hindupur India 13°49N 77°32E 245 H3
Hines Creek Canada 56°20N 118°40W 296 B5
Hinesville U.S.A. 31°51N 81°36W 316 D8
Hinganghat India 20°30N 78°52E 244 D4
Hingham U.S.A. 48°33N 110°25W 304 B8
Hinghwa = Xinghua China 32°58N 119°48E 229 A12
Hingir India 21°57N 83°41E 243 J10
Hingoli India 19°41N 77°15E 244 E3
Hinigaran Phil. 10°16N 122°50E 233 F4
Hinis Turkey 39°22N 41°43E 213 C9
Hinna = Imi Ethiopia 6°28N 42°10E 257 F5
Hinna Nigeria 10°25N 11°35E 263 C7
Hinnerup Denmark 56°16N 10°4E 163 H4
Hinnøya Norway 68°35N 15°50E 160 B16
Hino Japan 35°0N 136°15E 223 C8
Hinoba-an Phil. 9°35N 122°28E 233 G4
Hinojosa del Duque Spain 38°30N 5°9W 195 G5
Hinokage Japan 32°39N 131°24E 222 E3
Hinsdale U.S.A. 42°47N 72°29W 313 D12
Hinterrhein → Switz. 46°40N 9°25E 179 J5
Hinthada Burma 17°38N 95°26E 241 G5
Hinton Alta., Canada 53°26N 117°34W 296 C5
Hinton W. Va., U.S.A. 37°40N 80°54W 309 G13
Hinubuan = Antipolo Phil. 14°35N 121°10E 232 D3
Hinunangan Phil. 10°25N 125°12E 233 F5
Hios = Chios Greece 38°27N 26°9E 205 C8
Hirado Japan 33°22N 129°33E 222 D1
Hirado-Shima Japan 33°20N 129°30E 222 D1
Hirakata Japan 34°48N 135°38E 223 C7
Hirakud Dam India 21°32N 83°45E 244 D6
Hiran → India 23°6N 79°21E 243 H8
Hirapur India 24°22N 79°13E 243 G8
Hirara = Miyakojima Japan 24°48N 125°17E 221 M2
Hirata Japan 35°24N 132°49E 222 B4
Hiratsuka Japan 35°19N 139°21E 223 B11
Hirekerur India 14°28N 75°23E 245 G2
Hirfanlı Barajı Turkey 39°18N 33°31E 212 C5
Hirhafok Algeria 23°49N 5°45E 261 D6
Hiromi = Kihoku Japan 33°13N 132°34E 222 D4
Hiroo Japan 42°17N 143°19E 220 C11
Hirosaki Japan 40°34N 140°28E 220 D10
Hiroshima Japan 34°24N 132°30E 222 C4
Hiroshima □ Japan 34°50N 133°0E 222 C5
Hiroshima-Wan Japan 34°5N 132°20E 222 C4
Hirota Japan 34°35N 135°20E 133 A1
Hirschberg = Jelenia Góra Poland 50°50N 15°45E 185 H2
Hirschstetten Austria 48°14N 16°27E 142 A2
Hirson France 49°55N 4°4E 173 C11
Hirtshals Denmark 57°36N 9°57E 163 G3
Hisai Japan 34°40N 136°28E 223 C8
Hisar India 29°12N 75°45E 242 E6
Hisarcık Turkey 39°15N 29°14E 205 B11
Hisaria Bulgaria 42°30N 24°44E 203 D8
Hisb, Sha'ib = Ḥasb, W. → Iraq 31°45N 44°17E 246 D5
Ḥismá Si. Arabia 28°30N 36°0E 251 K7
Ḥiṣn al 'Abr Yemen 16°8N 47°14E 248 C4

Hispaniola *W. Indies* 19°0N 71°0W **321** C5
Hīt *Iraq* 33°38N 42°49E **213** F10
Hita *Japan* 33°20N 130°58E **222** D2
Hitachi *Japan* 36°36N 140°39E **223** A12
Hitachi-Ōta *Japan* 36°30N 140°30E **223** A12
Hitan, W. el *Egypt* 29°19N 30°10E **256** J7
Hitchin *U.K.* 51°58N 0°16W **169** F7
Hithadhoo *Maldives* 0°36S 73°5E **272** d
Hither Green *U.K.* 51°26N 0°0 **125** B3
Hitiaa *Tahiti* 17°36S 149°18W **289** e
Hitoyoshi *Japan* 32°13N 130°45E **222** E2
Hitra *Norway* 63°30N 8°45E **164** A5
Hitzacker *Germany* 53°9N 11°2E **178** B7
Hiu *Vanuatu* 13°10S 166°35E **287** C4
Hiuchi-Nada *Japan* 34°5N 133°20E **222** C5
Hiva Oa *French Polynesia* 9°45S 139°0W **289** f
Hixon *Canada* 53°25N 122°35W **296** C4
Hiyoshi *Japan* 35°32N 139°38E **140** B2
Ḩiyyon, N. ➜ *Israel* 30°25N 35°10E **251** H6
Hizma *West Bank* 31°50N 35°16E **123** B2
Hjalmar L. *Canada* 61°33N 109°25W **297** A7
Hjälmaren *Sweden* 59°18N 15°40E **162** E9
Hjältevad *Sweden* 57°38N 15°20E **163** G9
Hjalteyri *Iceland* 65°55N 18°18W **155** B8
Hjartdal *Norway* 59°37N 8°41E **164** E5
Hjelmelandsvågen *Norway* 59°14N 6°10E **164** E3
Hjelset *Norway* 62°48N 7°30E **164** B4
Hjerkinn *Norway* 62°13N 9°33E **164** B6
Hjo *Sweden* 58°22N 14°17E **163** F8
Hjørring *Denmark* 57°29N 9°59E **163** G3
Hjörsey *Iceland* 64°32N 22°11W **155** C4
Hjort Trench *S. Ocean* 58°0S 157°30E **151** B10
Hjortekær *Denmark* 55°47N 12°32E **118** A3
Hjortespring *Denmark* 55°44N 12°25E **118** A2
Hjortkvarn *Sweden* 58°54N 15°26E **163** F9
Hjukse *Norway* 59°31N 9°19E **164** E6
Hkakabo Razi *Burma* 28°25N 97°23E **228** C1
Hkakabo Razi △ *Burma* 28°0N 97°55E **241** A6
Hkamti *Burma* 26°0N 95°39E **241** C5
Hko-lam *Burma* 21°7N 98°5E **241** E7
Hko-ut *Burma* 20°58N 98°2E **241** E7
Hkyenhpa *Burma* 27°43N 97°25E **241** B6
Hlaingbwe *Burma* 17°8N 97°50E **241** G6
Hlinsko *Czechia* 49°45N 15°54E **180** B8
Hlobane *S. Africa* 27°42S 31°0E **271** C5
Hlohovec *Slovakia* 48°26N 17°49E **181** C10
Hlubočepy *Czechia* 50°2N 14°23E **135** B2
Hlučín *Czechia* 49°54N 18°11E **181** B11
Hluhluwe *S. Africa* 28°1S 32°15E **271** C5
Hluhluwe ⌂ *S. Africa* 22°10S 32°5E **271** B5
Hlukhiv *Ukraine* 51°40N 33°58E **189** G7
Hlwaze *Burma* 18°54N 96°37E **241** F6
Hlyboka *Ukraine* 48°5N 25°56E **183** B10
Hlybokaye *Belarus* 55°10N 27°45E **188** E4
Hnappadalssýsla *Iceland* 64°50N 22°30W **155** C4
Hnífsdalur *Iceland* 66°7N 23°8W **155** A3
Hnúšťa *Slovakia* 48°35N 19°58E **181** C12
Ho *Ghana* 6°37N 0°27E **263** D5
Ho Chi Minh City = Thanh Pho Ho Chi Minh *Vietnam* 10°58N 106°40E **237** G6
Ho Chung *Hong Kong, China* 22°21N 114°14E **122** A3
Ho Hoa Binh *Vietnam* 20°50N 105°0E **228** G5
Ho Thac Ba *Vietnam* 21°42N 105°1E **236** A5
Ho Thuong *Vietnam* 19°32N 105°48E **236** C5
Hoa Binh *Vietnam* 20°50N 105°20E **228** G5
Hoa Hiep *Vietnam* 11°34N 105°51E **237** G5
Hoai Nhon *Vietnam* 14°28N 109°1E **236** E7
Hoang Lien △ *Vietnam* 21°30N 105°32E **236** B5
Hoang Lien Son *Vietnam* 22°0N 104°0E **228** F4
Hoang Sa, Dao = Paracel Is. *S. China Sea* 15°50N 112°0E **230** A4
Hoanib ➜ *Namibia* 19°27S 12°46E **270** A2
Hoare B. *Canada* 65°17N 62°30W **295** D19
Hoarusib ➜ *Namibia* 19°3S 12°36E **270** A2
Hobart *Tas., Australia* 42°50S 147°21E **281** G4
Hobart *Ind., U.S.A.* 41°32N 87°15W **311** C9
Hobart *Okla., U.S.A.* 35°1N 99°6W **314** D5
Hobbs *U.S.A.* 32°42N 103°8W **305** K12
Hobbs Coast *Antarctica* 74°50S 131°0W **151** D14
Hobe Sound *U.S.A.* 27°4N 80°8W **317** H9
Hobo *Colombia* 2°35N 75°30W **328** C2
Hoboken *Ga., U.S.A.* 31°11N 82°8W **316** D7
Hoboken *New York, U.S.A.* **132** d1
Hobro *Denmark* 56°39N 9°46E **163** H3
Hobsons B. *Australia* 37°51S 144°55E **128** B1
Hoburgen *Sweden* 56°55N 18°7E **163** H12
Hobyo *Somalia* 5°25N 48°30E **267** C6
Hocalar *Turkey* 38°36N 30°0E **205** C11
Hochbrück *Germany* 48°14N 11°37E **131** A2
Hochelaga *Canada* 45°32N 73°33W **130** A2
Hochfeld *Namibia* 21°28S 17°58E **270** B2
Hochharz △ *Germany* 51°48N 10°38E **178** D6
Hochschwab *Austria* 47°35N 15°0E **180** D8
Höchstadt *Germany* 49°42N 10°47E **179** F6
Hochtaunus ⌂ *Germany* 50°20N 8°30E **179** E4
Hoch'uan = Hechuan *China* 30°2N 106°12E **228** B6
Hochwan = Hechuan *China* 30°2N 106°12E **228** B6
Hockenheim *Germany* 49°19N 8°32E **179** F4
Hockley = Levelland *U.S.A.* 33°35N 102°23W **314** E3
Hodaka-Dake *Japan* 36°17N 137°39E **223** A9
Hodeida = Al Ḩudaydah *Yemen* 14°50N 43°0E **248** D3
Hodgeville *Canada* 50°7N 106°58W **297** C7
Hodgson *Canada* 51°13N 97°36W **297** C9
Hodh El Gharbi □ *Mauritania* 16°30N 10°0W **262** B3
Hódmezővásárhely *Hungary* 46°28N 20°22E **182** D5
Hodna, Chott el *Algeria* 35°26N 4°43E **261** A5
Hodo-dan *N. Korea* 39°23N 127°32E **224** C3
Hodonín *Czechia* 48°50N 17°10E **181** C10
Hœdic, Î. de *France* 47°20N 2°53W **172** E4
Hoegi *S. Korea* 37°35N 127°3E **137** B2
Hoeilaart *Belgium* 50°46N 4°28E **116** B2
Hoek van Holland *Neths.* 52°0N 4°7E **170** C4
Hoengseong *S. Korea* 37°29N 127°59E **224** D3
Hoeryong *N. Korea* 42°30N 129°45E **224** A4
Hoeyang *N. Korea* 38°43N 127°36E **224** C3
Hof *Bayern, Germany* 50°19N 11°55E **179** E7
Hof *Austurland Iceland* 65°39N 15°0W **155** B11
Hof *Austurland Iceland* 64°33N 14°40W **155** C12
Hof *Vestfold, Norway* 59°32N 10°5E **164** E7
Hofburg *Vienna, Austria* **142** b1
Hofei = Hefei *China* 31°52N 117°18E **229** B11
Hoffell *Iceland* 64°23N 15°20W **155** C11
Hoffman I. *U.S.A.* 40°34N 74°3W **132** C1
Hofgarten *Munich, Germany* **131** a3
Hofgeismar *Germany* 51°29N 9°23E **178** D5
Hofheim *Germany* 50°5N 8°26E **179** E4
Hofmeyr *S. Africa* 31°39S 25°50E **270** D4
Höfn *Iceland* 64°15N 15°13W **155** C11
Hofors *Sweden* 60°31N 16°15E **162** D10
Hofsjökull *Iceland* 64°49N 18°48W **155** C8
Hofsós *Iceland* 65°53N 19°26W **155** B7
Hōfu *Japan* 34°3N 131°34E **222** C3
Hog Harbour *Vanuatu* 15°8S 167°6E **287** E5
Hog I. = Paradise I. *Bahamas* 25°6N 77°19W **153** b
Hog I. *Grenada* 12°0N 61°44W **323** q
Hog Pt. *Antigua & B.* 17°41N 61°47W **322** c
Hogan Group *Australia* 39°13S 147°1E **281** F4
Höganäs *Sweden* 56°12N 12°33E **163** H6
Hogansville *U.S.A.* 33°10N 84°55W **316** B5
Hogarth, Mt. *Australia* 21°48S 136°58E **280** C2
Hoge Kempen △ *Belgium* 51°6N 5°35E **170** C5
Hoge Veluwe △ *Neths.* 52°5N 5°46E **170** B5
Høgeloft *Norway* 61°3N 8°12E **164** C5
Hogenakai Falls *India* 12°6N 77°50E **245** H3
Hoggar = Ahaggar *Algeria* 23°0N 6°30E **261** D6
Högsäter *Sweden* 58°38N 12°5E **163** F6
Högsby *Sweden* 57°10N 16°1E **163** G10
Högsjö *Sweden* 59°4N 15°44E **162** E9
Hogsty Reef *Bahamas* 21°41N 73°48W **321** B5
Hoh ➜ *U.S.A.* 47°45N 124°29W **306** C2
Hoh Xil Shan *China* 36°30N 89°0E **218** D6
Hohd ech Chargui □ *Mauritania* 19°0N 7°15W **260** E3
Hohe Acht *Germany* 50°22N 7°0E **179** E3
Hohe Tauern *Austria* 47°11N 12°40E **180** D5
Hohe Tauern △ *Austria* 47°5N 12°20E **180** D5
Hohenau *Austria* 48°36N 16°55E **181** C9
Hohenbrunn *Germany* 48°2N 11°42E **131** B3
Hohenelbe = Vrchlabí *Czechia* 50°38N 15°37E **180** A8
Hohenems *Austria* 47°22N 9°42E **180** D2
Hohenloher Ebene *Germany* 49°14N 9°36E **179** F5
Hohenmauth = Vysoké Mýto *Czechia* 49°58N 16°10E **181** B9
Hohensalza = Inowrocław *Poland* 52°50N 18°12E **185** F5
Hohensalzburg = Lunino *Russia* 53°38N 45°18E **190** D7
Hohenschönhausen *Germany* 52°33N 13°30E **115** A4
Hohenstadt = Zábřeh *Czechia* 49°53N 16°52E **181** B9
Hohenstein = Olsztynek *Poland* 53°34N 20°19E **184** E7
Hohenwald *U.S.A.* 35°33N 87°33W **315** D11
Hohenwestedt *Germany* 54°5N 9°40E **178** A5
Hoher Rhön = Rhön *Germany* 50°24N 9°58E **178** E5
Hoher Vogelsberg ⌂ *Germany* 51°45N 9°35E **178** D5
Hohes Venn *Belgium* 50°30N 6°5E **170** D6
Hohes Venn-Eifel ⌂ *Europe* 50°30N 6°10E **178** E2
Hohhot *China* 40°52N 111°40E **226** D6
Hohoe *Ghana* 7°8N 0°32E **263** D5
Hoi An *Vietnam* 15°53N 108°19E **236** E7
Hoi Xuan *Vietnam* 20°25N 105°9E **228** G5
Hoihow = Haikou *China* 20°1N 110°16E **229** a
Hoisington *U.S.A.* 38°31N 98°47W **308** F4
Hojai *India* 26°2N 92°54E **241** B4
Hojambaz *Turkmenistan* 38°7N 65°0E **216** E6
Højer *Denmark* 54°58N 8°42E **163** K2
Hōjō *Japan* 33°58N 132°46E **222** D4
Hok *Sweden* 57°31N 14°16E **163** G8
Hok Tsui *Hong Kong, China* 22°12N 114°14E **122** B3
Hokang = Hegang *China* 47°20N 130°19E **219** B15
Hökensås *Sweden* 58°0N 14°5E **163** G8
Hökerum *Sweden* 57°51N 13°16E **163** G7
Hokianga Harbour *N.Z.* 35°31S 173°22E **284** B2
Hokitika *N.Z.* 42°42S 171°0E **285** C6
Hokkaidō □ *Japan* 43°30N 143°0E **220** C11
Hokksund *Norway* 59°48N 9°54E **164** E6
Hokuto *Japan* 41°49N 140°39E **220** D10
Hol-Hol *Djibouti* 11°20N 42°50E **257** E5
Hola *Kenya* 1°29S 40°2E **268** B4
Hola Prystan *Ukraine* 46°29N 32°32E **189** J7
Holakas *Greece* 35°57N 27°53E **206** F11
Holalkere *India* 14°2N 76°11E **245** G3
Hólar *Iceland* 65°44N 19°8W **155** B7
Holargos = Cholargos *Greece* 37°59N 23°48E **112** B2
Holašovice *Czechia* 48°57N 14°15E **180** C7
Holbæk *Denmark* 55°43N 11°43E **163** J5
Holborn *London, U.K.* **125** a4
Holbrook *N.S.W., Australia* 35°42S 147°18E **283** C7
Holbrook *Ariz., U.S.A.* 34°54N 110°10W **305** J8
Holcomb *U.S.A.* 42°54N 77°25W **312** D7
Holden *Mo., U.S.A.* 38°43N 94°0W **310** F3
Holden *Utah, U.S.A.* 39°6N 112°16W **304** G7
Holden, L. *U.S.A.* 28°30N 81°23W **133** B2
Holdenville *U.S.A.* 35°5N 96°24W **314** D6
Holdich *Argentina* 45°57S 68°13W **336** C3
Holdrege *U.S.A.* 40°26N 99°23W **308** E4
Hole-Narsipur *India* 12°48N 76°16E **245** H3
Holešov *Czechia* 49°20N 17°35E **181** B10
Holešovice *Czechia* 50°6N 14°28E **135** B2
Holetown *Barbados* 13°11N 59°38W **323** r
Holgate *U.S.A.* 41°15N 84°8W **311** C12
Holguín *Cuba* 20°50N 76°20W **320** B4
Holič *Slovakia* 48°49N 17°10E **181** C10
Holice *Czechia* 50°5N 16°0E **180** A8
Holiday *U.S.A.* 28°11N 82°44W **317** G7
Holiday Park *U.S.A.* 26°8N 80°7W **129** B3
Höljes *Sweden* 60°50N 12°35E **162** D6
Hollabrunn *Austria* 48°34N 16°5E **180** C9
Hollams Bird I. *Namibia* 24°40S 14°30E **270** B1
Holland = Netherlands ■ *Europe* 52°0N 5°30E **170** C5
Holland *Mich., U.S.A.* 42°47N 86°7W **311** B10
Holland *N.Y., U.S.A.* 42°38N 78°32W **312** D6
Holland B. *Jamaica* 17°57N 76°13W **320** a
Holland Centre *Canada* 44°23N 80°47W **312** B4
Holland Patent *U.S.A.* 43°14N 75°15W **313** C9
Holland Tunnel *New York, U.S.A.* **132** d1
Holland Village *Singapore* 1°18N 103°47E **138** B2
Hollandale *U.S.A.* 33°10N 90°51W **315** E9
Hollandia = Jayapura *Indonesia* 2°28S 140°38E **231** E10
Holley *U.S.A.* 43°14N 78°2W **312** C6
Hollfeld *Germany* 49°56N 11°18E **179** F7
Hollidaysburg *U.S.A.* 40°26N 78°24W **312** F6
Hollis *U.S.A.* 34°41N 99°55W **314** D5
Hollis Reservoir *Trin. & Tob.* 10°40N 61°10W **323** t
Hollister *Calif., U.S.A.* 36°51N 121°24W **306** J5
Hollister *Idaho, U.S.A.* 42°21N 114°35W **304** E6
Höllriegelskreuth *Germany* 48°2N 11°30E **131** B1
Höllviken *Sweden* 55°26N 12°58E **163** J6
Höllviksnäs = Höllviken *Sweden* 55°26N 12°58E **163** J6
Holly *U.S.A.* 42°48N 83°38W **311** B13
Holly Hill *Fla., U.S.A.* 29°16N 81°3W **317** F8
Holly Hill *S.C., U.S.A.* 33°19N 80°25W **316** B9
Holly Springs *Ga., U.S.A.* 34°10N 84°30W **316** A5
Holly Springs *Miss., U.S.A.* 34°46N 89°27W **315** D10
Hollywood *Wicklow, Ireland* 53°6N 6°35W **166** B6
Hollywood *Calif., U.S.A.* 34°5N 118°19W **126** B3
Hollywood *Fla., U.S.A.* 26°0N 80°8W **129** B2
Hollywood Bowl *U.S.A.* 34°7N 118°20W **126** B2
Holman = Ulukhaktok *Canada* 70°44N 117°44W **294** C8
Hólmavík *Iceland* 65°42N 21°40W **155** B5
Holmen *Norway* 59°40N 10°28E **164** E7
Holmen *Oppland, Norway* 60°40N 10°22E **164** D7
Holmen *Wis., U.S.A.* 43°58N 91°15W **308** D8
Holmenkollen *Norway* 59°57N 10°41E **164** E7
Holmes Beach *U.S.A.* 27°31N 82°43W **317** H7
Holmes Cr. ➜ *U.S.A.* 30°30N 85°50W **316** D4
Holmes Reefs *Australia* 16°27S 148°0E **280** B4
Holmestrand *Norway* 59°31N 10°14E **164** E7
Holmgård *Sweden* 59°14N 18°0E **139** B1
Holmlia *Norway* 59°49N 10°46E **133** B5
Holmsjö *Sweden* 56°25N 15°32E **163** H9
Holmsjön *Västernorrland, Sweden* 62°41N 16°33E **162** B10
Holmsjön *Västernorrland, Sweden* 62°26N 15°20E **162** B9
Holmsland Klit *Denmark* 56°0N 8°5E **163** J2
Holmsund *Sweden* 63°41N 20°20E **160** E19
Holocaust Memorial *Jerusalem* 31°47N 35°11E **123** B2
Holocaust Memorial Park *Boston, U.S.A.* **116** b2
Holod *Romania* 46°49N 22°8E **182** D7
Holon *Israel* 32°0N 34°46E **251** G5
Holopaw *U.S.A.* 28°8N 81°5W **317** G8
Holovne *Ukraine* 51°20N 24°3E **185** G11
Holøydal *Norway* 62°12N 11°27E **164** B8
Holozubyntsi *Ukraine* 48°50N 26°55E **183** B11
Holroyd ➜ *Australia* 14°10S 141°36E **280** A3
Holstebro *Denmark* 56°22N 8°37E **163** H2
Holsteinische Schweiz ⌂ *Germany* 54°8N 10°30E **178** A6
Holsteinsborg = Sisimiut *Greenland* 66°40N 53°30W **154** D5
Holsworthy *U.K.* 50°48N 4°22W **169** G3
Holt *Iceland* 63°33N 19°48W **155** D7
Holt *Fla., U.S.A.* 30°43N 86°45W **317** E3
Holt *Mich., U.S.A.* 42°39N 84°31W **311** B12
Holton *Nfld. & L., Canada* 54°31N 57°12W **299** B8
Holton *Kans., U.S.A.* 39°28N 95°44W **308** F6
Holts Summit *U.S.A.* 38°38N 92°7W **310** F4
Holtville *U.S.A.* 32°49N 115°23W **307** N11
Holualoa *U.S.A.* 19°37N 155°57W **302** D6
Holum *Norway* 58°6N 7°32E **164** F4
Holwerd *Neths.* 53°22N 5°54E **170** A5
Holy Cross *U.S.A.* 62°12N 159°46W **303** E8
Holy I. *Anglesey, U.K.* 53°17N 4°37W **168** D3
Holy I. *Northumberland, U.K.* 55°40N 1°47W **168** B6
Holyhead *U.K.* 53°18N 4°38W **168** D3
Holyoke *Colo., U.S.A.* 40°35N 102°18W **304** F12
Holyoke *Mass., U.S.A.* 42°12N 72°37W **313** D12
Holyrood *Canada* 47°27N 53°8W **299** C9
Holyrood House, Palace of *U.K.* 55°57N 3°10W **121** B3
Holysloot *Neths.* 52°25N 5°2E **112** A3
Holzkirchen *Germany* 47°52N 11°42E **179** H7
Holzminden *Germany* 51°50N 9°28E **178** D5
Homa Bay *Kenya* 0°36S 34°30E **268** C3
Homalin *Burma* 24°55N 95°0E **241** C5
Homand *Iran* 32°28N 59°37E **247** C8
Homathko ➜ *Canada* 51°0N 124°56W **296** C4
Homberg *Germany* 51°2N 9°25E **178** D5
Hombori *Mali* 15°20N 1°38W **263** B4
Hombori Tondo *Mali* 15°16N 1°40W **263** B4
Homburg *Germany* 49°28N 7°18E **179** F3
Home B. *Canada* 68°40N 67°10W **295** D18
Home Hill *Australia* 19°43S 147°25E **280** B4
Home Reef *Tonga* 18°59S 174°47W **287** P13
Homedale *U.S.A.* 43°37N 116°56W **304** E5
Homei *Taiwan* 24°7N 120°29E **225** B2
Homeland *U.S.A.* 30°51N 82°1W **316** E7
Homer *Alaska, U.S.A.* 59°39N 151°33W **303** G10
Homer *Ill., U.S.A.* 40°4N 87°57W **311** D9
Homer *La., U.S.A.* 32°48N 93°4W **314** E8
Homer *Mich., U.S.A.* 42°9N 84°49W **311** B12
Homer *N.Y., U.S.A.* 42°38N 76°10W **313** D8
Homer City *U.S.A.* 40°32N 79°10W **312** F5
Homert ⌂ *Germany* 51°15N 8°0E **178** D4
Homerton *U.K.* 51°32N 0°2W **125** A3
Homerville *U.S.A.* 31°2N 82°45W **316** D7
Homestead *Queens., Australia* 20°20S 145°40E **280** C4
Homestead *Fla., U.S.A.* 25°28N 80°29W **317** K9
Homestead ⌂ *U.S.A.* 40°17N 96°50W **308** E5
Hometown *U.S.A.* 41°44N 87°42W **119** C2
Homewood *U.S.A.* 41°34N 87°40W **311** C9
Hommelvik *Norway* 63°25N 10°48E **164** A7
Hommersåk *Norway* 58°56N 5°50E **164** F2
Homnabad *India* 17°45N 77°11E **244** F3
Homoine *Mozam.* 23°55S 35°8E **271** B6
Homoljske Planina *Serbia* 44°10N 21°45E **202** B5
Homonhon I. *Phil.* 10°44N 125°43E **233** F5
Homorod *Romania* 46°5N 25°15E **183** D10
Homosassa Springs *U.S.A.* 28°48N 82°35W **317** G7
Homs = Al Khums *Libya* 32°40N 14°17E **258** B2
Homs = Ḩimş *Syria* 34°40N 36°45E **250** D7
Homyel *Belarus* 52°28N 31°0E **177** B16
Homyel □ *Belarus* 52°40N 30°10E **189** F6
Hon Chong *Vietnam* 10°25N 104°30E **237** G5
Hon Hai *Vietnam* 10°0N 109°0E **237** H7
Hon Me *Vietnam* 19°23N 105°56E **236** C5
Honan = Henan □ *China* 34°0N 114°0E **226** H8
Honanchō *Japan* 35°40N 139°39E **140** A2
Hōnaunau *U.S.A.* 19°26N 155°55W **302** D6
Honavar *India* 14°17N 74°27E **245** G2
Honaz *Turkey* 37°46N 29°18E **205** D11
Honbetsu *Japan* 43°7N 143°37E **220** C11
Honcho *Japan* 35°40N 139°41E **140** A3
Honcut *U.S.A.* 39°20N 121°32W **306** F5
Honda *Colombia* 5°12N 74°45W **328** B3
Honda B. *Phil.* 9°53N 118°49E **233** G2
Hondarribia *Spain* 43°22N 1°47W **196** B3
Hondeklipbaai *S. Africa* 30°19S 17°17E **270** D2
Honden *Japan* 35°43N 139°50E **140** A4
Hondo *Japan* 32°27N 130°12E **222** E2
Hondo *Tex., U.S.A.* 29°21N 99°9W **314** G5
Hondo, Río ➜ *Belize* 18°25N 88°21W **319** D7
Hondo, Río ➜ *Calif., U.S.A.* 33°55N 118°11W **126** B4
Honduras ■ *Cent. Amer.* 14°40N 86°30W **320** D2
Honduras, G. de *Caribbean* 16°50N 87°0W **320** C2
Hønefoss *Norway* 60°10N 10°18E **164** D7
Honesdale *U.S.A.* 41°34N 75°16W **313** E9
Honey Harbour *Canada* 44°52N 79°49W **312** B5
Honey L. *U.S.A.* 40°15N 120°19W **306** E6
Honfleur *France* 49°25N 0°13E **172** C7
Høng *Denmark* 55°31N 11°18E **163** J5
Hong ➜ *Asia* 20°16N 106°34E **236** B5
Hong Gai *Vietnam* 20°57N 107°5E **228** G6
Hong He ➜ *China* 32°25N 115°35E **229** A10
Hong Hu *China* 29°54N 113°24E **229** C9
Hong Kong □ *China* 22°11N 114°14E **219** a
Hong Kong I. *China* 22°16N 114°12E **122** B2
Hong Kong Int. ✈ (HKG) *Hong Kong, China* 22°19N 113°57E **122** B1
Hong Kong Univ. *China* 22°16N 114°8E **122** B2
Honga *Japan* 15°9S 15°12E **265** F3
Hong'an *China* 31°20N 114°40E **229** B10
Hongcheon *S. Korea* 37°44N 127°53E **224** D3
Hongdo *S. Korea* 34°41N 125°12E **224** E2
Honghai Wan *China* 22°40N 115°0E **229** F10
Honghe *China* 23°25N 102°25E **228** F4
Honghu *China* 29°50N 113°30E **229** C9
Hongjie *S. Korea* 37°35N 126°56E **137** B1
Hongjiang *China* 27°7N 109°59E **228** D7
Hongjimun Tunnel *S. Korea* 37°37N 126°58E **137** B1
Honglong *China* 31°16N 121°29E **138** B1
Hongor *Mongolia* 45°45N 112°50E **226** B7
Hongqiao *China* 31°11N 121°22E **138** B1
Hongseong *S. Korea* 36°37N 126°38E **224** D3
Hongshan *China* 36°38N 117°58E **226** F9
Hongshui He ➜ *China* 23°48N 109°30E **228** F7
Hongtong *China* 36°16N 111°40E **226** F6
Honguedo, Détroit d' *Canada* 49°15N 64°0W **299** C7
Hongwon *N. Korea* 40°0N 127°56E **224** C3
Hongya *China* 29°57N 103°22E **228** C4
Hongyuan *China* 32°51N 102°40E **228** A4
Hongze Hu *China* 33°15N 118°35E **227** H10
Honiara *Solomon Is.* 9°27S 159°57E **287** M10
Honiton *U.K.* 50°47N 3°11W **169** G4
Honjō = Yurihonjō *Japan* 39°23N 140°3E **220** E10
Honjō *Japan* 36°14N 139°11E **223** A11
Honjyo *Japan* 35°41N 139°48E **140** A3
Honkawane *Japan* 35°5N 138°5E **223** B10
Honkorâb, Ras *Egypt* 24°35N 35°10E **256** C4
Honnali *India* 14°15N 75°40E **245** G2
Honningsvåg *Norway* 70°59N 25°59E **160** A21
Hönö *Sweden* 57°41N 11°39E **163** G5
Honoka'a *U.S.A.* 20°5N 155°28W **302** C6
Honokai Hale *U.S.A.* 21°20N 158°6W **302** K13
Honolulu *U.S.A.* 21°19N 157°52W **302** K14
Honolulu District *U.S.A.* 21°19N 157°46W **302** K14
Honolulu Int. ✈ (HNL) *U.S.A.* 21°19N 157°55W **302** K14
Honomu *U.S.A.* 19°52N 155°7W **302** D6
Honoré Mercier, Pont *Canada* 45°24N 73°39W **130** B1
Honouliuli *U.S.A.* 21°22N 158°2W **302** K13
Hönow *Germany* 52°32N 13°38E **115** A4
Honshū *Japan* 36°0N 138°0E **223** A8
Hontoria del Pinar *Spain* 41°50N 3°10W **196** D1
Honu'apo B. *U.S.A.* 19°5N 155°33W **302** D6
Hood, I. = Española, I. *Ecuador* 1°23S 89°39W **330** a
Hood, Mt. *U.S.A.* 45°23N 121°42W **304** D3
Hood, Pt. *Australia* 34°23S 119°34E **279** F2
Hood Pt. *Papua N. G.* 10°4S 147°45E **286** F4
Hood River *U.S.A.* 45°43N 121°31W **304** D3
Hoodsport *U.S.A.* 47°24N 123°9W **306** C3
Hooge *Germany* 54°34N 8°33E **178** A4
Hoogeveen *Neths.* 52°44N 6°28E **170** B6
Hoogezand-Sappemeer *Neths.* 53°9N 6°45E **170** A6
Hooghly = Hugli ➜ *India* 21°56N 88°4E **243** J13
Hooghly-Chinsura = Chunchura *India* 22°53N 88°27E **243** H13
Hook *U.K.* 51°22N 0°17W **125** B2
Hook Hd. *Ireland* 52°7N 6°56W **166** D5
Hook I. *Australia* 20°4S 149°0E **280** b
Hook of Holland = Hoek van Holland *Neths.* 52°0N 4°7E **170** C4
Hooker *U.S.A.* 36°52N 101°13W **314** C4
Hooker Creek = Lajamanu *Australia* 18°23S 130°38E **278** C5
Hooker Creek ◎ *Australia* 18°6S 130°23E **278** C5
Ho'olehua *U.S.A.* 21°10N 157°5W **302** B4
Hoonah *U.S.A.* 58°7N 135°27W **296** B1
Hoop *Bonaire* 12°7N 68°17W **322** h
Hooper Bay *U.S.A.* 61°32N 166°6W **303** F6
Hoopeston *U.S.A.* 40°28N 87°40W **311** D9
Hoopstad *S. Africa* 27°50S 25°55E **270** C4
Höör *Sweden* 55°56N 13°33E **163** J7
Hoorn *Neths.* 52°38N 5°4E **170** B5
Hoover *U.S.A.* 33°24N 86°49W **315** E11
Hoover Dam *U.S.A.* 36°1N 114°44W **307** K12
Hooversville *U.S.A.* 40°9N 78°55W **312** F6
Hop Bottom *U.S.A.* 41°42N 75°46W **313** E9
Hopa *Turkey* 41°28N 41°30E **213** B9
Hope *B.C., Canada* 49°25N 121°25W **296** D4
Hope *Ariz., U.S.A.* 33°43N 113°42W **307** M13
Hope *Ark., U.S.A.* 33°40N 93°36W **314** E8
Hope *Ind., U.S.A.* 39°18N 85°46W **311** E11
Hope, L. *S. Austral., Australia* 28°24S 139°18E **281** D2
Hope, L. *W. Austral., Australia* 32°35S 120°15E **279** F3
Hope, Pt. *U.S.A.* 68°21N 166°47W **303** B6
Hope Bay *Jamaica* 18°12N 76°34W **320** a
Hope I. *Canada* 44°55N 80°11W **312** B4
Hope Town *Bahamas* 26°35N 76°57W **320** A4
Hope Vale *Australia* 15°16S 145°20E **280** B4
Hope Vale ◎ *Australia* 15°8S 145°15E **280** B4
Hopedale *Nfld. & L., Canada* 55°28N 60°13W **299** A7
Hopedale *Mass., U.S.A.* 42°8N 71°33W **313** D13
Hopefield *S. Africa* 33°3S 18°22E **270** D2
Hopei = Hebei □ *China* 39°0N 116°0E **226** E9
Hopelchén *Mexico* 19°46N 89°51W **319** D7
Hopetoun *Vic., Australia* 35°42S 142°22E **282** C5
Hopetoun *W. Austral., Australia* 33°57S 120°7E **279** F3
Hopetown *S. Africa* 29°34S 24°3E **270** C3
Hopewell *U.S.A.* 37°18N 77°17W **309** G15
Hopfgarten *Austria* 47°27N 12°10E **180** D5
Hopin *Burma* 24°58N 96°30E **241** C6
Hoping *Changhua, Taiwan* 24°10N 120°56E **225** B2
Hoping *T'aitung, Taiwan* 23°4N 121°20E **225** C3
Hopkins *U.S.A.* 40°33N 94°49W **308** E6
Hopkins, L. *Australia* 24°15S 128°35E **278** D4
Hopkinsville *U.S.A.* 36°52N 87°29W **308** G10
Hopland *U.S.A.* 38°58N 123°7W **306** G3
Hopong *Burma* 20°47N 97°11E **241** E6
Hopwood's Ferry = Echuca *Australia* 36°10S 144°45E **283** D6
Hoque *Angola* 14°40S 13°55E **265** E2
Hoquiam *U.S.A.* 46°59N 123°53W **306** D3
Hora Hoverla *Ukraine* 48°7N 24°41E **183** B9
Hora Sfakion = Chora Sfakion *Greece* 35°15N 24°9E **207** E5
Hōrai *Japan* 34°58N 137°32E **223** C9
Horana *Sri Lanka* 6°43N 80°4E **245** L5
Horasan *Turkey* 40°3N 42°11E **213** B10
Horažďovice *Czechia* 49°19N 13°42E **180** B6
Horb *Germany* 48°26N 8°47E **179** G4
Hörby *Sweden* 55°51N 13°40E **163** J7
Horcajo de Santiago *Spain* 39°50N 3°1W **196** F1
Hordabø *Norway* 60°42N 4°54E **164** D1
Hordaland □ *Norway* 60°25N 6°15E **164** D3
Hordern Hills *Australia* 20°15S 130°0E **278** D5
Horezu *Romania* 45°6N 24°0E **183** E8
Horgen *Switz.* 47°15N 8°35E **179** H4
Horgos *China* 44°10N 80°25E **217** D10
Horgoš *Serbia* 46°10N 20°0E **182** D4
Horikiri *Japan* 35°44N 139°50E **140** A4
Horinchove *Ukraine* 48°16N 23°26E **183** B8
Horinger *China* 40°28N 111°48E **226** D6
Horizontina *Brazil* 27°37S 54°19W **335** B5
Horki *Belarus* 54°17N 30°59E **188** E6
Horlick Mts. *Antarctica* 84°0S 102°0W **151** E15
Horlivka *Ukraine* 48°19N 38°5E **189** H10
Hormak *Iran* 29°58N 60°51E **247** D9
Hormigueros *Puerto Rico* 18°8N 67°8W **321** b
Hormoz *Iran* 27°35N 55°0E **247** E7
Hormoz, Jaz.-ye *Iran* 27°8N 56°28E **247** E8
Hormozgān □ *Iran* 27°30N 56°0E **247** E8
Hormuz, Kūh-e *Iran* 27°27N 55°10E **247** E7
Hormuz, Str. of *The Gulf* 26°30N 56°30E **247** E8
Horn *Austria* 48°39N 15°40E **180** C8
Horn *Vestfirðir Iceland* 66°28N 22°25W **155** A4
Horn *Sweden* 57°54N 15°51E **163** G9
Horn ➜ *Canada* 61°30N 118°1W **296** A5
Horn, Cape = Hornos, C. de *Chile* 55°50S 67°30W **336** E3
Horn, Is. *Wall. & F. Is.* 14°16S 178°6W **277** C15
Horn Head *Ireland* 55°14N 8°0W **166** A3
Horn I. *Australia* 10°37S 142°17E **286** F2
Horn Plateau *Canada* 62°15N 119°15W **296** A5
Horn Pond *U.S.A.* 42°28N 71°9W **116** A1
Hornachuelos *Spain* 37°50N 5°14W **195** H5
Hornavan *Sweden* 66°15N 17°30E **160** C17
Hornbeck *U.S.A.* 31°20N 93°24W **314** F8
Hornbrook *U.S.A.* 41°55N 122°33W **304** F2
Hornburg *Germany* 52°2N 10°37E **178** C6
Hornby *N.Z.* 43°33S 172°33E **285** D7
Horncastle *U.K.* 53°13N 0°7W **168** D7
Hornchurch *U.K.* 51°33N 0°14E **125** A5
Horndal *Sweden* 60°18N 16°23E **162** D10
Hornell *U.S.A.* 42°20N 77°40W **312** D7
Hornell L. *Canada* 62°20N 119°25W **296** A5
Hornepayne *Canada* 49°14N 84°48W **298** C3
Horni *Czechia* 50°2N 14°33E **135** B3
Horní Planá *Czechia* 48°46N 14°2E **180** C7
Horní Počernice *Czechia* 50°6N 14°36E **135** B3
Hornindal *Norway* 61°58N 6°30E **164** C3
Hornindalsvatnet *Norway* 61°55N 6°20E **164** C3
Hornings Mills *Canada* 44°9N 80°12W **312** B4
Hornitos *U.S.A.* 37°30N 120°14W **306** H6
Hornopirén △ *Chile* 41°58S 72°17W **336** B2
Hornos, C. de *Chile* 55°50S 67°30W **336** E3
Hornos Is. *Papua N. G.* 2°12S 147°45E **286** B4
Hornoy-le-Bourg *France* 49°50N 1°54E **173** C8
Hornsby *Australia* 33°42S 151°2E **283** B9
Hornsea *U.K.* 53°55N 0°11W **168** D7
Hornsey *U.K.* 51°35N 0°7W **125** A3
Hornsjø *Norway* 61°19N 10°38E **164** C7
Hornslandet *Sweden* 61°35N 17°37E **162** C11
Hornslet *Denmark* 56°19N 10°19E **163** H4
Hörnum *Germany* 54°45N 8°17E **178** A4
Horobetsu = Noboribetsu *Japan* 42°24N 141°6E **220** C10
Horodenka *Ukraine* 48°41N 25°29E **183** B10
Horodnya *Ukraine* 51°55N 31°33E **189** G6
Horodok *Khmelnytskyy, Ukraine* 49°10N 26°34E **177** D14
Horodok *Lviv, Ukraine* 49°46N 23°32E **177** D12
Horodyshche *Ukraine* 49°17N 31°27E **189** H6
Horokhiv *Ukraine* 50°30N 24°45E **177** C13
Horoměřice *Czechia* 50°8N 14°20E **135** B1
Horonobe *Japan* 45°7N 141°47E **220** A10
Horovice *Czechia* 49°48N 13°53E **180** B6
Horqin Youyi Qianqi *China* 46°5N 122°3E **227** A12
Horqin Zuoyi Zhongqi *China* 44°8N 123°18E **227** B12
Horqueta *Paraguay* 23°15S 56°55W **334** A4
Horred *Sweden* 57°22N 12°28E **163** G6
Horse Cr. ➜ *U.S.A.* 41°57N 103°58W **304** F12
Horse I. *Canada* 53°20N 99°6W **297** C9
Horse Is. *Canada* 50°15N 55°50W **299** B8
Horsefly L. *Canada* 52°25N 121°0W **296** C4
Horseheads *U.S.A.* 42°10N 76°49W **312** D8
Horsens *Denmark* 55°52N 9°51E **163** J3
Horseshoe Bend ⌂ *U.S.A.* 32°59N 85°44W **316** C4
Horseshoe Lake *Canada* 45°17N 79°51W **312** A5
Horsham *Vic., Australia* 36°44S 142°13E **282** D5
Horsham *W. Susx., U.K.* 51°4N 0°20W **169** F7
Horšovský Týn *Czechia* 49°31N 12°58E **180** B5
Horta *Azores* 38°32N 28°38W **153** d1
Hortaleza *Spain* 40°28N 3°38W **127** B2
Horten *Norway* 59°25N 10°32E **164** E7
Hortense *U.S.A.* 31°20N 81°57W **316** D8
Horti *India* 17°7N 75°47E **244** F2
Hortobágy ➜ *Hungary* 47°30N 21°6E **182** C6
Hortobágyi △ *Hungary* 47°36N 21°10E **182** C6
Horton *Kans., U.S.A.* 39°40N 95°32W **308** F6
Horton *Mo., U.S.A.* 37°58N 94°22W **310** G2
Horton ➜ *Canada* 69°56N 126°52W **294** D6
Hortus Botanicus *Amsterdam, Neths.* **112** b3
Horwood L. *Canada* 48°5N 82°20W **298** C3
Hosaina *Ethiopia* 7°30N 37°47E **257** F4
Hosapete *India* 15°15N 76°20E **245** G3
Hosdrug = Kanhangad *India* 12°21N 74°58E **245** H2
Hosdurga *India* 13°49N 76°17E **245** H3
Hosenofu *Libya* 23°41N 21°4E **258** D4
Ḩoseynābād *Khuzestān, Iran* 32°45N 48°20E **247** C6
Ḩoseynābād *Kordestān, Iran* 35°33N 47°8E **213** E12
Hosford *U.S.A.* 30°23N 84°48W **316** E5
Hôsh ʼÎsa *Egypt* 30°55N 30°17E **256** H7
Hoshangabad *India* 22°45N 77°45E **242** H7
Hoshiarpur *India* 31°30N 75°58E **242** D6
Hoskins *Papua N. G.* 5°29S 150°27E **286** C6
Hoskote *India* 13°4N 77°48E **245** H3
Hosoyama *Japan* 35°36N 139°31E **140** B2
Hospet = Hosapete *India* 15°15N 76°20E **245** G3
Hossegor *France* 43°39N 1°25W **174** E2
Hostafranchs *Spain* 41°21N 2°8E **114** A1
Hoste, I. *Chile* 55°0S 69°0W **336** E3
Hostens *France* 44°30N 0°40W **174** D3
Hostivař *Czechia* 50°3N 14°31E **135** B3
Hosur *India* 12°43N 77°49E **245** H3
Hot *Thailand* 18°8N 98°29E **236** C2
Hot Creek Range *U.S.A.* 38°40N 116°20W **304** G5
Hot Springs = Truth or Consequences *U.S.A.* 33°8N 107°15W **305** K10
Hot Springs *Ark., U.S.A.* 34°31N 93°3W **314** D8
Hot Springs *S. Dak., U.S.A.* 43°26N 103°29W **308** D2
Hot Springs △ *U.S.A.* 34°31N 93°3W **314** D8
Hotagen *Sweden* 63°59N 14°12E **160** E16
Hotan *China* 37°25N 79°55E **217** E9
Hotan He ➜ *China* 40°22N 80°56E **217** D10
Hotazel *S. Africa* 27°17S 22°58E **270** C3
Hotchkiss *U.S.A.* 38°48N 107°43W **304** G10
Hôtel des Invalides *Paris, France* **134** c2
Hotham, C. *Australia* 12°2S 131°18E **278** B5
Hoting *Sweden* 64°8N 16°15E **160** D17
Hotolisht *Albania* 41°10N 20°25E **202** E4
Hotspur Seamount *Atl. Oc.* 17°55S 35°55W **333** E4
Hotte, Massif de la *Haiti* 18°30N 73°45W **321** C5
Hottentotsbaai *Namibia* 26°8S 14°59E **270** C1
Hou Hai *China* 22°32N 113°56E **219** a
Houailou *N. Cal.* 21°17S 165°38E **288** d
Houat, Î. de *France* 47°24N 2°58W **172** E4
Houbětin *Czechia* 50°6N 14°33E **135** B3
Houbi = Houpi *Taiwan* 23°22N 120°21E **225** C2
Houdan *France* 48°48N 1°35E **173** D8
Houei Sai *Laos* 20°18N 100°26E **228** G3
Houeillès *France* 44°12N 0°2E **174** D4
Houffalize *Belgium* 50°8N 5°48E **170** D5
Hougang *Singapore* 1°22N 103°53E **138** A3
Houghton *Gauteng, S. Africa* 26°10S 28°3E **123** B2
Houghton *Mich., U.S.A.* 47°7N 88°34W **308** B9
Houghton *N.Y., U.S.A.* 42°25N 78°10W **312** D6
Houghton L. *U.S.A.* 44°21N 84°44W **309** C11
Houghton-le-Spring *U.K.* 54°51N 1°28W **168** C6
Houhora Heads *N.Z.* 34°49S 173°9E **284** A2
Houilles *France* 48°56N 2°11E **134** A2
Houli *Taiwan* 24°19N 120°44E **225** B2
Houlton *U.S.A.* 46°8N 67°51W **309** B20
Houlung *Taiwan* 24°37N 120°47E **225** B2
Houma *China* 35°36N 111°20E **226** G6
Houma *La., U.S.A.* 29°36N 90°43W **315** G9
Houmt Souk = Djerba *Tunisia* 33°48N 10°54E **258** B2
Houndé *Burkina Faso* 11°34N 3°31W **262** C4
Hounslow □ *U.K.* 51°28N 0°21W **125** B1
Houpi *Taiwan* 23°22N 120°21E **225** C2
Hourtin *France* 45°11N 1°4W **174** C2
Hourtin-Carcans, L. d' *France* 45°10N 1°6W **174** C2
Housatonic ➜ *U.S.A.* 41°10N 73°7W **313** E11
House of Nobility = Riddarhuset *Stockholm, Sweden* **139** c2
House of Parliament = Riksdagshuset *Stockholm, Sweden* **139** b2
Houses of Parliament *London, U.K.* **125** c3
Houston *B.C., Canada* 54°25N 126°39W **296** C3
Houston *Fla., U.S.A.* 30°15N 82°54W **316** E7
Houston *Mo., U.S.A.* 37°22N 91°58W **308** G8
Houston *Tex., U.S.A.* 29°45N 95°21W **314** G7
Houston George Bush Intercontinental ✈ (IAH) *U.S.A.* 29°59N 95°20W **314** G7
Hout = Mogwadi ➜ *S. Africa* 23°4S 29°36E **271** B4
Hout Bay *S. Africa* 34°2S 18°23E **118** B1
Houtkraal *S. Africa* 30°23S 24°5E **270** D3
Houtman Abrolhos *Australia* 28°43S 113°48E **279** E1
Hov *Norway* 60°42N 10°20E **164** D7
Hovd = Dund-Us *Mongolia* 48°1N 91°38E **217** C12
Hovd □ *Mongolia* 48°2N 91°37E **217** C12
Hovda *Norway* 60°53N 9°11E **164** D6
Hovden *Aust-Agder, Norway* 59°33N 7°22E **164** E4
Hovden *Sogn og Fjordane, Norway* 61°41N 4°52E **164** C1
Hove *U.K.* 50°50N 0°10W **169** G7
Hove Å ➜ *Denmark* 55°36N 12°23E **118** B2
Hovedøya *Norway* 59°53N 10°43E **133** A3
Hovenweep ⌂ *U.S.A.* 37°20N 109°0W **305** H9
Hovet *Norway* 60°38N 8°8E **164** D5
Hoveyzeh *Iran* 31°27N 48°4E **247** D6
Hovgaard Ø *Greenland* 79°55N 18°50W **154** B9
Høvik *Norway* 59°54N 10°34E **133** A2
Hovin *Norway* 59°51N 9°0E **164** E6
Hovmantorp *Sweden* 56°47N 15°7E **163** H9
Hovorčovice *Czechia* 50°10N 14°31E **135** A3
Hövsgöl *Mongolia* 43°37N 109°39E **226** C5
Hövsgöl Nuur *Mongolia* 51°0N 100°30E **218** A9
Hovsta *Sweden* 59°22N 15°15E **162** E9
Howakil *Eritrea* 15°10N 40°16E **257** D5
Howar, Wadi ➜ *Sudan* 17°30N 27°8E **257** D2
Howard *Queens., Australia* 25°16S 152°32E **281** D5
Howard *Pa., U.S.A.* 41°1N 77°40W **312** F7
Howard *S. Dak., U.S.A.* 44°1N 97°32W **308** C5
Howard Beach *U.S.A.* 40°39N 73°50W **132** C2
Howe *U.S.A.* 43°48N 113°0W **304** E7
Howe, C. *Australia* 37°30S 150°0E **283** D9
Howe, West Cape *Australia* 35°8S 117°36E **279** G2
Howe I. *Canada* 44°16N 76°17W **313** B8
Howell *U.S.A.* 42°36N 83°56W **311** B13
Howick *Qué., Canada* 45°11N 73°51W **313** A11
Howick *N.Z.* 36°54S 174°56E **284** C3
Howick *KwaZulu Natal, S. Africa* 29°28S 30°14E **271** C5
Howick Group *Australia* 14°20S 145°30E **280** A4
Howitt, L. *Australia* 27°40S 138°40E **281** D2
Howland I. *Pac. Oc.* 0°48N 176°38W **288** G10
Howlong *Australia* 35°59S 146°38E **283** C7
Howrah = Haora *India* 22°34N 88°18E **124** B1
Howth *Ireland* 53°23N 6°7W **166** C5
Howth Hd. *Ireland* 53°22N 6°4W **166** C5
Höxter *Germany* 51°46N 9°22E **178** D5
Hoxtolgay *China* 46°35N 85°59E **217** C11
Hoxton *London, U.K.* **125** a5
Hoxud *China* 42°15N 86°51E **217** D11
Hoy *U.K.* 58°50N 3°15W **167** C5
Hoya *Niedersachsen, Germany* 52°49N 9°8E **178** C5
Hōya *Tōkyō, Japan* 35°44N 139°34E **140** A2
Høyanger *Norway* 61°13N 6°4E **164** C3
Hoyerswerda *Germany* 51°26N 14°14E **178** D10
Hōyo-Kaikyō *Japan* 33°20N 131°58E **222** D3
Hoyos *Spain* 40°9N 6°45W **194** E4
Hpa-an = Pa-an *Burma* 16°51N 97°40E **241** G6
Hpakant *Burma* 25°37N 96°20E **241** C6
Hpawlum *Burma* 27°12N 98°12E **241** B7
Hpettintha *Burma* 24°14N 95°23E **241** C5
Hpizow *Burma* 26°57N 98°24E **241** B7
Hpunan Pass *Asia* 27°30N 96°55E **241** B6
Hpyu = Pyu *Burma* 18°30N 96°28E **241** F6
Hradčany *Czechia* 50°5N 14°24E **135** B2
Hradec Králové *Czechia* 50°15N 15°50E **180** A8
Hrádek *Czechia* 48°46N 16°16E **181** C9
Hrafnseyri *Iceland* 65°46N 23°28W **155** B3
Hranice *Czechia* 49°34N 17°45E **181** B10
Hrazdan *Armenia* 40°30N 44°46E **191** K7
Hrebenka *Ukraine* 50°9N 32°22E **189** G7
Hrifunes *Iceland* 63°38N 18°30W **155** D8
Hrísey *Iceland* 66°0N 18°23W **155** B8
Hrisoupoli = Chrisoupoli *Greece* 40°58N 24°42E **203** F8
Hrodna *Belarus* 53°42N 23°52E **184** E10
Hrodna □ *Belarus* 53°20N 24°45E **188** F3
Hrodzyanka *Belarus* 53°31N 28°42E **177** B15
Hron ➜ *Slovakia* 47°49N 18°45E **181** D11
Hrubieszów *Poland* 50°49N 23°51E **185** H10
Hrubý Jeseník *Czechia* 50°5N 17°10E **181** A10
Hrvatska = Croatia ■ *Europe* 45°20N 16°0E **199** C13
Hrymayliv *Ukraine* 49°20N 26°5E **177** D14
Hrynyava *Ukraine* 47°59N 24°53E **183** C9
Hsa-paw *Burma* 19°1N 97°30E **241** F6
Hsenwi *Burma* 23°22N 97°55E **241** D6
Hsi-hkip *Burma* 20°25N 96°42E **241** E6
Hsiafu *Taiwan* 25°7N 121°27E **225** A3
Hsiamen = Xiamen *China* 24°25N 118°4E **229** E12
Hsian = Xi'an *China* 34°15N 109°0E **226** G5
Hsianghan *Taiwan* 24°48N 120°54E **225** B2
Hsiaochinmen Tao *Taiwan* 24°26N 118°14E **225** a
Hsiaohungt'ou Hsü *Taiwan* 21°57N 121°36E **225** D3
Hsiaokang *Taiwan* 22°34N 120°20E **225** D2
Hsiatahsi *Taiwan* 22°28N 120°56E **225** D2
Hsiaying *Taiwan* 23°14N 120°15E **225** C2
Hsichih *Taiwan* 25°4N 121°39E **225** A3
Hsikang *Taiwan* 23°7N 120°12E **225** C2
Hsilo *Taiwan* 23°48N 120°27E **225** C2
Hsinche *Taiwan* 24°10N 120°50E **225** B2
Hsinch'eng *Taiwan* 24°8N 121°39E **225** B3
Hsinchu *Taiwan* 24°48N 120°58E **225** B2
Hsinchu □ *Taiwan* 24°45N 121°10E **225** B3
Hsinchuang *Kaohsiung, Taiwan* 22°34N 120°29E **225** D2
Hsinchuang *T'aipei, Taiwan* 25°2N 121°27E **225** A3
Hsinfa *Taiwan* 23°10N 120°39E **225** C2
Hsinfeng *Taiwan* 24°54N 120°59E **225** B2
Hsinhailien = Lianyungang *China* 34°40N 119°11E **227** G10
Hsinhua *Taiwan* 23°2N 120°18E **225** C2
Hsini *Taiwan* 23°41N 120°51E **225** C2
Hsinkai = Bhamo *Burma* 24°15N 97°15E **241** C6
Hsinking = Changchun *China* 43°57N 125°17E **227** C13
Hsinpi *Taiwan* 22°28N 120°33E **225** D2
Hsinshih *Taiwan* 23°4N 120°17E **225** C2
Hsintien *Taiwan* 24°57N 121°32E **225** B3
Hsinwu *Taiwan* 24°59N 121°6E **225** B3
Hsinying *Taiwan* 23°21N 120°17E **225** C2
Hsinyuan *Taiwan* 22°23N 120°34E **225** D2
Hsipaw *Burma* 22°37N 97°18E **241** D6
Hsiukuluan Hsi ➜ *Taiwan* 23°28N 121°30E **225** C3
Hsiushui *Taiwan* 24°3N 120°30E **225** B2
Hsiyu *Taiwan* 23°36N 119°30E **225** C1
Hsopket *Burma* 23°11N 98°26E **228** F2
Hsüchou = Xuzhou *China* 34°18N 117°10E **227** G9
Hsüeh Shan *China* 24°24N 121°12E **225** B3
Hsüehchia *Taiwan* 23°14N 120°11E **225** C2
Hsühaitsun *Taiwan* 22°12N 120°52E **225** D2
Htawei = Dawei *Burma* 14°2N 98°12E **236** E2
Hu Xian *China* 34°8N 108°42E **226** G5
Hua Hin *Thailand* 12°34N 99°58E **236** F2
Hua Lamphong Railway Station *Bangkok, Thailand* **113** c2
Hua Muang *Laos* 20°13N 103°52E **236** B4
Hua Shan *China* 34°28N 110°4E **226** G6

Hua Xian Henan, China 35°30N 114°30E 226 G8
Hua Xian Shaanxi, China 34°30N 109°48E 226 G5
Hua Yü Taiwan 23°24N 119°19E 225 C1
Hua'an China 25°1N 117°32E 229 E11
Huab → Namibia 20°52S 13°25E 270 A2
Huacaya Bolivia 20°45S 63°43W 331 E5
Huachacalla Bolivia 18°45S 68°17W 330 D4
Huacheng China 24°4N 115°37E 229 E10
Huachinera Mexico 30°9N 108°55W 318 A3
Huacho Peru 11°10S 77°35W 330 C2
Huachón Peru 10°35S 76°0W 330 C2
Huade China 41°55N 113°59E 226 D7
Huadian China 43°0N 126°40E 227 C14
Huadu China 23°22N 113°12E 229 F9
Huahine, Î. French Polynesia 16°46S 150°58W 289 f
Huai Hat △ Thailand 16°52N 104°17E 236 D5
Huai He → China 33°0N 118°30E 229 A12
Huai Kha Khaeng ⌓ Thailand 15°20N 98°55E 236 E2
Huai Nam Dang △ Thailand 19°30N 98°30E 236 C2
Huai Yot Thailand 7°45N 99°37E 237 J2
Huai'an Hebei, China 40°30N 114°20E 226 D8
Huai'an Jiangsu, China 33°30N 119°10E 227 H10
Huaibei China 34°0N 116°48E 226 G9
Huaibin China 32°32N 115°27E 229 A10
Huaicho = Puerto Acosta Bolivia 15°32S 69°15W 330 D4
Huaide = Gongzhuling China 43°30N 124°40E 227 C13
Huaidezhen China 43°48N 124°50E 227 C13
Huaihua China 27°32N 109°57E 228 D7
Huaiji China 23°55N 112°12E 229 F9
Huainan China 32°38N 116°58E 229 A11
Huaining China 30°24N 116°40E 229 B11
Huairen China 39°48N 113°20E 226 E7
Huairou China 40°20N 116°35E 226 D9
Huaiyang China 33°40N 114°52E 226 H8
Huaiyin China 33°30N 119°2E 227 H10
Huaiyuan Anhui, China 32°55N 117°10E 229 A11
Huaiyuan Guangxi Zhuangzu, China 24°31N 108°22E 228 E7
Huajuapán de León Mexico 17°48N 97°46W 319 D5
Hualälai U.S.A. 19°42N 155°52W 302 D6
Hualapai Peak U.S.A. 35°5N 113°54W 307 K13
Hualian = Hualien Taiwan 23°59N 121°36E 225 C3
Hualien Taiwan 23°59N 121°36E 225 C3
Hualien □ Taiwan 23°45N 121°25E 225 C3
Huallaga → Peru 5°15S 75°30W 330 B2
Huallanca Peru 8°50S 77°56W 330 B2
Huamachuco Peru 7°50S 78°5W 330 B2
Huambo Angola 12°42S 15°54E 265 E3
Huambo □ Angola 13°0S 16°0E 265 E3
Huan Jiang → China 34°28N 109°0E 226 G5
Huan Xian China 36°33N 107°7E 226 F4
Huancabamba Peru 5°10S 79°15W 330 B2
Huancane Peru 15°10S 69°44W 330 D4
Huancapi Peru 13°40S 74°0W 330 C3
Huancavelica Peru 12°50S 75°5W 330 C2
Huancavelica □ Peru 13°0S 75°0W 330 C3
Huancayo Peru 12°5S 75°12W 330 C2
Huanchaca Bolivia 20°15S 66°40W 330 E4
Huanchaca, Serranía de Bolivia 14°30S 60°39W 331 C5
Huang Hai = Yellow Sea China 35°0N 123°0E 227 G12
Huang He → China 37°55N 118°50E 227 F10
Huang Xian China 37°38N 120°30E 227 F11
Huangchuan China 32°15N 115°10E 229 A10
Huangdao China 36°0N 120°7E 227 G11
Huanggang China 30°29N 114°52E 229 B10
Huangguoshu China 26°0N 105°40E 228 E5
Huanghua China 38°22N 117°20E 227 E9
Huanghuagang China 38°20N 117°54E 227 E9
Huanghuagang Mausoleum China 23°9N 113°17E 121 B2
Huangling China 35°34N 109°15E 226 G5
Huanglong China 35°30N 109°59E 226 G5
Huanglong ⌓ China 32°44N 103°50E 228 A4
Huanglongtan China 32°40N 110°33E 229 A8
Huangmei China 30°5N 115°56E 229 B10
Huangpi China 30°50N 114°22E 229 B10
Huangping China 26°52N 107°54E 228 D6
Huangpu China 31°14N 121°30E 138 B2
Huangpu Jiang → China 31°11N 121°29E 138 B1
Huangshan Anhui, China 30°8N 118°9E 229 B12
Huangshan Anhui, China 29°42N 118°25E 229 C12
Huangshi China 30°10N 115°3E 229 B10
Huangsongdian China 43°45N 127°25E 227 C14
Huangtugang China 39°49N 116°15E 114 C1
Huangyan China 28°38N 121°19E 229 C13
Huangyangsi China 26°33N 111°39E 229 D8
Huaning China 24°17N 102°56E 228 E4
Huanjiang China 24°50N 108°18E 228 E7
Huanren China 41°23N 125°20E 224 B2
Huanren Shuiku China 41°17N 125°34E 224 B2
Huanta Peru 12°55S 74°20W 330 C3
Huantai China 36°58N 117°56E 227 F9
Huánuco Peru 9°55S 76°15W 330 B2
Huánuco □ Peru 9°55S 76°14W 330 B2
Huanuni Bolivia 18°16S 66°51W 330 D4
Huanzo, Cordillera de Peru 14°35S 73°20W 330 C3
Huaping China 26°46N 101°25E 228 D3
Huara Chile 19°59S 69°47W 330 D4
Huaral Peru 11°32S 77°13W 330 C2
Huaraz Peru 9°30S 77°32W 330 B2
Huari Peru 9°14S 77°14W 330 B2
Huarmey Peru 10°5S 78°5W 330 C2
Huarochiri Peru 12°9S 76°15W 330 C2
Huarocondo Peru 13°26S 72°14W 330 C3
Huarong China 29°29N 112°30E 229 C9
Huascar Peru 11°59S 77°1W 124 A2
Huascarán, Nevado Peru 9°7S 77°37W 330 B2
Huasco Chile 28°30S 71°15W 334 B1
Huasco → Chile 28°27S 71°13W 334 B1
Huasna U.S.A. 35°6N 120°24W 307 K6
Huatabampo Mexico 26°50N 109°38W 318 B3
Huauchinango Mexico 20°12N 98°3W 319 C5
Huautla de Jiménez Mexico 18°8N 96°51W 319 D5
Huaxi China 26°25N 106°40E 228 D6
Huay Khwang Thailand 13°47N 100°33E 113 B2
Huayhuash, Cordillera Peru 10°30S 76°45W 330 B2
Huayin China 34°35N 110°5E 226 G6
Huaying China 30°8N 106°44E 228 B6
Huayllay Peru 11°3S 76°21W 330 C2
Huayuan China 28°37N 109°29E 228 C7
Huazhou China 21°33N 110°33E 229 G8
Hubballi India 15°22N 75°15E 245 G2
Hubbard Iowa, U.S.A. 42°18N 93°18W 310 B3
Hubbard Ohio, U.S.A. 41°9N 80°34W 312 E4
Hubbard Tex., U.S.A. 31°51N 96°48W 314 F6
Hubbard, Mt. N. Amer. 60°19N 139°4W 303 F13
Hubbard Glacier Canada 60°18N 139°22W 294 E4
Hubbart Pt. Canada 59°21N 94°41W 297 B10
Hubei □ China 31°0N 112°0E 229 B9
Hubli = Hubballi India 15°22N 75°15E 245 G2
Huch'ang N. Korea 41°25N 127°2E 224 B3
Huchow = Huzhou China 30°51N 120°8E 229 B13
Hucknall U.K. 53°3N 1°13W 168 D6
Huddersfield U.K. 53°39N 1°47W 168 D6
Huddinge Sweden 59°14N 18°0E 139 B2
Hude Germany 53°7N 8°26E 178 B4
Hudi Sudan 17°43N 34°18E 256 D3
Hudiksvall Sweden 61°43N 17°10E 162 C11
Hudson Ont., Canada 50°6N 92°9W 298 B1
Hudson Fla., U.S.A. 28°22N 82°42W 317 G7
Hudson Mass., U.S.A. 42°23N 71°34W 313 D13
Hudson Mich., U.S.A. 41°51N 84°21W 311 C12
Hudson N.Y., U.S.A. 42°15N 73°46W 313 D11
Hudson Wis., U.S.A. 44°58N 92°45W 308 C7
Hudson Wyo., U.S.A. 42°54N 108°35W 304 E9
Hudson → U.S.A. 40°42N 74°2W 313 F10
Hudson, C. Antarctica 68°21S 153°45E 151 C10
Hudson, Vol. Chile 46°4S 72°55W 336 C2
Hudson Bay Nunavut, Canada 60°0N 86°0W 295 F14
Hudson Bay Sask., Canada 52°51N 102°23W 297 C8
Hudson Falls U.S.A. 43°18N 73°35W 313 C11
Hudson Mts. Antarctica 74°32S 99°20W 151 D16
Hudson River Park New York, U.S.A. 132 e1
Hudson Str. Canada 62°0N 70°0W 295 E18
Hudson's Hope Canada 56°0N 121°54W 296 B4
Hudsonville U.S.A. 42°52N 85°52W 311 B11
Hue Vietnam 16°30N 107°35E 236 D6
Huebra → Spain 41°2N 6°48W 194 D4
Huechuraba Chile 33°22S 70°39W 137 B1
Huedin Romania 46°52N 23°2E 182 D8
Huehuetenango Guatemala 15°20N 91°28W 320 C1
Huejúcar Mexico 22°21N 103°13W 318 C4
Huélamo Spain 40°17N 1°48W 196 E3
Huelgoat France 48°22N 3°46W 172 D3
Huelma Spain 37°39N 3°28W 195 H7
Huelva Spain 37°18N 6°57W 195 H4
Huelva □ Spain 37°40N 7°0W 195 H4
Huelva → Spain 37°27N 6°0W 195 H5
Hueneme = Port Hueneme U.S.A. 34°7N 119°12W 307 L7
Huentelauquén Chile 31°38S 71°33W 334 C1
Huércal-Overa Spain 37°23N 1°57W 197 H3
Huerquehue △ Chile 39°6S 71°42W 336 A2
Huerta, Sa. de la Argentina 31°10S 67°30W 334 C2
Huertas, C. de las Spain 38°21N 0°24W 197 G4
Huerva → Spain 41°39N 0°52W 196 D4
Huesca Spain 42°8N 0°25W 196 C4
Huesca □ Spain 42°20N 0°1E 196 C5
Huéscar Spain 37°44N 2°35W 197 H2
Hueso Ballena, Pta. Chile 33°40S 78°46W 330 c
Huetamo Mexico 18°35N 100°53W 318 D4
Huete Spain 40°10N 2°43W 196 E2
Huevos I. Trin. & Tob. 10°42N 61°43W 323 t
Huger U.S.A. 33°6N 79°48W 316 B10
Hugh → Australia 25°1S 134°1E 280 D1
Hugh Taylor Birch State Recr. Area ⌓ U.S.A. 26°8N 80°6W 129 B3
Hughenden Australia 20°52S 144°10E 280 C3
Hughes U.S.A. 66°3N 154°15W 303 C9
Hughesville U.S.A. 41°14N 76°44W 313 E8
Hugli → India 21°56N 88°4E 243 J13
Hugo Colo., U.S.A. 39°8N 103°28W 304 G12
Hugo Okla., U.S.A. 34°1N 95°31W 314 D7
Hugoton U.S.A. 37°11N 101°21W 308 G3
Huguang Opera Museum Beijing, China 114 c2
Huhehaote = Hohhot China 40°52N 111°40E 226 D6
Huhsi Taiwan 23°35N 119°39E 225 C1
Hui Xian = Huixian China 35°27N 113°12E 226 G7
Hui Xian China 33°50N 106°4E 226 H4
Hui'an China 25°1N 118°43E 229 E12
Hui'anbu China 37°28N 106°38E 226 F4
Huiarau Ra. N.Z. 38°45S 176°55E 284 E5
Huichang China 25°32N 115°45E 229 E10
Huichapan Mexico 20°23N 99°39W 319 C5
Huichon N. Korea 40°10N 126°16E 224 B3
Huidong Guangdong, China 22°58N 114°43E 229 F10
Huidong Sichuan, China 26°34N 102°35E 228 D4
Huifa He → China 43°0N 127°50E 227 C14
Huíla Angola 15°4S 13°32E 265 F2
Huíla □ Angola 14°0S 15°0E 265 E2
Huila □ Colombia 2°30N 75°45W 328 C2
Huila, Nevado del Colombia 3°0N 76°0W 328 C2
Huilai China 23°0N 116°18E 229 F11
Huili China 26°35N 102°17E 228 D4
Huimin China 37°27N 117°28E 227 F9
Huinan China 42°40N 126°2E 224 A3
Huinca Renancó Argentina 34°51S 64°22W 334 C3
Huining China 35°38N 105°0E 226 G3
Huinong China 39°5N 106°35E 226 E4
Huiroa N.Z. 39°15S 174°30E 284 F3
Huishui China 26°7N 106°38E 228 D6
Huisne → France 47°59N 0°11E 172 E7
Huiting China 34°5N 116°5E 226 G9
Huitong China 26°51N 109°45E 228 D7
Huixian China 35°27N 113°12E 226 G7
Huixtla Mexico 15°9N 92°28W 319 D6
Huize China 26°24N 103°15E 228 D4
Huizhou China 23°0N 114°23E 229 F10
Huizingen Belgium 50°45N 4°17E 116 B1
Hukawng Valley Burma 26°30N 96°30E 241 B6
Hukeri India 16°14N 74°36E 245 F2
Hukou Jiangxi, China 29°45N 116°21E 229 C11
Huk'ou Taiwan 24°54N 121°2E 225 B3
Hukuntsi Botswana 23°58S 21°45E 270 B3
Hula Papua N. G. 10°5S 147°43E 286 F4
Ḩulayfā' Si. Arabia 25°58N 40°45E 246 E4
Huld = Ulaanjirem Mongolia 45°5N 105°30E 226 B3
Hulin China 45°48N 132°59E 219 B15
Hulin He → China 45°0N 122°10E 227 B12
Hull = Kingston upon Hull U.K. 53°45N 0°21W 168 D7
Hull Canada 45°26N 75°43W 313 A9
Hull → U.K. 53°44N 0°20W 168 D7
Hulst Neths. 51°17N 4°2E 170 C4
Hultschin = Hlučín Czechia 49°54N 18°11E 181 B11
Hultsfred Sweden 57°30N 15°52E 163 G9
Huludao China 40°45N 120°50E 227 D11
Hulun = Hailar China 49°10N 119°38E 219 B12
Hulun Nur China 49°0N 117°30E 219 B12
Hulunbuir = Hailar China 49°10N 119°38E 219 B12
Hulyaypole Ukraine 47°45N 36°21E 189 J9
Huma, Tanjung Malaysia 5°29N 100°16E 237 c
Humacao Puerto Rico 18°9N 65°50W 321 b
Humahuaca Argentina 23°10S 65°25W 334 A2
Humaitá = Porto Walter Brazil 8°15S 72°40W 330 B3
Humaitá Brazil 7°35S 63°1W 331 B5
Humaitá Paraguay 27°2S 58°31W 334 B4
Humansdorp S. Africa 34°2S 24°46E 270 D3
Humansville U.S.A. 37°48N 93°35W 310 G3
Humara, J. Sudan 16°16N 30°59E 257 D3
Humayun's Tomb India 28°35N 77°15E 120 B2
Humbe Angola 16°40S 14°55E 265 F2
Humbe, Serra do Angola 12°10S 15°25E 265 E2
Humber → Ont., Canada 43°47N 79°38W 141 A1
Humber → England, U.K. 53°42N 0°27W 168 D7
Humber B. Canada 43°37N 79°27W 141 B2
Humber Bay Canada 43°38N 79°29W 141 B2
Humber Bay Park Canada 43°37N 79°28W 141 B2
Humber College Canada 43°35N 79°30W 141 B1
Humber Summit Canada 43°45N 79°32W 141 A1
Humber Valley Village Canada 43°40N 79°31W 141 A1
Humberlea Canada 43°43N 79°31W 141 A1
Humberwood Park Canada 43°44N 79°37W 141 A1
Humboldt Sask., Canada 52°15N 105°9W 297 C7
Humboldt Iowa, U.S.A. 42°44N 94°13W 310 B2
Humboldt Tenn., U.S.A. 35°50N 88°55W 315 D10
Humboldt → U.S.A. 39°59N 118°36W 304 G4
Humboldt Gletscher = Sermersuaq Greenland 79°30N 62°0W 154 B4
Humboldt Mts. N.Z. 44°30S 168°15E 285 E3
Humboldt Park U.S.A. 41°54N 87°42W 119 B2
Humbolt, Mt. N. Cal. 21°53S 166°25E 288 d
Hume U.S.A. 36°48N 118°54W 306 J8
Hume, L. Australia 36°0S 147°5E 283 D7
Humen China 22°50N 113°40E 219 a
Humenné Slovakia 48°55N 21°50E 181 C14
Humera Spain 40°25N 3°46W 127 B1
Humeston U.S.A. 40°52N 93°30W 310 D3
Hummelsta Sweden 59°34N 16°58E 162 E10
Hummelvika Norway 63°29N 8°19E 164 A5
Hummingbird Centre Toronto, Canada 141 b3
Hummock Hill = Whyalla Australia 33°2S 137°30E 282 B2
Humpata Angola 15°2S 13°24E 265 F2
Humphreys, Mt. U.S.A. 37°17N 118°40W 306 H8
Humphreys Peak U.S.A. 35°21N 111°41W 305 J8
Humpolec Czechia 49°31N 15°20E 180 B8
Humptulips U.S.A. 47°14N 123°57W 306 C3
Humula Australia 35°30S 147°46E 283 C7
Hūn Libya 29°2N 16°0E 258 C3
Hun He → China 40°41N 122°8E 224 B1
Hun Jiang → China 40°50N 125°38E 227 D13
Húnaflói Iceland 65°50N 20°50W 155 B6
Hunan □ China 27°30N 112°0E 229 D9
Húnavatnssýsla Iceland 65°30N 20°25W 155 B6
Hunaydī Iraq 33°18N 44°29E 113 B2
Hunchun China 42°52N 130°28E 227 C16
Hundested Denmark 55°58N 11°52E 163 J5
Hundewali Pakistan 31°55N 72°38E 242 D5
Hundige Denmark 55°35N 12°18E 118 B1
Hundige Strand Denmark 55°35N 12°20E 118 B2
Hundorp Norway 61°33N 9°59E 164 C7
Hundred Islands △ Phil. 16°10N 120°2E 232 C3
Hundred Mile House Canada 51°38N 121°18W 296 C4
Hundvåg Norway 59°0N 5°43E 164 E2
Hunedoara Romania 45°40N 22°50E 182 E7
Hunedoara □ Romania 45°50N 22°54E 182 E7
Hunei Taiwan 22°53N 120°14E 225 D2
Hünfeld Germany 50°39N 9°46E 178 E5
Hung Hom Hong Kong, China 22°18N 114°11E 122 B3
Hung Yen Vietnam 20°39N 106°4E 228 G6
Hunga Ha'apai Tonga 20°41S 175°7W 287 Q13
Hungary ■ Europe 47°20N 19°20E 181 D12
Hungary, Plain of Europe 47°0N 20°0E 158 F10
Hungerford Australia 28°58S 144°24E 281 D3
Hŭngnam N. Korea 39°49N 127°45E 224 C3
Hungt'ou Hsü = Lan Yü Taiwan 22°4N 121°25E 225 D3
Huni Valley Ghana 5°33N 1°56W 262 D4
Hunjiang China 41°54N 126°26E 224 B3
Hunneberg Sweden 58°18N 12°30E 163 F6
Hunnebostrand Sweden 58°27N 11°18E 163 F5
Hunsberge Namibia 27°45S 17°12E 270 C2
Hunsrück Germany 49°56N 7°27E 179 F3
Hunstanton U.K. 52°56N 0°29E 168 E8
Hunsur India 12°16N 76°16E 245 H3
Hunte → Germany 53°14N 8°28E 178 B4
Hunter N.Z. 44°36S 171°2E 285 E6
Hunter N.Y., U.S.A. 42°13N 74°13W 313 D10
Hunter → N.S.W., Australia 32°52S 151°46E 283 B9
Hunter → N.Z. 44°21S 169°27E 285 E4
Hunter, C. Solomon Is. 9°48S 159°50E 287 M10
Hunter Hills, The N.Z. 44°26S 170°46E 285 E5
Hunter I. Tas., Australia 40°30S 144°45E 281 G3
Hunter I. B.C., Canada 51°55N 128°0W 296 C3
Hunter Mts. N.Z. 45°43S 167°25E 285 F2
Hunter Ra. Australia 32°45S 150°15E 283 B9
Hunters Hill Australia 33°50S 151°9E 139 B1
Hunters Pt. U.S.A. 37°43N 122°21W 136 B2
Hunters Road Zimbabwe 19°9S 29°49E 269 F2
Hunterville N.Z. 39°56S 175°35E 284 F4
Huntingburg U.S.A. 38°18N 86°57W 311 F10
Huntingdon Cambs., U.K. 52°20N 0°11W 169 E7
Huntingdon Pa., U.S.A. 40°30N 78°1W 312 F6
Huntington = Shelton U.S.A. 41°19N 73°5W 313 E11
Huntington Ind., U.S.A. 40°53N 85°30W 311 D11
Huntington N.Y., U.S.A. 40°52N 73°26W 313 F11
Huntington Oreg., U.S.A. 44°21N 117°16W 304 D5
Huntington Utah, U.S.A. 39°20N 110°58W 304 G8
Huntington Va., U.S.A. 38°47N 77°4W 143 C2
Huntington W. Va., U.S.A. 38°25N 82°27W 309 F12
Huntington Beach U.S.A. 33°40N 118°5W 307 M9
Huntington Park U.S.A. 33°58N 118°13W 126 C3
Huntley Jamaica 18°4N 77°35W 320 a
Huntley Ill., U.S.A. 42°10N 88°26W 311 B8
Huntly N.Z. 37°34S 175°11E 284 D4
Huntly Aberds., U.K. 57°27N 2°47W 167 D6
Huntsville Ont., Canada 45°20N 79°14W 312 A5
Huntsville Ala., U.S.A. 34°44N 86°35W 315 D11
Huntsville Mo., U.S.A. 39°26N 92°33W 310 E4
Huntsville Tex., U.S.A. 30°43N 95°33W 314 F7
Hunyani → Zimbabwe 15°57S 30°39E 269 F3
Hunyuan China 39°42N 113°42E 226 E7
Hunza → India 35°54N 74°20E 243 B6
Huo Shan China 36°26N 111°52E 226 F6
Huo Xian = Huozhou China 36°36N 111°42E 226 F6
Huocheng China 44°0N 80°48E 217 D10
Huolin Gol China 45°32N 119°38E 227 B10
Huon G. Papua N. G. 7°0S 147°30E 286 D4
Huon Pen. Papua N. G. 6°20S 147°30E 286 D4
Huong Khe Vietnam 18°13N 105°41E 236 C5
Huonville Australia 43°0S 147°5E 281 G4
Huoqiu China 32°20N 116°12E 229 A11
Huoshan China 31°25N 116°20E 229 B11
Huoshao Dao = Lütao Taiwan 22°40N 121°30E 225 D3
Huozhou China 36°36N 111°42E 226 F6
Hupeh = Hubei □ China 31°0N 112°0E 229 B9
Ḩūr Iran 30°50N 57°7E 247 D8
Hurānd Iran 38°51N 47°22E 213 C12
Ḩuraymīla Si. Arabia 25°8N 46°8E 246 E5
Hurbanovo Slovakia 47°51N 18°11E 181 D11
Hurd, C. Canada 45°13N 81°44W 312 A3
Hurdiyo Somalia 10°33N 51°6E 267 B7
Hure Qi China 42°45N 121°45E 227 C11
Hurezani Romania 44°49N 23°40E 183 F8
Hurghada Egypt 27°15N 33°50E 256 B3
Hurīya Iraq 33°21N 44°19E 113 A1
Hurley N. Mex., U.S.A. 32°42N 108°8W 305 K9
Hurley Wis., U.S.A. 46°27N 90°11W 308 B8
Huron Calif., U.S.A. 36°12N 120°6W 306 J6
Huron Ohio, U.S.A. 41°24N 82°33W 312 E2
Huron S. Dak., U.S.A. 44°22N 98°13W 308 C4
Huron, L. U.S.A. 44°30N 82°40W 312 B2
Huron East Canada 43°37N 81°18W 312 C3
Hurricane U.S.A. 37°11N 113°17W 305 H7
Hurso Ethiopia 9°35N 41°33E 257 F5
Hurst U.S.A. 32°49N 97°10W 120 B3
Hurstville Australia 33°57S 151°6E 139 B1
Hurtsboro U.S.A. 32°15N 85°25W 316 C4
Hurungwe ⌓ Zimbabwe 16°7S 29°5E 269 F2
Hurunui → N.Z. 42°54S 173°18E 285 C8
Hurup Denmark 56°46N 8°25E 163 H2
Húsafell Iceland 64°42N 20°53W 155 C6
Husan West Bank 31°42N 35°8E 123 B1
Húsavík Iceland 66°3N 17°21W 155 A9
Husby Sweden 59°24N 17°56E 139 A1
Huşi Romania 46°41N 28°7E 183 D13
Huskisson Australia 35°2S 150°41E 283 C9
Huskvarna Sweden 57°47N 14°15E 163 G8
Huslia U.S.A. 65°41N 156°24W 303 D8
Husnes Norway 59°52N 5°45E 164 E2
Hustad Norway 62°57N 7°6E 164 B4
Hustadvika Norway 63°0N 7°0E 164 A3
Hustontown U.S.A. 40°3N 78°2W 312 F6
Hustopeče Czechia 48°57N 16°43E 181 C9
Husum København, Denmark 55°42N 12°27E 118 A2
Husum Schleswig-Holstein, Germany 54°28N 9°4E 178 A5
Husum Sweden 63°21N 19°12E 162 A13
Huszt = Khust Ukraine 48°10N 23°18E 183 B8
Hutanopan Indonesia 0°40N 99°42E 234 B1
Hutchins U.S.A. 32°38N 96°42W 120 C5
Hutchinson Kans., U.S.A. 38°5N 97°56W 308 F5
Hutchinson Minn., U.S.A. 44°54N 94°22W 308 C6
Ḩūth Yemen 16°14N 43°58E 248 C3
Hutiao Xia China 27°13N 100°9E 228 D3
Hutjena Papua N. G. 5°23S 154°42E 286 C8
Hutsonville U.S.A. 39°7N 87°40W 311 E9
Hutte Sauvage, L. de la Canada 56°15N 64°45W 299 A7
Hütteldorf Austria 48°12N 16°15E 142 A1
Hüttenberg Austria 46°56N 14°33E 180 E7
Hüttener Berge ⌓ Germany 54°24N 9°40E 178 A5
Hutton, Mt. Australia 25°51S 148°20E 281 D4
Huvadu Atoll Maldives 0°30N 73°15E 272 d
Hüvösvölgy Hungary 47°32N 19°0E 117 A2
Huwaki Indonesia 7°55S 126°30E 231 F7
Huwei Taiwan 23°42N 120°26E 225 C2
Huwei Hsi → Taiwan 23°37N 120°22E 225 C2
Huwon Secret Garden S. Korea 37°34N 126°59E 137 B1
Huwun Ethiopia 4°23N 40°6E 257 G5
Huy Belgium 50°31N 5°15E 170 D5
Huzhou China 30°51N 120°8E 229 B13
Huzurabad India 18°12N 79°25E 244 E4
Huzurnagar India 16°54N 79°53E 244 F4
Hvalfjörður Iceland 64°20N 21°40W 155 C5
Hvalpsund Denmark 56°42N 9°11E 163 H3
Hvalstad Norway 59°51N 10°27E 133 A1
Hvalstrand Norway 59°50N 10°30E 133 A2
Hvammsfjörður Iceland 65°4N 22°5W 155 B4
Hvammstangi Iceland 65°24N 20°57W 155 B6
Hvammur Norðurland Vestra, Iceland 65°53N 19°51W 155 B7
Hvammur Vesturland, Iceland 64°50N 21°21W 155 C5
Hvannadalshnúkur Iceland 64°1N 16°41W 155 C10
Hvanneyri Iceland 64°34N 21°36W 155 C5
Hvar Croatia 43°11N 16°28E 199 E13
Hvarski Kanal Croatia 43°15N 16°35E 199 E13
Hveragerði Iceland 64°0N 21°12W 155 C5
Hvidovre Denmark 55°38N 12°27E 118 B2
Hvítá → Iceland 64°30N 21°58W 155 C5
Hvítárvatn Iceland 64°37N 19°50W 155 C7
Hvittingfoss Norway 59°29N 10°0E 164 E7
Hvizdets Ukraine 48°35N 25°17E 183 B10
Hvolsvöllur Iceland 63°45N 20°14W 155 D6
Hwacheon-Cheosuji S. Korea 38°5N 127°50E 224 C3
Hwagok S. Korea 37°32N 126°51E 137 B1
Hwainan = Huainan China 32°38N 116°58E 229 A11
Hwaiyin = Huaiyin China 33°30N 119°2E 227 H10
Hwang Ho = Huang He → China 37°55N 118°50E 227 F10
Hwange Zimbabwe 18°18S 26°30E 269 F2
Hwange △ Zimbabwe 19°0S 26°30E 270 A4
Hwanghaebuk-do □ N. Korea 38°30N 126°25E 224 C3
Hwanghaenam-do □ N. Korea 38°15N 125°30E 224 C2
Hwangju N. Korea 38°40N 125°46E 224 C2
Hwangshih = Huangshi China 30°10N 115°3E 229 B10
Hwaseong S. Korea 37°12N 126°48E 224 D3
Hwasun S. Korea 35°3N 126°59E 224 E3
Hwekum Burma 26°7N 95°22E 241 B5
Hwlffordd = Haverfordwest U.K. 51°48N 4°58W 169 F3
Hyaing Burma 22°39N 94°44E 241 D5
Hyannis Mass., U.S.A. 41°39N 70°17W 309 E18
Hyannis Nebr., U.S.A. 42°0N 101°46W 308 E3
Hyargas Nuur Mongolia 49°0N 93°0E 217 C12
Hyattsville U.S.A. 38°57N 76°57W 143 B3
Hybo Sweden 61°49N 16°15E 162 C10
Hydaburg U.S.A. 55°15N 132°50W 296 B2
Hyde N.Z. 45°18S 170°16E 285 F5
Hyde Park Sydney, Australia 139 b2
Hyde Park Guyana 6°30N 58°16W 329 B6
Hyde Park Gauteng, S. Africa 26°6S 28°2E 123 A2
Hyde Park London, U.K. 51°30N 0°10W 125 A2
Hyde Park Calif., U.S.A. 33°58N 118°19W 126 C3
Hyde Park Ill., U.S.A. 41°47N 87°35W 119 C3
Hyde Park Mass., U.S.A. 42°15N 71°7W 116 B2
Hyde Park N.Y., U.S.A. 41°47N 73°56W 313 E11
Hyden Australia 32°24S 118°53E 279 F2
Hyder U.S.A. 55°55N 130°5W 296 B2
Hyderabad India 17°22N 78°29E 244 F4
Hyderabad Pakistan 25°23N 68°24E 242 G3
Hydra Greece 37°20N 23°28E 204 D5
Hyen Norway 61°44N 5°56E 164 C2
Hyères France 43°8N 6°9E 175 E10
Hyères, Îs. d' France 43°0N 6°20E 175 F10
Hyesan N. Korea 41°20N 128°10E 224 B4
Hyland → Canada 59°52N 128°12W 296 B3
Hylestad Norway 59°6N 7°29E 164 E4
Hyllestad Norway 61°10N 5°17E 164 C2
Hyltebruk Sweden 56°59N 13°15E 163 H7
Hyndman Peak U.S.A. 43°45N 114°8W 304 E6
Hynnekleiv Norway 58°36N 8°25E 164 F5
Hyōgo □ Japan 35°15N 134°50E 222 B6
Hyrra Banda C.A.R. 5°58N 22°1E 264 A4
Hyrum U.S.A. 41°38N 111°51W 304 F8
Hysham U.S.A. 46°18N 107°14W 304 C10
Hythe U.K. 51°4N 1°5E 169 F9
Hyūga Japan 32°25N 131°35E 222 E3
Hyvinge = Hyvinkää Finland 60°38N 24°50E 188 B3
Hyvinkää Finland 60°38N 24°50E 188 B3

I

I-n-Akhmed Mali 19°49N 0°56W 261 E4
I-n-Azaoua Illizi, Algeria 25°42N 6°54E 261 C6
I-n-Azaoua Tamanrasset, Algeria 20°46N 7°32E 261 D6
I-n-Échaï Mali 20°10N 2°5W 260 D4
I-n-Ezzane Algeria 23°29N 11°15E 261 D7
I-n-Gall Niger 16°51N 7°1E 263 B6
I-n-Kelemet Algeria 26°57N 5°47E 261 C6
I-n-Oudad Algeria 20°17N 4°38E 261 D5
I-n-Ouzzal Algeria 20°41N 2°34E 261 D5
I-n-Tadreft Niger 19°5N 6°38E 263 B6
Iabès, Erg Algeria 27°30N 2°2W 261 C4
Iablaniţa Romania 44°57N 22°19E 182 F7
Iaco → Brazil 9°3S 68°34W 330 B4
Iacobeni Romania 47°25N 25°20E 183 C10
Iaçu Brazil 12°45S 40°13W 333 D3
Iakora Madag. 23°6S 46°40E 272 C2
Ialibu Papua N. G. 6°17S 143°59E 286 D2
Ialissos Greece 36°24N 28°10E 206 E12
Ialomiţa □ Romania 44°30N 27°30E 183 F12
Ialomiţa → Romania 44°42N 27°51E 183 F12
Ialoveni Moldova 46°56N 28°47E 183 D13
Ialpug → Moldova 45°41N 28°35E 183 E13
Iamonia L. U.S.A. 30°38N 84°14W 316 E5
Ianca Romania 45°6N 27°29E 183 E12
Iara Romania 46°31N 23°35E 183 D8
Iarda Ethiopia 11°9N 35°53E 257 E4
Iargara Moldova 46°24N 28°23E 183 D13
Iaşi Romania 47°10N 27°40E 183 C12
Iaşi □ Romania 47°20N 27°0E 183 C12
Iasmos Greece 41°8N 25°11E 203 E9
Iauaretê Colombia 0°36N 69°12W 328 C4
Ib → India 21°34N 83°48E 243 J10
Iba Phil. 15°22N 120°0E 232 D2
Ibadan Nigeria 7°22N 3°58E 263 D5
Ibagué Colombia 4°20N 75°20W 328 C2
Ibaiti Brazil 23°50S 50°10W 333 F1
Ibajay Phil. 11°49N 122°10E 233 F4
Iballë Albania 42°12N 20°2E 202 D4
Ibăneşti Botoşani, Romania 48°4N 26°22E 183 B11
Ibăneşti Mureş, Romania 46°45N 24°57E 183 D9
Ibanshe Dem. Rep. of the Congo 4°58S 21°30E 265 C4
Ibar → Serbia 43°43N 20°45E 202 C4
Ibara Japan 34°36N 133°28E 222 C5
Ibaraki Ibaraki, Japan 36°20N 140°30E 223 A12
Ibaraki Ōsaka, Japan 34°49N 135°34E 223 C7
Ibaraki □ Japan 36°10N 140°10E 223 A12
Ibarra Ecuador 0°21N 78°7W 328 C2
Ibb Yemen 14°2N 44°10E 248 D4
Ibb □ Yemen 14°2N 44°10E 248 D4
Ibba South Sudan 4°49N 29°2E 257 G2
Ibba, Bahr el → South Sudan 5°30N 28°55E 257 F2
Ibbenbüren Germany 52°16N 7°43E 178 C3
Ibeke Gembo Dem. Rep. of the Congo 1°24S 18°51E 264 C3
Ibembo Dem. Rep. of the Congo 2°35N 23°35E 264 B4
Ibenga → Congo 2°19N 18°9E 264 B3
Ibera, L. Argentina 28°30S 57°9W 334 B4
Iberia Peru 11°21S 69°35W 330 C4
Iberia Mo., U.S.A. 38°5N 92°18W 310 F4
Iberian Peninsula Europe 40°0N 5°0W 158 H5
Iberville Canada 45°19N 73°17W 313 A11
Iberville, Mt. d' Canada 58°50N 63°50W 295 F19
Ibese Nigeria 6°33N 3°28E 124 A2
Ibeto Nigeria 10°29N 5°8E 263 C6
Ibi Nigeria 8°15N 9°44E 263 D6
Ibi Spain 38°38N 0°34W 197 G4
Ibiá Brazil 19°30S 46°30W 333 E2
Ibiapaba, Sa. da Brazil 4°0S 41°30W 332 B3
Ibicaraí Brazil 14°51S 39°36W 333 D4
Ibicuí Brazil 14°51S 39°59W 333 D4
Ibicuí → Brazil 29°25S 56°47W 335 B4
Ibicuy Argentina 33°55S 59°10W 334 C4
Ibirapuera Brazil 23°36S 46°40W 137 B1
Ibirapuera, Parque do Brazil 23°35S 46°38W 137 B2
Ibitiara Brazil 12°39S 42°13W 333 D3
Ibiza = Eivissa Spain 38°54N 1°26E 206 D1
Ibiza ✕ (IBZ) Spain 38°53N 1°22E 197 G6
Íblei, Monti Italy 37°15N 14°45E 201 E7
Ibn Hāni', Ra's Syria 35°35N 35°43E 250 C6
Ibo Mozam. 12°22S 40°40E 269 E5
Ibonma Indonesia 3°29S 133°31E 231 E8
Ibotirama Brazil 12°13S 43°12W 333 D3
Iboundji Gabon 1°0S 11°51E 264 C2
Ibrā' Oman 22°41N 58°33E 249 B7
İbradı Turkey 37°4N 31°35E 250 A2
Ibrāhīm → Lebanon 34°4N 35°38E 250 D6
'Ibrī Oman 23°14N 56°30E 249 B7
İbriktepe Turkey 41°0N 26°30E 203 E10
Ibshawâi Egypt 29°21N 30°40E 256 J7
Ibu Indonesia 1°35N 127°33E 231 D7
Ibuki-Sanchi Japan 35°25N 136°18E 223 B8
Ibusuki Japan 31°12N 130°40E 222 F2
Ica Peru 14°0S 75°48W 330 C2
Ica □ Peru 14°20S 75°30W 330 C2
Iça → Brazil 2°55S 67°58W 330 A4
Icabarú Venezuela 4°20N 61°45W 329 C5
Icabarú → Venezuela 4°45N 62°15W 329 C5
Icacos Trin. & Tob. 10°3N 61°54W 323 t
Icacos Pt. Trin. & Tob. 10°3N 61°57W 323 t
Içana Brazil 0°21N 67°19W 328 C4
Içana → Brazil 0°26N 67°19W 328 C4
Icarai Brazil 22°54S 43°6W 135 B2
Icatu Brazil 2°46S 44°4W 332 B3
Icaturama = Santa Rosa de Viterbo Colombia 5°53N 72°59W 328 B3
İçel = Mersin Turkey 36°51N 34°36E 250 B5
Iceland ■ Europe 64°45N 19°0W 155 C8
Iceland Basin Atl. Oc. 61°0N 19°0W 150 C7
Icelandic Plateau Arctic 64°0N 10°0W 150 C7
Içerenköy Turkey 40°58N 29°6E 122 C2
İçeriçumra Turkey 37°34N 32°39E 212 D5
Ichalkaranji India 16°40N 74°33E 244 F2
Ich'ang = Yichang China 30°40N 111°20E 229 B8
Ichchapuram India 19°10N 84°40E 244 E7
Icheon S. Korea 37°17N 127°27E 224 D3
Ichgao Japan 35°32N 139°32E 140 B2
Ichhawar India 23°1N 77°1E 242 H7
Ichigat Muja-Cordillera del Condor ⌓ Peru 4°20S 77°30W 330 A2
Ichigaya Tokyo, Japan 140 a3
Ichihara Japan 35°28N 140°5E 223 B12
Ichikawa Japan 35°43N 139°54E 140 A4
Ichilo → Bolivia 15°57S 64°50W 331 D5
Ichinohe Japan 40°13N 141°17E 220 D10
Ichinomiya Gifu, Japan 35°18N 136°48E 223 B8
Ichinomiya Kumamoto, Japan 32°58N 131°5E 222 E3
Ichinoseki Japan 38°55N 141°8E 220 E10
Ichkeul △ Tunisia 37°5N 9°37E 258 A1
Ichnya Ukraine 50°52N 32°24E 189 G7
Icht Morocco 29°6N 8°54W 260 C3
Ichu Taiwan 23°20N 120°14E 225 C2
Ichun = Yichun China 47°44N 128°52E 219 B14
Ickenham U.K. 51°33N 0°26W 125 A1
Icó Brazil 6°24S 38°51W 332 C4
Icoca Angola 6°12S 16°20E 265 D3
Icod Canary Is. 28°22N 16°43W 153 e1
Içoguz Turkmenistan 40°11N 58°24E 216 D5
Iconi Comoros Is. 12°21S 43°51E 272 a
Icy C. U.S.A. 70°20N 161°52W 303 A7
Ida Grove U.S.A. 42°21N 95°28W 308 D6
Idaan Somalia 6°10N 48°55E 267 C6
Idabel U.S.A. 33°54N 94°50W 314 E7
Idaga Hamus Ethiopia 14°13N 39°48E 257 E4
Idah Nigeria 7°5N 6°40E 263 D6
Idaho □ U.S.A. 45°0N 115°0W 304 D6
Idaho City U.S.A. 43°50N 115°50W 304 E6
Idaho Falls U.S.A. 43°30N 112°2W 304 E7
Idalia △ Australia 24°49S 144°36E 280 C3
Idanha-a-Nova Portugal 39°50N 7°15W 194 F3
Idar-Oberstein Germany 49°43N 7°16E 179 F3
Iday Niger 14°54N 11°33E 259 F2
'Idd el Ghanam Sudan 11°30N 24°19E 259 F4
Iddo Nigeria 6°28N 3°22E 124 B2
Idelès Algeria 23°50N 5°53E 261 D6
Idensalmi = Iisalmi Finland 63°32N 27°10E 160 E22
Idfû Egypt 24°55N 32°49E 256 C3
Idi Indonesia 5°2N 97°37E 234 A1
Idi, Oros = Psiloritis, Oros Greece 35°15N 24°45E 207 E5
Idi Amin Dada, L. = Edward, L. Africa 0°25S 29°40E 268 C2
Idi-Oro Nigeria 6°31N 3°21E 124 A2
İdil Turkey 37°20N 41°53E 213 D9
Idiofa Dem. Rep. of the Congo 4°55S 19°42E 265 C3
Idjil = Fdérik Mauritania 22°40N 12°45W 260 D2
Idkerberget Sweden 60°22N 15°15E 162 D9
Idku Egypt 31°18N 30°17E 256 H7
Idku, Bahra el Egypt 31°18N 30°18E 256 H7
Idlib Syria 35°55N 36°36E 250 C7
Idlib □ Syria 35°45N 36°45E 250 C7
Idomeni Albania 41°7N 22°31E 202 E6
Idra = Hydra Greece 37°20N 23°28E 204 D5
Idre Sweden 61°52N 12°42E 162 C6
Idria U.S.A. 36°25N 120°41W 306 J6
Idrija Slovenia 46°0N 14°5E 199 C11
Idritsa Russia 56°17N 28°53E 188 D5
Idutywa = Dutywa S. Africa 32°8S 28°18E 271 D4
Ie Shima Japan 26°43N 127°48E 288 a
Ie Suido Japan 26°42N 127°51E 288 a
Ieper Belgium 50°51N 2°53E 170 D2
Ierapetra Greece 35°1N 25°44E 207 F6
Ierissos Greece 40°22N 23°52E 202 F7
Ierissos Kolpos Greece 40°27N 23°57E 202 F7
Iernut Romania 46°27N 24°15E 183 D9
Ieshima-Shotō Japan 34°40N 134°32E 222 C6
Iesi Italy 43°31N 13°14E 199 E10
Iet Ethiopia 4°33N 43°1E 267 D5
Ifac, Penyal d' Spain 38°38N 0°5E 197 G5
'Ifāl, W. al → Si. Arabia 28°7N 35°3E 251 K6
Ifanadiana Madag. 21°19S 47°39E 272 C2
Ife Nigeria 7°30N 4°31E 263 D5
Iférouâne Niger 19°5N 8°24E 259 E1
Ifetesene Algeria 25°30N 4°33E 261 C5
Iffley Australia 18°53S 141°12E 280 B3
Ifon Nigeria 6°58N 5°40E 263 D6
Iforas, Adrar des Africa 19°40N 1°40E 261 D5
Ifould, L. Australia 30°52S 132°6E 279 F5
Ifrane Morocco 33°33N 5°7W 260 B3
Ifugao □ Phil. 16°40N 121°10E 232 C3
Iga Japan 34°45N 136°10E 223 C8
Igalo Montenegro 42°28N 18°30E 202 D2
Iganga Uganda 0°37N 33°28E 268 B3
Iganmu Nigeria 6°28N 3°22E 124 B2
Igara-Paraná → Colombia 2°9S 71°47W 328 D3
Igarapava Brazil 20°3S 47°47W 333 F2
Igarapé-Açu Brazil 1°4S 47°33W 332 B2
Igarapé-Miri Brazil 1°59S 48°58W 332 B2
Igarka Russia 67°30N 86°33E 214 C9
Igatpuri India 19°40N 73°35E 244 E1
Igbetti Nigeria 8°44N 4°8E 263 D5
Igbo-Ora Nigeria 7°29N 3°15E 263 D5
Igbobi Nigeria 6°31N 3°22E 124 A2
Igboho Nigeria 8°53N 3°50E 263 D5
Igbologun Nigeria 6°24N 3°19E 124 B1
Igbor Nigeria 7°27N 8°34E 263 D6
Iğdır Turkey 39°55N 44°2E 213 C11
Igelfors Sweden 58°52N 15°41E 163 F9
Iggesund Sweden 61°39N 17°10E 162 C11
Ighil Izane = Relizane Algeria 35°44N 0°31E 261 A5
Igiugig U.S.A. 59°20N 155°55W 303 G9
Iglau = Jihlava Czechia 49°28N 15°35E 180 B8
Iglésias Italy 39°19N 8°32E 200 C1
Igli Algeria 30°25N 2°19W 261 B4
Igloolik = Iglulik Canada 69°20N 81°49W 295 D15
Igluligaarjuk = Chesterfield Inlet Canada 63°30N 90°45W 294 E13
Iglulik Canada 69°20N 81°49W 295 D15
'Igma, G. el Egypt 29°10N 34°0E 251 J5
Ignace Canada 49°30N 91°40W 298 C1
İğneada Turkey 41°52N 27°59E 203 E11
İğneada Burnu Turkey 41°53N 28°2E 203 E12
Igny France 48°44N 2°13E 134 B2
Igoumenitsa Greece 39°32N 20°18E 206 B10
Igrim Russia 63°12N 64°30E 214 C7
Iguaçu → Brazil 25°36S 54°36W 335 B5
Iguaçu, Cat. del Brazil 25°41S 54°26W 335 B5
Iguaçu △ Brazil 25°30S 54°0W 335 B5
Iguaçu Falls = Iguaçu, Cat. del Brazil 25°41S 54°26W 335 B5
Iguala Mexico 18°21N 99°32W 319 D5
Igualada Spain 41°37N 1°37E 196 D6
Iguape Brazil 24°43S 47°33W 333 F2
Iguaratinga = São Francisco do Maranhão Brazil 6°15S 42°52W 332 C3
Iguassu = Iguaçu → Brazil 25°36S 54°36W 335 B5
Iguatu Brazil 6°20S 39°18W 332 C4
Iguazú △ Argentina 25°42S 54°22W 335 B5
Iguéla Gabon 2°0S 9°16E 264 C1
Iguéla, Lagune Gabon 1°48S 9°16E 264 C2
Iguidi, Erg Africa 27°0N 6°0W 260 C3
Iguig Phil. 17°45N 121°44E 232 C3
Igumen = Cherven Belarus 53°45N 28°28E 177 B15
Iharana Madag. 13°25S 50°0E 272 A3
Ihavandiffulu Atoll Maldives 7°0N 72°50E 272 d
Ihbulag Mongolia 43°11N 107°10E 226 C4
Iheya-Shima Japan 27°4N 127°58E 221 L3
Ihiala Nigeria 5°51N 6°55E 263 D6
Ihirene, O. → Algeria 20°28N 4°37E 261 D5
Ihorombe □ Madag. 22°25S 46°10E 272 C2
Ihosy Madag. 22°24S 46°8E 272 C2
Ihotry, Farihy Madag. 21°56S 43°41E 272 C1
Ihu Papua N. G. 7°55S 145°24E 286 D3
Ihugh Nigeria 7°2N 9°0E 263 D6
Ii Finland 65°19N 25°22E 160 D21
Ii-Shima Japan 26°43N 127°47E 221 L3
Iida Japan 35°35N 137°50E 223 B9
Iijoki → Finland 65°20N 25°20E 160 D21
Iisalmi Finland 63°32N 27°10E 160 E22
Iiyama Japan 36°51N 138°22E 221 F9
Iizuka Japan 33°38N 130°42E 222 D2
IJ, Het → Neths. 52°23N 4°54E 112 A2
IJ-meer Neths. 52°23N 4°54E 112 A3
Ijâfene Mauritania 20°40N 8°0W 260 D3
IJberg Neths. 52°22N 5°0E 112 A3
Ijebu-Igbo Nigeria 6°56N 4°1E 263 D5
Ijebu-Ode Nigeria 6°47N 3°58E 263 D5
Ijesa-Tedo Nigeria 6°29N 3°19E 124 B1
Ijevan Armenia 40°52N 45°8E 191 K7
Ijill, Sebkhet Mauritania 22°47N 12°53W 260 D2
IJmuiden Neths. 52°28N 4°35E 170 B4
Ijo älv = Iijoki → Finland 65°20N 25°20E 160 D21
Ijora Nigeria 6°27N 3°22E 124 B2
IJssel → Neths. 52°35N 5°50E 170 B5
IJsselmeer Neths. 52°45N 5°20E 170 B5
Ijuí Brazil 28°23S 53°55W 335 B5
Ijuí → Brazil 27°58S 55°20W 335 B4
Ijūin Japan 31°37N 130°24E 222 F2
Ikalamavony Madag. 21°9S 46°35E 272 C2
Ikali Dem. Rep. of the Congo 2°2S 21°4E 264 C4
Ikamatua N.Z. 42°16S 171°41E 285 C6
Ikang Nigeria 4°49N 8°30E 263 E6
Ikanga Kenya 1°42S 38°4E 268 C4
Ikara Nigeria 11°12N 8°15E 263 C6
Ikare Nigeria 7°32N 5°40E 263 D6
Ikaria Greece 37°35N 26°10E 205 D8
Ikast Denmark 56°8N 9°10E 163 H3
Ikebe Japan 35°31N 139°34E 140 B2
Ikebukuro Japan 35°43N 139°42E 140 A3
Ikeda Japan 34°1N 133°48E 222 C5

Ikegami Japan 35°33N 139°42E 140 B3
Ikei-shima Japan 26°23N 127°59E 288 a
Ikeja Nigeria 6°35N 3°20E 124 A2
Ikela Dem. Rep. of the Congo 1°6S 23°6E 264 C4
Ikélemba Congo 1°12N 16°38E 264 B3
Ikélemba →
Dem. Rep. of the Congo 0°7N 18°17E 264 B3
Ikengo Dem. Rep. of the Congo 0°8S 18°8E 264 C3
Ikere Nigeria 7°25N 5°19E 263 D6
Ikeuchi Japan 34°35N 135°32E 133 B2
Ikhtiman Bulgaria 42°27N 23°48E 202 D7
Iki Japan 33°45N 129°42E 222 D1
Iki-Kaikyō Japan 33°40N 129°45E 222 D1
Ikimba L. Tanzania 1°30S 31°20E 268 C3
Ikire Nigeria 7°23N 4°15E 263 D5
Ikitsuki-Shima Japan 33°23N 129°26E 222 D1
İkizdere Turkey 40°46N 40°32E 213 B9
Iko Congo 0°35S 16°0E 264 C3
Ikom Nigeria 6°0N 8°42E 263 D6
Ikoma Japan 34°30N 135°40E 223 C7
Ikomu
Dem. Rep. of the Congo 1°54S 19°40E 264 C3
Ikongo Madag. 21°52S 47°27E 272 C2
Ikopa → Madag. 16°45S 46°40E 272 B2
Ikorodu Nigeria 6°35N 3°29E 124 A2
Ikorongo △ Tanzania 1°50S 34°53E 268 C3
Ikot Ekpene Nigeria 5°12N 7°40E 263 D6
Ikoyi Nigeria 6°27N 3°26E 124 B2
Ikparjuk = Arctic Bay
Canada 73°1N 85°7W 295 C14
Iksan S. Korea 35°59N 127°0E 224 E3
Ikuata Nigeria 6°24N 3°21E 124 B2
Ikungu Tanzania 1°33S 33°42E 268 C3
Ikuno Hyōgo, Japan 35°10N 134°48E 222 B6
Ikuno Ōsaka, Japan 34°40N 135°30E 133 A2
Ikuntji = Haasts Bluff
Australia 23°22S 132°0E 278 D5
Ikurun Nigeria 7°54N 4°40E 263 D5
Ikuta Japan 35°36N 139°32E 140 B2
Il-Kullana Malta 35°50N 14°24E 206 F7
Il-Munxar Malta 35°51N 14°34E 206 F8
Ila Dem. Rep. of the Congo 2°53S 21°7E 264 C4
Ila Nigeria 8°0N 4°39E 263 D5
Ila Oslo, Norway 59°57N 10°35E 133 A2
Ilafer Algeria 21°40N 1°58E 261 D5
Ilagan Phil. 17°7N 121°53E 232 C3
Ilaka Madag. 19°33S 48°52E 272 B2
Īlām Iran 33°36N 46°36E 213 F12
Ilam Nepal 26°58N 87°58E 243 F12
Īlām □ Iran 33°0N 47°0E 246 C5
Ilan Taiwan 24°45N 121°44E 225 B3
Ilan □ Taiwan 24°30N 121°35E 225 B3
Ilan, Mt. Phil. 10°26N 119°33E 233 F2
Ilanskiy Russia 56°14N 96°3E 215 D10
Ilaro Nigeria 6°53N 3°3E 263 D5
Ilatane Niger 16°30N 4°45E 263 B5
Ilave Peru 16°5S 69°40W 330 D4
Iława Poland 53°36N 19°34E 184 E6
Ilayangudi India 9°34N 78°37E 245 K4
Ile → Kazakhstan 45°53N 77°10E 217 C9
Île-à-la-Crosse Canada 55°27N 107°53W 297 B7
Île-à-la-Crosse, Lac
Canada 55°40N 107°45W 297 B7
Ile-Alatau △ Kazakhstan 43°5N 77°5E 217 D9
Île-de-France □ France 49°0N 2°20E 173 D9
Ileanda Romania 47°20N 23°38E 183 C8
Ilebo Dem. Rep. of the Congo 4°17S 20°55E 265 C4
Ilek Russia 51°32N 53°21E 216 B4
Ilek → Russia 51°30N 53°22E 186 D9
Ilemi Triangle Africa 5°0N 35°20E 257 G4
Iler, O. → Algeria 20°59N 3°14E 261 D5
Ilero Nigeria 8°0N 3°20E 263 D5
Ilesha Kwara, Nigeria 8°57N 3°28E 263 D5
Ilesha Oyo, Nigeria 7°37N 4°40E 263 D5
Ilet = Krasnogorskiy
Russia 56°10N 48°28E 190 B9
Iletskaya = Sol Iletsk
Russia 51°10N 55°0E 186 D10
Iletsky Gorodok = Ilek
Russia 51°32N 53°21E 216 B4
Ilford Man., Canada 56°4N 95°35W 297 B9
Ilford London, U.K. 51°33N 0°4E 125 A4
Ilfov □ Romania 44°36N 26°7E 183 F11
Ilfracombe Queens.,
Australia 23°30S 144°30E 280 C3
Ilfracombe Devon, U.K. 51°12N 4°8W 169 F3
Ilgaz Turkey 40°55N 33°37E 212 B5
Ilgaz Dağları Turkey 41°10N 33°50E 212 B5
Ilgın Turkey 38°16N 31°55E 212 C4
Ilha, Pta. da Azores 38°25N 28°3W 153 d1
Ilha Grande Brazil 0°27S 65°2W 329 D4
Ilha Grande, B. da Brazil 23°9S 44°30W 333 F3
Ilha Grande, Represa
Brazil 23°10S 53°5W 335 A5
Ilha Grande △ Brazil 23°10S 53°20W 335 A5
Ílhavo Portugal 40°33N 8°43W 194 E2
Ilhéus Brazil 14°49S 39°2W 333 D4
Ili = Ile → Kazakhstan 45°53N 77°10E 217 C9
Ilia Greece 37°45N 21°35E 204 D3
Ilia Romania 45°57N 22°40E 182 E7
Iliamna U.S.A. 59°45N 154°55W 303 G9
Iliamna L. U.S.A. 59°30N 155°0W 303 G9
Ilias, Profitis Greece 36°17N 27°56E 206 E11
Iliç Turkey 39°27N 38°33E 213 C8
Ilıca Turkey 39°52N 27°46E 205 B9
Ilig, Ras Somalia 7°47N 49°50E 267 C6
Iligan Phil. 8°12N 124°13E 233 G5
Iligan B. Phil. 8°25N 124°5E 233 G5
Iligan Pt. Phil. 18°25N 122°25E 232 B4
Ilin I. Phil. 12°14N 121°5E 232 E3
'Ilio Pt. U.S.A. 21°13N 157°16W 302 B4
Ilion U.S.A. 43°1N 75°2W 313 D9
Ilioupoli Greece 37°54N 23°47E 112 B2
Ilirska-Bistrica Slovenia 45°34N 14°14E 199 C11
Iliwa = Rewa → Guyana 3°19N 58°42W 329 C6
Iliysk = Qapshaghay
Kazakhstan 43°51N 77°14E 217 D9
Ilkal India 15°57N 76°8E 245 G3
Ilkenau = Olkusz Poland 50°18N 19°33E 185 H6
Ilkeston U.K. 52°58N 1°19W 168 E6
Ilkley U.K. 53°56N 1°48W 168 D6
Illampu = Ancohuma, Nevado
Bolivia 16°0S 68°50W 330 D4
Illana B. Phil. 7°35N 123°45E 233 H4
Illapel Chile 32°0S 71°10W 334 C1
Ille-et-Vilaine □ France 48°10N 1°30W 172 D5
Ille-sur-Têt France 42°40N 2°38E 174 F6
Illéla Niger 14°32N 5°20E 263 C6
Iller → Germany 48°23N 9°58E 179 G5
Illertissen Germany 48°12N 10°7E 179 G6
Illes Balears = Baleares, Is.
Spain 39°30N 3°0E 206 B4
Illescas Spain 40°8N 3°51W 194 E7
Illetas Spain 39°32N 2°35E 206 B3
Illichivsk Ukraine 46°20N 30°35E 189 J6
Illiers-Combray France 48°18N 1°15E 172 D8
Illimani, Nevado Bolivia 16°30S 67°50W 330 D4
Illinois □ U.S.A. 40°15N 89°30W 310 D7
Illinois → U.S.A. 38°58N 90°28W 310 F6
Illinois at Chicago, Univ. of
U.S.A. 41°52N 87°38W 119 B3
Illinois Institute of Technology
U.S.A. 41°50N 87°37W 119 B3
Illiopolis U.S.A. 39°51N 89°15W 310 E7
Illium = Troy Turkey 39°57N 26°12E 205 B8
Illizi Algeria 26°31N 8°32E 261 C6
Illizi □ Algeria 26°50N 8°10E 261 C6
Illkirch-Graffenstaden
France 48°34N 7°42E 173 D14
Íllora Spain 37°17N 3°53W 195 H7
Ilm → Germany 51°6N 11°40E 178 D7
Ilma, L. Australia 29°13S 127°46E 279 E4
Ilmajoki Finland 62°44N 22°34E 160 E20
Ilmen, Ozero Russia 58°15N 31°10E 188 C6
Ilmenau = Jordanów
Poland 49°41N 19°49E 185 J6
Ilmenau = Limanowa
Poland 49°42N 20°22E 185 J7
Ilmenau Germany 50°41N 10°54E 178 E6
Ilnytsya Ukraine 48°21N 23°5E 182 B8
Ilo Peru 17°40S 71°20W 330 D3
Ilobu Nigeria 7°45N 4°25E 263 D5
Iloc I. Phil. 11°17N 119°40E 233 F2
Ilocos Norte □ Phil. 18°10N 120°45E 232 B3
Ilocos Sur □ Phil. 17°20N 120°35E 232 C3
Iloilo Phil. 10°45N 122°33E 233 F4
Iloilo □ Phil. 11°0N 122°40E 233 F4
Ilomantsi Finland 62°38N 30°57E 160 E24
Ilora Nigeria 7°45N 3°50E 263 D5
Ilorin Nigeria 8°30N 4°35E 263 D5
Ilovatka Russia 50°30N 45°50E 190 E7
Ilovlya Russia 49°15N 44°2E 191 F7
Ilovlya → Russia 49°14N 44°0E 191 F7
Iłowa Poland 51°30N 15°10E 185 G2
Ilpendam Neths. 52°28N 4°57E 112 A2
Ilsos → Greece 37°55N 23°41E 112 B2
Ilubabor Ethiopia 7°25N 35°0E 257 F4
Ilulissat Greenland 69°12N 51°10W 154 D5
Ilva Mică Romania 47°17N 24°40E 183 C9
Ilwaco U.S.A. 46°19N 124°3W 306 D2
Ilyichevsk = Illichivsk
Ukraine 46°20N 30°35E 189 J6
Iłża Poland 51°10N 21°15E 185 G8
Iłżanka → Poland 51°14N 21°48E 185 G8
Imabari Japan 34°4N 133°0E 222 C5
Imagem e do Som, Museu da
Rio de J., Brazil 135 b3
Imaichi Japan 36°43N 139°46E 223 A11
Imaloto → Madag. 23°27S 45°13E 272 C2
İmamoğlu Turkey 37°15N 35°38E 212 D6
Iman = Dalnerechensk
Russia 45°50N 133°40E 220 B6
Imandra, Ozero Russia 67°30N 33°0E 160 C25
Imanombo Madag. 24°26S 45°49E 272 C2
Imari Japan 33°15N 129°52E 222 D1
Imasa Sudan 18°0N 36°12E 256 D4
Imatra Finland 61°12N 28°48E 188 B5
Imbâbah Egypt 30°3N 31°12E 117 A2
Imbabura □ Ecuador 0°30N 78°45W 328 C2
Imbaimadai Guyana 5°44N 60°17W 329 B5
Imbiah Lookout Singapore 1°16N 103°49E 138 B2
Imbonga
Dem. Rep. of the Congo 0°43S 19°44E 264 C3
Iménas Mali 16°20N 0°40E 263 B5
imeni 26 Bakinskikh Komissarov =
Neftçala Azerbaijan 39°19N 49°12E 213 C13
imeni 26 Bakinskikh Komissarov
Turkmenistan 39°22N 54°10E 247 B7
imeni Dvadtsati Shesti Bakinskikh
Komissarov = Neftçala
Azerbaijan 39°19N 49°12E 213 C13
imeni Dzerzhinskogo =
Naryan-Mar Russia 67°42N 53°12E 186 A9
imeni Ismail Samani, Pik
Tajikistan 39°0N 72°2E 217 E8
imeni Karl Libknekhta
Russia 51°40N 35°35E 189 G8
imeni Mikoyana = Kara-Balta
Kyrgyzstan 42°50N 73°49E 217 D8
imeni Petrovskogo G.I. =
Horodyshche Ukraine 49°17N 31°27E 189 H6
imeni Sverdlova = Sverdlovsk
Ukraine 48°5N 39°47E 189 H10
imeni Tovarishcha Khateyevicha =
Synelnykove Ukraine 48°25N 35°30E 189 H8
imeni Tretyego Internatsionala =
Novoshakhtinsk
Russia 47°46N 39°58E 189 J10
Imeri, Serra Brazil 0°50N 65°25W 328 C4
Imerimandroso Madag. 17°26S 48°35E 272 B2
Imese Dem. Rep. of the Congo 2°6N 18°9E 264 B3
Imfolozi △ S. Africa 28°18S 31°50E 271 C5
Imi Ethiopia 6°28N 42°10E 257 F5
Imielin Poland 52°9N 21°0E 143 C2
Imirim Brazil 23°29S 46°39W 137 A2
Imişli Azerbaijan 39°55N 48°4E 191 L9
Imitek Morocco 29°43N 8°10W 260 C3
Imitos Greece 37°55N 23°45E 112 B2
Imitos, Oros Greece 37°53N 23°48E 112 B2
Imizu Japan 36°47N 137°4E 223 A9
Imjado S. Korea 35°5N 126°5E 224 E3
Imjin-gang → N. Korea 37°47N 126°39E 224 D3
Imlay U.S.A. 40°40N 118°9W 304 F4
Imlay City U.S.A. 43°2N 83°5W 312 D1
Immaseri Sudan 15°40N 25°31E 257 D2
Immenstadt Germany 47°33N 10°13E 179 H6
Immingham U.K. 53°37N 0°13W 168 D7
Immokalee U.S.A. 26°25N 81°25W 317 J8
Imo □ Nigeria 5°30N 7°10E 263 D6
Imo → Nigeria 4°36N 7°35E 263 E6
Imola Italy 44°20N 11°42E 199 D8
Imotski Croatia 43°27N 17°12E 199 E14
Impé Congo 2°45S 15°16E 264 C3
Imperatorskaya Gavan = Vanino
Russia 48°50N 140°5E 215 E15
Imperatriz Amazonas, Brazil 5°18S 67°11W 330 B4
Imperatriz Maranhão,
Brazil 5°30S 47°29W 332 C2
Impéria Italy 43°53N 8°3E 198 E5
Imperial Sask., Canada 51°21N 105°28W 297 C7
Imperial Peru 13°4S 76°21W 330 C2
Imperial Calif., U.S.A. 32°51N 115°34W 307 N11
Imperial Nebr., U.S.A. 40°31N 101°39W 308 E3
Imperial Beach U.S.A. 32°35N 117°6W 307 N9
Imperial Dam U.S.A. 32°55N 114°25W 307 N12
Imperial Palace = Paço Imperial
Rio de J., Brazil 135 a2
Imperial Palace Museum Beijing, China 114 b3
Imperial Res. U.S.A. 32°53N 114°28W 307 N12
Imperial Valley U.S.A. 33°0N 115°30W 307 N11
Imperieuse Reef Australia 17°36S 118°50E 278 C2
Impfondo Congo 1°40N 18°0E 264 B3
Imphal India 24°48N 93°56E 241 C4
Imphy France 46°55N 3°16E 173 F10
Impulo Angola 13°51S 13°39E 265 E2
İmranlı Turkey 39°54N 38°7E 213 C8
İmroz = Gökçeada Turkey 40°10N 25°50E 203 F9
Imst Austria 47°15N 10°44E 180 D3
Imuris Mexico 30°47N 110°52W 318 A2
Imuruan B. Phil. 10°40N 119°10E 233 F2
Imus Phil. 14°26N 120°56E 232 D3
In Aleï Mali 17°42N 2°30W 262 B4
In Amenas Algeria 28°5N 9°33E 261 C6
In Amguel Algeria 23°41N 5°9E 261 D6
In Atei Algeria 20°33N 6°4E 261 D6
In Belbel Algeria 27°55N 1°12E 261 C5
In Delimane Mali 15°52N 1°31E 263 B5
In Ghar Algeria 27°10N 1°59E 261 C5
In Guezzam Algeria 19°37N 5°52E 261 E6
In Koufi Mali 19°11N 1°25E 263 B5
In Salah Algeria 27°10N 2°32E 261 C5
In Tallak Mali 16°19N 3°15E 263 B5
In Tebezas Mali 17°49N 1°53E 263 B5
Ina Japan 35°50N 137°55E 223 B8
Ina Ill., U.S.A. 38°9N 88°54W 311 F8
Ina-Bonchi Japan 35°45N 137°58E 223 B8
Inabanga Phil. 10°2N 124°4E 233 F5
Inaccessible I. Atl. Oc. 37°18S 12°40W 152 K10
Inagauan Phil. 9°33N 118°39E 233 G2
Inagi Japan 35°38N 139°31E 140 B2
Inajá Brazil 8°54S 37°49W 332 C4
Inambari → Peru 12°41S 69°44W 330 C4
Inangahua N.Z. 41°52S 171°59E 285 B6
Inanwatan Indonesia 2°8S 132°10E 231 E8
Iñapari Peru 11°0S 69°40W 330 C4
Inarajan Guam 13°16N 144°45E 302 d
Inari Finland 68°54N 27°1E 160 B22
Inarijärvi Finland 69°0N 28°0E 160 B23
Inawashiro-Ko Japan 37°29N 140°6E 220 F10
Inazawa Japan 35°15N 136°47E 223 B8
tInbhear Mór, An = Arklow
Ireland 52°48N 6°10W 166 D5
Inbin Burma 18°6N 95°16E 241 F5
Inca Spain 39°43N 2°54E 206 B3
Inca de Oro Chile 26°45S 69°54W 334 B2
Incahuasi Argentina 27°2S 68°18W 334 B2
Incahuasi Chile 29°12S 71°5W 334 B1
İnce Burun Turkey 42°7N 34°56E 212 A6
İncekum Burnu Turkey 36°13N 33°57E 250 B4
İncesu Turkey 38°38N 35°11E 212 C6
Inchcolm U.K. 56°2N 3°18W 121 A2
Incheon S. Korea 37°27N 126°40E 224 D3
Incheon Int. ✈ (ICN)
S. Korea 37°28N 126°26E 224 D3
Inchiri □ Mauritania 20°0N 15°0W 260 E2
Inchkeith U.K. 56°2N 3°8W 121 A3
Inchmickery U.K. 56°0N 3°16W 121 A2
Incio = A Cruz do Incio
Spain 42°39N 7°21W 194 C3
Incirano Italy 45°34N 9°9E 128 A1
İncirliova Turkey 37°50N 27°41E 205 D9
Incline Village U.S.A. 39°10N 119°58W 306 F7
Incomáti → Mozam. 25°46S 32°43E 271 C5
Incudine, Mte. France 41°50N 9°12E 175 G13
Inda Silase Ethiopia 14°10N 38°15E 257 E4
Indal Sweden 62°35N 17°5E 162 B11
Indalsälven → Sweden 62°36N 17°30E 162 B11
Indaw Burma 24°15N 96°5E 241 C6
Indawgyi, L. Burma 25°8N 96°20E 241 C6
Indbir Ethiopia 8°7N 37°52E 257 F4
Indefatigable, I. = Santa Cruz, I.
Ecuador 0°38S 90°23W 330 a
Independence Calif.,
U.S.A. 36°48N 118°12W 306 J8
Independence Iowa,
U.S.A. 42°28N 91°54W 310 B5
Independence Kans.,
U.S.A. 37°14N 95°42W 308 G6
Independence Ky.,
U.S.A. 38°57N 84°33W 311 F12
Independence Mo., U.S.A. 39°6N 94°25W 310 E2
Independence Avenue
Washington, D.C., U.S.A. 143 c2
Independence Fjord
Greenland 82°10N 29°0W 154 A8
Independence Mts.
U.S.A. 41°20N 116°0W 304 F5
Independência Brazil 5°23S 40°19W 332 C3
Independencia Santiago,
Chile 33°25S 70°39W 137 B2
Independencia Lima, Peru 11°59S 77°3W 124 A2
Independencia, I. Peru 14°16S 76°12W 330 C2
Independenţa Romania 45°25N 27°42E 183 E12
Inderbor Kazakhstan 48°33N 51°47E 216 C4
Index U.S.A. 47°50N 121°33W 306 C5
Indi India 17°10N 75°58E 244 F2
India ■ Asia 20°0N 78°0E 239 F11
India Gate Delhi, India 120 c2
Indialantic U.S.A. 28°6N 80°34W 317 G9
Indian → U.S.A. 27°59N 80°34W 317 G9
Indian Cabins Canada 59°52N 117°40W 296 B5
Indian Creek Village
U.S.A. 25°52N 80°8W 129 C3
Indian Harbour Canada 54°27N 57°13W 299 B8
Indian Harbour Beach
U.S.A. 28°10N 80°35W 317 G9
Indian Head Canada 50°30N 103°41W 297 C8
Indian L. U.S.A. 43°46N 74°16W 313 C10
Indian Lake U.S.A. 43°47N 74°16W 313 C10
Indian Ocean 5°0S 75°0E 273 E6
Indian Rocks Beach
U.S.A. 27°52N 82°51W 317 H7
Indian Springs U.S.A. 36°35N 115°40W 307 J11
Indian Town Pt.
Antigua & B. 17°6N 61°40W 322 b
Indian Walk Trin. & Tob. 10°16N 61°20W 323 t
Indiana U.S.A. 40°37N 79°9W 312 F5
Indiana □ U.S.A. 40°0N 86°0W 311 E11
Indiana Dunes △ U.S.A. 41°40N 87°0W 311 C9
Indianapolis U.S.A. 39°46N 86°9W 311 E10
Indianapolis Int. ✈ (IND)
U.S.A. 39°43N 86°17W 311 E10
Indianola Iowa, U.S.A. 41°22N 93°34W 310 C3
Indianola Miss., U.S.A. 33°27N 90°39W 315 E9
Indianópolis Brazil 23°35S 46°38W 137 B2
Indiantown U.S.A. 27°1N 80°28W 317 H9
Indiaporã Brazil 19°57S 50°17W 333 E1
Indiga Russia 67°38N 49°9E 186 A8
Indigirka → Russia 70°48N 148°54E 215 B15
Inđija Serbia 45°6N 20°7E 182 E5
Indio U.S.A. 33°43N 116°13W 307 M10
Indira Gandhi Canal India 28°0N 72°0E 242 F5
Indira Gandhi Int. ✈ (DEL)
India 28°34N 77°5E 120 B1
Indira Gandhi Memorial Museum
India 28°36N 77°12E 120 B2
Indira Pt. India 6°44N 93°49E 245 L11
Indira Sagar India 22°15N 76°40E 242 H7
Indispensable Str.
Solomon Is. 9°0S 160°30E 287 M11
Indo-China Asia 15°0N 102°0E 210 G12
Indonesia ■ Asia 5°0S 115°0E 235 C4
Indore India 22°42N 75°53E 242 H6
Indramayu Indonesia 6°20S 108°19E 235 D3
Indrapura = Kerinci
Indonesia 1°40S 101°15E 234 C2
Indravati → India 19°20N 80°20E 244 E5
Indre □ France 46°50N 1°39E 173 F8
Indre → France 47°16N 0°11E 172 E7
Indre Ålvik Norway 60°26N 6°26E 164 D3
Indre Arna Norway 60°26N 5°30E 164 D2
Indre-et-Loire □ France 47°20N 0°40E 172 E7
Indrio U.S.A. 27°31N 80°21W 317 H9
Indulkana Australia 26°58S 133°5E 281 D1
Indungo Angola 14°48S 16°17E 265 E3
Indura Belarus 53°26N 23°53E 184 E10
Indus → Pakistan 24°20N 67°47E 242 G2
Indus, Mouths of the
Pakistan 24°0N 68°0E 242 H3
Industria S. Africa 26°11S 27°58E 123 B1
Industrial Canal U.S.A. 30°4N 90°4W 131 A2
Industry U.S.A. 40°20N 90°36W 310 D6
İnebolu Turkey 41°55N 33°40E 212 B5
İnecik Turkey 40°56N 27°16E 203 F11
İnegöl Turkey 40°5N 29°31E 203 F13
Inés, Mt. Argentina 48°30S 69°40W 336 C3
Ineu Romania 46°26N 21°51E 182 D6
Inezgane Morocco 30°25N 9°29W 260 B3
Infanta Phil. 14°45N 121°39E 232 D3
Infantes = Villanueva de los
Infantes Spain 38°43N 3°1W 195 G7
Infiernillo, Presa del
Mexico 18°35N 101°50W 318 D4
Infiesto Spain 43°21N 5°21W 194 B5
Inga, Barrage d'
Dem. Rep. of the Congo 5°39S 13°39E 265 D2
Ingabu Burma 17°37N 95°20E 241 G5
Inganda
Dem. Rep. of the Congo 0°5S 20°57E 264 C4
Ingapirca Ecuador 2°38S 78°56W 328 D2
Ingaro Sweden 59°12N 18°45E 162 E12
Ingelstad Sweden 56°45N 14°56E 163 H8
Ingende
Dem. Rep. of the Congo 0°12S 18°57E 264 C3
Ingeniero Jacobacci
Argentina 41°20S 69°36W 336 B3
Ingenio Canary Is. 27°55N 15°26W 153 e1
Ingenio Santa Ana
Argentina 27°25S 65°40W 334 B2
Ingersoll Canada 43°4N 80°55W 312 C4
Ingham Australia 18°43S 146°10E 280 B4
Ingierstrand Norway 59°49N 10°46E 133 B3
Ingleborough U.K. 54°10N 2°22W 168 C5
Inglefield Land Greenland 78°30N 70°0W 154 B4
Inglewood Queens.,
Australia 28°25S 151°2E 281 D5
Inglewood Vic., Australia 36°29S 143°53E 282 D5
Inglewood N.Z. 39°9S 174°14E 284 F3
Inglewood Calif., U.S.A. 33°58N 118°21W 126 C3
Inglis U.S.A. 29°2N 82°40W 317 F7
Ingliston U.K. 55°56N 3°23W 121 B1
Ingolf Fjord Greenland 80°35N 17°30W 154 A9
Ingólfshöfði Iceland 63°48N 16°39W 155 D10
Ingolstadt Germany 48°46N 11°26E 179 G7
Ingomar U.S.A. 46°35N 107°23W 304 C10
Ingonish Canada 46°42N 60°18W 299 C7
Ingore Guinea-Biss. 12°24N 15°48W 262 C1
Ingraj Bazar India 24°58N 88°10E 243 G13
Ingrid Christensen Coast
Antarctica 69°30S 76°0E 151 C6
Ingul = Inhul → Ukraine 46°50N 32°0E 189 J7
Ingulec = Inhulec Ukraine 47°42N 33°14E 189 J7
Ingulets = Inhulets →
Ukraine 46°46N 32°47E 189 J7
Inguri = Enguri →
Georgia 42°27N 41°38E 191 J5
Ingushetia □ Russia 43°20N 44°50E 191 J7
Ingwavuma S. Africa 27°9S 31°59E 271 C5
Inhaca Mozam. 26°1S 32°57E 271 C5
Inhaca Pen. Mozam. 26°13S 32°55E 271 C5
Inhafenga Mozam. 20°36S 33°53E 271 B5
Inhambane Mozam. 23°54S 35°30E 271 B6
Inhambane □ Mozam. 22°30S 34°20E 271 B5
Inhambupe Brazil 11°47S 38°21W 333 D4
Inhaminga Mozam. 18°26S 35°0E 269 F4
Inharrime Mozam. 24°30S 35°0E 271 B6
Inharrime → Mozam. 24°30S 35°0E 271 B6
Inhaúma Brazil 22°51S 43°17W 135 B1
Inhisar Turkey 40°3N 30°23E 205 A12
Inhul → Ukraine 46°50N 32°0E 189 J7
Inhulec Ukraine 47°42N 33°14E 189 J7
Inhulets → Ukraine 46°46N 32°47E 189 J7
Inhuma Brazil 6°40S 41°42W 332 C3
Inhumas Brazil 16°22S 49°30W 333 E2
Iniesta Spain 39°27N 1°45W 197 F3
Ining = Yining China 43°58N 81°10E 217 D10
Inírida → Colombia 3°55N 67°52W 328 C4
Inis = Ennis Ireland 52°51N 8°59W 166 D3
Inishbofin Ireland 53°37N 10°13W 166 C1
Inisheer Ireland 53°3N 9°32W 166 C2
Inishfree B. Ireland 55°4N 8°23W 166 A3
Inishkea North Ireland 54°9N 10°11W 166 B1
Inishkea South Ireland 54°7N 10°12W 166 B1
Inishmaan Ireland 53°5N 9°35W 166 C2
Inishmore Ireland 53°8N 9°45W 166 C2
Inishmurray Ireland 54°26N 8°39W 166 B3
Inishowen Pen. Ireland 55°14N 7°15W 166 A4
Inishshark Ireland 53°37N 10°16W 166 C1
Inishturk Ireland 53°42N 10°7W 166 C1
Inishvickillane Ireland 52°3N 10°37W 166 D1
Initao Phil. 8°56N 124°20E 233 G5
Injāna Iraq 34°29N 44°38E 213 E11
Injibara Ethiopia 10°59N 37°0E 257 E4
Injinoo ✪ Australia 10°56S 142°15E 280 A3
Injune Australia 25°53S 148°32E 281 D4
Inkisi →
Dem. Rep. of the Congo 4°46S 14°52E 265 D3
Inklin → N. Amer. 58°50N 133°10W 296 B2
Inland Kaikoura Ra.
N.Z. 41°59S 173°41E 285 B8
Inland Sea = Setonaikai
Japan 34°20N 133°30E 222 C5
Inle L. Burma 20°30N 96°58E 241 E6
Inlet U.S.A. 43°45N 74°48W 313 C10
Inn → Austria 48°35N 13°28E 180 C6
Innamincka Australia 27°44S 140°46E 281 D3
Innbygda Norway 61°19N 12°17E 164 C9
Inner Hebrides U.K. 57°0N 6°30W 167 E2
Inner Mongolia = Nei Mongol
Zizhiqu □ China 42°0N 112°0E 226 D7
Inner Port Shelter
Hong Kong, China 22°22N 114°17E 122 A3
Inner Sound U.K. 57°30N 5°55W 167 D3
Innerkip Canada 43°13N 80°42W 312 C4
Innes △ Australia 35°52S 136°53E 282 C2
Innetalling I. Canada 56°0N 79°0W 298 A4
Innisfail Queens., Australia 17°33S 146°5E 280 B4
Innisfail Alta., Canada 52°2N 113°57W 296 C6
Innoko Nat. Wildlife Refuge △
U.S.A. 63°20N 158°25W 303 E8
In'noshima Japan 34°19N 133°10E 222 C5
Innsbruck Austria 47°16N 11°23E 180 D4
Innviertel Austria 48°15N 13°15E 180 C6
Innvik Norway 61°51N 6°37E 164 C3
Inny → Ireland 53°32N 7°51W 166 C4
Ino Japan 33°33N 133°26E 222 D5
Inocência Brazil 19°47S 51°48W 333 E1
Inongo
Dem. Rep. of the Congo 1°55S 18°30E 264 C3
Inoni Congo 3°4S 15°39E 264 C3
İnönü Turkey 39°48N 30°9E 205 B12
Inoucdjouac = Inukjuak
Canada 58°25N 78°15W 295 F16
Inousses Greece 38°33N 26°14E 205 C8
Inowrocław Poland 52°50N 18°12E 185 F5
Inquisivi Bolivia 16°50S 67°10W 330 D4
Inscription, C. Australia 25°29S 112°59E 279 E1
Insein Burma 16°50N 96°5E 241 G6
Insjön Sweden 60°41N 15°6E 162 D9
Ińsko Poland 53°25N 15°32E 184 E2
Insterberg = Chernyakhovsk
Russia 54°36N 21°48E 184 D8
Însurăţei Romania 44°50N 27°40E 183 F12
Inta Russia 66°5N 60°8E 186 A11
Intendente Alvear
Argentina 35°12S 63°32W 334 D3
İntepe Turkey 40°1N 26°20E 205 A8
Interlachen U.S.A. 29°37N 81°53W 317 F8
Interlagos Brazil 23°41S 46°42W 137 C1
Interlaken Switz. 46°41N 7°50E 179 J3
Interlaken N.Y., U.S.A. 42°37N 76°44W 313 D8
International Falls U.S.A. 48°36N 93°25W 308 A7
Interview I. India 12°55N 92°43E 245 H11
Intiyaco Argentina 28°43S 60°5W 334 B3
Întorsura Buzăului
Romania 45°41N 26°2E 183 E11
Intramuros Phil. 14°35N 120°57E 127 B1
Intrepid Air and Space Museum
New York, U.S.A. 132 b1
Intutu Peru 3°32S 74°48W 328 D3
Inubō-Zaki Japan 35°42N 140°52E 223 B12
Inukjuak Canada 58°25N 78°15W 295 F16
Inútil, B. Chile 53°30S 70°15W 336 D2
Inuvik Canada 68°16N 133°40W 294 D5
Inuyama Japan 35°23N 136°56E 223 B8
Invalides France 48°51N 2°18E 134 A2
Inveraray U.K. 56°14N 5°5W 167 E3
Inverbervie U.K. 56°51N 2°17W 167 E6
Invercargill N.Z. 46°24S 168°24E 285 G3
Inverclyde □ U.K. 55°55N 4°49W 167 F4
Inverell Australia 29°45S 151°8E 281 D5
Invergordon U.K. 57°41N 4°10W 167 D4
Inverkeithing U.K. 56°2N 3°24W 121 A1
Inverleigh Australia 38°6S 144°3E 282 E6
Inverloch Australia 38°38S 145°45E 281 F4
Invermere Canada 50°30N 116°2W 296 C5
Inverness N.S., Canada 46°15N 61°19W 299 C7
Inverness Highl., U.K. 57°29N 4°13W 167 D4
Inverness Ala., U.S.A. 32°1N 85°45W 316 C4
Inverness Fla., U.S.A. 28°50N 82°20W 317 G7
Inverurie U.K. 57°17N 2°23W 167 D6
Investigator Group
Australia 34°45S 134°20E 281 E1
Investigator Ridge Ind. Oc. 11°30S 98°10E 273 F8
Investigator Str. Australia 35°30S 137°0E 282 C2
Inya Russia 50°28N 86°37E 217 B11
Inyanga Zimbabwe 18°12S 32°40E 269 F3
Inyangani Zimbabwe 18°5S 32°50E 269 F3
Inyantue Zimbabwe 18°33S 26°39E 270 A4
Inyo Mts. U.S.A. 36°40N 118°0W 306 J9
Inyokern U.S.A. 35°39N 117°49W 307 K9
Inyonga Tanzania 6°45S 32°5E 268 D3
Inywa Burma 23°56N 96°17E 241 D6
Inza Russia 53°55N 46°25E 190 D8
Inzersdorf Austria 48°8N 16°21E 142 B2
Inzhavino Russia 52°22N 42°30E 190 D6
Inzia →
Dem. Rep. of the Congo 3°45S 17°57E 265 C3
Iō-Jima Japan 30°48N 130°18E 221 J5
Ioannina Greece 39°42N 20°47E 204 B2
Iokea Papua N. G. 8°25S 146°16E 286 E4
Iola U.S.A. 37°55N 95°24W 308 G6
Iolani Palace U.S.A. 21°18N 157°51W 302 K14
Ioma Papua N. G. 8°19S 147°52E 286 E4
Ion Corvin Romania 44°7N 27°50E 183 F12
Iona Angola 16°54S 12°34E 265 F2
Iona Argyll & Bute, U.K. 56°20N 6°25W 167 E2
Iona △ Angola 16°47S 12°20E 265 F2
Ione U.S.A. 38°21N 120°56W 306 G6
Iongo Angola 9°11S 17°45E 265 D3
Ionia U.S.A. 42°59N 85°4W 311 B11
Ionian Is. = Ionioi Nisoi
Greece 38°40N 20°0E 204 C2
Ionian Sea Medit. S. 37°30N 17°30E 193 D7
Ionioi Nisoi Greece 38°40N 20°0E 204 C2
Ionioi Nisoi □ Greece 38°40N 20°0E 207 B2
Iony, Ostrov Russia 56°24N 143°22E 215 D15
Ios Greece 36°41N 25°20E 205 E7
Iowa □ U.S.A. 42°18N 93°30W 310 C3
Iowa → U.S.A. 41°10N 91°1W 310 C5
Iowa City U.S.A. 41°40N 91°32W 310 C5
Iowa Falls U.S.A. 42°31N 93°16W 310 B3
Iowa Park U.S.A. 33°57N 98°40W 314 E5
Ipala Tanzania 4°30S 32°52E 268 C3
Ipameri Brazil 17°44S 48°9W 333 E2
Ipanema Minas Gerais,
Brazil 19°47S 41°44W 333 E3
Ipanema Rio de J., Brazil 22°59S 43°12W 135 B1
Ipatía Peru 9°17S 74°29W 330 B3
Ipati Greece 38°52N 22°14E 204 C4
Ipatinga Brazil 19°32S 42°30W 333 E3
Ipatovo Russia 45°45N 42°50E 191 H6
Ipek = Pejë Kosovo 42°40N 20°17E 202 D4
Ipel' → Europe 47°48N 18°53E 181 D11
Ipiales Colombia 0°50N 77°37W 328 C2
Ipiaú Brazil 14°8S 39°44W 333 D4
Ipil Phil. 7°47N 122°35E 233 H4
Ipin = Yibin China 28°45N 104°32E 228 C5
Ipirá Brazil 12°10S 39°44W 333 D4
Ipiranga Brazil 23°35S 46°36W 137 B2
Ipiranga → Brazil 23°37S 46°37W 137 B2
Ipixuna Brazil 7°0S 71°40W 330 B3
Ipixuna → Amazonas,
Brazil 7°11S 71°51W 330 B3
Ipixuna → Amazonas, Brazil 5°45S 63°2W 331 B5
Ipoh Malaysia 4°35N 101°5E 237 K3
Iponri Nigeria 6°28N 3°22E 124 B2
Iporá Brazil 16°28S 51°7W 331 D7
Ipota Vanuatu 18°52S 169°20E 287 H7
Ippy C.A.R. 6°5N 21°7E 264 A4
Ipsala Turkey 40°55N 26°23E 203 F10
Ipsario, Oros Greece 40°40N 24°40E 203 F8
Ipsos Greece 39°43N 19°48E 206 B9
Ipswich Queens., Australia 27°35S 152°40E 281 D5
Ipswich Suffolk, U.K. 52°4N 1°10E 169 E9
Ipswich Mass., U.S.A. 42°41N 70°50W 313 D14
Ipswich S. Dak., U.S.A. 45°27N 99°2W 308 C4
Ipu Brazil 4°23S 40°44W 332 B3
Ipueiras Brazil 4°33S 40°43W 332 B3
Ipuh Indonesia 3°0S 101°30E 234 C2
Ipupiara Brazil 11°49S 42°37W 333 D3
Iqaluit Canada 63°44N 68°31W 295 E18
Iqaluktuutiaq = Cambridge Bay
Canada 69°10N 105°0W 294 D11
Iquique Chile 20°19S 70°5W 330 E3
Iquitos Peru 3°45S 73°10W 328 D3
Ir Gannim = Bat Yam
Israel 32°2N 34°44E 251 F5
Irabu-Jima Japan 24°50N 125°10E 221 M2
Iracoubo Fr. Guiana 5°30N 53°10W 329 B7
Īrafshān Iran 26°42N 61°56E 247 E9
Irago-Suidō Japan 34°25N 137°0E 223 C8
Irahuan Phil. 9°48N 118°41E 233 G2
Iraklia Cyclades, Greece 36°50N 25°28E 205 E7
Iraklia Serres, Greece 41°10N 23°16E 202 E7
Iraklio Greece 35°20N 25°12E 207 E6
Iráklion = Iraklio Greece 35°20N 25°12E 207 E6
Irakliou, Kolpos Greece 35°23N 25°8E 207 E6
Irako-Zaki Japan 34°35N 137°1E 223 C9
Irala Paraguay 25°55S 54°35W 335 B5
Iran ■ Asia 33°0N 53°0E 247 C7
Iran, Pegunungan
Malaysia 2°20N 114°50E 235 B4
Iran Ra. = Iran, Pegunungan
Malaysia 2°20N 114°50E 235 B4
Iranamadu Tank Sri Lanka 9°23N 80°29E 245 K5
Īrānshahr Iran 27°15N 60°40E 247 E9
Irapa Venezuela 10°34N 62°35W 329 A5
Irapuato Mexico 20°41N 101°28W 318 C4
Iraq ■ Asia 33°0N 44°0E 213 F10
Irarrar, O. → Mali 20°0N 1°30E 261 E5
Irati Brazil 25°25S 50°38W 335 B5
Irazú, Volcan Costa Rica 9°59N 83°51W 320 D3
Irbes saurums Latvia 57°45N 22°5E 184 A9
Irbid Jordan 32°35N 35°48E 251 F6
Irbid □ Jordan 32°30N 35°50E 250 F6
Irbil = Arbīl Iraq 36°15N 44°5E 213 D11
Irebu Dem. Rep. of the Congo 0°40S 17°46E 264 C3
Irecê Brazil 11°18S 41°52W 332 D3
Iregua → Spain 42°27N 2°24E 196 C2
Ireland ■ Europe 53°50N 7°52W 166 C4
Ireland Island Bermuda 32°19N 64°50W 153 a
Irele Nigeria 7°40N 5°40E 263 D6
Ireng → Brazil 3°33N 59°51W 329 C6
Irerrer, O. → Algeria 19°25N 5°47E 261 E6
Irgiz = Yrghyz Kazakhstan 48°37N 61°16E 216 C6
Irgiz = Yrghyz →
Kazakhstan 48°6N 62°30E 216 C6
Irgiz, Bolshaya → Russia 52°10N 49°10E 190 D9
Irharhar, O. → Algeria 28°3N 6°15E 261 C6
Irherm Morocco 30°7N 8°18W 260 B3
Irhil M'Goun Morocco 31°30N 6°28W 260 B3
Iri = Iksan S. Korea 35°59N 127°0E 224 E3
Irian Barat = Papua □
Indonesia 4°0S 137°0E 231 E9
Irian Jaya = Papua □
Indonesia 4°0S 137°0E 231 E9
Irian Jaya Barat □
Indonesia 2°5S 132°50E 231 E8
Iriba Chad 15°7N 22°15E 259 E4
Irié Guinea 8°15N 9°10W 262 D3
Iriga Phil. 13°25N 123°25E 232 E4
Iriklinskoye Vdkhr. Russia 52°0N 59°0E 216 B5
Iringa Tanzania 7°48S 35°43E 268 D4
Iringa □ Tanzania 7°48S 35°43E 268 D4
Irinjalakuda India 10°21N 76°14E 245 J3
Iriomote △ Japan 24°29N 123°53E 221 M1
Iriomote-Jima Japan 24°19N 123°48E 221 M1
Iriona Honduras 15°57N 85°11W 320 C2
Iriri → Brazil 3°52S 52°37W 329 D7
Iriri Novo → Brazil 8°46S 53°22W 331 B7
Irish Sea Europe 53°38N 4°48W 168 D3
Irkeshtam Pass = Erkech-Tam Pass
Asia 39°46N 74°2E 217 E8
Irkutsk Russia 52°18N 104°20E 218 A9
Irlıganlı Turkey 37°53N 29°12E 205 D11
Irma Canada 52°55N 111°14W 297 C6
Irō-Zaki Japan 34°36N 138°51E 223 C10
Irois B. Trin. & Tob. 10°9N 61°45W 323 t
Iroise, Mer d' France 48°15N 4°45W 172 D2
Iron Baron Australia 32°58S 137°11E 282 B2
Iron Gate = Portile de Fier
Europe 44°44N 22°30E 182 F7
Iron Knob Australia 32°46S 137°8E 282 B2
Iron Mountain U.S.A. 45°49N 88°4W 308 C9
Iron Range △ Australia 12°34S 143°18E 280 A3
Iron River U.S.A. 46°6N 88°39W 308 B9
Irondequoit U.S.A. 43°13N 77°35W 312 C7
Ironton Mo., U.S.A. 37°36N 90°38W 308 G8
Ironton Ohio, U.S.A. 38°32N 82°41W 309 F12
Ironwood U.S.A. 46°27N 90°9W 308 B8
Ironwood Forest △
U.S.A. 32°32N 111°28W 305 K8
Iroquois Canada 44°51N 75°19W 313 B9
Iroquois → U.S.A. 41°5N 87°49W 311 C9
Iroquois Falls Canada 48°46N 80°41W 298 C3
Iroquois Point U.S.A. 21°19N 157°58W 302 K14
Irosin Phil. 12°42N 124°2E 232 E5
Irpin Ukraine 50°30N 30°15E 177 C16
Irqieqa, Ras I- Malta 35°56N 14°29E 206 F7
Irrara Cr. → Australia 29°35S 145°31E 281 D4
Irrawaddy = Ayeyawadi →
Burma 15°50N 95°6E 241 G5
Irrawaddy □ Burma 17°0N 95°0E 241 G5
Irrawaddy, Mouths of the
Burma 15°30N 95°0E 241 H5
Irricana Canada 51°19N 113°37W 296 C6
Irrunytju Australia 26°3S 128°56E 279 E4
Irshava Ukraine 48°19N 23°3E 182 B8
Irsina Italy 40°45N 16°14E 201 B9
Irtysh → Russia 61°4N 68°52E 214 C7
Irumu Dem. Rep. of the Congo 1°32N 29°53E 268 B2
Irún Spain 43°20N 1°52W 196 B3
Irunea = Pamplona-Iruña
Spain 42°48N 1°38W 196 C3
Irurzun Spain 42°55N 1°50W 196 C3
Irvine Alta., Canada 49°57N 110°16W 297 D6
Irvine N. Ayrs., U.K. 55°37N 4°41W 167 F4
Irvine Calif., U.S.A. 33°41N 117°46W 307 M9
Irvine Ky., U.S.A. 37°42N 83°58W 311 G13
Irvinestown U.K. 54°28N 7°39W 166 B4
Irving U.S.A. 32°48N 96°56W 120 B4
Irving Park U.S.A. 41°57N 87°42W 119 B2
Irvington U.S.A. 37°53N 86°17W 311 G10
Irvona U.S.A. 40°46N 78°33W 312 F6
Irwin → Australia 29°15S 114°54E 279 E1
Irwinton U.S.A. 32°49N 83°10W 316 C6
Irwinville U.S.A. 31°39N 83°23W 316 D6
Irymple Australia 34°14S 142°8E 282 C5
Is, Jebel Sudan 22°3N 35°28E 256 C4
Is-sur-Tille France 47°30N 5°8E 173 E12
Isa Nigeria 13°14N 6°24E 263 C6
Isa Khel Pakistan 32°41N 71°17E 242 C4
Isaac → Australia 22°55S 149°20E 280 C4
Isabel Rio de J., Brazil 22°55S 43°14W 135 B1
Isabel S. Dak., U.S.A. 45°24N 101°26W 308 C3
Isabel, I. Mexico 21°51N 105°55W 318 C3
Isabel Segunda Puerto Rico 18°9N 65°27W 321 b
Isabela Basilan, Phil. 6°40N 121°59E 233 H3
Isabela Negros, Phil. 10°12N 122°59E 233 F4
Isabela Puerto Rico 18°30N 67°2W 321 b
Isabela □ Phil. 17°0N 122°0E 232 C4
Isabela, Canal Ecuador 0°20S 90°55W 330 a
Isabela, I. Ecuador 0°30S 91°4W 330 a
Isabella, Cord. Nic. 13°30N 85°25W 320 D2
Isabella Ra. Australia 21°0S 121°4E 278 C3
Isaccea Romania 45°16N 28°28E 183 E13
Isachsen, C. Canada 79°20N 105°28W 295 B10
Isachsen Mt. Antarctica 72°8S 26°5E 151 D4
Ísafjarðardjúp Iceland 66°10N 23°0W 155 A3
Ísafjarðarsýsla Iceland 66°0N 23°0W 155 B3
Ísafjörður Iceland 66°5N 23°9W 155 A3
Isagarh India 24°48N 77°51E 242 G7
Isagatedo Nigeria 6°31N 3°19E 124 A1
Isahaya Japan 32°52N 130°2E 222 E2
Isaka Dem. Rep. of the Congo 2°33S 18°54E 264 C3
Isaka Tanzania 3°56S 32°59E 268 C3
Işalniţa Romania 44°24N 23°44E 183 F8
Isalo, Tangorombohitr'
Madag. 22°45S 45°15E 272 C2
Isalo △ Madag. 22°23S 45°16E 272 C2
Isan → India 26°51N 80°7E 243 F9
Isana = Içana → Brazil 0°26N 67°19W 328 C4
Isandja
Dem. Rep. of the Congo 2°59S 21°59E 264 C4
Isangano △ Zambia 11°8S 30°35E 269 E3
Isangi Dem. Rep. of the Congo 0°52N 24°10E 264 B4
Isanlu Makutu Nigeria 8°20N 5°50E 263 D6
Isar → Bayern, Germany 48°48N 12°57E 179 G8
Isar → Oberbayern,
Germany 48°15N 11°41E 131 A3
Isarco → Italy 46°27N 11°18E 199 B8
Isaris Greece 37°22N 22°0E 204 D3
Isarog, Mt. Phil. 13°39N 123°22E 232 E4
Isawa Japan 35°40N 138°35E 223 B10
Íscar Spain 41°22N 4°32W 194 D6
Iscayachi Bolivia 21°31S 65°3W 331 E4
İscehisar Turkey 38°51N 30°45E 205 C12
Íschia Italy 40°44N 13°57E 200 B6
Ischigualasto △ Argentina 30°0S 68°0W 334 B2
Iscuandé Colombia 2°28N 77°59W 328 C2
Isdell → Australia 16°27S 124°51E 278 C3
Ise Japan 34°25N 136°45E 223 C8
Ise-Shima △ Japan 34°25N 136°48E 223 C8
Ise-Wan Japan 34°43N 136°43E 223 C8
Isefjord Denmark 55°53N 11°50E 163 J5
Isel → Austria 46°50N 12°47E 180 E5
Iseo Italy 45°39N 10°3E 198 C7
Iseo, L. d' Italy 45°43N 10°4E 198 C7
Iseramagazi Tanzania 4°37S 32°10E 268 C3
Isère □ France 45°15N 5°40E 175 C9
Isère → France 44°59N 4°51E 175 D8
Iserlohn Germany 51°22N 7°41E 178 D3
Isérnia Italy 41°36N 14°14E 201 A7
Isesaki Japan 36°19N 139°12E 223 A11
Iseyin Nigeria 8°0N 3°36E 263 D5
Isfahan = Eşfahān Iran 32°39N 51°43E 247 C6
Isfjorden Norway 62°35N 7°49E 164 B4
Ishbīlīya Iraq 33°21N 44°26E 213 A2
Ishëm Albania 41°33N 19°34E 202 E3
Ishenga Oshwe
Dem. Rep. of the Congo 3°57S 22°33E 264 C4

Isherton Guyana 2°20N 59°25W 329 C6
Ishigaki Japan 24°26N 124°10E 221 M2
Ishigaki-Shima Japan 24°20N 124°10E 221 M2
Ishikari Japan 43°20N 141°15E 220 C10
Ishikari-Gawa → Japan 43°15N 141°23E 220 C10
Ishikari-Sammyaku Japan 43°30N 143°0E 220 C11
Ishikari-Wan Japan 43°25N 141°1E 220 C10
Ishikawa Japan 26°25N 127°49E 288 a
Ishikawa □ Japan 36°30N 136°30E 223 A8
Ishim Russia 56°10N 69°30E 214 D7
Ishim → Russia 57°45N 71°10E 214 D8
Ishimbay Russia 53°28N 56°2E 216 B5
Ishinomaki Japan 38°32N 141°20E 220 E10
Ishioka Japan 36°11N 140°16E 223 A12
Ishizuchi-Yama Japan 33°45N 133°6E 222 D5
Ishkashim Tajikistan 36°44N 71°37E 217 E8
Ishkoman Pakistan 36°30N 73°50E 243 A5
Ishøj Strand Denmark 55°36N 12°20E 118 B2
Ishpeming U.S.A. 46°29N 87°40W 308 B10
Ishurdi Bangla. 24°9N 89°3E 241 C2
Isiboro Sécure △ Bolivia 16°15S 65°50W 331 D4
Isigny-sur-Mer France 49°19N 1°6W 172 C5
Isıklar Dağı Turkey 40°45N 27°15E 203 F11
Işıklı Turkey 38°19N 29°51E 205 C11
Isil Kul Russia 54°55N 71°16E 217 B8
Ísili Italy 39°44N 9°6E 200 C2
iSimangaliso ⌓ S. Africa 27°50S 32°32E 271 C5
Isiolo Kenya 0°24N 37°33E 268 B4
Isiolo □ Kenya 1°0N 37°30E 268 B4
Isiro Dem. Rep. of the Congo 2°53N 27°40E 268 B2
Isisford Australia 24°15S 144°21E 280 C3
İskele = Trikomo Cyprus 35°17N 33°52E 207 E9
İskenderun Turkey 36°32N 36°10E 250 B7
İskenderun Körfezi Turkey 36°40N 35°50E 250 B6
İskilip Turkey 40°45N 34°29E 212 B6
Iskitim Russia 54°38N 83°18E 217 B10
Iskŭr → Bulgaria 43°45N 24°25E 203 C8
Iskŭr, Yazovir Bulgaria 42°23N 23°30E 202 D7
Iskushuban Somalia 10°18N 50°12E 267 B7
Iskut → Canada 56°45N 131°49W 296 B2
Isla → U.K. 56°32N 3°20W 167 E5
Isla Coiba ⌓ Panama 7°33N 81°36W 320 E4
Isla Cristina Spain 37°13N 7°17W 195 H3
Isla de Salamanca △ Colombia 10°59N 74°40W 328 A3
Isla Gorge △ Australia 25°10S 149°57E 280 D4
Isla Gorgona △ Colombia 2°59N 78°10W 328 C2
Isla Guamblin △ Chile 44°50S 75°4W 336 B1
Isla Isabel △ Mexico 21°54N 105°58W 318 C3
Isla Magdalena △ Chile 44°20S 73°13W 336 B2
Isla Tiburón y San Esteban ⌓ Mexico 29°0N 112°27W 318 B2
Isla Vista U.S.A. 34°25N 119°53W 307 L7
İslahiye Turkey 37°0N 36°35E 250 B7
Islam Headworks Pakistan 29°49N 72°33E 242 E5
Islamabad Pakistan 33°40N 73°10E 242 C5
Islamgarh Pakistan 27°51N 70°48E 242 F4
Islamkot Pakistan 24°42N 70°13E 242 G4
Islamorada U.S.A. 24°56N 80°37W 317 L9
Islampur Bihar, India 25°9N 85°12E 243 G11
Islampur Maharashtra, India 17°2N 74°20E 244 F2
Islampur Paschimbanga, India 26°16N 88°12E 243 F13
Island = Iceland ■ Europe 64°45N 19°0W 155 C8
Island B. Phil. 9°6N 118°10E 233 G2
Island Harbour Anguilla 18°12N 63°0W 322 a
Island L. Canada 53°47N 94°25W 297 C10
Island Lagoon Australia 31°30S 136°40E 282 A2
Island Park Canada 43°37N 79°22W 141 B2
Island Pond U.S.A. 44°49N 71°53W 313 B13
Islands, B. of Nfld. & L., Canada 49°11N 58°15W 299 C8
Islands, B. of N.Z. 35°15S 174°6E 284 B3
Islas Atlánticas de Galicia △ Spain 42°23N 8°55W 194 C2
Islay U.K. 55°46N 6°10W 167 F2
Isle → France 44°55N 0°15W 174 D3
Isle aux Morts Canada 47°35N 59°0W 299 C8
Isle of Hope U.S.A. 31°58N 81°5W 316 D8
Isle of Wight □ U.K. 50°41N 1°17W 169 G6
Isle Royale △ U.S.A. 48°0N 88°55W 308 B9
Isleton U.S.A. 38°10N 121°37W 306 G5
Islev Denmark 55°41N 12°27E 118 A2
Isleworth U.K. 51°28N 0°19W 125 B2
Islington Canada 43°38N 79°30W 141 B1
Islington □ U.K. 51°33N 0°5W 125 A3
Islote Pt. Trin. & Tob. 10°4N 61°47W 323 I
Ismail = Izmayil Ukraine 45°22N 28°46E 183 E13
Ismâ'ilîya Egypt 30°37N 32°18E 251 H3
Ismâ'ilîya □ Egypt 30°35N 32°15E 251 H3
Ismâ'ilîya, Qanâ el Egypt 30°7N 31°17E 117 A2
Ismâ'ilîya, Tir'at el → Egypt 30°4N 31°16E 251 H2
Ismaning Germany 48°13N 11°40E 131 A3
Ismayloskiy Park Russia 55°46N 37°46E 129 B3
Isna Egypt 25°17N 32°30E 256 B3
Isoanala Madag. 23°50S 45°44E 272 C2
Isojärvi △ Finland 61°40N 25°0E 160 F21
Ísola del Liri Italy 41°41N 13°34E 199 G10
Ísola della Scala Italy 45°16N 11°0E 198 C7
Ísola di Capo Rizzuto Italy 38°58N 17°6E 201 D10
Isolo Nigeria 6°31N 3°19E 124 A1
Isparta Turkey 37°47N 30°30E 205 D12
Isparta □ Turkey 38°0N 31°0E 212 D4
Isperikh Bulgaria 43°43N 26°50E 203 C10
Íspica Italy 36°47N 14°55E 201 F7
Ispir Turkey 40°28N 40°59E 213 B9
Israel ■ Asia 32°0N 34°50E 251 G5
Isratu Eritrea 16°20N 39°53E 257 D4
Issakly Russia 54°8N 51°32E 190 C10
Issano Guyana 5°49N 59°26W 329 B6
Issaouane, Erg Algeria 26°58N 8°42E 258 C1
Issia Ivory C. 6°33N 6°33W 262 D3
Issoire France 45°32N 3°15E 174 C7
Issoudun France 46°57N 1°59E 173 F8
Issy-les-Moulineaux France 48°49N 2°15E 134 B2
Issyk-Kul = Balykchy Kyrgyzstan 42°26N 76°12E 217 D9
Issyk-Kul, Ozero = Ysyk-Köl Kyrgyzstan 42°25N 77°15E 217 D9
Ist Croatia 44°17N 14°47E 199 D11
Istállós-kő Hungary 48°4N 20°26E 182 B5
İstanbul Turkey 41°0N 28°58E 122 C1
İstanbul □ Turkey 41°0N 29°0E 203 E12
İstanbul ✈ (IST) Turkey 40°59N 28°49E 203 F12
İstanbul Boğazı Turkey 41°5N 29°3E 122 B2
Istaravshān Tajikistan 39°55N 69°1E 217 E7
Isteren Norway 61°58N 11°47E 164 B8
Istiea Greece 38°57N 23°9E 204 C5
İstinye Turkey 41°6N 29°3E 122 B2
Istmina Colombia 5°10N 76°39W 328 B2
Isto, Mt. U.S.A. 69°12N 143°48W 303 B12
Istok = Burim Kosovo 42°45N 20°24E 202 D4
Istokpoga, L. U.S.A. 27°23N 81°17W 317 H8
Istra Croatia 45°10N 14°0E 199 C10
Istres France 43°31N 4°59E 175 E8
Istria = Istra Croatia 45°10N 14°0E 199 C10
Isugod Phil. 9°19N 118°5E 233 G2
Isulan Phil. 6°30N 124°29E 233 H5
Isumrud Str. Papua N. G. 4°50S 145°50E 286 D3
Itá Paraguay 25°29S 57°21W 334 B4
Itä Hakkila Finland 60°17N 25°7E 121 B3
Itabaiana Paraíba, Brazil 7°18S 35°19W 332 C4
Itabaiana Sergipe, Brazil 10°41S 37°37W 332 D4
Itabaianinha Brazil 11°16S 37°47W 332 D4
Itaberaba Brazil 12°32S 40°18W 333 D3
Itaberaí Brazil 16°2S 49°48W 333 E2
Itabira Brazil 19°37S 43°13W 333 E3
Itabirito Brazil 20°15S 43°48W 333 F3
Itaboca Brazil 4°50S 62°40W 329 D5
Itabuna Brazil 14°48S 39°16W 333 D4
Itacajá Brazil 8°19S 47°46W 332 C2
Itacaunas → Brazil 5°21S 49°8W 332 C2
Itacoatiara Brazil 2°58S 58°30W 329 D6
Itaewon S. Korea 37°32N 126°58E 137 B1
Itaguaí Brazil 22°15S 43°46W 335 A7
Itaguari → Brazil 14°11S 44°40W 333 D3
Itaguatins Brazil 5°47S 47°29W 332 C2
Itaim → Brazil 7°2S 42°2W 332 C3
Itainópolis Brazil 7°24S 41°31W 332 C3
Itaipú, Represa de Brazil 25°30S 54°30W 335 B5
Itäisen Suomenlahti △ Finland 60°25N 27°15E 160 F22
Itaituba Brazil 4°10S 55°50W 329 D6
Itajaí Brazil 27°50S 48°39W 335 B6
Itajany do Sul = Rio do Sul Brazil 27°13S 49°37W 335 B6
Itajubá Brazil 22°24S 45°30W 333 F2
Itajuípe Brazil 14°41S 39°22W 333 D4
Itaka Tanzania 8°50S 32°49E 269 D3
Itako Japan 35°56N 140°33E 223 B12
Itala ⌓ S. Africa 27°30S 31°7E 271 C5
Italy ■ Europe 42°0N 13°0E 192 C6
Itamaraju Brazil 17°4S 39°32W 333 E4
Itamarati Brazil 6°24S 68°15W 330 B4
Itamataré Brazil 2°16S 46°24W 332 B2
Itambacuri Brazil 18°1S 41°42W 333 E3
Itambé Brazil 15°15S 40°37W 333 E3
Itami Japan 34°46N 135°24E 133 A1
Itampolo Madag. 24°41S 43°57E 272 C1
Itanagar India 27°6N 93°37E 241 B4
Itandrano Madag. 21°47S 45°17E 272 C2
Itanhaém Brazil 24°11S 46°47W 333 F2
Itanhanga Brazil 22°59S 43°19W 135 B1
Itanhauã → Brazil 4°45S 63°48W 329 D5
Itanhém Brazil 17°9S 40°20W 333 E3
Itano Japan 34°7N 134°28E 222 C6
Itapaci Brazil 14°57S 49°34W 333 D2
Itapagé Brazil 3°41S 39°34W 332 B4
Itaparica = Petrolândia Brazil 9°5S 38°20W 332 C4
Itaparica, I. de Brazil 12°54S 38°42W 333 D4
Itaparica, Represa de Brazil 11°3S 42°47W 332 D3
Itapebi Brazil 15°56S 39°32W 333 E4
Itapecuru Mirim Brazil 3°24S 44°20W 332 B3
Itaperuna Brazil 21°10S 41°54W 333 F3
Itapetinga Brazil 15°15S 40°15W 333 E3
Itapetininga Brazil 23°36S 48°7W 335 A6
Itapeva Brazil 23°59S 48°59W 335 A6
Itapicuru → Bahia, Brazil 11°47S 37°32W 332 D4
Itapicuru → Maranhão, Brazil 2°52S 44°12W 332 B3
Itapipoca Brazil 3°30S 39°35W 332 B4
Itapira = Ubaitaba Brazil 14°18S 39°20W 333 D4
Itapiranga Brazil 2°45S 58°1W 329 D6
Itapiúna Brazil 4°33S 38°57W 332 B4
Itaporanga Paraíba, Brazil 7°18S 38°0W 332 C4
Itaporanga São Paulo, Brazil 23°42S 49°29W 333 F2
Itapuá □ Paraguay 26°40S 55°40W 335 B4
Itapuranga Brazil 15°40S 49°59W 333 E2
Itaquai → Brazil 4°20S 70°12W 330 A3
Itaqui Maranhão, Brazil 2°34S 44°22W 332 B3
Itaqui Rio Grande do S., Brazil 29°8S 56°30W 334 B4
Itararé Brazil 24°6S 49°23W 335 A6
Itarsi India 22°36N 77°51E 242 H7
Itarumã Brazil 18°42S 51°25W 333 E1
Itatí Argentina 27°16S 58°15W 334 B4
Itatiaia △ Brazil 22°22S 44°38W 335 A7
Itatira Brazil 4°30S 39°37W 332 B4
Itatuba Brazil 5°46S 63°20W 331 B5
Itatupã Brazil 0°37S 51°12W 329 D7
Itaueira Brazil 7°36S 43°2W 332 C3
Itaueira → Brazil 6°41S 42°55W 332 C3
Itaúna Brazil 20°4S 44°34W 333 F3
Itbayat Phil. 20°47N 121°51E 232 A3
Itbayat I. Phil. 20°45N 121°50E 232 A3
Itcha Ilgachuz ⌓ Canada 52°42N 124°58W 296 C3
Itchen → U.K. 50°55N 1°22W 169 G6
Itchouma Niger 20°14N 13°32E 261 D7
Ite Peru 17°55S 70°57W 330 D3
Itea Greece 38°25N 22°25E 204 C4
Itezhi Tezhi, L. Zambia 15°30S 25°30E 269 F2
Ithaca = Ithaki Greece 38°25N 20°40E 204 C2
Ithaca U.S.A. 42°27N 76°30W 313 D8
Ithaki Greece 38°25N 20°40E 204 C2
Ithakis, Stenon Greece 38°22N 20°39E 207 C2
Iti △ Greece 38°50N 22°15E 204 C4
Itimbiri → Dem. Rep. of the Congo 2°5N 22°44E 264 B4
Itinga Brazil 16°36S 41°47W 333 E3
Itiquira Brazil 17°12S 54°7W 331 D7
Itiquira → Brazil 17°18S 56°44W 331 D6
Itirucu Brazil 13°31S 40°9W 333 D3
Itiúba Brazil 10°43S 39°51W 332 D4
Itiyuro → Argentina 22°40S 63°50W 334 A3
Itkilik → U.S.A. 70°9N 150°56W 303 A10
Itō Japan 34°58N 139°5E 223 C11
Itogon Phil. 16°22N 120°41E 232 C3
Itoigawa Japan 37°2N 137°51E 221 F8
Itoko Dem. Rep. of the Congo 1°0S 21°48E 264 C4
Itoman Japan 26°7N 127°40E 288 a
Iton → France 49°9N 1°12E 172 C8
Itonamas → Bolivia 12°28S 64°24W 331 C5
Itri Italy 41°17N 13°32E 200 A6
Itsa Egypt 29°15N 30°47E 256 J7
Itsamia Comoros Is. 12°21S 43°52E 272 a
Itsandra Comoros Is. 11°40S 43°15E 272 a
Itsuki Japan 32°24N 130°50E 222 E2
Itsukushima Shrine Japan 34°17N 132°19E 222 C4
Íttiri Italy 40°36N 8°34E 200 B1
Ittoqqortoormiit Greenland 70°20N 23°0W 154 C8
Itu Brazil 23°17S 47°15W 335 A6
Itu Nigeria 5°10N 7°58E 263 D6
Itu Aba I. S. China Sea 10°23N 114°21E 230 B4
Ituaçu Brazil 13°50S 41°18W 333 D3
Ituango Colombia 7°4N 75°45W 328 B2
Ituí → Brazil 4°38S 70°19W 330 A3
Ituiutaba Brazil 19°0S 49°25W 333 E2
Itumbiara Brazil 18°20S 49°10W 333 E2
Ituna Canada 51°10N 103°24W 297 C8
Itunge Port Tanzania 9°40S 33°55E 269 D3
Ituni Guyana 5°28N 58°15W 329 B6
Itupiranga Brazil 5°9S 49°20W 332 C2
Iturama Brazil 19°44S 50°11W 333 E1
Iturbe Argentina 23°0S 65°25W 334 A2
Ituri Dem. Rep. of the Congo 2°30N 29°30E 268 B2
Ituri □ Dem. Rep. of the Congo 1°30N 29°0E 266 D2
Ituri → Dem. Rep. of the Congo 1°40N 27°1E 268 B2
Iturup, Ostrov Russia 45°0N 148°0E 215 E15
Ituverava Brazil 20°20S 47°47W 333 F2
Ituxi → Brazil 7°18S 64°51W 331 B5
Itzehoe Germany 53°55N 9°31E 178 B5
Iuka U.S.A. 34°48N 88°11W 311 F8
Iungsdalshytta Norway 60°49N 7°55E 164 D4
Ivahona Madag. 23°27S 46°10E 272 C2
Ivaí → Brazil 23°18S 53°42W 335 A5
Ivalo Finland 68°38N 27°35E 160 B22
Ivalojoki → Finland 68°40N 27°40E 160 B22
Ivanava Belarus 52°7N 25°29E 177 B13
Ivančice Czechia 49°6N 16°23E 181 B9
Ivane-Puste Ukraine 48°39N 26°10E 183 B11
Ivănești Romania 46°39N 27°27E 183 D12
Ivangorod = Dęblin Poland 51°34N 21°50E 185 G8
Ivangorod Russia 59°27N 28°13E 188 C5
Ivanhoe N.S.W., Australia 32°56S 144°20E 282 B6
Ivanhoe Vic., Australia 37°45S 145°3E 128 A2
Ivanhoe Ont., Canada 44°23N 77°28W 312 B7
Ivanhoe Calif., U.S.A. 36°23N 119°13W 306 J7
Ivanhoe Minn., U.S.A. 44°28N 96°15W 308 C5
Ivanhorod Ukraine 48°48N 29°50E 183 B14
Ivanić Grad Croatia 45°41N 16°25E 199 C13
Ivanjica Serbia 43°35N 20°12E 202 C4
Ivanjska Bos.-H. 44°55N 17°4E 182 F2
Ivankoyskoye Vdkhr. Russia 56°37N 36°32E 188 D9
Ivano-Frankivsk Ukraine 48°40N 24°40E 183 B9
Ivano-Frankivsk □ Ukraine 48°45N 24°30E 183 B9
Ivanof Bay U.S.A. 55°54N 159°29W 303 J8
Ivanovo = Ivanava Belarus 52°7N 25°29E 177 B13
Ivanovo Bulgaria 43°43N 25°58E 203 C9
Ivanovo Russia 57°5N 41°0E 188 D11
Ivanovo □ Russia 57°10N 41°50E 190 B5
Ivanšćica Croatia 46°12N 16°13E 199 B13
Ivashchenkovo = Chapayevsk Russia 53°0N 49°40E 190 D9
Ivato Madag. 20°37S 47°10E 272 C2
Ivatsevichy Belarus 52°43N 25°21E 177 B13
Ivaylovgrad Bulgaria 41°32N 26°8E 203 E10
Ivdel Russia 60°42N 60°24E 186 B11
Iveragh Pen. Ireland 51°52N 10°15W 166 E1
Ives Estates U.S.A. 25°58N 80°10W 129 C2
Ivgres = Komsomolsk Russia 57°2N 40°20E 188 D11
Ivindo → Gabon 0°9S 12°9E 264 C2
Ivinheima → Brazil 23°14S 53°42W 335 A5
Ivinhema Brazil 22°10S 53°37W 335 A5
Ivittuut Greenland 61°14N 48°12W 154 E6
Iviza = Eivissa Spain 38°54N 1°26E 206 D1
Ivohibe Madag. 22°31S 46°57E 272 C2
Ivolândia Brazil 16°34S 50°51W 333 E1
Ivory Coast W. Afr. 4°20N 5°0W 262 E4
Ivory Coast ■ Africa 7°30N 5°0W 262 D4
Ivösjön Sweden 56°8N 14°25E 163 H8
Ivrea Italy 45°28N 7°52E 198 C4
İvrindi Turkey 39°34N 27°30E 205 B9
Ivry-sur-Seine France 48°49N 2°22E 134 B3
Ivujivik Canada 62°24N 77°55W 295 E16
Ivvavik △ Canada 69°6N 139°30W 294 D4
Ivybridge U.K. 50°23N 3°56W 169 G4
Iwa Japan 36°5N 139°52E 223 A11
Iwai-Jima Japan 33°47N 131°58E 222 D3
Iwaizumi Japan 39°50N 141°45E 220 E10
Iwaki Japan 37°3N 140°55E 221 F10
Iwakuni Japan 34°15N 132°8E 222 C4
Iwami Japan 35°32N 134°15E 222 B6
Iwami Ginzan Japan 35°6N 132°26E 222 B4
Iwamizawa Japan 43°12N 141°46E 220 C10
Iwanai Japan 42°58N 140°30E 220 C10
Iwase Japan 36°21N 140°6E 223 A12
Iwata Japan 34°42N 137°51E 223 C9
Iwate □ Japan 39°30N 141°30E 220 E10
Iwate-San Japan 39°51N 141°0E 220 E10
Iwo Nigeria 7°39N 4°9E 263 D5
Iwo Jima Pac. Oc. 24°47N 141°20E 288 b
Iwŏn N. Korea 40°19N 128°39E 224 B4
Iwonicz-Zdrój Poland 49°37N 21°47E 185 J8
Iwungu Dem. Rep. of the Congo 5°16S 19°17E 265 D3
Ixelles Belgium 50°50N 4°22E 116 B2
Ixiamas Bolivia 13°50S 68°5W 330 C4
Ixopo S. Africa 30°11S 30°5E 271 D5
Ixtepec Mexico 16°34N 95°6W 319 D5
Ixtlán del Río Mexico 21°2N 104°22W 318 C4
Iyal Bakhit Sudan 13°20N 28°39E 257 E2
Iyo Japan 33°45N 132°45E 222 D4
Iyo-Mishima Japan 33°58N 133°30E 222 D5
Iyo-Nada Japan 33°40N 132°20E 222 D4
Izabal, L. de Guatemala 15°30N 89°10W 320 C2
Izamal Mexico 20°56N 89°1W 319 C7
Izberbash Russia 42°35N 47°52E 191 J8
Izbica Poland 50°53N 23°10E 185 H10
Izbica Kujawska Poland 52°25N 18°40E 185 F5
Izbiceni Romania 43°45N 24°40E 183 G9
Izembek Nat. Wildlife Refuge ⌓ U.S.A. 55°15N 162°45W 303 J7
Izena-Shima Japan 26°56N 127°56E 221 L3
Izgrev Bulgaria 43°36N 26°58E 203 C10
Izhevsk Russia 56°51N 53°14E 186 C9
Izhma = Sosnogorsk Russia 63°37N 53°51E 186 B9
Izhma → Russia 65°19N 52°54E 186 A9
Izileg Algeria 20°20N 6°4E 261 D6
Izkī Oman 22°56N 57°46E 249 B7
Izmayil Ukraine 45°22N 28°46E 183 E13
Izmaylovo Russia 55°47N 37°47E 129 B3
İzmir Turkey 38°25N 27°8E 205 C9
İzmir □ Turkey 38°15N 27°40E 205 C9
İzmir Adnan Menderes ✈ (ADB) Turkey 38°23N 27°6E 205 C9
İzmir Körfezi Turkey 38°30N 26°50E 205 C8
İzmit = Kocaeli Turkey 40°45N 29°50E 203 F13
Iznájar Spain 37°15N 4°19W 195 H6
Iznalloz Spain 37°24N 3°30W 195 H7
İznik Turkey 40°23N 29°46E 212 B3
İznik Gölü Turkey 40°27N 29°30E 203 F13
Izobilno-Tishchenskoye = Izobil'nyy Russia 45°25N 41°44E 191 H5
Izobil'nyy Russia 45°25N 41°44E 191 H5
Izola Slovenia 45°32N 13°39E 199 C10
Izozog, Bañados de Bolivia 18°48S 62°10W 331 D5
Izra Syria 32°51N 36°15E 250 F7
Iztacalco Mexico 19°23N 99°5W 128 B2
Iztapalapa Mexico 19°21N 99°6W 128 B2
Iztochni Rodopi Bulgaria 41°45N 25°30E 203 E9
Izu Japan 34°58N 138°56E 223 C10
Izu-Hantō Japan 34°45N 139°0E 223 C11
Izu-Shotō Japan 34°30N 140°0E 221 G10
Izúcar de Matamoros Mexico 18°36N 98°28W 319 D5
Izuhara Japan 34°12N 129°17E 222 C1
Izumi Kagoshima, Japan 32°5N 130°22E 222 E2
Izumi Ōsaka, Japan 34°28N 135°24E 223 C7
Izumi-Sano Japan 34°23N 135°18E 223 C7
Izumo Japan 35°20N 132°46E 222 B4
Izunokuni Japan 35°2N 138°55E 223 B10
Izyaslav Ukraine 50°5N 26°50E 177 C14
Izyum Ukraine 49°12N 37°19E 189 H9

J

J.F.K. Int. ✈ (JFK) U.S.A. 40°38N 73°47W 313 F11
J.F. Rodrigues Brazil 2°55S 50°20W 332 B1
J.P. Koch Fjord Greenland 82°45N 44°0W 154 A6
J. Strom Thurmond L. U.S.A. 33°40N 82°12W 316 B7
Ja-ela Sri Lanka 7°5N 79°53E 245 L4
Ja-eundo S. Korea 34°53N 126°2E 224 E3
Ja'ār Yemen 13°13N 45°18E 248 D4
Jaba Ethiopia 6°20N 35°7E 257 F4
Jaba West Bank 31°51N 35°16E 122 a
Jabal al Awliya' Sudan 15°14N 32°29E 266 A3
Jabal as Sirāj Afghan. 35°7N 69°16E 240 B3
Jabalón → Spain 38°53N 4°5W 195 G6
Jabalpur India 23°9N 79°58E 243 H8
Jabāliya Gaza Strip 31°32N 34°29E 251 G5
Jabbūl Syria 36°4N 37°30E 246 B3
Jabiru Australia 12°40S 132°53E 278 B5
Jablah Syria 35°20N 36°0E 250 C7
Jablanac Croatia 44°42N 14°56E 199 D11
Jablanica Bos.-H. 43°40N 17°45E 182 G2
Jablonec nad Nisou Czechia 50°43N 15°10E 180 A8
Jablonica Slovakia 48°37N 17°26E 181 C10
Jabłonowo Pomorskie Poland 53°23N 19°10E 184 E6
Jablunkov Czechia 49°35N 18°46E 181 B11
Jaboatão Brazil 8°7S 35°1W 332 C4
Jabonga Phil. 9°20N 125°32E 233 G5
Jabotabek = Jakarta Indonesia 6°9S 106°52E 122 A2
Jaboticabal Brazil 21°15S 48°17W 335 A6
Jabukovac Serbia 44°22N 22°21E 202 B6
Jaburu Brazil 5°30S 64°0W 331 B5
Jaca Spain 42°35N 0°33W 196 C4
Jacaré Brazil 22°53S 43°14W 135 B1
Jacaré → Brazil 10°3S 42°13W 332 D3
Jacareí Brazil 23°20S 46°0W 335 A6
Jacarèzinho Brazil 23°5S 49°58W 335 A6
Jaci-Paraná Brazil 9°15S 64°23W 331 B5
Jaciara Brazil 15°59S 54°57W 331 D7
Jacinto Brazil 16°10S 40°17W 333 E3
Jack River △ Australia 14°58S 144°19E 280 A3
Jackman U.S.A. 45°37N 70°15W 309 C18
Jacksboro U.S.A. 33°13N 98°10W 314 E5
Jackson Barbados 13°7N 59°36W 323 r
Jackson Ala., U.S.A. 31°31N 87°53W 315 F11
Jackson Calif., U.S.A. 38°21N 120°46W 306 G6
Jackson Ga., U.S.A. 33°20N 83°57W 316 B6
Jackson Ky., U.S.A. 37°33N 83°23W 309 G12
Jackson Mich., U.S.A. 42°15N 84°24W 311 B12
Jackson Minn., U.S.A. 43°37N 95°1W 308 D6
Jackson Miss., U.S.A. 32°18N 90°12W 315 E9
Jackson Mo., U.S.A. 37°23N 89°40W 308 G9
Jackson N.H., U.S.A. 44°10N 71°11W 313 B13
Jackson Ohio, U.S.A. 39°3N 82°39W 309 F12
Jackson S.C., U.S.A. 33°20N 81°47W 316 B8
Jackson Tenn., U.S.A. 35°37N 88°49W 315 D10
Jackson Wyo., U.S.A. 43°29N 110°46W 304 E8
Jackson, C. N.Z. 40°59S 174°20E 285 A9
Jackson B. N.Z. 43°58S 168°42E 285 D3
Jackson Center U.S.A. 40°27N 84°4W 311 D12
Jackson Hd. N.Z. 43°58S 168°37E 285 D3
Jackson Heights U.S.A. 40°44N 73°53W 132 B2
Jackson L. Fla., U.S.A. 30°30N 84°17W 316 E5
Jackson L. Ga., U.S.A. 33°19N 83°50W 316 B6
Jackson L. Wyo., U.S.A. 43°52N 110°36W 304 E8
Jackson Park U.S.A. 41°46N 87°34W 119 C3
Jacksons N.Z. 42°46S 171°32E 285 C6
Jackson's Arm Canada 49°52N 56°47W 299 C8
Jacksonville Ala., U.S.A. 33°49N 85°46W 316 B4
Jacksonville Ark., U.S.A. 34°52N 92°7W 314 D8
Jacksonville Calif., U.S.A. 37°52N 120°24W 306 H6
Jacksonville Fla., U.S.A. 30°20N 81°39W 316 E8
Jacksonville Ga., U.S.A. 31°49N 82°59W 316 D7
Jacksonville Ill., U.S.A. 39°44N 90°14W 310 E6
Jacksonville N.C., U.S.A. 34°45N 77°26W 315 D16
Jacksonville Tex., U.S.A. 31°58N 95°17W 314 F7
Jacksonville Beach U.S.A. 30°17N 81°24W 316 E8
Jacksonville Int. ✈ (JAX) U.S.A. 30°30N 81°41W 316 E8
Jacmel Haiti 18°14N 72°32W 321 C5
Jaco, Pte. Dominica 15°39N 61°24W 323 k
Jacob Lake U.S.A. 36°43N 112°13W 305 H7
Jacobabad Pakistan 28°20N 68°29E 242 E3
Jacobina Brazil 11°11S 40°30W 332 D3
Jacobshagen = Dobrzany Poland 53°22N 15°25E 184 E2
Jacon Javits Convention Center New York, U.S.A. 132 c1
Jacotet, B. Mauritius 20°30S 57°26E 272 e
Jacqueline Kennedy Onassis Res. New York, U.S.A. 132 a3
Jacques-Cartier Canada 45°31N 73°27W 130 A3
Jacques-Cartier, Dét. de Canada 50°0N 63°30W 299 C7
Jacques-Cartier, Mt. Canada 48°57N 66°0W 299 C6
Jacques-Cartier, Pont Canada 45°31N 73°32W 130 A2
Jacques-Cartier ⌓ Canada 47°15N 71°33W 299 C5
Jacqueville Ivory C. 5°12N 4°25W 262 D4
Jacuí → Brazil 30°2S 51°15W 335 C5
Jacumba U.S.A. 32°37N 116°11W 307 N10
Jacundá → Brazil 1°57S 50°26W 332 B1
Jadavpur India 22°28N 88°22E 124 C2
Jadcherla India 16°46N 78°9E 244 F4
Jade Germany 53°20N 8°14E 178 B4
Jade, Côte de France 46°40N 2°0W 172 F4
Jade Buddha Temple China 31°15N 121°25E 138 B1
Jade City Canada 59°15N 129°37W 296 B3
Jade Dragon Snow Mt. = Yulong Xueshan China 27°6N 100°10E 228 D3
Jade Island Beijing, China 114 b2
Jade Mt. = Yü Shan Taiwan 23°25N 120°52E 225 C2
Jadebusen Germany 53°29N 8°12E 178 B4
Jadotville = Likasi Dem. Rep. of the Congo 10°55S 26°48E 269 E2
Jadovnik Serbia 43°20N 19°45E 202 C3
Jadraque Spain 40°55N 2°55W 196 E2
Jādū Libya 32°0N 12°0E 258 B2
Jægersborg Denmark 55°45N 12°31E 118 A3
Jægersborg Dyrehave Denmark 55°46N 12°33E 118 A3
Jaén Peru 5°25S 78°40W 330 B2
Jaén Spain 37°44N 3°43W 195 H7
Jaén □ Spain 37°50N 3°30W 195 H7
Jæren Norway 58°42N 5°47E 164 F2
Jærens Rev Norway 58°45N 5°45E 164 F2
Jafarabad India 20°52N 71°22E 242 J4
Jaffa = Tel Aviv-Yafo Israel 32°4N 34°48E 251 F5
Jaffa, C. Australia 36°58S 139°40E 282 D3
Jaffna Sri Lanka 9°45N 80°2E 245 K5
Jaffrey U.S.A. 42°49N 72°2W 313 D12
Jagadhri India 30°10N 77°20E 242 D7
Jagadishpur Bihar, India 25°30N 84°21E 243 G11
Jagadishpur Paschimbanga, India 22°39N 88°17E 124 B1
Jagat Nepal 28°19N 84°53E 243 E11
Jagatpur India 28°44N 77°13E 120 A2
Jagdalpur India 19°3N 82°0E 244 E6
Jagdaqi China 50°25N 124°7E 219 A13
Jagersfontein S. Africa 29°44S 25°27E 270 C4
Jaghīn → Iran 27°17N 57°13E 247 E8
Jagna Phil. 9°39N 124°22E 233 G5
Jagodina Serbia 44°5N 21°15E 202 B5
Jagraon India 30°50N 75°25E 242 D6
Jagst → Germany 49°14N 9°10E 179 F5
Jagtial India 18°50N 79°0E 244 E4
Jaguaquara Brazil 13°32S 39°58W 333 D4
Jaguaré, Rib. do → Brazil 23°32S 46°45W 137 B1
Jaguariaíva Brazil 24°10S 49°50W 335 A6
Jaguaribe Brazil 5°53S 38°37W 332 C4
Jaguaribe → Brazil 4°25S 37°45W 332 B4
Jaguaruana Brazil 4°50S 37°47W 332 B4
Jagüey Grande Cuba 22°35N 81°7W 320 B3
Jagungal, Mt. Australia 36°8S 148°22E 283 D8
Jahanabad India 25°13N 84°59E 243 G11
Jahangirpur India 28°43N 77°12E 120 A2
Jahazpur India 25°37N 75°17E 242 G6
Jahrom Iran 28°30N 53°31E 247 D7
Jaicós Brazil 7°21S 41°8W 332 C3
Jaigarh India 17°17N 73°13E 244 F1
Jaijon India 31°21N 76°9E 242 D7
Jailolo Indonesia 1°5N 127°30E 231 D7
Jailolo, Selat Indonesia 0°5N 129°5E 231 D7
Jaintiapur Bangla. 25°8N 92°7E 241 C4
Jaipur Assam, India 27°16N 95°24E 241 B5
Jaipur Raj., India 27°0N 75°50E 242 F6
Jais India 26°15N 81°32E 243 F9
Jaisalmer India 26°55N 70°54E 242 F4
Jaisinghnagar India 23°38N 78°34E 243 H8
Jaitaran India 26°12N 73°56E 242 F5
Jaithari India 23°14N 78°37E 243 H8
Jājarkot Nepal 28°42N 82°14E 243 E10
Jājarm Iran 36°58N 56°27E 247 B8
Jajce Bos.-H. 44°19N 17°17E 182 F2
Jajpur India 20°53N 86°22E 244 D8
Jakam → India 23°54N 74°13E 242 H6
Jakar Dzong Bhutan 27°33N 90°43E 241 B3
Jakarta Indonesia 6°9S 106°52E 122 A2
Jakarta, Teluk Indonesia 6°5S 106°50E 122 A1
Jakarta Halim Perdana Kusuma Int. ✈ (HLP) Indonesia 6°16S 106°53E 122 B2
Jakarta Sukarno-Hatta Int. ✈ (CGK) Indonesia 6°7S 106°40E 231 G12
Jakhal India 29°48N 75°50E 242 E6
Jakharrah Libya 29°13N 21°34E 258 C4
Jakhau India 23°13N 68°43E 242 H3
Jakobshavn = Ilulissat Greenland 69°12N 51°10W 154 D5
Jakobstad = Pietarsaari Finland 63°40N 22°43E 160 E20
Jakupica Macedonia 41°45N 21°22E 202 E5
Jal U.S.A. 32°7N 103°12W 305 K12
Jalaihai Pt. Guam 13°18N 144°46E 302 d
Jalājil Si. Arabia 25°40N 45°27E 246 E5
Jalal-Abad Kyrgyzstan 40°56N 73°0E 217 D8
Jalal-Abad □ Kyrgyzstan 41°30N 72°30E 217 D8
Jalālābād Afghan. 34°30N 70°29E 242 B4
Jalalabad India 27°41N 79°42E 243 F8
Jalalpur Jattan Pakistan 32°38N 74°11E 242 C6
Jalama U.S.A. 34°29N 120°29W 307 L6
Jalan Kayu Singapore 1°24N 103°52E 138 A3
Jalandhar India 31°20N 75°40E 242 D6
Jalapa Guatemala 14°39N 89°59W 320 D2
Jalapa Enríquez = Xalapa Mexico 19°32N 96°55W 319 D5
Jalasjärvi Finland 62°29N 22°47E 160 E20
Jalaun India 26°8N 79°25E 243 F8
Jalāzin Afghan. 37°2N 64°49E 240 A2
Jaldak Afghan. 31°58N 66°43E 240 C2
Jaldhaka → Bangla. 26°16N 89°16E 241 B2
Jales Brazil 20°10S 50°33W 333 F1
Jalesar India 27°29N 78°19E 242 F8
Jaleswar Nepal 26°38N 85°48E 243 F11
Jalgaon India 21°0N 75°42E 244 D2
Jalībah Iraq 30°35N 46°32E 246 D5
Jalingo Nigeria 8°55N 11°25E 263 D7
Jalisco □ Mexico 20°20N 103°40W 318 D4
Jalkot Pakistan 35°14N 73°24E 243 B5
Jalna India 19°48N 75°38E 244 E2
Jalón → Spain 41°47N 1°4W 196 D3
Jalor India 25°21N 72°37E 242 G5
Jalpa Mexico 21°38N 102°58W 318 C4
Jalpaiguri India 26°32N 88°46E 241 B2
Jalpan Mexico 21°14N 99°29W 319 C5
Jālq Iran 27°35N 62°46E 247 E9
Jālū Libya 29°2N 21°33E 258 C4
Jaluit I. Marshall Is. 6°0N 169°30E 288 G8
Jalūlā Iraq 34°16N 45°10E 213 E11
Jam, Minaret of Afghan. 34°23N 64°30E 240 B2
Jamaame Somalia 0°4N 42°44E 267 D5
Jamaari Nigeria 11°44N 9°53E 263 C6
Jamaica ■ W. Indies 18°10N 77°30W 320 a
Jamaica B. U.S.A. 40°36N 73°50W 132 C3
Jamaica Channel Jamaica 17°0N 76°0W 321 C4
Jamaica Plain U.S.A. 42°18N 71°6W 116 B2
Jamakpuri India 28°37N 77°5E 120 B1
Jamalpur Bangla. 24°52N 89°56E 241 C2
Jamalpur India 25°18N 86°28E 243 G12
Jamalpurganj India 23°2N 87°59E 243 H13
Jamanota Aruba 12°29N 69°57W 322 f
Jamanxim → Brazil 4°43S 56°18W 331 A6
Jamari Brazil 8°45S 63°27W 331 B5
Jamari → Brazil 8°27S 63°30W 331 B5
Jamba Angola 14°40S 16°2E 265 E3
Jambewangi Indonesia 8°17S 114°7E 231 J17
Jambi Indonesia 1°38S 103°30E 234 C2
Jambi □ Indonesia 1°30S 102°30E 234 C2
Jambongan, Pulau Malaysia 6°45N 117°20E 235 A5
Jambusar India 22°3N 72°51E 242 H5
James U.S.A. 32°58N 83°29W 316 C6
James → S. Dak., U.S.A. 42°52N 97°18W 308 D5
James → Va., U.S.A. 36°56N 76°27W 309 G15
James, I. = San Salvador, I. Ecuador 0°16S 90°42W 330 a
James B. Canada 54°0N 80°0W 298 B3
James I. Gambia 13°19N 16°21W 262 C1
James Island U.S.A. 32°45N 79°55W 316 C10
James Ranges Australia 24°10S 132°30E 278 D5
James Ross I. Antarctica 63°58S 57°50W 151 C18
James Ross Str. Canada 69°40N 96°10W 294 D12
James Shoal S. China Sea 3°47N 112°10E 235 B4
Jamesabad Pakistan 25°17N 69°15E 242 G3
Jameson Land Greenland 71°0N 23°30W 154 C8
Jamesport U.S.A. 39°58N 93°48W 310 E3
Jamestown = Wawa Canada 47°59N 84°47W 298 C3
Jamestown S. Austral., Australia 33°10S 138°32E 282 B3
Jamestown St. Helena 15°55S 5°43W 153 h
Jamestown Eastern Cape, S. Africa 31°6S 26°45E 270 D4
Jamestown Ind., U.S.A. 39°56N 86°38W 311 E10
Jamestown Mo., U.S.A. 38°48N 92°30W 310 F4
Jamestown N. Dak., U.S.A. 46°54N 98°42W 308 B4
Jamestown N.Y., U.S.A. 42°6N 79°14W 312 D5
Jamestown Ohio, U.S.A. 39°39N 83°33W 311 E13
Jamestown Pa., U.S.A. 41°29N 80°27W 312 E4
Jamestown S.C., U.S.A. 33°17N 79°42W 316 B10
Jamīlābād Iran 34°24N 48°28E 247 C6
Jamira → India 21°35N 88°28E 243 J13
Jämjö Sweden 56°12N 15°49E 163 H9
Jamkhandi India 16°30N 75°15E 244 F2
Jamkhed India 18°43N 75°19E 244 E2
Jammalamadugu India 14°51N 78°25E 245 G4
Jammerbugten Denmark 57°15N 9°20E 163 G3
Jammu India 32°43N 74°54E 242 C6
Jammu & Kashmir □ India 34°25N 77°0E 243 B7
Jamnagar India 22°30N 70°6E 242 H4
Jamner India 20°45N 75°52E 244 D2
Jamni → India 25°13N 78°35E 243 G8
Jampur Pakistan 29°39N 70°40E 242 E4
Jamrud Pakistan 33°59N 71°24E 242 C4
Jämsä Finland 61°53N 25°10E 188 B3
Jamshedpur India 22°44N 86°12E 243 H12
Jamshīdīyeh Iran 35°42N 51°22E 141 A2
Jamsil S. Korea 37°30N 127°4E 137 B2
Jamtara India 23°59N 86°49E 243 H12
Jämtland Sweden 63°31N 14°0E 160 E16
Jämtland □ Sweden 63°0N 14°40E 162 B7
Jamuna → Bangla. 23°51N 89°45E 241 C2
Jamurki Bangla. 24°9N 90°2E 241 C3
Jamwon S. Korea 37°30N 127°0E 137 B2
Jan L. Canada 54°56N 102°55W 297 C8
Jan Mayen Arctic 71°0N 9°0W 150 B7
Janakkala Finland 60°54N 24°36E 188 B3
Janakpur Nepal 26°42N 85°55E 244 A7
Janaúba Brazil 15°48S 43°19W 333 E3
Janaucu, I. Brazil 0°30N 50°10W 332 A1
Jand Pakistan 33°30N 72°6E 242 C5
Jandaia Brazil 17°6S 50°7W 333 E1
Jandanku ☼ Australia 16°20S 135°45E 280 B2
Jandaq Iran 34°3N 54°22E 247 C7
Jandía Canary Is. 28°6N 14°21W 153 e2
Jandía, Pta. de Canary Is. 28°3N 14°31W 153 e2
Jandía △ Canary Is. 28°4N 14°19W 153 e2
Jandiatuba → Brazil 3°28S 68°42W 328 D4
Jandola Pakistan 32°20N 70°9E 242 C4
Jandowae Australia 26°45S 151°7E 281 D5
Jándula → Spain 38°3N 4°6W 195 G6
Jane Pk. N.Z. 45°15S 168°20E 285 F3
Janesville U.S.A. 42°41N 89°1W 310 B7
Jang Bogo Antarctica 74°37S 164°12E 151 D11
Janga Ghana 10°5N 1°0W 263 C4
Jangamo Mozam. 24°6S 35°21E 271 B6
Janghai India 25°33N 82°19E 243 G10
Jangheung S. Korea 34°41N 126°52E 224 E3
Janghowon S. Korea 37°7N 127°37E 224 D3
Jangipur India 24°28N 88°4E 243 G12
Jangoon India 17°44N 79°5E 244 F4
Jangsu S. Korea 35°38N 127°31E 224 E3
Janhtang Ga Burma 26°32N 96°38E 241 B6
Jani Khel Afghan. 32°46N 68°24E 240 B3
Janikowo Poland 52°45N 18°7E 185 F5
Janiuay Phil. 10°58N 122°30E 233 F4
Janja Bos.-H. 44°40N 19°14E 182 F4
Janjanbureh Gambia 13°30N 14°47W 262 C2
Janjevë Kosovo 42°35N 21°19E 202 D5
Janjgir India 22°1N 82°34E 243 J10
Janjina Croatia 42°58N 17°25E 199 F14
Janjina Madag. 20°30S 45°50E 272 C2
Jankau = Janikowo Poland 52°45N 18°7E 185 F5
Janki Poland 52°8N 20°52E 143 C1
Jannaale Somalia 1°48N 44°42E 267 D5
Janos Mexico 30°54N 108°10W 318 A3
Jánoshalma Hungary 46°18N 19°21E 182 D4
Jánosháza Hungary 47°8N 17°12E 182 C2
Jánossomorja Hungary 47°47N 17°11E 182 C2
Janów Poland 50°44N 19°27E 185 H6
Janów Lubelski Poland 50°48N 22°23E 185 H9
Janów Podlaski Poland 52°11N 23°11E 185 F10
Janowiec Wielkopolski Poland 52°45N 17°30E 185 F4
Jantho Indonesia 5°17N 95°38E 234 A1
Januária Brazil 15°25S 44°25W 333 E3
Janub = Southern △ South Sudan 6°50N 28°45E 257 F2
Janub al Batinah □ Oman 23°25N 57°25E 249 B7
Janub ash Sharqīyah □ Oman 22°0N 59°30E 249 B7
Janub Dârfûr □ Sudan 11°0N 24°0E 259 F4
Janub Kordofân □ Sudan 11°0N 31°0E 257 E3
Janûb Sînî □ Egypt 29°30N 33°50E 251 J4
Janubio Canary Is. 28°56N 13°50W 153 e2
Janville France 48°10N 1°50E 173 D8
Janwada India 18°0N 77°29E 244 E3
Janzé France 47°55N 1°28W 172 E5
Jaora India 23°40N 75°10E 242 H6
Japan ■ Asia 36°0N 136°0E 221 G8
Japan, Sea of Asia 40°0N 135°0E 220 E7
Japan Center San Francisco, U.S.A. 136 c1
Japan Trench Pac. Oc. 32°0N 142°0E 288 D6
Japen = Yapen Indonesia 1°50S 136°0E 231 E9
Japim Brazil 7°37S 72°54W 330 B3
Japla India 24°33N 84°1E 243 G11
Japurá Brazil 1°48S 66°34W 328 D4
Japura Indonesia 0°19S 102°21E 234 C2
Japurá → Brazil 3°8S 65°46W 328 D4
Jaquarão Brazil 32°34S 53°23W 335 C5
Jaqué Panama 7°27N 78°8W 320 E4
Jarābulus Syria 36°49N 38°1E 213 D8
Jaraguá Goiás, Brazil 15°45S 49°20W 333 E2
Jaraguá São Paulo, Brazil 23°27S 46°44W 137 A1
Jaraguá, Pico de Brazil 23°27S 46°46W 137 A1
Jaraguá do Sul Brazil 26°29S 49°4W 335 B6
Jaraguari Brazil 20°9S 54°35W 331 E7
Jaraicejo Spain 39°40N 5°49W 195 F5
Jaraíz de la Vera Spain 40°4N 5°45W 194 E5
Jarama → Spain 40°24N 3°32W 194 E7
Jaramānah Syria 33°29N 36°21E 250 E7
Jaramillo Argentina 47°10S 67°7W 336 C3
Jarandilla de la Vera Spain 40°8N 5°39W 194 E5
Jaranwala Pakistan 31°15N 73°26E 242 D5
Jarash Jordan 32°17N 35°54E 251 F6
Jarash □ Jordan 32°17N 35°54E 251 F6
Jarauçu → Brazil 1°48S 52°22W 329 D7
Järbo Sweden 60°43N 16°38E 162 D10
Jarboesville = Lexington Park U.S.A. 38°16N 76°27W 309 F15
Jardas al 'Abīd Libya 32°18N 20°59E 258 B4
Jardim Brazil 21°28S 56°2W 334 A4
Jardim Paulista Brazil 23°34S 46°41W 137 B1
Jardín → Spain 38°50N 2°10W 197 G2
Jardín América Argentina 27°3S 55°14W 335 B4
Jardin Botanique Brussels, Belgium 116 a3
Jardine River △ Australia 11°9S 142°21E 280 A3
Jardines de la Reina, Arch. de los Cuba 20°50N 78°50W 320 B4
Jargalang China 43°5N 122°55E 227 C12
Jargalant = Hovd □ Mongolia 48°2N 91°37E 217 C12
Jari → Brazil 1°9S 51°54W 329 D7
Jaria Janjail Bangla. 25°0N 90°40E 241 C3
Jarīr, W. al → Si. Arabia 25°38N 42°30E 246 E4
Järlåsa Sweden 59°53N 17°12E 162 E11
Jarlsberg og Larvik = Vestfold □ Norway 59°15N 10°0E 164 E7
Jarmen Germany 53°54N 13°20E 178 B9
Järna Sweden 59°6N 17°34E 162 E11
Jarnac France 45°40N 0°11W 174 C3
Jarny France 49°9N 5°53E 173 C12
Jaro Phil. 11°11N 124°47E 233 F5
Jarocin Poland 51°59N 17°29E 185 G4
Jaroměř Czechia 50°22N 15°52E 180 A8
Jarosław Poland 50°2N 22°42E 185 H9
Järpås Sweden 58°23N 12°57E 163 F6
Järpen Sweden 63°21N 13°26E 162 A7
Jarqo'rg'on Uzbekistan 37°31N 67°25E 240 A2
Jarrahdale Australia 32°24S 116°5E 279 F2
Jarrahi → Iran 30°49N 48°48E 247 D6
Jarso Ethiopia 5°15N 37°30E 257 F4
Jartai China 39°45N 105°48E 226 E3
Jaru Brazil 10°26S 62°27W 331 C5
Jaru → Brazil 10°5S 61°59W 331 C5
Jarud Qi China 44°28N 120°50E 227 B11
Järvatältet Sweden 59°25N 17°54E 139 A1
Järvenpää Finland 60°29N 25°5E 188 B3
Jarvis Canada 42°53N 80°6W 312 D4
Jarvis I. Pac. Oc. 0°15S 160°5W 289 H12
Jarvorník Czechia 50°23N 17°2E 181 A10
Järvsö Sweden 61°43N 16°10E 162 C10
Jarwa India 27°38N 82°30E 243 F10
Jaša Tomić Serbia 45°26N 20°50E 182 E5
Jasaan Phil. 8°39N 124°45E 233 G5
Jasdan India 22°2N 71°12E 242 H4
Jashpurnagar India 22°54N 84°9E 243 H11
Jasidih India 24°31N 86°39E 243 G12
Jasień Poland 51°46N 15°0E 185 G2
Jāsimīyah Iraq 33°45N 44°41E 213 F11
Jasin Malaysia 2°20N 102°26E 237 L4
Jāsk Iran 25°38N 57°45E 247 E8
Jaskhar India 18°54N 72°58E 130 B2

Jasliq Uzbekistan 43°58N 57°10E 216 D5
Jasło Poland 49°45N 21°30E 185 J8
Jasmund Germany 54°32N 13°35E 178 A9
Jasmund △ Germany 54°31N 13°38E 178 A9
Jaso India 24°30N 80°29E 243 G9
Jason Is. Falk. Is. 51°0S 61°0W 153 f
Jasonville U.S.A. 39°10N 87°12W 311 E9
Jasper Alta., Canada 52°55N 118°5W 296 C5
Jasper Ont., Canada 44°52N 75°57W 313 B9
Jasper Ala., U.S.A. 33°50N 87°17W 315 E11
Jasper Fla., U.S.A. 30°31N 82°57W 316 E7
Jasper Ind., U.S.A. 38°24N 86°56W 311 F10
Jasper Tex., U.S.A. 30°56N 94°1W 314 F7
Jasper △ Canada 52°50N 118°8W 296 C5
Jasrasar India 27°43N 73°49E 242 F5
Jassān Iraq 32°58N 45°52E 213 G11
Jassey = Iaşi Romania 47°10N 27°40E 183 C12
Jastarnia Poland 54°42N 18°40E 184 D5
Jastrebarsko Croatia 45°41N 15°39E 199 C12
Jastrow = Jastrowie Poland 53°26N 16°49E 184 E3
Jastrowie Poland 53°26N 16°49E 184 E3
Jastrzębie Zdrój Poland 49°57N 18°35E 185 J5
Jász-Nagykun-Szolnok □ Hungary 47°15N 20°30E 182 C5
Jászapáti Hungary 47°32N 20°10E 182 C5
Jászárokszállás Hungary 47°39N 19°58E 182 C4
Jászberény Hungary 47°30N 19°55E 182 C4
Jászkisér Hungary 47°27N 20°20E 182 C5
Jászladány Hungary 47°23N 20°10E 182 C5
Jataí Brazil 17°58S 51°48W 333 E1
Jatapu → Brazil 2°13S 58°17W 329 D6
Jath India 17°3N 75°13E 244 F2
Jati Pakistan 24°20N 68°19E 242 G3
Jatibarang Indonesia 6°28S 108°18E 235 D3
Jatiluwih Indonesia 8°23S 115°8E 231 J18
Jatinegara Indonesia 6°13S 106°52E 122 B2
Játiva = Xátiva Spain 38°59N 0°32W 197 G4
Jatobá = Petrolândia Brazil 9°5S 38°20W 332 C4
Jättendal Sweden 61°58N 17°15E 162 C11
Jaú Angola 15°12S 13°31E 265 F2
Jaú Brazil 22°10S 48°30W 335 A6
Jaú → Brazil 1°54S 61°26W 329 D5
Jauaperí → Brazil 1°26S 61°35W 329 D5
Jauer = Jawor Poland 51°4N 16°11E 185 G3
Jauja Peru 11°45S 75°15W 330 C2
Jaunpur India 25°46N 82°44E 243 G10
Jauru → Brazil 16°22S 57°46W 331 D6
Java = Jawa Indonesia 7°0S 110°0E 235 D4
Java Sea Indonesia 4°35S 107°15E 235 C3
Java Trench Ind. Oc. 9°0S 105°0E 234 D2
Javadi Hills India 12°40N 78°40E 245 H4
Javādīyeh Iran 35°39N 51°22E 141 B2
Javalambre, Sa. de Spain 40°6N 1°0W 196 E4
Javānrud Iran 34°47N 46°31E 213 E12
Jávea Spain 38°48N 0°10E 197 G5
Javhlant = Uliastay Mongolia 47°56N 97°28E 218 B8
Javier, I. Chile 47°5S 74°25W 336 C2
Javla India 17°18N 75°9E 244 F2
Jawa Indonesia 7°0S 110°0E 235 D4
Jawa Barat □ Indonesia 7°0S 107°0E 231 G12
Jawa Tengah □ Indonesia 7°0S 110°0E 235 D3
Jawa Timur □ Indonesia 8°0S 113°0E 235 D4
Jawad India 24°36N 74°51E 242 G6
Jawaharlal Nehru Port = Nhava Sheva India 18°58N 72°55E 130 B2
Jawf, W. al → Yemen 15°50N 45°30E 248 D4
Jawhar India 19°55N 73°14E 244 E1
Jawhar Somalia 2°48N 45°30E 267 D6
Jawor Poland 51°4N 16°11E 185 G3
Jaworowa Poland 52°9N 20°56E 143 C1
Jaworzno Poland 50°13N 19°11E 185 H6
Jaworzyna Śląska Poland 50°55N 16°28E 185 H3
Jawoyn ◎ Australia 14°16S 132°28E 278 B5
Jay U.S.A. 30°57N 87°9W 317 E2
Jay Peak U.S.A. 44°55N 72°32W 313 B12
Jaya, Puncak Indonesia 3°57S 137°17E 231 E9
Jayanca Peru 6°24S 79°50W 330 B2
Jayanti India 26°45N 89°40E 241 B2
Jayapura Indonesia 2°28S 140°38E 231 E10
Jayawijaya, Pegunungan Indonesia 5°0S 139°0E 231 F9
Jaynagar India 26°43N 86°9E 243 F12
Jaypur = Jeypore India 18°50N 82°38E 244 E6
Jayrūd Syria 33°49N 36°44E 250 E7
Jayton U.S.A. 33°15N 100°34W 314 E4
Jāz Mūrīān, Hāmūn-e Iran 27°20N 58°55E 247 E8
Jazīreh-ye Shīf Iran 29°4N 50°54E 247 D6
Jazminal Mexico 24°52N 101°24W 318 C4
Jazzīn Lebanon 33°31N 35°35E 250 E6
Jean U.S.A. 35°47N 115°20W 307 K11
Jean Lafitte Nat. Historical Park ⌓ U.S.A. 29°51N 90°9W 131 B1
Jean Marie River Canada 61°32N 120°38W 296 A4
Jean-Rabel Haiti 19°50N 73°5W 321 C5
Jeanerette U.S.A. 29°55N 91°40W 314 G9
Jeanette, Ostrov = Zhannetty, Ostrov Russia 76°43N 158°0E 215 B16
Jeanne-Mance, Parc Montréal, Canada 130 b1
Jeanneton, Morne Guadeloupe 16°14N 61°43W 322 e
Jeannette U.S.A. 40°20N 79°36W 312 F5
Jebāl Bārez, Kūh-e Iran 28°30N 58°20E 247 D8
Jebba Nigeria 9°9N 4°48E 263 D5
Jebel, Bahr el → South Sudan 9°30N 30°25E 257 F3
Jebel Ali = Minā' Jabal 'Alī U.A.E. 25°2N 55°8E 247 E7
Jebel Dud Sudan 13°25N 33°9E 257 E3
Jebel Elba △ Egypt 22°11N 36°22E 256 C4
Jebel Qerri Sudan 16°16N 32°50E 257 D3
Jeberos Peru 5°15S 76°10W 330 B2
Jebus Indonesia 1°43S 105°28E 234 C3
Jecheon S. Korea 37°8N 128°12E 224 D4
Jedburgh U.K. 55°29N 2°33W 167 F6
Jedda = Jiddah Si. Arabia 21°29N 39°10E 248 B2
Jeddore L. Canada 48°3N 55°55W 299 C8
Jedlesee Austria 48°15N 16°23E 142 A2
Jedlicze Poland 49°43N 21°40E 185 J8
Jędrzejów Poland 50°35N 20°15E 185 H7
Jedwabne Poland 53°17N 22°18E 185 E9
Jeetzel → Germany 53°9N 11°3E 178 B7
Jefferson Ga., U.S.A. 34°7N 83°35W 316 A6
Jefferson Iowa, U.S.A. 42°1N 94°23W 310 B2
Jefferson La., U.S.A. 29°57N 90°9W 131 B2
Jefferson Ohio, U.S.A. 41°44N 80°46W 312 E4
Jefferson Tex., U.S.A. 32°46N 94°21W 314 E7
Jefferson Wis., U.S.A. 43°0N 88°48W 311 B8
Jefferson, Mt. Nev., U.S.A. 38°47N 116°56W 304 G5
Jefferson, Mt. Oreg., U.S.A. 44°41N 121°48W 304 D3
Jefferson City Mo., U.S.A. 38°34N 92°10W 310 F4
Jefferson City Tenn., U.S.A. 36°7N 83°30W 315 C13
Jefferson Memorial Washington, D.C., U.S.A. 143 c1
Jefferson Park Calif., U.S.A. 34°2N 118°19W 126 B3
Jefferson Park Ill., U.S.A. 41°58N 87°46W 119 B2
Jeffersontown U.S.A. 38°12N 85°35W 311 F11
Jeffersonville Ga., U.S.A. 32°41N 83°20W 316 C6
Jeffersonville Ind., U.S.A. 38°17N 85°44W 311 F11
Jeffersonville Ohio, U.S.A. 39°39N 83°34W 311 E13
Jeffrey City U.S.A. 42°30N 107°49W 304 E10
Jega Nigeria 12°15N 4°23E 263 C5
Jegi S. Korea 37°34N 127°1E 137 B2
Jejevo Solomon Is. 8°6S 159°8E 287 M10
Jeju S. Korea 33°31N 126°32E 224 a
Jeju-do S. Korea 33°29N 126°34E 224 a
Jeju-do □ S. Korea 33°25N 126°30E 224 a
Jeju Haehyop S. Korea 33°50N 126°30E 227 H14
Jeju Int. ✈ (CJU) S. Korea 33°30N 126°30E 224 a
Jēkabpils Latvia 56°29N 25°57E 188 D3
Jekyll I. U.S.A. 31°4N 81°25W 316 D8
Jelambar Indonesia 6°9S 106°47E 122 A1
Jelcz-Laskowice Poland 51°2N 17°19E 185 G4
Jelenia Góra Poland 50°50N 15°45E 185 H2
Jelgava Latvia 56°41N 23°49E 184 B10
Jelica Serbia 43°50N 20°17E 202 C4
Jelli South Sudan 5°25N 31°45E 257 F3
Jelonki Poland 52°14N 20°54E 143 B1
Jelšava Slovakia 48°37N 20°15E 181 C13
Jema'a Mallam = Kafanchan Nigeria 9°40N 8°20E 263 D6
Jemaja Indonesia 3°5N 105°45E 234 B3
Jemaluang Malaysia 2°16N 103°52E 237 L4
Jember Indonesia 8°11S 113°41E 235 D4
Jempang, Danau Indonesia 0°25S 116°12E 235 C5
Jena Thüringen, Germany 50°54N 11°35E 178 E7
Jena La., U.S.A. 31°41N 92°8W 314 F8
Jenai Taiwan 24°2N 121°8E 225 B3
Jenbach Austria 47°24N 11°47E 180 D4
Jendouba Tunisia 36°29N 8°47E 258 A1
Jendouba □ Tunisia 36°34N 8°52E 261 A6
Jeneponto Indonesia 5°40S 119°44E 235 D5
Jengish Chokusu = Pobedy, Pik Asia 42°0N 79°58E 217 D9
Jenho Taiwan 23°54N 121°36E 225 C3
Jenin West Bank 32°28N 35°18E 251 F6
Jenison U.S.A. 42°54N 85°47W 311 B11
Jenkins U.S.A. 37°10N 82°38W 309 G12
Jenner U.S.A. 38°27N 123°7W 306 G3
Jennings Fla., U.S.A. 30°36N 83°6W 316 E6
Jennings La., U.S.A. 30°13N 92°40W 314 F8
Jennings Mo., U.S.A. 38°43N 90°15W 310 F6
Jenny Pt. Dominica 15°28N 61°15W 323 k
Jensen Beach U.S.A. 27°15N 80°14W 317 H9
Jente Taiwan 22°58N 120°16E 225 D2
Jenwu Taiwan 22°42N 120°20E 225 D2
Jeollabuk-do □ S. Korea 35°45N 127°15E 224 E3
Jeollanam-do □ S. Korea 34°45N 127°0E 224 E3
Jeong-eup S. Korea 35°35N 126°50E 224 E3
Jeongseon S. Korea 37°20N 128°45E 224 D4
Jeonju S. Korea 35°50N 127°4E 224 E3
Jepara Indonesia 7°40S 109°14E 235 D3
Jeparit Australia 36°8S 142°1E 282 D5
Jequié Brazil 13°51S 40°5W 333 D3
Jequitaí → Brazil 17°4S 44°50W 333 E3
Jequitinhonha Brazil 16°30S 41°0W 333 E3
Jequitinhonha → Brazil 15°51S 38°53W 333 E4
Jerada Morocco 34°17N 2°10W 261 B4
Jerantut Malaysia 3°56N 102°22E 237 L4
Jerejak, Pulau Malaysia 5°19N 100°19E 237 c
Jérémie Haiti 18°40N 74°10W 321 C5
Jeremoabo Brazil 10°4S 38°21W 332 D4
Jerez, Pta. Mexico 22°58N 97°40W 319 C5
Jerez de García Salinas Mexico 22°39N 103°0W 318 C4
Jerez de la Frontera Spain 36°41N 6°7W 195 J4
Jerez de los Caballeros Spain 38°20N 6°45W 195 G4
Jericho = El Arīḥā West Bank 31°52N 35°27E 251 G6
Jericho Australia 23°38S 146°6E 280 C4
Jerichow Germany 52°30N 12°1E 178 C8
Jerico Springs U.S.A. 37°37N 94°1W 310 G2
Jerid, Chott el = Djerid, Chott Tunisia 33°42N 8°30E 258 B1
Jerilderie Australia 35°20S 145°41E 283 C6
Jermyn U.S.A. 41°32N 75°33W 313 E9
Jerningham Junction Trin. & Tob. 10°33N 61°23W 323 t
Jerome U.S.A. 42°44N 114°31W 304 E6
Jerónimos, Mosteiro dos Portugal 38°41N 9°11W 126 A1
Jerramungup Australia 33°55S 118°55E 279 F2
Jersey U.K. 49°11N 2°7W 169 H5
Jersey City U.S.A. 40°42N 74°4W 132 B1
Jersey Shore U.S.A. 41°12N 77°15W 312 E7
Jerseyville U.S.A. 39°7N 90°20W 310 E6
Jerumenha Brazil 7°5S 43°30W 332 C3
Jerusalem Israel/West Bank 31°47N 35°10E 123 B2
Jervis B. Australia 35°8S 150°46E 283 C9
Jervis Bay △ Australia 35°9S 150°40E 283 C9
Jervis Inlet Canada 50°0N 123°57W 296 C4
Jerzu Italy 39°47N 9°31E 200 C2
Jesenice Slovenia 46°28N 14°3E 199 B11
Jeseník Czechia 50°14N 17°8E 181 A10
Jesenké Slovakia 48°20N 20°10E 181 C13
Jesi = Iesi Italy 43°31N 13°14E 199 E10
Jésolo Italy 45°32N 12°38E 199 C9
Jessamine, L. U.S.A. 28°28N 81°23W 133 B2
Jessel = Jasło Poland 49°45N 21°30E 185 J8
Jesselton = Kota Kinabalu Malaysia 6°0N 116°4E 235 A5
Jessheim Norway 60°9N 11°10E 164 D8
Jessnitz Germany 51°40N 12°18E 178 D8
Jessore Bangla. 23°10N 89°10E 241 D2
Jesup Ga., U.S.A. 31°36N 81°53W 316 D8
Jesup Iowa, U.S.A. 42°29N 92°4W 310 B4
Jesup, L. U.S.A. 28°43N 81°14W 317 G8
Jesús Peru 7°15S 78°25W 330 B2
Jésus, Î. Canada 45°36N 73°44W 130 A1
Jesús Carranza Mexico 17°26N 95°2W 319 D5
Jesús María Argentina 30°59S 64°5W 334 C3
Jesús María Lima, Peru 12°4S 77°3W 126 B2
Jetmore U.S.A. 38°4N 99°54W 308 F4
Jetpur India 21°45N 70°10E 242 J4
Jette Belgium 50°53N 4°20E 116 A1
Jeumont France 50°18N 4°6E 173 B11
Jeungdo S. Korea 34°56N 126°9E 224 E3
Jeungpyeong S. Korea 36°47N 127°34E 224 D3
Jevnaker Norway 60°15N 10°26E 164 D7
Jewell U.S.A. 45°20N 123°30W 306 E3
Jewett U.S.A. 40°22N 81°2W 312 F3
Jewett City U.S.A. 41°36N 71°59W 313 E13
Jewish Quarter Jerusalem 123 b3
Jey Iran 35°41N 51°20E 141 B2
Jeyḥūnābād Iran 34°58N 48°59E 247 C6
Jeypore India 18°50N 82°38E 244 E6
Jeziorak, Jezioro Poland 53°40N 19°35E 184 E6
Jeziorany Poland 53°58N 20°46E 184 E7
Jeziorka → Poland 52°8N 21°9E 185 F8
Jha Jha India 24°46N 86°22E 243 G12
Jhaarkand = Jharkhand □ India 24°0N 85°50E 243 H11
Jhabua India 22°46N 74°36E 242 H6
Jhajjar India 28°37N 76°42E 242 E7
Jhal Pakistan 28°17N 67°27E 242 E2
Jhal Jhao Pakistan 26°20N 65°35E 240 D2
Jhalakati Bangla. 22°39N 90°12E 241 D3
Jhalawar India 24°40N 76°10E 242 G7
Jhalida India 23°22N 85°58E 243 H11
Jhalrapatan India 24°33N 76°10E 242 G7
Jhang Maghiana Pakistan 31°15N 72°22E 242 D5
Jhang Sadr = Jhang Maghiana Pakistan 31°15N 72°22E 242 D5
Jhansi India 25°30N 78°36E 243 G8
Jhargram India 22°27N 86°59E 243 H12
Jharia India 23°45N 86°26E 243 H12
Jharkhand □ India 24°0N 85°50E 243 H11
Jharsuguda India 21°56N 84°5E 244 D7
Jhelum Pakistan 33°0N 73°45E 242 C5
Jhelum → Pakistan 31°20N 72°10E 242 D5
Jhenaidah Bangla. 23°33N 89°10E 241 D2
Jhilmilli India 23°24N 82°51E 243 H10
Jhudo Pakistan 24°58N 69°18E 242 G3
Jhunjhunun India 28°10N 75°30E 242 E6
Ji-Paraná Brazil 10°50S 61°58W 331 C5
Ji Xian China 36°7N 110°40E 226 F6
Ji Xian Henan, China 35°59N 113°12E 226 H7
Ji Xian Shaanxi, China 38°12N 110°28E 226 E6
Jiading = Chiehting Taiwan 22°54N 120°11E 225 D2
Jiadong = Chiatung Taiwan 22°25N 120°32E 225 D2
Jiahe China 25°38N 112°19E 229 E9
Jiaji = Qionghai China 19°15N 110°26E 229 a
Jiali = Chiali Taiwan 23°9N 120°10E 225 C2
Jialing Jiang → China 29°30N 106°20E 228 C6
Jiamusi China 46°40N 130°26E 219 B15
Jian = Chian Taiwan 23°59N 121°33E 225 C3
Ji'an Jiangxi, China 27°6N 114°59E 229 D10
Ji'an Jilin, China 41°5N 126°10E 227 D14
Jianchang China 40°55N 120°35E 227 D11
Jianchuan China 26°38N 99°55E 228 D2
Jiande China 29°23N 119°15E 229 C12
Jiang'an China 28°40N 105°3E 228 C5
Jiangbei China 29°40N 106°34E 228 C6
Jiangcheng China 22°36N 101°52E 228 F3
Jiangchuan China 24°8N 102°39E 228 E4
Jiangdi China 26°57N 103°37E 228 D4
Jiangdu China 32°27N 119°36E 229 A12
Jiange China 32°4N 105°32E 228 A5
Jianggao China 23°13N 113°13E 121 A2
Jianghua China 25°0N 111°47E 229 E8
Jiangjin China 29°14N 106°14E 228 C6
Jiangjun = Chiangchun Taiwan 23°12N 120°9E 225 C2
Jiangkou China 27°40N 108°49E 228 D7
Jiangle China 26°42N 117°23E 229 D11
Jiangmen China 22°32N 113°0E 229 F9
Jiangning China 31°55N 118°50E 229 B12
Jiangshan China 28°40N 118°37E 229 C12
Jiangsu □ China 33°0N 120°0E 227 H11
Jiangwan China 31°18N 121°28E 138 B1
Jiangxi □ China 27°30N 116°0E 229 D11
Jiangyan China 32°30N 120°10E 229 A13
Jiangyin China 31°54N 120°17E 229 B13
Jiangyong China 25°20N 111°22E 229 E8
Jiangyou China 31°44N 104°43E 228 B5
Jiangyuan China 42°2N 126°34E 227 C14
Jianhe China 26°37N 108°31E 228 D7
Jianli China 29°46N 112°56E 229 C9
Jianning China 26°50N 116°50E 229 D11
Jian'ou China 27°3N 118°17E 229 D12
Jianping China 41°53N 119°42E 227 D10
Jianshi China 30°37N 109°38E 228 B7
Jianshui China 23°36N 102°43E 228 F4
Jianyang Fujian, China 27°20N 118°5E 229 D12
Jianyang Sichuan, China 30°24N 104°33E 228 B5
Jiao Xian = Jiaozhou China 36°18N 120°1E 227 F11
Jiaohe Hebei, China 38°2N 116°20E 226 E9
Jiaohe Jilin, China 43°40N 127°22E 227 C14
Jiaoling China 24°41N 116°12E 229 E11
Jiaonan China 35°52N 119°58E 227 G10
Jiaoxi = Chiaohsi Taiwan 24°49N 121°46E 225 B3
Jiaozhou China 36°18N 120°1E 227 F11
Jiaozhou Wan China 36°5N 120°10E 227 F11
Jiaozuo China 35°16N 113°12E 226 G7
Jiawang China 34°28N 117°26E 227 G9
Jiaxiang China 35°25N 116°20E 226 G9
Jiaxing China 30°49N 120°45E 229 B13
Jiayi = Chiai Taiwan 23°29N 120°25E 225 C2
Jiayu China 29°55N 113°55E 229 C9
Jiayuguan China 39°49N 98°18E 218 D8
Jib West Bank 31°51N 35°11E 123 A2
Jibão, Serra do Brazil 14°48S 45°0W 333 D3
Jibeiyu = Chipei Tao Taiwan 23°45N 119°37E 225 C1
Jibiya Nigeria 13°5N 7°12E 263 C6
Jiblah Yemen 13°55N 44°9E 248 D4
Jibou Romania 47°15N 23°17E 183 C8
Jibuti = Djibouti ■ Africa 12°0N 43°0E 257 E5
Jicarón, I. Panama 7°10N 81°50W 320 E3
Jičín Czechia 50°25N 15°28E 180 A8
Jiddah Si. Arabia 21°29N 39°10E 248 B2
Jido India 29°2N 94°58E 241 A5
Jido S. Korea 35°4N 126°14E 224 E3
Jieshou China 33°18N 115°22E 226 H8
Jiexiu China 37°2N 111°55E 226 F6
Jieyang China 23°35N 116°21E 229 F11
Jigalong Australia 23°21S 120°47E 278 D3
Jigalong ◎ Australia 23°21S 120°46E 278 D3
Jigawa □ Nigeria 12°0N 9°45E 263 C6
Jigme Dorje △ Bhutan 28°0N 89°40E 241 B2
Jigme Singye Wangchuck Bhutan 27°20N 90°25E 241 B3
Jigni India 25°45N 79°25E 243 G8
Jihād Iraq 33°17N 44°19E 113 B1
Jihlava Czechia 49°28N 15°35E 180 B8
Jihlava → Czechia 48°55N 16°36E 181 C9
Jihnan Taiwan 24°22N 120°39E 225 B2
Jihočeský □ Czechia 49°8N 14°35E 180 B7
Jihomoravský □ Czechia 49°5N 16°30E 181 B9
Jihu = Chihu Taiwan 23°54N 120°24E 225 C2
Jiigley Somalia 5°25N 45°20E 267 C6
Jijel Algeria 36°52N 5°50E 261 A6
Jijel □ Algeria 36°45N 6°0E 261 A6
Jijiga Ethiopia 9°20N 42°50E 267 C5
Jikamshi Nigeria 12°12N 7°45E 263 C6
Jikau South Sudan 8°28N 33°47E 257 F3
Jilib Somalia 0°29N 42°46E 267 D5
Jilin China 43°44N 126°30E 227 C14
Jilin □ China 44°0N 127°0E 227 C14
Jiloca → Spain 41°21N 1°39W 196 D3
Jilong = Chilung Taiwan 25°3N 121°45E 225 A3
Jim Thompson's House Bangkok, Thailand 113 b3
Jim Thorpe U.S.A. 40°52N 75°44W 313 F9
Jima Ethiopia 7°40N 36°47E 257 F4
Jimbaran, Teluk Indonesia 8°46S 115°9E 231 K18
Jimbōchō Tokyo, Japan 140 a4
Jimbolia Romania 45°47N 20°43E 182 E5
Jimena de la Frontera Spain 36°27N 5°24W 195 J5
Jiménez Chihuahua, Mexico 27°8N 104°54W 318 B4
Jimenez Phil. 8°20N 123°50E 233 G4
Jimeta Nigeria 9°17N 12°28E 263 D7
Jimo China 36°23N 120°30E 227 F11
Jimsar China 43°59N 89°4E 217 D11
Jin Jiang → China 28°24N 115°48E 229 C10
Jin Xian = Jinzhou China 38°55N 121°42E 227 E11
Jinan China 36°38N 117°1E 226 F9
Jinchang China 38°30N 102°10E 218 D9
Jincheng China 35°29N 112°50E 226 G7
Jinchuan China 31°30N 102°3E 228 B4
Jind India 29°19N 76°22E 242 E7
Jindabyne Australia 36°25S 148°35E 283 D8
Jinding China 22°22N 113°33E 219 a
Jindo S. Korea 34°28N 126°15E 224 E3
Jindřichův Hradec Czechia 49°10N 15°2E 180 B8
Jing He → China 34°27N 109°4E 226 G5
Jing Shan China 31°20N 111°35E 229 B8
Jing Xian China 30°38N 118°25E 229 B12
Jing'an Jiangxi, China 28°50N 115°17E 229 C10
Jingan Shanghai, China 31°14N 121°25E 138 B1
Jingbian China 37°20N 108°30E 226 F5
Jingchuan China 35°20N 107°20E 226 G4
Jingde China 30°15N 118°27E 229 B12
Jingdezhen China 29°20N 117°11E 229 C11
Jingdong China 24°23N 100°47E 228 E3
Jinggangshan China 26°58N 114°15E 229 D10
Jinggu China 23°35N 100°41E 228 F3
Jinghai Guangdong, China 22°59N 116°31E 229 F11
Jinghai Tianjin, China 38°55N 116°55E 226 E9
Jinghong China 22°0N 100°45E 228 G3
Jinghong Dam China 22°10N 100°46E 228 F3
Jingjiang China 32°2N 120°16E 229 A13
Jingle China 38°20N 111°55E 226 E6
Jingmen China 31°0N 112°10E 229 B9
Jingning China 35°30N 105°43E 226 G3
Jingpo Hu China 43°55N 128°55E 227 C15
Jingshan China 31°1N 113°7E 229 B9
Jingtai China 37°10N 104°6E 226 F3
Jingtang China 39°10N 119°5E 227 E10
Jingu Outer Garden Tokyo, Japan 140 b2
Jingxi China 23°8N 106°27E 228 F6
Jingyang China 34°30N 108°50E 226 G5
Jingyu China 42°25N 126°45E 224 A3
Jingyuan China 36°30N 104°40E 226 F3
Jingzhou Hubei, China 30°21N 112°11E 229 B9
Jingzhou Hunan, China 26°33N 109°40E 228 D7
Jingziguan China 33°15N 111°0E 226 H6
Jinhua China 29°8N 119°38E 229 C12
Jining Nei Monggol Zizhiqu, China 41°5N 113°0E 226 D7
Jining Shandong, China 35°22N 116°34E 226 G9
Jinja Uganda 0°25N 33°12E 268 B3
Jinjang Malaysia 3°13N 101°39E 237 L3
Jinji China 37°58N 106°8E 226 F4
Jinjiang Fujian, China 24°43N 118°33E 229 E12
Jinjiang Yunnan, China 26°14N 100°34E 228 D3
Jinjini Ghana 7°26N 2°42W 262 D4
Jinju S. Korea 35°12N 128°2E 224 E4
Jinkou China 30°20N 114°8E 229 B10
Jinkouhe China 29°18N 103°4E 228 C4
Jinmu Jiao China 18°9N 109°34E 229 a
Jinnah Barrage Pakistan 32°58N 71°33E 242 C4
Jinnah Int. ✈ (KHI) Karachi, Pakistan 24°53N 67°9E 123 A2
Jinning China 24°38N 102°38E 228 E4
Jinočany Czechia 50°2N 14°16E 135 B1
Jinonice Czechia 50°3N 14°22E 135 B2
Jinotega Nic. 13°6N 85°59W 320 D2
Jinotepe Nic. 11°50N 86°10W 320 D2
Jinping Guizhou, China 26°41N 109°10E 228 D7
Jinping Yunnan, China 22°45N 103°18E 228 F4
Jinping Bend Dams China 28°1N 101°39E 228 C3
Jinqiao China 31°15N 121°36E 138 B2
Jinsha China 27°29N 106°12E 228 D6
Jinsha Jiang → China 28°50N 104°36E 228 C5
Jinshi China 29°40N 111°50E 229 C8
Jintan China 31°42N 119°36E 229 B12
Jintotolo Channel Phil. 11°48N 123°5E 233 F4
Jintotolo I. Phil. 11°51N 123°7E 233 F4
Jintur India 19°37N 76°42E 244 E3
Jinxi Jiangxi, China 27°56N 116°45E 229 D11
Jinxi Liaoning, China 40°52N 120°50E 227 D11
Jinxian China 28°26N 116°17E 229 C11
Jinxiang China 35°5N 116°22E 226 G9
Jinyang China 27°28N 103°5E 228 D4
Jinyun China 28°35N 120°5E 229 C13
Jinzhai China 31°40N 115°53E 229 B10
Jinzhong China 37°42N 112°46E 226 F7
Jinzhou Liaoning, China 38°55N 121°42E 227 E11
Jinzhou Liaoning, China 41°5N 121°3E 227 D11
Jiparaná → Brazil 8°3S 62°52W 331 B5
Jipijapa Ecuador 1°0S 80°40W 328 D1
Jiquilpan Mexico 19°59N 102°43W 318 D4
Jirau Brazil 9°18S 64°38W 331 B5
Jirisan S. Korea 35°20N 127°44E 224 E3
Jirisan △ S. Korea 35°15N 127°30E 224 E3
Jiroft Iran 28°45N 57°50E 247 D8
Jishan China 35°34N 110°58E 226 G6
Jishou China 28°21N 109°43E 228 C7
Jishui China 27°12N 115°8E 229 D10
Jisr ash Shughūr Syria 35°49N 36°18E 250 C7
Jitarning Australia 32°48S 117°57E 279 F2
Jitra Malaysia 6°16N 100°25E 237 J3
Jiu → Romania 43°47N 23°48E 183 G8
Jiudengkou China 39°56N 106°40E 226 E4
Jiujiang Guangdong, China 22°50N 113°0E 229 F9
Jiujiang Jiangxi, China 29°42N 115°58E 229 C10
Jiuling Shan China 28°40N 114°40E 229 C10
Jiulong = Kowloon Hong Kong, China 22°19N 114°11E 122 B3
Jiulong China 28°57N 101°31E 228 C3
Jiuquan China 39°50N 98°20E 218 D8
Jiutai China 44°10N 125°50E 227 B13
Jiuxincheng China 39°17N 115°59E 226 E8
Jiuzhaigou △ China 33°8N 103°52E 228 A4
Jiwaka □ Papua N. G. 5°50S 144°40E 286 C3
Jiwani Pakistan 25°1N 61°44E 240 D1
Jiwani, Ras Pakistan 25°1N 61°44E 240 D1
Jixi Anhui, China 30°5N 118°34E 229 B12
Jixi Heilongjiang, China 45°20N 130°50E 227 B16
Jiyang China 37°0N 117°12E 227 F9
Jiyuan China 35°7N 112°57E 226 G7
Jiyūgaoka Japan 35°35N 139°40E 140 B3
Jiz', W. → Yemen 16°12N 52°14E 249 C6
Jizā'ir Iraq 33°15N 44°23E 113 B2
Jīzān Si. Arabia 17°0N 42°20E 248 C3
Jize China 36°54N 114°56E 226 F8
Jizera → Czechia 50°10N 14°43E 180 A7
Jizhou China 37°35N 115°30E 226 F8
Jizīra Iraq 33°15N 44°25E 113 B2
Jizl, Wādī al → Si. Arabia 25°39N 38°25E 246 E3
Jizō-Zaki Japan 35°34N 133°20E 222 B5
Jizzax Uzbekistan 40°6N 67°50E 217 D7
Jizzax □ Uzbekistan 40°20N 67°40E 217 D7
Joaçaba Brazil 27°5S 51°31W 335 B5
Joaíma Brazil 16°39S 41°2W 333 E3
Joal Fadiout Senegal 14°9N 16°50W 262 C1
João Amaro Brazil 12°46S 40°22W 333 D3
João Belo = Xai-Xai Mozam. 25°6S 33°31E 271 C5
João Câmara Brazil 5°32S 35°48W 332 C4
João Neiva Brazil 19°45S 40°24W 333 E3
João Pessoa = Eirunepé Brazil 6°35S 69°53W 330 B4
João Pessoa = Porto Brazil 3°54S 42°42W 332 B3
João Pessoa Brazil 7°10S 34°52W 332 C5
João Pinheiro Brazil 17°45S 46°10W 333 E2
Joaquín V. González Argentina 25°10S 64°0W 334 B3
Jobat India 22°25N 74°34E 242 H6
Jobourg, Nez de France 49°41N 1°57W 172 C5
Jódar Spain 37°50N 3°21W 195 H7
Jodhpur India 26°23N 73°8E 242 F5
Jodiya India 22°42N 70°18E 242 H4
Joe Pool Lake U.S.A. 32°38N 96°59W 120 C4
Joensuu Finland 62°37N 29°49E 160 E23
Jōetsu Japan 37°12N 138°10E 221 F9
Jœuf France 49°12N 6°1E 173 C12
Jofane Mozam. 21°15S 34°18E 271 B5
Joffre, Morne = Moustique, Morne Guadeloupe 16°7N 61°44W 322 e
Jog Falls = Gersoppa Falls India 14°12N 74°46E 245 G2
Jogbani India 26°25N 87°15E 243 F12
Jõgeva Estonia 58°45N 26°24E 188 C4
Jogjakarta = Yogyakarta Indonesia 7°49S 110°22E 235 D4
Joglo Indonesia 6°13S 106°45E 122 B1
Jōhana Japan 36°30N 136°57E 223 A8
Johannesburg Gauteng, S. Africa 26°11S 28°2E 123 B2
Johannesburg Calif., U.S.A. 35°22N 117°38W 307 K9
Johannesburg, Univ. of S. Africa 26°11S 28°0E 123 B2
Johanneskirchen Germany 48°10N 11°38E 131 A2
Johannesstift Germany 52°34N 13°12E 115 A2
Johannisburg = Pisz Poland 53°38N 21°49E 184 E8
Johannisthal Germany 52°26N 13°30E 115 B4
Johansfors Sweden 56°42N 15°32E 163 H9
Johilla → India 23°37N 81°14E 243 H9
John Crow Mts. Jamaica 18°5N 76°25W 320 a
John Day U.S.A. 44°25N 118°57W 304 D4
John Day → U.S.A. 45°44N 120°39W 304 D3
John Day Fossil Beds ⌓ U.S.A. 44°33N 119°38W 304 D4
John D'or Prairie Canada 58°30N 115°8W 296 B5
John F. Kennedy Nat. Historic Site ⌓ U.S.A. 42°20N 71°7W 116 A2
John F. Kennedy Space Center U.S.A. 28°40N 80°42W 317 G9
John H. Kerr Res. U.S.A. 36°36N 78°18W 315 C15
John Hancock Center Chicago, U.S.A. 119 a2
John McLaren Park U.S.A. 37°43N 122°24W 136 B2
John o' Groats U.K. 58°38N 3°4W 167 C5
John U. Lloyd Beach ⌓ U.S.A. 26°4N 80°6W 129 B3
Johnnie U.S.A. 36°25N 116°5W 307 J10
Johns Creek U.S.A. 34°2N 84°12W 316 A5
Johns I. U.S.A. 32°47N 80°7W 316 C9
John's Ra. Australia 21°55S 133°23E 280 C1
Johnson U.S.A. 44°38N 72°41W 313 B12
Johnson City Kans., U.S.A. 37°34N 101°45W 308 G3
Johnson City N.Y., U.S.A. 42°7N 75°58W 313 D9
Johnson City Tenn., U.S.A. 36°19N 82°21W 315 C13
Johnson City Tex., U.S.A. 30°17N 98°25W 314 F5
Johnsonburg U.S.A. 41°29N 78°41W 312 E6
Johnsondale U.S.A. 35°58N 118°32W 307 K8
Johnsons Crossing Canada 60°29N 133°18W 296 A2
Johnsons Pt. Antigua & B. 17°2N 61°53W 322 b
Johnsonville N.Z. 41°13S 174°48E 284 H3
Johnston Iowa, U.S.A. 41°40N 93°42W 310 C3
Johnston S.C., U.S.A. 33°50N 81°48W 316 B8
Johnston, L. Australia 32°25S 120°30E 279 F3
Johnston Atoll Pac. Oc. 17°10N 169°8W 289 F11
Johnston City U.S.A. 37°49N 88°56W 310 G8
Johnston Falls = Mambilima Falls Zambia 10°31S 28°45E 269 E2
Johnstone Str. Canada 50°28N 126°0W 296 C3
Johnstown Kilkenny, Ireland 52°45N 7°33W 166 D4
Johnstown N.Y., U.S.A. 43°0N 74°22W 313 C10
Johnstown Ohio, U.S.A. 40°9N 82°41W 312 F2
Johnstown Pa., U.S.A. 40°20N 78°55W 312 F6
Johor □ Malaysia 2°5N 103°20E 237 M4
Johor, Selat Asia 1°28N 103°47E 237 d
Johor Bahru Malaysia 1°28N 103°46E 237 d
Johor Port Malaysia 1°26N 103°53E 237 d
Jõhvi Estonia 59°22N 27°27E 188 C4
Joigny France 47°58N 3°20E 173 E10
Joinville Brazil 26°15S 48°55W 335 B6
Joinville Haute-Marne, France 48°27N 5°10E 173 D12
Joinville I. Antarctica 65°0S 55°30W 151 C18
Joinville-le-Pont France 48°49N 2°27E 134 B3
Jojutla Mexico 18°37N 99°11W 319 D5
Jøkelbugten Greenland 78°25N 20°20W 154 B9
Jokkmokk Sweden 66°35N 19°50E 160 C18
Jökulsá á Bru → Iceland 65°40N 14°16W 155 B12
Jökulsá á Fjöllum → Iceland 66°10N 16°30W 155 A10
Jolfā Āzarbājān-e Sharqī, Iran 38°57N 45°38E 213 C11
Jolfā Eşfahan, Iran 32°58N 51°37E 247 C6
Joli-Bois Belgium 50°42N 4°24E 116 B2
Joliet U.S.A. 41°32N 88°5W 311 C8
Joliette Canada 46°3N 73°24W 298 C5
Jollas Finland 60°10N 25°5E 121 B3
Jolo Phil. 6°0N 121°0E 233 H3
Jolo Group Phil. 6°0N 121°9E 233 J3
Jolon U.S.A. 35°58N 121°9W 306 K5
Jølstravatnet Norway 61°32N 6°23E 164 C3
Jomalig I. Phil. 14°42N 122°22E 232 D4
Jombang Indonesia 7°33S 112°14E 235 D4
Jomda China 31°28N 98°12E 228 B2
Jonåker Sweden 58°45N 16°45E 163 F10
Jonava Lithuania 55°8N 24°12E 188 E3
Jondal Norway 60°16N 6°15E 164 D3
Jones Phil. 16°33N 121°42E 232 C3
Jones Sound Canada 76°0N 85°0W 295 B15
Jonesboro Ark., U.S.A. 35°50N 90°42W 315 D9
Jonesboro Ga., U.S.A. 33°31N 84°22W 316 B5
Jonesboro La., U.S.A. 32°15N 92°43W 314 E8
Jonesburg U.S.A. 38°51N 91°18W 310 F5
Jonesville Ind., U.S.A. 39°5N 85°54W 311 E11
Jonesville Mich., U.S.A. 41°59N 84°40W 311 C12
Jong → S. Leone 7°32N 12°23W 262 D2
Jonglei South Sudan 6°25N 31°30E 257 F3
Jonglei □ South Sudan 7°30N 32°30E 257 F3
Jonglei Canal South Sudan 9°20N 31°39E 266 C3
Jongmyo Royal Shrine S. Korea 37°34N 126°59E 137 B1
Jongno S. Korea 37°35N 126°59E 137 B1
Joniškis Lithuania 56°13N 23°35E 184 B10
Jönköping Sweden 57°45N 14°8E 163 G8
Jönköping □ Sweden 57°30N 14°30E 163 G8
Jonquière Canada 48°27N 71°14W 299 C5
Jonsered Sweden 57°45N 12°10E 163 G6
Jonstrup Denmark 55°45N 12°20E 118 A2
Jonzac France 45°27N 0°28W 174 C3
Joplin U.S.A. 37°6N 94°31W 308 G6
Joppa U.K. 55°57N 3°6W 121 B3
Jora India 26°20N 77°49E 242 F6
Jordan Guimaras, Phil. 10°40N 122°35E 233 F4
Jordan Mont., U.S.A. 47°19N 106°55W 304 C10
Jordan N.Y., U.S.A. 43°4N 76°29W 313 C8
Jordan ■ Asia 31°0N 36°0E 251 H7
Jordan → Asia 31°48N 35°32E 251 G6
Jordan Valley U.S.A. 42°59N 117°3W 304 E5
Jordânia Brazil 15°55S 40°11W 333 E3
Jordanów Poland 49°41N 19°49E 185 J6
Jordet Norway 61°25N 12°8E 164 C9
Jorge, C. Chile 51°40S 75°35W 336 D1
Jorge Chavez Int. ✈ (LIM) Lima, Peru 12°2S 77°8W 124 B2
Jorge Newbery ✈ (AEP) Argentina 34°34S 58°25W 117 B2
Jørgen Bronlund Fjord Greenland 82°30N 31°0W 154 A7
Jorhat India 26°45N 94°12E 241 B5
Jori → Norway 62°4N 9°25E 162 B3
Jorm Afghan. 36°50N 70°52E 240 A3
Jörn Sweden 65°4N 20°1E 160 D19
Jorong Indonesia 3°58S 114°56E 235 C4
Jørpeland Norway 59°3N 6°1E 164 E3
Jorquera → Chile 28°3S 69°58W 334 B2
Joru S. Leone 7°41N 11°3W 262 D2
Jos Nigeria 9°53N 8°51E 263 D6
Jos Plateau Nigeria 9°55N 9°0E 263 D6
Jošanička Banja Serbia 43°24N 20°47E 202 C4
Jose Abad Santos Phil. 5°55N 125°39E 233 J5
José Batlle y Ordóñez Uruguay 33°20S 55°10W 335 C4
José Bonifácio = Erechim Brazil 27°35S 52°15W 335 B5
José de San Martín Argentina 44°4S 70°26W 336 B2
Jose Panganiban Phil. 14°17N 122°41E 232 D4
Józefa Piłsudskiego Park Poland 52°15N 21°2E 143 B1
Joseni Romania 46°42N 25°29E 183 D10
Joseph, L. Canada 45°10N 79°44W 312 A5
Joseph Banks Group Australia 34°36S 136°16E 282 C2
Joseph Bonaparte G. Australia 14°35S 128°50E 278 B4
Joseph L. Canada 52°45N 65°18W 299 B6
Joshinath India 30°34N 79°34E 243 D8
Joshinetsu-Kōgen △ Japan 36°42N 138°32E 223 A10
Joshua Tree U.S.A. 34°8N 116°19W 307 L10
Joshua Tree △ U.S.A. 33°55N 116°0W 307 M10
Joss House B. Hong Kong, China 22°16N 114°17E 122 B3
Josselin France 47°57N 2°33W 172 E4
Jost Van Dyke I. Br. Virgin Is. 18°29N 64°47W 321 b
Jostedal Norway 61°35N 7°15E 164 C4
Jostedalsbreen Norway 61°40N 6°59E 164 C3
Jōtō Japan 34°42N 135°33E 133 A2
Jotunheimen Norway 61°35N 8°25E 164 C5
Jotunheimen △ Norway 61°32N 8°25E 164 C5
Joubertberge Namibia 18°30S 14°0E 270 A1
Joué-lès-Tours France 47°21N 0°40E 172 E7
Jourdanton U.S.A. 28°55N 98°33W 314 G5
Joutseno Finland 61°7N 28°31E 188 B5
Jouy-en-Josas France 48°46N 2°10E 134 B2
Jovellanos Cuba 22°40N 81°10W 320 B3
Jovellar Phil. 13°4N 123°36E 232 E4
Jowai India 25°26N 92°12E 241 C4
Jowkār Iran 34°25N 48°40E 213 E13
Jowzjān □ Afghan. 36°10N 66°0E 240 A2
Joya de Cerén El Salv. 13°49N 89°22W 320 D2
Joyeuse France 44°29N 4°16E 175 D8
Jōyō Japan 34°51N 135°46E 223 C7
Józefów Lubelskie, Poland 50°28N 23°2E 185 H10
Józefów Mazowieckie, Poland 52°10N 21°11E 185 F8
Ju Xian China 35°35N 118°20E 227 G10
Juan Aldama Mexico 24°19N 103°21W 318 C4
Juan Anchorena Argentina 34°30S 58°29W 117 A2
Juan Bautista Alberdi Argentina 34°26S 61°48W 334 C3
Juan de Bolas Jamaica 18°5N 77°9W 320 a
Juan de Fuca, Str. of N. Amer. 48°15N 124°0W 306 B3
Juan de Nova Ind. Oc. 17°3S 43°45E 271 A7
Juan Fernández, Arch. de Pac. Oc. 33°50S 80°0W 326 G2
Juan Fernández △ Chile 33°38S 78°52W 330 c
Juan González Romero Mexico 19°30N 99°3W 128 A2
Juan José Castelli Argentina 25°27S 60°57W 334 B3
Juan L. Lacaze Uruguay 34°26S 57°25W 334 C4
Juana Días Puerto Rico 18°3N 66°31W 321 b
Juangriego Venezuela 11°5N 63°58W 329 a
Juangriego, B. de Venezuela 11°6N 63°59W 329 a
Juanjuí Peru 7°10S 76°45W 330 B2
Juankoski Finland 63°3N 28°19E 160 E23
Juara Brazil 11°20S 57°25W 331 C6
Juárez Mexico 27°37N 100°44W 318 B4
Juárez, Sa. de Mexico 32°0N 115°50W 318 A1
Juárez Int. ✈ (MEX) Mexico 19°25N 99°5W 128 B2
Juatinga, Pta. da Brazil 23°17S 44°30W 333 F3
Juàzeiro Brazil 9°30S 40°30W 332 C3
Juàzeiro do Norte Brazil 7°10S 39°18W 332 C4
Juazohn Liberia 5°22N 8°50W 262 D3
Juba South Sudan 4°50N 31°35E 257 G3
Juba → Somalia 1°30N 42°35E 267 D5
Jubail = Al Jubayl Si. Arabia 27°0N 49°50E 247 E6
Jubany = Carlini Base Antarctica 62°30S 58°0W 151 C18
Jubayl Lebanon 34°5N 35°39E 250 D6
Jubbada Dhexe □ Somalia 2°0N 41°30E 267 D5
Jubbada Hoose □ Somalia 0°0 42°40E 267 E5
Jubbah Si. Arabia 28°2N 40°56E 246 D4
Jubbal India 31°5N 77°40E 242 D7
Jubbulpore = Jabalpur India 23°9N 79°58E 243 H8
Jübek Germany 54°33N 9°22E 178 A5
Jubilee L. Australia 29°0S 126°50E 279 E4
Juby, C. Morocco 28°0N 12°59W 260 C2
Júcar = Xúquer → Spain 39°5N 0°10W 197 F4
Júcaro Cuba 21°37N 78°51W 320 B4
Juchitán de Zaragoza Mexico 16°26N 95°1W 319 D5
Judaberg Norway 59°10N 5°51E 164 E2
Judea = Har Yehuda Israel 31°35N 34°57E 251 G5
Judeira West Bank 31°52N 35°12E 123 A2
Judenburg Austria 47°12N 14°38E 180 D7
Judith → U.S.A. 47°44N 109°39W 304 C9
Judith, Pt. U.S.A. 41°22N 71°29W 313 E13
Judith Gap U.S.A. 46°41N 109°45W 304 C9
Juelsminde Denmark 55°43N 10°1E 163 J4
Jufari → Brazil 1°13S 62°0W 329 D5
Juhdum West Bank 31°42N 35°15E 123 B2
Juhu India 19°5N 73°0E 130 A2
Juifang Taiwan 25°7N 121°48E 225 A3
Juigalpa Nic. 12°6N 85°26W 320 D2
Juillac France 45°20N 1°19E 174 C5
Juist Germany 53°40N 6°59E 178 B2
Juisui Taiwan 23°30N 121°22E 225 C3
Juiz de Fora Brazil 21°43S 43°19W 333 F3
Jūjā Japan 35°45N 139°43E 140 A3
Jujuy □ Argentina 23°20S 65°40W 334 A2
Jukao = Rugao China 32°23N 120°31E 229 A13
Jukskei → S. Africa 26°5S 28°6E 123 A2
Julesburg U.S.A. 40°59N 102°16W 304 F12
Juli Peru 16°10S 69°25W 330 D4
Julia Cr. → Australia 20°0S 141°11E 280 C3
Julia Creek Australia 20°39S 141°44E 280 C3
Juliaca Peru 15°25S 70°10W 330 D3
Julian U.S.A. 33°4N 116°38W 307 M10
Julian, L. Canada 54°25N 77°57W 298 B4
Julian Alps = Julijske Alpe Slovenia 46°15N 14°1E 199 B11
Juliana Top = Mandala, Puncak Indonesia 4°44S 140°20E 231 E10
Julianadorp Curaçao 12°9N 68°57W 322 g
Julianatop Suriname 3°40N 56°30W 329 C6
Julianehåb = Qaqortoq Greenland 60°43N 46°0W 154 E6
Julianów Poland 52°10N 21°9E 143 B2
Jülich Germany 50°55N 6°22E 178 E2
Juliette, L. U.S.A. 33°2N 83°50W 316 B6
Julijske Alpe Slovenia 46°15N 14°1E 199 B11
Julimes Mexico 28°25N 105°27W 318 B3
Jullundur = Jalandhar India 31°20N 75°40E 242 D6
Julu China 37°15N 115°2E 226 F8
Jumbo Zimbabwe 17°30S 30°58E 269 F3
Jumbo Pk. U.S.A. 36°12N 114°11W 307 J12
Jumeirah U.A.E. 25°11N 55°14E 119 B1
Jumentos Cays Bahamas 23°0N 75°40W 320 B4
Jumilla Spain 38°28N 1°19W 197 G3
Jumla Nepal 29°15N 82°13E 243 E10

Jumna = Yamuna → India 25°30N 81°53E 243 G9
Jumunjin S. Korea 37°55N 128°54E 224 D4
Junagadh India 21°30N 70°30E 242 J4
Junan China 35°12N 118°53E 227 G10
Juncos Puerto Rico 18°14N 65°55W 321 b
Junction Tex., U.S.A. 30°29N 99°46W 314 F5
Junction Utah, U.S.A. 38°14N 112°13W 305 G7
Junction B. Australia 11°52S 133°55E 280 A1
Junction City Ga., U.S.A. 32°36N 84°28W 316 C5
Junction City Kans., U.S.A. 39°2N 96°50W 308 F5
Junction City Oreg., U.S.A. 44°13N 123°12W 304 D2
Junction Pt. Australia 11°45S 133°50E 280 A1
Jundah Australia 24°46S 143°2E 280 C3
Jundiaí Brazil 24°30S 47°0W 335 A6
Juneau U.S.A. 58°18N 134°25W 296 B2
Junee Australia 34°53S 147°35E 283 C7
Jung S. Korea 37°33N 126°59E 137 B1
Jungar Qi China 39°49N 110°57E 226 E6
Jungbunzlau = Mladá Boleslav Czechia 50°27N 14°53E 180 A7
Jungfernheide, Volkspark Germany 52°32N 13°18E 115 A2
Jungfernsee Germany 52°25N 13°6E 115 B1
Jungfrau Switz. 46°32N 7°58E 179 J3
Junggar Pendi China 44°30N 86°0E 217 D11
Junghans, Teatro Venice, Italy 142 c2
Junghwa S. Korea 37°35N 127°3E 137 B2
Jungkat Indonesia 0°4N 109°13E 235 B3
Jungnang S. Korea 37°36N 127°5E 137 B2
Jungnangcheon → S. Korea 37°32N 126°55E 137 B1
Jungsdalshytta = Iungsdalshytta Norway 60°49N 7°55E 164 D4
Jungshahi Pakistan 24°52N 67°44E 242 G2
Juniata → U.S.A. 40°24N 77°1W 312 F7
Junín Argentina 34°33S 60°57W 334 C3
Junín Peru 11°12S 76°0W 330 C2
Junín □ Peru 11°30S 75°0W 330 C3
Junín, L. de Peru 11°2S 76°6W 330 C2
Junín de los Andes Argentina 39°45S 71°0W 336 A2
Juniper Green U.K. 55°54N 3°16W 121 B2
Jūniyah Lebanon 33°59N 35°38E 250 E6
Junk B. Hong Kong, China 22°17N 114°15E 122 B3
Junkerdal △ Norway 66°50N 15°50E 160 C16
Junlian China 28°8N 104°29E 228 C5
Junnar India 19°12N 73°58E 244 E1
Juno Beach U.S.A. 26°52N 80°3W 317 J9
Juntas Chile 28°24S 69°58W 334 B2
Juntura U.S.A. 43°45N 118°5W 304 E4
Juparanã, L. Brazil 19°16S 40°8W 333 E3
Jupiter U.S.A. 26°57N 80°6W 317 J9
Juquiá Brazil 24°19S 47°38W 333 F2
Jur → South Sudan 8°45N 29°15E 257 F2
Jura = Jura, Mts. du Europe 46°40N 6°5E 173 F13
Jura = Schwäbische Alb Germany 48°20N 9°30E 179 G5
Jura U.K. 56°0N 5°50W 167 F3
Jura □ France 46°47N 5°45E 173 F12
Jura □ Switz. 47°20N 7°20E 179 H3
Jūra → Lithuania 55°3N 22°9E 184 C9
Jura, Mts. du Europe 46°40N 6°5E 173 F13
Jura, Sd. of U.K. 55°57N 5°45W 167 F3
Juradó Colombia 7°7N 77°46W 328 B2
Jurassic Coast U.K. 50°42N 2°50W 169 G5
Jurbarkas Lithuania 55°4N 22°46E 184 C9
Jurien Bay Australia 30°18S 115°2E 279 F2
Jurilovca Romania 44°46N 28°52E 183 F13
Jūrmala Latvia 56°58N 23°34E 184 B10
Jurong Jiangsu, China 31°57N 119°9E 229 B12
Jurong Singapore 1°19N 103°42E 138 B2
Jurong, Selat Singapore 1°17N 103°42E 138 B2
Jurong Industrial Estate Singapore 1°19N 103°40E 138 B1
Juruá Brazil 3°27S 66°3W 328 D4
Juruá → Brazil 2°37S 65°44W 328 D4
Juruena Brazil 13°0S 58°10W 331 C6
Juruena → Brazil 7°20S 58°3W 331 B6
Juruena △ Brazil 8°30S 58°0W 331 B6
Jurujuba, Enseada de Brazil 22°54S 43°6W 135 B2
Juruti Brazil 2°9S 56°4W 329 D6
Jūsō Japan 34°42N 135°27E 133 A1
Jussey France 47°50N 5°55E 173 E12
Justice U.S.A. 41°44N 87°49W 119 C2
Justicia Madrid, Spain 127 a3
Justo Daract Argentina 33°52S 65°12W 334 C2
Jutaí Amazonas, Brazil 2°44S 66°57W 328 D4
Jutaí Amazonas, Brazil 5°11S 68°54W 330 B4
Jutaí → Brazil 2°43S 66°57W 328 D4
Jüterbog Germany 51°59N 13°5E 178 D9
Juticalpa Honduras 14°40N 86°12W 320 D2
Jutland = Jylland Denmark 56°25N 9°30E 163 H3
Juuka Finland 63°13N 29°17E 160 E23
Juventud, I. de la Cuba 21°40N 82°40W 320 B3
Juvigny-sous-Andaine France 48°32N 0°30W 172 D6
Juwangsan △ S. Korea 36°20N 129°15E 224 D4
Jūy Zar Iran 33°50N 46°18E 213 F12
Juye China 35°22N 116°5E 226 G9
Juzennecourt France 48°10N 4°58E 173 D11
Južni Brod = Brod Macedonia 41°32N 21°17E 202 E5
Jvari Georgia 42°42N 42°4E 191 J6
Jwalahari India 28°40N 77°6E 120 B1
Jyderup Denmark 55°40N 11°26E 163 J5
Jylland Denmark 56°25N 9°30E 163 H3
Jyväskylä Finland 62°14N 25°50E 188 A3

K

K2 Pakistan 35°58N 76°32E 243 B7
Ka → Nigeria 11°40N 4°10E 263 C5
Kaa-Iya △ Bolivia 18°35S 61°40W 331 D5
Ka'a'awa U.S.A. 21°33N 157°51W 302 J14
Kaakha = Kaka Turkmenistan 37°21N 59°36E 247 B8
Ka'ala U.S.A. 21°31N 158°9W 302 J13
Kaala-Gomén N. Cal. 20°40S 164°25E 288 d
Ka'alu'alu B. U.S.A. 18°58N 155°37W 302 E6
Kaap Plateau S. Africa 28°30S 24°0E 270 C3
Kaapkruis Namibia 21°55S 13°57E 270 B1
Kaapstad = Cape Town S. Africa 33°55S 18°22E 118 A1
Kaashidhoo Atoll Maldives 4°58N 73°28E 272 d
Kaashidhoo Channel Maldives 5°1N 73°28E 272 d
Kaatalon, Mt. Phil. 8°10N 124°52E 233 G5
Kaba Guinea 10°9N 11°40W 262 C2
Kabacan Phil. 7°8N 124°49E 233 H5
Kabachishche = Zelenodolsk Russia 55°55N 48°30E 190 C9
Kabaena Indonesia 5°15S 122°0E 231 F6
Kabala S. Leone 9°38N 11°37W 262 D2
Kabale Uganda 1°15S 30°0E 268 C3
Kabalo Dem. Rep. of the Congo 6°0S 27°0E 265 D5
Kabambare Dem. Rep. of the Congo 4°41S 27°39E 268 C2
Kabango Dem. Rep. of the Congo 8°35S 28°30E 269 D2
Kabanjahe Indonesia 3°6N 98°30E 234 B1
Kabankalan Phil. 9°59N 122°49E 233 G4
Kabara Fiji 18°59S 178°56W 287 B3
Kabara Mali 16°40N 2°50W 262 B4
Kabardinka Russia 44°40N 37°57E 189 K10
Kabardino-Balkaria □ Russia 43°30N 43°30E 191 J6
Kabarega Falls = Murchison Falls Uganda 2°15N 31°30E 268 B3
Kabarnet Kenya 0°30N 35°45E 268 B4
Kabasalan Phil. 7°47N 122°44E 233 H4
Kabat Indonesia 8°16S 114°19E 231 J17
Kabaty Poland 52°8N 21°4E 143 C2
Kabba Nigeria 7°50N 6°3E 263 D6
Kabbani → India 12°13N 76°54E 245 H3
Kabi Niger 13°30N 12°35E 259 F2
Kabin Buri Thailand 13°57N 101°43E 236 F3
Kabinakagami L. Canada 48°54N 84°25W 298 C3
Kabinda Dem. Rep. of the Congo 6°10S 24°29E 265 D4
Kabkabīyah Sudan 13°50N 24°0E 259 F4
Kablungu, C. Papua N. G. 6°20S 150°1E 286 D6
Kabna Sudan 19°6N 32°40E 256 D3
Kabo C.A.R. 7°35N 18°38E 264 A3
Kabompo Zambia 13°36S 24°14E 265 E4
Kabompo → Zambia 14°11S 23°11E 265 E4
Kabondo Dem. Rep. of the Congo 8°58S 25°40E 265 D5
Kabongo Dem. Rep. of the Congo 7°22S 25°33E 265 D5
Kabot Guinea 10°48N 14°57W 262 C2
Kabou Togo 9°28N 0°55E 263 D5
Kaboudia, Rass Tunisia 35°13N 11°10E 258 A2
Kabr Sudan 10°54N 26°50E 257 E2
Kabrīt, G. el Egypt 29°42N 33°16E 251 J4
Kabrousse Senegal 12°25N 16°45W 262 C1
Kabubu Dem. Rep. of the Congo 9°42S 24°40E 265 D4
Kabūd Gonbad Iran 37°5N 59°45E 247 B8
Kabudar Ahang Iran 35°11N 48°43E 213 E13
Kabugao Phil. 18°2N 121°11E 232 B3
Kābul Afghan. 34°28N 69°11E 242 B3
Kābul □ Afghan. 34°30N 69°0E 240 B3
Kābul → Pakistan 33°55N 72°14E 242 C5
Kabuli Papua N. G. 2°7S 146°40E 286 B4
Kabunga Dem. Rep. of the Congo 1°38S 28°3E 268 C2
Kaburuang Indonesia 3°50N 126°30E 231 D7
Kabushiya Sudan 16°54N 33°41E 257 D3
Kabwanga Dem. Rep. of the Congo 7°2S 22°36E 265 D4
Kabwe Zambia 14°30S 28°29E 269 E2
Kabwum Papua N. G. 6°11S 147°15E 286 D4
Kaçanik Kosovo 42°13N 21°12E 202 D5
Kačerginė Lithuania 54°56N 23°42E 184 D10
Kachar Kazakhstan 53°23N 62°55E 216 B6
Kachchh, Gulf of India 22°50N 69°15E 242 H3
Kachchh, Rann of India 24°0N 70°0E 242 H4
Kachchhidhana India 21°44N 78°46E 243 J8
Kachebera Zambia 13°50S 32°50E 269 E3
Kachia Nigeria 9°50N 7°55E 263 D6
Kachikau Botswana 18°8S 24°26E 270 A3
Kachin □ Burma 26°0N 97°30E 228 E1
Kachira, L. Uganda 0°40S 31°7E 268 C3
Kachīry Kazakhstan 53°10N 75°50E 217 B9
Kachisi Ethiopia 9°40N 37°50E 257 F4
Kachnara India 23°50N 75°6E 242 H6
Kachot Cambodia 11°30N 103°3E 237 G4
Kaçkar Turkey 40°45N 41°10E 213 B9
Kada Chad 19°20N 19°39E 259 E3
Kadaingti Burma 17°37N 97°32E 241 G6
Kadaiyanallur India 9°3N 77°22E 245 K3
Kadam, Mt. Uganda 1°45N 34°45E 268 B3
Kadan Czechia 50°23N 13°16E 180 A6
Kadan Kyun Burma 12°30N 98°20E 236 F2
Kadanai → Afghan. 31°22N 65°45E 242 D1
Kadapa India 14°30N 78°47E 245 G4
Kadarkút Hungary 46°13N 17°39E 182 D2
Kadavu Fiji 19°0S 178°15E 287 B2
Kadavu Passage Fiji 18°45S 178°0E 287 B2
Kade Ghana 6°7N 0°56W 263 D4
Kadéï → C.A.R. 3°31N 16°3E 264 B3
Kademlija = Triglav Slovenia 46°21N 13°50E 199 B10
Kadena Japan 26°22N 127°45E 288 a
Kadhimain = Al Kāẓimīyah Iraq 33°22N 44°18E 213 F11
Kadi India 23°18N 72°23E 242 H5
Kadiak I. = Kodiak I. U.S.A. 57°30N 152°45W 303 H9
Kadiana Mali 10°45N 6°30W 262 C3
Kadıköy Turkey 40°59N 29°1E 122 C2
Kadina Australia 33°55S 137°43E 282 B2
Kadınhanı Turkey 38°14N 32°13E 212 C5
Kadiolo Mali 10°35N 7°41W 262 C3
Kadipur India 26°10N 82°23E 243 F10
Kadirabad India 19°51N 75°54E 244 E2
Kadiri India 14°12N 78°13E 245 G4
Kadirli Turkey 37°23N 36°5E 212 D7
Kadiyevka = Stakhanov Ukraine 48°35N 38°40E 189 H10
Kadja, O. → Chad 12°2N 22°28E 259 F4
Kadmat I. India 11°14N 72°47E 245 J1
Kadodo Sudan 11°4N 29°31E 257 E2
Kadoka U.S.A. 43°50N 101°31W 308 D3
Kadom Russia 54°37N 42°30E 190 C6
Kadoma Osaka, Japan 34°44N 135°35E 133 A2
Kadoma Zimbabwe 18°20S 29°52E 269 F2
Kâdugli Sudan 11°0N 29°45E 257 E2
Kaduna Nigeria 10°30N 7°21E 263 C6
Kaduna □ Nigeria 11°0N 7°30E 263 C6
Kaduna → Nigeria 8°45N 5°48E 263 D6
Kadur India 13°34N 76°1E 245 H3
Kaduy Russia 59°12N 37°9E 188 C9
Kaédi Mauritania 16°9N 13°28W 262 B2
Kaélé Cameroon 10°7N 14°27E 259 F2
Ka'ena U.S.A. 21°34N 158°14W 302 J13
Ka'ena Pt. U.S.A. 21°35N 158°17W 302 J13
Kaeng Khoi Thailand 14°35N 101°0E 236 E3
Kaeng Krachan △ Thailand 12°57N 99°23E 236 F2
Kaeng Krung △ Thailand 9°30N 98°50E 237 H2
Kaeng Tana △ Thailand 15°25N 105°32E 236 E5
Kaeo N.Z. 35°6S 173°49E 284 B2
Kaesŏng N. Korea 37°58N 126°35E 224 D3
Kaesŏng □ N. Korea 38°0N 126°27E 224 D3
Kāf Si. Arabia 31°25N 37°29E 246 D3
Kafakumba Dem. Rep. of the Congo 9°38S 23°46E 265 D4
Kafan = Kapan Armenia 39°18N 46°27E 213 C12
Kafanchan Nigeria 9°40N 8°20E 263 D6
Kafareti Nigeria 10°25N 11°12E 263 C7
Kaffrine Senegal 14°8N 15°36W 262 C1
Kafia Kingi Sudan 9°20N 24°25E 264 A4
Kafin Nigeria 9°30N 7°4E 263 D6
Kafin Madaki Nigeria 10°41N 9°46E 263 C6
Kafinda Zambia 12°32S 30°20E 269 E3
Kafireas, Stenon Greece 37°55N 24°35E 204 E6
Kafr 'Aqab West Bank 31°52N 35°13E 123 A2
Kafr el Battikh Egypt 31°25N 31°44E 256 H7
Kafr el Dauwâr Egypt 31°8N 30°8E 256 H7
Kafr el Sheikh Egypt 31°15N 30°50E 251 G1
Kafr el Sheikh □ Egypt 31°30N 30°55E 251 G1
Kafr el Zaiyât Egypt 30°49N 30°48E 256 H7
Kafue Zambia 15°46S 28°9E 269 F2
Kafue → Zambia 15°12S 25°38E 269 F2
Kafue △ Zambia 15°12S 25°38E 269 F2
Kafue Flats Zambia 15°40S 27°25E 269 F2
Kafulwe Zambia 9°0S 29°1E 269 D2
Kafumba Dem. Rep. of the Congo 5°23S 18°55E 265 D3
Kaga Afghan. 34°14N 70°10E 242 B4
Kaga Japan 36°16N 136°15E 223 A8
Kaga Bandoro C.A.R. 7°0N 19°10E 264 A3
Kagamil I. U.S.A. 53°0N 169°43W 303 K5
Kaganovich = Tovarkovskiy Russia 53°40N 38°14E 188 F10
Kagarko Nigeria 9°28N 7°36E 263 D6
Kagawa □ Japan 34°15N 134°0E 222 C6
Kagera □ Tanzania 2°0S 31°30E 268 C3
Kagera → Uganda 0°57S 31°47E 268 C3
Kâğıthane Turkey 41°4N 28°58E 122 B1
Kâğıthane → Turkey 41°9N 28°56E 122 B1
Kağızman Turkey 40°5N 43°10E 213 B10
Kagmar Sudan 14°24N 30°25E 257 E3
Kagologolo Indonesia 1°9S 98°37E 234 C1
Kagopal Chad 8°16N 16°23E 259 G3
Kagoro Nigeria 9°36N 8°23E 263 D6
Kagoshima Japan 31°35N 130°33E 222 F2
Kagoshima □ Japan 31°30N 130°30E 222 F2
Kagoshima-Wan Japan 31°25N 130°40E 222 F2
Kagran Austria 48°14N 16°26E 142 A2
Kagua Papua N. G. 6°26S 143°48E 286 D2
Kagul = Cahul Moldova 45°50N 28°15E 183 E13
Kahak Iran 36°6N 49°46E 247 B6
Kāhala U.S.A. 21°16N 157°47W 302 K14
Kahalu'u U.S.A. 21°27N 157°50W 302 K14
Kahama Tanzania 4°8S 32°30E 268 C3
Kahan Pakistan 29°18N 68°54E 242 E3
Kahana U.S.A. 21°34N 157°53W 302 J14
Kahana B. U.S.A. 21°35N 157°50W 302 J14
Kahana Valley State Park ⌂ U.S.A. 21°32N 157°53W 302 J14
Kahang Malaysia 2°12N 103°32E 237 L4
Kahayan → Indonesia 3°40S 114°0E 235 C4
Kahe Tanzania 3°30S 37°25E 268 C4
Kahemba Dem. Rep. of the Congo 7°18S 18°55E 265 D3
Kaherekoau Mts. N.Z. 45°45S 167°15E 285 F2
Kahil, Djebel bou Algeria 34°26N 4°0E 261 B5
Kahnawake Canada 45°24N 73°40W 130 B1
Kahnūj Iran 27°55N 57°40E 247 E8
Kahoka U.S.A. 40°25N 91°44W 310 D5
Kaho'olawe U.S.A. 20°33N 156°37W 302 C5
Kahouanne Guadeloupe 16°15N 61°12W 322 e
Kahouanne, Îlet à Guadeloupe 16°22N 61°46W 322 e
Kahramanmaraş Turkey 37°37N 36°53E 212 D7
Kahramanmaraş □ Turkey 37°35N 36°33E 212 D7
Kâhta Turkey 37°46N 38°36E 213 D8
Kahuku U.S.A. 21°41N 157°57W 302 J14
Kahuku Pt. U.S.A. 21°43N 157°59W 302 J14
Kahul, Ozero Ukraine 45°24N 28°24E 183 E13
Kahului U.S.A. 20°54N 156°28W 302 C5
Kahului ✕ (OGG) U.S.A. 20°54N 156°26W 302 C5
Kahurangi △ N.Z. 41°10S 172°32E 285 B7
Kahurangi Pt. N.Z. 40°50S 172°10E 285 A7
Kahuta Pakistan 33°35N 73°24E 242 C5
Kahuzi-Biega △ Dem. Rep. of the Congo 1°50S 27°55E 268 C2
Kai Japan 35°42N 138°30E 223 B10
Kai, Kepulauan Indonesia 5°55S 132°45E 231 F8
Kai Besar Indonesia 5°35S 133°0E 231 F8
Kai Is. = Kai, Kepulauan Indonesia 5°55S 132°45E 231 F8
Kai Kecil Indonesia 5°45S 132°40E 231 F8
Kai Xian China 31°11N 108°21E 228 B7
Kaiama Nigeria 9°36N 4°1E 263 D5
Kaiapit Papua N. G. 6°18S 146°18E 286 D4
Kaiapoi N.Z. 43°24S 172°40E 285 D7
Kaidu He → China 41°46N 86°31E 218 C6
Kaieteur Falls Guyana 5°1N 59°10W 329 B6
Kaifeng China 34°48N 114°21E 226 G8
Kaihua China 29°12N 118°20E 229 C12
Kaijiang China 31°7N 107°55E 228 B6
Kaikohe N.Z. 35°25S 173°49E 284 B2
Kaikoura N.Z. 42°25S 173°43E 285 C8
Kaikoura Pen. N.Z. 42°25S 173°43E 285 C8
Kailahun S. Leone 8°18N 10°39W 262 D2
Kailash = Kangrinboqe Feng China 31°0N 81°25E 243 D9
Kailashahar India 24°19N 92°0E 241 C4
Kaili China 26°33N 107°59E 228 D6
Kailu China 43°38N 121°18E 227 C11
Kailua U.S.A. 21°24N 157°44W 302 K14
Kailua B. U.S.A. 21°25N 157°40W 302 K14
Kailua Kona U.S.A. 19°39N 155°59W 302 D6
Kaim → Papua N. G. 6°55S 141°33E 286 D1
Kaimaktsalan Oros = Voras Oros Greece 40°57N 21°45E 202 F5
Kaimana Indonesia 3°39S 133°45E 231 E8
Kaimanawa Mts. N.Z. 39°15S 175°56E 284 F4
Kaimata N.Z. 42°34S 171°28E 285 C6
Kaimes U.K. 55°54N 3°10W 121 B2
Kaimganj India 27°33N 79°24E 243 F8
Kaimon-Dake Japan 31°11N 130°32E 222 F2
Kaimur Hills India 24°30N 82°0E 243 G10
Kainab → Namibia 28°32S 19°34E 270 C2
Kainan Japan 34°9N 135°12E 223 C7
Kainantu Papua N. G. 6°18S 145°52E 286 D3
Kainji Dam Nigeria 9°55N 4°35E 263 D5
Kainji Lake △ Nigeria 10°5N 4°6E 263 C5
Kainji Res. Nigeria 10°1N 4°40E 263 C5
Kainsk = Samara Russia 53°8N 50°6E 190 D10
Kainuu □ Finland 64°30N 29°7E 160 D23
Kaipara Harbour N.Z. 36°25S 174°14E 284 C3
Kaiping China 22°23N 112°42E 229 F9
Kaipokok B. Canada 54°54N 59°47W 299 B8
Kaira India 22°45N 72°50E 242 H5
Kairana India 29°24N 77°15E 242 E7
Kairiru I. Papua N. G. 3°21S 143°34E 286 B2
Kaironi Indonesia 0°47S 133°40E 231 E8
Kairouan Tunisia 35°45N 10°5E 258 A2
Kairouan □ Tunisia 35°30N 9°46E 261 A6
Kairuku Papua N. G. 8°51S 146°35E 286 E4
Kaiser Wilhelm Gedächtniskirche Berlin, Germany 115 b2
Kaiser Wilhelm Kanal = Nord-Ostsee-Kanal Germany 54°12N 9°32E 178 A5
Kaiser-Wilhelmsland = Papua □ Indonesia 4°0S 137°0E 231 E9
Kaiserebersdorf Austria 48°9N 16°26E 142 B2
Kaiserslautern Germany 49°26N 7°45E 179 F3
Kaiserstuhl Germany 48°4N 7°40E 179 G3
Kaita Japan 34°22N 132°32E 222 C4
Kaitaia N.Z. 35°8S 173°17E 284 B2
Kaitangata N.Z. 46°17S 169°51E 285 G4
Kaithal India 29°48N 76°26E 242 E7
Kaitu → Pakistan 33°10N 70°30E 242 C4
Kaivoksela Finland 60°15N 24°53E 121 B2
Kaiwi Channel U.S.A. 21°15N 157°30W 302 K14
Kaiyang China 27°4N 106°59E 228 D6
Kaiyuan Liaoning, China 42°28N 124°1E 224 A2
Kaiyuan Yunnan, China 23°40N 103°12E 228 F4
Kaiyuh Mts. U.S.A. 64°30N 158°0W 303 D8
Kajaani Finland 64°17N 27°46E 160 D22
Kajabbi Australia 20°0S 140°1E 280 C3
Kajaki Afghan. 32°18N 65°5E 240 B2
Kajana = Kajaani Finland 64°17N 27°46E 160 D22
Kajang Malaysia 2°59N 101°48E 237 L3
Kajaran Armenia 39°10N 46°7E 213 C12
Kajiado Kenya 1°53S 36°48E 268 C4
Kajiado □ Kenya 2°0S 36°50E 268 C4
Kajo Kaji South Sudan 3°58N 31°40E 257 G3
Kajok South Sudan 8°19N 28°0E 257 F2
Kajuru Nigeria 10°15N 7°34E 263 C6
Kaka South Sudan 10°38N 32°10E 257 E3
Kaka Turkmenistan 37°21N 59°36E 247 B8
Kakabeka Falls Canada 48°24N 89°37W 298 C2
Kakadu △ Australia 12°0S 132°3E 278 B5
Kakamas S. Africa 28°45S 20°33E 270 C3
Kakamega Kenya 0°20N 34°46E 268 B3
Kakamigahara Japan 35°28N 136°48E 223 B8
Kakana India 9°7N 92°48E 245 K11
Kakanj Bos.-H. 44°4N 18°4E 182 F3
Kakanui Mts. N.Z. 45°10S 170°30E 285 F5
Kakata Liberia 6°35N 10°20W 262 D2
Kakching India 24°29N 94°0E 241 C5
Kakdwip India 21°53N 88°11E 243 J13
Kake = Akiōta Japan 34°36N 132°19E 222 C4
Kake U.S.A. 56°59N 133°57W 296 B2
Kakegawa Japan 34°45N 138°1E 223 C10
Kakeroma-Jima Japan 28°8N 129°14E 221 K4
Kākhak Iran 34°9N 58°38E 247 C8
Kakhib Russia 42°28N 46°34E 191 J8
Kakhonak U.S.A. 59°26N 154°51W 303 G9
Kakhovka Ukraine 46°45N 33°30E 189 J7
Kakhovske Vdskh. Ukraine 47°5N 34°0E 189 J7
Kakinada India 16°57N 82°11E 244 F6
Kakisa Canada 60°56N 117°25W 296 A5
Kakisa → Canada 61°3N 118°10W 296 A5
Kakisa L. Canada 60°56N 117°43W 296 A5
Kakisalmi = Priozersk Russia 61°2N 30°7E 188 B6
Kakogawa Japan 34°46N 134°51E 222 C6
Kaktovik U.S.A. 70°8N 143°38W 303 A12
Kakum △ Ghana 5°24N 1°20W 263 D4
Kakuma Kenya 3°43N 34°52E 268 B3
Kakwa → Canada 54°37N 118°28W 296 C5
Kāl Gūsheh Iran 30°59N 58°12E 247 D8
Kal Sefīd Iran 34°52N 47°23E 213 E12
Kala Nigeria 12°2N 14°40E 263 C7
Kala Oya → Sri Lanka 8°20N 79°45E 245 K4
Kalaa-Kebira Tunisia 35°59N 10°32E 258 A2
Kalaallit Nunaat = Greenland ☑ N. Amer. 66°0N 45°0W 154 D6
Kalabagh Pakistan 33°0N 71°28E 242 C4
Kalabahi Indonesia 8°13S 124°31E 231 F6
Kalabak = Radomir Bulgaria 42°37N 22°59E 202 D6
Kalabakan Malaysia 4°25N 117°29E 235 B5
Kalabana Mali 14°10N 8°35W 262 C3
Kalabo Zambia 14°58S 22°40E 265 E4
Kalaburagi India 17°20N 76°50E 244 F3
Kalach Russia 50°22N 41°0E 190 E5
Kalach na Donu Russia 48°43N 43°32E 191 F6
Kalachinsk Russia 55°3N 74°33E 217 A8
Kaladan → Burma 20°20N 93°5E 241 E4
Kaladar Canada 44°37N 77°5W 312 B7
Kalae U.S.A. 18°55N 155°41W 302 E6
Kalahari Africa 24°0S 21°30E 270 B3
Kalahari Gemsbok △ S. Africa 25°30S 20°30E 270 C3
Kalaheo U.S.A. 21°56N 159°32W 302 B2
Kalaikhum Tajikistan 38°28N 70°46E 217 E8
Kalajoki Finland 64°12N 24°10E 160 D21
Kalajun-Ku'erdening ⌂ China 43°10N 81°50E 217 D10
Kalakamati Botswana 20°40S 27°25E 271 B4
Kalakan Russia 55°15N 116°45E 215 D12
Kalakol Kenya 3°33N 35°54E 266 D4
K'alak'unlun Shank'ou = Karakoram Pass Asia 35°33N 77°50E 243 B7
Kalam Pakistan 35°34N 72°30E 243 B5
Kalama Dem. Rep. of the Congo 2°52S 28°35E 268 C2
Kalama Wash., U.S.A. 46°1N 122°51W 306 E4
Kalamaki Greece 37°52N 23°43E 112 B2
Kalamaloué △ Cameroon 12°9N 14°58E 259 F2
Kalamansig Phil. 6°33N 124°3E 233 H5
Kalamaria Greece 40°33N 22°55E 202 F6
Kalamata Greece 37°3N 22°10E 204 D4
Kalamazoo U.S.A. 42°17N 85°35W 311 B11
Kalamazoo → U.S.A. 42°40N 86°10W 311 B10
Kalamb India 18°3N 74°48E 244 E2
Kalambaka Greece 39°42N 21°39E 204 B3
Kalambo Falls Tanzania 8°37S 31°35E 269 D3
Kalamitsi Greece 38°45N 20°36E 207 B2
Kalamnuri India 19°40N 77°20E 244 E3
Kalamos Attiki, Greece 38°17N 23°52E 204 C5
Kalamos Lefkada, Greece 38°37N 20°55E 207 B2
Kalan = Tunceli Turkey 39°6N 39°31E 213 C8
Kalangadoo Australia 37°34S 140°41E 282 D4
Kalankalan Guinea 10°7N 8°54W 262 C3
Kalannie Australia 30°22S 117°5E 279 F2
Kalāntarī Iran 32°10N 54°8E 247 C7
Kalao Indonesia 7°21S 121°0E 231 F6
Kalaoa U.S.A. 19°43N 155°58W 302 D6
Kalaotoa Indonesia 7°20S 121°50E 231 F6
Kalapana U.S.A. 19°21N 154°59W 302 D7
Kälarne Sweden 62°59N 16°5E 162 B10
Kalasin Thailand 16°26N 103°30E 236 D4
Kalat Iran 25°29N 59°22E 247 E8
Kalat Pakistan 29°8N 66°31E 240 C2
Kalāteh Iran 36°33N 55°41E 247 B7
Kalāteh-ye Ganj Iran 27°31N 57°55E 247 E8
Kalathos Greece 36°9N 28°8E 206 E12
Kalatungan, Mt. Phil. 7°54N 124°50E 233 H5
Kalaupapa U.S.A. 21°12N 156°59W 302 B5
Kalaupapa ⌂ U.S.A. 21°10N 156°59W 302 B5
Kalaus → Russia 45°40N 44°7E 191 H7
Kalavrita Greece 38°3N 22°8E 204 C4
Kalaw Burma 20°38N 96°34E 241 E6
Kalawao County U.S.A. 21°11N 156°58W 302 B5
Kalbā U.A.E. 25°5N 56°22E 247 E8
Kalbadevi Mumbai, India 130 b2
Kalbān Oman 20°18N 58°38E 249 B7
Kalbarri Australia 27°40S 114°10E 279 E1
Kalbarri △ Australia 27°51S 114°30E 279 E1
Kalce Slovenia 45°54N 14°13E 176 F8
Kaldranaes Iceland 65°45N 21°25W 155 B5
Kale Antalya, Turkey 36°14N 30°0E 205 E12
Kale Denizli, Turkey 37°27N 28°49E 205 D10
Kaleburnu = Galinoporni Cyprus 35°31N 34°18E 207 E10
Kalecik Turkey 40°4N 33°26E 212 B5
Kalegauk Kyun Burma 15°33N 97°35E 236 E1
Kalehe Dem. Rep. of the Congo 2°6S 28°50E 268 C2
Kalema Tanzania 1°12S 31°55E 268 C3
Kalemie Dem. Rep. of the Congo 5°55S 29°9E 268 D2
Kalemyo Burma 23°11N 94°4E 241 D5
Kalety Poland 50°35N 18°52E 185 H5
Kalewa Burma 23°10N 94°15E 241 D5
Kaleybar Iran 38°47N 47°2E 213 C12
Kálfafell Iceland 63°57N 17°41W 155 D9
Kalgan = Zhangjiakou China 40°48N 114°55E 226 D8
Kalghatgi India 15°11N 74°58E 245 G2
Kalgoorlie-Boulder Australia 30°40S 121°22E 279 F3
Kalhovd Norway 60°4N 8°21E 164 D5
Kali → India 27°6N 79°55E 243 F8
Kali Sindh → India 25°32N 76°17E 242 G6
Kaliakra, Nos Bulgaria 43°21N 28°30E 203 C12
Kalianda Indonesia 5°50S 105°45E 234 D3
Kalibo Phil. 11°43N 122°22E 233 F4
Kaliganj Bangla. 22°25N 89°8E 241 D2
Kalihi U.S.A. 21°20N 157°53W 302 K14
Kalihi Valley U.S.A. 21°20N 157°52W 302 K14
Kalima Dem. Rep. of the Congo 2°33S 26°32E 268 C2
Kalimantan Indonesia 0°0 114°0E 235 C4
Kalimantan Barat □ Indonesia 0°0 110°30E 235 C4
Kalimantan Selatan □ Indonesia 2°30S 115°30E 235 C5
Kalimantan Tengah □ Indonesia 2°0S 113°30E 235 C4
Kalimantan Timur □ Indonesia 1°30N 116°30E 235 B5
Kalimantan Utara □ Indonesia 3°30N 117°0E 235 B5
Kálimnos Greece 37°0N 27°0E 205 D8
Kalimpong India 27°4N 88°35E 241 B2
Kalinadi → India 14°50N 74°7E 245 G2
Kalinga □ Phil. 17°30N 121°20E 232 C3
Kalinikinsk Russia 51°29N 44°28E 216 B2
Kalinin = Tver Russia 56°55N 35°59E 188 D8
Kaliningrad Russia 54°42N 20°32E 184 D7
Kaliningrad ✕ (KGD) Russia 54°45N 20°33E 184 D7
Kalininsk = Petrozavodsk Russia 61°41N 34°20E 188 B8
Kalininsk Russia 51°30N 44°40E 190 E7
Kalinkavichy Belarus 52°12N 29°20E 177 B15
Kalinkovichi = Kalinkavichy Belarus 52°12N 29°20E 177 B15
Kalinovik Bos.-H. 43°31N 18°25E 202 C2
Kalipetrovo Bulgaria 44°5N 27°14E 203 B11
Kalipur India 22°40N 88°17E 124 A1
Kalirachi Greece 40°40N 24°35E 203 F8
Kaliro Uganda 0°56N 33°30E 268 B3
Kalispell U.S.A. 48°12N 114°19W 304 B6
Kalisz Poland 51°45N 18°8E 185 G5
Kalisz Pomorski Poland 53°17N 15°55E 185 E2
Kalithea Greece 37°56N 23°43E 112 B2
Kaliua Tanzania 5°5S 31°48E 268 D3
Kalivelli Tank India 12°5N 79°50E 245 H4
Kalivia Thorikou Greece 37°50N 23°55E 204 D5
Kalix Sweden 65°53N 23°12E 160 D20
Kalixälven → Sweden 65°50N 23°11E 160 D20
Kalka India 30°46N 76°57E 242 D7
Kalkaji India 28°32N 77°12E 120 B2
Kalkal Ghat India 24°36N 92°20E 241 C4
Kalkan Turkey 36°15N 29°23E 205 E11
Kalkarindji Australia 17°30S 130°47E 278 C5
Kalkaska U.S.A. 44°44N 85°11W 309 C11
Kalkfeld Namibia 20°57S 16°14E 270 B2
Kalkfontein Botswana 22°4S 20°57E 270 B3
Kalkim Turkey 39°48N 27°13E 205 B9
Kalkrand Namibia 24°1S 17°35E 270 B2
Kallakkurichchi India 11°44N 79°1E 245 J4
Kallam India 18°36N 76°2E 244 E3
Kållandsö Sweden 58°40N 13°5E 163 F7
Kallavesi Finland 62°58N 27°30E 160 E22
Källby Sweden 58°30N 13°8E 163 F7
Kållered Sweden 57°32N 12°4E 163 G6
Kallidaikurichi India 8°38N 77°31E 245 K3
Kallies = Kalisz Pomorski Poland 53°17N 15°55E 185 E2
Kallimasia Greece 38°18N 26°6E 205 C8
Kallinge Sweden 56°15N 15°18E 163 H9
Kallmet Albania 41°51N 19°41E 202 E3
Kallsjön Sweden 63°38N 13°0E 160 E15
Kalmalo Nigeria 13°40N 5°20E 263 C6
Kalmanstunga Iceland 64°44N 20°48W 155 C6
Kalmar Sweden 56°40N 16°20E 163 H10
Kalmar □ Sweden 57°25N 16°15E 163 G10
Kalmar sund Sweden 56°40N 16°25E 163 H10
Kalmunai Sri Lanka 7°25N 81°49E 245 L5
Kalmykia □ Russia 46°5N 46°1E 191 G8
Kalna India 23°13N 88°25E 243 H13
Kalnai India 22°46N 83°30E 243 H10
Kalni → Bangla. 24°21N 91°13E 241 C3
Kalo Papua N. G. 10°1S 147°48E 286 E4
Kalo Nero Greece 37°20N 21°38E 204 D3
Kalocsa Hungary 46°32N 19°0E 182 D4
Kalofer Bulgaria 42°37N 24°59E 203 D8
Kaloko Channel U.S.A. 21°0N 157°0W 302 C5
Kalokhorio Cyprus 34°51N 33°2E 207 F9
Kaloko Dem. Rep. of the Congo 6°47S 25°48E 265 D5
Kaloko-Honokōhau ⌂ U.S.A. 19°40N 156°1W 302 D5
Kalol Gujarat, India 22°37N 73°31E 242 H5
Kalol Gujarat, India 23°15N 72°33E 242 H5
Kalolimnos Greece 37°4N 27°8E 205 D9
Kalomo Zambia 17°0S 26°30E 269 F2
Kalona U.S.A. 41°29N 91°43W 310 C5
Kaloni Greece 39°14N 26°12E 205 B8
Kaloni, Kolpos Greece 39°10N 26°10E 205 B8
Kalookan = Caloocan Phil. 14°39N 120°58E 127 B1
Kalpeni I. India 10°5N 73°38E 245 J1
Kalpi India 26°8N 79°47E 243 F8
Kalpitiya Sri Lanka 8°14N 79°46E 245 K4
Kalputhi I. India 10°49N 72°10E 245 J1
Kalrayan Hills India 11°45N 78°40E 245 J4
Kalsubai India 19°35N 73°45E 244 E1
Kaltag U.S.A. 64°20N 158°43W 303 D8
Kaltern = Caldaro Italy 46°25N 11°14E 198 B8
Kaltukatjara Australia 24°52S 129°5E 279 D4
Kaltungo Nigeria 9°48N 11°19E 263 D7
Kalu Pakistan 25°5N 67°39E 242 G2
Kaluga Russia 54°35N 36°10E 188 E9
Kaluga □ Russia 54°15N 34°50E 188 E8
Kalulong, Bukit Malaysia 3°14N 114°39E 235 B4
Kalulushi Zambia 12°50S 28°3E 269 E2
Kalumburu Australia 13°55S 126°35E 278 B4
Kalumburu ✪ Australia 14°17S 126°38E 278 B4
Kalundborg Denmark 55°41N 11°5E 163 J5
Kalush Ukraine 49°3N 24°23E 177 D13
Kałuszyn Poland 52°13N 21°52E 185 F8
Kalutara Sri Lanka 6°35N 80°0E 245 L5
Kalvåg Norway 61°46N 4°51E 164 C1
Kalvarija Lithuania 54°24N 23°14E 184 D10
Kalvebod Fælled Denmark 55°36N 12°33E 118 B3
Kalveboderne Denmark 55°37N 12°31E 118 B3
Kalwakurti India 16°41N 78°30E 244 F4
Kalya Russia 60°15N 59°59E 186 B10
Kalyan = Basavakalyan India 17°52N 76°57E 244 F3
Kalyan Maharashtra, India 19°15N 73°9E 244 E1
Kalyan Maharashtra, India 19°15N 73°9E 244 E1
Kalyandurg India 14°33N 77°6E 245 G3
Kalyansingapuram India 19°30N 83°19E 244 E6
Kalyazin Russia 57°15N 37°55E 188 D9
Kam Albania 42°17N 20°18E 202 D4
Kam → Nigeria 8°15N 1°10E 263 D7
Kam Shan Country Park ⌂ Hong Kong, China 22°21N 114°9E 122 A2
Kama Burma 19°1N 95°4E 241 F5
Kama Dem. Rep. of the Congo 3°30S 27°5E 268 C2
Kama Fukuoka, Japan 33°33N 130°49E 222 D2
Kama → Russia 55°45N 52°0E 186 C9
Kama Iwa Iwo Jima 24°47N 141°7E 288 b
Kamachumu Tanzania 1°37S 31°37E 268 C3
Kamae Japan 32°48N 131°56E 222 E3
Kamaing Burma 25°26N 96°35E 241 C6
Kamaishi Japan 39°16N 141°53E 220 E10
Kamakou U.S.A. 21°7N 156°52W 302 B5
Kamakura Japan 35°19N 139°33E 223 B11
Kamalapurum India 14°35N 78°39E 245 G4
Kamalété Gabon 0°43S 11°49E 264 C2
Kamalia Pakistan 30°44N 72°42E 242 D5
Kamamaung Burma 17°21N 97°40E 241 G6
Kaman India 27°39N 77°16E 242 F6
Kaman Turkey 39°22N 33°44E 212 C5
Kamana Dem. Rep. of the Congo 5°59S 24°58E 265 D4
Kamananui → U.S.A. 21°38N 158°4W 302 J13
Kamanjab Namibia 19°35S 14°51E 270 A2
Kamapanda Zambia 12°5S 24°0E 269 E1
Kamara Mali 14°38N 9°23W 262 C3
Kamarān Yemen 15°21N 42°35E 248 D3
Kamareddi India 18°19N 78°21E 244 E4
Kamarhati India 22°40N 88°23E 124 A2
Kamata Japan 35°33N 139°43E 140 B3
Kamativi Zimbabwe 18°20S 27°6E 270 A4
Kamba Dem. Rep. of the Congo 4°0S 22°22E 265 C4
Kamba Nigeria 11°50N 3°45E 263 C5
Kambalda West Australia 31°10S 121°37E 279 F3
Kambam India 9°45N 77°16E 245 K3
Kambangan, Nusa Indonesia 7°40S 108°10E 235 D3
Kambar Pakistan 27°37N 68°1E 242 F3
Kambarka Russia 56°15N 54°11E 186 C9
Kambia S. Leone 9°3N 12°53W 262 D2
Kambolé Togo 8°43N 1°39E 263 D5
Kambolé Zambia 8°47S 30°48E 269 D3
Kambos Cyprus 35°2N 32°44E 207 E8
Kambove Dem. Rep. of the Congo 10°51S 26°33E 269 E2
Kambuie Dem. Rep. of the Congo 6°59S 22°19E 265 D4
Kambwata Zambia 14°3S 23°43E 265 E4
Kamchatka, Poluostrov Russia 57°0N 160°0E 215 D17
Kamchatka Pen. = Kamchatka, Poluostrov Russia 57°0N 160°0E 215 D17
Kamchiya → Bulgaria 43°4N 27°44E 203 C11
Kame Ruins Zimbabwe 20°7S 28°25E 269 G2
Kameari Japan 35°45N 139°50E 140 A4
Kameda-Hantō Japan 41°50N 141°0E 220 D10
Kameido Japan 35°42N 139°50E 140 A4
Kamen Russia 53°50N 81°30E 217 B10
Kamen-Rybolov Russia 44°46N 132°2E 220 B5
Kamende Dem. Rep. of the Congo 6°26S 24°35E 265 D4
Kamenica Serbia 43°27N 22°27E 202 C6
Kamenica Serbia 44°25N 19°45E 202 B3
Kamenice nad Lipou Czechia 49°18N 15°2E 180 B8
Kamenjak, Rt Croatia 44°47N 13°55E 199 D10
Kamenka = Kamyanka Ukraine 49°3N 32°6E 189 H7
Kamenka Kazakhstan 51°7N 50°19E 190 E10
Kamenka Arkhangelsk, Russia 65°58N 44°0E 186 A7
Kamenka Penza, Russia 53°10N 44°5E 190 D6
Kamenka Voronezh, Russia 50°47N 39°20E 189 G10
Kamenka Bugskaya = Kamyanka-Buzka Ukraine 50°8N 24°16E 177 C13
Kamenka Dneprovskaya = Kamyanka-Dniprovska Ukraine 47°29N 34°28E 189 J8
Kamenka-Shevchenkovskaya = Kamyanka-Buzka Ukraine 50°8N 24°16E 177 C13
Kamennomostskiy Russia 44°18N 40°13E 191 H5
Kameno Bulgaria 42°34N 27°18E 203 D11
Kamenolomini Russia 47°40N 40°14E 191 G5
Kamensk-Shakhtinskiy Russia 48°23N 40°20E 191 F5
Kamensk Uralskiy Russia 56°25N 62°2E 214 D7
Kamenskaya = Kamensk-Shakhtinskiy Russia 48°23N 40°20E 191 F5
Kamenskiy Russia 50°48N 45°25E 190 E7
Kamenskoye = Dniprodzerzhynsk Ukraine 48°32N 34°37E 189 H8
Kamenskoye Russia 62°45N 165°30E 215 C17
Kamenyak Bulgaria 43°24N 26°57E 203 C10
Kamenz Germany 51°15N 14°5E 178 D10
Kameoka Japan 35°0N 135°35E 223 C7
Kamet India 30°55N 79°35E 243 D8
Kameyama Japan 34°51N 136°27E 223 C8
Kami Japan 33°36N 133°38E 222 D5
Kami-Itabashi Japan 35°45N 139°40E 140 A3
Kami-Jima Japan 32°27N 130°20E 222 E2
Kami-Koshiki-Jima Japan 31°50N 129°52E 222 F1
Kamiagata Japan 34°47N 129°24E 222 C1
Kamiah U.S.A. 46°14N 116°2W 304 C5
Kamień Krajeński Poland 53°32N 17°32E 184 E4
Kamień Pomorski Poland 53°57N 14°43E 184 E1
Kamienna → Poland 51°6N 21°47E 185 G8
Kamienna Góra Poland 50°47N 16°2E 185 H3
Kamieńsk Poland 51°12N 19°29E 185 G6
Kamieskroon S. Africa 30°9S 17°56E 270 D2
Kamikitazawa Japan 35°39N 139°36E 140 B2
Kamilukuak L. Canada 62°22N 101°40W 297 A8
Kamin-Kashyrskyy Ukraine 51°39N 24°56E 177 C13
Kamina Dem. Rep. of the Congo 8°45S 25°0E 265 D5
Kaminak L. Canada 62°10N 95°0W 297 A10
Kaminoyama Japan 38°9N 140°17E 220 E10
Kamioka Japan 36°25N 137°15E 223 A9
Kamiros Greece 36°20N 27°56E 206 E11
Kamishak Bay U.S.A. 59°15N 153°45W 303 G9
Kamisu Japan 35°50N 140°40E 223 B12
Kamitsuruma Japan 35°30N 139°26E 140 B1
Kamitsushima Japan 34°50N 129°28E 222 C1
Kamituga Dem. Rep. of the Congo 3°2S 28°10E 268 C2
Kamla → India 25°35N 86°36E 243 G12
Kamloops Canada 50°40N 120°20W 296 C4
Kamnik Slovenia 46°14N 14°37E 199 B11
Kamo Japan 37°39N 139°3E 220 F9
Kamo N.Z. 35°42S 174°20E 284 B3
Kamoa Mts. Guyana 1°30N 59°0W 329 C6
Kamogawa Japan 35°5N 140°5E 223 B12
Kamojima = Yoshinogawa Japan 34°4N 134°21E 222 C6
Kamoke Pakistan 32°4N 74°4E 242 C6
Kamo'oloa U.S.A. 21°34N 158°7W 302 J13
Kamoshida Japan 35°33N 139°31E 140 B2
Kamp → Austria 48°23N 15°42E 180 C8
Kampala Uganda 0°20N 32°30E 268 B3
Kampar Malaysia 4°18N 101°9E 237 K3
Kampar → Indonesia 0°30N 103°8E 234 B2
Kampen Neths. 52°33N 5°53E 170 B5
Kamphaeng Phet Thailand 16°28N 99°30E 236 D2
Kampinoski △ Poland 52°21N 20°40E 185 F7
Kampolombo, L. Zambia 11°37S 29°42E 269 E2
Kampong Cham Cambodia 12°0N 105°30E 237 G5
Kampong Chhnang Cambodia 12°20N 104°35E 237 F5
Kampong Landang Singapore 1°20N 103°55E 138 A3
Kampong Pengerang Malaysia 1°22N 104°7E 237 d
Kampong Punggai Malaysia 1°27N 104°18E 237 d
Kampong Saom Cambodia 10°38N 103°30E 237 G4
Kampong Saom, Chaak Cambodia 10°50N 103°32E 237 G4
Kampong Tanjong Langsat Malaysia 1°28N 104°1E 237 d
Kampong Tanjong Penjuru Singapore 1°18N 103°45E 138 B2
Kampong Telok Ramunia Malaysia 1°22N 104°15E 237 d
Kampot Cambodia 10°36N 104°10E 237 G5
Kampsville U.S.A. 39°18N 90°37W 310 E6
Kampti Burkina Faso 10°7N 3°25W 262 C4
Kampuchea = Cambodia ■ Asia 12°15N 105°0E 236 F5
Kampung Air Putih Malaysia 4°15N 103°10E 237 K4
Kampung Bali Indonesia 6°11S 106°48E 122 B1
Kampung Jerangau Malaysia 4°50N 103°10E 237 K4

Kampung Raja *Malaysia* 5°45N 102°35E **237** K4
Kampungbaru = Tolitoli *Indonesia* 1°5N 120°50E **231** D6
Kamrau, Teluk *Indonesia* 3°30S 133°36E **231** E8
Kamsack *Canada* 51°34N 101°54W **297** C8
Kamsar *Guinea* 10°40N 14°36W **262** C2
Kamskoye Ustye *Russia* 55°10N 49°20E **190** C9
Kamskoye Vdkhr. *Russia* 58°41N 56°7E **186** C10
Kamsuuma *Somalia* 0°15N 42°46E **267** D5
Kamthi *India* 21°9N 79°19E **244** D4
Kamuchawie L. *Canada* 56°18N 101°59W **297** B8
Kamuela *U.S.A.* 20°1N 155°41W **302** C6
Kamui-Misaki *Japan* 43°20N 140°21E **220** C10
Kamyanets-Podilskyy *Ukraine* 48°45N 26°40E **183** B11
Kamyanka *Ukraine* 49°3N 32°6E **189** H7
Kamyanka-Buzka *Ukraine* 50°8N 24°16E **177** C13
Kamyanka-Dniprovska *Ukraine* 47°29N 34°28E **189** J8
Kamyanyets *Belarus* 52°23N 23°49E **185** F10
Kamyanyuki *Belarus* 52°32N 23°49E **185** F10
Kāmyārān *Iran* 34°47N 46°56E **213** E12
Kamyshin *Russia* 50°10N 45°24E **190** E7
Kamyzyak *Russia* 46°4N 48°10E **191** G9
Kan = Gan Jiang → *China* 29°15N 116°0E **229** C11
Kan *Burma* 22°25N 94°5E **241** D5
Kan *South Sudan* 9°1N 31°47E **257** F3
Kanaaupscow → *Canada* 54°2N 76°30W **298** B4
Kanab *U.S.A.* 37°3N 112°32W **305** H7
Kanab Cr. → *U.S.A.* 36°24N 112°38W **305** H7
Kanacea *Lau Group, Fiji* 17°15S 179°6W **287** A3
Kanacea *Taveuni, Fiji* 16°59S 179°56E **287** A2
Kanaga I. *U.S.A.* 51°45N 177°22W **303** L3
Kanagawa □ *Japan* 35°20N 139°20E **223** B11
Kanagi *Japan* 40°54N 140°27E **220** D10
Kanairiktok → *Canada* 55°2N 60°18W **299** A7
Kanakanak *U.S.A.* 59°0N 158°32W **303** G8
Kanakapura *India* 12°33N 77°28E **245** H3
Kanalia *Greece* 39°30N 22°53E **204** B4
Kanamori *Japan* 35°31N 139°27E **140** B1
Kananga *Dem. Rep. of the Congo* 5°55S 22°18E **265** D4
Kanangra-Boyd △ *Australia* 33°57S 150°15E **283** B9
Kanash *Russia* 55°30N 47°32E **190** C8
Kanaskat *U.S.A.* 47°19N 121°54W **306** C5
Kanastraíon, Ákra = Paliouri, Akra *Greece* 39°57N 23°45E **202** G7
Kanawha → *U.S.A.* 38°50N 82°9W **309** F12
Kanazawa *Japan* 36°30N 136°38E **223** A8
Kanbalu *Burma* 23°12N 95°31E **241** D5
Kanchanaburi *Thailand* 14°2N 99°31E **236** E2
Kanchenjunga *Nepal* 27°50N 88°10E **243** F13
Kanchenjunga △ *India* 27°42N 88°8E **241** B2
Kanchipuram *India* 12°52N 79°45E **245** H4
Kanchow = Ganzhou *China* 25°51N 114°56E **229** E10
Kańczuga *Poland* 49°59N 22°25E **185** J9
Kanda *Tokyo, Japan* **140** a5
Kanda Kanda *Dem. Rep. of the Congo* 6°52S 23°48E **265** D4
Kandagach = Qandyaghash *Kazakhstan* 49°28N 57°25E **187** E10
Kandaghat *India* 30°59N 77°7E **242** D7
Kandahār *Kandahār, Afghan.* 31°32N 65°43E **240** C2
Kandahar *India* 18°52N 77°12E **244** E3
Kandahār □ *Afghan.* 31°0N 65°0E **240** C2
Kandala *Dem. Rep. of the Congo* 6°20S 19°40E **265** D3
Kandalaksha *Russia* 67°9N 32°30E **160** C25
Kandalakshskiy Zaliv *Russia* 66°0N 35°0E **186** A6
Kandang *Indonesia* 3°3N 97°19E **234** B1
Kandangan *Indonesia* 2°50S 115°20E **235** C5
Kandanos *Greece* 35°19N 23°44E **207** E4
Kandava *Latvia* 57°2N 22°46E **184** A9
Kandavu = Kadavu *Fiji* 19°0S 178°15E **287** B2
Kandavu Passage = Kadavu Passage *Fiji* 18°45S 178°0E **287** B2
Kandé = Kanté *Togo* 9°57N 1°3E **263** D5
Kandep *Papua N. G.* 5°54S 143°32E **286** C2
Kandhkot *Pakistan* 28°16N 69°8E **242** E3
Kandhla *India* 29°18N 77°19E **242** E7
Kandi *Benin* 11°7N 2°55E **263** C5
Kandi *India* 23°58N 88°5E **243** H13
Kandiaro *Pakistan* 27°4N 68°13E **242** F3
Kandila *Arkadia, Greece* 37°46N 22°22E **204** D4
Kandila *Etoloakarnania, Greece* 38°42N 20°56E **207** B2
Kandilli *Turkey* 41°4N 29°3E **122** B2
Kandıra *Turkey* 41°4N 30°9E **212** B4
Kandla *India* 23°0N 70°10E **242** H4
Kandor, O. → *Chad* 17°13N 20°52E **259** E4
Kandos *Australia* 32°45S 149°58E **283** B8
Kandreho *Madag.* 17°29S 46°6E **272** B2
Kandrian *Papua N. G.* 6°14S 149°37E **286** D5
Kandy *Sri Lanka* 7°18N 80°43E **245** L5
Kane *U.S.A.* 41°40N 78°49W **312** E6
Kane Basin *Greenland* 79°1N 70°0W **154** B4
Kaneilio Pt. *U.S.A.* 21°27N 158°12W **302** K13
Kanel *Senegal* 15°30N 13°18W **262** B2
Kanem □ *Chad* 15°0N 15°0E **259** F3
Kāne'ohe *U.S.A.* 21°25N 157°48W **302** K14
Kāne'ohe B. *U.S.A.* 21°30N 157°50W **302** K14
Kaneohe Station *U.S.A.* 21°27N 157°46W **302** K14
Kanevskaya *Russia* 46°3N 38°57E **191** G4
Kanfanar *Croatia* 45°7N 13°50E **199** C10
Kang *Botswana* 23°41S 22°50E **270** B3
Kangaamiut *Greenland* 65°50N 53°20W **154** D5
Kangaatsiaq *Greenland* 68°18N 53°28W **154** D5
Kangaba *Mali* 11°56N 8°25W **262** C3
Kangal *Turkey* 39°14N 37°23E **212** C7
Kangān *Fārs, Iran* 27°50N 52°3E **247** E7
Kangān *Hormozgān, Iran* 25°48N 57°28E **247** E8
Kangar *Malaysia* 6°27N 100°12E **237** J3
Kangaré *Mali* 11°36N 8°4W **262** C3
Kangaroo I. *Australia* 35°45S 137°0E **282** C2
Kangaroo Mts. *Australia* 23°29S 141°51E **280** C3
Kangasala *Finland* 61°28N 24°4E **188** B3
Kangāvar *Iran* 34°40N 48°0E **213** E12
Kangding *China* 30°2N 101°57E **228** B3
Kangdong *N. Korea* 39°9N 126°5E **224** C3
Kangean, Kepulauan *Indonesia* 6°55S 115°23E **235** D5
Kangean Is. = Kangean, Kepulauan *Indonesia* 6°55S 115°23E **235** D5
Kangen → *South Sudan* 6°47N 33°9E **257** F3
Kangerdlugssuak *Greenland* 68°10N 32°20W **154** D7
Kangerluarsoruseq *Greenland* 63°45N 51°27W **154** E5
Kangerluarsoruset = Kangerluarsoruseq *Greenland* 63°45N 51°27W **154** E5
Kangerlussuaq *Greenland* 66°59N 50°40W **154** D5
Kangertittivaq = Scoresby Sund *Greenland* 70°28N 21°46W **154** C8
Kanggye *N. Korea* 41°0N 126°35E **224** B3
Kanghsi *Taiwan* 23°34N 120°8E **225** C2
Kangikajik *Greenland* 70°7N 22°0W **154** C8
Kangilinnguit *Greenland* 61°20N 47°57W **154** E6
Kangiqliniq = Rankin Inlet *Canada* 62°30N 93°0W **294** E13
Kangiqsualujjuaq *Canada* 58°30N 65°59W **295** F18
Kangiqsujuaq *Canada* 61°30N 72°0W **295** E17
Kangiqtugaapik = Clyde River *Canada* 70°30N 68°30W **295** C18
Kangirsuk *Canada* 60°0N 70°0W **295** F18
Kangkar Chemaran *Malaysia* 1°34N 104°12E **237** d
Kangkar Sungai Tiram *Malaysia* 1°35N 103°55E **237** d
Kangkar Teberau *Malaysia* 1°32N 103°51E **237** d
Kango *Gabon* 0°11N 10°5E **264** B2
Kangoku Iwa *Iwo Jima* 24°48N 141°17E **288** b
Kangoya *Dem. Rep. of the Congo* 9°55S 22°48E **265** D4
Kangping *China* 42°43N 123°18E **227** C12
Kangpokpi *India* 25°8N 93°58E **241** C4
Kangra *India* 32°6N 76°16E **242** C7
Kangrinboqe Feng *China* 31°0N 81°25E **243** D9
Kangshan *Taiwan* 22°48N 120°17E **225** D2
Kangto *China* 27°50N 92°35E **241** B4
Kangtzu *Taiwan* 22°8N 120°52E **225** D2
Kangwon-do □ *N. Korea* 38°47N 127°35E **224** C3
Kangyidaung *Burma* 16°56N 94°54E **241** G5
Kanha △ *India* 22°15N 80°40E **243** H9
Kanhan → *India* 21°4N 79°34E **244** D4
Kanhangad *India* 12°21N 74°58E **245** H2
Kanhar → *India* 24°28N 83°8E **243** G10
Kani *Sagaing, Burma* 23°52N 95°22E **241** D5
Kani *Sagaing, Burma* 22°26N 94°51E **241** D5
Kani *Ivory C.* 8°29N 6°36W **262** D3
Kani *Japan* 35°25N 137°7E **223** B9
Kani-Keli *Mayotte* 12°57S 45°6E **272** b
Kaniama *Dem. Rep. of the Congo* 7°30S 24°12E **265** D4
Kaniapiskau = Caniapiscau → *Canada* 56°40N 69°30W **299** A6
Kaniapiskau, L. = Caniapiscau, L. *Canada* 54°10N 69°55W **299** B6
Kaniere, L. *N.Z.* 42°50S 171°10E **285** C6
Kanif *Micronesia* 9°31N 138°5E **287** R16
Kanigiri *India* 15°24N 79°31E **245** G4
Kanin, Poluostrov *Russia* 68°0N 45°0E **186** A8
Kanin Nos, Mys *Russia* 68°39N 43°32E **186** A7
Kanin Pen. = Kanin, Poluostrov *Russia* 68°0N 45°0E **186** A8
Kaninë *Albania* 40°23N 19°30E **202** F3
Kaniva *Australia* 36°22S 141°18E **282** D4
Kanjiža *Serbia* 46°3N 20°4E **182** D5
Kanjut Sar *Pakistan* 36°7N 75°25E **243** A6
Kankaanpää *Finland* 61°44N 22°50E **188** B2
Kankakee *U.S.A.* 41°7N 87°52W **311** C9
Kankakee → *U.S.A.* 41°23N 88°15W **311** C8
Kankan *Guinea* 10°23N 9°15W **262** C3
Kankendy = Xankändi *Azerbaijan* 39°52N 46°49E **213** C12
Kanker *India* 20°10N 81°40E **244** D5
Kankesanturai *Sri Lanka* 9°49N 80°2E **245** K5
Kankossa *Mauritania* 15°54N 11°31W **262** B2
Kankroli *India* 25°4N 73°53E **242** G5
Kankurgachi *India* 22°34N 88°23E **124** B2
Kanlıca *Turkey* 41°5N 29°3E **122** B2
Kanmaw Kyun *Burma* 11°40N 98°28E **237** G2
Kanmuri-Yama *Japan* 34°30N 132°4E **222** C4
Kannabe *Japan* 34°32N 133°23E **222** C5
Kannapolis *U.S.A.* 35°30N 80°37W **315** D14
Kannauj *India* 27°3N 79°56E **243** F8
Kanniyakumari *India* 8°5N 77°34E **245** K3
Kannur *India* 11°53N 75°27E **245** J2
Kannyakumari *India* 8°3N 77°40E **245** K3
Kano *Nigeria* 12°2N 8°30E **263** C6
Kano □ *Nigeria* 11°30N 8°30E **263** C6
Kanonerskiy, Ostrov *Russia* 59°53N 30°13E **137** B1
Kan'onji *Japan* 34°7N 133°39E **222** C5
Kanoroba *Ivory C.* 9°7N 6°8W **262** D3
Kanowha *U.S.A.* 42°57N 93°47W **310** B3
Kanowit *Malaysia* 2°14N 112°20E **235** B4
Kanoya *Japan* 31°25N 130°50E **222** F2
Kanpetlet *Burma* 21°10N 93°59E **241** E4
Kanpur *India* 26°28N 80°20E **243** F9
Kansai Int. ✈ (KIX) *Japan* 34°27N 135°12E **133** B2
Kansas *U.S.A.* 39°33N 87°56W **311** E9
Kansas □ *U.S.A.* 38°30N 99°0W **308** F4
Kansas → *U.S.A.* 39°7N 94°37W **308** F6
Kansas City *Kans., U.S.A.* 39°7N 94°38W **310** E2
Kansas City *Mo., U.S.A.* 39°6N 94°35W **310** E2
Kansas City Int. ✈ (MCI) *U.S.A.* 39°18N 94°43W **310** E2
Kansenia *Dem. Rep. of the Congo* 10°20S 26°0E **269** E2
Kansk *Russia* 56°20N 95°37E **215** D10
Kansu = Gansu □ *China* 36°0N 104°0E **226** G3
Kantaphor *India* 22°35N 76°34E **242** H7
Kantchari *Burkina Faso* 12°37N 1°37E **263** C5
Kantché *Niger* 13°31N 8°30E **259** F1
Kanté *Togo* 9°57N 1°3E **263** D5
Kantemirovka *Russia* 49°43N 39°55E **189** H10
Kanth = Kąty Wrocławskie *Poland* 51°2N 16°45E **185** G3
Kantharalak *Thailand* 14°39N 104°39E **236** E5
Kanthi = Contai *India* 21°54N 87°46E **243** J12
Kantishna *U.S.A.* 63°31N 150°57W **303** E10
Kantishna → *U.S.A.* 64°45N 149°58W **303** D10
Kantli → *India* 28°20N 75°30E **242** E6
Kantō □ *Japan* 36°15N 139°30E **223** A11
Kantō-Sanchi *Japan* 35°59N 138°50E **223** B10
Kantu-long *Burma* 19°57N 97°36E **241** F6
Kanturk *Ireland* 52°11N 8°54W **166** D3
Kanuma *Japan* 36°34N 139°42E **223** A11
Kanus *Namibia* 27°50S 18°39E **270** C2
Kanuti Nat. Wildlife Refuge ⌂ *U.S.A.* 66°25N 151°50W **303** C10
Kanye *Botswana* 24°55S 25°28E **270** B4
Kanzaki → *Japan* 34°41N 135°24E **133** A1
Kanzenze *Dem. Rep. of the Congo* 10°30S 25°12E **265** E5
Kanzi, Ras *Tanzania* 7°1S 39°33E **268** D4
Kanzoni, Chissioua *Comoros Is.* 12°23S 43°40E **272** a
Kao *Tonga* 19°40S 175°1W **287** P13
Kao Phara *Thailand* 8°3N 98°22E **237** a
Kaohsiung *Taiwan* 22°35N 120°16E **225** D2
Kaohsung □ *Taiwan* 23°0N 120°35E **225** D2
Kaoka *Solomon Is.* 9°42S 160°43E **287** M11
Kaokaona = Kirakira *Solomon Is.* 10°27S 161°56E **287** N11
Kaokoveld *Namibia* 19°15S 14°30E **270** A1
Kaolack *Senegal* 14°5N 16°8W **262** C1
Kaolack □ *Senegal* 14°0N 15°15W **262** C1
Kaolan = Lanzhou *China* 36°1N 103°52E **226** F2
Kaolo *Solomon Is.* 8°24S 159°38E **287** M10
Kaoma *Zambia* 14°47S 24°48E **265** E4
Kaoshan *China* 44°38N 124°50E **227** B13
Kaoshu *Taiwan* 22°49N 120°36E **225** D2
Kaouar *Niger* 19°5N 12°52E **259** E2
Kaoyao = Zhaoqing *China* 23°0N 112°20E **229** F9
Kapa'a *U.S.A.* 22°5N 159°19W **302** A2
Kapadvanj *India* 23°5N 73°0E **242** H5
Kapagere *Papua N. G.* 9°46S 147°42E **286** E4
Kapahulu *U.S.A.* 21°16N 157°49W **302** K14
Kapaklı *Turkey* 41°19N 27°59E **203** E11
Kapali Carsi *Turkey* 41°1N 28°58E **122** B1
Kapalua *U.S.A.* 20°59N 156°39W **302** C5
Kapan *Armenia* 39°18N 46°27E **213** C12
Kapanga *Bandundu, Dem. Rep. of the Congo* 5°4S 16°58E **265** D3
Kapanga *Katanga, Dem. Rep. of the Congo* 8°30S 22°40E **265** D4
Kapapa I. *U.S.A.* 21°29N 157°48W **302** K14
Kapatagan *Phil.* 7°52N 123°44E **233** H4
Kapchagai = Qapshaghay *Kazakhstan* 43°51N 77°14E **217** D9
Kapchagaiskoye Vdkhr. = Qapshaghay Bögeni *Kazakhstan* 43°45N 77°50E **217** D9
Kapedo *Kenya* 1°10N 36°6E **268** B4
Kapela = Velika Kapela *Croatia* 45°10N 15°5E **199** C12
Kapellerfeld *Austria* 48°18N 16°29E **142** A2
Kapellskär *Sweden* 59°44N 19°2E **162** E13
Kapelo, Akra *Greece* 36°9N 23°3E **204** E5
Kapema *Dem. Rep. of the Congo* 10°45S 28°22E **269** E2
Kapenguria *Kenya* 1°14N 35°7E **268** B4
Kapfenberg *Austria* 47°26N 15°18E **180** D8
Kapı Dağı *Turkey* 40°28N 27°50E **203** F11
Kapia *Dem. Rep. of the Congo* 4°17S 19°46E **265** C3
Kapiri Mposhi *Zambia* 13°59S 28°43E **269** E2
Kāpīsā □ *Afghan.* 35°0N 69°20E **240** B3
Kapiskau → *Canada* 52°47N 81°55W **298** B3
Kapit *Malaysia* 2°0N 112°55E **235** B4
Kapiti I. *N.Z.* 40°50S 174°56E **284** G3
Kapka, Massif du *Chad* 15°7N 21°45E **259** E4
Kaplan *U.S.A.* 30°0N 92°17W **314** F8
Kaplıca = Davlos *Cyprus* 35°25N 33°54E **207** E9
Kaplice *Czechia* 48°42N 14°30E **180** C7
Kapoe *Thailand* 9°34N 98°32E **237** H2
Kapoeta *South Sudan* 4°50N 33°35E **257** G3
Kapoho *U.S.A.* 19°30N 154°50W **302** D7
Kapolei *U.S.A.* 21°19N 158°5W **302** K13
Kápolnásnyék *Hungary* 47°16N 18°41E **182** C3
Kapombo *Dem. Rep. of the Congo* 10°40S 23°30E **265** E4
Kaponga *N.Z.* 39°29S 174°9E **284** F3
Kapos → *Hungary* 46°44N 18°30E **182** D3
Kaposvár *Hungary* 46°25N 17°47E **182** D2
Káposztásmegyer *Hungary* 47°35N 19°6E **117** A2
Kapotnya *Russia* 55°39N 37°48E **129** C3
Kapowsin *U.S.A.* 46°59N 122°13W **306** D4
Kapp *Norway* 60°43N 10°52E **164** D7
Käppala *Sweden* 59°21N 18°13E **139** A3
Kappeln *Germany* 54°40N 9°55E **178** A5
Kappelshamn *Sweden* 57°52N 18°47E **163** G12
Kapps *Namibia* 22°32S 17°18E **270** B2
Kaprije *Croatia* 43°42N 15°43E **199** E12
Kapsabet *Kenya* 0°12N 35°6E **268** B4
Kapsan *N. Korea* 41°4N 128°19E **224** B4
Kapsukas = Marijampolė *Lithuania* 54°33N 23°19E **184** D10
Kaptai *Bangla.* 22°21N 92°17E **241** D4
Kaptai L. *Bangla.* 22°40N 92°20E **241** D4
Kapuas → *Kalimantan Barat, Indonesia* 0°25S 109°20E **235** C3
Kapuas → *Kalimantan Tengah, Indonesia* 3°1S 114°19E **235** C4
Kapuas Hulu, Pegunungan *Malaysia* 1°30N 113°30E **235** B4
Kapuas Hulu Ra. = Kapuas Hulu, Pegunungan *Malaysia* 1°30N 113°30E **235** B4
Kapuk *Indonesia* 6°7S 106°44E **122** A1
Kapulo *Dem. Rep. of the Congo* 8°18S 29°15E **269** D2
Kapunda *Australia* 34°20S 138°56E **282** C3
Kapuni *N.Z.* 39°29S 174°8E **284** F3
Kapurthala *India* 31°23N 75°25E **242** D6
Kapuskasing *Canada* 49°25N 82°30W **298** C3
Kapuskasing → *Canada* 49°49N 82°0W **298** C3
Kapustin Yar *Russia* 48°37N 45°40E **191** F7
Kaputar, Mt. *Australia* 30°15S 150°10E **281** E5
Kaputir *Kenya* 2°5N 35°28E **268** B4
Kapuvár *Hungary* 47°36N 17°1E **182** C2
Käpylä *Finland* 60°13N 24°57E **121** B2
Kara *Russia* 69°10N 65°0E **214** C7
Karā, W. → *Si. Arabia* 20°45N 41°42E **256** C5
Kara Ada *Turkey* 36°58N 27°28E **205** E9
Kara-Balta *Kyrgyzstan* 42°50N 73°49E **217** D8
Kara Bogaz Gol, Zaliv = Garabogazköl Aylagy *Turkmenistan* 41°0N 53°30E **187** F9
Kara Burun *Turkey* 36°32N 27°58E **205** E9
Kara Kala = Garrygala *Turkmenistan* 38°31N 56°29E **247** B8
Kara Kalpak Republic = Qoraqalpog'istan □ *Uzbekistan* 43°0N 58°0E **216** D5
Kara-Köl *Kyrgyzstan* 41°40N 72°43E **217** D8
Kara Kum = Garagum *Turkmenistan* 39°30N 60°0E **247** B8
Kara-Saki *Japan* 34°41N 129°30E **222** C1
Kara Sea *Russia* 75°0N 70°0E **214** B8
Karaadilli *Turkey* 38°18N 30°37E **205** C12
Karabiğa *Turkey* 40°23N 27°17E **203** F11
Karabük *Turkey* 41°12N 32°37E **212** B5
Karabük □ *Turkey* 41°10N 32°30E **212** B5
Karaburun *Albania* 40°25N 19°20E **202** F3
Karaburun *Turkey* 38°41N 26°28E **205** C8
Karaburun-Sazan △ *Albania* 40°30N 19°21E **202** F3
Karabutak = Qarabutaq *Kazakhstan* 50°0N 60°14E **216** C6
Karacabey *Turkey* 40°12N 28°21E **203** F12
Karacakılavuz *Turkey* 41°8N 27°21E **203** E11
Karacaköy *Turkey* 41°24N 28°22E **203** E12
Karaçal Tepesi *Turkey* 36°21N 32°38E **250** B3
Karacasu *Turkey* 37°43N 28°35E **205** D10
Karachala = Qaraçala *Azerbaijan* 39°45N 48°53E **191** L9
Karachayevsk *Russia* 43°50N 41°55E **191** J5
Karachev *Russia* 53°10N 35°5E **189** F8
Karachey-Cherkessia □ *Russia* 43°40N 41°30E **191** J5
Karachi *Pakistan* 24°50N 67°0E **123** A2
Karad *India* 17°15N 74°10E **244** F2
Karadirek *Turkey* 38°34N 30°11E **205** C12
Karaga *Ghana* 9°58N 0°28W **263** D4
Karaganda = Qaraghandy *Kazakhstan* 49°50N 73°10E **217** C8
Karagayly = Qaraghayly *Kazakhstan* 49°26N 76°0E **214** E8
Karaginskiy, Ostrov *Russia* 58°45N 164°0E **215** D17
Karagiye, Vpadina *Kazakhstan* 43°27N 51°45E **187** F9
Karagiye Depression = Karagiye, Vpadina *Kazakhstan* 43°27N 51°45E **187** F9
Karagola Road *India* 25°29N 87°23E **243** G12
Karagüney Dağları *Turkey* 40°30N 34°40E **212** B6
Karahallı *Turkey* 38°21N 29°33E **205** C11
Kárahnjúkar *Iceland* 64°57N 15°46W **155** C11
Karaikal *India* 10°59N 79°50E **245** J4
Karaikkudi *India* 10°5N 78°45E **245** J4
Karaisali *Turkey* 37°16N 35°2E **212** D6
Karaiskakis *Greece* 38°35N 21°4E **207** B3
Karaitivu I. *Sri Lanka* 9°45N 79°52E **245** K4
Karaj *Iran* 35°48N 51°0E **247** C6
Karajarri ☼ *Australia* 19°0S 122°30E **278** C3
Karak *Malaysia* 3°25N 102°2E **237** L4
Karakalpakstan = Qoraqalpog'istan □ *Uzbekistan* 43°0N 58°0E **216** D5
Karakaya Barajı *Turkey* 38°31N 38°23E **213** C8
Karakelong *Indonesia* 4°35N 126°50E **231** D7
Karakitang *Indonesia* 3°14N 125°28E **231** D7
Karaklis = Vanadzor *Armenia* 40°48N 44°30E **191** K7
Karakoçan *Turkey* 38°57N 40°2E **213** C9
Karakol *Kyrgyzstan* 42°30N 78°20E **217** D9
Karakoram Pass *Asia* 35°33N 77°50E **243** B7
Karakoram Ra. *Pakistan* 35°30N 77°0E **243** B7
Karakul = Qorako'l *Uzbekistan* 39°32N 63°50E **216** E6
Karakul *Tajikistan* 39°2N 73°33E **217** E8
Karakul, Ozero *Tajikistan* 39°5N 73°25E **217** E8
Karakurt *Turkey* 40°10N 42°37E **213** B10
Karakuwisa *Namibia* 18°56S 19°40E **270** A2
Karal *Chad* 12°50N 14°46E **259** F2
Karalon *Russia* 57°5N 115°50E **215** D12
Karama *Jordan* 31°57N 35°35E **251** G6
Karaman *Balıkesir, Turkey* 39°39N 28°0E **205** B9
Karaman *Konya, Turkey* 37°14N 33°13E **212** D5
Karaman □ *Turkey* 37°5N 33°15E **250** A4
Karamanlı *Turkey* 37°23N 29°47E **205** D11
Karamay *China* 45°30N 84°58E **217** C10
Karambu *Indonesia* 3°53S 116°6E **235** C5
Karamea *N.Z.* 41°14S 172°6E **285** B7
Karamea → *N.Z.* 41°13S 172°26E **285** B7
Karamea Bight *N.Z.* 41°22S 171°40E **285** B6
Karamian *Indonesia* 5°5S 114°40E **235** D4
Karamnasa → *India* 25°31N 83°52E **243** G10
Karamürsel *Turkey* 40°41N 29°36E **203** F13
Karān *Si. Arabia* 27°43N 49°49E **247** E6
Karand *Iran* 34°16N 46°15E **213** E12
Karangana *Mali* 12°15N 5°4W **262** C3
Karanganyar *Indonesia* 7°38S 109°37E **235** D3
Karangasem = Amlapura *Indonesia* 8°27S 115°37E **231** J18
Karanja *Maharashtra, India* 21°11N 78°24E **244** D4
Karanja *Maharashtra, India* 20°29N 77°31E **244** D3
Karanjia *India* 21°47N 85°58E **243** J11
Karankasso *Burkina Faso* 10°50N 3°53W **262** C4
Karaova *Turkey* 37°5N 27°40E **205** D9
Karapınar *Turkey* 37°41N 33°30E **212** D5
Karapiro *N.Z.* 37°53S 175°32E **284** D4
Karas □ *Namibia* 27°0S 17°30E **270** C2
Karasburg *Namibia* 28°0S 18°44E **270** C2
Karasino *Russia* 66°50N 86°50E **214** C9
Karasjok *Norway* 69°27N 25°30E **160** B21
Karasu *Turkey* 41°4N 30°46E **212** B4
Karasu → *Antalya, Turkey* 36°18N 30°10E **205** E12
Karasu → *Hatay, Turkey* 36°20N 36°20E **250** B7
Karasubazar = Bilohirsk *Ukraine* 45°3N 34°35E **189** K8
Karasuk *Russia* 53°44N 78°2E **217** B9
Karasuyama *Japan* 36°39N 140°9E **223** A12
Karataş *Adana, Turkey* 36°36N 35°21E **250** B6
Karataş *Manisa, Turkey* 38°35N 28°16E **205** C10
Karataş Burnu *Turkey* 36°31N 35°24E **250** B6
Karatau, Khrebet = Qarataū *Kazakhstan* 43°30N 69°30E **217** D7
Karatax Shan *China* 35°57N 81°0E **217** E10
Karateki Shan *China* 40°40N 77°50E **217** D9
Karativu *Sri Lanka* 8°22N 79°47E **245** K4
Karatoprak = Turgutreis *Turkey* 37°2N 27°15E **205** D9
Karatoya → *India* 24°7N 89°36E **241** C2
Karatsu *Japan* 33°26N 129°58E **222** D1
Karaul *Russia* 70°6N 82°15E **214** B9
Karauli *India* 26°30N 77°4E **242** F7
Karavasta △ *Albania* 40°55N 19°29E **202** F3
Karavastasë, L. e *Albania* 40°55N 19°30E **202** F3
Karavia *Greece* 36°49N 23°37E **204** E5
Karavostasi *Cyprus* 35°8N 32°50E **207** E8
Karawa *Dem. Rep. of the Congo* 3°18N 20°17E **264** B4
Karawang *Indonesia* 6°30S 107°15E **235** D3
Karawanken *Europe* 46°30N 14°40E **180** E7
Karayazı *Turkey* 39°41N 42°9E **213** C10
Karazhal = Qarazhal *Kazakhstan* 48°2N 70°49E **214** E8
Karbalā' *Iraq* 32°36N 44°3E **213** F11
Karbalā' □ *Iraq* 32°30N 43°50E **213** F10
Kårböle *Sweden* 61°59N 15°22E **162** C9
Karcag *Hungary* 47°19N 20°57E **182** C5
Karcha → *Pakistan* 34°45N 76°10E **243** B7
Karchana *India* 25°17N 81°56E **243** G9
Karczew *Poland* 52°5N 21°15E **185** F8
Kardakata *Greece* 38°17N 20°28E **207** C1
Kardam *Bulgaria* 43°45N 28°6E **203** C12
Kardamila *Greece* 38°35N 26°5E **205** C8
Kardamili *Greece* 36°53N 22°13E **204** E4
Kardeljovo = Ploče *Croatia* 43°4N 17°26E **199** E14
Karditsa *Greece* 39°23N 21°54E **204** B3
Kärdla *Estonia* 59°0N 22°45E **188** C2
Kardzhali = Kŭrdzhali *Bulgaria* 41°38N 25°21E **203** E9
Kareeberge *S. Africa* 30°59S 21°50E **270** D3
Kareha → *India* 25°44N 86°21E **243** G12
Kareima *Sudan* 18°30N 31°49E **256** D3
Karelia □ *Russia* 65°30N 32°30E **186** A5
Karelian Republic = Karelia □ *Russia* 65°30N 32°30E **186** A5
Karelo-Finnish S.S.R. = Karelia □ *Russia* 65°30N 32°30E **186** A5
Karema *Papua N. G.* 9°12S 147°18E **286** E4
Karen = Kayin □ *Burma* 18°0N 97°30E **241** G6
Karenni = Kayah □ *Burma* 19°15N 97°15E **241** F6
Karera *India* 25°32N 78°9E **242** G8
Kārevāndar *Iran* 27°53N 60°44E **247** E9
Kargasok *Russia* 59°3N 80°53E **214** D9
Kargat *Russia* 55°10N 80°15E **214** D9
Kargi *Eastern, Kenya* 2°31N 37°34E **268** B4
Kargı *Turkey* 41°11N 34°30E **212** B6
Kargil *India* 34°32N 76°12E **243** B7
Kargopol *Russia* 61°30N 38°58E **188** B10
Kargowa *Poland* 52°5N 15°51E **185** F2
Karguéri *Niger* 13°27N 10°30E **259** F2
Karia *Greece* 38°45N 20°39E **207** B2
Karia ba Mohammed *Morocco* 34°22N 5°12W **260** B3
Karīān *Iran* 26°57N 57°14E **247** E8
Karianga *Madag.* 22°25S 47°22E **272** C2
Kariba *Zimbabwe* 16°28S 28°50E **269** F2
Kariba, L. *Zimbabwe* 16°40S 28°25E **269** F2
Kariba Dam *Zimbabwe* 16°30S 28°35E **269** F2
Kariba Gorge *Zambia* 16°30S 28°50E **269** F2
Karibib *Namibia* 22°0S 15°56E **270** B2
Karies *Greece* 40°14N 24°19E **203** F8
Karijini △ *Australia* 23°8S 118°15E **278** D2
Karikari, C. *N.Z.* 34°46S 173°24E **284** A2
Karimata, Kepulauan *Indonesia* 1°25S 109°0E **235** C3
Karimata, Selat *Indonesia* 2°0S 108°40E **235** C3
Karimata Is. = Karimata, Kepulauan *Indonesia* 1°25S 109°0E **235** C3
Karimganj *India* 24°52N 92°20E **241** C4
Karimnagar *India* 18°26N 79°10E **244** E4
Karimun, Pulau *Indonesia* 1°3N 103°22E **237** d
Karimun Kecil, Pulau *Indonesia* 1°8N 103°22E **237** d
Karimunjawa, Kepulauan *Indonesia* 5°50S 110°30E **235** D4
Karin *Bari, Somalia* 10°59N 49°13E **267** B6
Karin *Woqooyi Galbeed, Somalia* 10°50N 45°52E **267** B6
Karistos *Greece* 38°1N 24°29E **204** C6
Karīt *Iran* 33°29N 56°55E **247** C8
Kariya *Japan* 34°58N 137°1E **223** C9
Kariyangwe *Zimbabwe* 18°0S 27°38E **271** A4
Karjala *Finland* 62°0N 30°25E **188** A5
Karjat *India* 18°33N 75°0E **244** E2
Karkal *India* 13°15N 74°56E **245** H2
Karkar *Papua N. G.* 4°32S 145°57E **286** C3
Karkar I. *Papua N. G.* 4°40S 146°0E **286** C4
Karkaralinsk = Qarqaraly *Kazakhstan* 49°26N 75°30E **217** C9
Karkh *Iraq* 33°20N 44°22E **113** A2
Karkheh → *Iran* 31°2N 47°29E **246** D5
Karki *Azerbaijan* 39°47N 44°57E **213** C11
Karkinitska Zatoka *Ukraine* 45°56N 33°0E **189** K7
Karkinitskiy Zaliv = Karkinitska Zatoka *Ukraine* 45°56N 33°0E **189** K7
Karkuk = Kirkūk *Iraq* 35°30N 44°21E **213** E11
Karkur Tohl *Egypt* 22°5N 25°5E **256** C2
Karl Liebknecht = imeni Karl Libknekhta *Russia* 51°40N 35°35E **189** G8
Karl-Marx-Stadt = Chemnitz *Germany* 50°51N 12°54E **178** E8
Karla, L. = Volvi, L. *Greece* 40°40N 23°34E **202** F7
Karlantijpa North ☼ *Australia* 19°27S 133°33E **278** C5
Karlantijpa South ☼ *Australia* 20°31S 133°9E **278** D5
Karleby = Kokkola *Finland* 63°50N 23°8E **160** E20
Karlholmsbruk *Sweden* 60°31N 17°37E **162** D11
Karlin *Czechia* 50°5N 14°26E **135** B2
Karlino *Poland* 54°3N 15°53E **184** D2
Karlıova *Turkey* 39°17N 41°0E **213** C9
Karlivka *Ukraine* 49°29N 35°8E **189** H8
Karlobag *Croatia* 44°32N 15°5E **199** D12
Karlovac *Croatia* 45°31N 15°36E **199** C12
Karlovarský □ *Czechia* 50°10N 12°50E **180** A5
Karlovasi *Greece* 37°45N 26°42E **205** D8
Karlovka = Karlivka *Ukraine* 49°29N 35°8E **189** H8
Karlovo *Bulgaria* 42°38N 24°47E **203** D8
Karlovo náměstí *Prague, Czechia* **135** c1
Karlovy Vary *Czechia* 50°13N 12°51E **180** A5
Karlowitz = Sremski Karlovci *Serbia* 45°12N 19°56E **182** E4
Karlowitz = Velké Karlovice *Czechia* 49°20N 18°17E **181** B11
Karlsbad = Karlovy Vary *Czechia* 50°13N 12°51E **180** A5
Karlsborg *Sweden* 58°33N 14°33E **163** F8
Karlsburg = Alba-Iulia *Romania* 46°8N 23°39E **183** D8
Karlsena, Mys *Russia* 77°0N 67°42E **214** B7
Karlsfeld *Germany* 48°13N 11°28E **131** A1
Karlshamn *Sweden* 56°10N 14°51E **163** H8
Karlshorst *Germany* 52°29N 13°31E **115** B4
Karlshus *Norway* 59°21N 10°52E **164** E7
Karlskoga *Sweden* 59°28N 14°33E **162** E8
Karlskrona *Sweden* 56°10N 15°35E **163** H9
Karlsplatz *Munich, Germany* **131** b1
Karlsruhe *Germany* 49°0N 8°23E **179** F4
Karlstad = Karlovac *Croatia* 45°31N 15°36E **199** C12
Karlstad *Sweden* 59°23N 13°30E **162** E7
Karlstad *Minn., U.S.A.* 48°35N 96°31W **308** A5
Karlstadt *Germany* 49°57N 9°47E **179** F5
Karluk *U.S.A.* 57°34N 154°28W **303** H9
Karlův most *Prague, Czechia* **135** b1
Karma *Niger* 13°38N 1°52E **263** C5
Karmala *India* 18°25N 75°12E **244** E2
Karmi'el *Israel* 32°55N 35°18E **250** F6
Karmøy *Norway* 59°15N 5°15E **164** E2
Karnak *Egypt* 25°43N 32°39E **256** B3
Karnal *India* 29°42N 77°2E **242** E7
Karnali = Ghaghara → *India* 25°45N 84°40E **243** G11
Karnali → *Nepal* 28°45N 81°16E **243** E9
Karnaphuli Res. = Kaptai L. *Bangla.* 22°40N 92°20E **241** D4
Karnaprayag *India* 30°16N 79°15E **243** D8
Karnataka □ *India* 13°15N 77°0E **245** H3
Karnes City *U.S.A.* 28°53N 97°54W **314** G6
Karnische Alpen *Europe* 46°36N 13°0E **180** E6
Karnobat *Bulgaria* 42°39N 26°59E **203** D10
Kärnten □ *Austria* 46°52N 13°30E **180** E6
Karntner Strasse *Vienna, Austria* **142** b2
Karo *Mali* 12°16N 3°18W **262** C4
Karoi *Zimbabwe* 16°48S 29°45E **269** F2
Karol Bagh *India* 28°39N 77°11E **120** B2
Karolinenhof *Germany* 52°23N 13°38E **115** B4
Karon, Ao *Thailand* 7°51N 98°17E **237** a
Karonga *Malawi* 9°57S 33°55E **269** D3
Karoo △ *S. Africa* 32°18S 22°27E **270** D3
Karoonda *Australia* 35°1S 139°59E **282** C3
Karor *Pakistan* 31°15N 70°59E **242** D4
Karora *Sudan* 17°44N 38°15E **256** D4
Karosa *Indonesia* 1°48S 119°20E **235** C5
Karounga *Mali* 15°20N 7°35W **262** B3
Karousades *Greece* 39°47N 19°45E **206** B9
Karow *Germany* 52°36N 13°29E **115** A3
Karpacz *Poland* 50°46N 15°46E **185** H2
Karpasia *Cyprus* 35°32N 34°15E **207** E10
Karpathos *Greece* 35°37N 27°10E **205** F9
Karpathou, Stenon *Greece* 36°0N 27°30E **205** F9
Karpatsky △ *Ukraine* 48°20N 24°35E **183** B9
Karpenisi *Greece* 38°55N 21°40E **204** C3
Karpilovka = Aktsyabrski *Belarus* 52°38N 28°53E **177** B15
Karpinsk *Russia* 59°45N 60°1E **186** C11
Karpogory *Russia* 64°0N 44°27E **186** B7
Karpuz Burnu = Apostolos Andreas, C. *Cyprus* 35°42N 34°35E **207** E10
Karpuzlu *Turkey* 37°33N 27°51E **205** D9
Karrādah *Iraq* 33°17N 44°23E **113** B2
Karratha *Australia* 20°44S 116°52E **278** D2
Kars *Turkey* 40°40N 43°5E **213** B10
Kars □ *Turkey* 40°40N 43°0E **213** B10
Karsakpay *Kazakhstan* 47°55N 66°40E **217** C7
Karsha *Kazakhstan* 49°45N 51°35E **190** F10
Karshi = Qarshi *Uzbekistan* 38°53N 65°48E **217** E7
Karsiyang *India* 26°56N 88°18E **241** B2
Karsog *India* 31°23N 77°12E **242** D7
Kärsön *Sweden* 59°19N 17°54E **139** B1
Karst = Kras *Slovenia* 45°35N 14°0E **199** C10
Kartal *Turkey* 40°53N 29°11E **203** F13
Kartal Dağları *Turkey* 37°4N 36°55E **250** A7
Kartala *Comoros Is.* 11°45S 43°21E **272** a
Kartaly *Russia* 53°3N 60°40E **216** B6
Kartapur *India* 31°27N 75°32E **242** D6
Karthaus *U.S.A.* 41°8N 78°9W **312** E6
Kartuzy *Poland* 54°22N 18°10E **184** D5
Karuah *Australia* 32°37S 151°56E **283** B9
Karufa *Indonesia* 3°50S 133°20E **231** E8
Karula △ *Estonia* 57°43N 26°30E **188** D4
Karuma ⌂ *Uganda* 2°5N 32°15E **268** B3
Karumba *Australia* 17°31S 140°50E **280** B3
Karumo *Tanzania* 2°25S 32°50E **268** C3
Karumwa *Tanzania* 3°12S 32°38E **268** C3
Kārūn → *Iran* 30°26N 48°10E **247** D6
Karungu *Kenya* 0°50S 34°10E **268** C3
Karup *Denmark* 56°19N 9°10E **163** H3
Karur *India* 10°59N 78°2E **245** J4
Karviná *Czechia* 49°53N 18°31E **181** B11
Karwan → *India* 27°26N 78°4E **242** F8
Karwar *India* 14°55N 74°13E **245** G2
Karwendel ⌂ *Austria* 47°25N 11°30E **180** D4
Karwi *India* 25°12N 80°57E **243** G9
Karymskoye *Russia* 51°36N 114°21E **215** D12
Kas *Sudan* 12°30N 24°17E **259** F4
Kaş *Turkey* 36°11N 29°37E **205** E11
Kasaan *U.S.A.* 55°32N 132°24W **303** J14
Kasaba *Turkey* 36°18N 29°44E **205** E11
Kasabi *Zambia* 14°52S 23°45E **265** E4
Kasache *Malawi* 13°25S 34°20E **269** E3
Kasai *Hyōgo, Japan* 34°55N 134°52E **222** C6
Kasai *Tōkyō, Japan* 35°39N 139°52E **140** B4
Kasaï □ *Dem. Rep. of the Congo* 6°0S 21°0E **265** D4
Kasai → *Dem. Rep. of the Congo* 3°30S 16°10E **265** C3
Kasaï Central □ *Dem. Rep. of the Congo* 6°30S 22°30E **265** D4
Kasai-Oriental □ *Dem. Rep. of the Congo* 6°20S 23°20E **265** D4
Kasaji *Dem. Rep. of the Congo* 10°25S 23°27E **265** E4
Kasama *Japan* 36°23N 140°16E **223** A12
Kasama *Zambia* 10°16S 31°9E **269** E3
Kasan-dong *N. Korea* 41°18N 126°55E **224** B3
Kasane *Namibia* 17°34S 24°50E **270** A3
Kasanga *Tanzania* 8°30S 31°10E **269** D3
Kasangaie *Dem. Rep. of the Congo* 6°20S 22°42E **265** D4
Kasangulu *Dem. Rep. of the Congo* 4°33S 15°15E **265** C3
Kasanka △ *Zambia* 11°34S 30°15E **269** E3
Kasaoka *Japan* 34°30N 133°30E **222** C5
Kasar, Ras *Sudan* 18°2N 38°36E **256** D4
Kasaragod *India* 12°30N 74°58E **245** H2
Kasat *Burma* 15°56N 98°13E **241** G7
Kasba L. *Canada* 60°20N 102°10W **297** A8
Kasba Tadla *Morocco* 32°36N 6°17W **260** B3
Kaschau = Košice *Slovakia* 48°42N 21°15E **181** C14
Kaseda *Japan* 31°25N 130°19E **222** F2
Kāseh Garān *Iran* 34°5N 46°2E **246** C5
Kasempa *Zambia* 13°30S 25°44E **269** E2
Kasenga *Dem. Rep. of the Congo* 10°20S 28°45E **269** E2
Kasese *Uganda* 0°13N 30°3E **268** B3
Kasganj *India* 27°48N 78°42E **243** F8
Kashabowie *Canada* 48°40N 90°26W **298** C1
Kashaf *Iran* 35°58N 61°7E **247** C9
Kāshān *Iran* 34°5N 51°30E **247** C6
Kashechewan *Canada* 52°18N 81°37W **298** B3
Kashgān → *Iran* 33°5N 47°31E **213** F12
Kashgar = Kashi *China* 39°30N 76°2E **217** E9
Kashi *China* 39°30N 76°2E **217** E9
Kashihara *Japan* 34°27N 135°46E **223** C7
Kashiji Plain *Zambia* 13°12S 22°20E **265** E4
Kashima *Ibaraki, Japan* 35°58N 140°38E **223** B12
Kashima *Saga, Japan* 33°7N 130°6E **222** D2
Kashima-Nada *Japan* 36°0N 140°45E **223** B12
Kashimbo *Dem. Rep. of the Congo* 11°12S 26°19E **269** E2
Kashin *Russia* 57°20N 37°36E **188** D9
Kashing = Jiaxing *China* 30°49N 120°45E **229** B13
Kashipur *Odisha, India* 19°16N 83°3E **244** E6
Kashipur *Uttarakhand, India* 29°15N 79°0E **243** E8
Kashira *Russia* 54°45N 38°10E **188** E10
Kashiwa *Japan* 35°52N 139°59E **223** B11
Kashiwabara = Severo-Kurilsk *Russia* 50°40N 156°8E **215** D16
Kashiwazaki *Japan* 37°22N 138°33E **221** F9
Kashk-e Kohneh *Afghan.* 34°55N 62°30E **240** B1
Kashksaray *Iran* 38°27N 45°34E **213** C11
Kashkū'īyeh *Iran* 30°31N 55°40E **247** D7
Kāshmar *Iran* 35°16N 58°26E **247** C8
Kashmir *Asia* 34°0N 76°0E **243** C7
Kashmor *Pakistan* 28°28N 69°32E **242** E3
Kashpirovka *Russia* 53°0N 48°30E **190** D9
Kashun Noerh = Gaxun Nur *China* 42°22N 100°30E **218** C9
Kasiari *India* 22°8N 87°14E **243** H12
Kasilof *U.S.A.* 60°23N 151°18W **303** F10
Kasimov *Russia* 54°55N 41°20E **190** C5
Kasinge *Dem. Rep. of the Congo* 6°15S 26°58E **268** D2
Kasipur *India* 22°37N 88°22E **124** B2
Kasiruta *Indonesia* 0°25S 127°12E **231** E7
Kaskaskia → *U.S.A.* 37°58N 89°57W **310** G7
Kaskattama → *Canada* 57°3N 90°4W **297** B10
Kaskinen *Finland* 62°22N 21°15E **160** E19
Kaskö = Kaskinen *Finland* 62°22N 21°15E **160** E19
Kaslo *Canada* 49°55N 116°55W **296** D5
Kasmere L. *Canada* 59°34N 101°10W **297** B8
Kasongan *Indonesia* 2°0S 113°23E **235** C4
Kasongo *Dem. Rep. of the Congo* 4°30S 26°33E **268** C2
Kasongo Lunda *Dem. Rep. of the Congo* 6°35S 16°49E **265** D3
Kasos *Greece* 35°20N 26°55E **205** F8
Kasou, Stenon *Greece* 35°30N 26°30E **205** F8
Kaspi *Georgia* 41°59N 44°26E **191** K7
Kaspichan *Bulgaria* 43°18N 27°11E **203** C11
Kaspiysk *Russia* 42°52N 47°40E **191** J8
Kaspiyskiy *Russia* 45°22N 47°23E **191** H8
Kassab *Syria* 35°55N 35°59E **250** C6
Kassab ed Doleib *Sudan* 13°30N 33°35E **257** E3
Kassaba *Egypt* 22°40N 29°55E **256** C2
Kassalâ *Sudan* 15°30N 36°0E **257** D4
Kassalâ □ *Sudan* 15°20N 36°26E **257** D4
Kassandra *Greece* 40°0N 23°30E **202** F7
Kassandra Kolpos *Greece* 40°5N 23°30E **202** F7
Kassandras, Akra *Greece* 39°57N 23°30E **202** G7
Kassandria *Greece* 40°1N 23°27E **202** F7
Kassel *Germany* 51°18N 9°26E **178** D5
Kasserine *Tunisia* 35°10N 8°50E **258** A1
Kasserine □ *Tunisia* 35°15N 9°0E **258** A1
Kassinger *Sudan* 18°46N 31°51E **256** D3
Kassiopi *Greece* 39°48N 19°53E **206** B9
Kasson *U.S.A.* 44°2N 92°45W **308** C7
Kastamonu *Turkey* 41°25N 33°43E **212** B5
Kastamonu □ *Turkey* 41°20N 34°0E **212** B5
Kastav *Croatia* 45°22N 14°20E **199** C11
Kasteli = Kissamos *Greece* 35°29N 23°38E **207** E4
Kastellet *Copenhagen, Denmark* **118** a3
Kastelli *Greece* 35°12N 25°20E **207** E6
Kastellorizo = Megisti *Greece* 36°8N 29°34E **205** E11
Kastelo, Akra *Greece* 35°30N 27°15E **205** F9
Kasterlee *Belgium* 51°15N 4°59E **170** C4
Kastlösa *Sweden* 56°26N 16°25E **163** H10
Kastoria *Greece* 40°30N 21°19E **202** F5
Kastorias, L. *Greece* 40°30N 21°20E **202** F5
Kastorio *Greece* 37°10N 22°17E **204** D4
Kastornoye *Russia* 51°55N 38°2E **189** G10
Kastos *Greece* 38°35N 20°55E **207** B2
Kastro = Myrina *Greece* 39°53N 25°4E **205** B7
Kastrom Mefa'a = Umm al Rasas *Jordan* 31°30N 35°55E **251** G6
Kastrosikia *Greece* 39°6N 20°38E **207** A2
Kastrup *Denmark* 55°38N 12°39E **118** B3
Kastrup, København ✈ (CPH) *Denmark* 55°37N 12°39E **118** B3
Kastsyukovichy *Belarus* 53°20N 32°4E **189** F7
Kasubi Tombs *Uganda* 0°20N 32°30E **268** B3
Kasuga *Fukuoka, Japan* 33°32N 130°26E **222** D2
Kasuga *Tōkyō, Japan* 35°45N 139°38E **140** A2
Kasugai *Japan* 35°12N 136°59E **223** B8
Kasuge *Japan* 35°45N 139°49E **140** A3
Kasukabe *Japan* 35°58N 139°49E **223** B11
Kasulu *Tanzania* 4°37S 30°5E **268** C3
Kasumi *Japan* 35°38N 134°38E **222** B6
Kasumiga-Ura *Japan* 36°0N 140°25E **223** B12
Kasumigaseki *Tokyo, Japan* **140** b4
Kasumkent *Russia* 41°47N 48°15E **191** K9
Kasungu *Malawi* 13°0S 33°29E **269** E3
Kasungu △ *Malawi* 12°53S 33°9E **269** E3
Kasur *Pakistan* 31°5N 74°25E **242** D6
Kata, Ao *Thailand* 7°48N 98°18E **237** J2

Kata Archanes *Greece* 35°15N 25°10E **207** E6
Kata Tjuta *Australia* 25°20S 130°50E **279** E5
Kataba *Zambia* 16°5S 25°10E **269** F2
Katagum *Nigeria* 12°18N 10°21E **263** C7
Katahdin, Mt. *U.S.A.* 45°54N 68°56W **309** C19
Kataka = Cuttack *India* 20°25N 85°57E **244** D7
Katako Kombe *Dem. Rep. of the Congo* 3°25S 24°20E **264** C4
Katakolo *Greece* 37°38N 21°19E **204** D3
Katale *Tanzania* 4°52S 31°7E **268** C3
Katalla *U.S.A.* 60°12N 144°31W **303** F11
Katamatite *Australia* 36°6S 145°41E **283** D6
Katanda *Katanga, Dem. Rep. of the Congo* 7°52S 24°13E **265** D4
Katanda *Nord-Kivu, Dem. Rep. of the Congo* 0°55S 29°21E **268** C2
Katanga *Dem. Rep. of the Congo* 8°0S 25°0E **254** G6
Katangi *India* 21°56N 79°50E **244** D4
Katanning *Australia* 33°40S 117°33E **279** F2
Katapakishi *Dem. Rep. of the Congo* 8°15S 22°49E **265** D4
Katastari *Greece* 37°50N 20°45E **207** D2
Katavi □ *Tanzania* 6°0S 31°0E **268** D3
Katavi △ *Tanzania* 6°51S 31°3E **268** D3
Katavi Swamp *Tanzania* 6°50S 31°10E **268** D3
Katchall *India* 7°57N 93°22E **245** L11
Katchiungo *Angola* 12°35S 16°13E **265** E3
Katerini *Greece* 40°18N 22°37E **202** F6
Katghora *India* 22°30N 82°33E **243** H10
Katha *Burma* 24°10N 96°30E **241** C6
Katherîna, Gebel *Egypt* 28°30N 33°57E **251** K4
Katherine *Australia* 14°27S 132°20E **278** B5
Katherine Gorge = Nitmiluk △ *Australia* 14°6S 132°15E **278** B5
Kathi *India* 21°47N 74°3E **242** J6
Kathiawar *India* 22°20N 71°0E **242** H4
Kathikas *Cyprus* 34°55N 32°25E **207** F8
Kathleen *U.S.A.* 28°7N 82°2W **317** G7
Kathmandu *Nepal* 27°45N 85°20E **243** F11
Kathua *India* 32°23N 75°34E **242** C6
Kati *Mali* 12°41N 8°4W **262** C3
Kati Thanda-Lake Eyre *Australia* 29°30S 137°26E **276** F6
Kati Thanda-Lake Eyre (North) *Australia* 28°30S 137°20E **281** D2
Kati Thanda-Lake Eyre (South) *Australia* 29°18S 137°25E **281** D2
Katihar *India* 25°34N 87°36E **243** G12
Katikati *N.Z.* 37°32S 175°57E **284** D4
Katima Mulilo *Namibia* 17°28S 24°13E **270** A3
Katimbira *Malawi* 12°40S 34°0E **269** E3
Katingan = Mendawai → *Indonesia* 3°30S 113°0E **235** C4
Katiola *Ivory C.* 8°10N 5°10W **262** D3
Katipunan *Phil.* 8°31N 123°17E **233** G4
Katiti ☼ *Australia* 25°1S 131°11E **279** E5
Katla *Iceland* 63°36N 19°7W **155** D7
Katlabukh, Ozero *Ukraine* 45°28N 29°0E **183** E14
Katlanovo *Macedonia* 41°52N 21°40E **202** E5
Katmai △ *U.S.A.* 58°20N 155°0W **303** G9
Katmandu = Kathmandu *Nepal* 27°45N 85°20E **243** F11
Katni *India* 23°51N 80°24E **243** H9
Kato Achaia *Greece* 38°8N 21°33E **204** C3
Kato Chorio *Greece* 35°3N 25°47E **207** E6
Kato Korakiana *Greece* 39°42N 19°45E **206** B9
Kato Pyrgos *Cyprus* 35°11N 32°41E **207** E8
Katochi *Greece* 38°26N 21°15E **204** C3
Katol *India* 21°17N 78°38E **244** D4
Katompe *Dem. Rep. of the Congo* 6°2S 26°23E **265** D5
Katong *Singapore* 1°18N 103°53E **138** B3
Katonga → *Uganda* 0°34N 31°50E **268** B3
Katoomba *Australia* 33°41S 150°19E **283** B9
Katouna *Greece* 38°47N 21°7E **204** C3
Katowice *Poland* 50°17N 19°5E **185** H6
Katrancı Dağı *Turkey* 37°27N 30°25E **205** D12
Katrine, L. *U.K.* 56°15N 4°30W **167** E4
Katrineholm *Sweden* 59°0N 16°12E **162** E10
Katsepe *Madag.* 15°45S 46°15E **272** B2
Katsina *Nigeria* 13°0N 7°32E **263** C6
Katsina □ *Nigeria* 12°30N 7°30E **263** C6
Katsina Ala *Nigeria* 7°10N 9°30E **263** D6
Katsina Ala → *Nigeria* 7°10N 9°20E **263** D6
Katsumoto *Japan* 33°51N 129°42E **222** D1
Katsushika *Japan* 35°44N 139°51E **140** A4
Katsuta *Japan* 36°25N 140°31E **223** A12
Katsuura *Japan* 35°10N 140°20E **223** B12
Katsuyama *Fukui, Japan* 36°3N 136°30E **223** A8
Katsuyama *Okayama, Japan* 35°5N 133°41E **222** B5
Kattaqo'rg'on *Uzbekistan* 39°55N 66°15E **217** E7
Kattavia *Greece* 35°57N 27°46E **206** F11
Kattegat *Denmark* 56°40N 11°20E **163** H5
Katthammarsvik *Sweden* 57°26N 18°51E **163** G12
Kattowitz = Katowice *Poland* 50°17N 19°5E **185** H6
Katul, J. *Sudan* 14°12N 29°25E **257** E2
Katumba *Dem. Rep. of the Congo* 7°40S 25°17E **265** D5
Katun → *Russia* 52°25N 85°1E **217** B11
Katwa *India* 23°30N 88°5E **243** H13
Katwijk *Neths.* 52°12N 4°24E **170** B4
Kąty Wrocławskie *Poland* 51°2N 16°45E **185** G3
Ka'ū Desert *U.S.A.* 19°21N 155°19W **302** D6
Kau Pai Chau *Hong Kong, China* 22°12N 114°15E **122** B3
Kau Sai Chau *Hong Kong, China* 22°22N 114°19E **122** A3
Kau-Ye Kyun *Burma* 11°1N 98°32E **237** G2
Kau Yi Chau *Hong Kong, China* 22°17N 114°4E **122** B2
Kaua'i *U.S.A.* 22°3N 159°30W **302** A2
Kauai Channel *U.S.A.* 21°45N 158°50W **302** B3
Kauai Island Lihue Municipal ✈ **(LIH)** *U.S.A.* 21°58N 159°20W **302** B2
Kaub *Germany* 50°5N 7°46E **179** E3
Kaudom ⌓ *Namibia* 18°45S 20°51E **270** A3
Kauehi *French Polynesia* 15°49S 145°10W **289** f
Kaufbeuren *Germany* 47°53N 10°37E **179** H6
Kaufman *U.S.A.* 32°35N 96°19W **314** E6
Kauhajoki *Finland* 62°25N 22°10E **160** E20
Kauhaneva-Pohjankangas △ *Finland* 62°13N 22°20E **160** E20
Kaukauna *U.S.A.* 44°17N 88°17W **308** C9
Kaukauveld *Namibia* 20°0S 20°15E **270** B3
Kaukonahua → *U.S.A.* 21°35N 158°7W **302** J13
Ka'ula I. *U.S.A.* 21°40N 160°33W **302** B1
Kaulakahi Channel *U.S.A.* 22°0N 159°55W **302** B2
Kaulsdorf *Germany* 52°29N 13°34E **115** B4
Kaunā Pt. *U.S.A.* 19°2N 155°53W **302** D6
Kaunakakai *U.S.A.* 21°6N 157°1W **302** B4
Kaunas *Lithuania* 54°54N 23°54E **184** D10
Kaunas ✈ **(KUN)** *Lithuania* 54°57N 24°3E **184** D11
Kaunchi = Yangiyŭl *Uzbekistan* 41°0N 69°3E **217** D7
Kaunghein *Burma* 25°41N 95°26E **241** C5
Kaunia *Bangla.* 25°46N 89°26E **241** C2
Kauniainen *Finland* 60°13N 24°44E **121** B1
Kaunos *Turkey* 36°49N 28°39E **205** E10
Kaupangur *Iceland* 65°38N 18°2W **155** B8
Kaura Namoda *Nigeria* 12°37N 6°33E **263** C6
Kauru *Nigeria* 10°33N 8°12E **263** C6
Kautokeino *Norway* 69°0N 23°4E **160** B20
Kauwapur *India* 27°31N 82°18E **243** F10
Kavacha *Russia* 60°16N 169°51E **215** C17
Kavadarci *Macedonia* 41°26N 22°3E **202** E6
Kavajë *Albania* 41°11N 19°33E **202** E3
Kavak *Turkey* 41°4N 36°3E **212** B7
Kavak Dağı *Turkey* 37°10N 28°2E **205** D10
Kavaklı *Turkey* 41°39N 27°10E **203** E11
Kavaklıdere *Turkey* 37°27N 28°21E **205** D10
Kavaklii = Topolovgrad *Bulgaria* 42°5N 26°20E **203** D10
Kavala *Greece* 40°57N 24°28E **203** F8
Kavala Kolpos *Greece* 40°50N 24°25E **203** F8
Kavalerovo *Russia* 44°15N 135°4E **220** B7
Kavali *India* 14°55N 80°1E **245** G5
Kavango = Cubango → *Africa* 18°50S 22°25E **265** F4
Kavār *Iran* 29°11N 52°44E **247** D7
Kavaratti *India* 10°34N 72°37E **245** J1
Kavaratti I. *India* 10°33N 72°38E **245** J1
Kavarna *Bulgaria* 43°26N 28°22E **203** C12
Kavava *Dem. Rep. of the Congo* 8°52S 22°19E **265** D4
Kaveri = Cauvery → *India* 11°9N 78°52E **245** J4
Kavi *India* 22°12N 72°38E **242** H5
Kavieng *Papua N. G.* 2°36S 150°51E **286** B6
Kavimba *Botswana* 18°2S 24°38E **270** A3
Kavīr, Dasht-e *Iran* 34°30N 55°0E **247** C7
Kavīr △ *Iran* 34°40N 52°0E **247** C7
Kavirondo G. = Winam G. *Kenya* 0°20S 34°15E **268** C3
Kävlinge *Sweden* 55°47N 13°9E **163** J7
Kavos *Greece* 39°23N 20°3E **206** C10
Kavousi *Greece* 35°7N 25°51E **207** E6
Kavungo *Angola* 11°31S 23°3E **265** E4
Kaw *Fr. Guiana* 4°30N 52°15W **329** C7
Kawa *Sudan* 13°42N 32°34E **257** E3
Kawachi-Nagano *Japan* 34°28N 135°31E **223** C7
Kawagama L. *Canada* 45°18N 78°45W **312** A6
Kawagoe *Japan* 35°55N 139°29E **223** B11
Kawaguchi *Japan* 35°52N 139°45E **223** B11
Kawah Ijen △ *Indonesia* 8°3S 114°14E **235** D4
Kawaihae B. *U.S.A.* 20°0N 155°50W **302** C6
Kawaihoa Pt. *U.S.A.* 21°47N 160°12W **302** B1
Kawaikini *U.S.A.* 22°5N 159°29W **302** A2
Kawailoa *U.S.A.* 21°36N 158°3W **302** J13
Kawailoa Beach *U.S.A.* 21°37N 158°5W **302** J13
Kawakawa *N.Z.* 35°23S 174°6E **284** B3
Kawambwa *Zambia* 9°48S 29°3E **269** D2
Kawana *Zambia* 13°5S 25°58E **265** E5
Kawanabe *Japan* 31°23N 130°24E **222** F2
Kawanoe = Shikokochūō *Japan* 34°1N 133°34E **222** C5
Kawardha *India* 22°0N 81°17E **243** J9
Kawasaki *Japan* 35°31N 139°43E **140** B3
Kawasi *Indonesia* 1°38S 127°28E **231** E7
Kawau I. *N.Z.* 36°25S 174°52E **284** C3
Kawawa *Japan* 35°31N 139°33E **140** B2
Kawawachikamach *Canada* 54°48N 66°50W **299** B6
Kawęczyn *Poland* 52°16N 21°5E **143** B2
Kaweka Ra. *N.Z.* 39°17S 176°19E **284** F5
Kawela *U.S.A.* 21°42N 158°1W **302** J13
Kawerau *N.Z.* 38°7S 176°42E **284** E5
Kawhia *N.Z.* 38°4S 174°49E **284** E3
Kawhia Harbour *N.Z.* 38°5S 174°51E **284** E3
Kawio, Kepulauan *Indonesia* 4°30N 125°30E **231** D7
Kawkareik *Burma* 16°33N 98°14E **241** G7
Kawlin *Burma* 23°47N 95°41E **241** D5
Kawthaung *Burma* 10°5N 98°36E **237** H2
Kawthoolei = Kayin □ *Burma* 18°0N 97°30E **241** G6
Kawthule = Kayin □ *Burma* 18°0N 97°30E **241** G6
Kawya *Burma* 24°50N 94°58E **241** C5
Kaxgar He → *China* 39°45N 78°24E **217** E9
Kaxholmen *Sweden* 57°51N 14°19E **163** G8
Kaya *Burkina Faso* 13°4N 1°10W **263** C4
Kayah □ *Burma* 19°15N 97°15E **241** F6
Kayak I. *U.S.A.* 59°56N 144°23W **303** G11
Kayalıköy Barajı *Turkey* 41°50N 27°5E **203** E11
Kayamkulam *India* 9°10N 76°33E **245** K3
Kayan *Burma* 16°54N 96°34E **241** G6
Kayan → *Indonesia* 2°55N 117°35E **235** B5
Kayan Mentarang △ *Indonesia* 2°25N 115°30E **235** B5
Kaycee *U.S.A.* 43°43N 106°38W **304** E10
Kayeli *Indonesia* 3°20S 127°10E **231** E7
Kayenda *Dem. Rep. of the Congo* 10°48S 23°6E **265** E4
Kayenta *U.S.A.* 36°44N 110°15W **305** H8
Kayes *Congo* 4°25S 11°41E **265** C2
Kayes *Mali* 14°25N 11°30W **262** C2
Kayes □ *Mali* 14°0N 11°0W **262** C2
Kayı *Turkey* 39°12N 30°46E **205** B12
Kayima *S. Leone* 8°54N 11°15W **262** D2
Kayin □ *Burma* 18°0N 97°30E **241** G6
Kaymakçı *Turkey* 38°10N 28°8E **205** C10
Kayoa *Indonesia* 0°1N 127°28E **231** D7
Kayombo *Zambia* 13°3S 23°51E **265** E4
Kaysatskoye *Russia* 49°47N 46°49E **190** F8
Kayseri *Turkey* 38°45N 35°30E **212** C6
Kayseri □ *Turkey* 38°40N 36°0E **212** C7
Kaysville *U.S.A.* 41°2N 111°56W **304** F8
Kayts *Sri Lanka* 9°42N 79°51E **245** K4
Kayu Putih *Indonesia* 6°10S 106°53E **122** B2
Kayuagung *Indonesia* 3°24S 104°50E **234** C2
Kaz Dağı *Turkey* 39°42N 26°50E **205** B8
Kazachye *Russia* 70°52N 135°58E **215** B14
Kazakhstan ■ *Asia* 50°0N 70°0E **217** C8
Kazaly = Qazaly *Kazakhstan* 45°45N 62°6E **216** C6
Kazan *Russia* 55°50N 49°10E **190** C9
Kazan *Turkey* 40°14N 32°41E **212** B5
Kazan → *Canada* 64°2N 95°29W **297** A9
Kazan-Rettō *Pac. Oc.* 25°0N 141°0E **288** E6
Kazancı *Turkey* 36°29N 32°51E **250** B3
Kazanlăk *Bulgaria* 42°38N 25°20E **203** D9
Kazanlı *Turkey* 36°49N 34°43E **250** B5
Kazanskaya *Russia* 49°50N 41°10E **190** F5
Kazatin = Kozyatyn *Ukraine* 49°45N 28°50E **177** D15
Kazaure *Nigeria* 12°42N 8°28E **263** C6
Kazbek *Russia* 42°42N 44°30E **191** J7
Kāzerūn *Iran* 29°38N 51°40E **247** D6
Kazi Magomed = Qazımämmäd *Azerbaijan* 40°3N 49°0E **191** K9
Kazimierz Dolny *Poland* 51°19N 21°57E **185** G8
Kazimierza Wielka *Poland* 50°15N 20°30E **185** H7
Kazincbarcika *Hungary* 48°17N 20°36E **182** B5
Kazipet *India* 17°58N 79°30E **244** F4
Kaziranga △ *India* 26°40N 93°30E **241** B4
Kaziza *Dem. Rep. of the Congo* 10°42S 23°52E **265** E4
Kazlų Rūda *Lithuania* 54°46N 23°30E **184** D10
Kazo *Japan* 36°7N 139°36E **223** A11
Kaztalovka *Kazakhstan* 49°47N 48°43E **190** F9
Kazu *Burma* 25°27N 97°46E **241** C6
Kazuma Pan △ *Zimbabwe* 18°20S 25°48E **269** F2
Kazumba *Dem. Rep. of the Congo* 6°25S 22°5E **265** D4
Kazungula *Zambia* 17°35S 25°15E **265** F5
Kazuno *Japan* 40°10N 140°45E **220** D10
Kazym → *Russia* 63°54N 65°50E **214** C7
Kbely *Czechia* 50°8N 14°32E **135** B3
Kcynia *Poland* 53°0N 17°30E **185** F4
Ke-hsi Mansam *Burma* 21°56N 97°50E **241** E6
Ké-Macina *Mali* 13°58N 5°22W **262** C3
Kea *Greece* 37°35N 24°22E **204** D6
Kea'au *U.S.A.* 19°37N 155°2W **302** D6
Keady *U.K.* 54°15N 6°42W **166** B5
Keahi Pt. *U.S.A.* 21°19N 157°59W **302** K14
Keahole Pt. *U.S.A.* 19°44N 156°4W **302** D5
Kealaikahiki Channel *U.S.A.* 20°35N 156°50W **302** C5
Kealakekua *U.S.A.* 19°31N 155°55W **302** D6
Kearney *Mo., U.S.A.* 39°22N 94°22W **310** E2
Kearney *Nebr., U.S.A.* 40°42N 99°5W **308** E4
Kearney ☼ *Australia* 20°10S 128°4E **278** D4
Kearny *U.S.A.* 33°3N 110°55W **305** K8
Kearsarge, Mt. *U.S.A.* 43°22N 71°50W **313** C13
Keban *Turkey* 38°50N 38°50E **213** C8
Keban Barajı *Turkey* 38°41N 38°33E **213** C8
Kebara *Congo* 2°27S 14°25E **264** C2
Kebayoran Baru *Indonesia* 6°14S 106°47E **122** B1
Kebayoran Lama *Indonesia* 6°13S 106°46E **122** B1
Kebbi □ *Nigeria* 11°35N 4°0E **263** C5
Kébémèr *Senegal* 15°23N 16°34W **262** B1
Kébi *Ivory C.* 9°18N 6°37W **262** D3
Kebi, Mayo → *Cameroon* 9°18N 13°33E **264** A2
Kébili *Tunisia* 33°47N 9°0E **258** B1
Kébili □ *Tunisia* 33°30N 8°50E **261** B6
Kebnekaise *Sweden* 67°53N 18°33E **160** C18
Kebon Jeruk *Indonesia* 6°11S 106°46E **122** B1
Kebri Dehar *Ethiopia* 6°45N 44°17E **267** C5
Kebumen *Indonesia* 7°42S 109°40E **235** D3
Kecel *Hungary* 46°31N 19°16E **182** D4
Kechika → *Canada* 59°41N 127°12W **296** B3
Keçiborlu *Turkey* 37°57N 30°18E **205** D12
Kecskemét *Hungary* 46°57N 19°42E **182** D4
Kedada *Ethiopia* 5°25N 35°58E **257** F4
Kedah □ *Malaysia* 5°50N 100°40E **237** K3
Kėdainiai *Lithuania* 55°15N 24°2E **184** C11
Kedar *West Bank* 31°44N 35°18E **123** B2
Kedarnath *India* 30°44N 79°4E **243** D8
Kedgwick *Canada* 47°40N 67°20W **299** C6
Kediet Ijill *Mauritania* 22°38N 12°33W **260** D2
Kediri *Indonesia* 7°51S 112°1E **235** D4
Kedja *Dem. Rep. of the Congo* 4°50N 19°16E **264** B3
Kedjebi *Ghana* 8°12N 0°25E **263** D5
Kédougou *Senegal* 12°35N 12°10W **262** C2
Kedoya *Indonesia* 6°10S 106°45E **122** B1
Kedros Oros *Greece* 35°11N 24°37E **207** E5
Kędzierzyn-Koźle *Poland* 50°20N 18°12E **185** H5
Ke'ehi Lagoon *U.S.A.* 21°20N 157°54W **302** K14
Keeler *U.S.A.* 36°29N 117°52W **306** J9
Keeley L. *Canada* 54°54N 108°8W **297** C7
Keeling Is. = Cocos Is. *Ind. Oc.* 12°10S 96°55E **273** F8
Keelung = Chilung *Taiwan* 25°3N 121°45E **225** A3
Keenapusan *Phil.* 6°50N 118°50E **233** H2
Keene *Ont., Canada* 44°15N 78°10W **312** B6
Keene *Calif., U.S.A.* 35°13N 118°33W **307** K8
Keene *N.H., U.S.A.* 42°56N 72°17W **313** D12
Keene *N.Y., U.S.A.* 44°16N 73°46W **313** B11
Keep River △ *Australia* 15°49S 129°8E **278** C4
Keeper Hill *Ireland* 52°45N 8°16W **166** D3
Keepit, L. *Australia* 30°50S 150°30E **283** A9
Keerweer, C. *Australia* 14°0S 141°32E **280** A3
Keeseville *U.S.A.* 44°29N 73°30W **313** B11
Keetmanshoop *Namibia* 26°35S 18°8E **270** C2
Keewatin *Canada* 49°46N 94°34W **297** D10
Keewatin → *Canada* 56°29N 100°46W **297** B8
Kefa *Ethiopia* 6°55N 36°30E **257** F4
Kefalonia *Greece* 38°15N 20°30E **207** C2
Kefalonia ✈ **(EFL)** *Greece* 38°10N 20°30E **207** C1
Kefalos *Greece* 36°45N 26°59E **205** E8
Kefamenanu *Indonesia* 9°28S 124°29E **231** F6
Kefar Sava *Israel* 32°11N 34°54E **251** F5
Keffi *Nigeria* 8°55N 7°43E **263** D6
Keffin Hausa *Nigeria* 12°13N 9°59E **263** C6
Keflavík *Iceland* 64°2N 22°35W **155** C4
Keflavík ✈ **(KEF)** *Iceland* 64°0N 22°45W **155** C4
Keftya *Ethiopia* 13°54N 37°7E **257** E4
Keg River *Canada* 57°54N 117°55W **296** B5
Kegalla *Sri Lanka* 7°15N 80°21E **245** L5
Kegaska *Canada* 50°9N 61°18W **299** B7
Kehancha *Kenya* 1°11S 34°37E **268** C3
Keheili *Sudan* 19°25N 32°50E **256** D3
Kehena *U.S.A.* 19°23N 154°55W **302** D7
Kehl *Germany* 48°34N 7°50E **179** G3
Kei Ling Ha *Hong Kong, China* 22°25N 114°16E **122** A3
Keibul Lamjao △ *India* 24°30N 93°55E **241** C4
Keighley *U.K.* 53°52N 1°54W **168** D6
Keijo = Seoul *S. Korea* 37°31N 126°58E **137** B2
Keila *Estonia* 59°18N 24°25E **188** C3
Keilor *Australia* 37°42S 144°50E **128** A1
Keilor North *Australia* 37°44S 144°51E **128** A1
Keimoes *S. Africa* 28°41S 20°59E **270** C3
Keimola *Finland* 60°20N 24°49E **121** A1
Keita *Niger* 14°46N 5°56E **263** C6
Keïta, B. → *Chad* 9°14N 18°21E **259** G3
Keitele *Finland* 63°10N 26°20E **160** E22
Keith *S. Austral., Australia* 36°6S 140°20E **282** D4
Keith *Moray, U.K.* 57°32N 2°57W **167** D6
Keithsburg *U.S.A.* 41°6N 90°56W **310** C6
Keiyasi *Fiji* 17°53S 177°46E **287** A1
Keizer *U.S.A.* 44°57N 123°1W **304** D2
Kejimkujik △ *Canada* 44°25N 65°25W **299** D6
Kejserr Franz Joseph Fd. *Greenland* 73°30N 24°30W **154** C8
Kekaha *U.S.A.* 21°58N 159°43W **302** B2
Kekri *India* 26°0N 75°10E **242** G6
Keksgolm = Priozersk *Russia* 61°2N 30°7E **188** B6
Kelafo *Ethiopia* 5°37N 44°8E **267** C5
Kelam *Ethiopia* 4°48N 35°58E **257** G4
Kelamet *Eritrea* 16°0N 38°30E **257** D4
Kelan *China* 38°43N 111°31E **226** E6
Kelang = Klang *Malaysia* 3°2N 101°26E **237** L3
Kelani Ganga → *Sri Lanka* 6°58N 79°50E **245** L4
Kelantan □ *Malaysia* 5°10N 102°0E **237** K3
Kelantan → *Malaysia* 6°13N 102°14E **237** J4
Kelapa Gading *Indonesia* 6°9S 106°52E **122** A2
Kelberg *U.S.A.* 32°42N 96°36W **120** B6
Këlcyrë *Albania* 40°20N 20°12E **202** F4
Kelekçi *Turkey* 37°15N 29°20E **205** D11
Kelenföld *Hungary* 47°27N 19°2E **117** B2
Keles *Turkey* 39°54N 29°14E **203** G13
Keleti-főcsatorna *Hungary* 47°45N 21°20E **182** C6
Kelheim *Germany* 48°54N 11°52E **179** G7
Kelibia *Tunisia* 36°50N 11°3E **258** A2
Kelkit *Turkey* 40°7N 39°16E **213** B8
Kelkit → *Turkey* 40°45N 36°32E **212** B7
Kellé *Congo* 0°8S 14°38E **264** C2
Kellé *Niger* 14°16N 10°7E **263** C7
Keller *Ga., U.S.A.* 31°50N 81°15W **316** D8
Keller *Tex., U.S.A.* 32°56N 97°15W **120** A2
Kellerberrin *Australia* 31°36S 117°38E **279** F2
Kellett, C. *Canada* 72°0N 126°0W **150** B1
Kelleys I. *U.S.A.* 41°36N 82°42W **312** E2
Kellogg *U.S.A.* 47°32N 116°7W **304** C5
Kells *Ireland* 53°44N 6°53W **166** C5
Kelmė *Lithuania* 55°38N 22°56E **184** C9
Kelmentsi *Ukraine* 48°28N 26°50E **183** B11
Kélo *Chad* 9°10N 15°45E **259** G3
Kelokedhara *Cyprus* 34°48N 32°39E **207** F8
Kelowna *Canada* 49°50N 119°25W **296** D5
Kelsey Creek *Australia* 20°26S 148°31E **280** b
Kelseyville *U.S.A.* 38°59N 122°50W **306** G4
Kelso *N.Z.* 45°54S 169°15E **285** F4
Kelso *Borders, U.K.* 55°36N 2°26W **167** F6
Kelso *Wash., U.S.A.* 46°9N 122°54W **306** D4
Keluang = Kluang *Malaysia* 2°3N 103°18E **237** L4
Kelud *Indonesia* 7°56N 112°18E **231** H15
Kelvin *S. Africa* 26°4S 28°5E **123** A2
Kelvington *Canada* 52°10N 103°30W **297** C8
Kem *Russia* 65°0N 34°38E **186** B5
Kem → *Russia* 64°57N 34°41E **186** B5
Kem-Kem *Morocco* 30°40N 4°30W **260** B4
Kema *Indonesia* 1°22N 125°8E **231** D7
Kemah *Turkey* 39°32N 39°5E **213** C8
Kemaliye *Erzincan, Turkey* 39°16N 38°29E **213** C8
Kemaliye *Manisa, Turkey* 38°27N 28°25E **205** C10
Kemalpaşa *Turkey* 38°25N 27°27E **205** C9
Kemaman *Malaysia* 4°12N 103°18E **237** K4
Kemang *Indonesia* 6°15S 106°48E **122** B1
Kemano *Canada* 53°35N 128°0W **296** C3
Kemapyu *Burma* 18°49N 97°19E **241** F6
Kemasik *Malaysia* 4°25N 103°27E **237** K4
Kemayoran *Indonesia* 6°10S 106°51E **122** B2
Kembé *C.A.R.* 4°36N 21°54E **264** B4
Kembolcha *Ethiopia* 11°2N 39°42E **257** E4
Kemer *Antalya, Turkey* 36°36N 30°34E **205** E12
Kemer *Burdur, Turkey* 37°21N 30°4E **205** D12
Kemer *Muğla, Turkey* 36°40N 29°22E **205** E11
Kemer Barajı *Turkey* 37°30N 28°37E **205** D10
Kemerburgaz *Turkey* 41°9N 28°54E **122** B1
Kemerovo *Russia* 55°20N 86°5E **214** D9
Kemerovo □ *Russia* 55°0N 86°0E **217** B11
Ķemeru △ *Latvia* 56°58N 23°25E **184** B10
Kemi *Finland* 65°44N 24°34E **160** D21
Kemi älv = Kemijoki → *Finland* 65°47N 24°32E **160** D21
Kemi träsk = Kemijärvi *Finland* 66°43N 27°22E **160** C22
Kemijärvi *Finland* 66°43N 27°22E **160** C22
Kemijoki → *Finland* 65°47N 24°32E **160** D21
Kemmerer *U.S.A.* 41°48N 110°32W **304** F8
Kemmuna = Comino *Malta* 36°1N 14°20E **206** E7
Kémo □ *C.A.R.* 6°0N 19°0E **264** A3
Kemp, L. *U.S.A.* 33°46N 99°9W **314** E5
Kemp Land *Antarctica* 69°0S 55°0E **151** C5
Kempas *Malaysia* 1°33N 103°42E **237** d
Kempen = Kępno *Poland* 51°18N 17°58E **185** G4
Kempsey *Australia* 31°1S 152°50E **283** A10
Kempt, L. *Canada* 47°25N 74°22W **298** C5
Kempten *Germany* 47°45N 10°17E **179** H6
Kempton *Tas., Australia* 42°31S 147°12E **281** G4
Kempton *Ind., U.S.A.* 40°17N 86°14W **311** D10
Kempton Park Races *U.K.* 51°24N 0°23W **125** B1
Kemptville *Canada* 45°0N 75°38W **313** B9
Ken → *India* 25°13N 80°27E **243** G9
Kenadsa *Algeria* 31°48N 2°26W **261** B4
Kenai *U.S.A.* 60°33N 151°16W **303** F10
Kenai Fjords △ *U.S.A.* 59°40N 149°50W **303** G10
Kenai Mts. *U.S.A.* 60°0N 150°0W **303** G10
Kenai Nat. Wildlife Refuge ⌓ *U.S.A.* 60°20N 150°30W **303** F10
Kenamuke Swamp *South Sudan* 5°55N 33°48E **257** F3
Kenansville *U.S.A.* 27°53N 80°59W **317** H9
Kendai *India* 22°45N 82°37E **243** H10
Kendal *Indonesia* 6°56S 110°14E **235** D4
Kendal *Cumb., U.K.* 54°20N 2°44W **168** C5
Kendall *N.S.W., Australia* 31°35S 152°44E **283** A10
Kendall *Fla., U.S.A.* 25°40N 80°19W **129** D1
Kendall → *Australia* 14°4S 141°35E **280** A3
Kendallville *U.S.A.* 41°27N 85°16W **311** C11
Kendari *Indonesia* 3°50S 122°30E **231** E6
Kendawangan *Indonesia* 2°32S 110°17E **235** C4
Kende *Nigeria* 11°30N 4°12E **263** C5
Kendégué *Chad* 10°0N 18°36E **259** F3
Kendi, Pulau *Malaysia* 5°13N 100°11E **237** c
Kendrapara *India* 20°35N 86°30E **244** D8
Këndrevicës, Maja e *Albania* 40°15N 19°52E **202** F3
Kendrew *S. Africa* 32°32S 24°30E **270** D3
Kendrick *U.S.A.* 29°15N 82°10W **317** F7
Kene Thao *Laos* 17°44N 101°10E **236** D3
Kenedy *U.S.A.* 28°49N 97°51W **314** G6
Kenema *S. Leone* 7°50N 11°14W **262** D2
Keng Kok *Laos* 16°26N 105°12E **236** D5
Keng Tawng *Burma* 20°45N 98°18E **241** E7
Keng Tung *Burma* 21°18N 99°39E **236** B2
Kengani *Dem. Rep. of the Congo* 2°59S 17°36E **264** C3
Kenge *Dem. Rep. of the Congo* 4°50S 17°4E **265** C3
Kengeja *Tanzania* 5°26S 39°45E **268** D4
Kenhardt *S. Africa* 29°19S 21°12E **270** C3
Kéniéba *Mali* 12°54N 11°17W **262** C2
Kenilworth *Western Cape, S. Africa* 33°59S 18°27E **118** A1
Kenilworth *Ill., U.S.A.* 42°5N 87°43W **119** A2
Keningau *Malaysia* 5°20N 116°10E **235** A5
Kenitra *Morocco* 34°15N 6°40W **260** B3
Kenli *China* 37°30N 118°20E **227** F10
Kenmare *Kerry, Ireland* 51°53N 9°36W **166** E2
Kenmare *N. Dak., U.S.A.* 48°41N 102°5W **308** A2
Kenmare River → *Ireland* 51°48N 9°51W **166** E2
Kennebago Lake *U.S.A.* 45°4N 70°40W **313** A14
Kennebec *U.S.A.* 43°54N 99°52W **308** D4
Kennebec → *U.S.A.* 43°45N 69°46W **309** D19
Kennebunk *U.S.A.* 43°23N 70°33W **313** C14
Kennedale *U.S.A.* 32°38N 97°13W **120** C2
Kennedy *Zimbabwe* 18°52S 27°10E **270** A4
Kennedy, C. = Canaveral, C. *U.S.A.* 28°27N 80°32W **317** G9
Kennedy Channel *Arctic* 80°50N 66°0W **154** A4
Kennedy Entrance *U.S.A.* 59°1N 152°0W **303** G10
Kennedy Ra. *Australia* 24°45S 115°10E **279** D2
Kennedy Range △ *Australia* 24°34S 115°2E **279** D2
Kennedy Space Center *U.S.A.* 28°40N 80°42W **317** G9
Kennedy Town *Hong Kong, China* 22°16N 114°6E **122** B2
Kennemerduinen △ *Neths.* 52°27N 4°33E **170** B4
Kenner *U.S.A.* 29°59N 90°14W **131** A1
Kennesaw *U.S.A.* 34°1N 84°37W **316** A5
Kennet → *U.K.* 51°27N 0°57W **169** F7
Kenneth Hahn State Recreation Area ⌓ *Los Angeles, U.S.A.* 34°1N 118°21W **126** B2
Kenneth Ra. *Australia* 23°50S 117°8E **279** D2
Kennett *U.S.A.* 36°14N 90°3W **308** G8
Kennewick *U.S.A.* 46°12N 119°7W **304** C4
Kennington *London, U.K.* **125** c4
Kennisis Lake *Canada* 45°13N 78°36W **312** A6
Kenogami → *Canada* 51°6N 84°28W **298** B3
Kenora *Canada* 49°47N 94°29W **297** D10
Kenosha *U.S.A.* 42°35N 87°49W **311** B9
Kenozersky △ *Russia* 62°5N 38°10E **214** C1
Kensal Green *U.K.* 51°32N 0°13W **125** A2
Kensal Rise *London, U.K.* **125** a1
Kensington *N.S.W., Australia* 33°54S 151°13E **139** B2
Kensington *P.E.I., Canada* 46°28N 63°34W **299** C7
Kensington *Gauteng, S. Africa* 26°11S 28°6E **123** B2
Kensington *London, U.K.* 51°29N 0°10W **125** B2
Kensington *N.Y., U.S.A.* 40°38N 73°57W **132** C2
Kensington Palace *U.K.* 51°30N 0°11W **125** A2
Kent *Ohio, U.S.A.* 41°9N 81°22W **312** E3
Kent *Tex., U.S.A.* 31°4N 104°13W **314** F2
Kent *Wash., U.S.A.* 47°22N 122°14W **306** C4
Kent □ *U.K.* 51°12N 0°40E **169** F8
Kent Group *Australia* 39°30S 147°20E **281** F4
Kent Pen. *Canada* 68°30N 107°0W **294** D10
Kentaū *Kazakhstan* 43°32N 68°36E **217** D7
K'enting △ *Taiwan* 21°57N 120°48E **225** E2
Kentish Town *U.K.* 51°32N 0°8W **125** A3
Kentland *U.S.A.* 40°46N 87°27W **311** D9
Kenton *London, U.K.* 51°34N 0°17W **125** A2
Kenton *Ohio, U.S.A.* 40°39N 83°37W **311** D13
Kentucky □ *U.S.A.* 37°0N 84°0W **309** G11
Kentucky → *U.S.A.* 38°41N 85°11W **311** F11
Kentucky L. *U.S.A.* 37°1N 88°16W **308** G9
Kentville *Canada* 45°6N 64°29W **299** C7
Kentwood *La., U.S.A.* 30°56N 90°31W **315** F9
Kentwood *Mich., U.S.A.* 42°52N 85°39W **311** B11
Kenwood House *U.K.* 51°34N 0°9W **125** A3
Kenya ■ *Africa* 1°0N 38°0E **268** B4
Kenya, Mt. *Kenya* 0°10S 37°18E **268** C4
Kenyir, Tasik *Malaysia* 5°1N 102°54E **237** K4
Kenzou *Cameroon* 4°10N 15°2E **264** B3
Keo Neua, Deo *Vietnam* 18°23N 105°10E **236** C5
Keokuk *U.S.A.* 40°24N 91°24W **310** D5
Keoladeo △ *India* 27°0N 77°20E **242** F7
Keonjhargarh *India* 21°28N 85°35E **243** J11
Keosauqua *U.S.A.* 40°44N 91°58W **310** D5
Keota *U.S.A.* 41°22N 91°57W **310** C5
Kep *Cambodia* 10°29N 104°19E **237** G5
Kep *Vietnam* 21°24N 106°16E **236** B6
Kep △ *Cambodia* 10°30N 104°18E **237** G5
Kepa *Poland* 52°13N 21°3E **143** B2
Kepala Batas *Malaysia* 5°31N 100°26E **237** c
Kepez *Turkey* 40°5N 26°24E **203** F10
Kepi *Indonesia* 6°32S 139°19E **231** F9
Kępice *Poland* 54°16N 16°51E **184** D3
Kepler Mts. *N.Z.* 45°25S 167°20E **285** F2
Kępno *Poland* 51°18N 17°58E **185** G4
Keppel Harbour *Singapore* 1°15N 103°49E **138** B2
Keppel Pt. *Papua N. G.* 10°10S 147°58E **286** F4
Kepsut *Turkey* 39°40N 28°9E **205** B10
Kepuhi Pt. *U.S.A.* 21°29N 158°14W **302** K13
Kepulauan Karimunjawa △ *Indonesia* 5°50S 110°25E **235** D4
Kerala □ *India* 11°0N 76°15E **245** J3
Keram → *Papua N. G.* 4°7S 144°5E **286** C3
Kerama-Rettō *Japan* 26°5N 127°15E **221** L3
Keramikos *Athens, Greece* **112** b1
Keramoti *Greece* 40°52N 24°42E **203** F8
Keran *Pakistan* 34°35N 73°59E **243** B5
Keran △ *Togo* 10°9N 0°41E **263** C5
Kerang *Vic., Australia* 35°40S 143°55E **282** C5
Kerang *Indonesia* 2°15S 116°3E **235** C5
Keranyo *Ethiopia* 5°3N 38°18E **257** F4
Kerao → *South Sudan* 11°0N 32°41E **257** E3
Keratea *Greece* 37°48N 23°58E **204** D5
Keraudren, C. *Australia* 19°58S 119°45E **278** C2
Kerava *Finland* 60°25N 25°5E **188** B3
Keravat *Papua N. G.* 4°17S 152°2E **286** C7
Kerch *Ukraine* 45°20N 36°20E **189** K9
Kerchenskiy Proliv *Black Sea* 45°10N 36°30E **189** K9
Kerchoual *Mali* 17°12N 0°20E **263** B5
Kerema *Papua N. G.* 7°58S 145°50E **286** D3
Kerempe Burnu *Turkey* 42°2N 33°20E **212** A5
Keren *Eritrea* 15°45N 38°28E **257** D4
Kerepakupai-Meru = Angel Falls *Venezuela* 5°57N 62°30W **329** B5
Kerewan *Gambia* 13°29N 16°10W **262** C1
Kerguelen *Ind. Oc.* 49°15S 69°10E **273** J5
Kerguelen Plateau *S. Ocean* 55°0S 75°0E **273** K6
Keri *Greece* 37°40N 20°49E **207** D2
Keri Kera *Sudan* 12°21N 32°42E **257** E3
Kerian, Kuala *Malaysia* 5°10N 100°25E **237** c
Kericho *Kenya* 0°22S 35°15E **268** C4
Kerikeri *N.Z.* 35°12S 173°59E **284** B2
Kerinci *Indonesia* 1°40S 101°15E **234** C2
Kerinci Seblat △ *Indonesia* 2°30S 101°30E **234** C1
Kerintji = Kerinci *Indonesia* 1°40S 101°15E **234** C2
Keriya He → *China* 38°30N 82°10E **217** E10
Kerkenna, Îs. *Tunisia* 34°48N 11°11E **258** B2
Kerki = Atamyrat *Turkmenistan* 37°50N 65°12E **217** E7
Kerkini, L. *Greece* 41°12N 23°10E **202** E7
Kerkouane *Tunisia* 36°58N 11°2E **200** F4
Kerkrade *Neths.* 50°53N 6°4E **170** D6
Kerkyra *Greece* 39°38N 19°50E **206** B9
Kerkyra ✈ **(CFU)** *Greece* 39°35N 19°54E **204** B1
Kerkyras, Notio Steno *Greece* 39°34N 20°0E **206** B10
Kerma *Sudan* 19°33N 30°32E **256** D3
Kermadec Is. *Pac. Oc.* 30°0S 178°15W **277** G15
Kermadec Trench *Pac. Oc.* 30°30S 176°0W **277** G15
Kermān *Iran* 30°15N 57°1E **247** D8
Kerman *Calif., U.S.A.* 36°43N 120°4W **306** J6
Kermān □ *Iran* 30°0N 57°0E **247** D8
Kermān, Bīābān-e *Iran* 28°45N 59°45E **247** D8
Kermānshāh *Iran* 34°23N 47°0E **213** E12
Kermānshāh □ *Iran* 34°0N 46°30E **246** C5
Kermen *Bulgaria* 42°30N 26°16E **203** D10
Kermine = Navoiy *Uzbekistan* 40°9N 65°22E **216** D7
Kermit *U.S.A.* 31°52N 103°6W **314** F3
Kern → *U.S.A.* 35°16N 119°18W **307** K7
Kernavė *Lithuania* 54°53N 24°49E **188** E3
Kernhof *Austria* 47°49N 15°32E **180** D8
Kernow = Cornwall □ *U.K.* 50°26N 4°40W **169** G3
Kernville *U.S.A.* 35°45N 118°26W **307** K8
Keroh *Malaysia* 5°43N 101°1E **237** K3
Keros *Greece* 36°54N 25°40E **205** E7
Kérou *Benin* 10°50N 2°5E **263** C5
Kérouane *Guinea* 9°15N 9°0W **262** D3
Kerowagi *Papua N. G.* 5°51S 144°51E **286** C3
Kerpen *Germany* 50°51N 6°41E **178** E2
Kerrera *U.K.* 56°24N 5°33W **167** E3
Kerrobert *Canada* 51°56N 109°8W **297** C7
Kerrville *U.S.A.* 30°3N 99°8W **314** F5
Kerry □ *Ireland* 52°7N 9°35W **166** D2
Kerry Hd. *Ireland* 52°25N 9°56W **166** D2
Kersa *Ethiopia* 9°28N 41°48E **257** F5
Kertosono *Indonesia* 7°38S 112°9E **235** D4
Kerulen = Herlen → *Asia* 48°48N 117°0E **219** B12
Kervo = Kerava *Finland* 60°25N 25°5E **188** B3
Kerzaz *Algeria* 29°29N 1°37W **261** C4
Kesagami → *Canada* 51°40N 79°45W **298** B4
Kesagami L. *Canada* 50°23N 80°15W **298** B3
Keşan *Turkey* 40°49N 26°38E **203** F10
Kesariani *Greece* 37°57N 23°46E **112** B2
Kesennuma *Japan* 38°54N 141°35E **220** E10
Keshāvar *Iran* 36°50N 46°22E **213** D12
Keshit *Iran* 29°43N 58°17E **247** D8
Kesigi = Kosgi *India* 15°51N 77°16E **245** G3
Keşiş Dağ *Turkey* 39°47N 39°46E **213** C8
Keskal *India* 20°5N 81°35E **244** D5
Keskin *Turkey* 39°40N 33°36E **212** C5
Kestenga *Russia* 65°50N 31°45E **160** D24
Keswick *U.K.* 54°36N 3°8W **168** C4
Keszthely *Hungary* 46°50N 17°15E **182** D2
Ket → *Russia* 58°55N 81°32E **214** D9
Keta *Ghana* 5°49N 1°0E **263** D5
Keta Lagoon *Ghana* 5°55N 1°0E **263** D5
Ketapang *Jawa Timur, Indonesia* 8°9S 114°23E **231** J17
Ketapang *Kalimantan Barat, Indonesia* 1°55S 110°0E **235** C4
Ketchenery *Russia* 47°18N 44°32E **191** G7
Ketchikan *U.S.A.* 55°21N 131°39W **296** B2
Ketchum *U.S.A.* 43°41N 114°22W **304** E6
Kete Krachi *Ghana* 7°46N 0°1W **263** D4
Keti Bandar *Pakistan* 24°8N 67°27E **242** G2
Kétou *Benin* 7°25N 2°45E **263** D5
Ketri *India* 28°1N 75°50E **242** E6
Kętrzyn *Poland* 54°7N 21°22E **184** D8
Ketta *Congo* 1°28N 15°54E **264** B3
Kettering *Northants., U.K.* 52°24N 0°43W **169** E7
Kettering *Ohio, U.S.A.* 39°41N 84°10W **311** E12
Kettle → *Canada* 56°40N 89°34W **297** B11
Kettle Falls *U.S.A.* 48°37N 118°3W **304** B4
Kettle Point *Canada* 43°10N 82°1W **312** C2
Kettle Pt. *Canada* 43°13N 82°1W **312** C2
Kettleman City *U.S.A.* 36°1N 119°58W **306** J7
Kęty *Poland* 49°51N 19°16E **185** J6
Keuka L. *U.S.A.* 42°30N 77°9W **312** D7
Keung Shan *Hong Kong, China* 22°15N 113°53E **122** B1
Keuruu *Finland* 62°16N 24°41E **188** A3
Kevelaer *Germany* 51°36N 6°15E **178** D2
Kew *Vic., Australia* 37°48S 145°2E **128** A2
Kew *London, U.K.* 51°28N 0°17W **125** B2
Kew Gardens *Ont., Canada* 43°39N 79°18W **141** A3
Kew Gardens *London, U.K.* 51°28N 0°17W **125** B2
Kewanee *U.S.A.* 41°14N 89°56W **310** C7
Kewanna *U.S.A.* 41°1N 86°25W **311** C10
Keware *Nepal* 27°57N 83°47E **243** F10
Kewaunee *U.S.A.* 44°27N 87°31W **308** C10
Keweenaw B. *U.S.A.* 47°0N 88°15W **308** B9
Keweenaw Pen. *U.S.A.* 47°15N 88°15W **308** B9
Keweenaw Pt. *U.S.A.* 47°25N 87°43W **308** B10
Kexholm = Priozersk *Russia* 61°2N 30°7E **188** B6
Key, L. *Ireland* 54°0N 8°15W **166** C3
Key Biscayne *U.S.A.* 25°41N 80°9W **129** D3
Key Colony Beach *U.S.A.* 24°45N 80°57W **317** L9
Key Lake Mine *Canada* 57°5N 105°32W **297** B7
Key Largo *U.S.A.* 25°5N 80°27W **317** K9
Key West *U.S.A.* 24°33N 81°48W **317** L8
Keyala *South Sudan* 4°27N 32°52E **257** G3
Keynsham *U.K.* 51°24N 2°29W **169** F5
Keyser *U.S.A.* 39°26N 78°59W **309** F14
Keystone Heights *U.S.A.* 29°47N 82°2W **316** F7
Keytesville *U.S.A.* 39°26N 92°56W **310** E4
Kezhma *Russia* 58°59N 101°9E **215** D11
Kezi *Zimbabwe* 20°58S 28°32E **271** B4
Kežmarok *Slovakia* 49°10N 20°28E **181** B13
Kgalagadi □ *Botswana* 24°30S 22°0E **270** B3
Kgalagadi Transfrontier ⌓ *Africa* 25°10S 21°0E **270** C3
Khabarovsk *Russia* 48°30N 135°5E **219** B16
Khabr △ *Iran* 28°51N 56°22E **247** D8
Khābūr → *Syria* 35°17N 40°35E **213** E9
Khachmas = Xaçmaz *Azerbaijan* 41°31N 48°42E **191** K9
Khachrod *India* 23°25N 75°20E **242** H6
Khadari, W. el → *Sudan* 10°29N 27°15E **257** E2
Khadro *Pakistan* 26°11N 68°50E **242** F3
Khadyzhensk *Russia* 44°26N 39°32E **191** H4
Khadzhilyangar = Dahongliutan *China* 35°45N 79°20E **243** B8
Khaga *India* 25°47N 81°7E **243** G9
Khagaria *India* 25°30N 86°32E **243** G12
Khagrachari *Bangla.* 23°6N 91°58E **241** D3
Khaipur *Pakistan* 29°34N 72°17E **242** E5
Khair *India* 27°57N 77°46E **242** F7
Khairabad *India* 27°33N 80°47E **243** F9
Khairagarh *India* 21°27N 81°2E **243** J9
Khairpur *Pakistan* 27°32N 68°49E **242** F3
Khairpur Nathan Shah *Pakistan* 27°6N 67°44E **242** F2
Khairwara *India* 23°58N 73°38E **242** H5
Khaisor → *Pakistan* 31°17N 68°59E **242** D3
Khajuraho *India* 24°51N 79°55E **243** G8
Khajuri Kach *Pakistan* 32°4N 69°51E **242** C3
Khāk Dow *Afghan.* 34°57N 67°16E **240** B2
Khakassia □ *Russia* 53°0N 90°0E **217** B12
Khakhea *Botswana* 24°48S 23°22E **270** B3
Khalafābād *Iran* 30°54N 49°24E **247** D6
Khalīj *Iraq* 33°18N 44°28E **113** B2
Khalilabad *India* 26°48N 83°5E **243** F10
Khalīlī *Iran* 27°38N 53°17E **247** E7
Khalkhāl *Iran* 37°37N 48°32E **213** D13
Khalkís = Chalkida *Greece* 38°27N 23°42E **204** C5
Khalmer-Sede = Tazovskiy *Russia* 67°30N 78°44E **214** C8
Khalmer Yu *Russia* 67°58N 65°1E **214** C7
Khalturin *Russia* 58°40N 48°50E **186** C8
Kham Keut *Laos* 18°15N 104°43E **236** C5
Khamaria *India* 23°5N 80°48E **243** H9
Khambhaliya *India* 22°14N 69°41E **242** H3
Khambhat *India* 22°23N 72°33E **242** H5
Khambhat, G. of *India* 20°45N 72°30E **239** E10
Khamgaon *India* 20°42N 76°37E **244** D3
Khami Ruins = Kame Ruins *Zimbabwe* 20°7S 28°25E **269** G2
Khamīr *Iran* 26°57N 55°36E **247** E7
Khamir *Yemen* 16°2N 44°0E **248** C4
Khamīs Mushayţ *Si. Arabia* 18°18N 42°44E **248** C3
Khammam *India* 17°11N 80°6E **244** F5
Khamsa *Egypt* 30°27N 32°23E **251** H3
Khan → *Namibia* 22°37S 14°56E **270** B2
Khān Abū Shāmat *Syria* 33°39N 36°53E **250** E7
Khān al Baghdādī *Iraq* 33°51N 42°32E **213** G10
Khān al Ḩammād *Iraq* 32°19N 44°16E **213** G11
Khān Azād *Iraq* 33°7N 44°22E **246** C5
Khān Mujiddah *Iraq* 32°21N 43°48E **246** C4
Khān Shaykhūn *Syria* 35°26N 36°38E **212** E7
Khan Tengri, Pik *Asia* 42°12N 80°10E **217** D10
Khān Yūnis *Gaza Strip* 31°21N 34°18E **251** G5
Khānābād *Afghan.* 36°45N 69°5E **240** A3
Khanai *Pakistan* 30°30N 67°8E **242** D2
Khānaqīn *Iraq* 34°23N 45°25E **213** E11
Khanāşir *Syria* 35°45N 37°30E **250** C8
Khānbāghī *Iran* 36°10N 55°25E **247** B7
Khandwa *India* 21°49N 76°22E **244** D3
Khandyga *Russia* 62°42N 135°35E **215** C14
Khanewal *Pakistan* 30°20N 71°55E **242** D4
Khangah Dogran *Pakistan* 31°50N 73°37E **242** D5
Khangchendzonga = Kanchenjunga △ *India* 27°42N 88°8E **241** B2
Khanh Duong *Vietnam* 12°44N 108°44E **236** F7
Khaniá = Chania *Greece* 35°30N 24°4E **207** E5
Khaniadhana *India* 25°1N 78°8E **242** G8
Khanka, L. *Asia* 45°0N 132°24E **220** B6
Khankendy = Xankändi *Azerbaijan* 39°52N 46°49E **213** C12
Khanna *India* 30°42N 76°16E **242** D7
Khanozai *Pakistan* 30°37N 67°19E **242** D2
Khanpur *Pakistan* 28°42N 70°35E **242** E4
Khansā' *Iraq* 33°21N 44°28E **113** A2
Khanty-Mansiysk *Russia* 61°0N 69°0E **214** C7
Khanzira, Ras *Somalia* 10°52N 45°48E **267** B6
Khao Khitchakut △ *Thailand* 12°50N 102°10E **236** F4
Khao Laem △ *Thailand* 14°56N 98°31E **236** E2
Khao Laem Res. *Thailand* 14°50N 98°30E **236** E2
Khao Lak △ *Malaysia* 8°38N 98°18E **237** H2
Khao Luang △ *Thailand* 8°34N 99°42E **237** H2
Khao Nam Khang △ *Thailand* 6°32N 100°35E **237** J3
Khao Phlu *Thailand* 9°29N 99°59E **237** b
Khao Pu -Khao Ya △ *Thailand* 7°26N 99°57E **237** J2
Khao Sam Roi Yot △ *Thailand* 12°13N 99°57E **237** F2
Khao Sok △ *Thailand* 8°55N 98°38E **237** H2
Khao Yai △ *Thailand* 14°21N 101°29E **236** E3
Khaoen Si Nakarin △ *Thailand* 14°47N 99°0E **236** E2
Khapalu *Pakistan* 35°10N 76°20E **243** B7
Khapcheranga *Russia* 49°42N 112°24E **215** E12

Khaptao △ Nepal 29°20N 81°10E 243 E9
Kharabali Russia 47°25N 47°15E 191 G8
Kharagauli Georgia 42°1N 43°12E 191 J6
Kharaghoda India 23°11N 71°46E 242 H4
Kharagpur India 22°20N 87°25E 243 H12
Kharan Kalat Pakistan 28°34N 65°21E 240 C2
Kharānaq Iran 32°20N 54°45E 247 C7
Kharavli India 18°54N 72°55E 130 B2
Kharda India 18°40N 75°34E 244 E2
Khardung La India 34°20N 77°43E 243 B7
Kharg = Khārk, Jazīreh-ye Iran 29°15N 50°28E 247 D6
Khârga, El Wâhât el Egypt 25°10N 30°35E 256 B3
Khargon India 21°45N 75°40E 244 D2
Khari ➜ India 25°54N 74°31E 242 G6
Kharian Pakistan 32°49N 73°52E 242 C5
Khariar India 20°17N 82°46E 244 D6
Kharit, Wadi el ➜ Egypt 24°26N 33°3E 256 C3
Khārk, Jazīreh-ye Iran 29°15N 50°28E 247 D6
Kharkiv Ukraine 49°58N 36°20E 189 H9
Kharkiv □ Ukraine 48°20N 36°20E 189 H9
Kharkov = Kharkiv Ukraine 49°58N 36°20E 189 H9
Kharmanli Bulgaria 41°55N 25°55E 203 E9
Kharovsk Russia 59°56N 40°13E 188 C11
Kharsawangarh India 22°48N 85°50E 243 H11
Kharta Turkey 40°55N 29°7E 212 B3
Khartoum = El Khartûm Sudan 15°31N 32°35E 257 D3
Khartum Canada 45°15N 77°5W 312 A7
Khasan Russia 42°25N 130°40E 220 C5
Khasavyurt Russia 43°16N 46°40E 191 J8
Khāsh Iran 28°15N 61°15E 240 C1
Khāsh, Dasht-e Afghan. 31°50N 62°30E 240 C1
Khashm el Girba Sudan 14°59N 35°58E 257 E4
Khashum Sudan 12°27N 28°2E 257 E2
Khashuri Georgia 42°3N 43°35E 191 J6
Khasi Hills India 25°30N 91°30E 241 C3
Khaskovo Bulgaria 41°56N 25°30E 203 E9
Khaskovo □ Bulgaria 42°0N 25°40E 203 E9
Khat, Laem Thailand 8°6N 98°26E 237 a
Khatanga Russia 72°0N 102°20E 215 B11
Khatanga ➜ Russia 72°55N 106°0E 215 B11
Khatauli India 29°17N 77°43E 242 E7
Khatlon □ Tajikistan 37°50N 69°0E 217 E7
Khatra India 22°59N 86°51E 243 H12
Khātūnābād Iran 30°1N 55°25E 247 D7
Khatyrka Russia 62°3N 175°15E 215 C18
Khavda India 23°51N 69°43E 242 H3
Khawlaf, Ra's Yemen 12°40N 54°7E 249 D6
Khawr Fakkān U.A.E. 25°21N 56°22E 247 E8
Khay' Si. Arabia 18°45N 41°24E 248 C3
Khaybar, Ḥarrat Si. Arabia 25°30N 39°45E 246 E4
Khāzimiyah Iraq 34°46N 43°37E 246 C4
Khazzān Jabal al Awliyā Sudan 15°24N 32°20E 257 D3
Khe Bo Vietnam 19°8N 104°41E 236 C5
Khe Long Vietnam 21°29N 104°46E 236 B5
Khe Sanh Vietnam 16°37N 106°45E 236 D6
Khed Maharashtra, India 17°43N 73°27E 244 F1
Khed Maharashtra, India 18°51N 73°56E 244 E1
Khed Brahma India 24°7N 73°5E 242 G5
Khefren Egypt 29°58N 31°8E 117 B1
Khekra India 28°52N 77°20E 242 E7
Khem-Beldyr = Kyzyl Russia 51°50N 94°30E 217 B12
Khemarak Phouminville = Krong Kaoh Kong Cambodia 11°37N 102°59E 237 G4
Khemisset Morocco 33°50N 6°1W 260 B3
Khemmarat Thailand 16°10N 105°15E 236 D5
Khenāmān Iran 30°27N 56°29E 247 D8
Khenchela Algeria 35°28N 7°11E 261 A6
Khenchela □ Algeria 35°0N 7°0E 261 B6
Khenifra Morocco 32°58N 5°46W 260 B3
Kherrata Algeria 36°27N 5°13E 261 A6
Khersān ➜ Iran 31°33N 50°22E 247 D6
Kherson Ukraine 46°35N 32°35E 189 J7
Kherson □ Ukraine 46°15N 33°10E 189 J7
Kheta ➜ Russia 71°54N 102°6E 215 B11
Khewari Pakistan 26°36N 68°52E 242 F3
Khibinogorsk = Kirovsk Russia 67°32N 33°41E 186 A5
Khichripur India 28°37N 77°18E 120 B2
Khidirpur India 22°32N 88°19E 124 B1
Khilchipur India 24°2N 76°34E 242 G7
Khilok Russia 51°30N 110°45E 215 D12
Khimki Russia 55°50N 37°27E 188 E9
Khimki-Khovrino Russia 55°51N 37°31E 129 A2
Khios = Chios Greece 38°27N 26°9E 205 C8
Khirbet Batin Abu Lihyah West Bank 31°50N 35°6E 123 A1
Khirbet el-Misbah West Bank 31°53N 35°4E 123 A1
Khirbet Jub e-Rum West Bank 31°44N 35°16E 123 B2
Khirsadoh India 22°11N 78°47E 243 H8
Khiuma = Hiiumaa Estonia 58°50N 22°45E 188 C2
Khiva = Xiva Uzbekistan 41°30N 60°18E 216 D6
Khiwa = Xiva Uzbekistan 41°30N 60°18E 216 D6
Khlebarovo Bulgaria 43°37N 26°15E 203 C10
Khlong Khlung Thailand 16°12N 99°43E 236 D2
Khlong Lan △ Thailand 16°12N 99°13E 236 D2
Khlong Phanom △ Thailand 8°45N 98°38E 237 H2
Khlong San Thailand 13°43N 100°29E 113 B2
Khlong Toey Thailand 13°43N 100°36E 113 B2
Khmelnik Ukraine 49°33N 27°58E 177 D14
Khmelnytskyy Ukraine 49°23N 27°0E 177 D14
Khmelnytskyy □ Ukraine 49°50N 26°40E 177 D14
Khmer Rep. = Cambodia ■ Asia 12°15N 105°0E 236 F5
Khoai, Hon Vietnam 8°26N 104°50E 237 H5
Khobar = Al Khubar Si. Arabia 26°17N 50°12E 247 E6
Khodoriv Ukraine 49°24N 24°19E 177 D13
Khodzent = Khŭjand Tajikistan 40°17N 69°37E 217 D7
Khojak Pass Afghan. 30°51N 66°34E 242 D2
Khojayli = Xo'jayli Uzbekistan 42°29N 59°31E 216 D5
Khok Kloi Thailand 8°17N 98°19E 237 a
Khok Pho Thailand 6°43N 101°6E 237 J3
Khok Samrong Thailand 15°3N 100°43E 236 E3
Khokhropār Pakistan 25°42N 70°12E 240 D3
Kholm Afghan. 36°45N 67°40E 240 A2
Kholm Russia 57°10N 31°15E 188 D6
Kholmsk Russia 47°40N 142°5E 215 E15
Khomārlu Iran 39°6N 47°3E 213 C12
Khomas □ Namibia 23°30S 17°0E 270 B2
Khomas Hochland Namibia 22°40S 16°0E 270 B2
Khombole Senegal 14°43N 16°42W 262 C1
Khomeyn Iran 33°40N 50°7E 247 C6
Khomeyni Shahr Iran 32°41N 51°31E 247 C6
Khomodino Botswana 22°46S 23°52E 270 B3
Khon Kaen Thailand 16°30N 102°47E 236 D4
Khong ➜ Cambodia 13°32N 105°58E 236 F5
Khong Sedone Laos 15°34N 105°49E 236 E5
Khonsa India 26°57N 95°33E 241 B5
Khonuu Russia 66°30N 143°12E 215 C15
Khoper ➜ Russia 49°30N 42°20E 190 F6
Khor el 'Atash Sudan 13°20N 34°15E 257 E3
Khorāsān-e Janūb □ Iran 32°0N 59°0E 247 C8
Khorāsān-e Razavī □ Iran 35°0N 59°0E 247 C8
Khorāsān-e Shemālī □ Iran 37°0N 57°0E 247 B8
Khorat = Nakhon Ratchasima Thailand 14°59N 102°12E 236 E4
Khorat, Cao Nguyen Thailand 15°30N 102°50E 236 E4
Khorazm = Xorazm □ Uzbekistan 43°0N 60°0E 216 D6
Khorb el Ethel Algeria 28°30N 6°17W 260 C3
Khorel India 22°41N 88°18E 124 A1
Khorixas Namibia 20°16S 14°59E 270 B1
Khorol Ukraine 49°48N 33°15E 189 H7
Khorosovo Russia 55°46N 37°27E 129 B1
Khorramābād Khorāsān, Iran 35°6N 57°57E 247 C8
Khorramābād Lorestān, Iran 33°30N 48°25E 213 F13
Khorramdarreh Iran 36°11N 49°11E 213 D13
Khorramshahr Iran 30°29N 48°15E 247 D6
Khorugh Tajikistan 37°30N 71°36E 217 E8
Khosravi Iran 30°48N 51°28E 247 D6
Khosrowābād Khuzestān, Iran 30°10N 48°25E 247 D6
Khosrowābād Kordestān, Iran 35°31N 47°38E 213 E12
Khost Pakistan 30°13N 67°35E 242 D2
Khosūyeh Iran 28°32N 54°26E 247 D7
Khotan = Hotan China 37°25N 79°55E 217 E9
Khotang Nepal 27°1N 86°51E 243 F12
Khotyn Ukraine 48°31N 26°27E 183 B11
Khouribga Morocco 32°58N 6°57W 260 B3
Khowai Bangla. 24°5N 91°40E 241 C3
Khowst Afghan. 33°22N 69°58E 242 C3
Khowst □ Afghan. 33°20N 70°0E 240 B3
Khoyniki Belarus 51°54N 29°55E 177 C15
Khram, Ko Thailand 12°42N 100°47E 236 F3
Khrami ➜ Georgia 41°25N 45°0E 191 K7
Khrenovoye Russia 51°4N 40°16E 190 E5
Khromtaū Kazakhstan 50°17N 58°27E 216 B5
Khrysokhou B. Cyprus 35°6N 32°25E 207 E8
Khuan Wa Thailand 7°53N 98°17E 237 a
Khudrah, W. ➜ Yemen 18°10N 50°20E 249 C5
Khudzhand = Khŭjand Tajikistan 40°17N 69°37E 217 D7
Khuff Si. Arabia 24°55N 44°53E 246 E5
Khūgīānī Afghan. 31°34N 66°32E 242 D2
Khuis Botswana 26°40S 21°49E 270 C3
Khuiyala India 27°9N 70°25E 242 F4
Khŭjand Tajikistan 40°17N 69°37E 217 D7
Khujner India 23°47N 76°36E 242 H7
Khukhan Thailand 14°42N 104°12E 236 E5
Khulays Si. Arabia 22°9N 39°19E 248 B2
Khulna Bangla. 22°45N 89°34E 241 D2
Khulna □ Bangla. 22°25N 89°35E 241 D2
Khulo Georgia 41°33N 42°19E 191 K6
Khumago Botswana 20°26S 24°32E 270 B3
Khumrah Si. Arabia 21°22N 39°13E 248 B2
Khunjerab △ Pakistan 36°40N 75°30E 243 A6
Khunjerab Pass = Kinjirap Daban Asia 36°40N 75°25E 240 A4
Khūnsorkh Iran 27°9N 56°7E 247 E8
Khunti India 23°5N 85°17E 243 H11
Khūr Iran 32°55N 58°18E 247 C8
Khurai India 24°3N 78°23E 242 G8
Khurayṣah Yemen 15°33N 48°18E 249 D5
Khurayṣ Si. Arabia 25°6N 48°2E 247 E6
Khurda India 20°11N 85°37E 244 D7
Khureit Sudan 13°59N 26°3E 257 E2
Khurja India 28°15N 77°58E 242 E7
Khūrmāl Iraq 35°18N 46°2E 213 E12
Khurr, Wādī al Iraq 32°3N 43°52E 246 C4
Khūsf Iran 32°46N 58°53E 247 C8
Khushab Pakistan 32°20N 72°20E 242 C5
Khust Ukraine 48°10N 23°18E 183 B8
Khutse △ Botswana 23°31S 24°12E 270 B3
Khuwei Sudan 13°5N 29°14E 257 E2
Khuzdar Pakistan 27°52N 66°30E 242 F2
Khūzestān □ Iran 31°0N 49°0E 247 D6
Khvāf Iran 34°33N 60°8E 247 C9
Khvājeh Iran 38°9N 46°35E 246 B5
Khvājeh Moḥammad, Kūh-e Afghan. 36°22N 70°17E 240 A3
Khvalynsk Russia 52°30N 48°2E 190 D9
Khvalynsky △ Russia 52°30N 48°0E 190 D9
Khvānsār Iran 29°56N 54°8E 247 D7
Khvatovka Russia 52°24N 46°32E 190 D8
Khvor Iran 33°45N 55°0E 247 C7
Khvorgū Iran 27°34N 56°27E 247 E8
Khvormūj Iran 28°40N 51°30E 247 D6
Khvoy Iran 38°35N 45°0E 213 C11
Khvoynaya Russia 58°58N 34°28E 188 C8
Khwae Noi ➜ Thailand 14°1N 99°32E 236 E2
Khyber Pakhtunkhwa □ Pakistan 34°0N 72°0E 242 C4
Khyber Pass Afghan. 34°10N 71°8E 242 B4
Khyriv Ukraine 49°32N 22°50E 185 J9
Kia Fiji 16°16S 179°8E 287 A2
Kia Solomon Is. 7°32S 158°26E 287 L10
Kiabukwa Dem. Rep. of the Congo 8°40S 24°48E 265 D4
Kiadho ➜ India 19°37N 77°40E 244 E3
Kiama N.S.W., Australia 34°40S 150°50E 283 C9
Kiama Dem. Rep. of the Congo 7°19S 17°49E 265 D3
Kiamari Pakistan 24°49N 66°58E 123 B1
Kiamba Phil. 6°2N 124°46E 233 H5
Kiambi Dem. Rep. of the Congo 7°15S 28°0E 268 D2
Kiambu □ Kenya 1°10S 36°50E 268 C4
Kiamusze = Jiamusi China 46°40N 130°26E 219 B15
Kian = Ji'an China 41°5N 126°10E 227 D14
Kiana U.S.A. 66°58N 160°26W 303 C7
Kiang West △ Gambia 13°25N 15°50W 262 C1
Kiangara Madag. 17°58S 47°2E 272 B2
Kiangsi = Jiangxi □ China 27°30N 116°0E 229 D11
Kiangsu = Jiangsu □ China 33°0N 120°0E 227 H11
Kiato Greece 38°1N 22°45E 204 C4
Kibæk Denmark 56°2N 8°51E 163 H2
Kibale △ Uganda 0°16N 30°18E 268 B3
Kibanga Port Uganda 0°10N 32°58E 268 B3
Kibangou Congo 3°26S 12°22E 264 C2
Kibara Tanzania 2°8S 33°30E 268 C3
Kibare, Mts. Dem. Rep. of the Congo 8°25S 27°10E 268 D2
Kibawe Phil. 7°34N 125°0E 233 H5
Kibenga Dem. Rep. of the Congo 7°56S 17°30E 265 D3
Kibira △ Burundi 3°6S 30°24E 268 C3
Kiboga Uganda 0°58N 31°45E 268 B3
Kibombo Dem. Rep. of the Congo 3°57S 25°53E 265 C5
Kibondo Tanzania 3°35S 30°45E 268 C3
Kibre Mengist Ethiopia 5°54N 38°59E 257 F4
Kıbrıs = Cyprus ■ Asia 35°0N 33°0E 207 F9
Kibumbu Burundi 3°32S 29°45E 268 C2
Kibungo Rwanda 2°10S 30°32E 268 C3
Kibuye Burundi 3°39S 29°59E 268 C2
Kibuye Rwanda 2°3S 29°21E 268 C2
Kibwesa Tanzania 6°30S 29°58E 268 D2
Kibwezi Kenya 2°27S 37°57E 268 C4
Kıcasalih Turkey 41°23N 26°48E 203 E10
Kičevo Macedonia 41°34N 20°59E 202 E4
Kichha ➜ India 28°41N 79°18E 243 E8
Kichmengskiy Gorodok Russia 59°59N 45°48E 186 B8
Kicking Horse Pass Canada 51°28N 116°16W 296 C5
Kid, W. ➜ Egypt 28°9N 34°27E 251 K5
Kid I. Antigua & B. 17°42N 61°49W 322 c
Kidal Mali 18°26N 1°22E 263 B5
Kidal □ Mali 19°55N 1°5E 261 E5
Kidapawan Phil. 7°1N 125°3E 233 H5
Kidderminster U.K. 52°24N 2°15W 169 E5
Kidepo Valley △ Uganda 3°52N 33°50E 268 B3
Kidete Tanzania 6°25S 37°17E 268 D4
Kidira Senegal 14°28N 12°13W 262 C2
Kidnappers, C. N.Z. 39°38S 177°5E 284 F6
Kidsgrove U.K. 53°5N 2°14W 168 D5
Kidston Australia 18°52S 144°8E 280 B3
Kidugallo Tanzania 6°49S 38°15E 268 D4
Kidurong, Tanjong Malaysia 3°16N 113°3E 235 B4
Kiel Germany 54°19N 10°8E 178 A6
Kiel Canal = Nord-Ostsee-Kanal Germany 54°12N 9°32E 178 A5
Kiel-Kanal = Nord-Ostsee-Kanal Germany 54°12N 9°32E 178 A5
Kielce Poland 50°52N 20°42E 185 H7
Kielder Water U.K. 55°11N 2°31W 168 B5
Kieler Bucht Germany 54°35N 10°25E 178 A6
Kiembara Burkina Faso 13°15N 2°44W 262 C4
Kienge Dem. Rep. of the Congo 10°30S 27°30E 269 E2
Kierling Austria 48°18N 16°16E 142 A1
Kierlingbach ➜ Austria 48°18N 16°17E 142 A1
Kiessé Niger 13°29N 4°1E 263 C5
Kieta Papua N. G. 6°12S 155°36E 286 D8
Kiev = Kyyiv Ukraine 50°30N 30°28E 177 C16
Kifaya Guinea 12°10N 13°4W 262 C2
Kiffa Mauritania 16°37N 11°24W 262 B2
Kifisos ➜ Athina, Greece 37°58N 23°42E 112 B2
Kifisos ➜ Voiotia, Greece 38°35N 23°20E 204 C5
Kifissia Greece 38°4N 23°49E 204 C5
Kifrī Iraq 34°45N 45°0E 213 E11
Kigali Rwanda 1°59S 30°4E 268 C3
Kigarama Tanzania 1°1S 31°50E 268 C3
Kigelle South Sudan 8°40N 34°2E 257 F3
Kigezi △ Uganda 0°34S 29°55E 268 C2
Kiği Turkey 39°18N 40°21E 213 C9
Kigoma □ Tanzania 5°0S 30°0E 268 D3
Kigoma-Ujiji Tanzania 4°55S 29°36E 268 C2
Kigomasha, Ras Tanzania 4°58S 38°58E 268 C4
Kigosi △ Tanzania 4°10S 31°45E 268 C3
Kığzı Turkey 38°18N 43°25E 246 B4
Kīhei U.S.A. 20°47N 156°28W 302 C5
Kihikihi N.Z. 38°2S 175°22E 284 E4
Kihnu Estonia 58°9N 24°1E 188 C3
Kihoku Japan 33°13N 132°36E 222 D4
Kīholo B. U.S.A. 19°50N 155°55W 302 D6
Kii-Hantō Japan 34°0N 135°45E 223 D7
Kii-Nagashima Japan 34°12N 136°20E 223 C8
Kii-Sanchi Japan 34°20N 136°0E 223 D7
Kii-Suidō Japan 33°40N 134°45E 222 D6
Kiira Dam Uganda 0°25N 33°0E 268 B3
Kiire Japan 31°22N 130°33E 222 F2
Kijik U.S.A. 60°20N 154°20W 303 F9
Kikaiga-Shima Japan 28°19N 129°59E 221 K4
Kikiak = Rigolet Canada 54°10N 58°23W 299 B8
Kikinda Serbia 45°50N 20°30E 182 E5
Kikládhes = Kyklades Greece 37°0N 24°30E 204 E6
Kikoira Australia 33°39S 146°40E 283 B7
Kikombo Bandundu, Dem. Rep. of the Congo 5°37S 18°50E 265 D3
Kikombo Bandundu, Dem. Rep. of the Congo 5°49S 17°45E 265 D3
Kikongo Dem. Rep. of the Congo 4°16S 17°17E 265 C3
Kikori Papua N. G. 7°25S 144°15E 286 D3
Kikori ➜ Papua N. G. 7°38S 144°20E 286 D3
Kikuchi Japan 32°59N 130°47E 222 E2
Kikuna Japan 35°30N 139°37E 140 B2
Kikuyu Kenya 1°15S 36°40E 268 C4
Kikwit Dem. Rep. of the Congo 5°0S 18°45E 265 D3
Kil Sweden 59°30N 13°20E 162 E7
Kilafors Sweden 61°14N 16°36E 162 C10
Kilakkarai India 9°12N 78°47E 245 K4
Kilar India 33°6N 76°25E 242 C7
Kilauea U.S.A. 22°13N 159°25W 302 A2
Kīlauea Caldera U.S.A. 19°25N 155°17W 302 D6
Kilbeggan Ireland 53°22N 7°30W 166 C4
Kilbrannan Sd. U.K. 55°37N 5°26W 167 F3
Kilbuck Mts. U.S.A. 60°36N 159°53W 303 F8
Kilburn U.K. 51°32N 0°11W 125 A2
Kilchu N. Korea 40°57N 129°25E 224 B4
Kilcoy Australia 26°59S 152°30E 281 D5
Kildare Ireland 53°9N 6°55W 166 C5
Kildare □ Ireland 53°10N 6°50W 166 C5
Kildinstroy Russia 68°48N 33°6E 160 B25
Kileikli Sudan 11°25N 25°31E 257 E2
Kilembe Dem. Rep. of the Congo 5°42S 19°55E 265 D3
Kilen Norway 59°20N 8°49E 164 E5
Kilfinnane Ireland 52°21N 8°28W 166 D3
Kilgarvan Ireland 51°54N 9°27W 166 E2
Kilgore U.S.A. 32°23N 94°53W 314 E7
Kilgoris Kenya 1°0S 34°53E 268 C3
Kilibo Benin 8°32N 2°38E 263 D5
Kilifi Kenya 3°40S 39°48E 268 C4
Kilimanjaro Tanzania 3°7S 37°20E 268 C4
Kilimanjaro □ Tanzania 4°0S 38°0E 268 C4
Kilimanjaro △ Tanzania 3°2S 37°19E 268 C4
Kilimli Turkey 41°28N 31°50E 212 B4
Kilinailau Is. Papua N. G. 4°45S 155°20E 286 C8
Kilindini Kenya 4°4S 39°40E 268 C4
Kilinochchi Sri Lanka 9°24N 80°25E 245 K5
Kilis Turkey 36°42N 37°6E 250 B8
Kilis □ Turkey 36°50N 37°10E 212 D7
Kiliya Ukraine 45°28N 29°16E 183 E14
Kilkee Ireland 52°41N 9°39W 166 D2
Kilkeel U.K. 54°7N 5°55W 166 B5
Kilkenny Ireland 52°39N 7°15W 166 D4
Kilkenny □ Ireland 52°35N 7°15W 166 D4
Kilkieran B. Ireland 53°20N 9°41W 166 C2
Kilkis Greece 40°58N 22°57E 202 F6
Killala Ireland 54°13N 9°13W 166 B2
Killala B. Ireland 54°16N 9°8W 166 B2
Killaloe Ont., Canada 45°33N 77°25W 312 A7
Killaloe Clare, Ireland 52°48N 8°28W 166 D3
Killarney Queens., Australia 28°20S 152°18E 281 D5
Killarney Man., Canada 49°10N 99°40W 297 D9
Killarney Kerry, Ireland 52°4N 9°30W 166 D2
Killarney, L. Bahamas 25°3N 77°27W 153 b
Killarney △ Canada 46°2N 81°35W 298 C3
Killarney △ Ireland 52°0N 9°33W 166 D2
Killary Harbour Ireland 53°38N 9°52W 166 C2
Killdeer U.S.A. 47°22N 102°45W 308 B2
Killeberg Sweden 56°29N 14°5E 163 H8
Killeen U.S.A. 31°7N 97°44W 314 F6
Killin U.K. 56°28N 4°19W 167 E4
Killiney Ireland 53°15N 6°7W 121 B2
Killington Pk. U.S.A. 43°36N 72°49W 313 C12
Killini = Kyllini Greece 37°55N 21°8E 207 D3
Killini Greece 37°54N 22°25E 204 D4
Killiniq I. Canada 60°24N 64°37W 295 E19
Killorglin Ireland 52°6N 9°47W 166 D2
Killybegs Ireland 54°38N 8°26W 166 B3
Kilmarnock U.K. 55°37N 4°29W 167 F4
Kilmez Russia 56°58N 50°55E 190 B10
Kilmez ➜ Russia 56°58N 50°28E 190 B10
Kilmore Australia 37°25S 144°53E 283 D6
Kilmore Quay Ireland 52°10N 6°36W 166 D5
Kilo Finland 60°13N 24°47E 121 B1
Kilokri India 28°34N 77°15E 120 B2
Kilómetro 1082 = Joaquín V. González Argentina 25°10S 64°0W 334 B3
Kilondo Tanzania 9°45S 34°20E 269 D3
Kilosa Tanzania 6°48S 37°0E 268 D4
Kilrush Ireland 52°38N 9°29W 166 D2
Kiltan I. India 11°29N 73°0E 245 J1
Kilwa Kisiwani Tanzania 8°58S 39°32E 269 D4
Kilwa Kivinje Tanzania 8°45S 39°25E 269 D4
Kilwa Masoko Tanzania 8°55S 39°30E 269 D4
Kilwinning U.K. 55°39N 4°43W 167 F4
Kim U.S.A. 37°15N 103°21W 305 H12
Kim ➜ Cameroon 5°28N 11°7E 263 D7
Kimaam Indonesia 7°58S 138°53E 231 F9
Kimamba Tanzania 6°45S 37°10E 268 D4
Kimba Australia 33°8S 136°23E 282 B2
Kimball Nebr., U.S.A. 41°14N 103°40W 308 E2
Kimball S. Dak., U.S.A. 43°45N 98°57W 308 D4
Kimbanda Dem. Rep. of the Congo 4°16S 18°30E 265 C3
Kimbe Papua N. G. 5°33S 150°11E 286 C6
Kimbe B. Papua N. G. 5°15S 150°30E 286 C6
Kimberley W. Austral., Australia 16°20S 127°0E 278 C4
Kimberley B.C., Canada 49°40N 115°59W 296 D5
Kimberley Ont., Canada 44°23N 80°32W 312 B4
Kimberley Northern Cape, S. Africa 28°43S 24°46E 270 C3
Kimberly U.S.A. 42°32N 114°22W 304 E6
Kimbongo Dem. Rep. of the Congo 6°8S 18°1E 265 D3
Kimch'aek N. Korea 40°40N 129°10E 224 B4
Kimhae = Gimhae S. Korea 35°14N 128°53E 224 E4
Kimhwa N. Korea 38°25N 127°36E 224 C3
Kimi Greece 38°38N 24°6E 204 C6
Kimitsu Japan 35°19N 139°54E 223 B11
Kimjŏngsugŭp N. Korea 41°24N 127°45E 224 B3
Kimmirut Canada 62°50N 69°50W 295 E18
Kimolos Greece 36°48N 24°37E 204 E6
Kimongo Congo 4°27S 12°53E 265 C2
Kimovsk Russia 54°0N 38°29E 188 E10
Kimpangu Dem. Rep. of the Congo 5°52S 15°3E 265 D3
Kimparana Mali 12°48N 5°0W 262 C4
Kimpese Dem. Rep. of the Congo 5°33S 14°26E 265 D2
Kimry Russia 56°55N 37°15E 188 D9
Kimstad Sweden 58°35N 15°58E 163 F9
Kimvula Dem. Rep. of the Congo 5°44S 15°58E 265 D3
Kin Burma 22°46N 94°42E 241 D5
Kin-u Burma 22°46N 95°37E 241 D5
Kin-wan Japan 26°23N 127°55E 288 a
Kinabalian, Mt. Phil. 8°12N 125°26E 233 G5
Kinabalu, Gunung Malaysia 6°3N 116°14E 235 A5
Kinabalu △ Malaysia 6°0N 116°30E 235 A5
Kinango Kenya 4°8S 39°19E 268 C4
Kinard U.S.A. 30°16N 85°15W 316 E4
Kinaros Greece 36°59N 26°15E 205 E8
Kinaskan L. Canada 57°38N 130°8W 296 B2
Kinbasket L. Canada 52°0N 118°10W 296 C5
Kincaid U.S.A. 39°35N 89°25W 310 E7
Kincardine Canada 44°10N 81°40W 312 B3
Kinchafoonee Cr. ➜ U.S.A. 31°38N 84°10W 316 D5
Kinchega △ Australia 32°27S 142°15E 282 B5
Kincolith Canada 55°0N 129°57W 296 C3
Kincsem Park Budapest, Hungary 47°30N 19°8E 117 B2
Kinda Kasai-Or., Dem. Rep. of the Congo 9°18S 25°4E 265 D5
Kinda Katanga, Dem. Rep. of the Congo 4°47S 21°48E 265 C4
Kindambi Dem. Rep. of the Congo 5°6S 18°14E 265 D4
Kindberg Austria 47°30N 15°27E 180 D8
Kinde U.S.A. 43°56N 83°0W 312 C2
Kindele Dem. Rep. of the Congo 8°39S 24°10E 265 D4
Kinder Scout U.K. 53°24N 1°52W 168 D6
Kinderhook U.S.A. 39°42N 91°10W 310 E5
Kindersley Canada 51°30N 109°10W 297 C7
Kindi Iraq 33°18N 44°22E 113 B2
Kindia Guinea 10°0N 12°52W 262 D2
Kindongo Dem. Rep. of the Congo 3°58S 17°30E 264 C3
Kindu Dem. Rep. of the Congo 2°55S 25°50E 264 C5
Kinel Russia 53°15N 50°40E 190 D10
Kineshma Russia 57°30N 42°5E 190 B6
Kinesi Tanzania 1°25S 33°50E 268 C3
King, L. Australia 33°10S 119°35E 279 F2
King, Mt. Australia 25°10S 147°30E 280 D4
King Abdulaziz Int. ✕ (JED) Si. Arabia 21°41N 39°9E 248 B2
King Abdullah Economic City Si. Arabia 22°24N 39°5E 248 B2
King Christian I. Canada 77°48N 101°40W 295 B11
King City Calif., U.S.A. 36°13N 121°8W 306 J5
King City Mo., U.S.A. 40°3N 94°31W 310 D2
King Cove U.S.A. 55°3N 162°19W 303 J7
King Cr. ➜ Australia 24°35S 139°30E 280 C2
King Edward ➜ Australia 14°14S 126°35E 278 B4
King Edward Point S. Georgia 54°17S 36°30W 151 B1
King Frederick VI Land = Kong Frederik VI.s Kyst Greenland 63°0N 43°0W 154 E6
King George B. Falk. Is. 51°30S 60°30W 153 f
King George I. Antarctica 60°0S 60°0W 151 C18
King George Is. Canada 57°20N 80°30W 295 F15
King George Sd. Australia 35°5S 118°0E 279 G2
King George VI Falls Guyana 5°42N 61°5W 329 B5
King I. = Kadan Kyun Burma 12°30N 98°20E 236 F2
King I. Tas., Australia 39°50S 144°0E 281 F3
King I. B.C., Canada 52°10N 127°40W 296 C3
King Khalid Int. ✕ (RUH) Si. Arabia 24°57N 46°42E 246 E4
King Khalid Military City = Madinat al Malik Khālid al Askarīyah Si. Arabia 27°54N 45°31E 246 E5
King Leopold Ranges Australia 17°30S 125°45E 278 C4
King of Prussia U.S.A. 40°5N 75°23W 313 F9
King Salmon U.S.A. 58°42N 156°40W 303 G8
King Sd. Australia 16°50S 123°20E 278 C3
King Sejong Antarctica 62°30S 58°0W 151 C18
King Shaka Int. ✕ (DUR) S. Africa 29°37S 31°7E 271 C5
King William I. Canada 69°10N 97°25W 294 D12
King William's Town S. Africa 32°51S 27°22E 270 D4
Kingaok = Bathurst Inlet Canada 66°50N 108°1W 294 D10
Kingaroy Australia 26°32S 151°51E 281 D5
Kingdom City U.S.A. 38°56N 91°56W 310 F5
Kingfisher U.S.A. 35°52N 97°56W 314 D6
Kinghorn U.K. 56°5N 3°10W 121 A2
Kingirbān Iraq 34°40N 44°54E 246 C5
Kingisepp = Kuressaare Estonia 58°15N 22°30E 188 C2
Kingisepp Russia 59°25N 28°40E 188 C5
Kingking = Pantukan Phil. 7°9N 125°54E 233 H5
Kinglake △ Australia 37°30S 145°22E 283 D6
Kingman Ariz., U.S.A. 35°12N 114°4W 307 K12
Kingman Ind., U.S.A. 39°58N 87°18W 311 E9
Kingman Kans., U.S.A. 37°39N 98°7W 308 G4
Kingoonya Australia 30°55S 135°19E 281 E2
Kingri Pakistan 30°27N 69°49E 242 D3
Kings ➜ U.S.A. 36°3N 119°50W 306 J7
Kings Canyon Australia 24°15S 131°34E 278 D5
Kings Canyon △ U.S.A. 36°50N 118°40W 306 J8
Kings County = Offaly □ Ireland 53°15N 7°30W 166 C4
Kings Cross Sydney, Australia 139 c3
King's Cross London, U.K. 125 a4
Kings Domain Australia 37°49S 144°58E 128 A1
Kings Forest = Kongelunden Denmark 55°34N 12°34E 118 B3
King's Lynn U.K. 52°45N 0°24E 168 E8
Kings Park U.S.A. 40°53N 73°16W 313 F11
Kings Peak U.S.A. 40°46N 110°23W 304 F8
King's Trough Atl. Oc. 43°48N 22°0W 152 B9
Kingsbridge U.K. 50°17N 3°47W 169 G4
Kingsburg U.S.A. 36°31N 119°33W 306 J7
Kingsbury Vic., Australia 37°43S 145°2E 128 A2
Kingsbury London, U.K. 51°34N 0°15W 125 A2
Kingscote Australia 35°40S 137°38E 282 C2
Kingscourt Ireland 53°54N 6°48W 166 C5
Kingsford N.S.W., Australia 33°56S 151°14E 139 B2
Kingsford Mich., U.S.A. 45°48N 88°4W 308 C9
Kingsford Smith, Sydney ✕ (SYD) Australia 33°57S 151°11E 139 B2
Kingsland U.S.A. 30°48N 81°41W 316 E8
Kingsport U.S.A. 36°33N 82°33W 315 C13
Kingston Ont., Canada 44°14N 76°30W 313 B8
Kingston Jamaica 17°55N 76°50W 320 a
Kingston N.Z. 45°20S 168°43E 285 F3
Kingston N.H., U.S.A. 42°56N 71°3W 313 D13
Kingston N.Y., U.S.A. 41°56N 73°59W 313 E11
Kingston Pa., U.S.A. 41°16N 75°54W 313 E9
Kingston R.I., U.S.A. 41°29N 71°30W 313 E13
Kingston Pk. U.S.A. 35°44N 115°55W 307 K11
Kingston South East Australia 36°51S 139°55E 282 D3
Kingston upon Hull U.K. 53°45N 0°21W 168 D7
Kingston upon Hull □ U.K. 53°45N 0°21W 168 D7
Kingston-upon-Thames □ U.K. 51°24N 0°17W 125 B2
Kingston Vale U.K. 51°25N 0°25W 125 B2
Kingstown = Dún Laoghaire Ireland 53°17N 6°8W 166 C5
Kingstown N.S.W., Australia 30°29S 151°6E 283 A9
Kingstown St. Vincent 13°10N 61°10W 323 n
Kingstree U.S.A. 33°40N 79°50W 316 B10
Kingsville Ont., Canada 42°2N 82°45W 312 D2
Kingsville Tex., U.S.A. 27°31N 97°52W 314 H6
Kingsway Canada 43°38N 79°32W 141 B1
Kingtechen = Jingdezhen China 29°20N 117°11E 229 C11
Kingunda Dem. Rep. of the Congo 6°36S 16°58E 265 D3
Kingussie U.K. 57°6N 4°2W 167 D4
Kingwood U.S.A. 30°2N 95°16W 314 F7
Kinhwa = Jinhua China 29°8N 119°38E 229 C12
Kınık Antalya, Turkey 36°20N 29°20E 205 E11
Kınık İzmir, Turkey 39°6N 27°24E 205 B9
Kinistino Canada 52°57N 105°2W 297 C7
Kinjirap Daban Asia 36°40N 75°25E 240 A4
Kinkala Congo 4°18S 14°49E 265 C2
Kinki □ Japan 33°45N 136°0E 223 D8
Kinkony, Farihin' Madag. 16°8S 45°50E 272 B2
Kinleith N.Z. 38°20S 175°56E 284 E4
Kinlochleven U.K. 56°43N 5°0W 167 E4
Kinmen = Chinmen Taiwan 24°26N 118°19E 225 a
Kinmount Canada 44°48N 78°45W 312 B6
Kinmundy U.S.A. 38°46N 88°51W 311 F8
Kinn Norway 61°34N 4°45E 164 C1
Kinna Sweden 57°32N 12°42E 163 G6
Kinnairds Hd. U.K. 57°43N 2°1W 167 D6
Kinnared Sweden 57°2N 13°7E 163 G7
Kinnarodden = Nordkinn Norway 71°8N 27°40E 160 A22
Kinnarp Sweden 58°5N 13°32E 163 F7
Kinneviken Sweden 58°35N 13°15E 163 F7
Kinngait Canada 64°14N 76°32W 295 E16
Kinniyai Sri Lanka 8°29N 81°11E 245 K5
Kino Nuevo Mexico 28°52N 112°3W 318 B2
Kinogitan Phil. 9°0N 124°48E 233 G5
Kinoje ➜ Canada 52°8N 81°25W 298 B3
Kinokawa Japan 34°15N 135°20E 223 C7
Kinomoto Japan 35°30N 136°13E 223 B8
Kinoni Uganda 0°41S 30°28E 268 C3
Kinoosao Canada 57°5N 102°1W 297 B8
Kinross U.K. 56°13N 3°25W 167 E5
Kinsale Ireland 51°42N 8°31W 166 E3
Kinsale, Old Hd. of Ireland 51°37N 8°33W 166 E3
Kinsarvik Norway 60°22N 6°43E 164 D3
Kinsha = Chang Jiang ➜ China 31°48N 121°10E 229 B13
Kinshasa Dem. Rep. of the Congo 4°20S 15°15E 265 C3
Kinsley U.S.A. 37°55N 99°25W 308 G4
Kinsman U.S.A. 41°26N 80°35W 312 E4
Kinston Ala., U.S.A. 31°13N 86°10W 316 D3
Kinston N.C., U.S.A. 35°16N 77°35W 315 D16
Kintamani Indonesia 8°14S 115°19E 231 J18
Kintampo Ghana 8°5N 1°41W 263 D4
Kintap Indonesia 3°51S 115°13E 235 C5
Kintore U.K. 57°14N 2°20W 167 D6
Kintore Ra. Australia 23°15S 128°47E 278 D4
Kintshua Dem. Rep. of the Congo 4°27S 19°38E 265 C3
Kintyre U.K. 55°30N 5°35W 167 F3
Kintyre, Mull of U.K. 55°17N 5°47W 167 F3
Kinu-Gawa ➜ Japan 35°36N 139°57E 223 B11
Kinushseo ➜ Canada 55°15N 83°45W 298 A3
Kinuso Canada 55°20N 115°25W 296 B5
Kinvarra Ireland 53°8N 8°56W 166 C3
Kinwat India 19°38N 78°12E 244 E4
Kinyangiri Tanzania 4°25S 34°37E 268 C3
Kinyeti South Sudan 3°57N 32°54E 257 G3
Kinzia Dem. Rep. of the Congo 3°36S 18°26E 264 C3
Kinzig ➜ Germany 48°36N 7°49E 179 G3
Kinzua U.S.A. 41°52N 78°58W 312 E6
Kioni Greece 38°27N 20°41E 207 C2
Kiosk Canada 46°6N 78°53W 298 C4
Kiowa Kans., U.S.A. 37°1N 98°29W 308 G4
Kiowa Okla., U.S.A. 34°43N 95°54W 314 D7
Kipahigan L. Canada 55°20N 101°55W 297 B8
Kipanga Tanzania 6°15S 35°20E 268 D4
Kiparissia Greece 37°15N 21°40E 204 D3
Kiparissiakos Kolpos Greece 37°25N 21°25E 204 D3
Kipawa, L. Canada 46°50N 79°0W 298 C4
Kipembawe Tanzania 7°38S 33°27E 268 D3
Kipengere Ra. Tanzania 9°12S 34°15E 269 D3
Kipili Tanzania 7°28S 30°32E 268 D3
Kipini Kenya 2°30S 40°32E 268 C5
Kipling Canada 50°6N 102°38W 297 C8
Kipling Heights Canada 43°43N 79°34W 141 A1
Kipnuk U.S.A. 59°56N 164°3W 303 G6
Kippure Ireland 53°11N 6°21W 166 C5
Kipseli Athens, Greece 112 a3
Kipushi Dem. Rep. of the Congo 11°48S 27°12E 269 E2
Kira Uganda 0°24N 32°38E 268 B3
Kira Panagia Greece 39°17N 24°4E 204 B6
Kirakira Solomon Is. 10°27S 161°56E 287 N11
Kirandul India 18°33N 81°10E 244 E5
Kirane Mali 15°20N 10°20W 262 B2
Kiranomena Madag. 18°17S 46°2E 272 B2
Kiraz Turkey 38°14N 28°13E 205 C10
Kirazlı Turkey 40°2N 26°41E 203 F10
Kirchhain Germany 50°47N 8°56E 178 E4
Kirchheim Germany 48°39N 9°27E 179 G5
Kirchheimbolanden Germany 49°40N 8°0E 179 F3
Kirchschlag Austria 47°30N 16°19E 181 D9
Kirchstockbach Germany 48°1N 11°40E 131 B3
Kirchtrudering Germany 48°7N 11°40E 131 B3
Kirdâsa Egypt 30°2N 31°6E 251 H2
Kirdimi Chad 18°11N 18°31E 259 E3
Kireç Turkey 39°33N 28°22E 205 B10
Kirensk Russia 57°50N 107°55E 215 D11
Kirghiz Range Asia 42°40N 73°40E 217 D8
Kirghizia = Kyrgyzstan ■ Asia 42°0N 75°0E 217 D9
Kirgiz-Kulak = Chirchiq Uzbekistan 41°29N 69°35E 217 D7
Kirgiziya Steppe Eurasia 50°0N 55°0E 187 E10
Kiri Dem. Rep. of the Congo 1°29S 19°0E 264 C3
Kiri Buru India 22°0N 85°0E 244 D7
Kiribati ■ Pac. Oc. 3°0S 180°0E 277 A15
Kırıkhan Turkey 36°31N 36°21E 250 B7
Kirikiri Nigeria 6°26N 3°18E 124 B1
Kırıkkale Turkey 39°51N 33°32E 212 C5
Kirikopuni N.Z. 35°50S 174°1E 284 B3
Kirillov Russia 59°49N 38°24E 188 C10
Kirin = Jilin China 43°44N 126°30E 227 C14
Kirindi Oya ➜ Sri Lanka 6°15N 81°20E 245 L5
Kirindy Mitea △ Madag. 20°44S 44°10E 272 C1
Kirinyaga = Kenya, Mt. Kenya 0°10S 37°18E 268 C4
Kirinyaga □ Kenya 0°30S 37°20E 268 C4
Kirirom △ Cambodia 11°18N 104°5E 237 G5
Kirishi Russia 59°28N 32°0E 188 C7
Kirishima Japan 31°44N 130°46E 222 F2
Kirishima Yaku △ Japan 31°24N 130°50E 221 J5
Kirishima-Yama Japan 31°58N 130°55E 222 F2
Kiritimati Kiribati 1°58N 157°27W 289 G12
Kiriwina I. Papua N. G. 8°40S 151°6E 286 E6
Kirka Turkey 39°17N 30°33E 205 B12
Kırkağaç Turkey 39°8N 27°40E 205 B9
Kirkby U.K. 53°30N 2°54W 168 D5
Kirkby-in-Ashfield U.K. 53°6N 1°14W 168 D6
Kirkby Lonsdale U.K. 54°12N 2°36W 168 C5
Kirkby Stephen U.K. 54°29N 2°21W 168 C5
Kirkcaldy U.K. 56°7N 3°9W 167 E5
Kirkcudbright U.K. 54°50N 4°2W 167 G4
Kirke Værløse Denmark 55°47N 12°19E 118 A1
Kirkehamn Norway 58°14N 6°31E 164 F3
Kirkenær Norway 60°27N 12°3E 164 D9
Kirkenes Norway 69°40N 30°5E 160 B24
Kirkfield Canada 44°34N 78°59W 312 B6
Kirkhill U.K. 55°50N 3°13W 121 B2
Kirkintilloch U.K. 55°56N 4°8W 167 F4
Kirkjubæjarklaustur Iceland 63°47N 18°4W 155 D8
Kirkkonummi Finland 60°8N 24°26E 188 B3
Kirkland Ill., U.S.A. 42°6N 88°51W 311 B8
Kirkland Wash., U.S.A. 47°40N 122°12W 306 C4
Kirkland Lake Canada 48°9N 80°2W 298 C3
Kırklareli Turkey 41°44N 27°15E 203 E11
Kırklareli □ Turkey 41°45N 27°15E 203 E11
Kirklin U.S.A. 40°12N 86°22W 311 D10
Kirkliston U.K. 55°57N 3°24W 121 B1
Kirkliston Ra. N.Z. 44°25S 170°34E 285 E5
Kirknewton U.K. 55°53N 3°25W 121 B1
Kirknitz = Cerknica Slovenia 45°48N 14°21E 199 C11
Kirkpatrick, Mt. Antarctica 84°20S 166°25E 151 E11
Kirksville U.S.A. 40°12N 92°35W 310 D4
Kirkūk Iraq 35°30N 44°21E 213 E11
Kirkwall U.K. 58°59N 2°58W 167 C6
Kirkwood Eastern Cape, S. Africa 33°22S 25°15E 270 D4
Kirkwood Mo., U.S.A. 38°35N 90°24W 310 F6
Kirlampudi India 17°12N 82°12E 244 F6
Kirmasti = Mustafakemalpaşa Turkey 40°2N 28°24E 203 F12
Kirn Germany 49°47N 7°26E 179 F3
Kirobasi Turkey 36°43N 33°52E 250 B4
Kirov Kaluga, Russia 54°3N 34°20E 188 E8
Kirov Kirov, Russia 58°35N 49°40E 186 C8
Kirov Palace of Culture Russia 59°55N 30°16E 137 B1
Kirovabad = Gäncä Azerbaijan 40°45N 46°20E 191 K8
Kirovakan = Vanadzor Armenia 40°48N 44°30E 191 K7
Kirovo = Kirovohrad Ukraine 48°35N 32°20E 189 H7
Kirovo-Chepetsk Russia 58°28N 50°0E 186 C9
Kirovograd = Kirovohrad Ukraine 48°35N 32°20E 189 H7
Kirovohrad Ukraine 48°35N 32°20E 189 H7
Kirovohrad □ Ukraine 48°30N 31°30E 189 H6
Kirovsk Russia 67°32N 33°41E 186 A5
Kirovskiy = Balpyq Bī Kazakhstan 44°52N 78°12E 217 D9
Kirovskiy Astrakhan, Russia 45°51N 48°11E 191 H9
Kirovskiy Kamchatka, Russia 54°27N 155°42E 215 D16
Kirovskiy Primorsk, Russia 45°7N 133°30E 220 B6
Kirriemuir U.K. 56°41N 3°1W 167 E5
Kirsanov Russia 52°35N 42°40E 190 D6
Kırşehir Turkey 39°14N 34°5E 212 C6
Kirtachi Niger 12°52N 2°30E 263 C5
Kīrteh Afghan. 32°15N 63°0E 240 B1
Kirthar △ Pakistan 25°45N 67°30E 242 F2
Kirthar Range Pakistan 27°0N 67°0E 242 F2
Kirtland U.S.A. 36°44N 108°21W 305 H9
Kiruna Sweden 67°52N 20°15E 160 C19
Kirundu Dem. Rep. of the Congo 0°50S 25°35E 264 C5
Kirya Russia 55°5N 46°55E 190 C8
Kiryat Anavim Israel 31°49N 35°6E 123 B1
Kiryat Ha Yovel Israel 31°46N 35°10E 123 B1
Kiryū Japan 36°24N 139°20E 223 A11
Kisa Sweden 58°0N 15°39E 163 G9
Kisaga Tanzania 4°30S 34°23E 268 C3
Kisalföld Hungary 47°30N 17°0E 182 C2
Kisambo Dem. Rep. of the Congo 6°25S 18°14E 265 D3
Kisandji Dem. Rep. of the Congo 6°18S 19°16E 265 D3
Kisanga Dem. Rep. of the Congo 2°30N 26°35E 268 B2
Kisangani Dem. Rep. of the Congo 0°35N 25°15E 268 B2
Kisantu Dem. Rep. of the Congo 5°7S 15°5E 265 D3
Kisar Indonesia 8°5S 127°10E 231 F7
Kisaran Indonesia 3°0N 99°37E 234 B1
Kisarawe Tanzania 6°53S 39°0E 268 D4
Kisarazu Japan 35°23N 139°55E 223 B11
Kisbér Hungary 47°30N 18°2E 182 C3
Kiselevsk Russia 54°5N 86°39E 217 B11
Kish = Qeys Iran 26°32N 53°58E 249 A6
Kishanganga ➜ Pakistan 34°18N 73°28E 243 B5
Kishanganj India 26°3N 88°14E 241 B2
Kishangarh Raj., India 26°34N 74°52E 242 F6
Kishangarh Raj., India 27°50N 70°30E 242 F4
Kishb, Ḥarrat al Si. Arabia 22°30N 40°25E 248 B3
Kishi Nigeria 9°1N 3°52E 263 D5
Kishinev = Chişinău Moldova 47°2N 28°50E 183 C13
Kishiwada Japan 34°28N 135°22E 223 C7

Kishkareny = Lazo
Moldova 47°33N 28°2E **183 C13**
Kishkenekōl Kazakhstan 53°38N 72°20E **217 B8**
Kishorganj Bangla. 24°26N 90°40E **241 C3**
Kishtwar India 33°20N 75°48E **242 C6**
Kishwaukee ➤ U.S.A. 42°12N 89°8W **310 B7**
Kisielice Poland 53°36N 19°16E **184 E6**
Kisigo ➤ Tanzania 6°27S 34°17E **268 D3**
Kisii Kenya 0°40S 34°45E **268 C3**
Kisiju Tanzania 7°23S 39°19E **268 D4**
Kısıklı Turkey 41°1N 29°2E **122 B2**
Kisir Turkey 41°0N 43°5E **213 B10**
Kisizi Uganda 1°0S 29°58E **268 C2**
Kiska I. U.S.A. 51°59N 177°30E **303 L2**
Kiskomárom = Zalakomár
Hungary 46°33N 17°12E **182 D2**
Kiskőrei-víztároló
Hungary 47°31N 20°36E **182 C5**
Kiskőrös Hungary 46°37N 19°20E **182 D4**
Kiskundorozsma Hungary 46°16N 20°5E **182 D5**
Kiskunfélegyháza
Hungary 46°42N 19°53E **182 D4**
Kiskunhalas Hungary 46°28N 19°37E **182 D4**
Kiskunmajsa Hungary 46°30N 19°48E **182 D4**
Kiskunsági △ Hungary 46°39N 19°30E **182 D4**
Kislovodsk Russia 43°50N 42°45E **191 J6**
Kismaayo Somalia 0°22S 42°32E **267 E5**
Kismayu ➤ Somalia 1°25N 41°30E **267 D5**
Kiso-Gawa ➤ Japan 35°20N 136°45E **223 B8**
Kiso-Sammyaku Japan 35°45N 137°45E **223 B9**
Kisofukushima Japan 35°52N 137°43E **223 B9**
Kisoro Uganda 1°17S 29°48E **268 C2**
Kispest Hungary 47°27N 19°8E **117 B2**
Kissamos Greece 35°29N 23°38E **207 E4**
Kissamou, Kolpos Greece 35°30N 23°38E **207 E4**
Kissidougou Guinea 9°5N 10°5W **262 D2**
Kissimmee U.S.A. 28°18N 81°24W **317 G8**
Kissimmee ➤ U.S.A. 27°9N 80°52W **317 H8**
Kissimmee, L. U.S.A. 27°55N 81°17W **317 H8**
Kississing L. Canada 55°10N 101°20W **297 B8**
Kissónerga Cyprus 34°49N 32°24E **207 F8**
Kissu, J. Sudan 21°37N 25°10E **256 C2**
Kistanje Croatia 43°58N 15°55E **199 E12**
Kistna = Krishna ➤
India 15°57N 80°59E **245 G5**
Kisújszállás Hungary 47°12N 20°50E **182 C5**
Kisuki Japan 35°17N 132°54E **222 B4**
Kisumu Kenya 0°3S 34°45E **268 C3**
Kisvárda Hungary 48°14N 22°4E **182 B7**
Kiswani Tanzania 4°5S 37°57E **268 C4**
Kiswere Tanzania 9°27S 39°30E **269 D4**
Kit Carson U.S.A. 38°46N 102°48W **304 G12**
Kita Ōsaka, Japan 34°41N 135°30E **133 A2**
Kita Tōkyō, Japan 35°44N 139°44E **140 A3**
Kita Mali 13°5N 9°25W **262 C3**
Kita-Ura Japan 36°0N 140°34E **223 B12**
Kitaibaraki Japan 36°50N 140°45E **221 F10**
Kitakami Japan 39°20N 141°10E **220 E10**
Kitakami-Gawa ➤
Japan 38°25N 141°19E **220 E10**
Kitakata Japan 37°39N 139°52E **220 F9**
Kitakyūshū Japan 33°50N 130°50E **222 D2**
Kitale Kenya 1°0N 35°0E **268 B4**
Kitami Japan 43°48N 143°54E **220 C11**
Kitami-Sammyaku
Japan 44°22N 142°43E **220 B11**
Kitangiri, L. Tanzania 4°5S 34°20E **268 C3**
Kitanglad △ Phil. 8°5N 124°21E **233 G5**
Kitano Hana Iwo Jima 24°49N 141°20E **288 b**
Kitano-Kaikyō Japan 34°17N 134°58E **222 C6**
Kitaotao Phil. 7°40N 125°11E **233 H5**
Kitava I. Papua N. G. 8°40S 151°20E **286 D6**
Kitaya Tanzania 10°38S 40°8E **269 E5**
Kitazawa Japan 35°39N 139°40E **140 B3**
Kitcharao Phil. 9°27N 125°36E **233 G5**
Kitchener Canada 43°27N 80°29W **312 C4**
Kitee Finland 62°5N 30°8E **188 A6**
Kitega = Gitega Burundi 3°26S 29°56E **268 C2**
Kitengo
Dem. Rep. of the Congo 7°26S 24°8E **268 D4**
Kitgum Uganda 3°17N 32°52E **268 B3**
Kithira = Kythira Greece 36°8N 23°0E **204 E5**
Kithnos = Kythnos Greece 37°26N 24°27E **204 D6**
Kiti Cyprus 34°50N 33°34E **207 F9**
Kiti, C. Cyprus 34°48N 33°36E **207 F9**
Kitimat Canada 54°3N 128°38W **296 C3**
Kitinen ➤ Finland 67°14N 27°27E **160 C22**
Kitiyab Sudan 17°13N 33°35E **257 E3**
Kitombe
Dem. Rep. of the Congo 5°22S 18°59E **265 D3**
Kitridge Pt. Barbados 13°9N 59°25E **323 r**
Kitros Greece 40°22N 22°34E **202 F6**
Kitsman Ukraine 48°26N 25°46E **183 B10**
Kitsuki Japan 33°25N 131°37E **222 D3**

Kızılhisar Turkey 37°32N 29°17E **212 D3**
Kızılırmak Turkey 40°21N 33°58E **212 B5**
Kızılkaya Turkey 37°18N 30°27E **205 D12**
Kızılören Turkey 38°15N 30°10E **205 C12**
Kızıltepe Turkey 37°12N 40°35E **213 D9**
Kızıltoprak Turkey 40°58N 29°3E **122 C2**
Kızımkazi Tanzania 6°28S 39°30E **268 D4**
Kızlyar Russia 43°51N 46°40E **191 J8**
Kizuri Japan 34°38N 135°34E **133 B2**
Kizyl-Arvat = Serdar
Turkmenistan 39°4N 56°23E **247 B3**
Kjellerup Denmark 56°17N 9°25E **163 H3**
Kjellmyra Norway 60°30N 12°1E **164 D9**
Kjelsås Norway 59°57N 10°47E **133 A3**
Kjølen Norway 62°33N 8°45E **164 C5**
Kjölur Iceland 64°50N 19°25W **155 C7**
Kjósarsýsla Iceland 64°15N 21°30W **155 C5**
Kladanj Bos.-H. 44°14N 18°42E **182 F3**
Kladnica Serbia 43°23N 20°2E **202 C4**
Kladno Czechia 50°10N 14°7E **180 A7**
Kladovo Serbia 44°36N 22°33E **202 B6**
Kladow Germany 52°27N 13°9E **115 B1**
Klæbu Norway 63°18N 10°9E **164 A7**
Klaeng Thailand 12°47N 101°39E **236 F3**
Klagan Malaysia 5°58N 117°27E **235 A5**
Klagenfurt Austria 46°38N 14°20E **180 E7**
Klaipeda Lithuania 55°43N 21°10E **184 C8**
Klaipeda □ Lithuania 55°43N 21°7E **184 C8**
Klaksvík Færoe Is. 62°14N 6°35W **160 E9**
Klamath ➤ U.S.A. 41°33N 124°5W **304 F1**
Klamath Falls U.S.A. 42°13N 121°46W **304 E3**
Klamath Mts. U.S.A. 41°50N 123°20W **304 F2**
Klamono Indonesia 1°8S 131°30E **231 E8**
Klampenborg Denmark 55°46N 12°35E **133 A6**
Klampo Indonesia 0°7N 116°58E **235 B5**
Klang Malaysia 3°2N 101°26E **237 L3**
Klangklang Burma 22°41N 93°26E **241 D4**
Klanjec Croatia 46°3N 15°45E **199 B12**
Klappan ➤ Canada 58°0N 129°43W **296 B3**
Klara = Trysilelva ➤
Norway 61°2N 12°35E **164 C9**
Klarälven ➤ Sweden 59°23N 13°32E **162 E7**
Klässbol Sweden 59°33N 12°41E **162 E6**
Klaten Indonesia 7°43S 110°36E **235 D4**
Klatovy Czechia 49°23N 13°18E **180 B6**
Klausenburg = Cluj-Napoca
Romania 46°47N 23°38E **183 D8**
Klawer S. Africa 31°44S 18°36E **270 D2**
Klawock U.S.A. 55°33N 133°6W **303 J14**
Klazienaveen Neths. 52°44N 7°0E **170 B6**
Klé Mali 12°0N 6°28W **262 C3**
Klečany Czechia 50°10N 14°24E **135 A2**
Klecko Poland 52°38N 17°25E **185 B4**
Kleczew Poland 52°22N 18°9E **185 F5**
Kledering Austria 48°8N 16°26E **142 B2**
Kleena Kleene Canada 52°0N 124°59W **296 C4**
Klein Bonaire Bonaire 12°9N 68°18W **322 h**
Klein Jukskei ➤ S. Africa 26°6S 27°57E **135 A1**
Klein-Karas Namibia 27°33S 18°7E **270 C2**
Klein-Schlatten = Zlatna
Romania 46°8N 23°11E **183 D8**
Kleinbegin S. Africa 28°54S 21°40E **270 C3**
Kleinmachnow Germany 52°13N 13°14E **115 B2**
Kleinschönebeck
Germany 52°29N 13°42E **115 A3**
Klekovača Bos.-H. 44°25N 16°32E **199 D13**
Klembivka Ukraine 48°23N 28°25E **183 B13**
Klemetsrud Norway 59°50N 10°51E **133 A4**
Klender Indonesia 6°12S 106°54E **122 A2**
Klenovec Macedonia 41°32N 20°49E **206 A4**
Klenovec Slovakia 48°36N 19°54E **181 C12**
Klerksdorp S. Africa 26°53S 26°38E **270 C4**
Kleszczele Poland 52°35N 23°19E **185 F10**
Kletnya Russia 53°23N 33°12E **188 F7**
Kletsk = Klyetsk Belarus 53°5N 26°45E **177 B14**
Kletskiy Russia 49°16N 43°11E **191 F7**
Kleve Germany 51°47N 6°7E **178 D2**
Kličany Czechia 50°13N 14°22E **135 A2**
Klickitat U.S.A. 45°49N 121°9W **304 E4**
Klickitat ➤ U.S.A. 45°42N 121°17W **306 E5**
Klidhes Cyprus 35°42N 34°36E **207 E10**
Klimovichi Belarus 53°36N 32°0E **188 E9**
Klimovsk Russia 55°22N 37°28E **188 E9**
Klin Russia 56°20N 36°48E **188 D9**
Klinaklini ➤ Canada 51°21N 125°40W **296 C3**
Klinë Kosovo 42°37N 20°35E **202 C3**
Klintehamn Sweden 57°24N 18°12E **163 G12**
Klintsy Russia 52°50N 32°10E **189 F7**
Klip ➤ S. Africa 27°3S 29°3E **271 C4**
Klipdale S. Africa 34°19S 19°57E **270 D2**
Klippan Sweden 56°8N 13°6E **163 H7**
Klipplaat S. Africa 33°1S 24°22E **270 D3**
Klipriviersberg Nature Reserve ➤
S. Africa 26°18S 28°2E **123 B2**
Klishkivtsi Ukraine 48°26N 26°16E **183 B11**
Klisura Bulgaria 42°40N 24°28E **203 D8**
Kljajićevo Serbia 45°45N 19°17E **182 E4**
Ključ Bos.-H. 44°32N 16°48E **199 D13**
Klobuck Poland 50°55N 18°55E **185 H5**
Klockestrand Sweden 62°53N 17°45E **162 F11**
Kłodawa Poland 52°15N 18°55E **185 F5**
Kłodzko Poland 50°28N 16°38E **185 H3**
Kløfta Norway 60°4N 11°8E **163 D7**
Klondike Canada 64°0N 139°26W **294 E4**
Klondike Goldrush
U.S.A. 59°27N 135°19W **303 C14**
Klong Wang Chao △
Thailand 16°20N 99°9E **236 D2**
Klos Albania 41°28N 20°10E **202 E4**
Klosterneuburg Austria 48°18N 16°19E **142 A1**
Klosters Switz. 46°52N 9°52E **179 J5**
Klötze Germany 52°37N 11°10E **172 E5**
Klouto Togo 6°57N 0°44E **263 D5**
Kløvsjö Sweden 62°32N 14°11E **162 F8**
Kluane Canada 60°44N 139°30W **296 A1**
Kluane L. Canada 61°15N 138°40W **296 A1**
Kluang Malaysia 2°3N 103°18E **237 L4**
Kluczbork Poland 50°58N 18°12E **185 H5**
Klukhori = Karachayevsk
Russia 43°50N 41°55E **191 J5**
Klukwan U.S.A. 59°24N 135°54W **296 B1**
Klungkung Indonesia 8°32S 115°24E **231 K18**
Klyetsk Belarus 53°5N 26°45E **177 B14**
Klyuchevskaya, Sopka
Russia 55°50N 160°30E **215 D17**
Klyuchi Russia 56°18N 160°51E **215 D17**
Knaben Norway 58°40N 7°4E **164 F4**
Knappavelli Iceland 63°54N 36°W **155 D10**
Knaresborough U.K. 54°1N 1°28W **168 C6**
Knarvik Norway 60°32N 5°19E **164 D2**
Knee L. Man., Canada 55°3N 94°45W **298 A11**
Kneiss, Is. Tunisia 34°22N 10°18E **258 B2**
Knezha Bulgaria 43°30N 24°5E **203 C8**
Knight I. U.S.A. 60°21N 147°45W **303 F11**
Knight Inlet Canada 50°45N 125°40W **296 C3**
Knighton U.K. 52°21N 3°3W **169 E4**
Knights Ferry U.S.A. 37°50N 120°40W **306 H6**
Knights Landing U.S.A. 38°48N 121°43W **306 G5**
Knightsbridge London, U.K. **125 c2**
Knin Croatia 44°13N 16°17E **199 D13**
Knittelfeld Austria 47°13N 14°51E **180 D7**
Knivsta Sweden 59°43N 17°48E **162 E11**
Knjaževac Serbia 43°35N 22°18E **202 C6**
Knob, C. Australia 34°32S 119°16E **279 F2**

Knob Lake = Kawawachikamach
Canada 54°48N 66°50W **299 B6**
Knob Noster U.S.A. 38°46N 93°33W **310 F3**
Knock Ireland 53°48N 8°55W **166 C3**
Knockmealdown Mts.
Ireland 52°14N 7°56W **166 D4**
Knokke-Heist Belgium 51°21N 3°17E **170 C3**
Knossos Greece 35°16N 25°10E **205 D11**
Knowlton Canada 45°13N 72°31W **313 A12**
Knox U.S.A. 41°18N 86°37W **311 C10**
Knox Coast Antarctica 66°30S 108°0E **151 C8**
Knoxville Ga., U.S.A. 32°47N 83°59W **316 H6**
Knoxville Ill., U.S.A. 40°55N 90°17W **310 D6**
Knoxville Iowa, U.S.A. 41°19N 93°6W **310 C4**
Knoxville Pa., U.S.A. 41°57N 77°27W **312 E7**
Knoxville Tenn., U.S.A. 35°58N 83°55W **315 D13**
Knud Rasmussen Land
Greenland 78°0N 60°0W **154 B4**
Knysna S. Africa 34°2S 23°2E **270 D3**
Knyszyn Poland 53°20N 22°56E **184 E9**
Ko Kha Thailand 18°11N 99°24E **236 C2**
Kō-Saki Japan 34°5N 129°13E **222 C1**
Ko Tarutao △ Thailand 6°31N 99°26E **237 J2**
Ko Yao Thailand 8°7N 98°35E **237 a**
Koani Tanzania 6°8S 39°17E **268 D4**
Koartac = Quaqtaq
Canada 60°55N 69°40W **295 E18**
Koba Aru, Indonesia 6°37S 134°37E **231 F8**
Koba Bangka, Indonesia 2°26S 106°14E **234 C3**
Kóbánya Hungary 47°28N 19°9E **117 B2**
Kobarid Slovenia 46°15N 13°30E **199 B10**
Kobayashi Japan 31°56N 130°59E **222 F2**
Kobbegem Belgium 50°55N 4°15E **116 A1**
Kobdo = Hovd □
Mongolia 48°2N 91°37E **217 C12**
Kōbe Japan 34°41N 135°13E **223 C7**
Kobelyaky Ukraine 49°11N 34°9E **189 H8**
København Denmark 55°40N 12°26E **163 H6**
København ✈ (CPH)
Denmark 55°37N 12°39E **118 B3**
Kobenni Mauritania 15°58N 9°24W **262 B3**
Kōbi-Sho E. China Sea 25°56N 123°41E **221 M1**
Koblenz Germany 50°21N 7°36E **179 E3**
Kobo Dem. Rep. of the Congo 4°54S 17°9E **265 C3**
Kobo Ethiopia 12°2N 39°56E **257 E4**
Kobryn Belarus 52°15N 24°22E **177 B13**
Kobuchizawa Japan 35°52N 138°19E **223 B10**
Kobuk U.S.A. 66°54N 156°52W **303 C8**
Kobuk ➤ U.S.A. 66°54N 160°38W **303 C7**
Kobuk Valley △ U.S.A. 67°0N 160°0W **303 C7**
Kobuleti Georgia 41°55N 41°45E **191 K5**
Kobyletska Polyana Ukraine 48°3N 24°4E **183 B9**
Kobylin Poland 51°43N 17°12E **185 G4**
Kobylisy Czechia 50°7N 14°26E **135 A2**
Kobylka Poland 52°20N 21°10E **143 A3**
Kobyłkino Russia 54°8N 43°56E **188 D6**
Koca ➤ Turkey 40°8N 27°57E **203 F11**
Kocabaş Turkey 37°49N 29°20E **205 D11**
Kocaeli Turkey 40°45N 29°50E **203 F13**
Kocaeli □ Turkey 40°45N 29°55E **203 F13**
Kočane Serbia 43°12N 21°52E **202 C5**
Kočani Macedonia 41°55N 22°25E **202 E6**
Koçarlı Turkey 37°45N 27°43E **205 D9**
Koceljevo Serbia 44°28N 19°50E **202 B3**
Kočevje Slovenia 45°39N 14°50E **199 C11**
Kocgiri = Zara Turkey 39°58N 37°43E **212 C7**
Koch Bihar India 26°22N 89°29E **241 B2**
Kochas India 25°15N 83°56E **243 G10**
Kocher ➤ Germany 49°13N 9°12E **179 F5**
Kochi India 9°58N 76°20E **245 K3**
Kōchi Japan 33°30N 133°35E **222 D5**
Kōchi □ Japan 33°40N 133°30E **222 D5**
Kochiu = Gejiu China 23°20N 103°10E **228 F4**
Kochkor Kyrgyzstan 42°13N 75°46E **217 D9**
Kochubey Russia 44°23N 46°32E **191 H8**
Kock Poland 51°38N 22°27E **185 G9**
Kodaira Japan 35°43N 139°28E **140 A1**
Kodala India 19°38N 84°57E **244 E7**
Kodanaka Japan 35°34N 139°37E **140 B2**
Kodarma India 24°28N 85°36E **243 G11**
Koddiyar B. Sri Lanka 8°33N 81°15E **245 K5**
Kode Sweden 57°51N 11°51E **163 G5**
Kodenmacho Tokyo, Japan **140 a5**
Kodi Dem. Rep. of the Congo 3°34S 22°12E **264 C4**
Kodiak U.S.A. 57°47N 152°24W **303 H9**
Kodiak I. U.S.A. 57°30N 152°45W **303 H9**
Kodikkarai = Point Calimere
India 10°17N 79°49E **245 J4**
Kodinar India 20°46N 70°46E **242 J4**
Kodinsk Russia 58°40N 99°10E **215 D10**
Kodlipet India 12°48N 75°53E **245 H2**
Kodok South Sudan 9°53N 32°7E **257 F3**
Kodori ➤ Georgia 42°47N 41°10E **191 J5**
Kodoro Dem. Rep. of the Congo 11°26N 20°6E **264 B4**
Kodungallur = Cranganore
India 10°13N 76°13E **245 J3**
Kodyma Ukraine 48°9N 29°7E **183 B14**
Koedoesberge ➤ S. Africa 32°40S 20°11E **270 D3**
Koekelberg Belgium 50°52N 4°20E **116 A1**
Koes Namibia 26°0S 19°15E **270 C2**
Kofarnihon Tajikistan 38°33N 69°1E **217 F7**
Kofçaz Turkey 41°58N 27°12E **203 E11**
Koffiefontein S. Africa 29°30S 25°0E **270 C4**
Kofiau Indonesia 1°11S 129°50E **231 E7**
Köflach Austria 47°4N 15°5E **180 D8**
Koforidua Ghana 6°3N 0°17W **263 D4**
Kōfu Japan 35°40N 138°30E **223 B10**
Koga Fukuoka, Japan 33°45N 130°25E **222 D2**
Koga Ibaraki, Japan 36°11N 139°43E **140 A2**
Kogaluc ➤ Canada 56°12N 61°44W **299 A7**
Koganei Japan 35°42N 139°31E **140 A1**
Kogarah Australia 33°57S 151°8E **128 B1**
Køge Denmark 55°27N 12°11E **163 J6**
Køge Bugt Denmark 55°34N 12°2E **163 J6**
Kogi □ Nigeria 7°45N 6°45E **263 D6**
Kogin Baba Nigeria 7°55N 11°35E **263 D7**
Kogon Eq. Guin. 1°5N 9°42E **264 B1**
Kogon ➤ Guinea 39°43N 64°33E **216 E6**
Koh Ker Cambodia 13°30N 105°2E **236 F5**
Koh Wai Cambodia 11°54N 102°25E **237 H4**
Kohala Mts. U.S.A. 20°5N 155°45W **302 C6**
Kohat Pakistan 33°40N 71°29E **240 C3**
Kohima India 25°35N 94°10E **241 C5**
Kohkīlūyeh va Būyer Aḥmadi □
Iran 31°30N 50°30E **246 B4**
Kohler Ra. Antarctica 77°0S 110°0W **151 D15**
Kohlfurt = Węgliniec
Poland 51°18N 15°10E **185 G2**
Kohtla-Järve Estonia 59°20N 27°20E **188 C5**
Kohukohu N.Z. 35°22S 173°38E **286 B3**
Kohylnyk ➤ Ukraine 45°49N 29°40E **183 E14**
Koi Sanjaq Iraq 36°5N 44°38E **213 D11**
Koidu S. Leone 8°38N 10°59W **262 D2**
Koihoa India 8°12N 93°25E **245 K11**
Koikuntla India 15°14N 78°19E **245 G4**
Koillismaa Finland 65°44N 28°36E **160 D23**
Koimbani Comoros Is. 11°35S 43°21E **272 a**
Koin N. Korea 40°28N 126°18E **226 D5**
Koinare Bulgaria 43°11N 24°8E **203 C8**
Koivisto = Primorsk
Russia 60°22N 28°37E **188 B6**
Koivupää Finland 62°4N 26°37E **188 B6**
Koja Indonesia 6°5S 106°53E **122 A2**
Koja Utara Indonesia 6°5S 106°53E **122 A2**

Kojo N. Korea 38°58N 127°58E **224 C3**
Kojonup Australia 33°48S 117°10E **279 F2**
Kojūr Iran 36°23N 51°43E **247 B6**
Kokand = Qo'qon
Uzbekistan 40°31N 70°56E **217 D8**
Kokang Burma 23°45N 98°30E **228 F2**
Kokas Indonesia 2°42S 132°26E **231 E8**
Kokava Slovakia 48°35N 19°50E **181 C12**
Kokcha ➤ Afghan. 37°0N 69°42E **240 A7**
Kokchetav = Kökshetaū
Kazakhstan 53°20N 69°25E **217 B7**
Koke'e State Park
U.S.A. 22°6N 159°40W **302 A2**
Kokemäenjoki ➤ Finland 61°32N 21°44E **188 B1**
Kokerite Guyana 7°12N 59°35W **329 B6**
Kokhav Ya'akov
West Bank 31°53N 35°14E **123 A2**
Kokhma Russia 56°57N 41°9E **188 D5**
Koki Senegal 15°1N 15°59W **262 B1**
Kokiu = Gejiu China 23°20N 103°10E **228 F4**
Kokkilai Sri Lanka 9°0N 80°57E **245 K5**
Kokkina Cyprus 35°11N 32°36E **207 E8**
Kokkola Finland 63°50N 23°8E **160 E20**
Koko Nigeria 11°28N 4°29E **263 C6**
Koko Head U.S.A. 21°16N 157°43W **302 K14**
Koko Kyunzu Burma 14°10N 93°25E **245 G11**
Koko Nur = Qinghai Hu
China 36°40N 100°10E **218 D9**
Kokobunji Japan 35°42N 139°27E **140 A1**
Kokobunji-Temple Japan 35°44N 139°55E **140 a4**
Kokoda Papua N. G. 8°54S 147°47E **286 E4**
Kokologo Burkina Faso 12°11N 1°53E **262 C4**
Kokolopozo Ivory C. 5°8N 6°5W **262 D3**
Kokomo U.S.A. 40°29N 86°8W **311 D10**
Kokopo Papua N. G. 4°22S 152°19E **286 C7**
Kokoro Niger 14°12N 0°55E **263 C5**
Koksan N. Korea 38°46N 126°40E **224 C3**
Kökshetaū Kazakhstan 53°20N 69°25E **217 B7**
Koksoak ➤ Canada 58°30N 68°10W **295 F18**
Kokstad S. Africa 30°32S 29°29E **271 C5**
Kōktal Kazakhstan 44°8N 79°48E **217 D9**
Kokubu = Kirishima
Japan 31°44N 130°46E **222 F2**
Kokyar China 37°23N 77°10E **217 F9**
Kola Indonesia 5°35S 134°30E **231 F8**
Kola Russia 68°45N 33°8E **160 C25**
Kola Pen. = Kolskiy Poluostrov
Russia 67°30N 38°0E **186 A6**
Kolachel India 8°10N 77°15E **245 L3**
Kolachi ➤ Pakistan 27°8N 67°2E **242 F2**
Kolahoi India 34°12N 75°22E **243 B6**
Kolahun Liberia 8°15N 10°4W **262 D2**
Kolaka Indonesia 4°3S 121°46E **231 E6**
Kolar India 13°12N 78°15E **245 H4**
Kolar Gold Fields India 12°58N 78°16E **245 H4**
Kolarängen Sweden 59°16N 18°10E **139 B3**
Kolaras India 25°14N 77°36E **242 G6**
Kolarovgrad = Shumen
Bulgaria 43°18N 26°55E **203 C10**
Kolárovo Slovakia 47°54N 18°0E **181 D10**
Kolasib India 24°15N 92°45E **241 C4**
Kolašin Montenegro 42°50N 19°31E **202 D3**
Kolayat India 27°50N 72°50E **242 F5**
Kolbäck Sweden 59°34N 16°15E **162 E10**
Kolbäcksån ➤ Sweden 59°33N 16°15E **162 E10**
Kolbeinsstaðir Iceland 64°59N 22°16W **155 C4**
Kolberg = Kołobrzeg
Poland 54°10N 15°35E **184 D2**
Kolbermoor Germany 47°51N 12°4E **179 H8**
Kolbio Kenya 1°8S 41°12E **267 E5**
Kolbotn Norway 59°48N 10°48E **133 B3**
Kolbu Norway 60°39N 10°45E **164 D7**
Kolbuszowa Poland 50°14N 21°47E **185 H9**
Kolchugino = Leninsk-Kuznetskiy
Russia 54°44N 86°10E **217 B11**
Kolchugino Russia 56°17N 39°22E **188 D10**
Kolda Senegal 12°55N 14°57W **262 C2**
Kolda □ Senegal 13°5N 14°50W **262 C2**
Koldegi Sudan 12°3N 30°10E **257 E3**
Kolding Denmark 55°30N 9°29E **163 J3**
Kole Dem. Rep. of the Congo 3°16S 22°42E **264 C4**
Koléa Algeria 36°38N 2°46E **261 A5**
Kolepom = Dolak, Pulau
Indonesia 8°0S 138°30E **231 F9**
Kolguyev, Ostrov Russia 69°20N 48°30E **186 A8**
Kolhapur India 16°43N 74°15E **242 L4**
Kolia Ivory C. 9°46N 6°28W **262 D3**
Koliganek U.S.A. 59°48N 157°25W **303 G8**
Kolín Czechia 50°2N 15°9E **180 A8**
Kolka Latvia 57°46N 22°37E **184 A7**
Kolkas rags Latvia 57°46N 22°37E **184 A7**
Kolkata India 22°34N 88°21E **243 H13**
Kolkata Maidan India 22°33N 88°21E **124 B2**
Kolkata Netaji Subhash Chandra
Bose Int. ✈ (CCU) India 22°39N 88°26E **124 B2**
Kollam India 8°50N 76°38E **245 K3**
Kollegal India 12°9N 77°9E **245 H3**
Kolleru L. India 16°40N 81°10E **245 L6**
Kollum Neths. 53°17N 6°10E **170 A6**
Kolmanskop Namibia 26°45S 15°14E **270 C2**
Kolno Poland 53°25N 21°56E **184 E8**
Koło Poland 52°14N 18°40E **185 F5**
Kolo Warszawa, Poland 52°14N 20°54E **143 B2**
Koło Wielkopolskie, Poland 52°14N 18°40E **185 F5**
Kołobrzeg Poland 54°10N 15°35E **184 D2**
Kolochava Ukraine 48°26N 23°41E **183 B8**
Kologi Sudan 10°51N 30°23E **257 E3**
Kolokani Mali 13°35N 7°45W **262 C3**
Koloko Burkina Faso 11°5N 5°19W **262 C3**
Kolokani △ India 4°51N 21°40E **264 B4**
Kolombangara Solomon Is. 8°0S 157°5E **287 M9**
Kolomna Russia 55°8N 38°45E **188 D10**
Kolomyagi Russia 60°1N 30°18E **137 A1**
Kolomyya Ukraine 48°31N 25°2E **183 B10**
Kolondiéba Mali 11°5N 6°54W **262 C3**
Kolonodale Indonesia 2°0S 121°19E **231 E6**
Kolosib = Kolasib India 24°15N 92°45E **241 C4**
Kolpashevo Russia 58°20N 83°5E **216 D9**
Kolpino Russia 59°44N 30°39E **188 C6**
Kolpny Russia 52°14N 37°1E **188 F9**
Kolskiy Poluostrov Russia 67°30N 38°0E **186 A6**
Kolskiy Zaliv Russia 69°23N 34°0E **160 B25**
Kolsva Sweden 59°36N 15°53E **162 E9**
Kolubara ➤ Serbia 44°35N 20°15E **202 B4**
Kolumadulu Atoll Maldives 2°22N 73°7E **272 d**
Koluszki Poland 51°45N 19°46E **185 G6**
Kolva ➤ Russia 61°11N 56°57E **186 B10**
Kolwezi
Dem. Rep. of the Congo 10°40S 25°25E **269 E2**
Kolyma ➤ Russia 69°30N 161°0E **215 C17**
Kolymskoye Nagorye
Russia 63°0N 157°0E **215 C16**
Kôm Hamâda Egypt 30°54N 30°42E **256 H7**
Kôm Ombo Egypt 24°25N 32°52E **256 D3**
Koma Tou Yialou Cyprus 35°34N 34°8E **207 E10**
Komadugu Gana ➤
Nigeria 13°5N 12°24E **263 C7**
Komae Japan 35°38N 139°34E **140 B2**
Komagane Japan 35°43N 137°58E **223 B9**
Komaggas S. Africa 29°32S 17°32E **270 C2**
Komaki Japan 35°17N 136°55E **223 B8**
Komandorskiye Is. =
Komandorskiye Ostrova
Russia 55°0N 167°0E **215 D17**
Komandorskiye Ostrova
Russia 55°0N 167°0E **215 D17**

Kongernes Nordsjælland △
Denmark 56°5N 12°15E **163 H6**
Kongerslev Denmark 56°54N 10°6E **163 H4**
Kongkemul Indonesia 1°52N 116°10E **235 B5**
Konglu Burma 27°13N 97°57E **241 A6**
Kongmon = Jiangmen
China 22°32N 113°0E **229 F9**
Kongo Helsinki, Finland 60°20N 24°47E **132 B3**
Kongo Liberia 7°2N 11°6W **262 D2**
Kongo Central □
Dem. Rep. of the Congo 5°0S 15°0E **265 D2**
Kongola Namibia 17°45S 23°20E **270 A3**
Kongolo Kasai-Or.,
Dem. Rep. of the Congo 5°26S 24°49E **265 D4**
Kongolo Katanga,
Dem. Rep. of the Congo 5°22S 27°0E **268 D2**
Kongor South Sudan 7°1N 31°27E **257 F3**
Kongossambougou △ Mali 14°0N 8°30W **262 C3**
Kongoulou Cameroon 2°59N 11°7E **264 B2**
Kongoussi Burkina Faso 13°19N 1°32W **263 C4**
Kongsberg Norway 59°39N 9°39E **164 E6**
Kongsvinger Norway 60°12N 12°2E **164 D9**
Kongur Shan China 38°34N 75°18E **217 E9**
Kongwa Tanzania 6°11S 36°26E **268 D4**
Koni Dem. Rep. of the Congo 10°40S 27°11E **269 E2**
Koniakari Mali 14°35N 10°50W **262 C2**
Koniecpol Poland 50°46N 19°46E **185 H6**
Königgrätz = Hradec Králové
Czechia 50°15N 15°50E **180 A8**
Königs Wusterhausen
Germany 52°19N 13°38E **178 C9**
Königsberg = Chojna
Poland 52°58N 14°25E **185 F1**
Königsberg = Kaliningrad
Russia 54°42N 20°32E **184 D7**
Königsbrunn Germany 48°16N 10°53E **179 G6**
Königshütte = Chorzów
Poland 50°18N 18°57E **185 H5**
Königslutter Germany 52°15N 10°49E **178 C6**
Konin Poland 52°12N 18°15E **185 F5**
Königinhof an der Elbe = Dvůr
Králové nad Labem
Czechia 50°27N 15°50E **180 A8**
Koninklijk Paleis Amsterdam, Neths. **112 a2**
Konispol Albania 39°42N 20°10E **206 B10**
Konitsa Greece 40°5N 20°48E **204 A2**
Köniz Switz. 46°56N 7°25E **179 J3**
Konjic Bos.-H. 43°42N 17°58E **182 G2**
Konjkep Namibia 26°49S 17°15E **270 C2**
Konkö Japan 34°33N 133°36E **222 C4**
Konkouré ➤ Guinea 9°50N 13°42W **262 D2**
Konnagar India 22°42N 88°21E **124 A2**
Könnern Germany 51°41N 11°47E **178 D7**
Konnur India 16°14N 74°49E **245 F2**
Kono S. Leone 8°30N 11°5W **262 D2**
Konogogo Papua N. G. 3°29S 152°1E **288 B7**
Konongo Ghana 6°40N 1°15W **263 D4**
Konos Papua N. G. 3°10S 151°4E **286 B6**
Konosha Russia 61°0N 40°5E **186 C7**
Kōnosu Japan 36°3N 139°31E **223 A11**
Konotop Ukraine 51°12N 33°7E **189 G7**
Konqi He ➤ China 40°45N 90°10E **217 D11**
Konradshof = Skawina
Poland 49°59N 19°50E **185 J6**
Konradshöhe Germany 52°35N 13°13E **115 A2**
Konrei Palau 7°43N 134°36E **288 c**
Konsankoro Guinea 9°2N 9°0W **262 D3**
Końskie Poland 51°15N 20°23E **185 G7**
Konsmo Norway 58°16N 7°23E **164 F4**
Konstadt = Wołczyn Poland 51°1N 18°3E **185 G5**
Konstancin-Jeziorna Poland 52°5N 21°7E **143 B2**
Konstantinograd = Krasnohrad
Ukraine 49°27N 35°27E **189 H8**
Konstantinovka = Kostyantynivka
Ukraine 48°32N 37°39E **189 H9**
Konstantinovsk Russia 47°33N 41°10E **191 G5**
Konstantynów Łódźki
Poland 51°45N 19°20E **185 G6**
Konstanz Germany 47°40N 9°10E **179 H5**
Kont Iran 26°55N 61°50E **247 E9**
Kontagora Nigeria 10°23N 5°27E **263 C6**
Kontcha Cameroon 7°59N 12°15E **263 D7**
Kontiolahti Finland 62°46N 29°50E **160 E23**
Kontokali Greece 39°38N 19°51E **206 B9**
Konya Turkey 37°52N 32°35E **212 D5**
Konya Ovası Turkey 38°30N 33°0E **212 C5**
Konyin Burma 24°58N 94°42E **241 C5**
Konz Germany 49°42N 6°34E **179 F2**
Konza Kenya 1°45S 37°7E **268 C4**
Koo-wee-rup Australia 38°13S 145°28E **283 G6**
Koocanusa, L. Canada 49°20N 115°15W **304 B6**
Kookynie Australia 29°17S 121°22E **279 E3**
Ko'olau Range U.S.A. 21°35N 157°55W **302 J14**
Ko'olauloa District
U.S.A. 21°35N 157°55W **302 J14**
Ko'olaupoko District
U.S.A. 21°25N 157°50W **302 K14**
Koolyanobbing Australia 30°48S 119°36E **279 E2**
Koondrook Australia 35°33S 144°8E **282 E1**
Koonibba Australia 31°54S 133°25E **281 E1**
Koorawatha Australia 34°2S 148°33E **283 E4**
Koorda Australia 30°48S 117°35E **279 F2**
Kooskia U.S.A. 46°9N 115°59W **304 C6**
Kootenay ➤ U.S.A. 49°19N 117°39W **306 D5**
Kootenay △ Canada 51°0N 116°0W **304 C5**
Kootenay L. Canada 49°45N 116°50W **304 B5**
Kootingal Australia 31°1S 151°4E **283 A9**
Kootjieskolk S. Africa 31°15S 20°21E **270 D3**
Kopanica Czechia 50°3N 14°17E **135 B1**
Kopanovka Russia 47°28N 46°50E **191 G8**
Kopaonik ➤ Serbia 43°10N 20°50E **202 C3**
Kopaonik △ Serbia 43°10N 20°50E **202 C3**
Koparkhairna India 19°6N 72°59E **130 A2**
Kópasker Iceland 66°18N 16°27W **155 A10**
Kópavogur Iceland 64°6N 21°55W **155 C5**
Kopayhorod Ukraine 48°52N 27°53E **183 B12**
Kopenick Germany 52°27N 13°34E **115 B3**
Koper Slovenia 45°31N 13°44E **199 C10**
Kopervik Norway 59°17N 5°17E **164 E2**
Kopet Dagh Asia 38°0N 58°0E **247 B8**
Kopi Australia 33°24S 135°40E **281 E2**
Köping Sweden 59°31N 16°3E **162 E10**
Kopiste Croatia 42°48N 16°42E **199 F13**
Kopmanholmen Sweden 63°10N 18°35E **162 F12**
Koppal India 15°23N 76°5E **245 G3**
Koppang Norway 61°34N 11°3E **164 D8**
Kopparberg Sweden 59°52N 15°0E **162 E8**
Koppeh Dāgh = Kopet Dagh
Asia 38°0N 58°0E **247 B8**
Koppies S. Africa 27°20S 27°30E **271 C4**
Koppom Sweden 59°43N 12°10E **162 E6**
Koprivlen Bulgaria 41°31N 23°53E **206 B7**
Koprivnica Croatia 46°12N 16°45E **199 B13**
Köprivshtitsa Bulgaria 42°40N 24°19E **203 D8**
Köprü ➤ Turkey 36°48N 31°11E **212 D4**
Köprübaşı Turkey 38°44N 28°24E **205 C10**
Köprülü △ Turkey 37°20N 31°5E **246 B1**

Kopychyntsi Ukraine 49°7N 25°58E 177 D13
Kor Aban Somalia 3°58N 42°44E 267 D5
Kora △ Kenya 0°14S 38°44E 268 C4
Koraa Shiir Somalia 3°16N 46°6E 267 D8
Korahe Ethiopia 6°39N 44°5E 267 C6
Koral India 21°50N 73°12E 242 J5
Korangal India 17°6N 77°38E 244 E1
Korangi Pakistan 24°47N 67°8E 123 B2
Koraput India 18°50N 82°40E 244 B6
Korarou, L. Mali 15°15N 3°15W 262 B4
Korba India 22°20N 82°45E 243 H10
Korbach Germany 51°16N 8°52E 178 D4
Korbu, Gunung Malaysia 4°41N 101°18E 237 K3
Korçë Albania 40°37N 20°50E 202 F4
Korčula Croatia 42°56N 16°57E 199 F13
Korčulanski Kanal
   Croatia 43°3N 16°40E 199 E13
Kord Kūy Iran 36°48N 54°7E 247 B7
Kord Sheykh Iran 28°31N 52°53E 247 D7
Kordestān = Kurdistan
   Asia 37°20N 43°30E 213 D10
Kordestān □ Iran 36°0N 47°0E 246 C5
Kordie Burkina Faso 12°36N 2°22W 262 C4
Korē Mayroua Niger 13°18N 3°55E 262 C5
Korea, North ■ Asia 40°0N 127°0E 224 C3
Korea, South ■ Asia 36°0N 128°0E 224 C2
Korea Bay Korea 39°0N 124°0E 224 C2
Korea Strait Asia 34°0N 129°30E 227 H15
Koregaon India 17°40N 74°10E 244 F2
Korem Ethiopia 12°30N 39°32E 257 E4
Korennasa Japan 35°39N 139°29E 140 B1
Korenevo Russia 51°27N 34°55E 189 G8
Korenica = Titova Korenica
   Croatia 44°45N 15°41E 199 D12
Korenovsk Russia 45°30N 39°22E 191 H4
Korets Ukraine 50°40N 27°5E 177 C14
Korfantów Poland 50°29N 17°36E 185 H4
Körfez Turkey 40°47N 29°44E 203 F13
Korff Ice Rise Antarctica 79°0S 69°30W 151 D17
Korgalzhyn = Qorghalzhyn
   Kazakhstan 50°25N 69°11E 217 B7
Korgan Turkey 40°44N 37°13E 212 B7
Korgus Sudan 19°16N 33°29E 256 D3
Korhogo Ivory C. 9°29N 5°28E 262 D3
Koribundu S. Leone 7°41N 11°46W 262 D2
Koridalos Greece 37°59N 23°39E 112 B1
Korienzé Mali 15°22N 3°50W 262 B4
Korinthiakos Kolpos
   Greece 38°16N 22°30E 204 C4
Korinthos Greece 37°56N 22°56E 204 D4
Korioumé Mali 16°35N 3°0W 262 B4
Korissia, L. Greece 39°27N 19°53E 206 C9
Korithi Greece 37°55N 20°42E 207 D2
Kōriyama Japan 37°24N 140°23E 222 F10
Korkino Russia 54°54N 61°23E 216 B6
Korkuteli Turkey 37°4N 30°13E 205 D12
Korla China 41°45N 86°4E 217 D11
Kormakiti, C. Cyprus 35°23N 32°56E 207 E8
Körmend Hungary 47°5N 16°35E 182 C1
Kormor Iraq 35°8N 44°50E 213 E11
Kornat Croatia 43°50N 15°20E 199 E12
Kornat △ Croatia 43°50N 15°12E 199 E12
Korneshty = Corneşti
   Moldova 47°21N 28°1E 183 C13
Körnik Poland 52°15N 17°6E 185 F4
Kornsjø Norway 58°57N 11°39E 164 F8
Koro Fiji 17°19S 179°23E 287 C2
Koro Ivory C. 8°32N 7°30W 262 D3
Koro Mali 14°1N 2°58W 262 C4
Koro Sea Fiji 17°30S 179°45W 287 A3
Koro Toro Chad 16°5N 18°30E 259 D9
Koroba Papua N. G. 5°44S 142°47E 286 C2
Korobkovo = Gubkin
   Russia 51°17N 37°32E 189 G9
Korocha Russia 50°54N 37°19E 189 G9
Köroğlu Dağları Turkey 40°38N 33°0E 212 B5
Korogwe Tanzania 5°5S 38°25E 268 C4
Koroit Australia 38°18S 142°24E 282 E5
Koroleve Ukraine 48°9N 23°8E 183 B8
Korolevu Fiji 18°12S 177°46E 287 B1
Koromiri Cook Is. 21°15S 159°44W 289 h
Korona U.S.A. 29°25N 81°12W 317 F18
Koronadal Phil. 6°12N 124°51E 233 H15
Koronis Australia 38°25S 143°45E 282 D5
Koroni Greece 36°48N 21°57E 204 D4
Koronia, L. Greece 40°47N 23°10E 202 F7
Koronos Greece 37°12N 25°35E 205 D7
Koronowo Poland 53°19N 17°55E 185 E4
Koropelé C.A.R. 4°44N 17°11E 264 B3
Koropets Ukraine 48°56N 25°10E 183 B10
Koror Palau 7°20N 134°28E 288 c
Körös → Hungary 46°43N 20°12E 182 D5
Körös Maros △ Hungary 47°8N 20°52E 182 C5
Köröstarcsa Hungary 46°53N 21°3E 182 D6
Korosten Ukraine 50°54N 28°36E 177 C15
Korostyshev Russia 51°1N 39°2E 189 G6
Korotoyak Russia 51°1N 39°2E 189 G6
Korovou Fiji 17°47S 178°32E 287 A2
Koroyanitu △ Fiji 17°45S 177°39E 287 A1
Korraraika, Helodranon' i
   Madag. 17°45S 43°57E 272 B1
Korror I. Palau 7°20N 134°29E 288 c
Korsakov Russia 46°36N 142°42E 215 E15
Korsberga Sweden 57°19N 15°7E 163 G9
Korshiv Ukraine 48°39N 25°1E 183 B10
Korshunovo Russia 58°37N 110°10E 215 D12
Korsør Denmark 55°20N 11°9E 163 J5
Korsun Shevchenkovskiy
   Ukraine 49°26N 31°16E 189 H6
Korsze Poland 54°11N 21°9E 184 D8
Korti Sudan 18°6N 31°33E 256 D3
Kortrijk Belgium 50°50N 3°17E 170 D3
Korucu Turkey 39°28N 27°22E 205 B9
Korumburra Australia 38°26S 145°50E 283 C6
Korup △ Cameroon 5°15N 9°2E 264 A1
Korwai India 24°7N 78°5E 242 G8
Koryakskoye Nagorye
   Russia 61°0N 171°0E 215 C18
Koryukovka Ukraine 51°46N 32°16E 189 G7
Kos Greece 36°50N 27°15E 205 E9
Kosa Ethiopia 7°50N 36°50E 257 F4
Kosai Japan 34°42N 137°32E 223 C9
Kosan N. Korea 38°46N 127°25E 224 C2
Kosaya Gora Russia 54°10N 37°30E 188 E9
Kościan Poland 52°5N 16°40E 185 F3
Kościerzyna Poland 54°8N 17°59E 184 D4
Kosciuszko, Mt.
   Australia 36°27S 148°16E 283 D8
Kosciuszko △ Australia 36°30S 148°20E 283 D8
Kösely → Hungary 47°25N 21°5E 182 C6
Kosgi Andhra Pradesh, India 16°58N 77°43E 244 F13
Kosgi Andhra Pradesh, India 15°51N 77°16E 245 G3
Kosha Sudan 20°50N 30°30E 256 C2
Koshava Bulgaria 44°0N 22°52E 202 B7
Koshi Japan 32°53N 130°48E 222 F7
Koshigaya Japan 35°54N 139°48E 223 B11
K'oshih = Kashi China 39°30N 76°2E 217 E8
Koshiki-Kaikyō Japan 31°30N 129°49E 222 F1
Koshiki-Rettō Japan 31°45N 129°49E 222 F1
Koshim = Kazakhstan 49°50N 50°10E 190 E10
Koshkonong, L. U.S.A. 42°52N 88°58W 311 B8
Koshoku Japan 36°27N 138°6E 223 B10
Kōshū Japan 35°42N 138°44E 223 B10
Kosi India 27°48N 77°29E 242 F7

Kosi → India 28°41N 78°57E 243 E8
Košice Slovakia 48°42N 21°15E 181 C14
Košický □ Slovakia 48°45N 21°0E 181 C14
Kosino Russia 55°43N 37°50E 129 B4
Kosiv Ukraine 48°19N 25°6E 183 B10
Kosjerić Serbia 44°0N 19°55E 202 B3
Koskinou Greece 36°23N 28°13E 206 D12
Koslan Russia 63°34N 49°14E 186 B8
Köslin = Koszalin Poland 54°11N 16°8E 184 D3
Kosmach Ukraine 48°22N 24°48E 183 B9
Kosmos N. Korea 38°40N 128°22E 224 C4
Kosovo ■ Europe 42°30N 21°0E 202 D4
Kosovo Polje = Fushë Kosovë
   Kosovo 42°40N 21°5E 202 D5
Kosovska Kamenica = Dardanë
   Kosovo 42°35N 21°35E 202 D5
Kosovska Mitrovica = Mitrovicë
   Kosovo 42°54N 20°52E 202 D4
Kossou, L. de Ivory C. 6°59N 5°31W 262 D3
Kosta Sweden 56°50N 15°24E 163 H9
Kostajnica Bos.-H. 45°11N 16°33E 199 C13
Kostajnica Croatia 45°17N 16°30E 199 C13
Kostanjevica Slovenia 45°51N 15°27E 199 C12
Kostenets = Pernik
   Bulgaria 42°35N 23°2E 202 D7
Kostenets Bulgaria 42°15N 23°52E 202 D7
Koster S. Africa 25°52S 26°54E 270 C4
Kösterhavet △ Sweden 58°44N 10°56E 164 F7
Kösti Sudan 13°8N 32°43E 257 E3
Kostinbrod Bulgaria 42°49N 23°13E 202 D7
Kostolac Serbia 44°37N 21°15E 202 B5
Kostomuksha Russia 64°41N 30°49E 160 D24
Kostopil Ukraine 50°51N 26°22E 177 C14
Kostroma Russia 57°50N 40°58E 188 D11
Kostroma □ Russia 58°10N 42°50E 190 A6
Kostromskoye Vdkhr.
   Russia 57°52N 40°49E 188 D11
Kostryzhivka Ukraine 48°39N 25°43E 183 B10
Kostrzyn Lubuskie, Poland 52°35N 14°39E 185 F1
Kostrzyn Wielkopolskie,
   Poland 52°24N 17°14E 185 F4
Kostyantynivka Ukraine 48°32N 37°39E 189 H9
Kostyukovichi = Kastsyukovichy
   Belarus 53°20N 32°4E 189 F7
Kosugi Japan 36°34N 139°39E 140 B2
Koszalin Poland 54°11N 16°8E 184 D3
Kőszeg Hungary 47°23N 16°33E 182 C1
Kot Addu Pakistan 30°30N 71°0E 242 D4
Kot Kapura India 30°35N 74°50E 242 D6
Kot Moman Pakistan 32°13N 73°0E 242 C5
Kot Sultan Pakistan 30°46N 70°56E 242 D4
Kota India 25°14N 75°49E 242 G6
Kota Barrage India 25°6N 75°51E 242 G6
Kota Belud Malaysia 6°21N 116°26E 235 A5
Kota Kinabalu Malaysia 6°0N 116°4E 235 A5
Kota Tinggi Malaysia 1°44N 103°53E 237 M4
Kotaagung Indonesia 5°38S 104°29E 234 D2
Kotabaru Kalimantan Barat,
   Indonesia 0°49S 111°31E 235 C4
Kotabaru Kalimantan Selatan,
   Indonesia 3°20S 116°20E 235 C5
Kotabaru Sumatera Barat,
   Indonesia 1°7S 101°43E 234 C2
Kotabesi Indonesia 2°24S 112°58E 235 C4
Kotabumi Indonesia 4°49S 104°54E 234 C2
Kotajawa Indonesia 5°37S 104°19E 234 D2
Kotamobagu Indonesia 0°57N 124°31E 231 D6
Kotapad India 19°9N 82°21E 244 B6
Kotapinang Indonesia 1°53N 100°5E 237 M3
Kotawaringin Indonesia 2°28S 111°27E 235 C4
Kotcho L. Canada 59°7N 121°12W 296 B4
Kotdwara India 29°45N 78°32E 243 E8
Kotel Bulgaria 42°52N 26°26E 203 D10
Kotelnich Russia 58°22N 48°24E 190 A9
Kotelnikovo Russia 47°38N 43°8E 191 G6
Kotelny, Ostrov Russia 75°10N 139°0E 215 B14
Köthen Germany 51°45N 11°59E 178 D7
Kothapet India 19°21N 79°28E 244 E4
Kothari → India 25°20N 75°4E 242 G6
Kothi Chhattisgarh, India 23°21N 82°3E 243 H10
Kothi Mad. P., India 24°45N 80°40E 243 G9
Kotiro Pakistan 26°17N 67°13E 242 F2
Kotka Finland 60°28N 26°58E 188 B4
Kotlas Russia 61°17N 46°43E 186 B8
Kotlenska Planina
   Bulgaria 42°56N 26°30E 203 D10
Kotli Pakistan 33°30N 73°55E 242 C5
Kotlik U.S.A. 63°2N 163°33W 303 E7
Kotma India 23°12N 81°58E 243 H9
Kotmale → India 35°40N 139°48E 140 A3
Kotohira Japan 34°11N 133°49E 222 C5
Kotonkarfi Nigeria 8°6N 6°48E 263 D6
Kotonkoro Nigeria 11°3N 5°58E 263 C6
Kotor Montenegro 42°25N 18°47E 202 D2
Kotor Varoš Bos.-H. 44°38N 17°22E 182 F2
Kotoriba Croatia 46°23N 16°48E 199 B13
Kotovsk Russia 50°22N 44°45E 190 E7
Kotovsk Ukraine 47°45N 29°35E 177 E15
Kotputli India 27°43N 76°12E 242 F7
Kotri Pakistan 25°22N 68°22E 242 G3
Kotri → India 19°15N 80°35E 244 E5
Kötschach-Mauthen
   Austria 46°41N 13°1E 180 E6
Kottagudem India 17°30N 80°40E 244 F5
Kottayam India 9°35N 76°33E 245 K3
Kottur India 10°34N 76°56E 245 J3
Kottur India 14°45N 76°10E 245 G3
Kotu Group Tonga 20°0S 174°45W 287 Q13
Kotuy → Russia 71°54N 102°6E 215 B11
Kotyuzhany Ukraine 48°48N 27°42E 183 B12
Kotzebue U.S.A. 66°53N 162°39W 303 D7
Kotzebue Sound U.S.A. 66°20N 163°0W 303 C7
Kotzenau = Chocianów
   Poland 51°27N 15°55E 185 G2
Kouango C.A.R. 5°0N 20°10E 264 B4
Kouchibouguac △ Canada 46°50N 65°0W 299 C6
Koudougou Burkina Faso 12°10N 2°20W 262 C4
Koufey Niger 13°57N 7°56E 259 F11
Koufonisi Iraklio, Greece 34°56N 26°8E 207 F7
Koufonisi Notio Aigaio,
   Greece 36°57N 25°35E 205 D7
Kougaberge S. Africa 33°48S 23°50E 270 D3
K'ouihu Taiwan 23°35N 120°11E 225 C2
K'oubli Ivory C. 7°15N 7°14W 262 D3
Kouilou → Congo 4°10S 12°5E 264 C2
Kouilou → Congo 4°10S 12°5E 265 C2
Kouki C.A.R. 7°22N 17°3E 264 B3
Koukoulé, Mt. Comoros Is. 12°18S 43°41E 272 a
Koula Moutou Gabon 1°15S 12°25E 264 C2
Koulen = Kulen
   Cambodia 13°50N 104°40E 236 F5
Koulikoro Mali 12°40N 7°50W 262 C3
Koulikoro □ Mali 14°0N 7°45W 262 C3
Koumac N. Cal. 20°33S 164°17E 288 d
Koumala Australia 21°38S 149°15E 280 C4

Koumameveng Gabon 0°11N 11°51E 264 B2
Koumankou Mali 11°58N 6°56W 262 C3
Koumbia Burkina Faso 11°10N 3°50W 262 C4
Koumbia Guinea 11°48N 13°29W 262 C2
Koumboum Guinea 10°25N 13°0W 262 C2
Koumpenntoum Senegal 13°59N 14°34W 262 C2
Koumra Chad 8°50N 17°35E 259 G3
Koun-Fao Ivory C. 7°30N 3°15W 262 D4
Koundara Guinea 12°29N 13°18W 262 C2
Koundé C.A.R. 6°7N 14°38E 264 A2
Koungheul Senegal 14°0N 14°50W 262 C2
Koungou Mayotte 12°43S 45°12E 272 b
Koungoulou Congo 3°31S 13°20E 264 C2
Kountze U.S.A. 30°22N 94°19W 314 F7
Koupéla Burkina Faso 12°11N 0°21W 263 C4
Kouponia Greece 37°57N 23°47E 112 B2
Kourémalé Mali 11°59N 8°42W 262 C3
Kouri-shima Japan 26°42N 128°1E 288 a
Kouris → Cyprus 34°38N 32°54E 207 F8
Kourizo, P. de Chad 22°28N 15°27E 258 D2
Kourou Fr. Guiana 5°9N 52°39W 329 B7
Kourouba Mali 13°22N 10°57W 262 C2
Kouroudjel Mauritania 16°12N 11°30W 262 B2
Kouroukoto Mali 12°35N 10°55W 262 C2
Kouroussa Burkina Faso 11°35N 4°50W 262 C4
Kourouninkoto Mali 13°52N 9°35W 262 C3
Kouroussa Guinea 10°45N 9°45W 262 C3
Koussanar Senegal 13°52N 14°50W 262 C2
Koussané Mali 14°53N 11°14W 262 C2
Koussane Mali 14°10N 12°22W 262 C2
Kousseri Cameroon 12°0N 14°55E 259 F2
Koutiala Mali 12°25N 5°23W 262 C3
Kouto Ivory C. 9°53N 6°25W 262 D3
Kouts U.S.A. 41°19N 87°2W 311 C9
Kouvé Togo 6°25N 1°25E 263 D5
Kouvola Finland 60°52N 26°43E 188 B4
Kouyi Congo 2°29S 12°25E 264 C2
Kouyou → Congo 0°44S 16°38E 264 C3
Kovačica Serbia 45°5N 20°38E 182 E5
Kovdor Russia 67°34N 30°24E 160 C24
Kovel Ukraine 51°11N 24°38E 177 C13
Kovilpatti India 9°10N 77°50E 245 K3
Kovin Serbia 44°44N 20°59E 182 F5
Kovno = Kaunas
   Lithuania 54°54N 23°54E 184 D10
Kovrov Russia 56°25N 41°25E 190 B5
Kovur Andhra Pradesh, India 17°3N 81°39E 244 F5
Kovur Andhra Pradesh, India 14°30N 80°1E 245 G5
Kowal Poland 52°32N 19°7E 185 F6
Kowalewo Pomorskie
   Poland 53°10N 18°52E 185 E5
Kowanyama Australia 15°29S 141°44E 280 B3
Kowanyama △ Australia 15°20S 141°47E 280 B3
Kowlīnī Afghan. 36°10N 64°43E 240 A2
Kowloon
   Hong Kong, China 22°19N 114°11E 122 B3
Kowloon Peak
   Hong Kong, China 22°20N 114°13E 122 A3
Kowloon Tong
   Hong Kong, China 22°20N 114°10E 122 B3
Kowŏn N. Korea 39°26N 127°14E 224 C3
Kōyama Japan 31°20N 130°56E 222 F2
Koyampattur = Coimbatore
   India 11°2N 76°59E 245 J3
Köyceğiz Turkey 36°57N 28°40E 205 E10
Köyceğiz Gölü Turkey 36°56N 28°42E 205 E10
Köytendag Turkmenistan 37°30N 66°1E 240 A6
Koyuk U.S.A. 64°56N 161°9W 303 D7
Koyukuk U.S.A. 64°55N 157°32W 303 D8
Koyukuk → U.S.A. 64°55N 157°32W 303 D8
Koyukuk Nat. Wildlife Refuge △
   U.S.A. 65°55N 156°30W 303 D8
Koyulhisar Turkey 40°20N 37°52E 247 A7
Koyunyeri Turkey 40°50N 26°26E 203 F10
Koza = Okinawa Japan 26°19N 127°46E 288 a
Kozak Turkey 39°15N 27°6E 205 B9
Kozakli Turkey 39°13N 34°49E 212 C6
Kozan Turkey 37°35N 35°50E 212 D6
Kozani Greece 40°19N 21°47E 202 F5
Kozara Bos.-H. 45°0N 17°0E 199 D14
Kozara △ Bos.-H. 45°0N 17°0E 182 F2
Kozarac Bos.-H. 44°58N 16°48E 199 D13
Kozelets Ukraine 50°55N 31°7E 189 G6
Kozelsk Russia 54°2N 35°48E 188 E8
Kozhikode India 11°15N 75°43E 245 J2
Kozhva Russia 65°10N 57°0E 186 A10
Koziegłowy Poland 50°37N 19°8E 185 H6
Kozienice Poland 51°35N 21°34E 185 G8
Kozje Slovenia 46°5N 15°35E 199 B12
Kozłoduy Bulgaria 43°45N 23°42E 202 C7
Kozlov = Michurinsk
   Russia 52°58N 40°27E 190 D5
Kozlovets Bulgaria 43°30N 25°20E 203 C9
Kozłovka Russia 55°52N 48°14E 190 C9
Kozlu Turkey 41°26N 31°45E 212 B4
Kozluk Turkey 38°11N 41°31E 213 C9
Kozmin Poland 51°48N 17°27E 185 G4
Kozmodemyansk Russia 56°20N 46°36E 190 B8
Közu-Shima Japan 34°13N 139°10E 223 C11
Kożuchów Poland 51°45N 15°31E 185 G2
Kozyatyn Ukraine 49°45N 28°50E 177 D15
Kozyrevsk Russia 56°3N 159°51E 215 D16
Kpabia Ghana 9°10N 0°20W 263 D4
Kpalimé Togo 6°57N 0°44E 263 D5
Kpandae Ghana 8°30N 0°2E 263 D4
Kpessi Togo 8°4N 1°16E 263 D5
Kra, Isthmus of = Kra, Kho Khot
   Thailand 10°15N 99°30E 237 G2
Kra, Kho Khot Thailand 10°15N 99°30E 237 G2
Kra Buri Thailand 10°22N 98°46E 237 G2
Kraai → S. Africa 30°40S 26°45E 270 D4
Kraainem Belgium 50°52N 4°28E 116 A2
Krabi Thailand 8°4N 98°55E 237 H2
Kracheh = Kratie
   Cambodia 12°32N 106°10E 236 F6
Kragan Indonesia 6°43S 111°38E 235 D4
Kragerø Norway 58°52N 9°25E 164 F6
Kragujevac Serbia 44°2N 20°56E 202 B4
Krailling Germany 48°5N 11°25E 131 B1
Krainburg = Kranj
   Slovenia 46°16N 14°22E 199 B11
Krajenka Poland 53°18N 16°59E 185 E3
Krak Castle = Crac des Chevaliers
   Syria 34°47N 36°18E 250 D7
Krakatau = Rakata, Pulau
   Indonesia 6°10S 105°20E 234 D3
Krakatoa = Rakata, Pulau
   Indonesia 6°10S 105°20E 234 D3
Krakor Cambodia 12°32N 104°12E 236 F5
Kraków ✈ (KRK) Poland 50°5N 19°48E 185 H6
Kraksaan Indonesia 7°43S 113°23E 235 D4
Kralanh Cambodia 13°35N 103°25E 236 F4
Kralendijk Bonaire 12°9N 68°16W 322 h
Králíky Czechia 50°6N 16°45E 181 A9
Kraljevo Serbia 43°44N 20°41E 202 C4
Kralovéhradecký □
   Czechia 50°25N 15°50E 137 B1
Kralovský Chlmec
   Slovakia 48°27N 22°0E 181 C14
Kralupy nad Vltavou
   Czechia 50°13N 14°20E 180 A7
Kramatorsk Ukraine 48°50N 37°30E 189 H9
Kramfors Sweden 62°55N 17°48E 162 E11
Kramis, C. Algeria 36°26N 0°45E 261 A5
Krampnitz Germany 52°27N 13°3E 115 B1
Krampnitzsee Germany 52°27N 13°3E 115 B1
Krania Greece 39°53N 21°18E 202 G5

Krania Elassonas Greece 39°57N 22°2E 204 B4
Kranidi Greece 37°20N 23°10E 204 D5
Kranj Slovenia 46°16N 14°22E 199 B11
Kranji Industrial Estate
   Singapore 1°26N 103°45E 138 A2
Kranji Res. Singapore 1°26N 103°44E 138 A2
Kranjska Gora Slovenia 46°29N 13°48E 199 B10
Krankskop S. Africa 28°0S 30°47E 271 C5
Kranz = Zelenogradsk
   Russia 54°53N 20°29E 184 D7
Krapina Croatia 46°10N 15°52E 199 B12
Krapina → Croatia 45°50N 15°50E 199 C12
Krapkowice Poland 50°29N 17°56E 185 H4
Krappitz = Krapkowice
   Poland 50°29N 17°56E 185 H4
Kras Slovenia 45°35N 14°0E 199 C11
Krasavino Russia 60°58N 46°29E 186 B8
Krasieo Res. Thailand 14°49N 99°30E 236 E2
Kraskino Russia 42°44N 130°48E 220 C5
Kraslava Latvia 55°54N 27°10E 188 E4
Kraslice Czechia 50°19N 12°31E 180 A5
Krasnaya Gorbatka
   Russia 55°52N 41°45E 190 C5
Krasnaya Polyana Russia 43°40N 40°13E 191 H5
Krasnaya Sloboda =
   Krasnoslobodsk Russia 48°42N 44°33E 191 F7
Krasne Ukraine 46°7N 29°15E 183 D14
Krasni Okny Ukraine 47°32N 29°27E 183 C14
Kraśnik Poland 50°55N 22°15E 185 H9
Krasno-Presnenskaya
   Russia 55°45N 37°32E 129 B2
Krasnoarmeisk Ukraine 48°18N 37°11E 189 H9
Krasnoarmeysk = Tayynsha
   Kazakhstan 53°50N 69°45E 217 B7
Krasnoarmeysk Russia 51°0N 45°42E 190 E7
Krasnoarmeysk Russia 48°22N 44°12E 191 G6
Krasnoarmeysky Rudnik =
   Dobropole Ukraine 48°25N 37°2E 189 H9
Krasnobrod Poland 50°33N 23°12E 185 H10
Krasnodar Russia 45°5N 39°0E 191 H4
Krasnodar □ Russia 46°30N 39°0E 191 G4
Krasnodarskoye Vdkhr.
   Russia 45°1N 39°23E 191 H4
Krasnodon Ukraine 48°17N 39°44E 189 H10
Krasnogorskiy Russia 56°10N 48°28E 190 B9
Krasnograd = Krasnohrad
   Ukraine 49°27N 35°27E 189 H8
Krasnogvardeysk = Gatchina
   Russia 59°35N 30°9E 188 C6
Krasnogvardeysk Russia 45°32N 41°33E 191 H5
Krasnogvardeyskoye
   Russia 45°32N 41°33E 191 H5
Krasnohrad Ukraine 59°46N 60°12E 186 C11
Krasnokamensk Russia 50°3N 118°0E 215 D12
Krasnokamsk Russia 58°4N 55°48E 186 C10
Krasnokokshaysk = Yoshkar Ola
   Russia 56°38N 47°55E 190 B8
Krasnokutsk Ukraine 50°10N 35°0E 189 G8
Krasnolesny Russia 51°53N 39°35E 189 G10
Krasnoperekopsk Ukraine 46°0N 33°54E 189 K7
Krasnorechenskiy
   Russia 44°41N 135°14E 220 B7
Krasnoselkup Russia 65°20N 82°10E 214 C9
Krasnoslobodsk Mordvinia,
   Russia 54°25N 43°45E 190 C6
Krasnoslobodsk Volgograd,
   Russia 48°42N 44°33E 191 F7
Krasnoturinsk Russia 59°46N 60°12E 186 C11
Krasnoufimsk Russia 56°36N 57°38E 186 C10
Krasnouralsk Russia 58°21N 60°3E 186 C11
Krasnovishersk Russia 60°23N 57°3E 186 B10
Krasnovodsk = Türkmenbashi
   Turkmenistan 40°6N 53°5E 247 A7
Krasnoyarsk Russia 56°8N 93°0E 215 D10
Krasnoyarskoye Vdkhr.
   Russia 54°31N 21°56E 184 D8
Krasnoye = Krasnyy
   Russia 56°0N 92°30E 215 D10
Krasnoye = Ulan Erge
   Russia 46°22N 44°53E 191 G7
Kröpelin Germany 54°4N 11°47E 178 A7
Kropotkin Russia 45°28N 40°28E 191 H5
Kropp Germany 54°24N 9°32E 178 A5
Krosna Lithuania 54°32N 23°33E 184 D10
Krośniewice Poland 52°15N 19°11E 185 F6
Krosno Poland 49°42N 21°46E 185 J8
Krosno Odrzańskie Poland 52°3N 15°7E 185 F2
Krotoszyn Poland 51°42N 17°23E 185 G4
Krotovka Russia 53°18N 51°10E 190 D10
Krousonas Greece 35°13N 24°59E 207 E6
Krrabë Albania 41°13N 20°0E 202 E4
Krško Slovenia 45°57N 15°5E 199 C12
Krstača Serbia 42°45N 20°25E 202 D4
Kruger △ S. Africa 24°0S 31°40E 271 B5
Krugersdorp S. Africa 26°5S 27°46E 271 C4
Krui Indonesia 5°10S 103°55E 234 D2
Kruisfontein S. Africa 34°0S 24°43E 270 D3
Krujë Albania 41°32N 19°46E 202 E4
Krulevshchina = Krulyewshchyna
   Belarus 55°5N 27°45E 188 E4
Krulyewshchyna Belarus 55°5N 27°45E 188 E4
Krumbach Germany 48°13N 10°22E 179 G6
Krummë Albania 42°11N 20°25E 202 D4
Krummau = Český Krumlov
   Czechia 48°43N 14°21E 180 C7
Krumme Lanke Germany 52°27N 13°14E 115 B2
Krummensee Germany 52°35N 13°41E 115 A5
Krummhübel = Karpacz
   Poland 50°46N 15°46E 185 H2
Krumovgrad Bulgaria 41°29N 25°38E 203 E9
Krung Thep = Bangkok
   Thailand 13°45N 100°35E 113 B2
Krupanj Serbia 44°25N 19°22E 202 B3
Krupina Slovakia 48°22N 19°5E 181 C12
Krupinica → Slovakia 48°4N 18°55E 181 C11
Krupki Belarus 54°19N 29°8E 188 D5
Krusevac Serbia 43°35N 21°28E 202 C5
Kruševac Serbia 43°35N 21°28E 202 C5
Kruševo Macedonia 41°23N 21°19E 202 E5
Krushchyov = Svitlovodsk
   Ukraine 49°2N 33°13E 189 H7
Krushë e Madhe Kosovo 42°22N 20°42E 202 D4
Krushelnyksya Ukraine 49°7N 23°29E 185 J10
Kruszwica Poland 52°40N 18°20E 185 F5
Kruzenshterna, Proliv
   Russia 48°0N 154°0E 215 E16
Krychaw Belarus 53°40N 31°41E 188 F6
Krymskiy Poluostrov = Krymskyy
   Pivostriv Ukraine 45°0N 34°0E 189 K8
Krymskyy Pivostriv Ukraine 45°0N 34°0E 189 K8
Krynica Morska Poland 54°23N 19°25E 185 D6
Krynki Poland 53°17N 23°43E 185 E10
Krynychne Ukraine 45°32N 28°40E 183 E13
Kryvyy Rih Ukraine 47°51N 33°20E 189 J7
Kryzhopil Ukraine 48°23N 28°51E 183 B13
Krzanienec = Kremenets
   Ukraine 50°5N 25°43E 177 C13
Krzepice Poland 50°58N 18°50E 185 H5
Krzeszów Poland 50°24N 22°21E 185 H9
Krzna → Poland 51°59N 22°47E 185 F9
Krzywiń Poland 51°58N 16°50E 185 F3
Krzyż Wielkopolski Poland 52°52N 16°0E 185 F3
Krzeutal Germany 50°57N 8°0E 179 E5
Ksar Chellala Algeria 35°13N 2°19E 261 B6
Ksar el Boukhari Algeria 35°51N 2°52E 261 A5
Ksar el Kebir Morocco 35°0N 6°0W 260 B3

Ksar es Souk = Er Rachidia
   Morocco 31°58N 4°20W 260 B4
Ksar es Srhir Morocco 35°51N 5°34W 195 E3
Ksar Rhilane Tunisia 33°0N 9°39E 258 B1
Ksiaż Wielkopolski Poland 52°4N 17°14E 185 F4
Ksour, Mts. des Algeria 32°45N 0°30W 261 B4
Kstovo Russia 56°12N 44°13E 190 B7
Ku, W. el → Sudan 13°37N 25°15E 257 E2
Ku-Ring-Gai Chase △
   Australia 33°39S 151°14E 283 B9
Ku Tree Res. U.S.A. 21°30N 157°59W 302 J14
Kuah Malaysia 6°19N 99°51E 237 J2
Kuala Indonesia 2°55N 105°47E 234 B3
Kuala Belait Malaysia 4°35N 114°11E 235 A4
Kuala Berang Malaysia 5°5N 103°1E 237 K4
Kuala Dungun = Dungun
   Malaysia 4°45N 103°25E 237 K4
Kuala Kangsar Malaysia 4°46N 100°56E 237 K3
Kuala Kelawang Malaysia 2°56N 102°5E 237 L4
Kuala Kerai Malaysia 5°30N 102°12E 237 K4
Kuala Kubu Bharu
   Malaysia 3°34N 101°39E 237 L3
Kuala Lipis Malaysia 4°10N 102°3E 237 K4
Kuala Lumpur Malaysia 3°9N 101°41E 237 L3
Kuala Lumpur Int. ✈ (KUL)
   Malaysia 2°44N 101°42E 237 L3
Kuala Nerang Malaysia 6°16N 100°37E 237 J3
Kuala Pilah Malaysia 2°45N 102°15E 237 L4
Kuala Rompin Malaysia 2°49N 103°29E 237 L4
Kuala Selangor Malaysia 3°20N 101°15E 237 L3
Kuala Sepetang Malaysia 4°49N 100°28E 237 K3
Kuala Terengganu
   Malaysia 5°20N 103°8E 237 K4
Kualakapuas Indonesia 2°58S 110°46E 235 C4
Kualakapuas Indonesia 2°55S 114°20E 235 C4
Kualakurun Indonesia 1°10S 113°50E 235 C4
Kualapembuang Indonesia 3°14S 112°38E 235 C4
Kualapesaguan Indonesia 2°1S 110°7E 235 C4
Kualapu'u U.S.A. 21°9N 157°2W 302 B4
Kualasimpang Indonesia 4°17N 98°3E 234 B1
Kualatungkal Indonesia 0°49S 103°28E 234 C2
Kualoa Pt. U.S.A. 21°31N 157°50W 302 J14
Kuamut Malaysia 5°13N 117°30E 235 A5
Kuan Shan Taiwan 23°14N 120°54E 225 a
Kuanao Taiwan 24°31N 118°24E 225 a
Kuancheng China 40°37N 118°30E 227 D10
Kuandang Indonesia 0°56N 123°1E 231 D6
Kuandian China 40°45N 124°45E 226 G4
Kuando Kubango □
   Angola 16°25S 20°0E 265 F4
Kuangchou = Guangzhou
   China 23°6N 113°13E 121 B2
Kuangfu Taiwan 23°40N 121°25E 225 a
Kuanhsi Taiwan 24°48N 121°10E 225 a
Kuanmiao Taiwan 22°58N 120°19E 225 D2
Kuanshan Taiwan 23°3N 121°9E 225 C3
Kuantan Malaysia 3°49N 103°20E 237 L4
Kuanyin Ilan, Taiwan 24°23N 121°46E 225 A3
Kuanyin Taoyüan, Taiwan 25°2N 121°4E 225 A3
Kuapa Pond U.S.A. 21°17N 157°43W 302 K14
Kuapit Balinsasayao △
   Phil. 10°53N 124°55E 233 F5
Kuba = Quba Azerbaijan 41°21N 48°32E 191 K9
Kubah △ Malaysia 1°35N 110°9E 235 B4
Kuban → Russia 45°20N 37°30E 189 K9
Kuban Depression =
   Prikubanskaya Nizmennost
   Russia 45°39N 38°33E 191 H4
Kubaysah Iraq 33°35N 42°37E 213 C10
Kubenskoye, Ozero
   Russia 59°40N 39°25E 188 C10
Kuberle = Krasnoarmeyskiy
   Russia 47°0N 42°12E 191 G6
Kubokawa = Shimanto
   Japan 33°12N 133°8E 222 D5
Kubor, Mt. Papua N. G. 6°10S 144°44E 286 C3
Kubrat Bulgaria 43°49N 26°31E 203 C10
Kubu Indonesia 8°16S 115°35E 231 J18
Kubumesaai Indonesia 1°31N 115°6E 235 B5
Kubutabahan Indonesia 8°5S 115°10E 231 J18
Kucar, Tanjung
   Indonesia 8°39S 114°34E 231 K18
Kučevo Serbia 44°30N 21°40E 202 B5
Kuchaman India 27°13N 74°47E 242 F6
Kuchchaveli Sri Lanka 8°49N 81°6E 245 K5
Kuchenspitze Austria 47°7N 10°12E 180 D3
Kuchinda India 21°44N 84°21E 243 J11
Kuching Malaysia 1°33N 110°25E 235 B4
Kuchino-eruba-Jima
   Japan 30°28N 130°12E 221 J5
Kuchino-Shima Japan 29°57N 129°55E 221 K4
Kuchinotsu Japan 32°36N 130°11E 222 F7
Kuchl Austria 47°37N 13°10E 180 D6
Kuchnay Darvīshān
   Afghan. 30°59N 64°10E 240 C2
Kuchurhan → Ukraine 46°33N 29°57E 183 D14
Kucing = Kuching
   Malaysia 1°33N 110°25E 235 B4
Kuçovë Albania 40°47N 19°57E 202 F3
Küçükbahçe Turkey 38°33N 26°24E 205 C8
Küçükköy Balıkesir,
   Turkey 39°16N 26°42E 205 B8
Küçükköy İstanbul, Turkey 41°3N 28°52E 122 B1
Küçükkuyu Turkey 39°34N 26°34E 205 B8
Küçükmenderes →
   Turkey 37°57N 27°16E 205 D9
Küçüksu Turkey 41°5N 29°5E 122 B2
Kud → Pakistan 26°5N 66°20E 242 F2
Kuda India 23°10N 71°15E 242 H4
Kuda Indonesia 1°11N 112°58E 235 B4
Kudahuvadhoo Maldives 2°40N 72°54E 272 d
Kudahuvadhoo Channel
   Maldives 2°40N 72°54E 272 d
Kudaka-shima Japan 26°9N 127°53E 288 a
Kudal India 16°2N 73°43E 245 G1
Kudalier → India 18°35N 79°48E 244 E4
Kudamatsu Japan 34°0N 131°52E 222 D3
Kudankita Tokyo, Japan 35°... 140 a3
Kudarebe Aruba 12°37N 70°4W 322 f
Kudat Malaysia 6°55N 116°55E 235 A5
Kudirkos Naumiestis
   Lithuania 54°46N 22°53E 184 D9
Kudowa-Zdrój Poland 50°28N 16°18E 185 H3
Kudremukh India 13°15N 75°20E 245 H2
Kudryavtsi Russia 47°0N 40°0E 191 G5
Kudus Indonesia 6°48S 110°51E 235 D4
Kudymkar Russia 59°1N 54°39E 186 C9
Kueishan Tao Taiwan 24°51N 121°57E 225 a
Kueiyang = Guiyang
   China 26°32N 106°40E 228 D6
Kufra Oasis = Al Kufrah
   Libya 24°17N 23°15E 258 D4
Kufstein Austria 47°35N 12°11E 180 D5
Kugaaruk = Pelly Bay
   Canada 68°38N 89°50W 295 D14
Kugluktuk Canada 67°50N 115°5W 294 D8
Kugong I. Canada 56°18N 79°50W 298 B4
Küh Dasht Iran 33°32N 47°36E 213 F12
Küh-e Sorkh Iran 32°45N 58°0E 247 C8
Kühak Iran 27°12N 63°10E 247 E10
Kühbonān Iran 31°23N 56°19E 247 D8
Kühestak Iran 26°47N 57°2E 247 E8
Kühestān Afgh. 34°... 240 B3
Kūhīn Iran 36°22N 49°40E 246 B6
Kūhīrī Iran 26°55N 61°2E 247 E9
Kühistān-Badakhshon □
   Tajikistan 38°30N 73°0E 217 E8
Kuhmo Finland 64°7N 29°31E 160 D23

Kuhn Chae △ Thailand 19°8N 99°24E 236 C2
Kuhnsdorf Austria 46°37N 14°38E 180 E7
Kūhpāyeh Eşfahan, Iran 32°44N 52°20E 247 C7
Kūhpāyeh Kermān, Iran 30°35N 57°15E 247 D8
Kūhrān, Kūh-e Iran 26°46N 58°12E 247 E8
Kui Buri Thailand 12°3N 99°52E 237 F2
Kuiburi △ Thailand 12°10N 99°37E 237 F2
Kuichong China 22°38N 114°25E 219 a
Kuiseb → Namibia 22°59S 14°31E 270 B1
Kuito Angola 12°22S 16°55E 265 E3
Kuiu I. U.S.A. 57°45N 134°10W 296 B2
Kujalleq ☐ Greenland 61°0N 44°0W 154 E6
Kujang N. Korea 39°57N 126°1E 224 C3
Kujawsko-Pomorskie ☐ Poland 53°20N 18°30E 184 E5
Kuji Japan 40°11N 141°46E 220 D10
Kujū-San Japan 33°5N 131°15E 222 D3
Kuk Papua N. G. 5°47S 144°19E 286 C3
Kukarka = Sovetsk Russia 57°38N 48°53E 190 B9
Kukava Ukraine 48°37N 27°43E 183 B12
Kukavica Serbia 42°48N 21°57E 202 D5
Kukawa Nigeria 12°58N 13°27E 263 C7
Kuk'eng Taiwan 23°38N 120°33E 225 C2
Kukës Albania 42°5N 20°27E 202 D4
Kuki Japan 36°4N 139°40E 223 A11
Kukipi Papua N. G. 8°10S 146°6E 286 E4
Kukmor Russia 56°11N 50°54E 190 B10
Kükong = Shaoguan China 24°48N 113°35E 229 E9
Kuku Pt. Wake I. 19°18N 166°34E 302 b
Kukuan Taiwan 24°17N 121°2E 225 B3
Kukuihaele U.S.A. 20°5N 155°35W 302 C6
Kukup Malaysia 1°20N 103°27E 237 d
Kukup, Pulau Malaysia 1°18N 103°25E 237 d
Kukvidze Russia 50°40N 43°0E 190 E6
Kula Bulgaria 43°52N 22°36E 202 C6
Kula Serbia 45°37N 19°32E 182 E4
Kula Turkey 38°32N 28°40E 205 C10
Kula Gulf Solomon Is. 8°5S 157°18E 287 M9
K'ula Kangri Asia 28°14N 90°36E 241 A3
K'ula Shan Bhutan 28°14N 90°36E 241 A3
Kulachi Pakistan 31°56N 70°27E 242 D4
Kulai Malaysia 1°44N 103°35E 237 M4
Kulal, Mt. Kenya 2°43N 36°56E 266 D4
Kulaly Aral Kazakhstan 45°0N 50°5E 191 H10
Kulasekarappattinam India 8°20N 78°5E 245 K4
Kulassein I. Phil. 6°25N 120°41E 233 H3
Kulaura Bangla. 24°32N 92°3E 241 C4
Kulautuva Lithuania 54°56N 23°36E 184 D10
Kuldīga Latvia 56°58N 21°59E 184 B8
Kuldja = Yining China 43°58N 81°10E 217 D10
Kuldu Sudan 12°50N 28°30E 257 E2
Kulebaki Russia 55°22N 42°25E 190 C6
Kulen Cambodia 13°50N 104°40E 236 F5
Kulen Vakuf Bos.-H. 44°35N 16°2E 199 D13
Kulgam India 33°36N 75°2E 243 C6
Kulgera Australia 25°50S 133°18E 280 D1
Kulhudhuffushi Maldives 6°37N 73°3E 272 d
Kulim Malaysia 5°22N 100°34E 237 K3
Kulin Australia 32°40S 118°2E 279 F2
Kulittalai India 10°55N 78°25E 245 J4
Kulkayu = Hartley Bay Canada 53°25N 129°15W 296 C3
Kullen Sweden 56°18N 12°26E 163 H6
Kullu India 31°58N 77°6E 242 D7
Kulmbach Germany 50°6N 11°26E 179 E7
Kŭlob Tajikistan 37°55N 69°50E 217 E7
Kulosaari Finland 60°11N 25°0E 121 B3
Kulp Turkey 38°29N 41°2E 213 C9
Kulpawn → Ghana 10°20N 1°5W 263 D4
Kulsary = Qulsary Kazakhstan 46°59N 54°1E 187 E9
Kulti India 23°43N 86°50E 243 H12
Kulu Turkey 39°5N 33°4E 212 C5
Kulumadau Papua N. G. 9°3S 152°43E 286 E7
Kulunda Russia 52°35N 78°57E 217 B9
Kulundinskoye, Ozero Russia 53°0N 79°36E 217 B9
Kulungar Afghan. 34°0N 69°2E 242 C3
Kūlvand Iran 31°21N 54°35E 247 D7
Kulwin Australia 35°2S 142°42E 282 C5
Kulyab = Kŭlob Tajikistan 37°55N 69°50E 217 E7
Kuma Japan 33°39N 132°54E 222 D4
Kuma → Russia 44°55N 47°0E 191 H8
Kumafşarı Turkey 37°19N 29°32E 205 D11
Kumaganum Nigeria 13°8N 10°38E 263 C7
Kumagaya Japan 36°9N 139°22E 223 A11
Kumai Indonesia 2°44S 111°43E 235 C4
Kumai, Teluk Indonesia 3°0S 111°43E 235 C4
Kumalar Dağı Turkey 38°15N 30°20E 205 C12
Kumamba, Kepulauan Indonesia 1°36S 138°45E 231 E9
Kumamoto Japan 32°45N 130°45E 222 E2
Kumamoto ☐ Japan 32°55N 130°55E 222 E2
Kumano Japan 33°54N 136°5E 223 D8
Kumano-Nada Japan 33°47N 136°20E 223 D8
Kumanovo Macedonia 42°9N 21°42E 202 D5
Kumar → Afghan. 34°30N 70°28E 240 B3
Kumara N.Z. 42°37S 171°12E 285 C6
Kumarina Roadhouse Australia 24°41S 119°32E 279 D2
Kumarkhali Bangla. 23°51N 89°15E 241 D2
Kumasi Ghana 6°41N 1°38W 262 D4
Kumba Cameroon 4°36N 9°24E 263 E6
Kumbağ Turkey 40°51N 27°27E 203 F11
Kumbakonam India 10°58N 79°25E 245 J4
Kumbarilla Australia 27°15S 150°55E 281 D5
Kumbatine △ Australia 31°8S 152°35E 283 A10
Kumbhalgarh △ India 25°10N 73°35E 242 G5
Kumbhraj India 24°22N 77°3E 242 G7
Kumbia Australia 26°41S 151°39E 281 D5
Kumbo Cameroon 6°15N 10°36E 263 D7
Kumbukkan Oya → Sri Lanka 6°35N 81°40E 245 L5
Kŭmch'on N. Korea 38°10N 126°29E 224 C3
Kumdah Si. Arabia 20°23N 45°5E 248 B4
Kume-Shima Japan 26°20N 126°47E 221 L3
Kumeny Russia 58°10N 49°47E 190 A9
Kumertau Russia 52°45N 55°57E 186 D10
Kumharsain India 31°19N 77°27E 242 D7
Kumi Uganda 1°30N 33°58E 268 B3
Kumkale Turkey 39°59N 26°11E 203 G10
Kumkurgan = Qumqo'rg'on Uzbekistan 37°49N 67°35E 240 A2
Kumla Örebro, Sweden 59°8N 15°10E 162 E9
Kumla Stockholm, Sweden 59°13N 18°11E 139 B3
Kumlu Turkey 36°21N 36°27E 250 B7
Kumluca Turkey 36°22N 30°20E 205 E12
Kummerower See Germany 53°49N 12°51E 178 B8
Kumo Nigeria 10°1N 11°12E 263 C7
Kumo älv = Kokemäenjoki → Finland 61°32N 21°44E 188 B1
Kumon Bum Burma 26°30N 97°15E 241 B6
Kumotori-Yama Japan 35°51N 138°57E 223 B10
Kumta India 14°29N 74°25E 245 G2
Kumtag Shamo China 39°40N 92°0E 218 D7
Kumukahi, C. U.S.A. 19°31N 154°49W 302 D7
Kumul = Hami China 42°55N 93°25E 218 C7
Kumusi → Papua N. G. 8°16S 148°13E 286 E5
Kumyalı = Koma Tou Yialou Cyprus 35°25N 34°8E 207 E10
Kumylzhenskaya Russia 49°51N 42°38E 190 F6
Kuna U.S.A. 43°30N 116°25W 304 E5
Kunágota Hungary 46°26N 21°3E 182 D6
Kunak Malaysia 4°41N 118°15E 235 B5
Kunashir, Ostrov Russia 44°0N 146°0E 215 E15
Kunchaung Burma 23°50N 96°35E 241 D6
Kunchha Nepal 28°8N 84°20E 243 E11
Kunda Estonia 59°30N 26°34E 188 C4
Kunda India 25°43N 81°31E 243 G9
Kundar → Pakistan 31°56N 69°19E 242 D3
Kundelungu △ Dem. Rep. of the Congo 10°30S 27°40E 269 E2
Kundelungu Ouest △ Dem. Rep. of the Congo 9°55S 27°17E 269 D2
Kundian Pakistan 32°27N 71°28E 242 C4
Kundiawa Papua N. G. 6°2S 145°1E 286 D3
Kundla India 21°21N 71°25E 242 J4
Kundur Indonesia 0°45N 103°25E 234 B2
Kunene ☐ Namibia 20°0S 14°0E 270 A1
Kung, Ao Thailand 8°5N 98°24E 237 a
Kunga → Bangla. 21°46N 89°30E 241 E2
Kungälv Sweden 57°53N 11°59E 163 G5
Kungens kurva Sweden 59°15N 17°53E 139 B1
Kunghit I. Canada 52°6N 131°3W 296 C2
Kungkuan Taiwan 24°35N 120°44E 225 B2
Kungliao Taiwan 25°1N 121°54E 225 A3
Kungliga Slottet Stockholm, Sweden 139 b2
Kungrad = Qŭnghirot Uzbekistan 43°2N 58°50E 216 D5
Kungsängen Sweden 59°29N 17°45E 162 E11
Kungsbacka Sweden 57°30N 12°5E 163 G6
Kungsgården Sweden 60°37N 16°35E 162 D10
Kungshamn Sweden 58°22N 11°15E 163 F5
Kungshatt Sweden 59°17N 17°53E 139 B1
Kungsholmen Sweden 59°20N 18°2E 139 A2
Kungsör Sweden 59°25N 16°5E 162 E10
Kungssuliao Taiwan 24°37N 120°45E 225 B2
Kungu Dem. Rep. of the Congo 2°47N 19°12E 264 B3
Kungur Russia 57°25N 56°57E 186 C10
Kungurri Australia 21°4S 148°45E 280 b
Kungyangon Burma 16°27N 96°20E 241 G6
Kunhar → Pakistan 34°20N 73°30E 243 B5
Kunhegyes Hungary 47°22N 20°36E 182 C5
Kunia U.S.A. 21°28N 158°4W 302 K13
Kunigami Japan 26°46N 128°12E 288 a
Kunimi-Dake Japan 32°33N 131°1E 222 E3
Kuningan Jakarta, Indonesia 6°13S 106°49E 122 B1
Kuningan Jawa Barat, Indonesia 6°59S 108°29E 235 D3
Kunisaki Japan 33°33N 131°45E 222 D3
Kunitachi Japan 35°41N 139°27E 140 A1
Kunjirap Daban Pakistan 36°52N 75°27E 240 A4
Kunlara Australia 34°54S 139°55E 282 C3
Kunlong Burma 23°20N 98°50E 228 F2
Kunlun Antarctica 80°25S 77°7E 151 E6
Kunlun Shan Asia 36°0N 86°30E 217 E11
Kunlun Shankou China 35°38N 94°4E 218 D7
Kunmadaras Hungary 47°28N 20°45E 182 C5
Kunming China 25°1N 102°41E 228 E4
Kunming Changshui Int. ✈ (KMG) China 24°59N 102°45E 228 E4
Kunming Hu China 39°59N 116°13E 114 B1
Kunmunya ✪ Australia 15°26S 124°42E 278 C3
Kunnamkulam India 10°38N 76°7E 245 J3
Kunów Poland 50°57N 21°17E 185 H8
Kunratice Czechia 50°0N 14°28E 135 B2
Kunshan China 31°22N 120°58E 229 B13
Kunsthistorischesmuseum Vienna, Austria 142 b1
Kunszentmárton Hungary 46°50N 20°20E 182 D5
Kunszentmiklós Hungary 47°2N 19°8E 182 C4
Kuntaur Senegal 13°40N 14°48W 262 C2
Kunua Papua N. G. 5°46S 154°43E 286 C8
Kununurra Australia 15°40S 128°50E 278 C4
Kunwari → India 26°26N 79°11E 243 F8
Kunya-Urgench = Köneürgench Turkmenistan 42°19N 59°10E 216 D5
Künzelsau Germany 49°17N 9°42E 179 F5
Kunzulu Dem. Rep. of the Congo 3°28S 16°12E 264 C3
Kuohsing Taiwan 24°2N 120°51E 225 B2
Kuopio Finland 62°53N 27°35E 160 E22
Kupa → Croatia 45°28N 16°24E 199 C13
Kupang Indonesia 10°19S 123°39E 231 F6
Kupchino Russia 59°50N 30°23E 137 B2
Kupiano Papua N. G. 10°4S 148°14E 286 F5
Küpikipiki'ö Pt. U.S.A. 21°15N 157°47W 302 K14
Kupino Russia 54°21N 77°16E 217 B9
Kupreanof I. U.S.A. 56°50N 133°30W 296 B2
Kupres Bos.-H. 43°56N 17°15E 182 G2
Kupyansk Ukraine 49°52N 37°35E 189 H9
Kupyansk-Uzlovoi Ukraine 49°40N 37°43E 189 H9
Kuqa China 41°35N 82°30E 217 D10
Kür → Azerbaijan 39°29N 49°15E 213 C13
Kur → Bhutan 26°50N 91°0E 241 B3
Kür Dili Azerbaijan 39°3N 49°13E 213 C13
Kura = Kür → Azerbaijan 39°29N 49°15E 213 C13
Kurahashi-Jima Japan 34°8N 132°31E 222 C4
Kuramo Waters Nigeria 6°25N 3°26E 124 B2
Kuranda Australia 16°48S 145°35E 280 B4
Kuranga India 22°4N 69°10E 242 H3
Kurashiki Japan 34°40N 133°50E 222 C5
Kurayn Si. Arabia 27°39N 49°50E 247 E6
Kurayoshi Japan 35°26N 133°50E 222 B5
Kurbağalı → Turkey 40°58N 29°1E 122 C2
Kŭrchatov Kazakhstan 50°45N 78°32E 217 B9
Kurchatov Russia 51°40N 35°39E 189 G8
Kürdämir Azerbaijan 40°25N 48°3E 191 K9
Kurdistan Asia 37°20N 43°30E 213 D10
Kurduvadi India 18°8N 75°29E 244 E2
Kŭrdzhali Bulgaria 41°38N 25°21E 203 E9
Kŭrdzhali ☐ Bulgaria 41°38N 25°21E 203 E9
Kure Japan 34°14N 132°32E 222 C4
Küre Turkey 41°48N 33°43E 212 B5
Küre Dağları Turkey 41°50N 34°10E 212 B6
Kure I. U.S.A. 28°25N 178°25W 302 F8
Kuressaare Estonia 58°15N 22°30E 188 C2
Kurgan Russia 55°26N 65°18E 216 A7
Kurgan-Tyube = Qŭrghonteppa Tajikistan 37°50N 68°47E 217 E7
Kurganinsk Russia 44°54N 40°34E 191 H5
Kurgannaya = Kurganinsk Russia 44°54N 40°34E 191 H5
Kuri India 26°37N 70°43E 242 F4
Kuria Maria Is. = Ḩallāniyat, Jazā'ir al Oman 17°30N 55°58E 249 C6
Kurichchi India 11°36N 77°35E 245 J3
Kuridala Australia 21°16S 140°29E 280 C3
Kurigram Bangla. 25°49N 89°39E 241 C2
Kurihara Japan 35°45N 139°34E 140 A2
Kurikka Finland 62°36N 22°24E 160 E20
Kuril Basin Pac. Oc. 47°0N 150°0E 150 E15
Kuril Is. = Kurilskiye Ostrova Russia 45°0N 150°0E 215 E16
Kuril-Kamchatka Trench Pac. Oc. 44°0N 153°0E 288 C7
Kurilsk Russia 45°14N 147°53E 215 E15
Kurilskiye Ostrova Russia 45°0N 150°0E 215 E16
Kurino Japan 31°57N 130°43E 222 F2
Kurinskaya Kosa = Kür Dili Azerbaijan 39°3N 49°13E 213 C13
Kurisches Haff = Kurshskiy Zaliv Russia 55°9N 21°6E 184 C8
Kürkçü Turkey 36°34N 33°39E 250 B4
Kurkheda India 20°37N 80°12E 244 D5
Kurkur Egypt 23°50N 32°0E 256 C3
Kurla India 19°4N 72°52E 130 A2
Kurlkuta ✪ Australia 24°0S 127°5E 278 D4
Kurlovskiy Russia 55°25N 40°40E 190 C5
Kurmuk Sudan 10°33N 34°21E 257 E3
Kurmuri India 19°4N 72°53E 130 A2
Kurnool India 15°45N 78°0E 245 G4
Kuro-Shima Kagoshima, Japan 30°50N 129°57E 221 J4
Kuro-Shima Okinawa, Japan 24°14N 124°1E 221 M2
Kurobe-Gawe → Japan 36°55N 137°25E 223 A9
Kurogi Japan 33°12N 130°40E 222 D2
Kuror, J. Sudan 20°27N 31°30E 256 C3
Kurow N.Z. 44°44S 170°29E 285 E5
Kurów Poland 51°23N 22°12E 185 G9
Kurrajong Australia 33°33S 150°42E 283 B9
Kurram → Pakistan 32°36N 71°20E 242 C4
Kurri Kurri Australia 32°50S 151°28E 283 B9
Kurrimine Australia 17°47S 146°6E 280 B4
Kursavka Russia 44°29N 42°32E 191 H6
Kurse Korhi India 20°14N 80°46E 244 D5
Kurseong = Karsiyang India 26°56N 88°18E 241 B2
Kürshim Kazakhstan 48°34N 83°39E 217 C10
Kurshskaya Kosa ⌓ Russia 55°7N 20°45E 184 C7
Kurshskiy Zaliv Russia 55°9N 21°6E 184 C8
Kuršių Nerijos △ Lithuania 55°30N 21°6E 184 C8
Kursk Russia 51°42N 36°11E 189 G9
Kursk ☐ Russia 51°50N 36°10E 189 G9
Kursu = Salla Finland 66°50N 28°49E 160 C23
Kuršumlija Serbia 43°9N 21°19E 202 C5
Kuršumlijska Banja Serbia 43°3N 21°11E 202 C5
Kurşunlu Bursa, Turkey 40°3N 29°40E 203 F13
Kurşunlu Çankırı, Turkey 40°51N 33°15E 212 B5
Kurtalan Turkey 37°56N 41°44E 213 D9
Kurtbey Turkey 41°9N 26°35E 203 E10
Kurtistown U.S.A. 19°36N 155°4W 302 D6
Kuru South Sudan 7°43N 26°31E 257 F2
Kuru, Bahr el → South Sudan 8°10N 26°50E 257 F2
Kurucaşile Turkey 41°49N 32°42E 212 B5
Kuruçay Turkey 39°39N 38°29E 246 B3
Kurukshetra = Thanesar India 30°1N 76°52E 242 D7
Kuruktag China 41°0N 89°0E 217 D11
Kuruman S. Africa 27°28S 23°28E 270 C3
Kuruman → S. Africa 26°56S 20°39E 270 C3
Kurume Fukuoka, Japan 33°15N 130°30E 222 D2
Kurume Tōkyō, Japan 35°45N 139°31E 140 A2
Kurun → South Sudan 5°30N 34°17E 257 F3
Kurunegala Sri Lanka 7°30N 80°23E 245 L5
Kurupukari Guyana 4°43N 58°37W 329 C6
Kurya Russia 61°42N 57°9E 186 B10
Kuryanovo Russia 55°39N 37°42E 129 C3
Kus Gölü Turkey 40°10N 27°55E 203 F11
Kuşadası Turkey 37°52N 27°15E 212 D2
Kuşadası Körfezı Turkey 37°56N 27°0E 205 D8
Kusamba Indonesia 8°34S 115°27E 231 K18
Kusatsu Gumma, Japan 36°37N 138°36E 223 A10
Kusatsu Shiga, Japan 34°58N 135°57E 223 C7
Kusawa L. Canada 60°20N 136°13W 296 A1
Kusel Germany 49°32N 7°24E 179 F3
Kushaka Nigeria 10°32N 6°48E 263 C6
Kushalgarh India 23°10N 74°27E 242 H6
Kushalnagar India 12°14N 75°57E 245 H2
Kushchevskaya Russia 46°33N 39°35E 191 G4
Kusheriki Nigeria 10°33N 6°28E 263 C6
Kushikino Japan 31°44N 130°16E 222 F2
Kushima Japan 31°29N 131°14E 222 F3
Kushimoto Japan 33°28N 135°47E 223 D7
Kushiro Japan 43°0N 144°25E 220 C12
Kushiro-Gawa → Japan 42°59N 144°23E 220 C12
Kushiro Shitsugen △ Japan 43°9N 144°26E 220 C12
Kūshk Iran 28°46N 56°51E 247 D8
Kushka = Serhetabat Turkmenistan 35°20N 62°18E 247 C9
Kushmurun = Qusmuryn Kazakhstan 52°27N 64°36E 216 B6
Kushnytsya Ukraine 48°27N 23°15E 183 B8
Kushol India 33°40N 76°36E 243 C7
Kushtia Bangla. 23°55N 89°5E 241 D2
Kushva Russia 58°18N 59°45E 186 C10
Kuskan Turkey 36°29N 33°17E 250 B4
Kuskokwim → U.S.A. 60°5N 162°25W 303 F7
Kuskokwim B. U.S.A. 59°45N 162°25W 303 G7
Kuskokwim Mts. U.S.A. 62°30N 156°0W 303 E9
Kuskovo Russia 55°44N 37°48E 129 B3
Kusmi India 23°17N 83°55E 243 H10
Kusŏng N. Korea 39°59N 125°15E 224 C2
Kussharo-Ko Japan 43°38N 144°21E 220 C12
Kustanay = Qostanay Kazakhstan 53°10N 63°35E 216 B6
Küstenje = Constanța Romania 44°14N 28°38E 183 F13
Kustia India 22°31N 88°23E 124 B2
Küstrin = Kostrzyn Poland 52°35N 14°39E 185 F1
Kusu Japan 33°16N 131°9E 222 D3
Kut, Ko Thailand 11°40N 102°35E 237 G4
Kuta Indonesia 8°43S 115°11E 231 K18
Kutacane Indonesia 3°50N 97°50E 234 B1
Kütahya Turkey 39°30N 30°2E 205 B12
Kütahya ☐ Turkey 39°10N 29°30E 205 B11
Kutai △ Indonesia 0°23N 117°16E 235 B5
Kutaisi Georgia 42°19N 42°40E 191 J6
Kutaraja = Banda Aceh Indonesia 5°35N 95°20E 234 A1
Kutch, Gulf of = Kachchh, Gulf of India 22°50N 69°15E 242 H3
Kutch, Rann of = Kachchh, Rann of India 24°0N 70°0E 242 H4
Kutina Croatia 45°29N 16°48E 199 C13
Kutiyana India 21°36N 70°2E 242 J4
Kutjevo Croatia 45°23N 17°55E 182 E2
Kutkai Burma 23°27N 97°56E 241 D6
Kutkashen = Qäbälä Azerbaijan 40°58N 47°47E 191 K8
Kutná Hora Czechia 49°57N 15°16E 180 B8
Kutno Poland 52°15N 19°23E 185 F6
Kutru India 19°5N 80°46E 244 E5
Kutse Botswana 21°7S 22°16E 270 B3
Kuttabul Australia 21°1S 148°54E 280 b
Kutu Dem. Rep. of the Congo 2°40S 18°11E 264 C3
Kutu Moke Dem. Rep. of the Congo 3°12S 17°21E 264 C3
Kutum Sudan 14°10N 24°40E 257 E1
Kúty Slovakia 48°40N 17°3E 181 C10
Kuty Ukraine 48°16N 25°11E 183 B10
Kuujjuaq Canada 58°6N 68°15W 295 F18
Kuujjuarapik Canada 55°20N 77°35W 298 A4
Kuusamo Finland 65°57N 29°8E 160 D23
Kuusankoski Finland 60°55N 26°38E 188 B4
Kuvango Angola 14°28S 16°20E 265 E3
Kuvshinovo Russia 57°2N 34°11E 188 D8
Kuwait = Al Kuwayt Kuwait 29°30N 48°0E 246 D5
Kuwait ■ Asia 29°30N 47°30E 246 D5
Kuwana Japan 35°5N 136°43E 223 B8
Kuwana → India 26°25N 83°15E 243 F10
Kuwol-san N. Korea 38°30N 125°15E 224 C2
Kuybyshev = Samara Russia 53°8N 50°6E 190 D10
Kuybyshev Russia 55°27N 78°19E 214 D8
Kuybyshevka-Vostochnaya = Belogorsk Russia 51°0N 128°20E 215 D13
Kuybyshevo Ukraine 47°25N 36°40E 189 J9
Kuybyshevskoye Vdkhr. Russia 55°2N 49°30E 190 C9
Kuye He → China 38°23N 110°46E 226 E6
Kūyeh Iran 38°45N 47°57E 246 B5
Kuyto, Ozero Russia 65°6N 31°20E 160 D24
Kuytun China 44°25N 85°0E 217 D11
Kuyucak Turkey 37°55N 28°28E 205 D10
Kuyumba Russia 60°58N 96°59E 215 C10
Kuzey Anadolu Dağları Turkey 41°0N 36°45E 212 B7
Kuzguncuk Turkey 41°2N 29°2E 122 B2
Kuzhitturai India 8°18N 77°11E 245 K3
Kuzitrin → U.S.A. 65°10N 165°25W 303 D6
Kuzmin Serbia 45°2N 19°25E 182 E4
Kuznetsk Russia 53°12N 46°40E 190 D8
Kuznetsovo = Konakovo Russia 56°40N 36°51E 188 D9
Kuzomen Russia 66°22N 36°50E 186 A6
Kuzucubelen Turkey 36°51N 34°27E 250 B5
Kuzyminki Russia 55°42N 37°46E 129 B3
Kvænangen Norway 70°5N 21°15E 160 A19
Kværndrup Denmark 55°10N 10°31E 163 J4
Kvaløya Norway 69°40N 18°30E 160 B18
Kvam Norway 61°40N 9°42E 164 C6
Kvänum Sweden 58°18N 13°11E 163 F7
Kvareli = Qvareli Georgia 41°57N 45°47E 191 K7
Kvarner Croatia 44°50N 14°10E 199 D11
Kvarnerič Croatia 44°43N 14°37E 199 D11
Kvås Norway 58°16N 7°14E 164 F4
Kvernaland Norway 58°47N 5°45E 164 F2
Kvichak B. U.S.A. 58°48N 157°30W 303 G8
Kvicksund Sweden 59°27N 16°19E 162 E10
Kvikne Norway 62°35N 10°16E 164 B7
Kvillsfors Sweden 57°24N 15°29E 163 G9
Kvina → Norway 58°19N 6°55E 164 F3
Kvinlog Norway 58°31N 6°55E 164 F3
Kvirily = Zestaponi Georgia 42°6N 43°0E 191 J6
Kvismare kanal Sweden 59°11N 15°35E 162 E9
Kvissleby Sweden 62°18N 17°22E 162 B11
Kviteseid Norway 59°24N 8°29E 164 E5
Kvitøya Svalbard 80°8N 32°35E 154 A14
Kwabhaca S. Africa 30°51S 29°0E 271 D4
Kwai = Khwae Noi → Thailand 14°1N 99°32E 236 E2
Kwai Chung Hong Kong, China 22°22N 114°7E 122 A2
Kwajalein Marshall Is. 9°5N 167°20E 288 G8
Kwakhanai Botswana 21°39S 21°16E 270 B3
Kwakoegron Suriname 5°12N 55°25W 329 B6
Kwale Coast, Kenya 4°15S 39°31E 268 C4
Kwale Nigeria 5°46N 6°26E 263 D6
Kwamalasamutu Suriname 2°20N 56°47W 329 C6
KwaMashu S. Africa 29°45S 30°58E 271 C5
Kwamouth Dem. Rep. of the Congo 3°9S 16°12E 264 C3
Kwando → Africa 18°27S 23°32E 265 F4
Kwangchow = Guangzhou China 23°6N 113°13E 121 B2
Kwangdaeri N. Korea 40°34N 127°33E 227 D14
Kwango ☐ Dem. Rep. of the Congo 7°0S 18°0E 265 D3
Kwango → Dem. Rep. of the Congo 3°14S 17°22E 264 C3
Kwangsi-Chuang = Guangxi Zhuangzu Zizhiqu ☐ China 24°0N 109°0E 228 F7
Kwangtung = Guangdong ☐ China 23°0N 113°0E 229 F9
Kwanza Norte ☐ Angola 8°50S 14°30E 265 D2
Kwanza Sul ☐ Angola 10°50S 14°50E 265 E2
Kwara ☐ Nigeria 8°45N 4°30E 263 D6
Kwataboahegan → Canada 51°9N 80°50W 298 B3
Kwatisore Indonesia 3°18S 134°50E 231 E8
KwaZulu Natal ☐ S. Africa 29°0S 30°0E 271 C5
Kweichow = Guizhou ☐ China 27°0N 107°0E 228 D6
Kweilin = Guilin China 25°18N 110°15E 229 E8
Kweisui = Hohhot China 40°52N 111°40E 226 D6
Kweiyang = Guiyang China 26°32N 106°40E 228 D6
Kwekwe Zimbabwe 18°58S 29°48E 269 F2
Kweneng ☐ Botswana 24°0S 25°0E 270 B3
Kwenge → Dem. Rep. of the Congo 4°50S 18°44E 265 C3
Kwethluk U.S.A. 60°49N 161°26W 303 F7
Kwidzyn Poland 53°44N 18°55E 184 E5
Kwigillingok U.S.A. 59°51N 163°8W 303 G7
Kwiha Ethiopia 13°29N 39°32E 257 E4
Kwikila Papua N. G. 9°49S 147°38E 286 E4
Kwilu ☐ Dem. Rep. of the Congo 5°30S 19°0E 265 C3
Kwilu → Dem. Rep. of the Congo 3°22S 17°22E 265 C3
Kwinana Australia 32°15S 115°47E 279 F2
Kwinbet Burma 16°20N 94°14E 241 G5
Kwisa → Poland 51°34N 15°24E 185 G2
Kwoka Indonesia 0°31S 132°27E 231 E8
Kwolla Nigeria 9°0N 9°15E 263 D6
Kwun Tong Hong Kong, China 22°19N 114°13E 122 B3
Kya-in-Seikkyi Burma 16°2N 98°8E 241 G7
Kyabé Chad 9°30N 19°0E 259 G3
Kyabra Cr. → Australia 25°36S 142°55E 281 D3
Kyabram Australia 36°19S 145°4E 283 D6
Kyaikkami Burma 16°4N 97°34E 241 G6
Kyaiklat Burma 16°25N 95°40E 241 G5
Kyaikmaraw Burma 16°23N 97°44E 241 G6
Kyaikthin Burma 23°32N 95°40E 241 D5
Kyaikto Burma 17°20N 97°3E 236 D1
Kyaing Tong = Keng Tung Burma 21°18N 99°39E 236 B2
Kyakhta Russia 50°30N 106°25E 215 D11
Kyambura ⌓ Uganda 0°7S 30°9E 268 C3
Kyan-zaki Japan 26°5N 127°39E 288 a
Kyancutta Australia 33°8S 135°33E 281 E2
Kyangin Burma 18°20N 95°20E 241 F5
Kyaukhnyat Burma 18°15N 97°31E 241 F6
Kyaukki Burma 18°27N 96°56E 241 F6
Kyaukkyi Burma 18°15N 94°29E 241 F5
Kyaukme Burma 22°32N 97°2E 241 D6
Kyaukpadaung Burma 20°52N 95°8E 241 E5
Kyaukpyu Burma 19°28N 93°30E 241 F4
Kyaukse Burma 21°36N 96°10E 241 E6
Kyauktaga Burma 18°10N 96°37E 241 F6
Kyauktan Burma 16°38N 96°19E 241 G6
Kyauktaw Burma 20°51N 92°59E 241 E4
Kyaunggon Burma 17°6N 95°11E 241 G5
Kyawkku Burma 21°48N 96°56E 241 E6
Kybartai Lithuania 54°39N 22°45E 184 D9
Kyburz U.S.A. 38°47N 120°18W 306 G6
Kyeintali Burma 18°0N 94°29E 241 G5
Kyelang India 32°35N 77°2E 242 C7
Kyenjojo Uganda 0°40N 30°37E 268 B3
Kyidaunggan Burma 19°53N 96°12E 241 F6
Kyje Czechia 50°6N 14°33E 135 B3
Kyjov Czechia 49°1N 17°7E 181 B10
Kyklades Greece 37°0N 24°30E 204 E6
Kyle Sask., Canada 50°50N 108°2W 297 C7
Kyle Tex., U.S.A. 29°59N 97°53W 314 F6
Kyle Dam = Mutirikwe Dam Zimbabwe 20°15S 31°0E 269 G3
Kyle of Lochalsh U.K. 57°17N 5°44W 167 D3
Kyll → Germany 49°48N 6°41E 179 F2
Kyllburg Germany 50°2N 6°34E 179 E2
Kyllini Greece 37°55N 21°8E 207 D3
Kyllini, Akra Greece 37°57N 21°8E 207 D3
Kymijoki → Finland 60°30N 26°55E 188 B4
Kymmene älv = Kymijoki → Finland 60°30N 26°55E 188 B4
Kyneton Australia 37°10S 144°29E 282 D6
Kynuna Australia 21°37S 141°55E 280 C3
Kyō-ga-Saki Japan 35°45N 135°15E 223 B7
Kyoga, L. Uganda 1°35N 33°0E 268 B3
Kyogle Australia 28°40S 153°0E 281 D5
Kyom → South Sudan 8°58N 28°13E 257 F2
Kyŏngju = Gyeongju S. Korea 35°51N 129°14E 224 E4
Kyŏngsŏng N. Korea 41°35N 129°36E 224 B4
Kyōtamba Japan 35°6N 135°17E 223 B7
Kyōto Japan 35°0N 135°45E 223 C7
Kyōto ☐ Japan 35°15N 135°45E 223 B7
Kyparissovouno Cyprus 35°19N 33°10E 207 E9
Kyperounda Cyprus 34°56N 32°58E 207 F8
Kypros = Cyprus ■ Asia 35°0N 33°0E 207 F9
Kyrenia Cyprus 35°20N 33°20E 207 E9
Kyrgyzstan ■ Asia 42°0N 75°0E 217 D9
Kyritz Germany 52°56N 12°24E 178 C8
Kyrkhult Sweden 56°22N 14°34E 163 H8
Kyrksæterøra Norway 63°18N 9°5E 164 A6
Kyrnasivka Ukraine 48°35N 28°58E 183 B13
Kyrnychky Ukraine 45°42N 29°4E 183 E14
Kyro älv = Kyrönjoki → Finland 63°14N 21°45E 160 E19
Kyrönjoki → Finland 63°14N 21°45E 160 E19
Kystatyam Russia 67°20N 123°10E 215 C13
Kysucké Nové Mesto Slovakia 49°18N 18°47E 181 B11
Kytay, Ozero Ukraine 45°40N 29°13E 183 E14
Kythira Greece 36°8N 23°0E 204 E5
Kythnos Greece 37°26N 24°27E 204 D6
Kythréa Cyprus 35°15N 33°29E 207 E9
Kyu-hkok Burma 24°4N 98°4E 241 C7
Kyūhōji Japan 34°38N 135°33E 133 B2
Kyunhla Burma 23°25N 95°15E 241 D5
Kyuquot Sound Canada 50°2N 127°22W 296 D3
Kyurdamir = Kürdämir Azerbaijan 40°25N 48°3E 191 K9
Kyūshū Japan 33°0N 131°0E 222 E3
Kyūshū ☐ Japan 33°0N 131°0E 222 E3
Kyūshū-Palau Ridge Pac. Oc. 20°0N 136°0E 288 E5
Kyūshū-Sanchi Japan 32°35N 131°17E 222 E3
Kyūshū Trench Japan 31°35N 134°10E 222 F6
Kyustendil Bulgaria 42°16N 22°41E 202 D6
Kyustendil ☐ Bulgaria 42°16N 22°41E 202 D6
Kyusyur Russia 70°19N 127°30E 215 B13
Kywong Australia 34°58S 146°44E 283 C7
Kyyiv Ukraine 50°30N 30°28E 177 C16
Kyyiv ☐ Ukraine 50°5N 30°45E 189 G6
Kyyivske Vdskh. Ukraine 51°0N 30°25E 177 C16
Kyzyl Russia 51°50N 94°30E 217 B12
Kyzyl-Adyr Kyrgyzstan 42°39N 71°35E 217 D8
Kyzyl-Burun = Siyäzän Azerbaijan 41°3N 49°10E 191 K9
Kyzyl-Khoto = Kyzyl Russia 51°50N 94°30E 217 B12
Kyzyl Kum Uzbekistan 42°30N 65°0E 217 D7
Kyzyl-Kyya Kyrgyzstan 40°16N 72°8E 217 D8
Kyzyl Orda = Qyzylorda Kazakhstan 44°48N 65°28E 216 D7
Kyzyl-Suu Kyrgyzstan 42°20N 78°0E 217 D9

L

L.A. County Art Museum U.S.A. 34°4N 118°21W 126 B2
L.F. Wade Int. ✈ (BDA) Bermuda 32°22N 64°41W 153 a
La Albuera Spain 38°45N 6°49W 195 G4
La Alcarria Spain 40°31N 2°45W 196 E2
La Almarcha Spain 39°41N 2°24W 196 F2
La Almunia de Doña Godina Spain 41°29N 1°23W 196 D3
La Amistad △ Cent. Amer. 9°28N 83°18W 320 E3
La Asunción Venezuela 11°2N 63°51W 329 a
La Baie Canada 48°19N 70°53W 299 C5
La Banda Argentina 27°45S 64°10W 334 B3
La Bañeza Spain 42°17N 5°54W 194 C5
La Barca Mexico 20°17N 102°34W 318 C4
La Barceloneta Spain 41°22N 2°11E 114 A2
La Barge U.S.A. 42°16N 110°12W 304 E8
La Barra Nic. 12°54N 83°33W 320 D3
La Bastide-Puylaurent France 44°35N 3°55E 174 D7
La Baule France 47°17N 2°24W 172 E4
La Belle Fla., U.S.A. 26°46N 81°26W 317 J8
La Belle Mo., U.S.A. 40°7N 91°55W 310 D5
La Biche → Canada 59°57N 123°50W 296 B4
La Biche, L. Canada 54°50N 112°3W 296 C6
La Bisbal d'Empordà Spain 41°58N 3°2E 196 D8
La Blanca Chile 33°30S 70°40W 137 C2
La Boca Argentina 34°38S 58°22W 117 B2
La Brea Peru 4°40S 81°7W 330 A1
La Brea Trin. & Tob. 10°15N 61°37W 323 t
La Brède France 44°41N 0°32W 174 D3
La Bresse France 48°2N 6°53E 173 D13
La Bretèche France 48°51N 2°1E 134 A1
La Bureba Spain 42°36N 3°24W 194 C7
La Cal → Bolivia 17°27S 58°15W 331 D6
La Calera Chile 32°50S 71°10W 334 C1
La Calle = El Kala Algeria 36°53N 8°26E 261 A6
La Campana △ Chile 32°58S 71°14W 334 C1
La Campiña Lima, Peru 12°11S 77°0W 124 C2
La Campiña Spain 37°45N 4°45W 195 H6
La Canal = Sa Canal Spain 38°51N 1°23E 206 D1
La Cañiza = A Cañiza Spain 42°13N 8°16W 194 C2
La Canourgue France 44°26N 3°13E 174 D7
La Capelle France 49°59N 3°50E 173 C10
La Carlota Argentina 33°30S 63°20W 334 C3
La Carlota Phil. 10°25N 122°55E 233 F4
La Carlota Spain 37°40N 4°56W 195 H6
La Carolina Spain 38°17N 3°38W 195 G7
La Castellana Phil. 10°20N 123°3E 233 F4
La Cavalerie France 44°1N 3°10E 174 D7
La Ceiba Honduras 15°40N 86°50W 320 C2
La Ceiba Venezuela 9°28N 71°4W 328 C3
La Celle-St-Cloud France 48°50N 2°9E 134 A1
La Certosa, Isole Venice, Italy 142 b5
La Chaise-Dieu France 45°18N 3°42E 174 C7
La Chapelle d'Angillon France 47°21N 2°25E 173 E9
La Chapelle-St-Luc France 48°20N 4°3E 173 D11
La Chapelle-sur-Erdre France 47°18N 1°34W 172 E5
La Charité-sur-Loire France 47°10N 3°1E 173 E10
La Chartre-sur-le-Loir France 47°44N 0°34E 172 E7
La Châtaigneraie France 46°39N 0°44W 174 B3
La Châtre France 46°35N 2°0E 173 F9
La Chaux → Mauritius 20°23S 57°41E 272 e
La Chaux-de-Fonds Switz. 47°7N 6°50E 179 H2
La Chorrera Colombia 0°44S 73°1W 328 D3
La Chorrera Panama 8°53N 79°47W 320 c
La Ciotat France 43°10N 5°37E 175 E9
La Cisterna Chile 33°32S 70°39W 137 C2
La Ciudadela Mexico City, Mexico 128 c2
La Clayette France 46°17N 4°19E 173 F11
La Cocha Argentina 27°50S 65°40W 334 B2
La Concepción = Ri-Aba Eq. Guin. 3°28N 8°40E 263 E6
La Concepción Panama 8°31N 82°37W 320 E3
La Concepción Venezuela 10°30N 71°50W 328 A3
La Concordia Mexico 16°5N 92°38W 319 D6
La Constitución, Plaza de = Zócalo Mexico City, Mexico 128 b3
La Coruña = A Coruña Spain 43°20N 8°25W 194 B2
La Côte-St-André France 45°24N 5°15E 175 C9
La Courneuve France 48°55N 2°22E 134 A3
La Courtine France 45°41N 2°15E 174 C6
La Crau Bouches-du-Rhône, France 43°32N 4°40E 175 E8
La Crau Var, France 43°9N 6°4E 175 E10
La Crescent U.S.A. 43°50N 91°18W 308 D8
La Crete Canada 58°11N 116°24W 296 B5
La Crosse Fla., U.S.A. 29°51N 82°24W 316 F7
La Crosse Kans., U.S.A. 38°32N 99°18W 308 F4
La Crosse Wis., U.S.A. 43°48N 91°15W 308 D8
La Cruz Costa Rica 11°4N 85°39W 320 D2
La Cruz Sinaloa, Mexico 23°55N 106°54W 318 C3
La Cumbre, Volcán Ecuador 0°21S 91°32W 330 a
La Dehesa Chile 33°21S 70°33W 137 B2
La Désirade Guadeloupe 16°18N 61°3W 322 e
La Digue Seychelles 4°20S 55°51E 272 c
La Dorada Colombia 5°30N 74°40W 328 B3
La Encantada Peru 12°13S 77°1W 124 C2
La Esperanza Argentina 40°26S 68°32W 336 B3
La Esperanza Cuba 22°46N 83°44W 320 B3
La Esperanza Honduras 14°15N 88°10W 320 D2
La Estación Spain 40°27N 3°48W 127 B1
La Estrada = A Estrada Spain 42°43N 8°27W 194 C2
La Falaise, Gorges de Martinique 14°49N 61°10W 322 j
La Faouët France 48°2N 3°30W 172 D3
La Fayette U.S.A. 34°42N 85°17W 315 D12
La Fé Cuba 22°2N 84°15W 320 B3
La Fenice, Teatro Venice, Italy 142 b2
La Fère France 49°39N 3°21E 173 C10
La Ferté-Bernard France 48°10N 0°40E 172 D7
La Ferté-Gaucher France 48°47N 3°19E 173 D10
La Ferté-Macé France 48°35N 0°22W 172 D6
La Ferté-St-Aubin France 47°42N 1°57E 173 E8
La Ferté-sous-Jouarre France 48°56N 3°8E 173 D10
La Ferté-Vidame France 48°37N 0°53E 172 D7
La Flèche France 47°42N 0°4W 172 E6
La Floresta Spain 41°26N 2°3E 114 A1
La Florida Chile 33°33S 70°34W 137 C2
La Foa N. Cal. 21°43S 165°50E 288 d
La Follette U.S.A. 36°23N 84°7W 315 C12
La Fontaine U.S.A. 40°40N 85°43W 311 D11
La Fortuna Spain 40°21N 3°46W 127 B1
La França Spain 41°22N 2°9E 114 A1
La Fregeneda Spain 40°58N 6°54W 194 E4
La Fría Venezuela 8°13N 72°15W 328 B3
La Fuente Venezuela 11°4N 63°52W 329 a
La Fuente de San Esteban Spain 40°49N 6°15W 194 E4
La Gacilly France 47°45N 2°8W 172 E4
La Garenne-Colombes France 48°54N 2°15E 134 A2
La Gi Vietnam 10°40N 107°45E 237 G6
La Gineta Spain 39°8N 2°1W 197 F2
La Giudecca Venice, Italy 142 c2
La Giustiniana Italy 41°59N 12°24E 136 B1
La Glória Colombia 8°37N 73°48W 328 B3
La Goulette Tunisia 36°53N 10°18E 200 F3
La Gran Sabana Venezuela 5°30N 61°30W 329 B5
La Grand'Combe France 44°13N 4°2E 175 D8
La Grande U.S.A. 45°20N 118°5W 304 D4
La Grande → Canada 53°50N 79°0W 298 B5
La Grande 3, Rés. Canada 53°40N 75°10W 298 B4
La Grande 4, Rés. Canada 54°0N 73°15W 298 B5
La Grande-Motte France 43°23N 4°5E 175 E8
La Grange Calif., U.S.A. 37°42N 120°27W 306 H6
La Grange Ga., U.S.A. 33°2N 85°2W 316 B4
La Grange Ky., U.S.A. 38°24N 85°22W 311 F11
La Grange Mo., U.S.A. 40°3N 91°35W 310 D5
La Grange Tex., U.S.A. 29°54N 96°52W 314 G6
La Granja Chile 33°31S 70°38W 137 C2
La Grave France 45°3N 6°18E 175 C10
La Grazia, Isola Venice, Italy 142 c3
La Grita Venezuela 8°8N 71°59W 328 B3
La Guaira Venezuela 10°36N 66°56W 328 A4
La Guarda △ Mexico 29°20N 113°27W 318 B2
La Guardia = A Guarda Spain 41°56N 8°52W 194 D2
La Guardia Venezuela 11°0N 64°1W 329 a
La Guardia, New York ✈ (LGA) U.S.A. 40°46N 73°52W 132 B2
La Gudiña = A Gudiña Spain 42°4N 7°8W 194 C3
La Güera Mauritania 20°51N 17°0W 260 D1
La Guerche-de-Bretagne France 47°57N 1°16W 172 E5
La Guerche-sur-l'Aubois France 46°58N 2°56E 173 F9
La Habana Cuba 23°8N 82°22W 320 B3
La Harpe U.S.A. 40°35N 90°58W 310 D6
La Haute Vallée de Chevreuse ⌓ France 48°35N 1°58E 173 D8
La Haye-du-Puits France 49°17N 1°33W 172 C5
La Horqueta Venezuela 7°55N 60°20W 329 B5
La Horquetta Trin. & Tob. 10°36N 61°16W 323 t
La Horra Spain 41°44N 3°53W 194 D7
La Hulpe Belgium 50°43N 4°30E 116 B2
La Independencia Mexico 16°15N 92°1W 319 D6
La Isabela Dom. Rep. 19°58N 71°2W 321 C5
La Isleta Venezuela 10°54N 63°56W 329 a
La Jonquera Spain 42°25N 2°53E 196 C7
La Joya Peru 16°43S 71°52W 330 D3
La Junta U.S.A. 37°59N 103°33W 304 H12
La Laguna = San Cristóbal de La Laguna Canary Is. 28°28N 16°18W 153 e1
La Lézarde → Martinique 14°35N 61°1W 322 j
La Libertad = Puerto Libertad Mexico 29°55N 112°43W 318 B2
La Libertad Guatemala 16°47N 90°7W 320 C1
La Libertad ☐ Peru 8°0S 78°30W 330 B2
La Ligua Chile 32°30S 71°16W 334 C1
La Línea de la Concepción Spain 36°15N 5°23W 195 J5
La Llacuna Spain 41°24N 2°12E 114 A2
La Loche Canada 56°29N 109°26W 297 B7
La Loma Mexico 19°31N 99°11W 128 A1
La Londe-les-Maures France 43°8N 6°14E 175 E10
La Lora Spain 42°45N 4°0W 194 C7
La Loupe France 48°29N 1°0E 172 D8
La Louvière Belgium 50°27N 4°10E 170 D4
La Lucila Argentina 34°30S 58°29W 117 B2
La Lune Trin. & Tob. 10°3N 61°22W 323 t
La Machine France 46°54N 3°27E 173 F10
La Maddalena Italy 41°13N 9°24E 200 A2
La Maladrerie France 48°54N 2°1E 134 A1
La Malbaie Canada 47°40N 70°10W 299 C5
La Malinche △ Mexico 19°15N 98°3W 319 D5
La Mancha Spain 39°10N 2°54W 197 F2
La Manche → Martinique 14°33N 61°0W 322 j
La Mariña Spain 43°30N 7°40W 194 B3
La Martre, L. Canada 63°15N 117°55W 296 A5
La Merced Peru 11°3S 75°19W 330 C2
La Mercy ✈ (DUR) S. Africa 29°37S 31°7E 271 C5
La Mesa Baja Calif., Mexico 32°30N 116°57W 307 N10
La Mesa Calif., U.S.A. 32°46N 117°1W 307 N9
La Mesilla U.S.A. 32°16N 106°48W 305 K10
La Milla, Cerro Peru 12°2S 77°5W 124 B2
La Moille U.S.A. 41°32N 89°17W 310 C7
La Moine → U.S.A. 39°59N 90°31W 310 E6
La Monachina Italy 41°53N 12°21E 136 B1
La Montagne Réunion 20°53S 55°26E 272 f
La Monte U.S.A. 38°46N 93°26W 310 F3
La Moraleja Spain 40°30N 3°38W 127 A2
La Mothe-Achard France 46°37N 1°40W 172 F5
La Motte-Chalançon France 44°30N 5°21E 175 D9
La Motte-du-Caire France 44°20N 6°3E 175 D10
La Motte-Servolex France 45°35N 5°53E 175 C9

La Moure U.S.A. 46°21N 98°18W 308 B4
La Moustique ➛ Guadeloupe 16°10N 61°34W 322 e
La Muela Spain 41°36N 1°7W 196 D3
La Mure France 44°55N 5°48E 175 D9
La Negra Chile 23°46S 70°18W 334 A1
La Nopalera Mexico 19°18N 99°59W 128 C2
La Oliva Canary Is. 28°36N 13°57W 153 e2
La Oraya Peru 11°32S 75°54W 330 C2
La Orotava Canary Is. 28°22N 16°31W 153 e1
La Oroya Peru 11°32S 75°54W 330 C2
La Pacaudière France 46°11N 3°52E 173 F10
La Pagerie Martinique 14°32N 61°3W 322 j
La Palma Canary Is. 28°40N 17°50W 153 e1
La Palma Panama 8°15N 78°0W 320 E4
La Palma del Condado Spain 37°21N 6°38W 195 H4
La Palmyre France 45°43N 1°9W 174 C2
La Paloma Chile 30°35S 71°0W 334 C1
La Pampa □ Argentina 36°50S 66°0W 334 D2
La Paragua Venezuela 6°50N 63°20W 329 B5
La Pastora Trin. & Tob. 10°42N 61°19W 323 t
La Paternal Argentina 34°35S 58°26W 117 B2
La Paya △ Colombia 0°0 75°5W 328 C2
La Paz Entre Ríos, Argentina 30°50S 59°45W 334 C4
La Paz San Luis, Argentina 33°30S 67°20W 334 C2
La Paz Bolivia 16°20S 68°10W 330 D4
La Paz Honduras 14°20N 87°47W 320 D2
La Paz Baja Calif. S., Mexico 24°10N 110°18W 318 C2
La Paz Abra, Phil. 17°40N 120°41E 232 C3
La Paz Tarlac, Phil. 15°26N 120°45E 232 D3
La Paz □ Bolivia 15°30S 68°0W 330 D4
La Paz Centro Nic. 12°20N 86°41W 320 D2
La Pedrera Colombia 1°18S 69°43W 328 D4
La Pérade Canada 46°35N 72°12W 299 C5
La Perla Chihuahua, Mexico 28°18N 104°32W 318 B4
La Perla Lima, Peru 12°4S 77°7W 124 B2
La Perouse Australia 33°59S 151°14E 139 B2
La Perouse, Bahía Chile 27°5S 109°18W 330 b
La Perouse Str. Asia 45°40N 142°0E 220 B11
La Pesca Mexico 23°46N 97°47W 319 C5
La Piedad Mexico 20°21N 102°0W 318 C4
La Pine U.S.A. 43°40N 121°30W 304 E3
La Pisana Italy 41°51N 12°23E 136 B1
La Plaine Dominica 15°20N 61°15W 323 k
La Plaine des Cafres Réunion 21°13S 55°33E 272 f
La Plaine des Palmistes Réunion 21°7S 55°38E 272 f
La Plata Argentina 35°0S 57°55W 334 C4
La Plata Colombia 2°23N 75°53W 328 C2
La Plata Mo., U.S.A. 40°2N 92°29W 310 D4
La Plata, L. Argentina 44°55S 71°50W 336 B2
La Playa, Pta. Venezuela 10°48N 64°0W 329 a
La Plaza Venezuela 11°6N 63°52W 329 a
La Pobla de Lillet Spain 42°16N 1°59E 196 C6
La Pobla de Segur Spain 42°15N 0°58E 196 C5
La Pocatière Canada 47°22N 70°2W 299 C5
La Pola de Gordón Spain 42°51N 5°41W 194 C5
La Porta France 42°25N 9°21E 175 F13
La Porte U.S.A. 29°40N 95°1W 314 G7
La Porte City U.S.A. 42°19N 92°12W 310 B4
La Possession Réunion 20°55S 55°21E 272 f
La Prairie Canada 45°25N 73°29W 130 B3
La Presanella Italy 46°13N 10°40E 198 B7
La Puebla = Sa Pobla Spain 39°46N 3°1E 206 B4
La Puebla de Cazalla Spain 37°10N 5°20W 195 H5
La Puebla de los Infantes Spain 37°47N 5°24W 195 H5
La Puebla de Montalbán Spain 39°52N 4°22W 194 F6
La Puebla del Río Spain 37°16N 6°3W 195 H4
La Puerta de Segura Spain 38°22N 2°45W 195 G8
La Punta Peru 12°4S 77°10W 124 B1
La Puntigala Spain 41°27N 2°13E 114 A2
La Purísima Mexico 26°10N 112°4W 318 B2
La Push U.S.A. 47°55N 124°38W 306 C2
La Queue-en-Brie France 48°47N 2°34E 134 B4
La Quiaca Argentina 22°5S 65°35W 334 A2
La Rambla Barcelona, Spain 114 b2
La Reina Chile 33°26S 70°33W 137 B2
La Réole France 44°35N 0°1W 174 D3
La Republica, Plaza de Mexico City, Mexico 128 b1
La Restinga Canary Is. 27°38N 17°59W 153 e1
La Ribera Spain 41°21N 2°4E 114 A1
La Rinconada Peru 14°38S 69°27W 330 C4
La Rioja Argentina 29°20S 67°0W 334 B2
La Rioja □ Argentina 29°30S 67°0W 334 B2
La Rioja □ Spain 42°20N 2°20W 196 C2
La Rivière des Pluies Réunion 20°54S 55°31E 272 f
La Robla Spain 42°50N 5°41W 194 C5
La Roche N. Cal. 21°26S 168°2E 288 d
La Roche-Bernard France 47°31N 2°19W 172 E4
La Roche-Canillac France 45°12N 1°57E 174 C5
La Roche-en-Ardenne Belgium 50°11N 5°35E 170 D5
La Roche-sur-Foron France 46°4N 6°19E 173 F13
La Roche-sur-Yon France 46°40N 1°25W 172 F5
La Rochefoucauld France 45°44N 0°24E 174 C4
La Rochelle France 46°10N 1°9W 174 B2
La Roda Spain 39°13N 2°15W 197 F2
La Roda de Andalucía Spain 37°12N 4°46W 195 H6
La Romain Trin. & Tob. 10°15N 61°29W 323 t
La Romaine Canada 50°13N 60°40W 299 B7
La Romana Dom. Rep. 18°27N 68°57W 321 C6
La Ronge Canada 55°5N 105°20W 297 B7
La Rue U.S.A. 40°35N 83°23W 310 C6
La Rumorosa Mexico 32°34N 116°6W 307 N10
La Sabina = Sa Savina Spain 38°44N 1°25E 206 D1
La Sagra Spain 37°57N 2°35W 197 H2
La Sagrera Spain 41°25N 2°11E 114 A2
La Salada Argentina 34°43S 58°28W 117 C2
La Saline Réunion 21°4S 55°16E 272 f
La Salle U.S.A. 41°20N 89°6W 310 C7
La Sanabria Spain 42°0N 6°30W 194 C4
La Santa Canary Is. 29°5N 13°40W 153 e2
La Sarre Canada 48°45N 79°15W 298 C4
La Scala Italy 45°28N 9°11E 128 B2
La Scie Canada 49°57N 55°36W 299 C8
La Selva Spain 42°0N 2°45E 196 C7
La Selva Beach U.S.A. 36°56N 121°51W 306 J5
La Selva del Camp Spain 41°13N 1°8E 196 D6
La Serena Chile 29°55S 71°10W 334 B1
La Serena Spain 38°45N 5°40W 195 G5
La Seu d'Urgell Spain 42°22N 1°23E 196 C6
La Seyne-sur-Mer France 43°7N 5°52E 175 E9
La Sila Italy 39°15N 16°35E 201 C9
La Solana Spain 38°59N 3°14W 195 G7
La Soufrière St. Vincent 13°20N 61°11W 323 n
La Souterraine France 46°15N 1°30E 173 F8
La Spézia Italy 44°7N 9°50E 198 D6
La Storta Italy 41°59N 12°26E 136 A1
La Suze-sur-Sarthe France 47°53N 0°2E 172 E7
La Tagua Colombia 0°3N 74°40W 328 C3
La Taxonera Spain 41°25N 2°10E 114 A2
La Teste-de-Buch France 44°37N 1°8W 174 D2
La Tortuga, I. Venezuela 11°0N 65°22W 321 D6
La Tour-du-Pin France 45°33N 5°27E 175 C9
La Tranche-sur-Mer France 46°20N 1°27W 172 F5
La Tremblade France 45°46N 1°8W 174 C2
La Trinidad Phil. 16°28N 120°35E 232 C3
La Trinité Martinique 14°45N 60°58W 322 j
La Tuque Canada 47°30N 72°50W 298 C5
La Unión Chile 40°10S 73°0W 336 B2
La Unión Colombia 1°35N 77°5W 328 C2
La Unión El Salv. 13°20N 87°50W 320 D2
La Unión Guerrero, Mexico 17°58N 101°49W 318 D4
La Unión Peru 9°43S 76°45W 330 B2
La Unión Spain 37°38N 0°53W 197 H4
La Union □ Phil. 16°30N 120°25E 232 C3
La Urbana Venezuela 7°8N 66°56W 328 B4
La Vache B. Trin. & Tob. 10°45N 61°29W 323 t
La Vache Pt. Trin. & Tob. 10°47N 61°28W 323 t
La Vall d'Uixó Spain 39°49N 0°15W 196 F4
La Vecilla Spain 42°51N 5°27W 194 C5
La Vecindad Venezuela 11°4N 63°56W 329 a
La Vega Dom. Rep. 19°20N 70°30W 321 C5
La Vega Peru 10°41S 77°44W 330 C2
La Vela de Coro Venezuela 11°27N 69°34W 328 A4
La Veleta Spain 37°1N 3°22W 195 H7
La Venta Mexico 18°5N 94°3W 319 D6
La Venturosa Colombia 6°8N 68°48W 328 B4
La Vergne U.S.A. 36°1N 86°35W 315 C11
La Veronica Trin. & Tob. 10°42N 61°21W 323 t
La Victoria Lima, Peru 12°3S 77°2W 124 B2
La Victoria Venezuela 10°14N 67°20W 328 A4
La Villa Joiosa = Villajoyosa Spain 38°30N 0°12W 197 G4
La Vista U.S.A. 33°48N 84°21W 113 B2
La Voulte-sur-Rhône France 44°48N 4°46E 175 D8
Laa an der Thaya Austria 48°43N 16°23E 177 C9
Laaber, Grosse ➛ Germany 48°55N 12°30E 179 G8
Laage Germany 53°55N 12°21E 178 B8
Laajalahti Finland 60°11N 24°48E 121 B1
Laajasalo Finland 60°10N 25°1E 121 B3
Laaksolahti Finland 60°14N 24°45E 121 B1
Laas Dawaco Somalia 10°28N 49°0E 267 B6
Laascaanood = Las Anod Somalia 8°26N 47°19E 267 C6
Laasqoray Somalia 11°10N 48°20E 267 B6
Laatzen Germany 52°19N 9°48E 178 C5
Lā'au Pt. U.S.A. 21°6N 157°19W 302 B4
Laba ➛ Russia 45°11N 39°42E 191 H4
Labagou Nat. Forest Park ⌓ China 40°1N 116°22E 114 A2
Laban Burma 25°52N 96°40E 241 C6
Labasa Fiji 16°30S 179°27E 287 A2
Labason Phil. 8°4N 122°31E 233 G4
Labastide-Murat France 44°39N 1°33E 174 D5
Labastide-Rouairoux France 43°28N 2°39E 174 E6
Labbézenga Mali 15°2N 0°48E 263 B5
Labdah = Leptis Magna Libya 32°40N 14°12E 258 B2
Labe = Elbe ➛ Europe 53°50N 9°0E 178 B4
Labé Guinea 11°24N 12°16W 262 C2
Laberge, L. Canada 61°11N 135°12W 296 A1
Labes = Łobez Poland 53°38N 15°39E 184 E2
Labia, Palazzo Venice, Italy 142 a2
Labian, Tanjong Malaysia 5°9N 119°13E 235 A5
Labiau = Polessk Russia 54°50N 21°8E 184 D8
Labig Pt. = Iligan Pt. Phil. 18°25N 122°25E 232 B4
Labin Croatia 45°5N 14°8E 199 C11
Labinsk Russia 44°40N 40°48E 191 H5
Labis Malaysia 2°22N 103°2E 237 L4
Labiszyn Poland 52°57N 17°54E 185 F4
Lablâba, W. el ➛ Egypt 30°1N 31°19E 117 A2
Labo Phil. 14°9N 122°51E 232 D4
Laboe Germany 54°24N 10°13E 178 A6
Laborec ➛ Slovakia 48°37N 21°58E 181 C14
Laborie St. Lucia 13°45N 61°2W 323 m
Labouheyre France 44°13N 0°55W 174 D3
Laboulaye Argentina 34°10S 63°30W 334 C3
Labrador Canada 53°20N 61°0W 299 B7
Labrador City Canada 52°57N 66°55W 299 B6
Labrador Sea Atl. Oc. 57°0N 54°0W 295 F21
Lábrea Brazil 7°15S 64°51W 331 B5
Labruguière France 43°31N 2°16E 174 E6
Labuan □ Malaysia 5°20N 115°12E 235 A5
Labuan, Pulau Malaysia 5°21N 115°13E 235 A5
Labuha Indonesia 0°30S 127°30E 231 E7
Labuhan Indonesia 6°22S 105°50E 234 D3
Labuhanbajo Indonesia 8°28S 119°54E 235 D5
Labuhanbilik Indonesia 2°31N 100°10E 237 L3
Labuk, Telok Malaysia 6°10N 117°50E 235 A5
Labutta Burma 16°9N 94°46E 241 G5
Labyrinth, L. Australia 30°40S 135°11E 281 E2
Labytnangi Russia 66°39N 66°21E 186 A12
Laç Albania 41°38N 19°43E 202 E3
Lac □ Chad 13°30N 14°30E 259 F2
Lac Bay Bonaire 12°6N 68°13W 322 h
Lac-Bouchette Canada 48°16N 72°11W 299 C5
Lac-Édouard Canada 47°40N 72°16W 299 C5
Lac La Biche Canada 54°45N 111°58W 296 C6
Lac la Martre = Wha Ti Canada 63°8N 117°16W 294 E8
Lac La Ronge ⌓ Canada 55°9N 104°41W 297 B7
Lac-Mégantic Canada 45°35N 70°53W 299 D5
Lac Thien Vietnam 12°25N 108°11E 236 F7
Lacanau France 44°58N 1°5W 174 D2
Lacanau, L. de France 44°58N 1°7W 174 D2
Lacantún ➛ Mexico 16°36N 90°39W 319 D6
Lácara ➛ Spain 38°55N 6°25W 195 G4
Lacaune France 43°43N 2°40E 174 E6
Lacaune, Mts. de France 43°43N 2°50E 174 E6
Laccadive Is. = Lakshadweep Is. India 10°0N 72°30E 245 J1
Lacepede B. Australia 36°40S 139°40E 282 D3
Lacepede Is. Australia 16°55S 122°0E 278 C3
Lacerdónia Mozam. 18°3S 35°35E 269 F4
Lacey U.S.A. 47°7N 122°49W 306 C4
Lachania Greece 35°58N 27°54E 206 F11
Lachay, Pta. Peru 11°17S 77°44W 330 C2
Lachen India 27°46N 88°36E 241 B2
Lachhmangarh India 27°50N 75°4E 242 F6
Lachi Pakistan 33°25N 71°20E 242 C4
Lachia Taiwan 22°43N 120°53E 225 D2
Lachine Canada 45°26N 73°42W 130 B1
Lachine, Canal de Canada 45°26N 73°38W 130 B2
Lachlan ➛ Australia 34°22S 143°55E 282 C5
Lachoc Peru 12°50S 75°6W 330 C2
Lachute Canada 45°39N 74°21W 298 C5
Laçın Azerbaijan 39°38N 46°33E 213 C12
Lackagh Hills Ireland 54°16N 8°10W 166 B3
Lackawanna U.S.A. 42°50N 78°50W 312 D6
Lackawaxen U.S.A. 41°29N 74°59W 313 E10
Lacolle Canada 45°5N 73°22W 313 A11
Lacombe Canada 52°30N 113°44W 296 C6
Lacon U.S.A. 41°2N 89°24W 310 C7
Lacona Iowa, U.S.A. 41°12N 93°23W 310 C3
Lacona N.Y., U.S.A. 43°39N 76°10W 313 C8
Láconi Italy 39°54N 9°4E 200 C2
Laconia = Lakonia Greece 36°55N 22°30E 204 E4
Laconia U.S.A. 43°32N 71°28W 313 C13
Lacoochee U.S.A. 28°28N 82°11W 317 G7
Lacq France 43°25N 0°35W 174 E3
Lacre Punt Bonaire 12°1N 68°14W 322 h
Lacs □ Ivory C. 7°1N 4°46W 262 D4
Lad Phrao Thailand 13°47N 100°35E 113 B2
Ladakh Ra. India 34°0N 78°0E 243 C8
Ladário Brazil 19°1S 57°35W 331 D6
Ladd U.S.A. 41°23N 89°13W 310 C7
Laddonia U.S.A. 39°15N 91°39W 310 E5
Lądek-Zdrój Poland 50°21N 16°53E 185 H3
Ladera Heights U.S.A. 33°59N 118°22W 126 C2
Lâdik Turkey 40°57N 35°58E 212 B6
Ladismith S. Africa 33°28S 21°15E 270 D3
Ladispoli Italy 41°56N 12°5E 199 G9
Lādīz Iran 28°55N 61°15E 247 D9
Ladnun India 27°38N 74°25E 242 F6
Ladoga, L. = Ladozhskoye Ozero Russia 61°15N 30°30E 188 B6
Ladonas ➛ Greece 37°40N 21°50E 204 D3
Ladozhskoye Ozero Russia 61°15N 30°30E 188 B6
Ladrillero, G. Chile 49°20S 75°35W 336 C1
Ladson U.S.A. 32°59N 80°6W 316 C9
Ladushkin Russia 54°34N 20°10E 184 D7
Ládví Czechia 50°8N 14°27E 135 B2
Lady Poland 52°8N 20°57E 143 C1
Lady Elliott I. Australia 24°7S 152°42E 280 C5
Lady Frere S. Africa 31°42S 27°14E 270 D4
Lady Grey S. Africa 30°43S 27°13E 270 D4
Lady Lake U.S.A. 28°55N 81°55W 317 G8
Ladybrand S. Africa 29°9S 27°29E 270 C4
Ladysmith B.C., Canada 49°0N 123°49W 306 B3
Ladysmith KwaZulu Natal, S. Africa 28°32S 29°46E 271 C4
Ladysmith Wis., U.S.A. 45°28N 91°12W 308 C8
Ladyzhyn Ukraine 48°40N 29°15E 183 B14
Lae Papua N. G. 6°40S 147°2E 286 D4
Lae 'o Kealaikahiki U.S.A. 20°32N 156°42W 302 C5
Laem Chabang Thailand 13°5N 100°53E 236 F3
Laem Ngop Thailand 12°10N 102°26E 237 F4
Laem Son △ Thailand 9°29N 98°24E 237 H2
Lærdalsøyri Norway 61°6N 7°28E 164 C4
Laerma Greece 36°9N 27°57E 206 E11
Læsø Denmark 57°15N 11°5E 163 G5
Læsø Rende Denmark 57°20N 10°45E 163 G4
Lafayette Ala., U.S.A. 32°54N 85°24W 316 C4
Lafayette Ind., U.S.A. 40°25N 86°54W 311 D10
Lafayette La., U.S.A. 30°14N 92°1W 314 F8
Lafayette Tenn., U.S.A. 36°31N 86°2W 315 C11
Lafayette Park San Francisco, U.S.A. 136 b1
Lafayette Square New Orleans, U.S.A. 131 b2
Laferte ➛ Canada 61°53N 117°44W 296 A5
Lafia Nigeria 8°30N 8°34E 263 D6
Lafiagi Nigeria 8°52N 5°20E 263 D6
Lafkos Greece 39°9N 23°14E 204 B5
Lafleche Canada 49°45N 106°40W 297 D7
Lafon South Sudan 5°5N 32°29E 257 F3
Lafontaine Montréal, Canada 130 a1
Lafontaine, Parc Canada 45°33N 73°34W 130 A2
Laful India 7°10N 93°52E 245 L11
Lagaip ➛ Papua N. G. 5°4S 142°52E 286 C2
Lagan = Kaspiyskiy Russia 45°22N 47°23E 191 H8
Lagan Sweden 56°56N 13°58E 163 H7
Lagan ➛ Sweden 56°30N 12°58E 163 H6
Lagan ➛ Antrim, U.K. 54°36N 5°55W 166 B6
Lagana, Kolpas Greece 37°42N 20°53E 207 D2
Laganas Greece 37°44N 20°53E 207 D2
Lagangilang Phil. 17°37N 120°44E 232 C3
Lagarfljót ➛ Iceland 65°40N 14°18W 155 B12
Lagarto Brazil 10°54S 37°41W 332 D4
Lagawe Phil. 16°49N 121°6E 232 C3
Lagdo Cameroon 9°3N 13°44E 259 G2
Lagdo, L. de Cameroon 8°40N 14°0E 264 A2
Lage Germany 51°59N 8°48E 178 D4
Lågen ➛ Oppland, Norway 61°8N 10°25E 164 C7
Lågen ➛ Vestfold, Norway 59°3N 10°3E 164 E7
Lägerdorf Germany 53°53N 9°34E 178 B5
Lages Brazil 27°48S 50°20W 335 B5
Laggan = Lake Louise Canada 51°30N 116°10W 296 C5
Lagh Badana △ Somalia 1°16S 41°49E 267 E5
Laghmān □ Afghan. 34°20N 70°0E 240 B3
Laghouat Algeria 33°50N 2°59E 261 B5
Laghouat □ Algeria 33°35N 2°40E 261 B5
Lagnieu France 45°55N 5°20E 175 C9
Lagny-sur-Marne France 48°52N 2°44E 173 D9
Lago Italy 39°10N 16°9E 201 C9
Lago Agrio Ecuador 0°5N 76°52W 328 C2
Lago de Sanabria y Entorno ⌓ Spain 42°9N 6°45W 194 C4
Lago Posadas Argentina 47°30S 71°40W 336 C2
Lago Puelo △ Argentina 42°30S 71°45W 336 B2
Lago Ranco Chile 40°19S 72°30W 336 B2
Lagoa Azores 37°45N 25°20W 153 d3
Lagoa Rio de J., Brazil 22°58S 43°11W 135 B1
Lagôa Portugal 37°8N 8°27W 195 H2
Lagoa do Peixe △ Brazil 31°12S 50°55W 335 C5
Lagoa Vermelha Brazil 28°13S 51°32W 335 B5
Lagoaça Portugal 41°11N 6°44W 194 D4
Lagodekhi Georgia 41°50N 46°22E 191 K8
Lagona = Laguna Beach U.S.A. 33°33N 117°47W 307 M9
Lagónegro Italy 40°8N 15°45E 201 B8
Lagonoy G. Phil. 13°35N 123°50E 232 E4
Lagos Angola 16°3S 16°35E 265 F3
Lagos Greece 41°1N 25°6E 203 E9
Lagos Nigeria 6°25N 3°27E 124 B2
Lagos Portugal 37°5N 8°41W 195 H2
Lagos □ Nigeria 6°28N 3°25E 263 D5
Lagos de Moreno Mexico 21°21N 101°55W 318 C4
Lagos Harbour Nigeria 6°26N 3°23E 124 B2
Lagos-Ikeja ✕ (LOS) Nigeria 6°34N 3°19E 124 A1
Lagos Island Nigeria 6°26N 3°23E 124 B2
Lagos Lagoon Nigeria 6°30N 3°28E 124 B2
Lagrange = Bidyadanga Australia 18°45S 121°43E 278 C3
Lagrange U.S.A. 41°39N 85°25W 311 C11
Lagrange B. Australia 18°38S 121°42E 278 C3
Laguardia Spain 42°33N 2°35W 196 C2
Laguépie France 44°8N 1°57E 174 D5
Lagun Curaçao 12°19N 69°10W 322 g
Laguna = Padilla Bolivia 19°19S 64°20W 331 D5
Laguna Brazil 28°30S 48°50W 335 B6
Laguna N. Mex., U.S.A. 35°2N 107°25W 305 J10
Laguna □ Phil. 14°10N 121°20E 232 D3
Laguna, Sa. de la Mexico 23°35N 109°55W 318 C3
Laguna Beach U.S.A. 33°33N 117°47W 307 M9
Laguna Blanca △ Argentina 39°0S 70°5W 336 A2
Laguna de B. Phil. 14°29N 121°6E 127 C2
Laguna de Duero Spain 41°35N 4°43W 194 D6
Laguna de la Restinga △ Venezuela 11°0N 64°10W 329 a
Laguna de Lachuá △ Guatemala 15°55N 90°40W 320 C1
Laguna de Raya Venezuela 10°56N 64°7W 329 a
Laguna del Laja △ Chile 37°27S 71°20W 334 D1
Laguna del Tigre △ Guatemala 17°32N 90°56W 320 C1
Laguna Limpia Argentina 26°32S 59°45W 334 B4
Laguna San Rafael △ Chile 46°54S 73°31W 336 C2
Lagunas Chile 21°0S 69°45W 334 A2
Lagunas Peru 5°10S 75°35W 330 B2
Lagunas de Chacahua △ Mexico 16°0N 97°43W 319 D5
Lagunas de Montebello △ Mexico 16°4N 91°42W 319 D6
Lagunas de Ruidera ⌓ Spain 38°57N 2°52W 197 G2
Lagunes □ Ivory C. 5°47N 4°12W 262 D4
Lagunillas Bolivia 19°38S 63°43W 331 D5
Lahad Datu Malaysia 5°0N 118°20E 235 A5
Lahad Datu, Telok Malaysia 4°50N 118°20E 235 B5
Lahaina U.S.A. 20°53N 156°41W 302 C5
Lahan Sai Thailand 14°25N 102°52E 236 E4
Lahanam Laos 16°16N 105°16E 236 D5
Lahar India 26°12N 78°57E 243 F8
Laharpur India 27°43N 80°56E 243 F9
Lahat Indonesia 3°45S 103°30E 234 C2
Lahe Burma 26°20N 95°26E 241 B5
Lahewa Indonesia 1°22N 97°12E 234 B1
Laḥij Yemen 13°4N 44°53E 248 D4
Laḥij □ Yemen 13°0N 44°30E 248 D4
Lāhījān Iran 37°10N 50°6E 247 B6
Lahilahi Pt. U.S.A. 21°28N 158°13W 302 K13
Lahn = Wleń Poland 51°2N 15°39E 185 G2
Lahn ➛ Germany 50°19N 7°37E 179 E3
Lahnstein Germany 50°19N 7°37E 179 E3
Laholm Sweden 56°30N 13°2E 163 H7
Laholmsbukten Sweden 56°30N 12°45E 163 H6
Lahore Pakistan 31°32N 74°22E 242 D6
Lahpongsel Burma 27°7N 98°25E 241 B7
Lahr Germany 48°20N 7°53E 179 G3
Lahri Pakistan 29°11N 68°13E 242 E3
Lāhrūd Iran 38°30N 47°52E 213 C12
Lahti Finland 60°58N 25°40E 188 B3
Lahtis = Lahti Finland 60°58N 25°40E 188 B3
Lahugala Kitulana △ Sri Lanka 6°50N 81°40E 245 L5
Laï Chad 9°25N 16°18E 259 G3
Lai Chau Vietnam 22°5N 103°3E 228 F4
Lai Chi Wo Hong Kong, China 22°32N 114°15E 122 a
Lai-hka Burma 21°16N 97°40E 241 E6
Laiagam Papua N. G. 5°33S 143°30E 286 C2
Lai'an China 32°28N 118°30E 229 A12
Laibach = Ljubljana Slovenia 46°4N 14°33E 199 B11
Laibin China 23°42N 109°14E 228 F7
Lā'ie U.S.A. 21°39N 157°56W 302 J14
Laifeng China 29°27N 109°20E 228 C7
L'Aigle France 48°46N 0°38E 172 D7
Laignes France 47°50N 4°20E 173 E11
L'Aiguillon-sur-Mer France 46°20N 1°18W 174 B2
Laikipia □ Kenya 0°10N 36°40E 268 B4
Laila = Layla Si. Arabia 22°10N 46°40E 248 B4
Laim Germany 48°7N 11°30E 131 B2
Lainate Italy 45°34N 9°1E 128 A1
Laingsburg S. Africa 33°9S 20°52E 270 D3
Lainioälven ➛ Sweden 67°35N 22°40E 160 C20
Lainz Austria 48°10N 16°16E 142 B1
Lairg U.K. 58°2N 4°24W 167 C4
Laïri, B. de Chad 12°28N 16°45E 259 F3
Lais Indonesia 3°31S 102°3E 234 C2
Lais Phil. 6°20N 125°39E 233 H5
Laisamis Kenya 1°36N 37°48E 268 B4
Laissac France 44°23N 2°50E 174 D6
Láives Italy 46°26N 11°20E 199 B8
Laiwu China 36°15N 117°40E 227 F9
Laixi China 36°50N 120°31E 227 F11
Laiyang China 36°59N 120°45E 227 F11
Laiyuan China 39°20N 114°40E 226 E8
Laizhou China 37°8N 119°57E 227 F10
Laizhou Wan China 37°30N 119°30E 227 F10
Lajamanu Australia 18°23S 130°38E 278 C5
Lajeado = Guiratinga Brazil 16°21S 53°45W 331 D7
Lajedo Azores 39°23N 31°15W 153 d2
Lajere Nigeria 12°10N 11°25E 263 C7
Lajes Azores 38°46N 27°6W 153 d1
Lajes Rio Grande do N., Brazil 5°41S 36°14W 332 C4
Lajes das Flores Azores 39°23N 31°10W 153 d2
Lajes do Pico Azores 38°23N 28°16W 153 d1
Lajinha Brazil 20°9S 41°37W 333 F3
Lajkovac Serbia 44°27N 20°14E 202 B4
Lajosmizse Hungary 47°3N 19°32E 182 C4
Lak Sao Laos 18°11N 104°59E 236 C5
Lakaband Pakistan 31°2N 69°15E 242 D3
Lakamané Mali 14°35N 9°44W 262 C3
Lakatoro Vanuatu 16°6S 167°25E 287 F5
Lake U.S.A. 44°33N 110°24W 304 D8
Lake Alfred U.S.A. 28°6N 81°44W 317 G8
Lake Alpine U.S.A. 38°29N 120°0W 306 G7
Lake Andes U.S.A. 43°9N 98°32W 308 D4
Lake Arthur U.S.A. 30°5N 92°41W 314 F8
Lake Bindegolly △ Australia 28°0S 144°12E 281 D3
Lake Boga Australia 35°26S 143°38E 282 C5
Lake Buena Vista U.S.A. 28°23N 81°32W 133 B1
Lake Butig △ Phil. 7°45N 124°16E 233 H5
Lake Butler U.S.A. 30°1N 82°21W 316 E7
Lake Cain Hills U.S.A. 28°29N 81°28W 133 B2
Lake Cargelligo Australia 33°15S 146°22E 283 B7
Lake Charles U.S.A. 30°14N 93°13W 314 F8
Lake City Colo., U.S.A. 38°2N 107°19W 304 G10
Lake City Fla., U.S.A. 30°11N 82°38W 316 E7
Lake City Iowa, U.S.A. 42°16N 94°44W 310 B2
Lake City Mich., U.S.A. 44°20N 85°13W 309 C11
Lake City Minn., U.S.A. 44°27N 92°16W 308 C7
Lake City Pa., U.S.A. 42°1N 80°21W 312 D4
Lake City S.C., U.S.A. 33°52N 79°45W 316 B10
Lake Clark △ U.S.A. 61°0N 154°0W 303 F9
Lake Coleridge N.Z. 43°17S 171°30E 285 D6
Lake Cowichan Canada 48°49N 124°3W 296 D4
Lake District △ U.K. 54°30N 3°21W 168 C4
Lake Eildon △ Australia 37°10S 145°56E 283 D6
Lake Elsinore U.S.A. 33°38N 117°20W 307 M9
Lake Eyre △ Australia 28°40S 137°31E 281 D2
Lake Forest U.S.A. 42°15N 87°50W 311 B9
Lake Gairdner △ Australia 31°41S 135°51E 281 E2
Lake Geneva U.S.A. 42°36N 88°26W 311 B8
Lake George U.S.A. 43°26N 73°43W 313 C11
Lake Grace Australia 33°7S 118°28E 279 F2
Lake Gregory ◎ Australia 20°12S 127°27E 278 D4
Lake Harbor U.S.A. 26°42N 80°48W 317 J9
Lake Harbour = Kimmirut Canada 62°50N 69°50W 295 E18
Lake Havasu City U.S.A. 34°27N 114°22W 307 L12
Lake Helen U.S.A. 28°59N 81°14W 317 G8
Lake Hughes U.S.A. 34°41N 118°26W 307 L8
Lake Isabella U.S.A. 35°38N 118°28W 307 K8
Lake Jackson U.S.A. 29°3N 95°27W 314 G7
Lake King Australia 33°5S 119°45E 279 F2
Lake Kopiago Papua N. G. 5°23S 142°31E 286 C2
Lake Kutubu Papua N. G. 6°20S 143°18E 286 D2
Lake Lenore Canada 52°24N 104°59W 297 C8
Lake Louise Canada 51°30N 116°10W 296 C5
Lake Mackay ◎ Australia 21°48S 129°46E 278 D4
Lake Mburo △ Uganda 0°33S 30°56E 268 C3
Lake Mead △ U.S.A. 36°30N 114°22W 307 K12
Lake Meredith △ U.S.A. 35°50N 101°50W 314 D4
Lake Mills Iowa, U.S.A. 43°25N 93°32W 308 D7
Lake Mills Wis., U.S.A. 43°5N 88°55W 311 A8
Lake Murray Papua N. G. 6°48S 141°29E 286 D1
Lake Nakura △ Kenya 0°21S 36°8E 268 C4
Lake Odessa U.S.A. 42°47N 85°8W 311 B11
Lake Orion U.S.A. 42°47N 83°14W 311 B13
Lake Park Fla., U.S.A. 26°48N 80°3W 317 J9
Lake Park Ga., U.S.A. 30°41N 83°11W 316 E6
Lake Placid Fla., U.S.A. 27°18N 81°22W 317 H8
Lake Placid N.Y., U.S.A. 44°17N 73°59W 313 B11
Lake Pleasant U.S.A. 43°28N 74°25W 313 C10
Lake Point Tower Chicago, U.S.A. 119 b3
Lake Providence U.S.A. 32°48N 91°10W 314 E9
Lake Pukaki N.Z. 44°11S 170°8E 285 E5
Lake Roosevelt ⌓ U.S.A. 48°5N 118°14W 304 B4
Lake St. Peter Canada 45°18N 78°2W 312 A6
Lake Shore Drive Chicago, U.S.A. 119 a2
Lake Shore Park Chicago, U.S.A. 119 a2
Lake Stevens U.S.A. 48°1N 122°4W 306 B4
Lake Superior ⌓ Canada 47°45N 84°45W 298 C3
Lake Tekapo N.Z. 44°0S 170°30E 285 E5
Lake Torrens △ Australia 30°55S 137°40E 281 E2
Lake View U.S.A. 42°18N 95°3W 310 B1
Lake Villa U.S.A. 42°25N 88°5W 311 B8
Lake Village U.S.A. 33°20N 91°17W 314 E9
Lake Wales U.S.A. 27°54N 81°35W 317 H8
Lake Worth U.S.A. 26°37N 80°3W 317 J9
Lake Zurich U.S.A. 42°12N 88°5W 311 B8
Lakeba Fiji 18°13S 178°47W 287 B3
Lakeba Passage Fiji 18°0S 178°45W 287 B3
Lakefield = Rinyirru △ Australia 15°24S 144°26E 280 B3
Lakefield Canada 44°25N 78°16W 312 B6
Lakehurst U.S.A. 40°1N 74°19W 313 F10
Lakeland Queens., Australia 15°49S 144°57E 280 B3
Lakeland Fla., U.S.A. 28°3N 81°57W 317 G8
Lakeland Ga., U.S.A. 31°2N 83°4W 316 D6
Lakemba = Lakeba Fiji 18°13S 178°47W 287 B3
Lakemba Australia 33°55S 151°5E 139 B1
Lakepa Cook Is. 18°59S 169°48W 289 g
Lakeport Calif., U.S.A. 39°3N 122°55W 306 F4
Lakeport Mich., U.S.A. 43°7N 82°30W 312 C2
Lakes □ South Sudan 7°0N 30°0E 257 F3
Lakes Entrance Australia 37°50S 148°0E 283 D8
Lakeside Gauteng, S. Africa 26°5S 28°8E 123 A2
Lakeside Western Cape, S. Africa 34°5S 18°27E 118 B1
Lakeside Calif., U.S.A. 32°52N 116°55W 307 N10
Lakeside Nebr., U.S.A. 42°3N 102°26W 308 D2
Lakeview Ill., U.S.A. 41°56N 87°38W 119 B3
Lakeview La., U.S.A. 30°0N 90°6W 131 A2
Lakeview Oreg., U.S.A. 42°11N 120°21W 304 E3
Lakeville U.S.A. 44°39N 93°14W 308 C7
Lakewood Colo., U.S.A. 39°42N 105°4W 304 G11
Lakewood N.J., U.S.A. 40°6N 74°13W 313 F10
Lakewood N.Y., U.S.A. 42°6N 79°19W 312 D5
Lakewood Ohio, U.S.A. 41°28N 81°47W 312 E3
Lakewood Wash., U.S.A. 47°11N 122°32W 306 C4
Lakewood Park Fla., U.S.A. 27°33N 80°24W 317 H9
Lakewood Park Georgia, U.S.A. 33°43N 84°24W 113 B2
Lakha India 26°9N 70°54E 242 F4
Lakhimpur India 27°57N 80°46E 243 F9
Lakhipur Assam, India 24°48N 93°0E 241 C4
Lakhipur Assam, India 26°2N 90°18E 241 B3
Lakhisarai India 25°11N 86°5E 243 G12
Lakhnadon India 22°36N 79°36E 243 H8
Lakhnau = Lucknow India 26°50N 81°0E 243 F9
Lakhonpheng Laos 15°54N 105°34E 236 E5
Lakhpat India 23°48N 68°47E 242 H3
Lakhtinskiy Russia 59°59N 30°9E 137 B1
Lakhtinskiy Razliv, Oz. Russia 59°59N 30°12E 137 B1
Läki Azerbaijan 40°34N 47°22E 191 K8
Laki Iceland 64°4N 18°14W 155 C8
Lakin U.S.A. 37°57N 101°15W 308 G3
Lakitusaki ➛ Canada 54°21N 82°25W 298 B3
Lakka Greece 39°17N 20°9E 206 C10
Lakki Greece 35°24N 23°57E 207 E4
Lakki Pakistan 32°36N 70°55E 242 C4
Lakonia Greece 36°55N 22°30E 204 E4
Lakonikos Kolpos Greece 36°40N 22°40E 204 E4
Lakor Indonesia 8°15S 128°17E 231 F7
Lakota Ivory C. 5°50N 5°30W 262 D3
Lakota N. Dak., U.S.A. 48°2N 98°21W 308 A4
Laksar India 29°46N 78°3E 242 E8
Laksefjorden Norway 70°45N 26°50E 160 A22
Lakselv Norway 70°2N 25°0E 160 A21
Laksettipet India 18°52N 79°13E 244 E4
Lakshadweep □ India 10°0N 72°30E 245 J1
Lakshadweep Is. India 10°0N 72°30E 245 J1
Laksham Bangla. 23°14N 91°8E 241 D3
Lakshimpur Bangla. 22°58N 90°50E 241 D3
Lakshmanpur Chhattisgarh, India 22°58N 83°3E 243 H10
Lakshmanpur Paschimbanga, India 22°38N 88°16E 124 B1
Lakshmeshwar India 15°9N 75°28E 245 G2
Lakshmikantapur India 22°5N 88°20E 243 H13
Laksi Thailand 13°53N 100°35E 113 A2
Lakuramau Papua N. G. 2°54S 151°15E 286 B6
Lal-lo Phil. 18°12N 121°40E 232 B3
Lal Qila Delhi, India 120 a3
Lala Dem. Rep. of the Congo 4°10S 20°30E 265 C4
Lala Phil. 7°59N 123°46E 233 H4
Lala Musa Pakistan 32°40N 73°57E 242 C5
Lalaghat India 24°30N 92°40E 241 C4
Lalago Tanzania 3°28S 33°58E 268 C3
Lalang ➛ Indonesia 2°24S 104°39E 234 C2
Lalapanzi Zimbabwe 19°20S 30°15E 269 F3
Lalapaşa Turkey 41°49N 26°44E 203 E10
Lalara Gabon 0°19N 11°32E 264 B2
Lalbenque France 44°19N 1°34E 174 D5
Lalbert Australia 35°38S 143°20E 282 C5
L'Albufera Spain 39°20N 0°27W 197 F4
L'Alcora Spain 40°5N 0°14W 196 E4
L'Alfàs del Pi Spain 38°35N 0°5W 197 G4
Lalganj India 25°52N 85°13E 243 G11
Lalgola India 24°25N 88°15E 243 G13
Lālī Iran 32°21N 49°6E 247 C6
Lalibela Ethiopia 12°3N 39°0E 257 E4
Lalin Heilongjiang, China 45°12N 127°0E 227 B14
Lalín Spain 42°40N 8°5W 194 C2
Lalin He ➛ China 45°32N 125°40E 227 B13
Lalinde France 44°50N 0°44E 174 D4
Lalitpur India 24°42N 78°28E 243 G8
Lalitpur Nepal 27°40N 85°20E 243 F11
Lalkua India 29°5N 79°31E 243 E8
Lalm Norway 61°50N 9°17E 164 C6
Lalmanir Hat Bangla. 25°54N 89°27E 241 C2
Lalsot India 26°34N 76°20E 242 F7
Lam Nam Nan △ Thailand 17°55N 100°28E 236 D3
Lam Pao Res. Thailand 16°50N 103°15E 236 D4
Lam Tin Hong Kong, China 22°18N 114°14E 122 B3
Lama Kara Togo 9°30N 1°15E 263 D5
Lamae Thailand 9°51N 99°5E 237 H2
Lamag Malaysia 5°29N 117°49E 235 A5
Lamaing Burma 15°25N 97°53E 236 E1
Lamaipum Burma 25°40N 97°57E 241 C6
Lamap Vanuatu 16°26S 167°43E 287 F5
Lamar Colo., U.S.A. 38°5N 102°37W 304 G12
Lamar Mo., U.S.A. 37°30N 94°16W 308 G6
Lamarque Argentina 39°24S 65°40W 336 A3
Lamas Peru 6°28S 76°31W 330 B2
Lamastre France 44°59N 4°35E 175 D8
Lamayuru India 34°25N 76°56E 243 B7
Lambach Austria 48°6N 13°51E 180 C6
Lamballe France 48°29N 2°31W 172 D4
Lambaréné Gabon 0°41S 10°12E 264 C2
Lambasa = Labasa Fiji 16°30S 179°27E 287 A2
Lambay I. Ireland 53°29N 6°1W 166 C5
Lambayeque □ Peru 6°45S 80°0W 330 B2
Lambert Norway 59°52N 10°48E 133 A3
Lambert, C. Papua N. G. 4°11S 151°31E 286 C6
Lambert-St. Louis Int. ✕ (STL) U.S.A. 38°45N 90°22W 310 D4
Lambert's Bay S. Africa 32°5S 18°17E 270 D2
Lambertville U.S.A. 41°46N 83°35W 311 C13
Lambesc France 43°39N 5°16E 175 E9
Lambèse = Tazoult Algeria 35°29N 6°11E 261 A6
Lambeth Canada 42°54N 81°18W 312 D3
Lambeth □ U.K. 51°28N 0°6W 125 B3
Lambi Solomon Is. 9°22S 159°39E 287 M10
Lambia Greece 37°52N 21°53E 204 D3
Lambir Hills △ Malaysia 4°12N 114°1E 235 B4
Lambomakondro Madag. 22°41S 44°44E 272 C1
Lambon Papua N. G. 4°45S 152°48E 286 C7
Lambrate Italy 45°28N 9°16E 128 B2
Lambro ➛ Italy 45°8N 9°32E 198 C6
Lambro, Parco Italy 45°29N 9°14E 128 B2
Lambton Mills Canada 43°39N 79°30W 141 B1
Lambu Papua N. G. 3°18S 151°43E 286 B6
Lambunao Phil. 11°3N 122°29E 233 F4
Lamé Chad 9°15N 14°32E 259 G2
Lame Nigeria 10°30N 9°20E 263 C6
Lame Deer U.S.A. 45°37N 106°40W 304 D10
Lamego Portugal 41°5N 7°52W 194 D3
Lamentin Guadeloupe 16°16N 61°38W 322 e
Lamèque Canada 47°45N 64°38W 299 C7
Lameroo Australia 35°19S 140°33E 282 C4
Lamesa U.S.A. 32°44N 101°58W 314 E4
L'Ametlla de Mar Spain 40°53N 0°48E 196 E5
Lamezia Terme Italy 38°55N 16°16E 201 D9
Lami Fiji 18°7S 178°25E 287 B2
Lamia Greece 38°55N 22°26E 204 C4
Lamigan Pt. Phil. 6°48N 126°21E 233 H6
Lamine ➛ U.S.A. 38°59N 92°51W 310 F4
Lamington, Mt. Papua N. G. 8°57S 148°9E 286 E5
Lamington △ Australia 28°13S 153°12E 281 D5
Lamitan Phil. 6°39N 122°8E 233 H4
Lamlam, Mt. Guam 13°22N 144°41E 302 d
Lamma I. Hong Kong, China 22°12N 114°7E 122 B2
Lammermuir Hills U.K. 55°50N 2°40W 167 F6
Lammeulo Indonesia 5°14N 95°56E 234 A1
Lammhult Sweden 57°10N 14°35E 163 G8
Lamoille ➛ U.S.A. 44°38N 73°13W 313 B11
Lamon B. Phil. 14°30N 122°20E 232 D4
Lamongan Indonesia 7°7S 112°25E 235 D4
Lamoni U.S.A. 40°37N 93°56W 310 D3
Lamont Alta., Canada 53°46N 112°50W 296 C6
Lamont Calif., U.S.A. 35°15N 118°55W 307 K8
Lamont Fla., U.S.A. 30°23N 83°49W 316 E6
Lamont Iowa, U.S.A. 42°36N 91°39W 310 B5
Lamont Wyo., U.S.A. 42°13N 107°29W 304 E10
Lamotte-Beuvron France 47°36N 2°2E 173 E9
Lampa Peru 15°22S 70°22W 330 D3
Lampang Thailand 18°16N 99°32E 236 C2
Lampasas U.S.A. 31°4N 98°11W 314 F5
Lampazos de Naranjo Mexico 27°1N 100°31W 318 B4
Lampedusa Medit. S. 35°36N 12°40E 258 A2
Lampertheim Germany 49°35N 8°27E 179 F4
Lampeter U.K. 52°7N 4°4W 169 E3
Lamphun Thailand 18°40N 99°2E 236 C2
Lampione Medit. S. 35°33N 12°20E 258 A2
Lampman Canada 49°25N 102°50W 297 D8
Lamprechtshausen Austria 48°0N 12°58E 180 D5
Lampung □ Indonesia 5°30S 104°30E 234 D2
Lampung, Teluk Indonesia 5°40S 105°20E 234 D3
Lamta India 22°8N 80°7E 243 H9
Lamu Burma 19°14N 94°10E 241 F5
Lamu Coast, Kenya 2°16S 40°55E 268 C5
Lamud Peru 6°10S 77°57W 330 B2
Lamy U.S.A. 35°29N 105°53W 305 J11
Lan Xian China 38°15N 111°35E 226 E6
Lan Yü Taiwan 22°4N 121°25E 225 D3
Lāna'i U.S.A. 20°50N 156°55W 302 C5
Lāna'i City U.S.A. 20°50N 156°55W 302 C5
Lāna'ihale U.S.A. 20°49N 156°53W 302 C5
Lanak La China 34°27N 79°32E 243 B8
Lanak'o Shank'ou = Lanak La China 34°27N 79°32E 243 B8
Lanao, L. Phil. 7°52N 124°15E 233 H5
Lanao del Norte □ Phil. 8°0N 124°10E 233 H5
Lanao del Sur □ Phil. 7°40N 124°15E 233 H5
Lanark Ont., Canada 45°1N 76°22W 313 A8
Lanark S. Lanarks., U.K. 55°40N 3°47W 167 F5
Lanark Ill., U.S.A. 42°6N 89°50W 310 B7
Lanbi Kyun Burma 10°50N 98°20E 237 G2
Lancang China 22°36N 99°58E 228 F2
Lancang Jiang ➛ China 21°40N 101°10E 228 G3
Lancashire □ U.K. 53°50N 2°48W 168 D5
Lancaster Ont., Canada 45°10N 74°30W 313 A10
Lancaster Lancs., U.K. 54°3N 2°48W 168 C5
Lancaster Calif., U.S.A. 34°42N 118°8W 307 L8
Lancaster Ky., U.S.A. 37°37N 84°35W 309 G11
Lancaster Mo., U.S.A. 40°31N 92°32W 310 D4
Lancaster N.H., U.S.A. 44°29N 71°34W 313 B13
Lancaster Ohio, U.S.A. 39°43N 82°36W 309 F12
Lancaster Pa., U.S.A. 40°2N 76°19W 313 F8
Lancaster S.C., U.S.A. 34°43N 80°46W 315 D14
Lancaster Tex., U.S.A. 32°36N 96°45W 120 C5
Lancaster Wis., U.S.A. 42°51N 90°43W 310 B6
Lancaster, Récif = Neilson, Récif Pac. Oc. 27°1S 146°2W 289 f
Lancaster Sd. Canada 74°13N 84°0W 295 C15
Lancelin Australia 31°0S 115°18E 279 F2
Lanchow = Lanzhou China 36°1N 103°52E 226 F2
Lanchyn Ukraine 48°33N 24°45E 183 B9
Lanciano Italy 42°14N 14°23E 199 F11
Lanco Chile 39°24S 72°46W 336 A2
Lancones Peru 4°30S 80°30W 330 A1
Lancun China 36°25N 120°10E 227 F11
Łańcut Poland 50°10N 22°13E 185 H9
Land Between the Lakes ⌓ U.S.A. 36°25N 88°0W 315 C11
Landau Bayern, Germany 48°40N 12°41E 179 G8
Landau Rhld-Pfz., Germany 49°12N 8°6E 179 F4
Landay Afghan. 30°31N 63°47E 240 C1
Landeck Austria 47°9N 10°34E 180 D3
Lander U.S.A. 42°50N 108°44W 304 E9
Lander ➛ Australia 22°0S 132°0E 278 D5
Landerneau France 48°28N 4°17W 172 D2
Landeryd Sweden 57°7N 13°15E 163 G7
Landes France 44°0N 1°0W 174 D2
Landes □ France 43°57N 0°48W 174 E3
Landes de Gascogne ⌓ France 44°23N 0°50W 174 D3
Landeshut = Kamienna Góra Poland 50°47N 16°2E 185 H3
Landete Spain 39°56N 1°25W 196 F3
Landfall I. India 13°40N 93°2E 245 H11
Landi Kotal Pakistan 34°7N 71°6E 242 B4
Landianchang China 39°56N 116°17E 114 B1
Landisburg U.S.A. 40°21N 77°19W 312 F7
Landivisiau France 48°31N 4°6W 172 D2
Landmannalaugar Iceland 63°59N 19°4W 155 D7
Landquart Switz. 46°58N 9°32E 179 J5
Landrecies France 50°7N 3°40E 173 B10
Land's End U.K. 50°4N 5°44W 169 G2
Landsberg = Górowo Iławeckie Poland 54°17N 20°30E 184 D7
Landsberg Germany 48°2N 10°53E 179 G6
Landsberg an der Warthe = Gorzów Wielkopolski Poland 52°43N 15°15E 185 F2
Landsberg in Oberschlesien = Gorzów Śląski Poland 51°3N 18°22E 185 G5
Landsborough Cr. ➛ Australia 22°28S 144°35E 280 C3
Landsbro Sweden 57°24N 14°56E 163 G8
Landshut Germany 48°34N 12°8E 179 G8
Landskrona Sweden 55°53N 12°50E 163 J6
Landsmeer Neths. 52°26N 4°55E 112 A2
Landstrasse Austria 48°12N 16°23E 142 A2
Landstuhl Germany 49°24N 7°33E 179 F3
Landvetter Sweden 57°41N 12°17E 163 G6
Landwehr kanal Germany 52°29N 13°24E 115 B3
Lane U.S.A. 33°32N 79°53W 316 B10
Lane Cove Australia 33°48S 151°9E 139 A1
Lane Cove Nat. Park △ Australia 33°47S 151°8E 139 A1
Lanesboro U.S.A. 41°57N 75°34W 313 E9

Lanester *France* 47°46N 3°22W 172 E3
Lanett *U.S.A.* 32°52N 85°12W 316 C4
Lang Shan *China* 41°0N 106°30E 226 D4
Lang Son *Vietnam* 21°52N 106°42E 228 G6
Lang Suan *Thailand* 9°57N 99°4E 237 H2
Langå *Midtjylland, Denmark* 56°23N 9°54E 163 H3
Langa *Western Cape, S. Africa* 33°57S 18°31E 118 A2
La'nga Co *China* 30°45N 81°15E 243 D9
Langa-Langa *Dem. Rep. of the Congo* 3°50S 15°59E 264 C3
Langadas *Greece* 40°46N 23°6E 202 F7
Langadia *Greece* 37°43N 22°1E 204 D4
Långan → *Sweden* 63°19N 14°44E 162 A8
Langanes *Iceland* 66°20N 14°53W 155 A12
Langano, L. *Ethiopia* 7°36N 38°43E 257 F4
Langar *Afghan.* 37°2N 73°47E 240 A4
Langar *Iran* 35°23N 60°25E 247 C9
Langara I. *Canada* 54°14N 133°1W 296 C2
Langarūd *Iran* 37°11N 50°8E 247 B6
Långås *Sweden* 56°58N 12°26E 163 H6
Langatabbetje *Suriname* 4°59N 54°28W 329 C7
Langdai *China* 26°6N 105°21E 228 D5
Langdon *U.S.A.* 48°45N 98°22W 308 A4
Långe Jan = Ölands södra udde *Sweden* 56°12N 16°23E 163 H10
Langeac *France* 45°7N 3°29E 174 C7
Langeais *France* 47°20N 0°24E 172 E7
Langeb Baraka → *Sudan* 17°28N 36°50E 256 D4
Langeberg *S. Africa* 33°55S 21°0E 270 D3
Langeberge *S. Africa* 28°15S 22°33E 270 C3
Langeland *Denmark* 54°56N 10°48E 163 K4
Langelands Bælt *Denmark* 54°50N 10°55E 163 K4
Langen *Hessen, Germany* 49°59N 8°40E 179 F4
Langen *Niedersachsen, Germany* 53°36N 8°36E 178 B4
Langenbielau = Bielawa *Poland* 50°43N 16°37E 185 H3
Langenburg *Canada* 50°51N 101°43W 297 C8
Langeneß *Germany* 54°38N 8°36E 178 A4
Langenlois *Austria* 48°29N 15°40E 180 C8
Langenzersdorf *Austria* 48°18N 16°21E 142 A2
Langeoog *Germany* 53°45N 7°32E 178 B3
Langer See *Germany* 52°24N 13°37E 115 B4
Langeskov *Denmark* 55°22N 10°35E 163 J4
Langesund *Norway* 59°0N 9°45E 164 F6
Langevåg *Norway* 62°26N 6°13E 164 B3
Langfang *China* 39°30N 116°41E 226 E9
Langfoss *Norway* 59°51N 6°20E 164 E3
Langgapayung *Indonesia* 1°43N 99°58E 234 B1
Långhem *Sweden* 57°36N 13°14E 163 G7
Langhirano *Italy* 44°37N 10°16E 198 D7
Langholm *U.K.* 55°9N 3°0W 167 F5
Langisjór *Iceland* 64°11N 18°15W 155 C8
Langjökull *Iceland* 64°39N 20°12W 155 C6
Langkawi, Pulau *Malaysia* 6°25N 99°45E 237 J2
Langklip *S. Africa* 28°12S 20°20E 270 C3
Langkon *Malaysia* 6°30N 116°40E 235 A5
Langley *B.C., Canada* 49°7N 122°39W 306 A4
Langley *Va., U.S.A.* 38°57N 77°11W 143 B1
Langley Park *U.S.A.* 38°59N 76°58W 143 B3
Langnau *Switz.* 46°56N 7°47E 179 J3
Langogne *France* 44°43N 3°50E 174 D7
Langon *France* 44°33N 0°16W 174 D3
Langøya *Norway* 68°45N 14°50E 160 B16
Langreo *Spain* 43°18N 5°40W 194 B5
Langres *France* 47°52N 5°20E 173 E12
Langres, Plateau de *France* 47°45N 5°3E 173 E12
Langsa *Indonesia* 4°30N 97°57E 234 B1
Långsele *Sweden* 63°12N 17°4E 162 A11
Långshyttan *Sweden* 60°27N 16°2E 162 D10
Langtang △ *Nepal* 28°10N 85°30E 243 E11
Langtao *Burma* 27°15N 97°34E 241 B6
Langting *India* 25°31N 93°7E 241 C4
Langtou *China* 40°1N 124°19E 227 D13
Langtry *U.S.A.* 29°49N 101°34W 314 G4
Langu *Thailand* 6°53N 99°47E 237 J2
Langue de Barbarie △ *Senegal* 14°54N 16°30W 262 C1
Languedoc *France* 43°58N 3°55E 174 E7
Langwald *Germany* 48°10N 11°25E 131 A1
Langwang *China* 22°38N 113°27E 219 a
Langxi *China* 31°10N 119°12E 229 B12
Langzhong *China* 31°38N 105°58E 228 B5
Lanigan *Canada* 51°51N 105°2W 297 C7
Lanikai *U.S.A.* 21°23N 157°42W 302 K14
Lanín △ *Argentina* 40°0S 71°58W 336 A2
Lanjigarh *India* 19°43N 83°23E 244 E6
Lankao *China* 34°48N 114°50E 226 G8
Länkäran *Azerbaijan* 38°48N 48°52E 213 C13
Lankwitz *Germany* 52°25N 13°21E 115 B3
Lanmeur *France* 48°39N 3°43W 172 D3
Lannemezan *France* 43°8N 0°23E 174 E4
Lannilis *France* 48°35N 4°32W 172 D2
Lannion *France* 48°46N 3°29W 172 D3
L'Annonciation *Canada* 46°25N 74°55W 298 C5
L'Annunziatella *Italy* 41°49N 12°33E 136 C2
Lanouaille *France* 45°24N 1°9E 174 C5
Lanping *China* 26°28N 99°15E 228 D2
Lansang △ *Thailand* 16°45N 99°0E 236 D2
Lansdale *U.S.A.* 40°14N 75°17W 313 F9
Lansdowne *N.S.W., Australia* 31°48S 152°30E 283 A10
Lansdowne *Ont., Canada* 44°24N 76°1W 313 B8
Lansdowne *India* 29°50N 78°41E 243 E8
Lansdowne *Western Cape, S. Africa* 33°59S 18°30E 118 A2
Lansdowne House = Neskantaga *Canada* 52°14N 87°53W 298 B2
L'Anse *U.S.A.* 46°45N 88°27W 308 B9
L'Anse à l'Âne *Martinique* 14°32N 61°4W 322 j
L'Anse au Loup *Canada* 51°32N 56°50W 299 B8
L'Anse aux Epines *Grenada* 11°59N 61°45W 323 q
L'Anse aux Meadows *Canada* 51°36N 55°32W 299 B8
L'Anse Mitan *Martinique* 14°32N 61°3W 322 j
Lansford *U.S.A.* 40°50N 75°53W 313 F9
Lanshan *China* 25°24N 112°10E 229 E9
Lanshantou *China* 35°5N 119°20E 227 G10
Lånsi-Turunmaa *Finland* 60°18N 22°18E 188 B2
Lansing *Ont., Canada* 43°45N 79°24W 141 A2
Lansing *Mich., U.S.A.* 42°44N 84°33W 311 B12
Lanslebourg-Mont-Cenis *France* 45°17N 6°52E 175 C10
Lanta, Ko *Thailand* 7°35N 99°3E 237 J2
Lantana *U.S.A.* 26°35N 80°3W 317 J9
Lantau I. *Hong Kong, China* 22°15N 113°56E 122 B1
Lantau Pk. *Hong Kong, China* 22°15N 113°55E 122 B1
Lantewa *Nigeria* 12°16N 11°44E 263 C7
Lantian *China* 34°11N 109°20E 226 G5
Lanus *Argentina* 34°42S 58°23W 117 C2
Lanusei *Italy* 39°52N 9°34E 200 C2
Lanuza *Phil.* 9°14N 126°4E 233 G6
Lanxi *China* 29°13N 119°28E 229 C12
Lanyang Hsi → *Taiwan* 24°43N 121°49E 225 B3
Lanyü *Taiwan* 22°2N 121°33E 225 D3
Lanzarote *Canary Is.* 29°0N 13°40W 153 e2
Lanzarote ✈ (ACE) *Canary Is.* 28°57N 13°40W 153 e2
Lanzhou *China* 36°1N 103°52E 226 F2
Lanzo Torinese *Italy* 45°16N 7°28E 198 C4
Lao → *Italy* 39°47N 15°48E 201 C8
Lao Cai *Vietnam* 22°30N 103°57E 228 F4
Laoag *Phil.* 18°7N 120°34E 232 B3
Laoang *Phil.* 12°32N 125°8E 232 E5
Laoha He → *China* 43°25N 120°35E 227 C11
Laohekou *China* 32°22N 111°38E 229 A8
Laois □ *Ireland* 52°57N 7°27W 166 D4
Laon *France* 49°33N 3°35E 173 C10
Laona *U.S.A.* 45°34N 88°40W 308 C9
Laonung Hsi → *Taiwan* 22°47N 120°27E 225 D2
Laos ■ *Asia* 17°45N 105°0E 236 D5
Lapa *Paraná, Brazil* 25°46S 49°44W 335 B6
Lapa *Rio de J., Brazil* 22°54S 43°10W 135 B1
Lapac I. *Phil.* 5°32N 120°47E 233 J3
Lapai *Nigeria* 9°5N 6°32E 263 D6
Lapalisse *France* 46°15N 3°38E 173 F10
Laparan I. *Phil.* 5°57N 120°0E 233 J2
Lapeer *U.S.A.* 43°3N 83°19W 311 A13
Lapeyrade *France* 44°4N 0°3W 174 D3
Lapithos *Cyprus* 35°21N 33°11E 207 E9
Lapland = Lappland *Europe* 68°7N 24°0E 160 B21
LaPorte *Ind., U.S.A.* 41°36N 86°43W 311 C10
Laporte *Pa., U.S.A.* 41°25N 76°30W 313 E8
Lapovo *Serbia* 44°10N 21°7E 202 B5
Lappeenranta *Finland* 61°3N 28°12E 188 B5
Lappland *Europe* 68°7N 24°0E 160 B21
Lappo = Lapua *Finland* 62°58N 23°0E 160 E20
Laprida *Argentina* 37°34S 60°45W 334 D3
Lâpseki *Turkey* 40°20N 26°41E 203 F10
Laptev Sea *Russia* 76°0N 125°0E 215 B13
Lapu-Lapu *Phil.* 10°20N 123°55E 233 F4
Lapua *Finland* 62°58N 23°0E 160 E20
Lăpuş → *Romania* 47°25N 23°40E 183 C8
Lăpuş, Munţii *Romania* 47°20N 23°50E 183 C8
Lăpuşna *Moldova* 46°53N 28°25E 183 D13
Lapy *Poland* 52°59N 22°52E 185 F9
Laqiya Arba'in *Sudan* 20°1N 28°1E 256 C2
Laqiya Umran *Sudan* 19°55N 28°18E 256 D2
L'Aquila *Italy* 42°22N 13°22E 199 F10
Lār *Iran* 27°40N 54°14E 247 E7
Lara *Australia* 38°2S 144°26E 282 E6
Lara □ *Venezuela* 10°10N 69°50W 328 A4
Larabanga *Ghana* 9°16N 1°56W 262 D4
Larache *Morocco* 35°10N 6°5W 260 A3
Laragaran = Plaridel *Phil.* 8°37N 123°43E 233 G4
Laragne-Montéglin *France* 44°18N 5°49E 175 D9
Lārak *Iran* 26°51N 56°21E 247 E8
Laramie *U.S.A.* 41°19N 105°35W 304 F11
Laramie Mts. *U.S.A.* 42°0N 105°30W 304 F11
Laranda = Karaman *Turkey* 37°14N 33°13E 212 D5
Laranjal do Jari *Brazil* 0°51S 52°32W 329 D7
Laranjeiras *Brazil* 22°55S 43°10W 135 B1
Laranjeiras do Sul *Brazil* 25°23S 52°23W 335 B5
Larantuka *Indonesia* 8°21S 122°55E 231 F6
Larat *Indonesia* 7°0S 132°0E 231 F8
L'Arbresle *France* 45°50N 4°36E 175 C8
Lärbro *Sweden* 57°47N 18°50E 163 G12
Lårdal *Norway* 59°25N 8°10E 164 E5
Larde *Mozam.* 16°28S 39°43E 269 F4
Larder Lake *Canada* 48°5N 79°40W 298 C4
Lardos *Greece* 36°6N 28°1E 206 E12
Lardos, Akra = Lindos, Akra *Greece* 36°4N 28°10E 206 E12
Lardos, Ormos *Greece* 36°4N 28°2E 206 E12
Lare *Kenya* 0°20N 37°56E 268 C4
Laredo *Spain* 43°26N 3°28W 194 B7
Laredo *Tex., U.S.A.* 27°30N 99°30W 314 H5
Laredo Sd. *Canada* 52°30N 128°53W 296 C3
Larena *Phil.* 9°15N 123°35E 233 G4
Lares *Puerto Rico* 18°18N 66°53W 321 b
Large I. *Grenada* 12°24N 61°30W 323 q
Largentière *France* 44°34N 4°18E 175 D8
L'Argentière-la-Bessée *France* 44°47N 6°33E 175 D10
Largo *U.S.A.* 27°54N 82°47W 317 H7
Largo, Cayo *Cuba* 21°37N 81°28W 320 B3
Largo, Key *U.S.A.* 25°15N 80°15W 317 K9
Largs *U.K.* 55°47N 4°52W 167 F4
Lari *Italy* 43°34N 10°35E 198 E7
Lariang *Indonesia* 1°26S 119°17E 235 C5
Larimore *U.S.A.* 47°54N 97°38W 308 B5
Larino *Italy* 41°48N 14°54E 199 G11
Lario, Il = Como, L. di *Italy* 46°0N 9°11E 198 B6
Larisa *Greece* 39°36N 22°27E 204 B4
Larisis Station *Athens, Greece* 112 a1
Larissa = Larisa *Greece* 39°36N 22°27E 204 B4
Larkana *Pakistan* 27°32N 68°18E 242 F3
Larkins = South Miami *U.S.A.* 25°42N 80°17W 129 D1
Larnaca *Cyprus* 34°55N 33°38E 207 F9
Larnaca Bay *Cyprus* 34°53N 33°45E 207 F9
Larnaca Int. ✈ (LCA) *Cyprus* 34°50N 33°34E 207 F9
Larnare, Pte. *Martinique* 14°47N 61°13W 322 j
Larne *U.K.* 54°51N 5°51W 166 B6
Larned *U.S.A.* 38°11N 99°6W 308 F4
Laroquebrou *France* 44°58N 2°12E 174 D6
Larose *U.S.A.* 29°34N 90°23W 315 G9
Larose, Pte. *Martinique* 14°39N 60°53W 322 j
Larrimah *Australia* 15°35S 133°12E 278 C5
Larsen Bay *U.S.A.* 57°32N 153°59W 303 H9
Larsen Ice Shelf *Antarctica* 67°0S 62°0W 151 C17
Laruns *France* 43°0N 0°26W 174 F3
Larvik *Norway* 59°4N 10°2E 164 E7
Larzac, Causse du *France* 43°50N 3°17E 174 E7
Las Palmas *Argentina* 27°8S 58°45W 334 B4
Las Palmas → *Mexico* 32°31N 116°58W 307 N10
Las Palmas ✈ (LPA) *Canary Is.* 27°55N 15°25W 153 e1
Las Palmas de Gran Canaria *Canary Is.* 28°7N 15°26W 153 e1
Las Pedroñeras *Spain* 39°26N 2°40W 197 F2
Las Piedras *Puerto Rico* 18°11N 65°52W 321 b
Las Piedras *Uruguay* 34°44S 56°14W 335 C4
Las Pinas *Phil.* 14°29N 120°58E 127 C1
Las Pipinas *Argentina* 35°30S 57°19W 334 D4
Las Plumas *Argentina* 43°40S 67°15W 336 B3
Las Ramblas = La Rambla *Barcelona, Spain* 114 b2
Las Rejas *Chile* 33°27S 70°42W 137 B1
Las Rosas *Argentina* 32°30S 61°35W 334 C3
Las Rozas *Spain* 40°29N 3°52W 194 E7
Las Tablas *Panama* 7°49N 80°14W 320 E3
Las Toscas *Argentina* 28°21S 59°18W 334 B4
Las Tunas *Cuba* 20°58N 76°59W 320 B4
Las Varillas *Argentina* 31°50S 62°50W 334 C3
Las Vegas *N. Mex., U.S.A.* 35°36N 105°13W 305 J11
Las Vegas *Nev., U.S.A.* 36°10N 115°8W 124 A2
Las Vegas McCarran Int. ✈ (LAS) *U.S.A.* 36°5N 115°9W 124 B2
Lasa = Lhasa *China* 29°25N 90°58E 218 F7
LaSalle *Canada* 45°26N 73°38W 130 B2
LaSalle Street *Chicago, U.S.A.* 119 a1
LaSalle Street Station *Chicago, U.S.A.* 119 d1
Lasanga I. *Papua N. G.* 7°25S 147°15E 286 D4
Lasarte-Oria *Spain* 43°16N 2°1W 196 B2
Lascano *Uruguay* 33°35S 54°12W 335 C5
Lascelles *Australia* 35°34S 142°34E 282 C5
Lasek Bielański *Poland* 52°17N 20°57E 143 B1
Lasek Na Kole *Poland* 52°15N 20°56E 143 B1
Lash-e Joveyn *Afghan.* 31°45N 61°30E 240 C1
Lashburn *Canada* 53°10N 109°40W 297 C7
Lashio *Burma* 22°56N 97°45E 241 D6
Lashkar *India* 26°10N 78°10E 242 F8
Lashkar Gāh *Afghan.* 31°35N 64°21E 240 C2
Lasin *Poland* 53°30N 19°2E 184 E6
Lasithi *Greece* 35°11N 25°31E 207 E6
Lasithi □ *Greece* 35°5N 25°50E 207 D7
Lāsjerd *Iran* 35°24N 53°4E 247 C7
Lask *Poland* 51°34N 19°8E 185 G6
Laskarzew *Poland* 51°48N 21°36E 185 G8
Laško *Slovenia* 46°10N 15°16E 199 B12
Lassance *Brazil* 17°54S 44°34W 333 E3
Lassay-les-Châteaux *France* 48°27N 0°30W 172 D6
Lassen Pk. *U.S.A.* 40°29N 121°30W 304 F3
Lassen Volcanic △ *U.S.A.* 40°30N 121°20W 304 F3
Lassongo *Angola* 12°55S 22°46E 265 E4
Last Mountain L. *Canada* 51°5N 105°14W 297 C7
Lastchance Cr. → *U.S.A.* 40°2N 121°15W 306 E5
Lastoursville *Gabon* 0°55S 12°38E 264 C2
Lastovo *Croatia* 42°46N 16°55E 199 F13
Lastovski Kanal *Croatia* 42°50N 17°0E 199 F14
Lat Yao *Thailand* 15°45N 99°48E 236 E2
Lata Mt. *Amer. Samoa* 14°14S 169°27W 302 f
Latacunga *Ecuador* 0°50S 78°35W 328 D2
Latady I. *Antarctica* 70°45S 74°35W 151 D17
Latakia = Al Lādhiqīyah *Syria* 35°30N 35°45E 250 C6
Latchford *Canada* 47°20N 79°50W 298 C4
Late *Tonga* 18°48S 174°39W 287 P13
Latehar *India* 23°45N 84°30E 243 H11
Laterza *Italy* 40°37N 16°48E 201 B9
Latham *Australia* 29°44S 116°20E 279 E2
Lathen *Germany* 52°52N 7°19E 178 C3
Lathi *India* 27°43N 71°23E 242 F4
Lathi *Vanuatu* 14°57S 167°8E 287 D5
Lathrop *U.S.A.* 39°33N 94°20W 310 E2
Lathrop Wells *U.S.A.* 36°39N 116°24W 307 J10
Latiano *Italy* 40°33N 17°43E 201 B10
Latin, Quartier *Montréal, Canada* 130 b2
Latina *Italy* 41°28N 12°52E 200 A5
Latina *Madrid, Spain* 40°24N 3°44W 127 B1
Latisana *Italy* 45°47N 13°0E 199 C10
Latium = Lazio □ *Italy* 42°10N 12°30E 199 F9
Lato *Greece* 35°11N 25°39E 207 D7
Latorytsya → *Slovakia* 48°28N 21°50E 181 C14
Latouche Treville, C. *Australia* 18°27S 121°49E 278 C3
Latouma *Niger* 22°10N 14°50E 259 D2
Látrar *Iceland* 66°24N 23°2W 155 A3
Latrobe *Tas., Australia* 41°14S 146°30E 281 G4
Latrobe *Pa., U.S.A.* 40°19N 79°23W 312 F5
Latrónico *Italy* 40°5N 16°1E 201 B9
Latur *India* 18°25N 76°40E 244 E3
Latvia ■ *Europe* 56°50N 24°0E 188 D2
Lau *Nigeria* 9°11N 11°19E 263 D7
Lau Basin *Pac. Oc.* 20°0S 177°0W 277 E15
Lau Group *Fiji* 17°0S 178°30W 287 A3
Lau Ridge *Pac. Oc.* 21°0S 178°30W 277 E15
Lauban = Lubań *Poland* 51°5N 15°15E 185 G2
Lauca → *Bolivia* 19°9S 68°10W 330 D4
Lauchhammer *Germany* 51°29N 13°47E 178 D9
Lauda-Königshofen *Germany* 49°33N 9°42E 179 F5
Laudal *Norway* 58°15N 7°30E 164 F4
Laudat *Dominica* 15°20N 61°21W 323 k
Lauderdale Lakes *U.S.A.* 26°9N 80°12W 129 B1
Lauderhill *U.S.A.* 26°8N 80°12W 129 B2
Laudio = Llodio *Spain* 43°9N 2°58W 196 B2
Lauenburg = Lębork *Poland* 54°33N 17°46E 184 D4
Lauenburg *Germany* 53°22N 10°32E 178 B6
Lauenburgische Seen ⌓ *Germany* 53°38N 10°45E 178 B6
Lauf *Germany* 49°30N 11°16E 179 F7
Laufás *Iceland* 65°53N 18°4W 155 B8
Laugar *Iceland* 65°15N 21°48W 155 B5
Laugarás *Iceland* 64°7N 20°30W 155 C6
Laugarbakki *Iceland* 65°20N 20°55W 155 B6
Laugarvatn *Iceland* 64°13N 20°44W 155 C6
Lauge Koch Kyst *Greenland* 75°45N 57°45W 295 B20
Laughlin *U.S.A.* 35°10N 114°34W 307 K12
Lauhanvuori △ *Finland* 62°8N 22°4E 160 E20
Laujar de Andarax *Spain* 37°0N 2°54W 197 H2
Laukaa *Finland* 62°24N 25°56E 160 E21
Laukkaing *Burma* 23°52N 98°38E 241 D7
Laulau, Bahia *N. Marianas* 15°8N 145°45E 302 e
Launceston *Tas., Australia* 41°24S 147°8E 281 G4
Launceston *Corn., U.K.* 50°38N 4°22W 169 G3
Laune → *Ireland* 52°7N 9°47W 166 D2
Launglon Bok *Burma* 13°50N 97°54E 236 F1
Laupheim *Germany* 48°14N 9°52E 179 G5
Laura *Queens., Australia* 15°32S 144°32E 280 B3
Laura *S. Austral., Australia* 33°10S 138°18E 282 B3
Laureana di Borrello *Italy* 38°30N 16°5E 201 D9
Laurel *Fla., U.S.A.* 27°8N 82°27W 317 H7
Laurel *Ind., U.S.A.* 39°30N 85°11W 311 E11
Laurel *Miss., U.S.A.* 31°41N 89°8W 315 F10
Laurel *Mont., U.S.A.* 45°40N 108°46W 304 D9
Laurel Bay *U.S.A.* 32°27N 80°47W 316 C9
Laurel Hill *U.S.A.* 40°14N 79°6W 312 F5
Laurencekirk *U.K.* 56°50N 2°28W 167 E6
Laurens *Iowa, U.S.A.* 42°51N 94°52W 310 B2
Laurens *S.C., U.S.A.* 34°30N 82°1W 315 D13
Laurentian Plateau *Canada* 52°0N 70°0W 299 B6
Lauria *Italy* 40°2N 15°50E 201 B8
Laurie L. *Canada* 56°35N 101°57W 297 B8
Laurinburg *U.S.A.* 34°47N 79°28W 315 D15
Laurium *U.S.A.* 47°14N 88°27W 308 B9
Lausanne *Switz.* 46°32N 6°38E 179 J2
Laut *Indonesia* 4°45N 108°0E 235 B3
Laut, Pulau *Indonesia* 3°40S 116°10E 235 C5
Laut Kecil, Kepulauan *Indonesia* 4°45S 115°40E 235 C5
Lautaro *Chile* 38°31S 72°27W 336 A2
Lauterbach *Germany* 50°37N 9°24E 178 E5
Lauterecken *Germany* 49°38N 7°35E 179 F3
Lautoka *Fiji* 17°37S 177°27E 287 A1
L'Autre Bord *Guadeloupe* 16°20N 61°20W 322 e
Luuttasaari *Finland* 60°9N 24°52E 121 C2
Lauwersmeer △ *Neths.* 53°22N 6°11E 170 A6
Lauzès *France* 44°34N 1°35E 174 D5
Lava → *Russia* 54°37N 21°14E 184 D8
Lava, Nosy *Madag.* 14°33S 47°36E 272 A2
Lava Beds ⌓ *U.S.A.* 41°40N 121°30W 304 F3
Lavagh More *Ireland* 54°46N 8°6W 166 B3
Lavagna *Italy* 44°18N 9°20E 198 D6
Laval *France* 48°4N 0°48W 172 D6
Laval-des-Rapides *Canada* 45°33N 73°42W 130 A1
Lavalle *Argentina* 28°15S 65°15W 334 B2
Lāvān *Iran* 26°48N 53°22E 247 E7
Lavanggu *Solomon Is.* 11°36S 160°16E 287 N11
Lavant *Canada* 45°3N 76°42W 313 A8
Lāvar Meydān *Iran* 30°20N 54°30E 247 D7
Lavara *Greece* 41°19N 26°22E 203 E10
Lavardac *France* 44°12N 0°20E 174 D4
Lavaur *France* 43°40N 1°49E 174 E5
Lavelanet *France* 42°57N 1°51E 174 F5
Lavello *Italy* 41°3N 15°48E 201 A8
Laventille □ *Trin. & Tob.* 10°39N 61°30W 323 t
L'Averdy, C. *Papua N. G.* 5°33S 155°4E 286 C8
Lavers Hill *Australia* 38°40S 143°25E 282 E5
Laverton *Australia* 28°44S 122°29E 279 E3
Lavezzi, Îs. *France* 41°22N 9°16E 175 G13
Lavik *Norway* 61°6N 5°25E 164 C2
Lavis *Italy* 46°8N 11°7E 198 B8
Lavīzān *Iran* 35°47N 51°30E 141 A2
Lavos *Portugal* 40°6N 8°49W 194 E2
Lavoutte, Anse *St. Lucia* 14°5N 60°55W 323 m
Lavradio *Portugal* 38°40N 9°2W 126 A2
Lavras *Brazil* 21°20S 45°0W 333 F3
Lavre *Portugal* 38°46N 8°22W 195 G2
Lavrio *Greece* 37°40N 24°4E 204 D6
Lavris *Greece* 35°25N 24°40E 207 E5
Lavumisa *Swaziland* 27°20S 31°55E 271 C5
Lavushi Manda △ *Zambia* 12°46S 31°0E 269 E3
Law-Racoviţă *Antarctica* 69°23S 76°23E 151 C6
Lawa *Phil.* 6°12N 125°41E 233 H5
Lawa-an *Phil.* 11°51N 125°5E 233 F5
Lawachara △ *Bangla.* 24°20N 91°43E 241 C3
Lawak I. = Nanshan I. *S. China Sea* 10°45N 115°49E 230 B5
Lawaki *Fiji* 17°40S 178°35E 287 A2
Lawas *Malaysia* 4°55N 115°25E 235 B5
Lawdar *Yemen* 13°53N 45°52E 248 D4
Lawele *Indonesia* 5°13S 122°57E 231 F6
Lawit *Indonesia* 1°23N 112°55E 235 B4
Lawksawk *Burma* 21°15N 96°52E 241 E6
Lawn Hill = Boodjamulla △ *Australia* 18°15S 138°6E 280 B2
Lawndale *U.S.A.* 41°50N 87°42W 119 B2
Lawne L. *U.S.A.* 28°33N 81°26W 133 A2
Lawqah *Si. Arabia* 29°49N 42°45E 246 D4
Lawra *Ghana* 10°39N 2°51W 262 C4
Lawrence *N.Z.* 45°55S 169°41E 285 F4
Lawrence *Ind., U.S.A.* 39°50N 86°2W 311 E10
Lawrence *Kans., U.S.A.* 38°58N 95°14W 308 F6
Lawrence *Mass., U.S.A.* 42°43N 71°10W 313 D13
Lawrence Heights *Canada* 43°43N 79°25W 141 A2
Lawrenceburg *Ind., U.S.A.* 39°6N 84°52W 311 E12
Lawrenceburg *Ky., U.S.A.* 38°2N 84°54W 311 F12
Lawrenceburg *Tenn., U.S.A.* 35°14N 87°20W 315 D11
Lawrenceville *Ga., U.S.A.* 33°57N 83°59W 316 B6
Lawrenceville *Ill., U.S.A.* 38°44N 87°41W 311 F9
Lawrenceville *Pa., U.S.A.* 41°59N 77°8W 312 E7
Laws *U.S.A.* 37°24N 118°20W 306 H8
Lawson *U.S.A.* 39°26N 94°12W 310 E2
Lawtey *U.S.A.* 30°3N 82°5W 316 E7
Lawton *Mich., U.S.A.* 42°10N 85°50W 311 B11
Lawton *Okla., U.S.A.* 34°37N 98°25W 314 D5
Lawu *Indonesia* 7°40S 111°13E 235 D4
Lawz, J. al *Si. Arabia* 28°39N 35°18E 251 K6
Laxå *Sweden* 58°59N 14°37E 163 F8
Laxamýri *Iceland* 65°58N 17°24W 155 B9
Laxford, L. *U.K.* 58°24N 5°6W 167 C3
Laxiwa Dam *China* 36°4N 101°11E 218 D9
Laxou *France* 48°41N 6°8E 173 D13
Lay → *France* 46°18N 1°17W 174 B2
Layari *Pakistan* 24°52N 67°0E 123 A2
Layari → *Pakistan* 24°52N 66°58E 123 A1
Layla *Si. Arabia* 22°10N 46°40E 248 B4
Laylān *Iraq* 35°18N 44°31E 246 C5
Layon → *France* 47°20N 0°45W 172 E6
Layou *St. Vincent* 13°12N 61°17W 323 n
Layou → *Dominica* 15°23N 61°21W 323 k
Laysan I. *U.S.A.* 25°50N 171°50W 302 F9
Layton *Fla., U.S.A.* 24°50N 80°47W 317 L9
Layton *Utah, U.S.A.* 41°4N 111°58W 304 F8
Laytonville *U.S.A.* 39°41N 123°29W 304 G2
Laza *Burma* 26°30N 97°38E 241 B6
Lazarata *Greece* 38°47N 20°40E 207 B2
Lazarev *Russia* 52°13N 141°30E 215 D15
Lazarev Sea *S. Ocean* 67°30S 3°0W 151 C2
Lazarevac *Serbia* 44°23N 20°17E 202 B4
Lazarevskoye *Russia* 43°55N 39°21E 191 J4
Lazarivo *Madag.* 23°54S 44°59E 272 C1
Lázaro Cárdenas *Mexico* 17°55N 102°11W 318 D4
Lazdijai *Lithuania* 54°14N 23°31E 184 D10
Lazhuglung *China* 34°52N 81°24E 217 F10
Lazi *Phil.* 9°8N 123°38E 233 G4
Lazienki Palace *Warsaw, Poland* 143 c3
Lazienkowski Park *Poland* 52°13N 21°1E 143 B2
Lazio □ *Italy* 42°10N 12°30E 199 F9
Lazo *Moldova* 47°33N 28°2E 183 C13
Lazo *Russia* 43°25N 133°55E 220 C6
Lazy Lake *U.S.A.* 26°9N 80°8W 129 B2
Lbishchensk = Chapaev *Kazakhstan* 50°25N 51°10E 190 E10
Le Beausset *France* 43°12N 5°48E 175 E9
Le Bélier *Réunion* 21°2S 55°28E 272 f
Le Bic *Canada* 48°20N 68°41W 299 C6
Le Blanc *France* 46°37N 1°3E 174 B5
Le Blanc-Mesnil *France* 48°56N 2°27E 134 A3
Le Bleymard *France* 44°30N 3°42E 174 D7
Le Bourget *France* 48°56N 2°25E 134 A3
Le Bourgneuf-la-Fôret *France* 48°10N 0°59W 172 D6
Le Bugue *France* 44°55N 0°56E 174 D4
Le Carbet *Martinique* 14°42N 61°11W 322 j
Le Cateau Cambrésis *France* 50°7N 3°32E 173 B10
Le Caylar *France* 43°51N 3°19E 174 E7
Le Chambon-Feugerolles *France* 45°24N 4°19E 175 C8
Le Chameau *Guadeloupe* 15°51N 61°35W 322 e
Le Châtelet *France* 46°38N 2°16E 173 F9
Le Chenoi *Belgium* 50°41N 4°18E 116 B2
Le Chesnay *France* 48°49N 2°8E 134 B1
Le Chesne *France* 49°30N 4°45E 173 C11
Le Cheylard *France* 44°55N 4°25E 175 D8
Le Christ de Saclay *France* 48°43N 1°59E 134 B2
Le Claire *U.S.A.* 41°36N 90°21W 310 C6
Le Conquet *France* 48°21N 4°46W 172 D2
Le Creusot *France* 46°48N 4°24E 173 F11
Le Croisic *France* 47°18N 2°30W 172 E4
Le Diamant *Martinique* 14°28N 61°2W 322 j
Le Donjon *France* 46°22N 3°48E 173 F10
Le Dorat *France* 46°14N 1°5E 174 B5
Le François *Martinique* 14°38N 60°57W 322 j
Le Gosier *Guadeloupe* 16°14N 61°29W 322 e
Le Grand Brûlé *Réunion* 21°14S 55°47E 272 f
Le Grand-Lucé *France* 47°52N 0°28E 172 E7
Le Grand-Pressigny *France* 46°55N 0°48E 172 F7
Le Grand-Quevilly *France* 49°24N 1°3E 172 C8
Le Gris Gris *Mauritius* 20°31S 57°32E 272 d
Le Gros Morne *Réunion* 21°5S 55°28E 272 f
Le Havre *France* 49°30N 0°5E 172 C7
Le Kremlin-Bicêtre *France* 48°48N 2°21E 134 B3
Le Lamentin *Martinique* 14°35N 61°2W 322 j
Le Lavandou *France* 43°8N 6°22E 175 E10
Le Lion-d'Angers *France* 47°37N 0°43W 172 E6
Le Lorrain *Martinique* 14°48N 61°3W 322 j
Le Louroux-Béconnais *France* 47°30N 0°55W 172 E6
Le Luc *France* 43°23N 6°21E 175 E10
Le Lude *France* 47°39N 0°9E 172 E7
Le Maire, Estr. de *Argentina* 54°50S 65°0W 336 D4
Le Mans *France* 48°0N 0°10E 172 E7
Le Marigot *Martinique* 14°50N 61°4W 322 j
Le Marin *Martinique* 14°27N 60°55W 322 j
Le Mars *U.S.A.* 42°47N 96°10W 308 D5
Le Mayet-de-Montagne *France* 46°4N 3°40E 173 F10
Le Mêle-sur-Sarthe *France* 48°31N 0°22E 172 D7
Le Mesnil-le-Roi *France* 48°56N 2°7E 134 A1
Le Monastier-sur-Gazeille *France* 44°57N 3°59E 174 D7
Le Monêtier-les-Bains *France* 44°58N 6°30E 175 D10
Le Mont-Dore *France* 45°35N 2°49E 174 C6
Le Mont-St-Michel *France* 48°40N 1°30W 172 D5
Le Morne Brabant *Mauritius* 20°27S 57°19E 272 d
Le Morne Rouge *Martinique* 14°47N 61°8W 322 j
Le Morne-Vert *Martinique* 14°42N 61°8W 322 j
Le Moule *Guadeloupe* 16°20N 61°22W 322 e
Le Moyne, L. *Canada* 56°45N 68°47W 299 A6
Le Muy *France* 43°28N 6°34E 175 E10
Le Palais *France* 47°20N 3°10W 172 E3
Le Pecq *France* 48°53N 2°6E 134 A1
Le Perreux *France* 48°50N 2°29E 134 A3
Le Perthus *France* 42°30N 2°53E 174 F6
Le Pin *France* 48°54N 2°37E 134 A4
Le Plessis-Robinson *France* 48°47N 2°15E 134 B2
Le Plessis-Trévise *France* 48°48N 2°34E 134 B4
Le Port *Réunion* 20°56S 55°18E 272 f
Le Port-Marly *France* 48°52N 2°6E 134 A1
Le Pré-St-Gervais *France* 48°53N 2°23E 134 A3
Le Prêcheur *Martinique* 14°50N 61°12W 322 j
Le Puy-en-Velay *France* 45°3N 3°52E 174 C7
Le Raincy *France* 48°53N 2°31E 134 A4
Le Raysville *U.S.A.* 41°50N 76°10W 313 E8
Le Robert *Martinique* 14°40N 60°56W 322 j
Le Roy *Ill., U.S.A.* 40°21N 88°46W 311 D8
Le Roy *N.Y., U.S.A.* 42°58N 77°59W 312 D7
Le St-Esprit *Martinique* 14°34N 60°56W 322 j
Le Souffleur *Guadeloupe* 16°19N 61°2W 322 e
Le Sueur *U.S.A.* 44°28N 93°55W 308 C7
Le Tampon *Réunion* 21°16S 55°32E 272 f
Le Teil *France* 44°33N 4°40E 175 D8
Le Teilleul *France* 48°32N 0°53W 172 D6
Le Theil *France* 48°16N 0°42E 172 D7
Le Thillot *France* 47°53N 6°46E 173 E13
Le Thuy *Vietnam* 17°14N 106°49E 236 D6
Le Touquet-Paris-Plage *France* 50°30N 1°36E 173 B8
Le Tréport *France* 50°3N 1°20E 172 B8
Le Trou à Diable *Guadeloupe* 15°57N 61°14W 322 e
Le Val-André *France* 48°35N 2°32W 172 D4
Le Val-d'Ajol *France* 47°55N 6°30E 173 E13
Le Val Nature Park *Mauritius* 20°22S 57°37E 272 e
Le Vauclin *Martinique* 14°33N 60°52W 322 j
Le Verdon-sur-Mer *France* 45°33N 1°4W 174 C2
Le Vésinet *France* 48°54N 2°8E 134 A1
Le Vigan *France* 43°59N 3°36E 174 E7
Le Vignoble, Isola *Venice, Italy* 142 a4
Lea → *U.K.* 51°31N 0°1E 169 F8
Lea Bridge *U.K.* 51°33N 0°2W 125 A4
Lea Lea *Papua N. G.* 9°17S 146°59E 286 E4
Leach *Cambodia* 12°21N 103°46E 237 F4
Lead *U.S.A.* 44°21N 103°46W 308 C2
Leader *Canada* 50°50N 109°30W 297 C7
Leadville *U.S.A.* 39°15N 106°18W 304 G10
Leaf → *U.S.A.* 30°59N 88°44W 315 F10
Leaf Rapids *Canada* 56°30N 99°59W 297 B9
Leaghur, L. *Australia* 33°35S 143°3E 282 B5
League City *U.S.A.* 29°31N 95°6W 314 C7
Leaksville = Eden *U.S.A.* 36°29N 79°53W 315 C15
Lealui *Zambia* 15°10S 23°2E 265 F4
Leamington *Ont., Canada* 42°3N 82°36W 312 D2
Leamington *N.Z.* 37°55S 175°30E 284 D4
Leamington *Utah, U.S.A.* 39°32N 112°17W 304 G7
Leamington Spa = Royal Leamington Spa *U.K.* 52°18N 1°31W 169 E6
Le'an *China* 27°22N 115°48E 229 D10
Leander *U.S.A.* 30°34N 97°52W 314 F5
Leandro Norte Alem *Argentina* 27°34S 55°15W 335 B4
Leane, L. *Ireland* 52°2N 9°32W 166 D2
Learmonth *Australia* 22°13S 114°10E 278 D1
Leary *U.S.A.* 31°29N 84°31W 316 D5
Leasburg *U.S.A.* 38°2N 91°16W 310 F5
Leaside *Canada* 43°42N 79°22W 141 A2
Leask *Canada* 53°5N 106°45W 297 C7
Leatherhead *U.K.* 51°18N 0°20W 169 F7
Leavdnja = Lakselv *Norway* 70°2N 25°0E 160 A21
Leavenworth *Ind., U.S.A.* 38°12N 86°21W 311 F10
Leavenworth *Kans., U.S.A.* 39°19N 94°55W 308 F6
Leavenworth *Wash., U.S.A.* 47°36N 120°40W 304 C3
Leawood *U.S.A.* 38°58N 94°37W 310 F2
Łeba *Poland* 54°45N 17°32E 184 D4
Łeba → *Poland* 54°46N 17°33E 184 D4
Lebach *Germany* 49°25N 6°54E 179 F2
Lebak *Phil.* 6°32N 124°5E 233 H5
Lebam *U.S.A.* 46°34N 123°33W 306 D3
Lebane *Serbia* 42°56N 21°44E 202 D5
Lebango *Congo* 0°39N 14°21E 264 B2
Lebango → *Congo* 0°2N 14°52E 264 B2
Lebanon *Fla., U.S.A.* 29°10N 82°37W 317 F7
Lebanon *Ill., U.S.A.* 38°38N 89°49W 310 F7
Lebanon *Ind., U.S.A.* 40°3N 86°28W 311 D10
Lebanon *Kans., U.S.A.* 39°49N 98°33W 308 F4
Lebanon *Ky., U.S.A.* 37°34N 85°15W 309 G11
Lebanon *Mo., U.S.A.* 37°41N 92°40W 310 G4
Lebanon *N.H., U.S.A.* 43°39N 72°15W 313 C12
Lebanon *Ohio, U.S.A.* 39°26N 84°13W 311 E12
Lebanon *Oreg., U.S.A.* 44°32N 122°55W 304 D2
Lebanon *Pa., U.S.A.* 40°20N 76°26W 313 F8
Lebanon *Tenn., U.S.A.* 36°12N 86°18W 315 C11
Lebanon ■ *Asia* 34°0N 36°0E 250 E7
Lebanon Junction *U.S.A.* 37°50N 85°44W 311 G11
Lebap □ *Turkmenistan* 40°0N 63°0E 216 D6
Lebec *U.S.A.* 34°51N 118°52W 307 L8
Lebedyan *Russia* 53°0N 39°10E 189 F10
Lebedyn *Ukraine* 50°35N 34°30E 189 G8
Lebel-sur-Quévillon *Canada* 49°3N 76°59W 298 C4
Lebir *Israel* 22°59S 43°14W 135 B1
Lebo *Dem. Rep. of the Congo* 4°30N 23°58E 264 B4
Lebomboberge *S. Africa* 24°30S 32°0E 271 B5
Lębork *Poland* 54°33N 17°46E 184 D4
Lebowakgomo *S. Africa* 24°12S 29°30E 271 B4
Lebrija *Spain* 36°53N 6°5W 195 J4
Łebsko, Jezioro *Poland* 54°40N 17°25E 184 D4
Lebu *Chile* 37°40S 73°47W 334 D1
Leça da Palmeira *Portugal* 41°12N 8°42W 194 D2
Lecce *Italy* 40°23N 18°11E 201 B11
Lecco *Italy* 45°51N 9°23E 198 C6
Lecco, L. di *Italy* 45°55N 9°19E 198 C6
Lécera *Spain* 41°13N 0°43W 196 D4
Lech *Austria* 47°13N 10°9E 180 D3
Lech → *Germany* 48°43N 10°56E 179 G6
Lechang *China* 25°10N 113°20E 229 E9
Lechena *Greece* 37°57N 21°16E 204 D3
Lechtaler Alpen *Austria* 47°15N 10°30E 180 D3
Lecontes Mills *U.S.A.* 41°5N 78°17W 312 E6
Lectoure *France* 43°56N 0°38E 174 E4
Łęczna *Poland* 51°18N 22°53E 185 G9
Łęczyca *Poland* 52°5N 19°15E 185 F6
Ledang, Gunung *Malaysia* 2°22N 102°37E 237 L4
Ledesma *Spain* 41°6N 5°59W 194 D5
Lediba *Dem. Rep. of the Congo* 3°1S 16°34E 264 C3
Lednice *Czechia* 48°46N 16°46E 181 C9
Ledo *India* 27°18N 95°44E 241 B5
Lédo, Cabo *Angola* 9°43S 13°12E 265 D2
Ledong *China* 18°41N 109°5E 229 a
Leduc *Canada* 53°15N 113°30W 296 C6
Lee *London, U.K.* 51°27N 0°0 125 B4
Lee *Fla., U.S.A.* 30°25N 83°18W 316 E6
Lee *Mass., U.S.A.* 42°19N 73°15W 313 D11
Lee → *Ireland* 51°53N 8°56W 166 E3
Lee Vining *U.S.A.* 37°58N 119°7W 306 H7
Leech L. *U.S.A.* 47°10N 94°24W 308 B6
Leechburg *U.S.A.* 40°37N 79°36W 312 F5
Leeds *W. Yorks., U.K.* 53°48N 1°33W 168 D6
Leeds *Ala., U.S.A.* 33°33N 86°33W 315 E11
Leek *Neths.* 53°10N 6°24E 170 A6
Leek *Staffs., U.K.* 53°7N 2°1W 168 D5
Leeman *Australia* 29°57S 114°58E 279 E1
Leeper *U.S.A.* 41°22N 79°18W 312 E5
Leer *Germany* 53°13N 7°26E 178 B3
Lee's Summit *U.S.A.* 38°55N 94°23W 310 F2
Leesburg *Fla., U.S.A.* 28°49N 81°53W 317 G8
Leesburg *Ga., U.S.A.* 31°44N 84°10W 316 D5
Leesburg *Ohio, U.S.A.* 39°21N 83°33W 311 E13
Leeston *N.Z.* 43°45S 172°19E 285 D7
Leesville *U.S.A.* 31°8N 93°16W 314 F8
Leeton *Australia* 34°33S 146°23E 283 C7
Leetonia *U.S.A.* 40°53N 80°45W 312 F4
Leeu Gamka *S. Africa* 32°47S 21°59E 270 D3
Leeuwarden *Neths.* 53°15N 5°48E 170 A5
Leeuwin, C. *Australia* 34°20S 115°9E 279 F2
Leeuwin Naturaliste △ *Australia* 34°6S 115°3E 279 F2
Leeward Is. *Atl. Oc.* 16°30N 63°30W 321 C7
Léfini *Congo* 2°55S 15°39E 264 C3
Léfini → *Congo* 2°56S 16°9E 264 C3
Léfini ⌓ *Congo* 2°55S 15°20E 264 C3
Lefka *Cyprus* 35°6N 32°51E 207 E8
Lefkada *Greece* 38°40N 20°43E 207 B2
Lefkimi *Greece* 39°25N 20°3E 206 C10
Lefkimis, Akra *Greece* 39°29N 20°4E 206 C10
Lefkoniko *Cyprus* 35°18N 33°44E 207 E9
Lefkosia = Nicosia *Cyprus* 35°10N 33°25E 207 E9
Lefroy *Canada* 44°16N 79°34W 312 B5
Lefroy, L. *Australia* 31°21S 121°40E 279 F3
Łeg → *Poland* 50°42N 21°50E 185 H8
Leganés *Spain* 40°19N 3°45W 127 C1
Legazpi *Phil.* 13°10N 123°45E 232 E4
Legazpi *Madrid, Spain* 40°23N 3°41W 127 B1
Lège-Cap-Ferret *France* 44°48N 1°9W 174 D2
Lege Hida *Ethiopia* 7°56N 41°4E 257 F5
Legendre I. *Australia* 20°22S 116°55E 278 D2
Leghorn = Livorno *Italy* 43°33N 10°19E 198 E7
Legian *Indonesia* 8°42S 115°10E 231 K18
Legionowo *Poland* 52°25N 20°50E 185 F7
Legnago *Italy* 45°11N 11°18E 199 C8
Legnano *Italy* 45°36N 8°54E 198 C5
Legnica *Poland* 51°12N 16°10E 185 G3
Legrad *Croatia* 46°17N 16°51E 199 B13
Leh *India* 34°9N 77°35E 243 B7
Lehigh Acres *U.S.A.* 26°36N 81°39W 317 J8
Lehighton *U.S.A.* 40°50N 75°43W 313 F9
Lehliu *Romania* 44°29N 26°50E 183 F11
Leho *South Sudan* 7°7N 33°52E 257 F3
Lehrte *Germany* 52°22N 9°58E 178 C5
Lehtisaari *Finland* 60°10N 24°51E 121 B2
Lehua I. *U.S.A.* 22°1N 160°6W 302 A1
Lehututu *Botswana* 23°54S 21°55E 270 B3
Lei Shui → *China* 26°55N 112°35E 229 D9
Lei Yue Mun *Hong Kong, China* 22°17N 114°14E 122 B3
Leiah *Pakistan* 30°58N 70°58E 242 D4
Leião *Portugal* 38°43N 9°17W 126 A1
Leibnitz *Austria* 46°47N 15°34E 180 E8
Leibo *China* 28°11N 103°34E 228 C4
Leicester *U.K.* 52°38N 1°8W 169 E6
Leicester City □ *U.K.* 52°38N 1°8W 169 E6
Leicester Square *London, U.K.* 125 b3
Leicestershire □ *U.K.* 52°41N 1°17W 169 E6
Leichhardt *Australia* 33°53S 151°9E 139 B1
Leichhardt → *Australia* 17°35S 139°48E 280 B2
Leichhardt Ra. *Australia* 20°46S 147°40E 280 C4
Leiden *Neths.* 52°9N 4°30E 170 B4
Leie → *Belgium* 51°2N 3°45E 170 C3
Leifers = Láives *Italy* 46°26N 11°20E 199 B8
Leigh → *Australia* 38°18S 144°30E 282 E6
Leigh Creek *Australia* 30°38S 138°26E 282 A3
Leikang *Norway* 62°15N 5°47E 164 B2
Leikanger *Sogn og Fjordane, Norway* 62°8N 5°21E 164 B2
Leikanger *Sogn og Fjordane, Norway* 61°10N 6°51E 164 C3
Leiktho *Burma* 19°13N 96°35E 241 F6
Leimen *Germany* 49°21N 8°41E 179 F4
Leimus *Nic.* 14°40N 84°3W 320 D3
Leine → *Germany* 52°43N 9°36E 178 C5
Leinefelde-Worbris *Germany* 51°23N 10°19E 178 D6
Leinster *Australia* 27°51S 120°36E 279 E3
Leinster □ *Ireland* 53°3N 7°8W 166 C4
Leinster, Mt. *Ireland* 52°37N 6°46W 166 D5
Leipalingis *Lithuania* 54°5N 23°51E 184 D10
Leipe = Lipno *Poland* 52°49N 19°15E 185 F6
Leipzig *Germany* 51°18N 12°22E 178 D8
Leira *Norway* 60°58N 9°17E 164 D6
Leiria *Portugal* 39°46N 8°53W 194 F2
Leiria □ *Portugal* 39°46N 8°53W 194 F2
Leirvassbu *Norway* 61°33N 8°13E 164 C5
Leirvik *Norway* 59°47N 5°28E 164 E2
Leishan *China* 26°15N 108°20E 228 D7
Leisler, Mt. *Australia* 23°23S 129°20E 278 D4
Leisure City *U.S.A.* 25°30N 80°26W 317 K9
Leith *U.K.* 55°59N 3°11W 167 F5
Leith Hill *U.K.* 51°11N 0°22W 169 F7
Leitha → *Europe* 47°50N 17°15E 181 D10
Leitir Ceanainn = Letterkenny *Ireland* 54°57N 7°45W 166 B4
Leitrim *Ireland* 54°0N 8°5W 166 B3
Leitrim □ *Ireland* 54°8N 8°0W 166 B4
Leitza *Spain* 43°5N 1°55W 196 B3
Leixlip *Ireland* 53°22N 6°30W 166 C5
Leiyang *China* 26°27N 112°45E 229 D9
Leizhou *China* 20°52N 110°8E 229 G8
Leizhou Bandao *China* 21°0N 110°0E 228 G7
Leizhou Wan *China* 20°50N 110°20E 229 G8
Lek → *Neths.* 51°54N 4°35E 170 C4
Leka *Norway* 65°5N 11°35E 160 D14

Lekani Greece 41°10N 24°35E 203 E8
Lekbibaj Albania 42°17N 19°56E 202 D3
Lekeitio Spain 43°20N 2°32W 196 B2
Lékéti, Mt. Congo 2°34S 14°17E 264 C2
Lekki Nigeria 6°26N 3°28E 124 B2
Lekki Lagoon Nigeria 6°30N 4°7E 263 D5
Lekki Peninsula Nigeria 6°26N 3°29E 124 B2
Léko Mali 13°37N 9°2W 262 C3
Lékoli-Pandaka △ Congo 0°41N 14°50E 264 B2
Lékoni Gabon 1°35S 14°14E 264 C2
Lékoni → Gabon 1°11S 13°16E 264 C2
Lekou Burkina Faso 12°37N 3°40W 262 C4
Lékoumou □ Congo 2°0S 13°0E 264 C2
Leksand Sweden 60°44N 15°1E 162 D9
Leksura = Lentekhi
Georgia 42°47N 42°45E 191 J6
Leland Mich., U.S.A. 45°1N 85°45W 309 C11
Leland Miss., U.S.A. 33°24N 90°54W 315 E9
Lelång Sweden 59°10N 12°5E 162 E6
Lelepa Vanuatu 17°35S 168°14E 287 G6
Leleque Argentina 42°28S 71°0W 336 B2
Leli Solomon Is. 8°42S 161°4E 287 M11
Leling China 37°44N 117°13E 227 F9
Lélouma Guinea 11°11N 12°56W 262 C2
Lelu Burma 19°4N 95°30E 241 F5
Lelydorp Suriname 5°42N 55°14W 329 B6
Lelystad Neths. 52°30N 5°25E 170 B5
Lem Denmark 56°1N 8°24E 163 H2
Lema Nigeria 12°58N 4°13E 263 C5
Lema Shilindi Ethiopia 4°50N 42°6E 257 G5
Léman, L. Europe 46°26N 6°30E 173 F13
Lemankoa Papua N. G. 5°3S 154°34E 286 C8
Lembar Indonesia 8°45S 116°4E 231 K19
Lemberg = Lviv Ukraine 49°50N 24°0E 177 D13
Lembongan, Nusa
Indonesia 8°40S 115°27E 231 K18
Lembuak Indonesia 8°36S 116°11E 231 K19
Leme Brazil 22°58S 43°10W 135 B1
Lemera Dem. Rep. of the Congo 3°0S 28°55E 268 C2
Lemery Phil. 13°51N 120°56E 232 E3
Lemesós = Limassol Cyprus 34°42N 33°1E 207 F9
Lemfu Dem. Rep. of the Congo 5°18S 15°13E 265 D3
Lemhi Ra. U.S.A. 44°0N 113°0W 304 D7
Lemmenjoki △ Finland 68°40N 25°30E 160 B21
Lemmer Neths. 52°51N 5°43E 170 B5
Lemmon U.S.A. 45°57N 102°10W 308 C2
Lemmon, L. U.S.A. 32°41N 96°44W 120 B5
Lemon Grove U.S.A. 32°44N 117°1W 307 N9
Lemoore U.S.A. 36°18N 119°46W 306 J7
Lemotol B. Micronesia 7°21N 151°35E 287 T17
Lemoyne Canada 45°29N 73°29W 130 B3
Lempdes-sur-Allagnon
France 45°22N 3°17E 174 C7
Lemsid W. Sahara 26°33N 13°51W 260 C2
Lemukutan Indonesia 0°45N 108°43E 235 B3
Lemvig Denmark 56°33N 8°20E 163 H2
Lemyethna Burma 17°36N 95°9E 241 G5
Lena U.S.A. 42°23N 89°49W 310 B7
Lena → Russia 72°52N 126°40E 215 B13
Lena Pillars = Lenskiy Stolby
Russia 60°55N 126°0E 215 C13
Lenadoon Pt. Ireland 54°18N 9°3W 166 B2
Lenakel Vanuatu 19°38S 169°16E 287 J7
Lenart Slovenia 46°36N 15°48E 199 B12
Lenartovce Slovakia 48°18N 20°19E 181 C13
Lencloître France 46°50N 0°20E 172 F7
Lençóis Brazil 12°35S 41°24W 333 D3
Lençóis Maranhenses △
Brazil 2°30S 43°0W 332 B3
Lendava Slovenia 46°35N 16°25E 199 B13
Lendinara Italy 45°5N 11°36E 199 C8
Lenger Kazakhstan 42°12N 69°54E 217 D7
Lengerich Germany 52°11N 7°52E 178 C3
Lenggong Malaysia 5°6N 100°58E 237 K3
Lenggries Germany 47°41N 11°35E 179 H7
Léngoué Congo 1°15N 15°38E 264 B3
Lengshuijiang China 27°40N 111°26E 229 D8
Lengshuitan China 26°27N 111°35E 229 D8
Lengua de Vaca, Pta.
Chile 30°14S 71°38W 334 C1
Lengwe △ Malawi 16°14S 34°45E 269 F3
Lengwethen = Lunino
Russia 53°38N 45°18E 190 D7
Lengyeltóti Hungary 46°40N 17°40E 182 D2
Lengyeltótihács = Lengyeltóti
Hungary 46°40N 17°40E 182 D2
Lenhovda Sweden 57°0N 15°16E 163 G9
Lenin Mausoleum Moscow, Russia 129 b2
Lenina, Kanal → Russia 43°44N 45°17E 191 J7
Leninabad = Khŭjand
Tajikistan 40°17N 69°37E 217 D7
Leninakan = Gyumri
Armenia 40°47N 43°50E 191 K6
Lenine Ukraine 45°17N 35°46E 189 K8
Leningrad = Sankt-Peterburg
Russia 59°55N 30°20E 137 B1
Leningrad □ Russia 59°40N 32°0E 188 C7
Lenino = Leninsk-Kuznetskiy
Russia 54°44N 86°10E 217 B11
Lenino Russia 55°38N 37°39E 129 C2
Leninogorsk = Ridder
Kazakhstan 50°20N 83°30E 217 B10
Leninogorsk Russia 54°36N 52°30E 216 B4
Leninsk = Petrodvorets
Russia 59°52N 29°54E 188 C5
Leninsk Russia 48°40N 45°15E 191 F7
Leninsk-Kuznetskiy
Russia 54°44N 86°10E 217 B11
Leninsk-Turkmenskiy =
Türkmenabat
Turkmenistan 39°6N 63°34E 247 B9
Leninskiye Gory Russia 55°41N 37°32E 129 B2
Leninskoye Russia 58°23N 47°3E 190 A8
Lenk Switz. 46°27N 7°28E 179 J3
Lenkoran = Länkäran
Azerbaijan 38°48N 48°52E 213 C13
Lenmalu Indonesia 1°45S 130°15E 231 E8
Lennartsfors Sweden 59°20N 11°55E 162 E5
Lenne → Germany 51°25N 7°29E 178 D3
Lennestadt Germany 51°8N 8°2E 178 D4
Lennox Calif., U.S.A. 33°56N 118°20W 126 C2
Lennox S. Dak., U.S.A. 43°21N 96°53W 308 D5
Lennox, I. Chile 55°18S 66°50W 336 E3
Lennoxville Canada 45°22N 71°51W 313 A13
Leno Italy 45°22N 10°13E 198 C7
Lenoir U.S.A. 35°55N 81°32W 315 D14
Lenoir City U.S.A. 35°48N 84°16W 315 D12
Lenore L. Canada 52°30N 104°59W 297 C8
Lenox Ga., U.S.A. 31°16N 83°28W 316 D6
Lenox Iowa, U.S.A. 40°53N 94°34W 310 D2
Lenox Mass., U.S.A. 42°22N 73°17W 313 D11
Lens France 50°26N 2°50E 173 B9
Lensahn Germany 54°13N 10°53E 178 A6
Lensk Russia 60°48N 114°55E 215 C12
Lenskiy Stolby Russia 60°55N 126°0E 215 C13
Lensvik Norway 63°31N 9°48E 164 A6
Lentas Greece 34°56N 24°56E 207 F5
Lentekhi Georgia 42°47N 42°45E 191 J6
Lenti Hungary 46°37N 16°33E 182 D1
Lentini Italy 37°17N 15°0E 201 E8
Lentschütz = Łęczyca
Poland 52°5N 19°15E 185 F6
Lenwood U.S.A. 34°53N 117°7W 307 L9
Lenya Burma 11°33N 98°57E 237 G2
Lenzen Germany 53°5N 11°29E 178 B7
Léo Burkina Faso 11°3N 2°2W 262 C4
Leoben Austria 47°22N 15°5E 180 D8
Leobschütz = Głubczyce
Poland 50°13N 17°52E 185 H4
Leodhais = Lewis U.K. 58°9N 6°40W 167 C2
Leola U.S.A. 45°43N 98°56W 308 C4
Leominster Hereford, U.K. 52°14N 2°43W 169 E5
Leominster Mass., U.S.A. 42°32N 71°46W 313 D13
León = Cotopaxi □ Ecuador 0°5S 78°55W 328 D2
León Landes, France 43°53N 1°18W 174 E2
León Guanajuato, Mexico 21°6N 101°41W 318 C4
León Nic. 12°27N 86°51W 320 D2
León Spain 42°38N 5°34W 194 C5
Leon Iowa, U.S.A. 40°44N 93°45W 310 D3
León □ Spain 42°40N 5°55W 194 C5
Leon → U.S.A. 31°14N 97°28W 314 F6
León, Montes de Spain 42°30N 6°18W 194 C4
Leonardo da Vinci, Roma ✈ (FCO)
Italy 41°48N 12°15E 199 G9
Leonardtown U.S.A. 38°17N 76°38W 309 F15
Leonardville Namibia 23°29S 18°49E 270 B2
Leonárisso Cyprus 35°28N 34°8E 207 E10
Leonberg Germany 48°48N 9°1E 179 G5
Leonding Austria 48°16N 14°15E 180 C7
Leone Amer. Samoa 14°23S 170°48W 302 f
Leonessa Italy 42°34N 12°58E 199 F9
Leonforte Italy 37°38N 14°23E 201 E7
Leongatha Australia 38°30S 145°58E 283 E6
Leonia Fla., U.S.A. 30°55N 86°1W 316 E3
Leonia N.J., U.S.A. 40°51N 73°59W 132 A2
Leonidio Greece 37°9N 22°52E 204 D4
Leonora Australia 28°49S 121°19E 279 E3
Leopold II, L. = Mai-Ndombe, L.
Dem. Rep. of the Congo 2°0S 18°20E 264 C3
Leopoldau Austria 48°15N 16°26E 142 A2
Leopoldina = Aruanã
Brazil 14°54S 51°10W 333 D1
Leopoldina = Parnamirim
Brazil 8°5S 39°34W 332 C4
Leopoldina Brazil 21°28S 42°40W 333 F3
Leopoldo Bulhões Brazil 16°37S 48°46W 333 E2
Leopoldsburg Belgium 51°7N 5°13E 170 C5
Leopoldsdorf Austria 48°7N 16°23E 142 B2
Leopoldstadt Austria 48°13N 16°22E 142 A2
Leopoldville = Kinshasa
Dem. Rep. of the Congo 4°20S 15°15E 265 C3
Leoti U.S.A. 38°29N 101°21W 308 F3
Leova Moldova 46°28N 28°15E 183 D13
Leoville Canada 53°39N 107°33W 297 C7
Lepar Indonesia 2°57S 106°49E 234 C3
Lepe Spain 37°15N 7°12W 195 H3
Lepel = Lyepyel Belarus 54°50N 28°40E 188 E5
Lepenou Greece 38°42N 21°17E 204 C3
Leping China 28°47N 117°7E 229 C11
Lépo, L. do Angola 17°0S 19°0E 265 F3
Lepontine, Alpi Italy 46°22N 8°27E 198 B5
Leportovo Russia 55°46N 37°43E 129 B3
Leposavić Kosovo 43°6N 20°48E 202 C4
Leppävaara Finland 60°13N 24°49E 121 B1
Leppävirta Finland 62°29N 27°46E 160 E22
Lepsény Hungary 47°0N 18°15E 182 D3
Leptis Magna Libya 32°40N 14°12E 258 B2
Lequeitio = Lekeitio Spain 43°20N 2°32W 196 B2
Lercara Friddi Italy 37°45N 13°36E 200 E6
Léré C.A.R. 6°46N 17°25E 264 A3
Léré Chad 9°39N 14°13E 259 G2
Léré Mali 15°45N 4°55W 262 B4
Lere Bauchi, Nigeria 9°43N 9°18E 263 D6
Lere Kaduna, Nigeria 10°23N 8°35E 263 C6
Leribe Lesotho 28°51S 28°3E 271 C4
Lérici Italy 44°4N 9°55E 198 D6
Lérida = Lleida Spain 41°37N 0°39E 196 D5
Lérins, Îs. de France 43°31N 7°3E 175 E11
Lerma Spain 42°0N 3°47W 194 C7
Leros Greece 37°10N 26°50E 205 D8
Lérouville France 48°44N 5°30E 173 D12
Lerum Sweden 57°46N 12°16E 163 G6
Lerwick U.K. 60°9N 1°9W 167 A7
Leş Romania 46°58N 21°50E 182 D6
Les Abrets France 45°32N 5°35E 175 C9
Les Abymes Guadeloupe 16°17N 61°32W 322 e
Les Andelys France 49°15N 1°25E 172 C8
Les Anses-d'Arlets
Martinique 14°28N 61°6W 322 j
Les Avirons Réunion 21°14S 55°20E 272 f
Les Borges Blanques Spain 41°31N 0°52E 196 D5
Les Cayes Haiti 18°15N 73°46W 321 C5
Les Coteaux Canada 45°15N 74°13W 313 A10
Les Escoumins Canada 48°21N 69°24W 299 C6
Les Essarts France 46°47N 1°12W 172 F5
Les Grands Fonds
Guadeloupe 16°16N 61°26W 322 e
Les Herbiers France 46°52N 1°1W 172 F5
Les Lilas France 48°52N 2°25E 134 A3
Les Loges-en-Josas France 48°45N 2°8E 134 B1
Les Mangles Guadeloupe 16°23N 61°27W 322 e
Les Minquiers, Plateau des
Chan. Is. 48°58N 2°8W 172 D4
Les Moroubas C.A.R. 6°11N 20°13E 264 A4
Les Pavillons-sous-Bois
France 48°54N 2°30E 134 A4
Les Pieux France 49°30N 1°48W 172 C5
Les Ponts-de-Cé France 47°25N 0°30W 172 E6
Les Riceys France 47°59N 4°22E 173 E11
Les Sables-d'Olonne
France 46°30N 1°45W 174 B2
Les Tantes Grenada 12°19N 61°33W 323 q
Les Trois-Bassins Réunion 21°5S 55°18E 272 f
Les Trois-Îlets Martinique 14°32N 61°2W 322 j
Les Vans France 44°25N 4°7E 175 D8
Lesbos Greece 39°10N 26°20E 205 B8
L'Escala Spain 42°7N 3°8E 196 C8
L'Escalier Mauritius 20°28S 57°36E 272 e
Leschnitz = Leśnica
Poland 50°26N 18°11E 185 H5
Leshan China 29°33N 103°41E 228 C4
Leshukonskoye Russia 64°54N 45°46E 186 B9
Leshwe △
Dem. Rep. of the Congo 12°45S 29°30E 269 E2
Lésigny France 48°44N 2°37E 134 B4
Lésina Italy 41°52N 15°21E 199 G12
Lésina, L. di Italy 41°53N 15°26E 199 G12
Lesjaskog Norway 62°14N 8°22E 164 B5
Lesjaverk Norway 62°12N 8°34E 164 B5
Lesjöfors Sweden 59°58N 14°11E 162 E8
Leskhimstroy = Syeverodonetsk
Ukraine 48°58N 38°35E 189 H10
Lesko Poland 49°30N 22°23E 185 J9
Leskov I. Antarctica 56°0S 28°0W 151 B1
Leskovac Serbia 43°0N 21°58E 202 C5
Leskovik Albania 40°10N 20°34E 202 F4
Leslau = Włocławek
Poland 52°40N 19°3E 185 F6
Leslie Ga., U.S.A. 31°57N 84°5W 316 D5
Leslie Mich., U.S.A. 42°27N 84°26W 311 B12
Leśna Poland 51°1N 15°15E 185 G2
Lesneven France 48°35N 4°20W 172 D2
Leśnica Poland 50°26N 18°11E 185 H5
Lešnica Serbia 44°39N 19°20E 202 B3
Lesnoi = Umba Russia 66°42N 34°11E 186 A5
Lesnoye Russia 58°15N 35°18E 188 C8
Lesnozavodskaya Russia 59°51N 30°29E 137 B2
Lesopilnoye Russia 46°44N 134°20E 222 A7
Lesotho ■ Africa 29°40S 28°0E 271 C4
Lesozavodsk Russia 45°30N 133°29E 220 B6
Lesparre-Médoc France 45°18N 0°57W 174 C3
L'Espluga de Francolí Spain 41°24N 1°7E 196 D6
Lessay France 49°14N 1°30W 172 C5
Lesse → Belgium 50°15N 4°54E 170 D4
Lesse et Lomme △ Belgium 50°8N 5°9E 170 D5
Lessebo Sweden 56°45N 15°16E 163 H9
Lesser Antilles W. Indies 15°0N 61°0W 321 D7
Lesser Slave L. Canada 55°30N 115°25W 296 B5
Lesser Sunda Is. Indonesia 8°0S 120°0E 235 D5
Lessines Belgium 50°42N 3°50E 170 D3
Lester B. Pearson Int., Toronto ✈
(YYZ) Canada 43°46N 79°35W 141 A1
L'Esterre Grenada 12°28N 61°29W 323 q
Lestershire = Johnson City
U.S.A. 42°7N 75°58W 313 D9
Lestock Canada 51°19N 103°59W 297 C8
Lesuer I. Australia 13°50S 127°17E 278 B4
Lesueur △ Australia 30°11S 115°10E 279 F2
Lesung Indonesia 0°42N 114°42E 235 B4
Lésvos = Lesbos Greece 39°10N 26°20E 205 B8
Leszno Poland 51°50N 16°30E 185 G3
Letaba S. Africa 23°59S 31°50E 271 B5
Letälven → Sweden 59°5N 14°20E 162 E8
L'Étang-la-Ville France 48°52N 2°4E 134 A1
L'Étang-Salé Réunion 21°15S 55°23E 272 f
Létavértes Hungary 47°23N 21°55E 182 C6
Letchworth Garden City
U.K. 51°59N 0°13W 169 F7
Letea, Ostrovul Romania 45°18N 29°20E 183 E14
Lethbridge Canada 49°45N 112°45W 296 D6
Lethem Guyana 3°20N 59°50W 329 C6
Leti, Kepulauan Indonesia 8°10S 128°0E 231 F7
Leti Is. = Leti, Kepulauan
Indonesia 8°10S 128°0E 231 F7
Letiahau → Botswana 21°16S 24°0E 270 B3
Leticia Colombia 4°9S 70°0W 328 D4
Leting China 39°23N 118°55E 227 E10
Letjiesbos S. Africa 32°34S 22°16E 270 D3
Letlhakane Botswana 21°27S 25°30E 270 B4
Letlhakeng Botswana 24°0S 24°59E 270 B3
Letná Prague, Czechia 135 a2
Letňany Czechia 50°8N 14°30E 135 B3
Letopolis = Ausîm Egypt 30°7N 31°8E 117 A1
Letpadan Burma 17°45N 95°45E 241 G5
Letpan Burma 19°28N 94°10E 241 F5
Letsôk-aw Kyun Burma 11°30N 98°25E 237 G2
Letterkenny Ireland 54°57N 7°45W 166 B4
Leu Romania 44°10N 24°0E 183 F9
Léua Angola 11°34S 20°32E 265 E4
Leucadia U.S.A. 33°4N 117°18W 307 M9
Leucate France 42°56N 3°3E 174 F7
Leucate, Étang de France 42°50N 3°0E 174 F7
Leuchars U.K. 56°24N 2°53W 167 E6
Leuk Switz. 46°19N 7°37E 179 J3
Leuşeni Moldova 46°49N 28°12E 183 D13
Leuser, Gunung Indonesia 3°46N 97°12E 234 B1
Leusoalii Amer. Samoa 14°14S 169°25W 302 f
Leutkirch Germany 47°49N 10°1E 179 H6
Leutschau = Levoča
Slovakia 49°2N 20°35E 181 B13
Leuven Belgium 50°52N 4°42E 170 D4
Leuze-en-Hainaut Belgium 50°36N 3°37E 170 D3
Lev Tolstoy Russia 53°13N 39°29E 188 F10
Levallois-Perret France 48°53N 2°16E 134 A2
Levan Albania 40°40N 19°28E 202 F3
Levanger Norway 63°45N 11°19E 160 E14
Levant, Î. du France 43°3N 6°28E 175 E10
Lévanto Italy 44°10N 9°38E 198 D6
Lévanzo Italy 38°0N 12°20E 200 D5
Leveld Norway 60°44N 8°33E 164 D5
Levelland U.S.A. 33°35N 102°23W 314 E3
Levelock U.S.A. 59°7N 156°51W 303 G8
Leven U.K. 56°12N 3°0W 167 E6
Leven, L. U.K. 56°12N 3°22W 167 E5
Leven, Toraka Madag. 12°30S 47°45E 272 A2
Levent Turkey 41°5N 29°0E 122 B2
Leveque C. Australia 16°20S 123°0E 278 C3
Levera △ Grenada 12°13N 61°38W 323 q
Leverano Italy 40°17N 18°0E 201 B10
Leverger = Santo Antônio do
Leverger Brazil 15°52S 56°5W 331 D6
Leverkusen Germany 51°1N 7°1E 178 D3
Levice Slovakia 48°13N 18°35E 181 C11
Lévico Terme Italy 46°0N 11°18E 199 C8
Levie France 41°40N 9°7E 175 G13
Levier France 46°58N 6°8E 173 F13
Levin N.Z. 40°37S 175°18E 284 G4
Lévis Canada 46°48N 71°9W 299 C5
Lévis, L. Canada 62°37N 117°58W 296 A5
Levitha Greece 37°0N 26°28E 205 D8
Levittown N.Y., U.S.A. 40°44N 73°31W 313 F11
Levittown Pa., U.S.A. 40°9N 74°51W 313 F10
Levka Bulgaria 41°52N 26°15E 203 E10
Levka Oros Greece 35°18N 24°3E 207 E5
Levkás = Lefkada Greece 38°40N 20°43E 207 B2
Levoča Slovakia 49°2N 20°35E 181 B13
Levroux France 46°59N 1°38E 173 F8
Levski Bulgaria 43°21N 25°10E 203 C9
Levskigrad = Karlovo
Bulgaria 42°38N 24°47E 203 D8
Levuka Fiji 17°34S 179°0E 287 A2
Lewe Burma 19°38N 96°7E 241 F6
Lewes E. Sussex, U.K. 50°52N 0°1E 169 G8
Lewes Del., U.S.A. 38°46N 75°9W 309 F16
Lewin Brzeski Poland 50°45N 17°37E 185 H4
Lewis U.K. 58°9N 6°40W 167 C2
Lewis → U.S.A. 45°51N 122°48W 306 E4
Lewis, Butt of U.K. 58°31N 6°16W 167 C2
Lewis and Clark △
U.S.A. 46°8N 123°53W 306 D3
Lewis Pass N.Z. 42°31S 172°11E 285 C7
Lewis Ra. Australia 20°3S 128°50E 278 D4
Lewis Range U.S.A. 48°5N 113°5W 304 B7
Lewis Run U.S.A. 41°52N 78°40W 312 E6
Lewisburg Ohio, U.S.A. 39°51N 84°33W 311 E12
Lewisburg Pa., U.S.A. 40°58N 76°54W 312 F8
Lewisburg Tenn., U.S.A. 35°27N 86°48W 315 D11
Lewisburg W. Va.,
U.S.A. 37°48N 80°27W 309 G13
Lewisdale U.S.A. 38°58N 76°59W 143 B3
Lewisham □ U.K. 51°27N 0°1W 125 B3
Lewisport U.S.A. 37°56N 86°54W 311 G10
Lewisporte Canada 49°15N 55°3W 299 C8
Lewiston Idaho, U.S.A. 46°25N 117°1W 304 C5
Lewiston Maine, U.S.A. 44°6N 70°13W 309 C18
Lewiston N.Y., U.S.A. 43°11N 79°3W 312 C5
Lewistown Ill., U.S.A. 40°24N 90°9W 310 D6
Lewistown Mo., U.S.A. 40°5N 91°49W 310 D5
Lewistown Mont., U.S.A. 47°4N 109°26W 304 C9
Lewistown Pa., U.S.A. 40°36N 77°34W 312 F7
Lexington Ga., U.S.A. 33°52N 83°7W 316 B6
Lexington Ill., U.S.A. 40°39N 88°47W 311 D8
Lexington Ky., U.S.A. 38°3N 84°30W 311 F12
Lexington Mass., U.S.A. 42°25N 71°12W 116 A1
Lexington Mich., U.S.A. 43°16N 82°32W 312 C2
Lexington Mo., U.S.A. 39°11N 93°52W 310 E3
Lexington N.C., U.S.A. 35°49N 80°15W 315 D14
Lexington N.Y., U.S.A. 42°15N 74°22W 313 D10
Lexington Nebr., U.S.A. 40°47N 99°45W 308 E4
Lexington Ohio, U.S.A. 40°41N 82°35W 312 F2
Lexington S.C., U.S.A. 33°59N 81°11W 316 B8
Lexington Tenn., U.S.A. 35°39N 88°24W 315 D10
Lexington Va., U.S.A. 37°47N 79°27W 309 G14
Lexington Park U.S.A. 38°16N 76°27W 309 F15
Leyburn U.K. 54°19N 1°48W 168 C6
Leye China 24°48N 106°29E 228 E6
Leyeh Taiwan 23°28N 120°42E 225 C2
Leyland U.K. 53°42N 2°43W 168 D5
Leyte Phil. 10°30N 125°0E 233 F5
Leyte □ Phil. 11°0N 125°0E 233 F5
Leyte Gulf Phil. 10°50N 125°25E 233 F5
Leyton U.K. 51°33N 0°1W 125 A3
Leytonstone U.K. 51°34N 0°0 125 A4
Leżajsk Poland 50°16N 22°25E 185 H9
Lezay France 46°15N 0°1W 174 B3
Lezhë Albania 41°47N 19°39E 202 E3
Lezhi China 30°19N 104°58E 228 B5
Lézignan-Corbières France 43°13N 2°43E 174 E6
Lezoux France 45°49N 3°21E 174 C7
Lgov Russia 51°42N 35°16E 189 G8
Lhasa China 29°25N 90°58E 218 F7
L'Haÿ-les-Roses France 48°46N 2°20E 134 B3
Lhazê China 29°5N 87°38E 218 F6
L'Hermite, I. Chile 55°50S 68°0W 336 E3
Lhokkruet Indonesia 4°55N 95°24E 234 B1
Lhokseumawe Indonesia 5°10N 97°10E 234 A1
Lhoksukon Indonesia 5°2N 97°19E 234 A1
L'Hospitalet de Llobregat
Spain 41°21N 2°6E 114 A1
Lhotka Czechia 50°1N 14°26E 135 B2
Lhuntsi Dzong Bhutan 27°39N 91°10E 241 B3
Lhut, W. → Somalia 10°17N 50°9E 267 B7
Li Thailand 17°48N 98°57E 236 D2
Li Jiang → China 24°40N 110°40E 229 E8
Li Jiang △ China 24°38N 110°38E 229 E8
Li Shan China 35°30N 111°56E 226 G6
Li Shui → China 29°24N 112°1E 229 C9
Li Xian Gansu, China 34°10N 105°5E 226 G3
Li Xian Hebei, China 38°30N 115°35E 226 E8
Li Xian Hunan, China 29°36N 111°42E 229 C8
Li Yuba South Sudan 5°23N 27°25E 266 C2
Lia-Moya C.A.R. 6°54N 16°17E 264 A3
Liadi Greece 36°50N 26°11E 205 E8
Liamuiga, Mt.
St. Kitts & Nevis 17°22N 62°48W 322 d
Lian Phil. 14°3N 120°39E 232 D3
Liancheng China 25°42N 116°40E 229 E11
Liancourt Rocks Asia 37°15N 131°52E 221 F5
Liang Tao Taiwan 26°23N 128°28E 225 b
Lianga Phil. 8°38N 126°6E 233 G6
Lianga B. Phil. 8°37N 126°12E 233 G6
Liangcheng Nei Monggol Zizhiqu,
China 40°28N 112°25E 226 D7
Liangcheng Shandong,
China 35°32N 119°37E 227 G10
Liangdang China 33°56N 106°18E 226 H4
Lianghe China 24°50N 98°20E 228 E2
Lianghekou China 29°11N 108°44E 228 C7
Liangping China 30°38N 107°47E 228 B6
Liangpran Indonesia 1°4N 114°23E 235 B4
Liangshui He → China 39°48N 116°23E 114 C2
Lianhua China 27°3N 113°54E 229 D9
Lianhua Chi China 39°52N 116°16E 114 B1
Lianhua He → China 39°52N 116°13E 114 B1
Lianhua Shan China 23°40N 115°48E 229 F10
Lianjiang Fujian, China 26°12N 119°27E 229 D12
Lianjiang Guangdong,
China 21°40N 110°20E 229 G8
Lianping China 24°26N 114°30E 229 E10
Lianshan China 24°38N 112°8E 229 E9
Lianshanguan China 40°53N 123°43E 224 B1
Lianshui China 33°42N 119°20E 227 H10
Lianyuan China 27°40N 111°38E 229 D8
Lianyungang China 34°40N 119°11E 227 G10
Lianzhou China 24°51N 112°22E 229 E9
Liao He → China 41°0N 121°50E 227 D11
Liaocheng China 36°28N 115°58E 226 F8
Liaodong Bandao China 40°0N 122°30E 227 E12
Liaodong Wan China 40°20N 121°10E 227 D11
Liaoning □ China 41°40N 122°30E 224 B1
Liaotung, G. of = Liaodong Wan
China 40°20N 121°10E 227 D11
Liaoyang China 41°15N 122°58E 224 B1
Liaoyuan China 42°58N 125°2E 227 C13
Liaozhong China 41°23N 122°50E 224 B1
Liapades Greece 39°42N 19°40E 206 B9
Liard → Canada 61°51N 121°18W 296 A4
Liard River Canada 59°25N 126°5W 296 B3
Liari Pakistan 25°37N 66°30E 242 G2
Liat Indonesia 2°53S 107°5E 234 C3
Libanggaon Nepal 28°18N 82°38E 243 E10
Líbano Colombia 4°55N 75°4W 328 C2
Libau = Liepāja Latvia 56°30N 21°0E 184 B8
Libby U.S.A. 48°23N 115°33W 304 B6
Libčice nad Vltavou
Czechia 50°11N 14°22E 135 A2
Libeň Czechia 50°6N 14°27E 135 B2
Libenge
Dem. Rep. of the Congo 3°40N 18°55E 264 B3
Liberal U.S.A. 37°3N 100°55W 308 G3
Liberdade Acre, Brazil 10°5S 70°20W 330 C3
Liberdade São Paulo, Brazil 23°33S 46°37W 137 B2
Liberdade → Brazil 9°40S 52°17W 331 B7
Liberdade, Avenida da Lisbon, Portugal 126 b1
Liberec Czechia 50°47N 15°7E 180 A8
Liberecký □ Czechia 50°45N 15°0E 180 A8
Liberia Costa Rica 10°40N 85°30W 320 D2
Liberia ■ W. Afr. 6°30N 9°30W 262 D3
Libertà, Ponte della Venice, Italy 142 a1
Libertad Antique, Phil. 11°46N 121°55E 233 F3
Libertad Venezuela 8°20N 69°37W 328 B4
Libertador □ Chile 34°15S 70°45W 334 C1
Liberton U.K. 55°54N 3°9W 121 B3
Liberty Ind., U.S.A. 39°38N 84°56W 311 E12
Liberty Mo., U.S.A. 39°15N 94°25W 310 E2
Liberty N.Y., U.S.A. 41°48N 74°45W 313 E10
Liberty Pa., U.S.A. 41°34N 77°6W 312 E7
Liberty Tex., U.S.A. 30°3N 94°48W 314 F7
Liberty Center U.S.A. 41°27N 84°1W 311 C12
Liberty I. U.S.A. 40°41N 74°2W 132 B1
Liberty-Newark Int. ✈ (EWR)
U.S.A. 40°42N 74°10W 313 F10
Liberty Ōsaka Museum
Japan 34°38N 135°29E 133 B1
Liberty State Park △
U.S.A. 40°42N 74°2W 132 B1
Libertyville U.S.A. 42°18N 87°57W 311 B9
Libeznice Czechia 50°11N 14°29E 135 A2
Libiąż Poland 50°7N 19°21E 185 H6
Lîbîya, Sahrâ' Africa 25°0N 25°0E 258 C4
Libjo Phil. 10°12N 125°32E 233 F5
Libmanan Phil. 13°42N 123°4E 232 E4
Libo China 25°22N 107°53E 228 E6
Libobo, Tanjung Indonesia 0°54S 128°28E 231 E7
Libode S. Africa 31°33S 29°2E 271 D4
Libohovë Albania 40°3N 20°10E 202 F4
Liboi Kenya 0°24N 40°57E 267 D5
Libona Phil. 8°20N 124°44E 233 G5
Libonda Zambia 14°28S 23°12E 265 E4
Libong, Ko Thailand 7°15N 99°23E 237 J2
Libourne France 44°55N 0°14W 174 D3
Libramont Belgium 49°55N 5°23E 170 E5
Library of Congress
Washington, D.C., U.S.A. 143 b3
Librazhd Albania 41°12N 20°22E 202 E4
Libreville Gabon 0°25N 9°26E 264 B1
Libro Pt. Phil. 11°25N 119°28E 233 F2
Libuš Czechia 50°0N 14°27E 135 B2
Libya ■ N. Afr. 27°0N 17°0E 258 C3
Libyan Desert = Lîbîya, Sahrâ'
Africa 25°0N 25°0E 258 C4
Libyan Plateau = Ed Déffa
Egypt 30°40N 26°30E 256 A2
Licantén Chile 35°55S 72°0W 334 D1
Licata Italy 37°6N 13°56E 200 E6
Lice Turkey 38°27N 40°39E 213 C9
Licheng China 36°28N 113°20E 226 F7
Lichfield U.K. 52°41N 1°49W 169 E6
Lichia Taiwan 22°47N 121°3E 225 D3
Lichiao China 23°3N 113°18E 121 B2
Lichinga Mozam. 13°13S 35°11E 269 E4
Lichtenburg Berlin,
Germany 52°31N 13°30E 115 A4
Lichtenburg North West,
S. Africa 26°8S 26°8E 270 C4
Lichtenfels Germany 50°8N 11°4E 179 E7
Lichterfelde Germany 52°25N 13°19E 115 B2
Lichuan Hubei, China 30°18N 108°57E 228 B7
Lichuan Jiangxi, China 27°18N 116°55E 229 D11
Licking → U.S.A. 39°6N 84°30W 311 F12
Licosa, Punta Italy 40°15N 14°54E 201 B7
Licungo → Mozam. 17°40S 37°15E 269 F4
Lida Belarus 53°53N 25°15E 177 B13
Liden Sweden 62°42N 16°48E 162 B10
Lidhult Sweden 56°50N 13°27E 163 H7
Lidingö Sweden 59°21N 18°8E 139 A2
Lidköping Sweden 58°31N 13°7E 163 F7
Lido Niger 12°54N 3°44E 263 C5
Lido di Roma = Óstia, Lido di
Italy 41°43N 12°17E 199 G9
Lidoriki Greece 38°32N 22°12E 204 C4
Lidzbark Poland 53°15N 19°49E 185 E6
Lidzbark Warmiński
Poland 54°7N 20°34E 184 D7
Liebenthal = Lubomierz
Poland 51°1N 15°31E 185 G2
Liebenwalde Germany 52°52N 13°24E 178 C9
Lieberose Germany 51°59N 14°17E 178 D10
Liebig, Mt. Australia 23°18S 131°22E 278 D5
Liebling Romania 45°36N 21°20E 182 E6
Liechtenstein ■ Europe 47°8N 9°35E 179 H5
Liège Belgium 50°38N 5°35E 170 D5
Liège □ Belgium 50°32N 5°35E 170 D5
Liegnitz = Legnica Poland 51°12N 16°10E 185 G3
Lieksa Finland 63°18N 30°2E 160 E24
Lienart Dem. Rep. of the Congo 3°3N 25°31E 268 B2
Lienyünchiangshih = Lianyungang
China 34°40N 119°11E 227 G10
Lienz Austria 46°50N 12°46E 180 E5
Liepāja Latvia 56°30N 21°0E 184 B8
Liepājas ezers Latvia 56°27N 21°3E 184 B8
Lier Belgium 51°7N 4°34E 170 C4
Liernais France 47°13N 4°16E 173 E11
Lierne △ Norway 64°20N 13°50E 160 D15
Lieshi Lingyuan China 23°7N 113°16E 121 B2
Liesing Austria 48°8N 16°17E 142 B1
Liesing → Austria 48°8N 16°28E 142 B2
Liești Romania 45°38N 27°34E 183 E12
Lietuva = Lithuania ■
Europe 55°30N 24°0E 188 E2
Liévin France 50°24N 2°47E 173 B9
Lièvre → Canada 45°31N 75°26W 298 C4
Liezen Austria 47°34N 14°15E 180 D7
Liffey → Ireland 53°21N 6°13W 166 C5
Lifford Ireland 54°51N 7°29W 166 B4
Liffré France 48°12N 1°30W 172 D5
Lifjell Norway 59°27N 8°45E 164 E5
Lifou, Î. N. Cal. 20°53S 167°13E 288 d
Lifudzin Russia 44°21N 134°58E 220 B7
Lifuka Tonga 19°48S 174°21W 287 P13
Ligang = Likang Taiwan 22°47N 120°29E 225 D2
Ligao Phil. 13°14N 123°32E 232 E4
Ligasa Dem. Rep. of the Congo 0°44N 23°49E 264 B4
Lighthouse Point U.S.A. 26°15N 80°7W 317 J9
Lighthouse Pt. U.S.A. 29°54N 84°21W 316 F5
Lightning Ridge Australia 29°22S 148°0E 281 D4
Lignano Sabbiadoro Italy 45°42N 13°9E 199 C10
Ligny-en-Barrois France 48°36N 5°20E 173 D12
Ligonha → Mozam. 16°54S 39°9E 269 F4
Ligonier Ind., U.S.A. 41°28N 85°35W 311 C11
Ligonier Pa., U.S.A. 40°15N 79°14W 312 F5
Ligourio Greece 37°37N 23°4E 204 D5
Ligovo Russia 59°49N 30°10E 137 C1
Ligueil France 47°2N 0°49E 172 E7
Liguria □ Italy 44°30N 8°50E 198 D5
Ligurian Sea Medit. S. 43°20N 9°0E 198 E5
Lihir Group Papua N. G. 3°0S 152°35E 286 B7
Lihir I. Papua N. G. 3°5S 152°35E 286 B7
Lihou Reefs and Cays
Australia 17°25S 151°40E 280 B5
Lihu'e U.S.A. 21°59N 159°23W 302 B2
Lihué Calel △ Argentina 38°0S 65°10W 334 D2
Lijiang China 26°55N 100°20E 228 D3
Lijordet Norway 59°56N 10°36E 133 A2
Lik → Laos 18°31N 102°30E 236 C4
Likala Dem. Rep. of the Congo 0°9N 19°12E 264 B3
Likang Taiwan 22°47N 120°29E 225 D2
Likasi
Dem. Rep. of the Congo 10°55S 26°48E 269 E2
Likati Dem. Rep. of the Congo 3°20N 24°0E 264 B4
Likati →
Dem. Rep. of the Congo 2°53N 24°3E 264 B4
Likenäs Sweden 60°37N 13°3E 162 D7
Likete Dem. Rep. of the Congo 0°48S 21°31E 264 C4
Likhaya = Likhovskoy
Russia 48°10N 40°10E 191 F5
Likhoborka → Russia 55°50N 37°37E 129 A2
Likhoslavl Russia 57°12N 35°30E 188 D8
Likhovskoy Russia 48°10N 40°10E 191 F5
Likhvin = Chekalin
Russia 54°10N 36°10E 188 E9
Likimi Dem. Rep. of the Congo 2°44N 20°47E 264 B4
Likita Dem. Rep. of the Congo 4°15N 23°36E 264 B4
Liknes Norway 58°19N 6°59E 164 E3
Likokou Gabon 0°12S 12°48E 264 C2
Likoma I. Malawi 12°3S 34°45E 269 E3
Likouala □ Congo 2°0N 17°30E 264 B3
Likouala → Congo 0°2N 14°53E 264 C3
Likouala aux Herbes →
Congo 0°52S 17°8E 264 C3
Liku Cook Is. 19°2S 168°47W 289 g
Likumburu Tanzania 9°43S 35°8E 269 D4
Lilanga
Dem. Rep. of the Congo 0°34S 23°56E 264 C4
L'Île-Bouchard France 47°7N 0°26E 172 E7
L'Île-Rousse France 42°38N 8°57E 175 F12
Lilenga Dem. Rep. of the Congo 1°4N 22°2E 264 B4
Liling China 27°42N 113°29E 229 D9
Lilla Edet Sweden 58°9N 12°8E 163 F6
Lilla Värtan Sweden 59°20N 18°11E 139 A3
Lille France 50°38N 3°3E 173 B10
Lille Bælt Denmark 55°20N 9°45E 163 J3
Lille Værløse Denmark 55°47N 12°22E 118 A2
Lillebonne France 49°30N 0°32E 172 C7
Lillehammer Norway 61°8N 10°30E 164 C7
Lillesand Norway 58°15N 8°23E 164 F5
Lillestrøm Norway 59°58N 11°5E 164 E7
Lillhärdal Sweden 61°51N 14°5E 162 C8
Lillian Pt. Australia 27°40S 126°6E 279 E4
Lillo Spain 39°45N 3°20W 194 F7
Lillooet Canada 50°44N 121°57W 296 C4
Lillooet → Canada 49°15N 121°57W 296 D4
Lilongwe Malawi 14°0S 33°48E 269 E3
Liloy Phil. 8°4N 122°39E 233 G4
Liluah India 22°37N 88°19E 124 B1
Lim → Europe 43°45N 19°15E 202 C3
Lim Chu Kang Singapore 1°26N 103°43E 138 A2
Lima Brazil 4°36S 63°40W 329 D5
Lima Indonesia 3°39S 127°58E 231 E7
Lima Peru 12°3S 77°2W 124 B2
Lima Ill., U.S.A. 40°11N 91°23W 310 D5
Lima Mont., U.S.A. 44°38N 112°36W 304 D7
Lima N.Y., U.S.A. 42°54N 77°36W 312 D7
Lima Ohio, U.S.A. 40°44N 84°6W 311 D12
Lima □ Peru 12°3S 77°3W 330 C2
Lima → Portugal 41°41N 8°50W 194 D2
Lima Jorge Chavez Int. ✈ (LIM)
Lima, Peru 12°2S 77°8W 124 B2
Liman = Krasnyy Liman
Ukraine 48°58N 37°50E 189 H9
Liman Azerbaijan 38°53N 48°47E 213 C13
Liman Russia 45°45N 47°12E 191 H8
Limanowa Poland 49°42N 20°22E 185 J7
Limassol Cyprus 34°42N 33°1E 207 F9
Limavady U.K. 55°3N 6°56W 166 A5
Limay → Argentina 39°0S 68°0W 336 A3
Limay Mahuida
Argentina 37°10S 66°45W 334 D2
Limbach-Oberfrohna
Germany 50°52N 12°43E 178 E8
Limbang Malaysia 4°42N 115°6E 235 B5
Limbara, Mte. Italy 40°51N 9°10E 200 B2
Limbaži Latvia 57°31N 24°42E 188 D3
Limbdi India 22°34N 71°51E 242 H4
Limbe Cameroon 4°1N 9°10E 263 E6
Limbiate Italy 45°35N 9°7E 128 A1
Limbueta Angola 12°30S 18°42E 265 E3
Limbuhan = Pio V. Corpuz
Phil. 11°55N 124°2E 233 F5
Limburg Germany 50°22N 8°4E 179 E4
Limburg □ Belgium 51°2N 5°25E 170 C5
Limburg □ Neths. 51°20N 5°55E 170 C5
Lime Village U.S.A. 61°21N 155°28W 303 F9
Limedsforsen Sweden 60°52N 13°25E 162 D7
Limehouse U.K. 51°30N 0°1W 125 A3
Limeil-Brévannes France 48°44N 2°29E 134 B3
Limeira = Joaçaba Brazil 27°5S 51°31W 335 B5
Limeira Brazil 22°35S 47°28W 335 A6
Limenaria Greece 40°38N 24°32E 203 F8
Limenas = Thasos Greece 40°40N 24°40E 203 F8
Limenas Chersonisou
Greece 35°18N 25°21E 207 E6
Limerick Limerick, Ireland 52°40N 8°37W 166 D3
Limerick Maine, U.S.A. 43°41N 70°48W 313 C14
Limerick □ Ireland 52°30N 8°50W 166 D3
Limestone U.S.A. 42°2N 78°38W 312 D6
Limestone → Canada 56°31N 94°7W 297 B10
Limestone Hill = Lackawanna
U.S.A. 42°50N 78°50W 312 D6
Limfjorden Denmark 56°55N 9°0E 163 H3
Limia = Lima → Portugal 41°41N 8°50W 194 D2
Limingen Norway 64°48N 13°35E 160 D15
Limmared Sweden 57°34N 13°20E 163 G7
Limmen ✪ Australia 15°15S 135°30E 280 B2
Limmen Bight Australia 14°40S 135°35E 280 A2
Limmen Bight →
Australia 15°7S 135°44E 280 B2
Limni Greece 38°43N 23°18E 204 C5
Limnos Greece 39°50N 25°5E 205 B7
Limoeiro Brazil 7°52S 35°27W 332 C4
Limoeiro do Norte Brazil 5°5S 38°0W 332 C4
Limoges Ont., Canada 45°20N 75°16W 313 A9
Limoges Haute-Vienne,
France 45°50N 1°15E 174 C5
Limón Costa Rica 10°0N 83°2W 320 E3
Limon Colo., U.S.A. 39°16N 103°41W 304 G12
Limone Italy 45°48N 10°47E 198 C7
Limone Piemonte Italy 44°12N 7°34E 198 D4
Limonlu Turkey 36°34N 34°15E 250 B5
Limousin France 45°30N 1°30E 171 D4
Limousin, Plateaux du
France 45°45N 1°15E 174 C5
Limoux France 43°4N 2°12E 174 E6
Limpopo □ S. Africa 24°5S 29°0E 271 B4
Limpopo → Africa 25°5S 33°30E 271 C5
Lin Xian China 37°57N 110°58E 226 F6
Lin'an China 30°15N 119°42E 229 B12
Linao Pt. Phil. 6°46N 123°58E 233 H4
Linapacan Phil. 11°30N 119°52E 233 F2
Linapacan I. Phil. 11°27N 119°49E 233 F2
Linapacan Str. Phil. 11°37N 119°56E 233 F2
Linares Chile 35°50S 71°40W 334 D1
Linares Colombia 1°23N 77°31W 328 C2
Linares Nuevo León,
Mexico 24°52N 99°34W 319 C5
Linares Spain 38°10N 3°40W 195 G7
Linaria Greece 38°52N 24°31E 204 C6
Linaro, Capo Italy 42°2N 11°50E 199 F8
Linas Mte. Italy 39°25N 8°38E 200 C1
Linate, Milano ✈ (LIN)
Italy 45°27N 9°16E 128 B2
Linbian = Linpien
Taiwan 22°26N 120°30E 225 D2
Linbropark S. Africa 26°5S 28°7E 123 A2
Lincang China 23°58N 100°1E 228 F3
Lincheng China 37°25N 114°30E 226 F8
Linchuan China 27°57N 116°15E 229 D11
Lincoln = Beamsville
Canada 43°12N 79°28W 312 C5
Lincoln Argentina 34°55S 61°30W 334 C3
Lincoln N.Z. 43°38S 172°30E 285 D7
Lincoln Lincs., U.K. 53°14N 0°32W 168 D7
Lincoln Calif., U.S.A. 38°54N 121°17W 306 G5
Lincoln Ill., U.S.A. 40°9N 89°22W 310 D7
Lincoln Kans., U.S.A. 39°3N 98°9W 308 F4
Lincoln Maine, U.S.A. 45°22N 68°30W 309 C19
Lincoln N.H., U.S.A. 44°3N 71°40W 313 B13
Lincoln N. Mex., U.S.A. 33°30N 105°23W 305 K11
Lincoln Nebr., U.S.A. 40°49N 96°41W 308 E5
Lincoln Boyhood △
U.S.A. 38°7N 86°59W 311 F10
Lincoln Center for Performing Arts
New York, U.S.A. 132 b2
Lincoln City U.S.A. 44°57N 124°1W 304 D1
Lincoln Hav = Lincoln Sea
Arctic 84°0N 55°0W 154 A5
Lincoln Heights U.S.A. 34°4N 118°12W 126 B3
Lincoln Memorial U.S.A. 38°52N 77°4W 143 B2
Lincoln Park Calif.,
U.S.A. 37°47N 122°30W 136 B1
Lincoln Park Ga., U.S.A. 32°52N 84°20W 316 C5
Lincoln Park Ill., U.S.A. 41°57N 87°38W 119 B3
Lincoln Park Mich.,
U.S.A. 42°15N 83°11W 311 B13
Lincoln Park N.J., U.S.A. 40°55N 74°18W 132 B1
Lincoln Park Zoo U.S.A. 41°55N 87°38W 119 B3
Lincoln Sea Arctic 84°0N 55°0W 154 A5
Lincoln Tunnel New York, U.S.A. 132 c1
Lincolnshire □ U.K. 53°14N 0°32W 168 D7
Lincolnshire Wolds U.K. 53°26N 0°13W 168 D7
Lincolnton Ga., U.S.A. 33°48N 82°29W 316 B7
Lincolnton N.C., U.S.A. 35°29N 81°16W 315 D14
Lincolnwood U.S.A. 42°1N 87°43W 119 A2
Lind U.S.A. 46°58N 118°37W 304 C4
Linda U.S.A. 39°8N 121°34W 306 F5
Linda-a-Pastora Portugal 38°42N 9°15W 126 A1
Lindale U.S.A. 34°11N 85°11W 316 A4
Lindås Norway 60°44N 5°9E 164 D2
Lindau Germany 47°33N 9°42E 179 H5
Lindeman I. Australia 20°27S 149°3E 280 b
Lindeman Islands △
Australia 20°28S 149°5E 280 b
Linden = Gladstone
U.S.A. 39°13N 94°35W 310 E2
Linden Guyana 6°0N 58°10W 329 B6
Linden Gauteng, S. Africa 26°8S 28°0E 123 A2
Linden Ala., U.S.A. 32°18N 87°48W 315 E11
Linden Calif., U.S.A. 38°1N 121°5W 306 G5
Linden Ind., U.S.A. 40°11N 86°54W 311 D10
Linden Mich., U.S.A. 42°49N 83°47W 311 B13
Linden Tex., U.S.A. 33°1N 94°22W 314 E7
Lindenberg Germany 52°36N 13°31E 115 A4
Lindenhurst U.S.A. 40°41N 73°23W 313 F11
Lindenow Fjord Greenland 60°30N 43°25W 154 E6
Lindesberg Sweden 59°36N 15°15E 162 E9
Lindesnes Norway 57°58N 7°3E 164 G4
Lindi Tanzania 9°58S 39°38E 269 D4
Lindi □ Tanzania 9°40S 38°30E 269 D4
Lindi →
Dem. Rep. of the Congo 0°33N 25°5E 268 B2
Lindley U.S.A. 42°1N 77°8W 312 D7
Lindö Sweden 58°37N 16°15E 163 F10
Lindome Sweden 57°35N 12°5E 163 G6

Lindos Greece 36°6N 28°4E 206 E12
Lindos, Akra Greece 36°4N 28°10E 206 E12
Lindoso Portugal 41°52N 8°11W 194 D2
Lindow Germany 52°58N 12°59E 178 C8
Lindøya Norway 59°53N 10°42E 133 A3
Lindsay Ont., Canada 44°22N 78°43W 312 B6
Lindsay Calif., U.S.A. 36°12N 119°5W 306 J7
Lindsay Okla., U.S.A. 34°50N 97°38W 314 D6
Lindsborg U.S.A. 38°35N 97°40W 308 F5
Lindsdal Sweden 56°44N 16°18E 163 H10
Line Islands Pac. Oc. 7°0N 160°0W 289 H12
Linesville U.S.A. 41°39N 80°26W 312 E4
Lineville Ala., U.S.A. 33°19N 85°45W 316 B4
Lineville Iowa, U.S.A. 40°35N 93°32W 310 D3
Linfen China 36°3N 111°30E 226 F6
Ling Xian Hunan, China 26°29N 113°48E 229 D9
Ling Xian Shandong, China 37°22N 116°30E 226 F9
Lingal India 16°17N 78°31E 245 F4
Linganamakki Res. India 14°6N 74°52E 245 G2
Lingao China 19°56N 109°42E 229 a
Lingayen Phil. 16°1N 120°14E 232 C3
Lingayen G. Phil. 16°10N 120°15E 232 C3
Lingbao China 34°31N 110°51E 226 G6
Lingbi China 33°33N 117°33E 227 H9
Lingbo Sweden 61°3N 16°41E 162 C10
Lingchuan Guangxi Zhuangzu, China 25°26N 110°21E 229 E8
Lingchuan Shanxi, China 35°45N 113°12E 226 G7
Lingding Yang China 22°25N 113°44E 219 a
Lingen Germany 52°31N 7°19E 178 C3
Lingga Indonesia 0°12S 104°37E 234 C2
Lingga, Kepulauan Indonesia 0°10S 104°30E 234 C2
Lingga Arch. = Lingga, Kepulauan Indonesia 0°10S 104°30E 234 C2
Linghai China 41°11N 121°22E 227 D11
Linghed Sweden 60°48N 15°55E 162 D9
Linghem Sweden 58°26N 15°47E 163 F9
Lingig Phil. 8°2N 126°24E 233 G6
Lingle U.S.A. 42°8N 104°21W 304 E11
Lingomo Dem. Rep. of the Congo 0°38N 22°3E 264 B4
Lingqiu China 39°28N 114°22E 226 E8
Lingshan China 22°25N 109°18E 228 F7
Lingshi China 36°48N 111°48E 226 F6
Lingshou China 38°20N 114°20E 226 E8
Lingshui China 18°27N 110°0E 229 a
Lingsugur India 16°10N 76°31E 245 F3
Lingtai China 35°0N 107°40E 226 G4
Linguère Senegal 15°25N 15°5W 262 B1
Lingui China 25°12N 110°2E 229 E8
Lingunda Dem. Rep. of the Congo 0°49N 21°8E 264 C3
Lingwu China 38°6N 106°20E 226 E4
Lingyuan China 41°10N 119°15E 227 D10
Lingyun China 25°2N 106°35E 228 E6
Linhai China 28°50N 121°8E 229 C13
Linhares Brazil 19°25S 40°4W 333 E3
Linhe China 40°48N 107°20E 226 D4
Liniers Argentina 34°39S 58°30W 117 B1
Linjiang China 41°50N 127°0E 224 B3
Linkebeek Belgium 50°46N 4°20E 116 B2
Linköping Sweden 58°28N 15°36E 163 F9
Linkou China 45°15N 130°18E 227 B16
Linksfield S. Africa 26°9S 28°6E 123 A2
Linli China 29°27N 111°30E 229 C8
Linlithgow = West Lothian □ U.K. 55°54N 3°36W 167 F5
Linmeyer S. Africa 26°15S 28°4E 123 B2
Linn U.S.A. 38°29N 91°51W 310 F5
Linna Finland 60°20N 24°50E 121 A2
Linnansaari △ Finland 62°3N 28°40E 160 E23
Linnei Taiwan 23°45N 120°36E 225 C2
Linneus U.S.A. 39°53N 93°11W 310 E3
Linnhe, L. U.K. 56°36N 5°25W 167 E3
Linosa Medit. S. 35°51N 12°50E 258 A2
Linpien Taiwan 22°26N 120°30E 225 D2
Linqi China 35°45N 113°52E 226 G7
Linqing China 36°50N 115°42E 226 F8
Linqu China 36°25N 118°30E 227 F10
Linquan China 33°5N 115°17E 229 A10
Lins Brazil 21°40S 49°44W 335 A6
Linshu China 34°53N 118°38E 227 G10
Linshui China 30°21N 106°57E 228 B6
Linsia = Linxia China 35°36N 103°10E 218 D9
Linstead Jamaica 18°8N 77°2W 320 a
Linta → Madag. 25°2S 44°5E 272 D1
Lintao China 35°26N 103°58E 226 G2
Linth → Switz. 47°7N 9°7E 179 H5
Linthal Switz. 46°54N 9°0E 179 J5
Linton Ind., U.S.A. 39°2N 87°10W 311 F9
Linton N. Dak., U.S.A. 46°16N 100°14W 308 B3
Lintong China 34°20N 109°10E 226 G5
Lintuvaara Finland 60°14N 24°49E 121 B1
Linwood Canada 43°35N 80°43W 312 C4
Linwu China 25°19N 112°31E 229 E9
Linxi Hebei, China 39°42N 118°26E 227 E10
Linxi Liaoning, China 43°36N 118°2E 227 C10
Linxia China 35°36N 103°10E 218 D9
Linxiang China 29°28N 113°23E 229 C9
Linyanti → Africa 17°50S 25°5E 270 A4
Linyi Shandong, China 37°13N 116°54E 226 F9
Linyi Shandong, China 35°5N 118°21E 227 G10
Linying China 33°48N 113°56E 226 H7
Linyuan Taiwan 22°30N 120°23E 225 D2
Linz Austria 48°18N 14°18E 180 C7
Linz Rhld-Pfz., Germany 50°34N 7°17E 178 E3
Linzhenzhen China 36°30N 109°59E 226 F5
Linzhou China 36°4N 113°49E 226 F7
Linzi China 36°50N 118°20E 227 F10
Lioko Équateur, Dem. Rep. of the Congo 0°2N 22°4E 264 B4
Lioko Orientale, Dem. Rep. of the Congo 1°25N 23°7E 264 B4
Liomseter Norway 61°15N 9°35E 164 C6
Lion, G. du France 43°10N 4°0E 174 E7
Lion Rock Country Park ⌓ Hong Kong, China 22°21N 114°11E 122 A3
Lionel Town Jamaica 17°50N 77°15W 320 a
Lioni Italy 40°52N 15°11E 201 B8
Lions, G. of = Lion, G. du France 43°10N 4°0E 174 E7
Lion's Den Zimbabwe 17°15S 30°5E 269 F3
Lion's Head Ont., Canada 44°58N 81°15W 312 B3
Lion's Head Western Cape, S. Africa 33°56S 18°23E 118 A1
Liouesso Congo 1°2N 15°43E 264 B3
Lioumi Greece 38°0N 23°40E 112 B2
Liozno = Lyozna Belarus 55°0N 30°50E 188 E6
Lipa Phil. 13°57N 121°10E 232 E3
Lipali Mozam. 15°50S 35°50E 269 F4
Lipany Slovakia 49°9N 20°58E 181 B13
Lípari Italy 38°26N 14°58E 201 D7
Lípari, I. Italy 38°29N 14°56E 201 D7
Lípari, Is. = Eólie, Ís. Italy 38°30N 14°57E 201 D7
Lipatkain Indonesia 0°1N 101°12E 234 B2
Lipcani Moldova 48°14N 26°48E 183 B11
Liperi Finland 62°31N 29°24E 160 E23
Lipetsk Russia 52°37N 39°35E 189 F10
Lipetsk □ Russia 52°50N 38°50E 190 D4
Lipiany Poland 53°2N 14°58E 185 E1
Liping China 26°15N 109°7E 228 D7
Lipisi Greece 37°19N 26°50E 205 D8
Lipjan Kosovo 42°31N 21°7E 202 D5
Lipkany = Lipcani Moldova 48°14N 26°48E 183 B11
Lipník nad Bečvou Czechia 49°32N 17°36E 181 B10
Lipno Poland 52°49N 19°15E 185 F6
Lipova Romania 46°8N 21°42E 182 D6
Lipovets Ukraine 49°12N 29°1E 177 D15
Lippe → Germany 51°39N 6°36E 178 D2
Lippehne = Lipiany Poland 53°2N 14°58E 185 E1
Lippstadt Germany 51°41N 8°22E 178 D4
Lipscomb U.S.A. 36°14N 100°16W 314 C4
Lipsk Poland 53°44N 23°24E 184 E10
Lipsko Poland 51°9N 21°40E 185 G8
Liptovský Hrádok Slovakia 49°2N 19°44E 181 B12
Liptovský Milkuláš Slovakia 49°6N 19°35E 181 B12
Liptrap, C. Australia 38°50S 145°55E 283 E6
Lipu China 24°30N 110°22E 229 E8
Lira Uganda 2°17N 32°57E 268 B3
Liranga Congo 0°43S 17°32E 264 C3
Liri → Italy 41°25N 13°52E 200 A6
Liria = Lliria Spain 39°37N 0°35W 197 F4
Līsakovsk Kazakhstan 52°33N 62°37E 216 B6
Lisala Dem. Rep. of the Congo 2°12N 21°38E 264 B4
Lisboa Portugal 38°42N 9°8W 126 A2
Lisboa □ Portugal 39°0N 9°12W 195 F1
Lisboa ✈ (LIS) Portugal 38°46N 9°8W 126 A2
Lisbon = Lisboa Portugal 38°42N 9°8W 126 A2
Lisbon N. Dak., U.S.A. 46°27N 97°41W 308 B5
Lisbon N.H., U.S.A. 44°13N 71°55W 313 B13
Lisbon N.Y., U.S.A. 44°43N 75°19W 313 B9
Lisbon Ohio, U.S.A. 40°46N 80°46W 312 F4
Lisbon Falls U.S.A. 44°0N 70°4W 309 D18
Lisburn U.K. 54°31N 6°3W 166 B5
Lisburn, C. Vanuatu 15°39S 166°46E 287 E4
Lisburne, C. U.S.A. 68°53N 166°13W 303 B6
Liscannor B. Ireland 52°55N 9°24W 166 D2
Liscia → Italy 41°11N 9°9E 200 A2
Lisdoonvarna Ireland 53°2N 9°18W 166 C2
Lishan Taiwan 24°16N 121°14E 225 B3
Lishe Jiang → China 24°15N 101°35E 228 E3
Lishi China 37°31N 111°8E 226 F6
Lishu China 43°20N 124°18E 227 C13
Lishui Guangdong, China 23°12N 113°9E 121 A1
Lishui Jiangsu, China 31°38N 119°2E 229 B12
Lishui Zhejiang, China 28°28N 119°54E 229 C12
Lisianski I. U.S.A. 26°2N 174°0W 302 F9
Lisichansk = Lysychansk Ukraine 48°55N 38°30E 189 H10
Lisieux France 49°10N 0°12E 172 C7
Liski Russia 51°3N 39°30E 189 G10
L'Isle-Jourdain Gers, France 43°36N 1°5E 174 E5
L'Isle-Jourdain Vienne, France 46°13N 0°31E 174 B4
L'Isle-sur-la-Sorgue France 43°54N 5°2E 175 E9
Lisle-sur-Tarn France 43°52N 1°49E 174 E5
Lismore N.S.W., Australia 28°44S 153°21E 281 D5
Lismore Waterford, Ireland 52°8N 7°55W 166 D4
Lissa = Leszno Poland 51°50N 16°30E 185 G3
Lissos → Greece 41°15N 25°40E 203 E9
Lista Norway 58°7N 6°39E 164 F3
Lister, Mt. Antarctica 78°0S 162°0E 151 D11
Lister og Mandals = Vest-Agder □ Norway 58°30N 7°15E 164 F4
Liston Australia 28°39S 152°6E 281 D5
Listowel Ont., Canada 43°44N 80°58W 312 C4
Listowel Kerry, Ireland 52°27N 9°29W 166 D2
Lit Sweden 63°19N 14°51E 162 A8
Lit-et-Mixe France 44°2N 1°15W 174 D2
Litang Guangxi Zhuangzu, China 23°12N 109°8E 228 F7
Litang Sichuan, China 30°1N 100°17E 228 B3
Litang Malaysia 5°27N 118°31E 235 A5
Litang Qu → China 28°4N 101°32E 228 C3
Litani → Lebanon 33°20N 35°15E 250 E6
Litchfield Vic., Australia 36°18S 142°52E 282 D5
Litchfield Calif., U.S.A. 40°24N 120°23W 306 E6
Litchfield Conn., U.S.A. 41°45N 73°11W 313 E11
Litchfield Ill., U.S.A. 39°11N 89°39W 310 E7
Litchfield Minn., U.S.A. 45°8N 94°32W 308 C6
Litchfield △ Australia 13°14S 131°1E 278 B5
Liteni Romania 47°32N 26°32E 183 C11
Lithakia Greece 37°43N 20°50E 207 D2
Lithgow Australia 33°25S 150°8E 283 B9
Lithino, Akra Greece 34°55N 24°44E 207 F5
Lithuania ■ Europe 55°30N 24°0E 188 E2
Litija Slovenia 46°3N 14°50E 199 B11
Lititz U.S.A. 40°9N 76°18W 313 F8
Litochoro Greece 40°8N 22°34E 202 F6
Litoko Dem. Rep. of the Congo 1°13S 24°47E 264 C4
Litoměřice Czechia 50°33N 14°10E 180 A7
Litomyšl Czechia 49°52N 16°20E 181 B9
Litschau Austria 48°58N 15°4E 180 C8
Little Abaco Bahamas 26°50N 77°30W 320 A4
Little Andaman I. India 10°45N 92°30E 245 J11
Little Aral Sea = Northern Aral Sea Kazakhstan 46°20N 60°30E 216 C6
Little B. N.S.W., Australia 33°58S 151°15E 139 B2
Little B. Montserrat 16°43N 62°11W 323 p
Little Barrier I. N.Z. 36°12S 175°8E 284 C4
Little Basses Sri Lanka 6°24N 81°43E 245 L5
Little Belt Mts. U.S.A. 46°40N 110°45W 304 C8
Little Bighorn Battlefield ⌓ U.S.A. 45°34N 107°25W 304 D10
Little Blue → U.S.A. 39°42N 96°41W 308 F5
Little Buffalo → Canada 61°0N 113°46W 296 A6
Little Calumet → U.S.A. 41°39N 87°34W 119 D3
Little Cayman Cayman Is. 19°41N 80°3W 320 C3
Little Churchill → Canada 57°30N 95°22W 297 B9
Little Coco I. Burma 14°0N 93°13E 245 H11
Little Colorado → U.S.A. 36°12N 111°48W 305 H8
Little Current Canada 45°55N 82°0W 298 C3
Little Current → Canada 50°57N 84°36W 298 B3
Little Desert △ Australia 37°25S 141°30E 282 D4
Little Diomede I. U.S.A. 65°45N 168°56W 303 D5
Little Falls Minn., U.S.A. 45°59N 94°22W 308 C6
Little Falls N.Y., U.S.A. 43°3N 74°51W 313 C10
Little Ferry U.S.A. 40°50N 74°2W 132 A1
Little Fork → U.S.A. 48°31N 93°35W 308 A7
Little Grand Rapids Canada 52°0N 95°29W 297 C9
Little Haiti U.S.A. 25°50N 80°11W 129 C2
Little Havana U.S.A. 25°47N 80°15W 129 D1
Little Humboldt → U.S.A. 41°1N 117°43W 304 F5
Little Inagua I. Bahamas 21°40N 73°50W 321 B5
Little India Singapore 1°19N 103°51E 138 B3
Little Italy New York, U.S.A. 132 e2
Little Karoo S. Africa 33°45S 21°0E 270 D3
Little Khingan Mts. = Xiao Hinggan Ling China 49°0N 127°0E 219 B14
Little Lake U.S.A. 35°56N 117°55W 307 K9
Little Lake Conway U.S.A. 28°29N 81°21W 133 B2
Little Laut Is. = Laut Kecil, Kepulauan Indonesia 4°45S 115°40E 235 C5
Little London Jamaica 18°15N 78°13W 320 a
Little Mecatina = Petit-Mécatina → Canada 50°40N 59°30W 299 B8
Little Mermaid = Den Lille Havfrue Copenhagen, Denmark 118 a3
Little Minch U.K. 57°35N 6°45W 167 D2
Little Missouri → U.S.A. 47°36N 102°25W 308 B2
Little Nicobar India 7°20N 93°40E 245 L11
Little Ouse → U.K. 52°22N 1°12E 169 E9
Little Rann India 23°25N 71°25E 242 H4
Little Red → U.S.A. 35°11N 91°27W 314 D9
Little River N.Z. 43°45S 172°49E 285 D7
Little Rock U.S.A. 34°45N 92°17W 314 D8
Little Rouge → Canada 43°45N 79°11W 141 A4
Little Ruaha → Tanzania 7°57S 37°53E 268 D4
Little Sable Pt. U.S.A. 43°38N 86°33W 308 D10
Little Scarcies → S. Leone 8°50N 13°10W 262 D2
Little Sioux → U.S.A. 41°48N 96°4W 308 E5
Little Sitkin I. U.S.A. 51°57N 178°31E 303 L2
Little Smoky → Canada 54°44N 117°11W 296 C5
Little Snake → U.S.A. 40°27N 108°26W 304 F9
Little Sound Bermuda 32°15N 64°50W 153 a
Little Tokyo Los Angeles, U.S.A. 127 c2
Little Valley U.S.A. 42°15N 78°48W 312 D6
Little Wabash → U.S.A. 37°55N 88°5W 311 G8
Little White → U.S.A. 43°40N 100°40W 308 D3
Little York U.S.A. 41°1N 90°45W 310 C6
Little Zab = Zāb aş Şaghīr → Iraq 35°17N 43°29E 213 E10
Littlefield U.S.A. 33°55N 102°20W 314 E3
Littlehampton U.K. 50°49N 0°32W 169 G7
Littleton U.S.A. 44°18N 71°46W 313 B13
Littoral □ Cameroon 4°0N 10°0E 263 E7
Littoria = Latina Italy 41°28N 12°52E 200 A5
Litunga Angola 13°19S 16°48E 265 E3
Litvinov Czechia 50°36N 13°37E 180 A6
Liu He → Jilin, China 42°46N 126°13E 224 A3
Liu He → Liaoning, China 40°55N 121°35E 227 D11
Liu Jiang → China 23°55N 109°30E 228 F7
Liuba China 33°38N 106°55E 228 A6
Liucheng China 24°38N 109°14E 228 E7
Liuchia Taiwan 23°13N 120°21E 225 C2
Liuch'iu Taiwan 22°21N 120°23E 225 D2
Liuch'iu Yü Taiwan 22°21N 120°22E 225 D2
Liugou China 40°57N 118°15E 227 D10
Liuhang China 31°21N 121°21E 138 A1
Liuhe China 42°17N 125°43E 224 A2
Liuheng Dao China 29°40N 122°5E 229 C14
Liujiang China 24°26N 109°11E 228 E7
Liukang Tenggaja = Sabalana, Kepulauan Indonesia 6°45S 118°50E 231 F5
Liuli Tanzania 11°3S 34°38E 269 E3
Liupan Shan China 35°39N 106°12E 226 G4
Liupanshui China 26°38N 104°48E 228 D5
Liuqiu = Liuch'iu Taiwan 22°21N 120°23E 225 D2
Liurong Temple China 23°8N 113°15E 121 B2
Liuwa Plain Zambia 14°20S 22°30E 265 E4
Liuwa Plain △ Zambia 14°45S 22°35E 265 E4
Liuyang China 28°10N 113°37E 229 C9
Liuying Taiwan 23°17N 120°18E 225 C2
Liuzhou China 24°22N 109°22E 228 E7
Liuzhuang China 33°12N 120°18E 227 H11
Livada Romania 47°52N 23°5E 182 C8
Livadero Greece 40°2N 21°57E 202 F5
Livadhia Cyprus 34°57N 33°38E 207 F9
Livadhje Albania 39°47N 20°7E 206 B10
Livadi Greece 40°8N 22°9E 204 A4
Livadia Greece 38°27N 22°54E 204 C4
Livarot France 48°58N 0°9E 172 D7
Live Oak Calif., U.S.A. 39°17N 121°40W 306 F5
Live Oak Fla., U.S.A. 30°18N 82°59W 316 E7
Live Oak Manor U.S.A. 29°57N 90°14W 131 B1
Lively Canada 46°26N 81°9W 309 B13
Livengood U.S.A. 65°32N 148°33W 303 D10
Liveras Cyprus 35°23N 32°57E 207 E8
Livermore U.S.A. 37°41N 121°47W 306 H5
Livermore, Mt. U.S.A. 30°38N 104°11W 314 F2
Livermore Falls U.S.A. 44°29N 70°11W 309 C18
Liverpool N.S.W., Australia 33°54S 150°58E 283 B9
Liverpool N.S., Canada 44°5N 64°41W 299 D7
Liverpool Mersey., U.K. 53°25N 3°0W 168 D4
Liverpool N.Y., U.S.A. 43°6N 76°13W 313 C8
Liverpool Bay U.K. 53°30N 3°20W 168 D4
Liverpool Plains Australia 31°15S 150°15E 283 A9
Liverpool Ra. Australia 31°50S 150°30E 283 A9
Liverpool Street London, U.K. 125 a5
Livigno Italy 46°35N 10°10E 198 B7
Livingston Guatemala 15°50N 88°50W 320 C2
Livingston W. Loth., U.K. 55°54N 3°30W 167 F5
Livingston Ala., U.S.A. 32°35N 88°11W 315 E10
Livingston Calif., U.S.A. 37°23N 120°43W 306 H6
Livingston Mont., U.S.A. 45°40N 110°34W 304 D8
Livingston S.C., U.S.A. 33°38N 81°7W 316 B8
Livingston Tenn., U.S.A. 36°23N 85°19W 315 C12
Livingston Tex., U.S.A. 30°43N 94°56W 314 F7
Livingston Wis., U.S.A. 42°54N 90°26W 310 B6
Livingston, L. U.S.A. 30°50N 95°10W 314 F7
Livingston Manor U.S.A. 41°54N 74°50W 313 E10
Livingstone Zambia 17°46S 25°52E 269 F2
Livingstone △ Australia 35°22S 147°22E 283 C7
Livingstone Mts. N.Z. 45°15S 168°9E 285 F3
Livingstone Mts. Tanzania 9°40S 34°20E 269 D3
Livingstonia Malawi 10°38S 34°5E 269 E3
Livno Bos.-H. 43°50N 17°1E 182 G2
Livny Russia 52°30N 37°30E 189 F9
Livonia Mich., U.S.A. 42°23N 83°23W 311 B13
Livonia N.Y., U.S.A. 42°49N 77°40W 312 D7
Livorno Italy 43°33N 10°19E 198 E7
Livradois-Forez ⌓ France 44°0N 3°0E 174 E7
Livramento = Nossa Senhora do Livramento Brazil 15°48S 56°22W 331 D6
Livramento Brazil 30°55S 55°30W 335 C4
Livramento do Brumado Brazil 13°39S 41°50W 333 D3
Livron-sur-Drôme France 44°46N 4°51E 175 D8
Livry-Gargan France 48°55N 2°31E 134 A4
Livyntsi Ukraine 48°25N 26°37E 183 B11
Liwā' U.A.E. 23°0N 54°10E 249 B6
Liwale Tanzania 9°48S 37°58E 269 D4
Liwan China 23°3N 113°13E 121 B2
Liwiec → Poland 52°36N 21°34E 185 F8
Liwonde Malawi 15°4S 35°13E 269 F4
Liwonde △ Malawi 14°48S 35°20E 269 E4
Lixi China 26°23N 101°59E 228 D3
Lixian China 31°23N 103°13E 228 B4
Lixin China 33°8N 116°13E 229 A11
Lixouri Greece 38°12N 20°26E 207 C2
Liyang China 31°26N 119°28E 229 B12
Lizard → Trin. & Tob. 10°9N 61°1W 323 t
Lizard I. Australia 14°42S 145°30E 280 A4
Lizard Pt. U.K. 49°57N 5°13W 169 H2
Lizarda Brazil 9°36S 46°41W 332 C2
Lizarra = Estella Spain 42°40N 2°2W 196 C2
Lizella U.S.A. 32°48N 83°49W 316 C6
Lizzano Italy 40°23N 17°27E 201 B10
Ljan Norway 59°50N 10°46E 133 A3
Ljig Serbia 44°13N 20°18E 202 B4
Ljøra → Norway 61°24N 12°35E 164 C9
Ljørdalen Norway 61°23N 12°41E 164 C9
Ljosland Norway 58°47N 7°22E 164 F4
Ljubija Bos.-H. 44°55N 16°35E 199 D13
Ljubinje Bos.-H. 42°58N 18°5E 202 D2
Ljubišnja Europe 43°18N 19°6E 202 C3
Ljubljana Slovenia 46°4N 14°33E 199 B11
Ljubljana ✈ (LJU) Slovenia 46°14N 14°33E 199 B11
Ljubno Slovenia 46°25N 14°46E 199 B11
Ljubovija Serbia 44°11N 19°22E 202 B3
Ljugarn Sweden 57°20N 18°43E 163 G12
Ljung Sweden 57°59N 13°3E 163 G7
Ljungan → Sweden 62°18N 17°23E 162 B11
Ljungaverk Sweden 62°30N 16°5E 162 B10
Ljungby Sweden 56°49N 13°55E 163 H7
Ljungbyholm Sweden 56°39N 16°5E 163 H10
Ljungdalen Sweden 62°51N 12°47E 162 B6
Ljungsbro Sweden 58°31N 15°30E 163 F9
Ljungskile Sweden 58°14N 11°55E 163 F5
Ljusdal Sweden 61°46N 16°3E 162 C10
Ljusfallshammar Sweden 58°48N 15°30E 163 F9
Ljusnan → Sweden 61°12N 17°8E 162 C11
Ljusne Sweden 61°13N 17°7E 162 C11
Ljusterö Sweden 59°31N 18°37E 162 E12
Ljustorp Sweden 62°38N 17°19E 162 B11
Ljutomer Slovenia 46°31N 16°11E 199 B13
Llagostera Spain 41°50N 2°54E 196 D7
Llamellín Peru 9°0S 76°54W 330 B2
Llançà Spain 42°22N 3°9E 196 C8
Llancanelo, Salina Argentina 35°40S 69°8W 334 D2
Llandeilo U.K. 51°53N 3°59W 169 F4
Llandovery U.K. 51°59N 3°48W 169 F4
Llandrindod Wells U.K. 52°14N 3°22W 169 E4
Llandudno U.K. 53°19N 3°50W 168 D4
Llanelli U.K. 51°41N 4°10W 169 F3
Llanes Spain 43°25N 4°50W 194 B6
Llanfair-ym-Muallt = Builth Wells U.K. 52°9N 3°25W 169 E4
Llanganates △ Ecuador 0°51S 72°20W 328 D3
Llangollen U.K. 52°58N 3°11W 168 E4
Llanidloes U.K. 52°27N 3°31W 169 E4
Llano U.S.A. 30°45N 98°41W 314 F5
Llano → U.S.A. 30°39N 98°26W 314 F5
Llano de Can Gineu Spain 41°27N 2°10E 114 A2
Llano Estacado U.S.A. 33°30N 103°0W 314 E3
Llanos S. Amer. 5°0N 71°35W 326 C3
Llanos de Challe △ Chile 28°8S 71°1W 334 B1
Llanquihue, L. Chile 41°10S 72°50W 336 B1
Llanwrtyd Wells U.K. 52°7N 3°38W 169 E4
Llata Peru 9°25S 76°47W 330 B2
Llebeig, C. des Spain 39°33N 2°18E 206 B3
Lleida Spain 41°37N 0°39E 196 D5
Lleida □ Spain 42°6N 1°0E 196 C6
Llentrisca, C. Spain 38°52N 1°15E 206 D1
Llera de Canales Mexico 23°19N 99°1W 319 C5
Llerena Spain 38°17N 6°0W 195 G5
Llevant, Sa. de Spain 39°35N 3°17E 206 B4
Lleyn Peninsula U.K. 52°51N 4°36W 168 E3
Llica Bolivia 19°52S 68°16W 330 D4
Llico Chile 34°46S 72°5W 334 C1
Lliria Spain 39°37N 0°35W 197 F4
Llívia Spain 42°28N 1°59E 174 F5
Llobregat → Spain 41°19N 2°5E 196 D7
Llodio Spain 43°9N 2°58W 196 B2
Llogara △ Albania 40°13N 19°35E 202 F3
Llorente Phil. 11°25N 125°33E 233 F5
Lloret de Mar Spain 41°41N 2°53E 196 D7
Lloseta Spain 39°43N 2°52E 206 B3
Lloyd B. Australia 12°45S 143°27E 280 A3
Lloyd L. Canada 57°22N 108°57W 297 B7
Lloydminster Canada 53°17N 110°0W 297 C7
Llubí Spain 39°42N 3°0E 206 B4
Llucena del Cid Spain 40°9N 0°17W 196 E4
Llucmajor Spain 39°29N 2°53E 206 B3
Lluidas Vale Jamaica 18°6N 77°5W 320 a
Llullaillaco, Volcán S. Amer. 24°43S 68°30W 334 A2
Llullaillaco △ Chile 24°50S 68°51W 334 A2
Lo → Vietnam 21°18N 105°25E 236 B5
Lo Aranguiz Chile 33°23S 70°40W 137 B2
Lo Boza Chile 33°23S 70°43W 137 B1
Lo Espejo Chile 33°31S 70°42W 137 C1
Lo Hermida Chile 33°28S 70°33W 137 B2
Lo Prado Chile 33°26S 70°42W 137 B1
Lo So Shing Hong Kong, China 22°12N 114°7E 122 B2
Lo Wai Hong Kong, China 22°22N 114°8E 122 A2
Loa U.S.A. 38°24N 111°39W 304 G8
Loa → Chile 21°26S 70°41W 334 A1
Loagan Bunut △ Malaysia 3°32N 114°40E 235 B4
Loaita I. S. China Sea 10°41N 114°25E 230 B4
Loakulu Indonesia 0°31S 117°1E 235 C5
Loange → Dem. Rep. of the Congo 4°17S 20°2E 265 C4
Loango Congo 4°38S 11°50E 265 C2
Loanhead U.K. 55°53N 3°9W 121 B3
Loano Italy 44°8N 8°15E 198 D5
Loay Phil. 9°36N 124°1E 233 G5
Lobamba Swaziland 26°28S 31°12E 271 C5
Lobatse Botswana 25°12S 25°40E 270 C4
Lobau Wien, Austria 48°10N 16°31E 142 A3
Löbau Sachsen, Germany 51°5N 14°40E 178 D10
Lobaye □ C.A.R. 4°0N 17°30E 264 B3
Lobaye → C.A.R. 3°41N 18°35E 264 B3
Loben = Lubliniec Poland 50°43N 18°45E 185 H5
Lobenstein Germany 50°25N 11°39E 178 E7
Lobería Argentina 38°10S 58°40W 334 D4
Löberöd Sweden 55°47N 13°31E 163 J7
Łobez Poland 53°38N 15°39E 184 E2
Lobito Angola 12°18S 13°35E 265 E2
Lobo Phil. 13°39N 121°13E 232 E3
Lobo → Ivory C. 6°2N 6°45W 262 D3
Lobos Argentina 35°10S 59°0W 334 D4
Lobos, I. Mexico 27°20N 110°36W 318 B2
Lobos, I. de Canary Is. 28°45N 13°50W 153 e2
Lobos, Pt. U.S.A. 37°46N 122°30W 136 B1
Lobos de Afuera, Islas Peru 6°57S 80°42W 330 B1
Lobos de Tierra, I. Peru 6°27S 80°52W 330 B1
Łobżenica Poland 53°18N 17°15E 185 E4
Loc Binh Vietnam 21°46N 106°54E 236 B6
Loc Ninh Vietnam 11°50N 106°34E 237 G6
Locarno Switz. 46°10N 8°47E 179 J4
Loch Garman = Wexford Ireland 52°20N 6°28W 166 D5
Loch Lomond and the Trossachs △ U.K. 56°10N 4°40W 167 E4
Lochaber U.K. 56°59N 5°1W 167 E3
Locham Germany 48°7N 11°26E 131 B1
Locharbriggs U.K. 55°7N 3°35W 167 F5
Lochboisdale U.K. 57°9N 7°20W 167 D1
Loche, L. La Canada 56°30N 109°30W 297 B7
Lochem Neths. 52°9N 6°26E 170 B6
Loches France 47°7N 1°0E 172 E7
Lochgilphead U.K. 56°2N 5°26W 167 E3
Lochinvar △ Zambia 15°55S 27°15E 269 F2
Lochinver U.K. 58°9N 5°14W 167 C3
Lochkov Czechia 50°0N 14°21E 135 B2
Lochloosa L. U.S.A. 29°30N 82°7W 317 F7
Lochmaddy U.K. 57°36N 7°10W 167 D1
Lochnagar Queens., Australia 23°33S 145°38E 280 C4
Lochnagar Aberds., U.K. 56°57N 3°15W 167 E5
Łochów Poland 52°33N 21°42E 185 F8
Lochy, L. U.K. 57°0N 4°53W 167 E4
Lock Australia 33°34S 135°46E 281 E2
Lock Haven U.S.A. 41°8N 77°28W 312 E7
Lockeford U.S.A. 38°10N 121°9W 306 G5
Lockeport Canada 43°47N 65°4W 299 D6
Lockerbie U.K. 55°7N 3°21W 167 F5
Lockhart N.S.W., Australia 35°14S 146°40E 283 C7
Lockhart Tex., U.S.A. 29°53N 97°40W 314 G6
Lockhart, L. Australia 33°15S 119°3E 279 F2
Lockhart River Australia 12°58S 143°30E 280 A3
Lockhart River ☼ Australia 12°47S 143°20E 280 A3
Lockhausen Germany 48°10N 11°24E 131 A1
Lockney U.S.A. 34°7N 101°27W 314 D4
Lockport Ill., U.S.A. 41°35N 88°3W 311 C8
Lockport N.Y., U.S.A. 43°10N 78°42W 312 C6
Locminé France 47°54N 2°51W 172 E4
Locri Italy 38°14N 16°16E 201 D9
Locronan France 48°7N 4°15W 172 D2
Locust Cr. → U.S.A. 39°40N 93°17W 310 E3
Locust Grove U.S.A. 33°21N 84°7W 316 B5
Lod Israel 31°57N 34°54E 251 G5
Lodalskåpa Norway 61°47N 7°13E 164 C4
Lodeinoye Pole Russia 60°44N 33°33E 188 B7
Lodève France 43°44N 3°19E 174 E7
Lodge Bay Canada 52°14N 55°51W 299 B8
Lodge Grass U.S.A. 45°19N 107°22W 304 D10
Lodhran Pakistan 29°32N 71°30E 242 E4
Lodi Italy 45°19N 9°30E 198 C6
Lodi Calif., U.S.A. 38°8N 121°16W 306 G5
Lodi N.J., U.S.A. 40°52N 74°5W 132 A1
Lodi Ohio, U.S.A. 41°2N 82°1W 312 E3
Lodi Estate India 28°36N 77°15E 120 B2
Lodja Dem. Rep. of the Congo 3°30S 23°23E 264 C4
Lodosa Spain 42°25N 2°4W 196 C2
Lödöse Sweden 58°2N 12°9E 163 F6
Lodwar Kenya 3°7N 35°36E 268 B4
Łódź Poland 51°45N 19°27E 185 G6
Łódzkie □ Poland 51°30N 19°30E 185 G6
Loei Thailand 17°29N 101°35E 236 D3
Loengo Dem. Rep. of the Congo 4°48S 26°30E 265 C5
Loeriesfontein S. Africa 31°0S 19°26E 270 D2
Lofa → Liberia 6°35N 11°8W 262 D2
Lofa Mano △ Liberia 7°55N 10°25W 262 D2
Lofer Austria 47°35N 12°41E 180 D5
Lofoten Norway 68°30N 13°59E 160 B16
Lofsdalen Sweden 62°10N 13°20E 162 B7
Lofsen → Sweden 62°7N 13°57E 162 B7
Loftahammar Sweden 57°54N 16°41E 163 G10
Loga Niger 13°40N 3°15E 263 C5
Logan Iowa, U.S.A. 41°39N 95°47W 308 E6
Logan Ohio, U.S.A. 39°32N 82°25W 309 F12
Logan Utah, U.S.A. 41°44N 111°50W 304 F8
Logan W. Va., U.S.A. 37°51N 81°59W 309 G13
Logan, Mt. Canada 60°34N 140°23W 294 E3
Logan Int., Boston ✈ (BOS) U.S.A. 42°22N 71°1W 116 A2
Logan Martin L. U.S.A. 33°26N 86°20W 316 B3
Logan Square U.S.A. 41°55N 87°42W 119 B2
Logandale U.S.A. 36°36N 114°29W 307 J12
Logansport Ind., U.S.A. 40°45N 86°22W 311 D10
Logansport La., U.S.A. 31°58N 94°0W 314 F8
Loganville U.S.A. 33°50N 83°54W 316 B6
Logatec Slovenia 45°56N 14°15E 199 C11
Logirim South Sudan 4°43N 33°14E 257 G3
Lognes-Émerainville ✈ (XLG) France 48°49N 2°37E 134 B4
Logo South Sudan 5°20N 30°18E 257 F3
Logodoro Italy 40°35N 8°45E 200 B1
Logone → Chad 12°6N 15°2E 259 F3
Logone Gana Chad 11°36N 15°4E 259 F3
Logone Occidental □ Chad 8°30N 16°0E 259 G3
Logone Occidental → Chad 8°50N 16°0E 259 G3
Logone Oriental □ Chad 8°30N 16°30E 259 G3
Logone Oriental → Chad 9°7N 16°26E 259 G3
Logroño Spain 42°28N 2°27W 196 C2
Logrosán Spain 39°20N 5°32W 195 F5
Løgstør Denmark 56°58N 9°14E 163 H3
Logtak L. India 24°33N 93°50E 241 C4
Løgumkloster Denmark 55°4N 8°57E 163 J2
Loh Vanuatu 13°21S 166°38E 287 C4
Lohals Denmark 55°8N 10°55E 163 J4
Lohardaga India 23°27N 84°45E 243 H11
Loharia India 23°45N 74°14E 242 H6
Loharu India 28°27N 75°49E 242 E6
Lohja Finland 60°12N 24°5E 188 B3
Löhme Germany 52°37N 13°40E 115 A5
Löhne Germany 52°11N 8°40E 178 C4
Loho = Luohe China 33°32N 114°2E 226 H8
Lohr Germany 49°59N 9°35E 179 F5
Lohri Wah → Pakistan 27°27N 67°37E 242 F2
Loi-lem Burma 20°52N 97°28E 241 E6
Loikaw Burma 19°40N 97°17E 241 F6
Loimaa Finland 60°50N 23°5E 188 B2
Loir → France 47°33N 0°32W 172 E6
Loir-et-Cher □ France 47°40N 1°20E 172 E8
Loire □ France 45°40N 4°5E 175 C8
Loire → France 47°16N 2°10W 172 E4
Loire-Anjou-Touraine ⌓ France 47°14N 0°5W 172 E6
Loire-Atlantique □ France 47°25N 1°40W 172 E5
Loire Inférieure = Loire-Atlantique □ France 47°25N 1°40W 172 E5
Loiret □ France 47°55N 2°30E 173 E9
Loitz Germany 53°58N 13°8E 178 B9
Loja Ecuador 3°59S 79°16W 330 A2
Loja Spain 37°10N 4°10W 195 H6
Loja □ Ecuador 4°0S 79°13W 328 D2
Loje → Angola 7°49S 13°6E 265 D2
Loji = Kawasi Indonesia 1°38S 127°28E 231 E7
Lojo = Lohja Finland 60°12N 24°5E 188 B3
Løjt Kirkeby Denmark 55°7N 9°26E 163 J3
Lojung China 24°27N 109°36E 228 E7
Loka Dem. Rep. of the Congo 0°22N 18°2E 264 B3
Loka South Sudan 4°13N 31°0E 257 G3
Lokako Dem. Rep. of the Congo 0°57S 18°55E 264 C4
Lokandu Dem. Rep. of the Congo 2°30S 25°45E 264 C5
Lokaw Dem. Rep. of the Congo 2°40S 20°12E 264 C4
Løken Norway 59°48N 11°29E 164 E8
Lokeren Belgium 51°6N 3°59E 170 C3
Lokgwabe Botswana 24°10S 21°50E 270 B3
Lokhvytsya Ukraine 50°25N 33°18E 189 G7
Lokichar Kenya 2°23N 35°39E 268 B4
Lokichokio Kenya 4°19N 34°13E 268 B3
Lokitaung Kenya 4°12N 35°48E 268 B4
Lokkan tekojärvi Finland 67°55N 27°35E 160 C22
Løkken Denmark 57°22N 9°41E 163 G3
Løkken Sør-Trøndelag, Norway 63°9N 9°41E 164 A6
Loknya Russia 56°49N 30°4E 188 D6
Loko C.A.R. 3°38N 18°2E 264 B3
Loko Nigeria 8°1N 7°53E 263 D6
Lokoja Nigeria 7°47N 6°45E 263 D6
Lokolama Dem. Rep. of the Congo 2°35S 19°50E 264 C3
Lokolenge Dem. Rep. of the Congo 1°12N 22°38E 264 B4
Lokolo → Dem. Rep. of the Congo 1°43S 18°23E 264 C3
Lokot Russia 52°34N 34°36E 189 F8
Loktak L. = Logtak L. India 24°33N 93°50E 241 C4
Lokuru Solomon Is. 8°20S 157°0E 287 M9
Lol South Sudan 6°26N 29°37E 257 F2
Lol → South Sudan 9°13N 26°30E 257 F2
Lola Angola 14°19S 13°37E 265 E2
Lola Guinea 7°52N 8°29W 262 D3
Lola, Mt. U.S.A. 39°26N 120°22W 306 F6
Lolgorien Kenya 1°14S 34°48E 268 C3
Lolibai, Gebel South Sudan 3°50N 33°0E 257 G3
Lolimi South Sudan 4°35N 34°0E 257 G3
Loliondo Tanzania 2°2S 35°39E 268 C4
Lolland Denmark 54°45N 11°30E 163 K5
Lollar Germany 50°37N 8°43E 178 E4
Lolo U.S.A. 46°45N 114°5W 304 C6
Lolo → Gabon 0°18S 12°18E 264 C2
Lolobau I. Papua N. G. 4°55S 151°10E 286 C6
Lolodorf Cameroon 3°16N 10°49E 263 E7
Lolokhet Pakistan 24°54N 67°2E 123 A2
Loloma Zambia 13°24S 24°21E 265 E4
Loltong Vanuatu 15°32S 168°10E 287 E6
Lom Bulgaria 43°48N 23°12E 202 C7
Lom Oppland, Norway 61°50N 8°34E 164 C5
Lom → Bulgaria 43°45N 23°15E 202 C7
Lom → Cameroon 5°20N 13°24E 264 A2
Lom Kao Thailand 16°53N 101°14E 236 D3
Lom Sak Thailand 16°47N 101°15E 236 D3
Loma U.S.A. 47°56N 110°30W 304 C8
Loma Linda U.S.A. 34°3N 117°16W 307 L9
Loma Mansa S. Leone 9°13N 11°7W 262 D2
Loma Mts. S. Leone 9°10N 11°7W 262 D2
Lomako → Dem. Rep. of the Congo 0°50N 20°50E 264 B4
Lomaloma Fiji 17°17S 178°59W 287 A3
Lomami □ Dem. Rep. of the Congo 6°0S 25°0E 265 D4
Lomami → Dem. Rep. of the Congo 0°46N 24°16E 264 B4
Lomas Chapultepec Mexico 19°25N 99°12W 128 B1
Lomas de San Angel Inn Mexico 19°20N 99°13W 128 B1
Lomas de Zamora Argentina 34°45S 58°24W 334 C4
Lombadina Australia 16°31S 122°54E 278 C3
Lombard U.S.A. 41°53N 88°1W 311 C8
Lombárdia □ Italy 45°40N 9°30E 198 C6
Lombardy = Lombárdia □ Italy 45°40N 9°30E 198 C6
Lombardy East S. Africa 26°6S 28°7E 123 A2
Lombe Angola 9°27S 16°13E 265 D3
Lombez France 43°29N 0°55E 174 E4
Lomblen Indonesia 8°30S 123°32E 231 F6
Lombok Indonesia 8°45S 116°30E 235 D5
Lombok, Selat Indonesia 8°30S 115°50E 231 K18
Lomé Togo 6°9N 1°20E 263 D5
Lomela Dem. Rep. of the Congo 2°19S 23°15E 264 C4
Lomela → Dem. Rep. of the Congo 0°15S 20°40E 264 C4
Lomianki Poland 52°21N 20°54E 143 A1
Lomié Cameroon 3°13N 13°38E 264 B2
Lomma Sweden 55°43N 13°6E 163 J7
Lommel Belgium 51°14N 5°19E 170 C5
Lomond Canada 50°24N 112°36W 296 C6
Lomond, L. U.K. 56°8N 4°38W 167 E4
Lomonosov Ridge Arctic 88°0N 140°0E 150 A
Lomphat Cambodia 13°30N 106°59E 236 F6
Lompobatang Indonesia 5°24S 119°56E 231 F5
Lompoc U.S.A. 34°38N 120°28W 307 L6
Lomseggje Norway 61°49N 8°21E 164 C5
Lomus Reforma Mexico 19°24N 99°14W 128 B1
Łomża Poland 53°10N 22°2E 185 E9
Lon, Ko Thailand 7°47N 98°23E 237 a
Lonavale India 18°46N 73°29E 244 E1
Loncoche Chile 39°20S 72°50W 336 A2
Loncopué Argentina 38°4S 70°37W 336 A2
Londa India 15°30N 74°30E 245 G2
Londiani Kenya 0°10S 35°33E 268 C4
Londinières France 49°50N 1°25E 172 C8
London Ont., Canada 42°59N 81°15W 312 D3
London U.K. 51°30N 0°3W 125 B3
London Ky., U.S.A. 37°8N 84°5W 309 G11
London Ohio, U.S.A. 39°53N 83°27W 311 E13
London, Greater □ U.K. 51°36N 0°5W 169 F7
London Avenue Canal U.S.A. 30°3N 90°6W 131 A2
London Bridge Grenada 12°15N 61°35W 323 q
London Bridge London, U.K. 125 b5
London City ✈ (LCY) U.K. 51°30N 0°3E 125 A4
London Gateway U.K. 51°31N 0°29E 169 F8
London Gatwick ✈ (LGW) U.K. 51°10N 0°11W 169 F7
London Heathrow ✈ (LHR) U.K. 51°28N 0°27W 125 B1
London Mills U.S.A. 40°43N 90°11W 310 D6
London Stansted ✈ (STN) U.K. 51°54N 0°14E 169 F8
London Zoo U.K. 51°31N 0°9W 125 A3
Londonderry U.K. 55°0N 7°20W 166 B4
Londonderry □ U.K. 55°0N 7°20W 166 B4
Londonderry, C. Australia 13°45S 126°55E 278 B4
Londonderry, I. Chile 55°0S 71°0W 336 E2
Londres Argentina 27°46S 67°7W 334 B2
Londrina Brazil 23°18S 51°10W 335 A5
Londuimbale Angola 12°15S 15°19E 265 E3
Lone Pine U.S.A. 36°36N 118°4W 306 J8
Lonely Mine Zimbabwe 19°30S 28°49E 271 A4
Long, Î. Martinique 14°36N 60°51W 322 j
Long Akah Malaysia 3°19N 114°47E 235 B4
Long B. N.S.W., Australia 33°59S 151°15E 139 B2
Long B. Cornwall, Jamaica 18°20N 78°20W 320 a
Long B. S.C., U.S.A. 33°35N 78°45W 315 E15
Long Beach Calif., U.S.A. 33°46N 118°11W 307 M8
Long Beach N.Y., U.S.A. 40°35N 73°39W 313 F11
Long Beach Wash., U.S.A. 46°21N 124°3W 306 D2
Long Branch Ont., Canada 43°35N 79°31W 141 B1
Long Branch N.J., U.S.A. 40°18N 74°0W 313 F11
Long Cay Bahamas 25°6N 77°22W 153 b
Long Creek U.S.A. 44°43N 119°6W 304 D4
Long Ditton U.K. 51°22N 0°19W 125 B2
Long Eaton U.K. 52°53N 1°15W 168 E6
Long I. Antigua & B. 17°8N 61°45W 322 b
Long I. Queens., Australia 20°22S 148°51E 280 b
Long I. Bahamas 23°20N 75°10W 321 B4
Long I. Nunavut, Canada 54°50N 79°20W 298 B4
Long I. Cork, Ireland 51°30N 9°34W 166 E2
Long I. Papua N. G. 5°20S 147°5E 286 C4
Long I. N.Y., U.S.A. 40°45N 73°30W 313 F11
Long Island City U.S.A. 40°45N 73°56W 132 B2
Long Island Sd. U.S.A. 41°10N 73°0W 313 E12
Long L. Ont., Canada 49°30N 86°50W 298 C2
Long L. N.Y., U.S.A. 44°0N 74°23W 313 C10
Long Lake U.S.A. 43°58N 74°25W 313 C10
Long Mountain Mauritius 20°8S 57°33E 272 e
Long Point Canada 42°34N 80°25W 312 D4
Long Point B. Canada 42°40N 80°10W 312 D4
Long Prairie U.S.A. 45°59N 94°52W 308 C6
Long Prairie → U.S.A. 46°20N 94°36W 308 B6
Long Pt. Bahamas 25°1N 77°20W 153 b
Long Pt. Ont., Canada 42°35N 80°2W 312 D4
Long Pt. Ont., Canada 43°56N 76°53W 313 C8
Long Pt. Otago, N.Z. 46°34S 169°36E 285 G4
Long Range Mts. Canada 49°30N 57°30W 299 C8
Long Reef Australia 14°1S 125°48E 278 B4
Long Sault Canada 45°2N 74°53W 313 A10
Long Str. = Longa, Proliv Russia 70°0N 175°0E 215 C18
Long Street Cape Town, S. Africa 118 c2
Long Thanh Vietnam 10°47N 106°57E 237 G6
Long Xian China 34°55N 106°55E 226 G4
Long Xuyen Vietnam 10°19N 105°28E 237 G5
Longa Angola 14°42S 18°32E 265 E3
Longa Greece 36°53N 21°55E 204 E3
Longa → Angola 10°14S 13°29E 265 E2
Longa, Proliv Russia 70°0N 175°0E 215 C18
Longa Mavinga ⌓ Angola 16°20S 20°15E 265 F4
Longagung Indonesia 2°16N 115°16E 235 B5
Long'an China 23°10N 107°40E 228 F6
Longana Vanuatu 15°18S 168°0E 287 E5
Longarone Italy 46°16N 12°18E 199 B9
Longbenton U.K. 55°1N 1°31W 168 B6
Longberang Indonesia 3°43N 116°7E 235 B5
Longbia Indonesia 2°37N 116°42E 235 B5
Longboat Key U.S.A. 27°23N 82°39W 317 H7
Longboh Indonesia 0°52N 115°1E 235 B5
Longburn N.Z. 40°23S 175°35E 284 G4
Longchamp, Hippodrome de France 48°51N 2°13E 134 A2
Longchang China 29°18N 105°15E 228 C5
Longchuan Guangdong, China 24°5N 115°17E 229 E10
Longchuan Yunnan, China 24°23N 97°58E 228 E1
Longde China 35°30N 106°20E 226 G4
Longdenville Trin. & Tob. 10°31N 61°23W 323 t

Longeau-Percey France 47°47N 5°20E 173 E12
Longford Tas., Australia 41°32S 147°3E 281 G4
Longford Longf., Ireland 53°43N 7°49W 166 C4
Longford □ Ireland 53°42N 7°45W 166 C4
Longford, An = Longford Ireland 53°43N 7°49W 166 C4
Longgan Shan China 42°19N 126°30E 224 A3
Longhai China 24°25N 117°46E 229 E11
Longhua Guangdong, China 22°39N 114°0E 219 a
Longhua Hebei, China 41°18N 117°45E 227 D9
Longhua Pagoda China 31°10N 121°26E 138 B1
Longhua Park China 31°10N 121°26E 138 B1
Longhui China 27°7N 111°2E 229 D8
Longido Tanzania 2°43S 36°42E 268 C4
Longiram Indonesia 0°5S 115°45E 235 C5
Longjela Indonesia 2°28N 115°28E 235 B5
Longjing China 42°46N 129°25E 227 C15
Longkou Jiangxi, China 26°8N 115°10E 229 D10
Longkou Shandong, China 37°40N 120°18E 227 F11
Longlac Canada 49°45N 86°25W 298 C2
Longli China 26°25N 106°58E 228 D6
Longlin China 24°47N 105°20E 228 E5
Longling China 24°37N 98°39E 228 E2
Longmeadow U.S.A. 42°3N 72°34W 313 D12
Longmen China 23°40N 114°18E 229 F10
Longmen Shiku China 34°28N 112°28E 226 G7
Longming China 22°59N 107°7E 228 F6
Longmont U.S.A. 40°10N 105°6W 304 F11
Longnan China 24°55N 114°47E 229 E10
Longnawan Indonesia 1°51N 114°55E 235 B4
Longobucco Italy 39°27N 16°37E 201 C9
Longoni, B. de Mayotte 12°41S 45°8E 272 b
Longonot △ Kenya 0°55S 36°28E 266 E4
Longos Greece 39°16N 20°7E 206 C10
Longquan China 28°7N 119°10E 229 C12
Longreach Australia 23°28S 144°14E 280 C3
Longshan China 29°29N 109°25E 228 C7
Longsheng China 25°48N 110°0E 229 E8
Longtan = Lung'tan Taiwan 24°52N 121°12E 225 B3
Longtan Dam China 25°5N 107°0E 228 E6
Longtan Hu ➜ China 39°51N 116°24E 114 B2
Longtan Shuiku China 25°10N 106°50E 228 E6
Longué-Jumelles France 47°22N 0°8W 172 E6
Longue-Pointe Canada 45°35N 73°31W 130 A2
Longueau France 49°52N 2°21E 173 C9
Longueuil Canada 45°31N 73°29W 130 A3
Longuy Cameroon 3°5N 9°58E 264 B1
Longuyon France 49°27N 5°35E 173 C12
Longvic France 47°17N 5°4E 173 E12
Longview Tex., U.S.A. 32°30N 94°44W 314 E7
Longview Wash., U.S.A. 46°8N 122°57W 306 D4
Longwood St. Helena 15°57S 5°41W 153 h
Longwood Fla., U.S.A. 28°42N 81°21W 317 G8
Longwy France 49°30N 5°46E 173 C12
Longxi China 34°53N 104°40E 226 G3
Longxue Dao China 22°41N 113°38E 219 a
Longyan China 25°10N 117°0E 229 E11
Longyearbyen Svalbard 78°13N 15°40E 150 B8
Longyou China 29°1N 119°8E 229 C12
Longzhou China 22°22N 106°50E 228 F6
Loni India 28°45N 77°17E 120 A2
Lonigo Italy 45°23N 11°23E 199 C8
Löningen Germany 52°44N 7°46E 178 C3
Lonja ➜ Croatia 45°22N 16°40E 199 C13
Lonkala Dem. Rep. of the Congo 4°37S 23°14E 265 C4
Lonkin Burma 25°39N 96°22E 241 C6
Lonoke U.S.A. 34°47N 91°54W 314 D9
Lonquimay Chile 38°26S 71°14W 336 A2
Lons-le-Saunier France 46°40N 5°31E 173 F12
Lönsboda Sweden 56°24N 14°20E 163 H8
Lønset Norway 62°46N 7°24E 164 B4
Lonton Burma 25°6N 96°17E 241 C6
Looc Phil. 12°15N 121°59E 232 E3
Looe U.K. 50°22N 4°28W 169 G3
Loogootee U.S.A. 38°41N 86°55W 311 F10
Lookout, C. Canada 55°18N 83°56W 298 A3
Lookout, C. N.C., U.S.A. 34°35N 76°32W 315 D16
Loolmalasin Tanzania 3°0S 35°53E 268 C4
Loon ➜ Alta., Canada 57°8N 115°3W 296 B5
Loon ➜ Man., Canada 55°53N 101°59W 297 B8
Loon Lake Canada 54°2N 109°10W 297 C7
Loongana Australia 30°52S 127°5E 279 F4
Loop, The Chicago, U.S.A. 119 c1
Loop Hd. Ireland 52°34N 9°56W 166 D2
Lop China 37°3N 80°11E 217 E10
Lop Nor = Lop Nur China 40°20N 90°10E 217 D12
Lop Nur China 40°20N 90°10E 217 D12
Lopare Bos.-H. 44°39N 18°46E 182 F3
Lopatin Russia 43°50N 47°35E 191 J8
Lopatina, Gora Russia 50°47N 143°10E 215 D15
Lopatino = Volzhsk Russia 55°57N 48°23E 190 C9
Lopatka, Mys Russia 50°52N 156°40E 215 D16
Lopaye South Sudan 6°37N 33°40E 257 F3
Lopburi Thailand 14°48N 100°37E 236 E3
Lopé-Okanda ⌓ Gabon 0°45S 11°34E 264 C2
Lopevi Vanuatu 16°30S 168°21E 287 F6
Lopez Phil. 13°53N 122°15E 232 E4
Lopez Pa., U.S.A. 41°27N 76°20W 313 E8
Lopez, C. Gabon 0°47S 8°40E 264 C1
López de Filippis = Mariscal Estigarribia Paraguay 22°3S 60°40W 334 A3
Lopinot Trin. & Tob. 10°41N 61°19W 323 t
Lopori ➜ Dem. Rep. of the Congo 1°14N 19°49E 264 B3
Lopphavet Norway 70°27N 21°15E 160 A19
Lora Norway 62°8N 8°45E 164 B5
Lora ➜ Afghan. 31°35N 66°32E 240 C2
Lora ➜ Oppland, Norway 62°8N 8°42E 164 B5
Lora, Hāmūn-i- Pakistan 29°38N 64°58E 240 C2
Lora Cr. ➜ Australia 28°10S 135°22E 281 D2
Lora del Río Spain 37°39N 5°33W 195 H5
Lorain U.S.A. 41°28N 82°11W 312 E2
Loraine U.S.A. 40°9N 91°13W 310 D5
Loralai Pakistan 30°20N 68°41E 242 D3
Lorca Spain 37°41N 1°42W 197 H3
Lord Howe I. Pac. Oc. 31°33S 159°6E 277 G10
Lord Howe Rise Pac. Oc. 30°0S 162°30E 277 H12
Lord Howe Seamount Chain Pac. Oc. 28°0S 159°0E 277 F10
Lord Loughborough I. Burma 10°25N 97°54E 237 G1
Lord's Cricket Ground U.K. 51°31N 0°10W 125 A2
Lordsburg U.S.A. 32°21N 108°43W 305 K9
Lorengau Papua N. G. 2°1S 147°15E 286 B4
Lorestān □ Iran 33°30N 48°40E 247 C6
Loreto Bolivia 15°13S 64°40W 331 D5
Loreto Brazil 7°5S 45°10W 332 C2
Loreto Marche, Italy 43°26N 13°36E 199 E10
Loreto Piemonte, Italy 45°29N 9°12E 128 B2
Loreto Baja Calif. S., Mexico 26°0N 111°21W 318 B2
Loreto Surigao N., Phil. 10°21N 125°34E 232 F5
Loreto □ Peru 5°0S 75°0W 328 E3
Lorgues France 43°28N 6°22E 175 E10
Lorhosso = Loropéni Burkina Faso 10°17N 3°38W 262 C4
Lorian Swamp Kenya 0°40N 39°35E 267 D4
Lorica Colombia 9°14N 75°49W 328 B2
Lorient Morbihan, France 47°45N 3°23W 172 E3
Lorient St. Barts 17°54N 62°49W 322 a
Lorimor U.S.A. 41°8N 94°3W 310 C2
Lőrinci Hungary 47°44N 19°41E 182 C4
Lormi India 22°17N 81°41E 243 H9
Lorn U.K. 56°26N 5°10W 167 E3
Lorn, Firth of U.K. 56°20N 5°40W 167 E3
Lorne Australia 38°33S 143°59E 282 E5
Loronyo South Sudan 4°38N 32°38E 257 G3
Loropéni Burkina Faso 10°17N 3°38W 262 C4
Lorovouno Cyprus 35°8N 32°36E 207 E8
Lörrach Germany 47°36N 7°40E 179 H3
Lorrain ➜ Martinique 14°50N 61°3W 322 j
Lorraine = Baker U.S.A. 46°22N 104°17W 304 C11
Lorraine France 48°53N 6°0E 171 B7
Lorraine ⌓ France 48°55N 5°50E 173 D12
Los Sweden 61°45N 15°10E 162 C9
Los, Îles de Guinea 9°30N 13°50W 262 D2
Los Alamos Calif., U.S.A. 34°44N 120°17W 307 L6
Los Alamos N. Mex., U.S.A. 35°53N 106°19W 305 J10
Los Alcornocales ⌓ Spain 36°21N 5°32W 195 J5
Los Alerces △ Argentina 42°55S 71°55W 336 B2
Los Altos U.S.A. 37°23N 122°7W 306 H4
Los Andes Chile 32°50S 70°40W 334 C1
Los Angeles Chile 37°28S 72°23W 334 D1
Los Angeles Calif., U.S.A. 34°4N 118°15W 126 B3
Los Angeles Aqueduct U.S.A. 35°22N 118°5W 307 K9
Los Angeles Int. ✈ (LAX) U.S.A. 33°57N 118°25W 126 C2
Los Angeles Museum of the Holocaust U.S.A. 34°4N 118°21W 126 B2
Los Antiguos Argentina 46°35S 71°40W 336 C2
Los Bagres Venezuela 10°57N 63°58W 329 a
Los Banos U.S.A. 37°4N 120°51W 306 H6
Los Barrios Spain 36°11N 5°30W 195 J5
Los Blancos Argentina 23°40S 62°30W 334 A3
Los Cabos Int. ✈ (SJD) Mexico 23°9N 109°43W 318 C3
Los Cardones △ Argentina 25°8S 65°55W 334 B2
Los Cerrillos ✈ (ULC) Chile 33°29S 70°42W 137 B1
Los Chiles Costa Rica 11°2N 84°43W 320 D3
Los Corrales de Buelna Spain 43°16N 4°4W 194 B6
Los Cristianos Canary Is. 28°3N 16°42W 153 e1
Los Frailes, I. Venezuela 11°11N 63°44W 329 a
Los Gallardos Spain 37°10N 1°57W 197 H3
Los Gallos Pt. Trin. & Tob. 10°5N 61°55W 323 t
Los Gatos U.S.A. 37°14N 121°59W 306 H5
Los Glaciares △ Argentina 50°0S 73°55W 336 C2
Los Gómez Venezuela 10°57N 64°4W 329 a
Los Haïtises △ Dom. Rep. 19°4N 69°36W 321 C6
Los Hermanos, Is. Venezuela 11°45N 64°25W 321 D7
Los Huemules △ Chile 46°10S 73°23W 336 C2
Los Islotes Canary Is. 29°4N 13°44W 153 e2
Los Katios △ Colombia 7°50N 77°10W 328 B2
Los Lagos Chile 39°51S 72°50W 336 A2
Los Llanos de Aridane Canary Is. 28°38N 17°54W 153 e1
Los Loros Chile 27°50S 70°6W 334 B1
Los Lunas U.S.A. 34°48N 106°44W 305 J10
Los Menucos Argentina 40°50S 68°10W 336 B3
Los Mochis Mexico 25°45N 108°57W 318 B3
Los Monegros Spain 41°29N 0°13W 196 D4
Los Monos Argentina 46°1S 69°36W 336 C3
Los Muermos Chile 41°24S 73°29W 336 B2
Los Nevados △ Colombia 4°41N 75°21W 328 C2
Los Nietos Spain 37°39N 0°47W 197 H4
Los Nietos Calif., U.S.A. 33°57N 118°4W 126 C4
Los Olivos Lima, Peru 11°59S 77°5W 124 A2
Los Olivos Calif., U.S.A. 34°40N 120°7W 307 L6
Los Palacios Cuba 22°35N 83°15W 320 B3
Los Palacios y Villafranca Spain 37°10N 5°55W 195 H5
Los Queñes Chile 35°1S 70°48W 334 D1
Los Remedios △ Mexico 19°28N 99°17W 128 B1
Los Reyes Mexico 19°21N 99°6W 128 B2
Los Reyes de Salgado Mexico 19°35N 102°29W 318 D4
Los Ríos □ Ecuador 1°30S 79°25W 328 D2
Los Roques, Is. Venezuela 11°50N 66°45W 321 D6
Los Santos de Maimona Spain 38°27N 6°22W 195 G4
Los Teques Venezuela 10°21N 67°2W 328 A4
Los Testigos, Is. Venezuela 11°23N 63°6W 329 A4
Los Vilos Chile 32°10S 71°30W 334 C1
Los Yébenes Spain 39°36N 3°55W 195 F7
Loshan = Leshan China 29°33N 103°41E 228 C4
Losice Poland 52°13N 22°43E 185 F9
Lošinj Croatia 44°30N 14°30E 199 D11
Losiny Ostrov △ Russia 55°50N 37°45E 129 A3
Loskop Dam S. Africa 25°23S 29°20E 271 C4
Løsning Denmark 55°48N 9°42E 163 J3
Losombo Dem. Rep. of the Congo 1°2N 19°4E 264 B3
Lossiemouth U.K. 57°42N 3°17W 167 D5
Lossnen Sweden 62°26N 12°46E 162 B6
Lostwithiel U.K. 50°24N 4°41W 169 G3
Losuia Papua N. G. 8°30S 151°4E 286 E6
Lot Belgium 50°46N 4°16E 116 B1
Lot □ France 44°39N 1°40E 174 D5
Lot ➜ France 44°18N 0°20E 174 D4
Lot-et-Garonne □ France 44°22N 0°30E 174 D4
Lota Chile 37°5S 73°10W 334 D1
Lotagipi Swamp Kenya 4°36N 34°55E 266 B3
Løten Norway 60°51N 11°21E 164 D8
Lotfābād Iran 37°32N 59°20E 247 B8
Lothair S. Africa 26°22S 30°27E 271 C5
Loto Dem. Rep. of the Congo 2°48S 22°30E 264 C4
Lotoi ➜ Dem. Rep. of the Congo 1°35S 18°30E 264 C3
Lotorp Sweden 58°44N 15°50E 163 F9
Lötschbergtunnel Switz. 46°26N 7°43E 179 J3
Lotta ➜ Europe 68°42N 31°6E 160 B24
Lottefors Sweden 61°25N 16°24E 162 C10
Löttorp Sweden 57°10N 17°0E 163 G11
Lotung Taiwan 24°41N 121°46E 225 B3
Lotus River S. Africa 34°4S 18°31E 118 B2
Lotus Temple India 28°33N 77°15E 120 B2
Lötzen = Giżycko Poland 54°2N 21°48E 184 D8
Lou I. Papua N. G. 2°25S 147°22E 286 B4
Loubière Dominica 15°16N 61°23W 323 k
Loubomo Congo 4°9S 12°47E 264 C2
Loudéac France 48°11N 2°47W 172 D4
Loudi China 27°42N 111°59E 229 D8
Loudima Congo 4°6S 13°5E 264 C2
Loudonville U.S.A. 40°38N 82°14W 312 F2
Loudun France 47°3N 0°5E 172 E7
Loue ➜ France 47°1N 5°28E 173 E12
Louga Senegal 15°45N 16°5W 262 B1
Louga □ Senegal 15°10N 15°35W 262 B1
Loughborough U.K. 52°47N 1°11W 168 E6
Lougheed I. Canada 77°26N 105°6W 295 B10
Loughman U.S.A. 28°14N 81°34W 317 G8
Loughrea Ireland 53°12N 8°33W 166 C3
Loughros More B. Ireland 54°48N 8°32W 166 B3
Louhans France 46°38N 5°12E 173 F12
Louis Armstrong New Orleans Int. ✈ (MSY) U.S.A. 30°0N 90°15W 131 B1
Louis Armstrong Park New Orleans, U.S.A. 131 a2
Louis-Gentil = Youssoufia Morocco 32°16N 8°31W 260 B3
Louis Trichardt S. Africa 23°1S 29°43E 271 B4
Louis XIV, Pte. Canada 54°37N 79°45W 298 B4
Louisa U.S.A. 38°7N 82°36W 309 F12
Louisbourg Canada 45°55N 60°0W 299 C8
Louisburg U.S.A. 38°37N 94°41W 310 F2
Louisburgh Ireland 53°46N 9°49W 166 C2
Louise, L. U.S.A. 28°28N 81°32W 133 B1
Louise I. Canada 52°55N 131°50W 296 C2
Louiseville Canada 46°20N 72°56W 298 C5
Louisiade Arch. Papua N. G. 11°10S 153°0E 286 F7
Louisiana U.S.A. 39°27N 91°3W 310 E6
Louisiana □ U.S.A. 30°50N 92°0W 314 F9
Louisiana Superdome = Mercedes-Benz Superdome U.S.A. 29°56N 90°5W 131 b1
Louisville Ala., U.S.A. 31°47N 85°33W 316 D4
Louisville Ga., U.S.A. 33°0N 82°25W 316 B7
Louisville Ill., U.S.A. 38°46N 88°30W 311 F8
Louisville Ky., U.S.A. 38°15N 85°46W 311 F11
Louisville Miss., U.S.A. 33°7N 89°3W 315 E10
Louisville Ohio, U.S.A. 40°50N 81°16W 312 F3
Louisville Ridge Pac. Oc. 31°0S 172°30W 288 L10
Loukoléla Congo 1°4S 17°10E 264 C3
Loukouo Congo 3°38S 14°39E 264 C2
Loulay France 46°3N 0°30W 174 B3
Loulé Portugal 37°9N 8°0W 195 H3
Loulouni Mali 10°54N 5°36W 262 C3
Loum Cameroon 4°42N 9°44E 264 B1
Louny Czechia 50°20N 13°48E 180 A6
Loup City U.S.A. 41°17N 98°58W 308 E4
Loups Marins, Lacs des Canada 56°30N 73°45W 298 A5
Lourdes France 43°6N 0°3W 174 E3
Lourdes-de-Blanc-Sablon Canada 51°24N 57°12W 299 B8
Lourenço Brazil 2°30N 51°40W 329 C7
Lourenço Marques = Maputo Mozam. 25°58S 32°32E 271 C5
Loures Portugal 38°49N 9°10W 126 A1
Lourinhã Portugal 39°14N 9°17W 195 F1
Louros Greece 39°3N 20°47E 207 A2
Louroujina Cyprus 35°0N 33°28E 207 E12
Lousã Portugal 40°7N 8°14W 194 E2
Louta Burkina Faso 13°30N 3°10W 262 C4
Louth N.S.W., Australia 30°30S 145°8E 283 A6
Louth Louth, Ireland 53°58N 6°32W 166 C5
Louth Lincs., U.K. 53°22N 0°1W 168 D7
Louth □ Ireland 53°56N 6°34W 166 C5
Louth B. Australia 34°33S 135°56E 282 C1
Loutra Edipsou Greece 38°54N 23°2E 204 C5
Loutra Kyllinis Greece 37°52N 21°7E 207 D3
Loutraki Greece 37°58N 22°57E 204 D4
Loutropoli Thermis Greece 39°11N 26°29E 205 B8
Louvain = Leuven Belgium 50°52N 4°42E 170 D4
Louvale U.S.A. 32°10N 84°50W 316 C5
Louveciennes France 48°51N 2°8E 134 C1
Louviers France 49°12N 1°10E 172 C8
Louvre, Musée du Paris, France 134 b4
Louvre, Palais du Paris, France 134 b4
Louwsburg S. Africa 27°37S 31°7E 271 C5
Lovat ➜ Russia 58°14N 31°28E 188 C6
Lovćen Montenegro 42°23N 18°51E 202 D2
Lovćen △ Montenegro 42°20N 18°50E 202 D2
Lovech Bulgaria 43°8N 24°42E 203 C8
Lovech □ Bulgaria 43°0N 24°45E 203 D8
Loveland Colo., U.S.A. 40°24N 105°5W 304 F11
Loveland Ohio, U.S.A. 39°16N 84°16W 311 E12
Lovell U.S.A. 44°50N 108°24W 304 D9
Lovelock U.S.A. 40°11N 118°28W 304 F4
Lóvere Italy 45°49N 10°4E 198 C7
Lovers Leap Jamaica 17°52N 77°39W 320 a
Loves Park U.S.A. 42°19N 89°3W 310 B7
Lövestad Sweden 55°40N 13°54E 163 J7
Loviisa Finland 60°28N 26°12E 188 B4
Lovilia U.S.A. 41°8N 92°55W 310 C4
Lovina Indonesia 8°9S 115°1E 231 J18
Loving U.S.A. 32°17N 104°6W 305 K11
Lovington Ill., U.S.A. 39°43N 88°38W 311 E8
Lovington N. Mex., U.S.A. 32°57N 103°21W 305 K12
Lovisa = Loviisa Finland 60°28N 26°12E 188 B4
Lovosice Czechia 50°30N 14°2E 180 A7
Lovran Croatia 45°18N 14°15E 199 C11
Lovrin Romania 45°58N 20°48E 182 E5
Lövstabruk Sweden 60°25N 17°53E 162 D11
Lövstabukten Sweden 60°35N 17°45E 162 D11
Lóvua Lunda Norte, Angola 7°19S 20°12E 265 D4
Lóvua Moxico, Angola 11°33S 23°33E 265 E4
Lóvua ➜ Dem. Rep. of the Congo 6°6S 20°37E 265 D4
Low, L. Canada 52°29N 76°17W 298 B4
Low B. Antigua & B. 17°39N 61°51W 322 b
Low Pt. Australia 32°25S 127°25E 279 F4
Low Tatra = Nízké Tatry Slovakia 48°55N 19°30E 181 C12
Lowa Dem. Rep. of the Congo 1°25S 25°47E 268 C2
Lowa ➜ Dem. Rep. of the Congo 1°24S 25°51E 268 C2
Lowden U.S.A. 41°52N 90°56W 310 C6
Lowell Ind., U.S.A. 41°18N 87°25W 311 C9
Lowell Mass., U.S.A. 42°38N 71°19W 313 D13
Lowell Mich., U.S.A. 42°56N 85°20W 311 B11
Lowellville U.S.A. 41°2N 80°32W 312 E4
Löwen = Lewin Brzeski Poland 50°45N 17°37E 185 H4
Löwen ➜ Namibia 26°51S 18°17E 270 C2
Löwenberg = Lwówek Śląski Poland 51°7N 15°38E 185 G2
Löwenstadt = Brzeziny Poland 51°49N 19°42E 185 G6
Lower Alkali L. U.S.A. 41°16N 120°2W 304 F3
Lower Arrow L. Canada 49°40N 118°5W 296 D5
Lower Austria = Niederösterreich □ Austria 48°25N 15°40E 180 C8
Lower B. U.S.A. 40°32N 74°5W 132 C1
Lower California = Baja California Mexico 31°10N 115°12W 318 A1
Lower Don Lands Canada 43°38N 79°21W 141 B2
Lower East Side New York, U.S.A. 132 e1
Lower Glenelg △ Australia 38°4S 141°41E 282 E4
Lower Hutt N.Z. 41°10S 174°55E 284 H3
Lower Kalskag U.S.A. 61°31N 160°22W 303 F7
Lower Lake U.S.A. 38°55N 122°37W 306 G4
Lower Manhattan New York, U.S.A. 132 e1
Lower Manitou L. Canada 49°15N 93°0W 297 D10
Lower Manzanilla Trin. & Tob. 10°31N 61°3W 323 t
Lower New York B. = Lower B. U.S.A. 40°32N 74°5W 132 C1
Lower Paia U.S.A. 20°55N 156°23W 302 C5
Lower Peirce Res. Singapore 1°22N 103°49E 138 A2
Lower Post Canada 59°58N 128°30W 296 B3
Lower Red L. U.S.A. 47°58N 95°0W 308 B6
Lower Saxony = Niedersachsen □ Germany 52°50N 9°0E 178 C4
Lower Tunguska = Tunguska, Nizhnyaya ➜ Russia 65°48N 88°4E 215 C9
Lower Zambezi △ Zambia 15°25S 29°40E 269 F2
Lowestoft U.K. 52°29N 1°45E 169 E9
Lowgar □ Afghan. 34°0N 69°0E 240 B3
Łowicz Poland 52°6N 19°55E 185 F6
Lowly, Pt. Australia 33°0S 137°46E 282 B2
Lowry City U.S.A. 38°8N 93°44W 310 F3
Lowther I. Canada 74°33N 97°30W 295 C12
Lowville U.S.A. 43°47N 75°29W 313 C9
Loxton S. Austral., Australia 34°28S 140°31E 282 C4
Loxton Northern Cape, S. Africa 31°30S 22°22E 270 D3
Loyalton U.S.A. 39°41N 120°14W 306 F6
Loyalty Is. = Loyauté, Îs. N. Cal. 20°50S 166°30E 288 d
Loyang = Luoyang China 34°40N 112°26E 226 G7
Loyauté, Îs. N. Cal. 20°50S 166°30E 288 d
Loyev = Loyew Belarus 51°56N 30°46E 177 C16
Loyew Belarus 51°56N 30°46E 177 C16
Loyola Univ. U.S.A. 42°0N 87°39W 119 B3
Loyoro Uganda 3°22N 34°14E 268 B3
Lož Slovenia 45°43N 14°30E 199 C11
Lozère □ France 44°35N 3°30E 174 D7
Loznica Serbia 44°32N 19°12E 202 B3
Lozova Ukraine 49°0N 36°20E 189 H9
Ltalaltuma ⊛ Australia 23°57S 132°25E 278 D5
Lu India 26°58N 95°14E 241 B5
Lü Shan China 29°30N 115°55E 229 C10
Lü Shan △ China 29°26N 115°52E 229 C10
Lu Verne U.S.A. 42°55N 94°5W 310 B2
Lu Wo China 22°33N 114°6E 219 a
Lu Xun, Tomb of China 31°17N 121°29E 138 B1
Lu Xun Museum Beijing, China 114 b1
Lu Xun Park China 31°17N 121°28E 138 B1
Lua ➜ Dem. Rep. of the Congo 2°46N 18°26E 264 B3
Lua Makiki U.S.A. 20°33N 156°37W 302 C5
Luachimo Angola 7°23S 20°48E 265 D4
Luacono Angola 11°15S 21°37E 265 E4
Luajan ➜ India 24°44N 85°1E 243 G11
Lualaba □ Dem. Rep. of the Congo 9°30S 23°0E 265 D4
Lualaba ➜ Dem. Rep. of the Congo 0°26N 25°20E 264 B5
Luale Dem. Rep. of the Congo 1°9N 23°5E 264 B4
Luambe △ Zambia 12°30S 32°15E 269 E3
Luampa Zambia 15°4S 24°20E 265 F4
Lu'an China 31°45N 116°29E 229 B11
Luan Chau Vietnam 21°38N 103°24E 228 G4
Luan He ➜ China 39°20N 119°5E 227 E10
Luan Xian China 39°40N 118°40E 227 E10
Luancheng Guangxi Zhuangzu, China 22°48N 108°55E 228 F7
Luancheng Hebei, China 37°53N 114°40E 226 F8
Luanco Spain 43°37N 5°48W 194 B5
Luanda Angola 8°50S 13°15E 265 D2
Luando ➜ Angola 10°21S 16°27E 265 E3
Luando △ Angola 11°0S 17°32E 265 E3
Luang, Doi Thailand 18°30N 101°15E 236 C3
Luang, Thale Thailand 7°30N 100°15E 237 J3
Luang Nam Tha Laos 20°58N 101°30E 228 G3
Luang Prabang Laos 19°52N 102°10E 228 H4
Luanginga ➜ Zambia 15°11S 22°55E 265 F4
Luangwa Zambia 15°35S 30°16E 269 F3
Luangwa ➜ Zambia 14°25S 30°25E 269 E3
Luangwa Valley Zambia 13°30S 31°30E 269 E3
Luangwe = Loange ➜ Dem. Rep. of the Congo 4°17S 20°2E 265 C4
Luania-Bubi Dem. Rep. of the Congo 7°28S 24°49E 265 D4
Luanne China 40°55N 117°40E 227 D9
Luanping China 40°53N 117°23E 227 D9
Luanshya Zambia 13°3S 28°28E 269 E2
Luapula □ Zambia 11°0S 29°0E 269 E2
Luapula ➜ Africa 9°26S 28°33E 269 D2
Luar, Danau Indonesia 0°55N 112°15E 235 B4
Luarca Spain 43°32N 6°32W 194 B4
Luashi Dem. Rep. of the Congo 10°50S 23°36E 265 E4
Luatamba Angola 12°6S 20°19E 265 E4
Luatira Angola 12°52S 17°14E 265 E3
Luau Angola 10°40S 22°10E 265 E4
Luba Phil. 17°19N 120°42E 232 C3
Lubaczów Poland 50°10N 23°8E 185 H10
Lubalo Angola 9°10S 19°15E 265 D3
Lubamiti Dem. Rep. of the Congo 2°28S 17°47E 264 C3
Lubań Poland 51°5N 15°15E 185 G2
Lubana, Ozero = Lubānas Ezers Latvia 56°45N 27°0E 188 D4
Lubānas Ezers Latvia 56°45N 27°0E 188 D4
Lubang Phil. 13°52N 120°7E 232 E3
Lubang Is. Phil. 13°50N 120°12E 232 E3
Lubango Angola 14°55S 13°30E 265 E2
Lubao Dem. Rep. of the Congo 5°17S 25°42E 265 D5
Lubao Phil. 14°56N 120°36E 232 D3
Lübars Germany 52°37N 13°21E 115 A3
Lubartów Poland 51°28N 22°42E 185 G9
Lubawa Poland 53°30N 19°48E 184 E6
Lübbecke Germany 52°18N 8°37E 178 C4
Lübben Germany 51°56N 13°54E 178 D9
Lübbenau Germany 51°52N 13°57E 178 D9
Lubbock U.S.A. 33°35N 101°51W 314 E4
Lübeck Germany 53°52N 10°40E 178 B6
Lübecker Bucht Germany 54°3N 10°54E 178 A6
Lubefu Dem. Rep. of the Congo 4°47S 24°27E 265 C4
Lubefu ➜ Dem. Rep. of the Congo 4°10S 23°0E 265 C4
Lubelskie □ Poland 51°20N 22°50E 185 G9
Lüben = Lubin Poland 51°24N 16°11E 185 G3
Lubero = Luofu Dem. Rep. of the Congo 0°10S 29°15E 268 C2
Luberon ⌓ France 43°52N 5°25E 175 E9
Lubersac France 45°26N 1°23E 174 C5
Lubicon L. Canada 56°23N 115°56W 296 B5
Lubień Kujawski Poland 52°23N 19°9E 185 F6
Lubilash ➜ Dem. Rep. of the Congo 6°2S 23°45E 265 D4
Lubin Poland 51°24N 16°11E 185 G3
Lublin Poland 51°12N 22°38E 185 G9
Lubliniec Poland 50°43N 18°45E 185 H5
Lubnān = Lebanon ■ Asia 34°0N 36°0E 250 E7
Lubnān, Jabal Lebanon 33°45N 35°40E 250 E6
Lubniewice Poland 52°31N 15°15E 185 F2
Lubny Ukraine 50°3N 32°58E 189 G7
Lubomierz Poland 51°1N 15°31E 185 G2
Luboń Poland 52°21N 16°51E 185 F3
Lubondaie Dem. Rep. of the Congo 8°1S 26°32E 265 D4
Lubongola Dem. Rep. of the Congo 2°35S 27°50E 268 C2
L'ubotín Slovakia 49°17N 20°53E 181 B13
Lubraniec Poland 52°33N 18°50E 185 F5
Lubsko Poland 51°45N 14°57E 185 G1
Lübtheen Germany 53°18N 11°5E 178 B7
Lubuagan Phil. 17°21N 121°10E 232 C3
Lubudi Dem. Rep. of the Congo 6°51S 21°18E 265 D4
Lubudi ➜ Kasai-Occ., Dem. Rep. of the Congo 4°19S 20°23E 265 C4
Lubudi ➜ Katanga, Dem. Rep. of the Congo 9°0S 25°35E 265 D5
Lubuklinggau Indonesia 3°15S 102°55E 234 C2
Lubukpakam Indonesia 3°33N 98°52E 234 B1
Lubuksikaping Indonesia 0°10N 100°15E 234 B2
Lubumbashi Dem. Rep. of the Congo 11°40S 27°28E 269 E2
Lubunda Dem. Rep. of the Congo 5°12S 26°41E 265 D5
Lubungu Zambia 14°35S 26°24E 269 E2
Lubuskie □ Poland 52°10N 15°20E 185 F2
Lubutu Dem. Rep. of the Congo 0°45S 26°30E 268 C2
Lubyanka Moscow, Russia 129 a2
Luc-en-Diois France 44°36N 5°28E 175 D9
Lucala Angola 9°7S 15°58E 265 D3
Lucala ➜ Angola 9°38S 14°14E 265 D2
Lucan Ont., Canada 43°11N 81°24W 312 C3
Lucan Dublin, Ireland 53°22N 6°28W 166 C5
Lucania, Mt. Canada 61°1N 140°27W 294 E3
Lucapa Angola 8°25S 20°45E 265 D4
Lucas U.S.A. 41°2N 93°29W 310 C3
Lucas Channel = Main Channel Canada 45°21N 81°45W 312 A3
Lucban Phil. 14°6N 121°33E 232 D3
Lucca Italy 43°50N 10°29E 198 E7
Lucé France 48°26N 1°27E 172 D8
Luce Bay U.K. 54°45N 4°48W 167 G4
Lucea Jamaica 18°27N 78°10W 320 a
Lucedale U.S.A. 30°56N 88°35W 315 F10
Lucena Phil. 13°56N 121°37E 232 E3
Lucena Spain 37°27N 4°31W 195 H6
Lučenec Slovakia 48°18N 19°42E 181 C12
Lucera Italy 41°30N 15°20E 201 A8
Lucerne = Lake Worth U.S.A. 26°37N 80°3W 317 J9
Lucerne = Luzern Switz. 47°3N 8°18E 179 H4
Lucerne U.S.A. 39°6N 122°48W 306 F4
Lucerne Valley U.S.A. 34°27N 116°57W 307 L10
Luchena ➜ Spain 37°44N 1°50W 197 H3
Lucheng China 36°20N 113°11E 226 F7
Lucheringo ➜ Mozam. 11°43S 36°17E 269 E4
Luchow = Luzhou China 28°52N 105°20E 228 C5
Lüchow Germany 52°58N 11°8E 178 C7
Luchu Taiwan 22°52N 120°15E 225 D2
Luchuan China 22°21N 110°12E 229 F8
Lucia U.S.A. 36°2N 121°33W 306 J5
Luciara Brazil 10°45S 50°34W 333 D1
Lucie ➜ Suriname 3°35N 57°38W 329 C6
Lucinda Australia 18°32S 146°20E 280 B4
Lucindale Australia 36°58S 140°26E 282 D4
Lucira Angola 14°0S 12°35E 265 E2
Luciras, B. das Angola 13°52S 12°31E 265 E2
Luckau Germany 51°50N 13°42E 178 D9
Luckenwalde Germany 52°5N 13°10E 178 C9
Luckey U.S.A. 41°27N 83°29W 311 C13
Luckhoff S. Africa 29°44S 24°43E 270 C3
Lucknow Ont., Canada 43°57N 81°31W 312 C3
Lucknow India 26°50N 81°0E 243 F9
Luçon France 46°28N 1°10W 174 B2
Lucusse Angola 12°32S 20°48E 265 E4
Lucy, L. U.S.A. 28°34N 81°29W 133 A2
Lüda = Dalian China 38°50N 121°40E 227 E11
Luda Kamchiya ➜ Bulgaria 43°3N 27°29E 203 C11
Ludbreg Croatia 46°15N 16°38E 199 B13
Lüdenscheid Germany 51°13N 7°37E 178 D3
Lüderitz Namibia 26°41S 15°8E 270 C2
Lüderitzbaai Namibia 26°36S 15°8E 270 C2
Ludhiana India 30°57N 75°56E 242 D6
Ludian China 27°10N 103°33E 228 D4
Luding Qiao China 29°53N 102°12E 228 C4
Lüdinghausen Germany 51°46N 7°27E 178 D3
Ludington U.S.A. 43°57N 86°27W 308 D10
Ludlow Shrops., U.K. 52°22N 2°42W 169 E5
Ludlow Calif., U.S.A. 34°43N 116°10W 307 L10
Ludlow Pa., U.S.A. 41°43N 78°56W 312 E6
Ludlow Vt., U.S.A. 43°24N 72°42W 313 C12
Ludowici U.S.A. 31°43N 81°45W 316 D8
Luduș Romania 46°29N 24°5E 183 D9
Ludvika Sweden 60°8N 15°14E 162 D9
Ludwigsburg Germany 48°53N 9°11E 179 G5
Ludwigsfelde Germany 52°17N 13°17E 178 C9
Ludwigshafen Germany 49°29N 8°26E 179 F4
Ludwigslust Germany 53°19N 11°30E 178 B7
Ludza Latvia 56°32N 27°43E 188 D4
Lue Australia 32°38S 149°50E 283 B8
Luebo Dem. Rep. of the Congo 5°21S 21°23E 265 D4
Lueki Dem. Rep. of the Congo 3°20S 25°48E 264 C5
Luena Angola 12°13S 19°51E 265 E3
Luena Dem. Rep. of the Congo 9°28S 25°43E 269 D2
Luena Zambia 10°40S 30°25E 269 E3
Luena ➜ Angola 12°30S 22°34E 265 E4
Luena ➜ Zambia 14°46S 23°30E 265 E4
Luena Flats Zambia 14°47S 23°17E 265 E4
Luengué ⌓ Angola 16°55S 19°55E 265 F3
Luenha = Ruenya ➜ Africa 16°24S 33°48E 269 F3
Luepa Venezuela 5°43N 61°31W 329 B5
Lueta ➜ Dem. Rep. of the Congo 7°4S 21°40E 265 D4
Luete ➜ Zambia 15°46S 23°10E 265 F4
Lüeyang China 33°22N 106°10E 228 A6
Lufeng Guangdong, China 22°57N 115°38E 229 F10
Lufeng Yunnan, China 25°0N 102°5E 228 E4
Lufico Angola 6°24S 13°23E 265 D2
Lufira ➜ Dem. Rep. of the Congo 9°30S 27°0E 269 D2
Lufkin U.S.A. 31°21N 94°44W 314 F7
Lufupa Dem. Rep. of the Congo 10°37S 24°56E 265 E4
Luga Russia 58°40N 29°55E 188 C5
Luga ➜ Russia 59°40N 28°18E 188 C5
Lugang = Lukang Taiwan 24°1N 120°22E 225 B2
Lugano Switz. 46°1N 8°57E 179 J4
Lugano, L. di Switz. 46°0N 9°0E 198 C6
Lugansk = Luhansk Ukraine 48°38N 39°15E 189 H10
Luganville Vanuatu 15°27S 167°10E 287 E5
Lugard's Falls Kenya 3°6S 38°41E 268 C4
Lugela Mozam. 16°25S 36°43E 269 F4
Lugenda ➜ Mozam. 11°25S 38°33E 269 E4
Lugh = Luuq Somalia 3°48N 42°34E 267 D5
Lugina e Valbonës △ Albania 42°27N 19°53E 202 D3
Lugnaquilla Ireland 52°58N 6°28W 166 D5
Lugnvik Sweden 62°56N 17°55E 162 B11
Lugo Italy 44°25N 11°54E 199 D8
Lugo Spain 43°2N 7°35W 194 B3
Lugo □ Spain 43°0N 7°30W 194 C3
Lugoj Romania 45°42N 21°57E 182 E6
Lugovoy = Qulan Kazakhstan 42°55N 72°43E 214 E8
Lugu = Luku Taiwan 23°44N 120°45E 225 C2
Lugus I. Phil. 5°41N 120°50E 233 J3
Luhansk Ukraine 48°38N 39°15E 189 H10
Luhansk □ Ukraine 49°10N 38°40E 189 H10
Luhe China 32°19N 118°50E 229 A12
Luhe ➜ Germany 53°23N 10°13E 178 B6
Luhit ➜ India 27°48N 95°28E 241 B5
Luhu China 23°9N 113°16E 121 B2
Luhuo China 31°21N 100°48E 228 B3
Lui ➜ Angola 8°21S 17°33E 265 D3
Lui ➜ Zambia 16°18S 23°17E 265 F4
Luia Angola 8°10S 21°32E 265 D4
Luia ➜ Angola 8°32S 21°47E 265 D4
Luiana Angola 17°25S 22°59E 265 F4
Luiana ➜ Angola 17°24S 23°3E 265 F4
Luiana △ Angola 16°55S 22°20E 265 F4
Luichow = Liuzhou China 24°22N 109°22E 228 E7
Luichow Pen. = Leizhou Bandao China 21°0N 110°0E 228 G7
Luikuei Taiwan 23°0N 120°38E 225 D2
Luilaka ➜ Dem. Rep. of the Congo 0°52S 20°12E 264 C4
Luimneach = Limerick Ireland 52°40N 8°37W 166 D3
Luing U.K. 56°14N 5°39W 167 E3
Luino Italy 45°59N 8°44E 198 C5
Luío ➜ Angola 13°17S 21°37E 265 E4
Luís Correia Brazil 3°0S 41°35W 332 B3
Luís Gonçalves Brazil 5°37S 50°25W 333 C1
Luitpold Coast Antarctica 78°30S 32°0W 151 D1
Luiza Dem. Rep. of the Congo 7°40S 22°30E 265 D4
Luizi Dem. Rep. of the Congo 6°0S 27°25E 268 D2
Luján Argentina 34°45S 59°5W 334 C4
Lujiang China 31°20N 117°15E 229 B11
Luk Chau = George I. Hong Kong, China 22°13N 114°7E 122 B2
Lukang Taiwan 24°1N 120°22E 225 B2
Lukanga Bandundu, Dem. Rep. of the Congo 1°41S 18°9E 264 C3
Lukanga Équateur, Dem. Rep. of the Congo 1°0S 18°6E 264 C3
Lukanga Swamp Zambia 14°30S 27°40E 269 E2
Lukavac Bos.-H. 44°33N 18°32E 182 F3
Lukenie ➜ Dem. Rep. of the Congo 3°0S 18°50E 264 C3
Lŭki Bulgaria 41°50N 24°43E 203 E8
Lukk Libya 32°1N 24°46E 258 B4
Lukla Nepal 27°42N 86°43E 243 F12
Lukolela Équateur, Dem. Rep. of the Congo 1°10S 17°12E 264 C3
Lukolela Kasai-Or., Dem. Rep. of the Congo 5°23S 24°32E 265 D4
Lukosi Zimbabwe 18°30S 26°30E 269 F2
Lukovë Albania 39°59N 19°54E 202 G3
Lukovit Bulgaria 43°13N 24°11E 203 C8
Łuków Poland 51°55N 22°23E 185 G9
Lukoyanov Russia 55°2N 44°29E 190 C7
Luksefjell Norway 59°23N 9°34E 164 E6
Luku Taiwan 23°44N 120°45E 225 C2
Lukula Dem. Rep. of the Congo 5°31S 14°32E 265 D2
Lukulu Zambia 14°23S 23°15E 265 E4
Lukuni Dem. Rep. of the Congo 5°50S 17°16E 265 D3
Lukusuzi △ Zambia 12°43S 32°36E 269 E3
Lula Dem. Rep. of the Congo 5°22S 16°2E 265 D3
Lülang Shan China 38°0N 111°15E 226 F6
Luleå Sweden 65°35N 22°10E 160 D20
Luleälven ➜ Sweden 65°35N 22°10E 160 D20
Lüleburgaz Turkey 41°23N 27°22E 203 E11
Luliang China 25°0N 103°40E 228 E4
Lulima Dem. Rep. of the Congo 4°12S 25°36E 268 C2
Luling U.S.A. 29°41N 97°39W 314 G6
Lulong China 39°53N 118°51E 227 E10
Lulonga ➜ Dem. Rep. of the Congo 1°0N 18°10E 264 B3
Lulu U.S.A. 30°7N 82°29W 316 E7
Lulu ➜ Dem. Rep. of the Congo 1°18N 23°42E 264 B4
Lulua ➜ Dem. Rep. of the Congo 4°30S 20°30E 265 C4
Luluabourg = Kananga Dem. Rep. of the Congo 5°55S 22°18E 265 D4
Luma Amer. Samoa 14°16S 169°33W 302 f
Lumai Angola 13°13S 21°25E 265 E4
Lumajang Indonesia 8°8S 113°13E 235 D4
Lumaku, Gunong Malaysia 4°52N 115°38E 235 B5
Lumār Iran 33°33N 46°49E 213 F12
Lumbala ➜ Angola 12°39S 22°35E 265 E4
Lumbala Kaquengue Angola 12°39S 22°34E 265 E4
Lumbala N'guimbo Angola 14°18S 21°18E 265 E4
Lumbe ➜ Zambia 16°44S 23°41E 265 F4
Lumber City U.S.A. 31°56N 82°41W 316 D7
Lumberton N.C., U.S.A. 34°37N 79°0W 315 D15
Lumberton Tex., U.S.A. 30°16N 94°12W 314 F7
Lumbis Indonesia 4°18N 116°15E 235 B5
Lumding India 25°46N 93°10E 241 C4
Lumi Papua N. G. 3°30S 142°2E 286 B2
Lumiar Portugal 38°46N 9°10W 126 A2
Lumière, Côte de France 46°50N 2°10W 172 F4
Lumpkin U.S.A. 32°3N 84°48W 316 C5
Lumsden Sask., Canada 50°39N 104°52W 297 C8
Lumsden N.Z. 45°44S 168°27E 285 F3
Lumut Malaysia 4°13N 100°37E 237 K3
Lumut, Tanjung Indonesia 3°50S 105°58E 234 C3
Lumwana Zambia 11°50S 25°8E 269 E2
Luna India 23°43N 69°16E 242 H3
Luna Apayao, Phil. 18°18N 121°21E 232 B3
Lunan China 24°40N 103°18E 228 E4
Lunavada India 23°8N 73°37E 242 H5
Lunbei = Lunpei Taiwan 24°45N 120°21E 225 C2
Lunca Romania 47°22N 25°1E 183 C10
Lunca Corbului Romania 44°42N 24°45E 183 F9
Lund Sweden 55°44N 13°12E 163 J7
Lunda Norte □ Angola 8°0S 20°0E 265 D4
Lunda Sul □ Angola 10°0S 20°0E 265 E4
Lundamo Norway 63°9N 10°19E 164 A7
Lundazi Zambia 12°20S 33°7E 269 E3
Lunde Sweden 62°53N 17°51E 162 B11
Lundenburg = Břeclav Czechia 48°46N 16°53E 181 C9
Lunderskov Denmark 55°29N 9°19E 163 J3
Lundi ➜ Zimbabwe 21°43S 32°34E 269 G3
Lundtofte Denmark 55°47N 12°32E 118 A3
Lundu Malaysia 1°40N 109°50E 235 B3
Lundy U.K. 51°10N 4°41W 169 F3
Lune ➜ U.K. 54°0N 2°51W 168 C5
Lüneburg Germany 53°15N 10°24E 178 B6
Lüneburg Heath = Lüneburger Heide Germany 53°10N 10°12E 178 B6
Lüneburger Heide Germany 53°10N 10°12E 178 B6
Lunel France 43°39N 4°9E 175 E8
Lünen Germany 51°37N 7°32E 178 D3
Lunenburg Canada 44°22N 64°18W 299 D7
Lunéville France 48°36N 6°30E 173 D13
Lung Kwu Chau Hong Kong, China 22°23N 113°53E 122 A1
Lung Kwu Tan Hong Kong, China 22°23N 113°55E 122 A1
Lung Mei Hong Kong, China 22°23N 114°15E 122 A3
Lunga Dem. Rep. of the Congo 5°46S 12°14E 265 C4
Lunga ➜ Zambia 14°34S 26°25E 269 E2
Lunga Lunga Kenya 4°33S 39°7E 268 C4
Lungchin Taiwan 24°12N 120°31E 225 B2
Lunge Angola 12°13S 16°7E 265 E3
Lungga Solomon Is. 9°25S 160°3E 287 M11
Lungi S. Leone 8°40N 13°17W 262 D2
Lunglei India 22°55N 92°45E 241 D4
Lungngo Burma 21°57N 93°36E 241 E4
Lung'tan Taiwan 24°52N 121°12E 225 B3
Lungwebungu ➜ Zambia 14°19S 23°14E 265 E4
Luni India 26°0N 73°6E 242 G5
Luni ➜ India 24°41N 71°14E 242 G4
Luninets = Luninyets Belarus 52°15N 26°50E 177 B14
Luning U.S.A. 38°30N 118°11W 304 G4
Lunino Russia 53°38N 45°18E 190 D7
Luninyets Belarus 52°15N 26°50E 177 B14
Lunkaransar India 28°29N 73°44E 242 E5
Lunner Norway 60°19N 10°35E 164 D7
Lunpei Taiwan 24°45N 120°21E 225 C2
Lunsar S. Leone 8°41N 12°32W 262 D2
Lunsemfwa ➜ Zambia 14°54S 30°12E 269 E3
Lunsemfwa Falls Zambia 14°30S 29°6E 269 E2
Luntai China 41°46N 84°14E 217 D10
Luo He ➜ China 34°35N 110°20E 226 G6
Luocheng China 24°48N 108°53E 228 E7
Luochuan China 35°45N 109°26E 226 G5
Luoci China 25°19N 102°18E 228 E4
Luodian China 25°24N 106°43E 228 E6
Luoding China 22°45N 111°40E 229 F8
Luodong = Lotung Taiwan 24°41N 121°46E 225 B3
Luofu Dem. Rep. of the Congo 0°10S 29°15E 268 C2
Luohe China 33°32N 114°2E 226 H8
Luojiang Guangdong, China 23°5N 113°17E 121 B2
Luojiang Sichuan, China 31°18N 104°33E 228 B5
Luonan China 34°5N 110°10E 226 G6
Luoning China 34°35N 111°40E 226 G6
Luoshan China 32°13N 114°30E 229 A10
Luotian China 30°46N 115°22E 229 B10
Luoxiao Shan China 26°30N 114°1E 229 D10

Luoyang China 34°40N 112°26E **226** G7
Luoyuan China 26°28N 119°30E **229** F12
Luozi Dem. Rep. of the Congo 4°54S 14°0E **265** C2
Luozigou China 43°42N 130°18E **227** C16
Lupeni Romania 45°21N 23°13E **183** E8
Lupilichi Mozam. 11°47S 35°13E **269** E4
Lupire Angola 14°36S 19°20E **185** J9
Lupon Phil. 6°54N 126°3E **233** H7
Luputa Dem. Rep. of the Congo 7°7S 23°43E **265** D4
Luqa Malta 35°52N 14°29E **206** F7
Luquan Hebei, China 38°4N 114°17E **226** E8
Luquan Yunnan, China 25°35N 102°52E **228** E3
Luque Paraguay 25°19S 57°25W **334** B4
Luquembo Angola 10°44S 17°43E **265** G3
Luquillo Puerto Rico 18°23N 65°43W **321** b
Luquillo, Sierra de
    Puerto Rico 18°20N 65°47W **321** b
Lúras Italy 40°56N 9°10E **200** B2
Luray U.S.A. 38°40N 78°28W **309** F14
Lure France 47°40N 6°30E **173** E13
Luremo Angola 8°30S 17°50E **265** D3
Lurës △ Albania 41°47N 20°11E **202** E4
Lurgan U.K. 54°27N 6°20W **166** B5
Luribay Bolivia 17°6S 67°39W **330** D4
Lurín Peru 12°17S 76°52W **330** C2
Lúrio Mozam. 13°32S 40°30E **269** E5
Lusaka Zambia 15°28S 28°16E **269** F2
Lusaka ☐ Zambia 15°30S 29°0E **269** F2
Lusambo
    Dem. Rep. of the Congo 4°58S 23°28E **265** C4
Lusancay Is. and Reefs
    Papua N. G. 8°30S 150°30E **286** b
Lusangaye
    Dem. Rep. of the Congo 4°54S 26°0E **265** C5
Lusenga Plain △ Zambia 9°22S 29°14E **269** D2
Lusengo
    Dem. Rep. of the Congo 1°47N 19°31E **264** B3
Lushan Henan, China 33°45N 112°55E **226** H7
Lushan Sichuan, China 30°12N 102°52E **228** B4
Lushi China 34°3N 111°3E **226** G6
Lushnjë Albania 40°55N 19°41E **202** F3
Lushoto Tanzania 4°47S 38°20E **268** C4
Lushui China 25°58N 98°44E **228** E2
Lushuihe China 42°31N 127°47E **224** A3
Lüshun China 38°45N 121°15E **227** E11
Lusignan France 46°26N 0°8E **174** B4
Lusigny-sur-Barse France 48°16N 4°15E **173** D11
Lusiye Zambia 15°30S 23°57E **265** F4
Lusk U.S.A. 42°46N 104°27W **304** E11
Luso Portugal 40°23N 8°23W **194** E2
Lussac-les-Châteaux
    France 46°24N 0°43E **174** B4
Lustenau Austria 47°26N 9°39E **180** D2
Lustheim Germany 48°14N 11°41E **181** A2
Lustrafjorden Norway 61°23N 7°25E **164** C4
Lüt, Dasht-e Iran 31°30N 58°0E **247** D8
Luta = Dalian China 38°50N 121°40E **227** E11
Lütao Taiwan 22°40N 121°30E **225** D3
Lutembo Angola 13°26S 21°16E **265** G4
Lüshun China 38°45N 121°15E **227** E11
Lusignan France 46°26N 0°8E **174** B4
Lutherstadt Wittenberg
    Germany 51°53N 12°39E **178** D8
Luthersville U.S.A. 33°13N 84°45W **316** B5
Luti Solomon Is. 7°14S 157°0E **287** L9
Luton U.K. 51°53N 0°24W **169** F7
Luton ☐ U.K. 51°53N 0°24W **169** F7
Lutong Malaysia 4°28N 114°0E **235** B4
Lutsel K'e Canada 62°24N 110°44W **297** A6
Lutshima →
    Dem. Rep. of the Congo 3°10S 18°56E **265** C3
Lutsk Ukraine 50°50N 25°15E **177** C13
Luttenberg = Ljutomer
    Slovenia 46°31N 16°11E **199** B13
Lutto = Lotta → Europe 68°42N 31°6E **160** B24
Lutuai Angola 12°41S 20°7E **265** E4
Lutz U.S.A. 28°9N 82°28W **317** D12
Lützow Holmbukta
    Antarctica 69°10S 37°30E **151** C4
Lutzputs S. Africa 28°3S 20°40E **270** C3
Luuk Phil. 5°58N 121°18E **233** J4
Luuq Somalia 3°48N 42°34E **267** D5
Luverne Ala., U.S.A. 31°43N 86°16W **316** D3
Luverne Minn., U.S.A. 43°39N 96°13W **308** D5
Luvo Angola 5°51S 14°5E **265** D2
Luvua → Dem. Rep. of the Congo 6°50S 27°0E **265** D5
Luvua →
    Dem. Rep. of the Congo 6°50S 27°30E **268** D2
Luvuvhu → S. Africa 22°25S 31°18E **271** A5
Luwan China 31°12N 121°27E **138** B1
Luwegu → Tanzania 8°31S 37°23E **268** D4
Luwero Uganda 0°50N 32°28E **268** B3
Luwuk Indonesia 0°56S 122°47E **233** E6
Luxembourg Lux. 49°37N 6°9E **170** E6
Luxembourg ☐ Belgium 49°58N 5°30E **170** E5
Luxembourg ■ Europe 49°45N 6°0E **170** E6
Luxembourg ✕ (LUX) Lux. 49°37N 6°12E **170** E6
Luxembourg, Palais de Paris, France 134 c4
Luxeuil-les-Bains France 47°49N 6°24E **173** E13
Luxi Hunan, China 28°20N 110°7E **229** C8
Luxi Yunnan, China 24°40N 103°55E **228** E4
Luxi Yunnan, China 24°27N 98°36E **228** E2
Luxian China 29°9N 105°24E **228** C5
Luxor = El Uqsur Egypt 25°41N 32°38E **256** B3
Luy-de-Béarn → France 43°39N 0°48W **174** E3
Luy-de-France → France 43°39N 0°48W **174** E3
Luyeh Hualien, Taiwan 23°35N 121°32E **225** C3
Luyeh T'aitung, Taiwan 22°55N 121°8E **225** D3
Luyi China 33°50N 115°35E **226** H8
Luykau = Loikaw Burma 19°40N 97°17E **241** F6
Luz Brazil 39°27N 16°17E **201** C9
Luz, Estádio da
    Lisbon, Portugal 38°45N 9°11W **126** A1
Luz-St-Sauveur France 42°53N 0°0 **174** F4
Luza Russia 60°39N 47°10E **186** B8
Luzern Switz. 47°3N 8°18E **179** H4
Luzern ☐ Switz. 47°2N 7°55E **179** H3
Luzhai China 24°29N 109°42E **228** E7
Luzhany Ukraine 48°22N 25°47E **183** D10
Luzhi China 26°12N 105°16E **228** D5
Luzhniki Sports Centre
    Russia 55°43N 37°33E **129** B2
Luzhou China 28°52N 105°20E **228** C5
Luziânia Brazil 16°20S 48°0W **333** E2
Luziânia Brazil 3°28S 42°22W **332** B3
Lužnice → Czechia 49°14N 14°28E **180** C8
Luzon Phil. 16°0N 121°0E **232** C3
Luzon Strait Asia 21°0N 120°40E **229** G13
Luzy France 46°47N 3°58E **173** F10
Luzzi Italy 39°27N 16°17E **201** C9
Lviv Ukraine 49°50N 24°0E **177** D13
Lviv ☐ Ukraine 49°30N 23°45E **177** D12
Lvov = Lviv Ukraine 49°50N 24°0E **177** D13
Lwówek Poland 52°28N 16°10E **181** B9
Lwówek Śląski Poland 51°7N 15°38E **185** G2
Lyakhavichy Belarus 53°2N 26°32E **177** B14
Lyakhovskiye, Ostrova
    Russia 73°40N 141°0E **227** B15
Lyakhovichi =
    Lyakhavichy Belarus 53°2N 26°32E **177** B14
Lyaki = Läki Azerbaijan 40°34N 47°22E **191** K8
Lyal I. Canada 44°57N 81°24W **312** B3
Lyall Mt. N.Z. 45°16S 167°32E **285** F1
Lyallpur = Faisalabad
    Pakistan 31°30N 73°5E **242** D5
Lyaskovets Bulgaria 43°6N 25°44E **203** F10
Lyasnaya → Belarus 52°9N 23°31E **185** F10
Lybster U.K. 58°18N 3°15W **167** C5

Lycabettus Athens, Greece 112 b3
Lycaonia Turkey 38°0N 33°0E **212** D5
Lychen Germany 53°12N 13°18E **178** B9
Lychkova Russia 57°55N 32°24E **188** B7
Lycia Turkey 36°30N 29°30E **205** E11
Lyck = Elk Poland 53°50N 22°21E **184** E9
Lyckebyån → Sweden 56°12N 15°39E **163** H9
Lycksele Sweden 64°38N 18°40E **160** D18
Lycosura Greece 37°20N 22°3E **204** D4
Lydda = Lod Israel 31°57N 34°54E **251** G5
Lyddan I. Antarctica 74°0S 21°0W **151** D2
Lydenburg S. Africa 25°10S 30°29E **271** C5
Lydia Turkey 38°48N 28°19E **205** C10
Lydia → Poland 52°43N 20°26E **185** F7
Lyell I. Canada 52°40N 131°35W **296** C2
Lyell N.Z. 41°48S 172°4E **285** B7
Lyepyel Belarus 54°50N 28°40E **188** E5
Lyford Cay Bahamas 25°2N 77°33W **153** b
Lygnern Sweden 57°30N 12°15E **163** G6
Lykavittos Hill = Lycabettus
    Athens, Greece 112 b3
Lykens U.S.A. 40°34N 76°42W **313** F8
Lyman Ukraine 45°41N 29°45E **183** E14
Lyman Wyo., U.S.A. 41°20N 110°18W **304** F8
Lymanske Ukraine 46°40N 29°58E **183** D14
Lyme B. U.K. 50°42N 2°53W **169** G5
Lyme Regis U.K. 50°43N 2°57W **169** G5
Lymington U.K. 50°45N 1°32W **169** G6
Lyna → Poland 54°37N 21°14E **184** D8
Lynchburg Ohio, U.S.A. 39°15N 83°48W **311** E13
Lynchburg S.C., U.S.A. 34°3N 80°4W **316** A9
Lynchburg Va., U.S.A. 37°25N 79°9W **309** G14
Lynd → Australia 16°28S 143°18E **280** B3
Lynd Ra. Australia 25°30S 149°20E **281** D4
Lynden Ont., Canada 43°14N 80°9W **312** C4
Lynden Wash., U.S.A. 48°57N 122°27W **306** B4
Lynden Pindling Int. ✕ (NAS)
    Bahamas 25°2N 77°28W **153** b
Lyndhurst S. Austral.,
    Australia 30°15S 138°18E **281** E2
Lyndhurst N.J., U.S.A. 40°49N 74°7W **132** B1
Lyndon → Australia 23°29S 114°6E **279** D1
Lyndonville N.Y., U.S.A. 43°20N 78°23W **312** C6
Lyndonville Vt., U.S.A. 44°31N 72°1W **313** B12
Lyngdal Buskerud, Norway 59°54N 9°32E **164** E4
Lyngdal Vest-Agder, Norway 58°8N 7°7E **164** F1
Lyngen Norway 69°45N 20°30E **160** B19
Lyngør Norway 58°38N 9°8E **164** F6
Lynher Reef Australia 15°27S 121°55E **278** C3
Lynn I., U.S.A. 40°3N 84°56W **311** D12
Lynn Mass., U.S.A. 42°28N 70°57W **313** D14
Lynn Canal U.S.A. 58°50N 135°15W **303** G14
Lynn Haven U.S.A. 30°15N 85°39W **316** D6
Lynn Lake Canada 56°51N 101°3W **297** B8
Lynn Woods Res. U.S.A. 42°29N 71°0W **116** A2
Lynne U.S.A. 29°12N 81°55W **317** F8
Lynnville U.S.A. 38°12N 87°18W **311** F9
Lynnwood U.S.A. 47°49N 122°18W **306** C4
Lynton U.K. 51°13N 3°50W **169** F4
Lyntupy Belarus 55°4N 26°23E **188** E4
Lynx L. Canada 62°25N 106°15W **297** A7
Lyon France 45°46N 4°50E **175** C8
Lyon, Gare de Paris, France 134 c5
Lyon St-Exupery ✕ (LYS)
    France 45°44N 5°2E **175** C9
Lyonnais France 45°45N 4°15E **175** C8
Lyons = Lyon France 45°46N 4°50E **175** C8
Lyons Ga., U.S.A. 32°12N 82°19W **316** C7
Lyons Ill., U.S.A. 41°48N 87°49W **119** C2
Lyons Kans., U.S.A. 38°21N 98°12W **308** F4
Lyons N.Y., U.S.A. 43°5N 77°0W **312** C8
Lyons → Australia 25°2S 115°9E **279** E2
Lyons Falls U.S.A. 43°37N 75°22W **313** C9
Lyozna Belarus 55°0N 30°50E **188** E6
Lyra Reef Papua N. G. 1°50S 153°35E **286** A7
Lys = Leie → Belgium 51°2N 3°45E **170** C3
Lýsá nad Labem Czechia 50°11N 14°51E **180** A7
Lysaker Norway 59°54N 10°38E **133** A2
Lysekerselva → Norway 59°54N 10°38E **133** A2
Lysebotn Norway 59°3N 6°37E **164** E3
Lysefjorden Norway 59°0N 6°23E **164** E3
Lysekil Sweden 58°17N 11°26E **163** F15
Lysi Cyprus 35°6N 33°41E **207** E9
Lyskovo Russia 56°0N 45°3E **190** B7
Lysolaje Czechia 50°8N 14°22E **135** B2
Lystrup Denmark 56°14N 10°14E **163** H4
Lysva Russia 58°7N 57°49E **186** C10
Lysvik Sweden 60°1N 13°9E **162** D7
Lysychansk Ukraine 48°55N 38°30E **189** H10
Lytham St. Anne's U.K. 53°45N 3°0W **168** D4
Lyttelton N.Z. 43°35S 172°44E **285** D7
Lytton Canada 50°13N 121°31W **296** C4
Lyuban Russia 59°16N 31°18E **188** C6
Lyubertsy Russia 55°40N 37°51E **188** C9
Lyubim Russia 58°20N 40°39E **188** C11
Lyubiml Ukraine 51°11N 24°4E **185** C13
Lyubotyn Ukraine 50°0N 36°0E **189** H8
Lyubytino Russia 58°50N 33°16E **188** C7
Lyudao = Lütao Taiwan 22°40N 121°30E **225** D3
Lyudinovo Russia 53°52N 34°28E **188** F8

M

M.R. Štefánik, Bratislava ✕ (BTS)
    Slovakia 48°11N 17°9E **181** C10
Ma → Vietnam 19°47N 105°56E **228** H5
Ma, O. el → Algeria 27°45N 7°2W **260** C3
Ma Nam Wat
    Hong Kong, China 22°21N 114°16E **122** A3
Ma On Shan
    Hong Kong, China 22°23N 114°12E **122** A3
Ma On Shan Country Park △
    Hong Kong, China 22°21N 114°14E **122** A2
Ma Wan Hong Kong, China 22°21N 114°3E **122** A2
Ma Wan Channel
    Hong Kong, China 22°21N 114°4E **122** A2
Ma'adaba Jordan 31°43N 35°47E **251** H6
Maafushi Maldives 3°59N 73°27E **272** d
Maakhir Somalia 10°30N 47°30E **267** E4
Ma'ale Adumim
    West Bank 31°46N 35°17E **123** B2
Ma'ale Ha Khamisha
    Israel 31°49N 35°7E **123** B1
Ma'ale Mikhmas
    West Bank 31°52N 35°18E **123** A2
Ma'alot-Tarshiha Israel 33°1N 35°17E **250** B6
Maamba Zambia 17°17S 26°28E **270** A4
Maamba Zambia 32°10N 35°44E **251** H6
Ma'ān Jordan 30°0N 36°0E **251** J7
Ma'ān ☐ Jordan 30°0N 36°0E **251** J7
Maana'oba Solomon Is. 8°17S 160°50E **287** M11
Maanselkä Finland 63°52N 28°32E **160** C23
Ma'anshan China 31°44N 118°29E **229** B12
Maantiekylä Finland 60°20N 25°0E **121** A3
Maarianhamina = Mariehamn
    Finland 60°5N 19°55E **161** F18
Maarifa Iraq 33°15N 44°21E **262** C5
Maarianhamina = Mariehamn
    Finland 60°5N 19°55E **161** F18
Ma'arrat an Nu'mān
    Syria 35°43N 36°43E **250** C7
Maas → Neths. 51°45N 4°32E **170** C4
Maaseik Belgium 51°6N 5°45E **170** C5
Maasin Phil. 5°52N 125°0E **233** G6
Maasin Phil. 10°8N 124°50E **233** F5
Maasmechelen Belgium 50°58N 5°48E **170** D5
Maassluis Neths. 51°56N 4°16E **170** C4
Maave Mozam. 21°4S 34°47E **271** B5

Mababe Depression
    Botswana 18°50S 24°15E **270** A3
Mabaia Angola 7°12S 14°2E **265** D2
Mabalane Mozam. 23°37S 32°31E **271** B5
Mabanga
    Dem. Rep. of the Congo 1°30N 19°6E **264** B3
Mabaruma Guyana 8°10N 59°50W **326** B7
Mabato Pt. Phil. 14°29N 121°3E **127** C2
Mabein Burma 23°29N 96°37E **241** G20
Mabel L. U.S.A. 28°25N 81°32W **133** B1
Mabel L. Canada 50°35N 118°43W **296** C5
Mabenge
    Dem. Rep. of the Congo 3°9S 18°40E **264** C3
Maberly Canada 44°50N 76°32W **313** B8
Mabesi, S. Leone 7°10N 11°42W **262** D2
Mabian China 28°47N 103°37E **228** C4
Mabinay Phil. 9°48N 122°54E **233** G4
Mabirou Congo 1°3S 15°42E **264** C3
Mablethorpe U.K. 53°20N 0°15E **168** D8
Mableton U.S.A. 33°49N 84°35W **316** B5
Mably France 46°5N 4°4E **173** F11
Maboma
    Dem. Rep. of the Congo 2°30N 28°10E **268** B2
Mabonto S. Leone 8°53N 11°50W **262** D2
Maboukou →
    Dem. Rep. of the Congo 3°39S 12°31E **264** C2
Mabouya I. Grenada 12°29N 61°30W **323** q
Mabrouk Mali 19°29N 1°15W **261** B4
Mabrous Niger 21°14N 13°25E **259** D2
Mabuasehube → Botswana 25°5S 21°10E **270** C3
Mabuiag Australia 9°57S 142°11E **280** a
Mac Bac Vietnam 9°46N 106°7E **237** H6
Macachín Argentina 37°10S 63°43W **334** D3
Macaco, Morro do Brazil 22°56S 43°9W **135** B2
Macaé Brazil 22°20S 41°43W **333** F3
Macael Spain 37°20N 2°18W **197** H2
Macaíba Brazil 5°51S 35°21W **332** C4
Macajalar B. Phil. 8°55N 124°39E **233** G5
Macajuba Brazil 12°9S 40°22W **333** D3
McAlester U.S.A. 34°56N 95°46W **314** D7
McAllen U.S.A. 26°12N 98°14W **314** H5
McAlpin U.S.A. 30°8N 82°57W **316** F7
McAlpine L. Canada 66°32N 102°45W **294** D11
Macamic Canada 48°45N 79°0W **298** C4
Macanao, B. de Venezuela 11°2N 64°23W **329** a
Macanao, Pen. de
    Venezuela 11°0N 64°18W **329** a
Macao = Macau China 22°12N 113°33E **229** F9
Macão Portugal 39°35N 7°59W **195** F3
Macapá Brazil 0°5N 51°4W **329** C7
Macapé, Morne Dominica 15°20N 61°20W **323** k
Macará Ecuador 4°23S 79°57W **328** D2
Macarani Brazil 15°33S 40°24W **333** E3
Macarena, Serranía de la
    Colombia 2°45N 73°55W **328** C3
Macarao, Caño →
    Venezuela 9°47N 61°36W **329** B5
Macarthur Australia 38°5S 142°0E **282** E3
McArthur → Australia 15°54S 136°40E **280** B2
McArthur, Port Australia 16°4S 136°23E **280** B2
Macas Ecuador 2°19S 78°7W **328** D2
Macate Peru 8°48S 78°7W **330** C2
Macau Brazil 5°15S 36°40W **332** C4
Macau China 22°12N 113°33E **229** F9
Macaúbas Brazil 13°2S 42°42W **333** D3
Macauley I. Pac. Oc. 30°12S 178°28E **277** G15
Macaya → Colombia 0°59N 72°20W **328** C3
McBride Canada 53°20N 120°19W **296** C4
McCall U.S.A. 44°55N 116°6W **304** D6
McCamey U.S.A. 31°8N 102°14W **314** F3
McCammon U.S.A. 42°39N 112°12W **304** E7
McCarran Int., Las Vegas ✕ (LAS)
    U.S.A. 36°5N 115°9W **124** B2
McCarthy U.S.A. 61°26N 142°56W **303** F12
McCauley I. Canada 53°40N 130°15W **296** C2
McCleary U.S.A. 47°3N 123°16W **306** D3
Macclenny U.S.A. 30°17N 82°7W **316** E7
Macclesfield U.K. 53°15N 2°8W **168** D5
Macclesfield Bank
    S. China Sea 16°0N 114°30E **230** A4
M'Clintock Chan. Canada 72°0N 102°0W **294** C11
McClintock Ra. Australia 18°44S 127°38E **278** C4
McCloud U.S.A. 41°15N 122°8W **306** F4
McCluer I. Australia 11°5S 133°0E **280** A1
McClure U.S.A. 40°42N 77°19W **312** F7
McClure, L. U.S.A. 37°35N 120°16W **306** H6
M'Clure Str. Canada 75°0N 119°0W **295** C8
McClusky U.S.A. 47°29N 100°27W **308** B3
McComb U.S.A. 31°15N 90°27W **315** F9
McConnell Air. → Australia 15°54S 136°40E **280** B2
McCook U.S.A. 40°12N 100°38W **308** E3
McCook Ill., U.S.A. 41°47N 87°49W **119** C2
McCook Nebr., U.S.A. 40°12N 100°38W **308** E3
McCormick U.S.A. 33°55N 82°17W **316** B6
McCreary Canada 50°47N 99°29W **297** C9
McCullough Mt. U.S.A. 35°35N 115°13W **307** K11
McCusker → Canada 55°32N 108°39W **297** B7
McDavid U.S.A. 30°52N 87°19W **316** F2
McDermitt U.S.A. 41°59N 117°43W **304** F5
Macdonald, L. Australia 23°30S 129°0E **278** D4
Macdonald, Mt. Vanuatu 17°36S 168°23E **287** G6
McDonald Is. Ind. Oc. 53°0S 73°0E **273** K6
MacDonnell Ranges
    Australia 23°40S 133°0E **278** D5
McDonough U.S.A. 33°27N 84°9W **316** B5
McDougalls Well
    Australia 31°8S 141°15E **282** A4
Macdonnel L. Canada 52°15N 92°45W **298** B1
Macduff U.K. 57°40N 2°31W **167** D6
Maceda Spain 42°16N 7°39W **194** C3
Macedonia U.K. 41°19N 81°31W **312** E3
Macedonia ■ Europe 41°53N 21°40E **202** E5
Maceió Brazil 9°40S 35°41W **332** C4
Maceira Portugal 39°41N 8°55W **194** F2
Macenta Guinea 8°35N 9°32W **262** D3
Macerata Italy 43°18N 13°27E **199** C10
McFarland U.S.A. 35°41N 119°14W **307** K7
Macfarlane, L. Australia 32°0S 136°40E **282** B2
McGehee U.S.A. 33°38N 91°24W **315** D9
McGill U.S.A. 39°23N 114°47W **304** G6
McGill Univ. Montréal, Canada 130 b1
Macgillycuddy's Reeks
    Ireland 51°58N 9°45W **166** E2
McGrath U.S.A. 62°58N 155°36W **303** E9
McGraw U.S.A. 42°36N 76°8W **313** D8
McGregor U.S.A. 43°1N 91°11W **310** A5
McGregor → Canada 55°10N 122°0W **296** B4
McGregor Ra. Australia 27°0S 142°45E **281** D3
McGuire, Mt. Australia 20°18S 148°23E **280** b
Mach Pakistan 29°50N 67°20E **242** E2
Mâch Kowr Iran 25°48N 61°28E **247** E9
Machacalis Brazil 17°5S 40°45W **333** E3
Machado = Jiparaná →
    Brazil 8°3S 62°52W **334** B5
Machagai Argentina 26°56S 60°2W **334** B3
Machakos Kenya 1°30S 37°15E **268** C4
Machakos ☐ Kenya 1°30S 37°15E **268** C4
Machala Ecuador 3°20S 79°57W **328** D2
Machali Ecuador 1°24S 80°42W **328** D1
Machanga Mozam. 20°59S 35°0E **271** B6
Machattie, L. Australia 24°50S 139°48E **280** C2
Machault France 49°21N 4°29E **173** C11
Machava Mozam. 25°54S 32°28E **271** C5

Machecoul France 47°0N 1°49W **172** B3
MacTier Canada 45°8N 79°47W **312** A5
Macubela Mozam. 16°53S 37°49E **269** F4
Macugnaga Italy 45°58N 7°58E **198** C4
Macuira △ Colombia 12°9N 71°21W **328** A3
Macuje Colombia 0°24N 73°10W **328** C3
Macul Chile 33°30S 70°35W **137** C2
Macumba → Australia 27°52S 137°12E **281** D2
Macuro Venezuela 10°42N 61°55W **329** F9
Macuse Mozam. 17°45S 37°10E **269** F4
Macuspana Mexico 17°46N 92°36W **319** D6
Macusani Peru 14°4S 70°29W **330** C3
Macusse Angola 17°48S 20°23E **265** H4
Macy's on State Street Chicago, U.S.A. 119 C2
Mada → Nigeria 7°59N 7°55E **263** D6
Ma'dabā ☐ Jordan 31°43N 35°47E **251** H6
Madadeni S. Africa 27°43S 30°3E **271** C5
Madadi Chad 18°28N 20°45E **259** E9
Madagali Nigeria 10°56N 13°33E **263** C7
Madagascar ■ Africa 20°0S 47°0E **272** B8
Madagasi → Somalia 0°49N 42°58E **267** D5
Madā in Sālih Si. Arabia 26°46N 37°57E **246** E3
Madakasira India 13°56N 77°16E **245** H3
Madalena Azores 38°32N 28°32W **153** d1
Madama Niger 22°0N 13°40E **259** D2
Madame, I. Canada 45°30N 60°58W **299** C7
Madame Tussaud's London, U.K. 125 a3
Madan Bulgaria 41°30N 24°57E **203** E8
Madanapalle India 13°33N 78°28E **245** H4
Madang Papua N. G. 5°12S 145°49E **286** C3
Madang ☐ Papua N. G. 5°0S 145°30E **286** C3
Madaoua Niger 14°5N 6°27E **263** C6
Madaripur Bangla. 23°19N 90°15E **241** D3
Madauk Burma 17°56N 96°52E **241** G6
Madawaska Canada 45°30N 77°55W **312** A7
Madawaska → Canada 45°27N 76°21W **312** A7
Madaxmaroodi Somalia 2°39N 44°36E **267** D5
Madaya Burma 22°12N 96°10E **241** D6
Madbar South Sudan 6°17N 30°45E **257** F13
Maddalena Italy 41°16N 9°23E **200** A2
Maddalena, Arc Monastero della
    Venice, Italy 142 c2
Maddaloni Italy 41°2N 14°23E **201** A7
Maddela Phil. 16°21N 121°41E **232** C3
Madhab India 12°36N 77°4E **245** H3
Madeira Atl. Oc. 32°50N 17°0W **153** c
Madeira Ohio, U.S.A. 39°11N 84°21W **311** E12
Madeira → Brazil 3°22S 58°45W **329** D6
Madeleine, Îs. de la
    Canada 47°30N 61°40W **299** C7
Madera Chihuahua,
    Mexico 29°12N 108°7W **318** B3
Madera Calif., U.S.A. 36°57N 120°3W **306** J6
Madera Pa., U.S.A. 40°49N 78°26W **312** F6
Madgaon India 15°12N 73°58E **245** G1
Madha India 18°0N 75°30E **244** F2
Madhapura India 26°11N 86°23E **243** F12
Madhepura India 26°11N 86°23E **243** F12
Madhira India 16°55N 80°22E **244** F5
Madhubani India 26°21N 86°7E **243** F12
Madhudaha India 22°30N 88°24E **124** B2
Madhugiri India 13°40N 77°12E **245** H3
Madhumati → Bangla. 22°25N 89°52E **241** D2
Madhupur India 24°16N 86°39E **243** G12
Madhya Pradesh ☐ India 22°50N 78°0E **242** J8
Madhyamgram India 22°41N 88°26E **124** B2
Madidi → Bolivia 12°32S 66°52W **330** C4
Madikeri India 12°30N 75°45E **245** H2
Madikwe ≏ S. Africa 24°38S 26°25E **271** C4
Madill U.S.A. 34°6N 96°46W **314** D6
Madimba Angola 6°36S 14°23E **265** D2
Madimba
    Dem. Rep. of the Congo 4°58S 15°5E **265** D3
Madin Mexico, Mexico 19°32N 99°16W **128** A1
Ma'din Syria 35°45N 39°36E **213** E8
Madin, L. Mexico 19°31N 99°16W **128** A1
Madina Mali 13°25N 8°50W **262** C2
Madinani Ivory C. 9°37N 6°57W **262** D3
Madinat al Malik Khālid al
    Askarīyah Si. Arabia 25°54N 45°31E **246** E5
Madīnat ash Sha'b Yemen 12°50N 45°0E **248** E3
Madīnat al Thawrah
    Syria 35°50N 38°32E **213** E8
Madinat Masdar U.A.E. 24°26N 54°37E **247** E7
Mâdinet Nasr Egypt 30°4N 31°18E **117** A2
Madingo Congo 4°5S 11°25E **264** C2
Madingou Congo 4°10S 13°33E **264** C2
Madison Calif., U.S.A. 38°41N 121°59W **306** G5
Madison Fla., U.S.A. 30°28N 83°25W **316** E7
Madison Ga., U.S.A. 33°36N 83°28W **316** B6
Madison Ind., U.S.A. 38°44N 85°23W **311** F11
Madison Mo., U.S.A. 39°28N 92°13W **310** F4
Madison Nebr., U.S.A. 41°50N 97°27W **308** E6
Madison Ohio, U.S.A. 41°46N 81°3W **312** E3
Madison S. Dak., U.S.A. 44°0N 97°7W **308** C6
Madison Wis., U.S.A. 43°4N 89°24W **310** D7
Madison → U.S.A. 45°56N 111°31W **304** D8
Madison Avenue New York, U.S.A. 132 c2
Madison Heights U.S.A. 37°25N 79°8W **309** G14
Madison Square New York, U.S.A. 132 d2
Madison Square Garden
    New York, U.S.A. 132 c2
Madisonville Ky., U.S.A. 37°20N 87°30W **308** G10
Madisonville Tex., U.S.A. 30°57N 95°55W **314** F7
Madista Botswana 21°15S 25°6E **270** A4
Madiun Indonesia 7°38S 111°32E **235** D4
Madjingo Gabon 1°20N 14°4E **264** B2
Mado Gashi Kenya 0°44N 39°10E **268** B4
Madoc Canada 44°30N 77°28W **312** B7
Madon → France 48°36N 6°6E **173** D13
Madona Latvia 56°53N 26°5E **188** B4
Madonie Italy 37°50N 13°50E **200** E6
Madonna dell' Orto Venice, Italy 142 c2
Madou = Matou Taiwan 23°11N 120°15E **225** C2
Madra Dağı Turkey 39°23N 27°12E **205** B9
Madrakah, Ra's al Oman 19°0N 57°50E **249** D6
Madras = Chennai India 13°8N 80°19E **245** H5
Madras = Tamil Nadu ☐
    India 11°0N 77°0E **245** H3
Madras U.S.A. 44°38N 121°8W **304** D3
Madre, L. U.S.A. 26°0N 97°30W **314** H6
Madre, Sierra Phil. 17°0N 122°0E **232** C3
Madre de Dios ☐ Peru 12°0S 70°0W **330** C3
Madre de Dios → Bolivia 10°59S 66°8W **330** C4
Madre de Dios, I. Chile 50°20S 75°10W **336** D1
Madre del Sur, Sierra
    Mexico 17°30N 100°0W **319** D5
Madre Occidental, Sierra
    Mexico 27°0N 107°0W **318** B3
Madre Oriental, Sierra
    Mexico 25°0N 100°0W **318** C5

Madrid Barajas ✕ (MAD)
    Spain 40°26N 3°34W **127** B2
Madridejos Spain 39°28N 3°33W **195** F7
Madrigal de las Altas Torres
    Spain 41°5N 5°0W **194** D6
Madrona Spain 41°27N 2°1E **114** A1
Madrona, Sierra Spain 38°27N 4°16W **195** G6
Madroñera Spain 39°26N 5°42W **195** F5
Madrusah Libya 24°48N 14°58E **259** D2
Madu Sudan 14°37N 26°4E **257** E2
Madula
    Dem. Rep. of the Congo 0°27N 25°22E **264** B5
Maduo China 1°24S 20°44E **264** C4
Madupi Burma 21°36N 93°27E **241** E4
Madura W. Austral.,
    Australia 31°55S 127°0E **279** F4
Madura Indonesia 7°30S 114°0E **231** G15
Madura, Selat Indonesia 7°30S 113°20E **235** D4
Madura Oya △ Sri Lanka 7°20N 81°10E **245** K5
Madurai India 9°55N 78°10E **245** K4
Madurantakam India 12°30N 79°50E **245** H4
Madzhalis Russia 42°9N 47°47E **191** J8
Mae Chan Thailand 20°9N 99°52E **236** B2
Mae Charim △ Thailand 18°17N 100°59E **236** C3
Mae Hong Son Thailand 19°16N 97°56E **236** C2
Mae Khlong → Thailand 13°24N 100°0E **236** F3
Mae Moei △ Thailand 17°26N 98°7E **236** D2
Mae Phang △ Thailand 19°7N 99°13E **236** C2
Mae Phrik Thailand 17°27N 99°7E **236** D2
Mae Ping △ Thailand 17°37N 98°51E **236** D2
Mae Ramat Thailand 16°58N 98°31E **236** D2
Mae Rim Thailand 18°54N 98°57E **236** C2
Mae Sai Thailand 20°20N 99°55E **236** B2
Mae Sot Thailand 16°43N 98°34E **236** D2
Mae Suai Thailand 19°39N 99°33E **236** C2
Mae Tha Thailand 18°28N 99°8E **236** C2
Mae Tup Res. Thailand 17°52N 98°45E **236** D2
Mae Wa △ Thailand 45°30N 78°0W **312** A7
Mae Wong △ Thailand 15°54N 99°12E **236** E2
Mae Yom △ Thailand 18°43N 100°15E **236** C3
Maebaru Japan 33°33N 130°12E **222** D2
Maebashi Japan 36°24N 139°4E **223** A11
Maella Spain 41°8N 0°7E **196** D5
Maelpaeg L. Canada 48°20N 56°30W **299** C8
Maesawa Japan 35°44N 139°31E **140** A2
Maestra, Sierra Cuba 20°15N 77°0W **320** B4
Maestre di Campo I.
    Phil. 12°56N 121°42E **232** E3
Maetambe, Mt. Solomon Is. 7°3S 157°11E **287** L9
Maevatanana Madag. 16°56S 46°49E **272** B2
Maéwo Vanuatu 15°10S 168°10E **287** E6
Mafadi S. Africa 29°12S 29°21E **271** C4
Mafeking = Mafikeng
    S. Africa 25°50S 25°38E **270** C4
Mafeking Canada 52°40N 101°10W **297** C8
Maféré Ivory C. 5°30N 3°2W **262** D4
Mafeteng Lesotho 29°51S 27°15E **270** C4
Maffra Australia 37°53S 146°58E **283** D7
Mafia I. Tanzania 7°45S 39°50E **268** D4
Mafikeng S. Africa 25°50S 25°38E **270** C4
Mafra Brazil 26°10S 49°55W **335** B6
Mafra Portugal 38°55N 9°20W **195** G1
Mafungabusi Plateau
    Zimbabwe 18°30S 29°8E **269** F2
Magadan Russia 59°38N 150°50E **215** D16
Magadi Kenya 1°54S 36°19E **268** C4
Magadi Rift Valley, Kenya 1°54S 36°19E **268** C4
Magadi, L. Kenya 1°54S 36°19E **268** C4
Magaliesburg S. Africa 26°0S 27°32E **271** C4
Magallanes = Punta Arenas
    Chile 53°10S 71°0W **336** D2
Magallanes ☐ Chile 52°0S 73°0W **336** D2
Magallanes, Estrecho de
    Chile 52°30S 75°0W **336** D2
Magallanes y Antártica Chilena ☐
    Chile 52°30S 75°0W **336** D2
Magaluf Spain 39°29N 2°32E **208** B9
Maganoy = Shariff Aguak
    Phil. 6°51N 124°31E **233** H5
Magaria Niger 13°4N 9°5E **259** F1
Magarida Papua N. G. 10°18S 149°20E **286** F5
Magburaka S. Leone 8°47N 12°0W **262** D2
Magdagachi Russia 53°27N 125°48E **215** D13
Magdalen Is. = Madeleine, Îs. de la
    Canada 47°30N 61°40W **299** C7
Magdalena Argentina 35°5S 57°30W **334** D4
Magdalena Bolivia 13°13S 63°57W **330** C5
Magdalena Lima, Peru 12°5S 77°5W **124** B2
Magdalena N. Mex.,
    U.S.A. 34°7N 107°15W **305** J10
Magdalena ☐ Colombia 10°0N 74°0W **328** B7
Magdalena Colombia 11°6N 74°51W **328** A3
Magdalena, B. Mexico 24°35N 112°0W **318** C2
Magdalena, I. Mexico 24°40N 112°15W **318** C2
Magdalena, Llano de
    Mexico 25°0N 111°25W **318** C2
Magdalena Contreras
    Mexico 19°20N 99°13W **128** C1
Magdalena de Kino
    Mexico 30°38N 110°57W **318** A2
Magdeburg Germany 52°7N 11°38E **178** C7
Magdelaine Cays
    Australia 16°33S 150°18E **280** B5
Magdub Sudan 13°42N 25°5E **257** F2
Magee U.S.A. 31°52N 89°44W **315** F10
Magelang Indonesia 7°29S 110°13E **235** D4
Magellan's Str. = Magallanes,
    Estrecho de Chile 52°30S 75°0W **336** D2
Magelungen Sweden 59°13N 18°4E **139** B2
Magenta Italy 45°28N 8°53E **198** C5
Magenta, L. Australia 33°30S 119°2E **279** F2
Magerøya Norway 71°3N 25°40E **160** A21
Maggea Australia 34°23S 140°2E **282** C4
Maggia → Switz. 46°18N 8°36E **179** J4
Maggia Switz. 46°15N 8°42E **179** H4
Maggiorasca, Mte. Italy 44°33N 9°29E **198** D6
Maggiore, L. Italy 45°57N 8°39E **198** B5
Maggotty Jamaica 18°9N 77°46W **320** a
Maghâgha Egypt 28°38N 30°50E **256** B3
Maghama Mauritania 15°32N 12°57E **262** B2
Maghera U.K. 54°51N 6°41W **166** B5
Magherafelt U.K. 54°45N 6°37W **166** B5
Maghnia Algeria 34°50N 1°43W **261** B4
Maghreb Baghdad, Iraq 33°23N 44°22E **113** A2
Maghreb N. Africa 32°0N 4°0W **254** C3
Maginu Japan 35°35N 139°36E **140** B2
Magione Italy 43°8N 12°12E **199** E9
Magistralnyy Russia 56°16N 107°36E **215** D11
Maglaj Bos.-H. 44°33N 18°7E **182** F3
Magliana Italy 41°50N 12°26E **136** B1
Magliano in Toscana
    Italy 42°36N 11°18E **199** F8
Máglie Italy 40°7N 18°18E **201** B11
Magnac-Laval France 46°13N 1°11E **174** B5
Magnesia = Magnisia
    Greece 39°15N 23°0E **204** B5
Magnetic Pole (North)
    Arctic 85°9N 149°0W **150** A1
Magnetic Pole (South)
    Antarctica 64°8S 138°8E **151** C9
Magnisia Greece 39°15N 23°0E **204** B5
Magnitogorsk Russia 53°27N 59°4E **190** D10
Magnolia Ark., U.S.A. 33°16N 93°14W **314** E8
Magnolia Miss., U.S.A. 31°9N 90°28W **315** F9
Magnor Norway 59°56N 12°15E **164** F6
Magny-en-Vexin France 49°9N 1°47E **173** C8

Magny-les-Hameaux France 48°44N 2°3E 134 B1
Mago Fiji 17°26S 179°8W 287 A3
Mago △ Ethiopia 5°40N 36°18E 257 F4
Magog Canada 45°18N 72°9W 313 A12
Magong = Makung
Taiwan 23°34N 119°34E 225 C1
Magoro Uganda 1°45N 34°12E 268 B3
Magoye Zambia 16°1S 27°30E 269 F2
Magpet Phil. 7°6N 125°6E 233 H5
Magpie, L. Canada 51°0N 64°41W 299 B7
Magrath Canada 49°25N 112°50W 296 D6
Magre → Spain 39°11N 0°25W 197 F4
Magrur Sudan 14°1N 30°27E 257 E3
Magrur, Wadi → Sudan 16°5N 26°30E 257 D2
Magsingal Phil. 17°41N 120°25E 232 C3
Magta Lahjar Mauritania 17°28N 13°17W 262 B2
Magu Tanzania 2°30S 33°30E 268 C3
Maguan China 23°0N 104°21E 228 F5
Maguarinho, C. Brazil 0°15S 48°30W 332 B2
Magude Mozam. 25°2S 32°40E 271 C5
Maguindanao □ Phil. 7°5N 124°40E 233 H5
Magura Bangla. 23°26N 89°26E 241 D2
Magurski △ Poland 49°30N 21°30E 185 J8
Mağusa = Famagusta
Cyprus 35°8N 33°55E 207 E9
Maguse L. Canada 61°37N 95°10W 297 A9
Maguse Pt. Canada 61°20N 93°50W 297 A10
Magvana India 23°13N 69°22E 242 H3
Magway Burma 20°10N 95°0E 241 E5
Magway □ Burma 20°0N 95°0E 241 E5
Magwe South Sudan 4°8N 32°17E 257 G3
Magyarorszag = Hungary ■
Europe 47°20N 19°20E 181 D12
Maha Oya Sri Lanka 7°31N 81°22E 245 L5
Maha Sarakham
Thailand 16°12N 103°16E 236 D4
Mahābād Iran 36°50N 45°45E 213 D11
Mahabaleshwar India 17°58N 73°43E 244 F1
Mahabalipuram India 12°37N 80°11E 245 H5
Mahabharat Lekh Nepal 28°30N 82°0E 243 E10
Mahabo Madag. 20°23S 44°40E 272 C1
Mahad India 18°6N 73°29E 244 E1
Mahaddayweyne Somalia 2°58N 45°32E 267 D6
Mahadeo Hills India 22°20N 78°30E 243 H8
Mahadeopur India 18°48N 80°0E 244 E5
Mahaffey U.S.A. 40°53N 78°44W 312 F6
Mahagi
Dem. Rep. of the Congo 2°20N 31°0E 268 B3
Mahagnao Volcano △
Phil. 10°52N 124°51E 233 F5
Mahaica-Berbice □
Guyana 6°13N 57°51W 329 B6
Mahaicony Guyana 6°36N 57°48W 329 B6
Mahajamba → Madag. 15°33S 47°8E 272 B2
Mahajamba, Helodranon' i
Madag. 15°24S 47°5E 272 B2
Mahajan India 28°48N 73°56E 242 E5
Mahajanga Madag. 15°40S 46°25E 272 B2
Mahajilo → Madag. 19°42S 45°22E 272 B2
Mahakam → Indonesia 0°35S 117°17E 235 C5
Mahalapye Botswana 23°1S 26°51E 270 B4
Mahalaxmi Mumbai, India 130 a1
Mahalchhar Bangla. 22°55N 92°2E 241 D4
Mahale Mts. Tanzania 6°20S 30°0E 268 D3
Mahale Mts. △ Tanzania 6°10S 29°50E 268 D2
Maḩallāt Iran 33°55N 50°30E 247 C6
Māhān Iran 30°5N 57°18E 247 D8
Mahan → India 23°30N 82°50E 243 H10
Mahanadi → India 20°20N 86°25E 244 D8
Mahananda → India 25°12N 87°52E 243 G12
Mahanoro Madag. 19°54S 48°48E 272 B2
Mahanoy City U.S.A. 40°49N 76°9W 313 F8
Mahaplag Phil. 10°35N 124°57E 233 F5
Mahar, L. U.S.A. 25°46N 80°18W 129 D1
Maharashtra □ India 20°30N 75°30E 244 D2
Maharès Tunisia 34°32N 10°29E 258 B2
Maharivo → Madag. 20°26S 44°10E 272 C1
Mahasamund India 21°6N 82°6E 244 D6
Mahasham, W. → Egypt 30°15N 34°10E 251 H5
Mahasoa Madag. 22°12S 46°6E 272 C2
Mahasolo Madag. 19°7S 46°22E 272 B2
Mahattat ash Shīdīyah
Jordan 29°55N 35°55E 251 J6
Mahattat 'Unayzah
Jordan 30°30N 35°47E 251 H6
Mahaut Dominica 15°21N 61°24W 323 k
Mahaut Guadeloupe 16°11N 61°46W 322 e
Mahavavy → Madag. 15°57S 45°54E 272 B2
Mahaweli Ganga →
Sri Lanka 8°27N 81°13E 245 K5
Mahaxay Laos 17°22N 105°12E 236 D5
Mahbubabad India 17°42N 80°2E 244 F5
Mahbubnagar India 16°45N 77°59E 244 F3
Mahd adh Dhahab
Si. Arabia 23°30N 40°52E 248 B3
Mahda U.A.E. 25°20N 56°15E 247 E8
Maḩḑah Oman 24°24N 55°59E 247 E7
Mahdia Guyana 5°13N 59°8W 329 B6
Mahdia Tunisia 35°28N 11°0E 262 A7
Mahdia □ Tunisia 35°20N 10°35E 261 A7
Mahe Jammu & Kashmir,
India 33°10N 78°32E 243 C8
Mahé Puducherry, India 11°42N 75°34E 245 J2
Mahé Seychelles 5°0S 55°30E 277 c
Mahé ✕ (SEZ) Seychelles 4°40S 55°31E 272 c
Mahébourg Mauritius 20°24S 57°42E 272 e
Mahendra Giri India 8°20N 77°30E 245 K3
Mahendragarh India 28°17N 76°14E 242 E7
Mahendranagar Nepal 28°55N 80°20E 243 E9
Mahenge Tanzania 8°45S 36°41E 269 D4
Maheno N.Z. 45°10S 170°50E 285 F5
Mahesana India 23°39N 72°26E 242 H5
Maheshtala India 22°29N 88°15E 124 C1
Maheshwar India 22°11N 75°35E 242 H6
Maheskhali I. Bangla. 21°36N 91°56E 241 E3
Mahgawan India 26°29N 78°37E 243 F8
Mahi → India 22°15N 72°55E 242 H5
Mahia Pen. N.Z. 39°9S 177°55E 284 F6
Mahibadhoo Maldives 3°47N 72°58E 272 d
Mahighe Solomon Is. 8°30S 159°58E 287 M10
Mahikeng = Mafikeng
S. Africa 25°50S 25°38E 270 C4
Mahilyow Belarus 53°55N 30°18E 177 B16
Mahilyow □ Belarus 54°10N 30°50E 188 E6
Mahim Maharashtra, India 19°2N 72°50E 130 A2
Mahim Maharashtra, India 19°39N 72°44E 244 E1
Mahim B. India 19°2N 72°49E 130 A1
Mahina Tahiti 17°30S 149°27W 289 e
Mahipalpur India 28°32N 77°7E 120 B1
Mahirija Morocco 34°0N 3°16W 261 B4
Mahlaing Burma 21°6N 95°39E 241 E5
Mahlsdorf Germany 52°30N 13°37E 115 A4
Mahmiya Sudan 17°12N 33°43E 257 D3
Mahmoodabad Pakistan 24°51N 67°4E 123 A2
Mahmud Kot Pakistan 30°16N 71°0E 242 D4
Mahmudia Romania 45°5N 29°5E 183 E14
Mahmudiye Turkey 39°48N 30°15E 205 B12
Mahmutbey Turkey 41°3N 28°49E 203 E12
Mahmutlar Turkey 36°29N 32°5E 250 B3
Māhneshān Iran 36°44N 47°39E 213 D12
Mahnomen U.S.A. 47°19N 95°58W 308 B6
Maho Sri Lanka 7°49N 80°16E 245 L5
Mahoba India 25°15N 79°55E 243 G8
Mahomet U.S.A. 40°12N 88°24W 311 D8
Mahón = Maó Spain 39°53N 4°16E 206 B5
Mahon, Menorca ✕ (MAH)
Spain 39°50N 4°16E 196 F9
Mahone Bay Canada 44°27N 64°23W 299 D7
Mahongo ⌂ Namibia 18°0S 23°15E 270 B3
Mahopac U.S.A. 41°22N 73°45W 313 E11
Mahoua Chad 11°49N 18°26E 259 F3
Mahrāt, Jabal Yemen 17°0N 51°0E 249 C5
Mahrauli India 28°31N 77°10E 120 B2
Mährisch-Budwitz = Moravské
Budějovice Czechia 49°4N 15°49E 180 B8
Mährisch-Schönberg = Šumperk
Czechia 49°59N 16°59E 181 B9
Mährisch-Trubau = Moravská
Třebová Czechia 49°45N 16°40E 181 B9
Mahul India 19°0N 72°53E 130 A2
Mahuta Nigeria 11°32N 4°58E 263 C5
Mahuva India 21°5N 71°48E 242 J4
Mahya Dağı Turkey 41°47N 27°36E 203 E11
Mai-Ndombe □
Dem. Rep. of the Congo 2°30S 19°0E 264 C3
Mai-Ndombe, L.
Dem. Rep. of the Congo 2°0S 18°20E 264 C3
Mai Thon, Ko Thailand 7°40N 98°28E 237 a
Maia Amer. Samoa 14°13S 169°25W 302 g
Maia Azores 36°56N 25°1W 153 d4
Maia Portugal 41°14N 8°37W 194 D2
Maials Spain 41°22N 0°30E 196 D5
Maibong India 25°18N 93°10E 241 C4
Maicao Colombia 11°23N 72°13W 328 A3
Maîche France 47°16N 6°48E 173 E13
Maici → Brazil 6°30S 61°43W 331 B5
Maicuru → Brazil 2°14S 54°17W 329 D7
Máida Italy 38°51N 16°22E 201 D9
Maida Vale London, U.K. 125 a1
Maidan Khula Afghan. 33°36N 69°50E 242 C3
Maidenhead U.K. 51°31N 0°42W 169 F7
Maidstone Vic., Australia 37°47S 144°52E 128 A1
Maidstone Sask., Canada 53°5N 109°20W 297 C7
Maidstone Kent, U.K. 51°16N 0°32E 169 F8
Maiduguri Nigeria 12°0N 13°20E 263 C7
Maiella △ Italy 42°5N 14°5E 199 F11
Măieruş Romania 45°53N 25°31E 183 E10
Maigatari Nigeria 12°46N 9°27E 263 C6
Maigh Nuad = Maynooth
Ireland 53°23N 6°34W 166 C5
Maignelay Montigny
France 49°32N 2°30E 173 C9
Maigo Phil. 8°10N 123°57E 233 G4
Maigualida, Sierra
Venezuela 5°30N 65°10W 329 B4
Maigudo Ethiopia 7°30N 37°8E 257 F4
Maihar India 24°16N 80°45E 243 G9
Maihara Japan 35°19N 136°17E 223 B8
Maikala Ra. India 22°0N 81°0E 244 D5
Maiko △
Dem. Rep. of the Congo 0°30S 27°50E 268 C2
Mailani India 28°17N 80°21E 243 E9
Mā'ili U.S.A. 21°25N 158°11W 302 K13
Mā'ili Pt. U.S.A. 21°24N 158°11W 302 K13
Mailiao Taiwan 23°48N 120°13E 225 C2
Maillezais France 46°22N 0°45W 174 B3
Mailsi Pakistan 29°48N 72°15E 242 E5
Maimbung Phil. 5°56N 121°2E 233 J3
Main → Bayern, Germany 50°0N 8°18E 179 F4
Main → Antrim, U.K. 54°48N 6°18W 166 B5
Main Channel Canada 45°21N 81°45W 312 A3
Main Range △ Australia 28°11S 152°27E 281 D5
Main Ridge Trin. & Tob. 11°16N 60°40W 323 s
Mainburg Germany 48°38N 11°47E 179 G7
Maindargi India 17°28N 76°18E 244 F3
Maine France 48°20N 0°15W 172 D6
Maine □ U.S.A. 45°20N 69°0W 309 C19
Maine → Ireland 52°9N 9°45W 166 D2
Maine, G. of U.S.A. 43°0N 68°30W 301 G26
Maine-et-Loire □ France 47°31N 0°30W 172 E6
Maïne-Soroa Niger 13°13N 12°2E 263 C7
Maingkaing Burma 24°48N 95°16E 241 C5
Maingkwan Burma 26°15N 96°37E 241 B6
Mainistir na Corann = Midleton
Ireland 51°55N 8°10W 166 E3
Mainit Phil. 9°32N 125°32E 233 G5
Mainit, L. Phil. 9°31N 125°30E 233 G5
Mainland Orkney, U.K. 58°59N 3°8W 167 C5
Mainland Shet., U.K. 60°15N 1°22W 167 A7
Mainpuri India 27°18N 79°4E 243 F8
Maintal Germany 50°7N 8°52E 179 E4
Maintenon France 48°35N 1°35E 173 D8
Maintirano Madag. 18°3S 44°1E 272 B1
Mainz Germany 50°1N 8°14E 179 E4
Maio C. Verde Is. 15°10N 23°10W 153 j
Maipú Argentina 36°52S 57°50W 334 D4
Maipú Santiago, Chile 33°30S 70°45W 137 C1
Maiquetía Venezuela 10°36N 66°57W 328 A4
Máira → Italy 44°49N 7°38E 198 D4
Mairabari India 26°30N 92°22E 241 B4
Mairena del Aljarafe Spain 37°20N 6°6W 195 H4
Mairipotaba Brazil 17°18S 49°28W 333 E2
Maisi Cuba 20°17N 74°9W 321 B5
Maisí, Pta. de Cuba 20°10N 74°10W 321 B5
Maiskhal I. Bangla. 21°36N 91°56E 241 E3
Maison Coloniale
Guadeloupe 16°18N 61°16W 322 e
Maisonneuve, Parc
Canada 45°32N 73°33W 130 A2
Maisons-Alfort France 48°48N 2°26E 134 B2
Maisons-Laffitte France 48°57N 2°8E 134 A1
Maissoneuve Canada 45°32N 73°33W 130 A2
Maitland N.S.W.,
Australia 32°33S 151°36E 283 B9
Maitland S. Austral.,
Australia 34°23S 137°40E 282 C2
Maitland Western Cape,
S. Africa 33°53S 18°29E 118 A1
Maitland → Canada 43°45N 81°43W 312 C3
Maitland, Banjaran
Malaysia 4°55N 116°37E 235 B5
Maitri Antarctica 70°0S 3°0W 151 D3
Maitum Phil. 6°2N 124°30E 233 H5
Maiyema Nigeria 12°5N 4°25E 263 C5
Maiyuan China 25°34N 117°28E 229 E11
Maíz, Is. del Nic. 12°15N 83°4W 320 D3
Maizuru Japan 35°25N 135°22E 223 B7
Majagual Colombia 8°33N 74°38W 328 B3
Majalengka Indonesia 6°50S 108°13E 235 D3
Majanji Uganda 0°16N 34°0E 268 B3
Majari → Brazil 3°29N 60°58W 329 C5
Majdal Libya 25°51N 15°7E 258 C3
Majella = Maiella △ Italy 42°5N 14°5E 199 F11
Majene Indonesia 3°38S 118°57E 235 C5
Majes → Peru 16°40S 72°44W 330 D3
Majete △ Malawi 15°54S 34°34E 269 F3
Majevica Bos.-H. 44°45N 18°50E 182 F3
Maji Ethiopia 6°12N 35°30E 257 F4
Majiang China 26°28N 107°32E 228 D6
Majorca = Mallorca Spain 39°30N 3°0E 206 B4
Major's B. St. Kitts & Nevis 17°14N 62°38W 322 d
Majors Creek Australia 35°33S 149°45E 283 C8
Majuli I. India 26°58N 94°14E 241 B5
Majuriã Brazil 7°30S 64°55W 330 B4
Majuro Marshall Is. 7°9N 171°12E 288 G9
Mak, Ko Thailand 11°49N 102°29E 237 G4
Maka Senegal 13°40N 14°10W 262 C2
Mākaha Hawai'i, U.S.A. 21°29N 158°13W 302 K13
Makaha Zimbabwe 17°20S 32°39E 271 A5
Makahoa Pt. U.S.A. 21°41N 157°56W 302 J14
Makak Cameroon 3°36N 11°0E 263 E7
Makaka Congo 3°45S 13°39E 264 C2
Makakilo City U.S.A. 21°22N 158°5W 302 K13
Makakou Gabon 0°11S 12°12E 264 C2
Makalamabedi Botswana 20°19S 23°51E 270 B3
Makale Indonesia 3°6S 119°51E 235 C5
Makalu Nepal 27°55N 87°8E 243 F12
Makalu-Barun △ Nepal 27°45N 87°10E 243 F12
Makamba Burundi 4°8S 29°49E 268 C2
Makapu'u Pt. U.S.A. 21°19N 157°39W 302 K14
Makarewa Junction N.Z. 46°20S 168°21E 285 G3
Makari Cameroon 12°35N 14°28E 259 F2
Makarikari = Makgadikgadi Salt
Pans Botswana 20°40S 25°45E 270 B4
Makarov Basin Arctic 87°0N 150°0W 150 A
Makarovo Russia 57°40N 107°45E 215 D11
Makarska Croatia 43°20N 17°2E 199 E14
Makaryev Russia 57°52N 43°50E 190 B6
Makasar Indonesia 6°17S 106°52E 122 A2
Makassar Indonesia 5°10S 119°20E 235 D5
Makassar, Selat Indonesia 1°0S 118°20E 235 C5
Makassar, Str. of = Makassar, Selat
Indonesia 1°0S 118°20E 235 C5
Makat = Maqat
Kazakhstan 47°39N 53°19E 187 E9
Makati Phil. 14°33N 121°7E 127 B2
Makaw
Dem. Rep. of the Congo 3°29S 18°20E 264 C3
Makawao U.S.A. 20°52N 156°17W 302 C5
Makaya
Dem. Rep. of the Congo 3°21S 18°1E 264 C3
Makedonija = Macedonia ■
Europe 41°53N 21°40E 202 E5
Makefu Cook Is. 18°59S 169°55W 289 g
Makemo French Polynesia 16°35S 143°40W 289 f
Makeni S. Leone 8°55N 12°5W 262 D2
Makeyevka = Makiyivka
Ukraine 48°0N 38°0E 189 H9
Makgadikgadi △
Botswana 20°27S 24°47E 270 B3
Makgadikgadi Salt Pans
Botswana 20°40S 25°45E 270 B4
Makhachkala Russia 43°0N 47°30E 191 J8
Makhado = Louis Trichardt
S. Africa 23°1S 29°43E 271 B4
Makham, Ao Thailand 7°51N 98°25E 237 a
Makharadze = Ozurgeti
Georgia 41°55N 42°0E 191 K5
Makhfar al Buşayyah Iraq 30°0N 46°10E 246 D5
Makhmūr Iraq 35°46N 43°35E 213 E10
Makhtal India 16°30N 77°31E 245 E3
Makhyah, W. → Yemen 17°40N 49°1E 249 C5
Makian Indonesia 0°20N 127°20E 231 D7
Makira Solomon Is. 9°50S 160°50E 287 M11
Makindu Kenya 2°18S 37°50E 268 C4
Mäkiniitty Finland 60°20N 24°58E 121 A2
Makinka = Makinsk
Kazakhstan 52°37N 70°26E 217 B8
Makinsk Kazakhstan 52°37N 70°26E 217 B8
Makira = San Cristóbal
Solomon Is. 10°30S 161°0E 287 N11
Makiyivka Ukraine 48°0N 38°0E 189 H9
Makkah Si. Arabia 21°30N 39°54E 248 B2
Makkah □ Si. Arabia 21°30N 42°30E 248 B3
Makkovik Canada 55°10N 59°10W 299 A8
Makó Hungary 46°14N 20°33E 182 D5
Mako Senegal 12°52N 12°20W 262 C2
Makogai Fiji 17°28S 179°0E 287 A2
Makok Gabon 0°1S 9°35E 264 C1
Makokou Gabon 0°40N 12°50E 264 B2
Makongo
Dem. Rep. of the Congo 3°25N 26°17E 268 B2
Makoro
Dem. Rep. of the Congo 3°10N 29°59E 268 B2
Makoua Congo 0°5S 15°50E 264 C3
Maków Mazowiecki
Poland 52°52N 21°6E 185 F8
Maków Podhalański
Poland 49°43N 19°45E 185 J6
Makra Greece 36°15N 25°54E 205 E7
Makrai India 22°2N 77°0E 242 H7
Makran Asia 26°13N 61°30E 240 D1
Makran Coast Range
Pakistan 25°40N 64°0E 240 D2
Makrana India 27°2N 74°46E 242 F6
Makrany Belarus 51°48N 24°17E 185 G11
Makri Greece 40°52N 25°40E 203 F9
Makri India 19°46N 81°55E 244 E5
Makrigialos Greece 35°2N 25°59E 207 E6
Makthar Tunisia 35°48N 9°12E 258 A1
Mākū Iran 39°15N 44°31E 213 C11
Mākua U.S.A. 21°32N 158°13W 302 J13
Makueni □ Kenya 1°50S 37°40E 268 C4
Makum India 27°30N 95°23E 241 B5
Makumbi
Dem. Rep. of the Congo 5°50S 20°43E 265 D4
Makunda Botswana 22°30S 20°7E 270 B3
Makung Taiwan 23°34N 119°34E 225 C1
Makungo Somalia 0°49N 42°35E 267 D5
Makunudu Atoll Maldives 6°20N 72°35E 272 d
Makunza
Dem. Rep. of the Congo 8°52S 24°19E 265 D4
Makurazaki Japan 31°15N 130°20E 222 F2
Makurdi Nigeria 7°43N 8°35E 263 D6
Makushin Volcano
U.S.A. 53°53N 166°55W 303 K6
Makūyeh Iran 28°7N 53°9E 247 D7
Makwassie S. Africa 27°17S 26°0E 270 C4
Makwiro Zimbabwe 17°58S 30°25E 271 A5
Mal India 26°51N 88°45E 241 B2
Mâl Mauritania 16°58N 13°23W 262 B2
Mal B. Ireland 52°50N 9°30W 166 D2
Mala = Mallow Ireland 52°8N 8°39W 166 D3
Mala Peru 12°40S 76°38W 330 C2
Mala ✪ Australia 21°39S 130°45E 278 D5
Mala, Pta. Panama 7°28N 80°2W 320 E3
Mala Belozërka Ukraine 47°12N 34°56E 189 J8
Malá Fatra △ Slovakia 49°10N 19°0E 181 B12
Mala Kapela Croatia 44°45N 15°30E 199 D12
Mała Panew → Poland 50°43N 17°54E 185 H4
Malá Strana Czechia 50°4N 14°24E 135 B2
Mala Vyska Ukraine 48°39N 31°36E 189 H6
Malabang Phil. 7°36N 124°3E 233 H5
Malabar N.S.W., Australia 33°58S 151°14E 139 B2
Malabar Fla., U.S.A. 28°0N 80°34W 317 H9
Malabar Coast India 11°0N 75°0E 245 J2
Malabar Hill India 18°57N 72°48E 130 B1
Malabar Pt. India 18°56N 72°48E 130 B1
Malabo = Rey Malabo
Eq. Guin. 3°45N 8°50E 263 E6
Malabon Phil. 14°39N 120°56E 127 B1
Malabrigo = Puerto Chicama
Peru 7°45S 79°20W 330 B2
Malabrigo Pt. Phil. 13°36N 121°15E 232 E3
Malabu Nigeria 9°32N 12°48E 263 D7
Malabuñgan Phil. 9°3N 117°38E 233 G1
Malacañang Palace Phil. 14°35N 120°59E 127 B1
Malacca, Straits of Indonesia 3°0N 101°0E 237 L3
Malacky Slovakia 48°27N 17°0E 181 C10
Malad City U.S.A. 42°12N 112°15W 304 E7
Maladeta Spain 42°39N 0°39E 196 C5
Maladzyechna Belarus 54°20N 26°50E 177 A14
Málaga Colombia 6°42N 72°44W 328 B3
Málaga Spain 36°43N 4°23W 195 J6
Málaga □ Spain 36°38N 4°58W 195 J6
Malagarasi Tanzania 5°5S 30°50E 268 D3
Malagarasi → Tanzania 5°12S 29°47E 268 D2
Malagasy Rep. = Madagascar ■
Africa 20°0S 47°0E 272 B2
Malagón Spain 39°11N 3°52W 195 F7
Malagón → Spain 37°35N 7°29W 195 H3
Malah Syria 32°33N 36°54E 251 F7
Malahide Ireland 53°26N 6°9W 166 C5
Malaimbandy Madag. 20°20S 45°36E 272 C2
Malaita Solomon Is. 9°0S 161°0E 287 M11
Malakal South Sudan 9°33N 31°40E 257 F3
Malakal Harb. Palau 7°19N 134°27E 288 c
Malakanagiri India 18°21N 81°54E 244 E5
Malakand Pakistan 34°40N 71°55E 242 B4
Malakoff France 48°49N 2°18E 134 B2
Malakula Vanuatu 16°15S 167°30E 287 F5
Malakwal Pakistan 32°34N 73°13E 242 C5
Malalag Phil. 6°36N 125°24E 233 H5
Malalaua Papua N. G. 8°4S 146°10E 286 E4
Malam Chad 11°27N 20°59E 259 F4
Malamala Indonesia 3°21S 120°55E 231 E6
Malanda Australia 17°22S 145°35E 280 B4
Malang Indonesia 7°59S 112°45E 235 D4
Malanga Mozam. 13°28S 36°7E 269 E4
Malangas Phil. 7°37N 123°1E 233 H4
Malangen Norway 69°24N 18°37E 160 B18
Malangwa Nepal 26°52N 85°34E 243 F11
Malanje Angola 9°36S 16°17E 265 D3
Malanje □ Angola 9°30S 16°0E 265 D3
Malanut B. Phil. 9°15N 117°59E 233 G1
Malapatan Phil. 5°59N 125°18E 233 J5
Malappuram India 11°7N 76°11E 245 J3
Mälaren Sweden 59°30N 17°10E 162 E11
Malargüe Argentina 35°32S 69°30W 334 D2
Mälarhöjden Sweden 59°18N 17°58E 139 B1
Malartic Canada 48°9N 78°9W 298 C4
Malaryta Belarus 51°50N 24°3E 185 G11
Malasiqui Phil. 15°55N 120°24E 232 D3
Malaspina Glacier
U.S.A. 59°50N 140°30W 303 G12
Malate Phil. 14°34N 120°59E 127 B1
Malatya Turkey 38°25N 38°20E 213 C8
Malatya □ Turkey 38°15N 38°0E 212 C7
Malawali, Pulau Malaysia 7°3N 117°18E 235 A5
Malawi ■ Africa 11°55S 34°0E 269 E3
Malawi, L. Africa 12°30S 34°30E 269 E3
Malay Phil. 11°54N 121°55E 233 F3
Malay Pen. Asia 7°25N 100°0E 237 J3
Malay Quarter Cape Town, S. Africa 118 c2
Malaya Belozërka = Mala Belozërka
Ukraine 47°12N 34°56E 189 J8
Malaya Neva Russia 59°56N 30°16E 137 B1
Malaya Okhta Russia 59°55N 30°25E 137 B2
Malaya Vishera Russia 58°55N 32°25E 188 C7
Malaya Viska = Mala Vyska
Ukraine 48°39N 31°36E 189 H6
Malaybalay Phil. 8°5N 125°7E 233 G5
Malāyer Iran 34°19N 48°51E 213 E13
Malaysia ■ Asia 5°0N 110°0E 235 B4
Malazgirt Turkey 39°10N 42°33E 213 C10
Malbaza Niger 13°59N 5°38E 263 C6
Malbon Australia 21°5S 140°17E 280 C3
Malbooma Australia 30°41S 134°11E 281 E1
Malbork Poland 54°3N 19°1E 184 D6
Malca Dube Ethiopia 6°47N 42°4E 267 C5
Malcésine Italy 45°46N 10°48E 198 C7
Malchin Germany 53°44N 12°44E 178 B8
Malchow Berlin, Germany 52°34N 13°29E 115 A3
Malchow Mecklenburg-Vorpommern,
Germany 53°28N 12°25E 178 B8
Malcolm Australia 28°51S 121°25E 279 E3
Malcolm, Pt. Australia 33°48S 123°45E 279 F3
Malczyce Poland 51°14N 16°29E 185 G3
Maldah India 25°2N 88°9E 243 G13
Maldegem Belgium 51°14N 3°26E 170 C3
Malden London, U.K. 51°23N 0°15W 125 B2
Malden Mass., U.S.A. 42°26N 71°3W 116 A2
Malden Mo., U.S.A. 36°34N 89°57W 308 G9
Malden I. Kiribati 4°3S 155°1W 289 H12
Maldives ■ Ind. Oc. 5°0N 73°0E 272 d
Maldon Vic., Australia 37°0S 144°6E 282 D6
Maldon Essex, U.K. 51°44N 0°42E 169 F8
Maldonado Uruguay 34°59S 55°0W 335 C5
Maldonado, Pta. Mexico 16°20N 98°33W 319 D5
Malè Italy 46°21N 10°55E 198 B7
Malé Maldives 4°10N 73°28E 272 d
Malé ✕ (MLE) Maldives 4°11N 73°28E 272 d
Malé Atoll Maldives 4°45N 73°15E 272 d
Malé Karpaty Slovakia 48°30N 17°20E 181 C10
Maleas, Akra Greece 36°28N 23°7E 204 E5
Malebo, Pool Africa 4°17S 15°20E 265 C3
Malegaon India 20°30N 74°38E 244 D2
Malei Mozam. 17°12S 36°58E 269 F4
Maleizen Belgium 50°45N 4°31E 116 B3
Malek South Sudan 6°4N 31°36E 257 F3
Malek Kandī Iran 37°9N 46°6E 213 D12
Malela Bas-Congo,
Dem. Rep. of the Congo 5°59S 12°37E 265 D2
Malela Maniema,
Dem. Rep. of the Congo 4°22S 26°8E 265 C5
Malema Mozam. 14°57S 37°20E 269 E4
Maleme Greece 35°31N 23°49E 207 E4
Malendok I. Papua N. G. 3°28S 153°13E 286 B7
Maler Kotla India 30°32N 75°58E 242 D6
Målerås Sweden 56°54N 15°34E 163 H9
Males Greece 35°6N 25°35E 207 E6
Malesherbes France 48°15N 2°24E 173 D9
Maleshevska Planina
Europe 41°38N 23°7E 202 E7
Malešice Czechia 50°5N 14°30E 135 B3
Malesina Greece 38°37N 23°14E 204 C5
Malestroit France 47°49N 2°25W 172 E4
Malfa Italy 38°35N 14°50E 201 D7
Malgobek Russia 43°30N 44°34E 191 J7
Malgomaj Sweden 64°40N 16°30E 160 D17
Malgrat de Mar Spain 41°39N 2°46E 196 D7
Malha Sudan 15°8N 25°10E 257 D2
Malhada Brazil 14°21S 43°47W 333 D3
Malhargarh India 24°17N 74°59E 242 G6
Malheur → U.S.A. 44°4N 116°59W 304 D5
Malheur L. U.S.A. 43°20N 118°48W 304 E4
Mali Guinea 12°10N 12°20W 262 C2
Mali ■ Africa 17°0N 3°0W 262 B4
Mali → Burma 25°42N 97°30E 241 C6
Mali Kanal Serbia 45°36N 19°24E 182 E4
Mali Kyun Burma 13°0N 98°20E 236 F2
Malia Greece 35°17N 25°32E 207 E6
Malia, Kolpos Greece 35°19N 25°27E 207 E6
Malibran, Teatro Venice, Italy 142 b3
Malibu U.S.A. 34°2N 118°41W 307 L8
Maligaya = Gloria Phil. 12°59N 121°30E 232 E3
Maliku = Minicoy I. India 8°17N 73°2E 245 K1
Maliku Indonesia 0°39S 123°16E 231 E6
Malili Indonesia 2°42S 121°6E 231 E6
Målilla Sweden 57°23N 15°48E 163 G9
Malimba, Mts.
Dem. Rep. of the Congo 7°30S 29°30E 268 D2
Malin Hd. Ireland 55°23N 7°23W 166 A4
Malin Pen. Ireland 55°20N 7°17W 166 A4
Malindang, Mt. Phil. 8°13N 123°38E 233 G4
Malindi Kenya 3°12S 40°5E 268 C5
Malindi Marine ⌂ Kenya 3°15S 40°7E 268 C5
Malines = Mechelen
Belgium 51°2N 4°29E 170 C4
Malino Indonesia 1°0N 121°0E 231 D6
Malinyi Tanzania 8°56S 36°0E 269 D4
Malipo China 23°7N 104°42E 228 F5
Maliq Albania 40°45N 20°48E 202 F4
Malir → Pakistan 24°49N 67°4E 123 B2
Malita Phil. 6°19N 125°39E 233 H5
Maliwun Burma 10°17N 98°40E 237 G2
Maliya India 23°5N 70°46E 242 H4
Maljenik Serbia 43°54N 21°43E 202 C5
Malka Mari △ Kenya 4°11N 40°46E 268 B5
Malkapur India 20°53N 76°12E 244 D3
Malkara Turkey 40°53N 26°53E 203 F10
Malkhangiri = Malakanagiri
India 18°21N 81°54E 244 E5
Małkinia Górna Poland 52°42N 22°5E 185 F9
Malko Tŭrnovo Bulgaria 41°59N 27°31E 203 E11
Mall, The Washington, D.C., U.S.A. 143 b2
Mallacoota Australia 37°40S 149°40E 283 D8
Mallacoota Inlet
Australia 37°34S 149°40E 283 D8
Mallaig U.K. 57°0N 5°50W 167 D3
Mallala Australia 34°26S 138°30E 282 C3
Mallaoua Niger 13°2N 9°36E 263 C6
Mallard U.S.A. 42°56N 94°41W 310 B2
Mallawan India 27°4N 80°12E 243 F9
Mallawi Egypt 27°44N 30°44E 256 B3
Mallee Cliffs △ Australia 34°16S 142°32E 282 C5
Mallembe Gabon 3°34S 10°53E 264 C2
Mallemort France 43°43N 5°11E 175 E9
Malleny Mills U.K. 55°52N 3°20W 121 B2
Mállès Venosta Italy 46°41N 10°32E 198 B7
Mallicolo = Malakula
Vanuatu 16°15S 167°30E 287 F5
Mallorca Spain 39°30N 3°0E 206 B4
Mallorytown Canada 44°29N 75°53W 313 B9
Mallow Ireland 52°8N 8°39W 166 D3
Malmbäck Sweden 57°34N 14°28E 163 G8
Malmberget Sweden 67°11N 20°40E 160 C19
Malmédy Belgium 50°25N 6°2E 170 D6
Malmesbury S. Africa 33°28S 18°41E 270 D2
Malmi Finland 60°15N 24°59E 121 B2
Malmivaara = Malmberget
Sweden 67°11N 20°40E 160 C19
Malmköping Sweden 59°8N 16°44E 162 E10
Malmö Sweden 55°36N 12°59E 163 J7
Malmok Aruba 12°36N 70°4W 322 f
Malmøya Norway 59°52N 10°45E 133 A3
Malmslätt Sweden 58°27N 15°33E 163 F9
Malmyzh Russia 56°31N 50°41E 190 B10
Malnaş Romania 46°2N 25°49E 183 D10
Malo Vanuatu 15°40S 167°11E 287 E5
Malo Konare Bulgaria 42°12N 24°24E 203 D8
Maloarkhangelsk Russia 52°28N 36°30E 189 F9
Maloca Brazil 0°43N 55°57W 329 C6
Malolo Fiji 17°45S 177°11E 287 A1
Malolos Phil. 14°50N 120°49E 232 D3
Malolotja ⌂ Swaziland 26°4S 31°6E 271 C5
Malombe L. Malawi 14°40S 35°15E 269 E4
Malomice Poland 51°34N 15°29E 185 G2
Malomir Bulgaria 42°16N 26°32E 203 D10
Malone Fla., U.S.A. 30°57N 85°10W 316 E4
Malone N.Y., U.S.A. 44°51N 74°18W 313 B10
Malong China 25°24N 103°34E 228 E4
Malonga
Dem. Rep. of the Congo 10°24S 23°10E 265 E4
Małopolskie □ Poland 49°50N 20°20E 185 J7
Malorad Bulgaria 43°28N 23°41E 202 C7
Maloti Mts. = Drakensberg
S. Africa 31°0S 28°0E 271 D4
Måløv Denmark 55°44N 12°20E 118 A1
Måløy Norway 61°57N 5°6E 164 C2
Maloyaroslovets Russia 55°2N 36°20E 188 E9
Malpartida de Cáceres
Spain 39°26N 6°30W 195 F4
Malpaso Canary Is. 27°43N 18°3W 153 e1
Malpaso, Presa = Netzahualcóyotl,
Presa Mexico 17°8N 93°35W 319 D6
Malpelo, I. de Colombia 4°3N 81°35W 289 G19
Malpensa, Milano ✕ (MXP)
Italy 45°38N 8°43E 128 A1
Malpica de Bergantiños
Spain 43°19N 8°50W 194 B2
Malprabha → India 16°20N 76°5E 245 F3
Malpur India 23°21N 73°27E 242 H5
Malpura India 26°17N 75°23E 242 F6
Mals = Mállès Venosta
Italy 46°41N 10°32E 198 B7
Malsiras India 17°52N 74°55E 244 F2
Malta Brazil 6°54S 37°31W 332 C4
Malta Idaho, U.S.A. 42°18N 113°22W 304 E7
Malta Mont., U.S.A. 48°21N 107°52W 304 B10
Malta ■ Europe 35°55N 14°26E 206 F7
Malta ✕ (MLA) Malta 35°52N 14°29E 206 F7
Malta Freeport Malta 35°49N 14°32E 206 F8
Maltahöhe Namibia 24°55S 17°0E 270 B2
Maltepe Turkey 40°55N 29°8E 203 F13
Malton Ont., Canada 43°42N 79°38W 141 A1
Malton N. Yorks., U.K. 54°8N 0°49W 168 C7
Malu'a Solomon Is. 8°20S 160°38E 287 M11
Maludam △ Malaysia 1°39N 111°2E 235 B4
Maluko = Manolo Fortich
Phil. 8°28N 124°50E 233 G5
Maluku Indonesia 1°0S 127°0E 231 E7
Maluku □ Indonesia 3°0S 128°0E 231 E7
Maluku Sea = Molucca Sea
Indonesia 0°0 125°0E 231 E6
Malumfashi Nigeria 11°48N 7°39E 263 C6
Malunda Indonesia 3°0S 118°50E 235 C5
Malundo Angola 14°51S 22°0E 265 E4
Malung Sweden 60°42N 13°44E 162 D7
Malungon Phil. 6°16N 125°14E 233 H5
Malungsfors Sweden 60°44N 13°33E 162 D7
Malur India 13°0N 77°55E 245 H3
Maluso Phil. 6°33N 121°53E 233 H3
Maluwe Ghana 8°40N 2°17W 262 D4
Malvalli India 12°28N 77°8E 245 H3
Malvan India 16°2N 73°30E 245 F1
Malvern Vic., Australia 37°50S 145°2E 128 B2
Malvern Ont., Canada 43°47N 79°13W 141 A3
Malvern Gauteng, S. Africa 26°11S 28°5E 123 B2
Malvern Ark., U.S.A. 34°22N 92°49W 314 D8
Malvern Hills U.K. 52°0N 2°19W 169 E5
Malvik Norway 63°25N 10°40E 164 A7
Malvinas, Is. = Falkland Is. ☑
Atl. Oc. 51°30S 59°0W 153 f
Malwal South Sudan 9°19N 31°35E 257 F3
Malý Dunaj → Slovakia 47°45N 18°9E 181 D11
Malya Tanzania 3°5S 33°38E 268 C3
Malye Derbety Russia 47°57N 44°42E 191 G7
Malyn Ukraine 50°46N 29°3E 177 C15
Malyy Lyakhovskiy, Ostrov
Russia 74°7N 140°36E 215 B15
Malyy Taymyr, Ostrov
Russia 78°6N 107°15E 215 B11
Mama Russia 58°18N 112°54E 215 D12
Mamaku N.Z. 38°5S 176°8E 284 E5
Māmala B. U.S.A. 21°15N 157°55W 302 K14
Mamanguape Brazil 6°50S 35°4W 332 C4
Mamanuca Group Fiji 17°35S 177°5E 287 A1
Mamarr Mitlā Egypt 30°2N 32°54E 251 H3
Mamasa Indonesia 2°55S 119°20E 235 C5
Mambajao Phil. 9°15N 124°43E 233 G5
Mambasa
Dem. Rep. of the Congo 1°22N 29°3E 268 B2
Mamberamo → Indonesia 2°0S 137°50E 231 E9
Mambéré → C.A.R. 3°31N 16°3E 264 B3
Mambéré-Kadéï □ C.A.R. 4°30N 15°30E 264 B3
Mambili → Congo 0°6N 16°5E 264 B3
Mambilima Falls Zambia 10°31S 28°45E 269 E2
Mambirima
Dem. Rep. of the Congo 11°25S 27°33E 269 E2
Mambo Tanzania 4°52S 38°22E 268 C4
Mambrui Kenya 3°5S 40°5E 268 C5
Mamburao Phil. 13°13N 120°39E 232 E3
Mamedkala Russia 42°10N 48°7E 191 J9
Mameigwess L. Canada 52°35N 87°50W 298 B2
Mamers France 48°21N 0°22E 172 D7
Mamfé Cameroon 5°50N 9°15E 263 D6
Māmī, Ra's Yemen 12°32N 54°30E 249 D6
Mamili △ Namibia 18°2S 24°1E 270 B3
Mamiña Chile 20°5S 69°14W 330 E4
Mamlyutka Kazakhstan 54°56N 68°32E 217 B7
Mammoth U.S.A. 32°43N 110°39W 305 K8
Mammoth Cave △
U.S.A. 37°8N 86°13W 308 G10
Mammoth Lakes U.S.A. 37°39N 118°59W 306 H8
Mamonovo Russia 54°28N 19°55E 184 D6
Mamoré → Bolivia 10°23S 65°53W 331 C4
Mamou Guinea 10°15N 12°0W 262 C2
Mamoudzou Mayotte 12°48S 45°14E 272 b
Mampang Prapatan
Indonesia 6°15S 106°49E 122 B1
Mampikony Madag. 16°6S 47°38E 272 B2
Mampoko
Dem. Rep. of the Congo 0°51N 18°42E 264 B3
Mampong Ghana 7°6N 1°26W 263 D4
Mampukuji Japan 35°36N 139°31E 140 B2
Mamry, Jezioro Poland 54°5N 21°50E 184 D8
Mamuil Malal, Paso
S. Amer. 39°35S 71°28W 336 A2
Mamuju Indonesia 2°41S 118°50E 235 C5
Ma'mūl Oman 18°8N 55°16E 249 C6
Mamuno Botswana 22°16S 20°1E 270 B3
Mamuras Albania 41°34N 19°41E 202 E3
Man Ivory C. 7°30N 7°40W 262 D3
Man → India 17°31N 75°32E 244 F2
Man, I. of India 8°28N 93°36E 245 K11
Man, I. of U.K. 54°15N 4°30W 168 C3
Man-Bazar India 23°4N 86°39E 243 H12
Man Budrukh India 19°2N 72°55E 130 A2
Man Kat Burma 22°5N 98°1E 241 D7
Man Khurd India 19°3N 72°55E 130 A2
Man Na Burma 23°27N 97°19E 241 D6
Man of War B. Trin. & Tob. 11°19N 60°34W 323 s
Mana Fr. Guiana 5°45N 53°55W 329 B7
Mānā Hawai'i, U.S.A. 22°2N 159°47W 302 A2
Mana → Fr. Guiana 5°45N 53°55W 329 B7
Mana Pools △ Zimbabwe 15°56S 29°25E 269 F2
Manaar, G. of = Mannar, G. of
Asia 8°30N 79°0E 245 K4
Manabí □ Ecuador 0°40S 80°5W 328 D1
Manacacías → Colombia 4°23N 72°4W 328 C3
Manacapuru Brazil 3°16S 60°37W 329 D5
Manacapuru → Brazil 3°18S 60°37W 329 D5
Manacor Spain 39°34N 3°13E 206 B4
Manadas Azores 38°38N 28°6W 153 d1
Manado Indonesia 1°29N 124°51E 231 D6
Managua Nic. 12°6N 86°20W 320 D2
Managua, L. de Nic. 12°20N 86°30W 320 D2
Manaia N.Z. 39°33S 174°8E 284 F3
Manakara Madag. 22°8S 48°1E 272 C2
Manakau N.Z. 42°15S 173°42E 285 C8
Manākhah Yemen 15°5N 43°44E 248 D3
Manakhat Israel 31°45N 35°11E 123 B2
Manali India 32°16N 77°10E 242 C7
Manam I. Papua N. G. 4°5S 145°0E 286 C3
Manama = Al Manāmah
Bahrain 26°10N 50°30E 247 E6
Manambao → Madag. 17°35S 44°0E 272 B1
Manambato Madag. 13°43S 49°7E 272 A2
Manambolo → Madag. 19°18S 44°22E 272 B1
Manambolosy Madag. 16°2S 49°40E 272 B2
Mánamo, Caño →
Venezuela 9°55N 62°16W 329 B5
Mānana I. U.S.A. 21°20N 157°40W 302 K14
Mananara Madag. 16°10S 49°46E 272 B2
Mananara → Madag. 23°21S 47°42E 272 C2
Mananara △ Madag. 16°14S 49°45E 272 B2
Manangatang Australia 35°5S 142°54E 282 C5
Mananjary Madag. 21°13S 48°20E 272 C2
Manankoro Mali 10°28N 7°25W 262 C3
Manantali, L. de Mali 13°12N 10°28W 262 C2
Manantavadi India 11°49N 76°1E 245 J3
Manantenina Madag. 24°17S 47°19E 272 C2
Manaos = Manaus Brazil 3°0S 60°0W 329 D6
Manapire → Venezuela 7°42N 66°7W 328 B4
Manapla Phil. 10°58N 123°5E 233 F4
Manapouri N.Z. 45°34S 167°39E 285 F2
Manapouri, L. N.Z. 45°32S 167°32E 285 F2
Manapparai India 10°36N 78°25E 245 J4
Manaqil Sudan 14°15N 32°59E 257 E3
Manar → India 18°50N 77°20E 244 E3
Manār, Jabal Yemen 14°2N 44°17E 248 D4
Manaravolo Madag. 23°59S 45°39E 272 C2
Manas Xinjiang Uygur,
China 44°17N 86°10E 217 D11
Manas Somalia 2°57N 43°28E 267 D5
Manas → India 26°12N 90°40E 241 B3
Manas △ India 26°40N 91°0E 241 B3
Manas He → China 45°38N 85°12E 218 B3
Manas Hu China 45°45N 85°55E 217 C11
Manaslu Nepal 28°33N 84°33E 243 E11
Manasquan U.S.A. 40°8N 74°3W 313 F10
Manassa U.S.A. 37°11N 105°56W 305 H11
Manati Puerto Rico 18°26N 66°29W 321 d
Manati B. St. Helena 16°0S 5°46W 153 h
Manau Papua N. G. 8°4S 148°0E 286 E4
Manaus Brazil 3°0S 60°0W 329 D6
Manavgat Turkey 36°47N 31°26E 250 B2
Manavgat → Turkey 36°43N 31°27E 250 B2
Manawan = Rizal Phil. 17°51N 121°21E 232 C3
Manawan L. Canada 55°24N 103°14W 297 B8
Manawatu → N.Z. 40°28S 175°12E 284 G4
Manawatu-Wanganui □
N.Z. 39°50S 175°30E 284 F4
Manay Phil. 7°17N 126°33E 233 H6
Manbij Syria 36°31N 37°57E 212 D7
Mancha Real Spain 37°48N 3°39W 195 H7
Manche □ France 49°10N 1°20W 172 C5
Manchegorsk Russia 67°54N 32°58E 214 C4
Manchester Gt. Man., U.K. 53°29N 2°12W 168 D5
Manchester Calif.,
U.S.A. 38°58N 123°41W 306 G3
Manchester Conn.,
U.S.A. 41°47N 72°31W 313 E12
Manchester Ga., U.S.A. 32°51N 84°37W 316 C5
Manchester Iowa, U.S.A. 42°29N 91°27W 310 B5
Manchester Ky., U.S.A. 37°9N 83°46W 309 G12
Manchester Mich., U.S.A. 42°9N 84°2W 311 B12
Manchester N.H., U.S.A. 42°59N 71°28W 313 D13
Manchester N.Y., U.S.A. 42°56N 77°16W 312 D7
Manchester Ohio, U.S.A. 38°41N 83°36W 311 F13
Manchester Pa., U.S.A. 40°4N 76°43W 313 F8
Manchester Tenn., U.S.A. 35°29N 86°5W 315 D11
Manchester Vt., U.S.A. 43°10N 73°5W 313 C11
Manchester Int. ✕ (MAN)
U.K. 53°21N 2°17W 168 D5
Manchester L. Canada 61°28N 107°29W 297 A7
Manchhar L. Pakistan 26°25N 67°39E 242 F2
Manchineel Bay Grenada 12°26N 61°29W 323 q
Manchou Taiwan 22°1N 120°50E 225 D2
Manchuria = Dongbei
China 45°0N 125°0E 227 D13
Manchurian Plain China 47°0N 124°0E 210 D14
Manciano Italy 42°35N 11°31E 199 F8
Mancifa Ethiopia 6°53N 41°50E 257 F5
Máncora Peru 4°9S 81°1W 330 A1
Mand → India 21°42N 83°15E 243 J10
Mand → Iran 28°20N 52°30E 247 D7
Manda Ludewe, Tanzania 10°30S 34°40E 269 E3
Manda Mbeya, Tanzania 7°58S 32°29E 268 D3
Manda Mbeya, Tanzania 8°30S 32°49E 269 D3
Mandabé Madag. 21°0S 44°55E 272 C1
Mandaguari Brazil 23°32S 51°42W 335 A5
Mandah = Töhöm
Mongolia 44°27N 108°2E 226 B5
Mandai Singapore 1°24N 103°45E 138 A2
Mandal Norway 58°2N 7°25E 164 F4
Mandala, Puncak
Indonesia 4°44S 140°20E 231 E10
Mandalay Burma 22°0N 96°4E 241 E6
Mandalay □ Burma 22°0N 96°4E 241 E5
Mandale = Mandalay
Burma 22°0N 96°4E 241 E6

398 Mandalgarh INDEX

Mandalgarh India 25°12N 75°6E 242 G6
Mandalgovĭ Mongolia 45°45N 106°10E 226 B4
Mandalī Iraq 33°43N 45°28E 213 F11
Mandalselva → Norway 58°2N 7°28E 164 F4
Mandaluyong Phil. 14°35N 121°1E 127 B2
Mandan U.S.A. 46°50N 100°54W 308 B3
Mandaoli India 28°37N 77°17E 120 B2
Mandaon Phil. 12°13N 123°17E 232 E4
Mandaqui → Brazil 23°30S 46°40W 137 A2
Mandar, Teluk Indonesia 3°32S 119°21E 235 C5
Mandara Mts. W. Afr. 10°40N 13°40E 259 F2
Mándas Italy 39°40N 9°8E 200 C2
Mandasor = Mandsaur India 24°3N 75°8E 242 G6
Mandaue Phil. 10°20N 123°56E 233 F4
Mandel Afghan. 33°17N 61°53E 240 B1
Mandelieu-la-Napoule France 43°34N 6°57E 175 E10
Mandera Kenya 3°55N 41°53E 268 B5
Mandera □ Kenya 3°20N 40°40E 268 B5
Mandeville Jamaica 18°2N 77°31W 320 a
Mandi India 31°39N 76°58E 242 D7
Mandi Burewala Pakistan 30°9N 72°41E 242 D5
Mandi Dabwali India 29°58N 74°42E 242 E6
Mandiana Guinea 10°37N 8°39W 262 C3
Mandigos = Manica Mozam. 18°58S 32°59E 271 A5
Mandimba Mozam. 14°20S 35°40E 269 E4
Mandioli Indonesia 0°40S 127°20E 231 E7
Mandioré, L. S. Amer. 18°8S 57°33W 331 D6
Mandla India 22°39N 80°30E 243 H9
Mandø Denmark 55°18N 8°33E 163 J2
Mandoli India 28°41N 77°18E 120 A2
Mandorah Australia 12°32S 130°42E 278 B5
Mandoto Madag. 19°34S 46°17E 272 B2
Mandoudi Greece 38°48N 23°29E 204 C5
Mandoul Chad 9°40N 15°30E 259 G3
Mandra Greece 38°4N 23°30E 204 C5
Mandra Pakistan 33°23N 73°12E 242 C5
Mandraki Greece 36°36N 27°11E 205 E9
Mandrare → Madag. 25°10S 46°30E 272 D2
Mandritsara Madag. 15°50S 48°49E 272 B2
Mandronarivo Madag. 21°7S 45°38E 272 C2
Mandsaur India 24°3N 75°8E 242 G6
Mandurah Australia 32°36S 115°48E 279 F2
Mandúria Italy 40°24N 17°38E 201 B10
Mandvi Gujarat, India 22°51N 69°22E 242 H3
Mandvi Maharashtra, India 18°56N 72°50E 130 B2
Mandya India 12°30N 77°0E 245 H3
Mandzai Pakistan 30°55N 67°6E 242 D2
Mané Burkina Faso 12°59N 1°21W 263 C4
Maneh Iran 37°39N 57°7E 247 B8
Manenberg S. Africa 33°58S 18°33E 118 A2
Manengouba, Mts. Cameroon 5°0N 9°50E 263 E6
Maner → India 18°30N 79°40E 244 E4
Manera Madag. 22°55S 44°20E 272 C1
Manérbio Italy 45°21N 10°8E 198 C7
Maneroo Cr. → Australia 23°21S 143°53E 280 C3
Manfalût Egypt 27°20N 30°52E 256 B3
Manfred Australia 33°19S 143°45E 282 B5
Manfredónia Italy 41°38N 15°55E 199 G12
Manfredónia, G. di Italy 41°35N 16°5E 199 G13
Mang Kung Uk Hong Kong, China 22°18N 114°16E 122 B3
Mang-won S. Korea 37°33N 126°55E 137 B1
Manga Brazil 14°46S 43°56W 333 D3
Manga Burkina Faso 11°40N 1°4W 263 C4
Manga Congo 0°13S 16°5E 264 C3
Manga Niger 15°0N 14°0E 259 F2
Mangabeiras, Chapada das Brazil 10°0S 46°30W 332 D2
Mangai Dem. Rep. of the Congo 4°2S 19°33E 265 C3
Mangaia Cook Is. 21°55S 157°55W 289 K12
Mangakino N.Z. 38°22S 175°47E 284 E4
Mangal Phil. 6°25N 121°58E 233 H3
Mangalagiri India 16°26N 80°36E 245 F5
Mangaldai India 26°26N 92°2E 241 B4
Mangaldan Phil. 16°4N 120°24E 232 C3
Mangalia Romania 43°50N 28°35E 183 G13
Mangalmé Chad 12°26N 19°37E 259 F3
Mangalore = Mangaluru India 12°55N 74°47E 245 H2
Mangaluru India 12°55N 74°47E 245 H2
Mangalvedha India 17°31N 75°28E 244 F2
Mangan India 27°31N 88°32E 241 B2
Mangaon India 18°15N 73°20E 244 E1
Mangarrayi ⊙ Australia 15°55S 133°10E 280 B1
Mangawan India 24°41N 81°33E 243 G9
Mangaweka N.Z. 39°48S 175°47E 284 F4
Mangaweka, Mt. N.Z. 39°49S 176°5E 284 F5
Mange Dem. Rep. of the Congo 0°54N 20°30E 264 B4
Manger Norway 60°38N 5°3E 164 D2
Mangetti △ Namibia 18°43S 19°8E 270 A2
Manggar Indonesia 2°50S 108°10E 235 C3
Manggawitu Indonesia 4°8S 133°32E 231 E8
Mangghystaū Kazakhstan 43°40N 51°13E 216 D4
Mangghystaū □ Kazakhstan 45°0N 53°0E 216 D4
Mangghystaū Tübegi Kazakhstan 44°30N 52°30E 216 D4
Manggis Indonesia 8°29S 115°31E 231 J18
Mangin Taungdan Burma 24°15N 95°45E 241 C5
Mangindrano Madag. 14°17S 48°58E 272 A2
Mangkalihat, Tanjung Indonesia 1°2N 118°59E 235 B5
Mangkururrpa ⊙ Australia 20°35S 129°43E 278 D4
Mangla Pakistan 33°7N 73°39E 242 C5
Mangla Dam Pakistan 33°9N 73°44E 243 C5
Manglares, C. Colombia 1°36N 79°2W 328 C2
Manglaur India 29°44N 77°49E 242 E7
Mangle, B. de Venezuela 10°57N 64°10W 329 a
Mangle, Pta. Venezuela 10°52N 64°3W 329 a
Manglillo Venezuela 10°57N 64°19W 329 a
Manglisi Georgia 41°41N 44°22E 191 K7
Mangnai China 37°52N 91°43E 218 D7
Mangnai Zhen China 38°24N 90°14E 217 E12
Mango Togo 10°20N 0°30E 263 C5
Mango Tonga 20°17S 174°29W 287 O13
Mangoche Malawi 14°25S 35°16E 269 E4
Mangoky → Madag. 21°29S 43°41E 272 C1
Mangole Indonesia 1°50S 125°55E 231 E6
Mangolpuri India 28°41N 77°6E 120 A1
Mangombe Dem. Rep. of the Congo 1°20S 26°48E 268 C2
Mangonui N.Z. 35°1S 173°32E 284 B2
Mangoro → Madag. 20°0S 48°45E 272 C2
Mangrol Mad. P., India 21°7N 70°7E 242 J4
Mangrol Raj., India 25°20N 76°31E 242 G6
Mangrul Pir India 20°19N 77°21E 244 D3
Mangshi = Luxi China 24°27N 98°36E 228 E2
Manguaba = Pilar Brazil 9°36S 35°56W 332 C4
Mangualde Portugal 40°38N 7°48W 194 E3
Mangueigne Chad 10°30N 21°15E 259 F4
Mangueira, L. da Brazil 33°0S 52°50W 335 C5
Manguéni, Hamada Niger 22°35N 12°40E 258 D2
Mangui China 52°3N 122°3E 219 A13
Mangum U.S.A. 34°53N 99°30W 314 D5
Mangungu Dem. Rep. of the Congo 5°16S 19°36E 265 D3
Manguri Australia 28°58S 134°22E 281 A1
Mangyshlak, Poluostrov = Mangghystaū Tübegi Kazakhstan 44°30N 52°30E 216 D4
Manhattan Kans., U.S.A. 39°11N 96°35W 308 F5
Manhattan New York, U.S.A. 132 d2
Manhattan Beach U.S.A. 40°34N 73°56W 132 C2
Manhattan Bridge New York, U.S.A. 132 f2
Manhatten U.S.A. 41°26N 87°59W 311 C9
Manhiça Mozam. 25°23S 32°49E 271 C5
Manhuaçu Brazil 20°15S 42°2W 333 F3
Manhumirim Brazil 20°22S 41°57W 333 F3
Maní Colombia 4°49N 72°17W 328 C3
Mania → Madag. 19°42S 45°22E 272 B2
Maniago Italy 46°10N 12°43E 199 B9
Manica Mozam. 18°58S 32°59E 271 A5
Manica □ Mozam. 19°10S 33°45E 271 A5
Manicahan Phil. 7°1N 122°12E 233 H4
Manicaland □ Zimbabwe 19°0S 32°30E 269 F3
Manicoré Brazil 5°48S 61°16W 331 B5
Manicoré → Brazil 5°51S 61°19W 331 B5
Manicouagan → Canada 49°30N 68°30W 299 C6
Manicouagan, Rés. Canada 51°5N 68°40W 299 B6
Maniema □ Dem. Rep. of the Congo 3°0S 26°0E 268 C2
Manīfah Si. Arabia 27°44N 49°0E 247 E6
Manifold, C. Australia 22°41S 150°50E 280 C5
Maniganggo China 31°56N 99°10E 228 B2
Manigotagan Canada 51°6N 96°18W 297 C9
Manigotagan → Canada 51°7N 96°20W 297 C9
Manihari India 25°21N 87°38E 243 G12
Manihi French Polynesia 14°24S 145°56W 289 f
Manihiki Cook Is. 10°24S 161°1W 289 J11
Manihiki Plateau Pac. Oc. 11°0S 164°0W 289 J11
Maniitsoq Greenland 65°26N 52°55W 154 D5
Manika, Plateau de la Dem. Rep. of the Congo 10°0S 25°5E 269 E2
Manikchhari Bangla. 22°51N 91°50E 241 D3
Manikganj Bangla. 23°52N 90°0E 241 D3
Manikpur India 25°4N 81°7E 243 G9
Manila Phil. 14°35N 120°58E 127 B1
Manila Utah, U.S.A. 40°59N 109°43W 304 F9
Manila B. Phil. 14°40N 120°35E 232 D3
Manila Ninoy Aquino Int. ✕ (MNL) Phil. 14°31N 121°0E 127 B2
Manildra Australia 33°11S 148°41E 283 B8
Manilla Australia 30°45S 150°43E 283 A9
Manilva Spain 36°23N 5°15W 195 J5
Manimpé Mali 14°11N 5°28W 262 C3
Maningrida Australia 12°3S 134°13E 280 A1
Maninian Ivory C. 10°3N 7°52W 262 C3
Maninjau, Danau Indonesia 0°19S 100°11E 234 C2
Manipa, Selat Indonesia 3°20S 127°25E 231 E7
Manipur □ India 25°0N 94°0E 241 C5
Manipur → Burma 23°45N 94°20E 241 D5
Manisa Turkey 38°38N 27°30E 205 C9
Manisa □ Turkey 38°40N 28°0E 205 C9
Manistee U.S.A. 44°15N 86°19W 308 C10
Manistee → U.S.A. 44°15N 86°21W 308 C10
Manistique U.S.A. 45°57N 86°15W 308 C10
Manito U.S.A. 40°26N 89°47W 310 D7
Manitoba □ Canada 53°30N 97°0W 297 B9
Manitoba, L. Canada 51°0N 98°45W 297 C9
Manitou Canada 49°15N 98°32W 297 D9
Manitou, L. Canada 50°55N 65°17W 299 B6
Manitou Beach U.S.A. 41°58N 84°19W 311 C12
Manitou Is. U.S.A. 45°8N 86°0W 308 C10
Manitou L. Canada 52°43N 109°43W 297 C7
Manitou Springs U.S.A. 38°52N 104°55W 304 G11
Manitoulin I. Canada 45°40N 82°30W 298 C3
Manitouwadge Canada 49°8N 85°48W 298 C2
Manitowoc U.S.A. 44°5N 87°40W 308 C10
Manitsauá-Missu → Brazil 10°58S 53°20W 331 C7
Maniyachi India 8°51N 77°55E 245 K3
Manizales Colombia 5°5N 75°32W 328 B2
Manja Madag. 21°26S 44°20E 272 C1
Manjacaze Mozam. 24°45S 34°0E 271 B5
Manjakandriana Madag. 18°55S 47°47E 272 B2
Manjhand Pakistan 25°50N 68°10E 242 G3
Manjiang China 41°56N 127°35E 224 B3
Manjimup Australia 34°15S 116°6E 279 F2
Manjlegaon India 19°9N 76°14E 244 E3
Manjo Cameroon 4°50N 9°49E 264 B1
Manjra → India 18°49N 77°52E 244 E3
Mankato Kans., U.S.A. 39°47N 98°13W 308 F4
Mankato Minn., U.S.A. 44°10N 94°0W 308 C6
Mankayan Phil. 16°52N 120°47E 232 C3
Mankayane Swaziland 26°40S 31°4E 271 C5
Mankera Pakistan 31°23N 71°26E 242 D4
Mankim Cameroon 5°6N 12°3E 263 D7
Mankkaa Finland 60°11N 24°47E 121 B1
Mankono Ivory C. 8°1N 6°10W 262 D3
Mankota Canada 49°25N 107°5W 297 D7
Mankulam Sri Lanka 9°8N 80°26E 245 K5
Manlay = Üydzin Mongolia 44°9N 107°0E 226 B4
Manleluag △ Phil. 15°4N 120°17E 232 D3
Manley Hot Springs U.S.A. 65°0N 150°38W 303 D10
Manlleu Spain 42°2N 2°17E 196 C7
Manly Australia 33°47S 151°17E 139 A2
Manmad India 20°18N 74°28E 244 D2
Mann, L. U.S.A. 28°32N 81°35W 133 A2
Mann Ranges Australia 26°6S 130°5E 279 E5
Manna Indonesia 4°25S 102°55E 234 C2
Mannahill Australia 32°25S 140°0E 282 B4
Mannar Sri Lanka 9°1N 79°54E 245 K4
Mannar, G. of Asia 8°30N 79°0E 245 K4
Mannar I. Sri Lanka 9°5N 79°45E 245 K4
Mannargudi India 10°45N 79°51E 245 J4
Mannheim Germany 49°29N 8°29E 179 F4
Manning Alta., Canada 56°53N 117°39W 296 B5
Manning Oreg., U.S.A. 45°45N 123°13W 306 E3
Manning S.C., U.S.A. 33°42N 80°13W 316 B9
Manning → Australia 31°52S 152°43E 283 A10
Manning Str. Solomon Is. 7°30S 158°0E 287 L10
Mannswörth Austria 48°8N 16°30E 142 B3
Mannu → Italy 39°16N 9°0E 200 C2
Mannu, C. Italy 40°3N 8°21E 200 B1
Mannum Australia 34°50S 139°20E 282 C3
Mano S. Leone 8°3N 12°2W 262 D2
Mano → Liberia 6°56N 11°30W 262 D2
Manoa Bolivia 9°40S 65°27W 331 B4
Manoharpur India 22°23N 85°12E 243 H11
Manokotak U.S.A. 58°58N 159°3W 303 G8
Manokwari Indonesia 0°54S 134°0E 231 E8
Manolada Greece 38°4N 21°21E 204 C3
Manolo Fortich Phil. 8°28N 124°50E 233 G5
Manombo Madag. 22°57S 43°28E 272 C1
Manono Dem. Rep. of the Congo 7°15S 27°25E 268 D2
Manono Samoa 13°50S 172°5W 287 V19
Manoppello Italy 42°15N 14°3E 199 F11
Manor Park U.K. 51°32N 0°1E 125 A4
Manora Pakistan 24°47N 66°58E 123 B1
Manora Pt. Pakistan 24°47N 66°58E 123 B1
Manorhamilton Ireland 54°18N 8°11W 166 B3
Manosque France 43°49N 5°47E 175 E9
Manotick Canada 45°13N 75°41W 313 A9
Manouane → Canada 49°30N 71°10W 299 C5
Manouane, L. Canada 50°45N 70°45W 299 B5
Manovo-Gounda Saint Floris △ C.A.R. 9°30N 21°25E 264 A4
Mamp'o N. Korea 41°6N 126°24E 224 B3
Manpojin = Manp'o N. Korea 41°6N 126°24E 224 B3
Manpur Chhattisgarh, India 23°17N 83°35E 243 H10
Manpur Chhattisgarh, India 20°22N 80°43E 244 D5
Manpur Mad. P., India 22°26N 75°37E 242 H6
Manquehue, Cerro Chile 33°21S 70°35W 137 B2
Manra Kiribati 4°27S 171°15W 277 A16
Manresa Spain 41°48N 1°50E 196 D6
Mansa Gujarat, India 23°27N 72°45E 242 H5
Mansa Punjab, India 30°0N 75°27E 242 E6
Mansa Zambia 11°13S 28°55E 269 E2
Mansa Konko Gambia 13°28N 15°33W 262 C1
Mansalay Phil. 12°31N 121°26E 232 E3
Månsåsen Sweden 63°5N 14°18E 162 A8
Mansehra Pakistan 34°20N 73°15E 242 B5
Mansel I. Canada 62°0N 80°0W 295 E15
Mansfield Vic., Australia 37°4S 146°6E 283 D7
Mansfield Notts., U.K. 53°9N 1°11W 168 D6
Mansfield Ga., U.S.A. 33°31N 83°44W 316 B6
Mansfield La., U.S.A. 32°2N 93°43W 314 E8
Mansfield Mass., U.S.A. 42°2N 71°13W 313 D13
Mansfield Ohio, U.S.A. 40°45N 82°31W 312 F2
Mansfield Pa., U.S.A. 41°48N 77°5W 312 E7
Mansfield Tex., U.S.A. 32°33N 97°8W 120 C3
Mansfield, Mt. U.S.A. 44°33N 72°49W 313 B12
Mansi Burma 24°48N 95°52E 241 C5
Mansidão Brazil 10°43S 44°2W 332 D3
Mansilla de las Mulas Spain 42°30N 5°25W 194 C5
Mansle France 45°52N 0°12E 174 C4
Manso → Brazil 13°50S 47°0W 333 D2
Mansôa Guinea-Biss. 12°0N 15°20W 262 C1
Manson U.S.A. 42°32N 94°32W 310 B2
Manson Creek Canada 55°37N 124°32W 296 B4
Mansoura Algeria 36°1N 4°31E 261 A5
Manta Ecuador 1°0S 80°40W 328 D1
Manta, B. de Ecuador 0°54S 80°44W 328 D1
Mantalingajan, Mt. Phil. 8°55N 117°45E 233 G1
Mantantale Dem. Rep. of the Congo 2°10S 20°11E 264 C4
Mantare Tanzania 2°42S 33°13E 268 C3
Mantaro → Peru 12°16S 73°57W 330 C3
Manteca U.S.A. 37°48N 121°13W 306 H5
Mantecal Venezuela 7°34N 69°17W 328 B4
Mantena Brazil 18°47S 40°59W 333 E3
Manteno U.S.A. 41°15N 87°50W 311 C9
Manteo U.S.A. 35°55N 75°40W 315 D17
Mantes-la-Jolie France 48°58N 1°41E 173 D8
Mantha India 19°40N 76°23E 244 E3
Manthani India 18°40N 79°35E 244 E4
Manti U.S.A. 39°16N 111°38W 304 G8
Mantiqueira, Serra da Brazil 22°0S 44°0W 333 F3
Manton U.S.A. 44°25N 85°24W 309 C11
Mantorp Sweden 58°21N 15°20E 163 F9
Mántova Italy 45°9N 10°48E 198 C7
Mänttä Vilppula Finland 62°3N 24°40E 188 A3
Mantua = Mántova Italy 45°9N 10°48E 198 C7
Mantung Australia 34°35S 140°3E 282 C4
Manturovo Russia 58°23N 44°45E 190 A7
Manú Peru 12°10S 70°51W 330 C3
Manú → Peru 12°16S 70°55W 330 C3
Manu'a Is. Amer. Samoa 14°13S 169°35W 302 g
Manuel Alves → Brazil 11°19S 48°28W 333 D2
Manuel Alves Grande → Brazil 7°27S 47°35W 332 C2
Manuel Urbano Brazil 8°53S 69°18W 330 B4
Manui Indonesia 3°35S 123°5E 231 E6
Manukan Phil. 8°32N 123°12E 233 G4
Manukau N.Z. 37°0S 174°52E 284 D3
Manukau Harbour N.Z. 37°3S 174°45E 284 D3
Manunui N.Z. 38°54S 175°21E 284 E4
Manuoha N.Z. 38°39S 177°7E 284 E6
Manuripi → Bolivia 11°6S 67°36W 330 C4
Manus □ Papua N. G. 2°0S 147°0E 286 B4
Manus I. Papua N. G. 2°0S 147°0E 286 B4
Manvi India 15°57N 76°59E 245 G3
Manwan Dam China 24°44N 100°20E 228 E3
Manwath India 19°19N 76°32E 244 E3
Many U.S.A. 31°34N 93°29W 314 F8
Manyallaluk ⊙ Australia 14°16S 132°49E 278 B5
Manyani Kenya 3°5S 38°30E 268 C4
Manyara □ Tanzania 4°30S 37°10E 268 C4
Manyara, L. Tanzania 3°40S 35°50E 268 C4
Manyara △ Tanzania 3°35S 35°50E 268 C4
Manyas Turkey 40°2N 27°59E 203 F11
Manyas Gölü = Kus Gölü Turkey 40°10N 27°55E 203 F11
Manyava Ukraine 48°39N 24°21E 183 B9
Manych → Russia 47°13N 40°40E 191 G5
Manych-Gudilo, Ozero Russia 46°24N 42°38E 191 G6
Manyonga → Tanzania 4°10S 34°15E 268 C3
Manyoni Tanzania 5°45S 34°55E 268 D3
Manzai Pakistan 32°12N 70°15E 242 C4
Manzala, Bahra el Egypt 31°10N 31°56E 256 H7
Manzanar △ U.S.A. 36°44N 118°9W 306 J7
Manzanares Spain 39°2N 3°22W 195 F7
Manzanares, Canal de Spain 40°19N 3°38W 127 C2
Manzaneda Spain 42°12N 7°15W 194 C3
Manzanilla Pt. Trin. & Tob. 10°31N 61°1W 323 t
Manzanillo Cuba 20°20N 77°31W 320 B4
Manzanillo Colima, Mexico 19°3N 104°20W 318 D4
Manzanillo Venezuela 11°9N 63°54W 329 a
Manzanillo, Pta. Panama 9°30N 79°40W 322 E4
Manzano Mts. U.S.A. 34°40N 106°20W 305 J10
Manzarīyeh Iran 34°53N 50°50E 247 C6
Manzhouli China 49°35N 117°25E 219 B12
Manzini Swaziland 26°30S 31°25E 271 C5
Manzouli = Manzhouli China 49°35N 117°25E 219 B12
Manzur Vadisi △ Turkey 39°10N 39°30E 246 B3
Mao Chad 14°4N 15°19E 259 F3
Maó Spain 39°53N 4°16E 206 B5
Mao Mausoleum Beijing, China 114 c3
Maoka = Kholmsk Russia 47°40N 142°5E 215 E15
Maoke, Pegunungan Indonesia 3°40S 137°30E 231 E9
Maolin China 43°58N 123°30E 227 C12
Maoming China 21°50N 110°54E 229 G8
Maopi T'ou China 21°56N 120°43E 225 E2
Maouri, Dallol → Niger 12°5N 3°30E 263 C5
Maoxian China 31°41N 103°49E 228 B4
Maoxing China 45°28N 124°40E 227 B13
Map Micronesia 9°35N 138°10E 287 R16
Mapalma Dem. Rep. of the Congo 2°3N 24°30E 264 B4
Mapam Yumco China 30°45N 81°28E 227 B16
Mapastepec Mexico 15°26N 92°54W 319 D6
Mapfongui Gabon 1°15S 12°59E 264 C2
Maphrao, Ko Thailand 7°56N 98°26E 237 a
Mapia, Kepulauan Indonesia 0°50N 134°20E 231 D8
Mapimí Mexico 25°49N 103°51W 318 B4
Mapimí, Bolsón de Mexico 27°0N 104°15W 318 B4
Maping China 31°34N 113°32E 229 B9
Mapinga Tanzania 6°40S 39°12E 268 D4
Mapinhane Mozam. 22°20S 35°0E 271 B6
Mapire Venezuela 7°45N 64°42W 329 B5
Maple → U.S.A. 42°59N 84°57W 311 B12
Maple Creek Canada 49°55N 109°29W 297 D7
Maple Valley U.S.A. 47°25N 122°3W 306 C4
Mapleton U.S.A. 44°2N 123°52W 304 D2
Mapo S. Korea 37°32N 126°56E 137 B1
Mapoon ⊙ Australia 11°44S 142°8E 280 A3
Mapourika, L. N.Z. 43°16S 170°12E 285 D5
Mapri Papua N. G. 3°44S 143°3E 286 B2
Mapuca India 15°36N 73°46E 245 G1
Mapuera → Brazil 1°5S 57°2W 329 D6
Mapulanguene Mozam. 24°29S 32°6E 271 B5
Mapungubwe △ S. Africa 22°12S 29°22E 271 B4
Maputo Mozam. 25°58S 32°32E 271 C5
Maputo □ Mozam. 26°0S 32°25E 271 C5
Maputo, B. de Mozam. 25°50S 32°45E 271 C5
Maputo ⌓ Mozam. 26°23S 32°48E 271 C5
Maqanshy Kazakhstan 46°47N 82°1E 217 C10
Maqat Kazakhstan 47°39N 53°19E 187 E9
Maqên China 34°24N 100°6E 218 E9
Maqên Gangri China 34°55N 99°18E 218 E8
Maqiaohe China 44°40N 130°30E 227 B16
Maqnā Si. Arabia 28°25N 34°50E 251 K5
Maqran, W. → Si. Arabia 20°55N 47°12E 248 B4
Maqteïr Mauritania 21°50N 11°40W 260 D2
Maqu China 33°52N 101°42E 218 E9
Maquan He = Brahmaputra → Asia 23°40N 90°35E 241 D3
Maqueda Spain 40°4N 4°22W 194 E6
Maqueda Channel Phil. 13°42N 124°1E 232 E5
Maquela do Zombo Angola 6°0S 15°15E 265 D3
Maquinchao Argentina 41°15S 68°50W 336 B3
Maquoketa U.S.A. 42°4N 90°40W 310 B6
Mar Canada 44°49N 81°12W 312 B3
Mar, Serra do Brazil 25°30S 49°0W 335 B6
Mar Chiquita, L. Argentina 30°40S 62°50W 334 C3
Mar del Plata Argentina 38°0S 57°30W 334 D4
Mar Menor Spain 37°40N 0°45W 197 H4
Mar Vista U.S.A. 34°0N 118°25W 126 B2
Mara Guyana 6°0N 57°36W 329 B6
Mara India 28°11N 94°14E 241 A5
Mara Tanzania 1°30S 34°32E 268 C3
Mara □ Tanzania 1°45S 34°20E 268 C3
Mara Rosa Brazil 13°58S 49°9W 333 C2
Maraã Brazil 1°52S 65°25W 328 D4
Maraa Tahiti 17°46S 149°34W 289 e
Marabá Brazil 5°20S 49°5W 332 C2
Marabahan Indonesia 3°0S 114°45E 235 C4
Maraboon, L. Australia 23°41S 148°0E 280 C4
Maracá, I. de Brazil 2°10N 50°30W 329 C7
Maracaibo Venezuela 10°40N 71°37W 328 A3
Maracaibo, L. de Venezuela 9°40N 71°30W 328 B3
Maracaju Brazil 21°38S 55°9W 335 A4
Maracajú, Serra de Brazil 20°57S 55°1W 331 E6
Maracanã Brazil 0°46S 47°27W 332 B2
Maracanã, Estádio Rio de J., Brazil 22°54S 43°13W 135 B1
Maracanaú Brazil 3°52S 38°38W 332 B4
Maracás Brazil 13°26S 40°18W 333 D3
Maracas Trin. & Tob. 10°41N 61°24W 323 t
Maracas → Trin. & Tob. 10°34N 61°25W 323 t
Maracas B. Trin. & Tob. 10°45N 61°26W 323 t
Maracas Bay Village Trin. & Tob. 10°46N 61°28W 323 t
Maracas Falls Trin. & Tob. 10°44N 61°24W 323 t
Maracay Venezuela 10°15N 67°28W 328 A4
Maracena Spain 37°12N 3°38W 195 H7
Marādah Libya 29°15N 19°15E 258 C3
Maradi Niger 13°29N 7°20E 263 C6
Maradi □ Niger 14°15N 7°15E 263 C6
Marāgheh Iran 37°30N 46°12E 213 D12
Maragogipe Brazil 12°46S 38°55W 333 D4
Marāh Si. Arabia 25°0N 45°35E 246 E5
Marahoué △ Ivory C. 8°0N 7°8W 262 D3
Marais du Cotentin et du Bessin △ France 49°10N 1°30W 172 C5
Marais Poitevin, Val de Sèvre et Vendée △ France 46°18N 0°35W 174 B3
Maraisburg = Hofmeyr S. Africa 31°39S 25°50E 270 D4
Marajó, B. de Brazil 1°0S 48°30W 332 B2
Marajó, I. de Brazil 1°0S 49°30W 332 B2
Marākand Iran 38°51N 45°16E 246 B5
Marakele △ S. Africa 24°30S 25°30E 271 B4
Maralal Kenya 1°0N 36°38E 268 B4
Maralinga Australia 30°13S 131°32E 279 F5
Maralinga Tjarutja ⊙ Australia 29°30S 131°0E 279 E5
Maram India 25°25N 94°6E 241 C5
Marama Australia 35°10S 140°10E 282 C4
Maramag Phil. 7°46N 125°0E 233 H5
Maramaraereğlisi Turkey 40°57N 27°57E 203 F11
Maramasike Solomon Is. 9°30S 161°25E 287 M11
Marambio Antarctica 64°0S 56°0W 151 C18
Maramureș □ Romania 47°45N 24°0E 183 C9
Maran Malaysia 3°35N 102°45E 237 L4
Marana U.S.A. 32°27N 111°13W 305 K8
Maranboy Australia 14°40S 132°39E 278 B5
Maranchón Spain 41°6N 2°15W 196 D2
Marand Iran 38°30N 45°45E 213 C11
Marandochori Greece 38°38N 20°39E 207 B2
Maranello Italy 44°32N 10°52E 198 D7
Marang Malaysia 5°12N 103°13E 237 K4
Maranguape Brazil 3°55S 38°50W 332 B4
Maranhão = São Luís Brazil 2°39S 44°15W 332 B3
Maranhão □ Brazil 5°0S 46°0W 332 C2
Marano, L. di Italy 45°44N 13°10E 199 C10
Maranoa → Australia 27°50S 148°37E 281 D4
Marañón → Peru 4°30S 73°35W 330 A3
Marão Portugal 24°18S 34°2E 271 B5
Maraoli India 19°2N 72°53E 130 A2
Marapi → Brazil 0°37N 55°58W 329 C6
Marari Brazil 5°43S 67°47W 330 B4
Maraş = Kahramanmaraş Turkey 37°37N 36°53E 212 D7
Mărășești Romania 45°52N 27°14E 183 E12
Maratea Italy 39°59N 15°43E 201 C8
Marateca Portugal 38°34N 8°40W 195 G2
Marathasa Cyprus 34°59N 32°51E 207 F8
Marathia, Akra Greece 37°39N 20°50E 207 D2
Marathokambos Greece 37°43N 26°42E 205 D8
Marathon Queens., Australia 20°51S 143°32E 280 C3
Marathon Ont., Canada 48°44N 86°23W 298 C2
Marathon Fla., U.S.A. 24°43N 81°5W 317 L8
Marathon N.Y., U.S.A. 42°27N 76°2W 313 D8
Marathon Tex., U.S.A. 30°12N 103°15W 314 F3
Marathonas Greece 38°11N 23°58E 204 C5
Marathóvounos Cyprus 35°13N 33°37E 207 E9
Maratua Indonesia 2°10N 118°35E 235 B5
Maraú Brazil 14°6S 39°0W 333 D4
Marau Indonesia 2°9S 110°42E 235 C3
Marau Solomon Is. 10°31S 161°3E 287 N11
Maraval Trin. & Tob. 10°42N 61°31W 323 t
Maraval → Trin. & Tob. 10°39N 61°32W 323 t
Maravari Solomon Is. 7°50S 156°42E 287 L9
Maravatío Mexico 19°54N 100°27W 318 D4
Marawi City Phil. 8°0N 124°21E 233 G5
Marāwih U.A.E. 24°18N 53°18E 247 E7
Marazliyivka Ukraine 46°8N 30°3E 183 D15
Marbella Spain 36°30N 4°57W 195 J6
Marble Bar Australia 21°9S 119°44E 278 D2
Marblehead Mass., U.S.A. 42°29N 70°51W 313 D14
Marblehead Ohio, U.S.A. 41°32N 82°44W 312 E2
Mårbu Norway 60°11N 8°9E 164 D5
Marburg = Maribor Slovenia 46°36N 15°40E 199 B12
Marburg Germany 50°47N 8°46E 178 E4
Marca, Pta. do Angola 16°31S 11°43E 265 F2
Marcal → Hungary 47°41N 17°40E 182 C2
Marcali Hungary 46°35N 17°25E 182 D2
Marcapata Peru 13°31S 70°52W 330 C3
Marcaria Italy 45°7N 10°32E 198 C7
Mărcăuți Moldova 48°20N 27°14E 183 B12
Marcelin Poland 52°19N 20°59E 143 B1
Marceline U.S.A. 39°43N 92°57W 310 E4
March U.K. 52°33N 0°5E 169 E8
Marchal Dem. Rep. of the Congo 5°16S 14°58E 265 D2
Marchand = Rommani Morocco 33°31N 6°40W 260 B3
Marche France 46°5N 1°20E 174 B5
Marche □ Italy 43°30N 13°15E 199 E10
Marché Bonsecours Montréal, Canada 130 b3
Marche-en-Famenne Belgium 50°14N 5°19E 170 D5
Marchena Spain 37°18N 5°23W 195 H5
Marchena, Canal de Ecuador 0°19N 90°12W 330 a
Marchena, I. Ecuador 0°19N 90°29W 330 a
Marches = Marche □ Italy 43°30N 13°15E 199 E10
Marchesale ⌓ Italy 38°32N 16°13E 201 D9
Marciana Marina Italy 42°48N 10°12E 198 F7
Marcianise Italy 41°2N 14°17E 201 A7
Marcigny France 46°17N 4°2E 173 F11
Marcillat-en-Combraille France 46°12N 2°38E 173 F9
Marck France 50°57N 1°57E 173 B8
Marckolsheim France 48°10N 7°30E 173 D14
Marco Island U.S.A. 25°58N 81°44W 317 K8
Marco Rondon Brazil 12°0S 60°56W 331 C5
Marcona Peru 15°10S 75°0W 330 D3
Marcos Juárez Argentina 32°42S 62°5W 334 C3
Mărculești Moldova 47°52N 28°14E 183 C13
Marcus Baker, Mt. U.S.A. 61°26N 147°45W 303 F11
Marcus I. = Minami-Tori-Shima Pac. Oc. 24°20N 153°58E 288 E7
Marcy, Mt. U.S.A. 44°7N 73°56W 313 B11
Mardan Pakistan 34°20N 72°0E 242 B5
Mardarivka Ukraine 47°32N 29°44E 183 C14
Mardie Australia 21°12S 115°59E 278 D2
Mardin Turkey 37°20N 40°43E 213 D9
Mårdsjö Sweden 63°18N 15°35E 162 A9
Maré, Î. N. Cal. 21°30S 168°0E 277 E12
Mare e Brăila, I. Romania 45°0N 28°5E 183 F13
Marécchia → Italy 44°4N 12°34E 199 D9
Marechal Deodoro Brazil 9°43S 35°54W 332 C4
Marechal Floriano = Piranhas Brazil 9°27S 37°46W 332 C4
Maree, L. U.K. 57°40N 5°26W 167 D3
Mareeba Australia 16°59S 145°28E 280 B4
Mareeg Somalia 3°46N 47°18E 267 D6
Mareetsane S. Africa 26°9S 25°25E 270 C4
Mareil-Marly France 48°52N 2°4E 134 A1
Maremma Italy 42°30N 11°30E 199 F8
Maremma ⌓ Italy 42°35N 11°8E 198 F8
Maréna Kayes, Mali 14°36N 10°45W 262 C2
Maréna Koulikouro, Mali 13°55N 7°20W 262 C3
Marengo Ind., U.S.A. 38°22N 86°21W 311 F10
Marengo Iowa, U.S.A. 41°48N 92°4W 310 C4
Marennes France 45°49N 1°7W 174 C2
Marerano Madag. 21°23S 44°52E 272 C1
Marèttimo Italy 37°58N 12°4E 200 E5
Mareuil France 45°26N 0°29E 174 C4
Marfa U.S.A. 30°19N 104°1W 314 F2
Marganets = Marhanets Ukraine 47°40N 34°40E 189 J8
Margao = Madgaon India 15°12N 73°58E 245 G1
Margaret → Australia 18°9S 125°41E 278 C4
Margaret Bay Canada 51°20N 127°35W 296 C3
Margaret I. = Margitsziget Hungary 47°32N 19°3E 117 A2
Margaret L. Canada 58°56N 115°25W 296 B5
Margaret River Australia 33°57S 115°4E 279 F2
Margareten Austria 48°11N 16°20E 142 A2
Margarita, I. de Venezuela 11°0N 64°0W 329 a
Margariti Greece 39°22N 20°26E 204 B2
Margaritovo Russia 43°25N 134°45E 220 C7
Margate KwaZulu Natal, S. Africa 30°50S 30°20E 271 D5
Margate Kent, U.K. 51°23N 1°23E 169 F9
Margate Fla., U.S.A. 26°15N 80°12W 317 J9
Margeride, Mts. de la France 44°43N 3°38E 174 D7
Marggrabowa = Olecko Poland 54°2N 22°31E 184 D9
Margherita India 27°16N 95°40E 241 B5
Margherita di Savóia Italy 41°22N 16°9E 201 A9
Margherita Pk. Uganda 0°22N 29°51E 268 B3
Marghita Romania 47°22N 22°22E 182 C7
Marg'ilon Uzbekistan 40°27N 71°42E 217 D8
Margitsziget Hungary 47°32N 19°3E 117 A2
Margonin Poland 52°58N 17°5E 185 F4
Margosatubig Phil. 7°34N 123°10E 233 H4
Mārgow, Dasht-e Afghan. 30°40N 62°30E 240 C1
Marguerite Canada 52°30N 122°25W 296 C4
Marhanets Ukraine 47°40N 34°40E 189 J8
Marhoum Algeria 34°27N 0°11W 261 B4
Mari Papua N. G. 9°11S 141°42E 286 E1
Mārī Syria 36°29N 37°10E 250 B8
Mari El □ Russia 56°30N 48°0E 190 B8
Mari Indus Pakistan 32°57N 71°34E 242 C4
Mari Republic = Mari El □ Russia 56°30N 48°0E 190 B8
María Austria 48°11N 16°21E 142 A2
Maria, Îs. French Polynesia 21°48S 154°41W 289 L12
María, Sa. de Spain 37°39N 2°14W 197 H2
Maria Aurora Phil. 15°48N 121°28E 232 D3
María de la Salut Spain 39°40N 3°5E 206 B4
María Elena Chile 22°18S 69°40W 334 A2
María Grande Argentina 31°45S 59°55W 334 C4
Maria I. N. Terr., Australia 14°52S 135°45E 280 A2
Maria I. Tas., Australia 42°35S 148°0E 281 G4
Maria Is. St. Lucia 13°44N 60°56W 323 m
Maria Island △ Australia 42°38S 148°5E 281 G4
Maria Pereira = Mombaça Brazil 5°43S 39°45W 332 C4
Maria Theresiopel = Subotica Serbia 46°6N 19°39E 182 D4
Maria van Diemen, C. N.Z. 34°29S 172°40E 284 A1
Mariager Denmark 56°40N 9°59E 163 H3
Mariager Fjord Denmark 56°42N 10°19E 163 H4
Mariahilferstrasse Vienna, Austria 142 b1
Mariakani Kenya 3°50S 39°27E 268 C4
Mariala △ Australia 25°57S 145°2E 281 D4
Marian Australia 21°9S 148°57E 280 b
Marian L. Canada 63°0N 116°15W 296 A5
Mariana Islands Pac. Oc. 15°15N 145°48E 302 a
Mariana Trench Pac. Oc. 13°0N 145°0E 302 a
Mariani India 26°39N 94°19E 241 B5
Mariánica, Cord. = Morena, Sierra Spain 38°20N 4°0W 195 G7
Marianna Ark., U.S.A. 34°46N 90°46W 315 D9
Marianna Fla., U.S.A. 30°46N 85°14W 316 E4
Mariannelund Sweden 57°37N 15°35E 163 G9
Mariánské Lázně Czechia 49°58N 12°41E 180 B5
Marias → U.S.A. 47°56N 110°30W 304 C8
Marías, Is. Mexico 21°25N 106°28W 318 C3
Mariato, Punta Panama 7°12N 80°52W 320 E3
Mariazell Austria 47°47N 15°19E 180 D8
Ma'rib Yemen 15°25N 45°21E 248 D4
Ma'rib □ Yemen 15°25N 45°21E 248 D4
Maribo Denmark 54°48N 11°30E 163 K5
Maribor Slovenia 46°36N 15°40E 199 B12
Maricaban I. Phil. 13°39N 120°53E 232 E3
Maricao Puerto Rico 18°11N 66°59W 321 b
Marico → Africa 23°35S 26°57E 270 B4
Maricopa Ariz., U.S.A. 33°4N 112°3W 305 K7
Maricopa Calif., U.S.A. 35°4N 119°24W 307 K7
Maridalen Norway 59°59N 10°45E 133 A3
Maridalsvatnet Norway 59°59N 10°46E 133 A3
Maridi South Sudan 4°55N 29°25E 257 G2
Maridi, Wadi → South Sudan 6°15N 29°21E 257 F2
Marié → Brazil 0°27S 66°26W 328 D4
Marie Byrd Land Antarctica 79°30S 125°0W 151 D14
Marie-Galante Guadeloupe 15°56N 61°16W 322 e
Marie-Galante, Canal de Guadeloupe 16°0N 61°25W 322 e
Mariecourt = Kangiqsujuaq Canada 61°30N 72°0W 295 E17
Mariefred Sweden 59°15N 17°12E 162 E11
Mariehamn Finland 60°5N 19°55E 161 F18
Marieholm Sweden 55°53N 13°10E 163 J7
Mariembourg Belgium 50°6N 4°31E 170 D4
Marienbad = Mariánské Lázně Czechia 49°58N 12°41E 180 B5
Marienberg Germany 50°39N 13°9E 178 E9
Marienburg = Malbork Poland 54°3N 19°1E 184 D6
Mariendorf Germany 52°26N 13°23E 115 B3
Marienfelde Germany 52°24N 13°22E 115 B3
Marienplatz Munich, Germany 131 b2
Mariental Namibia 24°36S 18°0E 270 B2
Marienville U.S.A. 41°28N 79°8W 312 E5
Mariestad Sweden 58°43N 13°50E 163 F7
Marietta Ga., U.S.A. 33°57N 84°33W 316 B5
Marietta Ohio, U.S.A. 39°25N 81°27W 309 F13
Marieville Canada 45°26N 73°10W 313 A11
Mariga → Nigeria 9°40N 5°55E 263 C6
Marignane France 43°25N 5°13E 175 E9
Marigot Dominica 15°33N 61°18W 323 k
Marigot Guadeloupe 16°5N 61°46W 322 e
Marigot St.-Martin 18°4N 63°5W 322 a
Marigot Bay St. Lucia 13°58N 61°1W 323 m
Marihatag Phil. 8°48N 126°18E 233 G6
Mariinsk Russia 56°10N 87°20E 214 D9
Mariinsk Water = Volgo-Baltiyskiy Kanal Russia 60°0N 38°0E 188 B9
Mariinskiy Posad Russia 56°10N 47°45E 190 B8
Marijampolė Lithuania 54°33N 23°19E 184 D10
Marijampolė □ Lithuania 54°34N 23°21E 184 D10
Marikina Phil. 14°37N 121°5E 127 B2
Marikina → Phil. 14°33N 121°3E 127 B2
Marília Brazil 22°13S 50°0W 335 A6
Marimba Angola 8°28S 17°8E 265 D3
Marín Spain 42°23N 8°42W 194 C2
Marin, Cul-de-Sac du Martinique 14°27N 60°53W 322 j
Marin City U.S.A. 37°52N 122°30W 136 A1
Marin Pen. U.S.A. 37°50N 122°30W 136 A1
Marina U.S.A. 36°41N 121°48W 306 J5
Marina Bay Sands Singapore 1°17N 103°51E 138 B3
Marina del Rey U.S.A. 33°58N 118°27W 126 C2
Marinduque Phil. 13°25N 122°0E 231 B6
Marinduque □ Phil. 13°18N 122°0E 232 E4
Marine City U.S.A. 42°43N 82°30W 312 D2
Marine Drive Mumbai, India 130 b1
Marineland U.S.A. 29°40N 81°13W 316 F8
Marineo Italy 37°57N 13°25E 200 E6
Marinette U.S.A. 45°6N 87°38W 308 C10
Maringá Brazil 23°26S 52°2W 335 A5
Maringa → Dem. Rep. of the Congo 1°14N 19°48E 264 B3
Marinha Grande Portugal 39°45N 8°56W 194 F2
Marinho dos Abrolhos △ Brazil 17°50S 39°0W 333 E4
Marino Italy 41°46N 12°39E 199 G9
Marino di Campo Italy 42°46N 10°11E 198 F7
Marion Ala., U.S.A. 32°38N 87°19W 315 E11
Marion Ark., U.S.A. 35°13N 90°12W 308 H8
Marion Ill., U.S.A. 37°44N 88°56W 310 G8
Marion Ind., U.S.A. 40°32N 85°40W 311 D11
Marion Iowa, U.S.A. 42°2N 91°36W 310 B5
Marion Kans., U.S.A. 38°21N 97°1W 308 F5
Marion N.C., U.S.A. 35°41N 82°1W 315 D13
Marion Ohio, U.S.A. 40°35N 83°8W 312 F1
Marion S.C., U.S.A. 34°11N 79°24W 315 D15
Marion Va., U.S.A. 36°50N 81°31W 309 G13
Marion, L. U.S.A. 33°28N 80°10W 316 B9
Marion Bay Australia 35°12S 136°59E 282 C2
Marion I. Ind. Oc. 47°0S 38°0E 273 J2
Maripa Venezuela 7°26N 65°9W 329 B4
Maripasoula Fr. Guiana 3°40N 54°4W 329 C7
Maripipi I. Phil. 11°47N 124°19E 233 F5
Mariposa U.S.A. 37°29N 119°58W 306 H7
Mariscal Estigarribia Paraguay 22°3S 60°40W 334 A3
Marisco, Ponta do Brazil 23°1S 43°18W 135 C1
Maritas, Laguna de las Venezuela 10°55N 63°56W 329 a
Maritime Alps = Maritimes, Alpes Europe 44°10N 7°10E 175 D11
Maritimes, Alpes Europe 44°10N 7°10E 175 D11
Maritsa = Evros → Greece 41°40N 26°34E 203 F10
Maritsa Greece 36°22N 28°8E 206 E12
Marittima, Stazione Italy 142 b1
Mariupol Ukraine 47°5N 37°31E 189 J9
Marīvān Iran 35°30N 46°25E 213 E12
Mariveles Phil. 14°26N 120°29E 232 D3
Mariy Chodra △ Russia 56°10N 48°30E 190 B9
Marj 'Uyūn Lebanon 33°21N 35°34E 250 E6
Marjan = Wazikhwah Afghan. 32°11N 68°21E 240 B3
Mark Twain L. U.S.A. 39°28N 91°55W 310 E5
Marka Si. Arabia 18°14N 41°19E 256 D5
Marka Somalia 1°48N 44°50E 267 D5
Markam China 29°42N 98°38E 228 C2
Markapur India 15°44N 79°19E 245 G4
Markaryd Sweden 56°28N 13°35E 163 H7
Markat Albania 39°44N 20°12E 206 B10
Markazī □ Iran 34°0N 49°30E 247 C6
Markdale Canada 44°19N 80°39W 312 B4
Marked Tree U.S.A. 35°32N 90°25W 315 D9
Markelsdorfer Huk Germany 54°33N 11°4E 178 A7
Market Drayton U.K. 52°54N 2°29W 168 E5
Market Harborough U.K. 52°29N 0°55W 169 E7
Market Rasen U.K. 53°24N 0°20W 168 D7
Markham Ont., Canada 43°52N 79°16W 141 A2
Markham Ill., U.S.A. 41°36N 87°42W 119 D2
Markham → Papua N. G. 6°41S 147°2E 286 C4
Markham, Mt. Antarctica 83°0S 164°0E 151 E11
Marki Poland 52°19N 21°6E 143 B2
Märkisch Friedland = Mirosławiec Poland 53°20N 16°5E 184 E3
Märkische Schweiz △ Germany 52°34N 14°2E 178 C10
Markit China 38°54N 77°40E 217 E9
Markkleeberg Germany 51°16N 12°23E 178 D8
Markland Wood Canada 43°38N 79°34W 141 B1
Markleeville U.S.A. 38°42N 119°47W 306 G7
Markopoulo Greece 37°53N 23°57E 204 D5
Markounda C.A.R. 7°39N 16°55E 264 A3
Markovac Serbia 44°14N 21°7E 202 B5
Markovo Russia 64°40N 170°24E 215 C17
Markoye Burkina Faso 14°39N 0°2E 263 C5
Marks Russia 51°45N 46°50E 190 E8
Marksshtadt = Marks Russia 51°45N 46°50E 190 E8
Marksville U.S.A. 31°8N 92°4W 314 F8
Markt Schwaben Germany 48°11N 11°52E 179 G7
Marktoberdorf Germany 47°45N 10°37E 179 H6
Marktredwitz Germany 50°1N 12°6E 179 E8
Marl Germany 51°39N 7°4E 178 D3
Marla Australia 27°19S 133°33E 281 D1
Marlbank Canada 44°26N 77°6W 312 B7
Marlboro U.S.A. 41°36N 73°59W 313 E11
Marlborough Queens., Australia 22°46S 149°52E 280 C4
Marlborough Wilts., U.K. 51°25N 1°43W 169 F6

Marlborough Mass., U.S.A. 42°21N 71°33W 313 D13
Marlborough □ N.Z. 41°40S 173°50E 285 B8
Marlborough Downs U.K. 51°27N 1°53W 169 F6
Marle France 49°43N 3°47E 173 C10
Marlin U.S.A. 31°18N 96°54W 314 F6
Marlow Mecklenburg-Vorpommern, Germany 54°9N 12°33E 178 A8
Marlow Bucks., U.K. 51°34N 0°46W 169 F7
Marlow Okla., U.S.A. 34°39N 97°58W 314 D6
Marly, Forêt de France 48°52N 2°2E 134 A1
Marly-le-Roi France 48°52N 2°5E 134 A1
Marmagao India 15°25N 73°56E 245 G1
Marmande France 44°30N 0°10E 174 D4
Marmara Turkey 40°35N 27°34E 203 F11
Marmara, Sea of = Marmara Denizi Turkey 40°45N 28°15E 203 F12
Marmara Denizi Turkey 40°45N 28°15E 203 F12
Marmara Gölü Turkey 38°37N 28°2E 205 C10
Marmaris Turkey 36°50N 28°14E 205 E10
Marmaris Limanı Turkey 36°50N 28°19E 205 E10
Marmelos → Brazil 6°6S 61°46W 331 B5
Marmion, Mt. Australia 29°16S 119°50E 279 E2
Marmion L. Canada 48°55N 91°20W 298 C1
Marmolada, Mte. Italy 46°26N 11°51E 199 B8
Marmolejo Spain 38°3N 4°13W 195 G6
Marmora Canada 44°28N 77°41W 312 B7
Mármora, La Italy 39°59N 9°20E 200 C2
Marnay France 47°16N 5°48E 173 E12
Marne Germany 53°56N 9°2E 178 B5
Marne □ France 48°50N 4°10E 173 D11
Marne → France 48°47N 2°29E 173 D9
Marne-la-Vallée France 48°50N 2°37E 134 A4
Marneuli Georgia 41°30N 44°48E 191 K7
Marnia = Maghnia Algeria 34°50N 1°43W 261 B4
Marnoo Australia 36°40S 142°52E 282 D5
Maro Chad 8°30N 19°0E 259 G3
Maro Reef U.S.A. 25°25N 170°35W 302 F9
Maroa Ill., U.S.A. 40°2N 88°57W 310 D8
Maroa Venezuela 2°43N 67°33W 328 C4
Maroala Madag. 15°23S 47°59E 272 B2
Maroantsetra Madag. 15°26S 49°44E 272 B2
Maroelaboom Namibia 19°15S 18°53E 270 A2
Marofandilia Madag. 20°7S 44°34E 272 C1
Marojejy ⌂ Madag. 14°26S 49°21E 272 A2
Marokau French Polynesia 18°2S 142°17W 289 f
Marolambo Madag. 20°2S 48°7E 272 C2
Marolles-en-Brie France 48°44N 2°33E 134 B4
Maromandia Madag. 14°13S 48°5E 272 A2
Maromokotro Madag. 14°0S 49°0E 272 A2
Marondera Zimbabwe 18°5S 31°42E 269 F3
Maroni → Fr. Guiana 5°30N 54°0W 329 B7
Maronia Greece 40°53N 25°30E 203 F9
Maronne → France 45°5N 1°56E 174 C5
Maroochydore Australia 26°29S 153°5E 281 D5
Maroon Town Jamaica 18°22N 77°48W 320 a
Maroona Australia 37°27S 142°54E 282 D5
Maros Indonesia 5°0S 119°34E 235 C5
Maros → Hungary 46°15N 20°13E 182 D5
Marosakoa Madag. 15°26S 46°38E 272 B2
Maroseranana Madag. 18°32S 48°51E 272 B2
Maróstica Italy 45°44N 11°40E 199 C8
Marotandrano Madag. 16°10S 48°50E 272 B2
Marotiri, Îs. = Bass, Îs. de French Polynesia 27°55S 143°26W 289 f
Maroua Cameroon 10°40N 14°20E 259 F2
Maroubra Australia 33°56S 151°16E 139 B2
Marovato Madag. 15°48S 48°5E 272 B2
Marovoay Madag. 16°6S 46°39E 272 B2
Marowijne □ Suriname 4°0N 55°0W 329 C7
Marowijne → Suriname 5°45N 53°58W 329 B7
Marqakōl Kazakhstan 48°45N 85°45E 217 C11
Marquard S. Africa 28°40S 27°28E 270 C4
Marquesas Fracture Zone Pac. Oc. 9°0S 125°0W 289 H15
Marquesas Is. = Marquises, Îs. French Polynesia 9°30S 140°0W 289 f
Marquesas Keys U.S.A. 24°35N 82°10W 317 L7
Marquette U.S.A. 46°33N 87°24W 308 B10
Marquette Park U.S.A. 41°46N 87°42W 119 C2
Marquis St. Lucia 14°2N 60°54W 323 m
Marquis, C. St. Lucia 14°3N 60°54W 323 m
Marquis I. Grenada 12°5N 61°37W 323 q
Marquise France 50°50N 1°40E 173 B8
Marquises, Îs. French Polynesia 9°30S 140°0W 289 f
Marra, Gebel South Sudan 7°20N 27°35E 257 F2
Marra, Pta. da Angola 16°31S 11°43E 265 F2
Marra Cr. → Australia 30°8S 147°15E 283 A7
Marra-Marra △ Australia 33°30S 151°4E 283 B9
Marracuene Mozam. 25°45S 32°35E 271 C5
Marradi Italy 44°4N 11°37E 199 D8
Marrakech Morocco 31°9N 8°0W 260 B3
Marrakech-Tensift-Al Haouz □ Morocco 31°25N 8°40W 260 B3
Marratxí Spain 39°39N 2°48E 206 B3
Marrawah Australia 40°55S 144°42E 281 G3
Marrecas, Serra das Brazil 9°0S 41°0W 332 C3
Marree Australia 29°39S 138°1E 281 D2
Marrero U.S.A. 29°53N 90°6W 131 B2
Marrickville Australia 33°54S 151°9E 139 B1
Marrimane Mozam. 22°58S 33°34E 271 B5
Marromeu Mozam. 18°15S 36°25E 271 A6
Marromeu △ Mozam. 19°0S 36°0E 271 A6
Marroquí, Punta Spain 36°0N 5°37W 195 K5
Marrowie Cr. → Australia 33°23S 145°40E 283 B6
Marruás = Porto Brazil 3°54S 42°42W 332 B3
Marrubane Mozam. 18°0S 37°0E 269 F4
Marrúbiu Italy 39°40N 8°35E 200 C1
Marrupa Mozam. 13°8S 37°30E 269 E4
Mars B. Ascension I. 7°59S 14°24W 153 g
Mars Hill U.S.A. 46°31N 67°52W 309 B20
Marsa al Burayqah Libya 30°24N 19°37E 258 B3
Marsá 'Alam Egypt 25°5N 34°54E 256 B3
Marsá Matrûh Egypt 31°19N 27°9E 256 A2
Marsa Sha'b Sudan 22°52N 35°47E 256 C4
Marsabit Kenya 2°18N 38°0E 268 B4
Marsabit □ Kenya 3°0N 37°30E 268 B4
Marsabit △ Kenya 2°23N 37°56E 268 B4
Marsala Italy 37°48N 12°26E 200 E5
Marsalforn Malta 36°4N 14°16E 206 E7
Mârşani Romania 44°1N 24°1E 183 F9
Marsaskala Malta 35°52N 14°34E 206 F8
Marsaxlokk Malta 35°51N 14°33E 206 F8
Marsaxlokk Bay Malta 35°49N 14°33E 206 F8
Marsberg Germany 51°28N 8°52E 178 D4
Marsciano Italy 42°54N 12°20E 199 F9
Marsden Australia 33°47S 147°32E 283 B7
Marsden Point N.Z. 35°50S 174°31E 284 B3
Marseillan France 43°23N 3°31E 174 E7
Marseille France 43°18N 5°23E 175 E9
Marseille-Marignane ✕ (MRS) France 43°26N 5°14E 175 E9
Marseilles = Marseille France 43°18N 5°23E 175 E9
Marseilles U.S.A. 41°20N 88°43W 311 C8
Marsfield Australia 33°46S 151°7E 139 A1
Marsh Harbour Bahamas 26°33N 77°3W 320 A4
Marsh I. U.S.A. 29°34N 91°53W 314 G9
Marsha, L. U.S.A. 28°29N 81°29W 133 B2
Marshall Liberia 6°8N 10°22W 262 D2
Marshall Alaska, U.S.A. 61°53N 162°5W 303 F7
Marshall Ark., U.S.A. 35°55N 92°38W 314 D8
Marshall Ill., U.S.A. 39°23N 87°42W 311 E9
Marshall Mich., U.S.A. 42°16N 84°58W 311 B12
Marshall Minn., U.S.A. 44°27N 95°47W 308 C6
Marshall Mo., U.S.A. 39°7N 93°12W 310 E3
Marshall Tex., U.S.A. 32°33N 94°23W 314 E7
Marshall → Australia 22°59S 136°59E 280 C2
Marshall, C. Ecuador 0°1S 91°12W 330 a
Marshall Bennett Is. Papua N. G. 8°50S 151°55E 286 E6
Marshall Is. ■ Pac. Oc. 9°0N 171°0E 288 G9
Marshalltown U.S.A. 42°3N 92°55W 310 B4
Marshallville = Lewisporte Canada 49°15N 55°3W 299 C8
Marshallville U.S.A. 32°27N 83°56W 316 C6
Marshbrook Zimbabwe 18°33S 31°9E 271 A5
Marshfield = Coos Bay U.S.A. 43°22N 124°13W 304 E1
Marshfield Mo., U.S.A. 37°15N 92°54W 308 G7
Marshfield Vt., U.S.A. 44°20N 72°20W 313 B12
Marshfield Wis., U.S.A. 44°40N 90°10W 308 C8
Marshūn Iran 36°19N 49°23E 247 B6
Mársico Nuovo Italy 40°25N 15°44E 201 B8
Marsouins, R. des → Réunion 21°1S 55°44E 272 f
Märsta Sweden 59°37N 17°52E 162 E11
Marstal Denmark 54°51N 10°30E 163 K4
Marstrand Sweden 57°53N 11°35E 163 G5
Mart U.S.A. 31°33N 96°50W 314 F6
Marta → Italy 42°14N 11°42E 199 F8
Martaban Burma 16°30N 97°35E 241 G6
Martaban, G. of = Mottama, G. of Burma 16°5N 96°30E 241 G6
Martano Italy 40°12N 18°18E 201 B11
Martapura Kalimantan Selatan, Indonesia 3°22S 114°47E 235 C4
Martapura Sumatera Selatan, Indonesia 4°19S 104°22E 234 C2
Marte Nigeria 12°23N 13°46E 263 C7
Marte, Campo de Brazil 23°30S 46°38W 137 B2
Marte R. Gómez, Presa Mexico 26°10N 99°0W 319 B5
Martel France 44°57N 1°37E 174 D5
Martelange Belgium 49°49N 5°43E 170 E5
Martellago Italy 45°33N 12°9E 199 C9
Martés, Sierra Spain 39°20N 1°0W 197 F4
Martesana, Navíglio della Italy 45°31N 9°17E 128 A2
Martfű Hungary 47°1N 20°17E 182 C5
Marthaguy Cr. → Australia 30°16S 147°35E 283 A7
Marthapal India 19°24N 81°37E 244 E5
Martha's Vineyard U.S.A. 41°25N 70°38W 313 E14
Martigné-Ferchaud France 47°50N 1°20W 172 E5
Martigny Switz. 46°6N 7°3E 179 J3
Martigues France 43°24N 5°4E 175 E9
Martil Morocco 35°36N 5°15W 260 A3
Martin Slovakia 49°6N 18°58E 181 B11
Martin S. Dak., U.S.A. 43°11N 101°44W 308 D3
Martin Tenn., U.S.A. 36°21N 88°51W 315 C10
Martin → Spain 41°18N 0°19W 196 D4
Martin L. U.S.A. 32°41N 85°55W 316 C4
Martin Luther King Nat. Historic Site ⌂ U.S.A. 33°45N 84°22W 113 B2
Martin Pt. U.S.A. 70°8N 143°16W 303 A12
Martin Vaz Atl. Oc. 20°30S 28°51W 152 J9
Martina Franca Italy 40°42N 17°20E 201 B10
Martinborough N.Z. 41°14S 175°29E 284 H4
Martinez B. Aires, Argentina 34°29S 58°31W 117 A1
Martinez Calif., U.S.A. 38°1N 122°8W 306 G4
Martinez Ga., U.S.A. 33°31N 82°5W 316 B7
Martinho Campos Brazil 19°20S 45°13W 333 E2
Martinique ⊠ W. Indies 14°40N 61°0W 322 j
Martinique Channel St. Vincent 12°34N 61°25W 323 n
Martinique Passage W. Indies 15°15N 61°0W 321 C7
Martinkylä Finland 60°17N 24°51E 121 B2
Martino Greece 38°35N 23°12E 204 C5
Martinópolis Brazil 22°11S 51°12W 335 A5
Martins Ferry U.S.A. 40°6N 80°44W 312 F4
Martinsberg Austria 48°22N 15°9E 180 C8
Martinsburg Pa., U.S.A. 40°19N 78°20W 312 F6
Martinsburg W. Va., U.S.A. 39°27N 77°58W 309 F15
Martinsicuro Italy 42°54N 13°54E 199 F10
Martinsried Germany 48°6N 11°27E 131 B1
Martinsville Ill., U.S.A. 39°20N 87°53W 311 E9
Martinsville Ind., U.S.A. 39°26N 86°25W 311 E10
Martinsville Va., U.S.A. 36°41N 79°52W 309 G14
Marton N.Z. 40°4S 175°23E 284 G4
Martorell Spain 41°28N 1°56E 196 D6
Martos Spain 37°44N 3°58W 195 H7
Martu ✪ Australia 22°30S 122°30E 278 D3
Martûbah Libya 32°35N 22°46E 258 B4
Martuni Armenia 40°8N 45°20E 191 K7
Maru Nigeria 12°22N 6°22E 263 C6
Marudi Malaysia 4°11N 114°19E 235 B4
Maruf Afghan. 31°30N 67°6E 240 C2
Marugame Japan 34°15N 133°40E 222 C5
Marui = Pagwi Papua N. G. 4°4S 143°2E 286 C2
Maruia → N.Z. 41°47S 172°13E 285 B7
Maruim Brazil 10°45S 37°5W 332 D4
Maruko Japan 35°33N 139°40E 140 B3
Marulan Australia 34°43S 150°3E 283 C9
Marum, Mt. Vanuatu 16°15S 168°7E 287 F6
Marunga Angola 17°28S 20°2E 265 F4
Marungu, Mts. Dem. Rep. of the Congo 7°30S 30°0E 268 D3
Marunouchi Tokyo, Japan 140 b4
Maruoka = Sakai Japan 36°9N 136°16E 223 A8
Maruwa ✪ Australia 22°30S 127°30E 278 D4
Marv Dasht Iran 29°50N 52°40E 247 D7
Marvão = Castelo do Piauí Brazil 5°20S 41°33W 332 C3
Marvão Portugal 39°24N 7°20W 195 F3
Marvast Iran 30°30N 54°15E 247 D7
Marvejols France 44°33N 3°19E 174 D7
Marvel Loch Australia 31°28S 119°29E 279 F2
Marwar India 25°43N 73°45E 242 G5
Mary Turkmenistan 37°40N 61°50E 247 B9
Mary Esther U.S.A. 30°25N 86°40W 317 E3
Maryborough = Portlaoise Ireland 53°2N 7°18W 166 C4
Maryborough Queens., Australia 25°31S 152°37E 281 D5
Maryborough Vic., Australia 37°3S 143°44E 282 D5
Maryfield Canada 49°50N 101°35W 297 D8
Maryino = Pristen Russia 51°15N 36°44E 189 G9
Maryino Russia 55°40N 37°45E 129 B3
Maryland Singapore 1°19N 103°47E 138 B2
Maryland □ U.S.A. 39°0N 76°30W 309 F15
Maryland Junction Zimbabwe 17°45S 30°31E 269 F3
Marylebone London, U.K. 125 a2
Marymont Poland 52°16N 20°58E 143 B1
Maryport U.K. 54°44N 3°28W 168 C4
Mary's Harbour Canada 52°18N 55°51W 299 B8
Marysin Wawerski Poland 52°14N 21°9E 143 B2
Marystown Canada 47°10N 55°10W 299 C8
Marysville Calif., U.S.A. 39°9N 121°35W 306 F5
Marysville Kans., U.S.A. 39°51N 96°39W 308 F5
Marysville Mich., U.S.A. 42°54N 82°29W 312 D2
Marysville Ohio, U.S.A. 40°14N 83°22W 311 D13
Marysville Wash., U.S.A. 48°3N 122°11W 306 B4
Maryville Mo., U.S.A. 40°21N 94°52W 310 D2
Maryville Tenn., U.S.A. 35°46N 83°58W 315 D13
Marzahn Germany 52°32N 13°34E 115 A4
Marzo, Punta Colombia 6°50N 77°42W 328 B2
Masada Israel 31°18N 35°21E 251 G6
Mas'ada Syria 33°13N 35°45E 250 E6
Masahunga Tanzania 2°6S 33°18E 268 C3
Masai Malaysia 1°29N 103°55E 237 d
Masai Mara △ Kenya 1°25S 35°5E 268 C4
Masai Steppe Tanzania 4°30S 36°30E 268 C4
Masaka Uganda 0°21S 31°45E 268 C3
Masāl Iran 37°23N 49°8E 212 D10
Masalembo, Kepulauan Indonesia 5°35S 114°30E 235 D4
Masalima, Kepulauan Indonesia 5°4S 117°5E 235 D5
Masallı Azerbaijan 39°3N 48°40E 213 C13
Masalog Pt. N. Marianas 15°1N 145°40E 302 e
Masamba Indonesia 2°30S 120°15E 231 E6
Masan S. Korea 35°11N 128°32E 224 E4
Masandam, Ra's Oman 26°30N 56°30E 247 E8
Masasi Tanzania 10°45S 38°52E 269 E4
Masaya Nic. 12°0N 86°7W 320 D2
Masba Nigeria 11°35N 13°1E 263 C7
Masbate Phil. 12°21N 123°36E 232 E4
Masbate □ Phil. 12°20N 123°30E 232 E4
Masbate Pass. Phil. 12°30N 123°35E 232 E4
Máscali Italy 37°45N 15°12E 201 E8
Mascara Algeria 35°26N 0°6E 261 A5
Mascara □ Algeria 35°25N 0°10E 261 A5
Mascarene Is. Ind. Oc. 22°0S 55°0E 254 J9
Mascot Australia 33°55S 151°12E 139 B2
Mascota Mexico 20°32N 104°49W 318 C4
Mascoutah U.S.A. 38°29N 89°48W 310 F7
Masdar City = Madīnat Masdar U.A.E. 24°26N 54°37E 247 E7
Masefau B. Amer. Samoa 14°15S 170°37W 302 f
Masein Burma 23°22N 94°21E 241 D5
Masela Indonesia 8°9S 129°51E 231 F7
Maseru Lesotho 29°18S 27°30E 270 C4
Masfjorden Norway 60°48N 5°18E 164 D2
Mashaba Zimbabwe 20°2S 30°29E 269 G3
Mashābih Si. Arabia 25°35N 36°30E 246 E3
Mashan China 23°40N 108°11E 228 F7
Mashang China 36°48N 117°57E 227 F9
Mashar South Sudan 9°16N 26°51E 257 F2
Mashatu ⌂ Botswana 22°45S 29°5E 271 B4
Mashegu Nigeria 10°0N 5°35E 263 D6
Masherbrum Pakistan 35°38N 76°18E 243 B7
Mashhad Iran 36°20N 59°35E 247 B8
Mashi Nigeria 13°0N 7°54E 263 C6
Mashiki Japan 32°51N 130°53E 222 E2
Mashīz Iran 29°56N 56°37E 247 D8
Mashkel → Pakistan 26°2N 65°19E 240 D2
Māshkel, Hāmūn-i- Pakistan 28°20N 62°56E 240 C1
Mashki Chāh Pakistan 29°5N 62°30E 240 C1
Mashonaland Central □ Zimbabwe 17°30S 31°0E 271 A5
Mashonaland East □ Zimbabwe 18°0S 32°0E 271 A5
Mashonaland West □ Zimbabwe 17°30S 29°30E 271 A4
Mashrakh India 26°7N 84°48E 243 F11
Masi Manimba Dem. Rep. of the Congo 4°40S 17°54E 265 C3
Masindi Angola 11°6S 22°41E 265 E4
Masig Australia 9°45S 143°24E 280 a
Masindi Uganda 1°40N 31°43E 268 B3
Masindi Port Uganda 1°43N 32°2E 268 B3
Masinga Res. Kenya 0°58S 37°38E 268 C4
Masinloc Phil. 15°32N 119°57E 232 D2
Maşīrah, Jazīrat Oman 21°0N 58°50E 249 B7
Maşīrah, Khalīj Oman 20°10N 58°10E 249 B7
Maşīrah, Tur'at Oman 20°30N 58°40E 249 B7
Masísea Peru 8°35S 74°22W 330 B3
Masisi Dem. Rep. of the Congo 1°23S 28°49E 268 C2
Masjed Soleyman Iran 31°55N 49°18E 247 D6
Mask, L. Ireland 53°36N 9°22W 166 C2
Maskelyne Is. Vanuatu 16°32S 167°49E 287 F5
Maski India 15°56N 76°46E 245 G3
Maskin Oman 23°44N 56°52E 247 F8
Maslen Nos Bulgaria 42°18N 27°48E 203 D11
Maslinica Croatia 43°24N 16°13E 199 E13
Masmo Sweden 59°15N 17°53E 139 B1
Maşna'ah Yemen 14°27N 48°17E 249 D5
Masnou = El Masnou Spain 41°28N 2°20E 196 D7
Masoala, Saikanosy Madag. 15°45S 50°10E 272 B3
Masoala, Tanjon' i Madag. 15°59S 50°13E 272 B3
Masoala △ Madag. 15°30S 50°12E 272 B3
Masoarivo Madag. 19°3S 44°19E 272 B1
Masohi = Amahai Indonesia 3°20S 128°55E 231 E7
Masomeloka Madag. 20°17S 48°37E 272 C2
Mason Mich., U.S.A. 42°35N 84°27W 311 B12
Mason Nev., U.S.A. 38°56N 119°8W 306 G7
Mason Ohio, U.S.A. 39°22N 84°19W 311 E12
Mason Tex., U.S.A. 30°45N 99°14W 314 F5
Mason B. N.Z. 46°55S 167°45E 285 G2
Mason City Ill., U.S.A. 40°12N 89°42W 310 D7
Mason City Iowa, U.S.A. 43°9N 93°12W 310 A3
Mason Hall Trin. & Tob. 11°13N 60°43W 323 s
Maspalomas Canary Is. 27°46N 15°35W 153 e1
Maspalomas, Pta. Canary Is. 27°43N 15°36W 153 e1
Masqat Oman 23°37N 58°36E 249 B7
Maspeth U.S.A. 40°43N 73°55W 132 B2
Masr el Gedida Egypt 30°5N 31°21E 117 A2
Masr el Qadîma Egypt 30°0N 31°14E 117 A2
Massa Congo 3°45S 15°29E 264 C3
Massa Italy 44°1N 10°9E 198 D7
Massa, O. → Morocco 30°2N 9°40W 260 B3
Massa e Carrara □ Italy 44°10N 10°10E 198 D7
Massa Maríttima Italy 43°3N 10°52E 198 E7
Massachusetts □ U.S.A. 42°30N 72°0W 313 D13
Massachusetts Avenue Washington, D.C., U.S.A. 143 a2
Massachusetts B. U.S.A. 42°25N 70°50W 313 D14
Massachusetts Inst. of Tech. Boston, U.S.A. 42°21N 71°5W 116 A2
Massacre Dominica 15°20N 61°25W 323 k
Massafra Italy 40°35N 17°7E 201 B10
Massaguet Chad 12°28N 15°26E 259 F3
Massakory Chad 13°0N 15°49E 259 F3
Massamá Portugal 38°45N 9°16W 126 A1
Massamba Mozam. 15°58S 33°31E 269 F3
Massanella Spain 39°48N 2°51E 206 B3
Massangano Angola 9°40S 14°13E 265 D2
Massangena Mozam. 21°34S 33°0E 271 B5
Massango Angola 8°1S 16°10E 265 D3
Massapê Brazil 3°31S 40°19W 332 B3
Massat France 42°53N 1°21E 174 F5
Massawa = Mitsiwa Eritrea 15°35N 39°25E 257 D4
Massena U.S.A. 44°56N 74°54W 313 B10
Massenya Chad 11°21N 16°9E 259 F3
Masset Canada 54°2N 132°10W 296 C2
Masseube France 43°25N 0°34E 174 E4
Massey → Canada 43°42N 79°19W 141 A3
Massey Hall Toronto, Canada 141 a3
Massiac France 45°15N 3°11E 174 C7
Massif Central France 44°55N 3°0E 174 D7
Massif des Bauges ⌂ France 45°40N 6°10E 173 G13
Massigui Mali 11°48N 6°50W 262 C3
Massillon U.S.A. 40°48N 81°32W 312 F3
Massima Gabon 1°27S 11°33E 264 C2
Massinge, O. → Algeria 36°13N 2°12E 261 A5
Massinga Mozam. 23°15S 35°22E 271 B6
Massingir Mozam. 23°51S 32°4E 271 B5
Masson-Angers Canada 45°32N 75°25W 313 A9
Masson I. Antarctica 66°10S 93°20E 151 C7
Massouka Gabon 1°37S 9°56E 264 C1
Massow = Maszewo Poland 53°29N 15°3E 184 E2
Massy France 48°43N 2°16E 134 B2
Mastābah Si. Arabia 20°49N 39°26E 248 B2
Maştağa Azerbaijan 40°35N 50°1E 191 K10
Mastanli = Momchilgrad Bulgaria 41°33N 25°23E 203 E9
Masterton N.Z. 40°56S 175°39E 284 G4
Mastic U.S.A. 40°47N 72°54W 313 F12
Mastuj Pakistan 36°20N 72°36E 243 A5
Mastung Pakistan 29°50N 66°56E 240 C2
Mastūrah Si. Arabia 23°7N 38°52E 248 B2
Masty Belarus 53°27N 24°38E 177 B13
Masuda Japan 34°40N 131°51E 222 C3
Masuika Dem. Rep. of the Congo 7°37S 22°32E 265 D4
Masuku = Franceville Gabon 1°40S 13°32E 264 C2
Masurai Indonesia 2°30S 101°51E 234 C2
Masurian Lakes = Mazurski, Pojezierze Poland 53°50N 21°0E 184 E7
Masvingo Zimbabwe 20°8S 30°49E 269 G3
Masvingo □ Zimbabwe 21°0S 31°30E 269 G3
Maswa ⌂ Tanzania 2°58S 34°19E 268 C3
Maşyāf Syria 35°4N 36°20E 250 C7
Maszewo Poland 53°29N 15°3E 184 E2
Mat → Albania 41°40N 19°35E 202 E3
Mât → Réunion 20°57S 55°42E 272 f
Mata Israel 31°43N 35°4E 123 B1
Mata-au = Clutha → N.Z. 46°20S 169°49E 285 G4
Mata de São João Brazil 12°31S 38°17W 333 D4
Mata Redonda Venezuela 10°57N 64°7W 329 a
Mata-Utu Wall. & F. Is. 13°17S 176°8W 277 C15
Matabele Plain Zambia 16°20S 23°10E 265 F4
Matabeleland North □ Zimbabwe 19°0S 28°0E 269 F2
Matabeleland South □ Zimbabwe 21°0S 29°0E 269 G2
Matachel → Spain 38°50N 6°17W 195 G4
Matachewan Canada 47°56N 80°39W 298 C3
Matacuni → Venezuela 3°2N 65°16W 329 C4
Matadi Dem. Rep. of the Congo 5°52S 13°31E 265 D2
Matafao, Mt. Amer. Samoa 14°17S 170°42W 302 f
Matagalpa Nic. 13°0N 85°58W 320 D2
Matagami Canada 49°45N 77°34W 298 C4
Matagami, L. Canada 49°50N 77°40W 298 C4
Matagorda B. U.S.A. 28°40N 96°12W 314 G6
Matagorda I. U.S.A. 28°15N 96°30W 314 G6
Matahiva French Polynesia 17°32S 149°20W 289 f
Mataiea Tahiti 17°46S 149°25W 289 e
Matak Indonesia 3°18N 106°16E 234 B3
Matakana N.S.W., Australia 32°59S 145°54E 283 B6
Matakana N.Z. 36°21S 174°43E 284 C3
Matala Angola 14°46S 15°4E 265 E3
Matala Kriti, Greece 34°59N 24°45E 207 F5
Matalam Phil. 7°5N 124°54E 233 H5
Matalaque Peru 16°26S 70°49W 330 D3
Matale Sri Lanka 7°30N 80°37E 245 L5
Matam Senegal 15°34N 13°17W 262 B2
Matam □ Senegal 15°37N 13°19W 262 B2
Matamata N.Z. 37°48S 175°47E 284 D4
Matameye Niger 13°26N 8°28E 259 F1
Matamoros Coahuila, Mexico 25°32N 103°15W 318 B4
Matamoros Tamaulipas, Mexico 25°53N 97°30W 319 B5
Ma'ţan as Sarra Libya 21°45N 22°0E 259 D4
Ma'ţan Bishārah Libya 23°0N 22°32E 258 D4
Matandu → Tanzania 8°45S 34°19E 269 D3
Matane Canada 48°50N 67°33W 299 C6
Matang China 23°30N 104°7E 228 F5
Matankari Niger 13°46N 4°1E 263 C5
Matanomadh India 23°33N 68°57E 242 H3
Matanzas Cuba 23°0N 81°40W 320 B3
Matapa Botswana 23°11S 24°39E 270 B3
Matapan, C. = Tenaro, Akra Greece 36°22N 22°27E 204 E4
Matapédia Canada 48°0N 66°59W 299 C6
Matapo △ Zimbabwe 20°30S 29°40E 269 G2
Mataporquera Spain 42°52N 4°10W 194 C6
Matara Sri Lanka 5°58N 80°30E 245 M5
Mataram Indonesia 8°35S 116°7E 231 K19
Matarani Peru 17°0S 72°10W 330 D3
Mataranka Australia 14°55S 133°4E 278 B5
Matarinao B. Phil. 11°12N 125°33E 233 F5
Matarma, Râs Egypt 30°27N 32°44E 251 H3
Mataró Spain 41°32N 2°29E 196 D7
Matarraña → Spain 41°14N 0°22E 196 D5
Mataruška Banja Serbia 43°40N 20°40E 202 C4
Matasiete, Cerro Venezuela 11°3N 63°51W 329 a
Mataso Vanuatu 17°14S 168°26E 287 G6
Matata N.Z. 37°54S 176°48E 284 D5
Matatiele S. Africa 30°20S 28°49E 271 D4
Matatila Dam India 25°0N 78°22E 244 B4
Matatula, C. Amer. Samoa 14°15S 170°33W 302 f
Mataura N.Z. 46°11S 168°51E 285 G3
Mataura → N.Z. 46°34S 168°44E 285 G3
Matavai, B. de Tahiti 17°30S 149°23W 289 e
Matavera Cook Is. 21°13S 159°44W 289 h
Mataveri Chile 27°9S 109°27W 330 b
Mategua Bolivia 13°1S 62°48W 331 C5
Matehuala Mexico 23°39N 100°39W 318 C4
Mateke Dem. Rep. of the Congo 4°52S 24°25E 264 C3
Mateke Hills Zimbabwe 21°48S 31°0E 269 G3
Matelot Trin. & Tob. 10°50N 61°7W 323 t
Matera Italy 40°40N 16°36E 201 B9
Matese, Monti del Italy 41°27N 14°22E 201 A7
Matese △ Italy 41°24N 14°23E 201 A7
Mátészalka Hungary 47°58N 22°20E 182 C7
Matetsi Zimbabwe 18°12S 26°0E 269 F2
Mateur Tunisia 37°0N 9°40E 258 A1
Matfors Sweden 62°21N 17°2E 162 B11
Matha France 45°52N 0°20W 174 C3
Matheniko ⌂ Uganda 2°49N 34°27E 268 B3
Mathis U.S.A. 28°6N 97°50W 314 G6
Mathoura Australia 35°50S 144°55E 283 C6
Mathraki Greece 39°48N 19°31E 206 B9
Mathura India 27°30N 77°40E 242 F7
Mati Phil. 6°55N 126°15E 233 H6
Matiakoali Burkina Faso 12°28N 1°2E 263 C5
Matiali India 26°56N 88°49E 243 F13
Matías Romero Mexico 16°53N 95°2W 319 D5
Matibane Mozam. 14°49S 40°45E 269 E5
Matima Botswana 20°15S 24°26E 270 B3
Matinha Brazil 3°6S 45°2W 332 B2
Matinha Portugal 38°45N 9°6W 126 A2
Matinhos Brazil 25°49S 48°32W 333 G2
Matiri Ra. N.Z. 41°38S 172°20E 285 B7
Matjiesfontein S. Africa 33°14S 20°35E 270 D3
Matla → India 21°40N 88°40E 243 J13
Matlab Bazar Bangla. 23°20N 90°43E 241 D3
Matlamanyane Botswana 19°33S 25°57E 270 A4
Matli Pakistan 25°2N 68°39E 242 G3
Matlock U.K. 53°9N 1°33W 168 D6
Matmata Tunisia 33°37N 9°59E 258 B1
Matna Sudan 13°49N 35°10E 257 E4
Matnog Phil. 12°35N 124°5E 232 E5
Mato Dem. Rep. of the Congo 8°1S 24°2E 265 D4
Mato → Venezuela 7°9N 65°7W 329 B4
Mato, Serrania de Venezuela 6°25N 65°25W 328 B4
Mato Grosso □ Brazil 14°0S 55°0W 331 C7
Mato Grosso, Planalto do Brazil 15°0S 55°0W 331 D7
Mato Grosso do Sul □ Brazil 18°0S 55°0W 331 D7
Matobo = Matapo △ Zimbabwe 20°30S 29°40E 269 G2
Matochkin Shar, Proliv Russia 73°23N 55°12E 214 B6
Matola Mozam. 25°57S 32°27E 271 C5
Matong Papua N. G. 5°36S 151°50E 286 C6
Matopo Hills Zimbabwe 20°36S 28°20E 269 G2
Matopos Zimbabwe 20°20S 28°29E 269 G2
Matosinhos Portugal 41°11N 8°42W 194 D2
Matou Taiwan 23°11N 120°15E 225 G2
Matouba Guadeloupe 16°2N 61°41W 322 e
Matour France 46°19N 4°29E 173 F11
Matramam Indonesia 6°12S 106°51E 122 B2
Matroosberg S. Africa 33°23S 19°40E 270 D2
Maţruḩ Oman 23°37N 58°30E 249 B7
Matsalu △ Estonia 58°45N 23°36E 188 C2
Matsena Nigeria 13°5N 10°5E 263 C7
Matsesta Russia 43°34N 39°51E 191 J4
Matsu Tao Taiwan 26°8N 119°56E 225 b
Matsubara = Takahagi Japan 36°43N 140°45E 221 F10
Matsubara Japan 34°34N 135°33E 133 B2
Matsubase Japan 32°40N 130°40E 222 E2
Matsudo Japan 35°47N 139°54E 223 B11
Matsue Japan 35°25N 133°10E 222 B5
Matsum, Ko Thailand 9°22N 99°59E 237 b
Matsumae Japan 41°26N 140°7E 220 D10
Matsumae-Hantō Japan 41°30N 140°15E 220 D10
Matsumoto Japan 36°15N 138°0E 223 A10
Matsusaka Japan 34°34N 136°32E 223 C8
Matsushima Kumamoto, Japan 32°30N 130°25E 222 E2
Matsushima Miyagi, Japan 38°20N 141°10E 220 E10
Matsuura Japan 33°20N 129°49E 222 D1
Matsuyama Japan 33°45N 132°45E 222 D4
Matsuzaki Japan 34°43N 138°50E 223 C10
Mattagami → Canada 50°43N 81°29W 298 B3
Mattancheri India 9°50N 76°15E 245 K3
Mattapan U.S.A. 42°16N 71°6W 116 B2
Mattawa Canada 46°20N 78°45W 298 C4
Matterhorn Switz. 45°58N 7°39E 179 K3
Mattersburg Austria 47°44N 16°24E 181 D9
Matteson U.S.A. 41°30N 87°42W 311 C9
Matthew, Î. N. Cal. 22°29S 171°15E 277 E13
Matthew Town Bahamas 20°57N 73°40W 321 B5
Matthews U.S.A. 40°23N 85°30W 311 D11
Matthews Ridge Guyana 7°37N 60°10W 329 B5
Mattias Church Budapest, Hungary 117 b1
Mattice Canada 49°40N 83°20W 298 C3
Mattili India 18°33N 82°12E 244 E6
Mattituck U.S.A. 40°59N 72°32W 313 F12
Mattō = Hakusan Japan 36°31N 136°34E 223 A8
Mattoon U.S.A. 39°29N 88°23W 311 E8
Matuba Mozam. 24°28S 32°49E 271 B5
Matucana Peru 11°55S 76°25W 330 C2
Matugama Sri Lanka 6°31N 80°7E 245 L5
Matuguinao Phil. 12°5N 124°53E 232 E5
Matuka Papua N. G. 4°54S 145°47E 286 C3
Matuku Fiji 19°10S 179°44E 287 B2
Matūn = Khowst Afghan. 33°22N 69°58E 242 C3
Matura Trin. & Tob. 10°40N 61°4W 323 t
Matura B. Trin. & Tob. 10°39N 61°1W 323 t
Maturín Venezuela 9°45N 63°11W 329 B4
Matusadona △ Zimbabwe 16°58S 28°42E 269 F2
Matutum, Mt. Phil. 6°22N 125°5E 233 H5
Matveyev Kurgan Russia 47°35N 38°57E 189 J10
Matxitxako, C. Spain 43°28N 2°47W 196 B2
Mátyásföld Hungary 47°30N 19°12E 117 A3
Mau Mad. P., India 26°17N 78°41E 243 F8
Mau Ut. P., India 25°56N 83°33E 243 G10
Mau Ut. P., India 25°17N 81°23E 243 G9
Mau Escarpment Kenya 0°40S 36°0E 268 C4
Mau Ranipur India 25°16N 79°8E 243 G8
Mau Tso Ngam Hong Kong, China 22°22N 114°13E 122 A3
Maua Eastern, Kenya 0°14N 37°56E 268 C4
Maua Mozam. 13°53S 37°10E 269 E4
Mauban Phil. 14°12N 121°44E 232 D3
Maubeuge France 50°17N 3°57E 173 B10
Maubin Burma 16°44N 95°39E 241 G5
Maubourguet France 43°29N 0°1E 174 E4
Maud, Pt. Australia 23°6S 113°45E 278 D1
Maud Rise S. Ocean 66°0S 3°0E 151 C3
Maude Australia 34°29S 144°18E 282 C6
Maudin Sun Burma 16°0N 94°30E 241 G5
Mauer Austria 48°9N 16°16E 142 B1
Maués Brazil 3°20S 57°45W 329 D6
Maués-Acu → Brazil 3°22S 57°44W 329 D6
Maug Is. N. Marianas 20°1N 145°13E 302 a
Mauganj India 24°50N 81°55E 243 G9
Maughold Hd. I. of Man 54°18N 4°18W 168 C3
Mauguio France 43°37N 4°1E 174 E7
Maui U.S.A. 20°48N 156°20W 302 C5
Maulamyaing = Mawlamyine Burma 16°30N 97°40E 241 G6
Maule □ Chile 36°5S 72°30W 334 D1
Mauléon-Licharre France 43°14N 0°54W 174 E3
Maullín Chile 41°38S 73°37W 336 B2
Maulvi Bazar Bangla. 24°29N 91°42E 241 C3
Maumee U.S.A. 41°34N 83°39W 311 C13
Maumee → U.S.A. 41°42N 83°28W 311 C13
Maumere Indonesia 8°38S 122°13E 231 F6
Maumusson, Pertuis de France 45°48N 1°14W 174 C2
Maun Botswana 20°0S 23°26E 270 B3
Mauna Kea U.S.A. 19°50N 155°28W 302 D6
Mauna Loa U.S.A. 19°30N 155°35W 302 D6
Mauna Loa Forest Reserve U.S.A. 19°35N 155°33W 302 D6
Maunabo Puerto Rico 18°1N 65°54W 321 b
Maunaloa U.S.A. 21°8N 157°13W 302 B4
Maunalua B. U.S.A. 21°15N 157°45W 302 K14
Maunath Bhanjan = Mau India 25°56N 83°33E 243 G10
Maunawili U.S.A. 21°23N 157°46W 302 K14
Maunga Orito Chile 27°10S 109°25W 330 b
Maunga Puakatiki Chile 27°6S 109°15W 330 b
Maunga Terevaka Chile 27°5S 109°23W 330 b
Maungaroa Cook Is. 21°13S 159°48W 289 h
Maungatongatutti Cook Is. 21°14S 159°48W 289 h
Maungaturoto N.Z. 36°6S 174°23E 284 C3
Maungdaw Burma 20°50N 92°21E 241 E4
Maungmagan Kyunzu Burma 14°0N 97°48E 236 E1
Maungu Kenya 3°33S 38°45E 268 C4
Maupihaa French Polynesia 16°50S 153°55W 289 f
Maupin U.S.A. 45°11N 121°5W 304 D3
Maupiti French Polynesia 16°27S 152°15W 289 f
Maure-de-Bretagne France 47°9N 1°58W 172 E5
Maurepas, L. U.S.A. 30°15N 90°30W 315 F9
Maures France 43°15N 6°15E 175 E10
Mauriac France 45°13N 2°19E 174 C6
Maurice, L. Australia 29°30S 131°0E 279 E5
Maurice Bishop Int. ✕ (GND) Grenada 12°0N 61°46W 323 q
Mauriceville N.Z. 40°45S 175°42E 284 G4
Mauricie △ Canada 46°45N 73°0W 298 C5
Maurienne France 45°13N 6°30E 175 C10
Mauritania ■ Africa 20°50N 10°0W 260 D3
Mauritius ■ Ind. Oc. 20°0S 57°0E 272 e
Mauritius ✕ (MRU) Mauritius 20°25S 57°40E 272 e
Mauron France 48°9N 2°18W 172 D4
Maurs France 44°43N 2°12E 174 D6
Mauston U.S.A. 43°48N 90°5W 308 D8
Mauterndorf Austria 47°9N 13°40E 180 D6
Mauthen Austria 46°40N 13°0E 180 E6
Mauvezin France 43°44N 0°53E 174 E4
Mauzé-sur-le-Mignon France 46°12N 0°41W 174 B3
Mavaca → Venezuela 2°31N 65°11W 329 C4
Mavinga Angola 15°50S 20°21E 265 F4
Mavli India 24°45N 73°55E 242 G5
Mavoko = Athi River Kenya 1°28S 36°58E 268 C4
Mavrata Greece 38°4N 20°44E 207 C2
Mavrovë Albania 40°26N 19°32E 202 F3
Mavrovo △ Macedonia 41°36N 20°45E 202 E4
Mavuradonha Mts. Zimbabwe 16°30S 31°30E 269 F3
Mawa Dem. Rep. of the Congo 2°45N 26°40E 268 B2
Mawai India 22°30N 81°4E 243 H9
Mawana India 29°6N 77°58E 242 E7
Mawand Pakistan 29°33N 68°38E 242 E3
Mawat Iraq 35°54N 45°24E 213 E11
Mawjib, W. al → Jordan 31°28N 35°36E 251 G6
Mawkmai Burma 20°14N 97°37E 241 E6
Mawlaik Burma 23°40N 94°26E 241 D5
Mawlamyine Burma 16°30N 97°40E 241 G6
Mawlamyinegyun Burma 16°23N 95°16E 241 G5
Mawlawkho Burma 17°50N 97°38E 241 G6
Mawqaq Si. Arabia 27°25N 41°8E 246 E4
Mawson Antarctica 67°30S 62°53E 151 C6
Mawson Coast Antarctica 68°30S 63°0E 151 C6
Mawson Pk. Heard I. 53°6S 73°31E 273 K6
Mawsynram India 25°15N 91°30E 241 C3
Mawza' Yemen 13°16N 43°30E 248 D3
Max U.S.A. 47°49N 101°18W 308 B3
Maxambamba = Nova Iguaçu Brazil 22°45S 43°28W 333 F3
Maxcanú Mexico 20°35N 90°0W 319 C6
Maxesibeni S. Africa 30°49S 29°23E 271 D4
Maxeys U.S.A. 33°45N 83°11W 316 B6
Maxhamish L. Canada 59°50N 123°17W 296 B4
Maxhof Germany 48°4N 11°29E 131 B1
Maxixe Mozam. 23°54S 35°17E 271 B6
Maxville Canada 45°17N 74°51W 313 A10
Maxwell N.Z. 39°51S 174°49E 284 F3
Maxwell Calif., U.S.A. 39°17N 122°11W 306 F4
Maxwelton Australia 20°43S 142°41E 280 C3
MAXXI National Museum of 21st Century Arts Italy 41°56N 12°28E 136 B1
May, C. U.S.A. 38°56N 74°58W 309 F16
May Jirgui Niger 13°44N 8°8E 259 F1
May Pen Jamaica 17°58N 77°15W 320 a
May River Papua N. G. 4°19S 141°58E 286 C1
Maya Indonesia 1°10S 109°35E 235 C3
Maya → Russia 60°28N 134°28E 215 D14
Maya, Costa Mexico 18°44N 87°42W 319 D7
Maya Mts. Belize 16°30N 89°0W 320 C2
Mayabandar India 12°56N 92°56E 245 H11
Mayaguana I. Bahamas 22°30N 72°44W 321 B5
Mayagüez Puerto Rico 18°12N 67°9W 321 C6
Mayahi Niger 13°58N 7°40E 263 C6
Mayaky Ukraine 47°26N 29°33E 183 C14
Mayals = Maials Spain 41°22N 0°30E 196 D5
Mayama Congo 3°51S 14°54E 264 C2
Mayāmey Iran 36°24N 55°42E 247 B7
Mayang China 27°53N 109°49E 228 D7
Mayanup Australia 33°57S 116°27E 279 F2
Mayapán Mexico 20°29N 89°11W 319 C7
Mayari Cuba 20°40N 75°41W 321 B4
Mayaro Trin. & Tob. 10°17N 61°1W 323 t
Mayaro □ Trin. & Tob. 10°10N 61°5W 323 t
Mayaro B. Trin. & Tob. 10°14N 60°59W 323 t
Mayavaram = Mayiladuthurai India 11°3N 79°42E 245 J4
Maybell U.S.A. 40°31N 108°5W 304 F9
Maybio Phil. 5°50N 125°35E 233 J5
Maybole U.K. 55°21N 4°42W 167 F4
Maychew Ethiopia 12°50N 39°31E 257 E4
Maydān Iraq 34°55N 45°37E 213 E11
Maydan Ukraine 48°36N 23°29E 183 B8
Mayen Germany 50°19N 7°13E 179 E3
Mayenne France 48°20N 0°38W 172 D6
Mayenne □ France 48°10N 0°40W 172 D6
Mayenne → France 47°30N 0°32W 172 E6
Mayer U.S.A. 34°24N 112°14W 305 J7
Mayerthorpe Canada 53°57N 115°8W 296 C5
Maysville U.S.A. 34°0N 82°10W 316 A9
Mayfair Gauteng, S. Africa 26°11S 28°0E 123 B2
Mayfair London, U.K. 125 b3
Mayfield Ky., U.S.A. 36°44N 88°38W 308 G9
Mayfield N.Y., U.S.A. 43°6N 74°16W 313 C10
Mayhill U.S.A. 32°53N 105°29W 305 K11
Mayiladuthurai India 11°3N 79°42E 245 J4
Maykop Russia 44°35N 40°10E 191 H5
Mayma Russia 52°3N 85°55E 217 B11
Maymyo = Pyin-U-Lwin Burma 22°2N 96°28E 236 A1
Maynard Mass., U.S.A. 42°26N 71°27W 313 D13
Maynard Wash., U.S.A. 47°59N 122°55W 306 C4
Maynard Hills Australia 28°28S 119°49E 279 E2
Mayne → Australia 23°40S 141°55E 280 C3
Maynooth Ont., Canada 45°13N 77°56W 312 A7
Maynooth Kildare, Ireland 53°23N 6°34W 166 C5
Mayo Yukon, Canada 63°38N 135°57W 294 E4
Mayo Trin. & Tob. 10°21N 61°23W 323 t
Mayo Fla., U.S.A. 30°3N 83°10W 316 E6
Mayo □ Ireland 53°53N 9°3W 166 C2
Mayo → Argentina 45°45S 69°45W 336 C3
Mayo → Peru 6°38S 76°15W 330 B2
Mayo B. Phil. 6°56N 126°22E 233 H6
Mayo Daga Nigeria 6°59N 11°25E 263 D7
Mayo Faran Nigeria 8°57N 12°4E 263 D7
Mayo-Kébbi Est □ Chad 10°20N 15°30E 259 F3
Mayo-Kébbi Ouest □ Chad 9°40N 17°50E 259 G3
Mayoko Congo 2°18S 12°49E 264 C2
Mayoko Dem. Rep. of the Congo 1°6S 23°50E 264 C4
Mayon Volcano Phil. 13°15N 123°41E 232 E4
Mayor Buratovich Argentina 39°15S 62°37W 336 A4
Mayor I. N.Z. 37°16S 176°17E 284 D5
Mayor Pablo Lagerenza Paraguay 19°55S 60°47W 331 D5
Mayorga Spain 42°10N 5°16W 194 C5
Mayotte ⊠ Ind. Oc. 12°50S 45°10E 272 b
Mayoyao Phil. 16°59N 121°14E 232 C3
Mayqayyng Kazakhstan 51°27N 75°47E 217 B9
Mayraira Pt. Phil. 18°39N 120°51E 232 B3
Mayreau St. Vincent 12°39N 61°23W 323 n
Maysān □ Iraq 31°55N 47°15E 246 D5
Mayskiy Russia 43°47N 44°2E 191 J7
Maysville Ky., U.S.A. 38°39N 83°46W 311 F13
Maysville Mo., U.S.A. 39°53N 94°22W 310 E2
Maytiguid I. Phil. 11°3N 119°36E 233 F2
Mayu Indonesia 1°30N 126°30E 231 D7
Mayumba Gabon 3°25S 10°39E 264 C2
Mayuram = Mayiladuthurai India 11°3N 79°42E 245 J4
Mayville N. Dak., U.S.A. 47°30N 97°20W 308 B5
Mayville N.Y., U.S.A. 42°15N 79°30W 312 D5
Maywood Calif., U.S.A. 33°59N 118°12W 126 C3
Maywood Ill., U.S.A. 41°52N 87°51W 119 B1
Maywood N.J., U.S.A. 40°53N 74°3W 132 A1
Maywood Park Race Track U.S.A. 41°54N 87°50W 119 B1
Mazabuka Zambia 15°52S 27°44E 269 F2
Mazagān = El Jadida Morocco 33°11N 8°17W 260 B3
Mazagão Brazil 0°7S 51°16W 329 D7
Mazagaon Mumbai, India 130 a2
Mazamet France 43°30N 2°20E 174 E6
Mazán Peru 3°30S 73°0W 328 D3

Māzandarān □ *Iran* 36°30N 52°0E **247** B7
Mazapil *Mexico* 24°39N 101°34W **318** C4
Mazar *China* 36°32N 77°1E **217** E9
Mazar, O. → *Algeria* 31°50N 1°36E **261** B5
Mazār-e Sharīf *Afghan.* 36°41N 67°0E **240** A2
Mazara del Vallo *Italy* 37°39N 12°35E **200** E5
Mazarrón *Argentina* 47°10S 66°50W **336** C3
Mazarrón *Spain* 37°38N 1°19W **197** H3
Mazarrón, G. de *Spain* 37°27N 1°19W **197** H3
Mazaruni → *Guyana* 6°25N 58°35W **329** B6
Mazatán *Mexico* 29°0N 110°8W **318** B2
Mazatenango *Guatemala* 14°35N 91°30W **320** D1
Mazatlán *Mexico* 23°13N 106°25W **318** C3
Mažeikiai *Lithuania* 56°20N 22°20E **184** B9
Mazhaf, J. *Si. Arabia* 28°52N 35°5E **251** K6
Māzhān *Iran* 32°30N 59°0E **247** C8
Mazo Cruz *Peru* 16°45S 69°44W **330** D4
Mazoe *Mozam.* 16°42S 33°7E **269** F3
Mazoe → *Mozam.* 16°20S 33°30E **269** F3
Mazomanie *U.S.A.* 43°11N 89°48W **310** A7
Mazon *U.S.A.* 41°14N 88°25W **311** C8
Mazowe *Zimbabwe* 17°28S 30°58E **269** F3
Mazowieckie □ *Poland* 52°40N 21°0E **185** F8
Mazrûb *Sudan* 14°0N 29°20E **257** E2
Mazurski, Pojezierze
Poland 53°50N 21°0E **184** E7
Mazyr *Belarus* 51°59N 29°15E **177** B15
Mba *Fiji* 17°33S 177°41E **287** A1
Mbaba *Senegal* 14°59N 16°44W **262** C1
Mbabane *Swaziland* 26°18S 31°6E **271** C5
Mbaéré → *C.A.R.* 3°47N 17°31E **264** B3
Mbagne *Mauritania* 16°6N 14°47W **262** B2
Mbaïki *C.A.R.* 3°53N 18°1E **264** B3
Mbakana, Mt. de *Cameroon* 7°57N 15°6E **264** A3
Mbala *Zambia* 8°46S 31°24E **269** D3
Mbalabala *Zimbabwe* 20°27S 29°3E **271** B4
Mbalam *Cameroon* 2°13N 13°49E **264** B2
Mbale *Uganda* 1°8N 34°12E **268** B3
Mbali → *C.A.R.* 4°27N 18°20E **264** B3
Mbalmayo *Cameroon* 3°33N 11°33E **263** E7
Mbam → *Cameroon* 4°24N 11°17E **263** E7
Mbamba Bay *Tanzania* 11°13S 34°49E **269** E3
Mbandaka
Dem. Rep. of the Congo 0°1N 18°18E **264** B3
Mbandjok *Cameroon* 4°27N 11°54E **264** B2
Mbanga *Cameroon* 4°30N 9°33E **263** E6
Mbanika *Solomon Is.* 9°3S 159°13E **287** M10
Mbanza Congo *Angola* 6°18S 14°16E **265** D2
Mbanza Ngungu
Dem. Rep. of the Congo 5°12S 14°53E **265** D2
Mbarangandu *Tanzania* 10°11S 36°48E **269** D4
Mbarara *Uganda* 0°35S 30°40E **268** C3
Mbari → *C.A.R.* 4°34N 22°43E **264** B4
Mbatto *Ivory C.* 6°28N 4°22W **262** D4
Mbava *Solomon Is.* 7°47S 156°33E **287** L9
Mbé *Congo* 3°14S 15°50E **264** C3
Mbe *Eq. Guin.* 1°47N 9°56E **264** B1
Mbengga = Beqa *Fiji* 18°23S 178°8E **287** B2
Mbenguê *Gabon* 2°2S 11°7E **264** C2
Mbengui *Gabon* 2°3S 10°4E **264** C2
Mbéni *Comoros Is.* 11°30S 43°22E **272** a
Mbenkuru → *Tanzania* 9°25S 39°50E **269** D4
Mbéré → *Cameroon* 7°45N 15°36E **264** A3
Mberengwa *Zimbabwe* 20°29S 29°57E **269** C2
Mberengwa, Mt.
Zimbabwe 20°37S 29°55E **269** C2
Mberubu *Nigeria* 6°10N 7°38E **263** D6
Mbesuma *Zambia* 10°0S 32°2E **269** E3
Mbeya *Tanzania* 8°54S 33°29E **269** D3
Mbeya □ *Tanzania* 8°15S 33°30E **269** D3
Mbhashe → *S. Africa* 32°15S 28°54E **271** D4
Mbigou *Gabon* 1°53S 11°56E **264** C2
Mbini = Río Muni □
Eq. Guin. 1°30N 10°0E **264** B2
Mbini *Eq. Guin.* 1°35N 9°37E **264** B1
Mbini → *Eq. Guin.* 1°36N 9°37E **264** B1
Mbizi *Zimbabwe* 21°23S 31°1E **269** G3
Mboi *Dem. Rep. of the Congo* 6°57S 21°54E **265** D4
Mboki *C.A.R.* 5°19N 25°58E **257** F2
Mbokonimbeti
Solomon Is. 8°57S 160°7E **287** M11
Mboli *Dem. Rep. of the Congo* 4°8N 23°9E **264** B4
Mbombela *S. Africa* 25°29S 30°59E **271** C5
Mbomo *Congo* 0°25N 14°42E **264** B2
Mbomou = Bomu →
C.A.R. 4°40N 22°30E **264** B4
Mbomou □ *C.A.R.* 5°30N 23°30E **264** A4
M'bonge *Cameroon* 4°33N 9°5E **263** E6
Mboro *Senegal* 15°9N 16°54W **262** B1
Mboua *Cameroon* 4°25N 14°16E **264** A2
Mbouda *Cameroon* 5°38N 10°15E **264** B2
M'boukou, L. de *Cameroon* 6°23N 12°50E **263** D7
Mboune *Senegal* 14°42N 13°34W **262** C2
Mbouoma *Congo* 0°52S 15°4E **264** C3
Mbour *Senegal* 14°22N 16°54W **262** C1
Mbout *Mauritania* 16°1N 12°38W **262** B2
Mbrès *C.A.R.* 6°40N 19°48E **264** A3
M'Bridge → *Angola* 7°12S 12°51E **265** D2
Mbuji-Mayi
Dem. Rep. of the Congo 6°9S 23°40E **265** D4
Mbulu *Tanzania* 3°45S 35°30E **268** C4
Mbuma
Dem. Rep. of the Congo 3°23N 24°50E **264** B4
Mbuma *Solomon Is.* 8°59S 160°46E **287** M11
Mburucuyá *Argentina* 28°1S 58°14W **334** B4
Mburucuyá △ *Argentina* 28°1S 58°12W **334** B4
M'bwat *Cameroon* 6°29N 10°45E **264** A2
Mcherrah *Algeria* 27°0N 4°30W **260** C4
Mchinga *Tanzania* 9°44S 39°45E **269** D4
Mchinji *Malawi* 13°47S 32°58E **269** E3
Mdantsane *S. Africa* 32°56S 27°46E **271** D4
Mdennah *Mauritania* 24°37N 6°0W **260** D3
Me'a She' Arim *Jerusalem* **123** a2
Mead, L. *U.S.A.* 36°0N 114°44W **307** J12
Meade = Atqasuk →
U.S.A. 70°52N 155°55W **303** A9
Meade *U.S.A.* 37°17N 100°20W **308** G3
Meade River = Atqasuk →
U.S.A. 70°28N 157°24W **303** A9
Meadow Lake *Canada* 54°10N 108°26W **297** C7
Meadow Lake △ *Canada* 54°27N 109°0W **297** C7
Meadow Valley Wash →
U.S.A. 36°40N 114°34W **307** J12
Meadowbank Park
Australia 33°49S 151°6E **139** A1
Meadowlands Sports Complex
New York, U.S.A. 40°49N 74°5W **132** B1
Meadville *Mo., U.S.A.* 39°47N 93°18W **310** E3
Meadville *Pa., U.S.A.* 41°39N 80°9W **312** D4
Meaford *Canada* 44°36N 80°35W **312** B4
Meakan Dake *Japan* 45°15N 144°0E **220** C11
Mealhada *Portugal* 40°22N 8°27W **194** E2
Mealy Mts. *Canada* 53°10N 58°0W **298** B4
Meander River *Canada* 59°2N 117°42W **296** B5
Meares, C. *U.S.A.* 45°37N 124°0W **304** D1
Mearim → *Brazil* 3°4S 44°35W **332** B3
Meath □ *Ireland* 53°40N 6°57W **166** C5
Meath Park *Canada* 53°27N 105°22W **297** C7
Meaulne *France* 46°36N 2°36E **173** F9
Meaux *France* 48°58N 2°50E **173** D9
Mebechi-Gawa →
Japan 40°31N 141°31E **220** D10
Mebonden *Norway* 63°13N 11°2E **164** A8

Mebulu, Tanjung
Indonesia 8°50S 115°5E **231** K18
Mecanhelas *Mozam.* 15°12S 35°54E **269** F4
Mecaya → *Colombia* 0°29N 75°11W **328** C2
Mecca = Makkah
Si. Arabia 21°30N 39°54E **248** B2
Mecca *U.S.A.* 33°34N 116°5W **307** M10
Mechanicsburg *Ohio,*
U.S.A. 40°4N 83°33W **311** D13
Mechanicsburg *Pa., U.S.A.* 40°13N 77°1W **312** D7
Mechanicsville *U.S.A.* 41°54N 91°16W **310** C5
Mechanicville *U.S.A.* 42°54N 73°41W **313** D11
Mechara *Ethiopia* 8°36N 40°20E **257** F5
Mechelen *Belgium* 51°2N 4°29E **170** C4
Mecherchar = Eil Malk
Palau 7°10N 134°23E **288** c
Mecheria *Algeria* 33°35N 0°18W **261** B4
Mechernich *Germany* 50°35N 6°39E **178** E2
Mechetinskaya *Russia* 46°45N 40°32E **191** G5
Mēchŏlupy *Czechia* 50°3N 14°13E **135** B2
Mechra El Ksiri *Morocco* 34°34N 5°57W **260** B4
Mechra Benâbbou
Morocco 32°39N 7°48W **260** B3
Mēčice *Czechia* 50°11N 14°31E **135** A3
Mecidiye *Turkey* 40°38N 26°32E **203** F10
Mecidiyeköy *Turkey* 41°4N 29°0E **122** B2
Mecitözü *Turkey* 40°32N 35°17E **212** B6
Meckenheim *Germany* 50°37N 6°59E **178** E2
Mecklenburg *Germany* 53°33N 11°40E **178** B7
Mecklenburg-Vorpommern □
Germany 53°45N 12°15E **178** B8
Mecklenburger Bucht
Germany 54°20N 11°40E **178** A7
Meconta *Mozam.* 14°59S 39°50E **269** F4
Mecsek *Hungary* 46°10N 18°18E **182** D3
Mecubúri *Mozam.* 14°39S 38°54E **269** F4
Mecubúri → *Mozam.* 14°10S 40°30E **269** F5
Mecúfi *Mozam.* 13°20S 40°32E **269** F5
Mêda *Portugal* 40°57N 7°18W **194** E3
Medak *India* 18°1N 78°15E **244** F4
Medan *Indonesia* 3°40N 98°38E **234** B1
Medang *Indonesia* 8°9S 117°22E **235** D5
Médanos *Argentina* 38°50S 62°42W **336** A4
Médanos de Coro △
Venezuela 11°35N 69°44W **328** A4
Medanosa, Pta. *Argentina* 48°8S 66°0W **336** C3
Medart *U.S.A.* 30°5N 84°23W **316** E5
Medaryville *U.S.A.* 41°5N 86°55W **311** C9
Medawachchiya *Sri Lanka* 8°30N 80°30E **245** K5
Medchal *India* 17°37N 78°29E **244** F4
Mede *Italy* 45°6N 8°44E **198** C5
Médéa *Algeria* 36°12N 2°50E **261** A6
Médéa □ *Algeria* 36°0N 3°0E **261** A6
Mededa *Bos.-H.* 43°44N 19°10E **182** G4
Médégué *Gabon* 0°37N 10°8E **264** B2
Medeiros Neto *Brazil* 17°20S 40°14W **333** E3
Medellín *Colombia* 6°15N 75°35W **328** B2
Medelpad *Sweden* 62°33N 16°30E **162** B10
Medemblik *Neths.* 52°46N 5°8E **170** B5
Médenine *Tunisia* 33°21N 10°30E **261** B8
Médenine □ *Tunisia* 32°20N 10°0E **261** B7
Mederdra *Mauritania* 17°0N 15°38W **262** B1
Medford *Mass., U.S.A.* 42°25N 71°7W **116** A2
Medford *Oreg., U.S.A.* 42°19N 122°52W **304** E2
Medford *Wis., U.S.A.* 45°9N 90°20W **308** C8
Medgidia *Romania* 44°15N 28°19E **183** F13
Medi *South Sudan* 5°4N 30°42E **257** F3
Media Agua *Argentina* 31°58S 68°25W **334** C2
Media Luna *Argentina* 34°45S 66°44W **334** C2
Medianeira *Brazil* 25°17S 54°5W **335** B5
Mediapolis *U.S.A.* 41°0N 91°10W **310** E5
Medias *Romania* 46°9N 24°22E **183** D9
Medicilândia *Brazil* 3°33S 53°8W **329** D7
Medicina *Italy* 44°28N 11°38E **199** D8
Medicine Bow *U.S.A.* 41°54N 106°12W **304** F10
Medicine Bow Mts.
U.S.A. 40°40N 106°0W **304** F10
Medicine Hat *Canada* 50°0N 110°45W **297** D6
Medicine Lake *U.S.A.* 48°30N 104°30W **308** A2
Medicine Lodge *U.S.A.* 37°17N 98°35W **308** G4
Medina = Al Madīnah
Si. Arabia 24°35N 39°52E **246** E3
Medina *Brazil* 16°15S 41°29W **333** E3
Medina *Colombia* 4°30N 73°21W **328** C3
Medina *Mis. Or., Phil.* 8°55N 125°5E **233** G5
Medina *N. Dak., U.S.A.* 46°54N 99°18W **308** B4
Medina *N.Y., U.S.A.* 43°13N 78°23W **312** C6
Medina *Ohio, U.S.A.* 41°8N 81°52W **312** D3
Medina → *U.S.A.* 29°16N 98°29W **314** G5
Medina de Pomar *Spain* 42°56N 3°29W **194** C7
Medina de Ríoseco *Spain* 41°53N 5°3W **195** D6
Medina del Campo *Spain* 41°18N 4°55W **194** D6
Medina Gounas *Senegal* 13°8N 13°46E **262** C2
Medina L. *U.S.A.* 29°32N 98°56W **314** G5
Medina Sidonia *Spain* 36°28N 5°57W **195** F5
Medinaceli *Spain* 41°12N 2°30W **196** D2
Medinipur *India* 22°25N 87°21E **243** H12
Medio-Campidano □ *Italy* 39°35N 8°30E **200** C1
Mediodia *Spain* 40°22N 3°39W **133** B2
Mediterranean Sea *Europe* 35°0N 15°0E **193** E8
Medjerda, O. → *Tunisia* 37°7N 10°13E **258** A2
Mednogorsk *Russia* 51°24N 57°37E **216** B5
Medny = Mednogorsk
Russia 51°24N 57°37E **216** B5
Médoc *France* 45°10N 0°50W **172** D3
Medog *China* 29°19N 95°19E **241** A5
Médouneu *Gabon* 0°57N 10°47E **264** B2
Medulin *Croatia* 44°49N 13°55E **199** D10
Medveda *Serbia* 42°50N 21°32E **202** D5
Medvedevo *Russia* 56°37N 47°47E **190** B8
Medvedisa → *Tver, Russia* 57°5N 37°30E **188** B9
Medvedisa →
Russia 49°35N 42°41E **190** F6
Medvedok *Russia* 57°38N 50°22E **190** B9
Medvezhi, Ostrava *Russia* 71°0N 161°0E **215** B17
Medvezhye = Krasnogvardeyskoye
Russia 45°41N 38°12E **191** H5
Medvezhyegorsk *Russia* 63°0N 34°25E **186** B5
Medway □ *U.K.* 51°27N 0°46E **169** F8
Medway → *U.K.* 51°27N 0°48E **169** F8
Medzev *Slovakia* 48°43N 20°55E **181** C13
Medžitlija *Macedonia* 40°56N 21°26E **202** F5
Meekatharra *Australia* 26°32S 118°29E **279** E2
Meeker *U.S.A.* 40°2N 107°55W **304** F10
Meeniyan *Australia* 38°35S 146°0E **283** F4
Meersburg *Germany* 47°41N 9°16E **179** H5
Meerut *India* 29°1N 77°42E **242** E7
Meeteetse *U.S.A.* 44°9N 108°52W **304** D9
Mega *Ethiopia* 3°57N 38°19E **257** G4
Mega Sumatera Barat,
Indonesia 4°0S 101°2E **234** D2
Megalo *Ethiopia* 6°5N 40°47E **257** C5
Megalo Chorio *Greece* 36°27N 27°24E **205** E9
Megalopoli *Greece* 37°25N 22°7E **204** D4
Meganisi *Greece* 38°38N 20°46E **207** B2
Megasini *India* 21°38N 86°21E **243** J12
Megdova → = Tavropos →
Greece 39°10N 21°45E **204** B3
Megève *France* 45°51N 6°37E **175** C10
Meghalaya □ *India* 25°50N 91°0E **241** C8
Meghezez *Ethiopia* 9°18N 39°26E **257** F4
Meghna → *Bangla.* 22°50N 90°50E **241** D9
Megion *Russia* 61°3N 76°6E **214** C8
Mégiscane, L. *Canada* 48°35N 75°55W **298** C4
Megra *Russia* 60°11N 37°14E **188** B9

Meguro *Japan* 35°37N 139°42E **140** B3
Meguro → *Japan* 35°37N 139°45E **140** B3
Mehadia *Romania* 44°56N 22°23E **182** F7
Mehaïgueue, O. → *Algeria* 32°15N 2°59E **261** B5
Meharry, Mt. *Australia* 22°59S 118°35E **278** D2
Mehedeby *Sweden* 60°27N 17°25E **162** D11
Mehedinți □ *Romania* 44°40N 22°45E **182** F7
Mehekar *India* 20°9N 76°34E **244** D3
Mehndawal *India* 26°58N 83°5E **243** F10
Mehr Jān *Iran* 33°50N 55°6E **247** C7
Mehr *Iran* 26°45N 55°26E **247** E7
Mehrgarh *Pakistan* 29°30N 67°30E **242** E2
Mehriz *Iran* 31°35N 54°28E **247** D7
Mehrow *Germany* 52°34N 13°37E **115** A4
Mehtar Lam *Afghan.* 34°39N 70°11E **240** B3
Mehun-sur-Yèvre *France* 47°10N 2°13E **173** E9
Mei Jiang → *China* 24°25N 116°35E **229** E11
Mei Lanfang, Pantheon of
Beijing, China **114** a2
Mei Xian *China* 34°18N 107°55E **226** G5
Meia Ponte → *Brazil* 18°32S 49°36W **333** E2
Meicheng *China* 29°29N 119°16E **229** C12
Meichengzhen *China* 28°9N 111°40E **229** C8
Meichuan *China* 30°8N 115°31E **229** B10
Meichuan → *China* 30°6N 115°31E **229** B10
Meier *Cameroon* 22°52S 43°15W **135** B1
Meiganga *Cameroon* 6°30N 14°22E **264** A2
Meighen I. *Canada* 80°0N 99°30W **295** B12
Meigs *U.S.A.* 31°4N 84°6W **316** D5
Meigu *China* 28°16N 103°20E **228** C4
Meihekou *China* 42°32N 125°40E **224** A2
Meiji Shrine *Tokyo, Japan* **140** b1
Meiktila *Burma* 20°53N 95°54E **241** E5
Meili Xue Shan *China* 28°30N 98°23E **228** C2
Meimyu = Pyin-U-Lwin
Burma 22°2N 96°28E **236** A1
Meinerzhagen *Germany* 51°6N 7°38E **178** D3
Meiningen *Germany* 50°34N 10°25E **178** E6
Meinung *Taiwan* 22°54N 120°32E **225** G2
Meio → *Brazil* 13°36S 44°7W **333** D3
Meira, Serra de *Spain* 43°15N 7°15W **194** C3
Meise *Belgium* 50°56N 4°20E **116** A1
Meishan *Sichuan, China* 30°3N 103°23E **228** B4
Meishan *Taiwan* 23°35N 120°33E **225** C2
Meissen *Germany* 51°9N 13°29E **178** D9
Meissner *Germany* 51°14N 9°50E **178** D5
Meissner-Kaufunger Wald △
Germany 51°10N 9°45E **178** D5
Meitan *China* 27°45N 107°29E **228** D6
Meizhou *China* 24°16N 116°6E **229** E11
Meja *India* 25°9N 82°7E **243** G10
Mejillones *Chile* 23°10S 70°30W **334** A1
Mejiro *Japan* 35°43N 139°43E **140** A3
Mékambo *Gabon* 1°2N 13°50E **264** B2
Mekdela *Ethiopia* 11°24N 39°10E **257** E4
Mekele *Ethiopia* 13°33N 39°30E **257** E4
Mekerghene, Sebkra
Algeria 26°21N 1°30E **261** C5
Mékhé *Senegal* 15°7N 16°38W **262** B1
Mekhomiya = Razlog
Bulgaria 41°53N 23°28E **202** E7
Mekhtar *Pakistan* 30°30N 69°15E **240** C3
Meknès *Morocco* 33°57N 5°33W **260** B3
Meknès-Tafilalet □
Morocco 33°3N 5°35W **260** B3
Meko *Nigeria* 7°27N 2°52E **263** D5
Mekong → *Asia* 9°30N 106°15E **237** H6
Mekongga *Indonesia* 3°39S 121°15E **235** E6
Mekoryuk *U.S.A.* 60°23N 166°11W **303** F6
Mekrou → *Benin* 12°25N 2°50E **263** C5
Mekvari = Kür →
Azerbaijan 39°29N 49°15E **213** C13
Mel *Italy* 46°4N 12°5E **199** B9
Melagiri Hills *India* 12°20N 77°30E **245** H3
Melah, Oued el → *Algeria* 32°20N 2°28E **261** B5
Melaka *Malaysia* 2°15N 102°15E **237** L4
Melaka □ *Malaysia* 2°15N 102°15E **237** L4
Melaky → *Madag.* 18°10S 44°0E **272** B1
Melambes *Greece* 35°8N 24°40E **205** E5
Melanesia *Pac. Oc.* 0°0S 160°0E **288** G8
Melanesian Basin *Pac. Oc.* 0°0N 160°35E **288** G8
Melapalaiyam *India* 8°39N 77°44E **245** K3
Melawi → *Indonesia* 0°19S 111°12E **234** C4
Melbourne *Vic., Australia* 37°48S 144°58E **128** A1
Melbourne *U.S.A.* 28°5N 80°37W **317** G9
Melbourne *Iowa, U.S.A.* 41°57N 93°6W **310** C3
Melbourne ✈ (MEL)
Australia 37°40S 144°50E **128** A1
Melcher-Dallas *U.S.A.* 41°14N 93°15W **310** C3
Melchor Múzquiz
Mexico 27°53N 101°31W **318** B4
Melchor Ocampo
Mexico 24°51N 101°39W **318** C4
Meldal *Norway* 63°3N 9°4E **164** A6
Méldola *Italy* 44°7N 12°4E **199** D9
Meldorf *Germany* 54°5N 9°5E **178** A5
Mêlé *C.A.R.* 9°46N 21°33E **264** A4
Mele, B. *Vanuatu* 17°44S 168°14E **287** a6
Meleden *Somalia* 14°53N 48°0E **267** B6
Melegnano *Italy* 45°21N 9°19E **198** C6
Meleizem *Mauritania* 22°19N 11°24W **260** D2
Melekeok *Palau* 7°27N 134°38E **288** c
Melekess = Dimitrovgrad
Russia 54°14N 49°39E **190** C9
Melenci *Serbia* 45°32N 20°20E **182** C3
Melenki *Russia* 55°20N 41°37E **190** C5
Meleuz *Russia* 52°58N 55°55E **216** B5
Mélèzes → *Canada* 57°40N 69°29W **298** A5
Melfi *Chad* 11°0N 17°59E **259** F8
Melfi *Italy* 41°0N 15°39E **201** B8
Melfort *Sask., Canada* 52°50N 104°37W **297** C8
Melfort *Zimbabwe* 18°0S 31°25E **269** F3
Melgaço *Portugal* 42°7N 8°15W **194** C2
Melgar de Fernamental
Spain 42°27N 4°17W **194** C6
Melgraseyri *Iceland* 66°1N 22°27W **155** A4
Melhus *Norway* 63°17N 10°18E **164** A7
Meliadine *Canada* 61°27N 93°24E **294** D4
Melilla *N. Afr.* 35°21N 2°57W **261** A4
Melilli *Italy* 37°11N 15°7E **201** E8
Melilntang, Danau
Indonesia 0°18S 116°20E **235** C5
Melipilla *Chile* 33°42S 71°15W **334** C1
Melissa, Akra *Greece* 35°50N 139°18E **282** C2
Melissa Oros *Greece* 37°32N 26°4E **205** D8
Melitopol *Ukraine* 46°50N 35°22E **189** B8
Melk *Austria* 48°13N 15°20E **181** D8
Melk → *Austria* 48°13N 15°20E **181** D8
Melkki *Finland* 60°8N 24°53E **121** C2
Mellan Fryken *Sweden* 59°45N 13°10E **163** D7
Mellansel *Sweden* 63°26N 18°19E **160** E18
Mellbystrand *Sweden* 56°30N 12°56E **163** H6

Melle *Deux-Sèvres, France* 46°14N 0°10W **174** B3
Melle *Niedersachsen,*
Germany 52°12N 8°20E **178** C4
Mellègue, O. → *Tunisia* 36°36N 9°14E **258** A1
Mellen *U.S.A.* 46°20N 90°40W **308** B8
Mellerud *Sweden* 58°41N 12°28E **163** F6
Mellette *U.S.A.* 45°9N 98°30W **308** C4
Mellid = Melide *Spain* 42°55N 8°1W **194** C2
Mellieha *Malta* 35°59N 14°22E **206** F7
Mellit *Sudan* 14°7N 25°34E **257** E2
Mellizo Sur, Cerro *Chile* 48°33S 73°10W **336** C2
Mellrichstadt *Germany* 50°25N 10°17E **178** E6
Mellunkylä *Finland* 60°14N 25°5E **121** B3
Mellunmäki *Finland* 60°14N 25°5E **121** B3
Melnik *Bulgaria* 41°30N 23°25E **202** F7
Mělník *Czechia* 50°22N 14°23E **180** A7
Melnytsya Podilska
Ukraine 48°37N 26°10E **183** B11
Melo *Uruguay* 32°20S 54°10W **335** C5
Melolo *Indonesia* 9°53S 120°40E **235** F6
Melouprey *Cambodia* 13°48N 105°16E **236** F5
Melrhir, Chott *Algeria* 34°13N 6°30E **261** B6
Melrose *N.S.W., Australia* 32°42S 146°57E **283** B4
Melrose *Borders, U.K.* 55°36N 2°43W **167** F6
Melrose *Mass., U.S.A.* 42°27N 71°2W **116** A2
Melrose *Minn., U.S.A.* 45°40N 94°49W **308** C6
Melrose *N. Mex., U.S.A.* 34°26N 103°38W **305** J12
Melrose Park *U.S.A.* 26°6N 80°11W **119** B2
Melsetter = Chimanimani
Zimbabwe 19°48S 33°1E **269** F3
Melstone *U.S.A.* 46°36N 107°52W **304** C10
Melsungen *Germany* 51°7N 9°32E **178** D5
Melton *Australia* 37°41S 144°35E **282** D6
Melton Mowbray *U.K.* 52°47N 0°54W **168** E7
Melun *France* 48°32N 2°39E **173** D9
Melung *Nepal* 27°31N 86°3E **243** F12
Melur *India* 10°2N 78°23E **245** J4
Melut *South Sudan* 10°30N 32°13E **257** E3
Melville *Sask., Canada* 50°55N 102°50W **297** C8
Melville *Gauteng, S. Africa* 26°11S 28°1E **132** D3
Melville, L. *Canada*
U.S.A. 14°11S 144°30E **280** A2
Melville, C. *Phil.* 14°19N 117°0E **233** H1
Melville, C. *Canada* 53°30N 60°0W **298** B4
Melville B. *Greenland* 75°30N 63°0W **154** B4
Melville I. *N. Terr.,*
Australia 11°30S 131°0E **278** B5
Melville I. *Canada* 75°30N 112°0W **295** B9
Melville Pen. *Canada* 68°0N 84°0W **295** D15
Melvin, Lough *Ireland* 54°26N 8°10W **166** B3
Mélykút *Hungary* 46°11N 19°25E **182** D4
Memaliaj *Albania* 40°25N 19°56E **202** F3
Memba *Mozam.* 14°11S 40°30E **269** E5
Membalong *Indonesia* 3°9S 107°37E **235** C3
Memboro *Indonesia* 9°30S 119°30E **278** A2
Membrilla *Spain* 38°59N 3°21W **195** C7
Memel = Klaipėda
Lithuania 55°43N 21°10E **184** C8
Memel *S. Africa* 27°38S 29°36E **271** C4
Memmingen *Germany* 47°58N 10°10E **179** H6
Mempawah *Indonesia* 0°30N 109°5E **235** B3
Memphis *Egypt* 29°52N 31°12E **258** J7
Memphis *Mich., U.S.A.* 42°54N 82°46W **312** D2
Memphis *Mo., U.S.A.* 40°28N 92°10W **310** D3
Memphis *Tenn., U.S.A.* 35°8N 90°2W **315** D9
Memphis *Tex., U.S.A.* 34°44N 100°33W **314** D4
Memphrémagog, L.
N. Amer. 45°8N 72°17W **313** B12
Mena *Ukraine* 51°31N 32°13E **189** G7
Mena *Ark., U.S.A.* 34°35N 94°15W **315** D7
Mena → *Ethiopia* 5°40N 40°50E **257** F5
Menabe □ *Madag.* 20°20S 44°22E **272** B1
Menado = Manado
Indonesia 1°29N 124°51E **231** D6
Menai Strait *U.K.* 53°11N 4°13W **168** D3
Ménaka *Mali* 15°59N 2°18E **263** B5
Menan = Chao Phraya →
Thailand 13°40N 100°31E **236** F3
Menarandra → *Madag.* 25°17S 44°30E **272** D1
Menard *U.S.A.* 30°55N 99°47W **314** F5
Menard Fracture Zone
Pac. Oc. 43°0S 97°0W **289** M18
Menate *Indonesia* 0°12S 113°3E **235** C4
Menawashei *Sudan* 12°41N 24°59E **257** E1
Mendaña Fracture Zone
Pac. Oc. 16°0S 91°0W **289** J18
Mendawai *Indonesia* 3°30S 113°0E **235** C4
Mendawai → *Indonesia* 3°17S 113°3E **235** C4
Mende *France* 44°31N 3°30E **174** D7
Mendebo Mts. *Ethiopia* 7°0N 39°22E **257** F4
Mendeleyev Ridge *Arctic* 80°0N 178°0W **150** B17
Menden *Germany* 51°26N 7°47E **178** D3
Menderes → *Turkey* 37°25N 27°8E **205** D8
Mendez *Mexico* 25°7N 98°34W **319** C5
Mendham *U.S.A.* 33°35N 74°10E **243** D6
Mendi *Ethiopia* 9°47N 35°4E **257** F3
Mendi *Papua N. G.* 6°11S 143°39E **286** B7
Mendip Hills *U.K.* 51°17N 2°40W **169** F5
Mendocino *U.S.A.* 39°19N 123°48W **304** G2
Mendocino, C. *U.S.A.* 40°26N 124°25W **304** F1
Mendocino Fracture Zone
Pac. Oc. 40°0N 142°0W **289** D13
Mendol *Indonesia* 0°30N 103°13E **234** B2
Mendon *U.S.A.* 42°0N 85°27W **311** D11
Mendota *Calif., U.S.A.* 36°45N 120°23W **306** J6
Mendota *Ill., U.S.A.* 41°33N 89°7W **310** C7
Mendoyo *Indonesia* 8°23S 114°42E **231** J17
Mendoza *Argentina* 32°50S 68°52W **334** C2
Mendoza □ *Argentina* 33°0S 69°0W **334** C2
Mene Grande *Venezuela* 9°49N 70°56W **328** B3
Menemen *Turkey* 38°34N 27°3E **205** C9
Menen *Belgium* 50°47N 3°7E **170** D3
Menéndez, L. *Argentina* 42°40S 71°51W **336** B2
Menfi *Italy* 37°36N 12°58E **200** E5
Mengcheng *China* 33°12N 116°28E **228** H9
Mengdingjie *China* 23°31N 98°58E **228** F2
Mengè *Slovenia* 46°10N 14°35E **199** B11
Menggala *Indonesia* 4°30S 105°15E **234** E3
Menghai *China* 21°59N 100°20E **228** F3
Mengibar *Spain* 37°58N 3°48W **195** H7
Mengjin *China* 34°55N 112°45E **226** G7
Mengla *China* 21°20N 101°25E **228** G3
Menglian *China* 22°19N 99°27E **228** F2
Mengong *Cameroon* 2°36N 11°42E **264** B2
Mengshan *China* 24°0N 110°20E **229** E8
Mengyin *China* 35°40N 117°58E **227** G9
Mengzhe *China* 22°0N 100°26E **228** F3
Mengzi *China* 23°20N 103°22E **228** F4
Menihek *Canada* 54°28N 56°36W **298** B4
Menihek L. *Canada* 54°0N 66°35W **298** B4
Menin = Menen *Belgium* 50°47N 3°7E **170** D3
Menindee *Australia* 32°20S 142°25E **282** B3
Menindee L. *Australia* 32°20S 142°25E **282** B3
Meningie *Australia* 35°50S 139°18E **282** C2
Menjangan, Pulau
Indonesia 8°7S 114°31E **231** J17
Menkrour *Algeria* 29°19N 8°26E **261** C6
Menlo Park *U.S.A.* 37°27N 122°12W **306** H4
Mennenga → *Australia* 15°21S 131°16E **278** C5
Menominee *U.S.A.* 45°6N 87°37W **308** C9
Menominee → *U.S.A.* 45°6N 87°36W **308** C9
Menomonee Falls *U.S.A.* 43°11N 88°7W **311** A8
Menomonie *U.S.A.* 44°53N 91°55W **308** C7
Menongue *Angola* 14°48S 17°52E **265** G3

Mersing *Malaysia* 2°25N 103°50E **237** L4
Merta *India* 26°39N 74°4E **242** F5
Merta Road *India* 26°43N 73°55E **242** F5
Merthyr Tydfil *U.K.* 51°45N 3°22W **169** F4
Merthyr Tydfil □ *U.K.* 51°46N 3°21W **169** F4
Merti *Kenya* 1°4N 38°40E **268** B4
Mértola *Portugal* 37°40N 7°40W **195** H3
Merton □ *U.K.* 51°25N 0°13W **115** C2
Mertz Glacier *Antarctica* 67°30S 144°45E **151** C10
Mertzon *U.S.A.* 31°16N 100°49W **314** F4
Méru *Oise, France* 49°13N 2°8E **173** C9
Meru *Eastern, Kenya* 0°3N 37°40E **268** B4
Meru *Tanzania* 3°15S 36°46E **268** C4
Meru *Kenya* 0°5N 38°10E **268** B4
Meru Betiri △ *Indonesia* 8°27S 113°51E **235** D4
Merv = Mary
Turkmenistan 37°40N 61°50E **247** B9
Merville *France* 50°38N 2°38E **173** B9
Méry-sur-Seine *France* 48°31N 3°54E **173** D10
Merzifon *Turkey* 40°53N 35°32E **212** B6
Merzig *Germany* 49°26N 6°37E **179** F2
Merzouga, Erg Tin *Algeria* 24°0N 11°4E **261** D7
Mesa *U.S.A.* 33°25N 111°50W **305** K8
Mesa Verde △ *U.S.A.* 37°11N 108°29W **305** H9
Mesach Mellet *Libya* 24°30N 11°30E **258** D7
Mesada = Masada *Israel* 31°18N 35°21E **251** G6
Mesagne *Italy* 40°34N 17°48E **201** B10
Mesanagros *Greece* 36°1N 27°49E **206** E11
Mesaoría *Cyprus* 35°12N 33°14E **207** E9
Meschede *Germany* 51°20N 8°18E **178** D4
Mescit *Turkey* 40°21N 41°11E **213** B9
Mesemvria = Nesebŭr
Bulgaria 42°41N 27°46E **203** D11
Mesfinto *Ethiopia* 13°20N 37°22E **257** E4
Mesgārābād *Iran* 35°27N 51°30E **141** B3
Mesgouez, L. *Canada* 51°20N 75°0W **298** C4
Meshchovsk *Russia* 54°22N 35°17E **188** E8
Meshchyora □ *Russia* 55°30N 40°0E **190** C5
Meshchyorsky □ *Russia* 54°50N 41°0E **190** C5
Meshed = Mashhad *Iran* 36°20N 59°35E **247** B8
Meshgīn Shahr *Iran* 38°30N 47°45E **213** C12
Meshoppen *U.S.A.* 41°36N 76°3W **313** E8
Meshra er Req *South Sudan* 8°25N 29°18E **257** F2
Mesilinka → *Canada* 56°6N 124°30W **296** B4
Meslay-du-Maine *France* 47°58N 0°33W **172** E6
Mesocco *Switz.* 46°23N 9°12E **179** J5
Mesolongi *Greece* 38°21N 21°28E **204** C3
Mesongi *Greece* 39°35N 16°48E **201** C9
Mesopotamia = Al Jazirah
Iraq 33°30N 44°0E **213** E10
Mesopotamia *U.S.A.* 41°27N 80°57W **312** E4
Mesopotamo *Greece* 39°14N 20°22E **204** B2
Mesoraca *Italy* 39°5N 16°48E **201** C9
Mésou Volimais = Volimes
Greece 37°52N 20°39E **207** D2
Mesquite *Nev., U.S.A.* 36°47N 114°6E **314** E6
Mesquite *Tex., U.S.A.* 32°47N 96°36W **314** E6
Messac *France* 47°49N 1°50W **172** E5
Messalo → *Mozam.* 12°25S 39°15E **269** E4
Messaména *Cameroon* 3°48N 12°49E **264** B2
Messara, Kolpos *Greece* 35°6N 24°47E **205** E6
Messe *Austria* 48°13N 16°24E **142** A2
Messene *Greece* 37°12N 22°1E **204** D4
Messier, Canal *Chile* 48°20S 74°33W **336** C2
Messina = Musina *S. Africa* 22°20S 30°5E **271** B5
Messina *Italy* 38°11N 15°34E **201** D8
Messina, Str. di *Italy* 38°15N 15°35E **201** D8
Messiniakos Kolpos *Greece* 36°45N 22°5E **204** E4
Messkirch *Germany* 47°59N 9°7E **179** H5
Messlingen *Sweden* 62°40N 12°50E **162** B6
Mesta = Nestos → *Europe* 40°54N 24°49E **203** F8
Mesta, Akra *Greece* 38°16N 25°53E **205** C7
Mestanza *Spain* 38°35N 4°4W **195** H6
Mestersvig *Greenland* 72°10N 23°40W **154** C8
Mestre *Italy* 45°25N 12°15E **199** C9
Mestre, Espigão *Brazil* 12°30S 46°10W **333** D2
Mesudiye *Turkey* 40°30N 37°46E **212** B7
Meta □ *Colombia* 3°30N 73°0W **328** C3
Meta → *S. Amer.* 6°12N 67°28W **328** B4
Meta Incognita Pen.
Canada 62°45N 68°30W **295** E18
Metabetchouan *Canada* 48°26N 71°52W **299** C5
Metairie *U.S.A.* 29°59N 90°9W **131** A2
Metalici, Munții *Romania* 46°15N 22°50E **182** D7
Metaline Falls *U.S.A.* 48°52N 117°22W **304** B5
Metallifere, Colline *Italy* 43°10N 11°0E **198** E8
Metamora *U.S.A.* 40°47N 89°22W **310** D7
Metán *Argentina* 25°30S 65°0W **334** B3
Metangula *Mozam.* 12°40S 34°50E **269** E3
Metanópoli *Italy* 45°24N 9°15E **128** B2
Metauro → *Italy* 43°40N 13°13E **199** E10
Metema *Ethiopia* 12°56N 36°13E **257** E4
Metengobalame *Mozam.* 14°49S 34°30E **269** E3
Meteora *Greece* 39°40N 21°31E **204** B3
Methana *Greece* 37°35N 23°23E **204** D5
Methoni *Greece* 36°49N 21°42E **204** E3
Methven *N.Z.* 43°38S 171°40E **285** G3
Metil *Mozam.* 16°24S 39°0E **269** F4
Metkovets *Bulgaria* 43°37N 23°10E **202** E7
Metković *Croatia* 43°6N 17°39E **199** G14
Metlakatla *U.S.A.* 55°8N 131°35W **303** J15
Metlaoui *Tunisia* 34°24N 8°24E **261** B7
MetLife Stadium
New York, U.S.A. 40°48N 74°5W **132** B1
Metlika *Papua N. G.* 4°46S 152°55E **286** C7
Metlika *Slovenia* 45°40N 15°20E **199** C12
Metlili Chaamba *Algeria* 32°16N 3°38E **261** B5
Metro *Indonesia* 5°5S 105°20E **234** E3
Metro Toronto Zoo
Canada 43°48N 79°10W **141** A4
Metropolis *U.S.A.* 37°9N 88°44W **308** G9
Metropolitan □ *Chile* 33°30S 70°50W **334** C1
Metsovo *Greece* 39°48N 21°12E **204** B3
Metter *U.S.A.* 32°24N 82°3W **316** D7
Mettuppalaiyam *India* 11°18N 76°59E **245** J3
Mettur *India* 11°48N 77°47E **245** J3
Metu *Ethiopia* 8°18N 35°35E **257** F4
Metz *France* 49°8N 6°10E **173** C13
Metzingen *Germany* 48°31N 9°17E **179** G5
Meudon *France* 48°48N 2°14E **134** B2
Meulaboh *Indonesia* 4°11N 96°3E **234** B1
Meung-sur-Loire *France* 47°50N 1°40E **173** E8
Meureudu *Indonesia* 5°19N 96°10E **234** B1
Meurthe → *France* 48°47N 6°9E **173** D13
Meurthe-et-Moselle □
France 48°52N 6°0E **173** D13
Meuse □ *France* 49°8N 5°25E **173** C12
Meuse → *Europe* 50°45N 5°41E **170** D5
Meuselwitz *Germany* 51°2N 12°17E **178** D8
Meutapok, Mt. *Malaysia* 5°40N 117°0E **235** A5
Mevaseret Zion *Israel* 31°47N 35°6E **238** B1
Mevo Beitar *Israel* 31°43N 35°6E **123** B1
Mexia *U.S.A.* 31°41N 96°29W **314** F6
Mexiana, I. *Brazil* 0°0N 49°30W **332** B2
Mexicali *Mexico* 32°40N 115°30W **307** N11
Mexican Plateau *Mexico* 25°0N 105°0W **290** G9
Mexican Water *U.S.A.* 36°57N 109°32W **305** H9
Mexico *Maine, U.S.A.* 44°34N 70°33W **313** B14
Mexico *Mo., U.S.A.* 39°10N 91°53W **310** E4
Mexico *N.Y., U.S.A.* 43°28N 76°14W **313** C8
México □ *Mexico* 19°20N 99°30W **319** D5

Mexico ■ Cent. Amer. 25°0N 105°0W 318 C4
México, Ciudad de Mexico 19°24N 99°9W 128 B2
Mexico, G. of Cent. Amer. 25°0N 90°0W 319 C7
Mexico B. U.S.A. 43°35N 76°20W 313 C8
Mexico Beach U.S.A. 29°57N 85°25W 316 F4
Mexico City Int. ✈ (MEX) Mexico 19°25N 99°5W 128 B2
Meydān-e Naftūn Iran 31°56N 49°18E 247 D6
Meydani, Ra's-e Iran 25°24N 59°6E 247 E8
Meyenburg Germany 53°18N 12°14E 178 B8
Meyers Chuck U.S.A. 55°45N 132°15W 296 B2
Meyersdal S. Africa 26°17S 28°5E 123 B2
Meymac France 45°32N 2°10E 174 C6
Meymaneh Afghan. 35°53N 64°38E 240 B2
Meyo Cameroon 2°50N 11°1E 264 B2
Meyrueis France 44°12N 3°27E 174 D7
Meyssac France 45°3N 1°40E 174 C5
Meyzieu France 45°46N 4°59E 175 C8
Mezdra Bulgaria 43°12N 23°42E 202 C7
Mèze France 43°27N 3°36E 174 E7
Mezen Russia 65°50N 44°20E 186 A7
Mezen → Russia 65°44N 44°22E 186 A7
Mézenc, Mt. France 44°54N 4°11E 175 D8
Mezeş, Munţii Romania 47°5N 23°5E 182 C8
Mezha → Russia 55°44N 31°33E 188 E6
Mezhdurechensk Russia 53°41N 88°3E 217 B11
Mezhdurechenskiy Russia 59°36N 65°56E 214 D7
Mezhdurechye = Shali Russia 43°9N 45°55E 191 J7
Mezhevaya Utka = Sinegorskiy Russia 47°55N 40°52E 191 G5
Mézidon-Canon France 49°5N 0°1W 172 C6
Mézières-en-Brenne France 46°49N 1°13E 174 B5
Mézilhac France 44°49N 4°21E 175 D8
Mézin France 44°4N 0°16E 174 D4
Mezitli Turkey 36°45N 34°29E 250 B5
Mezőberény Hungary 46°49N 21°3E 182 D6
Mezőfalva Hungary 46°55N 18°49E 182 D3
Mezőhegyes Hungary 46°19N 20°49E 182 D5
Mezőkövácsháza Hungary 46°25N 20°57E 182 D5
Mezőkövesd Hungary 47°49N 20°35E 182 C5
Mézos France 44°5N 1°10W 174 D2
Mezőtúr Hungary 47°1N 20°41E 182 C5
Mezquital Mexico 23°29N 104°23W 318 C4
Mezzate Italy 45°26N 9°17E 128 B2
Mezzolombardo Italy 46°13N 11°5E 198 B8
Mfolozi → S. Africa 28°25S 32°26E 271 C5
Mgarr Malta 35°55N 14°22E 206 F7
Mgarr Gozo, Malta 36°2N 14°18E 206 E7
Mgeta Tanzania 8°22S 36°6E 269 D4
Mglin Russia 53°2N 32°50E 189 F7
Mhamid Morocco 29°49N 5°43W 260 C3
Mhlaba Hills Zimbabwe 18°30S 30°30E 269 F3
Mhow India 22°33N 75°50E 242 H6
Mi-Shima Japan 34°46N 131°9E 222 C3
Miadong S. Korea 37°36N 127°0E 137 B2
Miagao Phil. 10°39N 122°14E 233 F4
Miahuatlán Mexico 16°20N 96°36W 319 D5
Miaich South Sudan 9°30N 30°30E 257 F3
Miajadas Spain 39°9N 5°54W 195 F5
Miami Fla., U.S.A. 25°46N 80°11W 129 D2
Miami Okla., U.S.A. 36°53N 94°53W 314 C7
Miami Tex., U.S.A. 35°42N 100°38W 314 D4
Miami → U.S.A. 25°46N 80°11W 129 D1
Miami Beach U.S.A. 25°47N 80°7W 129 D3
Miami Canal U.S.A. 25°45N 80°12W 317 K9
Miami Gardens U.S.A. 25°56N 80°15W 129 C1
Miami Int. ✈ (MIA) U.S.A. 25°48N 80°17W 129 D1
Miami Lakes U.S.A. 25°54N 80°18W 129 C1
Miami Shores U.S.A. 25°51N 80°11W 129 C2
Miami Springs U.S.A. 25°49N 80°17W 129 D1
Miamisburg U.S.A. 39°38N 84°17W 311 E12
Mian Xian China 33°10N 106°32E 228 A6
Mianchi China 34°48N 111°48E 226 G6
Mīāndarreh Iran 35°37N 53°39E 247 C7
Mīāndowāb Iran 37°0N 46°5E 213 D12
Miandrivazo Madag. 19°31S 45°29E 272 B2
Mīāneh Iran 37°30N 47°40E 213 D12
Miangas, Pulau Indonesia 5°35N 126°34E 233 J6
Mianning China 28°32N 102°9E 228 C4
Mianwali Pakistan 32°38N 71°28E 242 C4
Mianyang China 31°22N 104°47E 228 B5
Mianzhu China 31°22N 104°7E 228 B5
Miao Ling China 26°5N 107°30E 228 D6
Miaodao Qundao China 38°10N 120°45E 227 E11
Miaoli Taiwan 24°37N 120°49E 225 B2
Miaoli □ Taiwan 24°30N 120°55E 225 B2
Miarinarivo Alaotra-Mangoro, Madag. 16°38S 48°15E 272 B2
Miarinarivo Itasy, Madag. 18°57S 46°55E 272 B2
Miariravaratra Madag. 20°13S 47°31E 272 C2
Miass Russia 54°59N 60°6E 186 D11
Miasteczko Krajeńskie Poland 53°7N 17°1E 185 E4
Miastko Poland 54°0N 16°58E 184 E3
Miasto Poland 52°15N 21°0E 143 B2
Mica S. Africa 24°10S 30°48E 271 B5
Micanopy U.S.A. 29°30N 82°17W 317 F7
Micăsasa Romania 46°7N 24°7E 183 D9
Micco U.S.A. 27°53N 80°30W 317 H9
Miccosukee U.S.A. 30°36N 84°3W 316 E5
Miccosukee, L. U.S.A. 30°33N 83°53W 316 E6
Michael, Mt. Papua N. G. 6°27S 145°22E 286 D3
Michalovce Slovakia 48°47N 21°58E 181 C14
Michałowice Poland 52°10N 20°52E 143 B1
Michigan □ U.S.A. 44°0N 85°0W 309 C11
Michigan, L. U.S.A. 44°0N 87°0W 308 D10
Michigan Avenue Chicago, U.S.A. 119 b2
Michigan Center U.S.A. 42°14N 84°20W 311 B12
Michigan City U.S.A. 41°43N 86°54W 311 C10
Michika Nigeria 10°36N 13°23E 263 C7
Michipicoten I. Canada 47°40N 85°40W 298 C2
Michle Czechia 50°3N 14°28E 135 B2
Michoacán □ Mexico 19°10N 101°50W 318 D4
Michurin Bulgaria 42°9N 27°51E 203 D11
Michurinsk Russia 52°58N 40°27E 190 D5
Miconje Angola 4°26S 12°48E 265 C2
Micoud St. Lucia 13°49N 60°54W 323 m
Micronesia Pac. Oc. 11°0N 160°0E 288 G7
Micronesia, Federated States of ■ Pac. Oc. 9°0N 150°0E 288 G7
Mid-Atlantic Ridge Atl. Oc. 0°0 20°0W 152 J10
Mid-City Calif., U.S.A. 34°4N 118°20W 126 B2
Mid City La., U.S.A. 29°58N 90°6W 131 B2
Mid-Indian Ocean Basin Ind. Oc. 10°0S 80°0E 273 F7
Mid-Indian Ridge Ind. Oc. 30°0S 75°0E 273 H6
Mid-Pacific Seamounts Pac. Oc. 18°0N 177°0W 288 F10
Midai Indonesia 3°0N 107°47E 235 B3
Midale Canada 49°25N 103°20W 297 D8
Middelburg Neths. 51°30N 3°36E 170 C3
Middelburg Eastern Cape, S. Africa 31°30S 25°0E 270 D4
Middelburg Mpumalanga, S. Africa 25°49S 29°28E 271 C4
Middelfart Denmark 55°30N 9°43E 163 J3
Middelpos S. Africa 31°55S 20°13E 270 D3
Middelwit S. Africa 24°51S 27°3E 270 B4
Middle → U.S.A. 41°26N 93°30W 310 C3
Middle Alkali L. U.S.A. 41°27N 120°5W 304 F3
Middle America Trench = Guatemala Trench Pac. Oc. 14°0N 95°0W 292 H10
Middle Andaman I. India 12°30N 92°50E 245 H11
Middle Bass I. U.S.A. 41°41N 82°48W 312 E2
Middle East Asia 35°0N 40°0E 210 E5
Middle Fork Feather → U.S.A. 38°33N 121°30W 306 F5
Middle Ground Midway Is. 28°14N 177°24W 302 c
Middle Harbour Australia 33°47S 151°14E 139 A2
Middle Hd. Australia 33°49S 151°16E 139 A2
Middle I. Australia 34°6S 123°11E 279 F3
Middle Island St. Kitts & Nevis 17°20N 62°48W 322 d
Middle Loup → U.S.A. 41°17N 98°24W 308 E4
Middle Park Australia 37°50S 144°57E 128 B1
Middle Raccoon → U.S.A. 41°35N 93°35W 310 C3
Middle Village U.S.A. 40°43N 73°52W 132 B2
Middleboro U.S.A. 41°54N 70°55W 313 E14
Middleburg Fla., U.S.A. 30°4N 81°52W 316 E8
Middleburg Pa., U.S.A. 40°47N 77°3W 312 F7
Middleburgh U.S.A. 42°36N 74°20W 313 D10
Middlebury Ind., U.S.A. 41°41N 85°42W 311 C11
Middlebury Vt., U.S.A. 44°1N 73°10W 313 B11
Middlefield U.S.A. 41°27N 81°4W 312 E3
Middlemarch N.Z. 45°30S 170°9E 285 F5
Middlemount Australia 22°50S 148°40E 280 C4
Middleport N.Y., U.S.A. 43°13N 78°29W 312 C6
Middleport Ohio, U.S.A. 39°0N 82°3W 309 F12
Middlesboro U.S.A. 36°36N 83°43W 309 G12
Middlesbrough U.K. 54°35N 1°13W 168 C6
Middlesbrough □ U.K. 54°28N 1°13W 168 C6
Middlesex Belize 17°2N 88°31W 320 C2
Middlesex N.J., U.S.A. 40°36N 74°30W 313 F10
Middlesex N.Y., U.S.A. 42°42N 77°16W 312 D7
Middlesex □ Jamaica 18°10N 77°5W 320 a
Middlesex Fells Reservation U.S.A. 42°27N 71°6W 116 A2
Middleton Queens., Australia 22°22S 141°32E 280 C3
Middleton N.S., Canada 44°57N 65°4W 299 D6
Middleton Wis., U.S.A. 43°6N 89°30W 310 A7
Middleton Cr. → Australia 22°35S 141°51E 280 C3
Middleton I. U.S.A. 59°26N 146°20W 303 G11
Middletown Armagh, U.K. 54°17N 6°51W 166 B5
Middletown Calif., U.S.A. 38°45N 122°37W 306 G4
Middletown Conn., U.S.A. 41°34N 72°39W 313 E12
Middletown Ky., U.S.A. 38°14N 85°32W 311 F11
Middletown N.Y., U.S.A. 41°27N 74°25W 313 E10
Middletown Ohio, U.S.A. 39°31N 84°24W 311 E12
Middletown Pa., U.S.A. 40°12N 76°44W 313 F8
Middleville U.S.A. 42°43N 85°28W 311 B11
Midelt Morocco 32°46N 4°44W 260 B4
Midge Point Australia 20°39S 148°43E 280 b
Midhirst N.Z. 39°17S 174°18E 284 F3
Miðsandur Iceland 64°24N 21°28W 155 C5
Midhurst Ont., Canada 44°26N 79°43W 312 B5
Midhurst W. Susx., U.K. 50°59N 0°44W 169 G7
Mīdī Yemen 16°19N 42°48E 248 C3
Midi, Canal du → France 43°45N 1°21E 174 E5
Midi, Gare du Brussels, Belgium 116 c1
Midi d'Ossau, Pic du France 42°50N 0°26W 174 F3
Midland W. Austral., Australia 31°54S 116°1E 279 F2
Midland Ont., Canada 44°45N 79°50W 312 B5
Midland Calif., U.S.A. 33°52N 114°48W 307 M12
Midland Mich., U.S.A. 43°37N 84°14W 309 D11
Midland Pa., U.S.A. 40°39N 80°27W 312 F4
Midland Tex., U.S.A. 32°0N 102°3W 314 F3
Midland Beach U.S.A. 40°34N 74°6W 132 C1
Midlands □ Zimbabwe 19°40S 29°0E 269 F2
Midleton Ireland 51°55N 8°10W 166 E3
Midlothian U.S.A. 41°37N 87°45W 119 D2
Midlothian □ U.K. 55°51N 3°5W 167 F5
Midnapore = Medinipur India 22°25N 87°21E 243 H12
Midongy, Tangorombohitr' i Madag. 23°30S 47°0E 272 C2
Midongy Atsimo Madag. 23°35S 47°1E 272 C2
Midongy de Sud △ Madag. 23°42S 47°6E 272 C2
Midori Japan 36°30N 139°15E 223 A11
Midou → France 43°54N 0°30W 174 E3
Midouze → France 43°48N 0°51W 174 E3
Midsayap Phil. 7°12N 124°32E 233 H5
Midsund Norway 62°41N 6°40E 164 B3
Midtgulen Norway 61°44N 5°11E 164 C2
Midu China 25°18N 100°30E 228 E3
Midville U.S.A. 32°49N 82°14W 316 C7
Midway Ala., U.S.A. 32°5N 85°31W 316 C4
Midway Fla., U.S.A. 30°30N 84°27W 316 E5
Midway, Chicago ✈ (MDW) U.S.A. 41°47N 87°45W 311 C9
Midway Is. Pac. Oc. 28°13N 177°22W 302 c
Midway Wells U.S.A. 32°41N 115°7W 307 N11
Midwest U.S.A. 42°0N 90°0W 301 G22
Midwest Wyo., U.S.A. 43°25N 106°16W 304 E10
Midwest City U.S.A. 35°27N 97°24W 314 D6
Midwood U.S.A. 40°37N 73°57W 132 C2
Midyat Turkey 37°25N 41°23E 213 D9
Midzŏr Bulgaria 43°24N 22°40E 202 C6
Mie Japan 32°58N 131°35E 222 E3
Mie □ Japan 34°30N 136°10E 223 C8
Miechów Poland 50°21N 20°5E 185 H7
Miedwie, Jezioro Poland 53°17N 14°54E 185 E1
Miedzeszyn Poland 52°10N 21°11E 143 B3
Międzybórz Poland 51°25N 17°34E 185 G4
Międzychód Poland 52°35N 15°53E 185 F2
Międzylesie Dolnośląskie, Poland 50°8N 16°40E 185 H3
Międzylesie Warszawa, Poland 52°12N 21°10E 143 B3
Międzyrzec Podlaski Poland 51°58N 22°45E 185 G9
Międzyrzecz Poland 52°26N 15°35E 185 F2
Międzyzdroje Poland 53°56N 14°26E 184 E1
Miejska Górka Poland 51°39N 16°58E 185 G3
Miélan France 43°27N 0°19E 174 E4
Mielau = Mława Poland 53°9N 20°25E 185 E7
Mielec Poland 50°15N 21°25E 185 H8
Mienga Angola 17°12S 19°48E 265 F3
Miercurea-Ciuc Romania 46°21N 25°48E 183 D10
Miercurea Sibiului Romania 45°53N 23°48E 183 E8
Mieres Spain 43°18N 5°48W 194 B5
Mieroszów Poland 50°40N 16°11E 185 H3
Mies = Stříbro Czechia 49°44N 13°0E 180 A6
Mieso Ethiopia 9°15N 40°43E 257 F5
Miessaari Finland 60°8N 24°47E 121 C1
Mieszkowice Poland 52°47N 14°30E 185 F1
Mifflintown U.S.A. 40°34N 77°24W 312 F7
Mifraz Hefa Israel 32°52N 35°0E 250 F6
Migang Shan China 35°32N 106°13E 226 G4
Migennes France 47°58N 3°31E 173 E10
Migliarino Italy 44°46N 11°56E 199 D8
Migliarino-San Rossore-Massaciuccoli ⌓ Italy 43°44N 10°20E 198 E7
Migori Kenya 1°4S 34°28E 268 C3
Migrash Harusim Jerusalem 123 b2
Miguasha △ Canada 48°5N 66°26W 299 C6
Miguel Alemán, Presa Mexico 18°15N 96°32W 319 D5
Miguel Alves Brazil 4°11S 42°55W 332 B3
Miguel Calmon Brazil 11°26S 40°36W 332 D3
Miguel Hidalgo Mexico 19°25N 99°12W 128 B1
Miguel Hidalgo, Presa Mexico 26°30N 108°34W 318 B3
Miguelturra Spain 38°58N 3°53W 195 G7
Mihăileni Romania 47°58N 26°9E 183 C11
Mihăileşti Romania 44°20N 25°54E 183 F10
Mihailovca Moldova 46°33N 28°56E 183 D13
Mihalgazi Turkey 40°2N 30°34E 205 A12
Mihaliççık Turkey 39°53N 31°30E 212 C4
Mihara Japan 34°24N 133°5E 222 C5
Mihara-Yama Japan 34°43N 139°23E 223 C11
Miheşu de Cîmpie Romania 46°41N 24°9E 183 D9
Mijas Spain 36°36N 4°40W 195 J6
Mikawa-Wan Japan 34°44N 137°13E 223 C9
Mikese Tanzania 6°48S 37°55E 268 D4
Mikha-Tskhakaya = Senaki Georgia 42°15N 42°1E 191 J6
Mikhailovka = Mykhaylivka Ukraine 47°12N 35°15E 189 J8
Mikhaylov Russia 54°14N 39°0E 188 E10
Mikhaylovgrad = Montana Bulgaria 43°27N 23°16E 202 C7
Mikhaylovka = Kimovsk Russia 54°0N 38°29E 188 E10
Mikhaylovka Russia 50°3N 43°5E 190 E6
Mikhaylovsk Russia 45°8N 42°0E 191 H5
Mikhnevo Russia 55°4N 37°59E 188 E9
Miki Hyōgo, Japan 34°48N 134°59E 222 C6
Miki Kagawa, Japan 34°12N 134°7E 222 C6
Mikir Hills India 26°10N 93°30E 241 B4
Mikkeli Finland 61°43N 27°15E 188 B4
Mikkwa → Canada 58°25N 114°46W 296 B6
Mikniya Sudan 17°0N 33°45E 257 D3
Mikołajki Poland 53°49N 21°37E 184 E8
Míkonos = Mykonos Greece 37°30N 25°25E 205 D7
Mikope Dem. Rep. of the Congo 4°58S 20°43E 265 C4
Mikoyan-Shakhar = Karachayevsk Russia 43°50N 41°55E 191 J5
Mikri Prespa, L. Greece 40°47N 21°3E 202 F5
Mikro Derio Greece 41°19N 26°6E 203 E10
Mikstat Poland 51°32N 17°59E 185 G4
Mikulov Czechia 48°48N 16°39E 181 C9
Mikumi Tanzania 7°26S 37°0E 268 D4
Mikumi △ Tanzania 7°35S 37°15E 268 D4
Mikun Russia 62°20N 50°0E 186 B9
Mikuni Japan 36°13N 136°9E 223 A8
Mikuni-Tōge Japan 36°50N 138°50E 223 A10
Mikura-Jima Japan 33°52N 139°36E 223 D11
Mila Algeria 36°27N 6°15E 261 A6
Mila □ Algeria 36°25N 6°10E 261 A6
Milaca U.S.A. 45°45N 93°39W 308 C7
Miladummadulu Atoll Maldives 5°50N 73°30E 272 d
Milagro Ecuador 2°11S 79°36W 328 D2
Milagros Phil. 12°13N 123°30E 232 E4
Milan = Milano Italy 45°28N 9°10E 128 B1
Milan Ga., U.S.A. 32°1N 83°4W 316 C6
Milan Ill., U.S.A. 41°27N 90°34W 310 C6
Milan Mich., U.S.A. 42°5N 83°41W 311 B13
Milan Mo., U.S.A. 40°12N 93°7W 310 D3
Milan Tenn., U.S.A. 35°55N 88°46W 315 D10
Miland Norway 59°54N 8°45E 164 E5
Milando Angola 8°45S 17°36E 265 D3
Milando ⌓ Angola 8°45S 17°10E 265 D3
Milanese, Parco Regionale ⌓ Italy 45°35N 9°5E 128 A1
Milang Australia 35°24S 138°58E 282 C3
Milange Mozam. 16°3S 35°45E 269 F4
Milano Italy 45°28N 9°10E 128 B1
Milano Due Italy 45°29N 9°16E 128 B2
Milano Linate ✈ (LIN) Italy 45°27N 9°16E 128 B2
Milano Malpense ✈ (MXP) Italy 45°38N 8°43E 128 A1
Milano San Felice Italy 45°28N 9°18E 128 B2
Milanoa Madag. 13°35S 49°47E 272 A2
Milâs Turkey 37°20N 27°50E 205 D9
Milatos Greece 35°18N 25°34E 207 E6
Milazzo Italy 38°13N 15°15E 201 D8
Milbank U.S.A. 45°13N 96°38W 308 C5
Milbanke Sd. Canada 52°19N 128°33W 296 C3
Milbertshofen Germany 48°10N 11°34E 131 A2
Milden Canada 51°29N 107°32W 297 C7
Mildenhall U.K. 52°21N 0°32E 169 E8
Mildmay Canada 44°3N 81°7W 312 B3
Mildura Australia 34°13S 142°9E 282 C5
Mile China 24°28N 103°20E 228 E4
Mile and a Quarter Barbados 13°16N 59°37W 323 r
Miles Australia 26°40S 150°9E 281 D5
Miles City U.S.A. 46°25N 105°51W 304 C11
Mileşti Moldova 47°13N 28°3E 183 C13
Milestone Canada 49°59N 104°31W 297 D8
Mileto Italy 38°36N 16°4E 201 D9
Miletto, Mte. Italy 41°27N 14°22E 201 A7
Miletus Turkey 37°30N 27°18E 205 D9
Milevsko Czechia 49°27N 14°21E 180 B7
Milford Calif., U.S.A. 40°10N 120°22W 306 E6
Milford Conn., U.S.A. 41°14N 73°3W 313 E11
Milford Del., U.S.A. 38°55N 75°26W 309 F16
Milford Ill., U.S.A. 40°38N 87°42W 311 D9
Milford Mass., U.S.A. 42°8N 71°31W 313 D13
Milford Mich., U.S.A. 42°35N 83°36W 311 B13
Milford N.H., U.S.A. 42°50N 71°39W 313 D13
Milford N.Y., U.S.A. 42°35N 74°56W 313 D10
Milford Pa., U.S.A. 41°19N 74°48W 313 E10
Milford Utah, U.S.A. 38°24N 113°1W 304 G7
Milford Haven U.K. 51°42N 5°7W 169 F2
Milford Sd. N.Z. 44°41S 167°47E 285 E2
Milḩ, Baḩr al = Razāzah, Buḩayrat ar Iraq 32°40N 43°35E 213 F10
Miliana Aïn Salah, Algeria 27°20N 2°32E 261 C5
Miliana Médéa, Algeria 36°20N 2°15E 261 A5
Milicz Poland 51°31N 17°19E 185 G4
Milies Greece 39°20N 23°9E 204 B5
Milikapiti Australia 11°26S 130°40E 278 B5
Mililani Town U.S.A. 21°28N 158°1W 302 K13
Miling Australia 30°30S 116°17E 279 F2
Militello in Val di Catánia Italy 37°16N 14°48E 201 E7
Militsch = Milicz Poland 51°31N 17°19E 185 G4
Milk, Wadi el → Sudan 17°55N 30°20E 256 D3
Milk River Canada 49°10N 112°5W 296 D6
Milk River Spa Jamaica 17°50N 77°22W 320 a
Mill → U.S.A. 42°57N 83°23W 312 D1
Mill Hill U.K. 51°37N 0°14W 125 A2
Mill I. Antarctica 66°0S 101°30E 151 C8
Mill I. Nunavut, Canada 63°58N 77°47W 295 E16
Mill Shoals U.S.A. 38°15N 88°21W 311 F8
Mill Valley U.S.A. 37°54N 122°32W 306 H4
Millárs → Spain 39°55N 0°1W 196 F4
Millau France 44°8N 3°4E 174 D7
Millbridge Canada 44°41N 77°36W 312 B7
Millbrook Ont., Canada 44°10N 78°29W 312 B6
Millbrook Ala., U.S.A. 32°29N 86°22W 315 E11
Millbrook N.Y., U.S.A. 41°47N 73°42W 313 E11
Mille Lacs, L. des Canada 48°45N 90°35W 298 C1
Mille Lacs L. U.S.A. 46°15N 93°39W 308 B7
Milledgeville Ga., U.S.A. 33°5N 83°14W 316 B6
Milledgeville Ill., U.S.A. 41°58N 89°46W 310 C7
Millen U.S.A. 32°48N 81°57W 316 C8
Millennium Dome U.K. 51°30N 0°0 125 A4
Millennium I. = Caroline I. Kiribati 9°58S 150°13W 289 H12
Millennium Park Chicago, U.S.A. 119 c2
Miller U.S.A. 44°31N 98°59W 308 C4
Miller Lake Canada 45°6N 81°26W 312 A3
Miller Meadow U.S.A. 41°51N 87°49W 119 B2
Millerhill U.K. 55°55N 3°5W 121 B3
Millerovo Russia 48°57N 40°28E 191 F5
Miller's Flat N.Z. 45°39S 169°23E 285 F4
Millers Point Sydney, Australia 139 a1
Millersburg Ind., U.S.A. 41°32N 85°42W 311 C11
Millersburg Ohio, U.S.A. 40°33N 81°55W 312 F3
Millersburg Pa., U.S.A. 40°32N 76°58W 312 F8
Millerton N.Z. 41°39S 171°54E 285 B6
Millerton N.Y., U.S.A. 41°57N 73°31W 313 E11
Millerton L. U.S.A. 37°1N 119°41W 306 J7
Millet St. Lucia 13°55N 60°59W 323 m
Millevaches, Plateau de France 45°45N 2°0E 174 C6
Millheim U.S.A. 40°54N 77°29W 312 F7
Millicent Australia 37°34S 140°21E 282 D4
Milligan U.S.A. 30°45N 86°38W 317 E3
Millington U.S.A. 35°20N 89°53W 315 D10
Millinocket U.S.A. 45°39N 68°43W 309 C19
Millmerran Australia 27°53S 151°16E 281 D5
Millom U.K. 54°13N 3°16W 168 C4
Mills L. Canada 61°30N 118°20W 296 A5
Millsboro U.S.A. 40°0N 80°0W 312 G5
Millstream Chichester △ Australia 21°35S 117°6E 278 D2
Millstreet Ireland 52°4N 9°4W 166 D2
Millthorpe Australia 33°26S 149°12E 283 B8
Millville N.J., U.S.A. 39°24N 75°2W 309 F16
Millville Pa., U.S.A. 41°7N 76°32W 313 E8
Millwood L. U.S.A. 33°42N 93°58W 314 E8
Milna Croatia 43°20N 16°28E 199 E13
Milne → Australia 21°10S 137°33E 280 C2
Milne Bay □ Papua N. G. 10°0S 152°30E 286 E7
Milne Land Greenland 70°40N 26°30W 154 C8
Milnerton S. Africa 33°53S 18°29E 118 A1
Milo U.S.A. 45°15N 68°59W 309 C19
Milo → Guinea 8°52N 9°0W 262 D3
Miloli'i U.S.A. 19°11N 155°55W 302 D6
Milon, Akra Greece 36°15N 28°11E 206 E12
Milon-la-Chapelle France 48°43N 2°3E 134 B1
Milos Greece 36°44N 24°25E 204 E6
Miłosław Poland 52°12N 17°32E 185 F4
Milot Albania 41°41N 19°43E 202 E3
Milparinka Australia 29°46S 141°57E 281 D3
Milpitas U.S.A. 37°26N 121°55W 306 H5
Milroy U.S.A. 39°30N 85°28W 311 E11
Miltenberg Germany 49°41N 9°16E 179 F5
Milton N.S.W., Australia 35°20S 150°27E 283 C9
Milton N.S., Canada 44°4N 64°45W 299 D7
Milton Ont., Canada 43°31N 79°53W 312 C5
Milton N.Z. 46°7S 169°59E 285 G4
Milton Calif., U.S.A. 38°3N 120°51W 306 G6
Milton Fla., U.S.A. 30°38N 87°3W 317 E2
Milton Iowa, U.S.A. 40°41N 92°10W 310 D4
Milton Mass., U.S.A. 42°14N 71°2W 116 B2
Milton Pa., U.S.A. 41°1N 76°51W 312 F8
Milton Vt., U.S.A. 44°38N 73°7W 313 B11
Milton Wis., U.S.A. 42°47N 88°56W 311 B8
Milton Bridge U.K. 55°51N 3°11W 121 B2
Milton-Freewater U.S.A. 45°56N 118°23W 304 D4
Milton Keynes U.K. 52°1N 0°44W 169 E7
Milton Keynes □ U.K. 52°1N 0°44W 169 E7
Milton Park Montréal, Canada 130 b1
Miltou Chad 10°14N 17°26E 259 F3
Miltown Malbay Ireland 52°52N 9°24W 166 D2
Miluo China 29°0N 112°59E 229 C9
Milverton Canada 43°34N 80°55W 312 C4
Milwaukee U.S.A. 43°2N 87°54W 311 A9
Milwaukee Deep Atl. Oc. 19°50N 68°0W 321 C6
Milwaukie U.S.A. 45°26N 122°38W 306 E4
Mim Ghana 6°57N 2°33W 262 D4
Mima Japan 34°4N 134°9E 222 C6
Mimaropa □ Phil. 11°30N 120°20E 233 F3
Mimico Canada 43°36N 79°29W 141 B2
Mimico Creek → Canada 43°37N 79°28W 141 B1
Mimili Australia 27°0S 132°42E 279 E5
Mimizan France 44°12N 1°13W 174 D2
Mimoň Czechia 50°38N 14°43E 180 A7
Mimongo Gabon 1°11S 11°36E 264 C2
Mimoso Brazil 15°10S 48°5W 333 E2
Mims U.S.A. 28°40N 80°51W 317 G9
Min Jiang → Fujian, China 26°0N 119°35E 229 E12
Min Jiang → Sichuan, China 28°45N 104°40E 228 C5
Min Xian China 34°25N 104°5E 226 G3
Mīnā' al Aḩmadī Kuwait 29°5N 48°10E 247 D6
Mīnā' Jabal 'Alī U.A.E. 25°2N 55°8E 247 E7
Mina Pirquitas Argentina 22°40S 66°30W 334 A2
Mina Raysūt = Raysūt Oman 16°56N 53°59E 249 C6
Mīnā Su'ud Si. Arabia 28°45N 48°28E 247 D6
Minago → Canada 54°33N 98°59W 297 C9
Minakami Japan 36°49N 138°59E 223 A10
Minaki Canada 49°59N 94°40W 297 D10
Minakuchi Japan 34°58N 136°10E 223 C8
Minalungao △ Phil. 15°2N 121°8E 232 D3
Minamata Japan 32°10N 130°30E 222 E2
Minami Japan 34°40N 135°30E 133 A2
Minami-Arapusa △ Japan 35°30N 138°9E 223 B10
Minami-Tori-Shima Pac. Oc. 24°20N 153°58E 288 E7
Minamiaizu Japan 37°12N 139°46E 221 F9
Minamiawaji Japan 34°10N 134°42E 222 C6
Minamisōma Japan 37°38N 140°58E 220 F10
Minamitsunashima Japan 35°32N 139°37E 140 B2
Minas Indonesia 0°50N 101°26E 234 B2
Minas Uruguay 34°20S 55°10W 335 C4
Minas, Sierra de las Guatemala 15°9N 89°31W 320 C2
Minas Basin Canada 45°20N 64°12W 299 C7
Minas de Riotinto Spain 37°42N 6°35W 195 H4
Minas Gerais □ Brazil 18°50S 46°0W 333 E2
Minas Novas Brazil 17°15S 42°36W 333 E3
Minatitlán Mexico 17°59N 94°31W 319 D6
Minato Ōsaka, Japan 34°39N 135°25E 133 B1
Minato Tokyo, Japan 140 c3
Minbu Burma 20°10N 94°52E 241 E5
Minbya Burma 20°22N 93°16E 241 E4
Minchinabad Pakistan 30°10N 73°34E 242 D5
Mincio → Italy 45°4N 10°59E 198 C7
Minčol Slovakia 49°15N 20°58E 181 B13
Mindanao Phil. 8°0N 125°0E 233 H5
Mindanao Sea = Bohol Sea Phil. 9°0N 124°0E 233 G5
Mindanao Trench Pac. Oc. 12°0N 126°6E 232 E5
Mindel → Germany 48°31N 10°23E 179 G6
Mindelheim Germany 48°2N 10°29E 179 G6
Mindelo C. Verde Is. 16°24N 25°0W 153 j
Minden Ont., Canada 44°55N 78°43W 312 B6
Minden Nordrhein-Westfalen, Germany 52°17N 8°55E 178 C4
Minden La., U.S.A. 32°37N 93°17W 314 E8
Minden Nev., U.S.A. 38°57N 119°46W 306 G7
Mindibungu = Billiluna Australia 19°37S 127°41E 278 C4
Mindiptana Indonesia 5°55S 140°22E 231 F10
Mindon Burma 19°21N 94°44E 241 F5
Mindona L. Australia 33°6S 142°6E 282 B5
Mindoro Phil. 13°0N 121°0E 232 E3
Mindoro Occidental □ Phil. 13°0N 120°55E 232 E3
Mindoro Oriental □ Phil. 13°0N 121°5E 232 E3
Mindoro Str. Phil. 12°30N 120°30E 232 E3
Mindouli Congo 4°12S 14°28E 265 C2
Mindourou Cameroon 3°29N 13°26E 264 B2
Mine Japan 34°12N 131°7E 222 C3
Minehead U.K. 51°12N 3°29W 169 F4
Mineiros Brazil 17°34S 52°34W 331 D7
Mineola N.Y., U.S.A. 40°44N 73°38W 313 F11
Mineola Tex., U.S.A. 32°40N 95°29W 314 E7
Mineral Bath Jamaica 17°58N 76°22W 320 a
Mineral King U.S.A. 36°27N 118°36W 306 J8
Mineral Point U.S.A. 42°52N 90°11W 310 B6
Mineral Wells U.S.A. 32°48N 98°7W 314 E5
Mineralnyye Vody Russia 44°15N 43°8E 191 H6
Miners Bay Canada 44°49N 78°46W 312 B6
Minersville U.S.A. 40°41N 76°16W 313 F8
Minerva N.Y., U.S.A. 43°47N 73°59W 313 C11
Minerva Ohio, U.S.A. 40°44N 81°6W 312 F3
Minervino Murge Italy 41°5N 16°5E 201 A9
Minetto U.S.A. 43°24N 76°28W 313 C8
Minfeng China 37°4N 82°46E 217 E10
Ming-Kush Kyrgyzstan 41°40N 74°28E 217 D8
Mingäçevir Azerbaijan 40°45N 47°0E 191 K8
Mingäçevir Su Anbarı Azerbaijan 40°57N 46°50E 191 K8
Mingala C.A.R. 5°6N 21°49E 264 A4
Mingan Canada 50°20N 64°0W 299 B7
Mingary Australia 32°8S 140°45E 282 B4
Mingchien Taiwan 23°50N 120°42E 225 C2
Mingechaur = Mingäçevir Azerbaijan 40°45N 47°0E 191 K8
Mingechaurskoye Vdkhr. = Mingäçevir Su Anbarı Azerbaijan 40°57N 46°50E 191 K8
Mingela Australia 19°52S 146°38E 280 B4
Mingenew Australia 29°12S 115°21E 279 E2
Mingera Cr. → Australia 20°38S 137°45E 280 C2
Minggang China 32°24N 114°3E 229 A10
Mingguang China 32°46N 117°59E 229 A11
Mingin Burma 22°50N 94°30E 241 D5
Mingir Moldova 46°40N 28°20E 183 D13
Minglanilla Spain 39°34N 1°38W 197 F3
Minglun China 25°10N 108°21E 228 E7
Mingo Congo 1°55S 15°1E 264 C3
Mingo Junction U.S.A. 40°19N 80°37W 312 F4
Mingora Pakistan 34°48N 72°22E 243 B5
Mingorría Spain 40°45N 4°40W 194 E6
Mingshan China 30°6N 103°10E 228 B4
Mingteke Daban = Mintaka Pass Pakistan 37°0N 74°58E 243 A6
Mingxi China 26°18N 117°12E 229 D11
Mingyuegue China 43°2N 128°50E 227 C15
Minhe China 36°9N 102°45E 218 D9
Minhla Bago, Burma 17°59N 95°43E 241 G5
Minhla Magway, Burma 19°58N 95°3E 241 F5
Minho = Miño → Spain 41°52N 8°40W 194 D2
Minhou China 26°0N 119°15E 229 E12
Minhsiung Taiwan 23°33N 120°35E 225 C2
Minićevo Serbia 43°42N 22°18E 182 G7
Minicoy I. India 8°17N 73°2E 245 K1
Minidoka U.S.A. 42°45N 113°29W 304 E7
Minier U.S.A. 40°26N 89°19W 310 D7
Minigwal, L. Australia 29°31S 123°14E 279 E3
Minilya → Australia 23°45S 114°0E 279 D1
Minilya Roadhouse Australia 23°55S 114°0E 279 D1
Mininera Australia 37°37S 142°58E 282 D5
Minipi L. Canada 52°25N 60°45W 299 B7
Minj Papua N. G. 5°54S 144°37E 286 C3
Minjilang Australia 11°8S 132°33E 278 B5
Mink L. Canada 61°54N 117°40W 296 A5
Minkammen South Sudan 6°3N 31°32E 257 F3
Minkebé Gabon 1°45N 12°45E 264 B2
Minlaton Australia 34°45S 137°35E 282 C2
Minna Nigeria 9°37N 6°30E 263 D6
Minna-shima Japan 26°39N 127°49E 288 a
Minneapolis Kans., U.S.A. 39°8N 97°42W 308 F5
Minneapolis Minn., U.S.A. 44°57N 93°16W 308 C7
Minneapolis-St. Paul Int. ✈ (MSP) U.S.A. 44°53N 93°13W 308 C7
Minnedosa Canada 50°14N 99°50W 297 C9
Minnesota □ U.S.A. 46°0N 94°15W 308 B6
Minnesota → U.S.A. 44°54N 93°9W 308 C7
Minnesund Norway 60°23N 11°14E 164 D8
Minnewaukan U.S.A. 48°4N 99°15W 308 A4
Minnipa Australia 32°51S 135°9E 281 E2
Minnitaki L. Canada 49°57N 92°10W 298 C1
Miño = A Carreira Spain 43°21N 8°12W 194 B2
Mino Japan 35°32N 136°55E 223 B8
Miño → Spain 41°52N 8°40W 194 D2
Mino-Kamo Japan 35°23N 137°2E 223 B9
Mino-Mikawa-Kōgen Japan 35°10N 137°23E 223 B9
Minoa Greece 35°6N 25°45E 207 E6
Minobu Japan 35°22N 138°26E 223 B10
Minobu-Sanchi Japan 35°14N 138°20E 223 B10
Minonk U.S.A. 40°54N 89°2W 310 D7
Minooka U.S.A. 41°27N 88°16W 311 C8
Minorca = Menorca Spain 40°0N 4°0E 206 B5
Minore Australia 32°14S 148°27E 283 B8
Minot U.S.A. 48°14N 101°18W 308 A3
Minqin China 38°38N 103°20E 226 E2
Minqing China 26°15N 118°50E 229 D12
Minsen Germany 53°41N 7°58E 178 B3
Minshât el Bekkarî Egypt 30°0N 31°8E 117 A1
Minsk Belarus 53°52N 27°30E 177 B14
Minsk □ Belarus 53°15N 27°30E 188 F4
Mińsk Mazowiecki Poland 52°10N 21°33E 185 F8
Minster U.S.A. 40°24N 84°23W 311 D12
Mintabie Australia 27°15S 133°7E 281 D1
Mintaka Pass Pakistan 37°0N 74°58E 243 A6
Minthami Burma 23°55N 94°16E 241 D5
Minto N.B., Canada 46°5N 66°5W 299 C6
Minto Alaska, U.S.A. 64°53N 149°10W 303 D10
Minto, L. Canada 57°13N 75°0W 298 A5
Minton Canada 49°10N 104°35W 297 D8
Mintoum Gabon 0°27N 12°16E 264 B2
Minturn U.S.A. 39°35N 106°26W 304 G10
Minturno Italy 41°15N 13°45E 200 A6
Minudasht Iran 37°17N 56°7E 247 B8
Minûf Egypt 30°26N 30°52E 256 H7
Minusinsk Russia 53°43N 91°20E 217 B12
Minutang India 28°15N 96°30E 241 A6
Minvoul Gabon 2°9N 12°8E 264 B2
Minwakh Yemen 16°48N 48°6E 249 C5
Minxiong = Minhsiung Taiwan 23°33N 120°35E 225 C2
Minya el Qamh Egypt 30°31N 31°21E 256 H7
Minya Konka = Gongga Shan China 29°40N 101°55E 228 C3
Minyip Australia 36°29S 142°36E 282 D5
Minzhong China 22°37N 113°30E 219 a
Mionica Bos.-H. 44°51N 18°29E 182 F3
Mionica Serbia 44°14N 20°6E 202 B4
Mioveni Romania 44°56N 24°54E 183 F9
Miquan China 43°58N 87°42E 217 D11
Miquelon Qué., Canada 49°25N 76°27W 298 C4
Miquelon St-P. & M. 47°8N 56°22W 299 C8
Mir Belarus 53°27N 26°28E 177 B14
Mir Niger 14°5N 11°59E 259 F2
Mīr Kūh Iran 26°22N 58°55E 247 E8
Mīr Shahdād Iran 26°15N 58°29E 247 E8
Mira Italy 45°26N 12°8E 199 C9
Mira Portugal 40°26N 8°44W 194 E2
Mira → Colombia 1°36N 79°1W 328 C2
Mira → Portugal 37°43N 8°47W 195 H2
Mira por vos Cay Bahamas 22°9N 74°30W 321 B5
Mīrābād Afghan. 30°25N 61°50E 240 C1
Mirabella Eclano Italy 41°2N 14°59E 201 A7
Mirabello, Kolpos Greece 35°10N 25°50E 207 E6
Miracema do Norte Brazil 9°33S 48°24W 332 C2
Mirador Brazil 6°22S 44°22W 332 C3
Mirador-Río Azul △ Guatemala 17°45N 89°50W 320 C1
Miraflores = Rovìra Colombia 4°15N 75°20W 328 C2
Miraflores Colombia 1°25N 72°13W 328 C3
Miraflores Lima, Peru 12°7S 77°2W 124 B2
Miraflores, L. Panama 9°1N 79°36W 320 c
Miraflores Locks Panama 9°0N 79°36W 320 c
Miraj India 16°50N 74°45E 244 F2
Miram Shah Pakistan 33°0N 70°2E 242 C4
Miramar Argentina 38°15S 57°50W 334 D4
Miramar Mozam. 23°50S 35°35E 271 B6
Miramar Fla., U.S.A. 25°59N 80°13W 129 C1
Miramas France 43°33N 4°59E 175 E8
Mirambeau France 45°23N 0°35W 174 C3
Miramichi Canada 47°2N 65°28W 299 C6
Miramichi B. Canada 47°15N 65°0W 299 C7
Miramont-de-Guyenne France 44°37N 0°21E 174 D4
Miranda Brazil 20°10S 56°15W 331 E6
Miranda □ Venezuela 10°15N 66°25W 328 A4
Miranda → Brazil 19°25S 57°20W 331 D6
Miranda de Ebro Spain 42°41N 2°57W 196 C2
Miranda do Corvo Portugal 40°6N 8°20W 194 E2
Miranda do Douro Portugal 41°30N 6°16W 194 D4
Mirande France 43°31N 0°25E 174 E4
Mirandela Portugal 41°32N 7°10W 194 D3
Mirándola Italy 44°53N 11°4E 198 D8
Mirandópolis Brazil 21°9S 51°6W 335 A5
Mirango Malawi 13°32S 34°58E 269 E3
Mirani Australia 21°8S 148°53E 280 b
Mirano Italy 45°30N 12°7E 199 C9
Miras Albania 40°30N 20°56E 202 F4
Mirassol Brazil 20°46S 49°28W 335 A6
Mirbāţ Oman 17°0N 54°45E 249 C6
Mirboo North Australia 38°24S 146°10E 283 E7
Mirear Egypt 23°15N 35°41E 256 C4
Mirebeau France 46°49N 0°10E 172 F7
Mirebeau-sur-Bèze France 47°25N 5°20E 173 E12
Mirecourt France 48°20N 6°10E 173 D13
Mires Greece 35°4N 24°56E 207 E5
Mirgorod = Myrhorod Ukraine 49°58N 33°37E 189 H7
Miri Malaysia 4°23N 113°59E 235 B4
Mirialguda India 16°52N 79°35E 244 F4
Miriam Vale Australia 24°20S 151°33E 280 C5
Miribel France 45°50N 4°57E 173 G11
Mirigama Sri Lanka 7°15N 80°8E 245 L5
Mirim, L. S. Amer. 32°45S 52°50W 335 C5
Mirimire Venezuela 11°10N 68°43W 328 A4
Miringoni Comoros Is. 12°17S 43°38E 272 a
Miriti Brazil 6°15S 59°0W 331 B6
Miriuwung Gajerrong ✿ Australia 15°0S 128°45E 278 C4
Mīrjāveh Iran 29°1N 61°30E 247 D9
Mirnyy Antarctica 66°50S 92°30E 151 C14
Mirnyy Russia 62°33N 113°53E 215 C12
Miroč Serbia 44°32N 22°16E 202 B6
Mirokhan Pakistan 27°46N 68°6E 242 F3
Mirond L. Canada 55°6N 102°47W 297 B8
Mirosławiec Poland 53°20N 16°5E 184 E3
Mirpur Pakistan 33°32N 73°56E 243 C5
Mirpur Batoro Pakistan 24°44N 68°16E 242 G3
Mirpur Bibiwari Pakistan 28°33N 67°44E 242 E2
Mirpur Khas Pakistan 25°30N 69°0E 242 G3
Mirpur Sakro Pakistan 24°33N 67°41E 242 G2
Mirria Niger 13°43N 9°7E 259 F1
Mirrool Australia 34°19S 147°10E 283 C7
Mirs Bay = Tai Pang Wan China 22°33N 114°24E 219 a
Mirsale Somalia 5°57N 47°59E 267 C6
Mirsk Poland 50°58N 15°23E 185 H2
Mirtağ Turkey 38°23N 41°56E 246 B4
Mirtoo Sea Greece 37°0N 23°20E 204 D5
Mirtou, Kolpos Greece 38°20N 20°27E 207 C1
Miryang S. Korea 35°31N 128°44E 224 E4
Mirzaani Georgia 41°24N 46°5E 191 K8
Mirzachul = Guliston Uzbekistan 40°29N 68°46E 217 D7
Mirzapur India 25°10N 82°34E 243 G10
Mirzapur-cum-Vindhyachal = Mirzapur India 25°10N 82°34E 243 G10
Mirzoyan = Taraz Kazakhstan 42°54N 71°22E 217 D8
Misaki Japan 34°18N 135°9E 223 C7
Misamis = Ozamiz Phil. 8°15N 123°50E 233 G4
Misamis Occidental □ Phil. 8°20N 123°42E 233 G4
Misamis Oriental □ Phil. 8°45N 125°0E 233 G5
Misantla Mexico 19°56N 96°50W 319 D5
Misawa Japan 40°41N 141°24E 220 D10
Miscou I. Canada 47°57N 64°31W 299 C7
Misdroy = Międzyzdroje Poland 53°56N 14°26E 184 E1
Misericordia = Itaporanga Brazil 7°18S 38°0W 332 C4
Misericordia, Sa. da Brazil 22°51S 43°17W 135 B1
Misha India 7°59N 93°20E 245 L10
Mish'āb, Ra's al Si. Arabia 28°15N 48°43E 247 D6
Mishagua → Peru 11°12S 72°58W 330 C3
Mishamo Tanzania 5°41S 30°41E 268 D3
Mishan China 45°37N 131°48E 220 B5
Mishawaka U.S.A. 41°40N 86°11W 311 C10
Mishbih, Gebel Egypt 22°38N 34°44E 256 C3
Mishima Japan 35°10N 138°52E 223 B10
Mishmi Hills India 29°0N 96°0E 241 A6
Mishō Japan 32°57N 132°35E 222 E4
Misima I. Papua N. G. 10°40S 152°45E 286 F7
Misión Mexico 32°6N 116°53W 307 N10
Misión Fagnano Argentina 54°32S 67°17W 336 D3
Misiones □ Argentina 27°0S 55°0W 335 B5
Misiones □ Paraguay 27°0S 56°0W 334 B4
Miskah Si. Arabia 24°49N 42°56E 246 E4
Miski, E. → Chad 20°0N 17°55E 259 E3
Miskitos, Cayos Nic. 14°26N 82°50W 320 D3
Miskolc Hungary 48°7N 20°50E 182 B5
Misoke Dem. Rep. of the Congo 0°42S 28°2E 268 C2
Misool Indonesia 1°52S 130°10E 231 E8
Mişr = Egypt ■ Africa 28°0N 31°0E 256 B3
Mişrātah Libya 32°24N 15°3E 258 B3
Mişrātah □ Libya 33°30N 15°0E 258 C3
Missanabie Canada 48°20N 84°6W 298 C3
Missão Catrimani Brazil 2°48N 62°18W 329 C5
Missão Velha Brazil 7°15S 39°10W 332 C4
Missinaibi → Canada 50°43N 81°29W 298 B3
Missinaibi L. Canada 48°23N 83°40W 298 C3
Mission B.C., Canada 49°10N 122°15W 296 D4
Mission Calif., U.S.A. 37°44N 122°25W 136 B2
Mission S. Dak., U.S.A. 43°18N 100°39W 308 D3
Mission Tex., U.S.A. 26°13N 98°20W 314 H5
Mission Beach Australia 17°53S 146°6E 280 B4
Mission Viejo U.S.A. 33°36N 117°40W 307 M9
Missirah Senegal 13°40N 16°30W 262 C1
Missisa L. Canada 52°20N 85°7W 298 B2
Missisicabi → Canada 51°14N 79°31W 298 B4
Mississagi → Canada 46°15N 83°9W 298 C3
Mississauga Canada 43°32N 79°35W 141 B1
Mississinewa L. U.S.A. 40°42N 85°52W 311 D10
Mississippi □ U.S.A. 33°0N 90°0W 315 E10
Mississippi → U.S.A. 29°9N 89°15W 315 G10
Mississippi L. Canada 45°5N 76°10W 313 A8
Mississippi River Delta U.S.A. 29°10N 89°15W 315 G10
Mississippi Sd. U.S.A. 30°20N 89°0W 315 F10
Missoula U.S.A. 46°52N 114°1W 304 C6
Missour Morocco 33°3N 4°0W 260 B4
Missouri □ U.S.A. 38°25N 92°30W 310 E3
Missouri → U.S.A. 38°49N 90°7W 310 F6
Missouri City U.S.A. 29°37N 95°32W 314 G7
Missouri Valley U.S.A. 41°34N 95°53W 308 E6
Mist U.S.A. 45°59N 123°15W 306 E3
Mistassibi → Canada 48°53N 72°13W 299 B5

Mistassini Canada 48°53N 72°12W 299 C5
Mistassini → Canada 48°42N 72°20W 299 C5
Mistassini, L. Canada 51°0N 73°30W 298 B5
Mistastin L. Canada 55°57N 63°20W 299 A7
Mistelbach Austria 48°34N 16°34E 181 C9
Misterbianco Italy 37°31N 15°1E 201 E8
Misteriosa Bank
Caribbean 18°50N 83°50W 320 C3
Misti, Volcán Peru 16°18S 71°24W 330 D3
Mistinibi, L. Canada 55°56N 64°17W 299 A7
Mistissini Canada 48°53N 72°12W 299 C5
Mistras = Mystras Greece 37°4N 22°22E 204 D4
Mistretta Italy 37°56N 14°22E 201 E7
Misty Fjords Nat. Monument ⌂
U.S.A. 55°40N 130°40W 303 J15
Misty L. Canada 58°53N 101°40W 297 B8
Misugi Japan 34°31N 136°16E 223 C8
Misumi Japan 32°37N 130°27E 222 E2
Misurata = Miṣrātah Libya 32°24N 15°3E 258 B3
Mît Ghamr Egypt 30°42N 31°12E 256 H7
Mitaka Japan 35°41N 139°34E 140 A2
Mitande Mozam. 14°6S 35°58E 269 E4
Mitatib Sudan 15°59N 36°12E 257 D4
Mitau = Jelgava Latvia 56°41N 23°49E 184 B10
Mitava = Jelgava Latvia 56°41N 23°49E 184 B10
Mitcham U.K. 51°23N 0°10W 125 B2
Mitcham Common U.K. 51°23N 0°8W 125 B3
Mitchell Queens.,
Australia 26°29S 147°58E 281 D4
Mitchell Ont., Canada 43°28N 81°12W 312 C3
Mitchell Ga., U.S.A. 33°13N 82°42W 316 B7
Mitchell Ind., U.S.A. 38°44N 86°28W 311 F10
Mitchell Nebr., U.S.A. 41°57N 103°49W 308 E2
Mitchell Oreg., U.S.A. 44°34N 120°9W 304 D3
Mitchell S. Dak., U.S.A. 43°43N 98°2W 308 D4
Mitchell → Australia 15°12S 141°35E 280 B3
Mitchell, Mt. U.S.A. 35°46N 82°16W 315 D13
Mitchell-Alice Rivers △
Australia 15°28S 142°5E 280 B3
Mitchell Museum of the American
Indian Chicago, U.S.A. 42°4N 87°43W 119 A2
Mitchell Ra. Australia 12°49S 135°36E 280 A2
Mitchell River △
Australia 37°37S 147°22E 283 D7
Mitchell's Plain S. Africa 34°4S 18°35E 118 B2
Mitchelstown Ireland 52°15N 8°16W 166 D3
Mitha Tiwana Pakistan 32°13N 72°6E 242 C5
Mithi Pakistan 24°44N 69°48E 242 G3
Mithimna Greece 39°20N 26°12E 205 B8
Mithrao Pakistan 27°28N 69°40E 242 F3
Mitiamo Australia 36°12S 144°15E 282 D6
Mitikas Etoloakarnania,
Greece 38°40N 20°56E 207 B2
Mitikas Preveza, Greece 39°0N 20°42E 207 B2
Mitilini Greece 39°6N 26°35E 205 B8
Mitilinii Greece 37°42N 26°56E 205 D8
Mitla Pass = Mamarr Mitlā
Egypt 30°2N 32°54E 251 H3
Mito Japan 36°20N 140°30E 223 A12
Mitra, Mt. Eq. Guin. 1°23N 9°19E 264 B1
Mitre, Mt. N.Z. 40°50S 175°30E 284 G4
Mitrofanovka Russia 49°58N 39°42E 189 H10
Mitrovicë Kosovo 42°54N 20°52E 202 D4
Mitrowitz = Sremska Mitrovica
Serbia 44°59N 19°38E 182 F4
Mitsamiouli Comoros Is. 11°20S 43°16E 272 a
Mitsang Gabon 0°42N 12°33E 264 B2
Mitsinjo Madag. 16°1S 45°52E 272 B2
Mitsio, Nosy Madag. 12°54S 48°36E 272 A2
Mitsiwa Eritrea 15°35N 39°25E 257 D4
Mitsiwa Channel Eritrea 15°30N 40°0E 257 D5
Mitsoudjé Comoros Is. 11°48S 43°16E 272 a
Mitsukaidō Japan 36°1N 139°59E 223 A11
Mitsushima Japan 34°15N 129°20E 222 C1
Mittagong Australia 34°28S 150°29E 283 C9
Mitte Germany 52°32N 13°24E 115 A3
Mittel Isarkanal →
Germany 48°12N 11°40E 131 A3
Mittel Schreiberhau = Szklarska
Poreba Poland 50°50N 15°33E 185 H2
Mittelberg Austria 47°20N 10°10E 180 D3
Mittelfranken □ Germany 49°25N 10°40E 179 F6
Mittellandkanal →
Germany 52°20N 8°28E 178 C4
Mittelwalde = Międzylesie
Poland 50°8N 16°40E 185 H3
Mittenwalde Germany 52°15N 13°31E 178 C9
Mittersill Austria 47°16N 12°29E 180 D5
Mitterteich Germany 49°57N 12°14E 179 F8
Mittimatalik = Pond Inlet
Canada 72°40N 77°0W 295 C16
Mittweida Germany 50°59N 12°59E 178 E8
Mitú Colombia 1°15N 70°13W 328 C3
Mituas Colombia 3°52N 68°49W 328 C4
Mitumba Tanzania 7°8S 31°2E 268 D3
Mitumba, Mts.
Dem. Rep. of the Congo 7°0S 27°30E 268 D2
Mitwaba
Dem. Rep. of the Congo 8°2S 27°17E 269 D2
Mityana Uganda 0°23N 32°2E 268 B3
Mitzic Gabon 0°45N 11°40E 264 B2
Miura Japan 35°12N 139°40E 223 B11
Mixcoac Mexico 19°23N 99°11W 128 B1
Mixteco → Mexico 18°11N 98°30W 319 D5
Miyagi □ Japan 38°15N 140°45E 220 E10
Miyāh, W. el → Egypt 25°0N 33°23E 256 C3
Miyāh, W. el → Syria 34°44N 39°57E 244 C3
Miyake-Jima Japan 34°5N 139°30E 223 C11
Miyako Japan 39°40N 141°59E 220 E10
Miyako-Jima Japan 24°45N 125°20E 221 M2
Miyako-Rettō Japan 24°24N 125°0E 221 M2
Miyakojima Okinawa,
Japan 24°48N 125°17E 221 M2
Miyakojima Ōsaka, Japan 34°42N 135°31E 133 A2
Miyakonojō Japan 31°40N 131°5E 222 F3
Miyān Rahan Iran 34°34N 47°26E 213 E12
Miyani India 21°50N 69°26E 242 J3
Miyanojō Japan 31°54N 130°27E 222 F2
Miyanoura-Dake Japan 30°20N 130°31E 221 J5
Miyata Japan 33°49N 130°42E 222 D2
Miyazaki Japan 31°56N 131°30E 222 F3
Miyazaki □ Japan 32°30N 131°30E 222 E3
Miyazu Japan 35°35N 135°10E 223 B7
Miyet, Bahr el = Dead Sea
Asia 31°30N 35°30E 251 G6
Miyi China 26°47N 102°9E 228 D4
Miyoshi Japan 34°48N 132°51E 222 C4
Miyun China 40°28N 116°50E 226 D9
Miyun Shuiku China 40°30N 117°0E 227 D9
Mizan Teferi Ethiopia 6°57N 35°3E 257 F4
Mizdah Libya 31°30N 13°0E 258 B2
Mizen Hd. Cork, Ireland 51°27N 9°50W 166 E2
Mizen Hd. Wicklow, Ireland 52°51N 6°4W 166 D5
Mizhhirya Ukraine 48°32N 23°30E 183 B8
Mizhi China 37°47N 110°12E 226 F6
Mizil Romania 44°59N 26°29E 183 F11
Mizo Hills = Mizoram □
India 23°30N 92°40E 241 D4
Mizonokuchi Japan 35°35N 139°34E 140 B2
Mizoram □ India 23°30N 92°40E 241 D4
Mizpe Ramon Israel 30°34N 34°49E 251 H5
Mizue Japan 35°41N 139°54E 140 A4
Mizuho = Kyōtamba
Japan 35°6N 135°17E 223 B7
Mizuho Antarctica 70°30S 41°0E 151 D5
Mizunami Japan 35°22N 137°15E 223 B9
Mizusawa = Ōshū Japan 39°8N 141°8E 220 E10
Mjällby Sweden 56°3N 14°40E 163 H8
Mjöbäck Sweden 57°28N 12°53E 163 G6
Mjölby Sweden 58°20N 15°10E 163 F9
Mjølfjell Norway 60°41N 6°55E 164 D3
Mjømna Norway 60°55N 4°55E 164 D1
Mjörn Sweden 57°55N 12°25E 163 G6
Mjøsa Norway 60°40N 11°0E 164 D8
Mkata Tanzania 5°45S 38°20E 268 D4
Mkhaya ⌂ Swaziland 26°34S 31°45E 271 C5
Mkhuze ⌂ S. Africa 29°27S 29°30E 271 C4
Mkoani Tanzania 5°22S 39°39E 268 D4
Mkokotoni Tanzania 5°55S 39°15E 268 D4
Mkomazi Tanzania 4°40S 38°7E 268 C4
Mkomazi → S. Africa 30°12S 30°50E 271 D5
Mkomazi ⌂ Tanzania 4°4S 30°2E 268 C3
Mkulwe Tanzania 8°37S 32°20E 269 D3
Mkumbi, Ras Tanzania 7°38S 39°55E 268 D4
Mkushi Zambia 14°25S 29°15E 269 E2
Mkushi River Zambia 13°32S 29°45E 269 E2
Mkuze S. Africa 27°10S 32°0E 271 C5
Mladá Boleslav Czechia 50°27N 14°53E 180 A7
Mladenovac Serbia 44°28N 20°44E 202 B4
Mlala Hills Tanzania 6°50S 31°40E 268 D3
M'lang Phil. 6°56N 124°52E 233 H5
Mlange = Mulanje, Mt.
Malawi 16°2S 35°33E 269 F4
Mlava → Serbia 44°45N 21°13E 202 B5
Mława Poland 53°9N 20°25E 185 E7
Mlawula ⌂ Swaziland 26°12S 32°2E 271 C5
Mliniště Bos.-H. 44°15N 16°50E 199 D13
Mljet Croatia 42°43N 17°30E 199 F14
Mljet △ Croatia 42°45N 17°25E 199 F14
Mljetski Kanal Croatia 42°48N 17°35E 199 F14
Młocinski, Park Poland 52°19N 20°57E 143 B1
Młociny Poland 52°18N 20°55E 143 B1
Mlynary Poland 54°12N 19°46E 184 D6
Mmabatho S. Africa 25°49S 25°30E 270 C4
Mme Cameroon 6°18N 10°14E 263 D7
Mnevniki Russia 55°45N 37°28E 129 B1
Mnichovo Hradiště
Czechia 50°32N 14°59E 180 A7
Mo Hordaland, Norway 60°49N 5°48E 164 D2
Mo Møre og Romsdal, Norway 63°0N 8°59E 164 A5
Mo Telemark, Norway 59°28N 7°50E 164 E4
Mo i Rana Norway 66°20N 14°7E 160 C16
Moa Queens., Australia 10°11S 142°16E 280 a
Moa Cuba 20°40N 74°56W 321 B4
Moa Indonesia 8°0S 128°0E 231 F7
Moa → S. Leone 6°59N 11°36W 262 D2
Moab U.S.A. 38°35N 109°33W 304 G9
Moabi Gabon 2°24S 10°59E 264 C2
Moaco → Brazil 7°41S 68°18W 330 B4
Moala Fiji 18°36S 179°53E 287 B2
Moama Australia 36°7S 144°46E 281 F3
Moamba Mozam. 25°36S 32°15E 271 C5
Moapa U.S.A. 36°40N 114°37W 307 J12
Moate Ireland 53°24N 7°44W 166 C4
Moba Dem. Rep. of the Congo 7°0S 29°48E 268 D2
Moba Lagos, Nigeria 6°26N 3°28E 124 B2
Mobara Japan 35°25N 140°18E 223 B12
Mobārakābād Iran 28°24N 53°20E 247 D7
Mobaye C.A.R. 4°25N 21°5E 264 B4
Mobayi
Dem. Rep. of the Congo 4°15N 21°8E 264 B4
Mobeka
Dem. Rep. of the Congo 1°52N 19°49E 264 B3
Mobenzélé Congo 0°56N 17°50E 264 B3
Moberly U.S.A. 39°25N 92°26W 310 F4
Moberly Lake Canada 55°50N 121°44W 296 B4
Mobile U.S.A. 30°41N 88°3W 315 F10
Mobile B. U.S.A. 30°30N 88°0W 315 F11
Mobridge U.S.A. 45°32N 100°26W 308 C3
Mobutu Sese Seko, L. = Albert, L.
Africa 1°30N 31°0E 268 B3
Moc Chau Vietnam 20°50N 104°38E 236 B5
Moc Hoa Vietnam 10°46N 105°56E 237 G5
Moca Puerto Rico 18°24N 67°10W 321 b
Mocabe Kasari
Dem. Rep. of the Congo 9°58S 26°12E 269 D2
Mocajuba Brazil 2°35S 49°30W 332 B2
Moçambique = Mozambique ■
Africa 19°0S 35°0E 269 F4
Moçambique Mozam. 15°3S 40°42E 269 F5
Moçâmedes = Namibe
Angola 15°7S 12°11E 265 F2
Mocanaqua U.S.A. 41°9N 76°8W 313 E8
Mocapra → Venezuela 7°56N 66°46W 328 B4
Mocco, Morro de Angola 12°28S 15°11E 265 E3
Moce Fiji 18°40S 178°29W 287 B3
Mocenigo, Palazzo Venice, Italy 142 b2
Mocha = Al Mukhā
Yemen 13°18N 43°15E 248 D3
Mocha, I. Chile 38°22S 73°56W 336 A2
Mochos Greece 35°16N 25°27E 207 E6
Mochudi Botswana 24°27S 26°7E 270 B4
Mocimboa da Praia
Mozam. 11°25S 40°20E 269 E5
Mociu Romania 46°46N 24°3E 183 D9
Möckeln Sweden 56°40N 14°15E 163 H8
Mockfjärd Sweden 60°30N 14°57E 162 D8
Moclips U.S.A. 47°14N 124°13W 306 C2
Mocoa Colombia 1°7N 76°35W 328 C2
Mococa Brazil 21°28S 47°0W 335 A6
Mocorito Mexico 25°29N 107°55W 318 B3
Moctezuma Mexico 29°48N 109°42W 318 B3
Moctezuma → Mexico 21°59N 98°34W 319 C5
Mocuba Mozam. 16°54S 36°57E 269 F4
Moczydło Poland 52°8N 21°2E 143 C2
Moda Burma 24°22N 96°29E 241 C6
Modane France 45°12N 6°40E 175 C10
Modasa India 23°30N 73°21E 242 H5
Modder → S. Africa 29°2S 24°37E 270 C3
Modderfontein = Niekerkshoop
S. Africa 29°19S 22°51E 270 C3
Modderfontein S. Africa 26°5S 28°10E 123 A2
Modderrivier S. Africa 29°2S 24°38E 270 C3
Módena Italy 44°40N 10°55E 198 D7
Modena Utah, U.S.A. 37°48N 113°56W 305 H7
Modernamuseet Stockholm, Sweden 139 b3
Modesto U.S.A. 37°39N 121°0W 306 H6
Möðrudalur Iceland 65°22N 15°53W 155 B11
Möðruvellir Iceland 65°46N 18°15W 155 B8
Módica Italy 36°52N 14°46E 201 F7
Modimolle S. Africa 24°42S 28°22E 271 B4
Modjadjiskloof S. Africa 23°42S 30°10E 271 B5
Modjamboli
Dem. Rep. of the Congo 2°28N 22°6E 264 B4
Mödling Austria 48°5N 16°17E 181 C9
Modo South Sudan 5°31N 30°33E 257 F3
Modoc U.S.A. 33°44N 82°13W 316 B7
Modra Slovakia 48°19N 17°20E 181 C10
Modřany Czechia 50°0N 14°24E 135 B2
Modriča Bos.-H. 44°57N 18°17E 182 F3
Moe Australia 38°12S 146°19E 283 E7
Moebase Mozam. 17°3S 38°41E 269 F4
Moëlan-sur-Mer France 47°49N 3°38W 172 E3
Moelv Norway 60°56N 10°43E 164 D7
Moen I. = Weno Pac. Oc. 7°27N 151°52E 287 T18
Moengo Suriname 5°45N 54°20W 329 B7
Moenjodaro = Mohenjodaro
Pakistan 27°19N 68°7E 242 F3
Moerewa N.Z. 35°8S 174°1E 284 B3
Moers Germany 51°27N 6°36E 178 D2
Moffat U.K. 55°21N 3°27W 167 F5
Moga India 30°48N 75°8E 242 D6
Mogadishu = Muqdisho
Somalia 2°2N 45°25E 267 D6
Mogador = Essaouira
Morocco 31°32N 9°42W 260 B3
Mogadouro Portugal 41°22N 6°47W 194 D4
Mogalakwena →
S. Africa 22°38S 28°40E 271 B4
Mogami-Gawa → Japan 38°45N 140°0E 220 E10
Mogán Canary Is. 27°53N 15°43W 153 e1
Mogandjo
Dem. Rep. of the Congo 1°23N 24°15E 264 B4
Mogaung Burma 25°20N 97°0E 241 C6
Mogen Norway 60°2N 7°52E 164 D4
Mogente = Moixent Spain 38°52N 0°45W 197 G4
Mogho Ethiopia 4°54N 40°16E 257 G5
Mogielnica Poland 51°42N 20°41E 185 G7
Mogige Ethiopia 5°24N 36°14E 257 F4
Mogilev = Mahilyow
Belarus 53°55N 30°18E 177 B16
Mogilev-Podolskiy = Mohyliv-
Podilskyy Ukraine 48°26N 27°48E 183 B12
Mogilno Poland 52°39N 17°55E 185 F4
Mogincual Mozam. 15°35S 40°25E 269 F5
Mogliano Véneto Italy 45°33N 12°14E 199 C9
Mogocha Russia 53°40N 119°50E 215 D12
Mogoditshane Botswana 24°37S 25°51E 270 B4
Mogok Burma 23°0N 96°40E 241 D6
Mogollon Rim U.S.A. 34°10N 110°50W 305 J8
Mógoro Italy 39°41N 8°47E 200 C1
Mograt Sudan 19°28N 33°16E 256 D3
Mogroum Chad 11°6N 15°25E 259 F3
Moguer Spain 37°15N 6°52W 195 H4
Mogumber Australia 31°2S 116°3E 279 F2
Mogwadi → S. Africa 23°4S 29°36E 271 B4
Mogyoród Hungary 47°35N 19°14E 117 A3
Mohács Hungary 45°58N 18°41E 182 E3
Mohaka → N.Z. 39°7S 177°12E 284 F6
Mohala India 20°35N 80°44E 244 D5
Mohales Hoek Lesotho 30°7S 27°26E 270 D4
Mohali = Ajitgarh India 30°47N 76°41E 242 D7
Mohali Congo 0°15N 15°29E 264 B3
Mohall U.S.A. 48°46N 101°31W 308 A3
Moḥammadābād Iran 37°52N 59°5E 247 B8
Mohammadia Algeria 35°33N 0°3E 261 A5
Mohammedia Morocco 33°44N 7°21W 260 B3
Mohammerah = Khorramshahr
Iran 30°29N 48°15E 247 D6
Mohana India 19°27N 84°16E 244 E7
Mohana → India 24°43N 85°0E 243 G11
Mohanganj Bangla. 24°54N 90°59E 241 C3
Mohanlalganj India 26°41N 80°58E 243 F9
Mohave, L. U.S.A. 35°12N 114°34W 307 K12
Mohawk → U.S.A. 42°47N 73°41W 313 D11
Moheda Sweden 57°1N 14°35E 163 G8
Mohéli Comoros Is. 12°20S 43°40E 272 a
Mohéli ✕ (NWA)
Comoros Is. 12°19S 43°47E 272 a
Mohenjodaro Pakistan 27°19N 68°7E 242 F3
Moher, Cliffs of Ireland 52°58N 9°27W 166 D2
Mohican, C. U.S.A. 60°12N 167°25W 303 F6
Mohicanville Res. U.S.A. 40°45N 82°9W 312 F2
Möhne → Germany 51°29N 7°57E 178 D3
Mohns Ridge Arctic 72°30N 5°0W 150 B7
Mohnyin Burma 24°47N 96°22E 241 C6
Mohoro Tanzania 8°6S 39°8E 268 D4
Mohrin = Moryń Poland 52°51N 14°22E 185 F1
Mohsenābād Iran 36°40N 59°35E 247 B8
Mohyliv-Podilskyy
Ukraine 48°26N 27°48E 183 B12
Moi Norway 58°27N 6°32E 164 F3
Moia South Sudan 5°3N 28°2E 257 F2
Moidart, L. U.K. 56°47N 5°52W 167 E3
Moinabad India 17°44N 77°16E 244 F3
Moinești Romania 46°28N 26°31E 183 D11
Moinho Velho, Cor. →
Brazil 23°35S 46°35W 137 B2
Moira → Canada 44°21N 77°24W 312 B7
Moirang India 24°30N 93°46E 241 C4
Moirans France 45°20N 5°33E 175 C9
Moirans-en-Montagne
France 46°26N 5°43E 173 F12
Moisaküla Estonia 58°3N 25°12E 188 C3
Moisie Canada 50°12N 66°1W 299 B6
Moisie → Canada 50°14N 66°5W 299 B6
Moissac France 44°7N 1°5E 174 D5
Moïssala Chad 8°21N 17°46E 259 G3
Moita Portugal 38°38N 8°58W 195 G2
Moixent Spain 38°52N 0°45W 197 G4
Möja Sweden 59°26N 18°55E 162 E12
Mojácar Spain 37°6N 1°55W 197 H3
Mojados Spain 41°26N 4°40W 196 D6
Mojave U.S.A. 35°3N 118°10W 307 K8
Mojave ⌂ U.S.A. 35°7N 115°32W 307 K11
Mojave Desert U.S.A. 35°0N 116°30W 307 L10
Moji das Cruzes Brazil 23°31S 46°11W 335 A6
Moji-Guaçu Brazil 22°22S 46°57W 333 F2
Moji-Guaçu → Brazil 20°53S 48°10W 335 A6
Mojiang China 23°37N 101°35E 228 F3
Mojjo → Ethiopia 7°55N 42°0E 257 F5
Mojkovac Montenegro 42°58N 19°35E 202 D3
Mojo Bolivia 21°48S 65°33W 334 A2
Mojo Ethiopia 8°35N 39°5E 257 F4
Mojokerto Indonesia 7°28S 112°26E 235 D4
Mojos, Llanos de Bolivia 15°10S 65°0W 331 D5
Moju Brazil 1°53S 48°46W 332 B2
Moju → Brazil 1°40S 48°25W 332 B2
Mok S. Korea 37°32N 126°52E 137 B1
Moka Mauritius 20°13S 57°29E 272 e
Mokai N.Z. 38°32S 175°56E 284 E4
Mokala ⌂ S. Africa 29°10S 24°10E 270 C3
Mokambo
Dem. Rep. of the Congo 12°25S 28°20E 269 E2
Mokameh India 25°24N 85°55E 243 G11
Mokau N.Z. 38°41N 91°53W 310 F5
Mökapu Peninsula
U.S.A. 21°25N 157°45W 302 K14
Mokau N.Z. 38°42S 174°39E 284 E3
Mokau → N.Z. 38°35S 174°35E 284 E3
Mokelumne → U.S.A. 38°13N 121°28W 306 G5
Mokelumne Hill U.S.A. 38°18N 120°43W 306 G6
Mokhotlong Lesotho 29°22S 29°2E 271 C4
Mokihinui → N.Z. 41°33S 171°58E 285 B6
Möklinta Sweden 60°4N 16°33E 162 D10
Moknine Tunisia 35°35N 10°58E 258 A2
Mokoan, L. Australia 36°27S 146°5E 283 D7
Mokokchung India 26°15N 94°30E 241 B5
Mökölea Rock U.S.A. 21°27N 157°44W 302 K14
Mokolo Cameroon 10°49N 13°54E 259 F2
Mokolo
Dem. Rep. of the Congo 1°55N 18°6E 264 B3
Mokolo → S. Africa 23°14S 27°43E 271 B4
Mokombe
Dem. Rep. of the Congo 0°14S 23°48E 264 C4
Mokopane S. Africa 24°10S 28°55E 271 B4
Mokotów Poland 52°12N 21°0E 143 B2
Mokpalin Burma 17°26N 96°53E 241 G6
Mokpo S. Korea 34°50N 126°25E 224 E3
Mokra Gora Europe 42°50N 20°30E 202 D4
Mokronog Slovenia 45°57N 15°9E 199 C12
Moksha → Russia 54°45N 41°53E 190 C6
Mokshan Russia 53°25N 44°35E 190 D7
Mokuauia I. U.S.A. 21°40N 157°56W 302 J14
Mokulē'ia U.S.A. 21°35N 158°9W 302 J13
Mokulua Is. U.S.A. 21°24N 157°42W 302 K14
Mokumanu U.S.A. 21°28N 157°43W 302 K14
Mokwa Nigeria 9°19N 5°0E 263 D6
Mol Belgium 51°11N 5°5E 170 C5
Mola di Bari Italy 41°4N 17°5E 201 A10
Molai Greece 36°49N 22°56E 204 E4
Molakalmuru India 14°55N 76°50E 245 G3
Molale Ethiopia 10°10N 39°41E 257 E4
Molaly Kazakhstan 45°27N 78°18E 217 C9
Molanda
Dem. Rep. of the Congo 2°28N 20°48E 264 B4
Molara Italy 40°52N 9°43E 200 B2
Molat Croatia 44°15N 14°50E 199 D11
Molave Phil. 8°5N 123°30E 233 G4
Molchanovo Russia 57°40N 83°50E 214 D9
Mold U.K. 53°9N 3°8W 168 D4
Moldava nad Bodvou
Slovakia 48°38N 21°0E 181 C14
Moldavia = Moldova ■
Europe 47°0N 28°0E 183 C13
Moldavia Romania 46°30N 27°0E 183 D12
Molde Norway 62°45N 7°9E 164 B4
Moldova ■ Europe 47°0N 28°0E 183 C13
Moldova Nouă Romania 44°45N 21°41E 182 F6
Moldoveanu, Vf. Romania 45°36N 24°45E 183 E9
Moldovița Romania 47°41N 25°32E 183 C10
Mole → U.K. 51°24N 0°21W 169 F7
Mole △ Ghana 9°43N 1°44W 263 D4
Molegbwe
Dem. Rep. of the Congo 4°12N 20°53E 264 B4
Molenbeek-St-Jean
Belgium 50°51N 4°19E 116 A1
Molepolole Botswana 24°28S 25°28E 270 B4
Molesworth N.Z. 42°5S 173°16E 285 C8
Molfetta Italy 41°12N 16°36E 201 A9
Moli'i Pond U.S.A. 21°31N 157°51W 302 J14
Molina de Aragón Spain 40°46N 1°52W 196 E3
Molina de Segura Spain 38°3N 1°12W 197 G3
Moline U.S.A. 41°30N 90°31W 310 C6
Molinella Italy 44°37N 11°40E 199 D8
Molino U.S.A. 30°43N 87°20W 317 E2
Molino de Rosas Mexico 19°21N 99°14W 128 B1
Molinos Argentina 25°28S 66°15W 334 B2
Moliro
Dem. Rep. of the Congo 8°12S 30°30E 268 D3
Moliterno Italy 40°14N 15°52E 201 B8
Molivos = Mithimna
Greece 39°20N 26°12E 205 B8
Molkom Sweden 59°37N 13°44E 162 E7
Mölle Sweden 56°17N 12°31E 163 H6
Molledo Spain 43°8N 4°6W 196 B6
Mollem Belgium 50°56N 4°13E 116 A1
Mollendo Peru 17°0S 72°0W 330 D3
Mollerin, L. Australia 30°30S 117°35E 279 F2
Mollerussa Spain 41°37N 0°54E 196 D5
Mollina Spain 37°8N 4°38W 195 H6
Mollins de Rey Spain 41°24N 2°1E 114 A1
Mölln Germany 53°39N 10°32E 178 B6
Mölltorp Sweden 58°30N 14°26E 163 F8
Mölndal Sweden 57°40N 12°3E 163 G5
Mölnlycke Sweden 57°40N 12°8E 163 G6
Molo Burma 23°22N 96°53E 241 D6
Molo Rift Valley, Kenya 0°15S 35°44E 268 C4
Molochansk Ukraine 47°15N 35°35E 189 J8
Molochnoye, Ozero
Ukraine 46°30N 35°20E 189 J8
Molodechno = Maladzyechna
Belarus 54°20N 26°50E 177 A14
Molodezhnaya Antarctica 67°40S 45°51E 151 C9
Molodove Ukraine 46°13N 29°39E 183 D14
Moloka'i U.S.A. 21°8N 157°0W 302 B4
Molokai Fracture Zone
Pac. Oc. 28°0N 125°0W 289 E15
Molokini I. U.S.A. 20°38N 156°30W 302 C5
Molong Australia 33°5S 148°54E 283 B8
Molopo → Africa 28°30S 20°12E 270 C3
Molos Greece 38°47N 22°37E 204 C4
Molotov = Perm Russia 58°0N 56°10E 186 C10
Molotov, Mys = Arkticheskiy, Mys
Russia 81°10N 95°0E 215 A10
Molotovsk = Nolinsk
Russia 57°28N 49°57E 190 B9
Molotovsk = Severodvinsk
Russia 64°27N 39°58E 186 B6
Molotovskoye =
Krasnogvardeyskoye
Russia 45°52N 41°33E 191 H5
Moloundou Cameroon 2°8N 15°15E 264 B3
Molowaie
Dem. Rep. of the Congo 5°47S 23°18E 265 D4
Molsheim France 48°33N 7°29E 173 D14
Molson L. Canada 54°22N 96°40W 297 C9
Molteno S. Africa 31°22S 26°22E 270 D4
Molu Indonesia 6°45S 131°40E 231 F8
Molucca Sea Indonesia 0°0 125°0E 231 E6
Moluccas = Maluku
Indonesia 1°0S 127°0E 231 E7
Molundo Phil. 7°57N 124°23E 233 H5
Moma Dem. Rep. of the Congo 1°35S 23°52E 264 C4
Moma Mozam. 16°47S 39°4E 269 F4
Momba Australia 30°58S 143°30E 282 A5
Mombaça Brazil 5°43S 39°45W 332 C4
Mombango
Dem. Rep. of the Congo 1°45N 24°26E 264 B4
Mombasa Kenya 4°3S 39°40E 268 C4
Mombetsu Japan 44°21N 143°22E 220 B11
Mombil Burma 27°46N 98°6E 241 B7
Momboyo →
Dem. Rep. of the Congo 0°16S 19°0E 264 C3
Mombuey Spain 42°3N 6°20W 194 C4
Momchilgrad Bulgaria 41°33N 25°23E 203 E9
Momence U.S.A. 41°10N 87°40W 311 C9
Momi Dem. Rep. of the Congo 1°42S 27°0E 268 C2
Momote Papua N. G. 2°4S 147°27E 286 B4
Mompog Pass. Phil. 13°34N 122°13E 232 E4
Mompós Colombia 9°14N 74°26W 328 B3
Møn Denmark 54°57N 12°20E 163 K6
Mon India 26°45N 95°6E 241 B5
Møn Hordaland, Norway 60°37N 6°31E 164 D3
Mon □ Burma 16°0N 97°30E 241 G6
Mona, Canal de la = Mona Passage
W. Indies 18°30N 67°45W 321 C6
Mona, Isla Puerto Rico 18°5N 67°54W 321 C6
Mona, Pta. Costa Rica 9°37N 82°36W 320 E3
Mona Passage W. Indies 18°30N 67°45W 321 C6
Mona Quimbundo Angola 9°55S 19°58E 265 D3
Monaca U.S.A. 40°41N 80°17W 312 F4
Monaco ■ Europe 43°46N 7°23E 175 E11
Monadhliath Mts. U.K. 57°10N 4°4W 167 D4
Monadnock, Mt. U.S.A. 42°52N 72°7W 313 D12
Monagas □ Venezuela 9°20N 63°0W 329 B5
Monaghan Ireland 54°15N 6°57W 166 B5
Monaghan □ Ireland 54°11N 6°56W 166 B5
Monahans U.S.A. 31°36N 102°54W 314 F3
Monapo Mozam. 14°56S 40°19E 269 E5
Monar, L. U.K. 57°26N 5°8W 167 D3
Monaragala Sri Lanka 6°52N 81°22E 245 L5
Monarch Mt. Canada 51°55N 125°57W 296 C3
Monashee Mts. Canada 51°0N 118°43W 296 C5
Monasterevin Ireland 53°8N 7°4W 166 C4
Monastir = Bitola
Macedonia 41°1N 21°20E 202 E5
Monastir Tunisia 35°50N 10°49E 258 A2
Monastir □ Tunisia 35°37N 10°45E 261 A7
Monbetsu = Hidaka
Japan 42°30N 142°10E 220 C11
Moncalieri Italy 45°0N 7°41E 198 D4
Moncalvo Italy 45°3N 8°16E 198 C5
Monção Portugal 42°4N 8°27W 194 C2
Moncarapacho Portugal 37°5N 7°46W 195 H3
Moncayo, Sierra del Spain 41°48N 1°50W 196 D3
Moncha-Guba = Monchegorsk
Russia 67°54N 32°58E 160 C25
Monchegorsk Russia 67°54N 32°58E 160 C25
Mönchengladbach
Germany 51°11N 6°27E 178 D2
Monchique Portugal 37°19N 8°38W 195 H2
Moncks Corner U.S.A. 33°12N 80°1W 316 B9
Monclova Mexico 26°54N 101°25W 318 B4
Moncontour France 48°22N 2°38W 172 D4
Moncton Canada 46°7N 64°51W 299 C7
Mondariz Spain 42°14N 8°27W 194 C2
Mondego → Portugal 40°9N 8°52W 194 E2
Mondego, C. Portugal 40°11N 8°54W 194 E2
Mondeodo Indonesia 3°34S 122°9E 231 E6
Mondeor S. Africa 26°16S 28°0E 123 B1
Mondeville France 49°10N 0°18W 172 C6
Mondimbi
Dem. Rep. of the Congo 1°48N 22°46E 264 B4
Mondjuku
Dem. Rep. of the Congo 1°41S 21°12E 264 C4
Mondlo S. Africa 27°59S 30°43E 271 C5
Mondo Chad 13°47N 15°32E 259 F3
Mondolfo Italy 43°45N 13°6E 199 E10
Mondoñedo Spain 43°25N 7°23W 194 B3
Mondovì Italy 44°23N 7°49E 198 D4
Mondragó Spain 39°21N 3°12E 206 B4
Mondragon = Arrasate
Spain 43°4N 2°30W 196 B2
Mondragon Phil. 12°31N 124°45E 232 E5
Mondragone Italy 41°7N 13°53E 200 A6
Mondrain I. Australia 34°9S 122°14E 279 F3
Moneague Jamaica 18°16N 77°7W 320 a
Moneda, Palacio de la
Chile 33°26S 70°39W 137 B2
Monemvasia Greece 36°41N 23°3E 204 E5
Monerò Brazil 22°48S 43°11W 135 A1
Moneron, Ostrov
Russia 46°15N 141°16E 220 A10
Monessen U.S.A. 40°9N 79°54W 312 F5
Monesterio Spain 38°6N 6°15W 195 G4
Monestier-de-Clermont
France 44°55N 5°38E 175 D9
Monett U.S.A. 36°55N 93°55W 308 G7
Moneymore U.K. 54°41N 6°40W 166 B5
Monfalcone Italy 45°49N 13°32E 199 C10
Monflanquin France 44°32N 0°47E 174 D4
Monforte Portugal 39°6N 7°25W 195 F3
Monforte de Lemos Spain 42°31N 7°33W 194 C3
Monfragüe ⌂ Spain 39°48N 5°52W 194 F5
Mong Hpayak Burma 20°52N 99°55E 236 B2
Mong Hsat Shan, Burma 21°54N 98°30E 228 G2
Mong Hsat Shan, Burma 20°31N 99°15E 236 B2
Mong Hta Burma 19°50N 98°35E 241 F7
Mong Ket Burma 23°8N 98°22E 241 D7
Mong Kok
Hong Kong, China 22°19N 114°10E 122 B3
Mong Kung Burma 21°35N 97°35E 241 E6
Mong Kyawt Burma 19°56N 98°45E 241 F7
Mong Long Burma 22°47N 96°37E 241 D6
Mong Mit Burma 23°7N 96°41E 241 D6
Mong Nai Burma 20°32N 97°46E 241 E6
Mong Pan Burma 20°19N 98°22E 241 E7
Mong Ping Burma 21°22N 99°2E 228 G2
Mong Pu Burma 20°55N 98°44E 241 E7
Mong Tai = Shan □
Burma 21°30N 98°30E 241 E7
Mong Ton Burma 20°17N 98°45E 241 E7
Mong Tung Burma 22°2N 97°41E 241 D6
Mong Yai Burma 22°21N 98°3E 241 D7
Mong Yang Burma 21°50N 99°41E 236 B2
Mong Yu Burma 23°30N 97°47E 241 D6
Monga
Dem. Rep. of the Congo 4°12N 22°49E 264 B4
Mongala →
Dem. Rep. of the Congo 1°53N 19°46E 264 B3
Mongalla South Sudan 5°8N 31°42E 257 F3
Mongandia Congo 0°45N 17°11E 264 B3
Mongers, L. Australia 29°25S 117°5E 279 E2
Mongga Solomon Is. 7°52S 157°0E 287 L9
Monghyr = Munger
India 25°23N 86°30E 243 G12
Mongibello = Etna Italy 37°50N 14°55E 201 E7
Mongla Bangla. 22°8N 89°35E 241 D2
Mongmong Guam 13°28N 144°45E 302 d
Mongnawng Burma 22°47N 96°59E 241 D6
Mongo Chad 12°14N 18°43E 259 F3
Mongo Eq. Guin. 1°52N 10°10E 264 B2
Mongó → S. Leone 9°35N 12°10W 262 D2
Mongolia ■ Asia 47°0N 103°0E 218 B9
Mongolia, Plateau of Asia 45°0N 105°0E 210 D12
Mongomo Eq. Guin. 1°38N 11°19E 264 B2
Mongonu Nigeria 12°40N 13°32E 263 C7
Mongororo Chad 12°3N 22°26E 259 F4
Mongstad Norway 60°49N 5°2E 164 D2
Mongu Zambia 15°16S 23°12E 265 F4
Môngua Angola 16°43S 15°20E 265 F3
Moniac U.S.A. 30°31N 82°14W 316 E7
Monifieth U.K. 56°30N 2°48W 167 E6
Monistrol-sur-Loire France 45°17N 4°11E 175 C8
Monkayo Phil. 7°50N 126°5E 233 H6
Monkey Bay Malawi 14°7S 35°1E 269 E4
Monkey Mia Australia 25°48S 113°43E 279 E1
Monkey River Belize 16°22N 88°29W 320 C2
Monkey Town Trin. & Tob. 10°12N 61°25W 323 t
Mońki Poland 53°23N 22°48E 184 E9
Monkland Canada 45°11N 74°52W 313 A10
Monkoto
Dem. Rep. of the Congo 1°38S 20°35E 264 C4
Monkton Canada 43°35N 81°5W 312 C3
Monmouth Monmouths.,
U.K. 51°48N 2°42W 169 F5
Monmouth Ill., U.S.A. 40°55N 90°39W 310 D6
Monmouth Oreg., U.S.A. 44°51N 123°14W 304 D2
Monmouthshire □ U.K. 51°48N 2°54W 169 F5
Monnickendam Neths. 52°28N 5°2E 112 A3
Mono Solomon Is. 7°20S 155°35E 287 L8
Mono → Togo 6°17N 1°51E 263 D5
Mono, Pta. Nic. 12°0N 83°30W 320 D3
Mono L. U.S.A. 38°1N 119°1W 306 H7
Monolith U.S.A. 35°7N 118°22W 307 K8
Monolithos Greece 36°7N 27°45E 206 E11
Monon U.S.A. 40°52N 86°53W 311 D10
Monona Iowa, U.S.A. 43°3N 91°23W 310 A5
Monona Wis., U.S.A. 43°4N 89°20W 310 A7
Monongahela U.S.A. 40°12N 79°56W 312 F5
Monópoli Italy 40°57N 17°18E 201 B10
Monor Hungary 47°21N 19°27E 182 C4
Monos I. Trin. & Tob. 10°42N 61°44W 323 t
Monóvar Spain 38°28N 0°53W 197 G4
Monowai N.Z. 45°53S 167°31E 285 F2
Monowai, L. N.Z. 45°53S 167°25E 285 F2
Monqoumba C.A.R. 3°33N 18°40E 264 B3
Monreal del Campo Spain 40°47N 1°20W 196 E3
Monreale Italy 38°5N 13°17E 200 D6
Monroe Ga., U.S.A. 33°47N 83°43W 316 B6
Monroe Iowa, U.S.A. 41°31N 93°6W 310 C3
Monroe La., U.S.A. 32°30N 92°7W 314 E8
Monroe Mich., U.S.A. 41°55N 83°24W 311 C13
Monroe N.C., U.S.A. 34°59N 80°33W 315 D14
Monroe N.Y., U.S.A. 41°20N 74°11W 313 E10
Monroe Ohio, U.S.A. 39°27N 84°22W 311 E11
Monroe Utah, U.S.A. 38°38N 112°7W 304 G7
Monroe Wash., U.S.A. 47°51N 121°58W 306 C5
Monroe Wis., U.S.A. 42°36N 89°38W 310 B7
Monroe, L. U.S.A. 28°50N 81°19W 317 G8
Monroe City Ind., U.S.A. 38°37N 87°20W 311 F9
Monroe City Mo., U.S.A. 39°39N 91°44W 310 E5
Monroe L. U.S.A. 39°1N 86°31W 311 E10
Monroeton U.S.A. 41°43N 76°29W 313 E8
Monroeville Ala., U.S.A. 31°31N 87°20W 315 F11
Monroeville Ind., U.S.A. 40°59N 84°52W 311 D11
Monroeville Pa., U.S.A. 40°26N 79°45W 312 F5
Monrovia Liberia 6°18N 10°47W 262 D2
Monrovia Calif., U.S.A. 34°9N 118°1W 126 B4
Mons Belgium 50°27N 3°58E 170 D3
Møns Klint Denmark 54°57N 12°33E 163 K6
Monsanto Portugal 38°44N 9°12W 126 A1
Monsanto, Parque Florestal de
Portugal 38°43N 9°11W 126 A1
Monsaraz Portugal 38°28N 7°22W 195 G3
Monse Indonesia 4°7S 123°15E 231 E6
Monsefú Peru 6°52S 79°52W 330 B2
Monségur France 44°38N 0°4E 174 D4
Monsélice Italy 45°14N 11°45E 199 C8
Mönsterås Sweden 57°3N 16°26E 163 G10
Mont Cenis, Col du France 45°15N 6°55E 175 C10
Mont-de-Marsan France 43°54N 0°31W 174 E3
Mont-Dore N. Cal. 22°16S 166°34E 288 d
Mont Fouari ⌂ Congo 2°52S 11°32E 264 C2
Mont-Joli Canada 48°37N 68°10W 299 C6
Mont-Laurier Canada 46°35N 75°30W 298 C4
Mont-Louis Canada 49°15N 65°44W 299 C6
Mont Peko △ Ivory C. 9°5N 7°15W 262 D3
Mont-roig del Camp Spain 41°5N 0°58E 196 D5
Mont-Royal Canada 45°30N 73°38W 130 A2
Mont-Royal, Parc Canada 45°30N 73°36W 130 A2
Mont-St-Michel, Le France 48°40N 1°30W 172 D5
Mont Sangbé △ Ivory C. 8°0N 7°10W 262 D3
Mont-Tremblant ⌂
Canada 46°30N 74°30W 298 C5
Montabaur Germany 50°25N 7°50E 178 E3
Montagnac = Remchi
Algeria 35°2N 1°26W 261 A4
Montagnac France 43°29N 3°28E 174 E7
Montagnana Italy 45°14N 11°28E 199 C8
Montagne Blanche
Mauritius 20°16S 57°39E 272 e
Montagne d'Ambre △
Madag. 12°37S 49°8E 272 A2
Montagne de Reims ⌂
France 49°8N 4°0E 173 C11
Montagnes □ Ivory C. 6°54N 7°50W 262 D3
Montagu S. Africa 33°45S 20°8E 270 D3
Montagu I. Antarctica 58°25S 26°20W 151 B1
Montague Canada 46°10N 62°39W 299 C7
Montague, I. Mexico 31°45N 114°48W 318 A2
Montague I. N.S.W.,
Australia 36°16S 150°13E 283 D9
Montague I. Alaska,
U.S.A. 60°0N 147°30W 303 G11
Montague Ra. Australia 27°15S 119°30E 279 E2
Montague Sd. Australia 14°28S 125°20E 278 B4
Montaigu France 46°59N 1°18W 172 F5
Montalbán Spain 40°50N 0°45W 196 E4
Montalbano Iónico Italy 40°17N 16°34E 201 B9
Montalbo Spain 39°53N 2°42W 196 F2
Montalcino Italy 43°3N 11°29E 199 E8
Montalegre Angola 8°45S 17°4E 265 D3
Montalegre Portugal 41°49N 7°47W 194 D3
Montalto Italy 38°10N 15°55E 201 D8
Montalto di Castro Italy 42°21N 11°37E 199 F8
Montalto Uffugo Italy 39°24N 16°9E 201 C9
Montalvo U.S.A. 34°15N 119°12W 307 L7
Montamarta Spain 41°39N 5°49W 194 D5
Montana Bulgaria 43°27N 23°16E 202 C7
Montaña Peru 6°0S 73°0W 330 B3
Montana □ Bulgaria 43°30N 23°10E 202 C7
Montana □ U.S.A. 47°0N 110°0W 304 C9
Montaña Clara, I.
Canary Is. 29°17N 13°33W 153 e2
Montañas de Malaga ⌂
Spain 36°48N 4°32W 195 J6
Montánchez Spain 39°15N 6°8W 195 F4
Montanhas do Tumucumaque △
Brazil 2°5N 53°0W 329 C7
Montañita Colombia 1°22N 75°28W 328 C2
Montargil Portugal 39°5N 8°10W 195 F2
Montargis France 47°59N 2°43E 173 E9
Montauban France 44°2N 1°21E 174 D5
Montauk U.S.A. 41°3N 71°57W 313 E13
Montauk Pt. U.S.A. 41°4N 71°51W 313 E13
Montbard France 47°38N 4°20E 173 E11
Montbarrey France 47°1N 5°39E 173 E12
Montbéliard France 47°31N 6°48E 173 E13
Montblanc Spain 41°23N 1°4E 196 D6
Montbrison France 45°36N 4°3E 175 C8
Montcada i Reixac Spain 41°29N 2°12W 114 A2
Montcalm, Pic de France 42°40N 1°25E 174 F5
Montceau-les-Mines
France 46°40N 4°23E 173 F11
Montcenis France 46°47N 4°23E 175 B8
Montchanin France 46°45N 4°28E 175 B8
Montclair U.S.A. 40°49N 74°12W 313 F10
Montcornet France 49°40N 4°1E 173 C11
Montcuq France 44°21N 1°13E 174 D5
Montdidier France 49°38N 2°35E 173 C9
Monte Albán Mexico 17°2N 96°46W 319 D5
Monte Alegre Brazil 2°0S 54°0W 329 D7
Monte Alegre de Goiás
Brazil 13°14S 47°10W 333 D2
Monte Alegre de Minas
Brazil 18°52S 48°52W 333 E2
Monte Alegre do Piauí
Brazil 9°46S 45°18W 332 C2
Monte Azul Brazil 15°9S 42°53W 333 E3
Monte-Carlo Monaco 43°44N 7°25E 175 E11
Monte Carmelo Brazil 18°43S 47°29W 333 E2
Monte Caseros Argentina 30°10S 57°50W 334 C4
Monte Chingolo
Argentina 34°43S 58°22W 117 C2
Monte Comán Argentina 34°40S 67°53W 334 C2
Monte Cristi Dom. Rep. 19°52N 71°39W 321 C5
Monte Cucco ⌂ Italy 43°22N 12°43E 199 E9
Monte Dinero Argentina 52°18S 68°33W 336 D3
Monte Dourado Brazil 0°52S 52°31W 329 D7
Monte Léon Argentina 50°15S 69°0W 336 D3
Monte Lindo → Paraguay 23°56S 57°12W 334 A4
Monte Palatino Rome, Italy 136 c3
Monte Pascoal △ Brazil 16°51S 39°21W 333 E4
Monte Patria Chile 30°42S 70°58W 334 C1
Monte Quemado
Argentina 25°53S 62°41W 334 B3
Monte Redondo Portugal 39°53N 8°50W 194 F2
Monte Rio U.S.A. 38°28N 123°0W 306 G4
Monte San Giovanni Campano
Italy 41°38N 13°31E 200 A6
Monte San Giuliano = Érice
Italy 38°2N 12°35E 200 D5
Monte San Savino Italy 43°20N 11°43E 199 E8
Monte Sant' Angelo
Italy 41°42N 15°59E 199 G12
Monte Santu, C. di Italy 40°5N 9°44E 200 B2
Monte Subasio ⌂ Italy 43°5N 12°40E 199 E9
Monte Vista U.S.A. 37°35N 106°9W 305 H10
Monteagudo Argentina 27°14S 54°8W 335 B5
Monteagudo Bolivia 19°49S 63°59W 331 D5
Montealegre del Castillo
Spain 38°48N 1°17W 197 G3
Montebello Qué., Canada 45°40N 74°55W 298 C5
Montebello Guadeloupe 16°10N 61°36W 322 e
Montebello Calif., U.S.A. 34°1N 118°8W 126 B4
Montebello Iónico Italy 37°59N 15°45E 201 E8
Montebello Is. Australia 20°30S 115°45E 278 D2
Montebelluna Italy 45°47N 12°3E 199 C9
Montebourg France 49°30N 1°20W 172 C5
Montecarlo Argentina 26°34S 54°47W 335 B5
Montecastrilli Italy 42°39N 12°29E 199 F9
Montecatini Terme Italy 43°53N 10°46E 198 E7
Montecito U.S.A. 34°26N 119°40W 307 L7
Montecristi Ecuador 1°0S 80°40W 328 D1
Montecristo Italy 42°20N 10°19E 198 F7
Montefalco Italy 42°54N 12°39E 199 F9
Montefiascone Italy 42°32N 12°2E 199 F9
Montefrío Spain 37°20N 4°0W 195 H7
Montegiórgio Italy 43°6N 13°33E 199 E10
Montego B. Jamaica 18°28N 77°56W 320 a

Montego Bay *Jamaica* 18°28N 77°55W 320 a
Montehermoso *Spain* 40°5N 6°21W 194 E4
Monteiro *Brazil* 7°48S 37°2W 332 C4
Montejícar *Spain* 37°33N 3°30W 195 H7
Montelbaanstoren *Amsterdam, Neths.* 112 b3
Monteleone di Calabria = Vibo Valéntia *Italy* 38°40N 16°6E 201 D9
Montelíbano *Colombia* 8°5N 75°29W 328 B2
Montélimar *France* 44°33N 4°45E 175 D8
Montella *Italy* 40°51N 15°1E 201 B8
Montellano *Spain* 36°59N 5°29W 195 J5
Montello *U.S.A.* 43°48N 89°20W 308 D9
Montemayor, Meseta de *Argentina* 44°20S 66°10W 336 B3
Montemor *Portugal* 38°49N 9°12W 126 A1
Montemor-o-Novo *Portugal* 38°40N 8°12W 195 G2
Montemor-o-Velho *Portugal* 40°11N 8°40W 194 E2
Montemorelos *Mexico* 25°12N 99°49W 319 B5
Montendre *France* 45°16N 0°26W 174 C3
Montenegro *Brazil* 29°39S 51°29W 335 B5
Montenegro ■ *Europe* 42°40N 19°20E 202 D3
Montenero di Bisáccia *Italy* 41°57N 14°47E 199 G11
Montepuez *Mozam.* 13°8S 38°59E 269 E4
Montepuez → *Mozam.* 12°32S 40°27E 269 E5
Montepulciano *Italy* 43°5N 11°47E 199 E8
Montereale *Italy* 42°31N 13°15E 199 F10
Montereau-Faut-Yonne *France* 48°22N 2°57E 173 D9
Monterey *Calif., U.S.A.* 36°37N 121°55W 306 J5
Monterey *Ind., U.S.A.* 41°11N 86°30W 311 C10
Monterey B. *U.S.A.* 36°45N 122°0W 306 J5
Monterey Hills *U.S.A.* 34°6N 118°10W 126 B3
Monterey Park *U.S.A.* 34°3N 118°7W 126 B4
Montería *Colombia* 8°46N 75°53W 328 B2
Montero *Bolivia* 17°20S 63°15W 331 D5
Monteros *Argentina* 27°11S 65°30W 334 B2
Monterotondo *Italy* 42°3N 12°37E 199 F9
Monterrey *Mexico* 25°40N 100°19W 318 B4
Montes Altos *Brazil* 5°50S 47°4W 332 C2
Montes Azules ⌓ *Mexico* 16°21N 91°3W 319 D6
Montes Claros *Brazil* 16°30S 43°50W 333 E3
Montesano *U.S.A.* 46°59N 123°36W 306 D3
Montesano sulla Marcellana *Italy* 40°16N 15°42E 201 B8
Montesárchio *Italy* 41°4N 14°38E 201 A7
Montescaglioso *Italy* 40°33N 16°40E 201 B9
Montesilvano *Italy* 42°29N 14°8E 199 F11
Montesinho ⌓ *Portugal* 41°54N 6°52W 194 D4
Montespaccato *Italy* 41°54N 12°23E 136 B1
Montesson *France* 48°54N 2°8E 134 A1
Montevarchi *Italy* 43°31N 11°34E 199 E8
Monteverde Nuovo *Italy* 41°52N 12°26E 136 B1
Montevideo *Uruguay* 34°50S 56°11W 335 C4
Montevideo *Minn., U.S.A.* 44°57N 95°43W 308 C6
Montezuma *Ga., U.S.A.* 32°18N 84°2W 316 C5
Montezuma *Ind., U.S.A.* 39°48N 87°22W 311 E9
Montezuma *Iowa, U.S.A.* 41°35N 92°32W 310 C4
Montezuma Castle ⌓ *U.S.A.* 34°39N 111°45W 305 J8
Montfaucon *France* 47°6N 1°7W 172 E5
Montfaucon-d'Argonne *France* 49°16N 5°8E 173 C12
Montfaucon-en-Velay *France* 45°11N 4°20E 175 C8
Montfermeil *France* 48°54N 2°33E 134 A4
Montfort-le-Gesnois *France* 48°3N 0°25E 172 D7
Montfort-sur-Meu *France* 48°9N 1°58W 172 D5
Montgenèvre *France* 44°56N 6°43E 175 D10
Montgó ⌓ *Spain* 38°48N 0°7W 197 G5
Montgomery = Sahiwal *Pakistan* 30°45N 73°8E 242 D5
Montgomery *Powys, U.K.* 52°34N 3°8W 169 E4
Montgomery *Ala., U.S.A.* 32°23N 86°19W 316 C3
Montgomery *Ill., U.S.A.* 41°44N 88°21W 311 C8
Montgomery *Pa., U.S.A.* 41°10N 76°53W 312 E8
Montgomery *W. Va., U.S.A.* 38°11N 81°19W 309 F13
Montgomery City *U.S.A.* 38°59N 91°30W 310 F5
Montguyon *France* 45°12N 0°12W 174 C3
Monthermé *France* 49°52N 4°42E 173 C11
Monthey *Switz.* 46°15N 6°56E 179 J2
Monthois *France* 49°19N 4°43E 173 C11
Monti *Italy* 40°49N 9°19E 200 B2
Monti Lucrétili ⌓ *Italy* 42°5N 12°50E 199 F9
Monti Picentini ⌓ *Italy* 40°45N 15°2E 201 B8
Monti Sibillini △ *Italy* 42°55N 13°15E 199 F10
Monti Simbruini ⌓ *Italy* 41°55N 13°13E 199 G10
Monticelli d'Ongina *Italy* 45°5N 9°56E 198 C6
Monticello *Ark., U.S.A.* 33°38N 91°47W 314 E9
Monticello *Fla., U.S.A.* 30°33N 83°52W 316 E6
Monticello *Ga., U.S.A.* 33°18N 83°40W 316 B6
Monticello *Ill., U.S.A.* 40°1N 88°34W 311 D8
Monticello *Ind., U.S.A.* 40°45N 86°46W 311 D10
Monticello *Iowa, U.S.A.* 42°15N 91°12W 310 B5
Monticello *Ky., U.S.A.* 36°50N 84°51W 309 G11
Monticello *Minn., U.S.A.* 45°18N 93°48W 308 C7
Monticello *Miss., U.S.A.* 31°33N 90°7W 315 F9
Monticello *Mo., U.S.A.* 40°7N 91°43W 310 D5
Monticello *N.Y., U.S.A.* 41°39N 74°42W 313 E10
Monticello *Utah, U.S.A.* 37°52N 109°21W 305 H9
Montichiari *Italy* 45°25N 10°23E 198 C7
Montier-en-Der *France* 48°30N 4°45E 173 D11
Montignac *France* 45°4N 1°10E 174 C5
Montigny-le-Bretonneux *France* 48°46N 2°1E 134 B1
Montigny-les-Metz *France* 49°7N 6°10E 173 C13
Montigny-sur-Aube *France* 47°57N 4°45E 173 E11
Montijo *Portugal* 38°41N 8°54W 195 G2
Montijo *Spain* 38°52N 6°39W 195 G4
Montilla *Spain* 37°36N 4°40W 195 H6
Montivilliers *France* 49°33N 0°12E 172 C7
Montjay-la-Tour *France* 48°54N 2°40E 134 A4
Montjuïc *Spain* 41°22N 2°10E 114 A2
Montjuïc, Parc de *Barcelona, Spain* 114 c1
Montluçon *France* 46°22N 2°36E 173 F9
Montmagny *Canada* 46°58N 70°34W 299 C5
Montmarault *France* 46°19N 2°57E 173 F9
Montmartre *Canada* 50°14N 103°27W 297 C8
Montmédy *France* 49°30N 5°20E 173 C12
Montmélian *France* 45°30N 6°4E 175 C10
Montmirail *France* 48°51N 3°30E 173 D10
Montmoreau-St-Cybard *France* 45°23N 0°8E 174 C4
Montmorillon *France* 46°26N 0°50E 174 B4
Montmort-Lucy *France* 48°55N 3°49E 173 D10
Monto *Australia* 24°52S 151°6E 280 C5
Montoire-sur-le-Loir *France* 47°45N 0°52E 172 E7
Montongbuwoh *Indonesia* 8°33S 116°4E 231 K19
Montório al Vomano *Italy* 42°35N 13°38E 199 F10
Montoro *Spain* 38°1N 4°27W 195 G6
Montour Falls *U.S.A.* 42°21N 76°51W 312 D8
Montoursville *U.S.A.* 41°15N 76°55W 312 E8
Montparnasse, Gare *Paris, France* 48°50N 2°19E 134 A2
Montpelier *Idaho, U.S.A.* 42°19N 111°18W 304 E8
Montpelier *Ind., U.S.A.* 40°33N 85°17W 311 D11
Montpelier *Ohio, U.S.A.* 41°35N 84°37W 311 C12
Montpelier *Vt., U.S.A.* 44°16N 72°35W 313 B12
Montpellier *France* 43°37N 3°52E 174 E7
Montpezat-de-Quercy *France* 44°15N 1°30E 174 D5
Montpon-Ménestérol *France* 45°0N 0°11E 174 D4
Montréal *Qué., Canada* 45°30N 73°33W 130 A2
Montréal *Aude, France* 43°13N 2°8E 174 E6
Montréal *Gers, France* 43°56N 0°11E 174 E4
Montreal → *Canada* 47°14N 84°39W 298 C3
Montréal, Î. de *Canada* 45°30N 73°40W 130 A2
Montréal, Univ. de *Canada* 45°29N 73°37W 130 B2
Montréal Est *Canada* 45°37N 73°31W 130 A2
Montréal L. *Canada* 54°20N 105°45W 297 C7
Montreal Lake *Canada* 54°3N 105°46W 297 C7
Montréal Nord *Canada* 45°36N 73°36W 130 A2
Montréal Ouest *Canada* 45°27N 73°39W 130 B1
Montréal Trudeau Int. ✕ (YUL) *Canada* 45°28N 73°44W 130 B1
Montredon-Labessonnié *France* 43°45N 2°18E 174 E6
Montrésor *France* 47°10N 1°10E 172 E8
Montret *France* 46°40N 5°7E 173 F12
Montreuil *Pas-de-Calais, France* 50°27N 1°45E 173 B8
Montreuil *Seine-St-Denis, France* 48°51N 2°27E 134 A3
Montreuil-Bellay *France* 47°8N 0°9W 172 E6
Montreux *Switz.* 46°26N 6°55E 179 J2
Montrevel-en-Bresse *France* 46°21N 5°8E 173 F12
Montrichard *France* 47°20N 1°10E 172 E8
Montrose *Angus, U.K.* 56°44N 2°27W 167 E6
Montrose *Colo., U.S.A.* 38°29N 107°53W 304 G10
Montrose *Pa., U.S.A.* 41°50N 75°53W 313 E9
Montrose, L. *U.S.A.* 38°18N 93°50W 310 F3
Montrouge *France* 48°48N 2°18E 134 B2
Monts, Pte. des *Canada* 49°20N 67°12W 299 C6
Montsalvy *France* 44°41N 2°30E 174 D6
Montsant, Serra de *Spain* 41°17N 1°0E 196 D6
Montsauche-les-Settons *France* 47°13N 4°2E 173 E11
Montsec, Serra del *Spain* 42°5N 0°45E 196 C5
Montseny ⌓ *Spain* 41°43N 2°22W 196 D2
Montserrat *B. Aires, Argentina* 34°37S 58°24W 117 B2
Montserrat *Spain* 41°36N 1°49E 196 D6
Montserrat ▨ *W. Indies* 16°40N 62°10W 323 p
Montserrat Hills *Trin. & Tob.* 10°23N 61°21W 323 t
Montuenga *Spain* 41°3N 4°38W 194 D6
Montuiri *Spain* 39°34N 2°59E 206 B3
Montvert-les-Bas *Réunion* 21°19S 55°32E 272 f
Monveda *Dem. Rep. of the Congo* 2°52N 21°30E 264 B4
Monyo *Burma* 17°59N 95°30E 241 G5
Monywa *Burma* 22°7N 95°11E 241 D5
Monza *Italy* 45°35N 9°16E 128 A2
Monza e Brianza □ *Italy* 45°30N 9°15E 198 C6
Monze *Zambia* 16°17S 27°29E 269 F2
Monze, C. *Pakistan* 24°47N 66°37E 242 G2
Monzón *Spain* 41°52N 0°10E 196 D5
Monzoro *Italy* 45°27N 9°2E 128 B1
Moóca *Brazil* 23°33S 46°35W 137 B2
Moodyville = North Vancouver *Canada* 49°19N 123°4W 306 A3
Mooers *U.S.A.* 44°58N 73°35W 313 B11
Mooi → *S. Africa* 28°45S 30°34E 271 C5
Mooi River *S. Africa* 29°13S 29°50E 271 C4
Mo'oka *Japan* 36°26N 140°1E 223 A12
Mookgopong *S. Africa* 24°31S 28°44E 271 B4
Moomba *Australia* 28°6S 140°12E 281 A3
Moonachie *U.S.A.* 40°50N 74°2W 132 B1
Moonah → *Australia* 22°3S 138°33E 280 C2
Moonda, L. *Australia* 25°52S 140°25E 280 D3
Moonee Ponds *Australia* 37°45S 144°53E 128 A1
Moonee Valley Racecourse *Australia* 37°45S 144°55E 128 A1
Moonie *Australia* 27°46S 150°20E 281 D5
Moonie → *Australia* 29°19S 148°43E 281 D4
Moonta *Australia* 34°6S 137°32E 282 C2
Moora *Australia* 30°37S 115°58E 279 F2
Moorcroft *U.S.A.* 44°16N 104°57W 304 D11
Moore → *Australia* 31°22S 115°30E 279 F2
Moore, L. *Australia* 29°50S 117°35E 279 E2
Moore Falls *Canada* 44°48N 78°48W 312 B6
Moore Haven *U.S.A.* 26°50N 81°6W 317 J8
Moore Park *Australia* 24°43S 152°17E 280 C5
Moore Res. *U.S.A.* 44°20N 71°53W 313 B13
Moore River △ *Australia* 31°7S 115°39E 279 F2
Moorea *French Polynesia* 17°30S 149°50W 289 e
Moorefield *U.S.A.* 39°4N 78°58W 309 F14
Mooresville *U.S.A.* 39°37N 86°22W 311 E10
Moorfoot Hills *U.K.* 55°44N 3°8W 167 F5
Moorhead *U.S.A.* 46°53N 96°45W 308 B5
Moorland *U.S.A.* 42°26N 94°18W 310 B2
Moormerland *Germany* 53°20N 7°20E 178 B3
Moornanyah L. *Australia* 33°15S 143°42E 282 B5
Mooroopna *Australia* 36°25S 145°22E 283 D6
Moorpark *U.S.A.* 34°17N 118°53W 307 L8
Moorreesburg *S. Africa* 33°6S 18°38E 270 D2
Moorrinya △ *Australia* 21°42S 144°58E 280 C3
Moosach *Germany* 48°10N 11°30E 131 A2
Moosburg *Germany* 48°27N 11°56E 179 G7
Moose → *Ont., Canada* 51°20N 80°25W 298 B3
Moose → *N.Y., U.S.A.* 43°38N 75°24W 313 C9
Moose Creek *Canada* 45°15N 74°58W 313 A10
Moose Factory *Canada* 51°16N 80°32W 298 B3
Moose Jaw *Canada* 50°24N 105°30W 297 C7
Moose Jaw → *Canada* 50°34N 105°18W 297 C7
Moose Lake *Man., Canada* 53°46N 100°8W 297 C8
Moose Lake *Minn., U.S.A.* 46°27N 92°46W 308 B7
Moose Mountain ⌓ *Canada* 49°48N 102°25W 297 D8
Moose Pass *U.S.A.* 60°29N 149°22W 303 F10
Moosehead L. *U.S.A.* 45°38N 69°40W 309 C19
Mooselookmeguntic L. *U.S.A.* 44°55N 70°49W 313 B14
Moosilauke, Mt. *U.S.A.* 44°3N 71°40W 313 B13
Moosomin *Canada* 50°9N 101°40W 297 C8
Moosonee *Canada* 51°17N 80°39W 298 B3
Moosup *U.S.A.* 41°43N 71°53W 313 E13
Mootwingee △ *Australia* 31°10S 142°30E 282 A5
Mopane *S. Africa* 22°37S 29°52E 271 B4
Mopeia Velha *Mozam.* 17°30S 35°40E 269 F4
Mopipi *Botswana* 21°6S 24°55E 270 B3
Mopoi *C.A.R.* 5°6N 26°54E 268 A2
Mopti *Mali* 14°30N 4°0W 262 C4
Mopti □ *Mali* 14°40N 4°0W 262 C4
Moqatta *Sudan* 14°38N 35°50E 257 E4
Moqor *Afghan.* 32°50N 67°42E 242 C2
Moquegua *Peru* 17°15S 70°46W 330 D3
Moquegua □ *Peru* 16°50S 70°55W 330 D3
Mór *Hungary* 47°25N 18°12E 182 C3
Mora *Cameroon* 11°2N 14°7E 259 F2
Mora *Maharashtra, India* 18°54N 72°55E 130 B2
Móra *Portugal* 38°55N 8°10W 195 G2
Mora *Spain* 39°41N 3°46W 195 F7
Mora *Sweden* 61°2N 14°38E 162 C8
Mora *Minn., U.S.A.* 45°53N 93°18W 308 C7
Mora *N. Mex., U.S.A.* 35°58N 105°20W 305 J11
Móra de Rubielos *Spain* 40°15N 0°45W 196 E4
Móra d'Ebre *Spain* 41°6N 0°38E 196 D5
Móra la Nova *Spain* 41°7N 0°39E 196 D5
Morača → *Montenegro* 42°20N 19°9E 202 D3
Morada Nova *Brazil* 5°7S 38°23W 332 C4
Morada Nova de Minas *Brazil* 18°37S 45°22W 333 E2
Moradabad *India* 28°50N 78°50E 243 E8
Morafenobe *Madag.* 17°50S 44°53E 272 B1
Morąg *Poland* 53°55N 19°56E 184 E6
Moral de Calatrava *Spain* 38°51N 3°33W 195 G7
Moraleda, Canal *Chile* 44°30S 73°30W 336 B2
Moraleja *Spain* 40°6N 6°43W 194 E4
Morales *Bolívar, Colombia* 8°16N 73°51W 328 B3
Morales *Cauca, Colombia* 2°45N 76°38W 328 C2
Moramanga *Madag.* 18°56S 48°12E 272 B2
Moran *Kans., U.S.A.* 37°55N 95°10W 308 G6
Moran *Wyo., U.S.A.* 43°50N 110°31W 304 E8
Moranbah *Australia* 22°1S 148°6E 280 C4
Morané *French Polynesia* 23°10S 137°7W 289 f
Morang = Biratnagar *Nepal* 26°27N 87°17E 243 F12
Moranhat *India* 27°10N 94°50E 241 B5
Morano Cálabro *Italy* 39°50N 16°8E 201 C9
Morant Bay *Jamaica* 17°53N 76°25W 320 a
Morant Cays *Jamaica* 17°22N 76°0W 320 C4
Morant Pt. *Jamaica* 17°55N 76°12W 320 a
Morar *India* 26°14N 78°14E 242 F8
Morar, L. *U.K.* 56°57N 5°40W 167 E3
Moratalaz *Spain* 40°24N 3°39W 127 B2
Moratalla *Spain* 38°14N 1°49W 197 G3
Moratuwa *Sri Lanka* 6°45N 79°55E 245 L4
Morava → *Slovakia* 48°10N 16°59E 181 C9
Moravia *Iowa, U.S.A.* 40°53N 92°49W 310 D4
Moravia *N.Y., U.S.A.* 42°43N 76°25W 313 D8
Moravian Hts. = Českomoravská Vrchovina *Czechia* 49°30N 15°40E 180 B8
Moravica → *Serbia* 43°52N 20°8E 202 C4
Moraviţa *Romania* 45°17N 21°14E 182 E6
Moravská Třebová *Czechia* 49°45N 16°40E 181 B9
Moravské Budějovice *Czechia* 49°4N 15°49E 180 B8
Moravskoslezský □ *Czechia* 49°55N 17°58E 181 B10
Morawa *Australia* 29°13S 116°0E 279 E2
Morawhanna *Guyana* 8°30N 59°40W 329 B6
Moray □ *U.K.* 57°31N 3°18W 167 D5
Moray Firth *U.K.* 57°40N 3°52W 167 D5
Morbach *Germany* 49°48N 7°6E 179 F3
Morbegno *Italy* 46°8N 9°34E 198 B6
Morbi *India* 22°50N 70°42E 242 H4
Morbihan □ *France* 47°55N 2°50W 172 E4
Mörby *Sweden* 59°23N 18°3E 139 A2
Mörbylånga *Sweden* 56°32N 16°22E 163 H10
Morcenx *France* 44°3N 0°55W 174 D3
Morcone *Italy* 41°20N 14°40E 201 A7
Mordelles *France* 48°5N 1°52W 172 D5
Morden *Man., Canada* 49°15N 98°10W 297 D9
Morden *London, U.K.* 51°24N 0°13W 125 B2
Mordoğan *Turkey* 38°30N 26°37E 205 C8
Mordovian Republic = Mordvinia □ *Russia* 54°20N 44°30E 190 C7
Mordovo *Russia* 52°6N 40°50E 190 D5
Mordvinia □ *Russia* 54°20N 44°30E 190 C7
Mordy *Poland* 52°13N 22°31E 185 F9
Møre og Romsdal □ *Norway* 62°30N 8°0E 164 B4
Moreau → *U.S.A.* 45°18N 100°43W 308 C3
Morebeng *S. Africa* 23°30S 29°55E 271 B4
Morecambe *U.K.* 54°5N 2°52W 168 C5
Morecambe B. *U.K.* 54°7N 3°0W 168 C5
Moree *Australia* 29°28S 149°54E 281 D4
Morée → *France* 48°57N 2°25E 134 A3
Morehead *Papua N. G.* 8°41S 141°41E 286 E1
Morehead *Ky., U.S.A.* 38°11N 83°26W 311 F13
Morehead City *U.S.A.* 34°43N 76°43W 315 D16
Morel → *India* 26°13N 76°36E 242 F7
Moreland *U.S.A.* 33°17N 84°46W 316 B5
Morelia *Mexico* 19°42N 101°7W 318 D4
Morella *Queens., Australia* 23°0S 143°52E 280 C3
Morella *Spain* 40°35N 0°5W 196 E4
Morelos *Mexico* 26°42N 107°40W 318 B3
Morelos □ *Mexico* 18°45N 99°0W 319 D5
Moremi ⌓ *Botswana* 19°18S 23°10E 270 A3
Morena *India* 26°30N 78°4E 242 F8
Morena, Sierra *Spain* 38°20N 4°0W 195 G7
Morenci *U.S.A.* 41°43N 84°13W 311 C12
Moreni *Romania* 44°59N 25°36E 183 F10
Moreno *Bolivia* 11°9S 66°15W 330 C4
Moreno Valley *U.S.A.* 33°56N 117°14W 307 M10
Moreru → *Brazil* 10°10S 59°15W 331 C6
Moresby I. *Canada* 52°30N 131°40W 296 C2
Morestel *France* 45°40N 5°28E 175 C9
Moreton I. *Australia* 27°10S 153°25E 281 D5
Moreton Island △ *Australia* 27°2S 153°24E 281 D5
Moreuil *France* 49°46N 2°30E 173 C9
Morez *France* 46°31N 6°2E 173 F13
Morgan *S. Austral., Australia* 34°2S 139°35E 282 C3
Morgan *Ga., U.S.A.* 31°32N 84°36W 316 D5
Morgan *Utah, U.S.A.* 41°2N 111°41W 304 F8
Morgan City *U.S.A.* 29°42N 91°12W 314 G9
Morgan Hill *U.S.A.* 37°8N 121°39W 306 H5
Morgan Park *U.S.A.* 41°41N 87°38W 119 C3
Morganfield *U.S.A.* 37°41N 87°55W 308 G10
Morgan's Port *U.S.A.* 29°40N 95°0W 314 G7
Morganton *U.S.A.* 35°45N 81°41W 315 D14
Morgantown *Ind., U.S.A.* 39°22N 86°16W 311 E10
Morgantown *W. Va., U.S.A.* 39°38N 79°57W 309 F14
Morgenzon *S. Africa* 26°45S 29°36E 271 C4
Morges *Switz.* 46°31N 6°29E 179 J2
Morghak *Iran* 29°7N 57°54E 247 D8
Morgongåva *Sweden* 59°57N 16°58E 162 E10
Morhange *France* 48°55N 6°38E 173 D13
Morhar → *India* 25°29N 85°11E 243 G11
Mori *China* 43°49N 90°11E 217 D12
Mori *Japan* 42°6N 140°35E 220 C10
Moriah *Trin. & Tob.* 11°15N 60°43W 323 s
Moriarty *U.S.A.* 34°59N 106°3W 305 J10
Moribaya *Guinea* 9°53N 9°32W 262 D3
Morice L. *Canada* 53°50N 127°40W 296 C3
Morichal Largo → *Venezuela* 9°27N 62°25W 329 B5
Morichal Viejo *Colombia* 2°13N 70°2W 328 C3
Moriguchi *Japan* 34°43N 135°34E 133 A2
Moriki *Nigeria* 12°52N 6°30E 263 C6
Morinville *Canada* 53°49N 113°41W 296 C6
Morioka *Japan* 39°45N 141°8E 220 E10
Moris *Mexico* 28°10N 108°32W 318 B3
Morisset *Australia* 33°6S 151°30E 283 B9
Morivione *Italy* 45°26N 9°12E 128 B2
Moriyama *Japan* 35°4N 135°59E 223 B7
Morlaàs *France* 43°21N 0°18W 174 E3
Morlaix *France* 48°36N 3°52W 172 D3
Mörlunda *Sweden* 57°19N 15°52E 163 G9
Mormanno *Italy* 39°53N 15°59E 201 C8
Mormant *France* 48°37N 2°52E 173 D9
Mormugao = Marmagao *India* 15°25N 73°56E 245 G1
Morne-à-l'Eau *Guadeloupe* 16°20N 61°27W 322 e
Morne des Esses *Martinique* 14°44N 61°1W 322 j
Morne Diablotins *Dominica* 15°30N 61°24W 323 k
Morne Fendue *Grenada* 12°12N 61°38W 323 q
Morne Raquette *Dominica* 15°27N 61°27W 323 k
Morne Trois Pitons △ *Dominica* 15°22N 61°20W 323 k
Morningside *Gauteng, S. Africa* 26°4S 28°3E 123 A2
Morningside *Edinburgh, U.K.* 55°56N 3°12W 121 B2
Morningside Park *Ont., Canada* 43°47N 79°12W 141 A3
Morningside Park *Fla., U.S.A.* 28°26N 81°24W 133 B2
Mornington *Australia* 38°15S 145°5E 283 E6
Mornington, I. *Chile* 49°50S 75°30W 336 C1
Mornington I. *Australia* 16°30S 139°30E 280 B2
Mornington Peninsula △ *Australia* 38°28S 144°53E 283 E6
Mornos → *Greece* 38°25N 21°50E 204 C3
Moro *Pakistan* 26°40N 68°0E 242 F2
Moro *Sudan* 10°50N 30°9E 257 E3
Moro → *Pakistan* 29°42N 67°22E 242 E2
Moro G. *Phil.* 6°30N 123°0E 233 H4
Morobe *Papua N. G.* 7°49S 147°38E 286 D4
Morobe □ *Papua N. G.* 7°0S 147°0E 286 D4
Morocco *U.S.A.* 40°57N 87°27W 311 D9
Morocco ■ *N. Afr.* 32°0N 5°50W 260 B3
Morococha *Peru* 11°40S 76°5W 330 C2
Morogoro *Tanzania* 6°50S 37°40E 268 D4
Morogoro □ *Tanzania* 8°0S 37°0E 268 D4
Moroleón *Mexico* 20°8N 101°12W 318 C4
Morombe *Madag.* 21°45S 43°22E 272 C1
Moron = Morong *Phil.* 14°41N 120°16E 232 D3
Morón *Argentina* 34°39S 58°37W 334 C4
Morón *Cuba* 22°8N 78°39W 320 B4
Mörön *Mongolia* 49°38N 100°9E 218 B9
Morón de Almazán *Spain* 41°29N 2°27W 196 D2
Morón de la Frontera *Spain* 37°6N 5°28W 195 H5
Morona → *Peru* 4°40S 77°10W 328 D2
Morona-Santiago □ *Ecuador* 2°30S 78°0W 328 D2
Morondava *Madag.* 20°17S 44°17E 272 C1
Morondo *Ivory C.* 8°57N 6°47W 262 D3
Morong *Phil.* 14°41N 120°16E 232 D3
Morongo Valley *U.S.A.* 34°3N 116°37W 307 L10
Moroni *Comoros Is.* 11°40S 43°16E 272 a
Moroni *Utah, U.S.A.* 39°32N 111°35W 304 G8
Moroni Iconi ✕ (YVA) *Comoros Is.* 11°32S 43°15E 272 a
Moronou *Ivory C.* 6°16N 4°59W 262 D4
Morotai *Indonesia* 2°10N 128°30E 231 D7
Moroto *Uganda* 2°28N 34°42E 268 B3
Moroto, Mt. *Uganda* 2°30N 34°43E 268 B3
Morozov *Bulgaria* 42°30N 25°10E 203 D9
Morozovsk *Russia* 48°25N 41°50E 191 F5
Morpeth *Ont., Canada* 42°23N 81°50W 312 D3
Morpeth *Northumberland, U.K.* 55°10N 1°41W 168 B6
Morphou *Cyprus* 35°12N 32°59E 207 E8
Morphou Bay *Cyprus* 35°15N 32°50E 207 E8
Morrelganj *Bangla.* 22°28N 89°51E 241 D2
Morrilton *U.S.A.* 35°9N 92°44W 314 D8
Morrinhos *Ceará, Brazil* 3°14S 40°7W 332 B3
Morrinhos *Minas Gerais, Brazil* 17°45S 49°10W 333 E2
Morrinsville *N.Z.* 37°40S 175°32E 284 D4
Morris *Man., Canada* 49°25N 97°22W 297 D9
Morris *Ill., U.S.A.* 41°22N 88°26W 311 C8
Morris *Minn., U.S.A.* 45°35N 95°55W 308 C6
Morris *N.Y., U.S.A.* 42°33N 75°15W 313 D9
Morris *Pa., U.S.A.* 41°35N 77°17W 312 E7
Morris, Mt. *Australia* 26°9S 131°4E 279 E5
Morris Jesup, Kap *Greenland* 83°40N 34°0W 154 A7
Morrisburg *Canada* 44°55N 75°7W 313 B9
Morrison *U.S.A.* 41°49N 89°58W 310 C7
Morrisonville *U.S.A.* 39°25N 89°27W 310 E7
Morristown *Ariz., U.S.A.* 33°51N 112°37W 305 K7
Morristown *Ind., U.S.A.* 39°40N 85°42W 311 E11
Morristown *N.J., U.S.A.* 40°48N 74°29W 313 F10
Morristown *N.Y., U.S.A.* 44°35N 75°39W 313 B9
Morristown *Tenn., U.S.A.* 36°13N 83°18W 315 C13
Morrisville *N.Y., U.S.A.* 42°53N 75°35W 313 D9
Morrisville *Pa., U.S.A.* 40°13N 74°47W 313 F10
Morrisville *Vt., U.S.A.* 44°34N 72°36W 313 B12
Morro, Pta. *Chile* 27°6S 71°0W 334 B1
Morro Bay *U.S.A.* 35°22N 120°51W 306 K6
Morro Chico *Chile* 52°2S 71°26W 336 D2
Morro del Jable *Canary Is.* 28°3N 14°23W 153 e2
Morro do Chapéu *Brazil* 11°33S 41°9W 333 D3
Morro Grande = Barão de Cocais *Brazil* 19°56S 43°28W 333 E3
Morro Jable, Pta. de *Canary Is.* 28°2N 14°20W 153 e2
Morro Solar, Cerro *Peru* 12°11S 77°1W 124 C2
Morrocoy △ *Venezuela* 10°48N 68°13W 328 A4
Morros *Brazil* 2°52S 44°3W 332 B3
Morrosquillo, G. de *Colombia* 9°35N 75°40W 320 E4
Morrow *U.S.A.* 39°21N 84°8W 311 E12
Mörrum *Sweden* 56°12N 14°45E 163 H8
Morrumbene *Mozam.* 23°31S 35°16E 271 B6
Mörrumsån → *Sweden* 56°10N 14°45E 163 H8
Mors *Denmark* 56°50N 8°45E 163 H2
Morshansk *Russia* 53°28N 41°50E 190 D5
Morsi *India* 21°21N 78°0E 244 D4
Mörsil *Sweden* 63°19N 13°40E 162 A7
Mortagne → *France* 48°33N 6°27E 173 D13
Mortagne-au-Perche *France* 48°31N 0°33E 172 D7
Mortagne-sur-Gironde *France* 45°28N 0°47W 174 C3
Mortagne-sur-Sèvre *France* 47°0N 0°59W 172 F6
Mortain *France* 48°40N 0°57W 172 D6
Mortara *Italy* 45°15N 8°44E 198 C5
Morteau *France* 47°3N 6°35E 173 E13
Morteros *Argentina* 30°50S 62°0W 334 C3
Mortes, R. das → *Brazil* 11°45S 50°44W 333 D1
Mortlach *Canada* 50°27N 106°4W 297 C7
Mortlake *N.S.W., Australia* 33°50S 151°6E 139 B1
Mortlake *Vic., Australia* 38°5S 142°50E 282 E5
Mortlake *London, U.K.* 51°27N 0°15W 125 B2
Morton *Ill., U.S.A.* 40°37N 89°28W 310 D7
Morton *Tex., U.S.A.* 33°44N 102°46W 314 E3
Morton *Wash., U.S.A.* 46°34N 122°17W 306 D4
Morton △ *Australia* 35°0S 150°12E 283 C9
Morton Grove *U.S.A.* 42°2N 87°46W 119 A2
Moruga *Trin. & Tob.* 10°4N 61°16W 323 t
Moruga → *Trin. & Tob.* 10°5N 61°16W 323 t
Morumbi *Brazil* 23°35S 46°42W 137 B1
Morundah *Australia* 34°57S 146°19E 283 C7
Morung *Sudan* 10°32N 31°3E 266 B3
Moruya *Australia* 35°58S 150°3E 283 C9
Morvan *France* 47°5N 4°3E 173 E11
Morvan ⌓ *France* 47°12N 4°3E 173 E11
Morvant *Trin. & Tob.* 10°40N 61°29W 323 t
Morven *Queens., Australia* 26°22S 147°5E 281 D4
Morven *N.Z.* 44°50S 171°6E 285 E6
Morven *Ga., U.S.A.* 30°57N 83°30W 316 E6
Morvern *U.K.* 56°38N 5°44W 167 E3
Morwell *Australia* 38°10S 146°22E 283 E7
Morwell △ *Australia* 38°14S 146°23E 283 E7
Moryń *Poland* 52°51N 14°22E 185 F1
Morzhovets, Ostrov *Russia* 66°44N 42°35E 186 A7
Morzine *France* 46°11N 6°42E 173 F13
Mosakahiken = Moose Lake *Canada* 53°46N 100°8W 297 C8
Mosalsk *Russia* 54°30N 34°55E 188 E8
Mosbach *Germany* 49°21N 9°9E 179 F5
Mosby *Norway* 58°12N 7°55E 164 F4
Moscavide *Portugal* 38°47N 9°6W 126 A2
Mošćenice *Croatia* 45°17N 14°16E 199 C11
Moschato *Greece* 37°55N 23°40E 112 B2
Mosciano Sant' Ángelo *Italy* 42°42N 13°52E 199 F10
Moscone Convention Center *San Francisco, U.S.A.* 136 c2
Moscos Is. *Burma* 14°0N 97°30E 236 F1
Moscow = Moskva *Russia* 55°45N 37°37E 129 B2
Moscow *Idaho, U.S.A.* 46°44N 117°0W 304 C5
Moscow *Mich., U.S.A.* 42°3N 84°30W 311 B12
Moscow *Pa., U.S.A.* 41°20N 75°31W 313 E9
Moscow Domodedovo Int. ✕ (DME) *Russia* 55°24N 37°54E 188 E9
Moscow Mills *U.S.A.* 38°57N 90°55W 310 F6
Moscow Sheremetyevo Int. ✕ (SVO) *Russia* 55°58N 37°25E 129 A1
Mosel → *Europe* 50°22N 7°36E 173 B14
Moselle = Mosel → *Europe* 50°22N 7°36E 173 B14
Moselle □ *France* 48°59N 6°33E 173 D13
Moses Lake *U.S.A.* 47°8N 119°17W 304 C4
Mosgiel *N.Z.* 45°53S 170°21E 285 F5
Moshaweng → *S. Africa* 26°35S 22°50E 270 C3
Moshchnyy, Ostrov *Russia* 60°1N 27°50E 188 B4
Moshi *Tanzania* 3°22S 37°18E 268 C4
Moshi → *Nigeria* 9°18N 4°38E 263 D5
Moshupa *Botswana* 24°46S 25°29E 270 B4
Mosi-oa-Tunya = Victoria Falls *Zimbabwe* 17°58S 25°52E 269 F2
Mosina *Poland* 52°15N 16°50E 185 F3
Mosite *Dem. Rep. of the Congo* 0°53N 23°40E 264 B4
Mosjøen *Norway* 65°51N 13°12E 160 D15
Moskenesøya *Norway* 67°58N 13°0E 160 C15
Moskenstraumen *Norway* 67°47N 12°45E 160 C15
Moskog *Norway* 61°26N 6°0E 164 C2
Moskva *Russia* 55°45N 37°37E 129 B2
Moskva □ *Russia* 56°20N 37°20E 188 D9
Moskva → *Russia* 55°5N 38°51E 188 E10
Moskvoretskiy *Russia* 55°42N 37°37E 129 B2
Moslavačka Gora *Croatia* 45°40N 16°37E 199 C13
Mosman *Australia* 33°49S 151°15E 139 B2
Moso *Vanuatu* 17°30S 168°15E 287 G6
Mosomane *Botswana* 24°2S 26°19E 270 B4
Mosonmagyaróvár *Hungary* 47°52N 17°18E 182 C2
Mošorin *Serbia* 45°19N 20°4E 182 E5
Mospyne *Ukraine* 47°52N 38°0E 189 J9
Mosqueiro *Brazil* 1°10S 48°28W 332 B2
Mosquera *Colombia* 2°35N 78°24W 328 C2
Mosquero *U.S.A.* 35°47N 103°58W 305 J12
Mosqueruela *Spain* 40°21N 0°27W 196 E4
Mosquitia *Honduras* 15°20N 84°10W 320 C3
Mosquito, Pta. *Venezuela* 10°53N 63°53W 329 a
Mosquito Coast = Mosquitos, Costa de *Nic.* 13°20N 83°35W 320 D3
Mosquito Creek L. *U.S.A.* 41°18N 80°46W 312 E4
Mosquito L. *Canada* 62°35N 103°20W 297 A8
Mosquitos, Costa de *Nic.* 13°20N 83°35W 320 D3
Mosquitos, G. de los *Panama* 9°15N 81°10W 320 E3
Moss *Norway* 59°27N 10°40E 164 E7
Moss Vale *Australia* 34°32S 150°25E 283 C9
Mossaka *Congo* 1°15S 16°45E 264 C3
Mossâmedes *Brazil* 16°7S 50°11W 333 E1
Mossbank *Canada* 49°56N 105°56W 297 D7
Mossburn *N.Z.* 45°41S 168°15E 285 F3
Mosselbaai *S. Africa* 34°11S 22°8E 270 D3
Mossendjo *Congo* 2°55S 12°42E 264 C2
Mossfellsbær *Iceland* 64°11N 21°45W 155 C5
Mossgiel *Australia* 33°15S 144°5E 282 B6
Mossingen *Germany* 48°24N 9°4E 179 G5
Mossman *Australia* 16°21S 145°15E 280 B4
Mossoró *Brazil* 5°10S 37°15W 332 C4
Mossuril *Mozam.* 14°58S 40°42E 269 E5
Mossy Head *U.S.A.* 30°45N 86°19W 317 E3
Mossy Point *Australia* 35°50S 150°11E 283 C9
Most *Czechia* 50°31N 13°38E 180 A6
Mosta *Malta* 35°55N 14°26E 206 F7
Mostaganem *Algeria* 35°54N 0°5E 261 A5
Mostaganem □ *Algeria* 35°40N 0°15E 261 A5
Mostar *Bos.-H.* 43°22N 17°50E 182 G2
Mostardas *Brazil* 31°2S 50°51W 335 C5
Mostefa, Rass *Tunisia* 36°55N 11°3E 258 A2
Mosteiros *Azores* 37°53N 25°49W 153 d3
Mosterhamn *Norway* 59°42N 5°21E 164 E2
Mostiska = Mostyska *Ukraine* 49°48N 23°4E 185 J10
Móstoles *Spain* 40°19N 3°53W 194 E7
Mosty = Masty *Belarus* 53°27N 24°38E 177 B13
Mostyska *Ukraine* 49°48N 23°4E 185 J10
Mosul = Al Mawşil *Iraq* 36°15N 43°5E 213 D10
Møsvatnet *Norway* 59°52N 8°5E 164 E5
Mota *Ethiopia* 11°5N 37°52E 257 E4
Mota *Vanuatu* 13°49S 167°42E 287 C5
Mota del Cuervo *Spain* 39°30N 2°52W 197 F2
Mota del Marqués *Spain* 41°38N 5°11W 194 D5
Mota Lava *Vanuatu* 13°40S 167°40E 287 C5
Motaba *Congo* 2°6N 18°2E 264 B3
Motagua → *Guatemala* 15°44N 88°14W 320 C2
Motala *Sweden* 58°32N 15°1E 163 F9
Motaze *Mozam.* 24°48S 32°52E 271 B5
Moţca *Romania* 47°15N 26°37E 183 C11
Motegi *Japan* 36°32N 140°11E 223 A12
Moth *India* 25°43N 78°57E 243 G8
Motherwell *U.K.* 55°47N 3°58W 167 F5
Moti Bagh *India* 28°33N 77°10E 120 B2
Motihari *India* 26°30N 84°55E 243 F11
Motilla del Palancar *Spain* 39°34N 1°55W 197 F3
Motiti I. *N.Z.* 37°38S 176°25E 284 D5
Motnik *Slovenia* 46°14N 14°54E 199 B11
Motobu *Japan* 26°39N 127°53E 288 a
Motocurunya *Venezuela* 4°24N 64°5W 329 C5
Motol *Czechia* 50°3N 14°21E 135 B2
Motovun *Croatia* 45°20N 13°50E 199 C10
Motozintla de Mendoza *Mexico* 15°22N 92°14W 319 D6
Motril *Spain* 36°31N 3°37W 195 J7
Motru *Romania* 44°48N 22°59E 182 F7
Motru → *Romania* 44°32N 23°31E 183 F8
Motsa *Israel* 31°47N 35°9E 123 B2
Motsa Ilit *Israel* 31°48N 35°9E 123 B1
Motspur Park *U.K.* 51°23N 0°14W 125 B2
Mott *U.S.A.* 46°23N 102°20W 308 B2
Mottama, G. of *Burma* 16°5N 96°30E 241 G6
Mottingham *U.K.* 51°26N 0°1E 125 B4
Möttling = Metlika *Slovenia* 45°40N 15°20E 199 C12
Móttola *Italy* 40°38N 17°2E 201 B10
Motu → *N.Z.* 37°52S 177°36E 284 D6
Motu Nui *Chile* 27°12S 109°28W 330 b
Motu Tapu *Cook Is.* 21°14S 159°43W 289 h
Motuba *Dem. Rep. of the Congo* 2°20N 18°34E 264 B3
Motueka *N.Z.* 41°7S 173°1E 285 B8
Motueka → *N.Z.* 41°5S 173°1E 285 B8
Motul *Mexico* 21°6N 89°17W 319 C7
Motupena Pt. *Papua N. G.* 6°30S 155°10E 286 D8
Mou *N. Cal.* 21°5S 167°26E 288 d
Mouanda *Gabon* 1°28S 13°7E 264 C2
Mouchalagane → *Canada* 50°56N 68°41W 299 B6
Mouchoir Bank *W. Indies* 20°57N 70°47W 321 B5
Mouding *China* 25°20N 101°28E 228 E3
Moudjeria *Mauritania* 17°50N 12°28W 262 B2
Moudon *Switz.* 46°40N 6°49E 179 J2
Moudros *Greece* 39°50N 25°18E 205 B7
Mougins *France* 43°36N 7°0E 175 E10
Mougoundou *Congo* 2°40S 12°41E 264 C2
Mouhoun = Black Volta → *Africa* 8°41N 1°33W 262 D4
Mouila *Gabon* 1°50S 11°0E 264 C2
Mouka *C.A.R.* 7°16N 21°52E 264 A4
Moukalaba ⌓ *Gabon* 2°50S 10°35E 264 C2
Moukambo *Gabon* 3°5S 11°38E 264 C2
Moul *Niger* 15°5N 13°11E 259 F2
Moulamein *Australia* 35°3S 144°1E 282 C6
Moule à Chique, C. *St. Lucia* 13°43N 60°57W 323 m
Moulhoulé *Djibouti* 11°58N 42°58E 267 B5
Mouliana *Greece* 35°10N 25°59E 207 E6
Moulin Rouge *Paris, France* 134 a3
Moulins *France* 46°35N 3°19E 173 F10
Moulmein = Mawlamyine *Burma* 16°30N 97°40E 241 G6
Moulouya, O. → *Morocco* 35°5N 2°25W 261 A4
Moulton *U.S.A.* 40°41N 92°41W 310 D4
Moultrie *U.S.A.* 31°11N 83°47W 316 D6
Moultrie, L. *U.S.A.* 33°20N 80°5W 316 B9
Mounana *Gabon* 1°18S 13°13E 264 C2
Mound City *Mo., U.S.A.* 40°7N 95°14W 308 E6
Mound City *S. Dak., U.S.A.* 45°44N 100°4W 308 C3
Moundou *Chad* 8°40N 16°10E 259 G3
Moundsville *U.S.A.* 39°55N 80°44W 312 G4
Mounembé *Congo* 3°20S 12°32E 264 C2
Moung *Cambodia* 12°46N 103°27E 236 F4
Moungoudi *Congo* 2°45S 11°46E 264 C2
Mount Airy *U.S.A.* 36°31N 80°37W 315 C14
Mount Albert *Canada* 44°8N 79°19W 312 B5
Mount Apo △ *Phil.* 7°0N 125°10E 233 H5
Mount Arayat △ *Phil.* 15°39N 120°44E 232 D3
Mount Aspiring △ *N.Z.* 44°19S 168°47E 285 E3
Mount Ayliff = Maxesibeni *S. Africa* 30°49S 29°23E 271 D4
Mount Ayr *U.S.A.* 40°43N 94°14W 310 D2
Mount Barker *S. Austral., Australia* 35°5S 138°52E 282 C3
Mount Barker *W. Austral., Australia* 34°38S 117°40E 279 F2
Mount Barnett Roadhouse *Australia* 16°39S 125°57E 278 C4
Mount Beauty *Australia* 36°47S 147°10E 283 D7
Mount Brydges *Canada* 42°54N 81°29W 312 D3
Mount Buffalo △ *Australia* 36°43S 146°46E 283 D7
Mount Burr *Australia* 37°34S 140°26E 281 F3
Mount Carleton ⌓ *Canada* 47°25N 66°55W 299 C6
Mount Carmel = Ha Karmel △ *Israel* 32°45N 35°5E 250 F6
Mount Carmel *Ill., U.S.A.* 38°25N 87°46W 311 F9
Mount Carmel *Pa., U.S.A.* 40°47N 76°26W 313 F8
Mount Carroll *U.S.A.* 42°6N 89°59W 310 B7
Mount Clemens *U.S.A.* 42°35N 82°53W 312 D2
Mount Cook *N.Z.* 43°44S 170°5E 285 D5
Mount Cook △ *N.Z.* 43°35S 170°15E 285 D5
Mount Coolon *Australia* 21°25S 147°25E 280 C4
Mount Darwin *Zimbabwe* 16°47S 31°38E 269 F3
Mount Dennis *Canada* 43°40N 79°28W 141 A2
Mount Desert I. *U.S.A.* 44°21N 68°20W 309 C19
Mount Dora *U.S.A.* 28°48N 81°38W 317 G8
Mount Ebenezer *Australia* 25°6S 132°34E 279 E5
Mount Eccles △ *Australia* 38°5S 141°54E 282 E4
Mount Eden *U.S.A.* 38°3N 85°9W 311 F11
Mount Edziza ⌓ *Canada* 57°30N 130°45W 296 B2
Mount Elgon △ *E. Afr.* 1°4N 34°42E 268 B3
Mount Field △ *Australia* 42°39S 146°35E 281 G4
Mount Fletcher *S. Africa* 30°40S 28°30E 271 D4
Mount Forest *Canada* 43°59N 80°43W 312 C4
Mount Frankland △ *Australia* 31°47S 116°37E 279 F2
Mount Frederick ◎ *Australia* 19°39S 129°18E 278 C4
Mount Frere = Kwabhaca *S. Africa* 30°51S 29°0E 271 D4
Mount Gambier *Australia* 37°50S 140°46E 282 D4
Mount Garnet *Australia* 17°37S 145°6E 280 B4
Mount Greenwood *U.S.A.* 41°42N 87°42W 119 C2
Mount Hagen *Papua N. G.* 5°52S 144°16E 286 C3
Mount Hamiguitan △ *Phil.* 6°44N 126°10E 233 H6
Mount Holly *U.S.A.* 39°59N 74°47W 313 G10
Mount Holly Springs *U.S.A.* 40°7N 77°12W 312 F7
Mount Hood Memorial Park ⌓ *U.S.A.* 42°26N 71°1W 116 A2
Mount Hope *N.S.W., Australia* 32°51S 145°51E 283 B6
Mount Hope *S. Austral., Australia* 34°7S 135°23E 281 E2
Mount Horeb *U.S.A.* 43°1N 89°44W 310 B7
Mount Iglit-Mount Baco △ *Phil.* 12°45N 121°8E 232 E3
Mount Isa *Australia* 20°42S 139°26E 280 C2
Mount Isarog △ *Phil.* 13°38N 123°24E 232 E4
Mount James ◎ *Australia* 24°51S 116°54E 279 D2
Mount Jewett *U.S.A.* 41°44N 78°39W 312 E6
Mount Ka'ala Nat. Area Reserve ⌓ *U.S.A.* 21°31N 158°7W 302 J13
Mount Kaputar △ *Australia* 30°16S 150°10E 281 E5
Mount Kenya △ *Kenya* 0°7S 37°21E 268 C4
Mount Kisco *U.S.A.* 41°12N 73°44W 313 E11
Mount Laguna *U.S.A.* 32°52N 116°25W 307 N10
Mount Larcom *Australia* 23°48S 150°59E 280 C5
Mount Lofty Ranges *Australia* 34°35S 139°5E 282 C3
Mount McKinley = Denali △ *U.S.A.* 63°30N 152°0W 303 E10
Mount Magnet *Australia* 28°2S 117°47E 279 E2
Mount Malindang △ *Phil.* 8°17N 123°32E 233 G4
Mount Manara *Australia* 32°29S 143°58E 282 B5
Mount Maunganui *N.Z.* 37°40S 176°14E 284 D5
Mount Molloy *Australia* 16°42S 145°20E 280 B4
Mount Morgan *Australia* 23°40S 150°25E 280 C5
Mount Morris *Mich., U.S.A.* 43°7N 83°42W 311 A13
Mount Morris *N.Y., U.S.A.* 42°44N 77°52W 312 D7
Mount Olive *U.S.A.* 39°4N 89°44W 310 E7
Mount Olivet *U.S.A.* 38°32N 84°2W 311 F12
Mount Olympus *U.S.A.* 34°7N 118°21W 126 B2
Mount Orab *U.S.A.* 39°2N 83°55W 311 E13
Mount Pearl *Canada* 47°31N 52°47W 299 C9
Mount Penn *U.S.A.* 40°20N 75°54W 313 F9
Mount Perry *Australia* 25°13S 151°42E 281 D5
Mount Pleasant *Iowa, U.S.A.* 40°58N 91°33W 310 D5
Mount Pleasant *Mich., U.S.A.* 43°36N 84°46W 309 D11
Mount Pleasant *Pa., U.S.A.* 40°9N 79°33W 312 F5
Mount Pleasant *S.C., U.S.A.* 32°47N 79°52W 316 C10
Mount Pleasant *Tenn., U.S.A.* 35°32N 87°12W 315 D11
Mount Pleasant *Tex., U.S.A.* 33°9N 94°58W 314 E7
Mount Pleasant *Utah, U.S.A.* 39°33N 111°27W 304 G8
Mount Pleasant ✕ (MPN) *Falk. Is.* 51°49S 58°23W 153 f
Mount Pocono *U.S.A.* 41°7N 75°22W 313 E9
Mount Pulaski *U.S.A.* 40°1N 89°17W 310 D7
Mount Pulog △ *Phil.* 16°35N 120°57E 232 C3
Mount Rainier *U.S.A.* 38°56N 76°57W 143 B3
Mount Rainier △ *U.S.A.* 46°55N 121°50W 306 D5
Mount Remarkable △ *Australia* 32°47S 138°3E 282 B3
Mount Revelstoke △ *Canada* 51°5N 118°30W 296 C5
Mount Robson ⌓ *Canada* 53°0N 119°0W 296 C5

Mount St. Helens ⌂ *U.S.A.* 46°14N 122°11W **306** D4
Mount Selinda *Zimbabwe* 20°24S 32°43E **271** B5
Mount Shasta *U.S.A.* 41°19N 122°19W **304** F2
Mount Signal *U.S.A.* 32°39N 115°37W **307** N11
Mount Somers *N.Z.* 43°45S 171°27E **285** D6
Mount Sterling *Ill., U.S.A.* 39°59N 90°45W **310** E6
Mount Sterling *Ky., U.S.A.* 38°4N 83°56W **311** F13
Mount Sterling *Ohio, U.S.A.* 39°43N 83°16W **311** E13
Mount Surprise *Australia* 18°10S 144°17E **280** B3
Mount Union *U.S.A.* 40°23N 77°53W **312** F7
Mount Upton *U.S.A.* 42°26N 75°23W **313** D9
Mount Vernon *Ga., U.S.A.* 32°11N 82°36W **316** C7
Mount Vernon *Ill., U.S.A.* 38°19N 88°55W **310** F8
Mount Vernon *Ind., U.S.A.* 37°56N 87°54W **311** G9
Mount Vernon *Iowa, U.S.A.* 41°55N 91°23W **310** C5
Mount Vernon *N.Y., U.S.A.* 40°54N 73°49W **132** A3
Mount Vernon *Ohio, U.S.A.* 40°23N 82°29W **312** F2
Mount Vernon *Wash., U.S.A.* 48°25N 122°20W **306** B4
Mount Vernon Square *Washington, D.C., U.S.A.* **143** a2
Mount Victor *Australia* 32°11S 139°44E **282** B3
Mount Washington *U.S.A.* 39°5N 84°24W **311** F11
Mount Wellington *N.Z.* 36°55S 174°52E **284** C3
Mount William △ *Australia* 40°56S 148°14E **281** G4
Mount Wynne *St. Vincent* 13°14N 61°16W **323** n
Mount Zion = Har Tsiyon *Jerusalem* **123** b3
Mount Zion *U.S.A.* 39°46N 88°53W **311** E8
Mounta, Akra *Greece* 38°3N 20°47E **207** C2
Mountain □ *Phil.* 17°20N 121°10E **232** C3
Mountain Ash *U.K.* 51°40N 3°23W **169** F4
Mountain Center *U.S.A.* 33°42N 116°44W **307** M10
Mountain City *Nev., U.S.A.* 41°50N 115°58W **304** F6
Mountain City *Tenn., U.S.A.* 36°29N 81°48W **315** C14
Mountain Creek L. *U.S.A.* 32°43N 96°56W **120** B4
Mountain Creek Lake Park *U.S.A.* 32°41N 96°58W **120** B4
Mountain Dale *U.S.A.* 41°41N 74°32W **313** E10
Mountain Grove *U.S.A.* 37°8N 92°16W **308** G7
Mountain Home *Ark., U.S.A.* 36°20N 92°23W **314** C8
Mountain Home *Idaho, U.S.A.* 43°8N 115°41W **304** E6
Mountain Iron *U.S.A.* 47°32N 92°37W **308** B7
Mountain Pass *U.S.A.* 35°29N 115°35W **307** K11
Mountain View *Ark., U.S.A.* 35°52N 92°7W **314** D8
Mountain View *Calif., U.S.A.* 37°23N 122°5W **306** H4
Mountain View *Hawai'i, U.S.A.* 19°33N 155°7W **302** D6
Mountain Village *U.S.A.* 62°5N 163°43W **303** E7
Mountain Zebra △ *S. Africa* 32°14S 25°27E **270** D4
Mountainair *U.S.A.* 34°31N 106°15W **305** J10
Mountbellew *Ireland* 53°28N 8°31W **166** C3
Mountlake Terrace *U.S.A.* 47°47N 122°18W **306** C4
Mountmellick *Ireland* 53°7N 7°20W **166** C4
Mountrath *Ireland* 53°0N 7°28W **166** D4
Moura *Queens., Australia* 24°35S 149°58E **280** C4
Moura *Brazil* 1°32S 61°38W **329** D5
Moura *Portugal* 38°7N 7°30W **195** G3
Mourão *Portugal* 38°22N 7°22W **195** G3
Mourdi, Dépression du *Chad* 18°10N 23°0E **259** E4
Mourdiah *Mali* 14°35N 7°25W **262** C3
Mourenx *France* 43°22N 0°38W **174** E3
Mouri *Ghana* 5°6N 1°14W **263** D4
Mourilyan *Australia* 17°35S 146°3E **280** B4
Mourmelon-le-Grand *France* 49°8N 4°22E **173** C11
Mourne → *U.K.* 54°52N 7°26W **166** B4
Mourne Mts. *U.K.* 54°10N 6°0W **166** B5
Mournies *Greece* 35°29N 24°1E **207** E5
Mouscron *Belgium* 50°45N 3°12E **170** D3
Mousgougou *Chad* 10°47N 16°9E **259** F3
Moussa 'Ali *Djibouti* 12°27N 42°24E **267** B5
Moussoro *Chad* 13°41N 16°35E **259** F3
Moustique, Morne *Guadeloupe* 16°7N 61°44W **322** e
Mouthe *France* 46°44N 6°12E **173** F13
Moutier *Switz.* 47°16N 7°21E **179** H3
Moûtiers *France* 45°29N 6°32E **175** C10
Moutong *Indonesia* 0°28N 121°13E **231** D6
Mouy *France* 49°18N 2°20E **173** C9
Mouydir, Monts du *Algeria* 25°30N 4°10E **261** C5
Mouyondzi *Congo* 4°1S 13°59E **264** C2
Mouzaki *Greece* 39°25N 21°37E **204** B3
Mouzarak *Chad* 13°17N 15°58E **259** F3
Mouzon *France* 49°36N 5°3E **173** C12
Movas *Mexico* 28°10N 109°25W **318** B3
Moville *Ireland* 55°11N 7°3W **166** A4
Mowandjum *Australia* 17°22S 123°40E **278** C3
Moweaqua *U.S.A.* 39°38N 89°1W **310** E7
Moxico □ *Angola* 12°0S 20°30E **265** E4
Moxotó → *Brazil* 9°19S 38°14W **332** C4
Moy → *Ireland* 54°8N 9°8W **166** B2
Moya *Comoros Is.* 12°18S 44°18E **272** a
Moyale *Ethiopia* 3°34N 39°5E **266** D4
Moyale *Kenya* 3°30N 39°4E **268** B4
Moyamba *S. Leone* 8°4N 12°30W **262** D2
Moyen Atlas *Morocco* 33°0N 5°0W **260** B4
Moyen-Chari □ *Chad* 9°0N 18°0E **259** G3
Moyen-Ogooué □ *Gabon* 0°30S 11°0E **264** C2
Moyo *Indonesia* 8°10S 117°40E **235** D5
Moyobamba *Peru* 6°0S 77°0W **330** B2
Moyowosi ⌂ *Tanzania* 3°50S 31°0E **268** C3
Møysalen △ *Norway* 68°32N 15°29E **160** B16
Moyto *Chad* 12°35N 16°33E **259** F3
Moyu *China* 37°15N 79°44E **217** E9
Moyyero → *Russia* 68°44N 103°42E **215** C11
Moyynqum *Zhambyl, Kazakhstan* 44°17N 72°57E **217** D8
Moyynqum *Zhambyl, Kazakhstan* 44°12N 71°0E **217** D8
Moyynty *Kazakhstan* 47°10N 73°18E **217** C8
Mozambique = Moçambique *Mozam.* 15°3S 40°42E **269** F5
Mozambique ■ *Africa* 19°0S 35°0E **269** F4
Mozambique Basin *Ind. Oc.* 30°0S 40°0E **273** G2
Mozambique Chan. *Africa* 17°30S 42°30E **271** A7
Mozarthaus *Vienna, Austria* **142** b2
Mozdok *Russia* 43°45N 44°48E **191** J7
Mozdūrān *Iran* 36°9N 60°35E **247** B9
Mozhaysk *Russia* 55°30N 36°2E **188** E9
Mozhga *Russia* 56°26N 52°15E **190** B11
Mozhnābād *Iran* 34°7N 60°6E **247** C9
Mozirje *Slovenia* 46°22N 14°58E **199** B11
Mozyr = Mazyr *Belarus* 51°59N 29°15E **177** B15
Mpanda *Tanzania* 6°23S 31°1E **268** D3
Mpé *Congo* 2°58S 14°38E **264** C2
Mpese *Dem. Rep. of the Congo* 5°16S 15°30E **265** D3
Mpésoba *Mali* 12°31N 5°39W **262** C3
Mphoeng *Zimbabwe* 21°10S 27°51E **269** G2
Mpika *Zambia* 11°51S 31°25E **269** E3
Mpoko → *C.A.R.* 4°19N 18°33E **264** B3
Mpouya *Congo* 2°38S 16°13E **264** C3
Mpulungu *Zambia* 8°51S 31°5E **269** D3
Mpumalanga *S. Africa* 29°50S 30°33E **271** C5
Mpumalanga □ *S. Africa* 26°0S 30°0E **271** C5
Mpwapwa *Tanzania* 6°23S 36°30E **268** D4
Mqabba *Malta* 35°51N 14°28E **206** F7
Mqanduli *S. Africa* 31°49S 28°45E **271** D4
Mqinvartsveri = Kazbek *Russia* 42°42N 44°30E **191** J7
Mrągowo *Poland* 53°52N 21°18E **184** E8
M'ramani *Comoros Is.* 12°20S 44°31E **272** a
Mramor *Serbia* 43°20N 21°45E **202** C5
Mrauk-u = Myohaung *Burma* 20°35N 93°11E **241** E4
Mrimina *Morocco* 29°50N 7°9W **260** C3
Mrkonjić Grad *Bos.-H.* 44°26N 17°4E **182** F2
Mrkopalj *Croatia* 45°21N 14°52E **199** C11
Mrocza *Poland* 53°16N 17°35E **185** E4
Msaken *Tunisia* 35°49N 10°33E **258** A2
Msambansovu *Zimbabwe* 15°50S 30°3E **269** F3
Msida *Malta* 35°54N 14°29E **206** F7
M'sila *Algeria* 35°46N 4°30E **261** A5
M'sila □ *Algeria* 35°20N 4°20E **261** A5
Msoro *Zambia* 13°35S 31°50E **269** E3
Msta → *Russia* 58°25N 31°20E **188** C6
Mstislavl = Mstsislaw *Belarus* 54°0N 31°50E **177** A16
Mstsislaw *Belarus* 54°0N 31°50E **177** A16
Mszana Dolna *Poland* 49°41N 20°5E **185** J7
Mszczonów *Poland* 51°58N 20°33E **185** G7
Mtama *Tanzania* 10°17S 39°21E **269** E4
Mtamvuna = Mthamvuna → *S. Africa* 31°6S 30°12E **271** D5
Mthamvuna → *S. Africa* 31°6S 30°12E **271** D5
Mthatha *S. Africa* 31°36S 28°49E **271** D4
Mtilikwe → *Zimbabwe* 21°9S 31°30E **269** G3
Mtima *Congo* 3°49S 12°7E **264** C2
Mtirala △ *Georgia* 41°50N 42°2E **191** K6
Mtito Andei *Kenya* 2°41S 38°10E **268** C4
Mtsamboro *Mayotte* 12°42S 45°4E **272** b
Mtsamboro, Î. *Mayotte* 12°38S 45°2E **272** b
Mtsangamouji *Mayotte* 12°45S 45°5E **272** b
Mtsapéré *Mayotte* 12°46S 45°11E **272** b
Mtsensk *Russia* 53°17N 36°36E **188** F9
Mtskheta *Georgia* 41°52N 44°45E **191** K7
Mtubatuba *S. Africa* 28°30S 32°8E **271** C5
Mtwalume *S. Africa* 30°30S 30°38E **271** D5
Mtwara □ *Tanzania* 10°20S 39°0E **269** E4
Mtwara-Mikindani *Tanzania* 10°20S 40°20E **269** E5
Mu → *Burma* 21°56N 95°38E **241** E5
Mu Gia, Deo *Vietnam* 17°40N 105°47E **236** D5
Mu Ko Chang △ *Thailand* 11°59N 102°22E **237** G4
Mu Ko Surin *Thailand* 9°30N 97°55E **237** H1
Mu-se *Burma* 23°59N 97°54E **241** D6
Mu Us Shamo *China* 39°0N 109°0E **226** E5
Muacandala *Angola* 10°2S 19°40E **265** E3
Muan *S. Korea* 34°59N 126°28E **224** E3
Muaná *Brazil* 1°25S 49°15W **332** B2
Muanda *Dem. Rep. of the Congo* 6°0S 12°20E **265** D2
Muang Beng *Laos* 20°23N 101°46E **228** G3
Muang Chiang Rai = Chiang Rai *Thailand* 19°52N 99°50E **228** H2
Muang Et *Laos* 20°49N 104°1E **236** B5
Muang Hiam *Laos* 20°5N 103°22E **236** B4
Muang Hongsa *Laos* 19°43N 101°20E **236** C3
Muang Houn *Laos* 20°8N 101°23E **228** G3
Muang Kau *Laos* 15°6N 105°47E **236** E5
Muang Khao *Laos* 19°38N 103°32E **236** C4
Muang Khong *Laos* 14°7N 105°51E **236** E5
Muang Khoua *Laos* 21°5N 102°31E **228** G4
Muang Liap *Laos* 18°29N 101°40E **236** C3
Muang Mai *Thailand* 8°5N 98°21E **237** a
Muang May *Laos* 14°49N 106°56E **236** E6
Muang Na Mo *Laos* 21°3N 101°49E **228** G3
Muang Ngeun *Laos* 20°36N 101°3E **228** G3
Muang Ngoi *Laos* 20°43N 102°41E **228** G4
Muang Nong *Laos* 16°22N 106°30E **236** D6
Muang Ou Neua *Laos* 22°18N 101°48E **228** F3
Muang Ou Tay *Laos* 22°7N 101°48E **228** F3
Muang Pak Beng *Laos* 19°54N 101°8E **228** H3
Muang Phalane *Laos* 16°39N 105°34E **236** D5
Muang Phiang *Laos* 19°6N 101°32E **236** C3
Muang Phine *Laos* 16°32N 106°2E **236** D6
Muang Phonhong *Laos* 18°30N 102°25E **236** C4
Muang Saiapoun *Laos* 18°24N 101°31E **236** C3
Muang Sing *Laos* 21°11N 101°9E **228** G3
Muang Son *Laos* 20°27N 103°19E **236** B4
Muang Soui *Laos* 19°33N 102°52E **236** C4
Muang Va *Laos* 21°53N 102°19E **228** G4
Muang Va *Laos* 18°18N 101°20E **236** C3
Muang Xai *Laos* 20°42N 101°59E **228** G3
Muang Xamteu *Laos* 19°59N 104°38E **236** C5
Muangai *Angola* 12°32S 19°55E **265** E3
Muar *Malaysia* 2°3N 102°34E **237** L4
Muara Takus *Indonesia* 0°20N 100°39E **234** B2
Muaraaman *Indonesia* 3°7S 102°12E **234** C2
Muarabadak *Indonesia* 0°20S 117°26E **235** C5
Muarabeliti *Indonesia* 3°15S 103°1E **234** C2
Muarabungo *Indonesia* 1°28S 102°52E **234** C2
Muaradua *Indonesia* 4°31S 104°4E **234** C2
Muaraenim *Indonesia* 3°40S 103°50E **234** C2
Muarajambi *Indonesia* 1°28S 103°40E **234** C2
Muarajuloi *Indonesia* 0°12S 114°3E **235** C4
Muarakaman *Indonesia* 0°2S 116°45E **235** C5
Muararupit *Indonesia* 2°43S 102°54E **234** C2
Muarasabak *Indonesia* 1°7S 103°51E **234** C2
Muarasiberut *Indonesia* 1°35S 99°12E **234** C1
Muaratebo *Indonesia* 1°30S 102°26E **234** C2
Muaratembesi *Indonesia* 1°42S 103°8E **234** C2
Muarateweh *Indonesia* 0°58S 114°52E **235** C4
Muarawahau *Indonesia* 1°1N 116°52E **235** B5
Mubarakpur *India* 26°6N 83°18E **243** F10
Mubarraz = Al Mubarraz *Si. Arabia* 25°30N 49°40E **247** E6
Mubende *Uganda* 0°33N 31°22E **268** B3
Mubi *Nigeria* 10°18N 13°16E **262** C7
Mucaba, Sa. de *Angola* 7°12S 15°0E **265** D3
Mucajaí *Brazil* 3°57S 57°32W **329** D6
Mucajaí → *Brazil* 2°25N 60°52W **329** C5
Mucajaí, Serra do *Brazil* 2°23N 61°10W **329** C5
Mucari *Angola* 9°30S 16°54E **265** D3
Muchachos, Roque de los *Canary Is.* 28°44N 17°52W **153** e1
Mücheln *Germany* 51°17N 11°47E **178** D7
Muchinga □ *Zambia* 12°0S 31°30E **269** E3
Muchinga Mts. *Zambia* 11°30S 31°30E **269** E3
Muchkapskiy *Russia* 51°52N 42°28E **190** E6
Muchuan *China* 28°57N 103°55E **228** C4
Muck *U.K.* 56°50N 6°15W **167** E2
Muckadilla *Australia* 26°35S 148°23E **281** D4
Muckalee Cr. → *U.S.A.* 31°38N 84°9W **316** D5
Muckaty ✪ *Australia* 18°37S 133°52E **280** B1
Muckle Flugga *U.K.* 60°51N 0°54W **167** A8
Muco → *Colombia* 4°15N 70°21W **328** C3
Mucoma *Angola* 15°18S 13°39E **265** F2
Muconda *Angola* 10°31S 21°15E **265** E4
Mucope *Angola* 16°24S 14°52E **265** F2
Mucugê *Brazil* 13°0S 41°23W **333** D3
Mucuim → *Brazil* 6°33S 64°18W **331** B5
Mucur *Turkey* 39°3N 34°22E **212** C4
Mucura *Brazil* 2°31S 62°43W **329** D5
Mucuri *Brazil* 18°0S 39°36W **333** E4
Mucurici *Brazil* 18°6S 40°31W **333** E3
Mucusso *Angola* 18°1S 21°25E **265** F4
Mucusso ⌂ *Angola* 17°27S 21°0E **265** F4
Mucussueje *Angola* 11°1S 21°56E **265** E4
Muda *Canary Is.* 28°34N 13°57W **153** e2
Mudanjiang *China* 44°38N 129°30E **227** B15
Mudanya *Turkey* 40°25N 28°50E **203** F12
Muddebihal *India* 16°20N 76°8E **245** F3
Muddus ⌂ *Sweden* 66°58N 20°15E **160** C19
Muddy Cr. → *U.S.A.* 38°24N 110°42W **304** G8
Mudeungsan *S. Korea* 35°7N 126°59E **224** E3
Mudgee *Australia* 32°32S 149°31E **283** B8
Mudhol *Karnataka, India* 16°21N 75°17E **245** F2
Mudhol *Telangana, India* 18°58N 77°55E **244** E3
Mudiata *Dem. Rep. of the Congo* 7°15S 22°1E **265** D4
Mudigere *India* 13°8N 75°38E **245** H2
Mūdiyah *Yemen* 13°56N 46°57E **248** D4
Mudjatik → *Canada* 56°1N 107°36W **297** B7
Mudu □ *Somalia* 7°0N 48°0E **267** C6
Mudukulattur *India* 9°21N 78°31E **245** K4
Mudumu △ *Namibia* 18°5S 23°29E **270** A3
Mudurnu *Turkey* 40°27N 31°12E **212** B4
Muecate *Mozam.* 14°55S 39°40E **269** E4
Mueda *Mozam.* 11°36S 39°28E **269** E4
Mueller Ranges *Australia* 18°18S 126°46E **278** C4
Muende *Mozam.* 14°28S 33°0E **269** E3
Muerto, Mar *Mexico* 16°10N 94°10W **319** D6
Mufu Shan *China* 29°20N 114°30E **229** C10
Mufulira *Zambia* 12°32S 28°15E **269** E2
Mufuma *Angola* 9°12S 16°29E **265** D3
Mufumbiro Range *Africa* 1°25S 29°30E **268** C2
Mugardos *Spain* 43°27N 8°15W **194** B2
Muge → *Portugal* 39°8N 8°44W **195** F2
Müggelberge *Germany* 52°25N 13°37E **115** B4
Müggelheim *Germany* 52°24N 13°40E **115** B5
Múggia *Italy* 45°36N 13°46E **199** C10
Muggiò *Italy* 45°35N 9°13E **128** A2
Mughal Gardens *Delhi, India* **120** c1
Mughal Sarai *India* 25°18N 83°7E **243** G10
Mughalzhar Taūy *Kazakhstan* 49°0N 58°40E **216** C5
Mughayrā' *Si. Arabia* 29°17N 37°41E **246** D3
Mugi *Japan* 33°40N 134°25E **222** D6
Mugia = Muxía *Spain* 43°3N 9°10W **194** B1
Mugila, Mts. *Dem. Rep. of the Congo* 7°0S 28°50E **268** D2
Muginga *Angola* 8°21S 17°36E **265** D3
Muğla *Turkey* 37°15N 28°22E **205** D10
Muğla □ *Turkey* 37°15N 28°20E **205** D10
Muglad *Sudan* 11°1N 27°50E **257** E2
Mŭglizh *Bulgaria* 42°37N 25°32E **203** D9
Mugodzhary = Mughalzhar Taūy *Kazakhstan* 49°0N 58°40E **216** C5
Mugu *Nepal* 29°45N 82°30E **243** E10
Mugu Karnali → *Nepal* 29°38N 81°51E **243** E9
Muhagiriya *Sudan* 12°0N 25°38E **259** F5
Muhala *Dem. Rep. of the Congo* 5°40S 28°43E **268** D2
Muhammad, Râs *Egypt* 27°44N 34°16E **251** L5
Muhammad Qol *Sudan* 20°53N 37°9E **256** C4
Muhammadabad *India* 26°4N 83°25E **243** F10
Muḩāyil *Si. Arabia* 18°33N 42°3E **248** C3
Muḩayriqah *Si. Arabia* 23°59N 45°4E **248** B4
Muhesi → *Tanzania* 7°0S 35°20E **268** D4
Mühlacker *Germany* 48°57N 8°51E **179** G4
Mühldorf *Germany* 48°14N 12°32E **179** G8
Mühleiten *Austria* 48°10N 16°33E **142** A3
Mühlenfliess → *Germany* 52°32N 13°42E **115** A5
Mühlhausen = Milevsko *Czechia* 49°27N 14°21E **180** B7
Mühlhausen *Germany* 51°12N 10°27E **178** D6
Mühlig Hofmann fjell *Antarctica* 72°30S 5°0E **151** D3
Mühlviertel *Austria* 48°30N 14°10E **180** C7
Muhoro *Kenya* 1°1S 34°7E **266** E3
Muhos *Finland* 64°47N 25°59E **160** D21
Muḩradah *Syria* 35°15N 36°35E **250** C7
Muhu *Estonia* 58°36N 23°11E **188** C2
Muhutwe *Tanzania* 1°35S 31°45E **268** C3
Mui Wo *Hong Kong, China* 22°16N 114°0E **122** B1
Muiden *Neths.* 52°20N 5°4E **112** A3
Muie *Angola* 14°23S 20°25E **265** E4
Muileann gCearr, An = Mullingar *Ireland* 53°31N 7°21W **166** C4
Muine Bheag = Bagenalstown *Ireland* 52°42N 6°58W **166** D5
Muineachán = Monaghan *Ireland* 54°15N 6°57W **166** B5
Muir, L. *Australia* 34°30S 116°40E **279** F2
Muir of Ord *U.K.* 57°32N 4°28W **167** D4
Muisné *Ecuador* 0°36N 80°2W **328** C1
Muizenberg *S. Africa* 34°5S 18°27E **118** B1
Mujahidpur *India* 28°33N 77°14E **120** B2
Mujeres, I. *Mexico* 21°13N 86°43W **320** B2
Mujui dos Campos *Brazil* 2°35S 54°41W **329** D7
Muka, Tanjung *Malaysia* 5°28N 100°11E **237** c
Mukacheve *Ukraine* 48°27N 22°45E **182** B7
Mukachevo = Mukacheve *Ukraine* 48°27N 22°45E **182** B7
Mukah *Malaysia* 2°55N 112°5E **235** B4
Mukandpur *India* 28°44N 77°11E **120** A2
Mukandwara *India* 24°49N 75°59E **242** G6
Mukawa *Papua N. G.* 9°38S 149°59E **286** E5
Mukawwa, Geziret *Egypt* 23°55N 35°53E **256** C4
Mukawwar *Sudan* 20°50N 37°17E **256** C4
Mukaylah *Si. Arabia* 19°16N 41°48E **248** C3
Mukdahan *Thailand* 16°32N 104°43E **236** D5
Mukdahan △ *Thailand* 16°26N 104°45E **236** D5
Mukden = Shenyang *China* 41°48N 123°27E **224** B1
Mukerian *India* 31°57N 75°37E **242** D6
Mukhavyets → *Belarus* 52°5N 23°39E **185** F10
Mukher *India* 18°42N 77°22E **244** E3
Mukhmas *West Bank* 31°52N 35°17E **123** A2
Mukhtolovo *Russia* 55°29N 43°15E **190** C6
Mukhtuya = Lensk *Russia* 60°48N 114°55E **215** C12
Mukinbudin *Australia* 30°55S 118°5E **279** F2
Mukishi *Kasai-Occ., Dem. Rep. of the Congo* 5°39S 21°3E **265** D4
Mukishi *Katanga, Dem. Rep. of the Congo* 8°30S 24°44E **265** D4
Muko *Japan* 34°55N 135°40E **223** C7
Muko → *Japan* 34°48N 135°22E **133** A1
Muko Phetra △ *Thailand* 6°57N 99°33E **237** J2
Mukojima *Japan* 35°43N 139°49E **140** A3
Mukomuko *Indonesia* 2°30S 101°10E **234** C2
Mukomwenze *Dem. Rep. of the Congo* 6°49S 27°15E **268** D2
Mukono *Uganda* 0°21N 32°45E **268** B3
Muktinath *Nepal* 28°49N 83°53E **243** E10
Muktsar *India* 30°30N 74°30E **242** D6
Mukur = Moqor *Afghan.* 32°50N 67°42E **242** C2
Mukutuwa → *Canada* 53°10N 97°24W **297** C9
Mukwela *Zambia* 17°0S 26°40E **269** F2
Mukwonago *U.S.A.* 42°52N 88°20W **311** B8
Mul *India* 20°4N 79°40E **244** D4
Mula *Spain* 38°3N 1°33W **197** G3
Mula → *India* 18°34N 74°21E **244** E2
Mula → *Pakistan* 27°57N 67°36E **242** F2
Mulaku Atoll *Maldives* 3°0N 73°30E **272** d
Mulamba *Dem. Rep. of the Congo* 6°21S 21°13E **265** D4
Mulanay *Phil.* 13°31N 122°24E **232** E4
Mulange *Dem. Rep. of the Congo* 3°40S 27°10E **268** C2
Mulanje, Mt. *Malawi* 16°2S 35°33E **269** F4
Mulâtre, Pte. *Dominica* 15°17N 61°15W **323** k
Mulatupo Sasardi *Panama* 8°57N 77°45W **328** B2
Mulbagal *India* 13°10N 78°24E **245** H4
Mulbarton *S. Africa* 26°17S 28°3E **123** B2
Mulberry *U.S.A.* 27°54N 81°59W **317** H8
Mulberry Grove *U.S.A.* 38°56N 89°16W **310** F7
Mulchatna → *U.S.A.* 59°40N 157°7W **303** G8
Mulchén *Chile* 37°45S 72°20W **334** D1
Mulde → *Germany* 51°53N 12°15E **178** D8
Muldraugh *U.S.A.* 37°56N 85°59W **311** G11
Mule Creek Junction *U.S.A.* 43°23N 104°13W **304** E11
Muleba *Tanzania* 1°50S 31°37E **268** C3
Mulegé *Mexico* 26°53N 111°59W **318** B2
Muleshoe *U.S.A.* 34°13N 102°43W **314** D3
Muletta, Gara *Ethiopia* 9°15N 41°44E **257** F5
Mulgrave *Canada* 45°38N 61°31W **299** C7
Mulgrave I. = Badu *Australia* 10°7S 142°11E **280** a
Mulhacén *Spain* 37°4N 3°20W **195** H7
Mülheim *Germany* 51°25N 6°54E **178** D2
Mulhouse *France* 47°40N 7°20E **173** E14
Muli *Sichuan, China* 27°52N 101°8E **228** D3
Muli *Maldives* 2°55N 73°34E **272** d
Mulifanua *Samoa* 13°50S 171°59W **287** V20
Muling *China* 44°35N 130°10E **227** B16
Mulki *India* 13°6N 74°48E **245** H2
Mull *U.K.* 56°25N 5°56W **167** E3
Mull, Sound of *U.K.* 56°30N 5°50W **167** E3
Mullach Íde = Malahide *Ireland* 53°26N 6°9W **166** C5
Mullaittivu *Sri Lanka* 9°15N 80°49E **245** K5
Mullen *U.S.A.* 42°3N 101°1W **308** D3
Mullengudgery *Australia* 31°43S 147°23E **281** B4
Mullens *U.S.A.* 37°35N 81°23W **309** G13
Muller, Pegunungan *Indonesia* 0°30N 113°30E **235** B4
Muller Ra. *Papua N. G.* 5°35S 142°20E **286** C2
Mullet Pen. *Ireland* 54°13N 10°2W **166** B1
Mulletbaai *St.-Maarten* 18°4N 63°7W **322** a
Mullewa *Australia* 28°29S 115°30E **279** E2
Müllheim *Germany* 47°47N 7°36E **179** H3
Mulligan → *Australia* 25°0S 139°0E **280** D2
Mullingar *Ireland* 53°31N 7°21W **166** C4
Mullins *U.S.A.* 34°12N 79°15W **315** D15
Mullsjö *Sweden* 57°56N 13°55E **163** G7
Mullumbimby *Australia* 28°30S 153°30E **281** D5
Mulobezi *Zambia* 16°45S 25°7E **269** F2
Mulondo *Angola* 15°41S 15°12E **265** F3
Mulonga Plain *Zambia* 16°20S 22°40E **265** F4
Mulroy B. *Ireland* 55°15N 7°46W **166** A4
Mulshi L. *India* 18°30N 73°48E **244** E1
Multai *India* 21°50N 78°21E **244** D4
Multan *Pakistan* 30°15N 71°36E **242** D4
Mulu, Gunung *Malaysia* 4°3N 114°56E **235** B4
Mulug *India* 18°11N 79°57E **244** E4
Mulumbe, Mts. *Dem. Rep. of the Congo* 8°40S 27°30E **269** D2
Mulundu *Dem. Rep. of the Congo* 6°40S 20°33E **265** D4
Mulungushi Dam *Zambia* 14°48S 28°48E **269** E2
Mulurulu L. *Australia* 33°15S 143°20E **282** B5
Mulvane *U.S.A.* 37°29N 97°15W **308** G5
Mulwad *Sudan* 18°45N 30°39E **256** D3
Mulwala *Australia* 35°59S 146°0E **283** C7
Mulwala, L. *Australia* 35°59S 146°1E **281** C4
Muma *Dem. Rep. of the Congo* 3°25N 23°21E **264** B4
Mumbai *India* 18°58N 72°50E **130** B2
Mumbai Chhatrapati Shivaji Int. ✕ **(BOM)** *India* 19°5N 72°51E **130** A2
Mumbai Harbour *India* 18°58N 72°55E **130** B2
Mumbeji *Zambia* 13°51S 23°39E **265** E4
Mumbondo *Angola* 10°9S 14°15E **265** E2
Mumbwa *Zambia* 15°0S 27°0E **269** F2
Mumeng *Papua N. G.* 7°1S 146°37E **286** D4
Mumias *Kenya* 0°20N 34°29E **268** C4
Mummel Gulf △ *Australia* 31°17S 151°51E **283** A9
Mumra *Russia* 45°45N 47°41E **191** H8
Mun → *Thailand* 15°19N 105°30E **236** E5
Mun-gyeong *S. Korea* 36°35N 128°12E **224** D4
Muna *Indonesia* 5°0S 122°30E **231** F6
Munabao *India* 25°45N 70°17E **242** G4
Munakata *Japan* 33°48N 130°38E **222** D2
Munamagi *Estonia* 57°43N 27°4E **188** D4
Munaung *Burma* 18°45N 93°40E **241** F4
Munaung I. = Cheduba I. *Burma* 18°45N 93°40E **241** F4
Muncan *Indonesia* 8°34S 115°11E **231** K18
Muncar *Indonesia* 8°26S 114°20E **231** J17
Munch-museum *Norway* 59°55N 10°46E **133** A3
Münchberg *Germany* 50°11N 11°47E **179** E7
Müncheberg *Germany* 52°30N 14°9E **178** C10
Münchehofe *Germany* 52°29N 13°40E **115** B5
München *Germany* 48°8N 11°34E **131** B2
München Franz Josef Strauss ✕ **(MUC)** *Germany* 48°21N 11°47E **131** A2
Munchen-Gladbach = Mönchengladbach *Germany* 51°11N 6°27E **178** D2
Munchique △ *Colombia* 2°44N 77°1W **328** C2
Muncho Lake *Canada* 59°0N 125°50W **296** B3
Munch'ŏn *N. Korea* 39°14N 127°19E **224** C3
Muncie *U.S.A.* 40°12N 85°23W **311** D11
Muncoonie L. West *Australia* 25°12S 138°40E **280** D2
Munda *Solomon Is.* 8°20S 157°16E **287** M9
Mundabbera *Australia* 25°36S 151°18E **281** D5
Mundakayam *India* 9°30N 76°50E **245** K3
Mundal *Sri Lanka* 7°48N 79°48E **245** L4
Munday *U.S.A.* 33°27N 99°38W **314** E5
Mundelein *U.S.A.* 42°16N 88°0W **311** B8
Mundemba *Cameroon* 4°57N 8°52E **264** B1
Münden *Germany* 51°25N 9°38E **178** D5
Münden ⌂ *Germany* 51°28N 9°42E **178** D5
Mundiwindi *Australia* 23°47S 120°9E **278** D3
Mundo → *Spain* 38°30N 2°15W **197** G2
Mundo Novo *Brazil* 11°50S 40°29W **333** D3
Mundo Nuevo *Trin. & Tob.* 10°28N 61°15W **323** t
Mundra *India* 22°54N 69°48E **242** H3
Mundrabilla *Australia* 31°52S 127°51E **279** F4
Munenga *Angola* 10°2S 14°56E **265** E2
Munera *Spain* 39°2N 2°29W **197** F2
Muneru → *India* 16°45N 80°3E **244** F5
Mungallala *Australia* 26°28S 147°34E **281** D4
Mungallala Cr. → *Australia* 28°53S 147°5E **281** D4
Mungana *Australia* 17°8S 144°27E **280** B3
Mungaoli *India* 24°24N 78°7E **242** G8
Mungari *Mozam.* 17°12S 33°30E **269** F3
Mungbere *Dem. Rep. of the Congo* 2°36N 28°28E **268** B2
Mungeli *India* 22°4N 81°41E **243** H9
Munger *India* 25°23N 86°30E **243** G12
Mungerannie *Australia* 28°1S 138°39E **281** A2
Mungilli ✪ *Australia* 25°14S 124°17E **279** E3
Mungkan Kandju △ *Australia* 13°35S 142°52E **280** A3
Mungkarta ✪ *Australia* 20°22S 134°2E **280** C1
Mungo *Angola* 11°49S 16°16E **265** E3
Mungo, L. *Australia* 33°45S 143°0E **282** B5
Mungo △ *Australia* 33°44S 143°6E **282** B5
Munhango *Angola* 12°10S 18°38E **265** E3
Munhango → *Angola* 11°17S 19°44E **265** E3
Munich = München *Germany* 48°8N 11°34E **131** B2
Munising *U.S.A.* 46°25N 86°40W **308** B10
Munka-Ljungby *Sweden* 56°16N 12°58E **163** H6
Munkebo *Denmark* 55°27N 10°34E **163** J4
Munkedal *Sweden* 58°28N 11°40E **163** F5
Munkfors *Sweden* 59°47N 13°30E **162** E7
Munkkiniemi *Finland* 60°11N 24°52E **121** B2
Munku-Sardyk *Russia* 51°45N 100°20E **215** D11
Münnerstadt *Germany* 50°14N 10°12E **179** E6
Munnsville *U.S.A.* 42°58N 75°35W **313** D9
Munoz *Phil.* 15°43N 120°54E **232** D3
Muñoz Gamero, Pen. *Chile* 52°30S 73°5W **336** D2
Munro *Argentina* 34°31S 58°31W **117** B1
Munroe L. *Canada* 59°13N 98°35W **297** B9
Munsan *S. Korea* 37°51N 126°48E **224** D3
Munshiganj *Bangla.* 23°33N 90°32E **241** D3
Munson *U.S.A.* 30°52N 86°52W **317** E3
Münster *Haut-Rhin, France* 48°2N 7°8E **173** D14
Münster *Niedersachsen, Germany* 52°58N 10°5E **178** C6
Münster *Nordrhein-Westfalen, Germany* 51°58N 7°37E **178** D3
Munster □ *Ireland* 52°18N 8°44W **166** D3
Münsterberg = Ziębice *Poland* 50°37N 17°2E **185** H4
Muntadgin *Australia* 31°45S 118°33E **279** F2
Muntele Mare, Vf. *Romania* 46°30N 23°12E **183** D8
Muntinlupa *Phil.* 14°27N 121°2E **127** C2
Muntok *Indonesia* 2°5S 105°10E **234** C3
Munzur Dağları *Turkey* 39°30N 39°10E **213** C8
Muong Nhie *Vietnam* 22°12N 102°28E **228** F4
Muong Sen *Vietnam* 19°24N 104°8E **236** C5
Muong Te *Vietnam* 22°24N 102°49E **228** F4
Muong Xia *Vietnam* 20°19N 104°50E **236** B5
Muonio *Finland* 67°57N 23°40E **160** C20
Muonio älv = Muonionjoki → *Finland* 67°11N 23°34E **160** C20
Muonioälven = Muonionjoki → *Finland* 67°11N 23°34E **160** C20
Muonionjoki → *Finland* 67°11N 23°34E **160** C20
Mupa *Angola* 16°5S 15°50E **265** F3
Mupa → *Mozam.* 18°58S 35°54E **269** F4
Mupa △ *Angola* 15°55S 15°35E **265** F3
Muping *China* 37°22N 121°36E **227** F11
Mupoi *South Sudan* 5°28N 27°40E **257** F2
Muqaddam, Wadi → *Sudan* 18°4N 31°30E **256** D3
Muqaybirah *Yemen* 13°20N 46°5E **248** D4
Muqdisho *Somalia* 2°2N 45°25E **267** D6
Muqshin *Oman* 19°35N 54°55E **249** C6
Muqshin, W. → *Oman* 19°44N 55°14E **249** C6
Muquequete *Angola* 14°50S 14°16E **265** E2
Mur → *Austria* 47°18N 16°52E **181** E9
Mûr-de-Bretagne *France* 48°12N 3°0W **172** D4
Muradiye *Manisa, Turkey* 38°39N 27°21E **205** C9
Muradiye *Van, Turkey* 39°0N 43°44E **213** C10
Murai Res. *Singapore* 1°23N 103°40E **138** A2
Murakami *Japan* 38°14N 139°29E **220** E9
Muralag = Prince of Wales I. *Australia* 10°40S 142°10E **280** a
Murallón, Cerro *Chile* 49°48S 73°30W **336** C2
Muranda *Rwanda* 1°52S 29°20E **268** C2
Murang'a *Kenya* 0°45S 37°9E **268** C4
Murano *Venice, Italy* **142** a4
Muranów *Poland* 52°14N 20°58E **143** B1
Murashi *Russia* 59°30N 49°0E **186** C8
Murat *France* 45°7N 2°53E **174** C6
Murat → *Turkey* 38°46N 40°0E **213** C9
Murat Bay = Ceduna *Australia* 32°7S 133°46E **281** E1
Murat Dağı *Turkey* 38°55N 29°43E **205** C11
Muratlı *Turkey* 41°10N 27°29E **203** E11
Murato *France* 42°35N 9°20E **175** F13
Murau *Austria* 47°6N 14°10E **180** D7
Muravera *Italy* 39°25N 9°34E **200** C2
Muravyevo = Mažeikiai *Lithuania* 56°20N 22°20E **184** B9
Muravyovsky = Korsakov *Russia* 46°36N 142°42E **215** E15
Murayama *Japan* 38°30N 140°25E **220** E10
Murça *Portugal* 41°24N 7°28W **194** D3
Murcaayo *Somalia* 11°41N 50°34E **267** B7
Murchison *N.Z.* 41°49S 172°21E **285** B7
Murchison → *Australia* 27°45S 114°0E **279** E1
Murchison, Mt. *Antarctica* 73°25S 166°20E **151** D11
Murchison, Mt. *N.Z.* 43°0S 171°22E **285** D6
Murchison Falls *Uganda* 2°15N 31°30E **268** B3
Murchison Falls △ *Uganda* 2°17N 31°48E **268** B3
Murchison Mts. *N.Z.* 45°13S 167°23E **285** F2
Murchison Ra. *Australia* 20°0S 134°10E **280** C1
Murchison Rapids *Malawi* 15°55S 34°35E **269** F3
Murchison Roadhouse *Australia* 27°39S 116°14E **279** E2
Murcia *Spain* 38°5N 1°10W **197** G3
Murcia □ *Spain* 37°50N 1°30W **197** H3
Murdo *U.S.A.* 43°53N 100°43W **308** D3
Murdoch Pt. *Australia* 14°37S 144°55E **280** A3
Mürefte *Turkey* 40°40N 27°14E **203** F11
Mureş □ *Romania* 46°45N 24°40E **183** D9
Mureş → *Romania* 46°15N 20°13E **182** D5
Mureşul = Mureş → *Romania* 46°15N 20°13E **182** D5
Muret *France* 43°30N 1°20E **174** E5
Murewa *Zimbabwe* 17°39S 31°47E **271** A5
Murfreesboro *N.C., U.S.A.* 36°27N 77°6W **315** C16
Murfreesboro *Tenn., U.S.A.* 35°51N 86°24W **315** D11
Murgap *Tajikistan* 38°10N 74°2E **217** E8
Murgap → *Turkmenistan* 38°18N 61°12E **247** B9
Murgenella *Australia* 11°34S 132°56E **278** B5
Murgeni *Romania* 46°12N 28°1E **183** D13
Murgha Kibzai *Pakistan* 30°44N 69°25E **242** D3
Murghob = Murgap *Tajikistan* 38°10N 74°2E **217** E8
Murgon *Australia* 26°15S 151°54E **281** D5
Muri *Cook Is.* 21°15S 159°43W **289** h
Muri *India* 23°22N 85°52E **243** H11
Muria *Indonesia* 6°36S 110°53E **235** D4
Muriaé *Brazil* 21°8S 42°23W **333** F3
Murias de Paredes *Spain* 42°52N 6°11W **194** C4
Murici *Brazil* 9°19S 35°56W **332** C4
Muriége *Angola* 9°58S 21°11E **265** D4
Muriel Mine *Zimbabwe* 17°14S 30°40E **269** F3
Murilo *Micronesia* 8°40N 152°11E **290** G7
Müritz *Germany* 53°25N 12°42E **178** B8
Müritz △ *Germany* 53°22N 12°52E **178** B8
Muriwai Beach *N.Z.* 36°50S 174°26E **284** C3
Murkong Selek *India* 27°44N 95°18E **241** B5
Murliganj *India* 25°54N 86°59E **243** G12
Murmansk *Russia* 68°57N 33°10E **160** B25
Murmashi *Russia* 68°47N 32°42E **160** B25
Murnau *Germany* 47°40N 11°12E **179** H7
Muro *Haute-Corse, France* 42°34N 8°54E **175** F12
Muro *Spain* 39°44N 3°3E **206** B4
Muro, C. di *France* 41°44N 8°37E **175** G12
Muro de Alcoy *Spain* 38°46N 0°26W **197** G4
Muro Lucano *Italy* 40°45N 15°29E **201** B8
Murom *Russia* 55°35N 42°3E **190** C6
Muroran *Japan* 42°25N 141°0E **220** C10
Muros *Spain* 42°45N 9°5W **194** C1
Muros e Noya, Ría de → *Spain* 42°45N 9°0W **194** C1
Muroto *Japan* 33°18N 134°9E **222** D6
Muroto-Misaki *Japan* 33°15N 134°10E **222** D6
Murovani Kurylivtsi *Ukraine* 48°44N 27°31E **183** B12
Murowana Goślina *Poland* 52°35N 17°0E **185** F3
Murphy *U.S.A.* 43°13N 116°33W **304** E5
Murphys *U.S.A.* 38°8N 120°28W **306** G6
Murphy's Station = Sunnyvale *U.S.A.* 37°23N 122°2W **306** H4
Murphysboro *U.S.A.* 37°46N 89°20W **310** G7
Murrat *Sudan* 18°51N 29°33E **256** D2
Murrat Wells *Sudan* 21°3N 32°55E **256** C3
Murray *Queens., Australia* 9°56S 144°2E **280** a
Murray *Iowa, U.S.A.* 41°3N 93°57W **310** C3
Murray *Ky., U.S.A.* 36°37N 88°19W **308** G9
Murray *Utah, U.S.A.* 40°40N 111°53W **304** F8
Murray → *Australia* 35°20S 139°22E **282** C3
Murray, L. *Papua N. G.* 7°0S 141°35E **286** D1
Murray, L. *S.C., U.S.A.* 34°3N 81°13W **316** A8
Murray Bridge *Australia* 35°6S 139°14E **282** C3
Murray Fracture Zone *Pac. Oc.* 35°0N 130°0W **289** D14
Murray Harbour *Canada* 46°0N 62°28W **299** C7
Murray River △ *Australia* 34°23S 140°32E **281** E3
Murray-Sunset △ *Australia* 34°45S 141°30E **282** C4
Murrayfield *U.K.* 55°57N 3°15W **121** B2
Murraysburg *S. Africa* 31°58S 23°47E **270** D3
Murrayville *U.S.A.* 39°35N 90°15W **310** E6
Murree *Pakistan* 33°56N 73°28E **242** C5
Murrieta *U.S.A.* 33°33N 117°13W **307** M9
Murro di Porco, Capo *Italy* 37°0N 15°20E **201** F8
Murrumbateman *Australia* 34°58S 149°0E **283** C8
Murrumbidgee → *Australia* 34°43S 143°12E **282** C5
Murrumburrah *Australia* 34°32S 148°22E **283** C8
Murrurundi *Australia* 31°42S 150°51E **283** A9
Murshid *Sudan* 21°40N 31°10E **256** C3
Murshidabad *India* 24°11N 88°19E **243** G13
Murska Sobota *Slovenia* 46°39N 16°12E **199** B13
Murtala Mohammed Int. ✕ **(LOS)** *Nigeria* 6°34N 3°19E **124** A1
Murtazapur *India* 20°40N 77°25E **244** D3
Murtle L. *Canada* 52°8N 119°38W **296** C5
Murtoa *Australia* 36°35S 142°28E **282** D5
Murtosa *Portugal* 40°44N 8°40W **194** E2
Muru → *Brazil* 8°9S 70°45W **330** B3
Murud *India* 18°19N 72°58E **244** E1
Murung → *Indonesia* 0°12N 114°3E **235** B4
Murungu *Tanzania* 4°12S 31°10E **268** C3
Murupara *N.Z.* 38°28S 176°42E **284** E5
Mururoa *French Polynesia* 21°52S 138°55W **289** f
Murwara *India* 23°46N 80°28E **243** H9
Murwillumbah *Australia* 28°18S 153°27E **281** D5
Mürz → *Austria* 47°30N 15°25E **180** D8
Murzūq *Libya* 25°53N 13°57E **258** C2
Murzūq □ *Libya* 25°0N 16°0E **258** D3
Murzūq, Idehān *Libya* 24°50N 13°51E **258** D2
Mürzzuschlag *Austria* 47°36N 15°41E **180** D8
Mus *India* 9°14N 92°47E **245** K11
Muş *Turkey* 38°45N 41°30E **213** C9
Muş □ *Turkey* 38°45N 41°30E **213** C9
Musa *Dem. Rep. of the Congo* 2°40N 19°18E **264** B3
Musa → *Papua N. G.* 9°3S 148°55E **286** E5
Mûsa, Gebel *Egypt* 28°33N 33°59E **251** K4
Musa Khel *Pakistan* 30°59N 69°52E **242** D3
Mūsá Qal'eh *Afghan.* 32°20N 64°50E **240** B2
Musabeyli *Turkey* 36°53N 36°55E **250** B7
Musadi *Dem. Rep. of the Congo* 2°31S 22°50E **264** C4
Musafirkhana *India* 26°22N 81°48E **243** F9
Musala *Bulgaria* 42°13N 23°37E **202** D7
Musala *Indonesia* 1°41N 98°28E **234** B1
Musan *N. Korea* 42°12N 129°12E **224** A4
Musandam □ *Oman* 26°0N 56°20E **249** A7
Musandam, Ra's *Oman* 26°20N 56°20E **249** A7
Musangu *Dem. Rep. of the Congo* 10°28S 23°55E **265** E4
Musasa *Tanzania* 3°25S 31°30E **268** C3
Musashino *Japan* 35°42N 139°33E **140** A2
Musaymīr *Yemen* 13°27N 44°37E **248** D4
Muscat = Masqat *Oman* 23°37N 58°36E **249** B7
Muscat & Oman = Oman ■ *Asia* 23°0N 58°0E **249** B7
Muscatatuck → *U.S.A.* 38°46N 86°10W **311** F10
Muscatine *U.S.A.* 41°25N 91°3W **310** C5
Muschu I. *Papua N. G.* 3°25S 143°35E **286** B2
Muscle Shoals *U.S.A.* 34°45N 87°40W **315** D11
Muscoda *U.S.A.* 43°11N 90°27W **310** A6
Musengezi = Unsengedsi → *Zimbabwe* 15°43S 31°14E **269** F3
Museumquartier *Vienna, Austria* **142** c1
Museumsinsel *Germany* 52°30N 13°25E **115** A3
Musgrave Harbour *Canada* 49°27N 53°58W **299** C9
Musgrave Ranges *Australia* 26°0S 132°0E **279** E5
Mushie *Dem. Rep. of the Congo* 2°56S 16°55E **264** C3
Mushima *Zambia* 14°10S 24°56E **265** E4
Mushin *Nigeria* 6°31N 3°21E **124** A2
Musi → *India* 16°41N 79°40E **244** F4
Musi → *Indonesia* 2°20S 104°56E **234** C2
Musiektheater *Amsterdam, Neths.* **112** b3
Musina *S. Africa* 22°20S 30°5E **271** B5
Musiri *India* 10°56N 78°27E **245** J4
Muskauer Park *Europe* 51°34N 14°43E **178** D10
Muskeg → *Canada* 60°20N 123°20W **296** A4
Muskego *U.S.A.* 42°55N 88°8W **311** B8
Muskegon *U.S.A.* 43°14N 86°16W **311** A10
Muskegon → *U.S.A.* 43°14N 86°21W **308** D10
Muskegon Heights *U.S.A.* 43°12N 86°16W **311** A10
Muskogee *U.S.A.* 35°45N 95°22W **314** D7
Muskoka, L. *Canada* 45°0N 79°25W **312** B5
Muskoka Falls *Canada* 44°59N 79°17W **312** B5
Muskwa → *Canada* 58°47N 122°48W **296** B4
Muslim Mindanao = Bangsamoro □ *Phil.* 8°0N 123°0E **233** H3
Muslim Quarter *Jerusalem* **123** a3
Muslimiyah *Syria* 36°19N 37°12E **246** B3
Musmar *Sudan* 18°13N 35°40E **256** D4
Musocco *Italy* 45°29N 9°8E **128** B1
Musofu *Zambia* 13°30S 29°0E **269** E2
Musoma *Tanzania* 1°30S 33°48E **268** C3
Musquaro, L. *Canada* 50°38N 61°5W **299** B7
Musquodoboit Harbour *Canada* 44°50N 63°9W **299** D7
Mussau I. *Papua N. G.* 1°30S 149°40E **286** A5
Musselburgh *U.K.* 55°57N 3°2W **167** F5
Musselshell → *U.S.A.* 47°21N 107°57W **304** C10
Mussende *Angola* 10°32S 16°5E **265** E3
Musserra *Angola* 7°37S 13°2E **265** D2
Mussidan *France* 45°2N 0°22E **174** C4
Mussolinea di Sardegna = Arborea *Italy* 39°46N 8°35E **200** C1
Mussolo *Angola* 9°59S 17°19E **265** D3
Mussomeli *Italy* 37°35N 13°45E **200** E6
Mussoorie *India* 30°27N 78°6E **242** D8
Mussuco *Angola* 17°2S 19°3E **265** F3
Mustafakemalpaşa *Turkey* 40°2N 28°24E **203** F12
Mustahil *Ethiopia* 5°16N 44°45E **267** C5
Mustang *Nepal* 29°10N 83°55E **243** E10
Mustansiriya *Iraq* 33°22N 44°24E **113** A2
Musters, L. *Argentina* 45°20S 69°25W **336** C3
Mustique I. *St. Vincent* 12°52N 61°11W **323** n
Musturud *Egypt* 30°8N 31°17E **117** A2
Musudan *N. Korea* 40°50N 129°43E **224** B4
Muswell Hill *U.K.* 51°35N 0°8W **125** A3
Muswellbrook *Australia* 32°16S 150°56E **283** B9
Muszyna *Poland* 49°22N 20°55E **185** J7
Mût *Egypt* 25°28N 28°58E **256** B2

Mut *Turkey* 36°40N 33°28E **250** B4
Mutalau *Cook Is.* 18°56S 169°50W **289** g
Mutanabi *Iraq* 33°19N 44°21E **113** B2
Mutanda

Dem. Rep. of the Congo 5°17S 16°34E **265** D3
Mutanda *Mozam.* 21°0S 33°34E **271** B5
Mutanda *Zambia* 12°24S 26°13E **269** D2
Mutanjiang = Mudanjiang

China 44°38N 129°30E **227** B15
Mutanshe *Taiwan* 22°9N 120°48E **225** D2
Mutare *Zimbabwe* 18°58S 32°38E **269** F3
Mutawintji △ *Australia* 31°10S 142°30E **281** E3
Mutha *Kenya* 1°48S 38°26E **268** C4
Muthana *Iraq* 33°19N 44°21E **113** B2
Muting *Indonesia* 7°23S 140°20E **231** F10
Mutirikwe Dam *Zimbabwe* 20°15S 31°10E **269** G3
Mutki = Mirtağ *Turkey* 38°23N 41°56E **246** B4
Mutoko *Kenya* 17°24S 32°13E **271** A5
Mutomo *Kenya* 1°51S 38°12E **268** C4
Mutoray *Russia* 60°56N 101°0E **215** C11
Mutoto

Dem. Rep. of the Congo 5°42S 22°42E **265** D4
Mutoxo *Angola* 12°17S 21°40E **268** G4
Mutsamudu *Comoros Is.* 12°10S 44°25E **272** a
Mutshatsha

Dem. Rep. of the Congo 10°35S 24°20E **265** E4
Mutsu *Japan* 41°5N 140°55E **220** D10
Mutsu-Wan *Japan* 41°5N 140°55E **220** D10
Muttaburra *Australia* 22°38S 144°29E **280** C3
Muttalip *Turkey* 39°50N 30°32E **205** B12
Mutton I. *Ireland* 52°49N 9°32W **166** D2
Muttra = Mathura *India* 27°30N 77°40E **242** F7
Muttukuru *India* 14°16N 80°6E **245** G5
Muttupet *India* 14°55S 37°0E **269** E4
Mutum Biyu *Nigeria* 8°40N 10°50E **263** D7
Mutumba *Burundi* 3°25S 29°21E **268** C2
Mutunópolis *Brazil* 13°40S 49°15W **333** D2
Mutur *Sri Lanka* 8°27N 81°16E **245** K5
Muweilih *Egypt* 30°42N 34°19E **251** H5
Muxía *Spain* 43°3N 9°10W **194** B1
Muxima *Angola* 9°33S 13°58E **265** D2
Muy Muy *Nic.* 12°39N 85°36W **320** D2
Muyinga *Burundi* 3°14S 30°33E **268** C3
Muÿnoq *Uzbekistan* 43°44N 59°10E **216** D3
Muyua = Woodlark I.

Papua N. G. 9°10S 152°50E **286** E7
Muyunkum, Peski = Moyynqum

Kazakhstan 44°12N 71°0E **217** D8
Muz Tag *China* 36°25N 87°25E **217** E11
Muzaffarabad *Pakistan* 34°25N 73°30E **243** B5
Muzaffargarh *Pakistan* 30°5N 71°14E **242** D4
Muzaffarnagar *India* 29°26N 77°40E **242** E7
Muzaffarpur *India* 26°7N 85°23E **243** F11
Muzafirpur *India* 28°58N 69°9E **242** D3
Mużakowski, Park = Muskauer

Park *Europe* 51°34N 14°43E **178** D10
Muzeze *Angola* 15°3S 17°43E **265** F3
Muzhi *Russia* 65°25N 64°40E **186** A11
Muzillac *France* 47°35N 2°30W **172** E4
Muzon, C. *U.S.A.* 54°40N 132°42W **303** J14
Muztor = Toktogul

Kyrgyzstan 41°50N 72°50E **217** D8
Muzūra *Egypt* 28°53N 30°48E **256** J7
Mvadhi-Ousyé *Gabon* 1°13N 13°12E **264** B2
Mvam *Gabon* 0°13S 9°39E **264** C1
Mvangan *Cameroon* 2°17N 11°43E **264** B2
Mvolo *South Sudan* 6°2N 29°53E **257** F2
Mvuma *Zimbabwe* 19°16S 30°30E **269** F3
Mvurwi *Zimbabwe* 17°0S 30°57E **269** F3
Mwabvi → *Malawi* 16°42S 35°0E **269** F3
Mwadi-Kalumbu

Dem. Rep. of the Congo 7°53S 18°43E **265** D3
Mwadui *Tanzania* 3°26S 33°32E **268** C3
Mwali = Mohéli *Comoros Is.* 12°20S 43°40E **272** a
Mwambo *Tanzania* 10°30S 40°22E **269** E5
Mwandi *Zambia* 17°30S 24°51E **269** F1
Mwanza *Katanga,*

Dem. Rep. of the Congo 7°55S 26°43E **265** D5
Mwanza *Tanzania* 2°30S 32°58E **268** C3
Mwanza *Zambia* 16°58S 24°28E **265** F4
Mwanza □ *Tanzania* 2°0S 33°0E **268** C3
Mwaya *Tanzania* 9°32S 33°55E **269** D3
Mweelrea *Ireland* 53°39N 9°49W **166** C2
Mweka

Dem. Rep. of the Congo 4°50S 21°34E **265** C4
Mwenandi

Dem. Rep. of the Congo 7°12S 18°51E **265** D3
Mwene-Ditu

Dem. Rep. of the Congo 6°35S 22°27E **265** D4
Mwenezi *Zimbabwe* 21°15S 30°48E **269** G3
Mwenezi → *Mozam.* 22°40S 31°50E **269** G3
Mwenga

Dem. Rep. of the Congo 3°1S 28°28E **268** C2
Mweru, L. *Zambia* 9°0S 28°40E **269** D2
Mweru Wantipa △ *Zambia* 8°39S 29°25E **269** D2
Mwetshi

Dem. Rep. of the Congo 4°50S 22°38E **265** D4
Mweza Range *Zimbabwe* 21°0S 30°0E **269** G3
Mwilambwe

Dem. Rep. of the Congo 8°7S 25°5E **265** D5
Mwimbi *Tanzania* 8°38S 31°39E **269** D3
Mwingi *Kenya* 0°56S 38°4E **268** C4
Mwinilunga *Zambia* 11°43S 24°25E **269** E4
My Son *Vietnam* 15°48N 108°7E **236** E7
My Tho *Vietnam* 10°29N 106°23E **237** G6
Mya, O. → *Algeria* 30°46N 4°54E **264** B6
Myajlar *India* 26°15N 70°20E **242** F4
Myakka → *U.S.A.* 26°56N 82°11W **317** J7
Myall Lakes △ *Australia* 32°25S 152°30E **283** B10
Myanaung *Burma* 18°18N 95°22E **241** F5
Myanmar = Burma ■ *Asia* 21°0N 96°30E **241** E6
Myaung *Burma* 21°55N 95°32E **241** E5
Myaungmya *Burma* 16°30N 94°40E **241** F5
Mycenae = Mykenes

Greece 37°43N 22°46E **204** D4
Myebon *Burma* 20°3N 93°22E **241** E4
Myedna *Belarus* 51°52N 23°42E **185** G10
Myeik = Mergui *Burma* 12°26N 98°34E **236** F2
Myeik Kyunzu *Burma* 11°30N 97°30E **237** G1
Myerstown *U.S.A.* 40°22N 76°19W **313** F8
Myingyan *Burma* 21°30N 95°20E **241** C6
Myitkyina *Burma* 25°24N 97°26E **241** C6
Myitson *Burma* 23°16N 96°34E **241** D6
Myittha *Burma* 21°25N 96°8E **241** E6
Myittha → *Burma* 23°30N 94°50E **241** C6
Myjava *Slovakia* 48°41N 17°37E **181** C10
Mykhaylivka *Ukraine* 47°12N 35°15E **189** A3
Mykines *Greece* 62°7N 7°5W **164** D2
Myking *Norway* 60°41N 5°19E **164** D2
Mykolayiv *Ukraine* 46°58N 32°0E **189** A3
Mykolayiv □ *Ukraine* 30°31N 31°50E **189** J6
Mykonos *Greece* 37°30N 25°25E **205** D7
Mylius Erichsen Land

Greenland 81°30N 27°0W **154** A18
Myllypuro *Finland* 60°13N 25°3E **121** B13
Mymensingh *Bangla.* 24°45N 90°24E **243** G4
Mymensingh □ *Bangla.* 24°50N 90°30E **241** C12
Mynydd Du *U.K.* 51°52N 3°50W **169** F4
Myo-gi *India* 21°27N 96°22E **241** E6
Myohaung *Burma* 19°16N 96°12E **241** F6
Myohla *Burma* 18°16N 95°12E **241** F5
Myotha *Burma* 21°41N 95°42E **241** E5
Myothit *Kachin, Burma* 25°4N 95°8E **241** C6
Myothit *Magway, Burma* 20°23N 94°43E **241** E5
Myrasysla *Iceland* 64°45N 21°30W **155** C5
Mýrdalsjökull *Iceland* 63°56N 19°5W **155** D5

Myrhorod *Ukraine* 49°58N 33°37E **189** H7
Mýri *Iceland* 65°23N 17°23W **155** B9
Myrina *Greece* 39°53N 25°4E **205** B7
Myrtle Beach *U.S.A.* 33°42N 78°53W **315** E15
Myrtle Creek *U.S.A.* 43°1N 123°17W **304** E2
Myrtle Grove *U.S.A.* 30°23N 87°17W **317** E2
Myrtle Point *U.S.A.* 43°4N 124°8W **304** E1
Myrtleford *Australia* 36°34S 146°44E **283** D7
Myrtoan Sea = Mirtoo Sea

Greece 37°0N 23°20E **204** D5
Myrtou *Cyprus* 35°18N 33°4E **207** E9
Myrviken *Sweden* 62°58N 14°20E **162** B8
Mysen *Norway* 59°33N 11°20E **164** E8
Mysia *Turkey* 39°50N 27°0E **203** G11
Myślenice *Poland* 49°51N 19°57E **185** J6
Myślibórz *Poland* 52°55N 14°50E **185** F1
Myslowice *Poland* 50°15N 19°12E **185** H6
Mysore = Karnataka □

India 13°15N 77°0E **245** H3
Mysore = Mysuru *India* 12°17N 76°41E **245** H3
Mystic *Conn., U.S.A.* 41°21N 71°58W **313** E13
Mystic *Iowa, U.S.A.* 40°47N 92°57W **310** D4
Mystic → *U.S.A.* 42°2N 71°3W **116** A2
Mystras *Greece* 37°4N 22°22E **204** D4
Mysuru *India* 12°17N 76°41E **245** H3
Myszków *Poland* 50°45N 19°22E **185** H6
Myszyniec *Poland* 53°23N 21°21E **184** E8
Mytilene = Mitilini *Greece* 39°6N 26°35E **205** B8
Mytishchi *Russia* 55°50N 37°50E **188** E9
Mývatn *Iceland* 65°36N 17°0W **155** B10
M'zab, Oued → *Algeria* 32°15N 5°0E **261** B6
M'zab Valley = M'zab, Oued →

Algeria 32°15N 5°0E **261** B6
Mże → *Czechia* 49°46N 13°24E **180** B6
Mzimba *Malawi* 11°55S 33°39E **269** E3
Mzimkulu → *S. Africa* 30°44S 30°28E **271** D5
Mzimvubu → *S. Africa* 31°38S 29°33E **271** D4
Mzuzu *Malawi* 11°30S 33°55E **269** E3

N

N.S.C.B. Int. ✈ (CCU)

India 22°38N 88°26E **124** B2
Na Clocha Liatha = Greystones

Ireland 53°9N 6°5W **166** C5
Na Haeo △ *Thailand* 17°31N 100°58E **236** D3
Na Hearadh = Harris *U.K.* 57°50N 6°55W **167** D2
Na Hearadh, Caolas = Harris, Sd. of

U.K. 57°44N 7°6W **167** D1
Na-lang *Burma* 22°42N 97°33E **241** D6
Na Noi *Thailand* 18°19N 100°43E **236** C3
Na Phao *Laos* 17°35N 105°44E **236** D5
Na Sam *Vietnam* 22°3N 106°37E **228** F6
Na Sceirí = Skerries *Ireland* 53°35N 6°6W **166** C5
Na Thon *Thailand* 9°32N 99°56E **237** b
Naab → *Germany* 49°1N 12°2E **179** F8
Nä'älehu *U.S.A.* 19°4N 155°35W **302** D6
Na'am *Sudan* 9°42N 28°27E **257** F2
Na'am → *South Sudan* 6°48N 29°57E **257** F2
Naama *Algeria* 33°16N 0°19E **261** B5
Naama □ *Algeria* 33°15N 0°45E **261** B5
Naantali *Finland* 60°29N 22°2E **188** B1
Naas *Ireland* 53°12N 6°40W **166** C5
Nababeep *S. Africa* 29°36S 17°46E **270** C2
Nabadwip = Navadwip

India 23°34N 88°20E **243** H13
Nabari *Japan* 34°37N 136°5E **223** C8
Nabawa *Australia* 28°30S 114°48E **279** E1
Nabberu, L. *Australia* 25°50S 120°30E **279** E3
Nabburg *Germany* 49°27N 12°11E **179** F8
Naberezhnaya Tower

Russia 55°45N 37°32E **129** B2
Naberezhnyye Chelny

Russia 55°42N 52°19E **190** C11
Nabesna *U.S.A.* 62°22N 143°0W **303** E12
Nabeul *Tunisia* 36°30N 10°44E **258** A2
Nabeul □ *Tunisia* 36°30N 10°40E **261** A7
Nabha *India* 30°26N 76°14E **242** D7
Nabi Sālih *Egypt* 28°37N 33°59E **251** K4
Nabīd *Iran* 29°40N 57°38E **247** D8
Nabire *Indonesia* 3°15S 135°26E **231** E9
Nabisar *Pakistan* 25°8N 69°40E **242** G3
Nabisipi → *Canada* 50°14N 62°13W **299** B7
Nabiswera *Uganda* 1°27N 32°15E **268** B3
Nâblus = Nābulus

West Bank 32°14N 35°15E **251** F4
Naboomspruit *S. Africa* 24°32S 28°40E **271** B4
Nabou *Burkina Faso* 11°25S 2°50W **262** C4
Nabouwalu *Fiji* 17°0S 178°45E **287** A2
Nabq *Egypt* 28°6N 34°25E **251** K5
Nabua *Phil.* 13°24N 123°22E **232** E4
Nābulus *West Bank* 32°14N 35°15E **251** F6
Nabunturan *Phil.* 7°35N 125°58E **233** H5
Nacala *Mozam.* 14°32S 40°34E **269** E5
Nacaome *Honduras* 13°31N 87°30W **320** D2
Nacaroa *Mozam.* 14°22S 39°56E **269** E4
Naches *U.S.A.* 46°44N 120°42W **304** C3
Naches → *U.S.A.* 46°38N 120°31W **304** C3
Nachicapau, L. *Canada* 56°40N 68°5W **299** A6
Nachikatsuura *Japan* 33°33N 135°58E **223** D7
Nachingwea *Tanzania* 10°23S 38°49E **269** E4
Nachna *India* 27°34N 71°41E **242** F4
Náchod *Czechia* 50°25N 16°8E **180** A9
Nachuge *India* 10°47N 92°21E **245** J11
Nacimiento, L. *U.S.A.* 35°46N 120°53W **306** K6
Nacka *Sweden* 59°19N 18°10E **189** B3
Nackara *Australia* 32°48S 139°12E **282** B3
Naco *Mexico* 31°19N 109°56E **318** A3
Nacogdoches *U.S.A.* 31°36N 94°39W **314** F7
Nácori Chico *Mexico* 29°40N 108°57W **318** B3
Nacozari de García

Mexico 30°24N 109°39W **318** A3
Nacula *Fiji* 16°54S 177°27E **287** A1
Nada = Danzhou *China* 19°31N 109°33E **229** a
Nådendal = Naantali

Finland 60°29N 22°2E **188** B1
Nadezhdinsky = Serov

Russia 59°29N 60°35E **186** C11
Nadi *Fiji* 17°42S 177°20E **287** A1
Nadi *Sudan* 18°40N 33°41E **256** D3
Nadiad *India* 22°41N 72°56E **242** H5
Nadlac *Romania* 46°10N 20°50E **182** D5
Nador *Morocco* 35°14N 2°58W **261** A4
Nador *Malta* 35°54N 14°22E **206** F7
Nadur *Gozo, Malta* 36°2N 14°18E **206** E7
Nadüshan *Iran* 32°2N 53°35E **247** C7
Nadvirna *Ukraine* 48°37N 24°30E **183** D7
Nadvoitsy *Russia* 63°52N 34°14E **186** B5
Nadvornaya = Nadvirna

Ukraine 48°37N 24°30E **183** D7
Nadym *Russia* 65°35N 72°42E **214** C8
Nadym → *Russia* 66°12N 72°0E **214** C8
Nærbø *Norway* 58°40N 5°39E **164** F2
Nærøyfjorden *Norway* 60°55N 6°55E **164** D5
Næstved *Denmark* 59°45N 117°23E **133** B1
Nafada *Nigeria* 11°8N 11°20E **263** C7
Nafarroa = Navarra □

Spain 42°40N 1°40W **196** C3
Nafpaktos *Greece* 38°24N 21°50E **204** C3
Nafplio *Greece* 37°33N 22°50E **204** D4
Naft-e Safid *Iran* 31°40N 49°17E **247** D6
Naft Pt. *N. Marianas* 15°5N 145°45E **302** e
Naftshahr *Iran* 34°0N 45°30E **213** E11
Nafud Desert = An Nafūd

Si. Arabia 28°15N 41°0E **246** D4

Nafūsah, Jabal *Libya* 32°12N 12°30E **258** B2
Nag Hammādi *Egypt* 26°2N 32°18E **256** B3
Naga *Japan* 26°34N 127°43E **288** a
Naga *Camarines S., Phil.* 13°38N 123°15E **232** D4
Naga *Cebu, Phil.* 10°13N 123°45E **233** F4
Naga *Zamboanga del S., Phil.* 7°46N 122°45E **233** H4
Naga, Kreb en *Africa* 24°12N 6°0W **260** D3
Naga Hills = Nagaland □

India 26°0N 94°30E **241** C5
Nagagami → *Canada* 50°23N 84°20W **298** B3
Nagahama *Ehime, Japan* 33°36N 132°29E **222** D4
Nagahama *Shiga, Japan* 35°23N 136°16E **223** B8
Nagai *Japan* 38°6N 140°2E **222** E10
Nagai I. *U.S.A.* 55°5N 160°0W **303** J8
Nagambie *Australia* 36°47S 145°10E **283** D6
Nagano *Japan* 36°40N 138°10E **223** A9
Nagano □ *Japan* 36°15N 138°0E **223** A10
Nagaoka *Japan* 37°27N 138°51E **221** F9
Nagaon *India* 26°20N 92°50E **241** B4
Nagappattinam *India* 10°46N 79°51E **245** J4
Nagar → *Bangla.* 24°27N 89°12E **241** C2
Nagar Karnul *India* 16°29N 78°20E **245** F4
Nagar Parkar *Pakistan* 24°28N 70°46E **242** G4
Nagara-Gawa → *Japan* 35°40N 136°43E **223** B8
Nagaram *India* 18°21N 80°24E **244** E5
Nagarhole △ *India* 12°0N 76°10E **245** J3
Nagari Hills *India* 13°3N 79°45E **245** H4
Nagarjuna Sagar *India* 16°56N 79°13E **245** F4
Nagasaki *Japan* 32°47N 129°50E **222** E1
Nagasaki □ *Japan* 32°50N 129°40E **222** E1
Nagato *Japan* 34°19N 131°5E **222** C3
Nagatsuta *Japan* 35°32N 139°31E **140** B2
Nagaur *India* 27°15N 73°45E **242** F5
Nagayo *Japan* 32°48N 129°50E **222** E1
Nagbhir *India* 20°34N 79°55E **244** D4
Nagda *India* 23°27N 75°25E **242** H6
Nagercoil *India* 8°12N 77°26E **245** K3
Nagina *India* 29°30N 78°30E **243** E8
Nagîneh *Iran* 34°20N 57°15E **247** C8
Nagir *Pakistan* 36°12N 74°42E **243** A6
Naglarby *Sweden* 60°25N 15°34E **162** D9
Nagles Mts. *Ireland* 52°8N 8°30W **166** D3
Nago-wan *Japan* 26°34N 127°57E **288** a
Nagod *India* 24°34N 80°36E **243** G9
Nagold *Germany* 48°32N 8°43E **179** G4
Nagold → *Germany* 48°52N 8°42E **179** F4
Nagoorin *Australia* 24°17S 151°15E **280** D5
Nagorno-Karabakh □

Azerbaijan 39°55N 46°45E **213** C12
Nagornyy *Russia* 55°58N 124°57E **215** D13
Nagoya *Indonesia* 1°15N 104°5E **234** B2
Nagoya *Japan* 35°10N 136°50E **223** B8
Nagoya ✈ (NGO) *Japan* 34°53N 136°45E **223** C8
Nagpartian = Burgos

Phil. 18°31N 120°39E **232** B3
Nagpur *India* 21°8N 79°10E **244** D4
Nagqu *China* 31°29N 92°3E **232** F4
Nags Head *St. Kitts & Nevis* 17°13N 62°38W **322** d
Nagua *Dom. Rep.* 19°23N 69°50W **321** C6
Naguabo *Puerto Rico* 18°13N 65°44W **321** b
Nagurunguru ☉

Australia 16°45S 129°45E **278** C4
Nagyatád *Hungary* 46°14N 17°22E **182** D2
Nagyecsed *Hungary* 47°53N 22°24E **182** C7
Nagykálló *Hungary* 47°53N 21°51E **182** C6
Nagykanizsa *Hungary* 46°28N 17°0E **182** D2
Nagykáta *Hungary* 47°25N 19°48E **182** C4
Nagykőrös *Hungary* 47°5N 19°48E **182** C4
Nagyszombat = Trnava

Slovakia 48°23N 17°35E **181** C10
Nagytétény *Hungary* 47°23N 18°59E **117** B1
Nagyvárad = Oradea

Romania 47°2N 21°58E **182** C6
Naha *Japan* 26°13N 127°42E **288** a
Nahabuan *Indonesia* 0°49N 114°45E **234** B4
Nahalin *West Bank* 31°41N 35°7E **123** B1
Nahan *India* 30°33N 77°18E **242** D7
Nahanni △ *Canada* 61°36N 125°41W **296** A4
Nahanni Butte *Canada* 61°2N 123°31W **296** A4
Nahargarh *Mad. P., India* 24°10N 75°14E **242** G6
Nahargarh *Raj., India* 24°55N 76°50E **242** G7
Nahariyya *Israel* 33°1N 35°5E **250** F6
Nahāvand *Iran* 34°10N 48°22E **213** E13
Nahe → *Germany* 49°58N 7°27E **183** F3
Nahîrne *Ukraine* 45°26N 28°27E **183** E13
Nahîya, W. → *Egypt* 28°55N 31°0E **256** B3
Nahuel Huapí, L. *Argentina* 41°0S 71°32W **336** B2
Nahuel Huapí △ *Argentina* 41°0S 71°59W **336** B2
Nahuelbuta △ *Chile* 37°44S 72°57W **334** D1
Nahunta *U.S.A.* 31°12N 81°59W **316** D8
Nai Yong *Thailand* 8°14N 98°22E **237** a
Naic *Mexico* 14°19N 120°46E **232** D3
Naicá *Mexico* 27°53N 105°31W **318** B3
Naicam *Canada* 52°30N 104°30W **297** C8
NaidAru *Maldives* 5°26N 73°0E **272** d
Naikoon △ *Canada* 53°55N 131°55W **296** C2
Naikul *India* 21°20N 84°58E **244** D7
Naila *Germany* 50°19N 11°42E **179** F7
Naimisharanya *India* 27°21N 80°30E **243** F9
Naimona'nyi Feng *China* 30°26N 81°18E **243** D9
Nain *St. Kitt & Nevis, Canada* 56°34N 61°40W **299** A7
Na'īn *Iran* 32°54N 53°0E **247** C7
Nain *Jamaica* 17°57N 77°38W **320** a
Naini Tal *India* 29°30N 79°30E **243** E8
Nainpur *India* 22°30N 80°10E **243** H9
Naintré *France* 46°46N 0°29E **172** F7
Nainwa *India* 25°46N 75°51E **242** G6
Naipu *Romania* 44°12N 25°47E **183** F10
Nairai *Fiji* 17°49S 179°15E **287** A2
Nairn *U.K.* 57°35N 3°53W **167** D5
Nairobi *Kenya* 1°17S 36°48E **268** C4
Nairobi □ *Kenya* 1°22S 36°50E **268** C4
Naissaar *Estonia* 59°34N 24°29E **188** A3
Naita, Mt. *Ethiopia* 5°30N 35°18E **257** F4
Naitaba *Fiji* 17°5S 179°10E **287** A3
Naivasha *Kenya* 0°40S 36°30E **268** C4
Naivasha, L. *Kenya* 0°48S 36°20E **268** C4
Najac *France* 44°14N 1°58E **174** D5
Najaf = An Najaf *Iraq* 32°3N 44°15E **213** G11
Najafābād *Iran* 32°40N 51°15E **247** C6
Najafgarh Drain → *India* 28°30N 77°6E **120** B1
Najd *Si. Arabia* 26°30N 42°0E **248** B3
Nájera *Spain* 42°26N 2°48W **196** C2
Najerilla → *Spain* 42°15N 2°49W **196** C2
Najibabad *India* 29°40N 78°20E **242** E8
Najin *N. Korea* 42°12N 130°15E **224** A5
Najmah *Si. Arabia* 26°42N 50°6E **247** E6
Najrān *Si. Arabia* 17°34N 44°18E **248** D4
Najrān □ *Si. Arabia* 18°30N 45°0E **248** C4
Naju *S. Korea* 35°3N 126°43E **224** E3
Naka-Gawa → *Japan* 36°20N 140°36E **223** A12
Nakadōri-Shima *Japan* 32°57N 129°4E **222** E1
Nakagüsuku-wan *Japan* 26°14N 127°53E **288** a
Nakaha → *Japan* 35°33N 139°37E **140** D2
Nakai = Naklo nad Notecią

Poland 53°9N 17°58E **185** E4
Nakalagba

Dem. Rep. of the Congo 2°50N 27°58E **268** B2
Nakalele Pt. *U.S.A.* 21°2N 156°35W **302** B5
Nakama *Japan* 33°56N 130°43E **222** D2

Nakambé = White Volta →

Ghana 9°10N 1°15W **263** D4
Nakaminato *Japan* 36°21N 140°36E **223** A12
Nakamura = Shimanto

Japan 32°59N 132°56E **222** E4
Nakanai Mts. *Papua N. G.* 5°40S 151°0E **286** D6
Nakano *Nagano, Japan* 36°45N 138°22E **223** A10
Nakano *Tōkyō, Japan* 35°42N 139°39E **140** A2
Nakano-Shima *Japan* 29°51N 129°52E **221** K4
Nakanojō *Japan* 36°35N 138°51E **223** A10
Nakashibetsu *Japan* 43°33N 144°59E **220** C12
Nakatsu *Japan* 33°34N 131°15E **222** D3
Nakatsugawa *Japan* 35°29N 137°30E **223** B9
Nakfa *Eritrea* 16°40N 38°32E **257** D4
Nakfa □ *Eritrea* 17°28N 38°55E **257** D4
Nakhichevan

Azerbaijan 39°12N 45°15E **213** C11
Nakhichevan Rep. = Naxçıvan □

Azerbaijan 39°25N 45°26E **213** C11
Nakhl *Egypt* 29°55N 33°43E **251** A4
Nakhl-e Taqī *Iran* 27°28N 52°36E **247** E7
Nakhodka *Russia* 42°53N 132°54E **220** C6
Nakhon Nayok *Thailand* 14°12N 101°13E **236** E3
Nakhon Pathom *Thailand* 13°49N 100°3E **236** F3
Nakhon Phanom

Thailand 17°23N 104°43E **236** D5
Nakhon Ratchasima

Thailand 14°59N 102°12E **236** E4
Nakhon Sawan *Thailand* 15°35N 100°10E **236** E3
Nakhon Si Thammarat

Thailand 8°29N 100°0E **237** H3
Nakhonle △ *India* 12°0N 76°10E **245** J3
Nakina *Canada* 50°10N 86°40W **298** B2
Nakina → *Canada* 26°40N 127°58E **288** a
Naknek *U.S.A.* 58°44N 157°1W **303** G8
Nako *Burkina Faso* 10°40N 3°4W **262** C4
Nakodar *India* 31°8N 75°31E **242** D6
Nakskov *Denmark* 54°50N 11°8E **163** K5
Naktong → *S. Korea* 35°7N 128°57E **224** E4
Nakuru *Kenya* 0°15S 36°4E **268** C4
Nakuru, L. *Kenya* 0°23S 36°5E **268** C4
Nakusp *Canada* 50°20N 117°45W **296** C5
Nal *Pakistan* 27°40N 66°12E **242** F2
Nal → *Pakistan* 25°20N 65°30E **242** G1
Nalázi *Mozam.* 24°3S 33°20E **271** C5
Nalchik *Russia* 43°30N 43°33E **191** J6
Nalęczów *Poland* 51°17N 22°9E **185** G9
Nalerigu *Ghana* 10°35N 0°25W **263** C4
Nalgonda *India* 17°6N 79°15E **244** F4
Nalhati *India* 24°17N 87°52E **243** G12
Nallamalai Hills *India* 15°30N 78°50E **245** G4
Nallıhan *Turkey* 40°11N 31°20E **212** B4
Nalolo *Zambia* 15°33S 23°7E **265** F4
Nalón → *Spain* 43°32N 6°4W **194** B4
Nalong *Burma* 24°44N 97°28E **241** C6
Nalubaale Dam *Uganda* 0°30N 33°5E **268** B3
Nalumasortoq *Greenland* 60°23N 44°28W **154** E6
Nalut *Libya* 31°54N 11°0E **258** B2
Nam Can *Vietnam* 8°46N 104°59E **237** H5
Nam-ch'on *N. Korea* 38°15N 126°26E **224** C3
Nam Co *China* 30°30N 90°45E **218** E7
Nam Dinh *Vietnam* 20°25N 106°5E **228** G6
Nam Du, Quan Dao

Vietnam 9°41N 104°21E **237** H5
Nam Hka → *Burma* 21°34N 95°41E **228** G2
Nam Loi → *Burma* 21°3N 98°27E **228** G3
Nam Nao △ *Thailand* 16°44N 101°32E **236** D3
Nam Ngum Res. *Laos* 18°35N 102°34E **236** C4
Nam Phan *Vietnam* 10°30N 106°0E **237** G6
Nam Phong *Thailand* 16°42N 102°52E **236** D4
Nam Theun Res. *Laos* 17°51N 105°3E **236** D5
Nam Tok *Thailand* 14°21N 99°4E **236** E2
Nam Un Res. *Thailand* 17°13N 103°44E **236** D4
Namachire *Japan* 11°26S 22°43E **265** E4
Namacunde *Angola* 17°18S 15°50E **265** F3
Namacurra *Mozam.* 17°30S 36°50E **271** A6
Namadgi △ *Australia* 35°42S 149°0E **283** F8
Namai B. *Palau* 7°31N 134°38E **288** c
Namak, Daryācheh-ye

Iran 34°30N 52°0E **247** C7
Namak, Kavir-e *Iran* 34°30N 57°30E **247** C8
Namakkal *India* 11°5N 78°13E **245** J4
Namakzār, Daryācheh-ye

Iran 34°0N 60°30E **247** B9
Namaland *Namibia* 26°0S 17°0E **270** B2
Namanga *Kenya* 2°33S 36°47E **268** C4
Namangan *Uzbekistan* 41°0N 71°40E **217** D8
Namangan □ *Uzbekistan* 41°0N 71°15E **217** D8
Namapa *Mozam.* 13°43S 39°50E **269** E4
Namaqua △ *S. Africa* 30°0S 17°30E **270** D2
Namaqualand *S. Africa* 30°0S 17°25E **270** D2
Namasagali *Uganda* 1°2N 33°0E **268** B3
Namatanai *Papua N. G.* 3°40S 152°29E **286** B7
Nambé *Indonesia* 1°2S 134°49E **231** E8
Nambour *Australia* 26°32S 152°58E **281** D5
Nambouwalu = Nabouwalu

Fiji 17°0S 178°45E **287** A2
Nambuangongo *Angola* 8°1S 14°12E **265** D2
Nambucca Heads

Australia 30°37S 153°0E **283** A10
Nambung △ *Australia* 30°30S 115°5E **279** F2
Namcha Barwa *China* 29°40N 95°10E **218** F8
Namche Bazar *Nepal* 27°51N 86°47E **243** F12
Namchonjŏm = Nam-ch'on

N. Korea 38°15N 126°26E **224** C3
Namdalen *Norway* 64°40N 12°45E **162** A7
Namdecunda *Mozam.* 14°54S 37°37E **269** E3
Nameh *Indonesia* 2°34N 116°21E **234** B5
Namen = Namur *Belgium* 50°27N 4°52E **170** D4
Namenalala △ *Fiji* 17°8S 179°9E **287** A2
Nameponda *Mozam.* 15°50S 39°50E **269** E4
Namerī △ *India* 26°55N 92°55E **241** B4
Nameríkawa *Japan* 36°46N 137°20E **223** A9
Náměšt nad Oslavou

Czechia 49°12N 16°10E **181** B9
Námestovo *Slovakia* 49°24N 19°25E **181** B12
Namew L. *Canada* 54°14N 101°56W **297** C8
Namgia *India* 31°48N 78°40E **243** D8
Namhkam *Burma* 23°50N 97°26E **241** D6
Namhsan *Burma* 22°48N 97°2E **241** D6
Namialo *Mozam.* 14°3S 39°40E **269** E4
Namib Desert *Namibia* 22°30S 15°0E **270** B2
Namib-Naukluft □

Namibia 24°40S 15°16E **270** B2
Namibe *Angola* 15°7S 12°11E **265** F2
Namibe □ *Angola* 16°35S 12°30E **265** F2
Namibia ■ *Africa* 22°0S 18°9E **270** B2
Namibia Abyssal Plain

Atl. Oc. 30°0S 5°0E **152** J12
Namibwoestyn = Namib Desert

Namibia 22°30S 15°0E **270** B2
Namīn *Iran* 38°30N 48°30E **213** C13
Namkhana = Lubango

Angola 14°55S 13°30E **265** D2
Namīnūs = Lüderitz

Namibia 26°41S 15°9E **270** D2
Nakahara → *Japan* 35°33N 139°37E **140** D2
Nakal = Naklo nad Notecią

Poland 53°9N 17°58E **185** E4
Nakalagba

Dem. Rep. of the Congo 2°50N 27°58E **268** B2
Namjeju *S. Korea* 33°11N 126°33E **224** F3
Namlan *Burma* 22°15N 97°34E **241** D6
Namlea *Indonesia* 3°18S 127°5E **231** E7
Namoi → *Australia* 30°12S 149°30E **283** A9
Namoia, O. en → *Algeria* 30°50N 5°15W **261** B4
Nampa *U.S.A.* 43°34N 116°34W **304** E5

Nanri Dao *China* 25°15N 119°25E **229** E12
Nansang *Burma* 20°53N 97°43E **241** E6
Nansei-Shotō = Ryūkyū-Rettō

Japan 26°0N 126°0E **221** M3
Nansen Basin *Arctic* 84°0N 50°0E **150** A10
Nansen Land *Greenland* 83°0N 43°0W **154** A6
Nansen Sd. *Canada* 81°0N 91°0W **295** A13
Nansha *China* 22°45N 113°34E **219** a
Nansha Port *China* 22°40N 113°40E **219** a
Nanshan *China* 22°45N 113°40E **219** a
Nanshan I. *S. China Sea* 10°45N 115°49E **230** B5
Nanshi *China* 31°12N 121°29E **138** B1
Nansio *Tanzania* 2°3S 33°4E **268** C3
Nant *France* 44°1N 3°18E **174** D7
Nantan *Japan* 35°6N 135°23E **223** B7
Nantawarrinna ☉

Australia 30°49S 138°58E **281** B2
Nanterre *France* 48°53N 2°12E **134** A2
Nantes *France* 47°12N 1°33W **172** E5
Nantiat *France* 46°1N 1°11E **174** B5
Nanticoke *U.S.A.* 41°12N 76°0W **313** E8
Nanton *Canada* 50°21N 113°46W **296** C6
Nanton *China* 32°1N 120°52E **229** A13
Nantou *China* 22°32N 113°55E **219** a
Nant'ou *Taiwan* 23°55N 120°41E **225** C3
Nant'ou □ *Taiwan* 23°50N 121°0E **225** C3
Nantua *France* 46°10N 5°35E **173** F12
Nantucket *U.S.A.* 41°17N 70°6W **309** E18
Nantucket I. *U.S.A.* 41°16N 70°5W **309** E18
Nantulo *Mozam.* 12°32S 38°45E **269** E4
Nantung = Nantong

China 32°1N 120°52E **229** A13
Nantwich *U.K.* 53°4N 2°31W **168** D5
Nanty Glo *U.S.A.* 40°28N 78°50W **312** F6
Nantze *Taiwan* 22°44N 120°16E **225** D2
Nanuku Passage *Fiji* 16°45S 179°15W **287** A3
Nanumanga *Pac. Oc.* 6°18S 176°22E **287** B14
Nanuque *Brazil* 17°50S 40°21W **333** E3
Nanusa, Kepulauan

Indonesia 4°45N 127°1E **231** D7
Nanutarra Roadhouse

Australia 22°32S 115°30E **278** D2
Nanwan *China* 21°57N 120°46E **225** E2
Nanxi *China* 28°54N 104°59E **228** C5
Nanxiong *China* 25°6N 114°15E **229** E10
Nanyang *China* 33°11N 112°30E **226** H7
Nanyi Hu *China* 31°5N 119°0E **229** B12
Nanyuan *China* 39°47N 116°23E **139** E6
Nanyuki *Kenya* 0°2N 37°4E **268** B4
Nanzhang *China* 31°45N 111°50E **229** B8
Nanzhao *China* 33°30N 112°20E **226** H7
Nanzi = Nantzu *Taiwan* 22°45N 120°16E **225** D2
Nao, C. de la *Spain* 38°44N 0°14E **197** G5
Naococane, L. *Canada* 52°50N 70°45W **299** B5
Naogaon *Bangla.* 24°52N 88°52E **241** C2
Naoné *Vanuatu* 15°0S 168°9E **287** E6
Naoussa *Cyclades, Greece* 37°7N 25°14E **205** F6
Naoussa *Imathia, Greece* 40°42N 22°9E **202** F6
Naozhou Dao *China* 20°55N 110°20E **228** G8
Napa *U.S.A.* 38°18N 122°17W **306** G4
Napa → *U.S.A.* 38°10N 122°19W **306** G4
Napaimiut *U.S.A.* 61°33N 158°42W **303** F8
Napakiak *U.S.A.* 60°42N 161°57W **303** F7
Nápali Coast *U.S.A.* 22°11N 159°39W **302** A2
Napanee *Canada* 44°15N 77°0W **312** B8
Napanoch *U.S.A.* 41°44N 74°22W **313** E10
Napaskiak *U.S.A.* 60°43N 161°55W **303** F7
Nape *Laos* 18°18N 105°6E **236** C5
Nape Pass = Keo Neua, Deo

Vietnam 18°23N 105°10E **236** C5
Naperville *U.S.A.* 41°46N 88°9W **311** C8
Napier *N.Z.* 39°30S 176°56E **284** F5
Napier Broome B.

Australia 14°2S 126°37E **278** B4
Napier Mole *Pakistan* 24°49N 66°58E **123** B1
Napier Pen. *Australia* 12°4S 135°43E **280** A2
Napierville *Canada* 45°11N 73°25W **313** A11
Napili-Honokowai

U.S.A. 20°58N 156°39W **302** C5
Naples = Nápoli *Italy* 40°50N 14°15E **207** B7
Naples *U.S.A.* 26°8N 81°48W **317** J8
Naples Park *U.S.A.* 26°17N 81°46W **317** J8
Napo *China* 23°22N 105°5E **228** F5
Napo → *Ecuador* 3°20S 72°40W **328** D3
Napo → *Peru* 3°20S 72°40W **328** D3
Napoleon *N. Dak., U.S.A.* 46°30N 99°46W **308** B4
Napoleon *Ohio, U.S.A.* 41°23N 84°8W **311** C12
Napoleon's Tomb *St. Helena* 15°56S 5°42W **153** h
Nápoli *Italy* 40°50N 14°15E **207** B7
Nápoli, G. di *Italy* 40°40N 14°10E **207** B7
Nápoli Capodichino ✈ (NAP)

Italy 40°53N 14°16E **201** B7
Napopo

Dem. Rep. of the Congo 4°15N 28°0E **268** B2
Nappanee *U.S.A.* 41°27N 86°0W **311** C11
Napperby *Australia* 33°9S 138°7E **282** B2
Naqadeh *Iran* 36°57N 45°23E **213** D11
Naqb, Ra's an *Jordan* 29°48N 35°44E **251** G4
Naqqāsh *Iran* 35°40N 49°6E **247** C6
Når *Sweden* 57°15N 18°45E **163** G10
Nara *Japan* 34°40N 135°49E **223** B7
Nara *Mali* 15°10N 7°20W **262** B3
Nara □ *Japan* 34°30N 136°0E **223** C8
Nara Canal *Pakistan* 24°30N 69°20E **242** G3
Nara Visa *U.S.A.* 35°37N 103°6W **305** J12
Naracoorte *Australia* 36°58S 140°45E **282** C4
Naradhan *Australia* 33°34S 146°17E **283** B7
Naraini *India* 25°11N 80°29E **243** G9
Naranjos *Mexico* 21°21N 97°41W **319** C5
Narasannapeta *India* 18°25N 84°5E **244** E7
Narasapur *India* 16°26N 81°40E **245** F5
Narasaraopet *India* 16°14N 80°4E **245** F5
Narathiwat *Thailand* 6°30N 101°48E **237** J3
Narayanadgadh = Bharatpur

Nepal 27°34N 84°10E **243** F11
Narayanganj *Bangla.* 23°40N 90°33E **241** D3
Narayanpet *India* 16°45N 77°30E **244** F3
Narbada = Narmada →

India 21°38N 72°36E **242** J5
Narberth *U.K.* 51°47N 4°44W **169** F3
Narbonne *France* 43°11N 3°0E **174** E7
Narborough, I. = Fernandina, I.

Ecuador 0°25S 91°30W **330** a
Narcea → *Spain* 43°33N 6°44W **194** B4
Narcondam I. *India* 13°30N 78°0W **328** G2
Nardin *Iran* 37°3N 55°59E **247** B7
Nardò *Italy* 40°1N 18°2E **209** B11
Narembeen *Australia* 32°7S 118°24E **279** F2
Nares Abyssal Plain

Atl. Oc. 22°0N 67°0W **152** G10
Nares Str. *Arctic* 80°0N 70°0W **295** B4
Naretha *Australia* 31°0S 124°45E **279** F3
Narew → *Poland* 52°26N 20°41E **185** F8
Nari → *Pakistan* 28°0N 67°40E **242** F2
Nariman Pt. *Mumbai, India* 18°55N 72°49E **130** A1
Narin *Afghan.* 36°5N 69°0E **248** A6
Narindra, Helodranon' i

Madag. 14°55S 47°30E **272** A2
Narino □ *Colombia* 1°30N 78°0W **328** C2
Narita *Japan* 35°47N 140°19E **223** B12
Narita, Tōkyō ✈ (NRT)

Japan 35°45N 140°23E **223** B12
Nariva → *Trin. & Tob.* 10°24N 61°4W **323** J
Nariva Swamp *Trin. & Tob.* 10°26N 61°4W **323** J
Närke *Sweden* 59°10N 15°0E **162** G8

406 Narmada INDEX

Narmada ~ India 21°38N 72°36E 242 J5
Narmada Canal India 22°20N 73°45E 244 C1
Nārmak Iran 35°42N 51°28E 141 A2
Narman Turkey 40°26N 41°57E 213 B9
Narnaul India 28°5N 76°11E 242 E7
Narni Italy 42°30N 12°30E 199 F9
Naro Ghana 10°22N 2°27W 262 C4
Naro Fominsk Russia 55°23N 36°43E 188 E9
Narochanski △ Belarus 54°55N 26°50E 188 E4
Narodnaya Russia 65°5N 59°58E 186 A10
Narodowy, Stadion Warsaw, Poland 143 b3
Narok Kenya 1°55S 35°52E 268 C4
Narok □ Kenya 1°15S 35°40E 268 C4
Narón Spain 43°32N 8°9W 194 B2
Narooma Australia 36°14S 150°4E 283 D9
Narowal Pakistan 32°6N 74°52E 242 C6
Narrabri Australia 30°19S 149°46E 281 E4
Narran ~ Australia 28°37S 148°12E 281 D4
Narrandera Australia 34°42S 146°31E 283 C7
Narrogin Australia 32°58S 117°14E 279 F2
Narromine Australia 32°12S 148°12E 283 B8
Narrow Hills ⌂ Canada 54°0N 104°37W 297 C8
Narrows, The St. Kitts & Nevis 17°12N 62°40W 322 d
Narsampet India 17°57N 79°58E 244 F4
Narsaq Greenland 60°57N 46°4W 154 E6
Narsimhapur India 22°54N 79°14E 243 H8
Narsingdi Bangla. 23°55N 90°43E 241 D3
Narsinghgarh India 23°45N 76°40E 242 H7
Narsinghpur India 20°28N 85°5E 244 D7
Narsipatnam India 17°40N 82°37E 244 F6
Nartes, L. e Albania 40°32N 19°25E 202 F3
Nartkala Russia 43°33N 43°51E 191 J6
Naruo Japan 34°43N 135°22E 133 A1
Narutō = Sanmu Kantō, Japan 34°11N 134°37E 222 C6
Narutō = Sanmu Shikoku, Japan 35°36N 140°25E 223 B12
Naruto-Kaikyō Japan 34°14N 134°39E 222 C6
Narva Estonia 59°23N 28°12E 188 C5
Narva ~ Russia 59°27N 28°2E 188 C4
Narva Bay = Narva Laht Estonia 59°35N 27°35E 161 G22
Narva Laht Estonia 59°35N 27°35E 161 G22
Narvacan Phil. 17°25N 120°28E 232 C3
Narvik Norway 68°28N 17°26E 160 B17
Narvskoye Vdkhr. Russia 59°18N 28°14E 188 C5
Narwana India 29°39N 76°6E 242 E7
Narwiański △ Poland 52°5N 22°53E 185 F9
Narwinbi ✪ Australia 16°7S 136°17E 280 B2
Naryan-Mar Russia 67°42N 53°12E 186 A9
Narym Russia 59°0N 81°30E 214 D9
Naryn Kyrgyzstan 41°26N 75°58E 217 D9
Naryn □ Kyrgyzstan 41°26N 75°58E 217 D9
Naryn ~ Uzbekistan 40°52N 71°36E 217 D8
Naryn Qum Kazakhstan 47°30N 49°0E 191 G9
Nås, An = Naas Ireland 53°12N 6°40W 166 C5
Nasa Norway 66°29N 15°23E 160 C16
Nasarawa Nigeria 8°32N 7°41E 263 D6
Nasarawa □ Nigeria 8°30N 8°20E 263 D6
Nasau Fiji 17°19S 179°27E 287 A2
Năsăud Romania 47°19N 24°29E 183 C9
Nasawa Vanuatu 15°12S 168°9E 287 E6
Naşb, W. ~ Egypt 28°29N 34°31E 251 K5
Näsby Sweden 59°25N 18°5E 139 A2
Näsbypark Sweden 59°25N 18°5E 139 A2
Nasca Peru 14°50S 74°57W 330 C3
Nasca Ridge Pac. Oc. 20°0S 80°0W 289 K19
Nascentes do Rio Parnaíba △ Brazil 10°0S 47°0W 332 C2
Naseby N.Z. 45°1S 170°10E 285 F5
Naselle U.S.A. 46°22N 123°49W 306 D3
Naser, Buheirat en Egypt 23°0N 32°30E 256 C3
Nashik = Nasik India 19°58N 73°50E 244 E1
Nashua Iowa, U.S.A. 42°57N 92°32W 310 B4
Nashua Mont., U.S.A. 48°8N 106°22W 304 B10
Nashua N.H., U.S.A. 42°45N 71°28W 313 D13
Nashville Ark., U.S.A. 33°57N 93°51W 314 E8
Nashville Ga., U.S.A. 31°12N 83°15W 316 D6
Nashville Ill., U.S.A. 38°21N 89°23W 310 F7
Nashville Ind., U.S.A. 39°12N 86°15W 311 E10
Nashville Mich., U.S.A. 42°36N 85°5W 311 B11
Nashville Tenn., U.S.A. 36°10N 86°47W 315 C11
Našice Croatia 45°32N 18°4E 182 E3
Nasielsk Poland 52°35N 20°50E 185 F7
Nasik India 19°58N 73°50E 244 E1
Nasinu Fiji 18°4S 178°30E 287 A2
Nasipit Phil. 8°57N 125°19E 233 G5
Nasir South Sudan 8°36N 33°4E 257 F3
Nasirabad = Mymensingh Bangla. 24°45N 90°24E 241 C3
Nasirabad India 26°15N 74°45E 242 F6
Nasirabad Pakistan 28°23N 68°24E 242 E3
Nasiri = Ahvāz Iran 31°20N 48°40E 247 D6
Nasiriyah = An Nāşirīyah Iraq 31°0N 46°15E 246 D5
Naskaupi ~ Canada 53°47N 60°51W 299 B7
Naso Italy 38°7N 14°47E 201 D7
Naso Pt. Phil. 10°25N 121°57E 233 F3
Naşrābād Iran 34°8N 51°26E 247 C6
Naşrīān-e Pā'īn Iran 32°52N 46°52E 246 C5
Nass ~ Canada 55°0N 129°40W 296 C3
Nassau Bahamas 25°5N 77°20W 153 b
Nassau N.Y., U.S.A. 42°31N 73°37W 313 D11
Nassau, B. Chile 55°20S 68°0W 336 E3
Nassau Lynden Pindling Int. ✈ (NAS) Bahamas 25°3N 77°28W 153 b
Nasser, L. = Naser, Buheirat en Egypt 23°0N 32°30E 256 C3
Nasser City = Kôm Ombo Egypt 24°25N 32°52E 256 C3
Nassian Ivory C. 8°28N 3°28W 262 D4
Nässjö Sweden 57°39N 14°42E 163 G8
Nastapoka ~ Canada 56°55N 76°33W 298 A4
Nastapoka, Is. Canada 56°55N 76°50W 298 A4
Nasugbu Phil. 14°5N 120°38E 232 D3
Näsum Sweden 56°10N 14°29E 163 H8
Nasushiobara Japan 36°58N 140°3E 221 F10
Näsviken Sweden 61°46N 16°52E 162 C10
Nat Ma Taung △ Burma 21°30N 93°35E 241 E4
Nata Botswana 20°12S 26°12E 270 B4
Nata ~ Botswana 20°14S 26°10E 270 B4
Natagaima Colombia 3°37N 75°6W 328 C2
Natal Brazil 5°47S 35°13W 332 C4
Natal Indonesia 0°35N 99°7E 234 B1
Natal Drakensberg = uKhahlamba Drakensberg ⌂ S. Africa 29°27S 29°30E 271 C4
Natalinci Serbia 44°15N 20°49E 182 F5
Naţanz Iran 33°30N 51°55E 247 C6
Natashquan Canada 50°14N 61°46W 299 B7
Natashquan ~ Canada 50°7N 61°50W 299 B7
Natchez U.S.A. 31°34N 91°24W 314 F9
Natchitoches U.S.A. 31°46N 93°5W 314 F8
Natewa B. Fiji 16°35S 179°40E 287 A2
Nathalia Australia 36°1S 145°13E 283 D6
Nathan Philips Square Toronto, Canada 141 b2
Nathdwara India 24°55N 73°50E 242 G5
Nathu La Asia 27°24N 88°49E 241 B2
Nati, Pta. Spain 40°3N 3°50E 206 A4
Natimuk Australia 36°42S 142°0E 282 D5
Nation ~ Canada 55°30N 123°32W 296 B4
National Arboretum Washington, D.C., U.S.A. 38°54N 76°59W 143 B2
National Art Gallery Beijing, China 114 b2
National Atomic Testing Museum U.S.A. 36°7N 115°9W 124 B2
National Capital District □ Papua N. G. 9°25S 147°10E 286 E4
National City U.S.A. 32°40N 117°5W 307 N9
National Grand Theatre Beijing, China 114 c2
National Maritime Museum London, U.K. 51°29N 0°0 125 B3
National September 11 Memorial and Museum New York, U.S.A. 132 e1
National University (N.U.S.) Singapore 1°19N 103°46E 138 B2
National Zoological Park Washington, D.C., U.S.A. 38°55N 77°4W 143 B2
Nationals Park U.S.A. 38°53N 77°1W 143 B2
Natitingou Benin 10°20N 1°26E 263 C5
Natividad, I. Mexico 27°52N 115°11W 318 B1
Natividade Brazil 11°43S 47°47W 333 D2
Nativity, Basilica of West Bank 31°42N 35°12E 123 B2
Natkyizin Burma 14°57N 97°59E 236 E1
Natmauk Burma 20°20N 95°24E 241 E5
Natogyi Burma 21°25N 95°39E 241 E5
Natolin Poland 52°8N 21°4E 143 C2
Natonin Phil. 17°6N 121°18E 232 C3
Nator Bangla. 24°21N 89°5E 241 C2
Natron, L. Tanzania 2°20S 36°0E 268 C4
Natrona Heights U.S.A. 40°37N 79°44W 312 F5
Natrûn, W. el ~ Egypt 30°25N 30°13E 256 H7
Nattai △ Australia 34°12S 150°22E 283 C9
Nättraby Sweden 56°13N 15°31E 163 H9
Natuashish Canada 55°55N 61°8W 299 A7
Natukanaoka Pan Namibia 18°40S 15°45E 270 A2
Natuna Besar, Kepulauan Indonesia 4°0N 108°15E 235 B3
Natuna Is. = Natuna Besar, Kepulauan Indonesia 4°0N 108°15E 235 B3
Natuna Selatan, Kepulauan Indonesia 2°45N 109°0E 235 B3
Natural Bridge U.S.A. 44°5N 75°30W 313 B9
Natural Bridges ⌂ U.S.A. 37°36N 110°0W 305 H9
Naturaliste, C. Tas., Australia 40°50S 148°15E 281 G4
Naturaliste, C. W. Austral., Australia 33°32S 115°0E 279 F2
Naturaliste Plateau Ind. Oc. 34°0S 112°0E 276 G1
Nau Qala Afghan. 34°5N 68°5E 242 B3
Naucalpan de Juárez Mexico 19°28N 99°14W 128 B1
Naucelle France 44°13N 2°20E 174 D6
Nauders Austria 46°54N 10°30E 180 E3
Nauen Germany 52°36N 12°52E 178 C8
Naugard = Nowogard Poland 53°41N 15°10E 184 E2
Naugatuck U.S.A. 41°30N 73°3W 313 E11
Naujaat = Repulse Bay Canada 66°30N 86°30W 295 D14
Naujan Phil. 13°20N 121°18E 232 E3
Naujan Lake △ Phil. 13°9N 121°20E 232 E3
Naujoji Akmenė Lithuania 56°19N 22°54E 184 B9
Naulila Angola 17°13S 14°39E 265 F2
Naumburg Germany 51°9N 11°47E 178 D7
Naumburg am Queis = Nowogrodziec Poland 51°12N 15°24E 185 G2
Naupada Andhra Pradesh, India 18°34N 84°18E 244 E7
Naupada Maharashtra, India 19°3N 72°50E 130 A2
Nā'ūr Jordan 31°53N 35°50E 251 G6
Nauru ■ Pac. Oc. 1°0S 166°0E 288 H8
Naushahra = Nowshera Pakistan 34°0N 72°0E 240 B4
Naushahro Pakistan 26°50N 68°7E 242 F3
Naushon I. U.S.A. 41°29N 70°45W 313 E14
Nausori Fiji 18°2S 178°32E 287 B2
Naustdal Norway 61°31N 5°43E 164 C2
Nauta Peru 4°31S 73°35W 328 D3
Nautanwa India 27°20N 83°25E 243 F10
Naute ⌂ Namibia 26°55S 17°57E 270 C2
Nautla Mexico 20°13N 96°47W 319 C5
Nauvoo U.S.A. 40°33N 91°23W 310 D5
Nava Coahuila, Mexico 28°25N 100°45W 318 B4
Nava Spain 43°21N 5°31W 194 B5
Nava del Rey Spain 41°22N 5°6W 194 D5
Navadwip India 23°34N 88°20E 243 H13
Navahermosa Spain 39°41N 4°28W 195 F6
Navahrudak Belarus 53°40N 25°50E 177 B13
Navai Fiji 17°36S 177°57E 287 A1
Navajo Res. U.S.A. 36°48N 107°36W 305 H10
Naval Phil. 11°34N 124°23E 233 F5
Navalcarnero Spain 40°17N 4°5W 194 E6
Navalgund India 15°34N 75°22E 245 G2
Navalmoral de la Mata Spain 39°52N 5°33W 194 F5
Navalvillar de Pela Spain 39°9N 5°24W 195 F5
Navan Ireland 53°39N 6°41W 166 C5
Navanagar = Jamnagar India 22°30N 70°6E 242 H4
Navapolatsk Belarus 55°32N 28°37E 188 E5
Navarin, Mys Russia 62°15N 179°5E 215 C18
Navarino, I. Chile 55°0S 67°40W 336 E3
Navarra □ Spain 42°40N 1°40W 196 C3
Navarre Fla., U.S.A. 30°24N 86°52W 317 E3
Navarre Ohio, U.S.A. 40°43N 81°31W 312 F3
Navarro ~ U.S.A. 39°11N 123°45W 306 F3
Navas de San Juan Spain 38°30N 3°19W 195 G7
Navasota U.S.A. 30°23N 96°5W 314 F6
Navassa I. W. Indies 18°30N 75°0W 321 C5
Nävekvarn Sweden 58°38N 16°49E 163 F10
Naver ~ U.K. 58°32N 4°14W 167 C4
Navet Trin. & Tob. 10°21N 61°10W 323 t
Navet ~ Trin. & Tob. 10°24N 61°5W 323 t
Navet Res. Trin. & Tob. 10°24N 61°15W 323 t
Navi Mumbai India 19°5N 73°0E 130 A2
Navia Spain 43°35N 6°42W 194 B4
Navia ~ Spain 43°15N 6°50W 194 B4
Navia de Suarna = A Pobre Spain 42°58N 7°3W 194 C3
Navibandar India 21°26N 69°48E 242 J3
Navidad Chile 33°57S 71°50W 334 C1
Navidad Bank W. Indies 20°0N 68°58W 321 B6
Navíglio di Pavia Italy 45°24N 9°9E 128 B1
Navíglio Grande Italy 45°25N 9°5E 128 B1
Navirai Brazil 23°8S 54°13W 335 A5
Naviti Fiji 17°7S 177°15E 287 A1
Navlakhi India 22°58N 70°28E 242 H4
Navlya Russia 52°53N 34°30E 189 B8
Năvodari Romania 44°19N 28°36E 183 F13
Navoiy Uzbekistan 40°9N 65°22E 216 D7
Navojoa Mexico 27°6N 109°26W 318 B3
Navolato Mexico 24°47N 107°42W 318 C3
Navona, Piazza Rome, Italy 136 b2
Navotas Phil. 14°39N 120°56E 127 B1
Navrongo Ghana 10°51N 1°3W 263 C4
Navsari India 20°57N 72°59E 244 D1
Navua Fiji 18°12S 178°11E 287 B2
Navy Pier Chicago, U.S.A. 119 b3
Nawa Kot Pakistan 28°21N 71°24E 242 E4
Nawab Khan Pakistan 30°17N 69°12E 242 D3
Nawabganj Bangla. 24°35N 88°14E 241 C2
Nawabganj Ut. P., India 26°56N 81°14E 243 F9
Nawabganj Ut. P., India 28°32N 79°40E 243 E8
Nawabshah Pakistan 26°15N 68°25E 242 F3
Nawada India 24°50N 85°33E 243 G11
Nāwah Afghan. 32°19N 67°53E 240 B2
Nawakot Nepal 27°55N 85°10E 243 F11
Nawalgarh India 27°50N 75°15E 242 F6
Nawanshahr India 32°33N 74°48E 243 C6
Nawapara India 20°46N 82°33E 244 D6
Nawar, Dasht-i- Afghan. 33°52N 68°0E 242 C3
Nawāsīf, Ḩarrat Si. Arabia 21°20N 42°10E 248 B3
Nawi Sudan 18°32N 30°50E 256 D3
Nawng Hpa Burma 22°30N 98°30E 241 D7
Nawoiy = Navoiy Uzbekistan 40°9N 65°22E 216 D7
Nawş, Ra's Oman 17°15N 55°16E 249 C6
Naxçıvan Azerbaijan 39°12N 45°15E 213 C11
Naxçıvan □ Azerbaijan 39°25N 45°26E 213 C11
Naxos Greece 37°8N 25°25E 205 D7
Naxxar Malta 35°55N 14°27E 206 F7
Nay France 43°10N 0°18W 174 E3
Nay, Mui Vietnam 12°54N 109°26E 236 F7
Nāy Band Būshehr, Iran 27°20N 52°40E 247 E7
Nāy Band Khorāsān, Iran 32°20N 57°34E 247 C8
Nay Pyi Taw = Naypyidaw Burma 19°44N 96°12E 241 F6
Naya ~ Colombia 3°13N 77°22W 328 C2
Nayagarh India 20°8N 85°6E 244 D7
Nayakhan Russia 61°56N 159°0E 215 C16
Nayarit □ Mexico 22°0N 105°0W 318 C4
Nayé Senegal 14°28N 12°12W 262 C2
Nayong China 26°50N 105°20E 228 D5
Nayoro Japan 44°21N 142°28E 220 B11
Naypyidaw Burma 19°44N 96°12E 241 F6
Nayudupeta India 13°54N 79°54E 245 H4
Nayyāl, W. ~ Si. Arabia 28°35N 39°4E 246 D3
Nazal Hikmat Beg Iraq 33°23N 44°25E 113 A2
Nazar Kahrīzī Iran 37°20N 46°45E 213 D12
Nazaré Bahia, Brazil 13°2S 39°0W 333 D4
Nazaré Pará, Brazil 6°25S 52°29W 331 B7
Nazaré Tocantins, Brazil 6°23S 47°40W 332 C2
Nazaré Portugal 39°36N 9°4W 195 F1
Nazareth = Nazerat Israel 32°42N 35°17E 250 F6
Nazareth U.S.A. 40°44N 75°19W 313 F9
Nazarovo Russia 57°2N 90°40E 215 D10
Nazas Mexico 25°14N 104°8W 318 B4
Nazas ~ Mexico 25°12N 104°12W 318 B4
Nazca = Nasca Peru 14°50S 74°57W 330 C3
Naze, The U.K. 51°53N 1°18E 169 F9
Nazerat Israel 32°42N 35°17E 250 F6
Nāzīk Iran 39°1N 45°4E 213 C11
Nazilli Turkey 37°55N 28°15E 205 D10
Nazimabad Pakistan 24°54N 67°1E 123 A2
Nazinon = Red Volta ~ Africa 10°34N 0°30W 263 C4
Nazir Hat Bangla. 22°35N 91°49E 241 D3
Nazko Canada 53°1N 123°37W 296 C4
Nazko ~ Canada 53°7N 123°34W 296 C4
Nazlet el Simmân Egypt 29°59N 31°9E 117 B1
Nāzlū Iran 37°41N 45°0E 213 D11
Nazret Ethiopia 8°32N 39°22E 257 F4
Ncama Eq. Guin. 1°55N 10°56E 264 B2
Nchanga Zambia 12°30S 27°49E 269 E2
Ncheu Malawi 14°50S 34°47E 269 E3
Ncue Eq. Guin. 2°1N 10°28E 264 B2
Ndala Tanzania 4°45S 33°15E 268 C3
Ndalatando Angola 9°12S 14°48E 265 D2
Ndali Benin 9°50N 2°46E 263 D5
Ndareda Tanzania 4°12S 35°30E 268 C4
Ndélé C.A.R. 8°25N 20°36E 264 A4
Ndendé Gabon 2°22S 11°23E 264 C2
Ndiael ⌂ Senegal 16°15N 16°0W 262 B1
Ndikinimeki Cameroon 4°46N 10°50E 263 E7
Ndim Cameroon 5°10N 10°41E 264 A2
Ndindi Gabon 3°46S 11°9E 264 C2
N'Dioum Senegal 16°31N 14°39W 262 B1
Ndjamena Chad 12°10N 15°0E 259 F3
Ndjolé Gabon 0°10S 10°45E 264 C2
Ndogo, Lagune Gabon 2°35S 10°0E 264 C2
Ndok Cameroon 7°57N 14°42E 264 A2
Ndola Zambia 13°0S 28°34E 269 E2
Ndomo ⌂ S. Africa 26°52S 32°15E 271 C5
Ndoto Mts. Kenya 2°0N 37°0E 268 B4
Ndoua, C. N. Cal. 22°24S 166°56E 288 d
Ndouba Congo 0°9S 14°4E 264 C2
Ndoukou C.A.R. 4°33N 20°39E 264 B4
Nduguti Tanzania 4°18S 34°41E 268 C3
Nea ~ Norway 63°15N 11°0E 164 A8
Nea Alexandria Greece 37°52N 23°46E 112 B2
Nea Alikarnassos Greece 35°19N 25°11E 207 E6
Nea Anchialos Greece 39°16N 22°49E 204 B4
Nea Artaki Greece 38°31N 23°38E 204 C5
Nea Epidavros Greece 37°40N 23°7E 204 D5
Nea Ionia Athina, Greece 38°3N 23°45E 112 A2
Nea Ionia Magnisia, Greece 39°21N 22°56E 204 B4
Nea Kalikratia Greece 40°21N 23°3E 202 F7
Nea Liosia Greece 38°3N 23°43E 112 A2
Nea Makri Greece 38°5N 23°59E 204 C5
Nea Moudania Greece 40°15N 23°17E 202 F7
Nea Peramos Attiki, Greece 38°0N 23°26E 204 C5
Nea Peramos Kavala, Greece 40°50N 24°18E 203 F8
Nea Samsounda Greece 39°55N 20°45E 207 A2
Nea Smirni Greece 37°54N 23°43E 112 B2
Nea Visa Greece 41°34N 26°33E 203 E10
Nea Zichni Greece 41°2N 23°49E 202 E7
Neagari = Nomi Japan 36°26N 136°25E 223 A8
Neagh, Lough U.K. 54°37N 6°25W 166 B5
Neah Bay U.S.A. 48°22N 124°37W 306 B2
Neale, L. Australia 24°15S 130°0E 278 D5
Neales ~ Australia 28°8S 136°47E 281 D2
Neamati India 26°50N 94°20E 241 B5
Neamţ □ Romania 47°0N 26°20E 183 C11
Neapoli Athens, Greece 112 a3
Neapoli Kozani, Greece 40°20N 21°24E 202 F5
Neapoli Kriti, Greece 35°15N 25°37E 207 E6
Neapoli Lakonia, Greece 36°27N 23°8E 204 E5
Near Is. U.S.A. 52°30N 174°0E 303 K1
Near North Chicago, U.S.A. 119 b1
Neath U.K. 51°39N 3°48W 169 F4
Neath Port Talbot □ U.K. 51°42N 3°45W 169 F4
Nebbi Uganda 2°28N 31°6E 268 B3
Nebbou Burkina Faso 11°9N 1°51W 263 C4
Nebelat el Hagana Sudan 12°13N 29°12E 257 E2
Nebine Cr. ~ Australia 29°27S 146°56E 281 D4
Nebitdag = Balkanabat Turkmenistan 39°30N 54°22E 247 B7
Nebka Algeria 27°28N 3°12W 260 C4
Neblina, Pico da Brazil 0°48N 66°0W 328 C4
Nebo Australia 21°42S 148°42E 280 C4
Nebolchy Russia 59°8N 33°18E 188 C7
Nebraska □ U.S.A. 41°30N 99°30W 308 E4
Nebraska City U.S.A. 40°41N 95°52W 308 E6
Nébrodi, Monti Italy 37°54N 14°35E 201 E7
Nebušice Czechia 50°6N 14°19E 135 B1
Necedah U.S.A. 44°2N 90°4W 308 C8
Nechako ~ Canada 53°55N 122°42W 296 C4
Neches ~ U.S.A. 29°58N 93°51W 314 G8
Nechisar △ Ethiopia 5°58N 37°55E 257 F4
Neckar ~ Germany 49°27N 8°29E 179 F4
Neckartal-Odenwald ⌂ Germany 49°30N 9°5E 179 F5
Necker I. U.S.A. 23°35N 164°42W 302 G11
Necochea Argentina 38°30S 58°50W 334 D4
Nectar Brook Australia 32°43S 137°57E 282 B2
Neda Spain 43°30N 8°9W 194 B2
Neda ~ Greece 37°25N 21°45E 204 D3
Nedalshytta Norway 62°59N 12°3E 164 B9
Nedelino Bulgaria 41°27N 25°3E 203 E9
Nedelišće Croatia 46°23N 16°22E 199 B13
Nederhorst Neths. 52°16N 5°3E 112 B3
Nederland = Netherlands ■ Europe 52°0N 5°30E 170 C5
Nedlitz Germany 52°25N 13°3E 115 B1
Nedoboyivtsi Ukraine 48°26N 26°21E 183 B11
Nedreberg Norway 60°59N 11°41E 164 D8
Nedroma Algeria 35°1N 1°45W 261 A4
Nedstrand Norway 59°21N 5°49E 164 E2
Nee Soon Singapore 1°24N 103°49E 138 A2
Needham U.S.A. 42°17N 71°14W 116 B1
Needham Heights U.S.A. 42°17N 71°14W 116 B1
Needles B.C., Canada 49°53N 118°7W 296 D5
Needles Calif., U.S.A. 34°51N 114°37W 307 L12
Needles, The U.K. 50°39N 1°35W 169 G6
Needles Pt. N.Z. 36°3S 175°25E 284 C4
Neembucú □ Paraguay 27°0S 58°0W 334 B4
Neemuch = Nimach India 24°30N 74°56E 242 G6
Neenah U.S.A. 44°11N 88°28W 308 C9
Neepawa Canada 50°15N 99°30W 297 C9
Neeses U.S.A. 33°33N 81°7W 316 B8
Nefta Tunisia 33°53N 7°50E 258 B1
Neftçala Azerbaijan 39°19N 49°12E 213 C13
Neftechala = Neftçala Azerbaijan 39°19N 49°12E 213 C13
Neftegorsk Krasnodar, Russia 44°25N 39°45E 191 H4
Neftegorsk Sakhalin, Russia 53°1N 142°58E 215 D15
Neftekumsk Russia 44°46N 44°50E 191 H7
Nefteyugansk Russia 61°5N 72°42E 214 C8
Nefyn U.K. 52°56N 4°31W 168 E3
Négala Mali 12°52N 8°30W 262 C3
Negapatam = Nagappattinam India 10°46N 79°51E 245 J4
Negara Indonesia 8°22S 114°37E 231 J17
Negaunee U.S.A. 46°30N 87°36W 308 B10
Negele Oromiya, Ethiopia 5°20N 39°36E 257 F4
Negele Oromiya, Ethiopia 7°21N 38°42E 266 C4
Negeri Sembilan □ Malaysia 2°45N 102°10E 237 L4
Negev Desert = Hanegev Israel 30°50N 35°0E 251 H6
Negoiul, Vf. Romania 45°38N 24°35E 183 E9
Negombo Sri Lanka 7°12N 79°50E 245 L4
Negotin Serbia 44°16N 22°37E 202 B6
Negotino Macedonia 41°29N 22°7E 202 E6
Negra, Peña Spain 42°11N 6°30W 194 C4
Negra, Pta. Mauritania 22°54N 16°18W 260 D1
Negra, Pta. Peru 6°6S 81°10W 330 B1
Negra Pt. Phil. 18°40N 120°50E 232 B3
Negra Pt. Trin. & Tob. 10°4N 61°23W 323 t
Negrais, C. = Maudin Sun Burma 16°0N 94°30E 241 G5
Nègres, Pte. des Martinique 14°35N 61°5W 322 j
Negreşti Romania 46°50N 27°30E 183 D12
Negreşti-Oaş Romania 47°52N 23°26E 183 C8
Negril Jamaica 18°22N 78°20W 320 a
Négrine Algeria 34°30N 7°30E 261 B6
Negro ~ Argentina 41°2S 62°47W 336 B4
Negro ~ Bolivia 14°11S 63°7W 331 C5
Negro ~ Brazil 3°0S 60°0W 329 D6
Negro ~ Uruguay 33°24S 58°22W 334 C4
Negro, C. = Tarf, Ras Morocco 35°40N 5°11W 260 A3
Negro, C. Venezuela 11°11N 63°53W 329 a
Negros Phil. 9°30N 122°40E 233 G4
Negros Occidental □ Phil. 10°0N 122°55E 233 F4
Negros Oriental □ Phil. 9°45N 123°0E 233 G4
Negru Vodă Romania 43°47N 28°21E 183 G13
Neguac Canada 47°15N 65°5W 299 C6
Nehalem ~ U.S.A. 45°40N 123°56W 306 E3
Nehāvand Iran 35°56N 49°31E 247 C6
Nehbandān Iran 31°35N 60°5E 247 D9
Nehe China 48°29N 124°50E 219 B13
Nehoiu Romania 45°24N 26°20E 183 E11
Nei Mongol Zizhiqu □ China 42°0N 112°0E 226 D7
Neiafu Tonga 18°39S 173°59W 287 P14
Neidenburg = Nidzica Poland 53°25N 20°28E 185 E7
Neiges, Piton des Réunion 21°5S 55°29E 272 f
Neijiang China 29°35N 104°55E 228 C5
Neikiang = Neijiang China 29°35N 104°55E 228 C5
Neilingding Dao China 22°25N 113°48E 219 a
Neill I. India 11°50N 93°3E 245 J11
Neillsville U.S.A. 44°34N 90°36W 308 C8
Neilson, Récif Pac. Oc. 27°1S 146°2W 289 f
Neilton U.S.A. 47°25N 123°53W 306 C3
Neipu Taiwan 22°37N 120°33E 225 D2
Neiqiu China 37°15N 114°30E 226 F8
Neisse = Nysa ~ Europe 52°4N 14°46E 178 C10
Neiva Colombia 2°56N 75°18W 328 C2
Neiwan Taiwan 24°42N 121°10E 225 B3
Neixiang China 33°10N 111°52E 226 H6
Nejanilini L. Canada 59°33N 97°48W 297 B9
Nejd = Najd Si. Arabia 26°30N 42°0E 248 A3
Nejo Ethiopia 9°30N 35°28E 257 F4
Nejrab Afghan. 34°58N 69°34E 240 B3
Nekā Iran 36°39N 53°19E 247 B7
Nekemte Ethiopia 9°4N 36°30E 257 F4
Nêkheb Egypt 25°10N 32°48E 256 B3
Nekso Denmark 55°4N 15°8E 163 J9
Nelamangala India 13°6N 77°24E 245 H3
Nelas Portugal 40°32N 7°52W 194 E3
Nelaug Norway 58°39N 8°40E 164 F5
Nelia Australia 20°39S 142°12E 280 C3
Nelidovo Russia 56°13N 32°49E 188 D7
Neligh U.S.A. 42°8N 98°2W 308 D4
Nelkan Russia 57°40N 136°4E 215 D14
Nellikuppam India 11°46N 79°43E 245 J4
Nellis Air Force Base ✕ (LSV) U.S.A. 36°14N 115°2W 124 A2
Nellore India 14°27N 79°59E 245 G4
Nelson B.C., Canada 49°30N 117°20W 296 D5
Nelson N.Z. 41°18S 173°16E 285 B8
Nelson Lancs., U.K. 53°50N 2°13W 168 D5
Nelson Ariz., U.S.A. 35°31N 113°19W 305 J7
Nelson Nev., U.S.A. 35°42N 114°49W 307 K12
Nelson □ N.Z. 41°20S 173°20E 285 B8
Nelson ~ Canada 54°33N 98°2W 297 C9
Nelson, C. Vic., Australia 38°26S 141°32E 282 E4
Nelson, C. Papua N. G. 9°0S 149°20E 286 E5
Nelson, Estrecho Chile 51°30S 75°0W 336 D2
Nelson Bay Australia 32°43S 152°9E 283 B10
Nelson Forks Canada 59°30N 124°0W 296 B4
Nelson House Canada 55°47N 98°51W 297 B9
Nelson L. Canada 55°48N 100°7W 297 B8
Nelson Lakes △ N.Z. 41°55S 172°44E 285 B7
Nelson Mandela ✕ (RAI) C. Verde Is. 14°55N 23°30W 153 j
Nelson's Dockyard Antigua & B. 17°1N 61°46W 322 b
Nelspoort S. Africa 32°7S 23°0E 270 D3
Nelspruit = Mbombela S. Africa 25°29S 30°59E 271 C5
Néma Mauritania 16°40N 7°15W 262 B3
Neman = Nemunas ~ Lithuania 55°25N 21°10E 184 C8
Neman Russia 55°2N 22°2E 184 C9
N'ematābād Iran 35°38N 51°21E 141 B2
Nembe Nigeria 4°32N 6°24E 263 E6
Nembrala Indonesia 10°53S 122°50E 278 B3
Nemea Greece 37°49N 22°40E 204 D4
Německý Brod = Havlíčkův Brod Czechia 49°36N 15°33E 180 B8
Nemeiben L. Canada 55°20N 105°20W 297 B7
Nemërçkë, Mal Albania 40°15N 20°15E 202 F4
Nemira, Vf. Romania 46°17N 26°19E 183 D11
Nemiscau Canada 51°18N 76°54W 298 B4
Nemiscau, L. Canada 51°25N 76°40W 298 B4
Nemours = Ghazaouet Algeria 35°8N 1°50W 261 A4
Nemours France 48°16N 2°40E 173 D9
Nemrut Dağı △ Turkey 38°0N 38°55E 213 C8
Nemšová Slovakia 48°58N 18°7E 181 C11
Nemunas ~ Lithuania 55°25N 21°10E 184 C8
Nemuro Japan 43°20N 145°35E 220 C12
Nemuro-Kaikyō Japan 43°30N 145°30E 220 C12
Nemyriv Ukraine 50°7N 23°27E 185 H10
Nen Jiang ~ China 45°28N 124°30E 227 B13
Nenagh Ireland 52°52N 8°11W 166 D3
Nenana U.S.A. 64°34N 149°5W 303 D10
Nenasi Malaysia 3°9N 103°23E 237 L4
Nendo Pac. Oc. 10°45S 165°54E 277 C12
Nene ~ U.K. 52°49N 0°11E 169 E8
Nengkao Shan Taiwan 23°58N 121°16E 225 C3
Nengonengo French Polynesia 18°47S 141°48W 289 f
Nenita Greece 38°14N 26°6E 205 C8
Nenjiang China 49°10N 125°10E 219 B14
Neno Malawi 15°25S 34°40E 269 F3
Neo Chori Greece 38°25N 21°17E 204 C3
Neochori Greece 39°4N 21°0E 204 B2
Neodesha U.S.A. 37°25N 95°41W 308 G6
Neoga U.S.A. 39°19N 88°27W 311 E8
Neon Petritsi Greece 41°16N 23°15E 202 E7
Neópolis Brazil 10°18S 36°35W 332 D4
Neora Valley △ India 27°0N 88°45E 241 B2
Neos Marmaras Greece 40°6N 23°47E 202 F7
Neosho U.S.A. 36°52N 94°22W 308 G6
Neosho ~ U.S.A. 36°48N 95°18W 314 C7
Nepal ■ Asia 28°0N 84°30E 243 F11
Nepalganj Nepal 28°5N 81°40E 243 E9
Nepalganj Road India 28°1N 81°41E 243 E9
Nepean B. Australia 35°42S 137°37E 282 C2
Nephi U.S.A. 39°43N 111°50W 304 G8
Nephin Ireland 54°1N 9°22W 166 B2
Nephin Beg Range Ireland 54°0N 9°40W 166 C2
Nepi Italy 42°14N 12°21E 199 F9
Nepomuk Czechia 49°29N 13°35E 180 B6
Neppel = Moses Lake U.S.A. 47°8N 119°17W 304 C4
Neptune U.S.A. 40°13N 74°2W 313 F10
Neptune Is. Australia 35°17S 136°10E 282 C2
Neqāb Iran 36°42N 57°25E 247 B8
Nera Italy 42°26N 12°24E 199 F9
Nera ~ Romania 44°48N 21°25E 182 F6
Nérac France 44°8N 0°21E 174 D4
Nerang Australia 27°58S 153°20E 281 D5
Nerastro, Sarīr Libya 24°20N 20°37E 258 D4
Neratovice Czechia 50°16N 14°31E 180 A7
Nerchinsk Russia 52°0N 116°39E 215 D12
Nereju Romania 45°43N 26°43E 183 E11
Nerekhta Russia 57°26N 40°38E 188 D11
Neresnytsya Ukraine 48°7N 23°46E 183 B8
Néret, L. Canada 54°45N 70°44W 299 B5
Neretvanski Kanal Croatia 43°7N 17°10E 199 E14
Nerima Japan 35°44N 139°40E 140 A3
Neringa Lithuania 55°20N 21°5E 184 C8
Neris ~ Lithuania 55°8N 24°16E 188 E3
Nerja Spain 36°43N 3°55W 195 J7
Nerl ~ Russia 56°11N 40°34E 188 D11
Nerpio Spain 38°11N 2°16W 197 G2
Nerva Spain 37°42N 6°30W 195 H4
Nervi Italy 44°23N 9°2E 198 D6
Neryungri Russia 57°38N 124°28E 215 D13
Nes Iceland 65°53N 17°24W 155 B9
Nes Buskerud, Norway 60°34N 9°59E 164 D6
Nesbyen Norway 60°34N 9°8E 164 D6
Nescopeck U.S.A. 41°3N 76°12W 313 E8
Nesebŭr Bulgaria 42°41N 27°46E 203 D11
Neset Norway 61°53N 10°7E 164 C7
Nesflaten Norway 59°38N 6°48E 164 E3
Nesjahverfi Iceland 64°20N 15°15W 155 C11
Neskantaga Canada 52°14N 87°53W 298 B2
Neskaupstaður Iceland 65°9N 13°42W 155 B13
Nesland Norway 59°31N 7°59E 164 E4
Neslandsvatn Norway 58°57N 9°10E 164 F6
Nesodden Norway 59°48N 10°41E 133 B3
Nesoddtangen Norway 59°48N 10°40E 133 A3
Nesøya Norway 59°52N 10°31E 133 A2
Ness, L. U.K. 57°15N 4°32W 167 D4
Ness City U.S.A. 38°27N 99°54W 308 F4
Nessebar = Nesebŭr Bulgaria 42°41N 27°46E 203 D11
Nesterov = Zhovkva Ukraine 50°4N 23°58E 177 C12
Nesterov Russia 54°38N 22°41E 184 D9
Nestorio Greece 40°24N 21°5E 202 F5
Nestos ~ Europe 40°54N 24°49E 203 F8
Nesttun Norway 60°19N 5°20E 164 D2
Nesvady Slovakia 47°56N 18°7E 181 D11
Nesvizh = Nyasvizh Belarus 53°14N 26°38E 177 B14
Netaji Subhash Chandra Bose Int. ✕ (CCU) India 22°38N 88°26E 124 B2
Netanya Israel 32°20N 34°51E 251 F5
Netarhat India 23°29N 84°16E 243 H11
Nete ~ Belgium 51°7N 4°14E 170 C4
Netherdale Australia 21°10S 148°33E 280 b
Netherlands ■ Europe 52°0N 5°30E 170 C5
Netherlands Antilles = ABC Islands W. Indies 12°15N 69°0W 322 g
Netherlands East Indies = Indonesia ■ Asia 5°0S 115°0E 235 C4
Netherlands Guiana = Suriname ■ S. Amer. 4°0N 56°0W 329 C6
Neto ~ Italy 39°12N 17°9E 201 C10
Netrakona Bangla. 24°53N 90°47E 241 C3
Netrang India 21°39N 73°21E 242 J5
Nettancourt France 48°51N 4°57E 173 D11
Nettilling L. Canada 66°30N 71°0W 295 D17
Nettuno Italy 41°27N 12°39E 200 A5
Netzahualcóyotl, Presa Mexico 17°8N 93°35W 319 D6
Neu Aubing Germany 48°8N 11°25E 131 B1
Neu-Bentschen = Zbąszynek Poland 52°16N 15°51E 185 F2
Neu Buch Germany 52°37N 13°31E 115 A4
Neu Buchhorst Germany 52°24N 13°44E 115 B5
Neu Fahrland Germany 52°26N 13°3E 115 B1
Neu-Isenburg Germany 50°3N 8°42E 179 E4
Neu-Langenburg = Tukuyu Tanzania 9°17S 33°35E 269 D3
Neu Lindenberg Germany 52°36N 13°33E 115 A4
Neu Mecklenberg = New Ireland Papua N. G. 3°20S 151°50E 286 B6
Neu Pommern = New Britain Papua N. G. 5°50S 150°20E 286 C6
Neu-Sandec = Nowy Sącz Poland 49°40N 20°41E 185 J7
Neu Sandez = Nowy Sącz Poland 49°40N 20°41E 185 J7
Neu-Ulm Germany 48°22N 10°0E 179 G6
Neubiberg Germany 48°4N 11°40E 131 B3
Neubrandenburg Germany 53°33N 13°15E 178 B9
Neubukow Germany 54°2N 11°39E 178 A7
Neuburg Germany 48°44N 11°11E 179 G7
Neuchâtel Switz. 47°0N 6°55E 179 J2
Neuchâtel □ Switz. 47°0N 6°55E 179 J2
Neuchâtel, Lac de Switz. 46°53N 6°50E 179 J2
Neudau Austria 47°11N 16°6E 180 D9
Neuenburg an der Elbe = Nymburk Czechia 50°10N 15°1E 180 A8
Neuenhagen Germany 52°32N 13°38E 115 A4
Neuenhaus Germany 52°30N 6°58E 178 C2
Neuessling Austria 48°15N 16°32E 142 A3
Neuf-Brisach France 48°1N 7°30E 173 D14
Neufahrn Bayern, Germany 48°41N 12°11E 179 G8
Neufahrn Bayern, Germany 48°18N 11°40E 179 G7
Neufchâteau Belgium 49°50N 5°25E 170 E5
Neufchâteau Vosges, France 48°21N 5°40E 173 D12
Neufchâtel-en-Bray France 49°44N 1°26E 172 C8
Neufchâtel-sur-Aisne France 49°26N 4°1E 173 C11
Neuhaus = Jindřichův Hradec Czechia 49°10N 15°2E 180 B8
Neuhaus Germany 53°17N 10°56E 178 B6
Neuhäusel = Nové Zámky Slovakia 48°2N 18°8E 181 C11
Neuhausen Germany 48°9N 11°32E 131 B2
Neuherberg Germany 48°13N 11°35E 131 A2
Neuhönow Germany 52°34N 13°44E 115 A5
Neuillé-Pont-Pierre France 47°33N 0°33E 172 E7
Neuilly-Plaisance France 48°51N 2°30E 134 A4
Neuilly-St-Front France 49°10N 3°15E 173 C10
Neuilly-sur-Marne France 48°51N 2°31E 134 A4
Neuilly-sur-Seine France 48°53N 2°15E 134 A2
Neukagran Austria 48°14N 16°27E 142 A2
Neukalen Germany 53°49N 12°46E 178 B8
Neukettenhof Austria 48°7N 16°28E 142 B2
Neukölln Germany 52°28N 13°25E 115 B3
Neumarkt = Nowy Targ Poland 49°29N 20°2E 185 J7
Neumarkt = Środa Śląska Poland 51°10N 16°36E 185 G3
Neumarkt Germany 49°16N 11°27E 179 F7
Neumarktl = Tržič Slovenia 46°22N 14°18E 199 B11
Neumayer III Antarctica 71°0S 68°30W 151 D17
Neumittelwalde = Międzybórz Poland 51°25N 17°34E 185 G4
Neumünster Germany 54°4N 9°58E 178 A5
Neung-sur-Beuvron France 47°30N 1°50E 173 E8
Neunkirchen Austria 47°43N 16°4E 180 D9
Neunkirchen Saarland, Germany 49°20N 7°9E 179 F3
Neuperlach Germany 48°6N 11°37E 131 B2
Neuquén Argentina 38°55S 68°0W 336 A3
Neuquén □ Argentina 38°0S 69°50W 334 D2
Neuquén ~ Argentina 38°59S 68°0W 336 A3
Neuried Germany 48°5N 11°27E 131 B1
Neuruppin Germany 52°55N 12°48E 178 C8
Neusalz an der Oder = Nowa Sól Poland 51°48N 15°44E 185 G2
Neusäss Germany 48°24N 10°50E 179 G6
Neusatz = Novi Sad Serbia 45°18N 19°52E 182 E4
Neuse ~ U.S.A. 35°6N 76°29W 315 D16
Neusiedl Austria 47°57N 16°50E 181 D9
Neusiedler See Austria 47°50N 16°47E 181 D9
Neusiedler See-Seewinkel △ Austria 47°50N 16°45E 181 D9
Neusohl = Banská Bystrica Slovakia 48°46N 19°14E 181 C12
Neuss Germany 51°11N 6°42E 178 D2
Neussargues-Moissac France 45°9N 3°0E 174 C7
Neustadt = Lwówek Poland 52°28N 16°10E 185 F3
Neustadt = Prudnik Poland 50°20N 17°38E 185 H4
Neustadt = Wejherowo Poland 54°35N 18°12E 184 D5
Neustadt Bayern, Germany 49°44N 12°10E 179 F8
Neustadt Bayern, Germany 48°48N 11°46E 179 G7
Neustadt Bayern, Germany 49°34N 10°37E 179 F6
Neustadt Bayern, Germany 50°19N 11°7E 179 E7
Neustadt Brandenburg, Germany 52°50N 12°27E 178 C8
Neustadt Hessen, Germany 50°51N 9°9E 178 E5
Neustadt Sachsen, Germany 51°2N 14°12E 178 D10
Neustadt Schleswig-Holstein, Germany 54°6N 10°49E 178 A6
Neustadt Thüringen, Germany 50°45N 11°43E 178 E7
Neustadt am Rübenberge Germany 52°30N 9°30E 178 C5
Neustadt an der Weinstrasse Germany 49°21N 8°10E 179 F4
Neustädtel = Nowe Miasteczko Poland 51°42N 15°42E 185 G2
Neustädtl = Novo Mesto Slovenia 45°47N 15°12E 199 C12
Neustettin = Szczecinek Poland 53°43N 16°41E 184 E3
Neustift am Walde Austria 48°14N 16°17E 142 A1
Neustrelitz Germany 53°21N 13°4E 178 B9
Neusüssenbrunn Austria 48°16N 16°29E 142 A2
Neutitschein = Nový Jičín Czechia 49°30N 18°2E 181 B11
Neuvic France 45°23N 2°16E 174 C6
Neuville-sur-Saône France 45°52N 4°51E 175 C8
Neuvy-le-Roi France 47°36N 0°36E 172 E7
Neuvy-St-Sépulchre France 46°35N 1°48E 173 F8
Neuvy-sur-Barangeon France 47°20N 2°15E 173 E9
Neuwaldegg Austria 48°14N 16°17E 142 A1
Neuwedell = Drawno Poland 53°13N 15°46E 185 E2
Neuwerk Germany 53°55N 8°30E 178 B4
Neuwied Germany 50°26N 7°29E 178 E3
Neva ~ Russia 59°56N 30°20E 188 C6
Nevada Iowa, U.S.A. 42°1N 93°27W 310 B3
Nevada Mo., U.S.A. 37°51N 94°22W 310 G2
Nevada □ U.S.A. 39°0N 117°0W 304 G5
Nevada City U.S.A. 39°16N 121°1W 306 F6
Nevado, Cerro Argentina 35°30S 68°32W 334 D2
Nevado de Colima = Volcán de Colima △ Mexico 19°30N 103°40W 318 D4
Nevado de Tres Cruces △ Chile 27°13S 69°5W 334 B2
Nevado del Huila △ Colombia 3°5N 75°58W 328 C2
Nevasa India 19°34N 75°0E 244 E2
Neve, Sa. da Angola 13°43S 13°10E 265 E2
Neve Ya'akov West Bank 31°50N 35°14E 123 A2
Nevel Russia 56°0N 29°55E 188 D5
Nevelsk Russia 46°40N 141°51E 215 E15
Nevers France 47°0N 3°9E 173 F10
Nevertire Australia 31°50S 147°44E 283 A7
Neves Brazil 22°51S 43°5W 132 B2
Nevesinje Bos.-H. 43°14N 18°6E 202 C2
Neville Canada 49°58N 107°39W 297 D7
Nevinnomyssk Russia 44°40N 42°0E 191 H6
Nevis St. Kitts & Nevis 17°0N 62°30W 322 d
Nevis Pk. St. Kitts & Nevis 17°9N 62°34W 322 d
Nevlunghavn Norway 58°58N 9°53E 164 F6
Nevoso, Mte. = Snežnik Slovenia 45°36N 14°35E 199 C11
Nevrokop = Gotse Delchev Bulgaria 41°36N 23°46E 202 E7
Nevşehir Turkey 38°33N 34°40E 212 C6
Nevşehir □ Turkey 38°50N 34°40E 212 C6
Nevskoye Russia 54°32N 22°39E 184 D9
Nevyansk Russia 57°30N 60°13E 186 C11
New ~ Guyana 3°20N 57°37W 329 C6
New ~ W. Va., U.S.A. 38°10N 81°12W 309 F13
New Aiyansh Canada 55°12N 129°4W 296 B3
New Albany Ind., U.S.A. 38°18N 85°49W 311 F11
New Albany Miss., U.S.A. 34°29N 89°0W 315 D10
New Albany Pa., U.S.A. 41°36N 76°27W 313 E8
New Amsterdam Guyana 6°15N 57°36W 329 B6
New Athens U.S.A. 38°19N 89°53W 310 F7
New Atlas = Akhali Atoni Georgia 43°7N 40°50E 191 J5
New Baghdād Iraq 33°18N 44°28E 113 B2
New Baltimore U.S.A. 42°41N 82°44W 312 D2
New Barakpur India 22°40N 88°26E 124 A2
New Barbadoes = Hackensack U.S.A. 40°52N 74°2W 132 A1
New Bedford U.S.A. 41°38N 70°56W 313 E14
New Berlin = North Canton U.S.A. 40°53N 81°24W 312 F3

New Berlin Ill., U.S.A. 39°44N 89°55W 310 E7
New Berlin N.Y., U.S.A. 42°37N 75°20W 313 D9
New Berlin Pa., U.S.A. 40°50N 76°57W 312 F8
New Berlin Wis., U.S.A. 42°59N 88°6W 311 B8
New Bern U.S.A. 35°7N 77°3W 315 D16
New Bethlehem U.S.A. 41°0N 79°20W 312 F5
New Bight Bahamas 24°19N 75°24W 321 B4
New Bloomfield U.S.A. 40°25N 77°11W 312 F7
New Boston U.S.A. 33°28N 94°25W 314 E7
New Braunfels U.S.A. 29°42N 98°8W 314 G5
New Brighton N.Z. 43°29S 172°43E 285 D7
New Brighton N.Y., U.S.A. 40°38N 74°5W 132 C1
New Brighton Pa., U.S.A. 40°42N 80°19W 312 F4
New Britain Papua N. G. 5°50S 150°20E 286 C6
New Britain Conn., U.S.A. 41°40N 72°47W 313 E12
New Britain Trench Pac. Oc. 6°0S 153°0E 276 J3
New Brockton U.S.A. 31°23N 85°56W 316 D4
New Brookland = West Columbia U.S.A. 33°59N 81°4W 316 B8
New Brunswick U.S.A. 40°30N 74°27W 313 F10
New Brunswick □ Canada 46°50N 66°30W 299 C6
New Buffalo U.S.A. 41°47N 86°45W 311 C10
New Bussa Nigeria 9°53N 4°31E 263 D5
New Caledonia ☒ Pac. Oc. 21°0S 165°0E 288 d
New Caledonia Trough Pac. Oc. 30°0S 165°0E 288 L8
New Canada S. Africa 26°12S 27°56E 123 B1
New Canada Dam S. Africa 26°12S 27°56E 123 B1
New Carlisle Ind., U.S.A. 41°45N 86°32W 311 C10
New Carlisle Ohio, U.S.A. 39°56N 84°2W 311 E12
New Castile = Castilla-La Mancha □ Spain 39°30N 3°30W 195 F7
New Castle Ind., U.S.A. 39°55N 85°22W 311 E11
New Castle Ky., U.S.A. 38°26N 85°10W 311 F11
New Castle Pa., U.S.A. 41°0N 80°21W 312 F4
New Chitose ✈ (CTS) Japan 42°46N 141°41E 220 C10
New City U.S.A. 41°9N 73°59W 313 E11
New Concord U.S.A. 39°59N 81°54W 312 G3
New Cross U.K. 51°28N 0°1W 125 B3
New Cumberland U.S.A. 40°30N 80°36W 312 F4
New Cuyama U.S.A. 34°57N 119°38W 307 L7
New Delhi India 28°36N 77°11E 120 B2
New Denver Canada 50°0N 117°25W 296 D5
New Don Pedro Res. U.S.A. 37°43N 120°24W 306 H6
New Dorp U.S.A. 40°34N 74°7W 132 C1
New Dorp Beach U.S.A. 40°33N 74°6W 132 C1
New Ellenton U.S.A. 33°28N 81°41W 316 B8
New England U.S.A. 43°0N 71°0W 301 G25
New England N. Dak., U.S.A. 46°32N 102°52W 308 B2
New England △ Australia 30°25S 152°30E 283 A10
New England Aquarium Boston, U.S.A. 116 b3
New England Ra. Australia 30°20S 151°45E 281 E5
New England Seamounts Atl. Oc. 38°0N 63°0W 152 C5
New Forest △ U.K. 50°53N 1°34W 169 G6
New Franklin U.S.A. 39°1N 92°44W 310 E4
New Galloway U.K. 55°5N 4°9W 167 F4
New Georgia Is. Solomon Is. 8°15S 157°30E 287 M9
New Georgia Sound Solomon Is. 8°0S 158°20E 287 L9
New Glarus U.S.A. 42°49N 89°38W 310 B7
New Glasgow Canada 45°35N 62°36W 299 C7
New Grant Trin. & Tob. 10°17N 61°19W 323 t
New Guinea Oceania 4°0S 136°0E 276 B7
New Halfa = Halfa al Jadidah Sudan 15°20N 35°35E 266 A4
New Hamburg Canada 43°23N 80°42W 312 C4
New Hampshire □ U.S.A. 44°0N 71°30W 313 C13
New Hampton U.S.A. 43°3N 92°19W 310 A4
New Hanover Papua N. G. 2°30S 150°10E 286 B6
New Hanover KwaZulu Natal, S. Africa 29°22S 30°31E 271 C5
New Harmony U.S.A. 38°8N 87°56W 311 F9
New Hartford U.S.A. 43°4N 75°18W 313 C9
New Haven Conn., U.S.A. 41°18N 72°55W 313 E12
New Haven Ill., U.S.A. 37°55N 88°8W 311 G8
New Haven Ind., U.S.A. 41°4N 85°1W 311 C11
New Haven Mich., U.S.A. 42°44N 82°48W 312 D2
New Haven Mo., U.S.A. 38°37N 91°13W 310 F5
New Haven N.Y., U.S.A. 43°28N 76°18W 313 C8
New Hazelton Canada 55°20N 127°30W 296 B3
New Hebrides = Vanuatu ■ Pac. Oc. 15°0S 168°0E 287 E6
New Holland U.S.A. 40°6N 76°5W 313 F8
New Iberia U.S.A. 30°1N 91°49W 314 F9
New Ireland Papua N. G. 3°20S 151°50E 286 B6
New Ireland □ Papua N. G. 3°0S 151°30E 286 B6
New Jersey □ U.S.A. 40°0N 74°30W 309 F16
New Kensington U.S.A. 40°34N 79°46W 312 F5
New Lexington U.S.A. 39°43N 82°13W 309 F12
New Liskeard Canada 47°31N 79°41W 298 C4
New London Conn., U.S.A. 41°22N 72°6W 313 E12
New London Iowa, U.S.A. 40°55N 91°24W 310 D5
New London Mo., U.S.A. 39°35N 91°24W 310 E5
New London Ohio, U.S.A. 41°5N 82°24W 312 E2
New London Wis., U.S.A. 44°23N 88°45W 308 C9
New Madrid U.S.A. 36°36N 89°32W 308 G9
New Malden U.K. 51°24N 0°15W 125 B2
New Martinsville U.S.A. 39°39N 80°52W 309 F13
New Meadows U.S.A. 44°58N 116°18W 304 D5
New Melones L. U.S.A. 37°57N 120°31W 306 H6
New Mexico □ U.S.A. 34°30N 106°0W 305 J11
New Miami U.S.A. 39°26N 84°32W 311 E12
New Milford Conn., U.S.A. 41°35N 73°25W 313 E11
New Milford N.Y., U.S.A. 40°56N 74°0W 132 A1
New Milford Pa., U.S.A. 41°52N 75°44W 313 E9
New Mumbai = Navi Mumbai India 19°5N 73°0E 130 A2
New Norcia Australia 30°57S 116°13E 279 F2
New Norfolk Australia 42°46S 147°2E 281 G4
New Orleans U.S.A. 29°57N 90°4W 131 B2
New Orleans Int. ✈ (MSY) U.S.A. 30°0N 90°15W 131 B1
New Palestine U.S.A. 39°45N 85°52W 311 E11
New Paris U.S.A. 39°51N 84°48W 311 E12
New Pekin U.S.A. 38°30N 86°0W 311 F10
New Philadelphia U.S.A. 40°30N 81°27W 312 F3
New Plymouth N.Z. 39°4S 174°5E 284 F3
New Plymouth Idaho, U.S.A. 43°58N 116°49W 304 E5
New Pomerania = New Britain Papua N. G. 5°50S 150°20E 286 C6
New Port Richey U.S.A. 28°16N 82°43W 317 G7
New Providence Bahamas 25°25N 77°35W 153 b
New Quay U.K. 52°13N 4°21W 169 E3
New Radnor U.K. 52°15N 3°9W 169 E4
New Richmond Qué., Canada 48°15N 65°45W 299 C6
New Richmond Ohio, U.S.A. 38°57N 84°17W 311 F12
New Richmond Wis., U.S.A. 45°7N 92°32W 308 C7
New River ➜ U.S.A. 26°6N 80°6W 129 B3
New River Gorge ⌓ U.S.A. 37°53N 81°5W 309 G13
New Roads U.S.A. 30°42N 91°26W 314 F9
New Rochelle U.S.A. 40°55N 73°46W 313 F11
New Rockford U.S.A. 47°41N 99°8W 308 B4
New Romney U.K. 50°59N 0°57E 169 G8
New Ross Ireland 52°23N 6°57W 166 D5
New Salem U.S.A. 46°51N 101°25W 308 B3
New Scone = Scone U.K. 56°25N 3°24W 167 E5
New Sharon U.S.A. 41°28N 92°39W 310 C4
New Siberian I. = Novaya Sibir, Ostrov Russia 75°10N 150°0E 215 B16
New Siberian Is. = Novosibirskiye Ostrova Russia 75°0N 142°0E 215 B15
New Smyrna Beach U.S.A. 29°1N 80°56W 317 F9
New South Wales □ Australia 33°0S 146°0E 283 B7
New Stuyahok U.S.A. 59°29N 157°20W 303 G8
New Tecumseth = Alliston Canada 44°9N 79°52W 312 B5
New Territories Hong Kong, China 22°23N 114°5E 122 A2
New Toronto Canada 43°35N 79°30W 141 B1
New Town = Nowe Miasto Warsaw, Poland 143 a2
New Town Edinburgh, U.K. 121 a2
New Town N. Dak., U.S.A. 47°59N 102°30W 308 B2
New Ulm U.S.A. 44°19N 94°28W 308 C6
New Utrecht U.S.A. 40°36N 73°59W 132 C2
New Vienna U.S.A. 39°19N 83°42W 311 E13
New Washington Phil. 11°39N 122°26E 233 F4
New Waterford Canada 46°13N 60°4W 299 C7
New Westminster Canada 49°13N 122°55W 306 A4
New York U.S.A. 40°43N 74°0W 132 B2
New York □ U.S.A. 43°0N 75°0W 313 D9
New York Avenue Washington, D.C., U.S.A. 143 a2
New York J.F. Kennedy Int. ✈ (JFK) U.S.A. 40°38N 73°47W 313 F11
New York La Guardia ✈ (LGA) U.S.A. 40°46N 73°52W 132 B2
New York University New York, U.S.A. 132 d2
New Zealand ■ Oceania 40°0S 176°0E 284 G5
Newaj ➜ India 24°24N 76°49E 242 G7
Newala Tanzania 10°58S 39°18E 269 E4
Newark Del., U.S.A. 39°41N 75°46W 309 F16
Newark N.J., U.S.A. 40°44N 74°10W 313 F10
Newark N.Y., U.S.A. 43°3N 77°6W 312 C7
Newark Ohio, U.S.A. 40°3N 82°24W 312 F2
Newark B. U.S.A. 40°40N 74°8W 132 B1
Newark Liberty Int. ✈ (EWR) U.S.A. 40°42N 74°10W 313 F10
Newark-on-Trent U.K. 53°5N 0°48W 168 D7
Newark Valley U.S.A. 42°14N 76°11W 313 D8
Newbattle U.K. 55°53N 3°4W 121 B3
Newberg U.S.A. 45°18N 122°58W 304 D2
Newberry Fla., U.S.A. 29°39N 82°37W 317 F7
Newberry Mich., U.S.A. 46°21N 85°30W 309 B11
Newberry S.C., U.S.A. 34°17N 81°37W 315 D14
Newberry Springs U.S.A. 34°50N 116°41W 307 L10
Newboro L. Canada 44°38N 76°20W 313 B8
Newbridge Ireland 53°11N 6°48W 166 C5
Newburg U.S.A. 37°55N 91°54W 310 G5
Newburgh Ont., Canada 44°19N 76°52W 312 B8
Newburgh Ind., U.S.A. 37°57N 87°24W 311 G9
Newburgh N.Y., U.S.A. 41°30N 74°1W 313 E10
Newbury W. Berkshire, U.K. 51°24N 1°20W 169 F6
Newbury N.H., U.S.A. 43°19N 72°3W 313 B12
Newbury Vt., U.S.A. 44°5N 72°4W 313 B12
Newbury Park U.K. 51°34N 0°5E 125 A4
Newburyport U.S.A. 42°49N 70°53W 313 D14
Newcastle N.S.W., Australia 33°0S 151°46E 283 B9
Newcastle N.B., Canada 47°1N 65°38W 299 C6
Newcastle Ont., Canada 43°55N 78°35W 298 D4
Newcastle Limerick, Ireland 52°27N 9°3W 166 D2
Newcastle St. Kitts & Nevis 17°14N 62°42W 322 d
Newcastle KwaZulu Natal, S. Africa 27°45S 29°58E 271 C4
Newcastle Down, U.K. 54°13N 5°54W 166 B6
Newcastle Calif., U.S.A. 38°53N 121°8W 306 G5
Newcastle Wyo., U.S.A. 43°50N 104°11W 304 E11
Newcastle Emlyn U.K. 52°2N 4°28W 169 E3
Newcastle Ra. Australia 15°45S 130°15E 278 C5
Newcastle-under-Lyme U.K. 53°1N 2°14W 168 D5
Newcastle-upon-Tyne U.K. 54°58N 1°36W 168 C6
Newcastle Waters Australia 17°30S 133°28E 280 B1
Newcomb U.S.A. 43°58N 74°10W 313 C10
Newcomerstown U.S.A. 40°16N 81°36W 312 F3
Newcraighall U.K. 55°56N 3°5W 121 B3
Newdegate Australia 33°6S 119°0E 279 F2
Newell Queens., Australia 16°20S 145°16E 280 B4
Newell Iowa, U.S.A. 42°36N 95°0W 310 B1
Newell S. Dak., U.S.A. 44°43N 103°25W 308 C2
Newenham, C. U.S.A. 58°39N 162°11W 303 G7
Newfane U.S.A. 43°17N 78°43W 312 C6
Newfield U.S.A. 42°18N 76°33W 313 D8
Newfound L. U.S.A. 43°40N 71°47W 313 C13
Newfoundland Canada 49°0N 55°0W 299 C8
Newfoundland Pa., U.S.A. 41°18N 75°19W 313 E9
Newfoundland & Labrador □ Canada 52°0N 58°0W 299 B8
Newhalen U.S.A. 59°43N 154°54W 303 G9
Newham □ U.K. 51°31N 0°3E 125 A4
Newhaven E. Sussex, U.K. 50°47N 0°3E 169 G8
Newhaven Edinburgh, U.K. 55°59N 3°11W 121 B2
Newington Edinburgh, U.K. 55°56N 3°10W 121 B2
Newington London, U.K. 125 c5
Newington Ga., U.S.A. 32°35N 81°30W 316 C8
Newkirk U.S.A. 36°53N 97°3W 314 C6
Newlands S. Africa 26°10S 27°57E 123 B1
Newlyn U.K. 50°6N 5°34W 169 G2
Newman W. Austral., Australia 23°18S 119°45E 278 D2
Newman Calif., U.S.A. 37°19N 121°1W 306 H5
Newman Ill., U.S.A. 39°48N 87°59W 311 E9
Newmarket Ont., Canada 44°3N 79°28W 312 B5
Newmarket Cork, Ireland 52°13N 9°0W 166 D2
Newmarket Jamaica 18°9N 77°55W 320 a
Newmarket Suffolk, U.K. 52°15N 0°25E 169 E8
Newmarket N.H., U.S.A. 43°5N 70°56W 313 C14
Newnan U.S.A. 33°23N 84°48W 316 B5
Newport = Nieuwpoort Curaçao 12°3N 68°49W 322 g
Newport Vic., Australia 37°50S 144°51E 128 B1
Newport Mayo, Ireland 53°53N 9°33W 166 C2
Newport I. of W., U.K. 50°42N 1°17W 169 G6
Newport Newport, U.K. 51°35N 3°0W 169 F5
Newport Ark., U.S.A. 35°37N 91°16W 314 D9
Newport Fla., U.S.A. 30°11N 84°10W 316 E5
Newport Ind., U.S.A. 39°53N 87°25W 311 E9
Newport Ky., U.S.A. 39°5N 84°29W 311 E12
Newport N.H., U.S.A. 43°22N 72°10W 313 C12
Newport N.Y., U.S.A. 43°11N 75°1W 313 C9
Newport Oreg., U.S.A. 44°39N 124°3W 304 D1
Newport Pa., U.S.A. 40°29N 77°8W 312 F7
Newport R.I., U.S.A. 41°29N 71°19W 313 E13
Newport Tenn., U.S.A. 35°58N 83°11W 315 D13
Newport Vt., U.S.A. 44°56N 72°13W 313 B12
Newport Wash., U.S.A. 48°11N 117°3W 304 B5
Newport □ U.K. 51°33N 3°1W 169 F4
Newport Beach U.S.A. 33°37N 117°56W 307 M9
Newport News U.S.A. 36°58N 76°25W 309 G15
Newport Pagnell U.K. 52°5N 0°43W 169 E7
Newquay U.K. 50°25N 5°6W 169 G2
Newry U.K. 54°11N 6°21W 166 B5
Newry Islands △ Australia 20°51S 148°56E 280 b
Newtok U.S.A. 60°56N 164°38W 303 F6
Newton Ga., U.S.A. 31°19N 84°20W 316 D5
Newton Ill., U.S.A. 38°59N 88°10W 311 F8
Newton Iowa, U.S.A. 41°42N 93°3W 310 C3
Newton Kans., U.S.A. 38°3N 97°21W 308 F5
Newton Mass., U.S.A. 42°21N 71°12W 116 B1
Newton Miss., U.S.A. 32°19N 89°10W 315 E10
Newton N.C., U.S.A. 35°40N 81°13W 315 D14
Newton N.J., U.S.A. 41°3N 74°45W 313 E10
Newton Tex., U.S.A. 30°51N 93°46W 314 F8
Newton Abbot U.K. 50°32N 3°37W 169 G4
Newton Aycliffe U.K. 54°37N 1°34W 168 C6
Newton Falls N.Y., U.S.A. 44°12N 74°59W 313 B10
Newton Falls Ohio, U.S.A. 41°11N 80°59W 312 E4
Newton L. U.S.A. 38°55N 88°15W 311 F8
Newton Stewart U.K. 54°57N 4°30W 167 G4
Newton Terrace Barbados 13°4N 59°32W 323 r
Newtonbrook Canada 43°47N 79°24W 141 A2
Newtongrange U.K. 55°53N 3°3W 121 B3
Newtonmore U.K. 57°4N 4°8W 167 D4
Newtontoppen Svalbard 79°0N 17°30E 154 B12
Newtonville U.S.A. 42°20N 71°11W 116 A1
Newtown N.S.W., Australia 33°54S 151°11E 139 B2
Newtown Powys, U.K. 52°31N 3°19W 169 E4
Newtown Ind., U.S.A. 40°13N 87°9W 311 D9
Newtown Mo., U.S.A. 40°22N 93°20W 310 D3
Newtownabbey U.K. 54°40N 5°56W 166 B6
Newtownards U.K. 54°36N 5°42W 166 B6
Newtownbarry = Bunclody Ireland 52°39N 6°40W 166 D5
Newtownstewart U.K. 54°43N 7°23W 166 B4
Newville U.S.A. 40°10N 77°24W 312 F7
Nexon France 45°41N 1°11E 174 C5
Neya Russia 58°21N 43°49E 190 A6
Neyrīz Iran 29°15N 54°19E 247 D7
Neyshābūr Iran 36°10N 58°50E 247 B8
Neyveli India 11°32N 79°29E 245 J4
Neyyattinkara India 8°26N 77°5E 245 K3
Nezametny = Aldan Russia 58°40N 125°30E 215 D13
Nezhin = Nizhyn Ukraine 51°5N 31°55E 189 G6
Nezperce U.S.A. 46°14N 116°14W 304 C5
Nezvysko Ukraine 48°46N 25°15E 183 B10
Nga, Laem Thailand 7°55N 98°27E 237 a
Ngaanyatjarra ◎ Australia 22°40S 127°0E 278 D4
Ngabang Indonesia 0°23N 109°55E 235 B3
Ngabe Congo 3°12S 16°12E 264 C3
Ngabordamlu, Tanjung Indonesia 6°56S 134°11E 231 F8
N'Gage Angola 7°46S 15°15E 265 D3
Ngaiphaipi Burma 22°14N 93°15E 241 D4
Ngala Nigeria 12°20N 14°11E 263 C7
Ngaliwurru Nungali ◎ Australia 15°42S 130°4E 278 C5
Ngalurrtju ◎ Australia 22°44S 132°5E 278 D5
Ngama Chad 11°45N 17°6E 259 F3
Ngambé Centre, Cameroon 5°48N 11°29E 263 D7
Ngambé Littoral, Cameroon 4°21N 10°40E 263 E7
Ngami Depression Botswana 20°30S 22°46E 270 B3
Ngamo Zimbabwe 19°3S 27°32E 269 F2
Ngamring China 29°14N 87°10E 218 F6
Nganbéto, L. de Togo 7°26N 1°25E 263 D5
Ngangala South Sudan 4°42N 31°55E 257 G3
Nganglong Kangri China 33°0N 81°0E 243 C9
Ngao Thailand 18°46N 99°59E 236 C2
Ngaoundéré Cameroon 7°15N 13°35E 264 A2
Ngapali Burma 18°26N 94°19E 241 F5
Ngapara N.Z. 44°57S 170°46E 285 E5
Ngape Burma 20°2N 94°28E 241 E5
Ngara Tanzania 2°29S 30°40E 268 C3
Ngardmau Palau 7°37N 134°34E 288 c
Ngardmau B. Palau 7°38N 134°34E 288 c
Ngardololok Palau 7°0N 134°14E 288 c
Ngaregur Palau 7°45N 134°37E 288 c
Ngarluma ◎ Australia 21°30S 118°30E 278 D2
Ngaruawahia N.Z. 37°42S 175°11E 284 D4
Ngaruroro ➜ N.Z. 39°34S 176°55E 284 F5
Ngatangiia Cook Is. 21°14S 159°43W 289 h
Ngatapa N.Z. 38°32S 177°45E 284 E6
Ngathainggyaung Burma 17°24N 95°5E 241 G5
Ngau Chi Wan Hong Kong, China 22°20N 114°12E 122 A3
Ngau Tau Kok Hong Kong, China 22°19N 114°12E 122 B3
Ngauruhoe, Mt. N.Z. 39°13S 175°45E 284 F4
Ngawi Indonesia 7°24S 111°26E 235 D4
Ngcobo S. Africa 31°37S 28°0E 271 D4
Ngele Dem. Rep. of the Congo 0°30S 20°22E 264 C4
Ngelebok Cameroon 4°16N 14°3E 264 B2
Ngeregong Palau 7°6N 134°21E 288 c
Ngergoi Palau 7°5N 134°15E 288 c
Ngerulmud = Melekeok Palau 7°27N 134°38E 288 c
Ngesebus I. Palau 7°3N 134°15E 288 c
Nggatokae Solomon Is. 8°45S 158°15E 287 M10
Nggela Pile Solomon Is. 9°5S 160°20E 287 M11
Nggela Sule Solomon Is. 9°2S 160°12E 287 M11
Nghia Lo Vietnam 21°33N 104°28E 228 G5
Ngidinga Dem. Rep. of the Congo 5°37S 15°17E 265 D3
Ngo Congo 2°29S 15°45E 264 C3
Ngoap Cameroon 4°9N 12°51E 264 B2
Ngobasangel Palau 7°16N 134°19E 288 c
Ngoboli South Sudan 4°57N 32°37E 257 G3
Ngol = Raqaba ez Zarqa ➜ South Sudan 9°14N 29°44E 257 F2
N'Gola Angola 14°10S 14°30E 265 E2
Ngoma Malawi 13°8S 33°45E 269 E3
Ngomahura Zimbabwe 20°26S 30°43E 269 G3
Ngomba Tanzania 8°20S 32°53E 269 D3
Ngomeni, Ras Kenya 2°59S 40°14E 268 C5
Ngong Kenya 1°22S 36°39E 268 C4
Ngong Ping Hong Kong, China 22°15N 113°54E 122 B1
Ngong Shuen Chau = Stonecutters I. Hong Kong, China 22°19N 114°8E 122 B2
Ngongotaha N.Z. 38°5S 176°12E 284 E5
Ngonye Falls Zambia 16°40S 23°25E 265 F4
Ngop South Sudan 6°17N 30°9E 257 F3
Ngoring Hu China 34°55N 97°5E 218 E8
Ngorkou Mali 15°40N 3°41W 262 B4
Ngorongoro Tanzania 3°11S 35°32E 268 C4
Ngorongoro ⌓ Tanzania 2°40S 35°30E 268 C4
Ngoto C.A.R. 3°59N 17°19E 264 B3
Ngounié □ Gabon 2°0S 11°0E 264 C2
Ngounie ➜ Gabon 0°37S 10°18E 264 C2
Ngouo, Dj. C.A.R. 7°55N 24°38E 264 A4
Ngoura Chad 12°44N 16°21E 259 F3
Ngouri Chad 13°38N 15°22E 259 F3
Ngourti Niger 15°19N 13°12E 259 E2
Ngoussou Gabon 3°0S 11°7E 264 C2
Ngozi Burundi 2°54S 29°50E 268 C2
Ngua Kok Wan Hong Kong, China 22°21N 114°5E 122 A2
Ngudu Tanzania 2°58S 33°25E 268 C3
Nguigmi Niger 14°20N 13°20E 259 F2
Nguila Cameroon 4°41N 11°43E 263 E7
Nguiu Australia 11°46S 130°38E 278 B5
Ngukurr Australia 14°44S 134°44E 280 A1
Ngum ➜ Laos 18°31N 102°32E 236 C4
Nguna Vanuatu 17°26S 168°22E 287 G6
Ngundu Zimbabwe 18°11S 31°15E 269 F3
Ngunga Tanzania 3°37S 33°37E 268 C3
Nguru Nigeria 12°56N 10°29E 263 C7
Nguru Mts. Tanzania 6°0S 37°30E 268 D4
Ngusi Malawi 14°0S 34°50E 269 E3
Nguyen Binh Vietnam 22°39N 105°56E 228 F5
Ngwaketse □ Botswana 25°0S 25°0E 270 C3
Ngwedaung Burma 19°31N 97°9E 241 F6
Ngwesaung Burma 16°52N 94°23E 241 G5
Nha Bang Vietnam 10°37N 105°0E 237 G5
Nha Trang Vietnam 12°16N 109°10E 237 F7
Nhacoongo Mozam. 24°18S 35°14E 271 B6
Nhamaabué Mozam. 17°25S 35°5E 269 F4
Nhambiquara Brazil 12°50S 59°49W 331 C6
Nhamundá Brazil 2°14S 56°43W 329 D6
Nhamundá ➜ Brazil 2°12S 56°41W 329 D6
Nhangulaze, L. Mozam. 24°0S 34°30E 271 B5
Nharêa Angola 11°38S 16°58E 265 E3
Nharnuwangga, Wajarri and Ngarlawangga ◎ Australia 24°50S 118°0E 279 D2
Nhava Sheva India 18°58N 72°55E 130 B2
Nhecolândia Brazil 19°17S 56°58W 331 D6
Nhill Australia 36°18S 141°40E 282 D4
Nho Quan Vietnam 20°18N 105°45E 228 G5
Nhulunbuy Australia 12°10S 137°20E 280 A2
Nhundo Angola 14°25S 21°23E 265 E4
Nia-nia Dem. Rep. of the Congo 1°30N 27°40E 268 B2
Niafounké Mali 16°0N 4°5W 262 B4
Niagara Falls Ont., Canada 43°7N 79°5W 312 C5
Niagara Falls N.Y., U.S.A. 43°5N 79°4W 312 C6
Niagara-on-the-Lake Canada 43°15N 79°4W 312 C5
Niah Malaysia 3°58N 113°46E 235 B4
Nialaha'u Pt. Solomon Is. 9°47S 161°34E 287 M11
Niamey Niger 13°27N 2°6E 263 C5
Niamtougou Togo 9°46N 1°6E 263 D5
Niandan-Koro Guinea 11°5N 9°15W 262 C3
Nianforando Guinea 9°37N 10°36W 262 D2
Niangara Dem. Rep. of the Congo 3°42N 27°50E 268 B2
Niangay, L. Mali 15°50N 3°0W 262 B4
Niangbo Ivory C. 8°49N 5°10W 262 D3
Niangoloko Burkina Faso 10°15N 4°55W 262 C4
Niangua ➜ U.S.A. 38°58N 92°48W 310 G4
Niantic U.S.A. 41°20N 72°11W 313 E12
Niari Congo 4°9S 14°9E 264 C2
Niari □ Congo 3°30S 12°0E 264 C2
Niaro Sudan 10°38N 31°31E 257 E3
Nias Indonesia 1°0N 97°30E 234 B1
Niassa □ Mozam. 13°30S 36°0E 269 E4
Niassa, L. = Malawi, L. Africa 12°30S 34°30E 269 E3
Niassa ⌓ Mozam. 12°4S 36°57E 269 E4
Nīāvarān Iran 35°47N 51°29E 141 A2
Nibāk Si. Arabia 24°25N 50°50E 247 E7
Nibe Denmark 56°59N 9°38E 163 H3
Nibra India 22°36N 88°15E 124 B1
Nicaragua ■ Cent. Amer. 11°40N 85°30W 320 D2
Nicaragua, L. de Nic. 12°0N 85°30W 320 D2
Nicastro Italy 38°59N 16°19E 201 D9
Nice France 43°42N 7°14E 175 E11
Nice-Côte-d'Azur ✈ (NCE) France 43°41N 7°12E 175 E11
Niceville U.S.A. 30°31N 86°30W 317 E3
Nichicun, L. Canada 53°5N 71°0W 299 B5
Nichinan Japan 31°38N 131°23E 222 F3
Nicholás, Canal Caribbean 23°30N 80°5W 320 B3
Nicholas Channel = Nicholás, Canal Caribbean 23°30N 80°5W 320 B3
Nicholasville U.S.A. 37°53N 84°34W 311 G12
Nicholls U.S.A. 31°31N 82°38W 316 D7
Nichols U.S.A. 42°1N 76°22W 313 D8
Nicholson W. Austral., Australia 18°2S 128°54E 278 C4
Nicholson Pa., U.S.A. 41°37N 75°47W 313 E9
Nicholson ➜ Australia 17°31S 139°36E 280 B2
Nicholson L. Canada 62°40N 102°40W 297 A8
Nicholson Ra. Australia 27°15S 116°45E 279 E2
Nicholville U.S.A. 44°41N 74°39W 313 B10
Nickerie ➜ Suriname 5°58N 57°0W 329 B6
Nico Pérez = José Batlle y Ordóñez Uruguay 33°20S 55°10W 335 C4
Nicobar Is. Ind. Oc. 8°0N 93°30E 245 L11
Nicola Canada 50°12N 120°40W 296 C4
Nicolls Town Bahamas 25°8N 78°0W 320 A4
Nicosia Cyprus 35°10N 33°25E 207 E9
Nicosia Italy 37°45N 14°24E 201 E7
Nicótera Italy 38°33N 15°56E 201 D8
Nicoya Costa Rica 10°9N 85°27W 320 D2
Nicoya, G. de Costa Rica 10°0N 85°0W 320 E3
Nicoya, Pen. de Costa Rica 9°45N 85°40W 320 E2
Nictheroy = Niterói Brazil 22°53S 43°7W 135 B2
Nida Lithuania 55°20N 21°4E 184 C8
Nidāl Iraq 33°19N 44°25E 113 B2
Nidaros = Trondheim Norway 63°36N 10°25E 164 A7
Nidd ➜ U.K. 53°59N 1°23W 168 D6
Nidda Germany 50°23N 9°1E 179 E5
Nidda ➜ Germany 50°17N 8°48E 179 E4
Niddrie Vic., Australia 37°44S 144°51E 128 A1
Niddrie Edinburgh, U.K. 55°56N 3°7W 121 B3
Nidri Greece 38°43N 20°42E 207 B2
Nidwalden □ Switz. 46°50N 8°25E 179 J4
Nidzica Poland 53°25N 20°28E 185 E7
Niebüll Germany 54°46N 8°48E 178 A4
Nied ➜ Germany 49°23N 6°40E 173 C13
Nieder Neuendorf Germany 52°36N 13°12E 115 A2
Niederaula Germany 50°47N 9°36E 178 E5
Niederbayern □ Germany 48°40N 12°50E 179 G8
Niederbronn-les-Bains France 48°57N 7°39E 173 D14
Niedere Tauern Austria 47°20N 14°0E 180 D7
Niederlausitz Germany 51°42N 13°59E 178 D9
Niederösterreich □ Austria 48°25N 15°40E 180 C8
Niedersachsen □ Germany 52°50N 9°0E 178 C4
Niedersächsisches Wattenmeer △ Germany 53°45N 7°30E 178 B3
Niederschöneweide Germany 52°27N 13°30E 115 B3
Niederschönhausen Germany 52°35N 13°25E 115 A3
Niefang Eq. Guin. 1°50N 10°14E 264 B2
Niekerkshoop S. Africa 29°19S 22°51E 270 C3
Niellé Ivory C. 10°5N 5°38W 262 C3
Niellim Chad 9°42N 17°49E 259 G3
Niem C.A.R. 6°12N 15°14E 264 A3
Niemba Dem. Rep. of the Congo 5°58S 28°24E 268 D2
Niemen = Nemunas ➜ Lithuania 55°25N 21°10E 184 C8
Niemeyer Brazil 22°59S 43°16W 135 B1
Niemodlin Poland 50°38N 17°38E 185 H4
Niemur Australia 35°17S 144°9E 282 C6
Nienburg Germany 52°39N 9°13E 178 C5
Niepołomice Poland 50°3N 20°13E 185 H7
Niers ➜ Germany 51°43N 5°57E 178 D1
Niesky Germany 51°17N 14°49E 178 D10
Nieszawa Poland 52°52N 18°50E 185 F5
Nieu Bethesda S. Africa 31°51S 24°34E 270 D3
Nieuw Amsterdam Suriname 5°53N 55°5W 329 B6
Nieuw Nickerie Suriname 6°0N 56°59W 329 B6
Nieuwe Kerk Amsterdam, Neths. 112 a2
Nieuwendam Neths. 52°23N 4°57E 112 A2
Nieuwoudtville S. Africa 31°23S 19°7E 270 D2
Nieuwpoort Belgium 51°8N 2°45E 170 C2
Nieuwpoort Curaçao 12°3N 68°49W 322 g
Nieves, Pico de las Canary Is. 27°57N 15°35W 153 e1
Nièvre □ France 47°10N 3°40E 173 E10
Nif Micronesia 9°28N 138°4E 287 S16
Niga Mali 13°38N 5°27W 262 C3
Niğde Turkey 37°58N 34°40E 212 D6
Niğde □ Turkey 38°0N 34°30E 212 D6
Nigel S. Africa 26°27S 28°25E 271 C4
Niger □ Nigeria 10°0N 5°30E 263 D6
Niger ■ W. Afr. 17°30N 10°0E 259 E2
Niger ➜ W. Afr. 5°33N 6°33E 263 D6
Niger Delta Africa 5°0N 6°0E 263 E6
Nigeria ■ W. Afr. 8°30N 8°0E 263 D6
Nighasin India 28°14N 80°52E 243 E9
Nightcaps N.Z. 45°57S 168°2E 285 F3
Nightmute U.S.A. 60°29N 164°44W 303 F6
Nigrita Greece 40°56N 23°29E 202 F7
Nihoa U.S.A. 23°6N 161°58W 302 G11
Nihon = Japan ■ Asia 36°0N 136°0E 221 G8
Nihonbashi Tokyo, Japan 140 b5
Nii-Jima Japan 34°20N 139°15E 223 C11
Niigata Japan 37°58N 139°0E 220 F9
Niigata □ Japan 37°15N 138°45E 221 F9
Niihama Japan 33°55N 133°16E 222 D5
Ni'ihau U.S.A. 21°54N 160°9W 302 B1
Niimi Japan 34°59N 133°28E 222 C5
Niipperi Finland 60°18N 24°45E 121 B1
Niislel Khureheh = Ulaanbaatar Mongolia 47°55N 106°53E 218 B10
Niitsu Japan 37°48N 139°7E 220 F9
Nij Laluk India 27°7N 93°56E 241 B4
Níjar Spain 36°53N 2°15W 197 J2
Nijil Jordan 30°32N 35°33E 251 H6
Nijkerk Neths. 52°13N 5°30E 170 B5
Nijmegen Neths. 51°50N 5°52E 170 C5
Nijverdal Neths. 52°22N 6°28E 170 B6
Nīk Pey Iran 36°50N 48°10E 213 D13
Nikao Cook Is. 21°12S 159°48W 289 h
Nikaweratiya Sri Lanka 7°45N 80°7E 245 L5
Nike Nigeria 6°26N 7°29E 263 D6
Nikea Greece 37°57N 23°38E 112 B1
Nikel Russia 69°24N 30°13E 160 B24
Nikiboko Bonaire 12°9N 68°16W 322 h
Nikiniki Indonesia 9°49S 124°30E 278 A3
Nikisiani Greece 40°57N 24°9E 203 F8
Nikiski U.S.A. 61°41N 151°18W 303 F10
Nikiti Greece 40°13N 23°43E 202 F7
Nikitinskiye promysly = Kirovskiy Russia 45°51N 48°11E 191 H9
Nikki Benin 9°58N 3°12E 263 D5
Nikkō Japan 36°45N 139°35E 223 A11
Nikkō △ Japan 36°56N 139°37E 221 F9
Nikolai U.S.A. 62°58N 154°10W 303 E9
Nikolainkaupunki = Vaasa Finland 63°6N 21°38E 160 E19
Nikolaistad = Vaasa Finland 63°6N 21°38E 160 E19
Nikolassee Germany 52°25N 13°12E 115 B2
Nikolayev = Mykolayiv Ukraine 46°58N 32°0E 189 J7
Nikolayevsk Russia 50°0N 45°35E 190 E7
Nikolayevsk-na-Amur Russia 53°8N 140°44E 215 D15
Nikolsburg = Mikulov Czechia 48°48N 16°39E 181 C9
Nikolsk Russia 53°49N 46°4E 190 D8
Nikolsk-Ussuriysky = Ussuriysk Russia 43°48N 131°59E 220 C5
Nikolskaya Pestravka = Nikolsk Russia 53°49N 46°4E 190 D8
Nikolski U.S.A. 52°56N 168°52W 303 K5
Nikolskiy Russia 55°49N 37°29E 129 B1
Nikolskoye = Ussuriysk Russia 43°48N 131°59E 220 C5
Nikolskoye Russia 55°12N 166°0E 215 D17
Nikolsky Khutor = Sursk Russia 53°3N 45°40E 190 D7
Nikopol Bulgaria 43°43N 24°54E 203 C8
Nikopol Ukraine 47°35N 34°25E 189 J8
Nikopolis Greece 39°5N 20°43E 207 A2
Niksar Turkey 40°31N 37°2E 212 B7
Nīkshahr Iran 26°15N 60°10E 247 E9
Nikšić Montenegro 42°50N 18°57E 202 D2
Nikumaroro Kiribati 4°40S 174°32W 277 A16
Nikunau Kiribati 1°22S 176°28E 277 A14
Nîl, Nahr en ➜ Africa 30°10N 31°6E 256 H7
Nîl el Abyad ➜ Sudan 15°38N 32°31E 257 D3
Nîl el Azraq ➜ Sudan 15°38N 32°31E 257 D3
Nila Indonesia 6°44S 129°31E 231 F7
Nilakkottai India 10°10N 77°52E 245 J3
Niland U.S.A. 33°14N 115°31W 307 M11
Nilanga India 18°6N 76°46E 244 E3
Nile = Nîl, Nahr en ➜ Africa 30°10N 31°6E 256 H7
Nile Delta Egypt 31°40N 31°0E 256 H7
Niles Ill., U.S.A. 42°1N 87°48W 119 A2
Niles Mich., U.S.A. 41°50N 86°15W 311 C10
Niles Ohio, U.S.A. 41°11N 80°46W 312 E4
Niles Center = Skokie U.S.A. 42°2N 87°43W 119 A2
Nileshwar India 12°15N 75°6E 245 H2
Nilgiri Hills India 11°30N 76°30E 245 J3
Nilo Peçanha Brazil 13°37S 39°6W 333 D4
Nilsebu Norway 59°11N 6°39E 164 E3
Nilüfer ➜ Turkey 40°18N 28°27E 203 F12
Nim Ka Thana India 27°44N 75°48E 242 F6
Nimach India 24°30N 74°56E 242 G6
Nimba, Mt. Africa 7°37N 8°25W 262 D3
Nimbahera India 24°37N 74°45E 242 G6
Nîmes France 43°50N 4°23E 175 E8
Nimfaíon, Ákra = Pines, Akra Greece 40°5N 24°20E 203 F8
Nimmitabel Australia 36°29S 149°15E 283 D8
Nīmrūz □ Afghan. 30°0N 62°0E 240 C1
Nimta India 22°40N 88°24E 124 A2
Nimule South Sudan 3°32N 32°3E 257 G3
Nimule △ South Sudan 3°38N 32°2E 257 G3
Nin Croatia 44°16N 15°12E 199 D12
Nīnawá Iraq 36°25N 43°10E 213 D10
Nīnawá □ Iraq 36°15N 43°0E 246 B4
Ninda Angola 14°47S 21°24E 265 E4
Nindigully Australia 28°21S 148°50E 281 D4
Nine Degree Channel India 9°0N 73°0E 245 K1
Ninepin Group China 22°16N 114°21E 219 a
Ninety Mile Beach N.Z. 34°48S 173°0E 284 A2
Ninety Mile Beach, The Australia 38°15S 147°24E 283 E7
Ninety Six U.S.A. 34°11N 82°1W 316 A7
Ninetyeast Ridge Ind. Oc. 1°0S 90°0E 273 E7
Nineveh = Nīnawá Iraq 36°25N 43°10E 213 D10
Ning Xian China 35°30N 107°58E 226 G4
Ningaloo Marine ⌓ Australia 22°23S 113°32E 278 D1
Ning'an China 44°22N 129°20E 227 B15
Ningbo China 29°51N 121°28E 229 C13
Ningcheng China 41°32N 119°53E 227 D10
Ningde China 26°38N 119°23E 229 D12
Ningdu China 26°25N 115°59E 229 D10
Ningerum Papua N. G. 5°41S 141°8E 286 C1
Ninggang China 26°42N 113°55E 229 D9
Ningguo China 30°35N 119°0E 229 B12
Ninghai China 29°15N 121°27E 229 C13
Ninghua China 26°14N 116°45E 229 D11
Ningi Nigeria 10°55N 9°30E 263 C6
Ningjin China 37°35N 114°57E 226 F8
Ningjing Shan China 31°0N 98°20E 228 C2
Ninglang China 27°20N 100°55E 228 D3
Ningling China 34°25N 115°22E 226 G8
Ningming China 22°8N 107°4E 228 F6
Ningnan China 27°5N 102°36E 228 D4
Ningpo = Ningbo China 29°51N 121°28E 229 C13
Ningqiang China 32°47N 106°15E 226 H4
Ningshan China 33°21N 108°21E 228 A7
Ningsia Hui A.R. = Ningxia Huizu Zizhiqu □ China 38°0N 106°0E 226 F4
Ningwu China 39°0N 112°18E 226 E7
Ningxia Huizu Zizhiqu □ China 38°0N 106°0E 226 F4
Ningxiang China 28°15N 112°30E 229 C9
Ningyang China 35°47N 116°45E 226 G9
Ningyuan China 25°37N 111°57E 229 E8
Ninh Binh Vietnam 20°15N 105°55E 228 G5
Ninh Giang Vietnam 20°44N 106°24E 236 B6
Ninh Hoa Vietnam 12°30N 109°7E 236 F7
Ninh Ma Vietnam 12°48N 109°21E 236 F7
Nini-Suhien △ Ghana 5°20N 2°34W 262 D4
Ninigo Group Papua N. G. 1°22S 144°17E 286 A3
Ninove Belgium 50°51N 4°2E 170 D4
Ninoy Aquino Int. ✈ (MNL) Phil. 14°31N 121°0E 127 B2
Nioaque Brazil 21°5S 55°50W 335 A4
Niobrara U.S.A. 42°45N 98°2W 308 D4
Niobrara ➜ U.S.A. 42°46N 98°3W 308 D4
Nioki Dem. Rep. of the Congo 2°47S 17°40E 264 C3
Niokolo-Koba △ Senegal 13°3N 13°2W 262 C2
Niono Mali 14°15N 6°0W 262 C3
Nionsamoridougou Guinea 8°45N 8°50W 262 D3
Nioro du Rip Senegal 13°40N 15°50W 262 C1
Nioro du Sahel Mali 15°15N 9°30W 262 B3
Niort France 46°19N 0°29W 174 B3
Nioumachoua Comoros Is. 12°21S 43°42E 272 a
Nipa Papua N. G. 6°9S 143°29E 286 D2
Nipani India 16°20N 74°25E 245 F2
Nipawin Canada 53°20N 104°0W 297 C8
Nipfjället Sweden 61°59N 12°50E 162 C6
Nipigon Canada 49°0N 88°17W 298 C2
Nipigon, L. Canada 49°50N 88°30W 298 C2
Nipishish L. Canada 54°12N 60°45W 299 B7
Nipissing, L. Canada 46°20N 80°0W 298 C4
Nipomo U.S.A. 35°3N 120°29W 307 K6
Nippa Japan 35°31N 139°36E 140 B2
Nippon = Japan ■ Asia 36°0N 136°0E 221 G8
Nippori Japan 35°43N 139°45E 140 A3
Nipton U.S.A. 35°28N 115°16W 307 K11
Niquelândia Brazil 14°33S 48°23W 333 D2
Nīr Iran 38°2N 47°59E 213 C12
Nira ➜ India 17°58N 75°8E 244 F2
Nirasaki Japan 35°42N 138°27E 223 B10
Nirayama = Izunokuni Japan 35°2N 138°55E 223 B10
Nirmal India 19°3N 78°20E 244 E4
Nirmali India 26°20N 86°35E 243 F12
Niš Serbia 43°19N 21°58E 202 C5
Nisa = Nysa ➜ Europe 52°4N 14°46E 178 C10
Nisa Portugal 39°30N 7°41W 195 F3
Nisa Turkmenistan 37°59N 58°11E 247 B8
Nişāb Si. Arabia 29°11N 44°43E 246 D5
Nişāb Yemen 14°25N 46°29E 248 D4
Nišava ➜ Serbia 43°20N 21°46E 202 C5
Niscemi Italy 37°9N 14°23E 201 E7
Nishi Japan 34°40N 135°28E 133 A1
Nishi-Sonogi-Hantō Japan 32°55N 129°45E 222 E1
Nishi-Tosa Japan 33°13N 132°46E 222 D4
Nishinari Japan 34°37N 135°28E 133 B1
Nishinomiya Japan 34°45N 135°20E 133 A1
Nishino'omote Japan 30°43N 130°59E 221 J5
Nishio Japan 34°52N 137°3E 223 C9
Nishiwaki Japan 34°59N 134°58E 222 C6
Nishiyodogawa Japan 34°41N 135°24E 133 A1
Nishon Tumani Uzbekistan 38°49N 65°47E 240 A2
Nishtūn Yemen 15°49N 52°14E 249 D6
Nisibin = Nusaybin Turkey 37°3N 41°10E 213 D9
Niška Banja Serbia 43°18N 22°1E 202 C6
Niskibi ➜ Canada 56°29N 88°9W 298 A2
Nisko Poland 50°35N 22°7E 185 H9
Nisporeni Moldova 47°4N 28°10E 183 C13
Nisqually ➜ U.S.A. 47°7N 122°42W 306 C4
Nissaki Greece 39°43N 19°52E 206 B9
Nissan ➜ Sweden 56°40N 12°51E 163 H6
Nissedal Norway 59°10N 8°30E 164 E5
Nisser Norway 59°7N 8°28E 164 E5
Nissiros Greece 36°35N 27°12E 205 E9
Nissum Bredning Denmark 56°40N 8°20E 163 H2
Nissum Fjord Denmark 56°20N 8°11E 163 H2
Nistru = Dnister ➜ Europe 46°18N 30°17E 177 E16
Nisutlin ➜ Canada 60°14N 132°34W 296 A2
Nitchequon Canada 53°10N 70°58W 299 B5
Niterói Brazil 22°53S 43°7W 135 B2
Nith ➜ Ont., Canada 43°12N 80°23W 312 C4
Nith ➜ Dumf. & Gall., U.K. 55°14N 3°33W 167 F5
Nitmiluk △ Australia 14°6S 132°15E 278 B5
Nitra Slovakia 48°19N 18°4E 181 C11
Nitra ➜ Slovakia 47°46N 18°10E 181 D11
Nitriansky □ Slovakia 48°10N 18°30E 181 C11
Nittenau Germany 49°12N 12°16E 179 F8
Niu Valley U.S.A. 21°19N 157°44W 302 K14
Niua Group Tonga 15°57S 173°45W 277 D16
Niuafo'ou Tonga 15°30S 175°58W 277 D15
Niuatoputapu Tonga 15°57S 173°45W 277 D16
Niue ☒ Pac. Oc. 19°2S 169°54W 289 g
Niulakita Pac. Oc. 10°45S 179°30E 277 C14
Niulan Jiang ➜ China 27°30N 103°5E 228 D4
Niulantsun Taiwan 25°1N 121°2E 225 A3
Niur Indonesia 0°26S 103°30E 234 C2
Niut Indonesia 0°55N 109°54E 235 B4
Niutao Pac. Oc. 6°7S 177°18E 277 B14
Niutou Shan China 29°5N 121°59E 229 C13
Niuzhuang China 40°58N 122°28E 224 B1
Nivala Finland 63°56N 24°57E 160 E21
Nivelles Belgium 50°35N 4°20E 170 D4
Nivernais France 47°15N 3°30E 173 E10
Niverville Canada 49°36N 97°3W 297 D9
Niwas India 23°3N 80°26E 243 H9
Nixa U.S.A. 37°3N 93°18W 308 G7
Nixon U.S.A. 29°16N 97°46W 314 G6
Nizam Sagar India 18°10N 77°58E 244 E3
Nizamabad India 18°45N 78°7E 244 E4
Nizamghat India 28°20N 95°45E 241 A5
Nizhne-Kolymsk Russia 68°34N 160°55E 215 C17
Nizhne-Svirskiy ⌓ Russia 60°30N 32°55E 188 B7
Nizhnegorskiy = Nyzhnohirskyy Ukraine 45°27N 34°38E 189 K8
Nizhnekamsk Russia 55°38N 51°49E 190 C10
Nizhneudinsk Russia 54°54N 99°3E 215 D10
Nizhnevartovsk Russia 60°56N 76°38E 214 C8
Nizhniy Bestyakh Russia 61°57N 129°54E 215 C13
Nizhniy Chir Russia 48°22N 43°5E 191 F6
Nizhniy Lomov Russia 53°34N 43°38E 190 D6
Nizhniy Novgorod Russia 56°20N 44°0E 190 B7
Nizhniy Novgorod □ Russia 56°30N 44°20E 190 B7
Nizhniy Tagil Russia 57°55N 59°57E 186 C10
Nizhniye Kresty = Cherskiy Russia 68°45N 161°18E 215 C17
Nizhyn Ukraine 51°5N 31°55E 189 G6
Nizina Mazowiecka Poland 52°30N 21°0E 185 F8
Nizip Turkey 37°5N 37°50E 212 D7
Nízké Tatry Slovakia 48°55N 19°30E 181 C12
Nízké Tatry △ Slovakia 48°55N 19°37E 181 C12
Nízký Jeseník Czechia 49°50N 17°30E 181 B10
Nizwá Oman 22°56N 57°32E 249 B7
Nizza Monferrato Italy 44°46N 8°21E 198 D5
Njakwa Malawi 11°1S 33°56E 269 E3

Njarðvíkur Iceland 63°59N 22°32W 155 D4
Njazidja = Grande Comore Comoros Is. 11°35S 43°20E 272 a
Njegoš Montenegro 42°53N 18°45E 202 D2
Njeru Uganda 0°27N 33°10E 268 B3
Njinjo Tanzania 8°48S 38°54E 269 D4
Njoko → Zambia 17°8S 24°4E 265 F4
Njombe Tanzania 9°20S 34°50E 269 D3
Njombe □ Tanzania 9°10S 34°50E 269 D3
Njombe → Tanzania 6°56S 35°6E 268 D4
Njurundabommen Sweden 62°15N 17°25E 162 B11
Nkambe Cameroon 6°35N 10°40E 263 D7
Nkana Zambia 12°50S 28°8E 269 E2
Nkandla S. Africa 28°37S 31°5E 271 C5
Nkawkaw Ghana 6°36N 0°49W 263 D4
Nkayi Congo 4°9S 13°17E 264 C2
Nkayi Zimbabwe 19°41S 29°20E 269 F2
Nkhotakota Malawi 12°56S 34°15E 269 E3
Nkhotakota ⌂ Malawi 12°50S 34°0E 269 E3
Nkolabona Gabon 1°14N 11°43E 264 B2
Nkomi, Lagune Gabon 1°35S 9°17E 264 C1
Nkondwe Tanzania 5°51S 30°51E 268 D3
Nkone Dem. Rep. of the Congo 1°2S 22°20E 264 C4
Nkongsamba Cameroon 4°55N 9°55E 263 E6
Nkoteng Cameroon 4°31N 12°2E 264 B2
Nkunga Dem. Rep. of the Congo 4°41S 18°34E 265 C3
Nkurenkuru Namibia 17°42S 18°32E 270 A2
Nkwanta Ghana 6°10N 2°10W 262 D4
Nmai → Burma 25°30N 97°25E 228 F2
No, L. South Sudan 9°30N 30°28E 266 C3
Noakhali Bangla. 22°48N 91°10E 241 D3
Noatak U.S.A. 67°34N 162°58W 303 C7
Noatak ⌂ U.S.A. 68°10N 160°0W 303 B8
Nob Hill San Francisco, U.S.A. 136 b1
Nobel Canada 45°25N 80°6W 312 A4
Nobeoka Japan 32°36N 131°41E 222 E3
Noble U.S.A. 38°42N 88°14W 311 F8
Noblejas Spain 39°58N 3°26W 194 F7
Noblesville U.S.A. 40°3N 86°1W 311 D11
Noboribetsu Japan 42°24N 141°6E 220 C10
Nocatee U.S.A. 27°10N 81°53W 317 H8
Noccundra Australia 27°50S 142°36E 281 D3
Noce → Italy 46°9N 11°4E 198 B8
Nocera Inferiore Italy 40°44N 14°38E 201 B7
Nocera Umbra Italy 43°5N 12°47E 199 E9
Noci Italy 40°48N 17°7E 201 B10
Nockeby Sweden 59°19N 17°56E 139 B1
Nocona U.S.A. 33°47N 97°44W 314 E6
Nocrich Romania 45°55N 24°26E 183 E9
Noda Japan 35°56N 139°52E 223 B11
Nodeland Norway 58°8N 7°51E 164 F4
Noel Kempff Mercado △ Bolivia 14°9S 60°49W 331 C5
Noel Park U.K. 51°35N 0°5W 125 A3
Nogal Valley = Nugaaleed, Dooxo Somalia 8°35N 48°35E 267 C6
Nogales Sonora, Mexico 31°19N 110°56W 318 A2
Nogales Ariz., U.S.A. 31°21N 110°56W 305 L8
Nogaro France 43°45N 0°2W 174 E3
Nogat → Poland 54°17N 19°17E 184 D6
Nōgata Japan 33°48N 130°44E 222 D2
Nogatino Russia 55°41N 37°41E 129 B3
Nogaysk = Prymorske Ukraine 46°48N 36°20E 189 J9
Nogent France 48°1N 5°20E 173 D12
Nogent-le-Rotrou France 48°20N 0°50E 172 D7
Nogent-sur-Marne France 48°50N 2°28E 134 A3
Nogent-sur-Seine France 48°30N 3°30E 173 D10
Noggara Ethiopia 13°54N 36°35E 257 E4
Noggerup Australia 33°32S 116°5E 279 F2
Noginsk Russia 64°30N 90°50E 215 C10
Nogliki Russia 51°50N 143°10E 215 D15
Nogoa → Australia 23°40S 147°55E 280 C4
Nogoyá Argentina 32°24S 59°48W 334 C4
Nógrád □ Hungary 48°0N 19°30E 182 C4
Noguera Pallaresa → Spain 41°55N 0°55E 196 D5
Noguera Ribagorçana → Spain 41°40N 0°43E 196 D5
Nohar India 29°11N 74°49E 242 E6
Nohfelden Germany 49°35N 7°7E 179 F3
Nohili Pt. U.S.A. 22°4N 159°47W 302 A2
Nohta India 23°40N 79°34E 243 H8
Nohwa S. Korea 34°10N 126°34E 224 E3
Nohwado S. Korea 34°12N 126°35E 224 E3
Noia Spain 42°48N 8°53W 194 C2
Noichi Japan 33°33N 133°42E 222 D5
Noida India 28°36N 77°19E 120 B2
Noipuos Papua N. G. 2°25S 150°7E 286 B6
Noire, Montagne France 43°28N 2°18E 174 E6
Noires, Mts. France 48°11N 3°40W 172 D3
Noirétable France 45°48N 3°46E 174 C7
Noirmoutier, Î. de France 46°58N 2°10W 172 F4
Noirmoutier-en-l'Île France 47°0N 2°14W 172 F4
Noiseau France 48°46N 2°32E 134 B4
Noisiel France 48°51N 2°37E 134 A4
Noisy-le-Grand France 48°50N 2°33E 134 A4
Noisy-le-Roi France 48°50N 2°3E 134 A1
Noisy-le-Sec France 48°53N 2°27E 134 A3
Nojane Botswana 23°15S 20°14E 270 B3
Nojima-Zaki Japan 34°54N 139°53E 223 C11
Nok Kundi Pakistan 28°50N 62°45E 240 C1
Nok Ta Phao, Ko Thailand 9°23N 99°40E 237 b
Nokaneng Botswana 19°40S 22°17E 270 A3
Nokia Finland 61°30N 23°30E 188 B2
Nokkala Finland 60°8N 24°45E 121 C1
Nokkeushi = Kitami Japan 43°48N 143°54E 220 C11
Nokomis Sask., Canada 51°35N 105°0W 297 C8
Nokomis Fla., U.S.A. 27°7N 82°27W 317 H7
Nokomis Ill., U.S.A. 39°18N 89°18W 310 E7
Nokomis L. Canada 57°0N 103°0W 297 B8
Nokou Chad 14°35N 14°47E 259 F2
Nokuku Vanuatu 14°54S 166°35E 287 D4
Nola C.A.R. 3°35N 16°4E 264 B3
Nola Italy 40°55N 14°33E 201 B7
Nolay France 46°58N 4°35E 173 F11
Noli, C. di Italy 44°12N 8°25E 198 D5
Nolinsk Russia 57°28N 49°57E 190 B9
Noma U.S.A. 30°59N 85°37W 316 E4
Noma Omuramba → Namibia 18°52S 20°53E 270 A3
Noma-Saki Japan 31°25N 130°7E 222 F2
Nomad Papua N. G. 6°19S 142°13E 286 D2
Nombre de Dios Panama 9°34N 79°28W 320 E4
Nome U.S.A. 64°30N 165°25W 303 D6
Nomentano Italy 41°55N 12°30E 136 B2
Nomgon Mongolia 42°50N 105°8E 226 C3
Nomi Japan 36°26N 136°25E 223 A8
Nomo-Zaki Japan 32°35N 129°44E 222 E1
Nomoneas Micronesia 7°24N 151°53E 287 T18
Nomuka Tonga 20°17S 174°48W 287 Q13
Nomuka Group Tonga 20°20S 174°48W 287 Q13
Nonacho L. Canada 61°42N 109°40W 297 A7
Nonakashinden Japan 35°44N 139°30E 140 A2
Nonancourt France 48°47N 1°11E 172 D8
Nonda Australia 20°40S 142°28E 280 C3
Nondalton U.S.A. 60°0N 154°51W 303 F9
None Italy 44°56N 7°32E 198 D4
Nong Chang Thailand 15°23N 99°51E 236 E2
Nong Han Res. Thailand 17°11N 104°9E 236 D5
Nong Het Laos 19°29N 103°59E 236 C4
Nong Khai Thailand 17°50N 102°46E 236 D4
Nong'an China 44°25N 125°5E 227 B13
Nongjrong India 25°29N 92°6E 241 C4
Nongminyundong Jiangxisuo China 23°7N 113°15E 121 B2
Nongoma S. Africa 27°58S 31°35E 271 C5
Nongpoh India 25°54N 91°53E 241 C3
Nongsa Indonesia 1°11N 104°8E 237 d
Nongstoin India 25°31N 91°16E 241 C3
Nonhyeon S. Korea 37°30N 127°1E 137 B2
Nono Ethiopia 8°32N 37°26E 266 C4
Nonoava Mexico 27°28N 106°44W 318 B3
Nonoc I. Phil. 9°51N 125°37E 233 G5
Nonoichi Japan 36°35N 136°35E 223 A8
Nonsan S. Korea 36°12N 127°5E 224 D3
Nonsuch B. Antigua & B. 17°3N 61°42W 322 b
Nonthaburi Thailand 13°50N 100°29E 113 A1
Nontron France 45°31N 0°40E 174 C4
Nonza France 42°47N 9°21E 175 F13
Noon Gun Cape Town, S. Africa 118 b1
Noonamah Australia 12°40S 131°4E 278 B5
Noondie, L. Australia 28°30S 119°30E 279 E2
Noonkanbah ✪ Australia 18°30S 124°50E 278 C3
Noord Aruba 12°34N 70°1W 322 f
Noord Brabant □ Neths. 51°40N 5°0E 170 C5
Noord Holland □ Neths. 52°30N 4°45E 170 B4
Noord Saliña Bonaire 12°11N 68°16W 322 h
Noordbeveland Neths. 51°35N 3°50E 170 C3
Noorderkerk Amsterdam, Neths. 112 a1
Noordgesig S. Africa 26°13S 27°56E 123 B1
Noordkaap Aruba 12°34N 70°1W 322 f
Noordoostpolder Neths. 52°45N 5°45E 170 B5
Noordpunt Bonaire 12°18N 68°23W 322 h
Noordpunt Curaçao 12°24N 69°10W 322 g
Noordwijk Neths. 52°14N 4°26E 170 B4
Noordzeekanaal Neths. 52°28N 4°47E 112 A1
Noorvik U.S.A. 66°50N 161°3W 303 C7
Noosa Heads Australia 26°25S 153°6E 281 D5
Nootka I. Canada 49°32N 126°42W 296 D3
Nopiming ⌂ Canada 50°30N 95°37W 297 C9
Nóqui Angola 5°55S 13°30E 265 D2
Nor-Bayzzet = Gavar Armenia 40°21N 45°7E 191 K7
Nora Eritrea 16°6N 40°4E 257 D5
Nora Sweden 59°32N 15°2E 162 E9
Nora Springs U.S.A. 43°9N 93°0W 310 A4
Norala Phil. 6°32N 124°40E 233 H5
Noralee Canada 53°59N 126°26W 296 C3
Noranda = Rouyn-Noranda Canada 48°20N 79°0W 298 C4
Norberg Sweden 60°4N 15°56E 162 D9
Norborne U.S.A. 39°18N 93°40W 310 E3
Nórcia Italy 42°48N 13°5E 199 F10
Norco U.S.A. 33°56N 117°33W 307 M9
Norcross U.S.A. 33°56N 84°13W 316 B5
Nord □ Cameroon 8°30N 14°0E 263 D7
Nord □ France 50°15N 3°30E 173 B10
Nord, Gare du Paris, France 134 a4
Nord, Pt. Comoros Is. 11°22S 43°19E 272 a
Nord-Kivu □ Dem. Rep. of the Congo 1°0S 29°0E 268 C2
Nord-Ostsee-Kanal Germany 54°12N 9°32E 178 A5
Nord-Ouest □ Cameroon 6°20N 10°30E 263 D7
Nord-Ubangi □ Dem. Rep. of the Congo 3°0N 21°0E 264 B4
Nordagutu Norway 59°25N 9°20E 164 E6
Nordaustlandet Svalbard 79°14N 23°0E 150 B9
Nordberg Norway 61°54N 8°10E 164 C5
Nordborg Denmark 55°5N 9°50E 163 J3
Nordby Denmark 55°27N 8°24E 163 J2
Norddeich Germany 53°36N 7°9E 178 B3
Nordegg Canada 52°29N 116°5W 296 C5
Norden Germany 53°35N 7°12E 178 B3
Nordenham Germany 53°30N 8°30E 178 B4
Nordenskjöld Sea = Laptev Sea Russia 76°0N 125°0E 215 B13
Norderhov Norway 60°7N 10°17E 164 D7
Norderney Germany 53°42N 7°9E 178 B3
Norderstedt Germany 53°42N 10°1E 178 B6
Nordeste Azores 37°50N 25°10W 153 d3
Nordfjord Norway 61°55N 5°30E 164 C2
Nordfjordeid Norway 61°54N 6°0E 164 C2
Nordfriesische Inseln Germany 54°40N 8°20E 178 A4
Nordhausen Germany 51°30N 10°47E 178 D6
Nordhorn Germany 52°26N 7°4E 178 C3
Norðoyar Færoe Is. 62°17N 6°35W 160 E9
Norðtunga Iceland 64°44N 21°24W 155 C5
Norður-múlasýsla Iceland 65°30N 15°0W 155 B11
Norðurbotn Iceland 65°36N 23°46W 155 B3
Norðurland Eystra □ Iceland 65°30N 17°0W 155 B9
Norðurland Vestra □ Iceland 65°30N 20°0W 155 B6
Nördinge-Nol Sweden 57°56N 12°5E 163 G6
Nordingrå Sweden 62°56N 18°17E 162 B12
Nordkapp Finnmark, Norway 71°10N 25°50E 160 A21
Nordkapp Svalbard 80°31N 20°0E 150 A9
Nordkinn Norway 71°8N 27°40E 160 A22
Nordkinnhalvøya Norway 70°55N 27°40E 160 A22
Nördlicher Teutoburger Wald-Wiehengebirge ⌂ Germany 52°18N 8°10E 178 C4
Nördlingen Germany 48°48N 10°30E 179 G6
Nordmarka Norway 59°58N 10°41E 133 A3
Nordmøre Norway 63°6N 8°15E 164 B4
Nordostrundingen Greenland 81°22N 11°40W 154 A9
Nordøyane Norway 62°40N 6°0E 164 B3
Nordrand-Siedlung Austria 48°16N 16°26E 142 A2
Nordre Bergenhus = Sogn og Fjordane □ Norway 61°40N 6°45E 164 C3
Nørdre Osa Norway 61°18N 11°45E 164 C8
Nordre Strømfjord Greenland 67°10N 53°35W 154 D5
Nordrhein-Westfalen □ Germany 51°45N 7°30E 178 D3
Nordsinni Norway 60°50N 9°57E 164 D6
Nørdstedalssæter Norway 61°40N 7°48E 164 C4
Nordstrand Schleswig-Holstein, Germany 54°30N 8°52E 178 A4
Nordstrand Oslo, Norway 59°52N 10°48E 133 A3
Nordvik Russia 74°2N 111°32E 215 B12
Nore → Ireland 52°25N 6°58W 166 D4
Norefjell Norway 60°16N 9°29E 164 D6
Noreland Canada 44°43N 78°48W 312 B6
Noresund Norway 60°11N 9°37E 164 D6
Norfolk = Simcoe Canada 42°50N 80°23W 312 D4
Norfolk N.Y., U.S.A. 44°48N 74°59W 313 B10
Norfolk Nebr., U.S.A. 42°2N 97°25W 308 D5
Norfolk Va., U.S.A. 36°50N 76°17W 309 G15
Norfolk □ U.K. 52°39N 0°54E 169 E8
Norfolk Basin Pac. Oc. 32°0S 170°0E 277 G13
Norfolk Broads △ U.K. 52°45N 1°30E 169 E9
Norfolk I. Pac. Oc. 28°58S 168°3E 277 F12
Norfolk Ridge Pac. Oc. 29°0S 168°0E 288 K8
Norfork L. U.S.A. 36°15N 92°14W 314 C8
Norge = Norway ■ Europe 63°0N 11°0E 160 E14
Norheimsund Norway 60°23N 6°6E 164 D3
Norilsk Russia 69°20N 88°6E 215 C9
Norland U.S.A. 25°57N 80°12W 129 C2
Norma, Mt. Australia 20°55S 140°42E 280 C3
Normal U.S.A. 40°31N 88°59W 310 D8
Norman U.S.A. 35°13N 97°26W 314 D6
Norman → Australia 19°18S 141°51E 280 B3
Norman Manley Int. ✈ (KIN) Jamaica 17°56N 76°47W 320 a
Norman Park U.S.A. 31°16N 83°41W 316 D6
Norman Wells Canada 65°17N 126°51W 294 D6
Normanby N.Z. 39°32S 174°18E 284 F3
Normanby → Australia 14°23S 144°10E 280 A3
Normanby I. Papua N. G. 10°5S 151°5E 286 F6
Normandie France 48°45N 0°10E 171 B4
Normandie □ France 49°0N 0°30E 172 D7
Normandie-Maine ⌂ France 48°30N 0°20W 172 D6
Normandin Canada 48°49N 72°31W 298 C5
Normandy = Normandie France 48°45N 0°10E 171 B4
Normanhurst, Mt. Australia 25°4S 122°30E 279 E3
Normanton Australia 17°40S 141°10E 280 B3
Normanville Australia 35°27S 138°18E 282 C3
Normétal Canada 49°0N 79°22W 298 C4
Norquay Canada 51°53N 102°5W 297 C8
Norquinco Argentina 41°51S 70°55W 336 B2
Norra Kvill △ Sweden 57°46N 15°35E 163 G9
Norra Ulvön Sweden 63°3N 18°40E 162 A12
Norrahammar Sweden 57°43N 14°7E 163 G8
Norrbottens län □ Sweden 66°50N 20°0E 160 C19
Norrdellen Sweden 61°53N 16°43E 162 C10
Nørre Aaby Denmark 55°27N 9°52E 163 J3
Nørre Alslev Denmark 54°54N 11°52E 163 K5
Nørrebro Copenhagen, Denmark 118 a1
Nørresundby Denmark 57°5N 9°52E 163 G3
Norrhult-Klavreström Sweden 57°7N 15°10E 163 G9
Norridge U.S.A. 41°57N 87°49W 119 B2
Norris City U.S.A. 37°59N 88°20W 311 G8
Norris Point Canada 49°31N 57°53W 299 C8
Norristown Ga., U.S.A. 32°30N 82°30W 316 C7
Norristown Pa., U.S.A. 40°7N 75°21W 313 F9
Norrköping Sweden 58°37N 16°11E 163 F10
Norrland Sweden 62°15N 15°45E 160 E16
Norrmalm Stockholm, Sweden 139 a1
Norrsundet Sweden 60°56N 17°8E 162 D11
Norrtälje Sweden 59°46N 18°42E 162 E12
Norseman Australia 32°8S 121°43E 279 F3
Norsewood N.Z. 40°3S 176°13E 284 G5
Norsjø Norway 59°18N 9°20E 164 E6
Norsk Russia 52°30N 130°5E 215 D14
Norsup Vanuatu 16°3S 167°24E 287 F5
Norte, C. Chile 27°3S 109°24W 330 b
Norte, Canal do → Brazil 0°40N 50°20W 329 C7
Norte, Pta. Argentina 42°5S 63°46W 336 B4
Norte, Pta. Chile 33°36S 78°54W 330 c
Norte, Pta. del Canary Is. 27°51N 17°57W 153 e1
Norte, Pta. do Azores 37°1N 25°4W 153 d4
Norte, Serra do Brazil 11°20S 59°0W 331 C6
Norte de Santander □ Colombia 8°0N 73°0W 328 B3
Norte Grande Azores 38°40N 28°4W 153 d1
Nortelândia Brazil 14°25S 56°48W 331 C6
North U.S.A. 33°37N 81°6W 316 B8
North, C. Canada 47°2N 60°20W 299 C7
North Adams U.S.A. 42°42N 73°7W 313 D11
North America 40°0N 100°0W 292 F10
North Andaman I. India 13°15N 92°55E 245 H11
North Arlington U.S.A. 40°47N 74°7W 132 B1
North Arm Canada 62°0N 114°30W 296 A5
North Atlanta U.S.A. 33°53N 84°19W 113 A3
North Augusta U.S.A. 33°30N 81°59W 316 B8
North Australian Basin Ind. Oc. 14°30S 116°30E 276 C2
North Ayrshire □ U.K. 55°45N 4°44W 167 F4
North Balabac Str. Phil. 8°8N 117°4E 233 G1
North Baltimore U.S.A. 41°11N 83°41W 311 C13
North Bass I. U.S.A. 41°40N 82°56W 312 E2
North Battleford Canada 52°50N 108°17W 297 C7
North Bay Canada 46°20N 79°30W 298 C4
North Bay Village U.S.A. 25°50N 80°9W 129 C3
North Beach San Francisco, U.S.A. 136 a2
North Belcher Is. Canada 56°50N 79°50W 298 A4
North Bend Oreg., U.S.A. 43°24N 124°14W 304 E1
North Bend Pa., U.S.A. 41°20N 77°42W 312 E7
North Bend Wash., U.S.A. 47°30N 121°47W 306 C5
North Bennington U.S.A. 42°56N 73°15W 313 D11
North Bergen U.S.A. 40°48N 74°0W 132 B1
North Berwick E. Loth., U.K. 56°4N 2°42W 167 E6
North Berwick Maine, U.S.A. 43°18N 70°44W 313 C14
North Borneo = Sabah □ Malaysia 6°0N 117°0E 235 A5
North Breakers Midway Is. 28°13N 177°24W 302 c
North Brother I. India 10°59N 92°40E 245 J11
North Bruce Canada 44°22N 81°26W 312 B3
North C. N.B., Canada 47°5N 64°0W 299 C7
North C. N.Z. 34°23S 173°4E 284 A2
North C. Papua N. G. 2°32S 150°50E 286 B6
North Canadian → U.S.A. 35°22N 95°37W 314 D7
North Canton U.S.A. 40°53N 81°24W 312 F3
North Cape = Nordkapp Norway 71°10N 25°50E 160 A21
North Caribou L. Canada 52°50N 90°40W 298 B1
North Carolina □ U.S.A. 35°30N 80°0W 315 D15
North Cascades △ U.S.A. 48°45N 121°10W 304 B3
North Cay Bahamas 25°6N 77°26W 153 b
North Channel Ont., Canada 46°0N 83°0W 298 C3
North Channel U.K. 55°13N 5°52W 167 F3
North Charleston U.S.A. 32°53N 79°58W 316 C10
North Cheam U.K. 51°22N 0°11W 125 B2
North Chicago U.S.A. 42°19N 87°51W 311 B9
North College Hill U.S.A. 39°13N 84°33W 311 E12
North Collins U.S.A. 42°35N 78°56W 312 D6
North Comino Channel Malta 36°1N 14°20E 206 E7
North Cotabato □ Phil. 7°10N 125°0E 233 H5
North Cray U.K. 51°25N 0°8E 125 B4
North Creek U.S.A. 43°42N 73°59W 313 C11
North Dakota □ U.S.A. 47°30N 100°15W 308 B3
North Decatur U.S.A. 33°48N 84°17W 113 B3
North Downs U.K. 51°19N 0°21E 169 F8
North Druid Hills U.S.A. 33°49N 84°17W 113 B3
North East U.S.A. 42°13N 79°50W 312 D5
North East □ Botswana 20°45S 27°30E 271 B4
North East B. Ascension I. 7°55S 14°21W 153 g
North East Frontier Agency = Arunachal Pradesh □ India 28°0N 95°0E 241 B5
North East Lincolnshire □ U.K. 53°34N 0°2W 168 D7
North End Boston, U.S.A. 116 a3
North Esk → Angus, U.K. 56°46N 2°24W 167 E6
North Esk → Midloth., U.K. 55°54N 3°4W 121 B2
North European Plain Europe 55°0N 25°0E 158 E10
North Fabius → U.S.A. 39°54N 91°30W 310 E5
North Foreland U.K. 51°22N 1°28E 169 F9
North Fork U.S.A. 37°14N 119°21W 306 H7
North Fork, Salt → U.S.A. 39°26N 91°53W 310 E5
North Fork American → U.S.A. 38°57N 120°59W 306 G5
North Fork Edisto → U.S.A. 33°16N 80°54W 316 B9
North Fork Feather → U.S.A. 38°33N 121°30W 306 F5
North Fork Grand → U.S.A. 45°47N 102°16W 308 C2
North Fork Red → U.S.A. 34°24N 99°14W 314 D5
North Fort Myers U.S.A. 26°41N 81°53W 317 J8
North Frisian Is. = Nordfriesische Inseln Germany 54°40N 8°20E 178 A4
North Gower Canada 45°8N 75°43W 313 A9
North Greenfield = West Allis U.S.A. 43°1N 88°0W 311 B8
North Gyle U.K. 55°57N 3°19W 121 B2
North Hackensack U.S.A. 40°54N 74°2W 132 A1
North Harbor Phil. 14°37N 120°57E 127 B1
North Hd. N.S.W., Australia 33°49S 151°18E 139 A2
North Hd. W. Austral., Australia 30°14S 114°59E 279 F1
North Henik L. Canada 61°45N 97°40W 297 A9
North Highlands U.S.A. 38°40N 121°23W 306 G5
North Hollywood U.S.A. 34°9N 118°22W 126 B2
North Horr Kenya 3°20N 37°8E 268 B4
North I. India 10°8N 72°20E 245 J1
North I. Rift Valley, Kenya 4°5N 36°5E 268 B4
North I. N.Z. 38°0S 175°0E 284 E4
North I. Seychelles 4°25S 55°13E 272 c
North Judson U.S.A. 41°13N 86°46W 311 C10
North Kingsville U.S.A. 41°54N 80°42W 312 E4
North Kitui ⌂ Kenya 0°15S 38°29E 268 C4
North Knife → Canada 58°53N 94°45W 297 B10
North Koel → India 24°45N 83°50E 243 G10
North Korea ■ Asia 40°0N 127°0E 224 C3
North L. N.S.W., Australia 32°30S 143°5E 282 B5
North L. Tex., U.S.A. 32°56N 96°58W 120 A4
North Lake Park U.S.A. 32°55N 96°58W 120 A4
North Lakhimpur India 27°14N 94°7E 241 B5
North Lanarkshire □ U.K. 55°52N 3°56W 167 F5
North Las Vegas U.S.A. 36°11N 115°7W 124 A1
North Las Vegas ✈ (VGT) U.S.A. 36°12N 115°11W 124 A1
North Lexington U.S.A. 42°27N 71°14W 116 A1
North Liberty Ind., U.S.A. 41°32N 86°26W 311 C10
North Liberty Iowa, U.S.A. 41°46N 91°35W 310 C5
North Lincolnshire □ U.K. 53°36N 0°30W 168 D7
North Little Rock U.S.A. 34°45N 92°16W 314 D8
North Loup → U.S.A. 41°17N 98°24W 308 E4
North Luangwa △ Zambia 11°49S 32°9E 269 E3
North Magnetic Pole Arctic 85°9N 149°0W 150 A1
North Malé Atoll Maldives 4°25N 73°30E 272 d
North Malosmadulu Atoll Maldives 5°37N 72°55E 272 d
North Manchester U.S.A. 41°0N 85°46W 311 D11
North Mankato U.S.A. 44°10N 94°2W 308 C6
North Miami U.S.A. 25°53N 80°11W 129 C2
North Miami Beach U.S.A. 25°55N 80°9W 129 C2
North Minch U.K. 58°5N 5°55W 167 C3
North Moose L. Canada 54°4N 100°12W 297 C8
North Myrtle Beach U.S.A. 33°48N 78°42W 315 E15
North Nahanni → Canada 62°15N 123°20W 296 A4
North Naples U.S.A. 26°12N 81°48W 317 J8
North Nazimabad Pakistan 24°55N 67°3E 123 A2
North New River Canal U.S.A. 26°30N 80°30W 317 J9
North Nilandu Atoll Maldives 3°14N 72°56E 272 d
North Olmsted U.S.A. 41°25N 81°56W 312 E3
North Ossetia-Alaniya □ Russia 43°30N 44°30E 191 J7
North Pagai, I. = Pagai Utara, Pulau Indonesia 2°35S 100°0E 234 C2
North Palisade U.S.A. 37°6N 118°31W 306 H8
North Paravar India 10°13N 76°14E 245 J3
North Perry ✈ (HWO) U.S.A. 26°0N 80°14W 129 B2
North Platte U.S.A. 41°8N 100°46W 308 E3
North Platte → U.S.A. 41°7N 100°42W 308 E3
North Point Hong Kong, China 22°17N 114°12E 122 B3
North Point Fla., U.S.A. 27°4N 82°10W 317 H7
North Point Park Boston, U.S.A. 116 a1
North Pole Arctic 90°0N 0°0 150 A
North Pole Alaska, U.S.A. 64°45N 147°21W 303 D11
North Portal Canada 49°0N 102°33W 297 D8
North Powder U.S.A. 45°2N 117°55W 304 D5
North Pt. Ascension I. 7°53S 14°23W 153 g
North Pt. Barbados 13°20N 59°37W 323 r
North Pt. Mich., U.S.A. 45°2N 83°16W 312 A1
North Pt. Vanuatu 14°56S 168°6E 287 D6
North Queensferry U.K. 56°1N 3°24W 121 A1
North Quincy U.S.A. 42°16N 71°1W 116 B2
North Reef I. India 13°5N 92°43E 245 H11
North Res. U.S.A. 42°27N 71°6W 116 A2
North Rhine Westphalia = Nordrhein-Westfalen □ Germany 51°45N 7°30E 178 D3
North Richland Hills U.S.A. 32°50N 97°13W 120 A2
North River Canada 53°49N 57°6W 299 B8
North Riverside U.S.A. 41°50N 87°48W 119 B2
North Rona Atl. Oc. 59°7N 5°49W 165 B4
North Ronaldsay U.K. 59°22N 2°26W 167 B6
North Salem U.S.A. 39°52N 86°39W 311 E10
North Saskatchewan → Canada 53°15N 105°5W 297 C7
North Saugus U.S.A. 42°29N 71°0W 116 A2
North Sea Europe 56°0N 4°0E 158 D6
North Seal → Canada 58°50N 98°7W 297 B9
North Sentinel I. India 11°33N 92°15E 245 J11
North Shields Australia 34°38S 135°52E 282 C1
North Shore U.S.A. 21°39N 158°30W 302 J13
North Shore Channel → U.S.A. 41°58N 87°42W 119 B2
North Slope U.S.A. 69°15N 152°0W 300 B9
North Somerset □ U.K. 51°24N 2°45W 169 F5
North Station Boston, U.S.A. 116 a2
North Sydney N.S.W., Australia 33°50S 151°13E 139 B2
North Sydney N.S., Canada 46°12N 60°15W 299 C7
North Syracuse U.S.A. 43°8N 76°7W 313 C8
North Taranaki Bight N.Z. 38°50S 174°15E 284 E3
North Thompson → Canada 50°40N 120°20W 296 C4
North Tonawanda U.S.A. 43°2N 78°53W 312 C6
North Troy U.S.A. 45°0N 72°24W 313 B12
North Twin I. Canada 53°20N 80°0W 298 B4
North Tyne → U.K. 55°0N 2°8W 168 B5
North Ubian I. Phil. 6°9N 120°27E 233 H3
North Uist U.K. 57°40N 7°15W 167 D1
North Union = Shaker Heights U.S.A. 41°28N 81°32W 312 E3
North Union St. Vincent 13°13N 61°8W 323 n
North Vancouver Canada 49°19N 123°4W 306 A3
North Vernon U.S.A. 39°0N 85°38W 311 F11
North Wabasca L. Canada 56°0N 113°55W 296 B6
North Walsham U.K. 52°50N 1°22E 168 E9
North Webster U.S.A. 41°25N 85°48W 311 C11
North West = Severo-Zapadnyy □ Russia 65°0N 40°0E 214 C4
North West □ Botswana 19°0S 22°30E 270 A3
North-West □ S. Africa 27°0S 25°0E 270 C4
North West Bluff Montserrat 16°49N 62°12W 323 p
North West C. Australia 21°45S 114°9E 278 D1
North West Frontier = Khyber Pakhtunkhwa □ Pakistan 34°0N 72°0E 242 C4
North West Highlands U.K. 57°33N 4°58W 167 D4
North West Pt. Jamaica 18°27N 78°13W 320 a
North West River Canada 53°30N 60°10W 299 B7
North Western □ Zambia 13°30S 25°30E 269 E2
North-Western Provinces and Oudh = Uttar Pradesh □ India 27°0N 80°0E 243 F9
North Wildwood U.S.A. 39°0N 74°48W 309 F16
North Woolwich U.K. 51°30N 0°3E 125 A4
North Yakima = Yakima U.S.A. 46°36N 120°31W 304 C3
North York Canada 43°45N 79°27W 141 A2
North York Moors U.K. 54°23N 0°53W 168 C7
North York Moors △ U.K. 54°27N 0°51W 168 C7
North Yorkshire □ U.K. 54°15N 1°25W 168 C6
Northallerton U.K. 54°20N 1°26W 168 C6
Northam W. Austral., Australia 31°35S 116°42E 279 F2
Northam Limpopo, S. Africa 24°56S 27°18E 270 B4
Northampton W. Austral., Australia 28°27S 114°33E 279 E1
Northampton Northants., U.K. 52°15N 0°53W 169 E7
Northampton Mass., U.S.A. 42°19N 72°38W 313 D12
Northampton Pa., U.S.A. 40°41N 75°30W 313 F9
Northamptonshire □ U.K. 52°16N 0°55W 169 E7
Northbridge N.S.W., Australia 33°49S 151°15E 139 A2
Northbridge Mass., U.S.A. 42°9N 71°39W 313 D13
Northbridge Park Australia 33°49S 151°15E 139 A2
Northbrook Ont., Canada 44°44N 77°9W 312 B7
Northbrook Ill., U.S.A. 42°7N 87°50W 119 A2
Northcliff S. Africa 26°8S 27°58E 123 A1
Northcliffe Australia 34°39S 116°7E 279 F2
Northcote Australia 37°46S 145°0E 128 A2
Northeast C. U.S.A. 63°18N 168°42W 303 E5
Northeast Pacific Basin Pac. Oc. 32°0N 145°0W 289 D13
Northeast Providence Channel W. Indies 26°0N 76°0W 320 A4
Northeastern Univ. U.S.A. 42°20N 71°4W 116 A2
Northeim Germany 51°42N 10°0E 178 D6
Northern = Limpopo □ S. Africa 24°5S 29°0E 271 B4
Northern □ Ghana 9°30N 1°0W 263 D4
Northern □ Malawi 11°0S 34°0E 269 E3
Northern □ Papua N. G. 9°0S 148°30E 286 E5
Northern □ S. Leone 9°15N 11°30W 262 D2
Northern □ Zambia 10°30S 30°30E 269 E3
Northern Aral Sea Kazakhstan 46°20N 60°30E 216 C6
Northern Areas = Gilgit-Baltistan □ Pakistan 36°30N 73°0E 243 A5
Northern Bahr el Ghazal □ South Sudan 8°0N 27°30E 257 F2
Northern Cape □ S. Africa 30°0S 20°0E 270 C3
Northern Circars India 17°30N 82°30E 244 F6
Northern Dvina = Dvina, Severnaya → Russia 64°32N 40°30E 186 B7
Northern Indian L. Canada 57°20N 97°20W 297 B9
Northern Ireland □ U.K. 54°45N 7°0W 166 B5
Northern Lau Group Fiji 17°30S 178°59W 287 A3
Northern Light L. Canada 48°15N 90°39W 298 C1
Northern Marianas ⊠ Pac. Oc. 17°0N 145°0E 302 a
Northern Province □ S. Africa 24°0S 29°0E 271 B4
Northern Range Trin. & Tob. 10°46N 61°15W 323 t
Northern Rhodesia = Zambia ■ Africa 15°0S 28°0E 269 F2
Northern Samar □ Phil. 12°30N 124°40E 232 E5
Northern Sporades = Voreios Sporades Greece 39°15N 23°30E 204 B5
Northern Territory □ Australia 20°0S 133°0E 278 D5
Northfield Ill., U.S.A. 42°5N 87°47W 119 A2
Northfield Minn., U.S.A. 44°27N 93°9W 308 C7
Northfield Vt., U.S.A. 44°9N 72°40W 313 B12
Northgate Canada 49°0N 102°16W 297 D8
Northland □ N.Z. 35°30S 173°30E 284 B2
Northmount Canada 43°46N 79°23W 141 A2
Northolt U.K. 51°32N 0°22W 125 A1
Northome U.S.A. 47°52N 94°17W 308 B6
Northport Ala., U.S.A. 33°14N 87°35W 315 E11
Northport N.Y., U.S.A. 40°54N 73°21W 313 F11
Northport Wash., U.S.A. 48°55N 117°48W 304 B5
Northumberland □ U.K. 55°12N 2°0W 168 B6
Northumberland, C. Australia 38°5S 140°40E 282 E4
Northumberland Heath U.K. 51°28N 0°10E 125 B5
Northumberland Is. Australia 21°30S 149°50E 280 C4
Northumberland Str. Canada 46°20N 64°0W 299 C7
Northville Ont., Canada 43°10N 81°56W 312 C3
Northville N.Y., U.S.A. 43°13N 74°11W 313 C10
Northway U.S.A. 62°58N 141°56W 303 E12
Northwest Atlantic Mid-Ocean Canyon Atl. Oc. 54°0N 48°0W 152 A7
Northwest Pacific Basin Pac. Oc. 32°0N 165°0E 288 D8
Northwest Providence Channel W. Indies 26°0N 78°0W 320 A4
Northwest Pt. Bahamas 25°4N 77°31W 153 b
Northwest Territories □ Canada 63°0N 118°0W 294 E8
Northwestern Hawaiian Is. Marine Nat. Monument = Papahānaumokuākea Marine Nat. Monument ⌂ U.S.A. 25°25N 170°35W 302 F9
Northwestern Univ. U.S.A. 42°3N 87°40W 119 A2
Northwich U.K. 53°15N 2°31W 168 D5
Northwood London, U.K. 51°36N 0°25W 125 A1
Northwood Iowa, U.S.A. 43°27N 93°13W 308 D7
Northwood N. Dak., U.S.A. 47°44N 97°34W 308 B5
Northwood Park Canada 43°45N 79°30W 141 A1
Norton Kans., U.S.A. 39°50N 99°53W 308 F4
Norton Zimbabwe 17°52S 30°40E 269 F3
Norton B. U.S.A. 64°45N 161°15W 303 D7
Norton Sd. U.S.A. 63°50N 164°0W 303 E7
Norton Shores U.S.A. 43°10N 86°16W 311 A10
Nortorf Germany 54°10N 9°50E 178 A5
Norwalk Calif., U.S.A. 33°54N 118°4W 307 M8
Norwalk Conn., U.S.A. 41°7N 73°22W 313 E11
Norwalk Iowa, U.S.A. 41°29N 93°41W 310 C3
Norwalk Ohio, U.S.A. 41°15N 82°37W 312 E2
Norway Maine, U.S.A. 44°13N 70°32W 309 C18
Norway Mich., U.S.A. 45°47N 87°55W 308 C10
Norway ■ Europe 63°0N 11°0E 160 E14
Norway House Canada 53°59N 97°50W 297 C9
Norwegian B. Canada 77°30N 90°0W 295 B14
Norwegian Basin Atl. Oc. 68°0N 2°0W 150 C7
Norwegian Sea Atl. Oc. 66°0N 1°0E 158 B6
Norwich Ont., Canada 42°59N 80°36W 312 D4
Norwich Norfolk, U.K. 52°38N 1°18E 169 E9
Norwich Conn., U.S.A. 41°31N 72°5W 313 E12
Norwich N.Y., U.S.A. 42°32N 75°32W 313 D9
Norwood Ont., Canada 44°23N 77°59W 312 B7
Norwood Gauteng, S. Africa 26°9S 28°4E 123 A2
Norwood N.Y., U.S.A. 44°45N 75°0W 313 B10
Norwood Ohio, U.S.A. 39°9N 84°27W 311 E12
Norwood Park U.S.A. 41°59N 87°48W 119 B2
Noryangjin S. Korea 37°30N 126°56E 137 B1
Nosappu-Misaki Japan 45°26N 141°39E 220 C12
Noshaq Pakistan 36°24N 71°49E 240 A3
Noshiro Japan 40°12N 140°0E 220 D10
Nosivka Ukraine 50°50N 31°37E 189 G6
Nosovka = Nosivka Ukraine 50°50N 31°37E 189 G6
Noşratābād Iran 29°55N 60°0E 247 D8
Noss Hd. U.K. 58°28N 3°3W 167 C5
Nossa Senhora da Glória Brazil 10°14S 37°25W 332 D4
Nossa Senhora das Dores Brazil 10°29S 37°13W 332 D4
Nossa Senhora de Candelária Rio de J., Brazil 135 a2
Nossa Senhora do Livramento Brazil 15°48S 56°22W 331 D6
Nossa Senhora do Ó Brazil 23°30S 46°41W 137 B1
Nossa Senhora do Socorro Brazil 10°52S 37°7W 332 D4
Nossebro Sweden 58°12N 12°43E 163 F6
Nossegem Belgium 50°53N 4°30E 116 A3
Nossob → S. Africa 26°55S 20°45E 270 C3
Nossombougou Mali 13°5N 7°55W 262 C3
Nosy Varika Madag. 20°35S 48°32E 272 C2
Notasulga U.S.A. 32°34N 85°41W 316 C4
Noteć → Poland 52°44N 15°26E 185 F2
Notikewin → Canada 57°2N 117°38W 296 B5
Notio Aigaio □ Greece 36°52N 25°34E 205 E7
Notios Aiyaíon = Notio Aigaio □ Greece 36°52N 25°34E 205 E7
Notios Evvoikos Kolpos Greece 38°20N 24°0E 204 C5
Noto Italy 36°53N 15°4E 201 F8
Noto, G. di Italy 36°50N 15°12E 201 F8
Noto, Val di Italy 37°14N 14°31E 201 E7
Noto-Hantō Japan 37°15N 136°40E 221 F8
Notodden Norway 59°35N 9°17E 164 E6
Notre-Dame Paris, France 134 c4
Notre-Dame, Basilique Montréal, Canada 130 c3
Notre-Dame, Bois France 48°45N 2°34E 134 B4
Notre Dame B. Canada 49°45N 55°30W 299 C8
Notre-Dame-de-Grace Canada 45°28N 73°38W 130 B2
Notre-Dame-de-Koartac = Quaqtaq Canada 60°55N 69°40W 295 E18
Notre-Dame-des-Bois Canada 45°24N 71°4W 313 A13
Notre-Dame-d'Ivugivic = Ivujivik Canada 62°24N 77°55W 295 E16
Notre-Dame-du-Nord Canada 47°36N 79°30W 298 C4
Notsé Togo 7°0N 1°17E 263 D5
Nottawasaga B. Canada 44°35N 80°15W 312 B4
Nottaway = Senneterre Canada 48°25N 77°15W 298 C4
Nottaway → Canada 51°22N 78°55W 298 B4
Notting Hill London, U.K. 125 b1
Nottingham U.K. 52°58N 1°10W 168 E6
Nottingham, City of □ U.K. 52°58N 1°10W 168 E6
Nottingham I. Canada 63°20N 77°55W 295 E16
Nottinghamshire □ U.K. 53°10N 1°3W 168 D6
Nottoway → U.S.A. 36°33N 76°55W 309 G15
Notwane → Botswana 23°35S 26°58E 270 B4
Nouabalé-Ndoki ⌂ Congo 2°32N 16°32E 264 B3
Nouâdhibou Mauritania 20°54N 17°0W 260 D1
Nouâdhibou, Dakhlet Mauritania 20°55N 16°52W 260 D1
Nouâdhibou, Râs Mauritania 20°50N 17°0W 260 D1
Nouakchott Mauritania 18°9N 15°58W 262 B1
Nouâmghâr Mauritania 19°20N 16°20W 262 B1
Nouméa N. Cal. 22°17S 166°30E 288 d
Nouna Burkina Faso 12°45N 3°52W 262 C4
Noupoort S. Africa 31°10S 24°57E 270 D3
Nouveau Comptoir = Wemindji Canada 53°0N 78°49W 298 B4
Nouvelle Amsterdam, Î. Ind. Oc. 38°30S 77°30E 273 H6
Nouvelle-Aquitaine □ France 45°0N 0°30E 174 C4
Nouvelle-Calédonie = New Caledonia ⊠ Pac. Oc. 21°0S 165°0E 288 d
Nouvelle France Mauritius 20°22S 57°33E 272 e
Nouzonville France 49°48N 4°44E 173 C11
Nová Baňa Slovakia 48°28N 18°39E 181 C11
Nová Bystřice Czechia 49°2N 15°8E 180 B8
Nova Cruz Brazil 6°28S 35°25W 332 C4
Nova Era Brazil 19°45S 43°3W 333 E3
Nova Esperança Brazil 23°8S 52°24W 335 A5
Nova Fontesvila = Vila Machado Mozam. 19°15S 34°14E 269 F3
Nova-Freixo = Cuamba Mozam. 14°45S 36°22E 269 E4
Nova Friburgo Brazil 22°16S 42°30W 333 F3
Nova Gaia = Cambundi-Catembo Angola 10°10S 17°35E 265 E3
Nova Gorica Slovenia 45°57N 13°39E 199 C10
Nova Gradiška Croatia 45°17N 17°28E 182 E2
Nova Granada Brazil 20°30S 49°20W 333 F2
Nova Iguaçu Brazil 22°45S 43°28W 333 F3
Nova Iorque Brazil 7°0S 44°5W 332 C3
Nova Kakhovka Ukraine 46°42N 33°27E 189 J7
Nova Lamego Guinea-Biss. 12°19N 14°11W 262 C2
Nova Lisboa = Huambo Angola 12°42S 15°54E 265 E3
Nova Lusitânia Mozam. 19°50S 34°34E 269 F3
Nova Mambone Mozam. 21°0S 35°3E 271 B6
Nova Milanese Italy 45°35N 9°12E 128 A2
Nova Odesa Ukraine 47°19N 31°47E 189 J6
Nova Olinda do Norte Brazil 3°45S 59°3W 329 D6
Nová Paka Czechia 50°29N 15°30E 180 A8
Nova Pavova Serbia 44°56N 20°14E 182 F5
Nova Ponte Brazil 19°8S 47°41W 333 E2
Nova Russas Brazil 4°42S 40°34W 332 B3
Nova Scotia □ Canada 45°10N 63°0W 299 C7
Nova Siri Italy 40°10N 16°35E 201 B9
Nova Sofala Mozam. 20°7S 34°42E 271 B5
Nova Ushytsya Ukraine 48°50N 27°17E 183 B12
Nova Varoš Serbia 43°29N 19°48E 202 C3
Nova Venécia Brazil 18°45S 40°24W 333 E3
Nova Vida Brazil 10°11S 62°47W 331 C5
Nova Zagora Bulgaria 42°32N 26°1E 203 D10
Novaci Macedonia 41°5N 21°29E 202 E5
Novaci Romania 45°10N 23°42E 183 E8
Novafeltria Italy 43°53N 12°17E 199 E9
Novar Canada 45°27N 79°15W 312 A5
Novara Italy 45°28N 8°38E 198 C5
Novate Milanese Italy 45°30N 9°8E 128 A1
Novato U.S.A. 38°6N 122°35W 306 G4
Novaya Aleksandriya = Puławy Poland 51°23N 21°59E 185 G8
Novaya Bukhara = Kogon Uzbekistan 39°43N 64°33E 216 E6
Novaya Derevnya Russia 60°0N 30°19E 137 A1
Novaya Kakhovka = Nova Kakhovka Ukraine 46°42N 33°27E 189 J7
Novaya Kazanka = Zhangaqala Kazakhstan 48°56N 49°36E 191 F9
Novaya Ladoga Russia 60°7N 32°16E 188 B7
Novaya Lyalya Russia 59°4N 60°45E 186 C11

Novaya Pismyanka = Ridder
Kazakhstan 50°20N 83°30E 217 B10
Novaya Sibir, Ostrov
Russia 75°10N 150°0E 215 B16
Novaya Zemlya Russia 75°0N 56°0E 214 B6
Nové Město Czechia 50°4N 14°25E 135 B2
Nové Město na Moravě
Czechia 49°34N 16°5E 180 B9
Nové Město nad Metují
Czechia 50°20N 16°10E 181 A9
Nové Město nad Váhom
Slovakia 48°45N 17°50E 181 C10
Nové Zámky Slovakia 48°2N 18°8E 181 C11
Novelda Spain 38°24N 0°45W 197 G4
Novellara Italy 44°51N 10°44E 198 D7
Novelty U.S.A. 40°1N 92°12W 310 D4
Noventa Vicentina Italy 45°17N 11°32E 199 C8
Novgorod = Velikiy Novgorod
Russia 58°30N 31°25E 188 C6
Novgorod □ Russia 58°50N 32°30E 188 C7
Novgorod-Severskiy = Novhorod-
Siverskyy Ukraine 52°2N 33°10E 189 G7
Novgradets = Suvorovo
Bulgaria 43°20N 27°35E 203 C11
Novhorod-Siverskyy
Ukraine 52°2N 33°10E 189 G7
Novi Bečej Serbia 45°36N 20°10E 182 E5
Novi Grad Bos.-H. 45°2N 16°22E 199 C13
Novi Iskar Bulgaria 42°48N 23°21E 202 D7
Novi Kneževac Serbia 46°4N 20°8E 182 D5
Novi Ligure Italy 44°46N 8°47E 198 D5
Novi Pazar Bulgaria 43°25N 27°15E 203 C11
Novi Pazar Serbia 43°12N 20°28E 202 C4
Novi Sad Serbia 45°18N 19°52E 182 E4
Novi Slankamen Serbia 45°8N 20°15E 182 E5
Novi Travnik Bos.-H. 44°10N 17°40E 182 F2
Novi Vinodolski Croatia 45°10N 14°48E 199 C11
Novigrad Istra, Croatia 45°19N 13°33E 199 C10
Novigrad Zadar, Croatia 44°10N 15°32E 199 D12
Novigradsko More
Croatia 44°12N 15°33E 199 D12
Novinger U.S.A. 40°14N 92°43W 310 D4
Novo Acôrdo Brazil 10°10S 46°48W 332 D2
Novo Airão Brazil 2°40S 60°59W 329 D5
Novo Aripuanã Brazil 5°8S 60°22W 329 E5
Novo Cruzeiro Brazil 17°29S 41°53W 333 E3
Novo Hamburgo Brazil 29°37S 51°7W 335 B5
Novo Horizonte Brazil 21°25S 49°10W 333 F2
Novo Ivanivka Ukraine 45°55N 29°5E 183 E14
Novo-Mariinsk = Anadyr
Russia 64°35N 177°20E 215 C18
Novo Mesto Slovenia 45°47N 15°12E 199 C12
Novo Miloševo Serbia 45°42N 20°20E 182 E5
Novo Nikolaevsk = Novosibirsk
Russia 55°0N 83°5E 217 B10
Novo Paraiso Brazil 1°17N 60°28W 329 C5
Novo-Starobinsk = Salihorsk
Belarus 52°51N 27°27E 177 B14
Novo Urgench = Urganch
Uzbekistan 41°40N 60°41E 216 D6
Novoaleksandrovsk = Zarasai
Lithuania 55°40N 26°20E 188 E4
Novoaleksandrovsk
Russia 45°29N 41°17E 191 H5
Novoaleksandrovskaya =
Novoaleksandrovsk
Russia 45°29N 41°17E 191 H5
Novoaleksandrovskoye
Russia 59°50N 30°31E 137 B2
Novoaltaysk Russia 53°30N 84°0E 217 B10
Novoannînskiy Russia 50°32N 42°39E 190 E6
Novoazovsk Ukraine 47°15N 38°4E 189 J10
Novocheboksarsk Russia 56°5N 47°27E 190 B8
Novocherkassk Russia 47°27N 40°15E 191 G5
Novodevichy Convent
Russia 55°43N 37°34E 129 B2
Novodevichye Russia 53°37N 48°50E 190 D9
Novodvinsk Russia 64°25N 40°42E 186 B7
Novogireyevo Russia 55°45N 37°46E 129 B3
Novogrudok = Navahrudak
Belarus 53°40N 25°50E 177 B13
Novohrad-Volynskyy
Ukraine 50°34N 27°35E 177 C14
Novokachalinsk Russia 45°5N 132°0E 220 B5
Novokazalinsk = Ayteke Bi
Kazakhstan 45°48N 62°6E 216 C6
Novokhopersk Russia 51°5N 41°39E 190 E5
Novokiyevskoye = Kraskino
Russia 42°44N 130°48E 220 C5
Novokuybyshevsk Russia 53°7N 49°58E 190 D9
Novokuznetsk Russia 53°45N 87°10E 217 B11
Novolazarevskaya
Antarctica 71°0S 12°0E 151 D3
Novolyalinsky = Novaya Lyalya
Russia 59°4N 60°45E 186 C11
Novomoskovsk Russia 54°5N 38°15E 188 E10
Novomoskovsk Ukraine 48°33N 35°17E 189 H8
Novomyrhorod Ukraine 48°45N 31°33E 189 H6
Novonikolayevka = Novoazovsk
Ukraine 47°15N 38°4E 189 J10
Novopolotsk = Navapolatsk
Belarus 55°32N 28°37E 188 E5
Novorossiysk Russia 44°43N 37°46E 189 K9
Novorybnoye Russia 72°50N 105°50E 215 B11
Novorzhev Russia 57°3N 29°25E 188 D5
Novosaratovka Russia 59°50N 30°32E 137 B3
Novosej Albania 41°56N 20°35E 202 E4
Novoselytsya Ukraine 48°14N 26°15E 183 B11
Novoshakhtinsk Russia 47°46N 39°58E 189 J10
Novosibirsk Russia 55°0N 83°5E 217 B10
Novosibirskiye Ostrova
Russia 75°0N 142°0E 215 B15
Novosibirskoye Vdkhr.
Russia 54°35N 82°35E 217 B10
Novosil Russia 52°59N 37°2E 189 F9
Novosokolniki Russia 56°20N 30°2E 188 D6
Novotitarovskaya Russia 45°17N 39°2E 191 H4
Novotroitsk Russia 51°10N 58°15E 186 D10
Novotroitskoye = Töle Bī
Kazakhstan 43°42N 73°46E 217 D8
Novoukrayinka Ukraine 48°25N 31°30E 189 H6
Novoulyanovsk Russia 54°8N 48°24E 190 C9
Novouzensk Russia 50°32N 48°17E 190 E9
Novovolynsk Ukraine 50°45N 24°4E 185 H11
Novovoronezh Russia 51°19N 39°13E 189 G10
Novoyavoriske Ukraine 49°53N 23°33E 185 J10
Novozybkov Russia 52°30N 32°0E 189 F6
Novska Croatia 45°19N 17°0E 199 C14
Nový Bor Czechia 50°46N 14°35E 180 A7
Novy Bug = Novyy Buh
Ukraine 47°34N 32°29E 189 J7
Nový Bydžov Czechia 50°14N 15°29E 180 A8
Novy Dvor Belarus 52°50N 24°21E 185 F11
Novy Dwór Mazowiecki
Poland 52°26N 20°44E 185 F7
Nový Jičín Czechia 49°30N 18°2E 181 B11
Novy Margelan = Farg'ona
Uzbekistan 40°23N 71°19E 217 D8
Novyy Bor Russia 66°43N 52°19E 186 A9
Novyy Buh Ukraine 47°34N 32°29E 189 J7
Novyy Oskol Russia 50°44N 37°55E 189 G9
Novyy Port Russia 67°40N 72°30E 214 C8
Novyy Urengoy Russia 65°48N 76°52E 214 C8
Nowa Deba Poland 50°26N 21°41E 185 H8
Nowa Nowa Australia 37°44S 148°3E 283 D8
Nowa Ruda Poland 50°35N 16°30E 185 H3
Nowa Sarzyna Poland 50°21N 22°21E 185 H9
Nowa Sól Poland 51°48N 15°44E 185 G2
Nowata U.S.A. 36°42N 95°38W 314 C7
Nowbarān Iran 35°8N 49°42E 247 C6
Nowe Poland 53°41N 18°44E 184 E5
Nowe-Babice Poland 52°15N 20°51E 143 B1
Nowe Miasteczko Poland 51°42N 15°42E 185 G2
Nowe Miasto Mazowieckie,
Poland 51°38N 20°34E 185 G7
Nowe Miasto Warsaw, Poland 143 a2
Nowe Miasto Lubawskie
Poland 53°27N 19°33E 184 E6
Nowe Skalmierzyce Poland 51°43N 18°0E 185 G4
Nowe Warpno Poland 53°42N 14°18E 184 E1
Nowendoc Australia 31°32S 151°44E 283 A9
Nowendoc △ Australia 31°33S 151°45E 283 A9
Nowghāb Iran 33°53N 59°4E 247 C8
Nowgong = Nagaon India 26°20N 92°50E 241 B4
Nowgong India 25°4N 79°27E 243 G8
Nowitna Nat. Wildlife Refuge ⌓
U.S.A. 64°40N 154°16W 303 D9
Nowogard Poland 53°41N 15°10E 184 E2
Nowogród Poland 53°14N 21°53E 185 E8
Nowogród Bobrzanski
Poland 51°48N 15°15E 185 G2
Nowogrodziec Poland 51°12N 15°24E 185 G2
Noworadomsk = Radomsko
Poland 51°5N 19°28E 185 G6
Nowra Australia 34°53S 150°35E 283 C9
Nowrangapur India 19°14N 82°33E 244 E6
Nowshāk = Noshaq
Pakistan 36°24N 71°49E 240 A3
Nowshera Pakistan 34°0N 72°0E 240 B4
Nowy Dwór Gdański
Poland 54°13N 19°7E 184 D6
Nowy Sącz Poland 49°40N 20°41E 185 J7
Nowy Staw Poland 54°13N 19°2E 184 D6
Nowy Targ Poland 49°29N 20°2E 185 J7
Nowy Tomyśl Poland 52°19N 16°10E 185 F3
Nowy Wiśnicz Poland 49°55N 20°28E 185 J7
Noxen U.S.A. 41°25N 76°4W 313 E8
Noyabr'sk Russia 64°34N 76°21E 214 C8
Noyant France 47°30N 0°6E 172 E7
Noyers France 47°40N 4°0E 173 E10
Nöykkiö Finland 60°10N 24°42E 121 B1
Noyon Oise, France 49°34N 2°59E 173 C9
Noyon Mongolia 43°2N 102°4E 226 C2
Nozay France 47°34N 1°38W 172 E5
Nqutu S. Africa 28°13S 30°32E 271 C5
Nsa Congo 2°22S 15°19E 264 C3
Nsa, O. en → Algeria 32°28N 5°24E 261 B6
Nsa, Plateau de Congo 2°26S 15°20E 264 C3
Nsanje Malawi 16°55S 35°12E 269 F4
Nsawam Ghana 5°50N 0°24W 263 D4
Nseluka Zambia 9°58S 31°16E 269 D3
Nsok Eq. Guin. 1°10N 11°19E 264 B2
Nsomba Zambia 10°45S 29°51E 269 E2
Nsontin
Dem. Rep. of the Congo 3°7S 17°56E 264 C3
Nsopzup Burma 25°51N 97°30E 241 C6
Nsukka Nigeria 6°51N 7°29E 263 D6
Ntaria ⊙ Australia 24°0S 132°41E 278 D5
Ntem → Cameroon 2°21N 9°49E 264 B2
Ntingui, Mt. Comoros Is. 12°12S 44°25E 272 a
Ntoum Gabon 0°22N 9°47E 264 B1
N'Tsama Congo 0°53S 14°44E 264 C2
Ntsaouéni Comoros Is. 11°27S 43°15E 272 a
Ntsoudjini Comoros Is. 11°39S 43°15E 272 a
Ntui Cameroon 4°27N 11°38E 263 E7
Ntungamo Uganda 0°56S 30°17E 268 C3
Nu Jiang → China 29°58N 97°25E 228 E2
Nu Shan China 26°0N 99°20E 228 E2
Nuakata I. Papua N. G. 10°17S 151°2E 286 F6
Nuba Mts. = Nubah, Jibalan
Sudan 12°0N 31°0E 257 E3
Nubah, Jibalan Sudan 12°0N 31°0E 257 E3
Nubia Africa 21°0N 32°0E 254 D7
Nubian Desert = Nûbîya, Es Sahrâ
en Sudan 21°30N 33°30E 256 C3
Nûbîya, Es Sahrâ en
Sudan 21°30N 33°30E 256 C3
Nubl Syria 36°22N 36°59E 250 B7
Nubledo Spain 43°31N 5°52W 194 B5
Nubrai Indonesia 2°10S 136°30E 231 E9
Nubra → India 34°35N 77°35E 243 B7
Nucet Romania 46°28N 22°35E 182 D7
Nueces → U.S.A. 27°51N 97°30W 314 H6
Nueltin L. Canada 60°30N 99°30W 297 A9
Nuestra Señora del Rosario de
Caá-Catí Argentina 27°45S 57°36W 334 B4
Nueva, I. Chile 55°13S 66°30W 336 E3
Nueva Antioquia Colombia 6°5N 69°26W 328 B4
Nueva Atzacoalco Mexico 19°29N 99°4W 128 B2
Nueva Carteya Spain 37°35N 4°28W 195 H6
Nueva Ciudad Guerrero
Mexico 26°34N 99°12W 319 B5
Nueva Ecija □ Phil. 15°35N 121°0E 232 D3
Nueva Esparta □ Venezuela 11°0N 64°0W 329 A5
Nueva Gerona Cuba 21°53N 82°49W 320 B3
Nueva Imperial Chile 38°45S 72°58W 336 A2
Nueva Loja = Lago Agrio
Ecuador 0°5N 76°52W 328 C2
Nueva Palmira Uruguay 33°52S 58°20W 334 C4
Nueva Pompeya
Argentina 34°40S 58°25W 117 C2
Nueva Rosita Mexico 27°57N 101°13W 318 B4
Nueva San Salvador
El Salv. 13°40N 89°18W 320 D2
Nueva Tabarca Spain 38°17N 0°30W 197 G4
Nueva Tenochtitlán
Mexico 19°27N 99°5W 128 B2
Nueva Vizcaya □ Phil. 16°20N 121°20E 232 C3
Nuéve de Julio Argentina 35°30S 61°0W 334 D3
Nuevitas Cuba 21°30N 77°20W 320 B4
Nuevo, G. Argentina 43°0S 64°30W 336 B4
Nuevo Casas Grandes
Mexico 30°25N 107°55W 318 A3
Nuevo Laredo Mexico 27°30N 99°31W 319 B5
Nuevo León □ Mexico 25°20N 100°0W 318 C5
Nuevo Mundo, Cerro
Bolivia 21°55S 66°53W 330 E4
Nuevo Rocafuerte Ecuador 0°55S 75°27W 328 D2
Nugaal □ Somalia 8°10N 49°0E 267 C6
Nugaal → Somalia 8°0N 49°47E 267 C6
Nugaaleed, Dooxo Somalia 8°35N 48°35E 267 C6
Nugget Pt. N.Z. 46°27S 169°50E 285 G4
Nugrus, Gebel Egypt 24°47N 34°35E 256 C3
Nuguria Is. Papua N. G. 3°20S 154°45E 286 B8
Nuhaka N.Z. 39°3S 177°45E 284 F6
Nui Pac. Oc. 7°15S 177°10E 277 B14
Nuijala Finland 60°12N 24°46E 121 B1
Nuits-St-Georges France 47°10N 4°56E 173 E11
Nukey Bluff Australia 32°26S 135°29E 281 E2
Nukha = Şaki Azerbaijan 41°10N 47°5E 191 K8
Nukhayb Iraq 32°4N 42°3E 213 F10
Nukheila Sudan 19°1N 26°21E 256 D2
Nukiki Solomon Is. 6°46S 156°35E 287 L9
Nuku Papua N. G. 3°41S 142°28E 286 B2
Nuku Hiva French Polynesia 8°54S 140°6W 289 f
Nuku'alofa Tonga 21°10S 175°12W 287 Q13
Nukuhu Papua N. G. 5°34S 149°22E 286 C5
Nukulaelae Tuvalu 9°23S 179°52E 277 B14
Nukunonu Pac. Oc. 9°12S 171°54W 277 B16
Nukus Uzbekistan 42°27N 59°41E 216 D5
Nulato U.S.A. 64°43N 158°6W 303 D8
Nules Spain 39°51N 0°9W 196 F4
Nullagine Australia 21°53S 120°7E 278 D3
Nullagine → Australia 21°20S 120°20E 278 D3
Nullarbor Australia 31°28S 130°55E 279 F5
Nullarbor △ Australia 32°39S 130°0E 279 F4
Nullarbor Plain Australia 31°10S 129°0E 279 F4
Numabukuro Japan 35°43N 139°39E 140 A2
Numalla, L. Australia 28°43S 144°20E 281 D3
Numan Nigeria 9°29N 12°3E 263 D7
Numanuma Papua N. G. 9°41S 150°55E 286 E6
Numata Japan 36°45N 139°4E 223 A11
Numatinna → South Sudan 7°38N 27°20E 257 F2
Numaykoos Lake ⌓
Canada 57°52N 95°58W 297 B9
Numazu Japan 35°7N 138°51E 223 B10
Numbulwar Australia 14°15S 135°45E 280 A2
Numedal Norway 60°6N 9°6E 164 D6
Numfoor Indonesia 1°0S 134°50E 231 E8
Numurkah Australia 36°5S 145°26E 283 D6
Nunaksaluk I. Canada 55°49N 60°20W 299 A7
Nunap Isua Greenland 59°48N 43°55W 154 F6
Nunatsiavut Canada 55°30N 62°0W 299 A7
Nunavik Canada 56°30N 71°0W 295 F17
Nunavik Greenland 71°50N 54°25W 154 C5
Nunavut □ Canada 66°0N 85°0W 295 D15
Nunda U.S.A. 42°35N 77°56W 312 D7
Nuneaton U.K. 52°32N 1°27W 169 E6
Nuñez Argentina 34°32S 58°27W 117 B2
Nungarin Australia 31°12S 118°6E 279 F2
Nungo Mozam. 13°23S 37°43E 269 E4
Nungwe Tanzania 2°48S 32°2E 268 C3
Nunhead U.K. 51°27N 0°3W 125 B3
Nunivak I. U.S.A. 60°10N 166°30W 303 F6
Nunkun India 33°57N 76°2E 243 C7
Ñuñoa Chile 33°27S 70°35W 137 B2
Nunukan Indonesia 4°4N 117°40E 235 B5
Nùoro Italy 40°20N 9°20E 200 B2
Nuozhadu Dam China 22°39N 100°25E 228 F3
Núpur Iceland 65°56N 23°36W 155 B3
Nuqayy, Jabal Libya 23°11N 19°30E 258 D3
Nuqūb Yemen 14°59N 45°48E 248 D4
Nuquí Colombia 5°42N 77°17W 328 B2
Nūr Iran 36°33N 52°1E 247 B7
Nur Dağı Turkey 36°54N 35°39E 250 B6
Nur Dağları Turkey 36°50N 36°23E 250 B7
Nura → Kazakhstan 50°30N 69°59E 217 B7
Nūrābād Hormozgān, Iran 27°47N 57°12E 247 E8
Nūrābād Lorestān, Iran 34°4N 47°58E 213 E12
Nure → Italy 45°3N 9°49E 198 C6
Nuremberg = Nürnberg
Germany 49°27N 11°3E 179 F7
Nuri Sonora, Mexico 28°5N 109°22W 318 B3
Nuri Sudan 18°29N 31°59E 256 D3
Nuriootpa Australia 34°27S 139°0E 282 C3
Nuristān □ Afghan. 35°20N 71°0E 217 E8
Nurlat Russia 54°29N 50°45E 190 C10
Nurmes Finland 63°33N 29°10E 160 E23
Nürnberg Germany 49°27N 11°3E 179 F7
Nurpur Pakistan 31°53N 71°54E 242 D4
Nurra, La Italy 40°45N 8°15E 200 B1
Nurran, L. = Terewah, L.
Australia 29°52S 147°35E 281 D4
Nurrari Lakes Australia 29°1S 130°5E 279 E5
Nurri Italy 39°43N 9°14E 200 C2
Nürtingen Germany 48°37N 9°19E 179 G5
Nurzec → Poland 52°37N 22°25E 185 F9
Nus Italy 45°45N 7°28E 198 C4
Nusa Dua Indonesia 8°48S 115°14E 231 K18
Nusa Tenggara Barat □
Indonesia 8°50S 117°30E 235 D5
Nusa Tenggara Timur □
Indonesia 9°30S 122°0E 231 F6
Nusaybin Turkey 37°3N 41°10E 213 D9
Nuşayrīyah, J. an Syria 35°20N 36°13E 250 C7
Nuşeirat Gaza Strip 31°27N 34°24E 251 G5
Nushki Pakistan 29°35N 66°0E 242 E2
Nusle Czechia 50°3N 14°26E 135 B2
Nussdorf Austria 48°15N 16°21E 142 A2
Nuuk Greenland 64°10N 51°35W 154 E5
Nuupere, Pte. Moorea 17°36S 149°47W 289 e
Nuussuaq Greenland 74°8N 57°3W 154 C5
Nu'uuli Amer. Samoa 14°19S 170°42W 302 f
Nuwakot Nepal 28°10N 83°55E 243 E10
Nuwara Eliya Sri Lanka 6°58N 80°48E 245 L5
Nuwayb'ī, W. an →
Si. Arabia 29°18N 34°57E 251 J5
Nuweiba' Egypt 28°59N 34°39E 251 K5
Nuweiveld S. Africa 31°8S 18°24E 270 D2
Nuweveldberge S. Africa 32°10S 21°45E 270 D3
Nuyts, Pt. Australia 35°4S 116°38E 279 G2
Nuyts Arch. Australia 32°35S 133°20E 281 E1
N'Vinda Angola 13°8S 19°2E 265 E3
Nxai Pan △ Botswana 19°50S 24°46E 270 A3
Nxaunxau Botswana 18°57S 21°4E 270 A3
Ny-Ålesund Svalbard 78°55N 11°56E 154 B12
Nyaake Liberia 4°52N 7°37W 262 E3
Nyabessan Cameroon 2°28N 10°24E 264 B2
Nyabing Australia 33°33S 118°9E 279 F2
Nyack U.S.A. 41°5N 73°55W 313 E11
Nyagan Russia 62°30N 65°38E 214 C7
Nyah West Australia 35°16S 143°21E 282 C5
Nyahanga Tanzania 2°20S 33°37E 268 C3
Nyahua Tanzania 5°25S 33°23E 268 D3
Nyahururu Kenya 0°2N 36°27E 268 B4
Nyainqêntanglha Shan
China 30°0N 90°0E 218 F7
Nyakanazi Tanzania 3°2S 31°10E 268 C3
Nyakrom Ghana 5°40N 0°50W 263 D4
Nyâlâ Sudan 12°2N 24°58E 257 E1
Nyalam China 28°32N 86°4E 218 F6
Nyamandhlovu Zimbabwe 19°55S 28°16E 269 F2
Nyambiti Tanzania 2°48S 33°27E 268 C3
Nyamira Kenya 0°36S 34°52E 268 B4
Nyamlell South Sudan 9°7N 26°59E 257 F2
Nyamwaga Tanzania 1°27S 34°33E 268 C3
Nyandekwa Tanzania 3°57S 32°32E 268 C3
Nyanding → South Sudan 8°40N 32°41E 257 F3
Nyandoma Russia 61°40N 40°12E 188 B11
Nyangana Namibia 18°0S 20°40E 270 A3
Nyanguge Tanzania 2°30S 33°12E 268 C3
Nyanji Zambia 14°25S 31°46E 269 E3
Nyankpala Ghana 9°21N 0°58W 263 D4
Nyanza Rwanda 2°20S 29°42E 268 C2
Nyanza □ Gabon 3°30S 11°0E 264 C2
Nyanza-Lac Burundi 4°21S 29°36E 268 C2
Nyaponges South Sudan 5°5N 33°45E 257 F3
Nyasa, L. = Malawi, L.
Africa 12°30S 34°30E 269 E3
Nyasaland = Malawi ■
Africa 11°55S 34°0E 269 E3
Nyasvizh Belarus 53°14N 26°38E 177 B14
Nyaungdon = Yandoon
Burma 17°0N 95°40E 241 G5
Nyaunglebin Burma 17°52N 96°42E 241 G6
Nyazepetrovsk Russia 56°3N 59°36E 186 C10
Nyazura Zimbabwe 18°40S 32°16E 269 F3
Nyazwidzi → Zimbabwe 20°0S 31°17E 269 G3
Nyborg Denmark 55°18N 10°47E 163 J4
Nybro Sweden 56°44N 15°55E 163 H9
Nyda Russia 66°40N 72°58E 214 C8
Nyeboe Land Greenland 82°0N 57°0W 154 A5
Nyengo Swamp Zambia 14°51S 22°7E 265 E4
Nyeri Kenya 0°23S 36°56E 268 C4
Nyerol South Sudan 8°41N 32°1E 257 F3
Nyhammar Sweden 60°17N 14°58E 162 D8
Nyika △ Malawi 10°30S 33°53E 269 E3
Nyimba Zambia 14°33S 30°50E 269 E3
Nyinahin Ghana 6°43N 2°3W 262 D4
Nyingchi China 29°32N 94°25E 218 F7
Nyíradony Hungary 47°41N 21°55E 182 C6
Nyiragongo
Dem. Rep. of the Congo 1°30S 29°15E 268 C2
Nyírbátor Hungary 47°49N 22°9E 182 C7
Nyíregyháza Hungary 47°58N 21°47E 182 C6
Nyiru, Mt. Kenya 2°8N 36°50E 268 B4
Nykarleby = Uusikaarlepyy
Finland 63°32N 22°31E 160 E20
Nykirke Norway 60°54N 10°19E 164 D7
Nykøbing Nordjylland,
Denmark 56°48N 8°51E 163 H2
Nykøbing Sjælland,
Denmark 54°56N 11°52E 163 K5
Nykøbing Sjælland,
Denmark 55°55N 11°40E 163 J5
Nyköping Sweden 58°45N 17°1E 163 F11
Nykroppa Sweden 59°37N 14°18E 162 E8
Nykvarn Sweden 59°11N 17°25E 162 E11
Nyland Sweden 63°1N 17°45E 162 A11
Nylstroom = Modimolle
S. Africa 24°42S 28°22E 271 B4
Nymagee Australia 32°7S 146°20E 283 B7
Nymboida △ Australia 29°38S 152°26E 281 D5
Nymburk Czechia 50°10N 15°1E 180 A8
Nymphenburg Germany 48°9N 11°30E 131 B2
Nymphenburg, Schloss
Germany 48°9N 11°30E 131 B2
Nynäshamn Sweden 58°54N 17°57E 163 F11
Nyngan Australia 31°30S 147°8E 283 A7
Nyoma Rap India 33°10N 78°40E 243 C8
Nyoman = Nemunas →
Lithuania 55°25N 21°10E 184 C8
Nyon Switz. 46°23N 6°14E 179 J2
Nyong → Cameroon 3°17N 9°54E 263 E6
Nyons France 44°22N 5°10E 175 D9
Nyou Burkina Faso 12°42N 2°1W 263 C4
Nýrsko Czechia 49°18N 13°9E 180 B6
Nysa Poland 50°30N 17°22E 185 H4
Nysa → Europe 52°4N 14°46E 178 C10
Nysa Kłodzka → Poland 50°49N 17°40E 185 H4
Nysætre Norway 62°2N 8°20E 164 B5
Nysäter Sweden 59°17N 12°47E 162 E6
Nyslott = Savonlinna
Finland 61°52N 28°53E 188 B5
Nyssa U.S.A. 43°53N 117°0W 304 E5
Nystad = Uusikaupunki
Finland 60°47N 21°25E 188 B1
Nysted Denmark 54°40N 11°44E 163 K5
Nyunzu
Dem. Rep. of the Congo 5°57S 27°58E 268 D2
Nyurba Russia 63°17N 118°28E 215 C12
Nyzhankovychi Ukraine 49°40N 22°49E 185 J9
Nyzhnohirskyy Ukraine 45°27N 34°38E 189 K8
Nyzhny Vorota Ukraine 48°46N 23°6E 182 B8
Nzébéla Guinea 8°9N 9°7W 262 D3
Nzega Tanzania 4°10S 33°12E 268 C3
Nzérékoré Guinea 7°49N 8°48W 262 D3
Nzeto Angola 7°10S 12°52E 265 D2
Nzilo, Chutes de
Dem. Rep. of the Congo 10°18S 25°27E 265 E5
Nzilo, L.
Dem. Rep. of the Congo 10°35S 25°39E 265 E5
N'zo → Ivory C. 6°15N 7°39W 262 D3
N'zo △ Ivory C. 6°15N 7°15W 262 D3
Nzubuka Tanzania 4°45S 32°50E 268 C3
Nzwani = Anjouan
Comoros Is. 12°15S 44°20E 272 a

O

O Barco Spain 42°23N 6°58W 194 C4
O Carballiño Spain 42°26N 8°5W 194 C2
O Castro de Ferreira Spain 42°31N 7°37W 194 C3
O Convento Spain 42°28N 8°41W 194 C2
O Corgo Spain 42°56N 7°25W 194 C3
O Le Pupū Pu'e △
Samoa 13°59S 171°43W 287 V20
O Pedrouzo Spain 42°56N 8°20W 194 C2
O Pino = O Pedrouzo
Spain 42°56N 8°20W 194 C2
O Porriño Spain 42°10N 8°37W 194 C2
O Real Spain 43°20N 8°19W 194 B2
O Seixo Spain 41°59N 8°46W 194 D2
Ō-Shima Hokkaidō, Japan 41°30N 139°22E 220 D9
Ō-Shima Nagasaki, Japan 33°29N 129°33E 222 D1
Ō-Shima Shizuoka, Japan 34°44N 139°24E 223 C11
O.R. Tambo Int. ✈ (JNB)
S. Africa 26°8S 28°15E 271 C4
Oa, Mull of U.K. 55°35N 6°20W 167 F2
Oacoma U.S.A. 43°48N 99°24W 308 D4
Oahe, L. U.S.A. 44°27N 100°24W 308 C3
Oahe Dam U.S.A. 44°27N 100°24W 308 C3
O'ahu U.S.A. 21°28N 157°58W 302 K14
Oak Creek U.S.A. 42°52N 87°55W 311 B9
Oak Forest U.S.A. 41°37N 87°47W 119 D2
Oak Grove U.S.A. 33°50N 84°18W 113 A3
Oak Harbor U.S.A. 48°18N 122°39W 306 B4
Oak Hill Fla., U.S.A. 28°52N 80°51W 317 G9
Oak Hill Mass., U.S.A. 42°18N 71°10W 116 B1
Oak Hill W. Va., U.S.A. 37°59N 81°9W 309 G13
Oak Island U.S.A. 33°55N 78°10W 315 E15
Oak Lawn U.S.A. 41°42N 87°45W 119 C2
Oak Park Ga., U.S.A. 32°22N 82°19W 316 C7
Oak Park Ill., U.S.A. 41°52N 87°47W 119 B2
Oak Ridge U.S.A. 36°1N 84°16W 315 C12
Oak Street Beach Chicago, U.S.A. 119 a2
Oak View Calif., U.S.A. 34°24N 119°18W 307 L7
Oak View Md., U.S.A. 39°1N 76°58W 143 A3
Oakan-Dake Japan 43°27N 144°10E 220 C12
Oakbank Australia 33°4S 140°33E 282 B4
Oakdale Calif., U.S.A. 37°46N 120°51W 306 H6
Oakdale Georgia, U.S.A. 33°51N 84°30W 113 A2
Oakdale La., U.S.A. 30°49N 92°40W 314 F8
Oakes U.S.A. 46°8N 98°6W 308 B4
Oakesdale U.S.A. 47°8N 117°15W 304 C5
Oakey Australia 27°25S 151°43E 281 D5
Oakfield Ga., U.S.A. 31°47N 83°58W 316 D6
Oakfield N.Y., U.S.A. 43°4N 78°16W 312 C6
Oakford U.S.A. 40°6N 89°58W 310 D7
Oakham U.K. 52°40N 0°43W 169 E7
Oakhurst U.S.A. 37°19N 119°40W 306 H7
Oakland Calif., U.S.A. 37°48N 122°18W 136 B3
Oakland Ill., U.S.A. 39°39N 88°2W 311 E8
Oakland Pa., U.S.A. 41°57N 75°36W 313 E9
Oakland City U.S.A. 38°20N 87°21W 311 F9
Oakland Park U.S.A. 26°10N 80°7W 129 A3
Oaklands Australia 35°34S 146°10E 283 C7
Oaklawn U.S.A. 38°46N 76°56W 143 C3
Oakleigh Australia 37°54S 145°5E 128 B2
Oakley Idaho, U.S.A. 42°15N 113°53W 304 E7
Oakley Kans., U.S.A. 39°8N 100°51W 308 F3
Oakover → Australia 21°0S 120°40E 278 D3
Oakridge U.S.A. 43°45N 122°28W 304 E2
Oaks, The Australia 34°3S 150°34E 283 C9
Oaktown U.S.A. 38°52N 87°27W 311 F9
Oakville Ont., Canada 43°27N 79°41W 312 C5
Oakville Wash., U.S.A. 46°51N 123°14W 306 D3
Oakwood U.S.A. 41°6N 84°23W 311 C12
Oakwood Beach U.S.A. 40°33N 74°7W 132 C1
Oamaru N.Z. 45°5S 170°59E 285 F5
Ōamishirasato Japan 35°31N 140°18E 223 B12
Oancea Romania 45°21N 27°42E 183 E12
Oarai Japan 36°21N 140°34E 223 A12
Oasis Calif., U.S.A. 37°29N 117°55W 306 H9
Oasis Calif., U.S.A. 33°28N 116°6W 307 M10
Oates Land Antarctica 69°0S 160°0E 151 C11
Oatley Australia 33°59S 151°4E 139 B1
Oatman U.S.A. 35°1N 114°19W 307 K12
Oaxaca Mexico 17°3N 96°43W 319 D5
Oaxaca □ Mexico 17°0N 96°30W 319 D5
Ob → Russia 66°45N 69°30E 214 C7
Oba Canada 49°4N 84°7W 298 C3
Obala Cameroon 4°9N 11°32E 263 E7
Obalende Nigeria 6°26N 3°25E 124 B2
Obama Fukui, Japan 35°30N 135°45E 223 B7
Obama Nagasaki, Japan 32°43N 130°13E 222 E2
Obama, Mt. Antigua & B. 17°2N 61°52W 322 b
Oban Nigeria 5°17N 8°33E 263 D6
Oban Argyll & Bute, U.K. 56°25N 5°29W 167 E3
Oba's Palace Nigeria 6°26N 3°22E 124 B2
Obbia = Hobyo Somalia 5°25N 48°30E 267 C6
Obdorsk = Salekhard
Russia 66°30N 66°35E 214 C7
Oberá Argentina 27°21S 55°2W 335 B4
Oberammergau Germany 47°36N 11°4E 179 H7
Oberasbach Germany 49°25N 10°57E 179 F6
Oberbayern □ Germany 48°5N 11°50E 179 G7
Oberburg = Gornji Grad
Slovenia 46°20N 14°52E 199 B11
Oberdonau = Oberösterreich □
Austria 48°10N 14°0E 180 C7
Oberdrauburg Austria 46°44N 12°58E 180 E5
Obere Donau ⌓ Germany 48°5N 9°0E 179 G5
Oberer Bayerischer Wald ⌓
Germany 49°15N 12°40E 179 F8
Oberföhring Germany 48°10N 11°37E 131 B2
Oberfranken □ Germany 50°10N 11°20E 179 E7
Oberglogau = Głogówek
Poland 50°21N 17°53E 185 H4
Oberhaching Germany 48°1N 11°35E 131 B2
Oberhausen Germany 51°28N 6°51E 178 D2
Oberkirch Germany 48°31N 8°4E 179 G4
Oberlaa Austria 48°8N 16°24E 142 B2
Oberlaibach = Vrhnika
Slovenia 45°58N 14°15E 199 C11
Oberlausitz Germany 51°16N 14°18E 178 D10
Oberlin Kans., U.S.A. 39°49N 100°32W 308 F3
Oberlin La., U.S.A. 30°37N 92°46W 314 F8
Oberlin Ohio, U.S.A. 41°18N 82°13W 312 E2
Oberlisse Austria 48°17N 16°26E 142 A2
Obermenzing Germany 48°10N 11°28E 131 A1
Obermoos Schwaige
Germany 48°14N 11°27E 131 A1
Obernai France 48°28N 7°30E 173 D14
Oberndorf Germany 48°17N 8°34E 179 G4
Obernigk = Oborniki Śląskie
Poland 51°17N 16°53E 185 G3
Oberon Australia 33°45S 149°52E 283 B8
Oberösterreich □ Austria 48°10N 14°0E 180 C7
Oberpfalz □ Germany 49°20N 12°10E 179 F8
Oberpfälzer Wald
Germany 49°30N 12°30E 179 F8
Oberpfälzer Wald ⌓
Germany 49°40N 12°20E 179 F8
Oberschleissheim
Germany 48°15N 11°33E 131 A2
Oberschöneweide
Germany 52°27N 13°31E 115 B4
Oberstdorf Germany 47°24N 10°15E 179 H6
Oberting Gabon 0°22S 9°46E 264 C1
Obertyn Ukraine 48°42N 25°10E 183 B10
Oberursel Germany 50°11N 8°35E 179 E4
Oberwart Austria 47°17N 16°12E 181 D9
Obi, Kepulauan Indonesia 1°23S 127°45E 231 E7
Obiaruku Nigeria 5°51N 6°9E 263 D6
Óbidos Brazil 1°50S 55°30W 329 D6
Óbidos Portugal 39°19N 9°10W 195 F1
Obihiro Japan 42°56N 143°12E 220 C11
Obilatu Indonesia 1°25S 127°20E 231 E7
Obilnoye Russia 47°32N 44°30E 191 G7
Obing Germany 48°0N 12°24E 179 G8
Objat France 45°16N 1°24E 174 C5
Oblong U.S.A. 39°0N 87°55W 311 F9
Obluchye Russia 49°1N 131°4E 215 E14
Obninsk Russia 55°8N 36°37E 188 E9
Obo C.A.R. 5°20N 26°32E 264 A5
Obock Djibouti 12°0N 43°20E 257 E5
Obodivka Ukraine 48°24N 29°15E 183 B14
Oborniki Poland 52°39N 16°50E 185 F3
Oborniki Śląskie Poland 51°17N 16°53E 185 G3
Obouya Congo 0°56S 15°43E 264 C3
Oboyan Russia 51°15N 36°21E 189 G9
Obozerskaya = Obozerskiy
Russia 63°34N 40°21E 186 B7
Obozerskiy Russia 63°34N 40°21E 186 B7
Obrenovac Serbia 44°40N 20°11E 202 B4
O'Brien U.S.A. 30°2N 82°57W 316 E7
Obrovac Croatia 44°11N 15°41E 199 D12
Obruk Turkey 38°7N 33°12E 212 C5
Obrzycko Poland 52°42N 16°32E 185 F3
Observatory Sydney, Australia 139 a1
Observatory Gauteng,
S. Africa 26°10S 28°4E 123 B2
Observatory Inlet
Canada 55°10N 129°54W 296 B3
Obshchi Syrt Russia 52°0N 53°0E 158 E16
Obskaya Guba Russia 69°0N 73°0E 214 C8
Obu Japan 35°0N 136°58E 223 B8
Obuasi Ghana 6°17N 1°40W 263 D4
Obubra Nigeria 6°8N 8°20E 263 D6
Óbuda Hungary 47°33N 19°2E 117 A2
Obudu Nigeria 6°38N 9°5E 263 D6
Obukhovo Russia 59°53N 30°22E 137 B2
Obura Papua N. G. 6°33S 145°58E 286 D3
Obvodnyy Kanal Russia 59°54N 30°20E 137 B1
Obwalden □ Switz. 46°55N 8°15E 179 J4
Obzor Bulgaria 42°50N 27°52E 203 D11
Ocala U.S.A. 29°11N 82°8W 317 F7
Ocamo → Venezuela 2°48N 65°14W 329 C4
Ocampo Chihuahua,
Mexico 28°11N 108°23W 318 B3
Ocampo Tamaulipas,
Mexico 22°50N 99°20W 319 C5
Ocaña Colombia 8°15N 73°20W 328 B3
Ocaña Spain 39°55N 3°30W 194 F7
Occidental, Cordillera
Colombia 5°0N 76°0W 328 C2
Occidental, Cordillera Peru 14°0S 74°0W 330 C3
Occidental, Grand Erg
Algeria 30°20N 1°0E 261 B5
Occitanie □ France 44°0N 2°0E 174 E5
Ocean City Md., U.S.A. 38°20N 75°5W 309 F16
Ocean City N.J., U.S.A. 39°17N 74°35W 309 F16
Ocean City Wash., U.S.A. 47°4N 124°10W 306 C2
Ocean Falls Canada 52°18N 127°48W 296 C3
Ocean I. = Banaba
Kiribati 0°45S 169°50E 288 H8
Ocean Park
Hong Kong, China 22°13N 114°10E 122 B3
Ocean Park Wash.,
U.S.A. 46°30N 124°3W 306 D2
Oceano U.S.A. 35°6N 120°37W 307 K6
Oceanport U.S.A. 40°19N 74°3W 313 F10
Oceanside U.S.A. 33°12N 117°23W 307 M9
Ochagavía Spain 42°55N 1°5W 196 C3
Ochakiv Ukraine 46°37N 31°33E 189 J6
Ochamchire Georgia 42°46N 41°32E 191 J5
Ochi, Oros Greece 38°5N 24°25E 204 C6
Ochiai Japan 35°1N 133°45E 222 B5
Ochil Hills U.K. 56°14N 3°40W 167 E5
Ochlocknee U.S.A. 30°58N 84°3W 316 E5
Ochlockonee → U.S.A. 29°59N 84°26W 316 F5
Ocho Rios Jamaica 18°24N 77°6W 320 a
Ochopee U.S.A. 25°54N 81°18W 317 K8
Ochota Poland 52°13N 20°58E 143 B1
Ochsenfurt Germany 49°40N 10°4E 179 F6
Ochsenhausen Germany 48°4N 9°57E 179 G5
Ocilla U.S.A. 31°36N 83°15W 316 D6
Ockelbo Sweden 60°54N 16°45E 162 D10
Ocmulgee → U.S.A. 31°58N 82°33W 316 D7
Ocmulgee ⌓ U.S.A. 32°49N 83°37W 316 C6
Ocna Mureş Romania 46°23N 23°55E 183 D8
Ocna Sibiului Romania 45°52N 24°2E 183 E9
Ocnele Mari Romania 45°8N 24°18E 183 E9
Ocniţa Moldova 48°25N 27°30E 183 B12
Ocoee U.S.A. 28°34N 81°32W 133 A1
Ocoña Peru 16°26S 73°8W 330 D3
Ocoña → Peru 16°28S 73°8W 330 D3
Oconee → U.S.A. 31°58N 82°33W 316 D7
Oconee, L. U.S.A. 33°28N 83°15W 316 B6
Oconomowoc U.S.A. 43°7N 88°30W 311 A8
Oconto U.S.A. 44°53N 87°52W 308 C10
Oconto Falls U.S.A. 44°52N 88°9W 308 C9
Ocosingo Mexico 16°53N 92°6W 319 D6
Ocotal Nic. 13°41N 86°31W 320 D2
Ocotlán Jalisco, Mexico 20°21N 102°46W 318 C4
Ocotlán Oaxaca, Mexico 16°48N 96°40W 319 D5
Ocreza → Portugal 39°32N 7°50W 195 F3
Ócsa Hungary 47°17N 19°15E 182 C4
Ocumare del Tuy
Venezuela 10°7N 66°46W 328 A4
Ocurí Bolivia 18°45S 65°50W 331 D4
Oda Ghana 5°50N 0°51W 263 D4
Ōda Shimane, Japan 35°11N 132°30E 222 B4
Oda, J. Sudan 20°21N 36°39E 256 C4
Ódáðahraun Iceland 65°5N 17°0W 155 B9
Ŏdaejin N. Korea 41°34N 129°40E 224 B4
Odaesan △ S. Korea 37°40N 128°30E 224 D4
Odaiba Japan 35°38N 139°47E 140 B3
Ödåkra Sweden 56°7N 12°45E 163 H6
Ōdana Japan 35°33N 139°35E 140 B2
Odate Japan 40°16N 140°34E 220 D10
Odawara Japan 35°20N 139°6E 223 B11
Odda Norway 60°3N 6°35E 164 D3
Odder = Xuddur Somalia 4°11N 43°52E 267 D5
Odder Denmark 55°58N 10°10E 163 J4
Odei → Canada 56°6N 96°54W 297 B9
Odell U.S.A. 41°0N 88°31W 311 C8
Odemira Portugal 37°35N 8°40W 195 H2
Ödemiş Turkey 38°15N 28°0E 205 C9
Öden-Stockach Germany 48°5N 11°41E 131 B3
Ödenburg = Sopron
Hungary 47°45N 16°32E 182 C1
Odendaalsrus S. Africa 27°48S 26°45E 270 C4
Odensbacken Sweden 59°10N 15°32E 162 E9
Odense Denmark 55°22N 10°23E 163 J4
Odenwald Germany 49°35N 9°0E 179 F5
Oder → Europe 53°33N 14°38E 178 B10
Oder-Havel Kanal
Germany 52°52N 14°2E 178 C10
Oderzo Italy 45°47N 12°29E 199 C9
Odesa Ukraine 46°30N 30°45E 189 J6
Odesa □ Ukraine 47°20N 29°55E 189 J5
Ödeshög Sweden 58°14N 14°39E 163 F8
Odessa = Odesa Ukraine 46°30N 30°45E 189 J6
Odessa Ont., Canada 44°17N 76°43W 313 B8
Odessa Mo., U.S.A. 39°0N 93°57W 310 F3
Odessa Tex., U.S.A. 31°52N 102°23W 314 F3
Odessa Wash., U.S.A. 47°20N 118°41W 304 C4
Odiakwe Botswana 20°12S 25°17E 270 B4
Odiel → Spain 37°10N 6°55W 195 H4
Odienné Ivory C. 9°30N 7°34W 262 D3
Odilampi Finland 60°18N 24°45E 121 B1
Odimba Gabon 2°2S 9°33E 264 C2
Odintsovo Russia 55°40N 37°16E 188 E9
Odiongan Phil. 12°24N 121°59E 232 E3
Odisha □ India 20°0N 84°0E 244 E7
Odivelas Portugal 38°47N 9°10W 126 A1
Odobeşti Romania 45°43N 27°4E 183 E12
Odolanów Poland 51°34N 17°40E 185 G4
Odolany Poland 52°13N 20°55E 143 B1
O'Donnell U.S.A. 32°58N 101°50W 314 E4
O'Donnell Pt. Canada 45°5N 80°5W 312 A4
Odorheiu Secuiesc
Romania 46°21N 25°21E 183 D10
Odoyevo Russia 53°56N 36°42E 188 F9
Odra = Oder → Europe 53°33N 14°38E 178 B10
Odra → Spain 42°14N 4°17W 194 C6
Odum U.S.A. 31°40N 82°2W 316 D7
Odžaci Serbia 45°30N 19°17E 182 E4
Odžak Bos.-H. 45°3N 18°18E 182 E3
Odzala Congo 0°37N 14°37E 264 B2
Odzala △ Congo 0°55N 14°55E 264 B2
Odzi Zimbabwe 19°0S 32°20E 271 A5
Odzi → Zimbabwe 19°45S 32°23E 271 A5
Oebisfelde Germany 52°27N 10°57E 178 C6
Oecussi = Pante Macassar
E. Timor 9°30S 123°58E 231 F6
Oedong S. Korea 35°42N 129°14E 224 E4
Oeiras Brazil 7°0S 42°8W 332 C3
Oeiras Portugal 38°41N 9°18W 126 A1
Oeiras do Para Brazil 1°58S 49°51W 329 D8
Oelrichs U.S.A. 43°11N 103°14W 308 D2
Oels in Schlesien = Oleśnica
Poland 51°13N 17°22E 185 G4
Oelsnitz Germany 50°24N 12°10E 179 E8
Oelwein U.S.A. 42°41N 91°55W 310 B5
Oenarodo S. Korea 34°26N 127°30E 224 E3
Oeno I. Pac. Oc. 24°0S 131°0W 289 K14
Oenpelli = Gunbalanya
Australia 12°20S 133°4E 278 B5
Oetz Austria 47°13N 10°53E 180 D3
Of Turkey 40°59N 40°23E 213 B9
O'Fallon U.S.A. 38°49N 90°42W 310 F6
Ofanto → Italy 41°22N 16°13E 201 A9
Offa Nigeria 8°13N 4°42E 263 D5
Offaly □ Ireland 53°15N 7°30W 166 C4
Offenbach Germany 50°6N 8°44E 179 E4
Offenburg Germany 48°28N 7°56E 179 G3
Officer Cr. → Australia 27°46S 132°30E 279 E5
Offida Italy 42°56N 13°41E 199 F10
Offoué → Gabon 0°4S 11°44E 264 C2
Ofidousa Greece 36°33N 26°8E 205 E8
Ofin Nigeria 6°32N 3°30E 124 A3
Ofolanga Tonga 19°38S 174°27W 287 P13
Ofotfjorden Norway 68°27N 17°0E 160 B17
Ofte Norway 59°30N 8°12E 164 E5
Ofu Amer. Samoa 14°11S 169°41W 302 g
Ōfunato Japan 39°4N 141°43E 220 E10
Oga Japan 39°55N 139°50E 220 E9
Oga-Hantō Japan 39°58N 139°47E 220 E9
Ogaden Ethiopia 7°30N 45°30E 267 C6
Ōgaki Japan 35°21N 136°37E 223 B8
Ogallala U.S.A. 41°8N 101°43W 308 E3
Ogan → Indonesia 3°1S 104°44E 234 C2
Ogasawara Gunto Pac. Oc. 27°0N 142°0E 288 E6
Ogawa Japan 35°44N 139°28E 140 A1
Ogbomosho Nigeria 8°1N 4°11E 263 D5
Ogden Iowa, U.S.A. 42°2N 94°2W 310 B2
Ogden Utah, U.S.A. 41°13N 111°58W 304 F8
Ogden Park U.S.A. 41°46N 87°39W 119 C2
Ogden Slip Chicago, U.S.A. 119 b3
Ogdensburg U.S.A. 44°42N 75°30W 313 B9
Ogea Driki Fiji 19°12S 178°27W 287 B3
Ogea Levu Fiji 19°8S 178°24W 287 B3
Ogeechee → U.S.A. 31°50N 81°3W 316 D8
Ogi Japan 33°20N 130°15E 222 D2
Ogikubo Japan 35°42N 139°37E 140 A2
Ogilby U.S.A. 32°49N 114°50W 307 N12
Ogilvie Transportation Center
Chicago, U.S.A. 41°52N 87°38W 119 B3
Oglat Beraber Algeria 30°15N 3°34W 260 B4
Oglat el Khnâchich Mali 21°51N 3°58W 260 D4
Oglesby U.S.A. 41°18N 89°4W 310 C7
Oglethorpe U.S.A. 32°18N 84°4W 316 C5
Ogliastra □ Italy 39°50N 9°35E 200 C2

Óglio → Italy 45°2N 10°39E **198** C7
Óglio Nord △ Italy 45°22N 9°54E **198** C6
Óglio Sud △ Italy 45°7N 10°18E **198** C7
Ogmore Australia 22°37S 149°35E **280** C4
Ognon → France 47°16N 5°28E **173** E12
Ogogoro Nigeria 6°25N 3°24E **124** B2
Ogoki → Canada 51°38N 85°58W **298** B2
Ogoki Canada 51°38N 85°57W **298** B2
Ogoki L. Canada 50°50N 87°10W **298** B2
Ogoki Res. Canada 50°45N 88°15W **298** B2
Ogoué → Gabon 1°0S 9°0E **264** C1
Ogooué-Ivindo □ Gabon 1°0N 13°0E **264** C2
Ogooué-Lolo □ Gabon 1°0S 12°0E **264** C1
Ogooué-Maritime □ Gabon 1°0S 9°0E **264** C1
Ogōri Fukuoka, Japan 33°24N 130°33E **222** D2
Ogōri Yamaguchi, Japan 34°6N 131°24E **222** C3
Ogosta → Bulgaria 43°48N 23°55E **202** F7
Ogou → Togo 7°50N 1°19E **263** D5
Ogoueïleten Nmâdi
    Mauritania 19°46N 11°1W **260** E2
Ogowe = Ogooué → Gabon 1°0S 9°0E **264** C1
Ogoyo Nigeria 6°25N 3°29E **124** B2
Ogr = Sharafa Sudan 11°59N 27°7E **257** E2
Ograźden Macedonia 41°30N 22°50E **202** E6
Ogre Latvia 56°49N 24°36E **188** D3
Ogrein Sudan 17°55N 34°50E **256** D3
Ogudu Nigeria 6°34N 3°24E **124** A2
Ogulin Croatia 45°16N 15°16E **199** C12
Ogun □ Nigeria 7°0N 3°0E **263** D5
Oguni Japan 33°11N 131°8E **222** D3
Ögur Iceland 66°2N 22°44W **155** A4
Ogurja Ada Turkmenistan 38°55N 53°2E **247** B7
Oguta Nigeria 5°44N 6°44E **263** D6
Ogwashi-Uku Nigeria 6°15N 6°30E **263** D6
Ogwe Nigeria 5°0N 7°14E **263** E6
Ohai N.Z. 45°55S 168°0E **285** F3
Ohakune N.Z. 39°24S 175°24E **284** F4
Ohanet Algeria 28°44N 8°46E **261** C6
Ohangwena □ Namibia 17°30S 17°0E **270** A2
Ōhara Japan 35°15N 140°23E **223** B12
O'Hare Int., Chicago ✈ (ORD)
    U.S.A. 41°59N 87°54W **311** C9
Ohata Japan 41°24N 141°10E **220** D10
Ohatchee U.S.A. 33°47N 86°0W **314** B3
Ohau, L. N.Z. 44°15S 169°53E **285** E4
Ohaupo N.Z. 37°56S 175°20E **284** E4
O'Higgins, C. Chile 27°5S 109°15W **330** b
O'Higgins, Parque Chile 33°27S 70°40W **337** B2
O'Higgins, Pta. Chile 33°41S 79°0W **330** c
Ohio □ U.S.A. 40°15N 82°45W **312** F2
Ohio → U.S.A. 36°59N 89°8W **308** G9
Ohio City U.S.A. 40°46N 84°37W **311** D12
Ohiwa Harbour N.Z. 37°55S 177°10E **284** D6
Ohlau = Oława Poland 50°57N 17°20E **185** H4
Ohře → Czechia 50°30N 14°10E **180** A7
Ohre → Sachsen-Anhalt,
    Germany 52°18N 11°46E **178** C7
Ohrid Macedonia 41°8N 20°52E **202** F5
Ohridsko Jezero Macedonia 41°8N 20°52E **202** E4
Ohrigstad S. Africa 24°39S 30°36E **271** B5
Öhringen Germany 49°12N 9°31E **179** F5
Ohura N.Z. 38°51S 174°59E **284** E3
Oi Qu → China 28°37N 98°16E **228** C2
Oiapoque Brazil 3°50N 51°50W **337** C8
Oiapoque → S. Amer. 4°8N 51°40W **329** C7
Oikou China 38°35N 117°42E **227** E9
Oil City U.S.A. 41°26N 79°42W **312** E5
Oil Springs Canada 42°47N 82°7W **312** D2
Oildale U.S.A. 35°25N 119°1W **307** K7
Oimachi Japan 35°35N 139°43E **146** B3
Oinousa = Inousses
    Greece 38°33N 26°14E **205** C8
Oise □ France 49°28N 2°30E **173** C9
Oise → France 49°0N 2°4E **173** C9
Oistins Barbados 13°4N 59°33W **323** r
Ōita Japan 33°14N 131°36E **222** D3
Ōita □ Japan 33°15N 131°30E **222** D3
Oiticica Brazil 5°3S 41°5W **332** C3
Ojai U.S.A. 34°27N 119°15W **307** L7
Ojcowski △ Poland 50°15N 19°50E **185** H6
Ojhar India 20°6N 73°56E **244** D1
Ojinaga Mexico 29°34N 104°25W **318** B4
Ojiya Japan 37°18N 138°48E **221** F9
Ojo Caliente Mexico 22°34N 102°15W **318** C4
Ojo de Liebre, L. Mexico 27°45N 114°15W **318** B2
Ojos del Salado, Cerro
    Argentina 27°0S 68°40W **338** B2
Ojota Nigeria 6°35N 3°23E **124** A2
Ojus U.S.A. 25°26N 80°9W **129** C3
Oka → France 7°9N 3°38E **263** D5
Oka → Russia 56°20N 43°59E **190** B7
Okaba Indonesia 8°6S 139°42E **231** F9
Okahandja Namibia 22°0S 16°59E **270** B2
Okahukura N.Z. 38°48S 175°14E **284** C4
Okaihau N.Z. 35°19S 173°47E **284** B7
Okakarara Namibia 20°35S 17°27E **270** B2
Okalakata Congo 0°18S 14°54E **264** C2
Okanagan L. Canada 50°0N 119°30W **296** D5
Okandja Gabon 0°35S 13°45E **264** C2
Okano → Gabon 0°5S 10°57E **264** C2
Okanogan U.S.A. 48°22N 119°35W **304** B4
Okanogan → U.S.A. 48°6N 119°44W **304** B4
Okanogan Range
    N. Amer. 49°0N 119°55W **296** D5
Okány Hungary 46°52N 21°21E **182** D6
Okapa Papua N. G. 38°5N 145°39E **286** D3
Okapi ○
    Dem. Rep. of the Congo 2°30N 27°20E **268** B2
Okaputa Namibia 20°5S 17°0E **270** B2
Okara Pakistan 30°50N 73°31E **242** D5
Okarito N.Z. 43°15S 170°9E **285** D5
Okarukambe = Steinhausen
    Namibia 21°49S 18°20E **270** B2
Okato N.Z. 39°12S 173°53E **284** F2
Okau Micronesia 9°32N 138°6E **287** R16
Okaukuejo Namibia 19°10S 16°0E **270** A2
Okavango = Cubango →
    Africa 18°50S 22°25E **265** F4
Okavango Delta Botswana 18°45S 22°45E **270** A3
Okavango Swamp = Okavango
    Delta Botswana 18°45S 22°45E **270** A3
Ōkawa Japan 33°9N 130°21E **222** D2
Okawville U.S.A. 38°26N 89°33E **307** J10
Okaya Japan 36°5N 138°10E **223** A10
Okayama Japan 34°40N 133°54E **222** C5
Okayama □ Japan 35°0N 133°50E **222** C5
Okazaki Japan 34°57N 137°10E **223** B9
Oke-Iho Nigeria 8°1N 3°18E **263** D5
Oke-Ira Nigeria 6°29N 3°22E **124** B2
Okęcie Poland 52°11N 20°56E **143** B1
Okęcie, Warszawa ✈ (WAW)
    Poland 52°9N 20°59E **143** B1
Okeechobee U.S.A. 27°15N 80°50W **317** E7
Okeechobee, L. U.S.A. 27°0N 80°50W **317** F7
Okefenokee ◇ U.S.A. 30°45N 82°18W **316** E7
Okefenokee Swamp
    U.S.A. 30°40N 82°20W **316** F6
Okehampton U.K. 50°44N 4°0W **169** G4
Okemos U.S.A. 42°43N 84°26W **311** B12
Okene Nigeria 7°32N 6°11E **263** D6
Okeogbe Nigeria 6°24N 3°23E **124** B2
Oker → Germany 52°32N 10°2E **178** C6
Okha India 22°43N 69°58E **244** H3
Okha Russia 53°40N 143°0E **215** D15
Okhla India 28°33N 77°16E **120** B2
Okhotsk Russia 59°20N 143°10E **215** D15
Okhotsk, Sea of Asia 55°0N 145°0E **215** D15

Okhotskiy Perevoz
    Russia 61°52N 135°35E **215** C14
Okhta → Russia 59°56N 30°25E **137** B2
Oki-no-Shima Japan 32°44N 132°33E **222** E4
Oki-Shotō Japan 36°5N 133°15E **222** A5
Okiep S. Africa 29°39S 17°53E **270** C2
Okigwi Nigeria 5°52N 7°20E **263** D6
Okija Nigeria 5°54N 6°55E **263** D6
Okinawa □ Japan 26°19N 127°46E **288** a
Okinawa □ Japan 26°40N 128°0E **288** a
Okinawa-Guntō Japan 26°40N 128°0E **221** L4
Okinawa-Jima Japan 26°32N 128°0E **221** L4
Okino-erabu-Shima
    Japan 27°21N 128°33E **221** L4
Okitipupa Ukraine 6°31N 4°50E **263** D5
Okkervil → Russia 59°56N 30°30E **137** B2
Oklahoma □ U.S.A. 35°20N 97°30W **314** D6
Oklahoma City U.S.A. 35°30N 97°30W **314** D6
Oklawaha → U.S.A. 29°28N 81°41W **317** F18
Okmulgee U.S.A. 35°37N 95°58W **314** D7
Oknitsa = Ocniţa
    Moldova 48°25N 27°30E **183** B12
Oko, W. → Sudan 21°15N 35°56E **256** C4
Okolo Uganda 2°37N 31°8E **268** B3
Okolona Ky., U.S.A. 38°8N 85°41W **311** F11
Okolona Miss., U.S.A. 34°0N 88°45W **315** E10
Okombahe Namibia 21°23S 15°22E **270** B2
Okonek Poland 53°32N 16°51E **184** E3
Okotoks Canada 50°43N 113°58W **296** C6
Okoyo Congo 1°28S 15°0E **264** C3
Okrika Nigeria 4°40N 7°10E **263** E6
Okrzeszyn Poland 52°8N 21°8E **143** C2
Oksapmin Papua N. G. 5°17S 142°15E **286** C2
Øksendalsøra Norway 62°42N 8°27E **164** B5
Oksovskiy Russia 62°33N 39°57E **186** B6
Oksval Norway 59°51N 10°40E **133** A3
Oktwin Burma 18°49N 96°26E **241** F6
Oktyabrsk = Qandyaghash
    Kazakhstan 49°28N 57°25E **187** E10
Oktyabrsk Russia 53°11N 48°40E **190** D9
Oktyabrskiy = Aktsyabrski
    Belarus 52°38N 28°53E **177** B15
Oktyabrskiy Bashkortostan,
    Russia 54°28N 53°28E **186** D9
Oktyabrskiy Kamchatka,
    Russia 52°39N 156°14E **215** D16
Oktyabrskiy Moskva,
    Russia 55°41N 37°35E **129** B2
Oktyabrskiy Rostov, Russia 47°30N 40°4E **191** G5
Oktyabrskoy Revolyutsii, Ostrov
    Russia 79°30N 97°0E **215** B10
Oktyabrskoye = Zhovtneve
    Ukraine 46°54N 32°3E **189** J7
Ōkubo Tokyo, Japan 140 a2
Okuchi Japan 32°4N 130°37E **222** E2
Okulovka Russia 58°25N 33°19E **188** C7
Ōkura Japan 35°35N 139°37E **140** B1
Okuru N.Z. 43°55S 168°55E **285** D3
Okushiri-Tō Japan 42°15N 139°30E **220** D10
Okuta Nigeria 9°14N 3°12E **263** D5
Okwa → Botswana 22°30S 23°0E **270** B3
Ola Russia 59°35N 151°17E **215** D16
Ola Ark., U.S.A. 35°2N 93°13W **314** D8
Ólafsfjörður Iceland 66°4N 18°39W **155** A8
Ólafsvík Iceland 64°53N 23°43W **155** C3
Olaine Latvia 56°48N 23°59E **184** B10
Olancha U.S.A. 36°17N 118°1W **307** J8
Olancha Pk. U.S.A. 36°16N 118°7W **307** J8
Olanchito Honduras 15°30N 86°30W **320** C2
Öland Sweden 56°45N 16°38E **163** H10
Ölands södra udde
    Sweden 57°22N 17°5E **163** G11
Ölands norra udde
    Sweden 56°12N 16°23E **163** H10
Olanta U.S.A. 33°56N 79°56W **316** B10
Olar U.S.A. 33°11N 81°11W **316** B8
Olargues France 43°34N 2°53E **174** E6
Olari Finland 60°10N 24°44E **121** B1
Olary Australia 32°18S 140°19E **282** B4
Olascoaga Argentina 35°15S 60°39W **334** D3
Olathe U.S.A. 38°53N 94°49W **308** F6
Olavarría Argentina 36°55S 60°20W **334** D3
Oława Poland 50°57N 17°20E **185** H4
Olbernhau Germany 50°40N 13°19E **178** E9
Ólbia Italy 40°55N 9°31E **200** B2
Ólbia, G. di Italy 40°55N 9°36E **200** B2
Olching Germany 48°12N 11°21E **179** G7
Old Admiralty
    Saint Petersburg, Russia 59°55N 30°20E **137** B1
Old Bahama Chan. = Bahama,
    Canal Viejo de
    W. Indies 22°10N 77°30W **320** B4
Old Baldy Pk. = San Antonio, Mt.
    U.S.A. 34°17N 117°38W **307** L9
Old Bar Australia 31°58S 152°35E **283** A10
Old Bridge U.S.A. 40°25N 74°22W **313** F10
Old Fort → Canada 58°36N 110°24W **296** B6
Old Harbor Alaska,
    U.S.A. 57°12N 153°18W **303** H9
Old Harbor Mass., U.S.A. 42°19N 71°1W **116** B3
Old Harbour Jamaica 17°56N 77°7W **320** a
Old Harbour Bay Jamaica 17°54N 77°6W **320** a
Old Ironsides = U.S.S. Constitution
    Boston, U.S.A. **116** a3
Old Mapoon ○ Australia 11°5S 142°22E **280** A3
Old Panamao Phil. 5°59N 121°13E **233** J4
Old Perlican Canada 48°5N 53°1W **299** C9
Old Road Bluff
    Antigua & B. 16°59N 61°50W **322** b
Old Road Town
    St. Kitts & Nevis 17°17N 62°47W **322** d
Old Roundhouse Toronto, Canada **141** c2
Old Shinyanga Tanzania 3°33S 33°27E **268** C3
Old Speck Mt. U.S.A. 44°34N 70°57W **313** B14
Old Town = Stare Miasto
    Warsaw, Poland **143** a2
Old Town Edinburgh, U.K. **121** b2
Old Town Fla., U.S.A. 29°36N 82°59W **317** F18
Old Town Ill., U.S.A. 41°54N 87°37W **119** B3
Old Town Maine, U.S.A. 44°56N 68°39W **309** C19
Old Town Hall = Altes Rathaus
    Munich, Germany **131** b3
Old Town Square Warsaw, Poland **143** a2
Old U.S. Mint New Orleans, U.S.A. **131** a3
Old Washington U.S.A. 40°2N 81°27W **312** F3
Old Wives L. Canada 50°5N 106°0W **296** C7
Oldbury U.K. 51°38N 2°33W **169** F5
Oldcastle Ireland 53°46N 7°10W **168** C4
Oldenburg Niedersachsen,
    Germany 53°9N 8°13E **178** B4
Oldenburg Schleswig-Holstein,
    Germany 54°17N 10°52E **178** A6

Oldenzaal Neths. 52°19N 6°53E **170** B6
Oldham U.K. 53°33N 2°7W **168** D5
Oldman → Canada 49°57N 111°42W **296** D6
Oldmeldrum U.K. 57°20N 2°19W **167** D6
Olds Canada 51°50N 114°10W **296** C6
Oldsmar U.S.A. 28°2N 82°39W **317** G7
Olduvai Gorge Tanzania 2°57S 35°23E **268** C4
Öldziyt Mongolia 44°40N 109°1E **226** B5
Ole Rømer Land
    Greenland 74°10N 24°0W **154** C8
Olean U.S.A. 42°5N 78°26W **312** D6
Oleby Sweden 60°8N 13°2E **162** D7
Olecko Poland 54°2N 22°31E **184** D9
Oléggio Italy 45°36N 8°38E **198** C5
Oleiros = O Real Spain 43°20N 8°19W **194** B2
Oleiros Portugal 39°56N 7°56W **194** F3
Olekma → Russia 60°22N 120°42E **215** C13
Olekminsk Russia 60°25N 120°30E **215** C13
Oleksandrivka Ukraine 48°55N 32°20E **189** H7
Oleksandriya Kirovohrad,
    Ukraine 48°42N 33°3E **189** H7
Oleksandriya Rivne,
    Ukraine 50°37N 26°19E **177** C14
Olema U.S.A. 38°3N 122°47W **306** G4
Ølen Norway 59°36N 5°48E **164** E2
Olenegorsk Russia 68°9N 33°18E **160** B25
Olenek → Russia 68°28N 112°18E **215** C12
Olenek → Russia 73°0N 120°10E **215** B13
Olenino Russia 56°15N 33°30E **188** D7
Olenya = Olenegorsk
    Russia 68°9N 33°18E **160** B25
Olga, L. Canada 49°47N 77°15W **298** C4
Olgas, The = Kata Tjuta
    Australia 25°20S 130°50E **279** E5
Olgino Russia 60°0N 30°10E **137** A1
Ölgiy Mongolia 48°56N 89°57E **217** C11
Ølgod Denmark 55°49N 8°36E **163** J2
Olhão Portugal 37°3N 7°48W **195** H3
Olhopil Ukraine 48°12N 29°30E **183** B14
Olhovatka Russia 54°30N 22°18E **184** D9
Olib Croatia 44°23N 14°44E **198** D11
Oliena Italy 40°16N 9°24E **200** B2
Oliete Spain 41°1N 0°41W **195** D11
Olifants = Elefantes →
    Africa 24°10S 32°40E **271** B5
Olifants → Namibia 25°30S 19°30E **270** B2
Olifantshoek S. Africa 27°57S 22°42E **270** C3
Ólimbos, Óros = Olymbos Oros
    Greece 40°6N 22°23E **202** F6
Olimbos, Óros = Olymbos Oros
    Greece 40°6N 22°23E **202** F6
Olímpia Brazil 20°44S 48°54W **335** A6
Olímpico, Estádio Mexico 19°20N 99°11W **128** C1
Olimpos-Beydağları △
    Turkey 36°36N 30°30E **205** E12
Olin U.S.A. 42°0N 91°9W **310** B5
Olinda Brazil 8°1S 34°51W **332** C5
Olite Spain 42°29N 1°40W **196** C3
Oliva Argentina 32°0S 63°38W **334** C3
Oliva Spain 38°58N 0°9W **197** G4
Oliva de la Frontera Spain 38°17N 6°54W **195** G4
Olivais Portugal 38°45N 9°7W **126** A2
Olivar de los Padres
    Mexico 19°21N 99°14W **128** B1
Olivares, Cerro los
    Argentina 30°18S 69°55W **334** C2
Olivares de Júcar Spain 39°46N 2°20W **196** F2
Olive Branch U.S.A. 34°57N 89°49W **315** D10
Olive Hill U.S.A. 38°18N 83°13W **311** F13
Olive Park Chicago, U.S.A. **119** B3
Olivehurst U.S.A. 39°6N 121°34W **306** F5
Oliveira Brazil 20°39S 44°50W **333** F3
Oliveira de Azeméis
    Portugal 40°49N 8°29W **194** E2
Oliveira do Douro Portugal 41°5N 8°29W **194** D2
Oliveira dos Brejinhos
    Brazil 12°19S 42°54W **333** D3
Olivenza Spain 38°41N 7°9W **195** G3
Oliver Canada 49°13N 119°37W **296** D5
Oliver L. Canada 56°56N 103°22W **297** B8
Olives, Mt. of West Bank 31°46N 35°15E **123** B2
Olivet Lorient, France 47°51N 1°55E **173** E8
Olivet Mich., U.S.A. 42°27N 84°56W **311** B12
Olívia, L., U.S.A. 38°31N 81°31W **133** A1
Olivine Ra. N.Z. 44°15S 168°30E **285** D5
Olivos Argentina 34°30S 58°28W **117** B2
Oljato U.S.A. 37°0N 110°20W **307** H8
Olkhovka Russia 49°48N 44°32E **190** F7
Ölkusz Poland 50°18N 19°33E **185** H6
Ollachea Peru 13°49S 70°29W **330** C3
Ollagüe Chile 21°15S 68°10W **334** A2
Ollombo Congo 1°18S 15°53E **264** C3
Olloua Congo 0°54S 14°36E **264** C2
Olmaliq Uzbekistan 40°50N 69°35E **217** D7
Olmedo Spain 41°20N 4°43W **194** D6
Olmeto France 41°43N 8°55E **175** G12
Olmos Argentina 34°50S 58°29W **117** B1
Olmütz = Olomouc
    Czechia 49°38N 17°12E **181** B10
Olney Ill., U.S.A. 38°44N 88°5W **311** F8
Olney Tex., U.S.A. 33°22N 98°45W **314** E5
Olofström Sweden 56°17N 14°32E **163** H8
Oloitokitok Kenya 2°56S 37°30E **268** C4
Ololi Congo 0°15S 14°36E **264** C2
Oloma Cameroon 3°29N 11°19E **263** E7
Olomane → Canada 50°14N 60°37W **299** B7
Olomouc Czechia 49°38N 17°12E **181** B10
Olomoucký □ Czechia 49°45N 17°5E **181** B10
Olona → Italy 45°29N 9°6E **128** B1
Olonets Russia 61°0N 32°54E **188** B7
Olongapo Phil. 14°50N 120°18E **232** D3
Olonkinbyen Norway 70°55N 8°43W **154** C10
Olonne-sur-Mer France 46°32N 1°47W **174** B2
Oloron, Gave d' → France 43°33N 1°5W **174** E2
Oloron-Ste-Marie France 43°8N 0°38W **174** E3
Olosega = Swains I.
    Amer. Samoa 11°11S 171°4W **289** J11
Olot Spain 42°11N 2°30E **196** C7
Olovo Bos.-H. 44°8N 18°35E **182** F3
Olovyannaya Russia 50°58N 115°35E **215** D12
Oloy → Russia 66°29N 159°29E **215** C16
Olsberg Germany 51°21N 8°31E **178** D4
Olshammar Sweden 58°45N 14°48E **163** F8
Olshany Ukraine 50°3N 35°53E **189** G8
Olsztyn Poland 53°48N 20°29E **184** E7
Olsztynek Poland 53°34N 20°19E **184** E7
Olt □ Romania 44°20N 24°30E **183** F8
Olt → Romania 43°43N 24°51E **183** G9
Oltedal Norway 58°49N 6°0E **164** F3
Olten Switz. 47°21N 7°53E **179** H3
Olteniţa Romania 44°7N 26°42E **183** F11
Olton U.S.A. 34°11N 102°8W **314** B3
Oltu Turkey 40°35N 41°58E **213** B9
Ōluan Pi Taiwan 21°53N 120°51E **225** E2
Oluanpi Taiwan 21°54N 120°51E **225** E2
Olula del Rio Spain 37°21N 2°18W **197** H2
Olur Turkey 40°49N 42°8E **213** B10
Olustee U.S.A. 30°12N 82°26W **316** E7
Olutanga Phil. 7°26N 122°56E **233** H4
Olutanga I. Phil. 7°22N 122°52E **233** H4
Olvega Spain 41°47N 2°0W **196** D2

Olvera Spain 36°55N 5°18W **195** J5
Olympos Cyprus 35°21N 33°45E **207** E9
Olymbos Óros Greece 40°6N 22°23E **202** F6
Olympia Greece 37°39N 21°39E **204** D3
Olympia London, U.K. **125** c1
Olympia Wash., U.S.A. 47°3N 122°53W **306** D4
Olympia, L. U.S.A. 43°6N 75°39W **313** C9
Olympic □ U.S.A. 47°45N 123°43W **306** C3
Olympic Dam Australia 30°30S 136°55E **282** A2
Olympic Green China 39°59N 116°23E **114** B2
Olympic Mts. U.S.A. 47°55N 123°45W **306** C3
Olympic Stadium = Turner Field
    Atlanta, U.S.A. 33°44N 84°23W **113** B2
Olympic Stadium Beijing,
    China 39°59N 116°23E **114** B2
Olympic Stadium Helsinki,
    Finland 60°11N 24°55E **121** B2
Olympique, Stade
    Montréal, Canada 45°33N 73°33W **130** A2
Olympus, Mt. = Olymbos Oros
    Greece 40°6N 22°23E **202** F6
Olympus, Mt. = Uludağ
    Turkey 40°4N 29°13E **203** F13
Olympus, Mt. U.S.A. 47°48N 123°43W **306** C3
Olyntorskiy, Mys
    Russia 59°55N 170°27E **215** D18
Om → Russia 54°59N 73°22E **217** B8
Om Hajer Eritrea 14°20N 36°41E **257** F4
Om Koi Thailand 17°48N 98°22E **236** D2
Ōma Japan 41°45N 141°5E **220** D10
Ōmachi Japan 36°30N 137°50E **223** A9
Omae-Zaki Japan 34°36N 138°14E **223** C10
Ōmagari = Daisen
    Japan 39°27N 140°29E **220** E10
Omagh U.K. 54°36N 7°19W **166** B4
Omagh □ U.K. 54°35N 7°15W **166** B4
Omaha U.S.A. 41°17N 95°58W **308** E6
Omaheke □ Namibia 21°30S 19°0E **270** B2
Omak U.S.A. 48°25N 119°31W **304** B4
Omalos Greece 35°19N 23°55E **207** E4
Omalur India 11°44N 78°4E **245** J4
Oman ■ Asia 23°0N 58°0E **249** C6
Oman, G. of Asia 24°30N 58°30E **247** E8
Omapere N.Z. 35°37S 173°22E **284** B2
Omar Combon Somalia 3°10N 45°47E **267** D6
Omaruru Namibia 21°26S 16°0E **270** B2
Omaruru → Namibia 22°7S 14°15E **270** B1
Omaruru → Namibia 16°45S 71°0W **330** D3
Omate Peru 8°30S 124°50E **231** F6
Ombai, Selat Indonesia 8°30S 124°50E **231** F6
Ombella-Mpoko □ C.A.R. 5°30N 17°30E **264** A3
Ombóone Gabon 1°35S 9°15E **264** C1
Ombrone → Italy 42°42N 11°5E **198** E8
Omchi Chad 21°22N 17°53E **259** D3
Omdurmân Sudan 15°40N 32°28E **257** D3
Ōme Japan 35°47N 139°15E **223** B11
Omega U.S.A. 31°21N 83°36W **316** D6
Omegna Italy 45°53N 8°24E **198** C5
Omemee Canada 44°18N 78°33W **312** B6
Omeo Australia 37°6S 147°36E **283** D7
Omeonga
    Dem. Rep. of the Congo 3°40S 24°22E **264** C4
Ometepe, I. de Nic. 11°32N 85°35W **320** D2
Ometepec Mexico 16°41N 98°25W **319** D5
Ōmi-Shima Ehime, Japan 34°15N 133°2E **222** C4
Ōmi-Shima Yamaguchi,
    Japan 34°25N 131°9E **222** C3
Omihachiman Japan 35°7N 136°3E **223** B8
Omineca → Canada 56°3N 124°16W **296** B4
Omineca Mts. Canada 56°30N 125°30W **296** B3
Omiš Croatia 43°28N 16°40E **199** E13
Omišalj Croatia 45°13N 14°32E **199** C11
Omitara Namibia 22°16S 18°2E **270** B2
Ōmiya = Saitama Japan 35°54N 139°38E **223** B11
Ommaney, C. U.S.A. 56°10N 134°40W **303** H14
Ommen Neths. 52°31N 6°26E **170** B6
Ōmnōgovĭ □ Mongolia 43°15N 104°0E **226** C2
Omo → Ethiopia 6°25N 36°10E **257** F4
Omo Valley Ethiopia 5°7N 36°0E **257** F4
Omodeo, L. Italy 40°8N 8°56E **200** B1
Omodhos Cyprus 34°51N 32°48E **207** F8
Omoï Congo 2°56S 13°13E **264** C2
Omoko Nigeria 5°19N 6°40E **263** D6
Omolon → Russia 68°42N 158°36E **215** C16
Omona Square Athens, Greece **112** b1
Omonia Square Athens, Greece **112** b1
Omono-Gawa → Japan 39°46N 140°3E **220** E10
Ōmori Japan 35°34N 139°43E **140** B3
Ompha Canada 45°0N 76°50W **313** B8
Omsk Russia 55°0N 73°12E **217** D8
Omsukchan Russia 62°32N 155°48E **215** C16
Ōmu Japan 44°34N 142°58E **220** B11
Omul, Vf. Romania 45°27N 25°29E **183** F10
Omulew → Poland 53°5N 21°33E **185** E8
Ōmura Japan 32°56N 129°57E **222** E1
Ōmura-Wan Japan 32°57N 129°52E **222** E1
Omuramba Omatako →
    Namibia 17°45S 20°25E **270** A2
Omuramba Ovambo →
    Namibia 18°45S 16°59E **270** A2
Omurtag Bulgaria 43°8N 26°26E **203** D11
Omusati □ Namibia 18°30S 15°0E **270** A1
Ōmuta Japan 33°5N 130°26E **222** D2
Omuthiya Namibia 17°43S 16°12E **270** A2
On-Take Japan 31°35N 130°39E **222** F2
On-Take Japan 32°46N 134°5E **222** E5
Ōna Spain 42°43N 3°25W **194** C7
Ona Fla., U.S.A. 27°29N 81°55W **317** H8
Ona Dikonde
    Dem. Rep. of the Congo 3°51S 24°11E **264** C4
Onaga U.S.A. 39°29N 96°10W **308** F5
Onalaska U.S.A. 43°53N 91°14W **308** D8
Onancock U.S.A. 37°43N 75°45W **309** G18
Onangue, L. Gabon 0°57S 10°4E **264** C1
Onaping L. Canada 47°3N 81°30W **312** A3
Onarga U.S.A. 40°43N 88°1W **311** E8
Onavas Mexico 28°31N 109°35W **318** B3
Onawa U.S.A. 42°2N 96°6W **308** D5
Oncócua Angola 16°30S 13°25E **270** A1
Onda Spain 39°55N 0°17W **196** F4
Ondangwa Namibia 17°57S 16°4E **270** A2
Ondarroa Spain 43°19N 2°25W **196** A2
Ondas → Brazil 13°25S 42°43W **333** D3
Ondava → Slovakia 48°27N 21°48E **181** C13
Ondjiva Angola 34°11N 132°32E **265** G3
Ondo Nigeria 7°4N 4°47E **263** D5
Ondo □ Nigeria 6°45N 5°0E **263** D6
Öndörhaan Mongolia 47°19N 110°39E **219** B11
Öndörörnes Iceland 64°52N 24°0W **155** C2
One and a Half Degree Channel
    Maldives 1°30N 73°0E **272** d
One Arm Point Australia 16°26S 123°3E **278** C3
One Arm Point ○
    Australia 16°31S 122°53E **278** C3
One Prudential Plaza Chicago, U.S.A. **119** c2
One Tree Australia 34°11S 144°43E **283** B3
One World Trade Center
    New York, U.S.A. 40°43N 74°1W **132** e2
Oneata Fiji 18°55S 178°24W **287** B2
Oneco U.S.A. 27°26N 82°32W **317** H7
Onega Russia 64°0N 38°10E **186** B6
Onega → Russia 63°58N 38°2E **186** B6

Onega, G. of = Onezhskaya Guba
    Russia 64°24N 36°38E **186** B6
Onega, L. = Onezhskoye Ozero
    Russia 61°44N 35°22E **188** B8
Oneida Ill., U.S.A. 41°4N 90°13W **310** C6
Oneida N.Y., U.S.A. 43°6N 75°39W **313** C9
Oneida L. U.S.A. 43°12N 75°54W **313** C9
O'Neill U.S.A. 42°27N 98°39W **308** D4
Onekotan, Ostrov
    Russia 49°25N 154°45E **215** E16
Onema
    Dem. Rep. of the Congo 4°35S 24°30E **265** C4
Oneonta U.S.A. 42°27N 75°4W **313** D9
Onerahi N.Z. 35°45S 174°22E **284** B3
Oneroa Cook Is. 21°15S 159°43W **289** h
Oneşti Romania 46°17N 26°47E **183** D11
Oracle U.S.A. 32°37N 110°46W **305** K8
Oracuzar Peru 4°42S 78°6W **328** D2
Oradea Romania 47°2N 21°58E **182** D6
Oradell U.S.A. 40°57N 74°1W **132** A1
Oradell Res. U.S.A. 40°57N 74°1W **132** A1
Öræfajökull Iceland 64°2N 16°39W **155** C10
Orahovac = Rahovec
    Kosovo 42°24N 20°40E **202** D4
Orahovica Croatia 45°35N 17°52E **182** E2
Orai India 25°58N 79°30E **243** G8
Oraiokastro Greece 40°44N 22°55E **202** F6
Oraison France 43°55N 5°55E **175** E9
Orаl → Kazakhstan 47°0N 51°48E **187** E9
Orаl Kazakhstan 51°20N 51°20E **190** E10
Oran Algeria 35°45N 0°39W **261** A4
Oran □ Algeria 35°0N 0°45W **261** A4
Orang ↯ India 26°37N 92°29E **241** B8
Orange N.S.W., Australia 33°15S 149°7E **283** B8
Orange Vaucluse, France 44°8N 4°47E **175** D8
Orange Calif., U.S.A. 33°47N 117°51W **307** M9
Orange Mass., U.S.A. 42°35N 72°19W **313** D12
Orange Tex., U.S.A. 30°6N 93°44W **314** F8
Orange → S. Africa 28°41S 16°28E **270** C2
Orange, C. Brazil 4°20N 51°30W **329** C7
Orange City U.S.A. 28°57N 81°18W **317** G8
Orange Cove U.S.A. 36°38N 119°19W **306** J7
Orange Free State = Free State □
    S. Africa 28°30S 27°0E **270** C4
Orange Grove U.S.A. 27°58N 97°56W **314** H6
Orange Hill Barbados 13°12N 59°36W **323** r
Orange Hill Jamaica 18°16N 77°59W **320** a
Orange Hill St. Vincent 13°19N 61°7W **323** h
Orange L. U.S.A. 29°25N 82°13W **317** F17
Orange Park U.S.A. 30°10N 81°42W **316** E8
Orange River Colony = Free State □
    S. Africa 28°30S 27°0E **270** C4
Orange Walk Belize 18°6N 88°33W **319** D7
Orangeburg U.S.A. 33°30N 80°52W **316** C8
Orangeville Ont., Canada 43°55N 80°5W **312** C4
Orangeville Ill., U.S.A. 42°28N 89°39W **310** A6
Orangi Pakistan 24°54N 67°0E **123** A2
Orango Guinea-Biss. 11°5N 16°0W **262** C1
Orani Italy 40°15N 9°11E **200** B2
Orani Phil. 14°49N 120°32E **232** D3
Oranienburg Germany 52°45N 13°14E **178** C9
Oranje = Orange →
    S. Africa 28°41S 16°28E **270** C2
Oranjemund Namibia 28°38S 16°29E **270** C2
Oranjerivier S. Africa 29°40S 24°12E **270** D3
Oranjestad Aruba 12°32N 70°2E **324** A3
Oranjestad St. Eustatius 17°28N 62°59W **322** a
Orap Vanuatu 15°58S 167°20E **287** E5
Oras Phil. 12°9N 125°22E **232** E6
Orașje Bos.-H. 45°3N 18°42E **182** E3
Orăştie Romania 45°50N 23°10E **183** E8
Orava → Slovakia 49°9N 19°8E **181** B12
Oraviţa Romania 45°6N 21°43E **182** E6
Orawia N.Z. 46°1S 167°50S **285** G2
Orb → France 43°15N 3°18E **174** E7
Orba → Italy 44°53N 8°37E **198** D5
Ørbæk Denmark 55°17N 10°39E **163** J4
Orbe Switz. 46°43N 6°32E **179** J2
Orbec France 49°1N 0°23E **172** C7
Orbetello Italy 42°27N 11°13E **199** F8
Órbigo → Spain 42°5N 5°42W **194** C5
Orbisonia U.S.A. 40°15N 77°54W **312** F7
Orbost Australia 37°40S 148°29E **283** D8
Ørbyhus Sweden 60°14N 17°43E **163** F11
Orcadas Antarctica 60°44S 44°37W **151** C18
Orcas I. U.S.A. 48°42N 122°56W **306** B4
Orce Spain 37°44N 2°28W **197** H2
Orce → Spain 37°44N 2°28W **197** H2
Orchard City U.S.A. 38°50N 107°58W **304** G10
Orchard Homes U.S.A. 46°55N 114°4W **304** C6
Orchard Road Singapore **138** a1
Orchid I. = Lan Yü
    Taiwan 22°4N 121°25E **225** D3
Orchies France 50°28N 3°14E **173** B10
Orchila, I. Venezuela 11°48N 66°10W **321** D6
Orchilla, Pta. Canary Is. 27°42N 18°10W **153** e1
Órcia → Italy 42°58N 11°21E **199** F8
Orco → Italy 45°10N 7°52E **198** B4
Orcopampa Peru 15°20S 72°23W **330** D3
Orcutt U.S.A. 34°52N 120°27W **307** L6
Ord □ U.S.A. 41°36N 98°56W **308** E4
Ord → Australia 15°33S 128°15E **278** C4
Ord, Mt. Australia 17°20S 125°34E **278** C4
Ord Mts. U.S.A. 34°39N 116°45W **307** L10
Ordenes = Ordes Spain 43°5N 8°29W **194** B2
Orderville U.S.A. 37°17N 112°38W **305** H7
Ordes Spain 43°5N 8°29W **194** B2
Ordesa y Monte Perdido △
    Spain 42°40N 0°10W **196** C5
Ording = Sankt Peter-Ording
    Germany 54°20N 8°36E **178** A4
Ordos = Mu Us Shamo
    China 39°0N 109°0E **226** E5
Ordrup Denmark 55°45N 12°34E **118** A3
Ordu Turkey 40°55N 37°53E **212** B7
Ordu □ Turkey 40°50N 37°40E **212** B7
Ordubad Azerbaijan 38°54N 46°1E **213** C12
Orduña Álava, Spain 42°58N 2°58W **196** C1
Orduña Granada, Spain 37°20N 3°30W **195** H7
Ordway U.S.A. 38°13N 103°46W **304** G12
Ordzhonikidze = Denisovka
    Kazakhstan 52°27N 61°39E **216** B6
Ordzhonikidze = Vladikavkaz
    Russia 43°0N 44°35E **191** J7
Ordzhonikidze = Yenakiyeve
    Ukraine 48°15N 38°15E **189** H10
Ordzhonikidze Ukraine 47°39N 34°3E **189** J8
Öre Dem. Rep. of the Congo 3°17N 29°30E **268** B2
Ore Mts. = Erzgebirge
    Germany 50°27N 12°55E **178** E8
Orealla Guyana 5°15N 57°23W **339** B8
Orebić Croatia 43°0N 17°11E **199** F14
Örebro Sweden 59°20N 15°18E **163** F9
Örebro □ Sweden 59°27N 15°0E **163** F9
Orecchiella △ Italy 44°16N 10°25E **198** D7
Ořech Czechia 50°1N 14°17E **135** B1
Oregon Ill., U.S.A. 42°1N 89°20W **310** B7
Oregon Ohio, U.S.A. 41°39N 83°29W **311** C13
Oregon Wis., U.S.A. 42°56N 89°23W **310** D7
Oregon □ U.S.A. 44°0N 121°0W **304** E3
Oregon Dunes △ U.S.A. 43°40N 124°10W **304** E1
Øregrund Sweden 60°21N 18°30E **162** D12

Öregrundsgrepen Sweden 60°25N 18°15E 162 D12
Oregun Nigeria 6°35N 3°22E 124 A2
Orekhov = Orikhiv Ukraine 47°30N 35°48E 189 J8
Orekhovo-Zuyevo Russia 55°50N 38°55E 188 E10
Orel Russia 52°57N 36°3E 189 F9
Orel □ Russia 52°30N 36°40E 189 F9
Orellana □ Ecuador 0°45S 76°25W 328 D2
Orellana, Canal de Spain 39°2N 6°0W 195 F5
Orellana, Embalse de Spain 39°5N 5°10W 195 F5
Orellana la Vieja Spain 39°1N 5°32W 195 F5
Orem U.S.A. 40°19N 111°42W 304 F8
Ören Turkey 37°3N 27°57E 205 D9
Orenburg Russia 51°45N 55°6E 186 D10
Örencik Turkey 39°16N 29°33E 205 B11
Orense = Ourense Spain 42°19N 7°55W 194 C3
Orepuki N.Z. 46°19S 167°46E 285 G2
Ørestad Denmark 55°38N 12°35E 118 B3
Orestes Pereyra Mexico 26°30N 105°39W 318 B3
Orestiada Greece 41°30N 26°33E 203 E10
Øresund Europe 55°45N 12°40E 163 J6
Oretana, Cordillera = Toledo, Montes de Spain 39°33N 4°20W 195 F6
Oreti → N.Z. 46°28S 168°14E 285 G3
Orfanos Kolpos Greece 40°33N 24°0E 202 F7
Orford Ness U.K. 52°5N 1°35E 169 E9
Organ Pipe Cactus ⌂ U.S.A. 32°0N 112°52W 305 K7
Organos, Pta. de los Canary Is. 28°12N 17°17W 153 e1
Organyà Spain 42°13N 1°20E 196 C6
Orgaz Spain 39°39N 3°53W 195 F7
Ørgenvika Norway 60°17N 9°42E 164 D6
Orgeyev = Orhei Moldova 47°24N 28°50E 183 C13
Orgiva Spain 36°53N 3°24W 195 J7
Orgūn Afghan. 32°55N 69°12E 240 B3
Orhaneli Turkey 39°54N 28°59E 203 G12
Orhaneli → Turkey 39°50N 28°55E 203 G12
Orhangazi Turkey 40°29N 29°18E 203 F13
Orhei Moldova 47°24N 28°50E 183 C13
Orhon Gol → Mongolia 50°21N 106°0E 218 A10
Ória Italy 40°30N 17°38E 201 B10
Orida Niger 21°20N 12°15E 261 D7
Orient Heights U.S.A. 42°23N 70°59W 116 A3
Oriental □ Morocco 33°0N 2°0W 261 B4
Oriental, Cordillera Bolivia 17°0S 66°0W 331 D4
Oriental, Cordillera Colombia 6°0N 73°0W 328 B3
Oriental, Grand Erg Algeria 30°0N 6°30E 261 B6
Oriental Pearl Tower Shanghai, China 31°14N 121°30E 138 B2
Oriente Argentina 38°44S 60°37W 334 D3
Orihuela Spain 38°7N 0°55W 197 G4
Orihuela del Tremedal Spain 40°33N 1°39W 196 E3
Orikhiv Ukraine 47°30N 35°48E 189 J8
Orikum Albania 40°20N 19°26E 202 F3
Oril → Ukraine 48°40N 34°39E 189 H8
Orillia Canada 44°40N 79°24W 312 B5
Orinduik Guyana 4°40N 60°3W 329 C5
Orinoco → Venezuela 9°15N 61°30W 329 B5
Orinoco, Delta del Venezuela 9°0N 61°30W 329 B5
Orion Canada 49°27N 110°49W 297 D6
Orion Ala., U.S.A. 31°58N 86°0W 316 D4
Orion Ill., U.S.A. 41°21N 90°23W 310 C6
Oriskany U.S.A. 43°10N 75°20W 313 C9
Orissa = Odisha □ India 20°0N 84°0E 244 E7
Orissaare Estonia 58°34N 23°5E 188 C2
Oristano Italy 39°54N 8°36E 200 C1
Oristano, G. di Italy 39°50N 8°29E 200 C1
Orituco → Venezuela 8°45N 67°27W 328 B4
Oriximina Brazil 1°45S 55°52W 329 D6
Orizaba Mexico 18°51N 97°6W 319 D5
Orizaba, Pico de Mexico 18°58N 97°15W 319 D5
Orizare Bulgaria 42°44N 27°39E 203 D11
Orizona Brazil 17°3S 48°18W 333 E2
Ørje Norway 59°29N 11°39E 164 E8
Orjen Bos.-H. 42°35N 18°34E 202 D2
Orjiva = Orgiva Spain 36°53N 3°24W 195 J7
Orkanger Norway 63°18N 9°52E 164 A6
Örkelljunga Sweden 56°17N 13°17E 163 H7
Örken Sweden 57°6N 15°1E 163 G9
Örkény Hungary 47°9N 19°26E 182 C4
Orkhaniye = Botevgrad Bulgaria 42°55N 23°47E 202 D7
Orkhon = Orhon Gol → Mongolia 50°21N 106°0E 218 A10
Orkla → Norway 63°18N 9°51E 164 A6
Orkney S. Africa 26°58S 26°40E 270 C4
Orkney □ U.K. 59°2N 3°13W 167 B5
Orkney Is. U.K. 59°0N 3°0W 167 B6
Orland Calif., U.S.A. 39°45N 122°12W 306 F4
Orland Ind., U.S.A. 41°47N 85°12W 311 C11
Orland Park U.S.A. 41°38N 87°52W 119 D2
Orlando U.S.A. 28°32N 81°22W 133 A2
Orlando, C. d' Italy 38°10N 14°43E 201 D7
Orlando Dam S. Africa 26°15S 27°55E 123 B1
Orlando East S. Africa 26°14S 27°55E 123 B1
Orlando Executive ✈ (ORL) U.S.A. 28°32N 81°20W 133 A2
Orlando Int. ✈ (MCO) U.S.A. 28°26N 81°19W 133 B3
Orléanais France 48°0N 2°0E 173 E9
Orléans Loiret, France 47°54N 1°52E 173 E8
Orleans Ind., U.S.A. 38°40N 86°27W 311 F10
Orleans Vt., U.S.A. 44°49N 72°12W 313 B12
Orléans, Î. d' Canada 46°54N 70°58W 299 C5
Orléansville = Ech Chéliff Algeria 36°10N 1°20E 261 A5
Orlice → Czechia 50°13N 15°50E 180 A8
Orlivka Ukraine 45°19N 28°27E 183 E13
Orlov = Khalturin Russia 58°40N 48°50E 186 C8
Orlov Slovakia 49°17N 20°51E 181 B13
Orlov Gay Russia 50°56N 48°19E 190 E9
Orlová Czechia 49°51N 18°26E 181 B11
Orlovat Serbia 45°14N 20°33E 182 E5
Orlovista U.S.A. 28°32N 81°27W 133 A2
Orlovskoye Polesye △ Russia 58°30N 35°30E 188 F8
Orly France 48°45N 2°23E 134 B3
Orly, Paris ✈ (ORY) France 48°44N 2°23E 134 B3
Ormara Pakistan 25°16N 64°33E 240 D2
Ormea Italy 44°9N 7°54E 198 D4
Ormesson-sur-Marne France 48°47N 2°32E 134 B4
Ormilia Greece 40°16N 23°39E 202 F7
Ormoc Phil. 11°0N 124°37E 233 F5
Ormond Vic., Australia 37°54S 145°1E 128 B2
Ormond N.Z. 38°33S 177°56E 284 E6
Ormond Beach U.S.A. 29°17N 81°3W 317 F8
Ormond-by-the-Sea U.S.A. 29°21N 81°4W 317 F8
Ormondville N.Z. 40°5S 176°19E 284 G5
Ormøya Norway 59°52N 10°45E 133 A3
Ormož Slovenia 46°25N 16°10E 199 B13
Ormskirk U.K. 53°35N 2°54W 168 D5
Ormstown Canada 45°8N 74°0W 313 A11
Ormtjernkampen △ Norway 61°12N 9°48E 164 C6
Ornans France 47°7N 6°10E 173 E13
Orne □ France 48°40N 0°5E 172 D7
Orne → France 49°18N 0°15W 172 C6
Orneta Poland 54°8N 20°9E 184 D7
Ornö Sweden 59°4N 18°24E 162 E12
Örnsköldsvik Sweden 63°17N 18°40E 162 A12
Oro = Northern □ Papua N. G. 9°0S 148°30E 286 E5
Oro N. Korea 40°1N 127°27E 224 B3
Oro → Mexico 25°35N 105°2W 318 B3
Oro Grande U.S.A. 34°36N 117°20W 307 L9
Oro Valley U.S.A. 32°26N 110°58W 305 K8
Orobie, Alpi Italy 46°7N 10°0E 198 B6
Orobie Bergamasche ⌂ Italy 46°0N 9°45E 198 C6
Orobie Valtellinesi ⌂ Italy 46°5N 9°45E 198 B6
Orocué Colombia 4°48N 71°20W 328 C3
Orodara Burkina Faso 11°0N 4°55W 262 C4
Orodo Nigeria 5°34N 7°4E 263 D6
Orofino U.S.A. 46°29N 116°15W 304 C5
Orohena, Mt. Tahiti 17°37S 149°28W 289 e
Orol Dengizi = Aral Sea Asia 45°0N 58°20E 216 C5
Oromiya □ Ethiopia 7°0N 40°0E 257 F5
Oromocto Canada 45°54N 66°29W 299 C6
Oron Nigeria 4°48N 8°14E 263 E6
Orona Kiribati 4°31S 172°11W 277 A16
Orongo Chile 27°11S 109°27W 330 b
Orono Ont., Canada 43°59N 78°37W 312 C6
Orono Maine, U.S.A. 44°53N 68°40W 309 C19
Oronsay U.K. 56°1N 6°15W 167 E2
Oropesa Spain 39°57N 5°10W 194 F5
Oropuche → Trin. & Tob. 10°36N 61°6W 323 t
Oropuche Lagoon Trin. & Tob. 10°14N 61°31W 323 t
Oroquieta Phil. 8°32N 123°44E 233 G4
Orós Brazil 6°15S 38°55W 332 C4
Orosei Italy 40°23N 9°42E 200 B2
Orosei, G. di Italy 40°15N 9°44E 200 B2
Orosháza Hungary 46°32N 20°42E 182 D5
Oroszlány Hungary 47°29N 18°19E 182 C3
Orote Pen. Guam 13°26N 144°38E 302 d
Orotukan Russia 62°16N 151°42E 215 C16
Oroville Calif., U.S.A. 39°31N 121°33W 306 F5
Oroville Wash., U.S.A. 48°56N 119°26W 304 B4
Oroville, L. U.S.A. 39°33N 121°29W 306 F5
Orpington U.K. 51°22N 0°6E 125 B4
Orrefors Sweden 56°50N 15°45E 163 H9
Orrick U.S.A. 39°13N 94°7W 310 E2
Orroroo Australia 32°43S 138°38E 282 B3
Orrviken Sweden 63°6N 14°26E 162 A8
Orrville U.S.A. 40°50N 81°46W 312 F3
Orsa Sweden 61°7N 14°37E 162 C8
Orsara di Púglia Italy 41°17N 15°16E 201 A8
Orsasjön Sweden 61°7N 14°37E 162 C8
Orsay, Musée d' Paris, France 134 b3
Orsha Belarus 54°30N 30°25E 188 E6
Örsjö Sweden 56°42N 15°45E 163 H9
Orsk Russia 51°12N 58°34E 216 B5
Orşova Romania 44°41N 22°25E 182 F7
Ørsta Norway 62°13N 6°8E 164 B3
Ørsted Denmark 56°30N 10°20E 163 H4
Örsundsbro Sweden 59°44N 17°18E 162 E11
Országos Levétár Budapest, Hungary 117 b1
Orta Turkey 40°38N 33°6E 212 B5
Orta, L. d' Italy 45°49N 8°24E 198 C5
Orta Nova Italy 41°19N 15°42E 201 A8
Ortaca Turkey 36°49N 28°45E 205 E10
Ortakent Turkey 37°5N 27°21E 205 D9
Ortaklar Turkey 37°53N 27°30E 205 D9
Ortaköy Çorum, Turkey 40°16N 35°15E 212 B6
Ortaköy İstanbul, Turkey 41°3N 29°1E 122 B2
Ortaköy Niğde, Turkey 38°44N 34°3E 212 C6
Orte Italy 42°27N 12°23E 199 F9
Ortegal, C. Spain 43°43N 7°52W 194 B3
Orteguaza → Colombia 0°43N 75°16W 328 C2
Ortelsburg = Szczytno Poland 53°33N 21°0E 184 E7
Orthez France 43°29N 0°48W 174 E3
Ortica Italy 45°28N 9°16E 128 B2
Ortigueira Spain 43°40N 7°50W 194 B3
Ortigueira, Ría de Spain 43°44N 7°45W 194 B3
Orting U.S.A. 47°6N 122°12W 306 C4
Ortisei Italy 46°34N 11°40E 199 B8
Ortles Italy 46°31N 10°33E 198 B7
Ortnevik Norway 61°6N 6°7E 164 C3
Ortoire → Trin. & Tob. 10°20N 61°0W 323 t
Ortón → Bolivia 10°50S 67°0W 330 C4
Ortona Italy 42°21N 14°24E 199 F11
Ortonville U.S.A. 45°19N 96°27W 308 C5
Oruba Nigeria 6°34N 3°24E 124 A2
Orukuizui Palau 7°10N 134°15E 288 c
Orūmīyeh Iran 37°40N 45°0E 213 D11
Orūmīyeh, Daryācheh-ye Iran 37°50N 45°30E 213 D11
Orune Italy 40°24N 9°22E 200 B2
Oruro Bolivia 18°0S 67°9W 330 D4
Oruro □ Bolivia 18°40S 67°30W 330 D4
Orust Sweden 58°10N 11°40E 163 F5
Oruzgān □ Afghan. 33°0N 66°0E 240 B2
Orvault France 47°17N 1°38W 172 E5
Orvieto Italy 42°43N 12°7E 199 F9
Orwell N.Y., U.S.A. 43°35N 75°50W 313 C9
Orwell Ohio, U.S.A. 41°32N 80°52W 312 E4
Orwell → U.K. 51°59N 1°18E 169 F9
Orwigsburg U.S.A. 40°38N 76°6W 313 F8
Oryakhovo Bulgaria 43°40N 23°57E 202 C7
Orynyn Ukraine 48°46N 26°24E 183 B11
Oryol = Orel Russia 52°57N 36°3E 189 F9
Orzinuovi Italy 45°24N 9°55E 198 C6
Orzyc → Poland 52°46N 21°14E 185 F8
Orzysz Poland 53°50N 21°58E 184 E8
Os Norway 62°30N 11°14E 164 B8
Osa Russia 57°17N 55°26E 186 C10
Osa → Poland 53°33N 18°46E 184 E5
Osa, Pen. de Costa Rica 8°0N 84°0W 320 E3
Osage U.S.A. 43°17N 92°49W 308 D7
Osage → U.S.A. 38°36N 91°57W 310 F5
Osage City U.S.A. 38°38N 95°50W 308 F6
Ōsaka Japan 34°42N 135°30E 133 B2
Ōsaka □ Japan 34°30N 135°30E 223 C7
Ōsaka Castle Japan 34°41N 135°30E 133 A2
Ōsaka Harbour Japan 34°38N 135°25E 133 B1
Ōsaka Itami Int. ✈ (ITM) Japan 34°46N 135°26E 133 A1
Ōsaka Kansai Int. ✈ (KIX) Japan 34°27N 135°12E 133 B2
Ōsaka-Wan Japan 34°30N 135°18E 223 C7
Osakarovka Kazakhstan 50°33N 72°34E 217 B8
Ōsaki Kagoshima, Japan 31°25N 131°2E 222 F3
Ōsaki Miyagi, Japan 38°34N 140°58E 220 E10
Ōsaki Tōkyō, Japan 35°36N 139°42E 140 B3
Osan S. Korea 37°11N 127°4E 224 D3
Osasco Brazil 23°31S 46°46W 137 B1
Osawatomie U.S.A. 38°31N 94°57W 308 F6
Osborn Plateau Ind. Oc. 14°45S 87°0E 273 F7
Osborne U.S.A. 39°26N 98°42W 308 F4
Osby Sweden 56°23N 13°59E 163 H7
Osceola Ark., U.S.A. 35°42N 89°58W 315 D10
Osceola Iowa, U.S.A. 41°2N 93°46W 310 C3
Osceola Mo., U.S.A. 38°3N 93°42W 310 F3
Oschatz Germany 51°17N 13°6E 178 D9
Oschersleben Germany 52°2N 11°14E 178 C7
Óschiri Italy 40°43N 9°6E 200 B2
Oscoda U.S.A. 44°26N 83°20W 312 B1
Osdorf Germany 52°24N 13°20E 115 B3
Osdorp Neths. 52°22N 4°47E 112 A1
Osečina Serbia 44°23N 19°34E 202 B3
Ösel = Saaremaa Estonia 58°30N 22°30E 188 C2
Osensjøen Norway 61°13N 11°50E 164 C8
Osery Russia 54°52N 38°28E 188 E10
Osgood U.S.A. 39°8N 85°18W 311 E11
Osgoode Canada 45°8N 75°36W 313 A9
Osgoode Hall Toronto, Canada 141 b2
Osh Kyrgyzstan 40°37N 72°49E 217 D8
Osh □ Kyrgyzstan 40°0N 73°0E 217 E8
Oshana □ Namibia 17°50S 15°40E 270 A2
Oshawa Canada 43°50N 78°50W 312 C6
Oshigambo Namibia 17°45S 16°5E 270 A2
Oshika-Hantō Japan 38°20N 141°30E 220 E10
Oshikoto □ Namibia 18°30S 17°0E 270 A2
Oshivelo Namibia 18°37S 17°10E 270 A2
Oshkosh Nebr., U.S.A. 41°24N 102°21W 308 E2
Oshkosh Wis., U.S.A. 44°1N 88°33W 308 C9
Oshmyany = Ashmyany Belarus 54°26N 25°52E 177 A13
Oshnovīyeh Iran 37°2N 45°6E 213 D11
Oshodi Nigeria 6°33N 3°21E 124 A2
Oshogbo Nigeria 7°48N 4°37E 263 D5
Oshtorīnān Iran 34°1N 48°38E 213 E13
Ōshū Japan 39°8N 141°8E 220 E10
Oshwe Dem. Rep. of the Congo 3°25S 19°28E 264 C3
Osi Nigeria 8°8N 5°14E 263 D6
Osieczna Poland 51°55N 16°40E 185 G3
Osijek Croatia 45°34N 18°41E 182 E3
Ósilo Italy 40°45N 8°40E 200 B1
Ósimo Italy 43°28N 13°30E 199 E10
Osintorf Belarus 54°40N 30°39E 188 E6
Osipenko = Berdyansk Ukraine 46°45N 36°50E 189 J9
Osipovichi = Asipovichy Belarus 53°19N 28°33E 177 B15
Osiyan India 26°43N 72°55E 242 F5
Osizweni S. Africa 27°49S 30°7E 271 C5
Oskaloosa U.S.A. 41°18N 92°39W 310 C4
Oskarshamn Sweden 57°15N 16°27E 163 G10
Oskarström Sweden 56°48N 12°58E 163 H6
Oskélanéo Canada 48°5N 75°15W 298 C4
Öskemen Kazakhstan 50°0N 82°36E 217 C10
Oskol → Ukraine 49°6N 37°25E 189 H9
Oskū Iran 37°54N 46°8E 213 D12
Oslo Norway 59°54N 10°43E 133 A3
Oslo □ Norway 59°54N 10°43E 164 D7
Oslo ✈ (OSL) Norway 60°11N 11°6E 133 A4
Oslob Phil. 9°31N 123°26E 233 G4
Oslofjorden Norway 59°20N 10°35E 164 E7
Osmanabad India 18°5N 76°10E 244 E3
Osmancık Turkey 40°58N 34°47E 212 B6
Osmaniye Turkey 37°5N 36°10E 250 A7
Osmanlı Turkey 41°35N 26°51E 203 E10
Osmannagar India 18°32N 79°20E 244 E4
Ösmo Sweden 58°58N 17°55E 162 F11
Osnabrück Germany 52°17N 8°3E 178 C4
Ośno Lubuskie Poland 52°28N 14°51E 185 F1
Osoblaha Czechia 50°17N 17°44E 181 A10
Osogbo = Oshogbo Nigeria 7°48N 4°37E 263 D5
Osogovska Planina Macedonia 42°10N 22°30E 202 D6
Ōsone Japan 35°31N 139°37E 140 B2
Osor Italy 44°42N 14°24E 199 D11
Osório Brazil 29°53S 50°17W 335 B5
Osório da Fonseca Brazil 3°52S 58°14W 329 D6
Osorno Chile 40°25S 73°0W 336 B2
Osorno Spain 42°24N 4°22W 194 C6
Osorno □ Chile 40°34S 73°9W 336 B2
Osorno, Vol. Chile 41°0S 72°30W 336 B2
Osorun Nigeria 6°33N 3°29E 124 A2
Osoyoos Canada 49°0N 119°30W 296 D5
Osøyro Norway 60°9N 5°30E 164 D2
Óspakseyri Iceland 65°27N 21°26W 155 B5
Ospiate Italy 45°32N 9°6E 128 A1
Ospika → Canada 56°20N 124°0W 296 B4
Osprey U.S.A. 27°12N 82°29W 317 H7
Osprey Reef Australia 13°52S 146°36E 280 A4
Oss Neths. 51°46N 5°32E 170 C5
Ossa, Mt. Australia 41°52S 146°3E 281 G4
Ossa, Oros Greece 39°47N 22°42E 204 B4
Ossa de Montiel Spain 38°58N 2°45W 197 G2
Ossabaw I. U.S.A. 31°50N 81°5W 316 D8
Ossabaw Sd. U.S.A. 31°50N 81°6W 316 D8
Osse → Lot-et-Garonne, France 44°7N 0°17E 174 D4
Osse → Nigeria 6°10N 5°20E 263 D6
Ossersee = Zarasai Lithuania 55°40N 26°20E 188 E4
Ossi Italy 40°40N 8°35E 200 B1
Ossining U.S.A. 41°10N 73°55W 313 E11
Ossipee U.S.A. 43°41N 71°7W 313 C13
Ossokmanuan L. Canada 53°25N 65°0W 299 B7
Ossora Russia 59°20N 163°13E 215 D17
Ostankino Russia 55°49N 37°37E 129 B2
Ostashkov Russia 57°4N 33°2E 188 D7
Östavall Sweden 62°26N 15°29E 162 B9
Østby Norway 61°15N 12°33E 164 C9
Oste → Germany 53°49N 9°2E 178 B5
Ostenburg = Pułtusk Poland 52°43N 21°6E 185 F8
Ostend = Oostende Belgium 51°15N 2°54E 170 C2
Ostend N.Z. 36°48S 175°2E 284 C4
Oster Ukraine 50°57N 30°53E 177 C16
Österbotten = Pohjanmaa □ Finland 62°58N 22°50E 160 E20
Østerbro Copenhagen, Denmark 118 a1
Osterburg Sachsen-Anhalt, Germany 52°47N 11°45E 178 C7
Osterburg Pa., U.S.A. 40°16N 78°31W 312 F6
Osterburken Germany 49°25N 9°26E 179 F5
Österbybruk Sweden 60°13N 17°55E 162 D11
Österbymo Sweden 57°49N 15°15E 163 G9
Österdalälven → Sweden 60°30N 15°7E 162 C7
Østerdalen Norway 61°40N 10°50E 162 C4
Österfärnebo Sweden 60°19N 16°48E 162 D10
Österforse Sweden 63°9N 17°3E 162 A11
Östergötland □ Sweden 58°35N 15°45E 163 F9
Osterholz-Scharmbeck Germany 53°13N 8°47E 178 B4
Østerild Denmark 57°2N 8°51E 163 G2
Osterley U.K. 51°28N 0°21W 125 B1
Osterley Park U.K. 51°29N 0°21W 125 B1
Östermalm Stockholm, Sweden 139 a3
Östermyra = Seinäjoki Finland 62°40N 22°51E 160 E20
Osterode Germany 51°43N 10°15E 178 D6
Osterode in Ostpreussen = Ostróda Poland 53°42N 19°58E 184 E6
Österreich = Austria ■ Europe 47°0N 14°0E 180 E7
Österreich ober der Ems = Oberösterreich □ Austria 48°10N 14°0E 180 C7
Österskär Sweden 59°26N 18°16E 139 A3
Östersund Sweden 63°10N 14°38E 162 A8
Östervåla Sweden 60°11N 17°11E 162 D11
Østfold □ Norway 59°25N 11°25E 164 E8
Ostfriesische Inseln Germany 53°42N 7°0E 178 B3
Ostfriesland Germany 53°20N 7°30E 178 B3
Östhammar Sweden 60°16N 18°22E 162 D12
Óstia, Lido di Italy 41°43N 12°17E 199 G9
Óstia Malpasso Italy 41°47N 12°26E 136 C1
Ostiense Italy 41°51N 12°29E 136 B1
Ostíglia Italy 45°4N 11°8E 199 C8
Östmark Sweden 60°17N 12°45E 162 D6
Østmarkkapellet Norway 59°52N 10°51E 133 A4
Østøya Norway 59°52N 10°34E 133 A2
Östra Husby Sweden 58°35N 16°33E 163 F10
Ostrava Czechia 49°51N 18°18E 181 B11
Ostróda Poland 53°42N 19°58E 184 E6
Ostrogozhsk Russia 50°55N 39°7E 189 G10
Ostroh Ukraine 50°20N 26°30E 177 C14
Ostrołęka Poland 53°4N 21°32E 185 E8
Ostrov Bulgaria 43°40N 24°9E 203 C8
Ostrov Czechia 50°18N 12°57E 180 A5
Ostrov Romania 44°6N 27°24E 183 F12
Ostrov Russia 57°25N 28°20E 188 D5
Ostrów Lubelski Poland 51°29N 22°51E 185 G9
Ostrów Mazowiecka Poland 52°50N 21°51E 185 F8
Ostrów Wielkopolski Poland 51°36N 17°44E 185 G4
Ostrowiec-Świętokrzyski Poland 50°55N 21°22E 185 H8
Ostrowo = Ostrów Wielkopolski Poland 51°36N 17°44E 185 G4
Ostrožac Bos.-H. 43°43N 17°49E 182 G2
Ostrzeszów Poland 51°25N 17°52E 185 G4
Ostseebad Kühlungsborn Germany 54°8N 11°44E 178 A7
Osttirol □ Austria 46°50N 12°30E 180 E5
Ostuni Italy 40°44N 17°35E 201 B10
Ostyako-Vogulsk = Khanty-Mansiysk Russia 61°0N 69°0E 214 C7
Osum → Albania 40°40N 20°10E 202 F4
Osŭm → Bulgaria 43°40N 24°50E 203 C8
Ōsumi-Hantō Japan 31°20N 130°55E 222 F2
Ōsumi-Kaikyō Japan 30°55N 131°0E 221 J5
Ōsumi-Shotō Japan 30°30N 130°0E 221 J5
Osun □ Nigeria 7°30N 4°30E 263 D5
Osuna Spain 37°14N 5°8W 195 H5
Oswegatchie → U.S.A. 44°42N 75°30W 313 B9
Oswego Ill., U.S.A. 41°41N 88°21W 311 C8
Oswego N.Y., U.S.A. 43°27N 76°31W 313 C8
Oswego → U.S.A. 43°27N 76°30W 313 C8
Oswestry U.K. 52°52N 3°3W 168 E4
Oświęcim Poland 50°2N 19°11E 185 H6
Ōta Fukui, Japan 35°57N 136°3E 223 B8
Ōta Gumma, Japan 36°18N 139°22E 223 A11
Ōta Tōkyō, Japan 35°34N 139°41E 140 B3
Ōta-Gawa → Japan 34°21N 132°18E 222 C4
Otaci Moldova 48°27N 27°47E 183 B12
Otago □ N.Z. 45°15S 170°0E 285 F5
Otago Harbour N.Z. 45°47S 170°42E 285 F5
Otago Pen. N.Z. 45°48S 170°39E 285 F5
Otaheite B. Trin. & Tob. 10°15N 61°30W 323 t
Otahuhu N.Z. 36°56S 174°51E 284 C3
Ōtake Japan 34°12N 132°13E 222 C4
Ōtaki Japan 35°17N 140°15E 223 B12
Otaki N.Z. 40°45S 175°10E 284 G4
Otane N.Z. 39°54S 176°39E 284 F5
Otaniemi Finland 60°11N 24°49E 121 B1
Otaru Japan 43°10N 141°0E 220 C10
Otaru-Wan = Ishikari-Wan Japan 43°25N 141°1E 220 C10
Otautau N.Z. 46°9S 168°1E 285 G3
Otava → Czechia 49°26N 14°12E 180 B7
Otavalo Ecuador 0°13N 78°20W 328 C2
Otavi Namibia 19°40S 17°24E 270 A2
Ōtawara Japan 36°50N 140°5E 221 F10
Otchinjau Angola 16°30S 13°56E 265 F2
Otego U.S.A. 42°23N 75°10W 313 D9
Oteiza = Marihatag Phil. 8°48N 126°18E 233 G6
Otelec Romania 45°36N 20°50E 182 E5
Otelnuk, L. Canada 56°9N 68°12W 299 A6
Oţelu Roşu Romania 45°32N 22°22E 182 E7
Otero de Rey = Outeiro de Rei Spain 43°6N 7°36W 194 B3
Othello U.S.A. 46°50N 119°10W 304 C4
Othoni Greece 39°52N 19°22E 206 B9
Othris, Oros Greece 39°2N 22°37E 204 B4
Oti → Africa 7°48N 0°8E 263 D5
Oti ⌂ Togo 10°40N 0°35E 263 C5
Otira N.Z. 42°49S 171°35E 285 C6
Otira Gorge N.Z. 42°53S 171°33E 285 C6
Otish, Mts. Canada 52°22N 70°30W 299 B5
Otishi △ Peru 11°40S 73°5W 330 C3
Otjinene Namibia 21°8S 18°46E 270 B2
Otjiwarongo Namibia 20°30S 16°33E 270 B2
Otjozondjupa □ Namibia 21°0S 17°0E 270 B2
Otmuchów Poland 50°28N 17°10E 185 H4
Oto Tolu Group Tonga 20°21S 174°32W 287 Q13
Otočac Croatia 44°53N 15°12E 199 D12
Otoineppu Japan 44°44N 142°16E 220 B11
Otok Croatia 43°42N 16°44E 199 E13
Otomavi = Korsakov Russia 46°36N 142°42E 215 E15
Oton Phil. 10°42N 122°29E 233 F4
Otopeni, Bucureşti ✈ (OTP) Romania 44°30N 26°11E 183 F11
Otorohanga N.Z. 38°12S 175°14E 284 E4
Otoskwin → Canada 52°13N 88°6W 298 B2
Ōtoyo Japan 33°43N 133°45E 222 D5
Otpor = Zabaykalsk Russia 49°40N 117°25E 215 E12
Otra → Norway 58°9N 8°1E 164 F5
Otradniy Russia 53°22N 51°21E 190 D10
Otranto Italy 40°9N 18°28E 201 B11
Otranto, C. d' Italy 40°7N 18°30E 201 B11
Otranto, Str. of Italy 40°15N 18°40E 201 B11
Otrobanda Curaçao 12°7N 68°57W 322 g
Otrokovice Czechia 49°12N 17°32E 181 B10
Otse S. Africa 25°2S 25°45E 270 C4
Otsego U.S.A. 42°27N 85°42W 311 B11
Otsego L. U.S.A. 42°45N 74°53W 313 D10
Ōtsu Japan 35°0N 135°50E 223 C7
Otsuka Japan 35°43N 139°44E 140 A3
Ōtsuki Japan 35°36N 138°57E 223 B10
Otta Norway 61°46N 9°32E 164 C6
Otta → Norway 61°46N 9°31E 164 C6
Ottakring Austria 48°12N 16°18E 142 A1
Ottapalam India 10°46N 76°23E 245 J3
Ottávia Italy 41°57N 12°24E 136 B1
Ottawa = Outaouais → Canada 45°27N 74°8W 298 C5
Ottawa Ont., Canada 45°26N 75°42W 313 A9
Ottawa Ill., U.S.A. 41°21N 88°51W 311 C8
Ottawa Kans., U.S.A. 38°37N 95°16W 308 F6
Ottawa Ohio, U.S.A. 41°1N 84°3W 311 C12
Ottawa Is. Canada 59°35N 80°10W 295 F15
Ottélé Cameroon 3°38N 11°19E 263 E7
Ottensheim Austria 48°21N 14°12E 180 C7
Otter Cr. → U.S.A. 44°13N 73°17W 313 B11
Otter Creek U.S.A. 29°19N 82°46W 317 F7
Otter Lake Canada 45°17N 79°56W 312 A5
Otterbäcken Sweden 58°57N 14°3E 163 F8
Otterbein U.S.A. 40°29N 87°6W 311 D9
Otterndorf Germany 53°48N 8°53E 178 B4
Otterøya Norway 62°45N 6°50E 164 B3
Otterup Denmark 55°30N 10°22E 163 J4
Otterville Ont., Canada 42°55N 80°36W 312 D4
Otterville Mo., U.S.A. 38°42N 93°0W 310 F4
Ottery S. Africa 34°1S 18°32E 118 B2
Ottery St. Mary U.K. 50°44N 3°17W 169 G4
Ottilien Reef Papua N. G. 4°33S 148°49E 286 C5
Ottmachau = Otmuchów Poland 50°28N 17°10E 185 H4
Otto Beit Bridge Zimbabwe 15°59S 28°56E 269 F2
Ottobrunn Germany 48°3N 11°40E 131 B3
Ottosdal S. Africa 26°46S 25°59E 270 C4
Ottoville U.S.A. 40°57N 84°22W 311 D12
Ottumwa U.S.A. 41°1N 92°25W 310 D4
Otukpa Nigeria 7°9N 7°41E 263 D6
Otuquis △ Bolivia 19°45S 58°44W 331 D6
Oturkpo Nigeria 7°16N 8°8E 263 D6
Otvazhnoye = Zhigulevsk Russia 53°28N 49°30E 190 D9
Otvazhny = Zhigulevsk Russia 53°28N 49°30E 190 D9
Otway, B. Chile 53°30S 74°0W 336 D2
Otway, C. Australia 38°52S 143°30E 282 E5
Otway, Seno de Chile 53°0S 71°30W 336 D2
Otway △ Australia 38°47S 143°34E 282 E5
Otwock Poland 52°5N 21°20E 185 F8
Otyniya Ukraine 48°44N 24°51E 183 B9
Ötztaler Ache → Austria 47°14N 10°50E 180 D3
Ötztaler Alpen Austria 46°56N 11°0E 180 E3
Ou → Laos 20°4N 102°13E 236 B4
Ou-Sammyaku Japan 39°20N 140°35E 220 E10
Ouachita → U.S.A. 31°38N 91°49W 314 F9
Ouachita, L. U.S.A. 34°34N 93°12W 314 D8
Ouachita Mts. U.S.A. 34°30N 94°30W 314 D7
Ouadâne Mauritania 20°50N 11°40W 260 D2
Ouadda C.A.R. 8°15N 22°20E 264 A4
Ouaddaï □ Chad 13°0N 21°0E 259 F4
Ouagadougou Burkina Faso 12°25N 1°30W 263 C4
Ouahigouya Burkina Faso 13°31N 2°25W 262 C4
Ouahran = Oran Algeria 35°45N 0°39W 261 A4
Ouaka □ C.A.R. 6°30N 21°0E 264 A4
Ouaka → C.A.R. 4°59N 19°56E 264 B3
Oualâta Mauritania 17°20N 6°55W 262 B3
Ouallah Comoros Is. 12°19S 43°39E 272 a
Ouallam Niger 14°23N 2°10E 263 C5
Ouallene Algeria 24°41N 1°11E 261 D5
Ouanary Fr. Guiana 4°13N 51°40W 329 C7
Ouanda Djallé C.A.R. 8°55N 22°53E 264 A4
Ouandago C.A.R. 7°13N 18°50E 264 A3
Ouandja C.A.R. 8°28N 23°17E 264 A4
Ouandjia, Bahr → C.A.R. 9°35N 21°43E 264 A4
Ouandjia-Vakaga ⌂ C.A.R. 9°2N 22°18E 264 A4
Ouangani Mayotte 12°50S 45°8E 272 b
Ouango C.A.R. 4°19N 22°30E 264 B4
Ouani Comoros Is. 12°9S 44°18E 272 a
Ouantonou C.A.R. 7°19N 15°18E 264 A3
Ouarâne Mauritania 21°0N 10°30W 260 D2
Ouargaye Burkina Faso 11°40N 0°5E 263 C5
Ouargla Algeria 31°59N 5°16E 261 B6
Ouargla □ Algeria 30°30N 6°10E 261 B6
Ouarkoye Burkina Faso 12°5N 3°40W 262 C4
Ouarkziz, Jebel Algeria 28°50N 8°0W 260 C3
Ouarra → C.A.R. 5°5N 24°26E 264 A4
Ouarzazate Morocco 30°55N 6°50W 260 B3
Ouassouas Mali 16°10N 1°23E 263 B5
Ouatagouna Mali 15°11N 0°43E 263 B5
Ouatere C.A.R. 5°30N 19°8E 264 A3
Oubangi → Dem. Rep. of the Congo 0°30S 17°50E 264 C3
Oubarakai, O. → Algeria 27°20N 9°0E 261 C6
Ouche → France 47°6N 5°16E 173 E12
Oud Zuid Amsterdam, Neths. 112 c1
Ouddorp Neths. 51°50N 3°57E 170 C3
Oude Kerk Amsterdam, Neths. 112 a2
Oude Rijn → Neths. 52°12N 4°24E 170 B4
Oudeïka Mali 17°30N 1°40W 263 B4
Oudenaarde Belgium 50°50N 3°37E 170 D3
Ouderkerk Neths. 52°18N 4°55E 112 B2
Oudon → France 47°41N 0°53W 172 E6
Oudtshoorn S. Africa 33°35S 22°14E 270 D3
Oued Zem Morocco 32°52N 6°34W 260 B3
Ouégoa N. Cal. 20°20S 164°26E 288 d
Oueita Chad 17°47N 20°39E 259 E4
Ouella Niger 14°48N 3°38E 263 C5
Ouellé Ivory C. 7°26N 4°1W 262 D4
Ouémé → Benin 6°30N 2°30E 263 D5
Ouenza Algeria 35°57N 8°4E 261 A6
Ouessa Burkina Faso 11°4N 2°47W 262 C4
Ouessant, Î. d' France 48°28N 5°6W 172 D1
Ouesso Congo 1°37N 16°5E 264 B3
Ouest □ Cameroon 5°30N 10°30E 263 D7
Ouest, Pte. de l' Canada 49°52N 64°40W 299 C7
Ouezzane Morocco 34°51N 5°35W 260 B3
Ougarou Burkina Faso 12°10N 0°58E 263 C5
Oughter, L. Ireland 54°1N 7°28W 166 B4
Oughterard Ireland 53°26N 9°18W 166 C2
Ouham □ C.A.R. 7°0N 17°30E 264 A3
Ouham → C.A.R. 6°35N 15°12E 264 A3
Ouham → Chad 9°18N 18°14E 259 G3
Ouham-Pendé □ C.A.R. 7°0N 16°0E 264 A3
Ouidah Benin 6°25N 2°0E 263 D5
Ouidi Niger 14°10N 13°0E 259 F2
Ouistreham France 49°17N 0°18W 172 C6
Oujda Morocco 34°41N 1°55W 261 B4
Oujeft Mauritania 20°2N 13°0W 260 D2
Oulad-Teïma Morocco 30°24N 9°12W 260 B3
Oulainen Finland 64°17N 24°47E 160 D21
Oulanka △ Finland 66°26N 29°25E 160 C23
Ould Yenjé Mauritania 15°38N 12°16W 262 B2
Ouled Djellal Algeria 34°28N 5°2E 261 B6
Ouled Naïl, Mts. des Algeria 34°30N 3°30E 261 B5
Ouli Cameroon 5°12N 14°33E 264 A2
Oullins France 45°43N 4°49E 175 C8
Oulmès Morocco 33°17N 6°0W 260 B3
Oulou, Bahr → C.A.R. 9°48N 21°32E 264 A4
Oulu Finland 65°1N 25°29E 160 D21
Oulujärvi Finland 64°25N 27°15E 160 D22
Oulujoki → Finland 65°1N 25°30E 160 D21
Oulunkylä Finland 60°13N 24°58E 121 B2
Oulx Italy 45°2N 6°50E 198 C3
Oum Chalouba Chad 15°48N 20°46E 259 E4
Oum-el-Bouaghi Algeria 35°55N 7°6E 261 A6
Oum-el-Bouaghi □ Algeria 35°50N 7°5E 261 A6
Oum el Ksi Algeria 29°4N 6°59W 260 C3
Oum-er-Rbia, O. → Morocco 33°19N 8°21W 260 B3
Oum Hadjer Chad 13°18N 19°41E 259 F3
Oum Hadjer, O. → Chad 16°38N 20°14E 259 E4
Oumé Ivory C. 6°21N 5°27W 262 D3
Oumm ed Droûs Guebli, Sebkhet Mauritania 24°3N 11°45W 260 D2
Oumm ed Droûs Telli, Sebkhet Mauritania 24°20N 11°30W 260 D2
Ounane, Dj. Algeria 25°4N 7°19E 261 C6
Ounasjoki → Finland 66°31N 25°40E 160 C21
Ounguati Namibia 22°0S 15°46E 270 B2
Ounianga Kébir Chad 19°4N 20°29E 259 E4
Ounianga Sérir Chad 18°54N 20°51E 259 E4
Ounissoui Niger 17°34N 12°13E 259 E2
Our → Lux. 49°55N 6°5E 170 E6
Oura, Akra Greece 38°10N 26°2E 205 C8
Oura-wan Japan 26°32N 128°4E 288 a
Ouranoupoli Greece 40°20N 23°59E 202 F7
Ourârene Niger 19°30N 7°10E 263 B6
Ourari, Tarso Chad 21°27N 17°27E 259 D3
Ouray U.S.A. 38°1N 107°40W 305 G10
Ourcq → France 49°1N 3°1E 173 C10
Ourcq, Canal de l' France 48°54N 2°28E 134 A3
Ourém Brazil 1°33S 47°6W 332 B2
Ourém Portugal 39°40N 8°35W 194 F2
Ourense Spain 42°19N 7°55W 194 C3
Ourense □ Spain 42°15N 7°51W 194 C3
Ouricuri Brazil 7°53S 40°5W 332 C3
Ourinhos Brazil 23°0S 49°54W 335 A6
Ourique Portugal 37°38N 8°16W 195 H2
Ouro Fino Brazil 22°16S 46°25W 335 A6
Ouro-Ndia Mali 15°8N 4°35W 262 B4
Ouro Prêto Brazil 20°20S 43°30W 333 F3
Ouro Prêto do Oeste Brazil 10°40S 62°18W 331 C5
Ouro Sogui Senegal 15°36N 13°19W 262 B2
Oursi Burkina Faso 14°41N 0°27W 263 C4
Ourthe → Belgium 50°29N 5°35E 170 D5
Ouse → E. Sussex, U.K. 50°47N 0°4E 169 G8
Ouse → N. Yorks., U.K. 53°44N 0°55W 168 D7
Oust France 42°52N 1°13E 174 F5
Oust → France 47°35N 2°6W 172 E4
Outamba-Kilimi △ S. Leone 9°50N 12°40W 262 D2
Outaouais → Canada 45°27N 74°8W 298 C5
Outapi Namibia 17°30S 15°0E 270 A2
Outardes → Canada 49°24N 69°30W 299 C6
Outat Oulad el Haj Morocco 33°22N 3°42W 261 B4
Outeiro de Rei Spain 43°6N 7°36W 194 B3
Outer Hebrides U.K. 57°30N 7°15W 167 D1
Outer Mission U.S.A. 37°43N 122°26W 136 B2
Outes = A Serra de Outes Spain 42°52N 8°55W 194 C2
Outjo Namibia 20°5S 16°7E 270 B2
Outlook Canada 51°30N 107°0W 297 C7
Outokumpu Finland 62°43N 29°1E 160 E23
Outreau France 50°40N 1°36E 173 B8
Outremont Canada 45°31N 73°36W 130 A2
Ouvéa, Î. N. Cal. 20°35S 166°35E 288 d
Ouvèze → France 43°59N 4°51E 175 E8
Ouyen Australia 35°1S 142°22E 282 C5
Ouzinkie U.S.A. 57°56N 152°30W 303 H9
Ouzouer-le-Marché France 47°54N 1°32E 173 E8
Ovacık Turkey 36°11N 33°40E 250 B4
Ovada Italy 44°38N 8°38E 198 D5
Ovahe Chile 27°5S 109°19W 330 b
Ovalau Fiji 17°40S 178°48E 287 A2
Ovalle Chile 30°33S 71°18W 334 C1
Ovamboland Namibia 18°30S 16°0E 270 A2
Ovan Gabon 0°19N 12°10E 264 B2
Ovanåker Sweden 61°22N 15°53E 162 C9
Ovar Portugal 40°51N 8°40W 194 E2
Ovau Solomon Is. 6°40S 156°8E 287 L9
Overath Germany 50°56N 7°17E 178 E3
Overflakkee Neths. 51°44N 4°10E 170 C4
Overijse Belgium 50°47N 4°32E 116 B3
Overijssel □ Neths. 52°25N 6°35E 170 B6
Overland U.S.A. 38°42N 90°21W 310 F6
Overland Park U.S.A. 38°58N 94°40W 308 F6
Overlander Roadhouse Australia 26°19S 114°28E 279 E1
Overton U.S.A. 36°33N 114°27W 307 J12
Övertorneå Sweden 66°23N 23°38E 160 C20
Överum Sweden 58°0N 16°20E 163 F10
Ovid Mich., U.S.A. 43°1N 84°22W 311 A12
Ovid N.Y., U.S.A. 42°41N 76°49W 313 D8
Ovidiopol Ukraine 46°15N 30°30E 189 J6
Ovidiu Romania 44°16N 28°34E 183 F13
Oviedo Spain 43°25N 5°50W 194 B5
Oviedo Fla., U.S.A. 28°40N 81°13W 317 G8
Oviksfjällen Sweden 63°0N 13°49E 162 A7
Ovišrags Latvia 57°33N 21°44E 184 A8
Ovoot Mongolia 45°21N 113°45E 226 B7
Övör Hangay □ Mongolia 45°0N 102°30E 226 B2
Ovoro Nigeria 5°26N 7°16E 263 D6
Øvre Anárjohka △ Norway 68°30N 24°40E 160 B21
Øvre Årdal Norway 61°19N 7°48E 164 C4
Øvre Dividal △ Norway 68°43N 19°50E 160 B18
Övre Fryken Sweden 60°0N 13°7E 162 E7
Øvre Pasvik ⌂ Norway 69°6N 28°54E 160 B23
Øvre Rendal Norway 61°54N 11°4E 164 C8
Øvre Rindal Norway 63°6N 9°10E 164 A6
Øvre Sirdal Norway 58°48N 6°43E 164 F3
Ovruch Ukraine 51°25N 28°45E 177 C15
Owaka N.Z. 46°27S 169°40E 285 G4
Owambo = Ovamboland Namibia 18°30S 16°0E 270 A2
Owando Congo 0°29S 15°55E 264 C3
Owariasahi Japan 35°10N 137°5E 223 B9
Owasco L. U.S.A. 42°50N 76°31W 313 D8
Owase Japan 34°7N 136°12E 223 C8
Owatonna U.S.A. 44°5N 93°14W 308 C7
Owbeh Afghan. 34°28N 63°10E 240 B1
Owego U.S.A. 42°6N 76°16W 313 D8
Owen Australia 34°15S 138°32E 282 C3
Owen, Mt. N.Z. 41°35S 172°33E 285 B7
Owen Falls Dam = Nalubaale Dam Uganda 0°30N 33°5E 268 B3
Owen Sound Canada 44°35N 80°55W 312 B4
Owen Stanley Ra. Papua N. G. 8°30S 147°0E 286 E4
Owendo Gabon 0°17N 9°30E 264 B1
Oweniny → Ireland 54°8N 9°34W 166 B2
Owens → U.S.A. 36°32N 117°59W 306 J9
Owens L. U.S.A. 36°26N 117°57W 307 J9
Owensboro U.S.A. 37°46N 87°7W 311 G9
Owensville Ind., U.S.A. 38°16N 87°41W 311 F9
Owensville Mo., U.S.A. 38°21N 91°30W 310 F5
Owenteik Guyana 4°27N 59°35W 329 C6
Owenton U.S.A. 38°32N 84°50W 311 F12
Owerri Nigeria 5°29N 7°0E 263 D6
Owhango N.Z. 39°0S 175°23E 284 F4
Owingsville U.S.A. 38°9N 83°46W 311 F13
Owl → Canada 57°51N 92°44W 297 B10
Owo Nigeria 7°10N 5°39E 263 D6
Oworonsoki Nigeria 6°32N 3°24E 124 A2
Owosso U.S.A. 43°0N 84°10W 311 B12
Owyhee U.S.A. 41°57N 116°6W 304 F5
Owyhee → U.S.A. 43°49N 117°2W 304 E5
Owyhee, L. U.S.A. 43°38N 117°14W 304 E5
Ox Mts. = Slieve Gamph Ireland 54°6N 9°0W 166 B3
Oxapampa Peru 10°33S 75°26W 330 C2
Öxarfjörður Iceland 66°15N 16°45W 155 A10
Oxbow Canada 49°14N 102°10W 297 D8
Oxelösund Sweden 58°43N 17°5E 163 F11
Oxford N.Z. 43°18S 172°11E 285 D7
Oxford Oxon., U.K. 51°46N 1°15W 169 F6
Oxford Ala., U.S.A. 33°36N 85°51W 316 B4
Oxford Iowa, U.S.A. 41°43N 91°47W 310 C5
Oxford Mass., U.S.A. 42°7N 71°52W 313 D13
Oxford Mich., U.S.A. 42°49N 83°16W 311 B13
Oxford Miss., U.S.A. 34°22N 89°31W 315 D10
Oxford N.C., U.S.A. 36°19N 78°35W 315 C15
Oxford N.Y., U.S.A. 42°27N 75°36W 313 D9
Oxford Ohio, U.S.A. 39°31N 84°45W 311 E12
Oxford L. Canada 54°51N 95°37W 297 C9
Oxford Street London, U.K. 125 b3
Oxfordshire □ U.K. 51°48N 1°16W 169 F6
Oxgangs U.K. 55°54N 3°13W 121 B2
Oxia Greece 38°18N 21°6E 207 C3
Oxie Sweden 55°33N 13°6E 163 J7
Oxilithos Greece 38°35N 24°7E 204 C6
Oxley Australia 34°11S 144°6E 282 C6
Oxley Wild Rivers △ Australia 30°57S 152°12E 283 A10
Oxnard U.S.A. 34°12N 119°11W 307 L7
Oxon Hill U.S.A. 38°48N 76°59W 143 C3
Oxsjövålen Sweden 62°34N 13°57E 162 B7
Oxus = Amudarya → Uzbekistan 43°58N 59°34E 216 D5
Oya Malaysia 2°55N 111°55E 235 B4
Oyabe Japan 36°47N 136°56E 223 A8
Oyala Eq. Guin. 1°35N 10°49E 264 B2
Oyama Japan 36°18N 139°48E 223 A11
Oyambre ⌂ Spain 43°22N 4°21W 194 B6
Oyapock → Fr. Guiana 4°8N 51°40W 329 C7
Øye Norway 58°16N 6°49E 164 F3
Oyem Gabon 1°34N 11°31E 264 B2
Oyen Canada 51°22N 110°28W 297 C6
Øyer Norway 61°16N 10°25E 164 C7
Øyeren Norway 59°50N 11°15E 164 E8
Oykel → U.K. 57°56N 4°26W 167 D4
Oymyakon Russia 63°25N 142°44E 215 C15
Oyo Congo 0°0 15°51E 264 C3
Oyo Nigeria 7°46N 3°56E 263 D5
Oyo Sudan 21°58N 36°10E 256 C4
Oyo □ Nigeria 8°15N 3°30E 263 D5
Oyodo Japan 34°42N 135°29E 133 A1
Oyón Peru 10°37S 76°47W 330 C2
Oyonnax France 46°16N 5°40E 173 F12
Oyrot = Gorno-Altay □ Russia 51°0N 86°0E 217 B11
Oyrot-Tura = Gorno-Altaysk Russia 51°50N 86°5E 217 B11
Øyslebø Norway 58°9N 7°34E 164 F4

Oyster Harbour = Ladysmith *Canada* 49°0N 123°49W **306** B3
Oyster Rock *India* 18°54N 72°49E **130** B1
Oyster Rocks *Pakistan* 24°48N 66°59E **123** B2
Øystese *Norway* 60°22N 6°9E **164** D3
Ōyūbari *Japan* 43°1N 142°5E **220** C11
Oyyl → *Kazakhstan* 49°4N 54°40E **216** C4
Özalp *Turkey* 38°39N 43°59E **213** C10
Ozamiz *Phil.* 8°15N 123°50E **233** G4
Ozar = Ojhar *India* 20°6N 73°56E **244** D1
Ozark *Ala., U.S.A.* 31°28N 85°39W **316** D4
Ozark *Ark., U.S.A.* 35°29N 93°50W **314** D8
Ozark *Mo., U.S.A.* 37°1N 93°12W **308** G7
Ozark Plateau *U.S.A.* 37°20N 91°40W **308** G8
Ozarks, L. of the *U.S.A.* 38°12N 92°38W **310** F4
Ożarów *Poland* 50°53N 21°40E **185** H8
Ózd *Hungary* 48°14N 20°15E **182** B5
Ozernovskiy *Russia* 51°30N 156°31E **215** D16
Ozernoye *Russia* 51°46N 51°28E **190** E10
Ozersk *Russia* 54°25N 22°0E **184** D8
Ozette, L. *U.S.A.* 48°6N 124°38W **306** B2
Ozieri *Italy* 40°35N 9°0E **200** B2
Ozimek *Poland* 50°41N 18°11E **185** H5
Ozinki *Russia* 51°12N 49°44E **190** E9
Ozoir-la-Ferrière *France* 48°46N 2°40E **134** B4
Ozona *U.S.A.* 30°43N 101°12W **314** F4
Ozone Park *U.S.A.* 40°40N 73°50W **132** B2
Ozorków *Poland* 51°57N 19°16E **185** G6
Ozren *Bos.-H.* 43°55N 18°29E **182** G3
Ōzu *Ehime, Japan* 33°30N 132°33E **222** D4
Ōzu *Kumamoto, Japan* 32°52N 130°52E **222** E2
Ozuluama *Mexico* 21°40N 97°51W **319** C5
Ozun *Romania* 45°47N 25°50E **183** E10
Ozurgeti *Georgia* 41°55N 42°0E **191** K5

P

Pa *Burkina Faso* 11°33N 3°19W **262** C4
Pa-an *Burma* 16°51N 97°40E **241** G6
Pa Mong Dam *Thailand* 18°0N 102°22E **236** D4
Pa Sak → *Thailand* 15°30N 101°0E **236** E3
Paama *Vanuatu* 16°28S 168°14E **287** F6
Paamiut *Greenland* 62°0N 49°43W **154** E16
Paanayarvi △ *Russia* 66°16N 30°10E **160** C24
Paar → *Germany* 48°46N 11°36E **179** G7
Paarl *S. Africa* 33°45S 18°56E **270** D2
Pa'auilo *U.S.A.* 20°2N 155°22W **302** C6
Pab Hills *Pakistan* 26°30N 66°45E **242** F2
Pabaidh = Pabbay *U.K.* 57°46N 7°14W **167** D1
Pabbay *U.K.* 57°46N 7°14W **167** D1
Pabean *Indonesia* 6°49S 115°19E **235** D5
Pabianice *Poland* 51°40N 19°20E **185** G6
Pabna *Bangla.* 24°1N 89°18E **241** C2
Pabo *Uganda* 3°1N 32°10E **268** B3
Pacaás Novos, Serra dos *Brazil* 10°45S 64°15W **331** C5
Pacaás Novos △ *Brazil* 11°0S 63°0W **331** C5
Pacaipampa *Peru* 5°35S 79°39W **330** B2
Pacaja → *Brazil* 1°56S 50°50W **332** B1
Pacajus *Brazil* 4°10S 38°31W **332** B4
Pacaraima, Sa. *S. Amer.* 4°0N 62°30W **329** C5
Pacarán *Peru* 12°50S 76°3W **330** C2
Pacaraos *Peru* 11°12S 76°42W **330** C2
Pacasmayo *Peru* 7°20S 79°35W **330** B2
Pace *U.S.A.* 30°36N 87°10W **317** E2
Paceco *Italy* 37°59N 12°33E **200** E5
Pachacamac *Peru* 12°14S 77°53W **330** C2
Pachang Hsi → *Taiwan* 23°20N 120°7E **225** C2
Pachao Yü *Taiwan* 23°22N 119°29E **225** C1
Pachia *Greece* 36°17N 25°50E **205** E7
Pachino *Italy* 36°43N 15°5E **201** F8
Pachitea → *Peru* 8°46S 74°33W **330** B3
Pachiza *Peru* 7°16S 76°46W **330** B2
Pachmarhi *India* 22°28N 78°26E **243** H8
Pachnai *India* 26°57N 92°19E **241** B4
Pachnes *Greece* 35°16N 24°4E **207** E5
Pacho *Colombia* 5°8N 74°10W **328** B3
Pachora *India* 20°38N 75°29E **244** D2
Pachpadra *India* 25°58N 72°10E **242** G5
Pachuca *Mexico* 20°7N 98°44W **319** C5
Pacific *U.S.A.* 38°29N 90°45W **310** F6
Pacific Antarctic Ridge *Pac. Oc.* 43°0S 115°0W **151** B13
Pacific City = Huntington Beach *U.S.A.* 33°40N 118°5W **307** M9
Pacific Grove *U.S.A.* 36°38N 121°56W **306** J5
Pacific Heights *U.S.A.* 37°47N 122°26W **136** B2
Pacific Manor *U.S.A.* 37°38N 122°27W **136** C2
Pacific Ocean 10°0N 140°0W **289** G14
Pacific Palisades *Calif., U.S.A.* 34°2N 118°32W **126** B1
Pacific Palisades *Hawai'i, U.S.A.* 21°25N 157°58W **302** K14
Pacific Rim △ *Canada* 48°40N 124°45W **306** B2
Pacifica *U.S.A.* 37°37N 122°27W **136** C2
Pacitan *Indonesia* 8°12S 111°7E **235** D4
Packsaddle *Australia* 30°36S 141°58E **282** A4
Packwood *U.S.A.* 46°36N 121°40W **306** D5
Paco *Phil.* 14°35N 120°59E **127** B1
Paco de Arcos *Portugal* 38°41N 9°17W **126** A1
Paço Imperial *Rio de J., Brazil* **135** a2
Pacov *Czechia* 49°27N 15°0E **180** B8
Pacoval *Brazil* 2°40S 54°11W **329** D7
Pacuí → *Brazil* 16°46S 45°1W **333** E2
Pacy-sur-Eure *France* 49°1N 1°23E **172** C8
Padaido, Kepulauan *Indonesia* 1°15S 136°30E **231** E9
Padali = Amursk *Russia* 50°14N 136°54E **215** D14
Padampur *India* 20°59N 83°4E **244** D6
Padang *Kalimantan Barat, Indonesia* 1°39S 108°55E **235** C3
Padang *Riau, Indonesia* 1°30N 102°30E **237** M4
Padang *Sumatera Barat, Indonesia* 1°0S 100°20E **234** C2
Padang Endau *Malaysia* 2°40N 103°38E **237** L4
Padang Lawas *Indonesia* 1°40N 99°56E **234** B1
Padangpanjang *Indonesia* 0°40S 100°20E **234** C2
Padangsidempuan *Indonesia* 1°30N 99°15E **234** B1
Padangtikar *Indonesia* 0°44S 109°15E **235** C3
Padauari → *Brazil* 0°15S 64°5W **329** D5
Padaung *Burma* 18°43N 95°9E **241** F5
Padborg *Denmark* 54°49N 9°21E **163** K3
Padcaya *Bolivia* 21°52S 64°48W **331** E5
Paddington *N.S.W., Australia* 33°53S 151°14E **139** B2
Paddington *London, U.K.* **125** b2
Paddle Prairie *Canada* 57°57N 117°29W **296** B5
Paderborn *Germany* 51°42N 8°45E **178** D4
Paderno *Italy* 45°33N 9°9E **128** A1
Paderoo *India* 18°5N 82°40E **244** E6
Padeş, Vf. *Romania* 45°40N 22°22E **182** E7
Padilla *Bolivia* 19°19S 64°20W **331** D5
Padina *Romania* 44°50N 27°8E **183** F12
Padjelanta △ *Sweden* 67°20N 16°35E **160** C17
Padma *India* 24°12N 85°22E **243** G11
Padma → *Bangla.* 23°22N 90°32E **241** D3
Pádova *Italy* 45°25N 11°53E **199** C8
Padra *India* 22°15N 73°7E **242** H5
Padrão, Pta. *Angola* 6°5S 12°20E **265** D2
Padrauna *India* 26°54N 83°59E **243** F10
Padre I. *U.S.A.* 27°10N 97°25W **314** H6
Padre Island ⌂ *U.S.A.* 27°0N 97°25W **314** H6
Padrón *Spain* 42°41N 8°39W **194** C2
Padstow *U.K.* 50°33N 4°58W **169** G3
Padthaway *Australia* 36°36S 140°31E **282** D4
Padua = Pádova *Italy* 45°25N 11°53E **199** C8
Paducah *Ky., U.S.A.* 37°5N 88°37W **308** G9
Paducah *Tex., U.S.A.* 34°1N 100°18W **314** D4
Padukka *Sri Lanka* 6°50N 80°5E **245** L5
Padul *Spain* 37°1N 3°38W **195** H7
Padwa *India* 18°27N 82°47E **244** E6
Paea *Tahiti* 17°41S 149°35W **289** e
Paekakariki *N.Z.* 40°59S 174°58E **284** G3
Paektu-san *N. Korea* 41°59N 128°4E **224** B4
Paengaroa *N.Z.* 37°49S 176°29E **284** D5
Paeroa *N.Z.* 37°23S 175°41E **284** D4
Paesana *Italy* 44°41N 7°16E **198** D4
Pafete *Phil.* 14°23N 121°29E **232** D3
Pafúri *Mozam.* 22°28S 31°17E **271** B5
Pag *Croatia* 44°25N 15°3E **199** D12
Paga *Gabon* 0°45S 10°21E **264** C2
Paga *Ghana* 11°1N 1°8W **263** C4
Pagadian *Phil.* 7°55N 123°30E **233** H4
Pagai Selatan, Pulau *Indonesia* 3°0S 100°15E **234** C2
Pagai Utara, Pulau *Indonesia* 2°35S 100°0E **234** C2
Pagalu = Annobón *Atl. Oc.* 1°25S 5°36E **255** G4
Pagalungan *Phil.* 7°4N 124°41E **233** H5
Pagan *Burma* 21°10N 94°52E **241** E5
Pagan *N. Marianas* 18°7N 145°46E **302** a
Pagara *India* 24°22N 80°1E **243** G9
Pagaralam *Indonesia* 4°1S 103°16E **234** C2
Pagasa I. = Thitu I. *S. China Sea* 11°3N 114°17E **230** B4
Pagastikos Kolpos *Greece* 39°15N 23°0E **204** B5
Pagatan *Indonesia* 3°33S 115°59E **235** C5
Page *U.S.A.* 36°57N 111°27W **305** H8
Pagėgiai *Lithuania* 55°9N 21°54E **184** C8
Pageri *Papua N. G.* 3°2S 141°10E **286** B1
Pageri *South Sudan* 4°0N 32°0E **257** G3
Paget, Mt. *S. Georgia* 54°26S 36°31W **326** H6
Paget I. *India* 13°26N 92°50E **245** H11
Pagewood *Australia* 33°56S 151°14E **139** B2
Pago B. *Guam* 13°25N 144°47E **302** d
Pago Pago *Amer. Samoa* 14°16S 170°43W **302** f
Pago Pago Harbor *Amer. Samoa* 14°17S 170°40W **302** f
Pagosa Springs *U.S.A.* 37°16N 107°1W **305** H10
Pagote *India* 18°53N 72°59E **130** B2
Pagri *China* 27°45N 89°10E **218** F6
Pagsanjan *Phil.* 14°16N 121°27E **232** D3
Pagua B. *Dominica* 15°32N 61°17W **323** k
Pagudpud *Phil.* 18°34N 120°47E **232** B3
Pagwa River *Canada* 50°2N 85°14W **298** B2
Pagwi *Papua N. G.* 4°4S 143°2E **286** C2
Pāhala *U.S.A.* 19°12N 155°29W **302** D6
Pahang □ *Malaysia* 3°30N 102°45E **237** L4
Pahang → *Malaysia* 3°30N 103°9E **237** L4
Paharpur *Bangla.* 24°51N 88°44E **241** C2
Pahia Pt. *N.Z.* 46°20S 167°41E **285** G2
Pahiatua *N.Z.* 40°27S 175°50E **284** G4
Pāhoa *U.S.A.* 19°30N 154°57W **302** D7
Pahokee *U.S.A.* 26°50N 80°40W **317** J9
Pahrump *U.S.A.* 36°12N 115°59W **307** J11
Pahute Mesa *U.S.A.* 37°20N 116°45W **306** H10
Pai *Thailand* 19°19N 98°27E **236** C2
Pai, I. do *Brazil* 22°59S 43°5W **135** B2
Paia *U.S.A.* 20°54N 156°22W **302** C5
Paichuan Liehtao *Taiwan* 25°58N 119°57E **225** b
Paicines *U.S.A.* 36°44N 121°17W **306** J5
Paide *Estonia* 58°53N 25°33E **188** C3
Paignton *U.K.* 50°26N 3°35W **169** G4
Paihia *N.Z.* 35°17S 174°6E **284** B3
Paiho *Taiwan* 23°21N 120°25E **225** C2
Paiján *Peru* 7°42S 79°20W **330** B2
Päijänne *Finland* 61°30N 25°30E **188** B3
Pailani *India* 25°45N 80°26E **243** G9
Pailin *Cambodia* 12°46N 102°36E **236** F4
Pailolo Channel *U.S.A.* 21°0N 156°40W **302** B5
Paimpol *France* 48°48N 3°4W **172** D3
Painan *Indonesia* 1°21S 100°34E **234** C2
Paine Grande, Cerro *Chile* 50°59S 73°4W **336** D2
Painesville *U.S.A.* 41°43N 81°15W **312** E3
Paint Hills = Wemindji *Canada* 53°0N 78°49W **298** B4
Paint L. *Canada* 55°28N 97°57W **297** B9
Painted Desert *U.S.A.* 36°0N 111°0W **305** H8
Paintsville *U.S.A.* 37°49N 82°48W **309** G12
País Vasco □ *Spain* 42°50N 2°45W **196** C2
Paisha *Taiwan* 23°40N 119°35E **225** C1
Paisley *Ont., Canada* 44°18N 81°16W **312** B3
Paisley *Renf., U.K.* 55°50N 4°25W **167** F4
Paisley *Oreg., U.S.A.* 42°42N 120°32W **304** E3
Païta *N. Cal.* 22°8S 166°22E **288** d
Paita *Peru* 5°11S 81°9W **330** B1
Paithan *India* 19°29N 75°23E **244** E2
Paiva → *Portugal* 41°4N 8°16W **194** D2
Paizhou *China* 30°12N 113°55E **229** B9
Pajá, Cerro *Ecuador* 1°17S 90°26W **330** a
Pájara *Canary Is.* 28°21N 14°6W **153** e2
Pajares *Spain* 43°1N 5°46W **194** B5
Pajares, Puerto de *Spain* 42°58N 5°46W **194** C5
Pajarito *Colombia* 5°17N 72°43W **328** B3
Pajęczno *Poland* 51°10N 19°0E **185** G5
Paju *S. Korea* 37°45N 126°46E **224** D3
Pak Kok *Hong Kong, China* 22°14N 114°7E **122** B2
Pak Kong *Hong Kong, China* 22°22N 114°15E **122** A3
Pak Lay *Laos* 18°15N 101°27E **236** C3
Pak Ou *Laos* 20°3N 102°12E **236** B4
Pak Phanang *Thailand* 8°21N 100°12E **237** H3
Pak Sane *Laos* 18°22N 103°39E **236** C4
Pak Song *Laos* 15°11N 106°14E **236** E6
Pak Suang *Laos* 19°58N 102°15E **228** H4
Pak Tam *Hong Kong, China* 22°25N 114°19E **122** A3
Pak Tam Chung *China* 22°24N 114°19E **219** a
Pak Thong Chai *Thailand* 14°43N 102°1E **236** E4
Pakala *India* 13°29N 79°8E **245** H4
Pakaraima Mts. *Guyana* 5°15N 60°0W **329** B6
Pakaur *India* 24°38N 87°51E **243** G12
Pakch'ŏn *N. Korea* 39°44N 125°35E **224** C2
Pakenham *Vic., Australia* 38°6S 145°30E **283** E6
Pakenham *Ont., Canada* 45°18N 76°18W **313** A8
Pakhoi = Beihai *China* 21°28N 109°6E **228** G7
Pakhuis *S. Africa* 32°9S 19°5E **270** D2
Pakila *Finland* 60°15N 24°55E **121** B2
Pakistan ■ *Asia* 30°0N 70°0E **242** E4
Pakkading *Laos* 18°19N 103°59E **236** C4
Paklay = Sayaboury *Laos* 19°15N 101°45E **236** C3
Paklenica △ *Croatia* 44°20N 15°29E **199** D12
Pakokku *Burma* 21°20N 95°0E **241** E5
Pakość *Poland* 52°48N 18°6E **185** F5
Pakowki L. *Canada* 49°20N 111°0W **297** D6
Pakpattan *Pakistan* 30°25N 73°27E **242** D5
Pakrac *Croatia* 45°27N 17°12E **182** E2
Pakruojis *Lithuania* 55°58N 23°52E **184** C10
Paks *Hungary* 46°38N 18°55E **182** D3
Paktīā □ *Afghan.* 33°30N 69°15E **240** B3
Paktīkā □ *Afghan.* 32°30N 69°0E **240** B3
Paku, Tanjung *Indonesia* 3°6S 106°31E **234** C3
Pakwach *Uganda* 2°28N 31°27E **268** B3
Pakxe *Laos* 15°5N 105°52E **236** E5
Pal Lahara *India* 21°27N 85°11E **243** J11
Pala *Chad* 9°25N 15°5E **259** G3
Pala *Dem. Rep. of the Congo* 6°45S 29°30E **268** D2
Pala *Calif., U.S.A.* 33°22N 117°5W **307** M9
Palabek *Uganda* 3°22N 32°33E **268** B3
Palacio Real *Madrid, Spain* **127** b1
Palacios *U.S.A.* 28°42N 96°13W **314** G6
Palafrugell *Spain* 41°55N 3°10E **196** D8
Palagiano *Italy* 40°35N 17°2E **201** B10
Palagonia *Italy* 37°19N 14°45E **201** E7
Palagruža *Croatia* 42°24N 16°15E **199** F13
Palais Royal *Brussels, Belgium* **116** b3
Palaiseau *France* 48°42N 2°14E **134** B2
Palakkad *India* 10°46N 76°42E **245** J3
Palakol *India* 16°31N 81°46E **245** F5
Palalankwe *India* 10°52N 92°29E **245** J11
Palam *India* 19°0N 77°0E **244** E3
Palamas *Greece* 39°26N 22°4E **204** B4
Palamós *Spain* 41°50N 3°10E **196** D8
Palampur *India* 32°10N 76°30E **242** C7
Palamut *Turkey* 38°59N 27°41E **205** C9
Palana *Tas., Australia* 39°45S 147°55E **281** F4
Palana *Russia* 59°10N 159°59E **215** D16
Palanan *Phil.* 17°8N 122°29E **232** C4
Palanan B. *Phil.* 17°9N 122°27E **232** C4
Palanan Pt. *Phil.* 17°17N 122°30E **232** C4
Palandri *Pakistan* 33°42N 73°40E **243** C5
Palanga *Lithuania* 55°58N 21°3E **184** C8
Palanganene *Dem. Rep. of the Congo* 6°32S 18°52E **265** D3
Palangkaraya *Indonesia* 2°16S 113°56E **235** C4
Palani *India* 10°30N 77°30E **245** J3
Palani Hills *India* 10°14N 77°33E **245** J3
Palanpur *India* 24°10N 72°25E **242** G5
Palaoa Pt. *U.S.A.* 20°44N 156°58W **302** C5
Palapag *Phil.* 12°33N 125°7E **232** E5
Palapye *Botswana* 22°30S 27°7E **270** B4
Palar → *India* 12°27N 80°13E **245** H5
Palas *Pakistan* 35°4N 73°14E **243** B5
Palas de Rei *Spain* 42°52N 7°52W **194** C3
Palasan I. *Phil.* 14°51N 122°2E **232** D4
Palasponga *India* 21°47N 85°34E **243** J11
Palatine *U.S.A.* 42°7N 88°3W **311** B8
Palatka *Russia* 60°6N 150°54E **215** C16
Palatka *Fla., U.S.A.* 29°39N 81°38W **316** F8
Palau *Italy* 41°11N 9°23E **200** A2
Palau ■ *Palau* 7°30N 134°30E **288** c
Palaui I. *Phil.* 18°32N 122°8E **232** B4
Palauk *Burma* 13°10N 98°40E **236** F2
Palaw *Burma* 12°58N 98°39E **236** F2
Palawan *Phil.* 9°30N 118°30E **233** G2
Palawan □ *Phil.* 10°0N 119°0E **233** G2
Palawan Passage *Phil.* 10°0N 118°0E **233** G2
Palayan *Phil.* 15°36N 121°8E **232** D3
Palayankottai *India* 8°45N 77°45E **245** K3
Palazze, Pte. *France* 42°28N 8°30E **175** F12
Palazzo San Gervásio *Italy* 40°56N 15°59E **201** B8
Palazzolo *Italy* 45°34N 9°9E **128** A1
Palazzolo Acréide *Italy* 37°4N 14°54E **201** F7
Palca *Chile* 19°7S 69°9W **330** D4
Paldiski *Estonia* 59°23N 24°9E **188** C3
Pale *Bos.-H.* 43°50N 18°38E **182** G3
Palekastro *Greece* 35°12N 26°15E **207** E7
Paleleh *Indonesia* 1°10N 121°50E **231** D6
Palembang *Indonesia* 3°0S 104°50E **234** C2
Palena → *Chile* 43°50S 73°50W **336** B2
Palena, L. *Chile* 43°55S 71°40W **336** B2
Palencia *Spain* 42°1N 4°34W **194** C6
Palencia □ *Spain* 42°31N 4°33W **194** C6
Paleng *Taiwan* 24°41N 121°23E **225** B3
Palenque *Mexico* 17°29N 92°1W **319** D6
Paleo Faliro *Greece* 37°53N 23°42E **112** B2
Paleochora *Greece* 35°16N 23°39E **207** E4
Paleokastritsa *Greece* 39°40N 19°41E **206** B9
Paleometokho *Cyprus* 35°7N 33°11E **207** E9
Paleopoli *Greece* 37°49N 24°50E **204** D6
Palermo *B. Aires, Argentina* 34°35S 58°24W **117** B2
Palermo *Colombia* 2°54N 75°26W **328** C2
Palermo *Italy* 38°7N 13°22E **200** D6
Palermo *Calif., U.S.A.* 39°26N 121°33W **306** F5
Palermo ✗ (PMO) *Italy* 38°11N 13°5E **200** D6
Paleros *Greece* 38°47N 20°53E **207** B2
Palestina = Jordânia *Brazil* 15°55S 40°11W **333** E3
Palestina *Chile* 23°50S 69°47W **334** A2
Palestine *Asia* 32°0N 35°0E **251** G6
Palestine *Ill., U.S.A.* 39°0N 87°37W **311** F9
Palestine *Tex., U.S.A.* 31°46N 95°38W **314** F7
Palestrina *Italy* 41°50N 12°53E **199** G9
Paletwa *Burma* 21°10N 92°50E **241** E4
Palghat = Palakkad *India* 10°46N 76°42E **245** J3
Palgrave, Mt. *Australia* 23°22S 115°58E **278** D2
Palhais *Portugal* 38°37N 9°2W **126** B2
Palhoça *Brazil* 27°38S 48°40W **335** B6
Pali *India* 25°50N 73°20E **242** G5
Pali *Taiwan* 25°8N 121°23E **225** A3
Pali-Aike △ *Chile* 52°6S 69°44W **336** D3
Palikea *U.S.A.* 21°26N 158°6W **302** K13
Palikir *Micronesia* 6°55N 158°9E **288** G7
Palimbang *Phil.* 6°12N 124°12E **233** H5
Palin, Mt. *Malaysia* 6°10N 117°10E **235** A5
Palinuro *Italy* 40°2N 15°17E **201** B8
Palinuro, C. *Italy* 40°2N 15°16E **201** B8
Paliouri, Akra *Greece* 39°57N 23°45E **202** G7
Palisades Park *U.S.A.* 40°50N 74°1W **132** A1
Palisades Res. *U.S.A.* 43°20N 111°12W **304** E8
Palisadoes, The *Jamaica* 17°57N 76°48W **320** a
Paliseul *Belgium* 49°54N 5°8E **170** E5
Palitana *India* 21°32N 71°49E **242** J4
Palizada *Mexico* 18°15N 92°5W **319** D6
Palk Bay *Asia* 9°30N 79°15E **245** K4
Palk Strait *Asia* 10°0N 79°45E **245** K4
Palkānah *Iraq* 35°49N 44°26E **246** C5
Palkonda *India* 18°36N 83°48E **244** E6
Palkonda Ra. *India* 13°50N 79°20E **245** H4
Palkot *India* 22°53N 84°39E **243** H11
Palla Road = Dinokwe *Botswana* 23°29S 26°37E **270** B4
Pallanza = Verbánia *Italy* 45°56N 8°33E **198** C5
Pallarenda *Australia* 19°12S 146°46E **280** B4
Pallas-Yllästunturi △ *Finland* 68°8N 24°15E **160** B21
Pallasovka *Russia* 50°4N 47°0E **190** E8
Palleru → *India* 16°45N 80°2E **244** F5
Pallës, Bishti i *Albania* 41°24N 19°24E **202** E3
Pallinup → *Australia* 34°27S 118°50E **279** F2
Pallisa *Uganda* 1°12N 33°43E **268** B3
Palliser, C. *N.Z.* 41°37S 175°14E **284** H4
Palliser, Îs. *French Polynesia* 15°30S 146°30W **289** f
Palliser B. *N.Z.* 41°26S 175°5E **284** H4
Pallu *India* 28°59N 74°14E **242** E6
Palm Bay *U.S.A.* 28°2N 80°35W **317** G9
Palm Beach *Aruba* 12°34N 70°2W **322** f
Palm Beach *Fla., U.S.A.* 26°43N 80°2W **317** J9
Palm Coast *U.S.A.* 29°35N 81°12W **317** F8
Palm Deira, The *U.A.E.* 25°17N 55°15E **119** A2
Palm Desert *U.S.A.* 33°43N 116°22W **307** M10
Palm-Grove △ *Australia* 24°57S 149°21E **280** C4
Palm Harbor *U.S.A.* 28°5N 82°46W **317** G7
Palm Is. *Australia* 18°40S 146°35E **280** B4
Palm Jumeirah, The *U.A.E.* 25°11N 55°11E **119** B1
Palm Springs *U.S.A.* 33°50N 116°33W **307** M10
Palm Valley *U.S.A.* 30°11N 81°23W **316** E8
Palma = Paraná *Brazil* 12°30S 47°48W **333** D2
Palma *Mozam.* 10°46S 40°29E **269** E5
Palma → *Brazil* 12°33S 47°52W **333** D2
Palma, B. de *Spain* 39°30N 2°39E **206** B3
Palma de Mallorca *Spain* 39°35N 2°39E **206** B3
Palma de Mallorca ✗ (PMI) *Spain* 39°34N 2°43E **197** F7
Palma del Río *Spain* 37°43N 5°17W **195** H5
Palma di Montechiaro *Italy* 37°11N 13°46E **200** E6
Palma Nova = Palmanova *Spain* 39°32N 2°34E **206** B3
Palma Soriano *Cuba* 20°15N 76°0W **320** B4
Palmaner *India* 13°12N 78°45E **245** H4
Palmanova *Spain* 39°32N 2°34E **206** B3
Palmares *Brazil* 8°41S 35°28W **332** C4
Palmarito *Venezuela* 7°37N 70°10W **328** B3
Palmarola *Italy* 40°56N 12°51E **200** B5
Palmas *Paraná, Brazil* 26°29S 52°0W **335** B5
Palmas *Tocantins, Brazil* 10°13S 48°16W **332** D2
Palmas, C. *Liberia* 4°27N 7°46W **262** E3
Pálmas, G. di *Italy* 39°0N 8°30E **200** D1
Palmas de Monte Alto *Brazil* 14°16S 43°10W **333** D3
Palmdale *Calif., U.S.A.* 34°35N 118°7W **307** L8
Palmdale *Fla., U.S.A.* 26°57N 81°19W **317** J8
Palmeira *Brazil* 25°25S 50°0W **333** G2
Palmeira das Missões *Brazil* 27°55S 53°17W **335** B5
Palmeira dos Índios *Brazil* 9°25S 36°37W **332** C4
Palmeirais *Brazil* 6°0S 43°0W **332** C3
Palmeiras *Brazil* 12°31S 41°34W **333** D3
Palmeiras → *Brazil* 12°22S 47°8W **333** D2
Palmeirinhas, Pta. das *Angola* 9°2S 12°57E **265** D2
Palmela *Portugal* 38°32N 8°57W **195** G2
Palmelo *Brazil* 17°20S 48°27W **333** E2
Palmer *Antarctica* 64°35S 65°0W **151** C17
Palmer *Alaska, U.S.A.* 61°36N 149°7W **303** F10
Palmer *Mass., U.S.A.* 42°9N 72°20W **313** D12
Palmer → *Australia* 16°0S 142°26E **280** B3
Palmer Arch. *Antarctica* 64°15S 65°0W **151** C17
Palmer Lake *U.S.A.* 39°7N 104°55W **304** G11
Palmer Land *Antarctica* 73°0S 63°0W **151** D18
Palmerston *N. Terr., Australia* 12°31S 130°59E **278** B5
Palmerston *Ont., Canada* 43°50N 80°51W **312** C4
Palmerston *N.Z.* 45°29S 170°43E **285** F5
Palmerston North *N.Z.* 40°21S 175°39E **284** G4
Palmerton *U.S.A.* 40°48N 75°37W **313** F9
Palmetto *Fla., U.S.A.* 27°31N 82°34W **317** H7
Palmetto *Ga., U.S.A.* 33°31N 84°40W **316** B5
Palmetto Pt. *Antigua & B.* 17°37N 61°51W **322** c
Palmetto Pt. *St. Kitts & Nevis* 17°18N 62°46W **322** d
Palmi *Italy* 38°21N 15°51E **201** D8
Palmira *Argentina* 32°59S 68°34W **334** C2
Palmira *Colombia* 3°32N 76°16W **328** C2
Palms *U.S.A.* 34°1N 118°24W **126** B2
Palmyra = Tudmur *Syria* 34°36N 38°15E **213** E8
Palmyra *Ill., U.S.A.* 39°26N 90°0W **310** E7
Palmyra *Mo., U.S.A.* 39°48N 91°32W **310** E5
Palmyra *N.J., U.S.A.* 40°0N 75°1W **313** F9
Palmyra *N.Y., U.S.A.* 43°5N 77°18W **312** C7
Palmyra *Pa., U.S.A.* 40°18N 76°36W **313** F8
Palmyra *Wis., U.S.A.* 42°52N 88°36W **311** B8
Palmyra Is. *Pac. Oc.* 5°52N 162°5W **289** G11
Palmyras = Santos Dumont *Brazil* 22°55S 43°10W **333** F3
Palmyras Pt. *India* 20°46N 87°1E **244** D8
Palo *Phil.* 11°10N 124°59E **233** F5
Palo Alto *U.S.A.* 37°27N 122°10W **306** H4
Palo Seco *Trin. & Tob.* 10°4N 61°36W **323** t
Palo Verde *U.S.A.* 33°26N 114°44W **307** M12
Palo Verde △ *Costa Rica* 10°21N 85°21W **320** D2
Paloh *Indonesia* 1°43N 109°18E **235** B3
Paloheinä *Finland* 60°15N 24°56E **121** B2
Paloich *South Sudan* 10°28N 32°32E **257** E3
Palomar Mt. *U.S.A.* 33°22N 116°50W **307** M10
Palomeras *Spain* 40°22N 3°39W **127** B2
Palompon *Phil.* 11°3N 124°23E **233** F5
Palopo *Indonesia* 3°0S 120°16E **231** E6
Palos, C. de *Spain* 37°38N 0°40W **197** H4
Palos de la Frontera *Spain* 37°14N 6°53W **195** H4
Palos Heights *U.S.A.* 41°39N 87°47W **119** D2
Palos Hills *U.S.A.* 41°42N 87°49W **119** C2
Palos Park *U.S.A.* 41°40N 87°50W **119** C1
Palos Verdes, Pt. *U.S.A.* 33°46N 118°25W **307** M8
Palos Verdes Estates *U.S.A.* 33°48N 118°23W **307** M8
Palpa *Peru* 14°30S 75°15W **330** C2
Palpara *India* 22°38N 88°22E **124** B2
Pålsboda *Sweden* 59°3N 15°22E **162** E9
Palu *Indonesia* 1°0S 119°52E **235** C5
Palu *Turkey* 38°45N 40°0E **213** C9
Paluan *Phil.* 13°26N 120°29E **232** E3
Paluke *Liberia* 5°2N 8°5W **262** D3
Paluma Ra. *Australia* 19°9S 146°22E **280** B4
Paluzza *Italy* 46°32N 13°1E **199** B10
Palwal *India* 28°8N 77°19E **242** E7
Pama *Burkina Faso* 11°19N 0°44E **263** C5
Pama → *C.A.R.* 4°23N 18°43E **264** B3
Pama ⌂ *Burkina Faso* 11°27N 0°40E **263** C5
Pamandzi *Mayotte* 12°47S 45°16E **272** b
Pamanukan *Indonesia* 6°16S 107°49E **235** D3
Pamban I. *India* 9°15N 79°20E **245** K4
Pamekasan *Indonesia* 7°10S 113°28E **235** D4
Pamenang *Indonesia* 8°24S 116°6E **231** J19
Pameungpeuk *Indonesia* 7°37S 107°43E **235** D3
Pamiers *France* 43°7N 1°39E **174** E5
Pamir *Tajikistan* 37°40N 73°0E **217** E8
Pamirsky Post = Murgap *Tajikistan* 38°10N 74°2E **217** E8
Pamlico → *U.S.A.* 35°20N 76°28W **315** D16
Pamlico Sd. *U.S.A.* 35°20N 76°0W **315** D17
Pampa *U.S.A.* 35°32N 100°58W **314** D4
Pampa de Agma *Argentina* 43°45S 69°40W **336** B3
Pampa de las Salinas *Argentina* 32°1S 66°58W **334** C2
Pampa Grande *Bolivia* 18°5S 64°6W **331** D5
Pampa Hermosa *Peru* 7°7S 75°4W **330** B2
Pampanga □ *Phil.* 15°4N 120°40E **232** D3
Pampanua *Indonesia* 4°16S 120°8E **231** E6
Pampas *Argentina* 35°0S 63°0W **334** D3
Pampas *Peru* 12°20S 74°50W **330** C3
Pampas → *Peru* 13°24S 73°12W **330** C3
Pampatar *Venezuela* 11°11N 63°48W **329** a
Pamphylia *Turkey* 37°0N 31°20E **250** B2
Pamplemousses *Mauritius* 20°6S 57°34E **272** e
Pamplona *Colombia* 7°23N 72°39W **328** B3
Pamplona *Phil.* 18°31N 121°20E **232** B3
Pamplona-Iruña *Spain* 42°48N 1°38W **196** C3
Pampoenpoort *S. Africa* 31°3S 22°40E **270** D3
Pamuk → *Turkey* 37°2N 34°29E **250** A5
Pamukçu *Turkey* 39°30N 27°54E **205** B9
Pamukkale *Turkey* 37°55N 29°8E **205** D11
Pan de Azúcar *Chile* 24°5S 68°10W **334** A2
Pan de Azúcar △ *Chile* 26°0S 70°40W **334** B1
Pan Xian *China* 25°46N 104°38E **228** E5
Pana *U.S.A.* 39°23N 89°5W **310** E7
Panabo *Phil.* 7°19N 125°42E **233** H5
Panaca *U.S.A.* 37°47N 114°23W **305** H6
Panacea *U.S.A.* 30°2N 84°23W **316** E5
Panadura *Sri Lanka* 6°47N 79°53E **245** L4
Panagyurishte *Bulgaria* 42°30N 24°15E **203** D8
Panaitan *Indonesia* 6°36S 105°12E **234** D3
Panajam *Indonesia* 1°15S 116°46E **235** C5
Panaji *India* 15°25N 73°50E **245** G1
Panamá *Panama* 9°0N 79°25W **320** c
Panamá *Sri Lanka* 6°45N 81°48E **245** L5
Panama ■ *Cent. Amer.* 8°48N 79°55W **320** E4
Panamá, G. de *Panama* 8°4N 79°20W **320** E4
Panama, Isthmus of *Cent. Amer.* 9°0N 79°0W **292** J12
Panama Basin *Pac. Oc.* 5°0N 83°30W **289** G19
Panama Canal *Panama* 9°10N 79°37W **320** c
Panama City *U.S.A.* 30°10N 85°40W **316** E4
Panama City Beach *U.S.A.* 30°11N 85°48W **316** E4
Panamint Range *U.S.A.* 36°20N 117°20W **307** J9
Panamint Springs *U.S.A.* 36°20N 117°28W **307** J9
Panão *Peru* 9°55S 75°55W **330** B2
Panaon I. *Phil.* 9°50N 125°13E **233** G5
Panare *Thailand* 6°51N 101°30E **237** J3
Panarea *Italy* 38°38N 15°4E **201** D8
Panaro → *Italy* 44°55N 11°25E **199** D8
Panay *Phil.* 11°10N 122°30E **233** F4
Panay G. *Phil.* 11°0N 122°30E **233** F4
Pančevo *Serbia* 44°52N 20°41E **182** F5
Panch'iao *Taiwan* 25°1N 121°27E **225** A3
Panchur *India* 22°32N 88°16E **124** B1
Panciu *Romania* 45°54N 27°8E **183** E12
Pancol *Phil.* 10°52N 119°25E **233** F2
Pancorbo, Desfiladero *Spain* 42°32N 3°5W **194** C7
Pâncota *Romania* 46°20N 21°45E **182** D6
Panda *Mozam.* 24°2S 34°45E **271** B5
Pandacan *Phil.* 14°35N 121°0E **127** B2
Pandan *Malaysia* 1°32N 103°46E **237** d
Pandan *Antique, Phil.* 11°45N 122°10E **233** F4
Pandan *Catanduanes, Phil.* 14°3N 124°10E **232** D5
Pandan, Selat *Singapore* 1°15N 103°44E **138** B2
Pandan B. *Phil.* 11°43N 122°0E **233** F4
Pandan Res. *Singapore* 1°18N 103°44E **138** B2
Pandan Tampoi = Tampoi *Malaysia* 1°30N 103°39E **237** d
Pandanan I. *Phil.* 8°17N 117°13E **233** G1
Pandegelang *Indonesia* 6°25S 106°5E **234** D3
Pandhana *India* 21°42N 76°13E **242** J7
Pandharkawada *India* 20°1N 78°32E **244** D4
Pandharpur *India* 17°41N 75°20E **244** F2
Pandhurna *India* 21°36N 78°35E **244** D4
Pando *Uruguay* 34°44S 56°0W **335** C4
Pando □ *Bolivia* 11°20S 67°40W **330** C4
Pando, L. = Hope, L. *Australia* 28°24S 139°18E **281** D2
Pandokratoras *Greece* 39°45N 19°50E **206** B9
Pandora *Costa Rica* 9°43N 83°3W **320** E3
Pandrup *Denmark* 57°14N 9°40E **163** G3
Pandu *Dem. Rep. of the Congo* 4°59N 19°16E **264** B3
Panepistimio *Athens, Greece* **112** b2
Panevéggio-Pale di San Martino ⌂ *Italy* 46°14N 11°46E **199** B8
Panevėžys *Lithuania* 55°42N 24°25E **188** E3
Panfilov = Zharkent *Kazakhstan* 44°10N 80°0E **217** D10
Panfilovo *Russia* 50°25N 42°46E **190** E6
Pang Sida △ *Thailand* 14°5N 102°17E **236** E4
Panga *Dem. Rep. of the Congo* 1°52N 26°18E **268** B2
Pangai *Tonga* 19°48S 174°21W **287** P13
Pangaíon Óros *Greece* 40°50N 24°0E **203** F8
Pangala *Congo* 3°16S 14°34E **264** C2
Pangalanes, Canal des = Ampangalana, Lakandranon' *Madag.* 22°48S 47°50E **272** C2
Pangandaran *Indonesia* 7°40S 108°39E **235** D3
Pangandaran △ *Indonesia* 7°43S 108°42E **235** D3
Pangani *Tanzania* 5°25S 38°58E **268** D4
Pangani → *Tanzania* 5°26S 38°58E **268** D4
Pangantocan *Phil.* 7°50N 124°49E **233** H5
Pangar Djerém ⌂ *Cameroon* 5°50N 13°10E **263** D7
Pangasinan □ *Phil.* 15°55N 120°20E **232** D3
Pangfou = Bengbu *China* 32°58N 117°20E **229** A11
Pangga, Tanjung *Indonesia* 8°54S 116°2E **231** K19
Panghsang = Bangkang *Burma* 22°4N 99°1E **228** F2
Pangil *Dem. Rep. of the Congo* 3°10S 26°35E **268** C2
Pangjiabu *China* 40°38N 115°26E **226** D8
Pangkah, Tanjung *Indonesia* 6°51S 112°33E **235** D4
Pangkai *Burma* 22°49N 98°39E **228** F2
Pangkajene *Indonesia* 4°46S 119°34E **235** C5
Pangkalanbrandan *Indonesia* 4°1N 98°20E **234** B1
Pangkalanbuun *Indonesia* 2°41S 111°37E **235** C4
Pangkalansusu *Indonesia* 4°2N 98°13E **234** B1
Pangkalpinang *Indonesia* 2°10S 106°10E **234** C3
Pangkoh *Indonesia* 3°5S 114°8E **235** C4
Pangkor, Pulau *Malaysia* 4°13N 100°34E **237** K3
Panglao *Phil.* 9°35N 123°45E **233** G4
Panglao I. *Phil.* 9°35N 123°48E **233** G4
Pangniqtuuq = Pangnirtung *Canada* 66°8N 65°43W **295** D18
Pangnirtung *Canada* 66°8N 65°43W **295** D18
Pango Aluquém *Angola* 8°43S 14°33E **265** D2
Pangody *Russia* 65°52N 74°27E **214** C8
Pangong Tso = Bangong Co *China* 33°45N 78°43E **243** C8
Pangrati *Greece* 37°56N 23°45E **112** B2
Pangsau Pass *Asia* 27°15N 96°10E **241** B6
Pangsua, Sungei → *Singapore* 1°25N 103°45E **138** A2
Pangtara *Burma* 20°57N 96°40E **241** E6
Panguipulli *Chile* 39°38S 72°20W **336** A2
Panguitch *U.S.A.* 37°50N 112°26W **305** H7
Panguna *Papua N. G.* 6°21S 155°25E **286** D8
Pangururan *Indonesia* 2°37N 98°42E **234** B1
Pangutaran *Phil.* 6°18N 120°34E **233** H3
Pangutaran Group *Phil.* 6°18N 120°34E **233** H3
Panhala *India* 16°49N 74°7E **244** F2
Panhandle *U.S.A.* 35°21N 101°23W **314** D4
Pani Mines *India* 22°29N 73°50E **242** H5
Pania-Mutombo *Dem. Rep. of the Congo* 5°11S 23°51E **265** D4
Pānī'au *U.S.A.* 21°56N 160°5W **302** B1
Panié, Mt. *N. Cal.* 20°36S 164°46E **288** d
Panihati *India* 22°41N 88°22E **124** A2
Panikota I. *India* 20°46N 71°21E **242** J4
Panipat *India* 29°25N 77°2E **242** E7
Paniqui *Phil.* 15°40N 120°34E **232** D3
Panitan *Phil.* 11°28N 122°46E **233** F4
Panj = Pyandzh → *Asia* 37°6N 68°20E **240** A2
Panjab *Afghan.* 34°23N 67°1E **240** B2
Panjakent *Tajikistan* 39°29N 67°37E **217** E7
Panjal Range = Pir Panjal Range *India* 32°30N 76°50E **242** C7
Panjang *Kepulauan Riau, Indonesia* 4°15N 108°12E **235** B3
Panjang *Lampung, Indonesia* 5°25S 105°20E **234** D3
Panjang, Bukit *Singapore* 1°22N 103°45E **138** A2
Panjgur *Pakistan* 27°0N 64°5E **240** D2
Panjhra → *India* 21°13N 74°57E **244** D2
Panjim = Panaji *India* 15°25N 73°50E **245** G1
Panjin *China* 41°3N 122°2E **227** D12
Panjnad → *Pakistan* 28°57N 70°30E **242** E4
Panjnad Barrage *Pakistan* 29°22N 71°15E **242** E4
Panjshīr □ *Afghan.* 35°50N 69°45E **240** B3
Panjwai *Afghan.* 31°26N 65°27E **242** D1
Panke → *Germany* 52°33N 13°22E **115** B3
Pankisi Gorge = Pankisis Kheoba *Georgia* 42°7N 45°15E **191** J7
Pankisis Kheoba *Georgia* 42°7N 45°15E **191** J7
Pankow *Germany* 52°34N 13°23E **115** A3
Pankshin *Nigeria* 9°16N 9°25E **263** D6
Panmunjŏm *N. Korea* 37°59N 126°38E **224** D3
Panna *India* 24°40N 80°15E **243** G9
Panna △ *India* 24°40N 80°0E **243** G8
Panna Hills *India* 24°40N 81°15E **243** G9
Pannawonica *Australia* 21°39S 116°19E **278** D2
Pannigi *Vanuatu* 15°58S 168°12E **287** E6
Pano Akil *Pakistan* 27°51N 69°7E **242** F3
Pano Lefkara *Cyprus* 34°53N 33°20E **207** F9
Pano Panayia *Cyprus* 34°55N 32°38E **207** F8
Panopah *Indonesia* 1°55S 111°10E **235** C4
Panora *U.S.A.* 41°42N 94°22W **310** C2
Panorama *Brazil* 21°21S 51°51W **335** A5
Panormos *Greece* 35°25N 24°41E **207** E5
Panruti *India* 11°46N 79°35E **245** J4
Pansemal *India* 21°39N 74°42E **244** D2
Panshan = Panjin *China* 41°3N 122°2E **227** D12
Panshi *China* 42°58N 126°5E **227** C14
Pantabangan L. *Phil.* 15°50N 121°9E **232** D3
Pantanal Matogrossense △ *Brazil* 17°35S 57°27W **331** D6
Pantanaw *Burma* 16°59N 95°28E **241** G5
Pantanos de Centla ⌂ *Mexico* 18°25N 92°25W **319** D6
Pantar *Indonesia* 8°28S 124°10E **231** F6
Pante Macassar *E. Timor* 9°30S 123°58E **231** F6
Pantego *U.S.A.* 32°42N 97°9W **120** B3
Pantelleria *Italy* 36°50N 11°57E **200** F4
Panthéon *Paris, France* **134** c4
Panthéon *Rome, Italy* **136** b2
Panthersville *U.S.A.* 33°43N 84°16W **113** B3
Panti *Indonesia* 0°22N 100°3E **234** B2
Pantin *France* 48°53N 2°24E **134** A3
Pantin Sakan *Burma* 18°38N 97°33E **241** F6
Pantitlán *Mexico* 19°24N 99°4W **128** B2
Pantoja *Peru* 0°58S 75°10W **328** D2
Pantón = O Castro de Ferreira *Spain* 42°31N 7°37W **194** C3
Pantukan *Phil.* 7°9N 125°54E **233** H5
Panu *Dem. Rep. of the Congo* 3°50S 19°10E **264** C3
Pánuco *Mexico* 22°3N 98°10W **319** C5
Panuitan I. *Phil.* 19°26N 121°30E **232** B3
Panukulan *Phil.* 14°56N 121°49E **232** D3
Panvel *India* 18°59N 73°4E **244** E1
Panyabungan *Indonesia* 0°51N 99°33E **234** B1
Panyam *Nigeria* 9°27N 9°8E **263** D6
Panyu *China* 23°1N 113°21E **121** B2
Panzhihua *China* 26°33N 101°44E **228** D3
Panzi *Dem. Rep. of the Congo* 7°17S 18°1E **265** D3
Pao → *Anzoátegui, Venezuela* 8°6N 64°17W **329** B5
Pao → *Apure, Venezuela* 8°33N 68°1W **328** B4
Paoay *Phil.* 18°3N 120°32E **232** B3
Paochi = Baoji *China* 34°20N 107°5E **226** G4
Paoki = Baoji *China* 34°20N 107°5E **226** G4
Páola *Italy* 39°21N 16°2E **201** C9
Paola *Malta* 35°52N 14°30E **206** F8
Paola *Kans., U.S.A.* 38°35N 94°53W **308** F6
Paoli *U.S.A.* 38°33N 86°28W **311** F10
Paonia *U.S.A.* 38°52N 107°36W **304** G10
Paopao *Moorea* 17°30S 149°49W **289** e
Paoting = Baoding *China* 38°50N 115°28E **226** E8
Paot'ou = Baotou *China* 40°32N 110°2E **226** D6
Paoua *C.A.R.* 7°9N 16°20E **264** A3
Pápa *Hungary* 47°22N 17°30E **182** C2
Pāpā *Hawai'i, U.S.A.* 19°13N 155°52W **302** D6
Papa Stour *U.K.* 60°20N 1°42W **167** A7
Papa Westray *U.K.* 59°20N 2°55W **167** B6
Pāpa'aloa *U.S.A.* 19°59N 155°13W **302** D6
Papadopoli, Palazzo *Venice, Italy* **142** b2
Papagayo → *Mexico* 16°46N 99°43W **319** D5
Papagayo, G. de *Costa Rica* 10°30N 85°50W **320** D2
Papagni → *India* 15°35N 77°45E **245** G3
Papahānaumokuākea Marine Nat. Monument ⌂ *U.S.A.* 25°25N 170°35W **302** F9
Papaïchton *Fr. Guiana* 3°48N 54°10W **329** C7
Pāpa'ikou *U.S.A.* 19°47N 155°6W **302** D6
Papakura *N.Z.* 37°4S 174°59E **284** D3
Papantla *Mexico* 20°27N 97°19W **319** C5
Papar *Malaysia* 5°45N 116°0E **235** A5
Papara *Tahiti* 17°43S 149°31W **289** e
Paparoa *N.Z.* 36°6S 174°16E **284** C3
Paparoa △ *N.Z.* 42°7S 171°26E **285** C6
Paparoa Ra. *N.Z.* 42°5S 171°35E **285** C6
Papatoetoe *N.Z.* 36°59S 174°51E **284** C3
Papatura *Solomon Is.* 7°32S 158°47E **287** L10
Papeete *Tahiti* 17°32S 149°34W **289** e
Papenburg *Germany* 53°5N 7°23E **178** B3
Papenoo *Tahiti* 17°30S 149°25W **289** e
Papenoo → *Tahiti* 17°30S 149°25W **289** e
Papetoai *Moorea* 17°29S 149°52W **289** e
Paphlagonia *Turkey* 41°30N 33°0E **212** B5
Paphos *Cyprus* 34°46N 32°25E **207** F8
Paphos ✗ (PFO) *Cyprus* 34°43N 32°30E **207** F8
Papien Chiang = Da → *Vietnam* 21°15N 105°20E **228** G5
Papikio Oros *Greece* 41°15N 25°13E **203** E9
Papiol *Spain* 41°25N 2°0E **114** A1
Paposo *Chile* 25°0S 70°30W **334** B1
Papoutsa *Cyprus* 34°54N 33°4E **207** F9
Papua □ *Indonesia* 4°0S 137°0E **231** E9
Papua, G. of *Papua N. G.* 9°0S 144°50E **286** E3
Papua New Guinea ■ *Oceania* 8°0S 145°0E **286** E3
Papudo *Chile* 32°29S 71°27W **334** C1
Papuk *Croatia* 45°30N 17°30E **182** E2
Papun *Burma* 18°2N 97°30E **241** F6
Papunya *Australia* 23°15S 131°54E **278** D5
Pará = Belém *Brazil* 1°20S 48°30W **332** B2
Pará □ *Brazil* 3°20S 52°0W **331** A7
Paraburdoo *Australia* 23°14S 117°32E **278** D2
Paracale *Phil.* 14°17N 122°48E **232** D4
Paracas, Pen. de *Peru* 13°53S 76°20W **330** C2
Paracatu *Brazil* 17°10S 46°50W **333** E2
Paracatu → *Brazil* 16°30S 45°4W **333** E2
Paracel Is. *S. China Sea* 15°50N 112°0E **230** A4
Parachilna *Australia* 31°10S 138°21E **282** A3
Parachinar *Pakistan* 33°55N 70°5E **242** C4
Paraćin *Serbia* 43°54N 21°27E **202** C5
Paracuru *Brazil* 3°24S 39°4W **332** B4
Parada, Punta *Peru* 15°22S 75°11W **330** D2
Paradas *Spain* 37°18N 5°29W **195** H5
Paradela *Spain* 42°44N 7°37W **194** C3
Paradera *Aruba* 12°32N 70°0W **322** f
Paradip *India* 20°15N 86°35E **244** D8
Paradise *Calif., U.S.A.* 39°46N 121°37W **306** F5
Paradise *Nev., U.S.A.* 36°5N 115°8W **124** B2
Paradise → *Canada* 53°27N 57°19W **299** B8
Paradise Hill *Canada* 53°32N 109°28W **297** C7
Paradise I. *Bahamas* 25°6N 77°19W **153** b
Paradise River *Canada* 53°27N 57°17W **299** B8
Paradise Valley *U.S.A.* 41°30N 117°32W **304** F5
Paradisi *Greece* 36°18N 28°7E **206** E12
Paragould *U.S.A.* 36°3N 90°29W **315** C9
Paragua = Palawan *Phil.* 9°30N 118°30E **233** G2
Paragua → *Bolivia* 13°34S 61°53W **331** C5
Paragua → *Venezuela* 6°55N 62°55W **329** B5
Paraguaçu = Paraguaçu Paulista *Brazil* 22°22S 50°35W **335** A5
Paraguaçú → *Brazil* 12°45S 38°54W **333** D4
Paraguaçu Paulista *Brazil* 22°22S 50°35W **335** A5
Paraguaipoa *Venezuela* 11°21N 71°57W **328** A3
Paraguaná, Pen. de *Venezuela* 12°0N 70°0W **328** A4
Paraguarí *Paraguay* 25°36S 57°0W **334** B4
Paraguarí □ *Paraguay* 26°0S 57°10W **334** B4
Paraguay ■ *S. Amer.* 23°0S 57°0W **334** A4
Paraguay → *Paraguay* 27°18S 58°38W **334** B4
Paraíba = João Pessoa *Brazil* 7°10S 34°52W **332** C5
Paraíba □ *Brazil* 7°0S 36°0W **332** C4
Paraíba do Sul → *Brazil* 21°37S 41°3W **333** F3
Paraíso *Brazil* 19°3S 52°59W **331** D7
Paraíso *Tabasco, Mexico* 18°24N 93°14W **319** D6
Paraíso *Panama* 9°3N 79°38W **320** c
Parak *Iran* 27°38N 52°25E **247** E7
Parakhino Paddubye *Russia* 58°26N 33°10E **188** C7

Parakou *Benin* 9°25N 2°40E **263 D5**
Parakylia *Australia* 30°24S 136°25E **282 A2**
Paralimni *Cyprus* 35°2N 33°58E **207 E9**
Paralio Astros *Greece* 37°25N 22°45E **204 D4**
Paralkote *India* 19°47N 80°41E **244 E5**
Param I. *Micronesia* 7°21N 151°47E **287 T18**
Parama I. *Papua N. G.* 9°0S 143°25E **286 E2**
Paramaribo *Suriname* 5°50N 55°10W **329 B6**
Parambu *Brazil* 6°13S 40°43W **332 C3**
Paramillo, Cerro *Colombia* 7°4N 75°55W **328 B2**
Paramillo △ *Colombia* 7°37N 76°13W **328 B2**
Paramirim *Brazil* 13°26S 42°15W **333 D3**
Paramirim ➜ *Brazil* 11°34S 43°18W **333 D3**
Paramithia *Greece* 39°30N 20°35E **204 B2**
Paramonga *Peru* 10°40S 77°50W **330 C2**
Paramount Studios
U.S.A. 34°5N 118°19W **126 B3**
Paramus *U.S.A.* 40°56N 74°2W **132 A1**
Paramushir, Ostrov
Russia 50°24N 156°0E **215 D16**
Paran ➜ *Israel* 30°20N 35°10E **251 H6**
Paraná *Argentina* 31°45S 60°30W **334 C3**
Paranã *Brazil* 12°30S 47°48W **333 D2**
Paraná □ *Brazil* 24°30S 51°0W **335 A5**
Paraná ➜ *Argentina* 33°43S 59°15W **334 C4**
Paranã ➜ *Brazil* 12°30S 48°14W **333 D2**
Paranaguá *Brazil* 25°30S 48°30W **335 B6**
Paranaíba *Brazil* 19°40S 51°11W **331 D7**
Paranaíba ➜ *Brazil* 20°6S 51°4W **333 F1**
Paranal, Cerro *Chile* 24°38S 70°24W **334 A1**
Paranapanema ➜ *Brazil* 22°40S 53°9W **335 A5**
Paranapiacaba, Serra do
Brazil 24°31S 48°35W **335 A6**
Paranaque *Phil.* 14°30N 120°59E **127 B1**
Paranas *Phil.* 11°42N 125°2E **233 F5**
Paranavaí *Brazil* 23°4S 52°56W **335 A5**
Parang *Maguindanao, Phil.* 7°23N 124°16E **233 H5**
Parang *Sulu, Phil.* 5°55N 120°54E **233 J3**
Parangippettai *India* 11°30N 79°38E **245 J4**
Parângul Mare, Vf.
Romania 45°20N 23°37E **183 E8**
Paranthan *Sri Lanka* 9°26N 80°24E **245 K5**
Paraoa *French Polynesia* 19°9S 140°43W **289 f**
Paraparaumu *N.Z.* 40°57S 175°3E **284 G4**
Parapetí ➜ *Bolivia* 18°58S 62°21W **331 D5**
Paraspori, Akra *Greece* 35°55N 27°15E **205 F9**
Parate Bueno *Venezuela* 10°59N 64°22W **329 a**
Paratinga *Brazil* 12°40S 43°10W **333 D3**
Paratoo *Australia* 32°42S 139°20E **282 B3**
Parauapebas *Brazil* 6°4S 49°54W **332 C2**
Paraúna *Brazil* 16°55S 50°26W **333 E1**
Paray-le-Monial *France* 46°27N 4°7E **173 F11**
Paray-Vieille-Poste *France* 48°42N 2°20E **134 B3**
Parbati ➜ *Mad. P., India* 25°50N 76°30E **242 G7**
Parbati ➜ *Raj., India* 26°54N 77°53E **242 F7**
Parbatipur *Bangla.* 25°39N 88°55E **241 C2**
Parbhani *India* 19°8N 76°52E **244 E3**
Parc des Princes
Paris, France 48°50N 2°15E **134 A2**
Parchim *Germany* 53°26N 11°52E **178 B7**
Parchwitz = Prochowice
Poland 51°17N 16°20E **185 G3**
Parco = Sinclair *U.S.A.* 41°47N 107°7W **304 F10**
Parczew *Poland* 51°40N 22°52E **185 G9**
Pardes Hanna-Karkur
Israel 32°28N 34°57E **251 F5**
Pardilla *Spain* 41°33N 3°43W **194 D7**
Pardisān Nature Park
Iran 35°44N 51°22E **141 A2**
Pardo ➜ *Bahia, Brazil* 15°40S 39°0W **333 E4**
Pardo ➜ *Mato Grosso, Brazil* 21°46S 52°9W **335 A5**
Pardo ➜ *Minas Gerais, Brazil* 15°48S 44°48W **333 E3**
Pardo ➜ *São Paulo, Brazil* 20°10S 48°38W **333 F2**
Pardoo Roadhouse
Australia 20°6S 119°3E **278 D2**
Pardubice *Czechia* 50°3N 15°45E **180 A8**
Pardubický □ *Czechia* 49°50N 16°0E **180 B8**
Pardubitz = Pardubice
Czechia 50°3N 15°45E **180 A8**
Pare *Indonesia* 7°43S 112°12E **231 G15**
Pare Mts. *Tanzania* 4°0S 37°45E **268 C4**
Parecis, Serra dos *Brazil* 13°0S 60°0W **331 C6**
Paredes de Nava *Spain* 42°9N 4°42W **194 C6**
Parel *India* 18°59N 72°49E **130 B1**
Parelhas *Brazil* 6°41S 36°39W **332 C4**
Paren *Russia* 62°30N 163°15E **215 C17**
Parenda *India* 18°16N 75°28E **244 E2**
Parengarenga Harbour
N.Z. 34°31S 173°0E **284 A2**
Parent *Canada* 47°55N 74°35W **298 C5**
Parent, L. *Canada* 48°31N 77°1W **298 C4**
Parentis-en-Born *France* 44°21N 1°4W **174 D2**
Parepare *Indonesia* 4°0S 119°40E **235 E5**
Parfino *Russia* 57°59N 31°34E **188 D6**
Parga *Greece* 39°15N 20°29E **204 B2**
Pargas = Länsi-Turunmaa
Finland 60°18N 22°18E **188 B2**
Pargi *India* 17°11N 77°53E **244 E3**
Pargo, Pta. do *Madeira* 32°49N 17°17W **153 c**
Parguera *Puerto Rico* 17°59N 67°3W **321 b**
Parham *Canada* 44°39N 76°43W **313 B8**
Pari *Brazil* 23°32S 46°36W **137 B2**
Paria ➜ *U.S.A.* 36°52N 111°36W **305 H8**
Paria, G. de *Venezuela* 10°30N 61°40W **323 t**
Paria, Pen. de *Venezuela* 10°50N 62°30W **329 A5**
Pariaguán *Venezuela* 8°51N 64°34W **329 B5**
Pariaman *Indonesia* 0°47S 100°11E **234 C2**
Paricatuba *Brazil* 4°26S 61°53W **329 D5**
Paricutín, Cerro *Mexico* 19°28N 102°15W **318 D4**
Parigi *Indonesia* 0°50S 120°5E **231 E6**
Parika *Guyana* 6°50N 58°20W **329 B6**
Parikia *Greece* 37°6N 25°11E **205 D7**
Parikkala *Finland* 61°33N 29°31E **188 B5**
Parima, Serra *Brazil* 2°30N 64°0W **329 C5**
Parinari *Peru* 4°35S 74°25W **330 A3**
Pariñas, Pta. *Peru* 4°30S 82°0W **330 A1**
Parincea *Romania* 46°27N 27°9E **183 D12**
Paringa *Australia* 34°10S 140°46E **282 C4**
Parintins *Brazil* 2°40S 56°50W **329 D6**
Parioli *Italy* 41°55N 12°29E **136 B1**
Paripārit Kyun *Burma* 14°52N 93°41E **245 G11**
Paris *Ont., Canada* 43°12N 80°25W **312 C4**
Paris *France* 48°53N 2°20E **134 A3**
Paris *Idaho, U.S.A.* 42°14N 111°24W **304 E8**
Paris *Ill., U.S.A.* 39°36N 87°42W **311 E9**
Paris *Ky., U.S.A.* 38°13N 84°15W **311 F12**
Paris *Mo., U.S.A.* 39°29N 92°0W **310 E5**
Paris *Tenn., U.S.A.* 36°18N 88°19W **315 C10**
Paris *Tex., U.S.A.* 33°40N 95°33W **314 E7**
Paris, Ville de □ *France* 48°50N 2°20E **173 D9**
Paris Charles de Gaulle ✈ (CDG)
France 49°0N 2°32E **173 D9**
Paris Orly ✈ (ORY) *France* 48°44N 2°23E **134 B3**
Parish *U.S.A.* 43°25N 76°8W **313 C8**
Parishville *U.S.A.* 44°38N 74°49W **313 B10**
Pariti *Indonesia* 10°1S 123°45E **278 B3**
Parjé *India* 18°54N 72°57E **130 B2**
Park *U.S.A.* 48°45N 122°18W **306 B4**
Park City *U.S.A.* 37°48N 97°20W **308 G5**
Pārk-e Āzādegān *Iran* 35°37N 51°28E **141 B2**
Pārk-e Mellat *Iran* 35°47N 51°24E **141 A2**
Park Falls *U.S.A.* 45°56N 90°27W **308 C8**
Park Forest *U.S.A.* 41°29N 87°40W **311 C9**
Park Head *Canada* 44°36N 81°9W **312 B3**
Park Hills *U.S.A.* 37°51N 90°51W **310 G6**
Park Range *U.S.A.* 40°41N 106°41W **304 F10**
Park Rapids *U.S.A.* 46°55N 95°4W **308 B6**
Park Ridge *U.S.A.* 42°2N 87°51W **119 A1**
Park River *U.S.A.* 48°24N 97°45W **308 A5**
Park Royal *U.K.* 51°31N 0°16W **125 A2**
Park Rynie *S. Africa* 30°25S 30°45E **271 D5**
Parkā Bandar *Iran* 25°55N 59°35E **247 E8**
Parkán = Štúrovo
Slovakia 47°48N 18°41E **181 D11**
Parkano *Finland* 62°1N 23°0E **188 A2**
Parkchester *U.S.A.* 40°49N 73°50W **132 B2**
Parkdale *Canada* 43°38N 79°25W **141 B2**
Parkent *Uzbekistan* 41°18N 69°40E **217 D7**
Parker *Ariz., U.S.A.* 34°9N 114°17W **307 L12**
Parker *Pa., U.S.A.* 41°5N 79°41W **312 E5**
Parker Center *Los Angeles, U.S.A.* **127 b2**
Parker Dam *U.S.A.* 34°18N 114°8W **307 L12**
Parkersburg *Iowa, U.S.A.* 42°35N 92°47W **310 B4**
Parkersburg *W. Va., U.S.A.* 39°16N 81°34W **309 F13**
Parkes *Australia* 33°9S 148°11E **283 B8**
Parkfield *U.S.A.* 35°54N 120°26W **306 K6**
Parkhill *Canada* 43°15N 81°38W **312 C3**
Parkhurst *S. Africa* 26°8S 28°1E **123 A2**
Parkland *U.S.A.* 47°9N 122°26W **306 C4**
Parklawn *U.S.A.* 38°50N 77°7W **143 B2**
Parkmore *S. Africa* 26°5S 28°2E **123 A2**
Parkside *U.S.A.* 37°44N 122°29W **136 B2**
Parkston *U.S.A.* 43°24N 97°59W **308 D5**
Parksville *Canada* 49°20N 124°21W **296 D4**
Parktown *S. Africa* 26°10S 28°2E **123 B2**
Parkview *S. Africa* 26°9S 28°1E **123 A2**
Parkville *U.S.A.* 40°38N 73°57W **132 C2**
Parkway *U.S.A.* 38°32N 121°26W **306 G5**
Parkwood *Gauteng, S. Africa* 26°9S 28°2E **123 A2**
Parkwood *Western Cape, S. Africa* 34°2S 18°30E **118 B1**
Parla *Spain* 40°14N 3°46W **194 E7**
Parlakimidi *India* 18°45N 84°5E **244 E7**
Parlatuvier *Trin. & Tob.* 11°18N 60°39W **323 s**
Parli *India* 18°50N 76°35E **244 E3**
Parliament *Budapest, Hungary* **117 b2**
Pârliţa *Moldova* 47°19N 27°52E **183 C12**
Parma *Italy* 44°48N 10°20E **198 D7**
Parma *Idaho, U.S.A.* 43°47N 116°57W **304 E5**
Parma *Ohio, U.S.A.* 41°24N 81°43W **312 E3**
Parma ➜ *Italy* 44°56N 10°26E **198 D7**
Parnaguá *Brazil* 10°10S 44°38W **332 D3**
Parnaíba *Brazil* 2°54S 41°47W **332 B3**
Parnaíba ➜ *Brazil* 3°0S 41°50W **332 B3**
Parnamirim *Pernambuco, Brazil* 8°5S 39°34W **332 C4**
Parnamirim *Rio Grande do N., Brazil* 5°55S 35°15W **332 C4**
Parnarama *Brazil* 5°31S 43°6W **332 C3**
Parnassos *Greece* 38°35N 22°30E **204 C4**
Parnassus *N.Z.* 42°42S 173°23E **285 C8**
Parndana *Australia* 35°48S 137°12E **282 C2**
Parner *India* 19°0N 74°26E **244 E2**
Parnitha *Greece* 38°14N 23°45E **204 C5**
Parnitha △ *Greece* 38°12N 23°44E **204 C5**
Parnonas Oros *Greece* 37°15N 22°45E **204 D4**
Pärnu *Estonia* 58°28N 24°33E **188 C3**
Pärnu ➜ *Estonia* 58°28N 24°33E **188 C3**
Paro Dzong *Bhutan* 27°32N 89°53E **241 B2**
Parola *India* 20°47N 75°7E **244 D2**
Paroo ➜ *Australia* 31°28S 143°32E **282 A5**
Paros *Greece* 37°5N 25°12E **205 D7**
Parow *S. Africa* 33°53S 18°37E **118 A2**
Parowan *U.S.A.* 37°51N 112°50W **305 H7**
Parpaillon *France* 44°30N 6°40E **175 D10**
Parque Chacabuco
Argentina 34°39S 58°26W **117 B2**
Parque Patricios
Argentina 34°39S 58°23W **117 B2**
Parral *Chile* 36°10S 71°52W **334 D1**
Parramatta *Australia* 33°48S 151°1E **283 B9**
Parramatta ➜ *Australia* 33°49S 151°3E **139 A1**
Parras *Mexico* 25°25N 102°11W **318 B4**
Parrett ➜ *U.K.* 51°12N 3°1W **169 F4**
Parris I. *U.S.A.* 32°20N 80°41W **316 C9**
Parrish *U.S.A.* 27°35N 82°26W **317 H7**
Parrott *U.S.A.* 31°54N 84°31W **316 D5**
Parrsboro *Canada* 45°30N 64°25W **299 C7**
Parry Channel *Canada* 74°15N 94°0W **295 C13**
Parry I. *Canada* 45°18N 80°10W **312 A4**
Parry Is. *Canada* 77°0N 110°0W **295 B10**
Parry Sound *Canada* 45°20N 80°0W **312 A5**
Parsābād *Iran* 39°39N 47°50E **213 C12**
Parsaloi *Kenya* 1°16N 36°51E **268 B4**
Parsberg *Germany* 49°10N 11°43E **179 F7**
Parsęta ➜ *Poland* 54°11N 15°34E **184 D2**
Parsnip ➜ *Canada* 55°10N 123°2W **296 B4**
Parsons *U.S.A.* 37°20N 95°16W **308 G6**
Parsons Ra. *Australia* 13°30S 135°15E **280 A2**
Partabpur *India* 20°0N 80°42E **244 E5**
Partanna *Italy* 37°43N 12°53E **200 E5**
Partenio △ *Italy* 40°56N 14°38E **201 B7**
Parthenay *France* 46°38N 0°16W **172 F6**
Parthenon *Athens, Greece* **112 c2**
Partinico *Italy* 38°3N 13°7E **200 D6**
Partizansk *Russia* 43°8N 133°9E **215 E14**
Partizánske *Slovakia* 48°38N 18°23E **181 C11**
Partridge I. *Canada* 55°59N 87°37W **298 A2**
Partry Mts. *Ireland* 53°40N 9°28W **166 C2**
Partur *India* 19°40N 76°14E **244 E3**
Paru ➜ *Brazil* 1°33S 52°38W **329 D7**
Parú ➜ *Venezuela* 4°20N 66°27W **328 C4**
Paru de Oeste ➜ *Brazil* 1°30N 56°0W **329 C6**
Parucito ➜ *Venezuela* 5°18N 65°59W **328 B4**
Parur = North Paravar
India 10°13N 76°14E **245 J3**
Paruro *Peru* 13°45S 71°50W **330 C3**
Parvān □ *Afghan.* 35°0N 69°0E **240 B3**
Parvatipuram *India* 18°50N 83°25E **244 E6**
Parvatsar *India* 26°52N 74°49E **242 F6**
Påryd *Sweden* 56°34N 15°55E **163 H9**
Parys *S. Africa* 26°52S 27°29E **270 C4**
Pas, Pta. des *Spain* 38°46N 1°26E **206 D1**
Pas, The *Canada* 53°45N 101°15W **297 C8**
Pas-de-Calais □ *France* 50°30N 2°10E **173 B9**
Paşabahçe *Turkey* 41°6N 29°5E **122 B2**
Pasada *Spain* 43°23N 5°40W **194 B5**
Pasadena *Nfld. & L., Canada* 49°1N 57°36W **299 C8**
Pasadena *Calif., U.S.A.* 34°9N 118°8W **126 B4**
Pasadena *Tex., U.S.A.* 29°43N 95°13W **314 G7**
Pasaje *Ecuador* 3°23S 79°50W **328 D2**
Pasaje ➜ *Argentina* 25°39S 63°56W **334 B3**
Paşalimanı *Turkey* 40°29N 27°36E **203 F11**
Pasar *Indonesia* 8°27S 114°54E **231 J17**
Pasar Minggu *Indonesia* 6°16S 106°49E **122 B1**
Pasargadae *Iran* 30°11N 53°10E **247 D7**
Pasarkuok *Indonesia* 1°27S 100°36E **234 C2**
Pasarsibuhuan *Indonesia* 1°3N 99°43E **234 B1**
Pasay *Phil.* 14°32N 120°59E **127 B1**
Pascagoula *U.S.A.* 30°21N 88°33W **315 F10**
Pascagoula ➜ *U.S.A.* 30°23N 88°37W **315 F10**
Paşcani *Romania* 47°14N 26°45E **183 C11**
Paschimbanga □ *India* 23°0N 88°0E **243 H13**
Pasco *U.S.A.* 46°14N 119°6W **304 C4**
Pasco □ *Peru* 10°40S 75°0W **330 C2**
Pasco I. *Australia* 20°57S 115°20E **278 D2**
Pascoag *U.S.A.* 41°57N 71°42W **313 E13**
Pascoe Vale *Australia* 37°43S 144°55E **128 A1**
Pascua, I. de *Chile* 27°7S 109°23W **330 b**
Paseo de la Reforma *Mexico City, Mexico* **128 b2**
Pasewalk *Germany* 53°30N 13°58E **178 B9**
Pasfield L. *Canada* 58°24N 105°20W **297 B7**
Pasha ➜ *Russia* 60°29N 32°55E **188 B7**
Pashmakli = Smolyan
Bulgaria 41°36N 24°38E **203 E8**
Pasig *Phil.* 14°33N 121°4E **127 B2**
Pasig ➜ *Phil.* 14°31N 121°6E **127 B2**
Pasighat *India* 28°4N 95°21E **241 A5**
Pasila *Finland* 60°12N 24°56E **121 B2**
Pasing *Germany* 48°8N 11°28E **131 B1**
Pasinler *Turkey* 39°59N 41°41E **213 C9**
Pasir Mas *Malaysia* 6°2N 102°8E **237 J4**
Pasir Panjang *Singapore* 1°18N 103°46E **138 B2**
Pasir Putih *Malaysia* 5°50N 102°24E **237 K4**
Pasir Ris *Singapore* 1°22N 103°56E **138 A3**
Pasirian *Indonesia* 8°13S 113°8E **235 D4**
Pasirkuning = Dabo
Indonesia 0°30S 104°33E **234 C2**
Pasirpengarayan
Indonesia 0°51N 100°16E **234 B2**
Påskallavik *Sweden* 57°10N 16°26E **163 G10**
Paskūh *Iran* 27°34N 61°39E **247 E9**
Pasłęk *Poland* 54°3N 19°41E **184 D6**
Pasłęka ➜ *Poland* 54°26N 19°46E **184 D6**
Pasley, C. *Australia* 33°52S 123°35E **279 F3**
Pašman *Croatia* 43°58N 15°20E **199 E12**
Pasmore ➜ *Australia* 31°5S 139°49E **282 A3**
Pasni *Pakistan* 25°15N 63°27E **240 D1**
Paso Bravo △ *Paraguay* 22°32S 57°5W **334 A4**
Paso Cantinela *Mexico* 32°33N 115°47W **307 N11**
Paso de Indios *Argentina* 43°55S 69°0W **336 B3**
Paso de los Indios
Argentina 38°32S 69°25W **336 A3**
Paso de los Libres
Argentina 29°44S 57°10W **334 B4**
Paso de los Toros
Uruguay 32°45S 56°30W **334 C4**
Paso Flores *Argentina* 40°35S 70°38W **336 B2**
Paso Robles *U.S.A.* 35°38N 120°41W **306 K6**
Pasorapa *Bolivia* 18°16S 64°37W **331 D5**
Paspébiac *Canada* 48°3N 65°17W **299 C6**
Pasrur *Pakistan* 32°16N 74°43E **242 C6**
Passage East *Ireland* 52°14N 7°0W **166 D5**
Passage West *Ireland* 51°52N 8°21W **166 E3**
Passaic *U.S.A.* 40°51N 74°7W **132 A1**
Passaic ➜ *U.S.A.* 40°42N 74°10W **132 B1**
Passam *Papua N. G.* 3°41S 143°38E **286 B2**
Passau *Germany* 48°34N 13°28E **179 G9**
Passenheim = Pasym
Poland 53°48N 20°49E **184 E7**
Passero, C. *Italy* 36°41N 15°10E **201 F8**
Passi *Phil.* 11°6N 122°38E **233 F4**
Passirana *Italy* 45°32N 9°2E **128 A1**
Passo Fundo *Brazil* 28°10S 52°20W **335 B5**
Passos *Brazil* 20°45S 46°37W **333 F2**
Passow *Germany* 53°8N 14°6E **178 B10**
Passy *France* 45°55N 6°41E **175 C10**
Pastavy *Belarus* 55°4N 26°50E **188 E4**
Pastaza □ *Ecuador* 2°0S 77°0W **328 D2**
Pastaza ➜ *Peru* 4°50S 76°52W **328 D2**
Pasto *Colombia* 1°13N 77°17W **328 C2**
Pastol B. *U.S.A.* 63°7N 163°15W **303 E7**
Pastos Bons *Brazil* 6°36S 44°5W **332 C3**
Pastrana *Spain* 40°27N 2°53W **196 E2**
Pasuquin *Phil.* 18°20N 120°37E **232 B3**
Pasuruan *Indonesia* 7°40S 112°44E **235 D4**
Pasym *Poland* 53°48N 20°49E **184 E7**
Pásztó *Hungary* 47°52N 19°43E **182 C4**
Pata *Phil.* 5°51N 121°10E **233 J3**
Pata I. *Phil.* 5°49N 121°10E **233 J3**
Patag I. = Flat I.
S. China Sea 10°49N 115°49E **230 B5**
Patagonia *Argentina* 45°0S 69°0W **336 C3**
Patagonia *Ariz., U.S.A.* 31°33N 110°45W **305 L8**
Patambar *Iran* 29°45N 60°17E **247 D9**
Patan = Lalitpur *Nepal* 27°40N 85°20E **243 F11**
Patan = Somnath *India* 20°53N 70°22E **242 J4**
Patan *Gujarat, India* 23°54N 72°14E **242 H5**
Patan *Maharashtra, India* 17°22N 73°57E **244 F1**
Patani *Indonesia* 0°20N 128°50E **231 D7**
Pătârlagele *Romania* 45°19N 26°21E **183 E11**
Pataudi *India* 28°18N 76°48E **242 E7**
Patchewollock *Australia* 35°22S 142°12E **282 C5**
Patchogue *U.S.A.* 40°46N 73°1W **313 F11**
Pate Coast, Kenya 2°10S 41°0E **268 C5**
Pate *Taiwan* 24°56N 121°17E **225 B3**
Patea *N.Z.* 39°45S 174°30E **284 F3**
Pategi *Nigeria* 8°50N 5°45E **263 D6**
Patel Nagar *India* 28°39N 77°10E **120 B1**
Patensie *S. Africa* 33°46S 24°49E **270 D3**
Paterna *Spain* 39°30N 0°26W **197 F4**
Paternion *Austria* 46°43N 13°38E **180 E6**
Paternò *Italy* 37°34N 14°54E **201 E7**
Pateros *Manila, Phil.* 14°32N 121°3E **127 B2**
Pateros *Wash., U.S.A.* 48°3N 119°54W **304 B4**
Paterson *N.S.W., Australia* 32°35S 151°36E **283 B9**
Paterson *N.J., U.S.A.* 40°54N 74°9W **313 F10**
Paterson Inlet *N.Z.* 46°56S 168°12E **285 G3**
Paterson Ra. *Australia* 21°45S 122°10E **278 D3**
Pathankot *India* 32°18N 75°45E **242 C6**
Pathardi *India* 19°10N 75°11E **244 E2**
Patharghata *Bangla.* 22°2N 89°58E **241 D2**
Pathein *Burma* 16°45N 94°30E **241 G5**
Pathfinder Res. *U.S.A.* 42°28N 106°51W **304 E10**
Pathiu *Thailand* 10°42N 99°19E **237 G2**
Pathri *India* 19°15N 76°27E **244 E3**
Pathum Thani *Thailand* 14°1N 100°32E **236 E3**
Pathumwan *Thailand* 13°44N 100°31E **113 B2**
Pati *Indonesia* 6°45S 111°1E **235 D4**
Pati Pt. *Guam* 13°35N 144°57E **302 d**
Patía *Colombia* 2°4N 77°4W **328 C2**
Patía ➜ *Colombia* 2°13N 78°40W **328 C2**
Patiala *Punjab, India* 30°23N 76°26E **242 D7**
Patiala *Ut. P., India* 27°43N 79°1E **243 F8**
Patine Kouka *Senegal* 12°45N 13°45W **262 C2**
Patipukur *India* 22°36N 88°24E **124 B2**
Patisia *Greece* 38°2N 23°45E **112 A2**
Patitiri *Greece* 39°8N 23°50E **204 B5**
Patkai Bum *India* 27°0N 95°30E **241 B5**
Patmos *Greece* 37°21N 26°36E **205 D8**
Patna *India* 25°35N 85°12E **243 G11**
Patnagarh *India* 20°43N 83°9E **244 D6**
Patnanongan I. *Phil.* 14°48N 122°11E **232 D4**
Patnongon *Phil.* 10°55N 122°0E **233 F4**
Patnos *Turkey* 39°13N 42°51E **213 C10**
Pato Branco *Brazil* 26°13S 52°40W **335 B5**
Patoka L. *U.S.A.* 38°20N 86°40W **311 F10**
Patong, Ao *Thailand* 7°54N 98°17E **237 a**
Patonga *Uganda* 2°45N 33°15E **268 B3**
Patos *Albania* 40°42N 19°38E **202 F3**
Patos *Brazil* 6°55S 37°16W **332 C4**
Patos, L. dos *Brazil* 31°20S 51°0W **335 C5**
Patos, Rio de los ➜
Argentina 31°18S 69°25W **334 C2**
Patos de Minas *Brazil* 18°35S 46°32W **333 E2**
Patquía *Argentina* 30°2S 66°55W **334 C2**
Patra *Greece* 38°14N 21°47E **204 C3**
Patraikos Kolpos *Greece* 38°17N 21°30E **204 C3**
Patras = Patra *Greece* 38°14N 21°47E **204 C3**
Patreksfjörður *Iceland* 65°35N 24°0W **155 B2**
Patriarsheye = Donskoy
Russia 53°55N 38°15E **188 F10**
Patricio Lynch, I. *Chile* 48°35S 75°30W **336 C1**
Patrocínio *Brazil* 18°57S 47°0W **333 E2**
Pattada *Italy* 40°35N 9°6E **200 B2**
Pattadakal *India* 16°1N 75°42E **245 F2**
Pattallassang *Indonesia* 5°26S 119°26E **235 D5**
Pattani *Thailand* 6°48N 101°15E **237 J3**
Pattaya *Thailand* 12°52N 100°55E **236 F3**
Patten *U.S.A.* 46°0N 68°38W **309 B19**
Patterson *Calif., U.S.A.* 37°28N 121°8W **306 H5**
Patterson *Ga., U.S.A.* 31°23N 82°8W **316 D7**
Patterson *La., U.S.A.* 29°42N 91°18W **314 G9**
Patterson, Mt. *U.S.A.* 38°29N 119°20W **306 G7**
Patteson, Passage
Vanuatu 15°26S 168°12E **287 E6**
Patti *Punjab, India* 31°17N 74°54E **242 D6**
Patti *Ut. P., India* 25°55N 82°12E **243 G10**
Patti *Italy* 38°8N 14°58E **201 D7**
Pattoki *Pakistan* 31°5N 73°52E **242 D5**
Patton = Monroeville
U.S.A. 40°26N 79°45W **312 F5**
Patton *U.S.A.* 40°38N 78°39W **312 F6**
Pattonsburg *U.S.A.* 40°3N 94°8W **310 D2**
Pattukkattai *India* 10°25N 79°20E **245 J4**
Patu *Brazil* 6°6S 37°38W **332 C4**
Patuakhali *Bangla.* 22°20N 90°25E **241 D3**
Patuanak *Canada* 55°55N 107°43W **297 B7**
Patuca ➜ *Honduras* 15°50N 84°18W **320 C3**
Patuca, Punta *Honduras* 15°49N 84°14W **320 C3**
Patuca △ *Honduras* 14°30N 85°30W **320 D2**
Pătulele *Romania* 44°21N 22°47E **182 F7**
Patur *India* 20°27N 76°56E **244 D3**
Patvinsuo △ *Finland* 63°7N 30°45E **160 E24**
Pátzcuaro *Mexico* 19°31N 101°38W **318 D4**
Pau *France* 43°19N 0°25W **174 E3**
Pau, Gave de ➜ *France* 43°33N 1°12W **174 E2**
Pau d'Arco *Brazil* 7°30S 49°22W **332 C2**
Pau dos Ferros *Brazil* 6°7S 38°10W **332 C4**
Pauanui *N.Z.* 37°1S 175°52E **284 D4**
Paucartambo *Peru* 13°19S 71°35W **330 C3**
Paudash *Canada* 44°59N 77°58W **312 B7**
Pauillac *France* 45°11N 0°46W **174 C3**
Pauini *Brazil* 7°40S 66°58W **330 B4**
Pauini ➜ *Brazil* 1°42S 62°50W **329 D5**
Pauk *Burma* 21°27N 94°30E **241 E5**
Paukkaung *Burma* 18°54N 95°33E **241 F5**
Pauktaw *Burma* 20°11N 93°4E **241 E4**
Paul I. *Canada* 56°30N 61°20W **299 A7**
Paul Isnard *Fr. Guiana* 4°47N 54°1W **329 C7**
Paul Revere Park *Boston, U.S.A.* **116 a2**
Paul Smiths *U.S.A.* 44°26N 74°15W **313 B10**
Paulatuk *Canada* 69°25N 124°0W **294 D7**
Paulding *U.S.A.* 41°8N 84°35W **311 C12**
Paulding Bay *S. Ocean* 66°0S 118°0E **151 C8**
Paulhan *France* 43°33N 3°28E **174 E7**
Paulis = Isiro
Dem. Rep. of the Congo 2°53N 27°40E **268 B2**
Paulista = Paulistana *Brazil* 8°9S 41°9W **332 C3**
Paulista *Brazil* 7°57S 34°53W **332 C5**
Paulistana *Brazil* 8°9S 41°9W **332 C3**
Paulström *Sweden* 57°28N 15°31E **163 G9**
Paulo Afonso *Brazil* 9°21S 38°15W **332 C4**
Paulo de Faria *Brazil* 20°2S 49°24W **333 F2**
Paulo E. Virginia, Gruta
Brazil 22°56S 43°16W **135 B1**
Paulpietersburg *S. Africa* 27°23S 30°50E **271 C5**
Pauls Valley *U.S.A.* 34°44N 97°13W **314 D6**
Paulshof *Germany* 52°34N 13°42E **115 A5**
Pauma Valley *U.S.A.* 33°16N 116°58W **307 M10**
Paung *Burma* 16°37N 94°28E **241 G5**
Paungde *Burma* 18°29N 95°30E **241 F5**
Pauni *India* 20°48N 79°40E **244 D4**
Pauri *India* 30°9N 78°47E **243 D8**
Pausa *Peru* 15°16S 73°22W **330 D3**
Pauto ➜ *Colombia* 5°9N 70°55W **328 B3**
Pavagada *India* 14°6N 77°16E **245 G3**
Pāveh *Iran* 35°3N 46°22E **213 E12**
Pavelets *Russia* 53°49N 39°14E **188 F10**
Pavia *Italy* 45°7N 9°8E **198 C6**
Pavilion *U.S.A.* 42°52N 78°1W **312 D6**
Pavilly *France* 49°34N 0°57E **172 C7**
Pāvilosta *Latvia* 56°53N 21°14E **184 B8**
Pavlikeni *Bulgaria* 43°14N 25°20E **203 C9**
Pavlodar *Kazakhstan* 52°33N 77°0E **217 B9**
Pavlograd = Pavlohrad
Ukraine 48°30N 35°52E **189 H8**
Pavlohrad *Ukraine* 48°30N 35°52E **189 H8**
Pavlovo *Russia* 55°58N 43°5E **190 C6**
Pavlovsk *Russia* 50°26N 40°5E **190 E5**
Pavlovskaya *Russia* 46°17N 39°47E **191 G4**
Pavlovskiy-Posad *Russia* 55°47N 38°42E **188 E10**
Pavo *U.S.A.* 30°58N 83°45W **316 E6**
Pavullo nel Frignano
Italy 44°20N 10°50E **198 D7**
Pavuvu *Solomon Is.* 9°4S 159°8E **287 M10**
Paw Paw *Ill., U.S.A.* 41°41N 88°59W **310 C8**
Paw Paw *Mich., U.S.A.* 42°13N 85°53W **311 B11**
Pawahku *Burma* 26°11N 98°40E **241 B7**
Pawai, Pulau *Singapore* 1°11N 103°44E **237 d**
Pawan ➜ *Indonesia* 1°55S 110°0E **235 C4**
Pawayan *India* 28°4N 80°6E **243 E9**
Pawhuska *U.S.A.* 36°40N 96°20W **314 C6**
Pawling *U.S.A.* 41°34N 73°36W **313 E11**
Pawnee *Ill., U.S.A.* 39°36N 89°35W **310 E7**
Pawnee *Okla., U.S.A.* 36°20N 96°48W **314 C6**
Pawnee City *U.S.A.* 40°7N 96°9W **308 E5**
Pawtucket *U.S.A.* 41°53N 71°23W **313 E13**
Paxi *Greece* 39°14N 20°12E **206 C10**
Paximadia *Greece* 35°0N 24°35E **207 F5**
Paxson *U.S.A.* 63°2N 145°30W **303 E11**
Paxton *U.S.A.* 40°27N 88°6W **310 D8**
Paya Lebar *Singapore* 1°21N 103°52E **138 A3**
Payagyi *Burma* 17°29N 96°32E **241 G6**
Payakumbuh *Indonesia* 0°20S 100°35E **234 C2**
Payapa = General Tinio
Phil. 15°39N 121°10E **232 D3**
Payas = Yakacık *Turkey* 36°46N 36°11E **250 B7**
Payerne *Switz.* 46°49N 6°56E **179 J2**
Payette *U.S.A.* 44°5N 116°56W **304 D5**
Paymogo *Spain* 37°44N 7°21W **195 H3**
Payne *U.S.A.* 41°5N 84°44W **311 C12**
Payne Bay = Kangirsuk
Canada 60°0N 70°0W **295 F18**
Payne L. *Canada* 59°30N 74°30W **295 F17**
Payne Pt. *Ascension I.* 7°57S 14°25W **153 g**
Paynes Find *Australia* 29°15S 117°42E **279 E2**
Paynesville *Liberia* 6°20N 10°45W **262 D2**
Paynesville *Minn., U.S.A.* 45°23N 94°43W **308 C6**
Payo Obispo = Chetumal
Mexico 18°30N 88°20W **319 D7**
Pays de la Loire □ *France* 47°45N 0°25W **172 E6**
Paysandú *Uruguay* 32°19S 58°8W **334 C4**
Payson *Ariz., U.S.A.* 34°14N 111°20W **305 J8**
Payson *Utah, U.S.A.* 40°3N 111°44W **304 F8**
Paz ➜ *Guatemala* 13°44N 90°10W **320 D1**
Paz, B. de la *Mexico* 24°9N 110°25W **318 C2**
Pāzanān *Iran* 30°35N 49°59E **247 D6**
Pazar *Turkey* 41°10N 40°50E **213 B9**
Pazarcık *Turkey* 37°30N 37°17E **212 D7**
Pazardzhik *Bulgaria* 42°12N 24°20E **203 D8**
Pazardzhik □ *Bulgaria* 42°12N 24°20E **203 D8**
Pazarköy *Turkey* 39°51N 27°24E **205 B9**
Pazarlar *Turkey* 38°59N 29°7E **205 C11**
Pazaryeri *Turkey* 40°0N 29°56E **205 B11**
Pazaryolu *Turkey* 40°21N 40°47E **213 B9**
Pazin *Croatia* 45°14N 13°56E **199 C10**
Pazña *Bolivia* 18°36S 66°55W **330 D4**
Pčinja ➜ *Macedonia* 41°50N 21°45E **202 E5**
Pe Ell *U.S.A.* 46°34N 123°18W **306 D3**
Pe ➜ *U.S.A.* 31°1N 85°51W **316 D4**
Peabody *U.S.A.* 42°31N 70°56W **313 D14**
Peace ➜ *Alta., Canada* 59°0N 111°25W **296 B6**
Peace ➜ *Fla., U.S.A.* 26°56N 82°6W **317 J7**
Peace Point *Canada* 59°7N 112°27W **296 B6**
Peace River *Canada* 56°15N 117°18W **296 B5**
Peach Springs *U.S.A.* 35°32N 113°25W **305 J7**
Peachland *Canada* 49°47N 119°45W **296 D5**
Peachtree City *U.S.A.* 33°25N 84°35W **316 B5**
Peacock Pt. *Wake I.* 19°16N 166°37E **302 b**
Peak, The = Kinder Scout
U.K. 53°24N 1°52W **168 D6**
Peak, The *Ascension I.* 7°57S 14°20W **153 g**
Peak Charles △ *Australia* 32°42S 121°10E **279 F3**
Peak District △ *U.K.* 53°24N 1°46W **168 D6**
Peak Hill *Australia* 32°47S 148°11E **283 B8**
Peak Ra. *Australia* 22°50S 148°20E **280 C4**
Peake *Australia* 35°25S 139°55E **282 C3**
Peake Cr. ➜ *Australia* 28°2S 136°7E **281 D2**
Peakhurst *Australia* 33°57S 151°3E **139 B1**
Peal de Becerro *Spain* 37°55N 3°7W **195 H7**
Peale, Mt. *U.S.A.* 38°26N 109°14W **304 G9**
Peale I. *Wake I.* 19°18N 166°37E **302 b**
Peania *Greece* 37°56N 23°50E **112 B3**
Pearblossom *U.S.A.* 34°30N 117°55W **307 L9**
Pearl *U.S.A.* 39°28N 90°38W **310 E6**
Pearl ➜ *U.S.A.* 30°11N 89°32W **315 F10**
Pearl and Hermes Reef
U.S.A. 27°55N 175°45W **302 F8**
Pearl Banks *Sri Lanka* 8°45N 79°45E **245 K4**
Pearl City *U.S.A.* 21°24N 157°59W **302 K14**
Pearl Harbor *U.S.A.* 21°21N 157°57W **302 K14**
Pearl Harbor Nat. Wildlife Refuge △
U.S.A. 21°23N 157°59W **302 K14**
Pearl River = Zhu Jiang ➜
China 22°45N 113°37E **229 F9**
Pearl River *U.S.A.* 41°4N 74°2W **313 E10**
Pearl River Bridge *China* 22°15N 113°48E **219 a**
Pearls *Grenada* 12°9N 61°37W **323 q**
Pearls Rock *Grenada* 12°9N 61°36W **323 q**
Pearsall *U.S.A.* 28°54N 99°6W **314 G5**
Pearson *U.S.A.* 31°18N 82°51W **316 D7**
Pearson Int. Toronto ✈ (YYZ)
Canada 43°46N 79°35W **141 A1**
Peary Chan. *Canada* 79°40N 101°30W **295 B11**
Peary Land *Greenland* 82°40N 33°0W **154 A7**
Pease ➜ *U.S.A.* 34°12N 99°2W **314 D5**
Peawanuck *Canada* 55°15N 85°12W **298 A2**
Pebane *Mozam.* 17°10S 38°8E **269 F4**
Pebas *Peru* 3°10S 71°46W **328 D3**
Pebble, I. *Falk. Is.* 51°20S 59°40W **153 f**
Pebble Beach *U.S.A.* 36°34N 121°57W **306 J5**
Peć = Pejë *Kosovo* 42°40N 20°17E **202 D4**
Peçanha *Brazil* 18°33S 42°34W **333 E3**
Pecatonica *U.S.A.* 42°19N 89°22W **310 B7**
Pecatonica ➜ *U.S.A.* 42°26N 89°12W **310 B7**
Péccioli *Italy* 43°33N 10°43E **198 E7**
Pechea *Romania* 45°36N 27°49E **183 E12**
Pechenga *Russia* 69°29N 31°4E **160 B24**
Pechenizhyn *Ukraine* 48°30N 24°48E **183 B9**
Pechiguera, Pta.
Canary Is. 28°51N 13°53W **153 e2**
Pechnezhskoye Vdkhr.
Ukraine 50°5N 36°54E **189 G9**
Pechora *Russia* 65°10N 57°11E **186 A10**
Pechora ➜ *Russia* 68°13N 54°15E **186 A9**
Pechorskaya Guba *Russia* 68°40N 54°0E **186 A9**
Pechory *Russia* 57°48N 27°40E **188 D4**
Pecica *Romania* 46°10N 21°3E **182 D6**
Pecka *Serbia* 44°18N 19°33E **202 B3**
Peckham *U.K.* 51°28N 0°3W **125 B3**
Pécora, C. *Italy* 39°27N 8°23E **200 C1**
Pecos *N. Mex., U.S.A.* 35°35N 105°41W **305 J11**
Pecos *Tex., U.S.A.* 31°26N 103°30W **314 F3**
Pecos ➜ *U.S.A.* 29°42N 101°22W **314 G4**
Pécs *Hungary* 46°5N 18°15E **182 D3**
Pedasí *Panama* 7°32N 80°2W **320 E3**
Pedda Bellala *India* 19°4N 78°49E **244 E4**
Peddapalli *India* 18°40N 79°24E **244 E4**
Peddapuram *India* 17°6N 82°8E **244 F6**
Pedder, L. *Australia* 42°55S 146°10E **281 G4**
Peddie *S. Africa* 33°14S 27°7E **271 D4**
Pedernales *Dom. Rep.* 18°2N 71°44W **321 C5**
Pedernales *Ecuador* 0°5N 80°3W **328 C1**
Pederstrup *Denmark* 55°44N 12°20E **118 A2**
Pedieos ➜ *Cyprus* 35°10N 33°54E **207 E9**
Pedirka Desert *Australia* 26°47S 134°11E **281 A1**
Pedra Azul *Brazil* 16°2S 41°17W **333 E3**
Pedra Branca *Brazil* 0°51N 51°58W **329 C7**
Pedra Grande, Recifes de
Brazil 17°45S 38°58W **333 E4**
Pedra Lume *C. Verde Is.* 16°40N 22°52W **153 j**
Pedralbes *Spain* 41°23N 2°7E **114 A1**
Pedras Negras *Brazil* 12°51S 62°54W **331 C5**
Pedras Tinhosas, I.
São Tomé & Principe 1°22N 7°17E **265 a**
Pedregal de San Angel, Jardines del
Mexico 19°19N 99°12W **128 C1**
Pedreguer *Spain* 38°48N 0°3E **197 G5**
Pedreiras *Brazil* 4°32S 44°40W **332 B3**
Pedro Afonso *Brazil* 9°0S 48°10W **332 C2**
Pedro Bank *Caribbean* 17°5N 78°20W **320 C4**
Pedro Bay *U.S.A.* 59°47N 154°7W **303 G9**
Pedro Cays *Jamaica* 17°5N 77°48W **320 C4**
Pedro Chico *Colombia* 1°4N 70°25W **328 C3**
Pedro de Valdivia *Chile* 22°55S 69°38W **334 A2**
Pedro Dorado *Colombia* 1°0N 70°14W **328 C3**
Pedro González *Venezuela* 11°7N 63°56W **329 a**
Pedro Juan Caballero
Paraguay 22°30S 55°40W **335 A4**
Pedro Miguel Locks *Panama* 9°1N 79°36W **320 c**
Pedro Muñoz *Spain* 39°25N 2°56W **195 F8**
Pedro Pt. = North West Pt.
Jamaica 18°27N 78°13W **320 a**
Pedrógão Grande *Portugal* 39°55N 8°9W **194 F2**
Pee Dee = Great Pee Dee ➜
U.S.A. 33°21N 79°10W **315 E15**
Peebinga *Australia* 34°52S 140°57E **282 C4**
Peebles *Borders, U.K.* 55°40N 3°11W **167 F5**
Peebles *Ohio, U.S.A.* 38°57N 83°24W **311 F13**
Peekskill *U.S.A.* 41°17N 73°55W **313 E11**
Peel *I. of Man* 54°13N 4°40W **168 C3**
Peel ➜ *N.S.W., Australia* 30°50S 150°29E **283 A9**
Peel ➜ *N.W.T., Canada* 67°0N 135°0W **294 D5**
Peel Sd. *Canada* 73°0N 96°0W **294 C12**
Peene ➜ *Germany* 54°9N 13°46E **178 A9**
Peera Peera Poolanna L.
Australia 26°30S 138°0E **281 D2**
Peerless Lake *Canada* 56°37N 114°40W **296 B6**
Peers *Canada* 53°40N 116°0W **296 C5**
Peery L. *Australia* 30°45S 143°35E **282 A5**
Pegasus Bay *N.Z.* 43°20S 173°10E **285 D8**
Peggau *Austria* 47°12N 15°21E **180 D8**
Peggy Guggenheim, Collezione
Venice, Italy **142 b2**
Pegnitz *Germany* 49°44N 11°31E **179 F7**
Pegnitz ➜ *Germany* 49°30N 10°59E **179 F6**
Pego *Spain* 38°51N 0°8W **197 G4**
Pegu = Bago *Burma* 17°20N 96°29E **241 G6**
Pegu Yoma *Burma* 19°0N 96°0E **241 F6**
Peguera *Spain* 39°32N 2°26E **206 B3**
Pehčevo *Macedonia* 41°41N 22°55E **202 E6**
Pehlivanköy *Turkey* 41°20N 26°55E **202 E10**
Pehuajó *Argentina* 35°45S 62°0W **334 D3**
Pei Xian *China* 34°44N 116°55E **226 G9**
Peian = Bei'an *China* 48°10N 126°20E **219 B14**
Peihai = Beihai *China* 21°28N 109°6E **228 G7**
Peikang *Taiwan* 23°34N 120°18E **225 C2**
Peikang Hsi ➜ *Taiwan* 24°2N 120°20E **225 C2**
Peikant'ang *Taiwan* 26°13N 120°0E **225 b**
Peimen *Taiwan* 23°16N 120°7E **225 C2**
Peinan *Taiwan* 22°47N 121°7E **225 D3**
Peinan Hsi ➜ *Taiwan* 22°46N 121°2E **225 D3**
Peinanchu Shan *Taiwan* 23°3N 120°52E **225 C2**
Peine *Chile* 23°45S 68°8W **334 A2**
Peine *Niedersachsen, Germany* 52°19N 10°14E **178 C6**
Peip'ing = Beijing *China* 39°53N 116°21E **114 B1**
Peipu *Taiwan* 24°2N 121°36E **225 B3**
Peipus, L. = Chudskoye, Ozero
Russia 58°13N 27°30E **188 C4**
Peissenberg *Germany* 47°48N 11°4E **179 H7**
Peitawu Shan *Taiwan* 22°38N 120°46E **225 D2**
Peitou *Changhua, Taiwan* 23°52N 120°30E **225 C2**
Peitou *T'aipei, Taiwan* 25°11N 121°27E **225 A3**
Peitun *Taiwan* 24°10N 120°41E **225 B2**
Peitz *Germany* 51°51N 14°24E **178 D10**
Peixe *Brazil* 12°0S 48°40W **333 D2**
Peixe ➜ *Brazil* 21°31S 51°58W **333 F1**
Peixoto de Azeredo ➜
Brazil 10°6S 55°31W **331 C6**
Pejantan, Pulau *Indonesia* 0°7N 107°13E **234 B3**
Pejë *Kosovo* 42°40N 20°17E **202 D4**
Pek ➜ *Serbia* 44°45N 21°29E **202 B5**
Pekalongan *Indonesia* 6°53S 109°40E **235 D3**
Pekan *Malaysia* 3°30N 103°25E **237 L4**
Pekan Nenas *Malaysia* 1°31N 103°24E **237 d**
Pekanbaru *Indonesia* 0°30N 101°15E **234 B2**
Pekin *U.S.A.* 40°35N 89°40W **310 D7**
Peking = Beijing *China* 39°53N 116°21E **114 B1**
Pekutatan *Indonesia* 8°25S 114°49E **231 J17**
Pela *Greece* 40°46N 22°23E **202 F6**
Pelabuhan Ratu, Teluk
Indonesia 7°5S 106°30E **234 D3**
Pelabuhanratu *Indonesia* 7°0S 106°32E **234 D3**
Pélagos = Kira Panagia
Greece 39°17N 24°4E **204 B6**
Pelaihari *Indonesia* 3°55S 114°45E **235 C4**
Pelat, Mt. *France* 44°16N 6°42E **175 D10**
Pelcowizna *Poland* 52°17N 21°0E **143 B2**
Pełczyce *Poland* 53°3N 15°16E **185 E2**
Peleaga, Vf. *Romania* 45°22N 22°55E **182 E7**
Pelechuco *Bolivia* 14°48S 69°4W **330 C4**
Pelée, Mt. *Martinique* 14°48N 61°10W **322 j**
Pelee, Pt. *Canada* 41°54N 82°31W **298 D3**
Pelee I. *Canada* 41°47N 82°40W **312 E2**
Pelejo *Peru* 6°10S 75°49W **330 B2**
Pelekech *Kenya* 3°52N 35°8E **268 B4**
Peleliu I. *Palau* 7°1N 134°15E **288 c**
Peleng *Indonesia* 1°20S 123°30E **231 E6**
Pelenge
Dem. Rep. of the Congo 2°44S 22°39E **264 C4**
Pelentong *Malaysia* 1°32N 103°49E **237 d**
Pélézi *Ivory C.* 7°17N 6°54W **262 D3**
Pelham *U.S.A.* 31°8N 84°9W **316 D5**
Pelhřimov *Czechia* 49°24N 15°12E **180 B8**
Pelican *U.S.A.* 57°58N 136°14W **296 B1**
Pelican L. *Canada* 52°28N 100°20W **297 C8**
Pelican Narrows *Canada* 55°10N 102°56W **297 B8**
Pelion *U.S.A.* 33°46N 81°15W **316 B8**
Pelister △ *Macedonia* 41°0N 21°10E **202 F5**
Pelješac *Croatia* 42°55N 17°25E **199 F14**
Pelkosenniemi *Finland* 67°6N 27°28E **160 C22**
Pell City *U.S.A.* 33°35N 86°17W **316 B3**
Pella *Greece* 40°52N 22°0E **202 F6**
Pella *Northern Cape, S. Africa* 29°1S 19°6E **270 C2**
Pella *Iowa, U.S.A.* 41°25N 92°55W **310 C4**
Pello *Finland* 66°47N 23°59E **160 C20**
Pellworm *Germany* 54°31N 8°39E **178 A4**
Pelly ➜ *Canada* 62°47N 137°19W **296 A1**
Pelly Bay *Canada* 68°38N 89°50W **295 D14**
Peloponnesos □ *Greece* 37°10N 22°0E **204 D4**
Peloponnisos Station *Athens, Greece* **112 a1**
Peloritani, Monti *Italy* 38°3N 15°20E **201 D8**
Pelorus ➜ *N.Z.* 41°16S 173°45E **285 B8**
Pelorus Sd. *N.Z.* 40°59S 173°59E **285 A8**
Pelotas *Brazil* 31°42S 52°23W **335 C5**
Pelotas ➜ *Brazil* 27°28S 51°55W **335 B5**
Pelovo *Bulgaria* 43°26N 24°17E **203 C8**
Pelplin *Poland* 53°55N 18°42E **184 E5**
Pelvoux, Massif du *France* 44°52N 6°20E **175 D10**
Pemalang *Indonesia* 6°53S 109°23E **235 D3**
Pemanggil, Pulau
Malaysia 2°37N 104°21E **237 L5**
Pematangsiantar *Indonesia* 2°57N 99°5E **234 B1**
Pemba *Mozam.* 12°58S 40°30E **269 E5**
Pemba *Zambia* 16°30S 27°28E **269 F2**
Pemba Channel *Tanzania* 5°0S 39°37E **268 D4**
Pemba I. *Tanzania* 5°0S 39°45E **268 D4**
Pemberton *W. Austral., Australia* 34°30S 116°0E **279 F2**
Pemberton *B.C., Canada* 50°25N 122°50W **296 C4**
Pembina ➜ *Canada* 54°45N 114°17W **296 C6**
Pembroke *Ont., Canada* 45°50N 77°7W **298 C4**
Pembroke *Trin. & Tob.* 11°13N 60°37W **323 s**
Pembroke *Pembs., U.K.* 51°41N 4°55W **169 F3**
Pembroke *Ga., U.S.A.* 32°8N 81°37W **316 C8**
Pembroke Park *U.S.A.* 25°59N 80°10W **129 C2**
Pembroke Pines *U.S.A.* 26°0N 80°13W **129 B1**
Pembrokeshire □ *U.K.* 51°52N 4°56W **169 F3**
Pembrokeshire Coast △
U.K. 51°50N 5°2W **169 F2**
Pembuang ➜ *Indonesia* 3°24S 112°33E **235 C4**
Pen *India* 18°45N 73°5E **244 E1**
Pen-y-bont ar Ogwr = Bridgend
U.K. 51°30N 3°34W **169 F4**
Pen-y-Ghent *U.K.* 54°10N 2°14W **168 C5**
Peña, Sierra de la *Spain* 42°32N 0°45W **196 C4**
Peña de Francia, Sierra de la
Spain 40°32N 6°10W **194 E4**
Penafiel *Portugal* 41°12N 8°17W **194 D2**
Peñafiel *Spain* 41°35N 4°7W **194 D6**
Peñaflor *Spain* 37°43N 5°21W **195 H5**
Penal *Trin. & Tob.* 10°9N 61°29W **323 t**
Peñalara *Spain* 40°51N 3°57W **194 E7**
Peñalolén *Chile* 33°28S 70°32W **137 B2**
Penalva *Brazil* 3°18S 45°10W **332 B2**
Penal/Debe □ *Trin. & Tob.* 10°14N 61°27W **323 t**
Penamacôr *Portugal* 40°10N 7°10W **194 E3**
Penang = Pinang *Malaysia* 5°25N 100°15E **237 c**
Penápolis *Brazil* 21°30S 50°0W **335 A6**
Peñaranda de Bracamonte
Spain 40°53N 5°13W **194 E5**
Peñarroya *Spain* 40°25N 0°40W **196 E4**
Peñarroya-Pueblonuevo
Spain 38°19N 5°16W **195 G5**
Penarth *U.K.* 51°26N 3°11W **169 F4**
Peñas, C. de *Spain* 43°42N 5°52W **194 B5**
Penas, G. de *Chile* 47°0S 75°0W **336 C2**
Peñas, Pta. *Venezuela* 11°17N 62°0W **329 A5**
Peñas de San Pedro *Spain* 38°44N 2°0W **197 G3**
Peñas del Chache
Canary Is. 29°6N 13°33W **153 e2**
Peñausende *Spain* 41°17N 5°52W **194 D5**
Pench ➜ *India* 21°17N 79°10E **244 D4**
Pench △ *India* 21°45N 79°20E **243 J8**
Pench'i = Benxi *China* 41°20N 123°48E **226 D12**
Pend Oreille ➜ *U.S.A.* 49°4N 117°37W **304 B5**
Pend Oreille, L. *U.S.A.* 48°10N 116°21W **304 B5**
Pendalofos *Greece* 40°14N 21°12E **202 F5**
Pendé ➜ *C.A.R.* 7°55N 16°36E **264 A3**
Pendembu *Eastern, S. Leone* 8°10N 10°42W **262 D2**
Pendembu *Northern, S. Leone* 9°7N 11°14W **262 D2**
Pendências *Brazil* 5°15S 36°43W **332 C4**
Pender B. *Australia* 16°45S 122°42E **278 C3**
Pendik *Turkey* 40°53N 29°13E **203 F13**
Pendjari ➜ *Benin* 10°55N 0°50E **263 C5**
Pendjari △ *Benin* 11°15N 1°32E **263 C5**
Pendleton *Ind., U.S.A.* 40°0N 85°45W **311 E11**
Pendleton *Oreg., U.S.A.* 45°40N 118°47W **304 D4**
Pendopo *Indonesia* 3°16S 103°52E **234 C2**
Pendra *India* 22°46N 81°57E **243 H9**
Pendzhikent = Panjakent
Tajikistan 39°29N 67°37E **217 E7**
Penebangan *Indonesia* 1°13S 109°15E **235 C3**
Peneda-Gerês △ *Portugal* 41°57N 8°15W **194 D2**

Penedo Brazil 10°15S 36°36W 332 D4
Penelokan Indonesia 8°17S 115°22E 231 J18
Penetanguishene Canada 44°50N 79°55W 312 B5
Penfield U.S.A. 41°13N 78°35W 312 E6
Penfro = Pembroke U.K. 51°41N 4°55W 169 F3
Peng Chau Hong Kong, China 22°17N 114°2E 122 B2
Peng Siang → Singapore 1°24N 103°43E 138 A2
Peng'an China 31°2N 106°22E 228 B6
Penganga → India 19°53N 79°9E 244 E4
Penge Kasai-Or., Dem. Rep. of the Congo 5°30S 24°33E 265 D4
Penge Sud-Kivu, Dem. Rep. of the Congo 4°27S 28°25E 268 C2
Penge London, U.K. 51°24N 0°3W 125 B3
P'enghu □ Taiwan 23°30N 119°30E 225 C1
P'enghu Ch'üntou Taiwan 23°34N 119°30E 225 C1
P'enghu Tao Taiwan 23°34N 119°37E 225 C1
Penglai China 37°48N 120°42E 227 F11
Pengshan China 30°14N 103°58E 228 B4
Pengshui China 29°17N 108°12E 228 C7
Penguin Australia 41°8S 146°6E 281 G4
Pengxi China 30°44N 105°45E 228 B5
Pengze China 29°52N 116°32E 229 C11
Pengzhou China 31°4N 103°32E 228 B4
Penha Brazil 22°49S 43°17W 135 A1
Penhalonga Zimbabwe 18°52S 32°40E 269 F3
Peniche Portugal 39°19N 9°22W 195 F1
Penicuik U.K. 55°50N 3°13W 121 B2
Penida, Nusa Indonesia 8°45S 115°30E 231 K18
Peninnes, Alpes = Pennine, Alpi Alps 46°4N 7°30E 179 J3
Peninsular Malaysia □ Malaysia 4°0N 102°0E 237 L4
Peñíscola Spain 40°22N 0°24E 196 E5
Penitente, Serra do Brazil 8°45S 46°20W 332 C2
Penjaringan Indonesia 6°7S 106°48E 122 A1
Pēnjwin Iraq 35°37N 45°56E 213 E11
Penki = Benxi China 41°20N 123°48E 224 B1
Penkridge U.K. 52°44N 2°6W 168 E5
Penmarch France 47°49N 4°21W 172 E2
Penmarch, Pte. de France 47°48N 4°22W 172 E2
Penn = Penn Hills U.S.A. 40°28N 79°52W 312 F5
Penn Hills U.S.A. 40°28N 79°52W 312 F5
Penn Station New York, U.S.A. 132 c2
Penn Yan U.S.A. 42°40N 77°3W 312 D7
Penna, Punta della Italy 42°10N 14°43E 199 F11
Pennant Canada 50°32N 108°14W 297 C7
Penne Italy 42°27N 13°55E 199 F10
Penner → India 14°35N 80°10E 245 G5
Penneshaw Australia 35°44S 137°56E 282 C2
Pennine, Alpi Alps 46°4N 7°30E 179 J3
Pennines U.K. 54°45N 2°27W 168 C5
Pennington U.S.A. 39°15N 121°47W 306 F5
Pennington → Nigeria 4°45N 5°35E 263 E6
Pennino, Mte. Italy 43°6N 12°53E 199 E9
Pennsburg U.S.A. 40°23N 75°29W 313 F9
Pennsylvania □ U.S.A. 40°45N 77°30W 309 E15
Pennsylvania Avenue Washington, D.C., U.S.A. 143 b2
Pennville U.S.A. 40°30N 85°9W 311 D11
Penny Canada 53°51N 121°20W 296 C4
Peno Russia 57°2N 32°49E 188 D7
Penobscot → U.S.A. 44°30N 68°48W 309 C19
Penobscot B. U.S.A. 44°35N 68°50W 309 C19
Penola Australia 37°25S 140°48E 282 D4
Penong Australia 31°56S 133°1E 279 F5
Penonomé Panama 8°31N 80°21W 320 E3
Penot, Mt. Vanuatu 16°20S 167°31E 287 E5
Penrhyn Cook Is. 9°0S 158°0W 289 H12
Penrith N.S.W., Australia 33°43S 150°38E 283 B9
Penrith Cumb., U.K. 54°40N 2°45W 168 C5
Penryn U.K. 50°9N 5°7W 169 G2
Pensacola U.S.A. 30°25N 87°13W 317 E2
Pensacola B. U.S.A. 30°25N 87°5W 317 E2
Pensacola Mts. Antarctica 84°0S 40°0W 151 E1
Pense Canada 50°25N 104°59W 297 C8
Penshurst Australia 37°49S 142°20E 282 D5
Pensiangan Malaysia 4°33N 116°19E 235 B5
Pentadaktylos Cyprus 35°20N 33°20E 207 E9
Pentagon U.S.A. 38°53N 77°3W 143 B2
Pentecost Vanuatu 15°42S 168°10E 287 E6
Pentecostes Brazil 3°48S 39°17W 332 B4
Pentecôte = Pentecost Vanuatu 15°42S 168°10E 287 E6
Penticton Canada 49°30N 119°38W 296 D5
Pentland Australia 20°32S 145°25E 280 C4
Pentland Firth U.K. 58°43N 3°10W 167 C5
Pentland Hills U.K. 55°48N 3°25W 167 F5
Penukonda India 14°5N 77°38E 245 G3
Penza Russia 53°15N 45°5E 190 D7
Penza □ Russia 52°50N 44°50E 190 D7
Penzance U.K. 50°7N 5°33W 169 G2
Penzberg Germany 47°45N 11°22E 179 H7
Penzhino Russia 63°30N 167°55E 215 C17
Penzhinskaya Guba Russia 61°30N 163°0E 215 C17
Penzing Austria 48°11N 16°18E 142 A1
Penzlin Germany 53°30N 13°5E 178 B9
People's Park China 31°13N 121°28E 138 B1
People's Square China 31°13N 121°28E 138 B1
Peoria Ariz., U.S.A. 33°43N 112°14W 305 K7
Peoria Ill., U.S.A. 40°42N 89°36W 310 D7
Peoria Heights U.S.A. 40°45N 89°35W 310 D7
Peotone U.S.A. 41°20N 87°48W 311 C9
Pepacton Res. U.S.A. 42°5N 74°58W 313 D10
Pepani → S. Africa 25°49S 22°47E 270 C3
Pepeekeo U.S.A. 19°51N 155°6W 302 D6
Pepel S. Leone 8°40N 13°5W 262 D2
Peqin Albania 41°3N 19°44E 202 E3
Pera Hd. Australia 12°55S 141°37E 280 A3
Perabumulih Indonesia 3°27S 104°15E 234 C2
Perachora Greece 38°2N 22°56E 204 C4
Perachori Greece 38°21N 20°43E 207 C2
Perak □ Malaysia 5°0N 101°0E 237 K3
Perak → Malaysia 4°0N 100°50E 237 K3
Perales del Alfambra Spain 40°38N 1°0W 196 E4
Perales del Puerto Spain 40°10N 6°40W 194 E4
Perales del Río Spain 40°18N 3°38W 127 C2
Peralta Spain 42°20N 1°48W 196 C3
Perama Epiros, Greece 39°42N 20°51E 204 B2
Perama Kerkyra, Greece 39°34N 19°54E 206 B9
Perama Kriti, Greece 35°20N 24°40E 207 E5
Perämeri △ Finland 65°35N 24°22E 160 D21
Perancak Indonesia 8°24S 114°37E 231 J17
Peräpohjola Finland 66°16N 26°10E 160 C22
Perast Montenegro 42°31N 18°47E 202 D2
Peratia Greece 38°49N 20°45E 207 B2
Peravillo Mexico City, Mexico 128 a3
Percé Canada 48°31N 64°13W 299 C7
Perche France 48°31N 1°1E 172 D8
Perche, Collines du France 48°30N 0°40E 171 B4
Perche ⌓ France 48°24N 0°46E 172 D7
Perchtoldsdorf Austria 48°7N 16°17E 142 B1
Percival Lakes Australia 21°25S 125°0E 278 D4
Percy Manche, France 48°55N 1°11W 172 D5
Percy Ill., U.S.A. 38°5N 89°41W 310 F7
Percy Is. Australia 21°39S 150°16E 280 C5
Perdido → Argentina 42°55S 67°0W 336 B3
Perdido, Mte. Spain 42°40N 0°5E 196 C5
Perdizes Brazil 23°32S 46°39W 137 B2
Perdu, Mt. = Perdido, Mte. Spain 42°40N 0°5E 196 C5
Perechyn Ukraine 48°44N 22°28E 182 B7
Perehinske Ukraine 48°49N 24°11E 183 B9
Pereira Colombia 4°49N 75°43W 328 C2
Perejil Spain 35°55N 5°25W 195 K5
Perelazovskiy Russia 49°8N 42°35E 191 F6
Peremul Par India 11°10N 72°4E 245 J1
Peremyshl = Przemyśl Poland 49°50N 22°45E 185 J9
Perené → Peru 11°9S 74°14W 330 C3
Perenjori Australia 29°26S 116°16E 279 E2
Peresecina Moldova 47°16N 28°46E 183 C13
Pereslavl-Zalesskiy Russia 56°45N 38°50E 188 D10
Peretu Romania 44°3N 25°5E 183 F10
Pereyaslav-Khmelnytskyy Ukraine 50°3N 31°28E 189 G6
Pereyma Ukraine 48°4N 29°30E 183 B14
Pérez, I. Mexico 22°24N 89°42W 319 C7
Perg Austria 48°15N 14°38E 180 C7
Pergamino Argentina 33°52S 60°30W 334 C3
Pergamon Turkey 39°8N 27°11E 205 B9
Pergamon Museum Berlin, Germany 115 a4
Pergau → Malaysia 5°23N 102°2E 237 K3
Perge Turkey 37°30N 30°56E 250 A1
Pergine Valsugana Italy 46°4N 11°14E 199 B8
Pérgola Italy 43°34N 12°50E 199 E9
Perham U.S.A. 46°36N 95°34W 308 B6
Perhentian, Kepulauan Malaysia 5°54N 102°42E 237 K4
Peri → Turkey 38°53N 39°52E 213 C8
Periam Romania 46°2N 20°52E 182 D5
Péribonka → Canada 48°45N 72°5W 299 C5
Péribonka, L. Canada 50°1N 71°10W 299 B5
Péribonka, La Centrale de Canada 49°30N 71°10W 299 C5
Perico Argentina 24°20S 65°5W 334 A2
Pericos Mexico 25°3N 107°42W 318 B3
Périers France 49°11N 1°25W 172 C5
Périgord France 45°0N 0°40E 174 D4
Périgord-Limousin ⌓ France 45°40N 0°50E 174 C4
Périgueux France 45°10N 0°42E 174 C4
Perijá, Sierra de Colombia 9°30N 73°3W 328 B3
Perijá △ Venezuela 9°30N 72°55W 328 B3
Peringat Malaysia 6°2N 102°17E 237 J4
Perisher Valley Australia 36°27S 148°25E 283 D8
Peristera Greece 39°15N 23°58E 204 B5
Peristeri Greece 38°1N 23°42E 112 A2
Peristerona → Cyprus 35°8N 33°5E 207 E9
Perito Moreno Argentina 46°36S 70°56W 336 C2
Perito Moreno △ Argentina 47°49S 72°17W 336 C2
Peritoró Brazil 4°20S 44°18W 332 B3
Perivale U.K. 51°31N 0°18W 125 A2
Perivol = Dragovishtitsa Bulgaria 42°22N 22°39E 202 D6
Periyakulam India 10°5N 77°30E 245 J3
Periyar → India 10°15N 76°10E 245 J3
Periyar, L. India 9°25N 77°10E 245 K3
Periyar △ India 9°25N 77°10E 245 K3
Perk Belgium 50°56N 4°30E 116 A2
Perkasie U.S.A. 40°22N 75°18W 313 F9
Perković Croatia 43°41N 16°10E 199 E13
Perlach Germany 48°5N 11°37E 131 B2
Perlacher Forst Germany 48°4N 11°34E 131 B2
Perlas, Arch. de las Panama 8°41N 79°7W 320 E4
Perlas, Punta de Nic. 12°30N 83°30W 320 D3
Perleberg Germany 53°5N 11°52E 178 B7
Perlez Serbia 45°11N 20°22E 182 E5
Perlis □ Malaysia 6°30N 100°15E 237 J2
Perm Russia 58°0N 56°10E 186 C10
Përmet Albania 40°15N 20°21E 202 F4
Permskoye = Komsomolsk-na-Amur Russia 50°30N 137°0E 219 A16
Pernambuco = Recife Brazil 8°0S 35°0W 332 C5
Pernambuco □ Brazil 8°0S 37°0W 332 C4
Pernambuco Abyssal Plain Atl. Oc. 5°0S 24°0W 152 G9
Pernatty Lagoon Australia 31°30S 137°12E 282 A2
Pernik Bulgaria 42°35N 23°2E 202 D7
Pernik □ Bulgaria 42°35N 23°2E 202 D7
Pernov = Pärnu Estonia 58°28N 24°33E 188 C3
Pero Italy 45°30N 9°5E 128 A1
Peron Is. Australia 13°9S 130°4E 278 B5
Peron Pen. Australia 26°0S 113°10E 279 E1
Péronne France 49°55N 2°57E 173 C9
Peropak, Bukit Singapore 1°19N 103°42E 138 B2
Perosa Argentina Italy 44°58N 7°10E 198 D4
Perovo Russia 55°44N 37°45E 129 B3
Perovsk = Qyzylorda Kazakhstan 44°48N 65°28E 216 D7
Perow Canada 54°35N 126°10W 296 C3
Perparim = Pogradec Albania 40°54N 20°37E 202 F4
Perpignan France 42°42N 2°53E 174 F6
Perrégaux = Mohammadia Algeria 35°33N 0°3E 261 A5
Perrine U.S.A. 25°36N 80°21W 317 K9
Perris U.S.A. 33°47N 117°14W 307 M9
Perros-Guirec France 48°49N 3°28W 172 D3
Perry Fla., U.S.A. 30°7N 83°35W 316 E6
Perry Ga., U.S.A. 32°28N 83°44W 316 C6
Perry Iowa, U.S.A. 41°51N 94°6W 310 C2
Perry Mich., U.S.A. 42°50N 84°13W 311 B12
Perry Mo., U.S.A. 39°26N 91°40W 310 E5
Perry N.Y., U.S.A. 42°42N 78°0W 312 D7
Perry Okla., U.S.A. 36°17N 97°14W 314 C6
Perrysburg U.S.A. 41°33N 83°38W 311 C13
Perryton U.S.A. 36°24N 100°48W 314 C4
Perryville Alaska, U.S.A. 55°55N 159°9W 303 J8
Perryville Mo., U.S.A. 37°43N 89°52W 310 G7
Persan France 49°9N 2°16E 173 C9
Persberg Sweden 59°47N 14°15E 162 E8
Perşembe Turkey 41°5N 37°46E 212 B7
Persepolis Iran 29°55N 52°50E 247 D7
Perseverancia Bolivia 14°44S 62°48W 331 C5
Pershing Square Los Angeles, U.S.A. 127 c1
Pershotravensk Ukraine 50°13N 27°40E 177 C14
Pershotravnevoye = Pershotravensk Ukraine 50°13N 27°40E 177 C14
Persia = Iran ■ Asia 33°0N 53°0E 247 C7
Persian Gulf Asia 27°0N 50°0E 247 E6
Perstorp Sweden 56°10N 13°25E 163 H7
Pertek Turkey 38°51N 39°19E 213 C8
Perth W. Austral., Australia 31°57S 115°52E 279 F2
Perth Ont., Canada 44°55N 76°15W 313 B8
Perth Perth & Kinr., U.K. 56°24N 3°26W 167 E5
Perth & Kinross □ U.K. 56°45N 3°55W 167 E5
Perth Amboy U.S.A. 40°30N 74°15W 313 F10
Perth-Andover Canada 46°44N 67°42W 299 C6
Pertuis France 43°42N 5°30E 175 E9
Pertusato, C. France 41°21N 9°11E 175 G13
Pertusella Italy 45°35N 9°3E 128 A1
Peru Ill., U.S.A. 41°20N 89°8W 310 C7
Peru Ind., U.S.A. 40°45N 86°4W 311 D10
Peru N.Y., U.S.A. 44°35N 73°32W 313 B11
Peru ■ S. Amer. 4°0S 75°0W 328 D3
Peru Basin Pac. Oc. 20°0S 95°0W 289 J18
Peru-Chile Trench Pac. Oc. 20°0S 72°0W 326 E3
Perugia Italy 43°7N 12°23E 199 E9
Perušić Croatia 44°40N 15°22E 199 D12
Peruvian Vale St. Vincent 13°11N 61°12W 323 n
Pervomaysk Russia 54°56N 43°58E 190 C6
Pervomaysk Ukraine 48°10N 30°46E 189 H6
Pervomayskiy Kazakhstan 50°16N 82°0E 217 B10
Pervouralsk Russia 56°59N 59°59E 186 C10
Pervouralskiy = Pervouralsk Russia 56°59N 59°59E 186 C10
Pesada Greece 38°7N 20°35E 207 C2
Pesagot West Bank 31°54N 35°13E 123 A2
Pesanggrahan, Kali → Indonesia 6°10S 106°44E 122 B1
Pésaro Italy 43°54N 12°55E 199 E9
Pésaro e Urbino □ Italy 43°45N 12°40E 199 E9
Pescadores = P'enghu Ch'üntou Taiwan 23°34N 119°30E 225 C1
Pescara Italy 42°28N 14°13E 199 F11
Pescara → Italy 42°28N 14°13E 199 F11
Peschanokopskoye Russia 46°14N 41°4E 191 G5
Peschanoye = Yashkul Russia 46°11N 45°21E 191 G7
Peschiera Borromeo Italy 45°26N 9°19E 128 B2
Péscia Italy 43°54N 10°41E 198 E7
Pescina Italy 42°2N 13°39E 199 F10
Pesek, Pulau Singapore 1°17N 103°41E 138 B2
Peshawar Pakistan 34°2N 71°37E 242 B4
Peshkopi Albania 41°41N 20°25E 202 E4
Peshtera Bulgaria 42°2N 24°18E 203 D8
Peshtigo U.S.A. 45°3N 87°45W 308 C10
Peski Russia 51°14N 42°29E 190 E6
Peski Turkmenistan 38°11N 63°22E 216 E6
Pêso da Régua Portugal 41°10N 7°47W 194 D3
Pesochnya = Kirov Russia 54°3N 34°20E 188 E8
Pesqueira Brazil 8°20S 36°42W 332 C4
Pessac France 44°48N 0°37W 174 D3
Pest Hungary 47°29N 19°4E 117 B2
Pest □ Hungary 47°29N 19°5E 182 C4
Pesterzsébet Hungary 47°26N 19°6E 117 B2
Pesthidegkút Hungary 47°33N 18°57E 117 A1
Pestimre Hungary 47°24N 19°11E 117 B3
Pestlőrinc Hungary 47°26N 19°11E 117 B3
Pestovo = Zavolzhye Russia 56°37N 43°26E 190 B6
Pestovo Russia 58°33N 35°42E 188 C8
Pestravka Russia 52°28N 49°57E 190 D9
Pestújhely Hungary 47°32N 19°7E 117 A2
Petah Tiqwa Israel 32°6N 34°53E 251 F5
Petalas Greece 38°25N 21°5E 207 C3
Petalidi Greece 36°57N 21°55E 204 E3
Petalii Greece 38°0N 24°15E 204 D6
Petaling Jaya Malaysia 3°4N 101°42E 237 L3
Petaloudes Greece 36°18N 28°5E 206 E12
Petaluma U.S.A. 38°14N 122°39W 306 G4
Pétange Lux. 49°33N 5°55E 170 E5
Petare Venezuela 10°29N 66°49W 321 D6
Petaro Pakistan 25°31N 68°18E 242 G3
Petas Helsinki, Finland 60°15N 24°50E 121 B2
Petas Greece 39°10N 21°2E 204 B3
Petatlán Mexico 17°31N 101°16W 318 D4
Petauke Zambia 14°14S 31°20E 269 E3
Petawawa Canada 45°54N 77°17W 298 C4
Petén Itzá, L. Guatemala 16°58N 89°50W 320 C2
Peter I. Br. Virgin Is. 18°22N 64°35W 321 b
Peter I. Øy Antarctica 69°0S 91°0W 151 C16
Peter Pond L. Canada 55°55N 108°44W 297 B7
Peterbell Canada 48°36N 83°21W 298 C3
Peterborough S. Austral., Australia 32°58S 138°51E 282 B3
Peterborough Ont., Canada 44°20N 78°20W 312 B6
Peterborough Peterborough, U.K. 52°35N 0°15W 169 E7
Peterborough N.H., U.S.A. 42°53N 71°57W 313 D13
Peterborough □ U.K. 52°35N 0°15W 169 E7
Peterculter U.K. 57°6N 2°16W 167 D6
Peterhead U.K. 57°31N 1°48W 167 D7
Peterhof = Petrodvorets Russia 59°52N 29°54E 188 C5
Peterlee U.K. 54°47N 1°20W 168 C6
Petermann ✪ Australia 24°58S 130°0E 279 E4
Petermann Bjerg Greenland 73°7N 28°25W 154 C8
Petermann Gletscher Greenland 80°30N 60°0W 154 A4
Petermann Ranges Australia 26°0S 130°30E 279 E5
Peter's Mine Guyana 6°14N 59°20W 329 B6
Petersburg = Peterborough Australia 32°58S 138°51E 282 B3
Petersburg Alaska, U.S.A. 56°48N 132°58W 303 H14
Petersburg Ill., U.S.A. 40°1N 89°51W 310 D7
Petersburg Ind., U.S.A. 38°30N 87°17W 311 F9
Petersburg Mich., U.S.A. 41°54N 83°43W 311 C13
Petersburg Pa., U.S.A. 40°34N 78°3W 312 F6
Petersburg Va., U.S.A. 37°14N 77°24W 309 G15
Petersburg W. Va., U.S.A. 39°1N 79°5W 309 F14
Petersfield U.K. 51°1N 0°56W 169 F7
Petershagen Germany 52°23N 8°58E 178 C4
Petilia Policastro Italy 39°7N 16°48E 201 C9
Petilla de Aragón Spain 42°28N 1°6W 196 C3
Petit Batanga Cameroon 3°15N 9°54E 264 B1
Petit-Bourg Guadeloupe 16°11N 61°37W 322 e
Petit-Canal Guadeloupe 16°25N 61°31W 322 e
Petit Cul-de-Sac Marin Guadeloupe 16°12N 61°33W 322 e
Petit Dominique Grenada 12°30N 61°24W 323 q
Petit-Goâve Haiti 18°27N 72°51W 321 C5
Petit Lac Manicouagan Canada 51°25N 67°40W 299 B6
Petit Loango ⌓ Gabon 2°20S 9°40E 264 C1
Petit-Mécatina → Canada 50°40N 59°30W 299 B8
Petit-Mécatina, Î. du Canada 50°30N 59°25W 299 B8
Petit Piton St. Lucia 13°51N 61°5W 322 f
Petit Raffray Mauritius 20°0S 57°36E 272 e
Petit-Saguenay Canada 48°15N 70°4W 299 C5
Petit Saint Bernard, Col du Italy 45°40N 6°52E 175 C10
Petit Soufrière B. Dominica 15°23N 61°15W 323 k
Petitcodiac Canada 45°57N 65°11W 299 C6
Petite Anse Martinique 14°28N 61°4W 322 j
Petite-Île Réunion 21°20S 55°35E 272 f
Petite Martinique Grenada 12°31N 61°23W 323 q
Petite Rivière Mauritius 20°11S 57°26E 272 e
Petite Savane Dominica 15°15N 61°17W 323 k
Petite Terre = Pamandzi Mayotte 12°47S 45°16E 272 b
Petite Terre, Îles de la Guadeloupe 16°13N 61°9W 322 e
Petites-Anses Guadeloupe 15°51N 61°38W 322 e
Petitjean = Sidi Kacem Morocco 34°12N 5°42W 260 B3
Petitot → Canada 60°14N 123°29W 296 A4
Petitsikapau L. Canada 54°37N 66°25W 299 B6
Petlad India 22°30N 72°45E 242 H5
Peto Mexico 20°8N 88°55W 319 C7
Petone N.Z. 41°13S 174°53E 284 H3
Petorca Chile 32°15S 70°56W 334 C1
Petoskey U.S.A. 45°22N 84°57W 309 C11
Petra Jordan 30°20N 35°22E 251 H6
Petra Spain 39°37N 3°6E 206 B4
Petra, Ostrov Russia 76°15N 118°30E 215 B12
Petra Velikogo, Zaliv Russia 42°40N 132°0E 220 C6
Petre, Pt. Canada 43°50N 77°9W 312 C7
Petrel = Petrer Spain 38°30N 0°46W 197 G4
Petrella, Monte Italy 41°18N 13°40E 200 A6
Petrer Spain 38°30N 0°46W 197 G4
Petreto-Bicchisano France 41°47N 8°58E 175 G12
Petrich Bulgaria 41°24N 23°13E 202 E7
Petrified Forest △ U.S.A. 35°0N 109°30W 305 J9
Petrijanec Croatia 46°23N 16°17E 199 B13
Petrikov = Pyetrikaw Belarus 52°11N 28°29E 177 B15
Petrila Romania 45°29N 23°29E 183 E8
Petrillo Music Shell Chicago, U.S.A. 119 c2
Petrinja Croatia 45°28N 16°18E 199 C13
Petrodvorets Russia 59°52N 29°54E 188 C5
Petrograd = Sankt-Peterburg Russia 59°55N 30°20E 137 B1
Petrogradskaya Storona Russia 59°56N 30°20E 137 B2
Petrolândia Brazil 9°5S 38°20W 332 C4
Petrolia Canada 42°54N 82°9W 312 D2
Petrolina Brazil 9°24S 40°30W 332 C3
Petromaryevka = Pervomaysk Ukraine 48°10N 30°46E 189 H6
Petropavl Kazakhstan 54°53N 69°13E 217 B7
Petropavlovsk = Petropavl Kazakhstan 54°53N 69°13E 217 B7
Petropavlovsk-Kamchatskiy Russia 53°3N 158°43E 215 D16
Petropavlovskiy = Akhtubinsk Russia 48°13N 46°7E 191 F8
Petropavlovsky = Severouralsk Russia 60°9N 59°57E 186 B10
Petrópolis Brazil 22°33S 43°9W 333 F3
Petroşani Romania 45°28N 23°20E 183 E8
Petroupoli Greece 38°3N 23°40E 112 A2
Petrova Gora Croatia 45°15N 15°45E 199 C12
Petrovac Montenegro 42°13N 18°57E 202 D2
Petrovac Serbia 44°22N 21°26E 202 B5
Petrovaradin Serbia 45°16N 19°55E 182 E4
Petrovgrad = Zrenjanin Serbia 45°22N 20°23E 182 E5
Petrovice Czechia 50°2N 14°33E 135 B3
Petrovsk Russia 52°22N 45°19E 190 D7
Petrovsk-Port = Makhachkala Russia 43°0N 47°30E 191 J8
Petrovsk-Zabaykalskiy Russia 51°20N 108°55E 215 D11
Petrovskaya Russia 45°25N 37°58E 189 K9
Petrovskiy Park Russia 55°47N 37°34E 129 B2
Petrovsko-Razumovskoye Russia 55°49N 37°34E 129 B2
Petrovskoye = Svetlograd Russia 45°25N 42°58E 191 H6
Petrovsky Stadium Saint Petersburg, Russia 59°57N 30°19E 137 B1
Petrovsky Zavod = Petrovsk-Zabaykalskiy Russia 51°20N 108°55E 215 D11
Petrozavodsk Russia 61°41N 34°20E 188 B8
Petrus Steyn S. Africa 27°38S 28°8E 271 C4
Petrusburg S. Africa 29°4S 25°26E 270 C4
Petsamo = Pechenga Russia 69°29N 31°4E 160 B24
Pettycur U.K. 56°4N 3°10W 121 A2
Petukhovo Russia 55°6N 67°58E 217 A7
Petuna = Fuyu China 45°12N 124°43E 227 B13
Petzeck Austria 46°57N 12°48E 180 E5
Peumo Chile 34°21S 71°12W 334 C1
Peureulak Indonesia 4°48N 97°45E 234 B1
Peusangan → Indonesia 5°16N 96°51E 234 A1
Peutie Belgium 50°56N 4°27E 116 A2
Pevek Russia 69°41N 171°19E 215 C18
Pevely U.S.A. 38°17N 90°24W 310 F6
Peveragno Italy 44°20N 7°37E 198 D4
Peyrehorade France 43°34N 1°7W 174 E2
Peyruis France 44°1N 5°56E 175 D9
Pézenas France 43°28N 3°24E 174 E7
Pezinok Slovakia 48°17N 17°17E 181 C10
Pfaffenhofen Germany 48°31N 11°31E 179 G7
Pfälzerwald ⌓ Germany 49°18N 9°55E 179 F5
Pfarrkirchen Germany 48°25N 12°56E 179 G8
Pfaueninsel Germany 52°26N 13°7E 115 B1
Pfeffenhausen Germany 48°39N 11°58E 179 G7
Pforzheim Germany 48°52N 8°41E 179 G4
Pfullendorf Germany 47°55N 9°15E 179 H5
Pfungstadt Germany 49°48N 8°35E 179 F4
Pha Taem △ Thailand 15°32N 105°30E 236 E5
Phaestos Greece 35°2N 24°50E 207 E5
Phagwara India 31°10N 75°40E 242 D6
Phala Botswana 23°45S 26°50E 270 B4
Phalaborwa S. Africa 23°57S 31°7E 271 B5
Phalera = Phulera India 26°52N 75°16E 242 F6
Phalodi India 27°12N 72°24E 242 F5
Phalsbourg France 48°46N 7°15E 173 D14
Phaltan India 17°59N 74°26E 244 F2
Phaluai, Ko Thailand 9°32N 99°41E 237 b
Phan Thailand 19°28N 99°43E 236 C2
Phan Rang -Thap Cham Vietnam 11°34N 109°0E 237 G7
Phan Ri Cua Vietnam 11°16N 108°40E 237 G7
Phan Si Pan Vietnam 22°18N 103°46E 236 A4
Phan Thiet Vietnam 11°1N 108°9E 237 G7
Phan Thiet, Vinh Vietnam 10°53N 108°5E 237 G7
Phan Wa, Laem Thailand 7°47N 98°25E 237 a
Phanae Greece 38°8N 25°57E 205 C7
Phanat Nikhom Thailand 13°27N 101°11E 236 F3
Phangan, Ko Thailand 9°45N 100°0E 237 H3
Phangnga Thailand 8°28N 98°30E 237 H2
Phangnga, Ao Thailand 8°16N 98°33E 237 a
Phanom Sarakham Thailand 13°45N 101°21E 236 F3
Phaphund India 26°36N 79°28E 243 F8
Pharenda India 27°5N 83°17E 243 F10
Pharr U.S.A. 26°12N 98°11W 314 H5
Phatthalung Thailand 7°39N 100°6E 237 J3
Phawngpui Blue Mountain △ India 22°45N 93°5E 241 D4
Phaya Thai Thailand 13°45N 100°37E 113 B2
Phayam, Ko Thailand 9°44N 98°25E 237 H2
Phayao Thailand 19°11N 99°55E 236 C2
Phelps U.S.A. 42°58N 77°3W 312 D7
Phelps L. Canada 59°15N 103°15W 297 B8
Phenix City U.S.A. 32°28N 85°1W 316 C4
Phet Buri = Phetchaburi Thailand 13°1N 99°55E 236 F2
Phetchabun Thailand 16°25N 101°8E 236 D3
Phetchabun, Thiu Khao Thailand 16°0N 101°20E 236 E3
Phetchaburi Thailand 13°1N 99°55E 236 F2
Phi Phi, Ko Thailand 7°45N 98°46E 237 J2
Phiafay Laos 14°48N 106°0E 236 E6
Phibun Mangsahan Thailand 15°14N 105°14E 236 E5
Phichai Thailand 17°22N 100°10E 236 D3
Phichit Thailand 16°26N 100°22E 236 D3
Phihai Pakistan 24°50N 67°8E 123 A2
Philadelphia Miss., U.S.A. 32°46N 89°7W 315 E10
Philadelphia N.Y., U.S.A. 44°9N 75°43W 313 B9
Philadelphia Pa., U.S.A. 39°57N 75°9W 313 G9
Philadelphia Int. ✕ (PHL) U.S.A. 39°51N 75°18W 313 G9
Philip U.S.A. 44°2N 101°40W 308 C3
Philip Smith Mts. U.S.A. 68°0N 148°0W 303 C10
Philipi Greece 41°1N 24°16E 203 E8
Philippeville = Skikda Algeria 36°50N 6°58E 261 A6
Philippeville Belgium 50°12N 4°33E 170 D4
Philippi U.S.A. 39°9N 80°3W 309 F13
Philippi L. Australia 24°20S 138°55E 280 C2
Philippine Basin Pac. Oc. 17°0N 132°0E 288 F5
Philippine Sea Pac. Oc. 18°0N 125°0E 288 F4
Philippine Trench = Mindanao Trench Pac. Oc. 12°0N 126°6E 232 E5
Philippines ■ Asia 12°0N 123°0E 232 E4
Philippolis S. Africa 30°15S 25°16E 270 D4
Philippopolis = Plovdiv Bulgaria 42°8N 24°44E 203 D8
Philipsburg Qué., Canada 45°2N 73°5W 313 A11
Philipsburg St.-Maarten 18°3N 63°5W 322 a
Philipsburg Mont., U.S.A. 46°20N 113°18W 304 C7
Philipsburg Pa., U.S.A. 40°54N 78°13W 312 F6
Philipstown = Daingean Ireland 53°18N 7°17W 166 C4
Philipstown S. Africa 30°28S 24°30E 270 D3
Phillip B. Australia 33°58S 151°14E 139 B2
Phillip I. Australia 38°30S 145°12E 283 E6
Phillips U.S.A. 45°42N 90°24W 308 C8
Phillipsburg Ga., U.S.A. 31°25N 83°30W 316 D6
Phillipsburg Kans., U.S.A. 39°45N 99°19W 308 F4
Phillipsburg N.J., U.S.A. 40°42N 75°12W 313 F9
Philmont U.S.A. 42°15N 73°39W 313 D11
Philomath Ga., U.S.A. 33°44N 82°59W 316 B7
Philomath Oreg., U.S.A. 44°32N 123°22W 304 D2
Phimai Thailand 15°13N 102°30E 236 E4
Phitsanulok Thailand 16°50N 100°12E 236 D3
Phnom Kulen △ Cambodia 13°38N 104°15E 236 F5
Phnom Penh Cambodia 11°33N 104°55E 237 G5
Phnum Penh = Phnom Penh Cambodia 11°33N 104°55E 237 G5
Pho, Laem Thailand 6°55N 101°19E 237 J3
Phocis = Fokida Greece 38°30N 22°15E 204 C4
Phoenicia U.S.A. 42°5N 74°14W 313 D10
Phoenix Mauritius 20°17S 57°30E 272 e
Phoenix Ariz., U.S.A. 33°26N 112°4W 305 K7
Phoenix Ill., U.S.A. 41°36N 87°37W 119 D3
Phoenix N.Y., U.S.A. 43°14N 76°18W 313 C8
Phoenix Is. Kiribati 3°30S 172°0W 277 A16
Phoenix Sky Harbour Int. ✕ (PHX) U.S.A. 33°26N 112°5W 305 K7
Phoenixville U.S.A. 40°8N 75°31W 313 F9
Phon Thailand 15°49N 102°36E 236 E4
Phong → Thailand 16°23N 102°56E 236 D4
Phong Nha -Ke Bang △ Vietnam 17°30N 106°10E 236 D6
Phong Saly Laos 21°42N 102°9E 228 G4
Phong Tho Vietnam 22°32N 103°21E 236 A4
Phonsavan Laos 19°27N 103°10E 236 C4
Phonum Thailand 8°49N 98°48E 237 H2
Phosphate Hill Australia 21°53S 139°58E 280 C2
Photharam Thailand 13°41N 99°51E 236 F2
Phra Kaeo Bangkok, Thailand 113 b1
Phra Khanong Thailand 13°40N 100°36E 113 B2
Phra Nakhon Thailand 13°45N 100°30E 113 B2
Phra Nakhon Si Ayutthaya Thailand 14°25N 100°30E 236 E3
Phra Pradaeng Thailand 13°39N 100°33E 113 C2
Phra Thong, Ko Thailand 9°5N 98°17E 237 H2
Phrae Thailand 18°7N 100°9E 236 C3
Phrom Phiram Thailand 17°2N 100°12E 236 D3
Phrom Thep, Laem Thailand 7°45N 98°19E 237 a
Phrygia Turkey 38°40N 30°0E 212 C4
Phthiotis = Fthiotida Greece 38°50N 22°25E 204 C4
Phu Bia Laos 19°10N 103°0E 236 C4
Phu Chong -Na Yoi △ Thailand 14°25N 105°30E 236 E5
Phu Hin Rong Kla △ Thailand 17°0N 100°59E 236 D3
Phu Kao -Phu Phan Kham △ Thailand 16°53N 102°31E 236 D4
Phu Kradung △ Thailand 17°2N 101°44E 236 D3
Phu Loi Laos 20°14N 103°14E 236 B4
Phu Luang △ Thailand 17°15N 101°29E 236 D3
Phu Ly Vietnam 20°35N 105°50E 228 G5
Phu My Vietnam 14°15N 109°5E 236 E7
Phu Pha Man △ Thailand 16°44N 101°50E 236 D3
Phu Phan △ Thailand 17°0N 103°56E 236 D4
Phu Quoc, Dao Vietnam 10°20N 104°0E 237 G4
Phu Sa Dok Bua △ Thailand 16°11N 104°45E 236 D5
Phu Sang △ Thailand 19°35N 100°19E 236 C3
Phu Tho Vietnam 21°24N 105°13E 228 G5
Phu Wiang △ Thailand 16°39N 102°23E 236 D4
Phuc Yen Vietnam 21°16N 105°45E 228 G5
Phuket Thailand 7°53N 98°24E 237 a
Phuket, Ko Thailand 8°0N 98°22E 237 a
Phul India 30°19N 75°14E 242 D6
Phulad India 25°38N 73°49E 242 G5
Phulbani India 20°28N 84°14E 244 D7
Phulbari India 25°55N 90°2E 241 C3
Phulchari Bangla. 25°11N 89°37E 241 C2
Phulera India 26°52N 75°16E 242 F6
Phulpur India 25°31N 82°49E 243 G10
Phunphin Thailand 9°7N 99°12E 237 b
Phuntsholing Bhutan 26°51N 89°23E 243 F13
Phuphrabat Thailand 17°40N 102°45E 236 D4
Phuthaditjhaba S. Africa 28°29S 28°48E 271 C4
Phyu = Pyu Burma 18°30N 96°28E 241 F6
Pia ✪ Australia 27°7S 116°23E 279 E2
Piaçabuçu Brazil 10°24S 36°25W 332 C4
Piacenza Italy 45°1N 9°40E 198 C6
Piai, Tanjung Malaysia 1°17N 103°30E 237 d
Piako → N.Z. 37°12S 175°30E 284 D4
Pian Cr. → Australia 30°2S 148°12E 281 E4
Pian-Upe ⌓ Uganda 1°44N 34°20E 268 B3
Piana France 42°15N 8°34E 175 F12
Pianella Italy 42°24N 14°2E 199 F11
Piangil Australia 35°5S 143°20E 282 C5
Pianosa Puglia, Italy 42°12N 15°44E 199 F12
Pianosa Toscana, Italy 42°35N 10°5E 198 F7
Piao'ertun China 41°50N 123°47E 227 D12
Piapot Canada 49°59N 109°8W 297 D7
Piarco Trin. & Tob. 10°35N 61°20W 323 t
Piarco Int. ✕ (POS) Trin. & Tob. 10°36N 61°20W 323 t
Pias Portugal 38°1N 7°29W 195 G3
Piaseczno Poland 52°5N 21°2E 185 F8
Piaski Poland 51°8N 22°52E 185 G9
Piastów Poland 52°12N 20°48E 185 F7
Piatã Brazil 13°9S 41°48W 333 D3
Piatra Romania 43°51N 25°9E 183 G10
Piatra Craiului △ Romania 45°30N 25°12E 183 E10
Piatra Neamţ Romania 46°56N 26°21E 183 D11
Piatra Olt Romania 44°22N 24°16E 183 F9
Piauí □ Brazil 7°0S 43°0W 332 C3
Piauí → Brazil 6°38S 42°42W 332 C3
Piave → Italy 45°32N 12°44E 199 C9
Piazza Ármerina Italy 37°21N 14°20E 201 E7
Pibor → South Sudan 7°35N 33°0E 257 F3
Pibor Post South Sudan 6°47N 33°3E 257 F3
Pic St-Loup France 43°47N 3°48E 174 E7
Pica Chile 20°35S 69°25W 330 E4
Picardie France 49°50N 3°0E 171 B5
Picardie, Plaine de France 50°0N 2°0E 173 C9
Picardy = Picardie France 49°50N 3°0E 171 B5
Picasso, Museu Barcelona, Spain 114 c2
Picayune U.S.A. 30°32N 89°41W 315 F10
Piccadilly London, U.K. 125 b3
Picerno Italy 40°38N 15°38E 201 B8
Pichhor India 25°58N 78°20E 243 G8
Pichilemu Chile 34°22S 72°0W 334 C1
Pichincha □ Ecuador 0°10S 78°40W 328 D2
Pichor India 25°11N 78°11E 242 G8
Pickerel L. Canada 48°40N 91°25W 298 C1
Pickering U.K. 54°15N 0°46W 168 C7
Pickering, Vale of U.K. 54°14N 0°45W 168 C7
Pickle Lake Canada 51°30N 90°12W 298 B1
Pickwick L. U.S.A. 35°4N 88°15W 315 D10
Picnic B. Hong Kong, China 22°13N 114°8E 122 B2
Pico Azores 38°28N 28°20W 153 d1
Pico, Ponta do Azores 38°28N 28°25W 153 d1
Pico Bonito △ Honduras 15°34N 86°48W 320 C2
Pico da Neblina △ Brazil 0°19N 66°28W 328 C4
Pico Rivera U.S.A. 33°59N 118°5W 126 C4
Pico Truncado Argentina 46°40S 68°0W 336 C3
Picos = Colinas Brazil 6°0S 44°10W 332 C3
Picos Brazil 7°5S 41°28W 332 C3
Picos, Pta. dos Spain 41°52N 8°53W 194 D2
Picos de Europa △ Spain 43°14N 4°59W 194 B6
Picota Peru 6°54S 76°24W 330 B2
Picton N.S.W., Australia 34°12S 150°34E 283 C9
Picton Ont., Canada 44°1N 77°9W 312 B7
Picton N.Z. 41°18S 174°3E 285 B9
Picton, I. Chile 55°2S 66°57W 336 E3
Pictou Canada 45°41N 62°42W 299 C7
Picture Butte Canada 49°55N 112°45W 296 D6
Pictured Rocks ⌓ U.S.A. 46°30N 86°30W 308 B10
Picuí Brazil 6°31S 36°21W 332 C4
Picún Leufú Argentina 39°30S 69°5W 336 A3
Pidbuzh Ukraine 49°19N 23°14E 185 J10
Pidurutalagala Sri Lanka 7°10N 80°50E 245 L5
Piechowice Poland 50°51N 15°36E 185 H2
Piedade Rio de J., Brazil 22°52S 43°18W 135 B1
Piedade Lisboa, Portugal 38°49N 9°16W 126 A1
Piedade, Cova da Portugal 38°40N 9°8W 126 A2
Piedecuesta Colombia 6°59N 73°3W 328 B3
Piedimonte Matese Italy 41°22N 14°22E 201 A7
Piedmont = Piemonte □ Italy 45°0N 8°0E 198 D5
Piedmont Ala., U.S.A. 33°55N 85°37W 316 B4
Piedmont S.C., U.S.A. 34°42N 82°28W 292 F11
Piedmont Park U.S.A. 33°47N 84°22W 113 B2
Piedra → Spain 41°18N 1°47W 196 D3
Piedra del Águila Argentina 40°2S 70°4W 336 B2
Piedra del Águila, Embalse Argentina 40°15S 70°4W 336 B2
Piedra Lais Venezuela 3°10N 65°50W 328 C4
Piedrabuena Spain 39°0N 4°10W 195 G6
Piedrahita Spain 40°28N 5°23W 194 E5
Piedralaves Spain 40°19N 4°42W 194 E6
Piedras, R. de las → Peru 12°30S 69°15W 330 C4
Piedras Blancas Spain 43°33N 5°58W 194 B5
Piedras Negras Mexico 28°42N 100°31W 318 B4
Piedras Pt. Phil. 10°11N 118°48E 233 F2
Piekar = Piekary Śląskie Poland 50°24N 18°57E 185 H5
Piekary Śląskie Poland 50°24N 18°57E 185 H5
Pieksämäki Finland 62°18N 27°10E 188 A4
Pielinen Finland 63°15N 29°40E 160 E23
Pieljekaise △ Sweden 66°20N 16°45E 160 C17
Piemonte □ Italy 45°0N 8°0E 198 D5
Pienaarsrivier S. Africa 25°15S 28°18E 271 C4
Pieniężno Poland 54°14N 20°8E 184 D7
Pieninský △ Europe 49°25N 20°28E 181 B13
Pieńsk Poland 51°16N 15°2E 185 G2
Pienza Italy 43°4N 11°40E 199 E8
Piercefield U.S.A. 44°13N 74°35W 313 B10
Pierceland Canada 54°20N 109°46W 297 C7
Pieria Greece 40°13N 22°25E 202 F6
Pierpont U.S.A. 41°45N 80°34W 312 E4
Pierre U.S.A. 44°22N 100°21W 308 C3
Pierre-Buffière France 45°41N 1°22E 174 C5
Pierre-de-Bresse France 46°54N 5°13E 173 F12
Pierre Elliott Trudeau Int. ✕ (YUL) Canada 45°28N 73°44W 130 B1
Pierrefonds Canada 45°29N 73°51W 313 A11
Pierrefontaine-les-Varans France 47°14N 6°32E 173 E13
Pierrefort France 44°55N 2°50E 174 D6
Pierrelatte France 44°23N 4°43E 175 D8
Pierson U.S.A. 29°14N 81°28W 317 F8
Piešťany Slovakia 48°38N 17°55E 181 C10
Piesting → Austria 48°6N 16°40E 181 C9
Pieszyce Poland 50°43N 16°33E 185 H3
Piet Retief S. Africa 27°1S 30°50E 271 C5
Pietarsaari Finland 63°40N 22°43E 160 E20
Pieter Both Mauritius 20°11S 57°32E 272 e
Pietermaritzburg S. Africa 29°35S 30°25E 271 C5
Pietersburg = Polokwane S. Africa 23°54S 29°25E 271 B4
Pietragalla Italy 40°45N 15°53E 201 B8
Pietralata Italy 41°55N 12°33E 136 B2
Pietrasanta Italy 43°57N 10°14E 198 E7
Pietroşiţa Romania 45°11N 25°26E 183 E10
Pietrosul, Vf. Maramureş, Romania 47°35N 24°43E 183 C9
Pietrosul, Vf. Suceava, Romania 47°12N 25°18E 183 C10
Pieve di Cadore Italy 46°26N 12°22E 199 B9
Pieve di Teco Italy 44°3N 7°56E 198 D4
Pievepélago Italy 44°12N 10°37E 198 D7
Pigaditsa Greece 39°59N 21°23E 202 G5
Pigeon Guadeloupe 16°9N 61°46W 322 e
Pigeon I. India 14°2N 74°20E 245 G2
Pigeon I. St. Lucia 14°6N 60°58W 323 m
Pigeon L. Canada 44°27N 78°30W 312 B6
Piges Greece 39°17N 21°25E 204 B3
Piggott U.S.A. 36°23N 90°11W 315 C9
Pigna Italy 43°56N 7°40E 198 E4
Pigüé Argentina 37°36S 62°25W 334 D3
Piha N.Z. 36°57S 174°28E 284 C3
Pihani India 27°36N 80°15E 243 F9
Pihlajamäki Finland 60°14N 24°58E 121 B2
Pihlajasaari Finland 60°8N 24°55E 121 C2
Pihlajavesi Finland 61°45N 28°45E 188 B5
Pijijiapan Mexico 15°42N 93°14W 319 D6
Pikalevo Russia 59°37N 34°9E 188 C8
Pikangikum Canada 51°49N 94°0W 297 C10
Pikes Peak U.S.A. 38°50N 105°3W 304 G11
Piketberg S. Africa 32°55S 18°40E 270 E2
Pikeville U.S.A. 37°29N 82°31W 309 G12
Pikit Phil. 7°4N 124°41E 233 H5
Pikou China 39°18N 122°22E 227 E12
Pikounda Congo 0°30N 16°44E 264 B3
Pikwitonei Canada 55°35N 97°9W 297 B9
Piła Poland 53°10N 16°48E 185 E3
Pila Spain 38°16N 1°11W 197 G3
Pilanesberg △ S. Africa 25°15S 27°4E 270 C4
Pilani India 28°22N 75°33E 242 E6
Pilar Brazil 9°36S 35°56W 332 C4
Pilar Paraguay 26°50S 58°20W 334 B4
Pilar Capiz, Phil. 11°29N 123°0E 233 F4
Pilar Sorsogon, Phil. 12°56N 123°40E 232 E4
Pilar de la Horadada Spain 37°52N 0°47W 197 H4
Pilares Brazil 22°52S 43°18W 135 B1
Pilas Group Phil. 6°45N 121°35E 233 H3
Pilat, Dune du France 44°35N 1°13W 174 D2
Pilat ⌓ France 45°20N 4°30E 175 C8
Pilawa Poland 51°57N 21°32E 185 G8
Pilaya → Bolivia 20°55S 64°4W 331 E5
Pilbara Australia 21°15S 118°16E 278 D2
Pilcomaya → Paraguay 25°21S 57°42W 334 B4
Pilea Greece 40°32N 22°59E 202 F6
Pilgrim's Rest S. Africa 24°55S 30°44E 271 B5
Pilgrimstad Sweden 62°57N 15°2E 162 B9
Pili Greece 36°50N 27°15E 205 E9
Pili Phil. 13°33N 123°19E 232 E4
Pilibhit India 28°40N 79°50E 243 E8
Pilica → Poland 51°52N 21°17E 185 G8
Pilio, Oros Greece 39°27N 23°3E 204 B5
Pilipinas = Philippines ■ Asia 12°0N 123°0E 232 E4
Pilis Hungary 47°17N 19°35E 182 C4
Pilisvörösvár Hungary 47°38N 18°56E 182 C3
Pilkhawa India 28°43N 77°42E 242 E7
Pillar B. Ascension I. 7°59S 14°21W 153 g
Pillaro Ecuador 1°10S 78°32W 328 D2
Pillau = Baltiysk Russia 54°41N 19°58E 184 D6
Pilliga Australia 30°21S 148°54E 281 E4
Pilos Greece 36°55N 21°42E 204 E3
Pilot Grove U.S.A. 38°53N 92°55W 310 F4
Pilot Mound Canada 49°15N 98°54W 297 D9
Pilot Point Alaska, U.S.A. 57°34N 157°35W 303 H8
Pilot Point Tex., U.S.A. 33°24N 96°58W 314 E6
Pilot Rock U.S.A. 45°29N 118°50W 304 D4
Pilot Station U.S.A. 61°56N 162°53W 303 F7

Pilote → Martinique 14°28N 60°55W 322 j
Pilsen = Plzeň Poland 49°58N 21°16E 185 J8
Pilsen = Plzeň Czechia 49°45N 13°22E 180 B6
Pilštanj Slovenia 46°8N 15°39E 199 B12
Piltene Latvia 57°13N 21°40E 184 A8
Pilton U.K. 55°58N 3°13W 121 B2
Pilzno Poland 49°58N 21°16E 185 J8
Pima U.S.A. 32°54N 109°50W 305 K9
Pimba Australia 31°18S 136°46E 282 A2
Pimenta Bueno Brazil 11°35S 61°10W 331 C5
Pimenteiras Brazil 13°40S 60°58W 331 C5
Pimentel Peru 6°45S 79°55W 330 B2
Pimlico London, U.K. 125 c3
Pimpri Chinchwad India 18°37N 73°47E 244 E1
Pimu Dem. Rep. of the Congo 1°42N 20°58E 264 B4
Pin Valley △ India 31°50N 77°50E 242 D7
Pina de Ebro Spain 41°29N 0°33W 196 D4
Pinamalayan Phil. 13°2N 121°29E 232 E3
Pinang Malaysia 5°25N 100°15E 237 c
Pinang □ Malaysia 5°20N 100°20E 237 K3
Pinar, C. des Spain 39°53N 3°12E 206 B4
Pinar del Río Cuba 22°26N 83°40W 320 B3
Pınarbaşı Çanakkale, Turkey 39°53N 26°15E 205 B8
Pınarbaşı Kayseri, Turkey 38°43N 36°23E 212 C7
Pınarhisar Turkey 41°37N 27°30E 203 E11
Pinatubo, Mt. Phil. 15°8N 120°21E 232 D3
Pinawa Canada 50°9N 95°50W 297 C9
Pincehely Hungary 46°41N 18°27E 182 D3
Pinchang China 31°36N 107°3E 228 B6
Pincher Creek Canada 49°30N 113°57W 296 D6
Pinchi L. Canada 54°38N 124°30W 296 C4
Pinckard U.S.A. 31°19N 85°33W 316 D4
Pinckneyville U.S.A. 38°5N 89°23W 310 F7
Pińczów Poland 50°32N 20°32E 185 H7
Pind Dadan Khan Pakistan 32°36N 73°7E 217 F8
Pindar Australia 28°30S 115°47E 279 E2
Pindaré → Brazil 3°17S 44°47W 332 B3
Pindaré-Mirim Brazil 3°37S 45°21W 332 B2
Pindera Downs ✪ Australia 29°24S 142°37E 281 A3
Pindi Gheb Pakistan 33°14N 72°21E 242 C5
Pindiga Nigeria 9°58N 10°53E 263 D7
Pindobal Brazil 3°16S 48°25W 332 B2
Pindos △ Greece 39°52N 21°11E 204 B3
Pindos Oros Greece 40°0N 21°0E 204 B3
Pindus Mts. = Pindos Oros Greece 40°0N 21°0E 204 B3
Pine → B.C., Canada 56°8N 120°43W 296 B4
Pine → Sask., Canada 58°50N 105°38W 297 B7
Pine Bluff U.S.A. 34°13N 92°1W 314 D8
Pine Bluffs U.S.A. 41°11N 104°4W 304 F11
Pine Castle U.S.A. 28°28N 81°22W 133 B2
Pine City U.S.A. 45°50N 92°59W 308 C7
Pine Cr. → U.S.A. 41°10N 77°16W 312 E7
Pine Creek Australia 13°50S 131°50E 278 B5
Pine Falls Canada 50°34N 96°11W 297 C9
Pine Flat L. U.S.A. 36°50N 119°20W 306 J7
Pine Grove Ont., Canada 43°47N 79°34W 141 A1
Pine Grove Pa., U.S.A. 40°33N 76°23W 313 F8
Pine Hill Australia 23°38S 146°57E 280 C4
Pine Hills U.S.A. 28°33N 81°27W 133 A2
Pine I. U.S.A. 26°36N 82°7W 317 J7
Pine Island U.S.A. 26°5N 80°16W 129 B1
Pine Island Glacier Antarctica 76°0S 100°0W 151 D15
Pine Level U.S.A. 32°4N 86°4W 316 C3
Pine Mountain U.S.A. 32°49N 84°51W 316 C5
Pine Pass Canada 55°25N 122°42W 296 B4
Pine Ridge N.S.W., Australia 31°30S 150°28E 283 A9
Pine Ridge S. Dak., U.S.A. 43°2N 102°33W 308 D2
Pine River Man., Canada 51°45N 100°30W 297 C8
Pine River Minn., U.S.A. 46°43N 94°24W 308 B6
Pine Valley U.S.A. 32°50N 116°32W 307 N10
Pinecrest Calif., U.S.A. 38°12N 120°1W 306 G6
Pinecrest Fla., U.S.A. 25°40N 80°18W 129 D1
Pineda de Mar Spain 41°37N 2°42E 196 D7
Pinedale Calif., U.S.A. 36°50N 119°48W 306 J7
Pinedale Wyo., U.S.A. 42°52N 109°52W 304 E9
Pinega → Russia 64°30N 44°19E 186 B8
Pinehouse L. Canada 55°32N 106°35W 297 B7
Pineimuta → Canada 52°8N 88°33W 298 B1
Pinellas Park U.S.A. 27°50N 82°41W 317 H7
Pinerolo Italy 44°53N 7°21E 198 D4
Pines, Akra Greece 40°5N 24°20E 203 F8
Pineto Italy 42°36N 14°4E 199 F11
Pinetop-Lakeside U.S.A. 34°9N 109°58W 305 J9
Pinetown S. Africa 29°48S 30°54E 271 C5
Pinetta U.S.A. 30°36N 83°21W 316 E6
Pineview U.S.A. 32°7N 83°30W 316 C6
Pineville La., U.S.A. 31°19N 92°26W 314 F8
Pineville S.C., U.S.A. 33°26N 80°1W 316 B9
Pinewood U.S.A. 33°44N 80°27W 316 B9
Pinewood Park U.S.A. 25°52N 80°13W 129 C2
Piney France 48°22N 4°21E 173 D11
Ping → Thailand 15°42N 100°9E 236 E3
Pingaring Australia 32°40S 118°32E 279 F2
Pingba China 26°23N 106°12E 228 D6
Pingbian China 23°0N 103°45E 228 F4
Pingchuan China 27°35N 101°55E 228 D3
Pingding China 37°47N 113°38E 226 F7
Pingdingshan China 33°43N 113°27E 226 H7
Pingdong = P'ingtung Taiwan 22°38N 120°30E 225 D2
Pingdu China 36°42N 119°59E 227 F10
Pingelly Australia 32°32S 117°5E 279 F2
Pingguo China 23°19N 107°36E 228 F6
Pinghe China 24°17N 117°21E 229 E11
Pinghu China 30°40N 121°2E 229 B13
Pingjiang China 28°45N 113°36E 229 C9
Pingle China 24°40N 110°40E 229 E8
Pingli China 32°27N 109°22E 228 A7
Pingliang China 35°35N 106°31E 226 G4
Pinglin Taiwan 24°56N 121°42E 225 B3
Pinglu China 39°31N 112°30E 226 E7
Pingluo China 38°52N 106°30E 226 E4
Pingnan Fujian, China 26°55N 119°0E 229 D12
Pingnan Guangxi Zhuangzu, China 23°33N 110°22E 229 F8
Pingo Gabon 1°19S 10°55E 264 C2
Pingquan China 41°1N 118°37E 227 D10
Pingrup Australia 33°32S 118°29E 279 F2
Pingshan China 28°39N 104°3E 228 C5
Pingtan China 25°31N 119°47E 229 E12
Pingtang China 25°49N 107°17E 228 E6
P'ingtung Taiwan 22°38N 120°30E 225 D2
P'ingtung □ Taiwan 22°30N 120°40E 225 D2
Pingwu China 32°25N 104°30E 226 H3
Pingxiang Guangxi Zhuangzu, China 22°6N 106°46E 228 F6
Pingxiang Jiangxi, China 27°43N 113°48E 229 D9
Pingyao China 37°12N 112°10E 226 F7
Pingyi China 35°30N 117°35E 227 G9
Pingyin China 36°20N 116°25E 226 F9
Pingyuan Guangdong, China 24°37N 115°57E 229 E10
Pingyuan Shandong, China 37°10N 116°22E 226 F9
Pingyuanjie China 23°45N 103°48E 228 F4
Pingzhou China 23°1N 113°11E 121 B2
Pinhal Novo Portugal 38°38N 8°55W 195 G2
Pinheiro Brazil 2°31S 45°5W 332 B2
Pinheiro Machado Brazil 31°34S 53°23W 335 C5
Pinheiros → Brazil 23°37S 46°44W 137 B1
Pinhel Portugal 40°50N 7°1W 194 E3
Pinhuá → Brazil 6°21S 65°0W 331 B5
Pini Indonesia 0°10N 98°40E 234 B1
Pinios → Ilia, Greece 37°48N 21°20E 204 D3
Pinios → Trikala, Greece 39°55N 22°41E 204 B4
Pinjarra Australia 32°37S 115°52E 279 F2
Pinjrapur Pakistan 24°53N 67°4E 123 A2
Pink Beach Bonaire 12°5N 68°17W 322 h
Pink Mountain Canada 57°3N 122°52W 296 B4
Pinkafeld Austria 47°22N 16°9E 181 D9
Pinlaung Burma 20°8N 96°47E 241 E6
Pinlebu Burma 24°5N 95°22E 241 C5
Pinnacle Is. = Senkaku-Shotō E. China Sea 25°45N 123°30E 221 M1
Pinnacles △ U.S.A. 36°25N 121°12W 306 J5
Pinnaroo Australia 35°17S 140°53E 282 C4
Pinneberg Germany 53°40N 9°48E 178 B5
Pinner U.K. 51°35N 0°22W 125 A1
Pinner Green U.K. 51°35N 0°23W 125 A1
Pino Hachado, Paso S. Amer. 38°39S 70°54W 336 A2
Pinon Hills U.S.A. 34°26N 117°39W 307 L9
Pinos Mexico 22°18N 101°34W 318 C4
Pinos, Mt. U.S.A. 34°49N 119°8W 307 L7
Pinos Pt. U.S.A. 36°38N 121°57W 305 H3
Pinos Puente Spain 37°15N 3°45W 195 H7
Pinrang Indonesia 3°46S 119°41E 235 C5
Pins, Î. des N. Cal. 22°37S 167°30E 288 d
Pins, Pte. aux Canada 42°15N 81°51W 312 D3
Pinsk Belarus 52°10N 26°1E 177 B14
Pinta, Canal de Ecuador 0°27N 90°38W 330 a
Pinta, I. Ecuador 0°35N 90°44W 330 a
Pintados Chile 20°35S 69°40W 330 E4
Pinturas → Argentina 46°30S 70°20W 336 C2
Pintuyan Phil. 9°57N 125°15E 233 G5
Pinukpuk Phil. 17°35N 121°22E 232 C3
Pinyang China 27°42N 120°31E 229 D13
Pinyug Russia 60°5N 48°0E 186 B8
Pio Duran Phil. 13°2N 123°25E 232 E4
Pio V. Corpuz Phil. 11°55N 124°2E 233 F5
Pio XII Brazil 3°53S 45°17W 332 B2
Pioche U.S.A. 37°56N 114°27W 305 H6
Pioltello Italy 45°30N 9°19E 128 A2
Piombino Italy 42°55N 10°32E 198 F7
Piombino, Canale di Italy 42°53N 10°30E 198 F7
Pioner, Ostrov Russia 79°50N 92°0E 215 B10
Pionerskiy Russia 54°56N 20°14E 184 D7
Pionki Poland 51°29N 21°28E 185 G8
Piopiotaki = Milford Sd. N.Z. 44°41S 167°47E 285 E2
Piorini → Brazil 3°23S 63°30W 329 D5
Piorini, L. Brazil 3°15S 62°35W 329 D5
Piotrków Trybunalski Poland 51°23N 19°43E 185 G6
Piove di Sacco Italy 45°18N 12°2E 199 C9
Pīp Iran 26°45N 60°10E 247 E9
Pipar India 26°25N 73°31E 242 F5
Pipar Road India 26°27N 73°27E 242 F5
Piparia Mad. P., India 22°45N 78°23E 242 H8
Piparia Mad. P., India 21°49N 77°37E 242 J7
Pipas Trin. & Tob. 10°20N 61°20W 323 t
Pipéri Greece 39°20N 24°19E 204 B6
Piperno = Priverno Italy 41°28N 13°11E 200 A6
Pipestone U.S.A. 44°0N 96°19W 308 D5
Pipestone → Canada 52°53N 89°23W 298 B2
Pipestone Cr. → Canada 49°38N 100°15W 297 D8
Pipiriki N.Z. 39°28S 175°5E 284 F4
Piplan Pakistan 32°17N 71°21E 242 C4
Piploda India 23°37N 74°56E 242 H6
Pipmuacan, Rés. Canada 49°45N 70°30W 299 C5
Pippingarra Australia 20°27S 118°42E 278 D2
Pipriac France 47°59N 1°58W 172 E5
Piqua U.S.A. 40°9N 84°15W 311 D12
Piquet Carneiro Brazil 5°48S 39°25W 332 C4
Piquiri → Brazil 24°3S 54°14W 335 A5
Pir Panjal Range India 32°30N 76°50E 242 C7
Pīr Sohrāb Iran 25°44N 60°54E 247 E9
Pira Benin 8°28N 1°48E 263 D5
Piracanjuba Brazil 17°18S 49°1W 333 E2
Piracicaba Brazil 22°45S 47°40W 335 A6
Piracuruca Brazil 3°50S 41°50W 332 B3
Pirae Tahiti 17°31S 149°32W 289 e
Piræus = Pireas Greece 37°57N 23°42E 112 B1
Piraiévs = Pireas Greece 37°57N 23°42E 112 B1
Pirajuçara → Brazil 23°33S 46°42W 137 B1
Pirajuí Brazil 21°59S 49°29W 335 A6
Piram I. India 21°36N 72°21E 242 J5
Piran Slovenia 45°31N 13°33E 199 C10
Pirané Argentina 25°42S 59°6W 334 B4
Piranhas Brazil 9°27S 37°46W 332 C4
Pirano = Piran Slovenia 45°31N 13°33E 199 C10
Pīrānshahr Iran 36°41N 45°8E 213 D11
Pirapemas Brazil 3°43S 44°14W 332 B3
Pirapora Brazil 17°20S 44°56W 333 E3
Pirara Guyana 3°37N 59°40W 329 C6
Pirawa India 24°10N 76°2E 242 G7
Piray → Bolivia 16°32S 63°45W 331 D5
Pirdop Bulgaria 42°40N 24°10E 203 D8
Pireas Greece 37°57N 23°42E 112 B1
Pires do Rio Brazil 17°18S 48°17W 333 E2
Pirganj Bangla. 25°51N 88°24E 241 C2
Pirgi Greece 38°13N 25°59E 205 C7
Pirgos Ilia, Greece 37°40N 21°27E 204 D3
Pirgos Kriti, Greece 35°0N 25°9E 207 E6
Pirgovo Bulgaria 43°44N 25°43E 203 C9
Piribebuy Paraguay 25°26S 57°2W 334 B4
Pirimapun Indonesia 6°20S 138°24E 231 F9
Pirin △ Bulgaria 41°48N 23°22E 202 E7
Pirin Planina Bulgaria 41°40N 23°30E 202 E7
Pirinçli Turkey 41°10N 28°52E 122 B1
Pirineos = Pyrénées Europe 42°45N 0°18E 174 F4
Piripiri Brazil 4°15S 41°46W 332 B3
Piritu Venezuela 9°23N 69°12W 328 B4
Pirituba Brazil 23°29S 46°44W 137 A1
Pirkkola Finland 60°14N 24°55E 121 B2
Pirlangimpi Australia 11°24S 130°26E 278 B5
Pirmasens Germany 49°12N 7°36E 179 F3
Pirna Germany 50°57N 13°56E 178 E9
Pirojpur Bangla. 22°35N 90°1E 241 D3
Pirot Serbia 43°9N 22°33E 202 C6
Piru Indonesia 3°4S 128°12E 231 E7
Piru Calif., U.S.A. 34°25N 118°48W 307 L8
Piryatin = Pyryatyn Ukraine 50°15N 32°25E 189 G7
Pisa Italy 43°43N 10°23E 198 E7
Pisa → Poland 53°14N 21°52E 185 E8
Pisa, Firenze ✈ (PSA) Italy 43°40N 10°22E 198 E7
Pisa Ra. N.Z. 44°52S 169°12E 285 E4
Pisac Peru 13°25S 71°50W 330 C3
Pisagua Chile 19°40S 70°15W 330 D3
Pisarovina Croatia 45°35N 15°50E 199 C12
Pisau, Tanjong Malaysia 6°4N 117°59E 235 A5
Pisba △ Colombia 10°39N 74°30W 328 A3
Pisco Peru 13°50S 76°12W 330 C2
Piscu Romania 45°30N 27°43E 183 E12
Písek Czechia 49°19N 14°10E 180 B7
Pisgat O'mer West Bank 31°49N 35°14E 123 B2
Pisgat Ze'ev West Bank 31°49N 35°14E 123 B2
Pishan China 37°30N 78°33E 217 E9
Pishcha Ukraine 51°35N 23°50E 185 G10
Pishchanka Ukraine 48°12N 28°54E 183 B13
Pīshīn Iran 26°6N 61°47E 247 E9
Pishin Pakistan 30°35N 67°0E 242 D2
Pishin Lora → Pakistan 29°9N 64°5E 242 E1
Pishpek = Bishkek Kyrgyzstan 42°54N 74°46E 217 D8
Pisidia Turkey 37°30N 31°40E 212 D4
Pising Indonesia 5°8S 121°53E 231 F6
Pisiou, Pte. Guadeloupe 15°59N 61°13W 322 e
Pismo Beach U.S.A. 35°9N 120°38W 307 K6
Písnice Czechia 49°59N 14°28E 135 C2
Piso, L. Liberia 6°50N 11°15W 262 D2
Pisogne Italy 45°45N 10°10E 198 C7
Pissila Burkina Faso 13°7N 0°50W 263 C4
Pissis, Cerro Argentina 27°45S 68°48W 334 B2
Pissos France 44°19N 0°49W 174 D3
Pissouri Cyprus 34°40N 32°42E 207 F8
Pisticci Italy 40°23N 16°33E 201 B9
Pistóia Italy 43°55N 10°54E 198 E7
Pistol B. Canada 62°25N 92°37W 297 A10
Pisuerga → Spain 41°33N 4°52W 194 D6
Pisz Poland 53°38N 21°49E 184 E8
Pit → U.S.A. 40°47N 122°6W 304 F2
Pita Guinea 11°5N 12°15W 262 C2
Pitalito Colombia 1°51N 76°2W 328 C2
Pitampura India 28°41N 77°7E 120 A1
Pitanga Brazil 24°46S 51°44W 333 F1
Pitangui Brazil 19°40S 44°54W 333 E3
Pitarpunga L. Australia 34°24S 143°30E 282 C5
Pitcairn I. Pac. Oc. 25°5S 130°5W 289 K14
Pitch Pt. Trin. & Tob. 10°15N 61°37W 323 t
Piteå Sweden 65°20N 21°25E 160 D19
Piteälven → Sweden 65°20N 21°25E 160 D19
Piterka Russia 50°41N 47°29E 190 E8
Pitești Romania 44°52N 24°54E 183 F9
Pithapuram India 17°10N 82°15E 244 F6
Pithara Australia 30°20S 116°35E 279 F2
Píthio Greece 41°24N 26°40E 203 E10
Pithiviers France 48°10N 2°13E 173 D9
Pithora India 21°16N 82°31E 244 D6
Pithoragarh India 29°35N 80°13E 243 E9
Pithoro Pakistan 25°31N 69°23E 242 G3
Piti Guam 13°28N 144°41E 302 d
Pitigliano Italy 42°38N 11°40E 199 F8
Pitkäjärvi Finland 60°15N 24°45E 121 B1
Pitkyaranta Russia 61°34N 31°37E 188 B6
Pitlochry U.K. 56°42N 3°44W 167 E5
Pitoa Cameroon 9°23N 13°32E 264 A2
Pitogo Phil. 13°47N 122°5E 232 E4
Piton, Pte. du Guadeloupe 16°30N 61°26W 322 e
Piton de la Petite Rivière Noire Mauritius 20°24S 57°23E 272 e
Pitons, Anses des St. Lucia 13°49N 61°4W 323 m
Pitou Taiwan 23°53N 120°27E 225 C2
Pitou Chiao Taiwan 25°8N 121°55E 225 A3
Pitrufquén Chile 38°59S 72°39W 336 A2
Pitschen = Byczyna Poland 51°7N 18°12E 185 G5
Pitsilia Cyprus 34°55N 33°0E 207 F9
Pitsunda = Bichvinta Georgia 43°9N 40°21E 191 J5
Pitt, Pta. Ecuador 0°43S 89°14W 330 a
Pitt I. B.C., Canada 53°30N 129°50W 296 C3
Pitt I. N.Z. 44°15S 176°15W 285 c
Pitti I. India 10°50N 72°38E 245 J1
Pittsburg Calif., U.S.A. 38°2N 121°53W 306 G5
Pittsburg Kans., U.S.A. 37°25N 94°42W 308 G6
Pittsburg Tex., U.S.A. 33°0N 94°59W 314 E7
Pittsburgh U.S.A. 40°26N 79°58W 312 F5
Pittsfield Ill., U.S.A. 39°36N 90°49W 310 E6
Pittsfield Maine, U.S.A. 44°47N 69°23W 309 C19
Pittsfield Mass., U.S.A. 42°27N 73°15W 313 D11
Pittsfield N.H., U.S.A. 43°18N 71°20W 313 C13
Pittston U.S.A. 41°19N 75°47W 313 E9
Pittsview U.S.A. 32°11N 85°10W 316 C4
Pittsworth Australia 27°41S 151°37E 281 D5
Pituri → Australia 22°35S 138°30E 280 C2
Pium Brazil 10°27S 49°11W 332 D2
Piumafua Mt. Amer. Samoa 14°11S 169°37W 302 f
Piumhi Brazil 20°28S 45°58W 333 F2
Piura Peru 5°15S 80°38W 330 B1
Piura □ Peru 5°10S 80°0W 330 B2
Piuthan Nepal 28°7N 82°56E 243 E10
Piva → Montenegro 43°20N 18°50E 202 C2
Pivijay Colombia 10°28N 74°37W 328 A3
Piwniczna Poland 49°27N 20°42E 185 J7
Pixian China 30°48N 103°52E 228 B4
Pixley U.S.A. 35°58N 119°18W 306 K7
Pizarra Spain 36°36N 4°42W 195 J6
Pizarro Colombia 4°58N 77°22W 328 C2
Pizhou = Pei Xian China 34°44N 116°55E 226 G9
Pizhou China 34°18N 117°57E 227 G9
Pizzo Italy 38°44N 16°10E 201 D9
Placentia Canada 47°20N 54°0W 299 C9
Placentia B. Canada 47°0N 54°40W 299 C9
Placer Masbate, Phil. 11°52N 123°55E 233 F4
Placer Surigao N., Phil. 9°36N 125°38E 233 G5
Placerville U.S.A. 38°44N 120°48W 306 G6
Placetas Cuba 22°15N 79°44W 320 B4
Plácido de Castro Brazil 10°20S 67°11W 330 C4
Plačkovica Macedonia 41°45N 22°30E 202 E6
Plaine des Jarres Laos 19°27N 103°10E 236 C4
Plaine Magnien Mauritius 20°25S 57°39E 272 e
Plaines des Papayes Mauritius 20°3S 57°34E 272 e
Plainfield Ill., U.S.A. 41°37N 88°12W 311 C8
Plainfield Ind., U.S.A. 39°42N 86°24W 311 E10
Plainfield N.J., U.S.A. 40°37N 74°25W 313 F10
Plainfield Ohio, U.S.A. 40°13N 81°43W 312 F3
Plainfield Vt., U.S.A. 44°17N 72°26W 313 B12
Plains Ga., U.S.A. 32°2N 84°24W 316 C5
Plains Mont., U.S.A. 47°28N 114°53W 304 C6
Plains Tex., U.S.A. 33°11N 102°50W 314 E3
Plainview Nebr., U.S.A. 42°21N 97°47W 308 D5
Plainview Tex., U.S.A. 34°11N 101°43W 314 D4
Plainwell U.S.A. 42°27N 85°38W 311 B11
Plaisance France 43°36N 0°3E 174 E4
Plaistow U.S.A. 42°50N 71°6W 313 D13
Plaju Indonesia 2°58S 104°49E 234 C2
Plaka Greece 40°0N 25°24E 205 B7
Plaka, Akra Greece 35°11N 26°19E 207 E7
Plakenska Planina Macedonia 41°14N 21°2E 202 E5
Plampang Indonesia 8°47S 117°46E 235 D5
Planá Czechia 49°50N 12°44E 180 B5
Plana Cays Bahamas 22°38N 73°30W 321 B5
Planada U.S.A. 37°16N 120°19W 306 H6
Planchón Peru 12°14S 69°11W 330 C4
Plancoët France 48°32N 2°13W 172 D4
Plandište Serbia 45°16N 21°10E 182 E6
Planegg Germany 48°6N 11°25E 131 B1
Planeta Rica Colombia 8°25N 75°36W 328 B2
Plano Ill., U.S.A. 41°40N 88°32W 311 C8
Plano Tex., U.S.A. 33°1N 96°42W 314 E6
Plant City U.S.A. 28°1N 82°7W 317 G7
Plantation U.S.A. 26°7N 80°14W 129 B2
Plantation Isles U.S.A. 26°6N 80°14W 129 B2
Plaquemine U.S.A. 30°17N 91°14W 314 F9
Plaridel Phil. 8°37N 123°43E 233 G4
Plasencia Spain 40°3N 6°8W 194 E4
Plaški Croatia 45°4N 15°22E 199 C12
Plassen Norway 61°9N 12°30E 164 C9
Plast Russia 54°22N 60°50E 216 B6
Plaster City U.S.A. 32°47N 115°51W 307 N11
Plaster Rock Canada 46°53N 67°22W 299 C6
Plastun Russia 44°45N 136°19E 220 B8
Plasy Czechia 49°56N 13°24E 180 B6
Plata, Río de la → S. Amer. 34°45S 57°30W 334 C4
Plátani → Italy 37°23N 13°16E 200 E6
Platanos Greece 35°28N 23°33E 207 E4
Plataria Greece 39°27N 20°16E 206 C10
Plateau □ Nigeria 8°30N 9°0E 263 D6
Plateau d'Ipassa △ Gabon 0°26N 12°40E 264 B2
Plateaux □ Congo 2°30S 15°30E 264 C3
Plathe = Płoty Poland 53°48N 15°18E 184 E2
Platinum U.S.A. 59°1N 161°49W 303 G7
Platja d'Aro Spain 41°49N 3°4E 196 D8
Plato Colombia 9°47N 74°47W 328 B3
Platte U.S.A. 43°23N 98°51W 308 D4
Platte → Mo., U.S.A. 39°16N 94°50W 310 E2
Platte → Nebr., U.S.A. 41°4N 95°53W 308 E6
Platte City U.S.A. 39°22N 94°47W 310 E2
Platteville U.S.A. 42°44N 90°29W 310 B6
Plattling Germany 48°46N 12°53E 179 G8
Plattsburg U.S.A. 39°34N 94°27W 310 E2
Plattsburgh U.S.A. 44°42N 73°28W 313 B11
Plattsmouth U.S.A. 41°1N 95°53W 308 E6
Plau Germany 53°27N 12°15E 178 B8
Plauen Germany 50°30N 12°8E 178 E8
Plauer See Germany 53°28N 12°17E 178 B8
Plav Montenegro 42°38N 19°57E 202 D3
Plavinas Latvia 56°35N 25°46E 188 D3
Plavnica Montenegro 42°20N 19°13E 202 D3
Plavno Croatia 44°9N 16°10E 199 D13
Plavsk Russia 53°40N 37°18E 188 F9
Playa Blanca Canary Is. 28°51N 13°50W 153 e2
Playa de las Americas Canary Is. 28°5N 16°43W 153 e1
Playa de Mogán Canary Is. 27°48N 15°47W 153 e1
Playa del Carmen Mexico 20°37N 87°4W 319 C7
Playa del Inglés Canary Is. 27°45N 15°33W 153 e1
Playas Ecuador 2°38S 80°23W 328 D1
Playgreen L. Canada 54°0N 98°15W 297 C9
Plaza Mayor Madrid, Spain 127 b2
Pleasant Bay Canada 46°51N 60°48W 299 C7
Pleasant Hill Calif., U.S.A. 37°57N 122°4W 306 H4
Pleasant Hill Ill., U.S.A. 39°27N 90°52W 310 E6
Pleasant Hill Mo., U.S.A. 38°47N 94°16W 310 F2
Pleasant Mount U.S.A. 41°44N 75°26W 313 E9
Pleasant Point N.Z. 44°16S 171°9E 285 c
Pleasant Prairie U.S.A. 42°33N 87°56W 311 B9
Pleasanton Calif., U.S.A. 37°39N 121°52W 306 H5
Pleasanton Tex., U.S.A. 28°58N 98°29W 314 G5
Pleasantville Iowa, U.S.A. 41°23N 93°18W 310 C3
Pleasantville N.J., U.S.A. 39°24N 74°32W 309 F16
Pleasantville Pa., U.S.A. 41°35N 79°34W 312 E5
Pleasure Island U.S.A. 28°21N 81°31W 133 B1
Pleasure Ridge Park U.S.A. 38°9N 85°50W 311 F11
Pléaux France 45°8N 2°13E 174 C6
Plei Ku Vietnam 13°57N 108°0E 236 F7
Plélan-le-Grand France 48°0N 2°7W 172 D4
Plenița Romania 44°14N 23°10E 183 F8
Plenty → Australia 23°25S 136°31E 280 C2
Plenty, B. of N.Z. 37°45S 177°0E 284 D6
Plentywood U.S.A. 48°47N 104°34W 304 B11
Plérin France 48°32N 2°46W 172 D4
Plesetsk Russia 62°43N 40°20E 186 B7
Pleshcheyevko Ozero △ Russia 56°45N 38°50E 188 D10
Pleskau = Pskov Russia 57°50N 28°25E 188 D5
Plessisville Canada 46°14N 71°47W 299 C5
Plestin-les-Grèves France 48°40N 3°39W 172 D3
Pleszew Poland 51°53N 17°47E 185 G4
Pleternica Croatia 45°17N 17°48E 182 E2
Plétipi, L. Canada 51°44N 70°6W 299 B5
Pleven Bulgaria 43°26N 24°37E 203 C8
Pleven □ Bulgaria 43°26N 24°37E 203 C8
Plevna Canada 44°58N 76°59W 312 B8
Plitvice Lakes = Plitvička Jezera △ Croatia 44°54N 15°35E 199 D12
Plitvička Jezera △ Croatia 44°54N 15°35E 199 D12
Plješevica Croatia 44°45N 15°45E 199 D12
Pljevlja Montenegro 43°21N 19°21E 202 C3
Ploaghe Italy 40°40N 8°45E 200 B1
Ploče Croatia 43°4N 17°26E 199 E14
Płock Poland 52°32N 19°40E 185 F6
Plöckenpass Italy 46°37N 12°57E 199 B9
Plöckenstein Germany 48°46N 13°51E 179 G9
Ploemeur France 47°44N 3°26W 172 E3
Ploërmel France 47°55N 2°26W 172 E4
Plöhnen = Płońsk Poland 52°37N 20°21E 185 F7
Ploiești Romania 44°57N 26°5E 183 F11
Plomari Greece 38°59N 26°22E 205 C8
Plombières-les-Bains France 47°58N 6°27E 173 E13
Plomin Croatia 45°8N 14°10E 199 C11
Plön Germany 54°9N 10°24E 178 A6
Plonge, Lac la Canada 55°8N 107°20W 297 B7
Płońsk Poland 52°37N 20°21E 185 F7
Plopeni Romania 45°4N 25°59E 183 E10
Plopișului, Munții Romania 47°5N 22°30E 182 C7
Plotsk = Płock Poland 52°32N 19°40E 185 F6
Płoty Poland 53°48N 15°18E 184 E2
Plouaret France 48°37N 3°28W 172 D3
Plouay France 47°55N 3°21W 172 E3
Ploučnice → Czechia 50°46N 14°13E 180 A7
Ploudalmézeau France 48°34N 4°41W 172 D2
Plouescat France 48°39N 4°10W 172 D2
Plougasnou France 48°42N 3°49W 172 D3
Plougastel-Daoulas France 48°22N 4°17W 172 D2
Plouguerneau France 48°36N 4°30W 172 D2
Plouha France 48°41N 2°57W 172 D4
Plouhinec France 48°0N 4°29W 172 E2
Plovdiv Bulgaria 42°8N 24°44E 203 D8
Plovdiv □ Bulgaria 42°15N 24°30E 203 D8
Plover Cove Res. China 22°28N 114°15E 219 a
Pluies, R. des → Réunion 20°52S 55°31E 272 f
Plum U.S.A. 40°29N 79°47W 312 F5
Plum I. U.S.A. 41°11N 72°12W 313 E12
Plumas U.S.A. 39°45N 120°4W 306 F6
Plummer U.S.A. 47°20N 116°53W 304 C5
Plumridge Lakes Australia 29°26S 125°16E 279 E4
Plumstead Western Cape, S. Africa 34°1S 18°28E 118 B1
Plumstead London, U.K. 51°29N 0°5E 125 B4
Plumtree Zimbabwe 20°27S 27°55E 269 G2
Plungė Lithuania 55°53N 21°59E 184 C8
Pluvigner France 47°46N 3°1W 172 E3
Plužine Montenegro 43°8N 18°51E 202 C2
Plymouth Montserrat 16°41N 62°12W 322 p
Plymouth Trin. & Tob. 11°14N 60°48W 323 s
Plymouth Plymouth, U.K. 50°22N 4°10W 169 G3
Plymouth Calif., U.S.A. 38°29N 120°51W 306 G6
Plymouth Ill., U.S.A. 40°18N 90°58W 310 D6
Plymouth Ind., U.S.A. 41°21N 86°19W 311 C10
Plymouth Mass., U.S.A. 41°57N 70°40W 313 E14
Plymouth N.C., U.S.A. 35°52N 76°43W 315 D16
Plymouth N.H., U.S.A. 43°46N 71°41W 313 C13
Plymouth Pa., U.S.A. 41°14N 75°57W 313 E9
Plymouth Wis., U.S.A. 43°45N 87°59W 308 D10
Plympton-Wyoming = Wyoming Canada 42°57N 82°7W 312 D2
Plynlimon = Pumlumon Fawr U.K. 52°28N 3°46W 169 E4
Plyussa Russia 58°28N 29°27E 188 C5
Plyussa → Russia 59°4N 28°6E 188 C5
Plyushchevo Russia 55°44N 37°45E 129 B3
Plzeň Czechia 49°45N 13°22E 180 B6
Plzeňský □ Czechia 49°35N 13°0E 180 B6
Pmere Nyente ✪ Australia 24°15S 136°10E 280 C2
Pniewy Poland 52°31N 16°16E 185 F3
Pnika Greece 112 c1
Pnyx = Pnika Greece 112 c1
Pô Burkina Faso 11°14N 1°5W 263 C4
Po → Italy 44°57N 12°4E 199 D9
Po, Delta del Italy 44°55N 12°30E 199 D9
Po Hai = Bo Hai China 39°0N 119°0E 227 E10
Po Toi China 22°10N 114°16E 219 a
Po Toi Is. Hong Kong, China 22°10N 114°16E 122 B3
Po Toi O Hong Kong, China 22°16N 114°17E 122 B3
Poasco Italy 45°24N 9°16E 128 B2
Pobé Benin 7°0N 2°56E 263 D5
Pobé Burkina Faso 13°53N 1°42W 263 C4
Pobeda Russia 65°12N 146°12E 215 C15
Pobedy, Pik Asia 42°0N 79°58E 217 D9
Pobiedziska Poland 52°29N 17°11E 185 F4
Pobladura del Valle Spain 42°6N 5°44W 194 C5
Poblet, Monasterio de Spain 41°22N 1°4E 196 D6
Pobra de Trives Spain 42°20N 7°10W 194 C3
Pocahontas Ark., U.S.A. 36°16N 90°58W 315 C9
Pocahontas Ill., U.S.A. 38°50N 89°33W 310 F7
Pocahontas Iowa, U.S.A. 42°44N 94°40W 310 B2
Pocatello U.S.A. 42°52N 112°27W 304 E7
Počátky Czechia 49°15N 15°14E 180 B8
Pocheon S. Korea 37°53N 127°13E 224 D3
Pochep Russia 52°58N 33°29E 189 F7
Pochinki Russia 54°41N 44°59E 190 C7
Pochinok Russia 54°28N 32°29E 188 E7
Pöchlarn Austria 48°12N 15°12E 180 C8
Poci Venezuela 5°57N 61°29W 329 B6
Pocinhos Brazil 7°4S 36°3W 332 C4
Pocking Germany 48°23N 13°19E 179 G9
Pocklington Reef Papua N. G. 10°51S 155°44E 286 F8
Poções Brazil 14°31S 40°21W 333 D3
Pocomoke City U.S.A. 38°5N 75°34W 309 F16
Poconé Brazil 16°15S 56°37W 331 D6
Poços de Caldas Brazil 21°50S 46°33W 335 A6
Podbaba Czechia 50°7N 14°22E 135 B2
Podbořany Czechia 50°14N 13°25E 180 A6
Poddębice Poland 51°54N 18°58E 185 G5
Poděbrady Czechia 50°9N 15°8E 180 A8
Podensac France 44°40N 0°22W 174 D3
Podenzano Italy 44°57N 9°41E 198 D6
Podgorač Croatia 45°27N 18°13E 182 E3
Podgorica Montenegro 42°30N 19°19E 202 D3
Podgorie Albania 40°49N 20°48E 202 F4
Podile India 15°37N 79°37E 245 G4
Podilska Vysochyna Ukraine 49°0N 28°0E 183 B13
Podkarpackie □ Poland 50°0N 22°10E 185 H9
Podkova Bulgaria 41°24N 25°24E 203 E9
Podlapača Croatia 44°37N 15°47E 199 D12
Podlaskie □ Poland 53°10N 23°0E 185 E10
Podocarpus △ Ecuador 4°13S 79°2W 328 D2
Podoleni Romania 46°46N 26°39E 183 D11
Podoli Czechia 50°2N 14°25E 135 B2
Podolínec Slovakia 49°16N 20°31E 181 B13
Podolsk Russia 55°25N 37°30E 188 E9
Podor Senegal 16°40N 15°2W 262 B1
Podporozhye Russia 60°55N 34°2E 188 B8
Podu Iloaiei Romania 47°13N 27°16E 183 C12
Podu Turcului Romania 46°11N 27°25E 183 D12
Podujevo = Besianë Kosovo 42°54N 21°10E 202 D5
Podyji △ Czechia 48°51N 15°57E 180 C8
Poechos Peru 4°41S 80°34W 328 D1
Poel Germany 54°0N 11°25E 178 A7
Pofadder S. Africa 29°10S 19°22E 270 C2
Poggiardo Italy 40°3N 18°23E 201 B11
Poggibonsi Italy 43°28N 11°9E 198 E8
Póggio Mirteto Italy 42°16N 12°41E 199 F9
Pogoanele Romania 44°55N 27°0E 183 F12
Pogorzela Poland 51°50N 17°12E 185 G4
Pogoso Dem. Rep. of the Congo 6°46S 17°12E 265 D3
Pogradec Albania 40°54N 20°37E 202 F4
Pogranichnyy Russia 44°25N 131°24E 220 B5
Poh Indonesia 0°46S 122°51E 231 E6
Pohang S. Korea 36°1N 129°23E 224 D4
Pohjanmaa □ Finland 62°58N 22°50E 160 E20
Pohjois-Pirkkala = Nokia Finland 61°30N 23°30E 188 B2
Pohnpei Micronesia 6°55N 158°10E 288 G7
Pohorelá Slovakia 48°50N 20°2E 181 C13
Pohořelice Czechia 48°59N 16°31E 181 C9
Pohorje Slovenia 46°30N 15°20E 199 B12
Pohri India 25°32N 77°22E 242 G6
Pōhue B. U.S.A. 19°0N 155°48W 302 E6
Poi Solomon Is. 10°9S 161°42E 287 N11
Poiana Mare Romania 43°57N 23°5E 182 G8
Poiana Ruscăi, Munții Romania 45°45N 22°25E 182 E7
Poiana Stampei Romania 47°19N 25°8E 183 C10
Poie Dem. Rep. of the Congo 2°50S 23°14E 264 C4
Poike, Peninsula Chile 27°6S 109°15W 330 b
Poindimié N. Cal. 20°56S 165°20E 288 d
Poinsett, C. Antarctica 65°42S 113°18E 151 C8
Point Arena U.S.A. 38°55N 123°41W 306 G3
Point Baker U.S.A. 56°21N 133°37W 296 B2
Point Calimere India 10°17N 79°49E 245 J4
Point Fortin Trin. & Tob. 10°10N 61°42W 323 t
Point Hope U.S.A. 68°21N 166°47W 303 B6
Point L. Canada 65°15N 113°4W 294 D9
Point Lay U.S.A. 69°46N 163°3W 303 B7
Point Lisas Trin. & Tob. 10°24N 61°29W 323 t
Point Pedro Sri Lanka 9°50N 80°15E 245 K5
Point Pelee △ Canada 41°57N 82°31W 312 E2
Point Pleasant N.J., U.S.A. 40°5N 74°4W 313 F10
Point Pleasant W. Va., U.S.A. 38°51N 82°8W 309 F12
Point Reyes △ U.S.A. 38°10N 122°55W 306 G2
Pointe-à-Pierre Trin. & Tob. 10°19N 61°28W 323 t
Pointe-à-Pitre Guadeloupe 16°15N 61°32W 322 e
Pointe-au-Pic = La Malbaie Canada 47°40N 70°10W 299 C5
Pointe-Aux-Trembles Canada 45°38N 73°30W 130 A2
Pointe-Claire Canada 45°26N 73°50W 313 A11
Pointe-Gatineau Canada 45°27N 75°41W 313 A9
Pointe Michel Dominica 15°15N 61°23W 323 k
Pointe-Noire Congo 4°48S 11°53E 265 C2
Pointe-Noire Guadeloupe 16°14N 61°47W 322 e
Poio = O Convento Spain 42°28N 8°41W 194 C2
Poipet Cambodia 13°39N 102°33E 236 F4
Poirino Italy 44°56N 7°48E 198 D4
Poisonbush Ra. Australia 22°30S 121°30E 278 D3
Poissonnier Pt. Australia 19°57S 119°10E 278 C2
Poissy France 48°55N 2°2E 134 A1
Poitiers France 46°35N 0°20E 172 F7
Poitou France 46°40N 0°10W 174 B3
Poix-de-Picardie France 49°47N 1°58E 173 C8
Poix-Terron France 49°38N 4°38E 173 C11
Pojoaque U.S.A. 35°54N 106°1W 305 J10
Pok Fu Lam Hong Kong, China 22°16N 114°7E 122 B2
Pōkaʻī B. U.S.A. 21°27N 158°12W 302 K13
Pokaran India 27°0N 71°50E 242 F4
Pokataroo Australia 29°30S 148°36E 281 D4
Pokcheong S. Korea 37°28N 127°8E 137 C2
Pokhara Nepal 28°14N 83°58E 243 E10
Pokhvistnevo Russia 53°30N 52°0E 190 D11
Pokigron Suriname 4°30N 55°22W 329 C6
Poko Dem. Rep. of the Congo 3°7N 26°52E 268 B2
Poko South Sudan 5°41N 31°55E 257 F3
Pokrov Russia 55°55N 39°7E 188 E10
Pokrovka = Kyzyl-Suu Kyrgyzstan 42°20N 78°0E 217 D9
Pokrovsk = Engels Russia 51°28N 46°6E 190 E8
Pokrovsk Russia 61°29N 129°0E 215 C13
Pokrovskoy = Priazovskoye Ukraine 46°44N 35°40E 189 J8
Pokrovskoye Russia 47°25N 38°54E 189 J10
Pol-e Dokhtar Iran 33°9N 47°42E 213 F12
Pol-e Khomrī Afghan. 35°56N 68°43E 240 B3
Pol-e Zahāb Iran 34°27N 45°51E 213 E11
Pola = Pula Croatia 44°54N 13°57E 199 D10
Pola Russia 57°55N 32°0E 188 D7
Pola de Allande Spain 43°16N 6°37W 194 B4
Pola de Lena Spain 43°10N 5°49W 194 B5
Pola de Siero Spain 43°24N 5°39W 194 B5
Pola de Somiedo Spain 43°5N 6°15W 194 B4
Pola I. Amer. Samoa 14°14S 170°40W 302 f
Polacca U.S.A. 35°50N 110°23W 305 J8
Polan Iran 25°30N 61°10E 247 E9
Pol'ana Slovakia 48°38N 19°29E 181 C12
Poland U.S.A. 43°13N 75°3W 313 C9
Poland ■ Europe 52°0N 20°0E 185 G3
Polanica-Zdrój Poland 50°24N 16°32E 185 H3
Połaniec Poland 50°26N 21°17E 185 H8
Polanów Poland 54°7N 16°41E 184 D3
Polar Bear ⌂ Canada 55°0N 83°45W 298 A2
Polatlı Turkey 39°36N 32°9E 212 C5
Polatsk Belarus 55°30N 28°50E 188 E5
Polavaram India 17°15N 81°38E 244 F5
Polcura Chile 37°17S 71°43W 334 D1
Połczyn-Zdrój Poland 53°47N 16°5E 184 E3
Poldasht Iran 39°20N 45°4E 213 C11
Poleski △ Poland 51°29N 23°5E 185 G10
Polessk Russia 54°50N 21°8E 184 D8
Polesye = Pripet Marshes Europe 52°10N 27°10E 177 B15
Polevskoy Russia 56°26N 60°11E 186 C11
Polewali Indonesia 3°25S 119°20E 235 C5
Polgar Hungary 47°54N 21°6E 182 C6
Poli Cameroon 8°34N 13°15E 263 C7
Policastro, G. di Italy 40°0N 15°35E 201 C8
Police Poland 53°33N 14°33E 184 E1
Police, Pte. Seychelles 4°51S 55°32E 272 c
Polichnitos Greece 39°6N 26°10E 205 B8
Polička Czechia 49°43N 16°15E 181 B9
Policoro Italy 40°13N 16°41E 201 B9
Poliegos Greece 36°45N 24°38E 204 E6
Poligiros Greece 40°23N 23°25E 202 F7
Polignano a Mare Italy 41°0N 17°13E 201 A9
Poligny France 46°50N 5°42E 173 F12
Polillo Phil. 14°43N 121°56E 232 D3
Polillo Is. Phil. 14°56N 122°0E 232 D4
Polillo Str. Phil. 14°44N 121°51E 232 D3
Polis Cyprus 35°2N 32°26E 207 E8
Polistena Italy 38°24N 16°4E 201 D9
Pölitz = Police Poland 53°33N 14°33E 184 E1
Polk U.S.A. 41°22N 79°56W 312 E5
Polkowice Poland 51°29N 16°3E 185 G3
Polkwitz = Polkowice Poland 51°29N 16°3E 185 G3
Polla Italy 40°31N 15°29E 201 B8
Pollachi India 10°35N 77°0E 245 J3
Pollença Spain 39°54N 3°1E 206 B4
Pollença, B. de Spain 39°53N 3°8E 206 B4
Pollfoss Norway 61°58N 7°54E 164 C4
Póllica Italy 40°11N 15°3E 201 B8
Pollino, Mte. Italy 39°55N 16°11E 201 C9
Pollino △ Italy 40°0N 16°12E 201 C9
Polna Russia 58°31N 28°5E 188 C5
Polnovat Russia 63°50N 65°54E 214 C7
Polo Ill., U.S.A. 41°59N 89°35W 310 C7
Polo Mo., U.S.A. 39°33N 94°3W 310 E2
Pology Ukraine 47°29N 36°15E 189 J9
Polokwane S. Africa 23°54S 29°25E 271 B4
Polokwane → S. Africa 22°25S 30°5E 271 B5
Polomolok Phil. 6°13N 125°3E 233 H5
Polonnaruwa Sri Lanka 7°56N 81°0E 245 L5
Polonne Ukraine 50°6N 27°30E 177 C14
Polonnoye = Polonne Ukraine 50°6N 27°30E 177 C14
Polski Trŭmbesh Bulgaria 43°20N 25°38E 203 C9
Polsko Kosovo Bulgaria 43°23N 25°38E 203 C9
Polson U.S.A. 47°41N 114°9W 304 C6
Poltár Slovakia 48°26N 19°48E 181 C12
Poltava Ukraine 49°35N 34°35E 189 H8
Poltava □ Ukraine 50°15N 33°15E 189 G7
Polton U.K. 55°52N 3°7W 121 B3
Poltoratsk = Ashgabat Turkmenistan 37°58N 58°24E 247 B8
Põltsamaa Estonia 58°39N 25°58E 188 C3
Polunochnoye Russia 60°52N 60°25E 214 C7
Polur India 12°32N 79°11E 245 H4
Põlva Estonia 58°3N 27°3E 188 C4
Polvoranca, Parque de Spain 40°19N 3°48W 127 C1
Polyana Ukraine 48°38N 22°58E 182 B7
Polyarny Russia 69°8N 33°20E 160 B25
Polyarnyye Zori Russia 67°22N 32°30E 160 C25
Polykastro Greece 41°0N 22°34E 202 E6
Polynesia Pac. Oc. 10°0S 162°0W 289 F11
Polynesian Cultural Center U.S.A. 21°38N 157°55W 302 J14
Polynésie française = French Polynesia ☑ Pac. Oc. 20°0S 145°0W 289 f
Polyustrovo Russia 59°57N 30°25E 137 B2
Pomabamba = Azurduy Bolivia 19°59S 64°29W 331 D5
Pomabamba Peru 8°50S 77°28W 330 B2
Pomarance Italy 43°18N 10°52E 198 E7
Pombal Brazil 6°45S 37°50W 332 C4
Pombal Portugal 39°55N 8°40W 194 F2
Pombia Greece 35°0N 24°51E 207 F5
Pombos, B. dos Angola 11°40S 13°47E 265 E2
Pomene Mozam. 22°53S 35°33E 271 B6
Pomeroon-Supenaam □ Guyana 7°5N 58°51W 329 B6
Pomeroy Ohio, U.S.A. 39°2N 82°2W 309 F12
Pomeroy Wash., U.S.A. 46°28N 117°36W 304 C5
Pomézia Italy 41°40N 12°30E 200 A5
Pomichna Ukraine 48°13N 31°36E 189 H6
Pomio Papua N. G. 5°32S 151°33E 286 C6
Pomme de Terre L. U.S.A. 37°54N 93°19W 310 G3
Pomme Rose Grenada 12°3N 61°39W 323 q
Pomona Queens., Australia 26°22S 152°52E 281 D5
Pomona Calif., U.S.A. 34°4N 117°45W 307 L9
Pomona Park U.S.A. 29°30N 81°36W 317 F8
Pomorie Bulgaria 42°32N 27°41E 203 D11
Pomorskie □ Poland 54°30N 18°0E 184 D5
Pomorskie, Pojezierze Poland 53°40N 16°37E 184 E3
Pomos Cyprus 35°9N 32°33E 207 E8
Pomos, C. Cyprus 35°10N 32°33E 207 E8
Pompano Beach U.S.A. 26°14N 80°7W 129 A3
Pompei Italy 40°45N 14°30E 201 B7
Pompey France 48°46N 6°6E 173 D13
Pompeys Pillar U.S.A. 45°59N 107°57W 304 D10
Pompeys Pillar △ U.S.A. 46°0N 108°0W 304 D10
Pompidou, Centre Paris, France 134 b4
Pomprap Thailand 13°44N 100°30E 113 B2
Pompton Lakes U.S.A. 41°0N 74°17W 313 F10
Ponape = Pohnpei Micronesia 6°55N 158°10E 288 G7
Ponask L. Canada 54°0N 92°41W 298 B1
Ponca U.S.A. 42°34N 96°43W 308 D5
Ponca City U.S.A. 36°42N 97°5W 314 C6
Ponce Puerto Rico 18°1N 66°37W 321 C6
Ponce de Leon U.S.A. 30°44N 85°56W 316 E4
Ponce de Leon B. U.S.A. 25°15N 81°10W 317 K8
Ponchatoula U.S.A. 30°26N 90°26W 315 F9
Poncheville, L. Canada 50°10N 76°55W 298 B4
Pond U.S.A. 35°43N 119°20W 307 K7
Pond Inlet Canada 72°40N 77°0W 295 C16
Pondicherry = Puducherry India 11°59N 79°50E 245 J4
Pondo Papua N. G. 4°33S 151°38E 286 C6
Pondok Gede Indonesia 6°17S 106°55E 122 A2
Pondok Indah Indonesia 6°16S 106°46E 122 B1
Ponds, I. of Canada 53°27N 55°52W 299 B8

416 Ponérihouen INDEX

Ponérihouen N. Cal. 21°5S 165°24E 288 d
Ponferrada Spain 42°32N 6°35W 194 C4
Pongo, Wadi → South Sudan 8°42N 27°40E 257 F2
Poniatowa Poland 51°11N 22°3E 185 G9
Poniec Poland 51°48N 16°50E 185 G3
Ponikva Slovenia 46°16N 15°26E 199 B12
Ponizovkino = Krasnyy Profintern Russia 57°45N 40°27E 188 D11
Ponnaiyar → India 11°50N 79°45E 245 J4
Ponnani India 10°45N 75°59E 245 J2
Ponneri India 13°20N 80°15E 245 H5
Ponnuru India 16°5N 80°34E 245 F5
Ponoka Canada 52°42N 113°40W 296 C6
Ponorogo Indonesia 7°52S 111°27E 235 D4
Ponot Phil. 8°25N 123°0E 233 G4
Ponoy Russia 67°0N 41°13E 186 A7
Ponoy → Russia 66°59N 41°17E 186 A7
Pons = Ponts Spain 41°55N 1°12E 196 D6
Pons France 45°35N 0°34W 174 C3
Ponsul → Portugal 39°40N 7°31W 194 F3
Pont-à-Mousson France 48°54N 6°1E 173 D13
Pont-Audemer France 49°21N 0°30E 172 C7
Pont-Aven France 47°51N 3°47W 172 E3
Pont Canavese Italy 45°25N 7°36E 198 C4
Pont Casse Dominica 15°22N 61°21W 323 k
Pont-d'Ain France 46°3N 5°21E 173 F12
Pont-de-Roide France 47°23N 6°45E 173 E13
Pont-de-Salars France 44°18N 2°44E 174 D6
Pont-de-Vaux France 46°26N 4°56E 173 F11
Pont-de-Veyle France 46°17N 4°53E 173 F11
Pont-du-Château France 45°47N 3°15E 173 G10
Pont du Gard France 43°57N 4°32E 175 E8
Pont-l'Abbé France 47°52N 4°15W 172 E2
Pont-l'Évêque France 49°18N 0°11E 172 C7
Pont-St-Esprit France 44°16N 4°40E 175 D8
Pont-St-Martin Italy 45°36N 7°48E 198 C4
Pont-Ste-Maxence France 49°18N 2°36E 173 C9
Pont-sur-Yonne France 48°18N 3°10E 173 D10
Pont-Viau Canada 45°35N 73°41W 130 A1
Ponta de Pedras Brazil 1°23S 48°52W 332 B2
Ponta Delgada Flores, Azores 39°31N 31°13W 153 d2
Ponta Delgada São Miguel, Azores 37°44N 25°40W 153 d3
Ponta Delgada ✕ (PDL) Azores 37°44N 25°41W 153 d3
Ponta do Pargo Madeira 32°49N 17°15W 153 c
Ponta do Sol Madeira 32°42N 17°7W 153 c
Ponta Grossa Brazil 25°7S 50°10W 335 B5
Ponta Porã Brazil 22°20S 55°35W 335 A4
Pontacq France 43°11N 0°8W 174 E3
Pontailler-sur-Saône France 47°13N 5°25E 173 E12
Pontal → Brazil 9°8S 40°12W 332 C3
Pontalina Brazil 17°31S 49°27W 333 E2
Pontardawe U.K. 51°43N 3°51W 169 F3
Pontarlier France 46°54N 6°20E 173 F13
Pontassieve Italy 43°46N 11°26E 199 E8
Pontault-Combault France 48°47N 2°36E 134 B4
Pontaumur France 45°52N 2°40E 174 C6
Pontcharra France 45°26N 6°1E 175 C10
Pontchartrain, L. U.S.A. 30°5N 90°5W 315 F9
Pontchâteau France 47°25N 2°5W 172 E4
Ponte Alta, Serra do Brazil 19°42S 47°40W 333 E2
Ponte Alta do Norte Brazil 10°45S 47°34W 332 D2
Ponte Branca Brazil 16°27S 52°40W 331 D7
Ponte da Barca Portugal 41°48N 8°25W 194 D2
Ponte de Lima Portugal 41°46N 8°35W 194 D2
Ponte de Sor Portugal 39°17N 8°1W 195 F2
Ponte dell'Ólio Italy 44°52N 9°39E 198 D6
Ponte di Legno Italy 46°16N 10°31E 198 B7
Ponte do Pungué Mozam. 19°30S 34°33E 269 F3
Ponte-Leccia France 42°28N 9°13E 175 F13
Ponte nelle Alpi Italy 46°11N 12°16E 199 B9
Ponte Nova Brazil 20°25S 42°54W 333 F3
Ponte Vedra Beach U.S.A. 30°15N 81°23W 316 E8
Ponteareas Spain 42°10N 8°28W 194 C2
Pontebba Italy 46°30N 13°18E 199 B10
Ponteceso Spain 43°15N 8°54W 194 B2
Pontecorvo Italy 41°27N 13°40E 200 A6
Pontedeume Spain 43°24N 8°10W 194 B2
Ponteix Canada 49°46N 107°29W 297 D7
Pontes e Lacerda Brazil 15°12S 59°22W 331 D6
Pontevedra Capiz, Phil. 11°29N 122°52E 233 F4
Pontevedra Neg. Occ., Phil. 10°22N 122°52E 233 F4
Pontevedra Spain 42°26N 8°40W 194 C2
Pontevedra □ Spain 42°25N 8°39W 194 C2
Pontevedra, R. de → Spain 42°22N 8°45W 194 C2
Pontevico Italy 45°16N 10°5E 198 C7
Pontiac Ill., U.S.A. 40°53N 88°38W 311 D8
Pontiac Mich., U.S.A. 42°38N 83°18W 311 B13
Pontian Kechil Malaysia 1°29N 103°23E 237 d
Pontianak Indonesia 0°3S 109°15E 235 C3
Pontine Is. = Ponziane, Ísole Italy 40°55N 12°57E 200 B5
Pontine Mts. = Kuzey Anadolu Dağları Turkey 41°0N 36°45E 212 B7
Pontinha Portugal 38°45N 9°11W 126 A1
Pontínia Italy 41°25N 13°2E 200 A6
Pontivy France 48°5N 2°58W 172 D4
Pontoise France 49°3N 2°5E 173 C9
Ponton → Canada 58°27N 116°11W 296 B5
Pontorson France 48°34N 1°30W 172 D5
Pontremóli Italy 44°22N 9°53E 198 D6
Pontrieux France 48°42N 3°10W 172 D3
Ponts Spain 41°55N 1°12E 196 D6
Pontypool Ont., Canada 44°6N 78°38W 312 B6
Pontypool Torf., U.K. 51°42N 3°2W 169 F4
Pontypridd U.K. 51°36N 3°20W 169 F4
Ponza Italy 40°54N 12°58E 200 B5
Ponziane, Ísole Italy 40°55N 12°57E 200 B5
Poochera Australia 32°43S 134°51E 281 E1
Pool □ Congo 3°30S 15°0E 264 C2
Poole Trin. & Tob. 10°17N 61°14W 323 t
Poole Poole, U.K. 50°43N 1°59W 169 G6
Poole □ U.K. 50°43N 1°59W 169 G6
Poole → Trin. & Tob. 10°15N 61°5W 323 t
Pooler U.S.A. 32°7N 81°15W 316 C8
Poona = Pune India 18°29N 73°57E 244 E1
Poonamallee India 13°3N 80°10E 245 H5
Pooncarie Australia 33°22S 142°31E 282 B5
Poopelloe L. Australia 31°40S 144°0E 282 A6
Poopó Bolivia 18°23S 66°59W 330 D4
Poopó, L. de Bolivia 18°30S 67°35W 330 D4
Poor Knights Is. N.Z. 35°29S 174°43E 284 B3
Poorman U.S.A. 64°5N 155°33W 303 D9
Popa Gabon 1°35S 12°32E 264 C2
Popa, Mt. Burma 20°55N 95°15E 241 E5
Popayán Colombia 2°27N 76°36W 328 C2
Poperinge Belgium 50°51N 2°42E 170 D2
Popiltah L. Australia 33°10S 141°42E 282 B4
Popina Bulgaria 44°7N 26°57E 203 B10
Popio L. Australia 33°10S 141°52E 282 B4
Poplar London, U.K. 51°30N 0°0 123 B3
Poplar Mont., U.S.A. 48°7N 105°12W 304 B11
Poplar → Canada 53°0N 97°19W 297 C9
Poplar Bluff U.S.A. 36°46N 90°24W 308 G8
Poplar Head = Dothan U.S.A. 31°13N 85°24W 316 D4
Poplarville U.S.A. 30°51N 89°32W 315 F10
Popocatépetl, Volcán Mexico 19°2N 98°38W 319 D5
Popokabaka Dem. Rep. of the Congo 5°41S 16°40E 265 D3
Pópoli Italy 42°10N 13°50E 199 F10
Popolo Dem. Rep. of the Congo 2°22N 21°8E 264 B4
Popolo, Porta del Rome, Italy 136 a2
Popomanaseu, Mt. Solomon Is. 9°40S 160°1E 287 M11
Popondetta Papua N. G. 8°48S 148°17E 286 E5
Popovača Croatia 45°30N 16°41E 199 C13
Popovo Bulgaria 43°21N 26°18E 203 C10
Poppberg Germany 49°26N 11°37E 179 F7
Poppi Italy 43°43N 11°46E 199 E8
Poprad Slovakia 49°3N 20°18E 181 B13
Poprad → Slovakia 49°38N 20°42E 181 B13
Poradaha Bangla. 23°51N 89°1E 241 D2
Porali → Pakistan 25°58N 66°26E 242 G2
Porangaba Brazil 8°48S 70°36W 330 B3
Porangahau N.Z. 40°17S 176°37E 284 G5
Porangatu Brazil 13°26S 49°10W 333 D2
Porbandar India 21°44N 69°43E 242 J3
Porce → Colombia 7°28N 74°53W 328 B3
Porcher I. Canada 53°50N 130°30W 296 C2
Porco Bolivia 19°50S 65°59W 331 D4
Porcos → Brazil 12°42S 45°7W 333 D2
Porcuna Spain 37°52N 4°11W 195 H6
Porcupine → Sask., Canada 59°11N 104°46W 297 B8
Porcupine → Alaska, U.S.A. 66°34N 145°19W 303 C11
Porcupine Abyssal Plain Atl. Oc. 48°0N 8°0W 152 B10
Porcupine Gorge △ Australia 20°22S 144°26E 280 C3
Pordenone Italy 45°57N 12°39E 199 C9
Pordim Bulgaria 43°23N 24°51E 203 C8
Pore Colombia 5°43N 72°0W 328 B3
Poreč Croatia 45°14N 13°36E 199 C10
Porecatu Brazil 22°43S 51°24W 333 F1
Porechye = Demidov Russia 55°16N 31°30E 188 E6
Poretskoye Russia 55°9N 46°21E 190 C8
Porgera Papua N. G. 5°28S 143°12E 286 C2
Pori Finland 61°29N 21°48E 188 B1
Pori Greece 35°58N 23°13E 204 F5
Porkhov Russia 57°45N 29°38E 188 D5
Porlamar Venezuela 10°57N 63°51W 329 a
Porlezza Italy 46°2N 9°7E 198 B6
Porma → Spain 42°29N 5°28W 194 C5
Pormpuraaw Australia 14°59S 141°26E 280 A3
Pormpuraaw ✪ Australia 14°55S 141°47E 280 A3
Pornic France 47°7N 2°5W 172 E4
Poronaysk Russia 49°13N 143°0E 219 B17
Poros Attiki, Greece 37°30N 23°30E 204 D5
Poros Kefalonia, Greece 38°9N 20°47E 207 C2
Poros Lefkada, Greece 38°38N 20°43E 207 B2
Poroshiri-Dake Japan 42°41N 142°52E 220 C11
Poroszló Hungary 47°39N 20°40E 182 C5
Poroto Mts. Tanzania 9°0S 33°30E 269 D3
Porpoise B. Antarctica 66°0S 127°0E 151 C9
Porpoise Pt. Ascension I. 7°54S 14°21W 153 g
Porquerolles, Î. de France 43°0N 6°13E 175 F10
Porrentruy Switz. 47°25N 7°6E 179 H3
Porreres Spain 39°31N 3°2E 206 B4
Porsangerfjorden Norway 70°40N 25°40E 160 A21
Porsgrunn Norway 59°10N 9°40E 164 E6
Port Adelaide Australia 34°50S 138°30E 282 C3
Port Alberni Canada 49°14N 124°50W 296 D4
Port Albert Australia 38°42S 146°42E 283 E7
Port Alexander U.S.A. 56°15N 134°38W 303 H14
Port Alfred S. Africa 33°36S 26°55E 270 D4
Port Alice Canada 50°20N 127°25W 296 C3
Port Allegany U.S.A. 41°48N 78°17W 312 E6
Port Allen U.S.A. 30°27N 91°12W 314 F9
Port Alma Queens., Australia 23°38S 150°53E 280 C5
Port Alma Ont., Canada 42°10N 82°14W 312 D2
Port Angeles U.S.A. 48°7N 123°27W 306 B3
Port Antonio Jamaica 18°10N 76°26W 320 a
Port Aransas U.S.A. 27°50N 97°4W 314 H6
Port Arthur Tas., Australia 43°7S 147°50E 281 G4
Port Arthur Tex., U.S.A. 29°54N 93°56W 314 G8
Port au Choix Canada 50°43N 57°22W 299 B8
Port au Port B. Canada 48°40N 58°50W 299 C8
Port-au-Prince Haiti 18°40N 72°20W 321 C5
Port Augusta Australia 32°30S 137°50E 282 B2
Port Austin U.S.A. 44°3N 83°1W 312 B2
Port Authority Bus Terminal New York, U.S.A. 132 c2
Port-aux-Français Kerguelen 49°21S 70°13E 273 J6
Port Bergé Vaovao Madag. 15°33S 47°40E 272 B2
Port Blair India 11°40N 92°45E 245 J11
Port Blandford Canada 48°20N 54°10W 299 C9
Port Botany Australia 33°58S 151°13E 139 B2
Port-Bouët Ivory C. 5°16N 3°57W 262 D4
Port Bradshaw Australia 12°30S 137°20E 280 A2
Port Broughton Australia 33°37S 137°56E 282 B2
Port Bruce Canada 42°39N 81°0W 312 D4
Port Burwell Canada 42°40N 80°48W 312 D4
Port Byron U.S.A. 41°36N 90°20W 310 C6
Port Campbell Vic., Australia 38°37S 143°1E 282 E5
Port Campbell India 11°56N 92°37E 245 J11
Port Campbell △ Australia 38°8S 143°6E 282 E5
Port Canning India 22°23N 88°40E 243 H13
Port Carling Canada 45°7N 79°35W 312 A5
Port-Cartier Canada 50°2N 66°50W 299 B6
Port Chalmers N.Z. 45°49S 170°30E 285 F5
Port Charles N.Z. 36°33S 175°30E 284 C4
Port Charlotte U.S.A. 26°59N 82°6W 317 J7
Port Chester U.S.A. 41°0N 73°40W 313 F11
Port Clements Canada 53°40N 132°10W 296 C2
Port Clinton U.S.A. 41°31N 82°56W 311 C14
Port Colborne Canada 42°50N 79°10W 312 D5
Port Coquitlam Canada 49°15N 122°45W 306 A4
Port Cornwallis India 13°17N 93°5E 245 H11
Port Credit Canada 43°33N 79°35W 312 C5
Port-Cros △ France 43°0N 6°24E 175 F10
Port Curtis Australia 23°57S 151°20E 280 C5
Port d'Alcúdia Spain 39°50N 3°7E 206 B4
Port Dalhousie Canada 43°13N 79°16W 312 C5
Port d'Andratx Spain 39°32N 2°23E 206 B3
Port Darwin N. Terr., Australia 12°24S 130°45E 278 B5
Port Darwin Falk. Is. 51°50S 59°0W 153 f
Port Davey Australia 43°16S 145°55E 281 G4
Port-de-Bouc France 43°24N 4°59E 175 E8
Port-de-Paix Haiti 19°50N 72°50W 321 C5
Port de Pollença Spain 39°54N 3°4E 206 B4
Port de Sóller Spain 39°48N 2°42E 206 B3
Port Dickson Malaysia 2°30N 101°49E 237 L3
Port Douglas Australia 16°30S 145°30E 280 B4
Port Dover Canada 42°47N 80°12W 312 D4
Port Edward Canada 54°12N 130°10W 296 C2
Port Elgin Canada 44°25N 81°25W 312 B3
Port Elizabeth S. Africa 33°58S 25°40E 270 D4
Port Ellen U.K. 55°38N 6°11W 167 F2
Port Elliot Australia 35°32S 138°41E 282 C3
Port-en-Bessin-Huppain France 49°21N 0°45W 172 C6
Port Erin I. of Man 54°5N 4°45W 168 C3
Port Essington Australia 11°15S 132°10E 278 B5
Port Etienne = Nouâdhibou Mauritania 20°54N 17°0W 260 D1
Port Ewen U.S.A. 41°54N 73°59W 313 E11
Port Fairy Australia 38°22S 142°12E 282 E5
Port Fitzroy N.Z. 36°8S 175°20E 284 C4
Port Florence = Kisumu Kenya 0°3S 34°45E 268 C3
Port Fouâd = Bûr Fuad Egypt 31°15N 32°20E 256 H8
Port Francqui = Ilebo Dem. Rep. of the Congo 4°17S 20°55E 265 C4
Port Gamble U.S.A. 47°51N 122°34W 306 C4
Port-Gentil Gabon 0°40S 8°50E 264 C1
Port Germein Australia 33°1S 138°1E 281 E2
Port Ghalib Egypt 25°20N 34°50E 246 E2
Port Gibson U.S.A. 31°58N 90°59W 314 F9
Port Glasgow U.K. 55°56N 4°41W 167 F4
Port-Gueydon = Azeffoun Algeria 36°51N 4°26E 261 A5
Port Harcourt Nigeria 4°40N 7°10E 263 E6
Port Hardy Canada 50°41N 127°30W 296 C3
Port Harrison = Inukjuak Canada 58°25N 78°15W 295 F16
Port Hawkesbury Canada 45°36N 61°22W 299 C7
Port Hedland Australia 20°25S 118°35E 278 D2
Port Heiden U.S.A. 56°55N 158°41W 303 H8
Port Henry U.S.A. 44°3N 73°28W 313 B11
Port Herald = Nsanje Malawi 16°55S 35°12E 269 F4
Port Hood Canada 46°0N 61°32W 299 C7
Port Hope Ont., Canada 43°56N 78°20W 312 C6
Port Hope Mich., U.S.A. 43°57N 82°43W 312 C2
Port Hope Simpson Canada 52°33N 56°18W 299 B8
Port Hueneme U.S.A. 34°7N 119°12W 307 L7
Port Huron U.S.A. 42°58N 82°26W 312 D2
Port Iliç = Liman Azerbaijan 38°53N 48°47E 213 C13
Port Jefferson U.S.A. 40°57N 73°3W 313 F11
Port Jervis U.S.A. 41°22N 74°41W 313 E10
Port-Joinville France 46°45N 2°23W 172 F4
Port Katon Russia 46°52N 38°46E 189 J10
Port Kavkaz Russia 45°20N 36°40E 189 K9
Port Kembla Australia 34°52S 150°49E 283 C9
Port Kenny Australia 33°10S 134°41E 281 E1
Port Klang Malaysia 3°0N 101°35E 237 L3
Port-la-Nouvelle France 43°1N 3°3E 174 E7
Port Láirge = Waterford Ireland 52°15N 7°8W 166 D4
Port Launay Seychelles 4°39S 55°24E 272 c
Port Lavaca U.S.A. 28°37N 96°38W 314 G6
Port Leyden U.S.A. 43°35N 75°21W 313 C9
Port Lincoln Australia 34°42S 135°52E 282 C1
Port Lions U.S.A. 57°52N 152°53W 303 H9
Port Loko S. Leone 8°48N 12°46W 262 D2
Port Louis Morbihan, France 47°42N 3°22W 172 E3
Port-Louis Guadeloupe 16°28N 61°32W 322 e
Port Louis Mauritius 20°10S 57°30E 272 e
Port Lyautey = Kenitra Morocco 34°15N 6°40W 260 B3
Port MacDonnell Australia 38°5S 140°48E 282 E4
Port McNeill Canada 50°35N 127°6W 296 C3
Port Macquarie Australia 31°25S 152°25E 283 A10
Port Maria Jamaica 18°22N 76°54W 320 a
Port Mathurin Rodrigues 19°41S 63°25E 273 F5
Port Matilda U.S.A. 40°48N 78°3W 312 F6
Port Mayaca U.S.A. 26°59N 80°36W 317 J9
Port McNicoll Canada 44°44N 79°48W 312 B5
Port Melbourne Australia 37°50S 144°54E 128 B1
Port Mellon Canada 49°32N 123°31W 296 D4
Port-Menier Canada 49°51N 64°15W 299 C7
Port Moller U.S.A. 55°59N 160°34W 303 J7
Port Moody Canada 49°17N 122°51W 306 A4
Port Morant Jamaica 17°54N 76°19W 320 a
Port Moresby Papua N. G. 9°24S 147°8E 286 E4
Port Mourant Guyana 6°15N 57°20W 329 B6
Port Muhammed Bin Qasim = Port Qasim Pakistan 24°46N 67°20E 242 G2
Port Musgrave Australia 11°55S 141°50E 280 A3
Port Narevin = Potnarvin Vanuatu 18°45S 169°10E 287 H7
Port-Navalo France 47°34N 2°54W 172 E4
Port Neches U.S.A. 30°0N 93°59W 314 G8
Port Nicholson N.Z. 41°20S 174°52E 284 H3
Port Nolloth S. Africa 29°17S 16°52E 270 C2
Port Nouveau-Québec = Kangiqsualujjuaq Canada 58°30N 65°59W 295 F18
Port of Climax Canada 49°10N 108°20W 297 D7
Port of Coronach Canada 49°7N 105°31W 297 D7
Port of Spain Trin. & Tob. 10°40N 61°31W 323 t
Port Olry Vanuatu 15°1S 167°4E 287 E5
Port Orange U.S.A. 29°9N 80°59W 317 F9
Port Orchard U.S.A. 47°32N 122°38W 306 C4
Port Orford U.S.A. 42°45N 124°30W 304 E1
Port Pegasus N.Z. 47°12S 167°41E 285 H2
Port Perry Canada 44°6N 78°56W 312 B6
Port Phillip B. Australia 38°10S 144°50E 283 E6
Port Pirie Australia 33°10S 138°1E 282 B3
Port Qasim Pakistan 24°46N 67°20E 242 G2
Port Rashid U.A.E. 25°16N 55°17E 119 A2
Port Renfrew Canada 48°30N 124°20W 306 B2
Port Richmond U.S.A. 40°38N 74°7W 132 C1
Port Roper Australia 14°45S 135°25E 280 A2
Port Rowan Canada 42°40N 80°30W 312 D4
Port Royal Jamaica 17°56N 76°51W 320 a
Port Royal Sd. U.S.A. 32°15N 80°40W 316 C9
Port Saeed U.A.E. 25°15N 55°20E 119 B2
Port Safaga = Bûr Safâga Egypt 26°43N 33°57E 246 E2
Port Said = Bûr Sa'îd Egypt 31°16N 32°18E 256 H8
Port St. Joe U.S.A. 29°49N 85°18W 316 F4
Port St. John U.S.A. 28°29N 80°47W 317 G9
Port St. Johns = Umzimvubu S. Africa 31°38S 29°33E 271 D4
Port-St-Louis-du-Rhône France 43°23N 4°49E 175 E8
Port St. Lucie U.S.A. 27°18N 80°21W 317 H9
Port-Ste-Marie France 44°15N 0°25E 174 D4
Port Salerno U.S.A. 27°9N 80°12W 317 H9
Port Sanilac U.S.A. 43°26N 82°33W 312 C2
Port Severn Canada 44°48N 79°43W 312 B5
Port Shelter Hong Kong, China 22°20N 114°17E 122 A3
Port Shepstone S. Africa 30°44S 30°28E 271 D5
Port Simpson Canada 54°30N 130°20W 296 C2
Port Stanley = Stanley Falk. Is. 51°40S 59°51W 153 f
Port Stanley Canada 42°40N 81°10W 312 D3
Port Sudan = Bûr Sûdân Sudan 19°32N 37°9E 256 D4
Port Sulphur U.S.A. 29°29N 89°42W 315 G10
Port-sur-Saône France 47°42N 6°2E 173 E13
Port Talbot U.K. 51°35N 3°47W 169 F4
Port Taufiq = Bûr Taufiq Egypt 29°54N 32°32E 256 J8
Port Townsend U.S.A. 48°7N 122°45W 306 B4
Port Union Canada 43°47N 79°7W 141 A4
Port-Vato Vanuatu 16°20S 168°17E 287 F6
Port-Vendres France 42°32N 3°8E 174 F7
Port Victoria Australia 34°30S 137°29E 282 C2
Port Vila Vanuatu 17°45S 168°18E 287 G6
Port Vladimir Russia 69°25N 33°6E 160 B25
Port Wakefield Australia 34°12S 138°10E 282 C3
Port Washington U.S.A. 43°23N 87°53W 308 D10
Port Weld = Kuala Sepetang Malaysia 4°49N 100°28E 237 K3
Port Wentworth U.S.A. 32°9N 81°10W 316 C8
Porta Orientalis Romania 45°6N 22°18E 177 F12
Portachuelo Bolivia 17°10S 63°20W 331 D5
Portacloy Ireland 54°20N 9°46W 166 B2
Portadown U.K. 54°25N 6°27W 166 B5
Portaferry U.K. 54°23N 5°33W 166 B6
Portage Ind., U.S.A. 41°34N 87°11W 311 C10
Portage Mich., U.S.A. 42°12N 85°35W 311 B11
Portage Pa., U.S.A. 40°23N 78°41W 312 F6
Portage Wis., U.S.A. 43°33N 89°28W 308 D9
Portage → U.S.A. 41°31N 83°5W 311 C14
Portage la Prairie Canada 49°58N 98°18W 297 D9
Portage Park U.S.A. 41°56N 87°45W 119 B2
Portageville U.S.A. 36°26N 89°42W 308 G9
Portal U.S.A. 32°33N 81°56W 316 C8
Portal de la Pau, Plaza Barcelona, Spain 114 c2
Portalegre Portugal 39°19N 7°25W 195 F3
Portalegre □ Portugal 39°20N 7°40W 195 F3
Portales U.S.A. 34°11N 103°20W 305 J12
Portarlington Ireland 53°9N 7°14W 166 C4
Portbou Spain 42°25N 3°9E 196 C8
Porteira Brazil 1°5S 57°4W 329 D6
Porteirinha Brazil 15°44S 43°2W 333 E3
Portel Brazil 1°57S 50°49W 332 B1
Portel Portugal 38°19N 7°41W 195 G3
Portela, Lisboa ✕ (LIS) Portugal 38°46N 9°8W 126 A2
Porter U.S.A. 41°36N 87°4W 311 C9
Porter, L. U.S.A. 28°30N 81°19W 133 A3
Porter L. N.W.T., Canada 61°41N 108°5W 297 A7
Porter L. Sask., Canada 56°20N 107°20W 297 B7
Porterville Western Cape, S. Africa 33°0S 19°0E 270 D2
Porterville Calif., U.S.A. 36°4N 119°1W 306 J8
Portes-lès-Valence France 44°52N 4°54E 175 D8
Porth Tywyn = Burry Port U.K. 51°41N 4°15W 169 F3
Porthcawl U.K. 51°29N 3°42W 169 F4
Porthill U.S.A. 48°59N 116°30W 304 B5
Porthmadog U.K. 52°55N 4°8W 168 E3
Portile de Fier Europe 44°44N 22°30E 182 F7
Portimão Portugal 37°8N 8°32W 195 H2
Portishead U.K. 51°29N 2°46W 169 F5
Portiţei, Gura Romania 44°41N 29°0E 183 F14
Portknockie U.K. 57°42N 2°51W 167 D6
Portland N.S.W., Australia 33°20S 150°0E 283 B9
Portland Vic., Australia 38°20S 141°35E 282 E4
Portland Ont., Canada 44°42N 76°12W 313 B8
Portland Conn., U.S.A. 41°34N 72°38W 313 E12
Portland Fla., U.S.A. 30°31N 86°12W 316 E3
Portland Ind., U.S.A. 40°26N 84°59W 311 D12
Portland Maine, U.S.A. 43°39N 70°16W 309 D18
Portland Mich., U.S.A. 42°52N 84°54W 311 B12
Portland Oreg., U.S.A. 45°32N 122°37W 306 E4
Portland Pa., U.S.A. 40°55N 75°6W 313 F9
Portland Tex., U.S.A. 27°53N 97°20W 314 H6
Portland, I. of U.K. 50°33N 2°26W 169 G5
Portland, Récif French Polynesia 23°42S 134°30W 289 f
Portland B. Australia 38°15S 141°45E 282 E4
Portland Bight Jamaica 17°52N 77°5W 320 a
Portland Bill U.K. 50°31N 2°28W 169 G5
Portland Canal U.S.A. 55°56N 130°0W 296 B2
Portland I. N.Z. 39°20S 177°51E 284 F6
Portland Int. ✕ (PDX) U.S.A. 45°35N 122°36W 306 E4
Portland Pt. Ascension I. 7°59S 14°25W 153 g
Portland Pt. Jamaica 17°42N 77°11W 320 a
Portlaoise Ireland 53°2N 7°18W 166 C4
Portmadoc = Porthmadog U.K. 52°55N 4°8W 168 E3
Portmore Jamaica 17°53N 76°53W 320 a
Porto Brazil 3°54S 42°42W 332 B3
Porto Corse-du-Sud, France 42°16N 8°42E 175 F12
Porto Portugal 41°8N 8°40W 194 D2
Porto □ Portugal 41°8N 8°20W 194 D2
Porto, G. de France 42°17N 8°34E 175 F12
Porto Acre Brazil 9°34S 67°31W 330 B4
Pôrto Alegre = Luzilândia Brazil 3°28S 42°22W 332 B3
Pôrto Alegre Pará, Brazil 4°22S 52°44W 329 D7
Pôrto Alegre Rio Grande do S., Brazil 30°5S 51°10W 335 C5
Porto Alegre São Tomé & Príncipe 0°2N 6°32E 265 a
Porto Amboim = Gunza Angola 10°50S 13°50E 265 E2
Porto Amélia = Pemba Mozam. 12°58S 40°30E 269 E5
Porto Azzurro Italy 42°46N 10°24E 198 F7
Porto Brandão Portugal 38°40N 9°12W 126 A1
Pôrto Cajueiro Brazil 11°3S 55°53W 331 C6
Porto Cervo Italy 41°8N 9°33E 200 A2
Porto Colom Spain 39°26N 3°15E 206 B4
Porto Cristo Spain 39°33N 3°20E 206 B4
Pôrto da Fôlha Brazil 9°55S 37°17W 332 C4
Porto de Moz Brazil 1°41S 52°13W 329 D7
Porto de Pedras Brazil 9°10S 35°17W 332 C4
Pôrto des Meinacos Brazil 12°33S 53°7W 331 C7
Pôrto dos Gaúchos Brazil 11°32S 57°16W 331 C6
Porto Empédocle Italy 37°17N 13°32E 200 E6
Porto Esperança Brazil 19°37S 57°29W 331 D6
Porto Espirdão Brazil 15°51S 58°28W 331 D6
Porto Formoso Azores 37°49N 25°25W 153 d3
Porto Franco Brazil 6°20S 47°24W 332 C2
Porto Grande Brazil 0°42N 51°24W 329 C7
Porto Inglês = Vila do Maio C. Verde Is. 15°21N 23°10W 153 j
Porto Jofre Brazil 17°20S 56°48W 331 D6
Porto Lengone = Porto Azzurro Italy 42°46N 10°24E 198 F7
Porto Maurizio = Impéria Italy 43°53N 8°3E 198 E5
Porto Mendes Brazil 24°30S 54°15W 335 A5
Porto Moniz Madeira 32°52N 17°11W 153 c
Porto Murtinho Brazil 21°45S 57°55W 331 E6
Porto Nacional Brazil 10°40S 48°30W 332 D2
Porto-Novo Benin 6°23N 2°42E 263 D5
Pôrto Novo Rio de J., Brazil 22°50S 43°7W 135 A2
Porto Novo Cr. → Nigeria 6°25N 3°22E 124 B2
Porto Primavera, Represa Brazil 22°10S 52°45W 335 A5
Porto San Giórgio Italy 43°11N 13°48E 199 E10
Porto Santana Brazil 0°3S 51°11W 329 D7
Porto Santo, I. de Madeira 33°45N 16°25W 260 B1
Porto Sant' Elpídio Italy 43°15N 13°43E 199 E10
Porto Santo Stéfano Italy 42°26N 11°7E 198 F8
Porto São José Brazil 22°43S 53°10W 335 A5
Porto Seguro = Guadalupe Brazil 6°44S 43°47W 332 C3
Porto Seguro Brazil 16°26S 39°5W 333 E4
Porto Tolle Italy 44°56N 12°22E 199 D9
Porto Tórres Italy 40°50N 8°24E 200 B1
Porto União Brazil 26°10S 51°10W 335 B5
Porto-Vecchio France 41°35N 9°16E 175 G13
Porto Velho Brazil 8°46S 63°54W 331 B5
Porto Viro Italy 45°1N 12°13E 199 C9
Porto Walter Brazil 8°15S 72°40W 330 B3
Portobello U.K. 55°57N 3°7W 121 B3
Portobelo Panama 9°35N 79°42W 320 E4
Portoferráio Italy 42°48N 10°20E 198 F7
Portofino Italy 44°18N 9°12E 198 D6
Portogruaro Italy 45°47N 12°50E 199 C9
Portola U.S.A. 39°49N 120°28W 306 F6
Portomaggiore Italy 44°42N 11°48E 199 D8
Portopetro Spain 39°22N 3°13E 206 B4
Portør Norway 58°48N 9°28E 164 F6
Portoscuso Italy 39°12N 8°24E 200 C1
Portovénere Italy 44°3N 9°51E 198 D6
Portoviejo Ecuador 1°7S 80°28W 328 D1
Portpatrick U.K. 54°51N 5°7W 167 G3
Portree U.K. 57°25N 6°12W 167 D2
Portrero U.S.A. 37°46N 122°25W 136 B3
Portrush U.K. 55°12N 6°40W 166 A5
Portsmouth Dominica 15°34N 61°27W 323 k
Portsmouth Portsmouth, U.K. 50°48N 1°6W 169 G6
Portsmouth N.H., U.S.A. 43°5N 70°45W 313 C14
Portsmouth Ohio, U.S.A. 38°44N 82°57W 309 F12
Portsmouth R.I., U.S.A. 41°36N 71°15W 313 E13
Portsmouth Va., U.S.A. 36°58N 76°23W 309 G15
Portsmouth □ U.K. 50°48N 1°6W 169 G6
Portsoy U.K. 57°41N 2°41W 167 D6
Portstewart U.K. 55°11N 6°43W 166 A5
Porttipahdan tekojärvi Finland 68°5N 26°40E 160 B22
Portugal ■ Europe 40°0N 8°0W 194 F3
Portugalete Spain 43°19N 3°4W 196 B1
Portuguesa □ Venezuela 9°10N 69°15W 328 B4
Portuguese East Africa = Mozambique ■ Africa 19°0S 35°0E 269 F4
Portuguese Guinea = Guinea-Bissau ■ Africa 12°0N 15°0W 262 C2
Portuguese Timor = East Timor ■ Asia 8°50S 126°0E 231 F7
Portuguese West Africa = Angola ■ Africa 12°0S 18°0E 265 E3
Portumna Ireland 53°6N 8°14W 166 C3
Portville U.S.A. 42°3N 78°20W 312 D6
Poruma Australia 10°2S 143°4E 280 a
Porus Jamaica 18°2N 77°25W 320 a
Porvenir Bolivia 11°10S 68°50W 330 C4
Porvenir Chile 53°10S 70°16W 336 D2
Porvoo Finland 60°24N 25°40E 188 B3
Porzuna Spain 39°9N 4°9W 195 F6
Pos Chiquito Aruba 12°27N 69°57W 322 f
Posada Italy 40°38N 9°43E 200 B2
Posada → Italy 40°39N 9°45E 200 B2
Posadas Argentina 27°30S 55°50W 335 B4
Posadas Spain 37°47N 5°11W 195 H5
Poschiavo Switz. 46°19N 10°4E 179 J6
Posen = Poznań Poland 52°25N 16°55E 185 F3
Posen U.S.A. 41°38N 87°42W 119 D2
Posets Spain 42°39N 0°25E 196 C5
Poseyville U.S.A. 38°10N 87°47W 311 F9
Poshan = Boshan China 36°28N 117°49E 227 F9
Posht-e Badam Iran 33°2N 55°23E 247 C7
Posidium Greece 35°30N 27°10E 205 F9
Poso Indonesia 1°20S 120°55E 231 E6
Poso, Danau Indonesia 1°52S 120°35E 231 E6
Posoegroenoe Suriname 4°23N 55°43W 329 C6
Posof Turkey 41°30N 42°43E 213 B10
Pospelikha Russia 51°57N 81°46E 217 B10
Posse Brazil 14°4S 46°18W 333 D2
Possedimenti Italiani dell'Egeo = Dodekanisa Greece 36°35N 27°0E 205 E8
Possel C.A.R. 5°5N 19°10E 264 A3
Possession I. Antarctica 72°4S 172°0E 151 D11
Pössneck Germany 50°42N 11°35E 178 E7
Possum Kingdom L. U.S.A. 32°52N 98°26W 314 E5
Post U.S.A. 33°12N 101°23W 314 E4
Post Falls U.S.A. 47°43N 116°57W 304 C5
Postavy = Pastavy Belarus 55°4N 26°50E 188 E4
Poste, R. du Mauritius 20°29S 57°36E 272 e
Poste de Flacq Mauritius 20°9S 57°43E 272 e
Poste de Flacq → Mauritius 20°9S 57°44E 272 e
Poste-de-la-Baleine = Kuujjuarapik Canada 55°20N 77°35W 298 A4
Postmasburg S. Africa 28°18S 23°5E 270 C3
Postojna Slovenia 45°46N 14°12E 199 C11
Poston U.S.A. 34°0N 114°24W 307 M12
Postumia = Postojna Slovenia 45°46N 14°12E 199 C11
Postville Nfld. & L., Canada 54°54N 59°47W 299 B8
Postville Iowa, U.S.A. 43°5N 91°34W 310 A5
Posyet Russia 42°39N 130°48E 220 C5
Potamos Antikythira, Greece 35°52N 23°15E 204 F5
Potamos Kythira, Greece 36°15N 22°58E 204 E4
Potaro-Siparuni □ Guyana 4°50N 59°19W 329 C6
Potchefstroom S. Africa 26°41S 27°7E 270 C4
Potcoava Romania 44°30N 24°39E 183 F9
Poté Brazil 17°49S 41°49W 333 E3
Poteau U.S.A. 35°3N 94°37W 314 D7
Poteet U.S.A. 29°2N 98°35W 314 G5
Potenza Italy 40°38N 15°48E 201 B8
Potenza → Italy 43°25N 13°40E 199 E10
Potenza Picena Italy 43°22N 13°37E 199 E10
Poteriteri, L. N.Z. 46°5S 167°10E 285 G2
Potgietersrus = Mokopane S. Africa 24°10S 28°55E 271 B4
Poti Georgia 42°10N 41°38E 191 J5
Potiraguá Brazil 15°36S 39°53W 333 E4
Potiskum Nigeria 11°39N 11°2E 263 C7
Potlogi Romania 44°34N 25°34E 183 F10
Potnavin Vanuatu 18°45S 169°10E 287 H7
Potomac → U.S.A. 38°0N 76°23W 309 F14
Potomac Overlook Reg. Park ⌓ U.S.A. 38°55N 77°6W 143 B2
Potomac Park Washington, D.C., U.S.A. 143 c1
Potosí Bolivia 19°38S 65°50W 331 D4
Potosi Mo., U.S.A. 37°56N 90°47W 310 G6
Potosí □ Bolivia 20°31S 67°0W 330 E4
Potosi Mt. U.S.A. 35°57N 115°29W 307 K11
Pototan Phil. 10°54N 122°38E 233 F4
Potrerillos Chile 26°30S 69°30W 334 B2
Potrero Pt. U.S.A. 37°45N 122°22W 136 B2
Potsdam Brandenburg, Germany 52°23N 13°3E 115 B1
Potsdam N.Y., U.S.A. 44°40N 74°59W 313 B10
Potsdamer Platz Berlin, Germany 115 b3
Pottangi India 18°34N 82°58E 244 E6
Pottenstein Germany 49°46N 11°24E 179 F7
Potters Village Antigua & B. 17°5N 61°49W 322 b
Pottersville U.S.A. 43°43N 73°50W 313 C11
Pottery Hill = Abu Ballas Egypt 24°26N 27°36E 256 C2
Pottstown U.S.A. 40°15N 75°39W 313 F9
Pottsville U.S.A. 40°41N 76°12W 313 F8
Pottuvil Sri Lanka 6°55N 81°50E 245 L5
Potzham Germany 48°1N 11°36E 131 B2
Pötzleinsdorf Austria 48°14N 16°17E 142 A1
P'otzu Taiwan 23°28N 120°15E 225 C2
Pouancé France 47°44N 1°10W 172 E5
Pouce Coupé Canada 55°40N 120°10W 296 B4
Pouébo N. Cal. 20°24S 164°36E 288 d
Poughkeepsie U.S.A. 41°42N 73°56W 313 E11
Pouilly-sur-Loire France 47°17N 2°57E 173 E9
Poulan U.S.A. 31°31N 83°47W 316 D6
Poulaphouca Res. Ireland 53°8N 6°30W 166 C5
Poulata Greece 38°14N 20°36E 207 C2
Poulsbo U.S.A. 47°44N 122°38W 306 C4
Poultney U.S.A. 43°31N 73°14W 313 C11
Poulton-le-Fylde U.K. 53°51N 2°58W 168 D5
Poum N. Cal. 20°14S 164°2E 288 d
Pounga-Nganda Gabon 2°58S 10°51E 264 C2
Pouso Alegre Mato Grosso, Brazil 11°46S 57°16W 331 C6
Pouso Alegre Minas Gerais, Brazil 22°14S 45°57W 335 A6
Pouso Alto = Piracanjuba Brazil 17°18S 49°1W 333 E2
Pout Senegal 14°45N 17°0W 262 C1
Pouthisat Cambodia 12°34N 103°50E 236 F4
Pouytenga Burkina Faso 12°15N 0°25W 263 C4
Pouzauges France 46°47N 0°50W 172 F6
Považská Bystrica Slovakia 49°8N 18°27E 181 B11
Povenets Russia 62°50N 34°50E 186 B5
Poverty B. N.Z. 38°43S 178°2E 284 E7
Poverty Point Nat. Monument ⌓ U.S.A. 32°39N 91°24W 314 E9
Povlen Serbia 44°9N 19°44E 202 B3
Póvoa de Lanhosa Portugal 41°33N 8°15W 194 D2
Póvoa de Santa Iria Portugal 38°51N 9°4W 195 G1
Póvoa de Santo Adriao Portugal 38°47N 9°9W 126 A2
Póvoa de Varzim Portugal 41°25N 8°46W 194 D2
Povoação Azores 37°45N 25°15W 153 d3
Povorino Russia 51°12N 42°5E 190 E6
Povorotnyy, Mys Russia 42°40N 133°2E 220 C6
Povungnituk = Puvirnituq Canada 60°2N 77°10W 295 E16
Powassan Canada 46°5N 79°25W 298 C4
Poway U.S.A. 32°58N 117°2W 307 N9
Powązki Poland 52°15N 20°58E 143 B1
Powder → U.S.A. 46°45N 105°26W 304 C11
Powder River U.S.A. 43°2N 106°59W 304 E10
Powder Springs U.S.A. 33°52N 84°41W 316 B5
Powell U.S.A. 44°45N 108°46W 304 D9
Powell, L. U.S.A. 36°57N 111°29W 305 H8
Powell River Canada 49°50N 124°35W 296 D4
Powelton U.S.A. 33°26N 82°52W 316 B7
Power House = Drayton Valley Canada 53°12N 114°58W 296 C6
Powers U.S.A. 45°41N 87°32W 308 C10
Powiśle Poland 52°14N 21°1E 143 B2
Pownal U.S.A. 42°45N 73°14W 313 D11
Powsin Poland 52°8N 21°6E 143 C2
Powsinek Poland 52°9N 21°6E 143 C2
Powys □ U.K. 52°20N 3°20W 169 E4
Poxoréo Brazil 15°50S 54°23W 331 D7
Poya N. Cal. 21°19S 165°7E 288 d
Poyan Res. Singapore 1°22N 103°40E 138 A2
Poyang Hu China 29°5N 116°20E 229 C11
Poyarkovo Russia 49°36N 128°41E 215 E13
Poysdorf Austria 48°40N 16°37E 181 C9
Poza de la Sal Spain 42°35N 3°31W 194 C7
Poza Rica Mexico 20°33N 97°27W 319 C5
Pozantı Turkey 37°25N 34°50E 212 D6
Požarevac Serbia 44°35N 21°18E 202 B5
Pozazal, Puerto Spain 42°56N 4°10W 194 C6
Požega Croatia 45°20N 17°40E 182 E2
Požega Serbia 43°53N 20°2E 202 C4
Poznań Poland 52°25N 16°55E 185 F3
Poznań ✕ (POZ) Poland 52°26N 16°45E 185 F3
Pozo U.S.A. 35°20N 120°24W 307 K6
Pozo Alcón Spain 37°42N 2°56W 195 H8
Pozo Almonte Chile 20°10S 69°50W 330 E4
Pozo Colorado Paraguay 23°30S 58°45W 334 A4
Pozo Negro Canary Is. 28°19N 13°55W 153 e2
Pozoblanco Spain 38°23N 4°51W 195 G6
Pozorrubio Phil. 16°7N 120°33E 232 C3
Pozuelo de Alarcón Spain 40°24N 3°49W 127 B1
Pozuzo Peru 10°5S 75°35W 330 C2
Pozzallo Italy 36°43N 14°51E 201 F7
Pozzomaggiore Italy 40°24N 8°39E 200 B1
Pozzuoli Italy 40°49N 14°7E 201 B7
Pra → Ghana 5°1N 1°37W 263 D4
Prabuty Poland 53°47N 19°15E 184 E6
Prača Bos.-H. 43°47N 18°43E 182 G3
Prachatice Czechia 49°1N 14°0E 180 B6
Prachin Buri Thailand 14°0N 101°25E 236 F3
Prachuap Khirikhan Thailand 11°49N 99°48E 237 G2
Pradelles France 44°46N 3°52E 174 D7
Pradera Colombia 3°25N 76°15W 328 C2
Prades France 42°38N 2°23E 174 F6
Prado Brazil 17°20S 39°13W 333 E4
Prado, Museo del Madrid, Spain 127 b3
Prado Churubusco Mexico 19°20N 99°8W 128 B2
Prado del Rey Spain 36°48N 5°33W 195 J5
Præstø Denmark 55°8N 12°2E 163 J6
Praga Poland 52°15N 21°2E 143 B2
Pragersko Slovenia 46°27N 15°42E 199 B12
Prague = Praha Czechia 50°4N 14°25E 135 B2
Praha Czechia 50°4N 14°25E 135 B2
Praha ✕ (PRG) Czechia 50°6N 14°16E 135 B1
Prahecq France 46°19N 0°26W 174 B3
Prahita → India 19°0N 79°55E 244 E4
Prahova □ Romania 45°10N 26°0E 183 E10
Prahova → Romania 44°50N 25°50E 183 F10
Prahovo Serbia 44°18N 22°39E 202 B6
Praia Azores 39°3N 27°58W 153 d1
Praia C. Verde Is. 15°2N 23°34W 153 j
Praia ✕ (RAI) C. Verde Is. 14°55N 23°30W 153 j
Praia a Mare Italy 39°50N 15°45E 201 C8
Praia da Vitória Azores 38°44N 27°4W 153 d1
Praia do Norte Azores 38°36N 28°46W 153 d1
Praia Grande Brazil 24°0S 46°24W 333 F2
Praid Romania 46°32N 25°10E 183 D10
Prainha Azores 38°27N 28°12W 153 d1
Prainha Pará, Brazil 1°45S 53°30W 329 D7
Prainha Nova Brazil 7°10S 60°30W 331 B5
Praires, R. des → Canada 45°38N 73°36W 130 A2
Prairie Australia 20°50S 144°35E 280 C3
Prairie City U.S.A. 44°28N 118°43W 304 D4
Prairie Dog Town Fork Red → U.S.A. 34°34N 99°58W 314 D5
Prairie du Chien U.S.A. 43°3N 91°9W 310 A5
Prairie du Rocher U.S.A. 38°5N 90°6W 310 F6
Prairie Village U.S.A. 38°58N 94°38W 310 F2
Prairies, L. of the Canada 51°16N 101°32W 297 C8
Pramanda Greece 39°32N 21°8E 204 B3
Prambanan Indonesia 7°45S 110°29E 235 D4
Prambanan △ Indonesia 7°45S 110°28E 231 G14
Prampram Ghana 5°43N 0°8E 263 D5
Pran Buri Thailand 12°23N 99°55E 236 F2
Prándarjökull Iceland 64°40N 14°55W 155 C12
Prang Ghana 8°1N 0°56W 263 D4
Prapat Indonesia 2°41N 98°58E 234 B1
Praslin St. Lucia 13°52N 60°54W 323 m
Praslin Seychelles 4°18S 55°45E 272 c
Prasonisi, Akra Greece 35°42N 27°46E 206 F11
Prassberg = Mozirje Slovenia 46°22N 14°58E 199 B11
Praszka Poland 51°5N 18°31E 185 G5
Prata Brazil 19°25S 48°54W 333 E2
Pratabpur India 23°28N 83°15E 243 H10
Pratapgarh Raj., India 24°2N 74°40E 242 G6
Pratapgarh Ut. P., India 25°56N 81°59E 243 G9
Pratas I. = Dongsha Dao S. China Sea 20°45N 116°43E 219 G12
Prater Austria 48°12N 16°25E 142 A2
Prato Italy 43°53N 11°6E 198 E8
Prátola Peligna Italy 42°6N 13°52E 199 F10
Prats-de-Mollo-la-Preste France 42°25N 2°27E 174 F6
Pratt U.S.A. 37°39N 98°44W 308 G4
Prattville U.S.A. 32°28N 86°29W 315 E11
Praust = Pruszcz Gdański Poland 54°17N 18°40E 184 D5
Pravara → India 19°35N 74°45E 244 E2
Pravdinsk Kaliningrad, Russia 54°27N 21°1E 184 D8
Pravdinsk Nizhniy Novgorod, Russia 56°29N 43°28E 190 B6
Pravets Bulgaria 42°53N 23°55E 202 D7
Pravia Spain 43°30N 6°12W 194 B4
Praya Indonesia 8°39S 116°17E 235 D5
Prayag = Allahabad India 25°25N 81°58E 243 G9
Pre-delta △ Argentina 32°10S 60°40W 334 C3
Pré-en-Pail France 48°28N 0°12W 172 D6
Preah Seihanu = Kampong Saom Cambodia 10°38N 103°30E 237 G4
Preah Vihear Cambodia 14°23N 104°41E 236 E5
Preau Trin. & Tob. 10°12N 61°19W 323 t

Preble U.S.A. 42°44N 76°8W 313 D8
Prêcheur Martinique 14°48N 61°13W 322 j
Precipice △ Australia 25°18S 150°5E 281 D5
Precordillera Argentina 30°0S 69°1W 334 C2
Precotto Italy 45°30N 9°13E 128 A2
Predáppio Italy 44°6N 11°59E 199 D8
Predazzo Italy 46°19N 11°36E 199 B8
Predeal Romania 45°30N 25°34E 183 E10
Predejane Serbia 42°51N 22°9E 202 D6
Preeceville Canada 51°57N 102°40W 297 C8
Preetz Germany 54°14N 10°18E 178 A6
Pregolya → Russia 54°41N 20°22E 184 D7
Pregrada Croatia 46°11N 15°45E 199 B12
Preiļi Latvia 56°18N 26°43E 188 D4
Preko Croatia 44°7N 15°10E 199 D12
Prelog Croatia 46°18N 16°32E 199 B13
Premer Australia 31°29S 149°56E 283 A8
Prémery France 47°10N 3°18E 173 E10
Premià de Mar Spain 41°29N 2°22E 196 D7
Premont U.S.A. 27°22N 98°7W 314 H5
Premuda Croatia 44°20N 14°36E 199 D11
Prenestino Labicano Italy 41°53N 12°33E 136 B2
Prentice U.S.A. 45°33N 90°17W 308 C8
Prenzlau Germany 53°19N 13°50E 178 B9
Prenzlauerberg Germany 52°32N 13°24E 115 A3
Preobrazheniye Russia 42°54N 133°54E 220 C6
Preparis I. = Pariparit Kyun Burma 14°52N 93°41E 245 G11
Preparis North Channel Ind. Oc. 15°27N 94°5E 245 G11
Preparis South Channel Ind. Oc. 14°33N 93°30E 245 G11
Přerov Czechia 49°28N 17°27E 181 B10
Prescott Ont., Canada 44°45N 75°30W 313 B9
Prescott Ariz., U.S.A. 34°33N 112°28W 305 J7
Prescott Ark., U.S.A. 33°48N 93°23W 314 E8
Prescott Valley U.S.A. 34°40N 112°18W 305 J7
Preservation Inlet N.Z. 46°8S 166°35E 285 G1
Preševo Serbia 42°19N 21°39E 202 D5
Presho U.S.A. 43°54N 100°3W 308 D3
Presicce Italy 39°54N 18°16E 201 C11
Presidencia de la Plaza Argentina 27°0S 59°50W 334 B4
Presidencia Roque Saenz Peña Argentina 26°45S 60°30W 334 B3
Président-Thiers, Récif French Polynesia 24°30S 146°0W 289 f
Presidente Dutra Brazil 5°15S 44°30W 332 C3
Presidente Epitácio Brazil 21°56S 52°6W 333 F1
Presidente Figueiredo Brazil 1°57S 60°2W 329 D5
Presidente Hayes ☐ Paraguay 24°0S 59°0W 334 A4
Presidente Juán Perón = Chaco ☐ Argentina 26°30S 61°0W 334 B3
Presidente Médici Brazil 11°17S 61°55W 331 C5
Presidente Prudente Brazil 22°5S 51°25W 335 A5
Presidente Ríos, L. Chile 46°28S 74°25W 336 C2
Presidente Vargas = Nova Era Brazil 19°45S 43°3W 333 E3
Presidio U.S.A. 29°34N 104°22W 314 G2
Preslav Bulgaria 43°10N 26°52E 203 C10
Preslavska Planina Bulgaria 43°10N 26°45E 203 C10
Prešov Slovakia 49°0N 21°15E 181 B14
Prešovský ☐ Slovakia 49°10N 21°0E 181 B13
Prespa Bulgaria 41°44N 24°55E 203 E8
Prespa, L. = Prespansko Jezero Macedonia 40°55N 21°0E 202 F5
Prespa △ Europe 40°48N 21°4E 202 F4
Prespansko Jezero Macedonia 40°55N 21°0E 202 F5
Presque I. U.S.A. 42°10N 80°6W 312 D4
Presque Isle U.S.A. 46°41N 68°1W 309 B19
Pressburg = Bratislava Slovakia 48°10N 17°7E 181 C10
Prestatyn U.K. 53°20N 3°24W 168 D4
Prestea Ghana 5°22N 2°7W 262 D4
Presteigne U.K. 52°17N 3°0W 169 E5
Přeštice Czechia 49°34N 13°20E 180 B6
Presto Bolivia 18°55S 64°56W 331 D5
Preston Vic., Australia 37°44S 145°0E 128 A1
Preston Ont., Canada 43°23N 80°21W 312 C4
Preston Lancs., U.K. 53°46N 2°42W 168 D5
Preston Ga., U.S.A. 32°4N 84°32W 316 C5
Preston Idaho, U.S.A. 42°6N 111°53W 304 E8
Preston Iowa, U.S.A. 42°3N 90°24W 310 B6
Preston Minn., U.S.A. 43°40N 92°5W 308 D7
Preston Mo., U.S.A. 37°56N 93°13W 310 G3
Preston, C. Australia 20°51S 116°12E 278 D2
Prestonsburg U.S.A. 37°40N 82°47W 309 G12
Prestranda Norway 59°6N 9°4E 162 E3
Prestwick U.K. 55°29N 4°37W 167 F4
Prêto → Amazonas, Brazil 0°8S 64°6W 329 D5
Prêto → Bahia, Brazil 11°21S 43°52W 332 D3
Prêto do Igapó-Açu → Brazil 4°26S 59°48W 329 D6
Pretoria S. Africa 25°44S 28°12E 271 C4
Pretos Forros, Sa. dos Brazil 22°54S 43°17W 135 B1
Preuilly-sur-Claise France 46°51N 0°56E 172 F7
Preussisch-Eylau = Bagrationovsk Russia 54°23N 20°39E 184 D7
Preussisch Friedland = Debrzno Poland 53°31N 17°14E 184 E4
Preussisch Holland = Pasłęk Poland 54°3N 19°41E 184 D6
Preussisch-Stargard = Starogard Gdański Poland 53°59N 18°30E 184 E5
Preveza Greece 38°57N 20°45E 207 B2
Preveza-Lefkada ✈ (PVK) Greece 38°57N 20°45E 207 B2
Préville Canada 45°28N 73°29W 130 B3
Prey Veng Cambodia 11°35N 105°29E 237 G5
Přezletice Czechia 50°9N 14°34E 135 B3
Priazovskoye Ukraine 46°44N 35°40E 189 J8
Pribalkhash = Balqash Kazakhstan 46°50N 74°50E 214 E8
Pribaykalsky △ Russia 52°30N 106°0E 215 D11
Pribilof Is. U.S.A. 57°0N 170°0W 303 H5
Priboj Serbia 43°35N 19°32E 202 C3
Příbram Czechia 49°41N 14°2E 180 B7
Price U.S.A. 39°36N 110°49W 304 G8
Price, C. India 13°34N 93°3E 245 H11
Price I. Canada 52°23N 128°41W 296 C3
Prichard U.S.A. 30°44N 88°5W 315 F10
Prickly Pear Cays Anguilla 18°16N 63°11W 322 a
Prickly Pt. Grenada 11°59N 61°45W 323 q
Priego Spain 40°26N 2°21W 196 E2
Priego de Córdoba Spain 37°27N 4°12W 195 H6
Priekule Latvia 56°26N 21°35E 184 B8
Priekule Lithuania 55°33N 21°19E 184 C8
Prielbrusye △ Russia 43°20N 42°37E 191 J6
Prien Germany 47°51N 12°20E 179 H8
Prienai Lithuania 54°38N 23°57E 184 D10
Prieska S. Africa 29°40S 22°42E 270 C3
Priest L. U.S.A. 48°35N 116°52W 304 B5
Priest River U.S.A. 48°11N 116°55W 304 B5
Priest Valley U.S.A. 36°10N 120°39W 306 J6
Prieto Diaz Phil. 13°2N 124°12E 232 E5
Prievidza Slovakia 48°46N 18°36E 181 C11
Prignitz Germany 53°6N 11°45E 178 B7
Prijedor Bos.-H. 44°58N 16°41E 199 D13
Prijepolje Serbia 43°27N 19°40E 202 C3
Prikaspiyskaya Nizmennost = Caspian Depression Eurasia 47°0N 48°0E 191 G9
Prikro Ivory C. 7°40N 3°59W 262 D4
Prikubanskaya Nizmennost Russia 45°39N 38°33E 191 H4
Prilep Macedonia 41°21N 21°32E 202 E5
Priluki = Pryluky Ukraine 50°30N 32°24E 189 G7
Prima Porta Italy 42°0N 12°30E 136 B1
Primavalle Italy 41°55N 12°25E 136 B1
Prime Hd. Antarctica 63°12S 48°57W 151 C18
Prime Seal I. Australia 40°3S 147°43E 281 G4
Primeira Cruz Brazil 2°30S 43°26W 332 B3
Primkenau = Przemków Poland 51°31N 15°48E 185 G2
Primo Tapia Mexico 32°16N 116°54W 307 N10
Primorsk Kaliningrad, Russia 54°44N 20°0E 184 D6
Primorsk St. Petersburg, Russia 60°22N 28°37E 188 B5
Primorskiy Kray ☐ Russia 45°0N 135°0E 220 B7
Primorsko Bulgaria 42°15N 27°44E 203 D11
Primorsko-Akhtarsk Russia 46°2N 38°10E 189 J10
Primrose S. Africa 26°11S 28°9E 123 B2
Primrose L. Canada 54°55N 109°45W 297 C7
Prince Albert Sask., Canada 53°15N 105°50W 297 C7
Prince Albert Western Cape, S. Africa 33°12S 22°2E 270 D3
Prince Albert △ Canada 54°0N 106°25W 297 C7
Prince Albert Mts. Antarctica 76°0S 161°30E 151 D11
Prince Albert Pen. Canada 72°30N 116°0W 294 C8
Prince Albert Sd. Canada 70°25N 115°0W 294 C9
Prince Alfred, C. Canada 74°20N 124°40W 150 B1
Prince Charles I. Canada 67°47N 76°12W 295 D16
Prince Charles Mts. Antarctica 72°0S 67°0E 151 D6
Prince Edward Fracture Zone Ind. Oc. 46°0S 35°0E 151 A4
Prince Edward I. ☐ Canada 46°20N 63°20W 299 C7
Prince Edward Is. Ind. Oc. 46°35S 38°0E 273 J2
Prince George Canada 53°55N 122°50W 296 C4
Prince of Wales, C. U.S.A. 65°36N 168°5W 303 D5
Prince of Wales I. Queens., Australia 10°40S 142°10E 286 F2
Prince of Wales I. Nunavut, Canada 73°0N 99°0W 294 C12
Prince of Wales I. Alaska, U.S.A. 55°47N 132°50W 303 J14
Prince of Wales Icefield Canada 78°15N 79°0W 295 B16
Prince of Wales Str. Canada 73°0N 117°0W 294 C8
Prince Patrick I. Canada 77°0N 120°0W 295 B8
Prince Regent Inlet Canada 73°0N 90°0W 295 C14
Prince Rupert Canada 54°20N 130°20W 296 C2
Prince Rupert B. Dominica 15°34N 61°29W 323 k
Prince Rupert Bluff Pt. Dominica 15°35N 61°29W 323 k
Prince William Sd. U.S.A. 60°40N 147°0W 303 F11
Princes Street Edinburgh, U.K. 121 b2
Princes Town Trin. & Tob. 10°16N 61°23W 323 t
Princesa Isabel Brazil 7°44S 38°0W 332 C4
Princess Charlotte B. Australia 14°25S 144°0E 280 A3
Princess Elizabeth Trough S. Ocean 64°10S 83°0E 151 C7
Princess May Ranges Australia 15°30S 125°30E 278 C4
Princess Royal I. Canada 53°0N 128°40W 296 C3
Princeton B.C., Canada 49°27N 120°30W 296 D4
Princeton Calif., U.S.A. 39°24N 122°1W 306 F4
Princeton Ill., U.S.A. 41°23N 89°28W 310 C7
Princeton Ind., U.S.A. 38°21N 87°34W 311 F9
Princeton Ky., U.S.A. 37°7N 87°53W 308 G10
Princeton Mo., U.S.A. 40°24N 93°35W 310 D3
Princeton N.J., U.S.A. 40°21N 74°39W 313 F10
Princeton W. Va., U.S.A. 37°22N 81°6W 309 G13
Princeville Hawai'i, U.S.A. 22°13N 159°29W 302 A2
Princeville Ill., U.S.A. 40°56N 89°46W 310 D7
Príncipe São Tomé & Príncipe 1°37N 7°25E 265 a
Principe da Beira Brazil 12°20S 64°30W 331 C5
Prineville U.S.A. 44°18N 120°51W 304 D3
Pringles Bay Dominica 15°21N 61°25W 323 k
Pringsewu Indonesia 5°24S 104°55E 234 D2
Prins Christian Sund Greenland 60°4N 43°10W 154 E6
Prins Harald Kyst Antarctica 70°0S 35°1E 151 D4
Prins Karls Forland Svalbard 78°30N 11°0E 154 B12
Prinsesse Astrid Kyst Antarctica 70°45S 12°30E 151 D3
Prinsesse Ragnhild Kyst Antarctica 70°15S 27°30E 151 D4
Printer's Row Chicago, U.S.A. 119 d2
Prinzapolca Nic. 13°20N 83°35W 320 D3
Prior, C. Spain 43°34N 8°17W 194 B2
Priozersk Russia 61°2N 30°7E 188 B6
Pripet = Prypyat → Europe 51°20N 30°15E 177 C16
Pripet Marshes Europe 52°10N 27°10E 177 B15
Pripyat Marshes = Pripet Marshes Europe 52°10N 27°10E 177 B15
Pripyats = Prypyat → Europe 51°20N 30°15E 177 C16
Prishib = Leninsk Russia 48°40N 45°15E 191 F7
Prishtinë Kosovo 42°40N 21°13E 202 D5
Prislop, Pasul Romania 47°37N 24°48E 183 C9
Pristen Russia 51°15N 36°44E 189 G9
Priština = Prishtinë Kosovo 42°40N 21°13E 202 D5
Pritzwalk Germany 53°9N 12°10E 178 B8
Privas France 44°45N 4°37E 175 D8
Priverno Italy 41°28N 13°11E 200 A6
Privolzhsk Russia 57°23N 41°16E 190 B5
Privolzhskaya Vozvyshennost Russia 51°0N 46°0E 190 E7
Privolzhskiy Russia 51°25N 46°3E 190 E8
Privolzhskiy ☐ Russia 56°0N 50°0E 214 D6
Privolzhye Russia 52°52N 48°33E 190 D9
Priyutnoye Russia 46°12N 43°40E 191 G6
Prizren Kosovo 42°13N 20°45E 202 D4
Prizzi Italy 37°43N 13°26E 200 E6
Prnjavor Bos.-H. 44°52N 17°43E 182 F2
Probolinggo Indonesia 7°46S 113°13E 235 D4
Prochowice Poland 51°17N 16°20E 185 G3
Proctor U.S.A. 43°40N 73°2W 313 C11
Proddatur India 14°45N 78°30E 245 G4
Prodhromos Cyprus 34°57N 32°50E 207 F8
Proença-a-Nova Portugal 39°45N 7°54W 194 F3
Profilia Greece 36°5N 27°51E 206 E11
Profondeville Belgium 50°23N 4°52E 170 D4
Progreso Coahuila, Mexico 27°28N 100°59W 318 B4
Progreso Yucatán, Mexico 21°20N 89°40W 319 C7
Progreso Nacional Mexico 19°30N 99°9W 128 A2
Progress Antarctica 66°22S 76°22E 151 C12
Progress Russia 49°45N 129°37E 215 E13
Prokhladnyy Russia 43°50N 44°2E 191 J7
Prokhorovka Russia 51°2N 36°44E 190 E3
Prokletije Albania 42°30N 19°45E 202 D3
Prokopyevsk Russia 54°0N 86°45E 217 B11
Prokuplje Serbia 43°16N 21°36E 202 C5
Proletarsk Russia 46°42N 41°50E 191 G5
Prome = Pye Burma 18°49N 95°13E 241 F5
Promise City U.S.A. 40°45N 93°9W 310 D3
Promzino = Surskoye Russia 54°30N 46°44E 190 C8
Prophet → Canada 58°48N 122°40W 296 B4
Prophet River Canada 58°6N 122°43W 296 B4
Prophetstown U.S.A. 41°40N 89°56W 310 C7
Propriá Brazil 10°13S 36°51W 332 D4
Propriano France 41°41N 8°52E 175 G12
Prosek Czechia 50°7N 14°30E 135 B3
Proserpine Australia 20°21S 148°36E 280 b
Proskurov = Khmelnytskyy Ukraine 49°23N 27°0E 177 D14
Prosna → Poland 52°6N 17°44E 185 F4
Prospect N.Y., U.S.A. 43°18N 75°9W 313 C9
Prospect Ohio, U.S.A. 40°27N 83°11W 311 D13
Prospect Hill Park U.S.A. 42°23N 71°13W 116 A1
Prosperidad Phil. 8°34N 125°52E 233 G5
Prosperity U.S.A. 30°51N 85°56W 316 E4
Prosperous B. St. Helena 15°56S 5°39W 153 h
Prosser U.S.A. 46°12N 119°46W 304 C4
Prossnitz = Prostějov Czechia 49°30N 17°9E 181 B10
Prostějov Czechia 49°30N 17°9E 181 B10
Prostki Poland 53°42N 22°25E 184 E9
Proston Australia 26°8S 151°32E 281 D5
Proszowice Poland 50°13N 20°16E 185 H7
Proti Greece 37°5N 21°32E 204 D3
Provadiya Bulgaria 43°12N 27°30E 203 C11
Provadiyska → Bulgaria 43°12N 27°42E 203 C11
Provence France 43°40N 5°46E 175 E9
Provence-Alpes-Côte d'Azur ☐ France 44°0N 6°15E 175 D10
Providence Ky., U.S.A. 37°24N 87°46W 308 G10
Providence R.I., U.S.A. 41°49N 71°24W 313 E13
Providence, C. N.Z. 45°59S 166°29E 285 F1
Providence Bay Canada 45°41N 82°15W 298 C3
Providence Mts. U.S.A. 35°10N 115°15W 307 K11
Providencia Chile 33°25S 70°36W 137 B2
Providencia, I. de Caribbean 13°25N 81°26W 320 D3
Providenciales Turks & Caicos 21°48N 72°15W 321 B5
Provideniya Russia 64°23N 173°18W 215 C19
Provincetown U.S.A. 42°3N 70°11W 309 D18
Provins France 48°33N 3°15E 173 D10
Provo = Providenciales Turks & Caicos 21°48N 72°15W 321 B5
Provo U.S.A. 40°14N 111°39W 304 F8
Provost Canada 52°25N 110°20W 297 C6
Prozor Bos.-H. 43°50N 17°34E 182 G2
Prrenjas Albania 41°4N 20°32E 202 E4
Prudentópolis Brazil 25°12S 50°57W 333 G1
Prudhoe Bay U.S.A. 70°18N 148°22W 303 A10
Prudhoe I. Australia 21°19S 149°41E 280 C4
Prud'homme Canada 52°20N 105°54W 297 C7
Prudnik Poland 50°20N 17°38E 185 H4
Průhonice Czechia 50°0N 14°33E 135 C3
Prüm Germany 50°12N 6°25E 179 E2
Prundu Romania 44°6N 26°14E 183 F11
Prundu Bârgăului Romania 47°13N 24°46E 183 C9
Pruszcz Gdański Poland 54°17N 18°40E 184 D5
Pruszków Poland 52°9N 20°49E 185 F7
Prut → Romania 45°28N 28°10E 183 E13
Pruzhany Belarus 52°33N 24°28E 177 B13
Prvič Croatia 44°55N 14°47E 199 D11
Prydz B. Antarctica 69°0S 74°0E 151 C6
Pryluky Ukraine 50°30N 32°24E 189 G7
Prymorske Ukraine 46°48N 36°20E 189 J9
Pryor U.S.A. 36°19N 95°19W 314 C7
Prypyat → Europe 51°20N 30°15E 177 C16
Prypyatsky △ Belarus 52°0N 28°0E 177 C14
Przasnysz Poland 53°2N 20°54E 185 E7
Przedbórz Poland 51°6N 19°53E 185 G6
Przedecz Poland 52°20N 18°53E 185 F5
Przemków Poland 51°31N 15°48E 185 G2
Przemyśl Poland 49°50N 22°45E 185 J9
Przeworsk Poland 50°6N 22°32E 185 H9
Przewóz Poland 51°28N 14°57E 185 G1
Przhevalsk = Karakol Kyrgyzstan 42°30N 78°20E 217 D9
Przysucha Poland 51°22N 20°38E 185 G7
Psachna Greece 38°34N 23°35E 204 C5
Psara Greece 38°37N 25°38E 205 C7
Psathoura Greece 39°30N 24°12E 204 B6
Pserimos Greece 36°56N 27°8E 205 E9
Psichiko Greece 38°1N 23°46E 112 A2
Psiloritis, Oros Greece 35°15N 24°45E 207 E5
Psira Greece 35°12N 25°52E 207 E6
Pskem → Uzbekistan 41°38N 70°1E 217 D7
Pskov Russia 57°50N 28°25E 188 D5
Pskov ☐ Russia 57°20N 29°0E 188 D5
Pskovskoye, Ozero Russia 58°0N 27°58E 188 D5
Psol → Ukraine 49°10N 33°37E 189 H7
Psunj Croatia 45°25N 17°19E 182 E2
Pteleos Greece 39°3N 22°57E 204 B4
Ptich = Ptsich → Belarus 52°9N 28°52E 177 B15
Ptichia = Vidos Greece 39°38N 19°55E 206 B9
Ptolemaida Greece 40°30N 21°43E 202 F5
Ptsich → Belarus 52°9N 28°52E 177 B15
Ptuj Slovenia 46°28N 15°50E 199 B12
Ptujska Gora Slovenia 46°23N 15°47E 199 B12
Pu Xian China 36°24N 111°6E 226 F6
Pua Thailand 19°11N 100°55E 236 C3
Pua'ena Pt. U.S.A. 21°36N 158°6W 302 J13
Puán Argentina 37°30S 62°45W 334 D3
Pu'an Guizhou, China 25°46N 104°57E 228 E5
Pu'apu'a Samoa 13°34S 172°9W 287 V19
Pubei China 22°16N 109°31E 228 F7
Pucacuro → Peru 3°20S 74°58W 328 D3
Pucallpa Peru 8°25S 74°30W 330 B3
Pucará Bolivia 18°43S 64°11W 331 D5
Pucará Cajamarca, Peru 6°0S 79°7W 330 B2
Pucará Puno, Peru 15°5S 70°24W 330 D3
Pucarani Bolivia 16°23S 68°30W 330 D4
Pucheng China 27°59N 118°31E 229 D12
Pucheni Romania 45°12N 25°17E 183 E10
Puchheim Germany 48°9N 11°21E 179 G7
Puch'on = Bucheon S. Korea 37°28N 126°45E 224 D3
Púchov Slovakia 49°8N 18°20E 181 B11
Pucio Pt. Phil. 11°46N 121°51E 233 F3
Pucioasa Romania 45°5N 25°25E 183 E10
Pučišća Croatia 43°22N 16°43E 199 E13
Puck Poland 54°45N 18°23E 184 D5
Pucka, Zatoka Poland 54°30N 18°40E 184 D5
Puçol Spain 39°37N 0°18W 197 F4
Pudasjärvi Finland 65°23N 26°53E 160 D22
Puding China 26°18N 105°44E 228 D5
Pudong New Area China 31°13N 121°30E 138 B2
Pudozh Russia 61°48N 36°32E 188 B9
Pudu = Suizhou China 31°42N 113°24E 229 B9
Puducherry India 11°59N 79°50E 245 J4
Pudukkottai India 10°28N 78°47E 245 J4
Pue Cook Is. 21°12S 159°45W 289 h
Puebla Mexico 19°3N 98°12W 319 D5
Puebla ☐ Mexico 18°50N 98°0W 319 D5
Puebla de Alcocer Spain 38°59N 5°14W 195 G5
Puebla de Don Fadrique Spain 37°58N 2°25W 197 H2
Puebla de Don Rodrigo Spain 39°5N 4°37W 195 F6
Puebla de Guzmán Spain 37°37N 7°15W 195 H3
Puebla de la Calzada Spain 38°54N 6°37W 195 G4
Puebla de Sanabria Spain 42°4N 6°38W 194 C4
Puebla de Trives = Pobra de Trives Spain 42°20N 7°10W 194 C3
Pueblo U.S.A. 38°16N 104°37W 304 G11
Pueblo Libre Peru 12°5S 77°4W 124 B2
Pueblo Nuevo = El Pobleneu Spain 41°23N 2°11E 114 A2
Pueblo Nuevo Spain 40°25N 3°37W 127 B2
Puelches Argentina 38°5S 65°51W 334 D2
Puelén Argentina 37°32S 67°38W 334 D2
Puente Alto Chile 33°32S 70°35W 334 C1
Puente-Genil Spain 37°22N 4°47W 195 H6
Puente la Reina Spain 42°40N 1°49W 196 C3
Puente San Miguel Spain 43°21N 4°5W 194 B6
Puenteareas = Ponteareas Spain 42°10N 8°28W 194 C2
Puentedeume = Pontedeume Spain 43°24N 8°10W 194 B2
Puentes de Garcia Rodriguez = As Pontes de García Rodríguez Spain 43°27N 7°50W 194 B3
Pu'er China 23°0N 101°15E 228 F3
Puerca, Pta. Puerto Rico 18°13N 65°36W 321 b
Puerco → U.S.A. 34°22N 107°50W 305 J10
Puerta del Sol, Plaza Madrid, Spain 127 b2
Puerto Acosta Bolivia 15°32S 69°15W 330 D4
Puerto Aisén Chile 45°27S 73°0W 336 C2
Puerto Ángel Mexico 15°40N 96°29W 319 D5
Puerto Arista Mexico 15°56N 93°48W 319 D6
Puerto Armuelles Panama 8°20N 82°51W 320 E3
Puerto Asis Colombia 0°30N 76°30W 328 C2
Puerto Ayacucho Venezuela 5°40N 67°35W 328 B4
Puerto Ayora Ecuador 0°45S 90°19W 330 a
Puerto Baquerizo Moreno Ecuador 0°54S 89°36W 330 a
Puerto Barrios Guatemala 15°40N 88°32W 320 C2
Puerto Bermejo Argentina 26°55S 58°34W 334 B4
Puerto Bermúdez Peru 10°20S 74°58W 330 C3
Puerto Bolívar Colombia 12°15N 71°59W 328 A3
Puerto Bolívar Ecuador 3°19S 79°55W 328 D2
Puerto Cabello Venezuela 10°28N 68°1W 328 A4
Puerto Cabezas Nic. 14°0N 83°30W 320 D3
Puerto Cabo Gracias á Dios Nic. 15°0N 83°10W 320 D3
Puerto Capaz = El Jebha Morocco 35°11N 4°43W 260 A4
Puerto Carreño Colombia 6°12N 67°22W 328 B4
Puerto Castilla Honduras 16°0N 86°0W 320 C2
Puerto Chicama Peru 7°45S 79°20W 330 B2
Puerto Cisnes Chile 44°45S 72°42W 336 B2
Puerto Coig Argentina 50°54S 69°15W 336 D3
Puerto Cortés Honduras 15°51N 88°0W 320 C2
Puerto Cumarebo Venezuela 11°29N 69°30W 328 A4
Puerto de Alcudia = Port d'Alcúdia Spain 39°50N 3°7E 206 B4
Puerto de Cabras = Puerto del Rosario Canary Is. 28°30N 13°52W 153 e2
Puerto de Cabrera Spain 39°8N 2°56E 206 B3
Puerto de la Cruz Canary Is. 28°24N 16°32W 153 e1
Puerto de los Angeles ⌓ Mexico 23°39N 105°45W 318 C3
Puerto de Mazarrón Spain 37°34N 1°15W 197 H3
Puerto de Sóller = Port de Sóller Spain 39°48N 2°42E 206 B3
Puerto de Somosierra Spain 41°9N 3°35W 194 D7
Puerto del Carmen Canary Is. 28°55N 13°38W 153 e2
Puerto del Rosario Canary Is. 28°30N 13°52W 153 e2
Puerto Deseado Argentina 47°55S 66°0W 336 C3
Puerto Escondido Mexico 15°50N 97°3W 319 D5
Puerto Gaitán Colombia 4°19N 72°4W 328 C3
Puerto Galera Phil. 13°30N 120°57E 232 E3
Puerto Guaraní Paraguay 21°18S 57°55W 331 E6
Puerto Heath Bolivia 12°34S 68°39W 330 C4
Puerto Huitoto Colombia 0°18N 74°3W 328 C3
Puerto Inca Peru 9°22S 74°54W 330 B3
Puerto Inírida Colombia 3°53N 67°52W 328 C4
Puerto Juárez Mexico 21°11N 86°49W 319 C7
Puerto La Cruz Venezuela 10°13N 64°38W 329 A5
Puerto Leguízamo Colombia 0°12S 74°46W 328 D3
Puerto Lempira Honduras 15°16N 83°46W 320 C3
Puerto Libertad Mexico 29°55N 112°43W 318 B2
Puerto Limón Colombia 3°23N 73°30W 328 C3
Puerto Lobos Argentina 42°0S 65°3W 336 B3
Puerto López Colombia 4°5N 72°58W 328 C3
Puerto Lumbreras Spain 37°34N 1°48W 197 H3
Puerto Madero Argentina 34°37S 58°21W 117 B2
Puerto Madryn Argentina 42°48S 65°4W 336 B3
Puerto Maldonado Peru 12°30S 69°10W 330 C4
Puerto Manatí Cuba 21°22N 76°50W 320 B4
Puerto Mariti Colombia 1°10S 69°59W 328 D4
Puerto Mercedes Colombia 1°11N 72°53W 328 C3
Puerto Mexico = Coatzacoalcos Mexico 18°7N 94°25W 319 D6
Puerto Miraña Colombia 1°20S 70°19W 328 D3
Puerto Montt Chile 41°28S 73°0W 336 B2
Puerto Morazán Nic. 12°51N 87°11W 320 D2
Puerto Morelos Mexico 20°50N 86°52W 319 C7
Puerto Nariño Colombia 4°56N 67°48W 328 C4
Puerto Natales Chile 51°45S 72°15W 336 D2
Puerto Nuevo Colombia 5°53N 69°56W 328 B4
Puerto Ordaz Venezuela 8°16N 62°44W 329 B5
Puerto Oscuro Chile 31°24S 71°35W 334 C1
Puerto Padre Cuba 21°13N 76°35W 320 B4
Puerto Páez Venezuela 6°13N 67°28W 328 B4
Puerto Peñasco Mexico 31°20N 113°33W 318 A2
Puerto Pinasco Paraguay 22°36S 57°50W 334 A4
Puerto Pirámides Argentina 42°35S 64°20W 336 B4
Puerto Piritu Venezuela 10°4N 65°3W 329 A4
Puerto Plata Dom. Rep. 19°48N 70°45W 321 C5
Puerto Pollensa = Port de Pollença Spain 39°54N 3°4E 206 B4
Puerto Portillo Peru 9°45S 72°42W 330 B3
Puerto Princesa Phil. 9°46N 118°45E 233 G2
Puerto Princesa Subterranean River △ Phil. 10°10N 118°55E 233 F2
Puerto Quepos Costa Rica 9°29N 84°6W 320 E3
Puerto Real Spain 36°33N 6°12W 195 J4
Puerto Rico Bolivia 11°5S 67°38W 330 C4
Puerto Rico Canary Is. 27°47N 15°42W 153 e1
Puerto Rico ☒ W. Indies 18°15N 66°45W 321 C6
Puerto Rico Trench Atl. Oc. 19°50N 66°0W 321 C6
Puerto Rondón Colombia 6°17N 71°6W 328 B3
Puerto Saavedra Chile 38°47S 73°24W 336 A2
Puerto San Julián Argentina 49°15S 67°45W 336 C3
Puerto Santa Cruz Argentina 50°0S 68°32W 336 D3
Puerto Sastre Paraguay 22°2S 57°55W 334 A4
Puerto Serrano Spain 36°56N 5°33W 195 J5
Puerto Siles Bolivia 12°48S 65°5W 331 C4
Puerto Suárez Bolivia 18°58S 57°52W 331 D6
Puerto Supe Peru 11°0S 77°30W 330 C2
Puerto Tejada Colombia 3°14N 76°24W 328 C2
Puerto Umbría Colombia 0°52N 76°33W 328 C2
Puerto Vallarta Mexico 20°37N 105°15W 318 C3
Puerto Varas Chile 41°19S 72°59W 336 B2
Puerto Velasco Ibarra Ecuador 1°17S 90°29W 330 a
Puerto Villamil Ecuador 0°56S 91°1W 330 a
Puerto Villazón Bolivia 13°32S 61°57W 331 C5
Puerto Wilches Colombia 7°21N 73°54W 328 B3
Puerto Williams Chile 54°56S 67°37W 336 D3
Puertollano Spain 38°43N 4°7W 195 G6
Puesto Cunambo Peru 2°10S 76°0W 328 D2
Pueu Tahiti 17°44S 149°13W 289 e
Pueyrredón, L. Argentina 47°20S 72°0W 336 C2
Púez Odle ⌓ Italy 46°37N 11°48E 199 B8
Puffin I. Ireland 51°50N 10°24W 166 E1
Pugachev Russia 52°0N 48°49E 190 D9
Pugal India 28°30N 72°48E 242 E5
Puge Sichuan, China 27°20N 102°31E 228 D4
Puge Tanzania 4°45S 33°11E 268 C3
Puget Sound U.S.A. 47°50N 122°30W 306 C4
Puget-Théniers France 43°58N 6°53E 175 E10
Púglia ☐ Italy 41°15N 16°15E 201 A9
Pugŏdong N. Korea 42°5N 130°0E 224 A5
Pugu Guangdong, China 23°10N 113°19E 121 A2
Pugu Tanzania 6°55S 39°4E 268 D4
Pūgūnzī Iran 25°49N 59°10E 247 E8
Puha N.Z. 38°30S 177°50E 284 E6
Puhuangyu China 39°50N 116°22E 114 B2
Pui Romania 45°30N 23°4E 182 E8
Pui O Wan Hong Kong, China 22°15N 113°58E 122 B1
Puica Peru 15°0S 72°33W 330 D3
Puieşti Romania 46°25N 27°33E 183 D12
Puig Major Spain 39°48N 2°47E 206 B3
Puigcerdà Spain 42°24N 1°50E 196 C6
Puigmal Spain 42°23N 2°7E 196 C7
Puigpunyent Spain 39°38N 2°32E 206 B3
Puijiang China 30°14N 103°30E 228 B4
Puisaye, Collines de la France 47°37N 3°20E 173 E10
Puiseaux France 48°11N 2°30E 173 D9
Puistola Finland 60°16N 25°2E 121 B3
Pujehun S. Leone 7°23N 11°45W 262 D2
Pujiang China 29°29N 119°54E 229 C12
Pujilí Ecuador 0°57S 78°41W 328 D2
Pujols France 44°48N 0°2W 174 D3
Pujon Indonesia 1°19S 114°19E 235 C4
Pujon-ho N. Korea 40°35N 127°35E 224 B3
Puka Puka French Polynesia 14°49S 138°48W 289 f
Puka Ruha French Polynesia 18°20S 137°2W 289 f
Pukaki, L. N.Z. 44°4S 170°1E 285 E5
Pukalani U.S.A. 20°51N 156°20W 302 C5
Pukapuka Cook Is. 10°53S 165°49W 289 J11
Pukaskwa △ Canada 48°20N 86°0W 298 C2
Pukatawagan Canada 55°45N 101°20W 297 B8
Pukchin N. Korea 40°12N 125°45E 224 B2
Pukch'ŏng N. Korea 40°14N 128°19E 224 B4
Pukë Albania 42°2N 19°53E 202 D3
Pukearuhe N.Z. 38°55S 174°31E 284 E3
Pukekohe N.Z. 37°12S 174°55E 284 D3
Puketeraki Ra. N.Z. 42°58S 172°13E 285 C7
Puketoi Ra. N.Z. 40°30S 176°5E 284 G5
Pukeuri N.Z. 45°4S 171°2E 285 F6
Pukhrayan India 26°14N 79°51E 243 F8
Pukinmäki Finland 60°15N 24°57E 121 B2
Puksubaek-san N. Korea 40°42N 127°45E 224 B3
Pula Croatia 44°54N 13°57E 199 D10
Pula Italy 39°1N 9°0E 200 C1
Pulacayo Bolivia 20°25S 66°41W 330 E4
Pulandian China 39°25N 121°58E 227 E11
Pulanduta Pt. Phil. 11°54N 123°9E 233 F4
Pulangpisau Indonesia 2°46S 114°13E 235 C4
Pulaski N.Y., U.S.A. 43°34N 76°8W 313 C8
Pulaski Tenn., U.S.A. 35°12N 87°2W 315 D11
Pulaski Va., U.S.A. 37°3N 80°47W 309 G13
Pulau → Indonesia 5°50S 138°15E 231 F9
Pulau Gili Indonesia 8°21S 116°1E 231 J19
Puławy Poland 51°23N 21°59E 185 G8
Pulga U.S.A. 39°48N 121°29W 306 F5
Pulgaon India 20°44N 78°21E 244 D4
Puli Taiwan 23°58N 120°57E 225 C2
Pulicat India 13°25N 80°19E 245 H5
Pulicat L. India 13°40N 80°15E 245 H5
Pulivendla India 14°25N 78°14E 245 G4
Puliyangudi India 9°11N 77°24E 245 K3
Pulkovo Int. ✈ (LED) Russia 59°48N 30°18E 137 C1
Pullach Germany 48°3N 11°31E 131 B1
Pullman U.S.A. 46°44N 117°10W 304 C5
Pullman Historic District U.S.A. 41°41N 87°36W 119 C3
Pulo Gadung Indonesia 6°11S 106°54E 122 B2
Pulog, Mt. Phil. 16°40N 120°50E 232 C3
Pulpí Spain 37°24N 1°44W 197 H3
Pułtusk Poland 52°43N 21°6E 185 F8
Pülümür Turkey 39°30N 39°51E 213 C8
Pumlumon Fawr U.K. 52°28N 3°46W 169 E4
Puna Bolivia 19°45S 65°28W 331 D4
Puná, I. Ecuador 2°55S 80°5W 328 D1
Punaauia Tahiti 17°37S 149°34W 289 e
Pūnak Iran 35°46N 51°20E 141 A2
Punakha Dzong Bhutan 27°42N 89°52E 241 B2
Punalur India 9°0N 76°56E 245 K3
Punalu'u U.S.A. 21°35N 157°53W 302 J14
Punasar India 27°6N 73°6E 242 F5
Punata Bolivia 17°32S 65°50W 331 D4
Punch India 33°48N 74°4E 243 C6
Punch → Pakistan 33°12N 73°40E 242 C5
Punchbowl Australia 33°55S 151°3E 139 B1
Punda Curaçao 12°6N 68°55W 322 g
Punda Maria S. Africa 22°40S 31°5E 271 B5
Punde India 18°53N 72°57E 130 B2
Pune India 18°29N 73°57E 244 E1
Punggol Singapore 1°23N 103°54E 138 A3
Punggol, Sungei → Singapore 1°24N 103°54E 138 A3
Punggol Pt. Singapore 1°24N 103°54E 138 A3
Pungo Andongo Angola 9°44S 15°35E 265 D3
P'ungsan N. Korea 40°50N 128°9E 224 B4
Pungsan S. Korea 36°34N 128°34E 224 D4
Pungue, Ponte de Mozam. 19°0S 34°0E 269 F3
Puning China 23°20N 116°12E 229 F11
Punjab ☐ India 31°0N 76°0E 242 D7
Punjab ☐ Pakistan 32°0N 72°30E 242 E6
Punjabi Bagh India 28°40N 77°6E 120 A1
Puno Peru 15°55S 70°3W 330 D3
Puno ☐ Peru 15°0S 70°0W 330 C3
Punpun → India 25°31N 85°18E 243 G11
Punta, Cerro de Puerto Rico 18°10N 66°37W 321 b
Punta Alta Argentina 38°53S 62°4W 336 A4
Punta Arenas Chile 53°10S 71°0W 336 D2
Punta Cana ✈ (PUJ) Dom. Rep. 18°34N 68°21W 321 C6
Punta Cardón Venezuela 11°38N 70°14W 328 A3
Punta Coles Peru 17°43S 71°23W 330 D3
Punta de Bombón Peru 17°10S 71°48W 330 D3
Punta de Piedras Venezuela 10°54N 64°5W 329 a
Punta del Díaz Chile 28°0S 70°45W 334 B1
Punta del Hidalgo Canary Is. 28°33N 16°19W 153 e1
Punta Delgado Argentina 42°43S 63°38W 336 B4
Punta Gorda Belize 16°10N 88°45W 320 C2
Punta Gorda Fla., U.S.A. 26°56N 82°3W 317 J7
Punta Prieta Mexico 28°58N 114°17W 318 B2
Punta Prima Spain 39°48N 4°16E 206 B5
Punta Umbría Spain 37°10N 6°56W 195 H4
Puntarenas Costa Rica 10°0N 84°50W 320 E3
Puntland Somalia 9°0N 50°0E 267 C6
Punto Fijo Venezuela 11°50N 70°13W 328 A3
Punxsutawney U.S.A. 40°57N 78°59W 312 F6
Punyu = Guangzhou China 23°6N 113°13E 121 B2
Puotila Finland 60°13N 25°6E 121 B3
Pupuan Indonesia 8°19S 115°0E 231 J18
Pūpūkea U.S.A. 21°40N 158°3W 302 J13
Puqi China 29°40N 113°50E 229 C9
Puquio Peru 14°45S 74°10W 330 C3
Pur → Russia 67°31N 77°55E 214 C8
Puracé, Vol. Colombia 2°21N 76°23W 328 C2
Puracé △ Colombia 2°10N 76°21W 328 C2
Puračić Bos.-H. 44°33N 18°28E 182 F3
Puralia = Puruliya India 23°17N 86°24E 243 H12
Purana Qila Delhi, India 120 c3
Puranpur India 28°31N 80°9E 243 E9
Purari → Papua N. G. 7°49S 145°0E 286 D3
Purbalingga Indonesia 7°23S 109°21E 235 D3
Purbeck, Isle of U.K. 50°39N 1°59W 169 G5
Purcell U.S.A. 35°1N 97°22W 314 D6
Purcell Mts. Canada 49°55N 116°15W 296 D5
Purdy Canada 45°19N 77°44W 312 A7
Puri India 19°50N 85°58E 244 E7
Purificación Colombia 3°51N 74°55W 328 C3
Purmerend Neths. 52°32N 4°58E 170 B4
Purna → India 19°6N 77°2E 244 E3
Purnia India 25°45N 87°31E 243 G12
Purnululu △ Australia 17°20S 128°20E 278 C4
Pursat = Pouthisat Cambodia 12°34N 103°50E 236 F4
Purukcahu Indonesia 0°35S 114°35E 235 C4
Puruliya India 23°17N 86°24E 243 H12
Purus → Brazil 3°42S 61°28W 329 D5
Purutu I. Papua N. G. 8°24S 143°27E 286 E2
Puruvesi Finland 61°50N 29°30E 188 B5
Purvis U.S.A. 31°9N 89°25W 315 F10
Pŭrvomay Bulgaria 42°8N 25°17E 203 D9
Purwa India 26°28N 80°47E 243 F9
Purwakarta Indonesia 6°35S 107°29E 235 D3
Purwo, Tanjung Indonesia 8°44S 114°21E 231 K18
Purwodadi Indonesia 7°7S 110°55E 235 D4
Purwokerto Indonesia 7°25S 109°14E 235 D3
Purworejo Indonesia 7°43S 110°2E 235 D4
Puryŏng N. Korea 42°5N 129°43E 224 A4
Pus → India 19°55N 77°55E 244 E3
Pusa India 25°59N 85°41E 243 G11
Pusad India 19°56N 77°36E 244 E3
Pusan = Busan S. Korea 35°5N 129°0E 224 E4
Pushkin Russia 59°45N 30°25E 188 C6
Pushkino Moskva, Russia 56°2N 37°49E 188 D9
Pushkino Saratov, Russia 51°16N 47°0E 190 E8
Püspökladány Hungary 47°19N 21°6E 182 C6
Pustoshka Russia 56°20N 29°30E 188 D5
Puszczykowo Poland 52°18N 16°49E 185 F3
Put-in-Bay U.S.A. 41°39N 82°49W 312 E2
Putahow L. Canada 59°54N 100°40W 297 B8
Putai Taiwan 23°23N 120°9E 225 C2
Putao Burma 27°28N 97°30E 241 B6
Putaruru N.Z. 38°2S 175°50E 284 E4
Putatan Malaysia 5°53N 116°3E 235 A5
Putbus Germany 54°22N 13°28E 178 A9
Puteaux France 48°53N 2°14E 134 A2
Puteran Indonesia 7°5S 114°0E 235 D4
Putian China 25°23N 119°0E 229 E12
Putignano Italy 40°51N 17°7E 201 B10
Putina Peru 14°55S 69°55W 330 C4
Puting, Tanjung Indonesia 3°31S 111°46E 235 C4
Putlitz Germany 53°15N 12°2E 178 B8
Putna Romania 47°50N 25°33E 183 C10
Putna → Romania 45°42N 27°26E 183 E12
Putnam U.S.A. 41°55N 71°55W 313 E13
Putney London, U.K. 51°27N 0°13W 125 B2
Putney Ga., U.S.A. 31°29N 84°8W 316 D5
Putnok Hungary 48°18N 20°26E 182 B5
Putorana, Gory Russia 69°0N 95°0E 215 C10
Putorino N.Z. 39°4S 176°58E 284 F5
Putrajaya Malaysia 2°55N 101°40E 237 L3
Putre Chile 18°12S 69°35W 330 D4
Puttalam Sri Lanka 8°1N 79°55E 245 K5
Puttalam Lagoon Sri Lanka 8°15N 79°45E 245 K4
Puttegga Norway 62°13N 7°42E 164 B4
Puttgarden Germany 54°30N 11°10E 178 A7
Püttlingen Germany 49°17N 6°53E 179 F2
Puttur Andhra Pradesh, India 13°27N 79°33E 245 H4
Puttur Karnataka, India 12°46N 75°12E 245 H2
Putty Australia 32°57S 150°42E 283 B9
Putumayo → S. Amer. 3°7S 67°58W 328 D4
Putuo Shanghai, China 31°15N 121°24E 138 B1
Putuo Zhejiang, China 29°56N 122°20E 229 C14
Putussibau Indonesia 0°50N 112°56E 235 B4
Pututahi N.Z. 38°39S 177°53E 284 E6
Putxet Spain 41°24N 2°8E 114 A1
Putyla Ukraine 48°0N 25°5E 183 B10
Pu'uanahulu U.S.A. 19°49N 155°51W 302 D6
Pu'uhonua o Hōnaunau ⌓ U.S.A. 19°25N 155°54W 302 D6
Pu'uka'aumakua U.S.A. 21°30N 157°54W 302 J14
Pu'ukeahiakahoe U.S.A. 21°23N 157°49W 302 K14
Pu'ukoholā Heiau ⌓ U.S.A. 20°1N 155°49W 302 C6
P'u'ula'ula U.S.A. 20°42N 156°15W 302 C5
Pu'u'oke'oke'o U.S.A. 19°13N 155°44W 302 D6
Pu'uwai U.S.A. 21°54N 160°12W 302 B1
Puvirnituq Canada 60°2N 77°10W 295 E16
Puxi China 31°12N 121°30E 138 B1
Puy-de-Dôme France 45°46N 2°57E 174 C6
Puy-de-Dôme ☐ France 45°40N 3°5E 174 C7
Puy-l'Évêque France 44°31N 1°9E 174 D5
Puyallup U.S.A. 47°12N 122°18W 306 C4
Puyang China 35°40N 115°1E 226 G8
Puyehue Chile 40°40S 72°37W 336 B2
Puyehue △ Chile 40°27S 72°6W 336 B2
Puylaurens France 43°35N 2°0E 174 E6
Puyo Ecuador 1°28S 77°59W 328 D2
Puysegur Pt. N.Z. 46°9S 166°37E 285 G1
Pūzeh Rīg Iran 27°20N 58°40E 247 E8
Puzhaykove Ukraine 48°7N 29°50E 183 B14
Puzi = P'otzu Taiwan 23°28N 120°15E 225 C2
Pwani ☐ Tanzania 7°0S 39°0E 268 D4
Pweto Dem. Rep. of the Congo 8°25S 28°51E 269 D2
Pwinbyu Burma 20°23N 94°40E 241 E5
Pwllheli U.K. 52°53N 4°25W 168 E3
Pyana → Russia 55°43N 46°1E 190 C8
Pyandzh → Asia 37°6N 68°20E 240 A2
Pyaozero, Ozero Russia 66°5N 30°58E 160 C24
Pyapon Burma 16°20N 95°40E 241 G5
Pyasina → Russia 73°30N 87°0E 215 B9
Pyatigorsk Russia 44°2N 43°6E 191 H6
Pyatykhatky Ukraine 48°28N 33°38E 189 H7
Pyawbwe Burma 20°35N 96°4E 241 E6
Pyay = Pye Burma 18°49N 95°13E 241 F5
Pyaye Burma 19°12N 95°10E 241 F5
Pydhuni Mumbai, India 130 b2
Pydna Greece 40°20N 22°34E 202 F6
Pye Burma 18°49N 95°13E 241 F5
Pyeongchang S. Korea 37°22N 128°23E 224 D4
Pyeonghae S. Korea 36°43N 129°26E 224 D4
Pyeongtaek S. Korea 37°1N 127°4E 224 D3
Pyetrikaw Belarus 52°11N 28°29E 177 B15
Pyhäjoki → Finland 64°28N 24°14E 160 D21
Pyhätunturi △ Finland 66°58N 27°5E 160 C22
Pyin-U-Lwin Burma 22°2N 96°28E 236 A1
Pyinbauk Burma 19°10N 95°12E 241 F5
Pyingaing Burma 23°9N 94°50E 241 D5
Pyinkayaing Burma 15°58N 94°24E 241 H5
Pyinmana Burma 19°45N 96°12E 241 F6
Pyinyaung Burma 20°49N 96°25E 241 E6
Pyla, C. Cyprus 34°56N 33°51E 207 F9
Pymatuning Res. U.S.A. 41°30N 80°28W 312 E4
Pyŏktong N. Korea 40°50N 125°50E 224 B2
P'yŏnganbuk-do ☐ N. Korea 40°0N 125°15E 224 C2
P'yŏngannam-do ☐ N. Korea 39°30N 126°24E 224 C3
P'yŏnggang N. Korea 38°24N 127°17E 224 C3
P'yŏngsong N. Korea 39°14N 125°52E 224 C2

P'yŏngyang N. Korea 39°0N 125°30E 224 C2
P'yŏngyang □ N. Korea 39°0N 125°50E 224 C2
Pyote U.S.A. 31°32N 103°8W 314 F3
Pyramid L. U.S.A. 40°1N 119°35W 304 F4
Pyramid Pk. U.S.A. 36°25N 116°37W 307 J10
Pyramid Pt. Ascension I. 7°55S 14°24W 153 g
Pyramids Egypt 29°58N 31°9E 117 B1
Pyrénées Europe 42°45N 0°18E 174 F4
Pyrénées △ France 42°52N 0°10W 174 F3
Pyrénées-Atlantiques □
  France 43°10N 0°50W 174 F3
Pyrénées-Orientales □
  France 42°35N 2°26E 174 F6
Pyry Poland 52°8N 21°10E 143 C1
Pyryatyn Ukraine 50°15N 32°25E 189 G7
Pyrzyce Poland 53°10N 14°55E 185 B4
Pyskowice Poland 50°24N 18°38E 185 H5
Pytalovo Russia 57°5N 27°58E 188 D4
Pyttegga = Puttegga
  Norway 62°13N 7°42E 164 B4
Pyu Burma 18°30N 96°28E 241 F6
Pyzdry Poland 52°11N 17°42E 185 F4

Q

Qaanaaq Greenland 77°30N 69°10W 154 B4
Qaasuitsup □ Greenland 74°0N 52°0W 154 C5
Qābālā Azerbaijan 40°58N 47°47E 191 K8
Qabanbay Kazakhstan 45°50N 80°37E 217 C10
Qabirri → Azerbaijan 41°3N 46°17E 191 K8
Qabr Hūd Yemen 16°9N 49°34E 249 C5
Qachasnek S. Africa 30°6S 28°42E 271 D4
Qādisiyah, Buhayrat al
  Iraq 34°20N 42°12E 213 E10
Qādub Yemen 12°37N 53°57E 249 D6
Qa'el Jafr Jordan 30°20N 36°25E 251 H7
Qa'emābād Iran 31°44N 60°2E 247 D9
Qā'emshahr Iran 36°30N 52°53E 247 B7
Qafê-Shtamë △ Albania 41°31N 19°54E 202 E3
Qagan Nur Jilin, China 45°15N 124°18E 227 B13
Qagan Nur Nei Monggol Zizhiqu,
  China 43°30N 114°55E 226 C8
Qahar Youyi Zhongqi
  China 41°12N 112°40E 226 D7
Qahremānshahr = Kermānshāh
  Iran 34°23N 47°0E 213 E12
Qaidam Pendi China 37°0N 95°0E 218 D8
Qaiyara Iraq 35°48N 43°17E 213 E10
Qajarīyeh Iran 31°1N 48°22E 247 D6
Qala Malta 36°2N 14°19E 206 E7
Qala, Ras il Malta 36°2N 14°20E 206 E7
Qala-i-Jadid = Spīn Būldak
  Afghan. 31°1N 66°25E 242 D2
Qala Point = Qala, Ras il
  Malta 36°2N 14°20E 206 E7
Qala Viala Pakistan 30°49N 67°17E 242 D2
Qala Yangi Afghan. 34°20N 66°30E 242 B2
Qalācheh Afghan. 35°30N 67°43E 240 B2
Qalaikhum = Kalaikhum
  Tajikistan 38°28N 70°46E 217 E8
Qalandiya West Bank 31°52N 35°12E 123 A2
Qalansīyah Yemen 12°41N 53°29E 249 D6
Qal'at al Akhḍar Si. Arabia 28°4N 37°9E 251 K8
Qal'at Bīshah Si. Arabia 20°0N 42°36E 248 C3
Qal'at Dīzah Iraq 36°11N 45°7E 213 D11
Qalāt-i-Ghilzai Iraq 32°15N 66°58E 240 B2
Qal'at Salah al Din Syria 34°46N 36°12E 250 D7
Qal'at Ṣāliḥ Iraq 31°31N 47°16E 246 D5
Qal'at Sukkar Iraq 31°51N 46°5E 213 G12
Qal'eh Morghi Iran 35°38N 51°22E 141 B2
Qal'eh-ye Now Afghan. 31°30N 64°21E 240 C2
Qal'eh-ye Now Afghan. 35°0N 63°5E 240 B1
Qal'eh-ye Panjeh Afghan. 37°0N 72°35E 240 A4
Qal'eh-ye Sarkari Afghan. 35°54N 67°17E 240 B2
Qal'eh-ye Vali Afghan. 35°46N 63°45E 240 B1
Qalyūb Egypt 30°12N 31°11E 251 H2
Qalyūbīya □ Egypt 30°18N 31°11E 251 H2
Qamani'tuaq = Baker Lake
  Canada 64°20N 96°3W 294 E12
Qamar, Ghubbat al
  Yemen 16°20N 52°30E 249 C6
Qamar, Jabal al Oman 16°48N 53°15E 249 C6
Qamdo China 31°15N 97°6E 228 B1
Qamea Fiji 16°45S 179°45W 287 A3
Qamīnis Libya 31°40N 20°1E 258 B4
Qammieh Point Malta 35°58N 14°19E 206 F7
Qamruddin Karez
  Pakistan 31°45N 68°20E 242 D3
Qandahār = Kandahār
  Afghan. 31°32N 65°43E 240 C2
Qandahār = Kandahār □
  Afghan. 31°0N 65°0E 240 C2
Qandala Somalia 11°30N 49°58E 267 B6
Qandyaghash Kazakhstan 49°28N 57°25E 187 E10
Qapān Iran 37°40N 55°47E 247 B7
Qapqal Iran 43°48N 81°5E 217 D10
Qapshaghay Kazakhstan 43°51N 77°14E 217 D9
Qapshaghay Bögeni
  Kazakhstan 43°45N 77°50E 217 D9
Qaqortoq Greenland 60°43N 46°0W 154 E6
Qāra Egypt 29°38N 26°30E 256 B2
Qarā', Jabal al Oman 17°15N 54°15E 249 C6
Qara Dāgh Iraq 35°18N 45°18E 213 E11
Qara Qash → China 35°0N 78°30E 243 B8
Qarabalyq Kazakhstan 53°45N 62°0E 216 D6
Qarabutaq Kazakhstan 50°0N 60°14E 216 D6
Qaraçala Azerbaijan 39°45N 48°53E 191 L9
Qaraçuxur Azerbaijan 40°25N 50°1E 191 K10
Qaraghandy Kazakhstan 49°50N 73°10E 217 C8
Qaraghayly Kazakhstan 49°26N 76°0E 214 E8
Qārah Si. Arabia 29°55N 40°3E 246 D4
Qarah Āghāj Iran 37°8N 46°58E 213 D12
Qaraoba Kazakhstan 47°6N 56°15E 216 C5
Qaraqiya Oyysy
  Kazakhstan 43°27N 51°45E 216 D4
Qaraqosh Iraq 36°16N 43°22E 213 D10
Qarataū Ongtüstik Qazaqstan,
  Kazakhstan 43°30N 69°30E 217 D7
Qarataū Zhambyl,
  Kazakhstan 43°10N 70°28E 217 D8
Qarāvol Afghan. 37°14N 68°46E 240 A3
Qarazhal Kazakhstan 48°2N 70°49E 214 E8
Qarchak Iran 35°25N 51°34E 247 C6
Qardho Somalia 9°30N 49°6E 267 C6
Qardud Sudan 10°20N 29°56E 257 E2
Qareh → Iran 39°25N 47°22E 213 C12
Qareh Tekān Iran 36°38N 49°29E 247 B6
Qarnein U.A.E. 24°56N 52°52E 247 E7
Qarokūl = Karakul, Ozero
  Tajikistan 39°5N 73°25E 217 F8
Qarqan He → China 39°30N 88°30E 217 E11
Qarqaraly Kazakhstan 49°26N 75°30E 217 C9
Qarqin Afghan. 37°24N 66°4E 240 A2
Qarrasa Sudan 14°38N 32°5E 257 E3
Qarshi Uzbekistan 38°53N 65°48E 217 F7
Qartaba Lebanon 34°4N 35°50E 250 D4
Qārūh Kuwait 28°49N 48°46E 247 D6
Qaryat al Gharab Iraq 31°27N 44°48E 246 D5
Qaryat al 'Ulyā Si. Arabia 27°33N 47°42E 246 E6
Qarynzharyq Oyysy
  Kazakhstan 42°55N 54°25E 216 D4
Qaşbah, Rās al Si. Arabia 28°2N 34°38E 251 K5
Qāsemābād Iran 35°46N 51°0E 141 A3
Qashqadaryo □ Uzbekistan 38°50N 65°18E 217 F7
Qasigiannguit Greenland 68°50N 51°18W 154 C5
Qasr 'Amra = Qasr 'Amra
  Jordan 31°48N 36°35E 246 D3
Qasr Bū Hadi Libya 31°1N 16°45E 258 B3
Qasr-e Fīrūzeh Iran 35°35N 51°31E 141 B3

Qasr-e Qand Iran 26°15N 60°45E 247 E9
Qasr-e Shīrīn Iran 34°31N 45°35E 213 E11
Qasr Farāfra Egypt 27°0N 28°1E 256 B2
Qasr Larocu Libya 26°32N 13°19E 258 C2
Qasuittuq = Resolute
  Canada 74°42N 94°54W 295 C13
Qa'ṭabah Yemen 13°51N 44°42E 248 D4
Qatanā Syria 33°26N 36°3E 250 B5
Qaṭānan, Ra's Yemen 12°21N 53°33E 249 D6
Qatane West Bank 31°50N 35°5E 123 B1
Qatar ■ Asia 25°30N 51°15E 247 E6
Qatlish Iran 37°50N 57°19E 247 B8
Qattâra Egypt 30°12N 27°3E 256 A2
Qattâra, Munkhafed el
  Egypt 29°30N 27°30E 256 B2
Qattâra Depression = Qattâra,
  Munkhafed el Egypt 29°30N 27°30E 256 B2
Qawām al Ḥamzah = Al Ḥamzah
  Iraq 31°43N 44°58E 246 D5
Qawra Point Malta 35°58N 14°26E 206 F7
Qāyen Iran 33°40N 59°10E 247 C8
Qaynar Kazakhstan 49°12N 77°22E 217 C9
Qazaly Kazakhstan 45°45N 62°6E 216 C6
Qazaqstan = Kazakhstan ■
  Asia 50°0N 70°0E 217 C8
Qazatyng Usaqshogylyghy
  Kazakhstan 50°0N 72°0E 217 C8
Qazax Azerbaijan 41°5N 45°21E 191 K7
Qazmämmäd Azerbaijan 40°3N 49°0E 191 K9
Qazvīn Iran 36°15N 50°0E 247 B6
Qazvīn □ Iran 36°20N 50°0E 247 B6
Qazyghurt Kazakhstan 41°45N 69°23E 217 D7
Qeisari = Caesarea Israel 32°30N 34°53E 251 F5
Qeissan Sudan 11°4N 34°40E 257 F3
Qena Egypt 26°10N 32°43E 256 B3
Qena, W. → Egypt 26°12N 32°44E 256 B3
Qeqertarsuaq Qaasuitsup,
  Greenland 69°45N 53°30W 154 C5
Qeqertarsuaq Qaasuitsup,
  Greenland 69°15N 53°38W 154 C5
Qeqertarsuatsiaat
  Greenland 63°45N 50°45W 154 C5
Qeqqata □ Greenland 66°30N 48°0W 154 D6
Qeshlāq Iran 34°55N 46°28E 213 E12
Qeshm Iran 26°55N 56°10E 247 E8
Qeydār Iran 36°N 48°35E 213 E13
Qeys Iran 26°32N 53°58E 249 A6
Qezel Owzen → Iran 36°45N 49°22E 247 B6
Qezi'ot Israel 30°52N 34°26E 251 H5
Qi Xian China 34°40N 114°48E 226 G8
Qian Gorlos China 45°5N 124°42E 227 B13
Qian Hai China 22°32N 113°54E 219 a
Qian Xian China 34°31N 108°15E 226 G5
Qian'an China 40°0N 118°41E 227 D12
Qianjiang Guangxi Zhuangzu,
  China 23°38N 108°58E 228 F7
Qianjiang Hubei, China 30°24N 112°55E 229 B9
Qianjiang Sichuan, China 29°33N 108°41E 228 C7
Qianjin China 47°34N 133°4E 219 B15
Qianmen China 39°51N 116°21E 114 B2
Qianshan Anhui, China 30°37N 116°35E 229 B11
Qianshan Guangdong,
  China 22°15N 113°31E 219 a
Qianwei China 29°13N 103°56E 228 C4
Qianxi China 27°3N 106°3E 228 D6
Qianyang Hunan, China 27°18N 110°10E 229 D8
Qianyang Shaanxi, China 34°40N 107°8E 226 G4
Qianyang Zhejiang,
  China 30°11N 119°25E 229 B12
Qi'ao China 22°25N 113°39E 219 a
Qi'ao Dao China 22°25N 113°38E 219 a
Qiaocun China 39°56N 112°56E 226 E7
Qiaojia China 26°56N 102°58E 228 D4
Qichun China 30°18N 115°25E 229 B10
Qidong Hunan, China 26°49N 112°7E 229 D9
Qidong Jiangsu, China 31°48N 121°38E 229 B13
Qiemo China 38°8N 85°32E 217 E11
Qijiang China 29°3N 106°35E 228 C6
Qijiaojing China 43°28N 91°36E 217 D12
Qikiqtaaluk = Baffin I.
  Canada 68°0N 75°0W 295 D17
Qila Safiullah Pakistan 30°45N 68°17E 242 D3
Qilian Shan China 38°30N 96°0E 218 D8
Qimei = Ch'imei Taiwan 23°12N 119°25E 225 c1
Qin He → China 35°1N 113°22E 226 G7
Qin Jiang → Guangxi Zhuangzu,
  China 21°53N 108°35E 228 F7
Qin Jiang → Jiangxi,
  China 26°15N 115°55E 229 D10
Qin Ling = Qinling Shandi
  China 33°30N 108°10E 226 H5
Qīnāb, W. → Yemen 15°30N 47°53E 249 C5
Qin'an China 34°48N 105°40E 226 G3
Qing Xian China 38°35N 116°45E 226 E9
Qingcheng China 37°15N 117°40E 227 F9
Qingcheng Shan China 30°50N 103°31E 228 B4
Qingchuan China 32°36N 105°9E 226 H3
Qingdao China 36°5N 120°20E 227 F11
Qingfeng China 35°52N 115°8E 226 G8
Qinghai □ China 36°0N 98°0E 218 D8
Qinghai Hu China 36°40N 100°10E 218 D9
Qinghe China 46°37N 90°25E 217 C12
Qinghecheng China 41°28N 124°15E 224 B2
Qinghemen China 41°48N 121°25E 227 D11
Qinghuayuan China 39°59N 116°19E 114 B1
Qingjian China 37°8N 110°8E 226 F6
Qingjiang = Huaiyin
  China 33°30N 119°2E 227 H10
Qingliu China 26°11N 116°48E 229 D11
Qinglong China 25°49N 105°12E 228 E5
Qingningsi China 31°16N 121°33E 138 B2
Qingping China 26°39N 107°47E 228 D6
Qingshui China 34°48N 106°8E 226 G4
Qingshuihe China 39°55N 111°35E 226 E6
Qingtian China 28°12N 120°15E 229 C13
Qingtongxia China 38°2N 106°3E 226 E4
Qingtongxia Shuiku
  China 37°50N 105°58E 226 E3
Qingxi China 29°31N 108°43E 228 D7
Qingxu China 37°34N 112°22E 226 F7
Qingyang Anhui, China 30°38N 117°50E 229 B11
Qingyang Gansu, China 36°2N 107°55E 226 F4
Qingyi Jiang → China 29°32N 103°44E 228 C4
Qingyuan Guangdong,
  China 23°40N 112°59E 229 F9
Qingyuan Liaoning, China 42°10N 124°55E 224 A2
Qingyuan Zhejiang, China 27°45N 119°3E 229 D12
Qingzhen China 26°32N 106°25E 228 D6
Qinhuangdao China 39°56N 119°30E 227 E10
Qinling Shandi China 33°50N 108°10E 226 H5
Qinshui = Ch'ingshui
  Taiwan 24°16N 120°34E 225 B2
Qinshui China 35°40N 112°8E 226 G7
Qinyang = Jiyuan China 35°7N 112°57E 226 G7
Qinyang China 35°8N 112°34E 226 G7
Qinyuan China 36°29N 112°20E 226 F7
Qinzhou China 21°58N 108°38E 228 G7
Qionghai China 19°15N 110°26E 229 F8
Qionglai China 30°25N 103°31E 228 B4
Qionglai Shan China 30°30N 102°30E 228 B4
Qiongshan China 19°51N 110°26E 229 a
Qiongzhou Haixia China 20°10N 110°15E 229 a
Qiqihar China 47°26N 124°0E 219 B13
Qira China 37°0N 80°48E 217 E10

Qiraïya, W. → Egypt 30°27N 34°0E 251 H5
Qiryat Ata Israel 32°47N 35°6E 250 F6
Qiryat Gat Israel 31°32N 34°46E 251 G5
Qiryat Mal'akhi Israel 31°44N 34°44E 251 G5
Qiryat Shemona Israel 33°13N 35°35E 250 E6
Qiryat Yam Israel 32°51N 35°4E 250 F6
Qīrzah, W. → Libya 30°56N 14°31E 258 B2
Qishan = Ch'ishan
  Taiwan 22°44N 120°31E 225 D2
Qishan China 34°25N 107°38E 226 G4
Qishn Yemen 15°26N 51°40E 249 D5
Qitai China 44°2N 89°35E 217 D11
Qitaihe China 45°48N 130°51E 220 B5
Qitbīt, W. → Oman 19°15N 54°23E 249 C6
Qiubei China 24°2N 104°12E 228 E5
Qixia China 37°17N 120°52E 227 F11
Qiyang China 26°35N 111°50E 229 D8
Qızılağac Körfäzi Azerbaijan 39°9N 49°13E 213 C13
Qobda Kazakhstan 50°5N 54°31E 216 B4
Qods Iran 35°45N 51°15E 247 C6
Qojūr Iran 36°12N 47°55E 246 B5
Qolhak Iran 35°45N 51°26E 141 A2
Qom Iran 34°40N 51°0E 247 C6
Qom □ Iran 34°40N 51°0E 247 C6
Qomolangma Feng = Everest, Mt.
  Nepal 28°5N 86°58E 243 E12
Qomsheh Iran 32°0N 51°55E 247 D6
Qong Muztag China 35°42N 82°22E 217 E10
Qoqek = Tacheng China 46°40N 82°58E 217 C10
Qoqon = Qo'qon
  Uzbekistan 40°31N 70°56E 217 D8
Qo'qon Uzbekistan 40°31N 70°56E 217 D8
Qorako'l Uzbekistan 39°32N 63°50E 216 E6
Qoraqalpog'iston □
  Uzbekistan 43°0N 58°0E 216 D5
Qorghalzhyn Kazakhstan 50°25N 69°11E 217 B7
Qormi Malta 35°53N 14°28E 206 F7
Qorveh Iran 35°10N 47°48E 213 E12
Qosshaghyl Kazakhstan 46°40N 54°0E 187 E9
Qostanay Kazakhstan 53°10N 63°35E 216 B6
Qotanqaraghay
  Kazakhstan 49°10N 85°36E 217 C11
Qotūr Iran 38°28N 44°25E 213 C11
Qoz Salsilgo C.A.R. 10°45N 22°56E 264 A4
Qrejten Point Malta 35°57N 14°27E 206 F7
Qu Jiang → China 30°1N 106°24E 228 B6
Qu Xian China 30°48N 106°58E 228 B6
Quabbin Res. U.S.A. 42°20N 72°20W 313 D12
Quadraro Italy 41°51N 12°33E 136 B2
Quaid-i-Azam Pakistan 24°50N 66°59E 123 A1
Quairading Australia 32°0S 117°21E 279 F2
Quakenbrück Germany 52°41N 7°57E 178 C3
Quakertown U.S.A. 40°26N 75°21W 313 F9
Qualicum Beach Canada 49°22N 124°26W 296 D4
Quambatook Australia 35°49S 143°34E 282 C5
Quambone Australia 30°57S 147°53E 283 A7
Quamby Australia 20°22S 140°17E 280 C3
Quan Long = Ca Mau
  Vietnam 9°7N 105°8E 237 H5
Quanah U.S.A. 34°18N 99°44W 314 D5
Quandialla Australia 34°1S 147°47E 283 C7
Quang Ngai Vietnam 15°13N 108°58E 236 E7
Quang Tri Vietnam 16°45N 107°13E 236 D6
Quang Yen Vietnam 20°56N 106°52E 234 B6
Quannan China 24°45N 114°33E 229 E10
Quanzhou Fujian, China 24°55N 118°34E 229 E12
Quanzhou Guangxi Zhuangzu,
  China 25°57N 111°5E 229 D9
Qu'Appelle → Canada 50°33N 103°53W 297 C8
Quaqtaq Canada 60°55N 69°40W 295 E18
Quaraí Brazil 30°15S 56°20W 334 C4
Quarré-les-Tombes France 47°21N 4°0E 173 E11
Quarteira Portugal 37°4N 8°6W 195 H2
Quarter, The Anguilla 18°13N 63°2W 322 a
Quartier D'Orléans
  St.-Martin 18°5N 63°2W 322 a
Quartier Militaire
  Mauritius 20°14S 57°35E 272 e
Quartiere Zingone Italy 45°25N 9°3E 128 B1
Quartu Sant'Elena Italy 39°15N 9°10E 200 C2
Quartzsite U.S.A. 33°40N 114°13W 307 M12
Quatre, I. St. Vincent 12°59N 61°15W 323 b
Quatre Bornes Mauritius 20°15S 57°28E 272 e
Quatsino Sd. Canada 50°25N 127°58W 296 C3
Quba Azerbaijan 41°21N 48°32E 191 K9
Qubeiba West Bank 31°50N 35°5E 123 A1
Qūchān Iran 37°10N 58°27E 247 B8
Quds Iraq 33°23N 44°24E 113 A2
Queanbeyan Australia 35°17S 149°14E 283 C8
Québec Canada 46°52N 71°13W 299 C5
Québec □ Canada 48°0N 74°0W 298 B6
Quebo Guinea-Biss. 11°46N 14°56W 262 C2
Quebrada del Condorito △
  Argentina 31°49S 64°40W 334 C3
Quebradillas Puerto Rico 18°29N 66°56W 321 b
Queen Alexandra Ra.
  Antarctica 85°0S 170°0E 151 E11
Queen Charlotte B. Falk. Is. 51°50S 60°40W 153 f
Queen Charlotte City
  Canada 53°15N 132°2W 296 C2
Queen Charlotte Is. = Haida Gwaii
  Canada 53°20N 132°10W 296 C2
Queen Charlotte Sd. B.C.,
  Canada 51°0N 128°0W 296 C3
Queen Charlotte Sd. N.Z. 41°10S 174°15E 285 B9
Queen Charlotte Strait
  Canada 50°45N 127°10W 296 C3
Queen Elizabeth △ Uganda 0°0 30°0E 268 C3
Queen Elizabeth Is. Canada 76°0N 95°0W 295 B13
Queen Elizabeth Land
  Antarctica 85°0S 60°0W 151 E17
Queen Elizabeth Nat. Park =
  Ruwenzori △ Canada 0°0 30°0E 268 B2
Queen Elizabeth Olympic Park
  London, U.K. 51°33N 0°1E 125 A3
Queen Mary Land
  Antarctica 70°0S 95°0E 151 D7
Queen Mary Res. U.K. 51°24N 0°27W 125 B1
Queen Maud G. Canada 68°15N 102°30W 294 D11
Queen Maud Land = Dronning
  Maud Land Antarctica 72°30S 12°0E 151 D3
Queen Maud Mts.
  Antarctica 86°0S 160°0W 151 E12
Queen Street Edinburgh, U.K. 121 a1
Queen Victoria Market
  Australia 37°47S 144°57W 128 A1
Queens Channel Australia 15°0S 129°30E 278 C4
Queens-Midtown Tunnel
  New York, U.S.A. 132 d2
Queen's Quay Terminal
  Toronto, Canada 141 c2
Queensboro Bridge New York, U.S.A. 132 c3
Queensbury U.K. 51°30N 0°16W 125 A2
Queenscliff Australia 38°16S 144°39E 282 D6
Queensferry U.K. 55°59N 3°23E 121 B1
Queensland □ Australia 31°46N 43°1W 316 D6
Queensland □ Australia 22°0S 142°0E 280 C3
Queensland Plateau
  Pac. Oc. 17°0S 150°0E 276 D8
Queenstown = Cobh
  Ireland 51°51N 8°17W 166 E3
Queenstown Australia 42°4S 145°35E 281 G4
Queenstown N.Z. 45°1S 168°40E 285 F3

Queenstown Singapore 1°18N 103°48E 138 B2
Queenstown Eastern Cape,
  S. Africa 31°52S 26°52E 270 D4
Queets U.S.A. 47°32N 124°19W 306 C2
Queguay Grande →
  Uruguay 32°9S 58°9W 334 C4
Queimada, Pta. da Azores 38°23N 28°14W 153 d1
Queimadas Brazil 11°0S 39°38W 332 D6
Queiros, C. Vanuatu 14°55S 167°1E 287 D5
Quela Angola 9°10S 16°56E 265 D3
Quelimane Mozam. 17°53S 36°58E 269 F4
Quellerina S. Africa 26°9S 27°56E 123 B1
Quellón Chile 43°7S 73°37W 336 B2
Quelo Angola 6°29S 12°36E 265 D2
Quelpart = Jeju-do
  S. Korea 33°29N 126°34E 224 a
Queluz Portugal 38°45N 9°14W 126 A1
Quemado N. Mex.,
  U.S.A. 34°20N 108°30W 305 J9
Quemado Tex., U.S.A. 28°56N 100°37W 314 G4
Quemoy = Chinmen
  Taiwan 24°26N 118°19E 225 a1
Quemú-Quemú Argentina 36°3S 63°36W 334 D3
Quepem India 15°13N 74°3E 245 G2
Quequén Argentina 38°30S 58°30W 334 D4
Querco Peru 13°50S 74°52W 330 C3
Querétaro Mexico 20°36N 100°23W 318 C4
Querétaro □ Mexico 21°0N 99°55W 318 C5
Querfurt Germany 51°23N 11°35E 178 D7
Quérigut France 42°42N 2°6E 174 F6
Querqueville France 49°40N 1°42W 172 C5
Quesada Spain 37°51N 3°4W 195 H7
Queshan China 32°55N 114°2E 229 A10
Quesnel Canada 53°0N 122°30W 296 C4
Quesnel → Canada 52°58N 122°29W 296 C4
Quesnel L. Canada 52°30N 121°20W 296 C4
Questa U.S.A. 36°42N 105°36W 305 H11
Questembert France 47°40N 2°28W 172 E4
Quetena Bolivia 22°10S 67°25W 330 E4
Quetico △ Canada 48°30N 91°45W 298 C1
Quetrequile Argentina 41°33S 69°22W 336 E3
Quetta Pakistan 30°15N 66°55E 242 D2
Quezaltenango
  Guatemala 14°50N 91°30W 320 D1
Quelát △ Chile 44°29S 72°24W 336 B2
Quevedo Ecuador 1°2S 79°29W 328 D2
Queyras △ France 44°45N 6°50E 175 D10
Quezon Phil. 9°15N 117°59E 233 G1
Quezon □ Phil. 14°0N 121°30E 232 D3
Quezon □ Phil. 14°0N 121°55E 232 D3
Quezon City Phil. 14°37N 121°2E 127 B2
Qufar Si. Arabia 27°26N 41°37E 246 E4
Qufu China 35°36N 116°58E 226 G9
Qui Nhon Vietnam 13°40N 109°13E 236 F7
Quibala Angola 10°46S 14°59E 265 E2
Quibaxe Angola 8°24S 14°27E 265 D2
Quibdó Colombia 5°42N 76°40W 328 B2
Quiberon France 47°29N 3°9W 172 E3
Quiberon, Presqu'île de
  France 47°30N 3°9W 172 E3
Quiçama △ Angola 9°41S 13°35E 265 D2
Quickborn Germany 53°42N 9°52E 178 B5
Quiet L. Canada 61°5N 133°5W 296 A2
Quiindy Paraguay 25°58S 57°14W 334 C4
Quilá Mexico 24°23N 107°13W 318 C3
Quilán, C. Chile 43°15S 74°30W 336 B2
Quilcene U.S.A. 47°49N 122°53W 306 C4
Quilengues Angola 14°12S 14°12E 265 E2
Quilon = Kollam India 8°50N 76°38E 245 K3
Quilpie Australia 26°35S 144°11E 281 D3
Quilpué Chile 33°5S 71°33W 334 C1
Quilua Mozam. 16°17S 39°54E 269 F4
Quimbele Angola 6°49S 16°25E 265 D3
Quimbonge Angola 8°36S 18°30E 265 D3
Quimili Argentina 27°40S 62°30W 334 B3
Quimper France 48°0N 4°9W 172 E2
Quimperlé France 47°53N 3°33W 172 E3
Quinam B. Trin. & Tob. 10°4N 61°30W 323 f
Quinault → U.S.A. 47°21N 124°18W 306 C2
Quince Mil Peru 13°15S 70°40W 330 C3
Quincy Calif., U.S.A. 39°56N 120°57W 306 F6
Quincy Ill., U.S.A. 39°56N 91°23W 316 F8
Quincy Mass., U.S.A. 42°14N 71°0W 313 D14
Quincy Mich., U.S.A. 41°57N 84°53W 311 D12
Quincy Wash., U.S.A. 47°14N 119°51W 304 C4
Quines Argentina 32°13S 65°48W 334 C3
Quinga Mozam. 15°49S 40°15E 269 F5
Quingey France 47°7N 5°52E 173 E12
Quinhagak U.S.A. 59°45N 161°54W 303 G7
Quinhámel Guinea-Biss. 11°53N 15°51W 262 C1
Quiniluban Group Phil. 11°27N 120°48E 233 F5
Quinta Normal Chile 33°26S 70°42W 137 B1
Quinta de la Serena
  Spain 38°45N 5°40W 195 G5
Quintana Roo □ Mexico 19°40N 88°30W 319 D7
Quintana Roo □ Quintana Roo,
  Mexico 20°15N 87°45W 319 C7
Quintanar de la Orden
  Spain 39°36N 3°5W 195 F7
Quintanar de la Sierra
  Spain 41°57N 2°55W 198 D7
Quintanar del Rey Spain 39°21N 1°56W 197 F3
Quintero Chile 32°45N 71°30W 334 C1
Quintin France 48°26N 2°56W 172 D4
Quinto Spain 41°25N 0°32W 198 D5
Quinto de Stampi Italy 45°24N 9°10E 128 B2
Quinto Romano Italy 45°29N 9°4E 128 B1
Quinzau Angola 6°51S 12°44E 265 D2
Quípar → Spain 38°15N 1°40W 197 G3
Quipeio Angola 12°27S 15°0E 265 E3
Quirihue Chile 36°15S 72°35W 334 D1
Quirima Angola 10°45S 18°6E 265 E3
Quirimbo Angola 10°36S 14°12E 265 E2
Quirindi Australia 31°28S 150°40E 283 B9
Quirino □ Phil. 16°15N 121°40E 232 C3
Quirinópolis Brazil 18°32S 50°30W 333 G8
Quiroga Spain 42°28N 7°18W 194 C3
Quissac France 43°55N 4°0E 175 G8
Quissanga Mozam. 12°24S 40°28E 269 E5
Quissico Mozam. 24°42S 34°44E 271 C5
Quitapa Angola 10°25S 15°5E 265 E3
Quitilipi Argentina 26°50S 60°13W 334 B3
Quitman U.S.A. 30°47N 83°34W 316 E6
Quito Ecuador 0°15S 78°35W 328 D2
Quitralco △ Chile 45°43S 73°25W 336 B2
Quixadá Brazil 4°55S 39°0W 332 C6
Quixaxe Mozam. 15°17S 40°4E 269 F5
Quixeramobim Brazil 5°12S 39°17W 332 C6

Quixico Angola 7°59S 14°25E 265 D2
Quixinge Angola 9°52S 14°23E 265 D3
Quizenga Angola 9°21S 15°28E 265 D3
Qujing China 25°32N 103°41E 228 E4
Qul'an, Jazā'ir Egypt 24°22N 35°31E 246 B3
Qulsary Kazakhstan 46°59N 54°1E 187 E9
Qumbu S. Africa 31°35N 28°48E 271 D4
Qumqo'rg'on Uzbekistan 37°49N 67°35E 240 A2
Qunayrita, Sabkhat al
  Libya 30°10N 21°0E 258 B4
Quneitra = Al Qunayṭirah
  Syria 33°5N 35°45E 250 F6
Qūnghirot Uzbekistan 43°2N 58°50E 216 D5
Qu'nyido China 31°15N 98°6E 228 B2
Quoin I. Australia 14°54S 129°32E 278 B4
Quoin Pt. S. Africa 34°46S 19°37E 270 D2
Quorn Australia 32°25S 138°5E 282 B3
Qurein Sudan 13°30N 34°50E 257 E3
Qŭrghonteppa Tajikistan 37°50N 68°47E 217 F7
Qurimbas △ Mozam. 12°20S 40°10E 269 E5
Qurnat as Sawdā' Lebanon 34°18N 36°6E 250 D7
Qurnah Iraq 43°12N 51°10E 216 D4
Quruq Tagh China 41°30N 90°0E 217 E12
Quryq Kazakhstan 43°12N 51°13E 186 F9
Qūs Egypt 25°55N 32°50E 256 B3
Qusar Azerbaijan 41°25N 48°26E 191 K9
Quşaybā' Si. Arabia 26°53N 43°35E 246 E4
Qusaybah Iraq 34°24N 40°59E 213 E9
Quşay'ir Yemen 14°55N 50°20E 249 D5
Quseir Egypt 26°7N 34°16E 246 E2
Quseir Amra = Qasr 'Amra
  Jordan 31°48N 36°35E 246 D3
Qūshkŭpir Iran 37°59N 45°3E 213 D11
Qusmuryn Kazakhstan 52°27N 64°36E 216 D6
Qusmuryn Köli
  Kazakhstan 52°41N 64°48E 216 B6
Qutang Gorge = Qutang Xia
  China 31°0N 109°40E 228 B7
Qutang Xia China 31°0N 109°40E 228 B7
Qutb Minar India 28°31N 77°11E 120 B2
Quthing Lesotho 30°25S 27°36E 271 D4
Qūṭīābād Iran 35°47N 48°30E 213 E13
Quttinirpaaq = Ellesmere I.
  Canada 79°30N 80°0W 295 B16
Quttinirpaaq Canada 82°13N 72°13W 295 A17
Quwayq → Syria 36°20N 37°10E 250 B7
Quwo China 35°38N 111°25E 226 G6
Quyang China 38°35N 114°40E 226 E8
Quynh Nhai Vietnam 21°49N 103°33E 236 B4
Quyon Canada 45°31N 76°14W 313 A8
Quzhou China 28°57N 118°54E 229 C12
Quzi China 36°12N 107°20E 226 F4
Qvareli Georgia 41°57N 45°47E 191 K7
Qytet Stalin = Kuçovë
  Albania 40°47N 19°57E 202 F3
Qyzylorda Kazakhstan 44°48N 65°28E 216 D6
Qyzylorda □ Kazakhstan 45°0N 65°0E 216 D6
Qyzylzhar Kazakhstan 48°17N 69°38E 217 C7

R

R.F.K. Memorial Stadium
  U.S.A. 38°52N 76°58W 143 B3
Ra, Ko Thailand 9°13N 98°16E 237 H2
Raab Austria 48°21N 13°39E 180 C6
Raahe Finland 64°40N 24°28E 160 D21
Raalte Neths. 52°23N 6°16E 178 C4
Ra'ananna Israel 32°10N 34°52E 251 F5
Raas Indonesia 7°8S 114°33E 235 D4
Raasay U.K. 57°25N 6°4W 167 D2
Raasay, Sd. of U.K. 57°30N 6°8W 167 D2
Raasdorf Austria 48°14N 16°33E 142 A3
Raasepori Finland 60°0N 23°26E 188 B2
Rab Croatia 44°45N 14°45E 199 D11
Raba Indonesia 8°36S 118°55E 235 D5
Rába → Hungary 47°38N 17°38E 182 C2
Rabaçal → Portugal 41°30N 7°12W 194 D3
Rabah Nigeria 13°5N 5°30E 263 C6
Rabai Kenya 3°50S 39°31E 268 C4
Rabak Sudan 13°9N 32°44E 257 E3
Rabaraba Papua N. G. 9°58S 149°49E 288 E5
Rabastens France 43°50N 1°43E 174 E5
Rabastens-de-Bigorre
  France 43°23N 0°9E 174 E4
Rahole = Kenya 0°5N 38°57E 268 B4
Rābḥolt Norway 60°16N 11°11E 164 D8
Rabon India 30°3N 76°7E 242 D7
Rabotev N.Z. 39°20S 173°49E 284 C7
Rahovec Kosovo 42°24N 20°39E 202 D4
Rahuri India 19°23N 74°39E 244 E2
Rai, Hon Vietnam 9°48N 104°38E 237 H5
Raiatéa, Î. French Polynesia 16°50S 151°25W 289 f
Raichur India 16°10N 77°20E 245 E3
Raiford U.S.A. 30°4N 82°14W 316 E7
Raiganj India 25°37N 88°10E 243 G13
Raigarh India 21°56N 83°25E 243 J10
Raijua Indonesia 10°37S 121°36E 231 F6
Raikot India 30°41N 75°42E 242 D6
Railton Australia 41°25S 146°28E 281 G4
Rainbow Bridge △ U.S.A. 37°5N 110°58W 305 H8
Rainbow City U.S.A. 33°57N 86°5W 316 E5
Rainbow Lake Canada 58°30N 119°23W 296 B5
Rainier U.S.A. 46°53N 122°41W 306 D4
Rainier, Mt. U.S.A. 46°52N 121°46W 306 D5
Rainy L. Canada 48°42N 93°10W 297 D10
Rainy River Canada 48°43N 94°29W 297 D10
Raippaluoto Finland 63°13N 21°14E 160 E19
Raipur India 21°17N 81°45E 244 D5
Rairakhol India 21°4N 84°21E 244 D7
Ra'is Si. Arabia 23°33N 38°43E 248 C2
Raisen India 23°20N 77°48E 242 H7
Raisio Finland 60°28N 22°11E 188 B2
Raivavae French Polynesia 23°52S 147°40W 289 f
Raj Ghat Delhi, India 120 B3
Raj Nandgaon India 21°5N 81°5E 243 J9
Raj Nilgiri India 21°28N 86°46E 243 J12
Raja, Ujung Indonesia 3°40N 96°25E 234 B1
Raja Ampat, Kepulauan
  Indonesia 0°30S 130°0E 231 E8
Rajah Sikatuna △ Phil. 9°42N 124°6E 233 G5
Rajahmahendravaram =
  Rajahmundry India 17°1N 81°48E 244 F5
Rajahmundry =
  Rajahmahendravaram
  India 17°1N 81°48E 244 F5
Rajaji △ India 30°10N 78°20E 242 D8
Rajakhera India 26°50N 77°50E 242 F7
Rajam India 18°44N 83°20E 244 E7
Rajang → Malaysia 2°30N 112°0E 235 B4
Rajanpur Pakistan 29°6N 70°19E 242 E4
Rajapalaiyam India 16°40N 73°31E 244 F1
Rajapur India 16°40N 73°31E 245 F1
Rajasthan □ India 26°45N 73°30E 242 F5
Rajasthan Canal = Indira Gandhi
  Canal India 28°0N 72°0E 242 F5
Rajbari India 23°47N 89°41E 243 H13
Rajendranagar India 17°1N 78°25E 245 F4
Rajgarh Mad. P., India 24°2N 76°45E 242 G7
Rajgarh Raj., India 27°14N 76°38E 242 F7
Rajgarh Raj., India 28°40N 75°25E 242 E6
Rajghat Dam India 24°45N 78°20E 243 G8
Rajgir India 25°2N 85°11E 243 G11
Rajgród Poland 53°42N 22°42E 184 E9
Rajim India 20°58N 81°53E 244 D5

Rajkot India 22°15N 70°56E 242 H4
Rajmahal Hills India 24°30N 87°30E 243 G12
Rajpath Delhi, India 120 c2
Rajpipla India 21°50N 73°30E 244 D1
Rajpur India 22°18N 74°21E 242 H6
Rajpura Delhi, India 28°41N 77°12E 120 A2
Rajpura Punjab, India 30°25N 76°32E 242 D7
Rajputana = Rajasthan □ India 26°45N 73°30E 242 F5
Rajsamand = Kankroli India 25°4N 73°53E 242 G5
Rajshahi Bangla. 24°22N 88°39E 241 C2
Rajshahi □ Bangla. 25°0N 89°0E 241 C2
Rājū Syria 36°40N 36°40E 250 B7
Rajula India 21°3N 71°26E 242 J4
Rajur India 20°7N 78°55E 244 D4
Rajura India 19°47N 79°22E 244 E4
Rakaia N.Z. 43°45S 172°1E 285 D7
Rakaia → N.Z. 43°36S 172°15E 285 D7
Rakan, Ra's Qatar 26°10N 51°20E 247 E6
Rakaposhi Pakistan 36°10N 74°25E 243 A6
Rakata, Pulau Indonesia 6°10S 105°20E 234 D3
Rakbah, Sahl Si. Arabia 22°15N 41°0E 256 C5
Rakhine □ Burma 19°0N 94°15E 241 F5
Rakhiv Ukraine 48°3N 24°12E 183 B9
Rakhni Pakistan 30°4N 69°56E 242 D3
Rakhni → Pakistan 29°31N 69°36E 242 E3
Rakhny-Lisovi Ukraine 48°47N 28°29E 183 B13
Rakhyūt Oman 16°44N 53°20E 249 C6
Rakiraki Fiji 17°22S 178°11E 287 A2
Rakitnoye Russia 50°57N 35°56E 189 G8
Rakitnoye Russia 45°36N 134°17E 220 B7
Rakitovo Bulgaria 41°59N 24°5E 203 E8
Rakiura = Stewart I. N.Z. 46°58S 167°54E 285 G2
Rakkestad Norway 59°25N 11°21E 164 E8
Rakoniewice Poland 52°10N 16°16E 185 F3
Rakops Botswana 21°1S 24°28E 270 B3
Rákos-patak → Hungary 47°29N 19°12E 117 B3
Rákoshegy Hungary 47°27N 19°14E 117 B3
Rákoskeresztúr Hungary 47°29N 19°15E 117 B3
Rákoskert Hungary 47°27N 19°18E 117 B3
Rákosliget Hungary 47°29N 19°16E 117 B3
Rákospalota Hungary 47°34N 19°7E 117 A2
Rákosszentmihály Hungary 47°31N 19°8E 117 A2
Rakovica Croatia 44°59N 15°38E 199 D12
Rakovník Czechia 50°6N 13°42E 180 A6
Rakovski Bulgaria 42°21N 24°57E 203 D8
Raków Poland 52°11N 20°56E 143 B1
Rakshan → Pakistan 27°10N 63°25E 240 D1
Rakvere Estonia 59°20N 26°25E 188 C4
Raleigh Fla., U.S.A. 29°25N 82°32W 317 F7
Raleigh N.C., U.S.A. 35°47N 78°39W 315 D15
Ralik Chain Pac. Oc. 8°0N 168°0E 288 G8
Ralja Serbia 44°33N 20°34E 202 B4
Rälla Sweden 56°40N 16°30E 163 H10
Ralls U.S.A. 33°41N 101°24W 314 E4
Ralston U.S.A. 41°30N 76°57W 312 E8
Ram West Bank 31°51N 35°14E 123 A2
Ram → Canada 62°1N 123°41W 296 A4
Rām Allāh West Bank 31°55N 35°10E 123 A2
Rama Nic. 12°9N 84°15W 320 D3
Ramacca Italy 37°23N 14°42E 201 E7
Ramachandrapuram India 16°50N 82°4E 244 F6
Ramadān Iraq 33°19N 44°20E 113 B2
Ramagiri Udayagiri India 19°5N 84°18E 244 E7
Ramagundam India 18°55N 79°15E 244 E4
Ramakona India 21°43N 78°50E 243 J8
Ramakrishna Puram India 28°32N 77°10E 120 B1
Ramalho, Serra do Brazil 13°45S 44°0W 333 D3
Rāmallāh = Rām Allāh West Bank 31°55N 35°10E 123 A2
Raman Thailand 6°29N 101°18E 237 J3
Ramanathapuram India 9°25N 78°55E 245 K4
Ramanathpur India 22°41N 88°24E 120 A1
Ramanujganj India 23°48N 83°42E 243 H10
Ramas C. India 15°5N 73°55E 245 G1
Ramat Allon West Bank 31°49N 35°12E 123 B2
Ramat Eshkol West Bank 31°48N 35°13E 123 B2
Ramat Gan Israel 32°4N 34°48E 251 F5
Ramat Razi'el Israel 31°46N 35°4E 123 B1
Ramat Shafet West Bank 31°48N 35°12E 123 B2
Ramatlhabama S. Africa 25°37S 25°33E 270 C4
Ramban India 33°14N 75°12E 243 C6
Rambervillers France 48°20N 6°38E 173 D13
Rambi = Rabi Fiji 16°30S 179°59W 287 A3
Rambipuji Indonesia 8°12S 113°37E 235 D4
Rambler Channel Hong Kong, China 22°21N 114°6E 122 A2
Rambouillet France 48°39N 1°50E 173 D8
Rambrai India 25°40N 91°19E 241 C3
Rambutyo I. Papua N. G. 2°18S 147°49E 286 B4
Ramdurg India 15°58N 75°22E 245 G2
Rame Hd. Australia 37°47S 149°30E 283 D8
Ramechhap Nepal 27°25N 86°10E 243 F12
Ramelton Ireland 55°2N 7°39W 166 A4
Ramenki Russia 55°41N 37°28E 129 B1
Ramenskoye Russia 55°32N 38°15E 188 E10
Ramer U.S.A. 32°3N 86°13W 316 C3
Ramersdorf Germany 48°6N 11°35E 131 B2
Rameses Station Egypt 30°3N 31°15E 117 A2
Rameswaram India 9°17N 79°18E 245 K4
Ramganga → India 27°5N 79°58E 243 F8
Ramgarh Bangla. 22°59N 91°44E 241 D3
Ramgarh Jharkhand, India 23°40N 85°35E 243 H11
Ramgarh Raj., India 27°16N 75°14E 242 F6
Ramgarh Raj., India 27°30N 70°36E 242 F4
Rāmhormoz Iran 31°15N 49°35E 247 D6
Ramīān Iran 37°3N 55°16E 247 B7
Ramiers Haiti 19°34N 72°14W 321 C5
Ramingining Australia 12°19S 135°3E 280 A2
Ramla Israel 31°55N 34°52E 251 G5
Ramlat Zalṭan Libya 28°30N 19°30E 258 C3
Ramlu Eritrea 13°32N 41°40E 257 E5
Ramm = Rum Jordan 29°39N 35°26E 251 J6
Râmna → Romania 45°36N 27°3E 183 E12
Ramnad = Ramanathapuram India 9°25N 78°55E 245 K4
Ramnagar Jammu & Kashmir, India 32°47N 75°18E 243 C6
Ramnagar Uttarakhand, India 29°24N 79°7E 243 E8
Ramnäs Sweden 59°46N 16°12E 162 E10
Râmnicu Sărat Romania 45°26N 27°3E 183 E12
Râmnicu Vâlcea Romania 45°9N 24°21E 183 E9
Ramnous Greece 38°12N 24°3E 204 C6
Ramon Isabela, Phil. 16°50N 121°31E 232 C3
Ramon Russia 51°55N 39°21E 189 G10
Ramona U.S.A. 33°2N 116°52W 310 M10
Ramonville-St-Agne France 43°33N 1°28E 174 E5
Ramore Canada 48°30N 80°25W 298 C3
Ramos Brazil 22°50S 43°14W 135 B1
Ramos → Nigeria 5°8N 5°22E 263 D6
Ramos I. Phil. 8°6N 117°1E 233 G1
Ramos Mejía Argentina 34°39S 58°33W 117 B1
Ramot West Bank 31°48N 35°13E 123 B2
Ramotswa Botswana 24°50S 25°52E 270 B4
Rampanalgas Trin. & Tob. 10°44N 60°59W 323 t
Rampart U.S.A. 65°30N 150°10W 303 D10
Rampur H.P., India 31°26N 77°43E 242 D7
Rampur Mad. P., India 23°25N 73°53E 242 H5
Rampur Odisha, India 21°48N 83°58E 244 D6
Rampur Ut. P., India 28°44N 77°18E 120 A2
Rampur Ut. P., India 28°50N 79°5E 243 E8
Rampur Hat India 24°10N 87°50E 243 G12
Rampura India 24°30N 75°27E 242 G6
Ramrama Tola India 21°52N 79°55E 243 J8
Ramree I. Burma 19°0N 93°40E 241 F5
Ramsagar △ Bangla. 25°33N 88°37E 241 C2
Rāmsar Iran 36°53N 50°41E 247 B6
Ramsey I. of Man 54°20N 4°22W 168 C3
Ramsey Ill., U.S.A. 39°8N 89°7W 310 E7
Ramsey N.J., U.S.A. 41°4N 74°9W 313 E10
Ramsey L. Canada 47°13N 82°15W 298 C3
Ramsgate N.S.W., Australia 33°58S 151°8E 139 B1
Ramsgate Kent, U.K. 51°20N 1°25E 169 F9
Ramshai India 26°44N 88°51E 241 B2
Ramsjö Sweden 62°11N 15°37E 162 B9
Ramstein Germany 49°27N 7°32E 179 F3
Ramtek India 21°20N 79°15E 244 D4
Ramu Kenya 3°55N 41°10E 268 B5
Ramu → Papua N. G. 4°0S 144°41E 286 C3
Ramvik Sweden 62°49N 17°51E 162 B11
Ramville, Î. = Chancel, Î. Martinique 14°41N 60°53W 322 j
Rana Pratap Sagar Dam India 24°58N 75°38E 242 G6
Ranaghat India 23°15N 88°35E 243 H13
Ranahu Pakistan 25°55N 69°45E 242 G3
Ranai Indonesia 3°55N 108°22E 235 B3
Ranau Malaysia 6°2N 116°40E 235 A5
Ranau, Danau Indonesia 4°49S 103°55E 234 C2
Rancagua Chile 34°10S 70°50W 334 C1
Rance → France 48°34N 1°59W 172 D5
Rancharia Brazil 22°15S 50°55W 333 F1
Rancheria → Canada 60°13N 129°7W 296 A3
Ranchester U.S.A. 44°54N 107°10W 304 D10
Ranchi India 23°19N 85°27E 243 H11
Rancho Cordova U.S.A. 38°36N 121°18W 306 G5
Rancho Cucamonga U.S.A. 34°10N 117°30W 307 L9
Rancho Park U.S.A. 34°3N 118°26W 126 B2
Ranco, L. Chile 40°15S 72°25W 336 B2
Rand Australia 35°33S 146°32E 283 C7
Rand ✈ (QRA) S. Africa 26°14S 28°8E 123 B2
Randaberg Norway 59°1N 5°36E 164 E2
Randabygda Norway 61°51N 6°20E 164 C3
Randalls I. U.S.A. 40°47N 73°55W 142 B2
Randalstown U.K. 54°45N 6°19W 166 B5
Randan France 46°2N 3°21E 173 F10
Randazzo Italy 37°53N 14°57E 201 E7
Randburg S. Africa 26°5S 27°57E 123 A1
Rander India 21°14N 72°47E 244 D1
Randers Denmark 56°29N 10°1E 163 H4
Randers Fjord Denmark 56°37N 10°20E 163 H4
Randfontein S. Africa 26°8S 27°45E 271 C4
Randhart S. Africa 26°16S 28°7E 123 B2
Randle U.S.A. 46°32N 121°57W 306 D5
Randolph Mass., U.S.A. 42°10N 71°2W 313 D13
Randolph N.Y., U.S.A. 42°10N 78°59W 312 D6
Randolph Utah, U.S.A. 41°40N 111°11W 304 F8
Randolph Vt., U.S.A. 43°55N 72°40W 313 C12
Randpark Ridge S. Africa 26°6S 27°58E 123 A1
Randsburg U.S.A. 35°22N 117°39W 307 K9
Randsfjorden Norway 60°25N 10°24E 164 D7
Randsverk Norway 61°44N 9°3E 164 C6
Randwick Australia 33°54S 151°14E 139 B2
Råneälven → Sweden 65°50N 22°20E 160 D20
Ranenburg = Chaplygin Russia 53°15N 40°0E 188 F11
Ranfurly N.Z. 45°7S 170°6E 285 F5
Rangae Thailand 6°19N 101°44E 237 J3
Rangamati Bangla. 22°38N 92°12E 241 D4
Rangapara India 26°49N 92°39E 241 B4
Rangárvallasýsla Iceland 63°55N 20°0W 155 D7
Rangataua N.Z. 39°26S 175°28E 284 F4
Rangaunu B. N.Z. 34°51S 173°15E 284 A2
Range, The Zimbabwe 19°2S 31°2E 269 F3
Rangeley U.S.A. 44°58N 70°39W 313 B14
Rangeley L. U.S.A. 44°55N 70°43W 313 B14
Rangely U.S.A. 40°5N 108°48W 304 F9
Ranger U.S.A. 32°28N 98°41W 314 E5
Rangia India 26°28N 91°38E 241 B3
Rangiora N.Z. 43°19S 172°36E 285 D7
Rangiroa French Polynesia 15°10S 147°35W 289 f
Rangitaiki N.Z. 38°52S 176°24E 284 E5
Rangitaiki → N.Z. 37°54S 176°49E 284 D5
Rangitata → N.Z. 43°45S 171°15E 285 D6
Rangitikei → N.Z. 40°17S 175°15E 284 G4
Rangitoto ke te tonga = D'Urville I. N.Z. 40°50S 173°55E 285 A8
Rangitoto Ra. N.Z. 38°25S 175°35E 284 E4
Rangkasbitung Indonesia 6°21S 106°15E 234 D3
Rangoon = Yangôn Burma 16°45N 96°20E 241 G6
Rangoon → Burma 16°28N 96°40E 241 G6
Rangpur Bangla. 25°42N 89°22E 241 C2
Rangpur □ Bangla. 26°0N 89°0E 241 C2
Rangpuri India 28°32N 77°8E 120 B1
Rangsang Indonesia 1°20N 103°5E 237 M4
Rangwe Kenya 0°36S 34°35E 266 E3
Rani-ki-Vav India 23°51N 72°6E 242 H4
Ranibennur India 14°35N 75°30E 245 G2
Raniganj India 27°3N 82°13E 243 F9
Ranikhet India 29°39N 79°25E 243 E8
Ranippettai India 12°56N 79°23E 245 H4
Raniwara India 24°50N 72°10E 242 G5
Rāniyah Iraq 36°15N 44°53E 213 D11
Ranka India 23°59N 83°47E 243 H10
Ranken → Australia 20°31S 137°36E 280 C2
Rankin Ill., U.S.A. 40°28N 87°54W 311 D9
Rankin Tex., U.S.A. 31°13N 101°56W 314 F4
Rankin Inlet Canada 62°30N 93°0W 294 E13
Rankins Springs Australia 33°49S 146°14E 283 B7
Rankovicevo = Kraljevo Serbia 43°44N 20°41E 202 C4
Rankweil Austria 47°17N 9°39E 180 D2
Rannersdorf Austria 48°7N 16°27E 142 B2
Rannoch, L. U.K. 56°41N 4°20W 167 E4
Rannoch Moor U.K. 56°38N 4°48W 167 E4
Rano Kau Chile 27°11S 109°26W 330 b
Rano Raraku, Volcán Chile 27°7S 109°17W 330 b
Ranobe → Madag. 17°10S 44°8E 272 B1
Ranobe, Helodranon' i Madag. 23°3S 43°33E 272 C1
Ranohira Madag. 22°29S 45°24E 272 C2
Ranomafana Anosy, Madag. 24°34S 47°0E 272 C2
Ranomafana Atsinanana, Madag. 18°57S 48°50E 272 B2
Ranomafana △ Madag. 21°16S 47°25E 272 C2
Ranomena Madag. 23°25S 47°17E 272 C2
Ranon Vanuatu 16°8S 168°7E 287 F6
Ranong Thailand 9°56N 98°40E 237 H2
Ranongga Solomon Is. 8°5S 156°35E 287 M9
Ranotsara Nord Madag. 22°48S 46°36E 272 C2
Ranpur India 20°5N 85°20E 244 D7
Rānsa Iran 33°39N 48°18E 247 C6
Ransbèche Belgium 50°56N 4°27E 116 B2
Ransdorp Neths. 52°24N 5°0E 112 A2
Ransiki Indonesia 1°30S 134°10E 231 E8
Ransom U.S.A. 41°9N 88°39W 311 C8
Rantabe Madag. 15°42S 49°39E 272 B2
Rantau Indonesia 2°56S 115°9E 235 C5
Rantau Abang Malaysia 4°52N 103°24E 237 K4
Rantauanjang Kalimantan Tengah, Indonesia 1°22S 112°4E 235 C4
Rantaupanjang Kalimantan Timur, Indonesia 2°9N 117°25E 235 B5
Rantauprapat Indonesia 2°15N 99°50E 234 B1
Rantaupulut Indonesia 1°55S 112°12E 235 C4
Rantemario Indonesia 3°15S 119°57E 231 E5
Ranthambore △ India 26°10N 76°30E 242 F7
Rantoul U.S.A. 40°19N 88°9W 311 D8
Ranum Denmark 56°54N 9°14E 163 H3
Ranvad India 18°53N 72°55E 130 B2
Ranyah, W. → Si. Arabia 21°18N 43°20E 248 B3
Raohe China 46°47N 134°0E 220 A7
Raon l'Étape France 48°24N 6°50E 173 D13
Raoping China 23°42N 117°1E 229 F11
Raoui, Erg er Algeria 29°0N 2°0W 261 C4
Raoul I. Pac. Oc. 29°16S 177°54W 277 F15
Raoyang China 38°15N 115°45E 226 E8
Rap, Ko Thailand 9°19N 99°58E 237 b
Rapa French Polynesia 27°35S 144°20W 289 f
Rapa Nui = Pascua, I. de Chile 27°7S 109°23W 330 b
Rapallo Italy 44°21N 9°14E 198 D6
Rapar India 23°34N 70°38E 242 H4
Rāpch Iran 25°40N 59°15E 247 E8
Rapel, Lago Chile 34°20S 71°14W 334 C1
Raper, C. Canada 69°44N 67°6W 295 D18
Rapid City U.S.A. 44°5N 103°14W 308 C2
Rapid River U.S.A. 45°55N 86°58W 308 C10
Rapla Estonia 59°1N 24°52E 188 C3
Raposo Portugal 38°40N 9°11W 126 A1
Rapti → India 26°18N 83°41E 243 F10
Rapu Rapu I. Phil. 13°12N 124°9E 232 E5
Raqaba ez Zarqa → South Sudan 9°14N 29°44E 257 F2
Rāqūbah Libya 28°58N 19°2E 258 C3
Raquette → U.S.A. 45°0N 74°42W 313 B10
Raquette Lake U.S.A. 43°49N 74°40W 313 C10
Rara △ Nepal 29°30N 82°10E 243 E10
Raraka French Polynesia 16°10S 144°54W 289 f
Raroia French Polynesia 16°1S 142°27W 289 f
Rarotonga Cook Is. 21°30S 160°0W 289 h
Ra's al 'Ayn Syria 36°45N 40°12E 213 D9
Ras al Hadd Oman 22°30N 59°50E 249 B7
Ra's Al Khair Si. Arabia 27°27N 49°18E 247 E6
Ra's al Khaymah U.A.E. 25°50N 55°59E 247 E7
Ra's aṭ Tib Tunisia 37°1N 11°2E 258 A2
Râs el Ma Algeria 34°26N 0°50W 261 B4
Râs el Mâ Mali 16°35N 4°30W 262 B4
Râs el Oued Algeria 35°57N 5°2E 261 A6
Râs Ghârib Egypt 28°6N 33°18E 256 B3
Ras Kōh Pakistan 28°43N 64°55E 240 C2
Ra's Lānūf Libya 30°46N 18°11E 258 B3
Râs Muhammad △ Egypt 27°45N 34°16E 256 B3
Ra's Shamrah Syria 35°35N 35°45E 250 C6
Râs Sudr Egypt 29°40N 32°42E 256 B3
Rasa, Pta. B. Aires, Argentina 36°20S 56°41W 334 D4
Rasa, Pta. Río Negro, Argentina 40°50S 62°15W 336 B4
Rasa I. Phil. 9°13N 118°26E 233 G2
Rasca, Pta. de la Canary Is. 27°59N 16°41W 153 e1
Rășcani Moldova 47°58N 27°33E 183 C12
Rasdhoo Maldives 4°17N 72°58E 272 d
Rasdu Atoll Maldives 4°18N 72°58E 272 d
Raseiniai Lithuania 55°25N 23°5E 184 C10
Rashad Sudan 11°55N 31°0E 257 E3
Rashîd Egypt 31°21N 30°22E 256 H7
Rashîd, Masabb Egypt 31°22N 30°17E 256 H7
Rashin = Najin N. Korea 42°12N 130°15E 224 A5
Rashmi India 25°4N 74°22E 242 G6
Rasht Iran 37°20N 49°40E 213 D13
Rashtrapati Bhawan Delhi, India 120 c1
Rasi Salai Thailand 15°20N 104°9E 236 E5
Rasipuram India 11°30N 78°15E 245 J4
Raška Serbia 43°19N 20°39E 202 C4
Raskot Nepal 29°14N 81°39E 243 E9
Râsnov Romania 45°35N 25°27E 183 E10
Rasŏn □ N. Korea 42°21N 130°23E 224 A5
Rason L. Australia 28°45S 124°25E 279 E3
Rașova Romania 44°15N 27°55E 183 F12
Rasovo Bulgaria 43°42N 23°17E 202 C7
Rasra India 25°50N 83°50E 243 G10
Rasskazovo Russia 52°35N 41°50E 190 D5
Rast Romania 43°53N 23°16E 183 G8
Rastaala Finland 60°15N 24°47E 121 B1
Rastatt Germany 48°50N 8°11E 179 G4
Rastede Germany 53°15N 8°12E 178 B4
Rastenburg = Kętrzyn Poland 54°7N 21°22E 184 D8
Rastila Finland 60°12N 25°7E 121 B3
Răstolița Romania 46°59N 24°58E 183 D9
Rastyapino = Dzerzhinsk Russia 56°14N 43°30E 190 B6
Rasua Garhi Nepal 28°17N 85°23E 243 E11
Rasul Pakistan 32°42N 73°34E 242 C5
Raszków Poland 51°43N 17°40E 185 G4
Raszyn Poland 52°9N 20°54E 143 C1
Rat → Canada 49°35N 97°10W 297 D9
Rat Buri = Ratchaburi Thailand 13°30N 99°54E 236 F2
Rat I. = Hawadax U.S.A. 51°48N 178°15E 303 L2
Rat I. St. Lucia 14°2N 60°58W 323 m
Rat Islands U.S.A. 52°0N 178°0E 303 L2
Rat L. Canada 56°10N 99°40W 297 B9
Ratak Chain Pac. Oc. 1°0N 170°0E 288 G8
Rätan Sweden 62°29N 14°33E 162 B8
Ratangarh India 28°5N 74°35E 242 E6
Raṭāwī Iraq 30°38N 47°13E 246 D5
Ratcatchers L. Australia 32°38S 143°12E 282 B5
Ratchaburi Thailand 13°30N 99°54E 236 F2
Rath India 25°36N 79°37E 243 G8
Rath Luirc = Charleville Ireland 52°21N 8°40W 166 D3
Rathangan Ireland 53°14N 7°0W 166 C4
Rathbun L. U.S.A. 40°54N 93°5W 310 D4
Rathdrum Ireland 52°56N 6°14W 166 D5
Rathedaung Burma 20°29N 92°45E 241 E4
Rathenow Germany 52°37N 12°19E 178 C8
Rathkeale Ireland 52°32N 8°56W 166 D3
Rathlin I. U.K. 55°18N 6°14W 166 A5
Ratho U.K. 55°55N 3°23W 121 B1
Ratho Station U.K. 55°56N 3°23W 121 B1
Ratibor = Racibórz Poland 50°7N 18°18E 185 H5
Rätikon Austria 47°0N 9°55E 180 D2
Ratingen Germany 51°18N 6°52E 178 D2
Ratlam India 23°20N 75°0E 242 H6
Ratmanova, Ostrov Russia 65°46N 169°6W 300 B6
Ratnagiri India 16°57N 73°18E 244 F1
Ratnapura Sri Lanka 6°40N 80°20E 245 L5
Rato Portugal 38°43N 9°8W 126 A2
Ratodero Pakistan 27°48N 68°18E 242 F3
Raton U.S.A. 36°54N 104°24W 305 H11
Ratschach = Radeče Slovenia 46°5N 15°14E 199 B12
Rattaphum Thailand 7°8N 100°16E 237 J3
Ratten Austria 47°28N 15°44E 180 D8
Rattray Hd. U.K. 57°38N 1°50W 167 D7
Rättvik Sweden 60°52N 15°7E 162 D9
Ratz, Mt. Canada 57°23N 132°12W 296 B2
Ratzebuhr = Okonek Poland 53°32N 16°51E 184 E3
Ratzeburg Germany 53°40N 10°46E 178 B6
Rau Indonesia 0°34N 100°1E 234 B2
Raub Malaysia 3°47N 101°52E 237 L3
Rauch Argentina 36°45S 59°5W 334 D4
Raudales Mexico 17°27N 93°39W 319 D6
Raudeberg Norway 61°59N 5°7E 164 C2
Raufarhöfn Iceland 66°27N 15°57W 155 A11
Raufoss Norway 60°44N 10°37E 164 D7
Rauhellern Norway 60°15N 7°50E 164 D4
Raukumara Ra. N.Z. 38°5S 177°55E 284 E6
Raul Soares Brazil 20°5S 42°22W 333 F3
Rauma Finland 61°10N 21°30E 188 B1
Rauma → Norway 62°34N 7°43E 164 B4
Raumo = Rauma Finland 61°10N 21°30E 188 B1
Raung, Gunung Indonesia 8°8S 114°3E 231 J17
Raurkela India 22°14N 84°50E 243 H11
Rausu-Dake Japan 44°4N 145°7E 220 B12
Răut → Moldova 47°15N 29°9E 183 C14
Rava-Ruska Ukraine 50°15N 23°42E 185 H10
Rava Russkaya = Rava-Ruska Ukraine 50°15N 23°42E 185 H10
Ravahere French Polynesia 18°14S 142°9W 289 f
Ravalli U.S.A. 47°17N 114°11W 304 C6
Ravānsar Iran 34°43N 46°40E 213 E12
Ravanusa Italy 37°16N 13°58E 200 E6
Rāvar Iran 31°20N 56°51E 247 D8
Ravelston U.K. 55°57N 3°14W 121 B2
Ravena U.S.A. 42°28N 73°49W 313 D11
Ravenel U.S.A. 32°46N 80°15W 316 C9
Ravenna Italy 44°25N 12°12E 199 D9
Ravenna Ky., U.S.A. 37°41N 83°57W 311 G13
Ravenna Nebr., U.S.A. 41°1N 98°55W 308 E4
Ravenna Ohio, U.S.A. 41°9N 81°15W 312 E3
Ravensburg Germany 47°46N 9°36E 179 H5
Ravenshoe Australia 17°37S 145°29E 280 B4
Ravensthorpe Australia 33°35S 120°2E 279 F3
Ravenswood Queens., Australia 20°6S 146°54E 280 C4
Ravenswood W. Va., U.S.A. 38°57N 81°46W 309 F13
Ravensworth Australia 32°26S 151°4E 283 B9
Ravenwood U.S.A. 40°22N 94°41W 310 D2
Raver India 21°15N 76°2E 244 D3
Ravi → Pakistan 30°35N 71°49E 242 D4
Ravine Chaude Guadeloupe 16°14N 61°40W 322 e
Ravna Gora Croatia 45°24N 14°50E 199 C11
Ravna Reka Serbia 44°1N 21°35E 202 B5
Ravne na Koroškem Slovenia 46°36N 14°59E 199 B11
Rawa Mazowiecka Poland 51°46N 20°12E 185 G7
Rawaki Kiribati 3°43S 170°43W 277 A16
Rawalpindi Pakistan 33°38N 73°8E 242 C5
Rawamangun Indonesia 6°11S 106°52E 122 B2
Rawang Malaysia 3°20N 101°35E 237 L3
Rawene N.Z. 35°25S 173°32E 284 B2
Rawi, Ko Thailand 6°33N 99°14E 237 J2
Rawicz Poland 51°36N 16°52E 185 G3
Rawitsch = Rawicz Poland 51°36N 16°52E 185 G3
Rawka → Poland 52°9N 20°8E 185 F7
Rawlinna Australia 30°58S 125°28E 279 F4
Rawlins U.S.A. 41°47N 107°14W 304 F10
Rawlinson Ra. Australia 24°40S 128°30E 279 D4
Rawson Argentina 43°15S 65°5W 336 B3
Raxaul India 26°59N 84°51E 243 F11
Ray U.S.A. 48°21N 103°10W 308 A2
Ray, C. Canada 47°33N 59°15W 299 C8
Ray City U.S.A. 31°5N 83°11W 316 D6
Ray Mts. U.S.A. 66°0N 152°0W 303 D10
Raya Ring, Ko Thailand 8°18N 98°29E 237 a
Rayachoti India 14°4N 78°50E 245 G4
Rayadurg India 14°40N 76°50E 245 G3
Rayagada India 19°15N 83°20E 244 E6
Raychikhinsk Russia 49°46N 129°25E 215 E13
Rāyen Iran 29°34N 57°26E 247 D8
Rayle U.S.A. 33°48N 82°54W 316 B7
Rayleigh U.K. 51°36N 0°37E 169 F8
Raymond Alta., Canada 49°30N 112°35W 296 D6
Raymond Calif., U.S.A. 37°13N 119°54W 306 H7
Raymond Ill., U.S.A. 39°19N 89°34W 310 E7
Raymond N.H., U.S.A. 43°2N 71°11W 313 C13
Raymond Wash., U.S.A. 46°41N 123°44W 306 D3
Raymond Terrace Australia 32°45S 151°44E 283 B9
Raymondville U.S.A. 26°29N 97°47W 314 H6
Raymore Canada 51°25N 104°31W 297 C8
Rayners Lane U.K. 51°34N 0°21W 125 A1
Raynes Park U.K. 51°24N 0°12W 125 B2
Rayón Mexico 29°43N 110°35W 318 B2
Rayong Thailand 12°40N 101°20E 236 F3
Raypur India 22°28N 88°22E 124 C2
Raystown L. U.S.A. 40°25N 78°5W 312 F6
Raysūt Oman 16°56N 53°59E 249 C6
Raytown U.S.A. 39°1N 94°28W 310 E2
Rayville U.S.A. 32°29N 91°46W 314 E9
Raz, Pte. du France 48°2N 4°47W 172 D2
Razan Iran 35°23N 49°2E 213 E13
Ražana Serbia 44°6N 19°55E 202 B3
Ražanj Serbia 43°40N 21°31E 202 C5
Razāzah, Buḥayrat ar Iraq 32°40N 43°35E 213 F10
Razdelna Bulgaria 43°13N 27°41E 203 C11
Razdel'naya = Rozdilna Ukraine 46°50N 30°2E 183 D15
Razdolnoye Russia 43°30N 131°52E 220 C5
Razdolnoye Ukraine 45°46N 33°29E 189 K7
Razeh Iran 32°47N 48°9E 247 C6
Razgrad Bulgaria 43°33N 26°34E 203 C10
Razgrad □ Bulgaria 43°33N 26°34E 203 C10
Razim, Lacul Romania 44°50N 29°0E 183 F14
Razlog Bulgaria 41°53N 23°28E 202 E7
Razmak Pakistan 32°45N 69°50E 242 C3
Rāznas Ezers △ Latvia 56°30N 27°30E 188 D4
Razzaza, L. = Razāzah, Buḥayrat ar Iraq 32°40N 43°35E 213 F10
Re, Cu Lao Vietnam 15°22N 109°8E 236 E7
Ré, Î. de France 46°12N 1°30W 174 B2
Reach Falls Jamaica 18°2N 76°18W 320 a
Reading Reading, U.K. 51°27N 0°58W 169 F7
Reading Mich., U.S.A. 41°50N 84°45W 311 C12
Reading Ohio, U.S.A. 39°13N 84°26W 311 E12
Reading Pa., U.S.A. 40°20N 75°56W 313 F9
Reading □ U.K. 51°27N 0°58W 169 F7
Real, Cordillera Bolivia 17°0S 67°10W 330 D4
Real Felipe, Fuerte Peru 12°4S 77°9W 124 B2
Realejo Alto Canary Is. 28°22N 16°34W 153 e1
Realicó Argentina 35°0S 64°15W 334 D3
Réalmont France 43°48N 2°10E 174 E6
Ream Cambodia 10°34N 103°39E 237 G4
Ream △ Cambodia 10°30N 103°45E 237 G4
Reams, L. U.S.A. 28°26N 81°34W 133 B1
Réao French Polynesia 18°31S 136°23W 289 f
Reay Forest U.K. 58°22N 4°55W 167 C4
Rebais France 48°50N 3°10E 173 D10
Rebecca, L. Australia 30°0S 122°15E 279 F3
Rebi Indonesia 6°23S 134°7E 231 F8
Rebiana Libya 24°12N 22°10E 258 D4
Rebiana, Sahrâ' Libya 24°30N 21°0E 258 D3
Reboly Russia 63°49N 30°47E 160 E24
Rebun-Tō Japan 45°23N 141°2E 220 B10
Recanati Italy 43°24N 13°32E 199 E10
Recaş Romania 45°46N 21°30E 182 E6
Recco Italy 44°22N 9°9E 198 D6
Recherche, Arch. of the Australia 34°15S 122°50E 279 F3
Rechna Doab Pakistan 31°35N 73°30E 242 D5
Rechytsa Belarus 52°21N 30°24E 177 B16
Recife Brazil 8°0S 35°0W 332 C5
Recife Seychelles 4°36S 55°42E 272 c
Recklinghausen Germany 51°37N 7°12E 178 D3
Reckong Peo India 31°32N 78°16E 242 D8
Reclining Buddha = Wat Pho Bangkok, Thailand 113 b1
Recoleta B. Aires, Argentina 34°36S 58°24W 117 B2
Recoleta Santiago, Chile 33°25S 70°40W 137 B2
Reconquista Argentina 29°10S 59°45W 334 B4
Recreio Brazil 8°0S 58°25W 331 B6
Recreo Argentina 29°25S 65°10W 334 B2
Recuay Peru 9°43S 77°28W 330 B2
Recz Poland 53°16N 15°31E 185 E2
Red = Hong → Asia 20°16N 106°34E 236 B5
Red → U.S.A. 31°1N 91°45W 314 F9
Red Bank U.S.A. 40°21N 74°5W 313 F10
Red Bay Canada 51°44N 56°25W 299 B8
Red Bluff U.S.A. 40°11N 122°15W 304 F2
Red Bluff Res. U.S.A. 31°54N 103°55W 305 L12
Red Bud U.S.A. 38°13N 89°59W 310 F7
Red Cliffs Australia 34°19S 142°11E 282 C5
Red Cloud U.S.A. 40°5N 98°32W 308 E4
Red Creek U.S.A. 43°14N 76°45W 313 C8
Red Deer Canada 52°20N 113°50W 296 C6
Red Deer → Alta., Canada 50°58N 110°0W 297 C7
Red Deer → Man., Canada 52°53N 101°1W 297 C8
Red Deer L. Canada 52°55N 101°20W 297 C8
Red Devil U.S.A. 61°46N 157°19W 303 F8
Red Fort = Lal Qila Delhi, India 120 a3
Red Hook U.S.A. 41°55N 73°53W 313 E11
Red Indian L. Canada 48°35N 57°0W 299 C8
Red L. Canada 51°3N 93°49W 297 C10
Red Lake Canada 51°3N 93°49W 297 C10
Red Lake Falls U.S.A. 47°53N 96°16W 308 B5
Red Lake Road Canada 49°59N 93°25W 297 C10
Red Lodge U.S.A. 45°11N 109°15W 304 D9
Red Mountain U.S.A. 35°37N 117°38W 307 K9
Red Oak U.S.A. 41°1N 95°14W 308 E6
Red River of the North → N. Amer. 49°0N 97°15W 308 A5
Red Rock Canada 48°55N 88°15W 298 C2
Red Rock, L. U.S.A. 41°22N 92°59W 310 C3
Red Rocks Pt. Australia 32°13S 127°32E 279 F4
Red Sea Asia 25°0N 36°0E 238 E3
Red Slate Mt. U.S.A. 37°31N 118°52W 306 H8
Red Square Moscow, Russia 129 b2
Red Sucker L. Canada 54°9N 93°40W 298 B1
Red Tower Pass = Turnu Roşu, P. Romania 45°33N 24°17E 183 E9
Red Volta → Africa 10°34N 0°30W 263 C4
Red Wing U.S.A. 44°34N 92°31W 308 C7
Reda Poland 54°40N 18°19E 184 D5
Redang, Pulau Malaysia 5°49N 103°2E 237 K4
Redange Lux. 49°46N 5°52E 170 E5
Redbridge □ U.K. 51°35N 0°7E 125 A4
Redcar U.K. 54°37N 1°4W 168 C6
Redcar & Cleveland □ U.K. 54°29N 1°0W 168 C7
Redcliff Canada 50°10N 110°50W 304 A8
Redcliffe Australia 27°12S 153°6E 281 D5
Redcliffe, Mt. Australia 28°30S 121°30E 279 E3
Reddersburg S. Africa 29°41S 26°10E 270 C4
Reddick Fla., U.S.A. 29°22N 82°12W 317 F7
Reddick Ill., U.S.A. 41°6N 88°15W 311 C8
Redding Calif., U.S.A. 40°35N 122°24W 304 F2
Redding Iowa, U.S.A. 40°36N 94°23W 310 D2
Redditch U.K. 52°18N 1°55W 169 E6
Redenção Brazil 4°13S 38°43W 332 B4
Redentore, Chiesa del Venice, Italy 142 c2
Redfern Australia 33°54S 151°12E 139 B2
Redfield U.S.A. 44°53N 98°31W 308 C4
Redford U.S.A. 44°38N 73°48W 313 B11
Redhead Trin. & Tob. 10°44N 60°58W 323 t
Redkey U.S.A. 40°21N 85°9W 311 D11
Redkino Russia 56°39N 36°16E 188 D9
Redlands U.S.A. 34°4N 117°11W 307 M9
Redmond Oreg., U.S.A. 44°17N 121°11W 304 D3
Redmond Wash., U.S.A. 47°40N 122°7W 306 C4
Redon France 47°40N 2°6W 172 E4
Redonda Antigua & B. 16°58N 62°19W 321 C7
Redonda, Pta. Chile 27°10S 109°22W 330 b
Redondela Spain 42°15N 8°38W 194 C2
Redondo Portugal 38°39N 7°37W 195 G3
Redondo Beach U.S.A. 33°50N 118°23W 307 M8
Redoubt Volcano U.S.A. 60°29N 152°45W 303 F9
Redpath Sugar Museum Toronto, Canada 141 c3
Redruth U.K. 50°14N 5°14W 169 G2
Redvers Canada 49°35N 101°40W 297 D8
Redwater Canada 53°55N 113°6W 296 C6
Redwood U.S.A. 44°18N 75°48W 313 B9
Redwood △ U.S.A. 41°40N 124°5W 304 F1
Redwood City U.S.A. 37°30N 122°15W 306 H4
Redwood Falls U.S.A. 44°32N 95°7W 308 C6
Ree, L. Ireland 53°35N 8°0W 166 C3
Reed City U.S.A. 43°53N 85°31W 309 D11
Reed L. Canada 54°38N 100°30W 297 C8
Reedley U.S.A. 36°36N 119°27W 306 J7
Reedsburg U.S.A. 43°32N 90°0W 308 D8
Reedsport U.S.A. 43°42N 124°6W 304 E1
Reedsville U.S.A. 40°39N 77°35W 312 F7
Reedy Creek Australia 36°58S 140°2E 282 D4
Reef Is. Pac. Oc. 10°15S 166°10E 277 C12
Reefton N.Z. 42°6S 171°51E 285 C6
Rees Germany 51°46N 6°24E 178 D2
Reese → U.S.A. 40°48N 117°4W 304 F5
Reetz = Recz Poland 53°16N 15°31E 185 E2
Refahiye Turkey 39°54N 38°47E 213 C8
Reflecting Pool Washington, D.C., U.S.A. 143 b1
Refshaleøen Denmark 55°41N 12°36E 118 A3
Reftele Sweden 57°11N 13°35E 163 G7
Refugio U.S.A. 28°18N 97°17W 314 G6
Rega → Poland 54°10N 15°18E 184 D2
Regalbuto Italy 37°39N 14°38E 201 E7
Regana, C. de Spain 39°25N 2°43E 206 B3
Regar = Tursunzoda Tajikistan 38°30N 68°14E 217 E7
Regen Germany 48°58N 13°8E 179 G9
Regen → Germany 49°1N 12°6E 179 F8
Regeneração Brazil 6°15S 42°41W 332 C3
Regensburg Germany 49°1N 12°6E 179 F8
Regenstauf Germany 49°7N 12°8E 179 F8
Regents Park Gauteng, S. Africa 26°14S 28°3E 123 B2
Regent's Park London, U.K. 125 a2
Regenwalde = Resko Poland 53°47N 15°25E 184 E2
Reggâne = Zaouiet Reggâne Algeria 26°32N 0°3E 261 C5
Reggello Italy 43°41N 11°32E 199 E8
Réggio di Calábria Italy 38°6N 15°39E 201 D8
Réggio nell'Emília Italy 44°43N 10°36E 198 D7
Reghin Romania 46°46N 24°42E 183 D9
Regina Sask., Canada 50°27N 104°35W 297 C8
Regina Fr. Guiana 4°19N 52°8W 329 C7
Regina Beach Canada 50°47N 105°0W 297 C8
Registro Brazil 24°29S 47°49W 335 A6
Rego Park U.S.A. 40°43N 73°51W 132 B2
Reguengos de Monsaraz Portugal 38°25N 7°32W 195 G3
Rehar → India 23°55N 82°40E 243 H10
Rehli India 23°38N 79°5E 243 H8
Rehoboth Namibia 23°15S 17°4E 270 B2
Rehovot Israel 31°54N 34°48E 251 G5
Rei, Costa Italy 39°15N 9°40E 200 C2
Reibell = Ksar Chellala Algeria 35°13N 2°19E 261 A5
Reichenau = Rychnov nad Kněžnou Czechia 50°10N 16°17E 181 A9
Reichenbach = Dzierżoniów Poland 50°45N 16°39E 185 H3
Reichenbach Germany 50°37N 12°17E 178 E8
Reichenberg = Liberec Czechia 50°47N 15°7E 180 A8
Reichshof = Rzeszów Poland 50°5N 21°58E 185 H8
Reichstag Berlin, Germany 115 a3
Reid Australia 30°49S 128°26E 279 F4
Reidsville Ga., U.S.A. 32°6N 82°7W 316 C7
Reidsville N.C., U.S.A. 36°21N 79°40W 315 C15
Reifnig = Ribnica Slovenia 45°45N 14°45E 199 C11
Reigate U.K. 51°14N 0°12W 169 F7
Reillo Spain 39°54N 1°53W 196 F3
Reims France 49°15N 4°1E 173 C11
Reina Adelaida, Arch. Chile 52°20S 74°0W 336 D2
Reina Beatrix Int. ✈ (AUA) Aruba 12°30N 70°1W 322 f
Reina Sofía, Centro de Arte Madrid, Spain 127 c3
Reina Sofía, Tenerife ✈ (TFS) Canary Is. 28°3N 16°33W 153 e1
Reinbeck U.S.A. 42°19N 92°36W 310 B4
Reinbek Germany 53°30N 10°16E 178 B6
Reindeer → Canada 55°36N 103°11W 297 B8
Reindeer I. Canada 52°30N 98°0W 297 C9
Reindeer L. Canada 57°15N 102°15W 297 B8
Reinga, C. N.Z. 34°25S 172°43E 284 A1
Reinheimen △ Norway 62°10N 7°45E 164 B4
Reinickendorf Germany 52°34N 13°22E 115 A3
Reinosa Spain 43°2N 4°15W 194 B6
Reinsvoll Norway 60°40N 10°38E 164 D7
Reitan Norway 62°49N 11°22E 164 B8
Reitz S. Africa 27°48S 28°29E 271 C4
Reivilo S. Africa 27°36S 24°8E 270 C3
Rejaf South Sudan 4°45N 31°35E 257 G3
Rejmyre Sweden 58°50N 15°55E 163 F9
Rejowiec Fabryczny Poland 51°5N 23°17E 185 G10
Reka → Slovenia 45°40N 14°0E 199 C11
Rekohu = Chatham I. N.Z. 43°50S 176°20W 285 a
Rekola Finland 60°19N 25°4E 121 B3
Rekovac Serbia 43°51N 21°3E 202 C5
Relámpago, Pta. Venezuela 11°3N 64°23W 329 a
Reliance Canada 63°0N 109°20W 297 A7
Relizane Algeria 35°44N 0°31E 261 A5
Relizane □ Algeria 35°45N 0°55E 261 A5
Remad, Oued → Algeria 33°28N 1°20W 261 B4
Rémalard France 48°26N 0°47E 172 D7
Remanso Brazil 9°41S 42°4W 332 C3
Remarkable, Mt. Australia 32°48S 138°10E 282 B3
Remarkables, The N.Z. 45°10S 168°50E 285 F3
Rembang Indonesia 6°42S 111°21E 235 D4
Rembau Malaysia 2°35N 102°6E 237 L4
Rembert U.S.A. 34°6N 80°32W 316 A9
Rembertów Poland 52°15N 21°9E 143 B2
Rembrandthuis Amsterdam, Neths. 112 b3
Rembrandtpark Neths. 52°22N 4°51E 112 A2
Rembrandtplein Amsterdam, Neths. 112 b2
Remchi Algeria 35°2N 1°26W 261 A4
Remedios Colombia 7°2N 74°41W 328 B3
Remedios Panama 8°15N 81°50W 320 E3
Remedios de Escalada Argentina 34°43S 58°24W 117 C2
Remeshk Iran 26°55N 58°50E 247 E8
Remetea Romania 46°45N 25°29E 183 D10
Remich Lux. 49°32N 6°22E 170 E6
Remington U.S.A. 40°46N 87°9W 311 D9
Rémire Fr. Guiana 4°53N 52°17W 329 C7
Remiremont France 48°2N 6°36E 173 D13
Remo Ethiopia 6°48N 41°20E 257 F5
Rémola, Estany del Spain 41°16N 2°4E 114 B1
Remontnoye Russia 46°34N 43°37E 191 G6
Remoulins France 43°55N 4°35E 175 E8
Rempang Indonesia 0°51N 104°10E 234 B2
Rempart → Mauritius 20°19S 57°22E 272 e
Remparts → Réunion 21°22S 55°37E 272 f
Remscheid Germany 51°11N 7°12E 178 D3
Ren Xian China 37°8N 114°40E 226 F8
Rena Norway 61°8N 11°20E 164 C8
Rena → Norway 61°8N 11°23E 164 C8
Renascença Brazil 3°50S 66°21W 328 D4
Renca Chile 33°24S 70°42W 137 B1
Rend Lake U.S.A. 38°2N 88°58W 310 F8
Rendang Indonesia 8°26S 115°25E 231 J18
Rende Italy 39°20N 16°11E 201 C9
Rendezvous Barbados 13°4N 59°35W 323 r
Rendina Greece 39°4N 21°58E 204 B3
Rendova Solomon Is. 8°33S 157°17E 287 M9
Rendsburg Germany 54°17N 9°39E 178 A5
René-Levasseur, Î. Canada 51°20N 68°40W 299 B6
Renfrew Canada 45°30N 76°40W 313 A8
Renfrewshire □ U.K. 55°49N 4°38W 167 F4
Rengat Indonesia 0°30S 102°45E 234 C2
Rengo Chile 34°24S 70°50W 334 C1
Renhua China 25°5N 113°40E 229 E9
Renhuai China 27°48N 106°24E 228 D6
Reni = Taranagar India 28°43N 74°50E 242 E6
Reni Ukraine 45°28N 28°15E 183 E13
Renigunta India 13°38N 79°30E 245 H4
Renk South Sudan 11°50N 32°50E 257 E3
Renland Greenland 71°10N 26°30W 154 C8
Renmark Australia 34°11S 140°43E 282 C4
Rennebu Norway 62°52N 9°49E 164 B6
Rennell Solomon Is. 11°40S 160°10E 287 N11
Rennell Sd. Canada 53°23N 132°35W 296 C2
Rennemoulin France 48°50N 2°2E 134 A1
Renner Springs Australia 18°20S 133°47E 280 B1
Rennes France 48°7N 1°41W 172 D5
Rennick Glacier Antarctica 70°30S 161°45E 151 D11
Rennie L. Canada 61°32N 105°35W 297 A7
Reno U.S.A. 39°31N 119°48W 306 F7
Reno → Italy 44°38N 12°16E 199 D9
Renovo U.S.A. 41°20N 77°45W 312 E7
Renqiu China 38°43N 116°5E 226 E9
Rens Denmark 54°54N 9°5E 163 K3
Renshou China 29°59N 104°9E 228 C5
Rensselaer Ind., U.S.A. 40°57N 87°9W 311 D9
Rensselaer N.Y., U.S.A. 42°38N 73°45W 313 D11
Renton U.S.A. 47°28N 122°12W 306 C4
Renukoot India 24°12N 83°2E 243 G10
Renwick N.Z. 41°30S 173°51E 285 B8
Renwick Gallery Washington, D.C., U.S.A. 143 a1
Renwu = Jenwu Taiwan 22°42N 120°20E 225 D2
Réo Burkina Faso 12°28N 2°35W 262 C4
Reocín = Puente San Miguel Spain 43°21N 4°5W 194 B6
Reotipur India 25°33N 83°45E 243 G10
Repalle India 16°2N 80°45E 245 F5
Répcelak Hungary 47°24N 17°1E 182 C2
Řeporyje Czechia 50°1N 14°18E 135 B1
Reppen = Rzepin Poland 52°20N 14°49E 185 F1
Republic Mo., U.S.A. 37°7N 93°29W 308 G7
Republic Wash., U.S.A. 48°39N 118°44W 304 B4
Republican → U.S.A. 39°4N 96°48W 308 F5
Republiek Suriname 5°30N 55°13W 329 B6
Republika Srpska □ Bos.-H. 44°56N 17°11E 199 D14
République, Place de la Paris, France 134 b5
Repulse B. Australia 20°35S 148°46E 280 b
Repulse Bay Nunavut, Canada 66°30N 86°30W 295 D14
Repulse Bay Hong Kong, China 22°13N 114°10E 122 B3
Repy Czechia 50°4N 14°17E 135 B1
Requena Peru 5°5S 73°52W 330 B3
Requena Spain 39°30N 1°4W 197 F3
Requin Bay Grenada 12°2N 61°39W 323 q
Réquista France 44°1N 2°32E 174 D6
Reşadiye Muğla, Turkey 36°45N 27°39E 205 E9
Reşadiye Tokat, Turkey 40°23N 37°20E 212 B7

Rodez France 44°21N 2°33E 174 D6
Ródhos = Rhodes Greece 36°15N 28°10E 206 E12
Rodi Gargánico Italy 41°55N 15°53E 199 G12
Rodia Greece 35°22N 25°1E 207 E6
Rodīna Kazakhstan 50°16N 66°53E 217 B7
Rodīna Romania 47°25N 24°50E 183 C9
Rodna ◎ Australia 23°45S 132°4E 278 D5
Rodnei, Munții Romania 47°35N 24°35E 183 C9
Rodney Canada 42°34N 81°41W 312 D3
Rodney, C. N.Z. 36°17S 174°50E 284 C3
Rodney B. St. Lucia 14°5N 60°58W 323 m
Rodniki Russia 57°7N 41°47E 190 B5
Rodolivos Greece 40°55N 24°0E 202 F7
Rodonit, Kepi i Albania 41°35N 19°27E 202 E3
Rodopi Greece 41°5N 25°30E 203 E9
Rodopi Planina Bulgaria 41°40N 24°20E 203 E8
Rodopos Greece 35°34N 23°45E 207 E4
Rødovre Denmark 55°40N 12°26E 118 A2
Rodrigo de Freitas, L. Brazil 22°58S 43°12W 135 B1
Rodrigues Ind. Oc. 19°45S 63°20E 273 F5
Roe → U.K. 55°6N 6°59W 166 A5
Roebling U.S.A. 40°7N 74°47W 313 F10
Roebourne Australia 20°44S 117°9E 278 D2
Roebuck B. Australia 18°5S 122°20E 278 C3
Roebuck Roadhouse Australia 17°59S 122°36E 278 C3
Roehampton U.K. 51°27N 0°15W 125 B2
Roermond Neths. 51°12N 6°0E 170 C6
Roes Welcome Sd. Canada 65°0N 87°0W 295 E14
Roeselare Belgium 50°57N 3°7E 170 D3
Rogachev = Ragachow Belarus 53°8N 30°5E 177 B16
Rogačica Serbia 44°4N 19°40E 202 B3
Rogagua, L. Bolivia 13°43S 66°50W 330 C4
Rogaland ☐ Norway 59°12N 6°20E 164 E3
Rogaška Slatina Slovenia 46°15N 15°42E 199 B12
Rogatec Slovenia 46°15N 15°46E 199 B12
Rogatica Bos.-H. 43°47N 19°0E 182 G4
Rogatyn Ukraine 49°24N 24°36E 177 D13
Rogen Sweden 62°20N 12°20E 162 B6
Rogers U.S.A. 36°20N 94°7W 314 C7
Rogers Centre Toronto, Canada 141 c1
Rogers City U.S.A. 45°25N 83°49W 309 C12
Rogers Park U.S.A. 42°0N 87°40W 119 A3
Rogersville Canada 46°44N 65°26W 299 C6
Roggan → Canada 54°24N 79°25W 298 B4
Roggan L. Canada 54°8N 77°50W 298 B4
Roggeveen Basin Pac. Oc. 31°30S 95°30W 289 L18
Roggeveldberge S. Africa 32°10S 20°10E 270 D3
Roggiano Gravina Italy 39°37N 16°9E 201 C9
Rogliano Haute-Corse, France 42°57N 9°30E 175 F13
Rogliano Italy 39°10N 16°19E 201 C9
Rogoaguado, L. Bolivia 13°0S 65°30W 331 C4
Rogojampi Indonesia 8°19S 114°17E 231 J17
Rogoźno Poland 52°45N 16°59E 185 F3
Rogue → U.S.A. 42°26N 124°26W 304 E1
Roha India 18°26N 73°7E 244 E1
Rohan France 48°4N 2°45W 172 D4
Rohnert Park U.S.A. 38°16N 122°40W 306 G4
Rohri Pakistan 27°45N 68°51E 242 F3
Rohri Canal Pakistan 26°15N 68°27E 242 F3
Rohtak India 28°55N 76°43E 242 E7
Rohtisch-Sauerbrunn = Rogaška Slatina Slovenia 46°15N 15°42E 199 B12
Roi Et Thailand 16°4N 103°40E 236 D4
Roi-Georges, Îs. du French Polynesia 14°32S 145°8W 289 f
Roihuvuori Finland 60°11N 25°2E 121 B3
Roing India 28°9N 95°51E 241 A5
Roissy-en-Brie France 48°48N 2°39E 134 B4
Roja Latvia 57°29N 22°43E 184 A9
Rojas Argentina 34°10S 60°45W 334 C3
Rojište Romania 44°4N 23°56E 183 F8
Rojo, C. Mexico 21°33N 97°20W 319 C5
Rokan → Indonesia 2°0N 100°50E 234 B2
Rokel → S. Leone 8°30N 12°48W 262 D2
Rokin Amsterdam, Neths. 112 b2
Rokiškis Lithuania 55°55N 25°35E 188 E3
Rokua △ Finland 64°30N 26°15E 160 D22
Rokycany Czechia 49°43N 13°35E 180 B6
Rokytka → Czechia 50°6N 14°27E 135 B3
Roland Garros Paris, France 48°51N 2°15E 134 A2
Rolândia Brazil 23°18S 51°23W 335 A5
Røldal Norway 59°47N 6°50E 164 E3
Rolfe U.S.A. 42°49N 94°31W 310 B2
Rolla Mo., U.S.A. 37°57N 91°46W 310 G5
Rolla N. Dak., U.S.A. 48°52N 99°37W 308 A4
Rolleston Queens., Australia 24°28S 148°35E 280 C4
Rolleston N.Z. 43°35S 172°24E 285 D7
Rolling Fork → U.S.A. 37°55N 85°50W 311 G11
Rollingstone Australia 19°2S 146°24E 280 B4
Rom Vest-Agder, Norway 58°8N 7°5E 164 F4
Rom South Sudan 9°54N 32°16E 257 F3
Roma Queens., Australia 26°32S 148°49E 281 D4
Roma Italy 41°54N 12°28E 136 B1
Roma Sweden 57°32N 18°26E 163 G12
Roma, Piazzale Venice, Italy 142 b2
Roma Fiumicino ✈ (FCO) Italy 41°48N 12°15E 199 G9
Roma-Los Saenz U.S.A. 26°24N 99°1W 314 H5
Roma Urbe ✈ Italy 41°57N 12°30E 136 B2
Római-Fürdő Hungary 47°34N 19°4E 117 A2
Romain, C. U.S.A. 33°0N 79°22W 315 E15
Romaine → Canada 50°18N 63°47W 299 B7
Romainville France 48°52N 2°26E 134 A3
Roman Bulgaria 43°8N 23°57E 202 C7
Roman Romania 46°57N 26°55E 183 D11
Roman Forum = Foro Romano Rome, Italy 136 c3
Roman-Kosh, Gora Ukraine 44°37N 34°15E 189 K8
Romanche → France 45°5N 5°43E 175 C9
Romang Indonesia 7°30S 127°20E 231 F7
Români Egypt 30°59N 32°38E 251 H3
Romania ■ Europe 46°0N 25°0E 183 D10
Romanija Bos.-H. 43°50N 18°45E 182 G3
Romano, C. U.S.A. 25°51N 81°41W 317 K8
Romano, Cayo Cuba 22°0N 77°30W 320 B4
Romano Banco Italy 45°25N 9°6E 128 B1
Romanov-Borisoglebsk = Tutayev Russia 57°53N 39°32E 188 D10
Romanovka = Basarabeasca Moldova 46°21N 28°58E 183 D13
Romanovna-Murmane = Murmansk Russia 68°57N 33°10E 160 B25
Romanovsk = Kropotkin Russia 45°28N 40°28E 191 H5
Romanovskiy Khutor = Kropotkin Russia 45°28N 40°28E 191 H5
Romans-sur-Isère France 45°3N 5°3E 175 C9
Romanshorn Switz. 47°33N 9°22E 179 H5
Romanzof C. U.S.A. 61°49N 166°6W 303 F6
Rombari South Sudan 4°31N 31°2E 257 G3
Romblon Phil. 12°33N 122°17E 232 E4
Romblon ☐ Phil. 12°30N 122°15E 232 E4
Romblon Pass. Phil. 12°27N 122°12E 232 E4
Rome = Roma Italy 41°54N 12°28E 136 B1
Rome Ga., U.S.A. 34°15N 85°10W 315 D12
Rome N.Y., U.S.A. 43°13N 75°27W 313 C9
Rome Pa., U.S.A. 41°51N 76°21W 313 E8
Romema Israel 31°48N 35°12E 123 B2
Romeoville U.S.A. 41°39N 88°3W 311 C8
Rometta Italy 38°10N 15°25E 201 D8
Romford U.K. 51°34N 0°11E 125 A5
Romilly-sur-Seine France 48°31N 3°44E 173 D10
Romiton Uzbekistan 39°56N 64°23E 216 E6
Rommani Morocco 33°31N 6°40W 260 B3
Romney U.S.A. 39°21N 78°45W 309 F14
Romney Marsh U.K. 51°2N 0°54E 169 F8
Romny Ukraine 50°48N 33°28E 189 G7
Rømø Denmark 55°10N 8°30E 163 J2
Romodan Ukraine 49°55N 33°15E 189 G7
Romodanovo Russia 54°26N 45°23E 190 C7
Romont Switz. 46°42N 6°54E 179 J2
Romorantin-Lanthenay France 47°21N 1°45E 173 E8
Rompin → Malaysia 2°49N 103°29E 237 L4
Romsdalen Norway 62°25N 7°52E 164 B4
Romsdalsfjorden Norway 62°38N 7°20E 164 B4
Romsey U.K. 51°0N 1°29W 169 G6
Ron India 15°40N 75°44E 245 G2
Ron Vietnam 17°53N 106°27E 236 D6
Rona U.K. 57°34N 5°59W 167 D3
Ronald Reagan Nat. Washington ✈ (DCA) U.S.A. 38°51N 77°2W 143 B2
Ronan U.S.A. 47°32N 114°6W 304 C6
Roncador, Cayos Caribbean 13°32N 80°4W 320 D3
Roncador, Serra do Brazil 12°30S 52°30W 333 D1
Ronciglione Italy 42°17N 12°13E 199 F9
Ronco → Italy 44°24N 12°12E 199 D9
Ronda Spain 36°46N 5°12W 195 J5
Ronda, Serranía de Spain 36°44N 5°3W 195 J5
Rondane Norway 61°57N 9°50E 164 C6
Rondane △ Norway 61°55N 9°44E 164 C6
Ronde, Pt. Dominica 15°33N 61°29W 323 k
Ronde I. Grenada 12°29N 61°36W 323 q
Rondebosch S. Africa 33°58S 18°28E 118 A1
Rondón Colombia 6°17N 71°6W 328 B3
Rondônia Brazil 10°52S 61°57W 331 C5
Rondônia ☐ Brazil 11°0S 63°0W 331 C5
Rondonópolis Brazil 16°28S 54°38W 331 D7
Rondslottet Norway 61°55N 9°45E 164 C6
Rondu Pakistan 35°32N 75°10E 243 B6
Rong, Koh Cambodia 10°45N 103°15E 237 G4
Rong Jiang → China 24°35N 109°20E 228 E7
Rong Xian China 22°50N 110°31E 229 F8
Rong'an China 25°14N 109°22E 228 E7
Rongchang China 29°20N 105°32E 228 C5
Rongcheng China 37°9N 122°23E 227 F12
Ronge, L. la Canada 55°6N 105°17W 297 B7
Rongjiang China 25°57N 108°28E 228 E7
Rongotea N.Z. 40°19S 175°25E 284 G4
Rongshui China 25°5N 109°12E 228 E7
Rongxian China 29°23N 104°22E 228 C5
Rønne Denmark 55°6N 14°43E 163 J8
Ronne Ice Shelf Antarctica 77°30S 60°0W 151 D18
Ronneby Sweden 56°12N 15°17E 163 H9
Ronnebyån → Sweden 56°11N 15°18E 163 H9
Rönneshytta Sweden 58°56N 15°2E 163 F9
Ronsard, C. Australia 24°46S 113°10E 279 D1
Ronse Belgium 50°45N 3°35E 170 D3
Ronuro → Brazil 11°56S 53°33W 331 C7
Roodepoort S. Africa 26°11S 27°54E 271 C4
Roodhouse U.S.A. 39°29N 90°24W 310 E6
Roof Butte U.S.A. 36°28N 109°5W 305 H9
Rooiboklaagte → Namibia 20°50S 21°0E 270 B3
Rooniu, Mt. Tahiti 17°49S 149°12W 289 e
Roopville U.S.A. 33°27N 85°8W 316 B4
Roorkee India 29°52N 77°59E 242 E7
Roosendaal Neths. 51°32N 4°29E 170 C4
Roosevelt U.S.A. 40°18N 109°59W 304 F9
Roosevelt → Brazil 7°35S 60°20W 331 B5
Roosevelt, Mt. Canada 58°26N 125°20W 296 B3
Roosevelt I. Antarctica 79°30S 162°0W 151 D12
Roosevelt I. New York, U.S.A. 132 c3
Ropczyce Poland 50°4N 21°38E 185 H8
Roper → Australia 14°43S 135°27E 280 A2
Roper Bar Australia 14°44S 134°44E 280 A1
Roper River = St. Vidgeon's ◎ Australia 14°47S 134°53E 280 A1
Roppongi Tokyo, Japan 140 c3
Roque Pérez Argentina 35°25S 59°24W 334 D4
Roquefort France 44°2N 0°20W 174 D3
Roquemaure France 44°3N 4°48E 175 D8
Roquetas de Mar Spain 36°46N 2°36W 197 J2
Roquetes Spain 40°50N 0°30E 196 E5
Roquevaire France 43°20N 5°36E 175 E9
Roraima ☐ Brazil 2°0N 61°30W 329 C5
Roraima, Mt. Venezuela 5°10N 60°40W 329 B5
Røros Norway 62°35N 11°23E 164 B8
Rorschach Switz. 47°28N 9°28E 179 H5
Ros Comáin = Roscommon Ireland 53°38N 8°11W 166 C3
Ros Mhic Thriúin = New Ross Ireland 52°23N 6°57W 166 D5
Rosa Zambia 9°33S 31°15E 269 D3
Rosa, C. Algeria 37°0N 8°16E 261 A6
Rosa, C. Galápagos Is., Ecuador 1°4S 91°10W 330 a
Rosa, Monte Europe 45°57N 7°53E 198 C4
Rosais, Pta. dos Azores 38°45N 28°19W 153 d1
Rosal de la Frontera Spain 37°59N 7°13W 195 H3
Rosales Phil. 15°54N 120°38E 232 D3
Rosalia U.S.A. 47°14N 117°22W 304 C5
Rosalie Dominica 15°22N 61°16W 323 k
Rosalie → Dominica 15°22N 61°15W 323 k
Rosalind Bank Caribbean 16°30N 80°30W 320 C3
Rosamond U.S.A. 34°52N 118°10W 307 L8
Rosans France 44°24N 5°29E 175 D9
Rosario Argentina 33°0S 60°40W 334 C3
Rosário Maranhão, Brazil 3°0S 44°15W 332 B3
Rosario Sinaloa, Mexico 22°58N 105°53W 318 C3
Rosário Paraguay 24°30S 57°35W 334 A4
Rosario Agusan del S., Phil. 8°24N 125°59E 233 G5
Rosario Batangas, Phil. 13°50N 121°12E 232 E3
Rosario, Villa del Venezuela 10°19N 72°19W 328 A3
Rosario de la Frontera Argentina 25°50S 65°0W 334 B3
Rosario de Lerma Argentina 24°59S 65°35W 334 A2
Rosario del Tala Argentina 32°20S 59°10W 334 C4
Rosário do Sul Brazil 30°15S 54°55W 335 C5
Rosário Oeste Brazil 14°50S 56°25W 331 C6
Rosarito Baja Calif., Mexico 32°20N 117°2W 307 N9
Rosarito Baja Calif., Mexico 28°38N 114°1W 318 B2
Rosarno Italy 38°29N 15°58E 201 D8
Rosas = Roses Spain 42°19N 3°10E 196 C8
Roscoe Mo., U.S.A. 37°58N 93°48W 310 G3
Roscoe N.Y., U.S.A. 41°56N 74°55W 313 E10
Roscoff France 48°44N 3°58W 172 D3
Roscommon Ireland 53°38N 8°11W 166 C3
Roscommon ☐ Ireland 53°49N 8°23W 166 C3
Roscrea Ireland 52°57N 7°49W 166 D4
Rose → Australia 14°16S 135°45E 280 A2
Rose, L. Bahamas 21°0N 73°30W 321 B5
Rose, L. Fla., U.S.A. 28°32N 81°30W 133 A1
Rose Belle Mauritius 20°24S 57°36E 272 e
Rose Blanche Canada 47°38N 58°45W 299 C8
Rose Bowl U.S.A. 34°9N 118°10W 126 B4
Rose Hall Great House Jamaica 18°31N 77°49W 320 a
Rose Hill = Port Mourant Guyana 6°15N 57°20W 329 B6
Rose Hill Mauritius 20°14S 57°27E 272 e
Rose Hill Va., U.S.A. 38°47N 77°6W 143 C2
Rose Pt. Canada 54°11N 131°39W 296 C2
Rose Rock Grenada 12°24N 61°28W 323 q
Rose Valley Canada 52°19N 103°49W 297 C8
Roseau Dominica 15°17N 61°24W 323 k
Roseau Minn., U.S.A. 48°51N 95°46W 308 A6
Rosebank Gauteng, S. Africa 26°8S 28°2E 123 A2
Rosebank N.Y., U.S.A. 40°36N 74°4W 132 C1
Rosebery N.S.W., Australia 33°55S 151°12E 139 B2
Rosebery Tas., Australia 41°46S 145°33E 281 G4
Rosebud Vic., Australia 38°21S 144°54E 282 E6
Rosebud S. Dak., U.S.A. 43°14N 100°51W 308 D3
Rosebud Tex., U.S.A. 31°4N 96°59W 314 F6
Roseburg U.S.A. 43°13N 123°20W 304 E2
Rosedal La Candelaria Mexico 19°20N 99°10W 128 B2
Rosedale U.S.A. 33°51N 91°2W 315 E9
Rosehearty U.K. 57°42N 2°7W 167 D6
Roseires Res. Sudan 11°51N 34°23E 266 B3
Roseland Calif., U.S.A. 38°25N 122°43W 306 G4
Roseland Ill., U.S.A. 41°42N 87°37W 119 C3
Rosemary Canada 50°46N 112°5W 296 C6
Rosemead U.S.A. 34°4N 118°4W 126 B4
Rosemont Qué., Canada 45°34N 73°33W 130 A2
Rosemont Ill., U.S.A. 41°59N 87°53W 119 B1
Rosenberg = Olesno Poland 50°51N 18°26E 185 H5
Rosenberg = Susz Poland 53°44N 19°20E 184 E6
Rosenberg U.S.A. 29°34N 95°49W 314 G7
Rosenborg Slot Copenhagen, Denmark 118 b2
Rosendaël France 51°3N 2°24E 173 A9
Rosendal Norway 59°59N 6°0E 164 E3
Rosendale U.S.A. 40°4N 94°51W 310 D2
Rosenheim Germany 47°51N 12°7E 179 H8
Rosenthal Germany 52°35N 13°22E 115 A3
Roses Spain 42°19N 3°10E 196 C8
Roses, G. de Spain 42°10N 3°15E 196 C8
Roseto degli Abruzzi Italy 42°41N 14°1E 199 F11
Rosetown Canada 51°35N 107°59W 297 C7
Rosetta = Rashîd Egypt 31°21N 30°22E 256 H7
Rosettenville S. Africa 26°15S 28°3E 123 B2
Roseville Calif., U.S.A. 38°45N 121°17W 306 G5
Roseville Ill., U.S.A. 40°44N 90°40W 310 D6
Roseville Mich., U.S.A. 42°30N 82°56W 312 D2
Roseville Pa., U.S.A. 41°51N 76°57W 313 E8
Rosewell U.K. 55°51N 3°8W 121 B3
Rosewood Australia 27°38S 152°36E 281 D5
Rosherville Dam S. Africa 26°13S 28°6E 123 B2
Roshkhvār Iran 34°58N 59°37E 247 C8
Rosières-en-Santerre France 49°49N 2°42E 173 C9
Rosignano Maríttimo Italy 43°24N 10°28E 198 E7
Rosignol Guyana 6°15N 57°30W 329 B6
Roşiori de Vede Romania 44°9N 25°0E 183 F10
Rositsa Bulgaria 43°57N 27°57E 203 C11
Rositsa → Bulgaria 43°10N 25°30E 203 C9
Rösjön Sweden 59°26N 18°0E 139 A2
Roskilde Denmark 55°38N 12°3E 163 J6
Roskovec Albania 40°44N 19°43E 202 F3
Roslags-Näsby Sweden 59°25N 18°2E 139 A2
Roslavl Russia 53°57N 32°55E 188 F7
Roslin U.K. 55°51N 3°11W 121 B3
Roslindale U.S.A. 42°17N 71°7W 116 B2
Rosmaninhal Portugal 39°44N 7°5W 194 F3
Rosmead S. Africa 31°29S 25°8E 270 D4
Rosnæs Denmark 55°44N 10°55E 163 J4
Rosny-sous-Bois France 48°52N 2°30E 134 A4
Rosolini Italy 36°49N 14°57E 201 F7
Rosporden France 47°57N 3°50W 172 E3
Ross Tas., Australia 42°2S 147°30E 281 G4
Ross N.Z. 42°53S 170°49E 285 E5
Ross Béthio Mauritania 16°15N 16°8W 262 B1
Ross Dependency Antarctica 76°0S 170°0W 151 D12
Ross I. Antarctica 77°30S 168°0E 151 D11
Ross Ice Shelf Antarctica 80°0S 180°0E 151 E12
Ross L. U.S.A. 48°44N 121°4W 304 B3
Ross-on-Wye U.K. 51°54N 2°34W 169 F5
Ross River N. Terr., Australia 23°44S 134°30E 280 C1
Ross River Yukon, Canada 62°30N 131°30W 296 A2
Ross Sea Antarctica 74°0S 178°0E 151 D11
Rossall Pt. U.K. 53°55N 3°3W 168 D4
Rossan Pt. Ireland 54°42N 8°47W 166 B3
Rossano Italy 39°36N 16°39E 201 C9
Rossburn Canada 50°40N 100°49W 297 C8
Rosseau Canada 45°16N 79°39W 312 A5
Rosseau, L. Canada 45°10N 79°35W 312 A5
Rössel = Reszel Poland 54°4N 21°10E 184 D8
Rossel I. Papua N. G. 11°21S 154°9E 286 F8
Rosses, The Ireland 55°2N 8°20W 166 A3
Rossford U.S.A. 41°36N 83°34W 311 C13
Rossignol, L. Canada 52°43N 73°40W 298 B5
Rossignol L. Canada 44°12N 65°10W 299 D6
Rossiya = Russia ■ Eurasia 62°0N 105°0E 215 C11
Rosskreppfjorden Norway 59°4N 7°10E 164 E4
Rossland Canada 49°6N 117°50W 296 D5
Rosslare Ireland 52°17N 6°24W 166 D5
Rosslare Europort = Rosslare Harbour Ireland 52°15N 6°20W 166 D5
Rosslare Harbour Ireland 52°15N 6°20W 166 D5
Rosslau Germany 51°52N 12°15E 178 D8
Rosslyn U.S.A. 38°53N 77°4W 143 B2
Rossmore Canada 44°8N 77°23W 312 B7
Rosso Mauritania 16°40N 15°45W 262 B1
Rosso, C. France 42°13N 8°32E 175 F12
Rossosh Russia 50°15N 39°28E 189 G10
Røssvatnet Norway 65°45N 14°5E 160 D16
Rossville Ill., U.S.A. 40°23N 87°40W 311 D9
Rossville Ind., U.S.A. 40°25N 86°36W 311 D10
Røst Norway 67°32N 12°10E 160 C15
Rostaq = Ar Rustāq Oman 23°23N 57°26E 249 B7
Rostāq Afghan. 37°7N 69°49E 240 A3
Rosthern Canada 52°40N 106°20W 297 C7
Rostock Germany 54°5N 12°8E 178 A8
Rostov Don, Russia 47°15N 39°45E 189 J10
Rostov Yaroslavl, Russia 57°14N 39°25E 188 D10
Rostov ☐ Russia 48°50N 41°10E 191 F5
Rostrenen France 48°14N 3°21W 172 D3
Roswell Ga., U.S.A. 34°2N 84°22W 316 A5
Roswell N. Mex., U.S.A. 33°24N 104°32W 305 K11
Rosyth U.K. 56°2N 3°25W 121 A1
Rot-Front = Dobropole Ukraine 48°25N 37°2E 189 H9
Rota N. Marianas 14°9N 145°12E 302 a
Rota Spain 36°37N 6°20W 195 J4
Rotan U.S.A. 32°51N 100°28W 314 E4
Rote Indonesia 10°50S 123°0E 231 F6
Rotenburg Hessen, Germany 50°59N 9°44E 178 E5
Rotenburg Niedersachsen, Germany 53°6N 9°25E 178 B5
Roth Germany 49°15N 11°5E 179 F7
Rothaargebirge Germany 51°2N 8°13E 178 D4
Rothaargebirge △ Germany 51°10N 8°15E 178 E4
Rothenburg ob der Tauber Germany 49°23N 10°11E 179 F6
Rother → U.K. 50°59N 0°45E 169 G8
Rothera Antarctica 67°34S 68°8W 151 C17
Rotherham U.K. 53°26N 1°20W 168 D6
Rotherhithe U.K. 51°29N 0°2W 125 B3
Rothes U.K. 57°32N 3°13W 167 D5
Rothesay N.B., Canada 45°23N 66°0W 299 C6
Rothesay Argyll & Bute, U.K. 55°50N 5°3W 167 F3
Rothneusiedl Austria 48°8N 16°23E 142 B2
Rothschmaige Germany 48°14N 11°27E 131 A1
Roti = Rote Indonesia 10°50S 123°0E 231 F6
Rotja, Pta. Spain 38°38N 1°35E 206 D2
Rotnes Norway 60°3N 10°51E 164 D7
Roto Australia 33°0S 145°30E 283 B6
Rotoaira, L. N.Z. 39°3S 175°45E 284 F4
Rotoehu, L. N.Z. 38°1S 176°32E 284 E5
Rotoiti, L. Bay of Plenty, N.Z. 38°2S 176°26E 284 E5
Rotoiti, L. W. Coast, N.Z. 41°51S 172°49E 285 B7
Rotoma, L. N.Z. 38°2S 176°35E 284 E5
Rotondo, Mte. France 42°14N 9°8E 175 F13
Rotoroa, L. N.Z. 41°55S 172°39E 285 B7
Rotorua N.Z. 38°9S 176°16E 284 E5
Rotorua, L. N.Z. 38°5S 176°18E 284 E5
Rott → Germany 48°27N 13°25E 179 G9
Rottenburg Germany 48°28N 8°55E 179 G4
Rottenmann Austria 47°31N 14°22E 180 D7
Rotterdam Neths. 51°55N 4°30E 170 C4
Rotterdam N.Y., U.S.A. 42°48N 74°1W 313 D10
Rottne Sweden 57°1N 14°54E 163 G8
Rottnest I. Australia 32°0S 115°27E 279 F2
Rottumeroog Neths. 53°33N 6°34E 170 A6
Rottweil Germany 48°9N 8°37E 179 G4
Rotuma Fiji 12°25S 177°5E 277 C14
Roubaix France 50°40N 3°10E 173 B10
Rouche Island St. Lucia 13°57N 60°52W 323 m
Roudnice nad Labem Czechia 50°25N 14°15E 180 A7
Rouen France 49°27N 1°4E 172 C8
Rouergue France 44°15N 2°0E 174 D5
Rouge Hill Canada 43°48N 79°6W 141 A4
Rough Ridge N.Z. 45°10S 169°55E 285 F4
Rouillac France 45°47N 0°4W 174 C3
Rouissat Algeria 31°55N 5°20E 261 B6
Rouleau Canada 50°10N 104°56W 297 C8
Roulers = Roeselare Belgium 50°57N 3°7E 170 D3
Roulpmaulpma ◎ Australia 23°52S 133°0E 278 D5
Round Hill Jamaica 17°50N 77°23W 320 a
Round Hill St. Kitts & Nevis 17°11N 62°36W 322 d
Round I. Hong Kong, China 22°13N 114°11E 122 B3
Round Mountain U.S.A. 38°43N 117°4W 304 G5
Round Mt. Australia 30°26S 152°16E 283 A10
Round Rock U.S.A. 30°31N 97°41W 314 F6
Roundhouse Park Toronto, Canada 141 c2
Roundup U.S.A. 46°27N 108°33W 304 C9
Roura Fr. Guiana 4°44N 52°20W 329 C7
Rousay U.K. 59°10N 3°2W 167 B5
Rouses Point U.S.A. 44°59N 73°22W 313 B11
Rouseville U.S.A. 41°28N 79°42W 312 E5
Rousse = Ruse Bulgaria 43°48N 25°59E 203 C9
Roussenski Lom △ Bulgaria 43°40N 26°10E 203 C10
Roussillac Swamp Trin. & Tob. 10°14N 61°35W 323 t
Roussillon Isère, France 45°24N 4°49E 175 C8
Roussillon Pyrénées-Or., France 42°30N 2°35E 174 F6
Rouxville S. Africa 30°25S 26°50E 270 D4
Rouyn-Noranda Canada 48°20N 79°0W 298 C4
Rovaniemi Finland 66°29N 25°41E 160 C21
Rovato Italy 45°34N 10°0E 198 C7
Rovenki Ukraine 48°5N 39°21E 189 H10
Rovereto Italy 45°53N 11°3E 198 C8
Roverud Norway 60°15N 12°3E 164 D9
Rovigno = Rovinj Croatia 45°5N 13°40E 199 C10
Rovigo Italy 45°4N 11°47E 199 C8
Rovinj Croatia 45°5N 13°40E 199 C10
Rovira Colombia 4°15N 75°20W 328 C2
Rovno = Rivne Ukraine 50°40N 26°10E 177 C14
Rovnoye Russia 50°52N 46°3E 190 E8
Rovuma = Ruvuma → Tanzania 10°29S 40°28E 269 E5
Row'ān Iran 35°8N 48°51E 247 C6
Rowena Australia 29°48S 148°55E 281 D4
Rowley I. Canada 69°6N 77°52W 295 D16
Rowley Shoals Australia 17°30S 119°0E 278 C2
Roxa Guinea-Biss. 11°15N 15°45W 262 C1
Roxas Capiz, Phil. 11°36N 122°49E 233 F4
Roxas Isabela, Phil. 17°8N 121°36E 232 C3
Roxas Mind. Or., Phil. 12°35N 121°31E 232 E3
Roxas Palawan, Phil. 10°20N 119°21E 232 F2
Roxboro U.S.A. 36°24N 78°59W 315 C15
Roxborough Trin. & Tob. 11°15N 60°35W 323 s
Roxburgh N.Z. 45°33S 169°19E 285 F4
Roxbury Mass., U.S.A. 42°19N 71°5W 116 B2
Roxbury N.Y., U.S.A. 42°17N 74°33W 313 D10
Roxbury Pa., U.S.A. 40°6N 77°39W 312 F7
Roxby Downs Australia 30°43S 136°46E 281 E2
Roxen Sweden 58°30N 15°40E 163 F9
Roxeth U.K. 51°33N 0°20W 125 A1
Roy Mont., U.S.A. 47°20N 108°58W 304 C9
Roy N. Mex., U.S.A. 35°57N 104°12W 305 J11
Roy Utah, U.S.A. 41°10N 112°2W 304 F7
Roy Hill Australia 22°41S 119°57E 278 D3
Roy Thomson Hall Toronto, Canada 141 b2
Royal △ Australia 34°5S 151°5E 283 C9
Royal Bardia △ Nepal 28°20N 81°20E 243 E9
Royal Botanic Gardens Sydney, Australia 139 b2
Royal Botanic Gardens Edinburgh, U.K. 55°58N 3°12W 121 B2
Royal Canal Ireland 53°30N 7°13W 166 C4
Royal Center U.S.A. 40°52N 86°30W 311 D10
Royal Chitawan △ Nepal 26°30N 84°30E 243 F11
Royal Exhibition Building Australia 37°48S 144°58E 128 A1
Royal Geographical Society Is. Canada 68°56N 100°15W 294 D11
Royal Leamington Spa U.K. 52°18N 1°31W 169 E6
Royal Manas △ Bhutan 26°45N 90°50E 241 B3
Royal Natal △ S. Africa 28°43S 28°51E 271 C4
Royal Oak U.S.A. 42°30N 83°9W 311 B13
Royal Observatory U.K. 55°55N 3°12W 121 B2
Royal Palace = Koninklijk Paleis Amsterdam, Neths. 112 a2
Royal Palace = Kungliga Slottet Stockholm, Sweden 139 b2
Royal Palace = Palacio Real Madrid, Spain 127 b1
Royal Palace = Palais Royal Brussels, Belgium 116 b3
Royal Palace = Slottet Oslo, Norway 133 a1
Royal Palm Beach U.S.A. 26°42N 80°14W 317 J9
Royal Park Australia 37°46S 144°57E 128 A1
Royal Tunbridge Wells U.K. 51°7N 0°16E 169 F8
Royal Turf Club Bangkok, Thailand 113 b2
Royale, Isle U.S.A. 48°0N 88°54W 308 B9
Royalla Australia 35°30S 149°9E 283 C8
Royan France 45°37N 1°2W 174 C2
Roye France 49°42N 2°48E 173 C9
Röylä Finland 60°18N 24°42E 121 B1
Royston U.K. 52°3N 0°0 169 E7
Rožaj Montenegro 42°50N 20°11E 202 D4
Różan Poland 52°52N 21°25E 185 F8
Rozas, Portilleros de las Spain 40°29N 3°49W 127 B1
Rozay-en-Brie France 48°41N 2°58E 173 D9
Rozdilna Ukraine 46°50N 30°2E 183 D15
Rozhnyativ Ukraine 48°56N 24°9E 183 B9
Rozhyshche Ukraine 50°54N 25°15E 177 C13
Rožmitál pod Třemšínem Czechia 49°36N 13°53E 180 B6
Rožňava Slovakia 48°37N 20°35E 181 C13
Rozogi Poland 53°28N 21°19E 184 E8
Rozoy-sur-Serre France 49°40N 4°8E 173 C11
Roztoczański △ Poland 50°37N 23°0E 185 H10
Roztoky Czechia 50°9N 14°23E 135 B2
Rozzano Italy 45°22N 9°10E 128 B1
Rrëshen Albania 41°47N 19°49E 202 E3
Rrogozhine Albania 41°4N 19°50E 202 E3
Rtanj Serbia 43°45N 21°50E 202 C5
Rtem, O. er → Algeria 33°29N 5°38E 261 B6
Rtishchevo Russia 52°18N 43°46E 190 D6
Rúa = A Rúa Spain 42°24N 7°6W 194 C3
Ruacaná Namibia 17°27S 14°21E 265 F2
Ruaha △ Tanzania 7°41S 34°30E 268 D3
Ruahine Ra. N.Z. 39°55S 176°2E 284 F5
Ruamahanga → N.Z. 41°24S 175°8E 284 H4
Ruapehu N.Z. 39°17S 175°35E 284 F4
Ruapuke I. N.Z. 46°46S 168°31E 285 G3
Ruâq, W. → Egypt 30°0N 33°49E 251 J4
Ruatoria N.Z. 37°55S 178°20E 284 D7
Ruavatu Solomon Is. 9°26S 160°26E 287 M11
Ruawai N.Z. 36°8S 173°59E 284 C2
Rub' al Khālī Si. Arabia 19°0N 48°0E 249 C5
Rubeho Mts. Tanzania 6°50S 36°25E 268 D4
Rubezhnoye = Rubizhne Ukraine 49°6N 38°25E 189 H10
Rubh a' Mhail U.K. 55°56N 6°8W 167 F2
Rubha Hunish U.K. 57°42N 6°20W 167 D2
Rubha Robhanais = Lewis, Butt of U.K. 58°31N 6°16W 167 C2
Rubí Spain 41°29N 2°2E 196 D7
Rubi → Dem. Rep. of the Congo 2°48N 23°54E 264 B4
Rubí → Barcelona, Spain 41°26N 2°0E 114 A1
Rubiataba Brazil 15°8S 49°48W 333 E2
Rubicon → U.S.A. 38°53N 121°4W 306 G5
Rubicone → Italy 44°8N 12°28E 199 D9
Rubik Albania 41°46N 19°47E 202 E3
Rubinéia Brazil 20°13S 51°2W 333 F1
Rubino Ivory C. 6°4N 4°18W 262 D4
Rubio Venezuela 7°43N 72°22W 328 B3
Rubizhne Ukraine 49°6N 38°25E 189 H10
Rubondo △ Tanzania 2°18S 31°58E 268 C3
Rubtsovsk Russia 51°30N 81°10E 217 B10
Ruby U.S.A. 64°45N 155°30W 303 D9
Ruby Beach = Jacksonville Beach U.S.A. 30°17N 81°24W 316 E8
Ruby L. U.S.A. 40°10N 115°28W 304 F6
Ruby Mts. U.S.A. 40°30N 115°20W 304 F6
Rubyvale Australia 23°25S 147°42E 280 C4
Rucheng China 25°33N 113°38E 229 E9
Ruciane-Nida Poland 53°40N 21°32E 184 E8
Rūd Sar Iran 37°8N 50°18E 247 B6
Ruda Sweden 57°6N 16°7E 163 G10
Ruda Śląska Poland 50°16N 18°50E 185 H5
Rudall Australia 33°43S 136°17E 282 B2
Rudall → Australia 22°34S 122°13E 278 D3
Rudall River △ Australia 22°38S 122°30E 278 D3
Rūdbār Afghan. 30°9N 62°36E 240 C1
Rudbar Iran 36°48N 49°23E 247 B6
Rüdersdorf Germany 52°27N 13°47E 178 C9
Rudewa Tanzania 10°7S 34°40E 269 E3
Rudkøbing Denmark 54°56N 10°41E 163 K4
Rudky Ukraine 49°38N 23°29E 185 J10
Rudna Poland 51°30N 16°17E 185 G3
Rudnik Bulgaria 42°36N 27°30E 203 D11
Rudnik Poland 50°26N 22°15E 185 H9
Rudnik Serbia 44°7N 20°35E 202 B4
Rudnya Russia 54°55N 31°7E 188 E6
Rudnytsa Ukraine 48°16N 28°54E 183 B13
Rudnyy Kazakhstan 52°57N 63°7E 216 B6
Rudo Bos.-H. 43°41N 19°23E 182 G4
Rudolfa, Ostrov Russia 81°45N 58°30E 214 A6
Rudolfsheim Austria 48°12N 16°20E 142 A2
Rudolfshöhe Germany 52°37N 13°44E 115 A5
Rudolstadt Germany 50°44N 11°19E 178 E7
Rudong China 32°20N 121°12E 229 A13
Rudow Germany 52°24N 13°29E 115 B3
Rudozem Bulgaria 41°29N 24°51E 203 E8
Rudrapur India 28°59N 79°24E 243 E8
Rudyard U.S.A. 46°14N 84°36W 309 B11
Rue France 50°15N 1°40E 173 B8
Rueil-Malmaison France 48°52N 2°11E 134 A2
Ruenya → Africa 16°24S 33°48E 269 F3
Rufa'a Sudan 14°44N 33°22E 257 E3
Ruffin U.S.A. 33°0N 80°49W 316 B9
Ruffling Pt. Br. Virgin Is. 18°44N 64°27W 321 b
Rufiji → Tanzania 7°50S 39°15E 268 D4
Rufino Argentina 34°20S 62°50W 334 C3
Rufisque Senegal 14°40N 17°15W 262 C1
Rufunsa Zambia 15°4S 29°34E 269 F2
Rugao China 32°23N 120°31E 229 A13
Rugby U.K. 52°23N 1°16W 169 E6
Rugby N. Dak., U.S.A. 48°22N 100°0W 308 A4
Rügen Germany 54°22N 13°24E 178 A9
Rügen △ Germany 54°25N 13°25E 178 A9
Rugles France 48°50N 0°40E 172 D7
Ruhea Bangla. 26°10N 88°25E 241 B2
Ruhengeri Rwanda 1°30S 29°36E 268 C2
Ruhla Germany 50°54N 10°23E 178 E6
Ruhland Germany 51°27N 13°51E 178 D9
Ruhnu Estonia 57°48N 23°15E 184 A10
Ruhr → Germany 51°27N 6°43E 178 D2
Ruhuhu → Tanzania 10°31S 34°34E 269 E3
Rui Barbosa Brazil 12°18S 40°27W 333 D3
Rui'an China 27°47N 120°40E 229 D13
Ruichang China 29°40N 115°39E 229 C10
Ruidoso U.S.A. 33°20N 105°41W 305 K11
Ruifang = Juifang Taiwan 25°7N 121°48E 225 A3
Ruijin China 25°48N 116°0E 229 E10
Ruili China 24°6N 97°46E 241 C6
Ruiru Kenya 1°9S 36°58E 268 C4
Ruisbroek Belgium 50°47N 4°18E 116 B1
Ruislip U.K. 51°34N 0°24W 125 A1
Ruivo, Pico Madeira 32°45N 16°56W 153 c
Ruj Bulgaria 42°52N 22°34E 202 D6
Rujen Macedonia 42°9N 22°30E 202 D6
Rujm Tal'at al Jamā'ah Jordan 30°24N 35°30E 251 H6
Ruk Pakistan 27°50N 68°42E 242 F3
Rukan-sho Japan 26°6N 127°32E 288 a
Rukhla Pakistan 32°27N 71°57E 242 C4
Rukumkot Nepal 28°37N 82°37E 243 E10
Rukwa ☐ Tanzania 7°0S 31°30E 268 D3
Rukwa, L. Tanzania 8°0S 32°20E 268 D3
Rulenge Burundi 2°43S 30°37E 268 C3
Rulhieres, C. Australia 13°56S 127°22E 278 B4
Rum Jordan 29°39N 35°26E 251 J6
Rùm Highl., U.K. 57°0N 6°20W 167 E2
Rum Cay Bahamas 23°40N 74°58W 321 B5
Rum Jungle Australia 13°0S 130°59E 278 B5
Ruma Serbia 45°0N 19°50E 182 E4
Ruma △ Kenya 0°39S 34°18E 268 C3
Rumāḥ Si. Arabia 25°29N 47°10E 246 E5
Rumah Kulit Malaysia 2°9N 114°14E 235 B4
Rumania = Romania ■ Europe 46°0N 25°0E 183 D10
Rumaylah Iraq 30°47N 47°37E 246 D5
Rumaylah, 'Urūq ar Si. Arabia 22°0N 48°30E 249 B5
Rumbek South Sudan 6°54N 29°37E 257 F2
Rumburk Czechia 50°57N 14°32E 180 A7
Rumelihisarı Turkey 41°4N 29°2E 122 B2
Rumford U.S.A. 44°33N 70°33W 313 B14
Rumia Poland 54°37N 18°25E 184 D5
Rumilly France 45°53N 5°56E 175 C9
Rummelsburg = Miastko Poland 54°0N 16°58E 184 E3
Rumoi Japan 43°56N 141°39E 220 C10
Rumonge Burundi 3°59S 29°26E 268 C2
Rumphi Malawi 11°1S 33°52E 269 E3
Rumson U.S.A. 40°23N 74°0W 313 F11
Rumung Micronesia 9°37N 138°9E 287 R16
Rumuruti Kenya 0°17N 36°32E 268 B4
Runan China 33°0N 114°30E 229 A10
Runanga N.Z. 42°25S 171°15E 285 C6
Runaway, C. N.Z. 37°32S 177°59E 284 D6
Runaway B. Antigua & B. 17°9N 61°51W 322 b
Runaway Bay Jamaica 18°27N 77°20W 320 a
Runcorn U.K. 53°21N 2°44W 168 D5
Rundu Namibia 17°52S 19°43E 270 A2
Rungis France 48°44N 2°20E 134 B3
Rungwa Tanzania 6°55S 33°32E 268 D3
Rungwa → Tanzania 7°36S 31°50E 268 D3
Rungwa △ Tanzania 6°53S 34°2E 268 D3
Rungwe Tanzania 9°11S 33°32E 269 D3
Runka Nigeria 12°28N 7°20E 263 C6
Runn Sweden 60°30N 15°40E 162 D9
Runton Ra. Australia 23°31S 123°6E 278 D3
Runu Micronesia 9°35N 138°8E 287 R16
Ruo Shui → China 41°0N 100°16E 218 C9
Ruokolahti Finland 61°17N 28°50E 188 B5
Ruoqiang China 38°55N 88°10E 217 E11
Rupa India 27°15N 92°21E 241 B4
Rupar India 31°2N 76°38E 242 D7
Rupat Indonesia 1°45N 101°40E 234 B2
Rupea Romania 46°2N 25°13E 183 D10
Rupen → India 23°28N 71°31E 242 H4
Rupert U.S.A. 42°37N 113°41W 304 E7
Rupert → Canada 51°29N 78°45W 298 B4
Rupert B. Canada 51°35N 79°0W 298 B4
Rupert House = Waskaganish Canada 51°30N 78°40W 298 B4
Rupnagar = Rupar India 31°2N 76°38E 242 D7
Rupsa India 21°37N 87°1E 243 J12
Rupununi → Guyana 4°3N 58°35W 329 C6
Rur → Germany 51°11N 5°59E 178 D1
Rurópolis Brazil 4°3S 54°59W 329 D7
Rurrenabaque Bolivia 14°30S 67°32W 330 C4
Rurutu French Polynesia 22°26S 151°20W 289 f
Rus → Spain 39°30N 2°30W 197 F2
Rusāfa Iraq 33°21N 44°23E 113 A2
Rusambo Zimbabwe 16°30S 32°4E 269 F3
Rusape Zimbabwe 18°35S 32°8E 269 F3
Ruschuk = Ruse Bulgaria 43°48N 25°59E 203 C9
Ruse Bulgaria 43°48N 25°59E 203 C9
Ruse ☐ Bulgaria 43°35N 25°40E 203 C9
Ruşeţu Romania 44°57N 27°14E 183 F12
Rush Ireland 53°31N 6°6W 166 C5
Rush Green U.K. 51°33N 0°10E 125 A5
Rushan China 36°56N 121°30E 227 F11
Rushden U.K. 52°18N 0°35W 169 E7
Rushikulya → India 19°23N 85°5E 244 E7
Rushmore, Mt. U.S.A. 43°53N 103°28W 308 D2
Rushville Ill., U.S.A. 40°7N 90°34W 310 D6
Rushville Ind., U.S.A. 39°37N 85°27W 311 E11
Rushville Nebr., U.S.A. 42°43N 102°28W 308 D2
Rushworth Australia 36°32S 145°1E 283 D6
Ruskin U.S.A. 27°43N 82°26W 317 H7
Russa India 22°29N 88°21E 124 C2
Russas Brazil 4°55S 37°50W 332 B4
Russell Man., Canada 50°50N 101°20W 297 C8
Russell N.Z. 35°16S 174°10E 284 B3
Russell Fla., U.S.A. 30°3N 81°45W 316 E8
Russell Kans., U.S.A. 38°54N 98°52W 308 F4
Russell N.Y., U.S.A. 44°27N 75°9W 313 B9
Russell Pa., U.S.A. 41°56N 79°8W 312 E5
Russell Cave △ U.S.A. 34°59N 85°49W 315 D12
Russell Is. Solomon Is. 9°4S 159°12E 287 M10
Russell L. Man., Canada 56°15N 101°30W 297 B8
Russell L. N.W.T., Canada 63°5N 115°44W 296 A5
Russellkonda India 19°57N 84°42E 244 E7
Russells Point U.S.A. 40°28N 83°54W 311 D13
Russellville Ala., U.S.A. 34°30N 87°44W 315 D11
Russellville Ark., U.S.A. 35°17N 93°8W 314 D8
Russellville Ky., U.S.A. 36°51N 86°53W 308 G10
Rüsselsheim Germany 49°59N 8°23E 179 F4
Russi Italy 44°22N 12°2E 199 D9
Russia ■ Eurasia 62°0N 105°0E 215 C11
Russian → U.S.A. 38°27N 123°8W 306 G3
Russian Hill San Francisco, U.S.A. 136 a1
Russian Mission U.S.A. 61°47N 161°19W 303 F7
Russiaville U.S.A. 40°25N 86°16W 311 D10
Russkaya Arktika △ Russia 73°40N 55°55E 214 B6
Russkiy, Ostrov Russia 43°0N 131°50E 220 C5
Russky Sever △ Russia 59°57N 38°34E 188 B10
Rust Austria 47°49N 16°42E 181 D9
Rustam Shahr Pakistan 26°58N 66°6E 242 F2
Rustavi Georgia 41°30N 45°0E 191 K7
Rustenburg S. Africa 25°41S 27°14E 270 C4
Ruston U.S.A. 32°32N 92°38W 314 E8
Rutana Burundi 3°55S 30°0E 268 C3
Rute Spain 37°19N 4°23W 195 H6
Ruteng Indonesia 8°35S 120°30E 231 F6
Rutenga Zimbabwe 21°15S 30°44E 269 G3
Ruth U.S.A. 43°42N 82°45W 312 C2
Rutherford Calif., U.S.A. 38°26N 122°24W 306 G4
Rutherford N.J., U.S.A. 40°49N 74°6W 132 B1
Rutherglen Australia 36°5S 146°29E 283 D7
Rutland U.S.A. 43°37N 72°58W 313 C12
Rutland ☐ U.K. 52°38N 0°40W 169 E7
Rutland I. India 11°25N 92°10E 245 J11
Rutland Water U.K. 52°39N 0°38W 169 E7
Rutledalen Norway 61°4N 5°10E 164 C2
Rutledge U.S.A. 33°38N 83°37W 316 B6
Rutledge → Canada 61°4N 112°0W 297 A6
Rutledge L. Canada 61°33N 110°47W 297 A6
Rutog China 33°27N 79°42E 217 F9
Rutqa, W. → Syria 34°30N 41°3E 213 E9
Rutshuru Dem. Rep. of the Congo 1°13S 29°25E 268 C2
Ruvo di Púglia Italy 41°7N 16°29E 201 A9
Ruvu Tanzania 6°49S 38°43E 268 D4
Ruvu → Tanzania 6°23S 38°52E 268 D4
Ruvuba △ Burundi 3°3S 29°33E 268 C2
Ruvuma ☐ Tanzania 10°20S 36°0E 269 E4
Ruvuma → Tanzania 10°29S 40°28E 269 E5
Ruwais U.A.E. 24°5N 52°50E 247 E7
Ruwenzori Africa 0°30N 29°55E 268 B2
Ruwenzori △ Uganda 0°20N 30°0E 268 B2
Ruya → Zimbabwe 16°27S 32°5E 271 A5
Ruyang China 34°9N 112°27E 226 G7
Ruyigi Burundi 3°29S 30°15E 268 C3
Ruyuan China 24°46N 113°16E 229 E9
Rūzaevka Kazakhstan 52°49N 66°56E 217 B7
Ruzayevka Russia 54°4N 45°0E 190 C7
Rūzhevo Konare Bulgaria 42°23N 24°46E 203 D8
Ruzhou China 34°11N 112°52E 226 G7
Ružomberok Slovakia 49°3N 19°17E 181 B12
Ruzyně Czechia 50°5N 14°17E 135 B1
Ruzyně, Praha ✈ (PRG) Czechia 50°6N 14°16E 135 B1
Rwanda ■ Africa 2°0S 30°0E 268 C3
Ryakhovo Bulgaria 43°58N 26°18E 203 C10
Ryan, L. U.K. 55°0N 5°2W 167 G3
Ryazan Russia 54°40N 39°40E 188 E10
Ryazan ☐ Russia 54°5N 39°30E 190 C4
Ryazhsk Russia 53°45N 40°3E 188 F11
Rybachiy Poluostrov Russia 69°43N 32°0E 160 B25
Rybachye = Balykchy Kyrgyzstan 42°26N 76°12E 217 D9
Rybatskaya Russia 59°59N 30°29E 137 B2
Rybinsk Russia 58°5N 38°50E 188 C10
Rybinskoye Vdkhr. Russia 58°30N 38°25E 188 C10
Rybnik Poland 50°6N 18°32E 185 H5
Rybnitsa = Rîbnița Moldova 47°45N 29°0E 183 C14
Rybnoye Russia 54°45N 39°30E 188 E10
Rychnov nad Kněžnou Czechia 50°10N 16°17E 181 A9
Rychwał Poland 52°4N 18°10E 185 F5

Rycroft Canada 55°45N 118°40W 296 B5
Ryd Sweden 56°27N 14°42E 163 H8
Rydaholm Sweden 56°59N 14°18E 163 H8
Rydboholm Sweden 59°26N 18°12E 139 A3
Ryde N.S.W., Australia 33°48S 151°6E 139 A1
Ryde I. of W., U.K. 50°43N 1°9W 169 G6
Ryderwood U.S.A. 46°23N 123°3W 306 D3
Rydzyna Poland 51°47N 16°39E 185 G3
Rye U.K. 50°57N 0°45E 169 G8
Rye → U.K. 54°11N 0°44W 168 C7
Rye Bay U.K. 50°52N 0°49E 169 G8
Rye Patch Res. U.S.A. 40°28N 118°19W 304 F4
Ryegate U.S.A. 46°18N 109°15W 304 C9
Ryerson University Toronto, Canada 141 a3
Ryfylke Norway 59°25N 6°25E 164 E3
Rykene Norway 58°24N 8°37E 164 F5
Ryki Poland 51°38N 21°56E 185 G8
Rykovo = Yenakiyeve
Ukraine 48°15N 38°15E 189 H10
Ryley Canada 53°17N 112°26W 296 C6
Rylsk Russia 51°36N 34°43E 189 G8
Rylstone Australia 32°46S 149°58E 283 B8
Rymanów Poland 49°35N 21°51E 185 J8
Ryn Poland 53°57N 21°34E 184 E8
Ryn Peski = Naryn Qum
Kazakhstan 47°30N 49°0E 191 G9
Ryogoku Japan 35°40N 139°48E 140 A3
Ryōhaku-Sanchi Japan 36°9N 136°49E 223 A8
Ryojun = Lüshun China 38°45N 121°15E 227 E11
Ryōtsu Japan 38°5N 138°26E 220 E9
Rypin Poland 53°3N 19°25E 185 E6
Ryssby Sweden 56°52N 14°10E 163 H8
Rysy Europe 49°10N 20°4E 181 B13
Ryūgasaki Japan 35°54N 140°11E 223 B12
Ryukyu Is. = Ryūkyū-Rettō
Japan 26°0N 126°0E 221 M3
Ryūkyū-Rettō Japan 26°0N 126°0E 221 M3
Ryūō = Kai Japan 35°42N 138°30E 223 B10
Rzepin Poland 52°20N 14°49E 185 F1
Rzeszów Poland 50°5N 21°58E 185 H8
Rzhev Russia 56°20N 34°20E 188 D8
Rzhevka Russia 59°59N 30°31E 137 B3

S

S.I.B.D. = Songdo
S. Korea 37°23N 126°39E 224 D3
Sa Cabaneta Spain 39°37N 2°45E 206 B3
Sa Canal Spain 38°51N 1°23E 206 D1
Sa Conillera Spain 38°59N 1°13E 206 D1
Sa Dec Vietnam 10°20N 105°46E 237 G5
Sa Dragonera Spain 39°35N 2°19E 206 B3
Sa Kaeo Thailand 13°49N 102°4E 236 F4
Sa-koi Burma 19°54N 97°3E 241 F6
Sa Mesquida Spain 39°55N 4°16E 206 B5
Sa Pa Vietnam 22°20N 103°47E 236 A4
Sa Pobla Spain 39°46N 3°1E 206 B4
Sa Savina Spain 38°44N 1°25E 206 D1
Sa'a Solomon Is. 9°43S 161°35E 287 M11
Sa'ādat Shahr Iran 30°10N 53°5E 247 D7
Sa'ādatābād Hormozgān,
Iran 28°3N 55°53E 247 D7
Sa'ādatābād Kermān, Iran 29°40N 55°51E 247 D7
Sa'ādatābād Tehrān, Iran 35°47N 51°22E 141 A2
Saadūn Iraq 33°19N 44°25E 113 B2
Saale → Germany 51°56N 11°54E 178 D7
Saaler Bodden Germany 54°20N 12°27E 178 A8
Saalfeld Germany 50°38N 11°21E 178 E7
Saalfelden Austria 47°25N 12°51E 180 D5
Saane → Switz. 47°8N 7°10E 179 H3
Saanich Canada 48°29N 123°26W 306 B3
Saar → Europe 49°41N 6°32E 170 E6
Saar-Hunsrück ⌂ Germany 49°30N 6°50E 179 F2
Saar in Mähren = Žďár nad Sázavou
Czechia 49°34N 15°57E 180 B8
Saarbrücken Germany 49°14N 6°59E 179 F2
Saarburg Germany 49°36N 6°32E 179 F2
Saaremaa Estonia 58°30N 22°30E 188 C2
Saarijärvi Finland 62°43N 25°16E 160 E21
Saarland ☐ Germany 49°20N 7°0E 179 F2
Saarlautern = Saarlouis
Germany 49°18N 6°45E 179 F2
Saarlouis Germany 49°18N 6°45E 179 F2
Saatlı Azerbaijan 39°55N 48°22E 213 C13
Saavedra Argentina 34°33S 58°29W 117 B2
Saaz = Žatec Czechia 50°20N 13°32E 180 A6
Sab 'Ābar Syria 33°46N 37°41E 212 F7
Saba W. Indies 17°38N 63°14W 322 a
Šabac Serbia 44°48N 19°42E 202 B3
Sabadell Spain 41°28N 2°7E 196 D7
Sabae Japan 35°57N 136°11E 223 B8
Sabah ☐ Malaysia 6°0N 117°0E 235 A5
Şabāḩ, Wadi → Si. Arabia 23°50N 48°30E 249 B5
Sabak Bernam Malaysia 3°46N 100°58E 237 L3
Sabalān, Kūhhā-ye Iran 38°15N 47°45E 213 C12
Sabalana, Kepulauan
Indonesia 6°45S 118°50E 231 F5
Sabalana, Kepuluauan
Indonesia 6°45S 118°49E 235 D5
Sabana, Arch. de Cuba 23°0N 80°0W 320 B3
Sabana de la Mar
Dom. Rep. 19°7N 69°24W 321 C6
Sabana Grande Puerto Rico 18°5N 66°58W 321 b
Sabana Westpunt = Westpunt
Curaçao 12°22N 69°10W 322 g
Sábanalarga Colombia 10°38N 74°55W 328 A3
Sabaneta Pt. N. Marianas 15°17N 145°49E 302 e
Sabang Indonesia 5°50N 95°15E 234 A1
Şabanözü Turkey 40°28N 33°16E 212 B5
Săbăoani Romania 47°1N 26°51E 183 C11
Sabari → India 17°35N 81°16E 244 F5
Sabarmati → India 22°18N 72°22E 242 H5
Saba'tayn, Ramlat as
Yemen 15°30N 46°10E 248 D4
Sabattis U.S.A. 44°6N 74°40W 313 B10
Sabáudia Italy 41°18N 13°1E 200 A6
Sabaya Bolivia 19°1S 68°23W 330 D4
Şabāyā, Jaza'ir Si. Arabia 18°35N 41°3E 248 C3
Saberania Indonesia 2°5S 138°18E 231 E9
Sabhā Libya 27°9N 14°29E 258 C2
Sabhar Bangla. 23°50N 90°15E 241 D3
Sabi → India 28°29N 76°44E 242 E7
Sabi Game Reserve = Kruger △
S. Africa 24°50S 26°17E 271 B4
Sabidana, J. Sudan 18°4N 36°50E 256 D4
Sabie S. Africa 25°10S 30°48E 271 C5
Sabina U.S.A. 39°29N 83°38W 311 E13
Sabinal U.S.A. 29°19N 99°28W 314 G5
Sabiñánigo Spain 42°31N 0°22W 196 C4
Sabinar, Punta del Spain 36°43N 2°44W 197 J2
Sabinas Mexico 27°51N 101°7W 318 B4
Sabinas → Mexico 27°37N 100°42W 318 B4
Sabinas Hidalgo Mexico 26°30N 100°10W 318 B4
Sabine → U.S.A. 29°59N 93°47W 314 G8
Sabine L. U.S.A. 29°53N 93°51W 314 G8
Sabine Pass U.S.A. 29°44N 93°54W 314 G8
Sabinópolis Brazil 18°40S 43°6W 333 E3
Sabinov Slovakia 49°6N 21°5E 181 B14
Sabirabad Azerbaijan 40°5N 48°30E 191 K9
Sabka Chad 19°15N 16°35E 259 E3
Sablayan Phil. 12°50N 120°50E 232 E3
Sable Canada 55°30N 68°21W 299 A6
Sable, C. N.S., Canada 43°29N 65°38W 299 D6
Sable, C. Fla., U.S.A. 25°9N 81°8W 317 K8
Sable I. N.S., Canada 44°0N 60°0W 299 D8
Sable I. Papua N. G. 3°38S 154°42E 286 B8
Sablé-sur-Sarthe France 47°50N 0°20W 172 E6
Saboeiro Brazil 6°32S 39°54W 332 C4
Saboli India 28°42N 77°18E 120 A2
Sabonkafi Niger 14°40N 8°45E 259 F1
Sabor → Portugal 41°10N 7°7W 194 D3
Sabou Burkina Faso 12°1N 2°15W 262 C4
Sabres France 44°9N 0°43W 174 D3
Sabrina Coast Antarctica 68°0S 120°0E 151 C9
Sabtang I. Phil. 20°19N 121°52E 232 A3
Sabugal Portugal 40°20N 7°5W 194 E3
Sabugo Portugal 38°49N 9°17W 126 A1
Sabula U.S.A. 42°4N 90°10W 310 B6
Sabulubek Indonesia 1°36S 98°40E 234 C1
Sabuncu Turkey 39°33N 30°12E 205 B12
Şabyā Si. Arabia 17°9N 42°37E 248 C3
Sabzevār Iran 36°15N 57°40E 247 B8
Sabzi Mand India 28°40N 77°12E 120 A2
Sabzvārān = Jiroft Iran 28°45N 57°50E 247 D8
Sac City U.S.A. 42°25N 95°0W 310 B2
Sacaba Bolivia 17°24S 66°2W 331 D4
Sacaolo Angola 12°58S 22°28E 265 E4
Sacatengo Angola 13°16S 21°20E 265 E4
Sacavém Portugal 38°47N 9°5W 126 A2
Sacca Fisola Venice, Italy 142 c1
Sacca San Biágio Venice, Italy 142 c1
Sacedón Spain 40°29N 2°41W 196 E2
Săcele Romania 45°37N 25°41E 183 E10
Sacheon S. Korea 35°0N 128°6E 224 E4
Sachigo → Canada 55°6N 88°58W 298 A2
Sachigo, L. Canada 53°50N 92°12W 298 B1
Sachimbo Angola 9°14S 20°16E 265 D4
Sachin India 21°5N 72°53E 244 D1
Sachkhere Georgia 42°25N 43°28E 191 J6
Sachsen ☐ Germany 50°55N 13°10E 178 E9
Sachsen-Anhalt ☐ Germany 52°0N 12°0E 178 D7
Sächsische Schweiz △
Germany 50°55N 14°10E 178 E10
Sacile Italy 45°57N 12°30E 199 C9
Sackets Harbor U.S.A. 43°57N 76°7W 313 C8
Sackville Canada 45°54N 64°22W 299 C7
Saclay France 48°43N 2°10E 134 B2
Saclay, Étang de France 48°44N 2°9E 134 B1
Saco Maine, U.S.A. 43°30N 70°27W 313 C14
Saco Mont., U.S.A. 48°28N 107°21W 304 B10
Sacol I. Phil. 6°58N 122°13E 233 H4
Sacomã Brazil 23°36S 46°35W 137 B2
Sacramento = Itatupã
Brazil 0°37S 51°12W 329 D7
Sacramento Brazil 19°53S 47°27W 333 E2
Sacramento Calif.,
U.S.A. 38°35N 121°29W 306 G5
Sacramento → U.S.A. 38°3N 121°56W 306 G5
Sacramento Mts.
U.S.A. 32°30N 105°30W 305 K11
Sacramento Valley
U.S.A. 39°30N 122°0W 306 G5
Sacratif, C. Spain 36°42N 3°28W 195 J7
Sacré Cœur Paris, France 134 a4
Sacrow Germany 52°25N 13°6E 115 B1
Sacrower See Germany 52°26N 13°6E 115 B1
Săcueni Romania 47°20N 22°5E 182 C7
Sada Mayotte 12°51S 45°6E 272 b
Sada Spain 43°22N 8°15W 194 B2
Sada-Misaki Japan 33°20N 132°5E 222 D4
Sada-Misaki-Hantō Japan 33°22N 132°1E 222 D4
Sádaba Spain 42°19N 1°12W 196 C3
Sadabad India 27°27N 78°3E 242 F8
Şa'dah Yemen 16°15N 43°37E 248 C3
Şa'dah ☐ Yemen 16°15N 43°37E 248 C3
Sadang S. Korea 37°29N 126°58E 137 C1
Sadani Tanzania 5°58S 38°35E 268 D4
Sadani ⌂ Tanzania 6°3S 38°47E 268 D4
Sadao Thailand 6°38N 100°26E 237 J3
Sadar Bazar Delhi, India 120 a1
Sadaseopet India 17°38N 77°59E 244 F3
Sadd el Aali Egypt 23°54N 32°54E 256 C3
Saddle → U.S.A. 40°51N 74°6W 132 A1
Saddle Brook U.S.A. 40°53N 74°5W 132 A1
Saddle Hill St. Kitts & Nevis 17°7N 62°33W 322 d
Saddle Mt. U.S.A. 45°58N 123°41W 306 E3
Saddle Pk. India 13°9N 93°1E 245 H11
Saddle Pt. St. Helena 15°57S 5°38W 153 h
Sade Nigeria 11°22N 10°45E 263 C7
Şadh Oman 17°3N 55°4E 249 C6
Sadhoowa Trin. & Tob. 10°8N 61°27W 323 t
Sadimi
Dem. Rep. of the Congo 9°25S 23°32E 265 D4
Sadiola Mali 13°50N 11°40W 262 C2
Sadiya India 27°50N 95°40E 241 B5
Sa'dīyah, Hawr as Iraq 32°15N 46°30E 213 F12
Sadlers St. Kitts & Nevis 17°24N 62°47W 322 d
Sado Japan 38°0N 138°25E 220 F9
Sado → Portugal 38°29N 8°55W 195 G2
Sadon Russia 42°52N 43°58E 191 J6
Sadovoye Russia 47°47N 44°31E 191 G7
Sadowara Japan 32°2N 131°26E 222 E3
Sadr Pakistan 24°51N 67°2E 123 A2
Sadr City Iraq 33°23N 44°27E 113 A2
Sadra India 23°21N 72°43E 242 H5
Sadrazamköy = Liveras
Cyprus 35°23N 32°57E 207 E8
Sadri India 25°11N 73°26E 242 G5
Sadyba Poland 52°11N 21°13E 143 B2
Sæbøvik Norway 59°47N 5°40E 164 E2
Sæby Denmark 57°21N 10°30E 163 G4
Saegertown U.S.A. 41°43N 80°9W 312 E4
Saelices Spain 39°55N 2°49W 196 F2
Sætre Norway 59°41N 10°33E 164 E7
Sævareid Norway 60°11N 5°46E 164 D2
Safaalan Turkey 41°26N 28°6E 203 E12
Şafājah Si. Arabia 26°25N 39°0E 246 E3
Šafárikovo = Tornal'a
Slovakia 48°25N 20°20E 181 C13
Safata B. Samoa 14°0S 171°50W 287 W20
Safdar Jang's Tomb India 28°35N 77°12E 120 B2
Safed Koh Afghan. 34°0N 70°0E 240 B3
Säffle Sweden 59°8N 12°55E 162 E6
Safford U.S.A. 32°50N 109°43W 305 K9
Saffron Walden U.K. 52°1N 0°16E 169 F7
Safi Morocco 32°18N 9°20W 260 B3
Safia Papua N. G. 9°35S 148°38E 286 E5
Safia, Hamada Mali 23°10N 4°15W 260 D4
Şafīābād Iran 36°45N 57°58E 247 B8
Safīd Dasht Iran 33°27N 48°11E 247 C6
Safīd Kūh Afghan. 34°45N 63°0E 240 B1
Safīd Rūd → Iran 37°23N 50°11E 247 B6
Safipur India 26°44N 80°21E 243 F9
Şāfītā Syria 34°48N 36°7E 250 D7
Safonovo Russia 55°4N 33°16E 188 E7
Safranbolu Turkey 41°15N 32°41E 212 B5
Saft el Laban Egypt 30°1N 31°10E 117 A2
Saft Rashîn Egypt 28°58N 30°55E 256 J7
Safune Samoa 13°25S 172°21W 287 V19
Şafwān Iraq 30°7N 47°43E 246 D5
Sag Harbor U.S.A. 41°0N 72°18W 313 E12
Sag Sag Papua N. G. 5°32S 148°23E 286 C5
Saga Kōchi, Japan 33°5N 133°6E 222 D5
Saga Saga, Japan 33°15N 130°16E 222 D3
Saga ☐ Japan 33°15N 130°20E 222 D2
Sagae Japan 38°22N 140°17E 220 E10
Sagaing Burma 21°52N 95°59E 241 E5
Sagaing ☐ Burma 23°55N 95°56E 241 D5
Sagala Mali 14°9N 6°38W 262 C3
Sagami-Nada Japan 34°58N 139°30E 223 C11
Sagami-Wan Japan 35°15N 139°25E 223 B11
Sagamihara Japan 35°33N 139°25E 223 B11
Sagamore U.S.A. 40°46N 79°14W 312 F5
Sagan = Żagań Poland 51°39N 15°22E 185 G2
Saganaga L. Canada 48°14N 90°52W 308 A8
Saganoseki Japan 33°15N 131°53E 222 D3
Saganthit Kyun Burma 11°56N 98°29E 237 G2
Sagar Karnataka, India 16°38N 76°48E 244 F3
Sagar Karnataka, India 14°14N 75°6E 245 G2
Sagar Mad. P., India 23°50N 78°44E 243 H8
Sagara Japan 34°41N 138°12E 223 C10
Sagara, L. Tanzania 5°20S 31°0E 268 D3
Sagarejo Georgia 41°44N 45°19E 191 K7
Sagarmatha = Everest, Mt.
Nepal 28°5N 86°58E 243 E12
Sagarmatha △ Nepal 27°55N 86°45E 243 F12
Sagavanirktok →
U.S.A. 70°19N 147°53W 303 A11
Sagay Phil. 10°57N 123°25E 233 F4
Sagene Norway 59°55N 10°46E 133 A3
Saghîr, El Bahr el → Egypt 31°8N 31°54E 251 G2
Sagiada Greece 39°38N 20°12E 206 B10
Saginaw Mich., U.S.A. 43°26N 83°56W 309 D12
Saginaw Tex., U.S.A. 32°51N 97°21W 120 A1
Saginaw B. U.S.A. 43°50N 83°40W 309 D12
Sagleipie Liberia 7°0N 8°52W 262 D3
Saglouc = Salluit Canada 62°14N 75°38W 295 E16
Sagone France 42°7N 8°42E 175 F12
Sagone, G. de France 42°4N 8°40E 175 F12
Sagrada Família, Templo de
Barcelona, Spain 114 a2
Sagres Portugal 37°0N 8°58W 195 J2
Sagu Burma 20°13N 94°46E 241 E5
Sagua la Grande Cuba 22°50N 80°10W 320 B3
Saguache U.S.A. 38°5N 106°8W 304 G10
Saguaro △ U.S.A. 32°12N 110°38W 305 K8
Saguenay → Canada 48°22N 71°0W 299 C5
Saguia el Hamra →
W. Sahara 27°24N 13°43W 260 C2
Sagunt Spain 39°42N 0°18W 196 F4
Sagunto = Sagunt Spain 39°42N 0°18W 196 F4
Sagvåg Norway 59°46N 5°25E 164 E2
Saha Sagara India 23°41N 74°1E 242 H6
Sahaba Sudan 18°57N 30°25E 256 D3
Sahagún Colombia 8°57N 75°27W 328 B2
Sahagún Spain 42°18N 5°2W 194 C5
Saḩam al Jawlān Syria 32°45N 35°55E 250 F6
Sahamandrevo Madag. 23°15S 45°35E 272 C2
Sahand, Kūh-e Iran 37°44N 46°27E 213 D12
Sahar, Mumbai ✕ (BOM)
India 19°5N 72°51E 130 A2
Sahara Africa 23°0N 5°0E 254 D4
Sahara, G. Egypt 28°2N 34°8E 251 K5
Saharan Atlas = Saharien, Atlas
Algeria 33°30N 1°0E 261 B5
Saharan Seamounts
Atl. Oc. 25°30N 19°50W 152 D10
Saharanpur India 29°58N 77°33E 242 E7
Saharien, Atlas Algeria 33°30N 1°0E 261 B5
Saharsa India 25°53N 86°36E 243 G12
Sahasinaka Madag. 21°49S 47°49E 272 C2
Sahaswan India 28°5N 78°45E 243 E8
Saheira, W. el → Egypt 30°5N 33°25E 251 H4
Sahel Africa 16°0N 5°0E 254 E3
Sahel, Canal du Mali 14°20N 6°0W 262 C3
Sahibganj India 25°12N 87°40E 243 G12
Sāḩilīyah Iraq 33°43N 42°42E 213 F10
Sahiwal Pakistan 30°45N 73°8E 242 D5
Şahneh Iran 34°29N 47°41E 213 E12
Sahrawi = Western Sahara ■
Africa 25°0N 13°0W 260 D2
Sahuaripa Mexico 29°3N 109°14W 318 B3
Sahuarita U.S.A. 31°57N 110°58W 305 L8
Sahuayo de Diaz Mexico 20°4N 102°43W 318 C4
Šahy Slovakia 48°4N 18°55E 181 C11
Sai → India 25°39N 82°47E 243 G10
Sai Buri Thailand 6°43N 101°45E 237 J3
Sai-Cinza Brazil 6°17S 57°42W 331 B6
Sai Kung
Hong Kong, China 22°23N 114°16E 122 A3
Sai Thong △ Thailand 15°56N 101°10E 236 E3
Sai Tso Wan
Hong Kong, China 22°16N 113°53E 122 B1
Sai Wan Ho
Hong Kong, China 22°17N 114°12E 122 B3
Sai Ying Pun
Hong Kong, China 22°17N 114°8E 122 B2
Sai Yok △ Thailand 14°25N 98°40E 236 E2
Saibai I. Australia 9°25S 142°40E 280 a
Sa'id Bundas South Sudan 8°24N 24°48E 259 G4
Saïda Algeria 34°50N 0°11E 261 B5
Saïda ☐ Algeria 34°40N 0°20E 261 B5
Sa'īdābād = Sīrjān Iran 29°30N 55°45E 247 D7
Sa'īdābād Iran 36°8N 54°11E 247 B7
Saidaiji Japan 34°39N 134°2E 222 C6
Saïdia Morocco 35°5N 2°14W 261 A4
Saidor Papua N. G. 5°40S 146°29E 286 C4
Saidpur Bangla. 25°48N 89°0E 241 C2
Saidpur India 25°33N 83°11E 243 G10
Saidu Sharif Pakistan 34°43N 72°24E 243 B5
Saignes France 45°20N 2°31E 174 C6
Saigō Japan 36°12N 133°20E 222 A5
Saigon = Thanh Pho Ho Chi Minh
Vietnam 10°58N 106°40E 237 G6
Saiha India 22°29N 92°58E 241 D4
Saijō Japan 33°55N 133°11E 222 D5
Saikai △ Japan 33°12N 129°36E 222 D1
Saikhoa Ghat India 27°50N 95°40E 241 B5
Saiki Japan 32°58N 131°51E 222 E3
Sailana India 23°28N 74°55E 242 H6
Saillans France 44°42N 5°12E 175 D9
Sailolof Indonesia 1°15S 130°46E 231 E8
Sailu India 19°28N 76°28E 244 E3
Saimaa Finland 61°15N 28°15E 188 B5
Saimbeyli Turkey 37°59N 36°6E 212 D7
Saimen = Saimaa Finland 61°15N 28°15E 188 B5
Şa'in Dezh Iran 36°40N 46°25E 213 D12
St. Abb's Head U.K. 55°55N 2°8W 167 F6
St-Affrique France 43°57N 2°53E 174 E6
St-Agrève France 45°0N 4°23E 175 C8
St-Aignan France 47°16N 1°22E 172 E8
St. Alban's Nfld. & L.,
Canada 47°51N 55°50W 299 C8
St. Albans Herts., U.K. 51°45N 0°19W 169 F7
St. Albans Vt., U.S.A. 44°49N 73°5W 313 B11
St. Albans W. Va., U.S.A. 38°23N 81°50W 309 F13
St. Alban's Head U.K. 50°34N 2°4W 169 G5
St. Albert Canada 53°37N 113°32W 296 C6
St-Amand-en-Puisaye
France 47°32N 3°5E 173 E10
St-Amand-les-Eaux
France 50°27N 3°25E 173 B10
St-Amand-Montrond
France 46°43N 2°30E 173 F9
St-Amarin France 47°54N 7°2E 173 E14
St-Amour France 46°26N 5°21E 173 F12
St-André Montréal, Canada 130 c1
St-André Réunion 20°57S 55°39E 272 f
St-André-de-Cubzac
France 44°59N 0°26W 174 D3
St-André-les-Alpes France 43°58N 6°30E 175 E10
St. Andrew Sd. U.S.A. 30°58N 81°25W 316 E8
St. Andrew's Nfld. & L.,
Canada 47°45N 59°15W 299 C8
St. Andrews N.Z. 44°33S 171°10E 285 E6
St. Andrews Fife, U.K. 56°20N 2°47W 167 E6
St. Andrews S.C., U.S.A. 32°47N 80°0W 316 C9
St-Anicet Canada 45°8N 74°22W 313 A10
St. Ann U.S.A. 41°1N 87°43W 311 C9
St. Annes Canada 49°40N 96°39W 297 D9
St. Anns B. Canada 46°22N 60°25W 299 C7
St. Ann's Bay Jamaica 18°26N 77°12W 320 a
St. Anthony Nfld. & L.,
Canada 51°22N 55°35W 299 B8
St. Anthony Idaho,
U.S.A. 43°58N 111°41W 304 E8
St-Antoine Canada 46°22N 64°45W 299 C7
St-Antonin-Noble-Val
France 44°10N 1°45E 174 D5
St-Arnaud = El Eulma
Algeria 36°9N 5°42E 261 A6
St. Arnaud Australia 36°40S 143°16E 282 D5
St. Arnaud Ra. N.Z. 42°1S 172°53E 285 C7
St-Astier France 45°8N 0°31E 174 C4
St-Aubin France 48°44N 2°8E 134 B1
St-Aubin-du-Cormier
France 48°15N 1°26W 172 D5
St-Augustin Canada 51°13N 58°38W 299 B8
St-Augustin → Canada 51°16N 58°40W 299 B8
St. Augustine U.S.A. 29°54N 81°19W 316 F8
St. Augustine Beach
U.S.A. 29°51N 81°16W 316 F8
St-Aulaye France 45°12N 0°9E 174 C4
St. Austell U.K. 50°20N 4°47W 169 G3
St-Avold France 49°6N 6°43E 173 C13
St. Barbe Canada 51°12N 56°46W 299 B8
St-Barthélemy ☒ W. Indies 17°50N 62°50W 322 a
St-Barthélemy Channel
St.-Martin 18°0N 63°0W 322 a
St. Barts = St-Barthélemy ☒
W. Indies 17°50N 62°50W 322 a
St. Basil's Cathedral Moscow, Russia 129 b3
St. Bathans N.Z. 44°53S 169°50E 285 E4
St. Bathan's, Mt. N.Z. 44°45S 169°45E 285 E4
St-Béat France 42°55N 0°41E 174 F4
St. Bees Hd. U.K. 54°31N 3°38W 168 C4
St. Bees I. Australia 20°56S 149°26E 280 b
St-Benoît Réunion 21°2S 55°43E 272 f
St-Benoît-du-Sault France 46°26N 1°24E 174 B5
St-Bonnet-en-Champsaur
France 44°40N 6°5E 175 D10
St-Brevin-les-Pins France 47°14N 2°10W 172 E4
St-Brice-en-Coglès France 48°25N 1°22W 172 D5
St. Bride's Canada 46°56N 54°10W 299 C9
St. Brides B. U.K. 51°49N 5°9W 169 F2
St-Brieuc France 48°30N 2°46W 172 D4
St-Calais France 47°55N 0°45E 172 E7
St-Cast-le-Guildo France 48°37N 2°18W 172 D4
St. Catharines Canada 43°10N 79°15W 312 C5
St. Catherine, Mt. Grenada 12°10N 61°40W 323 q
St. Catherine Pt. Bermuda 32°23N 64°40W 153 a
St. Catherines I. U.S.A. 31°40N 81°10W 316 D8
St. Catherine's Monastery
Egypt 28°34N 33°58E 251 K4
St. Catherine's Pt. U.K. 50°34N 1°18W 169 G6
St-Céré France 44°51N 1°54E 174 D5
St-Cergue Switz. 46°27N 6°10E 179 J2
St-Cernin France 45°5N 2°25E 174 C6
St-Chamond France 45°28N 4°31E 175 C8
St. Charles Ill., U.S.A. 41°54N 88°19W 311 C8
St. Charles Md., U.S.A. 38°36N 76°56W 309 F15
St. Charles Mo., U.S.A. 38°47N 90°29W 310 F6
St. Charles Va., U.S.A. 36°48N 83°4W 309 G12
St-Chély-d'Apcher France 44°48N 3°17E 174 D7
St-Chinian France 43°25N 2°56E 174 E6
St. Christopher = St. Kitts
W. Indies 17°20N 62°40W 322 d
St. Christopher-Nevis = St. Kitts &
Nevis ■ W. Indies 17°20N 62°40W 322 d
St-Ciers-sur-Gironde
France 45°17N 0°37W 174 C3
St. Clair Ga., U.S.A. 33°9N 82°13W 316 B7
St. Clair Mich., U.S.A. 42°50N 82°30W 312 D2
St. Clair Mo., U.S.A. 38°21N 90°59W 310 F6
St. Clair Pa., U.S.A. 40°43N 76°12W 313 F8
St. Clair → U.S.A. 42°38N 82°31W 312 D2
St. Clair, L. S. Austral.,
Australia 37°20S 139°55E 282 D3
St. Clair, L. N. Amer. 42°27N 82°39W 312 D2
St. Clair Shores U.S.A. 42°30N 82°53W 311 B14
St. Clairsville U.S.A. 40°5N 80°54W 312 F4
St-Claud France 45°54N 0°28E 174 C4
St. Claude Canada 49°40N 98°20W 297 D9
St-Claude Jura, France 46°22N 5°52E 173 F12
St-Claude Guadeloupe 16°3N 61°42W 322 e
St. Clears U.K. 51°49N 4°31W 169 F3
St-Clet Canada 45°21N 74°13W 313 A10
St. Cloud France 48°50N 2°12E 134 A2
St. Cloud Fla., U.S.A. 28°15N 81°17W 317 G8
St. Cloud Minn., U.S.A. 45°34N 94°10W 308 C6
St. Cricq, C. Australia 25°17S 113°6E 279 E1
St. Croix U.S. Virgin Is. 17°45N 64°45W 321 C7
St. Croix → U.S.A. 44°45N 92°48W 308 C7
St. Croix Falls U.S.A. 45°24N 92°38W 308 C7
St-Cyprien France 42°37N 3°2E 174 F7
St-Cyr-l'École France 48°47N 2°4E 134 B1
St-Cyr-l'École ✕ France 48°48N 2°4E 134 B1
St-Cyr-sur-Mer France 43°11N 5°43E 175 E9
St. David U.S.A. 40°30N 90°3W 310 D6
St. David's Nfld. & L.,
Canada 48°12N 58°52W 299 C8
St. David's Grenada 12°2N 61°40W 323 q
St. David's Pembs., U.K. 51°53N 5°16W 169 F2
St. David's Head U.K. 51°54N 5°19W 169 F2
St. David's I. Bermuda 32°21N 64°39W 153 a
St-Denis = Sig Algeria 35°32N 0°12W 261 A4
St-Denis Seine-St-Denis,
France 48°56N 2°20E 134 A3
St-Denis Réunion 20°52S 55°27E 272 f
St-Denis → Réunion 20°52S 55°27E 272 f
St-Denis ✕ (RUN) Réunion 20°53S 55°32E 272 f
St-Dié-en-Vosges France 48°17N 6°56E 173 D13
St-Dizier France 48°38N 4°56E 173 D11
St-Égrève France 45°14N 5°41E 175 C9
St. Elias, Mt. U.S.A. 60°18N 140°56W 303 F12
St. Elias Mts. N. Amer. 60°33N 139°28W 296 A1
St-Élie Fr. Guiana 4°49N 53°17W 329 C7
St. Elmo U.S.A. 39°2N 88°51W 311 E8
St-Eloy-les-Mines France 46°10N 2°51E 173 F9
St-Émilion France 44°53N 0°9W 174 D3
St-Étienne France 45°27N 4°22E 175 C8
St-Étienne → Réunion 21°17S 55°25E 272 f
St-Étienne-de-Tinée
France 44°16N 6°56E 175 D10
St-Étienne-du-Rouvray
France 49°23N 1°6E 172 C8
St. Eugène Canada 45°30N 74°28W 313 A10
St. Eustatius W. Indies 17°20N 63°0W 322 a
St-Exupery, Lyon ✕ (LYS)
France 45°44N 5°2E 175 C9
St-Fargeau France 47°39N 3°4E 173 E10
St-Félicien Canada 48°40N 72°25W 298 C5
St. Ferdinand = Florissant
U.S.A. 38°47N 90°19W 310 F6
St-Florent France 42°41N 9°18E 175 F13
St-Florent, G. de France 42°47N 9°12E 175 F13
St-Florent-sur-Cher France 46°59N 2°15E 173 F9
St-Florentin France 48°0N 3°45E 173 E10
St-Flour France 45°2N 3°6E 174 C7
St. Francis U.S.A. 39°47N 101°48W 308 F3
St. Francis → U.S.A. 34°38N 90°36W 315 D9
St. Francis, C. S. Africa 34°14S 24°49E 270 D3
St. Francisville Ill., U.S.A. 38°36N 87°39W 311 F9
St. Francisville La., U.S.A. 30°47N 91°23W 314 F9
St-François Guadeloupe 16°16N 61°18W 322 e
St-François, L. Canada 45°10N 74°22W 313 A10
St-Fulgent France 46°50N 1°10W 172 F5
St-Gabriel Canada 46°17N 73°24W 298 C5
St. Gallen = Sankt Gallen
Switz. 47°26N 9°22E 179 H5
St-Galmier France 45°35N 4°19E 173 G11
St-Gaudens France 43°6N 0°44E 174 E4
St-Gaultier France 46°39N 1°26E 172 F8
St-Gengoux-le-National
France 46°37N 4°40E 173 F11
St-Geniez-d'Olt France 44°27N 2°58E 174 D6
St. George Queens.,
Australia 28°1S 148°30E 281 D4
St. George N.B., Canada 45°11N 66°50W 299 C6
St. George Ont., Canada 43°15N 80°15W 312 C4
St. George Ga., U.S.A. 30°31N 82°2W 316 E7
St. George S.C., U.S.A. 33°11N 80°35W 316 B9
St. George Utah, U.S.A. 37°6N 113°35W 305 H7
St. George, C. Nfld. & L.,
Canada 48°30N 59°16W 299 C8
St. George, C. Papua N. G. 4°49S 152°53E 286 C7
St. George, C. Fla., U.S.A. 29°40N 85°5W 316 F4
St. George I. Alaska,
U.S.A. 56°35N 169°35W 303 H5
St. George I. Fla., U.S.A. 29°35N 84°55W 316 F5
St. George Ra. Australia 18°40S 125°0E 278 C4
St. George's Bermuda 32°22N 64°40W 153 a
St. George's Nfld. & L.,
Canada 48°26N 58°31W 299 C8
St-Georges Qué., Canada 46°8N 70°40W 299 C5
St-Georges Fr. Guiana 3°53N 51°50W 329 C7
St. George's Grenada 12°5N 61°43W 323 q
St. George's B. Canada 48°24N 58°53W 299 C8
St. Georges Basin N.S.W.,
Australia 35°7S 150°36E 283 C9
St. Georges Basin W. Austral.,
Australia 15°23S 125°2E 278 C4
St. George's Channel Europe 52°0N 6°0W 166 E6
St. George's Channel India 7°15N 93°43E 245 L11
St. George's Channel
Papua N. G. 4°10S 152°20E 286 C7
St. George's Harbour
Bermuda 32°33N 64°42W 153 a
St. Georges Hd. Australia 35°12S 150°42E 283 C9
St. George's I. Bermuda 32°23N 64°40W 153 a
St-Georges-lès-Baillargeaux
France 46°41N 0°22E 174 B4
St-Germain, Forêt de France 48°57N 2°5E 134 A1
St-Germain-de-Calberte
France 44°13N 3°48E 174 D7
St-Germain-en-Laye France 48°53N 2°4E 134 A1
St-Germain-Lembron
France 45°27N 3°14E 174 C7
St-Gervais-d'Auvergne
France 46°4N 2°50E 173 F9
St-Gervais-les-Bains
France 45°53N 6°42E 175 C10
St-Gildas, Pte. de France 47°8N 2°14W 172 E4
St. Giles Cathedral Edinburgh, U.K. 121 b2
St-Gilles Brussels, Belgium 50°49N 4°20E 116 B2
St-Gilles Gard, France 43°40N 4°26E 175 E8
St-Gilles Réunion 21°2S 55°14E 272 f
St-Gilles-les-Bains Réunion 21°2S 55°14E 272 f
St-Gilles-les-Hauts Réunion 21°2S 55°15E 272 f
St-Girons France 42°59N 1°8E 174 F5
St. Gotthard P. = San Gottardo, P.
del Switz. 46°33N 8°33E 179 J4
St. Helena Atl. Oc. 15°58S 5°42W 153 h
St. Helena Calif., U.S.A. 38°30N 122°28W 306 G4
St. Helena, Mt. U.S.A. 38°40N 122°36W 306 G4
St. Helena B. S. Africa 32°40S 18°10E 270 D2
St. Helena Sd. U.S.A. 32°15N 80°25W 316 C9
St. Helens Tas., Australia 41°20S 148°15E 281 G4
St. Helens Mersey., U.K. 53°27N 2°44W 168 D5
St. Helens Oreg., U.S.A. 45°52N 122°48W 306 E4
St. Helens, Mt. U.S.A. 46°12N 122°12W 306 D4
St. Helier Chan. Is., U.K. 49°10N 2°7W 169 H5
St. Helier London, U.K. 51°23N 0°11W 125 B2
St-Herblain France 47°13N 1°40W 172 E5
St-Hilaire-du-Harcouët
France 48°35N 1°5W 172 D5
St-Hillaire-de-Riez France 46°43N 1°57W 174 B2
St-Hippolyte France 47°19N 6°50E 173 E13
St-Hippolyte-du-Fort
France 43°58N 3°52E 174 E7
St-Honoré-les-Bains
France 46°54N 3°50E 173 F10
St-Hubert Canada 45°29N 73°25W 130 B3
St-Hubert, Galeries Royales
Brussels, Belgium 116 b2
St-Hyacinthe Canada 45°40N 72°58W 298 C5
St. Ignace U.S.A. 45°52N 84°44W 309 C11
St. Ignace I. Canada 48°45N 88°0W 298 C2
St. Ignatius U.S.A. 47°19N 114°6W 304 C6
St-Imier Switz. 47°9N 6°58E 179 H2
St. Isaac's Cathedral
Russia 59°55N 30°19E 137 B1
St. Ives Cambs., U.K. 52°20N 0°4W 169 E7
St. Ives Corn., U.K. 50°12N 5°30W 169 G2
St-Jacques Montréal, Canada 130 a2
St-Jacques → Canada 45°26N 73°29W 130 B3
St-James France 48°31N 1°20W 172 D5
St. James Minn., U.S.A. 43°59N 94°38W 308 D6
St. James Mo., U.S.A. 38°0N 91°37W 310 G5
St. James Cathedral Toronto, Canada 141 b3
St. James's London, U.K. 125 b3
St-Jean St. Barts 17°53N 62°50W 322 a
St-Jean → Canada 50°17N 64°20W 299 B7
St-Jean, L. Canada 48°40N 72°0W 299 C5
St-Jean Baptiste Montréal, Canada 130 a1
St-Jean-d'Angély France 45°57N 0°31W 174 C3
St-Jean-de-Braye France 47°53N 1°58E 173 E8
St-Jean-de-Luz France 43°23N 1°39W 174 E2
St-Jean-de-Maurienne
France 45°16N 6°21E 175 C10
St-Jean-de-Monts France 46°47N 2°4W 172 F4
St-Jean-du-Gard France 44°7N 3°52E 174 D7
St-Jean-en-Royans France 45°1N 5°18E 175 C9
St-Jean-Pied-de-Port
France 43°10N 1°14W 174 E2
St-Jean-Port-Joli Canada 47°15N 70°13W 299 C5
St-Jean-sur-Richelieu
Canada 45°20N 73°20W 313 A11
St-Jérôme Canada 45°47N 74°0W 298 C5
St. Joe U.S.A. 41°19N 84°54W 311 C12
St. John N.B., Canada 45°20N 66°8W 299 C6
St. John Kans., U.S.A. 38°0N 98°46W 308 F4
St. John → Liberia 6°40N 9°10W 262 D2
St. John → N. Amer. 45°12N 66°5W 309 C20
St. John, C. Canada 50°0N 55°32W 299 C8
St. John I. U.S. Virgin Is. 18°20N 64°42W 321 b
St. John's Antigua & B. 17°6N 61°51W 322 b
St. John's Nfld. & L.,
Canada 47°35N 52°40W 299 C9
St. Johns Montserrat 16°46N 62°11W 323 p
St. Johns Ariz., U.S.A. 34°30N 109°22W 305 J9
St. Johns Mich., U.S.A. 43°0N 84°33W 311 B12
St. Johns → U.S.A. 30°24N 81°24W 316 E8
St. John's Pt. Ireland 54°34N 8°27W 166 B3
St. Johnsbury U.S.A. 44°25N 72°1W 313 B12
St. Johnston Village
Antigua & B. 17°7N 61°50W 322 b
St. Johnsville U.S.A. 43°0N 74°43W 313 D10
St-Joost-Ten-Node Belgium 50°51N 4°21E 116 A2
St. Joseph Ont., Canada 43°24N 81°42W 312 C3
St. Joseph Dominica 15°24N 61°26W 323 k
St-Joseph Martinique 14°39N 61°4W 322 c
St-Joseph Réunion 21°22S 55°37E 272 f
St. Joseph Mayaro,
Trin. & Tob. 10°18N 60°59W 323 t
St. Joseph Tunapuna,
Trin. & Tob. 10°40N 61°25W 323 t
St. Joseph Ill., U.S.A. 40°7N 88°2W 311 D8
St. Joseph La., U.S.A. 31°55N 91°14W 314 F9
St. Joseph Mich., U.S.A. 42°6N 86°29W 311 B10
St. Joseph Mo., U.S.A. 39°46N 94°50W 310 E2
St. Joseph → U.S.A. 42°7N 86°29W 311 B10
St. Joseph, I. Canada 46°12N 83°58W 298 C3
St. Joseph, L. Canada 51°10N 90°35W 298 B1
St. Joseph Pt. U.S.A. 29°52N 85°24W 316 F4
St-Juéry France 43°57N 2°12E 174 E6
St. Julian's Malta 35°55N 14°29E 206 F7
St-Julien-Chapteuil France 45°2N 4°4E 175 C8
St-Julien-de-Vouvantes
France 47°38N 1°13W 172 E5
St-Julien-en-Genevois
France 46°9N 6°5E 173 F13
St-Junien France 45°53N 0°55E 174 C4
St-Just-en-Chaussée France 49°30N 2°25E 173 C9
St-Just-en-Chevalet France 45°55N 3°50E 174 C7
St. Kilda Vic., Australia 37°51S 144°58E 128 B1
St. Kilda N.Z. 45°53S 170°31E 285 F5
St. Kilda W. Isles, U.K. 57°49N 8°34W 165 C2
St. Kitts W. Indies 17°20N 62°40W 322 d
St. Kitts & Nevis ■
W. Indies 17°20N 62°40W 322 d
St-Lambert Qué., Canada 45°30N 73°29W 130 A3
St-Lambert Yvelines, France 48°43N 2°1E 134 B1
St. Laurent Canada 50°25N 97°58W 297 C9
St-Laurent Canada 45°30N 73°43W 130 A1
St-Laurent-de-la-Salanque
France 42°46N 2°59E 174 F6
St-Laurent-du-Maroni
Fr. Guiana 5°29N 54°3W 329 B7
St-Laurent-du-Pont France 45°23N 5°45E 175 C9
St-Laurent-en-Grandvaux
France 46°35N 5°58E 173 F12
St-Laurent-Médoc France 45°8N 0°49W 174 C3
St. Lawrence Queens.,
Australia 22°16S 149°31E 280 C4
St. Lawrence Nfld. & L.,
Canada 46°54N 55°23W 299 C8
St. Lawrence → Canada 49°30N 66°0W 299 C6
St. Lawrence, Gulf of
Canada 48°25N 62°0W 299 C7
St. Lawrence I. U.S.A. 63°30N 170°30W 303 E5
St. Lawrence Islands △
Canada 44°27N 75°52W 313 B9
St. Lawrence Market Toronto, Canada 141 b3
St-Lazare, Gare Paris, France 134 a3
St. Léonard Canada 47°12N 67°58W 299 C6
St-Léonard Canada 45°35N 73°34W 130 A2
St-Léonard-de-Noblat
France 45°49N 1°29E 174 C5
St-Leu Réunion 21°9S 55°18E 272 f
St. Lewis → Canada 52°26N 56°11W 299 B8
St-Lô France 49°7N 1°5W 172 C5
St-Louis Montréal, Canada 130 b2
St-Louis Haut-Rhin, France 47°30N 7°34E 173 E14
St-Louis Guadeloupe 15°56N 61°19W 322 e
St-Louis Réunion 21°16S 55°25E 272 f
St-Louis Senegal 16°8N 16°27W 262 B1
St. Louis U.S.A. 38°37N 90°11W 310 F6
St-Louis ☐ Senegal 16°20N 15°0W 262 B2
St. Louis → U.S.A. 46°44N 92°9W 308 B7
St. Louis Lambert Int. ✕ (STL)
U.S.A. 38°45N 90°22W 310 F6
St-Loup-sur-Semouse
France 47°53N 6°16E 173 E13
St-Luc Canada 45°22N 73°18W 313 A11
St. Lucia ■ W. Indies 14°0N 60°57W 323 m
St. Lucia, L. S. Africa 28°5S 32°30E 271 C5
St. Lucia △ S. Africa 28°6S 32°27E 271 C5
St. Lucia Channel
W. Indies 14°15N 61°0W 321 D7
St. Lucie U.S.A. 27°29N 80°20W 317 H9
St. Lucie Canal U.S.A. 27°10N 80°18W 317 H9
St. Maarten ☒ W. Indies 18°2N 63°5W 322 a
St. Magnus B. U.K. 60°25N 1°35W 167 A7
St-Maixent-l'École France 46°24N 0°12W 174 B3
St-Malo France 48°39N 2°1W 172 D4
St-Malo, G. de France 48°50N 2°30W 172 D4
St-Mandé France 48°50N 2°24E 134 A3
St-Mandrier-sur-Mer France 43°4N 5°57E 175 E9
St-Marc Haiti 19°10N 72°41W 321 C5
St-Marcellin France 45°9N 5°20E 175 C9
St-Marcouf, Îs. France 49°30N 1°10W 172 C5
St. Maries U.S.A. 47°19N 116°35W 304 C5
St. Mark B. Grenada 12°11N 61°42W 323 q
St. Marks U.S.A. 30°9N 84°12W 316 E5
St. Mark's Square = San Marco,
Piazza Venice, Italy 142 b3
St-Martin ☒ W. Indies 18°5N 63°5W 322 a
St-Martin, Bois France 48°48N 2°35E 134 B4
St-Martin, C. Martinique 14°52N 61°14W 322 j
St. Martin, L. Canada 51°40N 98°30W 297 C9
St-Martin-de-Crau France 43°38N 4°48E 175 E8
St-Martin-de-Ré France 46°12N 1°21W 174 B2
St-Martin-d'Hères France 45°9N 5°45E 175 C9
St-Martin-Vésubie France 44°4N 7°15E 175 D11
St. Martin's I. Bangla. 20°36N 92°20E 241 E4
St-Martory France 43°9N 0°56E 174 E4
St. Mary U.S.A. 37°53N 89°57W 310 G7
St. Mary, Mt. Papua N. G. 8°8S 147°2E 286 E4
St. Mary Cray U.K. 51°23N 0°7E 125 B4
St. Mary Is. India 13°20N 74°35E 245 H2
St. Mary Pk. Australia 31°32S 138°34E 282 A3
St. Marys Tas., Australia 41°35S 148°11E 281 G4
St. Marys Ont., Canada 43°20N 81°10W 312 C3
St. Mary's Trin. & Tob. 10°14N 61°33W 323 t
St. Mary's Corn., U.K. 49°55N 6°18W 169 H1
St. Mary's Orkney, U.K. 58°54N 2°54W 167 C6
St. Mary's Alaska, U.S.A. 62°4N 163°10W 303 E7
St. Marys Ga., U.S.A. 30°44N 81°33W 316 E8
St. Marys Ohio, U.S.A. 40°33N 84°24W 311 D12
St. Marys Pa., U.S.A. 41°26N 78°34W 312 E6
St. Marys → U.S.A. 30°43N 81°27W 316 E8
St. Mary's, C. Canada 46°50N 54°12W 299 C9
St. Mary's B. Canada 46°50N 53°50W 299 C9
St. Marys Bay Canada 44°25N 66°10W 299 D6
St. Mary's Cathedral
San Francisco, U.S.A. 136 c1
St-Mathieu, Pte. France 48°20N 4°45W 172 D2
St. Matthew I. U.S.A. 60°24N 172°42W 303 F4
St. Matthews Ky., U.S.A. 38°15N 85°39W 311 F11
St. Matthews S.C., U.S.A. 33°40N 80°46W 316 B9
St. Matthews, I. = Zadetkyi Kyun
Burma 10°0N 98°25E 237 G2
St. Matthias Group
Papua N. G. 1°30S 150°0E 286 A6
St-Maur-des-Fossés France 48°48N 2°29E 134 B3
St-Maurice France 48°49N 2°25E 134 A3
St-Maurice → Canada 46°21N 72°31W 298 C5
St. Mawes U.K. 50°10N 5°2W 169 G2
St-Maximin-la-Ste-Baume
France 43°27N 5°52E 175 E9
St-Médard-en-Jalles
France 44°53N 0°43W 174 D3
St-Méen-le-Grand France 48°11N 2°12W 172 D4
St. Meinrad U.S.A. 38°10N 86°49W 311 F10
St. Michael U.S.A. 63°29N 162°2W 303 E7
St. Michael's Cathedral Toronto, Canada 141 a3
St-Michel Canada 45°34N 73°37W 130 A2
St-Mihiel France 48°54N 5°32E 173 D12
St-Nazaire France 47°17N 2°12W 172 E4
St. Neots U.K. 52°14N 0°15W 169 E7
St-Nicolas-de-Port France 48°38N 6°18E 173 D13
St-Omer France 50°45N 2°15E 173 B9
St-Ouen France 48°56N 2°20E 134 A3
St-Palais-sur-Mer France 45°38N 1°5W 174 C2
St-Pamphile Canada 46°58N 69°48W 299 C6
St. Pancras International London, U.K. 125 a4
St-Pardoux-la-Rivière
France 45°29N 0°45E 174 C4
St. Paris U.S.A. 40°8N 83°58W 311 D13
St-Pascal Canada 47°32N 69°48W 299 C6
St. Patricks Barbados 13°6N 59°30W 323 r
St. Patrick's Cathedral New York, U.S.A. 132 e1
St. Patrick's Church Toronto, Canada 141 a1

St. Paul Canada 54°0N 111°17W 296 C6
St-Paul Réunion 20°59S 55°17E 272 f
St. Paul Alaska, U.S.A. 57°7N 170°17W 303 H5
St. Paul Ind., U.S.A. 39°26N 85°38W 311 E11
St. Paul Minn., U.S.A. 44°56N 93°5W 308 C7
St. Paul Nebr., U.S.A. 41°13N 98°27W 308 E4
St-Paul → Canada 51°27N 57°42W 299 B8
St. Paul → Liberia 6°25N 10°48W 262 D2
St. Paul, Î. Ind. Oc. 38°55S 77°34E 273 H6
St-Paul-de-Fenouillet France 42°48N 2°30E 174 F6
St. Paul I. N.S., Canada 47°12N 60°9W 299 C7
St. Paul I. Alaska, U.S.A. 57°10N 170°15W 303 H5
St-Paul-lès-Dax France 43°44N 1°3W 174 E2
St-Paul-sur-Ubaye France 44°31N 6°45E 175 D10
St. Pauls St. Helena 15°57S 5°43W 153 h
St. Paul's Bay Malta 35°57N 14°24E 206 F7
St. Paul's Cathedral London, U.K. 125 b4
St. Paul's Cray U.K. 51°23N 0°6E 125 B4
St-Péray France 44°57N 4°50E 175 D8
St. Pete Beach U.S.A. 27°43N 82°44W 317 H7
St. Peter U.S.A. 44°20N 93°57W 308 C7
St. Peter & St. Paul San Francisco, U.S.A. 136 a2
St. Peter Port U.K. 49°26N 2°33W 169 H5
St. Peters N.S.W., Australia 33°55S 151°11E 139 B2
St. Peters N.S., Canada 45°40N 60°53W 299 C7
St. Peters P.E.I., Canada 46°25N 62°35W 299 C7
St. Peters Montserrat 16°43N 62°13W 323 p
St. Peters Mo., U.S.A. 38°48N 90°37W 310 F6
St. Peter's Square = San Pietro, Piazza Rome, Italy 136 b1
St. Petersburg = Sankt-Peterburg Russia 59°55N 30°20E 137 B1
St. Petersburg U.S.A. 27°46N 82°40W 317 H7
St. Petersburg Pulkovo Int. ✕ (LED) Russia 59°48N 30°18E 137 C1
St-Philbert-de-Grand-Lieu France 47°2N 1°39W 172 E5
St-Phillippe Réunion 21°21S 55°44E 272 f
St-Pie Canada 45°30N 72°54W 313 A12
St-Pierre Qué., Canada 45°27N 73°38W 130 B2
St. Pierre Martinique 14°45N 61°10W 322 j
St. Pierre Mauritius 20°13S 57°31E 272 e
St-Pierre Réunion 21°19S 55°28E 272 f
St-Pierre St-P. & M. 46°46N 56°12W 299 C8
St-Pierre, L. Canada 46°12N 72°52W 298 C5
St-Pierre, Rade de Martinique 14°44N 61°11W 322 j
St-Pierre-de-la-Pointe-aux-Esquimaux = Havre-St.-Pierre Canada 50°18N 63°33W 299 B7
St-Pierre-d'Oléron France 45°57N 1°19W 174 C2
St-Pierre-en-Port France 49°48N 0°30E 172 C7
St-Pierre-et-Miquelon ☒ N. Amer. 46°55N 56°10W 299 C8
St-Pierre-le-Moûtier France 46°47N 3°7E 173 F10
St-Pierre-sur-Dives France 49°2N 0°1W 172 C6
St-Pieters Leew Belgium 50°47N 4°16E 116 B1
St-Pol-de-Léon France 48°41N 4°0W 172 D3
St-Pol-sur-Mer France 51°1N 2°20E 173 A9
St-Pol-sur-Ternoise France 50°23N 2°20E 173 B9
St-Pons France 43°30N 2°45E 174 E6
St-Pourçain-sur-Sioule France 46°18N 3°18E 173 F10
St-Priest France 45°42N 4°57E 175 C8
St-Quay-Portrieux France 48°39N 2°51W 172 D4
St-Quentin N.B., Canada 47°30N 67°23W 299 C6
St-Quentin Aisne, France 49°50N 3°16E 173 C10
St-Quentin, Étang de France 48°47N 2°0E 134 B1
St-Raphaël France 43°25N 6°46E 175 E10
St. Regis U.S.A. 47°18N 115°6W 304 C6
St. Regis Falls U.S.A. 44°40N 74°32W 313 B10
St-Renan France 48°26N 4°37W 172 D2
St. Robert U.S.A. 37°50N 92°11W 310 G4
St-Saëns France 49°41N 1°16E 172 C8
St-Savin France 46°34N 0°53E 174 B4
St-Savinien France 45°53N 0°42W 174 C3
St. Sebastien, Tanjon' i Madag. 12°26S 48°44E 272 A2
St-Seine-l'Abbaye France 47°26N 4°47E 173 E11
St-Sernin-sur-Rance France 43°54N 2°35E 174 E6
St-Sever France 43°45N 0°35W 174 E3
St-Siméon Canada 47°51N 69°54W 299 C6
St. Simons I. U.S.A. 31°12N 81°15W 316 D8
St. Simons Island U.S.A. 31°9N 81°22W 316 D8
St. Stephen N.B., Canada 45°16N 67°17W 299 C6
St. Stephen S.C., U.S.A. 33°24N 79°55W 316 B10
St. Stephen's Basilica Budapest, Hungary 117 b2
St. Stephen's Cathedral = Stephansdom Vienna, Austria 142 b2
St-Stevens-Woluwe Belgium 50°52N 4°26E 116 A2
St-Sulpice France 43°46N 1°41E 174 E5
St-Sulpice-Laurière France 46°3N 1°29E 174 B5
St-Sulpice-les-Feuilles France 46°19N 1°21E 174 B5
St-Syprien = St-Cyprien France 42°37N 3°2E 174 F7
St. Teresa U.S.A. 29°55N 84°27W 316 F5
St-Thégonnec France 48°31N 3°57W 172 D3
St. Thomas = Charlotte Amalie U.S. Virgin Is. 18°21N 64°56W 321 C7
St. Thomas Canada 42°45N 81°10W 312 D3
St. Thomas Bay Malta 35°51N 14°34E 206 F8
St. Thomas I. U.S. Virgin Is. 18°20N 64°55W 321 C7
St-Tite Canada 46°45N 72°34W 298 C5
St-Trond = Sint-Truiden Belgium 50°48N 5°10E 170 D5
St-Tropez France 43°17N 6°38E 175 E10
St-Vaast-la-Hougue France 49°35N 1°17W 172 C5
St-Valery-en-Caux France 49°52N 0°43E 172 C7
St-Valéry-sur-Somme France 50°11N 1°38E 173 B8
St-Vallier France 46°38N 4°22E 173 F11
St-Vallier-de-Thiey France 43°42N 6°51E 175 E10
St-Varent France 46°53N 0°13W 172 F6
St. Vaury France 46°12N 1°46E 174 B5
St. Vidgeon's ◎ Australia 14°47S 134°53E 280 A1
St. Vincent = São Vicente C. Verde Is. 17°0N 25°0W 153 j
St. Vincent Italy 45°45N 7°39E 198 C4
St. Vincent W. Indies 13°15N 61°10W 323 n
St. Vincent, G. Australia 35°0S 138°0E 282 C3
St. Vincent & the Grenadines ■ W. Indies 13°0N 61°10W 323 n
St-Vincent-de-Paul Canada 45°36N 73°39W 130 A2
St-Vincent-de-Tyrosse France 43°39N 1°19W 174 E2
St. Vincent I. U.S.A. 29°42N 85°3W 317 F4
St. Vincent Passage W. Indies 13°30N 61°0W 321 D7
St-Vith Belgium 50°17N 6°9E 170 D6
St-Vivien-de-Médoc France 45°25N 1°2W 174 C2
St. Walburg Canada 53°39N 109°12W 297 C7
St. Xavier Univ. U.S.A. 41°42N 87°42W 119 C2
St-Yrieix-la-Perche France 45°31N 1°12E 174 C5
Saintala India 20°26N 83°20E 244 D6
Ste-Adresse France 49°31N 0°5E 172 C7
Ste-Agathe-des-Monts Canada 46°3N 74°17W 298 C5
Ste-Anne Guadeloupe 16°13N 61°24W 322 e
Ste-Anne Martinique 14°25N 60°54W 322 j
Ste-Anne Réunion 21°4S 55°45E 272 f
Ste-Anne Seychelles 4°36S 55°31E 272 c
Ste-Anne, L. Canada 50°0N 67°42W 299 B6
Ste-Anne-des-Monts Canada 49°8N 66°30W 299 C6
Ste-Catherine Canada 45°24N 73°34W 130 B2
Ste-Croix Switz. 46°49N 6°34E 179 J2
Ste-Enimie France 44°22N 3°26E 174 D7
Ste-Foy-la-Grande France 44°50N 0°13E 174 D4
Ste. Genevieve U.S.A. 37°59N 90°2W 310 G6
Ste-Hélène, Î. Canada 45°31N 73°32W 130 A2
Ste-Hermine France 46°32N 1°4W 174 B2
Ste-Livrade-sur-Lot France 44°24N 0°36E 174 D4
Ste-Luce Martinique 14°28N 60°55W 322 j
Ste. Madeleine Trin. & Tob. 10°16N 61°26W 323 t
Ste-Marguerite Guadeloupe 16°23N 61°24W 322 e
Ste-Marguerite → Canada 50°9N 66°36W 299 B6
Ste-Marie Canada 46°26N 71°0W 299 C5
Ste. Marie Gabon 3°48S 11°1E 264 C2
Ste-Marie Guadeloupe 16°6N 61°33W 322 e
Ste-Marie Martinique 14°48N 61°1W 322 j
Ste-Marie Réunion 20°53S 55°33E 272 f
Ste-Marie, Ile = Boraha, Nosy Madag. 16°50S 49°55E 272 B2
Ste-Marie-aux-Mines France 48°15N 7°12E 173 D14
Ste-Marthe Guadeloupe 16°15N 61°15W 322 e
Ste-Maure-de-Touraine France 47°7N 0°37E 172 E7
Ste-Maxime France 43°19N 6°39E 175 E10
Ste-Menehould France 49°5N 4°54E 173 C11
Ste-Mère-Église France 49°24N 1°19W 172 C5
Ste-Rose Guadeloupe 16°20N 61°45W 322 e
Ste-Rose Réunion 21°8S 55°45E 272 f
Ste. Rose du Lac Canada 51°4N 99°30W 297 C9
Ste-Savine France 48°18N 4°3E 173 D11
Ste-Sigolène France 45°15N 4°14E 175 C8
Ste-Suzanne Réunion 20°54S 55°36E 272 f
Saintes France 45°45N 0°37W 174 C3
Saintes, Canal des Guadeloupe 15°55N 61°40W 322 e
Saintes, Îs. des Guadeloupe 15°50N 61°35W 322 e
Stes-Maries-de-la-Mer France 43°26N 4°26E 175 E8
Saintfield U.K. 54°28N 5°49W 166 B6
Saintonge France 45°40N 0°50W 174 C3
Saipal Nepal 29°50N 81°40E 243 E9
Saipan N. Marianas 15°12N 145°45E 302 e
Saipan Channel N. Marianas 15°5N 145°41E 302 e
Sairang India 23°50N 92°45E 241 D4
Sairecábur, Cerro Bolivia 22°43S 67°54W 334 A2
Sāitah Si. Arabia 16°36N 42°56E 248 C3
Saitama Japan 35°54N 139°38E 223 B11
Saitama □ Japan 36°25N 139°30E 223 A11
Saiteli = Kadınhanı Turkey 38°14N 32°13E 212 C5
Saiţi Moldova 46°30N 29°24E 183 D14
Saito Japan 32°3N 131°24E 222 E3
Saiwai Japan 35°32N 139°41E 140 B3
Saiyid Pakistan 33°7N 73°2E 242 C5
Saja-Besaya ⌓ Spain 43°10N 4°9W 194 B6
Sajama Bolivia 18°7S 69°0W 330 D4
Sajama, Nevado Bolivia 18°6S 68°54W 330 D4
Sajan Serbia 45°50N 20°20E 182 E5
Sajó → Hungary 47°56N 21°7E 182 C6
Sajókazinc = Kazincbarcika Hungary 48°17N 20°36E 182 B5
Sajószentpéter Hungary 48°12N 20°44E 182 B5
Sajum India 33°20N 79°0E 243 C8
Sak → S. Africa 30°52S 20°25E 270 D3
Saka Kenya 0°9S 39°20E 268 B4
Saka Kalat Pakistan 27°3N 65°3E 240 D2
Sakaba Nigeria 11°4N 5°35E 263 C6
Sakai Fukui, Japan 36°9N 136°16E 223 A8
Sakai Ōsaka, Japan 34°34N 135°27E 133 B1
Sakai Harbour Japan 34°36N 135°26E 133 B1
Sakaide Japan 34°19N 133°50E 222 C5
Sakaiminato Japan 35°38N 133°11E 222 B5
Sakākah Si. Arabia 30°0N 40°8E 246 D4
Sakakawea, L. U.S.A. 47°30N 101°25W 308 B3
Sakami → Canada 53°40N 76°40W 298 B4
Sakami, L. Canada 53°15N 77°0W 298 B4
Sakâne, 'Erg i-n Mali 20°30N 1°30W 260 D4
Sakania Dem. Rep. of the Congo 12°43S 28°30E 269 E2
Sakar I. Papua N. G. 5°25S 148°5E 286 C5
Sakaraha Madag. 22°55S 44°32E 272 C1
Sakartvelo = Georgia ■ Asia 42°0N 43°0E 191 J6
Sakarya Turkey 40°48N 30°25E 212 B4
Sakarya □ Turkey 40°45N 30°25E 212 B4
Sakarya → Turkey 41°7N 30°39E 212 B4
Sakashima-Guntō Japan 24°46N 124°0E 221 M2
Sakassou Ivory C. 7°29N 5°19W 262 D3
Sakata Japan 38°55N 139°50E 220 E9
Sakawa Japan 33°28N 133°11E 222 D5
Sakchu N. Korea 40°23N 125°2E 224 B2
Sakeny → Madag. 20°0S 45°25E 272 C2
Sakété Benin 6°40N 2°45E 263 D5
Sakha □ Russia 66°0N 130°0E 215 C14
Sakhalin Russia 51°0N 143°0E 215 D15
Sakhalinskiy Zaliv Russia 54°0N 141°0E 215 D15
Sakhi Gopal India 19°58N 85°50E 244 E7
Şaki Azerbaijan 41°10N 47°5E 191 K8
Šakiai Lithuania 54°59N 23°2E 184 D10
Sakiz-Adasi = Chios Greece 38°27N 26°9E 205 C8
Sakmara → Russia 51°46N 55°1E 216 B5
Sakoli India 21°5N 79°59E 244 D4
Sakon Nakhon Thailand 17°10N 104°9E 236 D5
Sakra, Pulau Singapore 1°15N 103°41E 138 B2
Sakrand Pakistan 26°10N 68°15E 242 F3
Sakri Maharashtra, India 26°13N 86°5E 243 F12
Sakri Maharashtra, India 21°2N 74°20E 244 D2
Sakrivier S. Africa 30°54S 20°28E 270 D3
Sakskøbing Denmark 54°49N 11°39E 163 K5
Sakti India 22°2N 82°58E 243 H10
Saku Japan 36°17N 138°31E 223 A10
Sakuma Japan 35°3N 137°49E 223 B9
Sakura Japan 35°43N 140°14E 223 B12
Sakurai Japan 34°30N 135°51E 223 C7
Sakurajima = On-Take Japan 31°35N 130°39E 222 F2
Saky Ukraine 45°9N 33°34E 189 K7
Sal → Russia 47°31N 40°45E 191 G5
Sal Rei C. Verde Is. 16°11N 22°53W 153 j
Sala Eritrea 16°53N 37°36E 257 D4
Šal'a Slovakia 48°10N 17°50E 181 C10
Sala Sweden 59°58N 16°35E 162 E10
Sala → Eritrea 16°53N 37°36E 257 D4
Sala, O. → Chad 17°0N 20°55E 259 E4
Sala Consilina Italy 40°23N 15°36E 201 B8
Sala-y-Gómez Pac. Oc. 26°28S 105°28W 289 K17
Sala-y-Gómez Ridge Pac. Oc. 25°0S 98°0W 289 K18
Salaberry-de-Valleyfield Canada 45°15N 74°8W 313 A10
Salacgrīva Latvia 57°45N 24°21E 184 A11
Salada, L. Mexico 32°20N 115°40W 305 K6
Saladas Argentina 28°15S 58°40W 334 B4
Saladillo Argentina 35°40S 59°55W 334 D4
Saladin's Castle = Qal'at Salah el Din Syria 34°46N 36°15E 250 D7
Salado → B. Aires, Argentina 35°44S 57°22W 334 D4
Salado → La Pampa, Argentina 37°30S 67°0W 336 A3
Salado → Río Negro, Argentina 41°34S 65°3W 336 B3
Salado → Santa Fe, Argentina 31°40S 60°41W 334 C3
Salado → Tamaulipas, Mexico 26°52N 99°19W 314 H5
Salaga Ghana 8°31N 0°31W 263 D4
Şalāh Syria 32°40N 36°45E 250 F7
Şalāḥ ad Dīn □ Iraq 34°35N 43°35E 246 C4
Salahin Somalia 2°57N 46°26E 267 D6
Sălaj □ Romania 47°15N 23°0E 182 C8
Salakos Greece 36°17N 27°57E 206 E11
Salal Chad 14°48N 17°12E 259 F3
Salala Liberia 6°42N 10°7W 262 D2
Salala Sudan 21°17N 36°16E 256 C4
Salālah Oman 16°56N 53°59E 249 C6
Salam Iraq 33°20N 44°20E 113 A2
Salamajärvi △ Finland 63°12N 24°50E 160 E21
Salamanca Chile 31°46S 70°59W 334 C1
Salamanca Madrid, Spain 40°25N 3°41W 127 B1
Salamanca Salamanca, Spain 40°58N 5°39W 194 E5
Salamanca N.Y., U.S.A. 42°10N 78°43W 312 D6
Salamanca □ Spain 40°57N 5°40W 194 E5
Salamat □ Chad 11°0N 20°30E 259 F4
Salamat, Bahr → Chad 9°20N 18°0E 259 G3
Salamatābād Iran 35°39N 47°50E 246 C5
Salamina Colombia 5°25N 75°29W 328 B2
Salamina Greece 37°56N 23°30E 204 D5
Salamis Cyprus 35°11N 33°54E 207 E9
Salamonie L. U.S.A. 40°46N 85°37W 311 D11
Salar de Atacama Chile 23°30S 68°25W 334 A2
Salar de Uyuni Bolivia 20°30S 67°45W 330 E4
Sălard Romania 47°12N 22°3E 182 C7
Salas Spain 43°25N 6°15W 194 B4
Salas de los Infantes Spain 42°2N 3°17W 194 C7
Salatiga Indonesia 7°19S 110°30E 235 D4
Salavat Russia 53°21N 55°55E 186 D10
Salaverry Peru 8°15S 79°0W 330 B2
Salawati Indonesia 1°7S 130°52E 231 E8
Salawin △ Thailand 18°18N 97°40E 236 C1
Salay Phil. 8°52N 124°47E 233 G5
Salaya India 22°19N 69°35E 242 H3
Salayar Indonesia 6°7S 120°30E 231 F6
Salazar → Spain 42°40N 1°20W 196 C3
Salazie Réunion 21°2S 55°33E 272 f
Salazie, Cirque de Réunion 21°3S 55°30E 272 f
Salbris France 47°25N 2°3E 173 E9
S'Albufera Spain 39°47N 3°7E 206 B4
S'Albufera d'es Grau Spain 39°56N 4°16E 206 B5
Salcantay, Nevado Peru 13°19S 72°33W 330 C3
Salcedo Phil. 11°9N 125°40E 233 F5
Salcia Romania 43°56N 24°55E 183 G9
Sălciua Romania 46°24N 23°26E 183 D8
Salcombe U.K. 50°14N 3°47W 169 G4
Saldaña Spain 42°32N 4°48W 194 C6
Saldanha S. Africa 33°0S 17°58E 270 D2
Saldanha B. S. Africa 33°6S 18°0E 270 D2
Saldus Latvia 56°38N 22°30E 184 B9
Sale Vic., Australia 38°6S 147°6E 283 E7
Sale Burma 20°50N 94°45E 241 E5
Sale Italy 44°59N 8°48E 198 D5
Salé Morocco 34°3N 6°48W 260 B3
Sale Gt. Man., U.K. 53°26N 2°19W 168 D5
Sale City U.S.A. 31°16N 84°1W 316 D5
Salée, Rivière Guadeloupe 16°17N 61°33W 322 e
Salegard = Salekhard Russia 66°30N 66°35E 214 C7
Saleh, Teluk Indonesia 8°34S 117°57E 235 D5
Salekhard Russia 66°30N 66°35E 214 C7
Salelologa Samoa 13°41S 172°11W 287 V19
Salem India 11°40N 78°11E 245 J4
Salem Montserrat 16°45N 62°13W 323 p
Salem Fla., U.S.A. 29°53N 83°25W 316 F6
Salem Ill., U.S.A. 38°38N 88°57W 310 F8
Salem Ind., U.S.A. 38°36N 86°6W 311 F10
Salem Mass., U.S.A. 42°31N 70°53W 313 D14
Salem Mo., U.S.A. 37°39N 91°32W 308 G8
Salem N.H., U.S.A. 42°45N 71°12W 313 D13
Salem N.J., U.S.A. 39°34N 75°28W 309 F16
Salem N.Y., U.S.A. 43°10N 73°20W 313 C11
Salem Ohio, U.S.A. 40°54N 80°52W 312 F4
Salem Oreg., U.S.A. 44°56N 123°2W 304 D2
Salem S. Dak., U.S.A. 43°44N 97°23W 308 D5
Salem Va., U.S.A. 37°18N 80°3W 309 G13
Salemi Italy 37°49N 12°48E 200 E5
Sälen Sweden 61°20N 13°10E 162 C7
Salernes France 43°34N 6°15E 175 E10
Salerno Italy 40°41N 14°47E 201 B7
Salerno, G. di Italy 40°32N 14°42E 201 B7
Sales Brazil 4°2S 63°40W 329 D5
Salford U.K. 53°30N 2°18W 168 D5
Salgótarján Hungary 48°5N 19°47E 182 B4
Salgueiro Brazil 8°4S 39°6W 332 C4
Salher India 20°40N 73°55E 244 D1
Salhus Norway 60°30N 5°15E 164 D2
Salhyr → Ukraine 45°38N 35°1E 189 K8
Salibabu Indonesia 3°51N 126°40E 231 D7
Salibea = Salybia Trin. & Tob. 10°43N 61°2W 323 t
Salibia Dominica 15°30N 61°16W 323 k
Salida U.S.A. 38°32N 106°0W 304 G11
Salies-de-Béarn France 43°28N 0°56W 174 E3
Salihli Turkey 38°28N 28°8E 212 C3
Salihorsk Belarus 52°51N 27°27E 177 B14
Salin Burma 20°35N 94°40E 241 E5
Salina Italy 38°34N 14°50E 201 D7
Salina Kans., U.S.A. 38°50N 97°37W 308 F5
Salina Utah, U.S.A. 38°58N 111°51W 304 G8
Salina Cruz Mexico 16°10N 95°12W 319 D5
Salina di Margherita di Savóia ⌓ Italy 41°23N 16°4E 201 A9
Salinas = Salinópolis Brazil 0°40S 47°20W 332 B2
Salinas Brazil 16°10S 42°10W 333 E3
Salinas Ecuador 2°10S 80°58W 328 D1
Salinas Calif., U.S.A. 36°40N 121°39W 306 J5
Salinas → Guatemala 16°28N 90°31W 319 D6
Salinas → Calif., U.S.A. 36°45N 121°48W 306 J5
Salinas, B. das Angola 14°11S 12°21E 265 E2
Salinas, B. de Nic. 11°4N 85°45W 320 D2
Salinas, Pampa de las Argentina 31°58S 66°42W 334 C2
Salinas Ambargasta Argentina 29°0S 65°0W 334 B3
Salinas de Hidalgo Mexico 22°38N 101°43W 318 C4
Salinas Grandes Argentina 30°0S 65°0W 334 C3
Salinas Pueblo Missions ⌓ U.S.A. 34°6N 106°4W 305 J10
Salinas Valley U.S.A. 36°15N 121°15W 306 J5
Saline U.S.A. 42°10N 83°47W 311 B13
Saline → Ark., U.S.A. 33°10N 92°8W 314 E8
Saline → Kans., U.S.A. 38°52N 97°30W 308 F5
Saline B. Trin. & Tob. 10°42N 61°2W 323 t
Saline di Trapani e Paceco ⌓ Italy 37°59N 12°28E 200 E5
Saline I. Grenada 12°26N 61°28W 323 q
Salines, C. de ses Spain 39°16N 3°4E 206 B4
Salines, Étang des Martinique 14°24N 60°52W 322 j
Salines, Pt. Grenada 12°0N 61°48W 323 q
Salines, Pte. de Martinique 14°23N 60°53W 322 j
Salinópolis Brazil 0°40S 47°20W 332 B2
Salins-les-Bains France 46°58N 5°52E 173 F12
Salir Portugal 37°14N 8°2W 195 H2
Salisbury = Harare Zimbabwe 17°43S 31°2E 269 F3
Salisbury S. Austral., Australia 34°46S 138°38E 282 C3
Salisbury Dominica 15°26N 61°27W 323 k
Salisbury Wilts., U.K. 51°4N 1°47W 169 F6
Salisbury Md., U.S.A. 38°22N 75°36W 309 F16
Salisbury Mo., U.S.A. 39°25N 92°48W 310 E4
Salisbury N.C., U.S.A. 35°40N 80°29W 315 D14
Salisbury I. Canada 63°30N 77°0W 295 E16
Salisbury Plain U.K. 51°14N 1°55W 169 F6
Săliște Romania 45°45N 23°56E 183 E8
Salitre → Brazil 9°29S 40°39W 332 C3
Salkehatchie → U.S.A. 32°37N 80°53W 316 C9
Şalkhad Syria 32°29N 36°43E 251 F7
Salkove Ukraine 48°15N 29°59E 183 B14
Salla Finland 66°50N 28°49E 160 C23
Sallanches France 45°55N 6°38E 175 C10
Sallent Spain 41°49N 1°54E 196 D6
Salles France 44°33N 0°52W 174 D3
Salles-Curan France 44°11N 2°48E 174 D6
Salling Denmark 56°40N 8°55E 163 H2
Salliq = Coral Harbour Canada 64°8N 83°10W 295 E15
Sallisaw U.S.A. 35°28N 94°47W 314 D7
Sallom Sudan 19°17N 37°6E 256 D4
Salluit Canada 62°14N 75°38W 295 E16
Sallyana Nepal 28°22N 82°10E 243 E10
Salmān Pak Iraq 33°6N 44°34E 213 G11
Salmannsdorf Austria 48°14N 16°14E 142 A1
Salmās Iran 38°11N 44°47E 213 C11
Salmedina Spain 40°18N 3°35W 127 C2
Salmerón Spain 40°33N 2°29W 196 E2
Salmo Canada 49°10N 117°20W 296 D5
Salmon U.S.A. 45°11N 113°54W 304 D7
Salmon → B.C., Canada 54°3N 122°40W 296 C4
Salmon → Idaho, U.S.A. 45°51N 116°47W 304 D5
Salmon Arm Canada 50°40N 119°15W 296 C5
Salmon Gums Australia 32°59S 121°38E 279 F3
Salmon Pt. Canada 43°52N 77°15W 312 C7
Salmon River Mts. U.S.A. 44°50N 115°30W 304 D6
Salmon River Res. U.S.A. 43°32N 75°55W 313 C9
Salo C.A.R. 3°10N 16°8E 264 B3
Salo Finland 60°22N 23°10E 188 B2
Salò Italy 45°36N 10°31E 198 C7
Salobreña Spain 36°44N 3°35W 195 J7
Salome U.S.A. 33°47N 113°37W 307 M13
Salomea Poland 52°11N 20°55E 143 B1
Salomon, C. Martinique 14°30N 61°6W 322 j
Salon India 26°2N 81°27E 243 F9
Salon-de-Provence France 43°39N 5°6E 175 E9
Salonga → Dem. Rep. of the Congo 0°10S 19°50E 264 C4
Salonga-Nord △ Dem. Rep. of the Congo 1°55S 21°45E 264 C4
Salonga-Sud △ Dem. Rep. of the Congo 2°25S 21°0E 264 C4
Salonica = Thessaloniki Greece 40°38N 22°58E 202 F6
Salonta Romania 46°49N 21°42E 182 D6
Salop = Shropshire □ U.K. 52°36N 2°45W 169 E5
Salor → Spain 39°39N 7°3W 195 F3
Salou Spain 41°4N 1°8E 196 D6
Salou, C. de Spain 41°3N 1°10E 196 D6
Saloum → Senegal 13°50N 16°45W 262 C1
Salpausselkä Finland 61°3N 26°15E 188 B4
Salsacate Argentina 31°20S 65°5W 334 C2
Salses France 42°50N 2°55E 174 F6
Salsette I. India 19°2N 72°53E 130 A2
Salsk Russia 46°28N 41°30E 191 G5
Salso → Italy 37°6N 13°57E 200 E6
Salsomaggiore Terme Italy 44°49N 9°59E 198 D6
Salt Spain 41°59N 2°47E 196 D7
Salt → Alta., Canada 60°0N 112°25W 296 B6
Salt → Ariz., U.S.A. 33°23N 112°19W 305 K7
Salt → Mo., U.S.A. 39°28N 91°4W 310 E5
Salt Cay Bahamas 25°6N 77°18W 153 b
Salt Flats = Witte Pan Bonaire 12°3N 68°17W 322 h
Salt Fork Red → U.S.A. 34°27N 99°21W 314 D5
Salt L. N.S.W., Australia 30°6S 142°8E 281 E3
Salt L. Hawai'i, U.S.A. 21°21N 157°55W 302 K14
Salt Lake City = Bidhan Nagar India 22°35N 88°25E 124 B2
Salt Lake City U.S.A. 40°45N 111°53W 304 F8
Salt Lake City Int. ✕ (SLC) U.S.A. 40°47N 111°58W 304 F7
Salt Lake Stadium Kolkata, India 22°34N 88°25E 124 B2
Salt Range Pakistan 32°30N 72°25E 242 C5
Salt River S. Africa 34°6S 18°28E 118 A1
Salt Springs U.S.A. 29°21N 81°44W 317 F8
Salt Water L. India 22°33N 88°26E 124 B2
Salta Argentina 24°57S 65°25W 334 A2
Salta □ Argentina 24°48S 65°30W 334 A2
Saltara Italy 43°45N 12°50E 199 E9
Saltash U.K. 50°24N 4°14W 169 G3
Saltburn-by-the-Sea U.K. 54°35N 0°58W 168 C7
Saltcoats U.K. 55°38N 4°47W 167 F4
Saltee Is. Ireland 52°7N 6°37W 166 D5
Salters U.S.A. 33°36N 79°51W 316 B10
Saltfjellet Norway 66°40N 15°15E 160 C16
Saltfjellet-Svartisen △ Norway 66°45N 15°10E 160 C16
Saltfjorden Norway 67°15N 14°10E 160 C16
Saltholm Denmark 55°38N 12°43E 163 J6
Salthólmavík Iceland 65°24N 21°57W 155 B5
Saltillo Mexico 25°25N 101°0W 318 B4
Salto Argentina 34°20S 60°15W 334 C3
Salto Uruguay 31°27S 57°50W 334 C4
Salto da Divisa Brazil 16°0S 39°57W 333 E4
Salto del Guaira Paraguay 24°3S 54°17W 335 A5
Salton City U.S.A. 33°18N 115°57W 307 M11
Salton Sea U.S.A. 33°15N 115°45W 307 M11
Saltpond Ghana 5°15N 1°3W 263 D4
Saltrød Norway 58°30N 8°49E 164 F5
Saltsburg U.S.A. 40°29N 79°27W 312 F5
Saltsjö-Duvnäs Sweden 59°18N 18°12E 139 B3
Saltsjöbaden Sweden 59°15N 18°20E 162 E12
Saluda U.S.A. 34°0N 81°47W 316 A8
Saluda → U.S.A. 34°1N 81°4W 316 A8
Salue Timpaus, Selat Indonesia 1°50S 123°50E 231 E6
Salug Phil. 8°7N 122°47E 233 G4
Salûm Egypt 31°31N 25°7E 256 A2
Salûm, Khâlig el Egypt 31°35N 25°24E 256 A2
Salur India 18°27N 83°18E 244 E6
Salut, Is. du Fr. Guiana 5°15N 52°35W 329 B7
Saluzzo Italy 44°39N 7°29E 198 D4
Salvación, B. Chile 50°50S 75°10W 336 D1
Salvador Brazil 13°0S 38°30W 333 D4
Salvador Canada 52°10N 109°32W 297 C7
Salvador, El ■ Cent. Amer. 13°50N 89°0W 320 D2
Salvador, L. U.S.A. 29°43N 90°15W 315 G9
Salvaterra Brazil 0°46S 48°31W 332 B2
Salvaterra de Magos Portugal 39°1N 8°47W 195 F2
Salvisa U.S.A. 37°54N 84°51W 311 G12
Sálvora, I. de Spain 42°30N 8°58W 194 C2
Salween → Burma 16°31N 97°37E 241 G6
Salyan Azerbaijan 39°33N 48°59E 213 C13
Salybia Trin. & Tob. 10°43N 61°2W 323 t
Salza → Austria 47°40N 14°43E 180 D7
Salzach → Austria 48°12N 12°56E 180 C5
Salzburg Austria 47°48N 13°2E 180 D6
Salzburg □ Austria 47°15N 13°0E 180 D6
Salzburgen = Château-Salins France 48°50N 6°30E 173 D13
Salzgitter Germany 52°9N 10°19E 178 C6
Salzkotten Germany 51°40N 8°37E 178 D4
Salzwedel Germany 52°52N 11°10E 178 C7
Sam Gabon 0°58N 11°16E 264 B2
Sam India 26°50N 70°31E 242 F4
Sam Neua Laos 20°29N 104°5E 228 G5
Sam Ngao Thailand 17°18N 99°0E 236 D2
Sam Rayburn Res. U.S.A. 31°4N 94°5W 314 F7
Sam Rong, Laem Thailand 9°35N 100°4E 237 b
Sam Son Vietnam 19°44N 105°54E 236 C5
Sama de Langreo = Langreo Spain 43°18N 5°40W 194 B5
Šamac Bos.-H. 45°3N 18°29E 182 E3
Samacimbo Angola 13°33S 16°59E 265 E3
Şamad Oman 22°48N 58°9E 249 B7
Samagaltay Russia 50°36N 95°3E 217 B13
Samā'il Oman 23°40N 57°50E 249 B7
Samaipata Bolivia 18°9S 63°52W 331 D5
Samal Phil. 7°5N 125°42E 233 H5
Samal I. Phil. 7°3N 125°44E 233 H5
Samales Group Phil. 6°0N 122°0E 233 J3
Samalga Pass U.S.A. 52°50N 169°0W 300 E6
Samalkot India 17°3N 82°13E 244 F6
Samâlût Egypt 28°20N 30°42E 256 B3
Samana India 30°10N 76°13E 242 D7
Samana Cays Bahamas 23°3N 73°45W 321 B5
Samandağ Turkey 36°5N 35°59E 250 B6
Samandıra Turkey 40°59N 29°13E 203 F13
Samanga Tanzania 8°20S 39°13E 269 D4
Samangān □ Afghan. 36°15N 68°3E 240 A3
Samangwa Dem. Rep. of the Congo 4°23S 24°10E 265 C4
Samani Japan 42°7N 142°56E 220 C11
Samanli Dağları Turkey 40°32N 29°10E 203 F13
Samannûd Egypt 30°57N 31°14E 251 H2
Samar Phil. 12°0N 125°0E 233 F5
Samar □ Phil. 11°50N 125°0E 233 F5
Samar Sea Phil. 12°0N 124°15E 232 E5
Samara Russia 53°8N 50°6E 190 D10
Samara → Russia 53°10N 50°4E 190 D10
Samara → Ukraine 48°28N 35°7E 189 H8
Samarai Papua N. G. 10°39S 150°41E 286 F6
Samaria West Bank 32°17N 35°12E 251 F6
Samaria △ Greece 35°17N 23°58E 207 E4
Samariapo Venezuela 5°15N 67°48W 328 B4
Samarinda Indonesia 0°30S 117°9E 235 C5
Samarkand = Samarqand Uzbekistan 39°40N 66°55E 217 E7
Samarkandsky = Temirtau Kazakhstan 50°5N 72°56E 217 B8
Samarqand Uzbekistan 39°40N 66°55E 217 E7
Samarqand □ Uzbekistan 39°35N 66°35E 217 E7
Sāmarrā' Iraq 34°12N 43°52E 213 E10
Samarskaya Luka △ Russia 53°30N 49°30E 190 D9
Samastipur India 25°50N 85°50E 243 G11
Samatya Turkey 40°59N 28°55E 122 C1
Samaúma Brazil 7°50S 60°2W 331 B5
Şamaxı Azerbaijan 40°38N 48°37E 191 K9
Samba Équateur, Dem. Rep. of the Congo 0°13N 21°25E 264 B4
Samba Maniema, Dem. Rep. of the Congo 4°38S 26°22E 265 C5
Samba Jammu & Kashmir, India 32°32N 75°10E 243 C6
Samba Caju Angola 8°46S 15°24E 265 D3
Sambaiba Brazil 7°8S 45°21W 332 C2
Sambalpur India 21°28N 84°4E 244 D7
Sambar, Tanjung Indonesia 2°59S 110°19E 235 C4
Sambas Indonesia 1°20N 109°20E 235 B3
Sambava Madag. 14°16S 50°10E 272 A3
Sambawizi Zimbabwe 18°24S 26°13E 269 F2
Sambhajinagar = Aurangabad India 19°50N 75°23E 244 E2
Sambhal India 28°35N 78°37E 243 E8
Sambhar India 26°52N 75°6E 242 F6
Sambhar L. India 26°55N 75°12E 242 F6
Sambir Ukraine 49°30N 23°10E 185 J10
Sambo Angola 13°3S 16°8E 265 E3
Sambo Indonesia 3°22S 118°52E 235 C5
Samboja Indonesia 1°1S 117°1E 235 C5
Sambor Cambodia 12°46N 106°0E 236 F6
Sambor Prei Kuk Cambodia 12°46N 105°58E 236 F5
Samborombón, B. Argentina 36°5S 57°20W 334 D4
Sambuca di Sicilia Italy 37°39N 13°7E 200 E6
Samburu □ Kenya 1°10N 36°40E 268 B4
Samburu △ Kenya 0°37N 37°31E 268 B4
Samcheok S. Korea 37°26N 129°10E 224 D4
Same Tanzania 4°2S 37°38E 268 C4
Samer France 50°38N 1°44E 173 B8
Samet, Ko Thailand 12°34N 101°27E 236 F3
Samfya Zambia 11°22S 29°31E 269 E2
Samḥah Yemen 12°15N 53°55E 249 D6
Samḥān, Jabal Oman 17°12N 54°55E 249 C6
Sami Greece 38°15N 20°39E 207 C2
Samka Burma 20°9N 96°57E 241 E6
Şamkir Azerbaijan 40°50N 46°0E 191 K8
Samland = Zemlandskiy Poluostrov Russia 54°50N 20°20E 184 D7
Şamlı Turkey 39°48N 27°51E 205 B9
Sammanturai Sri Lanka 7°36N 81°39E 245 L5
Sammanah Si. Arabia 25°10N 37°15E 246 E3
Samnū Libya 27°15N 14°55E 258 C2
Samo Alto Chile 30°22S 71°0W 334 C1
Samoa ■ Pac. Oc. 14°0S 172°0W 287 V20
Samoan Is. Pac. Oc. 14°0S 171°0W 287 V20
Samobor Croatia 45°47N 15°44E 199 C12
Samoëns France 46°5N 6°45E 173 F13
Samokov Bulgaria 42°18N 23°35E 202 D7
Šamorín Slovakia 48°2N 17°19E 181 C10
Samorogouan Burkina Faso 11°21N 4°57W 262 C4
Samos Greece 37°45N 26°50E 205 D8
Samoš Serbia 45°13N 20°46E 182 E5
Samos Spain 42°44N 7°20W 194 C3
Samoset U.S.A. 27°28N 82°33W 317 H7
Samosir Indonesia 2°55N 98°50E 234 B1
Samothráki = Mathraki Greece 39°48N 19°31E 206 B9
Samothraki Greece 40°28N 25°28E 203 F9
Samoylovka Russia 51°12N 43°43E 190 E6
Sampa Angola 10°38S 18°56E 265 E3
Sampa Ghana 8°0N 2°36W 262 D4
Sampacho Argentina 33°20S 64°50W 334 C3
Sampalan Indonesia 8°41S 115°34E 231 K18
Sampaloc Phil. 14°36N 120°59E 127 B1
Sampang Indonesia 7°11S 113°13E 235 D4
Samper de Calanda Spain 41°11N 0°28W 196 D4
Sampéyre Italy 44°34N 7°11E 198 D4
Samphan Thawong Thailand 13°44N 100°31E 113 B2
Sampit Indonesia 2°34S 113°0E 235 C4
Sampit → Indonesia 2°44S 112°54E 235 C4
Sampit, Teluk Indonesia 3°5S 113°3E 235 C4
Sampun Papua N. G. 5°21S 152°8E 286 C7
Samrong Cambodia 14°15N 103°30E 236 E4
Samseon S. Korea 37°34N 127°0E 137 B2
Samseong S. Korea 37°31N 127°2E 137 B2
Samsø Denmark 55°50N 10°35E 163 J4
Samsø Bælt Denmark 55°45N 10°45E 163 J4
Samson U.S.A. 31°7N 86°3W 316 D3
Samsun Turkey 41°15N 36°22E 212 B7
Samsun □ Turkey 41°10N 36°10E 212 B7
Samtah Si. Arabia 16°36N 42°56E 248 C3
Samtredia Georgia 42°7N 42°24E 191 J6
Samuel Smith Park Canada 43°35N 79°30W 141 B1
Samui, Ko Thailand 9°30N 100°0E 237 b
Samur → Russia 41°53N 48°32E 191 K9
Samurskiy Khrebet Russia 41°55N 47°11E 191 K8
Samusole Dem. Rep. of the Congo 10°2S 24°0E 265 E4
Samut Prakan Bangkok, Thailand 13°40N 100°36E 113 B2
Samut Sakhon Thailand 13°32N 100°17E 236 F3
Samut Songkhram Thailand 13°24N 100°1E 236 F3
Samwari Pakistan 28°30N 66°46E 242 E2
San Mali 13°15N 4°57W 262 C4
San → Cambodia 13°32N 105°57E 236 F5
San → Poland 50°45N 21°51E 185 H8
San Adrián Spain 42°20N 1°56W 196 C3
San Adrián, C. de Spain 43°21N 8°50W 194 B2
San Agustin Colombia 1°53N 76°16W 328 C2
San Agustin Romblon, Phil. 12°34N 122°6E 232 E4
San Agustin, C. Phil. 6°20N 126°13E 233 H6
San Agustín de Valle Fértil Argentina 30°35S 67°30W 334 C2
San Ambrosio Pac. Oc. 26°28S 79°53W 326 F3
San Andreas U.S.A. 38°12N 120°41W 306 G6
San Andres Catanduanes, Phil. 13°36N 124°6E 232 E5
San Andres Romblon, Phil. 13°19N 122°41E 232 E4
San Andres Romblon, Phil. 12°31N 122°2E 232 E4
San Andrès Barcelona, Spain 41°26N 2°11E 114 A2
San Andrés, I. de Caribbean 12°42N 81°46W 320 D3
San Andrés del Rabanedo Spain 42°37N 5°36W 194 C5
San Andres Mts. U.S.A. 33°0N 106°30W 305 K10
San Andrés Pt. Phil. 13°34N 121°52E 232 E3
San Andrés Tuxtla Mexico 18°27N 95°13W 319 D5
San Angel Mexico 19°20N 99°11W 128 B1
San Angelo U.S.A. 31°28N 100°26W 314 F4
San Angelo Raffaele Venice, Italy 142 b2
San Anselmo U.S.A. 37°59N 122°34W 306 H4
San Antonio Belize 16°15N 89°2W 320 C2
San Antonio Chile 33°40S 71°40W 334 C1
San Antonio Phil. 14°57N 120°5E 232 D3
San Antonio N. Mex., U.S.A. 33°55N 106°52W 305 K10
San Antonio Tex., U.S.A. 29°25N 98°29W 314 G5
San Antonio Amazonas, Venezuela 3°30N 66°44W 328 C4
San Antonio Nueva Esparta, Venezuela 10°57N 63°54W 329 a
San Antonio → U.S.A. 28°30N 96°54W 314 G6
San Antonio, C. Argentina 36°15S 56°40W 334 D4
San Antonio, C. de Cuba 21°50N 84°57W 320 B3
San Antonio, C. de Spain 38°48N 0°12E 197 G5
San Antonio, Mt. U.S.A. 34°17N 117°38W 307 L9
San Antonio B. Phil. 8°38N 117°35E 233 G1
San Antonio de los Baños Cuba 22°54N 82°31W 320 B3
San Antonio de los Cobres Argentina 24°10S 66°17W 334 A2
San Antonio Oeste Argentina 40°40S 65°0W 336 B4
San Arcángelo Italy 40°14N 16°14E 201 B9
San Ardo U.S.A. 36°1N 120°54W 306 J6
San Augustín Canary Is. 27°47N 15°32W 153 e1
San Augustine U.S.A. 31°32N 94°7W 314 F7
San Bartolomé Canary Is. 28°59N 13°37W 153 e2
San Bartolomé de Tirajana Canary Is. 27°54N 15°34W 153 e1
San Bartolomeo in Galdo Italy 41°24N 15°1E 201 A8
San Basilio Italy 41°56N 12°35E 136 B2
San Benedetto del Tronto Italy 42°57N 13°53E 199 F10
San Benedetto Po Italy 45°2N 10°55E 198 C7
San Benedicto, I. Mexico 19°18N 110°49W 318 D2
San Benito U.S.A. 26°8N 97°38W 314 H6
San Benito → U.S.A. 36°53N 121°34W 306 J5
San Benito Mt. U.S.A. 36°22N 120°37W 306 J6
San Bernardino U.S.A. 34°7N 117°19W 307 L9
San Bernardino Mts. U.S.A. 34°10N 116°45W 307 L10
San Bernardino Str. Phil. 12°30N 124°10E 232 E5
San Bernardo Chile 33°40S 70°50W 334 C1
San Bernardo, I. de Colombia 9°45N 75°50W 328 B2
San-Beyse = Choybalsan Mongolia 48°4N 114°30E 219 B11
San Biagio Venice, Italy 142 b4
San Blas Mexico 26°5N 108°46W 318 B3
San Blas, Arch. de Panama 9°50N 78°31W 320 E4
San Blas, C. U.S.A. 29°40N 85°21W 316 F4
San Bonifacio Italy 45°24N 11°16E 199 C8
San Borja Bolivia 14°50S 66°52W 330 C4
San Borja Lima, Peru 12°6S 76°59W 124 B3
San Bóvio Italy 45°27N 9°18E 128 B2
San Bruno, Pt. U.S.A. 37°39N 122°22W 136 C2
San Bruno Mountain State Park ⌓ U.S.A. 37°41N 122°26W 136 B2
San Buenaventura = Ventura U.S.A. 34°17N 119°18W 307 L7
San Buenaventura Bolivia 14°28S 67°35W 330 C4
San Buenaventura Coahuila, Mexico 27°5N 101°32W 318 B4
San Carlos = Butuku-Luba Eq. Guin. 3°29N 8°33E 263 E6
San Carlos = Sant Carles Spain 39°3N 1°34E 206 C2
San Carlos Argentina 33°50S 69°0W 334 C2
San Carlos Bolivia 17°24S 63°45W 331 D5
San Carlos Chile 36°10S 72°0W 334 D1
San Carlos Baja Calif. S., Mexico 24°47N 112°7W 318 C2
San Carlos Coahuila, Mexico 29°1N 100°51W 318 B4
San Carlos Nic. 11°12N 84°50W 320 D3
San Carlos Neg. Occ., Phil. 10°29N 123°25E 233 F4
San Carlos Pangasinan, Phil. 15°55N 120°20E 232 D3
San Carlos Uruguay 34°46S 54°58W 335 C5
San Carlos Ariz., U.S.A. 33°21N 110°27W 305 K8
San Carlos Amazonas, Venezuela 1°55N 67°4W 328 C4
San Carlos Cojedes, Venezuela 9°40N 68°36W 328 B4
San Carlos de Bariloche Argentina 41°10S 71°25W 336 B2
San Carlos de Bolívar Argentina 36°15S 61°6W 334 D3
San Carlos de la Rápita = Sant Carles de la Ràpita Spain 40°37N 0°35E 196 E5
San Carlos de Río Negro Venezuela 1°55N 67°4W 328 C4
San Carlos del Zulia Venezuela 9°1N 71°55W 328 B3
San Carlos L. U.S.A. 33°11N 110°32W 305 K8
San Carlos Park U.S.A. 26°28N 81°49W 317 J8
San Cataldo Italy 37°29N 13°59E 200 E6
San Celoni = Sant Celoni Spain 41°42N 2°30E 196 D7
San Clemente Chile 35°30S 71°29W 334 D1
San Clemente Spain 39°24N 2°25W 197 F2
San Clemente Calif., U.S.A. 33°26N 117°37W 307 M9
San Clemente I. U.S.A. 32°53N 118°29W 307 N8
San Cristóbal = Es Migjorn Gran Spain 39°57N 4°3E 206 B5
San Cristóbal B. Aires, Argentina 34°38S 58°23W 117 B2
San Cristóbal Santa Fe, Argentina 30°20S 61°10W 334 C3

San Cristóbal Colombia 2°18S 73°2W 328 D3
San Cristóbal Dom. Rep. 18°25N 70°6W 321 C5
San Cristóbal Solomon Is. 10°30S 161°0E 287 N11
San Cristóbal Madrid, Spain 40°25N 3°35W 127 B2
San Cristóbal Venezuela 7°46N 72°14W 328 B3
San Cristóbal, Cerro Chile 33°25S 70°38W 137 B2
San Cristóbal, I. Ecuador 0°50S 89°26W 330 a
San Cristóbal, Virgen del Chile 33°25S 70°38W 137 B2
San Cristóbal de La Laguna Canary Is. 28°28N 16°18W 153 e1
San Cristóbal de las Casas Mexico 16°45N 92°38W 319 D6
San Cristoforo Italy 45°26N 9°9E 128 B1
San Damiano d'Asti Italy 44°50N 8°4E 198 D5
San Daniele del Friuli Italy 46°9N 13°1E 199 B10
San Diego Calif., U.S.A. 32°42N 117°9W 307 N9
San Diego Tex., U.S.A. 27°46N 98°14W 314 H5
San Diego, C. Argentina 54°40S 65°10W 336 D3
San Diego de la Unión Mexico 21°28N 100°52W 318 C4
San Diego Int. ✕ (SAN) U.S.A. 32°44N 117°11W 307 N9
San Dimitri, Ras Malta 36°4N 14°11E 206 E6
San Dimitri Point = San Dimitri, Ras Malta 36°4N 14°11E 206 E6
San Donà di Piave Italy 45°38N 12°34E 199 C9
San Donato Milanese Italy 45°24N 9°16E 128 B2
Sân el Hagar Egypt 30°58N 31°52E 251 H2
San Estanislao Paraguay 24°39S 56°26W 334 A4
San Esteban △ Venezuela 10°24N 67°58W 328 A4
San Esteban de Gormaz Spain 41°34N 3°13W 196 D1
San Eugenio = Artigas Uruguay 30°20S 56°30W 334 C4
San Felice Circeo Italy 41°14N 13°5E 200 A6
San Felice sul Panaro Italy 44°50N 11°8E 199 D8
San Felipe Chile 32°43S 70°42W 334 C1
San Felipe Colombia 1°55N 67°6W 328 C4
San Felipe Baja Calif., Mexico 31°1N 114°52W 318 A2
San Felipe Phil. 15°4N 120°4E 232 D3
San Felipe Venezuela 10°20N 68°44W 328 A4
San Felipe ➔ U.S.A. 33°10N 115°49W 307 M11
San Félix Chile 28°56S 70°28W 334 B1
San Félix Pac. Oc. 26°23S 80°0W 326 F2
San Fernando = San Ferran Spain 38°42N 1°28E 206 D1
San Fernando Chile 34°30S 71°0W 334 C1
San Fernando Tamaulipas, Mexico 24°51N 98°10W 319 C5
San Fernando Cebu, Phil. 10°10N 123°42E 233 F4
San Fernando La Union, Phil. 16°40N 120°23E 232 C3
San Fernando Pampanga, Phil. 15°5N 120°37E 232 D3
San Fernando Romblon, Phil. 12°18N 122°36E 232 E4
San Fernando Cádiz, Spain 36°28N 6°17W 195 J4
San Fernando Trin. & Tob. 10°16N 61°28W 323 t
San Fernando Calif., U.S.A. 34°17N 118°26W 307 L8
San Fernando de Apure Venezuela 7°54N 67°15W 328 B4
San Fernando de Atabapo Venezuela 4°3N 67°42W 328 C4
San Fernando di Púglia Italy 41°18N 16°5E 201 A9
San Francesco di Paola Venice, Italy 142 b4
San Francique = Erin Trin. & Tob. 10°5N 61°39W 323 t
San Francisco Córdoba, Argentina 31°30S 62°5W 334 C3
San Francisco Bolivia 15°16S 65°31W 331 D4
San Francisco Peru 12°36S 73°49W 330 C3
San Francisco Agusan del S., Phil. 8°30N 125°56E 233 G5
San Francisco Cebu, Phil. 10°39N 124°23E 233 F5
San Francisco Quezon, Phil. 13°21N 122°31E 232 E4
San Francisco S. Leyte, Phil. 10°4N 125°9E 233 F5
San Francisco Calif., U.S.A. 37°46N 122°23W 136 B2
San Francisco ➔ U.S.A. 32°59N 109°22W 305 K9
San Francisco, C. de Colombia 6°18N 77°29W 328 B2
San Francisco, Paso de S. Amer. 27°0S 68°0W 334 B2
San Francisco B. U.S.A. 37°39N 122°14W 136 B3
San Francisco Culhuacán Mexico 19°19N 99°8W 128 C2
San Francisco de Macanao Venezuela 11°1N 64°17W 329 a
San Francisco de Macorís Dom. Rep. 19°19N 70°15W 321 C5
San Francisco del Monte de Oro Argentina 32°36S 66°8W 334 C2
San Francisco del Oro Mexico 26°52N 105°51W 318 B3
San Francisco della Vigna Venice, Italy 142 b3
San Francisco Int. ✕ (SFO) U.S.A. 37°37N 122°22W 306 H4
San Francisco Javier = Sant Francesc de Formentera Spain 38°42N 1°26E 206 D1
San Fratello Italy 38°1N 14°36E 201 D7
San Fruttuoso Italy 45°34N 9°14E 128 A2
San Gabriel Chile 33°47S 70°15W 334 C1
San Gabriel Ecuador 0°36N 77°49W 328 C2
San Gabriel Calif., U.S.A. 34°5N 118°5W 126 B4
San Gabriel ➔ U.S.A. 33°58N 118°5W 126 C4
San Gabriel Chilac Mexico 18°19N 97°21W 319 D5
San Gabriel Mts. U.S.A. 34°17N 117°38W 307 L9
San Gavino Monreale Italy 39°33N 8°47E 200 C1
San Gerardo Venice, Italy 142 c1
San Geremia Venice, Italy 142 a2
San German Puerto Rico 18°4N 67°4W 321 b
San Giacomo dall'Orio Venice, Italy 142 b2
San Gil Colombia 6°33N 73°8W 328 B3
San Giljan = St. Julian's Malta 35°55N 14°29E 206 F7
San Gimignano Italy 43°28N 11°2E 198 E8
San Giobbe Venice, Italy 142 a2
San Giorgio degli Schiavoni, Scuola di Venice, Italy 142 b3
San Giórgio di Nogaro Italy 45°50N 13°13E 199 C10
San Giórgio Iónico Italy 40°27N 17°23E 201 B10
San Giorgio Maggiore Venice, Italy 142 c3
San Giorgio Maggiore, Isola di Venice, Italy 142 c3
San Giovanni e Paolo Venice, Italy 142 b3
San Giovanni Bianco Italy 45°52N 9°39E 198 C6
San Giovanni in Bragora Venice, Italy 142 b3
San Giovanni in Fiore Italy 39°15N 16°42E 201 C9
San Giovanni in Persiceto Italy 44°38N 11°11E 199 D8
San Giovanni Rotondo Italy 41°42N 15°44E 199 G12
San Giovanni Valdarno Italy 43°34N 11°32E 199 E8
San Giuliano Milanese Italy 45°24N 9°17E 128 B2
San Giuliano Terme Italy 43°46N 10°26E 198 E7
San Gorgonio Mt. U.S.A. 34°6N 116°50W 307 L10
San Gottardo, P. del Switz. 46°33N 8°33E 179 J4
San Gregorio Uruguay 32°37S 55°40W 335 C4
San Gregorio Calif., U.S.A. 37°20N 122°23W 306 H4
San Guillermo △ Argentina 27°50S 69°45W 334 B2
San Guiseppe Lato Italy 37°57N 13°11E 200 E6
San Ignacio Belize 17°10N 89°5W 320 C2
San Ignacio Beni, Bolivia 14°53S 65°36W 331 C4
San Ignacio Santa Cruz, Bolivia 16°20S 60°55W 331 D5
San Ignacio Baja Calif. S., Mexico 27°27N 112°51W 318 B2
San Ignacio Paraguay 26°52S 57°3W 334 B4
San Ignacio Peru 5°8S 78°59W 330 B2
San Ignacio, L. Mexico 26°54N 113°13W 318 B2
San Ildefonso Phil. 15°4N 120°56E 232 D3
San Ildefonso, C. Phil. 16°0N 122°1E 232 C4
San Ildefonso Pen. Phil. 16°9N 122°5E 232 C4
San Isidro Argentina 34°29S 58°31W 334 C4
San Isidro Lima, Peru 12°5S 77°2W 124 B2
San Isidro Phil. 6°50N 126°5E 233 H6
San Isidro de Potot = Burgos Phil. 16°4N 119°52E 232 C2
San Jacinto Colombia 9°50N 75°8W 328 B2
San Jacinto Phil. 12°34N 123°44E 232 E4
San Jacinto Calif., U.S.A. 33°47N 116°57W 307 M10
San Jaime = Sant Jaume Spain 39°54N 4°4E 206 B5
San Javier Misiones, Argentina 27°55S 55°5W 335 B4
San Javier Santa Fe, Argentina 30°40S 59°55W 334 C4
San Javier Beni, Bolivia 14°34S 64°42W 331 C5
San Javier Santa Cruz, Bolivia 16°18S 62°30W 331 D5
San Javier Chile 35°40S 71°45W 334 D1
San Javier Spain 37°49N 0°50W 197 H4
San Jerónimo Lidice Mexico 19°19N 99°14W 128 C1
San Jerónimo Taviche Mexico 16°44N 96°35W 319 D5
San Joaquin Bolivia 13°4S 64°49W 331 C5
San Joaquin Santiago, Chile 33°29S 70°35W 137 B2
San Joaquin Phil. 10°35N 122°8E 233 F4
San Joaquin Calif., U.S.A. 36°36N 120°11W 306 J6
San Joaquin ➔ Bolivia 13°8S 63°41W 331 C5
San Joaquin ➔ Calif., U.S.A. 38°4N 121°51W 306 G5
San Joaquín, Cerro Ecuador 0°53S 89°30W 330 a
San Joaquin Valley U.S.A. 37°20N 121°0W 306 J6
San Jon U.S.A. 35°6N 103°20W 305 J12
San Jordi = Sant Jordi Spain 39°33N 2°46E 206 B3
San Jorge Argentina 31°54S 61°50W 334 C3
San Jorge Solomon Is. 8°28S 159°38E 287 M10
San Jorge, B. Mexico 31°20N 113°20W 318 A2
San Jorge, G. Argentina 46°0S 66°0W 336 C3
San José = San Josep Spain 38°55N 1°18E 206 D1
San José Argentina 32°12S 58°15W 334 C4
San José Costa Rica 9°55N 84°2W 320 E3
San José Guatemala 14°0N 90°50W 320 D1
San Jose Mind. Occ., Phil. 12°27N 121°4E 232 E3
San Jose Nueva Ecija, Phil. 15°45N 120°55E 232 D3
San Jose Calif., U.S.A. 37°20N 121°53W 306 H5
San Jose Ill., U.S.A. 40°18N 89°36W 310 D7
San Jose ➔ U.S.A. 34°25N 106°45W 305 J10
San José, G. Argentina 42°20S 64°18W 336 B4
San José, I. Mexico 25°0N 110°38W 318 C2
San José de Buenavista Phil. 10°45N 121°56E 233 F3
San José de Chiquitos Bolivia 17°53S 60°50W 331 D5
San José de Feliciano Argentina 30°26S 58°46W 334 C4
San José de Guanipa Venezuela 8°53N 64°9W 329 B5
San José de Jáchal Argentina 30°15S 68°46W 334 C2
San José de Mayo Uruguay 34°27S 56°40W 334 C4
San José de Ocuné Colombia 4°15N 70°20W 328 C3
San José de Uchapiamonas Bolivia 14°13S 68°5W 330 C4
San José del Cabo Mexico 23°3N 109°41W 318 C3
San José del Guaviare Colombia 2°35N 72°38W 328 C3
San José del Monte Phil. 14°49N 121°3E 232 D3
San José do Anauá Brazil 0°58N 61°22W 329 C5
San José Río Hondo Mexico 19°26N 99°14W 128 B1
San Josep Spain 38°55N 1°18E 206 D1
San Juan Argentina 31°30S 68°30W 334 C2
San Juan Antioquia, Colombia 8°46N 76°32W 328 B2
San Juan Curaçao 12°15N 69°6W 322 g
San Juan Ica, Peru 15°22S 75°7W 330 D2
San Juan Batangas, Phil. 13°50N 121°24E 232 E3
San Juan S. Leyte, Phil. 10°16N 125°10E 233 F5
San Juan Puerto Rico 18°28N 66°7W 321 C6
San Juan Trin. & Tob. 10°39N 61°29W 323 t
San Juan □ Argentina 31°9S 69°0W 334 C2
San Juan ➔ Argentina 32°20S 67°25W 334 C2
San Juan ➔ Bolivia 21°2S 65°19W 331 E4
San Juan ➔ Colombia 4°3N 77°27W 328 C2
San Juan ➔ Nic. 10°56N 83°42W 320 D3
San Juan ➔ Manila, Phil. 14°35N 121°0E 127 B2
San Juan ➔ Utah, U.S.A. 37°16N 110°26W 305 H8
San Juan ➔ Nueva Esparta, Venezuela 10°56N 63°57W 329 a
San Juan ➔ Sucre, Venezuela 10°14N 62°38W 329 A5
San Juan, C. Argentina 54°44S 63°44W 336 D4
San Juan, C. Eq. Guin. 1°5N 9°20E 264 B1
San Juan Bautista = Sant Joan de Labritja Spain 39°5N 1°31E 206 C2
San Juan Bautista = Villahermosa Mexico 17°59N 92°55W 319 D6
San Juan Bautista Chile 33°37S 78°50W 330 c
San Juan Bautista Paraguay 26°37S 57°6W 334 B4
San Juan Bautista Calif., U.S.A. 36°51N 121°32W 306 J5
San Juan Bautista Venezuela 11°1N 63°56W 329 a
San Juan Capistrano U.S.A. 33°30N 117°40W 307 M9
San Juan Cr. ➔ U.S.A. 35°40N 120°22W 306 J5
San Juan de Aragón Mexico 19°28N 99°4W 128 B2
San Juan de Aragón, Parque Mexico 19°27N 99°4W 128 B2
San Juan de Guadelupe Mexico 24°38N 102°44W 318 C4
San Juan de Guía, Cabo de Colombia 11°21N 73°59W 328 A3
San Juan de la Costa Mexico 24°20N 110°41W 318 C2
San Juan de los Lagos Mexico 21°15N 102°18W 318 C4
San Juan de los Morros Venezuela 9°55N 67°21W 328 B4
San Juan de Lurigancho Peru 11°59S 77°0W 124 A2
San Juan de Manapiare Venezuela 5°15N 66°5W 328 B4
San Juan de Villa Hermosa = Villahermosa Mexico 17°59N 92°55W 319 D6
San Juan del César Colombia 10°46N 73°1W 328 A3
San Juan del Monte Phil. 14°36N 121°1E 127 B2
San Juan del Norte Nic. 10°58N 83°40W 320 D3
San Juan del Norte, B. de Nic. 11°0N 83°40W 320 D3
San Juan del Rio Mexico 20°23N 100°0W 319 C5
San Juan del Sur Nic. 11°20N 85°51W 320 D2
San Juan I. U.S.A. 48°32N 123°5W 306 B3
San Juan Island △ U.S.A. 48°35N 123°8W 306 B4
San Juan Ixtacala Mexico 19°31N 99°10W 128 A1
San Juan Mts. U.S.A. 37°30N 107°0W 305 H10
San Julian Phil. 11°45N 125°27E 233 F5
San Just, Sierra de Spain 40°45N 0°49W 196 E4
San Just Desvern Spain 41°22N 2°4E 114 A1
San Justo B. Aires, Argentina 34°40S 58°33W 117 C1
San Justo Santa Fe, Argentina 30°47S 60°30W 334 C3
San Kamphaeng Thailand 18°45N 99°8E 236 C2
San Lázaro, C. Mexico 24°50N 112°18W 318 C2
San Leandro U.S.A. 37°42N 122°9W 306 H4
San Leonardo de Yagüe Spain 41°51N 3°5W 196 D1
San Lorenzo = Sant Llorenç des Cardassar Spain 39°37N 3°17E 206 B4
San Lorenzo Argentina 32°45S 60°45W 334 C3
San Lorenzo Beni, Bolivia 15°22S 65°48W 331 D4
San Lorenzo Tarija, Bolivia 21°26S 64°47W 331 E5
San Lorenzo Ecuador 1°15N 78°50W 328 C2
San Lorenzo Venice, Italy 142 b3
San Lorenzo Paraguay 25°20S 57°32W 334 B4
San Lorenzo ➔ Mexico 24°15N 107°24W 318 C3
San Lorenzo, I. Baja Calif., Mexico 28°38N 112°51W 318 B2
San Lorenzo, I. Peru 12°7S 77°15W 330 C2
San Lorenzo, Mte. Argentina 47°40S 72°20W 336 C2
San Lorenzo de la Parrilla Spain 39°51N 2°22W 196 F2
San Lorenzo de Morunys = Sant Llorenç de Morunys Spain 42°8N 1°35E 196 C6
San Lorenzo Tezonco Mexico 19°19N 99°3W 128 C2
San Lucas = Cabo San Lucas Mexico 22°53N 109°54W 318 C3
San Lucas Bolivia 20°5S 65°7W 331 E4
San Lucas Baja Calif. S., Mexico 27°10N 112°14W 318 B2
San Lucas Calif., U.S.A. 36°8N 121°1W 306 J5
San Lucas, C. Mexico 22°52N 109°53W 318 C3
San Lúcido Italy 39°18N 16°3E 201 C9
San Luis = Entre Rios Bolivia 21°30S 64°25W 334 A3
San Luis = Sevilla Colombia 4°16N 75°57W 328 C2
San Luis Argentina 33°20S 66°20W 334 C2
San Luis Pinar del Rio, Cuba 22°17N 83°46W 320 B3
San Luis Guatemala 16°14N 89°27W 320 C2
San Luis Lima, Peru 12°4S 77°0W 124 B2
San Luis Ariz., U.S.A. 32°29N 114°47W 305 K6
San Luis Colo., U.S.A. 37°12N 105°25W 305 H11
San Luis □ Argentina 34°0S 66°0W 334 C2
San Luis, I. Mexico 29°58N 114°26W 318 B2
San Luis, L. de Bolivia 13°45S 64°0W 331 C5
San Luis, Sierra de Argentina 32°30S 66°10W 334 C2
San Luis de la Paz Mexico 21°18N 100°31W 318 C4
San Luis Obispo U.S.A. 35°17N 120°40W 307 K6
San Luis Potosí Mexico 22°9N 100°59W 318 C4
San Luis Potosí □ Mexico 23°0N 101°0W 318 C4
San Luis Res. U.S.A. 37°4N 121°5W 306 H5
San Luis Río Colorado Mexico 32°29N 114°58W 318 A2
San Manuel Phil. 16°4N 120°40E 232 C3
San Manuel Ariz., U.S.A. 32°36N 110°38W 305 K8
San Marco Venice, Italy 142 b2
San Marco, C. Italy 39°51N 8°26E 200 C1
San Marco, Canale di Venice, Italy 142 b3
San Marco, Piazza Venice, Italy 142 b2
San Marco Argentano Italy 39°33N 16°7E 201 C9
San Marco in Lámis Italy 41°43N 15°38E 199 G12
San Marcos Colombia 8°39N 75°8W 328 B2
San Marcos Calif., U.S.A. 33°9N 117°10W 307 M9
San Marcos Tex., U.S.A. 29°53N 97°56W 314 G6
San Marcos, I. Mexico 27°13N 112°6W 318 B2
San Mariano Phil. 17°0N 122°2E 232 C4
San Marino San Marino 43°55N 12°30E 199 E9
San Marino Calif., U.S.A. 34°7N 118°5W 126 B4
San Marino ■ Europe 43°56N 12°25E 199 E9
San Martín = Tarapoto Peru 6°30S 76°20W 330 B2
San Martín Antarctica 68°11S 67°0W 151 C17
San Martín Argentina 33°5S 68°28W 334 C2
San Martín Colombia 3°42N 73°42W 328 C3
San Martín Barcelona, Spain 41°24N 2°11E 114 A2
San Martín □ Peru 7°0S 76°50W 330 B2
San Martín ➔ Bolivia 13°8S 63°43W 331 C5
San Martín, L. Argentina 48°50S 72°50W 336 C2
San Martín de la Vega Spain 40°13N 3°34W 194 E7
San Martín de los Andes Argentina 40°10S 71°20W 336 B2
San Martín de Porras Peru 12°1S 77°5W 124 B2
San Martín de Valdeiglesias Spain 40°21N 4°24W 194 E6
San Mateo = Sant Mateu Baleares, Spain 39°3N 1°23E 206 C1
San Mateo = Sant Mateu Valencia, Spain 40°28N 0°10E 196 E5
San Mateo Isabela, Phil. 16°54N 121°33E 232 C3
San Mateo Calif., U.S.A. 37°34N 122°19W 306 H4
San Mateo Tlaltenango Mexico 19°20N 99°16W 128 B1
San Matías Bolivia 16°25S 58°20W 331 D6
San Matías, G. Argentina 41°30S 64°0W 336 B4
San Michele, Isola di Venice, Italy 142 a3
San Miguel = Linapacan Phil. 11°30N 119°52E 233 F2
San Miguel = Sant Miquel Spain 39°3N 1°26E 206 C1
San Miguel = Sarrat Phil. 18°9N 120°39E 232 B3
San Miguel Bolivia 16°42S 61°1W 331 C5
San Miguel Brazil 28°35S 54°33W 335 B5
San Miguel Santiago, Chile 33°29S 70°39W 137 B2
San Miguel El Salv. 13°30N 88°12W 320 D2
San Miguel Panama 8°27N 78°55W 320 E4
San Miguel Lima, Peru 12°5S 77°6W 124 B2
San Miguel Bulacan, Phil. 15°9N 120°59E 232 D3
San Miguel Palawan, Phil. 11°30N 119°51E 233 F2
San Miguel Surigao S., Phil. 9°3N 125°59E 233 G5
San Miguel Calif., U.S.A. 35°45N 120°42W 306 K6
San Miguel ➔ Bolivia 13°52S 63°56W 331 C5
San Miguel ➔ Ecuador 0°25N 76°30W 328 C2
San Miguel, Golfo de Panama 8°22N 78°17W 328 B2
San Miguel B. Phil. 13°51N 123°11E 232 E4
San Miguel de Huachi Bolivia 15°40S 67°15W 330 D4
San Miguel de Tucumán Argentina 26°50S 65°20W 334 B2
San Miguel del Monte Argentina 35°23S 58°50W 334 D4
San Miguel I. U.S.A. 34°2N 120°23W 307 L6
San Miguel Is. Phil. 7°45N 118°28E 233 H2
San Miguelito Panama 9°2N 79°30W 320 c
San Millán de la Cogolla Spain 42°19N 2°51W 196 C2
San Miniato Italy 43°41N 10°51E 198 E7
San Narciso Phil. 13°34N 122°34E 232 E4
San Nicandro Garganico Italy 41°50N 15°34E 199 G12
San Nicolas = Sint Nicolaas Curaçao 12°17N 69°8W 322 g
San Nicolás B. Aires, Argentina 34°36S 58°22W 117 B2
San Nicolás Canary Is. 27°58N 15°47W 153 e1
San Nicolas Phil. 18°10N 120°36E 232 B3
San Nicolás de los Arroyos Argentina 33°25S 60°10W 334 C3
San Nicolas I. U.S.A. 33°15N 119°30W 307 M7
San Nicolo dei Mendicoli Venice, Italy 142 b1
San Onofre Colombia 9°44N 75°32W 328 B2
San Onofre Calif., U.S.A. 33°22N 117°34W 307 M9
San Onófrio Italy 41°57N 12°25E 136 B1
San Pablo Bolivia 21°43S 66°38W 334 A2
San Pablo Isabela, Phil. 17°27N 121°48E 232 C3
San Pablo Laguna, Phil. 14°11N 121°31E 232 D3
San Pablo Calif., U.S.A. 37°58N 122°21W 306 H4
San Pablo de Manta = Manta Ecuador 1°0S 80°40W 328 D1
San Pantalon Venice, Italy 142 b2
San Pàolo di Civitate Italy 41°44N 15°15E 199 G12
San Pascual Phil. 13°8N 122°59E 232 E4
San Pedro B. Aires, Argentina 33°40S 59°40W 334 C4
San Pedro Misiones, Argentina 26°30S 54°10W 335 B5
San Pedro Chile 33°54S 71°28W 334 C1
San Pedro Colombia 4°56N 71°53W 328 C3
San Pedro Ivory C. 4°50N 6°33W 262 E3
San Pedro Baja Calif. S., Mexico 23°55N 110°17W 318 C2
San Pedro Peru 14°49S 74°5W 330 C3
San Pedro □ Paraguay 24°0S 57°0W 334 A4
San Pedro ➔ Chihuahua, Mexico 28°21N 105°25W 318 B3
San Pedro ➔ Nayarit, Mexico 21°45N 105°30W 318 C3
San Pedro ➔ Ariz., U.S.A. 32°59N 110°47W 305 K8
San Pedro, Pta. Chile 25°30S 70°38W 334 B1
San Pedro, Sierra de Spain 39°18N 6°40W 195 F4
San Pedro B. Phil. 11°10N 125°10E 233 F5
San Pedro Channel U.S.A. 33°30N 118°25W 307 M8
San Pedro de Arimena Colombia 4°37N 71°42W 328 C3
San Pedro de Atacama Chile 22°55S 68°15W 334 A2
San Pedro de Coche Venezuela 10°47N 64°0W 329 a
San Pedro de Jujuy Argentina 24°12S 64°55W 334 A3
San Pedro de las Colonias Mexico 25°45N 102°59W 318 B4
San Pedro de Lloc Peru 7°15S 79°28W 330 B2
San Pedro de Macorís Dom. Rep. 18°30N 69°18W 321 C6
San Pedro del Norte Nic. 13°4N 84°33W 320 D3
San Pedro del Paraná Paraguay 26°43S 56°13W 334 B4
San Pedro del Pinatar Spain 37°50N 0°50W 197 H4
San Pedro Mártir Spain 41°23N 2°6E 114 A1
San Pedro Mártir, Sa. de Mexico 30°45N 115°13W 318 A1
San Pedro Ocampo = Melchor Ocampo Mexico 24°51N 101°39W 318 C4
San Pedro Pochutla Mexico 15°44N 96°28W 319 D5
San Pedro Sula Honduras 15°30N 88°0W 320 C2
San Pedro Tututepec Mexico 16°9N 97°38W 319 D5
San Pedro Zacatenco Mexico 19°30N 99°6W 128 A2
San Pietro Italy 39°8N 8°17E 200 C1
San Pietro, Isola di Venice, Italy 142 b4
San Pietro, Piazza Rome, Italy 136 b1
San Pietro di Castello Venice, Italy 142 b4
San Pietro Vernótico Italy 40°29N 18°0E 201 B11
San Po Kong Hong Kong, China 22°20N 114°11E 122 B3
San Polo Venice, Italy 142 b2
San Rafael Argentina 34°40S 68°21W 334 C2
San Rafael Bolivia 16°45S 60°34W 331 D5
San Rafael Trin. & Tob. 10°34N 61°16W 323 t
San Rafael Calif., U.S.A. 37°58N 122°32W 306 H4
San Rafael N. Mex., U.S.A. 35°7N 107°53W 305 J10
San Rafael Venezuela 10°58N 71°46W 328 A3
San Rafael Chamapa Mexico 19°27N 99°15W 128 B1
San Rafael Hills U.S.A. 34°10N 118°12W 126 A3
San Rafael Mt. U.S.A. 34°41N 119°52W 307 L7
San Rafael Mts. U.S.A. 34°40N 119°50W 307 L7
San Ramón Bolivia 13°17S 64°43W 331 C5
San Ramón de la Nueva Orán Argentina 23°10S 64°20W 334 A3
San Remo Italy 43°49N 7°46E 198 E4
San Román, C. Venezuela 12°12N 70°0W 328 A4
San Roque Argentina 28°25S 58°45W 334 B4
San Roque Manila, Phil. 14°37N 121°5E 127 B2
San Roque N. Samar, Phil. 12°37N 124°52E 232 E5
San Roque Spain 36°17N 5°21W 195 J5
San Rosendo Chile 37°16S 72°43W 334 D1
San Saba U.S.A. 31°12N 98°43W 314 F5
San Salvador El Salv. 13°40N 89°10W 320 D2
San Salvador Venice, Italy 142 b3
San Salvador, Canal de Ecuador 0°25S 90°30W 330 a
San Salvador, I. Ecuador 0°16S 90°42W 330 a
San Salvador de Jujuy Argentina 24°10S 64°48W 334 A3
San Salvador I. Bahamas 24°0N 74°30W 321 B5
San Salvo Italy 42°3N 14°44E 199 F11
San Sebastián = Donostia-San Sebastián Spain 43°17N 1°58W 196 B3
San Sebastián Argentina 53°10S 68°30W 336 D3
San Sebastián Puerto Rico 18°20N 66°59W 321 b
San Sebastián de la Gomera Canary Is. 28°5N 17°7W 153 e1
San Sebastiano Venice, Italy 142 b1
San Serra = Son Serra Spain 39°43N 3°13E 206 B4
San Serverino Marche Italy 43°13N 13°10E 199 E10
San Severo Italy 41°41N 15°23E 199 G12
San Simeon U.S.A. 35°39N 121°11W 306 K5
San Simeon Grande Venice, Italy 142 a2
San Simon U.S.A. 32°16N 109°14W 305 K9
San Siro Italy 45°28N 9°7E 128 B1
San Souci Australia 33°59S 151°8E 139 B1
San Stefano Venice, Italy 142 b2
San Stéfano di Cadore Italy 46°34N 12°33E 199 B9
San Stino di Livenza Italy 45°44N 12°41E 199 C9
San Tau Hong Kong, China 22°17N 113°55E 122 B1
San Telmo = Sant Elm Spain 39°35N 2°21E 206 B3
San Telmo B. Aires, Argentina 34°37S 58°23W 117 B2
San Telmo Baja Calif., Mexico 30°58N 116°6W 318 A1
San Teodoro Italy 40°46N 9°40E 200 B2
San Teodoro Phil. 13°26N 121°1E 232 E3
San Tiburcio Mexico 24°8N 101°32W 318 C4
San Trovaso Venice, Italy 142 c2
San Valentin, Mte. Chile 46°30S 73°30W 336 C2
San Vicenç dels Horts Spain 41°23N 2°0E 114 A1
San Vicente de Alcántara Spain 39°22N 7°8W 195 F3
San Vicente de Cañete Peru 13°8S 76°30W 330 C2
San Vicente de la Barquera Spain 43°23N 4°29W 194 B6
San Vicente del Caguán Colombia 2°7N 74°46W 328 C3
San Vicenzo Spain 42°58N 8°46W 194 C2
San Vincenzo Italy 43°6N 10°32E 198 E7
San Vito Costa Rica 8°50N 82°58W 320 E3
San Vito Italy 39°26N 9°32E 200 C2
San Vito, C. Italy 38°11N 12°41E 200 D5
San Vito al Tagliamento Italy 45°54N 12°52E 199 C9
San Vito Chietino Italy 42°18N 14°27E 199 F11
San Vito dei Normanni Italy 40°39N 17°42E 201 B10
San Yanaro Colombia 2°47N 69°42W 328 C4
San Zaccaria Venice, Italy 142 b3
Sana' = Ṣan'ā' Yemen 15°27N 44°12E 248 D4
Saña Peru 6°54S 79°36W 330 B2
Ṣan'ā' Yemen 15°27N 44°12E 248 D4
Ṣan'ā' □ Yemen 15°27N 44°12E 248 D4
Sana ➔ Bos.-H. 45°3N 16°23E 199 C13
Ṣan'ā' ✕ (SAH) = Ṣan'ā' Yemen 15°27N 44°12E 248 D4
Sanaag □ Somalia 10°30N 48°0E 267 B6
Sanaba Burkina Faso 12°25N 3°47W 262 C4
Sanae IV Antarctica 70°20S 9°0W 151 D2
Şanāfir Si. Arabia 27°56N 34°42E 251 L5
Sanaga ➔ Cameroon 3°35N 9°38E 263 E6
Sanak I. U.S.A. 54°25N 162°40W 303 J7
Sanalona, Presa Mexico 24°49N 107°7W 318 C3
Sanām Si. Arabia 23°40N 44°45E 248 B4
Sanana Indonesia 2°4S 125°58E 231 E7
Sanand India 22°59N 72°25E 242 H5
Sanandaj Iran 35°18N 47°1E 213 E12
Sanandita Bolivia 21°40S 63°45W 334 A3
Sanaroa I. Papua N. G. 9°37S 151°0E 286 E6
Sanary-sur-Mer France 43°7N 5°49E 175 E9
Sanāw Yemen 17°50N 51°5E 249 C5
Sanawad India 22°11N 76°5E 242 H7
Sanbancho Tokyo, Japan 140 a3
Sanbe-San Japan 35°6N 132°38E 222 B4
Sancellas = Sencelles Spain 39°39N 2°54E 206 B3
Sancergues France 47°10N 2°54E 173 E9
Sancerre France 47°20N 2°50E 173 E9
Sancerrois, Collines du France 47°20N 2°40E 173 E9
Sancha He ➔ China 26°48N 106°7E 228 D6
Sanchahe China 44°50N 126°2E 227 B14
Sánchez Dom. Rep. 19°15N 69°36W 321 C6
Sanchez Mira Phil. 18°34N 121°14E 232 B3
Sanchi India 23°28N 77°44E 242 H7
Sanchih Taiwan 25°15N 121°30E 225 A3
Sanchor India 24°45N 71°55E 242 G4
Sanch'ung Taiwan 25°4N 121°30E 225 A3
Sanco Pt. Phil. 8°15N 126°27E 233 G6
Sancoins France 46°47N 2°55E 173 F9
Sancti Spíritus Cuba 21°52N 79°33W 320 B4
Sancy, Puy de France 45°32N 2°50E 174 C6
Sand = Polokwane ➔ S. Africa 22°25S 30°5E 271 B5
Sand Norway 59°29N 6°16E 164 E3
Sand Bank B. St. Kitts & Nevis 17°15N 62°38W 322 d
Sand Cr. ➔ U.S.A. 39°3N 85°51W 311 E11
Sand Hills Guyana 6°27N 58°19W 329 B6
Sand Hills Nebr., U.S.A. 42°10N 101°30W 308 D3
Sand I. Midway Is. 28°12N 177°23W 302 g
Sand I. Hawai'i, U.S.A. 21°19N 157°53W 302 K14
Sand Islet Midway Is. 28°16N 177°22W 302 c
Sand Lakes △ Canada 57°51N 98°32W 297 B9
Sand Point U.S.A. 55°20N 160°30W 303 J7
Sand Springs U.S.A. 36°9N 96°7W 314 C6
Sanda Japan 34°53N 135°14E 223 C7
Sandai Indonesia 1°15S 110°31E 235 C4
Sandakan Malaysia 5°53N 118°4E 235 A5
Sandalwood Australia 34°55S 140°9E 282 C4
Sandan = Sambor Cambodia 12°46N 106°0E 236 F6
Sandane Norway 61°46N 6°13E 164 C3
Sandanski Bulgaria 41°35N 23°16E 202 E7
Sandaré Mali 14°40N 10°15W 262 C2
Sandared Sweden 57°43N 12°47E 163 G6
Sandarne Sweden 61°16N 17°9E 162 C11
Sandaun □ Papua N. G. 3°30S 142°0E 286 B2
Sanday U.K. 59°16N 2°31W 167 B6
Sande Møre og Romsdal, Norway 62°15N 5°27E 164 B2
Sande Sogn og Fjordane, Norway 61°20N 5°47E 164 C2
Sande Vestfold, Norway 59°36N 10°12E 162 E4
Sandefjord Norway 59°10N 10°15E 164 E7
Sandeid Norway 59°33N 5°52E 164 E2
Sanders Ariz., U.S.A. 35°13N 109°20W 305 J9
Sanders Ky., U.S.A. 38°40N 84°56W 311 F12
Sanderson Fla., U.S.A. 30°15N 82°16W 316 E7
Sanderson Tex., U.S.A. 30°9N 102°24W 314 F3
Sandersville U.S.A. 32°59N 82°48W 316 C7
Sandfire Roadhouse Australia 19°45S 121°15E 278 C3
Sandfloeggа Norway 59°58N 7°10E 164 E4
Sandfly L. Canada 55°43N 106°6W 297 B7
Sandfontein Namibia 23°48S 19°1E 270 B2
Sandhammaren Sweden 55°23N 14°14E 163 J8
Sandheads, The India 21°10N 88°20E 241 E2
Sandgerði Iceland 64°3N 22°42W 155 C4
Sandia Peru 14°10S 69°30W 330 C4
Sandıklı Turkey 38°28N 30°17E 205 C12
Sandila India 27°5N 80°31E 243 F9
Sandilands Bahamas 25°3N 77°19W 153 b
Sanding Indonesia 3°28S 100°40E 234 C2
Sanding, Selat Indonesia 3°24S 100°34E 234 C2
Sandnes Aust-Agder, Norway 58°53N 7°45E 164 F4
Sandnes Rogaland, Norway 58°50N 5°45E 164 F2
Sandnessjøen Norway 66°2N 12°38E 160 C15
Sandoa Dem. Rep. of the Congo 9°41S 23°0E 265 D4
Sandomierz Poland 50°40N 21°43E 185 H8
Sândominic Romania 46°35N 25°47E 183 D10
Sandona Colombia 1°17N 77°28W 328 C2
Sandongo Angola 15°30S 21°28E 265 F4
Sandoval U.S.A. 38°37N 89°7W 310 F7
Sandover ➔ Australia 21°43S 136°32E 280 C2
Sandoway = Thandwe Burma 18°20N 94°30E 241 F5
Sandown S. Africa 26°5S 28°4E 123 A2
Sandown Park Races U.K. 51°22N 0°21W 125 B1
Sandoy Færoe Is. 61°52N 6°46W 160 F9
Sandpoint U.S.A. 48°17N 116°33W 304 B5
Sandray U.K. 56°53N 7°31W 167 E1
Sandringham U.K. 52°51N 0°31E 168 E8
Sandstone Australia 27°59S 119°16E 279 E2
Sandton S. Africa 26°5S 28°4E 123 A2
Sandu China 26°0N 107°52E 228 E6
Sandumba Angola 13°45S 17°34E 265 E3
Sandur India 15°6N 76°33E 245 F3
Sandusky Mich., U.S.A. 43°25N 82°50W 312 C2
Sandusky Ohio, U.S.A. 41°27N 82°42W 312 E2
Sandusky ➔ U.S.A. 41°27N 83°0W 311 C14
Sandveld Namibia 21°25S 20°0E 270 B3
Sandvig Denmark 55°18N 14°47E 163 J8
Sandvika Norway 59°54N 10°31E 133 A2
Sandviken Sweden 60°38N 16°46E 162 D10
Sandwich U.S.A. 41°39N 88°37W 311 C8
Sandwich, C. Australia 18°14S 146°18E 280 B4
Sandwich B. Nfld. & L., Canada 53°40N 57°15W 299 B8
Sandwich B. Namibia 23°25S 14°20E 270 B1
Sandwip I. Bangla. 22°30N 91°25E 241 D3
Sandy Oreg., U.S.A. 45°24N 122°16W 306 E4
Sandy Pa., U.S.A. 41°6N 78°46W 312 E6
Sandy Utah, U.S.A. 40°32N 111°50W 304 F8
Sandy B. St. Helena 16°0S 5°43W 153 h
Sandy Bay Canada 55°31N 102°19W 297 B8
Sandy Bight Australia 33°50S 123°20E 279 F3
Sandy C. Queens., Australia 24°42S 153°15E 280 C5
Sandy C. Tas., Australia 41°25S 144°45E 281 G3
Sandy Cay Bahamas 23°13N 75°18W 321 B4
Sandy Cr. ➔ N.S.W., Australia 31°54S 145°18E 281 B4
Sandy Cr. ➔ Wyo., U.S.A. 41°51N 109°47W 304 F9
Sandy Creek U.S.A. 43°38N 76°5W 313 C8
Sandy Ground Village Anguilla 18°12N 63°6W 322 a
Sandy Hill B. Anguilla 18°13N 63°1W 322 a
Sandy I. Anguilla 18°13N 63°7W 322 a
Sandy I. Grenada 12°29N 61°29W 323 q
Sandy I. Grenada 12°13N 61°35W 323 q
Sandy L. Canada 53°2N 93°0W 298 B1
Sandy Lake Canada 53°0N 93°15W 298 B1
Sandy Point India 10°32N 92°22E 245 J11
Sandy Point Town St. Kitts & Nevis 17°22N 62°51W 322 d
Sandy Springs U.S.A. 33°56N 84°23W 316 B5
Sandy Valley U.S.A. 35°49N 115°38W 307 K11
Sånfjället △ Sweden 62°17N 13°35E 162 B7
Sanford Fla., U.S.A. 28°48N 81°16W 317 G8
Sanford Maine, U.S.A. 43°27N 70°47W 313 C14
Sanford N.C., U.S.A. 35°29N 79°10W 315 D15
Sanford ➔ Australia 27°22S 115°53E 279 E2
Sanford, Mt. U.S.A. 62°13N 144°8W 303 E11
Sang-i-Masha Afghan. 33°8N 67°27E 242 C2
Sanga Angola 11°9S 15°21E 265 E3
Sanga Mozam. 12°22S 35°21E 269 E4
Sanga ➔ Congo 1°5S 17°0E 264 C3
Sangaie Dem. Rep. of the Congo 6°48S 22°46E 265 D4
Sangamner India 19°37N 74°15E 244 E2
Sangamon ➔ U.S.A. 40°1N 90°26W 310 D6
Sangān Iran 34°23N 60°15E 247 C9
Sanganeb Atoll △ Sudan 19°33N 37°11E 256 D4
Sangar Afghan. 32°56N 65°30E 242 C1
Sangar Russia 64°2N 127°31E 215 C13
Sangar Sarai Afghan. 34°27N 70°35E 242 B4
Sangareddi India 17°38N 78°7E 244 F4
Sangaredi Guinea 11°7N 13°52W 262 C2
Sangarh ➔ Pakistan 30°43N 70°44E 242 D4
Sangasanga Indonesia 0°36S 117°13E 235 C5
Sangasso Mali 12°5N 5°35W 262 C3
Sangatte France 50°56N 1°44E 173 B8
Sangāw Iraq 35°17N 45°10E 213 E11
Sangay Ecuador 2°0S 78°20W 328 D2
Sangay △ Ecuador 2°15S 78°26W 328 D2
Sangbé Cameroon 6°3N 12°28E 264 A2
Sangchris L. U.S.A. 39°39N 89°29W 310 E7
Sangdong S. Korea 37°7N 128°49E 224 D4
Sange Dem. Rep. of the Congo 6°58S 28°21E 268 D2
Sangeang Indonesia 8°12S 119°6E 235 F5
Sangenjaya Japan 35°37N 139°39E 140 B2
Sângeorz-Băi Romania 47°22N 24°41E 183 C9
Sanger U.S.A. 36°42N 119°33W 306 J7
Sângera Moldova 46°55N 28°58E 183 D13
Sangerhausen Germany 51°28N 11°18E 178 D7
Sanggan He ➔ China 38°12N 117°15E 226 E9
Sanggau Kalimantan Barat, Indonesia 0°5N 110°30E 235 B4
Sanggau Kalimantan Barat, Indonesia 1°7N 109°36E 235 B3
Sanggye S. Korea 37°38N 127°3E 137 B2
Sangha □ Congo 1°0N 15°30E 264 B3
Sangha-Mbaéré □ C.A.R. 4°30N 16°30E 264 B3
Sanghar Pakistan 26°2N 68°57E 242 F3
Sangihe, Kepulauan Indonesia 3°0N 125°30E 231 D7
Sangihe, Pulau Indonesia 3°35N 125°30E 231 D7
Sangin Afghan. 32°4N 64°50E 240 B2
Sangiran Indonesia 7°25S 110°55E 235 D4
Sangiran △ Indonesia 7°27S 110°50E 231 G14
Sangju S. Korea 36°25N 128°10E 224 D4
Sangkapura Indonesia 5°52S 112°40E 235 D4
Sangkha Thailand 14°37N 103°52E 236 E4
Sangkhla Buri Thailand 14°57N 98°28E 236 E2
Sangkulirang Indonesia 0°59N 117°58E 235 B5
Sangla Pakistan 31°43N 73°23E 242 D5
Sangley Pt. Phil. 14°29N 120°54E 127 C1
Sangli India 16°55N 74°33E 244 F2
Sangmélima Cameroon 2°57N 12°1E 263 E7
Sango Angola 9°51S 15°44E 265 D2
Sango Zimbabwe 18°44S 31°44E 269 F3
Sangod India 24°55N 76°17E 242 G7
Sangole India 17°26N 75°12E 244 F2
Sangorodok = Ust-Vorkuta Russia 67°24N 64°0E 186 A11
Sangpang Bum Burma 26°30N 95°50E 241 B5
Sangre de Cristo Mts. U.S.A. 37°30N 105°20W 305 H11
Sangre Grande Trin. & Tob. 10°35N 61°8W 323 t
Sangro ➔ Italy 42°14N 14°32E 199 F11
Sangrur India 30°14N 75°50E 242 D6
Sangudo Canada 53°50N 114°54W 296 C6
Sangue ➔ Brazil 11°1S 58°39W 331 C6
Sangüesa Spain 42°37N 1°17W 196 C3
Sanguinaires, Îs. France 41°51N 8°36E 175 G12
Sangzhi China 29°25N 110°12E 229 C8
Sanhala Ivory C. 10°3N 6°51W 262 C3
Sanhsia Taiwan 24°56N 121°22E 225 B3
Sanhsien Hualien, Taiwan 23°8N 121°25E 225 C3
Sanhsien T'aitung, Taiwan 23°24N 121°19E 225 C3
Sanhsing Taiwan 24°40N 121°39E 225 B3
Sani Taiwan 24°24N 120°46E 225 B2
Sanibel U.S.A. 26°27N 82°1W 317 J7
Sanibel I. U.S.A. 26°26N 82°6W 317 J7
Sanikiluaq Canada 56°32N 79°14W 298 A4
Sanin-Kaigan △ Japan 35°39N 134°37E 222 B6
Sanirajak = Hall Beach Canada 68°46N 81°12W 295 D15
Sanjawi Pakistan 30°17N 68°21E 242 D3
Sanje Uganda 0°49S 31°30E 268 C3
Sanjiang China 25°48N 109°37E 228 E7
Sanjo Japan 37°37N 138°57E 220 F9
Sankarankovil India 9°10N 77°35E 245 K3
Sankeshwar India 16°23N 74°32E 245 F2
Sankh ➔ India 22°15N 84°48E 243 H11
Sankosh ➔ India 26°24N 89°47E 241 B2
Sankrail India 22°33N 88°13E 124 B1
Sankt Andrä Austria 46°46N 14°50E 180 E7
Sankt Anton Austria 47°8N 10°16E 179 H6
Sankt Augustin Germany 50°45N 7°10E 178 E3
Sankt Blasien Germany 47°47N 8°7E 179 H4
Sankt Gallen Switz. 47°26N 9°22E 179 H5
Sankt Gallen □ Switz. 47°25N 9°23E 179 H5
Sankt Goar Germany 50°12N 7°43E 179 E3
Sankt Ingbert Germany 49°16N 7°6E 179 F3
Sankt Johann im Pongau Austria 47°22N 13°12E 180 D6

Sankt Johann in Tirol Austria 47°30N 12°25E 180 D5
Sankt Marein = Smarje Slovenia 46°15N 15°34E 199 B12
Sankt Michel = Mikkeli Finland 61°43N 27°15E 188 B4
Sankt Moritz Switz. 46°30N 9°51E 179 J5
Sankt Peter-Ording Germany 54°20N 8°36E 178 A4
Sankt-Peterburg Russia 59°55N 30°20E 137 B1
Sankt Pölten Austria 48°12N 15°38E 180 C8
Sankt Ulrich = Ortisei Italy 46°34N 11°40E 199 B8
Sankt Valentin Austria 48°11N 14°33E 180 C7
Sankt Veit Austria 48°11N 16°16E 142 A1
Sankt Veit an der Glan Austria 46°47N 14°22E 180 E7
Sankt Wendel Germany 49°27N 7°9E 179 F3
Sankt Wolfgang Austria 47°43N 13°27E 180 D6
Sankuru □ Dem. Rep. of the Congo 5°0S 24°0E 265 C4
Sankuru → Dem. Rep. of the Congo 4°17S 20°25E 265 C4
Sanlihe China 39°53N 116°18E 114 B1
Sanlin China 31°9N 121°29E 138 C1
Sanlintang China 31°9N 121°29E 138 C1
Sanliurfa Turkey 37°12N 38°50E 213 D8
Sanliurfa □ Turkey 37°0N 39°0E 213 D8
Sanlúcar de Barrameda Spain 36°46N 6°21W 195 J4
Sanluri Italy 39°34N 8°54E 200 C1
Sânmartin Romania 46°19N 25°58E 183 D10
Sanmen China 29°5N 121°35E 229 C13
Sanmenxia China 34°47N 111°12E 226 G6
Sanming China 26°15N 117°40E 229 D11
Sanmu Kantō, Japan 34°11N 134°37E 222 C6
Sanmu Shikoku, Japan 35°36N 140°25E 223 B12
Sannan Japan 35°2N 135°1E 223 B7
Sannat Malta 36°1N 14°15E 206 E6
Sanndraigh = Sandray U.K. 56°53N 7°31W 167 E1
Sânnicolau Mare Romania 46°5N 20°39E 182 D5
Sannieshof S. Africa 26°30S 25°47E 270 C4
Sannīn, J. Lebanon 33°57N 35°52E 250 E6
Sanniquellie Liberia 7°19N 8°38W 262 D3
Sannûr Egypt 28°58N 31°3E 251 K2
Sannûr, W. → Egypt 28°59N 31°3E 251 K2
Sano Japan 36°19N 139°35E 223 A11
Sanok Poland 49°35N 22°10E 185 J9
Sanqingshan △ China 28°54N 118°3E 229 C12
Sanquhar U.K. 55°22N 3°54W 167 F5
Sanquianga △ Colombia 2°33N 78°14W 328 C2
Sanremo = San Remo Italy 43°49N 7°46E 198 E4
Sans Spain 41°22N 2°7E 114 A1
Sans Souci St. Vincent 13°13N 61°7W 323 n
Sans Souci Trin. & Tob. 10°50N 61°0W 323 t
Sansanding Mali 13°48N 6°0W 262 C3
Sansané Niger 13°50N 1°36E 263 C5
Sansepolcro Italy 43°34N 12°8E 199 E9
Sansha China 26°58N 120°12E 229 D13
Sanshui China 23°10N 112°56E 229 F9
Sanski Most Bos.-H. 44°46N 16°40E 199 D13
Sansom Park U.S.A. 32°48N 97°24W 120 B1
Sanssouci Germany 52°23N 13°2E 115 B1
Sansui China 26°58N 108°39E 228 D7
Sant Agusti Barcelona, Spain 114 c2
Sant Ambrogio, Basilica di Italy 45°27N 9°10E 128 B2
Sant Antoni de Portmany Spain 38°59N 1°19E 206 D1
Sant Boi de Llobregat Spain 41°20N 2°2E 114 A1
Sant Carles Spain 39°3N 1°34E 206 C2
Sant Carles de la Ràpita Spain 40°37N 0°35E 196 E5
Sant Celoni Spain 41°42N 2°30E 196 D7
Sant Cugat Spain 41°28N 2°5E 114 A1
Sant Elm Spain 39°35N 2°21E 206 B3
Sant Feliu de Guíxols Spain 41°45N 3°1E 196 D8
Sant Feliu de Llobregat Spain 41°22N 2°2E 114 A1
Sant Ferran Spain 38°42N 1°28E 206 D1
Sant Francesc de Formentera Spain 38°42N 1°26E 206 D1
Sant Jaume Spain 39°54N 4°4E 206 B5
Sant Joan Spain 39°36N 3°4E 206 B4
Sant Joan d'Alacant Spain 38°24N 0°26W 197 G4
Sant Joan de Labritja Spain 39°5N 1°31E 206 C2
Sant Joan Despi Spain 41°22N 2°2E 114 A1
Sant Jordi Ibiza, Spain 38°53N 1°24E 206 D1
Sant Jordi Mallorca, Spain 39°33N 2°46E 206 B3
Sant Jordi, G. de Spain 40°53N 1°2E 196 E6
Sant Llorenç de Morunys Spain 42°8N 1°35E 196 C6
Sant Llorenç del Munt y l'Obac ⌂ Spain 41°39N 1°55W 196 D3
Sant Llorenç des Cardassar Spain 39°37N 3°17E 206 B4
Sant Maria del Mar Barcelona, Spain 114 b3
Sant Mateu Baleares, Spain 39°3N 1°23E 206 C1
Sant Mateu Valencia, Spain 40°28N 0°10E 196 E5
Sant Miquel Spain 39°3N 1°26E 206 C1
Sant Pau del Camp Barcelona, Spain 114 c2
Sant Pere de Ribes Spain 41°16N 1°46E 196 D6
Sant Salvador Spain 39°27N 3°11E 206 B4
Sant Vicent del Raspeig Spain 38°24N 0°31W 197 G4
Santa Peru 8°59S 78°40W 330 B2
Sant' Ágata Militello Italy 38°2N 14°8E 201 D7
Santa Agnès Spain 39°3N 1°21E 206 C1
Santa Ana Beni, Bolivia 13°50S 65°40W 331 C4
Santa Ana La Paz, Bolivia 15°31S 67°30W 330 D4
Santa Ana Santa Cruz, Bolivia 18°43S 58°44W 331 D6
Santa Ana Santa Cruz, Bolivia 16°37S 60°43W 331 D5
Santa Ana Ecuador 1°16S 80°20W 328 D1
Santa Ana El Salv. 14°0N 89°31W 320 D2
Santa Ana Guam 13°32N 145°46E 302 d
Santa Ana Sonora, Mexico 30°33N 111°7W 318 A2
Santa Ana Cagayan, Phil. 18°28N 122°20E 232 B4
Santa Ana Manila, Phil. 14°34N 121°0E 127 B2
Santa Ana Solomon Is. 10°50S 162°30E 287 N12
Santa Ana Calif., U.S.A. 33°46N 117°52W 307 M9
Santa Ana → Venezuela 9°30N 71°57W 328 B3
Santa Ana de los Ríos de Cuenca = Cuenca Ecuador 2°50S 79°9W 328 D2
Sant' Andrea Venice, Italy 142 b1
Santa Anita Park U.S.A. 34°8N 118°5W 126 B4
Santa Bárbara Santa Maria, Azores 36°59N 25°4W 153 d4
Santa Bárbara Terciera, Azores 38°41N 27°20W 153 d1
Santa Bárbara Chile 37°40S 72°1W 334 D1
Santa Bárbara Colombia 5°53N 75°35W 328 B2
Santa Bárbara Curaçao 12°5N 68°51W 322 g
Santa Bárbara Honduras 14°53N 88°14W 320 D2
Santa Bárbara Chihuahua, Mexico 26°48N 105°49W 318 B3
Santa Barbara Phil. 10°50N 122°32E 233 F4
Santa Bárbara Spain 40°42N 0°29E 196 E5
Santa Barbara Calif., U.S.A. 34°25N 119°42W 307 L7
Santa Bárbara Amazonas, Venezuela 3°57N 67°6W 328 C4
Santa Bárbara Barinas, Venezuela 7°47N 71°10W 328 B3
Santa Bárbara, Mt. Spain 37°23N 2°50W 197 H2
Santa Bárbara, Serra de Azores 38°44N 27°19W 153 d1
Santa Barbara Channel U.S.A. 34°15N 120°0W 307 L7
Santa Barbara I. U.S.A. 33°29N 119°2W 307 M7
Santa Catalina Colombia 10°36N 75°17W 328 A2
Santa Catalina Neg. Or., Phil. 9°20N 122°52E 233 G4
Santa Catalina Solomon Is. 10°53S 162°29E 287 N12
Santa Catalina, Gulf of U.S.A. 33°10N 117°50W 307 N9
Santa Catalina, I. Mexico 25°40N 110°47W 318 B2
Santa Catalina de Armada Spain 43°2N 8°49W 194 B2
Santa Catalina I. U.S.A. 33°23N 118°25W 307 M8
Santa Catarina □ Brazil 27°25S 48°30W 335 B6
Santa Catarina, I. de Brazil 27°30S 48°40W 335 B6
Santa Caterina Venice, Italy 142 a3
Santa Caterina di Pittinuri Italy 40°6N 8°27E 200 B1
Santa Caterina Villarmosa Italy 37°35N 14°2E 201 E7
Santa Cecília Brazil 26°56S 50°18W 335 B5
Santa Clara Cuba 22°20N 80°0W 320 B4
Santa Clara Calif., U.S.A. 37°21N 121°57W 306 H5
Santa Clara N.Y., U.S.A. 44°38N 74°27W 313 B10
Santa Clara Utah, U.S.A. 37°8N 113°39W 305 H7
Santa Clara → Mexico 29°51N 107°6W 318 A3
Santa Clara, I. Chile 33°42S 79°0W 330 c
Santa Clara de Olimar Uruguay 32°50S 54°54W 335 C5
Santa Clara Valley U.S.A. 36°50N 121°30W 306 J5
Santa Clarita U.S.A. 34°24N 118°33W 307 L8
Santa Clotilde Peru 2°33S 73°45W 328 D3
Santa Coloma de Farners Spain 41°50N 2°39E 196 D7
Santa Coloma de Gramenet Spain 41°27N 2°13E 114 A2
Santa Comba = Santa Cataliña de Armada Spain 43°2N 8°49W 194 B2
Santa Croce Venice, Italy 142 b2
Santa Croce Camerina Italy 36°50N 14°31E 201 F7
Santa Croce di Magliano Italy 41°42N 14°59E 199 G11
Santa Cruz Aruba 12°30N 69°59W 322 f
Santa Cruz Bolivia 17°43S 63°10W 331 D5
Santa Cruz Brazil 6°13S 36°1W 332 C4
Santa Cruz Chile 34°38S 71°27W 334 C1
Santa Cruz Costa Rica 10°15N 85°35W 320 D2
Santa Cruz Curaçao 12°18N 69°7W 322 g
Santa Cruz Maharashtra, India 19°4N 72°51E 130 A1
Santa Cruz Jamaica 18°3N 77°43W 320 a
Santa Cruz Madeira 32°42N 16°46W 153 c
Santa Cruz Peru 5°40S 75°56W 330 B2
Santa Cruz Davao del S., Phil. 6°50N 125°25E 233 H5
Santa Cruz Laguna, Phil. 14°20N 121°24E 232 D3
Santa Cruz Manila, Phil. 14°36N 120°58E 127 B1
Santa Cruz Marinduque, Phil. 13°28N 122°2E 232 E4
Santa Cruz Mind. Occ., Phil. 13°4N 120°43E 232 E3
Santa Cruz Zambales, Phil. 15°46N 119°55E 232 D2
Santa Cruz Calif., U.S.A. 36°58N 122°1W 306 J4
Santa Cruz Venezuela 8°3N 64°27W 329 B5
Santa Cruz □ Argentina 49°0S 70°0W 336 C3
Santa Cruz □ Bolivia 17°43S 63°10W 331 D5
Santa Cruz → Argentina 50°10S 68°20W 336 D3
Santa Cruz, B. Curaçao 12°18N 69°10W 322 g
Santa Cruz, I. Ecuador 0°38S 90°23W 330 a
Santa Cruz, I. de Brazil 22°51S 43°7W 135 B2
Santa Cruz Cabrália Brazil 16°17S 39°2W 333 E4
Santa Cruz da Graciosa Azores 39°5N 28°1W 153 d1
Santa Cruz das Flores Azores 39°27N 31°7W 153 d2
Santa Cruz de Bravo = Felipe Carrillo Puerto Mexico 19°38N 88°3W 319 D7
Santa Cruz de la Palma Canary Is. 28°41N 17°46W 153 e1
Santa Cruz de la Palma ✈ (SPC) Canary Is. 28°40N 17°45W 153 e1
Santa Cruz de Mompox = Mompós Colombia 9°14N 74°26W 328 B3
Santa Cruz de Mudela Spain 38°39N 3°28W 195 G7
Santa Cruz de Olorde Spain 41°25N 2°3E 114 A1
Santa Cruz de Tenerife Canary Is. 28°28N 16°15W 153 e1
Santa Cruz del Norte Cuba 23°9N 81°55W 320 B3
Santa Cruz del Retamar Spain 40°8N 4°14W 194 E6
Santa Cruz del Sur Cuba 20°44N 78°0W 320 B4
Santa Cruz do Rio Pardo Brazil 22°54S 49°37W 335 A6
Santa Cruz do Sul Brazil 29°42S 52°25W 335 B5
Santa Cruz I. U.S.A. 34°1N 119°43W 307 M7
Santa Cruz Is. Solomon Is. 10°30S 166°0E 277 C12
Santa Cruz la Vieja △ Bolivia 17°55S 60°50W 331 D5
Santa Cruz Mts. Jamaica 17°58N 77°43W 320 a
Santa Efigénia Brazil 23°32S 46°38W 137 B2
Santa Elena Argentina 30°58S 59°47W 334 C4
Santa Elena Ecuador 2°16S 80°52W 328 D1
Sant' Elena Venice, Italy 142 c4
Santa Elena Camarines N., Phil. 14°12N 122°24E 232 D4
Santa Elena Manila, Phil. 14°38N 121°5E 127 B2
Santa Elena, C. Costa Rica 10°54N 85°56W 320 D2
Sant' Elena, Darsena di Venice, Italy 142 c4
Sant' Elena, Isola di Venice, Italy 142 c4
Santa Elena del Gomero Chile 33°28S 70°45W 137 B1
Sant' Eufèmia, G. di Italy 38°51N 16°4E 201 D9
Santa Eulalia Spain 41°25N 2°10E 114 A2
Santa Eulària des Riu Spain 38°59N 1°32E 206 D2
Santa Fé Argentina 31°35S 60°41W 334 C3
Santa Fe Nueva Viscaya, Phil. 16°10N 120°57E 232 C3
Santa Fe Romblon, Phil. 12°10N 122°0E 232 E4
Santa Fé Spain 37°11N 3°43W 195 H7
Santa Fe N. Mex., U.S.A. 35°41N 105°57W 305 J11
Santa Fé □ Argentina 31°50S 60°55W 334 C3
Santa Fé, Canal de Ecuador 0°48S 89°55W 330 a
Santa Fé, I. Ecuador 0°49S 90°5W 330 a
Santa Fé do Sul Brazil 20°13S 50°56W 333 F1
Santa Fe Springs U.S.A. 33°56N 118°3W 126 C4
Santa Filomena Brazil 9°6S 45°50W 332 C2
Santa Fiora Italy 42°50N 11°35E 199 F8
Santa Gertrudis Spain 39°0N 1°26E 206 C1
Santa Giulia France 41°32N 9°17E 175 G13
Santa Giustina Italy 46°10N 12°5E 199 B9
Santa Helena Brazil 2°14S 45°18W 332 B2
Santa Helena de Goiás Brazil 17°53S 50°35W 333 E1
Santa Inês Bahia, Brazil 13°17S 39°48W 333 D4
Santa Inês Maranhão, Brazil 3°39S 45°20W 332 B2
Santa Inés Extremadura, Spain 38°32N 5°37W 195 G5
Santa Inés, I. Chile 54°0S 73°0W 336 D2
Santa Iria da Azóia Portugal 38°49N 9°5W 126 A2
Santa Isabel = Rey Malabo Eq. Guin. 3°45N 8°50E 263 E6
Santa Isabel Argentina 36°10S 66°54W 334 D2
Santa Isabel Puerto Rico 17°58N 66°24W 321 b
Santa Isabel Solomon Is. 8°0S 159°0E 287 M10
Santa Isabel do Araguaia Brazil 6°7S 48°19W 332 C2
Santa Isabel do Morro Brazil 11°34S 50°40W 333 D1
Santa Isabel do Rio Negro Brazil 0°24S 65°2W 329 D4
Santa Julia Chile 33°30S 70°35W 137 C2
Santa Lucía Corrientes, Argentina 28°58S 59°5W 334 B4
Santa Lucía San Juan, Argentina 31°30S 68°30W 334 C2
Santa Lucia Phil. 17°7N 120°27E 232 C3
Santa Lucía Spain 37°35N 0°58W 197 H4
Santa Lucía Uruguay 34°27S 56°24W 334 C4
Santa Lucia, Stazione Venice, Italy 142 a2
Santa Lucía de Tirajana Canary Is. 27°55N 5°32W 153 e1
Santa Lucia Range U.S.A. 36°0N 121°20W 306 K5
Santa Luzia = Luziânia Brazil 16°20S 48°0W 333 E2
Santa Luzia Brazil 19°47S 43°52W 333 E3
Santa Luzia C. Verde Is. 16°50N 24°35W 153 j
Santa Margalida Spain 39°42N 3°6E 206 B4
Santa Margarita Argentina 38°28S 61°35W 334 D3
Santa Margarita Calif., U.S.A. 35°23N 120°37W 306 K6
Santa Margarita → U.S.A. 33°13N 117°23W 307 M9
Santa Margarita, I. Mexico 24°27N 111°50W 318 C2
Santa Margherita Italy 38°58N 8°58E 200 D1
Santa Margherita Ligure Italy 44°20N 9°11E 198 D6
Santa María Argentina 26°40S 66°0W 334 B2
Santa Maria Azores 36°58N 25°6W 153 d4
Santa Maria Brazil 29°40S 53°48W 335 B5
Santa Maria C. Verde Is. 16°31N 22°53W 153 j
Santa María Mexico City, Mexico 128 a1
Santa Maria Ilocos S., Phil. 17°22N 120°29E 232 C3
Santa Maria Isabela, Phil. 17°28N 121°45E 232 C3
Santa Maria Calif., U.S.A. 34°57N 120°26W 307 L6
Santa María → Mexico 31°0N 107°14W 318 A3
Santa María, B. de Mexico 25°4N 108°6W 318 B3
Santa Maria, C. de Portugal 36°58N 7°53W 195 J3
Santa Maria, I. Ecuador 1°17S 90°26W 330 a
Santa María, Vol. Guatemala 14°45N 91°33W 320 D1
Santa Maria Cápua Vétere Italy 41°5N 14°15E 201 A7
Santa Maria da Feira Portugal 40°55N 8°35W 194 E2
Santa Maria da Vitória Brazil 13°24S 44°12W 333 D3
Santa María de Guadalupe = Guadalupe Spain 39°27N 5°17W 195 F5
Santa María de Ipire Venezuela 8°49N 65°19W 329 B4
Santa Maria dei Frari Venice, Italy 142 b2
Santa Maria dei Miracoli Venice, Italy 142 b3
Santa Maria del Camí Spain 39°38N 2°47E 206 B3
Santa Maria della Misericórdia Venice, Italy 142 a3
Santa Maria della Pianto Venice, Italy 142 b3
Santa Maria della Salute Venice, Italy 142 c2
Santa Maria della Visitazione Venice, Italy 142 b3
Santa Maria delle Penitenti Venice, Italy 142 a2
Santa Maria di Léuca, C. Italy 39°47N 18°22E 201 C11
Santa Maria do Boiaçu Brazil 0°25S 61°48W 329 D5
Santa Maria do Suaçuí Brazil 18°12S 42°25W 333 E3
Santa Maria dos Marmelos Brazil 6°7S 61°51W 331 B5
Santa Maria Formosa Venice, Italy 142 b3
Santa María la Real de Nieva Spain 41°4N 4°24W 194 D6
Santa Maria Maggiore, Ex Chiesa di Venice, Italy 142 b1
Santa Marinella Italy 42°2N 11°52E 199 F8
Santa Marta Colombia 11°15N 74°13W 328 A3
Santa Marta, Sierra Nevada de Colombia 10°55N 73°50W 328 A3
Santa Marta de Tormes Spain 40°57N 5°38W 194 E5
Santa Marta Grande, C. Brazil 28°43S 48°50W 335 B6
Santa Martabaai = Sint Marthabaai Curaçao 12°17N 69°8W 322 g
Santa Maura = Lefkada Greece 38°40N 20°43E 207 B2
Santa Monica U.S.A. 34°1N 118°29W 126 B2
Santa Monica Mts. U.S.A. 34°6N 118°29W 126 B2
Santa Monica Mts. ⌂ U.S.A. 34°4N 118°44W 307 L8
Santa Olalla Spain 40°2N 4°25W 194 E6
Santa Olalla del Cala Spain 37°54N 6°14W 195 H4
Santa Paula U.S.A. 34°21N 119°4W 307 L7
Santa Pola Spain 38°13N 0°35W 197 G4
Santa Ponça Spain 39°30N 2°28E 206 B3
Santa Quitéria Brazil 4°20S 40°10W 332 B3
Santa Rita = Itumbiara Brazil 18°20S 49°10W 333 E2
Santa Rita Amazonas, Brazil 3°29S 69°19W 328 D4
Santa Rita Paraíba, Brazil 7°8S 34°58W 332 C5
Santa Rita Colombia 4°53N 68°24W 328 C4
Santa Rita Guam 13°23N 144°40E 302 d
Santa Rita Samar, Phil. 11°27N 124°56E 233 F5
Santa Rita Zulia, Venezuela 10°32N 71°32W 328 A3
Santa Rita de Cássia Brazil 11°0S 44°32W 332 D3
Santa Rita do Araguaia = Guiratinga Brazil 16°21S 53°45W 331 D7
Santa Rita do Araguaia Brazil 17°20S 53°12W 331 D7
Santa Rosa = Bella Unión Uruguay 30°15S 57°40W 334 C4
Santa Rosa La Pampa, Argentina 36°40S 64°17W 334 D3
Santa Rosa San Luis, Argentina 32°21S 65°10W 334 C2
Santa Rosa Beni, Bolivia 14°10S 66°53W 330 C4
Santa Rosa Pando, Bolivia 10°36S 67°20W 330 C4
Santa Rosa Santa Cruz, Bolivia 17°7S 63°35W 331 D5
Santa Rosa Brazil 27°52S 54°29W 335 B5
Santa Rosa Colombia 3°32N 69°48W 328 C4
Santa Rosa Curaçao 12°7N 68°53W 322 g
Santa Rosa El Oro, Ecuador 3°27S 79°58W 328 D2
Santa Rosa Galápagos Is., Ecuador 0°40S 90°25W 330 a
Santa Rosa Puno, Peru 14°30S 70°50W 330 C3
Santa Rosa San Martin, Peru 6°41S 76°37W 330 B2
Santa Rosa Phil. 15°25N 120°57E 232 D3
Santa Rosa Calif., U.S.A. 38°26N 122°43W 306 G4
Santa Rosa N. Mex., U.S.A. 34°57N 104°41W 305 J11
Santa Rosa Amazonas, Venezuela 1°29N 66°55W 328 C4
Santa Rosa, Mt. Guam 13°32N 144°55E 302 d
Santa Rosa and San Jacinto Mts. ⌂ U.S.A. 33°28N 116°20W 307 M10
Santa Rosa Beach U.S.A. 30°22N 86°14W 316 E3
Santa Rosa de Amanadona Venezuela 1°29N 66°55W 328 C4
Santa Rosa de Cabal Colombia 4°52N 75°38W 328 C2
Santa Rosa de Copán Honduras 14°47N 88°46W 320 D2
Santa Rosa de la Roca Bolivia 16°3S 61°34W 331 D5
Santa Rosa de Locobe Chile 33°25S 70°33W 137 B2
Santa Rosa de Osos Colombia 6°39N 75°28W 328 B2
Santa Rosa de Río Primero Argentina 31°8S 63°20W 334 C3
Santa Rosa de Viterbo Colombia 5°53N 72°59W 328 B3
Santa Rosa del Palmar Bolivia 16°54S 62°24W 331 D5
Santa Rosa I. Calif., U.S.A. 33°58N 120°6W 307 M6
Santa Rosa I. Fla., U.S.A. 30°20N 86°50W 317 E3
Santa Rosa Range U.S.A. 41°45N 117°40W 304 F5
Santa Rosalía Mexico 27°19N 112°17W 318 B2
Santa Stae Venice, Italy 142 b2
Santa Sylvina Argentina 27°50S 61°10W 334 B3
Santa Tecla = Nueva San Salvador El Salv. 13°40N 89°18W 320 D2
Santa Teresa Argentina 33°25S 60°47W 334 C3
Santa Teresa N. Terr., Australia 24°8S 134°22E 280 C1
Santa Teresa Brazil 19°55S 40°36W 333 E3
Santa Teresa Tamaulipas, Mexico 25°17N 97°51W 319 B5
Santa Teresa Venezuela 4°43N 61°4W 329 C5
Santa Teresa △ Uruguay 33°57S 53°31W 335 C5
Santa Teresa de la Ovalle Chile 33°22S 70°44W 137 B1
Santa Teresa di Riva Italy 37°57N 15°22E 201 E8
Santa Teresa Gallura Italy 41°14N 9°11E 200 A2
Santa Teresinha Brazil 10°28S 50°31W 332 D1
Santa Teresita Argentina 36°32S 56°41W 334 D4
Santa Uxía de Ribeira = Ribeira Spain 42°36N 8°58W 194 C2
Santa Vitória Brazil 18°50S 50°8W 333 E1
Santa Vitória do Palmar Brazil 33°32S 53°25W 335 C5
Santa Ynez → U.S.A. 34°41N 120°36W 307 L6
Santa Ynez Mts. U.S.A. 34°30N 120°0W 307 L6
Santa Ysabel U.S.A. 33°7N 116°40W 307 M10
Santadi Italy 39°5N 8°43E 200 C1
Santaella Spain 37°34N 4°51W 195 H6
Santahamina Finland 60°8N 25°2E 121 C3
Santahar Bangla. 24°48N 88°59E 241 C2
Santai China 31°5N 104°58E 228 B5
Santaluz Brazil 11°15S 39°22W 332 D4
Santan Indonesia 0°3S 117°28E 235 C5
Santana = Uruaçu Brazil 14°30S 49°10W 333 D2
Santana Bahia, Brazil 13°2S 44°5W 333 D3
Santana São Paulo, Brazil 23°29S 46°36W 137 A2
Santana Madeira 32°48N 16°52W 153 c
Sântana Romania 46°20N 21°30E 182 D6
Santana, Coxilha de Brazil 30°50S 55°35W 335 C4
Santana do Ipanema Brazil 9°22S 37°14W 332 C4
Santana do Livramento Brazil 30°55S 55°30W 335 C4
Santana do Paranaíba = Paranaíba Brazil 19°40S 51°11W 331 D7
Santander Colombia 3°1N 76°28W 328 C2
Santander Phil. 9°25N 123°20E 233 G4
Santander Spain 43°27N 3°51W 194 B7
Santander □ Colombia 7°0N 73°15W 328 B3
Santander Jiménez Mexico 24°13N 98°28W 319 C5
Santanilla, Is. Honduras 17°22N 83°57W 320 C3
Santanyí Spain 39°20N 3°5E 206 B4
Santaquin U.S.A. 39°59N 111°47W 304 G8
Santarcángelo di Romagna Italy 44°4N 12°26E 199 D9
Santarém Brazil 2°25S 54°42W 329 D7
Santarém Portugal 39°12N 8°42W 195 F2
Santarém □ Portugal 39°10N 8°40W 195 F2
Santaren Channel W. Indies 24°0N 79°30W 320 B4
Santee U.S.A. 32°50N 116°58W 307 N10
Santee → U.S.A. 33°7N 79°17W 315 E15
Santeny France 48°43N 2°34E 134 B4
Santéramo in Colle Italy 40°49N 16°45E 201 B9
Santerno → Italy 44°34N 11°58E 199 D8
Santhià Italy 45°22N 8°10E 198 C5
Santi Taiwan 22°43N 120°39E 225 D2
Santi-Quaranta = Sarandë Albania 39°52N 19°55E 206 B9
Santiago = Río Grande de Santiago → Mexico 21°36N 105°26W 318 C3
Santiago = São Tiago C. Verde Is. 15°0N 23°40W 153 j
Santiago Brazil 29°11S 54°52W 335 B5
Santiago Canary Is. 28°2N 17°12W 153 e1
Santiago Chile 33°26S 70°40W 137 B2
Santiago Panama 8°0N 81°0W 320 E3
Santiago Peru 14°11S 75°43W 330 C2
Santiago Ilocos S., Phil. 17°18N 120°27E 232 C3
Santiago Isabela, Phil. 16°41N 121°33E 232 C3
Santiago → Peru 4°27S 77°38W 328 D2
Santiago, C. Chile 50°46S 75°27W 336 D1
Santiago, I. = San Salvador, I. Ecuador 0°16S 90°42W 330 a
Santiago, Punta de Eq. Guin. 3°12N 8°40E 263 E6
Santiago, Sierra de Bolivia 18°25S 59°25W 331 D6
Santiago Benitez Int. ✈ (SCL) Santiago, Chile 33°33S 70°42W 137 B1
Santiago de Chiquitos Bolivia 18°19S 59°34W 331 D6
Santiago de Chuco Peru 8°9S 78°11W 330 B2
Santiago de Compostela Spain 42°52N 8°37W 194 C2
Santiago de Cuba Cuba 20°0N 75°49W 320 C4
Santiago de los Caballeros Dom. Rep. 19°30N 70°40W 321 C5
Santiago de Surco Peru 12°9S 77°0W 124 B2
Santiago del Estero Argentina 27°50S 64°15W 334 B3
Santiago del Estero □ Argentina 27°40S 63°15W 334 B3
Santiago del Teide Canary Is. 28°17N 16°48W 153 e1
Santiago do Boqueirão = Santiago Brazil 29°11S 54°52W 335 B5
Santiago do Cacém Portugal 38°1N 8°42W 195 G2
Santiago I. Phil. 16°23N 119°56E 232 C2
Santiago Ixcuintla Mexico 21°49N 105°13W 318 C3
Santiago Jamiltepec Mexico 16°17N 97°49W 319 D5
Santiago Papasquiaro Mexico 25°3N 105°25W 318 C3
Santiago Pinotepa Nacional Mexico 16°19N 98°1W 319 D5
Santiaguillo, L. de Mexico 24°48N 104°48W 318 C4
Santialing Taiwan 25°5N 121°51E 225 A3
Santiao Chiao Taiwan 25°1N 122°0E 225 A3
Santiaolun Taiwan 23°39N 120°9E 225 C2
Santiguila Mali 12°42N 7°25W 262 C3
Santillana del Mar Spain 43°24N 4°6W 194 B6
Santisteban del Puerto Spain 38°17N 3°15W 195 G7
Santo → Peru 8°56S 78°37W 330 B2
Santo Amaro Bahia, Brazil 12°30S 38°43W 333 D4
Santo Amaro São Paulo, Brazil 23°39S 46°42W 137 B1
Santo Amaro Lisboa, Portugal 38°42N 9°11W 126 A1
Santo Anastácio Brazil 21°58S 51°39W 335 A5
Santo André Brazil 23°39S 46°29W 335 A6
Santo André Lisboa, Portugal 38°38N 9°3W 126 B2
Santo Ângelo Brazil 28°15S 54°15W 335 B5
Sant' Angelo, Castel Rome, Italy 136 b1
Sant' Àngelo Lodigiano Italy 45°14N 9°25E 198 C6
Santo Antão C. Verde Is. 16°52N 25°10W 153 j
Santo Antão do Tojal Portugal 38°49N 9°9W 126 A2
Sant' Antíoco Italy 39°4N 8°27E 200 C1
Santo António São Tomé & Príncipe 1°37N 7°27E 265 a
Santo Antônio Brazil 2°24S 60°58W 329 D5
Santo Antônio, Qta. de Portugal 38°39N 9°15W 126 B1
Santo Antônio da Cachoeira = Itaguatins Brazil 5°47S 47°29W 332 C2
Santo Antônio de Jesus Brazil 12°58S 39°16W 333 D4
Santo Antônio do Abaixo = Santo Antônio do Leverger Brazil 15°52S 56°5W 331 D6
Santo Antônio do Içá Brazil 3°5S 67°57W 328 D4
Santo Antônio do Leverger Brazil 15°52S 56°5W 331 D6
Santo Corazón Bolivia 18°0S 58°45W 331 D6
Santo Cosimo e Damiano, Ex Chiesa di Venice, Italy 142 c2
Santo Domingo Dom. Rep. 18°30N 69°59W 321 C6
Santo Domingo Baja Calif. S., Mexico 25°29N 111°55W 318 B2
Santo Domingo Nic. 12°14N 84°59W 320 D3
Santo Domingo, Cay Bahamas 21°25N 75°45W 320 B4
Santo Domingo de la Calzada Spain 42°26N 2°57W 196 C2
Santo Domingo de los Colorados Ecuador 0°15S 79°9W 328 D2
Santo Domingo Pueblo U.S.A. 35°31N 106°22W 305 J10
Santo Domingo Tehuantepec = Tehuantepec Mexico 16°21N 95°13W 319 D5
Sant' Egídio alla Vibrata Italy 42°49N 13°42E 199 F10
Santo Nino I. Phil. 11°54N 124°26E 233 F5
Santo Stéfano di Camastro Italy 38°1N 14°22E 201 D7
Santo Tirso Portugal 41°21N 8°28W 194 D2
Santo Tomás Galápagos Is., Ecuador 0°51S 91°2W 330 a
Santo Tomás Baja Calif., Mexico 31°33N 116°24W 318 A1
Santo Tomás Peru 14°26S 72°8W 330 C3
Santo Tomas Phil. 7°32N 125°37E 233 H5
Santo Tomas, Univ. of Phil. 14°36N 120°59E 127 B1
Santo Tomás, Volcán Ecuador 0°48S 91°7W 330 a
Santo Tomé Argentina 28°40S 56°5W 335 B4
Santo Tomé de Guayana = Ciudad Guayana Venezuela 8°0N 62°30W 329 B5
Santomera Spain 38°4N 1°3W 197 G3
Santoña Spain 43°29N 3°27W 194 B7
Santorini Greece 36°23N 25°27E 205 E7
Santos Brazil 24°0S 46°20W 335 A6
Santos, Sierra de los Spain 38°7N 5°12W 195 G5
Santos Dumont Brazil 22°55S 43°10W 333 F3
Santos Dumont ✈ (SDU) Brazil 22°54S 43°9W 135 B2
Santoshpur India 22°31N 88°16E 124 B1
Santragachi India 22°35N 88°17E 124 B1
Santuario de Aves Laguna Colorada △ Bolivia 22°10S 67°45W 334 A2
Sanuki Japan 34°19N 134°10E 222 C6
Sanur Indonesia 8°41S 115°15E 231 K18
Sanwan Taiwan 24°39N 120°57E 225 B2
Sanwer India 22°59N 75°50E 242 H6
Sanxenxo Spain 42°24N 8°49W 194 C2
Sanxia = Sanhsia Taiwan 24°56N 121°22E 225 B3
Sanxia Shuiku China 30°3N 107°58E 228 B6
Sanxiang China 22°21N 113°25E 219 a
Sanxing = Sanhsing Taiwan 24°40N 121°36E 225 B3
Sanya China 18°14N 109°29E 229 a
San'yō Japan 34°2N 131°5E 222 C3
Sanyuan China 34°35N 108°58E 226 G5
Sanyuanli China 23°8N 113°14E 121 B2
Sanyuki-Sammyaku Japan 34°5N 134°0E 222 C6
Sanza Pombo Angola 7°18S 15°56E 265 D3
São Bartolomeu de Messines Portugal 37°15N 8°17W 195 H2
São Benedito = Beneditinos Brazil 5°27S 42°22W 332 C3
São Benedito Brazil 4°3S 40°53W 332 B3
São Benedito → Brazil 9°11S 57°2W 331 B6
São Bento Brazil 2°42S 44°50W 332 B3
São Bento do Norte Brazil 5°4S 36°2W 332 C4
São Bernardo do Campo Brazil 23°45S 46°34W 333 F2
São Borja Brazil 28°39S 56°0W 335 B4
São Brás de Alportel Portugal 37°8N 7°37W 195 H3
São Braz, C. de Angola 9°58S 13°19E 265 D2
São Caetano do Sul Brazil 23°37S 46°34W 137 B2
São Caitano Brazil 8°21S 36°6W 332 C4
São Carlos Brazil 22°0S 47°50W 335 A6
São Conrado Brazil 23°0S 43°17W 135 B1
São Cristóvão Rio de J., Brazil 22°53S 43°13W 135 B1
São Cristóvão Sergipe, Brazil 11°1S 37°15W 332 D4
São Domingos Brazil 13°25S 46°19W 333 D2
São Domingos Guinea-Biss. 12°19N 16°13W 262 C1
São Domingos da Boa Vista = São Domingos do Capim Brazil 1°41S 47°47W 332 B2
São Domingos do Capim Brazil 1°41S 47°47W 332 B2
São Domingos do Maranhão Brazil 5°42S 44°22W 332 C3
São Felipe = Eirunepé Brazil 6°35S 69°53W 330 B4
São Felipe = Içana Brazil 0°21N 67°19W 328 C4
São Félix Brazil 11°36S 50°39W 333 D1
São Félix do Xingu Brazil 6°38S 51°59W 331 B7
São Filipe C. Verde Is. 15°2N 24°30W 153 j
São Francisco = Itapagé Brazil 3°41S 39°34W 332 B4
São Francisco Brazil 16°0S 44°50W 333 E3
São Francisco → Brazil 10°30S 36°24W 332 D4
São Francisco do Maranhão Brazil 6°15S 42°52W 332 C3
São Francisco do Sul Brazil 26°15S 48°36W 335 B6
São Francisco Penitência Rio de J., Brazil 135 b1
São Gabriel Brazil 30°20S 54°20W 335 C5
São Gabriel da Cachoeira Brazil 0°8S 67°5W 328 D4
São Gabriel da Palha Brazil 18°47S 40°39W 333 E3
São Gonçalo = Araripina Brazil 7°33S 40°34W 332 C3
São Gonçalo Brazil 22°48S 43°5W 333 F3
São Gotardo Brazil 19°19S 46°3W 333 E2
Sao Hill Tanzania 8°20S 35°12E 269 D4
São João Guinea-Biss. 11°32N 15°25W 262 C1
São João da Baliza Brazil 0°52N 59°52W 329 C6
São João da Barra Brazil 21°38S 41°3W 333 F3
São João da Boa Vista Brazil 22°0S 46°52W 335 A6
São João da Madeira Portugal 40°54N 8°30W 194 E2
São João da Pesqueira Portugal 41°8N 7°24W 194 D3
São João da Ponte Brazil 15°56S 44°1W 333 E3
São João de Meriti Brazil 22°48S 43°21W 333 F3
São João de Montenegro = Montenegro Brazil 29°39S 51°29W 335 B5
São João del Rei Brazil 21°8S 44°15W 333 F3
São João do Araguaia Brazil 5°23S 48°46W 332 C2
São João do Paraíso Brazil 15°19S 42°1W 333 E3
São João do Piauí Brazil 8°21S 42°15W 332 C3
São João do Sul Angola 15°46S 12°0E 265 F2
São João dos Patos Brazil 6°30S 43°42W 332 C3
São Joaquim Amazonas, Brazil 0°1S 67°16W 328 D4
São Joaquim Sta. Catarina, Brazil 28°18S 49°56W 335 B6
São Joaquim △ Brazil 28°12S 49°37W 335 B6
São Joaquim da Barra Brazil 20°35S 47°53W 333 F2
São Jorge Azores 38°38N 28°3W 153 d1
São Jorge, Canal de Azores 38°30N 28°0W 153 d1
São Jorge, Castelo de Portugal 38°42N 9°8W 126 A2
São Jorge, Pta. de Azores 38°42N 27°3W 153 d1
São Jorge, Pta. de Madeira 32°50N 16°53W 153 c
São José Brazil 27°38S 48°39W 335 B5
São José, B. de Brazil 2°38S 44°4W 332 B3
São José da Lagoa = Nova Era Brazil 19°45S 43°3W 333 E3
São José da Laje Brazil 9°1S 36°3W 332 C4
São José de Mipibu Brazil 6°5S 35°15W 332 C4
São José de Tocantins = Niquelândia Brazil 14°33S 48°23W 333 D2
São José do Norte Brazil 32°1S 52°3W 335 C5
São José do Peixe Brazil 7°24S 42°34W 332 C3
São José do Rio Preto Brazil 20°50S 49°20W 335 A6
São José dos Campos Brazil 23°7S 45°52W 335 A6
São José dos Cocais = Nossa Senhora do Livramento Brazil 15°48S 56°22W 331 D6
São José dos Matões = Parnarama Brazil 5°31S 43°6W 332 C3
São Juliao do Tojal Portugal 38°49N 9°8W 126 A2
São Leopoldo Brazil 29°50S 51°10W 335 B5
São Lourenço Brazil 22°7S 45°3W 333 F2
São Lourenço → Brazil 17°53S 57°27W 331 D6
São Lourenço, Pantanal do Brazil 17°30S 56°20W 331 D6
São Lourenço, Pta. de Madeira 32°44N 16°39W 153 c
São Lourenço do Sul Brazil 31°22S 51°58W 335 C5
São Luís Brazil 2°39S 44°15W 332 B3
São Luís do Curu Brazil 3°40S 39°14W 332 B4
São Luís do Tapajós Brazil 4°25S 56°12W 329 D6
São Luís Gonzaga = Ipixuna Brazil 7°0S 71°40W 330 B3
São Luís Gonzaga Brazil 28°25S 55°0W 335 B5
São Marcos → Brazil 18°15S 47°37W 333 E2
São Marcos, B. de Brazil 2°0S 44°0W 332 B3
São Martinho da Cortiça Portugal 40°18N 8°8W 194 E2
São Mateus Azores 38°26N 28°27W 153 d1
São Mateus Brazil 18°44S 39°50W 333 E4
São Mateus → Brazil 18°35S 39°44W 333 E4
São Mateus do Sul Brazil 25°52S 50°23W 335 B5
São Miguel Azores 37°47N 25°30W 153 d3
São Miguel do Araguaia Brazil 13°19S 50°13W 333 D1
São Miguel do Guamá Brazil 1°37S 47°29W 332 B2
São Miguel do Oeste Brazil 26°45S 53°34W 335 B5
São Miguel dos Campos Brazil 9°47S 36°5W 332 C4
São Nicolau C. Verde Is. 16°20N 24°20W 153 j
São Nicolau → Angola 14°16S 12°22E 265 E2
São Nicolau → Brazil 5°45S 42°2W 332 C3
São Paulo Atl. Oc. 0°56N 29°22W 152 F9
São Paulo Brazil 23°32S 46°38W 137 B2
São Paulo □ Brazil 22°0S 49°0W 335 A6
São Paulo Congonhas ✈ (CGH) Brazil 23°38S 46°39W 137 B2
São Paulo de Olivença Brazil 3°27S 68°48W 328 D4
São Paulo-Guarulhos Int. ✈ (GRU) Brazil 23°26S 46°28W 333 F2
São Pedro Atl. Oc. 0°56N 29°22W 152 F9
São Pedro do Sul Portugal 40°46N 8°4W 194 E2
São Rafael Brazil 5°47S 36°55W 332 C4
São Raimundo das Mangabeiras Brazil 7°1S 45°29W 332 C2
São Raimundo Nonato Brazil 9°1S 42°42W 332 C3
São Romão Brazil 16°22S 45°4W 333 E2
São Roque Madeira 32°46N 16°48W 153 c
São Roque, C. de Brazil 5°30S 35°16W 332 C4
São Roque do Pico Azores 38°31N 28°19W 153 d1
São Salvador do Congo = Mbanza Congo Angola 6°18S 14°16E 265 D2
São Sebastião Azores 38°39N 27°6W 153 d1
São Sebastião, I. de Brazil 23°50S 45°18W 335 A6
São Sebastião do Paraíso Brazil 20°54S 46°59W 335 A6
São Simão Brazil 18°56S 50°30W 333 E1
São Teotónio Portugal 37°30N 8°42W 195 H2
São Tiago C. Verde Is. 15°0N 23°40W 153 j
São Tomé Brazil 5°58S 36°4W 332 C4
São Tomé São Tomé & Príncipe 0°10N 6°39E 265 a
São Tomé, C. de Brazil 22°0S 40°59W 333 F3
São Tomé, Pico de São Tomé & Príncipe 0°16N 6°33E 265 a
São Tomé & Príncipe ■ Africa 0°12N 6°39E 265 a
São Vicente = Araguatins Brazil 5°38S 48°7W 332 C2
São Vicente Brazil 23°57S 46°23W 335 A6
São Vicente C. Verde Is. 17°0N 25°0W 153 j
São Vicente Madeira 32°48N 17°3W 153 c
São Vicente, C. de Portugal 37°0N 9°0W 195 H1
Saona, I. Dom. Rep. 18°10N 68°40W 321 C6

Saône → France 45°44N 4°50E **173** G11
Saône-et-Loire □ France 46°30N 4°50E **173** F11
Saonek Indonesia 0°22S 130°55E **231** E8
Saoura, O. → Algeria 29°0N 0°55W **261** C4
Sapa India 22°30N 88°15E **124** B1
Sapam, Ao Thailand 8°0N 98°26E **237** a
Sapanca Turkey 40°41N 30°16E **212** B4
Sapanjang Indonesia 7°10S 115°50E **235** D5
Sapão → Brazil 11°1S 45°32W **332** D2
Saparua Indonesia 3°33S 128°40E **231** E7
Sapateiro, Cor. do → Brazil 23°35S 46°41W **137** B1
Sapé Brazil 7°6S 35°13W **332** C4
Sape Indonesia 8°34S 118°59E **235** D5
Sape, Teluk Indonesia 8°32S 119°4E **235** D5
Sapele Nigeria 5°50N 5°40E **263** D6
Sapelo I. U.S.A. 31°25N 81°12W **316** D8
Sapelo Sound U.S.A. 31°30N 81°10W **316** D8
Sapes Greece 41°2N 25°43E **203** E9
Şaphane Turkey 39°1N 29°13E **205** B11
Sapi ⌂ Zimbabwe 15°48S 29°42E **269** F2
Sapienza Greece 36°45N 21°43E **204** E3
Sapindji Dem. Rep. of the Congo 9°39S 23°12E **265** D4
Sapo △ Liberia 5°15N 8°30W **262** D3
Sapone Burkina Faso 12°3N 1°35W **263** C4
Saposoa Peru 6°55S 76°45W **330** B2
Sapotskina Belarus 53°49N 23°40E **184** E10
Sapouy Burkina Faso 11°34N 1°44W **263** C4
Sapozhok Russia 53°59N 40°41E **190** D5
Sapphire Australia 23°28S 147°43E **280** C4
Sappho U.S.A. 48°4N 124°16W **306** B2
Sapporo Japan 43°0N 141°21E **220** C10
Sapporo New Chitose ✕ (CTS) Japan 42°46N 141°41E **220** C10
Sapri Italy 40°4N 15°38E **201** B8
Sapt Kosi → Nepal 26°32N 86°56E **243** F12
Sapu Angola 12°28S 19°26E **265** E3
Sapudi Indonesia 7°6S 114°20E **235** D4
Sapulpa U.S.A. 35°59N 96°5W **314** D6
Sapulut Malaysia 4°42N 116°28E **235** B5
Saqqez Iran 36°15N 46°20E **213** D12
Sar Dasht Āzarbāyjān-e Gharbī, Iran 36°9N 45°28E **213** D11
Sar Dasht Khuzestān, Iran 32°32N 48°52E **247** C6
Sar-e Pol Afghan. 36°10N 66°0E **240** A2
Sar-e Pol □ Afghan. 36°20N 65°50E **240** A2
Sar Gachīneh = Yāsūj Iran 30°31N 51°31E **247** D6
Sar Passage Palau 7°12N 134°22E **288** c
Sar Planina Macedonia 42°0N 21°0E **202** E4
Sara Burkina Faso 11°40N 3°53W **262** C4
Sara Niger 20°46N 12°35E **259** D2
Sara Phil. 11°16N 123°1E **233** F4
Sara → Serbia 42°12N 21°0E **202** D5
Sara Buri = Saraburi Thailand 14°30N 100°55E **236** E3
Sarāb Iran 37°55N 47°40E **213** D12
Sarābādī Iraq 33°1N 44°48E **246** C5
Sarabit el Khâdim Egypt 29°2N 33°25E **251** J4
Sarābleh Iran 33°44N 46°34E **213** F12
Saraburi Thailand 14°30N 100°55E **236** E3
Saradiya India 21°34N 70°2E **242** J4
Saraféré Mali 15°50N 3°40W **262** B4
Saragossa = Zaragoza Spain 41°39N 0°53W **196** D4
Saraguro Ecuador 3°35S 79°16W **328** D2
Sarahs Turkmenistan 36°32N 61°13E **247** B9
Sarai Naurang Pakistan 32°50N 70°47E **242** C4
Saraikela India 22°42N 85°56E **243** H11
Saraipali India 21°20N 82°59E **244** D6
Saraiu Romania 44°43N 28°10E **183** F13
Sarajevo Bos.-H. 43°52N 18°26E **182** G3
Sarakhs = Sarahs Turkmenistan 36°32N 61°13E **247** B9
Sarakhs Iran 36°32N 61°9E **216** E6
Saramacca → Suriname 5°50N 55°55W **329** B6
Saramati Burma 25°44N 95°2E **241** C5
Saran, Gunung Indonesia 0°30S 111°25E **235** C4
Saranac U.S.A. 42°56N 85°13W **311** B11
Saranac Lake U.S.A. 44°20N 74°10W **313** B10
Saranac Lakes U.S.A. 44°20N 74°28W **313** B10
Saranda Tanzania 5°45S 34°59E **268** D3
Sarandë Albania 39°52N 19°55E **206** B9
Sarandi Argentina 34°40S 58°20W **117** C2
Sarandí del Yí Uruguay 33°18S 55°38W **335** C4
Sarandí Grande Uruguay 33°44S 56°20W **334** C4
Sarangani □ Phil. 5°45N 125°20E **233** J5
Sarangani B. Phil. 6°0N 125°13E **233** J5
Sarangani I. Phil. 5°26N 125°28E **233** J5
Sarangani Is. Phil. 5°25N 125°25E **233** J5
Sarangarh India 21°30N 83°5E **244** D6
Saranovo = Septemvri Bulgaria 42°13N 24°6E **203** D8
Saransk Russia 54°10N 45°10E **190** C7
Sarapul Russia 56°28N 53°48E **186** C9
Sarāqib Syria 35°52N 36°47E **250** C7
Sarar Plain = Bannaanka Saraar Somalia 9°25N 46°17E **267** C6
Sarasota U.S.A. 27°20N 82°32W **317** H7
Saraswati → India 22°46N 88°15E **124** A1
Sarata Ukraine 46°1N 29°40E **183** D14
Sarata → Ukraine 45°51N 29°41E **183** E14
Saratoga Calif., U.S.A. 37°16N 122°2W **306** H4
Saratoga Wyo., U.S.A. 41°27N 106°49W **304** F10
Saratoga ⌂ U.S.A. 43°0N 73°38W **313** D11
Saratoga L. U.S.A. 43°1N 73°44W **313** C11
Saratoga Springs U.S.A. 43°5N 73°47W **313** C11
Saratok Malaysia 1°55N 111°17E **235** B4
Saratov Russia 51°30N 46°2E **190** E7
Saratov □ Russia 51°50N 46°20E **190** E8
Saratovskoye Vdkhr. Russia 53°10N 48°35E **190** D9
Sarāvān Iran 27°25N 62°15E **247** E9
Saravane Laos 15°43N 106°25E **236** E6
Sarawak □ Malaysia 2°0N 113°0E **235** B4
Saray Tekirdağ, Turkey 41°26N 27°55E **203** E11
Saray Van, Turkey 38°38N 44°9E **213** C11
Saraya Senegal 12°50N 11°45W **262** C2
Saraycık Turkey 39°1N 29°49E **205** B11
Sarayköy Turkey 37°55N 28°54E **205** D10
Saraylar Turkey 40°39N 27°40E **203** F11
Sarayönü Turkey 38°16N 32°24E **212** C5
Sarbāz Iran 26°38N 61°19E **247** E9
Sarbisheh Iran 32°30N 59°40E **247** C8
Sárbogárd Hungary 46°50N 18°40E **182** D3
Sarca → Italy 45°52N 10°52E **198** C7
Sarcelles France 49°1N 2°23E **173** D9
Sarda → India 27°21N 81°23E **243** F9
Sardalas Libya 25°50N 10°34E **258** C2
Sardar Sarovar Dam India 21°50N 73°50E **244** D1
Sardarshahr India 28°30N 74°29E **242** E6
Sardegna □ Italy 40°0N 9°0E **200** B1
Sardhana India 29°9N 77°39E **242** E7
Sardina, Pta. Canary Is. 28°9N 15°44W **153** e1
Sardinata Colombia 8°5N 72°48W **328** B3
Sardinia = Sardegna □ Italy 40°0N 9°0E **200** B1
Sardinia U.S.A. 39°0N 83°49W **311** F13
Sardis Turkey 38°28N 27°58E **205** C10
Sardis Ga., U.S.A. 32°58N 81°46W **316** C8
Sardūīyeh = Dar Mazār Iran 29°14N 57°20E **247** D8
Sarecky potok → Czechia 50°7N 14°23E **135** B2
Sarek △ Sweden 67°22N 17°35E **160** C17
Saren Indonesia 8°26S 115°34E **231** J18
S'Arenal Spain 39°30N 2°45E **206** B3
Sarentino Italy 46°38N 11°21E **199** B8
Saréyamou Mali 16°7N 3°10W **262** B4
Sargasso Sea Atl. Oc. 27°0N 72°0W **292** G13
Sargent U.S.A. 33°26N 84°52W **316** B5
Sargodha Pakistan 32°10N 72°40E **242** C5
Sarh Chad 9°5N 18°23E **259** G3
Sarhala Ivory C. 8°22N 6°8W **262** D3
Sarhro, Jebel Morocco 31°6N 5°0W **260** B4
Sārī Iran 36°30N 53°4E **247** B7
Sari d'Orcino France 42°3N 8°49E **175** F12
Saria Greece 35°54N 27°17E **205** F9
Saria India 21°38N 83°22E **243** J10
Sariab Pakistan 30°6N 66°59E **242** D2
Sarıbeyler Turkey 39°24N 27°35E **205** B9
Saricumbe Angola 12°12S 19°46E **265** E3
Sarigan N. Marianas 16°43N 145°47E **302** a
Sarıgöl Turkey 38°14N 28°41E **212** C3
Sarıkamış Turkey 40°22N 42°35E **213** B10
Sarıkaya Turkey 39°29N 35°22E **212** C6
Sarikei Malaysia 2°8N 111°30E **235** B4
Sarıköy Turkey 40°12N 27°37E **203** F11
Sarila India 25°46N 79°41E **243** G8
Sarimbun Singapore 1°24N 103°40E **138** A2
Sarimbun Res. Singapore 1°25N 103°41E **138** A2
Sarina Australia 21°22S 149°13E **280** C4
Sariñena Spain 41°47N 0°10W **196** D4
Sarinleey Somalia 2°22N 42°17E **267** D5
Sarıoğlan Turkey 39°5N 35°59E **212** C6
Sariri Papua N. G. 9°11S 148°35E **286** E5
Sarita U.S.A. 27°13N 97°47W **314** H6
Sariwŏn N. Korea 38°31N 125°46E **224** C2
Sarıveliler Turkey 36°41N 32°37E **250** B3
Sarıyar Barajı Turkey 40°2N 31°33E **212** B4
Sarıyer Turkey 41°10N 29°3E **122** A2
Sarız Turkey 38°28N 36°30E **212** C7
Sarju → India 27°21N 81°23E **243** F9
Sark U.K. 49°25N 2°22W **169** H5
Sarkad Hungary 46°47N 21°23E **182** D6
Sarkari Tala India 27°39N 70°52E **242** F4
Şarkışla Turkey 39°21N 36°25E **212** C7
Şarköy Turkey 40°36N 27°6E **203** F11
Sarlat-la-Canéda France 44°54N 1°13E **174** D5
Sărmăşag Romania 47°21N 22°50E **182** C7
Sărmaşu Romania 46°45N 24°13E **183** D9
Sarmi Indonesia 1°49S 138°44E **231** E9
Sarmiento Argentina 45°35S 69°5W **336** C3
Sarmiento, Mt. Chile 54°27S 70°50W **336** D2
Sarmizegetusa Romania 45°31N 22°47E **182** E7
Särna Sweden 61°41N 13°8E **162** C7
Sarnano Italy 43°2N 13°18E **199** E10
Sarnen Switz. 46°53N 8°13E **179** J4
Sarnia Canada 42°58N 82°23W **312** D2
Sarno Italy 40°49N 14°37E **201** B7
Sarnthein = Sarentino Italy 46°38N 11°21E **199** B8
Särö Sweden 57°31N 11°57E **163** G5
Sarolangun Indonesia 2°19S 102°42E **234** C2
Saronikos Kolpos Greece 37°45N 23°45E **204** D5
Saronno Italy 45°38N 9°2E **198** C6
Saros Körfezi Turkey 40°30N 26°15E **203** F10
Sárospatak Hungary 48°18N 21°33E **182** B6
Sarov Russia 54°56N 43°19E **190** C6
Sarowbī Afghan. 34°36N 69°44E **240** B3
Sarpsborg Norway 59°16N 11°7E **164** E8
Sarqan Kazakhstan 45°24N 79°55E **217** C9
Sarracín Spain 42°15N 3°45W **194** C7
Sarralbe France 49°0N 7°1E **173** D14
Sarrat Phil. 18°9N 120°39E **232** B3
Sarre = Saar → Europe 49°41N 6°32E **170** E6
Sarre Italy 45°40N 7°15E **198** C4
Sarre-Union France 48°57N 7°4E **173** D14
Sarrebourg France 48°43N 7°3E **173** D14
Sarreguemines France 49°5N 7°4E **173** C14
Sarrià Barcelona, Spain 41°22N 2°8E **114** A1
Sarria Galicia, Spain 42°49N 7°29W **194** C3
Sarrión Spain 40°9N 0°49W **196** E4
Sarro Mali 13°40N 5°15W **262** C4
Sarroch Italy 39°4N 9°1E **200** C2
Sarsing Iraq 37°2N 43°20E **213** D10
Sarstedt Germany 52°14N 9°52E **178** C5
Sarsuna India 22°28N 88°17E **124** C1
Sartell U.S.A. 45°37N 94°12W **308** C6
Sartène France 41°38N 8°58E **175** G12
Sarthe □ France 48°10N 0°10E **172** D7
Sarthe → France 47°33N 0°31W **172** E6
Sartilly France 48°45N 1°28W **172** D5
Sartrouville France 48°56N 2°10E **134** A2
Saruhanlı Turkey 38°44N 27°36E **205** C9
Sărulești Romania 44°25N 26°39E **183** F11
Saruna → Pakistan 26°31N 67°7E **242** F2
Sarupeta India 26°30N 91°25E **243** F14
Sarur Azerbaijan 39°22N 45°5E **213** C11
Saruwaged Ra. Papua N. G. 6°13S 146°45E **286** D4
Sárvár Hungary 47°15N 16°56E **182** C1
Sarvar India 26°4N 75°0E **242** F6
Sarvestān Iran 29°20N 53°10E **247** D7
Särvfjället Sweden 62°42N 13°30E **162** B7
Sárvíz → Hungary 46°24N 18°41E **182** D3
Sary-Tash Kyrgyzstan 39°44N 73°15E **217** E8
Sarych, Mys Ukraine 44°25N 33°45E **189** K7
Saryesik-Atyraū Qumy Kazakhstan 45°30N 76°0E **217** C9
Sarykamyshskoye, Ozero = Saryqamysh Köli Turkmenistan 41°56N 57°25E **216** D5
Sarykemer Kazakhstan 43°0N 71°30E **217** D8
Sarykenggir → Kazakhstan 48°22N 67°59E **217** C7
Saryköl Kazakhstan 53°20N 65°12E **216** B7
Sarykolskiy Khrebet Tajikistan 38°30N 74°30E **217** E8
Saryözek Kazakhstan 44°22N 77°59E **217** D9
Saryqamysh Köli Turkmenistan 41°56N 57°25E **216** D5
Saryshaghan Kazakhstan 46°12N 73°38E **217** C8
Sarysū → Kazakhstan 45°12N 66°36E **217** C7
Sarzana Italy 44°7N 9°58E **198** D6
Sarzeau France 47°31N 2°48W **172** E4
Sasabeneh Ethiopia 7°59N 44°43E **267** C5
Sasad Hungary 47°28N 19°0E **117** B2
Sasamungga Solomon Is. 7°0S 156°50E **287** L9
Sasan Gir India 21°10N 70°36E **242** J4
Sasaram India 24°57N 84°5E **243** G11
Sasari, Mt. Solomon Is. 8°10S 159°30E **287** M10
Sasayama Japan 35°4N 135°13E **223** B7
Sasebo Japan 33°10N 129°43E **222** D1
Saser Kangri India 34°50N 77°50E **243** B7
Sashalom Hungary 47°30N 19°10E **117** A3
Saska Poland 52°14N 21°3E **143** B2
Saskatchewan □ Canada 54°40N 106°0W **297** C7
Saskatchewan → Canada 53°37N 100°40W **297** C8
Saskatoon Canada 52°10N 106°38W **297** C7
Saskylakh Russia 71°55N 114°1E **215** B12
Sasolburg S. Africa 26°46S 27°49E **271** C4
Sason Turkey 38°19N 41°24E **213** C9
Sasovo Russia 54°25N 41°55E **190** C5
Sassandra Ivory C. 4°55N 6°8W **262** E3
Sassandra → Ivory C. 4°58N 6°5W **262** E3
Sassandra-Marahoué □ Ivory C. 6°58N 6°26W **262** D3
Sássari Italy 40°43N 8°34E **200** B1
Sassie Australia 10°2S 142°51E **280** a
Sassnitz Germany 54°29N 13°39E **178** A9
Sasso Marconi Italy 44°24N 11°15E **199** D8
Sassocorvaro Italy 43°47N 12°30E **199** E9
Sassoferrato Italy 43°26N 12°51E **199** E9
Sassuolo Italy 44°33N 10°47E **198** D7
Sástago Spain 41°19N 0°21W **196** D4
Sastamala Finland 61°20N 22°54E **188** B2
Sastown Liberia 4°45N 8°27W **262** E3
Sasvad India 18°20N 74°2E **244** E2
Sasyk, Ozero Ukraine 45°45N 29°40E **183** E14
Sasykköl Kazakhstan 46°35N 81°0E **217** C10
Sata-Misaki Japan 31°0N 130°40E **222** F2
Satadougou Mali 12°25N 11°25W **262** C2
Satakunta □ Finland 61°45N 23°0E **160** F20
Satalice Czechia 50°7N 14°34E **135** B3
Satama-Soukoura Ivory C. 7°55N 4°27W **262** D4
Satara India 17°44N 73°58E **244** F1
Satara S. Africa 24°29S 31°47E **271** B5
Sätbaev Kazakhstan 48°10N 67°27E **216** C7
Satbarwa India 23°55N 84°16E **243** H11
Satellite Beach U.S.A. 28°10N 80°36W **317** G9
Säter Sweden 60°21N 15°45E **162** D9
Satevó Mexico 27°57N 106°7W **318** B3
Satgachi India 22°37N 88°25E **124** B2
Satilla → U.S.A. 30°59N 81°29W **316** E8
Satipo Peru 11°15S 74°25W **330** C3
Satka Russia 55°3N 59°1E **186** C10
Satkania Bangla. 22°4N 92°3E **241** D4
Satkhira Bangla. 22°43N 89°8E **241** D2
Satluj = Sutlej → Pakistan 29°23N 71°3E **242** E4
Satmala Hills Maharashtra, India 20°15N 74°40E **244** D2
Satmala Hills Telangana, India 19°45N 78°45E **244** E4
Satna India 24°35N 80°50E **243** G9
Šator Bos.-H. 44°11N 16°37E **199** D13
Sátoraljaújhely Hungary 48°25N 21°41E **182** B6
Satpukur India 22°37N 88°24E **124** B2
Satpura △ India 22°40N 78°15E **242** H8
Satpura Ra. India 21°25N 76°10E **244** D3
Sätra Sweden 59°17N 17°54E **139** B1
Satrup Germany 54°41N 9°36E **178** A5
Satsuma-Hantō Japan 31°25N 130°25E **222** F2
Satsuma-Sendai Japan 31°50N 130°20E **222** F2
Satsunan-Shotō Japan 30°0N 130°0E **221** K5
Sattahip Thailand 12°41N 100°54E **236** F3
Sattenapalle India 16°25N 80°6E **245** F5
Sattru Phai Bangkok, Thailand **113** b2
Satu Mare Romania 47°46N 22°55E **182** C7
Satu Mare □ Romania 47°45N 23°0E **182** C8
Satui Indonesia 3°50S 115°27E **235** C5
Satun Thailand 6°43N 100°2E **237** J3
Satupa'itea Samoa 13°45S 172°18W **287** V19
Saturnina → Brazil 12°15S 58°10W **331** C6
Sauce = Juan L. Lacaze Uruguay 34°26S 57°25W **334** C4
Sauce Argentina 30°5S 58°46W **334** C4
Sauceda Mexico 25°46N 101°19W **318** B4
Saucillo Mexico 28°1N 105°17W **318** B3
Sauda Norway 59°40N 6°20E **164** E3
Saudasjøen Norway 59°38N 6°17E **164** E3
Saúde Bahia, Brazil 10°56S 40°24W **332** D3
Saúde São Paulo, Brazil 23°36S 46°37W **137** B2
Sauðárkrókur Iceland 65°45N 19°40W **155** B7
Saudi Arabia ■ Asia 26°0N 44°0E **246** B3
Sauerland Germany 51°12N 7°59E **176** C4
Saugatuck U.S.A. 42°40N 86°12W **311** B10
Saugeen → Canada 44°30N 81°22W **312** B3
Saugerties U.S.A. 42°5N 73°57W **313** D11
Saugues France 44°58N 3°32E **174** D7
Saugus Calif., U.S.A. 34°25N 118°32W **307** L8
Saugus Mass., U.S.A. 42°28N 71°0W **116** A2
Saugus → U.S.A. 42°27N 70°58W **116** A2
Saujbulagh = Mahābād Iran 36°50N 45°45E **213** D11
Saujon France 45°41N 0°55W **174** C3
Sauk Centre U.S.A. 45°44N 94°57W **308** C6
Sauk City U.S.A. 43°17N 89°43W **310** A7
Sauk Rapids U.S.A. 45°35N 94°10W **308** C6
Saül Fr. Guiana 3°37N 53°12W **329** C7
Sauland Norway 59°37N 8°56E **164** E5
Saulgau Germany 48°1N 9°29E **179** G5
Saulieu France 47°17N 4°14E **173** E11
Sault France 44°6N 5°24E **175** D9
Sault-au-Récollet Canada 45°35N 73°39W **130** A2
Sault Ste. Marie Ont., Canada 46°30N 84°20W **298** C3
Sault Ste. Marie Mich., U.S.A. 46°30N 84°21W **309** B11
Saūmalkol Kazakhstan 53°17N 68°6E **217** B7
Saumlaki Indonesia 7°55S 131°20E **231** F8
Saumur France 47°15N 0°5W **172** E6
Saundatti India 15°47N 75°7E **245** G2
Saunders C. N.Z. 45°53S 170°45E **285** F5
Saunders I. Antarctica 57°48S 26°28W **151** B1
Saunders Pt. Australia 27°52S 125°38E **279** E4
Saunemin U.S.A. 40°54N 88°24W **311** D8
Saupite Angola 13°54S 17°43E **265** E3
Saurbær Norðurland Eystra, Iceland 65°27N 18°13W **155** B8
Saurbær Vesturland, Iceland 64°24N 21°35W **155** C5
Sauri Nigeria 11°42N 6°44E **263** C6
Saurimo Angola 9°40S 20°12E **265** D4
Sausalito U.S.A. 37°51N 122°29W **136** A2
Sautatá Colombia 7°50N 77°4W **328** B2
Sauteurs Grenada 12°14N 61°38W **323** q
Sauvage, Côte France 45°50N 1°30W **174** C2
Sauveterre-de-Béarn France 43°24N 0°57W **174** E3
Sauzé-Vaussais France 46°8N 0°8E **174** B4
Savá Honduras 15°32N 86°15W **320** C2
Sava Italy 40°24N 17°33E **201** B10
Sava □ Madag. 14°15S 50°10E **272** A2
Sava → Serbia 44°50N 20°26E **182** F5
Savage U.S.A. 47°27N 104°21W **304** C11
Savage I. = Niue ☒ Pac. Oc. 19°2S 169°54W **289** g
Savage River Australia 41°31S 145°14E **281** G4
Savai'i Samoa 13°28S 172°24W **287** V19
Savalou Benin 7°57N 1°58E **263** D5
Savane Mozam. 19°37S 35°8E **269** F4
Savanes □ Ivory C. 9°30N 6°0W **262** D3
Savaneta Aruba 12°27N 69°56W **322** f
Savanna U.S.A. 42°5N 90°8W **310** B6
Savanna-la-Mar Jamaica 18°10N 78°10W **320** a
Savannah Ga., U.S.A. 32°5N 81°6W **316** C8
Savannah Mo., U.S.A. 39°56N 94°50W **310** E2
Savannah Tenn., U.S.A. 35°14N 88°15W **315** D10
Savannah → U.S.A. 32°2N 80°53W **316** C9
Savannah Beach = Tybee Island U.S.A. 32°1N 80°51W **316** C9
Savannakhet Laos 16°30N 104°49E **236** D5
Savanne, Piton Mauritius 20°26S 57°29E **272** e
Savannes B. St. Lucia 13°45N 60°56W **323** m
Savant L. Canada 50°16N 90°44W **298** B1
Savant Lake Canada 50°14N 90°40W **298** B1
Savantvadi India 15°55N 73°54E **245** G1
Savanur India 14°59N 75°21E **245** G2
Savarkundla = Kundla India 21°21N 71°25E **242** J4
Săvârşin Romania 46°1N 22°14E **182** D7
Savaştepe Turkey 39°22N 27°42E **205** B9
Savda India 21°9N 75°56E **244** D2
Savé Benin 8°2N 2°29E **263** D5
Save → Haute-Garonne, France 43°47N 1°17E **174** E5
Save → Mozam. 21°16S 34°0E **271** B5
Sāveh Iran 35°2N 50°20E **247** C6
Savelugu Ghana 9°38N 0°54W **263** D4
Savenay France 47°20N 1°55W **172** E5
Săveni Romania 47°57N 26°52E **183** C11
Saverdun France 43°14N 1°34E **174** E5
Saverne France 48°43N 7°20E **173** D14
Savigliano Italy 44°38N 7°40E **198** D4
Savigny-sur-Braye France 47°53N 0°49E **172** E7
Sávio → Italy 44°19N 12°20E **199** D9
Šavnik Montenegro 42°59N 19°10E **202** D3
Savo Finland 62°45N 27°30E **160** E22
Savo Solomon Is. 9°8S 159°48E **287** M10
Savoie □ France 45°26N 6°25E **175** C10
Savolax = Savo Finland 62°45N 27°30E **160** E22
Savona Italy 44°17N 8°30E **198** D5
Savona N.Y., U.S.A. 42°17N 77°13W **312** D7
Savonet Curaçao 12°21N 69°7W **322** g
Savonlinna Finland 61°52N 28°53E **188** B5
Savoonga U.S.A. 63°42N 170°29W **303** E5
Savoy = Savoie □ France 45°26N 6°25E **175** C10
Şavşat Turkey 41°15N 42°20E **213** B10
Sävsjö Sweden 57°20N 14°40E **163** G8
Savur Turkey 37°34N 40°53E **246** B4
Savusavu Fiji 16°34S 179°15E **287** A2
Savusavu B. Fiji 16°45S 179°15E **287** A2
Savuti Botswana 18°37S 24°5E **270** A3
Sawah Besar Indonesia 6°8S 106°49E **122** A1
Sawahlunto Indonesia 0°40S 100°52E **234** C2
Sawai Indonesia 3°0S 129°5E **231** E7
Sawai Madhopur India 26°0N 76°25E **242** G7
Sawaleke Fiji 17°59S 179°18E **287** A2
Sawang Daen Din Thailand 17°28N 103°28E **236** D4
Sawankhalok Thailand 17°19N 99°50E **236** D2
Sawara Japan 35°55N 140°30E **223** B12
Sawatch Range U.S.A. 39°0N 106°30W **304** G10
Sawdā', Jabal as Libya 28°51N 15°12E **258** C3
Sawel Mt. U.K. 54°50N 7°2W **166** B4
Sawfajjin, W. → Libya 31°41N 14°44E **258** B2
Sawi Thailand 10°14N 99°5E **237** G2
Sawla Ghana 9°17N 2°25W **262** D4
Sawmills Zimbabwe 19°30S 28°2E **269** F2
Şawqirah Oman 18°7N 56°32E **249** C7
Şawqirah, Ghubbat Oman 18°35N 57°0E **249** C7
Sawtell Australia 30°19S 153°6E **283** A10
Sawtelle U.S.A. 34°2N 118°27W **126** B2
Sawtooth ⌂ U.S.A. 44°0N 114°50W **304** D6
Sawtooth Range U.S.A. 44°3N 114°58W **304** D6
Sawu Indonesia 10°35S 121°50E **231** F6
Sawu Sea Indonesia 9°30S 121°50E **231** F6
Saxby → Australia 18°25S 140°53E **280** B3
Saxmundham U.K. 52°13N 1°30E **169** E9
Saxon Switzerland = Sächsische Schweiz △ Germany 50°55N 14°10E **178** E10
Saxony = Sachsen □ Germany 50°55N 13°10E **178** E9
Saxony, Lower = Niedersachsen □ Germany 52°50N 9°0E **178** C4
Saxton U.S.A. 40°13N 78°15W **312** F6
Say Mali 13°50N 4°57W **262** C4
Say Niger 13°8N 2°22E **263** C5
Saya Nigeria 9°30N 3°18E **263** D5
Sayabec Canada 48°35N 67°41W **299** C6
Sayaboury Laos 19°15N 101°45E **236** C3
Sayán Peru 11°8S 77°12W **330** C2
Sayan, Vostochnyy Russia 54°0N 96°0E **215** D10
Sayan, Zapadnyy Russia 52°30N 94°0E **217** B12
Sayano-Shushenskoye Vdkhr. Russia 52°50N 91°22E **217** B12
Sayanogorsk Russia 53°5N 91°23E **215** D10
Saydā Lebanon 33°35N 35°25E **250** E6
Sayghān Afghan. 35°10N 67°55E **240** B2
Sayhandulaan = Öldziyt Mongolia 44°40N 109°1E **226** B5
Sayḥūt Yemen 15°12N 51°10E **249** D5
Saykhin Kazakhstan 48°50N 46°47E **191** F8
Saylac Somalia 11°21N 43°30E **267** B5
Saylorville L. U.S.A. 41°48N 93°46W **310** C3
Saynshand = Buyant-Uhaa Mongolia 44°55N 110°11E **226** B6
Sayō Japan 34°59N 134°22E **222** C6
Sayre Okla., U.S.A. 35°18N 99°38W **314** D5
Sayre Pa., U.S.A. 41°59N 76°32W **313** E8
Sayreville U.S.A. 40°28N 74°22W **313** F10
Sayula Mexico 19°52N 103°36W **318** D4
Say'ūn Yemen 15°56N 48°47E **249** D5
Sayward Canada 50°21N 125°55W **296** C3
Saza Japan 33°14N 129°39E **222** D1
Sazanit Albania 40°30N 19°20E **202** F3
Sázava → Czechia 49°53N 14°24E **180** B7
Sazin Pakistan 35°35N 73°30E **243** B5
Sazlika → Bulgaria 41°59N 25°50E **203** E9
Sbeïtla Tunisia 35°12N 9°7E **258** A1
Scaër France 48°2N 3°42W **172** D3
Scafell Pike U.K. 54°27N 3°14W **168** C4
Scald Law U.K. 55°50N 3°17W **121** B2
Scalea Italy 39°49N 15°47E **201** C8
Scalloway U.K. 60°9N 1°17W **167** A7
Scalpay U.K. 57°18N 6°0W **167** D3
Scalzi, Ponte degli Venice, Italy **142** b2
Scammon Bay U.S.A. 61°51N 165°35W **303** F6
Scandia Canada 50°20N 112°2W **296** C6
Scandiano Italy 44°36N 10°43E **198** D7
Scandicci Italy 43°45N 11°11E **199** E8
Scandinavia Europe 64°0N 12°0E **160** E15
Scansano Italy 42°41N 11°20E **199** F8
Scapa Flow U.K. 58°53N 3°3W **167** C5
Scappoose U.S.A. 45°45N 122°53W **306** E4
Scarámia, Capo Italy 36°47N 14°29E **201** F7
Scarba U.K. 56°11N 5°43W **167** E3
Scarborough Ont., Canada 43°44N 79°14W **141** A3
Scarborough Trin. & Tob. 11°11N 60°42W **323** s
Scarborough N. Yorks., U.K. 54°17N 0°24W **168** C7
Scarborough Bluffs Canada 43°42N 79°14W **141** B3
Scarborough Junction Canada 43°43N 79°15W **141** A3
Scarborough Shoal S. China Sea 15°0N 117°50E **232** D1
Scargill N.Z. 42°56S 172°58E **285** C7
Scariff I. Ireland 51°44N 10°15W **166** E1
Scarp U.K. 58°1N 7°8W **167** C1
Scarpanto = Karpathos Greece 35°37N 27°10E **205** F9
Scarpe-Escaut ⌂ France 50°26N 3°23E **173** B10
Scarsdale Australia 37°41S 143°39E **282** D5
Sceaux France 48°46N 2°17E **134** B2
Scebeli = Shabeelle → Somalia 2°0N 44°0E **267** D5
Šćedro Croatia 43°6N 16°43E **199** E13
Scenery, Mt. Saba 17°38N 63°14W **322** a
Schaal See Germany 53°36N 10°55E **178** B6
Schaalsee ⌂ Germany 53°40N 10°59E **178** B6
Schaerbeek Belgium 50°52N 4°22E **116** A2
Schaffhausen Switz. 47°42N 8°39E **179** H4
Schagen Neths. 52°49N 4°48E **170** B4
Schaghticoke U.S.A. 42°54N 73°35W **313** D11
Schärding Austria 48°27N 13°27E **180** C6
Scharfenberg Germany 52°35N 13°15E **115** A2
Scharfenwiese = Ostrołęka Poland 53°4N 21°32E **185** E8
Scharhörn Germany 53°57N 8°24E **178** B4
Schässburg = Sighişoara Romania 46°12N 24°50E **183** D9
Scheessel Germany 53°10N 9°29E **178** B5
Schefferville Canada 54°48N 66°50W **299** B6
Scheibbs Austria 48°1N 15°9E **180** C8
Scheldt = Schelde → Belgium 51°15N 4°16E **170** C4
Schelde → Belgium 51°15N 4°16E **170** C4
Schell City U.S.A. 38°1N 94°7W **310** F2
Schell Creek Ra. U.S.A. 39°25N 114°40W **304** G6
Schellsburg U.S.A. 40°3N 78°39W **312** F6
Schemnitz = Banská Štiavnica Slovakia 48°25N 18°55E **181** C11
Schenectady U.S.A. 42°49N 73°57W **313** D11
Schenevus U.S.A. 42°33N 74°50W **313** D10
Scherfede Germany 51°32N 9°2E **178** D5
Schesslitz Germany 49°58N 11°1E **179** F7
Schiavoni, Riva degli Venice, Italy **142** b3
Schiedam Neths. 51°55N 4°25E **170** C4
Schieratz = Sieradz Poland 51°37N 18°41E **185** G5
Schiermonnikoog Neths. 53°30N 6°15E **170** A6
Schiermonnikoog △ Neths. 53°30N 6°15E **170** A6
Schiller Woods U.S.A. 41°57N 87°51W **119** B1
Schiltigheim France 48°35N 7°45E **173** D14
Schinoussa Greece 36°53N 25°31E **205** E7
Schio Italy 45°43N 11°21E **199** C8
Schiphol, Amsterdam ✕ (AMS) Neths. 52°18N 4°45E **112** B1
Schippenbeil = Sępopol Poland 54°16N 21°2E **184** D8
Schivelbein = Świdwin Poland 53°47N 15°49E **184** E2
Schiza Greece 36°41N 21°40E **204** E3
Schlachtensee Germany 52°26N 13°13E **115** B2
Schladming Austria 47°23N 13°41E **180** D6
Schlanders = Silandro Italy 46°38N 10°46E **198** B7
Schlawa = Sława Poland 51°52N 16°2E **185** G3
Schlei → Germany 54°40N 10°0E **178** A5
Schleiden Germany 50°31N 6°28E **178** E2
Schleinitz Ra. Papua N. G. 3°0S 151°30E **286** B6
Schleiz Germany 50°35N 11°49E **178** E7
Schlesiersee = Sława Poland 51°52N 16°2E **185** G3
Schleswig Germany 54°31N 9°34E **178** A5
Schleswig-Holstein □ Germany 54°30N 9°30E **178** A5
Schlettstadt = Sélestat France 48°16N 7°26E **173** D14
Schlichtingsheim = Szlichtyngowa Poland 51°42N 16°15E **185** G3
Schlochau = Człuchów Poland 53°41N 17°22E **184** E4
Schloppe = Człopa Poland 53°6N 16°6E **185** E3
Schlossgarten Germany 52°31N 13°18E **115** A2
Schlüchtern Germany 50°20N 9°32E **179** E5
Schmalkalden Germany 50°44N 10°26E **178** E6
Schmargendorf Germany 52°28N 13°17E **115** B2
Schmölln Germany 50°54N 12°19E **178** E8
Schneeberg Austria 47°47N 15°48E **180** D8
Schneeberg Sachsen, Germany 50°35N 12°38E **178** E8
Schneidemühl = Piła Poland 53°10N 16°48E **185** E3
Schneider U.S.A. 41°13N 87°28W **311** C9
Schneverdingen Germany 53°7N 9°48E **178** B5
Schœlcher Martinique 14°36N 61°7W **322** j
Schofield Barracks U.S.A. 21°29N 158°7W **302** K13
Schoharie U.S.A. 42°40N 74°19W **313** D10
Schoharie Cr. → U.S.A. 42°57N 74°18W **313** D10
Schokland Neths. 52°38N 5°46E **170** B5
Scholls U.S.A. 45°24N 122°56W **306** E4
Schönau = Świerzawa Poland 51°1N 15°54E **185** G2
Schönberg Mecklenburg-Vorpommern, Germany 53°52N 10°56E **178** B6
Schönberg Schleswig-Holstein, Germany 54°23N 10°21E **178** A6
Schönblick Germany 52°27N 13°43E **115** B5
Schönbrunn Austria 48°10N 16°19E **142** A1
Schönbuch ⌂ Germany 48°35N 9°2E **179** G5
Schönebeck Germany 52°2N 11°44E **178** C7
Schöneberg Germany 52°28N 13°20E **115** B3
Schönefeld Germany 52°22N 13°33E **115** B4
Schöneiche Germany 52°28N 13°41E **115** B5
Schöngau Germany 47°47N 10°53E **179** H6
Schöningen Germany 52°8N 10°56E **178** C6
Schönlanke = Trzcianka Poland 53°3N 16°25E **185** E3
Schönstein = Šoštanj Slovenia 46°23N 15°4E **199** B12
Schönwalde Germany 52°37N 13°7E **115** A1
Schoolcraft U.S.A. 42°7N 85°38W **311** B11
Schopfheim Germany 47°38N 7°50E **179** H3
Schorndorf Germany 48°47N 9°32E **179** G5
Schortens Germany 53°31N 7°56E **178** B3
Schotschekloof Cape Town, S. Africa **118** b1
Schottegat Curaçao 12°7N 68°55W **322** g
Schouten I. Australia 42°20S 148°20E **281** G4
Schouten Is. = Supiori Indonesia 1°0S 136°0E **231** E9
Schouten Is. Papua N. G. 3°30S 144°30E **286** B3
Schouwen Neths. 51°43N 3°45E **170** C3
Schramberg Germany 48°13N 8°22E **179** G4
Schrankogel Austria 47°3N 11°7E **180** D4
Schreiber Canada 48°45N 87°20W **298** C2
Schrems Austria 48°47N 15°4E **180** C8
Schrobenhausen Germany 48°34N 11°16E **179** G7
Schroffenstein Namibia 27°11S 18°42E **270** C2
Schroon Lake U.S.A. 43°50N 73°46W **313** C11
Schröttersburg = Płock Poland 52°32N 19°40E **185** F6
Schruns Austria 47°5N 9°56E **180** D2
Schuchye = Shchūchīnsk Kazakhstan 52°56N 70°12E **217** B8
Schuler Canada 50°20N 110°6W **297** C6
Schulzendorf Germany 52°36N 13°16E **115** A2
Schumacher Canada 48°30N 81°16W **298** C3
Schurz U.S.A. 38°57N 118°49W **304** G4
Schuyler U.S.A. 41°27N 97°4W **308** E5
Schuylerville U.S.A. 43°6N 73°35W **313** C11
Schuylkill → U.S.A. 39°53N 75°12W **313** G9
Schuylkill Haven U.S.A. 40°37N 76°11W **313** F8
Schwabach Germany 49°19N 11°2E **179** F7
Schwaben □ Germany 48°15N 10°30E **179** G6
Schwabing Germany 48°10N 11°35E **131** B2
Schwäbisch-Fränkischer Wald ⌂ Germany 49°0N 9°30E **179** G5
Schwäbisch Gmünd Germany 48°49N 9°47E **179** G5
Schwäbisch Hall Germany 49°6N 9°44E **179** F5
Schwäbische Alb Germany 48°20N 9°30E **179** G5
Schwabmünchen Germany 48°10N 10°46E **179** G6
Schwalmstadt Germany 50°55N 9°10E **178** E5
Schwandorf Germany 49°20N 12°7E **179** F8
Schwanebeck Germany 52°37N 13°32E **115** A4
Schwanenwerder Germany 52°26N 13°10E **115** B2
Schwaner, Pegunungan Indonesia 1°0S 112°30E **235** C4
Schwanewede Germany 53°14N 8°36E **178** B4
Schwarmstedt Germany 52°39N 9°38E **178** C5
Schwarze Elster → Germany 51°48N 12°50E **178** D8
Schwarzenberg Germany 50°32N 12°47E **178** E8
Schwarzlackenau Austria 48°16N 16°23E **142** A2
Schwarzrand Namibia 25°37S 16°50E **270** C2
Schwarzwald Germany 48°30N 8°20E **179** G4
Schwatka Mts. U.S.A. 67°20N 156°30W **303** C8
Schwaz Austria 47°20N 11°44E **180** D4
Schwechat Austria 48°8N 16°28E **142** B3
Schwechat, Wien ✕ (VIE) Austria 48°5N 16°35E **142** B3
Schwedt Germany 53°3N 14°16E **178** B10
Schweidnitz = Świdnica Poland 50°50N 16°30E **185** H3
Schweinfurt Germany 50°3N 10°14E **179** E6
Schweiz = Switzerland ■ Europe 46°30N 8°0E **179** J4
Schweizer-Reneke S. Africa 27°11S 25°18E **270** C4
Schwenningen = Villingen-Schwenningen Germany 48°3N 8°26E **179** G4
Schwerin = Skwierzyna Poland 52°33N 15°30E **185** F2
Schwerin Germany 53°36N 11°22E **178** B7
Schweriner See Germany 53°43N 11°28E **178** B7
Schwetzingen Germany 49°23N 8°35E **179** F4
Schwiebus = Świebodzin Poland 52°15N 15°31E **185** F2
Schwyz Switz. 47°2N 8°39E **179** H4
Schwyz □ Switz. 47°2N 8°39E **179** H4
Sciacca Italy 37°31N 13°3E **200** E6
Scicli Italy 36°47N 14°42E **201** F7
Science and Industry, Museum of U.S.A. 41°47N 87°34W **119** C3
Sciliar-Catinaccio ⌂ Italy 46°28N 11°35E **199** B8
Scilla Italy 38°15N 15°43E **201** D8
Scilly, Isles of U.K. 49°56N 6°22W **169** H1
Ścinawa Poland 51°25N 16°26E **185** G3
Scione Greece 39°57N 23°36E **202** G7
Scioto → U.S.A. 38°44N 83°1W **311** D13
Scituate U.S.A. 42°12N 70°44W **313** D14
Scobey U.S.A. 48°47N 105°25W **304** B11
Scomenzera, Canale Venice, Italy **142** b1
Scone N.S.W., Australia 32°5S 150°52E **283** B9
Scone Perth & Kinr., U.K. 56°25N 3°24W **167** E5
Scopus, Mt. West Bank 31°48N 35°14E **123** B2
Scordia Italy 37°18N 14°51E **201** E7
Scoresby Sund Greenland 70°28N 21°46W **154** C8
Scoresbysund = Ittoqqortoormiit Greenland 70°20N 23°0W **154** C8
Scornicești Romania 44°34N 24°33E **183** F9
Scotia Calif., U.S.A. 40°29N 124°6W **304** F1
Scotia N.Y., U.S.A. 42°50N 73°58W **313** D11
Scotia Sea Antarctica 56°5S 56°0W **151** B18
Scotland Canada 43°1N 80°22W **312** C4
Scotland □ U.K. 57°0N 4°0W **167** E5
Scott Antarctica 77°50S 166°45E **151** D11
Scott C. Australia 13°30S 129°49E **278** B4
Scott Circle Washington, D.C., U.S.A. **143** a1
Scott City U.S.A. 38°29N 100°54W **308** F3
Scott Glacier Antarctica 66°15S 100°5E **151** C8
Scott I. Antarctica 67°0S 179°0E **151** C11
Scott Is. Canada 50°48N 128°40W **296** C3
Scott L. Canada 59°55N 106°18W **297** B7
Scott Monument Edinburgh, U.K. **121** b2
Scott Reef Australia 14°0S 121°50E **278** B3
Scottburgh S. Africa 30°15S 30°47E **271** D5
Scottdale Georgia, U.S.A. 33°47N 84°15W **113** B3
Scottdale Pa., U.S.A. 40°6N 79°35W **312** F5
Scottish Borders □ U.K. 55°35N 2°50W **167** F6
Scottish Parliament Edinburgh, U.K. 55°57N 3°10W **121** B2
Scotts Head N.S.W., Australia 30°45S 153°0E **283** A10
Scotts Head Dominica 15°13N 61°23W **323** k
Scotts Head Village Dominica 15°12N 61°22W **323** k
Scotts Valley U.S.A. 37°3N 122°1W **306** H4
Scottsbluff U.S.A. 41°52N 103°40W **308** E2
Scottsboro U.S.A. 34°40N 86°2W **315** D11
Scottsburg U.S.A. 38°41N 85°47W **311** F11
Scottsdale Tas., Australia 41°9S 147°31E **281** G4
Scottsdale Ariz., U.S.A. 33°40N 111°53W **305** K8
Scottsville Ky., U.S.A. 36°45N 86°11W **308** G10
Scottsville N.Y., U.S.A. 43°2N 77°47W **312** C7
Scottville U.S.A. 43°58N 86°17W **308** D10
Scranton U.S.A. 41°25N 75°40W **313** E9
Screven U.S.A. 31°29N 82°1W **316** D7
Scrub I. Anguilla 18°19N 62°55W **322** a
Scugog, L. Canada 44°10N 78°55W **312** B6
Sculeni Moldova 47°20N 27°37E **183** C12
Scunthorpe U.K. 53°36N 0°39W **168** D7
Scuol Schuls Switz. 46°48N 10°17E **179** J6
Scutari = Shkodër Albania 42°4N 19°32E **202** D3
Scutari = Üsküdar Turkey 41°1N 29°0E **122** B2
Sea Is. U.S.A. 31°30N 81°7W **316** D9
Sea Lake Australia 35°28S 142°55E **282** C5
Sea Point S. Africa 33°54S 18°23E **118** A1
Seabra = Tarauacá Brazil 8°6S 70°48W **330** B3
Seabra Brazil 12°25S 41°46W **333** D3
Seabrook, L. Australia 30°55S 119°40E **279** F2
Seacliff U.S.A. 37°47N 122°28W **136** B2
Seaford E. Sussex, U.K. 50°47N 0°7E **169** G8
Seaford Del., U.S.A. 38°39N 75°37W **309** F16
Seaforth N.S.W., Australia 33°48S 151°15E **139** A2
Seaforth Queens., Australia 20°55S 148°57E **280** b
Seaforth Ont., Canada 43°35N 81°25W **312** C3
Seaforth, L. U.K. 57°52N 6°36W **167** D2
Seagate U.S.A. 40°34N 74°0W **132** C1
Seagraves U.S.A. 32°57N 102°34W **314** E3
Seaham U.K. 54°50N 1°20W **168** C6
Seal → Canada 59°4N 94°48W **297** B10
Seal I. Anguilla 18°16N 63°9W **322** a
Seal L. Canada 54°20N 61°30W **299** B7
Seale U.S.A. 32°18N 85°10W **316** C4
Sealy U.S.A. 29°47N 96°9W **314** G6
Seaman U.S.A. 38°57N 83°34W **311** F13
Searchlight U.S.A. 35°28N 114°55W **307** K12
Searcy U.S.A. 35°15N 91°44W **314** D9
Searles L. U.S.A. 35°44N 117°21W **307** K9
Sears Tower = Willis Tower Chicago, U.S.A. **119** c1
Seascale U.K. 54°24N 3°29W **168** C4
Seaside Calif., U.S.A. 36°37N 121°50W **306** J5
Seaside Oreg., U.S.A. 46°0N 123°56W **306** E3
Seaspray Australia 38°25S 147°15E **283** E7
Seattle U.S.A. 47°36N 122°19W **306** C4
Seattle-Tacoma Int. ✕ (SEA) U.S.A. 47°27N 122°18W **306** C4
Seaward Kaikoura Ra. N.Z. 42°10S 173°44E **285** C8
SeaWorld U.S.A. 28°24N 81°28W **133** B2
Seba Indonesia 10°29S 121°50E **278** B3
Sebago L. U.S.A. 43°52N 70°34W **313** C14
Sebago Lake U.S.A. 43°51N 70°34W **313** C14
Sebakung Indonesia 1°37S 116°25E **235** C5
Sebangau △ Indonesia 2°34S 113°38E **235** C4
Sebangka Indonesia 0°7N 104°36E **234** B2
Sebastian U.S.A. 27°49N 80°28W **317** H9
Sebastián Vizcaíno, B. Mexico 28°0N 114°30W **318** B2
Sebastopol = Sevastopol Ukraine 44°35N 33°30E **189** K7
Sebastopol U.S.A. 38°24N 122°49W **306** G4
Sebatik Asia 4°10N 117°45E **235** B5
Sebba Burkina Faso 13°35N 0°32E **263** C5
Sebderat Eritrea 15°26N 36°42E **257** D4
Sebdou Algeria 34°38N 1°19W **261** B4
Sébé → Gabon 1°2S 13°6E **264** C2
Sébékoro Mali 12°58N 9°0W **262** C3
Seben Turkey 40°24N 31°34E **212** B4
Šeberov Czechia 50°0N 14°30E **135** B3
Sebeș Romania 45°58N 23°34E **183** E8
Sebeșului, Munții Romania 45°36N 23°40E **183** E8
Sebewaing U.S.A. 43°44N 83°27W **309** D12
Sebezh Russia 56°14N 28°22E **188** D5
Sebezhsky △ Russia 56°18N 28°30E **188** D5
Sebha = Sabhā Libya 27°9N 14°29E **258** C2
Sébi Mali 15°50N 4°12W **262** B4
Şebinkarahisar Turkey 40°22N 38°28E **213** B8
Sebino, L. di = Iseo, L. d' Italy 45°43N 10°4E **198** C7
Sebiș Romania 46°23N 22°13E **182** D7
Seblat Indonesia 3°14S 101°38E **234** C2
Sebnitz Germany 50°58N 14°15E **178** E10
Sebou, Oued → Morocco 34°16N 6°40W **260** B3
Sebring Fla., U.S.A. 27°30N 81°27W **317** H8

Sebring *Ohio, U.S.A.* 40°55N 81°2W **312** F3
Sebringville *Canada* 43°24N 81°4W **312** C3
Sebta = Ceuta *N. Afr.* 35°52N 5°18W **260** A3
Sebuku *Indonesia* 3°30S 116°25E **235** C5
Sebuku, Teluk *Indonesia* 4°0N 118°10E **235** B5
Sečanj *Serbia* 45°25N 20°47E **182** E5
Secauus *U.S.A.* 40°47N 74°3W **132** B1
Secchia → *Italy* 45°4N 11°10E **198** C6
Sechelt *Canada* 49°25N 123°42W **296** D4
Sechura *Peru* 5°33S 80°50W **330** B1
Sechura, Desierto de *Peru* 6°0S 80°30W **330** B1
Seclin *France* 50°33N 3°2E **173** B10
Second World War Memorial
  Washington, D.C., U.S.A. **143** b1
Secondigny *France* 46°37N 0°26W **172** F6
Sečovce *Slovakia* 48°42N 21°40E **181** C14
Secretary I. *N.Z.* 45°15S 166°56E **285** F1
Secunderabad *India* 17°28N 78°30E **244** F4
Sécure → *Bolivia* 15°10S 64°52W **331** D5
Security *U.S.A.* 38°45N 104°45W **304** G11
Sedalia *U.S.A.* 38°42N 93°14W **310** F3
Sedam *India* 17°11N 77°17E **244** E4
Sedan *S. Austral.,*
  Australia 34°34S 139°19E **282** C3
Sedan *Ardennes, France* 49°43N 4°57E **173** C11
Sedan *Kans., U.S.A.* 37°8N 96°11W **308** G6
Sedano *Spain* 42°43N 3°49W **194** C7
Sedaw *Burma* 22°19N 96°11E **241** D6
Sedbergh *U.K.* 54°20N 2°31W **168** C5
Seddinsee *Germany* 52°23N 13°41E **115** B5
Seddon *N.Z.* 41°40S 174°7E **285** B9
Seddonville *N.Z.* 41°33S 172°1E **285** B8
Sedé Boqér *Israel* 30°52N 34°47E **251** H5
Sedeh *Fārs, Iran* 30°45N 52°11E **247** D7
Sedeh *Khorāsān, Iran* 33°20N 59°14E **247** C8
Séderon *France* 44°12N 5°32E **175** D9
Sederot *Israel* 31°32N 34°37E **251** G5
Sédhiou *Senegal* 12°44N 15°30W **262** C1
Sedičiany *Czechia* 49°40N 14°25E **180** B7
Sedley *Canada* 50°10N 104°0W **297** C8
Sedom *Israel* 31°5N 35°20E **251** D4
Sedona *U.S.A.* 34°52N 111°46W **305** J8
Sedrata *Algeria* 36°7N 7°31E **261** A6
Sedro-Woolley *U.S.A.* 48°30N 122°14W **306** B3
Šeduva *Lithuania* 55°45N 23°45E **184** C10
Sędziszów *Poland* 50°35N 20°4E **185** H7
Sędziszów Małopolski
  Poland 50°5N 21°45E **185** H8
Seebad Ahlbeck *Germany* 53°56N 14°10E **178** B10
Seeberg *Germany* 52°33N 13°41E **115** A5
Seeburg = Jeziorany
  Poland 53°58N 20°46E **184** E7
Seeburg *Germany* 52°30N 13°7E **115** A1
Seefeld in Tirol *Austria* 47°19N 11°13E **180** D4
Seegefeld *Germany* 52°33N 13°6E **115** A1
Seehausen *Germany* 52°54N 11°45E **178** C7
Seeheim *Namibia* 26°50S 17°45E **270** D2
Seeheim-Jugenheim
  Germany 49°49N 8°40E **179** F4
Seehof *Germany* 52°34N 13°17E **115** B2
Seeis *Namibia* 22°29S 17°39E **270** C2
Seekoei → *S. Africa* 30°18S 25°1E **270** D4
Seeley's Bay *Canada* 44°29N 76°14W **313** B8
Seelow *Germany* 52°32N 14°23E **178** C10
Seemandra = Andhra Pradesh □
  India 18°0N 79°0E **244** F4
Sées *France* 48°38N 0°10E **172** D7
Seesen *Germany* 51°54N 10°10E **178** D6
Seevetal *Germany* 53°26N 10°1E **178** B6
Seewinkel = Neusiedler See-
  Seewinkel △ *Austria* 47°50N 16°45E **181** D9
Šefaatli *Turkey* 39°30N 34°45E **212** C6
Seferihisar *Turkey* 38°10N 26°50E **205** C8
Séfeto *Mali* 14°8N 9°49W **262** C3
Sefophe *Botswana* 22°11S 27°58E **271** B4
Sefrou *Morocco* 33°52N 4°52W **260** B4
Sefton *N.Z.* 43°15S 172°41E **285** D7
Sefuri-San *Japan* 33°28N 130°18E **222** D2
Sefwi Bekwai *Ghana* 6°10N 2°25W **262** D4
Seg-ozero *Russia* 63°20N 33°46E **186** B5
Segag *Ethiopia* 7°39N 42°50E **267** C5
Segamat *Malaysia* 2°30N 102°50E **237** L4
Segarcea *Romania* 44°6N 23°43E **183** F8
Ségbana *Benin* 10°55N 3°42E **263** C5
Segbwema *S. Leone* 8°0N 11°0W **262** D2
Segeltorp *Sweden* 59°16N 17°56E **139** B1
Segersta *Sweden* 61°16N 16°39E **162** G10
Segesta *Italy* 37°56N 12°50E **209** D5
Seget *Indonesia* 1°24S 130°58E **231** E8
Segewold = Sigulda
  Latvia 57°10N 24°55E **188** D3
Segezha *Russia* 63°44N 34°19E **186** B5
Seggueur, O. → *Algeria* 32°14N 1°48E **261** B5
Seghe *Solomon Is.* 8°32S 157°54E **287** M9
Segmon *Sweden* 59°17N 13°3E **162** E7
Segonzac *France* 45°36N 0°14W **174** C3
Segorbe *Spain* 39°50N 0°30W **196** F4
Ségou *Mali* 13°30N 6°16W **262** C3
Ségou □ *Mali* 14°0N 6°0W **262** C3
Segovia = Coco →
  Cent. Amer. 15°0N 83°8W **320** D3
Segovia *Colombia* 7°7N 74°42W **328** B3
Segovia *Spain* 40°57N 4°10W **194** E6
Segovia □ *Spain* 40°55N 4°10W **194** E6
Segrate *Italy* 45°29N 9°17E **128** B2
Segré *France* 47°40N 0°52W **172** E6
Segre → *Spain* 41°40N 0°43E **196** D5
Seguam I. *U.S.A.* 52°19N 172°30W **303** K4
Seguam Pass *U.S.A.* 52°0N 172°30W **303** K4
Séguédine *Niger* 20°9N 12°55E **259** D2
Séguéla *Ivory C.* 7°55N 6°40W **262** D3
Séguénon → *Ivory C.* 9°13N 7°7W **262** D3
Séguénéga *Burkina Faso* 13°25N 1°58W **263** C4
Seguin *U.S.A.* 29°34N 97°58W **314** G6
Segundo → *Argentina* 30°53S 62°44W **334** C3
Segura → *Spain* 38°3N 0°44W **197** G4
Segura, Sierra de *Spain* 38°5N 2°45W **197** G2
Seguro *Italy* 40°55N 9°17E **128** B2
Seh Konj, Küh-e *Iran* 30°6N 57°30E **247** D8
Seh Qal'eh *Iran* 33°40N 58°24E **247** C8
Sehithwa *Botswana* 20°30S 22°30E **270** B3
Sehlabathebe △ *Lesotho* 29°53S 29°7E **271** D4
Sehore *India* 23°10N 77°5E **242** H7
Sehulea *Papua N. G.* 9°58S 151°10E **286** E6
Sehwan *Pakistan* 26°28N 67°53E **242** F2
Seia *Portugal* 40°25N 7°43W **194** E3
Seica Mare *Romania* 46°1N 24°7E **183** D9
Seikan Tunnel *Japan* 41°28N 140°10E **220** E10
Seikpyu *Burma* 20°54N 94°48E **241** E5
Seil *U.K.* 56°18N 5°38W **167** E3
Seiland *Norway* 70°25N 23°15E **160** A20
Seilhac *France* 45°21N 1°43E **174** C5
Seiling *U.S.A.* 36°9N 98°56W **314** C6
Seille → *Moselle, France* 49°7N 6°11E **173** C13
Seille → *Saône-et-Loire,*
  France 46°31N 4°57E **173** F11
Sein, Î. de *France* 48°2N 4°52W **172** D2
Seinäjoki *Finland* 62°40N 22°51E **160** E20
Seine → *France* 49°26N 0°26E **172** C7
Seine, B. de la *France* 49°40N 0°40W **172** C6
Seine-et-Marne □ *France* 48°45N 3°0E **173** D10
Seine-Inférieure =
  Seine-Maritime □ *France* 49°40N 1°0E **172** C7
Seine-Maritime □ *France* 49°40N 1°0E **172** C7
Seine-St-Denis □ *France* 48°58N 2°24E **173** D9
Seini *Romania* 47°44N 23°21E **183** B8

Seirijai *Lithuania* 54°14N 23°49E **184** D10
Seis de Septiembre = Morón
  Argentina 34°39S 58°37W **334** C4
Seistan = Sīstān *Asia* 30°50N 61°0E **247** D9
Seistan, Daryācheh-ye = Sīstān,
  Daryācheh-ye *Iran* 31°0N 61°0E **247** D9
Seitler = Nyzhnohirskyy
  Ukraine 45°27N 34°38E **189** K8
Seitseminen △ *Finland* 61°55N 23°25E **160** F22
Seixal *Madeira* 32°48N 17°7W **153** c
Seixal Lisboa, Portugal 38°38N 9°5W **126** B2
Sejong *S. Korea* 36°35N 127°15E **224** D3
Sejong □ *S. Korea* 36°33N 127°16E **224** D3
Sejny *Poland* 54°6N 23°21E **184** D10
Sejong *S. Korea* 36°35N 127°15E **224** D3
Sejerø *Denmark* 55°54N 11°9E **163** J5
Sejerø Bugt *Denmark* 55°53N 11°15E **163** J5
Sejong *Poland* 54°6N 23°21E **184** D10
Sejong *S. Korea* 36°35N 127°15E **224** D3
Seka *Ethiopia* 8°10N 36°52E **257** F4
Sekadau *Indonesia* 0°1N 110°54E **235** C4
Sekayu *Indonesia* 2°51S 103°51E **234** C2
Seke *Tanzania* 3°20S 33°31E **268** E6
Seke-Banza
  Dem. Rep. of the Congo 5°20S 13°16E **265** D2
Sekenke *Tanzania* 4°18S 34°11E **268** C3
Sekharia *Tunisia* 34°20N 10°5E **258** B2
Seki *Japan* 35°29N 136°55E **223** G8
Seki *Turkey* 36°48N 29°35E **205** D12
Sekigahara *Japan* 35°22N 136°28E **223** B8
Sekondi-Takoradi *Ghana* 4°58N 1°45W **262** E4
Sekota *Ethiopia* 12°40N 39°2E **257** F4
Sekseül *Kazakhstan* 47°5N 61°9E **216** D6
Sekuma *Indonesia* 59°13N 38°30E **188** C10
Sekudai *Malaysia* 1°32N 103°39E **237** d
Sekuma *Botswana* 24°36S 23°50E **270** B3
Selah *U.S.A.* 46°39N 120°32W **304** C3
Selama *Malaysia* 5°12N 100°42E **237** K3
Selangor □ *Malaysia* 3°10N 101°30E **237** L3
Selárgius *Italy* 39°16N 9°10E **200** C2
Selaru *Indonesia* 8°9S 131°0E **231** F8
Selat, Selat *Malaysia* 5°15N 100°20E **237** c
Selatpanjang *Indonesia* 1°0N 102°43E **234** B2
Selawik *U.S.A.* 66°36N 160°0W **303** B7
Selawik → *U.S.A.* 66°35N 159°10W **303** C8
Selawik Nat. Wildlife Refuge △
  U.S.A. 66°35N 159°1W **303** C8
Selb *Germany* 50°10N 12°7E **179** E8
Selbusjøen *Norway* 63°15N 10°50E **164** A7
Selby *England, U.K.* 53°47N 1°5W **168** D6
Selby *S. Africa* 26°12S 28°2E **123** B2
Selby *N. Yorks., U.K.* 53°47N 1°5W **168** D6
Selby *S. Dak., U.S.A.* 45°31N 100°2W **308** C3
Selca *Croatia* 43°20N 16°50E **199** E13
Selçuk *Turkey* 37°56N 27°22E **205** D9
Sełdovia *U.S.A.* 59°26N 151°43W **303** D9
Sele → *Italy* 40°29N 14°56E **201** B7
Selebi-Phikwe *Botswana* 21°58S 27°48E **271** B4
Selemdzha → *Russia* 51°42N 128°53E **215** D13
Selendi *Manisa, Turkey* 38°43N 28°50E **205** C10
Selendi *Manisa, Turkey* 38°46N 27°53E **205** C9
Selevac *Serbia* 44°28N 20°52E **182** B5
Selenga = Selenge Mörön →
  Asia 52°16N 106°16E **218** A10
Selenge
  Dem. Rep. of the Congo 1°58S 18°11E **264** C3
Selenge Mörön → *Asia* 52°16N 106°16E **218** A10
Selenter See *Germany* 54°18N 10°26E **178** A6
Sélestat *France* 48°16N 7°26E **173** D14
Seletan, Tanjung
  Indonesia 4°10S 114°40E **235** C4
Seletar *Singapore* 1°22N 103°53E **138** A3
Seletar, Pulau *Singapore* 1°26N 103°51E **138** A3
Seletar Hills *Singapore* 1°23N 103°52E **138** A3
Seletar Res. *Singapore* 1°24N 103°48E **138** A2
Selevac *Serbia* 44°28N 20°52E **182** B5
Selfoss *Iceland* 63°56N 21°0W **155** D6
Selhurst *U.K.* 51°23N 0°5W **125** B3
Sélibabi *Mauritania* 15°10N 12°15W **262** B2
Seliger, Ozero *Russia* 57°15N 33°0E **188** D7
Seligman *U.S.A.* 35°20N 112°53W **305** J7
Selim *Turkey* 40°30N 42°46E **213** B10
Selima *Sudan* 21°22N 29°19E **256** C2
Selimiye *Turkey* 37°24N 27°40E **205** D9
Selinda Spillway →
  Botswana 18°35S 23°10E **270** A3
Selingué, L. de *Mali* 11°37N 8°14W **262** C3
Selinsgrove *U.S.A.* 40°48N 76°52W **312** F8
Selizharovo *Russia* 56°51N 33°27E **188** D7
Seljord *Norway* 59°30N 8°40E **164** E5
Selkirk *Man., Canada* 50°10N 96°55W **297** C9
Selkirk *Ont., Canada* 42°49N 79°56W **312** D5
Selkirk *U.K.* 55°33N 2°50W **167** F6
Selkirk *Borders, U.K.* 55°33N 2°50W **167** F6
Selkirk I. = Horse I.
  Canada 53°20N 99°6W **297** C9
Selkirk Mts. *Canada* 51°15N 117°40W **294** G8
Sellafield *U.K.* 54°25N 3°29W **168** C4
Sellama *Sudan* 12°51N 29°46E **257** E2
Sellegeti *Indonesia* 1°28S 103°31E **234** C2
Sellia *Greece* 35°12N 24°23E **207** E5
Sellières *France* 46°50N 5°32E **173** F12
Sells *U.S.A.* 31°55N 111°53W **305** L8
Sellye *Hungary* 45°52N 17°51E **182** E2
Selma *Ala., U.S.A.* 32°25N 87°1W **315** E11
Selma *Calif., U.S.A.* 36°34N 119°37W **306** J7
Selma *N.C., U.S.A.* 35°32N 78°17W **315** D15
Selmer *U.S.A.* 35°10N 88°36W **315** D10
Selongey *France* 47°36N 5°11E **173** E12
Selooné *France* 47°36N 5°11E **173** E12
Selouane *Morocco* 35°6N 2°57W **261** A4
Selous △ *Tanzania* 8°37S 37°42E **269** D4
Selowandoma Falls
  Zimbabwe 21°15S 31°50E **269** G3
Selsingen *Germany* 0°1S 130°5E **231** E8
Selsey Bill *U.K.* 50°43N 0°47W **169** G7
Seltso *Russia* 53°22N 34°4E **188** F8
Seltz *France* 48°54N 8°4E **173** D15
Selu *Indonesia* 7°32S 130°55E **231** F8
Sélune → *France* 48°38N 1°22W **172** D5
Selva = La Selva del Camp
  Spain 41°13N 1°8E **196** D6
Selva *Argentina* 29°50S 62°0W **334** B3
Selva Mallorca, Spain 39°46N 2°54E **206** B3
Selva Lancandona = Montes
  Azules △ *Mexico* 16°21N 91°3W **319** D6
Selvagens, Ilhas *Madeira* 30°5N 15°55W **260** B1
Selvas *Brazil* 6°30S 67°0W **330** B4
Selwyn *Australia* 21°32S 140°30W **279** D2
Selwyn → *Australia* 21°32S 140°0E **280** C2
Selwyn L. *Canada* 60°0N 104°30W **297** B8
Selwyn Mts. *Canada* 63°0N 130°0W **294** E5
Selwyn Ra. *Australia* 21°10S 140°0E **280** C3
Selwyn Passage *Vanuatu* 16°33S 168°12E **287** E6
Seman → *Albania* 40°45N 19°50E **203** D12
Semang, Teluk
  Indonesia 1°36S 104°42E **234** C2
Semarang *Indonesia* 7°0S 110°26E **235** D4
Semaraputra = Klungkung
  Indonesia 8°32S 115°24E **231** K18
Sematan *Malaysia* 1°48N 109°46E **235** B3
Semayang, Danau
  Indonesia 0°14S 116°28E **235** C5
Sembabule *Uganda* 0°4S 31°25E **268** C3
Sembawang *Singapore* 1°27N 103°49E **138** A3
Sembé *Congo* 1°39N 14°36E **264** B2
Sembilan *Indonesia* 1°59S 104°34E **234** C2
Sembung *Indonesia* 8°28S 115°11E **231** J18
Semedua *Indonesia* 3°10S 18°6E **264** C3
Semenic-Cheile Carașului △
  Romania 45°8N 22°5E **182** E7
Semenivka *Chernihiv,*
  Ukraine 52°8N 32°36E **189** F7
Semenivka *Kremenchuk,*
  Ukraine 49°37N 33°10E **189** H7
Semenov *Russia* 56°43N 44°30E **190** B7
Semera *Ethiopia* 11°48N 41°1E **257** E5
Semeru *Indonesia* 8°4S 112°55E **235** D4
Semey *Kazakhstan* 50°30N 80°10E **217** B10
Semichi Is. *U.S.A.* 52°42N 174°0E **303** K1
Semikarakorsk *Russia* 47°31N 40°48E **191** G5
Semiluki *Russia* 51°41N 39°2E **189** G10
Seminoe Res. *U.S.A.* 42°9N 106°55W **304** E10
Seminole *Fla., U.S.A.* 27°50N 82°47W **317** H17
Seminole *Okla., U.S.A.* 35°14N 96°41W **314** D6
Seminole *Tex., U.S.A.* 32°43N 102°39W **314** E3
Seminole, L. *U.S.A.* 30°43N 84°52W **316** F5
Seminole Draw →
  U.S.A. 32°27N 102°20W **314** E3
Semipalatinsk = Semey
  Kazakhstan 50°30N 80°10E **217** B10
Semirara I. *Phil.* 12°4N 121°23E **232** E3
Semirara Is. *Phil.* 12°0N 121°20E **233** F3
Semisopochnoi I. *U.S.A.* 51°55N 179°36E **303** L2
Semitau *Indonesia* 0°29N 111°57E **235** B4
Semliki → *Uganda* 0°49N 30°4E **268** B3
Semlin = Zemun *Serbia* 44°51N 20°25E **202** B4
Semmelweis Museum
  Budapest, Hungary **117** c2
Semmering P. *Austria* 47°41N 15°45E **180** D8
Semnān *Iran* 35°40N 53°23E **247** C7
Semnān □ *Iran* 36°0N 54°0E **247** C7
Sempang Mengayou, Tanjong
  Malaysia 7°0N 116°40E **235** A5
Sepanjung *Malaysia* 4°30N 118°33E **235** B5
Semuda *Indonesia* 2°51S 112°58E **235** C4
Semur-en-Auxois *France* 47°30N 4°20E **173** E11
Semunovka = Arsenev
  Russia 44°10N 133°15E **220** B6
Semyonovskoye = Bereznik
  Russia 62°51N 42°40E **186** B7
Sen → *Cambodia* 12°32N 104°28E **236** F5
Sena *Bolivia* 11°32S 67°11W **330** C4
Senā *Iran* 28°27N 51°36E **247** D6
Sena *Mozam.* 17°25S 35°0E **269** F4
Sena Madureira *Brazil* 9°5S 68°45W **330** B4
Senachwine L. *U.S.A.* 41°10N 89°18W **310** C7
Senador José Porfírio
  Brazil 2°35S 51°55W **329** D7
Senador Pompeu *Brazil* 5°40S 39°20W **332** C4
Senago *Italy* 45°34N 9°7E **128** A1
Senaja *Malaysia* 6°45N 117°3E **235** A5
Senaki *Georgia* 42°15N 42°1E **191** J6
Senang, Pulau *Singapore* 1°11N 103°52E **237** d
Senanga *Zambia* 16°7S 23°16E **268** H3
Senatobia *U.S.A.* 34°37N 89°58W **315** D10
Senayan Stadium = Gelora Bung
  Karno Stadium
  Jakarta, Indonesia 6°13S 106°47E **122** B1
Sencelles *Spain* 39°39N 2°54E **206** B3
Sendafa *Ethiopia* 9°11N 39°3E **257** F4
Sendai = Satsuma-Sendai
  Japan 31°50N 130°20E **222** E10
Sendai *Japan* 38°15N 140°53E **222** E10
Sendai-Wan *Japan* 38°15N 141°0E **222** E10
Senden *Bayern, Germany* 48°19N 10°4E **179** G6
Senden *Nordrhein-Westfalen,*
  Germany 51°52N 7°22E **178** D3
Sendhwa *India* 21°41N 75°6E **242** J6
Sendling *Germany* 48°7N 11°31E **131** B2
Sendlinger Tor Platz *Munich, Germany* **131** c1
Sendurjana *India* 21°32N 78°17E **244** D4
Sene → *Ghana* 7°30N 0°33W **263** D4
Senec *Slovakia* 48°12N 17°23E **181** C10
Seneca *Ill., U.S.A.* 41°19N 88°37W **311** C8
Seneca *S.C., U.S.A.* 34°41N 82°57W **315** D13
Seneca Falls *U.S.A.* 42°55N 76°48W **313** D8
Seneca L. *U.S.A.* 42°40N 76°54W **312** D8
Senecaville L. *U.S.A.* 39°55N 81°25W **312** G3
Senegal ■ *W. Afr.* 14°30N 14°30W **262** C2
Sénégal → *W. Afr.* 15°48N 16°32W **262** B1
Senegambia *Africa* 12°45N 12°0W **254** E2
Senegambia & Niger = Mali ■
  Africa 17°0N 3°0W **262** B4
Senekal *S. Africa* 28°20S 27°36E **271** D4
Senftenberg *Germany* 51°32N 14°0E **178** D10
Senga Hill *Zambia* 9°19S 31°11E **269** D3
Senge Khambab = Indus →
  Pakistan 24°20N 67°47E **242** G2
Sengerema *Tanzania* 2°42S 32°35E **268** C3
Sengeti *Indonesia* 1°28S 103°31E **234** C2
Senggigi *Indonesia* 8°29S 116°2E **231** J19
Sengiley *Russia* 53°58N 48°46E **190** D9
Sengua → *Zimbabwe* 17°7S 28°5E **269** F2
Senguerr → *Argentina* 45°35S 68°50W **336** D3
Senhor-do-Bonfim *Brazil* 10°30S 40°10W **332** D3
Senica *Slovakia* 48°41N 17°25E **181** C10
Senigállia *Italy* 43°43N 13°13E **199** E10
Senira *Burma* 25°32N 97°48E **241** C6
Senio → *Italy* 44°35N 12°15E **199** D9
Senirkent *Turkey* 38°6N 30°33E **205** C12
Senise *Italy* 40°9N 16°17E **201** B9
Senj *Croatia* 45°0N 14°58E **199** D11
Senja *Norway* 69°25N 17°30E **160** B17
Senju *Japan* 35°44N 139°48E **140** A3
Senkaku-Shotō
  E. China Sea 25°45N 123°30E **221** M1
Senkang *Singapore* 1°23N 103°53E **138** A3
Senlis *France* 49°13N 2°35E **173** C9
Senmonorom *Cambodia* 12°27N 107°12E **236** F6
Sennār *Sudan* 13°30N 33°35E **257** E3
Sennār □ *Sudan* 13°0N 34°0E **257** E3
Senneterre *Canada* 48°25N 77°15W **298** C4
Senno *Belarus* 54°45N 29°43E **188** E5
Sénnori *Italy* 40°47N 8°35E **200** B1
Seno *Laos* 16°35N 104°50E **236** D5
Senoia *U.S.A.* 33°18N 84°33W **316** E5
Senonches *France* 48°34N 1°2E **172** D8
Senorbi *Italy* 39°32N 9°8E **200** C2
Senožeče *Slovenia* 45°43N 14°3E **199** C11
Senqu = Orange →
  S. Africa 28°41S 16°28E **270** C2
Senriyama *Japan* 34°47N 135°30E **133** A2
Sens *France* 48°11N 3°15E **173** D10
Senta *Serbia* 45°55N 20°3E **182** E5
Sentarum, Danau
  Indonesia 0°51N 112°6E **235** B4
Sentery = Lubao
  Dem. Rep. of the Congo 5°17S 25°42E **265** D5
Sentinel *U.S.A.* 32°52N 113°13W **305** K7
Şentjur *Slovenia* 46°14N 15°24E **199** B12
Sentosa *Singapore* 1°16N 103°50E **138** A3
Sentry Hill *St.-Maarten* 18°2N 63°4W **322** a
Senwabarana *S. Africa* 23°7S 29°7E **271** B4
Senya Beraku *Ghana* 5°28N 0°31W **263** D4
Seo de Urgel = La Seu d'Urgell
  Spain 42°22N 1°23E **196** C6
Seobinggo *S. Korea* 37°31N 126°58E **137** B1
Seocho *S. Korea* 37°28N 127°0E **137** C1
Seodaemun *S. Korea* 37°34N 126°57E **137** B1
Seogwipo *S. Korea* 33°13N 126°34E **224** a
Seohara *India* 29°15N 78°33E **243** E8
Seokguram Grotto
  S. Korea 35°46N 129°20E **224** E4

Sémé *Senegal* 15°4N 13°41W **262** B2
Semith *Sudan* 12°43N 30°53E **257** E3
Semendua
  Dem. Rep. of the Congo 3°10S 18°6E **264** C3
Semenic-Cheile Carașului △
  Romania 45°8N 22°5E **182** E7
Semenivka *Chernihiv,*
  Ukraine 52°8N 32°36E **189** F7
Semenivka *Kremenchuk,*
  Ukraine 49°37N 33°10E **189** H7
Semenov *Russia* 56°43N 44°30E **190** B7
Semera *Ethiopia* 11°48N 41°1E **257** E5
Semeru *Indonesia* 8°4S 112°55E **235** D4
Semey *Kazakhstan* 50°30N 80°10E **217** B10
Semichi Is. *U.S.A.* 52°42N 174°0E **303** K1
Semikarakorsk *Russia* 47°31N 40°48E **191** G5
Semiluki *Russia* 51°41N 39°2E **189** G10
Seminoe Res. *U.S.A.* 42°9N 106°55W **304** E10
Seminole *Fla., U.S.A.* 27°50N 82°47W **317** H17
Seminole *Okla., U.S.A.* 35°14N 96°41W **314** D6
Seminole *Tex., U.S.A.* 32°43N 102°39W **314** E3
Seminole, L. *U.S.A.* 30°43N 84°52W **316** F5
Seminole Draw →
  U.S.A. 32°27N 102°20W **314** E3

Seokkwan *S. Korea* 37°35N 127°2E **137** B2
Seonath → *India* 21°44N 82°28E **243** J10
Seondha *India* 26°9N 78°48E **243** F8
Seongbuk *S. Korea* 37°35N 127°0E **137** B2
Seongdong *S. Korea* 37°33N 127°3E **137** B2
Seongmodo *S. Korea* 37°41N 126°19E **224** D3
Seongnam *S. Korea* 37°26N 127°8E **137** C2
Seongsu *S. Korea* 37°32N 127°2E **137** B2
Seoni *India* 22°5N 79°30E **243** H8
Seoni Malwa *India* 22°27N 77°28E **242** H7
Seonsan *S. Korea* 36°14N 128°17E **224** D4
Seonyudo *S. Korea* 35°49N 126°24E **224** E3
Seoraksan *S. Korea* 38°7N 128°28E **224** C4
Seoraksan ∩ *S. Korea* 38°15N 128°22E **224** C4
Seosan *S. Korea* 36°47N 126°27E **224** D3
Seoriuarayan *India* 21°45N 82°34E **244** D6
Seoul *S. Korea* 37°31N 126°58E **137** B2
Seoul Nat. Univ. *S. Korea* 37°32N 126°57E **137** C1
Seoul Tower *S. Korea* 37°32N 126°59E **137** B1
Sepang *Malaysia* 2°43N 101°50E **237** L3
Separation Pt. *N.Z.* 40°47S 172°59E **285** A7
Sepasu *Indonesia* 0°43N 117°34E **235** B5
Sepatini → *Brazil* 7°36S 65°24W **330** B4
Sepi *Solomon Is.* 8°31S 159°52E **287** M10
Sepīdān *Iran* 30°20N 52°5E **247** D7
Sepik → *Papua N. G.* 3°49S 144°30E **286** B3
Sepo-ri *N. Korea* 38°57N 127°25E **224** C3
Sepolia *Greece* 38°1N 23°42E **112** A2
Sepólno Krajeńskie
  Poland 53°26N 17°30E **184** E4
Sepone *Laos* 16°45N 106°13E **236** D6
Sępopol *Poland* 54°16N 21°2E **184** D8
Seppa *India* 27°16N 92°54E **241** B8
Sept-Îles *Canada* 50°13N 66°22W **299** B6
Septemvri *Bulgaria* 42°13N 24°6E **203** D8
Sepúlveda *Spain* 41°18N 3°45W **194** D7
Sepulveda Dam Rec. Area △
  U.S.A. 34°10N 118°28W **126** A2
Sequeros *Spain* 40°31N 6°2W **194** E4
Sequim *U.S.A.* 48°5N 123°6W **304** B2
Sequoia △ *U.S.A.* 36°30N 118°30W **306** J8
Serafimovich *Russia* 49°36N 42°43E **190** F6
Seraing *Belgium* 50°35N 5°32E **170** D5
Serakhis → *Cyprus* 35°13N 32°55E **211** D11
Seram *Indonesia* 3°10S 129°0E **231** E7
Seram Sea *Indonesia* 2°30S 128°30E **231** E7
Serampore = Shrirampur
  India 22°44N 88°21E **243** H13
Serangsara *Madag.* 18°30S 49°5E **272** B2
Serang *Indonesia* 6°8S 106°10E **234** D3
Serangoon *Singapore* 1°23N 103°54E **138** A3
Serangoon, Pulau
  Singapore 1°23N 103°55E **138** A3
Serangoon Harbour
  Singapore 1°23N 103°57E **138** A3
Serasan *Indonesia* 2°29N 109°4E **235** B3
Serasan, Selat *Indonesia* 2°20N 109°3E **235** B3
Seravezza *Italy* 43°59N 10°13E **198** E7
Seraya, Pulau *Indonesia* 1°16N 103°43E **138** B2
Serbál, G. *Egypt* 28°40N 33°35E **251** F4
Serbia ■ *Europe* 43°20N 20°0E **202** C4
Šercaia *Romania* 45°49N 25°9E **183** E10
Serchhip *India* 23°18N 92°51E **241** D4
Serdar *Turkmenistan* 39°4N 56°23E **247** B8
Serdo *Ethiopia* 11°56N 41°14E **257** E5
Serdobol = Sortavala
  Russia 61°42N 30°41E **188** B6
Serdobsk *Russia* 52°28N 44°10E **190** D7
Serebryansk *Kazakhstan* 49°41N 83°17E **217** C10
Sered' *Slovakia* 48°17N 17°44E **181** C10
Sereda = Furmanov *Russia* 57°10N 41°9E **190** B5
Seredka *Russia* 58°12N 28°10E **188** C5
Seredne *Ukraine* 48°32N 22°30E **182** B7
Şereflikoçhisar *Turkey* 38°15N 33°24E **212** C5
Seregno *Italy* 45°39N 9°12E **198** C6
Seremban *Malaysia* 2°43N 101°53E **237** L3
Serengeti △ *Tanzania* 2°11S 35°0E **268** C3
Serengeti Plain *Tanzania* 2°40S 35°0E **268** C4
Serenje *Zambia* 13°14S 30°15E **269** E3
Seret → *Ukraine* 48°37N 25°52E **183** B10
Sereth = Siret → *Romania* 45°24N 28°1E **183** E14
Sergach *Russia* 55°30N 45°30E **190** C8
Sergeevka *Kazakhstan* 53°52N 67°24E **217** B7
Sergipe □ *Brazil* 10°30S 37°30W **332** D4
Sergiyev Posad *Russia* 56°20N 38°10E **188** D10
Sergo = Stakhanov
  Ukraine 48°35N 38°40E **189** H10
Serhetabat *Turkmenistan* 35°20N 62°18E **247** D9
Seria *Brunei* 4°37N 114°23E **235** B4
Serian *Malaysia* 1°10N 110°31E **235** B4
Seriate *Italy* 45°41N 9°43E **198** C6
Seribu → *Indonesia* 5°32S 106°33E **234** D3
Sérifontaine *France* 49°20N 1°45E **173** C8
Sérifos *Greece* 37°9N 24°30E **206** D6
Sérigny → *Canada* 56°47N 66°0W **299** A5
Sérigny *France* 43°17N 3°17E **174** E7
Serik *Turkey* 36°55N 31°7E **250** B2
Seringapatam Reef
  Australia 13°38S 122°5E **278** B3
Serinhisar *Turkey* 37°36N 29°18E **205** D11
Seririt *Indonesia* 8°12S 114°56E **231** J17
Serishābād *Iran* 35°14N 47°36E **213** E12
Serkout *Algeria* 23°56N 6°47E **261** D6
Sermaize-les-Bains *France* 48°47N 4°54E **173** D11
Sermata *Indonesia* 8°15S 128°50E **231** F7
Sermersooq □ *Greenland* 62°30N 40°0W **154** D7
Sermersuaq *Greenland* 79°30N 62°0W **154** B4
Sérmide *Italy* 45°0N 11°18E **199** D8
Sernur *Russia* 56°52N 49°2E **190** B9
Serock *Poland* 52°31N 21°4E **185** F8
Seroe Colorado *Aruba* 12°25N 69°52W **322** f
Serón *Spain* 37°20N 2°29W **197** H2
Seròs *Spain* 41°27N 0°24E **196** D5
Serouenout *Algeria* 24°18N 7°25E **261** D6
Serov *Russia* 59°29N 60°35E **186** C11
Serowe *Botswana* 22°25S 26°43E **270** B4
Serpa *Portugal* 37°57N 7°38W **195** H3
Serpentara *Italy* 39°8N 9°36E **200** C2
Serpentine Lakes
  Australia 28°30S 129°10E **279** E4
Serpent's Mouth = Sierpe, Bocas
  la *Venezuela* 10°0N 61°30W **325** E15
Serpis → *Spain* 38°59N 0°9W **197** G4
Serpneve *Ukraine* 46°18N 29°1E **183** D14
Serpukhov *Russia* 54°55N 37°28E **188** E9
Serra da Bocaina △ *Brazil* 22°30S 44°40W **333** G5
Serra da Canastra △ *Brazil* 20°35S 46°50W **333** F2
Serra da Capivara △
  Brazil 8°42S 42°15W **332** D3
Serra das Confusões △
  Brazil 8°50S 43°50W **332** D3
Serra de Mesa, Barragem de
  Brazil 14°30S 48°30W **333** D2

Sevran *France* 48°56N 2°31E **134** A4
Sèvre-Nantaise → *France* 47°12N 1°33W **172** E5
Sèvre-Niortaise → *France* 46°28N 0°54W **174** B3
Sèvres *Paris, France* 48°49N 2°12E **134** B3
Sevsk *Russia* 52°10N 34°30E **189** F8
Sewa → *S. Leone* 7°20N 12°10W **262** D2
Sewani *India* 28°58N 75°39E **242** E6
Seward *Alaska, U.S.A.* 60°7N 149°27W **303** F10
Seward *Nebr., U.S.A.* 40°55N 97°6W **308** E5
Seward *Pa., U.S.A.* 40°25N 79°1W **312** F5
Seward Peninsula *U.S.A.* 65°30N 166°0W **303** D6
Sewell *Chile* 34°10S 70°23W **334** C1
Sewer *Indonesia* 5°53S 134°40E **231** F8
Sewickley *U.S.A.* 40°32N 80°12W **312** F4
Sewri *India* 18°59N 72°50E **130** B2
Sexsmith *Canada* 55°21N 118°47W **296** B5
Seychelles ■ *Ind. Oc.* 5°0S 56°0E **272** c
Seyðisfjörður *Iceland* 65°16N 13°57W **155** B13
Seydişehir *Turkey* 37°25N 31°51E **212** D4
Seydvān *Iran* 38°34N 45°2E **213** C11
Seyhan → *Turkey* 36°43N 34°53E **250** B5
Seyhan Baraji *Turkey* 37°2N 35°18E **212** D6
Seyitgazi *Turkey* 39°27N 30°43E **205** B12
Seyitömer *Turkey* 39°34N 29°52E **205** B11
Seym → *Ukraine* 51°27N 32°34E **189** G7
Seymen *Turkey* 41°6N 27°57E **203** E11
Seymour *Vic., Australia* 37°2S 145°10E **283** D6
Seymour *Eastern Cape,*
  S. Africa 32°33S 26°46E **271** D4
Seymour *Conn., U.S.A.* 41°24N 73°4W **313** E11
Seymour *Ind., U.S.A.* 38°58N 85°53W **311** F11
Seymour *Tex., U.S.A.* 33°35N 99°16W **314** E5
Seyne *France* 44°21N 6°22E **175** D10
Seyssel *France* 45°57N 5°50E **175** C9
Sezana *Slovenia* 45°43N 13°41E **199** C10
Sézanne *France* 48°40N 3°40E **173** D10
Sezze *Italy* 41°30N 13°3E **200** A6
Sfântu Gheorghe *Covasna,*
  Romania 45°52N 25°48E **183** E10
Sfântu Gheorghe *Tulcea,*
  Romania 44°53N 29°36E **183** F14
Sfântu Gheorghe, Brațul →
  Romania 44°53N 29°36E **183** F14
Sfax *Tunisia* 34°49N 10°48E **258** B2
Sfax □ *Tunisia* 34°40N 10°20E **261** B7
Sforzesco, Castello *Italy* 45°28N 9°10E **128** B2
Sha Chau
  Hong Kong, China 22°21N 113°53E **122** A1
Sha Kok Mei
  Hong Kong, China 22°23N 114°16E **122** A2
Sha Lo Wan
  Hong Kong, China 22°17N 113°54E **122** B1
Sha Tau Kok *China* 22°33N 114°13E **219** a
Sha Tin *Hong Kong, China* 22°23N 114°12E **122** A3
Sha Xi → *China* 26°35N 118°0E **229** D12
Sha Xian *China* 26°23N 117°45E **229** D11
Sha'ab *Iraq* 33°25N 44°26E **113** A2
Sha'ab North *Iraq* 33°25N 44°24E **113** A2
Shaanxi □ *China* 35°0N 109°0E **226** G5
Sha'ar Binyamin
  West Bank 31°52N 35°16E **123** A2
Shaba = Katanga □
  Dem. Rep. of the Congo 8°0S 25°0E **254** G6
Shaba → *Katanga □
  Dem. Rep. of the Congo 0°38N 37°48E **268** B4
Shabeellaha Dhexe □
  Somalia 3°0N 45°30E **267** D6
Shabeellaha Hoose □
  Somalia 1°0N 44°0E **267** D5
Shabeelle → *Somalia* 2°0N 44°0E **267** D5
Shabestar *Iran* 38°13N 45°41E **213** C11
Shabla *Bulgaria* 43°31N 28°32E **203** C12
Shabogamo L. *Canada* 53°15N 66°30W **299** B6
Shabrāmant *Egypt* 29°56N 31°11E **117** B2
Shabunda
  Dem. Rep. of the Congo 2°40S 27°16E **268** C2
Shabwah *Yemen* 15°22N 47°1E **248** D4
Shabwah □ *Yemen* 15°22N 47°1E **248** D4
Shache *China* 38°20N 77°10E **217** E9
Shackleton Fracture Zone
  S. Ocean 60°0S 60°0W **151** B18
Shackleton Ice Shelf
  Antarctica 66°0S 100°0E **151** C8
Shackleton Inlet
  Antarctica 83°0S 160°0E **151** E11
Shādegān *Iran* 30°40N 48°38E **247** D6
Shadi *Jiangxi, China* 26°7N 114°47E **229** D10
Shadi *Jammu & Kashmir,*
  India 33°24N 77°14E **243** C7
Shadrinsk *Russia* 56°5N 63°32E **214** D7
Shady Dale *U.S.A.* 33°24N 83°36W **316** E6
Shady Grove *U.S.A.* 30°17N 83°38W **316** F6
Shadyside *U.S.A.* 39°58N 80°45W **312** G4
Shafer, L. *U.S.A.* 40°46N 86°46W **311** D10
Shaffa *Nigeria* 10°30N 12°6E **263** C7
Shafter *U.S.A.* 35°30N 119°16W **307** K7
Shaftesbury *U.K.* 51°0N 2°11W **168** F5
Shaftsbury *U.S.A.* 43°0N 73°11W **313** D11
Shag Pt. *N.Z.* 45°29S 170°52E **285** F5
Shag Rocks *Atl. Oc.* 53°0S 41°0W **152** M7
Shagamu *Nigeria* 6°51N 3°39E **263** D5
Shagaluk *U.S.A.* 62°41N 159°34W **303** E8
Shagram *Pakistan* 36°24N 72°20E **243** A5
Shah Alam *Malaysia* 3°5N 101°32E **237** L3
Shah Alizai *Pakistan* 29°25N 66°33E **242** E2
Shah Bunder *Pakistan* 24°13N 67°56E **242** G2
Shāh Jūy *Afghan.* 32°31N 67°25E **240** C2
Shah Mosque *Iran* 37°17N 49°7E **247** C6
Shahabad *Karnataka, India* 17°10N 76°54E **244** F3
Shahabad *Punjab, India* 30°10N 76°55E **242** D7
Shahabad *Raj., India* 25°15N 77°11E **242** G7
Shahabad *Ut. P., India* 27°36N 79°56E **243** F8
Shahada *India* 21°33N 74°30E **244** D2
Shahadpur *Pakistan* 25°55N 68°35E **242** G3
Shahapur *India* 15°50N 74°34E **245** G2
Shahbā' *Syria* 32°52N 36°38E **251** C5
Shahbandar *Bangla.* 22°30N 90°45E **241** J17
Shahdād *Iran* 30°30N 57°40E **247** D8
Shahdād, Namakzār-e
  Iran 30°20N 58°20E **247** D8
Shahdadkot *Pakistan* 27°50N 67°55E **242** F2
Shahdara *India* 28°40N 77°18E **254** d
Shahe *China* 37°0N 114°32E **226** F8
Shahganj *India* 26°3N 82°44E **243** F10
Shahgarh *India* 27°15N 69°50E **242** F3
Shahjahanpur *India* 27°54N 79°57E **243** F8
Shahpur *Karnataka, India* 16°40N 76°48E **244** F3
Shahpur *Mad. P., India* 22°12N 77°58E **244** D1
Shahpur *Baluchistan,*
  Pakistan 28°46N 68°27E **242** E3
Shahpur *Punjab, Pakistan* 32°17N 72°26E **242** C5
Shahpur Chakar *Pakistan* 26°9N 68°39E **242** F3
Shahpura *Mad. P., India* 23°10N 80°45E **243** H9
Shahpura *Raj., India* 25°38N 74°56E **242** G6
Shahr-e Bābak *Iran* 30°7N 55°9E **247** D7
Shahr-e Kord *Iran* 32°15N 50°55E **247** C6
Shahr-e Rey *Iran* 35°35N 51°25E **247** C6
Shahr-i Sokhta *Iran* 30°45N 61°32E **247** D9
Shahrak = Golshahr *Iran* 34°41N 50°4E **247** C6
Shahrak-e Qods *Iran* 35°42N 51°1E **247** a
Shāhrakht *Iran* 33°38N 60°16E **247** C9
Shāhrezā = Qomsheh *Iran* 32°0N 51°55E **247** D6

Shahrig Pakistan 30°15N 67°40E 242 D2
Shahrisabz Uzbekistan 39°3N 66°50E 217 F7
Shāhrud = Emāmrūd Iran 36°30N 55°0E 247 B7
Shahukou China 40°20N 112°18E 226 D7
Shaikh Aomar Iraq 33°20N 44°23E 113 A2
Shaikhabad Afghan. 34°2N 68°45E 242 B3
Shajapur India 23°27N 76°21E 242 H7
Shajing China 22°44N 113°48E 219 a
Shajuwan Taiwan 23°13N 121°23E 225 C3
Shakargarh Pakistan 32°17N 75°10E 242 C6
Shakawe Botswana 18°28S 21°49E 270 A3
Shakenge Dem. Rep. of the Congo 6°14S 18°41E 265 D3
Shaker Heights U.S.A. 41°28N 81°32W 312 E3
Shakhrisyabz = Shahrisabz Uzbekistan 39°3N 66°50E 217 E7
Shakhtersk Russia 49°10N 142°8E 215 E15
Shakhtīnsk Kazakhstan 49°42N 72°35E 217 C8
Shakhty Russia 47°40N 40°16E 191 G5
Shakhtyorskoye = Pershotravensk Ukraine 50°13N 27°40E 177 C14
Shakhunya Russia 57°40N 46°46E 190 B8
Shaki Nigeria 8°41N 3°21E 263 D5
Shākir Egypt 27°30N 33°59E 256 B3
Shakotan-Hantō Japan 43°10N 140°30E 220 C10
Shaksam Valley Asia 36°0N 76°20E 243 A7
Shaktoolik U.S.A. 64°20N 161°9W 303 D7
Shakurbasti India 28°41N 77°6E 120 A1
Shala, L. Ethiopia 7°30N 38°30E 257 F4
Shali Russia 43°9N 45°55E 191 J7
Shalim Oman 18°7N 55°38E 249 C6
Shalkar Kōli Kazakhstan 50°35N 51°47E 190 E10
Shalkiya India 22°36N 88°21E 124 B2
Shallow Lake Canada 44°36N 81°5W 312 B3
Shalqar Kazakhstan 47°48N 59°39E 216 C5
Shalqar Kōli Kazakhstan 50°33N 51°40E 216 B4
Shalskiy Russia 61°48N 35°58E 188 B8
Shalu Taiwan 24°14N 120°34E 225 B2
Shaluli Shan China 30°40N 99°55E 228 B2
Shām Iran 26°39N 57°21E 247 E8
Shām, Bādiyat ash Asia 32°0N 40°0E 246 C3
Shām, J. ash Oman 23°14N 57°16E 249 B7
Sham Shui Po Hong Kong, China 22°19N 114°9E 122 B2
Sham Tseng Hong Kong, China 22°22N 114°3E 122 A2
Sham Wat Hong Kong, China 22°16N 113°53E 122 B1
Shamal al Batinah □ Oman 24°30N 56°20E 249 A7
Shamal ash Sharqīyah □ Oman 22°40N 58°30E 249 B7
Shamâl Bahr el Ghazal = Northern Bahr el Ghazal □ South Sudan 8°0N 27°30E 257 F2
Shamâl Dârfûr □ Sudan 15°0N 25°0E 257 E2
Shamâl Kordofân □ Sudan 15°0N 30°0E 257 E3
Shamâl Sînî □ Egypt 30°30N 33°30E 251 H4
Shamapur India 28°44N 77°8E 120 A1
Shamattawa Canada 55°51N 92°5W 298 A1
Shamattawa → Canada 55°1N 85°23W 298 A2
Shambe South Sudan 7°8N 30°46E 257 F3
Shambe △ South Sudan 6°57N 30°50E 257 F3
Shambu Ethiopia 9°32N 37°3E 257 F4
Shamgong Dzong Bhutan 27°13N 90°35E 241 B3
Shamian China 23°6N 113°13E 121 B2
Shamīl Iran 27°30N 56°55E 247 E8
Shamkhor = Şämkir Azerbaijan 40°50N 46°0E 191 K8
Shāmkūh Iran 35°47N 57°50E 247 C8
Shamli India 29°32N 77°18E 242 E7
Shammar, Jabal Si. Arabia 27°40N 41°0E 246 E4
Shamo = Gobi Asia 44°0N 110°0E 226 C6
Shamo, L. Ethiopia 5°45N 37°30E 257 F4
Shamokin U.S.A. 40°47N 76°34W 313 F8
Shamrock Ont., Canada 45°23N 76°50W 313 A8
Shamrock Tex., U.S.A. 35°13N 100°15W 314 D4
Shamva Zimbabwe 17°20S 31°32E 269 F3
Shan □ Burma 21°30N 98°30E 241 E7
Shan Mei Hong Kong, China 22°23N 114°11E 122 A3
Shan Xian China 34°50N 116°5E 226 G9
Shana = Kurilsk Russia 45°14N 147°53E 215 E15
Shanan → Ethiopia 8°0N 40°20E 257 F5
Shanchengzhen China 42°20N 125°20E 224 A2
Shāndak Iran 28°28N 60°27E 247 D9
Shandan China 38°45N 101°15E 218 D9
Shandon U.S.A. 35°39N 120°23W 306 K6
Shandong □ China 36°0N 118°0E 227 G10
Shandong Bandao China 37°0N 121°0E 227 F11
Shandur Pass Pakistan 36°4N 72°31E 243 A5
Shang Xian = Shangzhou China 33°50N 109°58E 226 H5
Shangalowe Dem. Rep. of the Congo 10°50S 26°30E 269 E2
Shangani Zimbabwe 19°41S 29°20E 271 A4
Shangani → Zimbabwe 18°41S 27°10E 269 F2
Shangbancheng China 40°50N 118°1E 227 D10
Shangcheng China 31°47N 115°26E 229 B10
Shangchuan Dao China 21°40N 112°50E 229 G9
Shangdu China 41°30N 113°30E 226 D7
Shanggao China 28°17N 114°55E 229 C10
Shanghai China 31°15N 121°26E 138 B2
Shanghai Hongqiao Int. ✕ (SHA) China 31°12N 121°20E 138 B1
Shanghai Pudong Int. ✕ (PVG) China 31°9N 121°47E 138 B2
Shanghai Shi □ China 31°0N 121°30E 229 B13
Shanghang China 25°2N 116°23E 229 E11
Shanghe China 37°20N 117°10E 227 F9
Shangjao = Shangrao China 28°25N 117°59E 229 C11
Shanglin China 23°27N 108°33E 228 F7
Shangnan China 33°32N 110°50E 226 H6
Shangqiu China 34°26N 115°36E 226 G8
Shangrao China 28°25N 117°59E 229 C11
Shangri-La = Zhongdian China 27°48N 99°42E 228 D2
Shangshui China 33°32N 114°35E 226 H8
Shangsi China 22°8N 107°58E 228 F6
Shangyi China 41°4N 113°57E 226 D7
Shangyou China 25°48N 114°32E 229 E10
Shangyu China 30°3N 120°52E 229 B13
Shangzhi China 45°22N 127°56E 227 B14
Shangzhou China 33°50N 109°58E 226 H5
Shanhetun China 44°33N 127°15E 227 B14
Shanhu Tan Taiwan 23°12N 120°23E 225 C2
Shanhua Taiwan 23°8N 120°17E 225 C2
Shani Nigeria 10°14N 12°2E 263 C7
Shānidar Iraq 36°48N 44°14E 213 D11
Shanklin U.K. 50°38N 1°11W 169 G6
Shanlin Taiwan 23°10N 120°32E 225 C2
Shannon N.Z. 40°33S 175°25E 284 G4
Shannon → Ireland 52°35N 9°30W 166 D2
Shannon ✕ (SNN) Ireland 52°42N 8°57W 166 D3
Shannon, Mouth of the Ireland 52°30N 9°55W 166 D2
Shannon △ Australia 34°35S 116°25E 279 F2
Shannon Ø Greenland 75°10N 18°30W 156 B9
Shannonbridge Ireland 53°17N 8°3W 166 C3
Shannontown U.S.A. 33°53N 80°21W 316 B9
Shanshan China 42°52N 90°10E 217 D12
Shanshang Taiwan 23°6N 120°21E 225 C2
Shansi = Shanxi □ China 37°0N 112°0E 226 F7
Shantar, Ostrov Bolshoy Russia 55°9N 137°40E 215 D14
Shantipur India 23°17N 88°25E 243 H13
Shantou China 23°18N 116°40E 229 F11
Shantung = Shandong □ China 36°0N 118°0E 227 G10
Shanwei China 22°48N 115°22E 229 F10
Shanxi □ China 37°0N 112°0E 226 F7
Shanyang China 33°31N 109°55E 226 H5
Shanyin China 39°25N 112°56E 226 E7
Shaodong China 27°15N 111°43E 229 D8
Shaoguan China 24°48N 113°35E 229 E9
Shaohing = Shaoxing China 30°0N 120°35E 229 C13
Shaoshan China 27°55N 112°33E 229 D9
Shaowu China 27°22N 117°28E 229 D11
Shaoxing China 30°0N 120°35E 229 C13
Shaoyang China 27°14N 111°25E 229 D8
Shap U.K. 54°32N 2°40W 168 C5
Shapinsay U.K. 59°3N 2°51W 167 B6
Shaqlāwah Iraq 36°23N 44°20E 213 D11
Shaqq el Gi'eifer → Sudan 15°16N 26°0E 257 D2
Shaqra' Si. Arabia 25°15N 45°16E 246 E5
Shar Kazakhstan 49°35N 81°2E 217 C10
Sharafa Sudan 11°59N 27°7E 257 E2
Sharafkhāneh Iran 38°11N 45°29E 213 C11
Sharashova Belarus 52°34N 24°12E 185 F11
Sharavati → India 14°20N 74°25E 245 G2
Sharbaqty Kazakhstan 51°23N 78°17E 217 B9
Sharbithāt, Ra's ash Oman 17°56N 56°21E 249 C7
Sharbot Lake Canada 44°46N 76°41W 313 B8
Shard Building London, U.K. 125 b5
Shardara, Step Kazakhstan 42°20N 68°0E 217 D7
Shargʻun Uzbekistan 38°35N 67°58E 240 A2
Sharhorod Ukraine 48°45N 28°5E 183 B13
Shari Japan 43°55N 144°40E 220 C12
Shariff Aguak Phil. 6°51N 124°31E 233 H5
Sharjah = Ash Shāriqah U.A.E. 25°23N 55°26E 247 E7
Shark B. Australia 25°30S 113°32E 279 E1
Shark Bay △ Australia 25°30S 113°30E 279 E1
Sharm el Sheikh Egypt 27°53N 34°18E 251 L5
Sharon Ont., Canada 44°6N 79°26W 312 B5
Sharon Mass., U.S.A. 42°7N 71°11W 313 D13
Sharon Pa., U.S.A. 41°14N 80°31W 312 E4
Sharon Wis., U.S.A. 42°30N 88°44W 311 B8
Sharon Springs Kans., U.S.A. 38°54N 101°45W 308 F3
Sharon Springs N.Y., U.S.A. 42°48N 74°37W 313 D10
Sharonville U.S.A. 39°16N 84°25W 311 E12
Sharp I. Hong Kong, China 22°21N 114°17E 122 A3
Sharp Pk. Phil. 5°58N 125°31E 233 J5
Sharp Pt. Australia 10°58S 142°43E 286 F2
Sharpe L. Canada 54°24N 93°40W 298 B1
Sharpes U.S.A. 28°26N 80°46W 317 G9
Sharpsville U.S.A. 41°15N 80°29W 312 E4
Sharq Dârfûr □ Sudan 11°0N 23°30E 267 E2
Sharq el Istiwa'iya = Eastern Equatoria □ South Sudan 5°0N 33°0E 257 G3
Sharqi, Al Jabal ash Lebanon 33°40N 36°10E 250 E7
Sharqîya, Es Sahrâ esh Egypt 27°30N 32°30E 256 B3
Sharr Kosovo 42°5N 20°41E 202 D4
Sharya Russia 58°22N 45°20E 190 A7
Shasha Ethiopia 6°29N 35°59E 257 F4
Shashemene Ethiopia 7°13N 38°33E 257 F4
Shashi Botswana 21°15S 27°27E 271 B4
Shashi → Africa 21°14S 29°20E 269 G2
Shasta, Mt. U.S.A. 41°25N 122°12W 304 F2
Shasta L. U.S.A. 40°43N 122°25W 304 F2
Shastrinagar India 28°40N 77°10E 120 A2
Shatawi Sudan 14°39N 32°6E 257 E3
Shāṭi', Wādī ash → Libya 27°30N 15°0E 252 C3
Shatilki = Svyetlahorsk Belarus 52°38N 29°46E 177 B15
Shatsk Russia 54°5N 41°45E 190 C5
Shatsk Ukraine 51°29N 23°55E 185 G10
Shatsky Rise Pac. Oc. 34°0N 157°0E 288 D7
Shatskyy △ Ukraine 51°30N 23°52E 185 G10
Shatt al Arab Asia 29°57N 48°34E 247 D6
Shatura Russia 55°33N 39°21E 188 E10
Shaturtof = Shatura Russia 55°33N 39°21E 188 E10
Shau Kei Wan Hong Kong, China 22°16N 114°13E 122 B3
Shaumyani = Shulaveri Georgia 41°22N 44°45E 191 K7
Shaunavon Canada 49°35N 108°25W 297 D7
Shaver L. U.S.A. 37°9N 119°18W 306 H7
Shavgar = Türkistan Kazakhstan 43°17N 68°16E 217 D7
Shavli = Šiauliai Lithuania 55°56N 23°15E 184 C10
Shaw → Australia 20°21S 119°17E 278 D2
Shaw I. Australia 20°30S 149°2E 280 b
Shawanaga Canada 45°31N 80°17W 312 A4
Shawangunk Mts. U.S.A. 41°35N 74°30W 313 E10
Shawano U.S.A. 44°47N 88°36W 308 C9
Shawinigan Canada 46°35N 72°50W 298 C5
Shawmari, J. ash Jordan 30°35N 36°35E 251 H7
Shawnee Ga., U.S.A. 32°29N 81°25W 316 C8
Shawnee Kans., U.S.A. 39°1N 94°43W 310 E2
Shawnee Okla., U.S.A. 35°20N 96°55W 314 D6
Shawocun China 39°53N 116°13E 114 B1
Shay Gap Australia 20°30S 120°10E 278 D3
Shayang China 30°42N 112°29E 229 B9
Shaybārā Si. Arabia 25°26N 36°47E 246 E3
Shayib el Banat, Gebel Egypt 26°59N 33°29E 256 B3
Shaykh, J. ash Lebanon 33°25N 35°50E 250 E6
Shaykh Miskīn Syria 32°49N 36°9E 250 F7
Shaykh Sa'd Iraq 32°34N 46°17E 213 F12
Shaykh 'Uthmān Yemen 12°52N 44°59E 248 D4
Shaytansky Zavod = Pervouralsk Russia 56°59N 59°59E 186 C10
Shayuan China 23°5N 113°15E 121 B2
Shāzand Iran 33°56N 49°24E 247 C6
Shazud Tajikistan 37°45N 72°25E 217 E8
Shcheglovo = Kemerovo Russia 55°20N 86°5E 214 D9
Shchekino Russia 54°1N 37°34E 188 E9
Shcherbakov = Rybinsk Russia 58°5N 38°50E 188 C10
Shchigry Russia 51°55N 36°58E 189 G9
Shchors Ukraine 51°48N 31°56E 189 G6
Shchūchīnsk Kazakhstan 52°56N 70°12E 217 B8
She Xian Anhui, China 29°50N 118°25E 229 C12
She Xian Hebei, China 36°30N 113°40E 226 F7
Shea Guyana 2°48N 59°4W 329 C6
Shebekino Russia 50°28N 36°54E 189 G9
Shebela → Ethiopia 7°32N 45°43E 267 C6
Shebele = Shabeelle → Somalia 2°0N 44°0E 267 D5
Shebele Ethiopia 8°8N 42°40E 267 C5
Shebenik-Jabllanicë △ Albania 41°12N 20°28E 202 E4
Sheberghān Afghan. 36°40N 65°45E 240 A2
Sheboygan U.S.A. 43°46N 87°45W 308 D10
Shebshi Mts. Nigeria 8°30N 12°0E 263 D7
Shediac Canada 46°14N 64°32W 299 C7
Sheelin, L. Ireland 53°48N 7°20W 166 C4
Sheen, L. U.S.A. 28°25N 81°31W 133 B1
Sheenjek → U.S.A. 66°45N 144°33W 303 C11
Sheep Haven Ireland 55°11N 7°52W 166 A4
Sheep Range U.S.A. 36°35N 115°15W 307 J11
Sheepshead Bay U.S.A. 40°35N 73°55W 132 C2
Sheerness U.K. 51°26N 0°47E 169 F8
Sheet Harbour Canada 44°56N 62°31W 299 D7
Sheffield N.Z. 43°23S 172°1E 285 D7
Sheffield S. Yorks., U.K. 53°23N 1°28W 168 D6
Sheffield Ala., U.S.A. 34°46N 87°41W 315 D11
Sheffield Ill., U.S.A. 41°21N 89°44W 310 C7
Sheffield Iowa, U.S.A. 42°54N 93°13W 310 B3
Sheffield Mass., U.S.A. 42°5N 73°21W 313 D11
Sheffield Pa., U.S.A. 41°42N 79°3W 312 E5
Shegaon India 20°48N 76°47E 244 D3
Shehojele Ethiopia 10°40N 35°9E 257 E4
Shehong China 30°54N 105°18E 228 B5
Shehuen → Argentina 49°35S 69°34W 336 C3
Shei-Pa △ Taiwan 24°36N 121°22E 225 B3
Shei Shan Taiwan 24°22N 121°15E 225 B3
Sheikh, W. el → Egypt 28°41N 33°41E 251 K4
Sheikh Zayed Canal Egypt 23°30N 30°15E 256 C3
Sheikh Zayed Road Dubai, U.A.E. 25°11N 55°15E 119 B2
Sheikhpura India 25°9N 85°53E 243 G11
Shek Hasan Ethiopia 12°5N 35°58E 257 E4
Shek Kong Hong Kong, China 22°26N 114°6E 122 A2
Shek Kwu Chau Hong Kong, China 22°12N 113°59E 122 B1
Shek O Hong Kong, China 22°13N 114°15E 122 B3
Shek O Country Park ⌂ Hong Kong, China 22°16N 114°14E 122 B3
Shek Pik Hong Kong, China 22°14N 113°53E 122 B1
Shek Pik Res. Hong Kong, China 22°14N 113°54E 122 B1
Shekhupura Pakistan 31°42N 73°58E 242 D5
Sheki = Şaki Azerbaijan 41°10N 47°5E 191 K8
Shekki = Zhongshan China 22°26N 113°20E 229 F9
Shekou China 22°30N 113°55E 219 a
Shelbina U.S.A. 39°47N 92°2W 310 E4
Shelburn U.S.A. 39°11N 87°24W 311 E9
Shelburne N.S., Canada 43°47N 65°20W 299 D6
Shelburne Ont., Canada 44°4N 80°15W 312 B4
Shelburne Vt., U.S.A. 44°23N 73°14W 313 B11
Shelburne B. Australia 11°50S 142°50E 286 F2
Shelburne Falls U.S.A. 42°36N 72°45W 313 D12
Shelby Mich., U.S.A. 43°37N 86°22W 308 D10
Shelby Miss., U.S.A. 33°57N 90°46W 315 E9
Shelby Mont., U.S.A. 48°30N 111°51W 304 B8
Shelby N.C., U.S.A. 35°17N 81°32W 315 D14
Shelby Ohio, U.S.A. 40°53N 82°40W 312 F2
Shelbyville Ill., U.S.A. 39°24N 88°48W 311 E8
Shelbyville Ind., U.S.A. 39°31N 85°47W 311 E11
Shelbyville Ky., U.S.A. 38°13N 85°14W 311 F11
Shelbyville Mo., U.S.A. 39°48N 92°2W 310 E4
Shelbyville Tenn., U.S.A. 35°29N 86°28W 315 D11
Shelbyville, L. U.S.A. 39°26N 88°46W 311 E8
Sheldon Ill., U.S.A. 40°46N 87°34W 311 D9
Sheldon Iowa, U.S.A. 43°11N 95°51W 308 D6
Sheldon Mo., U.S.A. 37°40N 94°18W 310 G2
Sheldon S.C., U.S.A. 32°36N 80°48W 316 C9
Sheldon Point U.S.A. 62°32N 164°52W 303 E6
Sheldrake Canada 50°20N 64°51W 299 B7
Shelek Kazakhstan 43°33N 78°17E 217 D9
Shelengo, Khawr → Sudan 10°33N 28°40E 257 E2
Shelikhova, Zaliv Russia 59°30N 157°0E 215 D16
Shelikof Strait U.S.A. 57°30N 155°0W 303 H9
Shell Beach = Huntington Beach U.S.A. 33°40N 118°5W 307 M9
Shell Lakes Australia 29°20S 127°30E 279 E4
Shellbrook Canada 53°13N 106°24W 297 C7
Shellharbour Australia 34°31S 150°51E 283 C9
Shellman U.S.A. 31°46N 84°37W 316 D5
Shellsburg U.S.A. 42°6N 91°52W 310 B5
Shelon → Russia 58°13N 30°47E 188 C6
Shelter Bay = Port-Cartier Canada 50°2N 66°50W 299 B6
Shelter I. Hong Kong, China 22°19N 114°17E 122 B3
Shelter I. N.Y., U.S.A. 41°4N 72°20W 313 E12
Shelton Conn., U.S.A. 41°19N 73°5W 313 E11
Shelton Wash., U.S.A. 47°13N 123°6W 306 C3
Shemakha = Şamaxı Azerbaijan 40°38N 48°37E 191 K9
Shemonaīkha Kazakhstan 50°37N 81°50E 217 B10
Shëmri Albania 42°7N 20°13E 202 D4
Shemsi Sudan 19°2N 29°57E 256 D2
Shen Xian China 36°15N 115°40E 226 F8
Shenandoah Iowa, U.S.A. 40°46N 95°22W 308 E6
Shenandoah Pa., U.S.A. 40°49N 76°12W 313 F8
Shenandoah Va., U.S.A. 38°29N 78°37W 309 F14
Shenandoah → U.S.A. 39°19N 77°44W 309 F15
Shenandoah △ U.S.A. 38°35N 78°22W 309 F14
Shenchi China 39°8N 112°10E 226 E7
Shencottah India 8°59N 77°18E 245 K3
Shendam Nigeria 8°49N 9°30E 263 D6
Shendî Sudan 16°46N 33°22E 257 D3
Shendurni India 20°39N 75°36E 244 D2
Shengang = Shenkang Taiwan 24°9N 120°39E 225 B2
Shenge S. Leone 7°54N 12°55W 262 D2
Shengfang China 39°3N 116°42E 226 E9
Shëngjergj Albania 41°17N 20°10E 202 E4
Shëngjin Albania 41°50N 19°35E 202 E3
Shengzhou China 29°35N 120°50E 229 C13
Shenjingzi China 44°40N 124°30E 227 B13
Shenkang Taiwan 24°9N 120°39E 225 B2
Shenmu China 38°50N 110°29E 226 E6
Shennongjia China 31°43N 110°44E 229 B8
Shenqiu China 33°25N 115°5E 226 H8
Shensi = Shaanxi □ China 35°0N 109°0E 226 G5
Shenyang China 41°48N 123°27E 224 B1
Shenzhen China 22°32N 114°5E 229 F10
Shenzhen Bao'an Int. ✕ (SZX) China 22°41N 113°49E 219 a
Shenzhen Shuiku China 22°34N 114°8E 219 a
Shenzhen Wan China 22°27N 113°55E 219 a
Sheo India 26°11N 71°15E 242 F4
Sheopur Kalan India 25°40N 76°40E 242 G7
Shepetivka Ukraine 50°10N 27°10E 177 C14
Shepherd Is. Vanuatu 16°55S 168°36E 287 F6
Shepherds Bush U.K. 51°30N 0°13W 125 A2
Shepherdsville U.S.A. 37°59N 85°43W 311 G11
Shepparton Australia 36°23S 145°26E 283 D6
Shepperton U.K. 51°23N 0°26W 125 B1
Sheppey, I. of U.K. 51°25N 0°48E 169 F8
Shepton Mallet U.K. 51°11N 2°33W 169 F5
Sheqi China 33°12N 112°57E 226 H7
Sher Khan Qala Afghan. 29°53N 66°13E 240 C2
Sher Qila Pakistan 36°7N 74°2E 243 A6
Sherab Sudan 10°44N 24°41E 257 E1
Sherborne U.K. 50°57N 2°31W 169 G5
Sherbro → S. Leone 7°45N 12°55W 262 D2
Sherbro I. S. Leone 7°30N 12°40W 262 D2
Sherbrooke N.S., Canada 45°8N 61°59W 299 C7
Sherbrooke Qué., Canada 45°28N 71°57W 313 A13
Sherburne U.S.A. 42°41N 75°30W 313 D9
Sherburne Reef Papua N. G. 3°20S 148°0E 286 B5
Sherda Chad 20°7N 16°46E 259 D3
Shereik Sudan 18°44N 33°47E 256 D3
Sheremetyevo Int., Moscow ✕ (SVO) Russia 55°58N 37°25E 129 A1
Shergaon India 27°7N 92°16E 241 B4
Shergarh India 26°20N 72°18E 242 F5
Sherghati India 24°34N 84°47E 243 G11
Sheridan Ark., U.S.A. 34°19N 92°24W 314 D8
Sheridan Ill., U.S.A. 41°32N 88°41W 311 C8
Sheridan Ind., U.S.A. 40°8N 86°13W 311 D10
Sheridan Wyo., U.S.A. 44°48N 106°58W 304 D10
Sheringham U.K. 52°56N 1°13E 168 E9
Sherkin I. Ireland 51°28N 9°26W 166 E2
Sherkot India 29°22N 78°35E 243 E8
Sherlovaya Gora Russia 50°34N 116°15E 215 D12
Sherman N.Y., U.S.A. 42°9N 79°35W 312 D5
Sherman Tex., U.S.A. 33°38N 96°36W 314 E6
Sherman Oaks U.S.A. 34°8N 118°29W 126 B2
Sherman Park U.S.A. 41°47N 87°39W 119 C2
Sherobod Uzbekistan 37°40N 67°1E 217 E7
Sherpur Bangla. 25°0N 90°0E 241 C3
Sherpur India 25°34N 83°47E 243 G10
Sherridon Canada 55°8N 101°5W 297 B8
Sherriffs St. Kitts & Nevis 17°10N 62°32W 322 d
Shertallai = Cherthala India 9°42N 76°20E 245 K3
Sherwood U.S.A. 41°17N 84°33W 311 C12
Sherwood, L. U.S.A. 28°33N 81°29W 133 A2
Sherwood Forest U.K. 53°6N 1°7W 168 D6
Sherwood Park Canada 53°31N 113°19W 296 C6
Sheslay → Canada 58°48N 132°5W 296 B2
Shet Bandar India 18°57N 72°55E 130 B2
Shete Boka △ Curaçao 12°22N 69°8W 322 g
Shethanei L. Canada 58°48N 97°50W 297 B9
Shetland □ U.K. 60°30N 1°30W 167 A7
Shetland Is. U.K. 60°30N 1°30W 167 A7
Shetou Taiwan 23°53N 120°35E 225 C2
Shetpe Kazakhstan 44°10N 52°7E 216 D4
Shetrunji → India 21°19N 72°7E 242 J5
Sheung Fa Shan Hong Kong, China 22°23N 114°5E 122 A2
Sheung Lau Wan Hong Kong, China 22°16N 114°16E 122 B3
Sheung Shui China 22°31N 114°7E 219 a
Sheung Wan Hong Kong, China 22°16N 114°9E 122 B2
Sheva India 18°56N 72°57E 130 B2
Sheva Nhava India 18°57N 72°57E 130 B2
Shevaroy Hills India 11°58N 78°12E 245 J4
Shevchenkovo = Dolynska Ukraine 48°6N 32°46E 189 H7
Shevchenkove Ukraine 45°33N 29°20E 183 E14
Shevgaon India 19°21N 75°14E 244 E2
Shevisheh Iran 35°21N 46°40E 213 E12
Shewa Ethiopia 9°33N 38°10E 257 F4
Shewa Gimira Ethiopia 7°4N 35°51E 257 F4
Shey-Phoksundo △ Nepal 29°30N 82°45E 243 E10
Sheyang China 33°48N 120°29E 227 H11
Sheyenne → U.S.A. 47°2N 96°50W 308 B5
Shiashkotan, Ostrov Russia 48°49N 154°6E 215 E16
Shiba Tokyo, Japan 140 c4
Shibām Yemen 15°59N 48°36E 249 D5
Shibata Japan 37°57N 139°20E 220 F9
Shibecha Japan 43°17N 144°36E 220 C12
Shibetsu Hokkaidō, Japan 43°30N 145°10E 220 C12
Shibetsu Hokkaidō, Japan 44°10N 142°23E 220 B11
Shibîn el Kôm Egypt 30°31N 30°55E 256 H7
Shibîn el Qanâtir Egypt 30°19N 31°19E 256 H7
Shibing China 27°2N 108°7E 228 D7
Shibogama L. Canada 53°35N 88°15W 298 B2
Shibpur India 22°34N 88°19E 124 B1
Shibukawa Japan 36°29N 139°0E 223 A11
Shibushi Japan 31°25N 131°8E 222 F3
Shibushi-Wan Japan 31°24N 131°8E 222 F3
Shibuya Tokyo, Japan 140 c1
Shicheng China 26°22N 116°20E 229 D11
Shicheng Dao China 39°31N 122°59E 224 C1
Shickshinny U.S.A. 41°9N 76°9W 313 E8
Shickshock Mts. = Chic-Chocs, Mts. Canada 48°55N 66°0W 299 C6
Shidād Si. Arabia 21°19N 40°3E 248 B3
Shidao China 36°50N 122°25E 227 F12
Shiderti → Kazakhstan 52°32N 74°50E 217 B8
Shidian China 24°40N 99°5E 228 E2
Shido = Sanuki Japan 34°19N 134°10E 222 C6
Shiel, L. U.K. 56°48N 5°34W 167 E3
Shield, C. Australia 13°20S 136°20E 280 A2
Shīeli Kazakhstan 44°20N 66°15E 217 D7
Shifang China 31°8N 104°10E 228 B5
Shiga □ Japan 35°20N 136°0E 223 B8
Shigaib Sudan 15°5N 23°35E 259 E4
Shigu China 26°51N 99°56E 228 D2
Shiguaigou China 40°52N 110°15E 226 D6
Shihan Yemen 17°42N 52°27E 249 C6
Shihan, W. → Yemen 17°24N 51°26E 249 C5
Shihchiachuangi = Shijiazhuang China 38°2N 114°28E 226 E8
Shihezi China 44°15N 86°2E 217 D11
Shihiu Taiwan 24°38N 121°10E 225 B3
Shihkengkeng Taiwan 24°1N 120°57E 225 B2
Shihmen Taiwan 25°17N 121°33E 225 A3
Shihmen Shuiku Taiwan 24°49N 121°21E 225 B3
Shihtan Taiwan 24°32N 120°55E 225 B2
Shiiba Japan 32°29N 131°4E 222 E3
Shiikh Somalia 9°56N 45°13E 267 C6
Shijak Albania 41°21N 19°33E 202 E3
Shijiazhuang China 38°2N 114°28E 226 E8
Shijiu Hu China 31°25N 118°50E 229 B12
Shikarpur India 28°17N 78°7E 242 E8
Shikarpur Pakistan 27°57N 68°39E 242 F3
Shikhrany = Kanash Russia 55°30N 47°32E 190 C8
Shikine-Jima Japan 34°19N 139°13E 223 C11
Shikohabad India 27°6N 78°36E 243 F8
Shikokochūō Japan 34°1N 133°34E 222 C5
Shikoku Japan 33°30N 133°30E 222 D5
Shikoku □ Japan 33°30N 133°30E 222 D5
Shikoku-Sanchi Japan 33°30N 133°30E 222 D5
Shikotan, Ostrov Asia 43°47N 146°44E 215 E15
Shikotsu-Ko Japan 42°45N 141°25E 220 C10
Shikotsu-Tōya △ Japan 44°4N 145°8E 220 C10
Shikuka = Poronaysk Russia 49°13N 143°0E 219 B17
Shilabo Ethiopia 6°5N 44°46E 267 C5
Shiliguri India 26°45N 88°25E 241 B2
Shilihe China 39°50N 116°25E 114 B2
Shiliu = Changjiang China 19°20N 108°55E 229 a
Shilka Russia 52°0N 115°55E 215 D12
Shilka → Russia 53°20N 121°26E 215 D13
Shillelagh Ireland 52°45N 6°32W 166 D5
Shillington U.S.A. 40°18N 75°58W 313 F9
Shillong India 25°35N 91°53E 241 C3
Shilo West Bank 32°4N 35°18E 251 F6
Shilong China 23°5N 113°52E 229 F9
Shilou China 37°0N 110°48E 226 F6
Shilovo Russia 54°25N 40°57E 190 C5
Shima-Hantō Japan 34°22N 136°45E 223 C8
Shimabara Japan 32°48N 130°20E 222 E2
Shimada Japan 34°49N 138°10E 223 C10
Shimane □ Japan 35°0N 132°30E 222 C4
Shimane-Hantō Japan 35°30N 133°0E 222 B5
Shimanovsk Russia 52°15N 127°30E 215 D13
Shimanto Kōchi, Japan 33°12N 133°8E 222 D5
Shimanto Kōchi, Japan 32°59N 132°56E 222 E4
Shimba Hills ⌂ Kenya 4°14S 39°25E 268 C4
Shimbiris Somalia 10°44N 47°14E 267 B6
Shimen China 29°35N 111°20E 229 C8
Shimenjie China 29°29N 116°48E 229 C11
Shimian China 29°17N 102°23E 228 C4
Shimizu Japan 35°0N 138°30E 223 B10
Shimla India 31°2N 77°9E 242 D7
Shimo-Jima Japan 32°15N 130°7E 222 E2
Shimo-Koshiki-Jima Japan 31°40N 129°43E 222 F1
Shimoda Japan 34°40N 138°57E 223 C10
Shimodate Japan 36°20N 139°55E 223 A11
Shimoga = Shivamogga India 13°57N 75°32E 245 H2
Shimogawara Japan 35°39N 139°27E 140 B1
Shimokita-Hantō Japan 41°20N 141°0E 220 D10
Shimoni Kenya 4°38S 39°20E 268 C4
Shimonita Japan 36°13N 138°47E 223 A10
Shimonoseki Japan 33°58N 130°55E 222 D2
Shimosalo Japan 35°45N 139°31E 140 A2
Shimoshakujii Japan 35°43N 139°35E 140 A2
Shimotsuma Japan 36°11N 139°58E 223 A11
Shimpuru Rapids Namibia 17°45S 19°55E 265 F3
Shimsha → India 13°15N 77°10E 245 H3
Shimsk Russia 58°15N 30°50E 188 C6
Shin, L. U.K. 58°5N 4°30W 167 C4
Shin-Nan'yō Japan 34°3N 131°49E 222 C3
Shin-Tone-Gawa → Japan 35°44N 140°51E 223 B12
Shinagawa Japan 35°36N 139°44E 140 B3
Shinan China 22°44N 109°53E 228 F7
Shināş Oman 24°46N 56°28E 247 E8
Shīndand Afghan. 33°12N 62°8E 240 B1
Shing Mun Country Park ⌂ Hong Kong, China 22°23N 114°8E 122 A2
Shing Mun Res. Hong Kong, China 22°23N 114°8E 122 A2
Shingbwiyang Burma 26°41N 96°13E 241 B6
Shinglehouse U.S.A. 41°58N 78°12W 312 E6
Shingū Japan 33°40N 135°55E 223 D7
Shingwidzi S. Africa 23°5S 31°25E 271 B5
Shinji Japan 35°24N 132°54E 222 B4
Shinji-Ko Japan 35°26N 132°57E 222 B4
Shinjō Japan 38°46N 140°18E 220 E10
Shinjuku Tokyo, Japan 140 a1
Shinjuku Nat. Garden Tokyo, Japan 140 a2
Shinkafe Nigeria 13°8N 6°29E 263 C6
Shinkoiwa Japan 35°43N 139°51E 140 A4
Shinminato = Imizu Japan 36°47N 137°4E 223 A9
Shinnakano Japan 35°41N 139°40E 140 A3
Shinshār Syria 34°36N 36°43E 250 D7
Shinshiro Japan 34°54N 137°30E 223 C9
Shintuya Peru 12°41S 71°15W 330 C3
Shinyanga Tanzania 3°45S 33°27E 268 C3
Shinyanga □ Tanzania 3°50S 33°0E 268 C3
Shio-no-Misaki Japan 33°25N 135°45E 223 D7
Shiogama Japan 38°19N 141°1E 220 E10
Shiojiri Japan 36°6N 137°58E 223 A9
Shipai China 23°8N 113°20E 121 B3
Shipchenski Prokhod Bulgaria 42°45N 25°15E 203 D9
Shiphoirt, L. = Seaforth, L. U.K. 57°52N 6°36W 167 D2
Shiping China 23°45N 102°23E 228 F4
Shippagan Canada 47°45N 64°45W 299 C7
Shippensburg U.S.A. 40°3N 77°31W 312 F7
Shippenville U.S.A. 41°15N 79°28W 312 E5
Shiprock U.S.A. 36°47N 108°41W 305 H9
Shiqian China 27°32N 108°13E 228 D7
Shiqma, N. → Israel 31°37N 34°30E 251 G5
Shiquan China 33°5N 108°15E 228 A7
Shiquan He = Indus → Pakistan 24°20N 67°47E 242 G2
Shīr Khān Afghan. 37°11N 68°36E 240 A3
Shīr Kūh Iran 31°39N 54°3E 247 D7
Shira'awh Qatar 25°2N 52°14E 247 E7
Shirabad = Sherobod Uzbekistan 37°40N 67°1E 217 E7
Shiragami-Misaki Japan 41°24N 140°12E 220 D10
Shirahama Japan 33°41N 135°20E 223 D7
Shirakawa Fukushima, Japan 37°7N 140°13E 221 F10
Shirakawa Gifu, Japan 36°17N 136°56E 223 A8
Shirane-San Gumma, Japan 36°48N 139°22E 223 A11
Shirane-San Yamanashi, Japan 35°42N 138°9E 223 B10
Shiraoi Japan 42°33N 141°21E 220 C10
Shirati Tanzania 1°8S 33°59E 266 E3
Shīrāz Iran 29°42N 52°30E 247 D7
Shirbīn Egypt 31°11N 31°32E 256 H7
Shire → Africa 17°42S 35°19E 269 F4
Shiren China 41°57N 126°34E 227 D14
Shiretoko △ Japan 44°15N 145°15E 220 B12
Shiretoko-Misaki Japan 44°21N 145°20E 220 B12
Shirinab → Pakistan 30°15N 66°28E 242 D2
Shirinashi → Japan 34°38N 135°27E 133 B1
Shiriya-Zaki Japan 41°25N 141°30E 220 D10
Shirley U.S.A. 39°53N 85°35W 311 E11
Shirogane Japan 35°37N 139°44E 140 B3
Shiroishi Japan 38°0N 140°37E 220 F10
Shirol India 16°47N 74°41E 244 F2
Shiroro Res. Nigeria 9°56N 6°54E 263 D6
Shirpur India 21°21N 74°57E 244 D2
Shirshov Ridge Pac. Oc. 58°0N 170°0E 288 B8
Shīrvān Iran 37°30N 57°50E 247 B8
Shirwa, L. = Chilwa, L. Malawi 15°15S 35°40E 269 F4
Shishaldin Volcano U.S.A. 54°45N 163°58W 303 J7
Shishi China 24°44N 118°37E 229 E12
Shishmaref U.S.A. 66°15N 166°4W 303 C6
Shishou China 29°38N 112°22E 229 C9
Shisur Oman 18°15N 53°39E 249 C6
Shitai China 30°12N 117°25E 229 B11
Shitata South Sudan 4°30N 30°10E 257 G3
Shitennoji Temple Japan 34°39N 135°31E 133 B2
Shithāthah Iraq 32°34N 43°28E 213 G10
Shivamogga India 13°57N 75°32E 245 H2
Shively U.S.A. 38°12N 85°49W 311 F11
Shivpuri India 25°26N 77°42E 242 G7
Shiweitang China 23°6N 113°12E 121 B2
Shixian China 43°5N 129°50E 227 C15
Shixing China 24°46N 114°5E 229 E10
Shiyan Guangdong, China 22°42N 113°56E 219 a
Shiyan Hubei, China 32°35N 110°45E 229 A8
Shiyan Shuiku China 22°42N 113°54E 219 a
Shiyata Egypt 29°25N 25°7E 256 B2
Shizhu China 29°58N 108°7E 228 C7
Shizong China 24°50N 104°0E 228 E5
Shizuishan China 39°15N 106°50E 226 E4
Shizuoka Japan 34°57N 138°24E 223 C10
Shizuoka □ Japan 35°15N 138°40E 223 C10
Shkhara Georgia 43°0N 43°8E 213 A10
Shklov = Shklow Belarus 54°16N 30°15E 177 A16
Shklow Belarus 54°16N 30°15E 177 A16
Shkodër Albania 42°4N 19°32E 202 D3
Shkodra = Shkodër Albania 42°4N 19°32E 202 D3
Shkumbini → Albania 41°2N 19°31E 202 E3
Shmidta, Ostrov Russia 81°0N 91°0E 215 A10
Shō-Gawa → Japan 36°47N 137°4E 223 A9
Shoal Cr. → U.S.A. 39°44N 93°32W 310 E3
Shoal L. Canada 49°33N 95°1W 297 D9
Shoal Lake Canada 50°30N 100°35W 297 C8
Shoalhaven → Australia 34°54S 150°42E 283 C9
Shoals U.S.A. 38°40N 86°47W 311 F10
Shōbara Japan 34°51N 133°1E 222 C5
Shōdo-Shima Japan 34°30N 134°15E 222 C6
Shogunle Nigeria 6°34N 3°20E 124 A2
Sholapur = Solapur India 17°43N 75°56E 244 F2
Shomolu Nigeria 6°32N 3°22E 124 A2
Shōmrōn West Bank 32°15N 35°13E 251 F6
Shonian Harb. Palau 7°10N 134°23E 288 c
Shonzhy Kazakhstan 43°32N 79°28E 217 D9
Shooters Hill U.K. 51°28N 0°4E 125 B4
Shoranur India 10°46N 76°19E 245 J3
Shorapur India 16°31N 76°48E 245 F3
Sho'rchi Uzbekistan 37°59N 67°47E 240 A2
Shoreditch London, U.K. 125 a5
Shoreham U.S.A. 43°53N 73°18W 313 C11
Shoreham-by-Sea U.K. 50°50N 0°16W 169 G7
Shorewood U.S.A. 43°5N 87°53W 311 A9
Shori → Pakistan 28°29N 69°44E 242 E3
Shorkot Pakistan 30°50N 72°0E 242 D4
Shorkot Road Pakistan 30°47N 72°15E 242 D5
Shorsky △ Russia 52°40N 88°0E 217 B11
Shorter U.S.A. 32°24N 85°57W 316 C4
Shorterville U.S.A. 31°34N 85°6W 316 D4
Shortland I. Solomon Is. 7°0S 155°45E 287 L8
Shortland Is. Solomon Is. 7°0S 156°0E 287 L8
Shortlands U.K. 51°23N 0°1E 125 B4
Shortt's I. India 20°47N 87°4E 244 D8
Shoshone Calif., U.S.A. 35°58N 116°16W 307 K10
Shoshone Idaho, U.S.A. 42°56N 114°25W 304 E6
Shoshone L. U.S.A. 44°22N 110°43W 304 D8
Shoshone Mts. U.S.A. 39°20N 117°25W 304 G5
Shoshong Botswana 22°56S 26°31E 270 B4
Shoshoni U.S.A. 43°14N 108°7W 304 E9
Shostka Ukraine 51°57N 33°32E 189 G7
Shotor Khūn Afghan. 34°19N 64°56E 240 B2
Shotover → N.Z. 44°59S 168°41E 285 E3
Shou Xian China 32°37N 116°42E 229 A11
Shouchang China 29°18N 119°12E 229 C12
Shouchia Taiwan 22°15N 120°50E 225 D2
Shoufeng Taiwan 23°52N 121°30E 225 C3
Shouguang China 37°52N 118°45E 227 F10
Shouning China 27°27N 119°31E 229 D12
Shouyang China 37°54N 113°8E 226 F7
Show Low U.S.A. 34°15N 110°2W 305 J8
Showa Japan 35°36N 139°29E 223 B10
Showak Sudan 14°23N 35°52E 257 E4
Showt Iran 39°12N 44°49E 213 C11
Shpola Ukraine 49°1N 31°30E 189 H6
Shpykiv Ukraine 48°47N 28°34E 183 B13
Shqipëria = Albania ■ Europe 41°0N 20°0E 202 E4
Shreveport U.S.A. 32°31N 93°45W 314 E8
Shrewsbury U.K. 52°43N 2°45W 169 E5
Shri Mohangarh India 27°17N 71°18E 242 F4
Shrigonda India 18°37N 74°41E 244 E2
Shrirampur India 22°44N 88°21E 243 H13
Shropshire □ U.K. 52°36N 2°45W 169 E5
Shtërpcë Kosovo 42°14N 21°1E 202 D5
Shū Kazakhstan 43°36N 73°42E 217 D8
Shū → Kazakhstan 45°0N 67°44E 217 D7
Shu'afat West Bank 31°49N 35°14E 123 B2
Shuangbai China 24°42N 101°38E 228 E3
Shuangcheng China 45°20N 126°15E 227 B14
Shuangfeng China 27°29N 112°11E 229 D9
Shuanggou China 34°2N 117°30E 227 G9
Shuangjiang China 23°26N 99°58E 228 F2
Shuangliao China 43°29N 123°30E 227 C12
Shuangshanzi China 40°20N 119°8E 227 D10
Shuangyang China 43°28N 125°40E 227 C13
Shuangyashan China 46°28N 131°5E 219 B15
Shu'b, Ra's Yemen 12°30N 53°25E 249 D6
Shubarqudyq Kazakhstan 49°13N 56°34E 216 C5
Shubarshi Kazakhstan 48°39N 57°11E 216 C5
Shubrâ Egypt 30°5N 31°14E 117 A2
Shubrâ el Kheima Egypt 30°4N 31°14E 117 A2
Shubrâ Khit Egypt 31°2N 30°42E 256 H7
Shucheng China 31°28N 116°57E 229 B11
Shugozero Russia 59°54N 34°10E 188 C8
Shuguri Falls Tanzania 8°33S 37°22E 269 D4
Shuhayr Yemen 14°41N 49°23E 249 D5
Shui Hau Hong Kong, China 22°13N 113°55E 122 B1
Shuiding = Huocheng China 44°0N 80°48E 217 D10
Shuiji China 27°13N 118°20E 229 D12
Shuikou China 23°10N 113°2E 121 A2
Shuili Taiwan 23°49N 120°51E 225 C3
Shuilien Taiwan 23°47N 121°34E 225 C3
Shuishang Taiwan 23°25N 120°23E 225 C2
Shuitiliao Taiwan 22°23N 120°35E 225 D2
Shujalpur India 23°18N 76°46E 242 H7
Shukpa Kunzang India 34°22N 78°22E 243 B8
Shulan China 44°28N 127°0E 227 B14
Shulaveri Georgia 41°22N 44°45E 191 K7
Shule China 39°25N 76°3E 217 E9
Shule He → China 40°20N 92°50E 218 C7
Shullsburg U.S.A. 42°35N 90°13W 310 B6
Shumagin Is. U.S.A. 55°7N 160°30W 303 J7
Shumanay Uzbekistan 42°38N 58°55E 216 D5
Shumen Bulgaria 43°18N 26°55E 203 C10
Shumerlya Russia 55°30N 46°25E 190 C8
Shumikha Russia 55°10N 63°15E 214 D7
Shûna, W. el → Egypt 29°38N 32°6E 251 J3
Shunān Japan 34°3N 131°50E 222 C3
Shunchang China 26°54N 117°48E 229 D11
Shunde China 22°42N 113°14E 229 F9
Shungay Kazakhstan 48°30N 46°45E 191 F8
Shungnak U.S.A. 66°52N 157°9W 303 C8
Shuo Xian = Shuozhou China 39°20N 112°33E 226 E7
Shuozhou China 39°20N 112°33E 226 E7
Shuqrā' Yemen 13°22N 45°44E 248 D4
Shūr → Fārs, Iran 28°30N 55°0E 247 D7
Shūr → Kermān, Iran 30°52N 57°37E 247 D8
Shūr → Yazd, Iran 31°45N 55°15E 247 D7
Shūr Āb Iran 34°23N 51°11E 247 C6
Shūr Gaz Iran 29°10N 59°20E 247 D8
Shūrāb Iran 33°43N 56°29E 247 C8
Shuri Japan 26°13N 127°43E 288 a
Shūrjestān Iran 31°24N 52°25E 247 D7
Shurkhua Burma 22°15N 93°38E 241 D4
Shurugwi Zimbabwe 19°40S 30°0E 269 F3
Shūsf Iran 31°50N 60°5E 247 D9
Shūsh Iran 32°11N 48°15E 213 F13
Shushenskoye Russia 53°19N 91°56E 217 B12
Shushensky Bor △ Russia 52°40N 91°15E 217 B12
Shūshtar Iran 32°0N 48°50E 247 C6
Shuswap L. Canada 50°55N 119°3W 296 C5
Shute Harbour △ Australia 20°17S 148°47E 280 b
Shuya Russia 56°50N 41°28E 190 B5
Shuyak I. U.S.A. 58°31N 152°30W 303 G9
Shuyang China 34°10N 118°42E 227 G10
Shuzenji = Izu Japan 34°58N 138°56E 223 C10
Shūzū Iran 29°52N 54°30E 247 D7
Shwangliao = Liaoyuan China 42°58N 125°2E 227 C13
Shwebo Burma 22°30N 95°45E 241 D5
Shwegu Burma 24°15N 96°26E 241 C6
Shwegun Burma 17°9N 97°39E 241 G6
Shwegyin Burma 17°55N 96°53E 241 G6
Shweli → Burma 23°45N 96°45E 241 D6
Shwenyaung Burma 20°46N 96°57E 241 E6
Shyamnagar India 13°21N 92°57E 245 H11
Shyghanaq Kazakhstan 45°6N 73°59E 217 C8
Shyghys Qazaqstan □ Kazakhstan 48°30N 82°0E 217 D10
Shymkent Kazakhstan 42°18N 69°36E 217 D7
Shyok India 34°13N 78°12E 243 B8
Shyok → Pakistan 35°13N 75°53E 243 B6
Shyroke Odesa, Ukraine 45°59N 30°5E 183 E15
Shyroke Ternopil, Ukraine 48°13N 23°6E 182 B8
Si Kiang = Xi Jiang → China 22°5N 113°20E 229 F9
Si Lanna △ Thailand 19°17N 99°12E 236 C2
Si Nakarin Res. Thailand 14°35N 99°0E 236 E2
Si-ngan = Xi'an China 34°15N 109°0E 226 G5
Si Phangnga Thailand 9°8N 98°29E 237 H2
Si Prachan Thailand 14°37N 100°9E 236 E3
Si Racha Thailand 13°10N 100°48E 236 F3
Si Sa Ket Thailand 15°8N 104°23E 236 E5
Siachen Glacier Asia 35°20N 77°30E 243 B7
Siah Cheshmeh Iran 39°3N 44°25E 213 C11
Siahaf → Pakistan 29°3N 68°57E 242 E3
Siahan Range Pakistan 27°30N 64°40E 240 D2
Siak → Indonesia 1°13N 102°9E 234 B2
Siak Sri Indrapura Indonesia 0°51N 102°0E 234 B2

Sialkot Pakistan 32°32N 74°30E 242 C6
Sialum Papua N. G. 6°5S 147°36E 286 D4
Siam = Thailand ■ Asia 16°0N 102°0E 236 E4
Sian = Xi'an China 34°15N 109°0E 226 G5
Sian Ka'an → Mexico 19°35N 87°40W 319 D7
Siangtan = Xiangtan
  China 27°51N 112°54E 229 D9
Sianów Poland 54°13N 16°18E 184 D3
Siantan Indonesia 3°10N 106°15E 234 B3
Siaolanyu = Hsiaohungt'ou Hsü
  Taiwan 21°57N 121°36E 225 E3
Siäpo → Venezuela 7°N 66°28W 328 C4
Siäreh Iran 28°5N 60°14E 247 D9
Siargao I. Phil. 9°52N 126°3E 233 G6
Siasi Phil. 5°34N 120°50E 233 J3
Siasi I. Phil. 5°33N 120°51E 233 J3
Siassi Papua N. G. 5°40S 147°51E 286 C4
Siatista Greece 40°15N 21°33E 202 F5
Siaton Phil. 9°4N 123°2E 233 G4
Siau Indonesia 2°50N 125°25E 231 D7
Šiauliai Lithuania 55°56N 23°15E 184 C10
Šiauliai □ Lithuania 55°56N 23°19E 184 C10
Siavonga Zambia 16°33S 28°42E 271 A4
Siaya Kenya 0°4N 34°17E 268 B3
Siazan' = Siyäzän
  Azerbaijan 41°3N 49°10E 191 K9
Sîbâi, Gebel el Egypt 25°45N 34°10E 246 B2
Sibang Gabon 0°25N 9°31E 264 B1
Sibang Bali. Indonesia 8°34S 115°13E 231 K18
Sibay Russia 52°42N 58°39E 186 D10
Sibay I. Phil. 11°51N 121°29E 233 E4
Sibayi, L. S. Africa 27°20S 32°45E 271 C5
Sibdu Sudan 10°57N 26°17E 257 E2
Šibenik Croatia 43°48N 15°54E 199 E12
Siberia = Sibirskiy □
  Russia 58°0N 90°0E 215 C10
Siberia Russia 60°0N 100°0E 210 B12
Siberië Curaçao 12°14N 69°9W 322 q
Siberut Indonesia 1°30S 99°0E 234 C1
Sierra de Bahoruco △
  Dom. Rep. 18°10N 71°25W 321 C5
Sierra de Baza △ Spain 37°20N 2°48W 197 H2
Sierra de Castril △ Spain 37°54N 2°50W 197 H2
Sierra de España △ Spain 37°50N 1°31W 197 H3
Silet Algeria 22°44N 4°37E 261 D5
Siletitengiz Köli
  Kazakhstan 53°20N 73°10E 217 B8
Silgarhi Doti Nepal 29°15N 81°0E 243 E9
Silghat India 26°35N 93°0E 241 B4
Silhouette Seychelles 4°29S 55°12E 272 c
Sili Burkina Faso 11°37N 2°30W 262 C4
Siliana Tunisia 36°5N 9°22E 261 A6
Siliana □ Tunisia 36°0N 9°20E 261 A6
Silicon Valley = Santa Clara Valley
  U.S.A. 36°50N 121°30W 306 J5
Silifke Turkey 36°22N 33°58E 250 B4
Siliguri = Shiliguri India 26°45N 88°25E 241 B2
Silili Somalia 11°0N 43°0E 267 B5
Siling Co China 31°50N 89°20E 218 G6
Silistra Bulgaria 44°6N 27°19E 203 B11
Silistra □ Bulgaria 44°6N 27°19E 203 B11
Silivri Turkey 41°4N 28°14E 203 E12
Siljan Telemark, Norway 59°18N 9°45E 164 C4
Siljan Sweden 60°55N 14°45E 162 D8
Siljansnäs Sweden 60°47N 14°52E 162 D8
Silkeborg Denmark 56°10N 9°32E 163 H3
Silkwood Australia 17°45S 146°2E 280 B4
Sillajhuay, Cordillera
  Chile 19°46S 68°40W 330 D4
Sillamäe Estonia 59°24N 27°45E 188 C4
Sillé-le-Guillaume France 48°10N 0°8W 172 D6
Silleda Spain 42°42N 8°14W 194 C2
Sillim S. Korea 37°28N 126°56E 137 C1
Sillod India 20°18N 75°39E 244 D2
Silloth U.K. 54°52N 3°23W 168 C4
Sillustani Peru 15°50S 70°7W 330 D3
Siloam Springs U.S.A. 36°11N 94°32W 314 C7
Silopi Turkey 37°15N 42°27E 213 D10
Siltou Chad 16°46N 15°33E 259 E3
Siluko Nigeria 6°35N 5°10E 263 D6
Siluö = Hsilo Taiwan 23°48N 120°27E 225 C2
Šilute Lithuania 55°21N 21°33E 184 C8
Silva Porto = Kuito
  Angola 12°22S 16°55E 265 E3
Silvan Turkey 38°7N 41°2E 213 C9
Silvani India 23°18N 78°25E 243 H8
Silvassa India 20°16N 73°1E 244 D1
Silver, L. U.S.A. 28°35N 81°23W 133 A2
Silver Bank W. Indies 20°30N 69°45W 321 B6
Silver Bank Passage
  W. Indies 20°0N 70°0W 321 B5
Silver City U.S.A. 32°46N 108°17W 305 K9
Silver Cr. → U.S.A. 43°16N 119°13W 304 E4
Silver Creek U.S.A. 42°33N 79°10W 312 D5
Silver Grove U.S.A. 39°2N 84°23W 311 L12
Silver Hill Montserrat 16°49N 62°11W 323 p
Silver Hill Md., U.S.A. 38°49N 76°55W 143 B3
Silver L. → U.S.A. 38°39N 120°6W 306 G6
Silver Lake Calif., U.S.A. 34°5N 118°15W 307 K9
Silver Lake Calif., U.S.A. 35°21N 116°7W 307 K10
Silver Lake Ind., U.S.A. 41°4N 85°53W 311 C11
Silver Lake Oreg., U.S.A. 43°8N 121°3W 304 E3
Silver Lake Wis., U.S.A. 42°33N 88°13W 311 B8
Silver Mine B.
  Hong Kong, China 22°16N 114°0E 122 B2
Silver Spring U.S.A. 38°59N 77°2W 143 A2
Silver Springs U.S.A. 29°13N 82°3W 317 F2
Silverdalen Sweden 57°32N 15°45E 163 G9
Silvermine Mts. Ireland 52°47N 8°15W 166 D3
Silvermine Nature Reserve
  S. Africa 34°6S 18°27E 118 B1
Silverstrand
  Hong Kong, China 22°19N 114°16E 122 B3
Silverton N.S.W.,
  Australia 31°52S 141°10E 282 A4
Silverton Colo., U.S.A. 37°49N 107°40W 305 H10
Silverton Tex., U.S.A. 34°28N 101°19W 314 D4
Silves Brazil 2°54S 58°27W 329 D6
Silves Portugal 37°11N 8°26W 195 H2
Silvi Marina Italy 42°34N 14°6E 199 F11
Silvia Colombia 2°37N 76°21W 328 C2
Silvies → U.S.A. 43°34N 119°2W 304 E4
Silvolantekojärvi Finland 60°17N 24°54E 121 B2
Silvretta-horn Switz. 46°50N 10°6E 179 C9
Silwa Bahari Egypt 24°45N 32°55E 256 C3
Silz Austria 47°16N 10°56E 180 D3
Sim, C. Morocco 31°26N 9°51W 260 B3
Simaltala India 24°43N 86°33E 243 G12
Simaluguri India 26°55N 94°46E 241 B5
Sim'än, J_ Syria 36°35N 36°53E 250 B7
Simanggang = Bandar Sri Aman
  Malaysia 1°15N 111°32E 235 B4
Simao China 22°47N 101°5E 228 F3
Simão Dias Brazil 10°44S 37°49W 332 D4
Simara I. Phil. 12°48N 122°3E 232 E4
Simard, L. Canada 47°40N 78°40W 298 C4
Simav Turkey 39°4N 28°58E 205 B10
Simav → Turkey 40°23N 28°31E 203 F12
Simba Tanzania 2°10S 37°36E 268 C4
Simbach Germany 48°16N 13°3E 179 G9
Simberi I. Papua N. G. 2°38S 152°0E 286 B7
Simbirsk = Ulyanovsk
  Russia 54°20N 48°25E 190 C9
Simbo Solomon Is. 8°16S 156°33E 287 M9
Simbo Tanzania 4°51S 29°41E 268 C2
Simcoe Canada 42°50N 80°20W 312 D4
Simcoe, L. Canada 44°25N 79°20W 312 B5
Simdega India 22°37N 84°31E 243 H11
Simeli Israel 31°35N 34°53E 250 D3
Simeni Portugal 27°50N 8°30W 260 C3
Simeto → Italy 37°24N 15°6E 201 E8
Simeulue Indonesia 2°45N 95°45E 234 B1
Simeto → Italy 37°24N 15°6E 201 E8
Simferopol Ukraine 44°55N 34°3E 189 K8
Simi Greece 36°35N 27°50E 207 D8
Simi Valley U.S.A. 34°16N 118°47W 307 L8
Simikot Nepal 30°0N 81°50E 243 E9
Simila Colombia 7°58N 73°57W 328 B3
Similaun Austria 46°47N 10°52E 180 C4
Similkameen → Canada 49°17N 119°38W 296 D5

Silacayoapan Mexico 17°30N 98°9W 319 D5
Šilalė Lithuania 55°28N 22°12E 184 C9
Silampur India 28°39N 77°16E 120 B2
Silandro Italy 46°38N 10°46E 198 B7
Silawad India 21°54N 74°54E 242 J6
Silay Phil. 10°47N 122°58E 233 F4
Silba Croatia 44°24N 14°41E 199 D11
Silchar India 24°49N 92°48E 241 C4
Silda Norway 62°5S 5°0E 164 B2
Şile Turkey 41°10N 29°37E 203 E13
Silent Valley △ India 11°10N 76°20E 245 J3
Siler City U.S.A. 35°44N 79°28W 315 D15
Sileru → India 17°49N 81°24E 244 F5
Silet Algeria 22°44N 4°37E 261 D5
Silagnahi = Tsonri Georgia 41°40N 45°57E 191 K7
Signal de Botrang Belgium 50°29N 6°4E 170 D6
Signal Hill S. Africa 34°5S 18°24E 118 A1
Signal Pk. U.S.A. 33°20N 114°2W 307 M12
Signy I. Antarctica 60°43S 45°36W 151 C18
Signy-l'Abbaye France 49°40N 4°25E 173 C11
Sigournay U.S.A. 41°20N 92°12W 310 C4
Sigsbee U.S.A. 31°16N 83°52W 316 B3
Sigsbee Deep Gulf of Mexico 25°0N 92°0W 152 D1
Sigsig Ecuador 3°0S 78°50W 328 D2
Sigtuna Sweden 59°37N 17°44E 162 E11
Sigüenza Spain 41°3N 2°40W 196 D2
Siguiri Guinea 11°31N 9°10W 262 C3
Sigulda Latvia 57°10N 24°55E 184 B4
Siguniangshan China 31°15N 103°10E 228 B4
Sihanoukville = Kampong Saom
  Cambodia 10°38N 103°30E 237 G4
Sihawa Indonesia 20°19N 81°55E 244 D1
Siheung S. Korea 37°28N 126°54E 137 C1
Sihong China 33°27N 118°18E 227 H10
Sihora India 23°29N 80°6E 243 H9
Sihu = Ssuhu Taiwan 23°38N 120°13E 225 C2
Sihuas Peru 8°40S 77°40W 330 B2
Sihui China 23°20N 112°40E 229 F9
Siikajoki → Finland 64°50N 24°43E 160 D21
Siilinjärvi Finland 63°4N 27°39E 160 E22
Siirt Turkey 37°57N 41°55E 213 D9
Siirt □ Turkey 37°50N 42°0E 213 D9
Sijarira Ra. = Chizarira Ra.
  Zimbabwe 17°36S 27°45E 269 F2
Sijunjung Indonesia 0°42S 100°58E 234 C2
Sikanni Chief → Canada 57°47N 122°15W 296 B4
Sikao Thailand 7°34N 99°21E 237 J2
Sikar India 27°33N 75°10E 242 F6
Sikasso Mali 11°18N 5°35W 262 C3
Sikasso □ Mali 10°55N 5°35W 262 C3
Sikátorpuszta Hungary 47°44N 19°37E 145 H7
Sikelenge Zambia 14°53S 24°14E 265 E4
Sikeston U.S.A. 36°53N 89°35W 308 G9
Sikhote Alin, Khrebet
  Russia 45°0N 136°0E 220 B8
Sikhote Alin Ra. = Sikhote Alin,
  Khrebet Russia 45°0N 136°0E 220 B8
Sikia Greece 40°3N 23°56E 202 F7
Sikinos Greece 36°40N 25°8E 207 D6
Sikkim □ India 27°50N 88°30E 241 B2
Siklós Hungary 45°50N 18°19E 145 H4
Sil → Spain 42°27N 7°43W 194 C3
Sila □ Chad 12°0N 21°0E 259 F4

Simlipal △ India 21°45N 86°30E 243 J12
Simmering Austria 48°10N 16°24E 142 A2
Simmering Heide Austria 48°10N 16°26E 142 A2
Simmern Germany 49°58N 7°30E 179 F3
Simmie Canada 49°56N 108°6W 297 D7
Simmler U.S.A. 35°21N 119°59W 307 K7
Simnas Lithuania 54°24N 23°39E 184 D10
Simo → Xining China 36°34N 101°40E 218 D9
Sining = Xining China 36°34N 101°40E 218 D9
Sinis Italy 38°55N 8°25E 200 C1
Siniscóla Italy 40°34N 9°41E 200 B2
Sinj Croatia 43°42N 16°39E 199 E13
Sinjai Indonesia 5°7S 120°20E 231 E6
Sinjajevina Montenegro 42°57N 19°22E 202 D3
Sinjär, Jabal Iraq 36°19N 41°52E 213 D9
Sinjär Syria 35°35N 37°0E 250 C8
Sinjär, Jabal Iraq 36°23N 41°47E 213 D9
Sinkat Sudan 18°55N 36°49E 256 C4
Sinki, Selat Singapore 1°15N 103°37E 121 B3
Sinkiang = Xinjiang Uygur
  Zizhiqu □ China 42°0N 86°0E 217 D11
Sinko Guinea 8°53N 8°16W 262 D3
Sinlumkaba Burma 24°16N 97°31E 241 C6
Sinmak N. Korea 38°25N 126°14E 224 C3
Sinmi-do N. Korea 39°33N 124°53E 224 C6
Sinnai Italy 39°18N 9°13E 200 C2
Sinnar India 19°48N 74°0E 244 E1
Sinni → Italy 40°8N 16°41E 201 B9
Sinnuris Egypt 29°26N 30°31E 256 A7
Sinoie, Lacul Romania 44°35N 28°50E 183 F13
Sinop Turkey 42°1N 35°11E 212 A6
Sinop □ Turkey 42°0N 35°0E 212 B6
Sinor India 21°55N 73°20E 242 J5
Sin'p'o N. Korea 40°0N 128°13E 224 C4
Sinsa S. Korea 37°31N 127°0E 137 B2
Sinsang N. Korea 39°38N 127°24E 224 C3
Sinsheim Germany 49°15N 8°52E 179 F4
Sinsiang = Xinxiang
  China 35°18N 113°50E 226 G7
Sinsk Russia 61°8N 126°48E 215 C13
Sint Annabaai Curaçao 12°6N 68°56W 322 a
Sint Christoffelberg Curaçao 12°20N 69°8W 322 a
Sint-Genesius-Rode
  Belgium 50°45N 4°22E 116 B2
Sint-Hubert Belgium 50°2N 5°23E 170 D5
Sint Jorisbaai Curaçao 12°7N 68°48W 322 a
Sint Marie, C. Curaçao 12°7N 69°3W 322 a
Sint Marthabaai Curaçao 12°17N 69°9W 322 a
Sint Michiel Curaçao 12°8N 69°0W 322 a
Sint Nicolaas Aruba 12°27N 69°54W 322 f
Sint Nicolaas Curaçao 12°17N 69°8W 322 a
Sint-Niklaas Belgium 51°10N 4°8E 170 C4
Sint-Truiden Belgium 50°48N 5°10E 170 D5
Sint Willibrordus Curaçao 12°14N 69°8W 322 g
Sintang Indonesia 0°5N 111°35E 235 B4
Sinton U.S.A. 28°2N 97°31W 314 G6
Sintra Portugal 38°47N 9°25W 195 G1
Sintra-Cascais △ Portugal 38°50N 9°25W 195 G1
Sinŭiju N. Korea 40°5N 124°24E 224 C6
Sinujif Somalia 8°33N 48°59E 267 C6
Sinyukha → Ukraine 48°3N 30°51E 189 H6
Sinzig Germany 50°32N 7°14E 178 E3
Sio → Hungary 46°20N 18°53E 182 E4
Siocon Phil. 7°40N 122°10E 233 H4
Siófok Hungary 46°54N 18°3E 182 D3
Sioma Zambia 16°40S 23°32E 265 F4
Sioma Ngwezi △ Zambia 17°14S 23°26E 265 F4
Sion Maharashtra, India 19°3N 72°52E 130 A2
Sion Switz. 46°14N 7°20E 179 C3
Sion Mills U.K. 54°48N 7°29W 166 B4
tSionainn, An = Shannon →
  Ireland 52°35N 9°30W 166 D2
Sioux Center U.S.A. 43°5N 96°11W 308 D5
Sioux City U.S.A. 42°30N 96°24W 308 D5
Sioux Falls U.S.A. 43°33N 96°44W 308 D5
Sioux Lookout Canada 50°10N 91°50W 298 B1
Sioux Narrows Canada 49°25N 94°10W 297 D10
Sipadan Malaysia 4°6N 118°38E 235 B5
Sipalay Phil. 9°45N 122°24E 233 G4
Šipan Croatia 42°43N 17°52E 202 D1
Sipang, Tanjong Malaysia 1°48N 110°20E 235 B4
Siparia Trin. & Tob. 10°8N 61°31W 323 t
Siparia △ Trin. & Tob. 10°9N 61°28W 323 t
Sipil Daği △ Turkey 38°38N 27°30E 205 C9
Sipiwesk L. Canada 55°5N 97°35W 297 B9
Siple I. Antarctica 73°40S 125°10W 151 D14
Sipocot Phil. 13°46N 122°58E 232 E4
Sipovo Bos.-H. 44°16N 17°6E 182 F2
Sippra → U.K. 51°29N 0°26W 125 B1
Sipsongpanna = Xishuangbanna
  China 22°5N 101°1E 228 F3
Sipul Papua N. G. 5°50S 151°15E 286 C6
Sipura Indonesia 2°18S 99°40E 234 C1
Sipura, Selat Indonesia 2°27S 99°54E 234 C1
Siqeil Egypt 30°7N 31°10E 117 A1
Siqirah Yemen 12°35N 54°20E 249 D6
Siqueira Campos Brazil 23°42S 49°50W 333 F2
Siquia → Nic. 12°30N 84°30E 320 D3
Siquijor Phil. 9°12N 123°35E 233 G4
Siquirres Costa Rica 10°6N 83°30W 320 D3
Siquisique Venezuela 10°34N 69°42W 328 A4
Sir Abu Nu'ayr U.A.E. 25°15N 54°18E 247 E7
Sir Edward Pellew Group
  Australia 15°40S 137°10E 280 B2
Sir Graham Moore Is.
  Australia 13°53S 126°34E 278 B4
Sir James MacBrien, Mt.
  Canada 62°7N 127°41W 294 E6
Sira Vest-Agder, Norway 58°24N 6°40E 164 F3
Sira → Norway 58°23N 6°34E 164 F3
Siracusa Italy 37°4N 15°17E 201 D8
Sirajganj Bangla. 24°25N 89°47E 241 C2
Sirakoro Mali 12°41N 9°14W 262 C3
Sīrān Turkey 40°11N 39°7E 213 B8
Sirasso Ivory C. 9°16N 6°6W 262 D3
Sirathu India 25°39N 81°19E 243 G9
Siraway Phil. 7°34N 122°3E 233 H4
Sirdaryakara Norway 36°9N 6°43E 164 F3
Sīrdān Iran 36°39N 49°12E 246 B6
Sīrdaryo □ Uzbekistan 40°30N 68°45E 217 D7
Sire Ethiopia 8°43N 37°8E 257 F4
Siren U.S.A. 45°47N 92°24W 308 C7
Sirente-Velino △ Italy 42°10N 13°12E 199 F10
Siret Romania 47°55N 26°5E 183 C11
Siret → Romania 45°24N 28°1E 183 F13
Siret Spain 38°56N 1°22E 196 G6
Sirevåg Norway 58°30N 5°48E 164 F2
Sirghāyā Syria 33°51N 36°8E 250 B7
Siria Romania 46°16N 21°38E 182 D6
Sirik Malaysia 2°40N 111°38E 235 B4
Sirik, Tanjung Malaysia 2°40N 111°38E 235 B4
Sirino, Monte Italy 40°7N 15°50E 201 B8
Sirjan Iran 29°30N 55°45E 247 D7
Sīrkali = Sirkazhi India 11°15N 79°41E 245 J4
Sirkazhi India 11°15N 79°41E 245 J4
Sirmaur India 24°51N 81°23E 243 G9
Sirmilik △ Canada 72°50N 80°35W 295 B11
Sirmione Italy 45°30N 10°36E 198 C7
Sirmur India 24°52N 77°39E 242 G7
Siros = Ermoupoli Greece 37°28N 24°57E 204 D6
Siroz = Serres Greece 41°5N 23°31E 202 E7
Sirpur India 19°29N 79°36E 244 E4
Sirr, Nafud as S. Arabia 25°33N 44°35E 246 E5
Sirrayn Si. Arabia 19°38N 40°36E 248 C3
Sirretta Pk. U.S.A. 35°56N 118°19W 307 K8
Sîrrî Iran 25°55N 54°32E 247 E7
Sirsa India 29°33N 75°4E 242 E6
Sirsa → India 26°51N 79°4E 243 F8
Sirsa = India 14°40N 74°49E 245 G2
Sirsilla India 18°23N 78°50E 244 E4
Sirte = Surt Libya 31°11N 16°39E 258 B3
Siruela Spain 38°58N 5°3W 195 G5
Siruguppa India 15°38N 76°54E 245 F3
Sirur India 18°50N 74°23E 244 E2
Sirvan Azerbaijan 39°58N 48°52E 191 L9
Şirvan = Iran 37°30N 57°50E 213 E12
Sisak Croatia 45°30N 16°21E 199 C13
Sisante Spain 39°25N 2°12W 197 F2
Sisargas, Is. Spain 43°21N 8°50W 194 B2
Sisco France 42°48N 9°22E 174 B2
Sishui China 35°42N 117°18E 227 G9
Sisian Armenia 39°31N 46°1E 213 C12
Sisiga India 37°54S 159°10E 287 L10
Sisimiut Greenland 66°40N 53°30W 154 D5
Sisipuk L. Canada 55°45N 101°50W 297 B8
Şişli Turkey 41°3N 28°58E 122 B1
Sisophon Cambodia 13°38N 102°59E 236 F4
Sisseton U.S.A. 45°40N 97°3W 308 C5
Sisson = Mount Shasta
  U.S.A. 41°19N 122°19W 304 F2
Sissonne France 49°34N 3°51E 173 C10
Sîstân Asia 30°50N 61°0E 247 D9
Sīstān, Daryācheh-ye Iran 31°0N 61°0E 247 D9
Sīstān va Balūchestān □
  Iran 27°0N 62°0E 247 E9
Sisteron France 44°12N 5°57E 175 D9
Sisters U.S.A. 44°18N 121°33W 304 D3
Sisters, The Grenada 12°18N 61°36W 323 q
Sisters Rocks Trin. & Tob. 7°56S 14°22W 153 g
Sisters Pk. Ascension I. 7°56S 14°22W 153 g
Siswa Bazar India 27°9N 83°46E 243 F10
Sitakili Mali 13°7N 11°14W 262 C2
Sitakunda Bangla. 22°37N 91°39E 241 D3
Sitamarhi India 26°37N 85°30E 243 F11
Sitampiky Madag. 16°41S 46°6E 272 B2
Sitangkai Phil. 4°40N 119°24E 233 J2
Sitapur India 27°38N 80°45E 243 F9
Siteki Swaziland 26°32S 31°58E 271 C5
Sitges Spain 41°17N 1°47E 196 D6
Sithonia Greece 40°0N 23°45E 202 F7
Sitia Greece 35°13N 26°6E 207 E7
Sitio d'Abadia Brazil 14°48S 46°16W 333 D2
Sitito-Ozima Ridge Pac. Oc. 23°0N 143°0E 288 E6
Sitka U.S.A. 57°3N 135°20W 303 H14
Sitka → U.S.A. 57°3N 135°19W 303 H14
Sitkaing = Sagaing
  Burma 21°52N 95°59E 241 G6
Sitkinak I. U.S.A. 56°33N 154°10W 303 H9
Sitoti Botswana 23°15S 23°40E 270 B3
Sitra Egypt 28°40N 26°53E 256 B2
Sittang Myit → Burma 17°20N 96°45E 241 G6
Sittard Neths. 51°0N 5°52E 170 C5
Sittaung Burma 24°10N 94°53E 241 C5
Sittensen Germany 53°17N 9°32E 178 B5
Sittingbourne U.K. 51°21N 0°45E 169 F8
Sittona Eritrea 14°25N 37°23E 257 E4
Sittoung = Sittang Myit →
  Burma 17°20N 96°45E 241 G6
Sittwe Burma 20°18N 92°45E 241 E4
Situbondo Indonesia 7°42S 113°56E 235 D4
Siu Kau Yi Chau
  Hong Kong, China 22°17N 114°3E 122 B2
Siufaalete Pt. Amer. Samoa 14°17S 169°29W 302 f
Siulagi Pt. Amer. Samoa 14°13S 169°30W 302 g
Si'umu Samoa 14°15S 171°48W 287 W20
Siuna Nic. 13°37N 84°45W 320 D3
Siuri India 23°50N 87°34E 243 H12
Sivtghiol, Lacul Romania 44°35N 28°35E 183 F13
Sivagiri India 9°50N 77°26E 245 K3
Sivagiri India 9°16N 77°26E 245 K3
Sivakasi India 9°24N 77°47E 245 K3
Sivand Iran 30°5N 52°55E 247 D7
Sivas Turkey 39°43N 36°58E 212 C7
Sivas □ Turkey 39°45N 37°0E 212 C7
Sivasagar India 27°0N 94°36E 241 B5
Sivasamudram India 12°18N 77°10E 245 H4
Sivash Turkey 38°31N 39°24E 205 C11
Siverek Turkey 37°50N 39°19E 213 D8
Sivomaskinskiy Russia 66°40N 62°35E 186 A11
Sivota Greece 39°24N 20°13E 206 C10
Sivrihisar Turkey 39°30N 31°35E 212 C4
Sivros Greece 38°40N 20°39E 206 C9
Sîwa Egypt 29°11N 25°31E 256 B2
Sîwa, El Wâhât es Egypt 29°10N 25°30E 256 B2
Siwa Oasis = Sîwa, El Wâhât es
  Egypt 29°10N 25°30E 256 B2
Siwalik Range Nepal 28°0N 83°0E 243 F10
Siwan India 26°13N 84°21E 243 F11
Siwana India 25°38N 72°25E 242 G5
Six Cross Roads Barbados 13°7N 59°28W 323 g
Six-Fours-les-Plages France 43°6N 5°49E 175 E9
Sixian China 33°42N 117°50E 227 H9
Sixmilebridge Ireland 52°44N 8°46W 166 D3
Sixth Cataract Sudan 16°20N 32°42E 257 D4
Siyabuswa S. Africa 25°7S 29°3E 271 C4
Siyah Kuh, Kavir-e Iran 32°55N 53°55E 247 C7
Siyâl, Jazâ'ir Egypt 22°49N 36°12E 256 C4
Siyang China 33°42N 118°40E 227 H10
Siyäzän Azerbaijan 41°3N 49°10E 191 K9
Siziwang Qi China 41°25N 111°40E 226 C9
Sjælland Denmark 55°30N 11°30E 163 J5
Sjællands Odde Denmark 55°58N 11°18E 163 J5
Själevad Sweden 63°18N 18°36E 162 A12
Sjelbukta Norway 69°56N 20°54E 161 D12
Sjenica Serbia 43°16N 20°0E 202 C3
Sjeverni Velebit △
  Croatia 44°30N 15°15E 199 D12
Sjöbo Sweden 55°37N 13°45E 163 J7
Sjöholt Norway 62°29N 6°50E 164 B2
Sjælland Norway 67°22N 11°18E 164 D4
Sjötorp Sweden 58°50N 14°0E 163 F7
Sjumen = Shumen
  Bulgaria 43°18N 26°55E 203 C10
Sjuntorp Sweden 58°12N 12°13E 163 F6
Skadarsko Jezero Europe 42°10N 19°20E 202 D3
Skadarsko Jezero △
  Montenegro 42°10N 19°20E 202 D3
Skadovsk Ukraine 46°17N 32°52E 189 J7
Skælskør Denmark 55°15N 11°18E 163 J5
Skærbæk Denmark 55°9N 8°45E 163 J2
Skaftafell Iceland 64°1N 17°0W 155 E5
Skagaffjarðarsýsla Iceland 65°30N 19°30W 155 D4
Skagafjörður Iceland 65°54N 19°35W 155 D4
Skagastølstindane Norway 61°28N 7°52E 164 C3
Skagaströnd Iceland 65°50N 20°19W 155 D3
Skagatá Iceland 66°5N 20°8W 155 D4
Skagen Denmark 57°43N 10°35E 163 G4
Skagern Sweden 59°0N 14°20E 163 F8
Skagerrak Denmark 57°30N 9°0E 163 G3
Skagit → U.S.A. 48°23N 122°22W 306 B4
Skagway U.S.A. 59°28N 135°19W 303 G14
Skala nad Zbruczem = Skala-
  Podilska Ukraine 48°50N 26°15E 183 B11

Skala-Podilska Ukraine 48°50N 26°15E 183 B11
Skalat Ukraine 49°23N 25°55E 177 D13
Skálavík Iceland 66°11N 23°29W 155 A3
Skalbmierz Poland 50°20N 20°25E 185 H7
Skälderviken Sweden 56°22N 12°30E 163 H6
Skålevik Norway 58°5N 8°1E 164 F5
Skalica Slovakia 48°50N 17°15E 181 C10
Skallingen Denmark 55°32N 8°13E 163 J2
Skalni Dol = Kamenyak
  Bulgaria 43°24N 26°57E 203 C10
Skanderborg Denmark 56°2N 9°55E 163 H3
Skåne Sweden 55°59N 13°30E 163 J7
Skåne □ Sweden 56°15N 14°0E 163 H7
Skaneateles U.S.A. 42°57N 76°26W 313 D8
Skaneateles L. U.S.A. 42°51N 76°22W 313 D8
Skånevik Norway 59°43N 5°53E 164 E2
Skänninge Sweden 58°24N 15°5E 163 F9
Skanör med Falsterbo
  Sweden 55°24N 12°50E 163 J6
Skansen Sweden 59°19N 18°7E 139 B2
Skantzoura Greece 39°5N 24°6E 204 B6
Skara Sweden 58°25N 13°30E 163 F7
Skärblacka Sweden 58°35N 15°54E 163 F9
Skarö Iceland 65°17N 22°19W 155 B4
Skardu Pakistan 35°20N 75°44E 243 B6
Skare Hordaland, Norway 59°55N 6°36E 164 E3
Skåre Sweden 59°26N 13°26E 162 E7
Skärhamn Sweden 57°59N 11°34E 163 G5
Skärholmen Sweden 59°16N 17°53E 139 B1
Skarnes Norway 60°15N 11°41E 164 D8
Skärpinge Sweden 59°26N 18°0E 139 A2
Skarpnäck Sweden 59°16N 18°7E 139 B2
Skarszewy Poland 54°4N 18°25E 184 D5
Skarvan og Roltdalen △
  Norway 63°16N 11°31E 160 E14
Skaryszew Poland 51°19N 21°15E 185 G8
Skaryszewski, Park Poland 52°15N 21°3E 143 B2
Skarżysko-Kamienna
  Poland 51°7N 20°52E 185 G7
Skattkärr Sweden 59°25N 13°40E 162 E7
Skattungbyn Sweden 61°10N 14°56E 162 C8
Skawina Poland 49°59N 19°50E 185 J6
Skebobruk Sweden 59°58N 18°36E 162 E12
Skee Sweden 58°56N 11°19E 163 F5
Skeena → Canada 54°9N 130°5W 296 C2
Skeena Mts. Canada 56°40N 128°30W 296 C3
Skegness U.K. 53°9N 0°20E 168 D8
Skei Norway 61°34N 6°28E 164 C3
Skeiðarársandur Iceland 63°54N 17°14W 155 D9
Skeiðflötur Iceland 63°26N 19°11W 155 D7
Skeleton Coast △ Namibia 20°0S 13°20E 270 B1
Skellefteå Sweden 64°45N 20°50E 160 D19
Skellefteälven → Sweden 64°45N 21°10E 160 D19
Skelleftehamn Sweden 64°40N 21°9E 160 D19
Skellig Michael = Great Skellig
  Ireland 51°47N 10°33W 166 E1
Skender Vakuf Bos.-H. 44°29N 17°22E 182 F2
Skënderaj Kosovo 42°45N 20°47E 202 D4
Skeppsholmen Stockholm, Sweden 139 C3
Skerries U.K. 53°35N 6°8W 166 C5
Skerries, The U.K. 53°25N 4°36W 168 D3
Skhidnytsya Ukraine 49°13N 23°20E 185 J10
Ski Norway 59°43N 10°52E 164 E7
Skiathos Greece 39°12N 23°30E 204 B5
Skibbereen Ireland 51°33N 9°16W 166 E2
Skiddaw U.K. 54°39N 3°9W 168 C4
Skidegate Canada 53°15N 132°1W 296 C2
Skidra Greece 40°46N 22°10E 202 F6
Skien Norway 59°12N 9°35E 164 E6
Skierniewice Poland 51°58N 20°10E 185 G7
Skikda Algeria 36°50N 6°58E 261 A6
Skikda □ Algeria 36°45N 6°50E 261 A6
Skillet Fork → U.S.A. 38°5N 88°5W 311 F8
Skillingaryd Sweden 57°27N 14°5E 163 G8
Skillinge Sweden 55°30N 14°16E 163 J8
Skilloura Cyprus 35°14N 33°10E 207 E9
Skinari, Akra Greece 37°56N 20°42E 207 D8
Skinnastaður Iceland 66°4N 16°27W 155 A10
Skinnskatteberg Sweden 59°50N 15°42E 162 E9
Skipton Vic., Australia 37°39S 143°40E 282 D5
Skipton N. Yorks., U.K. 53°58N 2°3W 168 D5
Skiptvet Norway 59°28N 11°11E 164 E8
Skiring, C. Senegal 12°26N 16°46W 262 C1
Skirmish Pt. Australia 11°59S 134°17E 280 A1
Skíros = Skyros Greece 38°55N 24°34E 204 C6
Skivarp Sweden 55°26N 13°34E 163 J7
Skive Denmark 56°33N 9°2E 163 H3
Skjærhalden Norway 59°2N 11°8E 164 E8
Skjálfandafljót → Iceland 65°59N 17°25W 155 A9
Skjálfandi Iceland 66°5N 17°30W 155 A9
Skjeberg Norway 59°12N 11°12E 164 E8
Skjern Denmark 55°57N 8°30E 163 H2
Skjern Å → Denmark 55°55N 8°30E 163 H2
Skjold Norway 59°31N 5°34E 164 E2
Skjolden Norway 61°29N 7°36E 164 C4
Skjöldólfsstaður Iceland 65°19N 15°7W 155 B11
Skjønhaug Norway 59°39N 11°19E 164 E8
Skobelev = Farg'ona
  Uzbekistan 40°23N 71°19E 217 D8
Škocjanske Jame Slovenia 45°40N 14°0E 199 C10
Skoczów Poland 49°49N 18°45E 185 J5
Skodje Norway 62°30N 6°43E 164 B3
Škofja Loka Slovenia 46°9N 14°19E 199 B11
Skógar Iceland 63°32N 19°28W 155 C4
Skógarnes Iceland 64°46N 22°34W 155 C4
Skoghall Sweden 59°20N 13°30E 162 E7
Skogskyrkogården Sweden 59°16N 18°5E 139 B2
Skogstorp Sweden 59°19N 16°29E 162 E10
Skoki Sweden 57°40N 17°11E 185 F4
Skokie U.S.A. 42°2N 87°43W 119 A2
Skokie → U.S.A. 42°3N 87°46W 119 A2
Skokie Heritage Museum
  Chicago, U.S.A. 42°2N 87°44W 119 A2
Skoklefall Norway 59°50N 10°40E 133 A3
Skole Ukraine 49°3N 23°30E 177 D12
Skollenborg Sweden 59°38N 9°43E 164 E6
Sköldinge Sweden 59°15N 16°28E 139 C2
Skopelos Greece 39°9N 23°47E 204 B5
Skopi Greece 35°11N 26°2E 207 E7
Skopin Russia 53°55N 39°32E 188 F10
Skopje Macedonia 42°1N 21°26E 202 E5
Skopje ✈ (SKP) Macedonia 41°59N 21°29E 202 E5
Skoppum Poland 59°23N 10°26E 164 E7
Skórcz Poland 53°47N 18°30E 184 E5
Skørping Denmark 56°50N 9°53E 163 H3
Skotfoss Norway 59°10N 9°30E 164 E6
Skotterud Norway 60°0N 12°7E 164 D8
Skövde Sweden 58°24N 13°50E 163 F7
Skovlunde Denmark 55°44N 12°24E 118 A2
Skovorodino Russia 54°0N 124°0E 215 D13
Skovshoved Denmark 55°45N 12°35E 118 A3
Skowhegan U.S.A. 44°46N 69°43W 309 C19
Skradin Croatia 43°52N 15°53E 199 E12
Skreia Norway 60°39N 10°56E 164 D7
Skrim Norway 59°31N 9°38E 164 E6
Skrunda Latvia 56°41N 22°1E 184 B9
Skrwa → Poland 52°34N 19°43E 185 F6
Skudeneshavn Norway 59°10N 5°10E 164 E2
Skuleskogen △ Sweden 63°6N 18°30E 162 A12
Skull Ireland 51°32N 9°34W 166 E2
Skultorp Sweden 58°24N 13°51E 163 F7
Skultuna Sweden 59°43N 16°25E 162 E10
Skunk → U.S.A. 40°42N 91°7W 310 D5
Skuodas Lithuania 56°16N 21°33E 184 B8
Skuru Sweden 59°18N 18°12E 139 B3
Skurup Sweden 55°28N 13°30E 163 J7
Skutskär Sweden 60°37N 17°25E 162 D11

Skútustaðir Iceland 65°34N 17°2W 155 B9
Skvyra Ukraine 49°44N 29°40E 177 D15
Skwierzyna Poland 52°33N 15°30E 185 F2
Sky Dome = Rogers Centre
  Toronto, Canada 141 c1
Sky Harbour Int., Phoenix ✈ (PHX)
  U.S.A. 33°26N 112°1W 305 K7
Sky Lake U.S.A. 28°27N 81°23W 133 B2
Skye U.K. 57°15N 6°10W 167 D2
Skykomish U.S.A. 47°42N 121°22W 304 C5
Skyring, Seno Chile 52°35S 72°0W 336 D3
Skyropoula Greece 38°50N 24°21E 204 C6
Skyros Greece 38°55N 24°34E 204 C6
Skyttorp Sweden 60°5N 17°44E 162 D11
Slade Green U.K. 51°27N 0°11E 125 B5
Slade Point Australia 21°4S 149°13E 280 b
Slade Pt. Australia 21°5S 149°13E 280 b
Slættaratindur Faroe Is. 62°18N 7°1W 160 E9
Slagelse Denmark 55°23N 11°19E 163 J5
Slamet Indonesia 7°16S 109°8E 235 D3
Slane Ireland 53°42N 6°33W 166 C5
Slaney → Ireland 52°26N 6°33W 166 D5
Slangberge S. Africa 31°32S 20°48E 270 D3
Slánic Romania 45°14N 25°58E 183 E10
Slano Croatia 42°48N 17°53E 202 D1
Slantsy Russia 59°7N 28°5E 188 C5
Slaný Czechia 50°13N 14°6E 180 A7
Śląsk Poland 51°0N 16°30E 176 C9
Śląskie □ Poland 50°30N 19°0E 185 H6
Slätbaken Sweden 58°25N 16°45E 163 F10
Slate Is. Canada 48°40N 87°0W 298 C2
Slater U.S.A. 39°13N 93°4W 310 E3
Slatina Croatia 45°42N 17°45E 182 E2
Slatina Romania 44°28N 24°22E 183 F9
Slatina Timiş Romania 45°15N 22°17E 182 E7
Slatington U.S.A. 40°45N 75°37W 313 F9
Slaton U.S.A. 33°26N 101°39W 314 E4
Slave → Canada 61°18N 113°39W 296 A6
Slave Coast W. Afr. 6°0N 2°30E 263 D5
Slave Lake Canada 55°17N 114°43W 296 B6
Slave Pt. Canada 61°11N 115°56W 296 A5
Slavgorod Russia 53°1N 78°37E 217 B9
Slavinja Serbia 43°9N 22°50E 202 C6
Slavkov u Brna Czechia 49°10N 16°52E 181 B9
Slavkovský Les Czechia 50°5N 12°44E 180 A5
Slavonia Europe 45°20N 17°40E 182 E2
Slavonski Brod Croatia 45°11N 18°1E 182 E3
Slavsk Russia 55°3N 21°41E 184 C8
Slavuta Ukraine 48°51N 23°27E 183 B8
Slavyanka Russia 42°53N 131°21E 220 C5
Slavyanovo Bulgaria 43°28N 24°52E 203 C8
Slavyansk = Slovyansk
  Ukraine 48°55N 37°36E 189 H9
Slavyansk-na-Kubani
  Russia 45°15N 38°11E 189 K10
Sława Poland 51°52N 16°2E 185 G3
Slawharad Belarus 53°27N 31°0E 177 B16
Sławno Poland 54°20N 16°41E 184 D3
Sławoborze Poland 53°55N 15°42E 184 D2
Slea Hd. Ireland 52°6N 10°27W 166 D1
Sleaford U.K. 53°0N 0°24W 168 D7
Sleaford B. Australia 34°55S 135°45E 281 E2
Sleat, Sd. of U.K. 57°5N 5°47W 167 D3
Sleðbrjótur Iceland 65°34N 14°30W 155 B12
Sleeper Is. Canada 58°30N 81°0W 295 F15
Sleeping Bear Dunes △
  U.S.A. 44°50N 86°5W 308 C10
Sleepy Eye U.S.A. 44°18N 94°43W 308 C6
Sleetmute U.S.A. 61°42N 157°10W 303 F8
Slemon L. Canada 63°13N 116°4W 296 A5
Slependen Norway 59°52N 10°30E 133 A2
Šlesin Poland 52°22N 18°14E 185 F5
Slide Mt. U.S.A. 42°0N 74°25W 313 E10
Slidell U.S.A. 30°17N 89°47W 315 F10
Slidre Norway 61°5N 8°58E 164 C5
Sligo Ireland 54°16N 8°28W 166 B3
Sligo U.S.A. 41°6N 79°29W 312 E5
Sligo □ Ireland 54°8N 8°42W 166 B3
Sligo B. Ireland 54°18N 8°40W 166 B3
Sligi Indonesia 6°11S 106°47E 122 B1
Slippery Rock U.S.A. 41°4N 80°3W 312 E4
Slite Sweden 57°42N 18°48E 163 G12
Slīteres Latvia 57°41N 22°21E 184 A9
Sliven Bulgaria 42°42N 26°19E 203 D10
Sliven □ Bulgaria 42°42N 26°19E 203 D10
Slivenec Czechia 50°1N 14°21E 135 B2
Slivnitsa Bulgaria 42°50N 23°2E 202 D7
Sljeme Croatia 45°57N 15°58E 199 C12
Sloan U.S.A. 35°57N 115°13W 307 K11
Sloansville U.S.A. 42°45N 74°22W 313 D10
Slobidka Ukraine 47°54N 29°21E 183 C14
Slobodskoy Russia 58°40N 50°6E 186 C9
Slobozia Moldova 46°45N 29°42E 183 D14
Slobozia Argeş, Romania 44°30N 25°14E 183 F10
Slobozia Ialomiţa,
  Romania 44°34N 27°23E 183 F12
Slocan Canada 49°48N 117°28W 296 D5
Slocomb U.S.A. 31°7N 85°36W 316 D4
Slomikhino = Zhalpaqtal
  Kazakhstan 49°42N 49°25E 190 F9
Słomniki Poland 50°16N 20°4E 185 H7
Slonim Belarus 53°4N 25°19E 177 B13
Slot, The = New Georgia Sound
  Solomon Is. 8°0S 158°0E 287 L9
Sloten Neths. 52°21N 4°48E 112 A1
Sloterdijk Neths. 52°23N 4°51E 112 A1
Sloterpark Neths. 52°22N 4°49E 112 A1
Slottet Oslo, Norway 133 a1
Slough U.K. 51°30N 0°36W 169 F7
Slough □ U.K. 51°30N 0°36W 169 F7
Sloughhouse U.S.A. 38°26N 121°12W 306 G5
Slovak Rep. = Slovakia ■
  Europe 48°30N 20°0E 181 C13
Slovakia ■ Europe 48°30N 20°0E 181 C13
Slovakian Ore Mts. = Slovenské
  Rudohorie Slovakia 48°45N 20°0E 181 C12
Slovenia ■ Europe 45°58N 14°30E 199 C11
Slovenija = Slovenia ■
  Europe 45°58N 14°30E 199 C11
Slovenj Gradec Slovenia 46°31N 15°5E 199 B12
Slovensko = Slovakia ■
  Europe 48°30N 20°0E 181 C13
Slovenska Bistrica
  Slovenia 46°24N 15°28E 199 B12
Slovenské Konjice
  Slovenia 46°20N 15°28E 199 B12
Slovenské Rudohorie
  Slovakia 48°45N 20°0E 181 C12
Slovyansk Ukraine 48°55N 37°36E 189 H9
Słowiński △ Poland 54°35N 17°26E 184 D4
Słubice Poland 52°22N 14°35E 185 F1
Sluch → Ukraine 51°37N 26°38E 177 C14
Sluhy Czechia 50°11N 14°33E 135 A3
Sluis Neths. 51°18N 3°23E 172 C3
Slunchev Bryag Bulgaria 42°40N 27°41E 203 D11
Slunj Croatia 45°6N 15°33E 199 C12

Słupca Poland 52°15N 17°52E 185 F4
Słupia → Poland 54°35N 16°51E 184 D3
Słupsk Poland 54°30N 17°3E 184 D4
Slurry S. Africa 25°49S 25°42E 270 C4
Slutsk = Pavlovsk Russia 50°26N 40°50E 190 E5
Slutsk Belarus 53°2N 27°31E 177 B14
Służew Poland 52°10N 21°1E 143 B2
Służewiec Poland 52°10N 21°0E 143 B2
Slyne Hd. Ireland 53°25N 10°10W 166 C1
Slyudyanka Russia 51°40N 103°40E 215 D11
Smaalenene = Østfold □
  Norway 59°25N 11°25E 164 E8
Småland Sweden 57°15N 15°25E 163 G9
Smålandsfarvandet
  Denmark 55°10N 11°20E 163 J5
Smålandsstenar Sweden 57°10N 13°25E 163 H7
Smaldeel = Theunissen
  S. Africa 28°26S 26°43E 270 C4
Smalltree L. Canada 61°0N 105°0W 297 A8
Smallwood Res. Canada 54°0N 68°0W 299 B7
Smara W. Sahara 26°48N 11°41W 260 C2
Smarhon Belarus 54°20N 26°24E 177 B14
Smarje Slovenia 46°15N 15°34E 199 B12
Smart Syndicate Dam
  S. Africa 30°45S 23°10E 270 D3
Smartville U.S.A. 39°13N 121°18W 306 F5
Smeaton Canada 53°30N 104°49W 297 C8
Smedby Sweden 56°38N 16°7E 163 H10
Smederevo Serbia 44°40N 20°57E 202 B4
Smederevska Palanka
  Serbia 44°22N 20°58E 202 B4
Smedjebacken Sweden 60°8N 15°25E 162 D9
Smela = Smila Ukraine 49°15N 31°58E 189 H6
Smeralda, Costa Italy 41°5N 9°35E 200 A2
Smerwick Harbour
  Ireland 52°12N 10°23W 166 D1
Smethport U.S.A. 41°49N 78°27W 312 E6
Smichov Czechia 50°4N 14°23E 135 B2
Smidovich Russia 48°36N 133°49E 215 E14
Smigiel Poland 52°1N 16°32E 185 F3
Smila Ukraine 49°15N 31°58E 189 H6
Smilyan Bulgaria 41°29N 24°46E 203 E8
Smith Canada 55°10N 114°0W 296 B6
Smith B. U.S.A. 70°30N 154°20W 303 A9
Smith Center U.S.A. 39°47N 98°47W 308 F4
Smith Forest Preserve
  U.S.A. 41°59N 87°45W 119 B2
Smith I. Nunavut, Canada 60°45N 78°25W 295 E16
Smith I. India 13°20N 93°4E 245 H11
Smith Islands △ Australia 20°40S 149°9E 280 b
Smith Sd. N. Amer. 78°25N 74°0W 154 B3
Smithburne → Australia 17°3S 140°57E 280 B3
Smithers Canada 54°45N 127°10W 296 C3
Smithfield Free State,
  S. Africa 30°9S 26°30E 271 D4
Smithfield N.C., U.S.A. 35°31N 78°21W 315 D15
Smithfield Utah, U.S.A. 41°50N 111°50W 304 F8
Smithfield Va., U.S.A. 36°59N 76°38W 316 C4
Smiths Falls Canada 44°55N 76°0W 313 B9
Smithsonian Institution
  Washington, D.C., U.S.A. 143 b2
Smithton Australia 40°53S 145°6E 281 G4
Smithville Ont., Canada 43°6N 79°33W 312 C5
Smithville Ga., U.S.A. 31°54N 84°15W 316 D5
Smithville Mo., U.S.A. 39°23N 94°35W 310 E2
Smithville Tex., U.S.A. 30°1N 97°10W 314 F6
Smoke Creek Desert
  U.S.A. 40°30N 119°40W 304 F4
Smoky → Canada 56°10N 117°21W 296 B5
Smoky Bay Australia 32°22S 134°13E 281 E1
Smoky Hill → U.S.A. 39°4N 96°48W 308 F5
Smoky Hills U.S.A. 39°15N 99°30W 308 F4
Smoky Lake Canada 54°10N 112°30W 296 C6
Smøla Norway 63°23N 8°3E 164 B3
Smolensk Russia 54°45N 32°5E 188 E7
Smolenskoye Poozerye △
  Russia 55°35N 31°50E 188 E6
Smolikas, Oros Greece 40°9N 20°58E 202 F4
Smolnik Slovakia 48°43N 20°44E 181 C13
Smolny Russia 59°56N 30°25E 137 B2
Smolny △ Russia 54°30N 47°10E 190 C7
Smolyan Bulgaria 41°36N 24°38E 203 E8
Smolyan □ Bulgaria 41°36N 24°38E 203 E8
Smooth Rock Falls
  Canada 49°17N 81°37W 298 C3
Smoothstone L. Canada 54°40N 106°50W 297 C7
Smorgon = Smarhon
  Belarus 54°20N 26°24E 177 A14
Smotrych Ukraine 48°57N 26°33E 183 B11
Smotrych → Ukraine 48°34N 26°39E 183 B11
Smulti Romania 45°57N 27°44E 183 E12
Smyadovo Bulgaria 43°2N 27°1E 203 C11
Smygehamn Sweden 55°21N 13°22E 163 J7
Smygehuk Sweden 55°20N 13°20E 163 J7
Smyley I. Antarctica 72°55S 78°0W 151 D17
Smyrna = İzmir Turkey 38°25N 27°8E 205 C9
Smyrna Del., U.S.A. 39°18N 75°36W 309 F16
Smyrna Ga., U.S.A. 33°53N 84°31W 316 B5
Smyrna Tenn., U.S.A. 35°59N 86°31W 316 C3
Snæfell Iceland 64°48N 15°34W 155 C11
Snaefell I. of Man 54°16N 4°27W 168 C3
Snæfellsjökull △ Iceland 64°49N 23°46W 155 C3
Snæfellsnes Iceland 64°48N 23°40W 155 C3
Snæfellsnessýsla Iceland 65°0N 23°0W 155 C3
Snake → U.S.A. 46°12N 119°2W 304 C4
Snake Creek Canal
  U.S.A. 25°57N 80°19W 129 C2
Snake I. = Zmiyiny, Ostriv
  Black Sea 45°15N 30°12E 189 K6
Snake I. Australia 38°47S 146°33E 282 E7
Snake Pt. Anguilla 18°17N 62°58W 322 a
Snake Range U.S.A. 39°0N 114°20W 304 G6
Snake River Plain U.S.A. 42°50N 114°0W 304 E7
Snásá Norway 64°12N 12°0E 160 D6
Snasahögarna Sweden 63°13N 12°12E 162 A6
Snåsavatnet Norway 64°12N 12°0E 160 D5
Snättringe Sweden 59°15N 17°58E 139 B1
Snedsted Denmark 56°55N 8°32E 163 H2
Sneek Neths. 53°2N 5°40E 170 A5
Sneem Ireland 51°50N 9°54W 166 E2
Sneeuberge S. Africa 31°46S 24°20E 270 D3
Snegurovka = Tetiyev
  Ukraine 49°22N 29°38E 177 D15
Snejbjerg Denmark 56°8N 8°54E 163 H2
Snelling Calif., U.S.A. 37°31N 120°26W 306 H6
Snelling S.C., U.S.A. 33°15N 81°27W 316 B8
Snells Beach N.Z. 36°25S 174°44E 284 C3
Snezhnoye Ukraine 48°0N 38°58E 189 H10
Snežka Europe 50°41N 15°50E 185 A4
Sniadowo Poland 53°2N 22°0E 185 E8
Śniardwy, Jezioro Poland 53°48N 21°50E 184 E8
Śnieżka Europe 50°44N 15°45E 180 A8
Snigirevka = Snihurivka
  Ukraine 47°2N 32°49E 189 J7
Snihurivka Ukraine 47°2N 32°49E 189 J7
Snillfjord Norway 63°24N 9°30E 164 A6
Snina Slovakia 48°58N 22°9E 181 C14
Snizort, L. U.K. 57°33N 6°28W 167 D2
Snøhetta Norway 62°19N 9°16E 164 B6
Snohomish U.S.A. 47°55N 122°6W 304 C4
Snonuten Norway 59°31N 6°52E 164 E3
Snoqualmie U.S.A. 47°31N 121°49W 304 C4
Snoqualmie Pass U.S.A. 47°25N 121°25W 304 C5
Snoul Cambodia 12°4N 106°26E 237 F6
Snov → Ukraine 51°48N 31°33E 189 G6

Snow Hill U.S.A. 38°11N 75°24W 309 F16
Snow Lake Canada 54°52N 100°3W 297 C8
Snow Mt. Calif., U.S.A. 39°23N 122°45W 306 F4
Snow Mt. Maine, U.S.A. 45°18N 70°48W 313 A14
Snow Shoe U.S.A. 41°2N 77°57W 312 E7
Snowbird L. Canada 60°45N 103°0W 297 A8
Snowdon U.K. 53°4N 4°5W 168 D3
Snowdonia U.K. 53°7N 3°59W 168 D4
Snowdoun U.S.A. 32°15N 86°18W 316 C3
Snowdrift = Łutsel K'e
  Canada 62°24N 110°44W 297 A6
Snowdrift → Canada 62°24N 110°44W 297 A6
Snowflake U.S.A. 34°30N 110°5W 305 J8
Snowshoe Pk. U.S.A. 48°13N 115°41W 304 B6
Snowtown Australia 33°46S 138°14E 282 C3
Snowville U.S.A. 41°58N 112°43W 304 F7
Snowy → Australia 37°46S 148°30E 283 D8
Snowy Mt. U.S.A. 43°42N 74°23W 313 C10
Snowy Mts. Australia 36°30S 148°20E 283 D8
Snowy River △ Australia 37°15S 147°29E 283 D7
Snug Corner Bahamas 22°33N 73°52W 321 B5
Snug Harbour Canada 45°22N 80°17W 312 A4
Snyatyn Ukraine 48°27N 25°38E 183 B10
Snyder Okla., U.S.A. 34°40N 98°57W 314 D5
Snyder Tex., U.S.A. 32°44N 100°55W 314 E4
So Kwun Wat
  Hong Kong, China 22°23N 114°0E 122 A2
Soacha Colombia 4°35N 74°13W 328 C3
Soahanina Madag. 18°42S 44°13E 272 B1
Soalala Madag. 16°6S 45°20E 272 B2
Soaloka Madag. 18°32S 45°15E 272 B2
Soamanonga Madag. 23°52S 44°47E 272 C1
Soan → Pakistan 33°1N 71°44E 242 C4
Soanierana-Ivongo
  Madag. 16°55S 49°35E 272 B2
Soanindraniny Madag. 19°54S 47°14E 272 B2
Soars Romania 45°56N 24°55E 183 E9
Soavina Madag. 20°23S 46°56E 272 C2
Soavinandriana Madag. 19°9S 46°45E 272 B2
Soba Nigeria 10°58N 8°4E 263 C6
Sobaeksan △ S. Korea 36°50N 128°25E 224 D4
Sobat → South Sudan 9°22N 31°33E 257 F3
Sobernheim Germany 49°47N 7°39E 178 D4
Sobhapur India 22°47N 78°17E 242 H8
Sobinka Russia 56°0N 40°0E 188 E11
Sobo-Yama Japan 32°51N 131°22E 222 E3
Søborg Denmark 55°43N 12°29E 118 A2
Sobótka Poland 50°54N 16°44E 185 H3
Sobra Croatia 42°44N 17°34E 199 F14
Sobradinho, Represa de
  Brazil 9°30S 42°0W 332 E3
Sobral Brazil 3°50S 40°20W 332 D3
Sobrance Slovakia 48°45N 22°11E 181 C14
Sobreda Portugal 38°39N 9°11W 126 B1
Sobreira Formosa Portugal 39°46N 7°51W 194 F3
Soc Giang Vietnam 22°54N 106°1E 228 F6
Soc Trang Vietnam 9°37N 105°50E 237 H5
Soča → Europe 46°20N 13°40E 180 E6
Socastee U.S.A. 33°41N 78°59W 315 E15
Soccer City Stadium
  Johannesburg, S. Africa 26°14S 27°59E 123 B1
Sochaczew □ Poland 52°15N 20°13E 185 F7
Sochaczew Poland 52°15N 20°13E 185 F7
Soch'e = Shache China 38°20N 77°10E 217 E9
Sochi Russia 43°35N 39°40E 191 J4
Sochi ✈ (AER) Russia 43°25N 39°57E 191 J4
Sochi □ Russia 43°40N 39°35E 191 J4
Sochos Greece 40°48N 23°22E 202 F7
Social City U.S.A. 33°39N 83°43W 316 B6
Society Hill U.S.A. 33°26N 85°27W 316 C4
Society Is. = Société, Îs. de la
  French Polynesia 17°0S 151°0W 289 f
Socompa, Portezuelo de
  Chile 24°27S 68°18W 334 A2
Socorro = Fronteiras Brazil 7°5S 40°37W 332 C3
Socorro Colombia 6°30N 73°16W 328 B3
Socorro Phil. 9°37N 125°58E 233 H7
Socorro N. Mex., U.S.A. 34°4N 106°54W 305 J10
Socorro Tex., U.S.A. 31°39N 106°18W 314 F1
Socorro, I. Mexico 18°45N 110°58W 318 D2
Socotra Yemen 12°30N 54°0E 249 E5
Socovos Spain 38°20N 1°58W 197 G3
Socuéllamos Spain 39°16N 2°47W 197 F2
Soda L. U.S.A. 35°10N 116°4W 307 K10
Soda Plains India 35°30N 79°0E 243 B8
Soda Springs U.S.A. 42°39N 111°36W 304 E8
Sodankylä Finland 67°29N 26°40E 160 C22
Soddy-Daisy U.S.A. 35°17N 85°10W 315 D12
Söderåkra Sweden 56°20N 16°5E 163 H10
Söderåsen △ Sweden 56°2N 13°13E 163 H7
Söderbärke Sweden 60°5N 15°35E 162 D9
Söderby Sweden 59°24N 18°12E 139 A3
Söderfors Sweden 60°23N 17°25E 162 D11
Söderhamn Sweden 61°18N 17°10E 162 D11
Söderköping Sweden 58°31N 16°20E 163 F10
Södermalm Sweden 59°18N 18°4E 139 B2
Södermanland Sweden 58°56N 16°55E 161 G17
Södermanland □ Sweden 59°10N 16°30E 162 E10
Södertälje Sweden 59°12N 17°39E 162 E11
Sodiri Sudan 14°27N 29°0E 257 E11
Sodo Ethiopia 7°0N 37°41E 257 F4
Sodpur India 22°42N 88°24E 245 H13
Södra Finnskoga Sweden 60°42N 12°34E 162 D6
Södra Sandby Sweden 55°43N 13°21E 163 J7
Södra Ulvön Sweden 63°0N 18°40E 162 A12
Södra Vi Sweden 57°45N 15°45E 163 G9
Sodražica Slovenia 45°46N 14°38E 199 C11
Sodus U.S.A. 43°14N 77°4W 312 C7
Sodwana Bay △ S. Africa 27°35S 32°47E 271 C6
Soe Indonesia 9°52S 124°17E 278 C2
Soekmekaar = Morebeng
  S. Africa 23°30S 29°55E 271 B4
Soest Germany 51°34N 8°7E 178 C4
Soest Neths. 52°9N 5°19E 170 B5
Soeurs, Î. des Canada 45°27N 73°32W 130 B2
Sofades Greece 39°20N 22°5E 204 B4
Sofala Guadeloupe 16°17N 61°43W 322 a
Sofala □ Mozam. 19°30S 34°30E 271 A5
Sofara Mali 13°59N 4°9W 262 C4
Sofia = Sofiya Bulgaria 42°45N 23°20E 202 D7
Sofia → Madag. 15°27S 47°23E 272 B2
Sofia □ Madag. 14°50S 48°0E 272 B2
Sofievka Ukraine 48°6N 33°55E 189 H7
Sofiko Greece 37°47N 23°3E 204 D5
Sofiya Bulgaria 42°45N 23°20E 202 D7
Sofiya □ Bulgaria 42°45N 23°20E 202 D7
Sofiya ✈ (SOF) Bulgaria 42°46N 23°23E 202 D7
Sofrana Greece 35°54N 26°19E 205 C7
Sôfu-Gan Japan 29°49N 140°21E 221 K10
Sogakofe Ghana 6°2N 0°39E 263 D5
Sogamoso Colombia 5°43N 72°56W 328 B3
Sogār Iran 25°53N 58°6E 247 E8
Sögel Germany 52°50N 7°31E 178 B4
Sogeri Papua N. G. 9°26S 147°35E 286 E4
Sogn og Fjordane □
  Norway 61°40N 6°0E 164 C3
Sognefjorden Norway 61°10N 5°50E 164 C2
Sogod Phil. 10°23N 124°59E 233 F7
Sögüt Bilecik, Turkey 40°2N 30°10E 205 B13
Sögüt Burdur, Turkey 37°2N 29°11E 205 D12
Sögüt Dağı Turkey 37°22N 29°0E 205 D12
Sögütük Turkey 36°40N 28°8E 205 D10
Soh Iran 33°26N 51°27E 247 C6

Somabhula Zimbabwe 19°42S 29°40E 271 A4
Somali = Sumale □ Ethiopia 7°0N 45°0E 267 C6
Somali Pen. Africa 7°0N 46°0E 254 F8
Somalia ■ Africa 7°0N 47°0E 267 C6
Somaliland □ Somalia 10°0N 46°0E 267 C6
Sombe Dzong Bhutan 27°13N 89°8E 241 B2
Somberton France 47°20N 4°40E 173 E11
Sombo Angola 8°42S 20°59E 265 D4
Sombor Serbia 45°46N 19°9E 182 E4
Sombra Canada 42°43N 82°29W 312 D2
Sombrerete Mexico 23°38N 103°39W 318 C4
Sombrero Channel India 7°41N 93°35E 245 L11
Somcuta Mare Romania 47°31N 23°28E 183 C8
Somdari India 25°47N 72°38E 242 G5
Someido → Spain 43°5N 6°11W 194 B4
Somers U.S.A. 48°5N 114°13W 304 B6
Somerset Bermuda 32°17N 64°52W 153 a
Somerset Ky., U.S.A. 37°5N 84°36W 309 G11
Somerset Mass., U.S.A. 41°47N 71°8W 313 E14
Somerset Md., U.S.A. 38°57N 77°5W 143 B2
Somerset Pa., U.S.A. 40°1N 79°5W 312 F5
Somerset □ U.K. 51°9N 3°0W 169 F5
Somerset East S. Africa 32°42S 25°35E 270 D4
Somerset I. Bermuda 32°17N 64°52W 153 a
Somerset I. Nunavut,
  Canada 73°30N 93°0W 294 C13
Somerset West S. Africa 34°8S 18°50E 270 D2
Somersworth U.S.A. 43°16N 70°52W 313 C14
Somerton U.S.A. 32°36N 114°43W 305 K6
Somerville Mass., U.S.A. 42°22N 71°5W 116 A2
Somerville N.J., U.S.A. 40°35N 74°38W 313 F10
Someş → Romania 47°49N 22°43E 182 C7
Someşul Mare → Romania 47°9N 23°55E 183 C8
Somme □ France 49°57N 2°20E 173 C9
Somme → France 50°11N 1°38E 173 B8
Somme, B. de la France 50°14N 1°33E 172 B3
Sommen Jönköping, Sweden 58°12N 14°58E 163 F8
Sommen Östergötland,
  Sweden 58°0N 15°15E 163 F9
Sommepy-Tahure France 49°15N 4°31E 173 C11
Sömmerda Germany 51°9N 11°7E 178 D7
Sommerfeld = Lubsko
  Poland 51°45N 14°57E 185 G1
Sommesous France 48°44N 4°12E 173 D11
Sommières France 43°47N 4°6E 175 E8
Somnath India 20°53N 70°22E 242 J4
Somogy □ Hungary 46°19N 17°30E 182 D2
Somogyszob Hungary 46°18N 17°20E 182 D2
Somosomo Fiji 16°47S 179°58W 287 A3
Somosomo Str. Fiji 16°0S 180°0E 287 A3
Somoto Nic. 13°28N 86°37W 320 D2
Sompolno Poland 52°26N 18°30E 185 F5
Somport, Túnel de Spain 42°48N 0°31W 196 C4
Somuncurá, Meseta de
  Argentina 41°30S 67°0W 336 B3
Somvarpet India 12°36N 75°52E 245 H2
Son → India 25°42N 84°52E 243 G11
Son, Laem Thailand 7°59N 98°16E 237 a
Son Ha Vietnam 15°3N 108°34E 236 E7
Son La Vietnam 21°20N 103°50E 228 G4
Son Morrell Spain 39°44N 3°20E 206 B4
Son Rapinya Spain 39°35N 2°37E 206 B3
Son Sardina Spain 39°37N 2°43E 206 B3
Son Serra Spain 39°43N 3°13E 206 B4
Son Servera Spain 39°37N 3°21E 206 B4
Son Tay Vietnam 21°8N 105°30E 228 G5
Son Tinh Vietnam 15°10N 108°40E 236 E7
Soná Panama 8°0N 81°20W 320 E3
Sonamarg India 34°18N 75°21E 243 B6
Sonamukhi India 23°18N 87°27E 243 H12
Sonar → India 24°24N 79°56E 243 G8
Sonari India 18°54N 72°59E 130 B2
Sonbhadra □ India 24°0N 83°0E 243 G10
Sönch'ŏn N. Korea 39°48N 124°55E 224 C2
Sondags → S. Africa 33°44S 25°51E 270 D4
Sóndalo Italy 46°20N 10°20E 198 B7
Sondeled Norway 58°36N 9°3E 164 F6
Sønder Felding Denmark 55°57N 8°47E 163 J2
Sønder Omme Denmark 55°50N 8°54E 163 J2
Sønderborg Denmark 54°55N 9°49E 163 K3
Sondershausen Germany 51°22N 10°51E 178 D6
Søndersø Denmark 55°29N 10°16E 163 J4
Søndre Bergenhus = Hordaland □
  Norway 60°25N 6°15E 164 D3
Søndre Strømfjord = Kangerlussuaq
  Greenland 67°0N 50°40W 154 C5
Søndre Strømhjem =
  Sør-Trøndelag □ Norway 63°0N 11°0E 164 A7
Sóndrio Italy 46°10N 9°52E 198 B6
Sondur → India 20°40N 82°1E 244 D6
Sone Mozam. 17°23S 34°55E 269 F3
Sonepur India 20°55N 83°50E 244 D6
Sonfim Brazil 6°0S 67°52W 330 B4
Song Nigeria 9°49N 12°39E 263 D7
Song Thailand 18°28N 100°11E 236 C3
Song Cau Vietnam 13°27N 109°18E 236 F7
Song-Köl Kyrgyzstan 41°50N 75°12E 217 D9
Song Ma Vietnam 20°56N 103°53E 228 G4
Song Qingling, Former Residence of
  Beijing, China 114 a2
Song Xian China 34°12N 112°8E 226 D7
Songad India 21°9N 73°33E 244 D1
Songan Indonesia 8°13S 115°24E 231 J18
Songavatnet Norway 59°52N 7°23E 164 E4
Songea Tanzania 10°40S 35°40E 269 E4
Songeons France 49°32N 1°50E 172 D4
Sönggan N. Korea 40°47N 126°34E 224 C3
Songgang China 22°46N 113°50E 219 a
Songhua Hu China 43°35N 126°50E 224 C2
Songhua Jiang →
  China 47°45N 132°30E 219 B15
Songimvelo △ S. Africa 25°50S 31°2E 271 C5
Songjiang Jilin, China 42°34N 128°20E 224 C4
Songjiang Shanghai,
  China 31°1N 121°12E 229 B13
Songjianghe China 42°10N 127°29E 224 C4
Söngjin = Kimch'aek
  N. Korea 40°40N 129°10E 224 C4
Songkan China 28°35N 106°52E 228 D6
Songkhla Thailand 7°13N 100°37E 238 C2
Songkhram → Thailand 17°28N 104°9E 236 D5
Songnim N. Korea 38°45N 125°39E 224 C2
Songnisan △ S. Korea 36°28N 127°45E 224 D3
Songo Angola 7°22S 14°51E 265 D2
Songo Mozam. 15°34S 32°38E 271 A5
Songololo = Mbanza Ngungu
  Dem. Rep. of the Congo 5°12S 14°53E 265 D2
Songpan China 32°40N 103°30E 228 B5
Songtao China 28°11N 109°10E 228 D7
Songwe
  Dem. Rep. of the Congo 3°20S 26°16E 268 C2
Songwe → Africa 9°44S 33°58E 269 F3
Songxi China 27°30N 118°42E 229 D12
Songzi China 30°12N 111°45E 229 B9
Sonhat India 23°29N 82°31E 243 H10
Sonid Youqi China 42°45N 112°48E 226 B7
Sonid Zuoqi China 43°50N 113°42E 226 B7
Sonipat India 29°0N 77°5E 242 E7
Sonkach India 22°59N 76°21E 242 H7
Sonkovo Russia 57°50N 37°5E 188 D9
Sonmiani Pakistan 25°25N 66°40E 242 G2
Sonmiani B. Pakistan 25°15N 66°30E 242 G2
Sonneberg Germany 50°22N 11°10E 179 E7

Sonnino Italy 41°25N 13°14E 200 A6
Sono → Minas Gerais, Brazil 17°2S 45°32W 333 E2
Sono → Tocantins, Brazil 9°58S 48°11W 332 C2
Sonobe = Nantan Japan 35°6N 135°28E 223 B7
Sonoma U.S.A. 38°18N 122°28W 306 G4
Sonora Calif., U.S.A. 37°59N 120°23W 306 H6
Sonora Tex., U.S.A. 30°34N 100°39W 314 F4
Sonora □ Mexico 29°20N 110°40W 318 B2
Sonora → Mexico 29°5N 110°55W 318 B2
Sonoran Desert U.S.A. 33°40N 113°30W 307 L12
Sonoyta Mexico 31°51N 112°50W 318 A2
Sonqor Iran 34°47N 47°36E 213 E12
Sonseca Spain 39°42N 3°57W 195 F7
Sonsón Colombia 5°43N 75°18W 328 B2
Sonsonate El Salv. 13°43N 89°44W 320 D2
Sonstorp Sweden 58°44N 15°38E 163 F9
Sonthofen Germany 47°30N 10°16E 179 H6
Sony Picture Studio U.S.A. 34°1N 118°4W 126 B2
Soo Japan 31°40N 131°5E 222 F3
Soochow = Suzhou China 31°19N 120°38E 229 B13
Sooke Canada 48°13N 123°43W 306 B3
Sool □ Somalia 8°40N 47°30E 267 C6
Soomaa △ Estonia 58°30N 28°5E 188 C3
Soomaaliya = Somalia ■ Africa 7°0N 47°0E 267 C6
Sop Hao Laos 20°33N 104°27E 228 G5
Sop Prap Thailand 17°53N 99°20E 236 D2
Sopachuy Bolivia 19°29S 64°31W 331 D5
Sopchoppy U.S.A. 30°4N 84°29W 316 E5
Sopelana Spain 43°23N 2°58W 196 B2
Soperton U.S.A. 32°23N 82°35W 316 C7
Sopi Indonesia 2°34N 128°28E 231 D7
Sopo, Nahr → South Sudan 8°40N 26°30E 257 F2
Sopot Bulgaria 42°39N 24°45E 203 D8
Sopot Poland 54°27N 18°31E 184 D5
Sopot Serbia 44°29N 20°30E 202 B4
Sopotnica Macedonia 41°18N 21°13E 202 E5
Sopron Hungary 47°45N 16°32E 182 C1
Sopur India 34°18N 74°27E 243 B6
Sør-Rondane Antarctica 72°0S 25°0E 151 D4
Sør-Trøndelag □ Norway 63°0N 11°0E 164 A7
Sora Italy 41°43N 13°37E 199 G10
Sorab India 14°23N 75°6E 245 G2
Sorada India 19°45N 84°26E 244 E7
Sorah Pakistan 27°13N 68°56E 242 F3
Söråker Sweden 62°30N 17°32E 162 B11
Sorang Kazakhstan 49°46N 72°51E 217 C8
Sorano Italy 42°41N 11°43E 199 F8
Soraon India 25°37N 81°51E 243 G9
Sorata Bolivia 15°50S 68°40W 330 D4
Sorbas Spain 37°6N 2°7W 197 H2
Sörbygden Sweden 62°48N 16°12E 162 B10
Sord = Swords Ireland 53°28N 6°13W 166 C5
Sordellen Sweden 61°48N 16°43E 162 C10
Sore France 44°18N 0°35W 174 D3
Søre Osa → Norway 61°18N 11°46E 164 C8
Sorel-Tracy Canada 46°0N 73°10W 298 C5
Soresina Italy 45°17N 9°51E 198 C6
Sørfjorden Norway 60°20N 6°37E 164 D3
Sörforsa Sweden 61°43N 16°58E 162 C10
Sórgono Italy 40°1N 9°6E 200 B2
Sorgues France 44°1N 4°53E 175 D8
Sorgun Turkey 39°46N 35°11E 212 C6
Sorgun → Turkey 36°36N 34°20E 250 B5
Sori Papua N. G. 1°58S 146°42E 286 A4
Soria Spain 41°43N 2°32W 196 D2
Soria □ Spain 41°46N 2°28W 196 D2
Soriano Uruguay 33°24S 58°19W 334 C4
Soriano nel Cimino Italy 42°25N 12°14E 199 F9
Sorkh, Kuh-e Iran 35°40N 58°30E 247 C8
Soro Denmark 55°26N 11°32E 163 J5
Soro Guinea 10°9N 9°48W 262 C3
Soroca Moldova 48°8N 28°12E 183 B13
Sorocaba Brazil 23°31S 47°27W 335 A6
Sorochinsk Russia 52°26N 53°10E 186 D9
Soroka = Belomorsk Russia 64°35N 34°54E 186 B5
Soroki = Soroca Moldova 48°8N 28°12E 183 B13
Sorokino = Krasnodon Ukraine 48°17N 39°44E 189 H10
Soroksár Hungary 47°24N 19°7E 117 B2
Soroksari Duna → Hungary 47°25N 19°5E 117 B2
Sorong Indonesia 0°55S 131°15E 231 E8
Soroni Greece 36°21N 28°1E 206 E12
Soroti Uganda 1°43N 33°35E 268 B3
Sørøya Norway 70°40N 22°30E 160 A20
Sørøyane Norway 62°25N 5°32E 164 B2
Sørøysundet Norway 70°25N 23°0E 160 A20
Sorraia → Portugal 38°55N 8°53W 195 G2
Sorrell Australia 42°47S 147°34E 281 G4
Sorrento Italy 40°37N 14°22E 201 B7
Sorsele Sweden 65°31N 17°30E 160 D17
Sörsjön Sweden 61°24N 13°5E 162 C7
Sorso Italy 40°48N 8°34E 200 B1
Sorsogon Phil. 13°0N 124°0E 232 E5
Sorsogon □ Phil. 12°50N 123°55E 232 E4
Sortavala Russia 61°42N 30°41E 188 B6
Sortino Italy 37°9N 15°2E 201 E8
Sortland Norway 68°42N 15°25E 160 B16
Sortot Sudan 19°3N 30°28E 256 D3
Sørum Norway 60°30N 10°17E 164 D7
Sørvågen Norway 67°53N 13°1E 160 C15
Sorvizhi Russia 57°52N 48°32E 190 B9
Sos del Rey Católico Spain 42°30N 1°13W 196 C3
Soscumica, L. Canada 50°15N 77°27W 298 B4
Sösdala Sweden 56°2N 13°41E 163 H7
Sosenka → Russia 55°46N 37°42E 129 B3
Sosna → Russia 52°42N 38°55E 189 F10
Sosnogorsk Russia 63°37N 53°51E 186 B9
Sosnovka Kirov, Russia 56°17N 51°17E 190 B10
Sosnovka St. Petersburg, Russia 60°0N 30°22E 137 B2
Sosnovka Tambov, Russia 53°13N 41°24E 190 D5
Sosnovyy Bor Russia 59°55N 29°6E 188 C5
Sosnowiec Poland 50°20N 19°10E 185 H6
Sosnowitz = Sosnowiec Poland 50°20N 19°10E 185 H6
Soso C.A.R. 3°55N 15°30E 264 B3
Sospel France 43°52N 7°27E 175 E11
Sospiri, Ponte dei Venice, Italy 142 b3
Sossus Vlei Namibia 24°40S 15°23E 270 B2
Šoštanj Slovenia 46°23N 15°4E 199 B12
Sŏsura N. Korea 42°16N 130°36E 224 A5
Sot → India 27°27N 79°37E 243 F8
Sotasæter Norway 61°49N 7°43E 164 C4
Sotavento C. Verde Is. 15°0N 24°0W 153 j
Sotik Kenya 0°41S 35°7E 268 C4
Sotkamo Finland 64°8N 28°23E 160 D23
Soto Curaçao 12°16N 69°6W 322 g
Soto Spain 43°32N 6°4W 194 B4
Soto la Marina Mexico 23°46N 98°13W 319 C5
Soto la Marina → Mexico 23°45N 97°45W 319 C5
Soto y Amío Spain 42°46N 5°53W 194 C5
Sotouboua Togo 8°34N 0°59E 263 D5
Sotrondio Spain 43°17N 5°36W 194 B5
Sotuf, Adrar W. Sahara 21°42N 15°36W 260 D1
Sotuta Mexico 20°36N 89°1W 319 C7
Souanké Congo 2°10N 14°3E 264 B2
Soubré Ivory C. 5°50N 6°35W 262 D3
Souda Greece 35°29N 24°4E 207 E5
Soudas, Ormos Greece 35°25N 24°10E 207 E5
Souderton U.S.A. 40°19N 75°19W 313 F9
Souflay Congo 2°1N 14°54E 264 B2
Soufli Greece 41°12N 26°18E 203 E10
Soufrière Dominica 15°13N 61°22W 323 k
Soufrière Guadeloupe 16°5N 61°40W 322 e
Soufrière St. Lucia 13°51N 61°3W 323 m
Soufrière Bay Dominica 15°13N 61°22W 323 k
Soufrière Bay St. Lucia 13°51N 61°4W 323 m
Soufrière Hills Volcano Montserrat 16°43N 62°10W 323 p
Souillac Lot, France 44°53N 1°29E 174 D5
Souillac Mauritius 20°31S 57°31E 272 e
Souilly France 49°3N 5°17E 173 C12
Souk-Ahras Algeria 36°23N 7°57E 261 A6
Souk-Ahras □ Algeria 36°10N 7°55E 261 A6
Souk el Arba du Rharb Morocco 34°43N 5°59W 260 B3
Soukhouma Laos 14°38N 105°48E 236 E5
Sŏul = Seoul S. Korea 37°31N 126°58E 137 B2
Soulac-sur-Mer France 45°30N 1°7W 174 C2
Soulougou Burkina Faso 13°1N 0°25E 263 C5
Soultz-sous-Forêts France 48°57N 7°52E 173 D14
Sound, The = Øresund Europe 55°45N 12°40E 163 J6
Sound, The U.K. 50°20N 4°10W 169 G3
Sound I. India 12°58N 92°59E 245 H11
Soundview U.S.A. 40°49N 73°53W 132 B2
Sounio, Akra Greece 37°37N 24°1E 204 D6
Sour el Ghozlane Algeria 36°10N 3°45E 261 A5
Sources, Mt. aux Lesotho 28°45S 28°50E 271 C4
Soure Brazil 0°35S 48°30W 332 B2
Soure Portugal 40°4N 8°38W 194 E2
Souris Man., Canada 49°40N 100°20W 297 D8
Souris P.E.I., Canada 46°21N 62°15W 299 C7
Souris → N. Amer. 49°40N 99°34W 308 A4
Sourou → Africa 12°45N 3°25W 262 C4
Sourpi Greece 39°6N 22°54E 204 B4
Sous, O. → Morocco 30°27N 9°31W 260 B3
Sous le Vent, Is. French Polynesia 16°30S 155°30W 289 f
Sous le Vent, Région Réunion 21°12S 55°20E 272 f
Sous-Massa △ Morocco 30°26N 9°35W 260 B3
Sous-Massa-Drâa □ Morocco 30°45N 6°30W 260 B3
Sousa Brazil 6°45S 38°10W 332 C4
Sousel Brazil 2°38S 52°29W 332 B1
Sousel Portugal 38°57N 7°40W 195 G3
Sousse Tunisia 35°50N 10°38E 258 A2
Sousse □ Tunisia 35°40N 10°30E 261 A7
Soustons France 43°45N 1°19W 174 E2
Sout → S. Africa 31°35S 18°24E 270 D2
South Africa ■ Africa 32°0S 23°0E 270 D3
South African National Museum of Military History S. Africa 26°10S 28°2E 123 A2
South America 10°0S 60°0W 326 E5
South Andaman India 11°45N 92°10E 245 J11
South Aulatsivik I. Canada 56°45N 61°30W 299 A7
South Australia □ Australia 32°0S 139°0E 282 B3
South Australian Basin Ind. Oc. 38°0S 126°0E 288 L4
South Ayrshire □ U.K. 55°18N 4°41W 167 F4
South Baldy Pk. U.S.A. 34°6N 107°11W 305 J10
South Bass I. U.S.A. 41°39N 82°49W 312 E2
South Bay U.S.A. 26°40N 80°43W 317 J9
South Beach Bahamas 25°1N 77°20W 153 b
South Beach Fla., U.S.A. 25°46N 80°7W 129 D3
South Beach N.Y., U.S.A. 40°35N 74°4W 132 C1
South Beach Harbor San Francisco, U.S.A. 136 c3
South Beloit U.S.A. 42°29N 89°2W 310 B7
South Bend Ind., U.S.A. 41°41N 86°15W 311 C10
South Bend Wash., U.S.A. 46°40N 123°48W 306 D3
South Bend Park U.S.A. 33°42N 84°23W 113 B2
South Boston Mass., U.S.A. 42°20N 71°2W 116 A2
South Boston Va., U.S.A. 36°42N 78°54W 309 G14
South Branch Canada 47°55N 59°2W 299 C8
South Branch Chicago River → Chicago, U.S.A. 119 d1
South Brook Canada 49°26N 56°5W 299 C8
South Brother I. India 10°56N 92°37E 245 J11
South Bruny I. Australia 43°20S 147°15E 281 G4
South C. = Kalae U.S.A. 18°55N 155°41W 302 E6
South Carolina □ U.S.A. 34°0N 81°0W 315 E14
South Channel Phil. 14°18N 120°37E 232 D3
South Charleston U.S.A. 38°22N 81°44W 309 F13
South China Sea Asia 10°0N 113°0E 230 C4
South Comino Channel Malta 36°0N 14°20E 206 F7
South Congaree U.S.A. 33°53N 81°9W 316 B8
South Cotabato □ Phil. 6°10N 125°0E 233 J5
South Cumberland Is. △ Australia 20°42S 149°11E 280 b
South Dakota □ U.S.A. 44°15N 100°0W 308 C4
South Dayton U.S.A. 42°21N 79°3W 312 D5
South Daytona U.S.A. 29°10N 81°0W 317 F8
South Decatur U.S.A. 33°44N 84°16W 113 B3
South Deerfield U.S.A. 42°29N 72°37W 313 D12
South Deering U.S.A. 41°42N 87°33W 119 C3
South Downs U.K. 50°52N 0°25W 169 G7
South Downs △ U.K. 50°50N 0°50W 169 G7
South Dublin □ Ireland 53°16N 6°24W 166 C5
South East □ Botswana 25°0S 25°40E 270 C4
South East B. Ascension I. 7°57S 14°18W 153 g
South East C. Australia 43°40S 146°50E 281 G4
South East Forest △ Australia 37°0S 149°30E 283 D8
South East Is. Australia 34°17S 123°30E 279 F3
South El Monte U.S.A. 34°3N 118°2W 126 B4
South Elgin U.S.A. 42°0N 88°18W 311 C8
South Esk → U.K. 56°43N 2°31W 167 E6
South Fiji Basin Pac. Oc. 26°0S 175°0E 288 K9
South Foreland U.K. 51°8N 1°24E 169 F9
South Fork American → U.S.A. 38°57N 120°59W 306 G5
South Fork Edisto → U.S.A. 33°16N 80°54W 316 B9
South Fork Feather → U.S.A. 39°17N 121°36W 306 F5
South Fork Grand → U.S.A. 45°43N 102°17W 308 C2
South Fork Licking → U.S.A. 38°40N 84°18W 311 F12
South Fork Milk → U.S.A. 48°4N 106°19W 304 B10
South Fork Republican → U.S.A. 40°3N 101°31W 308 E3
South Gate U.S.A. 33°56N 118°12W 126 C3
South Georgia Antarctica 54°30S 37°0W 151 B1
South Gloucestershire □ U.K. 51°32N 2°28W 169 F5
South Grand → U.S.A. 38°17N 93°25W 310 F3
South Hadley U.S.A. 42°16N 72°35W 313 D12
South Harbor Phil. 14°34N 120°58E 127 B1
South Harrow U.K. 51°33N 0°21W 125 A1
South Haven U.S.A. 42°24N 86°16W 311 B10
South Hd. Australia 33°50S 151°16E 139 B2
South Henik L. Canada 61°30N 97°20W 297 A9
South Hill Village Anguilla 18°11N 63°5W 322 a
South Hills S. Africa 26°14S 28°5E 123 B2
South Holland U.S.A. 41°36N 87°36W 119 D3
South Horr Kenya 2°12N 36°56E 268 B4
South I. India 10°3N 72°17E 245 J1
South I. Eastern, Kenya 2°35N 36°35E 268 B4
South I. N.Z. 44°0S 170°0E 285 E5
South Indian Lake Canada 56°47N 98°56W 297 B9
South Invercargill N.Z. 46°26S 168°23E 285 G3
South Island △ Kenya 2°39N 36°35E 268 B4
South Kensington London, U.K. 125 c2
South Kitui ⌓ Kenya 1°48S 38°46E 268 C4
South Knife → Canada 58°55N 94°37W 297 B10
South Koel → India 22°32N 85°14E 243 H11
South Korea ■ Asia 36°0N 128°0E 224 D4
South Lake Tahoe U.S.A. 38°57N 119°59W 306 G6
South Lanarkshire □ U.K. 55°37N 3°53W 167 F5
South Lawn U.S.A. 38°47N 77°0W 143 C2
South Loup → U.S.A. 41°4N 98°39W 308 E4
South Luangwa △ Zambia 13°0S 31°20E 269 E3
South Lyon U.S.A. 42°28N 83°39W 311 B13
South Magnetic Pole Antarctica 64°8S 138°8E 151 C9
South Malé Atoll Maldives 4°0N 73°25E 272 d
South Malosmadulu Atoll Maldives 5°12N 73°0E 272 d
South Miami U.S.A. 25°42N 80°17W 129 D1
South Milwaukee U.S.A. 42°55N 87°52W 311 B9
South Molton U.K. 51°1N 3°51W 169 F4
South Monroe U.S.A. 41°54N 83°26W 311 C13
South Moose L. Canada 53°49N 100°1W 297 C8
South Nahanni → Canada 61°3N 123°21W 296 A4
South Nation → Canada 45°34N 75°6W 313 A9
South Natuna Is. = Natuna Selatan, Kepulauan Indonesia 2°45N 109°0E 235 B3
South Negril Pt. Jamaica 18°16N 78°22W 320 a
South New Hebrides Trench Pac. Oc. 22°30S 170°0E 277 E13
South Newport U.S.A. 31°38N 81°24W 316 D8
South Nilandu Atoll Maldives 2°52N 72°57E 272 d
South Norwood U.K. 51°23N 0°3W 125 C3
South of Market San Francisco, U.S.A. 136 c2
South Orkney Is. Antarctica 63°0S 45°0W 151 C18
South Ossetia □ Georgia 42°21N 44°2E 191 J7
South Otselic U.S.A. 42°38N 75°46W 313 D9
South Ozone Park U.S.A. 40°41N 73°49W 132 B3
South Pagai, I. = Pagai Selatan, Pulau Indonesia 3°0S 100°15E 234 C2
South Paris U.S.A. 44°14N 70°31W 313 B14
South Pasadena U.S.A. 34°7N 118°8W 126 B4
South Pekin U.S.A. 40°30N 89°39W 310 D7
South Pittsburg U.S.A. 35°1N 85°42W 315 D12
South Platte → U.S.A. 41°7N 100°42W 308 E3
South Pole Antarctica 90°0S 0°0 151 E
South Ponte Vedra Beach U.S.A. 30°3N 81°20W 316 E8
South Porcupine Canada 48°30N 81°12W 298 C3
South Portland U.S.A. 43°38N 70°15W 309 D18
South Pt. Ascension I. 8°0S 14°24W 153 g
South Pt. Barbados 13°2N 59°32W 323 r
South Pt. Mich., U.S.A. 44°52N 83°19W 312 B1
South Res. U.S.A. 42°26N 71°6W 116 A2
South River Ont., Canada 45°52N 79°23W 298 C4
South River N.J., U.S.A. 40°27N 74°23W 313 F10
South Ronaldsay U.K. 58°48N 2°58W 167 C6
South Ruislip U.K. 51°33N 0°24W 125 A1
South Rukuru → Malawi 10°44S 34°14E 269 E3
South San Francisco U.S.A. 37°38N 122°26W 136 C2
South San Gabriel U.S.A. 34°3N 118°6W 126 B4
South Sandwich Is. Antarctica 57°0S 27°0W 151 B1
South Sandwich Trench Atl. Oc. 56°0S 24°0W 151 B1
South Saskatchewan → Canada 53°15N 105°5W 297 C7
South Seal → Canada 58°48N 98°8W 297 B9
South Sentinel I. India 10°59N 92°14E 245 J11
South Shetland Is. Antarctica 62°0S 59°0W 151 C18
South Shields U.K. 55°0N 1°25W 168 C6
South Shore U.S.A. 41°45N 87°34W 119 C3
South Sioux City U.S.A. 42°28N 96°24W 308 D5
South Sister U.S.A. 44°4N 121°51W 304 D3
South Solomon Trench Pac. Oc. 11°0S 164°30E 277 C11
South Soufrière Hills Montserrat 16°41N 62°10W 323 p
South Street Boston, U.S.A. 116 c2
South Sudan ■ Africa 8°0N 30°0E 257 F2
South Taranaki Bight N.Z. 39°40S 174°5E 284 F3
South Tasman Rise S. Ocean 48°0S 146°0E 151 A10
South Thompson → Canada 50°40N 120°20W 296 C4
South Twin I. Canada 53°7N 79°52W 298 B4
South Tyne → U.K. 54°59N 2°8W 168 C5
South Ubian Phil. 5°11N 120°30E 233 J3
South Uist U.K. 57°20N 7°15W 167 D1
South Valley U.S.A. 35°1N 106°41W 305 J10
South Venice U.S.A. 27°3N 82°25W 317 H7
South Verde I. Phil. 10°4N 119°13E 233 F2
South Wayne U.S.A. 42°34N 89°53W 310 B7
South Wellesley Is. Australia 16°58S 139°17E 280 B2
South West Africa = Namibia ■ Africa 22°0S 18°9E 270 B2
South West B. Ascension I. 7°58S 14°25W 153 g
South West B. Bahamas 25°0N 77°32W 153 b
South West C. Tas., Australia 43°34S 146°3E 281 G4
South West C. N.Z. 47°17S 167°28E 285 H2
South West Pt. Papua N. G. 2°14S 146°34E 286 B4
South West Pt. St. Helena 15°59S 5°48W 153 h
South West Rocks Australia 30°52S 153°3E 283 A10
South Whitley U.S.A. 41°5N 85°38W 311 C11
South Williamsport U.S.A. 41°13N 77°0W 312 E8
South Yemen = Yemen ■ Asia 15°0N 44°0E 248 D4
South Yorkshire □ U.K. 53°27N 1°36W 168 D6
Southall U.K. 51°30N 0°22W 125 A1
Southampton Ont., Canada 44°30N 81°25W 312 B3
Southampton Southampton, U.K. 50°54N 1°23W 169 G6
Southampton N.Y., U.S.A. 40°53N 72°23W 313 F12
Southampton □ U.K. 50°54N 1°23W 169 G6
Southampton I. Canada 64°30N 84°0W 295 E15
Southaven U.S.A. 34°59N 90°0W 315 D9
Southbank Canada 54°2N 125°46W 296 C3
Southborough U.K. 51°23N 0°3E 125 C4
Southbridge N.Z. 43°48S 172°16E 285 D7
Southbridge Mass., U.S.A. 42°5N 72°2W 313 D12
Southeast C. U.S.A. 62°56N 169°39W 303 E5
Southeast Indian Ridge Ind. Oc. 43°0S 80°0E 273 J10
Southend Sask., Canada 56°19N 103°22W 297 B8
Southend London, U.K. 51°25N 0°0 125 B3
Southend-on-Sea U.K. 51°32N 0°44E 169 F8
Southend-on-Sea □ U.K. 51°32N 0°44E 169 F8
Southern = Yedebub Biheraweb Bihereseboch na Hizboch □ Ethiopia 12°0N 36°0E 257 F4
Southern = Yuzhnyy □ Russia 44°0N 40°0E 214 E5
Southern □ Malawi 15°0S 35°0E 269 F4
Southern □ S. Leone 8°0N 12°30W 262 D2
Southern □ Zambia 16°20S 26°20E 269 F2
Southern △ South Sudan 6°50N 28°45E 257 F2
Southern Alps N.Z. 43°41S 170°11E 285 D5
Southern Aral Sea Asia 45°0N 58°0E 216 D5
Southern California, Univ. of U.S.A. 34°1N 118°17W 126 B3
Southern Cross Australia 31°12S 119°15E 279 F2
Southern Highlands □ Papua N. G. 6°30S 143°25E 286 D2
Southern Indian L. Canada 57°10N 98°30W 297 B9
Southern Lau Group Fiji 18°40S 178°40W 287 B3
Southern Leyte □ Phil. 10°30N 125°10E 233 F5
Southern Ocean 62°0S 60°0E 151 C6
Southern Pines U.S.A. 35°11N 79°24W 315 D15
Southern Rhodesia = Zimbabwe ■ Africa 19°0S 30°0E 269 F3
Southern Uplands U.K. 55°28N 3°52W 167 F5
Southfield U.S.A. 42°28N 83°15W 311 B13
Southfields U.K. 51°26N 0°11W 125 B2
Southington U.S.A. 41°36N 72°53W 313 E12
Southlake U.S.A. 32°56N 97°8W 120 A3
Southland □ N.Z. 45°30S 168°0E 285 F3
Southold U.S.A. 41°4N 72°26W 313 E12
Southport Queens., Australia 27°58S 153°25E 281 D5
Southport Mersey., U.K. 53°39N 3°0W 168 D4
Southport Fla., U.S.A. 30°17N 85°38W 316 E4
Southport La., U.S.A. 29°57N 90°8W 131 B2
Southport N.Y., U.S.A. 42°3N 76°49W 312 D8
Southwark □ U.K. 51°29N 0°6W 125 B3
Southwest △ Australia 43°8S 146°5E 281 G4
Southwest Museum Los Angeles, U.S.A. 34°6N 118°13W 126 B3
Southwest Pacific Basin Pac. Oc. 40°0S 140°0W 277 G17
Southwest Pt. U.S. Virgin Is. 17°40N 64°55W 321 b
Southwold U.K. 52°20N 1°41E 169 E9
Southwood △ Australia 27°48S 150°8E 281 D5
Soutpansberg S. Africa 23°0S 29°30E 271 B4
Souvigny France 46°33N 3°10E 173 F10
Søvang Denmark 55°34N 12°37E 118 B3
Sovata Romania 46°35N 25°3E 183 D10
Soverato Italy 38°41N 16°33E 201 D9
Sovetsk Kaliningrad, Russia 55°6N 21°50E 184 C8
Sovetsk Kirov, Russia 57°38N 48°53E 190 B9
Sovetskaya Gavan Russia 48°58N 140°18E 215 E15
Sovetskoye = Zelenokumsk Russia 44°24N 44°0E 191 H6
Sovicille Italy 43°17N 11°13E 199 E8
Søvik Norway 62°33N 6°17E 164 B3
Soweto S. Africa 26°14S 27°52E 123 B1
Sowhānak Iran 35°48N 51°31E 141 A3
Sowma'eh Sarā Iran 37°17N 49°18E 213 D13
Soya Japan 35°44N 139°55E 140 A4
Sōya-Kaikyō = La Perouse Str. Asia 45°40N 142°0E 220 B11
Sōya-Misaki Japan 45°30N 141°55E 220 B10
Soyangho S. Korea 37°57N 127°54E 224 D3
Soyaux France 45°39N 0°12E 174 C4
Søyland Norway 58°41N 5°36E 164 F2
Soyo Angola 6°13S 12°20E 265 D2
Sozaq Kazakhstan 44°8N 68°28E 217 D7
Sozh → Belarus 51°57N 30°48E 177 B16
Sozopol Bulgaria 42°23N 27°42E 203 D11
Spa Belgium 50°29N 5°53E 170 D5
Spaans Lagoen Aruba 12°28N 69°58W 322 f
Spaanse Water Curaçao 12°4N 68°51W 322 g
Spaatz I. Antarctica 73°10S 75°0W 151 D17
Spaccaforno = Ispica Italy 36°47N 14°55E 201 F7
Spagna, Piazza di Rome, Italy 136 b3
Spain ■ Europe 39°0N 4°0W 192 D3
Spalato = Split Croatia 43°31N 16°26E 199 E13
Spalding S. Austral., Australia 33°30S 138°37E 282 B3
Spalding Lincs., U.K. 52°48N 0°9W 168 E7
Spanaway U.S.A. 47°6N 122°26W 306 C4
Spandau Germany 52°33N 13°9E 115 A1
Spånga Sweden 59°23N 17°53E 139 A1
Spangler U.S.A. 40°39N 78°48W 312 F6
Spanische Reitschule Vienna, Austria 142 b1
Spanish Canada 46°12N 82°20W 298 C3
Spanish Fork U.S.A. 40°7N 111°39W 304 F8
Spanish Pt. Antigua & B. 17°33N 61°44W 322 c
Spanish Pt. Bermuda 32°18N 64°49W 153 a
Spanish Riding School = Spanische Reitschule Vienna, Austria 142 b1
Spanish Steps = Spagna, Piazza di Rome, Italy 136 b3
Spanish Town Br. Virgin Is. 18°26N 64°26W 321 b
Spanish Town Jamaica 18°0N 76°57W 320 a
Sparks Ga., U.S.A. 31°11N 83°26W 316 D6
Sparks Nev., U.S.A. 39°32N 119°45W 306 F7
Sparreholm Sweden 59°4N 16°49E 162 E10
Sparrow Bay Grenada 12°30N 61°27W 323 q
Sparta = Sparti Greece 37°5N 22°25E 204 D4
Sparta Ga., U.S.A. 33°17N 82°58W 316 B7
Sparta Ill., U.S.A. 38°8N 89°42W 310 F7
Sparta Mich., U.S.A. 43°10N 85°42W 311 A11
Sparta N.J., U.S.A. 41°2N 74°38W 313 E10
Sparta Wis., U.S.A. 43°56N 90°49W 308 D8
Spartanburg U.S.A. 34°56N 81°57W 315 D14
Spartel, C. Morocco 35°47N 5°56W 260 A3
Sparti Greece 37°5N 22°25E 204 D4
Spartivento, C. Calabria, Italy 37°55N 16°4E 201 E9
Spartivento, C. Sard., Italy 38°53N 8°50E 200 D1
Spartochori Greece 38°40N 20°46E 207 B2
Sparwood Canada 49°44N 114°53W 296 D6
Spas-Demensk Russia 54°20N 34°0E 188 E7
Spas-Klepiki Russia 55°10N 40°10E 188 E11
Spassk = Bednodemyanovsk Russia 53°55N 43°15E 190 D6
Spassk-Dalniy Russia 44°40N 132°48E 220 B6
Spassk-Ryazanskiy Russia 54°24N 40°25E 188 E11
Spatha, Akra Greece 35°42N 23°43E 207 E4
Spatsizi → Canada 57°42N 128°7W 296 B3
Spatsizi Plateau Wilderness ⌓ Canada 57°40N 128°0W 296 B3
Spean → U.K. 56°55N 4°59W 167 E4
Spearfish U.S.A. 44°30N 103°52W 308 C2
Spearman U.S.A. 36°12N 101°12W 314 C4
Spectacle I. U.S.A. 42°19N 70°59W 116 A3
Speculator U.S.A. 43°30N 74°22W 313 C10
Speed Australia 35°21S 142°27E 282 C5
Speedway U.S.A. 39°48N 86°16W 311 E10
Speery I. St. Helena 16°1S 5°46W 153 h
Speia Moldova 46°59N 29°19E 183 D14
Speicher-See Germany 48°12N 11°42E 131 A3
Speightstown Barbados 13°15N 59°39W 323 r
Speising Austria 48°10N 16°17E 142 B1
Speke Gulf Tanzania 2°20S 32°50E 268 C3
Spello Italy 42°59N 12°40E 199 F9
Spence Bay = Taloyoak Canada 69°32N 93°32W 294 D13
Spencer Idaho, U.S.A. 44°22N 112°11W 304 D7
Spencer Ind., U.S.A. 39°17N 86°46W 311 E10
Spencer Iowa, U.S.A. 43°9N 95°9W 308 D6
Spencer N.Y., U.S.A. 42°13N 76°30W 313 D8
Spencer Nebr., U.S.A. 42°53N 98°42W 308 D4
Spencer, C. Australia 35°20S 136°53E 282 C2
Spencer B. Namibia 25°30S 14°47E 270 C1
Spencer G. Australia 34°0S 137°20E 282 C2
Spencerville Ont., Canada 44°51N 75°33W 313 B9
Spencerville Ohio, U.S.A. 40°43N 84°21W 311 D12
Spences Bridge Canada 50°25N 121°20W 296 C4
Spennymoor U.K. 54°42N 1°36W 168 C6
Spenser Mts. N.Z. 42°15S 172°45E 285 C7
Spentrup Denmark 56°33N 10°2E 163 H4
Sperchios → Greece 38°57N 22°3E 204 C4
Sperillen Norway 60°28N 10°3E 164 D7
Sperrgebiet △ Namibia 27°38S 15°56E 270 C2
Sperrin Mts. U.K. 54°50N 7°0W 166 B5
Spessart Germany 49°56N 9°18E 179 F5
Spetalen Norway 59°18N 10°45E 164 E7
Spetses Greece 37°15N 23°10E 204 D5
Spey → U.K. 57°40N 3°6W 167 D5
Speyer Germany 49°29N 8°25E 179 F4
Speyside Trin. & Tob. 11°17N 60°32W 323 s
Spezand Pakistan 29°59N 67°0E 242 E2
Spezzano Albanese Italy 39°40N 16°19E 201 C9
Sphinx Egypt 29°58N 31°8E 117 B1
Spickard U.S.A. 40°14N 93°36W 310 D3
Spiddal Ireland 53°15N 9°18W 166 C2
Spiekeroog Germany 53°46N 7°42E 178 B3
Spiez Switz. 46°40N 7°40E 179 J3
Spili Greece 35°13N 24°31E 207 E5
Spilimbergo Italy 46°7N 12°54E 199 B9
Spīn Būldak Afghan. 31°1N 66°25E 242 D2
Spinaceto Italy 41°47N 12°28E 136 C1
Spinalonga Greece 35°18N 25°44E 207 E6
Spinazzola Italy 40°58N 16°5E 201 B9
Spineni Romania 44°43N 24°37E 183 F9
Spinifex ✪ Australia 28°30S 128°30E 279 E4
Spirding = Śniardwy, Jezioro Poland 53°48N 21°50E 184 E8
Spirit Lake U.S.A. 46°15N 122°9W 306 D4
Spirit River Canada 55°45N 118°50W 296 B5
Spiritwood Canada 53°24N 107°33W 297 C7
Spišská Nová Ves Slovakia 48°58N 20°34E 181 C13
Spišské Podhradie Slovakia 49°0N 20°48E 181 B13
Spit Junction Australia 33°49S 151°14E 139 A2
Spital Austria 47°42N 14°18E 180 D7
Spithead U.K. 50°45N 1°10W 169 G6
Spitsbergen = Svalbard Arctic 78°0N 17°0E 154 B12
Spittal an der Drau Austria 46°48N 13°31E 180 E6
Spjelkavik Norway 62°28N 6°22E 164 B3
Split Croatia 43°31N 16°26E 199 E13
Split ✈ (SPU) Croatia 43°33N 16°15E 199 E13
Split L. Canada 56°8N 96°15W 297 B9
Split Lake Canada 56°8N 96°15W 297 B9
Splitski Kanal Croatia 43°31N 16°20E 199 E13
Splügenpass Switz. 46°30N 9°20E 179 J5
Spofford U.S.A. 29°10N 100°25W 314 G4
Spokane U.S.A. 47°40N 117°24W 304 C5
Spoleto Italy 42°44N 12°44E 199 F9
Sponvika Norway 59°7N 11°15E 164 E8
Spoon → U.S.A. 40°19N 90°4W 310 D6
Spooner U.S.A. 45°50N 91°53W 308 C8
Spořilov Czechia 50°2N 14°29E 135 B3
Sporyy Navolok, Mys Russia 75°50N 68°40E 214 B7
Spot Pond U.S.A. 42°26N 71°4W 116 A2
Spotswood Australia 37°50S 144°52E 128 B1
Sprague U.S.A. 47°18N 117°59W 304 C5
Spratly I. S. China Sea 8°38N 111°55E 230 C4
Spratly Is. S. China Sea 8°20N 112°0E 230 C4
Spray U.S.A. 44°50N 119°48W 304 D4
Spreča → Bos.-H. 44°44N 18°6E 182 F3
Spree → Germany 52°32N 13°12E 178 C9
Spreewald Germany 51°58N 13°51E 178 D9
Spremberg Germany 51°34N 14°22E 178 D10
Sprengisandur Iceland 64°52N 18°7W 155 C8
Spring City U.S.A. 40°11N 75°33W 313 F9
Spring Cr. → U.S.A. 30°54N 84°45W 316 E5
Spring Creek U.S.A. 40°44N 115°35W 304 F6
Spring Garden Guyana 6°59N 58°31W 329 B6
Spring Garden Calif., U.S.A. 39°52N 120°47W 306 F6
Spring Green U.S.A. 43°11N 90°4W 310 A6
Spring Hill Ala., U.S.A. 31°42N 85°58W 316 D4
Spring Hill Fla., U.S.A. 28°27N 82°41W 317 G7
Spring Mts. U.S.A. 36°0N 115°45W 307 J11
Spring Temple Buddha China 33°46N 112°27E 226 H7
Spring Valley Calif., U.S.A. 32°44N 116°59W 307 N10
Spring Valley Ill., U.S.A. 41°20N 89°12W 310 C7
Spring Valley Nev., U.S.A. 36°6N 115°14W 124 B1
Springbok S. Africa 29°42S 17°54E 270 C2
Springboro U.S.A. 41°48N 80°22W 312 E4
Springdale Nfld. & L., Canada 49°30N 56°6W 299 C8
Springdale Ark., U.S.A. 36°11N 94°8W 314 C7
Springdale Ohio, U.S.A. 39°17N 84°29W 311 E12
Springe Germany 52°13N 9°33E 178 C5
Springeberg Germany 52°26N 13°43E 115 B5
Springer U.S.A. 36°22N 104°36W 305 H11
Springerville U.S.A. 34°8N 109°17W 305 J9
Springfield Ont., Canada 42°50N 80°56W 312 D4
Springfield Dominica 15°21N 61°23W 323 k
Springfield N.Z. 43°19S 171°56E 285 D6
Springfield Colo., U.S.A. 37°24N 102°37W 305 H12
Springfield Fla., U.S.A. 30°10N 85°37W 316 E4
Springfield Ga., U.S.A. 32°22N 81°18W 316 C8
Springfield Ill., U.S.A. 39°48N 89°39W 310 E7
Springfield Ky., U.S.A. 37°41N 85°13W 311 G11
Springfield Mass., U.S.A. 42°6N 72°35W 313 D12
Springfield Mo., U.S.A. 37°13N 93°17W 308 G7
Springfield Ohio, U.S.A. 39°55N 83°49W 311 E13
Springfield Oreg., U.S.A. 44°3N 123°1W 304 D2
Springfield S.C., U.S.A. 33°30N 81°17W 316 B8
Springfield Tenn., U.S.A. 36°31N 86°53W 315 C11
Springfield Va., U.S.A. 38°46N 77°10W 143 C1
Springfield Vt., U.S.A. 43°18N 72°29W 313 C12
Springfield, L. U.S.A. 39°46N 89°36W 310 E7
Springfontein S. Africa 30°15S 25°40E 270 D4
Springhill Canada 45°40N 64°4W 299 C7
Springhill La., U.S.A. 33°0N 93°28W 314 E8
Springhouse Canada 51°56N 122°7W 296 C4
Springlands = Corriverton Guyana 5°55N 57°20W 329 B6
Springs S. Africa 26°13S 28°25E 271 C4
Springsure Australia 24°8S 148°6E 280 C4
Springvale Ga., U.S.A. 31°50N 84°53W 316 D5
Springvale Maine, U.S.A. 43°28N 70°48W 313 C14
Springville Calif., U.S.A. 36°8N 118°49W 306 J8
Springville Iowa, U.S.A. 42°3N 91°27W 310 B5
Springville N.Y., U.S.A. 42°31N 78°40W 312 D6
Springville Utah, U.S.A. 40°10N 111°37W 304 F8
Springwater U.S.A. 42°38N 77°35W 312 D7
Sprottau = Szprotawa Poland 51°33N 15°35E 185 G2
Spruce-Creek U.S.A. 40°36N 78°9W 312 F6
Spruce Knob-Seneca Rocks ⌓ U.S.A. 38°50N 79°30W 309 F14
Spruce Mt. U.S.A. 44°12N 72°19W 313 B12
Sprucedale Canada 45°29N 79°28W 312 A5
Spur U.S.A. 33°28N 100°52W 314 E4
Spurn Hd. U.K. 53°35N 0°8E 168 D8
Spuž Montenegro 42°32N 19°10E 202 D3
Spuzzum Canada 49°37N 121°23W 296 D4
Spydeberg Norway 59°37N 11°5E 164 E8
Squam L. U.S.A. 43°45N 71°32W 313 C13
Squamish Canada 49°45N 123°10W 296 D4
Squantum U.S.A. 42°17N 71°0W 116 B2
Square Islands Canada 52°47N 55°47W 299 B8
Squillace, G. di Italy 38°43N 16°35E 201 D9
Squinzano Italy 40°26N 18°2E 201 B11
Squires, Mt. Australia 26°14S 127°28E 279 E4
Sragen Indonesia 7°26S 111°2E 235 D4
Srbac Bos.-H. 45°7N 17°30E 182 E2
Srbica = Skënderaj Kosovo 42°45N 20°47E 202 D4
Srbija = Serbia ■ Europe 43°20N 20°0E 202 C4
Srbobran Serbia 45°32N 19°48E 182 E4
Sre Ambel Cambodia 11°8N 103°46E 237 G4
Sre Khtum Cambodia 12°10N 106°52E 237 F6
Sre Umbell = Sre Ambel Cambodia 11°8N 103°46E 237 G4
Srebarna Bulgaria 44°6N 27°4E 203 B11
Srebrenica Bos.-H. 44°6N 19°18E 182 F4
Sredinnyy Khrebet Russia 57°0N 160°0E 215 D17
Sredinnyy Ra. = Sredinnyy Khrebet Russia 57°0N 160°0E 215 D17
Središče Slovenia 46°24N 16°17E 199 B13
Sredna Gora Bulgaria 42°40N 24°20E 203 D8
Srednaya Rogatka Russia 59°49N 30°22E 137 C2
Srednekolymsk Russia 67°27N 153°40E 215 C16
Sredni Rodopi Bulgaria 41°40N 24°45E 203 E8
Srednogorie Bulgaria 42°43N 24°10E 203 D8
Śrem Poland 52°6N 17°2E 185 F4
Sremska Mitrovica Serbia 44°59N 19°38E 182 F4
Sremski Karlovci Serbia 45°12N 19°56E 182 E4
Srepok → Cambodia 13°33N 106°16E 236 F6
Sretensk Russia 52°10N 117°40E 215 D12
Sri Aman = Bandar Sri Aman Malaysia 1°15N 111°32E 235 B4
Sri Kalahasti India 13°45N 79°44E 245 H4
Sri Ksetra Burma 18°48N 95°17E 241 F5
Sri Lanka ■ Asia 7°30N 80°50E 245 L5
Sri Pada = Adam's Peak Sri Lanka 6°48N 80°30E 245 L5
Sriharikota I. India 13°40N 80°20E 245 H5
Srikakulam India 18°14N 83°58E 244 E6
Srinagar India 34°5N 74°50E 243 B6
Sripur Bangla. 24°14N 90°30E 241 C3
Srivardhan India 18°4N 73°3E 244 E1
Srivilliputtur India 9°31N 77°40E 245 K3
Środa Śląska Poland 51°10N 16°36E 185 G3
Środa Wielkopolski Poland 52°15N 17°19E 185 F4
Śródmieście Poland 52°13N 21°4E 143 B2
Srono Indonesia 8°24S 114°16E 231 J17
Srpska Crnja Serbia 45°38N 20°44E 182 E5
Srpski Itebej Serbia 45°35N 20°44E 182 E5
Srungavarapukota India 18°7N 83°10E 244 E6
Ssese Is. = Sese Is. Uganda 0°20S 32°20E 268 C3
Ssuhu Taiwan 23°38N 120°13E 225 C2
St-Laurent-du Maroni □ Fr. Guiana 4°0N 53°45W 329 C7
Staaken Germany 52°31N 13°8E 115 A1
Staaten → Australia 16°24S 141°17E 280 B3
Staaten River △ Australia 16°15S 142°40E 280 B3
Stabbursdalen △ Norway 70°5N 24°15E 160 A21
Stabekk Norway 59°54N 10°36E 133 A2
Staberhuk Germany 54°23N 11°18E 178 A7
Stade Germany 53°35N 9°29E 178 B5
Stade de France Paris, France 48°55N 2°22E 134 A3
Staðarfell Iceland 65°7N 22°12W 155 B4
Staðarhólskirkja Iceland 65°23N 21°58W 155 B5
Staðastaður Iceland 64°49N 23°1W 155 C3
Stadhavet Norway 62°13N 5°0E 164 B2
Stadhuis Amsterdam, Neths. 112 b3
Staður Norðurland Vestra Iceland 65°9N 21°3W 155 B5
Staður Vestfirðir Iceland 66°15N 22°50W 155 A4
Stadlandet Norway 62°10N 5°10E 164 B2
Stadlau Austria 48°13N 16°27E 142 A2
Stadshuset Stockholm, Sweden 139 b1
Stadskanaal Neths. 53°4N 6°55E 170 A6
Stadsschouwburg Amsterdam, Neths. 112 c1
Stadtallendorf Germany 50°48N 9°1E 178 E5
Stadthagen Germany 52°19N 9°13E 178 C5
Stadtlohn Germany 51°59N 6°55E 178 D2
Stadtroda Germany 50°52N 11°44E 178 E7
Stafafell Iceland 64°25N 14°52W 155 C12
Staffa U.K. 56°27N 6°21W 167 E2
Staffanstorp Sweden 55°39N 13°13E 163 J7
Stafford Staffs., U.K. 52°49N 2°7W 168 E5
Stafford Kans., U.S.A. 37°58N 98°36W 308 G4
Stafford, L. U.S.A. 29°20N 82°29W 317 F7
Stafford Springs U.S.A. 41°57N 72°18W 313 E12
Staffordshire □ U.K. 52°53N 2°10W 168 E5
Stagnone Italy 37°53N 12°26E 200 E5
Stagnone di Marsala ⌓ Italy 37°52N 12°26E 200 E5
Staines-upon-Thames U.K. 51°26N 0°29W 169 F7
Stains France 48°57N 2°22E 134 A3
Stainz Austria 46°53N 15°17E 180 E8
Stakhanov Ukraine 48°35N 38°40E 189 H10
Stalać Serbia 43°43N 21°28E 202 C5
Stalin = Kuçovë Albania 40°47N 19°57E 202 F3
Stalin = Varna Bulgaria 43°13N 27°56E 203 C11
Stalin Pk. = Gerlachovský štít Slovakia 49°11N 20°7E 181 B13
Stalin Pk. = imeni Ismail Samani, Pik Tajikistan 39°0N 72°2E 217 E8
Stalin Pk. = Musala Bulgaria 42°13N 23°37E 202 D7
Stalinabad = Dushanbe Tajikistan 38°33N 68°48E 217 E7
Stalingrad = Volgograd Russia 48°40N 44°25E 191 F7
Staliniri = Tskhinvali Georgia 42°14N 44°1E 191 J7
Stalinogorsk = Novomoskovsk Russia 54°5N 38°15E 188 E10
Stalinogrod = Katowice Poland 50°17N 19°5E 185 H6
Stalinsk = Novokuznetsk Russia 53°45N 87°10E 217 B11
Stalinstadt = Eisenhüttenstadt Germany 52°9N 14°38E 178 C10
Stallarholmen Sweden 59°22N 17°12E 162 E11
Ställdalen Sweden 59°56N 14°56E 162 E8
Stalowa Wola Poland 50°34N 22°3E 185 H9
Stalybridge U.K. 53°28N 2°3W 168 D5
Stamford Queens., Australia 21°15S 143°46E 280 C3
Stamford Lincs., U.K. 52°39N 0°29W 169 E7
Stamford Conn., U.S.A. 41°3N 73°32W 313 E11
Stamford N.Y., U.S.A. 42°25N 74°38W 313 D10
Stamford Tex., U.S.A. 32°57N 99°48W 314 E5
Stamford Hill U.K. 51°34N 0°4W 125 A3
Stammersdorf Austria 48°18N 16°24E 142 A2
Stamnes Norway 60°40N 5°45E 164 D2
Stamping Ground U.S.A. 38°16N 84°41W 311 F12
Stampriet Namibia 24°20S 18°28E 270 B2
Stamps U.S.A. 33°22N 93°30W 314 E8
Stanberry U.S.A. 40°13N 94°35W 310 D2
Stančevo = Kalipetrovo Bulgaria 44°5N 27°14E 203 B11
Standerton S. Africa 26°55S 29°7E 271 C4
Standish U.S.A. 43°59N 83°57W 309 D12
Stanford S. Africa 34°26S 19°29E 270 D2
Stanford Mont., U.S.A. 47°9N 110°13W 304 C8
Stånga Sweden 57°17N 18°29E 163 G12
Stange Norway 60°43N 11°5E 164 D8
Stanger S. Africa 29°27S 31°14E 271 C5
Stängselåsen = Salpausselkä Finland 61°3N 26°15E 188 B4
Stangvik Norway 62°55N 8°28E 164 B5
Stanhope Vic., Australia 36°27S 144°59E 283 D6
Stanhope Iowa, U.S.A. 42°17N 93°48W 310 B3
Stanimaka = Asenovgrad Bulgaria 42°1N 24°51E 203 D8
Stanišić Serbia 45°56N 19°10E 182 E4
Stanislaus → U.S.A. 37°40N 121°14W 306 H5
Stanislav = Ivano-Frankivsk Ukraine 48°40N 24°40E 183 B9

Stanisławów = Ivano-Frankivsk Ukraine 48°40N 24°40E 183 B9
Stanisławów Poland 52°18N 21°33E 185 F8
Stanley Tas., Australia 40°46S 145°19E 281 G4
Stanley Hong Kong, China 22°13N 114°12E 122 B3
Stanley Falk. Is. 51°40S 59°51W 153 f
Stanley Durham, U.K. 54°53N 1°41W 168 C6
Stanley Idaho, U.S.A. 44°13N 114°56W 304 D6
Stanley N. Dak., U.S.A. 48°19N 102°23W 308 A2
Stanley N.Y., U.S.A. 42°48N 77°6W 312 D7
Stanley B. Hong Kong, China 22°13N 114°13E 122 B3
Stanley Falls = Boyoma, Chutes Dem. Rep. of the Congo 0°35N 25°23E 264 B5
Stanley Mission Canada 55°25N 104°33W 297 B8
Stanley Pen. Hong Kong, China 22°12N 114°12E 122 B3
Stanley Pool = Malebo, Pool Africa 4°17S 15°20E 265 C3
Stanley Res. India 11°50N 77°40E 245 J3
Stanleyville = Kisangani Dem. Rep. of the Congo 0°35N 25°15E 268 B2
Stanmore U.K. 51°37N 0°18W 125 A2
Stannards U.S.A. 42°5N 77°55W 312 D7
Stanovoy Khrebet Russia 55°0N 130°0E 215 D14
Stanovoy Ra. = Stanovoy Khrebet Russia 55°0N 130°0E 215 D14
Stansmore Ra. Australia 21°23S 128°33E 278 D4
Stansted, London ✈ (STN) U.K. 51°54N 0°14E 169 F8
Stanthorpe Australia 28°36S 151°59E 281 D5
Stanton Ky., U.S.A. 37°54N 83°52W 311 G13
Stanton Tex., U.S.A. 32°8N 101°48W 314 E4
Stantsiya Regar = Tursunzoda Tajikistan 38°30N 68°14E 217 E7
Stanwood U.S.A. 48°15N 122°23W 306 B4
Staples Ont., Canada 42°10N 82°35W 312 D2
Staples Minn., U.S.A. 46°21N 94°48W 308 B6
Stapleton N.Y., U.S.A. 40°36N 74°5W 132 C1
Stapleton Nebr., U.S.A. 41°29N 100°31W 308 E3
Stapodia Greece 37°24N 25°34E 205 D7
Stąporków Poland 51°9N 20°31E 185 G7
Star City Canada 52°50N 104°20W 297 C8
Star Harbour Solomon Is. 10°47S 162°19E 287 N12
Star Lake U.S.A. 44°10N 75°2W 313 B9
Stará Ďala = Hurbanovo Slovakia 47°51N 18°11E 181 D11
Stará L'ubovňa Slovakia 49°18N 20°42E 181 B13
Stara Moravica Serbia 45°50N 19°30E 182 E4
Stara Pazova Serbia 44°58N 20°10E 182 F5
Stara Planina Bulgaria 43°15N 23°0E 202 C7
Stara Sil Ukraine 49°29N 22°58E 185 J9
Stará Turá Slovakia 48°47N 17°42E 181 C10
Stara Ushytsya Ukraine 48°35N 27°8E 183 B12
Stara Zagora Bulgaria 42°26N 25°39E 203 D9
Stara Zagora □ Bulgaria 42°26N 25°39E 203 D9
Starachowice Poland 51°3N 21°2E 185 G8
Staraya Derevnya Russia 59°58N 30°15E 137 B1
Staraya Russa Russia 57°58N 31°23E 188 D6
Starbuck I. Kiribati 5°37S 155°55W 289 H12
Starchiojd Romania 45°19N 26°11E 183 E11
Starcke △ Australia 14°56S 145°2E 280 A4
Staré Město Czechia 50°5N 14°25E 135 B2
Stare Miasto Warsaw, Poland 143 a2
Stargard in Pommern = Stargard Szczeciński Poland 53°20N 15°0E 184 E2
Stargard Szczeciński Poland 53°20N 15°0E 184 E2
Stårheim Norway 61°56N 5°40E 164 C2
Stari Bar Montenegro 42°7N 19°10E 202 D3
Stari Bečej = Bečej Serbia 45°36N 20°3E 182 E5
Stari Grad Croatia 43°10N 16°38E 199 E13
Stari Trg Slovenia 45°29N 15°7E 199 C12
Staritsa Russia 56°33N 34°55E 188 D8
Starke U.S.A. 29°57N 82°7W 316 F7
Starke, L. U.S.A. 28°34N 81°32W 133 A1
Starkville U.S.A. 33°28N 88°49W 315 E10
Starnberg Germany 48°0N 11°21E 179 H7
Starnberger See Germany 47°54N 11°19E 179 H7
Staro Oryakhovo Bulgaria 42°59N 27°47E 203 D11
Starobilsk Ukraine 49°16N 39°0E 189 H10
Starodub Russia 52°30N 32°50E 189 F7
Starogard Gdański Poland 53°59N 18°30E 184 E5
Starokonstantinov = Starokonstyantyniv Ukraine 49°48N 27°10E 177 D14
Starokonstyantyniv Ukraine 49°48N 27°10E 177 D14
Starokozache Ukraine 46°20N 29°59E 183 D14
Starominskaya Russia 46°33N 39°0E 191 G4
Staroshcherbinovskaya Russia 46°40N 38°53E 191 G4
Starrs Mill U.S.A. 33°19N 84°31W 316 B5
Start Pt. U.K. 50°13N 3°39W 169 G4
Stary Sącz Poland 49°33N 20°35E 185 J7
Staryy Biryuzyak Russia 44°46N 46°50E 191 H8
Staryy Chartoriysk Ukraine 51°15N 25°54E 177 C13
Staryy Krym Ukraine 45°3N 35°8E 189 K8
Staryy Margilan = Marg'ilon Uzbekistan 40°27N 71°42E 217 D8
Staryy Oskol Russia 51°19N 37°55E 189 G9
Staryy Sambir Ukraine 49°27N 22°59E 185 J9
Stassfurt Germany 51°51N 11°35E 178 D7
Staszów Poland 50°33N 21°10E 185 H8
State Center U.S.A. 42°1N 93°10W 310 B3
State College U.S.A. 40°48N 77°52W 312 F7
State Street Chicago, U.S.A. 119 c2
Stateline U.S.A. 38°57N 119°56W 306 G7
Staten, I. = Estados, I. de Los Argentina 54°40S 64°30W 336 D4
Staten I. U.S.A. 40°35N 74°9W 313 F10
Staten Island Zoo U.S.A. 40°38N 74°6W 132 C1
Staten Islands Ferry Terminal U.S.A. 40°38N 74°4W 132 C1
Statenice Czechia 50°9N 14°19E 135 B1
Statenville U.S.A. 30°42N 83°2W 316 E6
Statesboro U.S.A. 32°27N 81°47W 316 C8
Statesville U.S.A. 35°47N 80°53W 315 D14
Statham U.S.A. 33°58N 83°35W 316 B6
Stathelle Norway 59°3N 9°41E 164 E6
Statia = St. Eustatius W. Indies 17°20N 63°0W 322 a
Stauffer U.S.A. 34°45N 119°3W 307 L7
Staunton Ill., U.S.A. 39°1N 89°47W 310 F7
Staunton Va., U.S.A. 38°9N 79°4W 309 F14
Stavanger = Rogaland □ Norway 59°12N 6°20E 164 E3
Stavanger Norway 58°57N 5°40E 164 F2
Stavelot Belgium 50°23N 5°55E 170 D5
Stavern Norway 59°0N 10°1E 164 F7
Stavoren Neths. 52°53N 5°22E 170 B5
Stavropol Russia 45°5N 42°0E 191 H6
Stavropol □ Russia 47°20N 42°50E 191 G6
Stavros Cyprus 35°1N 32°38E 207 E8
Stavros Ithaki, Greece 38°27N 20°39E 207 C2
Stavros Kriti, Greece 35°12N 24°45E 207 E5
Stavros Thessaloniki, Greece 40°39N 23°43E 202 F7
Stavros, Akra Greece 35°26N 24°58E 207 E5
Stavros Niarchos Cultural Centre Greece 37°56N 23°41E 112 B2
Stavroupoli Greece 41°12N 24°45E 203 E8
Stawell Australia 37°5S 142°47E 282 D5
Stawell ➜ Australia 20°20S 142°55E 280 C3
Stawiski Poland 53°22N 22°9E 184 E9
Stawiszyn Poland 51°56N 18°4E 185 G5
Stayner Canada 44°25N 80°5W 312 B4
Stayton U.S.A. 44°48N 122°48W 304 D2
Steamboat Springs U.S.A. 40°29N 106°50W 304 F10
Stean Norway 59°16N 8°33E 164 E5
Stebbins U.S.A. 63°31N 162°17W 303 E7
Steblevë Albania 41°23N 20°33E 202 E4
Stedelijk Museum Neths. 52°21N 4°52E 112 A2
Steele Ala., U.S.A. 33°56N 86°12W 316 B3
Steele N. Dak., U.S.A. 46°51N 99°55W 308 B4
Steele Creek Australia 37°44S 144°52E 128 A1
Steelton U.S.A. 40°14N 76°50W 312 F8
Steelville U.S.A. 37°58N 91°22W 310 G5
Steen River Canada 59°40N 117°12W 296 B5
Steenkool = Bintuni Indonesia 2°7S 133°32E 231 E8
Steenokkerzeel Belgium 50°55N 4°31E 116 A2
Steens Mt. U.S.A. 42°35N 118°40W 304 E4
Steenstrup Gletscher Greenland 75°15N 57°0W 154 B5
Steenwijk Neths. 52°47N 6°7E 170 B6
Steep Pt. Australia 26°8S 113°8E 279 E1
Steep Rock Canada 51°30N 98°48W 297 C9
Steer, L. U.S.A. 28°31N 81°30W 133 A2
Ştefan Vodă Moldova 46°27N 29°42E 183 D14
Ştefănesti Romania 47°44N 27°15E 183 C12
Stefanie △ Ethiopia 4°55N 36°55E 257 G4
Stefanie L. = Chew Bahir Ethiopia 4°40N 36°50E 257 G4
Stefansson Bay Antarctica 67°20S 59°8E 151 C5
Stefansson I. Canada 73°20N 105°45W 295 C10
Stege Denmark 54°59N 12°18E 163 K6
Stegi = Siteki Swaziland 26°32S 31°58E 271 C5
Steglitz Germany 52°27N 13°19E 115 B2
Stegman = Artesia U.S.A. 32°51N 104°24W 305 K11
Ştei Romania 46°32N 22°27E 182 D7
Steiermark □ Austria 47°26N 15°0E 180 D8
Steigerwald Germany 49°44N 10°26E 179 F6
Steigerwald ⌓ Germany 49°50N 10°30E 179 F6
Steilacoom U.S.A. 47°10N 122°36W 306 C4
Steilrandberge Namibia 17°45S 13°20E 270 A1
Stein = Kamnik Slovenia 46°14N 14°37E 199 B11
Steinbach Canada 49°32N 96°40W 297 D9
Steinfurt Germany 52°9N 7°20E 178 C3
Steinhatchee U.S.A. 29°40N 83°23W 316 F6
Steinhausen Namibia 21°49S 18°20E 270 B2
Steinheim Germany 51°51N 9°5E 178 D5
Steinhuder Meer Germany 52°29N 9°21E 178 C5
Steinhuder Meer ⌓ Germany 52°30N 9°16E 178 C5
Steinkjer Norway 64°1N 11°31E 160 D14
Steinkopf S. Africa 29°18S 17°43E 270 C2
Steinshamn Norway 62°47N 6°28E 164 B3
Steinwald ⌓ Germany 49°55N 12°8E 179 F8
Stellarton Canada 45°32N 62°30W 299 C7
Stellenbosch S. Africa 33°58S 18°50E 270 D2
Stélvio, Paso dello Italy 46°32N 10°27E 198 B7
Stenay France 49°29N 5°12E 173 C12
Stendal Germany 52°36N 11°53E 178 C7
Stende Latvia 57°11N 22°33E 184 A9
Stenen Koraal Curaçao 12°10N 68°56W 322 g
Stenhamra Sweden 59°20N 17°41E 162 E11
Stenshuvud △ Sweden 55°39N 14°15E 163 J8
Stenstorp Sweden 58°17N 13°45E 163 F7
Stenungsund Sweden 58°6N 11°50E 163 F5
Steornabhaigh = Stornoway U.K. 58°13N 6°23W 167 C2
Stepanakert = Xankändi Azerbaijan 39°52N 46°49E 213 C12
Stepanavan Armenia 41°1N 44°23E 191 K7
Stephansdom Vienna, Austria 142 b2
Stephens, C. N.Z. 40°42S 173°58E 285 A8
Stephens Creek Australia 31°50S 141°30E 282 A4
Stephens I. B.C., Canada 54°10N 130°45W 296 C2
Stephens I. N.Z. 40°40S 174°1E 285 A9
Stephens L. Canada 56°32N 95°0W 297 B9
Stephenville Nfld. & L., Canada 48°31N 58°35W 299 C8
Stephenville Tex., U.S.A. 32°13N 98°12W 314 E5
Stepney U.K. 51°30N 0°3W 125 A3
Stepnica Poland 53°38N 14°36E 184 E1
Stepnogorsk Kazakhstan 52°21N 71°53E 217 B8
Stepnoi = Elista Russia 46°16N 44°14E 191 G7
Steppe Asia 50°0N 50°0E 210 C7
Steps Pt. Amer. Samoa 14°23S 170°45W 302 f
Sterea Ellas □ Greece 38°50N 23°0E 204 C4
Sterkstroom S. Africa 31°32S 26°32E 270 D4
Sterling Alaska, U.S.A. 60°32N 150°46W 303 F10
Sterling Colo., U.S.A. 40°37N 103°13W 304 F12
Sterling Ga., U.S.A. 31°16N 81°34W 316 D8
Sterling Ill., U.S.A. 41°48N 89°42W 310 C7
Sterling Kans., U.S.A. 38°13N 98°12W 308 F4
Sterling City U.S.A. 31°51N 101°0W 314 F4
Sterling Heights U.S.A. 42°35N 83°2W 311 B13
Sterling Park U.S.A. 37°41N 122°27W 136 B2
Sterling Run U.S.A. 41°25N 78°12W 312 E6
Sterlitamak Russia 53°40N 56°0E 186 D10
Sternberg Germany 53°42N 11°50E 178 B7
Šternberk Czechia 49°45N 17°15E 181 B10
Sternes Greece 35°30N 24°9E 207 E5
Sterzing = Vipiteno Italy 46°54N 11°26E 199 B8
Stettin = Szczecin Poland 53°27N 14°27E 184 E1
Stettiner Haff Germany 53°47N 14°15E 178 B10
Stettler Canada 52°19N 112°40W 296 C6
Steubenville U.S.A. 40°22N 80°37W 312 F4
Stevenage U.K. 51°55N 0°13W 169 F7
Stevens Point U.S.A. 44°31N 89°34W 308 C9
Stevens Pottery U.S.A. 32°57N 83°17W 316 C6
Stevens Village U.S.A. 66°1N 149°6W 303 C10
Stevenson U.S.A. 45°42N 121°53W 306 E5
Stevenson ➜ Australia 27°6S 135°33E 281 D2
Stevenson L. Canada 53°55N 96°0W 297 C9
Stevensville U.S.A. 46°30N 114°5W 304 C6
Stevns Klint Denmark 55°17N 12°28E 163 J6
Steward U.S.A. 41°51N 89°1W 310 C7
Stewardson U.S.A. 39°16N 88°38W 311 E8
Stewart B.C., Canada 55°56N 129°57W 296 B3
Stewart Ga., U.S.A. 33°25N 83°52W 316 B6
Stewart Nev., U.S.A. 39°5N 119°46W 306 F7
Stewart ➜ Canada 63°19N 139°26W 294 E4
Stewart, C. Australia 11°57S 134°56E 280 A1
Stewart, I. Chile 54°50S 71°15W 336 D2
Stewart I. N.Z. 46°58S 167°54E 285 G2
Stewarts Point U.S.A. 38°39N 123°24W 306 G3
Stewartsville U.S.A. 39°45N 94°30W 310 E2
Stewartville U.S.A. 43°51N 92°29W 308 D7
Stewiacke Canada 45°9N 63°22W 299 C7
Steynsburg S. Africa 31°15S 25°49E 270 D4
Steyr Austria 48°3N 14°25E 180 C7
Steyr ➜ Austria 48°3N 14°25E 180 C7
Steytlerville S. Africa 33°17S 24°19E 270 D3
Stia Italy 43°48N 11°42E 199 E8
Sticklinge udde Sweden 59°23N 18°6E 139 A2
Stickney U.S.A. 41°49N 87°46W 119 C2
Stigler U.S.A. 35°15N 95°8W 314 D7
Stigliano Italy 40°24N 16°14E 201 B9
Stigtomta Sweden 58°47N 16°48E 163 F10
Stikine ➜ Canada 56°40N 132°30W 296 B2
Stilfontein S. Africa 26°51S 26°50E 270 C4
Stilida Greece 38°55N 22°47E 204 C4
Stillmore U.S.A. 32°27N 82°13W 316 C7
Stillwater N.Y., U.S.A. 42°55N 73°41W 313 D11
Stillwater Okla., U.S.A. 36°7N 97°4W 314 C6
Stillwater Range U.S.A. 39°50N 118°5W 304 G4
Stillwater Res. U.S.A. 43°54N 75°3W 313 C9
Stilo, Pta. Italy 38°25N 16°35E 201 D9
Stilwell U.S.A. 35°49N 94°38W 314 D7
Stînga Nistrului = Transnistria □ Moldova 47°20N 29°15E 183 C14
Štip Macedonia 41°42N 22°10E 202 E6
Stira Greece 38°9N 24°14E 204 C6
Stirling Ont., Canada 44°18N 77°33W 312 B7
Stirling N.Z. 46°14S 169°49E 285 G4
Stirling Stirling, U.K. 56°8N 3°57W 167 E5
Stirling □ U.K. 56°12N 4°18W 167 E4
Stirling Ra. Australia 34°23S 118°0E 279 F2
Stirling Range △ Australia 34°26S 118°20E 279 F2
Stittsville Canada 45°15N 75°55W 313 A9
Stjernøya Norway 70°20N 22°40E 160 A20
Stjørdalshalsen Norway 63°29N 10°51E 164 A7
Stock Island U.S.A. 24°32N 81°34W 317 L8
Stocka Sweden 61°53N 17°20E 162 C11
Stockach Germany 47°50N 9°1E 179 H5
Stockaryd Sweden 57°19N 14°36E 163 G8
Stockbridge Ga., U.S.A. 33°33N 84°14W 316 B5
Stockbridge Mich., U.S.A. 42°27N 84°11W 311 B12
Stockerau Austria 48°24N 16°12E 181 C9
Stockholm Sweden 59°19N 18°4E 139 B2
Stockholm □ Sweden 59°30N 18°20E 162 E12
Stockholm Arlanda ✈ (ARN) Sweden 59°41N 17°56E 139 A1
Stockport U.K. 53°25N 2°9W 168 D5
Stocksbridge U.K. 53°29N 1°35W 168 D6
Stocksund Sweden 59°23N 18°3E 139 A2
Stockton Calif., U.S.A. 37°58N 121°17W 306 H5
Stockton Ill., U.S.A. 42°21N 90°1W 310 B6
Stockton Kans., U.S.A. 39°26N 99°16W 308 F4
Stockton Mo., U.S.A. 37°42N 93°48W 310 G3
Stockton-on-Tees U.K. 54°35N 1°19W 168 C6
Stockton-on-Tees □ U.K. 54°35N 1°19W 168 C6
Stockton Plateau U.S.A. 30°30N 102°30W 314 F3
Stoclet, Palais Belgium 50°50N 4°24E 116 B2
Stoczek Łukowski Poland 51°58N 21°58E 185 G8
Stöde Sweden 62°28N 16°35E 162 B10
Stöðvarfjörður Iceland 64°49N 13°52W 155 C13
Stodůlky Czechia 50°3N 14°19E 135 B1
Stoeng Treng Cambodia 13°31N 105°58E 236 F5
Stoer, Pt. of U.K. 58°16N 5°23W 167 C3
Stogovo Macedonia 41°31N 20°38E 202 E4
Stoholm Denmark 56°30N 9°8E 163 H3
Stoke N.Z. 41°19S 173°14E 285 B8
Stoke Newington U.K. 51°33N 0°4W 125 A3
Stoke-on-Trent U.K. 53°1N 2°11W 168 D5
Stoke-on-Trent □ U.K. 53°1N 2°11W 168 D5
Stokes △ Australia 33°45S 121°11E 279 F3
Stokes Bay Canada 45°0N 81°28W 312 B3
Stokes Pt. Australia 40°10S 143°56E 281 G3
Stokes Ra. Australia 15°50S 130°50E 278 C5
Stokkseyri Iceland 63°50N 21°2W 155 D5
Stokksnes Iceland 64°14N 14°58W 155 C12
Stokmarknes Norway 68°34N 14°54E 160 B16
Stolac Bos.-H. 43°5N 17°59E 202 C1
Stolberg Germany 50°47N 6°13E 178 E2
Stolbovoy, Ostrov Russia 74°44N 135°14E 215 B14
Stolbtsy = Stowbtsy Belarus 53°30N 26°43E 177 B14
Stolin Belarus 51°53N 26°50E 177 C14
Stöllet Sweden 60°26N 13°15E 162 D7
Stolnici Romania 44°31N 24°48E 183 F9
Stolp = Słupsk Poland 54°30N 17°3E 184 D4
Stolpmünde = Ustka Poland 54°35N 16°55E 184 D3
Stomio Greece 35°21N 23°32E 207 E4
Ston Croatia 42°51N 17°43E 199 F14
Stone U.K. 52°55N 2°9W 168 E5
Stone Canyon Res. U.S.A. 34°6N 118°27W 126 B2
Stone Mountain U.S.A. 33°49N 84°10W 316 B5
Stone Zoo U.S.A. 42°28N 71°6W 116 A2
Stoneboro U.S.A. 41°20N 80°7W 312 E4
Stonebridge U.K. 51°32N 0°16W 125 A2
Stonecutters I. Hong Kong, China 22°19N 114°8E 122 B2
Stoneham U.S.A. 42°29N 71°5W 116 A2
Stonehaven U.K. 56°59N 2°12W 167 E6
Stonehenge Queens., Australia 24°22S 143°17E 280 C3
Stonehenge Wilts., U.K. 51°9N 1°45W 169 F6
Stonewall Canada 50°10N 97°19W 297 C9
Stongfjorden Norway 61°26N 5°10E 164 C2
Stonington U.S.A. 39°44N 89°12W 310 E7
Stony Brook Res. U.S.A. 42°15N 71°8W 116 B2
Stony Creek ➜ U.S.A. 41°38N 87°41W 119 C2
Stony Hill Jamaica 18°5N 76°48W 320 a
Stony I. U.S.A. 43°53N 76°19W 313 C8
Stony L. Man., Canada 58°51N 98°40W 297 B9
Stony L. Ont., Canada 44°30N 78°5W 312 B6
Stony Point U.S.A. 41°14N 73°59W 313 E11
Stony Pt. U.S.A. 43°50N 76°18W 313 C8
Stony Rapids Canada 59°16N 105°50W 297 B7
Stony River U.S.A. 61°47N 156°35W 303 F8
Stony Tunguska = Tunguska, Podkamennaya ➜ Russia 61°50N 90°13E 215 C10
Stonyford U.S.A. 39°23N 122°33W 306 F4
Stopnica Poland 50°27N 20°57E 185 H7
Storå Sweden 59°42N 15°6E 162 E9
Storå ➜ Denmark 56°20N 8°19E 163 H2
Stora Gla Sweden 59°30N 12°30E 162 E6
Stora Le Sweden 59°5N 11°55E 162 E5
Stora Lulevatten Sweden 67°10N 19°30E 160 C18
Stora Sjöfallet △ Sweden 67°36N 17°45E 160 C17
Stora Värtan Sweden 59°25N 18°7E 139 A2
Stóra-Vatnshorn Iceland 65°4N 21°33W 155 B5
Storavan Sweden 65°45N 18°10E 160 D18
Stord Norway 59°52N 5°23E 164 E2
Stordalen Norway 62°23N 7°0E 164 B4
Store Bælt Denmark 55°20N 11°0E 163 J4
Store Hareskov Denmark 55°46N 12°23E 118 A2
Store Heddinge Denmark 55°18N 12°23E 163 J6
Store Jukleggi = Høgeloft Norway 61°3N 8°12E 164 C5
Store Koldewey Greenland 76°30N 19°0W 154 B9
Store Magleby Denmark 55°35N 12°35E 118 B3
Store Mosse △ Sweden 57°18N 13°55E 163 G7
Store Sotra Norway 60°18N 5°4E 164 D1
Storebro Sweden 57°35N 15°52E 163 G9
Støren Norway 63°3N 10°18E 164 A7
Storerikvollen Norway 63°7N 11°58E 164 A8
Storfjellsætra Norway 61°40N 10°30E 164 C7
Storfjorden Norway 62°28N 6°35E 164 B3
Storfors Sweden 59°32N 14°17E 162 E8
Storholmen Sweden 59°23N 18°8E 139 A2
Storico Navale, Museo Venice, Italy 142 b3
Stóridalur Iceland 63°38N 19°57W 155 D7
Stórinúpur Iceland 64°3N 20°10W 155 C6
Storkerson Pen. Canada 72°30N 106°30W 294 C10
Storkyrkan Stockholm, Sweden 139 c2
Storli Norway 62°42N 9°5E 164 B6
Storlien Sweden 63°19N 12°6E 162 A6
Storm B. Australia 43°10S 147°30E 281 G4
Storm Lake U.S.A. 42°39N 95°13W 308 D6
Stormberge S. Africa 31°16S 26°17E 270 D4
Stormsrivier S. Africa 33°59S 23°52E 270 D3
Stornoway U.K. 58°13N 6°23W 167 C2
Storo Italy 45°51N 10°35E 198 C7
Storozhinets = Storozhynets Ukraine 48°14N 25°45E 183 B10
Storozhynets Ukraine 48°14N 25°45E 183 B10
Storrs U.S.A. 41°49N 72°15W 313 E12
Storsjøen Hedmark, Norway 60°20N 11°40E 164 D8
Storsjøen Hedmark, Norway 61°30N 11°14E 164 C8
Storsjön Gävleborg, Sweden 60°35N 16°45E 162 D10
Storsjön Jämtland, Sweden 62°48N 13°7E 162 B7
Storsjön Jämtland, Sweden 63°9N 14°30E 162 A8
Storsølnkletten Norway 61°59N 10°16E 164 C7
Storstrømmen Greenland 76°17N 22°25W 154 B8
Storuman Sweden 65°5N 17°10E 160 D17
Storuman, L. Sweden 65°13N 16°50E 160 D17
Stóruvellir Iceland 65°30N 17°29W 155 B9
Storvätteshågna Sweden 62°6N 12°30E 162 B6
Storviglen Norway 62°32N 12°2E 164 B9
Storvik Sweden 60°35N 16°33E 162 D10
Storvreta Sweden 59°58N 17°44E 162 E11
Story City U.S.A. 42°11N 93°36W 310 B3
Stouffville Canada 43°58N 79°15W 312 C5
Stoughton Sask., Canada 49°40N 103°0W 297 D8
Stoughton Wis., U.S.A. 42°55N 89°13W 310 B8
Stour ➜ Dorset, U.K. 50°43N 1°47W 169 G6
Stour ➜ Kent, U.K. 51°18N 1°22E 169 F9
Stour ➜ Suffolk, U.K. 51°57N 1°4E 169 F9
Stourbridge U.K. 52°28N 2°8W 169 E5
Stout L. Canada 52°0N 94°40W 297 C10
Stove Pipe Wells Village U.S.A. 36°35N 117°11W 307 J9
Støvring Denmark 56°54N 9°50E 163 H3
Stow U.S.A. 41°10N 81°27W 312 E3
Stowbtsy Belarus 53°30N 26°43E 177 B14
Stowmarket U.K. 52°12N 1°0E 169 E9
Stoyka Russia 59°57N 30°25E 137 B2
Strabane U.K. 54°50N 7°27W 166 B4
Stracin Macedonia 42°13N 22°2E 202 D6
Stradella Italy 45°5N 9°18E 198 C6
Strahan Australia 42°9S 145°20E 281 G4
Straiton U.K. 55°53N 3°9W 121 B3
Strajitsa Bulgaria 43°14N 25°58E 203 C9
Strakonice Czechia 49°15N 13°53E 180 B6
Straldzha Bulgaria 42°35N 26°40E 203 D10
Stralsund Germany 54°18N 13°4E 178 A9
Strand Hedmark, Norway 61°17N 11°17E 164 C8
Strand Western Cape, S. Africa 34°9S 18°48E 270 D2
Strand London, U.K. 125 b4
Stranda Møre og Romsdal, Norway 62°19N 6°58E 164 B3
Stranda Nord-Trøndelag, Norway 63°33N 10°14E 160 E14
Strandasýsla Iceland 65°45N 21°45W 155 B5
Strandby Denmark 57°30N 10°29E 163 G4
Strandfontein S. Africa 34°4S 18°34E 118 B2
Strangford L. U.K. 54°30N 5°37W 166 B6
Strängnäs Sweden 59°23N 17°2E 162 E11
Stranorlar Ireland 54°48N 7°46W 166 B4
Stranraer U.K. 54°54N 5°1W 167 G3
Strasbourg Sask., Canada 51°4N 104°55W 297 C8
Strasbourg Bas-Rhin, France 48°35N 7°42E 173 D14
Strasburg Germany 53°30N 13°43E 178 B9
Strășeni Moldova 47°8N 28°36E 183 C13
Strašnice Czechia 50°4N 14°28E 135 B2
Stråssa Sweden 59°44N 15°12E 162 E9
Strassburg = Aiud Romania 46°19N 23°44E 183 D8
Strasstrudering Germany 48°6N 11°41E 131 B3
Stratford N.S.W., Australia 32°7S 151°55E 283 B9
Stratford Vic., Australia 37°59S 147°7E 283 D7
Stratford Ont., Canada 43°23N 81°0W 312 C4
Stratford N.Z. 39°20S 174°19E 284 F3
Stratford London, U.K. 51°33N 0°0 125 A4
Stratford Calif., U.S.A. 36°11N 119°49W 306 J7
Stratford Conn., U.S.A. 41°12N 73°8W 313 E11
Stratford Tex., U.S.A. 36°20N 102°4W 314 C3
Stratford-upon-Avon U.K. 52°12N 1°42W 169 E6
Strath Spey U.K. 57°9N 3°49W 167 D5
Strathalbyn Australia 35°13S 138°53E 282 C3
Strathaven U.K. 55°40N 4°5W 167 F4
Strathcona ⌓ Canada 49°38N 125°40W 296 D3
Strathfield Australia 33°52S 151°5E 139 B1
Strathmore Alta., Canada 51°5N 113°18W 296 C6
Strathmore Angus, U.K. 56°37N 3°7W 167 E5
Strathmore Calif., U.S.A. 36°9N 119°4W 306 J7
Strathnaver Canada 53°20N 122°33W 296 C4
Strathpeffer U.K. 57°35N 4°32W 167 D4
Strathroy Canada 42°58N 81°38W 312 D3
Strathy Pt. U.K. 58°36N 4°1W 167 C4
Stratoni Greece 40°31N 23°49E 202 F7
Strattanville U.S.A. 41°12N 79°19W 312 E5
Stratton U.S.A. 45°8N 70°26W 313 A14
Stratton Mt. U.S.A. 43°4N 72°55W 313 C12
Straubing Germany 48°52N 12°34E 179 G8
Straumnes Iceland 66°26N 23°8W 155 A3
Strausberg Germany 52°35N 13°54E 178 C9
Strawberry ➜ U.S.A. 40°10N 110°24W 304 F8
Strawberry Point U.S.A. 42°41N 91°32W 310 B5
Strážnice Czechia 48°54N 17°19E 181 C10
Streaky B. Australia 32°48S 134°13E 281 E1
Streaky Bay Australia 32°51S 134°18E 281 E1
Streatham U.K. 51°25N 0°7W 125 B3
Streatham Vale U.K. 51°24N 0°8W 125 B3
Streator U.S.A. 41°8N 88°50W 311 C8
Strebersdorf Austria 48°17N 16°23E 142 A2
Středočeský □ Czechia 49°55N 14°30E 180 B7
Streetsboro U.S.A. 41°14N 81°21W 312 E3
Streetsville Canada 43°35N 79°42W 312 C5
Strehaia Romania 44°37N 23°10E 183 F8
Strehlen = Strzelin Poland 50°46N 17°2E 185 H4
Strelcha Bulgaria 42°25N 24°19E 203 D8
Streng ➜ Cambodia 13°12N 103°37E 236 F4
Stresa Italy 45°52N 8°28E 198 C5
Střešovice Czechia 50°5N 14°23E 135 B2
Streymoy Færoe Is. 62°8N 7°5W 160 E9
Strezhevoy Russia 60°42N 77°34E 214 C8
Stříbro Czechia 49°44N 13°0E 180 A6
Strickland ➜ Papua N. G. 7°35S 141°36E 286 D1
Striegau = Strzegom Poland 50°58N 16°20E 185 H3
Strilky Ukraine 49°20N 22°59E 185 J9
Strimonas ➜ Greece 40°46N 23°51E 202 F7
Strip, The Las Vegas, U.S.A. 36°7N 115°10W 124 B2
Střížkov Czechia 50°7N 14°28E 135 B2
Stroeder Argentina 40°12S 62°37W 336 B4
Strofades Greece 37°15N 21°0E 204 D3
Strokestown Ireland 53°47N 8°5W 166 C3
Stroma U.K. 58°41N 3°7W 167 C5
Strombeek-Bever Belgium 50°54N 4°21E 116 A2
Stromberg-Heuchelberg ⌓ Germany 49°2N 8°50E 179 F4
Strómboli Italy 38°47N 15°13E 201 D8
Stromeferry U.K. 57°21N 5°33W 167 D3
Strommen Norway 59°57N 11°0E 164 E7
Stromness U.K. 58°58N 3°17W 167 C5
Stromovka Czechia 50°6N 14°25E 135 B2
Strömsbruk Sweden 61°52N 17°18E 162 C11
Stromsburg U.S.A. 41°7N 97°36W 308 E5
Strömsnäsbruk Sweden 56°35N 13°45E 163 H7
Strömstad Sweden 58°56N 11°10E 163 F5
Strömsund Sweden 63°51N 15°33E 160 E16
Stronghurst U.S.A. 40°45N 90°55W 310 D6
Strongili Greece 36°6N 29°42E 205 E11
Stróngoli Italy 39°16N 17°3E 201 C10
Strongsville U.S.A. 41°19N 81°50W 312 E3
Stronie Śląskie Poland 50°18N 16°53E 185 H3
Stronsay U.K. 59°7N 2°35W 167 B6
Stropkov Slovakia 49°13N 21°39E 181 B14
Stroud U.K. 51°45N 2°13W 169 F5
Stroud Road Australia 32°18S 151°57E 283 B9
Stroudsburg U.S.A. 40°59N 75°12W 313 F9
Stroumbi Cyprus 34°53N 32°29E 207 F8
Štrpce = Shtërpcë Kosovo 42°14N 21°1E 202 D5
Struer Denmark 56°30N 8°35E 163 H2
Struga Macedonia 41°11N 20°44E 202 E4
Strugi Krasnyye Russia 58°21N 29°1E 188 C5
Strumica Macedonia 41°28N 22°41E 202 E6
Strumica ➜ Europe 41°20N 23°22E 202 E7
Strumok Ukraine 45°43N 29°27E 183 E14
Struthers U.S.A. 41°4N 80°39W 312 E4
Stryama Bulgaria 42°16N 24°54E 203 D8
Stryker U.S.A. 48°41N 114°46W 304 B6
Stryków Poland 51°55N 19°33E 185 G6
Stryn Norway 61°54N 6°43E 164 C3
Stryy Ukraine 49°16N 23°48E 177 D12
Strzegom Poland 50°58N 16°20E 185 H3
Strzelce Krajeńskie Poland 52°52N 15°33E 185 F2
Strzelce Opolskie Poland 50°31N 18°18E 185 H5
Strzelecki Cr. ➜ Australia 29°37S 139°59E 281 D2
Strzelecki Desert Australia 29°30S 140°0E 281 D3
Strzelin Poland 50°46N 17°2E 185 H4
Strzelno Poland 52°35N 18°9E 185 F5
Strzybnica Poland 50°28N 18°48E 185 H5
Strzyżów Poland 49°52N 21°47E 185 J8
Stuart Fla., U.S.A. 27°12N 80°15W 317 H9
Stuart Iowa, U.S.A. 41°30N 94°19W 310 C2
Stuart Nebr., U.S.A. 42°36N 99°8W 308 D4
Stuart ➜ Canada 54°0N 123°35W 296 C4
Stuart Bluff Ra. Australia 22°50S 131°52E 278 D5
Stuart I. U.S.A. 63°35N 162°30W 303 E7
Stuart L. Canada 54°30N 124°30W 296 C4
Stuart Mts. N.Z. 45°2S 167°39E 285 F2
Stuart Ra. Australia 29°10S 134°56E 281 D1
Stubbekøbing Denmark 54°53N 12°9E 163 K6
Stubbs St. Vincent 13°7N 61°9W 323 n
Stuben Austria 47°10N 10°8E 180 D3
Štubnianske Teplice = Turčianske Teplice Slovakia 48°52N 18°52E 181 C11
Studen Kladenets, Yazovir Bulgaria 41°37N 25°30E 203 E9
Studenica Serbia 43°29N 20°32E 202 C4
Studenka Czechia 49°44N 18°5E 181 B11
Studholme N.Z. 44°42S 171°9E 285 E6
Studio City U.S.A. 34°8N 118°24W 126 B2
Studley Park Trin. & Tob. 11°11N 60°40W 323 s
Stugudalen Norway 62°53N 11°53E 164 B8
Stugun Sweden 63°10N 15°40E 162 A9
Stuhlweissenburg = Székesfehérvár Hungary 47°15N 18°25E 182 C3
Stuhm = Sztum Poland 53°55N 19°1E 184 E6
Stuhr Germany 53°5N 8°44E 178 B4
Stull L. Canada 54°24N 92°34W 298 B1
Stung Treng = Stoeng Treng Cambodia 13°31N 105°58E 236 F5
Stupart ➜ Canada 56°0N 93°25W 298 A1
Stupava Slovakia 48°17N 17°2E 181 C10
Stupino Russia 54°57N 38°2E 188 E10
Stureby Sweden 59°15N 18°4E 139 B2
Sturge I. Antarctica 67°26S 164°47E 151 C11
Sturgeon B. Canada 52°0N 97°50W 297 C9
Sturgeon Bay U.S.A. 44°50N 87°23W 308 C10
Sturgeon Falls Canada 46°25N 79°57W 298 C4
Sturgeon L. Alta., Canada 55°6N 117°32W 296 B5
Sturgeon L. Ont., Canada 50°0N 90°45W 298 C1
Sturgeon L. Ont., Canada 44°28N 78°43W 312 B6
Sturgis Sask., Canada 51°56N 102°36W 297 C8
Sturgis Mich., U.S.A. 41°48N 85°25W 311 C11
Sturgis S. Dak., U.S.A. 44°25N 103°31W 308 C2
Sturkö Sweden 56°5N 15°42E 163 H9
Štúrovo Slovakia 47°48N 18°41E 181 D11
Sturt △ Australia 27°17S 141°37E 281 D3
Sturt Cr. ➜ Australia 19°8S 127°50E 278 C4
Sturt Stony Desert Australia 28°30S 141°0E 281 D3
Sturts Meadows Australia 31°18S 141°42E 282 A4
Stutterheim S. Africa 32°33S 27°28E 270 D4
Stuttgart Baden-W., Germany 48°48N 9°11E 179 G5
Stuttgart Ark., U.S.A. 34°30N 91°33W 314 D9
Stuttgart Echterdingen ✈ (STR) Germany 48°42N 9°11E 179 G5
Stutthof = Sztutowo Poland 54°20N 19°15E 184 D6
Stuvsta Sweden 59°15N 18°0E 139 B2
Stuyvesant U.S.A. 42°23N 73°45W 313 D11
Stuyvesant Town New York, U.S.A. 132 d2
Stykkishólmur Iceland 65°2N 22°40W 155 B4
Styria = Steiermark □ Austria 47°26N 15°0E 180 D8
Styrsö Sweden 57°37N 11°46E 163 G5
Su-no-Saki Japan 34°58N 139°45E 223 C11
Su Xian = Suzhou China 33°41N 116°59E 226 H9
Suakin Sudan 19°8N 37°20E 256 D4
Suakin Archipelago Sudan 18°42N 38°30E 256 D4
Suamico U.S.A. 44°38N 88°2W 308 C9
Suan N. Korea 38°42N 126°22E 224 C3
Suana Indonesia 8°44S 115°36E 231 K18
Süanhwa = Xuanhua China 40°40N 115°2E 226 D8
Suao Taiwan 24°36N 121°51E 225 B3
Suape Brazil 8°24S 35°0W 332 C5
Suapure ➜ Venezuela 6°48N 67°1W 328 B4
Suar India 29°2N 79°3E 243 E8
Suau Papua N. G. 10°37S 150°2E 286 F6
Suavanao Solomon Is. 7°35S 158°47E 287 L10
Şubā Si. Arabia 27°10N 35°40E 246 E2
Subang Indonesia 6°34S 107°45E 235 D3
Subankhata India 26°48N 91°25E 241 B3
Subansiri ➜ India 26°48N 93°50E 241 B4
Subarnagiri India 19°50N 83°51E 244 E6
Subarnarekha ➜ India 22°34N 87°24E 243 H12
Subay', Urūq Si. Arabia 22°15N 43°5E 256 C5
Subayhah Si. Arabia 30°2N 38°50E 246 D3
Subcetate Romania 45°36N 23°0E 182 E8
Subhepur India 28°44N 77°15E 120 A2
Subi Indonesia 2°58N 108°50E 235 B3
Subiaco Italy 41°56N 13°5E 199 G10
Subic B. Phil. 14°44N 120°12E 232 D3
Subotica Serbia 46°6N 19°39E 182 D4
Suburban Canal U.S.A. 30°2N 90°11W 131 B1
Suca Ethiopia 6°31N 39°14E 257 F4
Sucat Phil. 14°27N 121°2E 127 C2
Suceava Romania 47°38N 26°16E 183 C11
Suceava □ Romania 47°37N 25°40E 183 C10
Suceava ➜ Romania 47°32N 26°32E 183 C11
Sucha-Beskidzka Poland 49°44N 19°35E 185 J6
Suchan = Partizansk Russia 43°8N 133°9E 215 E14
Suchań Poland 53°18N 15°18E 185 E2
Suchdol Czechia 50°8N 14°22E 135 B2
Suchedniów Poland 51°3N 20°49E 185 G7
Suchil Mexico 23°39N 103°54W 318 C4
Suchou = Suzhou China 31°19N 120°38E 229 B13
Süchow = Xuzhou China 34°18N 117°10E 227 G9
Suchowola Poland 53°33N 23°3E 184 E10
Sucio ➜ Colombia 7°27N 77°7W 328 B2
Suck ➜ Ireland 53°17N 8°3W 166 C3
Suckling, Mt. Papua N. G. 9°49S 148°53E 286 E5
Sucre Bolivia 19°0S 65°15W 331 D4
Sucre Colombia 8°49N 74°44W 328 B3
Sucre □ Colombia 8°50N 75°40W 328 B2
Sucre □ Venezuela 10°25N 63°30W 329 A5
Sucuaro Colombia 4°34N 68°50W 328 C4
Sucumbíos □ Ecuador 0°6S 76°52W 328 D2
Sućuraj Croatia 43°10N 17°8E 199 E14
Sucuriju Brazil 1°39N 49°57W 332 A2
Sucuriú ➜ Brazil 20°47S 51°38W 331 E7
Sucy-en-Brie France 48°46N 2°31E 134 B4
Sud □ Cameroon 2°30N 11°45E 263 E7
Sud, Pte. Comoros Is. 11°53S 43°29E 272 a
Sud, Pte. du Canada 49°3N 62°14W 299 C7
Sud-Kivu □ Dem. Rep. of the Congo 3°0S 28°30E 268 C2
Sud-Ouest □ Cameroon 5°25N 9°20E 263 D6
Sud-Ouest, Pte. Qué., Canada 49°23N 63°36W 299 C7
Sud Ouest, Pte. Mauritius 20°28S 57°18E 272 e
Sud-Ubangi □ Dem. Rep. of the Congo 2°30N 19°0E 264 B3
Suda ➜ Russia 59°0N 37°40E 188 C9
Sudak Ukraine 44°51N 34°57E 189 K8
Sudan U.S.A. 34°4N 102°31W 314 D3
Sudan ■ Africa 15°0N 30°0E 257 E3
Sudauen = Suwałki Poland 54°8N 22°59E 184 D9
Sudbury U.K. 52°2N 0°45E 169 E8
Sudd South Sudan 8°20N 30°0E 257 F3
Suddie Guyana 7°8N 58°29W 329 B6
Sudeifel = Deutsch-Luxemburgischer ⌓ Germany 49°58N 6°12E 179 F2
Süderbrarup Germany 54°38N 9°45E 178 A5
Süderlügum Germany 54°52N 8°54E 178 A4
Süderoogsand Germany 54°27N 8°28E 178 A4
Sudeten Mts. = Sudety Europe 50°20N 16°45E 181 A9
Sudety Europe 50°20N 16°45E 181 A9
Súðavík Iceland 66°2N 23°0W 155 A3
Südheide ⌓ Germany 52°46N 10°10E 178 C6
Suður-múlasýsla Iceland 65°0N 14°30W 155 C12
Suður-þingeyjarsýsla Iceland 65°30N 17°0W 155 B9
Suðureyri Iceland 66°7N 23°32W 155 A3
Suðurland □ Iceland 64°30N 19°30W 155 C7
Suðurnes □ Iceland 63°50N 22°30W 155 D4
Suðuroy Færoe Is. 61°32N 6°50W 160 F9
Sudi Tanzania 10°11S 39°57E 269 E4
Sudirman, Pegunungan Indonesia 4°30S 137°0E 231 E9
Sudiți Romania 44°35N 27°38E 183 F12
Sudogda Russia 55°55N 40°50E 190 C5
Sudong, Pulau Singapore 1°13N 103°44E 237 d
Sudostroy = Severodvinsk Russia 64°27N 39°58E 186 B6
Sudova Vyshnya Ukraine 49°46N 23°22E 185 J10
Sudzha Russia 51°14N 35°17E 189 G8
Sue ➜ South Sudan 7°41N 28°3E 257 F2
Sue, L. U.S.A. 28°34N 81°21W 133 A2
Sueca Spain 39°12N 0°21W 197 F4
Sŭedinenie Bulgaria 42°16N 24°33E 203 D8
Suemez I. U.S.A. 55°15N 133°20W 296 B2
Sueyoshi = Soo Japan 31°40N 131°5E 222 F3
Suez = El Suweis Egypt 29°58N 32°31E 256 B3
Suez, G. of = Suweis, Khalîg el Egypt 28°40N 33°0E 256 J8
Suez Canal = Suweis, Qanâ es Egypt 31°0N 32°20E 256 H8
Suffield Canada 50°12N 111°10W 296 C6
Suffolk U.S.A. 36°44N 76°35W 309 G15
Suffolk □ U.K. 52°16N 1°0E 169 E9
Şufiān Iran 38°16N 45°58E 213 C11
Suga-no-Sen Japan 35°25N 134°25E 222 B6
Şugag Romania 45°47N 23°37E 183 E8
Sugaing = Sagaing Burma 21°52N 95°59E 241 E5
Sugamo Japan 35°44N 139°43E 140 A3
Sugar ➜ U.S.A. 42°26N 89°12W 310 B7
Sugar Cr. ➜ Ill., U.S.A. 40°9N 89°38W 310 D7
Sugar Cr. ➜ Ind., U.S.A. 39°51N 87°21W 311 E9
Sugar Grove U.S.A. 41°59N 79°20W 312 E5
Sugar Hill U.S.A. 34°6N 84°2W 316 A5
Sugar Loaf Grenada 12°13N 61°36W 323 q
Sugar Loaf Mt. = Açúcar, Pão de Brazil 22°56S 43°9W 135 B2
Sugar Loaf Pt. St. Helena 15°54S 5°42W 153 h
Sugarcreek U.S.A. 41°25N 79°52W 312 E5
Sugarive ➜ India 26°16N 86°24E 243 F12
Sugbai Passage Phil. 5°22N 120°33E 233 J3
Suge Japan 35°37N 139°32E 140 B2
Sughd □ Tajikistan 40°0N 69°0E 217 E7
Sugihwaras Indonesia 4°1S 103°46E 234 C2
Suginami Japan 35°41N 139°37E 140 A2
Suğla Gölü Turkey 37°20N 32°0E 212 D5
Sugluk = Salluit Canada 62°14N 75°38W 295 E16
Sugō Japan 35°34N 139°33E 140 B2
Sugun China 39°53N 76°47E 217 E9
Suha Reke = Therandë Kosovo 42°21N 20°50E 202 D4
Suhaia, Lacul Romania 43°45N 25°15E 183 G10
Şuḩār Oman 24°20N 56°40E 247 E8
Sühbaatar Mongolia 50°17N 106°10E 218 A10
Sühbaatar □ Mongolia 45°30N 114°0E 226 B8
Suheli Par India 10°5N 72°17E 245 J1
Suhl Germany 50°36N 10°42E 178 E6
Şuhut Turkey 38°31N 30°32E 205 C12
Sui Pakistan 28°37N 69°19E 242 E3
Sui Sai Wan Hong Kong, China 22°16N 114°14E 122 B3
Sui Xian China 34°25N 115°2E 226 G8
Suiá Missu ➜ Brazil 11°13S 53°15W 331 C7
Šuica Bos.-H. 43°52N 17°11E 182 G2
Suichang China 28°29N 119°15E 229 C12
Suichuan China 26°20N 114°32E 229 D10
Suide China 37°30N 110°12E 226 F6
Suifenhe China 44°25N 131°10E 227 B16
Suihua China 46°32N 126°55E 219 B14
Suijiang China 28°40N 103°59E 228 C4
Suining Hunan, China 26°35N 110°10E 229 D8
Suining Jiangsu, China 33°56N 117°58E 227 H9
Suining Sichuan, China 30°26N 105°35E 228 B5
Suiping China 33°10N 113°59E 226 H7
Suippes France 49°8N 4°30E 173 C11
Suir ➜ Ireland 52°16N 7°9W 166 D4
Suisse = Switzerland ■ Europe 46°30N 8°0E 179 J4
Suisun City U.S.A. 38°15N 122°2W 306 G4
Suita Japan 34°45N 135°30E 133 A2
Suitland U.S.A. 38°50N 76°55W 143 B3
Suixi China 21°19N 110°18E 229 G8
Suiyang Guizhou, China 27°58N 107°18E 228 D6
Suiyang Heilongjiang, China 44°30N 130°56E 227 B16
Suizhong China 40°21N 120°20E 227 D11
Suizhou China 31°42N 113°24E 229 B9
Sujangarh India 27°42N 74°31E 242 F6
Sujiatun China 41°39N 123°20E 227 D12
Sukabumi Indonesia 6°56S 106°50E 234 D3
Sukadana Kalimantan Barat, Indonesia 1°10S 110°0E 235 C4
Sukadana Lampung, Indonesia 5°5S 105°33E 234 D3
Sukadana, Teluk Indonesia 1°24S 109°50E 235 C3
Sukagawa Japan 37°17N 140°23E 221 F10
Sukamade Indonesia 8°30S 113°52E 235 D4
Sukamara Indonesia 2°43S 111°10E 235 C4
Sukaraja Indonesia 2°28S 110°25E 235 C4
Sukarnapura = Jayapura Indonesia 2°28S 140°38E 231 E10
Sukarno, Puntjak = Jaya, Puncak Indonesia 3°57S 137°17E 231 E9
Sukarno-Hatta Int., Jakarta ✈ (CGK) Indonesia 6°7S 106°40E 231 G12
Sukau Malaysia 5°32N 118°17E 235 A5
Sukawati Indonesia 8°35S 115°17E 231 K18
Sukchar India 22°42N 88°22E 124 A2
Sukch'ŏn N. Korea 39°22N 125°35E 224 C2
Sukhindol Bulgaria 43°11N 25°10E 203 C9
Sukhinichi Russia 54°8N 35°10E 188 E8
Sukhona ➜ Russia 61°15N 46°39E 186 C6

Sukhothai *Thailand* 17°1N 99°49E **236** D2
Sukhumi = Sokhumi *Georgia* 43°0N 41°0E **191** J5
Sukkertoppen = Maniitsoq *Greenland* 65°26N 52°55W **154** D5
Sukkur *Pakistan* 27°42N 68°54E **242** F3
Sukkur Barrage *Pakistan* 27°40N 68°50E **242** F3
Sukma *India* 18°24N 81°45E **244** E5
Sukovo *Serbia* 43°4N 22°37E **202** C6
Sukri → *India* 25°4N 71°43E **242** G4
Sukumo *Japan* 32°56N 132°44E **222** E4
Sukunka → *Canada* 55°45N 121°15W **296** B4
Sul, Canal do *Brazil* 0°10S 48°30W **332** B2
Sula *Norway* 61°7N 4°54E **164** C1
Sula → *Ukraine* 49°40N 32°41E **189** H7
Sula, Kepulauan *Indonesia* 1°45S 125°0E **231** E7
Sulaco → *Honduras* 15°2N 87°44W **320** C2
Sulaiman Range *Pakistan* 30°30N 69°50E **242** D3
Sulaiman-Too *Kyrgyzstan* 40°31N 72°46E **217** D8
Sulak → *Russia* 43°20N 47°34E **191** J8
Sulakyurt *Turkey* 40°9N 33°43E **212** B5
Sūlār *Iran* 31°53N 51°54E **247** D6
Sulawesi *Indonesia* 2°0S 120°0E **235** C5
Sulawesi Barat □ *Indonesia* 3°0S 119°0E **235** C5
Sulawesi Sea = Celebes Sea *Indonesia* 3°0N 123°0E **231** D6
Sulawesi Selatan □ *Indonesia* 2°30S 120°0E **231** E6
Sulawesi Tengah □ *Indonesia* 1°30S 121°0E **231** E6
Sulawesi Tenggara □ *Indonesia* 3°50S 122°0E **231** E6
Sulawesi Utara □ *Indonesia* 1°0N 124°0E **231** D6
Suldalsheiene *Norway* 59°28N 7°10E **164** E3
Suldalsosen *Norway* 59°29N 6°29E **164** E3
Sulechów *Poland* 52°5N 15°40E **185** F2
Sulęcin *Poland* 52°26N 15°10E **185** F2
Sulei *Solomon Is.* 8°3S 159°34E **287** M10
Suleja *Nigeria* 9°10N 7°10E **263** D6
Sulejów *Poland* 51°26N 19°53E **185** G6
Sulejówek *Poland* 52°13N 21°17E **185** F8
Süleymanlı *Turkey* 38°58N 27°47E **205** C9
Sulima *S. Leone* 6°58N 11°32W **262** D2
Sulina *Romania* 45°10N 29°40E **183** E14
Sulina, Braţul → *Romania* 45°10N 29°40E **183** E14
Sulingen *Germany* 52°41N 8°48E **178** C4
Sulița *Romania* 47°39N 26°59E **183** C11
Sulitjelma *Norway* 67°9N 16°3E **160** C17
Sułkowice *Poland* 49°50N 19°49E **185** J6
Sullana *Peru* 4°52S 80°39W **330** A1
Süller *Turkey* 38°9N 29°29E **205** C11
Sullivan *Ill., U.S.A.* 39°36N 88°37W **311** E8
Sullivan *Ind., U.S.A.* 39°6N 87°24W **311** E9
Sullivan *Mo., U.S.A.* 38°13N 91°10W **310** F5
Sullivan Bay *Canada* 50°55N 126°50W **296** C3
Sullivan I. = Lanbi Kyun *Burma* 10°50N 98°20E **237** G2
Sullom Voe *U.K.* 60°27N 1°20W **167** A7
Sullorsuaq *Greenland* 70°5N 53°0W **154** C5
Sully *U.S.A.* 41°34N 92°50W **310** C4
Sully-sur-Loire *France* 47°45N 2°20E **173** E9
Sulmierzyce *Poland* 51°37N 17°32E **185** G4
Sulmona *Italy* 42°3N 13°55E **199** F10
Süloğlu *Turkey* 41°44N 26°53E **203** E10
Sulphur *La., U.S.A.* 30°14N 93°23W **314** F8
Sulphur *Okla., U.S.A.* 34°31N 96°58W **314** D6
Sulphur Channel *Hong Kong, China* 22°15N 114°7E **122** B2
Sulphur Pt. *Canada* 60°56N 114°48W **296** A6
Sulphur Springs *U.S.A.* 33°8N 95°36W **314** E7
Sulsul *Ethiopia* 5°5N 44°50E **267** C5
Sultan *Ont., Canada* 47°36N 82°47W **298** C3
Sultan *Wash., U.S.A.* 47°52N 121°49W **306** C5
Sultan Dağları *Turkey* 38°20N 31°20E **212** C4
Sultan Hamud *Kenya* 2°1S 37°22E **268** C4
Sultan Kudarat *Phil.* 7°16N 124°18E **233** H5
Sultan Kudarat □ *Phil.* 6°30N 124°10E **233** H5
Sultan Naga Dimaporo *Phil.* 7°55N 123°44E **233** H4
Sultan sa Barongis *Phil.* 6°45N 124°35E **233** H5
Sultanābād = Arāk *Iran* 34°0N 49°40E **247** C6
Sultanahme Camil *Turkey* 41°0N 28°58E **122** B1
Sultanhisar *Turkey* 37°53N 28°9E **205** D10
Sultaniça *Turkey* 40°37N 26°8E **203** F10
Sultaniye *Turkey* 40°11N 28°12E **203** F12
Sultanpur *Mad. P., India* 23°9N 77°56E **242** H8
Sultanpur *Punjab, India* 31°13N 75°11E **242** D6
Sultanpur *Ut. P., India* 26°18N 82°4E **243** F10
Sulu □ *Phil.* 5°30N 120°30E **233** J3
Sulu Arch. *Phil.* 6°0N 121°0E **233** J3
Sulu Sea *E. Indies* 8°0N 120°0E **233** G3
Sülüklü *Turkey* 38°53N 32°20E **212** C5
Sululta *Ethiopia* 9°10N 38°43E **257** F4
Suluova *Turkey* 40°46N 35°32E **212** B6
Sulūq *Libya* 31°44N 20°14E **258** B4
Suluru *India* 13°42N 80°1E **245** H5
Sulzbach *Germany* 49°18N 7°3E **179** F3
Sulzbach-Rosenberg *Germany* 49°30N 11°44E **179** F7
Sulzberger Ice Shelf *Antarctica* 78°0S 150°0W **151** E13
Sumaco -Napo Galeras △ *Ecuador* 0°34S 77°38W **328** D2
Sumalata *Indonesia* 1°0N 122°31E **231** D6
Sumale □ *Ethiopia* 7°0N 45°0E **267** C6
Sumampa *Argentina* 29°25S 63°29W **334** B3
Sumapaz △ *Colombia* 3°49N 74°13W **328** C3
Sumaré *Brazil* 22°48S 47°17W **333** F2
Sumatera *Indonesia* 0°40N 100°20E **234** B2
Sumatera Barat □ *Indonesia* 1°0S 101°0E **234** B1
Sumatera Selatan □ *Indonesia* 3°0S 104°0E **234** C2
Sumatera Utara □ *Indonesia* 2°30N 98°0E **234** B1
Sumatra = Sumatera *Indonesia* 0°40N 100°20E **234** B2
Sumatra *U.S.A.* 30°1N 84°59W **316** E5
Sumava △ *Czechia* 49°0N 13°49E **180** C6
Sumba *Angola* 6°15S 12°38E **265** D2
Sumba *Indonesia* 9°45S 119°35E **231** F5
Sumba, Selat *Indonesia* 9°0S 118°40E **231** F5
Sumbawa *Indonesia* 8°26S 117°30E **235** D5
Sumbawa Besar *Indonesia* 8°30S 117°26E **235** D5
Sumbe *Angola* 11°10S 13°48E **265** E2
Sumbu △ *Zambia* 8°43S 30°22E **269** D3
Sumburgh Hd. *U.K.* 59°52N 1°17W **167** B7
Sumdeo *India* 31°26N 78°44E **243** D8
Sumdo *China* 35°6N 78°41E **243** B8
Sumé *Brazil* 7°39S 36°55W **332** C4
Sumedang *Indonesia* 6°52S 107°55E **235** D3
Sümeg *Hungary* 46°59N 17°20E **182** D2
Sumeih *Sudan* 9°50N 27°39E **257** F2
Šumen = Shumen *Bulgaria* 43°18N 26°55E **203** C10
Sumenep *Indonesia* 7°1S 113°52E **235** D4
Sumgait = Sumqayıt *Azerbaijan* 40°34N 49°38E **191** K9
Sumida *Japan* 35°42N 139°49E **140** A3
Sumida → *Japan* 35°39N 139°45E **140** A3
Sumisu-Jima *Japan* 31°27N 140°3E **223** F12
Sumiyoshi *Japan* 34°36N 135°30E **133** B2
Sumiyoshi Shrine *Japan* 34°36N 135°30E **133** B1
Summer L. *U.S.A.* 42°50N 120°45W **304** E3
Summerland *Canada* 49°32N 119°41W **296** D5
Summerland Key *U.S.A.* 24°40N 81°27W **317** L8
Summerside *Canada* 46°24N 63°47W **299** C7
Summersville *U.S.A.* 38°17N 80°51W **309** F13
Summerton *U.S.A.* 33°36N 80°20W **316** B9
Summertown *U.S.A.* 32°45N 82°16W **316** C7
Summerville *Ont., Canada* 43°37N 79°33W **141** B1
Summerville *Ga., U.S.A.* 34°29N 85°21W **315** D12
Summerville *S.C., U.S.A.* 33°1N 80°11W **316** B9
Summit *Alaska, U.S.A.* 63°20N 149°7W **303** E10
Summit *Ill., U.S.A.* 41°47N 87°47W **119** C2
Summit Lake *Canada* 54°20N 122°40W **296** C4
Summit Peak *U.S.A.* 37°21N 106°42W **305** H10
Sumner *N.Z.* 43°35S 172°48E **285** D7
Sumner *Ill., U.S.A.* 38°42N 87°53W **311** F9
Sumner *Iowa, U.S.A.* 42°51N 92°6W **310** B4
Sumner *Wash., U.S.A.* 47°12N 122°14W **306** C4
Sumner, L. *N.Z.* 42°42S 172°15E **285** C7
Sumner Tunnel *Boston, U.S.A.* **116** a3
Sumoto *Japan* 34°21N 134°54E **222** C6
Sumpangbinangae *Indonesia* 4°24S 119°36E **235** C5
Šumperk *Czechia* 49°59N 16°59E **181** B9
Sumprabum *Burma* 26°33N 97°36E **241** B6
Sumqayıt *Azerbaijan* 40°34N 49°38E **191** K9
Sumter *U.S.A.* 33°55N 80°21W **316** B9
Sumxi *China* 34°35N 80°22E **217** F10
Sumy *Ukraine* 50°57N 34°50E **189** G8
Sumy □ *Ukraine* 50°50N 33°50E **189** G7
Sun City *S. Africa* 25°17S 27°3E **270** C4
Sun City Center *U.S.A.* 27°43N 82°21W **317** H7
Sun Kosi → *Nepal* 26°59N 87°8E **243** F12
Sun Lakes *U.S.A.* 33°10N 111°52W **305** K8
Sun Prairie *U.S.A.* 43°11N 89°13W **310** A7
Sun Valley *U.S.A.* 43°42N 114°21W **304** E6
Sunagawa *Japan* 43°29N 141°55E **220** C10
Sunamachi *Japan* 35°40N 139°50E **140** A4
Sunamganj *Bangla.* 25°4N 91°24E **241** C3
Sunan *N. Korea* 39°15N 125°40E **224** C2
Sunart, L. *U.K.* 56°42N 5°43W **167** E3
Sunburst *U.S.A.* 48°53N 111°55W **304** B8
Sunbury *Vic., Australia* 37°35S 144°44E **283** D6
Sunbury *Pa., U.S.A.* 40°52N 76°48W **313** F8
Sunbury-on-Thames *U.K.* 51°25N 0°26W **125** B1
Sunchales *Argentina* 30°58S 61°35W **334** C3
Suncheon *S. Korea* 34°52N 127°31E **224** E3
Suncho Corral *Argentina* 27°55S 63°27W **334** B3
Sunch'on *N. Korea* 39°25N 125°56E **224** C2
Suncook *U.S.A.* 43°8N 71°27W **313** C13
Sunda, Selat *Indonesia* 6°20S 105°30E **234** D3
Sunda Is. *Indonesia* 5°0S 105°0E **288** H2
Sunda Str. = Sunda, Selat *Indonesia* 6°20S 105°30E **234** D3
Sunda Trench = Java Trench *Ind. Oc.* 9°0S 105°0E **234** D2
Sundance *Man., Canada* 56°32N 94°4W **297** B10
Sundance *Wyo., U.S.A.* 44°24N 104°23W **304** D11
Sundar Nagar *India* 31°32N 76°53E **242** D7
Sundarbans *Asia* 22°0N 89°0E **241** E2
Sundarbans △ *India* 22°0N 88°45E **241** E2
Sundargarh *India* 22°4N 84°5E **244** C7
Sundays = Sondags → *S. Africa* 33°44S 25°51E **270** D4
Sundbyberg *Sweden* 59°22N 17°57E **139** A1
Sundbyerne *Denmark* 55°39N 12°36E **118** B3
Sunderland *Ont., Canada* 44°16N 79°4W **312** B5
Sunderland *Tyne & W., U.K.* 54°55N 1°23W **168** C6
Sundi Lutete *Dem. Rep. of the Congo* 4°34S 14°14E **265** C2
Sundown △ *Australia* 28°49S 151°38E **281** D5
Sundre *Canada* 51°49N 114°38W **296** C6
Sunds *Denmark* 56°13N 9°1E **163** H3
Sundsvall *Sweden* 62°23N 17°17E **162** B11
Sundsvallsbukten *Sweden* 62°21N 17°25E **162** B11
Sungai Acheh *Malaysia* 5°8N 100°30E **237** c
Sungai Kolok *Thailand* 6°2N 101°58E **237** J3
Sungai Lembing *Malaysia* 3°55N 103°3E **237** L4
Sungai Petani *Malaysia* 5°37N 100°30E **237** K3
Sungai Siput *Malaysia* 4°49N 101°4E **234** B2
Sungaidurian *Indonesia* 0°6S 109°21E **235** C3
Sungaigerong *Indonesia* 2°59S 104°52E **234** C2
Sungailiat *Indonesia* 1°51S 106°8E **234** C3
Sungaipakning *Indonesia* 1°19N 102°8E **234** B2
Sungaipenuh *Indonesia* 2°1S 101°20E **234** C2
Sungari = Songhua Jiang → *China* 47°45N 132°30E **219** B15
Sungei Kadut Industrial Estate *Singapore* 1°24N 103°44E **138** A2
Sungei Selatar Res. *Singapore* 1°24N 103°51E **138** A3
Sungguminasa *Indonesia* 5°17S 119°30E **235** D5
Sunghua Chiang = Songhua Jiang → *China* 47°45N 132°30E **219** B15
Sungikai *Sudan* 12°20N 29°51E **257** E2
Sungsang *Indonesia* 2°22S 104°55E **234** C2
Sungu *Dem. Rep. of the Congo* 1°5S 17°21E **264** C3
Sungurlu *Turkey* 40°12N 34°21E **212** B6
Sunja *Croatia* 45°21N 16°35E **199** C13
Sunland Park *U.S.A.* 31°50N 106°40W **305** L10
Sunnansjö *Sweden* 60°13N 14°58E **162** D8
Sunndalsøra *Norway* 62°40N 8°33E **164** B5
Sunne *Sweden* 59°52N 13°5E **162** E7
Sunnemo *Sweden* 59°53N 13°44E **162** E7
Sunnfjord *Norway* 61°35N 5°45E **164** C2
Sunnmøre *Norway* 62°35N 6°30E **164** B3
Sunny Bay *Hong Kong, China* 22°20N 114°1E **122** B1
Sunny Isles Beach *U.S.A.* 25°55N 80°7W **129** C3
Sunnyside *U.S.A.* 46°20N 120°0W **304** C4
Sunnyvale *U.S.A.* 37°23N 122°2W **306** H4
Sunrise *U.S.A.* 26°8N 80°14W **129** B2
Sunrise Manor *U.S.A.* 36°12N 115°4W **124** A2
Sunrise Mountain Natural Area ⌓ *U.S.A.* 36°12N 114°58W **124** A2
Sunset Beach *U.S.A.* 21°40N 158°3W **302** J13
Sunset Park *N.Y., U.S.A.* 40°38N 73°59W **132** C2
Sunset Park *Nev., U.S.A.* 36°3N 115°6W **124** B2
Sunset Peak *Hong Kong, China* 22°15N 113°57E **122** B1
Sunshine Coast *Australia* 26°30S 153°0E **276** F9
Sunshine I. *Hong Kong, China* 22°16N 114°3E **122** B2
Sunshine Park *U.S.A.* 26°2N 80°13W **129** B2
Suntar *Russia* 62°15N 117°30E **215** C12
Sunter *Indonesia* 6°7S 106°51E **122** A2
Sunter, Kali → *Indonesia* 6°10S 106°53E **122** B2
Suntrana *U.S.A.* 63°52N 148°51W **303** E10
Sunwi-do *N. Korea* 37°43N 125°16E **224** D2
Sunyani *Ghana* 7°21N 2°22W **262** D4
Suō-Nada *Japan* 33°50N 131°30E **222** D3
Suomenlinna *Finland* 60°9N 24°59E **121** C2
Suomenselkä *Finland* 62°52N 24°0E **160** E21
Suomi = Finland ■ *Europe* 63°0N 27°0E **160** E22
Suomussalmi *Finland* 64°54N 29°10E **160** D23
Suoyarvi *Russia* 62°3N 32°20E **188** A7
Supai *U.S.A.* 36°15N 112°41W **305** H7
Supamo → *Venezuela* 6°48N 61°50W **329** B5
Supaul *India* 26°10N 86°40E **243** F12
Superagüi △ *Brazil* 25°6S 48°18W **333** G2
Superior *Ariz., U.S.A.* 33°18N 111°6W **305** K8
Superior *Mont., U.S.A.* 47°12N 114°53W **304** C6
Superior *Nebr., U.S.A.* 40°1N 98°4W **308** E4
Superior *Wis., U.S.A.* 46°44N 92°6W **308** B7
Superior, L. *N. Amer.* 47°0N 87°0W **298** C2
Supetar *Croatia* 43°25N 16°32E **199** E13
Suphan Buri *Thailand* 14°14N 100°10E **236** E3
Suphan Dağı *Turkey* 38°54N 42°48E **213** C10
Supiori *Indonesia* 1°0S 136°0E **231** E9
Supraśl *Poland* 53°13N 23°19E **185** E10
Supraśl → *Poland* 53°11N 22°57E **185** E9
Supreme Court *Washington, D.C., U.S.A.* **143** b3
Supsa *Georgia* 42°2N 41°49E **191** J5
Supung *N. Korea* 40°27N 124°54E **224** B2
Supung Shuiku *China* 40°35N 124°50E **224** B2
Sūq 'Abs *Yemen* 16°0N 43°12E **248** D3
Sūq al Jarrāḥī *Yemen* 14°10N 43°20E **248** D3
Sūq ash Shuyūkh *Iraq* 30°53N 46°28E **246** D5
Sūq Suwayq *Si. Arabia* 24°23N 38°27E **246** E3
Şuqaylabīyah *Syria* 35°23N 36°23E **250** C7
Suqian *China* 33°54N 118°8E **227** H10
Suquṭra = Socotra *Yemen* 12°30N 54°0E **249** D6
Sūr *Lebanon* 33°19N 35°16E **250** E6
Şūr *Oman* 22°34N 59°32E **249** B7
Sur, C. *Chile* 27°12S 109°26W **330** b
Sur, Pt. *U.S.A.* 36°18N 121°54W **306** J5
Sur Bahr *West Bank* 31°44N 35°13E **123** B2
Sura *India* 22°33N 88°24E **124** B2
Sura → *Russia* 56°6N 46°0E **190** C8
Surab *Pakistan* 28°25N 66°15E **242** E2
Surabaja = Surabaya *Indonesia* 7°17S 112°45E **235** D4
Surabaya *Indonesia* 7°17S 112°45E **235** D4
Surahammar *Sweden* 59°43N 16°13E **162** E10
Suraia *Romania* 45°40N 27°25E **183** E12
Surakarta *Indonesia* 7°35S 110°48E **235** D4
Suraksan *S. Korea* 37°40N 127°4E **137** A2
Surallah *Phil.* 6°22N 124°44E **233** H5
Šurany *Slovakia* 48°6N 18°10E **181** C11
Surat *Queens., Australia* 27°10S 149°6E **281** D4
Surat *India* 21°12N 72°55E **244** D1
Surat Thani *Thailand* 9°6N 99°20E **237** H2
Suratgarh *India* 29°18N 73°55E **242** E5
Surathkal *India* 12°58N 74°46E **245** H2
Suraxanı = Qaraçuxar *Azerbaijan* 40°25N 50°1E **191** K10
Şuraymilā *Si. Arabia* 25°7N 46°7E **246** E5
Suraż *Poland* 52°57N 22°57E **185** F9
Surazh *Belarus* 55°25N 30°44E **188** E6
Surazh *Russia* 53°5N 32°27E **189** F7
Surbiton *U.K.* 51°23N 0°17W **125** B2
Surduc *Romania* 47°15N 23°25E **183** C8
Surduc Pasul *Romania* 45°21N 23°23E **183** E8
Surdulica *Serbia* 42°41N 22°11E **202** D6
Surendranagar *India* 22°45N 71°40E **242** H4
Suresnes *France* 48°52N 2°13E **134** A2
Surf *U.S.A.* 34°41N 120°36W **307** L6
Surfers Paradise *Australia* 28°0S 153°25E **281** D5
Surfside *U.S.A.* 25°52N 80°7W **129** C3
Surgana *India* 20°34N 73°37E **244** D1
Surgères *France* 46°7N 0°47W **174** B3
Surgut *Russia* 61°14N 73°20E **214** C8
Sùria *Spain* 41°50N 1°45E **196** D6
Surian, Palazzo *Venice, Italy* **142** a2
Suriapet *India* 17°10N 79°40E **244** F4
Suribachi Yama *Iwo Jima* 24°45N 141°17E **288** b
Surigao *Phil.* 9°47N 125°29E **233** G5
Surigao del Norte □ *Phil.* 9°40N 125°40E **233** G5
Surigao del Sur □ *Phil.* 8°45N 126°0E **233** G6
Surigao Str. *Phil.* 10°15N 125°23E **233** F5
Surin *Thailand* 14°50N 103°34E **236** E4
Surinam = Suriname ■ *S. Amer.* 4°0N 56°0W **329** C6
Surinam *Mauritius* 20°30S 57°30E **272** e
Suriname ■ *S. Amer.* 4°0N 56°0W **329** C6
Suriname → *Suriname* 5°50N 55°15W **329** B6
Surjagarh *India* 19°36N 80°25E **244** E5
Surma → *Bangla.* 24°34N 91°14E **241** C3
Sūrmaq *Iran* 31°3N 52°48E **247** D7
Sürmene *Turkey* 41°0N 40°1E **213** B9
Surna → *Norway* 62°59N 8°40E **164** B5
Surnadalsøra *Norway* 62°58N 8°40E **164** B5
Surovikino *Russia* 48°32N 42°55E **191** F6
Surprise *U.S.A.* 33°38N 112°19W **305** K7
Surquillo *Peru* 12°6S 77°1W **124** B2
Surrency *U.S.A.* 31°44N 82°12W **316** D7
Surrey *Canada* 49°7N 122°45W **306** A4
Surrey □ *Jamaica* 18°5N 76°34W **320** a
Surrey □ *U.K.* 51°15N 0°31W **169** F7
Surrey Hills *Australia* 33°53S 151°13E **139** B2
Sursand *India* 26°39N 85°43E **243** F11
Sursar → *India* 26°14N 87°3E **243** F12
Sursee *Switz.* 47°11N 8°6E **179** H4
Sursk *Russia* 53°3N 45°40E **190** D7
Surskoye *Russia* 54°30N 46°44E **190** C8
Surt *Libya* 31°11N 16°39E **258** B3
Surt □ *Libya* 30°0N 17°30E **258** B3
Surt, Al Ḥamādah al *Libya* 30°0N 17°50E **258** C3
Surt, Khalīj *Libya* 31°40N 18°30E **258** B3
Surtanahu *Pakistan* 26°22N 70°0E **242** F4
Surte *Sweden* 57°50N 12°1E **163** G6
Surtsey *Iceland* 63°20N 20°30W **155** D6
Surubim *Brazil* 7°50S 35°45W **332** C4
Sürüç *Turkey* 36°58N 38°25E **213** D8
Surud, Ras *Somalia* 11°10N 47°30E **267** B6
Surud Ad *Somalia* 10°42N 47°9E **267** B6
Suruga-Wan *Japan* 34°45N 138°30E **223** C10
Surulangun *Indonesia* 2°37S 102°45E **234** C2
Surulere *Nigeria* 6°29N 3°21E **124** B2
Surumu → *Brazil* 3°22N 60°19W **329** C5
Surxondaryo □ *Uzbekistan* 38°0N 67°30E **217** E7
Susa = Sousse *Tunisia* 35°50N 10°38E **258** A2
Şuşa *Azerbaijan* 39°46N 46°45E **213** C12
Susa *Italy* 45°8N 7°3E **198** C4
Suså → *Denmark* 55°12N 11°42E **163** J5
Sušac *Croatia* 42°46N 16°30E **199** F13
Susaek *S. Korea* 37°34N 126°54E **137** B1
Sūsah *Libya* 32°52N 21°59E **258** B4
Susak *Croatia* 44°30N 14°18E **199** D11
Susaki *Japan* 33°22N 133°17E **222** D5
Susam-Adasi = Samos *Greece* 37°45N 26°50E **205** D8
Sūsangerd *Iran* 31°35N 48°6E **213** G13
Susanville *U.S.A.* 40°25N 120°39W **304** F3
Susch *Switz.* 46°46N 10°5E **179** J6
Suşehri *Turkey* 40°10N 38°6E **213** B8
Sušice *Czechia* 49°17N 13°30E **180** B6
Susleni *Moldova* 47°25N 28°59E **183** C13
Susner *India* 23°57N 76°5E **242** H7
Susong *China* 30°10N 116°5E **229** B11
Susono *Japan* 35°10N 138°55E **223** B10
Susquehanna *U.S.A.* 41°57N 75°36W **313** E9
Susquehanna → *U.S.A.* 39°33N 76°5W **313** G8
Susques *Argentina* 23°35S 66°25W **334** A2
Süssenbrunn *Austria* 48°16N 16°29E **142** A2
Sussex *N.B., Canada* 45°45N 65°37W **299** C6
Sussex *N.J., U.S.A.* 41°13N 74°37W **313** E10
Sussex, East □ *U.K.* 51°0N 0°20E **169** G8
Sussex, West □ *U.K.* 51°0N 0°30W **169** G7
Sussex Inlet *Australia* 35°10S 150°36E **283** C9
Sustut → *Canada* 56°20N 127°30W **296** B3
Susuman *Russia* 62°47N 148°10E **215** C15
Susunu *Indonesia* 3°7S 133°39E **231** E8
Susupe *N. Marianas* 14°58N 145°37E **302** e
Susurluk *Turkey* 39°54N 28°8E **205** B10
Susuz *Turkey* 40°46N 43°8E **213** B10
Susz *Poland* 53°44N 19°20E **184** E6
Sutay Uul *Asia* 46°35N 93°38E **218** B7
Sütçüler *Turkey* 37°29N 30°57E **212** D4
Şuteşti *Romania* 45°13N 27°27E **183** E12
Sutherland *N.S.W., Australia* 34°2S 151°4E **283** C9
Sutherland *Northern Cape, S. Africa* 32°24S 20°40E **270** D3
Sutherland *Highl., U.K.* 58°12N 4°50W **167** C4
Sutherland *Nebr., U.S.A.* 41°10N 101°8W **308** E3
Sutherland Falls *N.Z.* 44°48S 167°46E **285** E2
Sutherland Road *Barbados* 13°16N 59°39W **323** r
Sutherlin *U.S.A.* 43°23N 123°19W **304** E2
Suthri *India* 23°3N 68°55E **242** H3
Sutjeska △ *Bos.-H.* 43°50N 18°32E **182** G3
Sutlej → *Pakistan* 29°23N 71°3E **242** E4
Sutter *U.S.A.* 39°10N 121°45W **306** F5
Sutter Buttes *U.S.A.* 39°12N 121°49W **306** F5
Sutter Creek *U.S.A.* 38°24N 120°48W **306** G6
Sutton *Qué., Canada* 45°6N 72°37W **313** A12
Sutton *N.Z.* 45°34S 170°8E **285** F5
Sutton *London, U.K.* 51°21N 0°11W **125** B2
Sutton *Nebr., U.S.A.* 40°36N 97°52W **308** E5
Sutton *W. Va., U.S.A.* 38°40N 80°43W **309** F13
Sutton → *Canada* 55°15N 83°45W **298** A3
Sutton Coldfield *U.K.* 52°35N 1°49W **169** E6
Sutton in Ashfield *U.K.* 53°8N 1°16W **168** D6
Sutton L. *Canada* 54°15N 84°42W **298** B3
Suttor → *Australia* 21°36S 147°2E **280** C4
Suttsu *Japan* 42°48N 140°14E **220** C10
Sutwik I. *U.S.A.* 56°34N 157°12W **303** H8
Suva *Fiji* 18°6S 178°30E **287** B2
Suva Gora *Macedonia* 41°45N 21°3E **202** E5
Suva Planina *Serbia* 43°10N 22°5E **202** C6
Suva Reka = Therandë *Kosovo* 42°21N 20°50E **202** D4
Suvorov *Russia* 54°7N 36°30E **188** E9
Suvorov Is. = Suwarrow Is. *Cook Is.* 13°15S 163°5W **289** J11
Suvorove *Ukraine* 45°35N 28°59E **183** E13
Suvorovo *Bulgaria* 43°20N 27°35E **203** C11
Suwa *Japan* 36°2N 138°8E **223** A10
Suwa-Ko *Japan* 36°3N 138°5E **223** A10
Suwałki *Poland* 54°8N 22°59E **184** D9
Suwannaphum *Thailand* 15°33N 103°47E **236** E4
Suwannee *U.S.A.* 29°20N 83°9W **317** F6
Suwannee → *U.S.A.* 29°17N 83°10W **317** F6
Suwannee Sd. *U.S.A.* 29°20N 83°15W **317** F6
Suwanose-Jima *Japan* 29°38N 129°43E **221** K4
Suwarrow Is. *Cook Is.* 13°15S 163°5W **289** J11
Suwayqīyah, Hawr as *Iraq* 32°40N 46°3E **213** G12
Suweis, Khalîg el *Egypt* 28°40N 33°0E **256** J8
Suweis, Qanâ es *Egypt* 31°0N 32°20E **256** H8
Suwon *S. Korea* 37°17N 127°1E **224** D3
Suyu *S. Korea* 37°37N 127°0E **137** B2
Suzaka *Japan* 36°39N 138°19E **223** A10
Suzdal *Russia* 56°29N 40°26E **188** D11
Suzhou *Anhui, China* 33°41N 116°59E **226** H9
Suzhou *Jiangsu, China* 31°19N 120°38E **229** B13
Suzu *Japan* 37°25N 137°17E **221** F8
Suzu-Misaki *Japan* 37°31N 137°21E **221** F8
Suzuka *Japan* 34°55N 136°36E **223** C8
Suzuka-Sammyaku *Japan* 35°5N 136°30E **223** B8
Suzukishinden *Japan* 35°43N 139°31E **140** A2
Suzun *Russia* 53°47N 82°18E **217** B10
Suzzara *Italy* 44°59N 10°45E **198** D7
Svalbard *Arctic* 78°0N 17°0E **154** B12
Svalbard Radio = Longyearbyen *Svalbard* 78°13N 15°40E **150** B8
Svalbarð *Iceland* 66°12N 15°43W **155** A11
Svalbarðseyri *Iceland* 65°45N 18°5W **155** B8
Svalöv *Sweden* 55°57N 13°8E **163** J7
Svalyava *Ukraine* 48°33N 22°59E **182** B7
Svaneke *Denmark* 55°8N 15°8E **163** J9
Svanemøllen *Denmark* 55°43N 12°34E **118** A3
Svaneti *Georgia* 42°50N 42°45E **213** A10
Svängsta *Sweden* 56°16N 14°47E **163** H8
Svanskog *Sweden* 59°11N 12°33E **162** E6
Svappavaara *Sweden* 67°40N 21°3E **160** C19
Svärdsjö *Sweden* 60°45N 15°54E **162** D9
Svarstad *Norway* 59°27N 9°56E **164** E6
Svartå *Sweden* 59°8N 14°32E **162** E8
Svartárkot *Iceland* 65°20N 17°15W **155** B9
Svartevatn *Norway* 59°10N 6°56E **164** E3
Svartisen *Norway* 66°40N 13°59E **160** C15
Svartvik *Sweden* 62°19N 17°24E **162** B11
Svatove *Ukraine* 49°22N 38°15E **189** H10
Svatovo = Svatove *Ukraine* 49°22N 38°15E **189** H10
Svatsum *Norway* 61°20N 9°50E **164** C6
Svay Chek *Cambodia* 13°48N 102°58E **236** F4
Svay Rieng *Cambodia* 11°9N 105°45E **237** G5
Sveaborg = Suomenlinna *Finland* 60°9N 24°59E **121** C2
Svealand *Sweden* 60°20N 15°0E **162** D9
Svedala *Sweden* 55°30N 13°15E **163** J7
Sveg *Sweden* 62°2N 14°21E **162** B8
Sveindal *Norway* 58°29N 7°30E **164** F4
Sveinseyri *Iceland* 65°38N 23°51W **155** B3
Sveio *Norway* 59°33N 5°23E **164** E2
Svelgen *Norway* 61°46N 5°17E **164** C2
Svelvik *Norway* 59°37N 10°24E **164** E7
Svendborg *Denmark* 55°4N 10°35E **163** J4
Svene *Norway* 59°45N 9°31E **164** E6
Svenljunga *Sweden* 57°29N 13°5E **163** G7
Svenstavik *Sweden* 62°45N 14°26E **162** B8
Svenstrup *Denmark* 56°58N 9°50E **163** H3
Svenyhorodka *Ukraine* 49°4N 30°56E **189** H6
Sverdlov *Russia* 55°46N 37°36E **129** B2
Sverdlovsk = Yekaterinburg *Russia* 56°50N 60°30E **214** D7
Sverdlovsk *Ukraine* 48°5N 39°47E **189** H10
Sverdrup Chan. *Canada* 79°56N 96°25W **295** B12
Sverdrup Is. *Canada* 79°0N 97°0W **292** B10
Sverige = Sweden ■ *Europe* 57°0N 15°0E **161** H16
Sveshtari *Bulgaria* 43°40N 26°40E **203** C10
Svestad *Norway* 59°46N 10°36E **133** B2
Svetac *Croatia* 43°3N 15°43E **199** E12
Sveti Ivan = Zelina *Croatia* 45°57N 16°16E **199** C13
Sveti Nikola, Prokhad *Europe* 43°27N 22°6E **202** C6
Sveti Nikole *Macedonia* 41°51N 21°56E **202** E5
Sveti Rok *Croatia* 44°22N 15°39E **199** D12
Sveti Vrach = Sandanski *Bulgaria* 41°35N 23°16E **202** E7
Svetlaya *Russia* 46°33N 138°18E **220** A9
Svetlogorsk = Svyetlahorsk *Belarus* 52°38N 29°46E **177** B15
Svetlogorsk *Russia* 54°56N 20°10E **184** D7
Svetlograd *Russia* 45°25N 42°58E **191** H6
Svetlovodsk = Svitlovodsk *Ukraine* 49°2N 33°13E **189** H7
Svetlyy *Kaliningrad, Russia* 54°41N 20°8E **184** D7
Svetlyy *Orenburg, Russia* 50°48N 60°51E **216** B6
Svidník *Slovakia* 49°20N 21°37E **181** B14
Svignaskarð *Iceland* 64°40N 21°42W **155** C5
Svilaja Planina *Croatia* 43°49N 16°31E **199** E13
Svilajnac *Serbia* 44°15N 21°11E **202** B5
Svilengrad *Bulgaria* 41°49N 26°12E **203** E10
Svinafell *Iceland* 63°59N 16°51W **155** D10
Svinö *Finland* 60°7N 24°44E **121** C1
Svir → *Russia* 60°30N 32°48E **188** B7
Sviritsa *Russia* 60°29N 32°51E **188** B7
Svishtov *Bulgaria* 43°36N 25°23E **203** C9
Svislach *Belarus* 53°3N 24°2E **185** E11
Svitava → *Czechia* 49°11N 16°37E **181** B9
Svitavy *Czechia* 49°47N 16°28E **181** B9
Svitlovodsk *Ukraine* 49°2N 33°13E **189** H7
Svityaz, Ozero *Ukraine* 51°30N 23°50E **185** G10
Svizzera = Switzerland ■ *Europe* 46°30N 8°0E **179** J4
Svobodnyy *Russia* 51°20N 128°0E **215** D13
Svoge *Bulgaria* 42°59N 23°23E **202** D7
Svolvær *Norway* 68°15N 14°34E **160** B16
Svorkmo *Norway* 63°10N 9°46E **164** A6
Svoronata *Greece* 38°7N 20°31E **207** C2
Svratka → *Czechia* 49°11N 16°38E **181** B9
Svrljig *Serbia* 43°25N 22°6E **202** C6
Svullrya *Norway* 60°25N 12°23E **164** D9
Svyatogorovsky Rudnik = Dobropole *Ukraine* 48°25N 37°2E **189** H9
Svyetlahorsk *Belarus* 52°38N 29°46E **177** B15
Swa *Burma* 19°15N 96°17E **241** F6
Swa Tende *Dem. Rep. of the Congo* 7°9S 17°7E **265** D3
Swabian Alps = Schwäbische Alb *Germany* 48°20N 9°30E **179** G5
Swaffham *U.K.* 52°39N 0°42E **169** E8
Swains I. *Amer. Samoa* 11°11S 171°4W **289** J11
Swainsboro *U.S.A.* 32°36N 82°20W **316** C7
Swakop → *Namibia* 22°38S 14°36E **270** B2
Swakopmund *Namibia* 22°37S 14°30E **270** B1
Swale → *U.K.* 54°5N 1°20W **168** C6
Swamihalli *India* 14°52N 76°38E **245** G3
Swan → *W. Austral., Australia* 32°3S 115°45E **279** F2
Swan → *Man., Canada* 52°30N 100°45W **297** C8
Swan Hill *Australia* 35°20S 143°33E **282** C5
Swan Hills *Canada* 54°43N 115°24W **296** C5
Swan Is. = Santanilla, Is. *Honduras* 17°22N 83°57W **320** C3
Swan L. = Kalajun-Ku'erdening ⌓ *China* 43°10N 81°50E **217** D10
Swan L. *Man., Canada* 52°30N 100°40W **297** C8
Swan L. *Ont., Canada* 54°16N 91°11W **298** B1
Swan Ra. *U.S.A.* 48°0N 113°45W **304** C7
Swan Reach *Australia* 34°35S 139°37E **282** C3
Swan River *Canada* 52°10N 101°16W **297** C8
Swanage *U.K.* 50°36N 1°58W **169** G6
Swanley *U.K.* 51°23N 0°11E **125** B4
Swansea *N.S.W., Australia* 33°3S 151°35E **283** B9
Swansea *Tas., Australia* 42°8S 148°4E **281** G4
Swansea *Ont., Canada* 43°38N 79°28W **141** B2
Swansea *Swansea, U.K.* 51°37N 3°57W **169** F4
Swansea *S.C., U.S.A.* 33°44N 81°6W **316** B8
Swansea □ *U.K.* 51°38N 4°3W **169** F3
Swanton *U.S.A.* 41°35N 83°53W **311** C13
Swartberge *S. Africa* 33°20S 22°0E **270** D3
Swartmodder *S. Africa* 28°1S 20°32E **270** C3
Swartnossob → *Namibia* 23°8S 18°42E **270** B2
Swartruggens *S. Africa* 25°39S 26°42E **270** C4
Swarzędz *Poland* 52°25N 17°4E **185** F4
Swastika *Canada* 48°7N 80°6W **298** C3
Swat → *Pakistan* 34°40N 72°5E **243** B5
Swatow = Shantou *China* 23°18N 116°40E **229** F11
Swaziland ■ *Africa* 26°30S 31°30E **271** C5
Sweden ■ *Europe* 57°0N 15°0E **161** H16
Swedru *Ghana* 5°32N 0°41W **263** D4
Sweet Grass *U.S.A.* 48°59N 111°58W **304** B8
Sweet Home *U.S.A.* 44°24N 122°44W **304** D2
Sweet Springs *U.S.A.* 38°58N 93°25W **310** F3
Sweetwater *Nev., U.S.A.* 38°27N 119°9W **306** G7
Sweetwater *Tenn., U.S.A.* 35°36N 84°28W **315** D12
Sweetwater *Tex., U.S.A.* 32°28N 100°25W **314** E4
Sweetwater → *U.S.A.* 42°31N 107°2W **304** E10
Swellendam *S. Africa* 34°1S 20°26E **270** D3
Swider → *Poland* 52°6N 21°14E **185** F8
Świdnica *Poland* 50°50N 16°30E **185** H3
Świdnik *Poland* 51°13N 22°39E **185** G9
Świdwin *Poland* 53°47N 15°49E **184** E2
Świebodzice *Poland* 50°51N 16°20E **185** H3
Świebodzin *Poland* 52°15N 15°31E **185** F2
Świecie *Poland* 53°25N 18°30E **184** E5
Świerzawa *Poland* 51°1N 15°54E **185** G2
Świętokrzyski △ *Poland* 50°53N 20°59E **185** H7
Świętokrzyskie □ *Poland* 50°45N 20°45E **185** H7
Świętokrzyskie, Góry *Poland* 51°0N 20°30E **185** H7
Swift Current *Canada* 50°20N 107°45W **297** C7
Swift Current → *Canada* 50°38N 107°44W **297** C7
Swifts Creek *Australia* 37°17S 147°44E **283** D7
Swilly, L. *Ireland* 55°12N 7°33W **166** A4
Swinburne I. *U.S.A.* 40°33N 74°3W **132** C1
Swindon *U.K.* 51°34N 1°46W **169** F6
Swindon □ *U.K.* 51°34N 1°46W **169** F6
Swinemünde = Świnoujście *Poland* 53°54N 14°16E **184** E1
Swinford *Ireland* 53°57N 8°58W **166** C3
Świnoujście *Poland* 53°54N 14°16E **184** E1
Switzerland ■ *Europe* 46°30N 8°0E **179** J4
Swords *Ireland* 53°28N 6°13W **166** C5
Swoyerville *U.S.A.* 41°18N 75°53W **313** E9
Syasstroy *Russia* 60°9N 32°33E **188** B7
Sycamore *Ill., U.S.A.* 41°59N 88°41W **311** C8
Sycamore *Ohio, U.S.A.* 40°57N 83°10W **311** D13
Sychevka *Russia* 55°59N 34°16E **188** E8
Syców *Poland* 51°19N 17°40E **185** G4
Sydenham *S. Africa* 26°9S 28°5E **123** A2
Sydenham → *Canada* 42°33N 82°25W **312** D2
Sydney *N.S.W., Australia* 33°52S 151°12E **139** B2
Sydney *N.S., Canada* 46°7N 60°7W **299** C7
Sydney, Univ. of *Australia* 33°54S 151°11E **139** B2
Sydney Harbour △ *Australia* 33°50S 151°14E **139** B2
Sydney Harbour Bridge *Australia* 33°51S 151°12E **139** B2
Sydney Kingsford Smith ✈ **(SYD)** *Australia* 33°57S 151°11E **139** B2
Sydney L. *Canada* 50°41N 94°25W **297** C10
Sydney Mines *Canada* 46°18N 60°15W **299** C7
Sydprøven = Alluitsup Paa *Greenland* 60°30N 45°35W **154** E6
Sydra, G. of = Surt, Khalīj *Libya* 31°40N 18°30E **258** B3
Sydstranden *Denmark* 55°34N 12°38E **118** B3
Syeverodonetsk *Ukraine* 48°58N 38°35E **189** H10
Syfteland *Norway* 60°14N 5°27E **164** D2
Syke *Germany* 52°55N 8°50E **178** C4
Sykesville *U.S.A.* 41°3N 78°50W **312** E6
Sykkylven *Norway* 62°23N 6°35E **164** B3
Syktyvkar *Russia* 61°45N 50°40E **186** B9
Sylacauga *U.S.A.* 33°10N 86°15W **316** B3
Sylarna *Sweden* 63°2N 12°13E **164** A9
Sylhet *Bangla.* 24°54N 91°52E **241** C3
Sylhet □ *Bangla.* 24°50N 91°50E **241** C3
Sylt *Germany* 54°54N 8°22E **178** A4
Sylte *Norway* 62°18N 7°17E **164** B4
Sylvan Beach *U.S.A.* 43°12N 75°44W **313** C9
Sylvan Lake *Canada* 52°20N 114°3W **296** C6
Sylvania *N.S.W., Australia* 34°0S 151°7E **139** C1
Sylvania *Ga., U.S.A.* 32°45N 81°38W **316** C8
Sylvania *Ohio, U.S.A.* 41°43N 83°42W **311** C13
Sylvester *U.S.A.* 31°32N 83°50W **316** D6
Sym *Russia* 60°20N 88°18E **214** C9
Symphony Hall *San Francisco, U.S.A.* **136** c1
Synelnykove *Ukraine* 48°25N 35°30E **189** H8
Synevyr △ *Ukraine* 48°30N 23°40E **183** B8
Synevyrska Polyana *Ukraine* 48°35N 23°41E **183** B8
Synnervika *Norway* 62°25N 11°54E **164** B8
Synnfjell *Norway* 61°5N 9°46E **164** C6
Synnot Ra. *Australia* 16°30S 125°20E **278** C4
Syntagma Square *Athens, Greece* **112** b2
Synyak *Ukraine* 48°35N 22°51E **182** B7
Syon Park *U.K.* 51°28N 0°18W **125** B2
Syöte △ *Finland* 65°44N 27°58E **160** D22
Syowa *Antarctica* 68°50S 12°0E **151** C5
Syracuse = Siracusa *Italy* 37°4N 15°17E **201** E8
Syracuse *Ind., U.S.A.* 41°26N 85°45W **311** C11
Syracuse *Kans., U.S.A.* 37°59N 101°45W **308** G3
Syracuse *N.Y., U.S.A.* 43°3N 76°9W **313** C8
Syracuse *Nebr., U.S.A.* 40°39N 96°11W **308** E5
Syrdarya → *Kazakhstan* 46°3N 61°0E **216** C6
Syria ■ *Asia* 35°0N 38°0E **213** E8
Syriam *Burma* 16°44N 96°19E **241** G6
Syrian Desert = Shām, Bādiyat ash *Asia* 32°0N 40°0E **246** C3
Syros = Ermoupoli *Greece* 37°28N 24°57E **204** D6
Sysslebäck *Sweden* 60°44N 12°52E **162** D6
Syvden *Norway* 62°5N 5°44E **164** B2
Syzran *Russia* 53°12N 48°30E **190** D9
Szabolcs-Szatmár-Bereg □ *Hungary* 48°2N 21°45E **182** B6
Szadek *Poland* 51°41N 18°59E **185** G5
Szamocin *Poland* 53°2N 17°7E **185** E4
Szamos → *Hungary* 48°7N 22°20E **182** B7
Szamotuły *Poland* 52°37N 16°33E **185** F3
Száraz → *Hungary* 46°10N 21°15E **182** D6
Szarvas *Hungary* 46°50N 20°38E **182** D5
Százhalombatta *Hungary* 47°20N 18°58E **182** C3
Szczawnica *Poland* 49°26N 20°30E **185** J7
Szczebrzeszyn *Poland* 50°42N 22°59E **185** H9
Szczecin *Poland* 53°27N 14°27E **184** E1
Szczecinek *Poland* 53°43N 16°41E **184** E3
Szczeciński, Zalew = Stettiner Haff *Germany* 53°47N 14°15E **178** B10
Szczekociny *Poland* 50°38N 19°48E **185** H6
Szczęsliwice *Poland* 52°12N 20°57E **143** B1
Szczucin *Poland* 50°18N 21°4E **185** H8
Szczuczyn *Poland* 53°36N 22°19E **184** E9
Szczyrk *Poland* 49°43N 19°2E **185** J6
Szczytna *Poland* 50°25N 16°28E **185** H3
Szczytno *Poland* 53°33N 21°0E **184** E7
Széchnenyi-hegy *Hungary* 47°29N 18°57E **117** B1
Szechuan = Sichuan □ *China* 30°30N 103°0E **228** B5
Szechuan Basin = Sichuan Pendi *China* 31°0N 105°0E **228** B5
Szécsény *Hungary* 48°7N 19°30E **182** B4
Szeged *Hungary* 46°16N 20°10E **182** D5
Szeghalom *Hungary* 47°1N 21°10E **182** C6
Székesfehérvár *Hungary* 47°15N 18°25E **182** C3
Szekszárd *Hungary* 46°22N 18°42E **182** D3
Szendrő *Hungary* 48°24N 20°41E **182** B5
Szentendre *Hungary* 47°39N 19°4E **182** C4
Szentes *Hungary* 46°39N 20°21E **182** D5
Szentgotthárd *Hungary* 46°58N 16°19E **182** D1
Szentlőrinc *Hungary* 46°3N 18°1E **182** D3
Széphalom *Hungary* 47°34N 18°57E **117** A1
Szeping = Siping *China* 43°8N 124°21E **227** C13
Szerencs *Hungary* 48°10N 21°12E **182** B6
Szigetszentmiklós *Hungary* 47°21N 19°3E **182** C4
Szigetvár *Hungary* 46°3N 17°46E **182** D2
Szikszó *Hungary* 48°12N 20°56E **182** B5
Szklarska Poreba *Poland* 50°50N 15°33E **185** H2
Szkwa → *Poland* 53°11N 21°43E **185** E8
Szlichtyngowa *Poland* 51°42N 16°15E **185** G3
Szob *Hungary* 47°48N 18°53E **182** C3
Szolnok *Hungary* 47°10N 20°15E **182** C5
Szombathely *Hungary* 47°14N 16°38E **182** C1
Szprotawa *Poland* 51°33N 15°35E **185** G2
Sztálinváros = Dunaújváros *Hungary* 46°58N 18°57E **182** D3
Sztum *Poland* 53°55N 19°1E **184** E6
Sztutowo *Poland* 54°20N 19°15E **184** D6
Szubin *Poland* 53°1N 17°45E **185** E4
Szydłowiec *Poland* 51°15N 20°51E **185** G7
Szypliszki *Poland* 54°17N 23°2E **184** D10

T

Ta Khli *Thailand* 15°15N 100°21E **236** E3
Ta Lai *Vietnam* 11°24N 107°23E **237** G6
Ta Phraya △ *Thailand* 14°11N 102°49E **236** E4
Ta Pieh Shan = Dabie Shan *China* 31°20N 115°20E **229** B10
Taakoka *Cook Is.* 21°15S 159°43W **289** h
Taal, L. *Phil.* 13°56N 121°0E **232** E3
Taal Volcano *Phil.* 14°7N 120°59E **231** B6
Taal Volcano △ *Phil.* 14°1N 120°59E **232** D3
Taamisaari = Raasepori *Finland* 60°0N 23°26E **188** B2
Taan *Taiwan* 24°22N 120°35E **225** B2
Taastrup *Denmark* 55°39N 12°18E **118** B1
Tab *Hungary* 46°44N 18°2E **182** D3
Tabacal *Argentina* 23°15S 64°15W **334** A3
Tabaco *Phil.* 13°22N 123°44E **232** E4
Tabagné *Ivory C.* 7°59N 3°4W **262** D4
Ţābah *Si. Arabia* 26°55N 42°38E **246** E4
Tabajara *Brazil* 8°56S 62°8W **331** B5
Tabalo *Papua N. G.* 1°24S 149°40E **286** A5
Tabalos *Peru* 6°26S 76°37W **330** B2
Tabanan *Indonesia* 8°32S 115°8E **231** K18
Tabang *Indonesia* 0°34N 116°1E **235** B5
Tabankort *Niger* 17°44N 0°20E **263** B5
Tabaquite *Trin. & Tob.* 10°23N 61°18W **323** t
Tabaquite/Talparo □ *Trin. & Tob.* 10°28N 61°18W **323** t
Tabar I. *Papua N. G.* 2°56S 152°0E **286** B7
Tabar Is. *Papua N. G.* 2°50S 152°0E **286** B7
Tabarka *Tunisia* 36°56N 8°46E **258** A1
Ţabas *Khorāsān, Iran* 32°48N 60°12E **247** C9
Ţabas *Yazd, Iran* 33°35N 56°55E **247** C8
Tabasará, Serranía de *Panama* 8°35N 81°40W **320** E3
Tabasco □ *Mexico* 18°0N 92°40W **319** D6
Tabāsīn *Iran* 31°12N 57°54E **247** D8
Tabata *Japan* 35°44N 139°46E **140** A3
Tabatinga *Brazil* 4°16S 69°56W **330** A4
Tabatinga, Serra da *Brazil* 10°30S 44°0W **332** D3
Tabayin *Burma* 22°42N 95°20E **241** D5
Tabelbala *Algeria* 29°24N 3°15W **260** C4
Tabelbala, Kahal de *Algeria* 28°47N 2°0W **261** C4
Tabelembila *Algeria* 24°43N 4°16E **261** D5
Taber *Canada* 49°47N 112°8W **296** D6
Taberg *Sweden* 57°40N 14°6E **163** G8
Tabernacle *St. Kitts & Nevis* 17°23N 62°46W **322** d
Tabi *Angola* 8°10S 13°18E **265** D2
Tabina *Phil.* 7°28N 123°24E **233** H4
Tabira *Brazil* 7°35S 37°33W **332** C4
Tabiteuea *Kiribati* 1°25S 174°50E **277** A13
Tabla *Niger* 13°46N 3°1E **263** C5
Tablada *Argentina* 34°41S 58°32W **117** C1
Tablas de Daimiel △ *Spain* 39°9N 3°40W **195** F7
Tablas I. *Phil.* 12°25N 122°2E **232** E4
Tablas Str. *Phil.* 12°40N 121°48E **232** E3
Table, Pte. de la *Réunion* 21°14S 55°48E **272** f
Table B. *Nfld. & L., Canada* 53°40N 56°25W **299** B8
Table B. *Western Cape, S. Africa* 33°35S 18°25E **118** A1
Table C. *N.Z.* 39°6S 178°0E **284** F7
Table Grove *U.S.A.* 40°20N 90°27W **310** D6
Table I. *Burma* 14°12N 93°22E **245** G11
Table Mountain △ *S. Africa* 33°58S 18°28E **118** A1
Table Mt. *S. Africa* 33°58S 18°26E **118** A1
Table Rock L. *U.S.A.* 36°36N 93°19W **308** G7
Tableland *Trin. & Tob.* 10°16N 61°16W **323** t
Tabletop, Mt. *Australia* 23°24S 147°11E **280** C4
Taboão da Serra *Brazil* 23°36S 46°45W **137** B1
Tabocal *Brazil* 2°42S 57°40W **329** D6
Tabon Cave Complex *Phil.* 9°17N 118°5E **233** G2
Tábor *Czechia* 49°25N 14°39E **180** B7
Tabora *Tanzania* 5°2S 32°50E **268** D3
Tabora □ *Tanzania* 5°0S 33°0E **268** D3
Tabou *Ivory C.* 4°30N 7°20W **262** E3
Tabrīz *Iran* 38°7N 46°20E **213** C12
Tabuaeran *Kiribati* 3°51N 159°22W **289** G12
Tabubil *Papua N. G.* 5°20S 141°15E **286** C1
Tabuenca *Spain* 41°42N 1°33W **196** D3
Tabuk *Phil.* 17°24N 121°25E **232** C3
Tabūk *Si. Arabia* 28°23N 36°36E **251** K7
Tabūk □ *Si. Arabia* 27°40N 36°50E **246** E3
Tabunifi *Micronesia* 9°28N 138°4E **287** S16
Taburno-Camposauro ⌓ *Italy* 41°8N 14°37E **201** A7

Tabwemasana, Mt. *Vanuatu* 15°20S 166°44E **287** E4
Täby *Sweden* 59°26N 18°2E **139** A2
Tacámbaro de Codallos *Mexico* 19°14N 101°28W **318** D4
Tacarigua *Trin. & Tob.* 10°38N 61°22W **323** t
Tacarigua *Venezuela* 11°3N 63°54W **329** a
Tacarigua, Laguna de *Venezuela* 10°15N 65°50W **328** A4
Tacheng *Xinjiang Uygur, China* 46°40N 82°58E **217** C10
Tacheng *Taiwan* 23°51N 120°19E **225** C2
Tach'i *Taiwan* 24°53N 121°17E **225** B3
Tachia *Taiwan* 24°25N 120°28E **225** B2
Tachia Hsi → *Taiwan* 24°20N 120°33E **225** B3
Tachibana-Wan *Japan* 32°45N 130°7E **222** E2
Tachikawa *Japan* 35°42N 139°25E **223** B11
Tachilek *Burma* 20°26N 99°52E **236** B2
Tach'ing Shan = Daqing Shan *China* 40°40N 111°0E **226** D6
Táchira □ *Venezuela* 8°7N 72°15W **328** B3
Tachiumet *Libya* 26°19N 10°3E **258** C2
Tachoshui *Taiwan* 24°20N 121°44E **225** B3
Tachov *Czechia* 49°47N 12°39E **180** B5
Tácina → *Italy* 38°57N 16°55E **201** D9
Tacloban *Phil.* 11°15N 124°58E **233** F5
Tacna *Peru* 18°0S 70°20W **330** D3
Tacna □ *Peru* 17°40S 70°20W **330** D3
Tacoma *U.S.A.* 47°14N 122°26W **306** C4
Tacopaya = Zudañez *Bolivia* 19°6S 64°44W **331** D5
Tacuarembó *Uruguay* 31°45S 56°0W **335** C4
Tacuba *Mexico* 19°26N 99°11W **128** B1
Tacubaya *Mexico* 19°24N 99°10W **128** B1
Tacurong *Phil.* 6°40N 124°41E **233** H5
Tacutu = Takutu → *Guyana* 3°30N 60°29W **329** C5
Tada-u *Burma* 21°49N 95°58E **241** E5
Tadahadi *Solomon Is.* 10°18S 161°35E **287** N11
Tademaït, Plateau du *Algeria* 28°30N 2°30E **261** C5
Tādepallegudem *India* 16°50N 81°30E **244** F5
Tadéra *Niger* 20°29N 8°18E **261** D6
Tadine *N. Cal.* 21°33S 167°52E **288** d
Tadio, L. *Ivory C.* 5°10N 5°15W **262** D3
Tadjerdjeri, O. → *Algeria* 26°0N 8°0E **261** C6
Tadjerouna *Algeria* 33°31N 2°3E **261** B5
Tadjettaret, O. → *Algeria* 21°20N 7°22E **261** D6
Tadjmout *Laghouat, Algeria* 33°52N 2°30E **261** B5
Tadjmout *Saoura, Algeria* 25°37N 3°48E **261** C5
Tadjourah *Djibouti* 11°50N 42°55E **257** E5
Tadjourah, Golfe de *Djibouti* 11°50N 43°0E **257** E5
Tadla-Azilal □ *Morocco* 32°0N 6°30W **260** B3
Tadmor *N.Z.* 41°27S 172°45E **285** B7
Tadoba △ *India* 20°30N 78°20E **244** D4
Tadotsu *Japan* 34°16N 133°45E **222** C5
Tadoule L. *Canada* 58°36N 98°20W **297** B9
Tadoussac *Canada* 48°11N 69°42W **299** C6
Tadpatri *India* 14°55N 78°1E **245** G4
Tadrés △ *Niger* 16°0N 7°10E **263** B6
Tadzhikistan = Tajikistan ■ *Asia* 38°30N 70°0E **217** E8
Tae-an *S. Korea* 36°45N 126°17E **224** D3
Tae-an △ *S. Korea* 36°40N 126°0E **224** D3
Taebaek *S. Korea* 37°10N 128°59E **224** D4
Taebaeksan △ *S. Korea* 37°5N 128°54E **224** D4
T'aebaeksanmaek *S. Korea* 37°40N 128°50E **224** D4
Taedong-gang → *N. Korea* 38°41N 125°15E **224** C2
Taedong-man *N. Korea* 38°4N 125°7E **224** C2
Taegu = Daegu *S. Korea* 35°50N 128°37E **224** E4
Taegwan *N. Korea* 40°13N 125°12E **224** B2
Taehung *N. Korea* 40°5N 126°56E **224** B3
Taehwa-do *N. Korea* 39°26N 124°36E **224** C2
Taejŏn = Daejeon *S. Korea* 36°20N 127°28E **224** D3
Tælavåg *Norway* 60°15N 4°58E **164** D1
Taen, Ko *Thailand* 9°22N 99°57E **237** b
Tafalla *Spain* 42°30N 1°41W **196** C3
Tafar *South Sudan* 6°52N 28°15E **257** F2
Tafassasset, O. → *Algeria* 22°0N 9°57E **261** D6
Tafelbaai = Table B. *S. Africa* 33°35S 18°25E **118** A1
Tafelberg *Curaçao* 12°4N 68°50W **322** g
Tafelney, C. *Morocco* 31°3N 9°51W **260** B3
Tafermaar *Indonesia* 6°47S 134°10E **231** F8
Taffermit *Morocco* 29°37N 9°15W **260** C3
Tafi Viejo *Argentina* 26°43S 65°17W **334** B2
Tafihān *Iran* 29°25N 52°39E **247** D7
Tafilalet *Morocco* 31°20N 4°45W **260** B4
Tafiré *Ivory C.* 9°4N 5°4W **262** D3
Tafjord *Norway* 62°14N 7°24E **164** B4
Tafnidilt *Morocco* 28°47N 10°58W **260** C2
Tafo *Ghana* 6°15N 0°20W **263** D4
Tafraoute *Morocco* 29°50N 8°58W **260** C3
Tafresh *Iran* 34°45N 49°57E **247** C6
Taft *Iran* 31°45N 54°14E **247** D7
Taft *Phil.* 11°57N 125°30E **233** F5
Taft *Calif., U.S.A.* 35°8N 119°28W **307** K7
Taft *Fla., U.S.A.* 28°25N 81°21W **133** B2
Taftan *Pakistan* 29°0N 61°30E **240** C1
Taftān, Kūh-e *Iran* 28°40N 61°0E **247** D9
Tafu *Taiwan* 23°37N 121°23E **225** C3
Tafwap *India* 7°23N 93°43E **245** L11
Taga *Samoa* 13°46S 172°28W **287** V19
Taga Dzong *Bhutan* 27°5N 89°55E **241** B2
Tagana-an *Phil.* 9°42N 125°35E **233** G5
Taganay △ *Russia* 55°15N 59°48E **216** B5
Taganrog *Russia* 47°12N 38°50E **189** J10
Taganrogskiy Zaliv *Russia* 47°0N 38°30E **189** J10
Tagânt □ *Mauritania* 19°0N 10°0W **260** E3
Tagap Ga *Burma* 26°56N 96°13E **241** B6
Tagauayan I. *Phil.* 10°58N 121°13E **233** F3
Tagaung *Burma* 23°30N 96°2E **241** D6
Tagawa *Japan* 33°38N 130°51E **222** D2
Tagaytay *Phil.* 14°6N 120°56E **232** D3
Tagbilaran *Phil.* 9°39N 123°51E **233** G4
Tagdempt = Tiaret *Algeria* 35°20N 1°21E **261** A5
Tage *Papua N. G.* 6°19S 143°20E **286** D2
Tageren Canal *Micronesia* 9°33N 138°8E **287** R16
Tággia *Italy* 43°52N 7°51E **198** E4
Taghit *Algeria* 30°58N 2°0W **261** B4
Tagig → *Phil.* 14°31N 121°5E **127** B2
Tagish *Canada* 60°19N 134°16W **296** A2
Tagish L. *Canada* 60°10N 134°20W **296** A2
Tagkawayan *Phil.* 13°58N 122°32E **232** E4
Tagliacozzo *Italy* 42°4N 13°14E **199** F10
Tagliamento → *Italy* 45°38N 13°6E **199** C10
Táglio di Po *Italy* 45°0N 12°12E **199** C9
Tagna *Colombia* 2°24S 70°37W **328** D3
Tago *Phil.* 9°2N 126°13E **233** G6
Tago, Mt. *Phil.* 8°23N 125°5E **233** G5
Tagomago *Spain* 39°2N 1°39E **206** C2
Tagourâret *Mauritania* 17°45N 7°45W **262** B3
Taguatinga *Distrito Federal, Brazil* 15°51S 48°4W **333** E2
Taguatinga *Tocantins, Brazil* 12°27S 46°22W **333** D2
Tagudin *Phil.* 16°56N 120°27E **232** C3
Taguenout Chaggueret *Mali* 21°14N 0°48W **261** D4
Taguig *Phil.* 14°31N 121°4E **127** B2
Tagula *Papua N. G.* 11°22S 153°15E **286** F7
Tagula I. *Papua N. G.* 11°30S 153°30E **286** F7
Tagum *Phil.* 7°33N 125°53E **233** H5
Tagus = Tejo → *Europe* 38°40N 9°24W **195** F2
Tahakopa *N.Z.* 46°30S 169°23E **285** G4
Tahala *Morocco* 34°0N 4°28W **260** B4
Tahan, Gunung *Malaysia* 4°34N 102°17E **237** K4
Tahānah-ye sūr Gol *Afghan.* 31°43N 67°53E **240** C2
Tahara *Japan* 34°40N 137°16E **223** C9
Tahat *Algeria* 23°18N 5°33E **261** D6
Tāherī *Iran* 27°43N 52°20E **247** E7
Tahgong Pt. *N. Marianas* 15°6N 145°39E **302** e
Tahifet *Algeria* 22°58N 6°0E **261** D6
Tahiti *French Polynesia* 17°37S 149°27W **289** e
Tahlab → *Pakistan* 28°9N 62°45E **240** C1
Tahlequah *U.S.A.* 35°55N 94°58W **314** D7
Tahoe, L. *U.S.A.* 39°6N 120°2W **306** G6
Tahoe City *U.S.A.* 39°10N 120°9W **306** F6
Tahoka *U.S.A.* 33°10N 101°48W **314** E4
Taholah *U.S.A.* 47°21N 124°17W **306** C2
Tahora *N.Z.* 39°2S 174°49E **284** F3
Tahoua *Niger* 14°57N 5°16E **263** C6
Tahrir Square *Egypt* 30°2N 31°14E **117** A2
Tahrūd *Iran* 29°26N 57°49E **247** D8
Tahsis *Canada* 49°55N 126°40W **296** D3
Tahta *Egypt* 26°44N 31°32E **256** B3
Tahtaköprü *Turkey* 39°57N 29°39E **203** G13
Tahtalı Dağları *Turkey* 38°20N 36°0E **212** C7
Tahu *Taiwan* 24°26N 120°52E **225** B2
Tahuamanú → *Bolivia* 11°6S 67°36W **330** C4
Tahuata, I. *French Polynesia* 9°57S 139°5W **289** f
Tahulandang *Indonesia* 2°27N 125°23E **231** D7
Tahuna *Indonesia* 3°38N 125°30E **231** D7
Taï *Ivory C.* 5°55N 7°30W **262** D3
Taï △ *Ivory C.* 5°25N 7°5W **262** D3
Tai Ho *Hong Kong, China* 22°17N 113°58E **122** B1
Tai Hu *China* 31°5N 120°10E **229** B13
Tai Lam Chung Res. *Hong Kong, China* 22°23N 114°1E **122** A2
Tai Lam Country Park △ *Hong Kong, China* 22°23N 114°0E **122** A2
Tai Lo Shan *Hong Kong, China* 22°21N 114°1E **122** A3
Tai Long Wan Tsuen *Hong Kong, China* 22°13N 113°53E **122** B1
Tai Mo Shan *Hong Kong, China* 22°25N 114°7E **122** A2
Tai O *Hong Kong, China* 22°15N 113°52E **122** B1
Tai Pang Wan *China* 22°33N 114°24E **219** a
Tai Po *China* 22°27N 114°10E **219** a
Tai Po Tsai *Hong Kong, China* 22°20N 114°15E **122** A3
Tai Rom Yen △ *Thailand* 8°45N 99°30E **237** H2
Tai Seng *Singapore* 1°20N 103°53E **138** A3
Tai Shan *China* 36°25N 117°20E **227** F9
Tai Shui Hang *Hong Kong, China* 22°24N 114°12E **122** A3
Tai Tam B. *Hong Kong, China* 22°12N 114°13E **122** B3
Tai Tam Country Park △ *Hong Kong, China* 22°15N 114°12E **122** B3
Tai Tam Tuk Res. *Hong Kong, China* 22°14N 114°13E **122** B3
Tai Wai *Hong Kong, China* 22°22N 114°10E **122** A3
Tai Wan Tau *Hong Kong, China* 22°17N 114°17E **122** B3
Tai Wo Hau *Hong Kong, China* 22°21N 114°7E **122** A2
Tai Yue Shan = Lantau I. *Hong Kong, China* 22°15N 113°56E **122** B1
Tai'an *China* 36°12N 117°8E **227** F9
Taiarapu, Presqu'île de *Tahiti* 17°47S 149°14W **289** e
Taibai Shan *China* 33°57N 107°45E **226** H4
Taibei = T'aipei *Taiwan* 25°4N 121°29E **225** A3
Taibique *Canary Is.* 27°42N 17°58W **153** e1
Taibus Qi *China* 41°54N 115°22E **226** D8
Taicang *China* 31°30N 121°5E **229** B13
Taichow = Taizhou *China* 32°28N 119°55E **229** A12
T'aichung *Taiwan* 24°9N 120°37E **225** B2
Taidong = T'aitung *Taiwan* 22°43N 121°4E **225** D3
Taieri → *N.Z.* 46°3S 170°12E **285** G5
Taigu *China* 37°28N 112°30E **226** F7
Taihang Shan *China* 36°0N 113°30E **226** G7
Taihape *N.Z.* 39°41S 175°48E **284** F4
Taihe *Anhui, China* 33°20N 115°42E **226** H8
Taihe *Jiangxi, China* 26°47N 114°52E **229** D10
Taihoku = T'aipei *Taiwan* 25°4N 121°29E **225** A3
Taihsi *Taiwan* 23°51N 120°16E **225** C2
Taihu *China* 30°22N 116°20E **229** B11
Taijiang *China* 26°39N 108°21E **228** D7
Taikang *China* 34°5N 114°50E **226** G8
Taikkyi *Burma* 17°20N 96°0E **241** G6
Tailem Bend *Australia* 35°12S 139°29E **282** C3
Tailfingen *Germany* 48°15N 9°1E **179** G5
T'ailuko *Taiwan* 24°9N 121°37E **225** B3
T'aimali *Taiwan* 22°36N 121°0E **225** D3
Taimyr Peninsula = Taymyr, Poluostrov *Russia* 75°0N 100°0E **215** B11
Tain *U.K.* 57°49N 4°4W **167** D4
Tainaka *Japan* 34°36N 135°35E **133** B2
Tainan = T'ainan *Taiwan* 23°0N 120°10E **225** D2
T'ainan *Taiwan* 23°0N 120°10E **225** D2
T'ainan □ *Taiwan* 23°15N 120°20E **225** C2
Tainggyo *Burma* 17°49N 94°29E **241** G5
Taining *China* 26°54N 117°9E **229** D11
Taiobeiras *Brazil* 15°49S 42°14W **333** E3
Taipa *China* 22°10N 113°35E **219** a
T'aipei *Taiwan* 25°4N 121°29E **225** A3
T'aipei □ *Taiwan* 24°50N 121°35E **225** B3
Taiping *Anhui, China* 30°15N 118°6E **229** B12
Taiping *Malaysia* 4°51N 100°44E **237** K3
Taiping Dao = Itu Aba I. *S. China Sea* 10°23N 114°21E **230** B4
Taipingchuan *China* 44°23N 123°11E **227** B12
Taipingzhen *China* 33°35N 111°42E **226** H6
Taipu *Brazil* 5°37S 35°36W **332** C4
Tairenpokpi *India* 24°39N 93°40E **241** C4
Tairua *N.Z.* 37°0S 175°51E **284** D4
Tais *Indonesia* 4°6S 102°34E **234** C2
Taisha *Japan* 35°24N 132°40E **222** B4
Taishan *China* 22°14N 112°41E **229** F9
Taishō *Japan* 34°38N 135°27E **133** B1
Taishun *China* 27°30N 119°42E **229** D12
Taita Hills *Kenya* 3°25S 38°15E **268** C4
Taita-Taveta □ *Kenya* 3°20S 38°15E **268** C4
Taitao, C. *Chile* 45°53S 75°5W **336** C1
Taitao, Pen. de *Chile* 46°30S 75°0W **336** C2
T'aitung *Taiwan* 22°43N 121°4E **225** D3
T'aitung □ *Taiwan* 23°0N 121°0E **225** D3
Taivalkoski *Finland* 65°33N 28°12E **160** D23
Taiwan ■ *Asia* 23°30N 121°0E **225** C3
Taiwan Strait *Asia* 24°40N 120°0E **229** E12
Taiwan Taoyuan Int. ✈ **(TPE)** *Taiwan* 25°5N 121°13E **225** A3
Taiwei = Taihsi *Taiwan* 23°51N 120°16E **225** C2
Taixing *China* 32°11N 120°0E **229** A13
Taiyara *Sudan* 13°12N 30°47E **257** E3
Taiyiba *Israel* 32°36N 35°27E **250** C4
Taiyuan *China* 37°52N 112°33E **226** F7
Taizhong = T'aichung *Taiwan* 24°9N 120°37E **225** B2
Taizhou *Jiangsu, China* 32°28N 119°55E **229** A12
Taizhou *Zhejiang, China* 28°40N 121°24E **229** C13
Taizhou Liedao *China* 28°30N 121°55E **229** C13
Ta'izz *Yemen* 13°35N 44°2E **248** D4
Ta'izz □ *Yemen* 13°35N 44°24E **248** D4
Taj Mahal *India* 27°10N 78°2E **242** F8
Tājābād *Iran* 30°2N 54°24E **247** D7
Tajapuru, Furo do *Brazil* 1°50S 50°25W **332** B1
Tajarhī *Libya* 24°21N 14°28E **258** D2
Tajen *Taiwan* 22°17N 120°53E **225** D2
Tajikistan ■ *Asia* 38°30N 70°0E **217** E8
Tajima = Minamiaizu *Japan* 37°12N 139°46E **221** F9
Tajimi *Japan* 35°19N 137°8E **223** B9
Tajo = Tejo → *Europe* 38°40N 9°24W **195** F2
Tajrīsh *Iran* 35°48N 51°25E **141** A2
Tajumulco, Vol. *Guatemala* 15°2N 91°50W **320** C1
Tājūrā *Libya* 32°51N 13°21E **258** B2
Tak *Thailand* 16°52N 99°8E **236** D2
Takāb *Iran* 36°24N 47°7E **213** D12
Takabanare-shima *Japan* 26°22N 127°59E **288** a
Takabba *Kenya* 3°21N 40°13E **267** D5
Takachiho *Japan* 32°42N 131°18E **222** E3
Takachu *Botswana* 22°37S 21°58E **270** B3
Takada *Japan* 37°7N 138°15E **221** F9
Takahagi *Japan* 36°43N 140°45E **221** F10
Takahashi *Japan* 34°51N 133°39E **222** C5
Takaido *Japan* 35°40N 139°37E **140** A2
Takaishi *Japan* 35°36N 139°31E **140** B2
Takaka *N.Z.* 40°51S 172°50E **285** A7
Takaki = Yamato *Japan* 35°27N 139°25E **223** B11
Takalar *Indonesia* 5°28S 119°24E **235** D5
Takalous, O. → *Algeria* 22°36N 7°21E **261** D6
Takamaka *Seychelles* 4°50S 55°30E **272** c
Takamatsu *Japan* 34°20N 134°5E **222** C6
Takanabe *Japan* 32°8N 131°30E **222** E3
Takangkou *Taiwan* 23°28N 121°29E **225** C3
Takaoka *Japan* 36°47N 137°0E **223** A9
Takapau *N.Z.* 40°2S 176°21E **284** G5
Takapuna *N.Z.* 36°47S 174°47E **284** C3
Takarazuka *Japan* 34°47N 135°20E **133** A1
Takaroa *French Polynesia* 14°28S 144°58W **289** f
Takasago *Japan* 34°45N 134°48E **222** C6
Takasaki *Japan* 36°20N 139°0E **223** A11
Takashima *Japan* 35°24N 136°2E **223** B8
Takatsu *Japan* 35°36N 139°37E **140** B2
Takatsuki *Japan* 34°51N 135°37E **223** C7
Takaungu *Kenya* 3°38S 39°52E **268** C4
Takayama *Japan* 36°18N 137°11E **223** A9
Takayama-Bonchi *Japan* 36°0N 137°18E **223** B9
Take-Shima *Japan* 30°49N 130°26E **221** J5
Takefu = Echizen *Japan* 35°50N 136°10E **223** B8
Takehara *Japan* 34°21N 132°55E **222** C4
Takengon *Indonesia* 4°45N 96°50E **234** B1
Takeo *Cambodia* 10°59N 104°47E **237** G5
Takeo *Japan* 33°12N 130°1E **222** D2
Tåkern *Sweden* 58°22N 14°45E **163** F8
Takeshima = Liancourt Rocks *Asia* 37°15N 131°52E **221** F5
Takeshita *Japan* 35°33N 139°32E **140** B2
Tākestān *Iran* 36°0N 49°40E **247** C6
Taketa *Japan* 32°58N 131°24E **222** E3
Takh *India* 33°6N 77°32E **243** C7
Takhār □ *Afghan.* 36°40N 70°0E **240** A3
Takhiyatas *Uzbekistan* 42°20N 59°33E **216** D5
Takhmau *Cambodia* 11°29N 104°57E **237** G5
Takht-e Soleyman *Iran* 36°36N 47°14E **213** D12
Takht-Sulaiman *Pakistan* 31°40N 69°58E **242** D3
Taki *Papua N. G.* 6°29S 155°52E **286** D8
Takiéta *Niger* 13°41N 8°32E **263** C6
Takikawa *Japan* 43°33N 141°54E **220** C10
Takinegawa *Japan* 35°45N 139°44E **140** A3
Takla L. *Canada* 55°15N 125°45W **296** B3
Takla Landing *Canada* 55°30N 125°50W **296** B3
Taklamakan *China* 38°0N 83°0E **217** E10
Taklamakan Shamo = Taklamakan *China* 38°0N 83°0E **217** E10
Takoma Park *U.S.A.* 38°58N 77°0W **143** B2
Takotna *U.S.A.* 62°59N 156°4W **303** E8
Taksim *Turkey* 41°2N 28°58E **122** B1
Taksimo *Russia* 56°20N 114°52E **215** D12
Taku *Japan* 33°18N 130°3E **222** D2
Taku → *Canada* 58°30N 133°50W **296** B2
Takua Thung *Thailand* 8°24N 98°27E **237** a
Takum *India* 27°47N 93°37E **241** B4
Takum *Nigeria* 7°18N 9°36E **263** D6
Takume *French Polynesia* 15°49S 142°12W **289** f
Takundi *Dem. Rep. of the Congo* 4°45S 16°34E **265** C3
Takutu → *Guyana* 3°30N 60°29W **329** C5
Tal Halāl *Iran* 28°54N 55°1E **247** D7
Tala *Uruguay* 34°21S 55°46W **335** C4
Talachyn *Belarus* 54°25N 29°42E **188** E5
Talacogon *Phil.* 8°32N 125°39E **233** G5
Talagang *Pakistan* 32°55N 72°25E **242** C5
Talagante *Chile* 33°40S 70°50W **334** C1
Talaïhouhait *Algeria* 24°52N 1°5E **261** D5
Talaíde *Portugal* 38°44N 9°18W **126** A1
Talaimannar *Sri Lanka* 9°6N 79°43E **245** K4
Talaint *Morocco* 29°41N 9°40W **260** C3
Talak *Niger* 18°0N 5°0E **263** B6
Talakag *Phil.* 8°16N 124°37E **233** G5
Talamanca, Cordillera de *Cent. Amer.* 9°20N 83°20W **320** E3
Talampaya △ *Argentina* 29°43S 67°42W **334** B2
Talangbetutu *Indonesia* 2°53S 104°41E **234** C2
Talant *France* 47°19N 4°58E **173** E11
Talara *Peru* 4°38S 81°18W **330** A1
Talas *Kyrgyzstan* 42°30N 72°13E **217** D8
Talas *Turkey* 38°41N 35°33E **212** C6
Talas □ *Kyrgyzstan* 42°20N 72°0E **217** D8
Talas → *Kazakhstan* 44°0N 70°20E **217** D8
Talas Ala Too *Kyrgyzstan* 42°15N 72°0E **217** D8
Talasea *Papua N. G.* 5°20S 150°2E **286** C6
Talasskiy Alatau = Talas Ala Too *Kyrgyzstan* 42°15N 72°0E **217** D8
Talâta *Egypt* 30°36N 32°20E **251** H3
Talata Mafara *Nigeria* 12°38N 6°4E **263** C6
Talaud, Kepulauan *Indonesia* 4°30N 126°50E **231** D7
Talaud Is. = Talaud, Kepulauan *Indonesia* 4°30N 126°50E **231** D7
Talavera de la Reina *Spain* 39°55N 4°46W **194** F6
Talavera la Real *Spain* 38°53N 6°46W **195** G4
Talawgyi *Burma* 25°4N 97°19E **241** C6
Talayan *Phil.* 6°52N 124°24E **233** H5
Talayuela *Spain* 39°59N 5°36W **194** F5
Talbandh *India* 22°3N 86°20E **243** H12
Talbert, Sillon de *France* 48°53N 3°5W **172** D3
Talbot *Australia* 37°10S 143°44E **282** D5
Talbot, C. *Australia* 13°48S 126°43E **278** B4
Talbotton *U.S.A.* 32°41N 84°32W **316** C5
Talbragar → *Australia* 32°12S 148°37E **283** B8
Talca *Chile* 35°28S 71°40W **334** D1
Talcahuano *Chile* 36°40S 73°10W **334** D1
Talcher *India* 21°0N 85°18E **244** D7
Talcho *Niger* 14°44N 3°28E **263** C5
Taldy Kurgan = Taldyqorghan *Kazakhstan* 45°10N 78°45E **217** C9
Taldyqorghan *Kazakhstan* 45°10N 78°45E **217** C9
Tālesh *Iran* 37°58N 48°58E **213** D13
Tālesh, Kūhhā-ye *Iran* 37°42N 48°55E **213** D13
Talgar = Talghar *Kazakhstan* 43°19N 77°15E **217** D9
Talghar *Kazakhstan* 43°19N 77°15E **217** D9
Talguharai *Sudan* 18°19N 35°56E **256** D4
Talguppa *India* 14°13N 74°56E **245** G2
Tali Post *South Sudan* 5°55N 30°44E **257** F3
Taliabu *Indonesia* 1°50S 125°0E **231** E6
Taliao *Taiwan* 22°36N 120°23E **225** D2
Talibon *Phil.* 10°9N 124°20E **233** F5
Talichien *Taiwan* 24°58N 121°55E **225** B3
Taligānga *India* 22°30N 88°22E **124** B2
Talihina *U.S.A.* 34°45N 95°3W **314** D7
Talikota *India* 16°29N 76°17E **245** F3
Talikud I. *Phil.* 6°56N 125°41E **233** H5
Talin *Taiwan* 23°36N 120°27E **225** C2
Talipapa *Phil.* 14°41N 121°1E **127** A2
Talipaw *Phil.* 5°59N 121°7E **233** J3
Talipparamba *India* 12°3N 75°21E **245** H2
Talisay *Phil.* 10°44N 122°58E **233** F4
Talisayan *Phil.* 9°0N 124°55E **233** G5
Taliwang *Indonesia* 8°50S 116°55E **235** D5
Talkeetna *U.S.A.* 62°20N 150°6W **303** E10
Talkha *Egypt* 31°3N 31°22E **251** G2
Tálknafjörður *Iceland* 65°34N 24°0W **155** B2
Talkot *Nepal* 29°37N 81°19E **243** E9
Tall 'Afar *Iraq* 36°22N 42°27E **213** D10
Tall Kalakh *Syria* 34°41N 36°15E **250** D7
Tall Kayf *Iraq* 36°29N 43°7E **213** D10
Talla *Egypt* 28°5N 30°43E **256** B3
Talladega *U.S.A.* 33°26N 86°6W **316** B3
Tallaganda △ *Australia* 35°29S 149°37E **283** C8
Tallahassee *U.S.A.* 30°27N 84°17W **316** E5
Tallangatta *Australia* 36°15S 147°19E **283** D7
Tallapoosa *U.S.A.* 33°45N 85°17W **316** B4
Tallapoosa → *U.S.A.* 32°30N 86°16W **316** C3
Tallard *France* 44°28N 6°3E **175** D10
Tallarook *Australia* 37°5S 145°6E **283** D6
Tallassee *U.S.A.* 32°32N 85°54W **316** C4
Tällberg *Sweden* 60°51N 15°2E **162** D9
Tallering Pk. *Australia* 28°6S 115°37E **279** E2
Talli *Pakistan* 29°32N 68°8E **242** E3
Tallinn *Estonia* 59°22N 24°48E **188** C3
Tallkrogen *Sweden* 59°16N 18°4E **139** B2
Tallmadge *U.S.A.* 41°6N 81°27W **312** E3
Tallulah *U.S.A.* 32°25N 91°11W **314** E9
Tâlmaciu *Romania* 45°38N 24°19E **183** E9
Talmest *Morocco* 31°48N 9°21W **260** B3
Talmont-St-Hilaire *France* 46°27N 1°37W **174** B2
Talnakh *Russia* 69°29N 88°22E **215** C9
Talne *Ukraine* 48°50N 30°44E **189** H6
Talnoye = Talne *Ukraine* 48°50N 30°44E **189** H6
Taloda *India* 21°34N 74°11E **244** D2
Talodi *Sudan* 10°35N 30°22E **257** E3
Talofofo *Guam* 13°21N 144°45E **302** d
Tāloqān *Afghan.* 36°44N 69°33E **240** A3
Talovaya *Russia* 51°6N 40°45E **190** E5
Taloyoak *Canada* 69°32N 93°32W **294** D13
Talpa de Allende *Mexico* 20°23N 104°51W **318** C4
Talparo *Trin. & Tob.* 10°30N 61°17W **323** t
Talparo → *Trin. & Tob.* 10°34N 61°17W **323** t
Talquin, L. *U.S.A.* 30°23N 84°39W **316** E5
Talsi *Latvia* 57°10N 22°30E **184** A9
Talsinnt *Morocco* 32°33N 3°27W **260** B4
Taltal *Chile* 25°23S 70°33W **334** B1
Taltson → *Canada* 61°24N 112°46W **296** A6
Talu *Indonesia* 0°13N 99°58E **234** B1
Taluk *Indonesia* 0°31S 101°34E **234** C2
Talwood *Australia* 28°29S 149°29E **281** D4
Talyawalka Cr. → *Australia* 32°28S 142°22E **282** B5
Tam Dao △ *Vietnam* 21°45N 105°45E **236** B5
Tam Ky *Vietnam* 15°34N 108°29E **236** E7
Tam Quan *Vietnam* 14°35N 109°3E **236** E7
Tama *Tōkyō, Japan* 35°38N 139°26E **140** B1
Tama *Iowa, U.S.A.* 41°58N 92°35W **310** C4
Tama → *Japan* 35°32N 139°39E **140** B2
Tama △ *Ethiopia* 5°55N 36°5E **257** F4
Tama Abu, Banjaran *Malaysia* 3°50N 115°5E **235** B5
Tama Kyūryō *Japan* 35°34N 139°30E **140** B2
Tamada *Algeria* 21°31N 3°20E **261** D5
Tamaden *Japan* 35°39N 139°38E **140** B2
Tamagawa-josui → *Japan* 35°41N 139°47E **140** A1
Tamakautoga *Cook Is.* 19°5S 169°55W **289** g
Tamalameque *Colombia* 8°52N 73°49W **328** B3
Tamale *Ghana* 9°22N 0°50W **263** D4
Taman *Russia* 45°14N 36°41E **189** K9
Taman Negara △ *Malaysia* 4°38N 102°26E **237** K4
Taman Sari *Indonesia* 6°8S 106°48E **122** A1
T'aman Shan *Taiwan* 24°42N 121°27E **225** B3
Tamana *Japan* 32°58N 130°32E **222** E2
Tamana *Kiribati* 2°30S 175°59E **277** A14
Tamana, Mt. *Trin. & Tob.* 10°28N 61°12W **323** t
Tamanar *Morocco* 31°1N 9°46W **260** B3
Tamanduatei → *Brazil* 23°37S 46°37W **137** B2
Tamanhint *Libya* 27°13N 14°37E **258** C2
Tamani *Mali* 13°20N 6°50W **262** C3
Tamano *Japan* 34°29N 133°59E **222** C5
Tamanrasset *Algeria* 22°50N 5°30E **261** D6
Tamanrasset □ *Algeria* 23°45N 4°40E **261** D5
Tamanrasset, O. → *Algeria* 22°0N 2°0E **261** D5
Tamanthi *Burma* 25°19N 95°17E **241** C5
Tamaqua *U.S.A.* 40°48N 75°58W **313** F9
Tamar → *U.K.* 50°27N 4°15W **169** G3
Támara *Colombia* 5°50N 72°10W **328** B3
Tamarac *U.S.A.* 26°12N 80°15W **129** A1
Tamarin *Mauritius* 20°19S 57°20E **272** e
Tamarinda *Spain* 39°55N 3°49E **206** B4
Tamarite de Litera *Spain* 41°52N 0°25E **196** D5
Tamaroa *U.S.A.* 38°8N 89°14W **310** F7
Tamashima *Japan* 34°32N 133°40E **221** G6
Tamási *Hungary* 46°40N 18°18E **182** D3
Tamaské *Niger* 14°49N 5°43E **263** C6
Tamatave = Toamasina *Madag.* 18°10S 49°25E **272** B2
Tamaulipas □ *Mexico* 24°0N 98°45W **319** C5
Tamaulipas, Sierra de *Mexico* 23°30N 98°20W **319** C5
Tamazula *Mexico* 24°57N 106°57W **318** C3
Tamazunchale *Mexico* 21°16N 98°47W **319** C5
Tamba-Dabatou *Guinea* 11°50N 10°40W **262** C2
Tambach *Kenya* 0°36N 35°31E **268** B4
Tambacounda *Senegal* 13°45N 13°40W **262** C2
Tambacounda □ *Senegal* 14°0N 13°0W **262** C2
Tambaram *India* 12°55N 80°7E **245** H5
Tambea *Solomon Is.* 9°16S 159°41E **287** M10
Tambelan, Kepulauan *Indonesia* 1°0N 107°30E **235** B3
Tambellup *Australia* 34°4S 117°37E **279** F2
Tambo *Queens., Australia* 24°54S 146°14E **280** C4
Tambo *Peru* 12°57S 74°1W **330** C3
Tambo → *Peru* 10°42S 73°47W **330** C3
Tambo de Mora *Peru* 13°30S 76°8W **330** C2
Tambobamba *Peru* 13°54S 72°8W **330** C3
Tamboerskloof *S. Africa* 33°56S 18°25E **118** A1
Tambohorano *Madag.* 17°30S 43°58E **272** B1
Tambopata → *Peru* 13°21S 69°36W **330** C4
Tambora *Jakarta, Indonesia* 6°8S 106°47E **122** A1
Tambora *Nusa Tenggara Barat, Indonesia* 8°12S 118°5E **235** D5
Tamboritha, Mt. *Australia* 37°31S 146°40E **283** D7
Tamboura *C.A.R.* 5°10N 25°12E **264** A5
Tambov *Russia* 52°45N 41°28E **190** D5
Tambov □ *Russia* 52°50N 41°20E **190** D5
Tambre → *Spain* 42°49N 8°53W **194** C2
Tambuku *Indonesia* 7°8S 113°40E **235** D4
Tambul *Papua N. G.* 5°54S 143°54E **286** C2
Tambunar *Malaysia* 5°43N 116°24E **235** A5
Tambura *South Sudan* 5°40N 27°25E **257** F2
Tambuyukan, Gunong *Malaysia* 6°13N 116°39E **235** A5
Tâmchekket *Mauritania* 17°25N 10°40W **262** B2
Tame *Colombia* 6°28N 71°44W **328** B3
Tâmega → *Portugal* 41°5N 8°21W **194** D2
Tamegroute *Morocco* 30°15N 5°39W **260** B3
Tamelelt *Morocco* 31°50N 7°32W **260** B3
Tamenglong *India* 25°0N 93°35E **241** C4
Tamerza *Tunisia* 34°23N 7°58E **258** B1
Tamgak, Adrar *Niger* 19°12N 8°35E **259** E1
Tamgué, Massif du *Guinea* 12°0N 12°18W **262** C2
Tami Is. *Papua N. G.* 6°46S 147°55E **286** D4
Tamiahua, L. de *Mexico* 21°35N 97°35W **319** C5
Tamiami Canal *U.S.A.* 25°50N 81°0W **317** K8
Tamianglayang *Indonesia* 2°7S 115°10E **235** C5
Tamil Nadu □ *India* 11°0N 77°0E **245** J3
Tamiš → *Serbia* 44°51N 20°39E **182** F5
Tamiya *Egypt* 29°29N 30°58E **256** J7
Tamlelt, Plaine de *Morocco* 32°30N 2°20W **261** B4
Tamluk *India* 22°18N 87°58E **243** H12
Tammerfors = Tampere *Finland* 61°30N 23°50E **188** B2
Tammisalo *Finland* 60°11N 25°5E **121** B3
Tammūh *Egypt* 29°55N 31°15E **117** B2
Tämnaren *Sweden* 60°10N 17°25E **162** D11
Tampa *Angola* 15°30S 13°27E **265** F2
Tampa *Fla., U.S.A.* 27°56N 82°27W **317** H7
Tampa, Tanjung *Indonesia* 8°55S 116°12E **231** K19
Tampa B. *U.S.A.* 27°50N 82°30W **317** H7
Tampa Int. ✈ **(TPA)** *U.S.A.* 27°59N 82°32W **317** H7
Tamparan *Phil.* 7°53N 124°20E **233** H5
Tampere *Finland* 61°30N 23°50E **188** B2
Tampico *Tamaulipas, Mexico* 22°13N 97°51W **319** C5
Tampico *Ill., U.S.A.* 41°38N 89°47W **310** C7
Tampin *Malaysia* 2°28N 102°13E **237** L4
Tampines *Singapore* 1°21N 103°56E **138** A3
Tampoi *Malaysia* 1°30N 103°39E **237** d
Tamrah *Si. Arabia* 20°24N 45°25E **248** B4
Tamri *Morocco* 30°49N 9°50W **260** B3
Tamrida = Qādub *Yemen* 12°37N 53°57E **249** D6
Tamsagbulag *Mongolia* 47°14N 117°21E **219** B12
Tamsweg *Austria* 47°7N 13°49E **180** D6
Tamu *Burma* 24°13N 94°12E **241** C5
Tamu Massif *Pac. Oc.* 33°0N 158°0E **288** D7
Tamuja → *Spain* 39°38N 6°29W **195** F4
Tamuning *Guam* 13°29N 144°47E **302** d
Tamworth *N.S.W., Australia* 31°7S 150°58E **283** A9
Tamworth *Ont., Canada* 44°29N 77°0W **312** B8
Tamworth *Staffs., U.K.* 52°39N 1°41W **169** E6
Tan An *Vietnam* 10°32N 106°25E **237** G6
Tan Chau *Vietnam* 10°48N 105°12E **237** G5
T'an-do *N. Korea* 39°30N 124°41E **224** C2
Tan Hiep *Vietnam* 10°27N 106°21E **237** G6
Tan Iddah *Algeria* 26°33N 9°42E **261** C6
Tan-Tan *Morocco* 28°29N 11°1W **260** C2
Tan Yen *Vietnam* 22°4N 105°3E **236** A5
Tana → *Coast, Kenya* 2°32S 40°31E **268** C5
Tana → *Finnmark, Norway* 70°30N 28°14E **160** A23
Tana, L. *Ethiopia* 13°5N 37°30E **257** E4
Tana River □ *Kenya* 1°30S 39°30E **268** C4
Tana River Primate △ *Kenya* 1°55S 40°7E **268** C5
Tanabe *Japan* 33°44N 135°22E **223** D7
Tanabi *Brazil* 20°37S 49°37W **333** F2
Tanacross *U.S.A.* 63°23N 143°21W **303** E12
Tanafjorden *Norway* 70°45N 28°25E **160** A23
Tanaga I. *U.S.A.* 51°48N 177°53W **303** L3
Tanaga Volcano *U.S.A.* 51°53N 178°8W **303** L3
Tanah Abang *Indonesia* 6°12S 106°48E **122** B1
Tanah Kusir *Indonesia* 6°15S 106°46E **122** B1
Tanah Merah *Malaysia* 5°48N 102°9E **237** K4
Tanahbala *Indonesia* 0°30S 98°30E **234** C1
Tanahgrogot *Indonesia* 1°55S 116°15E **235** C5
Tanahjampea *Indonesia* 7°10S 120°35E **231** F6
Tanahmasa *Indonesia* 0°12S 98°39E **234** C1
Tanahmerah *Indonesia* 6°5S 140°16E **231** F10
Tanahputih *Indonesia* 1°40N 101°3E **234** B2
Tanakpur *India* 29°5N 80°7E **243** E9
Tanamalwila *Sri Lanka* 6°26N 81°8E **245** L5
Tanami Desert *Australia* 18°50S 132°0E **278** C5
Tanana *U.S.A.* 65°10N 152°4W **303** D9
Tanana → *U.S.A.* 65°10N 151°58W **303** D10
Tananarive = Antananarivo *Madag.* 18°55S 47°31E **272** B2
Tananger *Norway* 58°57N 5°37E **164** E2
Tanant *Morocco* 31°54N 6°56W **260** B3
Tanapag *N. Marianas* 15°14N 145°45E **302** e
Tánaro → *Italy* 44°55N 8°40E **198** D5
Tanauan *Phil.* 14°5N 121°10E **232** D3
Tanay *Phil.* 14°30N 121°17E **232** D3
Tanba-Sanchi *Japan* 35°7N 135°48E **223** B7
Tancheng *China* 34°25N 118°20E **227** G10
Tanch'ŏn *N. Korea* 40°27N 128°54E **224** B4
Tanda *Ut. P., India* 26°33N 82°35E **243** F10
Tanda *Ut. P., India* 28°57N 78°56E **243** E8
Tanda *Ivory C.* 7°48N 3°10W **262** D4
Tandag *Phil.* 9°4N 126°9E **233** G6
Tandaia *Tanzania* 9°25S 34°15E **269** D3
Tăndărei *Romania* 44°39N 27°40E **183** F12
Tandaué *Angola* 16°58S 18°5E **265** F3
Tandil *Argentina* 37°15S 59°6W **334** D4
Tandil, Sa. del *Argentina* 37°30S 59°0W **334** D4
Tandin *Burma* 19°33N 93°58E **241** F4
Tandjilé □ *Chad* 9°30N 16°30E **259** G3
Tandjilé → *Chad* 9°45N 16°30E **259** G3
Tandlianwala *Pakistan* 31°3N 73°9E **242** D5
Tando Adam *Pakistan* 25°45N 68°40E **242** G3
Tando Allahyar *Pakistan* 25°28N 68°43E **242** G3
Tando Bago *Pakistan* 24°47N 68°58E **242** G3
Tando Mohommed Khan *Pakistan* 25°8N 68°32E **242** G3
Tando-Zinze *Angola* 5°22S 12°30E **265** D2
Tandou-Bengou *Congo* 3°50S 11°44E **264** C2
Tandou L. *Australia* 32°40S 142°5E **282** B5
Tandoureh △ *Iran* 37°50N 59°0E **247** B8
Tandragee *U.K.* 54°21N 6°24W **166** B5
Tandsjöborg *Sweden* 61°42N 14°43E **162** C8
Tandubas *Phil.* 5°8N 120°20E **233** J3
Tandula → *India* 21°6N 81°14E **244** D5
Tandula Tank *India* 20°40N 81°12E **244** D5
Tandur *Telangana, India* 19°11N 79°30E **244** E4
Tandur *Telangana, India* 17°14N 77°35E **244** F3
Tane-ga-Shima *Japan* 30°30N 131°0E **221** J5
Taneatua *N.Z.* 38°4S 177°1E **284** E6
Tanen Tong Dan = Dawna Ra. *Burma* 16°30N 98°30E **236** D2
Tanew → *Poland* 50°29N 22°16E **185** H9
Tanezrouft *Algeria* 23°9N 0°11E **261** D5
Tanezzuft, W. → *Libya* 25°51N 10°19E **258** C2
Tang, Koh *Cambodia* 10°16N 103°7E **237** G4
Tang, Ra's-e *Iran* 25°21N 59°52E **247** E8
Tang Krasang *Cambodia* 12°34N 105°3E **236** F5
Tanga *Tanzania* 5°5S 39°2E **268** D4
Tanga □ *Tanzania* 5°20S 38°0E **268** D4
Tanga Is. *Papua N. G.* 3°20S 153°15E **286** B7
Tanga Langua *Grenada* 12°14N 61°39W **323** q
Tangail *Bangla.* 24°15N 89°55E **241** C2
Tangalla *Sri Lanka* 6°1N 80°48E **245** L5
Tanganyika = Tanzania ■ *Africa* 6°0S 34°0E **268** D3
Tanganyika □ *Dem. Rep. of the Congo* 6°30S 28°0E **268** D2
Tanganyika, L. *Africa* 6°40S 30°0E **268** D3
Tangará da Serra *Brazil* 14°50S 57°47W **331** C6
Tangarare *Solomon Is.* 9°36S 159°41E **287** M10
Tangasseri *India* 8°53N 76°35E **245** K3
Tangaza *Nigeria* 13°19N 4°55E **263** C5
Tangelo Park *U.S.A.* 28°27N 81°26W **133** B2
Tangen *Norway* 60°37N 11°15E **164** D8
Tanger *Morocco* 35°50N 5°49W **260** A3
Tanger-Med *Morocco* 35°53N 5°30W **195** K5
Tanger-Tétouan □ *Morocco* 35°50N 5°50W **260** A3
Tangerang *Indonesia* 6°11S 106°37E **234** D3
Tangerhütte *Germany* 52°26N 11°48E **178** C7
Tangermünde *Germany* 52°33N 11°58E **178** C7
Tanggu *China* 39°2N 117°40E **227** E9
Tanggula Shan *China* 32°40N 92°10E **218** E7
Tanggula Shankou *China* 32°42N 92°27E **218** E7
Tanghe *China* 32°47N 112°50E **229** A9
Tanghla Range = Tanggula Shan *China* 32°40N 92°10E **218** E7
Tangi *India* 19°56N 85°24E **244** E7
Tangier = Tanger *Morocco* 35°50N 5°49W **260** A3
Tangjia *China* 22°22N 113°35E **219** a
Tangjia Wan *China* 22°21N 113°36E **219** a
Tango-Hantō *Japan* 35°45N 135°10E **223** B7
Tangorin *Australia* 21°47S 144°12E **280** C3
Tangorombohitr'i Makay *Madag.* 21°0S 45°15E **272** C2
Tangra Yumco *China* 31°0N 86°38E **218** E6
Tangshan *China* 39°38N 118°10E **227** E10
Tangtou *China* 35°28N 118°30E **227** G10
Tangub *Phil.* 8°3N 123°44E **233** G4
Tanguen-Dassouri *Burkina Faso* 12°16N 1°42W **263** C4
Tanguiéta *Benin* 10°35N 1°21E **263** C5
Tangxi *China* 29°3N 119°25E **229** C12
Tangyan He → *China* 28°54N 108°19E **228** C7
Tangyin *China* 35°54N 114°21E **226** G8
Taniantaweng Shan *China* 31°20N 98°0E **228** B2
Taniao *Taiwan* 22°23N 120°53E **225** D2
Tanimbar, Kepulauan *Indonesia* 7°30S 131°30E **231** F8
Tanimbar Is. = Tanimbar, Kepulauan *Indonesia* 7°30S 131°30E **231** F8
Tanintharyi = Taninthayi *Burma* 12°6N 99°3E **237** F2
Taninthayi *Burma* 12°6N 99°3E **237** F2
Tanis *Egypt* 31°0N 31°54E **251** H2
Tanjay *Phil.* 9°30N 123°5E **233** G4
Tanjong Po *Malaysia* 1°45N 110°30E **235** B4
Tanjore = Thanjavur *India* 10°48N 79°12E **245** J4
Tanjung *Kalimantan Selatan, Indonesia* 2°10S 115°25E **235** C5
Tanjung *Nusa Tenggara Barat, Indonesia* 8°21S 116°9E **231** J19
Tanjung Datu △ *Malaysia* 2°13N 109°3E **235** B3
Tanjung Duren *Indonesia* 6°10S 106°46E **122** B1
Tanjung Malim *Malaysia* 3°42N 101°31E **237** L3
Tanjung Pelepas *Malaysia* 1°21N 103°33E **237** d
Tanjung Priok *Indonesia* 6°6S 106°52E **122** A2
Tanjung Puting △ *Indonesia* 2°54S 111°59E **235** C4
Tanjung Tokong *Malaysia* 5°28N 100°18E **237** c
Tanjungbalai *Kepulauan Riau, Indonesia* 1°0N 103°25E **234** B2
Tanjungbalai *Sumatera Utara, Indonesia* 2°55N 99°44E **234** B1
Tanjungbatu *Kalimantan Selatan, Indonesia* 3°0S 116°13E **235** C5
Tanjungbatu *Kalimantan Timur, Indonesia* 2°23N 118°3E **235** B5
Tanjungbatu *Kepulauan Riau, Indonesia* 0°37N 103°25E **234** B2
Tanjungisui *Indonesia* 0°30S 116°8E **235** C5
Tanjungkarang Telukbetung = Bandar Lampung *Indonesia* 5°20S 105°10E **234** D3
Tanjungpandan *Indonesia* 2°43S 107°38E **235** C3
Tanjungpinang *Indonesia* 1°5N 104°30E **234** B2
Tanjungraja *Indonesia* 3°21S 104°46E **234** C2
Tanjungredeb *Indonesia* 2°9N 117°29E **235** B5
Tanjungselor *Indonesia* 2°55N 117°25E **235** B5
Tank *Pakistan* 32°14N 70°25E **242** C4
Tankhala *India* 21°58N 73°47E **242** J5
Tankwa-Karoo △ *S. Africa* 32°14S 19°50E **270** D2
Tanlu *Taiwan* 22°12N 120°44E **225** D2
Tanna *Vanuatu* 19°30S 169°20E **287** J7
Tännäs *Sweden* 62°26N 12°42E **162** B6
Tannersville *U.S.A.* 41°3N 75°18W **313** E9
Tannis Bugt *Denmark* 57°40N 10°15E **163** G4
Tannu Ola *Asia* 51°0N 94°0E **217** B12
Tannum Sands *Australia* 23°57S 151°22E **280** C5
Tano → *Ghana* 5°7N 2°56W **262** D4
Tanombella *Algeria* 25°30N 5°49E **261** C6
Tanon Str. *Phil.* 10°20N 123°30E **233** F4
Tanout *Niger* 14°50N 8°55E **259** F1
Tanquinho *Brazil* 11°58S 39°6W **333** D4
Tanshui *Taiwan* 25°10N 121°28E **225** A3
Tanshui Kang → *Taiwan* 25°10N 121°25E **225** A3
Tansilla *Burkina Faso* 12°25N 4°23W **262** C4
Tansing *Nepal* 27°52N 83°33E **243** F10
Tanta *Egypt* 30°45N 30°57E **256** H7
Tantabin *Burma* 17°1N 95°59E **241** G5
Tantoyuca *Mexico* 21°21N 98°14W **319** C5
Tantung = Dandong *China* 40°10N 124°20E **224** B2
T'antzu *Taiwan* 24°13N 120°42E **225** B2
Tanuku *India* 16°45N 81°44E **244** F5
Tanum *Norway* 59°53N 10°28E **133** A1
Tanūmah *Si. Arabia* 18°58N 42°10E **248** C3
Tanumshede *Sweden* 58°42N 11°20E **163** F5
Tanunda *Australia* 34°30S 139°0E **282** C3
Tanur *India* 11°1N 75°52E **245** J2
Tanus *France* 44°8N 2°19E **174** D6
Tanzania ■ *Africa* 6°0S 34°0E **268** D3
Tanzawa-Sanchi *Japan* 35°27N 139°0E **223** B11
Tanzhou *China* 22°16N 113°28E **219** a
Tanzi = T'antzu *Taiwan* 24°13N 120°42E **225** B2
Tanzilla → *Canada* 58°8N 130°43W **296** B2
Tao, Ko *Thailand* 10°5N 99°52E **237** G2
Tao'an = Taonan *China* 45°22N 122°40E **227** B12
Tao'er He → *China* 45°45N 124°5E **227** B13
Taohua Dao *China* 29°50N 122°20E **229** C14
Taolanaro *Madag.* 25°2S 47°0E **272** D2
Taole *China* 38°48N 106°40E **226** E4
Taonan *China* 45°22N 122°40E **227** B12
Taora *Solomon Is.* 7°21S 157°30E **287** L9
Taormina *Italy* 37°51N 15°17E **201** E8
Taos *U.S.A.* 36°24N 105°35W **305** H11
Taoudenni *Mali* 22°40N 3°55W **260** D4
Taoudrart, Adrar *Algeria* 24°25N 2°24E **261** D5
Taounate *Morocco* 34°25N 4°41W **260** B4
Taourirt *Algeria* 26°37N 0°20E **261** C5
Taourirt *Morocco* 34°25N 2°53W **261** B4
Taouz *Morocco* 30°53N 4°0W **260** B4
Taoyuan *Hunan, China* 28°55N 111°16E **229** C8
T'aoyüan *Kaohsiung, Taiwan* 23°9N 120°46E **225** C2
T'aoyüan *Yünlin, Taiwan* 25°0N 121°4E **225** B3
T'aoyüan □ *Taiwan* 24°55N 121°15E **225** B3
Tap Shek Kok *Hong Kong, China* 22°23N 113°55E **122** A1
Tapa *Estonia* 59°15N 25°50E **161** G21
Tapa Shan = Daba Shan *China* 32°0N 109°0E **228** B7
Tapachula *Mexico* 14°54N 92°17W **319** E6
Tapada *Portugal* 38°49N 9°16W **126** A1
Tapah *Malaysia* 4°12N 101°15E **237** K3
Tapajós → *Brazil* 2°24S 54°41W **329** D7
Tapaktuan *Indonesia* 3°15N 97°10E **234** B1
Tapanahoni → *Suriname* 4°20N 54°25W **329** C7
Tapanila *Finland* 60°15N 25°2E **121** B3
Tapanui *N.Z.* 45°56S 169°18E **285** F4
Taparo Pt. *Trin. & Tob.* 10°3N 61°38W **323** t
Tapauá *Brazil* 5°40S 64°20W **331** B5
Tapauá → *Brazil* 5°40S 64°21W **331** B5
Tapaz *Phil.* 11°16N 122°32E **233** F4
Tapes *Brazil* 30°40S 51°23W **335** C5
Tapeta *Liberia* 6°29N 8°52W **262** D3
Taphan Hin *Thailand* 16°13N 100°26E **236** D3
Tapia de Casariego *Spain* 43°34N 6°56W **194** B4

Tapiales *Argentina* 34°42S 58°30W **117** C1
Tapiantana Channel *Phil.* 6°22N 122°1E **233** H4
Tapiantana Group *Phil.* 6°20N 122°0E **233** H4
Tapiau = Gvardeysk
Russia 54°39N 21°5E **184** D8
Tapilon = Daanbantayan
Phil. 11°17N 124°2E **233** F5
Taping *Taiwan* 24°6N 120°53E **225** B2
Tapini *Papua N. G.* 8°19S 147°0E **286** E4
Tapiola *Finland* 60°10N 24°48E **121** B1
Tapirai *Brazil* 19°52S 46°1W **333** E2
Tapirapé → *Brazil* 10°41S 50°38W **332** D1
Tapirapecó, Serra *Venezuela* 1°10N 65°0W **329** C5
Taplan *Australia* 34°33S 140°52E **282** C4
Taplejung *Nepal* 27°1N 86°16E **243** F12
Tapo-Capara △ *Venezuela* 7°55N 71°15W **328** B3
Tapochau, Mt.
N. Marianas 15°11N 145°44E **302** e
Tapoeripa *Suriname* 5°22N 56°34W **329** B6
Tapolca *Hungary* 46°53N 17°29E **182** D2
Tapsia *India* 22°32N 88°23E **124** B2
Tapti → *India* 21°8N 72°41E **244** D1
Tapu *Taiwan* 23°18N 120°35E **225** C2
Tapuae-o-Uenuku *N.Z.* 42°0S 173°39E **285** C8
Tapul *Phil.* 5°42N 120°55E **233** J3
Tapul Group *Phil.* 5°35N 120°50E **233** J3
Tapul I. *Phil.* 5°43N 120°55E **233** J3
Tapun *India* 27°35N 96°22E **241** B6
Tapurucuará *Brazil* 0°24S 65°2W **329** D4
Taputapu, C. *Amer. Samoa* 14°20S 170°51W **302** f
Taputimu *Amer. Samoa* 14°21S 170°46W **302** f
Ţaqţaq *Iraq* 35°53N 44°35E **213** E11
Taquara *Brazil* 29°36S 50°46W **335** B5
Taquari → *Brazil* 19°15S 57°17W **331** D6
Taquaritinga *Brazil* 21°24S 48°30W **333** F2
Tara *Queens., Australia* 27°17S 150°31E **281** D5
Tara *Ont., Canada* 44°28N 81°9W **312** B3
Tara *Maharashtra, India* 19°5N 72°49E **130** A1
Tara *Japan* 33°2N 130°11E **222** D2
Tara *Russia* 56°55N 74°24E **214** D8
Tara *Zambia* 16°58S 26°45E **269** F2
Tara → *Montenegro* 43°21N 18°51E **202** C2
Tara △ *Serbia* 43°55N 19°30E **202** C3
Tara-Dake *Japan* 32°58N 130°6E **222** E2
Taraba □ *Nigeria* 8°0N 10°30E **263** D7
Taraba → *Nigeria* 8°30N 10°15E **263** D7
Tarabuco *Bolivia* 19°10S 64°57W **331** D5
Tarābulus *Lebanon* 34°31N 35°50E **250** D6
Tarābulus *Libya* 32°49N 13°7E **258** B2
Tarābulus *Libya* 31°0N 13°0E **258** B2
Tarabya *Turkey* 41°8N 29°3E **122** B2
Taraclia *Taraclia, Moldova* 45°54N 28°40E **183** E13
Taraclia *Tighina, Moldova* 46°34N 29°7E **183** D14
Taradale *N.Z.* 39°33S 176°53E **284** F5
Taradehi *India* 23°18N 79°21E **243** H8
Tarāghīn *Libya* 26°0N 14°30E **258** C2
Taragi *Japan* 32°16N 130°56E **222** E2
Tarahouahout *Algeria* 22°41N 5°59E **261** D6
Tarajalejo *Canary Is.* 28°12N 14°7W **153** e2
Tarakan *Indonesia* 3°20N 117°35E **235** B5
Tarakit, Mt. *Kenya* 2°2N 35°10E **268** B4
Taralga *Australia* 34°26S 149°52E **283** C8
Tarama-Jima *Japan* 24°39N 124°42E **221** M2
Taramakau → *N.Z.* 42°34S 171°8E **285** C6
Taran, Mys *Russia* 54°56N 19°59E **184** D6
Tarana *India* 28°43N 74°50E **242** E6
Taranagar *India* 28°43N 74°50E **242** E6
Taranaki □ *N.Z.* 39°25S 174°30E **284** F3
Taranaki, Mt. *N.Z.* 39°17S 174°5E **284** F3
Tarancón *Spain* 40°1N 3°1W **196** E1
Tarangire △ *Tanzania* 4°21S 36°7E **268** C4
Taransay *U.K.* 57°54N 7°0W **167** D1
Táranto *Italy* 40°28N 17°14E **201** B10
Táranto, G. di *Italy* 40°8N 17°20E **201** B10
Tarapacá *Colombia* 2°56S 69°46W **328** D4
Tarapacá □ *Chile* 20°45S 69°30W **334** A2
Tarapoto *Peru* 6°30S 76°20W **330** B2
Taraquá *Brazil* 0°6N 68°28W **328** C4
Tarare *France* 45°54N 4°26E **175** C8
Tararua Ra. *N.Z.* 40°45S 175°25E **284** G4
Tarasag *Vanuatu* 14°12S 167°36E **287** D5
Tarasaigh = Taransay *U.K.* 57°54N 7°0W **167** D1
Tarascon *France* 43°48N 4°39E **175** E8
Tarascon-sur-Ariège
France 42°50N 1°36E **174** F5
Tarashcha *Ukraine* 49°30N 30°31E **177** D16
Tarata *Peru* 17°27S 70°2W **330** D3
Tarauacá *Brazil* 8°6S 70°48W **330** B3
Tarauacá → *Brazil* 6°42S 69°48W **330** B4
Taravao *Tahiti* 17°43S 149°18W **289** e
Taravao, Isthme de *Tahiti* 17°43S 149°19W **289** e
Taravo → *France* 41°42N 8°49E **175** G12
Tarawa *Kiribati* 1°30N 173°0E **288** G9
Tarawai I. *Papua N. G.* 3°13S 143°15E **286** B2
Tarawera *N.Z.* 39°2S 176°36E **284** F5
Tarawera, L. *N.Z.* 38°13S 176°27E **284** E5
Tarawera, Mt. *N.Z.* 38°14S 176°32E **284** E5
Taraz *Kazakhstan* 42°54N 71°22E **217** D8
Tarazona *Spain* 41°55N 1°43W **196** D3
Tarazona de la Mancha
Spain 39°16N 1°55W **197** F3
Tårbæk *Denmark* 55°46N 12°35E **118** A3
Tarbagatay, Khrebet
Kazakhstan 48°0N 83°0E **217** C10
Tarbaj *Kenya* 2°12N 40°8E **267** D5
Tarbat Ness *U.K.* 57°52N 3°47W **167** D5
Tarbela Dam *Pakistan* 34°8N 72°52E **242** B5
Tarbert *Kerry, Ireland* 52°34N 9°22W **166** D2
Tarbert *Argyll & Bute, U.K.* 55°52N 5°25W **167** F3
Tarbert *W. Isles, U.K.* 57°54N 6°49W **167** D2
Tarbes *France* 43°15N 0°3E **174** E4
Tarboro *U.S.A.* 35°54N 77°32W **315** D16
Tărcău, Munţii *Romania* 46°39N 26°7E **183** D11
Tarcento *Italy* 46°13N 13°13E **199** B10
Tarchomin *Poland* 52°19N 20°58E **143** B1
Tarcoola *Australia* 30°44S 134°36E **281** E1
Tarcoon *Australia* 30°15S 146°43E **281** E4
Tarcutta *Australia* 35°16S 147°44E **283** C7
Tardeo *India* 18°57N 72°48E **130** B1
Tardets-Sorholus *France* 43°8N 0°52W **174** E3
Tardoire → *France* 45°52N 0°14E **174** C4
Taredjerdja *Algeria* 25°12N 2°32E **261** C5
Taree *Australia* 31°50S 152°30E **283** A10
Tarella *Australia* 31°2S 143°2E **282** A5
Tarf, Ras *Morocco* 35°40N 5°11W **260** A3
Ţarfā, Ra's aţ *Si. Arabia* 17°2N 42°22E **248** C3
Tarfa, W. el → *Egypt* 28°25N 30°50E **256** B3
Tarfaya *Morocco* 27°55N 12°55W **260** C2
Târgovişte *Romania* 44°55N 25°27E **183** F10
Targówek *Poland* 52°16N 21°3E **143** B2
Târgu Bujor *Romania* 45°52N 27°54E **183** E12
Târgu Cărbuneşti
Romania 44°57N 23°31E **183** F8
Târgu Frumos *Romania* 47°12N 27°2E **183** C12
Târgu Jiu *Romania* 45°5N 23°19E **183** E8
Târgu Lăpuş *Romania* 47°27N 23°52E **183** C8
Târgu Mureş *Romania* 46°31N 24°38E **183** D9
Târgu Neamţ *Romania* 47°12N 26°25E **183** C11
Târgu Ocna *Romania* 46°16N 26°39E **183** D11
Târgu Secuiesc *Romania* 46°0N 26°10E **183** E11
Targuist *Morocco* 34°59N 4°14W **260** B4
Târguşor *Romania* 44°27N 28°25E **183** F13
Tărhăus, Vf. *Romania* 46°40N 26°8E **183** D11
Tarhbalt *Morocco* 30°39N 5°20W **260** B3
Tarhūnah *Libya* 32°27N 13°36E **258** B2
Tari *Papua N. G.* 5°54S 142°59E **286** C2
Táriba *Venezuela* 7°49N 72°13W **328** B3
Ţarif *U.A.E.* 24°3N 53°46E **247** E7
Tarifa *Spain* 36°1N 5°36W **195** J5
Tarigtig Pt. *Phil.* 16°25N 122°14E **232** C4
Tarija *Bolivia* 21°30S 64°40W **334** A3
Tarija □ *Bolivia* 21°30S 63°30W **334** A3
Tarik I. *Micronesia* 7°20N 151°46E **287** T18
Tariku → *Indonesia* 2°55S 138°26E **231** E9
Tarim *Yemen* 16°3N 49°0E **249** C5
Tarim Basin = Tarim Pendi
China 40°0N 84°0E **217** E10
Tarim He → *China* 39°30N 88°30E **217** E11
Tarim Pendi *China* 40°0N 84°0E **217** E10
Tarime *Tanzania* 1°21S 34°22E **266** E3
Taritatu → *Indonesia* 2°54S 138°27E **231** E9
Tarka → *S. Africa* 32°10S 26°0E **270** D4
Tarka La *Bhutan* 27°12N 89°44E **243** F13
Tarkastad *S. Africa* 32°0S 26°16E **270** D4
Tarkhankut, Mys *Ukraine* 45°25N 32°30E **189** K7
Tarko Sale *Russia* 64°55N 77°50E **214** C8
Tarkwa *Ghana* 5°20N 2°0W **262** D4
Tarlac *Phil.* 15°29N 120°35E **232** D3
Tarlac □ *Phil.* 15°30N 120°30E **232** D3
Tarm *Denmark* 55°56N 8°31E **163** J2
Tarma *Peru* 11°25S 75°45W **330** C2
Tarmiya *Iraq* 33°40N 44°23E **213** G11
Tarn □ *France* 43°49N 2°8E **174** E6
Tarn → *France* 44°5N 1°6E **174** D5
Tarn-et-Garonne □ *France* 44°8N 1°20E **174** D5
Tarna → *Hungary* 47°31N 19°59E **182** C4
Târnava Mare →
Romania 46°10N 23°43E **183** D8
Târnava Mică → *Romania* 46°9N 23°55E **183** D8
Târnăveni *Romania* 46°19N 24°13E **183** D9
Tårnby *Denmark* 55°37N 12°35E **118** B3
Tarnica *Poland* 49°4N 22°44E **185** J9
Tarnobrzeg *Poland* 50°35N 21°41E **185** H8
Tarnogród *Poland* 50°22N 22°45E **185** H9
Tarnopol = Ternopil
Ukraine 49°30N 25°40E **177** D13
Tarnos *France* 43°32N 1°28W **174** E2
Târnova *Moldova* 48°10N 27°40E **183** B12
Târnova *Romania* 45°23N 21°59E **182** E6
Tarnów *Poland* 50°3N 21°0E **185** H8
Tarnowitz = Tarnowskie Góry
Poland 50°27N 18°54E **185** H5
Tarnowskie Góry *Poland* 50°27N 18°54E **185** H5
Tärnsjö *Sweden* 60°9N 16°56E **162** D10
Taro *Solomon Is.* 6°43S 156°24E **287** L9
Táro → *Italy* 45°2N 10°15E **198** C7
Taroko △ *Taiwan* 24°10N 121°33E **225** B3
Ţārom *Iran* 28°11N 55°46E **247** D7
Taroom *Australia* 25°36S 149°48E **281** D4
Taroudannt *Morocco* 30°30N 8°52W **260** B3
Taroume *Cook Is.* 21°15S 159°45W **289** h
Tarp *Germany* 54°39N 9°24E **178** A5
Tarpeena *Australia* 37°37S 140°47E **282** D4
Tarpon Springs *U.S.A.* 28°9N 82°45W **317** G7
Tarqua Bay *Nigeria* 6°24N 3°23E **124** B2
Tarquínia *Italy* 42°15N 11°45E **199** F8
Tarra Bulga △ *Australia* 38°27S 146°31E **283** E7
Tarrafal *C. Verde Is.* 15°18N 23°39W **153** j
Tarragona *Spain* 41°5N 1°17E **196** D6
Tarragona □ *Spain* 41°5N 1°0E **196** D6
Tarraleah *Australia* 42°17S 146°26E **281** G4
Tarrasa = Terrassa *Spain* 41°34N 2°1E **196** D7
Tàrrega *Spain* 41°39N 1°9E **196** D6
Tarrytown *Ga., U.S.A.* 32°19N 82°34W **316** C7
Tarrytown *N.Y., U.S.A.* 41°4N 73°52W **313** E11
Tårs *Denmark* 57°23N 10°7E **163** G4
Tarsus *Turkey* 36°58N 34°55E **250** B5
Tarsus → *Turkey* 36°46N 34°52E **250** B5
Tartagal *Argentina* 22°30S 63°50W **334** A3
Tartane *Martinique* 14°45N 60°55W **322** j
Tärtär *Azerbaijan* 40°20N 46°58E **191** K8
Tärtär → *Azerbaijan* 40°26N 47°20E **191** K8
Tartas *France* 43°50N 0°49W **174** E3
Tartu *Estonia* 58°20N 26°44E **188** C4
Ţarţūs *Syria* 34°55N 35°55E **250** D6
Ţarţūs □ *Syria* 35°0N 36°0E **250** D7
Tarumirim *Brazil* 19°16S 41°59W **333** E3
Tarumizu *Japan* 31°29N 130°42E **222** F2
Tarussa *Russia* 54°44N 37°10E **188** E9
Tarutao = Ko Tarutao △
Thailand 6°31N 99°26E **237** J2
Tarutao, Ko *Thailand* 6°33N 99°40E **237** J2
Tarutung *Indonesia* 2°0N 98°54E **234** B1
Tarutyne *Ukraine* 46°12N 29°9E **183** D14
Tarvisio *Italy* 46°30N 13°35E **199** B10
Tarxien *Malta* 35°52N 14°31E **206** F8
Taşağıl *Turkey* 36°55N 31°14E **250** B2
Tasahku *Burma* 27°33N 97°52E **241** B6
Tasaret, O. → *Algeria* 26°25N 1°59E **261** C5
Tasāwah *Libya* 26°0N 13°30E **258** C2
Tasbōget *Kazakhstan* 44°46N 65°33E **216** D7
Tasek Merimbun △
Brunei 4°31N 114°41E **235** B4
Taseko → *Canada* 52°8N 123°45W **296** C4
Tasgaon *India* 17°2N 74°39E **244** F2
Tash-Kömür *Kyrgyzstan* 41°40N 72°10E **217** D8
Tashauz = Daşoguz
Turkmenistan 41°49N 59°58E **216** D5
Tashi Chho Dzong = Thimphu
Bhutan 27°31N 89°45E **241** B2
Tashino = Pervomaysk
Russia 54°56N 43°58E **190** C6
Ţashk, Daryācheh-ye
Iran 29°45N 53°35E **247** D7
Tashkent = Toshkent
Uzbekistan 41°20N 69°10E **217** D7
Tashtagol *Russia* 52°47N 87°53E **217** B11
Tashu *Taiwan* 22°41N 120°25E **225** D2
Tasiilaq *Greenland* 65°40N 37°20W **154** D7
Tasik Bera *Malaysia* 3°5N 102°38E **234** B2
Tasik Kenyir *Malaysia* 5°5N 102°45E **234** A2
Tasikmalaya *Indonesia* 7°18S 108°12E **235** D3
Tåsinge *Denmark* 55°0N 10°36E **163** J4
Tåsjön *Sweden* 64°15N 15°40E **160** D16
Task *Niger* 14°56N 10°46E **259** F2
Taskan *Russia* 62°59N 150°20E **215** C16
Taşkent *Turkey* 36°55N 32°29E **250** B3
Taşköprü *Turkey* 41°30N 34°15E **212** B6
Taskul *Papua N. G.* 2°32S 150°27E **286** B6
Taşlâc *Moldova* 47°4N 29°24E **183** C14
Taşlıçay *Turkey* 39°38N 43°22E **213** C10
Tasman □ *N.Z.* 41°30S 172°40E **285** B7
Tasman → *N.Z.* 43°48S 170°8E **285** D5
Tasman, Mt. *N.Z.* 43°34S 170°12E **285** D5
Tasman Abyssal Plain
Pac. Oc. 34°30S 153°15E **276** G9
Tasman B. *N.Z.* 40°59S 173°25E **285** A8
Tasman Basin *Pac. Oc.* 46°0S 158°0E **288** M7
Tasman Glacier *N.Z.* 43°37S 170°12E **285** D5
Tasman Mts. *N.Z.* 41°3S 172°25E **285** B7
Tasman Pen. *Australia* 43°10S 148°0E **281** G4
Tasman Sea *Pac. Oc.* 36°0S 160°0E **277** H10
Tasmania □ *Australia* 42°0S 146°30E **281** G4
Tasmanian Wilderness World
Heritage Area △
Australia 43°0S 146°0E **281** G4
Tåsnad *Romania* 47°30N 22°33E **182** C7
Taşova *Turkey* 40°45N 36°19E **212** B7
Tassili n'Ajjer *Algeria* 25°47N 8°1E **261** C6
Tassili n'Ajjer △ *Algeria* 26°5N 6°0E **258** C1
Tassili-oua-n-Ahaggar
Algeria 20°41N 5°30E **261** D6
Tassili Ti-n-Rerhoh *Algeria* 20°5N 3°55E **261** D5
Taşucu *Turkey* 36°19N 33°52E **250** B4
Taşucu Körfezi *Turkey* 36°16N 33°56E **250** B4
Tasūj *Iran* 38°18N 45°23E **213** C11
Tat Ton △ *Thailand* 15°57N 102°2E **236** E4
Tata *Hungary* 47°37N 18°19E **182** C3
Tata *Morocco* 29°46N 7°56W **260** C3
Tatabánya *Hungary* 47°32N 18°25E **182** C3
Tatakoto *French Polynesia* 17°20S 138°23W **289** f
Tatamá △ *Colombia* 5°5N 76°9W **328** B2
Tatamba *Solomon Is.* 8°21S 159°51E **287** M10
Tataouine *Tunisia* 32°57N 10°29E **258** B2
Tataouine □ *Tunisia* 32°0N 10°0E **261** B7
Tatar-Pazardzhik = Pazardzhik
Bulgaria 42°12N 24°20E **203** D8
Tatar Republic = Tatarstan □
Russia 55°30N 51°30E **190** C10
Tatarbunary *Ukraine* 45°50N 29°39E **183** E14
Tatarsk *Russia* 55°14N 76°0E **217** A9
Tatarskiy Proliv *Russia* 50°0N 141°0E **215** E15
Tatarstan □ *Russia* 55°30N 51°30E **190** C10
Tatatóváros = Tata
Hungary 47°37N 18°19E **182** C3
Tatatua, Pte. *Tahiti* 17°44S 149°8W **289** e
Tatau *Malaysia* 2°53N 112°51E **235** B4
Tatau I. *Papua N. G.* 2°48S 151°57E **286** B6
Tatebayashi *Japan* 36°15N 139°32E **223** A11
Tateshina-Yama *Japan* 36°8N 138°11E **223** A10
Tateyama *Chiba, Japan* 35°0N 139°50E **223** C11
Tateyama *Toyama, Japan* 36°40N 137°35E **223** A9
Tathlina L. *Canada* 60°33N 117°39W **296** A5
Tathlīth *Si. Arabia* 19°32N 43°30E **248** C3
Tathlīth, W. → *Si. Arabia* 20°35N 44°20E **248** B4
Tathong Channel
Hong Kong, China 22°15N 114°16E **122** B3
Tathong Pt.
Hong Kong, China 22°14N 114°17E **122** B3
Tathra *Australia* 36°44S 149°59E **283** D8
Tatinnai L. *Canada* 60°55N 97°40W **297** A9
Tatitlek *U.S.A.* 60°52N 146°41W **303** F11
Tatkon *Burma* 20°7N 96°13E **241** E6
Tatla Lake *Canada* 52°0N 124°20W **296** C4
Tatlisu = Akanthou
Cyprus 35°22N 33°45E **207** E9
Tatlısu *Turkey* 40°24N 27°55E **203** F11
Tatnam, C. *Canada* 57°16N 91°0W **297** B10
Tatra = Tatry *Slovakia* 49°20N 20°0E **181** B13
Tatranský △ *Slovakia* 49°10N 20°0E **181** B13
Tatry *Slovakia* 49°20N 20°0E **181** B13
Tatshenshini → *Canada* 59°28N 137°45W **296** B1
Tatshenshini-Alsek ⌓
Canada 59°55N 137°45W **296** B1
Tatsuno *Hyōgo, Japan* 34°52N 134°33E **222** C6
Tatsuno *Nagano, Japan* 35°58N 138°0E **223** B10
Tatta = Thatta *Pakistan* 24°42N 67°55E **242** G2
Tatuí *Brazil* 23°25S 47°53W **335** A6
Tatum *U.S.A.* 33°16N 103°19W **305** K12
Tat'ung = Datong *China* 40°6N 113°18E **226** D7
Tatura *Australia* 36°29S 145°16E **283** D6
Tatvan *Turkey* 38°31N 42°15E **213** C10
Ta'ū *Amer. Samoa* 14°15S 169°30W **302** g
Tau *Rogaland, Norway* 59°3N 5°55E **164** E2
Tauá *Brazil* 6°1S 40°26W **332** C3
Taubaté *Brazil* 23°0S 45°36W **335** A6
Tauberbischofsheim
Germany 49°37N 9°39E **179** F5
Taucha *Germany* 51°23N 12°29E **178** D8
Tauern *Austria* 47°15N 12°40E **176** E7
Tauern-tunnel *Austria* 47°0N 13°12E **180** D6
Taufikia *South Sudan* 9°24N 31°37E **257** F3
Taufkirchen *Germany* 48°2N 11°36E **131** B2
Taulé *France* 48°37N 3°55W **172** D3
Taumarunui *N.Z.* 38°53S 175°15E **284** E4
Taumaturgo *Brazil* 8°54S 72°51W **330** B3
Taung *S. Africa* 27°33S 24°47E **270** C3
Taungdwingyi *Burma* 20°1N 95°40E **241** E5
Taunggyi *Burma* 20°50N 97°0E **241** E6
Taungoo = Tounggoo
Burma 19°0N 96°30E **241** F6
Taungtha *Burma* 21°12N 95°25E **241** E5
Taungup *Burma* 18°51N 94°14E **241** F5
Taungup Pass *Burma* 18°40N 94°45E **241** F5
Taunsa *Pakistan* 30°42N 70°39E **242** D4
Taunsa Barrage *Pakistan* 30°42N 70°50E **242** D4
Taunton *Somst., U.K.* 51°1N 3°5W **169** F4
Taunton *Mass., U.S.A.* 41°54N 71°6W **313** E13
Taunus *Germany* 50°13N 8°34E **179** E4
Taupo *N.Z.* 38°41S 176°7E **284** E5
Taupo, L. *N.Z.* 38°46S 175°55E **284** E4
Tauragė *Lithuania* 55°14N 22°16E **184** C9
Tauragė □ *Lithuania* 55°15N 22°17E **184** C9
Tauranga *N.Z.* 37°42S 176°11E **284** D5
Tauranga Harb. *N.Z.* 37°30S 176°5E **284** D5
Taureau, Rés. *Canada* 46°46N 73°50W **298** C5
Tauri → *Papua N. G.* 8°8S 146°8E **286** E4
Taurianova *Italy* 38°21N 16°1E **201** D9
Tauroa Pt. *N.Z.* 35°10S 173°4E **284** B2
Taurus Mts. = Toros Dağları
Turkey 37°0N 32°30E **250** B3
Taus = Domažlice *Czechia* 49°28N 12°58E **180** B5
Tauste *Spain* 41°58N 1°18W **196** D3
Tautira *Tahiti* 17°44S 149°9W **289** e
Tauyskaya Guba
Russia 59°20N 150°20E **215** D16
Tauz = Tovuz *Azerbaijan* 41°0N 45°40E **191** K7
Tavan Bogd Uul
Mongolia 49°10N 87°49E **217** C11
Tavares *U.S.A.* 28°48N 81°44W **317** G8
Tavares, I. dos *Brazil* 22°49S 43°6W **135** A2
Tavas *Turkey* 37°34N 29°4E **205** D11
Tavastehus = Hämeenlinna
Finland 61°0N 24°28E **188** B3
Tavda *Russia* 58°7N 65°8E **214** D7
Tavda → *Russia* 57°47N 67°18E **214** D7
Taverner B. *Canada* 67°12N 72°25W **295** D17
Tavernes de la Valldigna
Spain 39°5N 0°13W **197** F4
Tavernier *U.S.A.* 25°1N 80°31W **317** K9
Taveta *Kenya* 3°23S 37°37E **268** C4
Taveuni *Fiji* 16°51S 179°58W **287** A3
Taviano *Italy* 39°59N 18°5E **201** C11
Tavignano → *France* 42°7N 9°33E **175** F13
Tavira *Portugal* 37°8N 7°40W **195** H3
Tavistock *Ont., Canada* 43°19N 80°50W **312** C4
Tavistock *Devon, U.K.* 50°33N 4°9W **169** G3
Tavolara *Italy* 40°54N 9°42E **200** B2
Távora → *Portugal* 41°8N 7°35W **194** D3
Tavoy = Dawei *Burma* 14°2N 98°12E **236** E2
Tavoy Pt. *Burma* 13°32N 98°10E **236** F2
Tavrichanka *Russia* 43°18N 131°59E **220** C5
Tavropos → *Greece* 39°10N 21°45E **204** B3
Tavros *Greece* 37°57N 23°43E **112** B2
Tavşanlı *Turkey* 39°32N 29°30E **205** B11
Tavua *Fiji* 17°37S 177°5E **287** A1
Tavuki *Fiji* 19°7S 178°8E **287** B2
Taw → *U.K.* 51°4N 4°4W **169** F3
Tawa → *India* 22°48N 77°48E **242** H8
Tawa Res. *India* 22°35N 78°5E **244** C4
Tawa Tawa Mal Reef
Papua N. G. 11°3S 152°55E **286** F7
Tawai *India* 27°48N 96°47E **241** B6
Tawang *India* 27°35N 91°52E **241** B3
Tawas City *U.S.A.* 44°16N 83°31W **309** C12
Tawau *Malaysia* 4°20N 117°55E **235** B5
Tawau Hills △ *Malaysia* 4°20N 117°54E **235** B5
Taweisha *Sudan* 12°19N 26°40E **257** E2
Tawi-tawi *Phil.* 5°10N 120°15E **233** J3
Tawi-tawi I. *Phil.* 5°10N 120°15E **233** J3
Tawngche *Burma* 26°34N 95°38E **241** B5
Tawu *Taiwan* 22°22N 120°54E **225** D2
Tāwūq *Iraq* 35°8N 44°26E **213** E11
Tāwurghā' *Libya* 32°1N 15°2E **258** B3
Tāwurghā', Sabkhat
Libya 31°51N 15°15E **258** B3
Taxco *Mexico* 18°33N 99°36W **319** D5
Taxila *Pakistan* 33°42N 72°52E **242** C5
Taxkorgan Tajik Zizhixian
China 37°49N 75°14E **217** E9
Tay → *U.K.* 56°37N 3°38W **167** E5
Tay, Firth of *U.K.* 56°25N 3°8W **167** E5
Tay, L. *W. Austral.,*
Australia 32°55S 120°48E **279** F3
Tay, L. *Perth & Kinr., U.K.* 56°32N 4°8W **167** E4
Tay ⌓ *U.K.* 56°43N 3°59W **167** E5
Tay Ninh *Vietnam* 11°20N 106°5E **237** G6
Tayabamba *Peru* 8°15S 77°16W **330** B2
Tayabas = Quezon *Phil.* 9°15N 117°59E **233** G1
Tayabas *Phil.* 14°1N 121°35E **232** D3
Tayabas B. *Phil.* 13°45N 121°45E **232** E3
Tayan *Indonesia* 0°1S 110°7E **235** C4
Taygetos Oros *Greece* 37°0N 22°23E **204** D4
Taylakova *Russia* 59°13N 74°0E **214** D8
Taylor *B.C., Canada* 56°13N 120°40W **296** B4
Taylor *Fla., U.S.A.* 30°26N 82°18W **316** E7
Taylor *Mich., U.S.A.* 42°14N 83°16W **311** B13
Taylor *Nebr., U.S.A.* 41°46N 99°23W **308** E4
Taylor *Pa., U.S.A.* 41°23N 75°43W **313** E9
Taylor *Tex., U.S.A.* 30°34N 97°25W **314** F6
Taylor, Mt. *N.Z.* 43°30S 171°20E **285** D6
Taylor, Mt. *N. Mex.,*
U.S.A. 35°14N 107°37W **305** J10
Taylorsville *U.S.A.* 38°2N 85°21W **311** F11
Taylorsville L. *U.S.A.* 38°0N 85°15W **311** G11
Taylorville *U.S.A.* 39°33N 89°18W **310** E7
Taymā *Si. Arabia* 27°35N 38°45E **246** E3
Taymyr, Oz. *Russia* 74°20N 102°0E **215** B11
Taymyr, Poluostrov
Russia 75°0N 100°0E **215** B11
Taypaq *Kazakhstan* 49°0N 51°47E **187** E9
Tayport *U.K.* 56°27N 2°52W **167** E6
Tayrona △ *Colombia* 11°20N 74°2W **328** A3
Tayshet *Russia* 55°58N 98°1E **215** D10
Taytay *Phil.* 10°45N 119°30E **233** F2
Taytay B. *Phil.* 10°55N 119°35E **233** F2
Tayuan *Taiwan* 25°3N 121°11E **225** A3
Tayug *Phil.* 16°2N 120°45E **232** C3
Tayüling *Taiwan* 24°11N 121°18E **225** B3
Täyyebād *Iran* 34°45N 60°45E **247** C9
Täyyebād □ *Iran* 34°44N 60°44E **247** C9
Tayynsha *Kazakhstan* 53°50N 69°45E **217** B7
Taz → *Russia* 67°32N 78°40E **214** C8
Taza *Morocco* 34°16N 4°6W **260** B4
Taza-Al Hoceïma-Taounate □
Morocco 34°15N 3°20W **261** B4
Tāza Khurmātū *Iraq* 35°18N 44°20E **213** E11
Taza-Taou □ *Morocco* 34°15N 4°10W **260** B4
Tazawa-Ko *Japan* 39°43N 140°40E **220** E10
Taze *Burma* 22°57N 95°24E **241** D5
Tazenakht *Morocco* 30°35N 7°12W **260** B3
Tazerbo *Libya* 25°45N 21°0E **258** C4
Tazin → *Canada* 59°48N 109°55W **297** B7
Tazin L. *Canada* 59°44N 108°42W **297** B7
Tazlina *U.S.A.* 62°4N 146°27W **303** E11
Tazouikert *Mali* 21°27N 1°16W **261** D4
Tazoult *Algeria* 35°29N 6°11E **261** A6
Tazovskiy *Russia* 67°30N 78°44E **214** C8
Tazrouk *Algeria* 23°24N 6°15E **261** D6
Tbilisi *Georgia* 41°43N 44°50E **191** K7
Tchad = Chad ■ *Africa* 15°0N 17°15E **259** F3
Tchad, L. *Chad* 13°30N 14°30E **259** F2
Tchaourou *Benin* 8°58N 2°40E **263** D5
Tch'eng-tou = Chengdu
China 30°38N 104°2E **228** B5
Tchentlo L. *Canada* 55°15N 125°0W **296** B4
Tchetti *Benin* 7°50N 1°40E **263** D5
Tchibanga *Gabon* 2°45S 11°0E **264** C2
Tchien *Liberia* 5°59N 8°15W **262** D3
Tchin Tabaraden *Niger* 15°58N 5°56E **263** B6
Tchogha Zanbil = Choghā Zanbīl
Iran 32°1N 48°32E **247** C6
Tcholliré *Cameroon* 8°24N 14°10E **264** A2
Tch'ong-k'ing = Chongqing
China 29°35N 106°25E **228** C6
Tchoupitoulas Street
New Orleans, U.S.A. **131** b2
Tczew *Poland* 54°8N 18°50E **184** D5
TD Garden *Boston, U.S.A.* **116** a2
Te Anau *N.Z.* 45°25S 167°43E **285** F2
Te Anau, L. *N.Z.* 45°15S 167°45E **285** F2
Te Araroa *N.Z.* 37°39S 178°25E **284** D7
Te Aroha *N.Z.* 37°32S 175°44E **284** D4
Te Awamutu *N.Z.* 38°1S 175°20E **284** E4
Te Ika-a-Māui = North I.
N.Z. 38°0S 175°0E **284** E4
Te Kaha *N.Z.* 37°44S 177°52E **284** D6
Te Karaka *N.Z.* 38°26S 177°53E **284** E6
Te Kauwhata *N.Z.* 37°25S 175°9E **284** D4
Te Kopuru *N.Z.* 36°2S 173°56E **284** C2
Te Kou *Cook Is.* 21°14S 159°46W **289** h
Te Kuiti *N.Z.* 38°20S 175°11E **284** E4
Te Manga *Cook Is.* 21°14S 159°45W **289** h
Te-n-Dghâmcha, Sebkhet
Mauritania 18°30N 15°55W **262** B1
Te Nggano, L.
Solomon Is. 11°40S 160°19E **287** N11
Te Puke *N.Z.* 37°46S 176°22E **284** D5
Te Teko *N.Z.* 38°2S 176°48E **284** E5
Te Waewae B. *N.Z.* 46°13S 167°33E **285** G2
Te Waipounamu = South I.
N.Z. 44°0S 170°0E **285** E5
Tea → *Brazil* 0°30S 65°9W **328** D4
Teaca *Romania* 46°55N 24°30E **183** D9
Teague *U.S.A.* 31°38N 96°17W **314** F6
Teahupoo *Tahiti* 17°50S 149°16W **289** e
Teaneck *U.S.A.* 40°53N 74°1W **132** A1
Teano *Italy* 41°15N 14°4E **201** A7
Teapa *Mexico* 17°33N 92°57W **319** D6
Teba *Spain* 36°59N 4°55W **195** J6
Tebakang *Malaysia* 1°6N 110°30E **235** B4
Tébarat *Niger* 14°49N 4°27E **263** C5
Teberau → *Malaysia* 1°30N 103°42E **237** d
Teberda *Russia* 43°30N 41°46E **191** J5
Tébessa *Algeria* 35°22N 8°8E **261** A6
Tébessa □ *Algeria* 35°0N 7°50E **261** B6
Tebet *Indonesia* 6°14S 106°50E **122** B2
Tebicuary → *Paraguay* 26°36S 58°16W **334** B4
Tebingtinggi *Riau, Indonesia* 1°0N 102°45E **234** B2
Tebingtinggi *Sumatera Selatan,*
Indonesia 3°36S 103°4E **234** C2
Tebingtinggi *Sumatera Utara,*
Indonesia 3°20N 99°9E **234** B1
Tébourba *Tunisia* 36°49N 9°51E **258** A1
Téboursouk *Tunisia* 36°29N 9°10E **258** A1
Tebulos *Georgia* 42°36N 45°17E **191** J7
Tecamachalco *Mexico* 19°25N 99°14W **128** B1
Tecate *Mexico* 32°34N 116°38W **307** N10
Tecer Dağları *Turkey* 39°27N 37°27E **212** C7
Tech → *France* 42°36N 3°3E **174** F7
Techiman *Ghana* 7°35N 1°58W **262** D4
Techirghiol *Romania* 44°4N 28°32E **183** F13
Techou = Dezhou *China* 37°26N 116°18E **226** F9
Tecka *Argentina* 43°29S 70°48W **336** B2
Tecomán *Mexico* 18°55N 103°53W **318** D4
Tecopa *U.S.A.* 35°51N 116°13W **307** K10
Tecoripa *Mexico* 28°37N 109°57W **318** B3
Tecuala *Mexico* 22°23N 105°27W **318** C3
Tecuci *Romania* 45°51N 27°27E **183** E12
Tecumseh *Ont., Canada* 42°19N 82°54W **312** D2
Tecumseh *Mich., U.S.A.* 42°0N 83°57W **311** B13
Tecumseh *Okla., U.S.A.* 35°15N 96°56W **314** D6
Ted *Somalia* 4°24N 43°55E **267** D5
Ted Williams Tunnel
Boston, U.S.A. 42°21N 71°1W **116** A2
Teddington *U.K.* 51°25N 0°20W **125** B1
Tedjert *Algeria* 21°23N 6°25E **261** D6
Tedzhen = Tejen
Turkmenistan 37°23N 60°31E **216** E6
Tees → *U.K.* 54°37N 1°10W **168** C6
Tees B. *U.K.* 54°40N 1°9W **168** C6
Teeswater *Canada* 43°59N 81°17W **312** C3
Tefé *Brazil* 3°25S 64°50W **329** D5
Tefé → *Brazil* 3°35S 64°47W **329** D5
Tefenni *Turkey* 37°18N 29°45E **205** D11
Tegal *Indonesia* 6°52S 109°8E **235** D3
Tegallalang *Indonesia* 8°27S 115°17E **231** J18
Tegalsari *Indonesia* 8°25S 114°8E **231** J17
Tegano, L. = Te Nggano, L.
Solomon Is. 11°40S 160°19E **287** N11
Tegel *Germany* 52°34N 13°16E **115** A2
Tegel, Berlin ✈ (TXL)
Germany 52°35N 13°14E **115** A2
Tegeler See *Germany* 52°34N 13°15E **115** A2
Tegelort *Germany* 52°34N 13°13E **115** A2
Tegernsee *Germany* 47°43N 11°46E **179** H7
Teggiano *Italy* 40°23N 15°32E **201** B8
Tegid, L. = Bala, L. *U.K.* 52°53N 3°37W **168** E4
Tegina *Nigeria* 10°5N 6°11E **263** C6
Tegua *Vanuatu* 13°15S 166°37E **287** C4
Tegucigalpa *Honduras* 14°5N 87°14W **320** D2
Teguidda i-n-Tessoum
Niger 17°25N 6°37E **263** B6
Teguise *Canary Is.* 29°3N 13°33W **153** e2
Tehachapi *U.S.A.* 35°8N 118°27W **307** K8
Tehachapi Mts. *U.S.A.* 35°0N 118°30W **307** L8
Tehamiyam *Sudan* 18°20N 36°32E **256** D4
Teheran = Tehrān *Iran* 35°41N 51°25E **141** A2
Tehilla *Sudan* 17°42N 36°6E **256** D4
Téhini *Ivory C.* 9°39N 3°40W **262** D4
Tehoru *Indonesia* 3°23S 129°30E **231** E7
Tehrān *Iran* 35°41N 51°25E **141** A2
Tehrān □ *Iran* 35°30N 51°30E **247** C6
Tehrān Mehrābād ✈ (THR)
Iran 35°41N 51°18E **141** A1
Tehrān Pārs *Iran* 35°44N 51°32E **141** A3
Tehri *India* 30°23N 78°29E **243** D8
Tehuacán *Mexico* 18°27N 97°23W **319** D5
Tehuantepec *Mexico* 16°21N 95°13W **319** D5
Tehuantepec, G. de
Mexico 15°50N 95°12W **319** D5
Tehuantepec, Istmo de
Mexico 17°15N 94°30W **319** D6
Tehuantepec Fracture Zone
Pac. Oc. 13°0N 97°0W **289** F18
Tei Tong Tsui
Hong Kong, China 22°16N 114°17E **122** B3
Teide, Pico del *Canary Is.* 28°15N 16°38W **153** e1
Teifi → *U.K.* 52°5N 4°41W **169** E3
Teigebyen *Norway* 60°12N 11°0E **162** D5
Teign → *U.K.* 50°32N 3°32W **169** G4
Teignmouth *U.K.* 50°33N 3°31W **169** G4
Teijo △ *Finland* 60°13N 22°56E **188** B2
Teinainano = Tarawa
Kiribati 1°30N 173°0E **288** G9
Teiuş *Romania* 46°12N 23°40E **183** D8
Teixeira *Brazil* 7°13S 37°15W **332** C4
Teixeira Pinto *Guinea-Biss.* 12°3N 16°0W **262** C1
Tejakula *Indonesia* 8°8S 115°20E **231** J18
Tejen *Turkmenistan* 37°23N 60°31E **216** E6
Tejen → *Turkmenistan* 37°24N 60°38E **247** B9
Tejo → *Europe* 38°40N 9°24W **195** F2
Tejo, Rio → *Portugal* 38°45N 9°3W **126** A2
Tejon Pass *U.S.A.* 34°49N 118°53W **307** L8
Tekamah *U.S.A.* 41°47N 96°13W **308** E5
Tekapo → *N.Z.* 44°13S 170°21E **285** E5
Tekapo, L. *N.Z.* 43°53S 170°33E **285** D5
Tekax *Mexico* 20°12N 89°17W **319** C7
Teke *Turkey* 41°4N 29°39E **203** E13
Tekeli *Kazakhstan* 44°50N 79°0E **217** D9
Tekeze → *Ethiopia* 14°20N 35°50E **257** E4
Tekeze Dam *Ethiopia* 13°10N 38°45E **257** E4
Tekija *Serbia* 44°42N 22°26E **202** B6
Tekirdağ *Turkey* 40°58N 27°30E **203** F11
Tekirdağ □ *Turkey* 41°0N 27°0E **203** E11
Tekirova *Turkey* 36°30N 30°32E **205** E12
Tekkali *India* 18°37N 84°15E **244** E7
Tekke *Turkey* 40°42N 36°12E **212** B7
Tekman *Turkey* 39°38N 41°29E **213** C9
Teknaf *Bangla.* 20°52N 92°18E **241** E4
Tekoa *U.S.A.* 47°14N 117°4W **304** C5
Tekokota *French Polynesia* 17°18S 142°34W **289** f
Tekong Besar, Pulau
Singapore 1°25N 104°3E **237** d
Tekouiât, O. → *Algeria* 22°25N 2°35E **261** D5
Tékro *Chad* 19°32N 20°56E **259** E4
Tekstilyshchik *Russia* 55°42N 37°41E **129** B3
Tel → *India* 20°50N 83°54E **244** D6
Tel Aviv-Yafo *Israel* 32°4N 34°48E **251** F5
Tel Lakhish *Israel* 31°34N 34°51E **251** G5
Tel Megiddo *Israel* 32°35N 35°11E **250** F6
Tela *Honduras* 15°40N 87°28W **320** C2
Télagh *Algeria* 34°51N 0°32W **261** B4
Telanaipura = Jambi
Indonesia 1°38S 103°30E **234** C2
Telangana □ *India* 17°30N 78°30E **244** F4
Telašćica ⌓ *Croatia* 43°55N 15°10E **199** E12
Telavi *Georgia* 42°0N 45°30E **191** J7
Telč *Czechia* 49°11N 15°28E **180** B8
Telciu *Romania* 47°25N 24°24E **183** C9
Telde *Canary Is.* 27°59N 15°25W **153** e1
Tele →
Dem. Rep. of the Congo 2°48N 23°54E **264** B4
Télé, L. *Congo* 1°20N 17°9E **264** B3
Telefomin *Papua N. G.* 5°10S 141°31E **286** C1
Telegraph Creek *Canada* 58°0N 131°10W **296** B2
Telegraph Hill *San Francisco, U.S.A.* **136** a2
Telekhany = Tsyelyakhany
Belarus 52°30N 25°46E **177** B13
Telemark *Norway* 59°15N 7°40E **161** G12
Telemark □ *Norway* 59°25N 8°30E **164** E5
Télemsès *Niger* 15°37N 4°44E **263** B5
Telen *Argentina* 36°15S 65°31W **334** D2
Telen → *Indonesia* 0°10S 117°20E **235** C5
Teleneşti *Moldova* 47°30N 28°22E **183** C13
Teleng *Iran* 25°47N 61°3E **247** E9
Teleño *Spain* 42°23N 6°22W **194** C4
Teleorman □ *Romania* 44°0N 25°0E **183** G10
Teleorman → *Romania* 43°52N 25°26E **183** G10
Telerhteba, Djebel *Algeria* 24°10N 6°51E **261** D6
Teles Pires → *Brazil* 7°21S 58°3W **331** B6
Telescope Pk. *U.S.A.* 36°10N 117°5W **307** J9
Telescope Pt. *Grenada* 12°7N 61°36W **323** q
Teletaye *Mali* 16°31N 1°30E **263** B5
Teletskoye, Oz. *Russia* 51°40N 87°30E **217** B11
Telford *U.K.* 52°40N 2°27W **169** E5
Telford and Wrekin □
U.K. 52°45N 2°27W **168** E5
Telfs *Austria* 47°19N 11°4E **180** D4
Telhal *Portugal* 38°49N 9°18W **126** A1
Télida *U.S.A.* 63°23N 153°16W **303** E9
Télimélé *Guinea* 10°54N 13°2W **262** C2
Teljo, J. *Sudan* 14°42N 25°26E **257** E2
Telkwa *Canada* 54°41N 127°5W **296** C3
Tell City *U.S.A.* 37°57N 86°46W **311** G10
Teller *U.S.A.* 65°16N 166°22W **303** D6
Tellicherry = Thalassery
India 11°45N 75°30E **245** J2
Telluride *U.S.A.* 37°56N 107°49W **305** H10
Telok Blangah *Singapore* 1°17N 103°49E **138** B2
Teloloapán *Mexico* 18°21N 99°51W **319** D5
Telpos Iz *Russia* 63°16N 59°13E **186** B10
Telsen *Argentina* 42°30S 66°50W **336** B3
Telšiai *Lithuania* 55°59N 22°14E **184** C9
Telšiai □ *Lithuania* 55°59N 22°15E **184** C9
Teltow *Germany* 52°23N 13°17E **115** B2
Teltow kanal *Germany* 52°26N 13°29E **115** B3
Teluk Anson = Teluk Intan
Malaysia 4°3N 101°0E **237** K3
Teluk Bahang *Malaysia* 5°28N 100°13E **237** c
Teluk Betung = Bandar Lampung
Indonesia 5°20S 105°10E **234** D3
Teluk Intan *Malaysia* 4°3N 101°0E **237** K3
Teluk Kumbar *Malaysia* 5°18N 100°14E **237** c
Telukbatang *Indonesia* 1°0S 109°46E **235** C3
Telukbayur *Kalimantan Timur,*
Indonesia 2°9N 117°24E **235** B5
Telukbayur *Sumatera Barat,*
Indonesia 0°59S 100°23E **234** C2
Telukbutun *Indonesia* 4°13N 108°12E **235** B3
Telukdalam *Indonesia* 0°33N 97°50E **234** B1
Tema *Ghana* 5°41N 0°0 **263** D5
Temagami, L. *Canada* 47°0N 80°10W **298** C3
Temasint *Algeria* 23°18N 7°40E **261** D6
Temantangi
French Polynesia 21°41S 140°40W **289** f
Temax *Mexico* 21°9N 88°56W **319** C7
Temba *S. Africa* 25°20S 28°17E **271** C4
Tembagapura *Indonesia* 4°20S 137°0E **231** E9
Tembe
Dem. Rep. of the Congo 0°16S 28°14E **268** C2
Tembe ⌓ *S. Africa* 26°51S 32°24E **271** C5
Tembesi → *Indonesia* 1°43S 103°6E **234** C2
Tembilahan *Indonesia* 0°19S 103°9E **234** C2
Temblador *Venezuela* 8°59N 62°44W **329** B5
Tembleque *Spain* 39°41N 3°30W **194** F7
Temblor Range *U.S.A.* 35°20N 119°50W **307** K7
Tembo Aluma *Angola* 7°42S 17°17E **265** D3
Teme → *U.K.* 52°11N 2°13W **169** E5
Temecula *U.S.A.* 33°30N 117°9W **307** M9
Temengor, Tasik *Malaysia* 5°24N 101°18E **237** K3
Temerloh *Malaysia* 3°27N 102°25E **237** L4
Temiang *Indonesia* 0°19N 104°23E **234** B2
Teminabuan *Indonesia* 1°26S 132°1E **231** E8
Temir *Kazakhstan* 49°1N 57°14E **187** E10
Temir-Khan-Shura = Buynaksk
Russia 42°48N 47°7E **191** J8
Temirtau *Kazakhstan* 50°5N 72°56E **217** B8
Temirtau *Russia* 53°10N 87°30E **217** B11
Témiscamie → *Canada* 50°59N 73°5W **299** B5
Témiscaming *Canada* 46°44N 79°5W **298** C4
Témiscamingue, L.
Canada 47°10N 79°25W **298** C4
Temnikov *Russia* 54°40N 43°11E **190** C6
Temo → *Italy* 40°17N 8°28E **200** B1
Temora *Australia* 34°30S 147°30E **283** C7
Temosachic *Mexico* 28°57N 107°51W **318** B3
Tempe *U.S.A.* 33°24N 111°54W **305** K8
Tempelburg = Czaplinek
Poland 53°34N 16°14E **184** E3
Tempelhof *Germany* 52°27N 13°23E **115** B3
Temperance *U.S.A.* 41°47N 83°34W **311** C13
Tempino *Indonesia* 1°46S 103°30E **234** C2
Témpio Pausânia *Italy* 40°54N 9°6E **200** B2
Tempiute *U.S.A.* 37°39N 115°38W **306** H11
Templar Bank *S. China Sea* 9°0N 117°30E **233** F1
Temple *U.S.A.* 31°6N 97°21W **314** F6
Temple B. *Australia* 12°15S 143°3E **286** G2
Temple City *U.S.A.* 34°6N 118°3W **126** B4
Temple Hills *U.S.A.* 38°48N 76°56W **143** C3
Temple Mount *Jerusalem* **123** b3
Temple of Heaven *China* 39°52N 116°23E **114** B2
Temple of the Dawn = Arun
Bangkok, Thailand **113** b1
Temple Terrace *U.S.A.* 28°2N 82°23W **317** G7
Templemore *Ireland* 52°47N 7°51W **166** D4
Templeton *U.S.A.* 35°33N 120°42W **306** K6
Templeton → *Australia* 21°0S 138°40E **280** C2
Templin *Germany* 53°7N 13°28E **178** B9
Templo Mayor *Mexico City, Mexico* **128** b3
Tempoal de Sánchez
Mexico 21°31N 98°23W **319** C5
Temppeliaukio Church
Finland 60°10N 24°56E **121** B2
Tempué *Angola* 13°27S 18°49E **265** E3
Temryuk *Russia* 45°15N 37°24E **189** K9
Temska → *Serbia* 43°17N 22°33E **202** C6
Temuco *Chile* 38°45S 72°40W **336** A2
Temuka *N.Z.* 44°14S 171°17E **285** E6
Ten Degree Channel *India* 10°0N 92°30E **245** K11
Ten Thousand Is. *U.S.A.* 25°55N 81°45W **317** K8
Tena *Ecuador* 0°59S 77°49W **328** D2
Tenabo *Mexico* 20°3N 90°14W **319** C6
Tenafly *U.S.A.* 40°54N 73°58W **132** A2
Tenaha *U.S.A.* 31°57N 94°15W **314** F7
Tenakee Springs *U.S.A.* 57°47N 135°13W **296** B1
Tenali *India* 16°15N 80°35E **245** F5
Tenancingo *Mexico* 18°58N 99°38W **319** D5
Tenango del Valle *Mexico* 19°7N 99°33W **319** D5
Tenaro, Akra *Greece* 36°22N 22°27E **204** E4
Tenasserim = Tanintharyi
Burma 12°6N 99°3E **237** F2
Tenasserim □ *Burma* 14°0N 98°30E **236** F2
Tenasserim → *Burma* 12°24N 98°37E **236** F2
Tenayuca, Piramide de
Mexico 19°31N 99°10W **128** A1
Tenby *U.K.* 51°40N 4°42W **169** F3
Tenda, Colle di *France* 44°7N 7°36E **175** D11
Tendaho *Ethiopia* 11°48N 40°54E **257** E5
Tende *France* 44°5N 7°35E **175** D11
Tendelti *Sudan* 13°1N 31°55E **257** E3
Tendjedi, Adrar *Algeria* 23°41N 7°32E **261** D6
Tendō *Japan* 38°20N 140°30E **220** E10
Tendrara *Morocco* 33°3N 1°58W **261** B4
Tendrovskaya Kosa
Ukraine 46°16N 31°35E **189** J6
Tendukhera *India* 23°24N 79°33E **243** H8
Teneguía, Volcán
Canary Is. 28°28N 17°51W **153** e1
Teneida *Egypt* 25°30N 29°19E **256** B2
Tenenkou *Mali* 14°28N 4°55W **262** C4
Tenente Marques →
Brazil 11°10S 59°56W **331** C6
Ténéré *Niger* 19°0N 10°30E **259** E2
Ténéré, Erg du *Niger* 17°35N 10°55E **259** E2
Tenerife *Canary Is.* 28°15N 16°35W **153** e1
Tenerife, Pico *Canary Is.* 27°43N 18°1W **153** e1
Tenerife Norte ✈ (TFN)
Canary Is. 28°28N 16°17W **153** e1
Tenerife Sur ✈ (TFS)
Canary Is. 28°3N 16°33W **153** e1
Ténès *Algeria* 36°31N 1°14E **261** A5
Teng Xian *Guangxi Zhuangzu,*
China 23°21N 110°56E **229** F8
Teng Xian *Shandong, China* 35°5N 117°10E **227** G9
Tengah → *Singapore* 1°23N 103°43E **138** A2
Tengah, Kepulauan
Indonesia 7°5S 118°15E **235** D5
Tengchong *China* 25°0N 98°28E **228** E2
Tengchowfu = Penglai
China 37°48N 120°42E **227** F11
Tenggarong *Indonesia* 0°24S 116°58E **235** C5
Tengger Feng *China* 43°20N 86°48E **217** D11
Tengger Shamo *China* 38°0N 104°10E **226** F3
Tenggol, Pulau *Malaysia* 4°48N 103°41E **237** K4
Tengi-Kharam = Dehqonobod
Uzbekistan 38°21N 66°30E **240** A2
Tengiz Köli *Kazakhstan* 50°30N 69°0E **217** B7
Tengzhou *China* 35°4N 117°9E **227** G9
Tenhult *Sweden* 57°41N 14°20E **163** G8
Teniente Enciso △ *Paraguay* 21°5S 61°8W **334** A3
Tenille *U.S.A.* 29°46N 83°19W **316** F6
Tenino *U.S.A.* 46°51N 122°51W **306** D4
Tenkasi *India* 8°55N 77°20E **245** K3

Tenke *Katanga, Dem. Rep. of the Congo* 11°22S 26°40E **269** E2
Tenke *Katanga, Dem. Rep. of the Congo* 10°32S 26°7E **269** E2
Tenkodogo *Burkina Faso* 11°54N 0°19W **263** C4
Tenna → *Italy* 43°14N 13°47E **199** E10
Tennant Creek *Australia* 19°30S 134°15E **280** B1
Tennessee □ *U.S.A.* 36°0N 86°30W **315** D11
Tennessee → *U.S.A.* 37°4N 88°34W **315** C10
Tennille *U.S.A.* 32°56N 82°48W **316** C7
Tennoji *Japan* 34°39N 135°30E **133** B2
Teno, Pta. de *Canary Is.* 28°21N 16°55W **153** e1
Tenojoki = Tana → *Norway* 70°30N 28°14E **160** A23
Tenom *Malaysia* 5°4N 115°57E **235** A5
Tenosique *Mexico* 17°29N 91°26W **319** D6
Tenri *Japan* 34°39N 135°49E **223** C7
Tenryū *Japan* 34°52N 137°49E **223** C9
Tenryū-Gawa → *Japan* 35°39N 137°48E **223** B9
Tensift, Oued → *Morocco* 32°3N 9°28W **260** B3
Tente *Indonesia* 8°35S 118°41E **235** D5
Tenterden *U.K.* 51°4N 0°42E **169** F8
Tenterfield *Australia* 29°0S 152°0E **281** D5
Tenuaiur, Uad → *W. Sahara* 21°36N 16°0W **260** D1
Teo = A Ramallosa *Spain* 42°45N 8°30W **194** C2
Teófilo Otoni *Brazil* 17°50S 41°30W **333** E3
Tepa *Indonesia* 7°52S 129°31E **231** F7
Tepa Pt. *Cook Is.* 19°6S 169°55W **289** g
Tepalcatepec → *Mexico* 18°35N 101°59W **318** D4
Tepalcates *Mexico* 19°23N 99°3W **128** B2
Tepecik *Bursa, Turkey* 40°7N 28°25E **203** F12
Tepecik *Kütahya, Turkey* 39°32N 29°28E **205** B11
Tepehuanes *Mexico* 25°21N 105°44W **318** B3
Tepelenë *Albania* 40°17N 20°2E **202** F4
Tepequem, Serra *Brazil* 3°45N 61°45W **329** C5
Tepetongo *Mexico* 22°28N 103°9W **318** C4
Tepeyac △ *Mexico* 19°30N 99°7W **128** B2
Tepic = Nayarit □ *Mexico* 22°0N 105°0W **318** C4
Tepic *Mexico* 21°30N 104°54W **318** C4
Teplá *Czechia* 49°59N 12°52E **180** B5
Teplice *Czechia* 50°40N 13°48E **180** A6
Teplitz = Teplice *Czechia* 50°40N 13°48E **180** A6
Teplyk *Ukraine* 48°40N 29°44E **183** B14
Tequila *Mexico* 20°54N 103°47W **318** C4
Ter → *Spain* 42°2N 3°12E **196** C8
Ter Apel *Neths.* 52°53N 7°5E **170** B7
Téra *Niger* 14°0N 0°45E **263** C5
Tera → *Spain* 41°54N 5°44W **194** D5
Tera Kora *Bonaire* 12°11N 68°14W **322** h
Teraina *Kiribati* 4°43N 160°25W **289** G12
Terakeka *South Sudan* 5°26N 31°45E **257** F3
Téramo *Italy* 42°39N 13°42E **199** F10
Terang *Australia* 38°15S 142°55E **282** E5
Terang, Teluk *Indonesia* 8°44S 116°0E **231** K19
Terawhiti, C. *N.Z.* 41°16S 174°38E **284** H3
Terazit, Massif de *Niger* 20°2N 8°30E **259** D1
Tercan *Turkey* 39°47N 40°23E **213** C9
Terceira *Azores* 38°43N 27°13W **153** d1
Tercero → *Argentina* 32°58S 61°47W **334** C3
Terdal *India* 16°33N 75°3E **244** F2
Terebovlya *Ukraine* 49°18N 25°44E **177** D13
Teregova *Romania* 45°10N 22°16E **182** E7
Tereida *Sudan* 10°35N 31°17E **257** E3
Terek → *Russia* 44°0N 47°30E **191** J8
Terengganu □ *Malaysia* 4°55N 103°0E **237** K4
Terenos *Brazil* 20°26S 54°50W **331** E7
Terepaima △ *Venezuela* 9°58N 69°17W **328** B4
Tereshka → *Russia* 51°48N 46°26E **190** E8
Teresina *Brazil* 5°9S 42°45W **332** C3
Teresinha *Brazil* 0°58N 52°2W **329** C7
Terespol *Poland* 52°5N 23°37E **185** F10
Teressa *India* 8°15N 93°10E **245** K11
Teresva *Ukraine* 48°0N 23°42E **183** B8
Terewah, L. *Australia* 29°52S 147°35E **281** D4
Terges → *Portugal* 37°49N 7°41W **195** H3
Tergnier *France* 49°40N 3°17E **173** C10
Terhazza *Mali* 23°38N 5°22W **260** D3
Teridgerie Cr. → *Australia* 30°25S 148°50E **283** A8
Terijoki = Zelenogorsk *Russia* 60°12N 29°43E **188** B5
Terlizzi *Italy* 41°8N 16°32E **201** A9
Termas de Río Hondo *Argentina* 27°29S 64°52W **334** B3
Terme *Turkey* 41°11N 37°0E **212** B7
Términi Imerese *Italy* 37°59N 13°42E **200** E6
Términos, L. de *Mexico* 18°37N 91°33W **319** D6
Termit, Massif de *Niger* 16°2N 11°20E **259** E2
Termiz *Uzbekistan* 37°15N 67°15E **217** E7
Térmoli *Italy* 42°0N 15°0E **199** F12
Ternate *Indonesia* 0°45N 127°25E **231** D7
Terneuzen *Neths.* 51°20N 3°50E **170** C3
Terney *Russia* 45°3N 136°37E **220** B8
Terni *Italy* 42°34N 12°37E **199** F9
Ternitz *Austria* 47°43N 16°2E **180** D9
Ternivka *Ukraine* 48°32N 29°58E **183** B14
Ternopil *Ukraine* 49°30N 25°40E **177** D13
Ternopil □ *Ukraine* 48°10N 25°10E **177** D13
Ternopol = Ternopil *Ukraine* 49°30N 25°40E **177** D13
Terowie *Australia* 33°8S 138°55E **282** B3
Terpni *Greece* 40°55N 23°26E **202** F7
Terra Bella *U.S.A.* 35°58N 119°3W **307** K7
Terra Nova △ *Canada* 48°33N 53°55W **299** C9
Terrace *Canada* 54°30N 128°35W **296** C3
Terrace Bay *Canada* 48°47N 87°5W **298** C2
Terracina *Italy* 41°17N 13°15E **200** A6
Terralba *Italy* 39°43N 8°39E **200** C1
Terranova di Sicilia = Gela *Italy* 37°4N 14°15E **201** E7
Terranova Pausania = Ólbia *Italy* 40°55N 9°31E **200** B2
Terrasini *Italy* 38°10N 13°4E **200** D6
Terrassa *Spain* 41°34N 2°1E **196** D7
Terrasson-la-Villedieu *France* 45°8N 1°18E **174** C5
Terrazzano *Italy* 45°32N 9°4E **128** A1
Terre-de-Bas *Guadeloupe* 15°51N 61°38W **322** e
Terre-de-Bas *Guadeloupe* 16°10N 61°7W **322** e
Terre-de-Haut *Guadeloupe* 15°52N 61°34W **322** e
Terre des Hommes *Canada* 45°31N 73°32W **130** A2
Terre Haute *U.S.A.* 39°28N 87°25W **311** E9
Terre Rouge *Mauritius* 20°7S 57°31E **272** e
Terrebonne B. *U.S.A.* 29°5N 90°35W **315** G9
Terrecht *Mali* 19°35N 0°22E **261** D4
Terrenceville *Canada* 47°40N 54°44W **299** C9
Terrick Terrick △ *Australia* 36°8S 144°13E **282** D6
Terrugem *Portugal* 38°41N 9°17W **126** A1
Terry *U.S.A.* 46°47N 105°19W **304** C11
Terrytown *U.S.A.* 29°54N 90°1W **131** B2
Terryville *U.S.A.* 41°41N 73°3W **313** E11
Terschelling *Neths.* 53°25N 5°20E **170** A5
Tersko-Kumskiy Kanal *Russia* 44°32N 44°38E **191** H7
Tertenia *Italy* 39°42N 9°34E **200** C2
Terter = Tärtär → *Azerbaijan* 40°26N 47°20E **191** K8
Teruel *Spain* 40°22N 1°8W **196** E3
Teruel □ *Spain* 40°48N 1°0W **196** E4
Tervel *Bulgaria* 43°45N 27°28E **203** C11
Tervola *Finland* 66°6N 24°49E **160** C21
Tervuren *Belgium* 50°49N 4°31E **116** B3
Tervuren, Park van *Belgium* 50°49N 4°31E **116** B3
Teryaweynya L. *Australia* 32°18S 143°22E **282** B5
Tešanj *Bos.-H.* 44°38N 18°1E **182** F3
Teschen = Cieszyn *Poland* 49°45N 18°35E **185** J5
Teseney *Eritrea* 15°5N 36°42E **257** D4
Tesha → *Russia* 55°38N 42°9E **190** C6
Teshekpuk L. *U.S.A.* 70°35N 153°26W **303** A9
Teshio *Japan* 44°53N 141°44E **220** B10
Teshio-Gawa → *Japan* 44°53N 141°45E **220** B10
Tešica *Serbia* 43°27N 21°45E **202** C5
Tesiyn Gol → *Mongolia* 50°40N 93°20E **218** A7
Teslić *Bos.-H.* 44°37N 17°54E **182** F2
Teslin *Canada* 60°10N 132°43W **296** A2
Teslin → *Canada* 61°34N 134°35W **296** A2
Teslin L. *Canada* 60°15N 132°57W **296** A2
Tesouro *Brazil* 16°4S 53°34W **331** D7
Tessalit *Mali* 20°12N 1°0E **261** D5
Tessaoua *Niger* 13°47N 7°56E **259** F1
Tessin *Germany* 54°2N 12°26E **178** A8
Tessit *Mali* 15°13N 0°18E **263** B5
Tessounfat *Mali* 22°53N 0°32E **261** D5
Test → *U.K.* 50°56N 1°29W **169** G6
Testa del Gargano *Italy* 41°50N 16°10E **199** G13
Testigos, Is. Los *Venezuela* 11°23N 63°7W **321** D7
Tét *Hungary* 47°30N 17°33E **182** C2
Têt → *France* 42°44N 3°2E **174** F7
Tetachuck L. *Canada* 53°18N 125°55W **296** C3
Tetas, Pta. *Chile* 23°31S 70°38W **334** A1
Tete *Mozam.* 16°13S 33°33E **269** F3
Tete □ *Mozam.* 15°15S 32°40E **269** F3
Tetenga, Caleta *Chile* 27°9S 109°19W **330** b
Tetepare *Solomon Is.* 8°45S 157°35E **287** M9
Teterev → *Ukraine* 51°1N 30°5E **177** C16
Teterow *Germany* 53°46N 12°34E **178** B8
Teteven *Bulgaria* 42°58N 24°17E **203** D8
Tethul → *Canada* 60°35N 112°12W **296** A6
Tetiyev *Ukraine* 49°22N 29°38E **177** D15
Tetlin *U.S.A.* 63°8N 142°31W **303** C12
Tetlin Junction *U.S.A.* 63°19N 142°36W **303** E12
Tetlin Nat. Wildlife Refuge △ *U.S.A.* 62°40N 141°50W **303** E12
Tetlit Zheh = Fort McPherson *Canada* 67°30N 134°55W **294** D5
Teton → *U.S.A.* 47°56N 110°31W **304** C8
Tétouan *Morocco* 35°35N 5°21W **260** A3
Tetovo *Macedonia* 42°1N 20°59E **202** D4
Tetschen = Děčín *Czechia* 50°47N 14°12E **180** A7
Tetuán = Tétouan *Morocco* 35°35N 5°21W **260** A3
Tetufera, Mt. *Tahiti* 17°40S 149°26W **289** e
Tetyukhe = Dalnegorsk *Russia* 44°32N 135°33E **220** B7
Tetyushi *Russia* 54°55N 48°49E **190** C9
Teuco → *Argentina* 25°35S 60°11W **334** B3
Teufelsberg *Germany* 52°29N 13°14E **115** B2
Teulada *Italy* 38°58N 8°46E **200** D1
Teulon *Canada* 50°23N 97°16W **297** C9
Teun *Indonesia* 6°59S 129°8E **231** F7
Teuri-Tō *Japan* 44°26N 141°19E **220** B10
Teutoburger Wald *Germany* 52°5N 8°22E **178** C4
Teutopolis *U.S.A.* 39°8N 88°29W **311** E8
Tevere → *Italy* 41°44N 12°14E **199** G9
Tevere △ *Italy* 42°46N 12°14E **199** F9
Teverya *Israel* 32°47N 35°32E **250** F6
Teviot → *U.K.* 55°29N 2°38W **167** F6
Tewantin *Australia* 26°27S 153°3E **281** D5
Teweh → *Indonesia* 0°58N 114°54E **235** C5
Tewkesbury *U.K.* 51°59N 2°9W **169** F5
Texada I. *Canada* 49°40N 124°25W **296** D4
Texarkana *Ark., U.S.A.* 33°26N 94°2W **314** E7
Texarkana *Tex., U.S.A.* 33°26N 94°3W **314** E7
Texas *Australia* 28°49S 151°9E **281** D5
Texas □ *U.S.A.* 31°40N 98°30W **314** F5
Texas City *U.S.A.* 29°24N 94°54W **314** G7
Texel *Neths.* 53°5N 4°50E **170** A4
Texline *U.S.A.* 36°23N 103°2W **314** C3
Texoma, L. *U.S.A.* 33°50N 96°34W **314** E6
Teykovo *Russia* 56°55N 40°30E **188** D11
Teyvareh *Afghan.* 33°30N 64°24E **240** B2
Teza → *Russia* 56°32N 41°53E **190** B5
Tezin *Afghan.* 34°24N 69°30E **242** B3
Teziutlán *Mexico* 19°49N 97°21W **319** D5
Tezpur *India* 26°40N 92°45E **241** B4
Tezu *India* 27°55N 96°10E **241** B6
Tezzeron L. *Canada* 54°43N 124°30W **296** C4
Tha-anne → *Canada* 60°31N 94°37W **297** A10
Tha Deua *Laos* 17°57N 102°53E **236** D4
Tha Deua *Laos* 19°26N 101°50E **236** C3
Tha Li *Thailand* 17°37N 101°25E **236** D3
Tha Pla *Thailand* 17°48N 100°32E **236** D3
Tha Rua *Thailand* 14°34N 100°44E **236** E3
Tha Sala *Thailand* 8°40N 99°56E **237** H2
Tha Song Yang *Thailand* 17°34N 97°55E **236** D1
Thaba Putsoa *Lesotho* 29°45S 28°0E **271** C4
Thaba-Tseka *Lesotho* 29°32S 28°36E **271** C4
Thabana Ntlenyana *Lesotho* 29°30S 29°16E **271** C4
Thabaung *Burma* 17°2N 94°48E **241** G5
Thabazimbi *S. Africa* 24°40S 27°21E **271** B4
Thabeikkyin *Burma* 22°53N 95°59E **241** D5
Thādiq *Si. Arabia* 25°18N 45°52E **246** E5
Thai Binh *Vietnam* 20°35N 106°1E **228** G6
Thai Muang *Thailand* 8°24N 98°16E **237** H2
Thai Nguyen *Vietnam* 21°35N 105°55E **228** G5
Thailand ■ *Asia* 16°0N 102°0E **236** E4
Thailand, G. of *Asia* 11°30N 101°0E **237** G3
Thakhek *Laos* 17°25N 104°45E **236** D5
Thakurgaon *Bangla.* 26°2N 88°34E **241** B2
Thal *Pakistan* 33°28N 70°33E **242** C4
Thal Desert *Pakistan* 31°10N 71°30E **242** D4
Thala *Tunisia* 35°35N 8°40E **258** A1
Thala La = Hkakabo Razi *Burma* 28°25N 97°23E **228** C1
Thalabarivat *Cambodia* 13°33N 105°57E **236** F5
Thalang = Amphoe Thalang *Thailand* 8°1N 98°20E **237** a
Thalara *Nepal* 29°29N 80°59E **243** E9
Thalassery *India* 11°45N 75°30E **245** J2
Thale Sap Songkhla *Thailand* 7°12N 100°28E **237** J3
Thalkirchen *Germany* 48°6N 11°32E **131** B2
Thallon *Australia* 28°39S 148°49E **281** D4
Thalu, Ko *Thailand* 9°26N 99°54E **237** b
Thalwil *Switz.* 47°17N 8°35E **179** H4
Tham Lot *Thailand* 19°34N 98°16E **236** C2
Thamarīt *Oman* 17°39N 54°2E **249** D6
Thames *N.Z.* 37°7S 175°34E **284** D4
Thames → *Ont., Canada* 42°20N 82°25W **312** D2
Thames → *U.K.* 51°29N 0°34E **169** F8
Thames → *Conn., U.S.A.* 41°18N 72°5W **313** E12
Thames, Firth of *N.Z.* 37°0S 175°25E **284** D4
Thames Ditton *U.K.* 51°23N 0°20W **125** B1
Thames Estuary *U.K.* 51°29N 0°52E **169** F8
Thamesford *Canada* 43°4N 81°0W **312** C3
Thamesmead *U.K.* 51°30N 0°7E **125** A4
Thamesville *Canada* 42°33N 81°59W **312** D3
Thāmit, W. → *Libya* 31°11N 16°8E **258** B3
Thamūd *Yemen* 17°18N 49°55E **249** C5
Than *India* 22°34N 71°11E **242** H4
Than Kyun *Burma* 9°49N 98°4E **237** H1
Than Uyen *Vietnam* 22°0N 103°54E **236** B4
Thana Cr. → *India* 19°4N 72°54E **130** B4
Thana Gazi *India* 27°25N 76°19E **242** F7
Thanbyuzayat *Burma* 15°58N 97°44E **241** G6
Thandaung *Burma* 19°4N 96°41E **241** F6
Thandla *India* 23°0N 74°34E **242** H6
Thandwe *Burma* 18°20N 94°30E **241** F5
Thane *India* 19°12N 72°59E **244** E1
Thanesar *India* 30°1N 76°52E **242** D7
Thanet, I. of *U.K.* 51°21N 1°20E **169** F9
Thangool *Australia* 24°38S 150°42E **280** C5
Thanh Hoa *Vietnam* 19°48N 105°46E **236** C5
Thanh Hung *Vietnam* 9°55N 105°43E **237** H5
Thanh Pho Ho Chi Minh *Vietnam* 10°58N 106°40E **237** G6
Thanh Thuy *Vietnam* 22°55N 104°51E **236** A5
Thanjavur *India* 10°48N 79°12E **245** J4
Thanlwin = Salween → *Burma* 16°31N 97°37E **241** G6
Thanlyin = Syriam *Burma* 16°44N 96°19E **241** G6
Thann *France* 47°48N 7°5E **173** E14
Thano Bula Khan *Pakistan* 25°22N 67°50E **242** G2
Thanya Buri *Thailand* 14°1N 100°45E **236** E3
Thaoge → *Botswana* 20°27S 22°36E **270** B3
Thaolintoa L. *Canada* 61°30N 96°25W **297** A9
Thaon-les-Vosges *France* 48°15N 6°24E **173** D13
Thap Lan △ *Thailand* 14°15N 102°16E **236** E4
Thap Sakae *Thailand* 11°30N 99°37E **237** G2
Thap Than *Thailand* 15°27N 99°54E **236** E2
Thar Desert *India* 28°0N 72°0E **242** F5
Tharad *India* 24°30N 71°44E **242** G4
Tharaka-Nithi □ *Kenya* 0°20S 38°0E **268** C4
Thargomindah *Australia* 27°58S 143°46E **281** D3
Tharp Fracture Zone *S. Ocean* 54°0S 135°0W **151** B14
Tharrawaddy *Burma* 17°38N 95°48E **241** G5
Tharrawaw *Burma* 17°41N 95°28E **241** G5
Tharthār, Buḥayrat ath *Iraq* 34°0N 43°15E **213** E10
Tharthar, L. = Tharthār, Buḥayrat ath *Iraq* 34°0N 43°15E **213** E10
Tharthār, W. ath → *Iraq* 34°32N 43°4E **213** E10
Thasopoula *Greece* 40°49N 24°45E **203** F8
Thasos *Greece* 40°40N 24°40E **203** F8
That Khe *Vietnam* 22°16N 106°28E **228** F6
Thatcher *Ariz., U.S.A.* 32°51N 109°46W **305** K9
Thatcher *Colo., U.S.A.* 37°33N 104°7W **305** H11
Thaton *Burma* 16°55N 97°22E **241** G6
Thatta *Pakistan* 24°42N 67°55E **242** G2
Thau, Bassin de *France* 43°23N 3°36E **174** E7
Thaungdut *Burma* 24°30N 94°40E **241** C5
Thawatti *Burma* 19°32N 96°16E **241** F6
Thayawthadangy Kyun *Burma* 12°19N 98°0E **236** F1
Thayer *U.S.A.* 36°31N 91°33W **308** G8
Thayetmyo *Burma* 19°20N 95°10E **241** F5
Thazi *Magway, Burma* 19°59N 95°3E **241** F5
Thazi *Mandalay, Burma* 21°0N 96°5E **241** E6
Thbeng Meanchey *Cambodia* 13°49N 104°58E **236** F5
The Bahamas ■ *N. Amer.* 24°0N 75°0W **321** B5
The Broads *U.K.* 52°45N 1°30E **168** E9
The Everglades *U.S.A.* 25°50N 81°0W **317** K9
The Gambia ■ *W. Afr.* 13°25N 16°0W **262** C1
The Gulf = Persian Gulf *Asia* 27°0N 50°0E **247** E6
The Hague = 's-Gravenhage *Neths.* 52°7N 4°17E **170** B4
The Pas *Canada* 53°45N 101°15W **297** C8
The Wash *U.K.* 52°58N 0°20E **168** E8
The Weald *U.K.* 51°4N 0°20E **169** F8
Thebes = Thiva *Greece* 38°19N 23°19E **204** C5
Thebes *Egypt* 25°40N 32°35E **256** B3
Thedford *U.S.A.* 41°59N 100°35W **308** E3
Thebine *Australia* 25°57S 152°34E **281** D5
Thègon *Burma* 18°39N 95°25E **241** F5
Thekulthili L. *Canada* 61°3N 110°0W **297** A7
Thelon → *Canada* 64°16N 96°4W **297** A8
Thénezay *France* 46°44N 0°2W **172** F6
Thenon *France* 45°9N 1°4E **174** C5
Theodore *Queens., Australia* 24°55S 150°3E **280** C5
Theodore *Sask., Canada* 51°26N 102°55W **297** C8
Theodore *Ala., U.S.A.* 30°33N 88°10W **315** F10
Theodore Roosevelt △ *U.S.A.* 47°0N 103°25W **308** B2
Theodore Roosevelt L. *U.S.A.* 33°40N 111°10W **305** K8
Thepha *Thailand* 6°52N 100°58E **237** J3
Thérain → *France* 49°15N 2°27E **173** C9
Therandë *Kosovo* 42°21N 20°50E **202** D4
Theresa *U.S.A.* 44°13N 75°48W **313** B9
Theressa *U.S.A.* 29°50N 82°4W **316** F7
Therma = Eagle Nest *U.S.A.* 36°33N 105°16W **305** H11
Thermaïkos Kolpos *Greece* 40°15N 22°45E **202** F6
Thermopolis *U.S.A.* 43°39N 108°13W **304** E9
Thermopylæ *Greece* 38°48N 22°35E **204** C4
Thesprotia *Greece* 39°27N 20°22E **204** B2
Thessalon *Canada* 46°20N 83°30W **298** C3
Thessalonica, Gulf of = Thermaïkos Kolpos *Greece* 40°15N 22°45E **202** F6
Thessaloniki *Greece* 40°38N 22°58E **202** F6
Thessaloniki ✕ (SKG) *Greece* 40°30N 23°0E **202** F7
Thessaly □ *Greece* 39°25N 22°0E **204** B4
Thetford *U.K.* 52°25N 0°45E **169** E8
Thetford Mines *Canada* 46°8N 71°18W **299** C5
Thethi △ *Albania* 42°24N 19°46E **202** D3
Theun → *Laos* 18°19N 104°0E **236** C5
Theunissen *S. Africa* 28°26S 26°43E **270** C4
Thevenard *Australia* 32°9S 133°38E **281** E1
Thiais *France* 48°46N 2°23E **134** B3
Thiamis → *Greece* 39°15N 20°6E **204** B2
Thibaud *Dominica* 15°36N 61°24W **323** k
Thiberville *France* 49°8N 0°27E **172** C7
Thibodaux *U.S.A.* 29°48N 90°49W **315** G9
Thicket Portage *Canada* 55°19N 97°42W **297** B9
Thief River Falls *U.S.A.* 48°7N 96°10W **308** A5
Thiel Mts. *Antarctica* 85°15S 91°0W **151** E16
Thiene *Italy* 45°42N 11°29E **199** C8
Thiérache *France* 49°51N 3°45E **173** C10
Thiers *France* 45°52N 3°33E **174** C7
Thiès *Senegal* 14°50N 16°51W **262** C1
Thiès □ *Senegal* 14°45N 16°50W **262** C1
Thiesi *Italy* 40°31N 8°43E **200** B1
Thika *Kenya* 1°1S 37°5E **268** C4
Thille-Boubacar *Senegal* 16°31N 15°5W **262** B1
Thimân, W. → *Egypt* 28°4N 33°45E **251** K4
Thimphu *Bhutan* 27°31N 89°45E **241** B2
Thina → *S. Africa* 31°18S 29°13E **271** D4
Thinadhoo *Maldives* 0°32N 72°56E **272** d
Thingangyun *Burma* 16°49N 96°12E **241** G6
Þingeyjarsýsla *Iceland* 65°40N 16°30W **155** B10
Þingeyri *Iceland* 65°52N 23°30W **155** B3
Þingmúli *Iceland* 65°2N 14°37W **155** B12
Þingvallavatn *Iceland* 64°11N 21°9W **155** C5
Þingvellir *Iceland* 64°15N 21°7W **155** C5
Þingvellir △ *Iceland* 64°16N 21°5W **155** C5
Thio *N. Cal.* 21°37S 166°14E **288** d
Thionville *France* 49°20N 6°10E **173** C13
Thira = Santorini *Greece* 36°23N 25°27E **205** E7
Thirasia *Greece* 36°26N 25°21E **205** E7
Third Cataract *Sudan* 19°42N 30°20E **256** D3
Thirsk *U.K.* 54°14N 1°19W **168** C6
Thiruvananthapuram *India* 8°41N 77°0E **245** K3
Thiruvarur *India* 10°46N 79°38E **245** J4
Thisio *Athens, Greece* **112** c1
Thisted *Denmark* 56°58N 8°40E **163** H2
Þistilfjörður *Iceland* 66°18N 15°24W **155** A11
Thistle I. *Australia* 35°0S 136°8E **282** C2
Thistletown *Canada* 43°44N 79°34W **141** A1
Thitgy *Burma* 18°15N 96°13E **241** F6
Thithia = Cicia *Fiji* 17°45S 179°18W **287** A3
Thitpokpin *Burma* 19°24N 95°58E **241** F5
Thitu I. *S. China Sea* 11°3N 114°17E **230** B4
Thiva *Greece* 38°19N 23°19E **204** C5
Thiviers *France* 45°25N 0°54E **174** C4
Þjórsá → *Iceland* 63°47N 20°48W **155** D6
Thlewiaza → *Canada* 60°29N 94°40W **297** A10
Thmar Puok *Cambodia* 13°57N 103°4E **236** F4
Tho Chu, Dao *Vietnam* 9°20N 103°28E **237** H4
Tho Vinh *Vietnam* 19°16N 105°42E **236** C5
Thoa → *Canada* 60°31N 109°47W **297** A7
Thoen *Thailand* 17°43N 99°12E **236** D2
Thoeng *Thailand* 19°41N 100°12E **236** C3
Thomas *U.S.A.* 35°45N 98°45W **314** D5
Thomas, L. *Australia* 26°4S 137°58E **281** D2
Thomas Circle *Washington, D.C., U.S.A.* **143** a1
Thomas Hill Res. *U.S.A.* 39°34N 92°39W **310** E4
Thomas Hubbard, C. *Canada* 82°0N 94°25W **295** A13
Thomaston *U.S.A.* 32°53N 84°20W **316** C5
Thomastown *Australia* 37°40S 145°2E **128** A2
Thomasville *Ala., U.S.A.* 31°55N 87°44W **315** F11
Thomasville *Ga., U.S.A.* 30°50N 83°59W **316** E6
Thomasville *N.C., U.S.A.* 35°53N 80°5W **315** D14
Thompson *Man., Canada* 55°45N 97°52W **297** B9
Thompson *Pa., U.S.A.* 41°52N 75°31W **313** E9
Thompson → *B.C., Canada* 50°15N 121°24W **296** C4
Thompson → *Mo., U.S.A.* 39°46N 93°37W **310** E3
Thompson Falls *U.S.A.* 47°36N 115°21W **304** C6
Thompson I. *U.S.A.* 42°19N 70°59W **116** B3
Thompson Pk. *U.S.A.* 41°0N 123°2W **304** F2
Thompson Sd. *N.Z.* 45°8S 166°46E **285** F1
Thompson Springs *U.S.A.* 38°58N 109°43W **304** G9
Thompsontown *U.S.A.* 40°33N 77°14W **312** F7
Thomson *Ga., U.S.A.* 33°28N 82°30W **316** B7
Thomson *Ill., U.S.A.* 41°58N 90°6W **310** C6
Thomson → *Australia* 25°11S 142°53E **280** C3
Thomson's Falls = Nyahururu *Kenya* 0°2N 36°27E **268** B4
Thon Buri *Thailand* 13°45N 100°29E **113** B1
Thônes *France* 45°54N 6°18E **175** C10
Thong Yang *Thailand* 9°28N 99°56E **237** b
Thongwa *Burma* 16°45N 96°33E **241** G6
Thonon-les-Bains *France* 46°22N 6°29E **173** F13
Thonze *Burma* 17°38N 95°47E **241** G5
Thoothukudi = Tuticorin *India* 8°50N 78°12E **245** K4
Thorez *Ukraine* 48°4N 38°34E **189** H10
Þórisjökull *Iceland* 64°32N 20°43W **155** C6
Þórisvatn *Iceland* 64°20N 18°55W **155** C8
Þórkötlustaðir *Iceland* 63°50N 22°24W **155** D4
Þorlákshöfn *Iceland* 63°51N 21°22W **155** D5
Thorn = Toruń *Poland* 53°2N 18°39E **185** E5
Thornaby on Tees *U.K.* 54°33N 1°18W **168** C6
Thornbury *Vic., Australia* 37°44S 145°1E **128** A2
Thornbury *Ont., Canada* 44°34N 80°26W **312** B4
Thornbury *N.Z.* 46°17S 168°9E **285** G3
Thorncliffe *Canada* 43°42N 79°20W **141** A2
Thorne *U.K.* 53°37N 0°57W **168** D7
Thornhill *Canada* 43°48N 79°25W **141** A2
Thornton *Ont., Canada* 44°16N 79°43W **312** B5
Thornton *Western Cape, S. Africa* 33°55S 18°32E **118** A2
Thornton *Colo., U.S.A.* 39°52N 104°58W **304** G11
Thornton *Iowa, U.S.A.* 42°57N 93°23W **310** B3
Thornton Heath *U.K.* 51°23N 0°6W **125** B3
Thorntown *U.S.A.* 40°8N 86°36W **311** D10
Thorold *Canada* 43°7N 79°12W **312** C5
Thorpes *Barbados* 13°9N 59°37W **323** r
Þórshöfn *Iceland* 66°12N 15°20W **155** A11
Thouarcé *France* 47°17N 0°30W **172** E6
Thouars *France* 47°0N 0°15W **172** F6
Thoubal *India* 24°38N 94°1E **241** C5
Thouet → *France* 47°17N 0°6W **172** E6
Thouin, C. *Australia* 20°20S 118°10E **278** D2
Thousand Islands *U.S.A.* 44°20N 76°0W **313** B9
Thousand Oaks *U.S.A.* 34°10N 118°50W **307** L8
Thrace *Europe* 41°0N 27°0E **203** F10
Thrace, Sea of *Greece* 40°30N 25°0E **203** F8
Thredbo *Australia* 36°31S 148°20E **283** D8
Three Fathoms Cove *Hong Kong, China* 22°25N 114°16E **122** A3
Three Forks *U.S.A.* 45°54N 111°33W **304** D8
Three Gorges Dam *China* 30°45N 111°15E **229** B8
Three Gorges Res. = Sanxia Shuiku *China* 30°3N 107°58E **228** B6
Three Hills *Canada* 51°43N 113°15W **296** C6
Three Hummock I. *Australia* 40°25S 144°55E **281** G3
Three Oaks *U.S.A.* 41°48N 86°36W **311** C10
Three Pagodas Pass *Asia* 15°20N 98°30E **236** E2
Three Points, C. *Ghana* 4°42N 2°6W **262** E4
Three Rivers *Calif., U.S.A.* 36°26N 118°54W **306** J8
Three Rivers *Mich., U.S.A.* 41°57N 85°38W **311** C11
Three Rivers *Tex., U.S.A.* 28°28N 98°11W **314** G5
Three Sisters Is. *Solomon Is.* 10°10S 161°57E **287** N11
Three Springs *Australia* 29°32S 115°45E **279** E2
Threipmuir Res. *U.K.* 55°51N 3°19W **121** B2
Thrissur *India* 10°30N 76°18E **245** J3
Throg's Neck *U.S.A.* 40°48N 73°49W **132** B3
Throssell, L. *Australia* 27°33S 124°10E **279** E3
Throssell Ra. *Australia* 22°3S 121°43E **278** D3
Thrumshing △ *Bhutan* 27°25N 90°50E **241** B3
Thrushton △ *Australia* 27°47S 147°40E **281** D4
Thu Dau Mot *Vietnam* 10°58N 106°39E **237** G6
Thua → *Kenya* 1°31S 39°30E **268** C4
Thuamal Rampur *India* 19°23N 82°56E **244** E6
Thuan Hoa *Vietnam* 8°58N 105°30E **237** H5
Thubun Lakes *Canada* 61°30N 112°0W **297** A6
Thueyts *France* 44°41N 4°9E **175** D8
Thugga = Dougga *Tunisia* 36°25N 9°13E **258** A1
Thuin *Belgium* 50°20N 4°17E **170** D4
Thuir *France* 42°38N 2°45E **174** F6
Thule = Qaanaaq *Greenland* 77°30N 69°10W **154** B4
Thule Air Base = Uummannaq *Greenland* 77°33N 68°52W **154** B4
Thun *Switz.* 46°45N 7°38E **179** J3
Thunder B. *U.S.A.* 45°0N 83°20W **312** B1
Thunder Bay *Canada* 48°20N 89°15W **298** C2
Thunderbolt *U.S.A.* 32°3N 81°4W **316** C8
Thunersee *Switz.* 46°43N 7°39E **179** J3
Thung Salaeng Luang △ *Thailand* 16°43N 100°50E **236** D3
Thung Song *Thailand* 8°10N 99°40E **237** H2
Thungyai △ *Thailand* 15°20N 98°55E **236** E2
Thunkar *Bhutan* 27°55N 91°0E **241** B3
Thuong Tra *Vietnam* 16°2N 107°42E **236** D6
Thur → *Switz.* 47°32N 9°10E **179** H5
Thurgau □ *Switz.* 47°34N 9°10E **179** H5
Thüringen □ *Germany* 51°0N 11°0E **178** D7
Thüringer Wald *Germany* 50°35N 11°0E **178** E6
Thuringowa △ *Australia* 19°18S 146°43E **280** B4
Thurles *Ireland* 52°41N 7°49W **166** D4
Thurn P. *Austria* 47°20N 12°25E **180** D5
Thurrock □ *U.K.* 51°31N 0°23E **169** F8
Thursday I. *Australia* 10°30S 142°3E **280** A3
Thurso *Qué., Canada* 45°36N 75°15W **298** C4
Thurso *Highl., U.K.* 58°36N 3°32W **167** C5
Thurso → *U.K.* 58°36N 3°32W **167** C5
Thurston I. *Antarctica* 72°0S 100°0W **151** D16
Thury-Harcourt *France* 48°59N 0°30W **172** D6
Thutade L. *Canada* 57°0N 126°55W **296** B3
Thy *Denmark* 56°52N 8°25E **163** H2
Thy △ *Denmark* 56°55N 8°25E **163** H2
Thyborøn *Denmark* 56°42N 8°12E **163** H2
Þykkvabæjarklaustur *Iceland* 63°30N 18°22W **155** D8
Þykkvibær *Iceland* 63°45N 20°37W **155** D6
Thyolo *Malawi* 16°7S 35°5E **269** F4
Thyssen-Bornemisza, Museo *Madrid, Spain* **127** b3
Ti-n-Amzi → *Niger* 18°20N 4°32E **263** B5
Ti-n-Barraouene, O. → *Africa* 18°40N 4°5E **261** E5
Ti-n-Rerhoh *Algeria* 20°40N 4°2E **261** D5
Ti-n-Tanetfirt *Algeria* 24°49N 3°48E **261** D5
Ti-n-Tarabine, O. → *Algeria* 21°16N 7°25E **261** D6
Ti-n-Toumma *Niger* 16°4N 12°40E **259** E2
Ti-n-Zaouatene *Algeria* 19°55N 2°55E **261** E5
Ti-Tree *Australia* 22°5S 133°22E **280** C1
Tiadiaye *Senegal* 14°25N 16°40W **262** C1
Tiahuanaco *Bolivia* 16°33S 68°42W **330** D4
Tian Shan *Asia* 40°30N 76°0E **217** D9
Tian Tan Buddha = Big Buddha *Hong Kong, China* 22°15N 113°54E **122** B1
Tian'anmen Square *Beijing, China* **114** c2
Tianchang *China* 32°40N 119°0E **229** A12
Tiancun *China* 39°54N 116°12E **114** B1
Tiandeng *China* 23°6N 107°7E **228** F6
Tiandong *China* 23°36N 107°8E **228** F6
Tian'e *China* 25°1N 107°9E **228** E6
Tianguá *Brazil* 3°44S 40°59W **332** B3
Tianhe *Guangdong, China* 23°8N 113°20E **121** B2
Tianhe *Guangxi Zhuangzu, China* 24°48N 108°40E **228** E7
Tianjin *China* 39°7N 117°12E **227** E9
Tianjin Shi □ *China* 39°8N 117°12E **227** E9
Tianjun *China* 38°0N 98°30E **218** D8
Tiankoura *Burkina Faso* 10°47N 3°17W **262** C4
Tianlin *China* 24°21N 106°12E **228** E6
Tianmen *China* 30°39N 113°9E **229** B9
Tianquan *China* 30°7N 102°43E **228** B4
Tianshifu *China* 41°17N 124°22E **224** B2
Tianshui *China* 34°32N 105°40E **226** G3
Tiantai *China* 29°10N 121°2E **229** C13
Tiantan Park *Beijing, China* **114** c3
Tianya *China* 18°18N 109°20E **229** a
Tianyang *China* 23°42N 106°53E **228** F6
Tianyar *Indonesia* 8°12S 115°30E **231** J18
Tianzhen *China* 40°24N 114°5E **226** D8
Tianzhong = T'ienchung *Taiwan* 23°52N 120°35E **225** C2
Tianzhu *China* 26°54N 109°11E **228** D7
Tianzhuangtai *China* 40°43N 122°5E **227** D12
Tiarei *Tahiti* 17°32S 149°20W **289** e
Tiaret *Algeria* 35°20N 1°21E **261** A5
Tiaret □ *Algeria* 34°30N 1°30E **261** B5
Tías *Canary Is.* 28°57N 13°39W **153** e2
Tiassalé *Ivory C.* 5°58N 4°57W **262** D4
Tibagi *Brazil* 24°30S 50°24W **335** A5
Tibagi → *Brazil* 22°47S 51°1W **335** A5
Tībastī, Sarīr *Libya* 22°50N 18°30E **258** D3
Tibati *Cameroon* 6°22N 12°30E **263** D7
Tibe *Ethiopia* 9°2N 37°12E **257** F4
Tiber = Tevere → *Italy* 41°44N 12°14E **199** G9
Tiber Res. *U.S.A.* 48°19N 111°6W **304** B8
Tiberias = Teverya *Israel* 32°47N 35°32E **250** F6
Tiberias, L. = Yam Kinneret *Israel* 32°45N 35°35E **250** F6
Tibesti *Chad* 21°0N 17°30E **259** D3
Tibet = Xizang Zizhiqu □ *China* 32°0N 88°0E **218** E6
Tibet, L. *U.S.A.* 28°27N 81°31W **133** B1
Tibet, Plateau of *Asia* 32°0N 86°0E **210** E10
Tibiao *Phil.* 11°17N 122°2E **233** F4
Tibidabo *Spain* 41°25N 2°6E **114** A2
Tibiri *Niger* 13°34N 7°4E **263** C6
Ţibleş, Vf. *Romania* 47°32N 24°15E **183** C9
Ţibleşului, Munţii *Romania* 47°38N 24°5E **183** C9
Tibnī *Syria* 35°36N 39°50E **213** E8
Tibooburra *Australia* 29°26S 142°1E **281** D3
Tibrikot *Nepal* 29°3N 82°48E **243** E10
Tibro *Sweden* 58°28N 14°10E **163** F8
Tiburon *U.S.A.* 37°52N 122°27W **136** A2
Tiburón, I. *Mexico* 29°0N 112°25W **318** B2
Tiburtino *Italy* 41°53N 12°30E **136** B2
Ticao I. *Phil.* 12°31N 123°42E **232** E4
Tice *U.S.A.* 26°40N 81°49W **317** J8
Tichît *Mauritania* 18°21N 9°29W **262** B3
Tichla *Mauritania* 21°36N 14°58W **260** D2
Ticho *Ethiopia* 7°50N 39°32E **257** F4
Ticino □ *Switz.* 46°20N 8°45E **179** J4
Ticino → *Italy* 45°9N 9°14E **198** C6
Ticleni *Romania* 44°53N 23°24E **183** F8
Ticomán *Mexico* 19°31N 99°8W **128** A2
Ticonderoga *U.S.A.* 43°51N 73°26W **313** C11
Ticul *Mexico* 20°24N 89°32W **319** C7
Tidaholm *Sweden* 58°12N 13°58E **163** F7
Tidal Basin *Washington, D.C., U.S.A.* **143** c1
Tidan *Sweden* 58°34N 14°1E **163** F8
Tiddim *Burma* 23°28N 93°45E **241** D4
Tiden *India* 7°15N 93°33E **245** L11
Tideridjaouine, Adrar *Algeria* 22°0N 2°15E **261** D5
Tidikelt *Algeria* 26°58N 1°30E **261** C5
Tidioute *U.S.A.* 41°41N 79°24W **312** E5
Tidjikja *Mauritania* 18°29N 11°35W **262** B2
Tidmore = Seminole *U.S.A.* 35°14N 96°41W **314** D6
Tidore *Indonesia* 0°40N 127°25E **231** D7
Tiébissou *Ivory C.* 7°9N 5°10W **262** D3
Tiéboro *Chad* 21°20N 17°7E **259** D3
Tiefa *China* 42°28N 123°26E **224** A1
Tiefensee *Germany* 52°24N 13°5E **115** B1
Tiegang Shuiku *China* 22°37N 113°53E **219** a
Tiel *Neths.* 51°53N 5°26E **170** C5
Tiel *Senegal* 14°55N 15°5W **262** C1
Tieli *China* 46°57N 128°3E **219** B14
Tieling *China* 42°20N 123°55E **224** A1
Tielt *Belgium* 51°0N 3°20E **170** C3
Tiemenguan *China* 41°49N 85°39E **217** D11
Tien Shan = Tian Shan *Asia* 40°30N 76°0E **217** D9
Tien-tsin = Tianjin *China* 39°7N 117°12E **227** E9
Tien Yen *Vietnam* 21°20N 107°24E **236** B6
T'ienching = Tianjin *China* 39°7N 117°12E **227** E9
T'ienchung *Taiwan* 23°52N 120°35E **225** C2
Tienen *Belgium* 50°48N 4°57E **170** D4
Tiéngbé *Ivory C.* 8°11N 5°43W **262** D3
Tientsin = Tianjin *China* 39°7N 117°12E **227** E9
Tiergarten *Germany* 52°31N 13°20E **115** A3
Tieri *Australia* 23°2S 148°21E **280** C4
Tierp *Sweden* 60°20N 17°30E **162** D11
Tierra Amarilla *Chile* 27°28S 70°18W **334** B1
Tierra Amarilla *N. Mex., U.S.A.* 36°42N 106°33W **305** H10
Tierra Colorada *Mexico* 17°11N 99°32W **319** D5
Tierra de Barros *Spain* 38°40N 6°30W **195** G4
Tierra de Campos *Spain* 42°10N 4°50W **194** C6
Tierra del Fuego □ *Argentina* 54°0S 67°45W **336** D3
Tierra del Fuego, I. Grande de *Argentina* 54°0S 69°0W **336** D3
Tierra del Fuego △ *Argentina* 54°50S 68°23W **336** D3
Tierradentro *Colombia* 2°35N 76°2W **328** C2
Tierralta *Colombia* 8°11N 76°4W **328** B2
Tiétar → *Spain* 39°50N 6°1W **194** F4
Tieté → *Brazil* 20°40S 51°35W **335** A5
Tifarati *W. Sahara* 26°9N 10°33W **260** C2
Tiffin *U.S.A.* 41°7N 83°11W **311** C13
Tiffin → *U.S.A.* 41°17N 84°23W **311** C12
Tiflèt *Morocco* 33°54N 6°20W **260** B3
Tiflis = Tbilisi *Georgia* 41°43N 44°50E **191** K7
Tifton *U.S.A.* 31°27N 83°31W **316** D6
Tifu *Indonesia* 3°39S 126°24E **231** E7
Tiga, Î. *N. Cal.* 21°7S 167°49E **288** d
Tiga Res. *Nigeria* 11°35N 8°30E **263** C6
Tigalda I. *U.S.A.* 54°6N 165°5W **303** J6
Tigaon *Phil.* 13°38N 123°30E **232** E4
Tigbauan *Phil.* 10°41N 122°27E **233** F4
Tiger Leaping Gorge = Hutiao Xia *China* 27°13N 100°9E **228** D3
Tigharghar, Adrar *Mali* 19°30N 1°13E **263** B5
Tighina = Bendery *Moldova* 46°50N 29°30E **183** D14
Tigil *Russia* 57°49N 158°40E **215** D16
Tigiria *India* 20°29N 85°31E **244** D7
Tignall *U.S.A.* 33°52N 82°44W **316** B7
Tignish *Canada* 46°58N 64°2W **299** C7
Tigray □ *Ethiopia* 13°35N 39°15E **257** E4
Tigre → *Peru* 4°30S 74°10W **328** D3
Tigre → *Venezuela* 9°20N 62°30W **329** B5
Tigre, Pta. de *Venezuela* 11°5N 64°11W **329** a
Tigris = Dijlah, Nahr → *Asia* 31°0N 47°25E **246** D5
Tiguentourine *Algeria* 27°52N 9°8E **261** C6
Tigveni *Romania* 45°10N 24°31E **183** E9
Tigyaing *Burma* 23°45N 96°10E **241** D6
Tigzerte, O. → *Morocco* 28°10N 9°37W **260** C3
Tîh, Gebel el *Egypt* 29°32N 33°26E **256** B3
Tihodaine, Erg de *Algeria* 25°15N 7°15E **261** C6
Tihwa = Ürümqi *China* 43°45N 87°45E **217** D11
Tiilikka △ *Finland* 63°40N 28°15E **160** E23
Tijara *India* 27°56N 76°31E **242** F7
Tijgerhof *S. Africa* 33°53S 18°30E **118** A2
Tījī *Libya* 32°0N 11°18E **258** B2
Tijuana *Mexico* 32°32N 117°1W **307** N9
Tijuca *Brazil* 22°56S 43°13W **135** B1
Tijuca, Pico da *Brazil* 22°56S 43°15W **135** B1
Tijuca △ *Brazil* 22°56S 43°14W **135** B1
Tikahau *French Polynesia* 15°0S 148°10W **289** f
Tikal *Guatemala* 17°13N 89°24W **320** C2
Tikamgarh *India* 24°44N 78°50E **243** G8
Tikaré *Burkina Faso* 13°15N 1°43W **263** C4
Tikchik Lakes *U.S.A.* 60°0N 159°0W **303** G8
Tikéi *French Polynesia* 14°58S 144°32W **289** f
Tikhonkaya = Birobidzhan *Russia* 48°50N 132°50E **219** B15
Tikhoretsk *Russia* 45°56N 40°5E **191** H5
Tikhvin *Russia* 59°35N 33°30E **188** C7
Tikirarjuaq = Whale Cove *Canada* 62°10N 92°34W **297** A10
Tikkadouine, Adrar *Algeria* 24°28N 1°30E **261** D5
Tikkurila *Finland* 60°17N 25°2E **121** B3
Tikmehdash *Iran* 37°16N 46°54E **213** D12
Tiko *Cameroon* 4°4N 9°20E **263** E6
Tikopia *Pac. Oc.* 12°19S 168°49E **277** C12
Tikrīt *Iraq* 34°35N 43°37E **213** E10
Tiksi *Russia* 71°40N 128°45E **215** B13
Tilā' al 'Alī *Jordan* 32°0N 35°52E **251** G6
Tiladummati Atoll *Maldives* 7°0N 73°20E **272** d
Tilak Nagar *India* 28°38N 77°5E **120** B1
Tilamuta *Indonesia* 0°32N 122°23E **231** D6
Tilanqiao *China* 31°15N 121°29E **138** B1
Tilburg *Neths.* 51°31N 5°6E **170** C5
Tilbury *Ont., Canada* 42°17N 82°23W **312** D2
Tilbury *Essex, U.K.* 51°27N 0°22E **169** F8
Tilcara *Argentina* 23°36S 65°23W **334** A2
Tilden *U.S.A.* 42°3N 97°50W **308** D5
Tilemsi, Vallée du *Mali* 17°42N 0°15E **263** B5
Tilhar *India* 28°0N 79°45E **243** F8
Tilia, O. → *Algeria* 27°32N 0°55E **261** C5
Tilichiki *Russia* 60°27N 166°5E **215** C17
Tililane *Algeria* 27°49N 0°6W **261** C4
Tilin *Burma* 21°41N 94°6E **241** E5
Tilissos *Greece* 35°20N 25°1E **207** E6
Till → *U.K.* 55°41N 2°13W **168** B5
Tillabéri *Niger* 14°28N 1°28E **263** C5
Tillamook *U.S.A.* 45°27N 123°51W **304** D2
Tillanchong I. *India* 8°30N 93°37E **245** K11
Tillberga *Sweden* 59°40N 16°39E **162** E10
Tillia *Niger* 16°8N 4°47E **263** B5
Tillman *U.S.A.* 32°28N 81°6W **316** C8
Tillsonburg *Canada* 42°53N 80°44W **312** D4
Tillyeria *Cyprus* 35°6N 32°40E **207** E8
Tilogne *Senegal* 16°0N 13°40W **262** B2
Tilos *Greece* 36°27N 27°27E **205** E9
Tilpa *Australia* 30°57S 144°24E **282** A6
Tilrhemt *Algeria* 33°9N 3°22E **261** B5
Tilsit = Sovetsk *Russia* 55°6N 21°50E **184** C8
Tilt → *U.K.* 56°46N 3°51W **167** E5
Tilton *U.S.A.* 43°27N 71°36W **313** C13
Tiltonsville *U.S.A.* 40°10N 80°41W **312** F4
Tim *Denmark* 56°12N 8°19E **163** H2
Tima *Egypt* 26°54N 31°25E **256** B3
Timah, Bukit *Singapore* 1°21N 103°46E **138** A2
Timanah *Asia* 19°0N 41°0E **248** C3
Timanfaya △ *Canary Is.* 29°0N 13°46W **153** e2
Timanskiy Kryazh *Russia* 65°58N 50°5E **186** A9
Timaru *N.Z.* 44°23S 171°14E **285** E6
Timashevo *Russia* 53°22N 51°9E **190** D10
Timashevsk *Russia* 45°35N 39°0E **191** H4
Timau *Kenya* 0°4N 37°15E **268** B4
Timbaki *Greece* 35°4N 24°45E **207** E5
Timbaúba *Brazil* 7°31S 35°19W **332** C4
Timbedgha *Mauritania* 16°17N 8°16W **262** B3
Timber Creek *Australia* 15°40S 130°29E **278** C5
Timber Lake *U.S.A.* 45°26N 101°5W **308** C3
Timber Mt. *U.S.A.* 37°6N 116°28W **306** H10
Timbío *Colombia* 2°20N 76°40W **328** C2
Timbiqui *Colombia* 2°46N 77°42W **328** C2
Timbo *Guinea* 10°35N 11°50W **262** C2
Timbo *Liberia* 5°35N 9°45W **262** D3
Timboon *Australia* 38°30S 142°58E **282** E5
Timbué, Ponta *Mozam.* 18°47S 36°22E **269** F4
Timbuktu = Tombouctou *Mali* 16°50N 3°0W **262** B4
Timdjaouine *Algeria* 21°37N 4°30E **261** D5
Timéiaouine *Algeria* 20°27N 1°50E **261** D5
Timellouline *Algeria* 29°22N 8°55E **261** C6
Times Square *New York, U.S.A.* **132** c2
Timétrine *Mali* 19°19N 0°34W **263** B4
Timétrine, Mts. *Mali* 19°25N 1°0W **263** B4
Timfi Oros *Greece* 39°59N 20°45E **204** B2
Timfristos, Oros *Greece* 38°57N 21°50E **204** C3
Timgad *Algeria* 35°29N 6°28E **261** A6
Timhadit *Morocco* 33°15N 5°4W **260** B3
Timi *Cyprus* 34°44N 32°31E **207** F8
Timia *Niger* 18°4N 8°40E **259** E1
Timika *Indonesia* 4°47S 136°32E **231** E9
Timimoun *Algeria* 29°14N 0°16E **261** C5
Timimoun, Sebkha de *Algeria* 28°50N 0°46E **261** C5
Timiris, Râs *Mauritania* 19°21N 16°30W **262** B1
Timiryazev Park *Russia* 55°49N 37°33E **129** B2
Timiș = Tamis → *Serbia* 44°51N 20°39E **182** F5
Timiș □ *Romania* 45°40N 21°30E **182** E6
Timiskaming, L. = Témiscamingue, L. *Canada* 47°10N 79°25W **298** C4
Timișoara *Romania* 45°43N 21°15E **182** E6
Timmersdala *Sweden* 58°32N 13°46E **163** F7
Timmins *Canada* 48°28N 81°25W **298** C3
Timmonsville *U.S.A.* 34°8N 79°57W **316** A10
Timok → *Serbia* 44°10N 22°40E **202** B6
Timoleague *Ireland* 51°39N 8°46W **166** E3
Timon *Brazil* 5°8S 42°52W **332** C3
Timor *Asia* 9°0S 125°0E **231** F7
Timor Leste = East Timor ■ *Asia* 8°50S 126°0E **231** F7
Timor Sea *Ind. Oc.* 12°0S 127°0E **278** B4

Timrå Sweden 62°29N 17°18E 162 B11
Timucuan ⌂ U.S.A. 30°28N 81°27W 316 E8
Tîn, Ra's at Libya 32°37N 23°8E 258 B4
Tin Alkoum Algeria 24°42N 10°17E 261 D7
Tin Amzi, O. → Algeria 18°20N 4°32E 261 D6
Tin Atanai Algeria 25°52N 1°37E 261 C5
Tin Can Bay Australia 25°56S 153°0E 281 D5
Tin Can I. Nigeria 6°26N 3°21E 124 B2
Tin Ethisane Mali 19°3N 0°52W 263 B4
Tin Gornai Mali 16°38N 0°38W 263 B4
Tin Mt. U.S.A. 36°50N 117°10W 306 J9
Tin Shui Wai China 22°28N 114°0E 219 a
Tina = Thina → S. Africa 31°18S 29°13E 271 D4
Tîna, Khalîg el Egypt 31°10N 32°40E 251 G3
Tinaca Pt. Phil. 5°30N 125°25E 233 J5
Tinaco Venezuela 9°42N 68°26W 328 B4
Tinajo Canary Is. 29°4N 13°42W 153 e2
Tinca Romania 46°46N 21°58E 182 D6
Tindal Australia 14°31S 132°22E 278 B5
Tindivanam India 12°15N 79°41E 245 H4
Tindouf Algeria 27°42N 8°10W 260 C3
Tindouf □ Algeria 27°25N 5°50W 260 C3
Tinée → France 43°55N 7°11E 175 E11
Tineo Spain 43°21N 6°27W 194 B4
Tinerhir Morocco 31°29N 5°31W 260 B3
Tinfouchi Algeria 28°52N 5°49W 260 C3
Tinfunque △ Paraguay 23°55S 60°17W 334 A3
Ting Jiang → China 24°45N 116°35E 229 E11
Ting Kau Hong Kong, China 22°22N 114°4E 122 A2
Tinggi, Pulau Malaysia 2°18N 104°7E 237 L5
Tinghert, Ḥamâdat Libya 29°0N 11°0E 258 C2
Tingi Mts. S. Leone 8°55N 10°47W 262 D2
Tingkan Taiwan 23°48N 120°52E 225 C2
Tingkawk Sakan Burma 26°4N 96°44E 241 B6
Tinglayan Phil. 17°15N 121°9E 232 C3
Tinglev Denmark 54°57N 9°13E 163 K3
Tingmerkpuk Mt. U.S.A. 68°34N 162°28W 303 B7
Tingo Maria Peru 9°10S 75°54W 330 B2
Tingrela Ivory C. 10°27N 6°25W 262 C3
Tingri China 28°34N 86°38E 218 F6
Tingsryd Sweden 56°31N 15°0E 163 H9
Tingstäde Sweden 57°44N 18°37E 163 G12
Tingvoll Norway 62°55N 8°12E 164 B5
Tingwon Group Papua N. G. 2°37S 149°42E 286 B5
Tinh Bien Vietnam 10°36N 104°57E 237 G5
Tinharé, I. de Brazil 13°30S 38°58W 333 D4
Tinian N. Marianas 15°0N 145°38E 302 e
Tinian Channel N. Marianas 14°54N 145°36E 302 e
Tinigua △ Colombia 2°30N 74°8W 328 C3
Tiniguiban Phil. 11°22N 119°30E 233 F2
Tinjar → Malaysia 4°4N 114°18E 235 B4
Tinkisso → Guinea 11°21N 9°10W 262 C3
Tinn = Atrå Norway 59°59N 8°45E 164 E5
Tinnevelly = Tirunelveli India 8°45N 77°45E 245 K3
Tinnoset Norway 59°43N 9°3E 164 E6
Tinnsjå Norway 59°55N 8°54E 164 E5
Tinogasta Argentina 28°5S 67°32W 334 B2
Tinos Greece 37°33N 25°8E 205 D7
Tiñoso, C. Spain 37°32N 1°6W 197 H3
Tinpahar India 24°59N 87°44E 243 G12
Tinputz Papua N. G. 5°35S 155°0E 286 C8
Tinrhert, Plateau du Algeria 29°30N 9°0E 258 C1
Tinsukia India 27°29N 95°20E 241 B5
Tinta Peru 14°3S 71°20W 330 C3
Tintamarre, Île St.-Martin 18°7N 63°2W 322 a
Tintâne Mauritania 16°18N 10°10W 262 B2
Tintina Argentina 27°2S 62°45W 334 B3
Tintinara Australia 35°48S 140°2E 282 C4
Tintioulé Guinea 10°13N 9°12W 262 C3
Tinto → Spain 37°12N 6°55W 195 H4
Tinui N.Z. 40°52S 176°5E 284 G5
Tinwald N.Z. 43°55S 171°43E 285 D6
Tiobraid Árann = Tipperary Ireland 52°28N 8°10W 166 D3
Tioga N. Dak., U.S.A. 48°24N 102°56W 308 A2
Tioga Pa., U.S.A. 41°55N 77°8W 312 E7
Tioman, Pulau Malaysia 2°50N 104°10E 237 L5
Tione di Trento Italy 46°2N 10°43E 198 B7
Tionesta U.S.A. 41°30N 79°28W 312 E5
Tior South Sudan 6°26N 31°11E 257 F3
Tiouliline Algeria 27°1N 0°2W 261 C4
Tipaza Algeria 36°35N 2°26E 261 A5
Tipaza □ Algeria 36°35N 2°25E 261 A5
Tipitapa Nic. 12°12N 86°5W 320 D2
Tipp City U.S.A. 39°58N 84°11W 311 E12
Tippecanoe → U.S.A. 40°30N 86°45W 311 D10
Tipperary Ireland 52°28N 8°10W 166 D3
Tipperary □ Ireland 52°37N 7°55W 166 D4
Tipton Calif., U.S.A. 36°4N 119°19W 306 J7
Tipton Ind., U.S.A. 40°17N 86°2W 311 D10
Tipton Iowa, U.S.A. 41°46N 91°8W 310 C5
Tipton Mo., U.S.A. 38°39N 92°47W 310 F4
Tipton Mt. U.S.A. 35°32N 114°12W 307 K12
Tiptonville U.S.A. 36°23N 89°29W 315 C10
Tiptur India 13°15N 76°26E 245 H3
Tiquié → Brazil 0°5N 68°25W 328 C4
Tiquina Bolivia 16°13S 68°50W 330 D4
Tira West Bank 31°52N 35°7E 123 A1
Tiracambu, Serra do Brazil 3°15S 46°30W 332 B2
Tirad Pass △ Phil. 17°3N 120°38E 232 C3
Tirahart, O. → Algeria 23°45N 3°10E 261 D5
Tīrān Iran 32°45N 51°8E 247 C6
Tīrān Si. Arabia 27°57N 34°32E 251 L5
Tīrān, Madīq Egypt 27°55N 34°30E 251 L5
Tiranë Albania 41°18N 19°49E 202 E3
Tiranë ✈ (TIA) Albania 41°57N 19°42E 202 E3
Tirano Italy 46°13N 10°10E 198 B7
Tirari Desert Australia 28°22S 138°7E 281 D2
Tiraspol Moldova 46°55N 29°35E 183 D14
Tirat Zevi Israel 32°26N 35°31E 251 F6
Tiratimine Algeria 25°56N 3°37E 261 C5
Tirau N.Z. 37°58S 175°46E 284 D4
Tirdout Mali 16°7N 1°5W 263 B4
Tire Turkey 38°5N 27°45E 205 C9
Tirebolu Turkey 40°58N 38°45E 213 B8
Tiree U.K. 56°31N 6°55W 167 E2
Tiree, Passage of U.K. 56°30N 6°30W 167 E2
Tîrgovişte = Târgovişte Romania 44°55N 25°27E 183 F10
Tîrgu Jiu = Târgu Jiu Romania 45°5N 23°19E 183 E8
Tîrgu Mureş = Târgu Mureş Romania 46°31N 24°38E 183 D9
Tirgua △ Venezuela 10°5N 68°48W 328 A4
Tirich Mir Pakistan 36°15N 71°55E 240 A3
Tiriolo Italy 38°57N 16°30E 201 D9
Tiririca, Serra da Brazil 17°6S 47°6W 333 E2
Tiriro Guinea 10°27N 8°40W 262 C3
Tiris Zemmour □ Mauritania 24°0N 9°0W 260 D3
Tiritiri o te Moana = Southern Alps N.Z. 43°41S 170°11E 285 D5
Tirna → India 18°4N 76°57E 244 E3
Tírnavos Greece 39°45N 22°18E 204 B4
Tirodi India 21°40N 79°44E 244 D4
Tirol □ Austria 47°3N 10°43E 180 D3
Tiros Brazil 19°0S 45°58W 333 E2
Tirrukkovil Sri Lanka 7°7N 81°51E 245 L5
Tirsa Egypt 29°57N 31°12E 117 B2
Tirschenreuth Germany 49°53N 12°19E 179 F8
Tirschtiegel = Trzciel Poland 52°23N 15°50E 185 F2
Tirso → Italy 39°53N 8°32E 200 C1
Tirstrup Denmark 56°18N 10°42E 163 H4
Tirtagangga Indonesia 8°24S 115°35E 231 J18
Tirthahalli India 13°42N 75°14E 245 H2
Tirua Pt. N.Z. 38°25S 174°40E 284 E3
Tiruchchendur India 8°30N 78°11E 245 K4
Tiruchchirappalli India 10°45N 78°45E 245 J4
Tirukkoyilur India 11°57N 79°12E 245 J4
Tirumangalam India 9°49N 77°58E 245 K3
Tirumayam India 10°14N 78°45E 245 J4
Tirunelveli India 8°45N 77°45E 245 K3
Tirupati India 13°39N 79°25E 245 H4
Tiruppattur Tamil Nadu, India 10°8N 78°37E 245 J4
Tiruppattur Tamil Nadu, India 12°30N 78°30E 245 H4
Tiruppur India 11°5N 77°22E 245 J3
Tirur India 10°54N 75°55E 245 J2
Tiruttani India 13°11N 79°58E 245 H4
Tirutturaippundi India 10°32N 79°41E 245 J4
Tiruvadaimarudur India 11°2N 79°27E 245 J4
Tiruvalla India 9°23N 76°34E 245 K3
Tiruvallar India 13°9N 79°57E 245 H4
Tiruvannamalai India 12°15N 79°5E 245 H4
Tiruvettipuram India 12°39N 79°33E 245 H4
Tiruvottiyur India 13°10N 80°22E 245 H5
Tis Issat Ethiopia 11°25N 37°45E 257 E4
Tisa India 32°50N 76°9E 242 C7
Tisa → Serbia 45°15N 20°17E 182 E5
Tisdale Canada 52°50N 104°0W 297 C8
Tishomingo U.S.A. 34°14N 96°41W 314 D6
Tishrīyaa Iraq 33°18N 44°24E 113 B2
Tisjön Sweden 60°56N 13°0E 162 D7
Tisnaren Sweden 58°58N 15°56E 163 F9
Tišnov Czechia 49°21N 16°25E 181 B9
Tisovec Slovakia 48°41N 19°56E 181 C12
Tissamaharama Sri Lanka 6°17N 81°17E 245 L5
Tissemsilt Algeria 35°35N 1°50E 261 A5
Tissemsilt □ Algeria 35°45N 1°45E 261 A5
Tissint Morocco 29°57N 7°16W 260 C3
Tista → India 25°23N 89°43E 241 C2
Tistedal Norway 59°8N 11°27E 164 E8
Tisza = Tisa → Serbia 45°15N 20°17E 182 E5
Tiszaföldvár Hungary 46°58N 20°14E 182 D5
Tiszafüred Hungary 47°38N 20°50E 182 C5
Tiszalök Hungary 48°1N 21°20E 182 B6
Tiszavasvári Hungary 47°58N 21°18E 182 C6
Tit Ahaggar, Algeria 23°0N 5°10E 261 D6
Tit Tademait, Algeria 27°0N 1°29E 261 C5
Tit-Ary Russia 71°55N 127°2E 215 B13
Titabar India 26°36N 94°12E 241 B5
Titaguas Spain 39°53N 1°6W 196 F3
Titao Burkina Faso 13°45N 2°5W 263 C4
Titel Serbia 45°10N 20°18E 182 E5
Tithwal Pakistan 34°21N 73°50E 243 B5
Titicaca, L. S. Amer. 15°30S 69°30W 330 D4
Titikaveka Cook Is. 21°16S 159°45W 289 h
Titisee Germany 47°54N 8°10E 179 H4
Titira Hd. N.Z. 43°36S 169°25E 285 D4
Titiut Burma 18°54N 95°16E 241 F5
Titiwa Nigeria 12°14N 12°53E 263 C7
Titlagarh India 20°15N 83°11E 244 D6
Tito Italy 40°35N 15°40E 201 B8
Titograd = Podgorica Montenegro 42°30N 19°19E 202 D3
Titova Korenica Croatia 44°45N 15°41E 199 D12
Titu Romania 44°39N 25°32E 183 F10
Titule Dem. Rep. of the Congo 3°15N 25°31E 268 B2
Titusville Fla., U.S.A. 28°37N 80°49W 317 G9
Titusville Pa., U.S.A. 41°38N 79°41W 312 E5
Tiu Keng Leng Hong Kong, China 22°18N 114°15E 122 B3
Tivaouane Senegal 14°56N 16°45W 262 C1
Tivat Montenegro 42°28N 18°43E 202 D2
Tivedens △ Sweden 58°45N 14°35E 163 F8
Tiverton Ont., Canada 44°16N 81°32W 312 B3
Tiverton Devon, U.K. 50°54N 3°29W 169 G4
Tivoli Grenada 12°10N 61°37W 323 q
Tivoli Italy 41°58N 12°45E 199 G9
Tiwanaku = Tiahuanaco Bolivia 16°33S 68°42W 330 D4
Tiwī Oman 22°45N 59°12E 249 B7
Tiwi ✪ Australia 11°33S 130°42E 278 B5
Tiyo Eritrea 14°41N 40°15E 257 E5
Tizapán Mexico 19°19N 99°13W 128 C1
Tizga Morocco 32°1N 5°9W 260 B3
Ti'zi N'Isli Morocco 32°28N 5°47W 260 B3
Tizi-Ouzou Algeria 36°42N 4°3E 261 A5
Tizi-Ouzou □ Algeria 36°35N 4°5E 261 A5
Tizimín Mexico 21°9N 88°9W 319 C7
Tiznados → Venezuela 8°16N 67°47W 328 B4
Tiznap He → China 38°21N 77°26E 217 E9
Tiznit Morocco 29°48N 9°45W 260 C3
Tjæreborg Denmark 55°28N 8°36E 163 J2
Tjällmo Sweden 58°43N 15°21E 163 F9
Tjeggelvas Sweden 66°37N 17°45E 160 C17
Tjieggelvas = Tjeggelvas Sweden 66°37N 17°45E 160 C17
Tjirebon = Cirebon Indonesia 6°45S 108°32E 235 D3
Tjirrkarli ✪ Australia 26°0S 125°28E 279 E4
Tjluring Indonesia 8°25S 114°13E 231 J17
Tjøme Norway 59°8N 10°26E 164 E7
Tjörn Sweden 58°0N 11°35E 163 F5
Tjukayirla Roadhouse Australia 27°9S 124°34E 279 E3
Tjurabalan ✪ Australia 19°50S 128°0E 278 C4
Tkibuli = Tqibuli Georgia 42°26N 43°0E 191 J6
Tkvarcheli = Tqvarcheli Georgia 42°47N 41°42E 191 J5
Tlacotalpan Mexico 18°37N 95°40W 319 D5
Tlahualilo de Zaragoza Mexico 26°7N 103°27W 318 B4
Tlalnepantla → Mexico 19°30N 99°18W 128 A1
Tlalpan Mexico 19°18N 99°10W 128 C2
Tlaquepaque Mexico 20°39N 103°19W 318 C4
Tlaxcala Mexico 19°19N 98°14W 319 D5
Tlaxcala □ Mexico 19°25N 98°10W 319 D5
Tlaxiaco Mexico 17°25N 97°35W 319 D5
Tlemcen Algeria 34°52N 1°21W 261 B4
Tlemcen □ Algeria 34°38N 1°30W 261 B4
Tleta Sidi Bouguedra Morocco 32°16N 9°59W 260 B3
Tlokweng Botswana 24°40S 25°58E 270 B4
Tlumach Ukraine 48°51N 25°0E 183 B10
Tłuszcz Poland 52°25N 21°25E 185 F8
Tlyarata Russia 42°9N 46°26E 191 J8
Tmassah Libya 26°19N 15°51E 258 C3
To Bong Vietnam 12°45N 109°16E 236 F7
To Kwa Wan Hong Kong, China 22°18N 114°11E 122 B3
To-Shima Japan 34°31N 139°17E 223 C11
Toa Payoh Singapore 1°20N 103°51E 138 A3
Toad → Canada 59°25N 124°57W 296 B4
Toad River Canada 58°51N 125°14W 296 B3
Toamasina Madag. 18°10S 49°25E 272 B2
Toay Argentina 36°43S 64°38W 334 D3
Toba China 31°19N 97°42E 228 B1
Toba Japan 34°30N 136°51E 223 C8
Toba, Danau Indonesia 2°30N 98°30E 234 B1
Toba Kakar Pakistan 31°30N 69°0E 242 D3
Toba Tek Singh Pakistan 30°55N 72°25E 242 D5
Tobago Trin. & Tob. 11°10N 60°30W 323 s
Tobarra Spain 38°37N 1°44W 197 G3
Tobelo Indonesia 1°45N 127°56E 231 D7
Tobercurry Ireland 54°3N 8°44W 166 B3
Tobermory Ont., Canada 45°12N 81°40W 312 A3
Tobermory Argyll & Bute, U.K. 56°38N 6°5W 167 E2
Tobi Palau 2°40N 131°10E 231 D8
Tobi-Shima Japan 41°12N 139°34E 220 D9
Tobias Fornier = Dao Phil. 10°30N 121°57E 233 F3
Tobiishi Hana Iwo Jima 24°45N 141°17E 288 b
Tobin, L. Australia 21°45S 125°49E 278 D4
Tobin L. Canada 53°35N 103°30W 297 C8
Toblach = Dobbiaco Italy 46°44N 12°14E 199 B9
Toboali Indonesia 3°0S 106°25E 234 C3
Tobol → Russia 58°10N 68°12E 214 D7
Toboli Indonesia 0°38S 120°5E 231 E6
Tobolsk Russia 58°15N 68°10E 214 D7
Tobor Senegal 12°40N 16°15W 262 C1
Toboso Phil. 10°43N 123°31E 233 F4
Tobruk = Tubruq Libya 32°7N 23°55E 258 B4
Tobyhanna U.S.A. 41°11N 75°25W 313 E9
Tobyl = Tobol → Russia 58°10N 68°12E 214 D7
Tobyl Kazakhstan 52°41N 62°34E 216 B6
Tocache Nuevo Peru 8°9S 76°26W 330 B2
Tocantínia Brazil 9°33S 48°22W 332 C2
Tocantinópolis Brazil 6°20S 47°25W 332 C2
Tocantins □ Brazil 10°0S 48°0W 332 D2
Tocantins → Brazil 1°45S 49°10W 332 B2
Toccoa U.S.A. 34°35N 83°19W 315 D13
Toce → Italy 45°56N 8°29E 198 C5
Tochi → Pakistan 32°49N 70°41E 242 C4
Tochigi Japan 36°25N 139°45E 223 A11
Tochigi □ Japan 36°45N 139°45E 223 A11
Tocina Spain 37°37N 5°44W 195 H5
Töcksfors Sweden 59°31N 11°52E 162 E5
Točná Czechia 49°58N 14°25E 135 C2
Toco Chile 22°5S 69°35W 330 E4
Toco Trin. & Tob. 10°49N 60°57W 323 t
Toco Hills U.S.A. 33°49N 84°20W 113 B2
Toconao Chile 23°11S 68°1W 334 A2
Tocopilla Chile 22°5S 70°10W 334 A1
Tocqueville = Râs el Oued Algeria 35°57N 5°2E 261 A6
Tocumwal Australia 35°51S 145°31E 283 C6
Tocuyo → Venezuela 11°3N 68°23W 328 A4
Tocuyo de la Costa Venezuela 11°2N 68°23W 328 A4
Todalen Norway 62°49N 8°44E 164 B5
Todd → Australia 24°52S 135°48E 280 C2
Todds Road Trin. & Tob. 10°28N 61°20W 323 t
Toddu Atoll Maldives 4°25N 72°57E 272 d
Todeli Indonesia 1°40S 124°29E 231 E6
Todenyang Kenya 4°35N 35°56E 268 B4
Todgarh India 25°42N 73°58E 242 G5
Todi Italy 42°47N 12°24E 199 F9
Todos os Santos, B. de Brazil 12°48S 38°38W 333 D4
Todos Santos Mexico 23°26N 110°13W 318 C2
Todt Hill U.S.A. 40°36N 74°6W 132 D1
Todtnau Germany 47°49N 7°56E 179 H3
Toe Hd. U.K. 57°50N 7°8W 167 D1
Toecé Burkina Faso 11°50N 1°16W 263 C4
Toetoes B. N.Z. 46°42S 168°41E 285 G3
Tofield Canada 53°25N 112°40W 296 C6
Tofino Canada 49°11N 125°55W 296 D3
Töfsingdalen △ Sweden 62°10N 12°28E 162 B6
Tofte Norway 59°33N 10°34E 164 E7
Tofua Tonga 19°45S 175°5W 287 P13
Toga Vanuatu 13°26S 166°42E 287 C4
Tōgane Japan 35°33N 140°22E 223 B12
Togba Mauritania 17°26N 10°12W 262 B2
Togbo C.A.R. 6°0N 17°27E 264 A3
Togdheer □ Somalia 9°20N 45°25E 267 C6
Togdheer → Somalia 6°26N 48°39E 267 C6
Togiak U.S.A. 59°4N 160°24W 303 G7
Togiak Nat. Wildlife Refuge ⌂ U.S.A. 59°20N 160°15W 303 G7
Togian, Kepulauan Indonesia 0°20S 121°50E 231 E6
Togliatti Russia 53°32N 49°24E 190 D9
Togo ■ W. Afr. 8°30N 1°35E 263 D5
Togo Wichale Somalia 9°22N 43°40E 267 C5
Tögrög Mongolia 47°25N 92°13E 217 C12
Togtoh China 40°15N 111°10E 226 D6
Tohiea, Mt. Moorea 17°33S 149°49W 289 e
Tohma → Turkey 38°29N 38°23E 212 C8
Tōhoku □ Japan 39°50N 141°45E 220 E10
Töhöm Mongolia 44°27N 108°2E 226 B5
Tohopekaliga, East L. U.S.A. 28°18N 81°15W 317 G8
Tohopekaliga, L. U.S.A. 28°12N 81°24W 317 G8
Toi Cook Is. 18°57S 169°51W 289 g
Toi Japan 34°54N 138°47E 223 C10
Toibalewe India 10°32N 92°30E 245 J11
Toiny St.-Martin 17°53N 62°47W 322 a
Toinya South Sudan 6°17N 29°46E 257 F2
Toiyabe Range U.S.A. 39°30N 117°0W 304 G5
Tojikiston = Tajikistan ■ Asia 38°30N 70°0E 217 E8
Tōjō Japan 34°53N 133°16E 222 C5
Tok U.S.A. 63°20N 142°59W 303 E12
Toka Guyana 3°58N 59°17W 329 C6
Tokaanu N.Z. 38°58S 175°46E 284 E4
Tokachi-Dake Japan 43°17N 142°5E 220 C11
Tokachi-Gawa → Japan 42°44N 143°42E 220 C11
Tōkagi Japan 35°42N 139°55E 140 A4
Tokai Japan 35°2N 136°55E 223 B8
Tokai Plantation S. Africa 34°3S 18°24E 118 B1
Tōkaichiba Japan 35°31N 139°30E 140 B2
Tokaj Hungary 48°8N 21°27E 182 B6
Tokala Indonesia 1°30S 121°40E 231 E6
Tōkamachi Japan 37°8N 138°43E 221 F9
Tokanui N.Z. 46°34S 168°56E 285 G3
Tokar Sudan 18°27N 37°56E 256 D4
Tokara-Rettō Japan 29°37N 129°43E 221 K4
Tokarahi N.Z. 44°56S 170°39E 285 E5
Tokashiki-Shima Japan 26°11N 127°21E 221 L3
Tokat Turkey 40°22N 36°35E 212 B7
Tokat □ Turkey 40°15N 36°30E 212 B7
Tŏkch'ŏn N. Korea 39°45N 126°18E 224 C3
Tokdo = Liancourt Rocks Asia 37°15N 131°52E 221 F5
Tokeland U.S.A. 46°42N 123°59W 306 D3
Tokelau Is. ☑ Pac. Oc. 9°0S 171°45W 277 B16
Toki Japan 35°18N 137°8E 223 B9
Toki Pt. Wake I. 19°19N 166°35E 302 b
Tokmak Kyrgyzstan 42°49N 75°15E 217 D9
Tokmak Ukraine 47°16N 35°42E 189 J8
Toko Ra. Australia 23°5S 138°20E 280 C2
Tokomaru Bay N.Z. 38°8S 178°22E 284 E7
Tokoname Japan 34°53N 136°51E 223 C8
Tokoro-Gawa → Japan 44°7N 144°5E 220 B12
Tokoroa N.Z. 38°13S 175°50E 284 E4
Tokorozawa Japan 35°47N 139°28E 223 B11
Toksook Bay U.S.A. 60°32N 165°0W 303 F6
Toksun China 42°47N 88°38E 217 D11
Toktogul Kyrgyzstan 41°50N 72°50E 217 D8
Toku Tonga 18°10S 174°11W 287 P13
Tokuji Japan 34°11N 131°42E 222 C3
Tokuno-Shima Japan 27°56N 128°55E 221 L4
Tokushima Japan 34°4N 134°34E 222 C6
Tokushima □ Japan 33°55N 134°0E 222 D6
Tokuyama = Shunān Japan 34°3N 131°50E 222 C3
Tōkyō Japan 35°43N 139°45E 140 B3
Tōkyō □ Japan 35°40N 139°30E 223 B11
Tōkyō B. = Tōkyō-Wan Japan 35°25N 139°50E 140 B4
Tōkyō Haneda ✈ (HND) Japan 35°33N 139°46E 140 B3
Tōkyō Harbour Japan 35°38N 139°46E 140 B3
Tōkyō Narita ✈ (NRT) Japan 35°45N 140°25E 223 B12
Tōkyō Sky Tree Japan 35°42N 139°49E 140 A3
Tōkyō-Wan Japan 35°25N 139°50E 140 B4
Tokzār Afghan. 35°52N 66°26E 240 B2
Tol I. Micronesia 7°20N 151°37E 287 U17
Tolaga Bay N.Z. 38°21S 178°20E 284 E7
Tolageak U.S.A. 70°3N 162°27W 303 A7
Tolbo Mongolia 48°25N 90°17E 217 C12
Tolbukhin = Dobrich Bulgaria 43°37N 27°49E 203 C11
Tolé C.A.R. 6°34N 16°1E 264 A3
Töle Bī Kazakhstan 43°42N 73°46E 217 D8
Toledo Brazil 24°44S 53°45W 335 A5
Toledo Phil. 10°23N 123°38E 233 F4
Toledo Spain 39°50N 4°2W 194 F6
Toledo Ill., U.S.A. 39°16N 88°15W 311 E8
Toledo Iowa, U.S.A. 42°0N 92°35W 310 C4
Toledo Ohio, U.S.A. 41°39N 83°33W 311 C13
Toledo Oreg., U.S.A. 44°37N 123°56W 304 D2
Toledo Wash., U.S.A. 46°26N 122°51W 306 D4
Toledo, Montes de Spain 39°33N 4°20W 195 F6
Toledo Bend Res. U.S.A. 31°11N 93°34W 314 F8
Tolentino Italy 43°12N 13°17E 199 E10
Tolfa Italy 42°9N 11°56E 199 F8
Tolga Algeria 34°40N 5°22E 261 B6
Tolga Queens., Australia 17°15S 145°29E 280 B4
Tolga Hedmark, Norway 62°26N 11°1E 164 B8
Tolhuaca △ Chile 38°15S 71°50W 336 A2
Toli China 45°57N 83°37E 217 C10
Toliara Madag. 23°21S 43°40E 272 C1
Tolima Colombia 4°40N 75°19W 328 C2
Tolima □ Colombia 3°45N 75°15W 328 C2
Tolitoli Indonesia 1°5N 120°50E 231 D6
Tolkmicko Poland 54°19N 19°31E 184 D6
Tollarp Sweden 55°55N 13°58E 163 J7
Tollensesee Germany 53°30N 13°13E 178 B9
Tollhouse U.S.A. 37°1N 119°24W 306 H7
Tollygunge = Taliganga India 22°30N 88°22E 124 B2
Tolmachevo Russia 58°56N 29°51E 188 C5
Tolmezzo Italy 46°24N 13°1E 199 B10
Tolmin Slovenia 46°11N 13°45E 199 B10
Tolna Hungary 46°25N 18°48E 182 D3
Tolna □ Hungary 46°30N 18°30E 182 D3
Tolo Dem. Rep. of the Congo 2°55S 18°34E 264 C3
Tolo, Teluk Indonesia 2°20S 122°10E 231 E6
Tolo Harbour Hong Kong, China 22°25N 114°13E 122 A3
Tolochin = Talachyn Belarus 54°25N 29°42E 188 E5
Tolokiwa I. Papua N. G. 5°19S 147°37E 286 C4
Tolong B. Phil. 9°20N 122°49E 233 G4
Tolono U.S.A. 39°59N 88°16W 311 E8
Tolosa Spain 43°8N 2°5W 196 B2
Tolox Spain 36°41N 4°54W 195 J6
Toltén Chile 39°13S 74°14W 336 A2
Toluca México, Mexico 19°17N 99°40W 319 D5
Toluca Ill., U.S.A. 41°0N 89°8W 310 C7
Tolworth U.K. 51°22N 0°17W 125 B2
Tolyatti = Togliatti Russia 53°32N 49°24E 190 D9
Tom Burke S. Africa 23°5S 28°0E 271 B4
Tom Price Australia 22°40S 117°48E 278 D2
Toma Burkina Faso 12°45N 2°53W 262 C4
Tomah U.S.A. 43°59N 90°30W 308 D8
Tomahawk U.S.A. 45°28N 89°44W 308 C9
Tomai Moldova 46°34N 28°19E 183 D13
Tomakomai Japan 42°38N 141°36E 220 C10
Tomales U.S.A. 38°15N 122°53W 306 G4
Tomales B. U.S.A. 38°15N 123°58W 306 G3
Tomanivi Fiji 17°37S 178°1E 287 A2
Tomar Portugal 39°36N 8°25W 195 F2
Tomaros, Oros Greece 39°29N 20°48E 204 B2
Tomarza Turkey 38°27N 35°48E 212 C6
Tomás Barrón Bolivia 17°35S 67°31W 330 D4
Tomashevka Belarus 51°33N 23°36E 185 G10
Tomashpil Ukraine 48°32N 28°31E 183 B13
Tomaszów Lubelski Poland 50°27N 23°25E 185 H10
Tomaszów Mazowiecki Poland 51°30N 20°2E 185 G7
Tomatlán Mexico 19°56N 105°15W 318 D3
Tomb of the Kings Jerusalem 123 a2
Tombador, Serra do Brazil 12°0S 58°0W 331 C6
Tombe South Sudan 5°53N 31°40E 257 F3
Tombeau Bay Mauritius 20°6S 57°30E 272 e
Tombel Cameroon 4°45N 9°40E 264 B1
Tombigbee → U.S.A. 31°8N 87°57W 315 F11
Tomboco Angola 6°48S 13°18E 265 D2
Tombouctou Mali 16°50N 3°0W 262 B4
Tombouctou □ Mali 20°0N 3°0W 262 B4
Tombstone U.S.A. 31°43N 110°4W 305 L8
Tombua Angola 15°55S 11°55E 265 F2
Tomé Chile 36°36S 72°57W 334 D1
Tome Japan 38°40N 141°20E 220 E10
Tomé-Açu Brazil 2°25S 48°9W 332 B2
Tomelilla Sweden 55°33N 13°58E 163 J7
Tomelloso Spain 39°10N 3°2W 195 F7
Tomil Micronesia 9°31N 138°9E 287 R16
Tomil Harbor Pac. Oc. 9°30N 138°10E 287 R16
Tomingley Australia 32°26S 148°16E 283 B8
Tomini Indonesia 0°30N 120°30E 231 D6
Tomini, Teluk Indonesia 0°10S 121°0E 231 E6
Tominian Mali 13°17N 4°35W 262 C4
Tomiño = O Seixo Spain 41°59N 8°46W 194 D2
Tomintoul U.K. 57°15N 3°23W 167 D5
Tomioka Japan 36°15N 138°54E 223 A10
Tomislavgrad Bos.-H. 43°42N 17°13E 182 G2
Tomkinson Ranges Australia 26°11S 129°5E 279 E4
Tommot Russia 59°4N 126°20E 215 D13
Tommy Thompson Park Canada 43°38N 79°20W 141 B3
Tomnop Ta Suos Cambodia 11°20N 104°15E 237 G5
Tomo Colombia 2°38N 67°32W 328 C4
Tomo → Colombia 5°20N 67°48W 328 B4
Tomobe Japan 36°20N 140°20E 223 A12
Tomorri △ Albania 40°43N 20°8E 202 F4
Tomra Norway 62°34N 6°56E 164 B3
Toms Place U.S.A. 37°34N 118°41W 306 H8
Toms River U.S.A. 39°58N 74°12W 313 G10
Tomsk Russia 56°30N 85°5E 214 D9
Tomtabacken Sweden 57°30N 14°30E 163 G8
Tömük Turkey 36°42N 34°23E 250 B5
Tomür Feng = Pobedy, Pik Asia 42°0N 79°58E 217 D9
Tona Spain 41°51N 2°14E 196 D7
Tonalá Chiapas, Mexico 16°4N 93°45W 319 D6
Tonalá Jalisco, Mexico 20°37N 103°14W 318 C4
Tonale, Passo del Italy 46°16N 10°35E 198 B7
Tonami Japan 36°40N 136°58E 223 A8
Tonantins Brazil 2°45S 67°45W 328 D4
Tonasket U.S.A. 48°42N 119°26W 304 B4
Tonate Fr. Guiana 5°0N 52°28W 329 C7
Tonawanda U.S.A. 43°1N 78°53W 312 D6
Tonb U.A.E. 26°15N 55°15E 247 E7
Tonbo Burma 18°31N 95°5E 241 F5
Tonbridge U.K. 51°11N 0°17E 169 F8
Tonda Papua N. G. 8°55S 141°34E 286 E1
Tondabayashi Japan 34°30N 135°36E 223 C7
Tondano Indonesia 1°35N 124°54E 231 D6
Tondela Portugal 40°31N 8°5W 194 E2
Tønder Denmark 54°58N 8°50E 163 K2
Tondern = Tønder Denmark 54°58N 8°50E 163 K2
Tondi India 9°45N 79°4E 245 K4
Tondi Kiwindi Niger 14°28N 2°2E 263 C5
Tondibi Mali 16°39N 0°14W 263 B4
Tondo Phil. 14°36N 120°57E 127 B1
Tondoro Namibia 17°45S 18°50E 270 A2
Tone → Australia 34°25S 116°25E 279 F2
Tone-Gawa → Japan 35°44N 140°51E 223 B12
Tonekābon Iran 36°45N 51°12E 247 B6
Tong Fuk Hong Kong, China 22°14N 113°56E 122 B1
Tong I. Papua N. G. 2°3S 147°47E 286 B4
Tong Xian China 39°55N 116°35E 226 E9
Tong-yeong S. Korea 34°50N 128°20E 224 E4
Tonga Cameroon 4°58N 10°42E 264 B2
Tonga South Sudan 9°28N 31°3E 257 F3
Tonga ■ Pac. Oc. 19°50S 174°30W 287 P13
Tonga Trench Pac. Oc. 18°0S 173°0W 277 D16
Tongaat S. Africa 29°33S 31°9E 271 C5
Tongala Australia 36°14S 144°56E 283 D6
Tong'an China 24°37N 118°8E 229 E12
Tongareva = Penrhyn Cook Is. 9°0S 158°0W 289 H12
Tongariro, Mt. N.Z. 39°8S 175°38E 284 F4
Tongariro △ N.Z. 39°8S 175°33E 284 F4
Tongass Nat. Forest U.S.A. 54°45N 133°0W 303 J14
Tongatapu Tonga 21°10S 175°10W 287 Q13
Tongatapu Group Tonga 21°0S 175°0W 287 Q13
Tongbai China 32°20N 113°23E 229 A9
Tongbinggo S. Korea 37°31N 126°58E 137 B1
Tongcheng Anhui, China 31°4N 116°56E 229 B11
Tongcheng Hubei, China 29°15N 113°50E 229 C9
Tongchuan China 35°6N 109°3E 226 G5
Tongdao China 26°10N 109°42E 228 D7
Tongeren Belgium 50°47N 5°28E 170 D5
Tonggu China 28°31N 114°20E 229 C10
Tonggu Jiao China 22°22N 113°37E 219 a
Tongguan China 34°40N 110°25E 226 G6
Tonghai China 24°10N 102°53E 228 E4
Tonghua China 41°42N 125°58E 224 B2
Tongi = Tungi Bangla. 23°53N 90°24E 241 D3
Tongjiang Heilongjiang, China 47°40N 132°27E 219 B15
Tongjiang Sichuan, China 31°58N 107°11E 228 B6
Tongjosŏn-man N. Korea 39°30N 128°0E 224 C4
Tongking, G. of = Tonkin, G. of Asia 20°0N 108°0E 236 C7
Tongliang China 29°50N 106°3E 228 C6
Tongliao China 43°38N 122°18E 227 C12
Tongling China 30°55N 117°48E 229 B11
Tonglu China 29°45N 119°37E 229 C12
Tongnan = Anyue China 30°9N 105°50E 228 B5
Tongoa Vanuatu 16°54S 168°34E 287 F6
Tongobory Madag. 23°32S 44°20E 272 C1
Tongoy Chile 30°16S 71°31W 334 C1
Tongqiao China 31°21N 121°22E 138 A1
Tongquil I. Phil. 6°2N 121°51E 233 H3
Tongren Guizhou, China 27°43N 109°11E 228 D7
Tongren Qinghai, China 35°25N 102°5E 218 D9
Tongres = Tongeren Belgium 50°47N 5°28E 170 D5
Tongsa Dzong Bhutan 27°31N 90°31E 241 B3
Tongsha Tao Taiwan 26°12N 128°28E 225 b
Tongshi China 18°50N 109°20E 229 a
Tongue U.K. 58°29N 4°25W 167 C4
Tongue → U.S.A. 46°25N 105°52W 304 C11
Tongwei China 35°0N 105°5E 226 G3
Tongxiang China 30°39N 120°34E 229 B13
Tongxiao = T'unghsiao Taiwan 24°29N 120°40E 225 B2
Tongxin China 36°59N 105°58E 226 F3
Tongyang N. Korea 39°9N 126°53E 224 C3
Tongyu China 44°45N 123°4E 227 B12
Tongzhou China 32°12N 121°2E 229 A13
Tongzi China 28°9N 106°49E 228 C6
Tonica U.S.A. 41°13N 89°4W 310 C7
Tonj South Sudan 7°20N 28°44E 257 F2
Tonj → South Sudan 7°31N 28°55E 257 F2
Tonk India 26°6N 75°54E 242 F6
Tonkawa U.S.A. 36°41N 97°18W 314 C6
Tonkin = Bac Phan Vietnam 22°0N 105°0E 228 G5
Tonkin, G. of Asia 20°0N 108°0E 236 C7
Tonlé Sap Cambodia 13°0N 104°0E 236 F5
Tonnay-Charente France 45°56N 0°55W 174 C3
Tonneins France 44°23N 0°19E 174 D4
Tonnerre France 47°51N 3°59E 173 E10
Tönning Germany 54°19N 8°56E 178 A4
Tono Japan 39°19N 141°32E 220 E10
Tonoas I. Micronesia 7°22N 151°52E 287 T18
Tonopah U.S.A. 38°4N 117°14W 305 G5
Tonoshō Japan 34°29N 134°11E 222 C6
Tonosí Panama 7°20N 80°20W 320 E3
Tons → Haryana, India 30°30N 77°39E 242 D7
Tons → Ut. P., India 26°1N 83°33E 243 F10
Tønsberg Norway 59°19N 10°25E 164 E7
Tonsina U.S.A. 61°39N 145°11W 303 F11
Tonstad Norway 58°40N 6°45E 164 F3
Tonto ⌂ U.S.A. 33°39N 111°7W 305 K8
Tonumea Tonga 20°30S 174°30W 287 Q13
Tonya Turkey 40°53N 39°16E 213 B8
Tonzang Burma 23°36N 93°42E 241 D4
Tonzi Burma 24°39N 94°57E 241 C5
Toobanna Australia 18°42S 146°9E 280 B4
Toodyay Australia 31°34S 116°28E 279 F2
Tooele U.S.A. 40°32N 112°18W 304 F7
Toompine Australia 27°15S 144°19E 281 D3
Toomsboro U.S.A. 32°50N 83°5W 316 C6
Toora Australia 38°39S 146°23E 283 E7
Toora-Khem Russia 52°28N 96°17E 217 B13
Toorak Australia 37°50S 145°1E 128 B2
Tootias Somalia 3°57N 43°57E 267 D5
Toowoomba Australia 27°32S 151°56E 281 D5
Top Springs Australia 16°37S 131°51E 278 C5
Topalu Romania 44°31N 28°3E 183 F13
Topanga State Park ⌂ U.S.A. 34°7N 118°31W 126 B1
Topaz U.S.A. 38°41N 119°30W 306 G7
Topeka U.S.A. 39°3N 95°40W 308 F6
Topkapi Turkey 41°1N 28°59E 122 B1
Topkapi Palaca Turkey 41°1N 28°59E 122 B2
Topl'a → Slovakia 48°45N 21°45E 181 C14
Topley Canada 54°49N 126°18W 296 C3
Toplica → Serbia 43°15N 21°49E 202 C5
Toplița Romania 46°55N 25°20E 183 D10
Topo Azores 38°33N 27°45W 153 d1
Topo, Pta. do Azores 38°33N 27°46W 153 d1
Topocalma, Pta. Chile 34°10S 72°2W 334 C1
Topock U.S.A. 34°46N 114°29W 307 L12
Topola Serbia 44°17N 20°41E 202 B4
Topolčani Macedonia 41°14N 21°25E 202 E5
Topoľčany Slovakia 48°35N 18°12E 181 C11
Topolnitsa → Bulgaria 42°11N 24°18E 203 D8
Topolobampo Mexico 25°36N 109°3W 318 B3
Topoloveni Romania 44°49N 25°5E 183 F10
Topolovgrad Bulgaria 42°5N 26°20E 203 D10
Topolvățu Mare Romania 45°46N 21°41E 182 E6
Topozero, Ozero Russia 65°35N 32°0E 160 D25
Toppenish U.S.A. 46°23N 120°19W 304 C3
Topraisar Romania 44°1N 28°27E 183 F13
Toprakkale Turkey 37°5N 36°8E 250 A7
Topusko Croatia 45°18N 15°59E 199 C12
Toquepala Peru 17°24S 70°25W 330 D3
Toqyraūyn → Kazakhstan 46°48N 75°24E 217 C9
Tor di Quinto Italy 41°56N 12°27E 136 B1
Tor Pignattara Italy 41°53N 12°31E 136 B2
Tor Sapienza Italy 41°53N 12°35E 136 B2
Torà Spain 41°49N 1°25E 196 D6
Tora Kit South Sudan 11°2N 32°36E 257 E3
Toranomon Tokyo, Japan 140 c3
Torata Peru 17°23S 70°1W 330 D3
Torbali Turkey 38°10N 27°21E 205 C9
Torbat-e Heydārīyeh Iran 35°15N 59°12E 247 C8
Torbat-e Jām Iran 35°16N 60°35E 247 C9
Torbay Canada 47°40N 52°42W 299 C9
Torbay □ U.K. 50°26N 3°31W 169 G4
Tørberget Norway 61°8N 12°7E 164 C9
Torbjörntorp Sweden 58°12N 13°36E 163 F7
Torcy France 48°51N 2°39E 134 A4
Tordesillas Spain 41°30N 5°0W 194 D6
Töreboda Sweden 58°41N 14°7E 163 F8
Torekov Sweden 56°26N 12°37E 163 H6
Torellò Spain 42°3N 2°16E 196 C7
Toreno Spain 42°42N 6°30W 194 C4
Torfaen □ U.K. 51°43N 3°3W 169 F4
Torfajökull Iceland 63°54N 19°0W 155 D7
Torgau Germany 51°34N 13°0E 178 D8
Torgelow Germany 53°37N 14°1E 178 B10
Torghay Kazakhstan 49°38N 63°29E 216 C6
Torghay → Kazakhstan 48°1N 62°45E 216 C6
Torghay Ustirti Asia 51°0N 63°0E 216 B6
Torghay Zhylghasy Kazakhstan 52°0N 64°30E 216 B6
Torgovaya = Salsk Russia 46°28N 41°30E 191 G5
Torhamn Sweden 56°6N 15°50E 163 H9
Torhout Belgium 51°5N 3°7E 170 C3
Torhovytsya Ukraine 48°36N 25°26E 183 B10
Tori Ethiopia 7°53N 33°35E 257 F3
Tori-Shima Japan 30°29N 140°19E 221 J10
Torigni-sur-Vire France 49°3N 0°58W 172 C6
Torija Spain 40°44N 3°2W 196 E1
Torilla Pen. Australia 22°29S 150°5E 280 C5
Torino Italy 45°3N 7°40E 198 C4
Torit South Sudan 4°27N 32°31E 257 G3
Torkamān Iran 37°35N 47°23E 213 D12
Torkovichi Russia 58°51N 30°21E 188 C6
Tormac Romania 45°30N 21°30E 182 E6
Tormes → Spain 41°18N 6°29W 194 D4
Tornado Mt. Canada 49°55N 114°40W 296 D6
Tornaľa Slovakia 48°25N 20°20E 181 C13
Torneå = Tornio Finland 65°50N 24°12E 160 D21
Torneälven → Europe 65°50N 24°12E 160 D21
Torneträsk Sweden 68°24N 19°15E 160 B18
Torngat Mountains Nat. Park △ Canada 59°0N 63°40W 295 F19
Torngat Mts. Canada 59°0N 63°40W 295 F19
Tornio Finland 65°50N 24°12E 160 D21
Tornionjoki = Torneälven → Europe 65°50N 24°12E 160 D21
Tornquist Argentina 38°8S 62°15W 334 D3
Toro Baleares, Spain 39°59N 4°8E 206 B5
Toro Zamora, Spain 41°35N 5°24W 194 D5
Torö Sweden 58°48N 17°50E 163 F11
Toro, Cerro del Chile 29°10S 69°50W 334 B2
Toro ⌂ Uganda 1°5N 30°22E 268 C3
Toro Pk. U.S.A. 33°34N 116°24W 307 M10
Torodi Niger 13°7N 1°47E 263 C5
Torokina Papua N. G. 6°14S 155°3E 286 D8
Törökszentmiklós Hungary 47°11N 20°27E 182 C5
Toronto N.S.W., Australia 33°0S 151°30E 283 B9
Toronto Ont., Canada 43°39N 79°20W 141 B2
Toronto Ohio, U.S.A. 40°28N 80°36W 312 F4
Toronto, Univ. of Canada 43°39N 79°23W 141 B2
Toronto City Centre ✈ (YTZ) Canada 43°38N 79°24W 141 B2
Toronto Harbour Canada 43°38N 79°21W 141 B2
Toronto I. Canada 43°37N 79°23W 141 B2
Toronto Lester B. Pearson Int. ✈ (YYZ) Canada 43°46N 79°35W 141 A1
Toropets Russia 56°30N 31°40E 188 D6
Tororo Uganda 0°45N 34°12E 268 B3
Toros Dağları Turkey 37°0N 32°30E 250 B3
Toros Monumental, Templo de Barcelona, Spain 114 a3
Torotoro Bolivia 18°7S 65°46W 331 D4
Torotoro △ Bolivia 18°8S 65°46W 331 D4
Torpa India 22°57N 85°6E 243 H11
Torpo Norway 60°40N 8°43E 164 D5
Torquay Vic., Australia 38°20S 144°19E 282 E6
Torquay Torbay, U.K. 50°27N 3°32W 169 G4
Torquemada Spain 42°2N 4°19W 194 C6
Torrais, Pta. Azores 39°43N 31°7W 153 d2
Torrance U.S.A. 33°50N 118°20W 307 M8
Torrão Portugal 38°16N 8°11W 195 G2
Torre Annunziata Italy 40°45N 14°27E 201 B7
Torre de Moncorvo Portugal 41°12N 7°8W 194 D3
Torre del Campo Spain 37°46N 3°53W 195 H7
Torre del Greco Italy 40°47N 14°22E 201 B7
Torre del Mar Spain 36°44N 4°6W 195 J6
Torre Latino-Americana Mexico City, Mexico 128 b2
Torre Lupara Italy 41°59N 12°39E 136 B2
Torre Nova Italy 41°51N 12°36E 136 B2
Torre-Pacheco Spain 37°44N 0°57W 197 H4
Torre Pellice Italy 44°49N 7°13E 198 D4
Torreblanca Spain 40°14N 0°12E 196 E5
Torrecampo Spain 38°29N 4°41W 195 G6
Torrecilla en Cameros Spain 42°15N 2°38W 196 C2
Torredembarra Spain 41°9N 1°24E 196 D6
Torredonjimeno Spain 37°46N 3°57W 195 H7
Torrejón de Ardoz Spain 40°27N 3°29W 194 E7
Torrejoncillo Spain 39°54N 6°28W 194 F4
Torrelaguna Spain 40°50N 3°38W 194 E7
Torrelavega Spain 43°20N 4°5W 194 B6
Torrellas → Spain 41°23N 2°1E 114 A1
Torremaggiore Italy 41°41N 15°17E 199 G12
Torremolinos Spain 36°38N 4°30W 195 J6
Torrens, L. Australia 31°0S 137°50E 282 A2
Torrens Cr. → Australia 22°23S 145°9E 280 C4
Torrens Creek Australia 20°48S 145°3E 280 C4
Torrent Spain 39°27N 0°28W 197 F4
Torrenueva Spain 38°38N 3°22W 195 G7
Torreón Mexico 25°33N 103°26W 318 B4
Torreperogil Spain 38°2N 3°17W 195 G7
Torres Brazil 29°21S 49°44W 335 B5
Torres Mexico 28°46N 110°47W 318 B2
Torres, Is. Vanuatu 13°15S 166°37E 287 C4
Torres del Paine △ Chile 51°3S 72°58W 336 G2
Torres Novas Portugal 39°27N 8°33W 195 F2
Torres Strait Australia 9°50S 142°20E 280 a
Torres Vedras Portugal 39°5N 9°15W 195 F1
Torrevécchia Italy 41°55N 12°25E 136 B1
Torrevieja Spain 37°59N 0°42W 197 H4
Torrey U.S.A. 38°18N 111°25W 304 G8
Torricelli Mts. Papua N. G. 3°23S 142°15E 286 B2
Torridge → U.K. 51°0N 4°13W 169 G3
Torridon, L. U.K. 57°35N 5°50W 167 D3
Torrijos Phil. 13°19N 122°5E 233 E4
Torrijos Spain 39°59N 4°18W 194 F6
Tørring Denmark 55°52N 9°29E 163 J3
Torrington Conn., U.S.A. 41°48N 73°7W 313 E11
Torrington Wyo., U.S.A. 42°4N 104°11W 304 E11
Torroella de Montgrí Spain 42°2N 3°8E 196 C8
Torrox Spain 36°46N 3°57W 195 J7
Torsås Sweden 56°24N 16°0E 163 H10
Torsby Sweden 60°7N 13°0E 162 D6
Torshälla Sweden 59°25N 16°28E 162 E10
Tórshavn Færoe Is. 62°5N 6°56W 160 E9
Torslanda Sweden 57°44N 11°45E 163 G5
Torsö Sweden 58°48N 13°45E 163 F7
Tortola Br. Virgin Is. 18°19N 64°45W 321 C7
Tórtoles de Esgueva Spain 41°49N 4°2W 194 D6
Tórtoli Italy 39°55N 9°39E 200 C2
Tortona Italy 44°54N 8°52E 198 D5
Tortorici Italy 38°2N 14°49E 201 D7
Tortosa Spain 40°49N 0°31E 196 E5
Tortosa, C. Spain 40°41N 0°52E 196 E5
Tortosendo Portugal 40°15N 7°31W 194 E3
Tortue, Î. de la Haiti 20°5N 72°57W 321 B5
Tortuga Trin. & Tob. 10°22N 61°24W 323 t
Tortuguero △ Costa Rica 10°31N 83°29W 320 D3
Tortum Turkey 40°19N 41°35E 213 B9

Ţorūd Iran 35°25N 55°5E 247 C7
Torul Turkey 40°34N 39°18E 213 B8
Toruń Poland 53°2N 18°39E 185 E5
Torun Ukraine 48°40N 23°34E 183 B8
Tory Hill Canada 44°58N 78°16W 312 B6
Tory I. Ireland 55°16N 8°13W 166 A3
Torysa ➝ Slovakia 48°39N 21°21E 181 C14
Torzhok Russia 57°5N 34°55E 188 D8
Torzym Poland 52°19N 15°5E 185 F2
Tosa Japan 33°24N 133°23E 222 D5
Tosa-Shimizu Japan 32°52N 132°58E 222 E4
Tosa-Wan Japan 33°15N 133°30E 222 D5
Tosa-Yamada = Kami
Japan 33°36N 133°38E 222 D5
Toscana □ Italy 43°25N 11°0E 198 E8
Toscanella = Tuscánia
Italy 42°25N 11°52E 199 F8
Toscano, Arcipelago Italy 42°30N 10°30E 198 F7
Toshima Japan 35°43N 139°43E 140 A3
Toshimaen Japan 35°43N 139°38E 140 A2
Toshka Egypt 22°30N 31°53E 256 C3
Toshka, Buheirat en Egypt 22°50N 31°0E 256 C3
Toshkent Uzbekistan 41°20N 69°10E 217 D7
Toshkent □ Uzbekistan 41°0N 69°40E 217 D7
Tosno Russia 59°38N 30°46E 188 C6
Tossa de Mar Spain 41°43N 2°56E 196 D7
Tösse Sweden 58°58N 12°39E 163 F6
Tostado Argentina 29°15S 61°50W 334 B3
Tostedt Germany 53°17N 9°42E 178 B5
Tostón, Pta. de Canary Is. 28°42N 14°2W 153 e2
Tosu Japan 33°22N 130°31E 222 D2
Tosya Turkey 41°1N 34°2E 212 B6
Toszek Poland 50°27N 18°32E 185 H5
Totak Norway 59°40N 8°0E 164 E5
Totana Spain 37°45N 1°30W 197 H3
Totebo Sweden 57°38N 16°12E 163 G10
Toteng Botswana 20°22S 22°58E 270 B3
Tôtes France 49°41N 1°2E 172 C8
Tótkomlós Hungary 46°24N 20°45E 182 D5
Totland Norway 61°56N 5°23E 164 C2
Totma Russia 60°0N 42°40E 186 C7
Totnes U.K. 50°26N 3°42W 169 G4
Totness Suriname 5°53N 56°19W 329 B6
Toto Angola 7°9S 14°16E 265 D2
Toto Nigeria 8°26N 7°5E 263 D6
Totonicapán Guatemala 14°58N 91°12W 320 D1
Totora Bolivia 17°42S 65°9W 331 D4
Totoya, I. Fiji 18°57S 179°50W 287 B3
Totten Glacier Antarctica 66°45S 116°10E 151 C8
Tottenham N.S.W.,
Australia 32°14S 147°21E 283 B7
Tottenham Vic., Australia 37°48S 144°51E 128 A1
Tottenham Ont., Canada 44°1N 79°49W 312 B5
Tottenham London, U.K. 51°35N 0°4W 125 A3
Tottori Japan 35°30N 134°15E 222 B6
Tottori □ Japan 35°30N 134°12E 222 B6
Touâret Niger 20°17N 7°8E 261 D6
Touat Algeria 27°27N 0°30E 261 C5
Touba Ivory C. 8°22N 7°40W 262 D3
Touba Senegal 14°50N 15°55W 262 C1
Toubkal, Djebel Morocco 31°0N 8°0W 260 B3
Toubkal △ Morocco 31°0N 8°2W 260 B3
Touboro Cameroon 7°47N 15°22E 264 A3
T'ouch'eng Taiwan 24°52N 121°49E 225 B3
Toucy France 47°44N 3°15E 173 E10
T'oufen Taiwan 24°41N 120°54E 225 B2
Tougan Burkina Faso 13°11N 2°58W 262 C4
Touggourt Algeria 33°6N 6°4E 261 B6
Tougouri Burkina Faso 13°20N 0°30W 263 C4
Tougué Guinea 11°25N 11°50W 262 C2
Toukoto Mali 13°27N 9°52W 262 C3
Toul France 48°40N 5°53E 173 D12
Toulepleu Ivory C. 6°32N 8°24W 262 D3
Touliu Taiwan 23°42N 120°31E 225 C2
Toulon Var, France 43°10N 5°55E 175 E9
Toulon Ill., U.S.A. 41°6N 89°52W 310 C7
Toulouse France 43°37N 1°27E 174 E5
Toulouse Blagnac ✈ (TLS)
France 43°37N 1°22E 174 E5
Toulouse Street New Orleans, U.S.A. 131 b2
Toummo Niger 22°45N 14°8E 258 D2
Toummo, Mts. de Africa 22°43N 14°12E 258 D2
Toumodi Ivory C. 6°32N 5°4W 262 D3
Tounan Taiwan 23°41N 120°28E 225 C2
Tounassine, Hamada
Algeria 28°48N 5°0W 260 C4
Tounggoo Burma 19°0N 96°30E 241 F6
Toungo Nigeria 8°20N 12°3E 263 D7
Touques ➝ France 49°22N 0°8E 172 C7
Touraine France 47°20N 0°30E 172 E7
Touran = Tūrān △ Iran 35°45N 56°30E 247 C8
Tourane = Da Nang
Vietnam 16°4N 108°13E 236 D7
Tourcoing France 50°42N 3°10E 173 B10
Touriñán, C. Spain 43°3N 9°18W 194 B1
Tourine Mauritania 22°23N 11°50W 260 D2
Tournai Belgium 50°35N 3°25E 170 D3
Tournan-en-Brie France 48°44N 2°46E 173 D9
Tournay France 43°13N 0°13E 174 E4
Tournon-St-Martin France 46°45N 0°58E 172 F7
Tournon-sur-Rhône France 45°4N 4°50E 175 C8
Tournus France 46°35N 4°54E 173 F11
Touros Brazil 5°12S 35°28W 332 C4
Tours France 47°22N 0°40E 172 E7
Tousidé, Pic Chad 21°1N 16°29E 259 D3
Toussoro, Mt. C.A.R. 9°7N 23°14E 264 A4
Toussus-le-Noble France 48°44N 2°6E 134 B1
Toussus-le-Noble ✈ (TNF)
France 48°44N 2°6E 134 B1
Touws ➝ S. Africa 33°45S 21°11E 270 D3
Touwsrivier S. Africa 33°20S 20°2E 270 D3
Tovar Venezuela 8°20N 71°46W 328 B3
Tovarkovskiy Russia 53°40N 38°14E 188 F10
Tovdal Norway 58°47N 8°10E 164 F5
Tovdalselva ➝ Norway 58°11N 8°7E 164 F5
Tovste Ukraine 48°50N 25°44E 183 B10
Tovuz Azerbaijan 41°0N 45°40E 191 K7
Towada Japan 40°37N 141°13E 220 D10
Towada-Hachimantai △
Japan 40°20N 140°55E 220 D10
Towada-Ko Japan 40°28N 140°55E 220 D10
Towanda Ill., U.S.A. 40°36N 88°53W 311 D8
Towanda Pa., U.S.A. 41°46N 76°27W 313 E8
Towarri △ Australia 31°50S 150°37E 283 A9
Towchāl Cable Car Iran 35°49N 51°24E 141 A2
Tower U.S.A. 47°48N 92°17W 308 B7
Tower, I. = Genovesa, I.
Ecuador 0°20N 89°58W 330 a
Tower Bridge London, U.K. 125 b5
Tower Hamlets □ U.K. 51°32N 0°2W 125 A3
Tower of London U.K. 51°30N 0°4W 125 A3
Towerhill Cr. ➝
Australia 22°28S 144°35E 280 C3
Towner U.S.A. 48°21N 100°25W 308 A3
Townsend Ga., U.S.A. 31°33N 81°31W 316 D8
Townsend Mont., U.S.A. 46°19N 111°31W 304 C8
Townshend I. Australia 22°10S 150°31E 280 C5
Townsville Australia 19°15S 146°45E 280 B4
Towot South Sudan 6°12N 34°25E 257 F3
Towra Pt. Australia 34°0S 151°10E 139 C2
Towraghondī Afghan. 35°13N 62°16E 240 B1
Towson U.S.A. 39°24N 76°36W 309 F15
Towuti, Danau Indonesia 2°45S 121°32E 231 E6
Toxkan He ➝ China 41°8N 80°11E 217 D10
Tōya-Ko Japan 42°35N 140°51E 220 C10
Toyama Japan 36°40N 137°15E 223 A9
Toyama □ Japan 36°45N 137°30E 223 A9
Toyama-Wan Japan 37°0N 137°30E 221 F8
Toyapakeh Indonesia 8°41S 115°29E 231 K18
Tøyen Norway 59°55N 10°47E 133 A3
Tōyō Ehime, Japan 33°56N 133°5E 222 D5
Tōyō Kōchi, Japan 33°26N 134°16E 222 D6
Toyohara = Yuzhno-Sakhalinsk
Russia 46°58N 142°45E 219 B17
Toyohashi Japan 34°45N 137°25E 223 C9
Toyokawa Japan 34°48N 137°27E 223 C9
Toyonaka Japan 34°46N 135°28E 133 A1
Toyooka Japan 35°35N 134°48E 222 B6
Toyota Japan 35°3N 137°7E 223 B9
Toyoura Japan 34°6N 130°57E 222 C2
Tozeur Tunisia 33°56N 8°8E 258 B1
Tozeur □ Tunisia 34°0N 8°5E 261 B6
Tqibuli Georgia 42°26N 43°0E 191 J6
Tqvarcheli Georgia 42°47N 41°42E 191 J5
Trá Li = Tralee Ireland 52°16N 9°42W 166 D2
Trá Mhór = Tramore
Ireland 52°10N 7°10W 166 D4
Tra On Vietnam 9°58N 105°55E 237 H5
Tra Vinh Vietnam 9°50N 106°15E 237 H6
Trabancos ➝ Spain 41°36N 5°15W 194 D5
Traben-Trarbach Germany 49°57N 7°7E 179 F3
Trabzon Turkey 41°0N 39°45E 213 B8
Trabzon □ Turkey 41°10N 39°45E 213 B8
Tracadie Canada 47°30N 64°55W 299 C7
Trachenburg = Żmigród
Poland 51°28N 16°53E 185 G3
Tracy Qué., Canada 46°1N 73°9W 298 C5
Tracy Calif., U.S.A. 37°44N 121°26W 306 H5
Tracy Minn., U.S.A. 44°14N 95°37W 308 C6
Tradate Italy 45°43N 8°54E 198 C5
Trade Town Liberia 5°40N 9°50W 262 D3
Traer U.S.A. 42°12N 92°28W 310 B4
Trafalgar Vic., Australia 38°14S 146°12E 283 E7
Trafalgar Dominica 15°19N 61°21W 323 k
Trafalgar, C. Spain 36°10N 6°2W 195 J4
Trafalgar Square London, U.K. 125 b3
Trafaria Portugal 38°40N 9°13W 126 A1
Tragonhsi Greece 37°27N 25°29E 205 D7
Traian Brăila, Romania 45°11N 27°44E 183 E12
Traian Tulcea, Romania 45°2N 28°15E 183 E13
Traição, Cor. ➝ Brazil 23°35S 46°41W 137 B2
Traiguén Chile 38°15S 72°41W 336 A2
Trail Canada 49°5N 117°40W 296 D5
Traill Ø Greenland 72°30N 23°0W 154 C8
Traimit Bangkok, Thailand 113 c2
Trainor L. Canada 60°24N 120°17W 296 A4
Traíra ➝ Brazil 1°4S 69°26W 328 D4
Trakai △ Lithuania 54°30N 25°10E 161 J21
Trákhonas Cyprus 35°12N 33°21E 207 E9
Tralee Ireland 52°16N 9°42W 166 D2
Tralee B. Ireland 52°17N 9°55W 166 D2
Tram Chim △ Vietnam 10°43N 105°31E 237 G5
Tramore Ireland 52°10N 7°10W 166 D4
Tramore B. Ireland 52°9N 7°10W 166 D4
Tramuntana, Serra de
Spain 39°48N 2°54E 206 B3
Tran Ninh, Cao Nguyen
Laos 19°30N 103°10E 236 C4
Tranås Sweden 58°3N 14°59E 163 F8
Tranbjerg Denmark 56°6N 10°9E 163 H4
Tranby Norway 59°49N 10°15E 164 E7
Trancas Argentina 26°11S 65°20W 334 B2
Trancoso Portugal 40°49N 7°21W 194 E3
Tranebjerg Denmark 55°51N 10°36E 163 J4
Tranegilde Denmark 55°37N 12°20E 118 B2
Tranemo Sweden 57°30N 13°20E 163 G7
Trang Thailand 7°33N 99°38E 237 J2
Trangahy Madag. 19°7S 44°31E 272 B1
Trangan Indonesia 6°40S 134°20E 231 F8
Trangie Australia 32°4S 148°0E 283 B8
Trångsund Sweden 59°13N 18°8E 139 B2
Trångsviken Sweden 63°19N 13°59E 162 A7
Trani Italy 41°17N 16°25E 201 A9
Tranoroa Madag. 24°42S 45°4E 272 C2
Tranqueras Uruguay 31°13S 55°45W 335 C4
Trans-Alaska Pipeline
U.S.A. 70°11N 148°27W 303 A10
Trans-Nzoia □ Kenya 1°10N 34°55E 268 B3
Transamerica Pyramid
San Francisco, U.S.A. 136 b2
Transantarctic Mts.
Antarctica 85°0S 170°0W 151 E12
Transbay Terminal
San Francisco, U.S.A. 136 b3
Transcarpathia = Zakarpattya □
Ukraine 48°20N 23°20E 183 B8
Transilvania Romania 46°30N 24°0E 183 D9
Transilvanian Alps = Carpații
Meridionali Romania 45°30N 25°0E 183 E9
Transjordan = Jordan ■
Asia 31°0N 36°0E 251 H7
Transnistria □ Moldova 47°20N 29°15E 183 C14
Transtrand Sweden 61°6N 13°20E 162 C7
Transtrandsfjällen Sweden 61°8N 13°0E 162 C6
Transylvania = Transilvania
Romania 46°30N 24°0E 183 D9
Trants Bay Montserrat 16°46N 62°9W 323 p
Trápani Italy 38°1N 12°29E 200 D5
Trappenfelde Germany 52°34N 13°39E 115 A4
Trapper Pk. U.S.A. 45°54N 114°18W 304 D6
Traralgon Australia 38°12S 146°34E 283 E7
Traryd Sweden 56°35N 13°45E 163 H7
Trarza □ Mauritania 18°0N 15°0W 260 E2
Trás-os-Montes = Cucumbi
Angola 10°17S 19°5E 265 E3
Trasacco Italy 41°57N 13°32E 199 G10
Trăscău, Munții Romania 46°14N 23°14E 183 D8
Trasimeno, L. Italy 43°8N 12°6E 199 E9
Träslövsläge Sweden 57°4N 12°16E 163 G6
Trastévere Italy 41°53N 12°28E 136 B1
Trasvase Tajo-Segura, Canal de
Spain 40°15N 2°55W 196 E2
Trat Thailand 12°14N 102°33E 237 F4
Tratani ➝ Pakistan 29°19N 68°20E 242 E3
Traun Austria 48°14N 14°15E 180 C7
Traunreut Germany 47°57N 12°36E 179 H8
Traunsee Austria 47°55N 13°50E 180 D6
Traunstein Germany 47°52N 12°37E 179 H8
Travellers L. Australia 33°20S 142°0E 282 B5
Travemünde Germany 53°57N 10°52E 178 B6
Travers, Mt. N.Z. 42°1S 172°45E 285 C7
Traverse City U.S.A. 44°46N 85°38W 309 C11
Travis, L. U.S.A. 30°24N 97°55W 314 F6
Travnik Bos.-H. 44°17N 17°39E 182 F2
Trawbreaga B. Ireland 55°20N 7°25W 166 A4
Trbovlje Slovenia 46°12N 15°5E 199 B12
Treasure I. U.S.A. 37°49N 122°22W 136 B2
Treasure Island U.S.A. 27°46N 82°46W 317 H7
Treasury Is. Solomon Is. 7°22S 155°37E 287 L8
Trébbia ➝ Italy 45°4N 9°41E 198 C6
Trebel ➝ Germany 53°54N 13°2E 178 B9
Trébeurden France 48°46N 3°35W 172 D3
Trebević △ Bos.-H. 43°20N 18°45E 182 G3
Třebíč Czechia 49°14N 15°55E 180 B8
Trebinje Bos.-H. 42°44N 18°22E 202 D2
Trebisacce Italy 39°52N 16°32E 201 C9
Trebišnjica ➝ Bos.-H. 42°47N 18°8E 202 D2
Trebišov Slovakia 48°38N 21°41E 181 C14
Trebitsch = Třebíč Czechia 49°14N 15°55E 180 B8
Trebižat ➝ Bos.-H. 43°15N 17°30E 199 E14
Trebnitz = Trzebnica
Poland 51°20N 17°1E 185 G4
Trebnje Slovenia 45°54N 15°1E 199 C12
Třeboň Czechia 49°1N 14°48E 180 B7
Trebonne Australia 18°37S 146°5E 280 B4
Třeboňsko △ Czechia 49°1N 14°49E 180 B7
Treboradice Czechia 50°9N 14°31E 135 B3
Třebotov Czechia 49°58N 14°17E 135 C1
Trebujena Spain 36°52N 6°11W 195 J4
Trecate Italy 45°26N 8°44E 198 C5
Tree Tops Park U.S.A. 26°4N 80°16W 129 B1
Trefaldwyn = Montgomery
U.K. 52°34N 3°8W 169 E4
Trefynwy = Monmouth
U.K. 51°48N 2°42W 169 F5
Tregaron U.K. 52°14N 3°56W 169 E4
Tregnago Italy 45°31N 11°10E 199 C8
Tregrosse Is. Australia 17°41S 150°43E 280 B5
Tréguier France 48°47N 3°16W 172 D3
Trégunc France 47°51N 3°51W 172 E3
Treherne Canada 49°38N 98°42W 297 D9
Tréia Italy 43°19N 13°19E 199 E10
Treignac France 45°32N 1°48E 174 C5
Treinta y Tres Uruguay 33°16S 54°17W 335 C5
Treis-karden Germany 50°10N 7°18E 179 E3
Treklyano Bulgaria 42°33N 22°36E 202 D6
Trelawney Zimbabwe 17°30S 30°30E 271 A5
Trélazé France 47°26N 0°30W 172 E6
Trelew Argentina 43°10S 65°20W 336 B3
Trélissac France 45°11N 0°47E 174 C4
Trelleborg Sweden 55°20N 13°10E 163 J7
Tremadog Bay U.K. 52°51N 4°18W 168 E3
Tremblay-en-France
France 48°56N 2°35E 134 A4
Tremblet Réunion 21°17S 55°48E 272 f
Trembowla = Terebovlya
Ukraine 49°18N 25°44E 177 D13
Tremedal = Monte Azul
Brazil 15°9S 42°53W 333 E3
Tremembe ➝ Brazil 23°27S 46°34W 137 A2
Trémiti Italy 42°8N 15°30E 199 F12
Tremont U.S.A. 40°50N 73°52W 132 A2
Tremonton U.S.A. 41°43N 112°10W 304 F7
Tremp Spain 42°10N 0°52E 196 C5
Trenche ➝ Canada 47°46N 72°53W 298 C5
Trenčiansky □ Slovakia 48°45N 18°20E 181 C11
Trenčín Slovakia 48°52N 18°4E 181 C11
Trengereid Norway 60°26N 5°37E 164 D2
Trenggalek Indonesia 8°3S 111°43E 235 D4
Trenno Italy 45°29N 9°6E 128 B1
Trenque Lauquen
Argentina 36°5S 62°45W 334 D3
Trent ➝ Ont., Canada 44°6N 77°34W 312 B7
Trent ➝ England, U.K. 53°41N 0°42W 168 D7
Trentino-Alto Adige □
Italy 46°30N 11°20E 199 B8
Trento Italy 46°4N 11°8E 198 B8
Trento Agusan del S., Phil. 8°3N 126°2E 233 G6
Trenton Ont., Canada 44°10N 77°34W 312 B7
Trenton Fla., U.S.A. 29°37N 82°49W 317 F7
Trenton Mich., U.S.A. 42°8N 83°11W 311 B13
Trenton Mo., U.S.A. 40°5N 93°37W 310 D3
Trenton N.J., U.S.A. 40°14N 74°46W 313 F10
Trenton Nebr., U.S.A. 40°11N 101°1W 308 E3
Trenton Ohio, U.S.A. 39°29N 84°28W 311 E12
Trenton S.C., U.S.A. 33°45N 81°51W 316 B8
Trepassey Canada 46°43N 53°25W 299 C9
Treptow Germany 52°29N 13°27E 115 B3
Treptow an der Rega = Trzebiatów
Poland 54°3N 15°18E 184 D2
Trepuzzi Italy 40°24N 18°4E 201 B11
Tres Arroyos Argentina 38°26S 60°20W 334 D3
Três Casas Brazil 6°59S 62°41W 331 B5
Três Corações Brazil 21°44S 45°15W 333 F2
Tres Equinas Colombia 0°43N 75°16W 328 C2
Três Lagoas Brazil 20°50S 51°43W 333 F1
Tres Lagos Argentina 49°35S 71°25W 336 C2
Tres Lomas Argentina 36°27S 62°51W 334 D3
Três Marias, Represa
Brazil 18°12S 45°15W 333 E2
Tres Montes, C. Chile 46°50S 75°30W 336 C1
Tres Pinos U.S.A. 36°48N 121°19W 306 J5
Três Pontas Brazil 21°23S 45°29W 333 F2
Tres Pontas, C. das Angola 10°28S 13°32E 265 E2
Tres Puentes Chile 27°50S 70°15W 334 B1
Tres Puntas, C. Argentina 47°0S 66°0W 336 C3
Três Rios Brazil 22°6S 43°15W 333 F3
Tres Rios, Sa. dos Brazil 22°56S 43°17W 135 B1
Tres Valles Mexico 18°15N 96°8W 319 D5
Tresco U.K. 49°57N 6°20W 169 H1
Tresfjord Norway 62°31N 7°7E 164 B4
Treska ➝ Macedonia 42°0N 21°20E 202 E5
Treskavica Bos.-H. 43°40N 18°20E 182 G3
Trespaderne Spain 42°47N 3°24W 194 C7
Tresticklan △ Sweden 59°0N 11°42E 163 F5
Trets France 43°27N 5°41E 175 E9
Treuburg = Olecko Poland 54°2N 22°31E 184 D9
Treuchtlingen Germany 48°58N 10°54E 179 G6
Treuenbrietzen Germany 52°5N 12°52E 178 C8
Treungen Norway 59°1N 8°31E 164 E5
Trèves = Trier Germany 49°45N 6°38E 179 F2
Trevi Italy 42°52N 12°45E 199 F9
Trevi, Fontana di Rome, Italy 136 b3
Treviglio Italy 45°31N 9°35E 198 C6
Trevinca, Peña Spain 42°15N 6°46W 194 C4
Treviño Spain 42°44N 2°45W 194 C8
Treviso Italy 45°40N 12°15E 199 C9
Trévoux France 45°57N 4°47E 175 C8
Trezzano sul Naviglio Italy 45°24N 9°4E 128 B1
Trgovište Serbia 42°20N 22°10E 202 D6
Triabunna Australia 42°30S 147°55E 281 G4
Trianda = Ialissos Greece 36°24N 28°10E 206 E12
Triangle Zimbabwe 21°2S 31°28E 271 B5
Triaucourt-en-Argonne
France 48°59N 5°2E 173 D12
Tribal Areas □ Pakistan 33°0N 70°0E 242 C4
Tribsees Germany 54°5N 12°44E 178 A8
Tribugá, G. de Colombia 5°45N 77°20W 328 B2
Tribulation, C. Australia 16°5S 145°29E 280 B4
Tribune U.S.A. 38°28N 101°45W 308 F3
Tribune Tower Chicago, U.S.A. 119 b2
Tricárico Italy 40°37N 16°9E 201 B9
Tricase Italy 39°56N 18°22E 201 C11
Trichinopoly = Tiruchchirappalli
India 10°45N 78°45E 245 J4
Trichonida, L. Greece 38°34N 21°30E 204 C3
Trichur = Thrissur India 10°30N 76°18E 245 J3
Trichy = Tiruchchirappalli
India 10°45N 78°45E 245 J4
Trida Australia 33°1S 145°1E 283 B6
Trier Germany 49°45N 6°38E 179 F2
Trieste Lazio, Italy 41°55N 12°30E 136 B2
Trieste Trieste, Italy 45°40N 13°46E 199 C10
Trieste, G. di Italy 45°40N 13°35E 199 C10
Trieux ➝ France 48°43N 3°9W 172 D3
Triggiano Italy 41°4N 16°55E 201 A9
Triglav Slovenia 46°21N 13°50E 199 B10
Triglavski △ Slovenia 46°20N 13°50E 199 B10
Trigno ➝ Italy 42°4N 14°48E 199 F11
Trigo de Morais = Guijá
Mozam. 24°27S 33°0E 271 B5
Trigueros Spain 37°24N 6°50W 195 H4
Trikala Greece 39°34N 21°47E 204 B3
Trikeri Greece 39°6N 23°5E 204 B5
Trikomo Cyprus 35°17N 33°52E 207 E9
Trikora, Puncak Indonesia 4°15S 138°45E 231 E9
Trilby U.S.A. 28°28N 82°12W 317 G7
Trilj Croatia 43°38N 16°42E 199 E13
Trillo Spain 40°42N 2°35W 196 E2
Trim Ireland 53°33N 6°48W 166 C5
Trimbak India 19°56N 73°33E 244 E1
Trimmu Dam Pakistan 31°10N 72°8E 242 D5
Trincomalee Sri Lanka 8°38N 81°15E 245 K5
Trindade Atl. Oc. 20°20S 29°50W 152 J9
Trindade Brazil 16°40S 49°30W 333 E2
Třinec Czechia 49°41N 18°39E 181 B11
Trinidad = Jose Abad Santos
Phil. 5°55N 125°39E 233 J5
Trinidad Bolivia 14°46S 64°50W 331 C5
Trinidad Colombia 5°25N 71°40W 328 B3
Trinidad Cuba 21°48N 80°0W 320 B4
Trinidad Paraguay 27°7S 55°47W 335 B4
Trinidad Trin. & Tob. 10°30N 61°15W 323 t
Trinidad Uruguay 33°30S 56°50W 334 C4
Trinidad Colo., U.S.A. 37°10N 104°31W 305 H11
Trinidad D.C., U.S.A. 38°54N 76°59W 143 B3
Trinidad, G. Chile 49°55S 75°25W 336 C1
Trinidad, I. Argentina 39°10S 62°0W 336 A4
Trinidad & Tobago ■
W. Indies 10°30N 61°20W 323 t
Trinitápoli Italy 41°21N 16°5E 201 A9
Trinité, Havre de
Martinique 14°44N 60°58W 322 j
Trinity Nfld. & L., Canada 48°59N 53°55W 299 C9
Trinity Edinburgh, U.K. 55°58N 3°12W 121 B2
Trinity Tex., U.S.A. 30°57N 95°22W 314 F7
Trinity ➝ Calif., U.S.A. 41°11N 123°42W 304 F2
Trinity ➝ Tex., U.S.A. 29°45N 94°43W 314 G7
Trinity B. Canada 48°20N 53°10W 299 C9
Trinity Church New York, U.S.A. 132 f1
Trinity Hills Trin. & Tob. 10°7N 61°7W 323 t
Trinity Is. U.S.A. 56°33N 154°25W 303 H9
Trinity Range U.S.A. 40°10N 118°40W 304 F4
Trinity River Greenbelt Park
U.S.A. 32°45N 96°48W 120 B4
Trinkat India 8°5N 93°30E 245 K11
Trinkitat Sudan 18°45N 37°51E 256 D4
Trino Italy 45°12N 8°18E 198 C5
Trinway U.S.A. 40°9N 82°1W 312 F2
Triolet Mauritius 20°4S 57°32E 272 e
Trionfale Italy 41°54N 12°26E 136 B1
Trionto, C. Italy 39°37N 16°43E 201 C9
Triora Italy 44°1N 7°46E 198 D4
Tripoli = Tarābulus
Lebanon 34°31N 35°50E 250 D6
Tripoli = Tarābulus Libya 32°49N 13°7E 258 B2
Tripoli Greece 37°31N 22°25E 204 D4
Tripoli Iowa, U.S.A. 42°49N 92°16W 310 B4
Tripolitania = Tarābulus
Libya 31°0N 13°0E 258 B2
Tripura □ India 24°0N 92°0E 241 D4
Tripylos Cyprus 34°59N 32°41E 207 F8
Trischen Germany 54°4N 8°40E 178 A4
Tristan da Cunha Atl. Oc. 37°6S 12°20W 255 K2
Trisul India 30°19N 79°47E 243 D8
Triton I. S. China Sea 15°47N 111°12E 230 A4
Triulzo Italy 45°25N 9°16E 128 B2
Trivandrum =
Thiruvananthapuram
India 8°41N 77°0E 245 K3
Trivento Italy 41°47N 14°33E 199 G11
Trizina Greece 37°25N 23°15E 204 D5
Trnava Slovakia 48°23N 17°35E 181 C10
Trnavský □ Slovakia 48°30N 17°45E 181 C10
Troarn France 49°11N 0°11W 172 C6
Trobriand Is. Papua N. G. 8°30S 151°0E 286 E6
Trocadero Paris, France 134 b1
Trochu Canada 51°50N 113°13W 296 C6
Trodely I. Canada 52°15N 79°26W 298 B4
Troebratskiy Kazakhstan 54°25N 66°4E 217 B7
Trogir Croatia 43°32N 16°15E 199 E13
Troglav Croatia 43°56N 16°36E 199 E13
Tróia Italy 41°22N 15°18E 201 A8
Troilus, L. Canada 50°50N 74°35W 298 B5
Troina Italy 37°47N 14°36E 201 E7
Trois Boutiques Mauritius 20°26S 57°38E 272 e
Trois Fourches, Cap des
Morocco 35°26N 2°58W 261 A4
Trois-Pistoles Canada 48°5N 69°10W 299 C6
Trois Pitons, Morne
Dominica 15°22N 61°20W 323 k
Trois-Rivières Qué.,
Canada 46°25N 72°34W 298 C5
Trois-Rivières Guadeloupe 15°57N 61°40W 322 e
Trois Rivières Martinique 14°28N 60°58W 322 j
Troisdorf Germany 50°48N 7°11E 178 E3
Troitsk Russia 54°10N 61°35E 216 B6
Troitsko Pechorsk
Russia 62°40N 56°10E 186 B10
Troitskosavsk = Kyakhta
Russia 50°30N 106°25E 215 D11
Troitskoye Russia 46°26N 44°15E 191 G7
Troitsky = Troitsk Russia 54°10N 61°35E 216 B6
Troja Czechia 50°7N 14°25E 135 B2
Troll Antarctica 72°0S 2°30E 151 D3
Trölladyngja Iceland 64°54N 17°16W 155 C9
Trollbäcken Sweden 59°14N 18°12E 139 B3
Trollhättan Sweden 58°17N 12°20E 163 F6
Trollheimen Norway 62°46N 9°1E 164 B6
Trombay India 19°2N 72°56E 130 A2
Trombetas ➝ Brazil 1°55S 55°35W 329 D6
Tromelin I. Ind. Oc. 15°52S 54°25E 273 F4
Tromøy Norway 58°27N 8°51E 164 F5
Tromsø Norway 69°40N 18°56E 160 B18
Tron Thailand 17°28N 100°7E 236 D3
Trona U.S.A. 35°46N 117°23W 307 K9
Tronador, Mte. Argentina 41°10S 71°50W 336 B2
Tronchetto Venice, Italy 142 b1
Trondelag Norway 64°17N 11°50E 160 D14
Trondheim Norway 63°36N 10°25E 164 A7
Trondheimsfjorden
Norway 63°35N 10°30E 160 E14
Trondheimsleia Norway 63°25N 8°30E 164 A5
Trondhjem = Trondheim
Norway 63°36N 10°25E 164 A7
Trönninge Sweden 56°37N 12°51E 163 H6
Tronto ➝ Italy 42°54N 13°55E 199 F10
Troodos Cyprus 34°55N 32°52E 207 F8
Troon U.K. 55°33N 4°39W 167 F4
Troparevo Russia 55°39N 37°29E 129 C1
Tropea Italy 38°41N 15°54E 201 D8
Tropic U.S.A. 37°37N 112°5W 305 H7
Tropojë Albania 42°23N 20°10E 202 D4
Troppau = Opava
Czechia 49°57N 17°58E 181 B10
Trosa Sweden 58°54N 17°33E 163 F11
Trostan U.K. 55°3N 6°10W 166 A5
Trostberg Germany 48°1N 12°33E 179 G8
Trostyanets Sumy, Ukraine 50°33N 34°59E 189 G8
Trostyanets Vinnyts'ka,
Ukraine 48°31N 29°11E 183 B14
Trotsk = Chapayevsk
Russia 53°0N 49°40E 190 D9
Trotsk = Gatchina Russia 59°35N 30°9E 188 C6
Trou Gras Pt. St. Lucia 13°51N 60°53W 323 m
Troumaka St. Vincent 13°16N 61°17W 323 n
Trout ➝ Canada 61°19N 119°51W 296 A5
Trout L. N.W.T., Canada 60°40N 121°14W 296 A4
Trout L. Ont., Canada 51°20N 93°15W 297 C10
Trout Lake N.W.T.,
Canada 56°30N 114°32W 296 B6
Trout Lake Wash., U.S.A. 46°0N 121°32W 306 E5
Trout River Canada 49°29N 58°8W 299 C8
Trout Run U.S.A. 41°23N 77°3W 312 E7
Trouville-sur-Mer France 49°21N 0°5E 172 C7
Trowbridge U.K. 51°18N 2°12W 169 F5
Troy Turkey 39°57N 26°12E 205 B8
Troy Ala., U.S.A. 31°48N 85°58W 316 D4
Troy Ill., U.S.A. 38°44N 89°54W 310 F7
Troy Ind., U.S.A. 37°59N 86°55W 311 G10
Troy Kans., U.S.A. 39°47N 95°5W 308 F6
Troy Mich., U.S.A. 42°37N 83°9W 311 B13
Troy Mo., U.S.A. 38°59N 90°59W 310 F6
Troy Mont., U.S.A. 48°28N 115°53W 304 B6
Troy N.Y., U.S.A. 42°44N 73°41W 313 D11
Troy Ohio, U.S.A. 40°2N 84°12W 311 D12
Troy Pa., U.S.A. 41°47N 76°47W 313 E8
Troyan Bulgaria 42°57N 24°43E 203 D8
Troyes France 48°19N 4°3E 173 D11
Trpanj Croatia 43°1N 17°15E 199 E14
Trstenik Serbia 43°36N 21°0E 202 C5
Trubchevsk Russia 52°33N 33°47E 189 F7
Truchas Pk. U.S.A. 35°58N 105°39W 305 J11
Trucial States = United Arab
Emirates ■ Asia 23°50N 54°0E 247 F7
Truckee U.S.A. 39°20N 120°11W 306 F6
Trudeau Int., Montréal ✈ (YUL)
Canada 45°28N 73°44W 130 B1
Trudfront Russia 45°56N 47°40E 191 H8
Trudovoye Russia 43°17N 132°5E 220 C6
Trudyashchikhsya, Ostrov
Russia 59°58N 30°18E 137 B1
Trujillo Colombia 4°10N 76°19W 328 C2
Trujillo Honduras 16°0N 86°0W 320 C2
Trujillo Peru 8°6S 79°0W 330 B2
Trujillo Spain 39°28N 5°55W 195 F5
Trujillo N. Mex., U.S.A. 35°32N 104°42W 305 J11
Trujillo Venezuela 9°22N 70°38W 328 B3
Trujillo □ Venezuela 9°25N 70°30W 328 B3
Trujillo, Mte. = Duarte, Pico
Dom. Rep. 19°2N 70°59W 321 C5
Trujillo Alto Puerto Rico 18°21N 66°1W 321 b
Truk Micronesia 7°25N 151°46E 287 T17
Trumann U.S.A. 35°41N 90°31W 315 D9
Trumansburg U.S.A. 42°33N 76°40W 313 D8
Trumbull, Mt. U.S.A. 36°25N 113°19W 305 H7
Trump Tower Chicago, U.S.A. 119 b2
Trŭn Bulgaria 42°51N 22°38E 202 D6
Trun Orne, France 48°50N 0°2E 172 D7
Trundle Australia 32°53S 147°35E 283 B7
Trung Lon, Hon Vietnam 8°36N 106°8E 237 H6
Trung Phan Vietnam 17°0N 109°0E 236 D6
Truong Sa, Dao = Spratly I.
S. China Sea 8°38N 111°55E 230 C4
Truro S. Austral., Australia 34°24S 139°9E 282 C3
Truro N.S., Canada 45°21N 63°14W 299 C7
Truro Corn., U.K. 50°16N 5°4W 169 G2
Trus Madi, Gunung
Malaysia 5°33N 116°31E 235 A5
Truskavets Ukraine 49°17N 23°30E 177 D12
Trŭstenik Bulgaria 43°31N 24°28E 203 C8
Trustrup Denmark 56°20N 10°46E 163 H4
Trutch Canada 57°44N 122°57W 296 B4
Truth or Consequences
U.S.A. 33°8N 107°15W 305 K10
Trutnov Czechia 50°37N 15°54E 180 A8
Truyère ➝ France 44°38N 2°34E 174 D6
Tryavna Bulgaria 42°54N 25°25E 203 D9
Tryonville U.S.A. 41°42N 79°48W 312 E5
Tryphena N.Z. 36°18S 175°28E 284 C4
Trysilelva ➝ Norway 61°2N 12°35E 164 C9
Tryvasshøgda Norway 59°59N 10°40E 133 A3
Trzcianka Poland 53°3N 16°25E 185 E3
Trzciel Poland 52°23N 15°50E 185 F2
Trzcińsko Zdrój Poland 52°58N 14°35E 185 F1
Trzebiatów Poland 54°3N 15°18E 184 D2
Trzebiez Poland 53°38N 14°31E 184 E1
Trzebnica Poland 51°20N 17°1E 185 G4
Trzemeszno Poland 52°33N 17°48E 185 F4
Tržič Slovenia 46°22N 14°18E 199 B11
Tsagaannur Mongolia 49°32N 89°42E 217 C11
Tsagan Aman Russia 47°34N 46°43E 191 G8
Tsala Apopka L. U.S.A. 28°53N 82°19W 317 G7
Tsamandas Greece 39°46N 20°21E 204 B2
Tsamkong = Zhanjiang
China 21°15N 110°20E 229 G8
Tsandi Namibia 17°42S 14°50E 270 A1
Tsangpo = Brahmaputra ➝
Asia 23°40N 90°35E 241 D3
Tsaochiao Taiwan 24°39N 120°51E 225 B2
Ts'aot'un Taiwan 23°58N 120°41E 225 C2
Tsaratanana Madag. 16°47S 47°39E 272 B2
Tsaratanana, Mt. de =
Maromokotro Madag. 14°0S 49°0E 272 A2
Tsaratanana ⌓ Madag. 13°57S 48°52E 272 A2
Tsarekonstantinovka =
Kuybyshevo Ukraine 47°25N 36°40E 189 J9
Tsarevo = Michurin
Bulgaria 42°9N 27°51E 203 D11
Tsarevo Bulgaria 42°28N 25°52E 203 D9
Tsaribrod = Dimitrovgrad
Serbia 43°2N 22°48E 202 C6
Tsaritsani Greece 39°53N 22°14E 204 B4
Tsarkasianos Greece 38°10N 20°40E 207 C2
Tsarskoye Selo = Pushkin
Russia 59°45N 30°25E 188 C6
Tsaryovokokshaysk = Yoshkar Ola
Russia 56°38N 47°55E 190 B8
Tsau Botswana 20°8S 22°22E 270 B3
Tsavo Kenya 2°59S 38°28E 268 C4
Tsavo East △ Kenya 2°44S 38°47E 268 C4
Tsavo West △ Kenya 3°19S 37°57E 268 C4
Tsawlaw Burma 26°9N 98°17E 241 B7
Tselinograd = Astana
Kazakhstan 51°10N 71°30E 217 B8
Tsementny = Fokino
Russia 53°30N 34°22E 188 F8
Tseng Lan Shue
Hong Kong, China 22°20N 114°14E 122 B3
Tsengwen Hsi ➝ Taiwan 23°8N 120°19E 225 C2
Tsengwen Shuiku
Taiwan 23°16N 120°34E 225 C2
Tsentralen Balkan △
Bulgaria 42°40N 24°45E 203 D8
Tsentralnyy □ Russia 52°0N 40°0E 214 D4
Tses Namibia 25°58S 18°8E 270 C2
Tsetserleg Mongolia 47°36N 101°32E 218 B9
Tseung Kwan
Hong Kong, China 22°19N 114°15E 122 B3
Tsévié Togo 6°25N 1°20E 263 D5
Tshabong Botswana 26°2S 22°29E 270 C3
Tshabuta
Dem. Rep. of the Congo 7°42S 23°7E 265 D4
Tshane Botswana 24°5S 21°54E 270 B3
Tshela Dem. Rep. of the Congo 4°57S 13°4E 265 C2
Tshesebe Botswana 21°51S 27°32E 271 B4
Tshibeke
Dem. Rep. of the Congo 2°40S 28°35E 268 C2
Tshibinda
Dem. Rep. of the Congo 2°23S 28°43E 268 C2
Tshikapa
Dem. Rep. of the Congo 6°28S 20°48E 265 D4
Tshilenge
Dem. Rep. of the Congo 6°17S 23°48E 265 D4
Tshindjambo
Dem. Rep. of the Congo 10°52S 22°43E 265 E4
Tshinota
Dem. Rep. of the Congo 7°2S 20°58E 265 D4
Tshinsenda
Dem. Rep. of the Congo 12°20S 28°0E 269 E2
Tshitadi
Dem. Rep. of the Congo 6°46S 21°43E 265 D4
Tshofa
Dem. Rep. of the Congo 5°13S 25°16E 265 D5
Tshopo □
Dem. Rep. of the Congo 1°0N 25°0E 264 B4
Tshuapa □
Dem. Rep. of the Congo 0°0 22°0E 264 B4
Tshuapa ➝
Dem. Rep. of the Congo 0°14S 20°42E 264 C4
Tshumbiri
Dem. Rep. of the Congo 2°38S 16°18E 264 C3
Tshwane = Pretoria
S. Africa 25°44S 28°12E 271 C4
Tshwane Botswana 22°24S 22°1E 270 B3
Tsiaotso = Jiaozuo China 35°16N 113°12E 226 G7
Tsibirihina ➝ Madag. 19°42S 44°31E 272 B1
Tsigara Botswana 20°22S 25°54E 270 B4
Tsihombe Madag. 25°10S 45°41E 272 D2
Tsiigehtchic Canada 67°15N 134°0W 294 D5
Ts'il-os ⌓ Canada 51°9N 123°59W 296 C4
Tsim Sha Tsui
Hong Kong, China 22°18N 114°10E 122 B3
Tsimanampetsotse △
Madag. 24°9S 43°50E 272 C1
Tsimlyansk Russia 47°40N 42°6E 191 G6
Tsimlyansk Res. = Tsimlyanskoye
Vdkhr. Russia 48°0N 43°0E 191 F6
Tsimlyanskoye Vdkhr.
Russia 48°0N 43°0E 191 F6
Tsinan = Jinan China 36°38N 117°1E 226 F9
Tsineng S. Africa 27°5S 23°5E 270 C3
Tsing Lung Tau
Hong Kong, China 22°22N 114°3E 122 A2
Tsing Yi Hong Kong, China 22°21N 114°6E 122 A2
Tsinghai = Qinghai □
China 36°0N 98°0E 218 D8
Tsingshih = Jinshi China 29°40N 111°50E 229 C8
Tsingtao = Qingdao
China 36°5N 120°20E 227 F11
Tsingy de Bemaraha ⌓
Madag. 18°35S 44°55E 272 B1
Tsingy de Namoraka ⌓
Madag. 16°29S 45°25E 272 B2
Tsining = Jining China 35°22N 116°34E 226 G9
Tsinjoarivo Madag. 19°37S 47°40E 272 B2
Tsinjomitondraka Madag. 15°40S 47°8E 272 B2
Tsinling Shan = Qinling Shandi
China 33°50N 108°10E 226 H5
Tsirigo = Kythira Greece 36°8N 23°0E 204 E5
Tsiroanomandidy Madag. 18°46S 46°2E 272 B2
Tsis I. Micronesia 7°17N 151°49E 287 U18
Tsiteli-Tsqaro = Dedoplis Tsqaro
Georgia 41°33N 46°0E 191 K8
Tsitondroina Madag. 21°19S 46°0E 272 C2
Tsitsihar = Qiqihar
China 47°26N 124°0E 219 B13
Tsitsikamma △ S. Africa 34°3S 23°40E 270 D3
Tsivilsk Russia 55°50N 47°25E 190 C8
Tsivory Madag. 24°4S 46°5E 272 C2
Tskhinvali Georgia 42°14N 44°1E 191 J7
Tsna ➝ Russia 54°55N 41°58E 190 C6
Tsnori Georgia 41°40N 45°57E 191 K7
Tso Moriri, L. India 32°50N 78°20E 243 C8
Tsobis Namibia 19°27S 17°30E 270 A2
Tsodilo Hills Botswana 18°49S 21°43E 270 A3
Tsogni Gabon 2°48S 10°10E 264 C2
Tsogttsetsiy = Baruunsuu
Mongolia 43°43N 105°35E 226 C3
Tsolo S. Africa 31°18S 28°37E 271 D4
Tsomo S. Africa 32°0S 27°42E 271 D4
Tsoukalades Greece 38°41N 20°47E 207 B2
Tsova West Bank 31°47N 35°6E 123 B1
Tsoying Taiwan 22°41N 120°17E 225 D2
Tsu Japan 34°45N 136°25E 223 C8
Tsu L. Canada 60°40N 111°52W 296 A6
Tsubata Japan 36°40N 136°44E 223 A8
Tsuchiura Japan 36°5N 140°15E 223 A12
Tsuen Wan
Hong Kong, China 22°22N 114°6E 122 A2
Tsugaru-Hantō Japan 41°0N 140°30E 220 D10
Tsugaru-Kaikyō Japan 41°35N 141°0E 220 D10
Tsuken-jima Japan 26°15N 127°56E 288 a
Tsukiji Tokyo, Japan 140 c5
Tsukuba Japan 36°2N 140°4E 223 A12
Tsukumi Japan 33°4N 131°52E 222 D3
Tsukushi-Sanchi Japan 33°25N 130°30E 222 D2
Tsumeb Namibia 19°9S 17°44E 270 A2
Tsumis Namibia 23°39S 17°29E 270 B2
Tsuna = Awaji Japan 34°28N 134°56E 222 C6
Tsuno-Shima Japan 34°21N 130°52E 222 C2
Tsur Hadassa Israel 31°43N 35°6E 123 B1
Tsuru Japan 35°31N 138°57E 223 B10
Tsuruga Japan 35°45N 136°2E 223 B8
Tsuruga-Wan Japan 35°50N 136°3E 223 B8
Tsurugi Japan 36°29N 136°37E 223 A8
Tsurugi-San Japan 33°51N 134°6E 222 D6
Tsurumi ➝ Japan 35°32N 139°40E 140 B3
Tsurumi-Saki Japan 32°56N 132°5E 222 E4
Tsuruoka Japan 38°44N 139°50E 220 E9
Tsurusaki Japan 33°14N 131°41E 222 D3
Tsushima Ehime, Japan 33°7N 132°32E 222 D4
Tsushima Gifu, Japan 35°10N 136°43E 223 B8
Tsushima Nagasaki, Japan 34°20N 129°20E 222 C1
Tsuyama Japan 35°3N 134°0E 222 B6
Tsvetkovo Ukraine 49°8N 31°33E 189 H6
Tsyelyakhany Belarus 52°30N 25°46E 177 B13
Tsz Wan Shan
Hong Kong, China 22°20N 114°11E 122 A3
Tu ➝ Burma 21°50N 96°15E 241 E6
Tua Dem. Rep. of the Congo 3°38S 16°38E 264 C3
Tua ➝ Papua N. G. 6°30S 144°28E 286 D3
Tua ➝ Portugal 41°13N 7°26W 194 D3
Tuaheni Pt. N.Z. 38°43S 178°4E 284 E7
Tuai N.Z. 38°47S 177°10E 284 E6
Tuaim = Tuam Ireland 53°31N 8°51W 166 C3
Tuakau N.Z. 37°16S 174°59E 284 D3
Tual Indonesia 5°38S 132°44E 231 F8
Tualatin U.S.A. 45°23N 122°45W 306 E4
Tuam Ireland 53°31N 8°51W 166 C3
Tuamarina N.Z. 41°25S 173°59E 285 B8
Tuamotu, Îs.
French Polynesia 17°0S 144°0W 289 f
Tuamotu Arch. = Tuamotu, Îs.
French Polynesia 17°0S 144°0W 289 f
Tuamotu Ridge Pac. Oc. 20°0S 138°0W 289 K14
Tuan Giao Vietnam 21°35N 103°25E 236 B4
Tuanfeng China 30°38N 114°52E 229 B10
Tuangku Indonesia 2°10N 97°16E 234 B1
Tuanxi China 27°28N 107°8E 228 D6
Tuao Phil. 17°45N 121°22E 232 C3
Tuapa Cook Is. 18°57S 169°54W 289 g
Tuapse Russia 44°5N 39°10E 191 H4
Tuaran Malaysia 6°10N 116°13E 235 A5
Tuas Singapore 1°19N 103°39E 138 B1
Tuatapere N.Z. 46°8S 167°41E 285 G2
Tuba City U.S.A. 36°8N 111°14W 305 H8
Tuban Indonesia 6°54S 112°3E 235 D4
Tubani Botswana 24°46S 24°18E 270 B3
Tubarão Brazil 28°30S 49°0W 335 B6
Ṭūbās West Bank 32°20N 35°22E 251 F6
Tubas ➝ Namibia 22°54S 14°35E 270 B2
Tubau Malaysia 3°10N 113°40E 235 B4
Tubbataha Reefs ⌓ Phil. 8°53N 119°53E 233 G2
Tubigon Phil. 9°57N 123°58E 233 G4
Tübingen Germany 48°31N 9°4E 179 G5
Tubmanburg = Bomi
Liberia 7°1N 10°38W 262 D2
Tubod Phil. 8°3N 123°48E 233 G4
Tubou Fiji 18°13S 178°48W 287 B3
Tubruq Libya 32°7N 23°55E 258 B4
Tubuaï French Polynesia 23°18S 149°30W 289 f
Tubuaï, Îs. French Polynesia 25°0S 150°0W 289 f
Tuburan Basilan, Phil. 6°39N 122°16E 233 H4
Tuburan Cebu, Phil. 10°44N 123°49E 233 F4
Tuc Trung Vietnam 11°1N 107°12E 237 G6
Tucacas Venezuela 10°48N 68°19W 328 A4
Tucano Brazil 10°58S 38°48W 332 D4
T'uch'ang Taiwan 24°35N 121°29E 225 B3
Tuchitua Canada 60°55N 129°13W 296 A3
Tuchodi ➝ Canada 58°17N 123°42W 296 B4
Tuchola Poland 53°33N 17°52E 184 E4
Tuchoměřice Czechia 50°7N 14°16E 135 B1
Tuchów Poland 49°54N 21°1E 185 J8
Tuckahoe U.S.A. 40°56N 73°49W 132 A3

Tuckanarra Australia 27°7S 118°5E 279 E2
Tucker U.S.A. 33°51N 84°13W 316 B5
Tuckers Town Bermuda 32°20N 64°42W 153 a
Tucson U.S.A. 32°13N 110°58W 305 K8
Tucumán □ Argentina 26°48S 66°2W 334 B2
Tucumcari U.S.A. 35°10N 103°44W 305 J12
Tucunaré Brazil 5°18S 55°51W 331 B6
Tucupido Venezuela 9°17N 65°47W 328 B4
Tucupita Venezuela 9°2N 62°3W 329 B5
Tucuruí Brazil 3°42S 49°44W 332 B2
Tucuruí, Represa de Brazil 4°0S 49°30W 332 B2
Tucuruvi Brazil 23°28S 46°35W 137 A2
Tuczno Poland 53°13N 16°10E 185 E3
Tuddal Norway 59°46N 8°49E 164 E5
Tudela Spain 42°4N 1°39W 196 C3
Tudmur Syria 34°36N 38°15E 213 E8
Tudor, L. Canada 55°50N 65°25W 299 A6
Tudora Romania 47°31N 26°45E 183 C11
Tuella → Portugal 41°30N 7°12W 194 D3
Tuen Mun Hong Kong, China 22°23N 113°57E 122 A1
Tuensang India 26°17N 94°50E 241 B5
Tueré → Brazil 2°48S 50°59W 332 B1
Tufanbeyli Turkey 38°15N 36°13E 212 C7
Tufello Italy 41°56N 12°32E 136 B2
Tüffer = Laško Slovenia 46°10N 15°16E 199 B12
Tufi Papua N. G. 9°8S 149°19E 286 E5
Tufnell Park U.K. 51°33N 0°8W 125 A3
Tufsingdal Norway 62°18N 11°44E 164 B8
Tufts Abyssal Plain Pac. Oc. 47°0N 140°0W 289 C14
Tufts Univ. U.S.A. 42°24N 71°7W 116 A2
Tufu Pt. Amer. Samoa 14°13S 169°30W 302 g
Tug Hill Plateau U.S.A. 43°45N 75°50W 313 C9
Tugaya Phil. 7°53N 124°10E 233 H5
Tugela → S. Africa 29°14S 31°30E 271 C5
Tugela Falls S. Africa 28°42S 29°51E 271 C4
Tughlakabad India 28°30N 77°16E 120 B2
Tugidak I. U.S.A. 56°30N 154°40W 303 H9
Tuguegarao Phil. 17°35N 121°42E 232 C3
Tugur Russia 53°44N 136°45E 215 D14
Tui Spain 42°3N 8°39W 194 C2
Tuileries, Jardin des Paris, France 134 b3
Tuineje Canary Is. 28°19N 14°3W 153 e2
Tukangbesi, Kepulauan Indonesia 6°0S 124°0E 231 F6
Tukarak I. Canada 56°15N 78°45W 298 A4
Tukayyid Iraq 29°47N 45°36E 246 D5
Tûkh Egypt 30°21N 31°12E 256 H7
Tukhlya Ukraine 48°55N 23°28E 183 B8
Tukituki → N.Z. 39°36S 176°56E 284 F5
Tukobo Ghana 5°1N 2°47W 262 D4
Tūkrah Libya 32°30N 20°37E 258 B4
Tuktoyaktuk Canada 69°27N 133°2W 294 D5
Tuktuk Indonesia 2°37N 98°54E 234 B1
Tuktut Nogait △ Canada 69°15N 122°0W 294 D7
Tuku Taiwan 23°41N 120°23E 225 C2
Tukums Latvia 56°58N 23°10E 184 B10
Tukuran Phil. 7°51N 123°34E 233 H4
Tukuyu Tanzania 9°17S 33°35E 269 D3
Tula Amer. Samoa 14°15S 170°34W 302 f
Tula Hidalgo, Mexico 20°3N 99°21W 319 C5
Tula Tamaulipas, Mexico 23°0N 99°43W 319 C5
Tula Nigeria 9°51N 11°27E 263 D7
Tula Russia 54°13N 37°38E 188 E9
Tula □ Russia 53°45N 37°30E 188 F9
Tulach Mhór = Tullamore Ireland 53°16N 7°31W 166 C4
Tulagi Solomon Is. 9°5S 160°10E 287 M11
Tūlak Afghan. 33°55N 63°40E 240 B1
Tulan Taiwan 22°53N 121°13E 225 D3
Tulancingo Mexico 20°5N 98°22W 319 C5
Tulangbawang → Indonesia 4°24S 105°52E 234 C3
Tulare Serbia 42°48N 21°28E 202 D5
Tulare Calif., U.S.A. 36°13N 119°21W 306 J7
Tulare Lake Bed U.S.A. 36°0N 119°48W 306 K7
Tularosa U.S.A. 33°5N 106°1W 305 K10
Tulbagh S. Africa 33°16S 19°6E 270 D2
Tulcán Ecuador 0°48N 77°43W 328 C2
Tulcea Romania 45°13N 28°46E 183 E13
Tulcea □ Romania 45°0N 28°30E 183 E13
Tulchyn Ukraine 48°41N 28°49E 183 B13
Tüledi Araldary Kazakhstan 45°2N 50°16E 191 H10
Tūleh Iran 34°35N 52°33E 247 C7
Tulemalu L. Canada 62°58N 99°25W 297 A9
Tulgheş Romania 46°58N 25°45E 183 D10
Tuli Zimbabwe 21°58S 29°13E 269 G2
Tulia U.S.A. 34°32N 101°46W 314 D4
Tuliszków Poland 52°5N 18°18E 185 F5
Tulita Canada 64°57N 125°30W 294 E6
Ţūlkarm West Bank 32°19N 35°2E 251 F6
Tulla Ireland 52°53N 8°46W 166 D3
Tullahoma U.S.A. 35°22N 86°13W 315 D11
Tullamarine Australia 37°41S 144°50E 128 A1
Tullamore N.S.W., Australia 32°39S 147°36E 283 B7
Tullamore Offaly, Ireland 53°16N 7°31W 166 C4
Tulle France 45°16N 1°46E 174 C5
Tulln an der Donau Austria 48°20N 16°4E 180 C9
Tullow Ireland 52°49N 6°45W 166 D5
Tullus Sudan 11°7N 24°31E 257 E1
Tully Queens., Australia 17°56S 145°55E 280 B4
Tully N.Y., U.S.A. 42°48N 76°7W 313 D8
Ţulmaythah Libya 32°40N 20°55E 258 B4
Tulnici Romania 45°51N 26°38E 183 E11
Tulovo Bulgaria 42°33N 25°32E 203 D9
Tulsa U.S.A. 36°10N 95°55W 314 C7
Tulse Hill U.K. 51°26N 0°6W 125 B3
Tulsequah Canada 58°39N 133°35W 296 B2
Tulu Milki Ethiopia 9°55N 38°20E 257 F4
Tulu Welel Ethiopia 8°56N 34°47E 257 F3
Tuluá Colombia 4°6N 76°11W 328 C2
Tuluceşti Romania 45°34N 28°2E 183 E13
Tuluksak U.S.A. 61°6N 160°58W 303 F7
Tulum Mexico 20°13N 87°28W 319 C7
Tulun Russia 54°32N 100°35E 215 D11
Tulungagung Indonesia 8°5S 111°54E 235 D4
Tuluran I. Phil. 10°58N 119°16E 233 F2
Tuma Russia 55°10N 40°30E 188 E11
Tuma → Nic. 13°6N 84°35W 320 D3
Tumacacori ⌓ U.S.A. 31°35N 111°6W 305 L8
Tumaco Colombia 1°50N 78°45W 328 C2
Tumaco, Ensenada Colombia 1°55N 78°45W 328 C2
Tumakuru India 13°18N 77°6E 245 H3
Tumatumari Guyana 5°20N 58°55W 329 B6
Tumauini Phil. 17°17N 121°49E 232 C3
Tumba Dem. Rep. of the Congo 3°10S 23°36E 264 C4
Tumba Sweden 59°12N 17°48E 162 E11
Tumba, L. Dem. Rep. of the Congo 0°50S 18°0E 264 C3
Tumbangsamba Indonesia 1°27S 113°7E 235 C4
Tumbarumba Australia 35°44S 148°0E 283 C8
Tumbaya Argentina 23°50S 65°26W 334 A2
Tumbes Peru 3°37S 80°27W 330 A1
Tumbes □ Peru 3°50S 80°30W 330 A1
Tumbler Ridge Canada 55°8N 121°0W 296 B4
Tumbur South Sudan 4°20N 31°34E 257 G3
Tumbwe Dem. Rep. of the Congo 11°25S 27°15E 269 E2
Tumby Bay Australia 34°21S 136°8E 282 C2
Tumd Youqi China 40°30N 110°30E 226 D6
Tumen China 43°0N 129°50E 224 A4
Tumen Jiang → China 42°20N 130°35E 224 A5
Tumeremo Venezuela 7°18N 61°30W 329 B5
Tumindao I. Phil. 4°41N 119°24E 233 J2
Tumiritinga Brazil 18°58S 41°38W 333 E3
Tumkur = Tumakuru India 13°18N 77°6E 245 H3
Tumon B. Guam 13°31N 144°48E 302 d
Tump Pakistan 26°7N 62°16E 240 D1
Tumpat Malaysia 6°11N 102°10E 237 J4
Tumsar India 21°26N 79°45E 244 D4
Tumu Ghana 10°56N 1°56W 262 C4
Tumucumaque, Serra Brazil 2°0N 55°0W 329 C7
Tumupasa Bolivia 14°9S 67°55W 330 C4
Tumut Australia 35°16S 148°13E 283 C8
Tumwater U.S.A. 47°1N 122°54W 306 C4
Tumxuk China 41°22N 79°58E 217 D9
Tun Sweden 58°26N 12°43E 163 F6
Tuna India 22°59N 70°5E 242 H4
Tunapuna Trin. & Tob. 10°38N 61°24W 323 t
Tunas de Zaza Cuba 21°39N 79°34W 320 B4
Tunbridge Wells = Royal Tunbridge Wells U.K. 51°7N 0°16E 169 F8
Tunçbilek Turkey 39°37N 29°29E 205 B11
Tunceli Turkey 39°6N 39°31E 213 C8
Tunceli □ Turkey 39°5N 39°35E 213 C8
Tunchang China 19°21N 110°5E 229 a
Tuncurry Australia 32°17S 152°29E 283 B10
Tundla India 27°12N 78°17E 242 F8
Tundubai Sudan 18°36N 28°35E 256 D2
Tunduru Tanzania 11°8S 37°25E 269 E4
Tundzha → Bulgaria 41°40N 26°35E 203 E10
Tung Chung Hong Kong, China 22°17N 113°57E 122 B1
Tung Lung Chau Hong Kong, China 22°15N 114°17E 122 B3
Tung O Hong Kong, China 22°11N 114°8E 122 B2
Tunga → India 15°0N 75°50E 245 G2
Tunga Pass Asia 29°0N 94°14E 241 A5
Tungabhadra → India 15°57N 78°15E 245 G4
Tungabhadra Dam India 15°0N 75°50E 245 G2
Tungao Taiwan 24°31N 121°50E 225 B3
Tungaru Sudan 10°9N 30°52E 257 E3
Tungawan Phil. 7°30N 122°20E 233 H4
Tungchi Yü Taiwan 23°15N 119°40E 225 C1
Tungch'uan = Dongchuan China 26°8N 103°1E 228 D4
Tungho Taiwan 22°58N 121°18E 225 D3
T'unghsiao Taiwan 24°29N 120°40E 225 B2
Tunghwa = Tonghua China 41°42N 125°58E 224 B2
Tungi Bangla. 23°53N 90°24E 241 D3
Tungkang Taiwan 22°27N 120°26E 225 D2
Tungku Malaysia 5°1N 118°53E 235 A5
Tungla Nic. 13°24N 84°21W 320 D3
T'unglo Taiwan 24°30N 120°47E 225 B2
Tungnafellsjökull Iceland 64°45N 17°55W 155 C9
Tungsha Tao = Dongsha Dao S. China Sea 20°45N 116°43E 219 G12
Tungshan Taiwan 24°38N 121°47E 225 B3
Tungshih Changhua, Taiwan 24°12N 120°43E 225 B2
Tungshih Chiai, Taiwan 23°27N 120°8E 225 C2
Tungsten Canada 61°57N 128°16W 296 A3
Tungufell Iceland 64°17N 20°10W 155 C6
Tungurahua □ Ecuador 1°15S 78°35W 328 D2
Tunguska, Nizhnyaya → Russia 65°48N 88°4E 215 C9
Tunguska, Podkamennaya → Russia 61°50N 90°13E 215 C10
Tungyin Tao Taiwan 26°22N 128°29E 225 b
Tuni India 17°22N 82°36E 244 F6
Tunia Colombia 2°41N 76°31W 328 C2
Tunica U.S.A. 34°41N 90°23W 315 D9
Tunis Baghdād, Iraq 33°23N 44°21E 113 A2
Tunis Tunisia 36°50N 10°11E 258 A2
Tunis □ Tunisia 36°46N 10°10E 261 A7
Tunis ✈ (TUN) Tunisia 36°52N 10°14E 200 F3
Tunis, Golfe de Tunisia 37°0N 10°30E 258 A2
Tunisia ■ Africa 33°30N 9°10E 258 B1
Tunja Colombia 5°33N 73°25W 328 B3
Tunkhannock U.S.A. 41°32N 75°57W 313 E9
Tunkinsky △ Russia 51°30N 102°0E 215 D11
Tunliu China 36°13N 112°52E 226 F7
Tunnel Creek △ Australia 17°41S 125°18E 278 C4
Tunnsjøen Norway 64°45N 13°25E 160 D15
Tunø Denmark 55°57N 10°27E 163 J4
Tuntutuliak U.S.A. 60°22N 162°38W 303 F7
Tununak U.S.A. 60°37N 165°15W 303 F6
Tunungayualok I. Canada 56°0N 61°0W 299 A7
Tunuyán Argentina 33°35S 69°0W 334 C2
Tunuyán → Argentina 33°33S 67°30W 334 C2
Tunxi = Huangshan China 29°42N 118°25E 229 C12
Tuo Jiang → China 28°50N 105°35E 228 C5
Tuolumne U.S.A. 37°58N 120°15W 306 H6
Tuolumne → U.S.A. 37°36N 121°13W 306 H5
Tuomarila Finland 60°11N 24°41E 121 B1
Tüp Kyrgyzstan 42°45N 78°20E 217 D9
Tūp Āghāj Iran 36°3N 47°50E 213 D12
Tupã Brazil 21°57S 50°28W 335 A5
Tupaciguara Brazil 18°35S 48°42W 333 E2
Tupelo U.S.A. 34°16N 88°43W 315 D10
Tupik Russia 55°42N 33°22E 188 E7
Tupinambarana, I. Brazil 3°0S 58°0W 329 D6
Tupirama Brazil 8°58S 48°12W 332 C2
Tupiratins Brazil 8°23S 48°8W 332 C2
Tupiza Bolivia 21°30S 65°40W 334 A2
Tupižnica Serbia 43°43N 22°10E 202 C6
Tupman U.S.A. 35°18N 119°21W 307 K7
Tupper Canada 55°32N 120°1W 296 B4
Tupper L. U.S.A. 44°10N 74°32W 313 B10
Tupper Lake U.S.A. 44°14N 74°28W 313 B10
Tüpqarghan Muyis Kazakhstan 44°40N 50°19E 191 H10
Tupungato, Cerro S. Amer. 33°15S 69°50W 334 C2
Tuquan China 45°18N 121°38E 227 B11
Túquerres Colombia 1°5N 77°37W 328 C2
Tura India 25°30N 90°16E 241 C3
Tura Russia 64°20N 100°17E 215 C11
Turabah Ḥā'il, Si. Arabia 28°20N 43°15E 246 D4
Turabah Makkah, Si. Arabia 21°15N 41°34E 248 B3
Turagua, Serranía Venezuela 7°20N 64°35W 329 B5
Turakina N.Z. 40°3S 175°16E 284 G4
Turakina → N.Z. 40°5S 175°8E 284 G4
Turakirae Hd. N.Z. 41°26S 174°56E 284 H3
Turama → Papua N. G. 7°40S 143°50E 286 D2
Tūrān Iran 35°39N 56°42E 247 C8
Turan Russia 51°55N 94°0E 217 B12
Tūrān △ Iran 35°45N 56°30E 247 C8
Turan Lowland Asia 43°30N 62°0E 216 D6
Turangi N.Z. 38°59S 175°48E 284 E4
Ţurayf Si. Arabia 31°41N 38°39E 246 D3
Turbaco Colombia 10°21N 75°25W 328 A2
Turbacz Poland 49°30N 20°8E 185 J7
Turbat Pakistan 25°59N 63°4E 240 D1
Turbe Bos.-H. 44°15N 17°35E 182 F2
Turbeville U.S.A. 33°54N 80°1W 316 B9
Turbo Colombia 8°6N 76°43W 328 B2
Turčianske Teplice Slovakia 48°52N 18°52E 181 C11
Turco Bolivia 18°10S 68°11W 330 D4
Turcoaia Romania 45°7N 28°11E 183 E13
Turda Romania 46°34N 23°47E 183 D8
Tureberg Sweden 59°25N 17°55E 139 A1
Turéia French Polynesia 20°50S 138°32W 289 f
Turek Poland 52°3N 18°30E 185 F5
Turfan = Turpan China 43°58N 89°10E 217 D11
Turfan Basin = Turpan Pendi China 42°40N 89°25E 217 D11
Turfan Depression = Turpan Pendi China 42°40N 89°25E 217 D11
Turffontein S. Africa 26°14S 28°2E 123 B2
Turgayskaya Stolovaya Strana = Torghay Ustirti Asia 51°0N 63°0E 216 B6
Turgeon → Canada 50°0N 78°56W 298 C4
Tŭrgovishte Bulgaria 43°17N 26°38E 203 C10
Tŭrgovishte □ Bulgaria 43°17N 26°38E 203 C10
Turgut Turkey 37°22N 28°4E 205 D10
Turgutlu Turkey 38°30N 27°43E 205 C9
Turgutreis Turkey 37°2N 27°15E 205 D9
Turgwe → Zimbabwe 21°31S 32°15E 271 B5
Turhal Turkey 40°24N 36°5E 212 B7
Turia → Spain 39°27N 0°19W 197 F4
Turiaçu Brazil 1°40S 45°19W 332 B2
Turiaçu → Brazil 1°36S 45°19W 332 B2
Turiec → Slovakia 49°7N 18°55E 181 B11
Turin = Torino Italy 45°3N 7°40E 198 C4
Turinskaya Kultbaza = Tura Russia 64°20N 100°17E 215 C11
Türk Telekom Arena Istanbul, Turkey 41°5N 28°59E 122 B1
Turka Ukraine 49°10N 23°2E 185 J10
Turkana □ Kenya 3°10N 35°20E 268 B4
Turkana, L. Africa 3°30N 36°5E 268 B4
Turkayel Ethiopia 8°7N 45°21E 267 C6
Türkeli Turkey 40°30N 27°30E 203 F11
Turkestan = Türkistan Kazakhstan 43°17N 68°16E 217 D7
Turkestan Range Asia 39°35N 69°0E 217 E7
Túrkeve Hungary 47°6N 20°44E 182 C5
Turkey ■ Eurasia 39°0N 36°0E 212 C7
Turkey → U.S.A. 42°43N 91°2W 310 B5
Turkey Creek = Warmun Australia 17°2S 128°12E 278 C4
Turkey L. U.S.A. 28°30N 81°28W 133 A2
Turkey Lake Park U.S.A. 28°30N 81°28W 133 A2
Turki Russia 52°0N 43°15E 190 D6
Türkistan Kazakhstan 43°17N 68°16E 217 D7
Türkmenabat Turkmenistan 39°6N 63°34E 247 B9
Türkmenbashi Turkmenistan 40°5N 53°5E 247 A7
Turkmenistan ■ Asia 39°0N 59°0E 216 E5
Türkmenli Turkey 39°45N 26°30E 205 B8
Türkoğlu Turkey 37°23N 36°50E 212 D7
Turks & Caicos Is. ☒ W. Indies 21°20N 71°20W 321 B5
Turks Island Passage Turks & Caicos 21°25N 71°19W 321 B5
Turku Finland 60°30N 22°19E 188 B2
Turkwel → Kenya 3°6N 36°6E 268 B4
Turlock U.S.A. 37°30N 120°51W 306 H6
Turnagain Australia 9°34S 142°17E 280 a
Turnagain → Canada 59°12N 127°35W 296 B3
Turnagain, C. N.Z. 40°28S 176°38E 284 G5
Turneffe Is. Belize 17°20N 87°50W 320 C2
Turner U.S.A. 48°51N 108°24W 304 B9
Turner Field Atlanta, U.S.A. 33°44N 84°23W 113 B2
Turner Pt. Australia 11°47S 133°32E 280 A1
Turner Valley Canada 50°40N 114°17W 296 C6
Turners Falls U.S.A. 42°36N 72°33W 313 D12
Turner's Pen. S. Leone 7°22N 12°24W 262 D2
Turnham Green U.K. 51°29N 0°16W 125 B2
Turnhouse U.K. 55°57N 3°20W 121 B1
Turnhout Belgium 51°19N 4°57E 170 C4
Türnitz Austria 47°55N 15°29E 180 D8
Turnor L. Canada 56°35N 108°35W 297 B7
Turnov Czechia 50°34N 15°10E 180 A8
Tŭrnovo = Veliko Tŭrnovo Bulgaria 43°5N 25°41E 203 C9
Turnu Măgurele Romania 43°46N 24°56E 183 G9
Turnu Roşu, P. Romania 45°33N 24°17E 183 E9
Turobin Poland 50°50N 22°44E 185 H9
Tuross Head Australia 36°3S 150°8E 283 D9
Turpan China 43°58N 89°10E 217 D11
Turpan Pendi China 42°40N 89°25E 217 D11
Turrawan Australia 30°28S 149°53E 283 A8
Turrës, Kala e Albania 41°10N 19°28E 202 E3
Turriff U.K. 57°32N 2°27W 167 D6
Tursāq Iraq 33°27N 45°47E 213 F11
Tursi Italy 40°15N 16°28E 201 B9
Tursunzoda Tajikistan 38°30N 68°14E 217 E7
Turtle Beach St. Kitts & Nevis 17°14N 62°38W 322 d
Turtle Head I. Australia 10°56S 142°37E 286 F2
Turtle Is. Phil. 6°7N 118°14E 233 H2
Turtle Is. S. Leone 7°40N 13°0W 262 D2
Turtle Islands Phil. 6°13N 118°6E 235 A5
Turtle L. Canada 53°36N 108°38W 297 C7
Turtle Lake U.S.A. 47°31N 100°53W 308 B3
Turtleford Canada 53°23N 108°57W 297 C7
Turtucaia = Tutrakan Bulgaria 44°2N 26°40E 203 B10
Turua N.Z. 37°14S 175°35E 284 D4
Turukhansk Russia 65°21N 88°5E 215 C9
Turyinskiye Rudniki = Krasnoturinsk Russia 59°46N 60°12E 186 C11
Turzovka Slovakia 49°25N 18°35E 181 B11
Tuscaloosa U.S.A. 33°12N 87°34W 315 E11
Tuscánia Italy 42°25N 11°52E 199 F8
Tuscany = Toscana □ Italy 43°25N 11°0E 198 E8
Tuscarawas → U.S.A. 40°24N 81°25W 312 F3
Tuscarora Mt. U.S.A. 40°55N 77°55W 312 F7
Tuscola Ill., U.S.A. 39°48N 88°17W 311 E8
Tuscola Tex., U.S.A. 32°12N 99°48W 314 E5
Tuscolana, Via Italy 41°52N 12°31E 136 B2
Tuscumbia Ala., U.S.A. 34°44N 87°42W 315 D11
Tuscumbia Mo., U.S.A. 38°14N 92°28W 310 F4
Tuskegee U.S.A. 32°25N 85°42W 316 C4
Tusket Wedge = Wedgeport Canada 43°44N 65°59W 299 D6
Tustna Norway 63°10N 8°5E 164 A5
Tuszyn Poland 51°36N 19°33E 185 G6
Tutak Turkey 39°31N 42°46E 213 C10
Tutayev Russia 57°53N 39°32E 188 D10
Tuticorin India 8°50N 78°12E 245 K4
Tutin Serbia 42°58N 20°20E 202 D4
Tutóia Brazil 2°45S 42°20W 332 B3
Tutong Brunei 4°47N 114°40E 235 B4
Tutova → Romania 46°7N 27°30E 183 D12
Tutrakan Bulgaria 44°2N 26°40E 203 B10
Tuttle Creek L. U.S.A. 39°15N 96°36W 308 F5
Tuttlingen Germany 47°58N 8°48E 179 H4
Tutuala E. Timor 8°25S 127°15E 231 F7
Tutuba Vanuatu 15°33S 167°16E 287 E5
Tutubeia Papua N. G. 9°34S 150°40E 286 E6
Tutuila Amer. Samoa 14°19S 170°50W 302 f
Tutuko, Mt. N.Z. 44°35S 168°1E 285 E3
Tutun Egypt 29°9N 30°46E 256 J7
Tütz = Tuczno Poland 53°13N 16°10E 185 E3
Tuul Gol → Mongolia 48°30N 104°25E 218 B9
Tuva □ Russia 51°30N 95°0E 217 B12
Tuvalu ■ Pac. Oc. 8°0S 178°0E 277 B14
Tuvuca Fiji 17°40S 178°48W 287 A3
Tūwal Si. Arabia 22°17N 39°6E 248 B2
Tuxer Alpen Austria 47°10N 11°45E 180 D4
Tuxpan Mexico 20°57N 97°24W 319 C5
Tuxtla Gutiérrez Mexico 16°45N 93°7W 319 D6
Tuy = Tui Spain 42°3N 8°39W 194 C2
Tuy Duc Vietnam 12°15N 107°27E 237 F6
Tuy Phong Vietnam 11°14N 108°43E 237 G7
Tuya L. Canada 59°7N 130°35W 296 B2
Tuyen Hoa Vietnam 17°50N 106°10E 236 D6
Tuyen Quang Vietnam 21°50N 105°10E 228 G5
Tuymazy Russia 54°36N 53°42E 216 B4
Tūysarkān Iran 34°33N 48°27E 213 E13
Tuyün = Duyun China 26°18N 107°29E 228 D6
Tuz Gölü Turkey 38°42N 33°18E 212 C5
Ţūz Khurmātū Iraq 34°56N 44°38E 213 E11
Tuzi Montenegro 42°22N 19°20E 202 D3
Tuzigoot △ U.S.A. 34°46N 112°2W 305 J7
Tuzla Bos.-H. 44°34N 18°41E 182 F3
Tuzla Turkey 36°42N 35°6E 250 B6
Tuzlov → Russia 47°17N 39°57E 189 J10
Tuzluca Turkey 40°3N 43°39E 213 B10
Tuzly Ukraine 45°54N 30°6E 183 E15
Tvååker Sweden 57°4N 12°25E 163 G6
Tvardiţa Moldova 46°9N 28°58E 183 D13
Tvedestrand Norway 58°38N 8°58E 164 F5
Tver Russia 56°55N 35°59E 188 D8
Tver □ Russia 56°50N 35°0E 188 D8
Tvrdošin Slovakia 49°21N 19°35E 181 B12
Tvrdošovce Slovakia 48°6N 18°4E 181 C11
Tvŭrditsa Bulgaria 42°42N 25°53E 203 D9
Twain U.S.A. 40°1N 121°3W 306 E5
Twain Harte U.S.A. 38°2N 120°14W 306 G6
Twardogóra Poland 51°23N 17°28E 185 G4
Twee River Namibia 25°27S 19°27E 270 C2
Tweed Canada 44°29N 77°19W 312 B7
Tweed → U.K. 55°45N 2°0W 167 F6
Tweed Heads Australia 28°10S 153°31E 281 D5
Tweedsmuir ⌓ Canada 53°0N 126°20W 296 C3
Twelve Apostles S. Africa 33°58S 18°23E 118 A1
Twentieth Century Fox Studios U.S.A. 34°4N 118°25W 126 B2
Twentynine Palms U.S.A. 34°8N 116°3W 307 L10
Tweya Dem. Rep. of the Congo 0°54S 18°58E 264 C3
Twickenham U.K. 51°26N 0°20W 125 B1
Twickenham Rugby Ground U.K. 51°27N 0°20W 125 B1
Twillingate Canada 49°42N 54°45W 299 C9
Twin Bridges U.S.A. 45°33N 112°20W 304 D7
Twin City U.S.A. 32°35N 82°10W 316 C7
Twin Falls Canada 53°30N 64°32W 299 B7
Twin Falls Idaho, U.S.A. 42°34N 114°28W 304 E6
Twin Hills U.S.A. 59°23N 159°58W 303 G8
Twin Lakes U.S.A. 30°43N 83°13W 316 E6
Twin Peaks U.S.A. 37°45N 122°26W 136 B2
Twin Valley U.S.A. 47°16N 96°16W 308 B5
Twinnge Burma 23°10N 96°2E 241 D6
Twins, The Hong Kong, China 22°15N 114°12E 122 B3
Twinsburg U.S.A. 41°19N 81°26W 312 E3
Twistringen Germany 52°48N 8°37E 178 C4
Twitchell Res. U.S.A. 34°59N 120°19W 307 L6
Two Boats Village Ascension I. 7°56S 14°22W 153 g
Two Harbors U.S.A. 47°2N 91°40W 308 B8
Two Hills Canada 53°43N 111°52W 296 C6
Two Rivers U.S.A. 44°9N 87°34W 308 C10
Two Rocks Australia 31°30S 115°35E 279 F2
Two Thumb Ra. N.Z. 43°45S 170°44E 285 D5
Twofold B. Australia 37°8S 149°59E 283 D8
Twyfelfontein Namibia 20°34S 14°22E 270 B1
Ty Ty U.S.A. 31°28N 83°39W 316 D6
Tyachiv Ukraine 48°1N 23°35E 177 D12
Tybee Island U.S.A. 32°1N 80°51W 316 C9
Tychy Poland 50°9N 18°59E 185 H5
Tyczyn Poland 49°58N 22°2E 185 J9
Tydal Norway 63°4N 11°34E 164 A8
Tyin Norway 61°18N 8°15E 164 C5
Tykocin Poland 53°13N 22°46E 185 E9
Tyler Minn., U.S.A. 44°17N 96°8W 308 C5
Tyler Tex., U.S.A. 32°21N 95°18W 314 E7
Tyligul → Ukraine 47°4N 30°57E 189 J6
Tylldal Norway 62°8N 10°48E 164 B7
Tymanivka Ukraine 48°34N 28°50E 183 B13
Týn nad Vltavou Czechia 49°13N 14°26E 180 B7
Tynda Russia 55°10N 124°43E 215 D13
Tyndall U.S.A. 43°0N 97°50W 308 D5
Tyndinsky = Tynda Russia 55°10N 124°43E 215 D13
Tyne → U.K. 54°59N 1°32W 168 C6
Tyne & Wear □ U.K. 55°6N 1°17W 168 B6
Týnec nad Sázavou Czechia 49°50N 14°36E 180 B7
Tynemouth U.K. 55°1N 1°26W 168 B6
Tynset Norway 62°17N 10°47E 164 B7
Tyonek U.S.A. 61°4N 151°8W 303 F10
Tyre = Sūr Lebanon 33°19N 35°16E 250 E6
Tyresta △ Sweden 59°12N 18°14E 162 E12
Tyrifjorden Norway 60°2N 10°8E 164 D7
Tyringe Sweden 56°9N 13°35E 163 H7
Tyristrand Norway 60°4N 10°6E 164 D7
Tyrnyauz Russia 43°21N 42°45E 191 J6
Tyrol = Tirol □ Austria 47°3N 10°43E 180 D3
Tyrone U.S.A. 40°40N 78°14W 312 F6
Tyrone □ U.K. 54°38N 7°11W 166 B4
Tyrrel Bay Grenada 12°27N 61°28W 323 q
Tyrrell → Australia 35°26S 142°51E 282 C5
Tyrrell, L. Australia 35°20S 142°50E 282 C5
Tyrrell L. Canada 63°7N 105°27W 297 A7
Tyrrhenian Sea Medit. S. 40°0N 12°30E 192 D6
Tysfjorden Norway 68°7N 16°25E 160 B17
Tysmenytsya Ukraine 48°54N 24°51E 183 B9
Tysnes Norway 60°1N 5°30E 164 D2
Tysnesøya Norway 60°0N 5°35E 164 D2
Tysse Norway 60°23N 5°47E 164 D2
Tyssedal Norway 60°7N 6°35E 164 D3
Tystberga Sweden 58°51N 17°15E 163 F11
Tytuvėnai Lithuania 55°36N 23°12E 184 C10
Tyub Karagan, Mys = Tüpqarghan Muyis Kazakhstan 44°40N 50°19E 191 H10
Tyuleni, Ostrova = Tüledi Araldary Kazakhstan 45°2N 50°16E 191 H10
Tyuleniy Russia 44°28N 47°30E 191 H8
Tyuleniy, Mys Azerbaijan 40°12N 50°22E 191 K10
Tyulgan Russia 52°22N 56°12E 186 D10
Tyumen Russia 57°11N 65°29E 214 D7
Tyup = Tüp Kyrgyzstan 42°45N 78°20E 217 D9
Tywi → U.K. 51°48N 4°21W 169 F3
Tywyn U.K. 52°35N 4°5W 169 E3
Tzaneen S. Africa 23°47S 30°9E 271 B5
Tzermiado Greece 35°12N 25°29E 207 E6
Tzia = Kea Greece 37°35N 24°22E 204 D6
Tzoumérka, Óros = Athamanon Oros Greece 39°30N 21°26E 204 B3
Tzukong = Zigong China 29°15N 104°48E 228 C5
Tzukuan Taiwan 22°46N 120°16E 225 D2
Tzupo = Boshan China 36°28N 117°49E 227 F9
Tzutung Taiwan 23°45N 120°30E 225 C2

U

U.S.A. = United States of America ■ N. Amer. 37°0N 96°0W 301 H20
U.S. Capitol Washington, D.C., U.S.A. 143 b3
U.S. Cellular Field Chicago, U.S.A. 41°50N 87°37W 119 C3
U.S.S. Arizona ⌓ U.S.A. 21°22N 157°57W 302 K14
U.S.S. Constitution Boston, U.S.A. 116 a3
U.S. Virgin Is. ☒ W. Indies 18°20N 65°0W 321 C7
Ua Huka French Polynesia 8°55S 139°32W 289 f
Ua Pu French Polynesia 9°25S 140°0W 289 f
Uachadi, Sierra = Uasadi-jidi Venezuela 4°54N 65°18W 329 C4
Uad Atui → W. Sahara 20°4N 15°59W 260 D2
Uad el Jat → W. Sahara 26°47N 13°3W 260 C2
Uaimh, An = Navan Ireland 53°39N 6°41W 166 C5
Uainambi Colombia 1°43N 69°51W 328 C4
Uamba Angola 7°21S 16°10E 265 D3
Uanle Uen = Wanleweyne Somalia 2°37N 44°54E 267 D5
Uasadi-jidi Venezuela 4°54N 65°18W 329 C4
Uasin Gishu □ Kenya 0°30N 35°15E 268 B4
Uati-Paraná → Brazil 1°51S 65°37W 328 D4
Uatumã → Brazil 2°26S 57°37W 329 D6
Uauá Brazil 9°50S 39°28W 332 C4
Uaupés Brazil 0°8S 67°5W 328 D4
Uaupés → Brazil 0°2N 67°16W 328 C4
Uaxactún Guatemala 17°25N 89°29W 320 C2
Ub Serbia 44°28N 20°6E 202 B4
Ubá Brazil 21°8S 43°0W 333 F3
Uba Nigeria 10°29N 13°13E 263 C7
Ubai Papua N. G. 5°39S 150°38E 286 C6
Ubaitaba Brazil 14°18S 39°20W 333 D4
Ubajara △ Brazil 3°55S 40°50W 332 B3
Ubangi = Oubangi → Dem. Rep. of the Congo 0°30S 17°50E 264 C3
Ubaté Colombia 5°19N 73°49W 328 B3
Ubauro Pakistan 28°15N 69°45E 242 E3
Ubay Phil. 10°3N 124°28E 233 F5
Ubaye → France 44°28N 6°18E 175 D10
Ubayyiḍ, W. al → Iraq 32°34N 43°48E 213 F10
Ube Japan 33°56N 131°15E 222 D3
Úbeda Spain 38°3N 3°23W 195 G7
Ubeidiya West Bank 31°43N 35°17E 123 B2
Uberaba Brazil 19°50S 47°55W 333 E2
Uberaba → Brazil 23°35S 46°41W 137 B2
Uberaba, L. Brazil 17°30S 57°50W 331 D6
Uberlândia Minas Gerais, Brazil 19°0S 48°20W 333 E2
Uberlândia Roraïma, Brazil 0°48N 59°20W 329 C6
Überlingen Germany 47°46N 9°10E 179 H5
Ubiaja Nigeria 6°41N 6°22E 263 D6
Ubin, Pulau Singapore 1°24N 103°57E 138 A3
Ubly U.S.A. 43°42N 82°55W 312 C2
Ubolratna Res. Thailand 16°45N 102°30E 236 D4
Ubombo S. Africa 27°31S 32°4E 271 C5
Ubon Ratchathani Thailand 15°15N 104°50E 236 E5
Ubondo Dem. Rep. of the Congo 0°55S 25°42E 268 C2
Ubort → Belarus 52°6N 28°30E 177 B15
Ubrique Spain 36°41N 5°27W 195 J5
Ubud Indonesia 8°30S 115°16E 231 J18
Ubuna Solomon Is. 10°11S 161°24E 287 N11
Ubundu Dem. Rep. of the Congo 0°22S 25°30E 264 C5
Ucar Azerbaijan 40°31N 47°39E 191 K8
Ucayali → Peru 4°30S 73°30W 328 D3
Uccle Belgium 50°48N 4°22E 116 B2
Uchab Namibia 19°47S 17°42E 270 A2
Uchiko Japan 33°33N 132°39E 222 D4
Uchiura-Wan Japan 42°25N 140°40E 220 C10
Uchiza Peru 8°25S 76°20W 330 B2
Uchquduq Uzbekistan 41°50N 62°50E 216 D6
Uchte Germany 52°30N 8°54E 178 C4
Uchur → Russia 58°48N 130°35E 215 D14
Uckermark Germany 53°5N 13°30E 178 B9
Ucluelet Canada 48°57N 125°32W 296 D3
Úcua Angola 8°43S 14°8E 265 D2
Uda → Russia 54°42N 135°14E 215 D14
Uda Walawe △ Sri Lanka 6°20N 81°0E 245 L5
Udachnyy Russia 66°25N 112°24E 215 C12
Udagamandalam India 11°30N 76°44E 245 J3
Udainagar India 22°33N 76°13E 242 H7
Udaipur Raj., India 24°36N 73°44E 242 G5
Udaipur Tripura, India 23°32N 91°30E 241 D3
Udaipur Garhi Nepal 27°0N 86°35E 243 F12
Udala India 21°35N 86°34E 243 J12
Udalguri India 26°46N 92°8E 241 B4
Udayagiri Andhra Pradesh, India 14°52N 79°19E 245 G4
Udayagiri Odisha, India 20°8N 84°23E 244 D7
Udbina Croatia 44°31N 15°47E 199 D12
Uddeholm Sweden 60°1N 13°38E 162 D7
Uddevalla Sweden 58°21N 11°55E 163 F5
Uddheden Sweden 59°57N 12°54E 162 E6
Uddjaure Sweden 65°56N 17°49E 160 D17
Udegeyskaya Legenda △ Russia 45°45N 135°30E 220 B7
Udelnaya Russia 60°0N 30°21E 137 A2
Udelnoe Russia 59°58N 30°20E 137 B1
Uden Neths. 51°40N 5°37E 170 C5
Udgir India 18°25N 77°5E 244 E3
Udhampur India 33°0N 75°5E 243 C6
Udi Nigeria 6°17N 7°21E 263 D6
Údine Italy 46°3N 13°14E 199 B10
Udintsev Fracture Zone S. Ocean 57°0S 145°0W 151 B13
Udlding Germany 48°15N 11°25E 131 A1
Udmurtia □ Russia 57°30N 52°30E 186 C9
Udon Thani Thailand 17°29N 102°46E 236 D4
Udong Cambodia 11°48N 104°45E 237 G5
Udot I. Micronesia 7°22N 151°42E 287 T17
Udskaya Guba Russia 54°50N 135°45E 215 D14
Udu Pt. Fiji 16°9S 179°57W 287 A3
Udumalaippettai India 10°35N 77°15E 245 J3
Udupi India 13°25N 74°42E 245 H2
Udva India 20°5N 73°0E 244 D1
Udvoy Balkan Bulgaria 42°50N 26°50E 203 D10
Udzungwa △ Tanzania 7°52S 36°35E 268 D4
Udzungwa Range Tanzania 9°30S 35°10E 269 D4
Ueckermünde Germany 53°44N 14°1E 178 B10
Ueda Japan 36°24N 138°16E 223 A10
Uedineniya, Os. Russia 78°0N 85°0E 150 B12
Uele → Dem. Rep. of the Congo 3°45N 24°45E 264 B4
Uelen Russia 66°10N 170°0W 215 C19
Uelzen Germany 52°57N 10°32E 178 C6
Ueno Mie, Japan 34°45N 136°8E 223 C8
Ueno Tōkyō, Japan 35°42N 139°46E 140 A3
Uetersen Germany 53°40N 9°40E 178 B5
Uetze Germany 52°28N 10°11E 178 C6
Ufa Russia 54°45N 55°55E 186 D10
Ufa → Russia 54°40N 56°0E 186 D10
Uffenheim Germany 49°33N 10°14E 179 F6
Ugab → Namibia 20°55S 13°30E 270 B1
Ugalla → Tanzania 5°8S 30°42E 268 D3
Ugalla River ⌓ Tanzania 5°50S 31°54E 268 D3
Uganda ■ Africa 2°0N 32°0E 268 B3
Ugento Italy 39°56N 18°10E 201 C11
Ugep Nigeria 5°53N 8°2E 263 D6
Ughelli Nigeria 5°33N 6°0E 263 D6
Ugie S. Africa 31°10S 28°13E 271 D4
Ugíjar Spain 36°58N 3°7W 195 J7
Ugine France 45°45N 6°25E 175 C10
Uglegorsk Russia 49°5N 142°2E 215 E15
Uglich Russia 57°33N 38°20E 188 D10
Ugljan Croatia 44°12N 15°10E 199 D12
Ugljane Croatia 43°35N 16°46E 199 E13
Ugolny = Beringovskiy Russia 63°3N 179°19E 215 C18
Ugolny = Karpinsk Russia 59°45N 60°1E 186 C11
Ugolnye Kopi = Kopeysk Russia 55°7N 61°37E 216 A6
Ugolnye Kopi Russia 64°44N 177°42E 215 C18
Ugoofaaru Maldives 5°40N 73°0E 272 d
Ugra → Russia 54°30N 36°7E 188 E9
Ugra △ Russia 54°45N 35°30E 188 E8
Ugŭrchin Bulgaria 43°6N 24°26E 203 C8
Uh → Slovakia 48°37N 22°0E 181 C15
Uherské Hradiště Czechia 49°4N 17°30E 181 B10
Uherský Brod Czechia 49°1N 17°40E 181 B10
Úhlava → Czechia 49°45N 13°24E 180 B6
Uhlenhorst Namibia 23°45S 17°55E 270 B2
Uhniv Ukraine 50°22N 23°45E 185 H10
Üholičky Czechia 50°9N 14°19E 135 B1
Uhrichsville U.S.A. 40°24N 81°21W 312 F3
Uhřiněves Czechia 50°2N 14°35E 135 B3
Uibhist a Deas = South Uist U.K. 57°20N 7°15W 167 D1
Uibhist a Tuath = North Uist U.K. 57°40N 7°15W 167 D1
Uiche Angola 12°2S 20°51E 265 E4
Uido S. Korea 34°36N 125°50E 224 E2
Uig U.K. 57°35N 6°21W 167 D2
Uíge Angola 7°30S 14°40E 265 D2
Uíge □ Angola 7°0S 16°0E 265 D3
Uiha Tonga 19°54S 174°25W 287 P13
Uijeongbu S. Korea 37°44N 127°2E 224 D3
Ŭiju N. Korea 40°15N 124°35E 224 B2
Uinta Mts. U.S.A. 40°45N 110°30W 304 F8
Uiryeong S. Korea 35°19N 128°15E 224 E4
Uis Namibia 21°8S 14°49E 270 B1
Uiseong S. Korea 36°21N 128°45E 224 D4
Uitenhage S. Africa 33°40S 25°28E 270 D4
Uithoorn Neths. 52°14N 4°50E 112 B1
Uithuizen Neths. 53°24N 6°41E 170 A6
Ujazd Poland 50°23N 18°21E 185 H5
Ujazdów Poland 52°13N 21°1E 143 B2
Ujazdowski Castle Warsaw, Poland 143 c3
Újfehértó Hungary 47°49N 21°41E 182 C6
Ujh → India 32°10N 75°18E 242 C6
Ujhani India 28°0N 79°6E 243 F8
Uji Japan 34°53N 135°48E 223 C7
Uji-guntō Japan 31°15N 129°25E 221 J4
Ujiyamada = Ise Japan 34°25N 136°45E 223 C8
Ujjain India 23°9N 75°43E 242 H6
Újpalota Hungary 47°32N 19°8E 117 A2
Újpest Hungary 47°35N 19°4E 117 A2
Ujście Poland 53°3N 16°45E 185 E3
Ujście Warty △ Poland 52°35N 14°44E 185 F1
Újszász Hungary 47°19N 20°7E 182 C5
Ujung Kulon △ Indonesia 6°46S 105°19E 234 D3
Ujung Pandang = Makassar Indonesia 5°10S 119°20E 235 D5
Uka Russia 57°50N 162°0E 215 D17
Ukai Sagar India 21°20N 73°43E 244 D1
Ukara I. Tanzania 1°50S 33°0E 268 C3
Uke-Shima Japan 28°2N 129°14E 221 K4
Ukerewe I. Tanzania 2°0S 33°0E 268 C3
uKhahlamba Drakensberg ⌓ S. Africa 29°27S 29°30E 271 C4
Ukholovo Russia 53°47N 40°30E 190 D5
Ukhrul India 25°10N 94°25E 241 C5
Ukhta Russia 63°34N 53°41E 186 B9
Uki Ni Masi Solomon Is. 10°15S 161°47E 287 N11
Ukiah U.S.A. 39°9N 123°13W 306 F3
Ukita Japan 35°40N 139°51E 140 A4
Ukkusiksalik △ Canada 65°20N 89°30W 294 D14
Ukmergė Lithuania 55°15N 24°45E 188 E3
Ukraine ■ Europe 49°0N 32°0E 189 H7
Uku Angola 11°24S 14°22E 265 E2
Ukwi Botswana 23°29S 20°30E 270 B3
Ula Turkey 37°6N 28°25E 212 D3
Ulaan Nuur Mongolia 44°30N 103°40E 226 B2
Ulaan-Uul Mongolia 46°4N 100°49E 218 B9
Ulaanbaatar Mongolia 47°55N 106°53E 218 B10
Ulaangom Mongolia 50°5N 92°10E 217 B12
Ulaanjirem Mongolia 45°5N 105°30E 226 B3
Ulak I. U.S.A. 51°22N 178°57W 303 L3
Ulala = Gorno-Altaysk Russia 51°50N 86°5E 217 B11
Ulalu I. Micronesia 7°23N 151°41E 287 T17
Ulamambri Australia 31°19S 149°23E 283 A8
Ulamba Dem. Rep. of the Congo 9°3S 23°38E 265 D4
Ulamona Papua N. G. 5°0S 151°15E 286 C6
Ulan Bator = Ulaanbaatar Mongolia 47°55N 106°53E 218 B10
Ulan Erge Russia 46°19N 44°53E 191 G7
Ulan Khol Russia 45°18N 47°4E 191 H8
Ulan Ude Russia 51°45N 107°40E 219 A10
Ulanhad = Chifeng China 42°18N 118°58E 227 C10
Ulanhot = Horqin Youyi Qianqi China 46°5N 122°3E 227 A12
Ulanów Poland 50°30N 22°16E 185 H9
Ulansuhai Nur China 40°53N 108°51E 226 D5
Ulaş Sivas, Turkey 39°26N 37°2E 212 C7
Ulaş Tekirdağ, Turkey 41°14N 27°42E 203 E11
Ulawa Solomon Is. 9°46S 161°57E 287 M11
Ulawun, Mt. Papua N. G. 5°3S 151°20E 286 C6
Ulaya Morogoro, Tanzania 7°3S 36°55E 268 D4
Ulaya Tabora, Tanzania 4°25S 33°30E 268 C3
Ulcinj Montenegro 41°58N 19°10E 202 E3
Ulco S. Africa 28°21S 24°15E 270 C3
Ule älv = Oulujoki → Finland 65°1N 25°30E 160 D21
Ule träsk = Oulujärvi Finland 64°25N 27°15E 160 D22
Uleåborg = Oulu Finland 65°1N 25°29E 160 D21
Ulefoss Norway 59°17N 9°16E 164 E6
Uleta U.S.A. 25°27N 80°10W 129 C2
Ulëz Albania 41°46N 19°54E 202 E3
Ulfborg Denmark 56°16N 8°20E 163 H2
Ulhasnagar India 19°15N 73°10E 244 E1
Uliastay Mongolia 47°56N 97°28E 218 B8
Uljin S. Korea 36°59N 129°24E 224 D4
Uljma Serbia 45°2N 21°10E 182 E6
Ülken Kazakhstan 45°12N 73°58E 217 C8
Ülken Borsyq Qumy Kazakhstan 47°0N 59°11E 216 C5
Ulla → Spain 42°39N 8°44W 194 C2
Ulladulla Australia 35°21S 150°29E 283 C9
Ullal India 12°48N 74°51E 245 H2
Ullapool U.K. 57°54N 5°9W 167 D3
Ullared Sweden 57°8N 12°42E 163 G6
Ulldecona Spain 40°36N 0°20E 196 E5
Ullerup Denmark 55°34N 12°36E 118 B3
Ulleungdo S. Korea 37°30N 130°30E 224 D5
Ullevål Norway 59°56N 10°46E 133 A3
Ullswater Ont., Canada 45°12N 79°29W 312 A5
Ullswater Cumb., U.K. 54°34N 2°52W 168 C5
Ulm Germany 48°23N 9°58E 179 G5
Ulmarra Australia 29°37S 153°4E 281 D5
Ulmeni Buzău, Romania 45°4N 26°40E 183 E11
Ulmeni Maramureş, Romania 47°28N 23°18E 183 C8
Ulonguè Mozam. 14°37S 34°19E 269 E3
Ulricehamn Sweden 57°46N 13°26E 163 G7
Ulrika Sweden 58°5N 15°23E 163 F9
Ulriksdal Sweden 59°23N 17°59E 139 A1
Ulsan S. Korea 35°20N 129°15E 224 E4
Ulsberg Norway 62°45N 10°0E 164 B6
Ulsta U.K. 60°30N 1°9W 167 A7
Ulsteinvik Norway 62°21N 5°53E 164 B2
Ulster □ U.K. 54°35N 6°30W 166 B5
Ulstrem Bulgaria 42°1N 26°27E 203 D10
Ultima Australia 35°30S 143°18E 282 C5
Ulu Temburong △ Brunei 4°27N 115°15E 235 B5
Ulubat Gölü Turkey 40°9N 28°35E 203 F12
Ulubey Turkey 38°25N 29°18E 205 C11
Uluborlu Turkey 38°4N 30°28E 205 C12
Uluçinar Turkey 36°24N 35°53E 250 B6
Uludağ Turkey 40°4N 29°13E 203 F13
Uludağ △ Turkey 40°5N 29°12E 203 F13
Uludere Turkey 37°28N 42°42E 213 D10
Ulugqat China 39°48N 74°15E 217 E8
Uluguru Mts. Tanzania 7°15S 37°40E 268 D4
Ulukhaktok Canada 70°44N 117°44W 294 C8
Ulukışla = Marathóvounos Cyprus 35°13N 33°37E 207 E9
Ulukışla Turkey 37°33N 34°28E 212 D6
Ulundi S. Africa 28°20S 31°25E 271 C5
Ulungur He → China 47°1N 87°24E 217 C11

Ulungur Hu China 47°20N 87°10E 217 C11
Ulupalakua U.S.A. 20°39N 156°24W 302 C5
Uluru Australia 25°23S 131°5E 279 E5
Uluru-Kata Tjuta △ Australia 25°19S 131°1E 279 E5
Uluwatu Indonesia 8°50S 115°5E 231 K18
Ulva U.K. 56°29N 6°13W 167 E2
Ulverston U.K. 54°13N 3°5W 168 C4
Ulverstone Australia 41°11S 146°11E 281 G4
Ulvik Norway 60°35N 6°54E 164 D3
Ulya Russia 59°10N 142°0E 215 D15
Ulyanka Russia 59°50N 30°14E 137 B1
Ulyanovo Russia 54°50N 22°6E 184 D9
Ulyanovsk Russia 54°20N 48°25E 190 C9
Ulyanovsk □ Russia 54°5N 48°5E 190 C9
Ulyasutay = Uliastay Mongolia 47°56N 97°28E 218 B8
Ulysses Kans., U.S.A. 37°35N 101°22W 308 G3
Ulysses Pa., U.S.A. 41°54N 77°46W 312 E7
Ulysses, Mt. Canada 57°20N 124°5W 296 B4
Ulysses S. Grant Nat. Historic Site ⌓ U.S.A. 38°33N 90°28W 310 F6
Ulytau Kazakhstan 48°39N 67°1E 217 C7
Ulyzhylanshyq → Kazakhstan 48°51N 63°46E 216 C6
Um Al Khanazir I. Iraq 33°17N 44°22E 113 B2
Umag Croatia 45°26N 13°31E 199 C10
Umala Bolivia 17°25S 68°5W 330 D4
'Umān = Oman ■ Asia 23°0N 58°0E 249 B7
Uman Ukraine 48°40N 30°12E 177 D16
Uman I. Micronesia 7°17N 151°52E 287 U18
Umaria India 23°35N 80°50E 243 H9
Umarkhed India 19°37N 77°46E 244 E3
Umarkot Pakistan 25°15N 69°40E 242 G3
Umarpada India 21°27N 73°30E 242 J5
Umatac Guam 13°18N 144°39E 302 d
Umatilla U.S.A. 45°55N 119°21W 304 D4
Umba Russia 66°42N 34°11E 186 A5
Umbagog L. U.S.A. 44°46N 71°3W 313 B13
Umbakumba Australia 13°47S 136°50E 280 A2
Umbértide Italy 43°18N 12°20E 199 E9
Umboi I. Papua N. G. 5°40S 148°0E 286 C5
Umbrella Mts. N.Z. 45°35S 169°5E 285 F4
Umbria □ Italy 42°53N 12°30E 199 F9
Umeå Sweden 63°45N 20°20E 160 E19
Umeälven → Sweden 63°45N 20°20E 160 E19
Umeda Japan 34°41N 135°29E 133 A1
Umera Indonesia 0°12S 129°37E 231 E7
Umerkhadi Mumbai, India 130 b2
Umfuli → Zimbabwe 17°30S 29°23E 269 F2
Umfurudzi ⌓ Zimbabwe 17°6S 31°40E 269 F3
Umgusa Zimbabwe 19°29S 27°52E 269 F2
Umgwenya → Mozam. 25°14S 32°18E 271 C5
Umiat U.S.A. 69°22N 152°8W 303 B9
Umiray Phil. 15°13N 121°25E 232 D3
Umiujaq Canada 56°33N 76°33W 298 A4
Umka Serbia 44°40N 20°19E 202 B4
Umkomaas S. Africa 30°13S 30°48E 271 D5
Umm ad Daraj, J. Jordan 32°18N 35°48E 251 F6
Umm al Arānib Libya 26°10N 14°43E 258 C2
Umm al Khashab Si. Arabia 17°23N 42°32E 256 D5
Umm al Qaywayn U.A.E. 25°30N 55°35E 247 E7
Umm al Qittayn Jordan 32°18N 36°40E 251 F7
Umm al Rasas Jordan 31°30N 35°55E 251 G6
Umm al Sheif U.A.E. 25°9N 55°13E 119 B1
Umm al'Abīd Libya 27°31N 15°2E 258 C3
Umm Arda Sudan 15°17N 32°31E 257 D3
Umm Bāb Qatar 25°12N 50°48E 247 E6
Umm Badr Sudan 14°13N 27°58E 257 E2
Umm Bel Sudan 13°35N 28°0E 257 E2
Umm Birkah Si. Arabia 27°44N 36°31E 256 B4
Umm Boim Sudan 11°43N 25°27E 257 E2
Umm Dam Sudan 13°45N 30°59E 257 E3
Umm Debi Sudan 14°37N 30°23E 257 E3
Umm Dubban Sudan 15°23N 32°52E 257 D3
Umm Durman = Omdurmân Sudan 15°40N 32°28E 257 D3
Umm el Fahm Israel 32°31N 35°9E 251 F6
Umm el Ketef, Khalîg Egypt 23°40N 35°35E 246 F2
Umm Gafala Sudan 13°22N 27°15E 257 E2
Umm Gimala Sudan 11°27N 28°12E 257 E2
Umm Inderaba Sudan 17°30N 33°13E 256 D3
Umm Isheirât, G. Egypt 28°21N 34°18E 251 K5
Umm Keddada Sudan 13°33N 26°35E 257 E2
Umm Koweika Sudan 13°10N 32°16E 257 E3
Umm Lajj Si. Arabia 25°0N 37°23E 246 E3
Umm Merwa Sudan 18°4N 32°30E 256 D3
Umm Qantur Sudan 14°17N 31°22E 257 E3
Umm Qasr Iraq 30°1N 47°58E 246 D5
Umm Qurein Sudan 9°58N 28°55E 257 F2
Umm Ruwaba Sudan 12°50N 31°20E 257 E3
Umm Sa'id Qatar 25°0N 51°33E 247 E6
Umm Saiyala Sudan 14°25N 31°10E 257 E3
Umm Shanqa Sudan 13°14N 27°14E 266 B2
Umm Shugeira Sudan 13°34N 29°37E 266 B2
Umm Shutur South Sudan 7°17N 33°14E 257 F3
Umm Sidr Sudan 14°29N 25°10E 257 E2
Umm Suqeim U.A.E. 25°11N 55°14E 119 B1
Umm Tais △ Qatar 26°7N 51°15E 247 E6
Umm Urūmah Si. Arabia 25°43N 36°35E 256 B4
Umm Zehetir Egypt 28°48N 32°31E 256 J8
Umnak I. U.S.A. 53°15N 168°20W 303 K5
Umniati → Zimbabwe 16°49S 28°45E 269 F2
Umpqua → U.S.A. 43°40N 124°12W 304 E1
Umpulo Angola 12°38S 17°42E 265 E3
Ümraniye Turkey 41°1N 29°4E 122 B2
Umred India 20°51N 79°18E 244 D4
Umreth India 22°41N 73°4E 242 H5
Umri India 19°2N 77°39E 244 E3
Umtata = Mthatha S. Africa 31°36S 28°49E 271 D4
Umuahia Nigeria 5°31N 7°26E 263 D6
Umuarama Brazil 23°45S 53°20W 335 A5
Umuda I. Papua N. G. 8°29S 143°46E 286 E2
Umurbey Turkey 40°13N 26°36E 203 F10
Umvukwe Ra. Zimbabwe 16°45S 30°45E 269 F3
Umzimvubu S. Africa 31°38S 29°33E 271 D4
Umzingwane → Zimbabwe 22°12S 29°56E 269 G2
Umzinto = eMuziwezinto S. Africa 30°15S 30°45E 271 D5
Una India 20°46N 71°8E 242 J4
Una → Bos.-H. 45°0N 16°20E 199 D13
Unac → Bos.-H. 44°30N 16°9E 199 D13
Unaðsdalur Iceland 66°7N 22°36W 155 A4
Unadilla Ga., U.S.A. 32°16N 83°44W 316 C6
Unadilla N.Y., U.S.A. 42°20N 75°19W 313 D9
Unaí Brazil 16°23S 46°53W 333 E2
Unalakleet U.S.A. 63°52N 160°47W 303 E7
Unalaska U.S.A. 53°53N 166°32W 303 K6
Unalaska I. U.S.A. 53°35N 166°50W 303 K6
'Unayzah Si. Arabia 26°6N 43°58E 246 E4
'Unayzah, J. Asia 32°12N 39°18E 213 F8
Uncastillo Spain 42°21N 1°8W 196 C3
Uncía Bolivia 18°25S 66°40W 330 D4
Uncompahgre Peak U.S.A. 38°4N 107°28W 304 G10
Uncompahgre Plateau U.S.A. 38°20N 108°15W 304 G9
Undara Volcanic △ Australia 18°14S 144°41E 280 B3
Unden Sweden 58°45N 14°25E 163 F8
Underbool Australia 35°10S 141°51E 282 C4
Underground Atlanta U.S.A. 33°45N 84°24W 113 B2
Underhill, L. U.S.A. 28°32N 81°20W 133 A3
Undersaker Sweden 63°19N 13°21E 162 A7
Underwood Canada 44°18N 81°29W 312 B3
Undredal Norway 60°57N 7°6E 164 D4
Unea I. Papua N. G. 4°53S 149°9E 286 C5
Unecha Russia 52°50N 32°37E 189 F7
Uneiuxi → Brazil 0°37S 65°34W 328 D4
Unětický potok → Czechia 50°9N 14°24E 135 B2
Unga I. U.S.A. 55°15N 160°40W 303 J7
Ungarie Australia 33°38S 146°56E 283 B7
Ungarisch-Hradisch = Uherské Hradiště Czechia 49°4N 17°30E 181 B10
Ungarisch-Ostra = Uherský Brod Czechia 49°1N 17°40E 181 B10
Ungarra Australia 34°12S 136°2E 282 C2
Ungat Papua N. G. 2°40S 150°15E 286 B6
Ungava, Pén. d' Canada 60°0N 74°0W 295 F17
Ungava B. Canada 59°30N 67°30W 295 F18
Ungeny = Ungheni Moldova 47°11N 27°51E 183 C12
Unggi N. Korea 42°16N 130°28E 224 A5
Ungheni Moldova 47°11N 27°51E 183 C12
Unguala → Ethiopia 8°6N 41°9E 257 F5
Unguja = Zanzibar Tanzania 6°12S 39°12E 268 D4
Ungvár = Uzhhorod Ukraine 48°36N 22°18E 182 B7
Ungwana B. Kenya 2°45S 40°20E 268 C5
Ungwatiri Sudan 16°52N 36°10E 257 D4
Unhos Portugal 38°49N 9°7W 126 A2
Uni Russia 57°46N 51°31E 190 B10
União Brazil 4°35S 42°52W 332 B3
União da Vitória Brazil 26°13S 51°5W 335 B5
União dos Palmares Brazil 9°10S 36°2W 332 C4
Uničov Czechia 49°46N 17°8E 181 B10
Unidad Santa Fe Mexico 19°23N 99°13W 128 B1
Uniejów Poland 51°59N 18°46E 185 G5
Unije Croatia 44°40N 14°15E 199 D11
Unimak I. U.S.A. 54°45N 164°0W 303 J7
Unimak Pass. U.S.A. 54°15N 164°30W 303 J6
Unini → Brazil 1°41S 61°31W 329 D5
Union Miss., U.S.A. 32°34N 89°7W 315 E10
Union Mo., U.S.A. 38°27N 91°0W 310 F6
Union Ohio, U.S.A. 39°55N 84°12W 311 E12
Union S.C., U.S.A. 34°43N 81°37W 315 D14
Union City Calif., U.S.A. 37°36N 122°1W 306 H4
Union City Ga., U.S.A. 33°35N 84°33W 316 B5
Union City New York, U.S.A. 132 b1
Union City Ohio, U.S.A. 40°12N 84°48W 311 D12
Union City Pa., U.S.A. 41°54N 79°51W 312 E5
Union City Tenn., U.S.A. 36°26N 89°3W 315 C10
Union Dale U.S.A. 41°43N 75°29W 313 E9
Union Gap U.S.A. 46°33N 120°28W 304 C3
Union Grove U.S.A. 42°41N 88°3W 311 B8
Union I. St. Vincent 12°36N 61°26W 323 n
Union Park U.S.A. 28°34N 81°17W 317 G8
Union Passenger Terminal New Orleans, U.S.A. 131 b1
Union Point U.S.A. 33°37N 83°4W 316 B6
Union Port U.S.A. 40°48N 73°51W 132 B2
Union Springs Ala., U.S.A. 32°9N 85°43W 316 C4
Union Springs N.Y., U.S.A. 42°50N 76°41W 313 D8
Union Square Hong Kong, China 22°19N 114°9E 122 B2
Union Square San Francisco, U.S.A. 136 b2
Union Star U.S.A. 39°59N 94°36W 310 E2
Union Station Toronto, Canada 141 c2
Union Station Chicago, U.S.A. 119 c1
Union Station Los Angeles, U.S.A. 127 b3
Union Station Washington, D.C., U.S.A. 143 b3
Union Station Plaza Washington, D.C., U.S.A. 143 b3
Uniondale S. Africa 33°39S 23°7E 270 D3
Uniontown Ky., U.S.A. 37°47N 87°56W 311 G9
Uniontown Pa., U.S.A. 39°54N 79°44W 309 F14
Unionville Ga., U.S.A. 31°26N 83°30W 316 D6
Unionville Mo., U.S.A. 40°29N 93°1W 310 D3
Unirea Romania 44°15N 27°35E 183 F12
United Arab Emirates ■ Asia 23°50N 54°0E 247 F7
United Arab Republic = Egypt ■ Africa 28°0N 31°0E 256 B3
United Center U.S.A. 41°53N 87°41W 119 B2
United Kingdom ■ Europe 53°0N 2°0W 165 E6
United Nations Headquarters New York, U.S.A. 132 c3
United Provinces = Uttar Pradesh □ India 27°0N 80°0E 243 F9
United States of America ■ N. Amer. 37°0N 96°0W 301 H20
Unity Canada 52°30N 109°5W 297 C7
Unity □ South Sudan 8°30N 30°0E 257 F3
Universal Studios Calif., U.S.A. 34°9N 118°21W 126 B2
Universal Studios Fla., U.S.A. 28°29N 81°29W 133 B2
Universales, Mtes. Spain 40°18N 1°33W 196 E3
Universidad Spain 40°27N 3°44W 127 B1
University City U.S.A. 38°39N 90°18W 310 F6
University Park Md., U.S.A. 38°58N 76°56W 143 B3
University Park N. Mex., U.S.A. 32°17N 106°45W 305 K10
University Park Tex., U.S.A. 32°51N 96°48W 120 A5
University Place U.S.A. 47°14N 122°33W 306 C4
Unjha India 23°46N 72°24E 242 H5
Unmet Vanuatu 16°8S 167°15E 287 F5
Unna Germany 51°32N 7°42E 178 D3
Unnao India 26°35N 80°30E 243 F9
Uno, Ilha Guinea-Biss. 11°15N 16°13W 262 C1
Unruhstadt = Kargowa Poland 52°5N 15°51E 185 F2
Unsan N. Korea 40°6N 125°54E 224 B2
Unsengedsi → Zimbabwe 15°43S 31°14E 269 F3
Unst U.K. 60°44N 0°53W 167 A8
Unstrut → Germany 51°10N 11°48E 178 D7
Unter den Linden Berlin, Germany 115 a4
Unterbiberg Germany 48°6N 11°38E 131 B2
Unterdrauburg = Dravograd Slovenia 46°36N 15°5E 199 B12
Unterföhring Germany 48°11N 11°38E 131 A3
Unterfranken □ Germany 50°0N 10°0E 179 F5
Unterhaching Germany 48°3N 11°37E 131 B2
Unterlaa Austria 48°8N 16°24E 142 B2
Untermenzing Germany 48°10N 11°28E 131 A1
Unterschleissheim Germany 48°17N 11°34E 179 G7
Unuk → Canada 56°5N 131°3W 296 B2
Ünye Turkey 41°5N 37°15E 212 B7
Unzen-Amakusa △ Japan 32°15N 130°10E 222 E2
Unzen-Dake Japan 32°45N 130°17E 222 E2
Unzha Russia 58°0N 44°0E 190 A7
Unzha → Russia 57°49N 43°47E 190 B6
Uong Bi Vietnam 21°2N 106°47E 236 B6
Uotsuri-Shima E. China Sea 25°45N 123°29E 221 M1
Uozu Japan 36°48N 137°24E 223 A9
Upata Venezuela 8°1N 62°24W 329 B5
Upatoi Cr. → U.S.A. 32°22N 84°58W 316 C5
Upemba, L. Dem. Rep. of the Congo 8°30S 26°20E 269 D2
Upemba △ Dem. Rep. of the Congo 9°0S 26°35E 269 D2
Upernavik Greenland 72°49N 56°20W 154 C5
Upington S. Africa 28°25S 21°15E 270 C3
Upleta India 21°46N 70°16E 242 J4
'Upolu Samoa 13°58S 172°0W 287 V20
Upolu Pt. U.S.A. 20°16N 155°52W 302 C6
Upongkor Vanuatu 18°50S 168°59E 287 H6
Upper Alkali L. U.S.A. 41°47N 120°8W 304 F3
Upper Arlington U.S.A. 40°0N 83°4W 311 E13
Upper Arrow L. Canada 50°30N 117°50W 296 C5
Upper Austria = Oberösterreich □ Austria 48°10N 14°0E 180 C7
Upper B. U.S.A. 40°40N 74°3W 132 C1
Upper Daly ☼ Australia 14°26S 131°3E 278 B5
Upper Darby U.S.A. 39°55N 75°16W 309 F16
Upper Demerara-Berbice □ Guyana 5°22N 58°14W 329 B6
Upper East □ Ghana 10°30N 1°0W 263 C4
Upper East Side New York, U.S.A. 132 b3
Upper Elmers End U.K. 51°23N 0°1W 125 B3
Upper Foster L. Canada 56°47N 105°20W 297 B7
Upper Hutt N.Z. 41°8S 175°5E 284 H4
Upper Klamath L. U.S.A. 42°25N 121°55W 304 E3
Upper Lake U.S.A. 39°10N 122°54W 306 F4
Upper Liard Canada 60°3N 128°54W 296 A3
Upper Manilla Australia 30°38S 150°40E 283 A9
Upper Manzanilla Trin. & Tob. 10°31N 61°4W 323 t
Upper Missouri Breaks ⌓ U.S.A. 47°50N 109°55W 304 C9
Upper Musquodoboit Canada 45°10N 62°58W 299 C7
Upper New York B. = Upper B. U.S.A. 40°40N 74°3W 132 C1
Upper Nile □ South Sudan 9°30N 33°0E 257 F3
Upper Norwood U.K. 51°24N 0°6W 125 B3
Upper Peirce Res. Singapore 1°22N 103°47E 138 A2
Upper Red L. U.S.A. 48°8N 94°45W 308 A6
Upper Sandusky U.S.A. 40°50N 83°17W 311 D13
Upper Senegal & Niger = Mali ■ Africa 17°0N 3°0W 262 B4
Upper Sydenham U.K. 51°26N 0°4W 125 B3
Upper Takutu-Upper Essequibo □ Guyana 2°40N 58°59W 329 C6
Upper Tooting U.K. 51°25N 0°9W 125 B3
Upper Volta = Burkina Faso ■ Africa 12°0N 1°0W 262 C4
Upper West □ Ghana 10°30N 2°20W 262 C4
Upper West Side New York, U.S.A. 132 a2
Upphärad Sweden 58°9N 12°19E 163 F6
Uppland Sweden 59°59N 17°48E 162 D12
Upplands-Väsby Sweden 59°31N 17°54E 162 E11
Uppsala Sweden 59°53N 17°38E 162 E11
Uppsala □ Sweden 60°0N 17°30E 162 D11
Upshi India 33°48N 77°52E 243 C7
Upton London, U.K. 51°32N 0°1E 125 A4
Upton Wyo., U.S.A. 44°6N 104°38W 304 D11
Uptown U.S.A. 41°58N 87°40W 119 B2
Uqsuqtuuq = Gjoa Haven Canada 68°38N 95°53W 294 D12
Ur Iraq 30°55N 46°25E 246 D5
Ur Kut Somalia 3°31N 42°47E 267 D5
Ura-Tyube = Istaravshān Tajikistan 39°55N 69°1E 217 E7
Urabá, G. de Colombia 8°25N 76°53W 328 B2
Urad Qianqi China 40°40N 108°30E 226 D5
Uraga-Suidō Japan 35°13N 139°45E 223 B11
Urahoro Japan 42°50N 143°40E 220 C11
Urakawa Japan 42°9N 142°47E 220 C11
Ural = Uralskiy □ Russia 64°0N 70°0E 214 C7
Ural = Zhayyq → Kazakhstan 47°0N 51°48E 187 E9
Ural Australia 33°21S 146°12E 283 B7
Ural Mts. = Uralskie Gory Eurasia 60°0N 59°0E 186 C10
Uralla Australia 30°37S 151°29E 283 A9
Uralmedstroy = Krasnouralsk Russia 58°21N 60°3E 186 C11
Uralsk = Oral Kazakhstan 51°20N 51°20E 190 E10
Uralskie Gory Eurasia 60°0N 59°0E 186 C10
Uralskiy □ Russia 64°0N 70°0E 214 C7
Urambo Tanzania 5°4S 32°0E 268 D3
Uran India 18°53N 72°56E 130 B2
Urana Australia 35°15S 146°21E 283 C7
Urana, L. Australia 35°16S 146°10E 283 C7
Urandangi Australia 21°32S 138°14E 280 C2
Uranga Australia 30°31S 153°1E 283 A10
Uranium City Canada 59°34N 108°37W 297 B7
Urapuntja = Utopia Australia 22°14S 134°33E 280 C1
Uraricaá → Brazil 3°20N 61°56W 329 C5
Uraricoera Brazil 3°27N 60°59W 329 C5
Uraricoera → Brazil 3°2N 60°30W 329 C5
Urasoe Japan 26°15N 127°43E 288 a
Uravakonda India 14°57N 77°12E 245 G3
Urawa = Saitama Japan 35°54N 139°38E 223 B11
Uray Russia 60°5N 65°15E 214 C7
Urayasu Japan 35°39N 139°53E 140 B4
'Uray'irah Si. Arabia 25°57N 48°53E 247 E6
Urbakh = Pushkino Russia 51°16N 47°0E 190 E8
Urbana Ill., U.S.A. 40°7N 88°12W 311 D8
Urbana Ohio, U.S.A. 40°7N 83°45W 311 D13
Urbandale U.S.A. 41°38N 93°43W 310 C3
Urbánia Italy 43°40N 12°31E 199 E9
Urbano Santos Brazil 3°12S 43°23W 332 B3
Urbe ✕ Italy 41°57N 12°30E 136 B2
Urbel → Spain 42°21N 3°40W 194 C7
Urbino Italy 43°43N 12°38E 199 E9
Urbión, Picos de Spain 42°1N 2°52W 196 C2
Urca Brazil 22°56S 43°9W 135 B2
Urcos Peru 13°40S 71°38W 330 C3
Urdaneta Phil. 15°59N 120°34E 232 D3
Urdinarrain Argentina 32°37S 58°52W 334 C4
Urdos France 42°51N 0°35W 174 F3
Ure → U.K. 54°5N 1°20W 168 C6
Uren Russia 57°35N 45°55E 190 B7
Urengoy Russia 65°58N 78°22E 214 C8
Ureparapara Vanuatu 13°32S 167°20E 287 C5
Ures Mexico 29°26N 110°24W 318 B2
Ureshino Japan 33°6N 129°59E 222 D1
Urewera △ N.Z. 38°29S 177°7E 284 E6
Urfa = Sanliurfa Turkey 37°12N 38°50E 213 D8
Urga = Ulaanbaatar Mongolia 47°55N 106°53E 218 B10
Urganch Uzbekistan 41°40N 60°41E 216 D6
Urgench = Urganch Uzbekistan 41°40N 60°41E 216 D6
Ürgüp Turkey 38°38N 34°56E 212 C6
Urho Kekkonen △ Finland 68°20N 27°40E 160 B22
Uri India 34°8N 74°2E 243 B6
Uri □ Switz. 46°43N 8°35E 179 J4
Uribante → Venezuela 7°25N 71°50W 328 B3
Uribe Colombia 3°13N 74°24W 328 C3
Uribia Colombia 11°43N 72°16W 328 A3
Uricani Romania 45°20N 23°9E 182 E8
Urimba Angola 10°56S 16°32E 265 E3
Uriondo Bolivia 21°41S 64°41W 334 A3
Urique Mexico 27°13N 107°55W 318 B3
Urique → Mexico 26°29N 107°58W 318 B3
Uritsk Russia 59°49N 30°10E 137 C1
Urk Neths. 52°39N 5°36E 170 B5
Urkiola ⌓ Spain 43°6N 1°2W 196 B3
Urla Turkey 38°20N 26°47E 205 C8
Urlaţi Romania 44°59N 26°15E 183 F11
Urmia = Orūmīyeh Iran 37°40N 45°0E 213 D11
Urmia, L. = Orūmīyeh, Daryācheh-ye Iran 37°50N 45°30E 213 D11
Urmston Road Hong Kong, China 22°22N 113°55E 122 A1
Üröm Hungary 47°35N 19°1E 117 A2
Uromi Nigeria 6°42N 6°20E 263 D6
Uroševac = Ferizaj Kosovo 42°23N 21°10E 202 D5
Ŭroteppa = Istaravshān Tajikistan 39°55N 69°1E 217 E7
Uroyan, Montanas de Puerto Rico 18°12N 66°50W 321 b
Urrampinyi Iltjiltarri ☼ Australia 24°20S 132°10E 278 D5
Urrao Colombia 6°20N 76°11W 328 B2
Urshult Sweden 56°31N 14°50E 163 H8
Ursus Poland 52°11N 20°52E 143 B1
Ursvik Sweden 59°23N 17°57E 139 A1
Uru Uru, L. Bolivia 18°6S 67°8W 330 D4
Uruaçu Brazil 14°30S 49°10W 333 D2
Uruanã Brazil 15°30S 49°41W 333 E2
Uruapan Mexico 19°24N 102°3W 318 D4
Uruará Brazil 3°42S 53°51W 329 D7
Uruará → Brazil 2°6S 53°38W 329 D7
Urubamba Peru 13°20S 72°10W 330 C3
Urubamba → Peru 10°43S 73°48W 330 C3
Urubaxi → Brazil 0°31S 64°50W 329 D5
Urubu → Brazil 2°55S 58°25W 329 D6
Urucará Brazil 2°32S 57°45W 329 D6
Uruçuí Brazil 7°20S 44°28W 332 C3
Uruçuí, Serra do Brazil 9°0S 44°45W 332 C3
Uruçuí Prêto → Brazil 7°20S 44°38W 332 C3
Urucuia → Brazil 16°8S 45°5W 333 E2
Uruguai → Brazil 26°0S 53°30W 335 B5
Uruguaiana Brazil 29°50S 57°0W 334 B4
Uruguay ■ S. Amer. 32°30S 56°30W 334 C4
Uruguay → S. Amer. 34°12S 58°18W 334 C4
Urukthapel I. Palau 7°17N 134°25E 288 c
Uruma Japan 26°21N 127°52E 288 a
Urumchi = Ürümqi China 43°45N 87°45E 217 D11
Ürümqi China 43°45N 87°45E 217 D11
Uruna ☼ Australia 24°3S 133°1E 278 D5
Urundi = Burundi ■ Africa 3°15S 30°0E 268 C3
Urup → Russia 45°0N 41°10E 191 H5
Urup, Ostrov Russia 46°0N 151°0E 215 E16
Urus-Martan Russia 43°8N 45°33E 191 J7
Urutaí Brazil 17°28S 48°12W 333 E2
Uryupinsk Russia 50°45N 41°58E 190 E5
Ürzhar Kazakhstan 47°5N 81°38E 217 C10
Urzhum Russia 57°10N 49°56E 190 B9
Urziceni Romania 44°40N 26°42E 183 F11
Usa Japan 33°31N 131°21E 222 D3
Usa → Russia 66°16N 59°49E 186 A10
Uşak Turkey 38°43N 29°28E 205 C11
Uşak □ Turkey 38°30N 29°0E 205 C11
Usakos Namibia 21°54S 15°31E 270 B2
Usborne, Mt. Falk. Is. 51°40S 59°55W 153 f
Ušće Serbia 43°30N 20°39E 202 C4
Usedom Germany 53°55N 14°2E 178 B10
Usedom ⌓ Germany 53°55N 14°0E 178 B10
Useless Loop Australia 26°8S 113°23E 279 E1
Usera Spain 40°22N 3°42W 127 B1
'Usfān Si. Arabia 21°58N 39°27E 248 B2
Ushakova, Ostrov Russia 82°0N 80°0E 215 A8
Ushakovo Russia 54°37N 20°16E 184 D7
Ushant = Ouessant, Î. d' France 48°28N 5°6W 172 D1
Üsharal Kazakhstan 46°10N 80°56E 217 C10
Ushashi Tanzania 1°59S 33°57E 268 C3
Ushat South Sudan 7°59N 29°28E 257 F2
'Ushayrah Ar Riyāḍ, Si. Arabia 25°35N 45°47E 246 E5
'Ushayrah Makkah, Si. Arabia 21°46N 40°42E 256 C5
Ushibuka Japan 32°11N 130°1E 222 E2
Ushigome Japan 35°42N 139°44E 140 A3
Üshtöbe Kazakhstan 45°16N 78°0E 217 C9
Ushuaia Argentina 54°50S 68°23W 336 D3
Ushumun Russia 52°47N 126°32E 215 D13
Ushytsya → Ukraine 48°35N 27°8E 183 B12
Usina Brazil 22°57S 43°17W 135 B1
Usino Papua N. G. 5°32S 145°23E 286 C3
Usinsk Russia 65°57N 57°27E 186 A10
Usk Canada 54°38N 128°26W 296 C3
Usk → U.K. 51°33N 2°58W 169 F5
Uska India 27°12N 83°7E 243 F10
Uskedalen Norway 59°56N 5°53E 164 E2
Üsküb = Skopje Macedonia 42°1N 21°26E 202 D5
Üsküdar Turkey 41°1N 29°0E 122 B2
Uslar Germany 51°39N 9°38E 178 D5
Usman Russia 52°5N 39°48E 189 F10
Usoke Tanzania 5°8S 32°24E 268 D3
Usolye-Sibirskoye Russia 52°48N 103°40E 215 D11
Usolye-Solikamskoye = Berezniki Russia 59°24N 56°46E 186 C10
Usoro Nigeria 5°33N 6°11E 263 D6
Uspallata, P. de Argentina 32°37S 69°22W 334 C2
Uspenka = Kirovskiy Russia 45°7N 133°30E 220 B6
Ussel France 45°32N 2°18E 174 C6
Usson-du-Poitou France 46°16N 0°31E 174 B4
Ussuriysk Russia 43°48N 131°59E 220 C5
Ussurka Russia 45°12N 133°31E 220 B6
Ust-Aldan = Batamay Russia 63°30N 129°15E 215 C13
Ust-Amginskoye = Khandyga Russia 62°42N 135°35E 215 C14
Ust-Buzulukskaya Russia 50°8N 42°11E 190 E6
Ust-Chaun Russia 68°47N 170°30E 215 C18
Ust-Chorna Ukraine 48°19N 23°56E 183 B8
Ust-Donetskiy Russia 47°35N 40°55E 191 G5
Ust-Dzheguta Russia 44°5N 41°58E 191 H5
Ust-Ilimpeya = Yukta Russia 63°26N 105°42E 215 C11
Ust-Ilimsk Russia 58°3N 102°39E 215 D11
Ust-Ishim Russia 57°45N 71°10E 214 D8
Ust-Kamchatsk Russia 56°10N 162°28E 215 D17
Ust-Kamenogorsk = Öskemen Kazakhstan 50°0N 82°36E 217 C10
Ust-Khayryuzovo Russia 57°15N 156°45E 215 D16
Ust-Kut Russia 56°50N 105°42E 215 D11
Ust-Kuyga Russia 70°1N 135°43E 215 B14
Ust-Labinsk Russia 45°15N 39°41E 191 H4
Ust-Luga Russia 59°35N 28°20E 188 C5
Ust-Maya Russia 60°30N 134°28E 215 C14
Ust-Medveditskaya = Serafimovich Russia 49°36N 42°43E 190 F6
Ust-Mil Russia 59°40N 133°11E 215 D14
Ust-Nera Russia 64°35N 143°15E 215 C15
Ust-Nyukzha Russia 56°34N 121°37E 215 D13
Ust-Olenek Russia 73°0N 120°5E 215 B12
Ust-Omchug Russia 61°9N 149°38E 215 C15
Ust-Port Russia 69°40N 84°26E 214 C9
Ust' Shchugor Russia 64°16N 57°36E 186 B10
Ust-Slavyanka Russia 59°51N 30°32E 137 C3
Ust-Sysolsk = Syktyvkar Russia 61°45N 50°40E 186 B9
Ust-Tsilma Russia 65°28N 52°11E 186 A9
Ust-Urt = Ustyurt Plateau Asia 44°0N 55°0E 216 D5
Ust-Usa Russia 66°2N 56°57E 186 A10
Ust-Vorkuta Russia 67°24N 64°0E 186 A11
Ust-Zhuya = Chara Russia 56°54N 118°20E 215 D12
Ustaoset Norway 60°30N 8°2E 164 D5
Ustaritz France 43°24N 1°27W 174 E2
Ustecký □ Czechia 50°30N 14°0E 180 A7
Uster Switz. 47°22N 8°43E 179 H4
Ústí nad Labem Czechia 50°41N 14°3E 180 A7
Ústí nad Orlicí Czechia 49°58N 16°24E 181 B9
Ústica Italy 38°42N 13°11E 200 D6
Ustinov = Izhevsk Russia 56°51N 53°14E 186 C9
Ustka Poland 54°35N 16°55E 184 D3
Ustroń Poland 49°43N 18°48E 185 J5
Ustrzyki Dolne Poland 49°27N 22°40E 185 J9
Ustupo Panama 9°27N 78°34W 328 B2
Ustyluh Ukraine 50°51N 24°10E 185 H11
Ustyurt Plateau Asia 44°0N 55°0E 216 D5
Ustyuzhna Russia 58°50N 36°32E 188 C9
Usu China 44°27N 84°40E 217 D10
Usuki Japan 33°8N 131°49E 222 D3
Usulután El Salv. 13°25N 88°28W 320 D2
Usumacinta → Mexico 18°24N 92°38W 319 D6
Usumbura = Bujumbura Burundi 3°16S 29°18E 268 C2
Usure Tanzania 4°40S 34°22E 268 C3
Usutuo → Mozam. 26°48S 32°7E 271 C5
Uta Indonesia 4°33S 136°0E 231 E9
Utah □ U.S.A. 39°20N 111°30W 304 G8
Utah L. U.S.A. 40°12N 111°48W 304 F8
Utansjö Sweden 62°46N 17°55E 162 B11
Utara, Selat Malaysia 5°28N 100°20E 237 c
Utarni India 26°5N 71°58E 242 F4
Utatlan Guatemala 15°2N 91°11W 320 C1
Ute Creek → U.S.A. 35°21N 103°50W 305 J12
Utebo Spain 41°43N 1°0W 196 D3
Utegi Tanzania 1°19S 34°13E 266 E3
Uteke Sweden 59°24N 18°15E 139 A3
Utena Lithuania 55°27N 25°40E 188 E3
Utete Tanzania 8°0S 38°45E 268 D4
Uthai Thani Thailand 15°22N 100°3E 236 E3
Uthal Pakistan 25°44N 66°40E 242 G2
Utiariti Brazil 13°0S 58°10W 331 C6
Utica N.Y., U.S.A. 43°6N 75°14W 313 C9
Utica Ohio, U.S.A. 40°14N 82°27W 312 F2
Utiel Spain 39°37N 1°11W 197 F3
Utikuma L. Canada 55°50N 115°30W 296 B5
Utila Honduras 16°6N 86°56W 320 C2
Utinga Brazil 12°6S 41°5W 333 D3
Utkela India 20°6N 83°10E 244 D6
Utlängen Sweden 56°2N 15°48E 163 H9
Utne Norway 60°25N 6°37E 164 D3
Utnur India 19°22N 78°46E 244 E4
Uto Japan 32°41N 130°40E 222 E2
Utö Sweden 58°56N 18°16E 162 F12
Utopia Australia 22°14S 134°33E 280 C1
Utrata Poland 52°15N 21°4E 143 B2
Utraula India 27°19N 82°25E 243 F10
Utrecht Neths. 52°5N 5°8E 170 B5
Utrecht KwaZulu Natal, S. Africa 27°38S 30°20E 271 C5
Utrecht □ Neths. 52°6N 5°7E 170 B5
Utrera Spain 37°12N 5°48W 195 H5
Utría △ Colombia 5°57N 77°21W 328 B2
Utsira Norway 59°19N 4°53E 164 E1
Utsjoki → Finland 69°51N 26°59E 160 B22
Utsunomiya Japan 36°30N 139°50E 223 A11
Uttar Pradesh □ India 27°0N 80°0E 243 F9
Uttaradit Thailand 17°36N 100°5E 236 D3
Uttarakhand □ India 30°0N 79°30E 243 D8
Uttaranchal = Uttarakhand □ India 30°0N 79°30E 243 D8
Uttarpara India 22°39N 88°21E 124 B1
Utterslev Mose Denmark 55°42N 12°29E 118 A2
Utterson Canada 45°12N 79°19W 312 A5
Uttoxeter U.K. 52°54N 1°52W 168 E6
Utuado Puerto Rico 18°16N 66°42W 321 b
Uummannaq Qaasuitsup, Greenland 70°58N 52°17W 150 B5
Uummannaq Qaasuitsup, Greenland 77°33N 68°52W 154 B4
Uummannarsuaq = Nunap Isua Greenland 59°48N 43°55W 154 F6
Uunartoq Qeqertoq Greenland 71°33N 21°47W 154 C8
Uusikaarlepyy Finland 63°32N 22°31E 160 E20
Uusikaupunki Finland 60°47N 21°25E 188 B1
Uva Russia 56°59N 52°13E 190 B11
Uvá → Colombia 3°41N 70°3W 328 C3
Uvac → Serbia 43°35N 19°30E 202 C3
Uvalda U.S.A. 32°2N 82°31W 316 C7
Uvalde U.S.A. 29°13N 99°47W 314 G5
Uvarovo Russia 51°59N 42°14E 190 E6
Uvat Russia 59°5N 68°50E 214 D7
Uvdal Norway 60°17N 8°48E 164 D5
Uvéa, I. Wall. & F. Is. 13°18S 176°10W 277 C15
Uvinza Tanzania 5°5S 30°24E 268 D3
Uvira Dem. Rep. of the Congo 3°22S 29°3E 268 C2
Uvs □ Mongolia 49°38N 93°0E 217 C12
Uvs Nuur Mongolia 50°20N 92°30E 217 B12
Uwa Japan 33°22N 132°31E 222 D4
'Uwairidh, Ḩarrat al Si. Arabia 26°50N 38°0E 246 E3
Uwajima Japan 33°10N 132°35E 222 D4
Uwanda ⌓ Tanzania 7°46S 32°0E 268 D3
Uweinat, Jebel Sudan 21°54N 24°58E 256 C1
Uxbridge Canada 44°6N 79°7W 312 B5
Uxin Qi China 38°50N 109°5E 226 E5
Uxmal Mexico 20°22N 89°46W 319 C7
Uyak U.S.A. 57°38N 154°0W 303 H9
Üydzin Mongolia 44°9N 107°0E 226 B4
Uyo Nigeria 5°1N 7°53E 263 D6
Uyu → Burma 24°51N 94°57E 241 C5
Üyüklü Tepe Turkey 37°5N 27°21E 205 D9
Uyûn Mûsa Egypt 29°53N 32°40E 251 J3
Uyuni Bolivia 20°28S 66°47W 330 E4
Uzbekistan ■ Asia 41°30N 65°0E 217 D7
Uzboy → Turkmenistan 39°30N 55°0E 247 B7
Uzen, Mal → Kazakhstan 49°4N 49°44E 191 F9
Uzerche France 45°25N 1°34E 174 C5
Uzès France 44°1N 4°26E 175 D8
Uzh → Ukraine 51°15N 30°12E 177 C16
Uzhgorod = Uzhhorod Ukraine 48°36N 22°18E 182 B7
Uzhhorod Ukraine 48°36N 22°18E 182 B7
Uzhok Ukraine 48°59N 22°52E 182 B7
Užice Serbia 43°55N 19°50E 202 C3
Uzlovaya Russia 54°0N 38°5E 188 F10
Üzümlü Turkey 36°44N 29°14E 205 E11
Uzuncaburç Turkey 36°35N 33°57E 250 B4
Uzunköprü Turkey 41°16N 26°43E 203 E10
Uzunkuyu Turkey 38°17N 26°33E 205 C8

V

V.C. Bird Int. ✕ (ANU) Antigua & B. 17°8N 61°47W 322 b
Vaal → S. Africa 29°4S 23°38E 270 C3
Vaal Dam S. Africa 27°0S 28°14E 271 C4
Vaalwater S. Africa 24°15S 28°8E 271 B4
Vaasa Finland 63°6N 21°38E 160 E19
Vabre France 43°42N 2°24E 174 E6
Vác Hungary 47°49N 19°10E 182 C4
Vacaos, Mare aux Mauritius 20°22S 57°30E 272 e
Vacaria Brazil 28°31S 50°52W 335 B5
Vacaville U.S.A. 38°21N 121°59W 306 G5
Vaccarès, Étang de France 43°32N 4°34E 175 E8
Vach = Vakh → Russia 60°45N 76°45E 214 C8
Vache, Î. à Haiti 18°2N 73°35W 321 C5
Väckelsång Sweden 56°37N 14°58E 163 H8
Vaclavské náměstí Prague, Czechia 135 b2
Vacoas Mauritius 20°18S 57°29E 272 e
Vada India 19°39N 73°8E 244 E1
Vadakara India 11°35N 75°40E 245 J2
Vadaul India 19°2N 72°55E 130 A2
Väddö Sweden 60°0N 18°50E 162 D12
Vadehavet △ Denmark 55°20N 8°30E 163 J2
Väderstad Sweden 58°19N 14°55E 163 F8
Vadheim Norway 61°13N 5°49E 164 C2
Vadnagar India 23°47N 72°40E 242 H5
Vado Ligure Italy 44°17N 8°26E 198 D5
Vadodara India 22°20N 73°10E 242 H5
Vadsø Norway 70°3N 29°50E 160 A23
Vadstena Sweden 58°28N 14°54E 163 F8
Vaduj India 17°36N 74°27E 244 F2
Vaduz Liech. 47°8N 9°31E 179 H5
Vadvetjåkka △ Sweden 68°30N 18°28E 160 B18
Værlandet Norway 61°18N 4°44E 164 C1
Værøy Norway 67°40N 12°40E 160 C15
Vagalat Albania 39°44N 20°8E 206 B10
Vågåmo Norway 61°52N 9°6E 164 C6
Vágar Fœroe Is. 62°5N 7°15W 160 E9
Vaggeryd Sweden 57°30N 14°10E 163 G8
Vagharshapat = Ejmiatsin Armenia 40°12N 44°19E 191 K7
Vaghena Solomon Is. 7°25S 157°45E 287 L9
Vaghia Greece 38°19N 23°11E 204 C5
Vagia, Akra Greece 36°15N 28°11E 206 E12
Vagney France 48°1N 6°43E 173 D13
Vagnhärad Sweden 58°57N 17°33E 163 F11
Vagos Portugal 40°33N 8°42W 194 E2
Vågsfjorden Norway 68°50N 16°50E 160 B17
Váh → Slovakia 47°43N 18°7E 181 D11
Vahitahi French Polynesia 18°44S 138°52W 289 f
Vahsel B. Antarctica 75°0S 35°0W 151 D1
Váhtjer = Gällivare Sweden 67°9N 20°40E 160 C19
Vaï Greece 35°15N 26°18E 207 E7
Vaiaku = Fongafale Tuvalu 8°31S 179°13E 277 B14
Vaiea Cook Is. 19°6S 169°54W 289 g
Vaigai → India 9°15N 79°10E 245 K4
Vaiges France 48°2N 0°30W 172 D6
Vaihingen Germany 48°54N 8°57E 179 G4
Vaihiria, L. Tahiti 17°40S 149°25W 289 e
Vaijapur India 19°58N 74°45E 244 E2
Vaikam India 9°45N 76°25E 245 K3
Vail U.S.A. 39°40N 106°20W 304 G10
Vailala → Papua N. G. 7°57S 145°25E 286 D3
Vailhau, Récif Comoros Is. 11°48S 43°4E 272 a
Vailly-sur-Aisne France 49°24N 3°31E 173 C10
Vailoatai Amer. Samoa 14°21S 170°46W 302 f
Vaippar → India 9°0N 78°25E 245 K4
Vairaatea French Polynesia 19°19S 139°20W 289 f
Vairao Tahiti 17°47S 149°17W 289 e
Vaires-sur-Marne France 48°52N 2°38E 134 A4
Vaisali → India 26°28N 78°53E 243 F8
Vaison-la-Romaine France 44°14N 5°4E 175 D9
Vaitogi Amer. Samoa 14°24S 170°44W 302 f
Vaitupu Pac. Oc. 7°28S 178°41E 277 B14
Vajpur India 21°24N 73°17E 244 D1
Vakaga □ C.A.R. 10°0N 22°30E 264 A4
Vakaga → C.A.R. 9°48N 21°32E 264 A4
Vakarai Sri Lanka 8°8N 81°26E 245 K5
Vakarel Bulgaria 42°35N 23°40E 202 D7
Vakfikebir Turkey 41°2N 39°17E 213 B8
Vakh → Russia 60°45N 76°45E 214 C8
Vakhsh → Tajikistan 37°6N 68°18E 217 E7
Vakhtan Russia 57°53N 46°47E 190 B8
Vakinankaratra □ Madag. 20°0S 47°0E 272 B2
Vaksdal Norway 60°29N 5°45E 164 D2
Vakuta I. Papua N. G. 8°51S 151°10E 286 E6
Vál Hungary 47°22N 18°40E 182 C3
Val Camónica Italy 45°57N 10°17E 198 C7
Val-de-Marne □ France 48°45N 2°28E 173 D9
Val-d'Isère France 45°27N 6°59E 175 C10
Val-d'Oise □ France 49°5N 2°10E 173 C9
Val-d'Or Canada 48°7N 77°47W 298 C4
Val Grande △ Italy 46°3N 8°25E 198 B5
Val Marie Canada 49°15N 107°45W 297 D7
Val Thorens France 45°20N 6°33E 175 C10
Valaam Russia 61°22N 30°57E 188 B6
Valadares Portugal 41°5N 8°38W 194 D2
Valahia Romania 44°35N 25°0E 183 F9
Valaichenai Sri Lanka 7°54N 81°32E 245 L5
Valais □ Switz. 46°12N 7°45E 179 J3
Valais, Alpes du Switz. 46°5N 7°35E 179 J3
Valandovo Macedonia 41°19N 22°34E 202 E6
Valašské Meziříčí Czechia 49°29N 17°59E 181 B10
Valatie U.S.A. 42°24N 73°40W 313 D11
Valaxa Greece 38°50N 24°29E 204 C6
Vålberg Sweden 59°23N 13°11E 162 E7
Valbo Sweden 60°40N 17°0E 162 D10
Valbondione Italy 46°2N 10°1E 198 B7
Valby Denmark 55°39N 12°29E 118 B2
Valcamonica = Val Camónica Italy 45°57N 10°17E 198 C7
Vălcani Romania 46°0N 20°26E 182 D5
Valcannuta Italy 41°52N 12°25E 136 B1
Vâlcea □ Romania 45°0N 24°10E 183 F9
Valcheta Argentina 40°40S 66°8W 336 B3
Valdagno Italy 45°39N 11°18E 199 C8
Valdahon France 47°8N 6°21E 173 E13
Valdai Hills = Valdayskaya Vozvyshennost Russia 57°0N 33°30E 188 D7
Valday Russia 57°58N 33°9E 188 D7
Valdayskaya Vozvyshennost Russia 57°0N 33°30E 188 D7
Valdaysky △ Russia 57°30N 33°0E 188 D7
Valdeazogues → Spain 38°45N 4°55W 195 G6
Valdecañas, Embalse de Spain 39°45N 5°25W 194 F5
Valdelatas Spain 40°31N 3°42W 127 A1
Valdemarsvik Sweden 58°14N 16°40E 163 F10
Valdemoro Spain 40°12N 3°40W 194 E7
Valdepeñas Spain 38°43N 3°25W 195 G7
Valderaduey → Spain 41°31N 5°42W 194 D5
Valdérice Italy 38°4N 12°37E 200 D5
Valderrobres Spain 40°53N 0°9E 196 E5
Valdés, Pen. Argentina 42°30S 63°45W 336 B4
Valdez Ecuador 1°15N 79°0W 328 C2
Valdez Alaska, U.S.A. 61°7N 146°16W 303 F11
Valdgeym = Dobropole Ukraine 48°25N 37°2E 189 H9
Valdivia Chile 39°50S 73°14W 336 A2
Valdivia Colombia 7°11N 75°27W 328 B2
Valdivia Abyssal Plain S. Ocean 62°30S 70°0E 151 C6
Valdobbiádene Italy 45°54N 12°0E 199 C8
Valdosta U.S.A. 30°50N 83°17W 316 E6
Valdoviño = Aviño Spain 43°36N 8°8W 194 B2
Valdres Norway 61°5N 9°5E 164 C6
Vale Georgia 41°30N 42°58E 191 K6
Vale Oreg., U.S.A. 43°59N 117°15W 304 E5
Vale of Glamorgan □ U.K. 51°28N 3°25W 169 F4
Valea lui Mihai Romania 47°32N 22°11E 182 C7
Valea Mărului Romania 45°49N 27°42E 183 E12
Valemount Canada 52°50N 119°15W 296 C5
Valença = Valença do Piauí Brazil 6°20S 41°45W 332 C3
Valença Brazil 13°20S 39°5W 333 D4
Valença Portugal 42°1N 8°34W 194 C2
Valença do Piauí Brazil 6°20S 41°45W 332 C3
Valençay France 47°9N 1°34E 173 E8
Valence France 44°57N 4°54E 175 D8
Valence d'Agen France 44°6N 0°53E 174 D4
Valencia Phil. 7°57N 125°3E 233 H5
Valencia Spain 39°27N 0°23W 197 F4
Valencia Trin. & Tob. 10°39N 61°11W 323 t
Valencia N. Mex., U.S.A. 34°48N 106°43W 305 J10
Valencia Venezuela 10°11N 68°0W 328 A4
Valencia □ Spain 39°20N 0°40W 197 F4
Valencia ✕ (VLC) Spain 39°20N 0°26W 197 F4
Valencia, G. de Spain 39°30N 0°20E 197 F5
Valencia de Alcántara Spain 39°25N 7°14W 195 F3
Valencia de Don Juan Spain 42°17N 5°31W 194 C5
Valencia I. Ireland 51°54N 10°22W 166 E1

Valenciennes France 50°20N 3°34E 173 B10
Văleni Romania 44°15N 24°45E 183 F9
Vălenii de Munte Romania 45°11N 26°2E 183 E11
Valensole France 43°50N 5°59E 175 E9
Valentigney France 47°27N 6°51E 173 E13
Valentim, Sa. do Brazil 6°0S 43°30W 332 C3
Valentin Russia 43°8N 134°17E 220 C7
Valentine Nebr., U.S.A. 42°52N 100°33W 308 D3
Valentine Tex., U.S.A. 30°35N 104°30W 314 F2
Valenton France 48°44N 2°27E 134 B3
Valenza Italy 45°1N 8°38E 198 C5
Våler Hedmark, Norway 60°41N 11°50E 164 D8
Våler Østfold, Norway 59°29N 10°51E 164 E7
Valera Piemonte, Italy 45°33N 9°3E 128 A1
Valera Venezuela 9°19N 70°37W 328 B3
Valesdir Vanuatu 16°47S 168°10E 287 F6
Valestrand Norway 59°40N 5°26E 164 E2
Valga Estonia 57°47N 26°2E 188 D4
Valguarnera Caropepe Italy 37°30N 14°23E 201 E7
Valier U.S.A. 48°18N 112°16W 304 B7
Valinco, G. de France 41°40N 8°52E 175 G12
Valjevo Serbia 44°18N 19°53E 202 B3
Valka Latvia 57°46N 26°3E 188 D3
Valkeakoski Finland 61°16N 24°2E 188 B2
Valkenswaard Neths. 51°21N 5°29E 170 C5
Vall de Uxó = La Vall d'Uixó Spain 39°49N 0°15W 196 F4
Valla Sweden 59°2N 16°20E 162 E10
Valladolid Yucatán, Mexico 20°41N 88°12W 319 C7
Valladolid Spain 41°38N 4°43W 194 D6
Valladolid □ Spain 41°38N 4°43W 194 D6
Vallata Italy 41°2N 15°15E 201 A8
Vallcarca Spain 41°25N 2°9E 114 A1
Valldemossa Spain 39°43N 2°37E 206 B3
Valldoreix Spain 41°27N 2°3E 114 A1
Valle Norway 59°13N 7°33E 164 E4
Valle d'Aosta □ Italy 45°45N 7°15E 198 C4
Valle de la Pascua Venezuela 9°13N 66°0W 328 B4
Valle de las Palmas Mexico 32°20N 116°43W 307 N10
Valle de Santiago Mexico 20°23N 101°12W 318 C4
Valle de Villaverde Spain 43°15N 3°15W 194 B7
Valle de Zaragoza Mexico 27°25N 105°50W 318 B3
Valle del Cauca □ Colombia 3°45N 76°30W 328 C2
Valle del Ticino ⌓ Italy 45°22N 9°0E 198 C6
Valle Fértil, Sierra del Argentina 30°20S 68°0W 334 C2
Valle Gran Rey Canary Is. 28°5N 17°20W 153 e1
Valle Hermoso Mexico 25°35N 97°40W 319 B5
Valle Nacional Mexico 17°47N 96°18W 319 D5
Vallecas Spain 40°22N 3°37W 127 B2
Vallecas, Cumbres de Spain 40°20N 3°33W 127 B2
Valledupar Colombia 10°29N 73°15W 328 A3
Vallée de Mai ⌓ Seychelles 4°19S 55°44E 272 c
Vallée du Bandama □ Ivory C. 8°0N 5°0W 262 D3
Vallegrande Bolivia 18°30S 64°10W 331 D5
Vallehermoso Canary Is. 28°10N 17°15W 153 e1
Vallejo U.S.A. 38°7N 122°14W 306 G4
Vallenar Chile 28°30S 70°50W 334 B1
Vallensbæk Denmark 55°38N 12°21E 118 B2
Vallensbæk Strand Denmark 55°36N 12°23E 118 B2
Vallentuna Sweden 59°32N 18°5E 162 E12
Vallentunasjön Sweden 59°27N 18°1E 139 A2
Valleranello Italy 41°46N 12°29E 136 C1
Valleraugue France 44°6N 3°39E 174 D7
Vallet France 47°10N 1°15W 172 E5
Valletta Malta 35°54N 14°31E 206 F8
Valley, The Anguilla 18°13N 63°4W 322 a
Valley Center U.S.A. 33°13N 117°2W 307 M9
Valley City U.S.A. 46°55N 98°0W 308 B5
Valley Falls Oreg., U.S.A. 42°29N 120°17W 304 E3
Valley Falls R.I., U.S.A. 41°54N 71°24W 313 E13
Valley Junction = West Des Moines U.S.A. 41°35N 93°43W 310 C3
Valley of Flowers △ India 30°50N 79°40E 243 D8
Valley of the Kings Egypt 25°41N 32°34E 256 B3
Valley Springs U.S.A. 38°12N 120°50W 306 G6
Valley Station U.S.A. 38°6N 85°52W 311 F11
Valley View U.S.A. 40°39N 76°33W 313 F8
Valley Wells U.S.A. 35°27N 115°46W 307 K11
Valleyview Canada 55°5N 117°17W 296 B5
Valli di Comácchio Italy 44°40N 12°15E 199 D9
Vallimanca, Arroyo Argentina 35°40S 59°10W 334 D4
Vallisaari Finland 60°7N 25°0E 121 C3
Vallo della Lucánia Italy 40°14N 15°16E 201 B8
Vallon-Pont-d'Arc France 44°24N 4°24E 175 D8
Vallorbe Switz. 46°42N 6°20E 179 J2
Valls Spain 41°18N 1°15E 196 D6
Vallvidrera Spain 41°24N 2°6E 114 A1
Vallvik Sweden 61°11N 17°10E 162 C11
Valmaseda = Balmaseda Spain 43°11N 3°12W 196 B1
Valmeyer U.S.A. 38°18N 90°19W 310 F6
Valmiera Latvia 57°37N 25°29E 188 D3
Valnera Spain 43°9N 3°40W 194 B7
Valognes France 49°30N 1°28W 172 C5
Valona = Vlorë Albania 40°32N 19°28E 202 F3
Valongo Portugal 41°8N 8°30W 194 D2
Valozhyn Belarus 54°3N 26°30E 177 A14
Valpaços Portugal 41°36N 7°17W 194 D3
Valparai India 10°22N 76°58E 245 J3
Valparaíso Chile 33°2S 71°40W 334 C1
Valparaíso Zacatecas, Mexico 22°46N 103°34W 318 C4
Valparaiso Fla., U.S.A. 30°29N 86°30W 317 E3
Valparaiso Ind., U.S.A. 41°28N 87°4W 311 C9
Valparaíso □ Chile 33°2S 71°40W 334 C1
Valpovo Croatia 45°39N 18°25E 182 E3
Valpoy India 15°32N 74°8E 245 G2
Valréas France 44°24N 5°0E 175 D9
Vals Switz. 46°39N 9°11E 179 J5
Vals → S. Africa 27°23S 26°30E 270 C4
Vals, Tanjung Indonesia 8°26S 137°25E 231 F9
Vals-les-Bains France 44°42N 4°24E 175 D8
Valsad India 20°40N 72°58E 244 D1
Valsamata Greece 38°10N 20°36E 207 C2
Valtellina Italy 46°11N 9°55E 198 B6
Valþjofsstaður Iceland 65°1N 14°59W 155 B12
Valti Greece 38°27N 21°7E 207 C3
Valuyki Russia 50°10N 38°5E 189 G10
Valverde Canary Is. 27°48N 17°55W 153 e1
Valverde del Camino Spain 37°35N 6°47W 195 H4
Valverde del Fresno Spain 40°15N 6°51W 194 E4
Valvidrera → Spain 41°25N 2°0E 114 A1
Vama Romania 47°34N 25°42E 183 C10
Vambori India 19°17N 74°44E 244 E2
Vamdrup Denmark 55°25N 9°17E 163 J3
Våmhus Sweden 61°7N 14°29E 162 C8
Vamizi, I. Mozam. 11°2S 40°40E 269 E5
Vammala = Sastamala Finland 61°20N 22°54E 188 B2
Vamos Greece 35°24N 24°13E 207 E5
Vamsadhara → India 18°21N 84°8E 244 E7
Van Turkey 38°30N 43°20E 213 C10
Van □ Turkey 38°30N 43°20E 213 C10
Van, L. = Van Gölü Turkey 38°30N 43°0E 213 C10
Van Alstyne U.S.A. 33°25N 96°35W 314 E6
Van Blommestein Meer Suriname 4°45N 55°5W 329 C6
Van Buren = Kettering U.S.A. 39°41N 84°10W 311 E12
Van Buren N.B., Canada 47°10N 67°55W 299 C6
Van Buren Ark., U.S.A. 35°26N 94°21W 314 D7
Van Buren Maine, U.S.A. 47°10N 67°58W 309 B20
Van Buren Mo., U.S.A. 37°0N 91°1W 308 G8
Van Canh Vietnam 13°37N 109°0E 236 F7
Van Diemen, C. N. Terr., Australia 11°9S 130°24E 278 B5
Van Diemen, C. Queens., Australia 16°30S 139°46E 280 B2
Van Diemen G. Australia 11°45S 132°0E 278 B5
Van Gogh Museum Amsterdam, Neths. 112 c1
Van Gölü Turkey 38°30N 43°0E 213 C10
Van Horn U.S.A. 31°3N 104°50W 314 F2
Van Horne U.S.A. 42°1N 92°5W 310 B4
Van Meter U.S.A. 41°32N 93°57W 310 C3
Van Ninh Vietnam 12°42N 109°14E 236 F7
Van Rees, Pegunungan Indonesia 2°35S 138°15E 231 E9
Van Tivu India 8°51N 78°15E 245 K4
Van Wert U.S.A. 40°52N 84°35W 311 D12
Van Yen Vietnam 21°4N 104°42E 228 G5
Van Zylsrus S. Africa 26°52S 22°4E 270 C3
Vanadzor Armenia 40°48N 44°30E 191 K7
Vanak Iran 35°45N 51°23E 141 A2
Vanavana French Polynesia 20°47S 139°9W 289 f
Vanavara Russia 60°22N 102°16E 215 C11
Vanceburg U.S.A. 38°36N 83°19W 311 F13
Vancouver B.C., Canada 49°15N 123°7W 306 A3
Vancouver Wash., U.S.A. 45°38N 122°40W 306 E4
Vancouver, C. Australia 35°2S 118°11E 279 G2
Vancouver, Mt. U.S.A. 60°20N 139°41W 303 F13
Vancouver I. Canada 49°50N 126°0W 306 B2
Vancouver Int. ✈ (YVR) Canada 49°10N 123°10W 306 A3
Vanda = Vantaa Finland 60°18N 24°56E 121 B2
Vandalia Ill., U.S.A. 38°58N 89°6W 310 F7
Vandalia Mo., U.S.A. 39°19N 91°29W 310 E5
Vandalia Ohio, U.S.A. 39°54N 84°12W 311 E12
Vandavasi India 12°30N 79°30E 245 H4
Vandellòs Spain 41°0N 0°55E 196 E5
Vandeloos B. Sri Lanka 8°0N 81°45E 245 L5
Vandenberg Village U.S.A. 34°43N 120°28W 307 L6
Vanderbijlpark S. Africa 26°42S 27°54E 271 C4
Vandergrift U.S.A. 40°36N 79°34W 312 F5
Vanderhoof Canada 54°0N 124°0W 296 C4
Vanderkloof Dam S. Africa 30°4S 24°40E 270 D3
Vanderlin I. Australia 15°44S 137°2E 280 B2
Vänern Sweden 58°47N 13°30E 163 F7
Vänersborg Sweden 58°26N 12°19E 163 F6
Vang Norway 61°7N 8°34E 164 C5
Vang Vieng Laos 18°58N 102°32E 236 C4
Vanga Kenya 4°35S 39°12E 268 C4
Vangaindrano Madag. 23°21S 47°36E 272 C2
Vänge Sweden 59°50N 17°20E 162 E11
Vangede Denmark 55°45N 12°30E 118 A3
Vangsnes Norway 61°9N 6°39E 164 C3
Vanguard Canada 49°55N 107°20W 297 D7
Vangunu Solomon Is. 8°40S 158°5E 287 M10
Vanikoro Pac. Oc. 11°39S 166°54E 277 C12
Vaniköy Turkey 41°3N 29°3E 122 B2
Vanimo Papua N. G. 2°42S 141°21E 286 B1
Vanino Russia 48°50N 140°5E 215 E15
Vanivilasa Sagara India 13°45N 76°30E 245 H3
Vaniyambadi India 12°46N 78°44E 245 H4
Vânju Mare Romania 44°25N 22°52E 182 F7
Vankleek Hill Canada 45°32N 74°40W 313 A10
Vanløse Denmark 55°41N 12°28E 118 A2
Vännäs Sweden 63°58N 19°48E 160 E18
Vannes France 47°40N 2°47W 172 E4
Vannøya Norway 70°6N 19°50E 160 A18
Vanoise, Massif de la France 45°25N 6°40E 175 C10
Vanrhynsdorp S. Africa 31°36S 18°44E 270 D2
Vansada India 20°47N 73°25E 244 D1
Vansbro Sweden 60°32N 14°15E 162 D8
Vanse Norway 58°6N 6°41E 164 F3
Vansittart B. Australia 14°3S 126°17E 278 B4
Vansittart I. Canada 65°50N 84°0W 295 D15
Vantaa Finland 60°18N 24°56E 121 B2
Vantaankoski Finland 60°18N 24°50E 121 B2
Vantaanpuisto Finland 60°18N 24°53E 121 B2
Vanua Balavu Fiji 17°12S 178°55W 287 A3
Vanua Lava Vanuatu 13°50S 167°30E 287 C5
Vanua Levu Fiji 16°33S 179°15E 287 A2
Vanua Vatu Fiji 18°22S 179°15W 287 B3
Vanuatu ■ Pac. Oc. 15°0S 168°0E 287 E6
Vanves France 48°49N 2°17E 134 B2
Vanwyksvlei S. Africa 30°18S 21°49E 270 D3
Vao N. Cal. 22°39S 167°32E 288 d
Vapi India 20°22N 72°54E 244 D1
Vapnyarka Ukraine 48°32N 28°45E 183 B13
Var □ France 43°27N 6°18E 175 E10
Var → France 43°39N 7°12E 175 E11
Vara Sweden 58°16N 12°55E 163 F6
Vara, Pico da Azores 37°48N 25°13W 153 d3
Varada → India 15°0N 75°40E 245 G2
Varadero Cuba 23°11N 81°11W 320 D3
Varades France 47°25N 1°1W 172 E5
Varáita → Italy 44°9N 7°53E 198 D4
Varaldsøy Norway 60°6N 5°59E 164 D2
Varalé Ivory C. 9°40N 3°17W 262 D4
Varallo Italy 45°49N 8°15E 198 C5
Varāmīn Iran 35°20N 51°39E 247 C6
Varāmīn □ Iran 35°18N 51°35E 247 B6
Varanasi India 25°22N 83°0E 243 G10
Varangerfjorden Norway 70°3N 29°25E 160 A23
Varangerhalvøya Norway 70°25N 29°30E 160 A23
Varano, Lago di Italy 41°53N 15°45E 199 G12
Varaždin Croatia 46°20N 16°20E 199 B13
Varazze Italy 44°22N 8°34E 198 D5
Varberg Sweden 57°6N 12°20E 163 G6
Varcar Vakuf = Mrkonjić Grad Bos.-H. 44°26N 17°4E 182 F2
Vardak □ Afghan. 34°0N 68°0E 240 B3
Vardar = Axios → Greece 40°57N 22°35E 202 F6
Varde Denmark 55°38N 8°29E 163 J2
Varde Å → Denmark 55°35N 8°19E 163 J2
Vardenis Armenia 40°10N 45°43E 191 K7
Vardø Norway 70°23N 31°5E 160 A24
Varedo Italy 45°35N 9°8E 128 A1
Varel Germany 53°23N 8°8E 178 B4
Varella, Mui = Nay, Mui Vietnam 12°54N 109°26E 236 F7
Varėna Lithuania 54°12N 24°30E 188 E3
Varennes-sur-Allier France 46°19N 3°24E 173 F10
Varennes-Vauzelles France 47°3N 3°9E 173 E10
Vareš Bos.-H. 44°12N 18°23E 182 F3
Varese Italy 45°48N 8°50E 198 C5
Vârfurile Romania 46°19N 22°31E 182 D7
Vårgårda Sweden 58°2N 12°49E 163 F6
Vargas Venezuela 10°36N 66°56W 328 A4
Vargem Bonita Brazil 20°20S 46°22W 333 F2
Vargem Grande Brazil 3°33S 43°56W 332 B3
Varginha Brazil 21°33S 45°25W 335 A6
Vargön Sweden 58°22N 12°20E 163 F6
Varhaug Norway 58°37N 5°41E 164 F2
Vari Greece 38°24N 20°35E 207 C2
Varillas Chile 24°0S 70°10W 334 A1
Varkaus Finland 62°19N 27°50E 188 A4
Varkiza Greece 37°50N 23°49E 112 C2
Värmdölandet Sweden 59°20N 18°33E 162 E12
Värmeln Sweden 59°35N 12°54E 162 E6
Värmland □ Sweden 60°0N 13°20E 162 E6
Värmlandsbro Sweden 59°11N 13°0E 162 E7
Varna Bulgaria 43°13N 27°56E 203 C11
Varna □ Bulgaria 43°20N 27°30E 203 C11
Varna → India 16°48N 74°32E 244 F2
Värnamo Sweden 57°10N 14°3E 163 G8
Várnjárga = Varangerhalvøya Norway 70°25N 29°30E 160 A23
Varnsdorf Czechia 50°55N 14°35E 180 A7
Varnville U.S.A. 32°51N 81°5W 316 C8
Várpalota Hungary 47°12N 18°8E 182 C3
Vars Ont., Canada 45°21N 75°21W 313 A9
Vars Hautes-Alpes, France 44°37N 6°42E 175 D10
Vartdal Norway 62°20N 6°8E 164 B3
Vartiokylä Finland 60°13N 25°6E 121 B3
Vartiosaari Finland 60°11N 25°5E 121 B3
Varto Turkey 39°10N 41°27E 213 C9
Varvarin Serbia 43°43N 21°20E 202 C5
Varysburg U.S.A. 42°46N 78°19W 312 D6
Varzaneh Iran 32°25N 52°40E 247 C7
Varzaqān Iran 38°29N 46°40E 213 C12
Várzea Alegre Brazil 6°47S 39°17W 332 C4
Várzea da Palma Brazil 17°36S 44°44W 333 E3
Várzea Grande Brazil 15°39S 56°8W 331 D6
Varzi Italy 44°49N 9°12E 198 D6
Varzo Italy 46°12N 8°15E 198 B5
Varzy France 47°22N 3°20E 173 E10
Vas □ Hungary 47°10N 16°55E 182 C1
Vasa = Vaasa Finland 63°6N 21°38E 160 E19
Vasa Barris → Brazil 11°10S 37°10W 332 D4
Vasai-Virar India 19°28N 72°48E 244 E1
Vasamuseet Stockholm, Sweden 139 b3
Vásárosnamény Hungary 48°9N 22°19E 182 B7
Vascâo → Portugal 37°31N 7°31W 195 H3
Vaşcău Romania 46°28N 22°30E 182 D7
Vasco S. Africa 33°54S 18°34E 118 A2
Vascongadas = País Vasco □ Spain 42°50N 2°45W 196 C2
Vasfenārd Iran 35°38N 51°20E 141 B2
Vashi India 19°4N 72°59E 130 A2
Vāshīr Afghan. 32°16N 63°51E 240 B1
Vashkivtsi Ukraine 48°23N 25°31E 183 B10
Vasht = Khāsh Iran 28°15N 61°15E 240 C1
Vasilevichi Belarus 52°15N 29°50E 177 B16
Vasilika Greece 40°29N 23°8E 202 F7
Vasiliki Greece 38°37N 20°36E 207 B2
Vasiliko = Michurin Bulgaria 42°9N 27°51E 203 D11
Vasiliko Greece 38°25N 23°40E 204 C5
Vasilikos Greece 37°43N 20°59E 207 D2
Vasilkov = Vasylkiv Ukraine 50°7N 30°15E 177 C16
Vasilyevskiy, Ostrov Russia 59°55N 30°16E 137 B1
Vasilyova Sloboda = Chkolovsk Russia 56°50N 43°10E 190 B6
Vasilyovo = Chkolovsk Russia 56°50N 43°10E 190 B6
Väskinde Sweden 57°40N 18°20E 163 G10
Vaslui Romania 46°38N 27°42E 183 D12
Vaslui □ Romania 46°30N 27°45E 183 D12
Väsman Sweden 60°9N 15°5E 162 D9
Vassar Man., Canada 49°10N 95°55W 297 D9
Vassar Mich., U.S.A. 43°22N 83°35W 309 D12
Vassfaret Norway 60°38N 9°28E 164 D6
Västerås Sweden 59°37N 16°38E 162 E10
Västerbotten Sweden 64°36N 20°4E 160 D19
Västerdalälven → Sweden 60°30N 15°7E 162 D8
Västergötland Sweden 58°0N 13°10E 163 F7
Västerhaninge Sweden 59°7N 18°6E 162 E12
Västervik Sweden 57°43N 16°33E 163 G10
Västmanland Sweden 59°45N 16°20E 161 G17
Västmanland □ Sweden 59°45N 16°20E 162 E10
Vasto Italy 42°8N 14°40E 199 F11
Västra Götaland □ Sweden 58°0N 13°0E 163 F6
Vasvár Hungary 47°3N 16°47E 182 C1
Vasylivka Ukraine 45°38N 28°50E 183 E13
Vasylkiv Ukraine 50°7N 30°15E 177 C16
Vat Phou Laos 14°51N 105°49E 236 E5
Vatan France 47°4N 1°50E 173 E8
Vaté = Efate, I. Vanuatu 17°40S 168°25E 287 G6
Vatersay U.K. 56°55N 7°32W 167 E1
Vathi Greece 38°41N 20°47E 207 B2
Vathia Greece 36°29N 22°29E 204 E4
Vati Greece 36°3N 27°53E 206 E11
Vatia Amer. Samoa 14°15S 170°40W 302 f
Vatican City ■ Europe 41°54N 12°27E 136 B1
Vaticano, C. Italy 38°37N 15°50E 201 D8
Vatili Cyprus 35°6N 33°40E 207 E9
Vatin Serbia 45°12N 21°20E 182 E6
Vatiu = Atiu Cook Is. 20°0S 158°10W 289 J12
Vatnajökull Iceland 64°30N 16°48W 155 C10
Vatnajökull △ Iceland 64°24N 16°48W 155 C10
Vatnås Norway 59°58N 9°37E 164 E6
Vatnsfjörður Iceland 65°56N 22°30W 155 B4
Vato Sweden 59°50N 19°0E 162 E12
Vatolakkos Greece 35°27N 23°53E 207 E4
Vatoloha Madag. 17°52S 47°48E 272 B2
Vatomandry Madag. 19°20S 48°59E 272 B2
Vatovavy-Fitovinany □ Madag. 22°10S 48°0E 272 C2
Vatra-Dornei Romania 47°22N 25°22E 183 C10
Vatrak → India 23°9N 73°2E 242 H5
Vattaru Atoll Maldives 3°16N 73°25E 272 d
Vättern Sweden 58°25N 14°30E 163 F8
Vatu Vara Fiji 17°26S 179°31W 287 A3
Vatulele Fiji 18°33S 177°37E 287 B1
Vauclin, Mt. du Martinique 14°33N 60°53W 322 j
Vauclin, Pte. de Martinique 14°34N 60°49W 322 j
Vaucluse Australia 33°51S 151°15E 139 B2
Vaucluse □ France 43°50N 5°20E 175 E9
Vaucluse House Australia 33°51S 151°15E 139 B2
Vaucouleurs France 48°37N 5°40E 173 D12
Vaucresson France 48°50N 2°9E 134 A1
Vaud □ Switz. 46°35N 6°30E 179 J2
Vaudreuil-Dorion Canada 45°23N 74°3W 313 A10
Vaughan Canada 43°50N 79°32W 141 A1
Vaughn Mont., U.S.A. 47°33N 111°33W 304 C8
Vaughn N. Mex., U.S.A. 34°36N 105°13W 305 J11
Vauhallan France 48°44N 2°12E 134 B2
Vaujours France 48°56N 2°34E 134 A4
Vaujours L. Canada 55°27N 74°15W 298 A5
Vaupés = Uaupés → Brazil 0°2N 67°16W 328 C4
Vaupés □ Colombia 1°0N 71°0W 328 C3
Vauvert France 43°42N 4°17E 175 E8
Vauxhall Alta., Canada 50°5N 112°9W 296 C6
Vauxhall London, U.K. 125 c4
Vav India 24°22N 71°31E 242 G4
Vavatenina Madag. 17°28S 49°12E 272 B2
Vava'u Tonga 18°36S 174°0W 287 P14
Vava'u Group Tonga 18°40S 174°0W 287 P14
Vavoua Ivory C. 7°23N 6°29W 262 D3
Vavuniya Sri Lanka 8°45N 80°30E 245 K5
Vawkavysk Belarus 53°9N 24°30E 177 B13
Vaxholm Sweden 59°25N 18°20E 162 E12
Växjö Sweden 56°52N 14°50E 163 H8
Våxtorp Sweden 56°25N 13°8E 163 H7
Vayalpad India 13°39N 78°38E 245 H4
Vayenga = Severomorsk Russia 69°5N 33°27E 160 B25
Vaygach, Ostrov Russia 70°0N 60°0E 214 C7
Veadeiros Brazil 14°7S 47°31W 333 D2
Veaikevárri = Svappavaara Sweden 67°40N 21°3E 160 C19
Vechelde Germany 52°16N 10°22E 178 C6
Vechta Germany 52°44N 8°17E 178 C4
Vechte → Neths. 52°34N 6°6E 170 B6
Vecsés Hungary 47°26N 19°19E 117 B3
Vedaranniyam India 10°25N 79°50E 245 J4
Vedavågen Norway 59°17N 5°12E 164 E2
Veddige Sweden 57°17N 12°20E 163 G6
Vedea → Romania 43°42N 25°41E 183 G10
Vedi Armenia 39°54N 44°43E 213 C11
Vedia Argentina 34°30S 61°31W 334 C3
Vedrette di Ries-Aurina ⌓ Italy 46°54N 12°5E 199 B9
Vedum Sweden 58°11N 13°0E 163 F7
Veedersburg U.S.A. 40°7N 87°16W 311 D9
Veendam Neths. 53°5N 6°52E 170 A6
Veenendaal Neths. 52°2N 5°34E 170 B5
Vefsna → Norway 65°48N 13°10E 160 D15
Vega Nordland, Norway 65°40N 11°55E 160 D14
Vega Tex., U.S.A. 35°15N 102°26W 314 D3
Vega Alta Puerto Rico 18°25N 66°20W 321 b
Vega Baja Puerto Rico 18°27N 66°23W 321 b
Vega de Ribadeo = Vegadeo Spain 43°27N 7°4W 194 B3
Vegadeo Spain 43°27N 7°4W 194 B3
Vegårshei Norway 58°44N 8°51E 164 F5
Vegas Verde = North Las Vegas U.S.A. 36°11N 115°7W 124 A1
Veggli Norway 60°3N 9°9E 164 D6
Veglia = Krk Croatia 45°8N 14°40E 199 C11
Vegoritida, L. Greece 40°45N 21°45E 202 F5
Vegreville Canada 53°30N 112°5W 296 C6
Veiholmen Norway 63°31N 7°58E 164 A4
Veimandu Channel Maldives 2°10N 73°20E 272 d
Veinge Sweden 56°33N 13°4E 163 H7
Veisiejai Lithuania 54°6N 23°42E 184 D10
Vejbystrand Sweden 56°19N 12°45E 163 H6
Vejen Denmark 55°30N 9°9E 163 J3
Vejer de la Frontera Spain 36°15N 5°59W 195 J5
Vejle Denmark 55°43N 9°30E 163 J3
Vejle Fjord Denmark 55°40N 9°50E 163 J3
Vela Luka Croatia 42°59N 16°44E 199 F13
Velachha India 21°26N 73°1E 244 D1
Velanai I. Sri Lanka 9°45N 79°45E 245 K4
Velas Azores 38°41N 28°13W 153 d1
Velas, C. Costa Rica 10°21N 85°52W 320 D2
Velasco, Sierra de Argentina 29°20S 67°10W 334 B2
Velay, Mts. du France 45°0N 3°40E 174 D7
Velbert Germany 51°20N 7°3E 178 D3
Velddrif S. Africa 32°42S 18°11E 270 D2
Velebit Planina Croatia 44°50N 15°20E 199 D12
Velebitski Kanal Croatia 44°45N 14°55E 199 D11
Veleka → Bulgaria 42°4N 27°58E 203 D11
Veleň Czechia 50°10N 14°33E 135 A3
Velencei-tó Hungary 47°13N 18°36E 182 C3
Velenje Slovenia 46°23N 15°8E 199 B12
Veles Macedonia 41°46N 21°47E 202 E5
Veleslavin Czechia 50°5N 14°21E 135 B2
Velestino Greece 39°23N 22°43E 204 B4
Vélez Colombia 6°1N 73°41W 328 B3
Vélez-Málaga Spain 36°48N 4°5W 195 J6
Vélez Rubio Spain 37°41N 2°5W 197 H2
Velhas → Brazil 17°13S 44°49W 333 E3
Velika Croatia 45°27N 17°40E 182 E2
Velika Gorica Croatia 45°44N 16°5E 199 C13
Velika Kapela Croatia 45°10N 15°5E 199 C12
Velika Kikinda = Kikinda Serbia 45°50N 20°30E 182 E5
Velika Kladuša Bos.-H. 45°11N 15°48E 199 C12
Velika Kruša = Krushë e Madhe Kosovo 42°19N 20°39E 202 D4
Velika Morava → Serbia 44°43N 21°3E 202 B5
Velika Plana Serbia 44°20N 21°4E 202 B5
Velikaya → Russia 57°48N 28°10E 188 D5
Velikaya Kema Russia 45°30N 137°12E 220 B8
Velikaya Lepetikha Ukraine 47°2N 33°58E 189 J7
Velike Lašče Slovenia 45°49N 14°45E 199 C11
Veliki Jastrebac Serbia 43°25N 21°30E 202 C5
Veliki Kanal Serbia 45°45N 19°15E 182 E4
Veliki Popović Serbia 44°8N 21°18E 202 B5
Veliki Ustyug Russia 60°47N 46°20E 186 B8
Velikiy Novgorod Russia 58°30N 31°25E 188 C6
Velikiye Luki Russia 56°25N 30°32E 188 D6
Veliko Gradište Serbia 44°46N 21°29E 202 B5
Veliko Tŭrnovo Bulgaria 43°5N 25°41E 203 C9
Veliko Tŭrnovo □ Bulgaria 43°5N 25°41E 203 C9
Velikonda Range India 14°45N 79°10E 245 G4
Vélingara Kolda, Senegal 13°12N 14°5W 262 C2
Vélingara Louga, Senegal 15°0N 14°40W 262 B2
Velingrad Bulgaria 42°4N 23°58E 202 D7
Velino, Mte. Italy 42°9N 13°23E 199 F10
Velizh Russia 55°36N 31°11E 188 E6
Vélizy-Villacoublay France 48°47N 2°11E 134 B2
Velka-Chuchle Czechia 50°0N 14°23E 135 B2
Vel'ké Kapušany Slovakia 48°34N 22°5E 181 C15
Velké Karlovice Czechia 49°20N 18°17E 181 B11
Velké Meziříčí Czechia 49°21N 16°1E 180 B9
Velké Přilepy Czechia 50°9N 14°19E 135 B1
Vel'ký Javorník Slovakia 49°19N 18°22E 181 B11
Vel'ký Krtíš Slovakia 48°12N 19°21E 181 C12
Vel'ký Meder Slovakia 47°52N 17°46E 181 D10
Vel'ký Tribeč Slovakia 48°28N 18°15E 181 C11
Vella G. Solomon Is. 8°0S 156°50E 287 M9
Vella Lavella Solomon Is. 7°45S 156°40E 287 L9
Vellar → India 11°30N 79°36E 245 J4
Velletri Italy 41°41N 12°47E 200 A5
Vellinge Sweden 55°29N 13°2E 163 J6
Vellmar Germany 51°22N 9°28E 178 D5
Vellore India 12°57N 79°10E 245 H4
Velopoula Greece 36°55N 23°27E 204 E5
Velsk Russia 61°10N 42°0E 188 B11
Velten Germany 52°42N 13°10E 178 C9
Veluwezoom △ Neths. 52°5N 6°0E 170 B6
Velva U.S.A. 48°4N 100°56W 308 A3
Velvendos Greece 40°15N 22°6E 202 F6
Velyka Mykhaylivka Ukraine 47°4N 29°52E 183 C14
Velyki Luchky Ukraine 48°25N 22°34E 182 B7
Velykyy Bereznyy Ukraine 48°54N 22°28E 182 B7
Velykyy Bychkiv Ukraine 47°58N 24°1E 183 C9
Vemb Denmark 56°21N 8°21E 163 H2
Vembanad L. India 9°36N 76°15E 245 K3
Vemdalen Sweden 62°27N 13°51E 162 B7
Ven Sweden 55°55N 12°45E 163 J6
Venaco France 42°14N 9°11E 175 F13
Venado Mexico 22°56N 101°6W 318 C4
Venado Tuerto Argentina 33°50S 62°0W 334 C3
Venafro Italy 41°29N 14°2E 201 A7
Venarey-les-Laumes France 47°32N 4°26E 173 E11
Venaría Italy 45°8N 7°38E 198 C4
Venčane Serbia 44°24N 20°28E 202 B4
Vence France 43°43N 7°6E 175 E11
Venda Seca Portugal 38°46N 9°15W 126 A1
Vendas Novas Portugal 38°39N 8°27W 195 G2
Vendée □ France 46°50N 1°35W 172 F5
Vendée → France 46°20N 1°10W 172 F5
Vendéen, Bocage France 46°40N 1°20W 174 B2
Vendeuvre-sur-Barse France 48°14N 4°28E 173 D11
Vendicari ⌓ Italy 36°49N 15°6E 201 F8
Vendôme France 47°47N 1°3E 172 E8
Vendramin Calergi, Palazzo Venice, Italy 142 a2
Vendrell = El Vendrell Spain 41°10N 1°30E 196 D6
Vendsyssel Denmark 57°22N 10°0E 163 G4
Vendychany Ukraine 48°38N 27°48E 183 B12
Venelles France 43°35N 5°28E 175 E9
Véneta, L. Italy 45°23N 12°25E 199 C9
Venetian Islands U.S.A. 25°47N 80°9W 129 D3
Venetie U.S.A. 67°1N 146°25W 303 C11
Véneto □ Italy 45°30N 12°0E 199 C9
Venev Russia 54°22N 38°17E 188 E10
Venézia Italy 45°27N 12°21E 199 C9
Venézia, G. di Italy 45°15N 13°0E 199 C10
Venézia, Palazzo Rome, Italy 136 c2
Venézia Lido Italy 45°25N 12°22E 199 C9
Venézia Tridentina = Trentino-Alto Adige □ Italy 46°30N 11°20E 199 B8
Venezuela ■ S. Amer. 8°0N 66°0W 328 B4
Venezuela, G. de Venezuela 11°30N 71°0W 328 A3
Venezuelan Basin Cent. Amer. 14°0N 68°0W 321 C6
Vengurla India 15°53N 73°45E 245 G1
Vengurla Rocks India 15°55N 73°22E 245 G1
Venice = Venézia Italy 45°27N 12°21E 199 C9
Venice Calif., U.S.A. 33°59N 118°27W 126 C2
Venice Fla., U.S.A. 27°6N 82°27W 317 H7
Vénissieux France 45°42N 4°53E 175 C8
Venjan Sweden 60°57N 13°55E 162 D7
Venjansjön Sweden 60°54N 14°0E 162 D8
Venkatagiri India 14°0N 79°35E 245 H4
Venkatapuram India 18°20N 80°30E 244 E5
Venlo Neths. 51°22N 6°11E 170 C6
Vennachar Junction Canada 45°5N 77°14W 312 A7
Vennesla Norway 58°15N 7°59E 164 F4
Venosa Italy 40°58N 15°49E 201 B8
Venray Neths. 51°31N 6°0E 170 C6
Vent, Îs. du French Polynesia 17°30S 149°30W 289 f
Venta Lithuania 56°12N 22°42E 184 B9
Venta → Latvia 57°24N 21°33E 184 A8
Venta de Baños Spain 41°55N 4°30W 194 D6
Venta de Cardeña = Cardeña Spain 38°16N 4°20W 195 G6
Ventana, Sa. de la Argentina 38°0S 62°30W 334 D3
Ventas Spain 40°26N 3°40W 127 B1
Ventersburg S. Africa 28°7S 27°9E 270 C4
Ventersburgweg = Hennenman S. Africa 27°59S 27°1E 270 C4
Venterstad S. Africa 30°47S 25°48E 270 D4
Ventimíglia Italy 43°47N 7°36E 198 E4
Ventnor U.K. 50°36N 1°12W 169 G6
Ventorro del Cano Spain 40°23N 3°49W 127 B1
Ventoténe Italy 40°47N 13°25E 200 B6
Ventoux, Mt. France 44°10N 5°17E 175 D9
Ventspils Latvia 57°25N 21°32E 184 A8
Ventuarí → Venezuela 3°58N 67°2W 328 C4
Ventucopa U.S.A. 34°50N 119°29W 307 L7
Ventura U.S.A. 34°17N 119°18W 307 L7
Venus U.S.A. 27°4N 81°22W 317 H8
Vénus, Pte. Tahiti 17°29S 149°29W 289 e
Venus B. Australia 38°40S 145°42E 283 E6
Venustiano Carranza Baja Calif., Mexico 30°25N 115°53W 318 A1
Venustiano Carranza Distrito Federal, Mexico 19°25N 99°5W 128 B2
Venustiano Carranza, Presa Mexico 27°30N 100°37W 318 B4
Vera Argentina 29°30S 60°20W 334 B3
Vera Spain 37°15N 1°51W 197 H3
Veracruz Mexico 19°11N 96°8W 319 D5
Veracruz □ Mexico 19°0N 96°15W 319 D5
Veraval India 20°53N 70°27E 242 J4
Verbánia Italy 45°56N 8°33E 198 C5
Verbano, L. di = Maggiore, L. Italy 45°57N 8°39E 198 B5
Verbano Cusio Ossola ⌓ Italy 46°15N 8°20E 198 B5
Verbicaro Italy 39°45N 15°55E 201 C8
Verbier Switz. 46°6N 7°13E 179 J3
Vercelli Italy 45°19N 8°25E 198 C5
Verchovchevo Ukraine 48°32N 34°10E 189 H8
Vercors ⌓ France 45°0N 5°25E 175 D9
Verdalsøra Norway 63°48N 11°30E 160 E14
Verde → Argentina 41°56S 65°5W 336 B3
Verde → Goiás, Brazil 19°11S 50°44W 333 E1
Verde → Goiás, Brazil 18°1S 50°14W 333 E1
Verde → Mato Grosso, Brazil 11°54S 55°48W 331 C6
Verde → Mato Grosso do Sul, Brazil 21°25S 52°20W 331 E7
Verde → São Paulo, Brazil 23°29S 46°27W 137 A1
Verde → Chihuahua, Mexico 26°39N 107°11W 318 B3
Verde → Jalisco, Mexico 20°42N 103°14W 318 C4
Verde → Oaxaca, Mexico 15°59N 97°50W 319 D5
Verde → Paraguay 23°9S 57°37W 334 A4
Verde → Ariz., U.S.A. 33°33N 111°40W 305 K8
Verde, Cay Bahamas 23°0N 75°5W 321 B4
Verde Grande → Brazil 16°13S 43°49W 333 E3
Verde I. Phil. 13°33N 121°5E 232 E3
Verde Island Pass. Phil. 13°34N 120°51E 232 E3
Verde Pequeno → Brazil 14°48S 43°31W 333 D3
Verden Germany 52°55N 9°14E 178 C5
Verdi Athina, Greece 38°2N 23°40E 112 A2
Verdi Nev., U.S.A. 39°31N 119°59W 306 F7
Verdikoussa Greece 39°47N 21°59E 204 B3
Verdon → France 43°43N 5°46E 175 E9
Verdon ⌓ France 43°50N 6°5E 175 E10
Verdugo Mts. U.S.A. 34°10N 118°16W 126 A2
Verdun Qué., Canada 45°27N 73°35W 130 B2
Verdun Meuse, France 49°9N 5°24E 173 C12
Verdun-sur-le-Doubs France 46°54N 5°2E 173 F12
Vereeniging S. Africa 26°38S 27°57E 271 C4
Verga, C. Guinea 10°30N 14°10W 262 C2
Vergara = Bergara Spain 43°9N 2°28W 196 B2
Vergara Uruguay 32°56S 53°57W 335 C5
Vergato Italy 44°17N 11°7E 198 D8
Vergemont Cr. → Australia 24°16S 143°16E 280 C3
Vergennes U.S.A. 44°10N 73°15W 313 B11
Vergina = Aigai Greece 40°28N 22°19E 202 F6
Vergt France 45°2N 0°43E 174 C4
Vérhalom Hungary 47°31N 19°1E 117 A2
Veria Greece 40°34N 22°12E 202 F6
Verín Spain 41°57N 7°27W 194 D3
Verkhnedvinsk = Vyerkhnyadzvinsk Belarus 55°45N 27°58E 188 E4
Verkhnetulomskoye Vdkhr. Russia 68°36N 31°12E 160 B24
Verkhnevilyuysk Russia 63°27N 120°18E 215 C13
Verkhniy Baskunchak Russia 48°14N 46°44E 191 F8
Verkhovye Russia 52°55N 37°15E 189 F9
Verkhovyna Ukraine 48°9N 24°47E 183 B9
Verkhoyansk Russia 67°35N 133°25E 215 C14
Verkhoyansk Ra. = Verkhoyanskiy Khrebet Russia 66°0N 129°0E 215 C13
Verkhoyanskiy Khrebet Russia 66°0N 129°0E 215 C13
Verma Norway 62°21N 8°3E 164 B5
Vermeille, Côte France 42°50N 3°20E 174 F7
Vermelho → Brazil 23°30S 46°46W 137 B1
Vermenton France 47°40N 3°42E 173 E10
Vermilion Alta., Canada 53°20N 110°50W 297 C6
Vermilion Ohio, U.S.A. 41°25N 82°22W 312 E2
Vermilion → Alta., Canada 53°22N 110°51W 297 C6
Vermilion → Ill., U.S.A. 41°19N 89°4W 310 C7
Vermilion B. U.S.A. 29°42N 92°0W 314 G9
Vermilion Bay Canada 49°51N 93°34W 297 D10
Vermilion Cliffs Nat. Monument ⌓ U.S.A. 36°54N 112°5W 305 H8
Vermilion L. U.S.A. 47°53N 92°26W 308 B7
Vermillion U.S.A. 42°47N 96°56W 308 D5
Vermillion → Canada 47°38N 72°56W 298 C5
Vermont U.S.A. 40°18N 90°26W 310 D6
Vermont □ U.S.A. 44°0N 73°0W 313 C12
Vermont Knolls U.S.A. 33°57N 118°21W 126 C3
Vermosh Albania 42°35N 19°42E 202 D3
Verna U.S.A. 27°23N 82°16W 317 H7
Vernadsky Antarctica 65°0S 64°0W 151 C17
Vernal U.S.A. 40°27N 109°32W 304 F9
Vernalis U.S.A. 37°36N 121°17W 306 H5
Vernazza Italy 44°10N 9°45E 198 D6
Verner Canada 46°25N 80°8W 298 C3
Verneuil-sur-Avre France 48°45N 0°55E 172 D7
Verneukpan S. Africa 30°0S 21°0E 270 D3
Vernier Switz. 46°11N 6°12E 179 J2
Vérnio Italy 44°3N 11°9E 198 D8
Vernon B.C., Canada 50°20N 119°15W 296 C5
Vernon Eure, France 49°5N 1°30E 172 C8
Vernon Calif., U.S.A. 34°0N 118°13W 126 B3
Vernon Ill., U.S.A. 38°48N 89°5W 310 F7
Vernon Ind., U.S.A. 38°59N 85°36W 311 F11
Vernon Tex., U.S.A. 34°9N 99°17W 314 D5
Vernonia U.S.A. 45°52N 123°11W 306 E3
Vernou Guadeloupe 16°11N 61°39W 322 e
Verny = Almaty Kazakhstan 43°15N 76°57E 217 D9
Vero Beach U.S.A. 27°38N 80°24W 317 H9
Véroia = Veria Greece 40°34N 22°12E 202 F6
Véroli Italy 41°41N 13°25E 199 G10
Verona Ont., Canada 44°29N 76°42W 313 B8
Verona Italy 45°27N 10°59E 198 C7
Verona Wis., U.S.A. 42°59N 89°32W 310 B7
Verrès Italy 45°40N 7°42E 198 C4
Verrières-le-Buisson France 48°44N 2°16E 134 B2
Verron Ra. Papua N. G. 4°21S 152°46E 286 C7
Versailles B. Aires, Argentina 34°38S 58°31W 117 B1
Versailles Yvelines, France 48°48N 2°7E 134 B1
Versailles Ill., U.S.A. 39°53N 90°39W 310 E6
Versailles Ind., U.S.A. 39°4N 85°15W 311 E11
Versailles Ky., U.S.A. 38°3N 84°44W 311 F12
Versailles Mo., U.S.A. 38°26N 92°51W 310 F4
Versailles Ohio, U.S.A. 40°13N 84°29W 311 D12
Versalles Bolivia 12°44S 63°18W 331 C5
Versmold Germany 52°2N 8°9E 178 C4
Vert, C. Senegal 14°45N 17°30W 262 C1
Vertou France 47°10N 1°28W 172 E5
Vertus France 48°54N 4°2E 173 D11
Verulam S. Africa 29°38S 31°2E 271 C5
Verviers Belgium 50°37N 5°52E 170 D5
Vervins France 49°50N 3°53E 173 C10
Veržej Slovenia 46°34N 16°13E 199 B13
Verzy France 49°9N 4°10E 173 C11
Vescovato France 42°30N 9°27E 175 F13
Veselí nad Lužnicí Czechia 49°12N 14°43E 180 B7
Veselie Bulgaria 42°18N 27°38E 203 D11
Veselovskoye Vdkhr. Russia 46°58N 41°25E 191 G5
Veshenskaya Russia 49°35N 41°44E 190 F5
Veshnyaki Russia 55°43N 37°48E 129 B3
Vesle → France 49°23N 3°28E 173 C10
Vesolyy Posolok Russia 59°53N 30°28E 137 B2
Vesoul France 47°40N 6°11E 173 E13
Vessigebro Sweden 56°58N 12°40E 163 H6
Vest-Agder □ Norway 58°30N 7°15E 164 F4
Vestale, Toraka Madag. 16°20S 43°58E 272 B1
Vestbygd Norway 58°6N 6°34E 164 F3
Vesterålen Norway 68°45N 15°0E 160 B16
Vestfirðir □ Iceland 65°45N 22°30W 155 B4
Vestfjorden Norway 67°55N 14°0E 160 C16
Vestfold □ Norway 59°15N 10°0E 164 E7
Vestfossen Norway 59°44N 9°52E 164 E6
Vestmannaeyjar Iceland 63°27N 20°15W 155 D6
Vestnes Norway 62°39N 7°5E 164 B4
Vestra Finland 60°19N 24°46E 121 B1
Vestre Gausdal Norway 61°12N 10°8E 164 C7
Vestskoven Denmark 55°41N 12°23E 118 A2
Vestur-skaftafellssýsla Iceland 63°50N 18°30W 155 D8
Vesturland □ Iceland 64°50N 22°0W 155 C5
Vestvågøya Norway 68°18N 13°50E 160 B15
Vesuvio Italy 40°49N 14°26E 201 B7
Vesuvius, Mt. = Vesuvio Italy 40°49N 14°26E 201 B7
Vesyegonsk Russia 58°40N 37°16E 188 C9
Veszprém Hungary 47°8N 17°57E 182 C2
Veszprém □ Hungary 47°5N 17°55E 182 C2
Vésztő Hungary 46°55N 21°16E 182 D6
Vetapalem India 15°47N 80°18E 245 G5
Vetlanda Sweden 57°24N 15°3E 163 G9
Vetluga Russia 57°53N 45°45E 190 B7
Vetlugu → Russia 56°36N 46°4E 190 B8
Vetluzhskiy Kostroma, Russia 58°23N 45°26E 190 A7
Vetluzhskiy Nizhniy Novgorod, Russia 57°17N 45°12E 190 B7
Vetovo Bulgaria 43°42N 26°16E 203 C10
Vetralla Italy 42°20N 12°2E 199 F9
Vetren Bulgaria 42°15N 24°3E 203 D8
Vettore, Mte. Italy 42°49N 13°16E 199 F10
Veurne Belgium 51°5N 2°40E 170 C2
Vevay U.S.A. 38°45N 85°4W 311 F11
Veveno → South Sudan 6°40N 32°58E 257 F3
Vevey Switz. 46°28N 6°51E 179 J2
Vevi Greece 40°47N 21°38E 202 F5
Veynes France 44°32N 5°49E 175 D9
Veys Iran 31°30N 49°0E 247 D6
Vézelay France 47°27N 3°45E 173 E10
Vézelise France 48°30N 6°5E 173 D13
Vézère → France 44°53N 0°53E 174 D4
Vezhen Bulgaria 42°50N 24°20E 203 D8
Vezirköprü Turkey 41°8N 35°27E 212 B6
Vezzani France 42°10N 9°15E 175 F13
Vi Thanh Vietnam 9°42N 105°26E 237 H5
Viacha Bolivia 16°39S 68°18W 330 D4
Viadana Italy 44°56N 10°31E 198 D7
Vialar = Tissemsilt Algeria 35°35N 1°50E 261 A5
Viamão Brazil 30°5S 51°0W 335 C5
Viana Brazil 3°13S 44°55W 332 B3
Viana Spain 42°31N 2°22W 196 C2
Viana do Alentejo Portugal 38°17N 7°59W 195 G3
Viana do Bolo Spain 42°11N 7°6W 194 C3
Viana do Castelo Portugal 41°42N 8°50W 194 D2
Viana do Castelo □ Portugal 41°50N 8°30W 194 D2
Vianden Lux. 49°56N 6°12E 170 E6
Viangchan = Vientiane Laos 17°58N 102°36E 236 D4
Vianópolis Brazil 16°40S 48°35W 333 E2
Vianos Greece 35°2N 25°21E 207 E6
Viar → Spain 37°36N 5°50W 195 H5
Viaréggio Italy 43°52N 10°14E 198 E7
Viaur → France 44°8N 1°58E 174 D5
Vibble Sweden 57°37N 18°16E 163 G12
Vibo Valéntia Italy 38°40N 16°6E 201 D9
Viborg Denmark 56°27N 9°23E 163 H3
Vibraye France 48°3N 0°44E 172 D7
Vic Spain 41°58N 2°19E 196 D7
Vic, Étang de France 43°29N 3°50E 174 E7
Vic-en-Bigorre France 43°24N 0°3E 174 E4
Vic-Fezensac France 43°47N 0°19E 174 E4
Vic-le-Comte France 45°39N 3°14E 173 G10
Vic-sur-Cère France 44°59N 2°38E 174 D6
Vicálvaro Spain 40°24N 3°36W 127 B2
Vícar Spain 36°50N 2°38W 197 J2
Vicente Lopez Argentina 34°31S 58°30W 117 B2
Vicente Pérez Rosales △ Chile 41°11S 72°12W 336 B2
Vicenza Italy 45°33N 11°33E 199 C8

Vich = Vic Spain 41°58N 2°19E 196 D7
Vichada □ Colombia 5°0N 69°30W 328 C4
Vichada → Colombia 4°55N 67°50W 328 C4
Vichuga Russia 57°12N 41°55E 190 B5
Vichy France 46°9N 3°26E 173 F10
Vicksburg Ariz., U.S.A. 33°45N 113°45W 307 M13
Vicksburg Mich., U.S.A. 42°7N 85°32W 311 B11
Vicksburg Miss., U.S.A. 32°21N 90°53W 315 E9
Vico France 42°10N 8°49E 175 F12
Vico, L. di Italy 42°19N 12°10E 199 F9
Vico del Gargano Italy 41°54N 15°57E 199 G12
Viçosa Brazil 9°28S 36°14W 332 C4
Viçosa do Ceará Brazil 3°34S 41°5W 332 B3
Vicovu de Sus Romania 47°56N 25°41E 183 C10
Victor India 21°0N 71°30E 242 J4
Victor Emanuel Ra. Papua N. G. 5°20S 142°15E 286 C2
Victor Harbor Australia 35°30S 138°37E 282 C3
Victor Hugo = Hamadia Algeria 35°28N 1°57E 261 A5
Victoria = Bandar Labuan Malaysia 5°20N 115°14E 235 A5
Victoria Argentina 32°40S 60°10W 334 C3
Victoria B.C., Canada 48°30N 123°25W 306 B3
Victoria Chile 38°13S 72°20W 336 A2
Victoria Hong Kong, China 22°17N 114°11E 122 B2
Victoria Grenada 12°12N 61°42W 323 q
Victoria Guinea 10°50N 14°32W 262 C2
Victoria Gozo, Malta 36°3N 14°14E 206 E6
Victoria Mind. Or., Phil. 13°12N 121°12E 232 E3
Victoria Tarlac, Phil. 15°35N 120°41E 232 D3
Victoria Romania 45°44N 24°41E 183 E9
Victoria Seychelles 4°38S 55°28E 272 c
Victoria London, U.K. 125 c3
Victoria Kans., U.S.A. 38°52N 99°9W 308 F4
Victoria Tex., U.S.A. 28°48N 97°0W 314 G6
Victoria □ Australia 37°0S 144°0E 282 D6
Victoria → Australia 15°10S 129°40E 278 C4
Victoria, Grand L. Canada 47°31N 77°30W 298 C4
Victoria, L. Africa 1°0S 33°0E 268 C3
Victoria, L. N.S.W., Australia 33°57S 141°15E 282 B4
Victoria, Mt. = Tomanivi Fiji 17°37S 178°1E 287 A2
Victoria, Mt. Burma 21°14N 93°55E 241 E4
Victoria, Mt. Papua N. G. 8°55S 147°32E 286 E4
Victoria, Pont Canada 45°29N 73°32W 130 B2
Victoria and Alfred Waterfront Cape Town, S. Africa 118 a1
Victoria Beach Canada 50°40N 96°35W 297 C9
Victoria de Durango = Durango Mexico 24°3N 104°39W 318 C4
Victoria de las Tunas = Las Tunas Cuba 20°58N 76°59W 320 B4
Victoria Falls Zimbabwe 17°58S 25°52E 269 F2
Victoria Fjord Greenland 82°10N 46°0W 154 A6
Victoria Gardens India 18°58N 72°50E 130 B2
Victoria Harbour Ont., Canada 44°45N 79°45W 312 B5
Victoria Harbour Hong Kong, China 22°17N 114°10E 122 B3
Victoria I. Canada 71°0N 111°0W 294 C9
Victoria Island Nigeria 6°25N 3°25E 124 B2
Victoria L. Nfld. & L., Canada 48°20N 57°27W 299 C8
Victoria L. Gauteng, S. Africa 26°13S 28°9E 123 B2
Victoria Lawn Tennis Courts Australia 37°50S 145°1E 128 B2
Victoria Ld. Antarctica 75°0S 160°0E 151 D11
Victoria Nile → Uganda 2°14N 31°26E 268 B3
Victoria Park Singapore 1°19N 103°49E 138 B2
Victoria Peak Hong Kong, China 22°16N 114°8E 122 B2
Victoria Peaks Phil. 9°22N 118°20E 233 G2
Victoria Pk. Belize 16°48N 88°37W 319 D7
Victoria Ra. N.Z. 42°12S 172°7E 285 C7
Victoria River Australia 16°25S 131°0E 278 C5
Victoria Str. Canada 69°31N 100°30W 294 D11
Victoria Terminus = Chhatrapati Shivaji Terminus India 18°56N 72°50E 130 B2
Victoria Village Canada 43°46N 79°20W 141 A3
Victoria West S. Africa 31°25S 23°4E 270 D3
Victoria Wharf Cape Town, S. Africa 118 a2
Victorias Phil. 10°54N 123°5E 233 F4
Victoriaville Canada 46°4N 71°56W 299 C5
Victorica Argentina 36°20S 65°30W 334 D2
Victorville U.S.A. 34°32N 117°18W 307 L9
Vicuña Chile 30°0S 70°50W 334 C1
Vicuña Mackenna Argentina 33°53S 64°25W 334 C3
Vidal U.S.A. 34°7N 114°31W 307 L12
Vidalia U.S.A. 32°13N 82°25W 316 C7
Vidamlya Belarus 52°19N 23°47E 185 F10
Vidauban France 43°25N 6°27E 175 E10
Viddolatno = Vindelälven → Sweden 63°55N 19°50E 160 E18
Videbæk Denmark 56°6N 8°38E 163 H2
Videle Romania 44°17N 25°31E 183 F10
Videsæter Norway 61°57N 7°14E 164 C4
Vidette U.S.A. 33°2N 82°15W 316 B7
Vidigueira Portugal 38°12N 7°48W 195 G3
Vidin Bulgaria 43°59N 22°50E 202 C6
Vidin □ Bulgaria 43°59N 22°50E 202 C6
Vidio, C. Spain 43°35N 6°14W 194 B4
Vidisha India 23°28N 77°53E 242 H7
Vidos Greece 39°38N 19°55E 206 B9
Vidra Romania 45°56N 26°55E 183 E11
Viduša Bos.-H. 42°55N 18°21E 202 D2
Vidzy Belarus 55°23N 26°37E 188 E4
Viechtach Germany 49°4N 12°53E 179 F8
Viedma Argentina 40°50S 63°0W 336 B4
Viedma, L. Argentina 49°30S 72°30W 336 C2
Vieille Case Dominica 15°36N 61°24W 323 k
Vieira do Minho Portugal 41°38N 8°8W 194 D2
Vielha Spain 42°43N 0°44E 196 C5
Viella = Vielha Spain 42°43N 0°44E 196 C5
Vielle St-Girons France 43°56N 1°18W 174 E2
Vielsalm Belgium 50°17N 5°54E 170 D5
Vienenburg Germany 51°57N 10°34E 178 D6
Vieng Pou Kha Laos 20°41N 101°4E 228 G3
Vienna = Wien Austria 48°12N 16°22E 142 A2
Vienna Ont., Canada 42°41N 80°48W 312 D4
Vienna Ga., U.S.A. 32°6N 83°47W 316 C6
Vienna Ill., U.S.A. 37°25N 88°54W 308 G9
Vienna Mo., U.S.A. 38°11N 91°57W 310 F5
Vienne France 45°31N 4°53E 175 C8
Vienne □ France 46°30N 0°42E 174 B4
Vienne → France 47°13N 0°5E 172 E7
Vientiane Laos 17°58N 102°36E 236 D4
Vientos, Paso de los Caribbean 20°0N 74°0W 321 C5
Vieques Puerto Rico 18°8N 65°25W 321 b
Vierge Pt. St. Lucia 13°49N 60°53W 323 m
Vierkant Pt. Bonaire 12°7N 68°17W 322 h
Viernheim Germany 49°31N 8°35E 179 F4
Viersen Germany 51°15N 6°23E 178 D2
Vierwaldstättersee Switz. 47°0N 8°30E 179 J4
Vierzon France 47°13N 2°5E 173 E9
Vieste Italy 41°53N 16°10E 199 G13
Viet Quang Vietnam 22°30N 104°48E 228 F5
Viet Tri Vietnam 21°18N 105°25E 236 B5
Vietnam ■ Asia 19°0N 106°0E 236 C6
Vietnam Veterans Memorial Washington, D.C., U.S.A. 38°53N 77°2W 143 B2
Vietz = Witnica Poland 52°40N 14°54E 185 F1
Vieux-Boucau-les-Bains France 43°48N 1°23W 174 E2
Vieux Bourg Guadeloupe 16°20N 61°36W 322 e
Vieux Carré = French Quarter New Orleans, U.S.A. 131 a2
Vieux Fort Guadeloupe 15°57N 61°41W 322 e
Vieux Fort Marie-Galante, Guadeloupe 15°59N 61°17W 322 e
Vieux Fort St. Lucia 13°46N 60°58W 323 m
Vieux Fort, Pte. du Guadeloupe 15°57N 61°42W 322 e
Vieux Fort, R. du → Guadeloupe 15°59N 61°17W 322 e
Vieux Grand Port Mauritius 20°22S 57°42E 272 e
Vieux-Habitants Guadeloupe 16°4N 61°46W 322 e
Vieux-Habitants, Rivière des → Guadeloupe 16°3N 61°46W 322 e
Vieux-Montréal Montréal, Canada 130 b3
View Park U.S.A. 34°0N 118°20W 126 B3
Vif France 45°5N 5°41E 175 C9
Viga Phil. 13°52N 124°18E 232 E5
Vigan Phil. 17°35N 120°28E 232 C3
Vigário Geral Brazil 22°48S 43°18W 135 A1
Vigentino Italy 45°26N 9°13E 128 B2
Vigeland Norway 58°5N 7°18E 164 F4
Vigévano Italy 45°19N 8°51E 198 C5
Viggbyholm Sweden 59°26N 18°7E 139 A2
Vighignolo Italy 45°29N 9°2E 128 B1
Vigia = Almenara Brazil 16°11S 40°42W 333 E3
Vigia Brazil 0°50S 48°5W 332 B2
Vigla Greece 39°7N 20°50E 207 A2
Viglas, Akra Greece 35°54N 27°51E 206 F11
Vignemalle France 42°47N 0°10W 174 F3
Vigneulles-lès-Hattonchâtel France 48°59N 5°43E 173 D12
Vignola Italy 44°29N 11°1E 198 D8
Vigo Spain 42°12N 8°41W 194 C2
Vigo, Ría de Spain 42°15N 8°45W 194 C2
Vigrestad Norway 58°34N 5°42E 164 F2
Vigsø Bugt Denmark 57°8N 8°47E 163 G2
Vihiers France 47°10N 0°30W 172 E6
Vihiga Kenya 0°3N 34°44E 268 B3
Vihowa Pakistan 31°8N 70°30E 242 D4
Vihowa → Pakistan 31°8N 70°41E 242 D4
Viikki Finland 60°13N 25°1E 121 B3
Viipuri = Vyborg Russia 60°43N 28°47E 188 B5
Vijayadurg India 16°30N 73°25E 244 F1
Vijayapura India 16°50N 75°55E 244 F2
Vijayawada India 16°31N 80°39E 244 F5
Vijosë → Albania 40°37N 19°24E 202 F3
Vík Iceland 63°25N 19°1W 155 D7
Vik Sogn og Fjordane, Norway 61°21N 6°6E 164 C3
Vika Sweden 60°57N 14°28E 162 D8
Vikarabad India 17°20N 77°54E 244 E3
Vikarbyn Sweden 60°55N 15°1E 162 D9
Vike Norway 60°42N 5°35E 164 D2
Vikedal Norway 59°30N 5°55E 164 E2
Vikeke = Viqueque E. Timor 8°52S 126°23E 231 F7
Vikeland = Vigeland Norway 58°5N 7°18E 164 F4
Viken Skåne, Sweden 56°9N 12°34E 163 H6
Viken Västra Götaland, Sweden 58°39N 14°20E 163 F8
Vikersund Norway 59°58N 9°59E 164 E6
Vikeså Norway 58°38N 6°3E 164 F3
Vikevåg Norway 59°5N 5°41E 164 E2
Vikhammer Norway 63°26N 10°37E 164 A7
Vikhroli India 19°6N 72°55E 130 A2
Viking Canada 53°7N 111°50W 296 C6
Vikmanshyttan Sweden 60°18N 15°50E 162 D9
Vikna Norway 64°55N 10°58E 160 D14
Vikos-Aoos △ Greece 40°0N 20°45E 204 B2
Vikøyri Norway 61°4N 6°34E 164 C3
Vila Alferes Chamusca = Guijá Mozam. 24°27S 33°0E 271 B5
Vila António Enes = Angoche Mozam. 16°8S 39°55E 269 F4
Vila Baleira Madeira 33°4N 16°20W 260 B1
Vila Bela da Santissima Trindade Brazil 15°0S 59°57W 331 C6
Vila Cabral = Lichinga Mozam. 13°13S 35°11E 269 E4
Vila Cabral = Niassa □ Mozam. 13°30S 36°0E 269 E4
Vila da Maganja Mozam. 17°18S 37°30E 269 F4
Vila da Ribeira Brava C. Verde Is. 16°32N 24°25W 153 j
Vila de Rei Portugal 39°41N 8°9W 194 F2
Vila do Bispo Portugal 37°5N 8°53W 195 H2
Vila do Conde Portugal 41°21N 8°45W 194 D2
Vila do Maio C. Verde Is. 15°21N 23°10W 153 j
Vila do Porto Azores 36°56N 25°9W 153 d4
Vila Franca de Xira Portugal 38°57N 8°59W 195 G2
Vila Franca do Campo Azores 37°43N 25°26W 153 d3
Vila Gamito Mozam. 14°12S 33°0E 269 E3
Vila Gomes da Costa Mozam. 24°20S 33°37E 271 B5
Vila Guilherme Brazil 23°30S 46°38W 137 B2
Vila Isabel Brazil 22°54S 43°15W 135 B1
Vila Jaguára Brazil 23°30S 46°45W 137 B1
Vila Machado Mozam. 19°15S 34°14E 269 F3
Vila Madalena Brazil 23°32S 46°41W 137 B1
Vila Maria Brazil 23°31S 46°36W 137 B2
Vila Mariana Brazil 23°34S 46°36W 137 B2
Vila Mouzinho Mozam. 14°48S 34°25E 269 E3
Vila Nova de Famalicão Portugal 41°25N 8°32W 194 D2
Vila Nova de Foz Côa Portugal 41°5N 7°9W 194 D3
Vila Nova de Gaia Portugal 41°8N 8°37W 194 D2
Vila Nova de Gaza = Xai-Xai Mozam. 25°6S 33°31E 271 C5
Vila Nova do Corvo Azores 39°40N 31°8W 153 d2
Vila Nova Sintra C. Verde Is. 14°52N 24°42W 153 j
Vila Pereira de Eça = Ondjiva Angola 16°48S 15°50E 265 F3
Vila Pery = Manica Mozam. 18°58S 32°59E 271 A5
Vila Pouca de Aguiar Portugal 41°30N 7°38W 194 D3
Vila Prudente Brazil 23°35S 46°33W 137 B2
Vila Real Portugal 41°17N 7°48W 194 D3
Vila-Real Spain 39°55N 0°3W 196 F4
Vila Real □ Portugal 41°36N 7°35W 194 D3
Vila Real de Santo António Portugal 37°10N 7°28W 195 H3
Vila-seca Spain 41°7N 1°9E 196 D6
Vila Texeira da Silva = Luau Angola 10°40S 22°10E 265 E4
Vila Vasco da Gama Mozam. 14°54S 32°14E 269 E3
Vila Velha Amapá, Brazil 3°13N 51°13W 329 C7
Vila Velha Espírito Santo, Brazil 20°20S 40°17W 333 F3
Vila Velha Sergipe, Brazil 11°20S 38°9W 332 D4
Vila Velha Portugal 38°45N 7°27W 195 G3
Viladecans Spain 41°18N 2°1E 114 B1
Vilafranca del Maestrat = Villafranca del Cid Spain 40°26N 0°16W 196 E4
Vilafranca del Penedès Spain 41°21N 1°40E 196 D6
Vilagarcía de Arousa Spain 42°34N 8°46W 194 C2
Vilaine → France 47°30N 2°27W 172 E4
Vilakalaka Vanuatu 15°25S 167°42E 287 E5
Vilanandro, Tanjona Madag. 16°11S 44°27E 272 B1
Vilanculos Mozam. 22°1S 35°17E 271 B6
Vilanova i la Geltrú Spain 41°13N 1°40E 196 D6
Vilar Formoso Portugal 40°38N 6°45W 194 E4
Vilaseca-Salou = Vila-seca Spain 41°7N 1°9E 196 D6
Vilbjerg Denmark 56°12N 8°46E 163 H2
Vilcabamba, Cordillera Peru 13°0S 73°0W 330 C3
Vilcanchos Peru 13°40S 74°25W 330 C3
Vilcheka, Ostrov Russia 80°0N 58°31E 214 B6
Vilcheka, Zemlya Russia 80°30N 60°30E 150 A11
Vilches Spain 38°12N 3°30W 195 G7
Vile Parle India 19°6N 72°51E 130 A2
Vileyka Belarus 54°30N 26°53E 177 A14
Vilhelmina Sweden 64°35N 16°39E 160 D17
Vilhena Brazil 12°40S 60°5W 331 C5
Viliya = Neris → Lithuania 55°8N 24°16E 188 E3
Viljandi Estonia 58°28N 25°30E 188 C3
Viljoensdorp = Newcastle S. Africa 27°45S 29°58E 271 C4
Vilkaviškis Lithuania 54°39N 23°2E 184 D10
Vilkija Lithuania 55°3N 23°35E 184 C10
Vilkitskogo, Proliv Russia 78°0N 103°0E 215 B11
Vilkomir = Ukmergė Lithuania 55°15N 24°45E 188 E3
Vilkovo = Vylkove Ukraine 45°28N 29°32E 183 E14
Villa Abecia Bolivia 21°0S 68°18W 334 A2
Villa Adelina Argentina 34°31S 58°33W 117 B1
Villa Ana Argentina 28°28S 59°40W 334 B4
Villa Angela Argentina 27°34S 60°45W 334 B3
Villa Ballester Argentina 34°33S 58°33W 117 B1
Villa Barilari Argentina 34°42S 58°20W 117 C2
Villa Bella = Serra Talhada Brazil 7°59S 38°18W 332 C4
Villa Bella Bolivia 10°25S 65°22W 331 C4
Villa Borghese Rome, Italy 136 a3
Villa Bosch Argentina 34°35S 58°33W 117 B1
Villa Bruzual Venezuela 9°20N 69°6W 328 C4
Villa C. Colon Argentina 34°41S 58°21W 117 C2
Villa Cañás Argentina 34°0S 61°35W 334 C3
Villa Cecilia = Ciudad Madero Mexico 22°19N 97°50W 319 C5
Villa Cisneros = Dakhla W. Sahara 23°50N 15°53W 260 D1
Villa Ciudadela Argentina 34°38S 58°33W 117 B1
Villa Constitución Argentina 33°15S 60°20W 334 C3
Villa de Arriaga Mexico 21°56N 101°20W 318 C4
Villa de Cura Venezuela 10°2N 67°29W 328 A4
Villa de Guadalupe Mexico 19°29N 99°6W 128 B2
Villa de María Argentina 29°55S 63°43W 334 B3
Villa de Méndez Mexico 25°7N 98°34W 319 B5
Villa del Nevoso = Ilirska-Bistrica Slovenia 45°34N 14°14E 199 C11
Villa del Rio Spain 37°59N 4°17W 195 H6
Villa del Rosario Venezuela 10°19N 72°19W 328 A3
Villa Devoto Argentina 34°36S 58°31W 117 B1
Villa Diamante Argentina 34°41S 58°25W 117 C2
Villa Dolores Argentina 31°58S 65°15W 334 C2
Villa Dominico Argentina 34°41S 58°19W 117 C3
Villa Gesell Argentina 37°15S 56°55W 334 D4
Villa Grove U.S.A. 39°52N 88°10W 311 E8
Villa Guillermina Argentina 28°15S 59°29W 334 B4
Villa Hayes Paraguay 25°5S 57°20W 334 B4
Villa Hidalgo Mexico 24°15N 99°26W 319 C5
Villa Iris Argentina 38°12S 63°12W 334 D3
Villa Las Estrellas = Frei Antarctica 62°30S 58°0W 151 C18
Villa Lugano Argentina 34°41S 58°27W 117 C2
Villa Lynch Argentina 34°35S 58°31W 117 B1
Villa Madero Argentina 34°41S 58°30W 117 C1
Villa María Argentina 32°20S 63°10W 334 C3
Villa Mazán Argentina 28°40S 66°30W 334 B2
Villa Minozzo Italy 44°22N 10°28E 198 D7
Villa Montes Bolivia 21°10S 63°30W 334 A3
Villa Ocampo Argentina 28°30S 59°20W 334 B4
Villa Ocampo Durango, Mexico 26°27N 105°31W 318 B3
Villa Ojo de Agua Argentina 29°30S 63°44W 334 B3
Villa Regina Argentina 39°6S 67°4W 336 A3
Villa Rica U.S.A. 33°44N 84°55W 316 B5
Villa Sáenz Pena Argentina 34°37S 58°32W 117 B1
Villa San Giovanni Italy 38°13N 15°38E 201 D8
Villa San Martín Argentina 28°15S 64°9W 334 B3
Villa Sanjurjo = Al Hoceïma Morocco 35°8N 3°58W 261 A4
Villa Santina Italy 46°24N 12°55E 199 B9
Villa Unión Mexico 23°12N 106°14W 318 C3
Villa Urquiza Argentina 34°34S 58°28W 117 B2
Villaba Phil. 11°13N 124°24E 233 F5
Villablino Spain 42°57N 6°19W 194 C4
Villacarlos Spain 39°53N 4°17E 206 B5
Villacarriedo Spain 43°14N 3°48W 194 B7
Villacarrillo Spain 38°7N 3°3W 195 G7
Villacastín Spain 40°46N 4°25W 194 E6
Villach Austria 46°37N 13°51E 180 E6
Villacidro Italy 39°27N 8°44E 200 C1
Villada Spain 42°15N 4°59W 194 C6
Villadiego Spain 42°31N 4°1W 194 C6
Villadóssola Italy 46°4N 8°16E 198 B5
Villafeliche Spain 41°10N 1°30W 196 D3
Villafranca Spain 42°17N 1°46W 196 C3
Villafranca de los Barros Spain 38°35N 6°18W 195 G4
Villafranca de los Caballeros Spain 39°26N 3°21W 195 F7
Villafranca del Cid Spain 40°26N 0°16W 196 E4
Villafranca del Panadés = Vilafranca del Penedès Spain 41°21N 1°40E 196 D6
Villafranca di Verona Italy 45°21N 10°50E 198 C7
Villafranca Tirrena Italy 38°20N 15°25E 201 D8
Villagio Mussolini = Arboréa Italy 39°46N 8°35E 200 C1
Villagrán Mexico 24°29N 99°29W 319 C5
Villaguay Argentina 32°0S 59°0W 334 C4
Villaharta Spain 38°9N 4°54W 195 G6
Villahermosa Tabasco, Mexico 17°59N 92°55W 319 D6
Villahermosa Spain 38°46N 2°52W 197 G2
Villaines-la-Juhel France 48°21N 0°20W 172 D6
Villajoyosa Spain 38°30N 0°12W 197 G4
Villalba Puerto Rico 18°8N 66°30W 321 b
Villalba Spain 43°22N 7°40W 194 B3
Villalba de Guardo Spain 42°42N 4°49W 194 C6
Villalón de Campos Spain 42°5N 5°4W 194 C5
Villalpando Spain 41°51N 5°25W 194 D5
Villaluenga de la Sagra Spain 40°2N 3°54W 194 E7
Villamanán Spain 42°19N 5°35W 194 C5
Villamartín Spain 36°52N 5°38W 195 J5
Villamayor de Santiago Spain 39°50N 2°59W 196 F2
Villamblard France 45°2N 0°32E 174 C4
Villanova Monteleone Italy 40°30N 8°28E 200 B1
Villanueva Colombia 10°37N 72°59W 328 A3
Villanueva N. Mex., U.S.A. 35°16N 105°22W 305 J11
Villanueva de Castellón Spain 39°5N 0°31W 197 F4
Villanueva de Córdoba Spain 38°20N 4°38W 195 G6
Villanueva de la Fuente Spain 38°42N 2°42W 197 G2
Villanueva de la Serena Spain 38°59N 5°50W 195 G5
Villanueva de la Sierra Spain 40°12N 6°24W 194 E4
Villanueva de los Castillejos Spain 37°30N 7°15W 195 H3
Villanueva de los Infantes Spain 38°43N 3°1W 195 G7
Villanueva del Arzobispo Spain 38°10N 3°0W 197 G2
Villanueva del Fresno Spain 38°23N 7°10W 195 G3
Villanueva y Geltrú = Vilanova i la Geltrú Spain 41°13N 1°40E 196 D6
Villaputzu Italy 39°26N 9°34E 200 C2
Villaquilambre Spain 42°39N 5°34W 194 C5
Villar del Arzobispo Spain 39°44N 0°50W 196 F4
Villar del Rey Spain 39°7N 6°50W 195 F4
Villard-de-Lans France 45°3N 5°33E 175 C9
Villarramiel Spain 42°2N 4°55W 194 C6
Villarreal = Vila-Real Spain 39°55N 0°3W 196 F4
Villarrica Chile 39°15S 72°15W 336 A2
Villarrica Paraguay 25°40S 56°30W 334 B4
Villarrica △ Chile 39°24S 71°46W 336 A2
Villarrobledo Spain 39°18N 2°36W 197 F2
Villarroya de la Sierra Spain 41°27N 1°46W 196 D3
Villarrubia de los Ojos Spain 39°14N 3°36W 195 F7
Villars-les-Dombes France 46°0N 5°3E 173 F12
Villasayas Spain 41°24N 2°39W 196 D2
Villaseco de los Gamitos Spain 41°2N 6°7W 194 D4
Villasimius Italy 39°8N 9°31E 200 C2
Villastar Spain 40°17N 1°9W 196 E3
Villatobas Spain 39°54N 3°20W 194 F7
Villaverde Spain 40°21N 3°42W 127 B1
Villaverde Bajo Spain 40°20N 3°40W 127 B1
Villavicencio Argentina 32°28S 69°0W 334 C2
Villavicencio Colombia 4°9N 73°37W 328 C3
Villaviciosa Spain 43°32N 5°27W 194 B5
Villazón Bolivia 22°0S 65°35W 334 A2
Ville-d'Avray France 48°49N 2°11E 134 B2
Ville-Marie Canada 47°20N 79°30W 298 C4
Ville Platte U.S.A. 30°41N 92°17W 314 F8
Villecresnes France 48°43N 2°31E 134 B4
Villedieu-les-Poêles France 48°50N 1°13W 172 D5
Villefort France 44°28N 3°56E 174 D7
Villefranche-de-Lauragais France 43°25N 1°44E 174 E5
Villefranche-de-Rouergue France 44°21N 2°2E 174 D6
Villefranche-du-Périgord France 44°38N 1°5E 174 D5
Villefranche-sur-Saône France 45°59N 4°43E 175 C8
Villejuif France 48°47N 2°21E 134 B3
Villel Spain 40°14N 1°12W 196 E3
Villemomble France 48°52N 2°30E 134 A4
Villemur-sur-Tarn France 43°51N 1°31E 174 E5
Villena Spain 38°39N 0°52W 197 G4
Villenaux-la-Grande France 48°35N 3°33E 173 D10
Villenave-d'Ornon France 44°46N 0°33W 174 D3
Villeneuve-d'Ascq France 50°38N 3°9E 173 B10
Villeneuve-la-Garenne France 48°56N 2°19E 134 A2
Villeneuve-l'Archevêque France 48°14N 3°32E 173 D10
Villeneuve-le-Roi France 48°43N 2°24E 134 B3
Villeneuve-lès-Avignon France 43°58N 4°49E 175 E8
Villeneuve-St-Georges France 48°43N 2°27E 134 B3
Villeneuve-sur-Allier France 46°40N 3°13E 173 F10
Villeneuve-sur-Lot France 44°24N 0°42E 174 D4
Villeneuve-sur-Yonne France 48°5N 3°18E 173 D10
Villeparisis France 48°56N 2°36E 134 A4
Villeréal France 44°38N 0°45E 174 D4
Villers-Bocage France 49°3N 0°40W 172 C6
Villers-Cotterêts France 49°15N 3°4E 173 C10
Villers-sur-Mer France 49°21N 0°2W 172 C6
Villersexel France 47°33N 6°26E 173 E13
Villerupt France 49°28N 5°55E 173 C12
Villeurbanne France 45°46N 4°55E 175 C8
Villevaudé France 48°55N 2°39E 134 A4
Villiers S. Africa 27°2S 28°36E 271 C4
Villiers-le-Bâcle France 48°44N 2°8E 134 B1
Villiers-sur-Marne France 48°49N 2°32E 134 B4
Villingen-Schwenningen Germany 48°3N 8°26E 179 G4
Villinki Finland 60°9N 25°6E 121 C3
Villisca U.S.A. 40°56N 94°59W 310 D2
Villmanstrand = Lappeenranta Finland 61°3N 28°12E 188 B5
Villoresi, Canale Italy 45°33N 9°9E 128 A1
Villupuram India 11°59N 79°31E 245 J4
Vilna = Vilnius Lithuania 54°38N 25°19E 188 E3
Vilna Canada 54°7N 111°55W 296 C6
Vilnius Lithuania 54°38N 25°19E 188 E3
Vils Austria 47°33N 10°38E 180 D3
Vils → Bayern, Germany 48°37N 13°11E 179 G9
Vils → Bayern, Germany 49°10N 11°55E 179 F7
Vilsandi △ Estonia 58°23N 21°52E 188 C1
Vilsbiburg Germany 48°26N 12°22E 179 G8
Vilshofen Germany 48°37N 13°11E 179 G9
Vilusi Montenegro 42°44N 18°34E 202 D2
Vilvoorde Belgium 50°56N 4°26E 116 A2
Vilyuchinsk Russia 52°55N 158°24E 215 D16
Vilyuy → Russia 64°24N 126°26E 215 C13
Vilyuysk Russia 63°40N 121°35E 215 C13
Vilyuyskoye Vdkhr. Russia 63°0N 112°0E 215 C12
Vimianzo Spain 43°7N 9°2W 194 B1
Vimioso Portugal 41°35N 6°31W 194 D4
Vimmerby Sweden 57°40N 15°55E 163 G9
Vimodrone Italy 45°30N 9°16E 128 A2
Vimont Canada 45°36N 73°43W 130 A1
Vimoutiers France 48°57N 0°10E 172 D7
Vimperk Czechia 49°3N 13°46E 180 B6
Vina → Cameroon 7°45N 15°36E 264 A3
Viña del Mar Chile 33°0S 71°30W 334 C1
Vinanmek Mansion Bangkok, Thailand 113 a2
Vinarós Spain 40°30N 0°27E 196 E5
Vincendo Réunion 21°21S 55°41E 272 f
Vincennes Val-de-Marne, France 48°51N 2°26E 134 A3
Vincennes Ind., U.S.A. 38°41N 87°32W 311 F9
Vincennes, Bois de France 48°49N 2°26E 134 B3
Vincennes Bay S. Ocean 66°0S 109°0E 151 C8
Vincent U.S.A. 34°33N 118°11W 307 L8
Vinces Ecuador 1°32S 79°45W 328 D2
Vinchina Argentina 28°45S 68°15W 334 B2
Vindava = Ventspils Latvia 57°25N 21°32E 184 A8
Vindelälven → Sweden 63°55N 19°50E 160 E18
Vindeln Sweden 64°12N 19°43E 160 D18
Vinderup Denmark 56°29N 8°45E 163 H2
Vindhya Ra. India 22°50N 77°0E 242 H7
Vine Grove U.S.A. 37°49N 85°59W 311 G11
Vineland Fla., U.S.A. 28°23N 81°30W 133 B1
Vineland N.J., U.S.A. 39°29N 75°2W 309 F16
Vineuil France 47°35N 1°22E 172 E8
Vinga Romania 46°1N 21°14E 182 D6
Vingåker Sweden 59°2N 15°52E 162 E9
Vingelen Norway 62°25N 10°52E 164 B7
Vingnes Norway 61°7N 10°26E 164 C7
Vinh Vietnam 18°45N 105°38E 236 C5
Vinh Loi = Bac Lieu Vietnam 9°17N 105°43E 237 H5
Vinh Long Vietnam 10°16N 105°57E 237 G5
Vinh Moc Vietnam 21°18N 105°1E 236 B5
Vinh Yen Vietnam 21°21N 105°35E 228 G5
Vinhais Portugal 41°50N 7°5W 194 D3
Vinica Croatia 46°20N 16°9E 199 B13
Vinica Macedonia 41°53N 22°30E 202 E6
Vinica Slovenia 45°28N 15°16E 199 C12
Vinings U.S.A. 33°53N 84°29W 113 A2
Vinita U.S.A. 36°39N 95°9W 314 C7
Vinje Sør-Trøndelag, Norway 63°12N 9°0E 164 A5
Vinje Telemark, Norway 59°37N 7°51E 164 E4
Vinjo Norway 60°48N 6°30E 164 D3
Vinkovci Croatia 45°19N 18°48E 182 E3
Vinnitsa = Vinnytsya Ukraine 49°15N 28°30E 177 D15
Vinnytsya Ukraine 49°15N 28°30E 177 D15
Vinnytsya □ Ukraine 49°20N 28°15E 177 D15
Vinodelnoye = Ipatovo Russia 45°45N 42°50E 191 H6
Vinohrady Prague, Czechia 135 c3
Vinoř Czechia 50°8N 14°34E 135 B3
Vinslöv Sweden 56°7N 13°55E 163 H7
Vinson Massif Antarctica 78°35S 85°25W 151 D16
Vinstra Norway 61°37N 9°44E 164 C6
Vinstra → Norway 61°37N 9°44E 164 C6
Vintar Phil. 18°14N 120°39E 232 B3
Vintjärn Sweden 60°50N 16°4E 162 D10
Vinton Calif., U.S.A. 39°48N 120°10W 306 F6
Vinton Iowa, U.S.A. 42°10N 92°1W 310 B4
Vinton La., U.S.A. 30°11N 93°35W 314 F8
Vințu de Jos Romania 46°0N 23°30E 183 D8
Vinukonda India 16°4N 79°45E 245 F4
Viöl Germany 54°34N 9°11E 178 A5
Viola U.S.A. 41°12N 90°35W 310 C6
Violet Hill Hong Kong, China 22°15N 114°11E 122 B3
Violet Town Australia 36°38S 145°42E 283 D6
Violet Valley ⊙ Australia 17°10S 127°55E 278 C4
Vioolsdrif S. Africa 28°46S 17°39E 270 C2
Viotia Greece 38°20N 23°0E 204 C5
Vipacco = Vipava Slovenia 45°51N 13°58E 199 C10
Vipava Slovenia 45°51N 13°58E 199 C10
Vipiteno Italy 46°54N 11°26E 199 B8
Viqueque E. Timor 8°52S 126°23E 231 F7
Vir Croatia 44°17N 15°3E 199 D12
Virac Phil. 13°30N 124°20E 232 E5
Virachey Cambodia 13°59N 106°49E 236 F6
Virachey △ Cambodia 14°14N 106°55E 236 E6
Virago Sd. Canada 54°0N 132°30W 296 C2
Virajpet = Virarajendrapet India 12°10N 75°50E 245 H2
Viramgam India 23°5N 72°0E 242 H5
Viranşehir Turkey 37°13N 39°45E 213 D8
Virányos Hungary 47°31N 18°59E 117 A1
Virarajendrapet India 12°10N 75°50E 245 H2
Virawah Pakistan 24°31N 70°46E 242 G4
Virbalis Lithuania 54°39N 22°49E 184 D9
Virden Man., Canada 49°50N 100°56W 297 D8
Virden Ill., U.S.A. 39°30N 89°46W 310 E7
Vire France 48°50N 0°53W 172 D6
Vire → France 49°20N 1°7W 172 C5
Virei Angola 15°43S 12°54E 265 F2
Virgem da Lapa Brazil 16°49S 42°21W 333 E3
Virgenes, C. Argentina 52°19S 68°21W 336 D3
Virgin → U.S.A. 36°28N 114°21W 305 H6
Virgin Gorda Br. Virgin Is. 18°30N 64°26W 321 C7
Virgin Is. (British) ⊘ W. Indies 18°30N 64°30W 321 C7
Virgin Is. (U.S.) ⊘ W. Indies 18°20N 65°0W 321 C7
Virgin Islands △ U.S. Virgin Is. 18°21N 64°43W 321 b
Virginia Free State, S. Africa 28°8S 26°55E 270 C4
Virginia Ill., U.S.A. 39°57N 90°13W 310 E6
Virginia Minn., U.S.A. 47°31N 92°32W 308 B7
Virginia □ U.S.A. 37°30N 78°45W 309 G14
Virginia, L. U.S.A. 28°35N 81°20W 133 A2
Virginia Beach U.S.A. 36°49N 76°9W 309 F16
Virginia City Mont., U.S.A. 45°18N 111°56W 304 D8
Virginia City Nev., U.S.A. 39°19N 119°39W 306 F7
Virginia Falls Canada 61°38N 125°42W 296 A3
Virginia Gardens U.S.A. 25°48N 80°18W 129 D1
Virginia Key U.S.A. 25°44N 80°9W 129 D3
Virginiatown Canada 48°9N 79°36W 298 C4
Virje Croatia 46°4N 16°59E 199 B13
Viroflay France 48°48N 2°10E 134 B2
Vironas Greece 37°55N 23°46E 112 B2
Viroqua U.S.A. 43°34N 90°53W 308 D8
Virovitica Croatia 45°51N 17°21E 182 E2
Virpazar Montenegro 42°14N 19°6E 202 D3
Virpur India 21°51N 70°42E 242 J4
Virsbo Sweden 59°52N 16°2E 162 E10
Virserum Sweden 57°20N 15°35E 163 G9
Virton Belgium 49°35N 5°32E 170 E5
Virú Peru 8°25S 78°45W 330 B2
Virudhunagar India 9°30N 77°58E 245 K3
Virum Denmark 55°47N 12°27E 118 A2
Virunga △ Dem. Rep. of the Congo 0°5N 29°38E 268 B2
Vis Croatia 43°4N 16°10E 199 E13
Visalia U.S.A. 36°20N 119°18W 306 J7
Visayan Sea Phil. 11°30N 123°30E 233 F4
Visayas □ Phil. 9°30N 122°45E 233 G4
Visby Sweden 57°37N 18°18E 163 G12
Viscount Melville Sd. Canada 74°10N 108°0W 295 C10
Visé Belgium 50°44N 5°41E 170 D5
Vise, Ostrov Russia 79°33N 76°50E 214 B8
Višegrad Bos.-H. 43°47N 19°17E 182 G4
Viseu Brazil 1°10S 46°5W 332 B2
Viseu Portugal 40°40N 7°55W 194 E3
Viseu □ Portugal 40°40N 7°55W 194 E3
Vișeu de Sus Romania 47°45N 24°25E 183 C9
Vishakhapatnam India 17°45N 83°20E 244 F6
Vișina Romania 43°52N 24°27E 183 G9
Vișinești Moldova 46°20N 28°27E 183 D13
Visingsö Sweden 58°2N 14°20E 163 F8
Visitacion Valley U.S.A. 37°42N 122°23W 136 B2
Viskafors Sweden 57°37N 12°50E 163 G6
Viskan → Sweden 57°14N 12°12E 163 G6
Viški Kanal Croatia 43°4N 16°5E 199 E13
Vislanda Sweden 56°46N 14°30E 163 H8
Visnagar India 23°45N 72°32E 242 H5
Višnja Gora Slovenia 45°58N 14°45E 199 C11
Viso, Mte. Italy 44°38N 7°5E 198 D4
Viso del Marqués Spain 38°32N 3°34W 195 G7
Visoko Bos.-H. 43°58N 18°10E 182 G3
Visokoi I. Antarctica 56°43S 27°15W 151 B1
Visp Switz. 46°17N 7°52E 179 J3
Vissefjärda Sweden 56°32N 15°35E 163 H9
Visselhövede Germany 52°59N 9°34E 178 C5
Vissenbjerg Denmark 55°23N 10°7E 163 J4
Vista U.S.A. 33°12N 117°14W 307 M9
Vista Alegre Santiago, Chile 33°30S 70°43W 137 C1
Vista Alegre Lima, Peru 12°9S 76°59W 124 B3
Vista Grove U.S.A. 33°51N 84°16W 113 A3
Vistabella Trin. & Tob. 10°17N 61°27W 323 t
Vistonida, L. Greece 41°0N 25°7E 203 E9
Vistonikos, Ormos = Vistonida, L. Greece 41°0N 25°7E 203 E9
Vistula = Wisła → Poland 54°22N 18°55E 184 D5
Vistula Lagoon = Wiślany, Zalew Poland 54°20N 19°50E 184 D6
Vistula Spit Europe 54°25N 19°35E 184 D6
Vit → Bulgaria 43°30N 24°30E 203 C8
Vita India 17°17N 74°33E 244 F2
Vitacura Chile 33°23S 70°35W 137 B2
Vitanje Slovenia 46°25N 15°18E 199 B12
Vitebsk = Vitsyebsk Belarus 55°10N 30°15E 188 E6
Viterbo Italy 42°25N 12°6E 199 F9
Vitez Bos.-H. 44°10N 17°48E 182 F2
Viti Levu Fiji 17°30S 177°30E 287 A1
Vitiaz Str. Papua N. G. 5°40S 147°10E 286 C4
Vitiaz Trench Pac. Oc. 10°0S 170°0E 277 C13
Vitigudino Spain 41°1N 6°26W 194 D4
Vitim Russia 59°28N 112°35E 215 D12
Vitim → Russia 59°26N 112°34E 215 D12
Vitina Bos.-H. 43°17N 17°29E 199 E14
Vitina Greece 37°40N 22°10E 204 D4
Vitínia Italy 41°47N 12°24E 136 C1
Vítkov Czechia 49°46N 17°45E 181 B10
Vitória = Vitória de Santo Antão Brazil 8°10S 35°20W 332 C4
Vitória Espírito Santo, Brazil 20°20S 40°22W 333 F3
Vitória Pará, Brazil 2°54S 52°1W 329 D7
Vitória da Conquista Brazil 14°51S 40°51W 333 D3
Vitória de Santo Antão Brazil 8°10S 35°20W 332 C4
Vitoria-Gasteiz Spain 42°50N 2°41W 196 C2
Vitória Seamount Atl. Oc. 20°0S 44°0W 333 F4
Vitorino Freire Brazil 4°4S 45°10W 332 B2
Vitosha △ Bulgaria 42°36N 23°18E 202 D7
Vitré France 48°8N 1°12W 172 D5
Vitry-le-François France 48°43N 4°33E 173 D11
Vitry-sur-Seine France 48°47N 2°23E 134 B3
Vitsand Sweden 60°20N 13°0E 162 D7
Vitsi, Oros Greece 40°40N 21°25E 202 F5
Vitsyebsk Belarus 55°10N 30°15E 188 E6
Vitsyebsk □ Belarus 55°10N 28°50E 188 E5
Vittaryd Sweden 56°58N 13°57E 163 H7
Vitteaux France 47°24N 4°30E 173 E11
Vittel France 48°12N 5°57E 173 D12
Vittória Italy 36°57N 14°32E 201 F7
Vittório = Vittório Véneto Italy 45°59N 12°18E 199 C9
Vittório Véneto Italy 45°59N 12°18E 199 C9
Vittoriosa Malta 35°54N 14°31E 206 F8
Vittsjö Sweden 56°20N 13°40E 163 H7
Viveiro Spain 43°39N 7°38W 194 B3
Vivian U.S.A. 32°53N 93°59W 314 E8
Viviers France 44°30N 4°40E 175 D8
Vivonne S. Austral., Australia 35°59S 137°9E 282 C2
Vivonne Vienne, France 46°25N 0°15E 174 B4
Vivonne B. Australia 35°59S 137°9E 282 C2
Viwa Fiji 17°10S 177°58E 287 A1
Vizagapatam = Vishakhapatnam India 17°45N 83°20E 244 F6
Vizandino, Moussio Athens, Greece 112 b3
Vizcaíno, Desierto de Mexico 27°30N 113°45W 318 B2
Vizcaíno, Sierra Mexico 27°30N 114°0W 318 B2
Vize Turkey 41°34N 27°45E 203 E11
Vizianagaram India 18°6N 83°30E 244 E6
Vizille France 45°5N 5°46E 175 C9
Viziñada Croatia 45°20N 13°46E 199 C10
Viziru Romania 45°0N 27°43E 183 E12
Vizlinsky Zaliv = Wiślany, Zalew Poland 54°20N 19°50E 184 D6
Vizzini Italy 37°10N 14°45E 201 E7
Vlaardingen Neths. 51°55N 4°21E 170 C4
Vlachiotis Greece 36°52N 22°42E 204 E4
Vlădeasa, Vf. Romania 46°47N 22°50E 182 D7
Vladičin Han Serbia 42°42N 22°1E 202 D6
Vladikavkaz Russia 43°0N 44°35E 191 J7
Vladimir Russia 56°15N 40°30E 188 D11
Vladimir □ Russia 56°5N 40°10E 190 B5
Vladimir Volynskiy = Volodymyr-Volynskyy Ukraine 50°50N 24°18E 177 C13
Vladimirci Serbia 44°36N 19°50E 202 B3
Vladimirovac Serbia 45°1N 20°53E 182 E5
Vladimirovka = Yuzhno-Sakhalinsk Russia 46°58N 142°45E 219 B17
Vladimirovka Russia 48°27N 46°10E 191 F8
Vladimirovo Bulgaria 43°32N 23°22E 202 C7
Vladislavovka Ukraine 45°12N 35°29E 189 K8
Vladivostok Russia 43°10N 131°53E 220 C5
Vladykino Russia 55°51N 37°35E 129 A2
Vlăhița Romania 46°21N 25°31E 183 D10
Vlasenica Bos.-H. 44°11N 18°59E 182 F3
Vlašić Bos.-H. 44°19N 17°37E 182 F2
Vlašim Czechia 49°40N 14°53E 180 B7
Vlasinsko Jezero Serbia 42°44N 22°22E 202 D6
Vlasotince Serbia 42°59N 22°7E 202 D6
Vlieland Neths. 53°16N 4°55E 170 A4
Vlissingen Neths. 51°26N 3°34E 170 C3
Vlkolínec Slovakia 49°1N 19°16E 181 B12
Vlorë Albania 40°32N 19°28E 202 F3
Vlorës, Gjiri i Albania 40°29N 19°27E 202 F3
Vltava → Czechia 50°21N 14°30E 180 A7
Vo Dat Vietnam 11°9N 107°31E 237 G6
Voćin Croatia 45°37N 17°33E 182 E2
Vöcklabruck Austria 48°1N 13°39E 180 C6
Vodice Croatia 43°47N 15°47E 199 E12
Vodlozersky △ Russia 62°40N 37°5E 214 C1
Vodňany Czechia 49°9N 14°11E 180 B7
Vodnjan Croatia 44°59N 13°52E 199 D10
Vodopyanovo = Donskoy Russia 53°55N 38°15E 188 F10
Voe U.K. 60°21N 1°16W 167 A7
Vogan Togo 6°23N 1°30E 263 D5
Vogar Iceland 63°58N 22°22W 155 D4
Vogel Pk. Nigeria 8°24N 11°47E 263 D7
Vogelkop = Doberai, Jazirah Indonesia 1°25S 133°0E 231 E8
Vogelsberg Germany 50°31N 9°12E 178 E5
Voghera Italy 44°59N 9°1E 198 D6
Voh N. Cal. 20°58S 164°42E 288 d
Vohibinany Madag. 18°49S 49°4E 272 B2
Vohilava Madag. 21°4S 48°0E 272 C2
Vohimarina = Iharana Madag. 13°25S 50°0E 272 A3
Vohimena, Tanjon' i Madag. 25°36S 45°8E 272 D2
Vohipeno Madag. 22°22S 47°51E 272 C2
Voi Kenya 3°25S 38°32E 268 C4
Void-Vacon France 48°40N 5°36E 173 D12
Voinești Iași, Romania 47°5N 27°27E 183 C12
Voinești Prahova, Romania 45°5N 25°14E 183 E10
Voinjama Liberia 8°25N 9°44W 262 D3
Voiron France 45°22N 5°35E 175 C9
Voisey B. Canada 56°15N 61°50W 299 A7
Voitsberg Austria 47°3N 15°9E 180 D8
Vojens Denmark 55°16N 9°18E 163 J3
Vojmsjön Sweden 65°0N 16°24E 160 D17
Vojnić Croatia 45°19N 15°43E 199 C12
Vojnik Italy 46°18N 15°19E 199 B12
Vojvodina □ Serbia 45°20N 20°0E 182 E5
Vokeo I. Papua N. G. 3°14S 144°2E 286 B3
Vokhtoga Russia 58°46N 41°8E 188 C11
Vokovice Czechia 50°5N 14°21E 135 B2
Volary Czechia 48°54N 13°52E 180 C6
Volborg U.S.A. 45°51N 105°41W 304 D11
Volcán de Colima △ Mexico 19°30N 103°40W 318 D4
Volcano U.S.A. 19°26N 155°14W 302 D6
Volcano Is. = Kazan-Rettō Pac. Oc. 25°0N 141°0E 288 E6
Volcans △ Rwanda 1°30S 29°26E 268 C2
Volcans d'Auvergne ⌓ France 45°20N 2°40E 174 C6
Volchansk = Vovchansk Ukraine 50°17N 36°58E 189 G9

Volchikha *Russia* 52°2N 80°23E **217** B10
Volchya → *Ukraine* 48°32N 36°0E **189** H8
Volda *Norway* 62°9N 6°5E **164** B3
Volga = Privolzhskiy □
Russia 56°0N 50°0E **214** D6
Volga *Russia* 58°5N 38°16E **188** C10
Volga → *Russia* 46°0N 48°30E **191** G9
Volga Hts. = Privolzhskaya
Russia 51°0N 46°0E **190** E7
Volgelsdorf *Germany* 52°32N 13°44E **115** B5
Volgo-Baltiyskiy Kanal
Russia 60°0N 38°0E **188** B9
Volgo-Donskoy Kanal
Russia 48°40N 43°37E **191** F7
Volgodonsk *Russia* 47°33N 42°5E **191** G6
Volgograd *Russia* 48°40N 44°25E **191** F7
Volgogradskoye Vdkhr.
Russia 50°0N 45°20E **190** E8
Volgorechensk *Russia* 57°28N 41°14E **190** B5
Volimes *Greece* 37°52N 20°29E **207** D2
Volintiri *Moldova* 46°26N 29°37E **183** D14
Volissos *Greece* 38°29N 25°54E **205** C7
Volkach *Germany* 49°52N 10°14E **179** F6
Völkermarkt *Austria* 46°39N 14°39E **180** E7
Volkhonka-Zil *Russia* 55°39N 37°37E **129** C2
Volkhov *Russia* 59°55N 32°15E **188** C7
Volkhov → *Russia* 60°8N 32°20E **188** B7
Volkhovstroy = Volkhov
Russia 59°55N 32°15E **188** C7
Völklingen *Germany* 49°15N 6°50E **179** E5
Volkovysk = Vawkavysk
Belarus 53°9N 24°30E **177** B13
Volksrust *S. Africa* 27°24S 29°53E **271** C4
Voll *Norway* 62°31N 7°27E **164** B4
Vollen *Norway* 59°48N 10°21E **133** B1
Volnovakha *Ukraine* 47°35N 37°30E **189** J9
Volochanka *Russia* 71°0N 94°28E **215** B10
Volodarsk *Russia* 56°12N 43°15E **190** B6
Volodarskoye *Russia* 59°54N 30°23E **137** B2
Volodymyr-Volynskyy
Ukraine 50°50N 24°18E **177** C13
Vologda *Russia* 59°10N 39°45E **188** C10
Vologda □ *Russia* 60°15N 39°0E **188** B10
Volokolamsk *Russia* 56°5N 35°57E **188** D8
Volokonovka *Russia* 50°33N 37°52E **189** G9
Volos *Greece* 39°24N 22°59E **204** B4
Vološinovo = Novi Bečej
Serbia 45°36N 20°10E **182** C5
Volosovo *Russia* 59°27N 29°32E **188** C5
Volovets *Ukraine* 48°43N 23°11E **183** B8
Volovo *Russia* 53°35N 38°1E **188** F10
Volozhin = Valozhyn
Belarus 54°3N 26°30E **177** A14
Volsk *Russia* 52°5N 47°22E **190** D8
Volta □ *Ghana* 7°0N 0°30E **263** D5
Volta → *Ghana* 5°46N 0°41E **263** D5
Volta, L. *Ghana* 7°30N 0°0 **263** D5
Volta Blanche = White Volta →
Ghana 9°10N 1°15W **263** D4
Volta Redonda *Brazil* 22°31S 44°5W **333** F3
Voltaire, C. *Australia* 14°16S 125°35E **278** B4
Volterra *Italy* 43°24N 10°51E **198** F7
Voltri *Italy* 44°26N 8°45E **198** D5
Volturno → *Italy* 41°1N 13°55E **200** A6
Volubilis *Morocco* 34°2N 5°33W **260** B3
Voluntar *Romania* 44°30N 26°11E **183** F11
Volvi, L. *Greece* 40°40N 23°34E **202** F7
Volyn □ *Ukraine* 51°15N 24°30E **177** C13
Volyně *Czechia* 49°10N 13°53E **180** B6
Volynkina-Derevnya
Russia 59°53N 30°18E **137** B1
Volzhsk *Russia* 55°57N 48°23E **190** C9
Volzhskiy *Russia* 48°56N 44°46E **191** F7
Vomo *Fiji* 17°30S 177°15E **287** A11
Vonavona *Solomon Is.* 8°15S 157°5E **287** M9
Vondelpark *Neths.* 52°21N 4°52E **112** A2
Vondrozo *Madag.* 22°49S 47°20E **272** C2
Vonitsa *Greece* 38°53N 20°53E **207** B2
Vopnafjörður *Iceland* 65°45N 14°50W **155** B12
Vorarlberg □ *Austria* 47°20N 10°0E **180** D2
Voras Oros *Greece* 40°57N 21°45E **202** F5
Vorbasse *Denmark* 55°39N 9°6E **163** J3
Vorchdorf *Austria* 48°0N 13°55E **180** C6
Vorderrhein → *Switz.* 46°49N 9°25E **179** D5
Vordingborg *Denmark* 55°0N 11°54E **163** J5
Vorë *Albania* 41°23N 19°40E **202** E3
Voreio Aigaio □ *Greece* 38°50N 25°30E **205** C7
Voreios Sporades *Greece* 39°15N 23°30E **204** B5
Voreppe *France* 45°18N 5°39E **175** C9
Vori *Greece* 35°4N 24°49E **207** E5
Vorios Evoikos Kolpos
Greece 38°45N 23°15E **204** C5
Vorkuta *Russia* 67°48N 64°20E **186** A11
Vorma → *Norway* 60°9N 11°29E **164** D8
Vormsi *Estonia* 59°1N 23°13E **188** C2
Vorona → *Russia* 51°22N 42°3E **190** D7
Voronezh *Russia* 51°40N 39°10E **188** G10
Voronezh *Ukraine* 51°47N 33°28E **189** G7
Voronezh □ *Russia* 51°30N 39°30E **190** E4
Voronezh → *Russia* 51°56N 37°17E **188** G9
Vorontsovo-Aleksandrovskoye =
Zelenokumsk *Russia* 44°24N 44°0E **191** H6
Voroshilov = Ussuriysk
Russia 43°48N 131°59E **220** C5
Voroshilovgrad = Luhansk
Ukraine 48°38N 39°15E **189** H10
Voroshilovsk = Alchevsk
Ukraine 48°30N 38°45E **189** H10
Voroshilovsk = Stavropol
Russia 45°5N 42°0E **191** H6
Vorpommersche
Boddenlandschaft △
Germany 54°25N 12°32E **178** A8
Vorskla → *Ukraine* 48°50N 34°10E **189** H8
Võrts järv *Estonia* 58°16N 26°3E **188** C4
Võru *Estonia* 57°48N 26°54E **188** D4
Vösendorf *Austria* 48°7N 16°20E **142** B2
Vosges *France* 48°20N 7°10E **173** D14
Vosges □ *France* 48°12N 6°20E **173** D13
Vosges du Nord △ *France* 48°40N 7°45E **173** D14
Voskopojë *Albania* 40°35N 20°33E **202** F4
Voskresensk *Russia* 55°19N 38°43E **188** E10
Voskresenskoye *Russia* 56°51N 45°30E **190** B7
Voss *Norway* 60°38N 6°26E **164** D3
Vostochnyy Port *Russia* 42°44N 133°4E **220** C6
Vostok = Neftegorsk
Russia 44°25N 39°45E **191** H4
Vostok *Antarctica* 78°30S 106°50E **151** D8
Vostok I. *Kiribati* 10°5S 152°23W **289** J12
Votice *Czechia* 49°38N 14°39E **180** B7
Votkinsk *Russia* 57°0N 53°55E **186** C9
Votkinskoye Vdkhr.
Russia 57°22N 55°12E **186** C10
Votuporanga *Brazil* 20°24S 49°59W **333** F2
Vouga → *Portugal* 40°41N 8°40W **194** E2
Vouillé *France* 46°38N 0°10E **172** F7
Voula *Greece* 37°49N 23°45E **112** C2
Vouliagmeni *Greece* 37°50N 23°46E **112** C2
Voulou *C.A.R.* 8°33N 22°36E **264** A4
Vouxa, Akra *Greece* 35°37N 23°32E **207** E4
Vouzela *Portugal* 40°43N 8°7W **194** E2
Vouziers *France* 49°22N 4°40E **173** C11
Vovchansk *Ukraine* 50°17N 36°58E **189** G9
Vovchyn *Belarus* 52°10N 23°10E **185** F10
Voyageurs △ *U.S.A.* 48°32N 93°0W **308** A7
Voynitsa *Russia* 65°10N 30°20E **160** D24

Voyvozh *Russia* 62°56N 54°56E **186** B9
Vozhe, Ozero *Russia* 60°45N 39°0E **188** B10
Vozhega *Russia* 60°29N 40°12E **188** B11
Voznesensk *Ukraine* 47°35N 31°21E **189** J6
Voznesenye *Russia* 61°0N 35°28E **188** B8
Vozrozhdeniya I. *Asia* 45°10N 59°20E **216** C5
Vrá *Denmark* 57°21N 9°56E **163** H3
Vrable *Slovakia* 48°15N 18°16E **181** C11
Vraćevšnica *Serbia* 44°2N 20°34E **202** B4
Vrachneika *Greece* 38°10N 21°40E **204** C3
Vrådal *Norway* 59°20N 8°25E **164** E5
Vrancea □ *Romania* 45°50N 26°45E **183** E11
Vrancei, Munţii *Romania* 46°0N 26°30E **183** E11
Vrangel, Ostrov *Russia* 71°0N 180°0E **215** B18
Vranje *Serbia* 42°34N 21°54E **202** C6
Vranjska Banja *Serbia* 42°34N 22°1E **202** C6
Vranov nad Topľou
Slovakia 48°53N 21°40E **181** C14
Vransko *Slovenia* 46°17N 14°58E **199** B11
Vransko Jezero *Croatia* 43°53N 15°34E **199** E12
Vrapčište *Macedonia* 41°50N 20°53E **202** E4
Vratsa *Bulgaria* 43°15N 23°30E **202** C7
Vratsa □ *Bulgaria* 43°15N 23°30E **202** C7
Vråvatn *Norway* 59°20N 8°8E **164** E5
Vrbas *Serbia* 45°40N 19°40E **182** E4
Vrbas → *Bos.-H.* 45°8N 17°29E **182** E2
Vrbnik *Croatia* 45°4N 14°40E **199** C11
Vrbovec *Croatia* 45°53N 16°28E **199** C13
Vrbovsko *Croatia* 45°24N 15°5E **199** C12
Vrchlabí *Czechia* 50°38N 15°37E **180** A8
Vredefort *S. Africa* 27°0N 27°22E **270** C4
Vrede *S. Africa* 27°24S 29°6E **271** C4
Vredefort *S. Africa* 27°0S 27°22E **270** C4
Vredenhoek *S. Africa* 33°57S 18°25E **118** A1
Vredenburg *S. Africa* 32°56N 18°0E **270** D2
Vredendal *S. Africa* 31°41S 18°35E **270** D2
Vretstorp *Sweden* 59°1N 14°53E **168** D6
Vrgorac *Croatia* 43°12N 17°20E **199** E14
Vrhnika *Slovenia* 45°58N 14°15E **199** C11
Vriddhachalam *India* 11°30N 79°20E **245** J4
Vridi *Ivory C.* 5°15N 4°3W **262** D4
Vrigstad *Sweden* 57°22N 14°28E **163** G8
Vrindavan *India* 27°37N 77°40E **242** F7
Vrisses *Greece* 35°23N 24°13E **207** E5
Vrnograč *Bos.-H.* 45°10N 15°57E **199** C12
Vrondados *Greece* 38°25N 26°7E **205** C8
Vrpolje *Croatia* 45°13N 18°24E **182** E3
Vršac *Serbia* 45°8N 21°20E **182** E6
Vršačka Kanal *Serbia* 45°15N 21°10E **182** E6
Vršovice *Czechia* 50°4N 14°28E **135** B2
Vrútky *Slovakia* 49°7N 18°55E **181** B11
Vryburg *S. Africa* 26°55S 24°45E **270** C3
Vryheid *S. Africa* 27°45S 30°47E **271** C5
Vsetín *Czechia* 49°20N 18°0E **181** B11
Vu Liet *Vietnam* 18°43N 105°23E **236** C5
Vūcha → *Bulgaria* 42°10N 24°26E **203** D8
Vučitrn = Vushtrri
Kosovo 42°49N 20°59E **202** D4
Vuga *South Sudan* 5°21N 29°40E **257** F2
Vukovar *Croatia* 45°21N 18°59E **182** E3
Vuktyl *Russia* 63°52N 57°20E **214** C6
Vulcan *Alta., Canada* 50°25N 113°15W **296** C6
Vulcan *Romania* 45°23N 23°17E **183** E8
Vulcănești *Moldova* 45°41N 28°18E **183** E13
Vulcano *Italy* 38°24N 14°58E **201** D7
Vúlchedruma *Bulgaria* 43°42N 23°27E **202** C7
Vulkaneshty = Vulcănești
Moldova 45°41N 28°18E **183** E13
Vunduzi → *Mozam.* 18°56S 34°1E **269** F3
Vung Tau *Vietnam* 10°21N 107°4E **237** G6
Vunidawa *Fiji* 17°50S 178°21E **287** A2
Vunisea *Fiji* 19°3S 178°10E **287** B2
Vuntut △ *Canada* 68°25N 139°41W **294** D4
Vurango → *Solomon Is.* 6°39S 156°38E **287** L9
Vürbitsa *Bulgaria* 42°59N 26°40E **203** D10
Vürshets *Bulgaria* 43°13N 23°23E **202** C7
Vushtrri *Kosovo* 42°49N 20°59E **202** D4
Vutcani *Romania* 46°26N 27°59E **183** D12
Vuzlove *Ukraine* 48°22N 22°54E **182** B7
Vwaza △ *Malawi* 10°58S 33°25E **269** E3
Vyara *India* 21°8N 73°28E **244** F1
Vyartsilya *Russia* 62°8N 30°45E **188** A6
Vyatka = Kirov *Russia* 58°35N 49°40E **186** C8
Vyatka → *Russia* 55°37N 51°28E **190** C10
Vyatskiye Polyany *Russia* 56°14N 51°5E **190** B10
Vyazemskiy *Russia* 47°32N 134°45E **215** E14
Vyazma *Russia* 55°10N 34°15E **188** E8
Vyazniki *Russia* 56°10N 42°10E **190** B6
Vyborg *Russia* 60°43N 28°47E **188** B5
Vyborgskaya Storona
Russia 59°57N 30°22E **137** B2
Vychegda → *Russia* 61°18N 46°36E **186** B8
Vychodné Beskydy
Europe 49°30N 22°0E **181** B15
Vyerkhnyadzvinsk
Belarus 55°45N 27°58E **188** E4
Vyg-ozero *Russia* 63°47N 34°29E **186** B5
Vyhoda *Ukraine* 48°56N 23°53E **183** B8
Vykhino *Russia* 55°43N 37°49E **129** C4
Vyksa *Russia* 55°19N 42°11E **190** C6
Výlkove *Ukraine* 45°28N 29°32E **183** E14
Vylok *Ukraine* 48°6N 22°50E **182** B7
Vynohradiv *Ukraine* 48°9N 23°2E **182** B7
Vypin *India* 10°10N 76°15E **245** J3
Vyrnwy, L. *U.K.* 52°48N 3°31W **168** E4
Výšehrad *Czechia* 50°3N 14°25E **135** B2
Vyshkiv *Ukraine* 48°44N 23°39E **183** B8
Vyshkove *Ukraine* 48°3N 23°25E **183** B8
Vyshniy Volochek *Russia* 57°30N 34°30E **188** D8
Vyshzha = imeni 26 Bakinskikh
Komissarov
Turkmenistan 39°22N 54°10E **247** B7
Vyškov *Czechia* 49°17N 17°0E **181** B9
Vysočina □ *Czechia* 49°30N 15°30E **180** B8
Vysokoye *Belarus* 52°22N 23°22E **185** F10
Vysoké Mýto *Czechia* 49°58N 16°10E **181** B9
Vysokovsk *Russia* 56°22N 36°30E **188** D8
Vyšší Brod *Czechia* 48°37N 14°19E **180** C7
Vytegra *Russia* 61°0N 36°27E **188** B9
Vyzhnytsya *Ukraine* 48°35N 25°11E **183** B10
Vyzhnytsya → *Ukraine* 48°7N 25°15E **183** B10

W

W du Benin △ *Benin* 11°57N 2°43E **263** C5
W du Burkina Faso △
Burkina Faso 11°52N 2°50E **263** C5
W du Niger △ *Niger* 13°31N 2°26E **263** C5
W.A.C. Bennett Dam
Canada 56°2N 122°6W **296** B4
Wa *Ghana* 10°7N 2°25W **262** C4
Waag = Váh → *Slovakia* 47°43N 18°7E **181** C9
Waal → *Neths.* 51°37N 5°0E **170** C5
Waalwijk *Neths.* 51°42N 5°4E **170** C5
Waanyi-Garawa ◎
Australia 18°2S 137°33E **280** B2
Waat *South Sudan* 8°10N 32°7E **257** F3
Wabag *Papua N. G.* 5°32S 143°40E **286** D2
Wabakimi △ *Canada* 50°43N 89°29W **300** B2
Wabana *Canada* 47°40N 53°0W **309** C9
Wabasca → *Canada* 58°22N 115°20W **296** B5
Wabasca-Desmarais
Canada 55°57N 113°56W **296** B6
Wabash *U.S.A.* 40°48N 85°49W **311** D11
Wabash → *U.S.A.* 37°48N 88°2W **311** G8
Wabasso *U.S.A.* 27°45N 80°26W **317** H9

Wabawng *Burma* 26°20N 97°25E **241** B6
Wabi → *Ethiopia* 7°45N 40°50E **257** F5
Wabigoon L. *Canada* 49°44N 92°44W **297** D10
Wabowden *Canada* 54°55N 98°38W **297** C9
Wabrzezno *Poland* 53°16N 18°57E **185** C5
Wabu Hu *China* 32°20N 116°50E **229** H1
Wabuda I. *Papua N. G.* 8°23S 143°37E **286** E2
Wabuk Pt. *Canada* 55°20N 85°5W **298** A2
Wabush *Canada* 52°55N 66°52W **309** B6
Waccasassa B. *U.S.A.* 29°10N 82°50W **317** F7
Wachau *Austria* 48°21N 15°26E **180** C8
Wachock *Poland* 51°4N 21°1E **185** G8
Wachtersberg *Germany* 48°2N 11°42E **131** B3
Wacissa *U.S.A.* 30°22N 83°59W **316** E6
Waco *U.S.A.* 31°33N 97°9W **314** F6
Waconichi, L. *Canada* 50°8N 74°0W **298** B5
Wad Banda *Sudan* 13°10N 27°56E **257** E6
Wad el Haddad *Sudan* 13°50N 33°30E **257** E3
Wad en Nau *Sudan* 14°10N 33°34E **257** E3
Wad Hamid *Sudan* 16°30N 32°45E **257** D3
Wad Medani *Sudan* 14°28N 33°30E **257** E3
Wad Thana *Pakistan* 27°22N 66°23E **242** F2
Wadai = Ouaddaï □ *Chad* 13°0N 21°0E **259** F4
Wadala *India* 19°1N 72°51E **130** A2
Wadayama *Japan* 35°19N 134°52E **222** B6
Wadbilliga △ *Australia* 36°25S 149°35E **283** D8
Waddān *Libya* 29°9N 16°10E **258** C8
Waddeneilanden *Neths.* 53°25N 5°10E **170** A5
Waddenzee *Neths.* 53°6N 5°10E **170** A5
Waddi, Chappal *Nigeria* 7°2N 11°43E **263** D7
Waddington *U.S.A.* 44°52N 75°12W **313** B9
Waddington, Mt.
Canada 51°23N 125°15W **296** C3
Waddy Pt. *Australia* 24°58S 153°21E **281** C5
Wadebridge *U.K.* 50°31N 4°51W **169** G3
Wadena *Sask., Canada* 51°57N 103°47W **297** C8
Wadena *Minn., U.S.A.* 46°26N 95°8W **306** B7
Wädenswil *Switz.* 47°14N 8°40E **179** H4
Wadern *Germany* 49°32N 6°53E **179** F2
Wadeye *Australia* 14°28S 129°52E **278** B4
Wadgaon *India* 18°44N 73°39E **244** E1
Wadhams *Canada* 51°30N 127°30W **296** C3
Wadhwan *India* 22°42N 71°41E **242** H4
Wadi *India* 17°4N 76°59E **244** F3
Wadi Al-Arayis *West Bank* 31°43N 35°15E **123** B2
Wadi al Ḥayat □ *Libya* 26°26N 12°30E **258** C2
Wadi aş Sir *Jordan* 31°56N 35°49E **258** D4
Wadi ash Shāṭī □ *Libya* 27°30N 13°37E **258** C2
Wadi Feirān *Egypt* 28°42N 33°19E **261** K4
Wadi Fira □ *Chad* 15°0N 21°0E **259** F4
Wadi Fukin *West Bank* 31°42N 35°6E **123** B1
Wadi Gemâl, I. *Egypt* 24°35N 35°10E **256** C4
Wadi Halfa *Sudan* 21°53N 31°19E **256** C3
Wādī Mūsā *Jordan* 30°19N 35°29E **251** H6
Wādī Rum △ *Jordan* 29°30N 35°20E **251** J6
Wadian *China* 32°42N 112°29E **229** A9
Wadley *Poland* 51°31N 19°23E **185** G6
Wadley *Ala., U.S.A.* 33°7N 85°34W **316** B4
Wadley *Ga., U.S.A.* 32°52N 82°24W **316** C7
Wadowice *Poland* 49°52N 19°30E **185** J6
Wadsworth *Nev., U.S.A.* 39°38N 119°17W **304** G4
Wadsworth *Ohio, U.S.A.* 41°1N 81°44W **312** E13
Waduk Pluit *Indonesia* 6°5S 106°46E **122** A1
Waegwan *S. Korea* 35°59N 128°23E **224** E4
Wafangdian *China* 39°38N 121°58E **227** E11
Wafania
Dem. Rep. of the Congo 1°23S 20°22E **264** C4
Wafrah *Kuwait* 28°33N 47°56E **246** D5
Wagadugu = Ouagadougou
Burkina Faso 12°25N 1°30W **263** C4
Wagait ◎ *Australia* 13°1S 130°5E **278** B5
Wageima = Wakema
Burma 16°30N 95°11E **241** G5
Wagener *U.S.A.* 33°39N 81°22W **316** B8
Wageningen *Neths.* 51°58N 5°40E **170** C5
Wageningen *Suriname* 5°50N 56°50W **329** B6
Wager B. *Canada* 65°26N 88°40W **295** D14
Wagga Wagga *Australia* 35°7S 147°24E **283** C7
Waggaman *U.S.A.* 29°55N 90°12W **331** B1
Waghai *India* 20°46N 73°29E **244** D1
Waghete *Indonesia* 4°10S 135°50E **239** E9
Wagin *Australia* 33°17S 117°25E **279** F2
Wagner *U.S.A.* 43°5N 98°18W **308** D4
Wagon Mound *U.S.A.* 36°1N 104°42W **305** H11
Wagoner *U.S.A.* 35°58N 95°22W **314** C7
Wagrowiec *Poland* 52°48N 17°11E **185** F4
Wah *Pakistan* 33°45N 72°40E **242** C5
Wah Fu *Hong Kong, China* 22°15N 114°8E **122** B2
Wahai *Indonesia* 2°48S 129°35E **239** E7
Waharoa *N.Z.* 37°46S 175°45E **284** D4
Wahda = Unity □
South Sudan 8°30N 30°0E **257** F3
Wahda *Iraq* 33°18N 44°28E **113** B2
Wahiawā *U.S.A.* 21°30N 158°2W **302** K13
Wahiawā District
U.S.A. 21°31N 157°58W **302** J14
Wahiawā Res. *U.S.A.* 21°30N 158°3W **302** K13
Wahībah, Ramlat al
Oman 21°15N 58°45E **249** B7
Wahnai *Afghan.* 32°40N 65°50E **242** C1
Wahni *Ethiopia* 12°40N 36°39E **257** E4
Wahoo *U.S.A.* 41°13N 96°37W **308** E5
Wahpeton *U.S.A.* 46°16N 96°36W **308** B5
Wahran = Oran *Algeria* 35°45N 0°39W **260** A5
Wahroonga *Australia* 33°43S 151°7E **121** A3
Wai *India* 17°56N 73°57E **244** F1
Wai'ale'ale *U.S.A.* 22°4N 159°30W **302** J2
Waiale'e *U.S.A.* 21°41N 158°1W **302** J13
Waialua *U.S.A.* 21°34N 158°8W **302** J13
Waialua B. *U.S.A.* 21°35N 158°8W **302** J13
Waialua District *U.S.A.* 21°35N 158°5W **302** J13
Wai'anae *U.S.A.* 21°27N 158°11W **302** K13
Wai'anae Coast *U.S.A.* 21°26N 158°11W **302** K13
Wai'anae District
U.S.A. 21°28N 158°10W **302** K13
Wai'anae Range
U.S.A. 21°30N 158°10W **302** K13
Waiau *Taiwan* 24°54N 121°51E **225** B3
Waiapu → *N.Z.* 37°47S 178°29E **284** D7
Waiau → *N.Z.* 42°39S 173°5E **285** C8
Waiau → *Southland, N.Z.* 46°12S 167°38E **285** G2
Waiau → *Canterbury,
N.Z.* 42°47S 173°22E **285** C8
Waiawa Ganga → *Sri Lanka* 8°15N 81°0E **245** L5
Waibeem *Indonesia* 0°30S 132°59E **281** E8
Waiblingen *Germany* 48°49N 9°18E **179** G5
Waidhofen an der Thaya
Austria 48°49N 15°17E **180** C8

Waikane *U.S.A.* 21°30N 157°51W **302** J14
Waikare, L. *N.Z.* 37°26S 175°13E **284** D4
Waikareiti, I. *N.Z.* 38°43S 177°10E **284** E6
Waikaremoana, L. *N.Z.* 38°42S 177°12E **284** E6
Waikaremoana *N.Z.* 38°49S 177°9E **284** E6
Waikari *N.Z.* 42°58S 172°41E **285** D7
Waikato → *N.Z.* 37°23S 174°43E **284** D3
Waikelo *Indonesia* 9°24S 119°19E **278** A2
Waikerie *Australia* 34°9S 140°0E **282** C4
Waikiki *U.S.A.* 37°5S 174°16E **284** B3
Waikiki *U.S.A.* 21°17N 157°50W **302** J14
Waikokopu *N.Z.* 39°3S 177°52E **284** E6
Waikouaiti *N.Z.* 45°36S 170°41E **285** F5
Waikouaiti Downs *N.Z.* 45°30S 170°30E **285** F5
Wailing Wall = Western Wall
Jerusalem **123** b3
Wailua *U.S.A.* 22°3N 159°20W **302** J2
Wailuku *U.S.A.* 20°53N 156°30W **302** K6
Waimakariri → *N.Z.* 43°24S 172°42E **285** D7
Waimalu *U.S.A.* 21°24N 157°57W **302** K14
Waimānalo *U.S.A.* 21°21N 157°43W **302** K14
Waimānalo B. *U.S.A.* 21°20N 157°40W **302** K14
Waimānalo Beach
U.S.A. 21°21N 157°42W **302** K14
Waimangaroa *N.Z.* 41°43S 171°46E **285** B6
Waimano → *U.S.A.* 21°25N 157°58W **302** K14
Waimarie *N.Z.* 41°35S 171°58E **285** B6
Waimate *N.Z.* 44°45S 171°3E **285** F4
Waimea *Hawai'i, U.S.A.* 21°58N 159°40W **302** B2
Waimea *Hawai'i, U.S.A.* 21°39N 158°3W **302** J13
Waimea B. *U.S.A.* 21°40N 158°5W **302** J13
Waimea Plain *N.Z.* 45°55S 168°35E **285** F3
Wainganga → *India* 18°50N 79°55E **244** E4
Waingapu *Indonesia* 9°35S 120°11E **231** F6
Waingmaw *Burma* 25°21N 97°26E **241** C6
Waini → *Guyana* 8°20N 59°50W **329** B6
Wainuiomata *N.Z.* 41°17S 174°56E **284** H3
Wainwright *Alta.,
Canada* 52°50N 110°50W **297** C6
Wainwright *Alaska,
U.S.A.* 70°38N 160°2W **303** A7
Waiotapu *N.Z.* 38°21S 176°25E **284** E6
Waiouru *N.Z.* 39°28S 175°41E **284** E5
Waipa → *N.Z.* 38°16S 175°21E **284** E4
Waipahi *N.Z.* 46°6S 169°15E **285** G4
Waipahu *U.S.A.* 21°23N 158°1W **302** K13
Waipara *N.Z.* 43°3S 172°46E **285** D7
Waipawa *N.Z.* 39°56S 176°38E **284** F6
Waipi'o *U.S.A.* 21°25N 158°0W **302** K14
Waipi'o Acres *U.S.A.* 21°28N 158°1W **302** K13
Waipi'o Peninsula
U.S.A. 21°20N 158°0W **302** K14
Waipiro *N.Z.* 38°2S 178°22E **284** E7
Waipiro Bay *N.Z.* 38°1S 178°21E **284** E7
Waipu *N.Z.* 35°59S 174°29E **284** C4
Waipukurau *N.Z.* 40°1S 176°33E **284** F6
Wairakei *N.Z.* 38°37S 176°6E **284** E5
Wairarapa, L. *N.Z.* 41°14S 175°15E **284** H4
Wairau → *N.Z.* 41°32S 174°7E **285** B9
Wairio *N.Z.* 45°59S 168°3E **285** F3
Wairoa → *Hawke's Bay,
N.Z.* 39°4S 177°25E **284** F6
Wairoa → *Northland, N.Z.* 36°5S 173°59E **284** C2
Wairuamata *Taiwan* 23°29N 120°1E **225** C2
Waïsisi *Vanuatu* 19°32S 169°22E **287** J7
Waitaki → *N.Z.* 44°56S 171°7E **285** E6
Waitaki Plains *N.Z.* 44°22S 170°0E **285** E5
Waitangi *N.Z.* 35°16S 174°5E **284** C4
Waitara *N.Z.* 38°59S 174°15E **284** E3
Waitiki Landing *N.Z.* 34°31S 172°50E **284** A1
Waitoa *N.Z.* 37°37S 175°37E **284** D4
Waitomo Caves *N.Z.* 38°16S 175°7E **284** E4
Waitotara *N.Z.* 39°49S 174°44E **284** F3
Waitotara → *N.Z.* 39°51S 174°41E **284** F3
Waitsburg *U.S.A.* 46°16N 118°9W **304** C4
Waitzen = Vác *Hungary* 47°49N 19°10E **182** C4
Waiuku *N.Z.* 37°15S 174°45E **284** D3
Wajima *Japan* 37°30N 137°0E **221** F8
Wajir *Kenya* 1°42N 40°5E **268** B5
Wajir □ *Kenya* 1°45N 40°5E **268** B5
Waka *Dem. Rep. of the Congo* 1°1N 20°13E **264** B4
Waka *Ethiopia* 7°9N 37°20E **257** F4
Waka-Kungo *Angola* 11°21S 15°7E **265** H3
Wakarusa *U.S.A.* 41°32N 86°1W **311** C10
Wakasa *Japan* 35°20N 134°24E **222** B6
Wakasa-Wan *Japan* 35°40N 135°30E **223** B7
Wakatipu, L. *N.Z.* 45°5S 168°33E **285** F2
Wakaw *Canada* 52°39N 105°44W **297** C7
Wakaya *Fiji* 17°37S 179°0E **287** A2
Wakayama *Japan* 34°15N 135°15E **223** C7
Wakayama □ *Japan* 33°50N 135°30E **223** D7
Wake *Japan* 34°48N 134°8E **222** C6
Wake Forest *U.S.A.* 35°59N 78°30W **315** D15
Wake I. *Pac. Oc.* 19°18N 166°36E **322** b
WaKeeney *U.S.A.* 39°1N 99°53W **308** F4
Wakefield *Jamaica* 18°26N 77°42W **320** a
Wakefield *N.Z.* 41°24S 173°5E **285** B8
Wakefield *W. Yorks., U.K.* 53°41N 1°29W **168** D6
Wakefield *Mass., U.S.A.* 42°30N 71°4W **313** D13
Wakefield *Mich., U.S.A.* 46°29N 89°56W **306** B9
Wakema *Burma* 16°30N 95°11E **241** G5
Wākhān *Afghan.* 37°0N 73°40E **247** B8
Wākhān □ *Afghan.* 37°8N 73°4E **240** A4
Waki = Mima *Japan* 34°4N 134°9E **222** c6
Wakkanai *Japan* 45°28N 141°35E **220** B10
Wakkerstroom *S. Africa* 27°24S 30°10E **271** C5
Wakool *Australia* 35°28S 144°23E **283** C6
Wakool → *Australia* 35°5S 143°33E **282** C5
Wakre *Indonesia* 0°19S 131°5E **231** E8
Waku *Papua N. G.* 6°5S 149°9E **286** C6
Wakuach, L. *Canada* 55°34N 67°32W **309** A6
Wakulla *U.S.A.* 30°14N 84°14W **316** E5
Wakunai *Papua N. G.* 5°52S 155°13E **286** C8
Walagunya ◎ *Australia* 23°10S 120°50E **278** D3
Walamba *Zambia* 13°30S 28°42E **269** E2
Walbrzych *Poland* 50°45N 16°18E **185** H3
Walbury Hill *U.K.* 51°21N 1°28W **169** F6
Walcha *Australia* 30°55S 151°31E **283** B9
Walcheren *Neths.* 51°30N 3°35E **170** C3
Walcott *U.S.A.* 41°46N 106°51W **304** F10
Walcz *Poland* 53°17N 16°27E **185** C3
Waldbröl *Germany* 50°52N 7°37E **178** E3
Waldburg Ra. *Australia* 24°40S 117°35E **279** D2
Waldeck *Germany* 51°12N 9°4E **178** D5
Walden *Colo., U.S.A.* 40°44N 106°17W **304** F10
Walden *N.Y., U.S.A.* 41°34N 74°11W **313** E10
Waldenberg = Walbrzych
Poland 50°45N 16°18E **185** H3
Waldersruh *Germany* 52°35N 13°37E **115** B4
Waldkirch *Germany* 48°6N 7°58E **179** G3
Waldkirchen *Germany* 48°43N 13°36E **180** C6
Waldkraiburg *Germany* 48°12N 12°18E **180** C5
Waldo *U.S.A.* 29°48N 82°10W **316** F7
Waldoboro *U.S.A.* 44°6N 69°22W **310** C13
Waldport *U.S.A.* 44°26N 124°4W **304** D1
Waldron *U.S.A.* 34°54N 94°5W **314** D8
Waldrudering *Germany* 48°6N 11°41E **131** B4
Waldviertel *Germany* 48°30N 15°30E **180** C8
Walebing *Australia* 30°41S 116°13E **279** F2
Walembele *Burkina Faso* 10°30N 1°58W **262** C4
Walensee *Switz.* 47°7N 9°13E **179** H5
Wales *U.K.* 52°19N 3°40W **169** E4
Wales □ *U.K.* 52°19N 3°40W **169** E4
Wales *U.S.A.* 65°37N 168°5W **303** B6
Wales I. *Canada* 68°1N 86°40W **295** D14

Walewale *Ghana* 10°21N 0°50W **263** C4
Walgett *Australia* 30°0S 148°5E **281** E4
Walgreen Coast
Antarctica 75°15S 105°0W **151** D15
Walhalla *Australia* 37°56S 146°29E **283** D7
Walis I. *Papua N. G.* 3°14S 143°18E **286** B2
Walkamin *Australia* 17°8S 145°25E **280** B4
Walker *Minn., U.S.A.* 47°6N 94°35W **306** B7
Walker *Mich., U.S.A.* 43°0N 85°46W **311** B11
Walker, L. *Canada* 50°20N 67°11W **309** B6
Walker L. *Man., Canada* 54°42N 95°57W **297** C9
Walker L. *Nev., U.S.A.* 38°42N 118°43W **304** G4
Walkerston *Australia* 21°11S 149°8E **280** b
Walkerton *Canada* 44°10N 81°10W **312** B3
Walkerton *Ind., U.S.A.* 41°28N 86°29W **311** C10
Wall *U.S.A.* 44°0N 102°8W **308** C2
Wall Street *New York,
U.S.A.* **132** f1
Walla Walla *N.S.W.,
Australia* 35°45S 146°54E **283** C7
Walla Walla *Wash.,
U.S.A.* 46°4N 118°20W **304** C4
Wallabout Bay *New York,
U.S.A.* **132** f2
Wallace *Idaho, U.S.A.* 47°28N 115°56W **304** C6
Wallace *N.C., U.S.A.* 34°44N 77°59W **315** D16
Wallaceburg *Canada* 42°34N 82°23W **312** D2
Wallacetown *N.Z.* 46°21S 168°19E **285** G3
Wallachia = Valahia
Romania 44°35N 25°0E **183** F9
Wallal *Australia* 26°32S 146°7E **281** D4
Wallam Cr. → *Australia* 28°40S 147°20E **281** D4
Wallambin, L. *Australia* 30°57S 117°35E **279** F2
Wallan *Australia* 37°26S 144°59E **283** D6
Wallangarra *Australia* 28°56S 151°58E **281** D5
Wallaroo *Australia* 33°56S 137°39E **282** B2
Wallasey *U.K.* 53°25N 3°2W **168** D4
Walldürn *Germany* 49°34N 9°22E **179** F5
Wallenhorst *Germany* 52°21N 8°1E **178** C4
Wallenpaupack, L.
U.S.A. 41°25N 75°15W **313** E9
Wallerawang *Australia* 33°25S 150°4E **283** B9
Wallingat △ *Australia* 32°14S 152°25E **283** B10
Wallingford *Conn.,
U.S.A.* 41°27N 72°50W **313** E12
Wallingford *Vt., U.S.A.* 43°28N 72°58W **313** C12
Wallis & Futuna, Is. □
Pac. Oc. 13°18S 176°10W **277** C15
Wallowa *U.S.A.* 45°34N 117°32W **304** D5
Wallowa Mts. *U.S.A.* 45°20N 117°30W **304** D5
Walls *U.K.* 60°14N 1°33W **167** A7
Walls of Jerusalem △
Australia 41°58S 146°15E **281** G4
Wallsend *Australia* 32°55S 151°40E **283** B9
Wallula *U.S.A.* 46°5N 118°54W **304** C4
Wallumbilla *Australia* 26°33S 149°9E **281** D4
Walmsley, L. *Canada* 63°25N 108°36W **297** A7
Walney, I. of *U.K.* 54°6N 3°15W **168** C4
Walnut *U.S.A.* 41°33N 89°36W **310** C7
Walnut Canyon △
U.S.A. 35°15N 111°20W **305** J8
Walnut Creek *U.S.A.* 37°54N 122°4W **306** H4
Walnut Grove *U.S.A.* 34°4N 86°18W **316** A3
Walnut Hill *U.S.A.* 30°53N 87°30W **317** D12
Walnut Ridge *U.S.A.* 36°4N 90°57W **315** C9
Walpeup *Australia* 35°7S 142°2E **282** C5
Walpole *W. Austral.,
Australia* 34°58S 116°44E **279** F2
Walpole *Mass., U.S.A.* 42°9N 71°15W **313** D13
Walpole-Nornalup △
Australia 35°0S 116°45E **279** G2
Wals *Austria* 47°47N 12°58E **180** D5
Walsall *U.K.* 52°35N 1°58W **169** E6
Walsenburg *U.S.A.* 37°38N 104°47W **305** H11
Walsh *U.S.A.* 37°23N 102°17W **305** H12
Walsh → *Australia* 16°31S 143°42E **280** B3
Walsingham *Canada* 42°40N 80°31W **312** D4
Walsrode *Germany* 52°51N 9°35E **178** C5
Walt Disney Concert Hall
Los Angeles, U.S.A. **127** b1
Walt Disney World Resort
U.S.A. 28°22N 81°33W **133** B1
Waltair *India* 17°44N 83°23E **244** F6
Walter F. George Res.
U.S.A. 31°38N 85°4W **316** D4
Walterboro *U.S.A.* 32°55N 80°40W **316** D8
Walters *U.S.A.* 34°22N 98°19W **314** D5
Waltershausen Gletscher
Greenland 73°54N 24°25W **154** C8
Waltham *U.S.A.* 42°23N 71°14W **116** A1
Waltham Forest □ *U.K.* 51°35N 0°0 **125** A3
Walthamstow *U.K.* 51°34N 0°1W **125** A3
Waltman *U.S.A.* 43°4N 107°12W **304** E9
Walton *Ky., U.S.A.* 38°52N 84°37W **311** F12
Walton *N.Y., U.S.A.* 42°10N 75°8W **313** D9
Walton-on-Thames *U.K.* 51°23N 0°24W **125** C2
Walton-on-the-Naze *U.K.* 51°51N 1°17E **169** F9
Waltonville *U.S.A.* 38°13N 89°2W **310** F7
Walu *Burma* 26°28N 98°2E **241** B7
Walvis Bay *Namibia* 23°0S 14°28E **270** B1
Walvis Ridge *Atl. Oc.* 26°0S 5°0E **152** J12
Walvisbaai = Walvis Bay
Namibia 23°0S 14°28E **270** B1
Walwa *Australia* 35°59S 147°44E **283** C7
Wamba *Équateur,
Dem. Rep. of the Congo* 1°37S 22°30E **264** C4
Wamba *Orientale,
Dem. Rep. of the Congo* 2°10N 27°57E **268** B2
Wamba *Rift Valley, Kenya* 0°58N 37°19E **268** B4
Wamba *Nigeria* 8°57N 8°42E **263** D6
Wamba →
Dem. Rep. of the Congo 3°56S 17°12E **265** C3
Wambardi ◎ *Australia* 16°0S 130°50E **278** C5
Wambeek *Belgium* 50°55N 4°3E **116** A3
Wamego *U.S.A.* 39°12N 96°18W **308** F5
Wamena *Indonesia* 4°4S 138°57E **231** F9
Wampana Karlantijpa ◎
Australia 17°45S 132°10E **278** C5
Wampaya ◎ *Australia* 17°20S 135°0E **280** B2
Wampsville *U.S.A.* 43°4N 75°42W **313** C9
Wamsutter *U.S.A.* 41°40N 107°58W **304** F9
Wamulan *Indonesia* 3°27S 126°7E **231** E7
Wan Chai
Hong Kong, China 22°16N 114°10E **122** B3
Wan Hat *Burma* 20°14N 97°53E **241** B6
Wan Kinghao *Burma* 21°34N 98°17E **241** B7
Wan Lai-kam *Burma* 21°13N 98°22E **241** B7
Wan Tup *Burma* 21°8N 98°17E **241** B7
Wan Xian *China* 38°47N 115°7E **226** E8
Wana *Pakistan* 32°20N 69°32E **242** C3
Wanaaring *Australia* 29°38S 144°9E **281** E3
Wanaka *N.Z.* 44°42S 169°9E **285** F2
Wanaka L. *N.Z.* 44°33S 169°7E **285** F2
Wan'an *China* 26°26N 114°49E **229** D10
Wanapiri *Indonesia* 4°30S 135°59E **231** E9
Wanapitei L. *Canada* 46°45N 80°40W **312** A5
Wanbi *Australia* 34°46S 140°17E **282** C4
Wandan = Wantan
Taiwan 22°34N 120°29E **225** C2
Wandel Sea = McKinley Sea
Arctic 82°0N 0°0 **154** A11
Wanderer *Zimbabwe* 19°36S 29°45E **271** A4
Wandhari *Pakistan* 27°42N 66°48E **242** F2
Wanding *China* 24°5N 98°4E **241** C7
Wandle → *U.K.* 51°28N 0°11W **125** C3
Wando *S. Korea* 34°11N 126°41E **224** E3
Wandoan *Australia* 26°5S 149°55E **281** D4
Wandsworth *U.K.* 51°27N 0°11W **125** C3
Warner Brothers Studios
U.S.A. 34°9N 118°20W **126** B2

Warner Mts. *U.S.A.* 41°40N 120°15W **304** F3
Warner Robins *U.S.A.* 32°37N 83°36W **316** C6
Warnes *Bolivia* 17°30S 63°10W **331** D5
Warnow → *Germany* 54°6N 12°9E **178** A8
Waroona *Australia* 32°50S 115°58E **279** F2
Warora *India* 20°14N 79°1E **244** D4
Warrabah △ *Australia* 30°31S 150°56E **283** A10
Warrabri ✪ *Australia* 21°1S 134°19E **280** C1
Warracknabeal *Australia* 36°9S 142°26E **282** D5
Warragul *Australia* 38°10S 145°58E **283** E6
Warrap = Warab *South Sudan* 8°8N 28°37E **257** F2
Warrâq el 'Arab *Egypt* 30°4N 31°11E **117** A2
Warrego → *Australia* 30°24S 145°21E **281** E4
Warrego Ra. *Australia* 24°58S 146°0E **280** C4
Warren *N.S.W., Australia* 31°42S 147°51E **283** A7
Warren *Ark., U.S.A.* 33°37N 92°4W **314** E8
Warren *Ill., U.S.A.* 42°29N 90°0W **310** B7
Warren *Ind., U.S.A.* 40°41N 85°26W **311** D11
Warren *Mich., U.S.A.* 42°28N 83°1W **311** B13
Warren *Minn., U.S.A.* 48°12N 96°46W **308** A5
Warren *Ohio, U.S.A.* 41°14N 80°49W **312** E4
Warren *Pa., U.S.A.* 41°51N 79°9W **312** E5
Warrenpoint *U.K.* 54°6N 6°15W **166** B5
Warrensburg *Ill., U.S.A.* 39°56N 89°4W **310** E7
Warrensburg *Mo., U.S.A.* 38°46N 93°44W **310** F3
Warrensburg *N.Y., U.S.A.* 43°29N 73°46W **313** C11
Warrenton *Northern Cape, S. Africa* 28°9S 24°47E **270** C3
Warrenton *Ga., U.S.A.* 33°24N 82°40W **316** B7
Warrenton *Mo., U.S.A.* 38°49N 91°9W **310** F5
Warrenton *Oreg., U.S.A.* 46°10N 123°56W **306** D3
Warrenville *U.S.A.* 33°33N 81°48W **316** B8
Warri *Nigeria* 5°30N 5°41E **263** D6
Warringal Park *Australia* 37°45S 145°4E **128** A2
Warrington *N.Z.* 45°43S 170°35E **285** F5
Warrington *Warrington, U.K.* 53°24N 2°35W **168** D5
Warrington *Fla., U.S.A.* 30°23N 87°17W **317** E2
Warrington □ *U.K.* 53°24N 2°35W **168** D5
Warriston *U.K.* 55°58N 3°11W **121** B2
Warrnambool *Australia* 38°25S 142°30E **282** E5
Warroad *U.S.A.* 48°54N 95°19W **308** A6
Warrumbungle △ *Australia* 31°18S 149°1E **283** A8
Warruwi *Australia* 11°36S 133°20E **280** A1
Warsak Dam *Pakistan* 34°11N 71°19E **242** B4
Warsaw = Warszawa *Poland* 52°14N 21°0E **143** B2
Warsaw *Ill., U.S.A.* 40°22N 91°26W **310** D5
Warsaw *Ind., U.S.A.* 41°14N 85°51W **311** C11
Warsaw *Ky., U.S.A.* 38°47N 84°54W **311** F12
Warsaw *Mo., U.S.A.* 38°15N 93°23W **310** F3
Warsaw *N.Y., U.S.A.* 42°45N 78°8W **312** D6
Warsaw *Ohio, U.S.A.* 40°20N 82°0W **312** F3
Warsaw Chopin ✈ **(WAW)** *Poland* 52°9N 20°59E **143** B1
Warshiikh *Somalia* 2°28N 45°55E **267** D6
Warstein *Germany* 51°26N 8°22E **178** D4
Warszawa *Poland* 52°14N 21°0E **143** B2
Warta *Poland* 51°43N 18°38E **185** G5
Warta → *Poland* 52°35N 14°39E **185** F1
Wartenberg *Germany* 52°34N 13°31E **115** A4
Wartenburg = Barczewo *Poland* 53°50N 20°42E **184** E7
Warthbrücken = Koło *Poland* 52°14N 18°40E **185** F5
Warthe = Warta → *Poland* 52°35N 14°39E **185** F1
Warthen *U.S.A.* 33°6N 82°48W **316** B7
Warthenau = Zawiercie *Poland* 50°30N 19°24E **185** H6
Waru *Indonesia* 3°30S 130°36E **231** E8
Warud *India* 21°30N 78°16E **244** D4
Warumungu ✪ *Australia* 19°15S 134°44E **280** B1
Warwick *Queens., Australia* 28°10S 152°1E **281** D5
Warwick *Warks., U.K.* 52°18N 1°35W **169** E6
Warwick *Ga., U.S.A.* 31°50N 83°57W **316** D6
Warwick *N.Y., U.S.A.* 41°16N 74°22W **313** E10
Warwick *R.I., U.S.A.* 41°42N 71°28W **313** E13
Warwickshire □ *U.K.* 52°14N 1°38W **169** E6
Wasaga Beach *Canada* 44°31N 80°1W **312** B4
Wasagaming *Canada* 50°39N 99°58W **297** C9
Wasatch Ra. *U.S.A.* 40°0N 111°30W **304** F8
Wasbank *S. Africa* 28°15S 30°9E **271** C5
Wasco *Calif., U.S.A.* 35°36N 119°20W **307** K7
Wasco *Oreg., U.S.A.* 45°36N 120°42W **304** D3
Wase *Nigeria* 9°4N 9°54E **263** D6
Waseca *U.S.A.* 44°5N 93°30W **308** C7
Wasekamio L. *Canada* 56°45N 108°45W **297** B7
Wasgomuwa △ *Sri Lanka* 7°45N 81°0E **245** L5
Wash, The *U.K.* 52°58N 0°20E **168** E8
Washago *Canada* 44°45N 79°20W **312** B5
Washburn *Ill., U.S.A.* 40°55N 89°17W **310** D7
Washburn *N. Dak., U.S.A.* 47°17N 101°2W **308** B3
Washburn *Wis., U.S.A.* 46°40N 90°54W **308** B8
Washim *India* 20°3N 77°0E **244** D3
Washington *Bonaire* 12°17N 68°23W **322** h
Washington *Tyne & W., U.K.* 54°55N 1°30W **168** C6
Washington *D.C., U.S.A.* 38°53N 77°2W **143** B2
Washington *Ga., U.S.A.* 33°44N 82°44W **316** B7
Washington *Ill., U.S.A.* 40°42N 89°24W **310** D7
Washington *Ind., U.S.A.* 38°40N 87°10W **311** F9
Washington *Iowa, U.S.A.* 41°18N 91°42W **310** C5
Washington *Mo., U.S.A.* 38°33N 91°1W **310** F5
Washington *N.C., U.S.A.* 35°33N 77°3W **315** D16
Washington *N.J., U.S.A.* 40°46N 74°59W **313** F10
Washington *Pa., U.S.A.* 40°10N 80°15W **312** F4
Washington *Utah, U.S.A.* 37°8N 113°31W **305** H7
Washington □ *U.S.A.* 47°30N 120°30W **304** C3
Washington, Mt. *U.S.A.* 44°16N 71°18W **313** B13
Washington Court House *U.S.A.* 39°32N 83°26W **311** E13
Washington Dulles Int. ✈ **(IAD)** *U.S.A.* 38°57N 77°27W **309** F15
Washington Heights *U.S.A.* 40°51N 73°56W **132** A2
Washington I. *U.S.A.* 45°23N 86°54W **308** C10
Washington Land *Greenland* 80°30N 66°0W **154** A4
Washington Monument *Washington, D.C., U.S.A.* **143** b1
Washington Park *U.S.A.* 41°47N 87°36W **119** C3
Washington Ronald Reagan Nat. ✈ **(DCA)** *U.S.A.* 38°51N 77°2W **143** B2
Washington Slagbaai △ *Bonaire* 12°16N 68°23W **322** h
Washougal *U.S.A.* 45°35N 122°21W **306** E4
Washpool △ *Australia* 29°22S 152°20E **281** D5
Washuk *Pakistan* 27°42N 64°45E **240** D2
Wasian *Indonesia* 1°47S 133°19E **231** E8
Wasilków *Poland* 53°12N 23°13E **185** E10
Wasilla *U.S.A.* 61°35N 149°26W **303** F10
Wasini Marine ⌓ *Kenya* 4°33S 39°14E **268** C4
Wasior *Indonesia* 2°43S 134°30E **231** E8
Wasiri *Indonesia* 7°30S 126°30E **231** F7
Wāsiţ □ *Iraq* 32°50N 45°50E **213** F11
Wasjabo *Suriname* 5°13N 57°11W **329** B6
Waskaganish *Canada* 51°30N 78°40W **298** B4
Waskaiowaka L. *Canada* 56°33N 96°23W **297** B9
Waskesiu Lake *Canada* 53°55N 106°5W **297** C7
Wassaw I. *U.S.A.* 31°53N 80°58W **316** D9
Wassaw Sd. *U.S.A.* 31°55N 80°55W **316** D9
Wasserburg *Germany* 48°3N 12°14E **179** G8
Wasserkuppe *Germany* 50°29N 9°55E **178** E5
Wassy *France* 48°30N 4°58E **173** D11
Wasu *Papua N. G.* 5°58S 147°12E **286** C4
Wasua *Papua N. G.* 8°18S 142°52E **286** D1
Wasur △ *Indonesia* 8°41S 140°44E **231** F10
Waswanipi *Canada* 49°40N 76°29W **298** C4
Waswanipi, L. *Canada* 49°35N 76°40W **298** C4
Wat Pho *Bangkok, Thailand* **113** b1
Watagans △ *Australia* 33°0S 151°28E **283** B9
Watam *Papua N. G.* 3°55S 144°33E **286** B3
Watampone *Indonesia* 4°29S 120°25E **231** E6
Watamu *Kenya* 3°23S 40°0E **268** C5
Watansoppeng *Indonesia* 4°10S 119°56E **235** C5
Watarrka △ *Australia* 24°20S 131°30E **278** D5
Watauga *U.S.A.* 32°51N 97°15W **120** A2
Watee *Solomon Is.* 10°30S 162°2E **287** N12
Watenstadt-Salzgitter = Salzgitter *Germany* 52°9N 10°19E **178** C6
Water of Leith → *U.K.* 55°59N 3°10W **121** B1
Water Park Pt. *Australia* 22°56S 150°47E **280** C5
Water Tower Place *Chicago, U.S.A.* **119** a2
Water Valley *U.S.A.* 34°10N 89°38W **315** D10
Waterberg Plateau ⌓ *Namibia* 20°25S 17°18E **270** B2
Waterberge *S. Africa* 24°10S 28°0E **271** B4
Waterbury *Conn., U.S.A.* 41°33N 73°3W **313** E11
Waterbury *Vt., U.S.A.* 44°20N 72°46W **313** B12
Waterbury L. *Canada* 58°10N 104°22W **297** B8
Waterdown *Canada* 43°20N 79°53W **312** C5
Wateree → *U.S.A.* 33°45N 80°37W **316** B9
Waterford *Ont., Canada* 42°56N 80°17W **312** D4
Waterford *Waterford, Ireland* 52°15N 7°8W **166** D4
Waterford *Calif., U.S.A.* 37°38N 120°46W **306** H6
Waterford *Mich., U.S.A.* 42°45N 83°32W **311** B13
Waterford *Pa., U.S.A.* 41°57N 79°59W **312** E5
Waterford *Wis., U.S.A.* 42°46N 88°13W **311** B8
Waterford □ *Ireland* 52°10N 7°40W **166** D4
Waterford Harbour *Ireland* 52°8N 6°58W **166** D5
Watergraafsmeer *Neths.* 52°21N 4°56E **112** A2
Waterhen L. *Canada* 52°10N 99°40W **297** C9
Waterland *Neths.* 52°26N 4°58E **112** A2
Waterloo *Belgium* 50°43N 4°25E **116** B2
Waterloo *Ont., Canada* 43°30N 80°32W **312** C4
Waterloo *Qué., Canada* 45°22N 72°32W **313** A12
Waterloo *S. Leone* 8°26N 13°8W **262** D2
Waterloo *Trin. & Tob.* 10°28N 61°28W **323** t
Waterloo *London, U.K.* **125** b4
Waterloo *Ill., U.S.A.* 38°20N 90°9W **310** F6
Waterloo *Ind., U.S.A.* 41°26N 85°1W **311** C11
Waterloo *Iowa, U.S.A.* 42°30N 92°21W **310** B4
Waterloo *N.Y., U.S.A.* 42°54N 76°52W **312** D8
Waterloo *Wis., U.S.A.* 43°11N 88°59W **310** A8
Waterman *U.S.A.* 41°46N 88°47W **311** C8
Watermeal-Boitsfort *Belgium* 50°48N 4°25E **116** B2
Watersmeet *U.S.A.* 46°16N 89°11W **308** B9
Waterton Lakes △ *Canada* 48°45N 115°0W **296** D6
Watertown *Conn., U.S.A.* 41°36N 73°7W **313** E11
Watertown *Fla., U.S.A.* 30°11N 82°36W **316** E7
Watertown *Mass., U.S.A.* 42°22N 71°10W **116** A1
Watertown *N.Y., U.S.A.* 43°59N 75°55W **313** C9
Watertown *S. Dak., U.S.A.* 44°54N 97°7W **308** C5
Watertown *Wis., U.S.A.* 43°12N 88°43W **311** A8
Waterval-Boven = Emgwenya *S. Africa* 25°40S 30°18E **271** C5
Waterville *Qué., Canada* 45°16N 71°54W **313** A13
Waterville *Maine, U.S.A.* 44°33N 69°38W **309** C19
Waterville *N.Y., U.S.A.* 42°56N 75°23W **313** D9
Waterville *Pa., U.S.A.* 41°19N 77°21W **312** E7
Waterville *Wash., U.S.A.* 47°39N 120°4W **304** C3
Watervliet *Mich., U.S.A.* 42°11N 86°18W **311** B10
Watervliet *N.Y., U.S.A.* 42°44N 73°42W **313** D11
Wates *Indonesia* 7°51S 110°10E **235** D4
Watford *Ont., Canada* 42°57N 81°53W **312** D3
Watford *Herts., U.K.* 51°40N 0°24W **169** F7
Watford City *U.S.A.* 47°48N 103°17W **308** B2
Wathaman → *Canada* 57°16N 102°59W **297** B8
Wathaman L. *Canada* 56°58N 103°44W **297** B8
Watheroo *Australia* 30°15S 116°5E **279** F2
Watheroo △ *Australia* 30°19S 115°48E **279** F2
Wating *China* 35°40N 106°38E **226** G4
Watîr, W. → *Egypt* 29°0N 34°40E **251** K5
Watkins Glen *U.S.A.* 42°23N 76°52W **312** D8
Watkinsville *U.S.A.* 33°52N 83°25W **316** B6
Watling I. = San Salvador I. *Bahamas* 24°0N 74°30W **321** B5
Watom I. *Papua N. G.* 4°7S 152°4E **286** C7
Watonga *U.S.A.* 35°51N 98°25W **314** D5
Watrous *Sask., Canada* 51°40N 105°25W **297** C7
Watrous *N. Mex., U.S.A.* 35°48N 104°59W **305** J11
Watsa *Dem. Rep. of the Congo* 3°4N 29°30E **268** B2
Watseka *U.S.A.* 40°47N 87°44W **311** D9
Watsi Kenga *Dem. Rep. of the Congo* 0°49S 20°34E **264** C4
Watson *Canada* 52°10N 104°30W **297** C8
Watson Lake *Canada* 60°6N 128°49W **296** A3
Watsonia *Australia* 37°43S 145°6E **128** A2
Watsontown *U.S.A.* 41°5N 76°52W **312** E8
Watsonville *U.S.A.* 36°55N 121°45W **306** J5
Watt Mt. *Dominica* 15°19N 61°19W **323** k
Wattiwarriganna Cr. → *Australia* 28°57S 136°10E **281** D2
Watts *U.S.A.* 33°56N 118°15W **126** C3
Wattwil *Switz.* 47°18N 9°6E **179** H5
Watu *Dem. Rep. of the Congo* 3°18S 20°3E **264** C4
Watuata = Batuata *Indonesia* 6°12S 122°42E **231** F6
Watubela, Kepulauan *Indonesia* 4°28S 131°35E **231** E8
Watubela Is. = Watubela, Kepulauan *Indonesia* 4°28S 131°35E **231** E8
Wau *Papua N. G.* 7°21S 146°47E **286** D4
Wau *South Sudan* 7°45N 28°1E **257** F2
Waubamik *Canada* 45°27N 80°1W **312** A4
Waubay *U.S.A.* 45°20N 97°18W **308** C5
Waubra *Australia* 37°21S 143°39E **282** D5
Wauchope *N.S.W., Australia* 31°28S 152°45E **283** A10
Wauchope *N. Terr., Australia* 20°36S 134°15E **280** C1
Wauchula *U.S.A.* 27°33N 81°49W **317** H8
Waukarlycarly, L. *Australia* 21°18S 121°56E **278** D3
Waukeenah *U.S.A.* 30°25N 83°57W **316** E6
Waukegan *U.S.A.* 42°22N 87°50W **311** B9
Waukesha *U.S.A.* 43°1N 88°14W **311** B8
Waukon *U.S.A.* 43°16N 91°29W **308** D8
Waunakee *U.S.A.* 43°11N 89°27W **310** A7
Waupaca *U.S.A.* 44°21N 89°5W **308** C9
Waupun *U.S.A.* 43°38N 88°44W **308** D9
Waurika *U.S.A.* 34°10N 98°0W **314** D6
Wausau *Fla., U.S.A.* 30°38N 85°35W **316** E4
Wausau *Wis., U.S.A.* 44°58N 89°38W **308** C9
Wauseon *U.S.A.* 41°33N 84°8W **311** C12
Wautoma *U.S.A.* 44°4N 89°18W **308** C9
Wauwatosa *U.S.A.* 43°2N 88°0W **311** A9
Wave Hill = Kalkarindji *Australia* 17°30S 130°47E **278** C5
Wave Rock ⌓ *Australia* 32°26S 118°53E **279** F2
Waveland *U.S.A.* 39°53N 87°3W **311** E9
Waveney → *U.K.* 52°35N 1°39E **169** E9
Waverley *N.S.W., Australia* 33°53S 151°15E **139** B2
Waverley *N.Z.* 39°46S 174°37E **284** F3
Waverley *Gauteng, S. Africa* 26°7S 28°4E **123** A2
Waverley *Mass., U.S.A.* 42°23N 71°10W **116** A1
Waverley Station *Edinburgh, U.K.* **121** b3
Waverly *Ala., U.S.A.* 32°44N 85°35W **316** C4
Waverly *Fla., U.S.A.* 27°59N 81°37W **317** H8
Waverly *Ga., U.S.A.* 31°6N 81°43W **316** D8
Waverly *Ill., U.S.A.* 39°36N 89°57W **310** E7
Waverly *Iowa, U.S.A.* 42°44N 92°29W **310** B4
Waverly *Mo., U.S.A.* 39°13N 93°31W **310** E3
Waverly *N.Y., U.S.A.* 42°1N 76°32W **313** E8
Waverly Hall *U.S.A.* 32°41N 84°44W **316** C5
Wavre *Belgium* 50°43N 4°38E **170** D4
Wâw = Wau *South Sudan* 7°45N 28°1E **257** F2
Waw *Burma* 17°28N 96°41E **241** G6
Wāw al Kabīr *Libya* 25°20N 16°43E **258** C3
Wāw an Nāmūs *Libya* 24°55N 17°46E **258** D3
Wawa *Ont., Canada* 47°59N 84°47W **298** C3
Wawa *Nigeria* 9°54N 4°27E **263** D5
Wawa *Sudan* 20°30N 30°22E **256** C3
Wawanesa *Canada* 49°36N 99°40W **297** D9
Wawasee, L. *U.S.A.* 41°24N 85°42W **311** C11
Wawer *Poland* 52°13N 21°8E **143** B2
Wawoi → *Papua N. G.* 7°48S 143°16E **286** D2
Wawona *U.S.A.* 37°32N 119°39W **306** H7
Wawrzyszew *Poland* 52°17N 20°53E **143** B1
Waxahachie *U.S.A.* 32°24N 96°51W **314** E6
Waxxari *China* 38°42N 87°12E **217** E11
Way, L. *Australia* 26°45S 120°16E **279** E3
Way Kambas △ *Indonesia* 4°54S 105°43E **234** C3
Waya *Fiji* 17°19S 177°10E **287** A1
Waycross *U.S.A.* 31°13N 82°21W **316** D7
Wayi *South Sudan* 5°8N 30°10E **257** F3
Wayland *Mich., U.S.A.* 42°40N 85°39W **311** B11
Wayland *N.Y., U.S.A.* 42°34N 77°35W **312** D7
Wayne *Nebr., U.S.A.* 42°14N 97°1W **308** D5
Wayne *W. Va., U.S.A.* 38°13N 82°27W **309** F12
Wayne City *U.S.A.* 38°21N 88°35W **311** F8
Wayne County, Detroit ✈ **(DTW)** *U.S.A.* 42°13N 83°21W **311** B13
Wayne Lakes *U.S.A.* 40°1N 84°40W **311** D12
Waynesboro *Ga., U.S.A.* 33°6N 82°1W **316** B7
Waynesboro *Miss., U.S.A.* 31°40N 88°39W **315** F10
Waynesboro *Pa., U.S.A.* 39°45N 77°35W **309** F15
Waynesboro *Va., U.S.A.* 38°4N 78°53W **309** F14
Waynesburg *U.S.A.* 39°54N 80°11W **309** F13
Waynesville *Mo., U.S.A.* 37°50N 92°12W **310** G4
Waynesville *N.C., U.S.A.* 35°28N 82°58W **315** D13
Waynesville *Ohio, U.S.A.* 39°32N 84°5W **311** E12
Waynoka *U.S.A.* 36°35N 98°53W **314** C5
Wayside *U.S.A.* 33°4N 83°37W **316** B6
Waza *Afghan.* 33°22N 69°26E **240** B3
Waza △ *Cameroon* 11°15N 14°38E **259** F2
Wazikhwah *Afghan.* 32°11N 68°21E **240** B3
Wāzin *Libya* 31°58N 10°40E **258** B2
Wazirabad *Delhi, India* 28°43N 77°13E **120** A2
Wazirabad *Pakistan* 32°30N 74°8E **242** C6
Waziristan *Pakistan* 33°0N 70°0E **242** C4
Wazīrīya *Iraq* 33°22N 44°22E **113** A2
Wazirpur *India* 28°41N 77°10E **120** A2
Wda → *Poland* 53°25N 18°29E **184** E5
We *Indonesia* 5°51N 95°18E **234** A1
Wé *N. Cal.* 20°55S 167°16E **288** d
Weald, The *U.K.* 51°4N 0°20E **169** F8
Wealdstone *U.K.* 51°35N 0°17W **125** A1
Weam *Papua N. G.* 8°37S 141°8E **286** E1
Wear → *U.K.* 54°55N 1°23W **168** C6
Weatherford *Okla., U.S.A.* 35°32N 98°43W **314** D5
Weatherford *Tex., U.S.A.* 32°46N 97°48W **314** E6
Weaubleau *U.S.A.* 37°54N 93°32W **310** G3
Weaverville *U.S.A.* 40°44N 122°56W **304** F2
Webb City *U.S.A.* 37°9N 94°28W **308** G6
Webequie *Canada* 52°59N 87°21W **298** B2
Weber *N.Z.* 40°24S 176°20E **284** G5
Weber Basin *Indonesia* 6°0S 131°0E **276** B5
Webo = Nyaake *Liberia* 4°52N 7°37W **262** E3
Webster *Mass., U.S.A.* 42°3N 71°53W **313** D13
Webster *N.Y., U.S.A.* 43°13N 77°26W **312** C7
Webster *S. Dak., U.S.A.* 45°20N 97°31W **308** C5
Webster City *U.S.A.* 42°28N 93°49W **310** B3
Webster Springs *U.S.A.* 38°29N 80°25W **309** F13
Webuye *Kenya* 0°37N 34°46E **268** B3
Weda *Indonesia* 0°21N 127°50E **231** D7
Weda, Teluk *Indonesia* 0°20N 128°0E **231** D7
Weddell Abyssal Plain *S. Ocean* 65°0S 20°0W **151** C2
Weddell I. *Falk. Is.* 51°50S 61°0W **153** f
Weddell Sea *Antarctica* 72°30S 40°0W **151** D1
Wedderburn *Australia* 36°26S 143°33E **282** D5
Weddin Mts. △ *Australia* 33°59S 148°0E **283** C8
Wedding *Germany* 52°32N 13°21E **115** A3
Wedel *Germany* 53°34N 9°42E **178** B5
Wedemark *Germany* 52°32N 9°43E **178** C5
Wedgeport *Canada* 43°44N 65°59W **299** D6
Wednesday I. *Australia* 10°31S 142°16E **286** F2
Wedowee *U.S.A.* 33°19N 85°29W **316** B4
Wedza *Zimbabwe* 18°40S 31°33E **269** F3
Wee Waa *Australia* 30°11S 149°26E **281** E4
Weed *U.S.A.* 41°25N 122°23W **304** F2
Weed Heights *U.S.A.* 38°59N 119°13W **306** G7
Weedsport *U.S.A.* 43°2N 76°33W **313** C8
Weedville *U.S.A.* 41°17N 78°30W **312** E6
Weehawken *New York, U.S.A.* **132** b1
Weeki Wachee *U.S.A.* 28°32N 82°35W **317** G7
Weel Shimbirro *Somalia* 2°23N 44°14E **267** D5
Weenen *S. Africa* 28°48S 30°7E **271** C5
Weener *Germany* 53°9N 7°20E **178** B3
Weerribben △ *Neths.* 52°47N 5°58E **170** B5
Weert *Neths.* 51°15N 5°43E **170** C5
Weesp *Neths.* 52°18N 5°2E **112** B3
Węgierska-Górka *Poland* 49°36N 19°7E **185** J6
Węgliniec *Poland* 51°18N 15°10E **185** G2
Węgorzewo *Poland* 54°13N 21°43E **184** D8
Węgorzyno *Poland* 53°32N 15°33E **184** E2
Węgrów *Poland* 52°24N 22°0E **185** F9
Wei He → *Hebei, China* 36°10N 115°45E **226** F8
Wei He → *Shaanxi, China* 34°38N 110°15E **226** G6
Weichang *China* 41°58N 117°49E **227** D9
Weichuan *China* 34°20N 113°59E **226** G7
Weida *Germany* 50°46N 12°3E **178** E8
Weiden *Germany* 49°41N 12°10E **179** F8
Weidling *Austria* 48°17N 16°18E **142** A1
Weidlingbach *Austria* 48°16N 16°15E **142** A1
Weifang *China* 36°44N 119°7E **227** F10
Weihai *China* 37°30N 122°6E **227** F12
Weihui *China* 35°25N 114°3E **226** G8
Weil *Germany* 47°35N 7°37E **179** H3
Weilburg *Germany* 50°28N 8°17E **178** E4
Weilheim *Germany* 47°50N 11°9E **179** H7
Weimar *Germany* 50°58N 11°19E **178** E7
Weinan *China* 34°31N 109°29E **226** G5
Weingarten *Germany* 49°3N 8°31E **179** F4
Weinheim *Germany* 49°32N 8°39E **179** F4
Weining *China* 26°50N 104°17E **228** D5
Weipa *Australia* 12°40S 141°50E **280** A3
Weir → *Queens., Australia* 28°20S 149°50E **281** D4
Weir → *Man., Canada* 56°54N 93°21W **297** B10
Weir, L. *U.S.A.* 29°0N 81°57W **317** F8
Weir River *Canada* 56°49N 94°6W **297** B10
Weirsdale *U.S.A.* 28°59N 81°55W **317** G8
Weirton *U.S.A.* 40°24N 80°35W **312** F4
Weiser *U.S.A.* 44°15N 116°58W **304** D5
Weishan *Shandong, China* 34°47N 117°5E **227** G9
Weishan *Yunnan, China* 25°12N 100°20E **228** E3
Weishan Hu *China* 34°35N 117°14E **227** G9
Weissenburg *Germany* 49°2N 10°58E **179** F6
Weissenfels *Germany* 51°11N 12°0E **178** D7
Weissensee *Germany* 52°33N 13°27E **115** A3
Weisskirchen = Hranice *Czechia* 49°34N 17°45E **181** B10
Weisswasser *Germany* 51°30N 14°36E **178** D10
Weistritz = Bystrzyca → *Dolnośląskie, Poland* 51°12N 16°55E **185** G3
Weistritz = Bystrzyca → *Lubelskie, Poland* 51°21N 22°46E **185** G9
Weitra *Austria* 48°41N 14°54E **180** C7
Weixi *China* 27°10N 99°10E **228** D2
Weixin *China* 27°48N 105°3E **228** D5
Weiyuan *Gansu, China* 35°7N 104°10E **226** G3
Weiyuan *Sichuan, China* 29°35N 104°36E **228** C5
Weiz *Austria* 47°13N 15°39E **180** D8
Weizhou Dao *China* 21°0N 109°5E **228** G7
Wejherowo *Poland* 54°35N 18°12E **184** D5
Wekoewa Pt. *Bonaire* 12°13N 68°24W **322** h
Wekusko L. *Canada* 54°40N 99°50W **297** C9
Welch *U.S.A.* 37°26N 81°35W **309** G13
Welchman Hall *Barbados* 13°11N 59°34W **323** r
Weldya *Ethiopia* 11°50N 39°34E **257** E4
Welega *Ethiopia* 9°25N 34°20E **257** F3
Welford △ *Australia* 25°5S 143°16E **280** D3
Weligama *Sri Lanka* 5°58N 80°25E **245** M5
Welkite *Ethiopia* 8°15N 37°42E **257** F4
Welkom *S. Africa* 28°0S 26°46E **270** C4
Welland *Canada* 43°0N 79°15W **312** D5
Welland → *U.K.* 52°51N 0°5W **169** E7
Wellawaya *Sri Lanka* 6°44N 81°6E **245** L5
Welles Harbor *Midway Is.* 28°13N 177°25W **302** c
Wellesley Hills *U.S.A.* 42°18N 71°16W **116** B1
Wellesley Is. *Australia* 16°42S 139°30E **280** B2
Wellesley Islands ✪ *Australia* 16°32S 139°23E **280** B2
Welling *U.K.* 51°27N 0°6E **125** B4
Wellingborough *U.K.* 52°19N 0°41W **169** E7
Wellington *N.S.W., Australia* 32°35S 148°59E **283** B8
Wellington *Ont., Canada* 43°57N 77°20W **312** C7
Wellington *N.Z.* 41°19S 174°46E **284** H3
Wellington *Western Cape, S. Africa* 33°38S 19°1E **270** D2
Wellington *Somst., U.K.* 50°58N 3°13W **169** G4
Wellington *Telford & Wrekin, U.K.* 52°42N 2°30W **169** E5
Wellington *Colo., U.S.A.* 40°42N 105°0W **304** F11
Wellington *Fla., U.S.A.* 26°39N 80°15W **317** J9
Wellington *Kans., U.S.A.* 37°16N 97°24W **308** G5
Wellington *Mass., U.S.A.* 42°24N 71°5W **116** A2
Wellington *Mo., U.S.A.* 39°8N 93°59W **310** E3
Wellington *Nev., U.S.A.* 38°45N 119°23W **306** G7
Wellington *Ohio, U.S.A.* 41°10N 82°13W **312** E2
Wellington *Tex., U.S.A.* 34°51N 100°13W **314** D4
Wellington □ *N.Z.* 41°0S 175°30E **284** H4
Wellington, I. *Chile* 49°30S 75°0W **336** C2
Wellington, L. *Australia* 38°6S 147°20E **283** E7
Wellington Chan. *Canada* 75°0N 93°0W **295** C13
Wellman *U.S.A.* 41°28N 91°50W **310** C5
Wells *Somst., U.K.* 51°13N 2°39W **169** F5
Wells *Maine, U.S.A.* 43°20N 70°35W **313** C14
Wells *N.Y., U.S.A.* 43°24N 74°17W **313** C10
Wells *Nev., U.S.A.* 41°7N 114°58W **304** F6
Wells, L. *Australia* 26°44S 123°15E **279** E3
Wells, Mt. *Australia* 17°25S 127°8E **278** C4
Wells Fargo Center *Los Angeles, U.S.A.* **127** b1
Wells Gray ⌓ *Canada* 52°30N 120°15W **296** C4
Wells-next-the-Sea *U.K.* 52°57N 0°51E **168** E8
Wells River *U.S.A.* 44°9N 72°4W **313** B12
Wellsboro *U.S.A.* 41°45N 77°18W **312** E7
Wellsburg *U.S.A.* 40°16N 80°37W **312** F4
Wellsford *N.Z.* 36°16S 174°32E **284** C3
Wellston = Warner Robins *U.S.A.* 32°37N 83°36W **316** C6
Wellsville *Mo., U.S.A.* 39°4N 91°34W **310** E5
Wellsville *N.Y., U.S.A.* 42°7N 77°57W **312** D7
Wellsville *Ohio, U.S.A.* 40°36N 80°39W **312** F4
Wellsville *Utah, U.S.A.* 41°38N 111°56W **304** F8
Wellton *U.S.A.* 32°40N 114°8W **305** K6
Welmel, Wabi → *Ethiopia* 5°38N 40°47E **257** F5
Welo *Ethiopia* 11°50N 39°48E **257** E4
Welo *Somalia* 9°25N 48°55E **267** C6
Wels *Austria* 48°9N 14°1E **180** C7
Welshpool *Vic., Australia* 38°42S 146°26E **283** E7
Welshpool *Powys, U.K.* 52°39N 3°8W **169** E4
Weltevreden Park *S. Africa* 26°7S 27°56E **123** A1
Welungen = Wieluń *Poland* 51°15N 18°34E **185** G5
Welwitschia = Khorixas *Namibia* 20°16S 14°59E **270** B1
Welwyn Garden City *U.K.* 51°48N 0°12W **169** F7
Wem *U.K.* 52°52N 2°44W **168** E5
Wembere → *Tanzania* 4°10S 34°15E **268** C3
Wembley *U.K.* 51°33N 0°17W **125** A2
Wemindji *Canada* 53°0N 78°49W **298** B4
Wemmel *Belgium* 50°55N 4°18E **116** A1
Wemmer Pan *S. Africa* 26°13S 28°3E **123** B2
Wemyss *Canada* 44°52N 76°23W **313** B8
Wen Xian *Gansu, China* 32°43N 104°36E **226** H3
Wen Xian *Henan, China* 34°55N 113°5E **226** G7
Wenatchee *U.S.A.* 47°25N 120°19W **304** C3
Wenceslas Square = Vaclavské náměstí *Prague, Czechia* **135** b2
Wenchang *China* 19°38N 110°42E **229** a
Wencheng *China* 27°46N 120°4E **229** D13
Wenchi *Ghana* 7°46N 2°8W **262** D4
Wenchow = Wenzhou *China* 28°0N 120°38E **229** D13
Wenchuan *China* 31°22N 103°35E **228** B4
Wenden *U.S.A.* 33°49N 113°33W **307** M13
Wendeng *China* 37°15N 122°5E **227** F12
Wendenschloss *Germany* 52°24N 13°35E **115** B4
Wendesi *Indonesia* 2°30S 134°17E **231** E8
Wendo *Ethiopia* 6°40N 38°27E **257** F4
Wendover *U.S.A.* 40°44N 114°2W **304** F6
Weng'an *China* 27°5N 107°25E **228** D6
Wengcheng *China* 24°22N 113°50E **229** E9
Wengen *Switz.* 46°37N 7°55E **173** F14
Wengyuan *China* 24°20N 114°9E **229** E10
Wenling *China* 28°21N 121°20E **229** C13
Wenlock → *Australia* 12°2S 141°55E **286** G1
Wennington *U.K.* 51°30N 0°12E **125** A5
Weno *Pac. Oc.* 7°27N 151°52E **287** T18
Wenona *U.S.A.* 41°3N 89°3W **310** C7
Wenshan *China* 23°20N 104°18E **228** F5
Wenshang *China* 35°45N 116°30E **226** G9
Wenshui *China* 37°26N 112°1E **226** F7
Wensleydale *U.K.* 54°17N 2°0W **168** C6
Wensu *China* 41°15N 80°10E **217** D10
Wensum → *U.K.* 52°40N 1°15E **168** E8
Wentworth *Australia* 34°2S 141°54E **282** C4
Wentzel L. *Canada* 59°2N 114°28W **296** B6
Wentzville *U.S.A.* 38°49N 90°51W **310** F6
Wenut *Indonesia* 3°11S 133°19E **231** E8
Wenxi *China* 35°20N 111°10E **226** G6
Wenzhou *China* 28°0N 120°38E **229** D13
Weott *U.S.A.* 40°20N 123°55W **304** F2
Wepener *S. Africa* 29°42S 27°3E **270** C4
Werda *Botswana* 25°24S 23°15E **270** C3
Werdau *Germany* 50°44N 12°22E **178** E8
Werder *Ethiopia* 6°58N 45°1E **267** C6
Werder *Brandenburg, Germany* 52°23N 12°55E **178** C8
Werdohl *Germany* 51°15N 7°46E **178** D3
Wereilu *Ethiopia* 10°40N 39°28E **257** E4
Weri *Indonesia* 3°10S 132°38E **231** E8
Werneck *Germany* 49°58N 10°5E **179** F6
Werneuchen *Germany* 52°38N 13°44E **115** A5
Wernigerode *Germany* 51°50N 10°47E **178** D6
Werra → *Germany* 51°24N 9°39E **178** D5
Werribee *Australia* 37°54S 144°40E **282** D6
Werrikimbe △ *Australia* 31°11S 152°15E **283** A10
Werrimull *Australia* 34°25S 141°38E **282** C4
Werris Creek *Australia* 31°18S 150°38E **283** A9
Werschetz = Vršac *Serbia* 45°8N 21°20E **182** E6
Wertach → *Germany* 48°22N 10°54E **179** G6
Wertheim *Germany* 49°45N 9°32E **179** F5
Wertingen *Germany* 48°33N 10°41E **179** G6
Wesel *Germany* 51°39N 6°37E **178** D2
Weser → *Germany* 53°36N 8°28E **178** B4
Weserbergland *Germany* 52°12N 9°7E **178** C5
Weserbergland Schaumburg Hameln ⌓ *Germany* 52°8N 9°20E **178** C5
Wesermünde = Bremerhaven *Germany* 53°33N 8°36E **178** B4
Weslaco *U.S.A.* 26°10N 97°58W **314** H6
Weslemkoon L. *Canada* 45°2N 77°25W **312** A7
Wesley *Dominica* 15°33N 61°18W **323** k
Wesleyville *Nfld. & L., Canada* 49°9N 53°33W **299** C9
Wesleyville *Pa., U.S.A.* 42°9N 80°1W **312** D4
Wessel, C. *Australia* 10°59S 136°46E **280** A2
Wessel Is. *Australia* 11°10S 136°45E **280** A2
Wesselburen *Germany* 54°13N 8°54E **178** A4
Wessex *U.K.* 51°0N 2°0W **169** F5
Wessington Springs *U.S.A.* 44°5N 98°34W **308** C4
West *U.S.A.* 31°48N 97°6W **314** F6
West → *U.S.A.* 42°52N 72°33W **313** D12
West Allis *U.S.A.* 43°1N 88°0W **311** B9
West Antarctica *Antarctica* 80°0S 90°0W **151** D15
West Baines → *Australia* 15°38S 129°59E **278** C4
West Bank □ *Asia* 32°6N 35°13E **251** F6
West Bend *U.S.A.* 43°25N 88°11W **308** D9
West Bengal = Paschimbanga □ *India* 23°0N 88°0E **243** H13
West Berkshire □ *U.K.* 51°25N 1°17W **169** F6
West Beskids = Západné Beskydy *Europe* 49°30N 19°0E **181** B12
West Branch *U.S.A.* 44°17N 84°14W **309** C11
West Branch Susquehanna → *U.S.A.* 40°53N 76°48W **313** F8
West Bromwich *U.K.* 52°32N 1°59W **169** E6
West Burra *U.K.* 60°5N 1°21W **167** A7
West Canada Cr. → *U.S.A.* 43°1N 74°58W **313** C10
West Caroline Basin *Pac. Oc.* 4°0N 138°0E **288** G5
West Carrollton *U.S.A.* 39°40N 84°17W **311** E12
West Chazy *U.S.A.* 44°49N 73°28W **313** B11
West Chester *U.S.A.* 39°58N 75°36W **313** G9
West Chicago *U.S.A.* 41°53N 88°12W **311** C8
West Coast □ *N.Z.* 43°15S 170°30E **285** D5
West Coast ⌓ *Namibia* 21°53S 14°14E **270** B1
West Coast △ *S. Africa* 33°13S 18°0E **270** D2
West Columbia *S.C., U.S.A.* 33°59N 81°4W **316** B8
West Columbia *Tex., U.S.A.* 29°9N 95°39W **314** G7
West Covina *U.S.A.* 34°4N 117°54W **307** L9
West Des Moines *U.S.A.* 41°35N 93°43W **310** C3
West Don → *Canada* 43°44N 79°24W **141** A2
West Drayton *U.K.* 51°30N 0°28W **125** A1
West Dunbartonshire □ *U.K.* 55°59N 4°30W **167** F4
West End *Bahamas* 26°41N 78°58W **320** A4
West End *Boston, U.S.A.* **116** b1
West End Village *Anguilla* 18°10N 63°10W **322** a
West Falkland *Falk. Is.* 51°40S 60°0W **153** f
West Fargo *U.S.A.* 46°52N 96°54W **308** B5
West Fiji Basin *Pac. Oc.* 17°0S 173°0E **288** J9
West Fjord = Vestfjorden *Norway* 67°55N 14°0E **160** C16
West Fork Trinity → *U.S.A.* 32°48N 96°54W **314** E6
West Frankfort *U.S.A.* 37°54N 88°55W **310** G8
West Grand L. *U.S.A.* 45°14N 67°51W **309** C20
West Green *U.S.A.* 31°37N 82°44W **316** D7
West Ham *U.K.* 51°31N 0°1E **125** A4
West Harrow *U.K.* 51°34N 0°21W **125** A1
West Hartford *U.S.A.* 41°45N 72°44W **313** E12
West Haven *U.S.A.* 41°17N 72°57W **313** E12
West Hazleton *U.S.A.* 40°58N 76°0W **313** F9
West Heath *U.K.* 51°29N 0°7E **125** B4
West Hill *Canada* 43°46N 79°10W **141** A3
West Hollywood *U.S.A.* 34°5N 118°21W **126** B2
West Hurley *U.S.A.* 41°59N 74°7W **313** E10
West I. *India* 13°35N 92°54E **245** H11
West Ice Shelf *Antarctica* 67°0S 85°0E **151** C7
West Indies *Cent. Amer.* 15°0N 65°0W **321** D7
West Jefferson *U.S.A.* 39°57N 83°17W **311** E13
West Jordan *U.S.A.* 40°36N 111°56W **304** F8
West Kavango □ *Namibia* 18°0S 18°30E **270** A2
West Kensington *London, U.K.* **125** c1
West Kilburn *London, U.K.* **125** b1
West Lafayette *U.S.A.* 40°27N 86°55W **311** D10
West Lamma Channel *Hong Kong, China* 22°14N 114°4E **122** B2
West Liberty *Iowa, U.S.A.* 41°34N 91°16W **310** C5
West Liberty *Ky., U.S.A.* 37°55N 83°16W **311** G13
West Liberty *Ohio, U.S.A.* 40°15N 83°45W **311** D13
West Linn *U.S.A.* 45°21N 122°36W **306** E4
West Lorne *Canada* 42°36N 81°36W **312** D3
West Los Angeles, Univ. of *U.S.A.* 34°7N 118°23W **126** C2
West Lothian □ *U.K.* 55°54N 3°36W **167** F5
West Lunga → *Zambia* 13°6S 24°39E **265** E4
West Lunga △ *Zambia* 12°49S 24°47E **265** E4
West MacDonnell △ *Australia* 23°38S 132°59E **278** D5
West Mariana Basin *Pac. Oc.* 15°0N 137°0E **288** F5
West Medford *U.S.A.* 42°25N 71°7W **116** A2
West Memphis *U.S.A.* 35°8N 90°10W **315** D9
West Miami *U.S.A.* 25°45N 80°17W **129** D1
West Midlands □ *U.K.* 52°26N 2°0W **169** E6
West Mifflin *U.S.A.* 40°21N 79°52W **312** F5
West Milford *U.S.A.* 41°8N 74°22W **313** E10
West Milton *Ohio, U.S.A.* 39°58N 84°20W **311** E12
West Milton *Pa., U.S.A.* 41°1N 76°50W **312** E8
West Molesey *U.K.* 51°24N 0°22W **125** B1
West Monroe *U.S.A.* 32°31N 92°9W **314** E8
West New Britain □ *Papua N. G.* 5°0S 149°30E **286** C5
West New York *New York, U.S.A.* **132** a1
West Newton *U.S.A.* 40°14N 79°46W **312** F5
West Nicholson *Zimbabwe* 21°2S 29°20E **269** G2
West Odessa *U.S.A.* 31°50N 102°30W **314** F3
West of Twin Peaks *U.S.A.* 37°43N 122°27W **128** B2
West Palm Beach *U.S.A.* 26°43N 80°3W **317** J9
West Palm Beach Canal *U.S.A.* 26°40N 80°15W **317** J9
West Park *Gauteng, S. Africa* 26°9S 27°59E **123** A1
West Park *Fla., U.S.A.* 25°59N 80°12W **129** C2
West Pensacola *U.S.A.* 30°25N 87°16W **317** E2
West Plains *U.S.A.* 36°44N 91°51W **308** G8
West Point *Ga., U.S.A.* 32°53N 85°11W **316** C4
West Point *Iowa, U.S.A.* 40°43N 91°27W **310** D5
West Point *Ky., U.S.A.* 37°59N 85°57W **311** G11
West Point *Miss., U.S.A.* 33°36N 88°39W **315** E10
West Point *N.Y., U.S.A.* 41°24N 73°58W **313** E11
West Point *Nebr., U.S.A.* 41°51N 96°43W **308** E5
West Point *Va., U.S.A.* 37°32N 76°48W **309** G15
West Point L. *U.S.A.* 33°8N 85°0W **316** B4
West Pokot □ *Kenya* 1°15N 35°10E **268** B4
West Pt. = Ouest, Pte. de l' *Canada* 49°52N 64°40W **299** C7
West Pt. *Australia* 35°1S 135°56E **282** C1
West Ra. *Papua N. G.* 4°15S 141°30E **286** C1
West Road → *Canada* 53°18N 122°53W **296** C4
West Rouge *Canada* 43°48N 79°7W **141** A4
West Roxbury *U.S.A.* 42°16N 71°9W **116** B2
West Rutland *U.S.A.* 43°36N 73°3W **313** C11
West Salem *U.S.A.* 38°31N 88°1W **311** F8
West Schelde = Westerschelde → *Neths.* 51°25N 3°25E **170** C3
West Seneca *U.S.A.* 42°51N 78°48W **312** D6
West Sepik = Sandaun □ *Papua N. G.* 3°30S 142°0E **286** B2
West Siberian Plain *Russia* 62°0N 75°0E **210** B9
West Sussex □ *U.K.* 50°55N 0°30W **169** G7
West Terre Haute *U.S.A.* 39°28N 87°27W **311** E9
West-Terschelling *Neths.* 53°22N 5°13E **170** A5
West Town *U.S.A.* 41°53N 87°42W **119** B2
West Union *Iowa, U.S.A.* 42°57N 91°49W **310** B5
West Union *Ohio, U.S.A.* 38°48N 83°33W **311** F13
West Unity *U.S.A.* 41°35N 84°26W **311** C12
West Valley City *U.S.A.* 40°42N 111°58W **304** F8
West Virginia □ *U.S.A.* 38°45N 80°30W **309** F13
West-Vlaanderen □ *Belgium* 51°0N 3°0E **170** D2
West Walker → *U.S.A.* 38°54N 119°9W **306** G7
West Wharf *Pakistan* 24°49N 66°58E **123** B1
West Wyalong *Australia* 33°56S 147°10E **283** B7
West Yellowstone *U.S.A.* 44°40N 111°6W **304** D8
West Yorkshire □ *U.K.* 53°45N 1°40W **168** D6
Westall, Pt. *Australia* 32°55S 134°4E **281** E1
Westbay *U.S.A.* 30°18N 85°52W **316** E4
Westbourne Green *London, U.K.* **125** a1
Westbrook *U.S.A.* 43°41N 70°22W **309** D18
Westbury *Australia* 41°30S 146°51E **281** G4
Westby *U.S.A.* 48°52N 104°3W **304** B11
Westchester *Calif., U.S.A.* 33°57N 118°23W **126** C2
Westchester *N.Y., U.S.A.* 40°51N 73°51W **132** A2
Westcliff *S. Africa* 26°10S 28°1E **123** B2
Westdene *S. Africa* 26°10S 27°59E **123** B1
Westend *Helsinki, Finland* 60°9N 24°48E **121** C1
Westend *Calif., U.S.A.* 35°42N 117°24W **307** K9
Wester Hailes *U.K.* 55°55N 3°16W **121** B2
Westerham *Germany* 48°3N 11°22E **131** B2
Westerland *Germany* 54°54N 8°17E **178** A4
Westerly *U.S.A.* 41°22N 71°50W **313** E13
Western □ *Ghana* 5°30N 2°30W **262** D4
Western □ *Papua N. G.* 7°30S 142°0E **286** D2
Western □ *S. Leone* 8°30N 13°20W **262** D2
Western □ *Zambia* 15°0S 24°4E **265** F4
Western Addition *U.S.A.* 37°47N 122°25W **136** B2
Western Australia □ *Australia* 25°0S 118°0E **279** E2
Western Bahr el Ghazal □ *South Sudan* 7°30N 25°30E **257** F2
Western Cape □ *S. Africa* 34°0S 20°0E **270** D3
Western Dvina = Daugava → *Latvia* 57°4N 24°3E **188** D3
Western Equatoria □ *South Sudan* 5°0N 30°0E **257** G3
Western Ghats *India* 14°0N 75°0E **245** H2
Western Highlands □ *Papua N. G.* 5°45S 144°10E **286** C3
Western Isles = Eilean Siar □ *U.K.* 57°30N 7°10W **167** D1
Western Sahara ■ *Africa* 25°0N 13°0W **260** D2
Western Samoa = Samoa ■ *Pac. Oc.* 14°0S 172°0W **287** V20
Western Sierra Madre = Madre Occidental, Sierra *Mexico* 27°0N 107°0W **318** B3
Western Wall *Jerusalem* **123** b3
Westernport *U.S.A.* 39°29N 79°3W **309** F14
Westerschelde → *Neths.* 51°25N 3°25E **170** C3
Westerstede *Germany* 53°15N 7°55E **178** B3
Westerwald *Germany* 50°38N 7°56E **178** E3
Westfield *Ill., U.S.A.* 39°27N 88°0W **311** E8
Westfield *Ind., U.S.A.* 40°2N 86°8W **311** D10
Westfield *Mass., U.S.A.* 42°7N 72°45W **313** D12
Westfield *N.Y., U.S.A.* 42°20N 79°35W **312** D5
Westfield *Pa., U.S.A.* 41°55N 77°32W **312** E7
Westgate *La., U.S.A.* 30°0N 90°13W **131** A1
Westgate *Md., U.S.A.* 38°57N 77°6W **143** B2
Westhill *U.K.* 57°9N 2°19W **167** D6
Westhope *U.S.A.* 48°55N 101°1W **308** A3
Westlake *Western Cape, S. Africa* 34°4S 18°26E **118** B1
Westlake *Calif., U.S.A.* 34°4N 118°15W **126** B3
Westlake *Calif., U.S.A.* 37°42N 122°29W **136** B2
Westland *U.S.A.* 42°15N 83°20W **311** B13
Westland Bight *N.Z.* 42°55S 170°5E **285** C5
Westland Tai Poutini △ *N.Z.* 43°16S 170°16E **285** D5
Westlock *Canada* 54°9N 113°55W **296** C6
Westmar *Australia* 27°55S 149°44E **281** D4
Westmeath □ *Ireland* 53°33N 7°34W **166** C4
Westminster *London, U.K.* 51°30N 0°7W **125** A3
Westminster *Calif., U.S.A.* 33°45N 118°0W **307** M8
Westminster *Colo., U.S.A.* 39°50N 105°2W **304** G11
Westminster *Md., U.S.A.* 39°34N 76°59W **309** F15
Westmont *U.S.A.* 41°9N 78°58W **312** F6
Westmorland *U.S.A.* 33°2N 115°37W **307** M11
Westmount *Canada* 45°29N 73°35W **130** B2
Weston *Ont., Canada* 43°42N 79°30W **141** A1
Weston *Ohio, U.S.A.* 41°21N 83°47W **311** C13
Weston *Oreg., U.S.A.* 45°49N 118°26W **304** D4
Weston *W. Va., U.S.A.* 39°2N 80°28W **309** F13
Weston I. *Canada* 52°33N 79°36W **298** B4
Weston-super-Mare *U.K.* 51°21N 2°58W **169** F5
Westover *U.S.A.* 40°45N 78°40W **312** F6
Westphalia *U.S.A.* 38°26N 92°0W **310** F5
Westport *Ont., Canada* 44°40N 76°25W **313** B8
Westport *Mayo, Ireland* 53°48N 9°31W **166** C2
Westport *N.Z.* 41°46S 171°37E **285** B6
Westport *Ind., U.S.A.* 39°11N 85°34W **311** E11
Westport *N.Y., U.S.A.* 44°11N 73°26W **313** B11
Westport *Oreg., U.S.A.* 46°8N 123°23W **306** D3
Westport *Wash., U.S.A.* 46°53N 124°6W **306** D2
Westpunt *Curaçao* 12°22N 69°10W **322** g
Westray *Man., Canada* 53°36N 101°24W **297** C8
Westray *Orkney, U.K.* 59°18N 3°0W **167** B5
Westree *Canada* 47°26N 81°34W **298** C3
Westville *Calif., U.S.A.* 39°8N 120°42W **306** F6
Westville *Fla., U.S.A.* 30°46N 85°51W **316** E4
Westville *Ill., U.S.A.* 40°2N 87°38W **311** D9
Westville *Ind., U.S.A.* 41°32N 86°54W **311** C10
Westwego *U.S.A.* 29°54N 90°8W **131** B2
Westwood *U.S.A.* 40°18N 121°0W **304** F3
Westwood Lake *U.S.A.* 25°44N 80°23W **317** K9
Westwood Village *U.S.A.* 34°3N 118°26W **126** B2
Westzaan *Neths.* 52°28N 4°46E **112** A1
Wetar *Indonesia* 7°48S 126°30E **231** F7
Wetaskiwin *Canada* 52°55N 113°24W **296** C6
Wetherby *U.K.* 53°56N 1°23W **168** D6
Wethersfield *U.S.A.* 41°42N 72°40W **313** E12
Wetlet *Burma* 22°20N 95°53E **241** D5
Wetteren *Belgium* 51°0N 3°53E **170** D3
Wetton *S. Africa* 34°0S 18°31E **118** B2
Wetumpka *U.S.A.* 32°32N 86°13W **316** C3
Wetzlar *Germany* 50°32N 8°31E **178** E4
Wevok *U.S.A.* 68°53N 166°13W **303** B6
Wewahitchka *U.S.A.* 30°7N 85°12W **316** E4
Wewak *Papua N. G.* 3°38S 143°41E **286** B2
Wewoka *U.S.A.* 35°9N 96°30W **314** D6
Wexford *Wexford, Ireland* 52°20N 6°28W **166** D5
Wexford □ *Ireland* 52°20N 6°25W **166** D5
Wexford Harbour *Ireland* 52°20N 6°25W **166** D5
Weybridge *U.K.* 51°22N 0°27W **125** B1
Weyburn *Canada* 49°40N 103°50W **297** D8
Weyer Markt *Austria* 47°51N 14°40E **180** D7
Weyhe *Germany* 52°58N 8°49E **178** C4
Weyib → *Ethiopia* 7°15N 40°15E **257** F5

Weymouth N.S., Canada 44°30N 66°1W 299 D6
Weymouth Dorset, U.K. 50°37N 2°28W 169 G5
Weymouth Mass., U.S.A. 42°13N 70°58W 313 D14
Weymouth, C. Australia 12°37S 143°27E 280 A3
Wezembeek-Oppem Belgium 50°51N 4°29E 116 A2
Wha Ti Canada 63°8N 117°16W 294 E8
Whakaari N.Z. 37°30S 177°13E 284 D6
Whakamaru N.Z. 38°23S 175°50E 284 E4
Whakatane N.Z. 37°57S 177°1E 284 D6
Whakatane → N.Z. 37°57S 177°1E 284 D6
Whale = Baleine → Canada 58°15N 67°40W 299 A6
Whale B. Burma 11°37N 98°38E 237 G2
Whale Cove Canada 62°10N 92°34W 297 A10
Whale Pt. Ascension I. 7°57S 14°18W 153 g
Whale Valley = Hitan, W. el Egypt 29°19N 30°10E 256 J7
Whales, B. of Antarctica 78°0S 160°0W 151 D12
Whalsay U.K. 60°22N 0°59W 167 A8
Whangachu → N.Z. 40°3S 175°6E 284 G4
Whangamata N.Z. 37°12S 175°53E 284 D4
Whangamomona N.Z. 39°8S 174°44E 284 F3
Whanganui △ N.Z. 39°17S 174°53E 284 F3
Whangaparaoa Pen. N.Z. 36°40S 174°45E 284 C3
Whangarei N.Z. 35°43S 174°21E 284 B3
Whangarei Harb. N.Z. 35°45S 174°28E 284 B3
Whangaroa Harb. N.Z. 35°4S 173°46E 284 B2
Whangaruru Harb. N.Z. 35°24S 174°23E 284 B3
Wharanui N.Z. 41°55S 174°6E 285 B9
Wharekauri = Chatham Is. Pac. Oc. 44°0S 176°40W 285 a
Wharfe → U.K. 53°51N 1°9W 168 D6
Wharfedale U.K. 54°6N 2°1W 168 C5
Wharton N.J., U.S.A. 40°54N 74°35W 313 F10
Wharton Pa., U.S.A. 41°31N 78°1W 312 E6
Wharton Tex., U.S.A. 29°19N 96°6W 314 G6
Wharton Basin Ind. Oc. 22°0S 99°0E 273 G9
Whataroa N.Z. 43°18S 170°24E 285 D5
Whataroa → N.Z. 43°7S 170°16E 285 D5
Whatcom = Bellingham U.S.A. 48°46N 122°29W 306 B4
Wheatfield U.S.A. 41°13N 87°4W 311 C9
Wheatland Calif., U.S.A. 39°1N 121°25W 306 F5
Wheatland Ind., U.S.A. 38°40N 87°19W 311 F9
Wheatland Wyo., U.S.A. 42°3N 104°58W 304 E11
Wheatley Canada 42°6N 82°27W 312 D2
Wheaton Ill., U.S.A. 41°52N 88°6W 311 C8
Wheaton Md., U.S.A. 39°3N 77°3W 309 F15
Wheaton Minn., U.S.A. 45°48N 96°30W 308 C5
Wheelbarrow Pk. U.S.A. 37°26N 116°5W 306 H10
Wheeler Oreg., U.S.A. 45°41N 123°53W 304 D2
Wheeler Tex., U.S.A. 35°27N 100°16W 314 D4
Wheeler → Canada 57°2N 67°13W 299 A6
Wheeler L. U.S.A. 34°48N 87°23W 315 D11
Wheeler Pk. N. Mex., U.S.A. 36°34N 105°25W 305 H11
Wheeler Pk. Nev., U.S.A. 38°57N 114°15W 306 G6
Wheeler Ridge U.S.A. 35°0N 118°57W 307 L8
Wheelersburg U.S.A. 38°44N 82°51W 309 F12
Wheeling U.S.A. 40°4N 80°43W 312 F4
Whernside U.K. 54°14N 2°24W 168 C5
Whiddy I. Ireland 51°41N 9°31W 166 E2
Whim Creek Australia 20°50S 117°49E 278 D2
Whirlwind Reef Papua N. G. 4°42S 148°16E 286 C5
Whiskey Jack L. Canada 58°23N 101°55W 297 B8
Whiskeytown-Shasta-Trinity ⌂ U.S.A. 40°45N 122°15W 304 F2
Whistleduck Cr. → Australia 20°15S 135°18E 280 C2
Whistler Canada 50°7N 122°58W 296 C4
Whitby Ont., Canada 43°52N 78°56W 312 C6
Whitby N. Yorks., U.K. 54°29N 0°37W 168 C7
Whitcombe Pass N.Z. 43°13S 170°55E 285 D5
White → Ark., U.S.A. 33°57N 91°5W 314 E9
White → Ind., U.S.A. 38°25N 87°45W 311 F9
White → S. Dak., U.S.A. 43°42N 99°27W 308 D4
White → Tex., U.S.A. 33°14N 100°56W 314 E4
White → Utah, U.S.A. 40°4N 109°41W 304 F9
White → Vt., U.S.A. 43°37N 72°20W 313 C12
White → Wash., U.S.A. 47°12N 122°15W 306 C4
White, L. Australia 21°9S 128°56E 278 D4
White B. Canada 50°0N 56°35W 299 C8
White Bird U.S.A. 45°46N 116°18W 304 D5
White Butte U.S.A. 46°23N 103°18W 308 B2
White City Fla., U.S.A. 29°53N 85°13W 316 F4
White City Oreg., U.S.A. 42°26N 122°51W 304 E2
White Cliffs Australia 30°50S 143°10E 282 A5
White Cloud Hill = Baiyun Mountain Scenic Area ⌂ China 23°11N 113°17E 121 A2
White Desert = Beida, Es Sahrâ al Egypt 27°50N 28°45E 256 B2
White Hall U.S.A. 39°26N 90°24W 310 E6
White Haven U.S.A. 41°4N 75°47W 313 E9
White Horse, Vale of U.K. 51°37N 1°30W 169 F6
White House, The Washington, D.C., U.S.A. 143 b1
White I. = Whakaari N.Z. 37°30S 177°13E 284 D6
White I. Grenada 12°26N 61°28W 323 q
White L. Ont., Canada 45°18N 76°31W 313 A8
White L. La., U.S.A. 29°44N 92°30W 314 G8
White Lake Canada 45°21N 76°29W 313 A8
White Mountain U.S.A. 64°41N 163°24W 303 D7
White Mountain Peak U.S.A. 37°38N 118°15W 306 H8
White Mountains Nat. Recr. Area ⌂ U.S.A. 65°30N 147°40W 303 D11
White Mts. Alaska, U.S.A. 65°30N 146°30W 303 D11
White Mts. Calif., U.S.A. 37°30N 118°15W 306 H8
White Mts. N.H., U.S.A. 44°15N 71°15W 313 B13
White Mts. △ Australia 20°43S 145°12E 280 C4
White Nile = Nîl el Abyad → Sudan 15°38N 32°31E 257 D3
White Nile Dam = Khazzân Jabal al Awliyâ Sudan 15°24N 32°20E 257 D3
White Oak U.S.A. 31°2N 81°43W 316 D8
White Otter L. Canada 49°5N 91°55W 298 C1
White Pass U.S.A. 46°38N 121°24W 306 D5
White Pigeon U.S.A. 41°48N 85°39W 311 C11
White Plains Ga., U.S.A. 33°28N 83°1W 316 B6
White Plains N.Y., U.S.A. 41°2N 73°46W 313 E11
White River Ont., Canada 48°35N 85°20W 298 C2
White River S. Dak., U.S.A. 43°34N 100°45W 308 D3
White Rock B.C., Canada 49°2N 122°48W 306 A4
White Rock N. Mex., U.S.A. 35°50N 106°12W 305 J10
White Rock L. U.S.A. 32°48N 96°43W 120 A5
White Rocks Nat. Recr. Area ⌂ U.S.A. 43°22N 72°55W 313 C12
White Russia = Belarus ■ Europe 53°30N 27°0E 177 B14
White Sands ⌂ U.S.A. 32°46N 106°20W 305 K10
White Sea = Beloye More Russia 66°30N 38°0E 186 A6
White Springs U.S.A. 30°20N 82°45W 316 E7
White Sulphur Springs Mont., U.S.A. 46°33N 110°54W 304 C8
White Sulphur Springs W. Va., U.S.A. 37°48N 80°18W 309 G13
White Swan U.S.A. 46°23N 120°44W 306 D6
White Volta → Ghana 9°10N 1°15W 263 D4
Whitechapel U.K. 51°31N 0°3W 125 A3
Whitecliffs N.Z. 43°26S 171°55E 285 D6
Whitecourt Canada 54°10N 115°45W 296 C5
Whiteface Mt. U.S.A. 44°22N 73°54W 313 B11
Whitefield U.S.A. 44°23N 71°37W 313 B13
Whitefish U.S.A. 48°25N 114°20W 304 B6
Whitefish B. U.S.A. 46°40N 84°55W 298 C3
Whitefish Bay U.S.A. 43°6N 87°54W 311 A9
Whitefish L. Canada 62°41N 106°48W 297 A7
Whitefish Pt. U.S.A. 46°45N 84°59W 309 B11
Whitegull, L. = Goélands, L. aux Canada 55°27N 64°17W 299 A7
Whitehall London, U.K. 125 b3
Whitehall Mich., U.S.A. 43°24N 86°21W 308 D10
Whitehall Mont., U.S.A. 45°52N 112°6W 304 D7
Whitehall N.Y., U.S.A. 43°33N 73°24W 313 C11
Whitehall Wis., U.S.A. 44°22N 91°19W 308 C8
Whitehaven U.K. 54°33N 3°35W 168 C4
Whitehorse Canada 60°43N 135°3W 296 A1
Whiteman Ra. Papua N. G. 5°55S 150°0E 286 C6
Whitemark Australia 40°7S 148°3E 281 G4
Whiteplains Liberia 6°28N 10°40W 262 D2
Whiteriver U.S.A. 33°50N 109°58W 305 K9
Whitesand → Canada 60°9N 115°45W 296 A5
Whitesands S. Africa 34°23S 20°50E 270 D3
Whitesboro N.Y., U.S.A. 43°7N 75°18W 313 C9
Whitesboro Tex., U.S.A. 33°39N 96°54W 314 E6
Whiteshell ⌂ Canada 50°0N 95°40W 297 D9
Whiteside, Canal Chile 53°55S 70°15W 336 D2
Whiteville U.S.A. 34°20N 78°42W 315 D15
Whitewater U.S.A. 42°50N 88°44W 311 B8
Whitewater B. U.S.A. 25°15N 81°0W 317 K9
Whitewater Baldy U.S.A. 33°20N 108°39W 305 K9
Whitewater L. Canada 50°50N 89°10W 298 B2
Whitewood Queens., Australia 21°28S 143°30E 280 C3
Whitewood Sask., Canada 50°20N 102°20W 297 C8
Whitfield Australia 36°42S 146°24E 283 D7
Whithorn U.K. 54°44N 4°26W 167 G4
Whitianga N.Z. 36°47S 175°41E 284 C4
Whiting U.S.A. 41°41N 87°30W 311 C9
Whitman U.S.A. 42°5N 70°56W 313 D14
Whitmore Mts. Antarctica 82°35S 104°30W 151 E15
Whitmore Village U.S.A. 21°31N 158°1W 302 J13
Whitney Ont., Canada 45°31N 78°14W 312 A6
Whitney Nev., U.S.A. 36°4N 115°5W 124 B2
Whitney, Mt. U.S.A. 36°35N 118°18W 306 J8
Whitney Point U.S.A. 42°20N 75°58W 313 D9
Whitstable U.K. 51°21N 1°3E 169 F9
Whitsunday I. Australia 20°15S 149°4E 280 b
Whitsunday Islands △ Australia 20°15S 149°0E 280 b
Whittemore U.S.A. 43°4N 94°26W 310 C4
Whittier Alaska, U.S.A. 60°47N 148°41W 303 F10
Whittier Calif., U.S.A. 33°58N 118°2W 126 C4
Whittier Narrows Recreation Area ⌂ U.S.A. 34°2N 118°4W 126 B4
Whittlesea Australia 37°27S 145°9E 283 D6
Whitton U.K. 51°27N 0°21W 125 B1
Wholdaia L. Canada 60°43N 104°20W 297 A8
Whyalla Australia 33°2S 137°30E 282 B2
Wiang Kosai △ Thailand 17°54N 99°29E 236 D2
Wiang Sa Thailand 18°34N 100°45E 236 C3
Wiarton Canada 44°40N 81°10W 312 B3
Wiawso Ghana 6°10N 2°25W 262 D4
Wiay U.K. 57°24N 7°13W 167 D1
Wiązów Poland 50°50N 17°10E 185 H4
Wibaux U.S.A. 46°59N 104°11W 304 C11
Wichabai Guyana 2°57N 59°35W 329 C6
Wichian Buri Thailand 15°39N 101°7E 236 E3
Wichita U.S.A. 37°42N 97°20W 308 G5
Wichita Falls U.S.A. 33°54N 98°30W 314 E5
Wick U.K. 58°26N 3°5W 167 C5
Wickenburg U.S.A. 33°58N 112°44W 305 K7
Wickepin Australia 32°50S 117°30E 279 F2
Wickham Australia 20°42S 117°11E 278 D2
Wickham, C. Australia 39°35S 143°57E 281 F3
Wickliffe U.S.A. 41°36N 81°28W 312 E3
Wicklow Ireland 52°59N 6°3W 166 D5
Wicklow □ Ireland 52°57N 6°25W 166 D5
Wicklow Hd. Ireland 52°58N 6°0W 166 D6
Wicklow Mts. Ireland 52°58N 6°26W 166 C5
Wicklow Mts. △ Ireland 53°6N 6°21W 166 C5
Widawa Poland 51°27N 18°51E 185 G5
Widawka → Poland 51°27N 18°52E 185 G5
Wide B. Papua N. G. 5°5S 152°5E 286 C7
Wideawake ✈ (ASI) Ascension I. 7°58S 14°23W 153 g
Widgeegoara Cr. → Australia 28°51S 146°34E 281 D4
Widgiemooltha Australia 31°30S 121°34E 279 F3
Widnes U.K. 53°23N 2°45W 168 D5
Wido S. Korea 35°35N 126°17E 224 E3
Więcbork Poland 53°21N 17°30E 185 E4
Wieden Austria 48°11N 16°22E 142 A2
Wiehengebirge = Nördlicher Teutoburger Wald-Wiehengebirge ⌂ Germany 52°18N 8°10E 178 C4
Wiehl Germany 50°56N 7°34E 178 E3
Wiek Germany 54°37N 13°17E 178 A9
Wielbark Poland 53°24N 20°55E 184 E7
Wieleń Poland 52°53N 16°9E 185 F3
Wielichowo Poland 52°7N 16°22E 185 F3
Wieliczka Poland 50°0N 20°5E 185 J7
Wielkopolski △ Poland 52°18N 16°45E 185 F3
Wielkopolskie □ Poland 52°10N 17°30E 185 F4
Wieluń Poland 51°15N 18°34E 185 G5
Wien Austria 48°12N 16°22E 142 A2
Wien-Schwechat ✈ (VIE) Austria 48°7N 16°35E 142 B3
Wiener Neustadt Austria 47°49N 16°16E 181 D9
Wienerberg Austria 48°9N 16°21E 142 B2
Wieprz → Poland 51°34N 21°49E 185 G8
Wieprza → Poland 54°26N 16°25E 184 D3
Wieruszów Poland 51°19N 18°9E 185 G5
Wierzbno Poland 52°11N 21°1E 143 B2
Wiesbaden Germany 50°4N 8°14E 179 E4
Wiesental Germany 49°13N 8°31E 179 F4
Wiesloch Germany 49°17N 8°41E 179 F4
Wiesmoor Germany 53°24N 7°47E 178 B3
Wieżyca Poland 54°14N 18°8E 184 D5
Wigan U.K. 53°33N 2°38W 168 D5
Wiggins Colo., U.S.A. 40°14N 104°4W 304 F11
Wiggins Miss., U.S.A. 30°51N 89°8W 315 F10
Wight, I. of U.K. 50°41N 1°17W 169 G6
Wigierski △ Poland 54°5N 23°5E 184 D10
Wigry, Jezioro Poland 54°2N 23°8E 184 D10
Wigston U.K. 52°35N 1°6W 169 E6
Wigton U.K. 54°50N 3°10W 168 C4
Wigtown U.K. 54°53N 4°27W 167 G4
Wigtown B. U.K. 54°46N 4°15W 167 G4
Wijde Wormer Neths. 52°28N 4°52E 112 A2
Wik and Wikway People ✪ Australia 13°55S 142°28E 280 A3
Wil Switz. 47°28N 9°3E 179 H5
Wilamowice Poland 49°55N 19°9E 185 J6
Wilanów Poland 52°10N 21°4E 143 B2
Wilanówka → Poland 52°13N 21°6E 143 C2
Wilber U.S.A. 40°29N 96°58W 308 E5
Wilberforce Canada 45°2N 78°13W 312 A6
Wilberforce, C. Australia 11°54S 136°35E 280 A2
Wilburton U.S.A. 34°55N 95°19W 314 D7
Wilcannia Australia 31°30S 143°26E 282 A5
Wilcox U.S.A. 41°35N 78°41W 312 E6
Wildbad Germany 48°44N 8°33E 179 G4
Wildcat Cr. → U.S.A. 40°28N 86°52W 311 D10
Wildenschwert = Ústí nad Orlicí Czechia 49°58N 16°24E 181 B9
Wildeshausen Germany 52°54N 8°27E 178 C4
Wildeshauser Geest ⌂ Germany 52°54N 8°30E 178 C4
Wildomar U.S.A. 33°36N 117°16W 307 M9
Wildon Austria 46°52N 15°31E 180 E8
Wildrose U.S.A. 36°14N 117°11W 307 J9
Wilds, The S. Africa 26°10S 28°2E 123 B2
Wildspitze Austria 46°53N 10°53E 180 E3
Wildwood U.S.A. 28°52N 82°2W 317 G7
Wilga → Poland 51°52N 21°18E 185 G8
Wilge → S. Africa 27°3S 28°20E 271 C4
Wilhelm, Mt. Papua N. G. 5°50S 145°1E 286 C3
Wilhelm II Coast Antarctica 68°0S 90°0E 151 C7
Wilhelmina Geb. Suriname 3°50N 56°30W 329 C6
Wilhelmina Top = Trikora, Puncak Indonesia 4°15S 138°45E 231 E9
Wilhelmsburg Austria 48°6N 15°36E 180 C8
Wilhelmshagen Germany 52°26N 13°42E 115 B5
Wilhelmshaven Germany 53°31N 8°7E 178 B4
Wilhelmstal Namibia 21°58S 16°21E 270 B2
Wilis Indonesia 7°51S 111°48E 235 D4
Wilkes-Barre U.S.A. 41°15N 75°53W 313 E9
Wilkes I. Wake I. 19°18N 166°34E 302 b
Wilkes Land Antarctica 69°0S 120°0E 151 D9
Wilket Creek Park Canada 43°43N 79°21W 141 A2
Wilkie Canada 52°27N 108°42W 297 C7
Wilkieston U.K. 55°54N 3°24W 121 B1
Wilkins Ice Shelf Antarctica 70°30S 72°0W 151 C17
Wilkinsburg U.S.A. 40°26N 79°52W 312 F5
Wilkinson Lakes Australia 29°40S 132°39E 279 E5
Will Rogers State Historical Park ⌂ U.S.A. 34°2N 118°30W 126 B1
Willacoochee U.S.A. 31°20N 83°3W 316 D6
Willandra △ Australia 33°12S 145°0E 283 B6
Willandra Creek → Australia 33°22S 145°52E 283 B6
Willapa B. U.S.A. 46°40N 124°0W 306 D3
Willapa Hills U.S.A. 46°35N 123°25W 306 D3
Willard U.S.A. 41°3N 82°44W 312 E2
Willare Bridge Roadhouse Australia 17°43S 123°38E 278 C3
Willaumez Pen. Papua N. G. 5°15S 150°2E 286 C6
Willbriggie Australia 34°28S 146°2E 283 C7
Willcox U.S.A. 32°15N 109°50W 305 K9
Willemstad Curaçao 12°5N 68°55W 322 g
Willenberg = Wielbark Poland 53°24N 20°55E 184 E7
Willesden U.K. 51°32N 0°15W 125 A2
Willesden Green U.K. 51°32N 0°13W 125 A2
Willi Willi △ Australia 30°57S 152°27E 283 A10
William → Canada 59°8N 109°19W 297 B7
William, Mt. Australia 37°17S 142°35E 282 D5
William 'Bill' Dannelly Res. U.S.A. 32°6N 87°24W 315 E11
William Creek Australia 28°58S 136°22E 281 D2
Williamnagar India 25°31N 90°37E 241 C3
Williams W. Austral., Australia 33°2S 116°52E 279 F2
Williams Ariz., U.S.A. 35°15N 112°11W 305 J7
Williams Calif., U.S.A. 39°9N 122°9W 306 F4
Williams Harbour Canada 52°33N 55°47W 299 B8
Williams Lake Canada 52°10N 122°10W 296 C4
Williamsbridge U.S.A. 40°52N 73°51W 132 A2
Williamsburg Fla., U.S.A. 28°24N 81°26W 133 B2
Williamsburg Iowa, U.S.A. 41°40N 92°1W 310 C4
Williamsburg Ky., U.S.A. 36°44N 84°10W 309 G11
Williamsburg New York, U.S.A. 132 f3
Williamsburg Pa., U.S.A. 40°28N 78°12W 312 F6
Williamsburg Va., U.S.A. 37°16N 76°43W 309 G15
Williamsburg Bridge New York, U.S.A. 132 e2
Williamsfield U.S.A. 40°55N 90°1W 310 D6
Williamson N.Y., U.S.A. 43°14N 77°11W 312 C7
Williamson W. Va., U.S.A. 37°41N 82°17W 309 G12
Williamsport Ind., U.S.A. 40°17N 87°17W 311 D9
Williamsport Pa., U.S.A. 41°15N 77°1W 312 E7
Williamston Mich., U.S.A. 42°41N 84°17W 311 B12
Williamston N.C., U.S.A. 35°51N 77°4W 315 D16
Williamstown Vic., Australia 37°51S 144°52E 128 B1
Williamstown Ky., U.S.A. 38°38N 84°34W 311 F12
Williamstown Mass., U.S.A. 42°43N 73°12W 313 D11
Williamstown N.Y., U.S.A. 43°26N 75°53W 313 C9
Williamsville U.S.A. 39°57N 89°33W 310 E7
Willikies Antigua & B. 17°3N 61°42W 322 b
Willimantic U.S.A. 41°43N 72°13W 313 E12
Willingboro U.S.A. 40°3N 74°54W 309 E16
Willis, L. U.S.A. 28°23N 81°28W 133 B2
Willis Tower Chicago, U.S.A. 119 c1
Willisburg U.S.A. 37°49N 85°8W 311 G11
Williston Northern Cape, S. Africa 31°20S 20°53E 270 D3
Williston Fla., U.S.A. 29°23N 82°27W 317 F7
Williston N. Dak., U.S.A. 48°9N 103°37W 308 A2
Williston S.C., U.S.A. 33°24N 81°25W 316 B8
Williston L. Canada 56°0N 124°0W 296 B4
Willits U.S.A. 39°25N 123°21W 304 G2
Willmar U.S.A. 45°7N 95°3W 308 C6
Willmore Wilderness ⌂ Canada 53°45N 119°30W 296 C5
Willoughby N.S.W., Australia 33°48S 151°12E 139 A2
Willoughby Ohio, U.S.A. 41°39N 81°24W 312 E3
Willoughby B. Antigua & B. 17°2N 61°44W 322 b
Willow U.S.A. 61°45N 150°3W 303 F10
Willow Bunch Canada 49°20N 105°35W 297 D7
Willow L. Canada 62°10N 119°8W 296 A5
Willow Tree Australia 31°40S 150°45E 283 A9
Willow Wall, The China 42°10N 122°0E 227 C12
Willowdale Ont., Canada 43°46N 79°25W 141 A2
Willowdale La., U.S.A. 30°0N 90°12W 131 A1
Willowick U.S.A. 41°38N 81°28W 312 E3
Willowlake → Canada 62°42N 123°8W 296 A4
Willowmore S. Africa 33°15S 23°30E 270 D3
Willows U.S.A. 39°31N 122°12W 306 F4
Willowvale = Gatyana S. Africa 32°16S 28°31E 271 D4
Wills, L. Australia 21°25S 128°51E 278 D4
Wills Cr. → Australia 22°43S 140°2E 280 C3
Willsboro U.S.A. 44°21N 73°24W 313 B11
Willunga Australia 35°15S 138°30E 282 C3
Wilma U.S.A. 30°9N 84°58W 316 E5
Wilmer U.S.A. 32°35N 96°41W 120 C5
Wilmersdorf Berlin, Germany 115 c1
Wilmette U.S.A. 42°4N 87°42W 119 A2
Wilmington S. Austral., Australia 32°39S 138°7E 282 B3
Wilmington Kent, U.K. 51°25N 0°12E 125 B5
Wilmington Del., U.S.A. 39°45N 75°33W 309 F16
Wilmington Ill., U.S.A. 41°18N 88°9W 311 C8
Wilmington N.C., U.S.A. 34°14N 77°55W 315 D16
Wilmington Ohio, U.S.A. 39°27N 83°50W 311 E13
Wilmington Vt., U.S.A. 42°52N 72°52W 313 D12
Wilmslow U.K. 53°19N 2°13W 168 D5
Wilna = Vilnius Lithuania 54°38N 25°19E 188 E3
Wilpattu △ Sri Lanka 8°20N 79°50E 245 K4
Wilpena Australia 31°31S 138°37E 282 A3
Wilpena Cr. → Australia 31°25S 139°29E 282 A3
Wilsall U.S.A. 45°59N 110°38W 304 D8
Wilson N.C., U.S.A. 35°44N 77°55W 315 D16
Wilson N.Y., U.S.A. 43°19N 78°50W 312 C6
Wilson Pa., U.S.A. 40°41N 75°15W 313 F9
Wilson → Australia 16°48S 128°16E 278 C4
Wilson Bluff Australia 31°41S 129°0E 279 F4
Wilson Inlet Australia 35°0S 117°22E 279 G2
Wilson Str. Solomon Is. 8°0S 156°39E 287 M9
Wilsons Promontory Australia 38°59S 146°23E 283 E7
Wilsons Promontory △ Australia 38°59S 146°23E 283 D7
Wilster Germany 53°55N 9°23E 178 B5
Wilton Iowa, U.S.A. 41°35N 91°1W 310 C5
Wilton N. Dak., U.S.A. 47°10N 100°47W 308 B3
Wilton → Australia 14°45S 134°33E 280 A1
Wilton Manors U.S.A. 26°9N 80°8W 129 B3
Wiltshire □ U.K. 51°18N 1°53W 169 F6
Wiltz Lux. 49°57N 5°55E 170 E5
Wiluna Australia 26°36S 120°14E 279 E3
Wimbledon U.K. 51°25N 0°13W 125 B2
Wimbledon Common U.K. 51°26N 0°14W 125 B2
Wimbledon Park U.K. 51°25N 0°11W 125 B2
Wimbledon Tennis Ground U.K. 51°25N 0°12W 125 B2
Wimborne Minster U.K. 50°48N 1°59W 169 G6
Wimereux France 50°45N 1°37E 173 B8
Wimmera → Australia 36°8S 141°56E 282 D4
Winam G. Kenya 0°20S 34°15E 268 C3
Winamac U.S.A. 41°3N 86°36W 311 C10
Winburg S. Africa 28°30S 27°2E 270 C4
Winchelsea Australia 38°10S 144°1E 282 E6
Winchendon U.S.A. 42°41N 72°3W 313 D12
Winchester N.Z. 44°11S 171°17E 285 E6
Winchester Hants., U.K. 51°4N 1°18W 169 F6
Winchester Conn., U.S.A. 41°53N 73°9W 313 E11
Winchester Idaho, U.S.A. 46°14N 116°38W 304 C5
Winchester Ill., U.S.A. 39°38N 90°27W 310 E6
Winchester Ind., U.S.A. 40°10N 84°59W 311 D12
Winchester Ky., U.S.A. 37°59N 84°11W 311 G12
Winchester Mass., U.S.A. 42°26N 71°8W 116 A2
Winchester N.H., U.S.A. 42°46N 72°23W 313 D12
Winchester Nev., U.S.A. 36°7N 115°7W 124 B2
Winchester Ohio, U.S.A. 38°56N 83°39W 311 F13
Winchester Tenn., U.S.A. 35°11N 86°7W 315 D11
Winchester Va., U.S.A. 39°11N 78°10W 309 F14
Wind → U.S.A. 43°12N 108°12W 304 E9
Wind Cave △ U.S.A. 43°32N 103°17W 308 D2
Wind Point U.S.A. 42°47N 87°46W 311 B9
Wind River Range U.S.A. 43°0N 109°30W 304 E9
Windamere, L. Australia 32°48S 149°51E 283 B8
Windau = Ventspils Latvia 57°25N 21°32E 184 A8
Windber U.S.A. 40°14N 78°50W 312 F6
Winder U.S.A. 34°0N 83°45W 316 A6
Windermere Western Cape, S. Africa 33°55S 18°30E 118 A2
Windermere Cumb., U.K. 54°23N 2°55W 168 C5
Windermere Fla., U.S.A. 28°29N 81°32W 133 B1
Windfall U.S.A. 40°22N 85°57W 311 D11
Windhoek Namibia 22°35S 17°4E 270 B2
Windidda ✪ Australia 26°23S 122°12E 279 E3
Windisch-Feistritz = Slovenska Bistrica Slovenia 46°24N 15°35E 199 B12
Windischgarsten Austria 47°42N 14°21E 180 D7
Windischgratz = Slovenj Gradec Slovenia 46°31N 15°5E 199 B12
Windjana Gorge △ Australia 17°51S 125°0E 278 C3
Windom U.S.A. 43°52N 95°7W 308 D6
Windorah Australia 25°24S 142°36E 280 D3
Window Rock U.S.A. 35°41N 109°3W 305 J9
Windrush → U.K. 51°43N 1°24W 169 F6
Windsor N.S.W., Australia 33°37S 150°50E 283 B9
Windsor N.S., Canada 44°59N 64°5W 299 D7
Windsor Ont., Canada 42°18N 83°0W 312 D2
Windsor N.Z. 44°59S 170°49E 285 E5
Windsor Gauteng, S. Africa 26°7S 27°59E 123 A1
Windsor Windsor & Maidenhead, U.K. 51°29N 0°36W 169 F7
Windsor Calif., U.S.A. 38°33N 122°49W 306 G4
Windsor Colo., U.S.A. 40°29N 104°54W 304 F11
Windsor Conn., U.S.A. 41°50N 72°39W 313 E12
Windsor Ill., U.S.A. 39°26N 88°36W 311 E8
Windsor Mo., U.S.A. 38°32N 93°31W 310 F3
Windsor N.Y., U.S.A. 42°5N 75°37W 313 D9
Windsor Vt., U.S.A. 43°29N 72°24W 313 C12
Windsor, Gare Montréal, Canada 130 c2
Windsor & Maidenhead □ U.K. 51°29N 0°40W 169 F7
Windsor Caves Jamaica 18°21N 77°39W 320 a
Windsor Hills U.S.A. 33°59N 118°22W 126 C2
Windsorton S. Africa 28°16S 24°44E 270 C3
Windward Is. W. Indies 13°0N 61°0W 321 D7
Windward Passage = Vientos, Paso de los Caribbean 20°0N 74°0W 321 C5
Windward Side Saba 17°38N 63°14W 322 a
Winefred L. Canada 55°30N 110°30W 297 B6
Winejok South Sudan 9°1N 27°30E 257 F2
Winfield Iowa, U.S.A. 41°7N 91°26W 310 C5
Winfield Kans., U.S.A. 37°15N 96°59W 308 G5
Winfield Mo., U.S.A. 39°0N 90°44W 310 F6
Wingate Mts. Australia 14°25S 130°40E 278 B5
Wingellina = Irrunytju Australia 26°3S 128°56E 279 E4
Wingham N.S.W., Australia 31°48S 152°22E 283 A10
Wingham Ont., Canada 43°55N 81°20W 312 C3
Winisk → Canada 55°17N 85°5W 298 A2
Winisk L. Canada 52°55N 87°22W 298 B2
Wink U.S.A. 31°45N 103°9W 314 F3
Winkler Canada 49°10N 97°56W 297 D9
Winklern Austria 46°52N 12°52E 180 E5
Winlock U.S.A. 46°30N 122°56W 306 D4
Winneba Ghana 5°25N 0°36W 263 D4
Winnebago U.S.A. 42°16N 89°15W 310 B7
Winnebago, L. U.S.A. 44°0N 88°26W 308 D9
Winnecke Cr. → Australia 18°35S 131°34E 278 C5
Winnemucca U.S.A. 40°58N 117°44W 304 F5
Winnemucca L. U.S.A. 40°7N 119°21W 304 F4
Winner U.S.A. 43°22N 99°52W 308 D4
Winnetka U.S.A. 42°6N 87°45W 119 A2
Winnett U.S.A. 47°0N 108°21W 304 C9
Winnfield U.S.A. 31°56N 92°38W 314 F8
Winnibigoshish, L. U.S.A. 47°27N 94°13W 308 B6
Winning Germany 48°2N 11°37E 118 B2
Winnipeg Canada 49°54N 97°9W 297 D9
Winnipeg → Canada 50°38N 96°19W 297 C9
Winnipeg, L. Canada 52°0N 97°0W 297 C9
Winnipeg Beach Canada 50°30N 96°58W 297 C9
Winnipegosis Canada 51°39N 99°55W 297 C9
Winnipegosis L. Canada 52°30N 100°0W 297 C9
Winnipesaukee, L. U.S.A. 43°38N 71°21W 313 C13
Winnisquam L. U.S.A. 43°33N 71°31W 313 C13
Winnsboro La., U.S.A. 32°10N 91°43W 314 E9
Winnsboro S.C., U.S.A. 34°23N 81°5W 315 D14
Winnsboro Tex., U.S.A. 32°58N 95°17W 314 E7
Winokapau, L. Canada 53°15N 62°50W 299 B7
Winona Minn., U.S.A. 44°3N 91°39W 308 C8
Winona Miss., U.S.A. 33°29N 89°44W 315 E10
Winooski U.S.A. 44°29N 73°11W 313 B11
Winooski → U.S.A. 44°32N 73°17W 313 B11
Winschoten Neths. 53°9N 7°3E 170 A7
Winsen Germany 53°22N 10°13E 178 B6
Winsford U.K. 53°12N 2°31W 168 D5
Winslow = Bainbridge Island U.S.A. 47°38N 122°32W 306 C4
Winslow Ariz., U.S.A. 35°2N 110°42W 305 J8
Winslow Ind., U.S.A. 38°23N 87°13W 311 F9
Winslow Reef Kiribati 1°36S 174°57W 277 A16
Winsted U.S.A. 41°55N 73°4W 313 E11
Winston-Salem U.S.A. 36°6N 80°15W 315 C14
Winter Garden U.S.A. 28°34N 81°35W 317 G8
Winter Haven U.S.A. 28°1N 81°44W 317 G8
Winter Park U.S.A. 28°36N 81°20W 317 G8
Winterberg Germany 51°11N 8°33E 178 D4
Winterhaven U.S.A. 32°44N 114°38W 307 N12
Winters U.S.A. 38°32N 121°58W 306 G5
Winterset U.S.A. 41°20N 94°1W 310 C3
Wintersville U.S.A. 40°23N 80°42W 312 F4
Winterswijk Neths. 51°58N 6°43E 170 C6
Winterthur Switz. 47°30N 8°44E 179 H4
Winthrop U.S.A. 48°28N 120°10W 304 B3
Winton Queens., Australia 22°24S 143°3E 280 C3
Winton N.Z. 46°8S 168°20E 285 G3
Wintua Vanuatu 16°30S 167°26E 287 F5
Wipper → Germany 51°16N 11°12E 178 D7
Wirlyajarrayi ✪ Australia 21°45S 132°35E 278 D5
Wirraminna Australia 31°12S 136°13E 282 A2
Wirrulla Australia 32°24S 134°31E 281 E1
Wisbech U.K. 52°41N 0°9E 169 E8
Wisconsin □ U.S.A. 44°45N 89°30W 308 C9
Wisconsin → U.S.A. 43°0N 91°15W 310 A5
Wisconsin Rapids U.S.A. 44°23N 89°49W 308 C9
Wisdom U.S.A. 45°37N 113°27W 304 D7
Wiseman U.S.A. 67°25N 150°6W 303 C10
Wishaw U.K. 55°46N 3°54W 167 F5
Wishek U.S.A. 46°16N 99°33W 308 B4
Wisła Poland 49°38N 18°53E 185 J5
Wisła → Poland 54°22N 18°55E 184 D5
Wiślany, Zalew Poland 54°20N 19°50E 184 D6
Wisłok → Poland 50°13N 22°32E 185 H9
Wisłoka → Poland 50°27N 21°23E 185 H8
Wismar Mecklenburg-Vorpommern, Germany 53°54N 11°29E 178 B7
Wismar Guyana 5°59N 58°18W 329 B6
Wisner U.S.A. 41°59N 96°55W 308 E5
Wissant France 50°52N 1°40E 173 B8
Wissembourg France 49°2N 7°57E 173 C14
Wissous France 48°44N 2°19E 134 B2
Wisznice Poland 51°48N 23°13E 185 G10
Witbank = eMalahleni S. Africa 25°51S 29°14E 271 C4
Witches Gorge = Wu Xia China 31°2N 110°10E 229 B8
Witdraai S. Africa 26°58S 20°48E 270 C3
Witham U.K. 51°48N 0°40E 169 F8
Witham → U.K. 52°59N 0°2W 168 E7
Withernsea U.K. 53°44N 0°1E 168 D8
Withlacoochee → Fla., U.S.A. 30°24N 83°10W 316 E6
Withlacoochee → Fla., U.S.A. 29°0N 82°45W 317 G7
Witjira △ Australia 26°22S 135°37E 281 D2
Witkowo Poland 52°26N 17°45E 185 F4
Witless Bay Canada 47°17N 52°50W 299 C9
Witney U.K. 51°48N 1°28W 169 F6
Witnica Poland 52°40N 14°54E 185 F1
Witnossob → Namibia 23°55S 18°45E 270 C3
Witriver S. Africa 25°20S 31°0E 271 C5
Wittdün Germany 54°38N 8°23E 178 A4
Witte Pan Bonaire 12°3N 68°17W 322 h
Wittelsheim France 47°48N 7°14E 173 E14
Witten Germany 51°26N 7°20E 178 D3
Wittenau Germany 52°35N 13°19E 115 A2
Wittenberge Germany 53°0N 11°45E 178 B7
Wittenburg Germany 53°31N 11°4E 178 B7
Wittenoom Australia 22°15S 118°20E 278 D2
Witti, Banjaran Malaysia 5°11N 116°29E 235 A5
Wittingau = Třeboň Czechia 49°1N 14°48E 180 B7
Wittingen Germany 52°44N 10°44E 178 C6
Wittlich Germany 49°59N 6°53E 179 F2
Wittmund Germany 53°34N 7°46E 178 B3
Wittow Germany 54°38N 13°20E 178 A9
Wittstock Germany 53°10N 12°28E 178 B8
Witu Kenya 2°23S 40°26E 268 C5
Witu Is. Papua N. G. 4°50S 149°25E 286 C5
Witvlei Namibia 22°23S 18°32E 270 B2
Witwatersrand, Univ. of S. Africa 26°11S 28°1E 123 B2
Witzenhausen Germany 51°20N 9°51E 178 D5
Wiwon N. Korea 40°54N 126°3E 224 B3
Wixom U.S.A. 42°32N 83°32W 311 B13
Wkra → Poland 52°27N 20°44E 185 F7
Władysławowo Poland 54°48N 18°25E 184 D5
Wleń Poland 51°2N 15°39E 185 G2
Wlingi Indonesia 8°5S 112°25E 235 D4
Włochy Poland 52°12N 20°54E 143 B1
Włocławek Poland 52°40N 19°3E 185 F6
Włodawa Poland 51°33N 23°31E 185 G10
Włoszczowa Poland 50°50N 19°55E 185 H6
Wo Mei Hong Kong, China 22°21N 114°15E 122 A3
Wo Yi Hop Hong Kong, China 22°23N 114°8E 122 A3
Woburn Ont., Canada 43°46N 79°12W 141 A3
Woburn Mass., U.S.A. 42°29N 71°9W 116 A2
Wodian China 32°50N 112°35E 226 H7
Wodonga Australia 36°5S 146°50E 283 D7
Wodzisław Śląski Poland 50°1N 18°26E 185 H5
Wœrth France 48°57N 7°45E 173 D14
Wohlau = Wołów Poland 51°20N 16°38E 185 G3
Woinbogoin China 32°51N 98°39E 228 A2
Woippy France 49°10N 6°8E 173 C13
Woitape Papua N. G. 8°33S 147°15E 286 E4
Wojcieszow Poland 50°58N 15°55E 185 H2
Wokam Indonesia 5°45S 134°28E 231 F8
Wokha India 26°6N 94°16E 241 B5
Woking U.K. 51°19N 0°34W 169 F7
Wokingham U.K. 51°24N 0°49W 169 F7
Wokingham □ U.K. 51°25N 0°51W 169 F7
Woko △ Australia 31°46S 151°49E 283 A9
Wola Poland 52°14N 20°57E 143 B1
Wolbrom Poland 50°24N 19°45E 185 H6
Wolcottville U.S.A. 41°32N 85°22W 311 C11
Wolczyn Poland 51°1N 18°3E 185 G5
Woldegk Germany 53°27N 13°34E 178 B9
Woldenberg = Dobiegniew Poland 52°59N 15°45E 185 F2
Woldenberg Park New Orleans, U.S.A. 131 b3
Woleu-Ntem □ Gabon 2°0N 12°30E 264 B2
Wolf → Canada 60°17N 132°33W 296 A2
Wolf, Volcán Ecuador 0°1N 91°20W 330 a
Wolf Creek U.S.A. 47°0N 112°4W 304 C7
Wolf L. Canada 60°24N 131°40W 296 A2
Wolf Point U.S.A. 48°5N 105°39W 304 B11
Wolfe Creek Crater △ Australia 19°10S 127°47E 278 C4
Wolfe I. Canada 44°7N 76°20W 313 B8
Wolfeboro U.S.A. 43°35N 71°13W 313 C13
Wolfenbüttel Germany 52°10N 10°33E 178 C6
Wolfratshausen Germany 47°54N 11°24E 179 H7
Wolfsberg Austria 46°50N 14°52E 180 E7
Wolfsburg Germany 52°25N 10°48E 178 C6
Wolgast Germany 54°3N 13°44E 178 A9
Wolgok S. Korea 37°35N 127°1E 132 B2
Wolhusen Switz. 47°4N 8°4E 179 H4
Wolica Poland 52°7N 20°51E 143 C1
Wolin Poland 53°50N 14°37E 184 E1
Woliński △ Poland 53°57N 14°28E 184 E1
Wollaston U.S.A. 42°15N 71°2W 116 B2
Wollaston, Is. Chile 55°40S 67°30W 336 E3
Wollaston Forland Greenland 74°25N 19°40W 154 C9
Wollaston L. Canada 58°7N 103°10W 297 B8
Wollaston Lake Canada 58°3N 103°33W 297 B8
Wollaston Pen. Canada 69°30N 115°0W 294 D9
Wollemi △ Australia 33°0S 150°30E 283 B9
Wollongong Australia 34°25S 150°54E 283 C9
Wolmar = Valmiera Latvia 57°37N 25°29E 188 D3
Wolmaransstad S. Africa 27°12S 25°59E 270 C4
Wolmirstedt Germany 52°14N 11°37E 178 C7
Wolomin Poland 52°19N 21°15E 185 F8
Wołów Poland 51°20N 16°38E 185 G3
Wolseley S. Austral., Australia 36°23S 140°54E 282 D4
Wolseley Western Cape, S. Africa 33°26S 19°7E 270 D2
Wolsey U.S.A. 44°25N 98°28W 308 C4
Wolstenholme, C. Canada 62°35N 77°30W 292 C12
Wolsztyn Poland 52°8N 16°5E 185 F3
Woltersdorf Germany 52°27N 13°44E 115 B5
Woluwe-St-Lambert Belgium 50°50N 4°24E 116 A2
Woluwe-St-Pierre Belgium 50°50N 4°25E 116 A2
Wolvega Neths. 52°52N 6°0E 170 B6
Wolverhampton U.K. 52°35N 2°7W 169 E5
Wondai Australia 26°20S 151°49E 281 D5
Wonenara Papua N. G. 6°48S 145°53E 286 D3
Wong Chuk Hang Hong Kong, China 22°15N 114°10E 122 B3
Wong Chuk Wan Hong Kong, China 22°23N 114°17E 122 A3
Wong Chuk Yeung Hong Kong, China 22°24N 114°15E 122 A3
Wonga Wongué △ Gabon 0°29S 9°25E 264 C1
Wongalarroo L. Australia 31°32S 144°0E 282 A6
Wongan Hills Australia 30°51S 116°37E 279 F2
Wonju S. Korea 37°22N 127°58E 224 D3
Wonosari Indonesia 7°58S 110°36E 231 G14
Wonosobo Indonesia 7°22S 109°54E 235 D3
Wonowon Canada 56°44N 121°48W 296 B4
Wŏnsan N. Korea 39°11N 127°27E 224 C3
Wonthaggi Australia 38°37S 145°37E 283 E6
Wood Buffalo △ Canada 59°0N 113°41W 296 B6
Wood Green U.K. 51°36N 0°6W 125 A3
Wood Is. Australia 16°24S 123°19E 278 C3
Wood L. Canada 55°17N 103°17W 297 B8
Wood Ridge U.S.A. 40°50N 74°4W 132 A1
Wood River U.S.A. 38°52N 90°5W 310 F6
Wood-Tikchik State Park ⌂ U.S.A. 59°30N 158°30W 303 G8
Woodah, I. Australia 13°27S 136°10E 280 A2
Woodbine U.S.A. 30°58N 81°44W 316 E8
Woodbine Race Track Canada 43°43N 79°36W 141 A1
Woodbourne U.S.A. 41°46N 74°36W 313 E10
Woodbridge Ont., Canada 43°47N 79°36W 141 A1
Woodbridge Suffolk, U.K. 52°6N 1°20E 169 E9
Woodbridge B. Dominica 15°19N 61°25W 323 k
Woodburn N.S.W., Australia 29°6S 153°23E 281 A5
Woodburn Oreg., U.S.A. 45°9N 122°51W 304 D2
Woodbury U.S.A. 32°59N 84°35W 316 C5
Woodenbong Australia 28°24S 152°39E 281 D5
Woodend Australia 37°20S 144°33E 282 D6
Woodford Queens., Australia 26°58S 152°47E 281 D5
Woodford London, U.K. 51°36N 0°1E 125 A4
Woodford Bridge U.K. 51°36N 0°3E 125 A4
Woodford Green U.K. 51°36N 0°1E 125 A4
Woodfords U.S.A. 38°47N 119°50W 306 G7
Woodhaven U.S.A. 40°41N 73°51W 132 B2
Woodhouselee U.K. 55°52N 3°13W 121 B2
Woodlake U.S.A. 36°25N 119°6W 306 J7
Woodland Calif., U.S.A. 38°41N 121°46W 306 G5
Woodland Maine, U.S.A. 45°9N 67°25W 309 C20
Woodland Pa., U.S.A. 41°0N 78°21W 312 F6
Woodland Wash., U.S.A. 45°54N 122°45W 306 E4
Woodland Caribou ⌂ Canada 51°0N 94°45W 297 C10
Woodlands Singapore 1°26N 103°46E 138 A2
Woodlands, The U.S.A. 30°9N 95°29W 314 F7
Woodlark I. Papua N. G. 9°10S 152°50E 286 E7
Woodmont U.S.A. 38°59N 77°5W 143 B2
Woodonga Australia 36°10S 146°50E 281 F4
Woodridge Canada 49°20N 96°9W 297 D9
Woodroffe, Mt. Australia 26°20S 131°45E 279 E5
Woods, L. Australia 17°50S 133°30E 280 B1
Woods, L. of the N. Amer. 49°15N 94°45W 297 D10
Woods Bay Canada 45°8N 79°59W 312 A5
Woodside S. Austral., Australia 34°58S 138°52E 282 C3
Woodside Vic., Australia 38°31S 146°52E 283 E7
Woodside London, U.K. 51°23N 0°4W 125 B3
Woodside N.Y., U.S.A. 40°44N 73°54W 132 B2
Woodson U.S.A. 39°37N 90°14W 310 E6
Woodstock N.S.W., Australia 33°45S 148°53E 283 B8
Woodstock Queens., Australia 19°35S 146°50E 280 B4
Woodstock N.B., Canada 46°11N 67°37W 299 C6
Woodstock Ont., Canada 43°10N 80°45W 312 C4
Woodstock Western Cape, S. Africa 33°55S 18°27E 118 A1
Woodstock Oxon., U.K. 51°51N 1°20W 169 F6
Woodstock Ill., U.S.A. 42°19N 88°27W 311 B8
Woodstock N.Y., U.S.A. 42°2N 74°7W 313 D10
Woodstock Vt., U.S.A. 43°37N 72°31W 313 C12
Woodsville U.S.A. 44°9N 72°2W 313 B13
Woodview Canada 44°35N 78°8W 312 B6
Woodville N.Z. 40°20S 175°53E 284 G4
Woodville Fla., U.S.A. 30°19N 84°15W 316 E5
Woodville Ga., U.S.A. 33°40N 83°7W 316 B6
Woodville Miss., U.S.A. 31°6N 91°18W 314 F9
Woodville Ohio, U.S.A. 41°27N 83°22W 311 C13
Woodville Tex., U.S.A. 30°47N 94°25W 314 F7
Woodward U.S.A. 36°26N 99°24W 314 C5
Woody U.S.A. 35°42N 118°50W 307 K8
Woody → Canada 52°31N 100°51W 297 C8
Woody I. S. China Sea 16°50N 112°20E 230 A4
Woolacombe U.K. 51°10N 4°13W 169 F3
Woolamai, C. Australia 38°30S 145°23E 283 E6
Woolbrook Australia 30°56S 151°25E 283 A9
Wooler U.K. 55°33N 2°1W 168 B5
Woolgoolga Australia 30°6S 153°11E 281 E5
Woollahra Australia 33°53S 151°15E 139 B2
Woolloomooloo Sydney, Australia 139 b2
Wooloowere B. Australia 34°1S 151°8E 139 C1
Woolwich U.K. 51°29N 0°4E 125 B4
Woolworth Building New York, U.S.A. 132 e1
Woomargama △ Australia 35°50S 147°15E 283 C7
Woomera Australia 31°5S 136°50E 282 A2
Woonsocket R.I., U.S.A. 42°0N 71°31W 313 E13
Woonsocket S. Dak., U.S.A. 44°3N 98°17W 308 C4
Wooramel → Australia 25°47S 114°10E 279 E1
Wooramel Roadhouse Australia 25°45S 114°17E 279 E1
Wooroonooran △ Australia 16°25S 146°1E 280 B4
Wooster U.S.A. 40°48N 81°56W 312 F3
Woqooyi Galbeed □ Somalia 10°0N 44°30E 267 C5
Woraksan △ S. Korea 36°50N 128°5E 224 D4

Worcester Western Cape, S. Africa 33°39S 19°27E 270 D2
Worcester Worcs., U.K. 52°11N 2°12W 169 E5
Worcester Mass., U.S.A. 42°16N 71°48W 313 D13
Worcester N.Y., U.S.A. 42°36N 74°45W 313 D10
Worcestershire □ U.K. 52°13N 2°10W 169 E5
Worden U.S.A. 38°56N 89°50W 310 F7
Wörgl Austria 47°29N 12°3E 180 D5
Worker's Stadium China 39°55N 116°25E 114 B2
Workington U.K. 54°39N 3°33W 168 C4
Worksop U.K. 53°18N 1°7W 168 D6
Workum Neths. 52°59N 5°26E 170 B5
Worland U.S.A. 44°1N 107°57W 304 D10
World Bank Washington, D.C., U.S.A. 143 b1
World Financial Center New York, U.S.A. 132 e1
World Financial Centre Shanghai, China 31°14N 121°30E 138 B2
World Trade Center, Site of former = National September 11 Memorial and Museum New York, U.S.A. 132 e1
World War Two Memorial Washington, D.C., U.S.A. 143 b1
Worli India 19°1N 72°49E 130 A1
Wormhout France 50°52N 2°28E 173 B9
Worms Germany 49°37N 8°21E 179 F4
Woroba ◇ Ivory C. 8°19N 7°5W 262 D3
Worsley Canada 56°31N 119°8W 296 B5
Wörth Bayern, Germany 49°1N 12°24E 179 F8
Worth Ill., U.S.A. 41°41N 87°47W 119 C2
Wortham U.S.A. 31°47N 96°28W 314 F6
Wörther See Austria 46°37N 14°10E 180 E7
Worthing U.K. 50°49N 0°21W 169 G7
Worthington Ind., U.S.A. 39°7N 86°59W 311 E10
Worthington Minn., U.S.A. 43°37N 95°36W 308 D6
Worthington Ohio, U.S.A. 40°5N 83°1W 311 E3
Worthington Pa., U.S.A. 40°50N 79°38W 312 F5
Wosi Indonesia 0°15S 128°0E 231 E7
Wote Kenya 1°47S 37°38E 268 C4
Wotjalum ◇ Australia 16°30S 123°45E 278 C3
Wotjobaluk ◇ Australia 37°0S 142°0E 281 C3
Wou-han = Wuhan China 30°31N 114°18E 229 B10
Wour Chad 21°14N 16°0E 259 D3
Wousi = Wuxi China 31°33N 120°18E 229 B13
Wowoni Indonesia 4°5S 123°5E 231 E6
Woy Woy Australia 33°30S 151°19E 283 B9
Wrangel I. = Vrangelya, Ostrov Russia 71°0N 180°0E 215 B18
Wrangell U.S.A. 56°28N 132°23W 296 B2
Wrangell Mts. U.S.A. 61°30N 142°0W 303 F12
Wrangell-St. Elias △ U.S.A. 61°0N 142°0W 303 F12
Wrath, C. U.K. 58°38N 5°1W 167 C3
Wray U.S.A. 40°5N 102°13W 304 F12
Wrekin, The U.K. 52°41N 2°32W 169 E5
Wrens U.S.A. 33°12N 82°23W 316 B7
Wren's Nest U.S.A. 33°44N 84°25W 113 B2
Wrexham U.K. 53°3N 3°0W 168 D4
Wrexham □ U.K. 53°1N 2°58W 168 D5
Wriezen Germany 52°42N 14°7E 178 C10
Wright = Paranas Phil. 11°42N 125°2E 233 F5
Wright Fla., U.S.A. 30°37N 86°38W 317 E3
Wright Wyo., U.S.A. 43°45N 105°28W 304 E11
Wright Pt. Canada 43°48N 81°44W 312 C3
Wrightmyo India 11°47N 92°43E 245 J11
Wrightson, Mt. U.S.A. 31°42N 110°51W 305 L8
Wrightsville U.S.A. 32°44N 82°43W 316 C7
Wrightwood U.S.A. 34°22N 117°38W 307 L9
Wrigley Canada 63°16N 123°37W 294 E7
Wrigley Building Chicago, U.S.A. 119 b2
Wrigley Field U.S.A. 41°56N 87°39W 119 b2
Wrocław Poland 51°5N 17°5E 185 G4
Wronki Poland 52°41N 16°21E 185 F3
Września Poland 52°21N 17°36E 185 F4
Wschowa Poland 51°48N 16°20E 185 G3
Wu → Taiwan 24°9N 120°31E 225 B2
Wu Jiang → China 29°40N 107°20E 228 C6
Wu Kau Tang China 22°30N 114°14E 219 a
Wu Xia China 31°2N 110°10E 229 B8
Wu'an China 36°40N 114°5E 226 F8
Wubalawun ◇ Australia 15°28S 133°1E 278 C5
Wubin Australia 30°6S 116°37E 279 F2
Wubu China 37°28N 110°42E 226 F6
Wuchang China 44°55N 127°5E 227 B14
Wucheng China 37°12N 116°20E 226 F9
Wuch'i Taiwan 24°16N 120°31E 225 B2
Wuchieh Taiwan 24°41N 121°47E 225 B3
Wuchow = Wuzhou China 23°30N 111°18E 229 F8

Wuning China 29°17N 115°5E 229 C10
Wunna → India 20°18N 78°48E 244 D4
Wunnummin L. Canada 52°55N 89°10W 298 B2
Wunsiedel Germany 50°2N 12°0E 179 E8
Wunstorf Germany 52°25N 9°29E 178 C5
Wuntho Burma 23°55N 95°45E 241 D5
Wupatki △ U.S.A. 35°35N 111°20W 305 J8
Wuping China 25°5N 116°5E 229 E11
Wuppertal Nordrhein-Westfalen, Germany 51°16N 7°12E 178 D3
Wuppertal Western Cape, S. Africa 32°13S 19°12E 270 D2
Wuqi = Wuch'i Taiwan 24°16N 120°31E 225 B2
Wuqia China 39°40N 75°7E 217 E9
Wuqing China 39°23N 117°4E 227 E9
Würm → Germany 48°8N 11°27E 131 B1
Würm-kanal Germany 48°13N 11°29E 131 A1
Wurralibi ◇ Australia 15°43S 137°1E 280 B2
Wurtsboro U.S.A. 41°35N 74°29W 313 E10
Würzburg Germany 49°46N 9°55E 179 F5
Wurzen Germany 51°22N 12°44E 178 D8
Wushan Gansu, China 34°43N 104°53E 226 G3
Wushan Guangdong, China 23°9N 113°21E 121 B3
Wushi China 41°9N 79°13E 217 D9
Wusih = Wuxi China 31°33N 120°18E 229 B13
Wusong China 31°22N 121°29E 138 A1
Wutach → Germany 47°37N 8°15E 179 H4
Wutai China 38°40N 113°12E 226 E7
Wutai Shan China 39°3N 113°32E 226 E7
Wuting = Huimin China 37°27N 117°28E 227 F9
Wutonghaolai China 42°50N 120°5E 227 C11
Wutongqiao China 29°22N 103°50E 228 C4
Wutung Papua N. G. 2°37S 141°1E 286 B1
Wuwei Anhui, China 31°18N 117°54E 229 B11
Wuwei Gansu, China 37°57N 102°34E 218 D9
Wuxi Jiangsu, China 31°33N 120°18E 229 B13
Wuxi Sichuan, China 31°23N 109°35E 228 B7
Wuxiang China 36°49N 112°50E 226 F7
Wuxuan China 23°34N 109°38E 228 F7
Wuxue China 29°52N 115°33E 229 C10
Wuyang China 33°25N 113°35E 226 H7
Wuyi Hebei, China 37°46N 115°56E 226 F8
Wuyi Zhejiang, China 28°52N 119°50E 229 C12
Wuyishan China 27°0N 117°0E 229 D11
Wuyishan China 27°45N 118°0E 229 C12
Wuyishan △ China 27°55N 117°54E 229 D11
Wuyo Nigeria 10°23N 11°50E 263 C7
Wuyuan Jiangxi, China 29°15N 117°50E 229 C11
Wuyuan Nei Monggol Zizhiqu, China 41°2N 108°20E 226 D5
Wuzhai China 38°54N 111°48E 226 E6
Wuzhi Shan China 18°45N 109°3E 229 a
Wuzhishan = Tongshi China 18°50N 109°20E 229 a
Wuzhong China 38°2N 106°12E 226 E4
Wuzhou China 23°30N 111°18E 229 F8
Wyaaba Cr. → Australia 16°27S 141°35E 280 B3
Wyalkatchem Australia 31°8N 117°22E 279 F2
Wyalusing U.S.A. 41°40N 76°16W 313 E8
Wyandotte U.S.A. 42°12N 83°9W 311 B13
Wyandra Australia 27°12S 145°56E 281 D4
Wyangala, L. Australia 33°54S 149°0E 283 B8
Wyara, L. Australia 28°42S 144°14E 281 D3
Wycheproof Australia 36°5S 143°17E 282 D5
Wycliffe Well Australia 20°48S 134°14E 280 C1
Wyczółki Poland 52°9N 20°59E 143 C1
Wye → U.K. 51°38N 2°40W 169 F5
Wyemandoo Australia 28°28S 118°29E 279 E2
Wygoda Poland 52°16N 21°7E 143 B2
Wyk Germany 54°41N 8°33E 178 A4
Wymondham U.K. 52°35N 1°7E 169 E9
Wymore U.S.A. 40°7N 96°40W 308 E5
Wynberg S. Africa 34°2S 18°28E 118 B1
Wyndham W. Austral., Australia 15°33S 128°3E 278 C4
Wyndham N.Z. 46°20S 168°51E 291 M2
Wynne U.S.A. 35°14N 90°47W 315 D9
Wynyard Tas., Australia 41°5S 145°44E 281 G4
Wynyard Sask., Canada 51°45N 104°10W 297 C8
Wyola L. Australia 29°8S 130°17E 279 E5
Wyoming Ont., Canada 42°57N 82°7W 312 D2
Wyoming Ill., U.S.A. 41°4N 89°47W 310 C7
Wyoming Iowa, U.S.A. 42°4N 91°0W 310 B6
Wyoming Mich., U.S.A. 42°54N 85°42W 311 B11
Wyoming □ U.S.A. 43°0N 107°30W 304 E10
Wyomissing U.S.A. 40°20N 75°59W 313 F9
Wyong Australia 33°14S 151°24E 283 B9
Wyperfeld △ Australia 35°35S 141°42E 282 C4
Wyrzysk Poland 53°10N 17°17E 185 E4
Wyśmierzyce Poland 51°37N 20°50E 185 G4
Wysoka Poland 53°13N 17°2E 185 E4
Wysokie Mazowieckie Poland 52°55N 22°30E 185 F9
Wyszków Poland 52°36N 21°25E 185 F9
Wyszogród Poland 52°23N 20°9E 185 F8
Wytheville U.S.A. 36°57N 81°5W 309 G13
Wyżyna Małopolska Poland 50°45N 20°0E 185 H7

X

Xa-Cassau Angola 9°5S 20°15E 265 D4
Xa-Muteba Angola 9°34S 17°50E 265 D3
Xaafuun Somalia 10°25N 51°16E 267 B7
Xaafuun, Ras Somalia 10°27N 51°24E 267 B7
Xabregas Portugal 38°43N 9°6W 196 G2
Xacmaz Azerbaijan 41°31N 48°42E 191 K9
Xaghra Malta 36°3N 14°16E 206 E7
Xai-Xai Mozam. 25°6S 33°31E 271 C5
Xaidulla China 36°28N 77°59E 217 E9
Xaignabouri = Sayaboury Laos 19°15N 101°45E 236 C3
Xainza China 30°58N 88°35E 216 D6
Xalapa Mexico 19°32N 96°55W 319 D5
Xalin Somalia 9°6N 48°37E 267 C5
Xallas → Spain 42°54N 9°8W 194 C1
Xambioá Brazil 6°25S 48°40W 332 C2
Xangongo Angola 16°45S 15°5E 265 F3
Xankändi Azerbaijan 39°52N 46°49E 213 C12
Xanlar = Goygöl Azerbaijan 40°37N 46°12E 191 K8
Xanten Germany 51°39N 6°26E 178 D2
Xanthi Greece 41°10N 24°58E 205 E11
Xanthos Turkey 36°19N 29°18E 205 E11
Xapuri Brazil 10°35S 68°35W 330 C4
Xar Moron He → China 43°25N 120°35E 227 C11
Xarardheere Somalia 4°33N 47°38E 267 D6
Xarrë Albania 39°44N 20°3E 206 B1
Xàtiva Spain 38°59N 0°32W 197 G4
Xau, L. Botswana 21°15S 24°44E 270 C3
Xavantina Brazil 21°15S 52°48W 335 A5
Xayar China 41°13N 82°48E 217 D10
Xebert China 44°2N 112°0E 227 B11
Xenia U.S.A. 39°41N 83°56W 311 E13
Xeraco Spain 39°2N 0°13W 197 F4
Xertigny France 48°3N 6°24E 173 D13
Xewkija Malta 36°2N 14°15E 206 E7
Xhora S. Africa 31°55S 28°38E 271 D4
Xhumo Botswana 21°7S 24°35E 270 C3
Xi Jiang → China 22°5N 113°20E 229 F9

Xi Ujimqin Qi China 44°32N 117°40E 227 B9
Xi Xian Henan, China 32°20N 114°43E 229 A10
Xi Xian Shanxi, China 36°41N 110°58E 226 F6
Xia Xian China 35°8N 111°12E 226 G6
Xiachengzi China 44°40N 130°18E 227 B16
Xiachuan Dao China 21°40N 112°40E 229 G9
Xiaguan China 25°32N 100°16E 218 F9
Xiajiang China 27°30N 115°10E 229 D10
Xiajin China 36°56N 116°0E 226 F9
Xiakeng China 24°50N 115°40E 121 A2
Xiamen China 24°25N 118°4E 229 E12
Xiamen Gaoqi Int. ✈ (XMN) China 24°33N 118°8E 229 E12
Xi'an China 34°15N 109°0E 226 G5
Xian Xian China 38°12N 116°6E 226 E9
Xian Xianyang Int. ✈ (XIY) China 34°27N 108°45E 226 G5
Xianfeng China 29°40N 109°8E 228 C7
Xiang Jiang → China 28°55N 112°50E 229 C9
Xiang Khouang Laos 19°17N 103°25E 236 C4
Xiangcheng Henan, China 33°50N 113°27E 226 H7
Xiangcheng Sichuan, China 28°53N 99°47E 228 C2
Xiangdu China 23°13N 106°58E 228 F6
Xiangfan China 32°2N 112°8E 229 A9
Xianggang = Hong Kong □ China 22°11N 114°14E 219 a
Xianghuang Qi China 42°2N 113°50E 226 C7
Xiangjiaba Dam China 28°37N 104°17E 228 C5
Xiangning China 35°58N 110°50E 226 G6
Xiangquan China 36°30N 113°1E 226 F7
Xiangquan He = Sutlej → Pakistan 29°23N 71°3E 242 E4
Xiangshan = Hsiangshan Taiwan 24°48N 120°54E 225 B2
Xiangshan China 29°29N 121°51E 229 C13
Xiangshui China 34°12N 119°33E 227 G10
Xiangtan China 27°51N 112°54E 229 D9
Xiangxiang China 28°38N 112°25E 229 D9
Xiangyin China 28°38N 112°54E 229 C9
Xiangyun China 25°34N 100°35E 228 E3
Xiangzhou China 23°58N 109°40E 228 F7
Xianju China 28°51N 120°44E 229 C13
Xianning China 29°51N 114°16E 229 C10
Xianshui He → China 30°10N 100°59E 228 B3
Xiantao China 30°25N 113°25E 229 B9
Xianyang China 34°20N 108°40E 226 G5
Xianyou China 25°22N 118°38E 229 E12
Xiao Hinggan Ling China 49°0N 127°0E 219 B14
Xiaofeng China 30°35N 119°52E 229 B12
Xiaogan China 30°55N 113°45E 229 B9
Xiaogang China 22°34N 120°20E 225 D2
Xiaogang Park China 23°6N 113°16E 121 B2
Xiaojin China 30°59N 102°21E 228 B4
Xiaolan China 22°38N 113°13E 229 F9
Xiaoshan China 30°12N 120°18E 229 B13
Xiaoshan China 30°12N 120°18E 229 B13
Xiaowan Dam China 24°42N 100°5E 228 E3
Xiaowutai Shan China 39°51N 114°59E 226 E8
Xiaoyi China 37°8N 111°48E 226 F6
Xiapu China 26°54N 119°59E 229 D12
Xiashachong China 23°8N 113°9E 121 B1
Xiashan = Zhanjiang China 21°15N 110°20E 229 G8
Xiawa China 42°35N 120°38E 227 C11
Xiawa China 34°15N 116°10E 226 G9
Xichang Guangdong, China 23°9N 113°13E 121 B2
Xichang Sichuan, China 27°51N 102°19E 228 D4
Xicheng Beijing, China 114 b1
Xichou China 23°25N 104°42E 228 E5
Xichuan China 33°0N 111°30E 229 A8
Xidan China 39°52N 116°20E 114 B2
Xide China 28°8N 102°19E 228 C4
Xiemahe China 31°38N 111°12E 229 B8
Xi'ercun China 23°3N 113°1E 121 B2
Xifei He → China 32°45N 116°40E 229 A11
Xifeng Gansu, China 35°40N 107°40E 226 G4
Xifeng Guizhou, China 27°7N 106°42E 228 D6
Xifeng Liaoning, China 42°42N 124°45E 227 C13
Xifengzhen = Xifeng China 35°40N 107°40E 226 G4
Xigang = Hsikang Taiwan 23°7N 120°12E 225 C2
Xigazê China 29°5N 88°45E 218 F6
Xihe China 34°2N 105°20E 226 G3
Xihua China 33°45N 114°30E 226 H8
Xilaganí Greece 40°58N 25°28E 205 D11
Xiliao He → China 43°32N 123°35E 227 C12
Xilin China 24°30N 105°6E 228 E5
Xiling Gorge = Xiling Xia China 30°54N 110°48E 229 B8
Xiling Xia China 30°54N 110°48E 229 B8
Xilinhot China 43°52N 116°2E 226 C9
Xilokastro Greece 38°5N 22°38E 204 C4
Xiluodu Dam China 28°12N 103°33E 228 C5
Ximana Mozam. 19°24S 33°58E 271 B5
Xime Guinea-Biss. 11°59N 14°57W 262 C2
Ximeng China 22°50N 99°27E 228 F2
Ximiao China 40°59N 100°12E 218 D9
Xin Xian = Xinzhou China 38°22N 112°46E 226 E7
Xin'anjiang Shuiku China 29°33N 118°56E 229 C12
Xinavane Mozam. 25°2S 32°47E 271 C5
Xinbin China 41°40N 125°2E 227 C13
Xincai China 32°43N 114°58E 229 A10
Xincheng = Hsinch'eng Taiwan 24°8N 121°39E 225 B3
Xincheng Guangxi Zhuangzu, China 24°5N 108°39E 228 E7
Xincheng Jiangxi, China 26°48N 114°6E 229 D10
Xinchengzi China 42°2N 123°30E 227 C12
Xincun China 23°5N 113°2E 121 B2
Xindian = Hsintien Taiwan 24°57N 121°32E 225 B3
Xinfeng = Hsinfeng Taiwan 24°57N 121°0E 225 B3

Xinhua = Hsinhua Taiwan 23°2N 120°18E 225 C2
Xinhua China 27°42N 111°13E 229 D8
Xinhuang China 27°21N 109°12E 228 D7
Xinhui China 22°25N 113°0E 229 F9
Xining China 36°34N 101°40E 226 G3
Xinji China 37°55N 115°13E 226 F8
Xinjian China 35°34N 115°46E 229 B10
Xinjiang China 35°34N 111°11E 226 G6
Xinjiang Uygur Zizhiqu □ China 42°0N 86°0E 217 D11
Xinjin = Pulandian China 39°25N 121°58E 227 E11
Xinjin China 30°24N 103°47E 228 B4
Xinkai He → China 43°32N 123°35E 227 C12
Xinken China 22°39N 113°36E 219 a
Xinle China 38°25N 114°40E 226 E8
Xinlitun China 42°0N 122°8E 227 C12
Xinlong China 30°57N 100°12E 228 B3
Xinmi China 34°30N 113°25E 226 G7
Xinmin China 41°59N 122°50E 227 C12
Xinning China 26°28N 110°50E 229 D8
Xinping China 24°5N 101°59E 228 E3
Xinshao China 27°21N 111°26E 229 D8
Xinshi = Hsinshih Taiwan 23°5N 120°17E 225 C2
Xintai China 35°55N 117°45E 227 G9
Xintian China 25°55N 112°13E 229 E9
Xinwan China 22°47N 113°40E 219 a
Xinwu = Hsinwu Taiwan 24°59N 121°5E 225 B3
Xinxiang China 35°18N 113°50E 226 G7
Xinxing China 22°35N 112°5E 229 F9
Xinyang China 32°6N 114°3E 229 A10
Xinye China 32°30N 112°21E 229 A9
Xinyi Guangdong, China 22°25N 111°0E 229 F8
Xinyi Nei Monggol Zizhiqu, China 22°25N 111°10E 227 G10
Xinyin = Hsinying Taiwan 23°17N 120°17E 225 C2
Xinyu China 27°49N 114°58E 229 D10
Xinzhan China 43°50N 127°18E 227 C14
Xinzheng China 34°20N 113°45E 226 G7
Xinzhou Hainan, China 19°43N 109°17E 229 a
Xinzhou Hubei, China 30°50N 114°48E 229 B10
Xinzhou Shanxi, China 38°22N 112°46E 226 E7
Xinzhu = Hsinchu China 24°48N 120°58E 225 B2
Xinzhuang = Hsinchuang China 25°2N 121°27E 225 A3
Xinzo de Limia Spain 42°3N 7°47W 194 C3
Xiongyuecheng China 40°12N 122°5E 227 D12
Xiping Henan, China 33°22N 114°5E 226 H8
Xiping Henan, China 33°25N 111°8E 226 H6
Xiping Zhejiang, China 28°16N 119°29E 229 C12
Xique-Xique Brazil 10°50S 42°40W 332 D3
Xirdalan Azerbaijan 40°27N 49°45E 213 B13
Xiruá → Brazil 8°5S 67°50W 330 B4
Xisha Qundao = Paracel Is. S. China Sea 15°50N 112°0E 230 A4
Xishuangbanna China 22°5N 101°1E 228 F3
Xishui Guizhou, China 28°19N 106°9E 228 C6
Xishui Hubei, China 30°30N 115°15E 229 B10
Xitole Guinea-Biss. 11°43N 14°50W 262 C2
Xiu Shui → China 29°13N 116°0E 229 C10
Xiuning China 29°45N 118°10E 229 C12
Xiuren China 24°27N 110°12E 229 E8
Xiushan China 28°25N 108°57E 228 C7
Xiushui China 29°2N 114°33E 229 C10
Xiuwen China 26°49N 106°32E 228 D6
Xiuyan China 40°18N 123°11E 227 D12
Xiva Uzbekistan 41°30N 60°18E 216 D6
Xixabangma Feng China 28°20N 85°40E 243 E11
Xixia China 33°25N 111°29E 226 H6
Xixiang Guangdong, China 22°34N 113°52E 219 a
Xixiang Shaanxi, China 33°0N 107°44E 226 H4
Xixón = Gijón Spain 43°32N 5°42W 194 B5
Xiyang China 37°38N 113°38E 226 F7
Xizang Zizhiqu □ China 32°0N 88°0E 218 E6
Xizhi = Hsiehih Taiwan 25°4N 121°39E 225 A3
Xizhimen China 39°55N 116°19E 114 B1
Xlendi Malta 36°1N 14°12E 206 E6
Xochimilco, Parque Ecológico Mexico 19°18N 99°5W 128 C2
Xochob Mexico 19°21N 89°48W 319 D7
Xo'jayli Uzbekistan 42°29N 59°31E 216 D5
Xorazm □ Uzbekistan 43°0N 60°0E 216 D6
Xu Beihong Memorial Hall Beijing, China 114 a2
Xu Jiang → China 28°0N 116°25E 229 C11
Xuan Loc Vietnam 10°56N 107°14E 237 G6
Xuan'en China 30°0N 109°30E 228 C7
Xuanhan China 31°18N 107°38E 228 B6
Xuanhua China 40°40N 115°2E 226 D8
Xuanwei China 26°15N 103°59E 228 E5
Xuanzhou China 30°56N 118°43E 229 B12
Xuchang China 34°2N 113°48E 226 G7
Xudat Azerbaijan 41°38N 48°41E 191 K9
Xuddur Somalia 4°11N 43°52E 267 D5
Xuefeng Shan China 27°30N 110°40E 229 D8
Xuejia China 23°14N 120°10E 225 C2
Xuejiaping China 31°11N 110°16E 229 B8
Xun Jiang → China 23°35N 111°32E 229 F8
Xun Xian China 35°42N 114°33E 226 G8
Xundian China 25°36N 103°15E 228 E4
Xunwu China 24°54N 115°37E 229 E10
Xunyang China 32°48N 109°22E 226 H5
Xunyi China 35°8N 108°20E 226 G5
Xupu China 27°53N 110°32E 229 D8
Xúquer → Spain 39°5N 0°10W 197 F4
Xushui China 39°2N 115°40E 226 E8
Xuwen China 20°20N 110°10E 229 G8
Xuyi China 32°55N 118°32E 229 A12
Xuyong China 28°10N 105°22E 228 C5
Xuzhou China 34°18N 117°10E 227 G9
Xylophagou Cyprus 34°54N 33°51E 207 F9

Y

Y Drenewydd = Newtown U.K. 52°31N 3°19W 169 E4
Y Fenni = Abergavenny U.K. 51°49N 3°1W 169 F4
Y Gelli Gandryll = Hay-on-Wye U.K. 52°5N 3°8W 169 E4
Y Trallwng = Welshpool U.K. 52°39N 3°8W 169 E4
Y.S. Falls Jamaica 18°9N 77°49W 320 a
Ya Xian = Sanya China 18°14N 109°29E 229 B
Yaamba Australia 23°8S 150°22E 280 C5
Ya'an China 29°58N 103°5E 228 B4
Yaapeet Australia 35°45S 142°3E 282 C5
Yaba Nigeria 6°30N 3°22E 263 a
Yabassi Cameroon 4°30N 9°57E 263 D7
Yabayo Ivory C. 5°56N 6°36W 262 D3
Yabelo Ethiopia 4°50N 38°8E 267 G4
Yablanitsa Bulgaria 43°2N 24°5E 203 C8
Yablonovyy Khrebet Russia 53°0N 114°0E 215 D12
Yablonovyy Ra. = Yablonovyy Khrebet Russia 53°0N 114°0E 215 D12
Yabluniv Ukraine 48°24N 24°57E 183 B9

Yablunytsya Ukraine 48°19N 24°29E 183 B9
Yabrai Shan China 39°40N 103°0E 226 D2
Yabrūd Syria 33°58N 36°39E 250 E7
Yabucoa Puerto Rico 18°3N 65°53W 321 d
Yacambú △ Venezuela 9°42N 69°27W 328 B4
Yacata Fiji 17°15S 179°31W 287 A3
Yacheng China 18°22N 109°6E 229 B
Yackandandah Australia 36°18S 146°52E 283 D7
Yacuiba Bolivia 22°0S 63°43W 334 A3
Yacuma → Bolivia 13°38S 65°23W 334 C4
Yacurí △ Ecuador 4°42S 79°20W 330 A2
Yadgir India 16°45N 77°5E 244 F3
Yadkin → U.S.A. 35°23N 80°4W 315 D14
Yadong China 27°26N 88°58E 241 F12
Yadrin Russia 55°57N 46°12E 190 C8
Yaeyama-Rettō Japan 24°30N 123°40E 221 M1
Yafran Libya 32°4N 12°31E 259 B8
Yaftābād Iran 35°37N 51°17E 141 B1
Yagaba Ghana 10°14N 1°20W 262 C4
Yagasa Cluster Fiji 18°57S 178°28W 287 B3
Yağcılar Turkey 39°25N 28°23E 205 B10
Yagodnoye Russia 62°33N 149°40E 215 C15
Yaguas → Peru 2°45S 70°10W 328 D3
Yahara → Japan 35°44N 139°37E 140 A2
Yahila Dem. Rep. of the Congo 0°13N 24°28E 264 D4
Yahila Dem. Rep. of the Congo 0°13N 24°28E 264 D4
Yahk Canada 49°6N 116°10W 296 D5
Yaho Japan 35°40N 139°26E 140 A1
Yahotyn Ukraine 50°17N 31°46E 189 G6
Yahuma Dem. Rep. of the Congo 1°0N 23°10E 264 B4
Yahyalı Turkey 38°5N 35°12E 212 C6
Yaita Japan 36°48N 139°56E 141 F9
Yaiza Canary Is. 28°57N 13°46W 153 F6
Yajiang China 30°2N 100°57E 228 B3
Yajua Nigeria 11°27N 12°49E 263 C7
Yakacık Turkey 36°46N 36°11E 250 B7
Yakage Japan 34°37N 133°35E 142 G6
Yakamba Dem. Rep. of the Congo 2°42N 19°38E 264 B3
Yakapınar Turkey 36°57N 35°30E 250 B6
Yakeshi China 49°17N 120°44E 219 B13
Yakima U.S.A. 46°36N 120°31W 304 C3
Yakima → U.S.A. 46°15N 119°14W 304 C4
Yakishiri-Jima Japan 44°26N 141°25E 220 B10
Yako Burkina Faso 12°59N 2°15W 262 C4
Yakobi I. U.S.A. 58°0N 136°30W 296 B1
Yakoma Dem. Rep. of the Congo 4°5N 22°27E 264 B4
Yakoruda Bulgaria 42°1N 23°39E 202 D7
Yakossi C.A.R. 5°37N 23°19E 264 A4
Yakovlevka Russia 44°26N 133°28E 220 B6
Yakovlevskoye = Privolzhsk Russia 57°23N 41°16E 190 B5
Yaksu S. Korea 37°34N 127°1E 137 F2
Yaku-Shima Japan 30°20N 130°30E 221 J5
Yakumo Japan 42°15N 140°16E 220 C10
Yakutat U.S.A. 59°33N 139°44W 303 G13
Yakutat B. U.S.A. 59°45N 140°45W 303 G12
Yakutia = Sakha □ Russia 66°0N 130°0E 215 C14
Yakutsk Russia 62°5N 129°50E 215 C13
Yakymivka Ukraine 46°44N 35°0E 189 J8
Yala Thailand 6°33N 101°18E 237 J3
Yala Sri Lanka 6°20N 81°30E 245 L5
Yala △ Sri Lanka 6°20N 81°30E 245 L5
Yalata Australia 31°59S 132°7E 279 F5
Yalata ◇ Australia 31°35S 132°7E 279 F5
Yalboroo Australia 20°50S 148°40E 280 b
Yaleko Dem. Rep. of the Congo 0°4N 21°3E 264 D4
Yalgoo Australia 28°16S 116°39E 279 E2
Yalgorup △ Australia 32°39S 115°37E 279 F2
Yalinga C.A.R. 6°33N 23°10E 264 A4
Yalkabul, Pta. Mexico 21°32N 88°37W 319 C7
Yallahs Jamaica 17°53N 76°35W 320 a
Yallahs Hill Jamaica 17°54N 76°30W 320 a
Yalleroi Australia 24°3S 145°42E 280 C4
Yalobusha → U.S.A. 33°33N 90°10W 315 E9
Yaloké C.A.R. 5°19N 17°6E 264 A3
Yalong Jiang → China 26°40N 101°55E 228 D3
Yalova Turkey 40°41N 29°15E 203 F13
Yalpirakinu ◇ Australia 22°24S 132°12E 278 D5
Yalpuh, Ozero Ukraine 45°30N 28°41E 183 E13
Yalta Ukraine 44°30N 34°10E 189 K8
Yalvaç Turkey 38°17N 31°10E 212 C4
Yam Ha Melah = Dead Sea Asia 31°30N 35°30E 251 G6
Yam Kinneret Israel 32°45N 35°35E 250 C6
Yamada = Kama Japan 33°33N 130°49E 142 D2
Yamada Kanagawa, Japan 34°47N 135°21E 143 A2
Yamada Osaka, Japan 34°52N 135°33E 143 A2
Yamaga Japan 33°1N 130°40E 142 D2
Yamagata □ Japan 38°30N 140°0E 222 E10
Yamaguchi Japan 34°10N 131°32E 142 E3
Yamaguchi □ Japan 34°20N 131°40E 142 E3
Yamal, Poluostrov Russia 71°0N 70°0E 214 B8
Yamal Pen. = Yamal, Poluostrov Russia 71°0N 70°0E 214 B8
Yamana → Japan 36°15N 136°22E 223 A8
Yamanaka Japan 35°41N 138°40E 223 B10
Yamanashi □ Japan 35°40N 138°40E 223 B10
Yamantau, Gora Russia 54°15N 58°6E 186 D10
Yamasaki Japan 35°0N 134°32E 142 G3
Yamato Japan 34°36N 135°26E 133 B1
Yamato Ridge Sea of Japan 39°20N 135°0E 220 F7
Yamatotakada Japan 34°31N 135°37E 133 B2
Yamba Australia 29°26S 153°23E 281 D5
Yambarran Ra. Australia 15°10S 130°25E 278 C5
Yambata Dem. Rep. of the Congo 2°26N 21°58E 264 B4
Yambéring Guinea 11°50N 12°18W 262 C2
Yambio South Sudan 4°35N 28°16E 267 G2
Yambol Bulgaria 42°30N 26°30E 203 D10
Yamboyo Dem. Rep. of the Congo 0°40N 22°18E 264 D4
Yamburg Russia 68°21N 77°8E 214 C8
Yambuya Dem. Rep. of the Congo 1°17N 24°34E 264 B4
Yame Japan 33°13N 130°35E 142 D2
Yamethin Burma 20°29N 96°18E 241 E6
Y'Ami I. Phil. 21°6N 121°57E 232 A2
Yamma Yamma, L. Australia 26°16S 141°20E 281 D3
Yamoussoukro Ivory C. 6°49N 5°17W 262 D3
Yampa → U.S.A. 40°32N 108°59W 304 E9
Yampi Sd. Australia 16°8S 123°38E 278 C3
Yampil Moldova 48°15N 28°15E 177 D15
Yampol = Yampil Moldova 48°15N 28°15E 177 D15
Yamrat Nigeria 10°11N 9°55E 263 C6

Yamrukchal = Botev Bulgaria 42°44N 24°52E 203 D8
Yamu, Laem Thailand 7°59N 98°26E 237 a
Yamuna → India 25°30N 81°53E 243 G9
Yamunanagar India 30°7N 77°17E 242 D7
Yamzho Yumco China 28°48N 90°35E 218 F7
Yan Nigeria 10°5N 12°11E 263 C7
Yan Kit Singapore 1°21N 103°58E 138 d
Yan Oya → Sri Lanka 9°0N 81°10E 245 K5
Yana → Russia 71°30N 136°0E 215 B14
Yan'an China 36°35N 109°26E 226 F5
Yanaul Russia 56°25N 55°0E 186 C10
Yanbian China 27°0N 101°31E 228 D3
Yanbu 'al Baḥr Si. Arabia 24°5N 38°5E 248 E3
Yanchang China 36°43N 110°1E 226 F6
Yancheng = Yenchao Taiwan 22°46N 120°21E 225 D2
Yancheng Henan, China 33°35N 114°0E 226 H8
Yancheng Jiangsu, China 33°23N 120°8E 227 H11
Yanchep Australia 31°33S 115°37E 279 F2
Yanchi China 37°48N 107°20E 226 F4
Yanchuan China 36°51N 110°10E 226 F6
Yanco Cr. → Australia 35°14S 145°35E 283 C8
Yandang Shan China 28°0N 120°35E 229 D13
Yandeyarra ◇ Australia 21°17S 118°24E 278 D2
Yandicoogina Australia 22°45S 119°12E 278 D2
Yandina Solomon Is. 9°7S 159°13E 287 N10
Yandja Dem. Rep. of the Congo 1°41S 17°43E 264 C3
Yandongi Dem. Rep. of the Congo 2°51N 22°16E 264 B4
Yandoon Burma 17°0N 95°40E 241 G5
Yanfeng China 25°52N 101°58E 228 E3
Yanfolila Mali 11°11N 8°9W 262 C3
Yang Xian China 33°15N 107°30E 226 H4
Yang-yang S. Korea 38°4N 128°38E 224 C4
Yang-Yang Senegal 15°30N 15°20W 262 B1
Yangambi Dem. Rep. of the Congo 0°47N 24°24E 264 B4
Yangbi China 25°41N 99°58E 228 E2
Yangcheng China 35°28N 112°22E 226 G7
Yangch'ü = Taiyuan China 37°52N 112°33E 226 F7
Yangchuan = Yangquan China 37°58N 113°31E 226 F7
Yangchun China 22°11N 111°48E 229 F8
Yanggang-do □ N. Korea 41°15N 128°0E 224 B4
Yanggao China 40°21N 113°55E 226 D7
Yanggu China 36°8N 115°43E 226 F8
Yanghuayuan China 39°49N 116°18E 114 C1
Yangiyŭl Uzbekistan 41°0N 69°3E 217 D7
Yangjae China 37°29N 127°2E 137 C2
Yangjiang China 21°50N 111°59E 229 G8
Yangjiazhuang China 31°22N 121°25E 138 A1
Yangju S. Korea 37°47N 127°7E 224 D3
Yangliuqing China 39°2N 117°5E 227 E9
Yangmei Taiwan 24°55N 121°9E 225 B3
Yangmingshan △ Taiwan 25°9N 121°32E 225 A3
Yangôn Burma 16°45N 96°20E 241 G6
Yangon □ Burma 16°45N 96°20E 241 G6
Yangonde Dem. Rep. of the Congo 0°3N 22°43E 264 B4
Yangpingguan China 32°58N 106°5E 228 A6
Yangpu China 31°16N 121°32E 138 B2
Yangpu Park China 31°17N 121°31E 138 B2
Yangquan China 37°58N 113°31E 226 F7
Yangsan S. Korea 35°20N 129°2E 224 E4
Yangshan Guangdong, China 24°30N 112°40E 229 E9
Yangshan Shanghai, China 30°37N 122°4E 229 B14
Yangtse = Chang Jiang → China 31°48N 121°10E 229 B13
Yangtze Kiang = Chang Jiang → China 31°48N 121°10E 229 B13
Yangudi Rassa △ Ethiopia 10°50N 40°42E 257 F5
Yangxin China 29°50N 115°12E 229 C10
Yangyuan China 40°1N 114°10E 226 D8
Yangzhou China 32°21N 119°26E 229 A12
Yanhe China 28°31N 108°29E 228 C7
Yanji China 42°59N 129°30E 227 C15
Yanjin China 27°29N 104°33E 228 D5
Yankari △ Nigeria 9°50N 10°29E 263 C6
Yankton U.S.A. 42°53N 97°23W 308 D5
Yankunytjatjara-Antakirinja Australia 27°20S 134°30E 281 A1
Yannawa Thailand 13°42N 100°33E 113 B2
Yanonge Dem. Rep. of the Congo 0°35N 24°38E 264 B4
Yanov = Ivanava Belarus 52°7N 25°29E 177 B13
Yanqi China 42°5N 86°35E 217 D11
Yanqing China 40°30N 115°58E 226 D8
Yanshan Hebei, China 38°4N 117°22E 227 E9
Yanshan Jiangxi, China 28°15N 117°41E 229 C11
Yanshan Yunnan, China 23°35N 104°20E 228 E5
Yanshou China 45°28N 128°22E 227 B15
Yantabulla Australia 29°21S 145°0E 281 D4
Yantai China 37°34N 121°22E 227 F11
Yantarnyy Russia 54°52N 19°57E 184 D6
Yanting China 31°11N 105°24E 228 B5
Yantongshan China 43°17N 126°0E 227 C14
Yantra → Bulgaria 43°40N 25°37E 203 C9
Yanuca Fiji 18°24S 178°0E 287 B1
Yanunbeyan △ Australia 35°29S 149°24E 283 C8
Yanwa China 27°4N 98°35E 228 D1
Yanzhou China 35°35N 116°49E 226 G9
Yao Chad 12°56N 17°33E 259 F3
Yao Xian China 34°57N 108°58E 226 G5
Yao Yai, Ko Thailand 8°7N 98°37E 237 a
Yao'an China 25°30N 101°32E 228 E3
Yaoundé Cameroon 3°50N 11°35E 263 D7
Yaowan China 34°15N 118°3E 227 G10
Yap Pac. Oc. 9°30N 138°10E 287 R16
Yapacaná △ Venezuela 3°49N 66°43W 328 B4
Yapehe Dem. Rep. of the Congo 0°13S 24°28E 264 C4
Yapei Ghana 9°10N 1°10W 262 C4
Yapen Indonesia 1°50S 136°0E 231 E9
Yapen, Selat Indonesia 1°20S 136°10E 231 E9
Yapero Indonesia 4°59S 137°11E 231 E9
Yappar → Australia 18°22S 141°16E 280 B3
Yaqaga Fiji 16°35S 178°39E 287 A2
Yaqui → Mexico 27°37N 110°39W 318 B2
Yar Çalli = Naberezhnyye Chelny Russia 55°42N 52°19E 190 C11
Yar-Sale Russia 66°50N 70°50E 214 C8

Yaracuy □ Venezuela 10°20N 68°45W 328 A4
Yaracuy → Venezuela 10°33N 68°15W 328 A4
Yaraka Australia 24°53S 144°3E 280 C3
Yaransk Russia 57°22N 47°49E 190 B8
Yarbasan Turkey 38°59N 28°49E 205 C10
Yardımcı Burnu Turkey 36°13N 30°25E 205 E12
Yare → U.K. 52°35N 1°38E 169 E9
Yaremcha Ukraine 48°27N 24°33E 183 B9
Yaren Nauru 0°33S 166°55E 288 H8
Yarensk Russia 62°11N 49°15E 186 B8
Yarfa Si. Arabia 24°37N 38°35E 256 C4
Yarí → Colombia 0°20S 72°20W 328 D3
Yarīm Yemen 14°20N 44°22E 248 D4
Yaritagua Venezuela 10°5N 69°8W 328 A4
Yarkand = Shache China 38°20N 77°10E 217 E9
Yarkant He → China 40°26N 80°59E 217 D10
Yarker Canada 44°23N 76°46W 313 B8
Yarkhun → Pakistan 36°17N 72°30E 243 A5
Yarlung Ziangbo Jiang =
Brahmaputra → Asia 23°40N 90°35E 241 D3
Yarmouth Canada 43°50N 66°7W 299 D6
Yarmūk Iraq 33°18N 44°19E 113 B1
Yarmūk → Syria 32°42N 35°40E 250 F6
Yaroslavl Russia 57°35N 39°55E 188 D10
Yaroslavl □ Russia 59°20N 38°50E 188 C10
Yarra → Trin. & Tob. 10°48N 61°21W 323 t
Yarra Bend Park Australia 37°47S 145°0E 128 A2
Yarra Ranges △ Australia 37°40S 146°3E 283 D7
Yarra Yarra Lakes
Australia 29°40S 115°45E 279 E2
Yarram Australia 38°29S 146°39E 283 E7
Yarraman Australia 26°50S 152°0E 281 D5
Yarras Australia 31°25S 152°20E 283 A10
Yarraville Australia 37°48S 144°53E 128 A1
Yarrawonga Australia 36°0S 146°0E 283 D7
Yarrie Australia 20°40S 120°12E 278 D3
Yartsevo Sib., Russia 60°20N 90°0E 215 C10
Yartsevo Smolensk, Russia 55°6N 32°43E 188 E7
Yarumal Colombia 6°58N 75°24W 328 B2
Yasa Dem. Rep. of the Congo 3°50S 21°25E 264 C4
Yasawa Fiji 16°47S 177°31E 287 A1
Yasawa Group Fiji 17°0S 177°23E 287 A1
Yaselda Belarus 52°7N 26°28E 177 B14
Yasen Ukraine 48°45N 24°10E 183 B9
Yashbum Yemen 14°19N 46°56E 248 D4
Yashi Nigeria 12°23N 7°54E 263 C6
Yashikera Nigeria 9°44N 3°29E 263 D5
Yashiro-Jima Japan 33°55N 132°15E 222 D4
Yashkul Russia 46°11N 45°21E 191 G7
Yasi = Türkistan
Kazakhstan 43°17N 68°16E 217 D7
Yasin Pakistan 36°24N 73°23E 243 A5
Yasinovataya Ukraine 48°7N 37°57E 189 H9
Yasinski, L. Canada 53°16N 77°35W 298 B4
Yasinya Ukraine 48°16N 24°21E 183 B9
Yasnyy Russia 51°1N 59°58E 216 B5
Yasothon Thailand 15°50N 104°10E 236 E5
Yass Australia 34°49S 148°54E 283 C8
Yasugi Japan 35°26N 133°15E 222 B5
Yāsūj Iran 30°31N 51°31E 247 D6
Yasuní △ Ecuador 1°19S 76°3W 328 D2
Yat Niger 20°28N 13°27E 259 D2
Yata → Bolivia 10°29S 65°26W 331 C4
Yata → C.A.R. 10°23N 22°45E 264 A4
Yata-Ngaya ⌓ C.A.R. 9°15N 23°25E 264 A4
Yatağan Turkey 37°20N 28°10E 205 D10
Yatakala Niger 14°50N 0°22E 263 C5
Yaté N. Cal. 22°9S 166°57E 288 d
Yates Center U.S.A. 37°53N 95°44W 308 G6
Yates Pt. N.Z. 44°29S 167°49E 285 E2
Yathkyed L. Canada 62°40N 98°0W 297 A9
Yathong Australia 32°37S 145°33E 283 B6
Yatolemu
Dem. Rep. of the Congo 0°25N 24°35E 264 B4
Yatsuo Japan 36°34N 137°8E 223 A9
Yatsushiro Japan 32°30N 130°40E 222 E2
Yatsushiro-Kai Japan 32°30N 130°25E 222 E2
Yatta Plateau Kenya 2°0S 38°0E 268 C4
Yatua → Venezuela 1°30N 66°30W 328 C4
Yauca Peru 15°39S 74°35W 330 D3
Yauco Puerto Rico 18°2N 66°51W 321 b
Yauri Peru 14°47S 71°25W 330 C3
Yauya Peru 8°59S 77°17W 330 B2
Yauyos Peru 12°19S 75°50W 330 C2
Yauza → Russia 55°54N 37°43E 129 B4
Yaval India 21°10N 75°42E 244 D2
Yavarí → Peru 4°21S 70°2W 330 A3
Yávaros Mexico 26°42N 109°31W 318 B3
Yavatmal India 20°20N 78°15E 244 D4
Yavero → Peru 12°6S 72°57W 330 C3
Yavne Israel 31°52N 34°45E 251 G5
Yavoriv Ukraine 49°55N 23°20E 177 D12
Yavorov = Yavoriv
Ukraine 49°55N 23°20E 177 D12
Yavuzeli Turkey 37°18N 37°24E 212 D7
Yawatahama Japan 33°27N 132°24E 222 D4
Yawnghwe Burma 20°39N 96°56E 241 E6
Yawri B. S. Leone 8°22N 13°0W 262 D2
Yaxi China 27°33N 106°41E 228 D6
Yaxian = Sanya China 18°14N 109°29E 229 a
Yayama
Dem. Rep. of the Congo 1°16S 23°7E 264 C4
Yayladağı Turkey 35°54N 36°3E 250 C7
Yazd Iran 31°55N 54°27E 247 D7
Yazd □ Iran 32°0N 55°0E 247 D7
Yazd-e Khvāst Iran 31°31N 52°7E 247 D7
Yazdān Iran 33°30N 60°50E 240 B1
Yazıköy Turkey 36°40N 27°20E 205 E9
Yazman Pakistan 29°8N 71°45E 242 E4
Yazoo → U.S.A. 32°22N 90°54W 315 E9
Yazoo City U.S.A. 32°51N 90°25W 315 E9
Ybbs Austria 48°12N 15°4E 180 C8
Ybycuí △ Paraguay 26°5S 56°46W 334 B4
Ybytyruzú △ Paraguay 25°51S 56°11W 335 B4
Ye Burma 15°15N 97°15E 236 E1
Ye-ngan Burma 21°9N 96°27E 241 E6
Ye-u Burma 22°46N 95°26E 241 D5
Ye Xian = Laizhou China 37°8N 119°57E 227 F10
Ye Xian China 33°35N 113°25E 226 H7
Yea Australia 37°14S 145°26E 283 D6
Yeading U.K. 51°31N 0°23W 125 A1
Yebawmi Burma 25°15N 95°45E 241 C5
Yebbi-Souma Chad 21°7N 17°54E 259 D3
Yebyu Burma 14°15N 98°13E 236 E2
Yecheng China 37°54N 77°26E 217 E9
Yecheon S. Korea 36°39N 128°27E 224 D4
Yecla Spain 38°35N 1°5W 197 G3
Yécora Mexico 28°20N 108°58W 318 B3
Yedashe Burma 19°10N 96°20E 241 F6
Yedebub Biheroch Bihereseboch na
Hizboch □ Ethiopia 12°0N 36°0E 257 F4
Yedigöller △ Turkey 40°55N 31°55E 212 B4
Yedikule Turkey 40°59N 28°55E 122 C1
Yedintsy = Edineţ
Moldova 48°9N 27°18E 183 B12
Yedri Chad 22°25N 17°30E 259 D3
Yedseram → Nigeria 12°30N 14°5E 263 C7
Yeed Somalia 4°33N 43°2E 267 D5
Yefremov Russia 53°8N 38°3E 188 F10
Yegguéba Niger 19°59N 12°52E 259 E2
Yeghegnadzor Armenia 39°44N 45°19E 213 C11
Yegorlyk → Russia 46°35N 41°57E 191 G5
Yegorlykskaya Russia 46°35N 40°35E 191 G5
Yegoryevsk Russia 55°27N 38°55E 188 E10
Yegri-Dere = Ardino
Bulgaria 41°34N 25°9E 203 E9
Yegros Paraguay 26°20S 56°25W 334 B4
Yehbuah Indonesia 8°23S 114°45E 231 J17
Yehuda, Midbar Israel 31°35N 35°15E 251 G6
Yei South Sudan 4°9N 30°40E 257 G3
Yei, Nahr → South Sudan 6°15N 30°13E 257 F3
Yeji Ghana 8°13N 0°39W 263 D4
Yejmiadzin = Ejmiatsin
Armenia 40°12N 44°19E 191 K7
Yekaterinburg Russia 56°50N 60°30E 214 D7
Yekaterinenshtadt = Marks
Russia 51°45N 46°50E 190 E8
Yekaterinodar = Krasnodar
Russia 45°5N 39°0E 191 H4
Yekateriny, Proliv
Russia 44°30N 146°30E 215 E15
Yekumbe
Dem. Rep. of the Congo 1°2S 23°27E 264 C4
Yelabuga Russia 55°46N 52°2E 190 C11
Yelan Russia 50°55N 43°43E 190 E6
Yelandur India 12°6N 77°0E 245 H3
Yelarbon Australia 28°33S 150°38E 281 D5
Yelatma Russia 55°0N 41°45E 190 C5
Yelcho, L. Chile 43°18S 72°18W 336 B2
Yelenovka = Sevan
Armenia 40°33N 44°56E 191 K7
Yelenovskiye Karyery =
Dokuchayevsk Ukraine 47°44N 37°40E 189 J9
Yelets Russia 52°40N 38°30E 189 F10
Yélimané Mali 15°9N 10°34W 262 B2
Yelin = Lingshui China 18°27N 110°0E 229 a
Yelizavetgrad = Kirovohrad
Ukraine 48°35N 32°20E 189 H7
Yelizovo Russia 53°11N 158°23E 215 D16
Yell U.K. 60°35N 1°5W 167 A7
Yell Sd. U.K. 60°33N 1°15W 167 A7
Yellamanchilli = Elamanchili
India 17°33N 82°50E 244 F6
Yellandu India 17°39N 80°23E 244 F5
Yellapur India 14°58N 74°43E 245 G2
Yellareddi India 18°12N 78°2E 244 E4
Yellow = Huang He →
China 37°55N 118°50E 227 F10
Yellow → U.S.A. 30°30N 87°0W 317 E3
Yellow Sea China 35°0N 123°0E 227 G12
Yellowhead Pass Canada 52°53N 118°25W 296 C5
Yellowknife Canada 62°27N 114°29W 296 A6
Yellowknife → Canada 62°31N 114°19W 296 A6
Yellowstone → U.S.A. 47°59N 103°59W 304 C12
Yellowstone △ U.S.A. 44°40N 110°30W 304 D8
Yellowstone L. U.S.A. 44°27N 110°22W 304 D8
Yelnya Russia 54°35N 33°15E 188 E7
Yelsk Belarus 51°50N 29°10E 177 C15
Yelwa Nigeria 10°49N 4°41E 263 C5
Yemanzhelinsk Russia 54°58N 61°18E 216 B6
Yemassee U.S.A. 32°41N 80°51W 316 C9
Yembongo
Dem. Rep. of the Congo 3°12N 19°2E 264 B3
Yemen ■ Asia 15°0N 44°0E 248 D4
Yemin Moshe Jerusalem 123 b2
Yemmiganur India 15°44N 77°29E 245 G3
Yen Bai Vietnam 21°42N 104°52E 228 G5
Yenagoa Nigeria 4°58N 6°16E 263 E6
Yenakiyeve Ukraine 48°15N 38°15E 189 H10
Yenakiyevo = Yenakiyeve
Ukraine 48°15N 38°15E 189 H10
Yenangyat Burma 21°6N 94°48E 241 E5
Yenangyaung Burma 20°30N 95°0E 241 E5
Yenanma Burma 19°46N 94°49E 241 F5
Yenbo = Yanbu 'al Baḩr
Si. Arabia 24°5N 38°5E 246 E3
Yenchao Taiwan 22°46N 120°21E 225 D2
Yenda Australia 34°13S 146°14E 283 C7
Yende Millimou Guinea 8°55N 10°10W 262 D2
Yendegaia △ Chile 54°50S 68°45W 336 D3
Yendéré Burkina Faso 10°12N 4°59W 262 C4
Yendi Ghana 9°29N 0°1W 263 D4
Yengisar China 38°56N 76°9E 217 E9
Yengo Congo 0°22N 15°29E 264 B3
Yengo △ Australia 33°0S 150°55E 283 B9
Yéni Niger 13°30N 3°1E 263 C5
Yenı Erenköy = Yialousa
Cyprus 35°32N 34°10E 207 E10
Yeni-Pazar = Novi Pazar
Serbia 43°12N 20°28E 202 C4
Yenıbogaziçi = Áyios Seryios
Cyprus 35°12N 33°53E 207 E9
Yenice Ankara, Turkey 39°14N 32°42E 212 C5
Yenice Aydın, Turkey 37°49N 28°35E 205 D10
Yenice Çanakkale, Turkey 39°55N 27°17E 205 B9
Yenice Edirne, Turkey 40°42N 26°9E 203 F10
Yenice Kahramanmaraş,
Turkey 37°0N 35°4E 250 B6
Yenice → Turkey 37°37N 35°33E 212 D6
Yenifoça Turkey 38°44N 26°51E 205 C8
Yenihisar = Didim Turkey 37°22N 27°16E 205 D9
Yenikapı Turkey 41°0N 28°56E 122 B1
Yeniköy Bursa, Turkey 40°31N 29°22E 203 F13
Yeniköy Çanakkale, Turkey 39°55N 26°10E 205 B8
Yeniköy İstanbul, Turkey 41°6N 29°3E 122 B2
Yeniköy Kütahya, Turkey 38°52N 29°17E 205 C11
Yenipazar Turkey 37°49N 28°11E 205 D10
Yenişehir Turkey 40°16N 29°38E 203 F13
Yenisey → Russia 71°50N 82°40E 214 B9
Yeniseysk Russia 58°27N 92°13E 215 D10
Yeniseyskiy Zaliv Russia 72°20N 81°0E 214 B9
Yenki = Yanji China 42°59N 129°30E 227 C15
Yenne France 45°43N 5°44E 175 C9
Yenotayevka Russia 47°15N 47°0E 191 G8
Yenpu Taiwan 22°45N 120°35E 225 D2
Yenshui Taiwan 23°19N 120°16E 225 C2
Yenyuka Russia 57°57N 121°15E 215 D13
Yeo → U.K. 51°2N 2°49W 169 G5
Yeo, L. Australia 28°0S 124°30E 279 E3
Yeo I. Canada 45°24N 81°48W 312 A3
Yeoju S. Korea 37°20N 127°35E 224 D3
Yeola India 20°2N 74°30E 244 D2
Yeon-gi = Sejong
S. Korea 36°35N 127°15E 224 D3
Yeoncheon S. Korea 38°5N 127°4E 224 C3
Yeong-am S. Korea 34°47N 126°42E 224 E3
Yeong-ilman S. Korea 36°4N 129°28E 224 D4
Yeong-wol S. Korea 37°11N 128°28E 224 D4
Yeong-yang S. Korea 36°39N 129°7E 224 D4
Yeongcheon S. Korea 35°58N 128°56E 224 E4
Yeongdeok S. Korea 36°24N 129°22E 224 D4
Yeongdeungpo S. Korea 37°31N 126°54E 137 B1
Yeongdong Chungcheongbuk-do,
S. Korea 36°10N 127°46E 224 D3
Yeongdong Seoul, S. Korea 37°30N 127°1E 137 B2
Yeonggwang S. Korea 35°16N 126°30E 224 E3
Yeongheungdo S. Korea 37°15N 126°27E 224 D3
Yeongju S. Korea 36°50N 128°40E 224 D4
Yeongju △ S. Korea 35°45N 129°20E 224 D4
Yeonpyeongdo S. Korea 37°40N 125°45E 224 D2
Yeosu S. Korea 34°47N 127°45E 224 E3
Yeotmal = Yavatmal
India 20°20N 78°15E 244 D4
Yeouido S. Korea 37°31N 126°55E 137 B1
Yeovil U.K. 50°57N 2°38W 169 G5
Yepes Spain 39°55N 3°39W 194 F7
Yeppoon Australia 23°5S 150°47E 280 C5
Yerba Buena I. U.S.A. 37°48N 122°21W 136 B2
Yerbent Turkmenistan 39°19N 58°36E 247 B8
Yerbogachen Russia 61°16N 108°0E 215 C11
Yerevan Armenia 40°10N 44°31E 191 K7
Yerington U.S.A. 38°59N 119°10W 304 G4
Yerkesik Turkey 37°7N 28°19E 205 D10
Yerköy Turkey 39°38N 34°28E 212 C6
Yerla → India 16°50N 74°30E 244 F2
Yermo U.S.A. 34°54N 116°50W 307 L10
Yerolakkos Cyprus 35°11N 33°15E 207 E9
Yeropol Russia 65°15N 168°40E 215 C17
Yeroskipos Cyprus 34°46N 32°28E 207 F8
Yerres France 48°43N 2°30E 134 B4
Yershov Russia 51°23N 48°27E 190 E9
Yerupajá, Cerro Peru 10°16S 76°55W 330 C2
Yerushalayim = Jerusalem
Israel/West Bank 31°47N 35°10E 123 B2
Yerville France 49°40N 0°53E 172 C7
Yes Tor U.K. 50°41N 4°0W 169 G4
Yesagyo Burma 21°38N 95°14E 241 E5
Yesan S. Korea 36°41N 126°51E 224 D3
Yeshin Burma 23°43N 95°6E 241 D5
Yeşikent = Erzin Turkey 36°57N 36°11E 250 B7
Yeşil → Turkey 37°20N 33°16E 250 A4
Yeşildere Turkey 37°9N 33°31E 250 A4
Yeşilhisar Turkey 38°20N 35°5E 212 C6
Yeşilırmak → Turkey 41°22N 36°37E 212 B7
Yeşilkent Turkey 36°57N 36°12E 212 D7
Yeşilova Turkey 37°31N 29°46E 205 D11
Yeşilyurt Manisa, Turkey 38°22N 28°40E 205 C10
Yeşilyurt Muğla, Turkey 37°10N 28°20E 205 D10
Yeski Dzhumaya = Târgovişte
Romania 44°55N 25°27E 183 F10
Yesnogorsk Russia 54°32N 37°38E 188 E9
Yeso U.S.A. 34°26N 104°37W 305 J11
Yessentuki Russia 44°5N 42°53E 191 H6
Yessey Russia 68°29N 102°10E 215 C11
Yeste Spain 38°22N 2°19W 197 G2
Yetman Australia 28°56S 150°48E 281 D5
Yetti Mauritania 26°10N 7°50W 260 C3
Yeu, Î. d' France 46°42N 2°20W 172 F4
Yevdokimovskoye =
Krasnogvardeyskoye
Russia 45°52N 41°33E 191 H5
Yevlax Azerbaijan 40°39N 47°7E 191 K8
Yevpatoriya Ukraine 45°15N 33°20E 189 K7
Yeya → Russia 46°40N 38°40E 191 G4
Yeysk Russia 46°40N 38°12E 189 J10
Yezd = Yazd Iran 31°55N 54°27E 247 D7
Yezerishche Belarus 55°50N 30°0E 188 E5
Ygatimi Paraguay 24°5S 55°40W 335 A4
Yhati Paraguay 25°45S 56°35W 334 B4
Yhú Paraguay 25°0S 56°0W 335 B4
Yí → Uruguay 33°7S 57°8W 334 C4
Yi 'Allaq, G. Egypt 30°21N 33°31E 251 H4
Yi He → China 34°10N 118°8E 227 G10
Yi O San Tsuen
Hong Kong, China 22°14N 113°51E 122 B1
Yi Xian Anhui, China 29°55N 117°57E 229 C11
Yi Xian Hebei, China 39°20N 115°30E 226 E8
Yi Xian Liaoning, China 41°30N 121°22E 227 D11
Yialiás → Cyprus 35°9N 33°44E 207 E9
Yialousa Cyprus 35°32N 34°10E 207 E10
Yibin China 28°45N 104°32E 228 C5
Yichang China 30°40N 111°20E 229 B8
Yicheng Henan, China 31°41N 112°12E 229 B9
Yicheng Shanxi, China 35°42N 111°40E 226 G6
Yichuan China 36°2N 110°10E 226 F6
Yichun Heilongjiang,
China 47°44N 128°52E 219 B14
Yichun Jiangxi, China 27°48N 114°22E 229 D10
Yidu China 36°43N 118°28E 227 F10
Yidun China 30°22N 99°21E 228 B2
Yifag Ethiopia 12°4N 37°46E 257 E4
Yifeng China 28°22N 114°45E 229 C10
Yigo Guam 13°32N 144°53E 302 d
Yiheyuan China 39°59N 116°15E 114 B1
Yihuang China 27°30N 116°12E 229 D11
Yijun China 35°28N 109°8E 226 G5
Yilan = Ilan Taiwan 24°45N 121°44E 225 B3
Yılanlıkale Turkey 36°59N 35°47E 250 B6
Yıldız Dağları Turkey 41°48N 27°36E 203 E11
Yıldız Park Turkey 41°2N 29°1E 122 B2
Yıldızeli Turkey 39°51N 36°36E 212 C7
Yilehuli Shan China 51°20N 124°20E 219 A13
Yiliang Yunnan, China 27°38N 104°2E 228 D5
Yiliang Yunnan, China 24°56N 103°11E 228 E4
Yılmazköy = Skilloura
Cyprus 35°14N 33°10E 207 E9
Yilong China 31°34N 106°23E 228 B6
Yima China 34°44N 111°53E 226 G6
Yimen China 24°40N 102°10E 228 E4
Yimianpo China 45°7N 128°2E 227 B15
Yin Xu China 36°7N 114°18E 226 F8
Yi'nan China 35°31N 118°24E 227 G10
Yinchuan China 38°30N 106°15E 226 E4
Yindaik Burma 23°35N 95°22E 241 D5
Yindarlgooda, L.
Australia 30°40S 121°52E 279 F3
Yindjibarndi ❂ Australia 22°0S 118°35E 278 D2
Ying He → China 32°30N 116°30E 229 A11
Ying Xian China 39°32N 113°10E 226 E7
Yingcheng China 30°56N 113°35E 229 B9
Yingde China 24°10N 113°25E 229 E9
Yingjiang China 24°41N 97°55E 228 E1
Yingjing China 29°41N 102°52E 228 C4
Yingkiong India 28°37N 95°3E 241 A5
Yingkou China 40°37N 122°18E 224 B1
Yingkow = Yingkou
China 40°37N 122°18E 224 B1
Yingpanshui China 37°26N 104°18E 226 F3
Yingshan Hubei, China 30°41N 115°32E 229 B10
Yingshan Sichuan, China 31°4N 106°35E 228 B6
Yingshang China 32°38N 116°12E 229 A11
Yingtan China 28°12N 117°0E 229 C11
Yingualyalya ❂ Australia 18°49S 129°12E 278 C4
Yinhangzhen China 31°20N 121°31E 138 A2
Yining China 43°58N 81°10E 217 D10
Yiningarra ❂ Australia 20°53S 129°27E 278 D4
Yinjiang China 28°1N 108°21E 228 C7
Yinmabin Burma 22°10N 94°55E 241 D5
Yioúra = Giaros Greece 37°32N 24°40E 204 D6
Yipinglang China 25°10N 101°52E 228 E3
Yirba Muda Ethiopia 6°12N 38°42E 257 F4
Yirga Alem Ethiopia 6°48N 38°22E 257 F4
Yirol South Sudan 6°33N 30°30E 257 F3
Yirrkala Australia 12°14S 136°56E 280 A2
Yishan China 24°28N 108°38E 228 E7
Yishui China 35°47N 118°30E 227 G10
Yishun Singapore 1°26N 103°51E 138 A3
Yitong China 43°13N 125°20E 227 C13
Yiwu China 29°20N 120°3E 229 C13
Yixing China 31°21N 119°48E 229 B12
Yiyang Henan, China 34°27N 112°10E 226 G7
Yiyang Hunan, China 28°35N 112°18E 229 C9
Yiyang Jiangxi, China 28°22N 117°20E 229 C11
Yizhang China 25°27N 112°57E 229 E9
Yizheng China 32°18N 119°10E 229 A12
Yizhu = Ichu Taiwan 23°20N 120°14E 225 C2
Ylästö Finland 60°17N 24°54E 121 B2
Yli-Kitka Finland 66°8N 28°30E 160 C23
Yliki, L. Greece 38°24N 23°15E 204 C5
Ylitornio Finland 66°19N 23°39E 160 C20
Ylivieska Finland 64°4N 24°28E 160 D21
Ymer Ø Greenland 73°9N 24°20W 154 C8
Yngaren Sweden 58°50N 16°35E 163 F10
Yoakum U.S.A. 29°17N 97°9W 314 G6
Yob ⌓ Eritrea 17°15N 37°50E 257 D4
Yobe □ Nigeria 12°0N 11°30E 263 C7
Yoboki Djibouti 11°30N 42°6E 267 B5
Yobuko Japan 33°32N 129°54E 222 D1
Yodo → Japan 34°45N 135°35E 133 A2
Yog Pt. Phil. 14°6N 124°12E 232 D5
Yoğuntaş Turkey 41°50N 27°4E 203 E11
Yogyakarta Indonesia 7°49S 110°22E 235 D4
Yogyakarta □ Indonesia 7°48S 110°22E 235 D4
Yoho △ Canada 51°25N 116°30W 296 C5
Yojoa, L. de Honduras 14°53N 88°0W 320 D2
Yok Don △ Vietnam 12°50N 107°40E 236 F6
Yokadouma Cameroon 3°26N 14°55E 264 B2
Yōkaichi Japan 35°6N 136°12E 223 B8
Yōkaichiba Japan 35°42N 140°33E 223 B12
Yokkaichi Japan 34°55N 136°38E 223 C8
Yoko Cameroon 5°32N 12°20E 263 D7
Yokohama Japan 35°27N 139°28E 223 B11
Yokosuka Japan 35°20N 139°40E 223 B11
Yokote Japan 39°20N 140°30E 220 E10
Yola Nigeria 9°10N 12°29E 263 D7
Yolaina, Cordillera de Nic. 11°30N 84°0W 320 D3
Yolombo
Dem. Rep. of the Congo 1°36S 23°12E 264 C4
Ýolöten Turkmenistan 37°18N 62°21E 247 B9
Yom → Thailand 15°35N 100°1E 236 E3
Yombi Gabon 1°26S 10°37E 264 C2
Yona Guam 13°25N 144°46E 302 d
Yonago Japan 35°25N 133°19E 222 B5
Yonaguni-Jima Japan 24°27N 123°0E 221 M1
Yonaha-Dake Japan 26°43N 128°13E 288 a
Yŏnan N. Korea 37°55N 126°11E 224 D3
Yonezawa Japan 37°57N 140°4E 220 F10
Yong-in S. Korea 37°14N 127°12E 224 D3
Yong Peng Malaysia 2°0N 103°3E 237 M4
Yong Sata Thailand 7°8N 99°41E 237 J2
Yongama
Dem. Rep. of the Congo 0°2N 24°35E 264 B4
Yongamp'o N. Korea 39°56N 124°23E 224 C2
Yong'an China 25°59N 117°25E 229 E11
Yongchang China 38°17N 102°7E 218 D9
Yongcheng China 33°55N 116°20E 226 H9
Yongchuan China 29°17N 105°55E 228 C5
Yongchun China 25°16N 118°20E 229 E12
Yongde China 24°5N 99°25E 228 E2
Yongdeng China 36°38N 103°25E 226 F2
Yongding China 24°43N 116°45E 229 E11
Yongdingman China 39°50N 116°20E 114 B2
Yonge Street Toronto, Canada 141 b3
Yongfeng China 27°20N 115°22E 229 D10
Yongfu China 24°59N 109°59E 228 E7
Yongfucun China 23°8N 113°17E 121 B2
Yonggyap Pass Asia 29°17N 95°37E 241 A5
Yonghe China 36°46N 110°38E 226 F6
Yonghong India 26°28N 94°58E 241 B5
Yŏnghŭng N. Korea 39°31N 127°18E 224 C3
Yŏnghŭng-man N. Korea 39°14N 127°30E 224 C3
Yongji Jilin, China 43°33N 126°13E 227 C14
Yongji Shanxi, China 34°52N 110°28E 226 G6
Yongjia China 28°10N 120°45E 229 C13
Yongkang = Yungk'ang
Taiwan 23°2N 120°15E 225 C2
Yongkang Yunnan, China 24°9N 99°20E 228 E2
Yongkang Zhejiang, China 28°55N 120°2E 229 C13
Yongnian China 36°47N 114°29E 226 F8
Yongning Guangxi Zhuangzu,
China 22°44N 108°28E 228 F7
Yongning Ningxia Huizu,
China 38°15N 106°14E 226 E4
Yongping China 25°27N 99°38E 228 E2
Yongren China 26°4N 101°40E 228 D3
Yongsan S. Korea 37°32N 126°58E 137 B1
Yongshan China 28°11N 103°35E 228 C4
Yongsheng China 26°38N 100°46E 228 D3
Yongshun China 29°2N 109°51E 228 C7
Yongtai China 25°49N 118°58E 229 E12
Yongxin = Jinggangshan
China 26°58N 114°15E 229 D10
Yongxing China 26°9N 113°8E 229 D9
Yongxing Dao = Woody I.
S. China Sea 16°50N 112°20E 230 A4
Yongxiu China 29°2N 115°42E 229 C10
Yongzhou China 26°17N 111°37E 229 D8
Yonibana S. Leone 8°30N 12°19W 262 D2
Yonkers U.S.A. 40°56N 73°52W 132 A2
Yonne □ France 47°50N 3°40E 173 E10
Yonne → France 48°23N 2°58E 173 D9
Yopal Colombia 5°21N 72°23W 328 B3
York W. Austral., Australia 31°52S 116°47E 279 F2
York Ont., Canada 43°40N 79°26W 141 A2
York York, U.K. 53°58N 1°6W 168 D6
York Ala., U.S.A. 32°29N 88°18W 315 E10
York Nebr., U.S.A. 40°52N 97°36W 308 E5
York Pa., U.S.A. 39°58N 76°44W 309 F15
York, C. Australia 10°42S 142°31E 286 F2
York, City of □ U.K. 53°58N 1°6W 168 D6
York, Kap Greenland 75°55N 66°25W 154 B4
York, Vale of U.K. 54°15N 1°25W 168 C6
York I. Antigua & B. 17°2N 61°40W 322 b
York Mills Canada 43°45N 79°22W 141 A2
York Sd. Australia 15°0S 125°5E 278 C4
York Univ. Canada 43°43N 79°22W 141 A1
Yorke Pen. Australia 34°50S 137°40E 282 C2
Yorketown Australia 35°2S 137°33E 282 C2
Yorkshire Dales △ U.K. 54°12N 2°10W 168 C5
Yorkshire Wolds U.K. 54°8N 0°31W 168 C7
Yorkton Canada 51°11N 102°28W 297 C8
Yorkville Calif., U.S.A. 38°52N 123°13W 306 G3
Yorkville Ga., U.S.A. 33°55N 84°58W 316 B5
Yorkville Ill., U.S.A. 41°38N 88°27W 311 C8
Yoro Honduras 15°9N 87°7W 320 C2
Yoron-Jima Japan 27°2N 128°26E 221 L4
Yorosso Mali 12°17N 4°55W 262 C4
Yos Sudarso, Pulau = Dolak, Pulau
Indonesia 8°0S 138°30E 231 F9
Yosemite △ U.S.A. 37°45N 119°40W 306 H7
Yosemite Village U.S.A. 37°45N 119°35W 306 H7
Yoshida Japan 34°40N 132°42E 222 C4
Yoshimatsu Japan 32°0N 130°47E 222 F2
Yoshino-Kumano △
Japan 34°12N 135°55E 223 C7
Yoshinogawa Japan 34°4N 134°21E 222 C6
Yoshkar Ola Russia 56°38N 47°55E 190 B8
Yotala Bolivia 19°10S 65°17W 331 D4
Yotsuya Tokyo, Japan 140 a2
Yotvata Israel 29°55N 35°2E 251 J6
You Jiang → China 22°50N 108°6E 228 F6
You Xian China 27°1N 113°17E 229 D9
You'anmen China 39°51N 116°19E 114 B1
Youbou Canada 48°53N 124°13W 306 B2
Youghal Ireland 51°56N 7°52W 166 E4
Youghal B. Ireland 51°55N 7°49W 166 E4
Youkounkoun Guinea 12°35N 13°11W 262 C2
Young N.S.W., Australia 34°19S 148°18E 283 C8
Young Sask., Canada 51°47N 105°45W 297 C7
Young Uruguay 32°44S 57°36W 334 C4
Young I. Antarctica 66°25S 162°24E 151 C11
Young Ra. N.Z. 44°10S 169°30E 285 E4
Younghusband, L.
Australia 30°50S 136°5E 282 A2
Younghusband Pen.
Australia 36°0S 139°25E 282 D3
Youngsfield S. Africa 34°0S 18°30E 118 B1
Youngstown Alta.,
Canada 51°35N 111°10W 297 C6
Youngstown Fla., U.S.A. 30°22N 85°26W 316 E4
Youngstown N.Y., U.S.A. 43°15N 79°3W 312 C5
Youngstown Ohio, U.S.A. 41°6N 80°39W 312 E4
Youngsville U.S.A. 41°51N 79°19W 312 E5
Youngwood U.S.A. 40°14N 79°34W 312 F5
Youssoufia Morocco 32°16N 8°31W 260 B3
Youxi China 26°10N 118°13E 229 D12
Youyang China 28°47N 108°42E 228 C7
Youyu China 40°10N 112°20E 226 D7
Yozgat Turkey 39°51N 34°47E 212 C6
Yozgat □ Turkey 39°30N 35°0E 212 C6
Ypacaraí △ Paraguay 25°18S 57°19W 334 B4
Ypané → Paraguay 23°29S 57°19W 334 A4
Yport France 49°45N 0°15E 172 C7
Ypres = Ieper Belgium 50°51N 2°53E 170 D2
Ypsilanti U.S.A. 42°14N 83°37W 311 B13
Yr Wyddgrug = Mold U.K. 53°9N 3°8W 168 D4
Yreka U.S.A. 41°44N 122°38W 304 F2
Yrghyz Kazakhstan 48°37N 61°16E 216 C6
Yrghyz → Kazakhstan 48°6N 62°30E 216 C6
Ysabel Chan. Papua N. G. 2°0S 150°0E 286 B6
Yssingeaux France 45°9N 4°8E 175 C8
Ystabøhamn Norway 59°3N 5°23E 164 E2
Ystad Sweden 55°26N 13°50E 163 J7
Ystradgynlais U.K. 51°47N 3°46W 169 F4
Ysyk-Köl = Balykchy
Kyrgyzstan 42°26N 76°12E 217 D9
Ysyk-Köl Kyrgyzstan 42°25N 77°15E 217 D9
Ysyk-Köl □ Kyrgyzstan 42°0N 78°0E 217 D9
Ythan → U.K. 57°19N 1°59W 167 D7
Ytre Arna Norway 60°27N 5°25E 164 D2
Ytre Enebakk Norway 59°44N 11°0E 164 E8
Ytre Hvaler Norway 58°59N 10°48E 164 F7
Ytre Rendal Norway 61°46N 11°8E 164 C8
Ytteran Sweden 63°16N 14°7E 162 A8
Ytterhogdal Sweden 62°12N 14°56E 162 B8
Yttermalung Sweden 60°35N 13°51E 162 D7
Ytyk-Kyuyel Russia 62°30N 133°45E 215 C14
Yu Jiang → China 23°22N 110°3E 228 F7
Yü Shan Taiwan 23°25N 120°52E 225 C2
Yü Shan △ Taiwan 24°45N 121°12E 225 C3
Yu Xian = Yuzhou China 34°10N 113°28E 226 G7
Yu Xian Hebei, China 39°50N 114°35E 226 E8
Yu Xian Shanxi, China 38°5N 113°20E 226 E7
Yuan Jiang = Hong →
Asia 20°16N 106°34E 236 B5
Yuan Jiang → Hunan,
China 28°55N 111°50E 229 C8
Yuan Jiang → Yunnan,
China 22°20N 103°59E 228 F4
Yuan'an China 31°3N 111°34E 229 B8
Yüanch'ang Taiwan 23°39N 120°18E 225 C2
Yuancun China 23°7N 113°22E 121 B3
Yuanjiang Hunan, China 28°47N 112°21E 229 C9
Yuanjiang Yunnan, China 23°32N 102°0E 228 F4
Yüanli Taiwan 24°27N 120°39E 225 B2
Yüanlin Taiwan 23°58N 120°30E 225 C2
Yuanling China 28°29N 110°22E 229 C8
Yuanmingyuan Park
China 40°0N 116°17E 114 A1
Yuanmou China 25°42N 101°53E 228 E3
Yuanping China 38°42N 112°46E 226 E7
Yuanqu China 35°18N 111°40E 226 G6
Yuanshan Taiwan 24°45N 121°43E 225 B3
Yuanxiatian China 23°12N 113°17E 121 A2
Yuanyang Henan, China 35°3N 113°58E 226 G7
Yuanyang Yunnan, China 23°10N 102°43E 228 F4
Yuat → Papua N. G. 4°10S 143°52E 286 C2
Yuba → U.S.A. 39°8N 121°36W 306 F5
Yuba City U.S.A. 39°8N 121°37W 306 F5
Yūbari Japan 43°4N 141°59E 220 C10
Yubdo Ethiopia 8°58N 35°24E 257 F4
Yūbetsu Japan 44°13N 143°50E 220 B11
Yucatán □ Mexico 20°50N 89°0W 319 C7
Yucatán, Canal de
Caribbean 22°0N 86°30W 320 B2
Yucatán, Península de
Mexico 19°30N 89°0W 292 H11
Yucatan Basin Cent. Amer. 19°0N 86°0W 320 C3
Yucatan Channel = Yucatán, Canal
de Caribbean 22°0N 86°30W 320 B2
Yucca U.S.A. 34°52N 114°9W 307 L12
Yucca Valley U.S.A. 34°8N 116°27W 307 L10
Yucheng China 36°55N 116°32E 226 F9
Yüch'ih Taiwan 23°54N 120°56E 225 C2
Yuching Taiwan 23°7N 120°27E 225 C2
Yuci = Jinzhong China 37°42N 112°46E 226 F7
Yudu China 25°59N 115°30E 229 E10
Yuechi China 30°34N 106°25E 228 B6
Yuen Long China 22°26N 114°2E 219 a
Yuendumu Australia 22°16S 131°49E 278 D5
Yuendumu ❂ Australia 22°21S 131°40E 278 D5
Yueqing China 28°9N 120°59E 229 C13
Yueqing Wan China 28°5N 121°20E 229 C13
Yuexi Anhui, China 30°50N 116°20E 229 B11
Yuexi Sichuan, China 28°37N 102°26E 228 C4
Yuexiu China 23°8N 113°16E 121 B2
Yuexiu Park China 23°8N 113°16E 121 B2
Yueyang China 29°21N 113°5E 229 C9
Yufu-Dake Japan 33°17N 131°33E 222 D3
Yugan China 28°43N 116°37E 229 C11
Yuğluk Dağı Turkey 36°59N 33°50E 250 B4
Yugo-Zarad Russia 55°40N 37°30E 129 B2
Yugorenok Russia 59°47N 137°40E 215 D14
Yugyd Va △ Russia 62°25N 58°45E 214 C6
Yuhuan China 28°9N 121°12E 229 C13
Yühuan Dao China 28°5N 121°15E 229 C13
Yujiang China 28°10N 116°43E 229 C11
Yukhary Askipara
Azerbaijan 41°4N 45°1E 213 B11
Yukhnov Russia 54°44N 35°15E 188 E8
Yūki Japan 36°18N 139°53E 223 A11
Yukon U.S.A. 35°31N 97°45W 314 D6
Yukon □ Canada 63°0N 135°0W 294 E5
Yukon → U.S.A. 62°32N 163°54W 303 E7
Yukon-Charley Rivers ⌓
U.S.A. 65°15N 144°0W 303 D12
Yukon Delta Nat. Wildlife Refuge ⌓
U.S.A. 61°0N 163°0W 303 F7
Yukon Flats U.S.A. 66°40N 145°45W 303 C11
Yüksekova Turkey 37°34N 44°16E 213 D11
Yukta Russia 63°26N 105°42E 215 C11
Yukuhashi Japan 33°44N 130°59E 222 D2
Yulara Australia 25°10S 130°55E 279 E5
Yule → Australia 20°41S 118°17E 278 D2
Yuleba Australia 26°37S 149°24E 281 D4
Yulee U.S.A. 30°38N 81°36W 316 E8
Yuli China 41°19N 86°15E 217 D11
Yuli Nigeria 9°44N 10°12E 263 D7
Yüli Taiwan 23°20N 121°18E 225 C3
Yulin Guangxi Zhuangzu,
China 22°40N 110°8E 229 F8
Yulin Hainan, China 18°10N 109°31E 229 a
Yulin Shaanxi, China 38°20N 109°30E 226 E5
Yulong Xueshan China 27°6N 100°10E 228 D3
Yuma Ariz., U.S.A. 32°43N 114°37W 307 N12
Yuma Colo., U.S.A. 40°8N 102°43W 304 F12
Yuma, B. de Dom. Rep. 18°20N 68°35W 321 C6
Yumali Australia 35°32S 139°45E 282 C3
Yumbe Uganda 3°28N 31°15E 268 B3
Yumbi Équateur,
Dem. Rep. of the Congo 1°53S 16°34E 264 C3
Yumbi Maniema,
Dem. Rep. of the Congo 1°12S 26°15E 268 C2
Yumbo Colombia 3°35N 76°28W 328 C2
Yumen China 39°50N 97°30E 218 D8
Yumurtalık Turkey 36°45N 35°48E 250 B6
Yun Gui Gaoyuan China 26°0N 104°0E 228 E3
Yun Ling Shan China 27°0N 99°20E 228 D2
Yun Xian Hubei, China 32°50N 110°46E 229 A8
Yun Xian Yunnan, China 24°27N 100°8E 228 E3
Yuna Australia 28°20S 115°0E 279 E2
Yunak Turkey 38°49N 31°43E 212 C4
Yunan China 23°12N 111°30E 229 F8
Yunaska I. U.S.A. 52°38N 170°40W 303 K5
Yuncheng Henan, China 35°36N 115°57E 226 G8
Yuncheng Shanxi, China 35°2N 111°0E 226 G6
Yunfu China 22°50N 112°5E 229 F9
Yung Shue Wan
Hong Kong, China 22°13N 114°6E 122 B2
Yungan Taiwan 22°49N 120°12E 225 D2
Yungang Shiku China 40°6N 113°7E 226 D7
Yungas Bolivia 17°0S 66°0W 331 D4
Yungay Chile 37°10S 72°5W 334 D1
Yungay Peru 9°2S 77°45W 330 B2
Yungk'ang Taiwan 23°2N 120°15E 225 C2
Yungki = Jilin China 43°44N 126°30E 227 C14
Yungning = Nanning
China 22°48N 108°20E 228 F7
Yunhe China 28°8N 119°33E 229 C12
Yunkai Dashan China 22°30N 111°0E 229 F8
Yunkanjini ❂ Australia 22°33S 131°6E 278 D5
Yünlin □ Taiwan 23°40N 120°20E 225 C2
Yunling Shan China 28°30N 98°50E 218 F8
Yunlong China 25°57N 99°13E 228 E2
Yunmeng China 31°2N 113°43E 229 B9
Yunnan □ China 25°0N 102°0E 228 E4
Yunotsu Japan 35°5N 132°21E 222 B4
Yunquera de Henares
Spain 40°47N 3°11W 196 E1
Yunshui Taiwan 23°23N 120°31E 225 C2
Yunt Dağı Turkey 38°56N 27°13E 205 C9
Yunta Australia 32°34S 139°36E 281 E2
Yunxi China 33°0N 110°22E 229 A8
Yunxiao China 23°59N 117°18E 229 F11
Yunyang Chongqing, China 31°2N 108°51E 228 B7
Yunyang Henan, China 33°26N 112°42E 229 A9
Yupanqui Basin Pac. Oc. 19°0S 101°0W 289 J17
Yuping China 27°13N 108°56E 228 D7
Yupukarri Guyana 3°45N 59°20W 329 C6
Yuqing China 27°13N 107°53E 228 D6
Yuraygir △ Australia 29°45S 153°15E 281 D5
Yurga Russia 55°42N 84°51E 214 D9
Yurihonjō Japan 39°23N 140°3E 220 E10
Yurimaguas Peru 5°55S 76°7W 330 B2
Yurkiyka Ukraine 48°42N 28°35E 183 B13
Yurubí △ Venezuela 10°26N 68°42W 321 E6
Yurungkax He → China 38°5N 80°34E 217 E10
Yuryev = Tartu Estonia 58°20N 26°44E 188 C4
Yuryev-Polskiy Russia 56°30N 39°40E 188 D10
Yuryevets Russia 57°25N 43°2E 190 B6
Yuscarán Honduras 13°58N 86°45W 320 D2
Yûsef, Bahr → Egypt 28°25N 30°35E 256 B3
Yushan China 28°42N 118°10E 229 C12
Yushanzhen China 29°28N 108°22E 228 C7
Yushe China 37°4N 112°58E 226 F7
Yushu Jilin, China 44°43N 126°38E 227 B14
Yushu Qinghai, China 33°5N 96°55E 218 E8
Yūsofābād Iran 35°43N 51°24E 141 A2
Yusufeli Turkey 40°50N 41°33E 213 B9
Yutai China 35°0N 116°45E 226 G9
Yutian Hebei, China 39°53N 117°45E 227 E9
Yutian Sinkiang-Uigur,
China 36°52N 81°42E 217 E10
Yütze = Jinzhong China 37°42N 112°46E 226 F7
Yüweng Tao Taiwan 23°36N 119°30E 225 C1
Yuxarı Qarabağ =
Nagorno-Karabakh □
Azerbaijan 39°55N 46°45E 213 C12
Yuxi China 24°30N 102°35E 228 E4
Yuyao China 30°3N 121°10E 229 B13
Yuzawa Japan 39°10N 140°30E 220 E10
Yuzha Russia 56°34N 42°1E 190 B6
Yuzhno-Kurilsk Russia 44°1N 145°51E 215 E15
Yuzhno-Sakhalinsk
Russia 46°58N 142°45E 219 B17
Yuzhno-Sukhokumsk
Russia 44°40N 45°35E 191 H7
Yuzhnoukrainsk Ukraine 47°49N 31°11E 189 J6
Yuzhnouralsk Russia 54°26N 61°15E 216 B6
Yuzhnyy □ Russia 44°0N 40°0E 214 E5
Yuzhou China 34°10N 113°28E 226 G7
Yuzovka = Donetsk
Ukraine 48°0N 37°45E 189 J9
Yvelines □ France 48°40N 1°45E 173 D8
Yverdon-les-Bains Switz. 46°47N 6°39E 179 J2
Yvetot France 49°37N 0°44E 172 C7
Yzeure France 46°33N 3°22E 173 F10

Z

Za'abeel U.A.E. 25°13N 55°19E 119 B2
Zaandam Neths. 52°26N 4°49E 112 A1
Zaandijk Neths. 52°28N 4°49E 112 A1
Zaanstad Neths. 52°27N 4°50E 112 A1
Zab, Monts du Algeria 34°55N 5°0E 261 B6
Zāb al Kabīr → Iraq 36°1N 43°24E 213 D10
Zāb aş Şaghīr → Iraq 35°17N 43°29E 213 E10
Žabalj Serbia 45°21N 20°5E 182 E5
Žabari Serbia 44°22N 21°15E 202 B5
Zabarjad Egypt 23°40N 36°12E 256 C4
Zabaykalsk Russia 49°40N 117°25E 215 E12
Zabaykalsky △ Russia 53°40N 109°0E 215 D11
Zabbar Malta 35°53N 14°32E 206 F8
Záběhlice Czechia 50°3N 14°29E 135 B2
Zabīd Yemen 14°0N 43°10E 248 D3
Zabīd, W. → Yemen 14°7N 43°6E 248 D3
Zabki Poland 52°17N 21°6E 143 B2
Ząbkowice Śląskie Poland 50°35N 16°50E 185 H3
Žabljak Montenegro 43°18N 19°5E 202 C3
Zabłudów Poland 53°0N 23°19E 185 F9
Żabno Poland 50°9N 20°53E 185 H7
Zabol Iran 31°0N 61°32E 247 D9
Zābol □ Afghan. 32°0N 67°0E 240 C2
Zābolī Iran 27°10N 61°35E 247 E9
Zabolotiv Ukraine 48°28N 25°18E 183 B10
Zabolottya Ukraine 51°38N 24°16E 185 G11
Zabré Burkina Faso 11°12N 0°36W 263 C4
Zábřeh Czechia 49°53N 16°52E 181 B9
Zabrze Poland 50°18N 18°50E 185 H5
Zabuzhzhya Ukraine 51°21N 23°42E 185 G10
Zabzuga Ghana 9°20N 0°30E 263 D5
Zacapa Guatemala 14°59N 89°31W 320 D2
Zacapu Mexico 19°50N 101°43W 318 D4
Zacatecas Mexico 22°47N 102°35W 318 C4
Zacatecas □ Mexico 23°0N 103°0W 318 C4
Zacatecoluca El Salv. 13°29N 88°51W 320 D2
Zacharo Greece 37°30N 21°39E 204 D3
Zachary U.S.A. 30°39N 91°9W 314 F9
Zachodnio-Pomorskie □
Poland 53°40N 15°50E 184 E2
Żacisze Poland 52°17N 21°4E 143 B2
Zacoalco de Torres
Mexico 20°14N 103°35W 318 C4
Zacualtipán Mexico 20°39N 98°36W 319 C5
Zadar Croatia 44°8N 15°14E 199 D12
Zadawa Nigeria 11°33N 10°19E 263 C7
Zadetkyi Kyun Burma 10°0N 98°25E 237 G2
Zadonsk Russia 52°25N 38°56E 189 F10
Zafarqand Iran 33°11N 52°29E 247 C7
Zafra Spain 38°26N 6°30W 195 G4
Żagań Poland 51°39N 15°22E 185 G2
Zagaoua Chad 16°0N 21°10E 259 E4
Žagarė Lithuania 56°21N 23°15E 184 B10
Zagazig Egypt 30°40N 31°30E 256 H7
Zāgheh Iran 33°30N 48°42E 247 C6
Zaghouan Tunisia 36°23N 10°10E 258 A2
Zaghouan □ Tunisia 36°20N 10°0E 261 A7
Zaglou Algeria 27°17N 0°3W 261 C4
Zagnanado Benin 7°18N 2°28E 263 D5
Zagora Greece 39°27N 23°6E 204 B5
Zagora Morocco 30°22N 5°51W 260 B3
Zagorje ob Savi Slovenia 46°8N 15°0E 199 B11
Zagórów Poland 52°10N 17°54E 185 F4
Zagorsk = Sergiyev Posad
Russia 56°20N 38°10E 188 D10
Zagorsky = Krasnozavodsk
Russia 56°27N 38°25E 188 D10

Zagórz Poland 49°30N 22°14E 185 J9
Zagreb Croatia 45°50N 15°58E 199 C12
Zagreb ✈ (ZAG) Croatia 45°45N 16°4E 199 C13
Zāgros, Kūhhā-ye Iran 33°45N 48°5E 247 C6
Zagros Mts. = Zāgros, Kūhhā-ye Iran 33°45N 48°5E 247 C6
Žagubica Serbia 44°15N 21°47E 202 B5
Zaguinaso Ivory C. 10°1N 6°14W 262 C3
Zagyva → Hungary 47°5N 20°4E 182 C5
Zahamena △ Madag. 17°37S 48°49E 272 B2
Zāhedān Fārs, Iran 28°46N 53°52E 247 D7
Zāhedān Sīstān va Balūchestān, Iran 29°30N 60°50E 247 D9
Zahirabad India 17°43N 77°37E 244 F3
Zahlah Lebanon 33°52N 35°50E 250 E6
Zahna Germany 51°55N 12°49E 178 D8
Záhony Hungary 48°25N 22°11E 182 B7
Zahrā Iraq 33°22N 44°19E 113 A1
Zahrān al Janub Si. Arabia 17°40N 43°30E 248 C3
Zainsk Russia 55°18N 52°4E 190 C11
Zaïre = Congo → Africa 6°4S 12°24E 265 D2
Zaïre = Congo, Dem. Rep. of the ■ Africa 3°0S 23°0E 265 C4
Zaire □ Angola 7°0S 14°0E 265 D2
Zaječar Serbia 43°53N 22°18E 202 C6
Zaka Zimbabwe 20°20S 31°29E 271 B5
Zakamensk Russia 50°23N 103°17E 215 D11
Zakani Dem. Rep. of the Congo 2°33N 23°16E 264 B4
Zakarpattya □ Ukraine 48°20N 23°20E 183 B8
Zakataly = Zaqatala Azerbaijan 41°38N 46°35E 191 K8
Zakbayemé Cameroon 4°2N 10°34E 264 B2
Zakhodnaya Dzvina = Daugava → Latvia 57°4N 24°3E 188 D3
Zākhū Iraq 37°10N 42°50E 213 D10
Zakinthos = Zakynthos Greece 37°47N 20°54E 207 D2
Zakinthos, Diavlos Greece 37°50N 21°0E 207 D2
Zakopane Poland 49°18N 19°57E 185 J6
Zakouma Chad 10°54N 19°49E 259 F3
Zakouma △ Chad 10°52N 19°45E 259 F3
Zakroczym Poland 52°26N 20°38E 185 F7
Zakros Greece 35°6N 26°10E 207 E7
Zakynthos Greece 37°47N 20°54E 207 D2
Zakynthos ✈ (ZTH) Greece 37°45N 20°50E 207 D2
Zala Angola 7°52S 13°42E 265 D2
Zala Ethiopia 6°28N 37°13E 257 F4
Zala □ Hungary 46°42N 16°50E 182 D1
Zala → Hungary 46°43N 17°16E 182 D2
Zalaegerszeg Hungary 46°53N 16°47E 182 D1
Zalakomár Hungary 46°33N 17°10E 182 D2
Zalalövő Hungary 46°51N 16°35E 182 D1
Zalamea de la Serena Spain 38°40N 5°38W 195 G5
Zalamea la Real Spain 37°41N 6°38W 195 H4
Zalantun China 48°0N 122°43E 219 B13
Zalari Russia 53°33N 102°30E 215 D11
Zalău Romania 47°12N 23°3E 182 C8
Žalec Slovenia 46°16N 15°10E 199 B12
Zaleshchiki = Zalishchyky Ukraine 48°45N 25°45E 183 B10
Zalesye Russia 54°50N 21°31E 184 D8
Zalewo Poland 53°50N 19°41E 184 E6
Zalim Si. Arabia 22°43N 42°10E 248 B3
Zalingei Sudan 12°51N 23°29E 259 F4
Zalingei □ Sudan 12°0N 23°0E 259 F4
Zalishchyky Ukraine 48°45N 25°45E 183 B10
Zalmah, J. az Libya 25°30N 24°40E 258 C4
Žalov Czechia 50°10N 14°22E 135 A2
Zaltan Al Wāhāt, Libya 28°51N 19°52E 258 C3
Zaltan An Nuqāt al Khams, Libya 32°57N 11°52E 258 B2
Zalun Burma 17°29N 95°34E 241 G5
Załuski Poland 52°9N 20°55E 143 C1
Zama L. Canada 58°45N 119°5W 296 B5
Zambales □ Phil. 15°20N 120°10E 232 D3
Zambales Mts. Phil. 15°45N 120°5E 232 D3
Zambeke Dem. Rep. of the Congo 2°8N 25°17E 268 B2
Zambeze → Africa 18°35S 36°20E 269 F4
Zambezi = Zambeze → Africa 18°35S 36°20E 269 F4
Zambezi Zambia 13°30S 23°15E 265 E4
Zambezi □ Namibia 18°0S 23°30E 270 A3
Zambezi △ Zimbabwe 17°54S 25°41E 269 F2
Zambezia □ Mozam. 16°15S 37°30E 269 F4
Zambia ■ Africa 15°0S 28°0E 269 F2
Zamboanga Phil. 6°59N 122°3E 233 H4
Zamboanga del Norte □ Phil. 8°0N 123°0E 233 G4
Zamboanga del Sur □ Phil. 7°0N 122°0E 233 H3
Zamboanga Pen. Phil. 7°32N 122°16E 233 H4
Zamboanga Sibugay □ Phil. 7°40N 123°0E 233 H4
Zamboanguita Phil. 9°6N 123°11E 233 G4
Zambrano Colombia 9°45N 74°49W 328 B3
Zambrów Poland 52°59N 22°14E 185 F9
Zamdorf Germany 48°8N 11°35E 131 B2
Zamfara □ Nigeria 12°10N 6°0E 263 C6
Zamfara → Nigeria 12°5N 4°2E 263 C5
Zamora Ecuador 4°4S 78°58W 328 D2
Zamora Michoacan, Mexico 19°59N 102°16W 318 D4
Zamora Spain 41°30N 5°45W 194 D5
Zamora □ Spain 41°30N 5°46W 194 D5
Zamora → Ecuador 2°59S 78°13W 328 D2
Zamora-Chinchipe □ Ecuador 4°15S 78°50W 328 D2
Zamość Poland 50°43N 23°15E 185 H10
Zamtang China 32°26N 101°6E 228 A3
Zamuro, Sierra del Venezuela 4°0N 62°30W 329 C5
Zamzam, W. → Libya 30°58N 14°48E 258 B2
Zan Ghana 9°26N 0°17W 263 D4
Zanaga Congo 2°48S 13°48E 264 C2
Záncara → Spain 39°18N 3°18W 197 F1
Zanda China 31°32N 79°50E 218 E4
Zanderij Suriname 5°20N 55°16W 329 B6
Zandu Dem. Rep. of the Congo 5°11S 18°16E 265 D3
Zandvoort Neths. 52°22N 4°32E 170 B4
Zanesville U.S.A. 39°56N 82°1W 312 G2
Zanevka Russia 59°55N 30°31E 137 B3
Zangābād Iran 38°26N 46°44E 246 B5
Zangliveri Greece 40°36N 23°15E 202 F7
Zangoza = Sangüesa Spain 42°37N 1°17W 196 C3
Zangue → Mozam. 17°50S 35°21E 269 F4
Zanjān Iran 36°40N 48°35E 213 D13
Zanjān □ Iran 37°20N 49°30E 247 B6
Zanjān → Iran 37°8N 47°47E 247 B6
Zannone Italy 40°58N 13°3E 200 B6
Zanow = Sianów Poland 54°13N 16°18E 184 D3
Zante = Zakynthos Greece 37°47N 20°54E 207 D2
Zanthus Australia 31°2S 123°34E 279 F3
Zanzan □ Ivory C. 8°30N 3°30W 262 D4
Zanzibar Tanzania 6°12S 39°12E 268 D4
Zanzūr Libya 32°55N 13°1E 258 B2
Zaouatallaz Algeria 24°52N 8°26E 261 D6
Zaouiet El-Kala = Bordj Omar Driss Algeria 28°10N 6°40E 261 C6
Zaouiet Reggâne Algeria 26°32N 0°3E 261 C5
Zaoyang China 32°10N 112°45E 229 A9
Zaozernyy Kazakhstan 53°6N 71°9E 217 B8
Zaozhuang China 34°50N 117°35E 227 G9
Zap Suyu = Zāb al Kabīr → Iraq 36°1N 43°24E 213 D10
Zapadna Morava → Serbia 43°38N 21°30E 202 C5
Zapadnaya Dvina = Daugava → Latvia 57°4N 24°3E 188 D3
Zapadnaya Dvina Russia 56°15N 32°3E 188 D7
Západné Beskydy Europe 49°30N 19°0E 181 B12
Zapadni Rodopi Bulgaria 41°50N 24°0E 202 E7
Západočeský □ Czechia 49°35N 13°0E 180 B6
Zapala Argentina 39°0S 70°5W 336 A2
Zapaleri, Cerro Bolivia 22°49S 67°11W 334 A2
Zapata U.S.A. 26°55N 99°16W 314 F5
Zapatón → Spain 39°0N 6°49W 195 F4
Zapiga Chile 19°40S 69°55W 330 D4
Zapolyarnyy Russia 69°26N 30°51E 160 B24
Zapopán Mexico 20°43N 103°24W 318 C4
Zaporizhzhya Ukraine 47°50N 35°10E 189 J8
Zaporizhzhya □ Ukraine 46°55N 35°50E 189 J8
Zaporozhye = Zaporizhzhya Ukraine 47°50N 35°10E 189 J8
Zapote Phil. 14°27N 120°56E 127 C1
Zappeion Athens, Greece 112 c2
Zaqatala Azerbaijan 41°38N 46°35E 191 K8
Zara Turkey 39°58N 37°43E 212 C7
Zarafshon Uzbekistan 41°34N 64°12E 216 E6
Zaragoza Colombia 7°30N 74°52W 328 B3
Zaragoza Coahuila, Mexico 28°29N 100°55W 318 B4
Zaragoza Nuevo León, Mexico 23°58N 99°46W 319 C5
Zaragoza Spain 41°39N 0°53W 196 D4
Zaragoza □ Spain 41°35N 1°0W 196 D4
Zarand Kermān, Iran 30°46N 56°34E 247 D8
Zarand Markazī, Iran 35°18N 50°25E 247 C6
Zărandului, Munții Romania 46°14N 22°7E 182 D7
Zaranj Afghan. 30°55N 61°55E 240 C1
Zarasai Lithuania 55°40N 26°20E 188 E4
Zárate Argentina 34°7S 59°0W 334 C4
Zarautz Spain 43°17N 2°10W 196 B2
Zaraysk Russia 54°48N 38°53E 188 E10
Zaraza Venezuela 9°21N 65°19W 329 B4
Zard, Kūh-e Iran 32°22N 50°4E 247 C6
Zarechniy Russia 56°49N 61°20E 190 D7
Zāreh Iran 35°7N 49°9E 247 C6
Zari Nigeria 13°4N 12°45E 263 C7
Zaria Nigeria 11°0N 7°40E 263 C6
Zarineh → Iran 36°17N 46°26E 213 D12
Zarinsk Russia 53°43N 84°55E 217 B10
Żarki Poland 50°38N 19°23E 185 H6
Zarko Greece 39°38N 22°6E 204 B4
Zarneh Iran 33°55N 46°10E 246 C5
Zărnești Romania 45°33N 25°18E 183 E10
Zaros Greece 35°8N 24°54E 207 E5
Żarów Poland 50°56N 16°29E 185 H3
Zarqā', Nahr az → Jordan 32°10N 35°37E 251 F6
Zarrīn Iran 32°46N 54°37E 247 C7
Zarrīnābād Iran 36°25N 48°17E 213 D13
Zaruma Ecuador 3°40S 79°38W 328 D2
Żary Poland 51°37N 15°10E 185 G2
Zarza de Granadilla Spain 40°14N 6°3W 194 E4
Zarzaïtine Algeria 28°15N 9°34E 261 C6
Zarzal Colombia 4°24N 76°4W 328 C2
Zarzis Tunisia 33°31N 11°2E 258 B2
Zas Spain 43°4N 8°53W 194 B2
Zashaghan Kazakhstan 51°11N 51°20E 216 B4
Zaskar → India 34°13N 77°20E 242 B4
Zaskar Mts. India 33°15N 77°30E 243 C7
Zastavna Ukraine 48°31N 25°51E 183 B10
Zastron S. Africa 30°18S 27°7E 270 D4
Žatec Czechia 50°20N 13°32E 180 A6
Zaterechnyy Russia 44°48N 45°11E 191 H7
Zatishye = Elektrostal Russia 55°41N 38°32E 188 E10
Zator Poland 49°59N 19°28E 185 J6
Zatyshshya Ukraine 47°20N 29°51E 183 C14
Zavala Bos.-H. 42°50N 17°59E 202 D1
Zavāreh Iran 33°29N 52°28E 247 C7
Zave Zimbabwe 17°6S 30°1E 271 A5
Zaventem Belgium 50°53N 4°28E 116 A2
Zavetnoye Russia 47°13N 43°50E 191 G6
Zavidovići Bos.-H. 44°27N 18°10E 182 F3
Zavitaya = Zavitinsk Russia 50°10N 129°20E 215 D13
Zavitinsk Russia 50°10N 129°20E 215 D13
Zavodovski I. Antarctica 56°0S 27°45W 151 B1
Zavodskoy = Komsomolskiy Russia 54°27N 45°33E 190 E7
Zavolzhsk Russia 57°30N 42°3E 190 B6
Zavolzhye = Zavolzhsk Russia 57°30N 42°3E 190 B6
Zavolzhye Russia 56°37N 43°26E 190 B6
Zawady Poland 52°10N 21°6E 143 B2
Zawadzkie Poland 50°37N 18°28E 185 H5
Zawichost Poland 50°48N 21°51E 185 H8
Zawidów Poland 51°1N 15°1E 185 G2
Zawiercie Poland 50°30N 19°24E 185 H6
Zāwīyah, J. az Syria 35°45N 36°35E 250 C7
Zāwiyat al Baydā = Al Baydā Libya 32°50N 21°44E 258 B4
Zāwiyat Masūs Libya 31°35N 21°1E 258 B4
Zāwiyat Abū Musallam Egypt 29°56N 31°9E 117 B1
Zawrā' Park Iraq 33°18N 44°23E 113 B2
Zāwyet Shammas Egypt 31°30N 26°37E 256 A2
Zâwyet Um el Rakham Egypt 31°18N 27°1E 256 A2
Zâwyet Ungeîla Egypt 31°23N 26°42E 256 A2
Zāyā Iraq 33°33N 44°13E 246 C5
Zāyandeh → Iran 32°35N 52°0E 247 C7
Zaymah Si. Arabia 21°37N 40°6E 248 B3
Zaysan Kazakhstan 47°28N 84°52E 217 C10
Zaysan Köli Kazakhstan 48°0N 83°0E 217 C10
Zayü China 28°48N 97°27E 218 F8
Zazafotsy Madag. 21°11S 46°21E 272 C2
Zāzamt, W. → Libya 30°29N 14°30E 258 B2
Zazir, O. → Algeria 22°0N 5°40E 261 D6
Zázrivá Slovakia 49°16N 19°7E 181 B12
Zbarazh Ukraine 49°43N 25°44E 177 D13
Zbąszyń Poland 52°14N 15°56E 185 F2
Zbąszynek Poland 52°16N 15°51E 185 F2
Zblewo Poland 53°56N 18°19E 184 E5
Zbraslav Czechia 49°58N 14°23E 135 C2
Zbruch → Ukraine 48°32N 26°27E 183 B11
Žbuzany Czechia 50°1N 14°17E 135 B1
Žďár nad Sázavou Czechia 49°34N 15°57E 180 B8
Ždiby Czechia 50°9N 14°27E 135 B2
Zdolbuniv Ukraine 50°30N 26°15E 177 C14
Ždrelo Serbia 44°16N 21°28E 202 B5
Zduńska Wola Poland 51°37N 18°59E 185 G5
Zduny Poland 51°39N 17°21E 185 G4
Zearing U.S.A. 42°10N 93°18W 310 B3
Zeballos Canada 49°59N 126°50W 296 D3
Zebbug Malta 35°52N 14°26E 206 F7
Żebbuġ Gozo, Malta 36°4N 14°14E 206 E6
Zebediela S. Africa 24°20S 29°17E 271 B4
Zebila Ghana 10°55N 0°30W 263 C4
Zebulon U.S.A. 33°6N 84°21W 316 B5
Zeebrugge Belgium 51°19N 3°12E 170 C3
Zeehan Australia 41°52S 145°25E 281 G4
Zeekoevlei S. Africa 34°4S 18°31E 118 B2
Zeeland U.S.A. 42°49N 86°1W 311 B10
Zeeland □ Neths. 51°30N 3°50E 170 C3
Zeelandia St. Eustatius 17°30N 62°59W 322 a
Zeerust S. Africa 25°31S 26°4E 270 C4
Zefat Israel 32°58N 35°29E 250 E6
Zegdou Algeria 29°51N 4°45W 260 C4
Zege Ethiopia 11°43N 37°18E 257 E4
Zeggerene, Iracher Mali 16°49N 2°16E 263 B5
Zégoua Mali 10°32N 5°35W 262 C3
Zehak Iran 30°53N 61°42E 247 D9
Zehden = Cedynia Poland 52°53N 14°12E 185 F1
Zehdenick Germany 52°58N 13°20E 178 C9
Zehlendorf Germany 52°26N 13°16E 115 B2
Zeigler U.S.A. 37°54N 89°3W 310 G7
Zeil, Mt. Australia 23°30S 132°23E 278 D5
Zeila = Saylac Somalia 11°21N 43°30E 267 B5
Zeist Neths. 52°5N 5°15E 170 B5
Zeitz Germany 51°2N 12°7E 178 D8
Zejtun Malta 35°51N 14°32E 206 F8
Żelechów Poland 51°49N 21°54E 185 G8
Zelena Ukraine 48°3N 24°45E 183 B9
Zelená Hora Czechia 49°34N 15°56E 180 B8
Zelengora Bos.-H. 43°22N 18°30E 202 C2
Zelenodolsk Russia 55°55N 48°30E 190 C9
Zelenogorsk Russia 60°12N 29°43E 188 B5
Zelenograd Russia 56°1N 37°12E 188 D9
Zelenogradsk Russia 54°53N 20°29E 184 D7
Zelenokumsk Russia 44°24N 44°0E 191 H6
Zeleqa, W. → Egypt 29°7N 34°31E 251 J5
Železná Ruda Czechia 49°8N 13°15E 180 B6
Železnik Serbia 44°43N 20°23E 202 B4
Zelfana Algeria 32°27N 4°15E 261 B5
Zelienople U.S.A. 40°48N 80°8W 312 F4
Želiezovce Slovakia 48°3N 18°40E 181 C11
Zelina Croatia 45°57N 16°16E 199 C13
Zell Baden-W., Germany 47°42N 7°52E 179 H3
Zell Rhld-Pfz., Germany 50°1N 7°10E 179 E3
Zell am See Austria 47°19N 12°47E 180 D5
Zella-Mehlis Germany 50°39N 10°40E 178 E6
Zelmen = Rovnoye Russia 50°52N 46°3E 190 E8
Zelów Poland 51°28N 19°14E 185 G6
Zeltweg Austria 47°11N 14°45E 180 D7
Zelyony Dol = Zelenodolsk Russia 55°55N 48°30E 190 C9
Žemaitijos △ Lithuania 56°2N 21°55E 184 B8
Zembra, I. Tunisia 37°5N 10°56E 258 A2
Zemetchino Russia 53°30N 42°30E 190 D6
Zemgale = Jelgava Latvia 56°41N 23°49E 184 B10
Zémio C.A.R. 5°2N 25°5E 264 A5
Zemlandskiy Poluostrov Russia 54°50N 20°20E 184 D7
Zemlya Imperatora Nikolaya II = Severnaya Zemlya Russia 79°0N 100°0E 215 B11
Zemmora Algeria 35°44N 0°51E 261 A5
Zemmour W. Sahara 25°5N 12°0W 260 C2
Zemongo ⌂ C.A.R. 6°45N 25°5E 264 A5
Zemoul, O. → Algeria 29°15N 7°0W 260 C3
Zempelburg = Sępólno Krajeńskie Poland 53°26N 17°30E 184 E4
Zempléni-hegység Hungary 48°25N 21°25E 182 B6
Zemplínska šírava Slovakia 48°48N 22°0E 181 C15
Zempoala Mexico 19°27N 96°23W 319 D5
Zemun Serbia 44°51N 20°25E 202 B4
Zendeh Jān Afghan. 34°21N 61°45E 240 B1
Zengbé Cameroon 5°46N 13°4E 263 D7
Zengcheng China 23°13N 113°52E 229 F9
Zenica Bos.-H. 44°10N 17°57E 182 F2
Zenne → Belgium 51°4N 4°26E 116 A2
Zentsūji Japan 34°14N 133°47E 222 C5
Zenza → Angola 8°45S 13°24E 265 D2
Zenza do Itombe Angola 9°16S 14°13E 265 D2
Žepče Bos.-H. 44°28N 18°2E 182 F3
Zephyr Field U.S.A. 29°58N 90°12W 131 B1
Zephyrhills U.S.A. 28°14N 82°11W 317 G7
Zepu China 38°11N 77°16E 217 E9
Zeraf, Bahr ez → South Sudan 9°42N 30°52E 257 F3
Żerań Poland 52°18N 20°58E 143 B1
Zerbst Germany 51°58N 12°5E 178 D8
Zerhamra Algeria 29°58N 2°30W 261 C4
Żerków Poland 52°4N 17°32E 185 F4
Zermatt Switz. 46°2N 7°46E 179 J3
Zernez Switz. 46°42N 10°7E 179 J6
Zernograd Russia 46°52N 40°19E 191 G5
Zernovoy = Zernograd Russia 46°52N 40°19E 191 G5
Zero Milestone Washington, D.C., U.S.A. 143 b1
Zerqan Albania 41°27N 20°20E 202 E4
Zerzeń Poland 52°12N 21°7E 143 B2
Zestaponi Georgia 42°6N 43°0E 191 J6
Zetel Germany 53°25N 7°58E 178 B3
Zetland = Shetland □ U.K. 60°30N 1°30W 167 A7
Zeulenroda-Triebes Germany 50°39N 11°59E 178 E7
Zévallos Guadeloupe 16°18N 61°17W 322 e
Zeven Germany 53°17N 9°16E 178 B5
Zevenaar Neths. 51°56N 6°5E 170 C6
Zévio Italy 45°22N 11°8E 198 C8
Zeya Russia 53°48N 127°14E 215 D13
Zeya → Russia 51°42N 128°53E 215 D13
Zeyne Turkey 36°25N 33°31E 250 B4
Zeyskoye Vdkhr. Russia 54°30N 127°30E 215 D13
Zeytinbağı Turkey 40°24N 28°47E 203 F12
Zeytinburnu Turkey 40°58N 28°53E 122 C1
Zeytindağ Turkey 38°58N 27°4E 205 C9
Zghartā Lebanon 34°21N 35°53E 250 D6
Zgierz Poland 51°50N 19°27E 185 G6
Zgorzelec Poland 51°10N 15°0E 185 G2
Zgurița Moldova 48°8N 28°1E 183 B13
Zhabei China 31°16N 121°26E 138 B1
Zhabinka Belarus 52°13N 24°2E 185 F11
Zhabokrych Ukraine 48°23N 28°59E 183 B13
Zhalaghash Kazakhstan 45°5N 64°40E 216 C6
Zhalpaqtal Kazakhstan 49°42N 49°25E 190 F9
Zhaltyr Kazakhstan 51°37N 69°49E 217 B7
Zhambyl = Taraz Kazakhstan 42°54N 71°22E 217 D8
Zhambyl □ Kazakhstan 44°0N 72°0E 217 D8
Zhanatas Kazakhstan 43°35N 69°35E 217 D7
Zhangaly Kazakhstan 47°1N 50°37E 191 G10
Zhangaözen Kazakhstan 43°18N 52°48E 187 F9
Zhangaqala Kazakhstan 48°56N 49°36E 191 F9
Zhangatas = Zhanatas Kazakhstan 43°35N 69°35E 217 D7
Zhangbei China 41°10N 114°45E 226 D8
Zhangguangcai Ling China 45°0N 129°0E 227 B15
Zhangjiabian China 22°33N 113°28E 219 a
Zhangjiagang China 31°55N 120°30E 229 B13
Zhangjiajie China 29°11N 110°30E 229 C8
Zhangjiakou China 40°48N 114°55E 226 D8
Zhangping China 25°17N 117°23E 229 E11
Zhangpu China 24°8N 117°35E 229 E11
Zhangshu China 28°4N 115°29E 229 C10
Zhangwu China 42°43N 122°22E 227 C12
Zhangye China 38°50N 100°23E 218 D9
Zhangzhou China 24°30N 117°35E 229 E11
Zhanhua China 37°40N 118°8E 227 F10
Zhänibek Kazakhstan 49°25N 46°50E 190 F8
Zhanjiang China 21°15N 110°20E 229 G8
Zhannetty, Ostrov Russia 76°43N 158°0E 215 B16
Zhanyi China 25°38N 103°48E 228 E4
Zhanyu China 44°30N 122°30E 227 B12
Zhao Xian China 37°43N 114°45E 226 F8
Zhao'an China 23°41N 117°10E 229 F11
Zhaocheng China 36°22N 111°38E 226 F6
Zhaodong China 46°4N 125°59E 219 B13
Zhaojue China 28°1N 102°49E 228 C4
Zhaoping China 24°11N 110°48E 229 E8
Zhaoqing China 23°0N 112°20E 229 F9
Zhaotong China 27°20N 103°44E 228 D4
Zhaoyang Hu China 35°4N 116°47E 226 G9
Zhaoyuan Heilongjiang, China 45°27N 125°0E 227 B13
Zhaoyuan Shandong, China 37°20N 120°23E 227 F11
Zhar, Mali Kosovo 42°20N 21°0E 202 D5
Zhari Namco China 31°6N 85°36E 218 E6
Zharkent Kazakhstan 44°10N 80°0E 217 D10
Zharkovskiy Russia 55°56N 32°19E 188 E7
Zhashkiv Ukraine 49°15N 30°5E 177 D16
Zhashui China 33°40N 109°8E 226 H5
Zhaslyk = Jasliq Uzbekistan 43°58N 57°10E 216 D5
Zhayrang Kazakhstan 48°20N 70°10E 217 C8
Zhayylma Kazakhstan 51°37N 61°33E 216 B6
Zhayyq → Kazakhstan 47°0N 51°48E 187 E9
Zhdanov = Mariupol Ukraine 47°5N 37°31E 189 J9
Zhdanovo Russia 55°44N 37°41E 129 B3
Zhecheng China 34°7N 115°20E 226 G8
Zhegao China 31°46N 117°45E 229 B11
Zheji China 23°4N 113°15E 121 B2
Zhejiang □ China 29°0N 120°0E 229 C13
Zheleznodorozhnyy = Qūnghirot Uzbekistan 43°2N 58°50E 216 D5
Zheleznodorozhnyy Kaliningrad, Russia 54°22N 21°19E 184 D8
Zheleznodorozhnyy Komi, Russia 62°35N 50°55E 186 B9
Zheleznogorsk Russia 52°22N 35°23E 189 F8
Zheleznogorsk-Ilimskiy Russia 56°34N 104°8E 215 D11
Zheltyye Vody = Zhovti Vody Ukraine 48°21N 33°31E 189 H7
Zhen'an China 33°27N 109°9E 228 A7
Zhenba China 32°34N 107°58E 228 A6
Zhencheng China 25°22N 105°40E 228 E5
Zheng'an China 28°32N 107°27E 228 C6
Zhengding China 38°8N 114°32E 226 E8
Zhenghe China 27°20N 118°50E 229 D12
Zhengyang China 32°37N 114°22E 229 A10
Zhengyangguan China 32°30N 116°29E 229 A11
Zhengzhou China 34°45N 113°34E 226 G7
Zhenhai China 29°59N 121°42E 229 C13
Zhenjiang China 32°11N 119°26E 229 A12
Zhenkang China 23°58N 99°0E 228 F2
Zhenlai China 45°50N 123°5E 227 B12
Zhenning China 26°4N 105°45E 228 D5
Zhenping Henan, China 33°10N 112°16E 226 H7
Zhenping Shaanxi, China 31°59N 109°31E 228 B7
Zhenru China 31°16N 121°22E 138 B1
Zhenxiong China 27°27N 104°50E 228 D5
Zhenyuan Gansu, China 35°35N 107°30E 226 G4
Zhenyuan Guizhou, China 27°4N 108°21E 228 D7
Zhenyuan Yunnan, China 23°51N 100°59E 228 F3
Zherdevka Russia 51°56N 41°29E 190 E5
Zherebkove Ukraine 47°50N 29°52E 183 C14
Zhernovka Russia 59°56N 30°30E 137 B2
Zherong China 27°15N 119°52E 229 D12
Zhetiqara Kazakhstan 52°11N 61°12E 216 B6
Zhezdi Kazakhstan 48°3N 67°3E 217 C7
Zhezqazghan Kazakhstan 47°44N 67°40E 217 C7
Zhicheng China 30°25N 111°27E 229 B8
Zhicun China 23°0N 113°18E 121 B2
Zhidan China 36°48N 108°48E 226 F5
Zhigansk Russia 66°48N 123°27E 215 C13
Zhigulevsk Russia 53°28N 49°30E 190 D9
Zhijiang Hubei, China 30°28N 111°45E 229 B8
Zhijiang Hunan, China 27°27N 109°42E 228 D7
Zhijin China 26°37N 105°45E 228 D5
Zhilinda Russia 70°0N 114°20E 215 C12
Zhilino Russia 54°54N 21°54E 184 D8
Zhingli = Chungli Taiwan 24°57N 121°13E 225 B3
Zhirnovsk Russia 50°57N 44°49E 190 E7
Zhirnovsky = Zhirnovsk Russia 50°57N 44°49E 190 E7
Zhirnoye = Zhirnovsk Russia 50°57N 44°49E 190 E7
Zhitomir = Zhytomyr Ukraine 50°20N 28°40E 177 C15
Zhizdra Russia 53°45N 34°40E 188 F8
Zhlobin Belarus 52°55N 30°0E 177 B16
Zhmerynka Ukraine 49°2N 28°2E 177 D15
Zhob Pakistan 31°20N 69°31E 242 D3
Zhob → Pakistan 32°4N 69°50E 242 C3
Zhodzina Belarus 54°5N 28°17E 177 A15
Zhokhova, Ostrov Russia 76°4N 152°40E 215 B16
Zholkev = Zhovkva Ukraine 50°4N 23°58E 177 C12
Zholkva = Zhovkva Ukraine 50°4N 23°58E 177 C12
Zhongba China 29°39N 84°10E 218 F5
Zhongdian China 27°48N 99°42E 228 D2
Zhongdong China 22°48N 107°47E 228 F6
Zhongdu China 24°40N 109°40E 228 E7
Zhongguancun China 39°59N 116°18E 114 B1
Zhonghe = Chungho Taiwan 25°0N 121°28E 225 A3
Zhongjian Dao = Triton I. S. China Sea 15°47N 111°12E 230 A4
Zhongjiang China 30°53N 104°46E 228 B5
Zhongning China 37°29N 105°40E 226 F3
Zhongpu = Chungpu Taiwan 23°26N 120°31E 225 C2
Zhongsha Qundao = Macclesfield Bank S. China Sea 16°0N 114°30E 230 A4
Zhongshan Antarctica 69°0S 39°50E 151 C6
Zhongshan Guangdong, China 22°26N 113°20E 229 F9
Zhongshan Guangxi Zhuangzu, China 24°29N 111°18E 229 E8
Zhongshan Park Beijing, China 114 c3
Zhongshan Park Shanghai, China 31°13N 121°24E 138 B1
Zhongshankong China 22°35N 113°29E 219 a
Zhongtiao Shan China 35°0N 111°10E 226 G6
Zhongwei China 37°30N 105°12E 226 F3
Zhongxian China 30°18N 107°58E 228 B6
Zhongxiang China 31°12N 112°34E 229 B9
Zhongyang China 37°20N 111°11E 226 F6
Zhorany Ukraine 51°19N 23°58E 185 G10
Zhosaly Kazakhstan 45°29N 64°4E 216 C6
Zhoucun Guangdong, China 23°11N 113°11E 121 A2
Zhoucun Shandong, China 36°47N 117°48E 227 F9
Zhoujiadu China 31°11N 121°29E 138 B1
Zhoujiazhen China 31°16N 121°33E 138 B2
Zhoukou China 33°38N 114°38E 226 H8
Zhoukoudian China 39°41N 115°56E 226 E8
Zhouning China 27°12N 119°20E 229 D12
Zhoushan China 30°1N 122°6E 229 B14
Zhoushan Dao China 30°5N 122°10E 229 B14
Zhouzhi China 34°10N 108°12E 226 G5
Zhouzhuangzi China 39°51N 116°16E 114 B1
Zhovkva Ukraine 50°4N 23°58E 177 C12
Zhovti Vody Ukraine 48°21N 33°31E 189 H7
Zhovtneve Lubelskie, Ukraine 50°42N 24°12E 185 H11
Zhovtneve Mykolayiv, Ukraine 46°54N 32°3E 189 J7
Zhu Jiang → China 22°45N 113°37E 229 F9
Zhuanghe China 39°40N 123°0E 224 C1
Zhuangwei = Chuangwei Taiwan 24°45N 121°47E 225 B3
Zhubei = Chupei Taiwan 24°50N 121°0E 225 B3
Zhucheng China 36°0N 119°27E 227 G10
Zhudong = Chutung Taiwan 24°44N 121°5E 225 B3
Zhugqu China 33°40N 104°30E 226 H3
Zhuhai China 22°17N 113°34E 229 F9
Zhuji China 29°40N 120°10E 229 C13
Zhujiang Kou China 22°20N 113°45E 219 a
Zhukovka Russia 53°35N 33°50E 188 F7
Zhulebino Russia 55°42N 37°58E 129 B4
Zhumadian China 32°59N 114°2E 229 A10
Zhunan = Chunan Taiwan 24°41N 120°52E 225 B2
Zhuo Xian = Zhuozhou China 39°28N 115°58E 226 E8
Zhuolu China 40°20N 115°12E 226 D8
Zhuozhou China 39°28N 115°58E 226 E8
Zhuozi China 41°0N 112°25E 226 D7
Zhuqi = Chuch'i Taiwan 23°31N 120°32E 225 C2
Zhur Kosovo 42°13N 20°34E 202 D4
Zhushadi China 23°11N 113°22E 121 A3
Zhushan = Chushan Taiwan 23°45N 120°40E 225 C2
Zhushan China 32°15N 110°13E 229 A8
Zhuxi China 32°25N 109°40E 228 A7
Zhuzhou China 27°49N 113°12E 229 D9
Zhvanets Ukraine 48°33N 26°30E 183 B11
Zhympity Kazakhstan 50°16N 52°35E 216 B4
Zhytomyr Ukraine 50°20N 28°40E 177 C15
Zhytomyr □ Ukraine 50°50N 28°10E 177 C14
Zi Shui → China 28°40N 112°40E 229 C9
Žiar nad Hronom Slovakia 48°35N 18°53E 181 C11
Ziarat Pakistan 30°25N 67°49E 242 D2
Zibo China 36°47N 118°3E 227 F10
Zichang China 37°18N 109°40E 226 F5
Zidarovo Bulgaria 42°20N 27°24E 203 D11
Zidi = Wandhari Pakistan 27°42N 66°48E 242 F2
Ziębice Poland 50°37N 17°2E 185 H4
Ziebingen = Cybinka Poland 52°12N 14°46E 185 F1
Ziegenhals = Głuchołazy Poland 50°19N 17°24E 185 H4
Zielenzig = Sulęcin Poland 52°26N 15°10E 185 F2
Zielona Poland 52°14N 21°11E 143 B3
Zielona Góra Poland 51°57N 15°31E 185 G2
Zielonka Poland 52°18N 21°9E 143 B2
Zierikzee Neths. 51°40N 3°55E 170 C3
Ziesar Germany 52°16N 12°17E 178 C8
Zifta Egypt 30°43N 31°14E 256 H7
Zighan Libya 25°29N 22°8E 258 C4
Zigon Burma 18°20N 95°37E 241 F5
Zigong China 29°15N 104°48E 228 C5
Ziguéy Chad 14°43N 15°50E 259 F3
Ziguinchor Senegal 12°35N 16°20W 262 C1
Ziguinchor □ Senegal 12°45N 16°20W 262 C1
Zihuatanejo Mexico 17°39N 101°33W 318 D4
Zijin China 23°33N 115°8E 229 F10
Zile Turkey 40°15N 35°52E 212 B6
Žilina Slovakia 49°12N 18°42E 181 B11
Žilinský □ Slovakia 49°10N 19°0E 181 B12
Zillah Libya 28°30N 17°33E 258 C3
Zillertaler Alpen Austria 47°6N 11°45E 180 D4
Zima Russia 54°0N 102°5E 215 D11
Zimapán Mexico 20°45N 99°21W 319 C5
Zimba Zambia 17°20S 26°11E 269 F2
Zimbabwe Zimbabwe 20°16S 30°54E 269 G3
Zimbabwe ■ Africa 19°0S 30°0E 269 F3
Zimmi S. Leone 7°20N 11°20W 262 D2
Zimnicea Romania 43°40N 25°22E 183 G10
Zimovniki Russia 47°10N 42°25E 191 G6
Zina Cameroon 11°19N 14°54E 259 F2
Zinave △ Mozam. 21°35S 33°40E 271 B5
Zinder Niger 13°48N 9°0E 259 F1
Zinder □ Niger 15°0N 10°30E 263 C7
Zinga C.A.R. 3°49N 18°34E 264 B3
Zinga Tanzania 9°16S 38°49E 269 D4
Zingaro △ Italy 38°6N 12°53E 200 D5
Zingst Germany 54°26N 12°39E 178 A8
Ziniaré Burkina Faso 12°35N 1°18W 263 C4
Zinjibār Yemen 13°7N 45°23E 248 D4
Zinnowitz Germany 54°5N 13°54E 178 A9
Zinovyevsk = Kirovohrad Ukraine 48°35N 32°20E 189 H7
Zion St. Kitts & Nevis 17°8N 62°33W 322 d
Zion Ill., U.S.A. 42°27N 87°50W 311 B9
Zion △ U.S.A. 37°15N 113°5W 305 H7
Zionsville U.S.A. 39°57N 86°16W 311 E10
Zipaquirá Colombia 5°0N 74°0W 328 C3
Zirbitzkogel Austria 47°4N 14°34E 180 D7
Zirc Hungary 47°17N 17°52E 182 C2
Žiri Slovenia 46°5N 14°5E 199 B11
Žirje Croatia 43°39N 15°42E 199 E12
Zirke = Sieraków Poland 52°39N 16°2E 185 F3
Zirl Austria 47°17N 11°14E 180 D4
Zirndorf Germany 49°27N 10°57E 179 F6
Ziro India 27°37N 93°44E 241 B4
Ziros Greece 35°5N 26°8E 207 E7
Zirreh, Gowd-e Afghan. 29°45N 62°0E 240 C1
Zisterdorf Austria 48°33N 16°45E 181 C9
Zitácuaro Mexico 19°24N 100°22W 318 D4
Žitava → Slovakia 48°14N 18°21E 181 C11
Zitelle, Chiesa delle Venice, Italy 142 c3
Žitište Serbia 45°30N 20°32E 182 E5
Zitong China 31°37N 105°10E 228 B5
Zitsa Greece 39°47N 20°40E 204 B2
Zittau Germany 50°53N 14°48E 178 E10
Zitundo Mozam. 26°48S 32°47E 271 C5
Živinice Bos.-H. 44°27N 18°36E 182 F3
Ziwa Maghariba = Kagera □ Tanzania 2°0S 31°30E 268 C3
Ziway Ethiopia 7°56N 38°43E 266 C4
Ziway, L. Ethiopia 8°0N 38°50E 257 F4
Zixi China 27°45N 117°4E 229 D11
Zixing China 25°59N 113°21E 229 E9
Ziyamet = Leonárisso Cyprus 35°28N 34°8E 207 E10
Ziyang Shaanxi, China 32°32N 108°31E 226 H5
Ziyang Sichuan, China 30°6N 104°40E 228 B5
Ziyuan China 26°2N 110°40E 229 D8
Ziyun China 25°45N 106°5E 228 E6
Ziz, Oued → Morocco 31°40N 4°15W 260 B4
Zizhong China 29°48N 104°47E 228 C5
Zizhou = Ch'ich'ou Taiwan 23°45N 120°33E 225 C2
Zizhuyuan Park China 39°54N 116°18E 114 B1
Žižkov Czechia 50°5N 14°28E 135 B2
Zizur Mayor Spain 42°47N 1°41W 196 C3
Zlarin Croatia 43°42N 15°49E 199 E12
Zlatar Croatia 46°5N 16°3E 199 B13
Zlatar Serbia 43°25N 19°47E 202 C3
Zlataritsa Bulgaria 43°2N 25°55E 203 C9
Zlaté Moravce Slovakia 48°23N 18°24E 181 C11
Zlatibor Serbia 43°45N 19°43E 202 C3
Zlatitsa Bulgaria 42°41N 24°7E 203 D8
Zlatna Romania 46°8N 23°11E 183 D8
Zlatna Panega Bulgaria 43°5N 24°9E 203 C8
Zlatni Pyasŭtsi Bulgaria 43°17N 28°3E 203 C12
Zlatograd Bulgaria 41°22N 25°7E 203 E9
Zlatoust Russia 55°10N 59°40E 186 C10
Zletovo Macedonia 41°59N 22°17E 202 E6
Zličín Czechia 50°3N 14°17E 135 B1
Zlín Czechia 49°14N 17°40E 181 B10
Zlínský □ Czechia 49°20N 17°40E 181 B10
Zlītan Libya 32°32N 14°35E 258 B2
Złocieniec Poland 53°30N 16°1E 184 E3
Złoczew Poland 51°24N 18°35E 185 G5
Zlot Serbia 44°1N 21°58E 202 B5
Złotoryja Poland 51°8N 15°55E 185 G2
Złotów Poland 53°22N 17°2E 184 E4
Zmeinogorsk Kazakhstan 51°10N 82°13E 217 B10
Żmigród Poland 51°28N 16°53E 185 G3
Zmiinyi, Ostriv Black Sea 45°15N 30°12E 189 K6
Zmiyev Ukraine 49°39N 36°27E 189 H9
Znamenka = Znamyanka Ukraine 48°45N 32°30E 189 H7
Znamensk = Kapustin Yar Russia 48°37N 45°40E 191 F7
Znamensk Russia 54°36N 21°16E 184 D8
Znamyanka Ukraine 48°45N 32°30E 189 H7
Żnin Poland 52°51N 17°44E 185 F4
Znojmo Czechia 48°50N 16°2E 180 C9
Zobeyrī Iran 34°10N 46°40E 246 C5
Zobia Dem. Rep. of the Congo 3°0N 25°59E 268 B2
Zobten = Sobótka Poland 50°54N 16°44E 185 H3
Zócalo Mexico City, Mexico 128 b3
Zoetermeer Neths. 52°3N 4°30E 170 B4
Zogang China 29°55N 97°42E 228 C1
Zogno Italy 45°48N 9°40E 198 C6
Zografou Greece 37°58N 23°47E 112 B2
Zohreh → Iran 30°16N 51°15E 247 D6
Zolfo Springs U.S.A. 27°30N 81°48W 317 H8
Żoliborz Poland 52°16N 20°57E 143 B1
Zolochiv Ukraine 49°45N 24°51E 177 D13
Zolotonosha Ukraine 49°39N 32°5E 189 H7
Zolotyy Potik Ukraine 48°54N 25°20E 183 B10
Zomba Malawi 15°22S 35°19E 269 F4
Zongo Dem. Rep. of the Congo 4°20N 18°35E 264 B3
Zonguldak Turkey 41°28N 31°50E 212 B4
Zonguldak □ Turkey 41°20N 31°45E 212 B4
Zongyang China 30°42N 117°12E 229 B11
Zonnebloem S. Africa 33°56S 18°26E 118 A1
Zonqor Pt. Malta 35°52N 14°34E 206 F8
Zonza France 41°45N 9°11E 175 G13
Zoo Baba Niger 18°13N 13°2E 259 E2
Zorgo Burkina Faso 12°15N 0°35W 263 C4
Zorita Spain 39°17N 5°39W 195 F5
Zorleni Romania 46°14N 27°44E 183 D12
Zornitsa Bulgaria 42°23N 26°58E 203 D10
Zorritos Peru 3°43S 80°40W 330 A1
Żory Poland 50°3N 18°44E 185 H5
Zorzor Liberia 7°46N 9°28W 262 D3
Zossen Germany 52°13N 13°27E 178 C9
Zou Xiang China 35°30N 116°58E 226 G9
Zouan-Hounien Ivory C. 6°55N 8°15W 262 D3
Zouar Chad 20°30N 16°32E 259 D3
Zouérate = Zouîrât Mauritania 22°44N 12°21W 260 D2
Zouîrât Mauritania 22°44N 12°21W 260 D2
Zouri Gabon 1°1S 8°53E 264 C1
Zourika Niger 19°16N 7°52E 259 E1
Zourma Burkina Faso 11°20N 0°50W 263 C4
Zousfana, O. → Algeria 31°28N 2°17W 261 B4
Zoutkamp Neths. 53°20N 6°18E 170 A6
Zov Tigra △ Russia 43°25N 134°10E 220 C7
Zrenjanin Serbia 45°22N 20°23E 182 E5
Zuata → Venezuela 7°52N 65°22W 329 B4
Zuba Nigeria 9°11N 7°12E 263 D6
Zubayr Yemen 15°3N 42°10E 248 D3
Zubin Potok Kosovo 42°54N 20°41E 202 D4
Zubtsov Russia 56°10N 34°34E 188 D8
Zudañez Bolivia 19°6S 64°44W 331 D5
Zuénoula Ivory C. 7°34N 6°3W 262 D3
Zuera Spain 41°51N 0°49W 196 D4
Zuetina = Az Zuwaytīnah Libya 30°58N 20°7E 258 B4
Zufār Oman 17°40N 54°0E 249 C6
Zufār □ Oman 18°0N 54°0E 249 C6
Zug Switz. 47°10N 8°31E 179 H4
Zug W. Sahara 21°36N 14°9W 260 D2
Zugdidi Georgia 42°30N 41°55E 191 J5
Zugersee Switz. 47°7N 8°35E 179 H4
Zugliget Hungary 47°30N 18°59E 117 B1
Zugló Hungary 47°31N 19°8E 117 A2
Zugspitze Germany 47°25N 10°59E 179 H6
Zuhd, J. az Si. Arabia 28°20N 35°17E 251 K6
Zuid-Holland □ Neths. 52°0N 4°35E 170 C4
Zuidbeveland Neths. 51°30N 3°50E 170 C3
Zuiderwoude Neths. 52°26N 5°2E 112 A3
Zuidhorn Neths. 53°15N 6°23E 170 A6
Zújar Spain 37°34N 2°50W 195 H8
Zújar → Spain 39°1N 5°47W 195 G5
Żukowo Poland 54°21N 18°22E 184 D5
Zula Eritrea 15°17N 39°40E 257 D4
Zulia □ Venezuela 10°0N 72°10W 328 B3
Züllichau = Sulechów Poland 52°5N 15°40E 185 F2
Zülpich Germany 50°41N 6°39E 178 E2
Zülz = Biała Poland 50°24N 17°40E 185 H4
Zumaia Spain 43°19N 2°15W 196 B2
Zumárraga Spain 43°5N 2°19W 196 B2
Zumbi Brazil 22°49S 43°10W 135 A1
Zumbo Mozam. 15°35S 30°26E 269 F3
Zummo Nigeria 9°51N 12°59E 263 D7
Zumpango Mexico 19°48N 99°6W 319 D5
Zunderdorp Neths. 52°24N 4°58E 112 A2
Zundi Angola 10°28S 16°48E 265 E3
Zungeru Nigeria 9°48N 6°8E 263 D6
Zunhua China 40°18N 117°58E 227 D9
Zunheboto India 25°58N 94°31E 241 C5
Zuni Pueblo U.S.A. 35°4N 108°51W 305 J9
Zunyi China 27°42N 106°53E 228 D6
Zuo Jiang → China 22°50N 108°6E 228 F6
Zuoquan China 37°1N 113°27E 226 F7
Zuoying = Tsoying Taiwan 22°41N 120°17E 225 D2
Zuozhou China 22°42N 107°27E 228 F6
Županja Croatia 45°4N 18°43E 182 E3
Zurbāṭīyah Iraq 33°9N 46°3E 213 F12
Zürich Switz. 47°22N 8°32E 179 H4
Zürich □ Switz. 47°26N 8°40E 179 H4
Zürich ✈ (ZRH) Switz. 47°27N 8°32E 179 H4
Zürichsee Switz. 47°18N 8°40E 179 H4
Żuromin Poland 53°4N 19°51E 185 E6
Zurrieq Malta 35°50N 14°28E 206 F7
Žut Croatia 43°52N 15°17E 199 E12
Zutphen Neths. 52°9N 6°12E 170 B6
Zuurberg △ S. Africa 33°12S 25°32E 270 D4
Zuvuvu → Brazil 23°40S 46°42W 137 C1
Zuwārah Libya 32°58N 12°1E 258 B2
Zūzan Iran 34°22N 59°53E 247 C8
Žužemberk Slovenia 45°52N 14°56E 199 C11
Zvanka = Volkhov Russia 59°55N 32°15E 188 C7
Zvečan Kosovo 42°54N 20°50E 202 D4
Zvenigorodka = Svenyhorodka Ukraine 49°4N 30°56E 189 H6
Zvezdets Bulgaria 42°6N 27°26E 203 D11
Zvishavane Zimbabwe 20°17S 30°2E 269 G3
Zvolen Slovakia 48°33N 19°10E 181 C12
Zvonce Serbia 42°57N 22°34E 202 D6
Zvornik Bos.-H. 44°26N 19°5E 182 F4
Zwanenburg Neths. 52°23N 4°45E 112 A1
Zwedru = Tchien Liberia 5°59N 8°15W 262 D3
Zweibrücken Germany 49°15N 7°21E 179 F3
Zwenkau Germany 51°13N 12°20E 178 D8
Zwettl Austria 48°35N 15°9E 180 C8
Zwickau Germany 50°44N 12°30E 178 E8
Zwierzyniec Poland 50°36N 22°58E 185 H9
Zwiesel Germany 49°1N 13°13E 179 F9
Zwittau = Svitavy Czechia 49°47N 16°28E 181 B9
Zwoleń Poland 51°21N 21°36E 185 G8
Zwölfaxing Austria 48°6N 16°28E 142 B2
Zwolle Neths. 52°31N 6°6E 170 B6
Zwolle La., U.S.A. 31°38N 93°39W 314 F8
Żychlin Poland 52°15N 19°37E 185 F6
Żyrardów Poland 52°3N 20°28E 185 F7
Zyryan Kazakhstan 49°43N 84°20E 217 C10
Zyryanka Russia 65°45N 150°51E 215 C16
Zyryanovsk = Zyryan Kazakhstan 49°43N 84°20E 217 C10
Zyuratkul △ Russia 54°50N 58°56E 216 B5
Żywiec Poland 49°42N 19°10E 185 J6